# GALE DIRECTORY OF PUBLICATIONS AND BROADCAST MEDIA

ISSN 1048-7972

# 140th Edition

Published annually since 1869

# GALE DIRECTORY OF PUBLICATIONS AND BROADCAST MEDIA

(Formerly *Ayer Directory of Publications*)

An annual Guide to Publications and Broadcasting Stations
Including Newspapers, Magazines, Journals, Radio Stations,
Television Stations, and Cable Systems

**Volume 4**
**U.S. and Canada**
**Regional Market Index**

**Ken Karges,** Project Editor

Detroit • New York • San Francisco • San Diego • New Haven, Conn. • Waterville, Maine • London • Munich

## Gale Directory of Publications and Broadcast Media, 140th Edition

**Project Editor**
Ken Karges

**Editorial**
Tara Atterberry, Kim Hunt, Kristin B. Mallegg, Rishi Modi, Bonnie Sarkar, Erin Stradtner

**Editorial Support Services**
Emmanuel T. Barrido

**Data Capture**
Katrina Coach, Elizabeth Pilette, Beth Richardson, Beverly Jendrowski

**Product Design**
Cynthia Baldwin, Kate Scheible

**Composition and Electronic Prepress**
Evi Seoud

**Manufacturing**
Rita Wimberley

© 2005 Thomson Gale, a part of the Thomson Corporation

Thomson and Star logo are trademarks and Gale is a registered trademark used herein under license.

*For more information, contact*
Thomson Gale
27500 Drake Rd.
Farmington Hills, MI 48331-3535
Or you can visit our Internet site at
http://www.gale.com

**ALL RIGHTS RESERVED**
No part of this work covered by the copyright hereon may be reproduced or used in any form or by any means—graphic, electronic, or mechanical, including photocopying, recording, taping, Web distribution, or information storage retrieval systems—without the written permission of the publisher.

This publication is a creative work fully protected by all applicable copyright laws, as well as by misappropriation, trade secret, unfair competition, and other applicable laws. The authors and editors of this work have added value to the underlying factual material herein through one or more of the following: unique and original selection, coordination, expression, arrangement, and classification of the information.

For permission to use material from this product, submit your request via Web at http://www.gale-edit.com/permissions, or you may download our Permissions Request form and submit your request by fax or mail to:

*Permissions Department*
Thomson Gale
27500 Drake Rd.
Farmington Hills, MI 48331-3535
Permissions Hotline:
248-699-8006 or 800-877-4253, ext. 8006
Fax: 248-699-8074 or 800-762-4058

Since this page cannot legibly accommodate all copyright notices, the acknowledgments constitute an extension of the copyright notice.

While every effort has been made to ensure the reliability of the information presented in this publication, Thomson Gale does not guarantee the accuracy of the data contained herein. Thomson Gale accepts no payment for listing; and inclusion in the publication of any organization, agency, institution, publication, service, or individual does not imply endorsement of the publisher. Errors brought to the attention of the publisher and verified to the satisfaction of the publisher will be corrected in future editions.

```
ISBN 0-7876-8207-1 (set)
ISBN 0-7876-8209-8 (Volume 1)
ISBN 0-7876-8210-1 (Volume 2)
ISBN 0-7876-8211-X (Volume 3)
ISBN 0-7876-8212-8 (Volume 4)
ISBN 0-7876-8213-6 (Volume 5)
     ISSN 1048-7972
```

Printed in the United States of America
10 9 8 7 6 5 4 3 2 1

# Contents

**Volume 1: Alabama - New Hampshire**

| | |
|---|---|
| Introduction | ix |
| User's Guide | xi |
| Abbreviations | xvii |
| Industry Activity—New Listings and Cessations | xxi |

Descriptive Listings

| | |
|---|---|
| Alabama | 1 |
| Alaska | 29 |
| Arizona | 37 |
| Arkansas | 59 |
| California | 79 |
| Colorado | 239 |
| Connecticut | 273 |
| Delaware | 305 |
| District of Columbia | 311 |
| Florida | 349 |
| Georgia | 407 |
| Hawaii | 451 |
| Idaho | 459 |
| Illinois | 471 |
| Indiana | 581 |
| Iowa | 625 |
| Kansas | 669 |
| Kentucky | 703 |
| Louisiana | 735 |
| Maine | 759 |
| Maryland | 771 |
| Massachusetts | 819 |
| Michigan | 913 |
| Minnesota | 973 |
| Mississippi | 1025 |
| Missouri | 1045 |
| Montana | 1103 |
| Nebraska | 1115 |
| Nevada | 1141 |
| New Hampshire | 1149 |

**Volume 2: New Jersey - Wyoming and Canada**

| | |
|---|---|
| Introduction | ix |
| User's Guide | xi |
| Abbreviations | xvii |
| Industry Activity—New Listings and Cessations | xxi |

Descriptive Listings

| | |
|---|---|
| New Jersey | 1161 |
| New Mexico | 1229 |
| New York | 1243 |
| North Carolina | 1427 |
| North Dakota | 1469 |
| Ohio | 1481 |
| Oklahoma | 1555 |
| Oregon | 1583 |
| Pennsylvania | 1607 |
| Puerto Rico | 1707 |
| Rhode Island | 1713 |
| South Carolina | 1723 |
| South Dakota | 1741 |
| Tennessee | 1755 |
| Texas | 1787 |
| Utah | 1885 |
| Vermont | 1897 |
| Virginia | 1907 |
| Washington | 1969 |
| West Virginia | 2003 |
| Wisconsin | 2019 |
| Wyoming | 2075 |

*Canada*

| | |
|---|---|
| Alberta | 2083 |
| British Columbia | 2101 |
| Manitoba | 2123 |
| New Brunswick | 2133 |
| Newfoundland and Labrador | 2139 |
| Northwest Territories | 2143 |
| Nova Scotia | 2145 |
| Ontario | 2151 |
| Prince Edward Island | 2227 |
| Quebec | 2229 |
| Saskatchewan | 2255 |
| Yukon Territory | 2265 |

## CONTENTS

### Volume 3: Indexes

Introduction . . . . . . . . . . . . . . . . . . . . . . . . . . ix
User's Guide . . . . . . . . . . . . . . . . . . . . . . . . . . xi
Abbreviations . . . . . . . . . . . . . . . . . . . . . . . . xvii
Industry Activity—New Listings and Cessations . . . . xxi
Broadcast and Cable Networks . . . . . . . . . . . . 2267
News and Feature Syndicates . . . . . . . . . . . . . 2273
Publishers Index . . . . . . . . . . . . . . . . . . . . . . 2281
Subject Indexes

   *Index to Subject Terms* . . . . . . . . . . . . . . 2741

   *Agricultural Publications* . . . . . . . . . . . . . 2747
     Agricultural Publications (by State) . . . . . . . 2747
     Agricultural Publications (by Subject) . . . . . . 2753

   *Ethnic Publications* . . . . . . . . . . . . . . . . 2763
     Black Publications . . . . . . . . . . . . . . . . 2763
     Foreign Language Publications . . . . . . . . . . 2767
     Hispanic Publications . . . . . . . . . . . . . . 2775
     Jewish Publications . . . . . . . . . . . . . . . 2777

   *Fraternal Publications* . . . . . . . . . . . . . . 2779
     College Publications . . . . . . . . . . . . . . 2779
     Fraternal Publications . . . . . . . . . . . . . 2791
     Religious Publications . . . . . . . . . . . . . 2793
     Women's Publications . . . . . . . . . . . . . . 2801

   *Magazines* . . . . . . . . . . . . . . . . . . . . . 2805
     Daily Periodicals . . . . . . . . . . . . . . . . 2805
     Magazines of General Circulation . . . . . . . . 2807

   *Newspapers* . . . . . . . . . . . . . . . . . . . . 2863
     Daily Newspapers . . . . . . . . . . . . . . . . 2863
     Paid Community Newspapers . . . . . . . . . . . 2889
     Free Newspapers . . . . . . . . . . . . . . . . 2939
     Shopping Guides . . . . . . . . . . . . . . . . . 2953

   *Radio Station Formats* . . . . . . . . . . . . . . 2961

   *Trade, Technical, and Professional Publications* . . . . . . . . . . . . . . . . . . 3081

Newspaper Feature Editors . . . . . . . . . . . . . . 3241
   Names, addresses, and telephone numbers of the editors of features appearing in daily newspapers with circulations of 50,000 or more. Prefaced by a list of newspapers represented.

Master Name and Keyword Index . . . . . . . . . . . 3263

### Volume 4: Regional Market Index

Introduction . . . . . . . . . . . . . . . . . . . . . . . . . . ix
User's Guide . . . . . . . . . . . . . . . . . . . . . . . . . . xi
Abbreviations . . . . . . . . . . . . . . . . . . . . . . . . xvii
Industry Activity—New Listings and Cessations . . . . xxi
Regional Market Index

   Newspaper Index . . . . . . . . . . . . . . . . . . 3575
   Periodical Index . . . . . . . . . . . . . . . . . 3897
   Cable Index . . . . . . . . . . . . . . . . . . . . 4229
   Radio Index . . . . . . . . . . . . . . . . . . . . 4251

   Television Index . . . . . . . . . . . . . . . . . 4343

### Volume 5: International

Introduction . . . . . . . . . . . . . . . . . . . . . . . . . . ix
User's Guide . . . . . . . . . . . . . . . . . . . . . . . . . . xi
Abbreviations . . . . . . . . . . . . . . . . . . . . . . . . xvii
Industry Activity—New Listings and Cessations . . . . xxi
Descriptive Listings

   Albania . . . . . . . . . . . . . . . . . . . . . . . 4365
   Algeria . . . . . . . . . . . . . . . . . . . . . . . 4367
   Anguilla . . . . . . . . . . . . . . . . . . . . . . 4369
   Antigua-Barbuda . . . . . . . . . . . . . . . . . . 4371
   Argentina . . . . . . . . . . . . . . . . . . . . . 4373
   Australia . . . . . . . . . . . . . . . . . . . . . 4375
   Austria . . . . . . . . . . . . . . . . . . . . . . 4405
   Azerbaijan . . . . . . . . . . . . . . . . . . . . . 4409
   Bahamas . . . . . . . . . . . . . . . . . . . . . . 4411
   Bahrain . . . . . . . . . . . . . . . . . . . . . . 4413
   Bangladesh . . . . . . . . . . . . . . . . . . . . . 4415
   Barbados . . . . . . . . . . . . . . . . . . . . . . 4419
   Belarus . . . . . . . . . . . . . . . . . . . . . . 4421
   Belgium . . . . . . . . . . . . . . . . . . . . . . 4423
   Belize . . . . . . . . . . . . . . . . . . . . . . . 4429
   Bermuda . . . . . . . . . . . . . . . . . . . . . . 4431
   Bhutan . . . . . . . . . . . . . . . . . . . . . . . 4433
   Bolivia . . . . . . . . . . . . . . . . . . . . . . 4435
   Bosnia-Hercegovina . . . . . . . . . . . . . . . . . 4437
   Botswana . . . . . . . . . . . . . . . . . . . . . . 4439
   Brazil . . . . . . . . . . . . . . . . . . . . . . . 4441
   Brunei Darussalam . . . . . . . . . . . . . . . . . 4443
   Bulgaria . . . . . . . . . . . . . . . . . . . . . . 4445
   Cambodia . . . . . . . . . . . . . . . . . . . . . . 4447
   Cameroon . . . . . . . . . . . . . . . . . . . . . . 4449
   Cayman Islands . . . . . . . . . . . . . . . . . . . 4451
   Chile . . . . . . . . . . . . . . . . . . . . . . . 4453
   China, People's Republic of . . . . . . . . . . . . 4455
   Colombia . . . . . . . . . . . . . . . . . . . . . . 4515
   Costa Rica . . . . . . . . . . . . . . . . . . . . . 4517
   Cote d'Ivoire . . . . . . . . . . . . . . . . . . . 4519
   Croatia . . . . . . . . . . . . . . . . . . . . . . 4521
   Cuba . . . . . . . . . . . . . . . . . . . . . . . . 4523
   Cyprus . . . . . . . . . . . . . . . . . . . . . . . 4525
   Czech Republic . . . . . . . . . . . . . . . . . . . 4527
   Denmark . . . . . . . . . . . . . . . . . . . . . . 4529
   Dominica . . . . . . . . . . . . . . . . . . . . . . 4535
   Ecuador . . . . . . . . . . . . . . . . . . . . . . 4537
   Egypt . . . . . . . . . . . . . . . . . . . . . . . 4539
   El Salvador . . . . . . . . . . . . . . . . . . . . 4541
   England—*see United Kingdom*
   Estonia . . . . . . . . . . . . . . . . . . . . . . 4543
   Ethiopia . . . . . . . . . . . . . . . . . . . . . . 4545
   Faroe Islands . . . . . . . . . . . . . . . . . . . 4547
   Fiji . . . . . . . . . . . . . . . . . . . . . . . . 4549
   Finland . . . . . . . . . . . . . . . . . . . . . . 4551

# CONTENTS

| | |
|---|---|
| France | 4559 |
| Georgia | 4567 |
| Germany | 4569 |
| Ghana | 4589 |
| Greece | 4591 |
| Guatemala | 4593 |
| Guyana | 4595 |
| Honduras | 4597 |
| Hong Kong—*See China, People's Republic of* | |
| Hungary | 4601 |
| Iceland | 4603 |
| India | 4605 |
| Indonesia | 4669 |
| Iran | 4695 |
| Ireland | 4701 |
| Israel | 4707 |
| Italy | 4709 |
| Jamaica | 4717 |
| Japan | 4719 |
| Jordan | 4769 |
| Kazakhstan | 4771 |
| Kenya | 4773 |
| Kirgizstan | 4775 |
| Korea, Democratic People's Republic of | 4777 |
| Korea, Republic of | 4781 |
| Kuwait | 4797 |
| Lao People's Democratic Republic | 4801 |
| Latvia | 4803 |
| Lebanon | 4805 |
| Lithuania | 4811 |
| Luxembourg | 4813 |
| Macedonia | 4815 |
| Malaysia | 4817 |
| Maldives | 4827 |
| Malta | 4829 |
| Mauritius | 4831 |
| Mexico | 4833 |
| Moldova | 4835 |
| Monaco | 4837 |
| Mongolia | 4839 |
| Morocco | 4841 |
| Mozambique | 4843 |
| Myanmar | 4845 |
| Namibia | 4847 |
| Nepal | 4849 |
| Netherlands | 4853 |
| New Caledonia | 4875 |
| New Zealand | 4877 |
| Nicaragua | 4887 |
| Nigeria | 4889 |
| Northern Ireland—*see United Kingdom* | |
| Norway | 4891 |
| Oman | 4895 |
| Pakistan | 4897 |
| Panama | 4911 |
| Papua New Guinea | 4913 |
| Peru | 4915 |
| Philippines | 4917 |
| Poland | 4935 |
| Portugal | 4937 |
| Qatar | 4939 |
| Romania | 4941 |
| Russia | 4943 |
| Rwanda | 4989 |
| San Marino | 4991 |
| Saudi Arabia | 4993 |
| Scotland—*see United Kingdom* | |
| Senegal | 4995 |
| Serbia | 4997 |
| Seychelles | 4999 |
| Sierra Leone | 5001 |
| Singapore | 5003 |
| Slovakia | 5015 |
| Slovenia | 5017 |
| Republic of South Africa | 5019 |
| Spain | 5025 |
| Sri Lanka | 5035 |
| Sudan | 5043 |
| Swaziland | 5045 |
| Sweden | 5047 |
| Switzerland | 5053 |
| Syrian Arab Republic | 5063 |
| Taiwan | 5065 |
| Tajikistan | 5077 |
| United Republic of Tanzania | 5079 |
| Thailand | 5081 |
| Tonga | 5091 |
| Trinidad and Tobago | 5093 |
| Tunisia | 5095 |
| Turkey | 5097 |
| Turkmenistan | 5105 |
| Uganda | 5107 |
| Ukraine | 5109 |
| United Arab Emirates | 5111 |
| United Kingdom | 5115 |
| Uruguay | 5329 |
| Uzbekistan | 5331 |
| Vatican City | 5333 |
| Venezuela | 5335 |
| Vietnam | 5337 |
| Virgin Islands, British | 5343 |
| Virgin Islands of the United States | 5345 |
| Wales—*see United Kingdom* | |
| Yemen | 5347 |
| Zimbabwe | 5349 |
| Publishers Index | 5351 |
| Subject Indexes | |
| ***Index to Subject Terms*** | 5537 |

## CONTENTS

**Agricultural Publications** . . . . . . . . . . . . . 5543
Agricultural Pubs. (by Country). . . . . . . . . . 5543
Agricultural Pubs. (by Subject) . . . . . . . . . . 5547

**Foreign Language Publications** . . . . . . . . . 5553

**Fraternal Publications** . . . . . . . . . . . . . . . 5563
College Publications . . . . . . . . . . . . . . . . . 5563
Fraternal Publications . . . . . . . . . . . . . . . . 5565
Religious Publications . . . . . . . . . . . . . . . . 5567
Women's Publications . . . . . . . . . . . . . . . 5569

**Magazines** . . . . . . . . . . . . . . . . . . . . . . . 5573
Magazines of General Circulation . . . . . . . . 5573

**Newspapers** . . . . . . . . . . . . . . . . . . . . . 5593
Daily Newspapers . . . . . . . . . . . . . . . . . . 5593
Paid Community Newspapers . . . . . . . . . . 5597
Free Newspapers . . . . . . . . . . . . . . . . . . 5601

**Trade, Technical, and Professional Publications** . . . . . . . . . . . . . . . . . . . . . 5603

Master Index . . . . . . . . . . . . . . . . . . . . . . 5701

# Introduction

The *Gale Directory of Publications and Broadcast Media (GDPBM)* has been the definitive media source since its inception in 1869. Formerly the *Ayer Directory of Publications*, and now in its 140th edition, *GDPBM* has grown with U.S., Canadian, and international media, and increased its scope to include the communication technologies of the twentieth century. *GDPBM* now covers approximately 52,000 newspapers, magazines, journals, and other periodicals, as well as radio, television, and cable stations and systems. Organized to help users find facts fast, GDPBM covers the whole media picture—ad rates, circulation statistics, local programming, names of key personnel, and other useful, accurate information. In addition, *GDPBM* offers a geographic arrangement that provides easy access to listings. Only *GDPBM* presents print and broadcast entries in one geographic sort, then alphabetically within state, province, territory, region, or country; city; and media category (Print or Broadcast).

**Highlights of this Edition**

The 140th Edition of *Gale Directory of Publications and Broadcast Media* features approximately 5,500 new listings.

**Scope and Preparation**

The following categories of publications are **excluded** from the *Gale Directory of Publications and Broadcast Media*'s coverage of the U.S., Canadian, and international print and broadcast arenas: • newsletters • directories.

Information provided in *GDPBM* is obtained primarily through research of publication and publisher websites and questionnaire responses from organizations listed. Some clarification and verification of data is obtained through telephone calls. Other published sources are used to verify some information, such as the audited circulation data in publication listings.

Organizations identified as defunct are removed from the main body of entries and listed in the Master Name and Keyword Index as "Ceased." The same basic procedure is followed for listings that cannot be located either through web research, direct mail, email or subsequent attempts at telephone follow-up; these entries are listed in the Master Index as "Unable to locate." Efforts to clarify the status of such nonrespondents are ongoing.

**Free Update Issued Between Editions**

Approximately midway between main editions of *GDPBM,* a supplementary Update is sent free to all subscribers. It provides new listings as well as critical updates to listings of newspapers, magazines, journals, radio stations, television stations, and cable systems that are listed in the current edition of the *Directory*.

**Acknowledgments**

The editors are grateful to the many media professionals who generously responded to our requests for updated information, provided additional data by telephone, email or fax, and helped in the shaping of this edition with their comments and suggestions throughout the year.

**Available in Electronic Formats**

*Licensing.* Gale Directory of Publications and Broadcast Media is available for licensing. The complete database is provided in a fielded format and is deliverable on such media as disk or CD-ROM. For more information, contact Thomson Gale's Business Development Group at 1-800-877-GALE, or visit our web site at www.gale.com/bizdev.

*Online.* Gale Directory of Publications and Broadcast Media (along with *Directories in Print* and *Newsletters in Print*) is accessible as File 469: *Gale Database of Publications and Broadcast Media* through the Dialog Corporation's DIALOG service. *GDPBM* is also accessible as PUBBRD through LexisNexis. For more information, contact The Dialog Corporation, 11000 Regency Parkway, Ste. 400, Cary, NC 27511; phone: (919) 462-8600; toll-free: 800-3-DIALOG; or LexisNexis, P.O. Box 933, Dayton, OH 45401-0933; phone (937) 865-6800; toll-free: 800-227-4908.

The *Directory* is also available through InfoTrac as part of *Gale's Ready Reference Shelf*. For more information, call 1-800-877-GALE.

**Comments and Suggestions Welcome**

If you have questions, concerns, or comments about *Gale*

## INTRODUCTION

*Directory of Publications and Broadcast Media,* please contact:

Project Editor
*Gale Directory of Publications and Broadcast Media*
Thomson Gale
27500 Drake Rd.
Farmington Hills, MI 48331-3535
Phone: (248) 699-4253
Toll-free: 800-347-GALE
Fax: (248) 699-8075
URL: http://www.gale.com

# User's Guide

*Gale Directory of Publications and Broadcast Media* comprises five volumes:

- Volume 1 includes U.S. entries from Alabama to New Hampshire.
- Volume 2 encompasses U.S. listings from New Jersey to Wyoming and Canadian entries.
- Volume 3 contains U.S. and Canadian broadcast & cable networks, news & feature syndicates, and 21 indexes.
- Volume 4 contains the U.S. and Canadian regional market index.
- Volume 5 includes entries from Albania to Zimbabwe and 14 indexes to International listings.

The samples and notes below offer more details on specific content and how to use the *Directory*'s listings and indexes. Please note that entry information appearing in this section has been fabricated.

## Sample Entries

The samples that follow are fabricated entries in which each numbered section designates information that might appear in a listing. The numbered items are explained in the descriptive paragraphs following each sample.

### Sample Publication Listing

**❙1❙** 222
**❙2❙** American Computer Review
**❙3❙** Jane Doe Publishing Company, Inc.
**❙4❙** 199 E. 49th St.
  PO Box 724866
  Salem, NY 10528-5555
**❙5❙** Phone: (518)555-9277
**❙6❙** Fax: (518)555-9288
**❙7❙** Free: 800-555-5432
**❙8❙** Publication E-mail: acr@jdpci.com
**❙9❙** Publisher E-mail: jdpci@jdpci.com

❙10❙ Magazine for users of Super Software Plus products. ❙11❙ **Subtitle:** The Programmer's Friend. ❙12❙ **Founded:** June 1979. ❙13❙ **Freq:** Monthly (combined issue July/Aug.). ❙14❙ **Print Method:** Offset. ❙15❙ **Trim Size:** 8/12 x 11. ❙16❙ **Cols./Page:** 3. ❙17❙ **Col. Width:** 24 nonpareils. ❙18❙ **Col. Depth:** 294 agate lines. ❙19❙ **Key Personnel:** Ian Smith, Editor, phone (518)555-1201, fax (518)555-1202, ismith@jdpci.com; James Newman, Publisher; Steve Jones Jr., Advertising Mgr. ❙20❙ **ISSN:** 5555-6226. ❙21❙ **Subscription Rates:** $25; $30 Canada; $2.50 single issue. ❙22❙ **Remarks:** Color advertising not accepted. ❙23❙ **Online:** Lexis-Nexis **URL:** http://www.acrmagazine.com. ❙24❙ **Alternate Format(s):** Braille; CD-ROM; Microform. ❙25❙ **Formerly:** Computer Software Review (Dec. 13, 1986). ❙26❙ **Feature Editors:** Ann Walker, *Consumer Affairs, Editorials,* phone (518)555-2306, fax (518)555-2307, aw@jdpci.com. ❙27❙ **Additional Contact Information: Advertising:** 123 Main St., New York, NY 10016, (201)555-1900, fax: (201)555-1908. ❙28❙ **Ad Rates:** BW: $850, PCI: $.75 ❙29❙ **Circulation:** 25,000

## Description of Numbered Elements

❙1❙ **Symbol/Entry Number.** Each publication entry number is preceded by a symbol (a magazine or newspaper) representing the publishing industry. Entries are numbered sequentially. Entry numbers, rather than page numbers, are used in the index to refer to listings.

❙2❙ **Publication Title.** Publication names are listed *as they appear on the masthead or title page,* as provided by respondents.

❙3❙ **Publishing Company.** The name of the commercial publishing organization, association, or academic institution, as provided by respondents.

❙4❙ **Address.** Full mailing address information is provided wherever possible. This may include: street address; post office box; city; state or province; and ZIP or postal code. ZIP plus-four numbers are provided when known.

❙5❙ **Phone.** Phone numbers listed in this section are usually the respondent's switchboard number.

❙6❙ **Fax.** Facsimile numbers are listed when provided.

❙7❙ **Free.** Toll-free numbers are listed when provided.

❙8❙ **Publication E-mail.** Electronic mail addresses for the publication are included as provided by the listee.

❙9❙ **Publisher E-mail:** Electronic mail addresses for the publishing company are included as provided by the listee.

❙10❙ **Description.** Includes the type of publication (i.e., newspaper, magazine) as well as a brief statement of purpose, intended audience, or other relevant remarks.

❙11❙ **Subtitle.** Included as provided by the listee.

❙12❙ **Founded.** Date the periodical was first published.

❙13❙ **Frequency.** Indicates how often the publication is is-

# USER'S GUIDE

sued—daily, weekly, monthly, quarterly, etc. Explanatory remarks sometimes accompany this information (e.g., for weekly titles, the day of issuance; for collegiate titles, whether publication is limited to the academic year; whether certain issues are combined.)

**❙14❙ Print Method.** Though offset is most common, other methods are listed as provided.

**❙15❙ Trim Size.** Presented in inches unless otherwise noted.

**❙16❙ Number of Columns Per Page.** Usually one figure, but some publications list two or more, indicating a variation in style.

**❙17❙ Column Width.** Column sizes are given exactly as supplied, whether measured in inches, picas (6 picas to an inch), nonpareils (each 6 points, 72 points to an inch), or agate lines (14 to an inch).

**❙18❙ Column Depth.** Column sizes are given exactly as supplied, whether measured in inches, picas (6 picas to an inch), nonpareils (each 6 points, 72 points to an inch), or agate lines (14 to an inch).

**❙19❙ Key Personnel.** Presents the names and titles of contacts at each publication. May include phone, fax, and e-mail addresses if different than those for the publication and company.

**❙20❙ International Standard Serial Number (ISSN).** Included when provided. Occasionally, United States Publications Serial (USPS) numbers are reported rather than ISSNs.

**❙21❙ Subscription Rates.** Unless otherwise stated, prices shown in this section are the individual annual subscription rate. Other rates are listed when known, including multiyear rates, prices outside the United States, discount rates, library/institution rates, and single copy prices.

**❙22❙ Remarks.** Information listed in this section further explains the Ad Rates.

**❙23❙ Online.** If a publication is accessible online via computer, that information is listed here. If the publication is available online but the details of the URL (universal resource locator) or vendor are not known, the notation "Available Online" will be listed.

**❙24❙ Alternate Format(s).** Lists additional mediums in which a publication may be available (other than online), including CD-ROM and microform.

**❙25❙ Variant Name(s).** Lists former or variant names of the publication, including the year the change took place, when known.

**❙26❙ Feature Editors.** Lists the names and beats of any feature editors employed by the publication.

**❙27❙ Additional Contact Information.** Includes mailing, advertising, news, and subscription addresses and phone numbers when different from the editorial/publisher address and phone numbers.

**❙28❙ Ad Rates.** Respondents may provide non-contract (open) rates in any of six categories:

    GLR = general line rate
    BW = one-time black & white page rate
    4C = one-time four-color page rate
    SAU = standard advertising unit rate
    CNU = Canadian newspaper advertising unit rate
    PCI = per column inch rate

Occasionally, explanatory information about other types of advertising appears in the Remarks section of the entry.

**❙29❙ Circulation.** Figures represent various circulation numbers; the figures are accompanied by a symbol (except for sworn and estimated figures). Following are explanations of the eight circulation classifications used by *GDPBM*, the corresponding symbols, if any, are listed at the bottom of each right hand page. All circulation figures *except* publisher's reports and estimated figures appear in boldface type.

These audit bureaus are independent, nonprofit organizations (with the exception of VAC, which is for-profit) that verify circulation rates. Interested users may contact the association for more information.

- **ABC:** Audit Bureau of Circulations, 900 N. Meacham Rd., Schaumburg, IL 60173; (847)605-0909

- **CAC:** Certified Audit of Circulations, Inc., 155 Willowbrook Blvd., 4th Fl., Wayne, NJ 07470-7036; (973)785-3000

- **CCAB:** Canadian Circulations Audit Board, 90 Eglinton Ave. E, Ste. 980, Toronto, ON Canada M4P 2Y3; (416)487-2418

- **VAC:** Verified Audit Circulation, 517 Jacoby St., Ste. A, San Rafael, CA 94901; (800)775-3332

- **Post Office Statement:** These figures were verified from a U.S. Post Office form.

- **Publisher's Statement:** These figures were accompanied by the signature of the editor, publisher, or other officer.

- **Sworn Statement:** These figures, which appear in **boldface** without a symbol, were accompanied by the notarized signature of the editor, publisher, or other officer of the publication.

- **Estimated Figures:** These figures, which are shown in lightface without a symbol, are the unverified report of the listee.

The footer on every odd-numbered page contains a key to circulation and entry type symbols, as well as advertising abbreviations.

## *Sample Broadcast Listing*

❙1❙ 111
❙2❙ **WCAF-AM—1530**
❙3❙ 199 E. 49th St.
    PO Box 724866
    Salem, NY 10528-5555
❙4❙ Phone: (518)555-9277
❙5❙ Fax: (518)555-9288
❙6❙ Free: 800-555-5432
❙7❙ E-mail: wcaf@wcaf.com

    ❙8❙ **Format:** Classical. ❙9❙ **Simulcasts:** WCAF-FM. ❙10❙ **Network(s):** Westwood One Radio; ABC. ❙11❙ **Owner:** Affici Communications, Inc., at above address. ❚12❚ **Founded:** 1996. ❚13❚ **Formerly:** WCAH-AM (1992). ❚14❚ **Operating Hours:** Continuous; 90% local, 10% network. ❚15❚ **ADI:** Elmira, NY. ❚16❚ **Key Personnel:** James Smith, General Mgr., phone (518)555-1002, fax (518)555-1010, jsmith@wcaf.com; Don White, Program Dir. ❚17❚ **Cities Served:** Salem, NY. ❚18❚ **Postal Areas Served:** 10528; 10529. ❚19❚ **Local Programs:** Who's Beethoven? Clement Goebel, Contact, (518)555-1301, fax (518)555-1320. ❚20❚ **Wattage:** 5000. ❚21❚ **Ad Rates:** Underwriting available. $10-15 for 30 seconds; $30-35 for 60 seconds. Combined advertising rates available with WCAF-FM. ❚22❚ **Additional Contact Information:** Mailing address: PO Box 555, Elmira, NY, 10529. ❚23❚ **URL:** http://www.wcaf.com.

## Description of Numbered Elements

❚1❚ **Entry Number.** Each broadcast or cable entry is preceded by a symbol (a microphone) representing the broadcasting industry. Entries are numbered sequentially. Entry numbers (rather than page numbers) are used in the index to refer to listings.

❚2❚ **Call Letters and Frequency/Channel** or **Cable Company Name.**

❚3❚ **Address.** Location and studio addresses appear as supplied by the respondent. If provided, alternate addresses are listed in the Additional Contact Information section of the entries (see item 22 below).

❚4❚ **Phone.** Telephone numbers are listed as provided.

❚5❚ **Fax.** Facsimile numbers are listed when provided.

❚6❚ **Free.** Toll-free numbers are listed when provided.

❚7❚ **E-mail.** Electronic mail addresses are included as provided by the listee.

❚8❚ **Format.** For television station entries, this subheading indicates whether the station is commercial or public. Radio station entries contain industry-defined (and, in some cases, station-defined) formats as indicated by the listee.

❚9❚ **Simulcasts.** Lists stations that provide simulcasting.

❚10❚ **Network(s).** Notes national and regional networks with which a station is affiliated. The term "independent" is used if indicated by the listee.

❚11❚ **Owner.** Lists the name of an individual or company, supplemented by the address and telephone number, when provided by the listee. If the address is the same as that of the station or company, the notation "at above address" is used, referring to the station or cable company address.

❚12❚ **Founded.** In most cases, the year the station/company began operating, regardless of changes in call letters/names and ownership.

❚13❚ **Variant Name(s).** For radio and television stations, former call letters and the years in which there were changes are presented as provided by the listee. Former cable company names and the years in which they were changed are also noted when available.

❚14❚ **Operating Hours.** Lists on-air hours and often includes percentages of network and local programming.

❚15❚ **ADI (Area of Dominant Influence).** The Area of Dominant Influence is a standard market region defined by the Arbitron Ratings Company for U.S. television stations. Some respondents also list radio stations as having ADIs.

❚16❚ **Key Personnel.** Presents the names and titles of contacts at each station or cable company.

❚17❚ **Cities Served.** This heading is primarily found in cable system entries and provides information on channels and the number of subscribers.

❚18❚ **Postal Areas Served.** This heading is primarily found in cable system entries and provides information on the postal (zip) codes served by the system.

❚19❚ **Local Programs.** Lists names, air times, and contact personnel of locally-produced television and radio shows.

❚20❚ **Wattage.** Applicable to radio stations, the wattage may differ for day and night in the case of AM stations. Occasionally a station's ERP (effective radiated power) is given in addition to, or instead of, actual licensed wattage.

❚21❚ **Ad Rates.** Includes rates for 10, 15, 30, and 60 seconds as provided by respondents. Some stations price advertisement spots "per unit" regardless of length; these units vary.

❚22❚ **Additional Contact Information.** Includes mailing, advertising, news, and studio addresses and phone numbers when different from the station, owner, or company address and phone numbers.

❚23❚ **Online.** If a radio station or cable company is accessible online via computer, that information is listed here. If the station or company is available online but the details of the URL (universal resource locator) or vendor are not known, the notation "Available Online" will be listed.

## Index Notes

Volumes 3 and 5 of the *Gale Directory of Publications and Broadcast Media* each feature a publishers index, referring to main section listings by entry number. Both volumes also include an index to subject terms, multiple subject indexes, and a master name and keyword index. These indexes refer to main section listings in Volumes 1 and 2 (U.S. and Canada) and Volume 5 (International) by entry number and geographic location. Volume 4 features a regional market index to all U.S. and Canadian listings, divided by publication or broadcast type. This index also refers back to main section listings in the first two volumes by entry number.

*Publishers Index* The Publishers Indexes in Volumes 3 (U.S. and Canada) and 5 (International) provide an alphabetical listing of the more than 25,000 publishers whose publications are listed in *GDPBM*. Entries in these indexes include publisher name, address, phone and fax numbers, and periodicals published. Multiple addresses for publishers are listed geographically by state, province, or country.

*Index to Subject Terms* The Index to Subject Terms is a consolidated alphabetical listing of the nearly 1,000 subject terms appearing in the Subject Indexes. Terms listed in this index are followed by page numbers in the appropriate subject index. Multiple page number citations indicate repeated uses of the terms. Additionally, "see" and "see also" references are provided.

**Subject Indexes** Seventeen indexes in Volume 3 (U.S. and Canada) and twelve indexes in Volume 5 (International) group listings by broad type or subject. These indexes have been arranged under several major categories with bleed tabs to facilitate use. Citations are presented in one of two formats:

- geographically, by states, provinces, and countries
- by subject, and within subject, geographically

Major categories are noted in the Table of Contents. Subcategories, shown as subheadings in the indexes, are listed alphabetically in the Index to Subject Terms.

Citations in the indexes refer to entry number, and for publications, provide circulation figures. (Circulation symbols are explained in footnotes on odd-numbered pages.) Additionally, the Daily Newspapers Indexes provide complete address and telephone information, and the College Publications Indexes include the names of issuing colleges and universities.

**Master Name and Keyword Index** The two Master Indexes provide comprehensive listings of all entries, both print and broadcast, included in Volumes 1 and 2 (U.S. and Canada) and Volume 5 (International) of *GDPBM*. Citations in these indexes are interfiled alphabetically throughout, regardless of media type.

Publication citations include the following:

- titles
- keywords within titles
- titles of cessations
- former titles
- foreign-language titles
- alternate titles

Broadcast media citations include the following:

- station call letters
- cable company names (U.S. and Canada)
- former call letters
- former cable company names (U.S. and Canada)
- radio, television, and cable company cessations

Indexing is word-by-word rather than letter-by-letter. Thus, "New York" is listed before "News." Current listings in the Index include geographic information and entry number. Former names, whether publication or broadcast, are indicated by an * and do not include a geographic designation.

**Regional Market Index** Volume 4 of the *Gale Directory of Publications and Broadcast Media (GDPBM)* features a regional market index, referring to main section entries in Volumes 1 and 2 (U.S. and Canada) by entry number. This index is divided into five sections:

- Newspaper Index
- Periodical Index
- Cable Index
- Radio Index
- Television Index

Each section is arranged geographically by region and then sorted by circulation, number of subscribing households, or Area of Dominant Influence (ADI). *[Note: Occasionally an ADI will appear under a region other than that listed. This is the result of an ADI designation which covers multiple neighboring states and will be represented multiple times.]* Newspaper and Periodical Index citations include publication title, entry number (given in parentheses immediately following the title), publisher name, address, phone and fax numbers, publication subject, and circulation figures. Cable Index citations include cable company name, entry number (given in parentheses immediately following the title), address, phone and fax numbers, cities served and number of subscribing households. Radio and Television Index citations include station call letters, entry number (given in parentheses immediately following the title), address, phone and fax numbers, and station format.

The regions have been defined as follows:

**Great Lakes States**

Illinois
Indiana
Michigan
Minnesota
Ohio
Wisconsin

**Great Plains States**

Iowa
Kansas
Missouri
Nebraska
North Dakota
South Dakota

**Middle Atlantic States**

Delaware
District of Columbia
Maryland
Virginia
West Virginia

**Northeastern States**

Connecticut
Maine
Massachusetts
New Hampshire
New Jersey
New York
Pennsylvania

Rhode Island
Vermont

### South Central States

Arkansas
Louisiana
Oklahoma
Texas
New Mexico

### Southern States

Alabama
Florida
Georgia
Kentucky
Mississippi
North Carolina
Puerto Rico
South Carolina
Tennessee

### Western States

Alaska
Arizona
California
Colorado
Hawaii

Idaho
Montana
Nevada
Oregon
Utah
Washington
Wyoming

### Central Canadian Provinces

Ontario
Manitoba
Saskatchewan

### Eastern Canadian Provinces

Newfoundland and Labrador
Prince Edward Island
Nova Scotia
New Brunswick
Quebec

### Northern Canadian Provinces

Northern Territories
Yukon Territories

### Western Canadian Provinces

British Columbia
Alberta

# Abbreviations

## Geographic Abbreviations

### U.S. State and Territory Postal Codes

| | |
|---|---|
| AK | Alaska |
| AL | Alabama |
| AR | Arkansas |
| AZ | Arizona |
| CA | California |
| CO | Colorado |
| CT | Connecticut |
| DC | District of Columbia |
| DE | Delaware |
| FL | Florida |
| GA | Georgia |
| HI | Hawaii |
| IA | Iowa |
| ID | Idaho |
| IL | Illinois |
| IN | Indiana |
| KS | Kansas |
| KY | Kentucky |
| LA | Louisiana |
| MA | Massachusetts |
| MD | Maryland |
| ME | Maine |
| MI | Michigan |
| MN | Minnesota |
| MO | Missouri |
| MS | Mississippi |
| MT | Montana |
| NC | North Carolina |
| ND | North Dakota |
| NE | Nebraska |
| NH | New Hampshire |
| NJ | New Jersey |
| NM | New Mexico |
| NV | Nevada |
| NY | New York |
| OH | Ohio |
| OK | Oklahoma |
| OR | Oregon |
| PA | Pennsylvania |
| PR | Puerto Rico |
| RI | Rhode Island |
| SC | South Carolina |
| SD | South Dakota |
| TN | Tennessee |
| TX | Texas |
| UT | Utah |
| VA | Virginia |
| VT | Vermont |
| WA | Washington |
| WI | Wisconsin |
| WV | West Virginia |
| WY | Wyoming |

### Canadian Province and Territory Postal Codes

| | |
|---|---|
| AB | Alberta |
| BC | British Columbia |
| MB | Manitoba |
| NB | New Brunswick |
| NL | Newfoundland and Labrador |
| NS | Nova Scotia |
| NT | Northwest Territories |
| ON | Ontario |
| PE | Prince Edward Island |
| QC | Quebec |
| SK | Saskatchewan |
| YT | Yukon Territory |

### Australian State and Territory Codes

| | |
|---|---|
| ACT | Australian Capitol Territory |
| NSW | New South Wales |
| NT | Northern Territory |
| QLD | Queensland |
| SA | South Australia |
| TAS | Tasmania |
| VIC | Victoria |
| WA | Western Australia |

### Chinese Province and Region Codes

| | |
|---|---|
| AN | Anhui |
| FJ | Fujian |
| GS | Gansu |
| GD | Guangdong |
| GZ | Guangxi Zhuangzu |
| GH | Guizhou |
| HB | Hebei |
| HL | Heilongjiang |
| HN | Henan |
| HU | Hubeu |
| HA | Hunan |
| JS | Jiangsu |
| JX | Jiangxi |
| JI | Jilin |
| LI | Liaoning |
| NM | Nei Monggol Zizhiqu |
| NH | Ningxia Huizu |
| QI | Qinghai |
| SH | Shaanxi |
| SD | Shandong |
| SX | Shanxi |
| SI | Sichuan |
| XU | Xinjiang Uygur Zizhigu |
| XZ | Xizang |
| YU | Yunnan |
| ZH | Zhejiang |

### Indian State and Territory Codes

| | |
|---|---|
| AN | Andaman and Nicobar |
| AP | Andhra Pradesh |
| AR | Arunachal Pradesh |
| AS | Assam |
| BH | Bihar |
| CH | Chandigarh |
| DN | Dadra and Nagar Haveli |
| DH | Delhi |
| GD | Goa Daman and Diu |
| GJ | Gujarat |
| HY | Haryana |
| HP | Himachal Pradesh |
| JK | Jammu and Kashmir |
| KA | Karnataka |
| KE | Kerala |
| LC | Laccadive Minicoy and Amindivi |
| MP | Madhya Pradesh |
| MH | Maharashtra |
| MN | Manipur |
| MG | Meghalaya |
| MZ | Mizoram |
| MY | Mysore |
| NG | Nagaland |

## ABBREVIATIONS

| | | | | | | | |
|---|---|---|---|---|---|---|---|
| OR | Orissa | | SP | San Luis Potosi | | CMB | Cambodia |
| PN | Pondicherry | | SN | Sinaloa | | CMR | Cameroon |
| PJ | Punjab | | SR | Sonora | | CYM | Cayman Islands |
| RJ | Rajasthan | | TB | Tabasco | | CHL | Chile |
| SK | Sikkim | | TM | Tamaulipas | | CHN | People's Republic of China |
| TN | Tamil Nadu | | TL | Tlaxcala | | COL | Colombia |
| TR | Tripura | | VC | Veracruz | | CRI | Costa Rica |
| UP | Uttar Pradesh | | YU | Yucatan | | COT | Cote d'Ivoire |
| WB | West Bengal (W. Bengal) | | ZA | Zacatecas | | CTA | Croatia |

### Irish County Codes

### Nigerian States

| | | | | | | | |
|---|---|---|---|---|---|---|---|
| | | | | | | CUB | Cuba |
| | | | | | | CYP | Cyprus |
| CV | Cavan | | AN | Anambra | | CZE | Czech Republic |
| CA | Carlow | | BA | Bauchi | | DEN | Denmark |
| CL | Clare | | BE | Bendel | | DMA | Dominica |
| CK | Cork | | BN | Benue | | DOM | Dominican Republic |
| DO | Donegal | | BR | Borno | | ECU | Ecuador |
| DU | Dublin | | CR | Cross River | | EGY | Egypt |
| GL | Galway | | GO | Gongola | | ELS | El Salvador |
| KR | Kerry | | IM | Imo | | EST | Estonia |
| KL | Kildare | | KD | Kaduna | | ETH | Ethiopia |
| KK | Kilkenny | | KN | Kano | | FAR | Faroe Islands |
| LA | Laoighis | | KW | Kwara | | FIJ | Fiji |
| LE | Leitrim | | LG | Lagos | | FIN | Finland |
| LI | Limerick | | NG | Niger | | FRA | France |
| LO | Longford | | OG | Ogun | | GAB | Gabon |
| LU | Louth | | ON | Ondo | | GBR | United Kingdom |
| MA | Mayo | | OY | Oyo | | GMB | Gambia |
| ME | Meath | | PL | Plateau | | GRG | Georgia |
| MO | Monaghan | | RV | Rivers | | GER | Germany |
| OF | Offaly | | SK | Sokoto | | GHA | Ghana |
| RO | Roscommon | | | | | GRC | Greece |
| SL | Sligo | | | | | GUM | Guam |

### Country Abbreviations

For England, Northern Ireland, Scotland, and Wales, please see United Kingdom (GBR).

| | | | | | | | |
|---|---|---|---|---|---|---|---|
| TP | Tipperary | | | | | GTM | Guatemala |
| WA | Waterford | | | | | GIN | Guinea |
| WE | Westmeath | | | | | GUY | Guyana |
| WX | Wexford | | ALB | Albania | | HND | Honduras |
| WI | Wicklow | | ALG | Algeria | | HKG | Hong Kong |
| | | | ANG | Angola | | HUN | Hungary |

### Mexican State Codes

| | | | | | | | |
|---|---|---|---|---|---|---|---|
| | | | AIA | Anguilla | | ICE | Iceland |
| AG | Aguascalientes | | ATG | Antigua-Barbuda | | IND | India |
| BN | Baja California Norte | | ARG | Argentina | | IDN | Indonesia |
| BS | Baja California Sur | | AMA | Armenia | | IRN | Iran |
| CM | Campeche | | AUS | Australia | | IRQ | Iraq |
| CP | Chiapas | | AUT | Austria | | IRL | Ireland |
| CH | Chihuahua | | AJN | Azerbaijan | | ISR | Israel |
| CO | Coahuila | | BHS | Bahamas | | ITA | Italy |
| CL | Colima | | BHR | Bahrain | | JAM | Jamaica |
| DF | Distritto Federal | | BGD | Bangladesh | | JPN | Japan |
| DU | Durango | | BRB | Barbados | | JOR | Jordan |
| GJ | Guanajuato | | BLR | Belarus | | KAZ | Kazakhstan |
| GU | Guerrero | | BEL | Belgium | | KEN | Kenya |
| HD | Hidalgo | | BLZ | Belize | | KGA | Kirgizstan |
| JA | Jalisco | | BEN | Benin | | KOR | Republic of Korea |
| ME | Mexico | | BMU | Bermuda | | KWT | Kuwait |
| MI | Michoacan | | BTN | Bhutan | | LAT | Latvia |
| MO | Morelos | | BOL | Bolivia | | LBN | Lebanon |
| NY | Nayarit | | HBO | Bosnia-Hercegovina | | LIT | Lithuania |
| NL | Nuevo Leon | | BWA | Botswana | | LUX | Luxembourg |
| OX | Oaxaca | | BRZ | Brazil | | MEC | Macedonia |
| PU | Puebla | | BUL | Bulgaria | | MWI | Malawi |
| QT | Queretaro | | BFA | Burkina Faso | | MYS | Malaysia |
| QR | Quintana Roo | | BDI | Burundi | | MDV | Maldives |

xviii     Gale Directory of Publications and Broadcast Media, 140th Edition

# ABBREVIATIONS

| | | | | | |
|---|---|---|---|---|---|
| MLI | Mali | URY | Uruguay | E. | East |
| MAL | Malta | UZN | Uzbekistan | EC | East Central |
| MUS | Mauritius | VAT | Vatican City | ENE | East Northeast |
| MEX | Mexico | VEN | Venezuela | ERP | Effective Radiated Power |
| MDI | Moldova | VNM | Vietnam | ESE | East Southeast |
| MCO | Monaco | BVI | British Virgin Islands | Eve. | Evening |
| MNG | Mongolia | VIR | Virgin Islands of the United States | Exec. | Executive |
| MON | Montenegro | | | Expy. | Expressway |
| MOR | Morocco | YEM | Yemen | Fed. | Federation |
| MOZ | Mozambique | ZMB | Zambia | Fl. | Floor |
| NAM | Namibia | ZWE | Zimbabwe | FM | Frequency Modulation |
| NPL | Nepal | | | FPO | Fleet Post Office |
| NLD | Netherlands | **Miscellaneous Abbreviations** | | Fri. | Friday |
| NAT | Netherlands Antilles | & | And | Fwy. | Freeway |
| NCL | New Caledonia | 4C | One-Time Four Color Page Rate | Gen. | General |
| NZL | New Zealand | | | GLR | General Line Rate |
| NCG | Nicaragua | ABC | Audit Bureau of Circulations | Hd. | Head |
| NER | Niger | Acad. | Academy | Hwy. | Highway |
| NGA | Nigeria | Act. | Acting | Inc. | Incorporated |
| NOR | Norway | Adm. | Administrative, Administration | Info. | Information |
| OMN | Oman | Admin. | Administrator | Inst. | Institute |
| PAK | Pakistan | AFB | Air Force Base | Intl. | International |
| PAN | Panama | AM | Amplitude Modulation | ISSN | International Standard Serial Number |
| PNG | Papua New Guinea | Amer. | American | | |
| PER | Peru | APO | Army Post Office | Jr. | Junior |
| PHL | Philippines | Apt. | Apartment | Libn. | Librarian |
| POL | Poland | Assn. | Association | Ln. | Lane |
| PRT | Portugal | Assoc. | Associate | Ltd. | Limited |
| ROM | Romania | Asst. | Assistant | Mgr. | Manager |
| RUS | Russia | Ave. | Avenue | mi. | miles |
| RWA | Rwanda | Bldg. | Building | Mktg. | Marketing |
| SLC | St. Lucia | Blvd. | Boulevard | Mng. | Managing |
| SAU | Saudi Arabia | boul. | boulevard | Mon. | Monday |
| SEN | Senegal | BPA | Business Publications Audit of Circulations | Morn. | Morning |
| SER | Serbia | | | N. | North |
| SYC | Seychelles | BTA | Best Time Available | NAS | Naval Air Station |
| SLE | Sierra Leone | BW | One-time Black & White Page Rate | Natl. | National |
| SGP | Singapore | | | NC | North Central |
| SLK | Slovakia | C | Central | NE | Northeast |
| SVA | Slovenia | CAC | Certified Audit of Circulations | NNE | North Northeast |
| SLM | Solomon Islands | CCAB | Canadian Circulations Audit Board | NNW | North Northwest |
| SAF | Republic of South Africa | | | No. | Number |
| SPA | Spain | CEO | Chief Executive Officer | NW | Northwest |
| SRI | Sri Lanka | Chm. | Chairman | Orgn. | Organization |
| SDN | Sudan | Chwm. | Chairwoman | PCI | Per Column Inch Rate |
| SWZ | Swaziland | CNU | Canadian Newspaper Advertising Unit Rate | Pkwy. | Parkway |
| SWE | Sweden | | | Pl. | Place |
| SWI | Switzerland | c/o | Care of | PO | Post Office |
| SYR | Syrian Arab Republic | Col. | Column | Pres. | President |
| TWN | Taiwan | Coll. | College | Prof. | Professor |
| TDN | Tajikistan | Comm. | Committee | Rd. | Road |
| TZA | United Republic of Tanzania | Co. | Company | RFD | Rural Free Delivery |
| THA | Thailand | COO | Chief Operating Officer | Rm. | Room |
| TGO | Togo | Coord. | Coordinator | ROS | Run of Schedule |
| TGA | Tonga | Corp. | Corporation | RR | Rural Route |
| TTO | Trinidad and Tobago | Coun. | Council | Rte. | Route |
| TUN | Tunisia | CP | case postale | S. | South |
| TUR | Turkey | Ct. | Court | Sat. | Saturday |
| UGA | Uganda | Dept. | Department | SAU | Standard Advertising Unit Rate |
| URE | Ukraine | Dir. | Director | | |
| UAE | United Arab Emirates | Div. | Division | SC | South Central |
| GBR | United Kingdom | Dr. | Doctor, Drive | SE | Southeast |

## ABBREVIATIONS

| | | | | | |
|---|---|---|---|---|---|
| Sec. | Secretary | Supt. | Superintendent | VAC | Verified Audit Circulation |
| Soc. | Society | SW | Southwest | VP | Vice President |
| Sq. | Square | Terr. | Terrace | W. | West |
| Sr. | Senior | Thurs. | Thursday | WC | West Central |
| SSE | South Southeast | Tpke. | Turnpike | Wed. | Wednesday |
| SSW | South Southwest | Treas. | Treasurer | WNW | West Northwest |
| St. | Saint, Street | Tues. | Tuesday | WSW | West Southwest |
| Sta. | Station | Univ. | University | x/month | Times per Month |
| Ste. | Sainte, Suite | USPS | United States Publications Serial | x/week | Times per Week |
| Sun. | Sunday | | | x/year | Times per Year |

# Industry Activity

*An alphabetical listing of newly added and recently defunct media outlets. New listings precede cessations, and International citations follow those of the United States and Canada in each instance.*

## New Listings

### United States and Canada

L'actualite (Montreal, QC)
The A.A. Grapevine (La Vina) (Bakersfield, CA)
AACN Clinical Issues (Baltimore, MD)
abilities (Toronto, ON)
aboriginaltimes (Calgary, AB)
About Campus (Oxford, OH)
Abstracts in Hematology & Oncology (Manhasset, NY)
Academic Emergency Medicine (Lansing, MI)
Academic Medicine (Baltimore, MD)
Academic Radiology (Philadelphia, PA)
Academy of Florida Trial Lawyers Journal (Tallahassee, FL)
ACC Current Journal Review (Ann Arbor, MI)
The Access Project (Saint Louis, MO)
Accident & Emergency Nursing (Saint Louis, MO)
Accountability in Research (Baltimore, MD)
Accounting and Finance (Malden, MA)
ACM Transactions on Algorithms (Boulder, CO)
ACM Transactions on Applied Perception (Orlando, FL)
ACM Transactions on Architecture and Code Optimization (New York, NY)
ACM Transactions on Design Automation of Electronic Systems (Irvine, CA)
ACM Transactions on Embedded Computer Systems (Princeton, NJ)
ACM Transactions on Internet Technology (New York, NY)
ACM Transactions on Multimedia Computing, Communications and Applications (Ottawa, ON)
ACM Transactions on Sensor Networks (Redmond, WA)
ACM Transactions on Speech and Language Processing (Yorktown Heights, NY)
ACM Transactions on Storage (Sunnyvale, CA)
Acta Agriculturae Scandinavica – Section A, Animal Science (Philadelphia, PA)
Acta Agriculturae Scandinavica – Section B, Soil and Plant Science (Philadelphia, PA)
Acta Biochemica et Biophysica Sinica (Malden, MA)
Acta Borealia (Philadelphia, PA)
Acta Oto-Laryngologica (Philadelphia, PA)
Acta Pharmacologica Sinica (Malden, MA)
Acta Physiologica Scandinavica (Malden, MA)
Action Martial Arts (Calgary, AB)
Action Research (Thousand Oaks, CA)
Active Learning in Higher Education (Thousand Oaks, CA)
Acute Pain (Saint Louis, MO)
Adaptive Behavior (Thousand Oaks, CA)
Adbusters Magazine (Vancouver, BC)
Addiction Biology (Bethesda, MD)
Addictive Behaviors (Saint Louis, MO)
Additions and Decks (New York, NY)
Adhesives and Sealants Industry (Lapeer, MI)
Administrative Law Review (Washington, DC)
Adolescent Medicine Clinics (Saint Louis, MO)
Adult Education Quarterly (Athens, GA)
Advance for Audiologists (King of Prussia, PA)
Advance for Healthy Aging (King of Prussia, PA)
Advance for Imaging and Oncology Administrators (King of Prussia, PA)
Advance for LPNs (King of Prussia, PA)
Advance Magazine (Cincinnati, OH)
Advanced Engineering Materials (Hoboken, NJ)
Advanced Materials (Hoboken, NJ)
The AdvanceNews (Langley, BC)
Advances in Anesthesia (Saint Louis, MO)
Advances in Chronic Kidney Disease (Saint Louis, MO)
Advances in Dermatology (Saint Louis, MO)
Advances in Developing Human Resources (Thousand Oaks, CA)
Advances in Neonatal Care (Saint Louis, MO)
Advances in Nursing Science (Baltimore, MD)
Advances in Pediatrics (Saint Louis, MO)
Advances in Small Animal Medicine & Therapy (Saint Louis, MO)
Advances in Speech-Language Pathology (Philadelphia, PA)
Advances in Surgery (Saint Louis, MO)
Advances in Vascular Surgery (Saint Louis, MO)
Advancing Philanthropy (Orleans, ON)
Adventure Kayak Magazine (Palmer Rapids, ON)
Advisor's Edge (Toronto, ON)
The Advocate (Syracuse, NY)
Adweek's Marketing y Medios (New York, NY)
Aerosol Science and Technology (Pasadena, CA)
Ageing Research Reviews (Saint Louis, MO)
Aggression and Violent Behavior (Saint Louis, MO)
Aging Cell (Providence, RI)
Agricultural Economics (Malden, MA)
The AIDS Reader (Manhasset, NY)
Alabama Sheriffs' Star (Montgomery, AL)

## INDUSTRY ACTIVITY

Alaska Quarterly Review (Fairbanks, AK)
Alberta Golf (Burnaby, BC)
Alberta History (Calgary, AB)
AlbertaViews (Calgary, AB)
Alcohol (Omaha, NE)
Alexandria Lakes Area Visitor Guide (Alexandria, MN)
Alimentary Pharmacology and Therapeutics (Malden, MA)
Along the Saucony (Kutztown, PA)
Alzheimer's Care Quarterly (Baltimore, MD)
Amateur Gardening (New York, NY)
Amateur Photographer (New York, NY)
AMBUCS (Audubon, PA)
Ambulatory Surgery (Boston, MA)
AMC Guide to Outdoor Adventures (Boston, MA)
American Big Twin Dealer (Cleveland, OH)
American Business Law Journal (Malden, MA)
The American Dowser (San Lorenzo, CA)
American Heart Journal (Saint Louis, MO)
American History (Leesburg, VA)
American Institute of Chemical Engineers Journal (Hoboken, NJ)
American Jewish History (Baltimore, MD)
American Journal of Cardiology (Dallas, TX)
American Journal of Distance Education (University Park, PA)
The American Journal of Drug and Alcohol Abuse (Philadelphia, PA)
American Journal of Economics and Sociology (Malden, MA)
American Journal of Emergency Medicine (Saint Louis, MO)
American Journal of Evaluation (Thousand Oaks, CA)
American Journal of Hypertension (Saint Louis, MO)
American Journal of Medical Quality (Thousand Oaks, CA)
American Journal of Medicine (Tucson, AZ)
American Journal of Nursing (Baltimore, MD)
American Journal of Ophthalmology (Jacksonville, FL)
American Journal of Otolaryngology (Saint Louis, MO)
American Journal of Political Science (Malden, MA)
American Journal of Preventative Medicine (La Jolla, CA)

American Journal of Psychiatric Rehabilitation (Evanston, IL)
American Journal of Reproductive Immunology (Malden, MA)
American Journal of Sexuality Education (Binghamton, NY)
The American Journal of Sports Medicine (Rosemont, IL)
The American Journal of Surgery (Louisville, KY)
American Journal of Therapeutics (Baltimore, MD)
American Journal of Transplantation (Edmonton, AB)
American Law and Economics Review (Chicago, IL)
The American Organist (Livonia, MI)
The American Organist (Pittsford, NY)
The American Organist (Zion, IL)
The American Organist (published by AGO National) (Wilmington, NC)
American Organists (Washington, DC)
American Snowmobiler (Waukesha, WI)
The American Surgeon (Atlanta, GA)
The American Wanderer (North Mankato, MN)
The American Wanderer (Ambler, PA)
The American Wanderer (Yachats, OR)
America's Civil War (Leesburg, VA)
Amusement Business (Los Angeles, CA)
Amyloid: The Journal of Protein Folding Disorders (Philadelphia, PA)
Amyotrophic Lateral Sclerosis and Other Motor Neuron Disorders (Philadelphia, PA)
Analyses of Social Issues and Public Policy (Waltham, MA)
Analysis (Malden, MA)
Analysis of Social Issues and Public Policy (Washington, DC)
Analytical Letters (Philadelphia, PA)
Anatomical Science International (Malden, MA)
Ancient Biomolecules (Philadelphia, PA)
Anesthesiology Clinics of North America (Saint Louis, MO)
Angewandte Chemie (Hoboken, NJ)
Angewandte Chemie International Edition (Hoboken, NJ)
Animal Biotechnology (New York, NY)
Animal Biotechnology (Urbana, IL)
Animal Feed Science and Technology (Davis, CA)
Animal Genetics (Logan, UT)
Animal Science Journal (Malden, MA)
ANJEC Report (Mendham, NJ)
Annalen der Physik (Hoboken, NJ)

Annals of Behavioral Medicine (Mahwah, NJ)
Annals of Clinical Psychiatry (Iowa City, IA)
Annals of Diagnostic Pathology (Saint Louis, MO)
Annals of Epidemiology (Saint Louis, MO)
Annals of Noninvasive Electrocardiology (Rochester, NY)
Annals of Public and Cooperative Economics (Malden, MA)
Annals and Recollections (Rome, NY)
Annals of Thoracic Surgery (Philadelphia, PA)
Annual Bulletin of Historical Literature (Malden, MA)
Annual Buyers Guide (Stafford, CT)
Annual Program (El Paso, TX)
Annual Report (Roanoke, VA)
Annual Report (Santa Fe, NM)
Anthropological Theory (Thousand Oaks, CA)
Anthropology News (Arlington, VA)
Anthropology of Work Review (Berkeley, CA)
Anti-Cancer Drugs (Baltimore, MD)
Antioch Review (Waukegan, IL)
Antipode: A Radical Journal of Geography (Malden, MA)
Antique Review (Dubuque, IA)
Antitrust Law Journal (West Redding, CT)
Antitrust Law Magazine (Redding, CT)
Anxiety, Stress and Coping (Indiana, PA)
AOJT News (Brooklyn, NY)
Apartment Guide (Metairie, LA)
APLAR Journal of Rheumatology (Malden, MA)
Appalachia Journal (Boston, MA)
Appeal Magazine (Burnaby, BC)
Appliance Design (Troy, MI)
Applicable Analysis (Newark, DE)
Applied Animal Behaviour Science (Saint Louis, MO)
Applied Clinical Trials (Cleveland, OH)
Applied Environmental Education and Communication (Charlottesville, VA)
Applied Linguistics (Honolulu, HI)
Applied Neurology (New York, NY)
Applied Nursing Research (Berea, KY)
Applied Psychological Measurement (Thousand Oaks, CA)
Applied Psychology (Malden, MA)
Applied Radiation and Isotopes (Saint Louis, MO)
Applied Spectroscopy (Erie, PA)

# INDUSTRY ACTIVITY

apply (Bellevue, NE)
Aquaculture Research (Hagerman, ID)
Aquatic Ecosystem Health & Management (Burlington, ON)
Aramaic Studies (Thousand Oaks, CA)
Arc (Ottawa, ON)
Arcadia Weekly (Arcadia, CA)
Arch (Calgary, AB)
Archaeoastronomy (Austin, TX)
Archeological Papers of the AAA (Berkeley, CA)
Archetype (West Sacramento, CA)
Architecture (New York, NY)
Archiv der Pharmazie (Hoboken, NJ)
Archives of Agronomy and Soil Science (Philadelphia, PA)
Archives of Physiology and Biochemistry (Philadelphia, PA)
Archives of Phytopathology and Plant Protection (Philadelphia, PA)
Archives of Psychiatric Nursing (Saint Louis, MO)
Archives of Suicide Research (Windsor, ON)
Area (Malden, MA)
The Argonaut (San Francisco, CA)
Argus (West Paterson, NJ)
The Aristotelian Society Supplementary Volume (Malden, MA)
Arizona Food Industry (Phoenix, AZ)
Arizona Grocer (Phoenix, AZ)
Arizona Parks and Recreation (Phoenix, AZ)
Arizona Pharmacist (Tempe, AZ)
Armed Forces and Society (Thousand Oaks, CA)
The Art Book (Malden, MA)
Art History (Malden, MA)
Art Jewelry (Waukesha, WI)
Arteriosclerosis, Thrombosis, and Vascular Biology (Baltimore, MD)
Arthritis Awareness (Philadelphia, PA)
Arthritis Today (Beachwood, OH)
Arthritis Today - National Magazine (Indianapolis, IN)
Artificial Cells, Blood Substitutes, and Biotechnology (Montreal, QC)
Artificial Intelligence in Medicine (Saint Louis, MO)
Artificial Life (Portland, OR)
Artificial Organs: Replacement, Recovery, and Regeneration (Malden, MA)
Arts (Marysville, CA)
Arts Alive (Idaho Falls, ID)
Arts and Humanities in Higher Education (Thousand Oaks, CA)
Ashe (West Jefferson, NC)

Asia Pacific Journal of Human Resources (Thousand Oaks, CA)
Asia Pacific Viewpoint (Malden, MA)
Asian Economic Journal (Malden, MA)
Asian Economic Papers (Davis, CA)
Asian Journal of Andrology (Malden, MA)
Asian Journal of Management Cases (Thousand Oaks, CA)
Asian Journal of Social Psychology (Malden, MA)
Asian-Pacific Economic Literature (Malden, MA)
Asian SUNews (Phoenix, AZ)
Asian Survey (Oakland, CA)
Asphalt Contractor (Fort Atkinson, WI)
ASSEMBLY Magazine (Bensenville, IL)
Assessment (Thousand Oaks, CA)
Assessment Update (Indianapolis, IN)
Association Connection (Nashville, TN)
Association Source (Tallahassee, FL)
Asthma Journal (Saint Louis, MO)
The Astrophysical Journal (Tucson, AZ)
ATEA Journal (Wahpeton, ND)
ATLA Docket (Little Rock, AR)
Atlantic Journal of Communication (Madison, NJ)
Atlas of the Hand Clinics (Saint Louis, MO)
Atlas of the Oral & Maxillofacial Surgery Clinics of North America (Saint Louis, MO)
Atmosphere-Ocean (Ottawa, ON)
ATN (Appalachian Trailway News) (Blacksburg, VA)
ATPE News (Austin, TX)
ATV Rider (Los Angeles, CA)
Auburn Works (Auburn, WA)
Audio Ideas Guide (King City, ON)
Audiological Medicine (Philadelphia, PA)
Augmentative & Alternative Communication (Vancouver, BC)
Australasian Journal on Ageing (Malden, MA)
Australasian Journal of Dermatology (Malden, MA)
Australasian Psychiatry (Malden, MA)
Australasian Radiology (Malden, MA)
Australian Economic Papers (Malden, MA)
The Australian Economic Review (Malden, MA)
The Australian Journal of Agriculture and Resource Economics (Malden, MA)
Australian Journal of Earth Sciences (Malden, MA)
Australian Journal of Entomology (Malden, MA)

Australian Journal of Politics & History (Malden, MA)
Australian Journal of Psychology (Philadelphia, PA)
Australian Journal of Public Administration (Malden, MA)
Australian Journal of Rural Health (Malden, MA)
The Australian and New Zealand Journal of Obstetrics and Gynecology (Malden, MA)
Australian and New Zealand Journal of Psychiatry (Malden, MA)
Australian Psychologist (Philadelphia, PA)
Australian Social Work (Malden, MA)
Autism (Thousand Oaks, CA)
Auto Trader Magazine (Saint Catharines, ON)
Autoimmunity (Philadelphia, PA)
Autoimmunity (Irvine, CA)
Automotive Body Repair News (Cleveland, OH)
avenue (Calgary, AB)
AvenueWest (Calgary, AB)
Avian Pathology (Philadelphia, PA)
Aviation History (Leesburg, VA)
AzGS Journal (Phoenix, AZ)
Azusa/Irwindale Neighborhood News (Walnut, CA)
Back Stage (New York, NY)
Backbone (North Vancouver, BC)
Baldwin Park Neighborhood News (Walnut, CA)
B&C (New York, NY)
Bank Systems & Technology (New York, NY)
Banking and Financial Services Policy Report (Frederick, MD)
Bar Briefs (Mount Clemens, MI)
Bar Leader (Chicago, IL)
Barnlakaren (Philadelphia, PA)
Bartow Neighbor (Marietta, GA)
The Basenji (New Lenox, IL)
Basin Research (Malden, MA)
Bass Guide (Baxter, MN)
Batesville Herald-Tribune (Batesville, IN)
Bauen mit Textilien (Hoboken, NJ)
BC Home (Burnaby, BC)
Beaches Leader (Jacksonville Beach, FL)
Beadstyle (Waukesha, WI)
The Bean Bag (Scottsbluff, NE)
Becoming (Atlanta, GA)
BEEF (Overland Park, KS)
Behavioral and Cognitive Neuroscience Reviews (Thousand Oaks, CA)

## INDUSTRY ACTIVITY

Behavioral Sleep Medicine (Tuscaloosa, AL)
Behavioural Neurology (Baltimore, MD)
Behavioural Pharmacology (Baltimore, MD)
The Bel-Air View (Los Angeles, CA)
Bell Gardens Sun (Commerce, CA)
Bell Labs Technical Journal (Murray Hill, NJ)
Bellevue Visitor's Guide (Bellevue, NE)
Bellflower/Downey Post (Los Angeles, CA)
Benton County Pioneer (Bentonville, AR)
Bergen County Economic Development Book (Paramus, NJ)
Best Ideas for Christmas (New York, NY)
Best Read Guide Amarillo (Amarillo, TX)
Best Read Guide Branson (Branson, MO)
Best Read Guide Cape Cod (South Dennis, MA)
Best Read Guide Charleston (Augusta, GA)
Best Read Guide Clearwater, Tampa Bay, St. Pete (Augusta, GA)
Best Read Guide Daytona Beach (Augusta, GA)
Best Read Guide Hilton Head (Augusta, GA)
Best Read Guide Kentucky (Augusta, GA)
Best Read Guide Las Vegas (Augusta, GA)
Best Read Guide London (Augusta, GA)
Best Read Guide Martha's Vineyard (Edgartown, MA)
Best Read Guide New Hampshire (Augusta, GA)
Best Read Guide Newport (Newport, RI)
Best Read Guide St. Augustine (Augusta, GA)
Best Read Guide San Antonio (Augusta, GA)
Best Read Guide Savannah (Savannah, GA)
Best Read Guide Smoky Mountains (Augusta, GA)
Best Read Guide Southern Maine (Augusta, GA)
Bibliographic Index (Bronx, NY)
Bicycle Event Calendar (Indianapolis, IN)
Big Walnut News (Columbus, OH)
Bike (Dana Point, CA)
Billboard (New York, NY)
Billboard Radio Monitor (New York, NY)
Biocontrol Science and Technology (Lethbridge, AB)
Bioethics (Malden, MA)
Biological Journal of the Linnean Society (Malden, MA)
Biological Psychiatry (New York, NY)
Biological Psychology (Saint Louis, MO)
Biological Research for Nursing (Thousand Oaks, CA)
Biological Rhythm Research (Philadelphia, PA)
Biologie in unserer Zeit (Hoboken, NJ)
Biology of Blood and Marrow Transplantation (Saint Louis, MO)
BioMechanics (San Francisco, CA)
Biomedicine & Pharmacotherapy (Saint Louis, MO)
Biometrics (Malden, MA)
BioPharm International (Cleveland, OH)
Biophysical Neural Networks (Larchmont, NY)
Bioremediation Journal (Houston, TX)
Biorheology (Montreal, QC)
BIOS (Milwaukee, WI)
BioScience Technology (Rockaway, NJ)
Biosecurity and Bioterrorism (Larchmont, NY)
Biostatistics (Baltimore, MD)
Biotechnic and Histochemistry (Philadelphia, PA)
Biotropica (Malden, MA)
Biotropica (Storrs, CT)
Bipolar Disorders (Malden, MA)
Bird Keeper (New York, NY)
Birmingham Magazine (Birmingham, AL)
Birth (Malden, MA)
Birth Defects Research (Hoboken, NJ)
BJOG (Malden, MA)
BJU International (Malden, MA)
BlackFlash (Saskatoon, SK)
Blair Business Mirror (Altoona, PA)
Blood and Aphorisms (Toronto, ON)
Blood Coagulation and Fibrinolysis (Baltimore, MD)
Blood Pressure Monitoring (Baltimore, MD)
Blood Reviews (Saint Louis, MO)
Bluefield Daily Telegraph (Bluefield, WV)
Bluegrass Roots (Frankfort, KY)
Blues News (Walla Walla, WA)
Board Leadership (Hoboken, NJ)
The Boathouse (Deephaven, MN)
BoatWorks for the Hands-On Sailor (Boston, MA)
Body and Society (Thousand Oaks, CA)
Bone (New Haven, CT)
Book History (Baltimore, MD)
Boston-Panorama Magazine (Boston, MA)
Botanical Journal of the Linnean Society (Malden, MA)
Bowhunter (Harrisburg, PA)
Bowling Green (Bowling Green, KY)
Brachytherapy (New York, NY)
Brain, Behavior, and Evolution (Austin, TX)
Brain & Development (Saint Louis, MO)
Brandweek (New York, NY)
The Breast (Saint Louis, MO)
The Breast Journal (Jacksonville, FL)
The Bridge (Bridgehampton, NY)
Bridge Structures: Assessment, Design and Construction (Philadelphia, PA)
Brighter Horizons (Baytown, TX)
British Journal of Clinical Pharmacology (Malden, MA)
British Journal of Dermatology (Malden, MA)
British Journal of Educational Studies (Malden, MA)
British Journal of Educational Technology (Malden, MA)
British Journal of Haematology (Malden, MA)
British Journal of Industrial Relations (Malden, MA)
British Journal of Learning Disabilities (Malden, MA)
British Journal of Management (Malden, MA)
British Journal of Neurosurgery (Philadelphia, PA)
British Journal of Plastic Surgery (Saint Louis, MO)
The British Journal of Politics & International Relations (Malden, MA)
The British Journal of Sociology (Malden, MA)
British Journal of Special Education (Malden, MA)
British Journal of Surgery (Hoboken, NJ)
British Journal of Visual Impairment (Thousand Oaks, CA)
British Journalism Review (Thousand Oaks, CA)
British Poultry Abstracts (Philadelphia, PA)
The Broomfielder (Broomfield, CO)
Brownsville Magazine (Brownsville, TN)
Buck Fax (Dryden, MI)
The Buckeye (Westerville, OH)
BuilderMart Magazine (Baltimore, MD)
The Bulletin (Des Moines, IA)
The Bulletin (Princeton, NJ)
Bulletin d'Information (New York, NY)
Bulletin of Economic Research (Malden, MA)

# INDUSTRY ACTIVITY

Bulletin of Latin American Research (Malden, MA)
The Bulletin of MDHA (Okemos, MI)
Bulletin of Science, Technology and Society (Thousand Oaks, CA)
Bulletin of Volcanology (Montreal, QC)
Burbank Business Journal (Burbank, CA)
Burlingame Daily News (San Mateo, CA)
Burlington, Discover the Treasures (Burlington, WI)
Burnaby NewsLeader (Burnaby, BC)
Burnt toast (Ottawa, ON)
Business (Pico Rivera, CA)
Business to Business (Palm Desert, CA)
Business and Community Guide (Port Saint Lucie, FL)
Business Connection (Taylor, MI)
Business Directory (Bath, NY)
Business Ethics: A European Review (Malden, MA)
Business Focus (Whittier, CA)
Business Information Reviews (Thousand Oaks, CA)
Business Magazine (Albany, GA)
Business Network (Bloomington, IN)
Business News Quarterly (Rock Island, IL)
Business and Professional Directory (Bellmore, NY)
Business and Society Review (Malden, MA)
Business Strategy Review (Malden, MA)
Business Trends (London, ON)
Business 2.0 (New York, NY)
Business Wise (New Bern, NC)
Businessmatters (Wausau, WI)
Buyers Guide (Salt Lake City, UT)
C/C+ Users Journal (San Mateo, CA)
CA Grange News (Sacramento, CA)
Cage & Aviary Birds (New York, NY)
Calendar of Events (Hawley, PA)
Calgary Magazine (Calgary, AB)
Calgary's Child (Calgary, AB)
California Compatriot (Milpitas, CA)
California Country (Madera, CA)
California Enrolled Agent (Sacramento, CA)
California Garden Magazine (San Diego, CA)
The California-Hawaii Elk (Fresno, CA)
The California Parent Educator (Norwalk, CA)
The California Psychologist (Sacramento, CA)
The California School Psychologist (Sacramento, CA)

The California Tomato Grower (Stockton, CA)
Callaloo (College Station, TX)
Camden Co. Tribune & Georgian (Saint Marys, GA)
Camera Obscura (Santa Barbara, CA)
CanaData Construction Starts (Markham, ON)
Canadian Acoustics (Ottawa, ON)
Canadian Aviator (Vancouver, BC)
Canadian Children's Book News (Toronto, ON)
Canadian Children's Literature (Guelph, ON)
Canadian Classics (O'Leary, PE)
Canadian Contractor (Toronto, ON)
Canadian Cowboy Country (Edmonton, AB)
Canadian Criminal Law Review (Toronto, ON)
The Canadian Geographer/Le Geographie canadien (Malden, MA)
Canadian Healthcare Manager (Toronto, ON)
Canadian Homes and Cottages (Mississauga, ON)
Canadian Investment Review (Toronto, ON)
Canadian Journal of Administrative Law and Practice (Toronto, ON)
The Canadian Journal on Aging/Le Revue Canadienne du Vieillissement (Kingston, ON)
Canadian Journal of Agricultural Economics (Ottawa, ON)
Canadian Journal of Agricultural Economics (Malden, MA)
Canadian Journal of Criminology and Criminal Justice (Ottawa, ON)
The Canadian Journal of Film Studies (Kingston, ON)
Canadian Journal of Information and Library Science (London, ON)
Canadian Journal of Law and Society (Montreal, QC)
Canadian Journal of Marketing Research (North York, ON)
Canadian Journal of Mathematics (Vancouver, BC)
Canadian Journal of Netherlandic Studies (Delta, BC)
Canadian Journal of Program Evaluation (Ottawa, ON)
Canadian Journal of Science, Mathematics and Technology Education (Toronto, ON)
Canadian Journal of Women and the Law/Revue femmes et dro (Toronto, ON)

Canadian Meat Goat (Lancaster, ON)
Canadian Notes and Queries (Erin, ON)
The Canadian Philatelist (Toronto, ON)
Canadian Printer (Toronto, ON)
Canadian Review of American Studies (Ottawa, ON)
Canadian Screenwriter (Toronto, ON)
Canadian Sports Collector (Saint Catharines, ON)
Canadian Stories (Sweetser, IN)
Canadian Teddy Bear News (Water Valley, AB)
Canadian Woodworking Magazine (Burford, ON)
Cancer (Hoboken, NJ)
Cancer (Atlanta, GA)
Cancer Detection and Prevention (Worcester, MA)
Cancer Genetics and Cytogenetics (Phoenix, AZ)
Cancer Science (Malden, MA)
Canoe and Kayak (Kirkland, WA)
Canoeroots Magazine (Palmer Rapids, ON)
CanPlay (Toronto, ON)
The Canyon Courier (Evergreen, CO)
Cardiology Clinics (Saint Louis, MO)
Cardiology in Review (Baltimore, MD)
Cardiovascular Pathology (Toronto, ON)
Cardiovascular Radiation Medicine (Washington, DC)
Carolina Forestry Journal (Columbia, SC)
Carolinas Contacts (Charlotte, NC)
carousel (Guelph, ON)
Cascade Magazine (Denver, CO)
Cashiers Crossroads Chronicle (Athens, GA)
Casual Living (Greensboro, NC)
Catalysis Reviews (New York, NY)
Catalysis Reviews: Science and Engineering (Philadelphia, PA)
CatComm Journal (Washington, DC)
Catfish In-Sider Guide (Baxter, MN)
Catheterization and Cardiovascular Interventions (New Orleans, LA)
Catholic Family News (Niagara Falls, NY)
CDA Journal (Sacramento, CA)
Cell Communication and Adhesion (Bethesda, MD)
Cellular Microbiology (Berkeley, CA)
Cement Americas (Overland Park, KS)
Centaurus (Malden, MA)
Center of Tomorrow (Sterling, VA)
Central Nevada's Glorious Past (Tonopah, NV)
Century Limited (Rochester, NY)

## INDUSTRY ACTIVITY

Ceramic Industry (Powell, OH)
Cerebral Cortex (New Haven, CT)
Cerokee Tribune (Canton, GA)
Chalk and Cue (Mississauga, ON)
Chamber Digest (Southaven, MS)
The Chamber Guide (Palatine, IL)
Chamber Magazine (Rosenberg, TX)
Chamber Page in the Versailles Republican (Versailles, IN)
Chamber Review (Davison, MI)
Chamber Voice (Donaldsonville, LA)
Chamberletter (Hopkinsville, KY)
Chatter Box Luncheon Digest (Saint Catharines, ON)
The Chaucer Review (Baltimore, MD)
CheckUP (Calgary, AB)
ChemBioChem (Hoboken, NJ)
Chemical Engineering Communications (Troy, NY)
Chemical Engineering and Technology (Hoboken, NJ)
The Chemical Record (New York, NY)
Chemical Senses (Saint Augustine, FL)
Chemie-Ingenieur-Technik (Hoboken, NJ)
Chemie in unserer Zeit (Hoboken, NJ)
Cheminformatics (Troy, NY)
Chemistry - A European Journal (Hoboken, NJ)
Chemistry and Biodiversity (Hoboken, NJ)
ChemPhysChem (Hoboken, NJ)
Chest Surgery Clinics (Saint Louis, MO)
The Chesterton Review (Wilmington, DE)
The Chickasha Express Star (Chickasha, OK)
Child and Adolescent Mental Health (Malden, MA)
Child & Adolescent Psychiatric Clinics (Saint Louis, MO)
Child Development (Malden, MA)
Child Maltreatment (Detroit, MI)
Childhood (Thousand Oaks, CA)
Chinese Journal of Digestive Diseases (Malden, MA)
Christian Higher Education (Denton, TX)
Christian Mission (Fort Erie, ON)
Christmas Crafts (New York, NY)
Chronicles of Smith County, Texas (Tyler, TX)
Chronobiology International (Houston, TX)
Cincy Business Magazine (Cleveland, OH)
Cinema Scope (Toronto, ON)
Circuits, Systems & Signal Processing (Montreal, QC)
CITATIONS (Ventura, CA)

City Cyclist (New York, NY)
City Eagle (Syracuse, NY)
City Palate (Calgary, AB)
City & Society (Saint Cloud, MN)
CityArt (Toronto, ON)
Civil Engineering and Environmental Systems (Philadelphia, PA)
Civil War Times (Leesburg, VA)
Cladistics (New York, NY)
Claremore Progress (Claremore, OK)
Classic Boat (New York, NY)
Classical World (New York, NY)
The Classroom Teacher (Austin, TX)
Clean Energy Living (Austin, TX)
Climacteric (Philadelphia, PA)
Climbing (Carbondale, CO)
Clinical Acupuncture and Oriental Medicine (Saint Louis, MO)
Clinical and Applied Immunology Reviews (Chicago, IL)
Clinical Case Studies (Thousand Oaks, CA)
Clinical Child Psychology and Psychiatry (Thousand Oaks, CA)
Clinical Chiropractic (Saint Louis, MO)
Clinical & Developmental Immunology (Philadelphia, PA)
Clinical Dysmorphology (Baltimore, MD)
Clinical Effectiveness in Nursing (Saint Louis, MO)
Clinical Endocrinology (Malden, MA)
Clinical and Experimental Opthalmology (Malden, MA)
Clinical and Experimental Pharmacology and Physiology (Malden, MA)
Clinical Gastroenterology and Hepatology (Saint Louis, MO)
Clinical Genetics (Vancouver, BC)
Clinical Imaging (Saint Louis, MO)
Clinical Intensive Care (Philadelphia, PA)
Clinical Journal of Women's Health (Saint Louis, MO)
Clinical and Laboratory Haematology (Malden, MA)
Clinical Microbiology and Infection (Malden, MA)
Clinical Neurophysiology (Bethesda, MD)
Clinical Neuroscience Research (Irvine, CA)
Clinical Nurse Specialist (Baltimore, MD)
Clinical Otolaryngology and Allied Sciences (Malden, MA)
Clinical Pediatric Emergency Medicine (Saint Louis, MO)
Clinical Psychologist (Philadelphia, PA)
Clinical Pulmonary Medicine (Baltimore, MD)

Clinical Research and Regulatory Affairs (Philadelphia, PA)
The Clinical Teacher (Malden, MA)
Clinical Techniques in Equine Practice (Saint Louis, MO)
Clinical Techniques in Small Animal Practice (Saint Louis, MO)
Clinical Toxicology (Mineola, NY)
Clinical Transplantation (Minneapolis, MN)
Clinician's Research Digest (Washington, DC)
Clinics in Chest Medicine (Saint Louis, MO)
Clinics in Dermatology (Saint Louis, MO)
Clinics in Family Practice (Saint Louis, MO)
Clinics in Geriatric Medicine (Saint Louis, MO)
Clinics in Laboratory Medicine (Saint Louis, MO)
Clinics in Liver Disease (Saint Louis, MO)
Clinics in Occupational and Environmental Medicine (Saint Louis, MO)
Clinics in Perinatology (Saint Louis, MO)
Clinics in Plastic Surgery (Saint Louis, MO)
Clinics in Podiatric Medicine and Surgery (Saint Louis, MO)
Clinics in Sports Medicine (Saint Louis, MO)
Clues (Washington, DC)
Coachella Valley White Sheet (Palm Desert, CA)
Coal Preparation (Blacksburg, VA)
Coastline (Portsmouth, NH)
Cobb County Genealogical Society Quarterly (Marietta, GA)
Cochise Journal (Douglas, AZ)
The Cochrane Library (Hoboken, NJ)
CoDesign (Philadelphia, PA)
Coffeyville Journal (Coffeyville, KS)
Cognitive and Behavioral Neurology (Baltimore, MD)
Cognitive Science: A Multidisciplinary Journal (Bloomington, IN)
The Collected Letters of Thomas and Jane Welsh Carlyle (Durham, NC)
Collierville Magazine (Collierville, TN)
Collision Repair Product News (Fort Atkinson, WI)
The Colony Connection (The Colony, TX)
Colorado Mining: Today and Tomorrow (Denver, CO)
Columbine Community Courier (Littleton, CO)

# INDUSTRY ACTIVITY

Columbus Blues Alliance Magazine (Columbus, OH)
Combustion Science and Technology (Philadelphia, PA)
Combustion Theory and Modelling (Philadelphia, PA)
Combustion Theory & Modelling (Evanston, IL)
The Commemorative Trail (Huntington Beach, CA)
Comments on Inorganic Chemistry (College Station, TX)
Commerce Comet (Commerce, CA)
Commerce Journal (Commerce, TX)
Commerce Magazine (Baton Rouge, LA)
Commercial Property News (New York, NY)
Communications in Partial Differential Equations (Philadelphia, PA)
Communications in Statistics–Simulation and Computation (Hamilton, ON)
The Communicator (Westerville, OH)
Communio (Washington, DC)
Communique (East Arlington, VT)
Community Dentistry and Oral Epidemiology (Ann Arbor, MI)
Community Profile (Denton, TX)
Comparative American Studies (Thousand Oaks, CA)
Comparative Immunology, Microbiology & Infectious Diseases (Saint Louis, MO)
Comparative Literature Studies (Baltimore, MD)
Comparative Technology Transfer and Society (Colorado Springs, CO)
Compensation and Benefits Review (Thousand Oaks, CA)
Complementary Health Practice Review (Thousand Oaks, CA)
Complementary Therapies in Clinical Practice (Saint Louis, MO)
Complementary Therapies in Medicine (Saint Louis, MO)
Complex Variables (Philadelphia, PA)
Complexus (Farmington, CT)
Comprehensive Psychiatry (Saint Louis, MO)
Computational Intelligence (Edmonton, AB)
Computer-Aided Civil and Infrastructure Engineering (Columbus, OH)
Computer Methods in Biomechanics and Biomedical Engineering (Philadelphia, PA)
Computerized Medical Imaging and Graphics (Saint Louis, MO)
Computers in Entertainment (CIE) (Burbank, CA)
Concrete Concepts (Fort Atkinson, WI)

Concurrent Engineering (Thousand Oaks, CA)
Conflict Management and Peace Science (University Park, PA)
Conflict Resolution Quarterly (Washington, DC)
The Confluence (Wenatchee, WA)
Connecticut Woodlands (Rockfall, CT)
Connections (Santa Clara, CA)
Connections (Toronto, ON)
Connective Tissue Research (Chicago, IL)
Connector Specifier (Nashua, NH)
Consensus (Ottawa, ON)
Conservation Biology (Gainesville, FL)
Conservation in Practice (Seattle, WA)
Conservation and Society (Thousand Oaks, CA)
Constellations (Malden, MA)
Construction (Norcross, GA)
Construction Distribution (Fort Atkinson, WI)
Construction Journal (Dayton, OH)
Consultant (Darien, CT)
Consultant for Pediatricians (Manhasset, NY)
Consulting Psychology Journal: Practice and Research (Marshfield Hills, MA)
Consumer Resource Digest (Abilene, TX)
Contemporary Clinical Trials (Chicago, IL)
Contemporary OB/GYN (Montvale, NJ)
Contemporary Pediatrics (Montvale, NJ)
Contemporary Urology (Montvale, NJ)
Continuing Education in Radiologic Technology (Saint Louis, MO)
CONTINUUM (Baltimore, MD)
Contours (Champaign, IL)
Contours: A Journal of the African Diaspora (Durham, NC)
Contraception (Los Angeles, CA)
Contributions to Indian Sociology (Thousand Oaks, CA)
Contributions to Plasma Physics (Hoboken, NJ)
Controlled Clinical Trials (Saint Louis, MO)
Controlling Interest (Concord, NH)
Convenience Store News (New York, NY)
Conversations in Religion and Theology (Hartford, CT)
Cooperation and Conflict (Thousand Oaks, CA)
COPD: Journal of Chronic Obstructive Pulmonary Disease (Denver, CO)

Corn and Soybean Digest (Minneapolis, MN)
Cornell Hotel and Restaurant Administration Quarterly (Thousand Oaks, CA)
Cosmetic Surgery Times (Cleveland, OH)
CosmoGIRL! (New York, NY)
The Cottager (Victoria Beach, MB)
The Counseling Interviewer (Jackson, MO)
Countdown (Independence, OH)
Countdown (Perrysburg, OH)
Countdown (Oklahoma City, OK)
Countdown (Fort Lauderdale, FL)
Countdown (Irvine, CA)
Countdown (Shrewsbury, NJ)
Countdown (Birmingham, AL)
Countdown (East Greenbush, NY)
Countdown (Roanoke, VA)
Countdown (Cherry Hill, NJ)
Countdown Magazine (Wyomissing, PA)
Country Homes & Interiors (New York, NY)
Country Life (New York, NY)
County Lines (Raleigh, NC)
County News (Bismarck, ND)
Coupe (Toronto, ON)
Couteau Journal (Pipestone, MN)
Covina Neighborhood News (Walnut, CA)
CPER Magazine (Berkeley, CA)
CraftTrends (Golden, CO)
Crawford County Genealogy (Meadville, PA)
Creating Keepsakes (Bluffdale, UT)
Creative Machine Embroidery (Golden, CO)
Creativity and Innovation Management (Malden, MA)
Creditor Reporting System on Aid Activities (Washington, DC)
Crime and Justice (Castine, ME)
Crime, Media, Culture (Thousand Oaks, CA)
Criminal Justice (Thousand Oaks, CA)
Criminal Justice Policy Review (Thousand Oaks, CA)
Criminal Justice Review (Atlanta, GA)
Criminology (College Park, MD)
Criminology & Public Policy (New York, NY)
Critical Care Clinics (Saint Louis, MO)
Critical Care Nursing Clinics (Saint Louis, MO)
Critical Care Nursing Clinics of North America (Saint Louis, MO)

INDUSTRY ACTIVITY

Critical Care Nursing Quarterly (Baltimore, MD)
Critical Inquiry in Language Studies (Mahwah, NJ)
Critical Pathways in Cardiology (Baltimore, MD)
Critical Quarterly (Malden, MA)
Critical Reviews in Analytical Chemistry (Philadelphia, PA)
Critical Reviews in Biochemistry and Molecular Biology (Madison, WI)
Critical Reviews in Biotechnology (Philadelphia, PA)
Critical Reviews in Clinical Laboratory Sciences (Toronto, ON)
Critical Reviews in Computed Tomography (Baltimore, MD)
Critical Reviews in Food Science & Nutrition (Amherst, MA)
Critical Reviews in Microbiology (Louisville, KY)
Critical Reviews in Plant Sciences (Philadelphia, PA)
Critical Reviews in Solid State and Materials Sciences (Philadelphia, PA)
Critical Reviews in Toxicology (Albuquerque, NM)
Critical Social Policy (Thousand Oaks, CA)
Critique of Anthropology (Thousand Oaks, CA)
Crossings (Saint Cloud, MN)
Crossroads: The ACM Student Magazine (New York, NY)
Crosswinds (Exeter, NH)
CSAS Bulletin (Independence, KY)
CSAS Bulletin (Berkeley, CA)
CSPE Issues (Sacramento, CA)
CSREA Sentinel (New York, NY)
CT Jewish History (West Hartford, CT)
Cultural Diversity and Ethnic Minority Psychology (Washington, DC)
Cultural Dynamics (Thousand Oaks, CA)
Cultural Studies - Critical Methodologies (Thousand Oaks, CA)
Culture and Agriculture (San Antonio, TX)
Culture and Psychology (Worcester, MA)
The Culver City Observer (Culver City, CA)
Current Anaesthesia & Critical Care (Saint Louis, MO)
Current Directions in Psychological Science (Malden, MA)
Current Eye Research (Pittsburgh, PA)
Current Obstetrics & Gyncology (Saint Louis, MO)
Current Opinion in Allergy and Clinical Immunology (Baltimore, MD)

Current Opinion in Clinical Nutrition and Metabolic Care (Baltimore, MD)
Current Opinion in Critical Care (Baltimore, MD)
Current Opinion in Endocrinology and Diabetes (Baltimore, MD)
Current Opinion in Hematology (Baltimore, MD)
Current Opinion in Immunology (Saint Louis, MO)
Current Opinion in Infectious Diseases (Baltimore, MD)
Current Opinion in Internal Medicine (Baltimore, MD)
Current Opinion in Nephrology and Hypertension (Baltimore, MD)
Current Opinion in Neurobiology (Saint Louis, MO)
Current Opinion in Organ Transplantation Online (Baltimore, MD)
Current Opinion in Otolaryngology & Head and Neck Surgery (Baltimore, MD)
Current Opinion in Pulmonary Medicine (Baltimore, MD)
Current Opinion in Urology (Baltimore, MD)
Current Pediatrics (Saint Louis, MO)
Current Surgery (Greenville, NC)
Currents in Biblical Research (Thousand Oaks, CA)
Curtis's Botanical Magazine (Malden, MA)
Cushing Daily Citizen (Cushing, OK)
Custom Kitchens and Bath (New York, NY)
Custom Rodder (Anaheim, CA)
Cutaneous and Ocular Toxicology (Andover, MA)
CVPhoto (Montreal, QC)
Cycle Sport (Saint Paul, MN)
Cynthania Democrat (Cynthiana, KY)
Cytokine & Growth Factor (New York, NY)
Cytopathology (Malden, MA)
Cytotherapy (Philadelphia, PA)
Daily Bulletin (Ontario, CA)
The Daily Citizen (Dalton, GA)
Daily Iowegian & (Ad Express) (Centerville, IA)
The Daily Observer (Pembroke, ON)
The Daily Post (Lindsay, ON)
The Daily Southerner (Tarboro, NC)
Dalhousie Pier (Saint Catharines, ON)
Dance (Dallas, TX)
Dance Chronicle (Philadelphia, PA)
dANDelion (Calgary, AB)
Danville Boyle County (Danville, KY)

DB2 Magazine (San Mateo, CA)
Dealernews (Cleveland, OH)
Dearborn Business Journal (Dearborn, MI)
Decision Sciences (Malden, MA)
Declaration (Independence, VA)
Decorating Ideas (New York, NY)
The Delano Eagle (Osseo, MN)
Delaware County Genealogist and Historian (Muncie, IN)
Delaware News (Columbus, OH)
Delta Farm Press (Overland Park, KS)
Dementia (Thousand Oaks, CA)
Dental Abstracts (Saint Louis, MO)
Dental Clinics of North America (Saint Louis, MO)
Dental Practice Report (Northfield, IL)
Dental Products Report Europe (Northfield, IL)
Dental Traumatology (Malden, MA)
Der Reggeboge: The Rainbow (Kutztown, PA)
Dermatologic Clinics (Saint Louis, MO)
Dermatologic Therapy (Malden, MA)
Design Issues (Pittsburgh, PA)
Developing World Bioethics (Malden, MA)
Development and Change (Malden, MA)
Development, Growth and Differentiation (Malden, MA)
Development Policy Review (Malden, MA)
Developmental Science (Malden, MA)
Devil's Artisan (Erin, ON)
Devine News (Devine, TX)
The Diabetes Educator (Thousand Oaks, CA)
Diabetes Forecast (Houston, TX)
Diabetes, Obesity and Metabolism (Malden, MA)
Diabetic Medicine (Malden, MA)
Diagnostic Imaging Asia Pacific (San Francisco, CA)
Diagnostic Imaging Europe (San Francisco, CA)
Diagnostic Microbiology and Infectious Disease (North Liberty, IA)
Dialectica (Malden, MA)
Dialog (Malden, MA)
Differentiation (Malden, MA)
Digestive Endoscopy (Malden, MA)
Digestive and Liver Disease (Saint Louis, MO)
Digital Imaging Techniques (Melville, NY)
Digital Journal of Optometry (Albany, NY)
Digital Pipe Digest (Halton Hills, ON)

# INDUSTRY ACTIVITY

Dimensions of Early Childhood (Little Rock, AR)
Diplomat & International Canada (Ottawa, ON)
Diplomatic History (Malden, MA)
DIRECT (Overland Park, KS)
Direct Mail Rocket (Jonesboro, AR)
DIRT Sports (Cleveland, OH)
Disaster Management & Response (Saint Louis, MO)
Disasters (Malden, MA)
Discourse and Society (Thousand Oaks, CA)
Discourse Studies (Thousand Oaks, CA)
Discover Cannon Falls (Cannon Falls, MN)
Diseases of the Esophagus (Malden, MA)
Display & Design Ideas (New York, NY)
Dispute Resolution (Chicago, IL)
Dispute Resolution Times (Boston, MA)
Distinctly Denton (Denton, TX)
Diversity and Distributions (Malden, MA)
Domestic Animal Endocrinology (Saint Louis, MO)
Domino (New York, NY)
Downhomer (Saint John's, NL)
The Downtowner (Saint Catharines, ON)
Dreaming (Somerville, MA)
Dressage Today (Gaithersburg, MD)
Driven (Columbia, SC)
Driven (Frankfort, KY)
Drug and Alcohol Dependence (Richmond, VA)
Drug and Chemical Toxicology (Newark, DE)
Drug Delivery (Philadelphia, PA)
Drug Resistance Updates (Saint Louis, MO)
Drug Topics (Cleveland, OH)
Drying Technology (Philadelphia, PA)
Duarte View (Duarte, CA)
Dynamical Systems: An International Journal (Philadelphia, PA)
Eagle Rock Post (Los Angeles, CA)
Early Medieval Europe (Malden, MA)
Earth Save-Healthy People, Healthy Planet (Louisville, KY)
East European Politics and Societies (Thousand Oaks, CA)
Eating Light (New York, NY)
Eaton County Quest (Charlotte, MI)
Ecclesiology (Thousand Oaks, CA)
Echocardiography (Malden, MA)
Echoes (Waldron, AR)
Echography (Malden, MA)

Eco-Management and Auditing (Hoboken, NJ)
Ecological Entomology (Malden, MA)
Ecological Management and Restoration (Malden, MA)
Ecological Research (Malden, MA)
Ecology of Food and Nutrition (Amherst, MA)
Ecology of Freshwater Fish (Malden, MA)
Ecology Letters (Malden, MA)
Econometric Reviews (Dallas, TX)
Econometrica (Malden, MA)
Econometrics Journal (Malden, MA)
Economic Affairs (Malden, MA)
Economic History Review (Malden, MA)
Economic and Industrial Democracy (Thousand Oaks, CA)
Economic Inquiry (College Station, TX)
Economic Journal (Malden, MA)
Economic Notes (Malden, MA)
Economic Outlook (Malden, MA)
Economic Policy (Malden, MA)
Economic Policy Reforms (Washington, DC)
Economic Record (Malden, MA)
Economica (Malden, MA)
Economics & Politics (Malden, MA)
Economics of Transition (Malden, MA)
The Edge (Mc Lean, VA)
Edmond Living Magazine (Edmond, OK)
Edmonton's Media Magazine (Edmonton, AB)
Education, Citizenship and Social Justice (Thousand Oaks, CA)
Education for Health: Change in Learning and Practice (Philadelphia, PA)
Education and Urban Society (Thousand Oaks, CA)
Educational Administration Abstracts (Thousand Oaks, CA)
Educational Administration Quarterly (Thousand Oaks, CA)
Educational Management Administration and Leadership (Thousand Oaks, CA)
Educational Measurement: Issues and Practice (Malden, MA)
Educational Opportunities in South Dakota (Sioux Falls, SD)
Educational Philosophy and Theory (Malden, MA)
Educational Policy (Thousand Oaks, CA)
Educational Theory (Malden, MA)
Effingham Daily News (Effingham, IL)
Eighteenth Century Fiction (Hamilton, ON)
EJVES Extra (Saint Louis, MO)

The Eldersburg Eagle (Eldersburg, MD)
Electric Power Components and Systems (Lexington, KY)
Electrical Contracting Products (Arlington Heights, VA)
Electroanalysis (Tempe, AZ)
Electromagnetic Biology and Medicine (New York, NY)
Electromagnetic Biology and Medicine (Philadelphia, PA)
Electrophoresis (Hoboken, NJ)
Elegant Bride (New York, NY)
Elle Canada (Toronto, ON)
Elle Girl (New York, NY)
Elmwood Park Elm Leaves (Oak Park, IL)
eMagine (Plymouth, MN)
Embedded Computing Solutions (Manhasset, NY)
Emergency Medical Clinics (Saint Louis, MO)
Emergency Medical Product News (Fort Atkinson, WI)
Emergency Medicine Australasia (Malden, MA)
Emotion (Madison, WI)
Emotion (Washington, DC)
Emotional and Behavioural Difficulties (Thousand Oaks, CA)
Empire Outdoor Journal (Syracuse, NY)
Empirical Studies of the Arts (Amityville, NY)
Employee Assistance Quarterly (Orlando, FL)
Employment Guide (Syracuse, NY)
EMS Insider (Saint Louis, MO)
Endless Mountains Visitors Guide (Tunkhannock, PA)
Endocrine Research (West Amherst, NY)
Endocrinology and Metabolism Clinics (Saint Louis, MO)
Endodontic Topics (Malden, MA)
Endothelium: Journal of Endothelial Cell Research (Philadelphia, PA)
The Engineering Economist (Bethlehem, PA)
Engineering in Life Sciences (Hoboken, NJ)
English Literary Renaissance (Malden, MA)
Enid News & Eagle (Enid, OK)
Enterprise (Lansing, MI)
Enterprise and Society (Miami, FL)
Entertainment Magazine On-Line (EMOL.org) (Tucson, AZ)
Entomologia Experimental et Applicata (Malden, MA)
Entomological Science (Malden, MA)

Entrepreneurship Theory and Practice (Malden, MA)

Environment and Urbanization (Thousand Oaks, CA)

Environmental Claims Journal (Reston, VA)

Environmental Forensics (San Marcos, CA)

Environmental Microbiology (Malden, MA)

Environmental Progress (Toledo, OH)

Environmental Sciences (Philadelphia, PA)

EPBM: Early Pregnancy: Biology and Medicine (Cherry Hill, NJ)

Epilepsy and Behavior (Saint Louis, MO)

Epilepsy Currents (Malden, MA)

Epilepsy Research (Minneapolis, MN)

EPPO Bulletin (Malden, MA)

Equine Times (Camden, MI)

Equity & Excellence in Education (Amherst, MA)

Erie County Legal Journal (Erie, PA)

Erigenia (Westville, IL)

Essay and General Literature Index (Bronx, NY)

Essays on Canadian Writing (Toronto, ON)

Etched in Time (Roselle, IL)

Ethnicities (Thousand Oaks, CA)

Ethnography (Thousand Oaks, CA)

Ethnohistory (Madison, WI)

Ethology (Malden, MA)

Euro Tuner (Los Angeles, CA)

Europa Star (New York, NY)

Europa Star China (New York, NY)

Europa Star Espana (New York, NY)

Europa Star International (New York, NY)

european car (Anaheim, CA)

European Financial Management (Malden, MA)

European Heart Journal (Saint Louis, MO)

European History Quarterly (Thousand Oaks, CA)

European Journal of Archaeology (Thousand Oaks, CA)

European Journal of Cancer Care (Malden, MA)

European Journal of Cancer Prevention (Baltimore, MD)

European Journal of Cancer Surgery (Saint Louis, MO)

European Journal of Cardiovascular Prevention & Rehabilitation (Baltimore, MD)

European Journal of Clinical Investigation (Malden, MA)

European Journal of Communication (Thousand Oaks, CA)

European Journal of Criminology (Thousand Oaks, CA)

European Journal of Cultural Studies (Thousand Oaks, CA)

European Journal of Dental Education (Malden, MA)

European Journal of Education (Malden, MA)

European Journal of Emergency Medicine (Baltimore, MD)

European Journal of Haematology (Malden, MA)

European Journal of Industrial Relations (Thousand Oaks, CA)

European Journal of Inorganic Chemistry (Hoboken, NJ)

European Journal of International Relations (Thousand Oaks, CA)

European Journal of Lipid Science and Technology (Hoboken, NJ)

European Journal of Morphology (Philadelphia, PA)

European Journal of Neurology (Malden, MA)

European Journal of Neuroscience (Malden, MA)

European Journal of Oral Sciences (Malden, MA)

European Journal of Organic Chemistry (Hoboken, NJ)

European Journal of Paediatric Neurology (Saint Louis, MO)

European Journal of Pain (Saint Louis, MO)

European Journal of Philosophy (Malden, MA)

European Journal of Phycology (Philadelphia, PA)

European Journal of Political Research (Malden, MA)

European Journal of Political Theory (Thousand Oaks, CA)

European Journal of Radiology (Saint Louis, MO)

European Journal of Radiology Extra (Saint Louis, MO)

European Journal of Social Psychology (Hoboken, NJ)

European Journal of Social Theory (Thousand Oaks, CA)

European Journal of Soil Science (Malden, MA)

European Journal of Sport Science (Philadelphia, PA)

European Journal of Vascular and Endovascular Surgery (Saint Louis, MO)

European Law Journal (Malden, MA)

European Neuropsychopharmacology (Saint Louis, MO)

European Pharmaceutical Executive (Cleveland, OH)

European Physical Education Review (Thousand Oaks, CA)

European Psychiatry (Saint Louis, MO)

European Psychologist (Washington, DC)

European Transactions on Electrical Power (Hoboken, NJ)

European Urban and Regional Studies (Thousand Oaks, CA)

Evaluation (Thousand Oaks, CA)

Eventing (New York, NY)

Evergreen (Evergreen, CO)

Evidence-Based Gastroenterology (Baltimore, MD)

Evidence-based Healthcare (Saint Louis, MO)

Evidence-Based Healthcare & Public Health (Saint Louis, MO)

Evidence-Based Obstetrics and Gynecology (Saint Louis, MO)

Evidence-Based Ophthalmology (Baltimore, MD)

Evolution & Development (Malden, MA)

Evolution and Human Behavior (Hamilton, ON)

Exercise and Sport Sciences Reviews (Baltimore, MD)

existere (Toronto, ON)

Exogenous Dermatology (Farmington, CT)

Experience (Chicago, IL)

Experimental and Clinical Psychopharmacology (Belmont, MA)

Experimental and Clinical Psychopharmacology (Washington, DC)

Experimental Dermatology (Malden, MA)

Experimental Hematology (Saint Louis, MO)

Experimental Neurology (Saint Louis, MO)

Experimental Physiology (Malden, MA)

Expert Systems (Malden, MA)

Explore Maine's Oxford Hills (South Paris, ME)

Explore: The Journal of Science and Healing (Saint Louis, MO)

The EXPONENT (Des Moines, IA)

The Expositor (Brantford, ON)

Fabricating & Metalworking (Birmingham, AL)

Facial Plastic Surgery Clinics of North America (Saint Louis, MO)

FACT (La Jolla, CA)

The Fairy Garden Documentary (Port Saint Lucie, FL)

# INDUSTRY ACTIVITY

Faith Today (Markham, ON)
Families, Systems, & Health (Rochester, NY)
Family Business Review (Malden, MA)
Family & Community Health (Baltimore, MD)
Family Health (Edmonton, AB)
Family Health Matters (Princeton, NJ)
The Family Journal (Thousand Oaks, CA)
Family Process (Malden, MA)
Family Relations (Malden, MA)
Fantastic Flagler (Bunnell, FL)
Far North Oil and Gas Review (Yellowknife, NT)
Farm Talk (Parsons, KS)
Farming For Tomorrow (Calgary, AB)
FASHION18 (Toronto, ON)
Fastline de Mexico (Buckner, KY)
Fayette Tribune (Beckley) (Oak Hill, WV)
FCWG Quarterly (Hales Corners, WI)
Feminism and Psychology (Thousand Oaks, CA)
Feminist Teacher (Champaign, IL)
Feminist Theology (Thousand Oaks, CA)
Fernandina Beach News-Leader (Fernandina Beach, FL)
Ferroelectrics (Princeton, NJ)
Ferroelectrics Letters Section (Princeton, NJ)
Fertility and Sterility (Los Angeles, CA)
Fetal and Pediatric Pathology (Philadelphia, PA)
Field Methods (Thousand Oaks, CA)
5.0 Mustangs and Super Fords (Tampa, FL)
The Filson (Louisville, KY)
Financial Accountability and Management (Malden, MA)
Financial Markets, Institutions & Instruments (Malden, MA)
The Financial Review (Malden, MA)
Fire Chief (Chicago, IL)
Fire Rescue (Saint Louis, MO)
fireEMS (Tulsa, OK)
First Draft (Montgomery, AL)
First Hand News (Ann Arbor, MI)
First Language (Thousand Oaks, CA)
Fiscal Studies (Malden, MA)
Fish and Fisheries (Malden, MA)
Fisheries Management and Ecology (Malden, MA)
Fisheries Oceanography (La Jolla, CA)
Fleet Maintenance (Fort Atkinson, WI)
Fleet Owner (Overland Park, KS)
Fleur de Lis (Harahan, LA)
Florida Golfer (Tampa, FL)

The Florida Humanist (Bradenton, FL)
Florida Land Title News (Tallahassee, FL)
Fly Fisherman (Los Angeles, CA)
Flying Changes (Salem, OR)
FOCUS (Saint Paul, MN)
Focus on Business (Oakland, CA)
Folsom Magazine (Folsom, CA)
Food Biotechnology (Amherst, MA)
Food Engineering (West Chester, PA)
Food Science and Technology International (Thousand Oaks, CA)
Food Service Technology (Malden, MA)
Foodborne Pathogens and Disease (Knoxville, TN)
Foodservice Research International (Malden, MA)
The Foot (Saint Louis, MO)
Foot and Ankle Clinics (Baltimore, MD)
Foot and Ankle Surgery (Saint Louis, MO)
Forecast (Las Vegas, NV)
Foreign Policy Analysis (Malden, MA)
Forensic Science International (Saint Louis, MO)
Forest Landowner Magazine (Atlanta, GA)
Forest Pathology (Malden, MA)
Forever Young (Oakville, ON)
Forschung (Hoboken, NJ)
Forth Smith Regional Community Guide (Fort Smith, AR)
Forum (Chicago, IL)
Forum - State Magazine (Westmont, NJ)
Foundation Focus (Pittsburgh, PA)
Fragblast (Philadelphia, PA)
Franchise Law Journal (Chicago, IL)
Francophonies d'Amerique (Ottawa, ON)
Franklin County Citizen (Athens, GA)
Franklin Lakes/Oakland Suburban News (West Paterson, NJ)
Franklin Park Herald-Journal (Oak Park, IL)
Free Flight (Ottawa, ON)
Free Radical Research (Philadelphia, PA)
FreeFall (Calgary, AB)
FREEWorld (Montreal, QC)
French Cultural Studies (Thousand Oaks, CA)
Freshwater Biology (Malden, MA)
FRONT Magazine (Vancouver, BC)
Frozen Food Age (Melville, NY)
The Fruit Gardener (Fullerton, CA)
Fuel Cells (Hoboken, NJ)
Fullerenes, Nanotubes and Carbon Nanostructures (Philadelphia, PA)

Fun Times Guide (Gulfport, MS)
Functional Ecology (Malden, MA)
Fundamental & Clinical Pharmacology (Malden, MA)
FYI (Oak Forest, IL)
G-FAN (Steinbach, MB)
GA Lions Newspaper (Waycross, GA)
Gait & Posture (Saint Paul, MN)
Game and Fish (Marietta, GA)
Games and Culture (Thousand Oaks, CA)
Gardening and Deck Design (New York, NY)
Gardening and Outdoor Living (New York, NY)
Gastroenterology Clinics of North America (Saint Louis, MO)
Gastroenterology Nursing (Baltimore, MD)
Gastrointestinal Endoscopy Clinics of North America (Saint Louis, MO)
Gastrolenterology (Saint Louis, MO)
Gateways to Greater Nashua: Business, Lifestyle and Relocation Guide (Nashua, NH)
A Gathering of the Tribes (New York, NY)
Gazette (Thousand Oaks, CA)
GCHGS Quarterly (Paragould, AR)
The Gem (Boise, ID)
Gender & History (Malden, MA)
Gender, Technology and Development (Thousand Oaks, CA)
Gender, Work and Organization (Malden, MA)
General Hospital Psychiatry (Cambridge, MA)
General Informational Folder (Waterloo, IA)
Generation (Windsor, ON)
Generations (Baltimore, MD)
Genes, Brain and Behavior (Malden, MA)
Genes to Cells (Malden, MA)
Genesis: The Journal of Genetics and Development (Houston, TX)
Geobiology (Malden, MA)
Geofluids (Malden, MA)
Geografiska Annaler: Series A, Physical Geography (Malden, MA)
Geografiska Annaler: Series B, Human Geography (Malden, MA)
Geographical Analysis (Malden, MA)
Geographical Journal (Malden, MA)
Geographical Research (Malden, MA)
Geology Today (Malden, MA)
Geophysical Journal International (Malden, MA)

INDUSTRY ACTIVITY

Geophysical Prospective (Malden, MA)
Georgetown Independent and Free Press (Georgetown, ON)
Geriatric Times (Irvine, CA)
Geriatrics & Gerontology (Malden, MA)
German Economic Review (Malden, MA)
German Life and Letters (Malden, MA)
Gerodontology (Malden, MA)
Giles County Chamber Business Directory (Pulaski, TN)
Giles County Chamber Quality of Life Book (Pulaski, TN)
The Glass Club Bulletin (Millburn, NJ)
The Glen Rock Gazette (West Paterson, NJ)
Global Business Review (Thousand Oaks, CA)
Global Change Biology (Malden, MA)
Global Ecology and Biogeography (Malden, MA)
Global Media and Communication (Thousand Oaks, CA)
Global Networks (Malden, MA)
Global Social Policy (Thousand Oaks, CA)
Glow (Toronto, ON)
GLQ: A Journals of Lesbian and Gay Studies (New York, NY)
GM High Tech Performance (Anaheim, CA)
Goin' to Kansas City (Kansas City, MO)
Going Natural (Etobicoke, ON)
The Good Society (College Park, MD)
good times (Toronto, ON)
The Gourmet Retailer (New York, NY)
Governance (Malden, MA)
Government and Opposition (Malden, MA)
Government Security (Overland Park, KS)
Graft (Thousand Oaks, CA)
Grain Magazine (Saskatoon, SK)
Grand Lake Magazine (Jay, OK)
Grant County News and Express (Williamstown, KY)
Grass and Forage Science (Malden, MA)
Grassland Science (Malden, MA)
Grayson Journal Enquirer (Grayson, KY)
Great Escapes (Boston, MA)
Great Lakes Trail Rider (Rives Junction, MI)
Greater Omaha Official Visitors Guide (Omaha, NE)
Greater Wilkes-Barre Outlook (Wilkes-Barre, PA)
Green Diamond (Paxton, IL)
Green Mountain Granger (Hartford, VT)

Greensburg Daiy News/GB Times (Greensburg, IN)
Grey Room (New York, NY)
The Gridley Herald (Gridley, CA)
The Grimsby Lincoln News (Grimsby, ON)
Ground Support Magazine (Fort Atkinson, WI)
Ground Water (Malden, MA)
Ground Water Monitoring & Remediation (Malden, MA)
Groundwork (Rockville, MD)
Group Analysis (Thousand Oaks, CA)
Group Dynamics (Washington, DC)
Group Dynamics: Theory, Research, and Practice (College Park, MD)
Group Processes and Intergroup Relations (Thousand Oaks, CA)
Growth and Change (Malden, MA)
Growth Factors (Philadelphia, PA)
Guide (Leominster, MA)
Guide Book (Point Pleasant Beach, NJ)
Guide to the Licensed Guides of New York State (Lake Placid, NY)
Gyn. Obs. (Saint Louis, MO)
Gynecological Endocrinology (Philadelphia, PA)
Haemophilia (Malden, MA)
Hallym International Journal of Aging (Amityville, NY)
Halton Business Times (Burlington, ON)
Hand Clinics (Saint Louis, MO)
Harbor County Guide (New Buffalo, MI)
The Harpweaver (Saint Catharines, ON)
The Harvard International Journal of Press/Politics (Thousand Oaks, CA)
Harvard Review of Psychiatry (Belmont, MA)
Havre de Grace Chamber of Commerce Directory and Business Guide (Havre de Grace, MD)
Hawaii Hospitality (Honolulu, HI)
Hawk Mountain News (Kempton, PA)
Hazleton Area Image (Hazleton, PA)
HazMat Management Magazine (Toronto, ON)
HD-Journal (Lake Forest, CA)
Headache Currents (Malden, MA)
Headache & Pain (Manhasset, NY)
Headache: The Journal of Head and Face Pain (Malden, MA)
Health: (Thousand Oaks, CA)
Health Education and Behavior (Thousand Oaks, CA)
Health Education Research (Atlanta, GA)
Health Expectations (Malden, MA)
Health Informatics Journal (Thousand Oaks, CA)

Health Information & Libraries Journal (Malden, MA)
Health and Medicine Rhode Island (Providence, RI)
Health & Place (Saint Louis, MO)
Health Promotion Practice (Thousand Oaks, CA)
Health Services Research (Malden, MA)
Health and Social Care in the Community (Malden, MA)
Healthcare Traveler (Cleveland, OH)
Heart Failure Clnics (Saint Louis, MO)
Heart Rhythm (Indianapolis, IN)
Heat Transfer - Asian Research (Hoboken, NJ)
Helicobacter (Malden, MA)
Helvetica Chimica Acta (Hoboken, NJ)
Hematology/Oncology Clinics (Saint Louis, MO)
Hemodialysis International (Malden, MA)
Hemoglobin (Philadelphia, PA)
Hempstead Trails (Hope, AR)
Herald-Press (Palestine, TX)
Hereditas (Malden, MA)
Heritage Magazine (Ottawa, ON)
The Heythrop Journal (Malden, MA)
High Performance Polymers (Thousand Oaks, CA)
High Performance Pontiac (Anaheim, CA)
Higher Education Quarterly (Malden, MA)
The Highflyer (Carmel, IN)
HighGrader Magazine (Cobalt, ON)
The Highlands Voice (Charleston, WV)
Hinsdale/Clarendon Hills/Oak Brook Suburban Life (Oak Brook, IL)
Hispanic American Historical Review (College Park, MD)
Histoire Sociale/Social History (Ottawa, ON)
Histopathology (Malden, MA)
The Historian (Malden, MA)
Historic Marion (Salem, OR)
Historical Research (Malden, MA)
Historical Review (Winchester, TN)
Historical Society of Michigan Chronicle (East Lansing, MI)
History (Malden, MA)
History of the Human Sciences (Thousand Oaks, CA)
History of Photography (Philadelphia, PA)
History of Psychiatry (Thousand Oaks, CA)
History of Psychology (Bloomington, IN)
History of Psychology (Washington, DC)
History and Theory (Malden, MA)

# INDUSTRY ACTIVITY

HIV Medicine (Malden, MA)
Holiday Baking (New York, NY)
Holiday Cookies (New York, NY)
Holiday Cooking and Entertaining (New York, NY)
Holistic Nursing Practice (Baltimore, MD)
Hollywood Business (Hollywood, CA)
The Hollywood Reporter (New York, NY)
Holt Community News (Charlotte, MI)
Home Building (New York, NY)
Home Remodeling (New York, NY)
Home Remodeling New Project Ideas (New York, NY)
HomeCare (Overland Park, KS)
Homeopathy (Saint Louis, MO)
Homes & Gardens (New York, NY)
Homes Magazine (Thomasville, GA)
Homicide Studies (Thousand Oaks, CA)
Homily Service (Chicago, IL)
Honda Tuning (Anaheim, CA)
Hoosier Outdoor (Indianapolis, IN)
Horse & Hound (New York, NY)
Horse and Rider (Carrollton, TX)
Hospital Pharmacy (Baltimore, MD)
Hot Prospects (Bullhead City, AZ)
Hot Rod Bikes (Anaheim, CA)
House & Garden (New York, NY)
The Howard Journal of Criminal Justice (Malden, MA)
HPB: Journal of the International Hepato Pancreato Biliary Association (Philadelphia, PA)
Human Antibodies (San Diego, CA)
Human and Ecological Risk Assessment (Philadelphia, PA)
The Human Ecologist (Oakland, CA)
Human Immunology (Saint Louis, MO)
Human Nature (Somerset, NJ)
Human Pathology (Saint Louis, MO)
Human Relations (Thousand Oaks, CA)
Human Resource Development Review (Thousand Oaks, CA)
Human Rights (Chicago, IL)
Human Systems Management (New York, NY)
The Humanistic Psychologist (Oxford, OH)
The Hummingbird Connection (Newark, DE)
Huntingdon County Data Book (Huntingdon, PA)
Huntington Library Quarterly (San Marino, CA)
The Huntsville Item (Huntsville, TX)
The Hustler (Pine, CO)
HVVA Newsletter (West Hurley, NY)

Hypertension in Pregnancy (Philadelphia, PA)
Hypertension in Pregnancy (New York, NY)
Ibis (Malden, MA)
Ibsen Studies (Philadelphia, PA)
Ice Fishing Guide (Baxter, MN)
Ichnos: An International Journal for Plant and Animal Traces (Edmonton, AB)
IEEE/ACM Transactions on Computational Biology and Bioinformatica (New York, NY)
IFLA Journal (Thousand Oaks, CA)
Illness, Crisis & Loss (Amityville, NY)
Image (Bonham, TX)
Images (Libertyville, IL)
Images (Chapel Hill, NC)
Images of Asheboro/Randolph (Asheboro, NC)
Images of Clermont County (Milford, OH)
Images of the Franklin Area (Franklin, NC)
Images of Greenville Pitt County, NC (Greenville, NC)
Images of Henderson-Henderson County (Henderson, KY)
Images Journal (Jefferson City, MO)
Images of Richmond County (Rockingham, NC)
Images of Tuscarawas County (New Philadelphia, OH)
Imagine (Baltimore, MD)
Imaging Business (Melville, NY)
Imaging Decisions MRI (Malden, MA)
Immunity (Saint Louis, MO)
Immunological Investigations (Buffalo, NY)
Immunological Reviews (Malden, MA)
Immunology (Malden, MA)
Immunology and Allergy Clinics of North America (Saint Louis, MO)
Immunology and Cell Biology (Malden, MA)
Impact (Calgary, AB)
Imperial Valley White Sheet (Palm Desert, CA)
Implant Dentistry (Baltimore, MD)
Import Tuner (Anaheim, CA)
Impressions (Alpharetta, GA)
Improving Schools (Thousand Oaks, CA)
In Hamden (Hamden, CT)
In Port (Port Colborne, ON)
In Touch (Columbus, OH)
Independent Dealer (Orlando, FL)
Indian Journal of Gender Studies (Thousand Oaks, CA)
Indiana Genealogist (Fort Wayne, IN)

Indoor Air (Malden, MA)
Indoor and Built Environment (Thousand Oaks, CA)
Industrial Biotechnology (Larchmont, NY)
Industrial Guide (Simpsonville, SC)
Industrial Heating (Fort Myers, FL)
Industrial Machinery Digest (Birmingham, AL)
Industrial Relations: A Journal of Economy and Society (Malden, MA)
Industrial Relations Journal (Malden, MA)
Industrial WaterWorld (Tulsa, OK)
Infants & Young Children (Baltimore, MD)
Infections in Medicine (Manhasset, NY)
Infectious Disease Clinics of North America (Saint Louis, MO)
Infectious Diseases in Clinical Practice (Baltimore, MD)
Infectious Diseases in Obstetrics & Gynecology (Houston, TX)
Info Express (New York, NY)
Information Development (Thousand Oaks, CA)
Information Knowledge Systems Management (Atlanta, GA)
The Information Management Journal (Cincinnati, OH)
Information Systems Journal (Malden, MA)
Information Technologies and International Development (College Park, MD)
Information Technology for Development (Omaha, NE)
InfoStor Europe (Tulsa, OK)
Ingham County Community News (Charlotte, MI)
Ink Maker (Melville, NY)
Inlandport (Laredo, TX)
Innerview (Marysville, CA)
Inprint (Manassas, VA)
Insect Molecular Biology (Malden, MA)
Insect Science (Malden, MA)
Inside CSPE (Sacramento, CA)
Inside Gwinnett (Duluth, GA)
Inside MS (Pittsburgh, PA)
Inside SEMC (Atlanta, GA)
Inside Track (Toronto, ON)
Inspired House (Newtown, CT)
Insurance & Technology (New York, NY)
Integrated Ferroelectrics (Princeton, NJ)
Integrative Cancer Therapies (Thousand Oaks, CA)
Intelligent Data Analysis (Ottawa, ON)
Intensive Care and Critical Care Nursing (Saint Louis, MO)
Interface (Ocala, FL)

## INDUSTRY ACTIVITY

Internal Medicine Journal (Malden, MA)
International Affairs (Malden, MA)
International Clinical Psychopharmacology (Baltimore, MD)
International Criminal Justice Review (Atlanta, GA)
International Economic Review (Malden, MA)
International Endodontic Journal (Malden, MA)
International Finance (Malden, MA)
International Interactions (Philadelphia, PA)
International Journal of Andrology (Malden, MA)
International Journal of Antimicrobial Agents (Saint Louis, MO)
International Journal of Applied Ceramic Technology (Oak Ridge, TN)
International Journal of Applied Linguistics (Malden, MA)
International Journal of Aromatherapy (Saint Louis, MO)
International Journal of Art & Design Education (Malden, MA)
International Journal of Audiology (Philadelphia, PA)
International Journal of Auditing (Malden, MA)
International Journal of Behavioral Development (Thousand Oaks, CA)
International Journal of Cardiovascular Interventions (Philadelphia, PA)
International Journal of Clinical Practice (Malden, MA)
International Journal of Comparative Sociology (Thousand Oaks, CA)
International Journal of Computational Fluid Dynamics (Montreal, QC)
International Journal for Computational Methods in Engineering Science (College Station, TX)
International Journal of Consumer Studies (Malden, MA)
International Journal of Cosmetic Science (Malden, MA)
International Journal of Cross Cultural Management (Thousand Oaks, CA)
International Journal of Cultural Studies (Thousand Oaks, CA)
International Journal of Dairy Technology (Malden, MA)
International Journal of Damage Mechanics (Thousand Oaks, CA)
International Journal of Dental Hygiene (Malden, MA)
International Journal of Dermatology (Malden, MA)
International Journal of Developmental Neuroscience (Saint Louis, MO)

International Journal of Distributed Sensor Networks (Baton Rouge, LA)
International Journal of Economic Theory (Malden, MA)
International Journal of Environmental Analytical Chemistry (Philadelphia, PA)
International Journal of Environmental Studies (Philadelphia, PA)
International Journal for Equity and Health (Toronto, ON)
International Journal of Evidence-Based Healthcare (Malden, MA)
International Journal of Experimental Pathology (Malden, MA)
International Journal of Finance and Economics (Hoboken, NJ)
International Journal of Food Science and Technology (Malden, MA)
International Journal of Food Sciences and Nutrition (Philadelphia, PA)
International Journal of Fruit Science (Baton Rouge, LA)
International Journal of General Systems (Philadelphia, PA)
International Journal of Green Energy (Waterloo, ON)
International Journal of Green Energy (New York, NY)
International Journal of Gynecological Cancer (Malden, MA)
International Journal of Gynecology & Obstetrics (Chicago, IL)
International Journal of High Performance Computing Applications (Thousand Oaks, CA)
International Journal of Hybrid Intelligent Systems (Tulsa, OK)
International Journal of Immunogenetics (Malden, MA)
International Journal of Injury Control and Safety Promotion (Decatur, GA)
International Journal of Intelligence and Counter Intelligence (New York, NY)
International Journal of Japanese Sociology (Malden, MA)
International Journal of Logistics: Research and Applications (Philadelphia, PA)
International Journal of Lower Extremity Wounds (Thousand Oaks, CA)
International Journal of Management Reviews (Malden, MA)
The International Journal on Media Management (Mahwah, NJ)
International Journal of Medical Informatics (Framingham, MA)
International Journal of Mental Health Nursing (Malden, MA)
International Journal of Music Education (Thousand Oaks, CA)

International Journal of Nautical Archaeology (Malden, MA)
International Journal of Neuroscience (Chapel Hill, NC)
International Journal of Number Theory (Urbana, IL)
International Journal of Nursing Practice (Malden, MA)
International Journal of Nursing Terminologies and Classifications (Malden, MA)
International Journal of Obstetric Anesthesia (Saint Louis, MO)
International Journal of Offender Therapy and Comparative Criminology (Thousand Oaks, CA)
International Journal of Paediatric Dentistry (Malden, MA)
International Journal of Parallel, Emergent and Distributed Systems (Ottawa, ON)
International Journal of Pediatric Otorhinolaryngology (Bronx, NY)
International Journal of Phytoremediation (Philadelphia, PA)
International Journal of Polymer Analysis and Characterization (Wilmington, DE)
International Journal of Polymeric Materials (Morris Plains, NJ)
International Journal of Prisoner Health (Philadelphia, PA)
International Journal of Psychiatry in Clinical Practice (Philadelphia, PA)
International Journal for the Psychology of Religion (Mahwah, NJ)
International Journal of Psychophysiology (Saint Louis, MO)
International Journal of Radiation Oncology (Houston, TX)
International Journal of Rehabilitation Research (Baltimore, MD)
International Journal of RF and Microwave Computer-Aided Engineering (Roanoke, VA)
International Journal of Robotics Research (Thousand Oaks, CA)
International Journal of Rural Management (Thousand Oaks, CA)
International Journal of Selection and Assessment (Malden, MA)
International Journal of Self Help and Self Care (Amityville, NY)
International Journal of Social Psychiatry (Thousand Oaks, CA)
International Journal of Social Research Methodology (Philadelphia, PA)
International Journal of Social Welfare (Malden, MA)
International Journal of Stress Management (Tucson, AZ)

International Journal of Stroke (Malden, MA)

International Journal of Surface Mining, Reclamation and Environment (Calgary, AB)

International Journal of Systematic Theology (Malden, MA)

International Journal of Training and Development (Malden, MA)

International Journal of Transgenderism (Binghamton, NY)

International Journal of Urban and Regional Research (Malden, MA)

International Journal of Urology (Malden, MA)

The International Lawyer (Dallas, TX)

International Migration (Malden, MA)

International Nursing Review (Malden, MA)

International Ophthalmology Clinics (Baltimore, MD)

International Political Science Review (Thousand Oaks, CA)

International Politics and Society (Somerset, NJ)

International Regional Science Review (Thousand Oaks, CA)

International Relations (Thousand Oaks, CA)

International Relations in a Globalising World (Thousand Oaks, CA)

International Review of Administrative Sciences (Thousand Oaks, CA)

International Review of Finance (Malden, MA)

International Review for the Sociology of Sport (Thousand Oaks, CA)

International Small Business Journal (Thousand Oaks, CA)

International Social Science Journal (Malden, MA)

International Social Security Review (Malden, MA)

International Social Work (Thousand Oaks, CA)

International Sociology (Stony Brook, NY)

International Student Exchange of Iowa (Saint Charles, MO)

International Studies Perspectives (Malden, MA)

International Studies Quarterly (Malden, MA)

International Studies Review (Malden, MA)

International Transactions in Operational Research (Malden, MA)

International Wound Journal (Malden, MA)

The Interner Journal of Plastic Surgery (Sugar Land, TX)

The Internet Journal of Alternative Medicine (Sugar Land, TX)

The Internet Journal of Bioengineering (Sugar Land, TX)

The Internet Journal of Cardiology (Sugar Land, TX)

The Internet Journal of Cardiovascular Research (Sugar Land, TX)

The Internet Journal of Dental Science (Sugar Land, TX)

The Internet Journal of Dermatology (Sugar Land, TX)

The Internet Journal of Emergency Medicine (Sugar Land, TX)

The Internet Journal of Endocrinology (Sugar Land, TX)

The Internet Journal of Epidemiology (Sugar Land, TX)

The Internet Journal of Forensic Science (Sugar Land, TX)

The Internet Journal of Genomics and Proteomics (Sugar Land, TX)

The Internet Journal of Geriatrics and Gerontology (Sugar Land, TX)

Internet Journal of Hematology (Sugar Land, TX)

The Internet Journal of Informal Science Education (Sugar Land, TX)

The Internet Journal of Laboratory Medicine (Sugar Land, TX)

The Internet Journal of Medical Informatics (Sugar Land, TX)

The Internet Journal of Medical Simulation (Sugar Land, TX)

The Internet Journal of Medical Technology (Sugar Land, TX)

The Internet Journal of Mental Health (Sugar Land, TX)

The Internet Journal of Microbiology (Sugar Land, TX)

The Internet Journal of Nanotechnology (Sugar Land, TX)

The Internet Journal of Nephrology (Sugar Land, TX)

The Internet Journal of Neurology (Sugar Land, TX)

The Internet Journal of Nuclear Medicine (Sugar Land, TX)

The Internet Journal of Oncology (Sugar Land, TX)

The Internet Journal of Parasitic Diseases (Sugar Land, TX)

The Internet Journal of Pharmacology (Sugar Land, TX)

The Internet Journal of Rheumatology (Sugar Land, TX)

The Internet Journal of Third World Medicine (Sugar Land, TX)

The Internet Journal of Toxicology (Sugar Land, TX)

The Internet Journal of Tropical Medicine (Sugar Land, TX)

The Internet Journal of Urology (Sugar Land, TX)

The Internet Journal of Veterinary Medicine (Sugar Land, TX)

The Internet Journal of World Health and Societal Politics (Sugar Land, TX)

The Internet journal of Spine Surgery (Sugar Land, TX)

Inuktitut (Ottawa, ON)

Invertebrate Biology (Malden, MA)

Iowa Architect (Des Moines, IA)

Iowa Natural Heritage (Des Moines, IA)

Iowa's Pride (Iowa City, IA)

ISHN (Troy, MI)

The Island Arc (Malden, MA)

Island Guide (Put-in-Bay, OH)

Islands' Weekly (Bainbridge Island, WA)

Jacksonville Daily Progress (Jacksonville, TX)

Jane (New York, NY)

Japan Journal of Nursing Science (Malden, MA)

The Japanese Economic Review (Malden, MA)

Japanese Journal of Ophthalmology (Saint Louis, MO)

Japanese Psychological Research (Malden, MA)

Jasper News (Jasper, FL)

Jasper, TX (Jasper, TX)

JCMS: Journal of Common Market Studies (Malden, MA)

Jewish Exponent (Philadelphia, PA)

JGE: The Journal of General Education (Baltimore, MD)

The John Thurman Historical Society Quarterly (Athol, NY)

Joint Bone Spine (Saint Louis, MO)

JONA's Healthcare Law, Ethics, and Regulation (Baltimore, MD)

Journal (Concord, NH)

Journal (Vineland, NJ)

The Journal (Fort Smith, AR)

Journal (Harrisburg, PA)

Journal (Pierre, SD)

Journal of Aboriginal Health (Ottawa, ON)

Journal of the Acadian Entomological Society (Fredericton, NB)

Journal of Access Services (Gainesville, FL)

Journal of Accounting Research (Malden, MA)

## INDUSTRY ACTIVITY

The Journal of Adhesion (Williamsburg, VA)

Journal of Adolescent Health (San Francisco, CA)

Journal of Advanced Nursing (Malden, MA)

The Journal of Aesthetics and Art Criticism (Malden, MA)

Journal of Affordable Housing and Community Development Law (Chicago, IL)

Journal of African American Studies (Somerset, NJ)

Journal of Aging and Pharmacotherapy (Binghamton, NY)

Journal of Agrarian Change (Malden, MA)

Journal of Agronomy and Crop Science (Malden, MA)

Journal of Algebra and Its Applications (Athens, OH)

Journal of Alzheimer's Disease (Cleveland, OH)

The Journal of Ambulatory Care Management (Baltimore, MD)

Journal of the American Academy of Nurse Practitioners (Austin, TX)

Journal of the American Association for Medical Transcription (Baltimore, MD)

Journal of the American College of Cardiology (San Diego, CA)

Journal of the American College of Radiology (Reston, VA)

Journal of the American College of Surgeons (Saint Louis, MO)

The Journal of American Culture (Malden, MA)

Journal of the American Dietetic Association (Saint Louis, MO)

Journal of American Folklore (Columbia, MO)

Journal of the American Medical Directors Association (Sherman Oaks, CA)

Journal of the American Medical Informatics (Saint Louis, MO)

Journal of the American Musicological Society (Los Angeles, CA)

Journal of the American Psychiatric Nurses Association (Coopersburg, PA)

Journal of the American Society for Surgery of the Hand (Saint Louis, MO)

The Journal of Analytical Psychology (Malden, MA)

Journal of Anatomy (Malden, MA)

Journal of Anglican Studies (Thousand Oaks, CA)

Journal of Animal Breeding and Genetics (Malden, MA)

Journal of Animal Ecology (Malden, MA)

Journal of Animal Psychology and Nutrition (Malden, MA)

Journal of Anxiety Disorders (Saint Louis, MO)

Journal of Applied Corporate Finance (Malden, MA)

Journal of Applied Ecology (Malden, MA)

Journal of Applied Entomology (Malden, MA)

Journal of Applied Gerontology (Thousand Oaks, CA)

Journal of Applied Ichthyology (Malden, MA)

Journal of Applied Microbiology (Malden, MA)

Journal of Applied Philosophy (Malden, MA)

Journal of Applied Research in Intellectual Disabilities (Malden, MA)

Journal of Applied Sport Psychology (Corvallis, OR)

Journal of Archaeology (Boston, MA)

Journal of Architectural Education (Malden, MA)

Journal of Architectural Education (JAE) (Los Angeles, CA)

The Journal of Arthroscopic & Related Surgery (Winston-Salem, NC)

Journal of Asian and African Studies (Thousand Oaks, CA)

Journal of the Association for Laboratory Autmation (Princeton, NJ)

Journal of the Association of Nurses in AIDS Care (Kennesaw, GA)

Journal of the Association for Research of Mothering (Toronto, ON)

Journal of Attention Disorders (Thousand Oaks, CA)

Journal of Avian Biology (Malden, MA)

Journal of Behavior Therapy and Experimental Psychiatry (Saint Louis, MO)

The Journal of Behavioral Health Services & Research (Baltimore, MD)

Journal of Bioactive and Compatible Polymers (Thousand Oaks, CA)

Journal of Biogepgraphy (Malden, MA)

Journal of Biomaterials Applications (Thousand Oaks, CA)

Journal of Biomolecular Screening (Thousand Oaks, CA)

Journal of Broadcasting & Electronic Media (Tempe, AZ)

Journal of Burn Care & Rehabilitation (Baltimore, MD)

Journal of Business Communication (Thousand Oaks, CA)

Journal of Business Cycle Measurement and Analysis (Washington, DC)

Journal of Business and Finance Accounting (Malden, MA)

The Journal of Business Valuation (Toronto, ON)

Journal of Cancer Education (Denver, CO)

Journal of Cancer Pain and Symptom Palliation (Albany, NY)

Journal of Cardiac Surgery (Malden, MA)

The Journal of Cardiovascular Electrophysiology (Malden, MA)

Journal of Cardiovascular Magnetic Resonance (North Los Angeles, CA)

Journal of Cardiovascular Magnetic Resonance (New York, NY)

The Journal of Cardiovascular Nursing (Baltimore, MD)

Journal of Career Assessment (Thousand Oaks, CA)

Journal of Career Development (Thousand Oaks, CA)

Journal of Cataract & Refractive Surgery (Fairfax, VA)

Journal of Cellular Plastics (Thousand Oaks, CA)

Journal of Chemical Dependency Treatment (Binghamton, NY)

Journal of Child and Adolescent Psychiatric Nursing (Malden, MA)

Journal of Child Custody (Newport Beach, CA)

Journal of Child Health Care (Thousand Oaks, CA)

The Journal of Child Psychology and Psychiatry (Malden, MA)

Journal of Child Sexual Abuse (San Diego, CA)

Journal of Chinese Philosophy (Malden, MA)

Journal of Chronic Fatigue Syndrome (Binghamton, NY)

Journal of Classical Sociology (Thousand Oaks, CA)

Journal of Clinical Anesthesia (Boston, MA)

Journal of Clinical Engineering (Baltimore, MD)

Journal of Clinical Epidemiology (Ottawa, QC)

Journal of Clinical Neuroscience (Saint Louis, MO)

Journal of Clinical Nursing (Malden, MA)

Journal of Clinical Periodontology (Malden, MA)

The Journal of Clinical Pharmacology (Thousand Oaks, CA)

Journal of Clinical Pharmacy and Therapeutics (Malden, MA)
Journal of Clinical Psychology (Tuscaloosa, AL)
Journal of Clinical Virology (Denver, CO)
Journal of Cognition and Development (Mahwah, NJ)
Journal of Cognitive Neuroscience (Berkeley, CA)
Journal of College Student Development (Ames, IA)
Journal of College Student Retention: Research, Theory and Practice (Amityville, NY)
Journal of Colonialism and Colonial History (Baltimore, MD)
The Journal of Commonwealth Literature (Thousand Oaks, CA)
Journal of Community Practice (Binghamton, NY)
Journal of Comparative Pathology (Saint Louis, MO)
Journal of Comparative Psychology (Knoxville, TN)
Journal of Composite Materials (Thousand Oaks, CA)
Journal of Computational and Nonlinear Dynamics (New York, NY)
Journal of Computer Assisted Learning (Malden, MA)
Journal of Computer Security (Fairfax, VA)
Journal of Computing and Information Science in Engineering (New York, NY)
Journal of Consumer Affairs (Malden, MA)
Journal of Consumer Culture (Thousand Oaks, CA)
Journal of Contemporary Criminal Justice (Thousand Oaks, CA)
Journal of Contemporary History (Thousand Oaks, CA)
Journal of Contingencies and Crisis Management (Malden, MA)
Journal of Coordination Chemistry (Philadelphia, PA)
Journal of Cosmetic Dermatology (Malden, MA)
Journal of Cosmetic and Laser Therapy (Philadelphia, PA)
Journal of Couple and Relationship Therapy (Hammond, IN)
Journal of Creativity in Mental Health (Binghamton, NY)
Journal of Critical Care (Saint Louis, MO)
Journal of Crop Improvement (Wichita, KS)
Journal of Crystallography (Malden, MA)

Journal of Cutaneous Pathology (Malden, MA)
Journal of Dermatological Treatment (Philadelphia, PA)
Journal der Deutschen Dermatologischen Gesellschaft (Malden, MA)
Journal of Developing Societies (Thousand Oaks, CA)
Journal of Dietary Supplements (Salt Lake City, UT)
Journal of Difference Equations and Applications (San Antonio, TX)
Journal of Digital and Electronic Acquisitions (Bowling Green, OH)
Journal of Dispersion Science and Technology (Philadelphia, PA)
Journal of Divorce and Remarriage (Tucson, AZ)
The Journal of Drug Evaluation (Philadelphia, PA)
Journal of Drug Targeting (Philadelphia, PA)
Journal of Dual Diagnosis (Binghamton, NY)
Journal of E-Government (Binghamton, NY)
Journal of Early Childhood Literacy (Thousand Oaks, CA)
Journal of Early Childhood Research (Thousand Oaks, CA)
Journal of Ecology (Malden, MA)
Journal of Economic Geography (Toronto, ON)
Journal of Economic Surveys (Malden, MA)
Journal of Economics & Management Strategy (Malden, MA)
Journal of Education Finance (Champaign, IL)
Journal of Educational Measurement (Malden, MA)
Journal on Educational Resources in Computing (JERIC) (Villanova, PA)
Journal of Elastomers and Plastics (Thousand Oaks, CA)
Journal of Electrocardiology (Saint Louis, MO)
Journal of Electronic Packaging (New York, NY)
Journal of Electronic Resources in Libraries (Binghamton, NY)
Journal of Electronic Resources in Medical Libraries (Binghamton, NY)
Journal of Embedded Computing (Antigonish, NS)
Journal of Emergency Medical Services (Saint Louis, MO)
Journal of Emergency Medicine (San Diego, CA)

Journal of Emergency Nursing (Saint Louis, MO)
Journal of Emerging Market Finance (Thousand Oaks, CA)
Journal of Empirical Legal Studies (Malden, MA)
Journal of Energetic Materials (Philadelphia, PA)
Journal of Engineering Design (Philadelphia, PA)
Journal of Engineering Materials and Technology (New York, NY)
Journal of English Linguistics (Ann Arbor, MI)
Journal of Entrepreneurship (Thousand Oaks, CA)
The Journal of Environment and Development (Thousand Oaks, CA)
Journal of Environmental Engineering and Science (Ottawa, ON)
Journal of Environmental Science and Health, Part A (Philadelphia, PA)
Journal of Environmental Science and Health, Part B (Philadelphia, PA)
Journal of Environmental Science and Health, Part C (Philadelphia, PA)
Journal of Enzyme Inhibition and Medicinal Chemistry (Philadelphia, PA)
Journal of Equine Veterinary Science (Saint Louis, MO)
Journal of Ethnicity in Criminal Justice (Pomona, NJ)
The Journal of Eukaryotic Microbiology (Malden, MA)
Journal of the European Economic Association (JEEA) (Cambridge, MA)
Journal of European Social Policy (Thousand Oaks, CA)
Journal of European Studies (Thousand Oaks, CA)
Journal of Evaluation in Clinical Practice (Malden, MA)
Journal of Evidence-Based Social Work (Binghamton, NY)
Journal of Evolutionary Biology (Malden, MA)
Journal of Excellence (Chelsea, QC)
Journal of Experimental Nanoscience (Philadelphia, PA)
Journal of Experimental Psychology: Applied (Washington, DC)
Journal of Experimental Psychology: Applied (Atlanta, GA)
Journal of Experimental Psychology: General (Victoria, BC)
Journal of Experimental & Theoretical Artificial Intelligence (Philadelphia, PA)
Journal of Family History (Thousand Oaks, CA)
Journal of Family Therapy (Malden, MA)

## INDUSTRY ACTIVITY

Journal of Feline Medicine and Surgery (Saint Louis, MO)

The Journal of Finance (Malden, MA)

Journal of Financial Econometrics (Montreal, QC)

The Journal of Financial Research (Malden, MA)

Journal of Fire Protection Engineering (Thousand Oaks, CA)

Journal of Fire Sciences (Thousand Oaks, CA)

Journal of Fish Biology (Malden, MA)

Journal of Fish Diseases (Malden, MA)

Journal of Food Biochemistry (Malden, MA)

Journal of Food Biochemistry (Magalia, CA)

Journal of Food Lipids (Malden, MA)

Journal of Food Process Engineering (College Station, TX)

Journal of Food Processing and Preservation (Pullman, WA)

Journal of Food Quality (Athens, GA)

Journal of Fuel Cell Science and Technology (New York, NY)

Journal of Gastrointestinal Surgery (Baltimore, MD)

Journal of Gay and Lesbian Issues in Education (Johns Island, SC)

Journal of Gay and Lesbian Politics (Birmingham, AL)

Journal of Gay & Lesbian Psychotherapy (New York, NY)

Journal of Gene Medicine (Hoboken, NJ)

Journal of Geriatric Psychiatry and Neurology (Thousand Oaks, CA)

Journal of GLBT Family Studies (Denver, CO)

Journal of GLBT Issues in Counseling (Binghamton, NY)

Journal of Groups in Addiction and Recovery (Chicago, IL)

Journal of Hand Surgery (American Volume) (Saint Louis, MO)

The Journal of Head Trauma Rehabilitation (Baltimore, MD)

Journal of Health Management (Thousand Oaks, CA)

Journal of Health Psychology (Thousand Oaks, CA)

The Journal of Heart and Lung Transplantation (Birmingham, AL)

Journal of Hematotherapy & Stem Cell Research (Tampa, FL)

Journal of Hepatology (Saint Louis, MO)

Journal of High Speed Networks (Baltimore, MD)

Journal of Hispanic Higher Education (Thousand Oaks, CA)

Journal of the Historical Society (Boston, MA)

Journal of the History of the Behavioral Sciences (Toronto, ON)

Journal of the History of the Neurosciences (Philadelphia, PA)

Journal of HIV/AIDS Prevention in Children and Youth (Binghamton, NY)

Journal of Hospice and Palliative Nursing (Baltimore, MD)

Journal of Hospitality and Tourism Research (Thousand Oaks, CA)

Journal of Human Lactation (Thousand Oaks, CA)

Journal of Human Values (Thousand Oaks, CA)

Journal of the Illinois State Historical Society (Springfield, IL)

Journal of Immunoassay & Immunochemistry (Philadelphia, PA)

Journal of Immunotoxicology (Philadelphia, PA)

Journal of Immunotoxicology (Tuxedo, NY)

Journal of Industrial Hemp (Binghamton, NY)

Journal of Industrial Textiles (Thousand Oaks, CA)

Journal of Information & Knowledge Management (Tulsa, OK)

Journal of Information Science (Thousand Oaks, CA)

Journal of Intellectual & Developmental Disability (Philadelphia, PA)

Journal of Intellectual Disabilities (Thousand Oaks, CA)

Journal of Intelligent Material Systems and Structures (Thousand Oaks, CA)

Journal of Intelligent Transportation Systems (Philadelphia, PA)

Journal of Interconnection Networks (New York, NY)

Journal of Interlibrary Loan, Document Delivery, and Electronic Reserve (Binghamton, NY)

Journal of the International Association of Physicians in AIDS Care (Thousand Oaks, CA)

Journal of International Economic Law (Washington, DC)

Journal of International Wildlife Law & Policy (Philadelphia, PA)

Journal of the Internet in Technical Services (Binghamton, NY)

Journal of Interprofessional Care (Philadelphia, PA)

Journal of Labor Research (Somerset, NJ)

Journal of Land Use Science (Philadelphia, PA)

Journal of Latin American Geography (Austin, TX)

Journal of Librarianship and Information Science (Thousand Oaks, CA)

Journal of Liposome Research (Philadelphia, PA)

Journal of Liquid Chromatography and Related Technologies (Philadelphia, PA)

Journal of Literacy Research (Commerce, TX)

Journal of Lower Genital Tract Disease (Baltimore, MD)

Journal of Macromarketing (Mesa, AZ)

Journal of Macromolecular Science, Part A (Philadelphia, PA)

Journal of Macromolecular Science, Part B (Philadelphia, PA)

Journal of Macromolecular Science, Part C (Philadelphia, PA)

Journal of Maine Education (Brunswick, ME)

Journal of Management (Thousand Oaks, CA)

Journal of Management Information Systems (Saddle River, NJ)

Journal of Management Inquiry (Thousand Oaks, CA)

Journal of Manufacturing Science and Engineering (New York, NY)

Journal of Map and Geography Libraries (Binghamton, NY)

Journal of Marketing Education (Thousand Oaks, CA)

Journal of Material Culture (Thousand Oaks, CA)

Journal of Maternal-Fetal & Neonatal Medicine (Philadelphia, PA)

Journal of Mathematical Sociology (Philadelphia, PA)

Journal of Maxillofacial Surgery (Saint Louis, MO)

Journal of Mechanical Design (New York, NY)

Journal of Mechanics in Medicine and Biology (Ann Arbor, MI)

The Journal of Medical Risk (Philadelphia, PA)

Journal of Medicinal Food (Larchmont, NY)

Journal of Medicine and Philosophy (Philadelphia, PA)

Journal of Midwifery & Women's Health (Saint Louis, MO)

Journal of Military Ethics (Philadelphia, PA)

Journal of Minimally Invasive Gynecology (Santa Fe Springs, CA)

Journal of Molecular and Cellular Cardiology (Cleveland, OH)

Journal of Molecular Microbiology and Biotechnology (Farmington, CT)
Journal of Moral Philosophy (Thousand Oaks, CA)
Journal of Multilingual Communication Disorders (Philadelphia, PA)
Journal of Muscle Foods (Urbana, IL)
The Journal of Musicology (Bloomington, IN)
Journal of Natural Fibers (Binghamton, NY)
Journal of Neurogenetics (Philadelphia, PA)
Journal of Neuroimmunology (Bronx, NY)
Journal of the Neurological Sciences (Detroit, MI)
Journal of Neuropathic Pain and Symptom Palliation (Binghamton, NY)
Journal of Neuropathology & Experimental Neurology (Baltimore, MD)
Journal of NeuroVirology (Philadelphia, PA)
Journal of Neutron Research (Philadelphia, PA)
The Journal of New York Folklore (Schenectady, NY)
Journal of Nietzsche Studies (Baltimore, MD)
Journal of Nonparametric Statistics (Philadelphia, PA)
Journal of Nursing Care Quality (Baltimore, MD)
Journal of Nutritional Biochemistry (Lexington, KY)
Journal of Nutritional & Environmental Medicine (Philadelphia, PA)
Journal of Obstetrics and Gynaecology (Philadelphia, PA)
Journal of Occupational and Environmental Hygiene (Philadelphia, PA)
Journal of Occupational and Environmental Hygiene (Seattle, WA)
Journal of Occupational Health Psychology (Fairfax, VA)
Journal of Occupational Health Psychology (Washington, DC)
Journal Of Cardiovascular Magnetic Resonance (North Los Angeles, CA)
Journal Of Chronic Obstructive Pulmonary Disease (Denver, CO)
Journal of Offshore Mechanics and Arctic Engineering (New York, NY)
Journal of Organ Dysfunctions (Philadelphia, PA)
Journal of Orthopaedic Nursing (Saint Louis, MO)
The Journal of Osceola County Business (Kissimmee, FL)

Journal of Pain (Saint Louis, MO)
Journal of Pain and Symptom Management (New York, NY)
Journal of Palestine Studies (Washington, DC)
Journal of Patient Safety (Baltimore, MD)
Journal of Peace Research (Thousand Oaks, CA)
Journal of Pediatric and Adolescent Gynecology (Louisville, KY)
Journal of Pediatric Healthcare (Long Beach, CA)
Journal of Pediatric Oncology Nursing (Thousand Oaks, CA)
Journal of Pediatric Surgery (Saint Louis, MO)
Journal of Pentecostal Theology (Thousand Oaks, CA)
Journal of PeriAnesthesia Nursing (Saint Louis, MO)
The Journal of Perinatal & Neonatal Nursing (Baltimore, MD)
Journal of Physical Activity and Health (Dallas, TX)
Journal of Planning Education and Research (Thousand Oaks, CA)
Journal of Planning History (Thousand Oaks, CA)
Journal of Plant Interactions (Philadelphia, PA)
Journal of Plant Nutrition (Philadelphia, PA)
Journal of Plant Nutrition and Soil Science (Hoboken, NJ)
Journal of Plastic Film and Sheeting (Thousand Oaks, CA)
Journal of Policy History (Baltimore, MD)
Journal of Political Marketing (Chicago, IL)
Journal of Political Science Education (Philadelphia, PA)
Journal of Political Science Education (Kirksville, MO)
Journal of Psychiatric Practice (Baltimore, MD)
Journal of Psychopharmacology (Thousand Oaks, CA)
Journal of Psychosomatic Obstetrics & Gynecology (Philadelphia, PA)
Journal of Psychotherapy Integration (Garden City, NY)
Journal of Public Child Welfare (Athens, GA)
Journal of Public Health Management and Practice (Baltimore, MD)
Journal of Radio Studies (Charleston, SC)
Journal of Radiology Nursing (Miami, FL)

Journal of Rapid Methods and Automation in Microbiology (Houston, TX)
Journal of Receptors and Signal Transduction (Philadelphia, PA)
Journal of Receptors and Signal Transduction (New York, NY)
The Journal-Register (Medina, NY)
Journal of Rehabilitation Medicine (Philadelphia, PA)
Journal of Reinforced Plastics and Composites (Thousand Oaks, CA)
Journal of Religion, Spirituality and Aging (Waco, TX)
Journal of Renal Nutrition (Saint Louis, MO)
Journal of Reproductive Immunology (Salt Lake City, UT)
Journal of Research in International Education (Thousand Oaks, CA)
Journal of Research in Nursing (Thousand Oaks, CA)
Journal of the Riverside Historical Society (Riverside, CA)
Journal of Sandwich Structures and Materials (Thousand Oaks, CA)
Journal of Scandinavian Studies in Criminology and Crime Prevention (Philadelphia, PA)
Journal of School Choice (Binghamton, NY)
Journal of School Violence (Raleigh, NC)
Journal for the Scientific Study of Religion (Malden, MA)
Journal of Security Education (Binghamton, NY)
Journal of Sensory Studies (Scottsdale, AZ)
Journal of Separation Science (Hoboken, NJ)
Journal of Seventeenth-Century Music (Lancaster, PA)
Journal of Social Archaeology (Thousand Oaks, CA)
Journal of Social Issues (Washington, DC)
Journal of Social and Personal Relationships (Thousand Oaks, CA)
Journal of Social Work (Thousand Oaks, CA)
Journal of Social Work in Disability and Rehabilitation (Binghamton, NY)
Journal of Social Work in End-of-Life and Palliative Care (Tuscaloosa, AL)
Journal of the Society for the Anthropology of Europe (Berkeley, CA)
Journal of the Society for Gynecologic Investigation (New York, NY)

Journal of Sociology (Thousand Oaks, CA)
Journal of Solar Energy Engineering (New York, NY)
Journal for Specialists in Pediatric Nursing (Denver, CO)
Journal of Speculative Philosophy (Baltimore, MD)
Journal of Sports Economics (Thousand Oaks, CA)
Journal of Sports Sciences (Philadelphia, PA)
Journal of Statistical Computation and Simulation (Philadelphia, PA)
Journal of Studies in International Education (Thousand Oaks, CA)
Journal for the Study of the Historical Jesus (Thousand Oaks, CA)
Journal for the Study of the New Testament (Thousand Oaks, CA)
Journal for the Study of the Old Testament (Thousand Oaks, CA)
Journal for the Study of the Pseudepigrapha (Thousand Oaks, CA)
Journal of Substance Abuse Treatment (Philadelphia, PA)
Journal of Substance Use (Philadelphia, PA)
Journal of Sulfur Chemistry (Philadelphia, PA)
Journal of Surgical Research (Hershey, PA)
Journal of Teacher Education (Thousand Oaks, CA)
Journal of Texture Studies (Geneva, NY)
Journal of Theoretical and Computational Chemistry (New York, NY)
Journal of Theoretical Medicine (Philadelphia, PA)
Journal of Theoretical Politics (Thousand Oaks, CA)
Journal for the Theory of Social Behaviour (Malden, MA)
Journal of Thermal Envelope and Building Science (Thousand Oaks, CA)
Journal of Thermoplastic Composite Materials (Thousand Oaks, CA)
Journal of Toxicology and Environmental Health: A (Ottawa, ON)
Journal of Toxicology and Environmental Health: B (Ottawa, ON)
Journal of Transcultural Nursing (Thousand Oaks, CA)
Journal of Transformative Education (Thousand Oaks, CA)
Journal of Travel Research (Thousand Oaks, CA)
Journal of Turbulence (Philadelphia, PA)
Journal of Vacation Marketing (Thousand Oaks, CA)

Journal of Vegetable Science (Binghamton, NY)
Journal of Vibration and Acoustics (New York, NY)
Journal of Vibration and Control (Thousand Oaks, CA)
Journal of Vinyl and Additive Technology (Williamsburg, VA)
Journal of Visual Communication in Medicine (Philadelphia, PA)
Journal of Visual Culture (Thousand Oaks, CA)
Journal of Voice (Philadelphia, PA)
Journal of Website Promotion (Baton Rouge, LA)
Journal of Wide Bandgap Materials (Thousand Oaks, CA)
Journal of WOCN (Wound, Ostomy and Continence Nursing) (Baltimore, MD)
Journal of Women's History (Urbana, IL)
Journal of Women's Imaging (Baltimore, MD)
Journal of Wood Chemistry and Technology (Philadelphia, PA)
Journal of Workplace Behavioral Health (Orlando, FL)
Journal of X-Ray Science and Technology (Norman, OK)
Journalism (Thousand Oaks, CA)
JPO: Journal of Prosthetics and Orthotics (Baltimore, MD)
The Judge's Journal (Chicago, IL)
KABQ-FM (Albuquerque, NM)
KAKQ-FM (Fairbanks, AK)
Kansas City Nursing News (Overland Park, KS)
Kansas Review (Topeka, KS)
KAZX-FM (Farmington, NM)
KBGE-AM (Tyler, TX)
KBGO-FM (Waco, TX)
KBKO-AM (Santa Barbara, CA)
KBKO-FM (Bakersfield, CA)
KBME-AM (Houston, TX)
KBRQ-FM (Waco, TX)
KBTM-AM (Jonesboro, AR)
KBZS-FM (Wichita Falls, TX)
KCBL-AM (Fresno, CA)
KCNL-FM (San Jose, CA)
KCQL-AM (Farmington, NM)
KCQQ-FM (Davenport, IA)
KCRS-AM (Odessa, TX)
KDAG-FM (Farmington, NM)
KDBL-FM (Yakima, WA)
KDFO-AM (Bakersfield, CA)
KDFO-FM (Bakersfield, CA)
KDJE-FM (Little Rock, AR)
KDNN-FM (Honolulu, HI)

KDRB-FM (Des Moines, IA)
KDZA-FM (Pueblo, CO)
Keep on Truckin' News (Springfield, IL)
Kennel Up (Westerose, AB)
Kentucky Heritage (Frankfort, KY)
KEX-AM (Portland, OR)
Key Magazine Carmel/Monterey (Carmel, CA)
Key Magazine Milwaukee (Mequon, WI)
Key Magazine Oklahoma City (Shawnee, OK)
Key Magazine Santa Barbara/Ventura (Ventura, CA)
Key Magazine This Week in Chicago (Chicago, IL)
Key Magazine Tucson (Goodyear, AZ)
Keynotes (Harrisburg, PA)
KFAB-FM (Fargo, ND)
KFBX-AM (Fairbanks, AK)
KFI-AM (Los Angeles, CA)
KFMD-FM (Denver, CO)
KFMQ-FM (Gallup, NM)
KFMX-FM (Lubbock, TX)
KFNK-FM (Seattle, WA)
KFXN-AM (Minneapolis, MN)
KFXR-AM (Addison, TX)
KFXR-FM (Gallup, NM)
KFYR-AM (Bismarck, ND)
KGAB-AM (Cheyenne, WY)
KGET-AM (Bakersfield, CA)
KGVO-AM (Missoula, MT)
KHBZ-AM (Honolulu, HI)
KHBZ-FM (Oklahoma City, OK)
KHHO-AM (Seattle, WA)
KHHT-FM (Burbank, CA)
KHKN-FM (Little Rock, AR)
KHKZ-FM (Brownsville, TX)
KHTS-FM (San Diego, CA)
KHUS-FM (Omaha, NE)
KIAI-FM (Mason City, IA)
KIBT-FM (Colorado Springs, CO)
KIBZ-FM (Lincoln, NE)
KIGL-FM (Fayetteville, AR)
KIGN-FM (Cheyenne, WY)
KIIZ-FM (Harker Heights, TX)
Kirbyville Centennial Magazine 1995 (Kirbyville, TX)
Kiss Machine (Toronto, ON)
KIST-FM (Santa Barbara, CA)
Kitchens and Baths (New York, NY)
KIXA-FM (Victorville, CA)
KIXZ-FM (Spokane, WA)
KJMY-FM (Salt Lake City, UT)
KJQY-FM (Denver, CO)
KJR-AM (Seattle, WA)
KJR-FM (Seattle, WA)

# INDUSTRY ACTIVITY

KJZI-FM (Minneapolis, MN)
KKAM-AM (Lubbock, TX)
KKBX-FM (Fargo, ND)
KKCB-FM (Duluth, MN)
KKDM-FM (Des Moines, IA)
KKED-FM (Fairbanks, AK)
KKTL-AM (Casper, WY)
KKZN-AM (Denver, CO)
KLDJ-FM (Duluth, MN)
KLMY-FM (Lincoln, NE)
KLOO-FM (Albany, OR)
KLSD-AM (San Diego, CA)
KLTC-FM (Missoula, MT)
KLUB-FM (Victoria, TX)
KMFX-FM (Rochester, MN)
KMHK-FM (Billings, MT)
KMJI-FM (Texarkana, AR)
KMJM-AM (Cedar Rapids, IA)
KMMS-AM (Bozeman, MT)
KMMS-FM (Bozeman, MT)
KMRK-FM (Odessa, TX)
KMRQ-FM (Modesto, CA)
KMSX-FM (Little Rock, AR)
KMXF-FM (Fayetteville, AR)
KMYI-FM (San Diego, CA)
KMYT-FM (San Diego, CA)
KNFX-FM (Bryan, TX)
Knowledge and Process Management: The Journal of Corporate Transformation (Hoboken, NJ)
Knoxville Journal Express (Knoxville, GA)
KNRS-AM (Salt Lake City, UT)
KODJ-FM (Salt Lake City, UT)
KOSS-FM (Lancaster, CA)
KOSY-AM (Texarkana, AR)
KOSY-FM (Salt Lake City, UT)
KOY-AM (Tempe, AZ)
KPOJ-AM (Portland, OR)
KPRC-FM (Salinas, CA)
KPWW-FM (Texarkana, AR)
KQKE-AM (Concord, CA)
KQLF-FM (Fort Collins, CO)
KQNT-AM (Spokane, WA)
KQOL-FM (Las Vegas, NV)
KQVT-FM (Victoria, TX)
KQXX-AM (Brownsville, TX)
KRAB-FM (Bakersfield, CA)
KRSX-FM (Victorville, CA)
KRVK-FM (Casper, WY)
KRVO-FM (Portland, OR)
KSAS-FM (Boise, ID)
KSD-FM (Saint Louis, MO)
KSLI-AM (Abilene, TX)
KSLZ-FM (Saint Louis, MO)
KSME-FM (Fort Collins, CO)

KSMY-FM (Santa Maria, CA)
KSTT-FM (San Luis Obispo, CA)
KTBT-FM (Tulsa, OK)
KTBZ-AM (Tulsa, OK)
KTDD-AM (Riverside, CA)
KTHH-AM (Albany, OR)
KTHR-FM (Wichita, KS)
KTMQ-FM (San Diego, CA)
KTPI-AM (Lancaster, CA)
KTZN-AM (Anchorage, AK)
KTZR-FM (Tucson, AZ)
KULL-FM (Abilene, TX)
KURQ-FM (San Luis Obispo, CA)
KUSS-FM (San Diego, CA)
KUTI-AM (Yakima, WA)
KVBL-AM (Fresno, CA)
KVET-FM (Austin, TX)
KVNS-AM (Brownsville, TX)
KVVS-FM (Mojave, CA)
KWFM-AM (Tucson, AZ)
KWHF-FM (Jonesboro, AR)
KWID-FM (Las Vegas, NV)
KWMT-FM (Tucson, AZ)
KWYY-FM (Casper, WY)
KXLB-FM (Bozeman, MT)
KXMR-AM (Bismarck, ND)
KXRV-FM (Salt Lake City, UT)
KXTA-AM (Los Angeles, CA)
KXTC-FM (Gallup, NM)
KXUS-FM (Springfield, MO)
KXXM-FM (San Antonio, TX)
KYGL-FM (Texarkana, AR)
KYJT-FM (Yuma, AZ)
KYYW-AM (Abilene, TX)
KZCH-FM (Wichita, KS)
KZFX-AM (Salinas, CA)
La Bonne Vie (Chatham, ON)
L.A. Daily News (Woodland Hills, CA)
LABI Enterprise (Baton Rouge, LA)
The Labor Lawyer (Syracuse, NY)
Labor: Studies in Working-Class History of the Americas (Chicago, IL)
Lake Chelan Visitors Guide (Chelan, WA)
Lake County Visitors Guide (Hammond, IN)
Lake in the Hills Countryside (Algonquin, IL)
The Lake Los Angeles News (Lake Los Angeles, CA)
Lake Michigan Circle Tour and Lighthouse Guide (Grand Rapids, MI)
Lakeville Sun Current (Eden Prairie, MN)
Lamar County Genealogy & History (Paris, TX)

Language Assessment Quarterly (Mahwah, NJ)
Language Learning and Development (Mahwah, NJ)
Language and Literature (Thousand Oaks, CA)
Lansing City Community News (Charlotte, MI)
Lapeer Legacy (Lapeer, MI)
Laredo Economic Activity Index (Laredo, TX)
Laser Physics Letters (Hoboken, NJ)
Latina Magazine (New York, NY)
Law Enforcement Product News (Fort Atkinson, WI)
Law and Literature (Berkeley, CA)
LC-GC Asia Pacific (Cleveland, OH)
LC-GC Europe (Cleveland, OH)
Leader to Leader (Hoboken, NJ)
Leadership (Thousand Oaks, CA)
Leadership in Action (Hoboken, NJ)
League Peaks (Colorado Springs, CO)
Leaves and Saplings (El Cajon, CA)
Lebanon Enterprise (Lebanon, KY)
Lebensmittelchemie (Hoboken, NJ)
The Leeds News (Leeds, AL)
Legacy (Edmonton, AB)
Leonardo (San Francisco, CA)
Les Papetieres du Quebec (Toronto, ON)
Lethaia (Philadelphia, PA)
Lethbridge living (Lethbridge, AB)
Letter of Invitation (Stamford, CT)
Leukemia and Lymphoma (Philadelphia, PA)
Leukemia Research (Rochester, NY)
Lexington Snitch (Lexington, KY)
Library & Archival Security (Binghamton, NY)
License! (Cleveland, OH)
License! Europe (Cleveland, OH)
Life Learning (Toronto, ON)
Life on Mars (Mars, PA)
Life in the Valley (Salt Lake City, UT)
Lifelines (Plattsburgh, NY)
Lifestyles (Fort Walton Beach, FL)
LIGHTHOUSE (Burlington, ON)
LIGHTHOUSE (Calgary, AB)
Lightwave Europe (Nashua, NH)
Linear and Multilinear Algebra (Philadelphia, PA)
The Linking Ring (Cary, NC)
Lippincott's Case Management (Baltimore, MD)
Liquid Crystals (Philadelphia, PA)
Literary Review of Canada (Toronto, ON)

# INDUSTRY ACTIVITY

Litigation (Chicago, IL)
Liturgy (Philadelphia, PA)
Local 951 Journal (Grand Rapids, MI)
Lockport Union-Sun & Journal (Lockport, NY)
Locksmith Ledger International (Arlington Heights, IL)
The Logan Banner (Logan, WV)
Logopedics Phoniatrics Vocology (Philadelphia, PA)
Logos: A Journal of Catholic Thought and Culture (Saint Paul, MN)
Long Weekends (Cleveland, OH)
Los Angeles Wave (Los Angeles, CA)
Los Angeles Wave: East Edition (Los Angeles, CA)
Los Angeles Wave: Lynwood Edition (Los Angeles, CA)
Los Angeles Wave: Northeast Edition (Los Angeles, CA)
Los Angeles Wave: West Edition (Los Angeles, CA)
Los Gatos Daily News (Los Gatos, CA)
Lou Lou (Toronto, ON)
Louisiana Propane-Gas News (Baton Rouge, LA)
Louisville Snitch (Louisville, KY)
Lowrider (Anaheim, CA)
Lowrider Arte (Anaheim, CA)
Lupus Now (Des Moines, IA)
Lustre Magazine (Cedar Grove, NJ)
Lymphatic Research and Biology (Stanford, CA)
Lynch's Ferry Magazine (Lynchburg, VA)
M (Montgomery, AL)
Machining Science and Technology (Philadelphia, PA)
Macromolecular Bioscience (Hoboken, NJ)
Macromolecular Chemistry and Physics (Hoboken, NJ)
Macromolecular Materials and Engineering (Hoboken, NJ)
Macromolecular Rapid Communications (Hoboken, NJ)
Macromolecular Symposia (Hoboken, NJ)
Macromolecular Theory and Simulations (Hoboken, NJ)
MADDvocate (Columbia, SC)
MADDvocate (Frankfort, KY)
Madera County Farm Bureau News (Madera, CA)
Madison County Heritage (Oneida, NY)
Madison County Musings (Huntsville, AR)
Madison Magazine (Madison, FL)
MAG Newsletter (Phoenix, AZ)
Magazine (Colorado Springs, CO)

Magazine (Richmond, VA)
Magnetic Resonance Imaging (Nashville, TN)
Magnetic Resonance Imaging Clinics (Saint Louis, MO)
Magnetic Resonance in Medicine (Hershey, PA)
Mahwah Suburban News (West Paterson, NJ)
Mail Works (Montreal, QC)
Main Group Chemistry (Philadelphia, PA)
Maisonneuve (Montreal, QC)
Mama (Hyannis, MA)
Management Learning (Thousand Oaks, CA)
Management Research: The Journal of the Iberoamerican Academy of Management (Armonk, NY)
Mankato Free Press (Mankato, MN)
Manual Therapy (Saint Louis, MO)
Marana Community Profile and Membership Directory (Marana, AZ)
Marco Island (Marco Island, FL)
Marietta Daily Journal (Marietta, GA)
Marine Biology Research (Philadelphia, PA)
Marine and Freshwater Behaviour & Physiology (Philadelphia, PA)
Marketing Theory (Thousand Oaks, CA)
Marshall County Historical Society Quarterly (Plymouth, IN)
Maryknoll (East Walpole, MA)
Maryland Bar Journal (Baltimore, MD)
Maryland Messenger (Glen Burnie, MD)
Mass Communication & Society (Ithaca, NY)
Mass Spectrometry Reviews (Memphis, TN)
Massachusetts Law Review (Boston, MA)
Material History Review (Ottawa, ON)
Materials and Corrosion/Werkstoffe und Korrosion (Hoboken, NJ)
Materials and Manufacturing Processes (Philadelphia, PA)
Materialwissenschaft und Werkstofftechnik (Hoboken, NJ)
Mathematical and Computer Modelling of Dynamical Systems (Philadelphia, PA)
Mathematical Population Studies (Philadelphia, PA)
Mathematics and Mechanics of Solids (Thousand Oaks, CA)
Matrix Magazine (Montreal, QC)
Maturitas (Saint Louis, MO)
Mayo Free Press (Mayo, FL)
McAlester News-Capital (McAlester, OK)
McCall's Quick Quilts (Golden, CO)

McCall's Quilting (Golden, CO)
McCreary County Record (Whitley City, KY)
McKinney Living Magazine (McKinney, TX)
McKinney Living Magazine's Relocation & Referral Guide (McKinney, TX)
McLean County News (Calhoun, KY)
Mechanics of Advanced Materials and Structures (Philadelphia, PA)
Mechanics Based Design of Structures and Machines (Philadelphia, PA)
Media, Culture and Society (Thousand Oaks, CA)
Media Week (New York, NY)
Medical Anthropology (Philadelphia, PA)
Medical Care (Baltimore, MD)
Medical Care Research and Review (Thousand Oaks, CA)
Medical Clinics of North America (Saint Louis, MO)
Medical Decision Making (Thousand Oaks, CA)
Medical Economics (Montvale, NJ)
Medical Meetings (Overland Park, KS)
Medical Mycology (Philadelphia, PA)
Medical Teacher (Philadelphia, PA)
The Medieval History Journal (Thousand Oaks, CA)
Meeting News (New York, NY)
Meeting Planner Guide (Sacramento, CA)
Melanoma Research (Baltimore, MD)
Members Guide (Tampa, FL)
Members' Magazine (Toronto, ON)
Membership Directory/Buyers Guide (Lake Wales, FL)
Men and Masculinities (Thousand Oaks, CA)
Menifee County News (Morehead, KY)
Mennonite Health Journal (Goshen, IN)
Mental and Physical Disability Law Digest (Chicago, IL)
Mental and Physical Disability Law Reporter (Chicago, IL)
Mental Retardation in Developmental Disabilities Research Reviews (Baltimore, MD)
Merced Today (Merced, CA)
Mercer County History (Mercer, PA)
Mergent's Dividend Achievers (Hoboken, NJ)
Mergent's Handbook of Common Stocks (Hoboken, NJ)
Mergent's Handbook of NASDAQ Stocks (Hoboken, NJ)
Meta (Ottawa, ON)

Metabolism-Clinical and Experimental (Saint Louis, MO)
Mfg. (Pittsburgh, PA)
MFS: Modern Fiction Studies (West Lafayette, IN)
MHQ: The Quarterly Journal of Military History (Leesburg, VA)
Michigan Bicyclist (Lansing, MI)
Michigan Boating Annual (Livonia, MI)
Michigan Chess (Novi, MI)
Michigan Farm Edition (Buckner, KY)
Michigan Forward (Lansing, MI)
Michigan Historical Review (East Lansing, MI)
Michigan History Magazine (East Lansing, MI)
Michigan-Indiana Holstein News (Greens Fork, IN)
Microbial Ecology in Health and Disease (Philadelphia, PA)
Microcirculation (Philadelphia, PA)
Microscale Thermophysical Engineering (Philadelphia, PA)
Middle School Journal (Saginaw, MI)
Middlesex Magazine and Business Review (Middletown, CT)
Midland Park Suburban News (West Paterson, NJ)
Midwifery (Saint Louis, MO)
Military History (Leesburg, VA)
Mill Valley Business (Mill Valley, CA)
Mineral Processing and Extractive Metallurgy Review (Philadelphia, PA)
Mineral Wells Index (Mineral Wells, TX)
Minimally Invasive Therapy and Allied Technologies (Philadelphia, PA)
Minnesota Cities (Saint Paul, MN)
Minnesota Journal (Minneapolis, MN)
Minnesota Precision Manufacturing Journal (Plymouth, MN)
Minnetonka Sun Sailor (Eden Prairie, MN)
Missions Today (Scarborough, ON)
Missouri Architect (Jefferson City, MO)
Missouri Courier (Saint Louis, MO)
MIX (Overland Park, KS)
MLN: Modern Language Notes (Baltimore, MD)
Modern Bulk Transporter (Overland Park, KS)
Modern Judaism (Boston, MA)
Modern Uniforms (Overland Park, KS)
Molecular Crystals and Liquid Crystals (Philadelphia, PA)
Molecular Nutrition and Food Research (Hoboken, NJ)
Molecular Simulation (Philadelphia, PA)

Molecular Vision: a Peer-Reviewed Web Journals (Albany, NY)
Money Sense (Toronto, ON)
Moneysense (Toronto, ON)
Monrovia Weekly (Arcadia, CA)
Montage (Toronto, ON)
Montana English Journal (Helena, MT)
Montgomery County Story (Rockville, MD)
Montgomery Herald (Beckley) (Montgomery, WV)
Monthly Digest (Towson, MD)
Monthly Reporter (Madison, WI)
Motor Age (Cleveland, OH)
Motor Caravan (New York, NY)
Motorcycle Cruiser (Los Angeles, CA)
Mount Snow/Haystack Chamber - Guide to Southern Vermont (Wilmington, VT)
Mountain Country (Franconia, NH)
Mountain Life (Calgary, AB)
Mountain Traveler (Athens, GA)
MSBOA Journal (Ann Arbor, MI)
MSDN Magazine (San Francisco, CA)
Municipal Bulletin (Albany, NY)
The Murals of Lake Placid (Lake Placid, FL)
Murray-Calloway County Magazine (Murray, KY)
Murrieta Chamber of Commerce Business Directory and Community Resource Guide (Murrieta, CA)
Muscle Mustangs and Fast Fords (Anaheim, CA)
Muse (Ottawa, ON)
Museletter (Somerville, MA)
Music Education Technology (Overland Park, KS)
Music Theory Spectrum (Oberlin, OH)
Musical Quarterly (Annandale on Hudson, NY)
NACBA-Ledger (Tulsa, OK)
Nanomedicine: Nanotechnology, Biology, and Medicine (Baltimore, MD)
Nanotoxicology (Philadelphia, PA)
NAPA Bulletin (Berkeley, CA)
NASW Missouri Chapter Newspaper (Jefferson City, MO)
Nation (Montreal, QC)
National (Okotoks, AB)
National Floor Trends (NFT) (Woodland Hills, CA)
National Hog Farmer (Overland Park, KS)
National Institute Economic Review (Thousand Oaks, CA)
National Outdoor America (Milwaukee, WI)
The Natural Farmer (Barre, MA)

Natural Gas and Electricity (Hoboken, NJ)
Natural Product Research (Philadelphia, PA)
Natural Resources and Environment (Chicago, IL)
NEA News (Washington, DC)
NEARA Journal (Edgecomb, ME)
Nebraska Humanities (Lincoln, NE)
Nebraska School Law Reporter (Lincoln, NE)
The Nebraska Sheriff (Lincoln, NE)
The Negro Spiritual (Oakland, CA)
Nenana Messenger (Nenana, AK)
NEPA Bulletin (Boston, MA)
Nephron Clinical Practice (Farmington, CT)
Nephron Experimental Nephrology (Farmington, CT)
Nephron Physiology (Farmington, CT)
Net Results (Marietta, GA)
Network (Philadelphia, PA)
Neuro-Oncology (Durham, NC)
Neuro-Ophthalmology (Philadelphia, PA)
Neurodegenerative Diseases (Farmington, CT)
Neuroimaging Clinics of North America (New York, NY)
Neurologic Clinics (Saint Louis, MO)
Neurology Now (Baltimore, MD)
Neuropeptides (Saint Louis, MO)
NeuroRehabilitation (Richmond, VA)
NeuroReport (Baltimore, MD)
Neuroscience (Saint Louis, MO)
Neuroscience & Biobehavioral Reviews (Saint Louis, MO)
The Neuroscientist (Thousand Oaks, CA)
Neurosurgery Clinics of North America (San Francisco, CA)
Neutron News (Philadelphia, PA)
New Albany News (Columbus, OH)
The New American (Yakima, WA)
New Beginnings (Evansville, IN)
New Castle News (New Castle, PA)
New Directions for Philanthropic Fundraising (Hoboken, NJ)
New Directions for Teaching and Learning (Austin, TX)
The New Educator (Philadelphia, PA)
New Educator (New York, NY)
New England Theatre Journal (Boston, MA)
New Jersey Audubon (Bernardsville, NJ)
New Jersey English Journal (Caldwell, NJ)
New Labor Forum (Philadelphia, PA)
New Literary History (Charlottesville, VA)

INDUSTRY ACTIVITY

New Mathematics and Natural Computation (Durham, NC)
New Media and Society (Thousand Oaks, CA)
New Review of Hypermedia and Multimedia (Philadelphia, PA)
New Socialist (Toronto, ON)
New Technology Magazine (Toronto, ON)
New Times (San Jose, CA)
New Trail (Edmonton, AB)
New York Chinese American Association Annual Journal (Flushing, NY)
New York-City Guide Magazine (New York, NY)
New York Parent-Teacher (Albany, NY)
Newborn and Infant Nursing Reviews (Saint Louis, MO)
Newcomers Guide (Monroe, NC)
Newman Studies Journal (Pittsburgh, PA)
The News-Courier (Athens, AL)
News Daily (Jonesboro, GA)
The News-Enterprise (Elizabethtown, KY)
News Leader (Lavonia, GA)
Newsworthy (Minneapolis, MN)
Newton County Saga (Neosho, MO)
NGAT News (Austin, TX)
Niagara Gazette (Niagara Falls, NY)
Niagara this Week (Thorold, ON)
Nickle's Oil & Gas Statistics Quarterly (Toronto, ON)
Nicotine & Tobacco Research (Philadelphia, PA)
90210 Beverly Hills (Los Angeles, CA)
Nondestructive Testing and Evaluation (Philadelphia, PA)
NORA (Philadelphia, PA)
Nordic Journal of Psychiatry (Philadelphia, PA)
Norman Business Journal (Norman, OK)
North American Bird Bander (Hellertown, PA)
North American Dialogue (Arlington, VA)
North American Inns (Hamilton, ON)
North Augusta Lifestyle Guide (North Augusta, SC)
The North Jefferson News (Gardendale, AL)
Northeast-Midwest Economic Review (Washington, DC)
Northern Business Journal (Timmins, ON)
Northern Hi-Lites (Arlington Heights, IL)
Northern Horse Review (Calgary, AB)
Northern Kentucky Heritage Magazine (Covington, KY)
Northern Kentucky Snitch (Newport, KY)

Northlake Herald-Journal (Oak Park, IL)
NorthVIEW (Anchorage, AK)
Northwest Navigator (Bainbridge Island, WA)
Northwestern Journal of International Law & Business (Champaign, IL)
Norwegian Archaeological Review (Philadelphia, PA)
Nova Religio: The Journal of Alternative and Emergent Religions (New Orleans, LA)
Nuclear Law Bulletin (Washington, DC)
Nuclear Medicine and Biology (Bethesda, MD)
Nuclear Medicine Communications (Baltimore, MD)
Nuclear Physics News (Philadelphia, PA)
Nucleosides, Nucleotides and Nucleic Acids (Philadelphia, PA)
Nuevo Mundo (San Jose, CA)
Numerical Functional Analysis and Optimization (Philadelphia, PA)
Nurse Leader (Nashville, TN)
Nursing Administration Quarterly (Baltimore, MD)
Nursing Clinics of North America (Saint Louis, MO)
Nursing Made Incredibly Easy! (Baltimore, MD)
Nursing Research (Baltimore, MD)
Nursing Science Quarterly (Thousand Oaks, CA)
Nursing2005 (Baltimore, MD)
Nutrition (Syracuse, NY)
Nutrition Research (West Lafayette, IN)
Nutritional Anthropology (Berkeley, CA)
Nutritional Neuroscience (Philadelphia, PA)
Nutritional Neuroscience (New Orleans, LA)
NUVO Magazine (Vancouver, BC)
Oak Park Oak Leaves (Oak Park, IL)
Oakland Business Review (Oakland, CA)
Obesity Management (Denver, CO)
Objective Conseiller (Montreal, QC)
Obstetrics & Gynecology Clinics (Saint Louis, MO)
Occasional Papers of the Association of Senior Anthropologists (Washington, DC)
Occupational Ergonomics (Halifax, NS)
Ocean Yearbook (Halifax, NS)
October (New York, NY)
Ocular Immunology and Inflammation (Louisville, KY)
Ocular Immunology and Inflammation (Philadelphia, PA)

Ocular Surgery News Japan Edition (Thorofare, NJ)
OD Practitioner (South Orange, NJ)
OECD Economic Outlook (Washington, DC)
OECD Papers (Washington, DC)
Off-Road Retailer (Cleveland, OH)
The Official All Around Alton Visitors Guide (Alton, IL)
Official Buyer's Guide (DeFuniak Springs, FL)
Ohio Business (Cleveland, OH)
The Ohio Christian News (Columbus, OH)
Ohio Civil War Genealogy Journal (Mansfield, OH)
Ohio Entrepreneur (Cleveland, OH)
Ohio Genealogical Society Quarterly (Mansfield, OH)
Ohio Matters (Columbus, OH)
Ohio PHC Contractor (Chagrin Falls, OH)
Ohio Prairie Gazette (Huron, OH)
Oil & Gas Financial Journal (Houston, TX)
Okoboji Spirit (Arnolds Park, IA)
Old Wall Historical Society Journal (Wall, NJ)
On the Line (Concord, CA)
On Site (Fort Wayne, IN)
On Site (Ajax, ON)
On-Stream (Calgary, AB)
Oncology Hematology (Saint Louis, MO)
Oncology News International (Manhasset, NY)
Oneida Press (Canastota, NY)
Online Journal of Issues in Nursing (Salt Lake City, UT)
Operations & Fulfillment (Overland Park, KS)
Operative Techniques in Neurosurgery (Saint Louis, MO)
Operative Techniques in Orthopaedics (Saint Louis, MO)
Operative Techniques in Otolaryngology–Head and Neck Surgery (Saint Louis, MO)
Operative Techniques in Plastic and Reconstructive Surgery (Saint Louis, MO)
Operative Techniques in Sports Medicine (Saint Louis, MO)
Ophthalmic Epidemiology (Vancouver, BC)
Ophthalmic Epidemiology (Shreveport, LA)
Ophthalmic Epidemiology (Philadelphia, PA)
Ophthalmic Genetics (Philadelphia, PA)

Ophthalmic Genetics (Cleveland, OH)
Ophthalmology (Baltimore, MD)
Ophthalmology Clinics of North America (San Francisco, CA)
Ophthalmology Times International (Cleveland, OH)
Opinion-Tribune (Glenwood, IA)
Optimization (Philadelphia, PA)
Optimize (Manhasset, NY)
Optoelectronics Manufacturing (Nashua, NH)
Optometry and Vision Science (Baltimore, MD)
Opus (Toronto, ON)
Oral and Maxillofacial Surgery Clinics of North America (Saint Louis, MO)
The Orange Leader (Birmingham, AL)
The Oregon Clarion (Salem, OR)
The Oregon PeaceWorker (Albany, OR)
Organization (Thousand Oaks, CA)
Organization and Environment (Thousand Oaks, CA)
Organization Studies (Thousand Oaks, CA)
Organizational Research Methods (Thousand Oaks, CA)
Orthopaedic Nursing (Baltimore, MD)
Orthopedic Clinics of North America (Saint Louis, MO)
The Oskaloosa Herald (Oskaloosa, IA)
Osteoarthritis and Cartilage (Agua Dulce, CA)
Other Voices (Edmonton, AB)
Otorlaryngologic Clinics of North America (Saint Louis, MO)
Ottumwa Daily Courier (Ottumwa, IA)
Our Canada (Montreal, QC)
Our World (Calgary, AB)
Outlook (New Lenox, IL)
Outlook (Fairless Hills, PA)
Outpost (Toronto, ON)
Overland Journal (Independence, MO)
Pacific Golf (Burnaby, BC)
Pacific Palisades (Los Angeles, CA)
Packet & Times (Orillia, ON)
Paedriatric Respiratory Reviews (Saint Louis, MO)
Pain (San Francisco, CA)
Pain Management Nursing (Saint Louis, MO)
Palos Verdes View (Culver City, CA)
Pancreatology (Farmington, CT)
Paper Crafts (Bluffdale, UT)
Papers in Regional Science (West Lafayette, IN)
Parenting (Bethesda, MD)
Parenting (New York, NY)

Parker Country Magazine (Parker, CO)
Parkinsonism & Related Disorders (Vancouver, BC)
Parks and Recreation Canada (Ottawa, ON)
Party Politics (Thousand Oaks, CA)
Passport to the Legendary West (Billings, MT)
Pathfinder (Spokane, WA)
Patient Care (Montvale, NJ)
Patient Education and Counseling (Boston, MA)
Paulding Neighbor (Marietta, GA)
Paw Prints (Austin, TX)
PDN (Photo District News) (New York, NY)
The Peanut Patriot (Albany, GA)
PEB Exchange (Washington, DC)
Pediatric Blood and Cancer (Hoboken, NJ)
Pediatric Clinics of North America (Saint Louis, MO)
Pediatric Neurology (Saint Paul, MN)
Pegasus (Orlando, FL)
Pelham News (Pelham, ON)
Penguin Eggs (Edmonton, AB)
Perry County Community Profile Magazine (Tell City, IN)
Personalist Forum (Oklahoma City, OK)
Perspectives (Hamilton, NJ)
Perspectives in Biology and Medicine (Chicago, IL)
Perspectives in Psychiatric Care (Van Nuys, CA)
Perspectives on Science: Historical, Philosophical, Social (Blacksburg, VA)
Petaluma Business (Petaluma, CA)
Pharmaceutical Discovery (Cleveland, OH)
Pharmaceutical Executive (Cleveland, OH)
Pharmaceutical Statistics (Hoboken, NJ)
Pharmaceutical Technology (Cleveland, OH)
Pharmaceutical Technology Europe (Cleveland, OH)
Pharmacogenetics and Genomics (Baltimore, MD)
Pharmazie in unserer Zeit (Hoboken, NJ)
The Pharos-Tribune (Logansport, IN)
Philip Roth Studies (Washington, DC)
Philosophy in the Contemporary World (Green Bay, WI)
Philosophy and Rhetoric (Baltimore, MD)
Philosophy and Social Criticism (Thousand Oaks, CA)

Photomedicine and Laser Surgery (Rochester, NY)
Physical Biology (Philadelphia, PA)
Physical Medicine & Rehabilitation Clinics of North America (Saint Louis, MO)
Physical Therapy in Sport (Saint Louis, MO)
Piano Guild Notes (Fairport, NY)
Pickerington Times-Sun (Columbus, OH)
Pictorial Register (Albuquerque, NM)
Pioneer (Salt Lake City, UT)
Pioneer Days Family Festival (Orlando, FL)
Pioneer Trails (Pendleton, OR)
Pittsburgh Point Magazine (Pittsburgh, PA)
Planning Theory (Thousand Oaks, CA)
Plastic Surgical Nursing (Baltimore, MD)
PLG-TV (Bardstown, KY)
Plymouth Sun Sailor (Eden Prairie, MN)
PM (Bensenville, IL)
PMEA News (Hamburg, PA)
PN/Paraplegia News (Hines, IL)
Point of Care (Baltimore, MD)
Police Officers Journal (New York, NY)
Police Quarterly (Thousand Oaks, CA)
Policy Papers (Ottawa, ON)
Policy, Politics, and Nursing Practice (Thousand Oaks, CA)
Political Analysis (New York, NY)
Politics, Philosophy and Economics (Thousand Oaks, CA)
Polymer Composites (Hoboken, NJ)
Polymer Engineering and Science (Hoboken, NJ)
Popular Communication (Athens, OH)
Popular Hot Rodding (Anaheim, CA)
Population, Space and Place (Hoboken, NJ)
Port Colborne Leader (Port Colborne, ON)
Port Colborne Shopper (Port Colborne, ON)
Portland, Oregon: The Official Visitor Guide (Portland, OR)
Potentials (New York, NY)
POV (Point of View) (Toronto, ON)
Powder (Dana Point, CA)
Power Electronics Technology (Overland Park, KS)
PPA Literary Review (East Meadow, NY)
Practical Diabetes International (Hoboken, NJ)
Practical Horseman (Gaithersburg, MD)
Prairies North (Norquay, SK)
Prehospital Emergency Care (Saint Louis, MO)

## INDUSTRY ACTIVITY

- Premier Living Guide (West Des Moines, IA)
- Premiere (Los Angeles, CA)
- Prepared Foods (Bensenville, IL)
- Press for Conversion (Ottawa, ON)
- Preventative Veterinary Medicine (Ithaca, NY)
- Primary Care: Clinics in Office Practice (Berea, KY)
- Primary Care Update for OB/GYNS (Berea, KY)
- Prime (Syracuse, NY)
- Pro-Ado (Montreal, QC)
- Pro-Contractor (Calgary, AB)
- Pro-Teen (Montreal, QC)
- Probation Journal (Thousand Oaks, CA)
- Proceedings (Yellowstone National Park, WY)
- Proceedings of the American Catholic Philosophical Association (Charlottesville, VA)
- Proceedings of Annual Production Conference (Bethlehem, PA)
- Proceedings of NCHS (Sunbury, PA)
- Proceedings and Papers of the Greenville County Historical Society (Greenville, SC)
- Process Safety Progress (Hoboken, NJ)
- Professional Distributor (Fort Atkinson, WI)
- Professional Safety (Keithville, LA)
- Professional Tool & Equipment News (Melville, NY)
- Profit (Toronto, ON)
- Progress in Pediatric Cardiology (Kansas City, KS)
- Progress in Structural Engineering and Materials (Hoboken, NJ)
- Project (Ottawa, ON)
- PROMO (Overland Park, KS)
- Propellants, Explosives, Pyrotechnics (Hoboken, NJ)
- Proteins: Structure, Function, and Bioinformatics (Hoboken, NJ)
- Proteomics (Hoboken, NJ)
- Pryor Daily Times (Pryor, OK)
- Psychiatric Clinics of North America (Berea, KY)
- Psychiatric Genetics (Baltimore, MD)
- Psychiatric Times (Irvine, CA)
- Psychiatry (New York, NY)
- Psychiatry Research: Neuroimaging (New York, NY)
- Psychoanalytic Psychology (New York, NY)
- Psychoanalytic Psychology (Washington, DC)
- Psychological Methods (Washington, DC)
- Psychological Methods (Tempe, AZ)
- Psychological Services (Washington, DC)
- Psychology of Addictive Behaviors (Boston, MA)
- Psychology and Developing Societies (Thousand Oaks, CA)
- Psychology of Men & Masculinity (Iowa City, IA)
- Psychology of Men & Masculinity (Washington, DC)
- Psychology of Music (Thousand Oaks, CA)
- Psychology, Public Policy, and Law (Washington, DC)
- Psychology of Sport and Exercise (Berea, KY)
- Psychoneuroendocrinology (Madison, WI)
- Psychotherapy: Theory, Research, Practice, Training (College Park, MD)
- Psychotherapy: Theory, Research, Practice, Training (Washington, DC)
- P2: Pollution Prevention Review (Hoboken, NJ)
- Public (Toronto, ON)
- Public Health (Berea, KY)
- Public Integrity (Tallahassee, FL)
- The Public Lawyer (Chicago, IL)
- Public Performance and Management Review (Armonk, NY)
- Public Understanding of Science (Thousand Oaks, CA)
- Publication of the American Dialect Society (Durham, NC)
- Publications of the ASP (San Francisco, CA)
- Puget Sound Fresh Farm Guide (Seattle, WA)
- Pulp Magazine (San Bernardino, CA)
- Pulp & Paper Canada (Toronto, ON)
- Pulse Niagara (Saint Catharines, ON)
- Punishment and Society (Thousand Oaks, CA)
- Purchasing b2b (Toronto, ON)
- Purple Martin Update (Edinboro, PA)
- Pythian International (New Castle, IN)
- QSAR and Combinatorial Science (Hoboken, NJ)
- QUALITY (Bensenville, IL)
- Quality Assurance Journal (Hoboken, NJ)
- Quality of Life (Chatsworth, GA)
- Quality of Life (Rock Spring, GA)
- Quality of Life (Phenix City, AL)
- Quality of Life Magazine (Creve Coeur, MO)
- Quality Management in Health Care (Baltimore, MD)
- Quarterly (Mundelein, IL)
- The Quester (Vancouver, BC)
- Queue: Tomorrow's Computing Today (New York, NY)
- Quilter's Newsletter Magazine (Golden, CO)
- Quiltmaker (Golden, CO)
- Radical Philosophy Review (San Francisco, CA)
- Radiologic Clinics of North America (Berea, KY)
- Ralph (San Francisco, CA)
- Rampike Magazine (Windsor, ON)
- Ramsey Suburban News (West Paterson, NJ)
- Rapid Magazine (Palmer Rapids, ON)
- RDH (Nashua, NH)
- Real Estate Advertiser (Saint Catharines, ON)
- Real Estate Magazine (Kennewick, WA)
- Real Living with Multiple Sclerosis (Baltimore, MD)
- Real Property, Probate and Trust Journal (New York, NY)
- The Record (Hot Springs, AR)
- Records and Information Management Report (Armonk, NY)
- Redding Directions (Redding, CA)
- Redwood City Daily News (San Mateo, CA)
- The Reel News (Gig Harbor, WA)
- Reeves Journal (Troy, MI)
- Reflections (Richmond, MO)
- Refrigerated Transporter (Overland Park, KS)
- Region 4 Omnibus (Lincoln, NE)
- Regional Anesthesia and Pain Medicine (Berea, KY)
- Registered Rep. (Overland Park, KS)
- Rehab & Community Care Medicine (Toronto, ON)
- Rehabilitation Journal (Toronto, ON)
- Rehabilitation Psychology (Washington, DC)
- Rejuvenation Research (Larchmont, NY)
- Relatively Seeking (Columbus, KS)
- Relocation Guide (Ogden, UT)
- Remembering Our Past (Loogootee, IN)
- Remix (Mount Morris, IL)
- Rental Equipment Register (Overland Park, KS)
- Research in Human Development (Mahwah, NJ)
- Research in Social & Administrative Pharmacy (Pittsburgh, PA)
- Research in Veterinary Science (Berea, KY)
- Residential Design & Build (Arlington Heights, VA)

# INDUSTRY ACTIVITY

Resource Book (Livonia, MI)
Respiratory Care Clinics of North America (Berea, KY)
Retina (Baltimore, MD)
Review of General Psychology (Lewisburg, PA)
Review of General Psychology (Washington, DC)
The Review of Higher Education (Houston, TX)
Reviews in Medical Microbiology (Baltimore, MD)
Reviews in Toxicology (Raleigh, NC)
Revista Maryknoll (East Walpole, MA)
Revue d'Histoire de l'Amerique Francaise (Outremont, QC)
Reynoldsburg News (Columbus, OH)
Rhetoric Review (Tucson, AZ)
Rheumatic Disease Clinics of North America (Saint Louis, MO)
Rhode Island Independent Agent (Warwick, RI)
Rhubarb (Winnipeg, MB)
Richmond Magazine (Richmond, CA)
Richmond Register (Richmond, KY)
RINK Magazine (Larchmont, NY)
River Forest Forest Leaves (Oak Park, IL)
River Grove Messenger (Oak Park, IL)
River Teeth (Lincoln, NE)
Riverland News (Dunnellon, FL)
RN (Cleveland, OH)
Roadhouse Music Magazine (Tucson, AZ)
The Roaring Muse (Duluth, MN)
Robbinsdale Sun Post (Robbinsdale, MN)
Rod and Custom (Anaheim, CA)
The Rosamond News (Rosamond, CA)
Rosemead/El Monte Neighborhood News (Walnut, CA)
Rosemead Report (Rosemead, CA)
Rosemount Sun Current (Eden Prairie, MN)
Route 422 Business Advisor (Pottstown, PA)
Rugby World (New York, NY)
Rural Voices (Washington, DC)
RV Trade Digest (Melville, NY)
Ryerson Review of Journalism (Toronto, ON)
Sacramento Hispanic (Sacramento, CA)
SAE Journal (Tucson, AZ)
Safety Alert (Lincoln, NE)
St. Catharines Shopping News (Saint Catharines, ON)
St. Catharines Standard (Saint Catharines, ON)

St. Louis Nursing News (Overland Park, KS)
San Bernardino Green Sheet (Redlands, CA)
San Diego Snitch (San Diego, CA)
San Diego Tennis Yearbook (San Diego, CA)
San Mateo Daily News (San Mateo, CA)
Sanctuary (Lincoln, MA)
The Santa Monica Sun (Los Angeles, CA)
The S.A.R. Magazine (Saint Clair Shores, MI)
SAR Magazine (Boise, ID)
The SAR Magazine (Milpitas, CA)
The SAR Magazine (Newport Beach, CA)
Saskatoon StarPhoenix (Saskatoon, SK)
Savannah Snitch (Savannah, GA)
S.C. Nurse (Columbia, SC)
Scale Auto (Waukesha, WI)
The Scene: Diamond Bar (Walnut, CA)
Schizophrenia Research (Cincinnati, OH)
Schoharie County Historical Review (Schoharie, NY)
Science and Spirit (Quincy, MA)
The Sciences (New York, NY)
The SciTech Lawyer (Chicago, IL)
Scott's Fort Erie Shopper (Fort Erie, ON)
Scripsit (Merrifield, VA)
Scrye (Iola, WI)
Second Impressions (Saint Albert, AB)
Secure Enterprise (Manhasset, NY)
Security Dealer (Melville, NY)
Security Technology & Design (Cumming, GA)
SEE-The Berkshires (Adams, MA)
Seeds of Diversity (Toronto, ON)
Seizure–European Journal of Epilepsy (Saint Louis, MO)
SEL Studies in English Literature (Houston, TX)
Seminars in Anesthesia, Perioperative Medicine and Pain (Saint Louis, MO)
Seminars in Arthritis and Rheumatism (Saint Louis, MO)
Seminars in Arthroplasty (Saint Louis, MO)
Seminars in Avian and Exotic Pet Medicine (Saint Louis, MO)
Seminars in Breast Disease (Saint Louis, MO)
Seminars in Cerebrovascular Disease and Stroke (Saint Louis, MO)
Seminars in Cutaneous Medicine and Surgery (Saint Louis, MO)

Seminars in Diagnostic Pathology (Saint Louis, MO)
Seminars in Integrative Medicine (Saint Louis, MO)
Seminars in Oncology (Saint Louis, MO)
Seminars in Oncology Nursing (Columbia, MO)
Seminars in Orthodontics (Saint Louis, MO)
Seminars in Pain Medicine (Saint Louis, MO)
Seminars in Pediatric Neurology (Saint Louis, MO)
Seminars in Perinatology (Saint Louis, MO)
Seminars in Radiologic Technology (Birmingham, AL)
Seminars in Roentgenology (Saint Louis, MO)
Seminars in Spine Surgery (Saint Louis, MO)
Seminars in Ultrasound CT and MRI (Saint Louis, MO)
Seminars in Ultrasound CT and MRI (Holyoke, MA)
Seminars in Urologic Oncology (Saint Louis, MO)
Senior Life (South Bend Edition) (Milford, IN)
Senior Observer (Winter Park, FL)
The Seniors Review (Saint Catharines, ON)
The Sentinel-Echo (London, KY)
Seventeen (New York, NY)
Sexuality Reproduction & Menopause (Birmingham, AL)
Sexuality Research and Social Policy: Journal of the NSRC (San Francisco, CA)
SG (San Clemente, CA)
SGB (Sporting Goods Business) (New York, NY)
Share International (North Chelmsford, MA)
Share Owner (Toronto, ON)
SHAW: The Annual of Bernard Shaw Studies (Baltimore, MD)
Shelbyville Daily Union (Shelbyville, IL)
Shock (Baltimore, MD)
Shoot Monthly (New York, NY)
SHOP Etc. (New York, NY)
ShoreLines Magazine (Shawnigan Lake, BC)
Shorewood Sun Sailor (Eden Prairie, MN)
Short Story Index (Bronx, NY)
Sierra Madre Weekly (Arcadia, CA)
Sierra Magazine (Sacramento, CA)
Signal Magazine (Nellis AFB, NV)

## INDUSTRY ACTIVITY

Signal Transduction (Hoboken, NJ)
Signature (Lake Orion, MI)
SIMILE: Studies in Media & Information Literacy Education (Omaha, NE)
Simple Scrapbooks (Bluffdale, UT)
Simpsonville Membership Directory (Simpsonville, SC)
Sirena: poesia, arte y critica (Carlisle, PA)
Skaneateles Press (Skaneateles, NY)
Skateboarder (Dana Point, CA)
SkyNews (Yarker, ON)
Slam (New York, NY)
Sleep Medicine (Edison, NJ)
Sleep Medicine Reviews (Saint Louis, MO)
Small (Hoboken, NJ)
Small Ruminant Research (Saint Louis, MO)
Smart Home Owner Magazine (Portland, ME)
Smart Shopper Buy, Sell and Trade (Niagara Falls, ON)
Sno-Dak News (Bismarck, ND)
The Snow Scoop (Firestone, CO)
Snowboarder (Dana Point, CA)
Soap Opera Digest (New York, NY)
Soap Opera Weekly (New York, NY)
Social Philosophy Today (Charlottesville, VA)
Social Studies Texan (Fort Worth, TX)
Soft Materials (New York, NY)
Software Testing, Verification and Reliability (Hoboken, NJ)
Solid Surface Magazine (Fort Atkinson, WI)
Solutions (Toronto, ON)
Solvay Geddes Express (Syracuse, NY)
Someplace Special (Austin, MN)
Songwriters Magazine (Toronto, ON)
The Sound Historian (Waco, TX)
Sound and Vision (New York, NY)
South Carolina Snitch (Columbia, SC)
South Central Review (College Station, TX)
South Marion Citizen (Ocala, FL)
Southeast Farm Press (Overland Park, KS)
The Southern Baptist Educator (Jackson, TN)
Southern Changes (Atlanta, GA)
Southern Growth (Research Triangle Park, NC)
Southern Jewish History (Atlanta, GA)
Southern Medical Journal (Baltimore, MD)
Southern Oregon Heritage Today (Medford, OR)

Southwest Cycling News (Austin, TX)
Southwest Farm Press (Overland Park, KS)
Spanish River Papers (Boca Raton, FL)
Spatial Cognition & Computation (Pittsburgh, PA)
Special Events Magazine (Overland Park, KS)
Spectroscopy (Cleveland, OH)
Spectroscopy Europe (Hoboken, NJ)
Spencer Magnet (Taylorsville, KY)
The Spine Journal (La Grange, IL)
SPIRIT (Parry Sound, ON)
Spiritus: A Journal of Christian Spirituality (Los Angeles, CA)
Sport Compact Car (Anaheim, CA)
Sport Rider (Los Angeles, CA)
Sporting Gun (New York, NY)
Sports 'N Spokes (Hines, IL)
Sports Wrap Magazine (Fonthill, ON)
Spotlight La Puente (Walnut, CA)
Spray Journal (Bethel, CT)
SRO Magazine (Overland Park, KS)
The Standard Bearer (Grandville, MI)
The Star-Herald (Kosciusko, MS)
Star News (Syracuse, NY)
The State of California Labor (Los Angeles, CA)
The State and Local Tax Lawyer (Chicago, IL)
Step by Step Beads (Devon, PA)
Stereophile (New York, NY)
Sterling Heights Mirror (Royal Oak, MI)
Stillwater Gazette (Stillwater, MN)
The Stillwater Newspress (Stillwater, OK)
Stillwell Democrat Journal (Stillwater, OK)
Stitches Magazine (Overland Park, KS)
Stochastic Analysis and Applications (New York, NY)
Stock Car Racing (Tampa, FL)
Stone World (Paramus, NJ)
Storytelling (Washington, DC)
Strategic Change (Hoboken, NJ)
Street Chopper (Anaheim, CA)
Streetviews (Cheyenne, WY)
Studies in American Indian Literatures (Lincoln, NE)
Studies in Canadian Literature (SCL) (Frederiction, NB)
Studio Photography & Design Magazine (SP & D) (Melville, NY)
Su Guia (West Paterson, NJ)
Substance Abuse (New York, NY)
Substantive Law Journal (White Plains, NY)

Suburban News/Village Gazette (West Paterson, NJ)
Sun-News of the Northland (Liberty, MO)
Sunscripts (Tampa, FL)
Sunset (New York, NY)
Super Street (Los Angeles, CA)
Supply & Demand Chain Executive (Melville, NY)
Supply House Times (Bensenville, IL)
Surface Mount Technology (SMT) (Nashua, NH)
Surfer (San Juan Capistrano, CA)
Surgery for Obesity and Related Diseases (Saint Louis, MO)
Surgical Clinics of North America (Saint Louis, MO)
Surgical Neurology (Chicago, IL)
Surgical Oncology (Menlo Park, CA)
Surgical Oncology Clinics of North America (Saint Louis, MO)
Survey of Ophthalmology (Saint Louis, MO)
Suwannee Democrat (Live Oak, FL)
SWE Magazine (San Diego, CA)
Sylva Herald (Sylva, NC)
Symbolic Interaction (Las Vegas, NV)
Synchronicity (Calgary, AB)
Syracuse Parent (Syracuse, NY)
SysAdmin (Lawrence, KS)
Systems Engineering (Fairfax, VA)
Tahlequah Daily Press (Tahlequah, OK)
Tall Ships Challenge Official Souvenir Program (Newport, RI)
Teaching Artist Journal (Mahwah, NJ)
TechNet Magazine (San Francisco, CA)
TECHNews (New York, NY)
Techniques in Foot & Ankle Surgery (Baltimore, MD)
Techniques in Gastrointestinal Endoscopy (Saint Louis, MO)
Techniques in Knee Surgery (Baltimore, MD)
Techniques in Ophthalmology (Baltimore, MD)
Techniques in Shoulder & Elbow Surgery (Baltimore, MD)
Techniques in Vascular and Interventional Radiology (Saint Louis, MO)
Technology and Health Care (Mobile, AL)
Teen Times (Jefferson City, MO)
Teen Vogue (New York, NY)
Telfair Enterprise (McRae, GA)
Tennessee Nurse (Nashville, TN)
Texan FFA Magazine (Austin, TX)
Texas Mexico Border Coalition Journal (Rio Grande City, TX)

# INDUSTRY ACTIVITY

Texas Police Journal (Austin, TX)
Texas Sings! (Austin, TX)
Theatre Journal (Reisterstown, MD)
Theatre Topics (Kalamazoo, MI)
Theory into Practice (Mahwah, NJ)
Think Three (Toronto, ON)
This is Indianapolis Visitors Guide (Indianapolis, IN)
Thomasville Times-Enterprise (Thomasville, GA)
Thoracic Surgery Clinics (Saint Louis, MO)
3rd bed (Lincoln, RI)
Thrombosis Research (Washington, DC)
TILE Magazine (Troy, MI)
Toastmaster (Buena Park, CA)
Today's Kids in Motion (Toronto, ON)
Toot Your Horn (Saint Joseph, MO)
Topics in Clinical Nutrition (Baltimore, MD)
Topics in Emergency Medicine (Baltimore, MD)
Topics in Geriatric Rehabilitation (Baltimore, MD)
Topics in Language Disorders (Baltimore, MD)
Touchline (Monroeville, PA)
Tourism Brochure (Cleveland, GA)
Town & Country Travel (New York, NY)
The Towne Courier (Charlotte, MI)
Toxicology Mechanisms and Methods (West Point, PA)
The Tracer (Cincinnati, OH)
Trailer/Body Builders (Overland Park, KS)
Trails Advocate (Center Point, IA)
Training (Minneapolis, MN)
Transforming Anthropology (Durham, NC)
Transfusion and Apheresis Science (Ottawa, ON)
Transfusion Medicine and Hemotherapy (Farmington, CT)
Translorial (Berkeley, CA)
Transplantation Proceedings (Houston, TX)
Transplantation Reviews (Madison, WI)
Transportation Alternatives (New York, NY)
Travel Agent Guide (Anaheim, CA)
Travel Medicine and Infectious Disease (Saint Louis, MO)
Traveler's Guide (Santa Cruz, CA)
Treesearcher (Dodge City, KS)
Trends in Cardiovascular Medicine (Saint Louis, MO)
Treoir (Burr Ridge, IL)
Trial Reporter (Baltimore, MD)

Truck Logger (Vancouver, BC)
Tuberculosis (Fort Collins, CO)
Tucson Teen (Tucson, AZ)
Tuttle Times (Tuttle, OK)
Ubiquity (New York, NY)
Ultrasound in Obstetrics and Gynecology (Hoboken, NJ)
Underwater Naturalist (Broad Channel, NY)
Union Parish Community Guide (Farmerville, LA)
United States Dressage Federation (Lincoln, NE)
Universal Security Systems & Sourcebook (Fort Atkinson, WI)
Update (Phoenix, AZ)
Urban CNY (Syracuse, NY)
Urologic Clinics of North America (Saint Louis, MO)
Urologic Oncology (New York, NY)
Urology (Baltimore, MD)
Utah! Accommodations Guide: The Official Lodging Guide for Utah (Salt Lake City, UT)
Van Wert Community Guide (Van Wert, OH)
The Velvet Light Trap (Austin, TX)
Vermont Genealogy (Saint Albans, VT)
Vermont Registered Nurse (Winooski, VT)
The Veteran (Silver Spring, MD)
Veterinary Clinics of North America: Equine Practice (Fort Collins, CO)
Veterinary Clinics of North America: Exotic Animal Practice (College Station, TX)
Veterinary Clinics of North America: Food Animal Practice (Stillwater, OK)
Veterinary Clinics of North America: Small Animal Practice (Saint Louis, MO)
Veterinary Economics (Cleveland, OH)
Veterinary Immunology and Immunopathology (Amherst, MA)
Veterinary Journal (Saint Louis, MO)
Veterinary Medicine (Cleveland, OH)
Veterinary Microbiology (Saint Louis, MO)
Veterinary Parasitology (Saint Louis, MO)
Vette (Tampa, FL)
Vietnam (Leesburg, VA)
Views (Saint Paul, MN)
Viltis (Milwaukee, WI)
The Virginia Pulmonary (Richmond, VA)
Virginia Sheriff (Richmond, VA)
Visions (Goldsboro, NC)
The Visitor (Beverly Hills, FL)

Visitor Guide (Sacramento, CA)
Visual Anthropology Review (Glen Cove, NY)
Visual Anthropology Review (Berkeley, CA)
Visual Communication Quarterly (Mahwah, NJ)
The Voice (Rockford, IL)
The Voice (Raleigh, NC)
The Voice (Fort Worth, TX)
Voice Magazine (Saratoga Springs, NY)
Voices (Omaha, NE)
Voices (Berkeley, CA)
Voters' Guide (Albany, NY)
VOX (Atlanta, GA)
Voyaging (Los Angeles, CA)
Wabasha-Kellogg Area Getaway Guide (Wabasha, MN)
WACL-FM (Harrisonburg, VA)
Wafer News (Nashua, NH)
WAGH-FM (Columbus, GA)
Waldwick Suburban News (West Paterson, NJ)
Walleye Guide (Baxter, MN)
Wallpaper* (New York, NY)
Walls, Windows, and Floors (New York, NY)
WAMX-FM (Huntington, WV)
Ward's Auto World (Overland Park, KS)
Ward's Dealer Business (Overland Park, KS)
Watch Aficionado (New York, NY)
Waters (Vancouver, BC)
The Waters Edge (Muskegon, MI)
WATQ-FM (Eau Claire, WI)
Wauconda Courier (Algonquin, IL)
WBFA-FM (Columbus, GA)
WBGG-AM (Pittsburgh, PA)
WBHP-AM (Decatur, AL)
WBKS-FM (Huntington, WV)
WBLJ-FM (Williamsport, PA)
WBTJ-FM (Richmond, VA)
WBTT-FM (Fort Myers, FL)
WBUK-FM (Findlay, OH)
WBUL-FM (Lexington, KY)
WBUV-FM (Biloxi, MS)
WBVB-FM (Huntington, WV)
WBVD-FM (Melbourne, FL)
WBWT-FM (Tallahassee, FL)
WBYL-FM (Williamsport, PA)
WBZT-FM (Greenville, SC)
WBZW-FM (Ashland, OH)
WBZY-FM (Atlanta, GA)
WCDG-FM (Norfolk, VA)
WCET Journal (Mississauga, ON)
WCKT-FM (Fort Myers, FL)

# INDUSTRY ACTIVITY

WCPV-FM (Colchester, VT)
WCTH-FM (Tavernier, FL)
WCVS-FM (Springfield, IL)
WCVU-FM (Punta Gorda, FL)
WCZR-FM (Port Saint Lucie, FL)
WDAY-FM (Fargo, ND)
WDDV-FM (Venice, FL)
WDIZ-AM (Panama City, FL)
WDKF-FM (Dayton, OH)
WDSJ-FM (Dayton, OH)
WDTW-FM (Detroit, MI)
WDXB-FM (Birmingham, AL)
We Need Not Walk Alone (Oak Brook, IL)
WEBG-FM (Maitland, FL)
WEBL-FM (Macon, GA)
WEBZ-FM (Panama City, FL)
The Weekly News: Walnut (Walnut, CA)
WEEZ-AM (Hattiesburg, MS)
Weld County Genealogical Society Quarterly (Greeley, CO)
Welland Shopping News (Saint Catharines, ON)
West of the City Magazine (Oakville, ON)
West Covina Neighborhood News (Walnut, CA)
West Michigan: Carefree Travel (Grand Rapids, MI)
West Michigan: Carefree Travel-Winter/Fall Edition (Grand Rapids, MI)
West, OCJOGAM Carefree Travel-Winter/Fall Edition (Grand Rapids, MI)
Westchester/Marina Observer (Culver City, CA)
Western Farm Press (Overland Park, KS)
Western Petroleum Markets (Salt Lake City, UT)
Westland News (Columbus, OH)
The Westminster Eagle (Westminster, MD)
Westmoreland History (Greensburg, PA)
Westside Today (Los Angeles, CA)
WFBQ-FM (Indianapolis, IN)
WFBX-FM (Panama City, FL)
WFJX-FM (Columbus, OH)
WFKP-FM (Poughkeepsie, NY)
WFKS-FM (Jacksonville, FL)
WFLF-AM (Maitland, FL)
WFMF-FM (Baton Rouge, LA)
WFMX-FM (Statesville, NC)
WFRX-AM (Marion, IL)
WFXF-FM (Rochester, NY)
WFXJ-AM (Jacksonville, FL)
WFXJ-FM (Ashtabula, OH)
WFXN-AM (Davenport, IA)

WFXN-FM (Ashland, OH)
WFZX-FM (Ellsworth, ME)
WGBT-FM (Greensboro, NC)
WGMN-AM (Roanoke, VA)
WGRB-AM (Chicago, IL)
WGSQ-FM (Cookeville, TN)
WGXL-FM (Lebanon, NH)
WHAL-FM (Memphis, TN)
What Digital Camera (New York, NY)
What's Up Kids? (Ridgeville, ON)
Wheel Clicks (San Marino, CA)
WHERE Charleston (Charleston, SC)
WHERE Muskoka (Toronto, ON)
WHERE Ottawa (Ottawa, ON)
WHERE San Diego (San Diego, CA)
WHERE Singapore (Los Angeles, CA)
WHERE Vancouver (Vancouver, BC)
WHERE Winnipeg (Winnipeg, MB)
White County News-Telegraph (Cleveland, GA)
WHKF-FM (Harrisburg, PA)
WHLH-FM (Jackson, MS)
WHMJ-FM (Somerset, KY)
Who Weekly (New York, NY)
Who, What, Where, When (W4) (Doylestown, PA)
WHOS-AM (Decatur, AL)
Who's Who in Canadian Purebred Swine (Ottawa, ON)
WHP-AM (Harrisburg, PA)
WHTE-FM (Charlottesville, VA)
WHTK-AM (Rochester, NY)
WHYN-AM (Springfield, MA)
WIBB-FM (Macon, GA)
WIBT-FM (Charlotte, NC)
Wide-Format Imaging (Melville, NY)
WIGY-FM (Augusta, ME)
Wild West (Leesburg, VA)
Wilkin County Fair (Premium Book) (Breckenridge, MN)
Williamson County Magazine (Franklin, TN)
Williston Pioneer Sun-News (Williston, FL)
Wilmott Magazine (Hoboken, NJ)
WIMT-FM (Lima, OH)
Wind Energy (Albuquerque, NM)
Wired (San Francisco, CA)
Wireless Communications and Mobile Computing (Hoboken, NJ)
Wisconsin Police Journal (Madison, WI)
WISY-FM (Rochester, NY)
WITI FastTrack (Manhasset, NY)
WJZO-FM (Shelbyville, KY)
WKCI-AM (Staunton, VA)
WKEZ-FM (Tavernier, FL)

WKFS-FM (Cincinnati, OH)
WKGB-FM (Vestal, NY)
WKGS-FM (Rochester, NY)
WKMQ-AM (Tupelo, MS)
WKSC-FM (Chicago, IL)
WKSP-FM (Augusta, GA)
WKTU-FM (Jersey City, NJ)
WKUS-FM (Norfolk, VA)
WKXJ-FM (Chattanooga, TN)
WKZP-FM (Mc Minnville, TN)
WLAY-AM (Muscle Shoals, AL)
WLBW-FM (Salisbury, MD)
WLBY-AM (San Antonio, TX)
WLCG-AM (Macon, GA)
WLFJ-AM (Greenville, SC)
WLKT-FM (Lexington, KY)
WNSX-FM (Ellsworth, ME)
WNYGS Journal (Hamburg, NY)
Woman (New York, NY)
Woman Dentist Journal (Nashua, NH)
Woman and Home (New York, NY)
Women's FORUM (Calgary, AB)
Women's Health Issues (Washington, DC)
Women's Health Style (Livonia, MI)
Wood Digest's Finishing Magazine (Melville, NY)
Woodland Steward (Belchertown, MA)
WORK (Boston, MA)
World Championship Dragon Boat Festival (Vancouver, BC)
World History Connected (Champaign, IL)
World History Connected (Pullman, WA)
World War II (Leesburg, VA)
Wound Care Canada (Toronto, ON)
Written By (Los Angeles, CA)
Xtreme Video (Manhasset, NY)
Yachting (New York, NY)
Year Book of Allergy, Asthma, and Clinical Immunology (Saint Louis, MO)
Year Book of Anesthesiology and Pain Management (Saint Louis, MO)
Year Book of Cardiology (Saint Louis, MO)
Year Book of Dentistry (Saint Louis, MO)
Year Book of Dermatology and Dermatology Surgery (Saint Louis, MO)
Year Book of Diagnostic Radiology (Saint Louis, MO)
Year Book of Emergency Medicine (Saint Louis, MO)
Year Book of Endocrinology (Saint Louis, MO)

Year Book of Family Practice (Saint Louis, MO)
Year Book of Gastroenterology (Saint Louis, MO)
Year Book of Hand Surgery (Saint Louis, MO)
Year Book of Medicine (Saint Louis, MO)
Year Book of Neonatal and Perinatal Medicine (Saint Louis, MO)
Year Book of Neurology and Neurosurgery (Saint Louis, MO)
Year Book of Nuclear Medicine (Saint Louis, MO)
Year Book of Obstetrics, Gynecology, and Women's Health (Saint Louis, MO)
Year Book of Oncology (Saint Louis, MO)
Year Book of Ophthalmology (Saint Louis, MO)
Year Book of Otolaryngology-Head and Neck Surgery (Saint Louis, MO)
Year Book of Pathology and Laboratory Medicine (Saint Louis, MO)
Year Book of Pediatrics (Saint Louis, MO)
Year Book of Plastic and Aesthetic Surgery (Saint Louis, MO)
Year Book of Psychiatry and Applied Mental Health (Saint Louis, MO)
Year Book of Pulmonary Disease (Saint Louis, MO)
Year Book of Rheumatology, Arthritis, and Musculoskeletal Disease (Saint Louis, MO)
Year Book of Sports Medicine (Saint Louis, MO)
Year Book of Surgery (Saint Louis, MO)
Year Book of Urology (Saint Louis, MO)
Year Book of Vascular Surgery (Saint Louis, MO)
Yearbook of Comparative and General Literature (Bloomington, IN)
Yearbook of the National Society for the Study of Education (Stillwater, OK)
Yesteryears (Oskaloosa, KS)
York County Genealogical Society Journal (Eliot, ME)
Young Children (East Lansing, MI)
Youth Awareness Press (Tucson, AZ)
Yuma White Sheet (Yuma, AZ)
Zebrafish (West Lafayette, IN)

### International
AA Autofocus (Auckland, NZL)
AA Directions (Auckland, NZL)
AATA Quarterly (Redhill, GBR)
Abacus (Sydney, AUS)
ABC Coast-FM (Gold Coast City, QL, AUS)
ABC NewsRadio-AM (Sydney, NW, AUS)
ABC Northern Territory-AM (Alice Springs, NT, AUS)
ABC Radio National-AM (Sydney, NW, AUS)
Able Update (Wellington, NZL)
ABS-FM (Auburn, NW, AUS)
Academy (Ilford, GBR)
Access All Areas (London, GBR)
Accounting, Auditing & Accountability Journal (Sydney, AUS)
Accreditation and Quality Assurance (Tokyo, JPN)
ACM Transactions on Asian Language Information Processing (Hong Kong, CHN)
ACM Transactions on Computational Logic (Amsterdam, NLD)
Acta hydrochimica et hydrobiologica (Karlsruhe, GER)
Acta Agriculturae Scandinavica Section C (Frederiksberg, DEN)
Acta Anaesthesiologica Scandinavica (Trondheim, NOR)
Acta Archaeologica (Copenhagen, DEN)
Acta Biochimica et Biophysica Sinica (Oxford, GBR)
Acta Crystallographica Section A (Manchester, GBR)
Acta Crystallographica Section B (Manchester, GBR)
Acta Crystallographica Section C (Manchester, GBR)
Acta Crystallographica Section D (Manchester, GBR)
Acta Crystallographica Section F (Manchester, GBR)
Acta Dermato-Venereologica (Uppsala, SWE)
Acta Dermato-Venereologica (Abingdon, GBR)
Acta Diabetologica (Tokyo, JPN)
Acta Endoscopica (Tokyo, JPN)
Acta Geologica Sinica (Beijing, CHN)
Acta Informatica (Tokyo, JPN)
Acta Mathematica Sinica (Tokyo, JPN)
Acta Mathematicae Applicatae Sinica (Tokyo, JPN)
Acta Mechanica (Tokyo, JPN)
Acta Mechanica Sinica (Tokyo, JPN)
Acta Medica Austriaca (Vienna, AUT)
Acta Neurologica Scandanavica (Gothenburg, SWE)
Acta Neuropathologica (Tokyo, JPN)
Acta Obstetricia et Gynecologica (Gothenburg, SWE)
Acta Odontologica Scandinavica (Huddinge, SWE)
Acta Oncologica (Abingdon, GBR)
Acta Oncologica (Stockholm, SWE)
Acta Ophthalmologica Scandinavica (Reykjavik, ICE)
Acta Orthopaedica (Lund, SWE)
Acta Oto-Laryngologica (Abingdon, GBR)
Acta Paediatrica (Stockholm, SWE)
Acta Pharmacologica Sinica (Oxford, GBR)
Acta Psychiatrica Scandinavica (Aalborg, DEN)
Acta Radiologica (Abingdon, GBR)
Acta Sociologica (Copenhagen, DEN)
Acta Zoologica (Uppsala, SWE)
Action Packed (Adelaide, SA, AUS)
Ad Astra (Sydney, NW, AUS)
Addiction Abstracts (Abingdon, GBR)
Addiction Biology (Abingdon, GBR)
Adelphi Papers (Abingdon, GBR)
The Adelphi Papers (Oxford, GBR)
ADORANTEN (Tanumshede, SWE)
Adsorption Science & Technology (Brentwood, GBR)
Advanced Synthesis and Catalysis (Ostfildern, GER)
Advances in Gerontology (Saint Petersburg, RUS)
Advances in Physiotherapy (Utrecht, NLD)
Advances in Speech Language Pathology (Abingdon, GBR)
Advances in Structural Engineering (Brentwood, GBR)
The Adventure (Wellington, NZL)
Aequationes mathematicae (Graz, AUT)
Aerostat (Bristol, GBR)
AES Bug Club Magazine (London, GBR)
Africa Confidential (London, GBR)
Africa Research Bulletin: Economic, Financial and Technical (Devon, GBR)
Africa Research Bulletin: Political, Social and Cultural Series (Devon, GBR)
African Development Review (Tunis Belvedere, TUN)
African Journal of Ecology (Kampala, UGA)
Age and Ageing (London, GBR)
Agenda (Sydney, NW, AUS)
Agendas (South Melbourne, VI, AUS)
Agents News (Harpenden, GBR)
The Aging Male (Ramat Gan, ISR)
Aging and Mental Health (Abingdon, GBR)
Agreement (Amersham, GBR)
Agribusiness Connections (Kent Town, SA, AUS)

## INDUSTRY ACTIVITY

Agricultural Economics (Oxford, GBR)
Agricultural and Forest Entomolgy (Banchory, GBR)
AI Communications (Amsterdam, NLD)
AI & SOCIETY (Tokyo, JPN)
AIDS Abstracts (Abingdon, GBR)
AIDS Care (Abingdon, GBR)
Aikakauskirja (Helsinki, FIN)
AIPM Flash (Moscow, RUS)
Air & Space Law (The Hague, NLD)
Aircraft Engineering & Aerospace Technology (Bradford, GBR)
Al-An Kabout (Jerusalem, ISR)
Alcohol and Alcoholism (Oxford, GBR)
Alcohol and Alcoholism (Edinburgh, GBR)
Alcohol in Israel (Ramat Gan, ISR)
Algebra Colloquium (Beijing, CHN)
Algebra Uuniversalis (Tokyo, JPN)
Allergology International (Tokyo, JPN)
Allergy (Montpellier Cedex 5, FRA)
Allgemeines Statistisches Archive (Tokyo, JPN)
Aloft (Portsmouth, GBR)
ALT-J (Oxford, GBR)
Ambassador (London, GBR)
American Business Law Journal (Oxford, GBR)
American Journal on Addictions (Abingdon, GBR)
American Law and Economics Review (Oxford, GBR)
Amino Acids (Tokyo, JPN)
AMPO (Tokyo, JPN)
AMTA Journal (Melbourne, VI, AUS)
Amyloid: The Journal of Protein Folding Disorders (Abingdon, GBR)
Amyotrophic Lateral Sclerosis and Other Motor Neuron Disorders (Abingdon, GBR)
Anaesthesia (Nottingham, GBR)
Analytical and Bioanalytical Chemistry (Heidelberg, GER)
Anatomia, Histologia, Embryologia (Munich, GER)
Anatomy and Embryology (Tokyo, JPN)
andrologia (Giessen, GER)
Animal Cognition (Heidelberg, GER)
Animal Conservation (London, GBR)
Animal Health Research Reviews (Wallingford, GBR)
Animal Reproduction Science (Werribee, VI, AUS)
Annales Henri Poincare (Tokyo, JPN)
Annali di Matematica Pura ed Applicata (Tokyo, JPN)
Annals of the Arts and Social Sciences (Safat, KWT)

Annals of Botany (Bristol, GBR)
Annals of Botany (Oxford, GBR)
Annals of Combinatorics (Tokyo, JPN)
Annals of Finance (Tokyo, JPN)
Annals of Hematology (Hannover, GER)
Annals of Oncology (Viganello-Lugano, SWI)
Annals of Oncology (Oxford, GBR)
Annals of Regional Science (Tokyo, JPN)
Annual Report on European Development (Beijing, CHN)
Anomaly (Frome, GBR)
Anthropology Today (London, GBR)
Anti-corrosion Methods & Materials (Bradford, GBR)
Antichthon (Sydney, NW, AUS)
ANZ Journal of Surgery (Carlton South, VI, AUS)
Apex (Waitomo Caves, NZL)
APMIS (APMIS) (Copenhagen, DEN)
Applicable Algebra in Engineering, Communication and Computing (Tokyo, JPN)
Applied Bionics and Biomechanics (Cambridge, GBR)
Applied Financial Economics Letters (Abingdon, GBR)
Applied Linguistics (Oxford, GBR)
Applied Magnetic Resonance (Tokyo, JPN)
Applied Microbiology and Biotechnology (Tokyo, JPN)
Applied Numerical Analysis and Computational Mathematics (Athens, GRC)
Applied Ontology (Trento, ITA)
Applied Physics A (Tokyo, JPN)
Applied Physics B (Tokyo, JPN)
Aquaculture Nutrition (Sentrum, NOR)
Aquatic Insects (Stuttgart, GER)
Aquatic Resources, Culture and Development (Wallingford, GBR)
Aquatic Sciences (Dubendorf, SWI)
Arabian Archaeology and Epigraphy (Sydney, NW, AUS)
Arbitration (London, GBR)
Archaeologia Aeliana (Newcastle upon Tyne, GBR)
Archaeometry (Oxford, GBR)
Archiv der Mathematik (Saarbrucken, GER)
Archive of Applied Mechanics (Bremen, GER)
Archive for History of Exact Sciences (Tokyo, JPN)
Archive for Mathematical Logic (Munster, GER)

Archive for Rational Mechanics and Analysis (Oxford, GBR)
Archives of Animal Nutrition (Berlin, GER)
Archives of Dermatological Research (Tokyo, JPN)
Archives of Gerontology and Geriatrics (Debrecen, HUN)
Archives of Gynecology and Obstetrics (Tokyo, JPN)
Archives of Medical Research (Colonia Doctores, MEX)
Archives of Microbiology (Tokyo, JPN)
Archives of Oral Biology (Manchester, GBR)
Archives of Orthopaedic and Trauma Surgery (Tokyo, JPN)
Archives of Toxicology (Tokyo, JPN)
Archives of Women's Mental Health (Tokyo, JPN)
Art Libraries Journal (Bromsgrove, GBR)
The Artisan (York, GBR)
Arts Radio-FM (Curtin, AC, AUS)
Asia Bottled Water (Jakarta, IDN)
Asia Europe Journal (Tokyo, JPN)
Asia-Pacific Journal of Clinical Oncology (Carlton, VI, AUS)
Asia Pacific Journal of Education (Abingdon, GBR)
Asian Journal of Andrology (Oxford, GBR)
Asian Journal of Cell Biology (Faisalabad, PAK)
Asian Journal of Water, Environment and Pollution (Delhi, IND)
Asian Population Studies (Abingdon, GBR)
Asian Science Bulletin (Faisalabad, PAK)
Aslib Proceedings (Bradford, GBR)
Assembly Automation (Bradford, GBR)
ASTI Review (Dublin, DU, IRL)
Astronomical and Astrophysical Transactions (Moscow, RUS)
Astronomische Nachrichten (Potsdam, GER)
Astronomy and Astrophysics Review (Tokyo, JPN)
Astronomy and Geophysics (Leeds, GBR)
Astronomy Letters (Moscow, RUS)
Astronomy Reports (Moscow, RUS)
Asymptotic Analysis (Paris, FRA)
At The Sign Of (Wolverhampton, GBR)
Atherosclerosis (Glasgow, GBR)
Atmospheric Science Letters (Exeter, GBR)
Atomic Maximum Power Computing (Australia) Magazine (London, GBR)

Attachment & Human Development (Abingdon, GBR)
Attractions Management (Hitchin, GBR)
Augmentative & Alternative Communication (Abingdon, GBR)
Auris Nasus Larynx (Tokyo, JPN)
The AUSIMM Bulletin (Carlton, VI, AUS)
Australasian Journal on Ageing (South Melbourne, VI, AUS)
Australasian Sound Archive (Hepburn Springs, VI, AUS)
Australia Drama Education Magazine (Brisbane, QL, AUS)
Australian Archaeology (Sydney, NW, AUS)
Australian Biologist (Adelaide, SA, AUS)
Australian Economic History Review (Canberra, AUS)
Australian Gaming Magazine (Crows Nest, NW, AUS)
Australian Garden History (Melbourne, VI, AUS)
The Australian Health Consumer (Manuka, AC, AUS)
Australian Insolvency Journal (Sydney, NW, AUS)
Australian Journal of Earth Sciences (South Perth, WA, AUS)
Australian & New Zealand Journal of Statistics (Carlton, VI, AUS)
Australian Occupational Therapy Journal (Carlton South, VI, AUS)
Australian Organic Journal (Chermside, QL, AUS)
The Australian Orienteer (Glebe, NW, AUS)
Australian Pipeliner (Kingston, AC, AUS)
Australian Property Journal (Deakin, AC, AUS)
Australian Social Work (Kingston, AC, AUS)
Australian Stainless Magazine (Brisbane, QL, AUS)
Australian Universities Review (South Melbourne, VI, AUS)
Australian Veterinary Practitioner (Artarmon, NW, AUS)
Autonomic and Autacoid Pharmacology (Cardiff, GBR)
Autonomic Neuroscience (London, GBR)
Autosport Magazine (London, GBR)
Avoscene (Tauranga, NZL)
b-FM (Auckland, NZL)
B-ROCK-FM (Bathurst, NW, AUS)
Bailrigg-FM (Bailrigg, LC, GBR)
Balance (Brisbane, QL, AUS)
Baltic Journal of Management (Bradford, GBR)
Banci Estet Koko (Kota Kinabalu, MYS)

Basic & Clinical Pharmacology & Toxicology (Copenhagen, DEN)
Basic Research in Cardiology (Tokyo, JPN)
BAY-FM (Geelong, VI, AUS)
The Bay-FM (Lancaster, GBR)
BBC GMR-FM (Manchester, GBR)
BBC London-FM (London, GBR)
BBC Merseyside-FM (Liverpool, GBR)
BBC Northampton-FM (Northampton, NH, GBR)
BBC Radio Berkshire-FM (Reading, GBR)
BBC Radio Bristol-FM (Bristol, GBR)
BBC Radio Cambridgeshire-FM (Cambridgeshire, GBR)
BBC Radio Cleveland-FM (Middlesbrough, GBR)
BBC Radio Cumbria-FM (Carlisle, CM, GBR)
BBC Radio Dent-FM (Tunbridge Wells, KT, GBR)
BBC Radio Derby-FM (Derby, GBR)
BBC Radio Essex-FM (Chelmsford, EX, GBR)
BBC Radio 5-AM (London, GBR)
BBC Radio 4-FM (London, GBR)
BBC Radio Guernsey-FM (Sampson's, GBR)
BBC Radio Humberside-FM (Hull, GBR)
BBC Radio Lancashire-FM (Blackburn, LC, GBR)
BBC RAdio Leeds-FM (Leeds, GBR)
BBC Radio Leicester-FM (Leicester, LE, GBR)
BBC Radio Newcastle-FM (Newcastle Upon Tyne, GBR)
BBC Radio Norfolk-FM (Norwich, GBR)
BBC Radio Nottingham-FM (Nottingham, GBR)
BBC Radio 1-FM (London, GBR)
BBC Radio Oxford-FM (Oxford, GBR)
BBC Radio Scotland-FM (Glasgow, GBR)
BBC Radio Sheffield-FM (Sheffield, GBR)
BBC Radio Shropshire-FM (Shropshire, GBR)
BBC Radio Solent-FM (Southampton, GBR)
BBC Radio Stoke-FM (Stoke-On-Trent, ST, GBR)
BBC Radio 3-FM (London, GBR)
BBC Radio 2-FM (London, GBR)
BBC Radio Wiltshire-FM (Swindon, GBR)
BBC Radio WM-FM (Birmingham, GBR)
BBC Southern Counties-FM (Guilford, SR, GBR)

BBC 3CR-FM (Luton, GBR)
BCB-FM (Bradford, WY, GBR)
Beat 106-FM (Glasgow, GBR)
Behavioral Ecology and Sociobiology (Heidelberg, GER)
Behaviour Change (Nedlands, WA, AUS)
Behaviour and Information Technology (Abingdon, GBR)
Benchmarking (Bradford, GBR)
Berichte zur Wissenschaftsgeschichte (Marburg, GER)
BG Journal (Richmond, GBR)
Bibliotek for Laeger (Copenhagen, DEN)
biiBUSINESS (Camberley, GBR)
Bil & Motor (Frederiksberg, DEN)
BIM (London, GBR)
Bio-Medical Materials and Engineering (Utsunomiya, JPN)
Biocatalysis and Biotransformation (London, GBR)
BioControl (Wageningen, NLD)
BioEssays (Cambridge, GBR)
BioFactors (Braunschweig, GER)
Biofouling (Buckingham, GBR)
Bioinformatics (Oxford, GBR)
Biological Cybernetics (Tokyo, JPN)
Biology and Fertility of Soils (Tokyo, JPN)
Biomarkers (London, GBR)
Biomaterials (Liverpool, GBR)
Biomechanics and Modeling in Mechanobiology (Tokyo, JPN)
Biometrical Journal (Gottingen, GER)
Biometrika (Oxford, GBR)
Biophysical Reviews and Letters (Potsdam, GER)
Bioprocess and Biosystems Engineering (Tokyo, JPN)
Biostatistics (Oxford, GBR)
BioSynopsis (Chisinau, MDI)
Bird Conservation International (Cambridge, GBR)
Birds Eye View (Ta'Xbiex, MAL)
Black Theology (Poole, GBR)
Blast 1386-AM (Reading, BR, GBR)
Blastpipe (West Lothian, GBR)
Blood Pressure (Goteborg, SWE)
Blood Pressure (Abingdon, GBR)
BMHF Yearbook & Directory (Birmingham, GBR)
Body, Movement and Dance in Psychotherapy (Herts, GBR)
Boer Briefs (Armidale, NW, AUS)
Bokasafnid (Reykjavik, ICE)
Bokatidindi (Reykjavik, ICE)
Bondi-FM (Bondi Beach, NW, AUS)
B105-FM (Brisbane, QL, AUS)

INDUSTRY ACTIVITY

Bongo News (Accra, GHA)
Boobook (Hawthorn East, VI, AUS)
Bookbird: A journal of international children's literature (Dublin, IRL)
Booksellers News (Wellington, NZL)
Boreas (Arhus, DEN)
Botanicheski Zhurnal (Saint Petersburg, RUS)
The Bottle Street Gazette (Winchelsea, GBR)
Braford Annual (Rockhampton, QL, AUS)
Brain (Oxford, GBR)
Break In (Upper Hutt, NZL)
Breast Disease (Amsterdam, NLD)
Breeze-FM (Browns Plains, QL, AUS)
The Breeze-FM (Centreplace, NZL)
The Breeze-FM (Christchurch, NZL)
The Breeze-FM (Wellington, NZL)
Bridge Structures (Abingdon, GBR)
Brief Treatment and Crisis Intervention (Oxford, GBR)
Briefings in Bioinformatics (London, GBR)
Briefings in Functional Genomics & Proteomics (London, GBR)
Bright 106.4-FM (Burgess Hill, WS, GBR)
British Educational Research Journal (Edinburgh, GBR)
British Food Journal (Bradford, GBR)
British Journal of Anaesthesia (Oxford, GBR)
British Journal of Anaesthetic and Recovery Nursing (Cambridge, GBR)
British Journal of Educational Psychology (Leicester, GBR)
British Journal of Neurosurgery (Abingdon, GBR)
British Journal of Nutrition (Wallingford, GBR)
British Journal or Oral and Maxillofacial Surgery (Edinburgh, GBR)
British Journal of Play Therapy (Bristol, GBR)
British Medical Bulletin (Sheffield, GBR)
British Medical Bulletin (Oxford, GBR)
British Poultry Science (Roslin, GBR)
British Resorts Factpack (Southport, GBR)
BRMB-FM (Birmingham, GBR)
Build It (Birmingham, GBR)
Bulgarian Cardiology (Sofia, BUL)
Bulletin (Leamington Spa, GBR)
Bulletin (London, GBR)
The Bulletin (London, GBR)
Bulletin of the Brazilian Mathematical Society (Tokyo, JPN)

Bulletin of Engineering Geology and the Environment (Tokyo, JPN)
Bulletin of Entomological Research (Cardiff, GBR)
Burns (Salisbury, GBR)
Business Forums (Hanoi, VNM)
Business Process Management Journal (Riyadh, SAU)
Business Pulse (East Perth, WA, AUS)
Business Strategy and the Environment (West Yorkshire, GBR)
Butterflies (Tokyo, JPN)
BWP Update (Oxford, GBR)
Calcolo (Tokyo, JPN)
Calculus of Variations and Partial Differential Equation (Tokyo, JPN)
Cambridge Journal of Economics (Oxford, GBR)
Cambridge Journal of Economics (Cambridge, GBR)
Campus-Wide Information Systems (Bradford, GBR)
Canadian Journal of Agricultural Economics (Oxford, GBR)
Cancer Biomarkers (Amsterdam, NLD)
Cancer Chemotherapy and Pharmacology (Tokyo, JPN)
Cancer Immunology, Immunotherapy (Tokyo, JPN)
Cancer Letters (Heidelberg, GER)
Cancer Science (Oxford, GBR)
Cancer Treatment (Sheffield, GBR)
Capital-FM (London, GBR)
Caravan (Croydon, GBR)
Carcinogenesis (Oxford, GBR)
Cardiology in the Young (Cambridge, GBR)
Cardiovascular Research (Aulweg, GER)
Career Development International (Bradford, GBR)
CareerScope (Camberley, GBR)
Catchword (Gloucester, GBR)
CCHHR-AM (Hemel Hempstead, HF, GBR)
Cell Calcium (Manchester, GBR)
Cell Communication and Adhesion (Abingdon, GBR)
Cell Proliferation (London, GBR)
Cell and Tissue Research (Tokyo, JPN)
Cellular and Molecular Life Sciences (Tokyo, JPN)
Cellular Oncology (Amsterdam, NLD)
Central European Journal of Operations Research (Tokyo, JPN)
Central-FM (Falkirk, GBR)
Century-FM (Manchester, GBR)
Cephalalgia (Oxford, GBR)
The Cerebellum (Brussels, BEL)

Cerebellum (Abingdon, GBR)
CERN Courier (Bristol, GBR)
Chamaerops Magazine (Richmond, GBR)
Channel 103-FM (Jersey, GBR)
The Charles Lamb Bulletin (London, GBR)
Chelmer-FM (Chelmsford, GBR)
Chemical Senses (Oxford, GBR)
Chemistry in Australia (North Melbourne, VI, AUS)
Chemistry and Ecology (Ancona, ITA)
Chemkon - Chemie konkret, Forum fuer Unterricht und Didaktik (Oldenburg, GER)
Chemoecology (Brussels, BEL)
Child: Care, Health and Development (Oxford, GBR)
Child and Family Social Work (Heslington, GBR)
Child Language and Teaching Therapy (London, GBR)
Children and Society (London, GBR)
Children's Social and Economics Education (Stoke-On-Trent, GBR)
Child's Nervous System (Tokyo, JPN)
China-Britain Business Review (London, GBR)
China Information (Leiden, NLD)
China Oil & Gas (Tokyo, JPN)
Chinese Annals of Mathematics (Shanghai, CHN)
Chinese-German Journal of Clinical Oncology (Tokyo, JPN)
Chinese Journal of Agricultural Biotechnology (Wallingford, GBR)
Chinese Journal of Chemistry (Shanghai, CHN)
Chinese Journal of International Law (Oxford, GBR)
Chinese Physics (Beijing, CHN)
Chinese Physics Letters (Bristol, GBR)
Choice-FM (London, GBR)
Chromatographia (Tokyo, JPN)
Chromosoma (Martinsried, GER)
Circuit World (Bradford, GBR)
Circular (Wellington, NZL)
Citybeat-FM (Belfast, GBR)
Clare-FM (Ennis, CL, IRL)
Classic-FM (London, GBR)
Clean Technologies and Environmental Policy (Tokyo, JPN)
Clematis International (Waltham Cross, GBR)
The Clerk (Nottingham, GBR)
Clinical Autonomic Research (Tokyo, JPN)
Clinical Biomechanics (Huddersfield, GBR)

# INDUSTRY ACTIVITY

Clinical and Developmental Immunology (Abingdon, GBR)

Clinical & Experimental Allergy (South Kensington, London, GBR)

Clinical and Experimental Allergy Reviews (South Kensington, London, GBR)

Clinical and Experimental Dermatology (London, GBR)

Clinical Governance (Bradford, GBR)

Clinical Hemorheology and Microcirculation (Siena, ITA)

Clinical Intensive Care (Abingdon, GBR)

Clinical Neurology and Neurosurgery (Leiden, NLD)

Clinical Nutrition (Barcelona, SPA)

Clinical Oncology (Northwood, GBR)

Clinical Oral Implants Research (Bern, SWI)

Clinical Oral Investigations (Tokyo, JPN)

Clinical Physiology and Functional Imaging (Malmo, SWE)

Clinical Psychology (Oxford, GBR)

Clinical Radiology (London, GBR)

Clinical Radiology Extra (London, GBR)

Club Business International (Camberley, GBR)

Clyde 1-FM (Glasgow, GBR)

Clyde 2-AM (Glasgow, GBR)

Coast-FM (Warrnambool, VI, AUS)

Coatings Comet (Teddington, GBR)

Codes of Practice (Middlesex, GBR)

CoDesign (Abingdon, GBR)

Cognition, Technology & Work (Tokyo, JPN)

Cognitive Neuropsychiatry (Abingdon, GBR)

Cognitive Processing (Rome, ITA)

Collection Building (Bradford, GBR)

Colloid and Polymer Science (Aachen, GER)

Combinatorica (Tokyo, JPN)

Combustion and Flame (Calcutta, WB, IND)

Common Knowledge (Ramat Gan, ISR)

Communication Reports (Abingdon, GBR)

Communication Research Reports (Abingdon, GBR)

Communications Engineer Magazine (Stevenage-Hertfordshire, GBR)

Community Development Journal (Bristol, GBR)

Community Development Journal (Oxford, GBR)

Comparative Clinical Pathology (Tokyo, JPN)

Comparative and Functional Genomics (Manchester, GBR)

COMPEL (Bradford, GBR)

Computational Complexity (Tokyo, JPN)

Computational Linguistics (Sydney, NW, AUS)

Computational Management Science (Tokyo, JPN)

Computational Mechanics (Tokyo, JPN)

Computational Statistics (Berlin, GER)

Computational Mathematics and Mathematical Physics (Moscow, RUS)

Computer Graphics Forum (Bath, GBR)

Computer Journal (Egham, GBR)

Computer Methods in Biomechanics and Biomedical Engineering (Abingdon, GBR)

Computer Methods and Programs in Biomedicine (Uppsala, SWE)

Computing & Control Engineering Magazine (Stevenage-Hertfordshire, GBR)

Computing and Visualization in Science (Heidelberg, GER)

Congenital Anomalies (Hamamatsu, JPN)

Connect-FM (Telford Way, NH, GBR)

Connection Science (Sheffield, GBR)

Connective Tissue Research (Abingdon, GBR)

Consumer Choice (Dublin, DU, IRL)

Contact Dermatitis (Hellerup, DEN)

Contact Lens & Anterior Eye (Birmingham, GBR)

Contemporary Economic Policy (Oxford, GBR)

Continence (London, GBR)

Continual Medical Education Magazine (Ankara, TUR)

Continuing Education in Anaesthesia, Critical Care, and Pain (Oxford, GBR)

Continuing Education in Anesthesia, Critical Care & Pain (Leicester, GBR)

Continuum Mechanics and Thermodynamics (Tokyo, JPN)

Contributions to Mineralogy and Petrology (Tokyo, JPN)

Contributions to Political Economy (Oxford, GBR)

Contributions to Political Economy (Cambridge, GBR)

Convenience World (Randwick, NW, AUS)

Cool Blue-FM (Bay of Islands, NZL)

Cool Country Radio-FM (Saint Marys, NW, AUS)

Cool-FM (Belfast, GBR)

Cor et Vasa (Brno, CZE)

Coral Reefs (Tokyo, JPN)

Cork Campus Radio-FM (Cork, IRL)

Corporate Governance (Bradford, GBR)

Corporate Governance: An International Review (Edgbatson, GBR)

Corporate Reputation Review (London, GBR)

Corporate Social Responsibility and Environmental Management (Shipley, GBR)

COSMOS (Singapore, SGP)

Cotton World (Harare, ZWE)

Counselling and Psychotherapy Research (Abingdon, GBR)

Country Radio-FM (Rotorua, NZL)

Countryside Building (Stowmarket, GBR)

County Sound Radio-AM (Guilford, SR, GBR)

Cracking Matters (Farnham, GBR)

Craft Stamper (Croydon, GBR)

CRC-FM (Castlebar, MA, IRL)

Credit Union News (Manchester, GBR)

Crisis: The Journal of Crisis Intervention and Suicide Prevention (Gondrin, FRA)

Critical Perspectives on International Business (Bradford, GBR)

Critical Public Health (Abingdon, GBR)

CRMK-FM (Milton Keynes, GBR)

Crossroads-FM (Taranaki, NZL)

Crystal Research and Technology (Berlin, GER)

Crystallography Reports (Moscow, RUS)

Crystallography Reviews (Surrey, GBR)

CSI Adhyayan (Mumbai, MH, IND)

CSI Communications (Mumbai, MH, IND)

CSI Computer Science and Informatics (Mumbai, MH, IND)

CSI Digest (Mumbai, MH, IND)

CTR-FM (Maidstone, GBR)

Culture, Health and Sexuality (London, GBR)

CUR-AM (Cambridge, GBR)

Current Diagnostic Pathology (Liverpool, GBR)

Current Genetics (Goteborg, SWE)

Current Orthopaedics (Leeds, GBR)

Current Sociology (Loughborough, GBR)

Cycling Weekly (Croydon, GBR)

Cytotherapy (Abingdon, GBR)

Dat's News (Hobart, TA, AUS)

Day One Magazine (Epsom, GBR)

Decanter (London, GBR)

Decisions in Economics and Finance (Tokyo, JPN)

Dee-FM (Chester, GBR)

Dental Materials (Manchester, GBR)

Desidamos (Buenos Aires, ARG)

Deutsche Entomologische Zeitschrift (Berlin, GER)
Development Genes and Evolution (Tokyo, JPN)
Development and Learning in Organizations (Bradford, GBR)
Diabetes (Tampere, FIN)
Diabetes/Metabolism Research and Reviews (Rome, ITA)
Diabetes Research and Clinical Practice (Nagoya, JPN)
Diabetes Update (London, GBR)
Diabetessa Alert (Hilton, SA, AUS)
Dialectica (Oxford, GBR)
Dialectologia et Geolinguistica (Umea, SWE)
Dialog (Wiesbaden, GER)
Dine-Out (London, GBR)
Diogenes (Paris, FRA)
Disability and Society (Abingdon, GBR)
Disarmament Diplomacy (London, GBR)
Disaster Prevention and Management (Bradford, GBR)
Discrete & Computational Geometry (Tokyo, JPN)
Disease Markers (Amsterdam, NLD)
Disney Princess Magazine (Quezon City, PHL)
Divadelni Noviny (Prague, CZE)
Division of Labor & Transaction Costs (Clayton, VI, AUS)
DNA Sequence (Abingdon, GBR)
DNA Sequence (Cambridge, GBR)
Doff-laoio (Reykjavik, ICE)
Doklady Mathematics (Moscow, RUS)
Dream 100-FM (Colchester, EX, GBR)
Drug and Alcohol Findings (London, GBR)
Drug and Alcohol Review (Brisbane, AUS)
Drug and Alcohol Review (Abingdon, GBR)
Drugs (Abingdon, GBR)
Drugs: Education, Prevention & Policy (Enfield, GBR)
Dune-FM (Southport, MS, GBR)
Durbar (Huntingdon, GBR)
Eagle-FM (Goulburn, NW, AUS)
Early Child Development and Care (Middlesex, GBR)
Early Human Development (London, GBR)
Early Popular Visual Culture (Abingdon, GBR)
Easy Radio London-AM (Southall, GBR)
EAU Update Series (Brussels, BEL)
Echo-FM (Preston, VI, AUS)

Eclogae Geologicae Helvetia (Tokyo, JPN)
EcoHealth (Tokyo, JPN)
Ecological Research (Tokyo, JPN)
Economic Inquiry (Oxford, GBR)
Economics of Governance (Tokyo, JPN)
Ecosystems (Tokyo, JPN)
The Edge (Leicester, GBR)
Edge-FM (Auckland, NZL)
Edge-FM (Wangaratta, VI, AUS)
The Edge-FM (North Ryde, NW, AUS)
Education for Health (Abingdon, GBR)
Education for Information (Manchester, GBR)
Education Training (Bradford, GBR)
Educational Measurement: Issues and Practice (Oxford, GBR)
8CCC-FM (Alice Springs, NT, AUS)
88-FM (Springwood, QL, AUS)
Electrical Engineering (Tokyo, JPN)
Electronic Journal of Pathology and Histology (Heidelberg, GER)
Electronic Library (Bradford, GBR)
Electronics Letters (Stevenage-Hertfordshire, GBR)
Electronics Systems & Software Magazine (Stevenage-Hertfordshire, GBR)
ELT Journal (Oxford, GBR)
ELT Journal (Reepham, GBR)
Emergency Medicine (West Melbourne, VI, AUS)
Emergency Radiology (Tokyo, JPN)
Emotional and Behavioral Difficulties (Cumbria, GBR)
The Employer (Wellington, NZL)
ENA-FM (Adelaide, SA, AUS)
Endothelium (Abingdon, GBR)
Engineer Magazine (London, GBR)
Engineering Computations (Bradford, GBR)
Engineering with Computers (Tokyo, JPN)
Engineering, Construction and Architectural Management (Bradford, GBR)
Engineering Optimization (Liverpool, GBR)
English in Australia (Norwood, SA, AUS)
English Historical Review (Oxford, GBR)
Enterprise & Society (Oxford, GBR)
Environmental Chemistry Letters (Tokyo, JPN)
Environmental Geology (Tokyo, JPN)
Environmental Practice (Oxford, GBR)
Environmental Toxicology (Aranda, AC, AUS)
Epidemiologic Reviews (Oxford, GBR)

Equestrian Trade News (Wetherby, GBR)
Equine and Comparative Exercise Physiology (Wallingford, GBR)
Ergonomics SA (Auckland Park, SAF)
ESHRE Monographs (Oxford, GBR)
Esophagus (Tokyo, JPN)
Ethics and Education (Abingdon, GBR)
Ethnography & Education (Abingdon, GBR)
Ethnopolitics (Abingdon, GBR)
Europace (London, GBR)
European Archives of Oto-Rhino-Laryngology (Tokyo, JPN)
European Archives of Psychiatry and Clinical Neuroscience (Tokyo, JPN)
European Biophysics Journal (Oxford, GBR)
European Business Review (Bradford, GBR)
European Clinics in Obstetrics and Gynaecology (Tokyo, JPN)
European Environment: The Journal of European Environmental Policy (Shipley, GBR)
European Food Research and Technology (Tokyo, JPN)
European Heart Journal (Oxford, GBR)
European Information (Manchester, GBR)
European Journal of Ageing (Tokyo, JPN)
European Journal of Applied Physiology (Tokyo, JPN)
European Journal of Cancer (Edinburgh, GBR)
European Journal of Cardio-Thoracic Surgery (Martigny, SWI)
European Journal of Cardiovascular Nursing (Groningen, NLD)
European Journal of Cardiovascular Prevention & Rehabilitation (London, GBR)
European Journal of Contraception and Reproductive Health Care (Athens, GRC)
The European Journal of Contraception & Reproductive Health Care (Abingdon, GBR)
European Journal of Echocardiography (Rotterdam, NLD)
European Journal of Engineering Education (Paris, FRA)
European Journal of Heart Failure (Kingston Upon Hull, GBR)
European Journal of Immunology (Freiburg, GER)
European Journal of Innovation Management (Bradford, GBR)

# INDUSTRY ACTIVITY

European Journal of International Law (Florence, ITA)
European Journal of International Law (Oxford, GBR)
European Journal of Obstetrics & Gynecology (Leeds, GBR)
European Journal of Oncology Nursing (Manchester, GBR)
European Journal of Orthodontics (Oxford, GBR)
European Journal of Public Health (Oxford, GBR)
European Journal of Public Health (Utrecht, NLD)
European Journal of Sport Science (Abingdon, GBR)
European Journal of Ultrasound (Nottingham, GBR)
European Psychologist (Jena, GER)
European Research In Regional Science (London, GBR)
European Review of Agricultural Economics (Oxford, GBR)
European Review of Agricultural Economics (Wageningen, NLD)
European Sociological Review (Bamberg, GER)
European Sociological Review (Oxford, GBR)
European Transactions in Telecommunications (Milan, ITA)
European Union Politics (Konstanz, GER)
European Urology (Brussels, BEL)
European Urology (Arnhem, NLD)
European Vegetarian (Fischbach, GER)
European Weightlifter (San Marino, SMR)
Evidence-Based Cardiovascular Medicine (Sydney, AUS)
Evidence-based Complementary and Alternative Medicine (Oxford, GBR)
Evolutionary Computation (Orsay, FRA)
Experimental Thermal and Fluid Science (Bussum, NLD)
The Expository Times (Edinburgh, GBR)
Facilities (Bradford, GBR)
Fackoversattaren (Bastad, SWE)
Family Court Review (Oxford, GBR)
Family Practice (Oxford, GBR)
Family Practice (Birmingham, GBR)
The Farmer (Kingston, JAM)
Farmers Weekly (Sutton, GBR)
Farmland Market (Sutton, GBR)
Fatigue & Fracture of Engineering Materials & Structures (Sheffield, GBR)
FBI-FM (Strawberry Hills, NW, AUS)

FEBS Journal (Cambridge, GBR)
Feddes Repertorium (Berlin, GER)
Federation Focus (Edinburgh, GBR)
Feedback (Middlesex, GBR)
Fetal and Pediatric Pathology (Abingdon, GBR)
Fire Australia (Box Hill, VI, AUS)
Fire-FM (Bournemouth, DS, GBR)
Fiscal Studies (Oxford, GBR)
Fisheries Science (Tokyo, JPN)
5AA-AM (Adelaide, SA, AUS)
5DDD-FM (Stepney, SA, AUS)
5EBI-FM (Adelaide, SA, AUS)
5EZY-FM (Mount Barker, SA, AUS)
5MG-AM (Mount Gambier, SA, AUS)
5MU-AM (Murray Bridge, SA, AUS)
5RM-AM (Berri, SA, AUS)
5SE-AM (Mount Gambier, SA, AUS)
5UV-AM (Adelaide, SA, AUS)
5YYY-FM (Whyalla Norrie, SA, AUS)
Flipside Magazine (Stevenage-Hertfordshire, GBR)
Fly Navy (London, GBR)
Food and Agricultural Immunology (Chester, GBR)
Food and Chemical Toxicology (Carshalton, GBR)
Foreign Policy Analysis (Wellington, NZL)
Foresight (Bradford, GBR)
Forestry (Oxford, GBR)
Forschungsberichte aus Technik und Naturwissenschaften (Hannover, GER)
Fortattaren (Stockholm, SWE)
Fortschritte der Physik/Progress of Physics (Munich, GER)
Forum for Modern Language Studies (Fife, GBR)
Forum for Modern Language Studies (Oxford, GBR)
Fossils and Strata (Copenhagen, DEN)
4AM-AM (Mareeba, QL, AUS)
4BBB-FM (Brisbane, QL, AUS)
4BC-AM (Brisbane, QL, AUS)
4BH-AM (Brisbane City, QL, AUS)
4BI-AM (Brisbane City, QL, AUS)
4BU-AM (Bundaberg, QL, AUS)
4CA-FM (Cairns, QL, AUS)
4CBL-FM (Logan City DC, QL, AUS)
4CC-AM (Gladstone, QL, AUS)
4EB-FM (Brisbane, QL, AUS)
4GC-AM (Charters Towers, QL, AUS)
4GR-AM (Toowoomba, QL, AUS)
4GY-AM (Gympie, QL, AUS)
4HI-AM (Emerald, QL, AUS)
4KQ-AM (Stones Corner, QL, AUS)
4LG-AM (Longreach, QL, AUS)

4LM-AM (Mt. Isa, QL, AUS)
4MBS-FM (Coorparoo, QL, AUS)
4MMM-FM (Brisbane, QL, AUS)
4OUR-FM (Caboolture, QL, AUS)
4QN-AM (Townsville, QL, AUS)
4QR-AM (Brisbane, QL, AUS)
4RK-AM (Rockhampton, QL, AUS)
4TO-FM (Hyde Park, QL, AUS)
4ZR-AM (Roma, QL, AUS)
FOX-FM (Saint Kilda, VI, AUS)
Fox-FM (Cowley, OX, GBR)
Fractional Calculus and Applied Analysis (Sofia, BUL)
Free Radical Research (Abingdon, GBR)
Free Tibet (London, GBR)
French History (Oxford, GBR)
French History (Staffordshire, GBR)
Fresh-FM (Adelaide, SA, AUS)
Frontline (South Melbourne, VI, AUS)
Fruit Basket (Cavan, SA, AUS)
Fundamenta Informaticae (Amsterdam, NLD)
Galaxy 105-FM (Leeds, GBR)
Galaxy 105-106-FM (Wallsend, TW, GBR)
Galaxy 102-FM (Manchester, GBR)
Galaxy 102.2-FM (Birmingham, GBR)
The Galloway Journal (Castle Douglas, GBR)
Galway Bay-FM (Galway, IRL)
GAMM - Mitteilungen (Kaiserslautern, GER)
Gazzetta (Zurich, SWI)
Gekkan Oruta (Tokyo, JPN)
Genetics and Breeding (Sofia, BUL)
Geographical Analysis (Oxford, GBR)
Geologica Belgica (Brussels, BEL)
Geologisk Tidsskrift (Copenhagen, DEN)
Geophysical & Astrophysical Fluid Dynamics (Exeter, GBR)
Geotectonics (Moscow, RUS)
Geowissenschaftliche Reihe (Berlin, GER)
German History (London, GBR)
german research (Bonn, GER)
Gestalt Journal of Australia and New Zealand (Sydney, NW, AUS)
Ghana Journal of Science (Legon, GHA)
Gilbert & Sullivan News (London, GBR)
Glazed Expressions (Stoke-On-Trent, GBR)
Gleditschia (Berlin, GER)
Global Crime (Abingdon, GBR)
Global Environmental Politics (Sydney, NW, AUS)
Global Future (Burwood East, VI, AUS)
Global Public Health (Abingdon, GBR)

Gale Directory of Publications and Broadcast Media, 140th Edition

Glycobiology (Oxford, GBR)
GOLD 92.5-FM (Southport, QL, AUS)
GOLD 104.3-FM (Richmond, VI, AUS)
The Golf (Croydon, GBR)
Goolarri-FM (Broome, WA, AUS)
Goss Hawk (Ilkeston, GBR)
GP Growth Point (Reading, GBR)
Graduate Recruiter (Warwick, GBR)
Grana (Stockholm, SWE)
Grassland Science (Oxford, GBR)
Green's Business Law Bulletin (Edinburgh, GBR)
Greens Civil Practice Bulletin (Edinburgh, GBR)
Greens Criminal Law Bulletin (Edinburgh, GBR)
Green's Property Law Bulletin (Edinburgh, GBR)
The Grieg Companion (London, GBR)
Ground Water (Oxford, GBR)
Ground Water Monitoring and Remediation (Oxford, GBR)
Growth Factors (Abingdon, GBR)
Growth Hormone & IGF Research (Kommunehospitalet, DEN)
GT-FM (Pontypridd, GBR)
The Guitar Magazine (Croydon, GBR)
Guldsmedebladet (Virum, DEN)
Gulf-FM (Kadina, SA, AUS)
Handbook of Business Strategy (Bradford, GBR)
Headway News (Nottingham, GBR)
Health Club Management (Hitchin, GBR)
Health Education Research (Oxford, GBR)
Health Policy (Leuven, BEL)
Health Promotion International (Oxford, GBR)
Health Promotion International (Burwood, VI, AUS)
Heart-FM (Birmingham, GBR)
Heart 100.7-FM (Birmingham, GBR)
Heart 106.2-FM (London, GBR)
Hellenic Journal of Cardiology (Athens, GRC)
Hellenic Journal of Psychology (Thessaloniki, GRC)
Hellenic Radiology Journal (Athens, GRC)
Hematology (Whitechapel, GBR)
Hematology (Abingdon, GBR)
The Hematology Journal (Rotterdam, NLD)
Hepatology Research (Tokyo, JPN)
Herald of the Russian Academy of Sciences (Moscow, RUS)
The Herb Grower (South Lismore, NW, AUS)

Hertbeat-FM (Hertfordshire, GBR)
Hi Society (Wellington, NZL)
High Pressure Research (Paris, FRA)
Higher Education Research and Development (HERD) (Milperra, NW, AUS)
HISSAB (Addis Ababa, ETH)
Historical Biology (Dublin, IRL)
Historical Journal of Film, Radio and Television (Berlin, GER)
History Workshop Journal (London, GBR)
HO-FM (Hobart, TA, AUS)
Hokonui Gold-FM (Gore, NZL)
Holocaust and Genocide Studies (Oxford, GBR)
Homeless in Europe (Brussels, BEL)
Homeopathy in Practice (East Sussex, GBR)
Horse (London, GBR)
Horticultural Journal (Calcutta, IND)
HPB (Abingdon, GBR)
The Hub-AM (Bristol, GBR)
Human Communication Research (Oxford, GBR)
Human Fertility (Abingdon, GBR)
Human Fertility (York, GBR)
Human Genomics (London, GBR)
Human Molecular Genetics (Oxford, GBR)
Human Reproduction (Oxford, GBR)
Human Reproduction (Cambridge, GBR)
Human Reproduction Update (Oxford, GBR)
Human Resource Management International Digest (Bradford, GBR)
Human Rights Law Review (Oxford, GBR)
Hygiea Internationalis: An Interdisciplinary Journal for the History of Public Health (Linkoping, SWE)
Hypertension In Pregnancy (Abingdon, GBR)
I-Ways (Amsterdam, NLD)
IASSI Quarterly (New Delhi, DH, IND)
IEE Proceedings Circuits, Devices & Systems (Stevenage-Hertfordshire, GBR)
IEE Proceedings Communications (Stevenage-Hertfordshire, GBR)
IEE Proceedings Computers & Digital Techniques (Stevenage-Hertfordshire, GBR)
IEE Proceedings Control Theory & Applications (Stevenage-Hertfordshire, GBR)
IEE Proceedings Electric Power Applications (Stevenage-Hertfordshire, GBR)

IEE Proceedings Generation, Transmission & Distribution (Stevenage-Hertfordshire, GBR)
IEE Proceedings Microwaves, Antennas & Propagatio (Stevenage-Hertfordshire, GBR)
IEE Proceedings Nanobiotechnology (Stevenage-Hertfordshire, GBR)
IEE Proceedings Optoelectronics (Stevenage-Hertfordshire, GBR)
IEE Proceedings Radar, Sonar & Navigation (Stevenage-Hertfordshire, GBR)
IEE Proceedings Science, Measurement & Technology (Stevenage-Hertfordshire, GBR)
IEE Proceedings Software (Stevenage-Hertfordshire, GBR)
IEE Proceedings Vision, Image & Signal Processing (Stevenage-Hertfordshire, GBR)
IEE Review Magazine (Stevenage-Hertfordshire, GBR)
II-Merill (Ta'Xbiex, MAL)
IIA Digital Digest (Dublin, DU, IRL)
IIA Non-Members Update (Dublin, DU, IRL)
IIM Metal News (Calcutta, WB, IND)
IIM Transactions (Calcutta, WB, IND)
IMA Journal of Applied Mathematics (Oxford, GBR)
IMA Journal of Management Mathematics (Oxford, GBR)
IMA Journal of Mathematical Control and Information (Oxford, GBR)
IMA Journal of Numerical Analysis (Oxford, GBR)
IMA Journal of Numerical Analysis (Southend-On-Sea, GBR)
Imagine-FM (Stockport, GBR)
Immunogenetics (Tokyo, JPN)
Impact (Auckland, NZL)
In Brief (Saint Neots, GBR)
In Silico Biology (Gottingen, GER)
In Vitro Cellular and Developmental Biology - Plant (Selangor, MYS)
Indian Journal of Microbiology (New Delhi, IND)
Industria & Quimica (Buenos Aires, ARG)
Industrial & Commercial Training (Bradford, GBR)
Industrial and Corporate Change (Oxford, GBR)
Industrial and Corporate Change (Castellanza (VA), ITA)
Industrial Lubrication & Tribology (Bradford, GBR)
Infant Observation (Abingdon, GBR)

Infectious Diseases in Obstetrics & Gynecology (Abingdon, GBR)
Infectology (Sofia, BUL)
Inflammation Research (Tokyo, JPN)
Informatica (Amsterdam, NLD)
Information Management & Computer Security (Bradford, GBR)
Information Polity (Glasgow, GBR)
Information Services & Use (Amsterdam, NLD)
Information Technology Journal (Faisalabad, PAK)
i98-FM (Wollongong, NW, AUS)
Injury (Coventry, GBR)
Injury Prevention (London, GBR)
INNOTECH Journal (Quezon City, PHL)
Insect Science (Oxford, GBR)
Inside Housing (Westwood Way, GBR)
Insight (London, GBR)
Integral Transforms and Special Functions (Moscow, RUS)
Interiors Focus (Solihull, GBR)
Interlending and Document Supply (Bradford, GBR)
International Boat Industry (Croydon, GBR)
International and Comparative Law Quarterly (Oxford, GBR)
International Contact Lens Clinic (Birmingham, GBR)
International Hatchery Practice (Driffield, GBR)
International Immunology (Osaka, JPN)
International Immunology (Oxford, GBR)
International Journal of Aeroacoustics (Brentwood, GBR)
International Journal of Angiology (Tokyo, JPN)
International Journal of Applied Electromagnetics and Mechanics (Sendai, JPN)
International Journal of Art Therapy (Abingdon, GBR)
International Journal of Artificial Intelligence in Education (Glasgow, GBR)
International Journal of Asian Management (Tokyo, JPN)
International Journal of Audiology (Abingdon, GBR)
International Journal of Behavioural Development (Jena, GER)
International Journal of Botany (Faisalabad, PAK)
International Journal of Cancer Research (Faisalabad, PAK)
International Journal of Cardiology (Sydney, NW, AUS)
International Journal of Cardiovascular Interventions (Abingdon, GBR)
International Journal of Cardiovascular Inventions (Abingdon, GBR)
International Journal of Clothing Science & Technology (Bradford, GBR)
International Journal of Colorectal Disease (Tokyo, JPN)
International Journal of Computational Methods in Engineering Science & Mechanics (Abingdon, GBR)
International Journal of Computer Mathematics (Leicestershire, GBR)
International Journal of Constitutional Law (Oxford, GBR)
International Journal of Contemporary Hospitality Management (Bradford, GBR)
International Journal of Cooperative Information Systems (Tilburg, NLD)
International Journal of Dairy Science (Faisalabad, PAK)
International Journal of Disaster Medicine (Abingdon, GBR)
International Journal of Disaster Medicine (Linkoping, SWE)
International Journal of Disclosure and Governance (London, GBR)
International Journal of Drug Policy (London, GBR)
International Journal of Economic Theory (Oxford, GBR)
International Journal of Educational Advancement (London, GBR)
International Journal of Educational Management (Bradford, GBR)
International Journal of Emerging Markets (Bradford, GBR)
International Journal of Entrepreneurial Behaviour & Research (Bradford, GBR)
International Journal of Environmental Health Research (Paisley, GBR)
International Journal of Epidemiology (Bristol, GBR)
International Journal of Food Properties (Muscat, OMN)
International Journal of Food Sciences & Nutrition (Abingdon, GBR)
International Journal of Health Care Quality Assurance (Bradford, GBR)
International Journal of Image and Graphics (Kowloon, CHN)
International Journal of Information Acquisition (Singapore, SGP)
International Journal of Injury Control and Safety Promotion (Amsterdam, NLD)
International Journal of Knowledge-Based and Intelligent Engineering Systems (Amsterdam, NLD)
International Journal of Lexicography (Leiden, NLD)
International Journal of Lexicography (Oxford, GBR)
International Journal of Nanoscience (Rueschlikon, SWI)
International Journal of Neuroscience (Abingdon, GBR)
International Journal of Numerical Methods for Heat and Fluid Flow (Bradford, GBR)
International Journal of Nursing Studies (London, GBR)
International Journal of Nursing Terminologies and Classifications (Oxford, GBR)
International Journal Of Bank Marketing (Bradford, GBR)
International Journal or Oral & Maxillofacial Surgery (Guildford, GBR)
International Journal of Pattern Recognition and Artificial Intelligence (Munich, GER)
International Journal of Pharmacology (Faisalabad, PAK)
International Journal of Prisoner Health (Abingdon, GBR)
International Journal of Productivity and Performance Management (Bradford, GBR)
International Journal of Psychiatry in Clinical Practice (Abingdon, GBR)
International Journal of Public Sector Management (Bradford, GBR)
International Journal for Quality in Health Care (Oxford, GBR)
International Journal for Quality in Health Care (Geneva, SWI)
International Journal of Risk and Safety in Medicine (Amsterdam, NLD)
International Journal of Service Industry Management (Bradford, GBR)
International Journal of Space Structures (Brentwood, GBR)
International Journal of Sustainability in Higher Education (Bradford, GBR)
International Journal for Technology in Mathematics Education (Plymouth, GBR)
International Journal of Toxicology (Abingdon, GBR)
International Journal of Tropical Insect Science (Wallingford, GBR)
International Journal of Uncertainty, Fuzziness and Knowledge-Based Systems (Paris, FRA)

International Journal of Virology (Faisalabad, PAK)

International Journal on Wireless and Optical Communications (Singapore, SGP)

International Journal of Zoological Research (Faisalabad, PAK)

International Pig Topics (Driffield, GBR)

International Poultry Production (Driffield, GBR)

International Relations of the Asia-Pacific (Tokyo, JPN)

International Relations of the Asia-Pacific (Oxford, GBR)

International Review of Hydrobiology (Berlin, GER)

International Review of Psychiatry (Abingdon, GBR)

International Reviews Of Immunology (Abingdon, GBR)

The Internet Journal of Otorhinolaryngology (London, GBR)

Internet Research (Bradford, GBR)

Intervention Research (Amsterdam, NLD)

Invicta-FM (Whitstable, KT, GBR)

Irish Family History Society (Naas, KL, IRL)

Irish Mountain Log (Dublin, DU, IRL)

Irrigation and Drainage (London, GBR)

Irrigation and Drainage (Marseille, FRA)

Island-FM (Guernsey, CI, GBR)

Isle of Wight Radio-FM (Newport, IW, GBR)

Isokinetics and Exercise Science (Tel Aviv, ISR)

Isotopes in Environmental and Health Studies (Abingdon, GBR)

Issues (Sydney, NW, AUS)

IUBMB Life (Bern, SWI)

Japan Heterocerists Journal (Tokyo, JPN)

Japan Racing Journal (Tokyo, JPN)

Japanese Journal of Clinical Oncology (Oxford, GBR)

Japanese Journal of Ophthalmology (Tokyo, JPN)

Japanese Journal of Radiological Technology (Kyoto, JPN)

Jazz-FM (London, GBR)

Jewellery Time (Christchurch, NZL)

Journal of Affective Disorders (Canterbury, GBR)

Journal of African Economics (Oxford, GBR)

Journal of Agronomy (Faisalabad, PAK)

Journal of the American Ceramic Society (Oxford, GBR)

Journal of Antimicrobial Chemotherapy (Oxford, GBR)

Journal of Applied Corporate Finance (Oxford, GBR)

Journal of Applied Sciences (Faisalabad, PAK)

Journal of Architectural Education (Oxford, GBR)

Journal of the Argentine Chemical Society (Buenos Aires, ARG)

Journal of Asian Natural Products Research (Beijing, CHN)

Journal of Atmospheric and Ocean Science (European Way, GBR)

Journal of Back and Musculoskeletal Rehabilitation (Enschede, NLD)

Journal of Banking Regulation (London, GBR)

Journal of Basic Microbiology (Jena, GER)

Journal of Biochemistry (Oxford, GBR)

Journal of Biomechanics (Eindhoven, NLD)

Journal of Biopharmaceutical Statistics (Taipei, TWN)

Journal of Bodywork and Movement Therapies (London, GBR)

Journal of Bond Trading and Management (London, GBR)

Journal of Brand Management (London, GBR)

The Journal of the British Association of Teachers of the Deaf (High Wycombe, BK, GBR)

The Journal of British Podiatric Medicine (London, GBR)

Journal of Building Appraisal (London, GBR)

Journal of Carbohydrate Chemistry (Zurich, SWI)

Journal of Chemical Sciences (Bangalore, KA, IND)

Journal of Child and Adolescent Psychiatric Nursing (Oxford, GBR)

Journal of China Particuology (Beijing, CHN)

Journal of Civil Society (Abingdon, GBR)

Journal of Clinical Forensic Medicine (London, GBR)

Journal of Commercial Biotechnology (London, GBR)

Journal of Communication Management (London, GBR)

The Journal of the Communications Network (Sunbury-On-Thames, GBR)

Journal of Competition Law and Economics (Oxford, GBR)

Journal of Computational Methods in Sciences and Engineering (Amsterdam, NLD)

Journal of Computer and Systems Sciences International (Moscow, RUS)

Journal of Conflict and Security Law (Oxford, GBR)

Journal of Corporate Real Estate (London, GBR)

Journal of Cosmetic and Laser Therapy (Abingdon, GBR)

Journal of Cosmology and Astroparticle Physics (Bristol, GBR)

Journal of Cranio-Maxillofacial Surgery (Rostock, GER)

Journal of Criminal Justice Education (Abingdon, GBR)

Journal of Cystic Fibrosis (The Hague, NLD)

Journal of Database Marketing and Customer Strategy Management (London, GBR)

Journal of Deaf Studies and Deaf Education (Oxford, GBR)

Journal of Dentistry (Birmingham, GBR)

Journal of Derivatives Accounting (Singapore, SGP)

Journal of Dermatological Science (Sapporo, JPN)

Journal of Dermatological Treatment (Abingdon, GBR)

Journal of Design History (Oxford, GBR)

Journal of Developmental Entrepreneurship (Singapore, SGP)

Journal of Digital Asset Management (London, GBR)

Journal of Digital Information (Oxford, GBR)

Journal of Drug Evaluation (Abingdon, GBR)

Journal of Drug Targeting (Abingdon, GBR)

Journal of Early Childhood Teacher Education (Abingdon, GBR)

Journal of Earth System Science (Bangalore, KA, IND)

Journal of Economic Geography (Oxford, GBR)

Journal of Economics Studies (Bradford, GBR)

Journal of Educational Administration (Bradford, GBR)

Journal of Educational Measurement (Oxford, GBR)

Journal of Electron Microscopy (Oxford, GBR)

Journal of Electron Microscopy (Tokyo, JPN)

Journal of Entomology (Faisalabad, PAK)

Journal of Environmental Sciences (Amsterdam, NLD)

Journal of Enzyme Inhibition (Abingdon, GBR)

Journal of Enzyme Inhibition and Medicinal Chemistry (Abingdon, GBR)

Journal of Epidemiology (Oxford, GBR)

Journal of Eukaryotic Microbiology (Oxford, GBR)

Journal of Experimental Botany (Oxford, GBR)

Journal of Experimental Nanoscience (Abingdon, GBR)

Journal of Facilities Management (London, GBR)

Journal of Fashion Marketing and Management (Bradford, GBR)

Journal of Financial Crime (London, GBR)

Journal of Financial Econometrics (Oxford, GBR)

Journal of Financial Regulation and Compliance (London, GBR)

Journal of Financial Services Marketing (London, GBR)

Journal of Food Lipids (Oxford, GBR)

Journal of Food Safety (Oxford, GBR)

Journal of Forest Research (Tokyo, JPN)

The Journal of Further and Higher Education (London, GBR)

Journal of General Plant Pathology (Tokyo, JPN)

Journal of Generic Medicines (London, GBR)

Journal of Geophysics and Engineering (Bristol, GBR)

Journal of the Ghana Science Association (Legon, GHA)

Journal of Global Ethics (Abingdon, GBR)

Journal of Grey System (Wuhan, CHN)

Journal of Hand Surgery (British & European Volume) (Oakham, GBR)

Journal of Headache and Pain (Tokyo, JPN)

Journal of Health, Organization and Management (Bradford, GBR)

Journal of Helminthology (Wallingford, GBR)

Journal of High Energy Physics (Bristol, GBR)

Journal of Higher Education Policy and Management (O'Connor, AC, AUS)

Journal of the History of Collections (Oxford, GBR)

Journal of Holistic Healthcare (Hove, GBR)

Journal of Hospital Infection (London, GBR)

Journal of the ICRU (Oxford, GBR)

Journal of the Indian Society of Soil Science (New Delhi, DH, IND)

Journal of Infection (Harlow, GBR)

Journal of the Institution of Occupational Safety and Health (Wigston, GBR)

Journal of Integrated Design & Process Science (Hagen, GER)

Journal of Integrative Neuroscience (Singapore, SGP)

Journal of Integrative Plant Biology (Oxford, GBR)

Journal of Intellectual and Development Disability (Abingdon, GBR)

Journal of Intellectual and Developmental Disability (Ryde, AUS)

Journal of International Criminal Justice (Oxford, GBR)

Journal of Interprofessional Care (Abingdon, GBR)

Journal of Investigative Psychology and Offender Profiling (Liverpool, GBR)

Journal of Islamic Studies (Oxford, GBR)

Journal of the Israel Heart Society (Ramat Gan, ISR)

Journal of the Kilvert Society (Kinnersley, GBR)

Journal of Knowledge Management (Bradford, GBR)

Journal of Korean Radiological Society (Seoul, KOR)

Journal of Legal Studies Education (Oxford, GBR)

Journal of Logic and Computation (London, GBR)

Journal of Manufacturing Technology Management (Bradford, GBR)

Journal of Marketing (Johannesburg, SAF)

Journal of Material Cycles and Waste Management (Tokyo, JPN)

Journal of Mathematics (Lower Hutt, NZL)

Journal of Medical Engineering and Technology (Cardiff, GBR)

Journal of Medical Marketing (London, GBR)

Journal of Medical Ultrasonics (Tokyo, JPN)

Journal of Mental Health (Abingdon, GBR)

Journal of Micromechanics and Microengineering (Bristol, GBR)

Journal of Molecular Medicine (Tokyo, JPN)

Journal of Molluscan Studies (Oxford, GBR)

Journal of Money Laundering Control (London, GBR)

Journal of Multilingual Communication Disorders (Abingdon, GBR)

Journal of the National Cancer Institute (Oxford, GBR)

Journal of the Nepal Dental Association (Lalitpur, NPL)

Journal of Neural Engineering (Bristol, GBR)

Journal News (London, GBR)

Journal of Nuclear and Radiochemical Sciences (Ibaraki, JPN)

Journal of Nutritional & Environmental Medicine (Abingdon, GBR)

Journal of Oceanography (Tokyo, JPN)

The Journal Of The British Association Of Psychotherapists (London, GBR)

Journal Of Workplace Learning (Bradford, GBR)

Journal of Optics A (Bristol, GBR)

Journal of Optics B (Bristol, GBR)

Journal of Organ Dysfunctions (Abingdon, GBR)

Journal of Organizational Change Management (Bradford, GBR)

Journal of Pediatric Neurology (Amsterdam, NLD)

Journal of Petrology (Leeds, GBR)

Journal of the Planetary Gemologists Association (Bangkok, THA)

Journal of Plankton Research (Oxford, GBR)

Journal of Plant Interactions (Abingdon, GBR)

The Journal of Positive Psychology (Abingdon, GBR)

Journal of Postcolonial Writing (Abingdon, GBR)

Journal of Product and Brand Management (Bradford, GBR)

Journal of Property Investment & Finance (Bradford, GBR)

Journal of Psychiatric Research (Munich, GER)

Journal of Psychosomatic Research (Manchester, GBR)

Journal of Public Administration Research and Theory (Oxford, GBR)

Journal of Public Health (Oxford, GBR)

Journal of Quality in Maintenance Engineering (Bradford, GBR)

Journal of Refugee Studies (Brighton, GBR)

Journal of Rehabilitation Medicine (Abingdon, GBR)

Journal of Reproductive and Infant Psychology (Abingdon, GBR)

Journal of Retail and Leisure Property (London, GBR)

Journal of Revenue and Pricing Managemen (London, GBR)

Journal of School Health (Oxford, GBR)

Journal of Semantics (Oxford, GBR)

## INDUSTRY ACTIVITY

Journal of Semitic Studies (Manchester, GBR)
Journal of Sexual Aggression (Oxfordshire, GBR)
Journal of Small Business and Enterprise Development (Bradford, GBR)
Journal of Southeast European and Black Sea Studies (Athens, GRC)
Journal of Statistical Mechanics: Theory and Experiment (Bristol, GBR)
Journal of the Stephenson Locomotive Society (Chigwell, GBR)
Journal of Strain Analysis for Engineering Design (London, GBR)
Journal of Structural Control and Health Monitoring (Pavia, ITA)
Journal of Structural and Functional Genomics (Tokyo, JPN)
Journal of Substance Use (Abingdon, GBR)
Journal of Supply Chain Management (Oxford, GBR)
Journal of Symbolic Logic (Wellington, NZL)
Journal of Systems Architecture (Saint Augustin, GER)
Journal of Systems Science and Information (Beijing, CHN)
Journal of the Textile Institutes (Cambridge, GBR)
Journal of Textile Research (Beijing, CHN)
Journal of Theoretical Medicine (Abingdon, GBR)
Journal of Thrombosis and Thrombolysis (Tokyo, JPN)
Journal of the Tiles and Architectural Ceramic Society (Stoke-On-Trent, GBR)
Journal of Travel and Tourism Marketing (Kowloon, HKG)
Journal of Tropical Pediatrics (Oxford, GBR)
Journal of Turfgrass Science (Bingley, WY, GBR)
Journal of Urban Health (Oxford, GBR)
Journal of Vestibular Research (Amsterdam, NLD)
Journal of Visual Communication in Medicine (Abingdon, GBR)
Journal of Workplace Learning (Bradford, GBR)
Joy-FM (South Melbourne, VI, AUS)
Just Country-FM (Christchurch, NZL)
Justice Quarterly (Abingdon, GBR)
K-ROCK-FM (Geelong, VI, AUS)
Kaffa Coffee (Addis Ababa, ETH)
Kagaku-to Kyoiku (Tokyo, JPN)

KCR-FM (Prescot, MS, GBR)
Kello and Kulta (Espoo, FIN)
Key 103-FM (Manchester, GBR)
KGB-FM (South Yarra, VI, AUS)
KIK-FM (Mareeba, QL, AUS)
Killi-News (Wymondham, GBR)
Kiwi Parent (Lower Hutt, NZL)
KIX-FM (Kingscote, SA, AUS)
KM-FM (Rochester, KT, GBR)
KO-FM (Charlestown, NW, AUS)
K1-FM (Bournemouth, GBR)
Koori Radio-FM (Strawberry Hills, NW, AUS)
Korean Journal of Radiology (Seoul, KOR)
Krasnogruda: Nations Cultures and Small Homelands of Central-Eastern Europe (Sejny, POL)
Kruhl Ruze (Zagreb, CTA)
Lace (Stourbridge, GBR)
Land Degradation and Development (Swansea, GBR)
Landscape and Ecological Engineering (Tokyo, JPN)
Laser Physics (Moscow, RUS)
Lasers in Medical Science (Tokyo, JPN)
Latin America Quarterly Magazine (La Paz, BOL)
Latin American and Caribbean Ethnic Studies (Abingdon, GBR)
Latin American Politics, Economy & Society (Tokyo, JPN)
Law, Probability and Risk (Edinburgh, GBR)
LBC-AM (London, GBR)
LCR-AM (Loughborough, GBR)
Leadership in Health Services (Bradford, GBR)
Learning Organization (Bradford, GBR)
Legal Medicine (Sugitani, JPN)
Leisure Management Magazine (Camberley, GBR)
Leisure Opportunities (Camberley, GBR)
Leukemia and Lymphoma (Abingdon, GBR)
Library Association Record (London, GBR)
Library Management (Bradford, GBR)
Library Review (Bradford, GBR)
LIFE-FM (Hendon Common, SA, AUS)
Life-FM (Auckland, NZL)
Light Box (London, GBR)
Light-FM (Mont Albert, VI, AUS)
Lincs-FM (Lincoln, GBR)
Literary and Linguistic Computing (London, GBR)
Literature and Theology (Stirling, GBR)

Lithuanian Journal of Cardiology (Vilnius, LIT)
Lithuanian Journal of Physics (Vilnius, LIT)
Live 95-FM (Limerick, IRL)
Livestock Production Science (Paris, FRA)
LMS Journal of Computation and Mathematics (London, GBR)
Local Transport Today (London, GBR)
Lochbroom-FM (Ross Shire, GBR)
Logic Journal of the IGPL (Oxford, GBR)
Logopedics Phoniatrics Vocology (Abingdon, GBR)
The London Bird Report (London, GBR)
London Greek Radio-FM (London, GBR)
The London Naturalist (London, GBR)
Low Frequency Noise & Vibration (Brentwood, GBR)
Lung Cancer (Copenhagen, DEN)
Lyric-FM (Limerick, IRL)
Made in Germany (Lima, PER)
Magic-AM (Sheffield, GBR)
Magic-FM (Osborne Park, WA, AUS)
Magic 105.4-FM (London, GBR)
Magic 1152-AM (Newcastle, GBR)
Magic 1161-AM (Hull, GBR)
Magic 693-AM (South Melbourne, VI, AUS)
Mai-FM (Auckland, NZL)
Malaysian Cocoa Monitor (Kota Kinabalu, MYS)
Management of Environmental Quality (Bradford, GBR)
Management and Organization Review (Oxford, GBR)
Management Research News (Bradford, GBR)
Managerial Auditing Journal (Bradford, GBR)
Managerial Law (Bradford, GBR)
Managing Service Quality (Bradford, GBR)
Manufacturing Engineer Magazine (Stevenage-Hertfordshire, GBR)
Manx Radio-AM (Douglas, GBR)
Maternal and Child Nutrition (Preston, GBR)
Mathematica Plus (Sofia, BUL)
Mathematical Medicine and Biology (Nottingham, GBR)
Mathematics in School (Leicester, GBR)
Mathematische Nachrichten (Regensburg, GER)
MBR – Mountain Bike Rider (Croydon, GBR)
MCR-FM (London, GBR)

# INDUSTRY ACTIVITY

Measuring Business Excellence (Bradford, GBR)
Meat Processing Global Edition (Paris, FRA)
Media Week (Croydon, GBR)
Medical & Biological Engineering & Computing (Stevenage-Hertfordshire, GBR)
Medical Engineering and Physics (Highfield, GBR)
Medical Entomology and Zoology (Tokyo, JPN)
Medical Hypotheses (Newcastle Upon Tyne, GBR)
Medical Image Analysis (Sophia Antipolis Cedex, FRA)
Medical Informatics and the Internet in Medicine (Guildford, GBR)
Medical Journal of the Islamic Academy of Sciences (Amman, JOR)
Medical Law Review (Manchester, GBR)
Medical Microbiology and Immunology (Tokyo, JPN)
Medical Mycology (Abingdon, GBR)
Mediterranean Studies (Aldershot, GBR)
MegaLine (Penang, MYS)
Mental Health Matters (Gladesville, NW, AUS)
Mental Health, Religion and Culture (Abingdon, GBR)
Metro Radio-FM (Newcastle, GBR)
Metrologia (Bristol, GBR)
MIA MIA (North Mackay, QL, AUS)
Microbial Ecology in Health and Disease (Abingdon, GBR)
Microcirculation (Abingdon, GBR)
Microelectronics International (Bradford, GBR)
Military Balance (Abingdon, GBR)
Military In Scale (Croydon, GBR)
Minimally Invasive Therapy and Allied Technologies (Abingdon, GBR)
Minimally Invasive Therapy & Allied Technologies (Tubingen, GER)
Mitteilungen der Fachgruppe Umweltchemie und Okotoxikologie (Marseburg, GER)
Mix-FM (Maroochydore, QL, AUS)
MIX-FM (Richmond, VI, AUS)
Mix 94.5-FM (Subiaco, WA, AUS)
Mix 96-FM (Aylesbury, BK, GBR)
MIX 101.1-FM (Richmond, VI, AUS)
Mix 105.3-FM (The Lakes, QL, AUS)
Mix 104.9-FM (Darwin, NT, AUS)
Mix 106.5-FM (North Ryde, NW, AUS)
MIX 102.3-FM (North Adelaide, SA, AUS)

MLQ - Mathematical Logic Quarterly (Greifswald, GER)
MMM-FM (Saint Kilda, VI, AUS)
Mobile Information Systems (Clayton, VI, AUS)
Mobilities (Abingdon, GBR)
MOCA News (Solihull, GBR)
Model Assisted Statistics and Applications (Amsterdam, NLD)
Model Collector (Croydon, GBR)
Model Helicopter World (Croydon, GBR)
Modelling and Simulation in Materials Science and Engineering (Bristol, GBR)
Modern Prose, Modern Poetry (Moscow, RUS)
Modern Rheumatology (Tokyo, JPN)
Molecular Biology and Evolution (Oxford, GBR)
Molecular Human Reproduction (Cambridge, GBR)
More-FM (Wellington, NZL)
Motorcycling GB (Rugby, GBR)
Motorsports Now! (Slough, GBR)
MS Voice (Wellington, NZL)
The Mulcher-FM (Taranaki, NZL)
Multiagent and Grid Systems (Glasgow, GBR)
Muratho (Pretoria, SAF)
Murdoch-FM (Perth, WA, AUS)
The Muses Journal (Powys, GBR)
Musicae Scientiae (Liege, BEL)
Mutagenesis (Sutton, GBR)
Mycoscience (Tokyo, JPN)
Nanotechnology (Bristol, GBR)
Nanotoxicology (Abingdon, GBR)
National Safety (Malvern, VI, AUS)
Nephrology Dialysis Transplantation (Paris, FRA)
Network: Computation in Neural Systems (Abingdon, GBR)
Neuroembryology (Rostock, GER)
Neuroforum (Berlin, GER)
Neuromuscular Disorders (London, GBR)
Neuropsychiatric Disease and Treatment (Randwick, NW, AUS)
New-FM (Sandgate, NW, AUS)
The New Innkeeper (Camberley, GBR)
New Library World (Bradford, GBR)
New Zealand Geographer (Oxford, GBR)
New Zealand Population Review (Hamilton, NZL)
New Zealand Studies in Applied Linguistics (Auckland, NZL)
News and Views (Belfast, GBR)
News and Views (London, GBR)
NEWSLI (London, GBR)

NewsTalk 106-FM (Dublin, IRL)
NGV Worldwide (Auckland, NZL)
Nicotine and Tobacco Research (Abingdon, GBR)
Nigerian Medical Journal (Lagos, NGA)
98.5-FM (Shepparton, VI, AUS)
999-AM (Palmerston North, NZL)
973-FM (Coorparoo DC, QL, AUS)
91.6-FM (Dublin, IRL)
96.5-FM (Milton BC, QL, AUS)
96.5-FM (Geraklton, WA, AUS)
96.1-FM (North Ryde, NW, AUS)
96.2-FM (Oldham, GBR)
92.9-FM (Subiaco, WA, AUS)
98-FM (Geraldton, WA, AUS)
95-FM (Limerick, IRL)
90-FM (Auckland, NZL)
96-FM (Patrick's Place, CK, IRL)
96-FM (East Perth, WA, AUS)
NJ (Brisbane, QL, AUS)
NKO Magazine (Accra, GHA)
Nonproliferation Review (Abingdon, GBR)
Noosa 96.1-FM (Noosa Junction, QL, AUS)
Nordic Journal for Architectural Research (Stockholm, SWE)
Nordic Journal of Psychiatry (Helsinki, FIN)
NORM News (Staffordshire, GBR)
Northsound Two-AM (Aberdeen, GBR)
Notas Rojas (Taipei, TWN)
Nova-FM (Richmond, VI, AUS)
Nuclear Fusion (Vienna, AUT)
Nuclear Science Journal of Malaysia (Kajang, MYS)
Nucleic Acids Research (Oxford, GBR)
Nurse Education in Practice (Salford, GBR)
Nursing Forum (Oxford, GBR)
Nursing Home News (Birmingham, GBR)
Nutrition, Metabolism, & Cardiovascular Diseases (Napoli, ITA)
Nutrition Research Reviews (Wallingford, GBR)
NX-FM (Charlestown, NW, AUS)
Oak 107-FM (Loughborough, LE, GBR)
Oasis-FM (St. Albans, HF, GBR)
Ocean-FM (West Fareham, HM, GBR)
Ocean-FM (Hants, GBR)
Oceanology (Moscow, RUS)
OCLC Systems and Services (Bradford, GBR)
Odontology (Tokyo, JPN)
Olive Press (Pendle Hill, NW, AUS)
On the Horizon (Bradford, GBR)
100-FM (Darwin, NT, AUS)
104-FM (Ballsbridge, DU, IRL)

## INDUSTRY ACTIVITY

107-FM (Hobart, TA, AUS)
103-FM (Patrick's Place, CK, IRL)
103-FM (Hobart, TA, AUS)
104.7-FM (Grafton, NW, AUS)
104.6-FM (Auckland, NZL)
101.7-FM (South Perth, WA, AUS)
107.8-FM (Surbiton, SR, GBR)
1075-FM (Orange, NW, AUS)
107.4-FM (Portsmouth, HM, GBR)
1XX-FM (Whakatane, NZL)
The Open Book (Havant, GBR)
Open Society (Auckland, NZL)
Ophthalmic and Physiological Optics (London, GBR)
Optometry in Practice (London, GBR)
Oral Oncology (London, GBR)
The Osteopath (London, GBR)
Outlooks on Pest Management (Hemel Hempstead, GBR)
Oxford Art Journal (Hertfordshire, GBR)
Pacific Economic Review (Hong Kong, CHN)
Pacific Waves (Darwin, NT, AUS)
Pan American Journal of Public Health (Geneva, SWI)
Paper and Timberland (Helsinki, FIN)
Parasitology Research (Tokyo, JPN)
Parity (Fitzroy, VI, AUS)
Parrot Society of Australia News (Salisbury, QL, AUS)
Particle and Particle Systems Characterization (Erlangen, GER)
Patchwork & Quilting (Croydon, GBR)
Pathophysiology (Kuopio, FIN)
Pathophysiology of Haemostasis and Thrombosis (Maastricht, NLD)
Pattern Recognition and Image Analysis (Moscow, RUS)
PAYadvice (Solihull, GBR)
PBA-FM (Salisbury, SA, AUS)
Peak-FM (Chesterfield, GBR)
Pediatric Rehabilitation (Abingdon, GBR)
Pegasus-FM (Christchurch, NZL)
PEN International (London, GBR)
Pensions (London, GBR)
Performance Measurements and Metrics (Bradford, GBR)
Personnel Psychology (Oxford, GBR)
PESTALK (Moorabbin, VI, AUS)
Petroleum Chemistry (Moscow, RUS)
Petrology (Moscow, RUS)
Pharmaceuticals Policy and Law (Granada, SPA)
Pharmacy Education (London, GBR)
The Philippine Natural Law Journal (Quezon City, PHL)
Philosophia Mathematica (Oxford, GBR)

The Photographer (Ware, GBR)
physica status solidi (a) (Garching, GER)
physica status solidi (b) (Garching, GER)
physica status solidi (c) (Garching, GER)
Physics of Metals and Metallography (Ekaterinburg, RUS)
Physics of Particles and Nuclei Letters (Moscow, RUS)
Physics of the Solid State (Saint Petersburg, RUS)
Physik Journal (Weinheim, GER)
Physik in unserer Zeit (Leimen, GER)
Physiotherapy Theory and Practice (Abingdon, GBR)
Picon News (Godalming, GBR)
Pigment & Resin Technology (Bradford, GBR)
Pioneer (Dublin, DU, IRL)
Place Branding (London, GBR)
Placenta (Auenbruggerplatz 14, AUT)
Plant and Cell Physiology (Tokyo, JPN)
Plant Genetic Resources (Wallingford, GBR)
Plasma Physics Reports (Moscow, RUS)
Plasma Sources Science and Technology (Bristol, GBR)
Platelets (Abingdon, GBR)
Play Action (Bognor Regis, GBR)
Play Therapy (Bristol, GBR)
Plymouth Sound-FM (Plymouth, DN, GBR)
PNC (London, GBR)
Policing (Bradford, GBR)
Popular Flying (Northants, GBR)
Practical Boat Owner (Poole, GBR)
Practical Crafts (Croydon, GBR)
The Practising Administrator (Winmalee, NW, AUS)
Pramana Journal of Physics (Bangalore, KA, IND)
Prediction (Croydon, GBR)
Premier Radio-AM (London, GBR)
Prenatal Diagnosis (Cambridge, GBR)
Problems of Aging & Longevity (Kiev, URE)
Proceedings (London, GBR)
Proceedings - Mathematical Sciences (Bangalore, KA, IND)
Proceedings of the Nutrition Society (Wallingford, GBR)
Professionalism in Practice (Derby, GBR)
Programme Report 2000-2001 (Kathmandu, NPL)
Progress in Nuclear Magnetic Resonance Spectroscopy (Southampton, GBR)
Progress in Osteoporosis (Tokyo, JPN)

Prostaglandins, Leukotrienes and Essential Fatty Acids (Stirling, GBR)
Prosthetics & Orthotics International (Abingdon, GBR)
Protein Engineering Design and Selection (Oxford, GBR)
PRWeek Magazine (London, GBR)
Psychology and Health (Abingdon, GBR)
Psychology, Health and Medicine (Abingdon, GBR)
Psychology, Public Policy, and Law (Sydney, NW, AUS)
Psychosomatic Obstetrics and Gynecology (Abingdon, GBR)
Public Health Nutrition (Southampton, GBR)
Public Opinion Quarterly (Oxford, GBR)
Publications of the Astronomical Society of Australia (Sydney, NW, AUS)
Pulse (Swansea, GBR)
Pulse-FM (Bradford, WY, GBR)
Pulse Radio-FM (London, GBR)
Pump-FM (Karratha, WA, AUS)
QJM (Southampton, GBR)
Qualitative Market Research (Bradford, GBR)
Qualitative Research in Organizations and Management (Bradford, GBR)
Quality Assurance in Education (Bradford, GBR)
Quarterly Journal (Surbiton, GBR)
Quarterly Journal of Experimental Psychology (Abingdon, GBR)
Quarterly Journal of Mathematics (Oxford, GBR)
Quarterly Journal of Mechanics and Applied Mathematics (London, GBR)
The Quay-FM (Portsmouth, HM, GBR)
Quiet (Sheffield, GBR)
Quiet & Electric Flight International (Croydon, GBR)
R/C Jet International (Croydon, GBR)
R/C Model World (Croydon, GBR)
Radiation Protection Dosimetry (Oxford, GBR)
Radical Economics (London, GBR)
Radio Active-FM (Wellington, NZL)
Radio Adelaide-FM (Adelaide, SA, AUS)
Radio Caroline-FM (Maidstone, KT, GBR)
Radio Control-FM (Palmerston North, NZL)
Radio Foyle-FM (London, GBR)
Radio Humberside (Hull, GBR)
Radio Kerry-FM (Tralee, KR, IRL)
Radio Latics-AM (Oldham, GBR)
Radio Metro-FM (Surfers Paradise, QL, AUS)

## INDUSTRY ACTIVITY

Radio 1-FM (Dublin, IRL)
Radio Rhema-AM (Auckland, NZL)
Radio Sport-AM (Melbourne, VI, AUS)
Radio Tarana-AM (Auckland, NZL)
Radio T9 (Sarajevo, HBO)
Radio 2-AM (Homebush, NW, AUS)
Radio Ulster-FM (London, GBR)
Radio Wave 96.5-FM (Blackpool, LC, GBR)
Radiology (Salford, GBR)
Radiotherapy and Oncology (Aarhus, DEN)
Rapid Prototyping Journal (Bradford, GBR)
Rare Earth Bulletin (Brentwood, GBR)
RDU-FM (Christchurch, NZL)
Reach (Dublin, DU, IRL)
Reading 107-FM (Reading, BR, GBR)
Real Radio-FM (Cardiff, GBR)
Rebel-FM (Beaudesert, QL, AUS)
ReCALL Journal (Limerick, LI, IRL)
Red Cross News (Wellington, NZL)
Red Dragon-FM (Cardiff, GBR)
Red-FM (Bishopstown, CK, IRL)
Reference Reviews (Bradford, GBR)
Reflective Practice (Abingdon, GBR)
Renewable Agriculture and Food Systems (Wallingford, GBR)
The Reparation Report (London, GBR)
Reportback (London, GBR)
Reports on Progress in Physics (Bristol, GBR)
Reproductive Health Matters (London, GBR)
Research in Sports Medicine (Abingdon, GBR)
Resonance-FM (London, GBR)
Resource Management & Recovery (London, GBR)
Respiratory Medicine (Lund, SWE)
Restorative Neurology and Neuroscience (Magdeburg, GER)
Resuscitation (Wiltshire, GBR)
Reviews in Gynaecological Practice (Bristol, GBR)
Revista Latinoamericana De Ciencias De La Comunicacion (Sao Paulo, SP, BRZ)
Rhema-FM (Belmont, VI, AUS)
Rheumatology International (Tokyo, JPN)
Rhythm-FM (Darlinghurst, NW, AUS)
Rider Haggard Journal (Whitley Bay, GBR)
The River-FM (Albury, NW, AUS)
River 94.9-FM (Ipswich, QL, AUS)
RJ Magazine (Birmingham, GBR)
RMT News (London, GBR)

RNZ-FM (Wellington, NZL)
The Rock-FM (Auckland, NZL)
Rookwood Sound-AM (Cardiff, GBR)
Roska (Prague, CZE)
Russian Journal of Bioorganic Chemistry (Moscow, RUS)
Russian Journal of Biotechnology (Moscow, RUS)
Russian Metallurgy (Moscow, RUS)
SA-FM (Unley, SA, AUS)
SAA: Special Publication (Canberra, AC, AUS)
The Safety and Health Practitioner (Wigston, GBR)
Safety Management (London, GBR)
SAGA 105.7-FM (Birmingham, GBR)
SAGA 106.6-FM (East Midlands, GBR)
SANE News (South Melbourne, VI, AUS)
Sarcoma (Abingdon, GBR)
Scandinavian Cardiovascular Journal (Abingdon, GBR)
Scandinavian Journal of Clinical and Laboratory Investigation (Oslo, NOR)
Scandinavian Journal of Disability Research (Abingdon, GBR)
Scandinavian Journal of Gastroenterology (Abingdon, GBR)
Scandinavian Journal of Infectious Diseases (Abingdon, GBR)
Scandinavian Journal of Laboratory Animal Science (Stockholm, SWE)
Scandinavian Journal of Nutrition (Abingdon, GBR)
Scandinavian Journal of Occupational Therapy (Abingdon, GBR)
Scandinavian Journal of Primary Health Care (Abingdon, GBR)
Scandinavian Journal of Public Health (Abingdon, GBR)
Scandinavian Journal of Rheumatology (Abingdon, GBR)
Scandinavian Journal of Urology and Nephrology (Abingdon, GBR)
Scandinavianinavian Cardiovascular Journal (Abingdon, GBR)
Schizophrenia Bulletin (Oxford, GBR)
The Scottish Beekeeper (Dunblane, GBR)
Scrapbook Magic (Croydon, GBR)
The Sculpture Journal (London, GBR)
Sculpture Magazine (Accra, GHA)
Sea-FM (Southport, QL, AUS)
Sea-FM (Warragul, VI, AUS)
Sea 99.5-FM (Cairns, QL, AUS)
Seafarer (London, GBR)
Seed Science Research (Wallingford, GBR)

Seminars in Cardiology (Vilnius, LIT)
Seminars in Fetal & Neonatal Medicine (Leeds, GBR)
SEN-AM (Richmond, VI, AUS)
Sensor Review (Bradford, GBR)
Serdica Mathematical Journal (Sofia, BUL)
7HO-FM (Hobart, TA, AUS)
Seventh Wave (London, GBR)
7ZR-AM (Hobart, TA, AUS)
Sewing World (Croydon, GBR)
Sex Education (London, GBR)
Sexual Addiction & Compulsivity (Abingdon, GBR)
Shakespeare (Abingdon, GBR)
Shakespeare Southern Africa (Grahamstown, SAF)
Ships and Offshore Structures (Cambridge, GBR)
Shopping Centers (Rio de Janeiro, RJ, BRZ)
Shopping - Centros Comerciais em Revista (Lisbon, PRT)
Signal 1-FM (Stoke-On-Trent, GBR)
Sikh Formations: Religion, Culture, Theory (Abingdon, GBR)
Silk-FM (Macclesfield, CH, GBR)
Similia (Hastings, VI, AUS)
Singapore Journal of Physics (Singapore, SGP)
6AL-AM (Albany, WA, AUS)
6IX-AM (East Perth, WA, AUS)
6PR-AM (East Perth, WA, AUS)
Skogssport (Farsta, SWE)
SKY Journal of Linguistics (Helsinki, FIN)
Smart Materials and Structures (Bristol, GBR)
Social Influence (Abingdon, GBR)
Social Politics (Stockholm, SWE)
Socialism and Democracy (Abingdon, GBR)
Society and Business Review (Bradford, GBR)
Society of Fellows Journal (London, GBR)
Socio-Economic Review (London, GBR)
The Sociological Quarterly (Oxford, GBR)
Soil Use and Management (Wallingford, GBR)
Sokiu Sporias (Vilnius, LIT)
Soldering & Surface Mount Technology (Bradford, GBR)
Solid Gold-FM (Auckland, NZL)
Sonshine-FM (Morley, WA, AUS)
Sotsiologicheski Problemi (Sofia, BUL)

# INDUSTRY ACTIVITY

South African Journal of Economics (Lynnwood Ridge, SAF)
South African Journal of Marine Science (Umhlanga, SAF)
South East Radio-FM (Wexford, IRL)
Southeast European Politics (Tirana, ALB)
Southern African Forestry Journal (Menlo Park, SAF)
Southern African Treasurer (Cresta, SAF)
Southern-FM (Brighton, GBR)
Southern-FM (Moorabbin, VI, AUS)
Souvenir (London, GBR)
Space Communications (Amsterdam, NLD)
Special Anniversary Magazine (Melbourne, VI, AUS)
Spectra (London, GBR)
Speculum (Bath, GBR)
Speedup Journal (Fribourg, SWI)
Spices India (Kochi, KE, IND)
Sport in History (Abingdon, GBR)
Sport 927-AM (Melbourne, VI, AUS)
Sports Management (Hitchin, GBR)
Stamp Magazine (Croydon, GBR)
Stampi (Milan, ITA)
Star and Furrow (Stroud, GBR)
Star 1045-FM (Erina, NW, AUS)
Star 107.9-FM (Cambridge, GBR)
Star 106.6-FM (Slough, BR, GBR)
Starch/Staerke (Hamburg, GER)
Statistical Journal of the United Nations Economic Commission for Europe (Amsterdam, NLD)
Storylines (Reading, GBR)
Strabismus (Rotterdam, NLD)
Strategic Survey (Abingdon, GBR)
Stratigraphy and Geological Correlation (Moscow, RUS)
Street-FM (Surfers Paradise, QL, AUS)
Strength, Fracture and Complexity (Amsterdam, NLD)
Stress, Trauma, and Crisis (Abingdon, GBR)
Structural Survey (Bradford, GBR)
Structure & Infrastructure Engineering (Abingdon, GBR)
Student & Graduate Magazine (Stevenage-Hertfordshire, GBR)
Studies on Russian Economic Development (Moscow, RUS)
Studying Teacher Education (Abingdon, GBR)
Suara TEEAM (Kuala Lumpur, MYS)
Subcity Radio-FM (Glasgow, GBR)
Sun-FM (Shepparton, VI, AUS)
Sunrise Radio-AM (Middlesex, GBR)

Suo- Mires and Peat (Helsinki, FIN)
Superbike (Croydon, GBR)
Surface Coatings International (Wembley, GBR)
Surge-AM (Southampton, GBR)
Sustainable Development (Shipley, GBR)
Sustainments Relational News (Newtown, NW, AUS)
Swedish Book Review (Sutton, GBR)
SWR-FM (Doonside, NW, AUS)
Synthesis and Reactivity in Inorganic, Metal-Organic, and Nano-Metal Chemistry (Abingdon, GBR)
Systematic and Applied Acarology (Canberra, AC, AUS)
Systems Biology (Stevenage-Hertfordshire, GBR)
TAG Bulletin (Plymouth, GBR)
Tahi-FM (Tauranga, NZL)
Talking Politics (Manchester, GBR)
TalkSPORT-AM (London, GBR)
Tall Poppies (Waitomo Caves, NZL)
TDD (Reykjavik, ICE)
Teaching Mathematics and Its Applications (West Sussex, GBR)
Team Performance Management (Bradford, GBR)
Techniques in Coloproctology (Tokyo, JPN)
Technology and Disability (Hoensbroek, NLD)
Tesseract (Singapore, SGP)
TEXT (Ormskirk, GBR)
Themescene (Swindon, GBR)
Theoretical Issues in Ergonomics Science (Abingdon, GBR)
Theriogenology (Milan, ITA)
Thermal Engineering (Moscow, RUS)
The Thermal and Nuclear Power (Tokyo, JPN)
Thermophysics and Aeromechanics (Novosibirsk, RUS)
Think: Philosophy for Everyone (London, GBR)
Third Sector Magazine (London, GBR)
3AW-AM (South Melbourne, VI, AUS)
3BA-FM (Ballarat, VI, AUS)
3EE-AM (South Melbourne, VI, AUS)
3FOX-FM (Saint Kilda, VI, AUS)
3GG-AM (Warragul, VI, AUS)
3GV-AM (Traralgon, VI, AUS)
3HHH-FM (Horsham, VI, AUS)
3INR-FM (Heidelberg, VI, AUS)
3LO-AM (Melbourne, VI, AUS)
3PBS-FM (Fitzroy MDC, VI, AUS)
3RRR-FM (Melbourne, VI, AUS)
3SCB-FM (Moorabbin, VI, AUS)

3SR-FM (Shepparton, VI, AUS)
3SRA-FM (Melbourne, VI, AUS)
3TR-FM (Traralgon, VI, AUS)
3TT-FM (Richmond, VI, AUS)
3WBC-FM (Box Hill, VI, AUS)
3WM-AM (Horsham, VI, AUS)
3WRB-FM (Sunshine, VI, AUS)
3XX-AM (South Yarra, VI, AUS)
3YB-AM (Warrnambool, VI, AUS)
Tissue & Cell (Siena, ITA)
TMJ Science (Rosny Park, TA, AUS)
Today-FM (Dublin, IRL)
Today's Technician (Nottingham, GBR)
Tourism and Hospitality Research (London, GBR)
Toxicologic Pathology (Abingdon, GBR)
Training and Management Development Methods (Bradford, GBR)
Transplant International (Vienna, AUT)
Transplant International (Tokyo, JPN)
Transportant (Auckland, NZL)
Travel Guide International (Chepstow, GBR)
Treasury Management (Hyderabad, IND)
Tree News (London, GBR)
Triangle (Matlock, GBR)
TT-FM (Richmond, VI, AUS)
TUBA-AR (Ankara, TUR)
Tube 103.8-FM (London, GBR)
TUNE-FM (Armidale, NW, AUS)
Turk Psikoloji Dergisi (Turkish Journal of Psychology) (Ankara, TUR)
Twentieth Century British History (York, GBR)
2-FM (Donnybrook, DU, IRL)
Two Lochs Radio-FM (Gairloch, GBR)
2AAA-FM (Wagga Wagga, NW, AUS)
2BR-FM (Nelson, GBR)
2BS-AM (Bathurst, NW, AUS)
2CH-AM (Sydney, NW, AUS)
2CN-AM (Canberra, AC, AUS)
2CR-FM (Bournemouth, DS, GBR)
2CS-AM (Coffs Harbour, NW, AUS)
2DAY-FM (Bondi Junction, NW, AUS)
2DU-AM (Dubbo, NW, AUS)
2EC-FM (Bega, NW, AUS)
2GB-AM (Pyrmont, NW, AUS)
2GO-FM (Gosford, NW, AUS)
2HBS-FM (Napier, NZL)
2HD-AM (Sandgate, NW, AUS)
2HHH-FM (Waitara, NW, AUS)
2JJJ-FM (Sydney, NW, AUS)
2KO-FM (Charlestown, NW, AUS)
2KY-AM (Parramatta, NW, AUS)
2MBS-FM (Saint Leonards, NW, AUS)
2MC-FM (Port Macquarie, NW, AUS)

# INDUSTRY ACTIVITY

2MM-AM (Sydney, NW, AUS)
2MMM-FM (Bondi Junction, NW, AUS)
2NUR-FM (Callaghan, NW, AUS)
2RDJ-FM (Burwood North, NW, AUS)
2RE-AM (Taree, NW, AUS)
2RRR-FM (Gladesville, NW, AUS)
2SM-AM (Pyrmont, NW, AUS)
2SSR-FM (Sutherland, NW, AUS)
2ST-FM (North Nowra, NW, AUS)
2UE-AM (Sydney, NW, AUS)
2WKT-FM (Bowral, NW, AUS)
2WS-FM (North Ryde, NW, AUS)
2XL-AM (Cooma, NW, AUS)
Ugeskrift for Laeger (Copenhagen, DEN)
Ulster Folklife (Holywood, GBR)
Ultrasound in Medicine & Biology (Bristol, GBR)
Ultrasound Review of Obstetrics & Gynecology (Abingdon, GBR)
Uncut (London, GBR)
UP-FM (Auckland, NZL)
Upsala Journal of Medical Sciences (Upsala, SWE)
URN-AM (Nottingham, GBR)
Urological Research (Tokyo, JPN)
URY-AM (York, GBR)
Vakuum in Forschung und Praxis (Niederzier, GER)
Valley-FM (Erindale, AC, AUS)
Venue Thailand (Bangkok, THA)
Vibe 105-FM (Bury St. Edmunds, SU, GBR)
Vibe 101-FM (Bristol, GBR)
Vietnam Commerce and Industry (Hanoi, VNM)
VINE (Bradford, GBR)
Virgin Radio-AM (London, GBR)
Virtual and Physical Prototyping (Abingdon, GBR)
Vision 100-FM (Manawatu, NZL)
Visual Impairment Research (Abingdon, GBR)
The Vitreous Enameller (Cannock, GBR)
VolksWorld (Croydon, GBR)
Water and Wastes in New Zealand (Wellington, NZL)
Wave-FM (Warrawong, NW, AUS)
The Wave-FM (Swansea, GBR)
Waves in Random and Complex Media (Abingdon, GBR)
Wayfarer News (Colchester, GBR)
WDM in Action (London, GBR)
Web Intelligence and Agent Systems (Kowloon Tong, CHN)
Webuser (London, GBR)
Wessex-FM (Dorchester, DS, GBR)
WHERE Budapest (Budapest, HUN)

WHERE Hong Kong (Hong Kong, CHN)
WHERE London (London, GBR)
WHERE Macau (Hong Kong, CHN)
WHERE Moscow (Moscow, RUS)
WHERE Rome (Rome, ITA)
WHERE St. Petersburg (Saint Petersburg, RUS)
White Cane (Singapore, SGP)
Wicket Women (London, GBR)
Wire-FM (Warrington, GBR)
Wish-FM (Iwgan, GBR)
Withichiwit (Thai Ageways) (Chiang Mai, THA)
WLR-FM (Waterford, IRL)
The Wolf-FM (Wolverhampton, GBR)
Women in Management Review (Bradford, GBR)
Women's Oncology Review (Abingdon, GBR)
World Bank Research Observer (Oxford, GBR)
World Food Regulation Review (Hemel Hempstead, GBR)
World Soccer (London, GBR)
World's Poultry Science Journal (Wallingford, GBR)
WoundCare (Hartford, GBR)
WS-FM (North Ryde, NW, AUS)
X-FM (London, GBR)
Xpression-FM (Exeter, GBR)
XS-FM (Palmerston North, NZL)
Yachting Monthly (London, GBR)
Yachting World (London, GBR)
Yearbook of NZACL (Wellington, NZL)
Yorkshire Coast Radio-FM (Scarborough, GBR)
ZAAC - Zeitschrift fuer Anorganische und Allgemeine Chemie (Berlin, GER)
ZAMM - Zeitschrift fuer Angewandte Mathematik und Mechanik (Saale, GER)
ZB-AM (Auckland, NZL)
Zeitschrift des Deutschen Vereins fur Kunstwissenschaft (Berlin, GER)
ZFR (Vogtsburg, GER)
Zoologische Reihe (Berlin, GER)

## Cessations

### United States and Canada

AAA World–Maryland (Philadelphia, PA)
AACN's Clinical Issues in Critical Care Nursing (New York, NY)
ACCA Express (Montclair, NJ)
Access (Greenwood, IN)
Action (New York, NY)
The AD-PAK (Raleigh Edition) (Raleigh, NC)

The Advantage (Albemarle, NC)
Adventure Road (Chicago, IL)
Adventure West (Incline Village, NV)
Advertiser - North and South Edition (Jefferson, WI)
Advisor (Mitchell, SD)
The Advocate (San Pablo, CA)
AFDS Today (Kingsport, TN)
African Herald (Dallas, TX)
AgriAmerica Network (Jefferson City, MO)
Air Cargo News (La Guardia Airport, NY)
Akademiska Dzive/Academic Life (Minneapolis, MN)
The Akron Reporter (Akron, OH)
Al-Arabiyya (Williamsburg, VA)
Alaska Highway News (Delta Junction, AK)
The Alaskan Viewpoint (Seward, AK)
Alba de America (Westminster, CA)
Albion (Boone, NC)
Albion News (Albion, PA)
The Alexandria Journal (Alexandria, VA)
ALON (New York, NY)
Alternative Cinema (Montclair, NJ)
Alumni Gazette (Williamsburg, VA)
Alverno Today (Milwaukee, WI)
aMagazine (New York, NY)
Amass (Los Angeles, CA)
American Art Journal (New York, NY)
American Baby (New York, NY)
American Beef Cattleman (Allen, KS)
American Ceramics (New York, NY)
American Clean Car (Chicago, IL)
American Federation of Musicians (San Diego, CA)
American Fern Journal (Little Rock, AR)
American Flint (Toledo, OH)
American Indian Basketry Magazine (Portland, OR)
American Journal of Addictions (Arlington, VA)
American Journal of Chinese Medicine (Garden City, NY)
American Journal of Comparative Law (Berkeley, CA)
American Journal of Dance Therapy (Columbia, MD)
The American Mother (Dover, DE)
American Paint and Coatings Journal (Loveland, CO)
American Review of Respiratory Disease (New York, NY)
American Rowing (Indianapolis, IN)
American Sports (Rosemead, CA)
American Visions (Washington, DC)

Gale Directory of Publications and Broadcast Media, 140th Edition  lxvii

## INDUSTRY ACTIVITY

American Woodworker (Eagan, MN)
Amherst Press (Littlefield, TX)
Andrews County News (Andrews, TX)
Angel Advisor (New York, NY)
Angolite (Angola, LA)
Animal Watch (New York, NY)
Animaltown News (Chatham, NJ)
Annals of Software Engineering (Norwell, MA)
Ansearchin' News (Memphis, TN)
Antique Journal for California & Nevada (El Cajon, CA)
The Apache County Reporter (Eagar, AZ)
Apparel Industry International (Roswell, GA)
Applied Microwave & Wireless (Norcross, GA)
The Aquaculture News (Natchez, MS)
Aquarium Sciences and Conservation (Norwell, MA)
Aquatica (Hayward, CA)
Arabian Horse Express (Kenilworth, IL)
Archives of Family Medicine (Philadelphia, PA)
The Argyle Sun (Lake Dallas, TX)
Aristos (New York, NY)
Arizona Cattlelog (Albuquerque, NM)
Arizona Farm Bureau News (Higley, AZ)
Arizona Trends (Scottsdale, AZ)
Arizoo (Phoenix, AZ)
Arkansas Family Historian (Hot Springs, AR)
Arkansas Living (Little Rock, AR)
The Arlington Journal (Alexandria, VA)
Art, Antiquity and Law (Norwell, MA)
Artique (Quakertown, PA)
ARTS ALIVE! Magazine (Allentown, PA)
Arts & Crafts (Iola, WI)
AS/400 Systems Management (Chicago, IL)
Ashcroft Journal (Ashcroft, BC)
Asia Pacific Journal of Environmental Law (Norwell, MA)
Asia Pacific Law Review (Norwell, MA)
At the Shore (Pleasantville, NJ)
Augustana College Magazine (Rock Island, IL)
Augustana Observer (Rock Island, IL)
Austin Chronicle (Pekin, IN)
AutoCAD User (Toronto, ON)
The Automotive Messenger (Hazelwood, MO)
Automotive & Transportation Interiors (Roswell, GA)
Avenue (New York, NY)
Azle News (Azle, TX)

Badminton USA Magazine (Colorado Springs, CO)
Balance (Alexandria, VA)
BAM Magazine (Concord, CA)
The Bancroft Register (Bancroft, IA)
Bandwagon (Columbus, OH)
Banner (Deer Lodge, MT)
Basic Education (Washington, DC)
Bay Area Reporter (San Francisco, CA)
Bay Sports Review (Albany, CA)
Be Magazine (Seattle, WA)
The Beacon (Spirit Lake, IA)
The Beacon (March Air Force Base, CA)
Beans & Bears! (Iola, WI)
Beeville Bee–Picayune (Beeville, TX)
The Benning Leader (Columbus, GA)
Benton County Daily Record (Bentonville, AR)
Biography (New York, NY)
Birmingham World (Birmingham, AL)
Birth Gazette (Summertown, TN)
Black Books Bulletin: Words Work (Chicago, IL)
Black River Tribune (Ludlow, VT)
Black Voice/Carta Latina (New Brunswick, NJ)
Blade-Empire (Kansas City, MO)
The Blitz (Oakland, CA)
The Bloomfield News (Bloomfield, IN)
Bloomville Gazette (Attica, OH)
Blue Ridge Leader (Purcellville, VA)
Boardwatch Magazine (New York, NY)
Boise Weekly (Boise, ID)
Bonkers? (Palm Beach, FL)
Book (New York, NY)
Booster (Germantown, OH)
Bowling Magazine (Greendale, WI)
Bowling Proprietor (Arlington, TX)
Boynton Beach Times (Deerfield Beach, FL)
Brain and Mind (Norwell, MA)
Bridgeport News-Blade (Bridgeport, NE)
Bridgewater Townsman (Needham, MA)
The Bristol BayTimes (Dillingham, AK)
The Broadcaster (Rockville, CT)
Broken Bow News (Broken Bow, OK)
The Brookings Review (Washington, DC)
Brooklyn New York Recorder (Brooklyn, NY)
Broome Pennysaver (Owego, NY)
Buffalo Law Review (Buffalo, NY)
BuffaloBeat (Buffalo, NY)
Builder/Dealer (Erie, PA)
The Bulletin (Sarasota, FL)
The Bulletin (New York, NY)

Bulletin of Bibliography (Raleigh, NC)
Bulletin/Progress Enterprise (Bridgewater, NS)
Bulletin de la Societe Americaine de Philosophie de Langue Francaise (DeKalb, IL)
The Burley Tobacco Farmer (Raleigh, NC)
The Bush Blade (Anchor Point, AK)
The Business Advocate (Washington, DC)
Business Atlanta (Atlanta, GA)
Business Digest (New Milford, CT)
Business Forum (Los Angeles, CA)
Business Geographics (Norwalk, CT)
Business & Industry (Carlisle, IA)
Business Monthly (Hemlock, MI)
The Business Picture (South Pasadena, CA)
Business Woman (Norwalk, CT)
The Cache Citizen (Logan, UT)
Cactus and Succulent Journal (Monrovia, CA)
California Cattleman (Sacramento, CA)
California Chronicles (Peterborough, NH)
California Voice (San Francisco, CA)
Cambridge Daily Reporter (Cambridge, ON)
Campbell County Recorder (Fort Thomas, KY)
Campbell Publication (Winchester, IL)
Campus.ca (Toronto, ON)
The Canadian Baptist (Etobicoke, ON)
Canadian Computer Wholesaler (Vancouver, BC)
Canadian Defence Quarterly (Toronto, ON)
Canadian Ethnic Studies Journal (Calgary, AB)
The Canadian Firefighter (Toronto, ON)
The Canadian Journal of Herbalism (Port Burwell, ON)
Canadian Journal of Information and Library Science (Toronto, ON)
Canadian Journal of Regional Science (Montreal, QC)
Canadian Journal of Women and the Law/Revue Femmes et Droit (Toronto, ON)
Canadian Review of American Studies (Ottawa, ON)
Canadian Speeches (Woodville, ON)
Canyon Shopper (Flagstaff, AZ)
Capital Times (Middletown, PA)
Cardiovascular Reviews & Reports (Darien, CT)
The Carolinian (Raleigh, NC)
Cartoonist Profiles (Fairfield, CT)

# INDUSTRY ACTIVITY

The Cashton Record (Cashton, WI)
Cat World International (Phoenix, AZ)
CATS (New York, NY)
Catskill Shopper-Sullivan & Ulster County Editions (Liberty, NY)
CATTECH (Norwell, MA)
Cellular & Mobile International (Overland Park, KS)
Central Coast Times (Paso Robles, CA)
Centre D'Etudes de L'Asie de L'Est/Cahiers (Montreal, QC)
The Champion (Kissimmee, FL)
Chapel News (Chapel Hill, NC)
Char-Jay (Shelton, WA)
Chemeketa Courier (Salem, OR)
Cherokee Advocate (Washington, DC)
Cherokee Daily Times (Cherokee, IA)
The Chesley Enterprise (Chesley, ON)
Chester Herald (Lincoln, NE)
Chevy Outdoors (Warren, MI)
Chic Magazine (Beverly Hills, CA)
The Chicago Computer Guide (Chicago, IL)
Chicago History (Chicago, IL)
Chicago Life (Chicago, IL)
Chicago South Shore Scene (Chicago, IL)
Children's Services (Mahwah, NJ)
China Telecom (Brighton, MA)
Chinese American Daily News (Monterey Park, CA)
Chinese Times (San Francisco, CA)
Chips-O-Wood (Mathiston, MS)
Choices (Malden, MA)
Chokio Review (Chokio, MN)
Chosun Daily (Flushing, NY)
Christian Conquest Magazine (Mobile, AL)
Christian Social Action (Washington, DC)
Christmas Helps & Holiday Baking (New York, NY)
Chronicle Extra (Geneva, IL)
Chronos (Jersey City, NJ)
Church History (Durham, NC)
Church News (Salt Lake City, UT)
Cinematograph (San Francisco, CA)
Cissna Park News (Cissna Park, IL)
Citizen Gazette (Burnet, TX)
Citizens Centre Report (Edmonton, AB)
Clark County Journal (Jeffersonville, IN)
Classic American Homes (New York, NY)
The Clay Times Journal (Lineville, AL)
The Cleveland Daily Banner (Cleveland, TN)
Cleveland Enterprise Magazine (Cleveland, OH)

Cleveland Small Business News (Cleveland, OH)
Client/Server Computing (Westborough, MA)
Clinical and Applied Thrombosis/Hemostasis (Baltimore, MD)
Clinical Kinesiology (Toledo, OH)
Clinician Reviews (Clifton, NJ)
Co-Op City News (Bronx, NY)
Coalgate Record-Register (Coalgate, OK)
Collectibles Canada (Saint Catharines, ON)
Collectibles, Flea Market Finds (New York, NY)
Collector's Mart (Iola, WI)
Collectors' Showcase (Tulsa, OK)
College Services (Charlottesville, VA)
The Collegian (Coffeyville, KS)
The Collegian (Toledo, OH)
Collegian (Ashland, OH)
Colleton Shopper (Walterboro, SC)
Colonial Homes (New York, NY)
The Colony Leader (Lewisville, TX)
The Columns (Fairmont, WV)
Comda Key (Scarborough, ON)
The Comedy Magazine (Seattle, WA)
Commerce Magazine (Charleston, SC)
Common Lives/Lesbian Lives (Iowa City, IA)
Commonwealth Progress (Ahoskie, NC)
Community Focus (Philadelphia, PA)
Community Forum (Hackettstown, NJ)
Community News E/W (Green Bay, WI)
Community Relations Report (Bartlesville, OK)
Compressed Air (Davidson, NC)
Compressor Tech Two (Waukesha, WI)
Computer Buyer's Guide & Handbook (New York, NY)
Computer Design (Nashua, NH)
Computer Law Reporter (Washington, DC)
Computer Shopper (New York, NY)
Comunicaciones (New York, NY)
Cong Thuong (New York, NY)
Connecticut Family (Mamaroneck, NY)
The Connection (Grosse Pointe Farms, MI)
Connexions (Berkeley, CA)
Construction Equipment Operation and Maintenance (Cedar Rapids, IA)
Consumer Comments (Washington, DC)
Contemporary Dialysis & Nephrology (New York, NY)
Contemporary Jewry (Melrose Park, PA)
Contemporary Surgery (Torrance, CA)

Contractor Marketing (Fairborn, OH)
Control Ad-Lits (Itasca, IL)
COPI Press (Houston, TX)
Copperopolis Herald (Copperopolis, CA)
Cornerstone (Union, MO)
Corning Pennysaver (Horseheads, NY)
Country Charm Magazine (Palmerston, ON)
Country Music (Westport, CT)
County Line Advertiser (Chillicothe, OH)
The Courier (Cobleskill, NY)
The Courier (Freeport, NY)
Coverings (Picton, ON)
Craft Supply (Iola, WI)
Crafting Traditions (Greendale, WI)
Cranberries (Rochester, MA)
Cranbrook Daily Townsman (Cranbrook, BC)
The Crane News (Crane, TX)
Crawdaddy! (Encinitas, CA)
Crazy for Cross Stitch (Berne, IN)
Crescent International (Markham, ON)
The Cresset (Valparaiso, IN)
Crown Jewels of the Wire (Saint Charles, IL)
CT LIFE (Wallingford, CT)
The Culinarian (San Francisco, CA)
Cumberland Poetry Review (Nashville, TN)
Current Index to Journals in Education (Phoenix, AZ)
Current Problems in Dermatology (Saint Louis, MO)
Current Problems in Obstetrics, Gynecology and Fertility (Saint Louis, MO)
CVC Report (New York, NY)
The Daily Advocate (Greenville, OH)
The Daily Citizen-News (Dalton, GA)
The Daily Courier (Kelowna, BC)
Daily Herald (Roanoke Rapids, NC)
The Daily Item (Sunbury, PA)
The Daily News (Halifax, NS)
The Daily Record (Wooster, OH)
The Daily Sundial (Northridge, CA)
Dansville-Wayland Pennysaver (Canisteo, NY)
Davidson Leader (Davidson, SK)
Davie County Enterprise-Record (Clemmons, NC)
Defense Counsel Journal (Chicago, IL)
The Delphos Republican (Glasco, KS)
The Delta Reporter (Escanaba, MI)
Desert Wings (Edwards AFB, CA)
Design Book Review (Berkeley, CA)
Designer/Builder (Santa Fe, NM)
Devon Dispatch (Devon, AB)

## INDUSTRY ACTIVITY

Diabetes (Saint Louis, MO)
The Dickey County Leader (Ellendale, ND)
Disability Studies Quarterly (Chicago, IL)
Distinguished Home Plans (Saint Paul, MN)
District Energy (Westborough, MA)
Dixie News (Florence, KY)
Document Management (Scottsdale, AZ)
Dodge Construction News (Illinois, Indiana, Wisconsin Edition) (Columbus, OH)
The Doll Artisan (Iola, WI)
Dollmaking (Iola, WI)
Double Take (Somerville, MA)
Dowline (Princeton, NJ)
Dunnville Shoppers Guide (Dunnville, ON)
The Durand Express (Owosso, MI)
The Durham Chronicle (Durham, ON)
Dutton Advance (Dutton, ON)
Dwight Star & Herald (Tinley Park, IL)
The Eagle Valley Enterprise (Eagle, CO)
EAP Association Exchange (Arlington, VA)
The Earlville Leader (Earlville, IL)
Earth (Los Angeles, CA)
Earth Work (Charlestown, NH)
East Boston Times (East Boston, MA)
East European Quarterly (Bradenton, FL)
East Metro Plus (Conyers, GA)
East Tennessee Senior Living (Springfield, MO)
East Texas Catholic (Beaumont, TX)
Eastern Aftermarket Journal (Boynton Beach, FL)
Eastern Economic Journal (Easton, PA)
Eastern Itascan (Nashwauk, MN)
Eastern Kansas Senior Star (Garnett, KS)
EBay Magazine (Iola, WI)
EC.COM Magazine (Saratoga, CA)
L'Echo de la Lievre (Mont-Laurier, QC)
Economic Planning in Free Societies (Mount Royal, QC)
Economic Review (Cleveland, OH)
Edgewood Reminder (Edgewood, IA)
Editorial Pace (Westmont, IL)
EIDOS (Boston, MA)
El Editor Permian Basin (Odessa, TX)
El Hospital (Cincinnati, OH)
El Informador (Vista, CA)
El Manana News (Chicago, IL)
El Paso Times-Journal (Peoria, IL)
El Pregonero (Washington, DC)
The El Reno Daily Tribune (El Reno, OK)

El Sol de Hialeah (Hialeah, FL)
El Tiempo Libre (Las Vegas, NV)
El Vaquero (Glendale, CA)
Elk Grove-Laguna Neighbors (Elk Grove, CA)
The Ellenville Press (Ellenville, NY)
Elmvale Lance (Elmvale, ON)
Elroy Wonewoc Keystone Tribune (Portage, WI)
EM: Ebony Man (Chicago, IL)
Empire State Food Service News (Skaneateles, NY)
Employee Benefits Journal (Brookfield, WI)
Employment Opportunities (Englewood) (New York, NY)
Energy & Environmental Management (Cleveland, OH)
Energy Manager (Toronto, ON)
Energy Times (Melville, NY)
Engineers (Washington, DC)
English Digest (New York, NY)
Enlace, U.S.A. (McAllen, TX)
The Enterprise (Lutcher, LA)
Enterprise Engineering Modeling World (Exton, PA)
Enterprise-Journal (San Mateo, CA)
Enterprise Systems Journal (Chatsworth, CA)
Environ (Fort Collins, CO)
Environmental Ethics (Denton, TX)
EOS/ESD Technology (Framingham, MA)
EPA Administrative Law Reporter (Washington, DC)
Equestrian (Lexington, KY)
ESP Magazine (High Point, NC)
Essex Reporter (Colchester, VT)
Estelline Journal (Castlewood, SD)
Estevan This Week (Weyburn, SK)
ETC: A Review of General Semantics (Concord, CA)
European Access (Ann Arbor, MI)
Evaluation Practice (Berkeley, CA)
Evart Review (Reed City, MI)
The Evening News (New Glasgow, NS)
The Evening World (Bloomfield, IN)
Everest World (Horton, KS)
Everett Business Journal (Wenatchee, WA)
Excalibur (Takoma Park, MD)
Executive Intelligence Review (Washington, DC)
Executive Technology (New York, NY)
Exercise Immunology Review (Champaign, IL)
Exhibit Marketing Magazine (Florham Park, NJ)

Exhibitor Times (Phoenix, AZ)
Expert Evidence (Norwell, MA)
Explorer (Los Angeles, CA)
The Expressline (Wilkes Barre, PA)
Extra (Hickory, NC)
Extra Equity for Homebuyers (Greens Farms, CT)
Eyewitness (Wayne, MI)
Facilities Design & Management (New York, NY)
Families, Systems & Health (Rochester, NY)
Family Court Review (Thousand Oaks, CA)
Family Life (New York, NY)
Far Northeast Citizen Sentinel (Horsham, PA)
Farm Supply Retailing (Englewood, CO)
The Fast Track (Meadville, PA)
Fastline–Ontario Farm Edition (Buckner, KY)
Fax Mainichi U.S.A. (Santa Monica, CA)
Femme-Lines (New York, NY)
Fenestration (New York, NY)
Fermata (Burnaby, BC)
FIBERARTS (Asheville, NC)
Fiction Forum (Golden, CO)
Fifth Column (Montreal, QC)
The Filipino-American Headliner (Santa Clara, CA)
Filles d'Aujourd'hui (Outremont, QC)
Financing Operations (New York, NY)
Fine Print (Leakey, TX)
Fireside Guard (Centralia, MO)
Fireweed (Toronto, ON)
First Class Executive Travel (Los Angeles, CA)
The First Informer (Summerside, PE)
The Fisherman (New Westminster, BC)
The Fisherman-Long Island Edition (Shirley, NY)
Fleurs, Plantes et Jardins (Quebec, QC)
Floating Island (Cedarville, CA)
Florida Administrative Weekly (Tallahassee, FL)
Florida Hotel & Motel Journal (Tallahassee, FL)
Florida Rental Association News (Tallahassee, FL)
The Flue Cured Tobacco Farmer (Raleigh, NC)
Flushing Pennysaver (Ontario, ON)
Fly! (Ambler, PA)
FOCUS: Journal for Respiratory Care Managers and Educators (Rhinebeck, NY)
Food Chemical News (Washington, DC)

# INDUSTRY ACTIVITY

Food Distributor (Falls Church, VA)
Food Extra (Greenville, SC)
Foothills Sentinel (Yuma, AZ)
For Patients Only (Woodland Hills, CA)
Foreign Language Annals (Alexandria, VA)
The Formalist (Evansville, IN)
The Fort Bend Mirror (Rosenberg, TX)
Fort Bragg Paraglide (Raeford, NC)
Fort Devens Dispatch (Devens, MA)
Fort Fairfield Review (Fort Fairfield, ME)
Ft. Polk Guardian (Sulphur, LA)
Fort Smith Historical Society Journal (Fort Smith, AR)
Fort Wayne Journal-Gazette (Fort Wayne, IN)
Fourth Estate (Walla Walla, WA)
France-Amerique (New York, NY)
Franklin Focus (Somerville, NJ)
Franklin News Weekly (Franklin, TX)
Free Press (100 Mile House, BC)
Free Press & Economist (Shelburne, ON)
Freebies (Santa Barbara, CA)
The Freer Press (Freer, TX)
Freie Zeitung (Kenilworth, NJ)
Friendly Woman (Cincinnati, OH)
Gazette (Port Jervis, NY)
The Gazette (Colorado Springs, CO)
The Gazette (Saint Petersburg, FL)
The General (Baltimore, MD)
Generations (Winnipeg, MB)
Genessee Country Express (Dansville, NY)
Genoa Leader-Times (Genoa, NE)
Genre (Norman, OK)
GEO Europe (Palm Springs, CA)
George Sand Studies (Medford, MA)
Georgia Food Connection (Smyrna, GA)
Georgia Trend (Norcross, GA)
Giddings Times and News (Giddings, TX)
The Gila Monster (Thatcher, AZ)
Glasgow Republican (Glasgow, KY)
Glass Collector's Digest (Marietta, OH)
Glass Digest (New York, NY)
Glass Industry (New York, NY)
Glass New England (Franklin, MA)
The Gleaner (Camden, NJ)
God's Word Today (Saint Paul, MN)
Going Places (Minot) (Minot, ND)
Gold River News (Sacramento, CA)
Golden Gate Gazette (Naples, FL)
GOLF NEWS Magazine (Rancho Mirage, CA)
Good News (Asheville, NC)

Good News Magazine (Tucson, AZ)
Grain & Feed Marketing (Seattle, WA)
Grand Street (New York, NY)
Great American Crafts (Iola, WI)
Great Lakes Pilot News (Ann Arbor, MI)
Great Plains Quarterly (Lincoln, NE)
Green Acres (Troy, KS)
Green County Spectrum (Xenia, OH)
Greenhorn Valley-News (Colorado City, CO)
The Greyhound Review (Abilene, KS)
Guernsey Breeders' Journal (Reynoldsburg, OH)
The Gulf Breeze Sentinel (Gulf Breeze, FL)
Gunfighter (Boise, ID)
Half Tones to Jubilee (Pensacola, FL)
Hallelujah! (Vancouver, BC)
Hamlin Herald (Hamlin, TX)
The Hanska Herald (Hanska, MN)
Hardware Age's Home Improvement Market (New York, NY)
Harmony (Deerfield, IL)
Harrington Journal (Harrington, DE)
Harrow & Colchester South This Week (Harrow, ON)
Hart's Lubricants World (Houston, TX)
Hawaii Pacific Review (Honolulu, HI)
Hawkinsville Dispatch and News (Hawkinsville, GA)
Headliner (Sonoma, CA)
Health Care Weekly Review (Southfield, MI)
Healthcare Product News (Vancouver, BC)
Heartland Retailer (Omaha, NE)
Hellenic Hamilton News (Hamilton, ON)
The Hellenic News (London, ON)
Henderson Independent (Henderson, MN)
The Herald-News (Reed City, MI)
Herpetologica (Blacksburg, VA)
Hesperia (Princeton, NJ)
High Performance Mopar (Saddle Brook, NJ)
Highland Park Herald (Somerville, NJ)
Highland Shopping Guide (Howell, MI)
Highlights of Agricultural Research (Auburn, AL)
The Hills Crescent (Hills, MN)
Hillsboro Banner (Hillsboro, ND)
Hit Parader (Paramus, NJ)
Hlas Naroda (Voice of the Nation) (Chicago, IL)
Home Automation (Worcester, MA)
Home & Condo (Naples, FL)

Home Healthcare Consultant (Princeton, NJ)
Home with Homeland (Forrest City, AR)
Home Mechanix (New York, NY)
Home-Office Computing (Danbury, CT)
Home PC (Manhasset, NY)
Homestead Hotline (Clayton, NJ)
HomeStyles Publishing and Marketing Inc. (Saint Paul, MN)
Hope (Brooklin, ME)
Hora de Cierre (Miami, FL)
Horizon (Salt Lake City, UT)
The Horn Speaker (Mabank, TX)
The Horsetrader (Fort Worth, TX)
Hospital for Joint Diseases Bulletin (New York, NY)
Hot House (Dover, NJ)
House Beautiful Kitchen/Baths (New York, NY)
Housing Operations Manager (Olney, MD)
Howard (Washington, DC)
HR Executive Review (New York, NY)
Humanist in Canada (Ottawa, ON)
Hungarian Word (Amerikai Magyar SZO) (New York, NY)
Huntington Beach/Fountain Valley Independent (Huntington Beach, CA)
Huntington Library Quarterly (San Marino, CA)
Huron County Press & Newsweekly (Sebewaing, MI)
Hurricane Alice (Providence, RI)
Hydrological Science and Technology (Saint Paul, MN)
ICR: The International Cookbook Revue (New York, NY)
The Idaho World (Garden Valley, ID)
The IDB (Washington, DC)
Illinois Research (Urbana, IL)
Illinois Wildlife (Edwardsville, IL)
Impact (Austin) (Austin, TX)
Imperial Valley Press (El Centro, CA)
Imprinting Business (South Plainfield, NJ)
In Pittsburgh Newsweekly (Philadelphia, PA)
Income Opportunities (New York, NY)
Incursion Music Review (Toronto, ON)
Independent Bulletin (Chicago, IL)
Independent Cable of System Idaho (Soda Springs, ID)
Independent Republican (Goshen, NY)
The Index (Hermitage, MO)
India in New York (New York, NY)
Indiana Builder Magazine (Spencer, IN)
Indiana Libraries (Bloomington, IN)

Gale Directory of Publications and Broadcast Media, 140th Edition     lxxi

## INDUSTRY ACTIVITY

Indo-Pacific Fishes (Honolulu, HI)
The Industrial Physicist (College Park, MD)
Info (Gary, IN)
Informal Logic (Windsor, ON)
InfoText (Santa Ana, CA)
L'Ingenieur (Montreal, QC)
Inland Architect (Chicago, IL)
Inland Register (Spokane, WA)
The Institutional Distribution (New York, NY)
Integrated Communications Design (Nashua, NH)
Interim (Las Vegas, NV)
The Interior News (Smithers, BC)
INTERIORS (New York, NY)
The International Citizen (Windsor, ON)
International Daily News (Monterey Park, CA)
International Instrumentation and Controls (Great Neck, NY)
International Journal of Acarology (West Bloomfield, MI)
International Journal of Cognitive Ergonomics (Mahwah, NJ)
International Journal of Occupational Medicine, Immunology and Toxicology (Princeton, NJ)
International Journal of Rehabilitation and Health (New York, NY)
International Journal of Trauma Nursing (Saint Louis, MO)
International Musician (New York, NY)
Interservice (Washington, DC)
Iowa Pork Today (Cedar Rapids, IA)
Iowegian (Centerville, IA)
Irish America Magazine (New York, NY)
Irondequoit Shopper (Rochester, NY)
Island Life Magazine (Sanibel, FL)
Islander (South Hero, VT)
Italica (Columbus, OH)
Ivey Business Quarterly (Toronto, ON)
JADARA (Lusby, MD)
Jamaica Shopping & Entertainment Guide (Jamaica, NY)
The Jambar (Youngstown, OH)
The Japanese Daily Sun-Nikkan San (New York, NY)
Jasonville Leader (Jasonville, IN)
Jefferson County Advertiser (Jefferson, WI)
The Jefferson County Transcript (Golden, CO)
JNMS: Journal of the Neuromusculoskeletal System (Brooklandville, MD)
The Jotter (Janesville, WI)
The Journal (Voorhees, NJ)

Journal of Agricultural & Resource Economics (Fort Collins, CO)
Journal of the American College of Dentists (San Diego, CA)
Journal of the American Medical Women's Association (New York, NY)
Journal of the American Psychiatric Nurses Association (Saint Louis, MO)
Journal of the American Water Resources Association (Middleburg, VA)
Journal of the Association for Communication Administration (JACA) (Washington, DC)
Journal of Business Strategies (Huntsville, TX)
Journal of Caribbean Studies (Lexington, KY)
Journal of Clinical Activities, Assignments & Handouts in Psychotherapy (Hammond, IN)
The Journal of Comparative Asian Development (Chicago, IL)
Journal of Computer-Assisted Microscopy (Norwell, MA)
Journal of Corporation Law (Iowa City, IA)
Journal of Country Music (Nashville, TN)
Journal of Critical Inquiry into Curriculum and Instruction (San Francisco, CA)
Journal of Dentistry for Children (Chicago, IL)
Journal of Druze Studies (San Diego, CA)
Journal of the Early Republic (West Lafayette, IN)
Journal of Educational Relations (Camp Hill, PA)
Journal of Foraminiferal Research (Newark, DE)
Journal of Forensic Economics (Kansas City, MO)
The Journal (Greenbrook-North Plainfield Edition) (Somerville, NJ)
Journal of Healthcare Safety, Compliance & Infection Control (Weston, MA)
Journal of the History of International Law (Norwell, MA)
Journal of HIV/AIDS Prevention and Education for Adolescents & Children (West Hartford, CT)
Journal of Housing Research (Washington, DC)
Journal of Hypnotherapy (Kenner, LA)
Journal of Intergroup Relations (Nashville, TN)
Journal of International Wildlife Law and Policy (El Cerrito, CA)

Journal of Investigative Medicine (Philadelphia, PA)
Journal of Jewish Education (New York, NY)
Journal of Land Resouces and Environmental Law (Salt Lake City, UT)
Journal of Materials Synthesis and Processing (Norwell, MA)
Journal of Mayan Linguistics (Baton Rouge, LA)
The Journal of Medical Practice Management (Chicago, IL)
Journal of Modern Physics B (River Edge, NJ)
Journal of Network Industries (Norwell, MA)
Journal of Outcome Measurement (Naperville, IL)
Journal of Paralegal Education and Practice (Mt. Royal, NJ)
Journal of Peace & Justice Studies (Villanova, PA)
Journal of Personnel Evaluation in Education (Norwell, MA)
Journal of Pharmacoepidemiology (Jackson, MS)
Journal of Psychiatric Research (Arlington, VA)
Journal of Psychotherapy in Independent Practice (Fort Lauderdale, FL)
Journal of Radiosurgery (Norwell, MA)
Journal of Reducing Space Mission Cost (Norwell, MA)
Journal Review (Crawfordsville, IN)
Journal of the Royal Astronomical Society of Canada (R.A.S.C.) (Toronto, ON)
Journal de St. Michel (Montreal, QC)
Journal of Science Teacher Education (Norwell, MA)
The Journal of Services Marketing (Santa Barbara, CA)
Journal of Social and Behavioral Sciences (Washington, DC)
Journal of Social Distress and the Homeless (Norwell, MA)
Journal of Social and Evolutionary Systems (Berkeley, CA)
Journal of Sport Behavior (Mobile, AL)
Journal of Systems Integration (Norwell, MA)
Journal of Systems Integration (Norwell, MA)
Journal of Systems Management (Cleveland, OH)
Journal of Tau Alpha Pi National Honor Society - Engineering Technologies (Washington, DC)

## INDUSTRY ACTIVITY

Journal of Turkish Studies/Turkluk Bilgisi Arastirmalari (Duxbury, MA)
Journal for Vocational Special Needs Education (Pittsburgh, PA)
Journal of WOCN (Wound, Ostomy, and Continence Nursing) (Saint Louis, MO)
Junior Magazine (Pittsburgh, PA)
Junior Statement (San Mateo, CA)
KANADA KURIER (Winnipeg, MB)
Kansas City Wyandotte Echo (Kansas City, KS)
Kansas Food Dealers Bulletin (Shawnee Mission, KS)
KCTS E-zine (Seattle, WA)
The Keystone (Kutztown, PA)
Kidpreneurs News (New York, NY)
Kids Courier (Hamburg, NY)
Kidstuff (Lake Park, FL)
Kidsworld (Toronto, ON)
Kitchenware News (Yarmouth, ME)
KLKE-TV (Lincoln, NE)
Knitting Digest (Berne, IN)
Knowledge Management (Irvine, CA)
Korea Post (Columbia, MD)
Korea Times (Los Angeles, CA)
Korean Southeast News (Doraville, GA)
La Bobina (Columbia, SC)
La Latina Presencia (Gardner, KS)
La Replique (Victoriaville, QC)
La Semana (Orlando, FL)
La Villa News (Malvern, AR)
Labor Legislation in Nova Scotia (Halifax, NS)
Labradorian (Happy Valley, NL)
Lacja's World (Cooper City, FL)
Lacon Home Journal (Tarrytown, NY)
Laiks (Time) (Brooklyn, NY)
Lake Michigan Journal (Benton Harbor, MI)
The Lake News (Lake Cowichan, BC)
The Laker (Tampa, FL)
Lakeside Review (Layton, UT)
Lamar County News (Jackson, MS)
Landscape Design (Chicago, IL)
Landscape & Irrigation (Chicago, IL)
Langford Bugle (Britton, SD)
Lanier County News (Lakeland, GA)
The Lantern (Baytown, TX)
Latin American Jewish Studies (Swarthmore, PA)
Latitudes (Winter Park, FL)
Laubach Litscape (Syracuse, NY)
The Laurel Review (Maryville) (Maryville, MO)
Law Library Journal (Carbondale, IL)
Le Courrier des Moulins (Laval, QC)
Le Magazine Jeunesse (Montreal, QC)

Le Magazine L'agent de voyages (Ville D'Anjou, QC)
Le Misanthrope (Montreal, QC)
Le Regional Hull-Aylmer (Hull, QC)
Le Reveil (Jonquiere, QC)
Le Temiscamien (Ville-Marie, QC)
Lead Detection and Abatement Contractor (Bethesda, MD)
The Leader (Moline, IL)
Leader (Lemmon, SD)
Leader-Journal (Saint James, MO)
Leader & State Register (Seaford, DE)
Lefthander Magazine (Topeka, KS)
The Legal History Review (Norwell, MA)
Leiden Journal of International Law (Norwell, MA)
The Leland Progress (Leland, MS)
Letters in Peptide Science (Norwell, MA)
Lewis County Herald (Hohenwald, TN)
Lewisville News (Lewisville, TX)
Librarians at Liberty (Gainesville, FL)
Lifestyle (Oakland, CA)
The Lighthouse (Point Mugu NAWC, CA)
Lighthouse Syndications (Canyon, TX)
Lincoln New Era (Lincoln, MO)
Lincoln Review (Washington, DC)
The Lindale News (Lindale, TX)
The Linden Herald (Copperopolis, CA)
The Linden World (Saint Charles, MO)
Linguistic Notes from La Jolla (La Jolla, CA)
The Link (Montreal, QC)
The Listowel Banner (Listowel, ON)
Literature and Psychology (Providence, RI)
The Living Light (Washington, DC)
Loafer's Choice (Plantation, FL)
Logger and Lumberman (Wadley, GA)
Long Beach Independent Voice (Lynbrook, NY)
The Longboat Observer (Longboat Key, FL)
The Longview Current (Lees Summit, MO)
Los Angeles Times–Ventura County Edition (Ventura, CA)
Lost River Star (Merrill, OR)
Lottery Player's Magazine (Marlton, NJ)
Lynn–Linn Lineage Quarterly (McHenry, IL)
Lynx Eye (Los Osos, CA)
Lyrical Iowa (Des Moines, IA)
Machine Translation (Norwell, MA)
Magazine Le Clap (Sainte-Foy, QC)
Magyar Naplo (Toronto, ON)
Maine Times (Bangor, ME)

Maison d'Aujourd'hui (Montreal, QC)
Managed Care/Innovations (Saint Louis, MO)
The Mancos Times (Mancos, CO)
Manglarama Journal (Silver Spring, MD)
Manila Mail (Daly City, CA)
Manistee County Pioneer Press (Big Rapids, MI)
Marine Fish Monthly (Luttrell, TN)
Marine Performance and Fisheries Product News (Stonington, ME)
Mark Twain Regional News (Mexico, MO)
Marketing Asst. (Ipswich, MA)
Martial Arts Presents (Burbank, CA)
MascuLines (New York, NY)
Mason County News (Mason, TX)
Maumee Valley Herald (Toledo, OH)
The Mayflower Quarterly (Marmora, NJ)
MCC Post (Flint, MI)
McCormick Messenger (Mc Cormick, SC)
McIntosh County Democrat (Checotah, OK)
Media Studies Journal (Nashville, TN)
Medical Economics for Surgeons (Duluth, MN)
Medical Gazette (San Antonio, TX)
Medical Industry Information Report (Mission Viejo, CA)
Medicine & Global Survival (Cambridge, MA)
Meeting Planners MarketPlace (Norwood, MA)
Meie Elu (Toronto, ON)
Mekeel's Weekly Stamp News (Hollis, NH)
Melrose Chronicle (Melrose, WI)
Memory Magic (Iola, WI)
The Mercedes Enterprise (Mercedes, TX)
Methods in Cell Science (Burlington, VT)
The Metro Courier (Augusta, GA)
MetroToday (Toronto, ON)
Metuchen Edison Review (Somerville, NJ)
Michael's Create! (Iola, WI)
Michigan Academician (Alma, MI)
Michigan Historical Review (Mount Pleasant, MI)
Michigan Natural Resources Magazine (West Bloomfield, MI)
Micro Computer Journal (Port Washington, NY)
Mid-America Weekly Trucking (Fort Dodge, IA)
Middle Tennessee Shopper (Columbia, TN)

## INDUSTRY ACTIVITY

Middlesex Buyer's Guide (Somerville, NJ)
Middlesex Chronicle (Somerville, NJ)
Midwestern States Salvage Guide (Moore, OK)
Migration World Magazine (Staten Island, NY)
Milford Herald-News (Milford, IL)
The Militant (New York, NY)
Military Sun Press (Kaneohe, HI)
The Milton Daily Standard/The Lewisburg Daily Journal (Milton, PA)
Milton Shopping News (Oakville, ON)
Miner's News (Boise, ID)
Ministry (Silver Spring, MD)
Minnesota Parent (Norfolk, VA)
Mission Valley Review (Woodland Hills, CA)
Missouri Speech & Theatre Journal (Saint Louis, MO)
MIT Sloan Management Review (Cambridge, MA)
The Mitchell Tribune (Mitchell, IN)
Mode (Irvine, CA)
Modern Medicine (New York, NY)
Molecular Engineering (Norwell, MA)
The Moncton Provider (Moncton, NB)
Monday Morning (Louisville, KY)
Money Saver (Nevada, IA)
Moneyworld (Ocala, FL)
Monkeyshines on America (Greensboro, NC)
Monkeyshines on Health and Science (Greensboro, NC)
Monroe Area Shopping News (Monroe, WI)
Monroe County Sun (Clarendon, AR)
Moody Magazine (Chicago, IL)
Morning Sun (Pittsburg, KS)
Motocycliste (Montreal, QC)
Motorboating (New York, NY)
Motoring Road Magazine (Franklin, MA)
The Mount Hope Clarion (Mount Hope, KS)
Mount Olive Review (Mount Olive, NC)
Mountain Bike Action (Valencia, CA)
Mountain Sports & Living (New York, NY)
MSP Airport News (Saint Paul, MN)
Multi-County Star (Covington, GA)
Museum News (Washington, DC)
Music and Dance News (Saint Joseph, MN)
Mustang Daily (San Luis Obispo, CA)
Mutual Broadcasting System, Inc. (Silver Spring, MD)
Mutual Funds (Chicago, IL)

NAFTA (Norwell, MA)
Naples Times (Bonita Springs, FL)
Nasinec (Granger, TX)
National Croquet Calendar (Monmouth, OR)
National Development/Desarrollo Nacional (Milford, CT)
National Gardening (South Burlington, VT)
The National Hobby News (New Philadelphia, OH)
National Inner City (Mobile, AL)
The National Record (Hollywood, CA)
Nature Study (Dingmans Ferry, PA)
Naugatuck News (Naugatuck, CT)
Nautical Research Journal (Newburyport, MA)
Navioneer (Grand Junction, CO)
NE AR Tribune (Jonesboro, AR)
Neighbors (Fresno, CA)
New Art Examiner (Chicago, IL)
New College of California Journal of Public Interest Law (San Francisco, CA)
New Covenant (Huntington, IN)
New England Economic Review (Boston, MA)
New England Golf (Hubbardston, MA)
The New Era (Davenport, OK)
New Jersey Outdoors (Trenton, NJ)
The New Korea (Los Angeles, CA)
The New Morning (Pleasantville, NY)
New Richland Star (New Richland, MN)
New Rochelle Standard-Star (New Rochelle, NY)
New Sharon Star (Fremont, IA)
New Town News (New Town, ND)
The New York Evening Express (New York, NY)
The New York Voice/Harlem U.S.A. (Forest Hills, NY)
The News Gazette (Winchester, IN)
News-Herald (Ravena, NY)
News-Wave (Whitehall, WI)
Newton County News (Granby, MO)
Newton County News (Newton, TX)
Niagara Farmers' Monthly (Smithville, ON)
The Niagara Index (Niagara University, NY)
The Niagara Journal (Niagara, WI)
Nicholas County News Leader (Richwood, WV)
Night Roses (Prospect Heights, IL)
The Nikkei Weekly (New York, NY)
99 North Magazine (Squamish, BC)
Ninnau (Basking Ridge, NJ)

Nonlinear Dynamics, Psychology, and Life Sciences (Norwell, MA)
North American Lily Society Quarterly (Owatonna, MN)
North Beach Now (San Francisco, CA)
North Delta Sentinel (Delta, BC)
North Iowa Times (Black Earth, WI)
North Island Televiewer (Port Hardy, BC)
North Miami Beach News (Miami, FL)
Northeast Detroiter Harper Woods Herald (Birmingham, MI)
Northern Gardener (Falcon Heights, MN)
The Northern Light (Williams, MN)
Northern New York Business Journal (Potsdam, NY)
Northstar (Amherst, NY)
Northumberland News (Cobourg, ON)
Northwest Christian Journal (Renton, WA)
Northwest Comic News (Eugene, OR)
The Northwest Dispatch (Tacoma, WA)
Northwest Metro Times (Bethany, OK)
Northwest Shopper (Des Moines, IA)
Northwesterner (Santa Rosa, CA)
Norwich Gazette (Norwich, ON)
Norwood-Young America Times (Norwood, MN)
Notes on Linguistics (Dallas, TX)
Notes on Literacy (Dallas, TX)
Noticias del Mundo (Long Island City, NY)
Nouveau Quartier Libre (Montreal, QC)
Novy Domov (New Homeland) (Scarborough, ON)
Nueces County Record Star (Robstown, TX)
Nueva Vista (Midland, TX)
Nut Grower (Fresno, CA)
Nutrition Science News (Boulder, CO)
NYC Poetry Calendar (New York, NY)
The Oak Ridger (Oak Ridge, TN)
Oblong Gem (Oblong, IL)
The Observer (Newark, NJ)
Office Systems 96 (Spring House, PA)
offspring (New York, NY)
Ohio County Engineer (Columbus, OH)
The Ohio Journal of Science (Kent, OH)
Ohio Records & Pioneer Families (Mansfield, OH)
Ohio Sportsman (Port Clinton, OH)
Okeechobee Shoppers Guide (Okeechobee, FL)
Oklahoma Entertainment News (Oklahoma City, OK)
Oklahoma Farmers Union News & Views (Oklahoma City, OK)

## INDUSTRY ACTIVITY

Oklahoma Grocers Journal (Oklahoma City, OK)
The Oklahoma Hornet (Waukomis, OK)
Old News (Marietta, PA)
Old-Time Crochet (Berne, IN)
On-Stage Studies (Boulder, CO)
Online USA (Santa Monica, CA)
Ontario Tennis Association (Toronto, ON)
Operation Update (New York, NY)
OR Manager (Santa Fe, NM)
Orchid Isle Television (Birmingham, AL)
Oregon Pharmacist (Wilsonville, OR)
The Orthodox Catholic Voice (Akron, OH)
Oshkosh Buyers' Guide (Oshkosh, WI)
The Oswegonian (Oswego, NY)
The Other Side of the Lake (Paducah, KY)
O2 (Devon, PA)
Our Home Town (Vanderbilt, MI)
Our Paper (Indianapolis, IN)
The Outdoor Press (Spokane, WA)
Outstate Business (Boyne City, MI)
Outyouth (New York, NY)
The Overton Press (Overton, TX)
Owen County History & Genealogy (Gosport, IN)
P S C Clarion (New York, NY)
P & T Community (Yardley, PA)
The Pan-Pacific Entomologist (San Jose, CA)
Panther Prints (Charlottetown, PE)
Panthers' Plus, Canadian Grey Panthers (Toronto, ON)
The Paper Cut (Montreal, QC)
The Paramount Journal (Paramount, CA)
Parchment (Toronto, ON)
Parent & Child (Bethesda, MD)
Parenting's Healthy Pregnancy (New York, NY)
The Park Stylus (Parkville, MO)
Parker County Shopper (Weatherford, TX)
Parsippany News (West Caldwell, NJ)
Pasadena Broadcaster (Pasadena, TX)
Paths of Learning (Brandon, VT)
Patient Care (Toronto, ON)
Patriots of the Heartland (Springfield, IL)
Patron Magazine (Mississauga, ON)
The Paullina Times (Paullina, IA)
PCI Journal (Chicago, IL)
Peabody Gazette-Bulletin (Peabody, KS)
Peace and Freedom (Philadelphia, PA)
The Peak (Burnaby, BC)
The Peanut Farmer (Raleigh, NC)
Pecan South (Bryan, TX)

PEI Magazine (Atlanta, GA)
Pembroke Magazine (Pembroke, NC)
Pen Tip Illustrations (Parsippany, NJ)
Pennsylvania Medicine (Harrisburg, PA)
The Pennsylvania Police Criminal Law Bulletin (Pittsburgh, PA)
Pennysaver (Reno, NV)
Penticton Herald (Penticton, BC)
Peptide Research (Westborough, MA)
Periodico Horizonte (Fajardo, PR)
Perspectives in Mexican American Studies (Tucson, AZ)
Perspectives in Religious Studies (Kansas City, KS)
Petlife: Your Companion Animal Magazine (Fort Worth, TX)
The Pflugerville Pflag (Pflugerville, TX)
Pharmaceutical Laboratory (New York, NY)
The Philadelphia Tribune (Philadelphia, PA)
Phillips County Historical Review (Helena, AR)
The Phoenix (Milpitas, CA)
Phoenix Magazine (Phoenix, AZ)
Photographer's Forum (Santa Barbara, CA)
Phylaxis Magazine (Fort Leavenworth, KS)
Physiological Chemistry and Physics and Medical NMR (Melville, NY)
Piano Technicians Journal (Kansas City, MO)
Pillsbury Classic Cookbooks (Minneapolis, MN)
Pinewood Country Creations (Cochrane, ON)
Piscataway Review (Somerville, NJ)
Pittsburgh Parent (Bakerstown, PA)
Pixel Vision (New York, NY)
Plant Molecular Biology Reporter (Athens, GA)
The Plantagenet Connection (Arvada, CO)
The Plantsman (Loudon, NH)
Pleasure Boatings Caribbean Sports & Travel Magazine (Miami, FL)
Pleiades Magazine (Edgewater, CO)
Poem (Huntsville, AL)
Point Of Purchase (Alpharetta, GA)
A Policy for the Moment of Truth (Washington, DC)
Policy and Practice of Public Human Services (Washington, DC)
Polymer Preprints (Newark, NJ)
Poptronics (Boulder, CO)
Popular Home Automation (Framingham, MA)

Portland Parent (Seattle, WA)
Pottsville Republican (Pottsville, PA)
PPI Detailed Report (Chicago, IL)
Pratfall (Burbank, CA)
Praying (Kansas City, MO)
Pre-Vue Entertainment Magazine (La Jolla, CA)
Premiere (Boulder, CO)
Prensa Hispana (Hispanic Press) (Avon Park, FL)
Prepared Foods (Bensenville, IL)
The Presidency (Washington, DC)
The Press-Enterprise (Riverside, CA)
Pretre et Pasteur (Montreal, QC)
Prime (Madison, WI)
Prime Times (Setauket, NY)
Primroses (Juneau, AK)
Processing (Itasca, IL)
Produce Business (Boca Raton, FL)
The Produce News (Englewood Cliffs, NJ)
Professional Ethics (Gainesville, FL)
Progress Enterprise 1 Bulletin (Lunneburg, NS)
Propaneorist (Oklahoma City, OK)
The Prospector (Yuma, AZ)
Provident Book Finder (Scottdale, PA)
Provincial Judges Journal/Journal des Juges Provinciaux (Grand Bank, NL)
Psyche (Cambridge, MA)
Psychoanalytic Books (New York, NY)
The Psychotherapy Patient (New York, NY)
Psychotherapy Research (Oxford, OH)
Public Perspective (Storrs, CT)
Public Relations Quarterly (Rhinebeck, NY)
Public Safety Product News (Denver, CO)
Pulse! (West Sacramento, CA)
The Punch List (New York, NY)
Puncture (Portland, OR)
Q Journal (Cambridge, MA)
Quantitative Microbiology (Norwell, MA)
The Quarterly (New York, NY)
Quarterly Labour Force Statistics (Washington, DC)
Quebec Info (Sainte-Foy, QC)
Queens Bar Bulletin (Jamiaca, NY)
Quick & Easy Plastic Canvas (Big Sandy, TX)
Quick & Easy Quilting (Berne, IN)
The Racquette (Potsdam, NY)
RAE Cable (Bottineau, ND)
The Ranger (Tacoma, WA)
Rare Coin Review (Irvine, CA)
Ratite Marketplace (Bowie, TX)

## INDUSTRY ACTIVITY

The Rawlins County Square Deal (Atwood, KS)
Raymondville Chronicle and Willacy County News (Raymondville, TX)
Real Estate Northwest (Edmonds, WA)
Real Estate Today (Chicago, IL)
The Record (New Westminster, BC)
Recreational Ice Skating (Dallas, TX)
Renaissance Magazine (Nantucket, MA)
Renaissance Quarterly (New York, NY)
The Reporter (Spokane, WA)
Republican Liberty (Gainesville, FL)
The Republican Woman (Alexandria, VA)
Residences (Westmount, QC)
Response (New York, NY)
Retail News (Sandusky, OH)
Retail Operations & Construction (Roswell, GA)
Review-Herald (Bishop, CA)
The Review Times (Greenfield, OH)
Revista de Critica Literaria Latinoamericana (Hanover, NH)
The Rhode Island Builder Report (East Providence, RI)
The Rhode Island Gourmet Guide (East Greenwich, RI)
The Rhode Island Parents' Paper (Jamaica Plain, MA)
River Valley Shopper (Spring Valley, MN)
RLE Currents (Cambridge, MA)
Rock Garden Quarterly (Denver, CO)
The Rocket (Fairbury, IL)
Rotary Review (Los Angeles, CA)
Ruah (Oakland, CA)
Running Wild (Shutesbury, MA)
Rural Pennysaver, Inc. (Conklin, NY)
Rural Special Education Quarterly (Morgantown, WV)
Russell's Official National Motor Coach Guide (Cedar Rapids, IA)
RV West Magazine (Woodinville, WA)
The Sabbath Watchman (Downey, CA)
Sacramento Lawyer (Sacramento, CA)
St. Lawrence (Canton, NY)
Salesian (New Rochelle, NY)
The Salina Sun (Gunnison, UT)
Salut Dimanche (Louiseville, QC)
SAMPE Journal (Covina, CA)
San Diego Computer Journal (San Diego, CA)
San Diego Navy Dispatch (San Diego, CA)
San Diego Parent (San Diego, CA)
San Francisco (San Francisco, CA)
The San Juan Record (Monticello, UT)

San Saba News and Star (San Saba, TX)
The Sanderson Times (Sanderson, TX)
Sanford Herald (Sanford, FL)
The Saponifier (Silvana, WA)
Saskatchewan History (Saskatoon, SK)
Satellite Entertainment Guide (Edmonton, AB)
Satellite TV Week (Fortuna, CA)
Scanning Microscopy (Elk Grove Village, IL)
SCD's Price Guide Weekly (Iola, WI)
Science Fiction Eye (Asheville, NC)
Science Weekly (Silver Spring, MD)
Scintilla (Santa Cruz, CA)
Scottsdale Progress Tribune (Scottsdale, AZ)
The SDC Magazine (Delhi, CA)
Seagoville Suburbia News (Seagoville, TX)
Seattle Compass (Seattle, WA)
The Seattle Press (Seattle, WA)
Sebring Shopping Guide (Sebring, FL)
The Second Line (New Orleans, LA)
Seconds (New York, NY)
Seed & Crops Digest (Cedar Falls, IA)
Semeia (Saskatoon, SK)
SENGA (New Orleans, LA)
Senior Scene (Tacoma, WA)
Sentinel (Cortez, CO)
Sephardic Scholar (New York, NY)
Sepsis (Norwell, MA)
Server/Workstation Expert (Newton Center, MA)
Server/Workstation Expert (Newton Center, MA)
Service and Contracting (S & C) (Elgin, IL)
ServiceInsights (Arlington, TX)
Setonian (Greensburg, PA)
Seventeen (New York, NY)
73 Amateur Radio Today (Peterborough, NH)
Share International (North Hollywood, CA)
Shelby County News-Gazette (Windsor, IL)
Shelter (Cordova, TN)
The Shield (Hornel Heights, ON)
Shing Wah News (Toronto, ON)
The Shopper (Zone I) (Durant, OK)
The Shopper's Helper (Greenwich, OH)
Shopping News South (Bristol, RI)
Shoreeast Magazine (Pleasantville, NJ)
Si Magazine (Los Angeles, CA)
Sierra County Sentinel (Truth or Consequences, NM)

Sign Language Studies (Burtonsville, MD)
The Signal (Merced, CA)
Silver Magazine (Shaker Heights, OH)
Silver World (Lake City, CO)
Sioux Rapids Bulletin-Press (Sioux Rapids, IA)
Sister City News (Washington, DC)
Sister Miriam Teresa League of Prayer Bulletin (Convent Station, NJ)
Skin Diver (Los Angeles, CA)
The Skyline (Alpine, TX)
Slant 6 News (Salem, OR)
Slater Main Street News (Slater, MO)
SLV Saturday Want Ads (Monte Vista, CO)
Small Pond Magazine of Literature (Stratford, CT)
Small Publisher (Princeton, WV)
The Smallholder (Argenta, BC)
Smart Shoppers (Cornwall, ON)
Smith County News (Tyler, TX)
Smith University Funding Report (Monroe, NY)
Snake River Echoes (Rexburg, ID)
Snicker (Saint Louis, MO)
Soap Opera Update (Englewood Cliffs, NJ)
Soccer Jr. (New York, NY)
Social Register Observer (New York, NY)
Somerset County Buyer's Guide (Somerville, NJ)
Somerset Pulaski News Journal (Somerset, KY)
The Soroptimist of the Americas Magazine (Philadelphia, PA)
The Sound Shore Review (White Plains, NY)
South Central Review (College Station, TX)
South Florida Times (West Palm Beach, FL)
The South Hill Enterprise (South Hill, VA)
South Lincoln County News (Waldport, OR)
South OKC Leader (Moore, OK)
South Shore Baby Journal (Kingston, MA)
South Shore Gazette (South Shore, SD)
South Shore Record (Lynbrook, NY)
South Texas Informer & Business Journal (Corpus Christi, TX)
The South Texas Reporter (Roma, TX)
Southern California Business Trends (Los Angeles, CA)

Southern California Senior Life (Inland Empire Edition) (Los Angeles, CA)
Southern Folklore (Bowling Green, KY)
Southern Genealogists Exchange Quarterly (Jacksonville, FL)
Southern Growth Magazine (Research Triangle Park, NC)
Southern New Jersey Swapper (Cinnaminson, NJ)
Southwest Computer Monthly (Glendale, AZ)
Southwest Stockman (Wheat Ridge, CO)
Space and Time Magazine (New York, NY)
Spartan Daily (San Jose, CA)
Special Libraries Association, Geography & Map Division (Topton, PA)
The Spectator (Jackson, MI)
The Spectrum (Saint George, UT)
Spokane, Washington, Official Gazette (Spokane, WA)
Sports Business (Woodbridge, ON)
Sportwear International (New York, NY)
The Spotlight (Washington, DC)
Spring Mills TV Co. (Spring Mills, PA)
Springfield Parent, Inc. (Springfield, MO)
SR (Studies in Religion)/(Sciences Religieuses) (Edmonton, AB)
Stages (New York, NY)
Stamp Wholesaler (Iola, WI)
Standard & Poor's A.S.E. Stock Reports (New York, NY)
Stanford French & Italian Studies (Saratoga, CA)
Stanstead Historical Society Journal (Stanstead, QC)
Star Review (Burleson, TX)
Star Trek Communicator (Aurora, CO)
Star Wars Insider (Aurora, CO)
The Steamboat Whistle (Steamboat Springs, CO)
Steward Anthropological Society Journal (Urbana, IL)
Stock Car Racing (Tampa, FL)
The Stock Market Magazine (Yonkers, NY)
Stockbridge Town Crier (Stockbridge, MI)
Store Equipment & Design (New York, NY)
Storm Lake Times (Storm Lake, IA)
Storyette Magazine (Marina del Rey, CA)
Stratford Star (Stratford, TX)
Strictly Hunterdon (Bridgewater, NJ)
Studies in Music (London, ON)
Suburban Leader (Chicago, IL)
Sumter Shopper (Fruitland Park, FL)
Sun-News (Lowden, IA)

The Sun Visitor (Yuma, AZ)
Sunshine (Pharr, TX)
Super Shopper (Clarksville, VA)
SuperOnda (Santa Barbara, CA)
Surprises (Minneapolis, MN)
Swea City Herald-Press (Swea City, IA)
The Tahlequah Times Journal (Tahlequah, OK)
Tape/Disc Business (Purchase, NY)
Target (Gibson City, IL)
The Tattnall Journal (Reidsville, GA)
The Tawakoni News (Quinlan, TX)
TCI Cablevision of Nevada, Inc. (Carson City, NV)
Technocrat (Butte, MT)
Technology & Conservation of Art, Architecture & Antiquities (Somerville, MA)
Technology Review (Cambridge, MA)
The Telephone Pioneer (Denver, CO)
Temas (New York, NY)
Temple Law Review (Philadelphia, PA)
The Temple Terrace Beacon (Tampa, FL)
Tennis Buyer's Guide (New York, NY)
Teviskes Ziburiai (The Lights of Homeland) (Mississauga, ON)
Texas City Sun (Pearland, TX)
Texas Food Merchant (Austin, TX)
Textile World Latina (Atlanta, GA)
TG Magazine (Toronto, ON)
Thanatos (Tallahassee, FL)
Thoi Bao (San Jose, CA)
The Thomas Tribune (New York, NY)
Thomaston Times (Thomaston, GA)
Thorold News (Thorold, ON)
Thunderbolt (Glendale, AZ)
TIEMPO (Waco, TX)
Tiger Beat Magazine (New York, NY)
Timber Bulletin (Bellevue, WA)
TIMES: in harness (Harrisburg, PA)
Times (Wheeler, TX)
The Times (Thomasville, NC)
Times (Springfield, SD)
The Times At The Jersey Shore (Ocean Grove, NJ)
Times-Leader (Union City, PA)
The Times News (Lehighton, PA)
Timesaver (Rochester, NY)
To Dragma (Brentwood, TN)
Today in San Diego (San Diego, CA)
Today's Internist (Washington, DC)
Toledo Jewish News (Sylvania, OH)
Tonkawa News (Tonkawa, OK)
TopCats! (Bridgewater, NJ)
Totem Times (Lazo, BC)

Tourisme Jeunesse (Montreal, QC)
Town & Country News (Blue Springs, MO)
Town & County Advertiser (Britt, IA)
Townsfolk (Chicago, IL)
Trade Fax (Iola, WI)
Tradewinds (Los Angeles, CA)
Transactions of the Society for Computer Simulation International (San Diego, CA)
Translog: Journal of Military Transportation Management (Alexandria, VA)
Transportation Human Factors (Mahwah, NJ)
Trends in the Hotel Industry (New York, NY)
Tri-City Journal (Oak Park, IL)
Tri-City Labor Review (Rock Island, IL)
Tri-County News (South Bend, IN)
The Tri-County News (Irene, SD)
Tri-County News (Junction City, OR)
Tri-County Shoppers News (Springfield, OH)
Tri-County Weekly (Jamesport, MO)
The Trial Lawyer (New York, NY)
Triangle Pointer (Chapel Hill, NC)
Tribune (Throckmorton, TX)
Tribune (Trenton, TX)
Tribune (Grand Haven, MI)
The Tribune (Monument, CO)
Trinity Journal (Weaverville, CA)
The Trinity Standard (Trinity, TX)
TriQuarterly (Evanston, IL)
Tuba Frenzy (Chapel Hill, NC)
Tucson Gourmet (Tucson, AZ)
TV Crosswords (New York, NY)
TV Hebdo (Montreal, QC)
TV Plus (Shelby, NC)
Twin City Trade Lines Shopper's Guide (Eau Claire, MI)
Tyler Cableguide (Tyler, TX)
UMBC Review (Baltimore, MD)
L'Union (Woonsocket, RI)
U.S. Japan Business News (Los Angeles, CA)
U.S. Piper (Birmingham, AL)
University Times (Los Angeles, CA)
Update (San Diego, CA)
Urban Ecology (Oakland, CA)
The Urban Latino News (San Francisco, CA)
USA Cycling Magazine (Colorado Springs, CO)
USRowing (Indianapolis, IN)
Utah Genealogical Association (Salt Lake City, UT)

## INDUSTRY ACTIVITY

The Utica Herald (Utica, OH)
Vacation Ownership World (Bothell, WA)
Vail International Dance Festival (Avon, CO)
The Valierian (Valier, MT)
Valley of the Moon Visitor's News (Sonoma, CA)
Valley News (Beardsley, MN)
Valley News Dispatch (Pittsburgh, PA)
Valley Times (Eagle, ID)
Value Shopper (Somerville, NJ)
VANTAGE (Schaumburg, IL)
Varpelis (The Little Bell) (Brooklyn, NY)
Vertex National SalesTax Manuals (Berwyn, PA)
Veterinary and Human Toxicology (Manhattan, KS)
Victimology (Arlington, VA)
Victorian Homes (Brooklyn, NY)
Victorian Review (Lethbridge, AB)
Vida Social (Miami, FL)
Vietnam War Generation Journal (Tucson, AZ)
The Villager (Bronxville, NY)
Virginia Builder (Moon, VA)
Virginia Parent News (Reston, VA)
Vision (Mayaguez, PR)
Vista USA (Warren, MI)
Visual Arts Research (Champaign, IL)
Vivre (Cochrane, ON)
The Voice (Vancouver, BC)
The Voice (Indianapolis, IN)
The VOICE for Education (Harrisburg, PA)
Voices of Experience (Seattle, WA)
Voices in Italian Americana (Lafayette, IN)
Voz Fronteriza (La Jolla, CA)
A Voz de Portugal (Montreal, QC)
Voz de Portugal (Hayward, CA)
VW Trends (Anaheim, CA)
The Wagnerian (Staten Island, NY)
The Waldron News - Bulletin (Waldron, AR)
Wall & Window Trends (Melville, NY)
The Walton Log (Destin, FL)
War Whoop (Abilene, TX)
Warsaw-Faison News (Warsaw, NC)
Water Engineering & Management (Des Plaines, IL)
The Water Log Maritime Journal (Mount Pleasant, SC)
Waterbirds (Honolulu, HI)
The Waterford Post (Waterford, WI)
Waterfront Southern California News (Irvine, CA)
Watkins Patriot (Eden Valley, MN)

The Watson Witness (Watson, SK)
The Way (Philadelphia, PA)
WCLA-FM (Claxton, GA)
WebNet Journal (Norfolk, VA)
The Weekly News (Hasbrouck Heights, NJ)
Wessington Times Enterprise (Wessington, SD)
West Carrollton Times (Kettering, OH)
West Lincoln Review (Smithville, ON)
West Valley Eagle (Salt Lake City, UT)
Westchester Star (Los Angeles, CA)
The Westford Eagle (Concord, MA)
WFIV-AM (Cape Canaveral, FL)
What's New in Advertising and Marketing (Richmond, VA)
Wheelers (Yucca Valley, CA)
White River Gazette (Fishers, IN)
Whitehall Times (Granville, NY)
Whitetail Business (Iola, WI)
Whitman Academic Journal (Walla Walla, WA)
WHLB-AM (Hibbing, MN)
WHOF-AM (Ocala, FL)
The Willapa Harbor Herald (Raymond, WA)
Williston Sun-Suwannee Valley News (Williston, FL)
Windham Independent (Windham, NH)
Windows Magazine (Manhasset, NY)
Windsor Review (Windsor, ON)
Windward Sun-Press (Kaneohe, HI)
The Winnsboro News (Winnsboro, TX)
Wireless Integration (Nashua, NH)
Wisconsin Beverage Business (Northfield, IL)
Wisconsin Home Gallery Magazine (Cedarburg, WI)
WKYR-AM (Burkesville, KY)
WNYC Program Guide (New York, NY)
The Wolfe City Mirror (Wolfe City, TX)
The Women's Review of Books (Wellesley, MA)
WomenWise (Concord, NH)
WOODALL's Northeast Summers (Ventura, CA)
WOODALL's Texas RV (Ventura, CA)
The Wooden Horse (Saint Petersburg, FL)
Woods County Enterprise (Waynoka, OK)
Worcester County Messenger (Pocomoke City, MD)
Working Woman (New York, NY)
Worklife Report (Kingston, ON)
The World Bank Economic Review (Washington, DC)

World Broadcast News (Overland Park, KS)
World Tribune (Santa Monica, CA)
Worldprofit Online Magazine (Edmonton, AB)
Worthington Times (Worthington, IN)
Writing For Our Lives (Los Gatos, CA)
WRKN-AM (Brandon, MS)
WWIH-FM (High Point, NC)
www.industry.net (Englewood, CO)
Xavierian Weekly (Antigonish, NS)
Yesterday's Island (Nantucket, MA)
Yomiuri America (New York, NY)
York Gazette (Toronto, ON)
Young Judaean (New York, NY)
Your Life Matters (Las Vegas, NV)
Your Money (Skokie, IL)
Yugntruf (New York, NY)
Zephyrhills Shopper (Clermont, FL)

*International*

Agricultural Chemistry (Moscow, RUS)
Bamtock Society (Bristol, GBR)
BEC42 (Taipei, TWN)
Brownie (London, GBR)
China in Focus (Cheltenham, GC, GBR)
Club Sandwich (Westcliff-On-Sea, GBR)
The Dawn (Anglesea, VI, AUS)
Design News (Tokyo, JPN)
Digital Technology Law Journal (Perth, WA, AUS)
Doklady Biochemistry (Moscow, RUS)
Doklady Botanical Sciences (Moscow, RUS)
Doklady Chemical Technology (Moscow, RUS)
Elsa Journal (Hong Kong, CHN)
Engineering Service, Management (Bracknell, GBR)
The English Teacher Online (Bangkok, THA)
Environmental Geoscience (Moscow, RUS)
Evening News (Dannevirke, NZL)
FORTH Dimensions (Milan, ITA)
GEC Journal of Technology (Chelmsford, GBR)
Genomika (London, GBR)
Global Change & Human Health (Bussum, NLD)
The Globe (London, GBR)
Hospitality Industry International (Croydon, GBR)
The Independent Newspaper (Dominica) (Roseau, DMA)
Indian Journal of Social Sciences (Hyderabad, AP, IND)
Indian Records (Calcutta, WB, IND)

# INDUSTRY ACTIVITY

IndiaWorld (Mumbai, MH, IND)

International Journal of Development Banking (Mumbai, MH, IND)

Jane's Asian Infrastructure Monthly (Coulsdon, GBR)

The Journal of Electroacoustic Music (London, GBR)

Journal of European Society of Veterinary Pathology (Giessen, GER)

The Library Association Record (London, GBR)

Mineral Resources Engineering (Singapore, SGP)

National Radio of Cambodia - Phnom Penh (Phnom Penh, CMB)

National Radio of Cambodia - Sihanoukville (Phnom Penh, CMB)

National Radio of Cambodia - Steung Treng (Phnom Penh, CMB)

National Television and Radio Broadcasting Company - Akstafa (Baku, AJN)

National Television and Radio Broadcasting Company - Astara (Baku, AJN)

National Television and Radio Broadcasting Company - Baki (Baki, AJN)

National Television and Radio Broadcasting Company - Danaci (Baku, AJN)

National Television and Radio Broadcasting Company - Duzdag (Baku, AJN)

National Television and Radio Broadcasting Company - Ganca (Baku, AJN)

National Television and Radio Broadcasting Company - Geokcay (Baku, AJN)

National Television and Radio Broadcasting Company - Jebrayl (Baku, AJN)

National Television and Radio Broadcasting Company - Kuba (Baku, AJN)

National Television and Radio Broadcasting Company - Lenkoran (Baku, AJN)

National Television and Radio Broadcasting Company - Lerik (Baku, AJN)

National Television and Radio Broadcasting Company - Ordubad (Baku, AJN)

National Television and Radio Broadcasting Company - Pirsaqat (Baki, AJN)

National Television and Radio Broadcasting Company - Sarur (Baku, AJN)

National Television and Radio Broadcasting Company - Susa (Baku, AJN)

NIRA Review (Tokyo, JPN)

Philippine Economic Journal (Quezon City, PHL)

Philippine Journal of Labor and Industrial Relations (Quezon City, PHL)

Philippine Review of Economics and Business (Quezon City, PHL)

Progress in Reproduction (London, GBR)

Radio Nationale Lao - Houa Phanh (Vientiane, LAO)

Radio Nationale Lao - Muang Hay (Vientiane, LAO)

Radio Nationale Lao - Pakse (Vientiane, LAO)

Radio Nationale Lao - Phonsavan (Vientiane, LAO)

Radio Sara - Baki (Baku, AJN)

Radio TV Malaysia Kota Kinabalu (Kota Kinabalu, MYS)

RTEC-Khon Kaen (Bangkok, THA)

RTEC-Lampang (Bangkok, THA)

RTEC-Nakhon Phanom (Bangkok, THA)

RTEC-Phattalung (Bangkok, THA)

RTEC-Rayong (Bangkok, THA)

RTEC-Uttaradit (Bangkok, THA)

Russian Academy of Sciences Journal of Journals (Moscow, RUS)

Russian Journal of Zoology (Moscow, RUS)

St. Gabriel (Rome, ITA)

Sankhya Series B (Calcutta, WB, IND)

Seeing (Shoreham-By-Sea, GBR)

Social Science Probings (New Delhi, DH, IND)

South Asian Bibliographer (New Delhi, DH, IND)

Sri Lanka Broadcasting Corporation - Ekala (Colombo, SRI)

3rd Magazine (Collingwood, VI, AUS)

Tool and Tillage (Frederiksberg, DEN)

Tribal Arts (Paris, FRA)

Urethane Abstracts (London, GBR)

Voice of Kuanghua (Taipei, TWN)

Voice of the Strait (Fuzhou, FJ, CHN)

Water and Energy Abstracts (New Delhi, DH, IND)

Xinjiang People's Broadcasting Station (Urumqi, XU, CHN)

027.8 School Library Bulletin (Hobart, TA, AUS)

# Newspaper Index

Index entries are arranged geographically by region. Within region in this index, citations appear in descending order of circulation. Citations include publication title, entry number (given in parentheses immediately following the title), publisher name, address, phone and fax numbers, publication subject, and circulation figures.

## Great Lakes States

**Chicago Tribune  (8139)**
Tribune Publishing
435 N. Michigan Ave.
Chicago, IL 60611-4041
Phone: (312)222-4150
Fax: (312)222-3935
**Subject(s):** Daily Newspapers
**Circ:** (Sat.)★545,538
(Mon.-Fri.)★600,988
(Sun.)★963,927

**REALTOR Magazine  (8393)**
National Association of Realtors
430 N Michigan Ave.
Chicago, IL 60611-4087
Phone: (312)329-8200
Fax: (312)329-5978
**Subject(s):** Real Estate
**Circ:** (Free)1,077
(Paid)763,219

**The Detroit News  (15178)**
Gannett Company Inc.
615 W. Lafayette Blvd.
Detroit, MI 48226
Phone: (313)222-2300
Fax: (800)678-4115
**Subject(s):** Daily Newspapers
**Circ:** (Mon.-Fri.)237,991
(Sat.)546,342
(Sun.)738,248

**Today's Realtor  (8428)**
National Association of Realtors
430 N Michigan Ave.
Chicago, IL 60611-4087
Phone: (312)329-8200
Fax: (312)329-5978
**Subject(s):** Real Estate
**Circ:** (Free)1,323
(Paid)725,000

**Detroit Free Press  (15175)**
Knight-Ridder Inc.
600 W. Fort St.
Detroit, MI 48226
Phone: (313)222-5981
Fax: (800)678-6400
**Subject(s):** Daily Newspapers
**Circ:** (Sat.)★510,736
(Mon.-Fri.)★573,053
(Sun.)★710,036

**St. Paul Pioneer Press  (16612)**
Knight-Ridder Inc.
345 Cedar St.
Saint Paul, MN 55101
Phone: (651)228-5500
Fax: (800)950-9080
**Subject(s):** Daily Newspapers
**Circ:** (Mon.-Fri.)533,000
(Sun.)681,000

**Star Tribune  (16347)**
425 Portland Ave.
Minneapolis, MN 55488
Phone: (612)673-4000
Fax: (612)673-7138
**Subject(s):** Daily Newspapers
**Circ:** (Mon.-Sat.)★381,094
(Sun.)★678,650

**The Fear Finder  (15685)**
Halloween Events Inc.
18 S. Perry
Pontiac, MI 48342
Phone: (248)332-7662
**Subject(s):** Paid Community Newspapers; Entertainment; Local, State, and Regional Publications
**Circ:** (Combined)500,000

**The Wall Street Journal (Midwest Edition)  (8443)**
Dow Jones & Company Inc.
1 S Wacker Dr., Ste. 2100
Chicago, IL 60606
Phone: (312)750-4000
Fax: (312)750-4153
**Subject(s):** Daily Newspapers; Business
**Circ:** (Mon.-Fri.)492,514

**Chicago Sun-Times  (8138)**
Chicago Sun-Times Inc.
401 N Wabash Ave.
Chicago, IL 60611-3593
Phone: (312)321-3000
Fax: (312)321-3084
**Subject(s):** Daily Newspapers
**Circ:** (Sat.)287,863
(Sun.)378,371
(Mon.-Fri.)486,936

**Plain Dealer  (24479)**
Newhouse Services
1801 Superior Ave.
Cleveland, OH 44114-2198
Phone: (216)999-6000
Fax: (216)344-4620
**Subject(s):** Daily Newspapers
**Circ:** (Mon.-Sat.)★354,309
(Sun.)★479,131

**The Penny Saver  (9452)**
Penny Saver Publications Inc.
6901 W 159th St.
Tinley Park, IL 60477
Phone: (708)633-6890
Fax: (708)633-4919
**Subject(s):** Shopping Guides
**Circ:** 450,000

**Milwaukee Journal Sentinel  (33317)**
Journal Sentinel Inc.
PO Box 661
Milwaukee, WI 53201
Phone: (414)224-2000
Fax: (414)224-2469
**Subject(s):** Daily Newspapers
**Circ:** (Sat.)★227,387
(Mon.-Fri.)★240,581
(Sun.)★435,127

**The Indianapolis Star  (9873)**
Gannett Company Inc.
307 N. Pennsylvania St.
Indianapolis, IN 46204
Phone: (317)444-4000
Fax: (800)669-7827
**Subject(s):** Daily Newspapers
**Circ:** (Mon.-Sat.)251,601
(Sun.)365,546

**The Columbus Dispatch  (24541)**
The Dispatch Printing Co.
34 S. 3rd St.
Columbus, OH 43215
Phone: (614)461-5000
Fax: (614)461-7580
**Subject(s):** Daily Newspapers
**Circ:** (Mon.-Sat.)★251,045
(Sun.)★361,304

**Cincinnati Enquirer  (24297)**
Gannett Company Inc.
312 Elm St.
Cincinnati, OH 45202
Phone: (513)721-2700
Fax: (513)721-2703
**Subject(s):** Daily Newspapers
**Circ:** (Mon.-Thurs.)195,360
(Sat.)210,217
(Fri.)218,667
(Sun.)311,425

**Batavia Sun  (9032)**
Sun Publications
1500 W. Ogden Ave.
PO Box 269
Naperville, IL 60566-0269
Phone: (630)355-0063
Fax: (630)416-5163
**Subject(s):** Paid Community Newspapers
**Circ:** (Combined)280,876

**The Bolingbrook Sun  (9033)**
Sun Publications
1500 W. Ogden Ave.
PO Box 269
Naperville, IL 60566-0269
Phone: (630)355-0063
Fax: (630)416-5163
**Subject(s):** Paid Community Newspapers
**Circ:** (Combined)280,786

**The Fox Valley Villages/60504 Sun  (9035)**
Sun Publications
1500 W. Ogden Ave.
PO Box 269
Naperville, IL 60566-0269
Phone: (630)355-0063
Fax: (630)416-5163
**Subject(s):** Free Newspapers
**Circ:** (Combined)280,786

**Geneva Sun  (9036)**
Sun Publications
1500 W. Ogden Ave.
PO Box 269
Naperville, IL 60566-0269
Phone: (630)355-0063

**Circulation:** ★ = ABC; △ = BPA; ♦ = CAC; • = CCAB; □ = VAC; ⊕ = PO Statement; ‡ = Publisher's Report; Boldface figures = sworn; Light figures = estimated.

## Great Lakes States

Fax: (630)416-5163
**Subject(s):** Paid Community Newspapers

**Circ:** (Combined)280,786

**Homer/Lockport/Lemont Sun (9038)**
Sun Publications
1500 W. Ogden Ave.
PO Box 269
Naperville, IL 60566-0269
Phone: (630)355-0063
Fax: (630)416-5163
**Subject(s):** Paid Community Newspapers

**Circ:** (Combined)280,786

**Lincoln-Way Sun (9040)**
Sun Publications
1500 W. Ogden Ave.
PO Box 269
Naperville, IL 60566-0269
Phone: (630)355-0063
Fax: (630)416-5163
**Subject(s):** Paid Community Newspapers

**Circ:** (Combined)280,786

**The Lisle Sun (9041)**
Sun Publications
1500 W. Ogden Ave.
PO Box 269
Naperville, IL 60566-0269
Phone: (630)355-0063
Fax: (630)416-5163
**Subject(s):** Paid Community Newspapers

**Circ:** (Combined)280,786

**Plainfield Sun (9044)**
Sun Publications
1500 W. Ogden Ave.
PO Box 269
Naperville, IL 60566-0269
Phone: (630)355-0063
Fax: (630)416-5163
**Subject(s):** Paid Community Newspapers

**Circ:** (Combined)280,786

**St. Charles Sun (9045)**
Sun Publications
1500 W. Ogden Ave.
PO Box 269
Naperville, IL 60566-0269
Phone: (630)355-0063
Fax: (630)416-5163
**Subject(s):** Paid Community Newspapers

**Circ:** (Combined)280,786

**Wheaton Sun (9047)**
Sun Publications
1500 W. Ogden Ave.
PO Box 269
Naperville, IL 60566-0269
Phone: (630)355-0063
Fax: (630)416-5163
**Subject(s):** Paid Community Newspapers

**Circ:** (Combined)280,786

**This Week Publications (33418)**
Community Newspaper
15700 W. Cleveland Ave.
New Berlin, WI 53151
Phone: (262)798-1234
Fax: (262)798-1222
**Subject(s):** Shopping Guides

**Circ:** (Free)242,182

**The Onion (33323)**
Onion Inc.
544 E. Ogden Ave., No. 700-388
Milwaukee, WI 53202
Phone: (414)272-1372
Fax: (414)272-3555
**Subject(s):** Paid Community Newspapers; Entertainment

**Circ:** (Paid)20,489
(Controlled)240,000

**The Advertiser (7840)**
Lakes Area Advertiser Inc.
236 Rte. 173
Antioch, IL 60002
Phone: (847)395-4444
Fax: (847)395-2814
**Subject(s):** Shopping Guides

**Circ:** (Paid)‡234
(Free)‡200,000

**The Blade (25086)**
The Toledo Blade Co.
541 N. Superior St.
Toledo, OH 43660
Phone: (419)724-6000
Fax: (419)724-6439
**Subject(s):** Daily Newspapers

**Circ:** (Mon.-Sat.)‡140,000
(Sun.)‡194,000

**The Grand Rapids Press (15339)**
Booth Newspapers Inc.
155 Michigan St. NW
Grand Rapids, MI 49503-2302
Phone: (616)459-1400
Fax: (616)459-1502
**Subject(s):** Daily Newspapers

**Circ:** (Mon.-Sat.)★138,126
(Sun.)★189,690

**Ads Express (32999)**
Milwaukee Express News
103 N 10437 Washington Dr.
Germantown, WI 53022
Phone: (262)238-6397
Fax: (262)242-9450
**Subject(s):** Shopping Guides

**Circ:** (Free)‡189,600

**Lakes Area Advertiser (7842)**
Lakes Area Advertiser Inc.
236 Rte. 173
Antioch, IL 60002
Phone: (847)395-4444
Fax: (847)395-2814
**Subject(s):** Free Newspapers

**Circ:** (Paid)❑7991
(Free)❑186,846

**Dayton Daily News (24649)**
Dayton Newspapers Inc.
45 S. Ludlow St.
Dayton, OH 45402
Phone: (937)223-1515
Fax: (937)225-2489
**Subject(s):** Daily Newspapers

**Circ:** (Mon.)★122,639
(Sat.)★129,296
(Fri.)★137,758
(Thurs.)★178,099
(Sun.)★185,122

**Wisconsin State Journal (33229)**
Capital Newspapers Inc.
1901 Fish Hatchery Rd.
PO Box 8058
Madison, WI 53713
Phone: (608)252-6200
Fax: (608)252-6119
**Subject(s):** Daily Newspapers

**Circ:** (Mon.-Fri.)★89,569
(Sat.)★100,187
(Sun.)★154,427

**Daily Herald (7852)**
Paddock Publications
PO Box 280
Arlington Heights, IL 60006
Phone: (847)427-4300
Fax: (847)427-1301
**Subject(s):** Daily Newspapers

**Circ:** (Sun.)144,218
(Mon.-Sat.)145,902

**ADA News (8053)**
ADA Publishing
211 E Chicago Ave.
Chicago, IL 60611-2678
Phone: (312)440-2500
Fax: (312)440-3538
**Subject(s):** Dentistry

**Circ:** 140,000

**Chicago Reader (8134)**
Chicago Reader Inc.
11 E Illinois
Chicago, IL 60611
Phone: (312)828-0350
Fax: (312)828-0305
**Subject(s):** Free Newspapers; Alternative and Underground

**Circ:** (Paid)291
(Non-paid)133,158

**The Hoosier Legionnaire (9857)**
The American Legion, Indiana Dept.
777 N Meridian St.
Indianapolis, IN 46204
Phone: (317)630-1300
Fax: (317)237-9891
**Subject(s):** Veterans

**Circ:** (Free)‡133,000

**La Raza (8299)**
Rossi Publications Inc.
6001 N. Clark St.
Chicago, IL 60660
Phone: (773)273-2900
Fax: (773)273-2926
**Subject(s):** Spanish; Hispanic Publications; Paid Community Newspapers

**Circ:** (Paid)12,159
(Non-paid)130,686

**The Journal Gazette (9720)**
The Journal Gazette Co.
600 W. Main St.
PO Box 88
Fort Wayne, IN 46802
Phone: (260)461-8444
Fax: (260)461-8648
**Subject(s):** Daily Newspapers

**Circ:** (Mon.-Sat.)57,995
(Sun.)130,347

**UTU News (24493)**
United Transportation Union
14600 Detroit Ave.
Cleveland, OH 44107-4250
Phone: (216)228-9400
Fax: (216)228-5755
**Subject(s):** Labor

**Circ:** (Controlled)130,000

**Spectator (32927)**
University of Wisconsin-Eau Claire
Hibbard Humanities Hall, 108
Eau Claire, WI 54701
Phone: (715)836-2637
Fax: (715)836-5958
**Subject(s):** College Publications

**Circ:** (Mon.-Fri.)107,137
(Sat.)127,707

**Shopper Stopper (33479)**
Capital Newspapers Inc.
1640 LaDawn Dr.
Portage, WI 53901-0470
Phone: (608)745-3500
Fax: (608)745-3530
**Subject(s):** Shopping Guides

**Circ:** (Paid)27
(Free)125,790

**N'DIGO (8349)**
Hartman Group Publishing Inc.
19 N. Sangamon
Chicago, IL 60607
Phone: (312)822-0202
Fax: (312)822-0288
**Subject(s):** Free Newspapers; Black Publications

**Circ:** (Combined)125,000

**Network Marketing Business Journal (9450)**
Money Maker's Monthly
6827 W. 171st St.
Tinley Park, IL 60477
Phone: (708)633-8888
Fax: (708)633-8889
**Subject(s):** Business; Selling and Salesmanship; Advertising and Marketing

**Circ:** (Paid)‡125,000
(Non-paid)‡125,000

**Eaton Rapids Community News (15111)**
Community Newspapers
239 S Cochran
Charlotte, MI 48813
Phone: (517)543-9913
Fax: (517)543-3677
**Subject(s):** Free Newspapers

**Circ:** (Paid)1,305
(Non-paid)120,193

**City Pages (16282)**
City Pages Inc.
PO Box 59183
Minneapolis, MN 55459-0183
Phone: (612)375-1015

Fax: (612)372-3737
**Subject(s):** Alternative and Underground; Entertainment; Free Newspapers
**Circ:** (Free)116,697

**Minnesota Legionnaire** (16599)
Minnesota American Legion Publishing Co.
20 W. 12th St., Rm. 300A
Saint Paul, MN 55155-2069
Phone: (651)291-1800
Fax: (651)291-1057
**Subject(s):** Veterans
**Circ:** ‡116,000

**Semana** (33617)
Spanish Publications Inc.
20975 Swenson Dr., Ste. 125
Waukesha, WI 53186
Phone: (262)798-7956
Fax: (262)798-5260
**Subject(s):** Free Newspapers
**Circ:** (Non-paid)109,768

**The Flint Journal** (15287)
200 E. 1st St.
Flint, MI 48502-1925
**Subject(s):** Daily Newspapers
**Circ:** (Mon.-Sat.)84,437
(Sun.)103,720

**Metro Times** (15188)
Metro Times Inc.
733 St. Antoine
Detroit, MI 48226
Phone: (313)961-4060
Fax: (313)961-6598
**Subject(s):** Free Newspapers
**Circ:** (Paid)◻25
(Free)◻102,082

**The Vindicator** (25209)
The Vindicator Printing Co.
Vindicator Sq. No. 107
PO Box 780
Youngstown, OH 44501
Phone: (330)747-1471
Fax: (330)747-6712
**Subject(s):** Daily Newspapers
**Circ:** (Mon.-Sat.)70,231
(Sun.)100,736

**The Times** (10053)
Howard Publications
601 W 45th Ave.
Munster, IN 46321
Phone: (219)933-3333
Fax: (219)933-3249
**Subject(s):** Daily Newspapers
**Circ:** (Mon.-Sat.)85,506
(Sun.)93,201

**Lansing State Journal** (15512)
120 E. Lenawee
Lansing, MI 48919
**Subject(s):** Daily Newspapers
**Circ:** (Mon.-Sat.)★70,725
(Sun.)★90,502

**Journal Star** (9213)
The Peoria Journal Star Inc.
1 News Plz.
Peoria, IL 61643
Phone: (309)686-3000
Fax: (309)686-3296
**Subject(s):** Daily Newspapers
**Circ:** (Mon.-Fri.)★68,089
(Sat.)★76,879
(Sun.)★87,188

**The Repository** (24241)
500 Market Ave. S
Canton, OH 44702-2112
Phone: (216)454-5611
Fax: (216)454-5610
**Subject(s):** Daily Newspapers
**Circ:** (Mon.-Sat.)★65,598
(Sun.)★86,572

**Our Sunday Visitor** (9808)
Our Sunday Visitor Publishing
200 Noll Plz.
Huntington, IN 46750
Phone: (260)356-8400
Fax: (260)356-8472

**Subject(s):** Religious Publications
**Circ:** 85,000

**Flashes Kalamazoo Shopper** (15468)
Flashes Publishers
7837 Sprinkle Rd.
Kalamazoo, MI 49002
Phone: (616)324-1000
Fax: (616)324-1005
**Subject(s):** Shopping Guides
**Circ:** (Free)84,950

**Franklin/Hales Corners Enterprise** (33032)
Community Newspaper
15700 W. Cleveland Ave.
New Berlin, WI 53151
Phone: (262)798-1234
Fax: (262)798-1222
**Subject(s):** Shopping Guides
**Circ:** (Free)‡84,490

**Greenfield/Greendale Enterprise** (33028)
Community Newspaper
15700 W. Cleveland Ave.
New Berlin, WI 53151
Phone: (262)798-1234
Fax: (262)798-1222
**Subject(s):** Shopping Guides
**Circ:** (Free)‡84,490

**New Berlin Enterprise** (33411)
Community Newspaper
15700 W. Cleveland Ave.
New Berlin, WI 53151
Phone: (262)798-1234
Fax: (262)798-1222
**Subject(s):** Shopping Guides
**Circ:** (Free)‡84,490

**Chicago Metro News** (8133)
3437 S Indiana Ave.
Chicago, IL 60616-3840
**Subject(s):** Paid Community Newspapers; Black Publications
**Circ:** (Free)500
(Paid)84,000

**Exito!** (8192)
Chicago Tribune
820 N. Orleans St., Ste. 400
Chicago, IL 60610-3051
Phone: (312)654-3009
Fax: (312)654-3029
**Subject(s):** Paid Community Newspapers
**Circ:** (Free)83,497

**Green Bay Press-Gazette** (33007)
PO Box 23430
Green Bay, WI 54305-3430
**Subject(s):** Daily Newspapers
**Circ:** (Mon.-Fri.)★57,662
(Sat.)★68,944
(Sun.)★83,395

**Coin World** (25039)
Amos Press Inc.
PO Box 150
Sidney, OH 45365-0150
Phone: (937)498-0812
Fax: (800)673-8311
**Subject(s):** Collecting
**Circ:** (Non-paid)‡1,000
(Paid)‡83,051

**South Bend Tribune** (10164)
225 W. Colfax Ave.
South Bend, IN 46626
Phone: (574)235-6161
Fax: (574)236-1765
**Subject(s):** Daily Newspapers
**Circ:** (Mon.-Sat.)‡63,441
(Sun.)‡82,748

**Market Journal** (8754)
PO Box 410
Grayslake, IL 60030-0410
Phone: (847)223-3280
Fax: (847)223-9390
**Subject(s):** Shopping Guides
**Circ:** (Free)82,387

**Oakland Press** (15686)
Oakland Press Co.
48 W Huron St., No. 436009
PO Box 9
Pontiac, MI 48342-2101
Phone: (248)332-8181
Fax: (248)332-8284
**Subject(s):** Daily Newspapers
**Circ:** (Mon.-Sat.)★66,140
(Thurs.)★78,213
(Sun.)★80,737

**FarmWeek** (7914)
Illinois Agricultural Association
1701 Towanda Ave.
Bloomington, IL 61701
Phone: (309)557-2111
Fax: (800)557-2559
**Subject(s):** Farm Newspapers
**Circ:** (Paid)80,608

**The News-Herald** (15797)
Heritage Newspapers Inc.
1 Heritage Pl., Ste. 100
Southgate, MI 48195
Phone: (734)246-0810
Fax: (734)284-2117
**Subject(s):** Paid Community Newspapers
**Circ:** (Sun.)♦56,989
(Wed.)♦80,000

**The Cincinnati Post** (24300)
E.W. Scripps Co.
125 E. Court St.
Cincinnati, OH 45202
Phone: (513)352-2000
Fax: (513)621-3962
**Subject(s):** Daily Newspapers
**Circ:** (Mon.-Fri.)55,807
(Sat.)79,903

**Kalamazoo Flashes** (14975)
Flashes Publishers Inc.
595 Jenner Dr.
Allegan, MI 49010
Phone: (269)673-1602
Fax: (269)673-6768
**Subject(s):** Shopping Guides
**Circ:** (Combined)79,850

**Minnesota Educator** (16596)
Education Minnesota
41 Sherburne Ave.
Saint Paul, MN 55103
Phone: (651)227-9541
Fax: (651)292-4802
**Subject(s):** Education
**Circ:** ‡78,000

**Rockford Register Star** (9305)
Gannett Company Inc.
99 E. State St.
Rockford, IL 61104
Phone: (815)987-1200
Fax: (800)383-7827
**Subject(s):** Daily Newspapers
**Circ:** (Mon.-Sat.)★64,518
(Sun.)★77,183

**The Council Chronicle** (9470)
National Council of Teachers of English
1111 W. Kenyon Rd.
Urbana, IL 61801-1096
Phone: (217)328-3870
Fax: (217)328-9645
**Subject(s):** Education
**Circ:** (Paid)77,000

**The Catholic New World** (8118)
New World Publications
721 N LaSalle St.
Chicago, IL 60610
Phone: (312)655-7777
Fax: (312)642-7350
**Subject(s):** Religious Publications
**Circ:** ‡75,000

**The Post-Crescent** (32812)
PO Box 59
Appleton, WI 54912
Phone: (920)733-4411
Fax: (920)733-1945

Circulation: ★ = ABC; △ = BPA; ♦ = CAC; • = CCAB; ◻ = VAC; ⊕ = PO Statement; ‡ = Publisher's Report; Boldface figures = sworn; Light figures = estimated.

**Subject(s):** Daily Newspapers

**Circ:** (Mon.-Fri.)56,218
(Sat.)67,587
(Sun.)74,804

**Post-Tribune (10020)**
Post-Tribune Publishing
1433 E. 83rd Ave.
Merrillville, IN 46410-6307
Phone: (219)648-3000
**Subject(s):** Daily Newspapers

**Circ:** (Mon.-Sat.)★65,621
(Sun.)★73,795

**Kalamazoo Gazette (15474)**
Booth Newspapers
401 S. Burdick St.
Kalamazoo, MI 49007
Phone: (616)345-3511
Fax: (616)388-8447
**Subject(s):** Daily Newspapers

**Circ:** (Mon.-Fri.)★56,276
(Sat.)★62,350
(Sun.)★72,945

**The Criterion (9843)**
1400 N. Meridian St.
Indianapolis, IN 46202
Phone: (317)236-1570
Fax: (317)236-1434
**Subject(s):** Religious Publications; Paid Community Newspapers

**Circ:** (Combined)72,500

**This Week Life & Times (15995)**
12190 County Rd. 11
Burnsville, MN 55337
Phone: (952)894-1111
Fax: (952)846-2010
**Subject(s):** Free Newspapers

**Circ:** (Free)72,494

**Broward Jewish Journal (8110)**
Tribune Co.
435 N Michigan Ave.
Chicago, IL 60611
Phone: (312)222-9100
Fax: (312)222-4674
**Subject(s):** Jewish Publications; Free Newspapers

**Circ:** (Free)72,000

**Kenosha News (33115)**
Division of United Communications Corp.
5800 7th Ave.
Lower Level
Kenosha, WI 53140
Phone: (262)657-1000
Fax: (262)656-1255
**Subject(s):** Shopping Guides

**Circ:** (Free)‡70,000

**New City (8351)**
New City Communications Inc.
770 N. Halsted, Ste. 306
Chicago, IL 60622
Phone: (312)243-8786
Fax: (312)243-8802
**Subject(s):** Free Newspapers

**Circ:** (Paid)40
(Free)70,000

**The Review (33474)**
The Plymouth Review
PO Box 317, 113 E Mill St.
Plymouth, WI 53073
Phone: (920)893-6411
Fax: (920)893-5505
**Subject(s):** Paid Community Newspapers

**Circ:** ‡69,000

**The Macomb Daily (15607)**
100 Macomb Daily Dr.
PO Box 707
Mount Clemens, MI 48046
Phone: (810)469-4510
Fax: (810)469-2892
**Subject(s):** Daily Newspapers

**Circ:** (Mon.-Sat.)★42,463
(Thurs.)★54,342
(Sun.)★68,860

**Monday Green Sheet (15435)**
Hometown Newspapers
323 E Grand River
PO Box 230
Howell, MI 48843
Phone: (517)548-2000
Fax: (248)437-9460
**Subject(s):** Shopping Guides

**Circ:** (Non-paid)66,174

**Catholic Herald (33295)**
Milwaukee Catholic Press Apostolate Inc.
3501 S Lake Dr.
PO Box 070913
Milwaukee, WI 53207-0913
Phone: (414)769-3500
Fax: (414)769-3468
**Subject(s):** Religious Publications

**Circ:** (Free)‡2,012
(Paid)‡65,813

**Currents (24269)**
Chagrin Valley Publishing Co.
525 E Wash St.
PO Box 150
Chagrin Falls, OH 44022
Phone: (440)247-5335
Fax: (440)247-5615
**Subject(s):** Lifestyle; Art; Entertainment

**Circ:** 65,000

**State Journal-Register (9408)**
1 Copley Plz.
PO Box 219
Springfield, IL 62701-1927
Phone: (217)788-1300
Fax: (217)788-1372
**Subject(s):** Daily Newspapers

**Circ:** (Mon.-Sat.)★55,334
(Sun.)★64,548

**Heritage Sunday (15796)**
Heritage Newspapers Inc.
1 Heritage Pl., Ste. 100
Southgate, MI 48195
Phone: (734)246-0810
Fax: (734)284-2117
**Subject(s):** Paid Community Newspapers

**Circ:** (Non-paid)♦16,069
(Paid)♦64,432

**The Ann Arbor News (14996)**
340 E Huron St.
PO Box 1147
Ann Arbor, MI 48106-1147
Phone: (734)994-6989
Fax: (734)994-6702
**Subject(s):** Daily Newspapers

**Circ:** (Mon.-Sat.)★50,815
(Sun.)★64,212

**The Suburban News (15798)**
Heritage Newspapers Inc.
1 Heritage Dr., Ste. 100
Southgate, MI 48195-3407
Phone: (734)246-0800
**Subject(s):** Free Newspapers

**Circ:** (Paid)693
(Non-paid)63,965

**Belleville News-Democrat (7890)**
Knight-Ridder Inc.
120 S. Illinois St.
PO Box 427
Belleville, IL 62222-0427
Phone: (618)234-1000
Fax: (618)234-9597
**Subject(s):** Daily Newspapers

**Circ:** (Mon.-Sat.)★53,694
(Sun.)★63,906

**Anoka County Shopper (16025)**
4101 Coon Rapids Blvd.
PO Box 99
Coon Rapids, MN 55433
Phone: (763)421-4444
Fax: (763)421-4315
**Subject(s):** Shopping Guides

**Circ:** (Free)62,553

**Gun List (33082)**
Krause Publications Inc.
700 E. State St.
Iola, WI 54990-0001
Phone: (715)445-2214

Fax: (715)445-4087
**Subject(s):** Firearms

**Circ:** (Paid)62,514

**The Voice News (15631)**
Advisor & Source Newspapers
51180 Bedford St.
PO Box 760
New Baltimore, MI 48047
Phone: (586)716-8100
Fax: (586)716-8918
**Subject(s):** Free Newspapers

**Circ:** (Free)62,024

**Shepherd Express (33335)**
Alternative Publications Inc.
413 N 2nd St., No. 150
Milwaukee, WI 53203-3110
Phone: (414)276-2222
Fax: (414)276-3312
**Subject(s):** Free Newspapers

**Circ:** (Paid)76
(Free)60,845

**Shopper (32839)**
Helmer Printing Inc.
N6402 790th St.
PO Box 40
Beldenville, WI 54003
Phone: (715)273-4601
Fax: (715)273-4769
**Subject(s):** Shopping Guides

**Circ:** (Paid)62
(Free)60,727

**Old Cars Weekly (33090)**
Krause Publications Inc.
700 E. State St.
Iola, WI 54990-0001
Phone: (715)445-2214
Fax: (715)445-4087
**Subject(s):** Automotive (Consumer)

**Circ:** (Paid)‡60,514

**Warren Weekly (15882)**
C & G Publishing
13650 E Eleven Mile Rd.
Warren, MI 48089
Phone: (586)498-8000
Fax: (586)498-9631
**Subject(s):** Paid Community Newspapers

**Circ:** (Non-paid)60,514

**Isthmus (33189)**
Isthmus Publishing
101 King St.
Madison, WI 53703
Phone: (608)251-5627
Fax: (608)251-4732
**Subject(s):** Free Newspapers

**Circ:** (Paid)519
(Free)60,508

**Milwaukee Labor Press, AFL-CIO (33318)**
Milwaukee County Labor Council AFL-CIO
633 S Hawley Rd.
Milwaukee, WI 53214
Phone: (414)771-7070
Fax: (414)771-0509
**Subject(s):** Labor

**Circ:** (Free)‡642
(Paid)‡60,000

**Minneapolis Labor Review (16314)**
MPLS Central Labor Union Council
312 Central Ave., Ste. 54d2
Minneapolis, MN 55414-1077
Phone: (612)379-4725
Fax: (612)379-1307
**Subject(s):** Labor

**Circ:** ‡60,000

**Scotsman (15999)**
ECM Group
234 S Main St.
PO Box 352
Cambridge, MN 55008-0352
Phone: (763)689-1981
Fax: (763)689-4372
**Subject(s):** Shopping Guides

**Circ:** (Paid)‡100
(Free)‡60,000

Gale Directory of Publications & Broadcast Media/140th Ed.  Great Lakes States

**Newspaper Index**

**The News-Herald (25177)**
7085 Mentor Ave.
Willoughby, OH 44094
Phone: (440)951-0000
Fax: (440)975-2293
**Subject(s):** Daily Newspapers

**Circ:** (Mon.-Sat.)48,033
(Sun.)59,506

**Pennysaver (33492)**
The Journal Times
PO Box 1735
Racine, WI 53401
Phone: (414)634-3111
Fax: (414)631-1705
**Subject(s):** Shopping Guides

**Circ:** (Free)‡59,321

**Daily Southtown (9449)**
Midwest Suburban Publishing
6901 W 159th St.
Tinley Park, IL 60477-1604
Phone: (708)633-6880
Fax: (708)633-6999
**Subject(s):** Daily Newspapers

**Circ:** (Sat.)41,841
(Mon.-Fri.)52,567
(Sun.)58,678

**Chicago Crusader (8125)**
Crusader Newspapers
6429 S Martin Luther King Dr.
Chicago, IL 60637
Phone: (773)752-2500
Fax: (773)752-2817
**Subject(s):** Paid Community Newspapers; Black Publications

**Circ:** (Paid)‡57,000

**Aslip/Crestwood/Blue Island (7921)**
Star Newspapers
6901 W. 159th St.
Tinley Park, IL 60477
Phone: (708)802-8800
Fax: (708)802-8088
**Subject(s):** Paid Community Newspapers

**Circ:** (Thurs.)54,309
(Sun.)56,355

**Burnham/Calumet City Star (7939)**
Star Newspapers
6901 W. 159th St.
Tinley Park, IL 60477
Phone: (708)802-8800
Fax: (708)802-8088
**Subject(s):** Paid Community Newspapers

**Circ:** (Thurs.)54,209
(Sun.)56,355

**Chicago Heights Area (9448)**
Star Newspapers
6901 W. 159th St.
Tinley Park, IL 60477
Phone: (708)802-8800
Fax: (708)802-8088
**Subject(s):** Paid Community Newspapers

**Circ:** (Thurs.)54,209
(Sun.)56,355

**Crete/University Park (9460)**
Star Newspapers
6901 W. 159th St.
Tinley Park, IL 60477
Phone: (708)802-8800
Fax: (708)802-8088
**Subject(s):** Paid Community Newspapers

**Circ:** (Thurs.)54,209
(Sun.)56,355

**Frankfort/Mokena (8981)**
Star Newspapers
6901 W. 159th St.
Tinley Park, IL 60477
Phone: (708)802-8800
Fax: (708)802-8088
**Subject(s):** Paid Community Newspapers

**Circ:** (Thurs.)54,209
(Sun.)56,355

**Harvey/Markham (8771)**
Star Newspapers
6901 W. 159th St.
Tinley Park, IL 60477
Phone: (708)802-8800
Fax: (708)802-8088
**Subject(s):** Paid Community Newspapers

**Circ:** (Thurs.)54,209
(Sun.)56,355

**Hazel Crest Country Club Hills (8517)**
Star Newspapers
6901 W. 159th St.
Tinley Park, IL 60477
Phone: (708)802-8800
Fax: (708)802-8088
**Subject(s):** Paid Community Newspapers

**Circ:** (Thurs.)54,209
(Sun.)56,355

**Homer Glenlemont.Lockport (8798)**
Star Newspapers
6901 W. 159th St.
Tinley Park, IL 60477
Phone: (708)802-8800
Fax: (708)802-8088
**Subject(s):** Paid Community Newspapers

**Circ:** (Thurs.)54,209
(Sun.)56,355

**Homewood/Flossmoor (8799)**
Star Newspapers
6901 W. 159th St.
Tinley Park, IL 60477
Phone: (708)802-8800
Fax: (708)802-8088
**Subject(s):** Paid Community Newspapers

**Circ:** (Thurs.)54,209
(Sun.)56,355

**Lansing/Lynwood (8857)**
Star Newspapers
6901 W. 159th St.
Tinley Park, IL 60477
Phone: (708)802-8800
Fax: (708)802-8088
**Subject(s):** Paid Community Newspapers

**Circ:** (Thurs.)54,209
(Sun.)56,355

**Matteson/Richton (8943)**
Star Newspapers
6901 W. 159th St.
Tinley Park, IL 60477
Phone: (708)802-8800
Fax: (708)802-8088
**Subject(s):** Paid Community Newspapers

**Circ:** (Thurs.)54,209
(Sun.)56,355

**Oak Forest/Midlothian Star (9163)**
Star Newspapers
6901 W. 159th St.
Tinley Park, IL 60477
Phone: (708)802-8800
Fax: (708)802-8088
**Subject(s):** Paid Community Newspapers

**Circ:** (Thurs.)54,209
(Sun.)56,355

**Oak Lawn (9164)**
Star Newspapers
6901 W. 159th St.
Tinley Park, IL 60477
Phone: (708)802-8800
Fax: (708)802-8088
**Subject(s):** Paid Community Newspapers

**Circ:** (Thurs.)52,209
(Sun.)56,355

**Orland Park Star (9185)**
Star Newspapers
6901 W. 159th St.
Tinley Park, IL 60477
Phone: (708)802-8800
Fax: (708)802-8088
**Subject(s):** Paid Community Newspapers

**Circ:** (Thurs.)54,209
(Sun.)56,355

**South Holland/Dolton (9383)**
Star Newspapers
6901 W. 159th St.
Tinley Park, IL 60477
Phone: (708)802-8800
Fax: (708)802-8088
**Subject(s):** Paid Community Newspapers

**Circ:** (Thurs.)54,209
(Sun.)56,355

**Tinley Park (9453)**
Star Newspapers
6901 W. 159th St.
Tinley Park, IL 60477
Phone: (708)802-8800
Fax: (708)802-8088
**Subject(s):** Paid Community Newspapers

**Circ:** (Thurs.)54,209
(Sun.)56,355

**Worth/Chicago Ridge (9454)**
Star Newspapers
6901 W. 159th St.
Tinley Park, IL 60477
Phone: (708)802-8800
Fax: (708)802-8088
**Subject(s):** Paid Community Newspapers

**Circ:** (Thurs.)54,209
(Sun.)56,355

**Palos Area (9451)**
Star Newspapers
6901 W. 159th St.
Tinley Park, IL 60477
Phone: (708)802-8800
Fax: (708)802-8088
**Subject(s):** Paid Community Newspapers

**Circ:** (Thurs.)54,209
(Sun.)56,255

**Park Forest (9198)**
Star Newspapers
6901 W. 159th St.
Tinley Park, IL 60477
Phone: (708)802-8800
Fax: (708)802-8088
**Subject(s):** Paid Community Newspapers

**Circ:** (Thurs.)54,209
(Sun.)56,255

**The Saginaw News (15723)**
203 S. Washington Ave.
Saginaw, MI 48607
**Subject(s):** Daily Newspapers

**Circ:** (Mon.-Sat.)★46,439
(Sun.)★55,690

**Tradin' Times (25025)**
Trader Publishing Co.
20200 Detroit Rd.
Rocky River, OH 44116-2422
Phone: (440)333-7355
**Subject(s):** Shopping Guides

**Circ:** (Free)55,043

**phenomeNEWS (15780)**
18444 W. 10 Mile, Ste. 105
Southfield, MI 48075
Phone: (248)569-3888
Fax: (248)569-4512
**Subject(s):** Free Newspapers; New Age

**Circ:** (Free)55,000

**Pro Football Weekly (9286)**
302 Saunders Rd., No. 100
Riverwoods, IL 60015-3897
Phone: (847)940-1100
Fax: (847)940-1108
**Subject(s):** (Football)

**Circ:** (Non-paid)‡342
(Paid)‡55,000

**The Bargain Bulletin (32806)**
306 W Washington St.
Appleton, WI 54912
Phone: (920)733-3460
Fax: (920)996-7233
**Subject(s):** Shopping Guides

**Circ:** (Wed.)54,152

**The Pantagraph (7915)**
301 W. Washington St.
PO Box 2907
Bloomington, IL 61702-2907
Phone: (309)829-9000
Fax: (309)829-8497
**Subject(s):** Daily Newspapers

**Circ:** (Mon.-Sat.)47,919
(Sun.)52,247

**Stateline Shopping News (32845)**
Community Shoppers Inc.
1550 Huebbe Pkwy.
Beloit, WI 53511
Phone: (608)365-1663

Circulation: ★ = ABC; △ = BPA; ♦ = CAC; ◆ = CCAB; ▫ = VAC; ⊕ = PO Statement; ‡ = Publisher's Report; Boldface figures = sworn; Light figures = estimated.

3579

Fax: (608)365-7045
**Subject(s):** Shopping Guides
**Circ:** (Wed.)34,585
(Sun.)51,868

**Battle Creek Shopper News  (15043)**
J-Ad Corp.
1361 E. Columbia Ave.
Battle Creek, MI 49014
Phone: (269)965-3955
Fax: (269)968-8586
**Subject(s):** Free Newspapers
**Circ:** (Free)‡51,855

**Michigan Citizen  (15402)**
New Day Publishing Enterprises
211 Glendale, Ste. 216
Highland Park, MI 48203
Phone: (313)869-0033
Fax: (313)869-0430
**Subject(s):** Black Publications; Paid Community Newspapers
**Circ:** (Free)918
(Paid)51,442

**The Muskegon Chronicle & The Sunday Chronicle  (15621)**
981 3rd St.
PO Box 59
Muskegon, MI 49443-0059
Phone: (231)722-3161
**Subject(s):** Daily Newspapers
**Circ:** (Mon.-Sat.)★45,138
(Sun.)★50,470

**Columbus Alive  (24539)**
Columbus Alive Inc.
1079 N. High St.
Columbus, OH 43201-2439
Phone: (614)221-2449
Fax: (614)221-2456
**Subject(s):** Free Newspapers
**Circ:** (Combined)50,000

**Villager  (16616)**
Villager Communications Inc.
757 Snelling Ave. S.
Saint Paul, MN 55116-2296
Phone: (651)699-1462
Fax: (651)699-6501
**Subject(s):** Free Newspapers
**Circ:** (Paid)‡400
(Free)‡49,600

**Algonquin Countryside  (7828)**
Pioneer Press Newspapers
c/o Andrea Brown
1485 Merchant Dr.
Algonquin, IL 60102-5917
Phone: (847)458-5300
Fax: (847)458-5325
**Subject(s):** Paid Community Newspapers
**Circ:** (Combined)49,572

**Arlington Heights Post  (7849)**
Pioneer Press Newspapers
c/o MArc Alberts
291 N. Dunton Ave.
Arlington Heights, IL 60004
Phone: (847)797-5100
Fax: (847)797-5151
**Subject(s):** Paid Community Newspapers
**Circ:** (Combined)49,572

**Buffalo Grove Countryside  (7933)**
Pioneer Press Newspapers
c/o Marc Alberts
291 N. Dunton Ave.
Arlington Heights, IL 60004
Phone: (847)797-5100
Fax: (847)797-5151
**Subject(s):** Free Newspapers
**Circ:** (Combined)49,572

**Cary-Grove Countryside  (7994)**
Pioneer Press Newspapers
c/o Andrea Brown
1485 Merchant Dr.
Algonquin, IL 60102
Phone: (847)458-5300
Fax: (847)458-5325
**Subject(s):** Paid Community Newspapers
**Circ:** (Combined)49,572

**Elk Grove Times  (8638)**
Pioneer Press Newspapers
c/o Marc Alberts
291 N. Dunton Ave.
Arlington Heights, IL 60004
Phone: (847)797-5100
Fax: (847)797-5151
**Subject(s):** Paid Community Newspapers
**Circ:** (Combined)49,572

**Lake Zurich Courier  (7830)**
Pioneer Press Newspapers
c/o Andrea Brown
1485 Merchant Dr.
Algonquin, IL 60102
Phone: (847)458-5300
Fax: (847)458-5325
**Subject(s):** Paid Community Newspapers
**Circ:** (Combined)49,572

**Palatine Countryside  (9191)**
Pioneer Press Newspapers
c/o Marc Alberts
291 N. Dunton Ave.
Arlington Heights, IL 60004
Phone: (847)797-5100
Fax: (847)797-5151
**Subject(s):** Paid Community Newspapers
**Circ:** (Combined)49,572

**Rolling Meadows Review  (9322)**
Pioneer Press Newspapers
c/o Marc Alberts
291 N. Dunton Ave.
Arlington Heights, IL 60004
Phone: (847)797-5100
Fax: (847)797-5151
**Subject(s):** Paid Community Newspapers
**Circ:** (Combined)49,572

**Schaumburg Review  (9359)**
Pioneer Press Newspapers
c/o Marc Alberts
291 N. Dunton Ave.
Arlington Heights, IL 60004
Phone: (847)797-5100
Fax: (847)797-5151
**Subject(s):** Paid Community Newspapers
**Circ:** (Combined)49,572

**Wheeling Countryside  (9531)**
Pioneer Press Newspapers
c/o Marc Alberts
291 N. Dunton Ave.
Arlington Heights, IL 60004
Phone: (847)797-5100
Fax: (847)797-5151
**Subject(s):** Paid Community Newspapers
**Circ:** (Combined)49,572

**Inside  (8239)**
Inside Publications
4159 N. Western Ave.
Chicago, IL 60618
Phone: (773)313-2000
**Subject(s):** Free Newspapers
**Circ:** (Free)‡49,500

**Eastside Messenger  (24549)**
Columbus Messenger Co.
3378 Sullivant Ave.
Columbus, OH 43204-1887
Phone: (614)272-5422
Fax: (614)272-0684
**Subject(s):** Free Newspapers
**Circ:** (Non-paid)49,491

**The News-Gazette  (8023)**
News-Gazette Inc.
15 Main St.
PO Box 677
Champaign, IL 61824-0677
Phone: (217)351-5266
Fax: (217)351-5291
**Subject(s):** Daily Newspapers
**Circ:** (Mon.-Fri.)43,149
(Sat.)45,625
(Sun.)49,180

**The Sunday Post (Washington County)  (33648)**
PO Box 478
100 S. 6th Ave.
West Bend, WI 53095
Phone: (262)306-5000
Fax: (262)334-6252

**Subject(s):** Shopping Guides
**Circ:** (Free)‡48,100

**Michigan Chronicle  (15190)**
Real Times Inc.
479 Ledyard St.
Detroit, MI 48201
Phone: (313)963-5522
Fax: (313)963-8788
**Subject(s):** Paid Community Newspapers; Black Publications
**Circ:** ‡47,428

**The Monitor  (15191)**
Downtown Detroit Monitor Inc.
33490 Groesbeck
Fraser, MI 48026
Phone: (586)296-6007
Fax: (586)296-6072
**Subject(s):** Free Newspapers
**Circ:** (Free)‡47,000

**Shopping News  (16550)**
Gannett Company Inc.
3413 3rd St. N
Saint Cloud, MN 56303-0768
Phone: (320)252-4400
Fax: (320)252-1031
**Subject(s):** Shopping Guides
**Circ:** (Combined)47,000

**Brooklyn Center Sun-Post  (15987)**
Minnesota Sun Publications
10917 Valley View Rd.
Eden Prairie, MN 55344
Phone: (952)829-0797
Fax: (952)392-6868
**Subject(s):** Free Newspapers
**Circ:** (Paid)♦2,167
(Non-paid)♦46,929

**Post-Bulletin  (16517)**
18 1st Ave. SE
PO Box 6118
Rochester, MN 55903-6118
Phone: (507)285-7600
Fax: (507)281-7436
**Subject(s):** Daily Newspapers
**Circ:** (Mon.-Fri.)★43,351
(Sat.)★46,688

**Action Advertiser  (32949)**
Action Publications
N6637 Rolling Meadows Dr.
Fond du Lac, WI 54937
Phone: (920)922-8640
Fax: (920)922-0125
**Subject(s):** Shopping Guides; Free Newspapers
**Circ:** (Wed.)34,853
(Sun.)46,659

**Skyway News  (16342)**
Skyway Publications Inc.
1115 Hennipen Ave. S.
Minneapolis, MN 55403
Phone: (612)825-9205
Fax: (612)825-0929
**Subject(s):** Free Newspapers
**Circ:** (Free)44,546

**St. Cloud Visitor  (16549)**
305 7th Ave. N
PO Box 1068
Saint Cloud, MN 56302
Phone: (320)251-3022
Fax: (320)251-0424
**Subject(s):** Religious Publications
**Circ:** (Non-paid)185
(Paid)44,500

**Herald-Times  (9589)**
Herald-Times Inc.
1900 S. Walnut St.
PO Box 909
Bloomington, IN 47402
Phone: (812)332-4401
Fax: (812)331-4285
**Subject(s):** Daily Newspapers
**Circ:** (Mon.-Sat.)★27,526
(Sun.)★44,442

**The Bay City Times  (15052)**
311 5th St.
Bay City, MI 48708
Phone: (989)895-8551
Fax: (989)895-5910

**Subject(s):** Daily Newspapers

Circ: (Mon.-Sat.)★34,581
(Sun.)★44,407

**Back of the Yards Journal (8093)**
Back of the Yards Journal Inc.
1751 West 47th Street
Chicago, IL 60609
Phone: (773)927-7200
Fax: (773)927-7940
**Subject(s):** Paid Community Newspapers; Spanish

Circ: (Combined)44,000

**The Advisor (15254)**
Advisor & Source Newspapers
48075 Van Dyke Ave.
Shelby Township, MI 48317
Phone: (586)731-1000
Fax: (586)731-8172
**Subject(s):** Free Newspapers

Circ: (Free)‡43,822

**Duluth Budgeteer News (16055)**
222 W. Superior St.
Duluth, MN 55802
Phone: (218)723-1207
Fax: (218)727-7348
**Subject(s):** Free Newspapers

Circ: (Paid)260
(Non-paid)43,785

**Journal and Courier (9976)**
Federated Publications Inc.
217 N. 6th St.
Lafayette, IN 47901-1448
Phone: (317)423-5511
Fax: (317)742-5633
**Subject(s):** Daily Newspapers

Circ: (Mon.-Sat.)37,370
(Sun.)43,641

**West Side Leader (24110)**
Leader Publications
3075 Smith Rd., Ste. 204
Akron, OH 44333
Phone: (330)665-0909
Fax: (330)665-0908
**Subject(s):** Paid Community Newspapers

Circ: (Combined)43,600

**Central Shopper (24837)**
Ogden Newspapers
308 W Maple St.
Lisbon, OH 44432
Phone: (330)424-9541
Fax: (330)424-0048
**Subject(s):** Shopping Guides

Circ: (Free)‡43,588

**The Lima News (24829)**
3515 Elida Rd.
Lima, OH 45807
Phone: (419)223-1010
Fax: (419)229-0426
**Subject(s):** Daily Newspapers

Circ: (Mon.-Sat.)35,266
(Sun.)43,525

**The Advisor (15605)**
Advisor & Source Newspapers
48075 Van Dyke Ave.
Shelby Township, MI 48317
Phone: (586)731-1000
Fax: (586)731-8172
**Subject(s):** Free Newspapers

Circ: (Non-paid)43,313

**Call and Post (24382)**
11800 Shaker Blvd.
Box 6237
Cleveland, OH 44120
Phone: (216)791-7600
Fax: (216)451-0404
**Subject(s):** Paid Community Newspapers; Black Publications

Circ: ‡43,283

**The Trading Post (25023)**
Trogdon Publishing Inc.
12555 Benner Rd.
Rittman, OH 44270
Phone: (330)925-3040
Fax: (330)927-6890
**Subject(s):** Shopping Guides

Circ: (Non-paid)43,273

**Evanston Review (8670)**
Pioneer Press Newspapers
c/o Gary Taylor
1601 Sherman Ave., Ste. 500
Evanston, IL 60201
Phone: (847)866-6501
Fax: (847)866-0965
**Subject(s):** Paid Community Newspapers

Circ: (Combined)43,110

**Glencoe News (8736)**
Pioneer Press Newspapers
c/o Brett Johnson
3701 W. Lake Ave.
Glenview, IL 60026
Phone: (847)486-9200
Fax: (847)486-7451
**Subject(s):** Paid Community Newspapers

Circ: (Combined)43,110

**Glenview Announcements (8737)**
Pioneer Press Newspapers
c/o Brett Johnson
3701 W. Lake Ave.
Glenview, IL 60025
Phone: (847)486-9200
Fax: (847)486-7451
**Subject(s):** Paid Community Newspapers

Circ: (Combined)43,110

**Morton Grove Champion Review (9000)**
Pioneer Press Newspapers
c/o Gary Taylor
1601 Sherman Ave., Ste. 500
Evanston, IL 60201
Phone: (847)866-6501
Fax: (847)866-0965
**Subject(s):** Paid Community Newspapers

Circ: (Combined)43,110

**Northbrook Star (8741)**
Pioneer Press Newspapers
c/o Brett Johnson
3701 W. Lake Ave.
Glenview, IL 60026
Phone: (847)486-9200
Fax: (847)486-7451
**Subject(s):** Paid Community Newspapers

Circ: (Combined)43,110

**Skokie Review (9379)**
Pioneer Press Newspapers
Gary Taylor
1601 Sherman Ave., Ste. 500
Evanston, IL 60201
Phone: (847)866-6501
Fax: (847)866-0965
**Subject(s):** Paid Community Newspapers

Circ: (Combined)43,110

**Wilmette Life (8743)**
Pioneer Press Newspapers
c/o Brett Johnson
3701 W. Lake Ave.
Glenview, IL 60026
Phone: (847)486-9200
Fax: (847)486-7451
**Subject(s):** Paid Community Newspapers

Circ: (Combined)43,110

**Winnetka Talk (9535)**
Pioneer Press Newspapers
c/o Brett Johnson
3701 W. Lake Ave.
Glenview, IL 60026
Phone: (847)486-9200
Fax: (847)486-7451
**Subject(s):** Paid Community Newspapers

Circ: (Combined)43,110

**Times Herald (15687)**
The Times Herald Co.
911 Military St.
Port Huron, MI 48060
Phone: (810)985-7171
Fax: (810)989-6294
**Subject(s):** Daily Newspapers

Circ: (Mon.-Sat.)30,987
(Sun.)43,096

**Journal (8916)**
Rock Valley Publishing
11512 N 2nd St.
Machesney Park, IL 61115
Phone: (815)877-4044

Fax: (815)654-4857
**Subject(s):** Shopping Guides

Circ: (Paid)43,000

**Crain's Chicago Business (8163)**
Crain Communications Inc.
360 N. Michigan Ave.
Chicago, IL 60601-3806
Phone: (312)649-5411
Fax: (312)280-3150
**Subject(s):** Banking, Finance, and Investments; Business

Circ: (Non-paid)★7,778
(Paid)★42,912

**The Joliet Herald News (8830)**
Sun Publications
300 Caterpillar Dr.
Joliet, IL 60436
Phone: (815)729-6161
**Subject(s):** Daily Newspapers

Circ: (Mon.-Sat.)37,462
(Sun.)42,902

**Today's Advantage (7835)**
192A Open Square Mall Dr
PO Box 8003
Alton, IL 62002
Phone: (618)463-0612
Fax: (618)463-0733
**Subject(s):** Free Newspapers

Circ: (Free)‡42,216

**La Crosse Tribune (33123)**
Lee Enterprises Inc.
401 N. 3rd St.
La Crosse, WI 54601-3281
Phone: (608)782-9723
Fax: (800)262-0420
**Subject(s):** Daily Newspapers

Circ: (Mon.-Fri.)★31,852
(Sat.)★39,081
(Sun.)★41,432

**Holly Herald (15431)**
Hometown Communication Network
PO Box 230
Howell, MI 48844-0230
Phone: (734)665-4081
Fax: (248)634-8233
**Subject(s):** Paid Community Newspapers

Circ: (Combined)41,300

**Herald-News (8829)**
Copley Newspapers/Copley Press
300 Caterpillar Dr.
Joliet, IL 60436
Phone: (815)729-6161
Fax: (815)729-6063
**Subject(s):** Daily Newspapers

Circ: (Mon.-Sat.)37,723
(Sun.)41,286

**The Dispatch and the Rock Island Argus (8983)**
Moline Dispatch Publishing Co.
1720 5th Ave.
Moline, IL 61265
Phone: (309)764-4344
Fax: (309)797-0311
**Subject(s):** Daily Newspapers

Circ: (Sun.)34,144
(Mon.-Sat.)‡41,203

**Herald & Review (8536)**
Herald & Review Newspapers
601 E. William St.
Decatur, IL 62525
Phone: (217)429-5151
**Subject(s):** Daily Newspapers

Circ: (Mon.-Fri.)33,688
(Sat.)40,277
(Sun.)41,052

**News Journal (24857)**
70 W 4th St.
PO Box 25
Mansfield, OH 44903
Phone: (419)522-3311
Fax: (419)522-2672
**Subject(s):** Daily Newspapers

Circ: (Mon.-Sat.)★31,345
(Sun.)★40,836

Circulation: ★ = ABC; △ = BPA; ♦ = CAC; ● = CCAB; ❑ = VAC; ⊕ = PO Statement; ‡ = Publisher's Report; Boldface figures = sworn; Light figures = estimated.

3581

# Great Lakes States

**Wausau Buyers' Guide  (33633)**
ADD Inc.
PO Box 1516
Wausau, WI 54402-1516
Phone: (715)842-5989
Fax: (715)842-5989
**Subject(s):** Shopping Guides

Circ: (Combined)40,624

**Thrifty Nickel Want Ads  (9692)**
1301 E Morgan Ave.
Evansville, IN 47711
Phone: (812)428-8484
Fax: (812)428-8491
**Subject(s):** Shopping Guides

Circ: (Free)‡40,500

**The Calumet Press  (9800)**
8411 Kennedy Ave.
Highland, IN 46322
Phone: (219)838-0717
Fax: (219)838-1338
**Subject(s):** Paid Community Newspapers

Circ: (Free)40,340

**Cincinnati CityBeat  (24296)**
Lightborne Publishing Inc.
23 E. Seventh St., Ste. 617
Cincinnati, OH 45202
Phone: (513)665-4369
Fax: (513)665-4369
**Subject(s):** Paid Community Newspapers

Circ: (Paid)25
 (Free)40,287

**The Northeastern Shopper  (15817)**
129 East North St.
Box 447
Tawas City, MI 48764-0447
Phone: (989)362-6111
Fax: (989)362-7080
**Subject(s):** Shopping Guides

Circ: (Free)‡40,252

**Walworth County Shopper Advertiser & Shopper Sunday  (32909)**
Community Shoppers Inc.
120 N Wright St.
PO Box 367
Delavan, WI 53115-0367
Phone: (262)728-3424
Fax: (262)728-5479
**Subject(s):** Shopping Guides

Circ: (Wed.)40,202
 (Sun.)40,246

**The Shopper Diversified  (16159)**
Liberty Group
Box 267
301 3rd Ave West
Halstad, MN 56548
Phone: (218)456-2133
Fax: (218)456-2567
**Subject(s):** Shopping Guides

Circ: (Free)‡40,220

**The Drummer  (15989)**
Wright County Journal Press
108 Central Ave.
PO Box 159
Buffalo, MN 55313
Phone: (763)682-1221
Fax: (763)682-5458
**Subject(s):** Shopping Guides

Circ: (Non-paid)40,100

**Midwest Foodservice News  (25003)**
Pinnacle Publishing Group
8205-F Estates Pky.
Plain City, OH 43064
Phone: (614)873-1120
Fax: (614)873-1650
**Subject(s):** Hotels, Motels, Restaurants, and Clubs

Circ: (Controlled)‡40,000

**Milwaukee Courier  (33316)**
2431 W Hopkins St.
PO Box 06279
Milwaukee, WI 53206-1298
Phone: (414)449-4860
Fax: (414)449-4872
**Subject(s):** Black Publications; Paid Community Newspapers

Circ: 40,000

**Minnesota Women's Press  (16600)**
Minnesota Women's Press Inc.
771 Raymond Ave.
Saint Paul, MN 55114-1522
Phone: (651)646-3968
Fax: (651)646-2186
**Subject(s):** Women's Interests

Circ: (Paid)500
 (Free)40,000

**People's Weekly World  (8373)**
Long View Publishing Company Inc.
3339 S. Halsetd St.
Chicago, IL 60608
Phone: (773)446-9920
Fax: (773)446-9928
**Subject(s):** Politics; Labor

Circ: (Non-paid)‡1,500
 (Paid)‡40,000

**Southwest Journal  (16345)**
1115 Hennepin Ave. S.
Minneapolis, MN 55403
Phone: (612)825-9205
Fax: (612)825-0929
**Subject(s):** Free Newspapers

Circ: (Non-paid)40,000

**Catholic Exponent  (25207)**
Catholic Exponent Inc.
144 W Wood St.
Youngstown, OH 44503
Phone: (330)744-5251
Fax: (330)744-5252
**Subject(s):** Religious Publications

Circ: 39,500

**Home Magazine  (16239)**
215 Maxfield
PO Box 2
Mankato, MN 56001
Phone: (507)387-7953
Fax: (507)387-4775
**Subject(s):** Shopping Guides

Circ: (Combined)39,316

**The Jackson Citizen Patriot  (15454)**
Booth Newspapers
214 S Jackson St.
Jackson, MI 49201-2282
Phone: (517)781-2300
Fax: (517)787-9711
**Subject(s):** Daily Newspapers

Circ: (Mon.-Sat.)★34,208
 (Sun.)★39,075

**Traverse City Record-Eagle  (15831)**
Herald & Record Co.
120 W. Front St.
PO Box 632
Traverse City, MI 49685
Phone: (231)946-2000
Fax: (231)946-8273
**Subject(s):** Daily Newspapers

Circ: (Mon.-Sat.)★28,235
 (Sun.)★39,032

**Deerfield Review  (8547)**
Pioneer Press Newspapers
c/o Arnold Grahl
2383 N. Delany Rd.
Waukegan, IL 60087
Phone: (847)599-6900
Fax: (847)599-6902
**Subject(s):** Paid Community Newspapers

Circ: (Combined)38,946

**Grayslake Review  (8752)**
Pioneer Press Newspapers
c/o Arnold Grahl
2383 N. Delany Rd.
Waukegan, IL 60087
Phone: (847)599-6900
Fax: (847)599-6902
**Subject(s):** Paid Community Newspapers

Circ: (Combined)38,946

**Gurnee Review  (8762)**
Pioneer Press Newspapers
c/o Arnold Grahl
2383 N. Delany Rd.
Waukegan, IL 60087
Phone: (847)599-6900
Fax: (847)599-6902
**Subject(s):** Paid Community Newspapers

Circ: (Combined)38,946

**Highland Park News  (8782)**
Pioneer Press Newspapers
c/o Arnold Grahl
2383 N. Delany Rd.
Waukegan, IL 60087
Phone: (847)599-6900
Fax: (847)599-6902
**Subject(s):** Paid Community Newspapers

Circ: (Combined)38,946

**Lake Forester  (8853)**
Pioneer Press Newspapers
c/o Arnold Grahl
2383 N. Delany Rd.
Waukegan, IL 60087
Phone: (847)599-6900
Fax: (847)599-6902
**Subject(s):** Paid Community Newspapers

Circ: (Combined)38,946

**Libertyville Review  (8873)**
Pioneer Press Newspapers
2383 N. Delany Rd.
Waukegan, IL 60087
Phone: (847)599-6900
Fax: (847)599-6902
**Subject(s):** Paid Community Newspapers

Circ: (Combined)38,946

**Mundelein Review  (9029)**
Pioneer Press Newspapers
c/o Arnlod Grahl
2383 N. Delany Rd.
Waukegan, IL 60087
Phone: (847)599-6900
Fax: (847)599-6902
**Subject(s):** Paid Community Newspapers

Circ: (Combined)38,946

**The Review of Lake Villa/Lindenhurst  (8900)**
Pioneer Press Newspapers
c/o Arnold Grahl
2383 N. Delany Rd.
Waukegan, IL 60087
Phone: (847)599-6900
Fax: (847)599-6902
**Subject(s):** Paid Community Newspapers

Circ: (Combined)38,946

**Vernon Hills Review  (9513)**
Pioneer Press Newspapers
c/o Arnold Grahl
2383 N. Delany Rd.
Waukegan, IL 60087
Phone: (847)599-6900
Fax: (847)599-6902
**Subject(s):** Paid Community Newspapers

Circ: (Combined)38,946

**Tribune-Star  (10193)**
222 S. 7th St.
PO Box 149
Terre Haute, IN 47808
Phone: (812)231-4200
Fax: (812)231-4321
**Subject(s):** Daily Newspapers

Circ: (Mon.-Sat.)30,954
 (Sun.)38,813

**Northwest Herald  (8523)**
Northwest Newspapers
7717 South Rt. 31
Crystal Lake, IL 60014
**Subject(s):** Daily Newspapers

Circ: (Mon.-Sat.)★37,241
 (Sun.)★38,417

**The Morning Journal  (24842)**
The Lorain Journal Co.
1657 Broadway
Lorain, OH 44052
Phone: (216)245-6901
Fax: (216)245-5637
**Subject(s):** Daily Newspapers

Circ: (Mon.-Sat.)34,311
 (Sun.)38,106

**Leader-Telegram (32926)**
Eau Claire Press Co.
701 S. Farwell St.
PO Box 570
Eau Claire, WI 54701
Phone: (715)833-9200
Fax: (715)858-7310
**Subject(s)**: Daily Newspapers
**Circ**: (Mon.-Fri.)★26,901
(Sat.)★31,824
(Sun.)★37,682

**The Buy Line (15382)**
109 N Lafayette St.
PO Box 340
Greenville, MI 48838
Phone: (616)754-9301
Fax: (616)754-8559
**Subject(s)**: Shopping Guides
**Circ**: (Free)‡37,605

**The Star Press (10046)**
Muncie Newspapers
345 S. High
Muncie, IN 47305
Phone: (765)747-5754
Fax: (765)747-5748
**Subject(s)**: Daily Newspapers
**Circ**: (Mon.-Sat.)33,625
(Sun.)37,504

**Des Plaines Times (8579)**
Pioneer Press Newspapers
c/o Lloyd H.Weston
130 S. Prospect Ave.
Park Ridge, IL 60068
Phone: (847)696-3133
Fax: (847)696-3229
**Subject(s)**: Paid Community Newspapers
**Circ**: (Combined)37,449

**Edgebrook Times Review (8620)**
Pioneer Press Newspapers
c/o Lloyd H.Weston
130 S. Prospect Ave.
Park Ridge, IL 60068
Phone: (847)696-3133
Fax: (847)696-3229
**Subject(s)**: Paid Community Newspapers
**Circ**: (Combined)37,449

**Edison-Norwood Times Review (8182)**
Pioneer Press Newspapers
c/o Lloyd H. Weston
130 S. Prospect Ave.
Park Ridge, IL 60068
Phone: (847)696-3133
Fax: (847)696-3229
**Subject(s)**: Paid Community Newspapers
**Circ**: (Combined)37,449

**Mount Prospect Times (9020)**
Pioneer Press Newspapers
c/o Lloyd H. Weston
130 S. Prospect Ave.
Park Ridge, IL 60068
Phone: (847)696-3133
Fax: (847)696-3229
**Subject(s)**: Paid Community Newspapers
**Circ**: (Combined)37,449

**Niles Herald-Spectator (9063)**
Pioneer Press Newspapers
c/o Lloyd H. Weston
130 S. Prospect Ave.
Park Ridge, IL 60068
Phone: (847)696-3133
Fax: (847)696-3229
**Subject(s)**: Paid Community Newspapers
**Circ**: (Combined)37,449

**Norridge—Harwood Heights News (8773)**
Pioneer Press Newspapers
c/o Lloyd H. Weston
130 S. Prospect Ave.
Park Ridge, IL 60068
Phone: (847)696-3133
Fax: (847)696-3229
**Subject(s)**: Paid Community Newspapers
**Circ**: (Combined)37,449

**Park Ridge Herald—Advocate (9201)**
Pioneer Press Newspapers
c/o Lloyd H. Weston
130 S. Prospect Ave.
Park Ridge, IL 60068
Phone: (847)696-3133
Fax: (847)696-3229
**Subject(s)**: Paid Community Newspapers
**Circ**: (Combined)37,449

**Access (14960)**
Access Communications
155 N Winter St.
Adrian, MI 49221
Phone: (517)263-0800
Fax: (517)263-8809
**Subject(s)**: Shopping Guides
**Circ**: (Free)37,435

**Tribune Chronicle (25137)**
240 Franklin St. SE
PO Box 1431
Warren, OH 44482
Phone: (216)841-1600
Fax: (216)841-1721
**Subject(s)**: Daily Newspapers
**Circ**: (Mon.-Sat.)★32,938
(Sun.)★37,185

**Grant, Iowa, Lafayette Shopping News (33467)**
Woodward Communications
41 Means Drive
PO Box 500
Platteville, WI 53818-0500
Phone: (608)348-3388
Fax: (800)236-2537
**Subject(s)**: Shopping Guides
**Circ**: (Paid)102
(Free)37,158

**Union Advocate (16613)**
411 Main St.
Rm. 202
Saint Paul, MN 55102-1044
Phone: (651)222-3787
Fax: (651)293-1989
**Subject(s)**: Labor
**Circ**: ‡37,153

**Battle Creek Enquirer (15042)**
Gannett Company Inc.
155 W. Van Buren St.
Battle Creek, MI 49017-3093
Phone: (616)964-0299
Fax: (616)964-8242
**Subject(s)**: Daily Newspapers
**Circ**: (Mon.-Sat.)26,000
(Sun.)37,000

**The Newark-Licking Advertiser (24943)**
Add Inc.
195 Union St.
Newark, OH 43058
Phone: (740)522-2502
Fax: (740)522-2498
**Subject(s)**: Shopping Guides
**Circ**: (Non-paid)♦36,918

**St. Cloud Times (16548)**
St. Cloud Newspapers Inc.
3000 N 7th St.
Saint Cloud, MN 56301
Phone: (320)255-8700
Fax: (320)255-8773
**Subject(s)**: Daily Newspapers
**Circ**: (Mon.-Sat.)★27,776
(Sun.)★36,733

**Hendrick County Flyer/Weekend Edition (9557)**
Thomson Indiana Inc.
8109 Kingston Rd., Ste. 500
Avon, IN 46123
Phone: (317)272-5800
Fax: (317)272-5887
**Subject(s)**: Paid Community Newspapers
**Circ**: (Combined)36,500

**The New Star (8353)**
St. Nicholas Diocesan Press
2208 W Chicago Ave.
Chicago, IL 60622
Phone: (773)227-3970
**Subject(s)**: Religious Publications; Ukrainian
**Circ**: (Controlled)2,035
(Paid)36,129

**Southern Illinoisan (7955)**
710 N Illinois
Carbondale, IL 62901
Phone: (618)529-5454
Fax: (618)457-2935
**Subject(s)**: Daily Newspapers
**Circ**: (Mon.-Sat.)★27,671
(Sun.)★36,014

**Springfield News-Sun (25055)**
Springfield Newspapers Inc.
202 N Limestone St.
Springfield, OH 45501
Phone: (937)328-0300
Fax: (937)328-0227
**Subject(s)**: Daily Newspapers
**Circ**: (Mon.-Sat.)★28,929
(Sun.)★35,510

**Farm World (9964)**
Mayhill Publications
27 N. Jefferson St.
PO Box 90
Knightstown, IN 46148
Fax: (765)345-3398
**Subject(s)**: Farm Newspapers
**Circ**: (Paid)35,141

**The Hendricks County Flyer (9558)**
Thomson Indiana Inc.
8109 Kingston Rd., Ste. 500
Avon, IN 46123
Phone: (317)272-5800
Fax: (317)272-5887
**Subject(s)**: Free Newspapers
**Circ**: (Combined)35,100

**The Bargaineer (9546)**
Zion-Benton News
2719 Elisha Ave.
Zion, IL 60099
Phone: (847)746-9000
Fax: (847)746-9150
**Subject(s)**: Shopping Guides
**Circ**: (Paid)5,000
(Non-paid)35,000

**Grand Marais Pilot & Pictured Rocks Review (15765)**
PO Box 123
Seney, MI 49883
Phone: (906)499-3318
Fax: (906)499-3321
**Subject(s)**: Paid Community Newspapers
**Circ**: ‡35,000

**The Michigan Catholic (15189)**
305 Michigan Ave.
Detroit, MI 48226
Phone: (313)224-8000
Fax: (313)224-8009
**Subject(s)**: Religious Publications
**Circ**: ‡35,000

**Milwaukee Community Journal (33315)**
Milwaukee Community Journal Inc.
3612 N Martin Luther King Dr.
Milwaukee, WI 53212
Phone: (414)265-5300
Fax: (414)265-1536
**Subject(s)**: Free Newspapers; Black Publications
**Circ**: (Paid)4,960
(Free)35,000

**Skywrighter (25199)**
Times Community Newspapers
1865 Fourth St.
ASC/PAI Bldg. 4
Wright Patterson AFB, OH 45433-1729
Phone: (937)255-7000
Fax: (937)656-4022
**Subject(s)**: Military and Navy; Free Newspapers
**Circ**: (Free)‡35,000

**The Voice of Agriculture (16617)**
Minnesota Farm Bureau Federation
3080 Eagandale Pl.
PO Box 64370
Saint Paul, MN 55164-4370
Phone: (651)905-2100
Fax: (651)905-2159
**Subject(s)**: Farm Bureau, Grange, and Cooperative Associations; Farm Newspapers; Free Newspapers
**Circ**: (Combined)35,000

---

Circulation: ★ = ABC; △ = BPA; ♦ = CAC; ● = CCAB; ▫ = VAC; ⊕ = PO Statement; ‡ = Publisher's Report; Boldface figures = sworn; Light figures = estimated.

# Great Lakes States

**The Wanderer (16619)**
Wanderer Press
201 Ohio St.
Saint Paul, MN 55107
Phone: (612)224-5733
Fax: (612)224-9666
**Subject(s):** Religious Publications
**Circ:** ‡35,000

**Rock Island Argus (9294)**
Moline Dispatch Publishing Co.
1724 4th Ave.
Rock Island, IL 61201-8713
Phone: (309)786-7639
Fax: (309)786-7639
**Subject(s):** Daily Newspapers
**Circ:** (Mon.-Sat.)★31,742
(Sun.)★34,977

**The Source (15808)**
Advisor & Source Newspapers
48075 Van Dyke
Shelby Township, MI 48317
Phone: (586)731-8172
Fax: (586)731-8172
**Subject(s):** Free Newspapers
**Circ:** (Non-paid)34,706

**Northeaster & Northnews (16332)**
Northeaster
2304 Central Ave. NE
Minneapolis, MN 55418
Phone: (612)788-9003
Fax: (612)788-3199
**Subject(s):** Paid Community Newspapers
**Circ:** (Non-paid)‡34,500

**50 Plus Lifestyles (33179)**
PO Box 44327
Madison, WI 53744
Phone: (608)274-5200
Fax: (608)274-5492
**Subject(s):** Senior Citizens' Interests; Health; Banking, Finance, and Investments
**Circ:** ‡5,300
(Controlled)‡34,300

**The Paper (Elkhart County Edition) (9768)**
The Papers Inc.
134 S. Main St.
Goshen, IN 46526
Phone: (219)534-2591
Fax: (219)533-4280
**Subject(s):** Free Newspapers
**Circ:** (Free)34,020

**The Hometown Advertiser (33568)**
Hometown News Group Publications
207 E. Main St.
PO Box 645
Sun Prairie, WI 53590
Phone: (608)837-2521
Fax: (608)825-4460
**Subject(s):** Shopping Guides
**Circ:** (Free)33,918

**Lancaster Fairfield Advertiser (24822)**
Add Inc.—Ohio Group
760 Linden Ave., No. 2353
PO Box 2353
Zanesville, OH 43701-3355
Phone: (740)453-0615
Fax: (740)453-9504
**Subject(s):** Shopping Guides
**Circ:** (Free)◆33,734

**ISBA Bar News (8247)**
Illinois State Bar Association
20 S. Clark St., Ste. 900
Chicago, IL 60603-1802
Phone: (312)726-8775
Fax: (312)726-1422
**Subject(s):** Law
**Circ:** (Controlled)‡33,600

**Wisconsin Hi-Liter (32874)**
Southern Lakes Newspapers
140 Commerce St.
Burlington, WI 53105-0437
Phone: (262)763-3511
Fax: (262)763-2238
**Subject(s):** Shopping Guides
**Circ:** (Paid)10
(Free)33,450

**The Daily Journal (8833)**
Small Newspaper Group
8 Dearborn Sq.
Kankakee, IL 60901
Phone: (815)937-3300
Fax: (815)937-3301
**Subject(s):** Daily Newspapers
**Circ:** (Mon.-Fri.)29,038
(Sun.)33,331

**Early Bird (33508)**
Chronotype Publishing Co.
28 S. Main St.
P.O. Box 30
Rice Lake, WI 54868
Phone: (715)234-2121
Fax: (715)234-5232
**Subject(s):** Shopping Guides
**Circ:** (Free)‡33,000

**The State News (15248)**
State News Inc.
345 Student Service Bldg.
East Lansing, MI 48824
Phone: (517)355-3447
Fax: (517)353-2599
**Subject(s):** College Publications; Daily Newspapers
**Circ:** ‡33,000

**Toledo Herald (25079)**
Herald Newspapers
5739 N Main St.
Sylvania, OH 43560
Phone: (419)885-9222
Fax: (419)885-0764
**Subject(s):** Paid Community Newspapers
**Circ:** (Paid)316
(Non-paid)33,000

**Catholic Universe Bulletin (24384)**
Catholic Universe Bulletin Publishing Company Inc.
1027 Superior Ave.
Cleveland, OH 44114-2556
Phone: (216)696-6525
Fax: (216)696-6519
**Subject(s):** Religious Publications
**Circ:** ‡32,485

**St. Croix Valley Peach (16130)**
ECM Publishers Inc. (Forest Lake)
880 SW 15th St.
Forest Lake, MN 55025
Phone: (651)464-4601
Fax: (651)464-4605
**Subject(s):** Shopping Guides
**Circ:** (Free)‡32,435

**The Week (32910)**
Walworth County Publishers
1436 Mound Rd.
PO Box 366
Delavan, WI 53115-0366
Phone: (262)728-5505
Fax: (262)728-5706
**Subject(s):** Free Newspapers
**Circ:** (Paid)◆186
(Non-paid)◆32,422

**Lake Area Sunday Post (33431)**
Conley Publishing Co.
212 E Wisconsin Ave.
Oconomowoc, WI 53066
Phone: (262)567-5511
Fax: (262)567-4422
**Subject(s):** Shopping Guides
**Circ:** (Combined)32,313

**Eagan Sun Current (16083)**
Minnesota Sun Publications
10917 Valley View Rd.
Eden Prairie, MN 55344
Phone: (952)829-0797
Fax: (952)392-6868
**Subject(s):** Free Newspapers
**Circ:** (Paid)166
(Non-paid)32,102

**Tuscarawas Bargain Hunter (24914)**
Graphic Publications Inc.
7368 County Rd. 623
PO Box 358
Millersburg, OH 44654
Phone: (330)674-2300
Fax: (330)674-2461

**Subject(s):** Free Newspapers
**Circ:** (Free)32,000

**Southeast DuPage Progress (8609)**
Liberty Suburban Chicago Newspapers
922 Warren Ave.
Downers Grove, IL 60515
Phone: (630)969-0188
Fax: (630)969-0228
**Subject(s):** Free Newspapers
**Circ:** (Non-paid)31,800

**Beacon-News (9195)**
Beacon News Publishing
PO Box 100
Paris, IL 61944
Phone: (217)465-6424
Fax: (217)463-1232
**Subject(s):** Daily Newspapers
**Circ:** (Mon.-Sat.)28,389
(Sun.)31,710

**The Catholic Outlook (16048)**
c/o Carlson and Kirwan
118 E Superior St.
Duluth, MN 55802
Phone: (218)722-7220
Fax: (218)722-3358
**Subject(s):** Religious Publications
**Circ:** 31,484

**The Truth (9681)**
Truth Publishing Company Inc.
421 S 2nd St.
Box 487
Elkhart, IN 46516-3227
Phone: (574)294-1661
Fax: (574)294-3895
**Subject(s):** Daily Newspapers
**Circ:** (Mon.-Sat.)27,761
(Sun.)31,438

**The Journal Times (33491)**
212 4th St.
Racine, WI 53403-1066
Phone: (262)634-3322
Fax: (262)631-1702
**Subject(s):** Daily Newspapers
**Circ:** (Mon.-Sat.)★29,217
(Sun.)★31,336

**Maywood Herald (8949)**
Pioneer Press Newspapers
c/o Dan Obermaier
1140 Lake St.
Oak Park, IL 60301
Phone: (708)383-3200
Fax: (708)383-3678
**Subject(s):** Paid Community Newspapers
**Circ:** (Combined)31,238

**Melrose Park Herald (8953)**
Pioneer Press Newspapers
1140 Lake St.
Oak Park, IL 60301
Phone: (708)383-3200
Fax: (708)383-3678
**Subject(s):** Paid Community Newspapers
**Circ:** (Combined)31,238

**West Proviso Herald (9259)**
Pioneer Press Newspapers
c/o Dan Obermaier
1140 Lake St.
Oak Park, IL 60301
Phone: (708)383-3200
Fax: (708)383-3678
**Subject(s):** Paid Community Newspapers
**Circ:** (Combined)31,238

**Lakeland Shopping Guide (15928)**
Echo Press
225 7th Ave. E.
PO Box 549
Alexandria, MN 56308
Phone: (320)763-3133
Fax: (320)763-3258
**Subject(s):** Shopping Guides
**Circ:** (Free)31,000

**Lapeer Buyer's Guide** (15542)
Lapeer County Buyer's Guide
PO Box 66
Lapeer, MI 48446-0066
**Subject(s):** Shopping Guides
**Circ:** (Free)30,775

**The Beacon-News** (7872)
101 S. River St.
Aurora, IL 60506
Phone: (630)844-5844
Fax: (630)844-5818
**Subject(s):** Daily Newspapers
**Circ:** (Mon.-Sat.)28,641
(Sun.)30,764

**Your Family Shopper** (32889)
321 Frenette Drive
PO Box 69
Chippewa Falls, WI 54729
Phone: (715)723-2839
Fax: (715)723-9644
**Subject(s):** Shopping Guides
**Circ:** (Non-paid)30,699

**Star Buyer's Guide** (15754)
Morningstar Publications
356 Sanilac Ave.
Sandusky, MI 48471-1151
Phone: (810)648-9900
Fax: (810)664-7572
**Subject(s):** Shopping Guides
**Circ:** (Free)30,293

**West Boca Community News** (8444)
Tribune Co.
435 N Michigan Ave.
Chicago, IL 60611
Phone: (312)222-9100
Fax: (312)222-4674
**Subject(s):** Free Newspapers
**Circ:** (Non-paid)30,240

**Mid-America Boating** (24523)
Recreation Press Inc.
3091 Mayfield Rd., Ste. 315
Cleveland Heights, OH 44118-1732
Phone: (216)371-5750
Fax: (216)371-5440
**Subject(s):** (Boating and Yachting); Paid Community Newspapers
**Circ:** (Combined)30,084

**The Herald-Palladium** (15743)
3450 Hollywood Rd.
PO Box 128
Saint Joseph, MI 49085
Phone: (269)429-2400
Fax: (269)429-4398
**Subject(s):** Daily Newspapers
**Circ:** (Mon.-Sat.)28,179
(Sun.)30,065

**Brighton Park-McKinley Park Life** (8108)
Litotype Publication
2949 W Pope John Paul II Dr.
Chicago, IL 60632
Phone: (773)523-3663
Fax: (773)523-3983
**Subject(s):** Free Newspapers
**Circ:** (Free)‡30,000

**The Christian Century** (8144)
104 S Michigan Ave., Ste. 700
Chicago, IL 60603
Phone: (312)263-7510
Fax: (312)263-7540
**Subject(s):** Religious Publications
**Circ:** ‡30,000

**Cotton & Quail Antique Gazette** (33072)
Krause Publications Inc.
700 E. State St.
Iola, WI 54990-0001
Phone: (715)445-2214
Fax: (715)445-4087
**Subject(s):** Antiques; Collecting
**Circ:** (Combined)30,000

**Dearborn Heights Press & Guide** (15149)
Heritage Newspapers Inc.
15340 Michigan Ave.
Dearborn, MI 48126-2917
Phone: (313)943-4250
Fax: (313)846-5531

**Subject(s):** Paid Community Newspapers
**Circ:** (Sun.)22,000
(Wed.)30,000

**Dearborn Press & Guide** (15150)
Heritage Newspapers Inc.
15340 Michigan Ave.
Dearborn, MI 48126-2917
Phone: (313)943-4250
Fax: (313)846-5531
**Subject(s):** Paid Community Newspapers
**Circ:** (Sun.)22,000
(Wed.)30,000

**The MidWeek** (8560)
The Midweek Inc.
650 Peace Rd.
PO Box 546
DeKalb, IL 60115
Phone: (815)758-0696
Fax: (815)758-1418
**Subject(s):** Free Newspapers
**Circ:** (Free)‡30,000

**The National Psychologist** (24571)
Ohio Psychology Publications Inc.
6100 Channingway Blvd., Ste. 303
Columbus, OH 43232
Phone: (614)861-1999
Fax: (614)861-1996
**Subject(s):** Psychology and Psychiatry
**Circ:** (Combined)30,000

**Ohio Baptist Messenger** (24577)
State Convention of Baptists in Ohio
1680 E. Broad St.
Columbus, OH 43203
Phone: (614)258-8491
Fax: (614)827-1860
**Subject(s):** Religious Publications
**Circ:** ‡30,000

**The Scene** (32814)
Scene Publications
300 N. Appleton St., Ste. 2
Appleton, WI 54911
Phone: (920)733-5743
Fax: (920)733-5783
**Subject(s):** Free Newspapers
**Circ:** (Non-paid)30,000

**Warrendale-West Detroit Press & Guide** (15156)
Heritage Newspapers Inc.
15340 Michigan Ave.
Dearborn, MI 48126-2917
Phone: (313)943-4250
Fax: (313)846-5531
**Subject(s):** Paid Community Newspapers
**Circ:** (Sun.)22,000
(Wed.)30,000

**Illinois Times** (9398)
Central Illinois Communications, LLC
PO Box 5256
Springfield, IL 62704
Phone: (217)753-2226
Fax: (217)753-2281
**Subject(s):** Free Newspapers
**Circ:** (Paid)60
(Free)29,940

**The Paper (Goshen Edition)** (9769)
The Papers Inc.
134 S. Main St.
Goshen, IN 46526
Phone: (219)534-2591
Fax: (219)533-4280
**Subject(s):** Free Newspapers
**Circ:** (Free)29,759

**The Herald** (9319)
Rock Valley Publishing
555 N. Blackhawk
Rockton, IL 61072
**Subject(s):** Free Newspapers
**Circ:** (Paid)3,680
(Free)29,482

**Burnsville/Savage Sun Current** (15993)
Minnesota Sun Publications
10917 Valley View Rd.
Eden Prairie, MN 55344
Phone: (952)829-0797
Fax: (952)392-6868

**Subject(s):** Free Newspapers
**Circ:** (Paid)298
(Non-paid)29,312

**The Telegraph** (7834)
Journal Register Co.
111 E. Broadway
PO Box 278
Alton, IL 62002-0278
Phone: (618)463-2563
**Subject(s):** Daily Newspapers
**Circ:** (Mon.-Sat.)27,134
(Sun.)29,010

**Tri County Citizen** (32836)
Citizen Publishing Co.
805 Park Ave.
Beaver Dam, WI 53916
Phone: (920)885-7800
Fax: (920)887-8790
**Subject(s):** Free Newspapers
**Circ:** (Free)‡29,000

**Catholic Post** (9211)
409 N Monroe St
PO Box 1722
Peoria, IL 61603
Phone: (309)673-3603
Fax: (309)673-0334
**Subject(s):** Religious Publications
**Circ:** 28,900

**Kettering-Oakwood Times** (24817)
Times Community Newspapers
3085 Woodman Dr., Ste. 170
Kettering, OH 45420-1159
Phone: (937)294-7000
Fax: (937)294-2981
**Subject(s):** Paid Community Newspapers
**Circ:** (Sat.)2,144
(Wed.)28,867

**The Sunday Reminder** (16709)
West Central Tribune
2208 Trott Ave. SW
PO Box 839
Willmar, MN 56201
Phone: (320)235-1150
Fax: (320)235-6769
**Subject(s):** Shopping Guides
**Circ:** (Non-paid)28,800

**The Sheboygan Press** (33537)
632 Center Ave.
Sheboygan, WI 53081
Phone: (920)457-7711
Fax: (920)457-0178
**Subject(s):** Daily Newspapers
**Circ:** (Mon.-Sat.)27,055
(Sun.)28,678

**Hastings Reminder** (15396)
J-Ad Corp.
1351 N M-43 Hwy.
PO Box 188
Hastings, MI 49058-0188
Phone: (269)945-9554
Fax: (269)945-5192
**Subject(s):** Free Newspapers
**Circ:** (Free)28,450

**The Janesville Sunday Messenger** (33106)
Community Shoppers Inc.
1506 Creston Park Dr.
Janesville, WI 53545
Phone: (608)752-1007
Fax: (608)752-1007
**Subject(s):** Free Newspapers
**Circ:** (Free)28,360

**Royal Oak Mirror** (15716)
Mirror Newspapers
1523 N Main
PO Box 430
Royal Oak, MI 48067-0430
Phone: (248)546-4900
Fax: (248)398-2353
**Subject(s):** Free Newspapers
**Circ:** (Combined)28,345

# Great Lakes States

**The Catholic Moment (9975)**
The Times
PO Box 1603
610 Lingle Ave
Lafayette, IN 47901
Phone: (765)742-2050
Fax: (765)742-7513
**Subject(s):** Religious Publications
**Circ:** ‡28,309

**Buyers Guide (15608)**
Mt. Pleasant Buyers Guide
711 W Pickard St.
PO Box 447
Mount Pleasant, MI 48804-0447
Phone: (989)779-6000
Fax: (989)779-6012
**Subject(s):** Shopping Guides
**Circ:** (Free)‡28,259

**Action Shopper (15572)**
307 S Front St., Ste. 101
PO Box 610
Marquette, MI 49855
Phone: (906)228-8920
Fax: (906)228-5777
**Subject(s):** Free Newspapers
**Circ:** (Free)‡28,000

**Ohio State Lantern (24590)**
Ohio State University
School of Journalism
242 W. 18th Ave.
Columbus, OH 43210
Phone: (614)292-2031
Fax: (614)292-3722
**Subject(s):** College Publications
**Circ:** (Free)‡28,000

**The Wayne Journal (24915)**
Graphic Publications Inc.
7368 County Rd. 623
PO Box 358
Millersburg, OH 44654
Phone: (330)674-2300
Fax: (330)674-2461
**Subject(s):** Free Newspapers
**Circ:** (Free)28,000

**Midland Buyer's Guide (15611)**
Morning Star Publishing Co.
PO Box 464
215 N. Main St.
Mount Pleasant, MI 48804-0464
**Subject(s):** Shopping Guides
**Circ:** (Free)27,901

**Northwestern (33452)**
Oshkosh Northwestern Co.
224 State St.
PO Box 2926
Oshkosh, WI 54901-4839
Phone: (920)235-7700
Fax: (920)235-1316
**Subject(s):** Daily Newspapers
**Circ:** (Mon.-Sat.)24,291
(Sun.)27,884

**Holland Flashes Shopping Guide (15414)**
Flashes Publishers
437 136th Ave.
Holland, MI 49424
Phone: (616)396-2394
Fax: (616)396-4710
**Subject(s):** Shopping Guides
**Circ:** (Free)27,540

**Super Shopper (15673)**
Petoskey News-Review, Super Shopper, and Graphic
319 State St.
PO Box 528
Petoskey, MI 49770-0528
Phone: (231)347-2544
Fax: (231)347-6833
**Subject(s):** Shopping Guides
**Circ:** ‡27,500

**The Early Bird (24755)**
Ball Publishing Co.
5312 Sebring-Warner Rd.
Greenville, OH 45331-9702
Phone: (937)548-3330
Fax: (937)548-3376

**Subject(s):** Free Newspapers
**Circ:** (Paid)42
(Non-paid)27,376

**Sandusky Register (25033)**
Sandusky Newspapers Inc.
314 W Market St.
Sandusky, OH 44870-2410
Phone: (419)625-5500
**Subject(s):** Daily Newspapers
**Circ:** (Mon.-Sat.)★23,213
(Sun.)★27,252

**Wheaton Gazette (16701)**
1114 Broadway
Wheaton, MN 56296
Phone: (320)563-8146
Fax: (320)563-8147
**Subject(s):** Paid Community Newspapers
**Circ:** (Combined)27,127

**The Quincy Herald Whig (9260)**
ABC Quincy Newspaper Inc.
130 S. 5th St.
PO Box 909
Quincy, IL 62301
Phone: (217)223-5100
Fax: (217)223-9757
**Subject(s):** Daily Newspapers
**Circ:** (Mon.-Sat.)★22,939
(Sun.)★27,118

**Chicago's Northwest Side Press (8142)**
NADIG Newspapers Inc.
4937 N Milwaukee Ave.
Chicago, IL 60630
Phone: (773)286-6100
Fax: (773)286-8151
**Subject(s):** Free Newspapers
**Circ:** (Paid)9,000
(Free)‡27,000

**El Dia Newspaper (8504)**
5718 W Cermak Rd.
Cicero, IL 60804-2444
Phone: (708)652-6396
Fax: (708)652-6653
**Subject(s):** Paid Community Newspapers; Hispanic Publications; Spanish
**Circ:** (Paid)3,000
(Free)27,000

**Gary New Crusader (9758)**
1549 Broadway St.
Gary, IN 46407
Phone: (219)885-4357
Fax: (219)883-3317
**Subject(s):** Paid Community Newspapers; Black Publications
**Circ:** ‡27,000

**Hometown News (15638)**
Hometown
314 E Main St.
PO Box 549
Niles, MI 49120
Phone: (269)684-6802
Fax: (269)684-6115
**Subject(s):** Free Newspapers
**Circ:** (Free)‡27,000

**The Minnesota Daily (16317)**
University of Minnesota
10 Murphy Hall
206 Church St. SE
Minneapolis, MN 55414-3070
Phone: (612)627-4080
Fax: (612)627-4159
**Subject(s):** College Publications
**Circ:** (Free)‡27,000

**New Brighton-Mounds View Bulletin (16415)**
Lillie Suburban Newspapers
PO Box 120608
New Brighton, MN 55112
Phone: (651)633-2777
Fax: (651)633-3846
**Subject(s):** Free Newspapers
**Circ:** (Paid)129
(Free)27,000

**The St. Anthony Bulletin (16543)**
Lillie Suburban Newspapers
PO Box 120608
New Brighton, MN 55112
Phone: (651)633-2777

Fax: (651)633-3846
**Subject(s):** Free Newspapers
**Circ:** (Paid)129
(Free)27,000

**Shoreview-Arden Hills Bulletin (16645)**
Lillie Suburban Newspapers
PO Box 120608
New Brighton, MN 55112
Phone: (651)633-2777
Fax: (651)633-3846
**Subject(s):** Free Newspapers
**Circ:** (Paid)129
(Free)27,000

**Times-Herald (15159)**
13730 Michigan Ave.
Dearborn, MI 48126
Phone: (313)584-4000
Fax: (313)584-1357
**Subject(s):** Paid Community Newspapers
**Circ:** ‡27,000

**The Ross County Advertiser (24275)**
Add Inc.—Ohio Group
147 W Water St.
P.O. Box 6355
Chillicothe, OH 45601
Phone: (740)773-5010
Fax: (740)773-5021
**Subject(s):** Shopping Guides
**Circ:** (Non-paid)◆26,937

**Great Dane Shopping News (33444)**
Woodward Communications
845 Market Street
Oregon, WI 53575
Phone: (608)873-6671
**Subject(s):** Shopping Guides
**Circ:** (Free)‡26,750

**Palm Beach Jewish Journal South (9520)**
Tribune Co.
435 N Michigan Ave.
Chicago, IL 60611
Phone: (312)222-9100
Fax: (312)222-4674
**Subject(s):** Free Newspapers; Jewish Publications
**Circ:** (Combined)26,500

**Prairie Catholic (16423)**
1400 6th St. N.
New Ulm, MN 56073
Phone: (507)359-2966
Fax: (507)354-3667
**Subject(s):** Religious Publications
**Circ:** (Combined)⊕26,500

**The Sun (24955)**
Sun Newspapers
28895 Lorain Rd.
North Olmsted, OH 44070-4042
Phone: (440)777-3800
Fax: (440)777-8423
**Subject(s):** Paid Community Newspapers
**Circ:** (Paid)26,189

**The Herald/Country Market (7927)**
B & B Publishing Co.
500 Brown Blvd.
Bourbonnais, IL 60914
Phone: (815)933-1131
Fax: (815)933-3785
**Subject(s):** Free Newspapers
**Circ:** (Paid)‡5,100
(Free)‡26,000

**The Janesville Gazette (33105)**
PO Box 5001
Janesville, WI 53547-5001
Phone: (608)754-3311
Fax: (608)754-8179
**Subject(s):** Daily Newspapers
**Circ:** (Mon.-Sat.)★22,656
(Sun.)★26,008

**Anderson Herald-Bulletin (9550)**
1133 Jackson St.
Anderson, IN 46016-1466
Phone: (317)643-5371
Fax: (317)649-3271
**Subject(s):** Daily Newspapers
**Circ:** (Mon.-Sat.)★24,005
(Sun.)★25,568

# Gale Directory of Publications & Broadcast Media/140th Ed. — Great Lakes States

**Arrow Shopper** (32946)
15811 Bridge St.
Ettrick, WI 54627
Phone: (608)525-5771
Fax: (608)525-2617
**Subject(s):** Shopping Guides
**Circ:** (Free)‡25,482

**The Doings** (8793)
Hollinger International Inc.
440 E Ogden Ave.
PO Box 151
Hinsdale, IL 60521
Phone: (630)887-0600
Fax: (630)887-9646
**Subject(s):** Paid Community Newspapers
**Circ:** (Paid)25,467

**The Compass** (33005)
Green Bay Register Inc.
1825 Riverside Dr.
Box 23825
Green Bay, WI 54305-3825
Phone: (920)437-7531
Fax: (920)437-0694
**Subject(s):** Religious Publications
**Circ:** ‡25,060

**The Country Today** (32922)
Eau Claire Press Co.
701 S Farwell St.
Eau Claire, WI 54701
Phone: (715)833-9270
Fax: (715)858-7307
**Subject(s):** Farm Newspapers
**Circ:** (Free)‡2,903
(Paid)‡25,000

**The Electron** (24405)
Cleveland Institute of Electronics
1776 E 17th St.
Cleveland, OH 44114
Phone: (216)781-9400
Fax: (216)781-0331
**Subject(s):** Electronics Engineering
**Circ:** ‡25,000

**Harmony** (9371)
Eintracnt Inc.
9456 N Lawler Ave.
Skokie, IL 60077
Phone: (847)677-9456
Fax: (847)677-9471
**Subject(s):** German; Paid Community Newspapers; Ethnic Publications
**Circ:** ‡25,000

**Heartland** (8225)
Heartland Publications
19 S. LaSalle St., Ste. 903
Chicago, IL 60603
Phone: (312)377-4000
Fax: (312)377-5000
**Subject(s):** Paid Community Newspapers; Travel and Tourism
**Circ:** (Combined)25,000

**Narod Polish** (8347)
Polish Roman Catholic Union of America
984 N Milwaukee Ave.
Chicago, IL 60622-4101
Phone: (773)782-2600
Fax: (773)278-4595
**Subject(s):** Polish; Religious Publications
**Circ:** (Non-paid)‡25,000

**Northwest Leader** (8356)
Leader
6008 W Belmont Ave.
Chicago, IL 60634-5195
Phone: (773)283-7900
Fax: (773)283-7761
**Subject(s):** Paid Community Newspapers
**Circ:** 25,000

**Southwest Farm Press** (16344)
7900 International Dr., 3rd Fl.
Minneapolis, MN 55425-1510
Phone: (952)851-9329
Fax: (952)851-4601
**Subject(s):** Paid Community Newspapers; Farm Newspapers
**Circ:** (Non-paid)21,666
(Paid)25,009

**The UP Catholic** (15575)
347 Rock St.
PO Box 548
Marquette, MI 49855
Phone: (906)227-9131
Fax: (906)226-6941
**Subject(s):** Religious Publications
**Circ:** (Paid)25,000

**West Michigan Senior Times** (15416)
54 W 8th St.
Holland, MI 49423
Phone: (616)546-4356
**Subject(s):** Free Newspapers; Senior Citizens' Interests
**Circ:** (Free)25,000

**Bloomington Sun Current** (16087)
Minnesota Sun Publications
10917 Valley View Rd.
Eden Prairie, MN 55344
Phone: (952)829-0797
Fax: (952)392-6868
**Circ:** (Paid)2,384
(Non-paid)24,968

**The Monroe Evening News/The Monroe Sunday News** (15599)
Monroe Publishing Co.
20 W. 1st St.
Monroe, MI 48161
Phone: (734)242-1100
**Subject(s):** Daily Newspapers
**Circ:** (Mon.-Sat.)22,325
(Sun.)24,891

**Dunn County Reminder** (33275)
PO Box 40
710 Main Street
Menomonie, WI 54751-0040
Phone: (715)235-9011
Fax: (715)235-0936
**Subject(s):** Shopping Guides
**Circ:** (Free)‡24,850

**Chronicle-Telegram** (24710)
Lorain County Printing & Publishing
225 E Ave.
PO Box 4010
Elyria, OH 44036
Phone: (216)329-7000
Fax: (216)329-7282
**Subject(s):** Daily Newspapers
**Circ:** (Mon.-Sat.)★23,385
(Sun.)★24,705

**The Countyline** (24224)
Bryan Publishing Co.
127 S Walnut St.
PO Box 471
Bryan, OH 43506
Phone: (419)636-1111
Fax: (419)636-8937
**Subject(s):** Shopping Guides
**Circ:** (Free)‡24,650

**The Spotlight** (9914)
4217 S Meridian St.
Indianapolis, IN 46217-3313
Phone: (317)788-4554
Fax: (317)788-4570
**Subject(s):** Free Newspapers
**Circ:** (Wed.)24,609

**Cuyahoga Falls News-Press** (25068)
Record Publishing Co.
1619 Commerce Dr.
Stow, OH 44224
Phone: (330)688-0088
Fax: (330)688-1588
**Subject(s):** Free Newspapers
**Circ:** (Paid)‡2,335
(Free)‡24,571

**The Cincinnati Herald** (24298)
354 Hearne Ave.
Cincinnati, OH 45229
Phone: (513)961-3331
Fax: (513)961-0304
**Subject(s):** Paid Community Newspapers; Black Publications
**Circ:** ‡24,500

**Troy-Somerset Gazette** (15867)
Gazette Newspapers Inc.
1903 E. Wattles
Troy, MI 48098
Phone: (248)524-4868
Fax: (248)524-9140
**Subject(s):** Free Newspapers
**Circ:** (Free)‡24,500

**Winona Post** (16720)
64 E 2nd St.
PO Box 27
Winona, MN 55987-0027
Phone: (507)452-1262
Fax: (507)454-6409
**Subject(s):** Free Newspapers
**Circ:** (Free)‡24,440

**Waste News** (24109)
Crain Communications Inc.
1725 Merriman Rd.
Akron, OH 44313
Phone: (330)836-9180
Fax: (330)836-1692
**Subject(s):** Waste Management and Recycling
**Circ:** (Paid)16,231
(Non-paid)24,147

**Suburban LIFE Citizen** (9159)
Liberty Suburban Chicago Newspapers
709 Enterprise Dr.
Oak Brook, IL 60523
Phone: (630)368-1100
Fax: (630)368-1188
**Subject(s):** Paid Community Newspapers
**Circ:** (Paid)24,119

**Catholic Telegraph** (24293)
100 E 8th St.
Cincinnati, OH 45202
Phone: (513)421-3131
Fax: (513)381-2242
**Subject(s):** Religious Publications
**Circ:** (Free)‡400
(Paid)‡24,100

**Free Press** (16238)
Free Press Co.
418 S. 2nd St.
Mankato, MN 56001
Phone: (507)625-4451
Fax: (507)388-4355
**Subject(s):** Daily Newspapers
**Circ:** (Mon.-Sat.)24,058

**Journal-News** (24760)
228 Court St. & Journal Sq.
Hamilton, OH 45011
Phone: (513)863-8200
Fax: (513)896-9489
**Subject(s):** Daily Newspapers
**Circ:** (Mon.-Sat.)★21,649
(Sun.)★24,047

**Shoppers Fair** (15120)
Cheboygan Daily Tribune Inc.
308 N. Main St.
PO Box 290
Cheboygan, MI 49721
Phone: (231)627-7144
Fax: (231)627-5331
**Subject(s):** Shopping Guides
**Circ:** (Free)‡24,000

**Sanilac County News** (15753)
432 S Sandusky Rd.
Sandusky, MI 48471
Phone: (810)648-4000
Fax: (810)648-4002
**Subject(s):** Free Newspapers
**Circ:** (Paid)‡9,400
(Free)‡23,900

**Stevens Point Buyers' Guide** (33556)
Add Inc.
71 Sunset Blvd.
Stevens Point, WI 54481
Phone: (715)344-4700
Fax: (715)344-5117
**Subject(s):** Shopping Guides
**Circ:** (Combined)23,754

Circulation: ★ = ABC; △ = BPA; ♦ = CAC; ● = CCAB; ▫ = VAC; ⊕ = PO Statement; ‡ = Publisher's Report; Boldface figures = sworn; Light figures = estimated.

**Kokomo Tribune** (9970)
300 N Union St.
Kokomo, IN 46901
Phone: (765)459-3121
Fax: (765)456-3815
**Subject(s):** Daily Newspapers

Circ: (Mon.-Sat.)★21,751
(Sun.)★23,615

**Downers Grove Reporter** (8602)
Liberty Suburban Chicago Newspapers
922 Warren Ave.
Downers Grove, IL 60515
Phone: (630)257-5300
Fax: (630)969-0228
**Subject(s):** Paid Community Newspapers

Circ: (Wed.)5,146
(Fri.)23,570

**Miami County Advocate** (25113)
TDN Publishing Co.
224 S. Market St.
Troy, OH 45373
Phone: (937)339-9535
Fax: (937)339-8413
**Subject(s):** Shopping Guides

Circ: (Non-paid)♦23,440

**The Republic** (9656)
333 2nd St.
Columbus, IN 47201-6795
Phone: (812)372-7811
Fax: (812)379-5608
**Subject(s):** Daily Newspapers

Circ: (Non-paid)♦58
(Sun.)♦175
(Paid)♦20,961
(Sun.)♦23,439

**Times-Reporter** (24939)
629 Wabash Ave. NW
PO Box 667
New Philadelphia, OH 44663
Phone: (330)364-5577
Fax: (330)364-8449
**Subject(s):** Daily Newspapers

Circ: (Mon.-Sat.)★23,328
(Sun.)★23,401

**South-West Review** (16437)
Lillie Suburban Newspapers
2515 E 7th Ave.
North Saint Paul, MN 55109
Phone: (651)777-8800
Fax: (651)777-8288
**Subject(s):** Free Newspapers

Circ: (Free)23,389

**Northern Watch** (16660)
Thief River Falls Times Inc.
324 Main Ave. N
PO Box 100
Thief River Falls, MN 56701
Phone: (218)681-4450
Fax: (218)681-4455
**Subject(s):** Free Newspapers

Circ: (Combined)‡23,200

**Clermont Community Journal** (24847)
Press Community Newspapers
394 Wards Corner Rd.
Loveland, OH 45140
Phone: (513)248-8600
Fax: (513)248-1938
**Subject(s):** Free Newspapers

Circ: (Combined)23,199

**The Shawano Shopper** (33532)
109 1/2 S Main St.
PO Box 476
Shawano, WI 54166
Phone: (715)526-6188
Fax: (715)526-6420
**Subject(s):** Shopping Guides

Circ: (Non-paid)23,112

**Southwest News-Herald** (8413)
Vondrac Publishing
6225 S Kedzie Ave.
Chicago, IL 60629-3397
Phone: (312)476-4800
Fax: (312)475-7811
**Subject(s):** Paid Community Newspapers

Circ: ‡23,083

**The Courier** (24724)
The Findlay Publishing Co.
701 W. Sandusky St.
Findlay, OH 45840
Phone: (419)422-5151
Fax: (419)422-2937
**Subject(s):** Daily Newspapers

Circ: (Mon.-Sat.)23,052

**Neenah/Menasha Buyers' Guide** (33272)
1486 Kentwood Center
Menasha, WI 54952
Phone: (920)729-7610
Fax: (920)982-7672
**Subject(s):** Shopping Guides

Circ: (Non-paid)23,030

**Shoppers Advantage** (15098)
Caro Publishing Co.
344 N State St.
PO Box 106
Caro, MI 48723
Phone: (989)673-7671
Fax: (989)673-5662
**Subject(s):** Shopping Guides

Circ: (Non-paid)23,023

**Minnesota Christian Chronicle** (16316)
World Newspaper Publishing Inc.
7317 Cahill Rd., Ste. 201
Minneapolis, MN 55439
Phone: (952)562-1234
Fax: (952)941-3010
**Subject(s):** Paid Community Newspapers; Religious Publications

Circ: (Paid)23,000

**Sunday Home Journal** (8750)
Granite City Journal
1815 Delmar
Granite City, IL 62040
Phone: (618)877-7700
Fax: (618)876-4240
**Subject(s):** Free Newspapers

Circ: (Free)23,000

**Wayzata/Orono/Long Lake Sun-Sailor** (16487)
Minnesota Sun Publications
10917 Valley View Rd.
Eden Prairie, MN 55344
Phone: (952)829-0797
Fax: (952)392-6868
**Subject(s):** Free Newspapers

Circ: (Paid)23,000

**Wisconsin State Farmer** (33626)
Waupaca County Publishing Co.
PO Box 152
717 10th St.
Waupaca, WI 54981-1934
Phone: (715)258-5546
Fax: (715)258-8162
**Subject(s):** General Agriculture

Circ: (Non-paid)‡4,000
(Paid)‡23,000

**M & M Journal** (8789)
Hillsboro Journal Inc.
PO Box 100
Hillsboro, IL 62049
Phone: (217)532-3933
Fax: (217)532-3632
**Subject(s):** Paid Community Newspapers

Circ: (Combined)22,985

**Clear-Ridge Reporter** (8147)
Vondrac Publishing
6225 S Kedzie Ave.
Chicago, IL 60629-3397
Phone: (312)476-4800
Fax: (312)475-7811
**Subject(s):** Shopping Guides

Circ: 22,900

**Telegraph Herald** (8705)
Woodward Communications
1342 S. Harlem Ave.
PO Box 607
Freeport, IL 61032-0604
Phone: (815)235-4106
Fax: (815)235-7077
**Subject(s):** Shopping Guides

Circ: (Non-paid)22,861

**The Montrose Sun** (24897)
Sun Newspapers
2795 Medina Rd.
Medina, OH 44256-8163
Phone: (330)725-1147
Fax: (330)725-2314
**Subject(s):** Paid Community Newspapers

Circ: (Combined)‡22,741

**West Akron Sun** (24898)
Sun Newspapers
2795 Medina Rd.
Medina, OH 44256-8163
Phone: (330)725-1147
Fax: (330)725-2314
**Subject(s):** Paid Community Newspapers

Circ: (Combined)‡22,741

**Wisconsin Rapids Buyers' Guide** (33666)
Add Inc.
180 1st St. N.
Wisconsin Rapids, WI 54494-4156
Phone: (715)424-1230
Fax: (715)423-5070
**Subject(s):** Shopping Guides

Circ: (Combined)22,711

**The Advocate** (24942)
22 N 1st St.
Newark, OH 43055-5608
Phone: (740)345-4053
Fax: (740)345-1634
**Subject(s):** Daily Newspapers

Circ: (Mon.-Sat.)21,764
(Sun.)22,687

**Walker/Westside Advance** (15875)
Advance Newspapers
2141 Port Sheldon Rd.
PO Box 9
Jenison, MI 49428-9301
Phone: (616)669-2700
Fax: (616)669-1162
**Subject(s):** Free Newspapers

Circ: (Paid)❏200
(Free)❏22,654

**Bargain Hunter** (15915)
Messenger Publications Inc.
213 Minnesota Ave. N
PO Box 259
Aitkin, MN 56431-0259
Phone: (218)927-3761
Fax: (218)927-3763
**Subject(s):** Shopping Guides

Circ: (Free)‡22,600

**Chicago Weekend** (8141)
Citizen Newspapers
806 E. 78th St.
Chicago, IL 60619
Phone: (773)783-1251
Fax: (773)783-1301
**Subject(s):** Paid Community Newspapers; Black Publications

Circ: (Free)‡2,053
(Paid)‡22,583

**Parma Sun Post** (24988)
Sun Newspapers
32 Park St.
Berea, OH 44017-1516
Phone: (216)986-7550
Fax: (216)986-7551
**Subject(s):** Paid Community Newspapers

Circ: (Paid)22,579

**Catholic Explorer** (9323)
402 S. Independence Blvd.
Romeoville, IL 60446-2264
Phone: (815)838-6475
Fax: (815)834-4067
**Subject(s):** Religious Publications

Circ: ‡22,500

**The Coal City Courant** (9534)
The Free Press Newspapers
PO Box 327
Wilmington, IL 60481
Phone: (815)476-7966
Fax: (815)476-7002
**Subject(s):** Paid Community Newspapers

Circ: 22,500

**Daily Egyptian (7947)**
Southern Illinois University at Carbondale
1247 Communications Bldg.
PO Box 6887
Carbondale, IL 62901
Phone: (618)536-3311
Fax: (618)453-3248
**Subject(s):** College Publications

Circ: (Free)‡22,500

**East St. Louis Monitor (8618)**
East St. Louis Monitor Publishing Inc.
1501 State St.
PO Box 2137
East Saint Louis, IL 62205
Phone: (618)271-0468
Fax: (618)271-0468
**Subject(s):** Paid Community Newspapers; Black Publications

Circ: ‡22,500

**The Southside Times (9566)**
301 Main St.
Beech Grove, IN 46107
Phone: (317)787-3291
Fax: (317)787-3325
**Subject(s):** Free Newspapers

Circ: (Free)‡22,500

**Senior Times (14977)**
Flashes Publishers Inc.
595 Jenner Dr.
Allegan, MI 49010
Phone: (269)673-1602
Fax: (269)673-6768
**Subject(s):** Free Newspapers; Senior Citizens' Interests

Circ: (Free)22,450

**Berlin/Ripon Buyers' Guide (32849)**
Buyers' Guide Group
321 Watson St.
Po Box 301
Ripon, WI 54971
Phone: (715)258-8450
Fax: (715)258-8469
**Subject(s):** Shopping Guides

Circ: (Free)‡22,400

**Echoland Shopper (16466)**
Echo Publishing & Printing Inc.
PO Box 240
4285 West Lake Street
Pequot Lakes, MN 56472
Phone: (218)568-8521
Fax: (218)568-5407
**Subject(s):** Shopping Guides

Circ: (Free)‡22,373

**Pompano Times (8382)**
Tribune Co.
435 N Michigan Ave.
Chicago, IL 60611
Phone: (312)222-9100
Fax: (312)222-4674
**Subject(s):** Shopping Guides

Circ: (Combined)22,130

**Palladium-Item (10128)**
Palladium Publishing
1175 N A St.
PO Box 308
Richmond, IN 47374-3226
Phone: (765)962-1575
Fax: (765)973-4570
**Subject(s):** Daily Newspapers

Circ: (Mon.-Sat.)★17,833
 (Sun.)★22,122

**The Paper (Kosciusko Edition) (10234)**
The Papers Inc.
114 W. Market St.
Warsaw, IN 46580
**Subject(s):** Free Newspapers

Circ: (Free)22,100

**Marshfield Buyers' Guide (33260)**
Buyers' Guide Group
1213 S Central Ave. Ste. B
Marshfield, WI 54449
Phone: (715)384-4440
Fax: (715)384-4085
**Subject(s):** Shopping Guides

Circ: (Combined)22,086

**Shopper Stopper Reminder (33481)**
Capital Newspapers
1640 LaDawn Blvd.
PO Box 470
Portage, WI 53901
Phone: (608)742-2111
Fax: (608)742-8346
**Subject(s):** Shopping Guides

Circ: (Non-paid)22,065

**Echoes (10188)**
Rose-Hulman Institute of Technology
5500 Wabash Ave.
Terre Haute, IN 47803
Phone: (812)877-8258
Fax: (812)877-8362
**Subject(s):** College Publications

Circ: (Free)22,000

**The Octopus (8026)**
2603 W Bradley Ave.
Champaign, IL 61821-1829
Fax: (217)398-0946
**Subject(s):** Free Newspapers; Alternative and Underground

Circ: (Combined)22,000

**Middletown Journal (24903)**
52 S. Broad St.
PO Box 490
Middletown, OH 45042
Phone: (513)422-3611
Fax: (513)422-8698
**Subject(s):** Daily Newspapers

Circ: (Mon.-Sat.)★19,924
 (Sun.)★21,994

**The Star Beacon (24138)**
Thomsom Newspaper
PO Box 2100
Ashtabula, OH 44005-2100
Phone: (440)998-2323
Fax: (440)998-7938
**Subject(s):** Daily Newspapers

Circ: (Mon.-Sat.)20,607
 (Sun.)21,977

**The Capital Times (33161)**
1901 Fish Hatchery Rd.
PO Box 8060
Madison, WI 53708
Phone: (608)252-6400
Fax: (608)252-6445
**Subject(s):** Daily Newspapers

Circ: (Mon.-Fri.)19,408
 (Sat.)21,956

**The Republic (9752)**
Home News Enterprises L.L.C.
2575 N Morton St.
Franklin, IN 46131
Phone: (317)736-7101
Fax: (317)736-2759
**Subject(s):** Daily Newspapers

Circ: (Combined)21,912

**The Post-Journal and Metro Rockford Journal (9302)**
Rock Valley Publishing
11512 N 2nd St.
Machesney Park, IL 61115
Phone: (815)877-4044
Fax: (815)654-4857
**Subject(s):** Paid Community Newspapers

Circ: ‡21,855

**Times-Recorder Midweek (25228)**
Thompson Newspaper
34 S 4th St.
Zanesville, OH 43701
Phone: (740)452-4561
Fax: (740)452-4561
**Subject(s):** Shopping Guides

Circ: (Mon.-Sat.)21,806

**Fox Valley Shopping News (9541)**
PO Box 609
Yorkville, IL 60560-0609
Phone: (630)553-7431
Fax: (630)553-0310
**Subject(s):** Shopping Guides

Circ: (Paid)228
 (Free)21,773

**The Centerville-Bellbrook Times (24265)**
Times Community Newspapers
3085 Woodman Dr., Ste. 170
Kettering, OH 45420-1159
Phone: (937)294-7000
Fax: (937)294-2981
**Subject(s):** Paid Community Newspapers

Circ: (Sat.)2,548
 (Wed.)21,766

**Palm Beach Jewish Journal North (8369)**
Tribune Co.
435 N Michigan Ave.
Chicago, IL 60611
Phone: (312)222-9100
Fax: (312)222-4674
**Subject(s):** Free Newspapers; Jewish Publications

Circ: (Combined)21,575

**Agri News (16509)**
Post-Bulletin
18 1st Ave. SE
PO Box 6118
Rochester, MN 55903-6118
Phone: (507)285-7600
Fax: (507)281-7436
**Subject(s):** Farm Newspapers

Circ: (Paid)‡21,500

**Door County Advocate (33562)**
Door County Publishing Co.
Box 130
Sturgeon Bay, WI 54235-0130
Phone: (920)743-5817
**Subject(s):** Paid Community Newspapers

Circ: (Paid)12,600
 (Combined)21,500

**Lombardian (8909)**
116 S Main St.
Lombard, IL 60148-2628
Phone: (630)627-7010
Fax: (630)627-7027
**Subject(s):** Paid Community Newspapers

Circ: ‡21,500

**Villa Park Review/Lombardian (8911)**
Lombardian
116 S Main St.
Lombard, IL 60148-2628
Phone: (630)627-7010
Fax: (630)627-7027
**Subject(s):** Paid Community Newspapers

Circ: 13,500
 ‡21,500

**Hot Sheet (TMC) (33055)**
Hudson Star-Observer
226 Locust St.
Hudson, WI 54016-1668
Phone: (715)386-9333
Fax: (715)386-9891
**Subject(s):** Shopping Guides

Circ: (Free)‡21,472

**Star Republican (25182)**
Brown Publishing Co.
47 S S. St.
Wilmington, OH 45177
Phone: (937)382-2574
**Subject(s):** Paid Community Newspapers

Circ: (Paid)‡200
 (Free)‡21,400

**Virginia Manney Shopper (16678)**
Manney's Shopper Inc.
626 1/2 2nd Ave.
PO Box 66
Two Harbors, MN 55616
Phone: (218)834-5551
Fax: (218)834-2555
**Subject(s):** Shopping Guides

Circ: (Free)‡21,406

**The Naperville Sun (9042)**
Sun Publications
1500 W. Ogden Ave.
PO Box 269
Naperville, IL 60566-0269
Phone: (630)355-0063
Fax: (630)416-5163
**Subject(s):** Paid Community Newspapers

Circ: (Sun.)20,828
 (Wed.)21,234
 (Fri.)21,234

Circulation: ★ = ABC; △ = BPA; ♦ = CAC; • = CCAB; ❑ = VAC; ⊕ = PO Statement; ‡ = Publisher's Report; Boldface figures = sworn; Light figures = estimated.

**Chronicle-Tribune** (10010)
Gannett Company Inc.
PO Box 309
Marion, IN 46952-0309
**Subject(s):** Daily Newspapers
**Circ:** (Mon.-Sat.)18,928
(Sun.)21,199

**The Times Leader** (24878)
200 S 4th St.
Martins Ferry, OH 43935
Phone: (740)633-1131
Fax: (740)633-1122
**Subject(s):** Daily Newspapers
**Circ:** (Mon.-Fri.)18,355
(Sun.)21,037

**Superior Manney Shopper** (33572)
Manney's Shopper Inc.
1105 Tower Ave.
Superior, WI 54880
Phone: (715)394-5571
Fax: (715)394-2751
**Subject(s):** Shopping Guides
**Circ:** (Free)‡20,933

**Countryside/Indian Head Park/Willow Springs/Burr Ridge/Pleasantdale Suburban Life** (9086)
Liberty Suburban Chicago Newspapers
7222 W. Cermak Rd., Ste. 505
North Riverside, IL 60546
Phone: (708)447-9810
**Subject(s):** Paid Community Newspapers
**Circ:** (Paid)20,850

**Hillside/Broadview/Berkeley/Westchester Suburban Life** (9090)
Liberty Suburban Chicago Newspapers
7222 W. Cermak Rd., Ste. 505
North Riverside, IL 60546
Phone: (708)447-9810
**Subject(s):** Paid Community Newspapers
**Circ:** (Paid)20,850

**The Midweek** (16123)
The Midweek Inc.
PO Box 651
Fergus Falls, MN 56538
Phone: (218)739-3308
**Subject(s):** Shopping Guides
**Circ:** (Non-paid)20,853

**North Riverside/Riverside/Riverside Lawn Suburban Life** (9095)
Liberty Suburban Chicago Newspapers
7222 W. Cermak Rd., Ste. 505
North Riverside, IL 60546
Phone: (708)447-9810
**Subject(s):** Paid Community Newspapers
**Circ:** (Paid)20,850

**Western Springs Suburban Life** (9101)
Liberty Suburban Chicago Newspapers
7222 W. Cermak Rd., Ste. 505
North Riverside, IL 60546
Phone: (708)447-9810
**Subject(s):** Paid Community Newspapers
**Circ:** (Paid)20,850

**The Reporter (Fond du Lac)** (32952)
The Reporter
PO Box 630
33 W. 2nd St.
Fond du Lac, WI 54936-0630
Phone: (920)922-4600
Fax: (920)922-3552
**Subject(s):** Daily Newspapers
**Circ:** (Mon.-Fri.)19,000
(Sun.)20,807

**River Valley News Shopper** (15429)
The Pioneer Group
491 Shaw St.
PO Box 407
Howard City, MI 49329
Phone: (231)937-4740
Fax: (231)937-4048
**Subject(s):** Shopping Guides
**Circ:** (Free)‡20,600

**Tire Business** (24105)
Crain Communications Inc.
1725 Merriman Rd., Ste. 300
Akron, OH 44313-5283
Phone: (330)836-9180

Fax: (330)836-2831
**Subject(s):** Automotive (Trade)
**Circ:** (Paid)★7,628
(Non-paid)★20,601

**Chatham-Southeast Citizen** (8122)
Citizen Newspapers
806 E. 78th St.
Chicago, IL 60619
Phone: (773)783-1251
Fax: (773)783-1301
**Subject(s):** Paid Community Newspapers; Black Publications
**Circ:** (Free)‡9,365
(Paid)‡20,597

**The Press, Metro Edition** (24910)
Douthit Communications Inc.
PO Box 169
Millbury, OH 43447
Phone: (419)836-2221
Fax: (419)836-1319
**Subject(s):** Free Newspapers
**Circ:** (Free)‡20,564

**The Detroit Jewish News** (15176)
29200 Northwestern Hwy., Ste.110
Southfield, MI 48034
Phone: (248)354-6060
Fax: (248)354-6069
**Subject(s):** Jewish Publications
**Circ:** (Free)300
(Paid)20,555

**Wild Rivers Advertiser - South** (32996)
Inter-County Co-op Publishing Association
303 N Wisconsin Ave.
PO Box 490
Frederic, WI 54837
Phone: (715)327-4236
Fax: (715)327-4870
**Subject(s):** Shopping Guides
**Circ:** (Free)‡20,551

**Wyoming Advance** (15900)
Advance Newspapers
2141 Port Sheldon Rd.
PO Box 9
Jenison, MI 49428-9301
Phone: (616)669-2700
Fax: (616)669-1162
**Subject(s):** Paid Community Newspapers
**Circ:** (Paid)❏1,397
(Free)❏20,548

**The Times Recorder** (25227)
Thomson Newspapers
34 S 4th St.
Zanesville, OH 43701
Phone: (614)452-4561
Fax: (614)452-0750
**Subject(s):** Daily Newspapers
**Circ:** (Sun.)★20,295
(Mon.-Sat.)★20,428

**Calumet County Shopper** (32885)
Calumet Publishing
19 E Main St.
Chilton, WI 53014
Phone: (920)849-4551
Fax: (920)849-4651
**Subject(s):** Shopping Guides
**Circ:** (Free)‡20,400

**North Woods Trader** (32916)
Eagle River Publications Inc.
346 W Division St.
PO Box 1929
Eagle River, WI 54521
Phone: (715)479-4421
Fax: (715)479-6242
**Subject(s):** Shopping Guides
**Circ:** (Free)‡20,300

**Cadillac News** (15086)
130 N. Mitchell St.
PO Box 640
Cadillac, MI 49601
Phone: (231)775-6565
Fax: (231)775-8790
**Subject(s):** Daily Newspapers
**Circ:** (Mon.-Fri.)‡1,0218
(Sat.)‡11,500
(Free)‡2,0225

**The Holland Sentinel** (15415)
54 W 8th St.
Holland, MI 49423
Phone: (616)392-2311
Fax: (616)392-3526
**Subject(s):** Daily Newspapers
**Circ:** (Mon.-Sat.)★18,746
(Sun.)★20,201

**Indianhead Advertiser** (32991)
Inter-County Co-op Publishing Association
303 N Wisconsin Ave.
PO Box 490
Frederic, WI 54837
Phone: (715)327-4236
Fax: (715)327-4870
**Subject(s):** Shopping Guides
**Circ:** (Free)‡20,188

**East Side Review** (16433)
Lillie Suburban Newspapers
2515 7th Ave. East
North Saint Paul, MN 55109
Phone: (612)777-8800
Fax: (612)777-8288
**Subject(s):** Free Newspapers
**Circ:** (Free)20,128

**Peoria Times Observer** (9217)
Times Newspapers
1616 W Pioneer Pkwy.
Peoria, IL 61615
Phone: (309)692-6600
Fax: (309)690-3399
**Subject(s):** Paid Community Newspapers
**Circ:** (Paid)150
(Free)20,100

**The Pickaway County Advertiser** (24369)
Add Inc.—Ohio Group
1204 N Court St.
Circleville, OH 43113
Phone: (740)477-3386
Fax: (740)474-9750
**Subject(s):** Shopping Guides
**Circ:** (Non-paid)♦20,010

**AHA News** (8058)
Health Forum L.L.C.
1 N Franklin, 29th Fl.
Chicago, IL 60606
Phone: (312)893-6800
Fax: (312)422-4506
**Subject(s):** Hospitals and Healthcare Institutions
**Circ:** (Paid)20,000

**Buyers Express** (33122)
1523 Rose St.
La Crosse, WI 54603
Phone: (608)791-7171
Fax: (608)791-7107
**Subject(s):** Shopping Guides
**Circ:** (Free)‡20,000

**Courier-Press** (33485)
Howe Printing Company Inc.
132 S. Beaumont Rd.
PO Box 149
Prairie du Chien, WI 53821
Phone: (608)326-2441
Fax: (608)326-2443
**Subject(s):** Paid Community Newspapers
**Circ:** (Combined)‡20,000

**The Daily Illini** (8009)
Illini Media Co.
57 E. Green St.
Champaign, IL 61820
Phone: (217)333-3733
Fax: (217)244-6616
**Subject(s):** College Publications
**Circ:** ‡20,000

**The East Side Herald** (9847)
East Side Suburban Newspapers
4309 E Michigan St., No. 11042
Indianapolis, IN 46201-3652
Phone: (317)356-2487
Fax: (317)356-5871
**Subject(s):** Free Newspapers
**Circ:** (Paid)50
(Free)20,000

**Hi-Lites Shoppers Guide (15309)**
Hi-Lites Graphics Inc.
1212 Locust
Fremont, MI 49412
Phone: (616)924-0630
Fax: (616)924-5580
**Subject(s):** Shopping Guides
**Circ:** (Free)20,000

**In These Times (8236)**
Institute for Public Affairs Inc.
2040 N. Milwaukee Ave.
Chicago, IL 60647
Phone: (773)772-0100
Fax: (773)772-4180
**Subject(s):** Politics; Paid Community Newspapers
**Circ:** ‡20,000

**The Mature American (33313)**
Alternative Publications Inc.
413 N 2nd St., No. 150
Milwaukee, WI 53203-3110
Phone: (414)276-2222
Fax: (414)276-3312
**Subject(s):** Senior Citizens' Interests
**Circ:** (Controlled)20,000

**The Niles Bugle (9062)**
Bugle Publications
7400 Waukekan Rd.
Niles, IL 60714
Phone: (847)588-1900
Fax: (847)588-1911
**Subject(s):** Free Newspapers
**Circ:** (Free)‡20,000

**Outlines (8366)**
Lambda Publications Inc.
1115 W Belmont Ave., Ste. 2-D
Chicago, IL 60657
Phone: (773)871-7610
Fax: (773)871-7609
**Subject(s):** Gay and Lesbian Interests
**Circ:** (Paid)1,000
(Non-paid)20,000

**The Rock River Times (9304)**
128 N. Church St.
Rockford, IL 61107
Phone: (815)964-9767
Fax: (815)964-9825
**Subject(s):** Free Newspapers
**Circ:** (Free)‡20,000

**Tempo (33120)**
Delta Publications Inc.
606 Fremont St.
Kiel, WI 53042
Phone: (920)894-2828
Fax: (920)894-2161
**Subject(s):** Shopping Guides
**Circ:** (Free)‡20,000

**Ashtabula Star-Beacon (24137)**
4626 Park Ave.
PO Box 2100
Ashtabula, OH 44004
Phone: (440)994-3241
Fax: (440)992-9655
**Subject(s):** Daily Newspapers
**Circ:** (Mon.-Sat.)★**18,747**
(Sun.)★**19,905**

**Tri-County South Advisor (32994)**
Inter-County Co-op Publishing Association
303 N Wisconsin Ave.
PO Box 490
Frederic, WI 54837
Phone: (715)327-4236
Fax: (715)327-4870
**Subject(s):** Shopping Guides
**Circ:** (Free)‡19,836

**Alpena Star (14988)**
Morningstar Publications
431 N. Ripley Blvd.
PO Box 464
Alpena, MI 49707
Phone: (989)356-2121
Fax: (989)354-8275
**Subject(s):** Shopping Guides
**Circ:** (Combined)19,800

**Northern Star (15320)**
Morningstar Publications
1966 S. Otsego Ave.
P. O. Box 620
Gaylord, MI 49735
Phone: (989)732-5125
Fax: (989)732-9323
**Subject(s):** Shopping Guides
**Circ:** (Non-paid)19,800

**Tri-County Buyers' Guide (15760)**
American Publishing of Michigan
109 Arlington St.
Sault Sainte Marie, MI 49783-1901
Phone: (906)632-2235
Fax: (906)632-1222
**Subject(s):** Shopping Guides
**Circ:** (Free)‡19,770

**Commercial-News (8528)**
Gannett Company Inc.
17 W. North St.
Danville, IL 61833
Phone: (217)446-1000
Fax: (217)446-6648
**Subject(s):** Daily Newspapers
**Circ:** (Mon.-Sat.)17,733
(Sun.)19,629

**South End Citizen (8411)**
Citizen Newspapers
806 E. 78th St.
Chicago, IL 60619
Phone: (773)783-1251
Fax: (773)783-1301
**Subject(s):** Paid Community Newspapers; Black Publications
**Circ:** (Paid)‡9,121
(Free)‡19,586

**Wisconsin-Iowa Shopping News (33486)**
Woodward Communications
405 Marquette
PO Box 97
Prairie du Chien, WI 53821-0097
Phone: (608)326-2457
**Subject(s):** Shopping Guides
**Circ:** (Paid)54
(Non-paid)19,564

**Fairfield Echo (24719)**
The Journal News
5120 Dixie Hwy.
Fairfield, OH 45014
Phone: (513)863-3478
Fax: (513)829-7950
**Subject(s):** Free Newspapers
**Circ:** (Free)‡19,500

**Northfield Advance (15343)**
Advance Newspapers
2141 Port Sheldon Rd.
PO Box 9
Jenison, MI 49428-9301
Phone: (616)669-2700
Fax: (616)669-1162
**Subject(s):** Paid Community Newspapers
**Circ:** (Paid)▫5
(Free)▫**19,495**

**Daily Journal (9749)**
Home News Enterprises L.L.C.
2575 N Morton St.
Franklin, IN 46131
Phone: (317)736-7101
Fax: (317)736-2759
**Subject(s):** Daily Newspapers
**Circ:** (Mon.-Fri.)♦**18,487**
(Sat.)♦**19,453**

**Nursery News (8361)**
Cenflo Inc.
205 W Wacker Dr., Ste. 1040
Chicago, IL 60606-3508
Phone: (312)739-5000
Fax: (312)739-0739
**Subject(s):** Seed and Nursery Trade
**Circ:** (Paid)‡2,246
(Non-paid)‡19,446

**Rhinelander/Hodag Buyers' Guide (33501)**
Add Inc.
24 Rives St.
PO Box 558
Rhinelander, WI 54501
Phone: (715)369-3331

Fax: (715)369-2691
**Subject(s):** Shopping Guides
**Circ:** (Combined)19,438

**The Daily Tribune (15712)**
Independent Newspapers Inc.
210 E. 3rd St.
Royal Oak, MI 48068
Phone: (248)541-3000
Fax: (248)541-3096
**Subject(s):** Daily Newspapers
**Circ:** (Mon.-Fri.)16,148
(Sun.)19,342

**The Farmers' Advance (15094)**
Camden Publications Inc.
331 E. Bell St.
Camden, MI 49232
Phone: (517)368-5201
Fax: (517)368-5131
**Subject(s):** Farm Newspapers
**Circ:** (Free)‡2,512
(Paid)‡19,315

**Crain's Cleveland Business (24393)**
Crain Communications Inc.
700 W. St. Clair, Ste. 310
Cleveland, OH 44113
Phone: (216)522-1383
Fax: (216)694-4264
**Subject(s):** Business; Local, State, and Regional Publications
**Circ:** (Paid)★**19,287**

**Henry County Advertiser Shopper (8720)**
Geneseo Republic
108 W 1st St.
Geneseo, IL 61254-0209
Phone: (309)944-2119
Fax: (309)944-5615
**Subject(s):** Shopping Guides
**Circ:** (Free)19,200

**Brooklyn Park Sun-Post (16088)**
Minnesota Sun Publications
10917 Valley View Rd.
Eden Prairie, MN 55344
Phone: (952)829-0797
Fax: (952)392-6868
**Subject(s):** Free Newspapers
**Circ:** (Paid)513
(Non-paid)19,170

**Deerfield Beach Times (8170)**
Tribune Co.
435 N Michigan Ave.
Chicago, IL 60611
Phone: (312)222-9100
Fax: (312)222-4674
**Subject(s):** Free Newspapers
**Circ:** (Free)19,133

**The Steubenville Register (25062)**
Diocese of Steubenville
422 Washington St.
PO Box 160
Steubenville, OH 43952-2181
Phone: (740)282-3631
Fax: (740)282-3238
**Subject(s):** Religious Publications
**Circ:** (Free)⊕120
(Paid)⊕**19,096**

**Sanilac County Buyer's Guide (15752)**
356 E Sanilac Ave.
PO Box 72
Sandusky, MI 48471-0072
Phone: (810)648-9900
Fax: (810)648-4526
**Subject(s):** Shopping Guides
**Circ:** (Free)19,086

**Petoskey/Charlevoix Star (15670)**
Morningstar Publications
1327 Spring St.
PO Box 826
Petoskey, MI 49770
Phone: (231)347-8186
Fax: (231)347-5744
**Subject(s):** Free Newspapers; Shopping Guides
**Circ:** (Non-paid)19,070

**Monday Marketeer** (33257)
Citizen Publishing Co.
51 E. John St.
PO Box 394
Markesan, WI 53946
Phone: (920)398-2334
Fax: (920)398-3835
**Subject(s):** Shopping Guides

Circ: (Free)‡19,000

**The Monitor** (16602)
Minnesota State University Student Association
106 Como Ave.
Saint Paul, MN 55103
Phone: (651)224-1518
Fax: (651)224-9753
**Subject(s):** College Publications

Circ: (Non-paid)‡19,000

**The Toledo Journal** (25092)
3021 Douglas Rd.
PO Box 2536
Toledo, OH 43606
Phone: (419)472-4521
Fax: (419)472-1602
**Subject(s):** Paid Community Newspapers; Black Publications

Circ: 19,000

**News-Tribune** (8849)
News-Tribune Publication
426 2nd St.
La Salle, IL 61301
Phone: (815)223-3200
Fax: (815)223-2543
**Subject(s):** Daily Newspapers

Circ: (Mon.-Sat.)18,953

**Chagrin Herald Sun** (24267)
Sun Newspapers
3355 Richmond Rd., Ste. 171
Beachwood, OH 44122-4171
Phone: (216)986-5890
Fax: (216)464-8816
**Subject(s):** Paid Community Newspapers

Circ: (Paid)18,897

**Solon Herald Sun** (25050)
Sun Newspapers
3355 Richmond Rd., Ste. 171
Beachwood, OH 44122-4171
Phone: (216)986-5890
Fax: (216)464-8816
**Subject(s):** Paid Community Newspapers

Circ: (Paid)18,897

**Crescent-News** (24691)
Defiance Publishing Co.
624 W Second St.
PO Box 249
Defiance, OH 43512
Phone: (419)784-5441
Fax: (419)784-1492
**Subject(s):** Daily Newspapers

Circ: (Mon.-Fri.)★17,652
(Sun.)★18,872

**The Reporter** (9194)
Regional Publishing Corp.
12247 S Harlem Ave.
Palos Heights, IL 60463-0932
Phone: (708)448-6161
Fax: (708)448-4012
**Subject(s):** Paid Community Newspapers

Circ: (Paid)⊕18,873

**The Thumb Blanket** (15037)
County Press
55 Westland Dr.
Bad Axe, MI 48413
Phone: (989)269-8109
Fax: (989)269-8109
**Subject(s):** Shopping Guides

Circ: (Non-paid)18,859

**Record-Courier** (25019)
126 N. Chestnut St.
PO Box 1201
Ravenna, OH 44266
Phone: (330)296-9657
Fax: (330)296-2698
**Subject(s):** Daily Newspapers

Circ: (Mon.-Sat.)★18,359
(Sun.)★18,810

**Marshall Community Advisor** (15588)
J-Ad Corp.
215 W. Michigan
Marshall, MI 49068-0111
Phone: (616)781-5444
Fax: (616)781-7766
**Subject(s):** Free Newspapers

Circ: (Free)18,791

**Regional News** (9193)
Regional Publishing Corp.
12247 S Harlem Ave.
Palos Heights, IL 60463-0932
Phone: (708)448-6161
Fax: (708)448-4012
**Subject(s):** Paid Community Newspapers

Circ: (Paid)⊕18,782

**Morrison County Record** (16218)
216 SE 1st St.
Little Falls, MN 56345
Phone: (320)632-2345
Fax: (320)632-2348
**Subject(s):** Paid Community Newspapers; Shopping Guides

Circ: (Paid)543
(Free)18,746

**News & Advertiser** (10266)
The News Gazette
Box 429
Winchester, IN 47394
Phone: (765)584-4501
Fax: (765)584-3066
**Subject(s):** Paid Community Newspapers

Circ: ‡18,688

**Good Morning Advertiser** (33660)
Hometown News Group Publications
136 W. Main St.
Whitewater, WI 53190
Phone: (262)473-2711
Fax: (262)753-0001
**Subject(s):** Shopping Guides

Circ: ‡18,645

**The AD-vertiser** (15668)
The AD-vertiser Inc.
1327 Spring St.
PO Box 826
Petoskey, MI 49770
Phone: (231)347-8186
Fax: (231)347-5744
**Subject(s):** Shopping Guides

Circ: (Free)‡18,592

**Farm and Home News** (10054)
The Pilot Company Inc.
158 W Market St.
PO Box 230
Nappanee, IN 46550-0230
Phone: (574)773-3127
Fax: (574)936-3844
**Subject(s):** Shopping Guides

Circ: (Free)18,500

**Penasee Globe** (15885)
Wayland Printing Inc.
133 E Superior
Wayland, MI 49348
Phone: (269)792-2271
Fax: (269)792-2030
**Subject(s):** Free Newspapers

Circ: (Free)‡18,500

**Rantoul Press** (9272)
East Central Communications Inc.
1332 Harmon Dr. E
PO Box 5110
Rantoul, IL 61866
Phone: (217)892-9613
Fax: (217)892-9451
**Subject(s):** Paid Community Newspapers

Circ: (Paid)♦7,459
(Non-paid)♦18,508

**Shoreline Chronicle** (33538)
PO Box 358
Sheboygan, WI 53082-0358
Phone: (920)459-8820
Fax: (920)459-7449
**Subject(s):** Shopping Guides

Circ: (Non-paid)18,379

**Northside Topics** (10075)
Topics Newspapers Inc.
PO Box 1478
Noblesville, IN 46061
Phone: (317)598-6397
Fax: (317)598-6360
**Subject(s):** Free Newspapers

Circ: (Paid)65
(Non-paid)18,323

**Wild Rivers Advertiser - North** (32995)
Inter-County Co-op Publishing Association
303 N Wisconsin Ave.
PO Box 490
Frederic, WI 54837
Phone: (715)327-4236
Fax: (715)327-4870
**Subject(s):** Shopping Guides

Circ: (Free)‡18,305

**Search Shopper** (16215)
PO Box 748
Lindstrom, MN 55045-0748
Phone: (651)257-5115
Fax: (651)257-5500
**Subject(s):** Shopping Guides

Circ: (Free)‡18,277

**Dispatch** (15978)
The Brainerd Daily Dispatch
506 James St.
PO Box 974
Brainerd, MN 56401
Phone: (218)829-4705
Fax: (218)829-7735
**Subject(s):** Daily Newspapers

Circ: (Mon.-Fri.)13,994
(Sun.)18,261

**County Press** (15541)
1521 Imlay City Rd.
Lapeer, MI 48446
Phone: (810)664-0811
Fax: (810)664-5852
**Subject(s):** Paid Community Newspapers

Circ: (Wed.)16,865
(Sun.)18,100

**Midland Daily News** (15590)
PO Box 432
Midland, MI 48640-5161
Phone: (517)835-7171
Fax: (517)835-6991
**Subject(s):** Daily Newspapers

Circ: (Mon.-Sat.)★16,439
(Sun.)★18,054

**The Advertiser** (9777)
Daily Reporter
22 W New Rd.
PO Box 279
Greenfield, IN 46140
Phone: (317)462-5528
Fax: (317)467-6009
**Subject(s):** Shopping Guides

Circ: (Non-paid)‡18,000

**Cass River Trader** (15873)
Bilbey Publications L.L.C.
PO Box 1653
Vassar, MI 48768
Phone: (989)823-8651
Fax: (989)823-2531
**Subject(s):** Shopping Guides

Circ: (Free)18,000

**Courier** (9502)
100 Ford Ln.
PO Box 349
Washington, IL 61571
Phone: (309)444-3139
Fax: (309)444-8505
**Subject(s):** Free Newspapers

Circ: (Paid)‡500
(Free)‡18,000

**Downtowner Newspaper** (24306)
Taylor Communications Inc.
128 E 6th St.
Cincinnati, OH 45202
Phone: (513)241-9906
Fax: (513)241-7235
**Subject(s):** Free Newspapers

Circ: (Free)‡18,000

**The Holmes County Bargain Hunter (24912)**
Graphic Publications Inc.
7368 County Rd. 623
PO Box 358
Millersburg, OH 44654
Phone: (330)674-2300
Fax: (330)674-2461
**Subject(s):** Free Newspapers

Circ: (Free)18,000

**The Michigan Daily (15013)**
420 Maynard St.
Ann Arbor, MI 48109-1327
**Subject(s):** College Publications

Circ: (Free)‡18,000

**Lake County Buyer's Guide (33043)**
PO Box 200
Hartland, WI 53029
Phone: (262)367-3272
Fax: (262)367-7414
**Subject(s):** Shopping Guides

Circ: (Free)17,902

**The Evergreen Shopping Guide (33550)**
Murphy McGinnis Media Inc.
PO Box 338
Spooner, WI 54801
Phone: (715)635-2181
Fax: (715)635-2186
**Subject(s):** Shopping Guides

Circ: (Non-paid)♦17,778

**Herald-Times Reporter (33246)**
902 Franklin St.
Manitowoc, WI 54220
Phone: (920)684-4433
Fax: (920)684-4416
**Subject(s):** Daily Newspapers

Circ: (Sun.)17,495
(Mon.-Sat.)17,771

**The Press, Suburban Edition (24911)**
Photo Journal Press
POB 169
Millbury, OH 43447
Phone: (419)836-2221
Fax: (419)836-1319
**Subject(s):** Free Newspapers

Circ: ‡17,764

**West Shore Shoppers Guide (15566)**
The Pioneer Group
75 Maple St.
PO Box 317
Manistee, MI 49660
Phone: (616)723-3592
Fax: (616)723-4733
**Subject(s):** Shopping Guides

Circ: (Free)17,700

**The Bonus Paper (33437)**
Shellman Publishing Inc.
107 S Main St.
PO Box 128
Oconto Falls, WI 54154-0128
Phone: (920)848-3427
Fax: (920)848-3430
**Subject(s):** Shopping Guides

Circ: (Free)‡17,658

**Hyde Park Herald (8232)**
Herald Newspaper Inc.
5240 S Harper St
Chicago, IL 60615
Phone: (773)643-8533
Fax: (773)643-8542
**Subject(s):** Free Newspapers

Circ: (Paid)‡9,000
(Free)‡17,600

**St. Johns Reminder (15741)**
109 W Higham St.
PO Box 473
Saint Johns, MI 48879-0473
Phone: (989)224-8356
Fax: (989)224-9458
**Subject(s):** Shopping Guides

Circ: (Free)17,600

**Northland News (24575)**
Suburban News Publications
5257 Sinclair Rd.
PO Box 29912
Columbus, OH 43229
Phone: (614)785-1212
Fax: (614)785-1881
**Subject(s):** Free Newspapers

Circ: (Paid)3,830
(Non-paid)17,553

**The Sun Press (24174)**
Sun Newspapers
3355 Richmond Rd., Ste. 171
Beachwood, OH 44122-4171
Phone: (216)986-5890
Fax: (216)464-8816
**Subject(s):** Paid Community Newspapers

Circ: (Paid)17,538

**Boone County Shopper, Inc. (7893)**
Boone County Shopper Inc.
112 Leonard Ct.
Belvidere, IL 61008
Phone: (815)544-2166
Fax: (815)544-5558
**Subject(s):** Shopping Guides

Circ: (Paid)‡70
(Free)‡17,515

**Northwest Indiana Catholic (10019)**
9292 Broadway
Merrillville, IN 46410
Phone: (219)769-9292
Fax: (219)738-9034
**Subject(s):** Religious Publications

Circ: (Paid)‡17,500

**The Courier News (8631)**
Copley Newspapers/Copley Press
300 Lake St.
Elgin, IL 60120
Phone: (847)888-7780
Fax: (708)888-7714
**Subject(s):** Daily Newspapers

Circ: (Mon.-Sat.)16,121
(Sun.)17,331

**Edina Sun Current (16097)**
Minnesota Sun Publications
10917 Valley View Rd.
Eden Prairie, MN 55344
Phone: (952)829-0797
Fax: (952)392-6868
**Subject(s):** Free Newspapers

Circ: (Paid)1,337
(Non-paid)17,301

**Geneva Republican (9088)**
Liberty Suburban Chicago Newspapers
7222 W. Cermak Rd., Ste. 505
North Riverside, IL 60546
Phone: (708)447-9810
**Subject(s):** Paid Community Newspapers

Circ: (Combined)17,300

**St. Charles Republican (9097)**
Liberty Suburban Chicago Newspapers
7222 W. Cermak Rd., Ste. 505
North Riverside, IL 60546
Phone: (708)447-9810
**Subject(s):** Paid Community Newspapers

Circ: (Combined)17,300

**The Shopper (33393)**
News Publishing
614 Hewett St.
PO Box 149
Neillsville, WI 54456
Phone: (715)743-2600
Fax: (715)743-5460
**Subject(s):** Shopping Guides

Circ: (Free)17,300

**The Free Enterprise (24746)**
Gazette Newspapers
2899 Hubbard Rd.
Madison, OH 44057-2933
Phone: (440)428-0790
Fax: (440)428-0786
**Subject(s):** Shopping Guides

Circ: (Free)17,269

**Gladwin Buyers Guide (15324)**
Morning Star Publishing Co.
311 E Superior
PO Box 425
Alma, MI 48801
Phone: (989)463-6071
Fax: (989)463-3338
**Subject(s):** Shopping Guides

Circ: (Free)17,200

**West Geauga Sun (25127)**
Sun Newspapers
5510 Cloverleaf Pkwy.
Valley View, OH 44125-4887
Phone: (216)986-2600
Fax: (216)986-2380
**Subject(s):** Paid Community Newspapers

Circ: (Paid)17,164

**West Central Tribune (16710)**
2208 Trott Ave. SW
PO Box 839
Willmar, MN 56201
Phone: (320)235-1150
Fax: (320)235-6769
**Subject(s):** Daily Newspapers

Circ: (Paid)17,134

**Three Rivers Commercial-News (15824)**
Three Rivers Commerical News
124 N Main St.
PO Box 130
Three Rivers, MI 49093
Phone: (269)279-7488
Fax: (269)279-6007
**Subject(s):** Daily Newspapers

Circ: (Paid)4,503
(Free)‡17,100

**The Athens News (24144)**
Athens News Inc.
14 N. Court St.
Athens, OH 45701
Phone: (740)594-8219
Fax: (740)592-5695
**Subject(s):** Free Newspapers

Circ: (Paid)❏13
(Free)❏17,062

**The Mining Journal (15574)**
PO Box 430
Marquette, MI 49855
Phone: (906)228-2500
Fax: (906)228-5556
**Subject(s):** Daily Newspapers

Circ: (Mon.-Sat.)★**14,963**
(Sun.)★**17,046**

**The Graphic (15669)**
Petoskey News-Review, Super Shopper, and Graphic
319 State St.
PO Box 528
Petoskey, MI 49770-0528
Phone: (231)347-2544
Fax: (231)347-6833
**Subject(s):** Free Newspapers

Circ: (Free)17,000

**Hyde Park Citizen (8231)**
Citizen Newspapers
806 E. 78th St.
Chicago, IL 60619
Phone: (773)783-1251
Fax: (773)783-1301
**Subject(s):** Paid Community Newspapers; Black Publications

Circ: ‡17,000

**Image (9779)**
Indy Suburban Newspapers
119 W N St.
Greenfield, IN 46140
Phone: (317)462-7368
Fax: (317)462-7779
**Subject(s):** Paid Community Newspapers

Circ: ‡17,000

**Indiana Daily Student (9593)**
Indiana University
Ernie Pyle Hall, Rm. 120
Bloomington, IN 47405
Phone: (812)855-0763
Fax: (812)855-8009
**Subject(s):** College Publications

Circ: ‡17,000

Circulation: ★ = ABC; △ = BPA; ♦ = CAC; • = CCAB; ❏ = VAC; ⊕ = PO Statement; ‡ = Publisher's Report; Boldface figures = sworn; Light figures = estimated.

# Great Lakes States

**Brainerd Daily Dispatch (15977)**
Morris Communications Corp.
Brainerd Daily Dispatch
506 James St.
PO Box 974
Brainerd, MN 56401
Phone: (218)829-4705
Fax: (218)829-7735
**Subject(s):** Daily Newspapers
Circ: (Mon.-Fri.)13,049
 (Sun.)16,990

**The Banner-Gazette (10104)**
Green Banner Publications Inc.
PO Box 38
Pekin, IN 47165-0038
Phone: (812)967-3176
Fax: (812)967-3194
**Subject(s):** Free Newspapers
Circ: (Paid)86
 (Free)16,952

**The Giveaway (10150)**
Green Banner Publications Inc.
183 East McClain St.
Scottsburg, IN 47170
Phone: (812)752-3171
Fax: (812)752-6486
**Subject(s):** Free Newspapers
Circ: (Paid)90
 (Free)16,873

**Livingston County Press and Argus (15433)**
Hometown Newspapers
PO Box 230
Howell, MI 48844
**Subject(s):** Paid Community Newspapers
Circ: (Mon.-Sat.)15,335
 (Sun.)16,801

**Elk River Star News (16103)**
ECM Publishing
506 Freeport
PO Box 330
Elk River, MN 55330
Phone: (763)241-8146
Fax: (763)441-6401
**Subject(s):** Free Newspapers
Circ: (Paid)‡16,718

**Northern Michigan News (15087)**
130 N Mitchell St.
PO Box 640
Cadillac, MI 49601-1856
Phone: (231)775-6565
Fax: (231)775-8790
**Subject(s):** Free Newspapers
Circ: (Paid)‡9,747
 (Free)‡16,638

**Skyline (8897)**
Lerner Communications Inc.
7331 N Lincoln Ave.
Lincolnwood, IL 60712
Phone: (847)329-2000
Fax: (847)329-2060
**Subject(s):** Free Newspapers
Circ: (Paid)40
 (Non-paid)16,610

**The Goshen News (9764)**
PO Box 569
Goshen, IN 46526-0569
Phone: (219)533-2151
Fax: (219)533-0839
**Subject(s):** Daily Newspapers
Circ: (Sun.)16,246
 (Mon.-Sat.)16,517

**Tri-County North Advertiser (32993)**
Inter-County Co-op Publishing Association
303 N Wisconsin Ave.
PO Box 490
Frederic, WI 54837
Phone: (715)327-4236
Fax: (715)327-4870
**Subject(s):** Shopping Guides
Circ: (Free)‡16,513

**Foto News (33280)**
Foto News Publications Inc.
805 E Main St.
Merrill, WI 54452
Phone: (715)536-7121
Fax: (715)539-3686

**Subject(s):** Free Newspapers
Circ: 251
 (Free)16,500

**Lake Front News (25006)**
Lake Front Publications
PO Box K
127 W Perry St
Port Clinton, OH 43452
Phone: (419)734-1280
Fax: (419)732-3664
**Subject(s):** Free Newspapers
Circ: (Free)‡16,500

**Shopper Stopper Extra (33480)**
Capital Newspapers
1640, Ladawn Dr.
Portage, WI 53901
Phone: (608)745-3500
Fax: (608)745-3530
**Subject(s):** Shopping Guides
Circ: (Non-paid)16,500

**The Daily Telegram (14961)**
133 N Winter St.
Adrian, MI 49221
Phone: (517)265-5111
Fax: (517)263-4152
**Subject(s):** Daily Newspapers
Circ: (Mon.-Sat.)15,361
 (Sun.)16,489

**Herald-Star (25061)**
401 Herald-Star
Steubenville, OH 43952
Phone: (740)283-4711
Fax: (740)282-4261
**Subject(s):** Daily Newspapers
Circ: (Mon.-Sat.)★14,435
 (Sun.)★16,460

**North Country Sun (15448)**
North Country Sun Inc.
PO Box 425
Ironwood, MI 49938
Phone: (906)932-3530
Fax: (906)932-3074
**Subject(s):** Shopping Guides
Circ: (Non-paid)16,430

**Brown County Press (24920)**
2919 South High St.
Mount Orab, OH 45154
Phone: (937)444-3441
Fax: (937)444-2652
**Subject(s):** Free Newspapers
Circ: (Free)‡16,350

**Allegan Flashes (14974)**
Flashes Publishers Inc.
595 Jenner Dr.
Allegan, MI 49010
Phone: (269)673-1602
Fax: (269)673-6768
**Subject(s):** Shopping Guides
Circ: (Paid)7
 (Free)16,340

**Rockford/Cedar Springs Advance (15703)**
Advance Newspapers
2141 Port Sheldon Rd.
PO Box 9
Jenison, MI 49428-9301
Phone: (616)669-2700
Fax: (616)669-1162
**Subject(s):** Free Newspapers
Circ: (Paid)❏125
 (Free)❏16,307

**Lake Area Press (16043)**
Forum Communications Co.
511 Washington Ave.
Detroit Lakes, MN 56501-3007
Phone: (218)847-3151
Fax: (218)847-9409
**Subject(s):** Free Newspapers
Circ: (Free)❏16,241

**The Paper (10228)**
Highways 24 & 13 N
PO Box 603
Wabash, IN 46992
Phone: (260)563-8326
Fax: (260)563-2863

**Subject(s):** Paid Community Newspapers
Circ: (Tues.)16,225

**Kentwood Advance (15497)**
Advance Newspapers
2141 Port Sheldon Rd.
PO Box 9
Jenison, MI 49428-9301
Phone: (616)669-2700
Fax: (616)669-1162
**Subject(s):** Paid Community Newspapers
Circ: (Paid)❏271
 (Free)❏16,148

**Waupaca Buyers' Guide (33624)**
Add Inc.
600 Industrial Dr
PO Box 609
Waupaca, WI 54981-0609
Phone: (715)258-3207
Fax: (715)258-4877
**Subject(s):** Shopping Guides
Circ: (Combined)16,062

**Anglican Advance (8078)**
Diocese of Chicago
65 E Huron St.
Chicago, IL 60611
Phone: (312)751-4207
Fax: (312)787-4534
**Subject(s):** Religious Publications
Circ: 16,000

**Chicago Standard News (8498)**
Standard Newspapers
615 S Halsted
Chicago Heights, IL 60411
Phone: (708)755-5021
Fax: (708)755-5020
**Subject(s):** Black Publications; Paid Community Newspapers
Circ: 16,000

**Cleveland Jewish News (24165)**
Cleveland Jewish Publication Co.
23880 Commerce Pk., No. 1
Beachwood, OH 44122
Phone: (216)454-8200
Fax: (216)454-8100
**Subject(s):** Paid Community Newspapers; Jewish Publications
Circ: (Paid)16,000

**Decatur Voice of the Black Community (8535)**
625 E Wood St.
Decatur, IL 62523
Phone: (217)423-2231
**Subject(s):** Paid Community Newspapers; Black Publications
Circ: (Non-paid)‡3,000
 (Paid)‡16,000

**Mississippi Monitor (16718)**
Upper Mississippi Basin Stakeholder Network
360 Vila St., 7
Winona, MN 55987
**Subject(s):** Free Newspapers
Circ: (Non-paid)16,000

**Muslim Journal (8800)**
Muslim Journal Enterprises Inc.
1141 W. 175st. St.
Homewood, IL 60430
Phone: (708)647-9600
Fax: (708)647-0754
**Subject(s):** Black Publications; Religious Publications
Circ: ‡16,000

**The Northern Star (8562)**
Northern Illinois University
Campus Life Bldg., Ste. 130
DeKalb, IL 60115
Phone: (815)753-0101
Fax: (815)753-0708
**Subject(s):** College Publications
Circ: (Fri.)12,000
 (Free)‡16,000

**Tech Center News (15880)**
Springer Publications
31201 Chicago Rd., Ste. A-101
Warren, MI 48093
Phone: (586)939-6800
Fax: (586)939-5850
**Subject(s):** Free Newspapers
Circ: (Controlled)‡16,000

**Welfare Warriors** (33341)
2711 W Michigan Ave.
Milwaukee, WI 53208
Phone: (414)342-6662
Fax: (414)342-6667
**Subject(s):** Free Newspapers; Women's Interests
**Circ:** (Paid)250
 (Non-paid)16,000

**Portsmouth Daily Times** (25008)
APMS
637 6th St.
Portsmouth, OH 45662
Phone: (740)353-3101
Fax: (740)353-7280
**Subject(s):** Daily Newspapers
**Circ:** (Sun.)15,830
 (Mon.-Sat.)15,944

**Roseville Review** (16436)
Lillie Suburban Newspapers
2515 E 7th Ave.
North Saint Paul, MN 55109
Phone: (651)777-8800
Fax: (651)777-8288
**Subject(s):** Free Newspapers
**Circ:** (Free)15,866

**Hilliard Northwest News** (24769)
Suburban News Publications
5257 Sinclair Rd.
PO Box 29912
Columbus, OH 43229
Phone: (614)785-1212
Fax: (614)785-1881
**Subject(s):** Free Newspapers
**Circ:** (Paid)3,585
 (Non-paid)15,774

**Straits Area Star** (15121)
Morningstar Publications
222 N. Main St.
Cheboygan, MI 49721
Phone: (231)627-3151
Fax: (231)627-6244
**Subject(s):** Shopping Guides
**Circ:** (Free)15,767

**Daily Vidette** (9068)
Illinois State University
University and Locust
Campus Box 0890
Normal, IL 61790-0890
Phone: (309)438-8742
Fax: (309)438-5211
**Subject(s):** College Publications
**Circ:** (Paid)‡300
 (Free)‡15,700

**Chillicothe Gazette** (24273)
50 W Main St.
Chillicothe, OH 45601
Fax: (740)772-9501
**Subject(s):** Daily Newspapers
**Circ:** (Mon.-Fri.)★**15,329**
 (Sat.)★**15,555**
 (Sun.)★**15,589**

**The Register-Mail** (8712)
140 S Prairie St.
PO Box 310
Galesburg, IL 61402-0310
Phone: (309)343-7181
Fax: (309)342-5171
**Subject(s):** Daily Newspapers
**Circ:** (Sun.)14,734
 (Mon.-Sat.)15,573

**Door Reminder** (33545)
PO Box 198
Country Walk Drive
Sister Bay, WI 54234
Phone: (920)854-2662
Fax: (920)854-2788
**Subject(s):** Shopping Guides
**Circ:** (Non-paid)15,544

**Southern Minnesota Peach** (16230)
Madelia Media Inc.
112 W Main St.
Madelia, MN 56062-1440
Phone: (507)642-3636
Fax: (507)642-3535
**Subject(s):** Shopping Guides
**Circ:** (Non-paid)‡15,500

**Stow Sentry** (25071)
Record Publishing Co.
1619 Commerce Dr.
Stow, OH 44224
Phone: (330)688-0088
Fax: (330)688-1588
**Subject(s):** Paid Community Newspapers
**Circ:** (Paid)‡15,433

**Action Shopper** (32950)
Action Publications
N6637 Rolling Meadows Dr.
Fond du Lac, WI 54937
Phone: (920)922-8640
Fax: (920)922-0125
**Subject(s):** Shopping Guides
**Circ:** (Wed.)15,414

**South Advance** (15801)
Advance Newspapers
2141 Port Sheldon Rd.
PO Box 9
Jenison, MI 49428-9301
Phone: (616)669-2700
Fax: (616)669-1162
**Subject(s):** Paid Community Newspapers
**Circ:** (Paid)❏271
 (Free)❏15,376

**Medina County Gazette** (24895)
885 W Liberty St.
Medina, OH 44258
Phone: (330)725-4166
Fax: (330)725-4299
**Subject(s):** Daily Newspapers
**Circ:** (Mon.-Sat.)15,356

**Morning Sentinel** (8001)
Centralia Press Ltd.
PO Box 627
Centralia, IL 62801
Phone: (800)371-9892
**Subject(s):** Daily Newspapers
**Circ:** (Combined)15,319

**Rochester Eccentric** (15701)
Observer & Eccentric Newspapers
36251 Schoolcraft Rd.
Livonia, MI 48150
Phone: (734)591-2300
Fax: (734)953-2232
**Subject(s):** Paid Community Newspapers
**Circ:** (Thurs.)15,190
 (Sun.)15,276

**The Independent** (24882)
Copley Ohio Newspapers Inc.
50 N Ave. NW
Massillon, OH 44647
Phone: (330)833-2631
Fax: (330)833-2635
**Subject(s):** Daily Newspapers
**Circ:** (Sun.)‡14,559
 (Mon.-Sat.)‡15,216

**Cumberland Courier** (9844)
The Lawrence Community Journal
7968 Pendleton Pke.
Indianapolis, IN 46226
Fax: (317)542-1137
**Subject(s):** Free Newspapers
**Circ:** (Non-paid)15,200

**Daily Globe** (16732)
300 11th St.
PO Box 639
Worthington, MN 56187
Phone: (507)376-9711
Fax: (507)376-5202
**Subject(s):** Daily Newspapers
**Circ:** (Paid)12,330
 (Free)15,200

**West Life** (25165)
PICT
26933 Westwood Dr.
Westlake, OH 44145
Phone: (440)871-6157
Fax: (440)871-0157
**Subject(s):** Paid Community Newspapers
**Circ:** ‡15,200

**Grand Valley West Advance** (15461)
Advance Newspapers
2141 Port Sheldon Rd.
PO Box 9
Jenison, MI 49428-9301
Phone: (616)669-2700
Fax: (616)669-1162
**Subject(s):** Paid Community Newspapers
**Circ:** (Paid)❏2,098
 (Free)❏15,117

**Charlotte Shopping Guide** (15107)
Community Newspapers
239 S Cochran
Charlotte, MI 48813
Phone: (517)543-9913
Fax: (517)543-3677
**Subject(s):** Free Newspapers
**Circ:** (Paid)46
 (Non-paid)15,107

**SE DuPage Suburban LIFE/Reporter** (8608)
Liberty Suburban Chicago Newspapers
922 Warren Ave.
Downers Grove, IL 60515
Phone: (630)969-0188
Fax: (630)969-0228
**Subject(s):** Paid Community Newspapers
**Circ:** (Paid)15,100

**The Hoosier Topics** (9653)
Hoosier Topics
PO Box 496
1 N. Main St.
Cloverdale, IN 46120
Phone: (765)795-4438
Fax: (765)795-3121
**Subject(s):** Shopping Guides
**Circ:** (Combined)15,092

**The News Sun** (24189)
Sun Newspapers
32 Park St.
Berea, OH 44017-1516
Phone: (216)986-7550
Fax: (216)986-7551
**Subject(s):** Paid Community Newspapers
**Circ:** (Paid)15,062

**Heartland Trader** (25142)
PO Box 376
Wauseon, OH 43567
Phone: (419)335-2010
Fax: (419)335-2030
**Subject(s):** Free Newspapers
**Circ:** (Free)15,053

**News Republic Cent Saver** (32831)
Independent Media Group Inc.
219 First St.
PO Box 9
Baraboo, WI 53913-0009
Phone: (608)356-4808
Fax: (608)356-0344
**Subject(s):** Free Newspapers
**Circ:** (Combined)15,054

**ASDA News** (8090)
Alliance of the American Dental Association
211 E Chicago Ave., Ste. 730
Chicago, IL 60611
Phone: (312)440-2795
Fax: (312)440-2820
**Subject(s):** Dentistry
**Circ:** 15,000

**The Buchtelite** (24094)
University of Akron
303 Buchtel Ave.
Akron, OH 44325
Phone: (330)972-7111
Fax: (330)972-7810
**Subject(s):** College Publications
**Circ:** (Free)‡15,000

**Elmhurst Press** (9087)
Liberty Suburban Chicago Newspapers
7222 W. Cermak Rd., Ste. 505
North Riverside, IL 60546
Phone: (708)447-9810
**Subject(s):** Paid Community Newspapers
**Circ:** (Combined)15,000

Circulation: ★ = ABC; △ = BPA; ♦ = CAC; • = CCAB; ❏ = VAC; ⊕ = PO Statement; ‡ = Publisher's Report; Boldface figures = sworn; Light figures = estimated.

# Great Lakes States
## Gale Directory of Publications & Broadcast Media/140th Ed.

**The Enquirer Express (7960)**
Macoupin County Enquirer Inc.
PO Box 200
Carlinville, IL 62626-0200
Phone: (217)854-2534
Fax: (217)854-2535
**Subject(s):** Shopping Guides
**Circ:** (Free)15,000

**Gay People's Chronicle (24417)**
KWIR Publications
PO Box 5426
Cleveland, OH 44101-0426
Phone: (216)631-8646
Fax: (216)631-1052
**Subject(s):** Gay and Lesbian Interests; Paid Community Newspapers
**Circ:** (Controlled)15,000

**The Labor Paper (33116)**
Union Cooperative Publishing Co.
3030 39th Ave., Ste. 110
Kenosha, WI 53144-4210
Phone: (262)657-6116
Fax: (262)657-6153
**Subject(s):** Labor; Paid Community Newspapers
**Circ:** 15,000

**Lombard Spectator (9094)**
Liberty Suburban Chicago Newspapers
7222 W. Cermak Rd., Ste. 505
North Riverside, IL 60546
Phone: (708)447-9810
**Subject(s):** Free Newspapers
**Circ:** (Combined)15,000

**Middleton Times-Tribune (33285)**
News Publishing Inc.
7507 Hubbard Ave.
Middleton, WI 53562
Phone: (608)827-5797
Fax: (608)831-7765
**Subject(s):** Paid Community Newspapers
**Circ:** (Paid)⊕3,300
(Non-paid)⊕15,000

**National Catholic Register (9014)**
Circle Media
PO Box 373
Mount Morris, IL 61054
Phone: (815)288-5600
Fax: (815)288-5157
**Subject(s):** Religious Publications
**Circ:** (Free)453
(Paid)15,000

**South Suburban Standard (8501)**
Standard Newspapers
615 S Halsted
Chicago Heights, IL 60411
Phone: (708)755-5021
Fax: (708)755-5020
**Subject(s):** Black Publications; Paid Community Newspapers
**Circ:** 15,000

**Villa Park/Oakbrook Terrace Argus (9098)**
Liberty Suburban Chicago Newspapers
7222 W. Cermak Rd., Ste. 505
North Riverside, IL 60546
Phone: (708)447-9810
**Subject(s):** Paid Community Newspapers
**Circ:** (Combined)15,000

**Westside Flyer (9559)**
Thomson Indiana Inc.
8109 Kingston Rd., Ste. 500
Avon, IN 46123
Phone: (317)272-5800
Fax: (317)272-5887
**Subject(s):** Paid Community Newspapers
**Circ:** 15,000

**Booster (24533)**
Suburban News Publications
5257 Sinclair Rd.
PO Box 29912
Columbus, OH 43229
Phone: (614)785-1212
Fax: (614)785-1881
**Subject(s):** Free Newspapers
**Circ:** (Paid)3,389
(Free)14,979

**Rural Rambler (33457)**
PO Box 105
Oxford, WI 53952
**Subject(s):** Shopping Guides
**Circ:** ‡14,926

**Central Michigan Life (15609)**
Central Michigan University
8 Anspach Hall
Mount Pleasant, MI 48859
Phone: (989)774-3493
Fax: (989)774-7805
**Subject(s):** College Publications
**Circ:** (Paid)‡700
(Free)‡14,900

**Intercom (16682)**
Wadena Pioneer Journal
314 S Jefferson
PO Box 31
Wadena, MN 56482
Phone: (218)631-2561
Fax: (218)631-1621
**Subject(s):** Free Newspapers
**Circ:** (Non-paid)14,883

**Apple Valley/Rosemount Sun Current (15933)**
Minnesota Sun Publications
10917 Valley View Rd.
Eden Prairie, MN 55344
Phone: (952)829-0797
Fax: (952)392-6868
**Subject(s):** Free Newspapers
**Circ:** (Paid)256
(Non-paid)14,869

**Tri-County Tab (33657)**
Whitehall Times Inc.
36435 Main St.
Whitehall, WI 54773
Phone: (715)538-4765
Fax: (715)538-4540
**Subject(s):** Shopping Guides
**Circ:** (Free)‡14,848

**Labor World (16059)**
Duluth AFL-CIO Central Labor Body
2002 London Rd., No. 110
Duluth, MN 55812
Phone: (218)728-4469
Fax: (218)724-1413
**Subject(s):** Labor
**Circ:** (Paid)‡14,800

**Evergreen Country Shopper (32823)**
La Pean Publications
PO Box 408
Ashland, WI 54806
Phone: (715)682-8131
Fax: (715)682-6400
**Subject(s):** Shopping Guides
**Circ:** (Non-paid)14,760

**Action Plus Shopper (9680)**
827 S Halleck St.
Box 110
DeMotte, IN 46310
Phone: (219)987-5111
Fax: (219)987-5119
**Subject(s):** Shopping Guides
**Circ:** (Free)‡14,750

**Ada/Cascade/Forest Hills Advance (14958)**
Advance Newspapers
2141 Port Sheldon Rd.
PO Box 9
Jenison, MI 49428-9301
Phone: (616)669-2700
Fax: (616)669-1162
**Subject(s):** Paid Community Newspapers
**Circ:** (Paid)❑119
(Free)❑14,696

**Grosse Pointe News (15386)**
Anteebo Publishers
96 Kercheval Ave.
Grosse Pointe Farms, MI 48236
Phone: (313)882-0294
Fax: (313)882-1585
**Subject(s):** Paid Community Newspapers
**Circ:** (Thurs.)14,693

**The Daily Gazette (9428)**
PO Box 498
Sterling, IL 61081
Phone: (815)625-3600
Fax: (815)625-9390
**Subject(s):** Daily Newspapers
**Circ:** 14,639

**Eagle-Gazette (24821)**
138 W. Chestnut St.
Lancaster, OH 43130
Phone: (740)681-4344
Fax: (740)681-4456
**Subject(s):** Daily Newspapers
**Circ:** (Mon.-Sat.)★14,195
(Sun.)★14,585

**Thrif-T-Nickel Weekly News-Tab (9187)**
F.W. Gray & Associates Ltd.
Box 279
801 Canal St., No. 279
Ottawa, IL 61350-4901
Phone: (815)433-5595
Fax: (815)433-5596
**Subject(s):** Free Newspapers
**Circ:** (Paid)‡12
(Free)‡14,539

**Marshfield News-Herald (33261)**
111 W. 3rd St.
Marshfield, WI 54449
Phone: (715)384-3131
Fax: (715)387-4175
**Subject(s):** Daily Newspapers
**Circ:** (Mon.-Fri.)13,712
(Sat.)14,512

**Jersey County Shopper (7988)**
Carrollton Gazette Patriot Inc.
PO Box 231
Carrollton, IL 62016
Phone: (217)942-3626
Fax: (217)942-3699
**Subject(s):** Shopping Guides
**Circ:** (Free)14,491

**Kane County Chronicle (8722)**
Chronicle Newspapers Inc.
1000 Randall Rd.
Geneva, IL 60134
Phone: (630)232-9222
Fax: (630)232-4976
**Subject(s):** Daily Newspapers
**Circ:** (Mon.-Sat.)14,440

**Beloit Daily News (32841)**
Beloit Daily News Publishing Co.
149 State St.
Beloit, WI 53511
Phone: (608)365-8811
Fax: (608)365-1420
**Subject(s):** Daily Newspapers
**Circ:** (Non-paid)‡382
(Paid)‡14,411

**The Vegetable Growers News (15802)**
Great American Publishing Co.
75 Applewood Dr., Ste. A
PO Box 128
Sparta, MI 49345
Phone: (616)887-9008
Fax: (616)887-2666
**Subject(s):** Farm Newspapers; General Agriculture
**Circ:** (Combined)‡14,415

**Waukesha County Freeman (33619)**
PO Box 7
Waukesha, WI 53187
Phone: (414)542-2501
Fax: (414)542-6082
**Subject(s):** Daily Newspapers
**Circ:** (Mon.-Sat.)★14,395

**Centralia Sentinel (8000)**
Centralia Press Ltd.
PO Box 627
Centralia, IL 62801
**Subject(s):** Daily Newspapers
**Circ:** (Non-paid)♦378
(Paid)♦14,367

**Gale Directory of Publications & Broadcast Media/140th Ed.**                  **Great Lakes States**

**South St. Paul/Inver Grove Heights Sun Current** (16649)
Minnesota Sun Publications
10917 Valley View Rd.
Eden Prairie, MN 55344
Phone: (952)829-0797
Fax: (952)392-6868
**Subject(s):** Free Newspapers

Circ: (Paid)224
      (Non-paid)14,362

**Central County Trade Lines Shopper's Guide** (15257)
Paxton Media Group
115 Main St.
Eau Claire, MI 49111
Phone: (269)926-0588
Fax: (269)926-1051
**Subject(s):** Shopping Guides

Circ: (Free)14,324

**Owatonna Area Shopper** (16457)
Huckle Publishing Inc.
135 W Pearl
Owatonna, MN 55060
Phone: (507)451-2840
**Subject(s):** Free Newspapers

Circ: (Free)14,167

**The Sun Herald** (24956)
Sun Newspapers
28895 Lorain Rd.
North Olmsted, OH 44070-4042
Phone: (440)777-3800
Fax: (440)777-8423
**Subject(s):** Paid Community Newspapers

Circ: (Paid)14,163

**The Coshocton County Advertiser** (24633)
Add Inc.—Ohio Group
1104 Fairy Falls Dr.
Coshocton, OH 43812
Phone: (740)622-4122
Fax: (740)623-0618
**Subject(s):** Shopping Guides

Circ: (Non-paid)♦14,137

**The Clinton County News** (15740)
Community Newspapers
320 N. Clinton
Saint Johns, MI 48879
Phone: (989)224-2361
Fax: (989)224-4452
**Subject(s):** Free Newspapers

Circ: (Combined)14,115

**Command Post** (8622)
Edwardsville Publishing Company Inc.
117 N 2nd St.
PO Box 70
Edwardsville, IL 62025-1938
Phone: (618)656-4700
Fax: (618)656-7618
**Subject(s):** Paid Community Newspapers; Military and Navy

Circ: ‡14,100

**Monroe County Clarion Journal** (8516)
Pulitzer Publishing
212 W. Locust
Columbia, IL 62236
Phone: (314)487-8955
**Subject(s):** Free Newspapers

Circ: (Sun.)14,094
      (Wed.)14,094

**Times-Sentinel** (24741)
Ohio Valley Publishing
825 3rd Ave.
Gallipolis, OH 45631
Phone: (740)446-2342
Fax: (740)446-3008

Circ: (Sun.)10,918
      (Mon.-Sat.)14,083

**The Weekly Shopper** (9122)
Liberty Group Publishing Co.
3000 Dundee Rd., Ste. 202
Northbrook, IL 60062
Phone: (847)272-2244
Fax: (847)272-6244
**Subject(s):** Shopping Guides

Circ: (Non-paid)♦14,050

**Freeport Journal-Standard** (8704)
The Journal-Standard
27 S State Ave.
PO Box 330
Freeport, IL 61032
Phone: (815)232-1171
Fax: (815)232-3601
**Subject(s):** Daily Newspapers

Circ: (Mon.-Sat.)★13,488
      (Sun.)★14,035

**Pennysaver** (9118)
Liberty Group Publishing
3000 Dundee Rd., Ste. 202
Northbrook, IL 60062
Phone: (847)272-2244
Fax: (847)272-6244
**Subject(s):** Shopping Guides

Circ: (Free)‡14,019

**Ball State Daily News** (10044)
AJ 276, Ball State Univ.
Muncie, IN 47306-0481
**Subject(s):** College Publications

Circ: 14,000

**The Chagrin Valley Times** (24268)
Chagrin Valley Publishing Co.
525 E Wash St.
PO Box 150
Chagrin Falls, OH 44022
Phone: (440)247-5335
Fax: (440)247-5615
**Subject(s):** Paid Community Newspapers

Circ: (Free)4,000
      (Paid)‡14,000

**The Circle** (16281)
PO Box 6026
Minneapolis, MN 55406
Phone: (612)722-3686
Fax: (612)722-3773
**Subject(s):** Paid Community Newspapers

Circ: (Paid)1,000
      (Non-paid)14,000

**EL CENTRAL Newspaper** (15181)
4124 W Vernor
Detroit, MI 48209
Phone: (313)841-0100
Fax: (313)841-0155
**Subject(s):** Free Newspapers; Spanish

Circ: (Combined)14,000

**The Post** (24151)
Ohio University
20 E Union St.
Athens, OH 45701
Phone: (740)593-4000
Fax: (740)593-0561
**Subject(s):** College Publications

Circ: (Paid)76
      (Free)14,000

**Resorter** (33138)
Lake Geneva Printing and Publishing
315 Broad St.
PO Box 937
Lake Geneva, WI 53147
Phone: (262)248-4444
Fax: (262)248-4476
**Subject(s):** Free Newspapers

Circ: (Combined)‡14,000

**The Edmore Advertiser** (14983)
Morning Star Publishing Co.
311 E. Superior
PO Box 425
Alma, MI 48801
**Subject(s):** Shopping Guides

Circ: (Free)13,997

**The Heartland Shopping News** (16122)
The Midweek Inc.
PO Box 651
Fergus Falls, MN 56538
Phone: (218)739-3308
**Subject(s):** Shopping Guides

Circ: (Non-paid)13,971

**Clintonville Shopper's Guide** (32894)
17 9th St.
PO Box 330
Clintonville, WI 54929-0330
Phone: (715)823-3107

Fax: (715)823-1364
**Subject(s):** Shopping Guides

Circ: (Free)13,948

**The Echo** (9626)
News Banner Publications Inc.
125 N Johnson St.
PO Box 436
Bluffton, IN 46714
Phone: (260)824-0224
Fax: (260)824-0700
**Subject(s):** Shopping Guides

Circ: (Controlled)‡13,930

**The Grand Blanc News** (15328)
The Flint Journal
200 E. 1st St.
Flint, MI 48502-1925
**Subject(s):** Paid Community Newspapers

Circ: (Combined)13,935

**White Bear Press** (16708)
Press Publications
4779 Bloom Ave.
White Bear Lake, MN 55110
Phone: (651)407-1200
Fax: (651)429-1242
**Subject(s):** Free Newspapers

Circ: (Paid)4,784
      (Free)13,929

**Vincennes Sun-Commercial** (10222)
702 Main St.
Vincennes, IN 47591
Phone: (812)886-9955
Fax: (812)885-2002
**Subject(s):** Daily Newspapers

Circ: (Mon.-Fri.)12,195
      (Sun.)13,887

**New London Buyers' Guide** (33422)
ADD Inc.
112 Naston St.
PO Box 283
New London, WI 54961
Phone: (920)982-2511
Fax: (920)982-7672
**Subject(s):** Shopping Guides

Circ: (Combined)13,859

**Farmer's Exchange** (10067)
Exchange Publishing Corp.
POB 45
New Paris, IN 46553
**Subject(s):** Farm Newspapers

Circ: (Free)‡800
      (Paid)‡13,800

**Hopkins/East Minnetonka Sailor-Sun** (16179)
Minnesota Sun Publications
10917 Valley View Rd.
Eden Prairie, MN 55344
Phone: (952)829-0797
Fax: (952)392-6868
**Subject(s):** Free Newspapers

Circ: (Non-paid)♦13,481
      (Paid)13,803

**The Loudonville Times and The Loudonville Mohican Area Shopper** (24844)
Ashland Publishing Company L.L.C.
255 W Main
Loudonville, OH 44842
Phone: (419)994-5600
Fax: (419)994-5826
**Subject(s):** Shopping Guides

Circ: (Free)‡13,800

**The News-Messenger** (24733)
Gannett Satellite Information Network
1700 Cedar St.
PO Box 1230
Fremont, OH 43420
Phone: (419)332-5511
Fax: (419)332-9750
**Subject(s):** Daily Newspapers

Circ: (Mon.-Sat.)13,800

**The Marion Star** (24874)
150 Court St.
Marion, OH 43302
Phone: (614)387-0400
Fax: (614)382-2210

---

Circulation: ★ = ABC; △ = BPA; ♦ = CAC; • = CCAB; ☐ = VAC; ⊕ = PO Statement; ‡ = Publisher's Report; Boldface figures = sworn; Light figures = estimated.

3597

**Great Lakes States**

Subject(s): Daily Newspapers
Circ: (Mon.-Sat.)★13,695
(Sun.)★13,788

**Woodford Star** (8658)
Woodford County Journal
1926 S Main St.
PO Box 36
Eureka, IL 61530
Phone: (309)467-3314
Fax: (309)467-4563
Subject(s): Shopping Guides
Circ: (Free)‡13,746

**Athletes in Action** (25200)
651 Taylor Dr.
Xenia, OH 45385
Phone: (937)352-1000
Fax: (937)352-1091
Subject(s): (General Sports); Religious Publications
Circ: (Free)300
(Paid)13,700

**The Times-Mail** (9563)
The Times News
813 16th St.
PO Box 849
Bedford, IN 47421
Phone: (812)275-3355
Fax: (812)275-4191
Subject(s): Daily Newspapers
Circ: (Mon.-Sat.)13,681

**Central County** (15058)
Paxton Media Group
88 W. Main 100
Benton Harbor, MI 49022
Phone: (269)926-0588
Fax: (269)926-1051
Subject(s): Shopping Guides
Circ: (Non-paid)13,633

**The Sidney Daily News** (25044)
Amos Press Inc.
911 Vandemark Rd.
PO Box 4129
Sidney, OH 45365
Phone: (937)498-2111
Fax: (937)498-0812
Subject(s): Daily Newspapers
Circ: (Mon.-Sat.)13,638

**Waterford Spinal Column Newsweekly** (15884)
Spinal Column Publications
7196 Cooley Lake Rd.
PO Box 14
Union Lake, MI 48387-0014
Phone: (248)360-7355
Fax: (248)360-4711
Subject(s): Free Newspapers
Circ: (Free)‡13,600

**Grand Valley East Advance** (15460)
Advance Newspapers
2141 Port Sheldon Rd.
PO Box 9
Jenison, MI 49428-9301
Phone: (616)669-2700
Fax: (616)669-1162
Subject(s): Paid Community Newspapers
Circ: (Paid)❏4,515
(Free)❏13,588

**Dublin News** (24702)
Suburban News Publications
5257 Sinclair Rd.
PO Box 29912
Columbus, OH 43229
Phone: (614)785-1212
Fax: (614)785-1881
Subject(s): Free Newspapers
Circ: (Paid)4,370
(Non-paid)13,534

**Stoplight** (32888)
Independent Media Group Inc.
321 Frenette Dr.
PO Box 69
Chippewa Falls, WI 54729-0069
Subject(s): Shopping Guides
Circ: (Controlled)13,538

**West Sherburne Tribune** (15965)
29 S Lake St.
PO Box 276
Big Lake, MN 55309
Phone: (763)263-3602
Fax: (763)263-8458
Subject(s): Free Newspapers
Circ: (Paid)188
(Non-paid)13,536

**The Beacon** (25004)
Schaffner Publications Inc.
205 SE Catawba Rd., Ste. G
Port Clinton, OH 43452
Phone: (419)732-2154
Fax: (419)734-5382
Subject(s): Free Newspapers
Circ: (Free)‡13,500

**Chicago Chronicle** (8124)
University of Chicago
5801 S. Ellis Ave., Rm. 200
Chicago, IL 60637-1473
Phone: (773)702-8360
Fax: (773)702-8324
Subject(s): College Publications
Circ: (Paid)500
(Free)13,500

**Shoppers News** (10125)
Kankakee Valley Publishing Co.
PO Box 298
117 N. Rensselaer
Rensselaer, IN 47978-0298
Phone: (219)866-5111
Fax: (219)866-3775
Subject(s): Shopping Guides
Circ: (Free)‡13,500

**Town and Country Shopper** (16030)
E.C.M. Publishers Inc.
4095 Coon Rapids Blvd.
Coon Rapids, MN 55433
Phone: (763)712-2400
Fax: (763)712-2480
Subject(s): Shopping Guides
Circ: (Free)12,098
(Free)‡13,420

**The Perry County Advertiser** (24935)
Add Inc.—Ohio Group
116 S Main St.
New Lexington, OH 43764
Phone: (740)342-5483
Fax: (740)342-5305
Subject(s): Shopping Guides
Circ: (Non-paid)♦13,411

**Becker County Record** (16041)
Forum Communications Co.
511 Washington Ave.
Detroit Lakes, MN 56501-3007
Phone: (218)847-3151
Fax: (218)847-9409
Subject(s): Free Newspapers
Circ: (Paid)❏259
(Free)❏13,327

**The Grand Ledge Independent** (15112)
Community Newspapers
239 S Cochran
Charlotte, MI 48813
Phone: (517)543-9913
Fax: (517)543-3677
Subject(s): Free Newspapers
Circ: (Paid)259
(Non-paid)13,314

**The Indianapolis Recorder** (9872)
The George P. Stewart Printing Inc.
2901 N Tacoma Ave.
PO Box 18499
Indianapolis, IN 46218-2700
Phone: (317)924-5143
Fax: (317)924-5148
Subject(s): Paid Community Newspapers; Black Publications
Circ: 13,300

**Wisconsin Rapids Daily Tribune** (33667)
Gannett Company Inc.
220 First Ave. S.
Wisconsin Rapids, WI 54495
Phone: (715)423-7200
Subject(s): Daily Newspapers
Circ: (Mon.-Sat.)13,278

**The Daily Jeffersonian** (24234)
The Jeffersonian Company Inc.
831 Wheeling Ave.
PO Box 10
Cambridge, OH 43725
Phone: (740)439-3531
Fax: (740)432-6219
Subject(s): Daily Newspapers
Circ: (Mon.-Fri.)★12,875
(Sun.)★13,256

**Antigo Area Shoppers Guide** (32801)
Antigo Shoppers Guide
Civic Bldg.
809 5th Ave.
Antigo, WI 54409
Phone: (715)623-5024
Fax: (715)623-5389
Subject(s): Shopping Guides
Circ: (Paid)25
(Non-paid)13,174

**Petoskey Star Advertiser** (15672)
Morningstar Publications
P. O. Box 826
Petoskey, MI 49770
Phone: (989)779-6008
Fax: (231)347-5744
Subject(s): Shopping Guides
Circ: (Non-paid)13,161

**Shoppers Review** (16259)
Marshall Independent
508 W. Main St.
Marshall, MN 56258
Phone: (507)537-1551
Fax: (507)537-1557
Subject(s): Shopping Guides
Circ: (Free)‡13,103

**The Advertiser** (14981)
Morningstar Publications
311 E. Superior
PO Box 425
Alma, MI 48801-0425
Phone: (989)463-6071
Fax: (989)463-3338
Subject(s): Shopping Guides
Circ: (Free)13,080

**Westerville News & Public Opinion** (25162)
Suburban News Publications
5257 Sinclair Rd.
PO Box 29912
Columbus, OH 43229
Phone: (614)785-1212
Fax: (614)785-1881
Subject(s): Free Newspapers
Circ: (Paid)7,697
(Non-paid)13,087

**Cambridge Star** (15997)
North Star Media
930 South Cleveland
Cambridge, MN 55008
Phone: (763)689-1181
Fax: (763)689-1185
Subject(s): Paid Community Newspapers
Circ: (Paid)603
(Free)13,065

**Times-Record/Bulletin** (33388)
Mukwonago Publications
PO Box 204
Mukwonago, WI 53149
Phone: (262)363-4045
Fax: (262)363-8573
Subject(s): Shopping Guides
Circ: (Free)‡13,050

**The Sun & News** (15398)
J-Ad Corp.
1351 N M-43 Hwy.
PO Box 188
Hastings, MI 49058-0188
Phone: (269)945-9554
Fax: (269)945-5192
Subject(s): Free Newspapers
Circ: ‡13,025

**The Chicago Maroon** (8131)
Ida Noyes Hall
1212 E. 59th St.
Lower Level
Chicago, IL 60637
Phone: (773)702-1403
Fax: (773)702-3032
**Subject(s):** College Publications
**Circ:** ‡13,000

**Oshkosh Advance-Titan** (33454)
University of Wisconsin-Oshkosh
800 Algoma Blvd.
Oshkosh, WI 54901
Phone: (920)424-1234
**Subject(s):** College Publications
**Circ:** (Free)‡13,000

**The Sagamore** (9909)
Indiana University-Purdue University at Indianapolis
425 University Blvd.
Indianapolis, IN 46202-5143
Phone: (317)274-4591
**Subject(s):** College Publications
**Circ:** (Free)‡13,000

**The Sentinel** (24799)
Gazette Printing Company Inc.
34 S. Chestnut St.
Jefferson, OH 44047
Phone: (440)576-9115
Fax: (440)576-4337
**Subject(s):** Paid Community Newspapers
**Circ:** (Free)‡13,000

**Sun Publications** (9046)
1500 W. Ogden Ave.
PO Box 269
Naperville, IL 60566-0269
Phone: (630)355-0063
Fax: (630)416-5163
**Subject(s):** Paid Community Newspapers
**Circ:** ‡13,000

**The Guernsey-Noble Advertiser** (24235)
Add Inc.—Ohio Group
61234 Southgate Pkwy.
Cambridge, OH 43725
Phone: (740)432-7077
Fax: (740)439-7072
**Subject(s):** Shopping Guides
**Circ:** (Non-paid)♦12,923

**The Morning Sun** (15612)
Morning Star Publishing Co.
PO Box 447
Mount Pleasant, MI 48804-0447
Phone: (989)779-6050
Fax: (989)779-6051
**Subject(s):** Daily Newspapers
**Circ:** (Sat.)★10,710
(Mon.-Fri.)★11,329
(Sun.)★12,873

**The Herald** (9949)
216 E 4th St
PO Box 31
Jasper, IN 47547-0031
Phone: (812)482-2424
Fax: (812)482-4104
**Subject(s):** Daily Newspapers
**Circ:** (Paid)‡12,865

**Town and Country Shopper** (16559)
St. James Publishing Company Inc.
604 1st Ave. S.
PO Box 67
Saint James, MN 56081-3221
Phone: (507)375-3161
Fax: (507)375-3221
**Subject(s):** Shopping Guides
**Circ:** (Free)‡12,860

**Richland Center Shopping News** (33512)
Woodward Communications
174 N. Main
PO Box 272
Richland Center, WI 53581-0272
Phone: (608)647-2911
Fax: (608)647-7238
**Subject(s):** Shopping Guides
**Circ:** (Free)‡12,828

**South Suburban Citizen** (8412)
Citizen Newspapers
806 E. 78th St.
Chicago, IL 60619
Phone: (773)783-1251
Fax: (773)783-1301
**Subject(s):** Paid Community Newspapers; Black Publications
**Circ:** (Paid)8,750
(Free)‡12,750

**The Review** (24119)
Alliance Publishing Company Inc.
40 S Linden Ave.
PO Box 2180
Alliance, OH 44601
Phone: (330)868-5222
Fax: (330)821-8258
**Subject(s):** Daily Newspapers
**Circ:** (Mon.-Sat.)★12,733

**Business Courier** (24292)
Cincinnati Business Courier
101 W. 7th St.
Cincinnati, OH 45202
Phone: (513)621-6665
Fax: (513)621-2462
**Subject(s):** Business; Local, State, and Regional Publications
**Circ:** (Paid)12,701

**Woodbury-South Maplewood Review** (16438)
Lillie Suburban Newspapers
2515 E 7th Ave.
North Saint Paul, MN 55109
Phone: (651)777-8800
Fax: (651)777-8288
**Subject(s):** Free Newspapers
**Circ:** (Free)12,674

**The Daily Times** (9186)
Ottawa Publishing Co.
110 W Jefferson St.
Ottawa, IL 61350
Phone: (815)433-2000
Fax: (815)433-1626
**Subject(s):** Daily Newspapers
**Circ:** (Mon.-Sat.)12,654

**Madison Messenger** (24850)
Columbus Messenger Co.
78 S. Main St.
London, OH 43140
Phone: (740)852-0809
Fax: (740)852-0814
**Subject(s):** Free Newspapers
**Circ:** (Non-paid)♦12,649

**The Clarion** (9665)
O'Bannon Publishing Co.
301 N Capitol Ave.
Corydon, IN 47112
Phone: (812)738-2211
Fax: (812)738-1909
**Subject(s):** Paid Community Newspapers
**Circ:** (Free)170
(Paid)12,569

**Worthington News** (25197)
Suburban News Publications
5257 Sinclair Rd.
PO Box 29912
Columbus, OH 43229
Phone: (614)785-1212
Fax: (614)785-1881
**Subject(s):** Free Newspapers
**Circ:** (Paid)5,856
(Non-paid)12,569

**The Herald** (9503)
Knight-Ridder
114 North main St.
PO Box 147
Waterloo, IL 62298
Phone: (618)337-7300
Fax: (618)939-3815
**Subject(s):** Free Newspapers
**Circ:** (Paid)‡100
(Free)‡12,500

**The Observer** (10090)
University of Notre Dame
024 South Dining Hall
PO Box Q
Notre Dame, IN 46556
Phone: (219)631-7471
Fax: (219)239-6927

**Subject(s):** College Publications; Daily Newspapers
**Circ:** 12,500

**Shoppers Guide** (15661)
Community Shoppers Guide Inc.
117 N Farmer St.
PO Box 168
Otsego, MI 49078-0168
Phone: (269)694-9431
Fax: (269)694-9145
**Subject(s):** Shopping Guides
**Circ:** (Free)‡12,500

**Spotlight - Advertiser** (10218)
The Ripley Publishing Co.
115 S Washington St.
PO Box 158
Versailles, IN 47042
Phone: (812)689-6364
Fax: (812)689-6508
**Subject(s):** Shopping Guides
**Circ:** (Combined)12,500

**UWM Post** (33339)
University of Wisconsin-Milwaukee
2200 E. Kenwood Blvd.
Ste. EG80
Milwaukee, WI 53201
**Subject(s):** College Publications
**Circ:** (Free)12,500

**Western Herald** (15481)
Western Michigan University
1903 W. Michigan Ave.
Kalamazoo, MI 49008
Phone: (269)387-2092
Fax: (269)387-2267
**Subject(s):** College Publications
**Circ:** (Combined)12,500

**Clare County Buyers Guide** (14982)
Morning Star Publishing Co.
311 E Superior
PO Box 425
Alma, MI 48801
Phone: (989)463-6071
Fax: (989)463-3338
**Subject(s):** Shopping Guides
**Circ:** (Free)‡12,470

**Prairie Advocate** (8856)
Acres of Sky Communications Inc.
446 S. Broad St.
PO Box 84
Lanark, IL 61046
Phone: (815)493-2560
Fax: (815)493-2561
**Subject(s):** Free Newspapers
**Circ:** (Paid)2,300
(Free)12,400

**Eden Prairie Sun Current** (16090)
Minnesota Sun Publications
10917 Valley View Rd.
Eden Prairie, MN 55344
Phone: (952)829-0797
Fax: (952)392-6868
**Subject(s):** Free Newspapers
**Circ:** (Paid)379
(Free)12,361

**The Kewaunee County Star** (32794)
Door County Publishing Co.
602 Third St.
PO Box 68
Algoma, WI 54201
Phone: (920)487-2222
Fax: (920)487-3194
**Subject(s):** Shopping Guides
**Circ:** (Free)‡12,300

**Winona Daily News** (16719)
Lee Enterprises Inc.
601 Franklin St.
PO Box 5147
Winona, MN 55987-3822
Phone: (507)453-3510
Fax: (507)454-1440
**Subject(s):** Daily Newspapers
**Circ:** (Mon.-Sat.)11,545
(Sun.)12,258

Circulation: ★ = ABC; △ = BPA; ♦ = CAC; • = CCAB; ☐ = VAC; ⊕ = PO Statement; ‡ = Publisher's Report; Boldface figures = sworn; Light figures = estimated.

**The Sunriser News  (10100)**
News Banner Publications Inc.
105 N. Jefferson
PO Box 365
Ossian, IN 46777
Phone: (219)622-4108
Fax: (219)622-4108
**Subject(s):** Shopping Guides

Circ: (Controlled)‡12,242

**Rocky Fork Enterprise  (25196)**
CNS/This Week Newspapers
670 Lakeview Plaza Blvd., Ste. F
Worthington, OH 43085
Phone: (614)438-8100
Fax: (614)875-6028
**Subject(s):** Paid Community Newspapers

Circ: (Combined)12,211

**La Porte Herald-Argus  (9989)**
LaPorte Herald-Argus
701 State St.
LaPorte, IN 46350
Phone: (219)362-2161
Fax: (219)362-2166
**Subject(s):** Daily Newspapers

Circ: (Mon.-Sat.)★**12,209**

**Forest Lake Times  (16129)**
ECM Publishers Inc. (Forest Lake)
880 SW 15th St.
Forest Lake, MN 55025
Phone: (651)464-4601
Fax: (651)464-4605
**Subject(s):**

Circ: (Paid)798
      (Free)12,195

**The Sun Messenger  (24173)**
Sun Newspapers
3355 Richmond Rd., Ste. 171
Beachwood, OH 44122-4171
Phone: (216)986-5890
Fax: (216)464-8816
**Subject(s):** Paid Community Newspapers

Circ: (Paid)12,171

**Gahanna News  (24737)**
Suburban News Publications
5257 Sinclair Rd.
PO Box 29912
Columbus, OH 43229
Phone: (614)785-1212
Fax: (614)785-1881
**Subject(s):** Free Newspapers

Circ: (Paid)1,286
      (Free)12,121

**Sparta/Kent City Advance  (15463)**
Advance Newspapers
2141 Port Sheldon Rd.
PO Box 9
Jenison, MI 49428-9301
Phone: (616)669-2700
Fax: (616)669-1162
**Subject(s):** Paid Community Newspapers

Circ: (Paid)❑123
      (Free)❑**12,123**

**Sentinel-Tribune  (24212)**
The Sentinel Co.
300 E Poe Rd.
PO Box 88
Bowling Green, OH 43402
Phone: (419)352-4611
Fax: (419)354-0314
**Subject(s):** Daily Newspapers

Circ: (Mon.-Sat.)12,119

**Seymour Buyers' Guide and Times Press  (33530)**
ADD Inc.
205 N. Main St.
PO Box 276
Seymour, WI 54165
Phone: (920)833-2517
Fax: (920)833-2454
**Subject(s):** Shopping Guides

Circ: (Combined)12,100

**Ashland Times-Gazette  (24131)**
Dix Communications
40 E 2nd St.
Ashland, OH 44805
Phone: (419)281-0581
Fax: (419)281-5591

**Subject(s):** Daily Newspapers

Circ: (Mon.-Sat.)★**12,092**

**Daily Citizen  (32835)**
Citizen Publishing Co.
805 Park Ave.
Beaver Dam, WI 53916
Phone: (920)887-0321
Fax: (928)871-0150
**Subject(s):** Daily Newspapers

Circ: (Mon.-Fri.)★**10,328**
      (Sat.)★**12,084**

**Rhinelander Our Town  (33502)**
ADD Inc.
24 W Rives
Rhinelander, WI 54501
Phone: (715)369-3331
Fax: (715)369-4859
**Subject(s):** Free Newspapers

Circ: (Free)‡12,048

**The Leader  (9646)**
Green Banner Publications Inc.
382 Main Cross St.
Charlestown, IN 47111
Phone: (812)967-3176
Fax: (812)256-3377
**Subject(s):** Free Newspapers

Circ: (Paid)28
      (Free)12,027

**Grand Rapids Advance  (15337)**
Advance Newspapers
2141 Port Sheldon Rd.
PO Box 9
Jenison, MI 49428-9301
Phone: (616)669-2700
Fax: (616)669-1162
**Subject(s):** Paid Community Newspapers

Circ: (Paid)❑12
      (Free)❑**12,010**

**The Argus-Press  (15663)**
The Argus-Press Co.
201 E Exchange St.
PO Box 399
Owosso, MI 48867
Phone: (989)725-5136
**Subject(s):** Daily Newspapers

Circ: (Paid)‡12,000

**Courier-Times  (10061)**
201 S 14th St.
New Castle, IN 47362-3328
Phone: (765)529-1111
Fax: (765)529-1731
**Subject(s):** Daily Newspapers

Circ: 12,000

**Daily Kent Stater  (24806)**
Kent State University Student Publication Policy Committee
101 Taylor Hall
PO Box 5190
Kent, OH 44242
Phone: (330)672-2584
**Subject(s):** College Publications

Circ: (Free)‡12,000

**The Lake County Gazette  (24797)**
Gazette Printing Company Inc.
34 S Chestnut St.
Jefferson, OH 44047
Phone: (440)576-9115
Fax: (440)576-4337
**Subject(s):** Paid Community Newspapers

Circ: (Combined)12,000

**Nightlines Weekly  (8355)**
Lambda Publications Inc.
1115 W Belmont Ave., Ste. 2-D
Chicago, IL 60657
Phone: (773)871-7610
Fax: (773)871-7609
**Subject(s):** Gay and Lesbian Interests

Circ: (Non-paid)12,000

**Northfield Shopper  (16442)**
Northfield News
115 W. 5th St.
PO Box 58
Northfield, MN 55057
Phone: (507)645-5615
Fax: (507)645-6005

**Subject(s):** Shopping Guides

Circ: (Free)12,000

**Oak Lawn Independent  (8973)**
Southwest Messenger Press Inc.
3840 W 147th St.
PO Box 548
Midlothian, IL 60445
Phone: (708)388-2425
Fax: (708)385-7811
**Subject(s):** Free Newspapers

Circ: (Free)‡1,800
      (Paid)‡12,000

**Prairie/Valley Shopping News  (33146)**
The Lodi Enterprise
146 S Main St.
PO Box 16
Lodi, WI 53555
Phone: (608)592-3261
Fax: (608)592-3866
**Subject(s):** Shopping Guides

Circ: (Free)‡12,000

**Spotlite  (24926)**
Napoleon Inc.
595 E Riverview
PO Box 567
Napoleon, OH 43545
Phone: (419)592-5055
Fax: (419)592-9778
**Subject(s):** Shopping Guides

Circ: (Free)‡12,000

**Toledo Union Journal  (25094)**
UAW Local 12
2300 Ashland Ave.
Toledo, OH 43620
Phone: (419)241-9126
**Subject(s):** Labor

Circ: ‡12,000

**The Athens Messenger  (24143)**
The Messenger Publishing Co.
9300 Johnson Rd.
PO Box 4210
Athens, OH 45701
Phone: (740)592-6612
Fax: (740)592-4647
**Subject(s):** Daily Newspapers

Circ: (Mon.-Sat.)★**10,111**
      (Sun.)★**11,963**

**The Daily Ledger  (9709)**
Topics Newspapers Inc.
13095 Publisher's Dr.
Fishers, IN 46038
Phone: (317)598-6300
Fax: (317)444-5541
**Subject(s):** Free Newspapers

Circ: (Paid)11,963

**LaPorte Herald-Argus  (9991)**
701 State. St.
LaPorte, IN 46350
Phone: (219)362-2161
Fax: (219)362-2166
**Subject(s):** Daily Newspapers

Circ: (Paid)11,949

**The New Albany Tribune  (10058)**
CNHI
303 Scribner Dr.
PO Box 997
New Albany, IN 47150
Phone: (812)944-6481
Fax: (812)949-6585
**Subject(s):** Daily Newspapers

Circ: (Mon.-Fri.)11,919

**The Daily Press  (15260)**
600 Ludington St.
Escanaba, MI 49829-0828
Phone: (906)786-2021
Fax: (906)786-3752
**Subject(s):** Daily Newspapers

Circ: 11,842

**Register-News  (9024)**
911 Broadway St.
PO Box 489
Mount Vernon, IL 62864
Phone: (618)242-0113
Fax: (618)242-8286

**Subject(s):** Daily Newspapers
**Circ:** (Sat.)10,688
(Tues.-Fri.)10,688
(Mon.)11,821

**Euclid Sun Journal (24716)**
Sun Newspapers
3355 Richmond Rd., Ste. 171
Beachwood, OH 44122-4171
Phone: (216)986-5890
Fax: (216)464-8816
**Subject(s):** Paid Community Newspapers
**Circ:** (Paid)11,810

**Sun Scoop Journal (24717)**
Sun Newspapers
3355 Richmond Rd., Ste. 171
Beachwood, OH 44122-4171
Phone: (216)986-5890
Fax: (216)464-8816
**Subject(s):** Paid Community Newspapers
**Circ:** (Paid)11,810

**Fairmont Photo Press (16114)**
112 E 1st St.
PO Box 973
Fairmont, MN 56031
Phone: (507)238-9456
Fax: (507)238-9457
**Subject(s):** Shopping Guides; Free Newspapers
**Circ:** (Free)11,800

**The Medina Sun (24896)**
Sun Newspapers
5510 Cloverleaf Pkwy.
Valley View, OH 44125-4887
Phone: (216)986-2600
Fax: (216)986-2380
**Subject(s):** Paid Community Newspapers
**Circ:** (Thurs.)11,777

**Oconomowoc Buyers Guide (33432)**
Lake Country Publications
108 N. Main St
Oconomowoc, WI 53066
Phone: (262)567-0885
Fax: (262)567-7869
**Subject(s):** Free Newspapers
**Circ:** (Non-paid)11,754

**Times-Union (10235)**
Reub Williams and Sons Inc.
PO Box 1448
Warsaw, IN 46581-1448
Phone: (219)267-3111
Fax: (219)267-7784
**Subject(s):** Daily Newspapers; Free Newspapers
**Circ:** (Mon.-Sat.)11,650

**The Sun Star (25075)**
Sun Newspapers
32 Park St.
Berea, OH 44017-1516
Phone: (216)986-7550
Fax: (216)986-7551
**Subject(s):** Paid Community Newspapers
**Circ:** (Paid)11,631

**Greene County Shopper (7986)**
Carrollton Gazette Patriot Inc.
PO Box 231
Carrollton, IL 62016
Phone: (217)942-3626
Fax: (217)942-3699
**Subject(s):** Shopping Guides
**Circ:** (Free)11,613

**Birmingham Eccentric (15070)**
Observer & Eccentric Newspapers
36251 Schoolcraft Rd.
Livonia, MI 48150
Phone: (734)591-2300
Fax: (734)953-2232
**Subject(s):** Paid Community Newspapers
**Circ:** (Sun.)11,562
(Thurs.)11,600

**The Word (9924)**
Word Publications
110 E Washington St., Ste. 1402
Indianapolis, IN 46204
Phone: (317)725-8840
Fax: (317)687-8840
**Subject(s):** Free Newspapers; Gay and Lesbian Interests
**Circ:** (Paid)11,600

**St. Louis Park Sun-Sailor (16563)**
Minnesota Sun Publications
10917 Valley View Rd.
Eden Prairie, MN 55344
Phone: (952)829-0797
Fax: (952)392-6868
**Subject(s):** Free Newspapers
**Circ:** (Paid)♦797
(Non-paid)♦11,590

**The Catholic Weekly (15721)**
GLS Diocesan Reports
1520 Court St.
PO Box 1405
Saginaw, MI 48605-1405
Phone: (989)793-7661
Fax: (989)793-7663
**Subject(s):** Religious Publications
**Circ:** (Free)⊕583
(Paid)⊕11,546

**Ogle County Life (9183)**
311 W Washington
PO Box 378
Oregon, IL 61061
Phone: (815)732-2156
Fax: (815)732-6154
**Subject(s):** Paid Community Newspapers
**Circ:** (Paid)‡1,324
(Free)‡11,535

**Advertiser-Tribune (25080)**
320 Nelson St.
PO Box 778
Tiffin, OH 44883-0778
Phone: (419)448-3200
Fax: (419)447-3274
**Subject(s):** Daily Newspapers
**Circ:** (Mon.-Sat.)10,944
(Sun.)11,520

**Berwyn/Stickney/Forest View LIFE (9082)**
Liberty Suburban Chicago Newspapers
7222 W. Cermak Rd., Ste. 505
North Riverside, IL 60546
Phone: (708)447-9810
**Subject(s):** Paid Community Newspapers
**Circ:** (Paid)11,500

**Bi-County Herald (15437)**
115 S Church St.
PO Box 87
Hudson, MI 49247
Phone: (517)448-2201
Fax: (517)448-2201
**Subject(s):** Shopping Guides
**Circ:** (Free)‡11,500

**Cicero Life (7911)**
Liberty Suburban Chicago Newspapers
3208 Grove Ave.
Berwyn, IL 60402-3025
Phone: (708)484-1234
Fax: (708)484-7778
**Subject(s):** Paid Community Newspapers
**Circ:** (Paid)11,500

**Farmers' Weekly Review (8827)**
100 Manhattan Rd.
Joliet, IL 60433
Phone: (815)727-4811
Fax: (815)727-5570
**Subject(s):** Paid Community Newspapers; Farm Newspapers
**Circ:** 11,500

**Farmington Observer (15265)**
Observer & Eccentric Newspapers
36251 Schoolcraft Rd.
Livonia, MI 48150
Phone: (734)591-2300
Fax: (734)953-2232
**Subject(s):** Paid Community Newspapers
**Circ:** (Sun.)11,362
(Thurs.)11,507

**Mendota Shopping Guide (8958)**
504 9th St.
Mendota, IL 61342-1794
Phone: (815)539-7476
Fax: (815)539-7477

**Subject(s):** Shopping Guides
**Circ:** (Free)‡11,500

**Community Press of Mason (24849)**
Press Community Newspapers
394 Wards Corner Rd.
Loveland, OH 45140
Phone: (513)248-8600
Fax: (513)248-1938
**Subject(s):** Free Newspapers
**Circ:** (Non-paid)11,419

**Daily Reporter (9778)**
22 W New Rd.
PO Box 279
Greenfield, IN 46140
Phone: (317)462-5528
Fax: (317)467-6009
**Subject(s):** Daily Newspapers
**Circ:** (Non-paid)87
(Paid)11,400

**Journal-Gazette (8944)**
Mid-Illinois Newspapers Inc.
100 Broadway
Mattoon, IL 61938
Phone: (217)235-5656
Fax: (217)235-1925
**Subject(s):** Daily Newspapers
**Circ:** (Mon.-Sat.)11,386

**The Daily Chronicle (8557)**
Lee Enterprises Inc.
1586 Barber Greene Rd.
DeKalb, IL 60115-7900
Phone: (815)756-4841
**Subject(s):** Daily Newspapers
**Circ:** (Mon.-Fri.)10,616
(Sun.)11,365

**Home Town News (15432)**
Hometown Newspapers
323 E Grand River
PO Box 230
Howell, MI 48843
Phone: (517)548-2000
Fax: (248)437-9460
**Subject(s):** Paid Community Newspapers
**Circ:** (Paid)10,503
(Free)11,321

**Photo Star (25181)**
307 State St.
P O Box B
Willshire, OH 45898
Phone: (419)495-2696
Fax: (419)495-2143
**Subject(s):** Free Newspapers
**Circ:** (Paid)200
(Free)11,300

**Pleasant Ridge/Ferndale Mirror (15715)**
Mirror Newspapers
1523 N Main
PO Box 430
Royal Oak, MI 48067-0430
Phone: (248)546-4900
Fax: (248)398-2353
**Subject(s):** Free Newspapers
**Circ:** (Combined)11,307

**Glen Ellyn News (9089)**
Liberty Suburban Chicago Newspapers
7222 W. Cermak Rd., Ste. 505
North Riverside, IL 60546
Phone: (708)447-9810
**Subject(s):** Paid Community Newspapers
**Circ:** (Combined)11,250

**Huber Heights Courier (24776)**
Suburban Newspapers
7089 Taylorsville Rd.
Huber Heights, OH 45424
Phone: (937)236-4990
Fax: (937)236-4176
**Subject(s):** Paid Community Newspapers
**Circ:** 11,250

**Wheaton Leader (9103)**
Liberty Suburban Chicago Newspapers
7222 W. Cermak Rd., Ste. 505
North Riverside, IL 60546
Phone: (708)447-9810

---

Circulation: ★ = ABC; Δ = BPA; ♦ = CAC; • = CCAB; □ = VAC; ⊕ = PO Statement; ‡ = Publisher's Report; Boldface figures = sworn; Light figures = estimated.

## Great Lakes States

**Subject(s):** Paid Community Newspapers

Circ: (Combined)11,250

**Comics Buyer's Guide (33070)**
Krause Publications Inc.
700 E. State St.
Iola, WI 54990-0001
Phone: (715)445-2214
Fax: (715)445-4087
**Subject(s):** Comics and Comic Technique

Circ: (Paid)11,218

**Bloomingdale/Glendale Heights Press (9083)**
Liberty Suburban Chicago Newspapers
7222 W. Cermak Rd., Ste. 505
North Riverside, IL 60546
Phone: (708)447-9810
**Subject(s):** Paid Community Newspapers

Circ: (Combined)11,200

**Carol Stream Press (9085)**
Liberty Suburban Chicago Newspapers
7222 W. Cermak Rd., Ste. 505
North Riverside, IL 60546
Phone: (708)447-9810
**Subject(s):** Paid Community Newspapers

Circ: (Combined)11,200

**Itasca/Roselle Press: Serving Bartlett/Hanover Park/Steamwood Press (9091)**
Liberty Suburban Chicago Newspapers
7222 W. Cermak Rd., Ste. 505
North Riverside, IL 60546
Phone: (708)447-9810
**Subject(s):** Paid Community Newspapers

Circ: (Combined)11,200

**The Washington County Edition (10147)**
Green Banner Publications Inc.
105 East Walnut
Salem, IN 47167
Phone: (812)883-5555
Fax: (812)883-3658
**Subject(s):** Free Newspapers

Circ: (Free)11,192

**Flower News (8204)**
Cenflo Inc.
205 W Wacker Dr., Ste. 1040
Chicago, IL 60606-3508
Phone: (312)739-5000
Fax: (312)739-0739
**Subject(s):** Florists and Floriculture

Circ: (Paid)‡5,941
(Non-paid)‡11,188

**Mesabi Daily News (16677)**
Murphy McGinnis Media Inc.
704 7th Ave. S
Virginia, MN 55792
Phone: (218)741-5544
Fax: (218)741-1005
**Subject(s):** Daily Newspapers

Circ: (Mon.-Sat.)♦9,642
(Sun.)♦11,173

**The Extra Shopper (33464)**
Murphy McGinnis Media Inc.
115 N Lake Ave.
PO BOX 170
Phillips, WI 54555
Phone: (715)339-3036
Fax: (715)339-4300
**Subject(s):** Shopping Guides

Circ: (Non-paid)♦11,163

**West Side Sun News (24957)**
Sun Newspapers
28895 Lorain Rd.
North Olmsted, OH 44070-4042
Phone: (440)777-3800
Fax: (440)777-8423
**Subject(s):** Paid Community Newspapers

Circ: (Paid)11,137

**The Borderline (16533)**
106 W Center St.
PO Box 220
Roseau, MN 56751-0220
Phone: (218)463-1521
Fax: (218)463-1530
**Subject(s):** Shopping Guides

Circ: (Free)11,125

**Tele Guia de Chicago (8506)**
Tele Guia Publications
3116 S Austin Blvd.
Cicero, IL 60804
Phone: (708)656-6666
Fax: (708)656-6679
**Subject(s):** Paid Community Newspapers; Hispanic Publications

Circ: (Paid)9,516
(Non-paid)11,121

**The Jackson County Advertiser (24790)**
Add Inc.—Ohio Group
300 Morton St.
Jackson, OH 45640
Phone: (740)286-7571
Fax: (740)286-4766
**Subject(s):** Shopping Guides

Circ: (Non-paid)11,103

**The Marietta Times (24871)**
700 Channel Ln.
PO Box 635
Marietta, OH 45750
Phone: (614)373-2121
Fax: (614)373-6251
**Subject(s):** Daily Newspapers

Circ: (Mon.-Sat.)★11,089

**Brighton Argus (15430)**
Hometown Newspapers
323 E Grand River
PO Box 230
Howell, MI 48843
Phone: (517)548-2000
Fax: (248)437-9460
**Subject(s):** Paid Community Newspapers

Circ: (Non-paid)485
(Paid)11,065

**South Washington County Bulletin (16031)**
7584 80th St., S.
Cottage Grove, MN 55016
Phone: (651)459-3434
Fax: (651)459-9491
**Subject(s):** Paid Community Newspapers

Circ: ⊕11,048

**Alpena News (14987)**
Alpena News Publishing Co.
130 Park Pl.
PO Box 367
Alpena, MI 49707
Phone: (989)354-3111
Fax: (989)354-2096
**Subject(s):** Daily Newspapers

Circ: (Mon.-Sat.)★11,025

**Harrison Daily Times (8931)**
American Publishing Co.
1120 N Carbon, Ste. 100
Marion, IL 62959
Phone: (618)993-1711
Fax: (618)997-5209
**Subject(s):** Daily Newspapers

Circ: (Controlled)127
(Paid)11,011

**Bartlett Examiner (7881)**
Examiner Publications
4N781 Gerber Rd.
Bartlett, IL 60103
Phone: (630)830-4145
**Subject(s):** Paid Community Newspapers

Circ: 11,000

**Burlington Standard Press (32872)**
Southern Lakes Newspapers
140 Commerce St.
Burlington, WI 53105-0437
Phone: (262)763-3511
Fax: (262)763-2238
**Subject(s):** Paid Community Newspapers

Circ: (Paid)‡5,600
(Free)‡11,000

**The Davison Index (15145)**
220 N Main St.
PO Box 100
Davison, MI 48423-0100
Phone: (810)653-3511
Fax: (810)653-3077
**Subject(s):** Paid Community Newspapers

Circ: 11,000

**Eden Prairie News (16089)**
Southwest Suburban Publishing
PO Box 44220
Eden Prairie, MN 55344
Phone: (952)934-5045
Fax: (952)934-7960
**Subject(s):** Paid Community Newspapers

Circ: (Free)11,000

**Edgebrook Reporter (8181)**
NADIG Newspapers Inc.
4937 N Milwaukee Ave.
Chicago, IL 60630
Phone: (773)286-6100
Fax: (773)286-8151
**Subject(s):** Free Newspapers

Circ: (Free)‡11,000

**Kanabec County Times (16406)**
107 Park St. South
Mora, MN 55051
Phone: (320)679-2661
Fax: (320)679-2663
**Subject(s):** Free Newspapers

Circ: (Paid)‡3,000
(Free)‡11,000

**South County Gazette and Shopper (15823)**
American Publishing Company of Michigan
110 N. Elm St.
Three Oaks, MI 49128
Phone: (616)756-2421
Fax: (616)756-7220
**Subject(s):** Free Newspapers

Circ: (Combined)‡11,002

**Tri-County Shoppers Guide (15066)**
The Pioneer Group
502 N State St.
Big Rapids, MI 49307
Phone: (231)796-4831
Fax: (231)796-1152
**Subject(s):** Shopping Guides

Circ: (Free)‡10,990

**Petoskey News-Review (15671)**
Petoskey News-Review, Super Shopper, and Graphic
319 State St.
PO Box 528
Petoskey, MI 49770-0528
Phone: (231)347-2544
Fax: (231)347-6833
**Subject(s):** Daily Newspapers

Circ: (Mon.-Fri.)★10,983

**Polish Daily News (8381)**
Alliance Printers and Publishers Inc.
5711 N Milwaukee
Chicago, IL 60646
Phone: (773)763-3343
Fax: (773)763-3825
**Subject(s):** Daily Newspapers; Polish

Circ: (Free)‡203
(Paid)‡10,847

**The Pioneer (15954)**
The Pioneer/Advertiser
1320 Neilson Ave. SE
Bemidji, MN 56601
Phone: (218)751-3740
Fax: (218)751-2193
**Subject(s):** Daily Newspapers

Circ: (Mon.-Fri.)10,270
(Sun.)10,838

**The Times (24605)**
Suburban News Publications
5257 Sinclair Rd.
PO Box 29912
Columbus, OH 43229
Phone: (614)785-1212
Fax: (614)785-1881
**Subject(s):** Paid Community Newspapers

Circ: 10,835

**The Troy Daily News (25118)**
TDN Publishing Co.
224 S. Market St.
Troy, OH 45373
Phone: (937)339-9535
Fax: (937)339-8413
**Subject(s):** Daily Newspapers

Circ: (Mon.-Sat.)10,838

**The Peshtigo Times (33462)**
PO Box 187
Peshtigo, WI 54157
Phone: (715)582-4541
Fax: (715)582-4662
**Subject(s):** Paid Community Newspapers
**Circ:** ‡10,817

**Madison Press (24851)**
Central Ohio Printing
30 S Oak St.
PO Box 390
London, OH 43140-1079
Phone: (740)852-1616
Fax: (740)852-1620
**Subject(s):** Daily Newspapers
**Circ:** (Paid)‡6,500
⊕10,800

**The Flint Township News (15288)**
The Flint Journal
200 E. 1st St.
Flint, MI 48502-1925
**Subject(s):** Paid Community Newspapers
**Circ:** (Combined)10,779

**The Swartz Creek News (15816)**
The Flint Journal
200 E. First St.
Flint, MI 48502-1925
**Subject(s):** Paid Community Newspapers
**Circ:** (Combined)10,779

**Ottawa Advance (15140)**
Advance Newspapers
2141 Port Sheldon Rd.
PO Box 9
Jenison, MI 49428-9301
Phone: (616)669-2700
Fax: (616)669-1162
**Subject(s):** Paid Community Newspapers
**Circ:** (Paid)❏70
(Free)❏10,703

**County News (15998)**
ECM Group
234 S Main St.
PO Box 352
Cambridge, MN 55008-0352
Phone: (763)689-1981
Fax: (763)689-4372
**Subject(s):** Paid Community Newspapers
**Circ:** 10,600

**Herald Journal Shopper (16729)**
Herald Journal Publishing
PO Box 129
Winsted, MN 55395
Phone: (320)485-2535
Fax: (320)485-2878
**Subject(s):** Shopping Guides
**Circ:** (Free)‡10,575

**Mora Advertisers (16407)**
Karabee Publications
107 Park St. South
Mora, MN 55051
Phone: (320)679-2661
Fax: (320)679-2663
**Subject(s):** Shopping Guides
**Circ:** (Paid)‡192
(Free)❏10,554

**Grove City News (24758)**
Suburban News Publications
5257 Sinclair Rd.
PO Box 29912
Columbus, OH 43229
Phone: (614)785-1212
Fax: (614)785-1881
**Subject(s):** Free Newspapers
**Circ:** (Paid)41
(Non-paid)10,521

**The Bryan Times (24223)**
Bryan Publishing Co.
127 S Walnut St.
PO Box 471
Bryan, OH 43506
Phone: (419)636-1111
Fax: (419)636-8937
**Subject(s):** Daily Newspapers
**Circ:** (Mon.-Sat.)★10,515

**Canton Observer (15096)**
Observer & Eccentric Newspapers
36251 Schoolcraft Rd.
Livonia, MI 48150
Phone: (734)591-2300
Fax: (734)953-2232
**Subject(s):** Free Newspapers
**Circ:** (Thurs.)9,864
(Sun.)10,518

**The Daily News (33647)**
Conley Publishing
100 S. 6th Ave.
PO Box 478
West Bend, WI 53095-0478
Phone: (262)306-5000
Fax: (262)338-1984
**Subject(s):** Daily Newspapers
**Circ:** (Mon.-Fri.)10,501

**The Evening News (9954)**
221 Spring St.
Jeffersonville, IN 47130
Phone: (812)283-6636
Fax: (812)284-7081
**Subject(s):** Daily Newspapers
**Circ:** (Paid)10,500

**Green Bay News-Chronicle (33006)**
133 S Monroe St.
PO Box 2467
Green Bay, WI 54306
Phone: (920)432-2941
Fax: (920)432-8581
**Subject(s):** Daily Newspapers
**Circ:** 7,400
‡10,500

**Lakeland Times (33376)**
Box 790
Minocqua, WI 54548
Phone: (715)356-5236
Fax: (715)358-2121
**Subject(s):** Paid Community Newspapers
**Circ:** 10,500

**Miami Valley Sunday News (25117)**
TDN Publishing Co.
224 S. Market St.
Troy, OH 45373
Phone: (937)339-9535
Fax: (937)339-8413
**Subject(s):** Paid Community Newspapers
**Circ:** (Sun.)10,465

**Troy Eccentric (15866)**
Observer & Eccentric Newspapers
36251 Schoolcraft Rd.
Livonia, MI 48150
Phone: (734)591-2300
Fax: (734)953-2232
**Subject(s):** Paid Community Newspapers
**Circ:** (Thurs.)10,309
(Sun.)10,415

**Downers Grove Progress (8601)**
Liberty Suburban Chicago Newspapers
922 Warren Ave.
Downers Grove, IL 60515
Phone: (630)969-0885
Fax: (630)969-0228
**Subject(s):** Free Newspapers
**Circ:** (Combined)10,400

**The Shelbyville News (10159)**
Shelbyville Newspapers Inc.
123 E Washington St.
PO Box 750
Shelbyville, IN 46176
Phone: (317)398-6631
Fax: (317)398-0194
**Subject(s):** Daily Newspapers
**Circ:** (Mon.-Sat.)10,409

**West Bloomfield Eccentric (15890)**
Observer & Eccentric Newspapers
36251 Schoolcraft Rd.
Livonia, MI 48150
Phone: (734)591-2300
Fax: (734)953-2232
**Subject(s):** Paid Community Newspapers
**Circ:** (Sun.)10,403
(Thurs.)10,404

**Westmont Progress (9102)**
Liberty Suburban Chicago Newspapers
7222 W. Cermak Rd., Ste. 505
North Riverside, IL 60546
Phone: (708)447-9810
**Subject(s):** Paid Community Newspapers
**Circ:** (Combined)10,400

**Woodridge Progress (9105)**
Liberty Suburban Chicago Newspapers
7222 W. Cermak Rd., Ste. 505
North Riverside, IL 60546
Phone: (708)447-9810
**Subject(s):** Free Newspapers
**Circ:** (Combined)10,400

**Woodbury Bulletin (16731)**
8420 City Centre Dr.
Woodbury, MN 55125
Phone: (651)730-4007
Fax: (651)702-0977
**Subject(s):** Paid Community Newspapers
**Circ:** (Paid)10,396

**Record-News (24867)**
Record Publishing Co.
1619 Commerce Dr.
Stow, OH 44224
Phone: (330)688-0088
Fax: (330)688-1588
**Subject(s):** Free Newspapers
**Circ:** (Paid)‡100
(Free)‡10,367

**Livewire (16188)**
Livewire Printing Co.
310 2nd St.
PO Box 208
Jackson, MN 56143
Phone: (507)847-3771
Fax: (507)847-5822
**Subject(s):** Shopping Guides
**Circ:** (Paid)321
(Free)10,333

**North DuPage Press (8731)**
Liberty Suburban Chicago Newspapers
460 Pennsylvania Ave.
Glen Ellyn, IL 60137
Phone: (630)469-0100
Fax: (630)469-4772
**Subject(s):** Free Newspapers
**Circ:** (Combined)10,285

**Crystal Robbinsdale Sun Post (16036)**
Minnesota Sun Publications
10917 Valley View Rd.
Eden Prairie, MN 55344
Phone: (952)829-0797
Fax: (952)392-6868
**Subject(s):** Paid Community Newspapers
**Circ:** (Paid)707
(Non-paid)10,250

**St. Croix Valley Press (16704)**
Press Publications
4779 Bloom Ave.
White Bear Lake, MN 55110
Phone: (651)407-1200
Fax: (651)429-1242
**Subject(s):** Free Newspapers
**Circ:** (Paid)181
(Free)10,247

**Seymour Daily Tribune (10154)**
The Tribune
100 St. Louis Ave.
PO Box 447
Seymour, IN 47274
Phone: (812)522-4871
Fax: (812)522-7691
**Subject(s):** Daily Newspapers
**Circ:** (Mon.-Sat.)10,235

**The Daily Standard (24261)**
123 E Market St.
PO Box 140
Celina, OH 45822
Phone: (419)586-2371
Fax: (419)586-6271
**Subject(s):** Daily Newspapers
**Circ:** (Free)‡50
(Paid)‡10,200

## Great Lakes States

**Midlothian-Bremen Messenger (8971)**
Southwest Messenger Press Inc.
3840 W 147th St.
PO Box 548
Midlothian, IL 60445
Phone: (708)388-2425
Fax: (708)385-7811
**Subject(s):** Free Newspapers
**Circ:** (Free)‡500
(Paid)‡10,200

**The Three Lakes News (32917)**
Eagle River Publications Inc.
346 W Division St.
PO Box 1929
Eagle River, WI 54521
Phone: (715)479-4421
Fax: (715)479-6242
**Subject(s):** Paid Community Newspapers
**Circ:** (Paid)⊕10,200

**Vilas County News Review (32919)**
Eagle River Publications Inc.
346 W Division St.
PO Box 1929
Eagle River, WI 54521
Phone: (715)479-4421
Fax: (715)479-6242
**Subject(s):** Paid Community Newspapers
**Circ:** (Paid)⊕10,200

**Whitehall News (25167)**
Suburban News Publications
5257 Sinclair Rd.
PO Box 29912
Columbus, OH 43229
Phone: (614)785-1212
Fax: (614)785-1881
**Subject(s):** Free Newspapers
**Circ:** (Paid)76
(Non-paid)10,179

**The Echo/Press (15927)**
Echo Press
225 7th Ave. E.
PO Box 549
Alexandria, MN 56308
Phone: (320)763-3133
Fax: (320)763-3258
**Subject(s):** Paid Community Newspapers
**Circ:** (Wed.)9,388
(Fri.)10,167

**Itasca Shopper (16150)**
Murphy McGinnis Media Inc.
301 1st Ave. NW
PO Box 220
Grand Rapids, MN 55744
Phone: (218)326-6623
Fax: (218)326-6627
**Subject(s):** Shopping Guides
**Circ:** (Non-paid)♦10,140

**Luverne Announcer (16225)**
Announcer-Star Herald
PO Box 837
Luverne, MN 56156-0837
Phone: (507)283-2333
Fax: (507)283-2335
**Subject(s):** Shopping Guides
**Circ:** (Free)10,122

**New Hope/Golden Valley Sun-Post (16417)**
Minnesota Sun Publications
10917 Valley View Rd.
Eden Prairie, MN 55344
Phone: (952)829-0797
Fax: (952)392-6868
**Subject(s):** Free Newspapers
**Circ:** (Paid)1,106
(Non-paid)10,092

**West DuPage Press (9340)**
Liberty Suburban Chicago Newspapers
1519 Main St.
Saint Charles, IL 60174
Phone: (630)513-5050
Fax: (630)513-6660
**Subject(s):** Free Newspapers
**Circ:** (Combined)10,094

**The Pike County Advertiser (25143)**
Add Inc.—Ohio Group
201 E Emmitt Ave., Ste. B
Waverly, OH 45690
Phone: (740)947-7084
Fax: (740)947-7916
**Subject(s):** Shopping Guides
**Circ:** (Non-paid)10,062

**The Daily Mining Gazette (15423)**
PO Box 368
Houghton, MI 49931
Phone: (906)482-1500
Fax: (906)482-2726
**Subject(s):** Daily Newspapers
**Circ:** (Mon.-Sat.)★10,027

**Penny Saver (24637)**
Arens Publications
395 S. High St.
Covington, OH 45318
Phone: (937)473-2028
Fax: (937)473-3299
**Subject(s):** Shopping Guides
**Circ:** (Combined)10,021

**Albion Recorder (14968)**
125 Cass St.
Albion, MI 49224-1755
Phone: (517)629-0041
Fax: (517)629-5790
**Subject(s):** Daily Newspapers
**Circ:** (Paid)3,100
(Non-paid)10,000

**Blaine Banner (15968)**
12570 Radisson Rd. NE
Blaine, MN 55449
Phone: (763)755-3832
Fax: (763)755-3832
**Subject(s):** Free Newspapers
**Circ:** (Non-paid)‡10,000

**Contact (16468)**
PO Box 288
Perham, MN 56573
Phone: (218)346-5900
Fax: (218)346-5901
**Subject(s):** Shopping Guides
**Circ:** (Free)10,000

**The Daily Cardinal (33171)**
The Daily Cardinal Newspaper Corp.
2142 Vilas Communication Hall
821 Univ. Ave.
Madison, WI 53706-1497
Phone: (608)262-8000
Fax: (608)262-8100
**Subject(s):** College Publications
**Circ:** (Free)‡10,000

**Eastern Echo (15903)**
Eastern Michigan University
Eastern Echo
Ypsilanti, MI 48197
Phone: (734)487-0397
Fax: (734)487-1241
**Subject(s):** College Publications
**Circ:** (Free)‡10,000

**Flashes Shoppers Guide & News (15256)**
115 Grand St.
PO Box 156
Eaton Rapids, MI 48827-0156
Phone: (517)663-2361
Fax: (517)663-2381
**Subject(s):** Shopping Guides
**Circ:** (Free)‡10,000

**Homeless Grapevine (24425)**
NE Ohio Coalition for the Homeless
3631 Perkins Ave., Ste. 3A-3
Cleveland, OH 44114
Phone: (216)432-0540
**Subject(s):** Paid Community Newspapers; Social and Political Issues
**Circ:** (Paid)10,000

**Lac du Flambeau News (33133)**
Lac du Flambeau Band of Lake Superior Chippewa Indians
PO Box 67
Lac du Flambeau, WI 54538
Phone: (715)588-9272
Fax: (715)588-9408
**Subject(s):** Native American Interests
**Circ:** (Paid)500
(Non-paid)10,000

**The Link (9889)**
Synod of Lincoln Trails
1100 W 42nd St.
Indianapolis, IN 46208
Phone: (317)923-3681
**Subject(s):** Religious Publications
**Circ:** (Non-paid)10,000

**The Miami Student (24980)**
Miami University
17 Macmillan Hall
Oxford, OH 45056
Phone: (513)529-2210
Fax: (513)529-1893
**Subject(s):** College Publications
**Circ:** (Free)10,000

**The Press (24157)**
PO Box 300
158 Lear Rd.
Avon Lake, OH 44012
Phone: (440)933-5100
Fax: (440)933-7904
**Subject(s):** Paid Community Newspapers
**Circ:** ‡10,000

**Savannah Journal Illinois Dispatch (9345)**
Times-Journal
PO Box 218
Savanna, IL 61074
Phone: (815)273-2277
Fax: (815)273-2715
**Subject(s):** Free Newspapers
**Circ:** (Free)‡10,000

**The South End (15200)**
Wayne State University Student Newspapers Publishing Board
5425 Woodward Ave. Ste. 101
Detroit, MI 48202
Phone: (313)577-7878
Fax: (313)993-8108
**Subject(s):** College Publications
**Circ:** (Free)‡10,000

**The Swanton Enterprise (25077)**
Gazette Publishing Co.
97 N Main St.
PO Box 180
Swanton, OH 43558
Phone: (419)826-3580
Fax: (419)826-3590
**Subject(s):** Paid Community Newspapers
**Circ:** (Combined)‡10,000

**University of Cincinnati News Record (24341)**
University of Cincinnati
PO Box 210135
Cincinnati, OH 45221-0135
Phone: (513)556-5900
Fax: (513)556-5922
**Subject(s):** College Publications
**Circ:** (Free)‡10,000

**Rubber & Plastics News (24103)**
Crain Communications Inc.
1725 Merriman Rd.
Akron, OH 44313-9180
Phone: (330)836-9180
Fax: (330)836-2831
**Subject(s):** Plastic and Composition Materials; Rubber Trade
**Circ:** (Paid)△6,322
(Non-paid)△9,995

**Freeway Shoppers Guide (15698)**
The Pioneer Group
101 W. Slosson
Reed City, MI 49677
Phone: (231)832-5566
Fax: (231)832-5558
**Subject(s):** Shopping Guides
**Circ:** (Free)‡9,971

**News-Sun (9957)**
102 N Main St.
PO Box 39
Kendallville, IN 46755
Phone: (219)347-0400
Fax: (219)347-2693

**Subject(s):** Daily Newspapers
**Circ:** (Mon.-Sat.)9,953

**Fairview Heights/O'Fallon Journal (9441)**
Suburban Journal
5050 Old Collinsville Rd.
Swansea, IL 62226-2009
Phone: (618)622-5050
**Subject(s):** Free Newspapers
**Circ:** (Wed.)9,760
(Sun.)9,940

**West Bloomfield Spinal Column Newsweekly (15891)**
Spinal Column Publications
7196 Cooley Lake Rd.
PO Box 14
Union Lake, MI 48387-0014
Phone: (248)360-7355
Fax: (248)360-4711
**Subject(s):** Free Newspapers
**Circ:** (Free)‡9,900

**White Lake Beacon (15897)**
432 Spring St.
PO Box 98
Whitehall, MI 49461
Phone: (231)894-5356
Fax: (231)894-2174
**Subject(s):** Free Newspapers
**Circ:** (Paid)‡815
(Free)‡9,885

**Osseo-Maple Grove Press (16454)**
Sun Press and News Publications
33 2nd St. NE
Box 280
Osseo, MN 55369
Phone: (763)425-3323
Fax: (763)425-2945
**Subject(s):** Paid Community Newspapers
**Circ:** (Paid)4,649
(Free)9,871

**Zeeland Flashes Shopping Guide (14978)**
Flashes Publishers
595 Jenner Dr.
Allegan, MI 49010-1567
Phone: (269)324-1602
Fax: (269)673-6768
**Subject(s):** Shopping Guides
**Circ:** (Paid)2
(Controlled)9,853

**The Review (24703)**
210 E. 4th St.
East Liverpool, OH 43920
Phone: (330)385-4545
Fax: (330)385-7114
**Subject(s):** Daily Newspapers
**Circ:** (Mon.-Sat.)9,838

**Commerce Spinal Column Newsweekly (15139)**
Spinal Column Publications
7196 Cooley Lake Rd.
PO Box 14
Union Lake, MI 48387-0014
Phone: (248)360-7355
Fax: (248)360-4711
**Subject(s):** Free Newspapers
**Circ:** (Free)‡9,800

**Carson City Gazette (15102)**
Greenville News Inc.
211 W. Main
Carson City, MI 48811-9728
Phone: (989)584-3967
Fax: (989)584-3591
**Subject(s):** Free Newspapers
**Circ:** (Paid)‡273
(Free)‡9,730

**Upper Arlington News (25123)**
Suburban News Publications
5257 Sinclair Rd.
PO Box 29912
Columbus, OH 43229
Phone: (614)785-1212
Fax: (614)785-1881
**Subject(s):** Free Newspapers
**Circ:** (Paid)6,174
(Non-paid)9,718

**Business Ledger (9144)**
Ledger Publishing Co.
600 Enterprise Dr., Ste. 100
Oak Brook, IL 60523
Phone: (630)571-8911
Fax: (630)571-4053
**Subject(s):** Local, State, and Regional Publications
**Circ:** (Paid)1,300
(Controlled)9,700

**Shoreview Press (16705)**
Press Publications
4779 Bloom Ave.
White Bear Lake, MN 55110
Phone: (651)407-1200
Fax: (651)429-1242
**Subject(s):** Paid Community Newspapers
**Circ:** (Paid)212
(Non-paid)9,701

**Mt. Vernon News (24922)**
Progressive Communication Corp.
18 E Vine
Mount Vernon, OH 43050
Phone: (740)397-5333
Fax: (740)397-1321
**Subject(s):** Daily Newspapers
**Circ:** (Mon.-Sat.)9,634

**Kewaunee County Sunday Chronicle (32795)**
Tri-County Publishing
203 Ellis St.
PO Box 68
Algoma, WI 54201
Phone: (920)487-2222
Fax: (920)487-3194
**Subject(s):** Shopping Guides
**Circ:** (Non-paid)9,600

**KMA Chief II (33386)**
Mukwonago Publications
555 Bay View Rd., Ste. 1
Mukwonago, WI 53149
**Subject(s):** Shopping Guides
**Circ:** (Free)‡9,600

**The Shopping News (24968)**
Gazette Publishing Company Inc.
42 S. Main St.
Oberlin, OH 44074
Phone: (440)775-1611
Fax: (440)774-2167
**Subject(s):** Shopping Guides
**Circ:** (Free)‡9,600

**The Madison Courier (10006)**
310 Courier Sq.
Madison, IN 47250
Phone: (812)265-3641
Fax: (812)273-6903
**Subject(s):** Daily Newspapers
**Circ:** (Free)56
(Paid)9,596

**The Daily Sentinel (24739)**
Ohio Valley Publishing
825 3rd Ave.
Gallipolis, OH 45631
Phone: (740)446-2342
Fax: (740)446-3008
**Subject(s):** Daily Newspapers
**Circ:** (Mon.-Fri.)★4,044
(Sun.)★9,582

**West Saint Paul/Mendota Heights Sun Current (16699)**
Minnesota Sun Publications
10917 Valley View Rd.
Eden Prairie, MN 55344
Phone: (952)829-0797
Fax: (952)392-6868
**Subject(s):** Free Newspapers
**Circ:** (Paid)200
(Non-paid)9,552

**Stillwater Valley Advertiser (24638)**
Arens Publications
395 S. High St.
Covington, OH 45318
Phone: (937)473-2028
Fax: (937)473-3299
**Subject(s):** Shopping Guides; Free Newspapers
**Circ:** (Combined)9,539

**The BG News (24199)**
Bowling Green State University
214 West Hall
Bowling Green State University
Bowling Green, OH 43403
Phone: (419)372-6966
Fax: (419)372-0202
**Subject(s):** College Publications
**Circ:** (Free)‡9,500

**Hocking Valley Advertiser (24838)**
51 S., Spring St.
PO Box 247
Logan, OH 43138
Phone: (740)385-1969
Fax: (740)385-8458
**Subject(s):** Shopping Guides
**Circ:** (Non-paid)9,506

**Sunday Square Shooter (16656)**
Devlin Newspapers Inc.
PO Box 100
Staples, MN 56479
Phone: (218)894-1112
Fax: (218)894-3570
**Subject(s):** Shopping Guides
**Circ:** (Free)‡9,500

**Worthington Globe (16733)**
Forum Communications Co.
PO Box 639
Worthington, MN 56187
Phone: (507)376-9711
**Subject(s):** Daily Newspapers
**Circ:** (Free)❑88
(Paid)❑9,422

**Fergus Fall Daily Journal (16121)**
Boone Newspaper
914 E Channing Ave.
PO Box 506
Fergus Falls, MN 56537
Phone: (218)736-7511
Fax: (218)736-5919
**Subject(s):** Daily Newspapers
**Circ:** (Mon.-Sat.)9,409

**Rice Lake Chronotype (33509)**
Chronotype Publishing Co.
PO Box 30
Rice Lake, WI 54868
**Subject(s):** Paid Community Newspapers
**Circ:** (Free)152
(Paid)9,400

**Illinois Spirit Shopping Guide (9506)**
PO Box 250
1492 E Walnut
Watseka, IL 60970
Phone: (815)432-5227
Fax: (815)432-5159
**Subject(s):** Shopping Guides
**Circ:** (Free)‡9,362

**Morning Star: The Shopping Guide (14970)**
Salesmen Publications
125 E Cass St.
Albion, MI 49224
Phone: (517)629-2127
Fax: (517)629-5210
**Subject(s):** Shopping Guides
**Circ:** (Free)9,366

**The Star Press (25054)**
Miller Publishing Co.
PO Box 147
Springboro, OH 45066
Phone: (937)748-2550
Fax: (937)746-6013
**Subject(s):** Paid Community Newspapers
**Circ:** (Paid)2,744
(Free)9,321

**Hudson Hub-Times (25070)**
Record Publishing Co.
1619 Commerce Dr.
Stow, OH 44224
Phone: (330)688-0088
Fax: (330)688-1588
**Subject(s):** Free Newspapers
**Circ:** (Paid)‡468
(Free)‡9,296

Circulation: ★ = ABC; △ = BPA; ◆ = CAC; ● = CCAB; ❑ = VAC; ⊕ = PO Statement; ‡ = Publisher's Report; Boldface figures = sworn; Light figures = estimated.

## Great Lakes States

**Evening News** (15758)
American Publishing of Michigan
109 Arlington St.
Sault Sainte Marie, MI 49783-1901
Phone: (906)632-2235
Fax: (906)632-1222
**Subject(s):** Daily Newspapers
**Circ:** 9,213

**Bolingbrook/Romeoville Reporter** (9084)
Liberty Suburban Chicago Newspapers
7222 W. Cermak Rd., Ste. 505
North Riverside, IL 60546
Phone: (708)447-9810
**Subject(s):** Paid Community Newspapers
**Circ:** (Combined)9,200

**The Laker** (16412)
J.D. Barreth Pub.
2365 Commerce Blvd.
PO Box 82
Mound, MN 55364-0082
Phone: (952)472-1140
Fax: (952)472-0516
**Subject(s):** Paid Community Newspapers
**Circ:** ‡9,200

**Lisle Reporter** (9093)
Liberty Suburban Chicago Newspapers
7222 W. Cermak Rd., Ste. 505
North Riverside, IL 60546
Phone: (708)447-9810
**Subject(s):** Paid Community Newspapers
**Circ:** (Combined)9,200

**Mt. Horeb Mail** (33385)
News Publishing Company Inc.
118 E. Main St.
POB 88
Mount Horeb, WI 53572
**Subject(s):** Paid Community Newspapers
**Circ:** (Paid)2,900
(Non-paid)9,209

**Naperville Reporter** (8605)
Liberty Suburban Chicago Newspapers
922 Warren Ave.
Downers Grove, IL 60515-3690
Phone: (630)969-0885
Fax: (630)969-0228
**Subject(s):** Paid Community Newspapers
**Circ:** (Combined)9,200

**Bexley News** (24191)
Suburban News Publications
5257 Sinclair Rd.
PO Box 29912
Columbus, OH 43229
Phone: (614)785-1212
Fax: (614)785-1881
**Subject(s):** Free Newspapers
**Circ:** (Paid)330
(Non-paid)9,160

**Lakeshore Flashes Shopping Guide** (14976)
Flashes Publishers Inc.
595 Jenner Dr.
Allegan, MI 49010
Phone: (269)673-1602
Fax: (269)673-6768
**Subject(s):** Shopping Guides
**Circ:** (Paid)2
(Controlled)9,128

**The Weekly Reminder** (24993)
PO Box 180
Paulding, OH 45879-0180
Phone: (419)399-4015
Fax: (419)399-4030
**Subject(s):** Shopping Guides
**Circ:** (Free)‡9,100

**Four Seasons Shopper** (33045)
Murphy McGinnis Media Inc.
15617 B Hwy. 63
PO Box 919
Hayward, WI 54843
Phone: (715)634-4881
Fax: (715)634-8191
**Subject(s):** Shopping Guides
**Circ:** (Non-paid)♦9,094

**Clare County Review** (15126)
431 N. McEwan St.
Clare, MI 48617-1402
Phone: (989)386-4414
Fax: (989)386-2412
**Subject(s):** Free Newspapers
**Circ:** (Paid)‡918
(Non-paid)‡9,082

**The Bellefontaine Examiner** (24180)
Hubbard Publishing Co.
127 E Chillicothe Ave.
Bellefontaine, OH 43311
Phone: (937)592-3060
Fax: (937)592-4463
**Subject(s):** Daily Newspapers
**Circ:** (Mon.-Sat.)9,062

**Cannon Shopper** (16002)
Beacon
Box 366
Cannon Falls, MN 55009
Phone: (507)263-3991
**Subject(s):** Shopping Guides
**Circ:** (Free)‡9,064

**Huntington Woods/Berkley Mirror** (15714)
Mirror Newspapers
1523 N Main
PO Box 430
Royal Oak, MI 48067-0430
Phone: (248)546-4900
Fax: (248)398-2353
**Subject(s):** Free Newspapers
**Circ:** (Combined)9,038

**Ludington Daily News** (15559)
202 N. Rath Ave.
PO Box 340
Ludington, MI 49431-0340
Phone: (231)845-5181
Fax: (231)843-4011
**Subject(s):** Daily Newspapers
**Circ:** (Mon.-Sat.)★9,032

**Boardman News** (24194)
6221 Market St.
Boardman, OH 44512
Phone: (330)758-6397
Fax: (330)758-2658
**Subject(s):** Paid Community Newspapers
**Circ:** ‡9,000

**Daily Eastern News** (8044)
Eastern Illinois University
600 Lincoln Ave.
Charleston, IL 61920-3099
Phone: (217)581-2812
Fax: (217)581-2923
**Subject(s):** College Publications
**Circ:** ‡9,000

**Ely Echo** (16105)
Milestones Inc.
15 E. Chapman St.
Ely, MN 55731
Phone: (218)365-3141
Fax: (218)365-3142
**Subject(s):** Paid Community Newspapers
**Circ:** 9,000

**The Griffin Report of Food Marketing** (8217)
Griffin Publishing Company Inc.
PO Box 377572
Chicago, IL 60637
Phone: (773)493-1574
**Subject(s):** Food and Grocery Trade
**Circ:** (Paid)3,500
(Free)9,000

**North Country Saver** (16107)
Milestones Inc.
15 E. Chapman St.
Ely, MN 55731
Phone: (218)365-3141
Fax: (218)365-3142
**Subject(s):** Shopping Guides
**Circ:** (Free)9,000

**Washington Times-Herald** (10238)
Community Newspaper Holdings Inc.
102 E. Van Trees St.
PO Box 471
Washington, IN 47501
Phone: (812)254-0480
Fax: (812)254-7517
**Subject(s):** Daily Newspapers
**Circ:** (Mon.-Sat.)9,005

**The Telegraph** (8597)
Dixon Telegraph Inc.
113-115 S Peoria Ave.
Dixon, IL 61021
Phone: (815)284-2222
Fax: (815)284-2870
**Subject(s):** Daily Newspapers
**Circ:** (Mon.-Sat.)★8,972

**Shopping Reminder** (32898)
Citizen Newspapers L.L.C.
101 S. Ludington St.
PO Box 188
Columbus, WI 53925
**Subject(s):** Shopping Guides
**Circ:** (Non-paid)8,926

**The Clio Messenger** (15132)
The Flint Journal
200 E. 1st St.
Flint, MI 48502-1925
**Subject(s):** Paid Community Newspapers
**Circ:** (Combined)8,889

**Lake to Lake Shopper** (32866)
Zander Press Inc.
425 W. Ryan St.
Brillion, WI 54110
Phone: (920)756-2222
Fax: (920)756-2701
**Subject(s):** Shopping Guides
**Circ:** (Free)‡8,855

**The Davison Flagstaff** (15144)
The Flint Journal
200 E. 1st St.
Flint, MI 48502-1925
**Subject(s):** Paid Community Newspapers
**Circ:** (Combined)8,808

**Marinette Eagle-Star** (33251)
Eagle Printing Co.
PO Box 77
Marinette, WI 54143
Phone: (715)735-6611
Fax: (715)735-0229
**Subject(s):** Daily Newspapers
**Circ:** ‡8,800

**Putnam County Sentinel** (24971)
PO Box 149
224 E Main St.
Ottawa, OH 45875
Phone: (419)523-5709
Fax: (419)523-3512
**Subject(s):** Paid Community Newspapers
**Circ:** ‡8,800

**Murphysboro American** (8991)
Liberty Group
PO Box 650
Monmouth, IL 61462
Phone: (309)734-3176
Fax: (309)734-4649
**Subject(s):** Paid Community Newspapers
**Circ:** (Combined)8,770

**Whitewater Valley Market Guide** (9663)
Connersville News Examiner
406 Central Ave.
PO Box 287
Connersville, IN 47331
Phone: (765)825-0581
Fax: (765)825-4599
**Subject(s):** Shopping Guides
**Circ:** (Free)8,747

**County Ledger-Press** (32829)
Metro Newspaper
PO Box 129
Balsam Lake, WI 54810
Phone: (715)485-3121
Fax: (715)485-3037
**Subject(s):** Paid Community Newspapers
**Circ:** 8,716

**Star Gazette Extra** (7888)
Beardstown Newspapers Inc.
1210 Wall St.
Beardstown, IL 62618
Phone: (217)323-1010
Fax: (217)323-5402
**Subject(s):** Shopping Guides
**Circ:** (Free)‡8,700

**Lake Country Reporter** (33042)
440 Cardinal Ln.
PO Box 200
Hartland, WI 53029
Phone: (262)367-3272
Fax: (262)367-7414
**Subject(s):** Paid Community Newspapers
**Circ:** 8,690

**Shopping Guide News** (10139)
PO Box 229
Rochester, IN 46975
Phone: (574)223-5417
Fax: (574)223-8330
**Subject(s):** Shopping Guides
**Circ:** (Paid)37
(Free)8,682

**The Daily News** (15383)
109 N. Lafayette
Greenville, MI 48838
Phone: (616)754-9301
Fax: (616)754-8559
**Subject(s):** Daily Newspapers
**Circ:** (Paid)8,649

**Norwalk Reflector** (24959)
Reflector-Herald Inc.
61 E. Monroe St.
Norwalk, OH 44857
Phone: (419)668-3771
Fax: (419)668-2424
**Subject(s):** Daily Newspapers
**Circ:** (Mon.-Sat.)★8,633

**Richfield Sun Current** (16507)
Minnesota Sun Publications
10917 Valley View Rd.
Eden Prairie, MN 55344
Phone: (952)829-0797
Fax: (952)392-6868
**Subject(s):** Free Newspapers
**Circ:** (Paid)1,113
(Non-paid)8,611

**Detroit Lutheran** (15848)
Lutheran Center Association
6336 Donaldson Dr.
Troy, MI 48085-1532
Phone: (248)879-7610
Fax: (248)879-7610
**Subject(s):** Religious Publications
**Circ:** (Free)‡45
(Paid)‡8,600

**The Times-Record** (7826)
219 S College Rd.
Aledo, IL 61231
Phone: (309)582-5112
Fax: (309)582-5319
**Subject(s):** Paid Community Newspapers
**Circ:** (Paid)3,500
(Non-paid)8,600

**Ironwood Daily Globe** (15447)
Globe Publishing Co.
118 E McLeod Ave.
Ironwood, MI 49938
Phone: (906)932-2211
Fax: (906)932-5358
**Subject(s):** Daily Newspapers
**Circ:** ‡8,585

**Delta Waverly Community News** (15108)
Community Newspapers
239 S Cochran
Charlotte, MI 48813
Phone: (517)543-9913
Fax: (517)543-3677
**Subject(s):** Free Newspapers
**Circ:** (Paid)56
(Non-paid)8,565

**Gazette** (24694)
The Delaware Gazette Co.
18 E. William St.
PO Box 100
Delaware, OH 43015
Phone: (740)363-1161
Fax: (740)363-6262
**Subject(s):** Daily Newspapers
**Circ:** (Paid)⊕8,534

**Ad-Visor** (15422)
10575 Main St.
Honor, MI 49640-9761
Phone: (231)325-8600
Fax: (231)325-8602
**Subject(s):** Paid Community Newspapers
**Circ:** 8,500

**Belleville Recorder** (32840)
619 River St.
PO Box 50
Belleville, WI 53508
Phone: (608)424-3232
**Subject(s):** Paid Community Newspapers
**Circ:** (Combined)‡8,500

**Highland News Leader** (8781)
PO Box 250
Highland, IL 62249
Phone: (618)654-2366
**Subject(s):** Paid Community Newspapers
**Circ:** (Paid)6,500
(Free)‡8,500

**Lawrence Community Journal** (9887)
The Lawrence Community Journal
7968 Pendleton Pke.
Indianapolis, IN 46226
Fax: (317)542-1137
**Subject(s):** Paid Community Newspapers
**Circ:** (Paid)4,700
(Non-paid)8,500

**Macomb Journal** (8920)
203 N. Randolph St.
Macomb, IL 61455
Phone: (309)833-2114
Fax: (309)833-2346
**Subject(s):** Daily Newspapers
**Circ:** 7,800
(Sun.)8,500

**Wednesday Journal of Oak Park & River Forest** (9174)
Wednesday Journal Inc.
141 S. Oak Park Ave.
Oak Park, IL 60302
Phone: (708)524-8300
Fax: (708)524-0447
**Subject(s):** Paid Community Newspapers
**Circ:** (Free)3,000
(Paid)8,500

**Tuscola County Advertiser** (15099)
A Division of Caro Publishing
PO Box 106
Caro, MI 48723
Phone: (989)673-3181
Fax: (989)673-5662
**Subject(s):** Paid Community Newspapers
**Circ:** (Sat.)7,709
(Wed.)8,423

**Connersville News-Examiner** (9661)
406 Central Ave.
PO Box 287
Connersville, IN 47331
Phone: (765)825-0581
Fax: (765)825-4599
**Subject(s):** Daily Newspapers
**Circ:** (Paid)8,362

**Sentinel** (16115)
64 Downtown Plz.
PO Box 681
Fairmont, MN 56031
Phone: (507)235-3303
Fax: (507)235-3718
**Subject(s):** Daily Newspapers
**Circ:** (Mon.-Sat.)8,336

**Washington Times-Reporter** (9222)
Times Newspapers
1616 W Pioneer Pkwy.
Peoria, IL 61615
Phone: (309)692-6600
Fax: (309)690-3399
**Subject(s):** Free Newspapers
**Circ:** (Paid)100
(Free)8,330

**Herald-Press** (9806)
Huntington Newspapers Inc.
7 N Jefferson St.
Huntington, IN 46750-2839
Phone: (260)356-6700
Fax: (260)356-9026
**Subject(s):** Daily Newspapers
**Circ:** (Mon.-Fri.)‡7,200
(Sun.)‡8,300

**The Corydon Democrat** (9666)
O'Bannon Publishing Company Inc.
301 N Capitol Ave
Corydon, IN 47112
Phone: (812)738-2211
Fax: (812)738-1909
**Subject(s):** Paid Community Newspapers
**Circ:** 8,289

**Lakewood Sun Post** (24819)
Sun Newspapers
28895 Lorain Rd.
North Olmsted, OH 44070-4042
Phone: (440)777-3800
Fax: (440)777-8423
**Subject(s):** Paid Community Newspapers
**Circ:** (Paid)8,281

**News Graphic** (32882)
Lakeshore Newspapers Inc.
N 19 W 6733 Commerce Ct.
PO Box 47
Cedarburg, WI 53012
Phone: (262)375-5100
Fax: (262)375-5107
**Subject(s):** Paid Community Newspapers
**Circ:** (Mon.)8,237
(Thurs.)8,237

**Gladwin County Record and Beaverton Clarion** (15325)
700 E. Cedar
Gladwin, MI 48624
Phone: (989)426-9411
Fax: (989)426-2023
**Subject(s):** Free Newspapers; Free Newspapers
**Circ:** (Free)‡60
(Paid)‡8,200

**The Indianapolis Herald** (9870)
East Side Suburban Newspapers
4309 E Michigan St., No. 11042
Indianapolis, IN 46201-3652
Phone: (317)356-2487
Fax: (317)356-5871
**Subject(s):** Paid Community Newspapers
**Circ:** (Combined)8,200

**Marshall Independent** (16258)
508 W. Main St.
Marshall, MN 56258
Phone: (507)537-1551
Fax: (507)537-1557
**Subject(s):** Daily Newspapers
**Circ:** (Mon.-Sat.)8,174

**Southfield Eccentric** (15781)
Observer & Eccentric Newspapers
36251 Schoolcraft Rd.
Livonia, MI 48150
Phone: (734)591-2300
Fax: (734)953-2232
**Subject(s):** Paid Community Newspapers
**Circ:** (Thurs.)8,029
(Sun.)8,120

**Darien Du Page Progress** (8600)
Liberty Suburban Chicago Newspapers
922 Warren Ave.
Downers Grove, IL 60515
Phone: (630)257-5300
Fax: (630)969-0228
**Subject(s):** Paid Community Newspapers
**Circ:** (Combined)8,089

Circulation: ★ = ABC; △ = BPA; ♦ = CAC; • = CCAB; □ = VAC; ⊕ = PO Statement; ‡ = Publisher's Report; Boldface figures = sworn; Light figures = estimated.

## Great Lakes States

**Romeo-Washington Source (15768)**
Advisor & Source Newspapers
48075 Van Dyke Ave.
Shelby Township, MI 48317
Phone: (586)731-1000
Fax: (586)731-8172
Subject(s): Free Newspapers

Circ: (Non-paid)8,086

**Extra Shopping Guide (8801)**
Chronicle
308 E Main St.
Hoopeston, IL 60942
Phone: (217)283-5111
Fax: (217)283-5846
Subject(s): Paid Community Newspapers

Circ: 1,935
        8,056

**Garfield-Maple Sun (24868)**
Sun Newspapers
5510 Cloverleaf Pkwy.
Valley View, OH 44125-4887
Phone: (216)986-2600
Fax: (216)986-2380
Subject(s): Paid Community Newspapers

Circ: (Paid)8,057

**Des Plaines Valley News (9438)**
PO Box 348
6257 South Archer Rd
Summit, IL 60501-0348
Phone: (708)594-9340
Fax: (708)594-9494
Subject(s): Paid Community Newspapers

Circ: ‡8,000

**Detroit Auto Scene (15878)**
Springer Publications
31201 Chicago Rd., Ste. A-101
Warren, MI 48093
Phone: (586)939-6800
Fax: (586)939-5850
Subject(s): Free Newspapers

Circ: (Free)8,000

**KentonTimes (24814)**
Hardin County Publishing Co.
201 E Columbus St.
Kenton, OH 43326
Phone: (419)673-4066
Fax: (419)673-1125
Subject(s): Daily Newspapers

Circ: (Paid)8,000

**Mendota Reporter (8957)**
News Media Corp.
703 Illinois Ave.
PO Box 300
Mendota, IL 61342
Phone: (815)539-9396
Fax: (815)539-7862
Subject(s): Paid Community Newspapers

Circ: (Paid)‡4,400
        (Free)‡8,000

**North Country Angler (16106)**
Milestones Inc.
15 E. Chapman St.
Ely, MN 55731
Phone: (218)365-3141
Fax: (218)365-3142
Subject(s): (Hunting, Fishing, and Game Management)

Circ: (Free)‡8,000

**Pro-Life Action News (8384)**
Pro-Life Action League
6160 N. Cicero Ave. Suite 600
Chicago, IL 60646
Phone: (773)777-2900
Fax: (773)777-3061
Subject(s): Free Newspapers

Circ: (Paid)⊕8,000

**Twin Valley News & Advisor (25148)**
Twin Valley Publications Inc.
PO Box 24
West Alexandria, OH 45381
Phone: (937)839-4733
Fax: (937)839-5351
Subject(s): Shopping Guides; Paid Community Newspapers

Circ: (Paid)‡600
        (Free)‡8,000

**U.S. Auto Scene (15881)**
Springer Publications
31201 Chicago Rd., Ste. A-101
Warren, MI 48093
Phone: (586)939-6800
Fax: (586)939-5850
Subject(s): Automotive (Consumer); Automotive (Trade)

Circ: 8,000

**Two Harbors Manney Shopper (16673)**
Manney's Shopper Inc.
626 1/2 2nd Ave.
PO Box 66
Two Harbors, MN 55616
Phone: (218)834-5551
Fax: (218)834-2555
Subject(s): Shopping Guides

Circ: (Free)‡7,981

**Neighbors (33258)**
51 E John St.
PO Box 397
Markesan, WI 53946
Phone: (920)398-2334
Fax: (920)398-3835
Subject(s): Paid Community Newspapers

Circ: (Paid)‡7,960

**Tribune (15920)**
Albert Lea Publishing Co.
808 W Front St., No. 60
Albert Lea, MN 56007
Phone: (507)373-1411
Fax: (507)373-0333
Subject(s): Daily Newspapers

Circ: (Mon.-Fri.)7,708
        (Sun.)7,940

**Forest Hills Journal-Press (24730)**
Press Community Newspapers
394 Wards Corner Rd.
Loveland, OH 45140
Phone: (513)248-8600
Fax: (513)248-1938
Subject(s): Paid Community Newspapers

Circ: (Non-paid)5,276
        (Paid)7,923

**Barberton Herald (24158)**
Richardson Publishing Company Luc.
70 4th St. NW
PO Box 831
Barberton, OH 44203
Phone: (330)753-1068
Fax: (330)753-1021
Subject(s): Paid Community Newspapers

Circ: ‡7,900

**Pike Press (9246)**
Pike County Publishing Co.
115 W Jefferson
Box 70
Pittsfield, IL 62363
Phone: (217)285-2345
Fax: (217)285-5222
Subject(s): Paid Community Newspapers

Circ: ‡7,900

**Dearborn County Register (9995)**
Register Publications
126 W High St.
PO Box 328
Lawrenceburg, IN 47025
Phone: (812)537-0063
Fax: (812)537-5576
Subject(s): Paid Community Newspapers

Circ: (Free)‡32
        (Paid)‡7,861

**Republican-Eagle (16497)**
2760 North. Service Dr.
Po Box 82
Red Wing, MN 55066-0082
Phone: (651)388-8235
Fax: (651)388-8912
Subject(s): Daily Newspapers

Circ: (Mon.-Sat.)7,852

**Wayne County Press (8688)**
213 E Main St.
PO Box F
Fairfield, IL 62837
Phone: (618)842-2662
Fax: (618)842-7912

Subject(s): Paid Community Newspapers

Circ: ‡7,850

**Carol Stream Examiner (7969)**
Examiner Publications
4N781 Gerber Rd.
Bartlett, IL 60103
Phone: (630)830-4145
Subject(s): Paid Community Newspapers

Circ: (Paid)7,800

**Madison county journals (8515)**
Madison County Publications
2 Executive Dr.
Collinsville, IL 62234
Phone: (618)344-0264
Fax: (618)344-3831
Subject(s): Paid Community Newspapers

Circ: ‡7,800

**Morris Daily Herald (8997)**
Shaw Newspapers
1804 N Division St.
Morris, IL 60450
Phone: (815)942-3221
Fax: (815)942-0988
Subject(s): Daily Newspapers

Circ: ‡7,800

**Ogden Leader (9177)**
The Leader
115 E Ave.
PO Box 97
Ogden, IL 61859
Phone: (217)582-2373
Fax: (217)582-2237
Subject(s): Free Newspapers

Circ: (Free)7,800

**Point and Shoreland Journal (24998)**
Welch Publishing Co.
117 E 2nd St.
PO Box 267
Perrysburg, OH 43552
Phone: (419)874-4491
Fax: (419)874-7311
Subject(s): Free Newspapers

Circ: (Free)7,800

**Warrenville Post (9099)**
Liberty Suburban Chicago Newspapers
7222 W. Cermak Rd., Ste. 505
North Riverside, IL 60546
Phone: (708)447-9810
Subject(s): Paid Community Newspapers

Circ: (Combined)7,800

**West Chicago Press (9100)**
Liberty Suburban Chicago Newspapers
7222 W. Cermak Rd., Ste. 505
North Riverside, IL 60546
Phone: (708)447-9810
Subject(s): Paid Community Newspapers

Circ: (Combined)7,800

**Winfield Press (9104)**
Liberty Suburban Chicago Newspapers
7222 W. Cermak Rd., Ste. 505
North Riverside, IL 60546
Phone: (708)447-9810
Subject(s): Paid Community Newspapers

Circ: (Combined)7,800

**Iosco County News Herald (15253)**
News-Press Publishing Company Inc.
110 W State St.
Box 72
East Tawas, MI 48730-0072
Phone: (989)362-3456
Fax: (989)362-6601
Subject(s): Paid Community Newspapers

Circ: ‡7,790

**News (16118)**
PO Box 249
Faribault, MN 55021
Phone: (507)334-1853
Fax: (507)334-8569
Subject(s): Daily Newspapers

Circ: ‡7,772

**Huron Daily Tribune (15036)**
211 N. Heisterman St.
Bad Axe, MI 48413
Phone: (989)269-6461
Fax: (989)269-9893
**Subject(s):** Daily Newspapers
**Circ:** (Mon.-Fri.)★**7,264**
(Sun.)★**7,768**

**Twinsburg Bulletin (24177)**
Record Publishing Co.
711 Broadway
PO Box 46059
Bedford, OH 44146-0059
Phone: (440)232-4055
Fax: (440)232-8861
**Subject(s):** Free Newspapers
**Circ:** (Paid)687
(Free)7,765

**Lincolnland Shopping Guide (10184)**
News Publishing Co.
PO Box 309
Tell City, IN 47586
Phone: (812)547-3424
Fax: (812)547-2847
**Subject(s):** Shopping Guides
**Circ:** (Non-paid)7,759

**DeWitt Bath Review (15109)**
Community Newspapers
239 S Cochran
Charlotte, MI 48813
Phone: (517)543-9913
Fax: (517)543-3677
**Subject(s):** Free Newspapers
**Circ:** (Paid)28
(Non-paid)7,746

**Herald-Review (16149)**
Murphy McGinnis Media Inc.
301 1st Ave. NW
PO Box 220
Grand Rapids, MN 55744
Phone: (218)326-6623
Fax: (218)326-6627
**Subject(s):** Paid Community Newspapers
**Circ:** (Non-paid)♦**202**
(Paid)♦**7,714**

**Westland Observer (15895)**
Observer & Eccentric Newspapers
36251 Schoolcraft Rd.
Livonia, MI 48150
Phone: (734)591-2300
Fax: (734)953-2232
**Subject(s):** Paid Community Newspapers
**Circ:** (Thurs.)6,832
(Sun.)7,706

**Lakewood News (15501)**
J-Ad Corp.
1351 N M-43 Hwy.
PO Box 188
Hastings, MI 49058-0188
Phone: (269)945-9554
Fax: (269)945-5192
**Subject(s):** Paid Community Newspapers
**Circ:** (Free)7,695

**Reporter-Times (10017)**
Hoosier-Times Inc.
dba Reporter-Times
60 S Jefferson St.
PO Box 1636
Martinsville, IN 46151
Phone: (765)342-3311
Fax: (765)342-1446
**Subject(s):** Daily Newspapers
**Circ:** (Paid)7,695

**Sturgis Journal (15811)**
Hometown Communications Inc.
209 John St.
Box 660
Sturgis, MI 49091-1459
Fax: (269)651-2296
**Subject(s):** Daily Newspapers
**Circ:** ‡7,687

**Home Shopper (8653)**
116 S Magnolia
Box 289
Elmwood, IL 61529
Phone: (309)742-2511
Fax: (309)742-2511
**Subject(s):** Shopping Guides
**Circ:** (Free)‡7,635

**The Houghton Lake Resorter (15428)**
PO Box 248
Houghton Lake, MI 48629
Phone: (989)366-5341
Fax: (989)366-4472
**Subject(s):** Paid Community Newspapers
**Circ:** (Non-paid)⊕**50**
(Paid)⊕**7,635**

**Barrington Courier-Review (7850)**
Pioneer Press Newspapers
c/o Marc Alberts
291 N. Dunton Ave.
Arlington Heights, IL 60004
Phone: (847)797-5100
Fax: (847)797-5151
**Subject(s):** Paid Community Newspapers
**Circ:** (Thurs.)7,604

**Lawrence Times (10073)**
Topics Newspapers Inc.
PO Box 1478
Noblesville, IN 46060
Phone: (317)598-6397
Fax: (317)598-6360
**Subject(s):** Free Newspapers
**Circ:** (Paid)143
(Non-paid)7,560

**Oceana's Herald-Journal (15391)**
Oceana's Herald
123 State St.
Hart, MI 49420-0190
Phone: (231)861-2126
Fax: (231)873-4775
**Subject(s):** Paid Community Newspapers
**Circ:** ‡7,560

**Chippewa Herald (32886)**
Chippewa Publishing Co.
321 Frenette Dr.
PO Box 69
Chippewa Falls, WI 54729
Phone: (715)723-5515
Fax: (715)723-9644
**Subject(s):** Daily Newspapers
**Circ:** ‡7,541

**The Shopper (9505)**
Republic Times L.L.C.
114 N Main
PO Box 147
Waterloo, IL 62298
Phone: (618)939-3814
Fax: (618)939-3815
**Subject(s):** Shopping Guides
**Circ:** (Free)‡7,548

**Mount Vernon Democrat (10042)**
Landmark Community Newspapers Inc.
231 A Main St.
PO Box 767
Mount Vernon, IN 47620
Phone: (812)838-4811
Fax: (812)838-3696
**Subject(s):** Daily Newspapers
**Circ:** (Paid)3,268
(Free)7,527

**Presque Isle Star (14989)**
Morningstar Publications
431 N. Ripley Blvd.
PO Box 464
Alpena, MI 49707
Phone: (989)356-2121
Fax: (989)354-8275
**Subject(s):** Shopping Guides
**Circ:** (Free)7,522

**East Allen Courier (9772)**
Box 77
Grabill, IN 46741-0077
Phone: (219)627-2728
Fax: (219)627-2519
**Subject(s):** Free Newspapers
**Circ:** (Paid)‡450
(Free)‡7,500

**The Flushing Observer (15302)**
The Flint Journal
200 E. 1st St.
Flint, MI 48502-1925
**Subject(s):** Paid Community Newspapers
**Circ:** ‡7,500

**Hudson Star-Observer (33056)**
226 Locust St.
Hudson, WI 54016-1668
Phone: (715)386-9333
Fax: (715)386-9891
**Subject(s):** Paid Community Newspapers
**Circ:** (Paid)‡7,500

**Lake City Shopper (16205)**
Lake City Graphic
111 S 8th St.
PO Box 469
Lake City, MN 55041
Phone: (651)345-3316
Fax: (651)345-4200
**Subject(s):** Shopping Guides
**Circ:** (Free)‡7,500

**Marquette Tribune (33311)**
Marquette Journal
1131 W Wisconsin Ave.
Milwaukee, WI 53233
Phone: (414)288-7171
Fax: (414)288-1979
**Subject(s):** College Publications
**Circ:** ‡7,500

**Mason City Banner Times (8942)**
126 N Tonica St.
PO Box 71
Mason City, IL 62664
Phone: (217)482-3276
Fax: (217)482-3277
**Subject(s):** Free Newspapers
**Circ:** (Paid)2,100
(Free)7,500

**Milford Times (15594)**
Hometown Newspapers
405 N. Main St.
Milford, MI 48381
Phone: (810)685-1507
**Subject(s):** Free Newspapers
**Circ:** (Combined)7,500

**Milwaukee Times (33320)**
1938 MLK Jr. Dr.
Milwaukee, WI 53212
Phone: (414)263-5088
Fax: (414)263-4445
**Subject(s):** Paid Community Newspapers; Black Publications
**Circ:** (Non-paid)‡7,500

**Perrysburg Messenger Journal (24997)**
Welch Publishing Co.
117 E 2nd St.
PO Box 267
Perrysburg, OH 43552
Phone: (419)874-4491
Fax: (419)874-7311
**Subject(s):** Paid Community Newspapers
**Circ:** (Paid)5,600
(Free)‡7,500

**Reporter (16242)**
Minnesota State University, Mankato
293 CSU
Mankato, MN 56001
Phone: (507)389-1776
Fax: (507)389-5812
**Subject(s):** College Publications
**Circ:** (Free)7,500

**Times-Indicator (15310)**
T.I. Publications
44 W. Main St.
PO Box 7
Fremont, MI 49412-0007
Phone: (231)924-4400
Fax: (231)924-4066
**Subject(s):** Paid Community Newspapers
**Circ:** 7,500

**Tri-County Press (9252)**
113 North Franklin St.
Polo, IL 61064
Phone: (815)946-2364
Fax: (815)732-4238

## Great Lakes States

**Subject(s):** Paid Community Newspapers
**Circ:** (Combined)7,500

**Valley (16213)**
Le Sueur Publishing
101 Bridge St.
Le Sueur, MN 56058
Phone: (507)665-3334
**Subject(s):** Free Newspapers
**Circ:** (Free)‡7,500

**Wilmington News-Journal (25183)**
Brown Publishing Co.
47 S. South St.
Wilmington, OH 45177
Phone: (937)382-2574
Fax: (937)382-4392
**Subject(s):** Daily Newspapers
**Circ:** ‡7,500

**The Perry County News (10186)**
News Publishing Co.
PO Box 309
Tell City, IN 47586
Phone: (812)547-3424
Fax: (812)547-2847
**Subject(s):** Paid Community Newspapers
**Circ:** 7,490

**Mount Greenwood Express (8972)**
Southwest Messenger Press Inc.
3840 W 147th St.
PO Box 548
Midlothian, IL 60445
Phone: (708)388-2425
Fax: (708)385-7811
**Subject(s):** Free Newspapers
**Circ:** (Free)‡300
(Paid)‡7,471

**The Daily Telegram (33570)**
1226 Ogden Ave.
Superior, WI 54880
Phone: (715)394-4411
Fax: (715)394-9404
**Subject(s):** Daily Newspapers
**Circ:** (Non-paid)♦252
(Paid)♦7,415

**The Free Press-Standard (24254)**
Carrollton Publishing Company Inc.
43 E Main St.
PO Box 37
Carrollton, OH 44615-9982
Phone: (330)627-5591
Fax: (330)627-3195
**Subject(s):** Paid Community Newspapers
**Circ:** ⊕7,414

**News Gazette (8917)**
Rock Valley Publishing
11512 N 2nd St.
Machesney Park, IL 61115
Phone: (815)877-4044
Fax: (815)654-4857
**Subject(s):** Paid Community Newspapers
**Circ:** ‡7,400

**The Co-Pilot (16686)**
Murphy McGinnis Media Inc.
PO Box 190
Walker, MN 56484
Phone: (218)547-1000
Fax: (218)547-3000
**Subject(s):** Shopping Guides
**Circ:** (Non-paid)♦7,382

**Hillsdale Daily News (15404)**
Morris Communications Corp.
33 McCollum St.
PO Box 287
Hillsdale, MI 49242-0287
Phone: (517)437-7351
Fax: (517)437-3963
**Subject(s):** Daily Newspapers
**Circ:** (Combined)⊕7,373

**Schiller Park/Uptown News-Star (8896)**
Lerner Communications Inc.
7331 N Lincoln Ave.
Lincolnwood, IL 60712
Phone: (847)329-2000
Fax: (847)329-2060

**Subject(s):** Free Newspapers
**Circ:** (Paid)341
(Free)7,345

**Chippewa Herald Telegram (32887)**
Independent Media Group Inc.
321 Frenette Dr.
PO Box 69
Chippewa Falls, WI 54729-0069
**Subject(s):** Daily Newspapers
**Circ:** (Free)31
(Paid)7,325

**Owatonna People's Press (16458)**
Box 346
135 W Pearl St.
Owatonna, MN 55060-0346
Phone: (507)451-2840
Fax: (507)444-3282
**Subject(s):** Daily Newspapers
**Circ:** (Tues.-Fri.)★7,076
(Sun.)★7,323

**Prior Lake American (16493)**
Southwest Suburban Publishing
14093 Commerce Ave. NE
PO Box 538
Prior Lake, MN 55372
Phone: (952)447-6669
Fax: (952)447-6671
**Subject(s):** Paid Community Newspapers
**Circ:** ⊕7,300

**Coshocton Tribune (24634)**
550 Main St.
PO Box 10
Coshocton, OH 43812
Phone: (740)622-1122
Fax: (740)622-7341
**Subject(s):** Daily Newspapers
**Circ:** (Mon.-Sat.)★6,896
(Sun.)★7,229

**Redford Observer (15697)**
Observer & Eccentric Newspapers
36251 Schoolcraft Rd.
Livonia, MI 48150
Phone: (734)591-2300
Fax: (734)953-2232
**Subject(s):** Paid Community Newspapers
**Circ:** (Thurs.)6,608
(Sun.)7,224

**Iron River Reporter (15445)**
Northland Publishers Inc.
801 W Adams
PO Box 311
Iron River, MI 49935
Phone: (906)265-9927
Fax: (906)265-5755
**Subject(s):** Paid Community Newspapers
**Circ:** ‡7,200

**The Lebanon Reporter (9997)**
117 E Washington St.
Lebanon, IN 46052
Phone: (765)482-5400
Fax: (765)482-4652
**Subject(s):** Daily Newspapers
**Circ:** 7,200

**The Message (9690)**
PO Box 4169
Evansville, IN 47724-0169
Phone: (812)424-5536
Fax: (812)424-0972
**Subject(s):** Religious Publications
**Circ:** (Controlled)‡7,200

**The Times (10041)**
Reporter-Times Inc.
PO Box 308
Mooresville, IN 46158
Phone: (317)831-7068
Fax: (317)831-7068
**Subject(s):** Paid Community Newspapers
**Circ:** (Paid)⊕7,200

**Tribune (24787)**
Ironton Publications Inc.
2903 S. Fifth St.
PO Box 647
Ironton, OH 45638
Phone: (740)532-1441
Fax: (740)532-1506

**Subject(s):** Daily Newspapers
**Circ:** (Mon.-Fri.)6,200
(Sun.)7,200

**Waupaca County Post (33625)**
Waupaca County Publishing Co.
PO Box 152
717 10th St.
Waupaca, WI 54981-1934
Phone: (715)258-5546
Fax: (715)258-8162
**Subject(s):** Paid Community Newspapers
**Circ:** 7,200

**The Daily Ledger (7941)**
Liberty Group Pub.
53 W Elm St.
PO Box 540
Canton, IL 61520
Phone: (309)647-5100
Fax: (309)647-4665
**Subject(s):** Daily Newspapers
**Circ:** ‡7,183

**Westland Eagle (15889)**
The Journal Newspapers
35540 Michigan Ave.
PO Box 578
Wayne, MI 48184
Phone: (734)467-1900
Fax: (734)729-1840
**Subject(s):** Paid Community Newspapers
**Circ:** (Combined)7,185

**Farmland News (24128)**
104 Depot St.
PO Box 240
Archbold, OH 43502-0240
Phone: (419)445-9456
Fax: (419)445-4444
**Subject(s):** Paid Community Newspapers; Farm Newspapers
**Circ:** 7,107

**Gratiot County Herald (15453)**
MacDonald Publications
123 N. Main St.
Ithaca, MI 48847
Phone: (989)875-4151
Fax: (989)875-3159
**Subject(s):** Paid Community Newspapers
**Circ:** ‡7,100

**The Sun Courier (24216)**
Sun Newspapers
5510 Cloverleaf Pkwy.
Valley View, OH 44125-4887
Phone: (216)986-2600
Fax: (216)986-2380
**Subject(s):** Paid Community Newspapers
**Circ:** (Paid)7,032

**Times-Courier (8046)**
Howard Publications
2110 Woodfall Dr., No. 10
Charleston, IL 61920-3058
Phone: (217)345-7085
Fax: (217)345-7090
**Subject(s):** Daily Newspapers
**Circ:** (Mon.-Sat.)7,029

**Gaylord Herald Times (15318)**
Otsego County Herald Times Inc.
PO Box 598
Gaylord, MI 49734
Phone: (989)732-1111
Fax: (989)732-3490
**Subject(s):** Paid Community Newspapers
**Circ:** (Free)‡140
(Paid)‡7,010

**American Jewish World (16561)**
American Jewish World Publishing Inc.
4509 Minnetonka Blvd.
Saint Louis Park, MN 55416-4027
Phone: (952)259-5280
Fax: (952)920-6205
**Subject(s):** Jewish Publications
**Circ:** ‡7,000

**Bureau County Republican (9256)**
800 Ace Road
PO Box 340
Princeton, IL 61356
Phone: (815)875-4461
Fax: (815)875-1235

**Subject(s):** Paid Community Newspapers

**Circ:** 7,000

**The County Journal (9236)**
Willis Publishing Co.
PO Box 369
Percy, IL 62272
Phone: (618)497-8272
Fax: (618)497-2607
**Subject(s):** Paid Community Newspapers

**Circ:** 7,000

**The Daily Northwestern (8668)**
Northwestern University Students Publishing Co.
1999 S Campus Dr., Norris Center
Evanston, IL 60208
Phone: (847)491-7206
Fax: (847)491-9905
**Subject(s):** College Publications

**Circ:** (Paid)‡300
    (Free)‡7,000

**Hanover Park Examiner (8765)**
Examiner Publications
4N781 Gerber Rd.
Bartlett, IL 60103
Phone: (630)830-4145
**Subject(s):** Paid Community Newspapers

**Circ:** 7,000

**The Hastings Banner (15395)**
J-Ad Corp.
PO Box B
Hastings, MI 49058
**Subject(s):** Paid Community Newspapers

**Circ:** ‡7,000

**Independent-Register (32867)**
The Independent-Register Inc.
922 Exchange St.
PO Box 255
Brodhead, WI 53520
Phone: (608)897-2193
Fax: (608)897-4137
**Subject(s):** Paid Community Newspapers

**Circ:** (Paid)‡2,000
    (Free)‡7,000

**Lake Geneva Regional News (33137)**
Lake Geneva Printing and Publishing
315 Broad St.
PO Box 937
Lake Geneva, WI 53147
Phone: (262)248-4444
Fax: (262)248-4476
**Subject(s):** Paid Community Newspapers

**Circ:** ‡7,000

**Leslie Local Independent (15546)**
S. & G. Publications
109 Carney
Box 617
Leslie, MI 49251-0617
Phone: (517)589-8228
Fax: (517)589-8526
**Subject(s):** Free Newspapers

**Circ:** (Paid)‡1,600
    (Free)‡7,000

**Loyola Phoenix (8318)**
Loyola Phoenix Loyola University of Chicago
6525 N. Sheridan Rd.
Chicago, IL 60626
Phone: (773)508-7110
Fax: (773)508-7121
**Subject(s):** College Publications

**Circ:** (Free)7,000

**Midwest Racing News (33314)**
6646 W Fairview Ave.
Milwaukee, WI 53213
Phone: (414)778-4700
Fax: (414)778-4688
**Subject(s):** (Auto Racing)

**Circ:** ‡7,000

**News from Indian Country (33046)**
Indian Country Communications Inc.
8558N County Rd., K
Hayward, WI 54843-5800
Phone: (715)634-5226
Fax: (715)634-3243
**Subject(s):** Native American Interests

**Circ:** ‡7,000

**News & Letters (8354)**
36 S. Wabash, Rm. 1440
Rm. 1440
Chicago, IL 60603
Phone: (312)236-0799
Fax: (312)236-0725
**Subject(s):** Agnostic and Free Thought; Alternative and Underground

**Circ:** ‡7,000

**The North Ridgeville Press & Light (25032)**
Douthit Communications Inc.
520 Warren St.
Sandusky, OH 44870
Phone: (419)625-5825
Fax: (419)625-2834
**Subject(s):** Paid Community Newspapers

**Circ:** 7,000

**Review (9459)**
Tuscola Review Inc.
PO Box 350
Tuscola, IL 61953
Phone: (217)253-2358
**Subject(s):** Paid Community Newspapers

**Circ:** ‡7,000

**Royal Purple (33661)**
UW - Whitewater
800 W. Main St.
Whitewater, WI 53190-1790
Phone: (262)472-1234
Fax: (262)472-5101
**Subject(s):** College Publications

**Circ:** ‡7,000

**St. Charles Examiner (7882)**
Examiner Publications
4N781 Gerber Rd.
Bartlett, IL 60103
Phone: (630)830-4145
**Subject(s):** Paid Community Newspapers

**Circ:** 7,000

**The St. Ignace News (15739)**
Maurer Publishing Co.
359 Reagon St.
PO Box 277
Saint Ignace, MI 49781
Phone: (906)643-9150
Fax: (906)643-9122
**Subject(s):** Paid Community Newspapers

**Circ:** 7,000

**Speedway Town Press (9913)**
Speedway-Northwest Press Inc.
1564 Main St.
Indianapolis, IN 46224-6527
Phone: (317)241-4345
Fax: (317)241-4386
**Subject(s):** Free Newspapers

**Circ:** (Free)7,000

**Streamwood Examiner (9433)**
Examiner Publications
4N781 Gerber Rd.
Bartlett, IL 60103
Phone: (630)830-4145
**Subject(s):** Paid Community Newspapers

**Circ:** (Paid)7,000

**Times (9744)**
Frankfort Times Inc.
251 E Clinton St., No. 9
Frankfort, IN 46041-1906
Phone: (765)659-4622
Fax: (765)654-7031
**Subject(s):** Daily Newspapers

**Circ:** (Paid)7,000

**University Chronicle (16551)**
St. Cloud State University
13 Stewart Hall
720 4th Ave. S.
Saint Cloud, MN 56301-4498
Phone: (320)308-0121
**Subject(s):** College Publications

**Circ:** (Free)‡7,000

**West Side Messenger (9923)**
Speedway-Northwest Press Inc.
1564 Main St.
Indianapolis, IN 46224-6527
Phone: (317)241-4345
Fax: (317)241-4386

**Subject(s):** Free Newspapers

**Circ:** (Combined)‡7,000

**Western Star (24827)**
200 Harmon Ave.
PO Box 29
Lebanon, OH 45036
Phone: (513)932-3010
Fax: (513)932-6056
**Subject(s):** Paid Community Newspapers

**Circ:** (Free)245
    (Paid)7,000

**Peru Daily Tribune (10106)**
Nixon Newspapers Inc.
26 W 3rd St.
PO Box 87
Peru, IN 46970-2155
Phone: (317)472-4438
**Subject(s):** Daily Newspapers

**Circ:** (Non-paid)33
    (Paid)6,975

**The Romeo Observer (15706)**
124 W St. Clair
Box 96
Romeo, MI 48065-0096
Phone: (586)752-3524
Fax: (586)752-0548
**Subject(s):** Paid Community Newspapers

**Circ:** (Free)6,650
    (Paid)6,971

**State Journal/The Courier (8875)**
Copley Corp.
601 Pulaski St.
P.O. Box 40
Lincoln, IL 62656-2825
Phone: (217)732-2101
Fax: (217)732-7039
**Subject(s):** Daily Newspapers

**Circ:** (Mon.-Sat.)6,940

**Chicago Daily Law Bulletin (8126)**
Law Bulletin Publishing Co.
415 N. State
Chicago, IL 60610
Phone: (312)644-7800
Fax: (312)644-4255
**Subject(s):** Daily Periodicals; Law

**Circ:** ‡6,900

**Olympia Review (8980)**
Rickard Publishing Co.
PO Box 710
102 South Main
Minier, IL 61759-0710
Phone: (309)392-2414
Fax: (309)392-2169
**Subject(s):** Free Newspapers; Free Newspapers

**Circ:** (Free)‡6,900

**Quad Community Press (16703)**
Press Publications
4779 Bloom Ave.
White Bear Lake, MN 55110
Phone: (651)407-1200
Fax: (651)429-1242
**Subject(s):** Free Newspapers

**Circ:** (Paid)2,291
    (Free)6,894

**The Bucyrus Telegraph-Forum (24228)**
PO Box 471
Bucyrus, OH 44820
Phone: (419)562-3333
**Subject(s):** Daily Newspapers

**Circ:** (Mon.-Sat.)★6,865

**Antigo Daily Journal (32802)**
Berner Brothers Publishing Company Inc.
612 Superior St.
Antigo, WI 54409
Phone: (715)623-4191
Fax: (715)623-4193
**Subject(s):** Daily Newspapers

**Circ:** (Free)17
    (Paid)⊕6,841

**Salem News (25030)**
161 N. Lincoln Ave.
Salem, OH 44460
Phone: (330)332-4601
Fax: (330)332-3084

# Great Lakes States

**Subject(s):** Daily Newspapers
**Circ:** (Sun.)★6,369
(Mon.-Sat.)★6,830

**Robinson Daily News (9288)**
302 S Cross St.
PO Box 639
Robinson, IL 62454
Phone: (618)544-2101
Fax: (618)544-9533
**Subject(s):** Daily Newspapers
**Circ:** (Paid)⊕6,825

**Daily Leader (9253)**
Liberty Group
318 N Main St.
PO Box 170
Pontiac, IL 61764-0170
Phone: (815)842-1153
Fax: (815)842-4388
**Subject(s):** Daily Newspapers
**Circ:** ‡6,800

**Eaton Register-Herald (24705)**
Brown Publishing Co.
1332 N. Barron St.
Eaton, OH 45320-1016
Phone: (937)456-5553
Fax: (937)456-3558
**Subject(s):** Paid Community Newspapers
**Circ:** 6,800

**The Greensburg Daily News (9782)**
CHNI Media L.L.C.
135 S Franklin St.
PO Box 106
Greensburg, IN 47240
Phone: (812)663-3111
Fax: (812)663-2985
**Subject(s):** Daily Newspapers
**Circ:** ‡6,750

**The Tribune (24921)**
Central Ohio Printing
30 S Oak St.
PO Box 390
London, OH 43140-1079
Phone: (740)852-1616
Fax: (740)852-1620
**Subject(s):** Free Newspapers
**Circ:** (Free)‡6,750

**Hibbing Daily Tribune (16172)**
Daily Tribune
2142 1st Ave.
PO Box 38
Hibbing, MN 55746-1805
Phone: (218)262-1011
Fax: (218)262-4318
**Subject(s):** Daily Newspapers
**Circ:** (Mon.-Fri.)6,048
(Sun.)6,747

**Sawyer County Record (33047)**
Murphy McGinnis Media Inc.
15617B Highway 63
Hayward, WI 54843
Phone: (715)634-4881
Fax: (715)634-8191
**Subject(s):** Paid Community Newspapers
**Circ:** (Non-paid)♦35
(Paid)♦6,735

**Montgomery County News (8790)**
PO Box 250
Hillsboro, IL 62049
Phone: (217)532-3929
Fax: (217)532-3522
**Subject(s):** Paid Community Newspapers
**Circ:** 6,700

**Shawano Leader (33531)**
1464 E. Green Bay St.
Shawano, WI 54166
Phone: (715)526-2121
Fax: (715)524-3941
**Subject(s):** Daily Newspapers
**Circ:** (Paid)6,700

**The Telegram (25147)**
The Telegram Publishing Company Inc.
12 S Ohio Ave.
PO Box 111
Wellston, OH 45692
Phone: (740)384-6102

**Subject(s):** Free Newspapers
**Circ:** (Paid)‡6,700

**Tallmadge Express (25072)**
Record Publishing Co.
1619 Commerce Dr.
Stow, OH 44224
Phone: (330)688-0088
Fax: (330)688-1588
**Subject(s):** Free Newspapers
**Circ:** (Free)‡5,281
(Paid)‡6,674

**The Countryman (15705)**
The Romeo Observer
124 W St. Clair
Box 96
Romeo, MI 48065-0096
Phone: (586)752-3524
Fax: (586)752-0548
**Subject(s):** Free Newspapers
**Circ:** (Non-paid)‡6,650

**North Vernon Plain Dealer (10079)**
North Vernon Plain Dealer & Sun
528 E O&M Ave.
PO Box 988
North Vernon, IN 47265
Phone: (812)346-3973
Fax: (812)346-8368
**Subject(s):** Paid Community Newspapers
**Circ:** 6,657

**Princeton Daily Clarion (10120)**
Princeton Publishing Inc.
100 N Gibson
PO Box 30
Princeton, IN 47670
Phone: (812)385-2525
Fax: (812)386-6199
**Subject(s):** Daily Newspapers
**Circ:** ‡6,640

**The Evening Leader (25028)**
American Publishing of Ohio
102 E Spring St.
Saint Marys, OH 45885
Phone: (419)394-7414
Fax: (419)394-7202
**Subject(s):** Daily Newspapers
**Circ:** 6,600

**Ftichburg Star (33443)**
Fitchburg Star
PO Box 26
Oregon, WI 53575-0026
Phone: (608)273-3576
Fax: (608)835-0130
**Subject(s):** Paid Community Newspapers
**Circ:** (Free)‡6,600

**Pine Cone Press-Citizen (16224)**
PO Box 401
Longville, MN 56655-0401
Phone: (218)363-2002
Fax: (218)363-3043
**Subject(s):** Free Newspapers
**Circ:** (Paid)‡384
(Non-paid)‡6,609

**The Beverly Review (8099)**
TR Communications Inc.
10546 S Western Ave.
Chicago, IL 60643
Phone: (773)238-3366
Fax: (773)238-1492
**Subject(s):** Paid Community Newspapers
**Circ:** ‡6,500

**The Enterprise (9249)**
Perry Co.
15507 S Route 59
Plainfield, IL 60544
Phone: (815)436-2431
Fax: (815)436-2592
**Subject(s):** Paid Community Newspapers
**Circ:** 6,500

**The Indiana Statesman (10189)**
Indiana State University
HMSU No. 719
Terre Haute, IN 47809
Phone: (812)237-3025
Fax: (812)237-7629

**Subject(s):** College Publications
**Circ:** (Free)‡6,500

**Kandiyohi County Times (16650)**
Kandiyohi Publishing
PO Box 910
Spicer, MN 56288
Phone: (320)796-2945
Fax: (320)796-6375
**Subject(s):** Paid Community Newspapers
**Circ:** 6,500

**The Oakwood Register (24658)**
Oakwood Register
435 Patterson Rd.
Dayton, OH 45419
Phone: (937)294-2662
Fax: (937)294-8375
**Subject(s):** Free Newspapers
**Circ:** (Paid)‡500
(Non-paid)‡6,500

**Press-Gazette (24770)**
Brown Publishing Co.
209 S. High St.
PO Box 40
Hillsboro, OH 45133
Phone: (513)393-3456
Fax: (513)393-2059
**Subject(s):** Paid Community Newspapers
**Circ:** (Paid)‡6,500

**Times Advocate (9521)**
PO Box 427
West Salem, IL 62476-0427
Phone: (618)456-8808
Fax: (618)456-8809
**Subject(s):** Paid Community Newspapers
**Circ:** (Paid)2,400
(Free)6,500

**Vermilion Photo Journal (25132)**
630 N Main St.
PO Box 23
Vermilion, OH 44089
Phone: (440)967-5268
Fax: (440)967-2535
**Subject(s):** Paid Community Newspapers
**Circ:** 6,500

**Waushara Argus (33644)**
The Wautoma Newspaper Inc.
PO Box 838
Wautoma, WI 54982
Phone: (920)787-3334
Fax: (920)787-2883
**Subject(s):** Paid Community Newspapers
**Circ:** 6,500

**Western Courier (8923)**
Western Illinois University
1 University Cir.
Macomb, IL 61455-1330
Phone: (309)298-1876
Fax: (309)298-2309
**Subject(s):** College Publications
**Circ:** (Free)‡6,500

**Northern Ogle Tempo (8918)**
Rock Valley Publishing
11512 N 2nd St.
Machesney Park, IL 61115
Phone: (815)877-4044
Fax: (815)654-4857
**Subject(s):** Paid Community Newspapers
**Circ:** (Free)71
(Paid)6,488

**Breeze-Courier (9442)**
212 S Main St.
PO Box 440
Taylorville, IL 62568
Phone: (217)824-2233
Fax: (217)824-2026
**Subject(s):** Daily Newspapers
**Circ:** (Mon.-Fri.)6,382
(Sun.)6,456

**Brunswick Sun Times (24221)**
Sun Newspapers
2795 Medina Rd.
Medina, OH 44256-8163
Phone: (330)725-1147
Fax: (330)725-2314

**Subject(s):** Paid Community Newspapers

**Circ:** (Paid)6,419

**The Daily Press (32822)**
Murphy McGinnis Media Inc.
122 3rd St. W
Ashland, WI 54806
Phone: (715)682-2313
Fax: (715)682-4699
**Subject(s):** Daily Newspapers

**Circ:** (Non-paid)29
(Paid)6,418

**Harrison News Herald (24232)**
130 N. Main St.
PO Box 127
Cadiz, OH 43907
Phone: (740)942-2118
Fax: (740)942-4667
**Subject(s):** Paid Community Newspapers

**Circ:** ‡6,400

**Indiana Spirit Shopping Guide (9959)**
Twin States Publishing
PO Box 107
Kentland, IN 47951
Phone: (219)474-5531
Fax: (219)474-5354
**Subject(s):** Shopping Guides

**Circ:** (Free)‡6,409

**The Monroe Times (33380)**
Monroe Publishing L.L.C.
1065 4th Ave. W
PO Box 230
Monroe, WI 53566
Phone: (608)328-4202
Fax: (608)328-4217
**Subject(s):** Daily Newspapers

**Circ:** (Paid)6,400

**Town & Country (9362)**
F.W. Gray & Associates Ltd.
Box 279
801 Canal St., No. 279
Ottawa, IL 61350-4901
Phone: (815)433-5595
Fax: (815)433-5596
**Subject(s):** Free Newspapers

**Circ:** (Paid)‡29
(Free)‡6,403

**The Journal Press (9996)**
Register Publications
126 W High St.
PO Box 328
Lawrenceburg, IN 47025
Phone: (812)537-0063
Fax: (812)537-5576
**Subject(s):** Paid Community Newspapers

**Circ:** (Free)35
(Paid)6,391

**Brookfield News (33397)**
Community Newspapers
15700 W Cleveland Ave.
New Berlin, WI 53151
Phone: (262)938-5000
Fax: (262)938-5001
**Subject(s):** Paid Community Newspapers

**Circ:** 6,340

**Clarkston Eccentric (15128)**
Observer & Eccentric Newspapers
36251 Schoolcraft Rd.
Livonia, MI 48150
Phone: (734)591-2300
Fax: (734)953-2232
**Subject(s):** Paid Community Newspapers

**Circ:** (Thurs.)6,347

**Marysville Journal-Tribune (24879)**
Marysville Newspapers Inc.
207 N. Main St.
PO Box 226
Marysville, OH 43040
Phone: (937)644-9111
Fax: (937)644-9211
**Subject(s):** Daily Newspapers

**Circ:** ‡6,337

**Uptown News-Star (8898)**
Lerner Communications Inc.
7331 N Lincoln Ave.
Lincolnwood, IL 60712
Phone: (847)329-2000
Fax: (847)329-2060
**Subject(s):** Paid Community Newspapers

**Circ:** (Combined)6,333

**Havana Mason County Democrat (8774)**
Martin Publishing Inc.
217 W Market St.
Havana, IL 62644
Phone: (309)543-3311
Fax: (309)543-6844
**Subject(s):** Paid Community Newspapers

**Circ:** (Combined)6,300

**The Star News (33269)**
Central Wisconsin Publications Inc.
116 S Wisconsin Ave.
PO Box 180
Medford, WI 54451
Phone: (715)748-2626
Fax: (715)748-2699
**Subject(s):** Paid Community Newspapers

**Circ:** (Free)‡159
(Paid)‡6,307

**Westosha Report (33585)**
Southern Lakes Newspapers
PO Box 992
Twin Lakes, WI 53181-0992
Phone: (414)877-2813
Fax: (414)877-3619
**Subject(s):** Free Newspapers

**Circ:** (Free)‡6,000
(Paid)‡6,300

**Brooklyn Sun Journal (24219)**
Sun Newspapers
5510 Cloverleaf Pkwy.
Valley View, OH 44125-4887
Phone: (216)986-2600
Fax: (216)986-2380
**Subject(s):** Paid Community Newspapers

**Circ:** (Paid)‡6,298

**Wauwatosa News-Times (33419)**
Community Newspapers
15700 W Cleveland Ave.
New Berlin, WI 53151
Phone: (262)938-5000
Fax: (262)938-5001
**Subject(s):** Paid Community Newspapers

**Circ:** 6,286

**Circleville Herald (24368)**
Brown Publishing Co.
PO Box 498
210 N Court St.
Circleville, OH 43113
Phone: (614)474-3131
Fax: (614)474-9525
**Subject(s):** Daily Newspapers

**Circ:** (Mon.-Sat.)★6,251

**The Friend (8207)**
Lithuanian Catholic Press Society
4545 W 63rd St.
Chicago, IL 60629-5589
Phone: (773)585-9500
Fax: (773)585-8284
**Subject(s):** Lithuanian; Religious Publications

**Circ:** ‡6,200

**Murray County Wheel/Herald (16646)**
Wheel Beers
PO Box 263
2734 Broadway St.
Slayton, MN 56172
Phone: (507)836-8726
Fax: (507)836-8942
**Subject(s):** Shopping Guides

**Circ:** (Paid)‡960
(Free)6,200

**The South Lyon Herald (15771)**
Hometown Newspapers
101 N. Lafayette
South Lyon, MI 48178
Phone: (248)437-2011
Fax: (248)437-3386

**Subject(s):** Paid Community Newspapers

**Circ:** (Non-paid)102
(Paid)6,200

**Tri-City Times (15439)**
Page One Corp.
PO Box 278
Imlay City, MI 48444
Phone: (810)724-0254
Fax: (810)724-8552
**Subject(s):** Paid Community Newspapers

**Circ:** 6,200

**Plymouth Observer (15683)**
Observer & Eccentric Newspapers
36251 Schoolcraft Rd.
Livonia, MI 48150
Phone: (734)591-2300
Fax: (734)953-2232
**Subject(s):** Paid Community Newspapers

**Circ:** (Thurs.)5,882
(Sun.)6,187

**Aitkin Independent Age (15914)**
Messenger Publications Inc.
213 Minnesota Ave. N
PO Box 259
Aitkin, MN 56431-0259
Phone: (218)927-3761
Fax: (218)927-3763
**Subject(s):** Paid Community Newspapers

**Circ:** ‡6,175

**Urbana Daily Citizen (25126)**
Brown Publishing Co.
220 E. Court St.
PO Box 191
Urbana, OH 43078
Phone: (937)652-1331
Fax: (937)652-1336
**Subject(s):** Daily Newspapers

**Circ:** (Mon.-Sat.)6,174

**Breese Journal (7930)**
8060 Old Hwy. 50
PO Box 405
Breese, IL 62230
Phone: (618)526-7211
Fax: (618)526-2590
**Subject(s):** Paid Community Newspapers

**Circ:** 6,165

**Port Clinton News Herald (25007)**
News Herald
115 W 2nd St.
PO Box 550
Port Clinton, OH 43452
Phone: (419)734-3141
Fax: (419)734-4662
**Subject(s):** Daily Newspapers

**Circ:** (Mon.-Sat.)6,164

**Arenac County Independent (15806)**
203 E Cedar St.
PO Box 699
Standish, MI 48658
Phone: (989)846-4531
Fax: (989)846-9868
**Subject(s):** Paid Community Newspapers

**Circ:** ‡6,156

**Morresville/Decatur Times (10040)**
Schurz Communications Inc.
23 E Main St.
Mooresville, IN 46158
Phone: (317)831-0280
Fax: (317)831-7068
**Subject(s):** Paid Community Newspapers

**Circ:** (Combined)6,144

**North Crow River News (16453)**
Sun Press and News Publications
33 2nd St. NE
Box 280
Osseo, MN 55369
Phone: (763)425-3323
Fax: (763)425-2945
**Subject(s):** Paid Community Newspapers

**Circ:** (Paid)2,943
(Free)6,123

**The Salem Democrat  (10145)**
Leader Publishing Company of Salem Inc.
117-119 E Walnut St.
PO Box 509
Salem, IN 47167
Phone: (812)883-3281
Fax: (812)883-4446
**Subject(s):** Paid Community Newspapers; Paid Community Newspapers

Circ: (Free)176
(Paid)6,100

**The Salem Leader  (10146)**
Leader Publishing Company of Salem Inc.
117-119 E Walnut St.
PO Box 509
Salem, IN 47167
Phone: (812)883-3281
Fax: (812)883-4446
**Subject(s):** Free Newspapers

Circ: (Free)176
(Paid)6,100

**Northwest Columbus News  (24576)**
Suburban News Publications
5257 Sinclair Rd.
PO Box 29912
Columbus, OH 43229
Phone: (614)785-1212
Fax: (614)785-1881
**Subject(s):** Free Newspapers

Circ: (Paid)880
(Non-paid)6,065

**North Town News-Star  (8895)**
Lerner Communications Inc.
7331 N Lincoln Ave.
Lincolnwood, IL 60712
Phone: (847)329-2000
Fax: (847)329-2060
**Subject(s):** Paid Community Newspapers

Circ: (Paid)♦6,040

**Olentangy Valley News  (25017)**
Suburban News Publications
5257 Sinclair Rd.
PO Box 29912
Columbus, OH 43229
Phone: (614)785-1212
Fax: (614)785-1881
**Subject(s):** Free Newspapers

Circ: (Paid)1,389
(Non-paid)6,029

**Addison Press  (9080)**
Liberty Suburban Chicago Newspapers
7222 W. Cermak Rd., Ste. 505
North Riverside, IL 60546
Phone: (708)447-9810
**Subject(s):** Paid Community Newspapers

Circ: (Combined)6,000

**Bensenville/Wood Dale Press  (9081)**
Liberty Suburban Chicago Newspapers
7222 W. Cermak Rd., Ste. 505
North Riverside, IL 60546
Phone: (708)447-9810
**Subject(s):** Paid Community Newspapers

Circ: (Combined)6,000

**The Exponent  (15082)**
Exponent
160 S Main
Brooklyn, MI 49230
Phone: (517)592-2122
Fax: (517)592-3241
**Subject(s):** Free Newspapers

Circ: (Paid)‡6,000

**Ferris State Torch  (15063)**
Ferris State University
805 Campus Dr.
Rankin Ctr.
Box 15
Big Rapids, MI 49307
Phone: (231)591-2609
Fax: (231)591-3617
**Subject(s):** College Publications

Circ: (Free)‡6,000

**La Prensa Nacional  (25091)**
La Prensa Publications Inc.
616 Adams St.
Toledo, OH 43604
Phone: (419)242-7744

Fax: (419)255-7700
**Subject(s):** Paid Community Newspapers; Hispanic Publications

Circ: (Paid)6,000

**Lemont Reporter/Metropolitan  (9092)**
Liberty Suburban Chicago Newspapers
7222 W. Cermak Rd., Ste. 505
North Riverside, IL 60546
Phone: (708)447-9810
**Subject(s):** Paid Community Newspapers

Circ: (Combined)6,000

**North Vernon Sun  (10080)**
North Vernon Plain Dealer & Sun
528 E O&M Ave.
PO Box 988
North Vernon, IN 47265
Phone: (812)346-3973
Fax: (812)346-8368
**Subject(s):** Paid Community Newspapers

Circ: 6,000

**Northwestern Illinois Farmer  (8865)**
Box 536
Lena, IL 61048-0536
Phone: (815)369-2811
Fax: (815)369-2816
**Subject(s):** Farm Newspapers

Circ: ‡6,000

**Record-Herald  (25139)**
138 S Fayette St.
Washington Court House, OH 43160
Phone: (740)335-3611
Fax: (740)335-5728
**Subject(s):** Daily Newspapers

Circ: (Paid)‡6,000

**The Solon Times  (25051)**
Chagrin Valley Publishing Co.
525 E Wash St.
PO Box 150
Chagrin Falls, OH 44022
Phone: (440)247-5335
Fax: (440)247-5615
**Subject(s):** Paid Community Newspapers

Circ: ‡6,000

**Star  (24220)**
14 Mulberry St.
Brookville, OH 45309
Phone: (937)833-2545
**Subject(s):** Paid Community Newspapers

Circ: (Paid)300
(Free)6,000

**Tempo  (8426)**
Chicago State University
Tempo SUB 230
9501h at King Dr.
Chicago, IL 60628-1598
Phone: (773)995-2000
Fax: (773)995-3593
**Subject(s):** College Publications

Circ: (Free)6,000

**UMD Statesman  (16068)**
University of Minnesota
118 Kirby Student Ctr.
Duluth, MN 55812
Phone: (218)726-8154
Fax: (218)726-8246
**Subject(s):** College Publications

Circ: 6,000

**The Verona Press  (33588)**
Schroeder Publications
120 W Verona Ave.
Verona, WI 53593
Phone: (608)845-9559
Fax: (608)845-9550
**Subject(s):** Paid Community Newspapers

Circ: (Paid)‡1,937
(Free)‡6,000

**Waynedale News  (9725)**
2700 Lower Huntington Rd.
Fort Wayne, IN 46809
Phone: (260)747-4535
Fax: (260)747-5529
**Subject(s):** Free Newspapers

Circ: (Free)‡6,000

**The Catholic Times  (15301)**
GLS Diocesan Reports
104 1/2 E. Main St.
Flushing, MI 48433-2024
Phone: (810)659-4670
Fax: (810)659-4859
**Subject(s):** Religious Publications

Circ: (Non-paid)157
(Paid)5,975

**Clawson Mirror  (15711)**
Mirror Newspapers
1523 N Main
PO Box 430
Royal Oak, MI 48067-0430
Phone: (248)546-4900
Fax: (248)398-2353
**Subject(s):** Paid Community Newspapers

Circ: (Combined)5,953

**Vernon County Broadcaster  (33591)**
PO Box 472
Viroqua, WI 54665
Phone: (608)637-3137
Fax: (608)637-8557
**Subject(s):** Paid Community Newspapers

Circ: ‡5,950

**Decatur Daily Democrat  (9679)**
Decatur Publishing Company Inc.
141 S 2nd St.
PO Box 1001
Decatur, IN 46733
Phone: (260)724-2121
Fax: (260)724-7981
**Subject(s):** Daily Newspapers

Circ: ‡5,939

**West Minnetonka/Deephaven Sun-Sailor  (16391)**
Minnesota Sun Publications
10917 Valley View Rd.
Eden Prairie, MN 55344
Phone: (952)829-0797
Fax: (952)392-6868
**Subject(s):** Free Newspapers

Circ: (Paid)407
(Non-paid)5,935

**The Commercial Review  (10114)**
309 W Main
PO Box 1049
Portland, IN 47371
Phone: (260)726-8141
Fax: (260)726-8143
**Subject(s):** Daily Newspapers

Circ: 5,922

**The Boscobel Dial  (32863)**
Southwest Publishers L.L.C.
901 Wisconisn Ave.
Boscobel, WI 53805-1531
Phone: (608)375-4458
Fax: (608)375-2369
**Subject(s):** Paid Community Newspapers

Circ: (Paid)‡5,900

**Democrat  (9634)**
Whitewater Publications Inc.
531 Main St.
Brookville, IN 47012
Phone: (317)647-4221
Fax: (317)647-4811
**Subject(s):** Paid Community Newspapers

Circ: ‡5,900

**Oscoda Press  (15660)**
News Press Publishing Co.
311 S State St.
PO Box 663
Oscoda, MI 48750
Phone: (989)739-2054
Fax: (989)739-3201
**Subject(s):** Paid Community Newspapers

Circ: 5,900

**Prairie Shopper  (8841)**
McGirgan Productions
101 Jefferson
PO Box 27
La Fayette, IL 61449-0027
Phone: (309)995-3877
Fax: (309)995-3975
**Subject(s):** Shopping Guides

Circ: (Free)5,900

**White Lake Spinal Column Newsweekly (15896)**
Spinal Column Publications
7196 Cooley Lake Rd.
PO Box 14
Union Lake, MI 48387-0014
Phone: (248)360-7355
Fax: (248)360-4711
**Subject(s):** Free Newspapers

Circ: (Free)‡5,900

**Manistee News Advocate (15565)**
The Pioneer Group
75 Maple St.
PO Box 317
Manistee, MI 49660
Phone: (616)723-3592
Fax: (616)723-4733
**Subject(s):** Daily Newspapers

Circ: ‡5,898

**Harrison Press (24763)**
Register Publications
307 Harrison Ave.
Harrison, OH 45030
Phone: (513)367-4582
**Subject(s):** Paid Community Newspapers

Circ: (Non-paid)⊕41
 (Non-paid)40
 (Paid)5,509
 (Paid)⊕**5,875**

**Star-Courier (8837)**
Liberty Group Publishing
105 E Central Blvd.
Kewanee, IL 61443-0836
Phone: (309)852-2181
Fax: (309)852-0010
**Subject(s):** Daily Newspapers

Circ: (Mon.-Sat.)5,872

**The Pioneer (15065)**
The Pioneer Group
502 N State St.
Big Rapids, MI 49307
Phone: (231)796-4831
Fax: (231)796-1152
**Subject(s):** Daily Newspapers

Circ: (Free)24
 (Paid)5,859

**Litchfield News-Herald (8906)**
Litchfield News-Herald Inc.
112 E Ryder St.
PO Box 160
Litchfield, IL 62056
Phone: (217)324-2121
Fax: (217)324-2122
**Subject(s):** Daily Newspapers

Circ: ‡5,800

**Scottsdale Ashburn Independent (8976)**
Southwest Messenger Press Inc.
3840 W 147th St.
PO Box 548
Midlothian, IL 60445
Phone: (708)388-2425
Fax: (708)385-7811
**Subject(s):** Free Newspapers

Circ: (Free)‡5,800

**The Tecumseh Herald (15822)**
PO Box 218
110 E Logan
Tecumseh, MI 49286
Phone: (517)423-2174
Fax: (517)423-6258
**Subject(s):** Paid Community Newspapers

Circ: ‡5,800

**Northfield News (16441)**
115 W. 5th St.
PO Box 58
Northfield, MN 55057
Phone: (507)645-5615
Fax: (507)645-6005
**Subject(s):** Paid Community Newspapers

Circ: (Free)375
 (Paid)5,790

**Horizons (24987)**
1900 Carlton Rd.
Parma, OH 44134-3129
Phone: (216)741-3312
Fax: (216)741-9356

**Subject(s):** Religious Publications

Circ: (Non-paid)295
 (Paid)5,779

**Park Rapids Enterprise (16460)**
PO Box 111
Park Rapids, MN 56470
Phone: (218)732-3364
Fax: (218)732-8757
**Subject(s):** Free Newspapers

Circ: (Combined)5,767

**Ladysmith News (33134)**
Bell Press Inc.
PO Box 189
Ladysmith, WI 54848
Phone: (715)532-5591
Fax: (715)532-6644
**Subject(s):** Paid Community Newspapers

Circ: (Paid)5,750

**Burbank Stickney Independent (8967)**
Southwest Messenger Press Inc.
3840 W 147th St.
PO Box 548
Midlothian, IL 60445
Phone: (708)388-2425
Fax: (708)385-7811
**Subject(s):** Free Newspapers

Circ: (Free)‡200
 (Paid)‡5,700

**La Grange Standard (9987)**
LaGrange Publishing Co.
State Rd. 9 S
PO Box 148
LaGrange, IN 46761
Phone: (260)463-2167
Fax: (260)463-2734
**Subject(s):** Paid Community Newspapers

Circ: ‡5,706

**Northwest Signal (24925)**
Napoleon Inc.
595 E Riverview
PO Box 567
Napoleon, OH 43545
Phone: (419)592-5055
Fax: (419)592-9778
**Subject(s):** Daily Newspapers

Circ: ‡5,704

**Aurora Advocate (25067)**
Record Publishing Co.
1619 Commerce Dr.
Stow, OH 44224
Phone: (330)688-0088
Fax: (330)688-1588
**Subject(s):** Free Newspapers

Circ: (Free)‡5,680

**Bluffton News-Banner (9625)**
News Banner Publications Inc.
125 N Johnson St.
PO Box 436
Bluffton, IN 46714
Phone: (260)824-0224
Fax: (260)824-0700
**Subject(s):** Paid Community Newspapers

Circ: (Paid)‡5,640

**Republic Times (9504)**
Republic Times L.L.C.
114 N Main
PO Box 147
Waterloo, IL 62298
Phone: (618)939-3814
Fax: (618)939-3815
**Subject(s):** Paid Community Newspapers

Circ: ‡5,629

**The Spencer County Journal-Democrat (10141)**
Landmark Community Newspapers Inc.
PO Box 6
Rockport, IN 47635
Phone: (812)649-9196
Fax: (812)649-9197
**Subject(s):** Paid Community Newspapers

Circ: 5,625

**Antrim County News (15055)**
Up North Publications Inc.
206 N. Bridge St.
PO Box 337
Bellaire, MI 49615
Phone: (231)533-8523
**Subject(s):** Paid Community Newspapers

Circ: ‡5,600

**Hastings Star Gazette (16161)**
Trade Winds
PO Box 277
Hastings, MN 55033
Phone: (651)437-6153
Fax: (651)437-5911
**Subject(s):** Paid Community Newspapers

Circ: ‡5,600

**Mille Lacs Messenger (16185)**
280, W. Main St.
PO Box 26
Isle, MN 56342
Phone: (320)676-3123
Fax: (320)676-8450
**Subject(s):** Paid Community Newspapers

Circ: 5,600

**The Saline Reporter (15750)**
Heritage Newspapers Inc.
106 W Michigan Ave.
Saline, MI 48176
Phone: (734)429-7380
Fax: (734)429-3621
**Subject(s):** Paid Community Newspapers

Circ: (Non-paid)♦94
 (Paid)♦**5,600**

**Excelsior/Shorewood/Chanhassen Sun-Sailor (16112)**
Minnesota Sun Publications
10917 Valley View Rd.
Eden Prairie, MN 55344
Phone: (952)829-0797
Fax: (952)392-6868
**Subject(s):** Free Newspapers

Circ: (Paid)♦513
 (Non-paid)♦**5,586**

**Hutchinson Leader (16181)**
Hutchinson Leader Inc.
36 Washington Ave. W.
Hutchinson, MN 55350
Phone: (320)587-5000
Fax: (320)587-6104
**Subject(s):** Paid Community Newspapers

Circ: (Paid)‡5,564

**Gibson County Today (10119)**
Princeton Publishing Inc.
100 N Gibson
PO Box 30
Princeton, IN 47670
Phone: (812)385-2525
Fax: (812)386-6199
**Subject(s):** Shopping Guides

Circ: (Free)‡5,534

**Anoka County Union (16026)**
Anoka County Shopper
4101 Coon Rapids Blvd.
PO Box 99
Coon Rapids, MN 55433
Phone: (763)421-4444
Fax: (763)421-4315
**Subject(s):** Paid Community Newspapers

Circ: (Paid)‡5,515

**The Advertiser (8651)**
116 S Magnolia
PO Box 289
Elmwood, IL 61529
Phone: (309)742-2521
Fax: (309)742-2511
**Subject(s):** Shopping Guides

Circ: (Free)‡5,500

**The Allegan County News (14973)**
Kaechele Publications Inc.
231 Trowbridge
PO Box 189
Allegan, MI 49010
Phone: (269)673-5534
Fax: (269)673-5535
**Subject(s):** Paid Community Newspapers

Circ: 5,500

**Fulton Press (8709)**
The Fulton Press
PO Box 30
Fulton, IL 61252
Phone: (815)589-2424
Fax: (815)589-2568
**Subject(s):** Paid Community Newspapers

**Circ:** (Combined)5,500

**Moorhead State University Advocate (16400)**
Moorhead State University
1104 7th Ave. S.
Moorhead, MN 56563-0001
Phone: (218)236-2204
Fax: (218)477-5086
**Subject(s):** College Publications

**Circ:** (Free)‡5,500

**Poultry Press (9662)**
PO Box 542
Connersville, IN 47331
Phone: (765)827-0932
Fax: (765)827-4186
**Subject(s):** Poultry and Pigeons

**Circ:** ‡5,500

**Times Journal (24791)**
Brown Publishing Co.
1 Acy Ave., Ste. D
PO Box 270
Jackson, OH 45640
Phone: (740)286-2187
Fax: (740)286-5854
**Subject(s):** Paid Community Newspapers

**Circ:** (Tues.)5,325
(Thurs.)5,325
(Sun.)5,492

**The Press-Dispatch (10110)**
PO Box 68
Petersburg, IN 47567
Phone: (812)354-8500
Fax: (812)354-2014
**Subject(s):** Paid Community Newspapers

**Circ:** 5,472

**Shakopee Valley News (16644)**
Southwest Suburban Publishing
c/o Patrick Minelli,
327 Marschall Rd.
Ste. 125
PO Box 8
Shakopee, MN 55379-0008
Phone: (952)445-3333
Fax: (952)445-3335
**Subject(s):** Paid Community Newspapers

**Circ:** (Free)344
(Paid)5,450

**Savage Pacer (16640)**
Southwest Suburban Publishing
14093 Commerce Ave.
PO Box 376
Prior Lake, MN 55372
Phone: (952)440-1234
Fax: (952)447-6671
**Subject(s):** Paid Community Newspapers

**Circ:** (Paid)5,440

**Jefferson Park/Portage Park Times (8889)**
Lerner Communications Inc.
7331 N Lincoln Ave.
Lincolnwood, IL 60712
Phone: (847)329-2000
Fax: (847)329-2060
**Subject(s):** Free Newspapers

**Circ:** (Paid)♦5,415

**Cadence (15459)**
Valley Media Inc.
PO Box 9
Jenison, MI 49429-0009
Phone: (616)669-2700
Fax: (616)669-4848
**Subject(s):** Paid Community Newspapers

**Circ:** ‡5,400

**The Journal Express (32804)**
Berner Brothers Publishing Company Inc.
612 Superior St.
Antigo, WI 54409
Phone: (715)623-4191
Fax: (715)623-4193
**Subject(s):** Shopping Guides

**Circ:** (Free)‡5,400

**The Northville Record (15641)**
Hometown Newspapers
104 W. Main
Northville, MI 48167-1521
Phone: (313)369-1700
Fax: (810)349-1050
**Subject(s):** Paid Community Newspapers

**Circ:** (Combined)5,405

**The Star and the Hometown Advertiser (33569)**
Hometown News Group Publications
207 E. Main St.
PO Box 645
Sun Prairie, WI 53590
Phone: (608)837-2521
Fax: (608)825-4460
**Subject(s):** Paid Community Newspapers

**Circ:** ‡5,400

**Thief River Falls Times (16661)**
Thief River Falls Times Inc.
324 Main Ave. N
PO Box 100
Thief River Falls, MN 56701
Phone: (218)681-4450
Fax: (218)681-4455
**Subject(s):** Paid Community Newspapers

**Circ:** ‡5,400

**The Daily Clintonian (9652)**
Clinton Color Crafters
422 S Main St.
P.O Box 309
Clinton, IN 47842-0309
Phone: (765)832-2443
**Subject(s):** Daily Newspapers

**Circ:** (Free)⊕24
(Paid)⊕5,385

**Freethought Today (33183)**
Freedom From Religion Foundation Inc.
PO Box 750
Madison, WI 53701
Phone: (608)256-8900
Fax: (608)256-1116
**Subject(s):** Atheism

**Circ:** (Non-paid)‡300
(Paid)‡5,300

**Journal and Monitor-Herald (33578)**
Tomah Journal Newspapers
1108 Superior Ave.
PO Box 190
Tomah, WI 54660-0190
Phone: (608)372-4123
Fax: (608)372-2791
**Subject(s):** Paid Community Newspapers

**Circ:** 5,300

**The Nashville News (9049)**
Riccon Inc.
211 W St. Louis St.
PO Box 47
Nashville, IL 62263-0047
Phone: (618)327-3411
Fax: (618)327-3299
**Subject(s):** Paid Community Newspapers

**Circ:** ‡5,300

**Vandalia Leader Union (9492)**
Landmark Community Newspapers Inc.
229 S. 5th St.
Vandalia, IL 62471
Phone: (618)283-3374
Fax: (618)283-0977
**Subject(s):** Paid Community Newspapers

**Circ:** 5,300

**Salem Times-Commoner (9342)**
120 S Broadway
PO Box 548
Salem, IL 62881
Phone: (618)548-3330
Fax: (618)548-3593
**Subject(s):** Paid Community Newspapers

**Circ:** (Free)123
(Paid)5,264

**The Brazil Times (9630)**
The Brazil Times Publishing Corp.
100 N Meridian St.
PO Box 429
Brazil, IN 47834
Phone: (812)446-2216
Fax: (812)446-0938

**Subject(s):** Daily Newspapers

**Circ:** (Paid)‡5,242

**Portage Daily Register (33478)**
Capital Newspapers
1640, Ladawn Dr.
PO Box 470
Portage, WI 53901
Phone: (608)745-3500
Fax: (608)745-3530
**Subject(s):** Daily Newspapers

**Circ:** (Mon.-Sat.)★5,221

**The Daily Register (8767)**
American Publishing
35 S. Vine St.
Harrisburg, IL 62946
Phone: (618)253-7146
Fax: (618)252-0863
**Subject(s):** Daily Newspapers

**Circ:** (Combined)5,201

**Lake County Business Journal (25176)**
PO Box 656
Willoughby, OH 44096
Phone: (440)975-9580
Fax: (440)975-9299
**Subject(s):** Free Newspapers

**Circ:** (Paid)500
(Non-paid)5,200

**Monroe County Democrat (33546)**
Monroe County Publishers Inc.
1302 River Rd.
PO Box 252
Sparta, WI 54656-0252
Phone: (608)269-3186
Fax: (608)269-6876
**Subject(s):** Paid Community Newspapers

**Circ:** 5,200

**Vandalia Drummer News (25131)**
Times Community Newspapers
320 James Bohanan Dr.
Vandalia, OH 45377
Phone: (937)890-6030
**Subject(s):** Paid Community Newspapers

**Circ:** ‡5,200

**The Versailles Republican (10219)**
The Ripley Publishing Co.
115 S Washington St.
PO Box 158
Versailles, IN 47042
Phone: (812)689-6364
Fax: (812)689-6508
**Subject(s):** Paid Community Newspapers

**Circ:** ‡5,200

**Westville Indicator (10263)**
Box 828
Westville, IN 46391
Phone: (219)785-2234
Fax: (219)785-2242
**Subject(s):** Paid Community Newspapers

**Circ:** ‡5,200

**Community Journal (North) (24848)**
Press Community Newspapers
394 Wards Corner Rd.
Loveland, OH 45140
Phone: (513)248-8600
Fax: (513)248-1938
**Subject(s):** Paid Community Newspapers

**Circ:** (Paid)1,771
(Non-paid)5,116

**Frankenmuth News (15303)**
231 Hubinger
PO Box 252
Frankenmuth, MI 48734-1703
Phone: (989)652-3246
Fax: (989)652-2417
**Subject(s):** Paid Community Newspapers

**Circ:** ‡5,100

**Galena Gazette and Advertiser (8710)**
Galena Gazette Publications Inc.
716 S Bench St.
Galena, IL 61036-0319
Phone: (815)777-0019
Fax: (815)777-3809
**Subject(s):** Paid Community Newspapers

**Circ:** ‡5,100

**The Morgan County Advertiser (24934)**
Add Inc.—Ohio Group
116 S Main St.
New Lexington, OH 43764
Phone: (740)342-5483
Fax: (740)342-5305
**Subject(s):** Shopping Guides
**Circ:** (Non-paid)♦5,101

**Redwood Gazette (16499)**
Redwood Gazette Inc.
219 S Washington
PO Box 299
Redwood Falls, MN 56283
Phone: (507)637-2929
Fax: (507)637-3175
**Subject(s):** Paid Community Newspapers
**Circ:** ‡5,100

**Edwardsville Intelligencer (8623)**
Edwardsville Publishing Company Inc.
117 N 2nd St.
PO Box 70
Edwardsville, IL 62025-1938
Phone: (618)656-4700
Fax: (618)656-7618
**Subject(s):** Daily Newspapers
**Circ:** (Mon.-Sat.)★5,092

**Champlin Dayton Press (16451)**
Sun Press and News Publications
33 2nd St. NE
Box 280
Osseo, MN 55369
Phone: (763)425-3323
Fax: (763)425-2945
**Subject(s):** Paid Community Newspapers
**Circ:** (Paid)1,986
(Free)5,056

**Heartland Publications (24740)**
Ohio Valley Publishing
825 3rd Ave.
Gallipolis, OH 45631
Phone: (740)446-2342
Fax: (740)446-3008
**Subject(s):** Daily Newspapers
**Circ:** (Mon.-Fri.)5,014

**The Akron Legal News (24092)**
60 S Summit St.
Akron, OH 44308
Phone: (330)376-0917
Fax: (330)376-7001
**Subject(s):** Daily Newspapers; Law
**Circ:** ‡5,000

**The Alger County Shopper (15618)**
113 W Superior St.
Munising, MI 49862-1123
Phone: (906)387-3282
Fax: (906)387-4054
**Subject(s):** Shopping Guides
**Circ:** ‡5,000

**The American Legion Press (24995)**
Welch Publishing Co.
117 E 2nd St.
PO Box 267
Perrysburg, OH 43552
Phone: (419)874-4491
Fax: (419)874-7311
**Subject(s):** Veterans
**Circ:** ‡5,000

**Carroll County Comet (9710)**
Carroll Papers Inc.
14 E Main
Flora, IN 46929-0026
Phone: (574)967-4135
Fax: (574)967-3384
**Subject(s):** Paid Community Newspapers
**Circ:** (Free)‡35
(Paid)‡5,000

**The Carroll News (25122)**
John Carroll University
20700 N Park Blvd.
University Heights, OH 44118
Phone: (216)397-4398
Fax: (216)397-1729
**Subject(s):** College Publications; Free Newspapers
**Circ:** (Free)‡5,000

**The Cauldron (24385)**
Cleveland State University
2121 Euclid Ave., Rm. 10
Cleveland, OH 44115
Phone: (216)687-2475
Fax: (216)687-5155
**Subject(s):** College Publications
**Circ:** ‡5,000

**Chesterton Tribune (9647)**
193 S Calumet Road
PO Box 919
Chesterton, IN 46304
Phone: (219)926-1131
Fax: (219)926-6389
**Subject(s):** Daily Newspapers
**Circ:** ⊕5,000

**Chicago Shimpo (8137)**
4670 N Manor Ave.
Chicago, IL 60625
Phone: (773)478-6170
Fax: (773)478-9360
**Subject(s):** Paid Community Newspapers; Japanese; Ethnic Publications
**Circ:** (Combined)5,000

**Clarion (24645)**
Sinclair Community College
444 W 3rd St.
Atten: Clarion Newspaper
Rm 8027
Dayton, OH 45402-1460
Phone: (937)512-2744
Fax: (937)512-4590
**Subject(s):** College Publications
**Circ:** (Free)‡5,000

**Courier (8728)**
College of DuPage
425 Fawell Blvd.
Glen Ellyn, IL 60137
Phone: (630)942-2379
Fax: (630)942-3747
**Subject(s):** College Publications
**Circ:** (Free)‡5,000

**Crawford County Avalanche (15379)**
102 Michigan Ave.
PO Box 490
Grayling, MI 49738
Phone: (517)348-6811
Fax: (517)348-6806
**Subject(s):** Paid Community Newspapers
**Circ:** ‡5,000

**The Enquirer-Democrat (7959)**
Macoupin County Enquirer Inc.
PO Box 200
Carlinville, IL 62626-0200
Phone: (217)854-2534
Fax: (217)854-2535
**Subject(s):** Paid Community Newspapers
**Circ:** (Combined)5,000

**Fifth Avenue Journal (9278)**
Triton College
2000 N 5th Ave.
River Grove, IL 60171-1995
Phone: (708)456-0300
Fax: (708)583-3140
**Subject(s):** College Publications
**Circ:** (Free)‡5,000

**Flyer News (24651)**
University of Dayton
300 College Park
Dayton, OH 45469-1659
Phone: (937)229-3241
Fax: (937)229-3063
**Subject(s):** College Publications
**Circ:** (Paid)‡20
(Free)‡5,000

**Herald (8960)**
214 E Partridge
Box 229
Metamora, IL 61548
Phone: (309)367-2335
Fax: (309)367-4277
**Subject(s):** Paid Community Newspapers
**Circ:** 5,000

**Journal & Noble County Leader (24233)**
Journal Leader
PO Box 315
309 Main Street
Caldwell, OH 43724-0390
Phone: (740)732-2341
Fax: (740)732-7288
**Subject(s):** Paid Community Newspapers
**Circ:** ‡5,000

**The Lafayette Leader (9977)**
514 Main St.
PO Box 908
Lafayette, IN 47902-0908
Phone: (765)429-8474
Fax: (765)742-5156
**Subject(s):** Paid Community Newspapers
**Circ:** ‡5,000

**Michigan Tech Lode (15424)**
Michigan Technological University
106 Memorial Union Bldg.
Houghton, MI 49931
Phone: (906)487-2404
**Subject(s):** College Publications
**Circ:** (Free)5,000

**New Buffalo Times (15633)**
P.O. Box 369
102 S. Whittaker
New Buffalo, MI 49117
Phone: (616)469-1100
Fax: (616)469-6397
**Subject(s):** Paid Community Newspapers
**Circ:** ‡5,000

**The New Senior Life Styles Vista (24798)**
Gazette Printing Company Inc.
34 S Chestnut St.
Jefferson, OH 44047
Phone: (440)576-9115
Fax: (440)576-4337
**Subject(s):** Free Newspapers; Senior Citizens' Interests; Local, State, and Regional Publications
**Circ:** (Non-paid)5,000

**The News (33424)**
PO Box 338
New Richmond, WI 54017-0338
Phone: (715)246-6881
Fax: (715)246-7117
**Subject(s):** Paid Community Newspapers
**Circ:** (Paid)5,000

**The Northeast Herald (9899)**
East Side Suburban Newspapers
4309 E Michigan St., No. 11042
Indianapolis, IN 46201-3652
Phone: (317)356-2487
Fax: (317)356-5871
**Subject(s):** Free Newspapers
**Circ:** (Paid)101
(Free)5,000

**Oconomowoc Enterprise (33433)**
212 E. Wisconsin Ave.
PO Box B
Oconomowoc, WI 53066
Phone: (262)567-5511
Fax: (262)542-8259
**Subject(s):** Paid Community Newspapers
**Circ:** 5,000

**Pataskala Standard (24991)**
350 S Main St.
PO Box 7
Pataskala, OH 43062-0007
Phone: (740)927-2991
Fax: (740)927-2930
**Subject(s):** Paid Community Newspapers
**Circ:** (Free)12
(Paid)5,000

**Scott County Journal (10151)**
Green Banner Publications Inc.
PO Box 159
Scottsburg, IN 47170
Phone: (812)967-3176
Fax: (812)752-2611
**Subject(s):** Paid Community Newspapers
**Circ:** 5000

Circulation: ★ = ABC; △ = BPA; ♦ = CAC; • = CCAB; ▢ = VAC; ⊕ = PO Statement; ‡ = Publisher's Report; Boldface figures = sworn; Light figures = estimated.

**Great Lakes States**      Gale Directory of Publications & Broadcast Media/140th Ed.

**The Sparta Herald** (33547)
Monroe County Publishers Inc.
1302 River Rd.
PO Box 252
Sparta, WI 54656-0252
Phone: (608)269-3186
Fax: (608)269-6876
**Subject(s):** Paid Community Newspapers
**Circ:** 5,000

**Varsity News** (15202)
University of Detroit-Mercy
3800 Puritan
Detroit, MI 48238
Phone: (313)993-3300
Fax: (313)993-1120
**Subject(s):** College Publications
**Circ:** (Free)‡5,000

**Winonan** (16721)
Winona State University
PO Box 5838
Winona, MN 55987
Phone: (507)457-2525
Fax: (507)457-5317
**Subject(s):** College Publications
**Circ:** (Free)‡5,000

**Amery Free Press** (32799)
Sondreal Enterprises
PO Box 338
Amery, WI 54001
**Subject(s):** Paid Community Newspapers
**Circ:** (Non-paid)34
    (Paid)4,969

**Novi News** (15646)
Hometown Newspapers
104 W. Main
Northville, MI 48167
Phone: (810)349-1700
Fax: (810)349-1050
**Subject(s):** Paid Community Newspapers
**Circ:** (Combined)4,954

**Wayland-Weston Town Crier** (15886)
Cummins Publishing Company Inc.
2563 Ashburton Ct.
Rochester, MI 48306-4926
**Subject(s):** Paid Community Newspapers
**Circ:** (Non-paid)169
    (Paid)4,951

**Union Banner** (7962)
671 10th St.
PO Box 220
Carlyle, IL 62231
Phone: (618)594-3131
Fax: (618)594-3115
**Subject(s):** Paid Community Newspapers
**Circ:** (Free)‡89
    (Paid)‡4,931

**EXTRA** (8195)
EXTRA Publications Inc.
3906 W N Ave.
Chicago, IL 60647
Phone: (773)252-3534
Fax: (773)252-6031
**Subject(s):** Paid Community Newspapers
**Circ:** ‡4,926

**West Allis Star** (33420)
Community Newspapers
15700 W Cleveland Ave.
New Berlin, WI 53151
Phone: (262)938-5000
Fax: (262)938-5001
**Subject(s):** Paid Community Newspapers
**Circ:** 4,926

**The Chelsea Standard** (15124)
Heritage Newspapers Inc.
20750 Old U.S. 12
Chelsea, MI 48118
Phone: (734)475-1371
**Subject(s):** Paid Community Newspapers
**Circ:** (Non-paid)♦30
    (Paid)♦4,900

**Monroe County Beacon** (25186)
103 E Court St.
PO Box 70
Woodsfield, OH 43793-0070
Phone: (740)472-0734
Fax: (740)472-0735
**Subject(s):** Paid Community Newspapers
**Circ:** ‡4,900

**Osgood Journal** (10217)
The Ripley Publishing Co.
115 S Washington St.
PO Box 158
Versailles, IN 47042
Phone: (812)689-6364
Fax: (812)689-6508
**Subject(s):** Paid Community Newspapers
**Circ:** (Free)‡41
    (Paid)‡4,900

**Total Shopper** (16642)
Review-Messenger
112 Minnesota Ave. W
PO Box 309
Sebeka, MN 56477
Phone: (218)837-5558
Fax: (218)837-5560
**Subject(s):** Shopping Guides
**Circ:** (Free)4,900

**The Post & Mail** (9654)
Columbia City Publishing Co.
PO Box 128
Columbia City, IN 46725
Phone: (260)248-5112
Fax: (260)244-7598
**Subject(s):** Daily Newspapers
**Circ:** ‡4,867

**Fox Lake Press** (8751)
Lakeland Media Inc.
30 S Whitney St.
PO Box 268
Grayslake, IL 60030-0268
Phone: (847)223-8161
Fax: (847)223-8810
**Subject(s):** Paid Community Newspapers
**Circ:** ‡4,856

**News-Leader** (9290)
211 Hwy. 38 East
PO Box 46
Rochelle, IL 61068
Phone: (815)562-4171
Fax: (815)562-2161
**Subject(s):** Paid Community Newspapers
**Circ:** (Non-paid)‡150
    (Paid)‡4,850

**Barnesville Enterprise** (24159)
Jeffersonian Co.
166 E Main
PO Box 30
Barnesville, OH 43713
Phone: (740)425-1912
Fax: (740)425-2545
**Subject(s):** Paid Community Newspapers
**Circ:** 4,825

**Daily Register** (33477)
Capital Newspapers
1640 LaDawn Blvd.
PO Box 470
Portage, WI 53901
Phone: (608)742-2111
Fax: (608)742-8346
**Subject(s):** Daily Newspapers
**Circ:** (Free)16
    (Paid)4,829

**Garden City Observer** (15316)
Observer & Eccentric Newspapers
36251 Schoolcraft Rd.
Livonia, MI 48150
Phone: (734)591-2300
Fax: (734)953-2232
**Subject(s):** Paid Community Newspapers
**Circ:** (Thurs.)4,343
    (Sun.)4,823

**Maple Valley News** (15397)
J-Ad Corp.
1351 N M-43 Hwy.
PO Box 188
Hastings, MI 49058-0188
Phone: (269)945-9554
Fax: (269)945-5192
**Subject(s):** Free Newspapers
**Circ:** (Free)‡4,825

**Detroit Lakes Tribune** (16042)
Forum Communications Co.
511 Washington Ave.
Detroit Lakes, MN 56501-3007
Phone: (218)847-3151
Fax: (218)847-9409
**Subject(s):** Paid Community Newspapers
**Circ:** (Free)❑24
    (Paid)❑4,806

**Fulton Democrat** (8866)
165 W Lincoln
PO Box 191
Lewistown, IL 61542
Phone: (309)547-3055
Fax: (309)543-6844
**Subject(s):** Free Newspapers
**Circ:** (Free)4,800

**Posey County News** (10118)
PO Box 250
Poseyville, IN 47633
Phone: (812)985-7989
Fax: (812)874-6397
**Subject(s):** Paid Community Newspapers
**Circ:** ‡4,800

**Canton Eagle** (15095)
The Journal Newspapers
35540 Michigan Ave.
PO Box 578
Wayne, MI 48184
Phone: (734)467-1900
Fax: (734)729-1840
**Subject(s):** Paid Community Newspapers
**Circ:** (Combined)4,798

**The Delavan Enterprise** (32908)
Walworth County Publishers
1436 Mound Rd.
PO Box 366
Delavan, WI 53115-0366
Phone: (262)728-5505
Fax: (262)728-5706
**Subject(s):** Paid Community Newspapers
**Circ:** ‡4,752

**Oconto County Times-Herald** (33438)
Shellman Publishing Inc.
107 S Main St.
PO Box 128
Oconto Falls, WI 54154-0128
Phone: (920)848-3427
Fax: (920)848-3430
**Subject(s):** Paid Community Newspapers
**Circ:** (Free)‡150
    (Paid)‡4,729

**Spooner Advocate** (33551)
Murphy McGinnis Media Inc.
PO Box 338
Spooner, WI 54801
Phone: (715)635-2181
Fax: (715)635-2186
**Subject(s):** Daily Newspapers
**Circ:** (Non-paid)♦24
    (Paid)♦4,726

**Grayslake Times** (8753)
Lakeland Media Inc.
30 S Whitney St.
PO Box 268
Grayslake, IL 60030-0268
Phone: (847)223-8161
Fax: (847)223-8810
**Subject(s):** Paid Community Newspapers
**Circ:** ‡4,712

**Chief-Union** (25124)
The Harding Publishing Co.
111 W Wyandot Ave.
PO Box 180
Upper Sandusky, OH 43351
Phone: (419)294-2332
Fax: (419)294-5608
**Subject(s):** Daily Newspapers
**Circ:** ‡4,700

**Daily Times** (10176)
Daily News
PO Box 130
Sullivan, IN 47882
Phone: (812)268-6356
Fax: (812)268-3110

Subject(s): Daily Newspapers
Circ: ‡4,700

**The Dodgeville Chronicle (32912)**
J. Patrick and T. Michael Reilly
106 W Merrimac St.
Dodgeville, WI 53533
Phone: (608)935-2331
Fax: (608)935-9531
Subject(s): Paid Community Newspapers
Circ: (Free)200
(Paid)4,700

**Metropolis Planet (8961)**
111 E 5th St.
Box 820
Metropolis, IL 62960-0820
Phone: (618)524-2141
Fax: (618)524-4727
Subject(s): Paid Community Newspapers
Circ: (Free)50
(Paid)4,700

**Pierce County Herald (32944)**
Rivertown Newspaper Group
126 S Chestnut St.
Ellsworth, WI 54011-4117
Phone: (715)273-4334
Fax: (715)273-4335
Subject(s): Paid Community Newspapers
Circ: 4,700

**Times Advantage (9631)**
The Brazil Times Publishing Corp.
100 N Meridian St.
PO Box 429
Brazil, IN 47834
Phone: (812)446-2216
Fax: (812)446-0938
Subject(s): Shopping Guides
Circ: (Paid)500
(Free)‡4,700

**Uinta County Herald (9291)**
News Media Corp.
211 Hwy. 38 E.
Rochelle, IL 61068
Phone: (815)562-2061
Fax: (815)562-7048
Subject(s): Paid Community Newspapers
Circ: ‡4,700

**Bridgeport News (8107)**
3252 S Halsted
Chicago, IL 60608-6698
Phone: (312)842-5883
Fax: (312)842-5097
Subject(s): Free Newspapers
Circ: (Combined)4,680

**Gurnee Press (8761)**
Lakeland Media Inc.
30 S Whitney St.
PO Box 268
Grayslake, IL 60030-0268
Phone: (847)223-8161
Fax: (847)223-8810
Subject(s): Paid Community Newspapers
Circ: 4,618

**River Falls Journal (33523)**
The River Falls Journal
2815 Praire Dr.
PO Box 25
River Falls, WI 54022
Phone: (715)425-1561
Fax: (715)425-5666
Subject(s): Paid Community Newspapers
Circ: ‡4,600

**Stoughton Courier Hub (33561)**
Woodward Communications
135 W Main St., Ste. 102
Stoughton, WI 53589-2135
Subject(s): Paid Community Newspapers
Circ: ⊕4,600

**Marquette County Tribune (33383)**
News Publishing Company Inc.
PO Box 188
120 Underwood Ave.
Marquette County Tribune
Montello, WI 53949
Phone: (608)297-2424
Fax: (608)297-9283

Subject(s): Paid Community Newspapers
Circ: (Free)‡44
(Paid)‡4,585

**Morgan County Herald (24892)**
89 W Main St.
Box 268
McConnelsville, OH 43756
Phone: (740)962-3377
Fax: (740)962-6861
Subject(s): Paid Community Newspapers
Circ: ‡4,582

**American News (16392)**
Montevideo Publishing Co.
PO Box 99
223 1st St.
Montevideo, MN 56265
Phone: (320)269-2156
Fax: (320)269-2159
Subject(s): Paid Community Newspapers
Circ: (Free)30
(Paid)4,566

**Banner Journal (32857)**
409 E Main St.
Black River Falls, WI 54615
Phone: (715)284-4304
Fax: (715)284-4634
Subject(s): Paid Community Newspapers
Circ: ‡4,560

**Oak Creek Pictorial (33412)**
Community Newspapers
15700 W Cleveland Ave.
New Berlin, WI 53151
Phone: (262)938-5000
Fax: (262)938-5001
Subject(s): Paid Community Newspapers
Circ: 4,566

**Daily Tribune (15119)**
Cheboygan Daily Tribune Inc.
308 N. Main St.
PO Box 290
Cheboygan, MI 49721
Phone: (231)627-7144
Fax: (231)627-5331
Subject(s): Daily Newspapers
Circ: (Non-paid)450
(Paid)4,550

**Gazette-Democrat (7838)**
Reppert Publications
PO Box 529
Anna, IL 62906
Phone: (618)833-2158
Fax: (618)833-5813
Subject(s): Paid Community Newspapers
Circ: (Thurs.)4,558

**Logan Daily News (24839)**
Brown Publishing Co.
72 E Main St.
PO Box 758
Logan, OH 43138-0758
Fax: (614)385-4514
Subject(s): Daily Newspapers
Circ: (Mon.-Sat.)4,533

**The Herald-Tribune (9561)**
CNHI
701 Tekulve Road
PO Box 89
Batesville, IN 47006
Phone: (812)934-4343
Fax: (812)934-6406
Subject(s): Paid Community Newspapers
Circ: ‡4,500

**Holmes County Hub (24913)**
25 N Clay St.
PO Box 151
Millersburg, OH 44654-0151
Phone: (330)674-1811
Fax: (330)674-3780
Subject(s): Paid Community Newspapers
Circ: ‡4,500

**The News Democrat (24747)**
Brown Publishing
111 W. Cherry St.
PO Box 169
Georgetown, OH 45121-0169
Phone: (513)378-6161

Fax: (513)378-2004
Subject(s): Paid Community Newspapers
Circ: (Free)200
(Paid)4,500

**Palos Citizen (8975)**
Southwest Messenger Press Inc.
3840 W 147th St.
PO Box 548
Midlothian, IL 60445
Phone: (708)388-2425
Fax: (708)385-7811
Subject(s): Paid Community Newspapers
Circ: (Free)‡500
(Paid)‡4,500

**Stearns-Morrison Enterprise (15918)**
Stearn-Morrison
PO Box 310
Albany, MN 56307
Phone: (320)845-2700
Fax: (320)845-4805
Subject(s): Paid Community Newspapers
Circ: 4,500

**The Tribune (24800)**
Gazette Printing Company Inc.
34 S Chestnut St.
Jefferson, OH 44047
Phone: (440)576-9115
Fax: (440)576-4337
Subject(s): Paid Community Newspapers
Circ: (Paid)4,500

**Clearwater Tribune (15964)**
West Sherburne Tribune
29 S Lake St.
PO Box 276
Big Lake, MN 55309
Phone: (763)263-3602
Fax: (763)263-8458
Subject(s): Free Newspapers
Circ: (Non-paid)4,476

**Inter-County Leader (32992)**
Inter-County Co-op Publishing Association
303 N Wisconsin Ave.
PO Box 490
Frederic, WI 54837
Phone: (715)327-4236
Fax: (715)327-4870
Subject(s): Paid Community Newspapers
Circ: ‡4,478

**Lake Orion Eccentric (15503)**
Observer & Eccentric Newspapers
36251 Schoolcraft Rd.
Livonia, MI 48150
Phone: (734)591-2300
Fax: (734)953-2232
Subject(s): Paid Community Newspapers
Circ: (Thurs.)4,460

**Wayzata Sun-Sailor (16390)**
Minnesota Sun Publications
13911 Ridgedale Dr.
Minnetonka, MN 55305
Phone: (612)546-7484
Fax: (612)546-7484
Subject(s): Free Newspapers
Circ: (Paid)272
(Non-paid)4,461

**Benzie County Record-Patriot (15304)**
The Pioneer Group
417 Main St.
PO Box 673
Frankfort, MI 49635
Phone: (616)352-9659
Fax: (616)352-7874
Subject(s): Paid Community Newspapers
Circ: ‡4,427

**Evergreen Park Courier (8969)**
Southwest Messenger Press Inc.
3840 W 147th St.
PO Box 548
Midlothian, IL 60445
Phone: (708)388-2425
Fax: (708)385-7811
Subject(s): Free Newspapers
Circ: (Free)‡500
(Paid)‡4,410

**German Village Gazette (24553)**
Suburban News Publications
5257 Sinclair Rd.
PO Box 29912
Columbus, OH 43229
Phone: (614)785-1212
Fax: (614)785-1881
**Subject(s):** Free Newspapers
**Circ:** (Paid)30
(Non-paid)4,418

**Round Lake News (9330)**
Lakeland Media Inc.
30 S Whitney St.
PO Box 268
Grayslake, IL 60030-0268
Phone: (847)223-8161
Fax: (847)223-8810
**Subject(s):** Paid Community Newspapers
**Circ:** ‡4,410

**Beacon (16001)**
Box 366
Cannon Falls, MN 55009
Phone: (507)263-3991
**Subject(s):** Paid Community Newspapers
**Circ:** ‡4,400

**The Bee (33463)**
Murphy McGinnis Media Inc.
115 N Lake Ave.
PO BOX 170
Phillips, WI 54555
Phone: (715)339-3036
Fax: (715)339-4300
**Subject(s):** Paid Community Newspapers
**Circ:** (Non-paid)♦10
(Paid)♦4,405

**Brown County Democrat (10056)**
Home News Enterprizes
147 East Main St.
PO Box 277
Nashville, IN 47448
Phone: (812)988-2221
Fax: (812)988-6502
**Subject(s):** Paid Community Newspapers
**Circ:** ‡4,406

**The News Leader (24917)**
Alliance Publishing Company Inc.
PO Box 30
177 Curry St.
Minerva, OH 44657
Phone: (330)868-5164
Fax: (330)868-3273
**Subject(s):** Paid Community Newspapers
**Circ:** ‡4,400

**The News Leader (24853)**
Alliance Publishing Company Inc.
PO Box 527
Malvern, OH 44644
Phone: (330)868-3408
Fax: (330)868-3273
**Subject(s):** Paid Community Newspapers
**Circ:** ‡4,400

**News-Sun (9707)**
PO Box 25
Fairmount, IN 46928
Phone: (317)948-4164
**Subject(s):** Free Newspapers
**Circ:** (Mon.-Sat.)4,400

**The Oxford Press (24981)**
15 S. Beech St.
Oxford, OH 45056
Phone: (513)523-4139
Fax: (513)523-1935
**Subject(s):** Paid Community Newspapers
**Circ:** ‡4,400

**Perry County Tribune (24936)**
Hirt Media
PO Box 312
New Lexington, OH 43764
Phone: (740)342-4121
Fax: (740)342-4131
**Subject(s):** Paid Community Newspapers
**Circ:** ‡4,400

**Presque Isle County Advance (15656)**
Presque Newspaper
PO Box 176
Onaway, MI 49765-0176
Phone: (989)733-6543
Fax: (989)733-6572
**Subject(s):** Paid Community Newspapers
**Circ:** 4,400

**Tomahawk Leader (33582)**
PO Box 345
Tomahawk, WI 54487
Phone: (715)453-2151
Fax: (715)453-1865
**Subject(s):** Paid Community Newspapers
**Circ:** (Paid)‡4,377

**Phillips Bee (33465)**
Price County Publications
115 N Lake Ave.
PO Box 170
Phillips, WI 54555
Phone: (715)339-3036
Fax: (715)339-4300
**Subject(s):** Free Newspapers
**Circ:** (Paid)4,346

**Franklin-Hales Corners Hub (33402)**
Community Newspapers
15700 W Cleveland Ave.
New Berlin, WI 53151
Phone: (262)938-5000
Fax: (262)938-5001
**Subject(s):** Paid Community Newspapers
**Circ:** 4,324

**The Courier-Wedge (32915)**
Valley Publications
103 W Main St
Durand, WI 54736
Phone: (715)672-4252
Fax: (715)672-4254
**Subject(s):** Paid Community Newspapers
**Circ:** 4,300

**Evansville Review (32947)**
Evansville Review Ltd.
PO Box 77
Evansville, WI 53536
Phone: (608)882-5220
Fax: (608)882-5221
**Subject(s):** Paid Community Newspapers
**Circ:** 4,300

**New Berlin Citizen (33410)**
Community Newspapers
15700 W Cleveland Ave.
New Berlin, WI 53151
Phone: (262)938-5000
Fax: (262)938-5001
**Subject(s):** Paid Community Newspapers
**Circ:** 4,309

**New Prague Times (16419)**
200 E Main St.
PO Box 25
New Prague, MN 56071
Phone: (952)758-4435
Fax: (952)758-4135
**Subject(s):** Paid Community Newspapers
**Circ:** 4,300

**Oconto County Reporter (33434)**
PO Box 200
Oconto, WI 54153
Phone: (920)834-4242
Fax: (920)834-4878
**Subject(s):** Paid Community Newspapers
**Circ:** 4,300

**Paulding Progress (24992)**
Eagle Print
113 S. William St.
PO Box 180
Paulding, OH 45879
Phone: (419)399-4015
Fax: (419)399-4030
**Subject(s):** Paid Community Newspapers
**Circ:** ‡4,300

**The Chanhassen Villager (16005)**
Southwest Suburban Publishing
80 W. 78th St.
No. 170
PO Box 99
Chanhassen, MN 55317
Phone: (952)934-5045
Fax: (952)934-7690
**Subject(s):** Free Newspapers
**Circ:** (Paid)‡85
(Free)‡4,290

**Crosby-Ironton Courier (16035)**
Crosby-Ironton Courier Inc.
12 E Main St.
PO Box 67
Crosby, MN 56441-0067
Phone: (218)546-5029
Fax: (218)546-8352
**Subject(s):** Paid Community Newspapers
**Circ:** (Free)51
(Paid)4,282

**Milford Miami Advertiser (24909)**
Press Community Newspapers
394 Wards Corner Rd.
Loveland, OH 45140
Phone: (513)248-8600
Fax: (513)248-1938
**Subject(s):** Paid Community Newspapers
**Circ:** (Paid)4,108
(Non-paid)4,282

**Bedford Sun Banner (24175)**
Sun Newspapers
3355 Richmond Rd., Ste. 171
Beachwood, OH 44122-4171
Phone: (216)986-5890
Fax: (216)464-8816
**Subject(s):** Paid Community Newspapers
**Circ:** (Paid)4,274

**Dunn County News, Shopper, and Reminder (33274)**
Lee Enterprises
710 E Main St.
Menomonie, WI 54751
Phone: (715)235-3411
Fax: (715)235-0936
**Subject(s):** Paid Community Newspapers
**Circ:** (Wed.)4,273
(Sun.)4,273

**Baraboo News Republic (32830)**
219 1st St.
PO Box 9
Baraboo, WI 53913
Phone: (608)356-4808
Fax: (608)356-0344
**Subject(s):** Daily Newspapers
**Circ:** (Mon.-Sat.)★4,257

**Glen Ellyn Press (8729)**
Liberty Surburban Chicago Newspapers
709 Enterprise Dr.
Oak Brook, IL 60523-8814
Phone: (708)352-9852
Fax: (708)834-0910
**Subject(s):** Free Newspapers; Free Newspapers
**Circ:** (Paid)‡219
(Free)‡4,252

**L'Anse Sentinel (15507)**
L'Anse Sentinel Inc.
202 N Main
PO Box 7
Lanse, MI 49946
Phone: (906)524-6194
Fax: (906)524-6197
**Subject(s):** Paid Community Newspapers
**Circ:** ‡4,241

**The Monroe Guardian (15600)**
Heritage Newspapers Inc.
15649 S. Telegraph Rd.
Monroe, MI 48161
Phone: (734)243-2100
**Subject(s):** Paid Community Newspapers
**Circ:** (Paid)♦801
(Non-paid)♦4,242

**The Leader (9967)**
15 N. Main St.
PO Box 38
Knox, IN 46534
Phone: (574)772-2101

Fax: (574)772-7041
**Subject(s):** Paid Community Newspapers
**Circ:** ‡4,237

**Boonville Standard (9628)**
Warrick Publishing Co.
204 W. Locust St.
PO Box 266
Boonville, IN 47601
Phone: (812)897-2330
Fax: (812)897-3703
**Subject(s):** Paid Community Newspapers
**Circ:** (Paid)4,219

**Chaska Herald (16006)**
Southwest Suburban Publishing
123 W. 2nd St.
PO Box 113
Chaska, MN 55318
Phone: (952)448-2650
Fax: (952)448-3146
**Subject(s):** Paid Community Newspapers
**Circ:** (Free)400
(Paid)4,200

**Coon Rapids Herald (16028)**
Anoka County Shopper
4101 Coon Rapids Blvd.
PO Box 99
Coon Rapids, MN 55433
Phone: (763)421-4444
Fax: (763)421-4315
**Subject(s):** Paid Community Newspapers
**Circ:** (Paid)‡4,200

**The County Journal (33594)**
PO Box 637
324 West Bayfield Street
Washburn, WI 54891-0637
Phone: (715)373-5500
Fax: (715)373-5546
**Subject(s):** Paid Community Newspapers
**Circ:** 4,200

**The Gazette (24796)**
Gazette Printing Company Inc.
34 S. Chestnut St.
Jefferson, OH 44047
Phone: (440)576-9115
Fax: (440)576-4337
**Subject(s):** Paid Community Newspapers
**Circ:** (Paid)‡4,200

**Platteville Journal (33468)**
1190 W Hwy. 151
Platteville, WI 53818-0266
Phone: (608)348-3006
Fax: (608)348-7979
**Subject(s):** Paid Community Newspapers
**Circ:** (Paid)‡4,200

**Willard Times Junction (25169)**
211 Myrtle Ave.
PO Box 368
Willard, OH 44890
Phone: (419)935-0184
Fax: (419)933-2031
**Subject(s):** Paid Community Newspapers
**Circ:** (Paid)⊕**4,200**

**Crookston Daily Times (16033)**
Crookston Times Printing Co.
124 S Broadway St.
PO Box 615
Crookston, MN 56716
Phone: (218)281-2730
Fax: (218)281-7234
**Subject(s):** Daily Newspapers
**Circ:** (Free)250
(Paid)4,195

**Fairborn Daily Herald (24718)**
Times Community Newspapers
PO Box 1352
Fairborn, OH 45324-1352
**Subject(s):** Daily Newspapers
**Circ:** (Paid)4,197

**The Booster (8885)**
Lerner Communications Inc.
7331 N Lincoln Ave.
Lincolnwood, IL 60712
Phone: (847)329-2000
Fax: (847)329-2060

**Subject(s):** Paid Community Newspapers
**Circ:** (Paid)4,188

**Lake County Star (15041)**
The Pioneer Group
851 Michigan
PO Box 399
Baldwin, MI 49304-0399
Phone: (231)745-4635
Fax: (231)745-7733
**Subject(s):** Shopping Guides
**Circ:** (Free)‡4,154

**Novi Spinal Column Newsweekly (15647)**
Spinal Column Publications
7196 Cooley Lake Rd.
PO Box 14
Union Lake, MI 48387-0014
Phone: (248)360-7355
Fax: (248)360-4711
**Subject(s):** Free Newspapers
**Circ:** (Free)‡4,150

**Antioch News (7841)**
Lakeland Media Inc.
30 S Whitney St.
PO Box 268
Grayslake, IL 60030-0268
Phone: (847)223-8161
Fax: (847)223-8810
**Subject(s):** Paid Community Newspapers
**Circ:** 4,132

**The Mayville News (33267)**
Wisconsin Free Press
PO Box 271
Mayville, WI 53050-0271
Phone: (920)387-2211
Fax: (920)387-5515
**Subject(s):** Paid Community Newspapers
**Circ:** 4,085
4,120

**The News Record (16688)**
Grimsrud Publishing Inc.
225 Main St.
PO Box 97
Zumbrota, MN 55992
Phone: (507)732-7617
Fax: (507)732-7619
**Subject(s):** Paid Community Newspapers
**Circ:** 4,123

**Tri-Village News (24606)**
Suburban News Publications
5257 Sinclair Rd.
PO Box 29912
Columbus, OH 43229
Phone: (614)785-1212
Fax: (614)785-1881
**Subject(s):** Free Newspapers
**Circ:** (Paid)368
(Non-paid)4,112

**Daily Republican Register (9001)**
115 E 4th St.
PO Box 550
Mount Carmel, IL 62863-0550
Phone: (618)262-5144
Fax: (618)263-4437
**Subject(s):** Daily Newspapers
**Circ:** (Free)⊕63
(Paid)⊕**4,094**

**East Grand Rapids Cadence (15336)**
Advance Newspapers
2141 Port Sheldon Rd.
PO Box 9
Jenison, MI 49428-9301
Phone: (616)669-2700
Fax: (616)669-1162
**Subject(s):** Paid Community Newspapers
**Circ:** (Paid)❑423
(Free)❑**4,097**

**Beverly News (8965)**
Southwest Messenger Press Inc.
3840 W 147th St.
PO Box 548
Midlothian, IL 60445
Phone: (708)388-2425
Fax: (708)385-7811
**Subject(s):** Free Newspapers
**Circ:** (Free)‡100
(Paid)‡4,080

**The Courier-Leader (15667)**
PO Box 129
Paw Paw, MI 49079-0129
Phone: (616)657-3072
Fax: (616)657-5723
**Subject(s):** Paid Community Newspapers; Farm Newspapers
**Circ:** (Free)45
(Paid)⊕**4,069**

**Southwestern Shoppers Guide (7932)**
Bunker Hill Publications
PO Box 606
Brighton, IL 62012
Phone: (618)372-8451
Fax: (618)372-4925
**Subject(s):** Shopping Guides
**Circ:** (Free)‡4,044

**Shelby Daily Globe (25038)**
Shelby Daily Globe Inc.
37 W Main St.
PO Box 647
Shelby, OH 44875-0647
Phone: (419)342-4276
Fax: (419)342-4246
**Subject(s):** Daily Newspapers
**Circ:** (Non-paid)⊕20
(Paid)⊕**4,035**

**Berlin Journal (32848)**
Berlin Journal Newspapers
PO Box 10
Berlin, WI 54923-0010
Phone: (920)361-1515
Fax: (920)361-1518
**Subject(s):** Paid Community Newspapers
**Circ:** ‡4,000

**Calhoun News-Herald (8766)**
310 S County Rd.
PO Box 367
Hardin, IL 62047
Phone: (618)576-2345
Fax: (618)576-2245
**Subject(s):** Paid Community Newspapers
**Circ:** ‡4,000

**The Concordian (16399)**
Concordia College
FPO 104, Concordia College 901 8th St., S.
Moorhead, MN 56562
Phone: (218)299-3826
Fax: (218)299-4313
**Subject(s):** College Publications
**Circ:** ‡4000

**Daily Record (8858)**
1209 State St.
PO Box 559
Lawrenceville, IL 62439
Phone: (618)943-2331
Fax: (618)943-3976
**Subject(s):** Daily Newspapers
**Circ:** (Paid)4,005

**Daily Review Atlas (9111)**
Liberty Group Publishing
3000 Dundee Rd., Ste. 202
Northbrook, IL 60062
Phone: (847)272-2244
Fax: (847)272-6244
**Subject(s):** Daily Newspapers
**Circ:** ‡4,000

**The Edgerton Reporter (32942)**
The Reporter Company Inc.
21 N Henry St.
Edgerton, WI 53534
Phone: (608)884-3367
Fax: (608)884-8187
**Subject(s):** Paid Community Newspapers
**Circ:** ‡4,000

**The Elburn Herald (8630)**
Kaneland Publications Inc.
123 N Main St.
Elburn, IL 60119
Phone: (630)365-6446
Fax: (630)365-2251
**Subject(s):** Paid Community Newspapers
**Circ:** 4,000

**Grant County Herald Independent (33141)**
208 W Cherry St.
Lancaster, WI 53813
Phone: (608)723-2151
Fax: (608)723-7272
Subject(s): Paid Community Newspapers
Circ: ‡4,000

**The Greenwood and Southside Challenger (9786)**
PO Box 708
Greenwood, IN 46142
Phone: (317)888-3376
Fax: (317)888-3377
Subject(s): Paid Community Newspapers
Circ: ‡4,000

**Hancock County Journal Pilot (7992)**
31 N Washington
PO Box 478
Carthage, IL 62321-0478
Phone: (217)357-2149
Fax: (217)357-2177
Subject(s): Paid Community Newspapers
Circ: (Paid)‡4,000

**The Journal (25076)**
23 Lowellville Rd.
Struthers, OH 44471
Phone: (330)755-2155
Fax: (330)755-0320
Subject(s): Paid Community Newspapers
Circ: ‡4,000

**Newton Press-Mentor (9056)**
700 W Washington
PO Box 151
Newton, IL 62448-0151
Phone: (618)783-2324
Fax: (618)783-2325
Subject(s): Paid Community Newspapers
Circ: ‡4,000

**O'Fallon Progress (9137)**
PO Box 970
1840 Greenmoun Rd., Ste. 200
O Fallon, IL 62269-0970
Phone: (618)632-3643
Fax: (618)632-6438
Subject(s): Paid Community Newspapers
Circ: 4,000

**Pioneer-Tribune (15569)**
212 Walnut St.
Manistique, MI 49854
Phone: (906)341-5200
Fax: (906)341-5914
Subject(s): Paid Community Newspapers
Circ: 4,000

**The Pointer (33555)**
University of Wisconsin-Stevens Point
104 CAC
Stevens Point, WI 54481
Subject(s): College Publications
Circ: 4,000

**The Progressor-Times (24252)**
1198 E Findlay St.
PO Box 37
Carey, OH 43316
Phone: (419)396-7567
Fax: (419)396-7527
Subject(s): Paid Community Newspapers
Circ: (Combined)‡4,000

**Richland Observer (33513)**
172 E Court St.
Box 31
Richland Center, WI 53581-0031
Phone: (608)647-6141
Fax: (608)647-6143
Subject(s): Paid Community Newspapers
Circ: 4,000

**Sauk-Prairie Star (33528)**
News Publishing Black Earth
801 Water St.
PO Box 606
Sauk City, WI 53583
Phone: (608)643-3444
Fax: (608)643-4988
Subject(s): Paid Community Newspapers
Circ: 4,000

**Tri-County News (33121)**
Delta Publications Inc.
606 Fremont St.
Kiel, WI 53042
Phone: (920)894-2828
Fax: (920)894-2161
Subject(s): Paid Community Newspapers
Circ: (Free)200
(Paid)4,000

**Triad (33654)**
Foxxy Shopper
PO Box 847
West Salem, WI 54669
Phone: (608)786-1950
Fax: (608)269-1488
Subject(s): Paid Community Newspapers
Circ: (Free)‡4,000

**Zionsville Times Sentinel (10268)**
250 S Elm St.
Zionsville, IN 46077-1601
Phone: (317)873-6397
Fax: (317)873-6259
Subject(s): Paid Community Newspapers
Circ: ‡4,000

**Rushville Republican (10143)**
Rushville Newspapers Inc.
PO Box 189
306 North Main St.
Rushville, IN 46173-0189
Phone: (765)932-2222
Fax: (765)932-4358
Subject(s): Daily Newspapers
Circ: ‡3,983

**Highland Spinal Column Newsweekly (15400)**
Spinal Column Publications
7196 Cooley Lake Rd.
PO Box 14
Union Lake, MI 48387-0014
Phone: (248)360-7355
Fax: (248)360-4711
Subject(s): Free Newspapers
Circ: (Free)‡3,950

**Marion Daily Republican (8932)**
Liberty Group
502 W Jackson St.
PO Box 490
Marion, IL 62959-0490
Phone: (618)993-2626
Fax: (618)993-8326
Subject(s): Daily Newspapers
Circ: (Paid)3,958

**The Leader and the Kalkaskian (15495)**
318 N. Cedar St.
Kalkaska, MI 49646
Phone: (231)258-4600
Fax: (231)258-4603
Subject(s): Paid Community Newspapers
Circ: 3,900

**Staunton Star-Times (9426)**
Star-Times Publishing Company Inc.
108 W Main St.
PO Box 180
Staunton, IL 62088
Phone: (618)635-2000
Fax: (618)635-5281
Subject(s): Paid Community Newspapers
Circ: (Paid)‡3,891

**Pioneer Journal (16683)**
Wadena Pioneer Journal
314 S Jefferson
PO Box 31
Wadena, MN 56482
Phone: (218)631-2561
Fax: (218)631-1621
Subject(s): Paid Community Newspapers
Circ: (Combined)3,875

**Bloomer Advance (32861)**
PO Box 25
Bloomer, WI 54724
Phone: (715)568-3100
Fax: (715)568-3111
Subject(s): Paid Community Newspapers
Circ: ‡3,850

**Oakland City Journal Dollar Saver (10096)**
Princeton Publishing Inc.
222 N. Main St.
PO Box 187
Oakland City, IN 47660
Phone: (812)749-3913
Subject(s): Shopping Guides
Circ: (Free)‡3,850

**Chicago County Press (16214)**
12615 Lake Blvd.
(Hwy. 8, west end of town)
PO Box 748
Lindstrom, MN 55045
Phone: (651)257-5115
Fax: (651)257-5500
Subject(s): Paid Community Newspapers
Circ: (Free)‡30
(Paid)‡3,835

**Vadnais Heights Press (16707)**
Press Publications
4779 Bloom Ave.
White Bear Lake, MN 55110
Phone: (651)407-1200
Fax: (651)429-1242
Subject(s): Free Newspapers
Circ: (Paid)316
(Non-paid)3,833

**Geneseo Republic (8719)**
108 W 1st St.
Geneseo, IL 61254-0209
Phone: (309)944-2119
Fax: (309)944-5615
Subject(s): Paid Community Newspapers
Circ: 3,821

**The Clermont Sun (24160)**
465 E Main St.
PO Box 366
Batavia, OH 45103
Phone: (513)732-2511
Fax: (513)732-6344
Subject(s): Paid Community Newspapers
Circ: 3,800

**Cottonwood County Citizen (16714)**
260 10th St.
PO Box 309
Windom, MN 56101-0309
Phone: (507)831-3455
Fax: (507)831-3740
Subject(s): Paid Community Newspapers
Circ: ‡3,806

**The Jackson County Banner (9635)**
116 E Cross St.
PO Box G
Brownstown, IN 47220
Phone: (812)358-2111
Fax: (812)358-5606
Subject(s): Paid Community Newspapers
Circ: (Free)5
(Paid)3,800

**Litchfield Independent-Review (16216)**
PO Box 921
217 N. Sibley Ave.
Litchfield, MN 55355
Phone: (320)693-3266
Fax: (320)693-9177
Subject(s): Paid Community Newspapers
Circ: 3,800

**The News Bulletin (9216)**
Legal Record Corp.
PO Box 563
Peoria, IL 61651-0563
Phone: (309)672-1600
Fax: (888)568-7488
Subject(s): Daily Periodicals
Circ: (Paid)2,000
(Free)3,800

**News Progress (9437)**
100 W Monroe St.
PO Box 290
Sullivan, IL 61951-0290
Phone: (217)728-7381
Fax: (217)728-2020
Subject(s): Paid Community Newspapers
Circ: (Free)‡154
(Paid)‡3,800

**Minnesota Spokesman** (16323)
Minnesota Spokesman-Recorder
3744 4th Ave. S
Minneapolis, MN 55409
Phone: (612)827-4021
Fax: (612)827-0577
**Subject(s):** Paid Community Newspapers; Black Publications

Circ: (Free)‡517
(Paid)‡3,790

**Orland Township Messenger** (8974)
Southwest Messenger Press Inc.
3840 W 147th St.
PO Box 548
Midlothian, IL 60445
Phone: (708)388-2425
Fax: (708)385-7811
**Subject(s):** Free Newspapers

Circ: (Free)‡200
(Paid)‡3,788

**Burnett County Sentinel** (33004)
114 Madison Ave.
Box 397
Grantsburg, WI 54840-0397
Phone: (715)463-2341
Fax: (715)463-5138
**Subject(s):** Paid Community Newspapers

Circ: (Combined)3,750

**Daily Clay County Advocate-Press** (8697)
Clay County Advocate Press Inc.
105 W N Ave.
PO Box 519
Flora, IL 62839-1613
Phone: (618)662-2108
Fax: (618)662-2939
**Subject(s):** Daily Newspapers

Circ: (Free)50
(Paid)3,750

**The Marcolian** (24870)
Marietta College
Campus Mail Box A-20
Marietta, OH 45750-4000
Phone: (740)376-4555
**Subject(s):** College Publications

Circ: (Paid)‡250
(Free)‡3,750

**OCCurrence** (8586)
Oakton Community College
1600 E Golf Rd.
Des Plaines, IL 60016
Phone: (847)635-1600
Fax: (847)635-2610
**Subject(s):** College Publications

Circ: (Free)‡3,750

**The Ontonagon Herald** (15657)
326 River St.
Ontonagon, MI 49953
Phone: (906)884-2826
Fax: (906)884-2939
**Subject(s):** Paid Community Newspapers

Circ: 3,750

**The Review-Republican** (10264)
Kankakee Valley Publishing
38 N Monroe
Box 216
Williamsport, IN 47993
Phone: (765)762-3322
Fax: (765)762-6418
**Subject(s):** Paid Community Newspapers

Circ: ‡3,750

**Tri County Today** (9544)
C/O Fox Alley Shopping News
PO Box 609
Yorkville, IL 60560
Phone: (815)786-2125
Fax: (815)553-0310
**Subject(s):** Paid Community Newspapers

Circ: 3,735

**Waseca County News** (16693)
PO Box 465
Waseca, MN 56093
Phone: (507)835-3380
Fax: (507)835-3435
**Subject(s):** Paid Community Newspapers

Circ: (Paid)‡3,727

**Pipestone County Star** (16480)
Pipestone Publishing Co.
115 2nd St. NE
Box 277
Pipestone, MN 56164-0277
Phone: (507)825-3333
Fax: (507)825-2168
**Subject(s):** Paid Community Newspapers

Circ: (Non-paid)99
(Paid)3,714

**The Advocate-Tribune** (16155)
PO Box 99
713 Prentice
Granite Falls, MN 56241-0099
Phone: (320)564-2126
Fax: (320)564-4293
**Subject(s):** Free Newspapers

Circ: (Free)‡100
(Paid)‡3,700

**The Ripon Commonwealth Express** (33516)
Ripon Community Printer
PO Box 344
Ripon, WI 54971
Phone: (920)748-3017
Fax: (920)748-3028
**Subject(s):** Paid Community Newspapers

Circ: ‡3,700

**The Vinton County Advertiser** (24792)
Add Inc.—Ohio Group
300 Morton St.
Jackson, OH 45640
Phone: (740)286-7571
Fax: (740)286-4766
**Subject(s):** Shopping Guides

Circ: (Non-paid)3,690

**Bedford Times-Register** (24176)
Record Publishing Co.
711 Broadway Ave.
PO Box 46059
Bedford, OH 44146-0059
Phone: (440)232-8861
Fax: (440)232-8861
**Subject(s):** Paid Community Newspapers

Circ: ‡3,674

**Princeton Union-Eagle** (16029)
E.C.M. Publishers Inc.
4095 Coon Rapids Blvd.
Coon Rapids, MN 55433
Phone: (763)712-2400
Fax: (763)712-2480
**Subject(s):** Paid Community Newspapers

Circ: (Free)70
(Paid)3,666

**The Clark County Press** (33392)
News Publishing
614 Hewett St.
PO Box 149
Neillsville, WI 54456
Phone: (715)743-2600
Fax: (715)743-5460
**Subject(s):** Paid Community Newspapers

Circ: (Paid)3,650

**Cook News-Herald** (16024)
Cook News
PO Box 1179
Cook, MN 55723
Phone: (218)666-5944
Fax: (218)666-5609
**Subject(s):** Paid Community Newspapers

Circ: 3,652

**The Ortonville Independent** (16448)
Kaercher Publications
P O Box 336
29 North West Second Street
Ortonville, MN 56278-0336
Phone: (320)839-6163
Fax: (320)839-3761
**Subject(s):** Paid Community Newspapers

Circ: ‡3,650

**South Milwaukee Voice Graphic** (33416)
Community Newspapers
15700 W Cleveland Ave.
New Berlin, WI 53151
Phone: (262)938-5000
Fax: (262)938-5001

**Subject(s):** Paid Community Newspapers

Circ: 3,645

**Cook County News-Herald** (16147)
Murphy McGinnis Media Inc.
PO Box 757
Grand Marais, MN 55604
Phone: (218)387-1025
Fax: (218)387-2539
**Subject(s):** Paid Community Newspapers

Circ: (Non-paid)♦193
(Paid)♦3,617

**Wauconda Leader** (9511)
Lakeland Media Inc.
30 S Whitney St.
PO Box 268
Grayslake, IL 60030-0268
Phone: (847)223-8161
Fax: (847)223-8810
**Subject(s):** Paid Community Newspapers

Circ: ‡3,615

**The Chetek Alert** (32883)
312 Knapp St.
PO Box 5
Chetek, WI 54728
Phone: (715)924-4118
Fax: (715)924-4122
**Subject(s):** Paid Community Newspapers

Circ: ‡3,600

**Chicago Ridge Citizen** (8968)
Southwest Messenger Press Inc.
3840 W 147th St.
PO Box 548
Midlothian, IL 60445
Phone: (708)388-2425
Fax: (708)385-7811
**Subject(s):** Free Newspapers

Circ: (Free)‡300
(Paid)‡3,600

**The Dexter Leader** (15221)
Heritage Newspapers Inc.
8005 Main St.
Dexter, MI 48130
Phone: (734)475-1371
**Subject(s):** Paid Community Newspapers

Circ: (Non-paid)♦21
(Paid)♦3,600

**Kendall County Record** (9542)
Kendall County Record Inc.
222 S Bridge St.
PO Box J
Yorkville, IL 60560
Phone: (630)553-7034
Fax: (630)553-7085
**Subject(s):** Paid Community Newspapers

Circ: ‡3,600

**The Mackinac Island Town Crier** (15562)
Maurer Publishing Co.
359 Reagon St.
PO Box 277
Saint Ignace, MI 49781
Phone: (906)643-9150
Fax: (906)643-9122
**Subject(s):** Paid Community Newspapers

Circ: ‡3,600

**Newberry News** (15635)
Newberry News Inc.
PO Box 46
Newberry, MI 49868
Phone: (906)293-8401
Fax: (906)293-8815
**Subject(s):** Paid Community Newspapers

Circ: 3,600

**Piatt County Journal-Republican** (8994)
East Central Communications Inc.
118 E Washington
PO Box 110
Monticello, IL 61856
Phone: (217)762-2511
Fax: (217)762-8591
**Subject(s):** Paid Community Newspapers

Circ: (Non-paid)98
(Paid)3,608

# Great Lakes States

**Pulaski County Journal (10265)**
PO Box 19
Winamac, IN 46996-0019
Phone: (574)946-6628
Fax: (574)946-7471
**Subject(s):** Paid Community Newspapers
**Circ:** 3600

**Rensselaer Republican (10124)**
Kankakee Valley Publishing Co.
PO Box 298
117 N. Rensselaer
Rensselaer, IN 47978-0298
Phone: (219)866-5111
Fax: (219)866-3775
**Subject(s):** Daily Newspapers
**Circ:** ‡3,600

**Sleepy Eye Herald-Dispatch (16648)**
115 2nd Ave. NE
Sleepy Eye, MN 56085
Phone: (507)794-3511
Fax: (507)794-5031
**Subject(s):** Paid Community Newspapers
**Circ:** (Free)‡310
   (Paid)‡3,600

**Delano Eagle (16040)**
Sun Press and News Publications
PO Box 168
Delano, MN 55328-0168
Phone: (763)972-6171
**Subject(s):** Paid Community Newspapers
**Circ:** (Paid)1,331
   (Free)3,598

**Drum Corps World (33173)**
Sights and Sounds Inc.
1410 Northport Dr., Lower Level
PO Box 8052
Madison, WI 53708-8052
Phone: (608)241-2292
Fax: (608)241-4974
**Subject(s):** Music and Musical Instruments
**Circ:** ‡3,582

**Grove City Record (24759)**
The Grove City Record
4048 Broadway
Grove City, OH 43123
Phone: (614)875-2307
Fax: (614)875-6028
**Subject(s):** Paid Community Newspapers
**Circ:** (Paid)‡3,587

**Muskego Sun (33409)**
Community Newspapers
15700 W Cleveland Ave.
New Berlin, WI 53151
Phone: (262)938-5000
Fax: (262)938-5001
**Subject(s):** Paid Community Newspapers
**Circ:** 3,574

**Sun-Tribune (16409)**
Morris Sun-Tribune
108 E 6th St.
PO Box 470
Morris, MN 56267
Phone: (320)589-2525
**Subject(s):** Paid Community Newspapers
**Circ:** (Free)‡62
   (Paid)‡3,568

**World (10174)**
Spencer Evening World
114 E Franklin St.
P.O. Box 226
Spencer, IN 47460
Phone: (812)829-2255
Fax: (812)829-4666
**Subject(s):** Daily Newspapers
**Circ:** (Paid)‡3,550

**Hickory Hills Citizen (8970)**
Southwest Messenger Press Inc.
3840 W 147th St.
PO Box 548
Midlothian, IL 60445
Phone: (708)388-2425
Fax: (708)385-7811
**Subject(s):** Free Newspapers
**Circ:** (Free)‡400
   (Paid)‡3,530

**Pine City Pioneer (16472)**
405 SE 2nd Ave.
Pine City, MN 55063
Phone: (320)629-6771
Fax: (320)629-6772
**Subject(s):** Paid Community Newspapers
**Circ:** ‡3,532

**The Beacher (10023)**
911 Franklin St.
Michigan City, IN 46360
Phone: (219)879-0088
Fax: (219)879-8070
**Subject(s):** Local, State, and Regional Publications
**Circ:** 3,500

**Belle Plaine Herald (15951)**
113 East Main
PO Box 7
Belle Plaine, MN 56011
Phone: (952)873-2261
Fax: (952)873-2262
**Subject(s):** Paid Community Newspapers
**Circ:** 3,500

**Blade (8687)**
Liberty Group
125 W Locust St.
Fairbury, IL 61739
Phone: (815)692-2366
Fax: (815)692-3782
**Subject(s):** Paid Community Newspapers
**Circ:** ‡3,500

**Chimes (15333)**
Calvin College
3201 Burton SE
Grand Rapids, MI 49546
Phone: (616)526-6000
**Subject(s):** College Publications
**Circ:** (Paid)‡90
   (Free)‡3,500

**Clinton Daily Journal (8510)**
Rt. 54 W.
PO Box 615
Clinton, IL 61727
Phone: (217)935-3171
Fax: (217)935-6086
**Subject(s):** Daily Newspapers
**Circ:** (Non-paid)‡250
   (Paid)‡3,500

**The Collegiate (15335)**
Grand Rapids Community College
143 Bostwick NE
Grand Rapids, MI 49503-3295
Phone: (616)234-4000
Fax: (616)234-4158
**Subject(s):** College Publications
**Circ:** (Free)‡3,500

**Courier (9380)**
South Suburban College
15800 S State St., Rm. 3234
South Holland, IL 60473
Phone: (708)596-2000
Fax: (708)210-5776
**Subject(s):** College Publications
**Circ:** ‡3,500

**Enterprise Dispatch (16016)**
JEB Company, L.L.C.
225 Millard Ave.
Cokato, MN 55321
**Subject(s):** Paid Community Newspapers
**Circ:** 3,500

**Exponent (33466)**
University of Wisconsin-Platteville
1 University Plz.
Platteville, WI 53818
Phone: (608)342-1471
Fax: (608)342-1671
**Subject(s):** College Publications
**Circ:** ‡3,500

**The Ferdinand News (9708)**
Dubois Spencer Counties Publishing Company Inc.
PO Box 38
Ferdinand, IN 47532
Phone: (812)367-2041
Fax: (812)367-2371

**Subject(s):** Paid Community Newspapers
**Circ:** (Wed.)‡3,500

**Herald (16635)**
Sauk Centre Publishers Inc.
522 Sinclair Lewis Ave.
Sauk Centre, MN 56378
Phone: (320)352-6577
Fax: (320)352-5647
**Subject(s):** Paid Community Newspapers
**Circ:** 3,500

**The Manchester Signal (24854)**
414 E 7th Street
Manchester, OH 45144-1402
Phone: (937)549-2800
Fax: (937)549-3611
**Subject(s):** Paid Community Newspapers
**Circ:** (Paid)‡3,500

**The Newcomerstown News (24947)**
The Jeffersonion Co.
PO Box 30
Newcomerstown, OH 43832
Phone: (740)498-7117
Fax: (740)498-5624
**Subject(s):** Paid Community Newspapers
**Circ:** ‡3,500

**The Oberlin Review (24967)**
Oberlin College
135 W. Lorain St.
Wilder Box 90
Oberlin, OH 44074
Phone: (440)775-8123
Fax: (440)775-6733
**Subject(s):** College Publications
**Circ:** (Free)3,500

**Our Hope (9802)**
Croatian Catholic Union of U.S.A.
PO Box 602
Hobart, IN 46342-0602
Phone: (219)942-1191
Fax: (219)942-8808
**Subject(s):** Religious Publications; Ethnic Publications; Croatian
**Circ:** (Paid)‡50
   (Free)‡3,500

**Randolph County Herald Tribune (8049)**
Liberty Group Publishing
624 State St.
PO Box 269
Chester, IL 62233
Phone: (618)826-2385
Fax: (618)826-5181
**Subject(s):** Paid Community Newspapers
**Circ:** 3,500

**Sylvania Herald (25078)**
Herald Newspapers
5739 N Main St.
Sylvania, OH 43560
Phone: (419)885-9222
Fax: (419)885-0764
**Subject(s):** Paid Community Newspapers
**Circ:** 3,500

**Western Guard (16232)**
PO Box 187
Madison, MN 56256-0183
Phone: (320)598-7521
Fax: (320)598-7523
**Subject(s):** Paid Community Newspapers
**Circ:** ‡3,500

**Zion Benton News (9547)**
2719 Elisha Ave.
Zion, IL 60099
Phone: (847)746-9000
Fax: (847)746-9150
**Subject(s):** Paid Community Newspapers
**Circ:** ‡3,500

**Greenfield Observer (33406)**
Community Newspapers
15700 W Cleveland Ave.
New Berlin, WI 53151
Phone: (262)938-5000
Fax: (262)938-5001
**Subject(s):** Paid Community Newspapers
**Circ:** 3,469

**Lake County News-Chronicle (16672)**
Lake County Publications, In.
109 Waterfront Dr.
PO Box 158
Two Harbors, MN 55616
Phone: (218)834-2141
Fax: (218)834-2144
**Subject(s):** Paid Community Newspapers
**Circ:** (Non-paid)♦37
(Paid)♦3,468

**Mondovi Herald-News (33379)**
PO Box 67
Mondovi, WI 54755
Phone: (715)926-4970
Fax: (715)926-4928
**Subject(s):** Paid Community Newspapers
**Circ:** (Free)‡48
(Paid)‡3,460

**Cass City Chronicle (15103)**
6550 Main St.
Cass City, MI 48726
Phone: (989)872-2010
Fax: (989)872-3810
**Subject(s):** Paid Community Newspapers
**Circ:** ‡3,454

**Howard Lake-Waverly Montrose Herald Journal (16180)**
Herald Journal Publishing
PO Box 190
Howard Lake, MN 55349
**Subject(s):** Paid Community Newspapers
**Circ:** (Paid)‡3,450

**Perham Enterprise Bulletin (16469)**
222 2nd Ave. SE
PO Box 288
Perham, MN 56573
Phone: (218)346-5900
Fax: (218)346-5901
**Subject(s):** Paid Community Newspapers
**Circ:** 3,450

**Times (16397)**
Monticello Times Inc.
116 E. River St.
P.O. Box 420
Monticello, MN 55362
Phone: (763)295-3131
Fax: (763)295-3080
**Subject(s):** Paid Community Newspapers
**Circ:** ‡3,450

**Winsted-Lester Prairie Herald Journal (16730)**
Herald Journal Publishing
PO Box 129
Winsted, MN 55395
Phone: (320)485-2535
Fax: (320)485-2878
**Subject(s):** Paid Community Newspapers
**Circ:** (Paid)3,450

**Cudahy Reminder/Enterprise (33399)**
Community Newspapers
15700 W Cleveland Ave.
New Berlin, WI 53151
Phone: (262)938-5000
Fax: (262)938-5001
**Subject(s):** Paid Community Newspapers
**Circ:** 3,434

**Review-Messenger (16641)**
112 Minnesota Ave. W
PO Box 309
Sebeka, MN 56477
Phone: (218)837-5558
Fax: (218)837-5560
**Subject(s):** Paid Community Newspapers
**Circ:** ‡3,421

**Alcona County Review (15390)**
111 Lake St.
PO Box 548
Harrisville, MI 48740
Phone: (989)724-6384
Fax: (989)724-6655
**Subject(s):** Paid Community Newspapers
**Circ:** ‡3,400

**The Call-Leader (9689)**
Elwood Publishing Co.
317 South Anderson St.
P.O. Box 85
Elwood, IN 46036
Phone: (765)552-3355
Fax: (765)552-3358
**Subject(s):** Daily Newspapers
**Circ:** (Paid)‡3,400

**The Clarkston News (15129)**
Sherman Publications Inc.
5 S. Main
Clarkston, MI 48346
Phone: (248)625-3370
Fax: (248)625-0706
**Subject(s):** Paid Community Newspapers
**Circ:** (Paid)3,400

**De Pere Journal (32906)**
126 S Broadway
PO Box 5066
De Pere, WI 54115-5066
Phone: (920)336-4221
**Subject(s):** Paid Community Newspapers
**Circ:** 3,400

**Lake Orion Review (15504)**
30 N Broadway
Lake Orion, MI 48362
Phone: (248)693-8331
Fax: (248)693-5712
**Subject(s):** Paid Community Newspapers
**Circ:** 3,400

**The Menard Time (8955)**
Box 711
Menard, IL 62259
Phone: (618)826-5071
Fax: (618)826-2000
**Subject(s):** Police, Penology, and Penal Institutions
**Circ:** (Non-paid)‡3,400

**Elmwood Park/River Grove Times (8887)**
Lerner Communications Inc.
7331 N Lincoln Ave.
Lincolnwood, IL 60712
Phone: (847)329-2000
Fax: (847)329-2060
**Subject(s):** Free Newspapers
**Circ:** (Paid)♦3,399

**Plainview News (16483)**
Stump Publishing Co.
409 W Broadway, No. 457
Plainview, MN 55964
Phone: (507)534-3121
Fax: (507)534-3920
**Subject(s):** Paid Community Newspapers
**Circ:** 3,380

**Pelican Rapids Press (16465)**
29 W Mill
Box 632
Pelican Rapids, MN 56572-0632
Phone: (218)863-1421
Fax: (218)863-1423
**Subject(s):** Paid Community Newspapers
**Circ:** (Free)26
(Paid)3,369

**Carmi Times (7964)**
American Publishing Co.
323 E Main St.
PO Box 190
Carmi, IL 62821
Phone: (618)382-4176
Fax: (618)384-2163
**Subject(s):** Daily Newspapers
**Circ:** 3,350

**Times (9331)**
PO Box 226
110 E Lafayette
Rushville, IL 62681
Phone: (217)322-3321
Fax: (217)322-2770
**Subject(s):** Paid Community Newspapers
**Circ:** (Free)‡50
(Paid)‡3,325

**Republican Journal (32904)**
316 S Main St.
PO Box 20
Darlington, WI 53530
Phone: (608)776-4425
Fax: (608)776-4301
**Subject(s):** Paid Community Newspapers
**Circ:** 3,316

**Cass County Star-Gazette (7887)**
Beardstown Newspapers Inc.
1210 Wall St.
Beardstown, IL 62618
Phone: (217)323-1010
Fax: (217)323-5402
**Subject(s):** Paid Community Newspapers
**Circ:** (Combined)3,300

**Loogootee Tribune (10003)**
PO Box 277
104 W Maine St.
Loogootee, IN 47553-0277
Phone: (812)295-2500
Fax: (812)295-5221
**Subject(s):** Paid Community Newspapers
**Circ:** 3,300

**The Mail-Journal (10027)**
The Papers Inc.
206 S Main St.
PO Box 188
Milford, IN 46542-0188
Phone: (574)658-4111
Fax: (574)658-4701
**Subject(s):** Paid Community Newspapers
**Circ:** (Free)40
(Paid)3,300

**The Milton Courier (33288)**
Hometown News Group Publications
513 Vernal Ave.
PO Box 69
Milton, WI 53563
Phone: (608)868-2442
Fax: (608)868-4664
**Subject(s):** Paid Community Newspapers
**Circ:** ‡3,300

**The Daily American (9517)**
Liberty Group
Daily American
PO Box 617
West Frankfort, IL 62896
Phone: (618)932-2146
**Subject(s):** Daily Newspapers
**Circ:** (Combined)3,297

**The Oxford Leader (15666)**
Sherman Publications Inc.
PO Box 108
Oxford, MI 48371
Phone: (248)628-4801
Fax: (248)628-9750
**Subject(s):** Paid Community Newspapers
**Circ:** (Free)‡36
(Paid)‡3,297

**Manito Review (8941)**
Banner Times Publications
PO Box 71
Mason City, IL 62664
Phone: (217)482-3276
Fax: (217)482-3277
**Subject(s):** Free Newspapers
**Circ:** (Free)3,250

**The Pine Knot (16014)**
Cloquet Newspapers
813 Cloquet Ave.
Cloquet, MN 55720-1613
Phone: (218)879-6761
Fax: (218)879-6696
**Subject(s):** Paid Community Newspapers
**Circ:** (Non-paid)40
(Paid)3,221

**Akron Jewish News (24091)**
Jewish Community Board of Akron
750 White Pond Dr.
Akron, OH 44320
Phone: (330)869-2424
Fax: (330)867-8498
**Subject(s):** Free Newspapers; Jewish Publications
**Circ:** (Non-paid)3,200

Circulation: ★ = ABC; △ = BPA; ♦ = CAC; • = CCAB; ❏ = VAC; ⊕ = PO Statement; ‡ = Publisher's Report; Boldface figures = sworn; Light figures = estimated.

**Great Lakes States**      **Gale Directory of Publications & Broadcast Media/140th Ed.**

**The Clare Sentinel (15127)**
112 W 4th St.
P O BOX 237
Clare, MI 48617
Phone: (989)386-9937
Fax: (989)386-9311
**Subject(s):** Paid Community Newspapers
**Circ:** ‡3,200

**The Cornell & Lake Holcombe Courier (32899)**
Trygg J. Hansen Publications
121 Main St.
PO Box 546
Cornell, WI 54732
Phone: (715)239-6688
Fax: (715)239-6200
**Subject(s):** Paid Community Newspapers
**Circ:** (Paid)‡3,200

**Cumberland Advocate (32903)**
1375 2nd Ave.
PO Box 637
Cumberland, WI 54829
Phone: (715)822-4469
Fax: (715)822-4451
**Subject(s):** Paid Community Newspapers
**Circ:** ‡3,200

**The Glencoe Enterprise (16140)**
831 11th Street
P.O. Box 97
Glencoe, MN 55336
Phone: (320)864-4715
Fax: (320)864-4715
**Subject(s):** Paid Community Newspapers
**Circ:** ‡3,200

**Lake City Graphic (16204)**
111 S 8th St.
PO Box 469
Lake City, MN 55041
Phone: (651)345-3316
Fax: (651)345-4200
**Subject(s):** Paid Community Newspapers
**Circ:** ‡3,200

**Long Prairie Leader (16221)**
PO Box 479
Long Prairie, MN 56347
Phone: (320)732-2151
Fax: (320)732-2152
**Subject(s):** Paid Community Newspapers
**Circ:** 3,200

**Republican (10101)**
Orange County Publishing Company Inc.
PO Box 190
Paoli, IN 47454
Phone: (812)723-2572
Fax: (812)723-2592
**Subject(s):** Paid Community Newspapers
**Circ:** 3,200

**Swift County Monitor-News (15961)**
101 12th St. S
PO Box 227
Benson, MN 56215
Phone: (320)843-4111
Fax: (320)843-3246
**Subject(s):** Paid Community Newspapers
**Circ:** 3,200

**Kankakee Valley Post News (10123)**
Kankakee Valley Publishing Co.
PO Box 298
117 N. Rensselaer
Rensselaer, IN 47978-0298
Phone: (219)866-5111
Fax: (219)866-3775
**Subject(s):** Paid Community Newspapers
**Circ:** ‡3,192

**McLeod County Chronicle (16141)**
McLeod Publishing Inc.
PO Box 188
Glencoe, MN 55336
Phone: (320)864-5518
Fax: (320)864-5510
**Subject(s):** Paid Community Newspapers
**Circ:** (Free)56
     (Paid)‡3,181

**Journal-Register (7824)**
19 W Main St.
PO Box 10
Albion, IL 62806
Phone: (618)445-2355
Fax: (618)445-3459
**Subject(s):** Paid Community Newspapers
**Circ:** ‡3,162

**The Petersburg Observer (9245)**
Petersburg Observer
235 E Sangamon Ave.
Petersburg, IL 62675-1245
Phone: (217)632-2236
Fax: (217)632-2237
**Subject(s):** Paid Community Newspapers
**Circ:** ‡3,150

**Rockford Area News Leader (16455)**
Sun Press and News Publications
33 2nd St. NE
Box 280
Osseo, MN 55369
Phone: (763)425-3323
Fax: (763)425-2945
**Subject(s):** Paid Community Newspapers
**Circ:** (Paid)1,189
     (Free)3,149

**South Crow River News (16456)**
Sun Press and News Publications
33 2nd St. NE
Box 280
Osseo, MN 55369
Phone: (763)425-3323
Fax: (763)425-2945
**Subject(s):** Paid Community Newspapers
**Circ:** (Paid)1,189
     (Free)3,149

**Sheaf (16689)**
127 W Johnson Ave.
PO Box 45
Warren, MN 56762
Phone: (218)745-5174
Fax: (218)745-5175
**Subject(s):** Paid Community Newspapers
**Circ:** (Non-paid)129
     (Paid)3,133

**Kewaskum Statesman (33118)**
355Main St.
PO Box 98
Kewaskum, WI 53040-0098
Phone: (262)626-2626
Fax: (262)626-1382
**Subject(s):** Paid Community Newspapers
**Circ:** ‡3,125

**New London Press-Star (33423)**
ADD Inc.
112 Naston St.
PO Box 283
New London, WI 54961
Phone: (920)982-2511
Fax: (920)982-7672
**Subject(s):** Paid Community Newspapers
**Circ:** (Paid)‡3,117

**Arthur Graphic Clarion (7859)**
PO Box 19
113 E Illinos St.
Arthur, IL 61911
Phone: (217)543-2151
Fax: (217)543-2152
**Subject(s):** Paid Community Newspapers
**Circ:** ‡3,100

**Ledger-Sentinel (9543)**
Kendall County Record Inc.
222 S Bridge St.
PO Box J
Yorkville, IL 60560
Phone: (630)553-7034
Fax: (630)553-7085
**Subject(s):** Paid Community Newspapers
**Circ:** ‡3,100

**The Louisville Herald (24845)**
The Louisville Herald Inc.
PO Box 170
Louisville, OH 44641-0170
Phone: (330)875-5610
Fax: (330)875-4475

**Subject(s):** Paid Community Newspapers
**Circ:** (Paid)‡3,100

**Tribune Press Reporter (33001)**
Tribune Press
105 Misty Ct.
P O Box 38
Glenwood City, WI 54013
Phone: (715)265-4646
Fax: (715)265-7496
**Subject(s):** Paid Community Newspapers
**Circ:** ‡3,100

**The Munising News (15619)**
Peterson Publishing Inc.
113 W Superior St.
Munising, MI 49862
Phone: (906)387-3282
Fax: (906)387-4054
**Subject(s):** Paid Community Newspapers
**Circ:** (Free)‡65
     (Paid)‡3,075

**Sun Banner Pride (25135)**
Sun Newspapers
2795 Medina Rd.
Medina, OH 44256-8163
Phone: (330)725-1147
Fax: (330)725-2314
**Subject(s):** Paid Community Newspapers
**Circ:** (Paid)3,062

**The Ile Camera (15385)**
Heritage Newspapers Inc.
8545 Macomb St.
PO Box 233
Grosse Ile, MI 48138
Phone: (734)676-0515
Fax: (734)676-0638
**Subject(s):** Paid Community Newspapers
**Circ:** (Non-paid)10
     (Paid)3,059

**Oxford Eccentric (15665)**
Observer & Eccentric Newspapers
36251 Schoolcraft Rd.
Livonia, MI 48150
Phone: (734)591-2300
Fax: (734)953-2232
**Subject(s):** Paid Community Newspapers
**Circ:** (Thurs.)3,048

**Mundelein News (8755)**
Lakeland Media Inc.
30 S Whitney St.
PO Box 268
Grayslake, IL 60030-0268
Phone: (847)223-8161
Fax: (847)223-8810
**Subject(s):** Paid Community Newspapers
**Circ:** ‡3,020

**Attica Hub (24156)**
Seneca Publishing Inc.
26 N Main St.
PO Box 516
Attica, OH 44807
Phone: (419)426-3491
Fax: (419)426-2003
**Subject(s):** Paid Community Newspapers
**Circ:** (Free)‡43
     (Paid)‡3,000

**Barron News Shield (32833)**
219 E LaSalle
PO Box 100
Barron, WI 54812
Phone: (715)537-3117
Fax: (715)537-5640
**Subject(s):** Paid Community Newspapers
**Circ:** 3,000

**Beacon (16266)**
Melrose Beacon
PO Box 186
Melrose, MN 56352-0186
Phone: (320)256-3240
Fax: (320)256-3363
**Subject(s):** Paid Community Newspapers
**Circ:** 3,000

**The Blazer (8825)**
Joliet Junior College
1215 Houbolt Ave.
Joliet, IL 60431-8938
Phone: (815)729-9020
Fax: (815)744-5507
**Subject(s):** College Publications
**Circ:** (Free)‡3,000

**Bulletin (32828)**
PO Box 76
Baldwin, WI 54002
Phone: (715)684-2484
Fax: (715)684-4937
**Subject(s):** Paid Community Newspapers
**Circ:** ‡3,000

**The De Pauw (9773)**
De Pauw University
609 S Locust St.
Greencastle, IN 46135
Phone: (765)658-5998
Fax: (765)658-5991
**Subject(s):** College Publications
**Circ:** (Paid)400
 (Free)3,000

**The Exponent (24187)**
Baldwin-Wallace College
275 Eastland Rd.
Berea, OH 44017
Phone: (440)826-2900
Fax: (440)826-2388
**Subject(s):** College Publications
**Circ:** 3,000

**Franklin Challenger (9750)**
Challenger Newspapers
PO Box 73
Franklin, IN 46131
Phone: (317)888-3376
Fax: (317)888-3377
**Subject(s):** Paid Community Newspapers
**Circ:** (Paid)‡3,000

**The GSU Innovator (9461)**
Governors State University
Student Life Campus Ctr.
University Pkwy.
University Park, IL 60466-3186
Phone: (708)534-5000
Fax: (708)534-8953
**Subject(s):** College Publications
**Circ:** (Free)‡3,000

**The Lake Mills Leader (33139)**
Hometown News Group Publications
320 N. Main St.
PO Box 310
Lake Mills, WI 53551
Phone: (920)648-2334
Fax: (920)648-8187
**Subject(s):** Paid Community Newspapers
**Circ:** ‡3,000

**Mauston Star Times (33265)**
Capital Newspapers
201 E. State St.
PO Box 220
Mauston, WI 53948
Phone: (608)847-7341
Fax: (608)847-4867
**Subject(s):** Paid Community Newspapers
**Circ:** (Combined)3000

**Milan News-Leader (15749)**
Heritage Newspapers Inc.
106 W Michigan Ave.
Saline, MI 48176
Phone: (734)429-7380
Fax: (734)429-3621
**Subject(s):** Paid Community Newspapers
**Circ:** (Non-paid)♦66
 (Paid)♦3,000

**The Mosaic (24767)**
Cuyahoga Community College
4250 Richmond Rd.
Highland Hills, OH 44122
Phone: (216)987-2344
Fax: (216)987-2104
**Subject(s):** College Publications
**Circ:** (Free)‡3,000

**Neighbors (33629)**
Citizen Newspapers L.L.C.
1118 1/2 W. Main St.
Waupun, WI 53963
Phone: (920)324-5555
Fax: (920)324-8582
**Subject(s):** Paid Community Newspapers
**Circ:** ‡3,000

**The Ottawa County Exponent (24960)**
158 W Water St.
PO Box 70
Oak Harbor, OH 43449-0070
Phone: (419)898-5361
Fax: (419)898-0501
**Subject(s):** Paid Community Newspapers
**Circ:** 3,000

**Rock County Star Herald (16226)**
Announcer-Star Herald
PO Box 837
Luverne, MN 56156-0837
Phone: (507)283-2333
Fax: (507)283-2335
**Subject(s):** Paid Community Newspapers
**Circ:** 3,000

**Springs Valley Herald (9755)**
PO Box 311
French Lick, IN 47432
Phone: (812)936-9630
Fax: (812)936-9559
**Subject(s):** Paid Community Newspapers
**Circ:** ‡3,000

**Valley Courier (24342)**
218 W Benson St.
Cincinnati, OH 45215-3206
Phone: (513)821-4575
Fax: (513)761-3304
**Subject(s):** Paid Community Newspapers
**Circ:** (Free)‡200
 (Paid)‡3,000

**The Woodstock Independent (9538)**
671 E. Calhoun St.
Woodstock, IL 60098
Phone: (815)388-8040
Fax: (815)338-8177
**Subject(s):** Paid Community Newspapers
**Circ:** (Paid)⊕3,000

**Yale Expositor (15902)**
21 S Main St.
PO Box 158
Yale, MI 48097
Phone: (810)387-2300
Fax: (810)387-2300
**Subject(s):** Paid Community Newspapers
**Circ:** 3,000

**Archbold Buckeye (24127)**
Archbold Buckeye Inc.
207 N Defiance St.
Archbold, OH 43502
Phone: (419)445-4466
Fax: (419)445-4177
**Subject(s):** Paid Community Newspapers
**Circ:** (Free)⊕80
 (Paid)⊕2,988

**The Pilot-Independent (16687)**
Murphy McGinnis Media Inc.
PO Box 190
Walker, MN 56484
Phone: (218)547-1000
Fax: (218)547-3000
**Subject(s):** Paid Community Newspapers
**Circ:** (Non-paid)♦43
 (Paid)♦2,988

**Whitefish Bay Herald (33421)**
Community Newspapers
15700 W Cleveland Ave.
New Berlin, WI 53151
Phone: (262)938-5000
Fax: (262)938-5001
**Subject(s):** Paid Community Newspapers
**Circ:** 2,988

**Appleton Press (15934)**
241 W Snelling
Appleton, MN 56208
Phone: (320)289-1323
**Subject(s):** Paid Community Newspapers
**Circ:** 2,950

**Greendale Village Life (33405)**
Community Newspapers
15700 W Cleveland Ave.
New Berlin, WI 53151
Phone: (262)938-5000
Fax: (262)938-5001
**Subject(s):** Paid Community Newspapers
**Circ:** 2,947

**The Park Falls Herald (33458)**
Murphy McGinnis Media Inc.
259 2nd Ave. N
Park Falls, WI 54552-1217
Phone: (715)762-4940
Fax: (715)762-2757
**Subject(s):** Paid Community Newspapers
**Circ:** (Non-paid)♦7
 (Paid)♦2,916

**Bluffton News (24192)**
101 N. Main St.
Bluffton, OH 45817
Phone: (419)358-8010
Fax: (419)358-5027
**Subject(s):** Paid Community Newspapers
**Circ:** 2,900

**Caledonia Argus (15996)**
121 W Main St.
Box 227
Caledonia, MN 55921
Phone: (507)724-3475
Fax: (507)725-8610
**Subject(s):** Paid Community Newspapers
**Circ:** (Paid)2,900

**The Democrat-Message (9023)**
The Democrat-Message Inc.
110 W Main St
PO Box 71
Mount Sterling, IL 62353-0071
Phone: (217)773-3371
Fax: (217)773-3369
**Subject(s):** Paid Community Newspapers
**Circ:** (Paid)2,900

**Forest Park Review (9167)**
Wednesday Journal Inc.
141 S. Oak Park Ave.
Oak Park, IL 60302
Phone: (708)524-8300
Fax: (708)524-0447
**Subject(s):** Paid Community Newspapers
**Circ:** 2,900

**The Freeburg Tribune (8703)**
820 S State
Box 98
Freeburg, IL 62243
Phone: (618)539-3320
**Subject(s):** Shopping Guides
**Circ:** ‡2,900

**Greene Prairie Press (7987)**
516 N Main St.
PO Box 265
Carrollton, IL 62016
Phone: (217)942-9100
Fax: (217)942-6543
**Subject(s):** Paid Community Newspapers
**Circ:** 2,900

**Whitewater Register (33662)**
162 W. Main
PO Box 327
Whitewater, WI 53190
Phone: (262)473-3363
Fax: (262)473-5635
**Subject(s):** Paid Community Newspapers
**Circ:** (Paid)‡2900

**Henry News-Republican (8775)**
Henry News-Republican Inc.
709 3rd St.
PO Box 190
Henry, IL 61537
Phone: (309)364-3250
Fax: (309)364-3858
**Subject(s):** Paid Community Newspapers
**Circ:** 2,850

## Great Lakes States

**Nordonia Hills Sun** (24958)
Sun Newspapers
5510 Cloverleaf Pkwy.
Valley View, OH 44125-4887
Phone: (216)986-2600
Fax: (216)986-2380
**Subject(s):** Paid Community Newspapers
**Circ:** (Combined)2,854

**The Sounder** (33497)
Times Printing Company Inc.
405 2nd St.
PO Box 346
Random Lake, WI 53075-0346
Phone: (920)994-9244
Fax: (920)994-4817
**Subject(s):** Paid Community Newspapers
**Circ:** 2,852

**Star-Gazette** (16405)
308 Elm St.
Box 449
Moose Lake, MN 55767
Phone: (218)485-4406
Fax: (218)485-0237
**Subject(s):** Paid Community Newspapers
**Circ:** (Paid)2,850

**Tricounty Times** (7925)
Beardstown Newspapers
PO Box 320
Bluffs, IL 62621-0320
Phone: (217)323-1010
Fax: (217)754-3369
**Subject(s):** Paid Community Newspapers
**Circ:** ‡2,850

**The Twinsburg Sun** (25120)
Sun Newspapers
5510 Cloverleaf Pkwy.
Valley View, OH 44125-4887
Phone: (216)986-2600
Fax: (216)986-2380
**Subject(s):** Paid Community Newspapers
**Circ:** (Combined)2,854

**Vevay Reveille-Enterprise** (10220)
Vevay Newspapers Inc.
111 W Market St.
PO Box 157
Vevay, IN 47043
Phone: (812)427-2311
Fax: (812)427-2793
**Subject(s):** Paid Community Newspapers
**Circ:** ‡2,842

**De Forest Times-Tribune** (32905)
Times-Tribune
PO Box 585
De Forest, WI 53532
Phone: (608)846-5576
Fax: (608)846-5757
**Subject(s):** Paid Community Newspapers
**Circ:** 2,825

**Iron County Miner** (33057)
216 Copper St.
Hurley, WI 54534-1339
Phone: (715)561-3405
**Subject(s):** Paid Community Newspapers
**Circ:** ‡2,827

**Columbus Journal-Republican** (32897)
Citizen Newspapers L.L.C.
101 S. Ludington St.
PO Box 188
Columbus, WI 53925
Phone: (920)623-3160
**Subject(s):** Paid Community Newspapers
**Circ:** 2,800

**The Courier (Conneaut)** (24795)
Gazette Printing Company Inc.
34 S Chestnut St.
Jefferson, OH 44047
Phone: (440)576-9115
Fax: (440)576-4337
**Subject(s):** Paid Community Newspapers
**Circ:** (Paid)2,800

**Crothersville Times** (9672)
510 Moore St., Ste. 100
PO Box 141
Crothersville, IN 47229
Phone: (812)793-2188

Fax: (812)793-2188
**Subject(s):** Paid Community Newspapers
**Circ:** ‡2,800

**Hartford City News Times** (9798)
American Publishing Co.
123 S Jefferson St.
Hartford City, IN 47348
Phone: (317)348-0110
Fax: (317)348-0112
**Subject(s):** Daily Newspapers
**Circ:** ‡2,800

**Pioneer** (16235)
PO Box 219
Mahnomen, MN 56557
Phone: (218)935-5296
Fax: (218)935-2555
**Subject(s):** Paid Community Newspapers
**Circ:** ‡2,800

**The Richwood Gazette** (25021)
Marysville Newspapers Inc.
PO Box 187
Richwood, OH 43344
Phone: (614)943-2214
**Subject(s):** Paid Community Newspapers
**Circ:** ‡2,800

**Star** (8724)
PO Box 7
Gilman, IL 60938
Phone: (815)265-7332
Fax: (815)265-7880
**Subject(s):** Paid Community Newspapers
**Circ:** 2,800

**The Thirteen Towns** (16132)
The Thirteen Towns of Fosston Inc.
118 N Johnson
Fosston, MN 56542
Phone: (218)435-1313
Fax: (218)435-1309
**Subject(s):** Paid Community Newspapers
**Circ:** (Paid)‡2,800

**Plaindealer** (16558)
St. James Publishing Company Inc.
604 1st Ave. S.
PO Box 67
Saint James, MN 56081-3221
Phone: (507)375-3161
Fax: (507)375-3221
**Subject(s):** Paid Community Newspapers
**Circ:** 2,790

**Cloquet Journal** (16013)
813 Cloquet Ave.
Cloquet, MN 55720
Phone: (218)879-1950
Fax: (218)879-2078
**Subject(s):** Paid Community Newspapers
**Circ:** (Non-paid)37
(Paid)2,780

**Journal** (10097)
Odon Journal
102 1/2 W Main St.
P.O Box 307
Odon, IN 47562-0307
Phone: (812)636-7350
Fax: (812)636-7359
**Subject(s):** Paid Community Newspapers
**Circ:** 2,782

**Norridge Times** (8894)
Lerner Communications Inc.
7331 N Lincoln Ave.
Lincolnwood, IL 60712
Phone: (847)329-2000
Fax: (847)329-2060
**Subject(s):** Free Newspapers
**Circ:** (Paid)♦2,762

**Tipton Tribune** (10207)
Elwood Publishing Co.
116 South Main St.,Ste. A
PO Box 248
Tipton, IN 46072
Phone: (317)675-2115
Fax: (317)675-4147
**Subject(s):** Daily Newspapers
**Circ:** (Free)⊕128
(Paid)⊕2,761

**The Elkhorn Independent** (32943)
11 W Walworth St.
Elkhorn, WI 53121
Phone: (262)723-2250
Fax: (262)723-7424
**Subject(s):** Paid Community Newspapers
**Circ:** ‡2,750

**Nappanee Advance-News** (10055)
The Pilot Company Inc.
158 W Market St.
PO Box 230
Nappanee, IN 46550-0230
Phone: (574)773-3127
Fax: (574)936-3844
**Subject(s):** Paid Community Newspapers
**Circ:** (Free)150
(Paid)2,750

**Romulus Roman** (15707)
The Journal Newspapers
35540 Michigan Ave.
PO Box 578
Wayne, MI 48184
Phone: (734)467-1900
Fax: (734)729-1840
**Subject(s):** Paid Community Newspapers
**Circ:** (Paid)1,084
(Non-paid)2,758

**The Cambridge News** (32878)
Hometown News Group Publications
201 W. N. St.
PO Box 8
Cambridge, WI 53523
Phone: (608)423-3213
Fax: (608)423-7802
**Subject(s):** Paid Community Newspapers
**Circ:** ‡2,745

**The Independent** (32907)
Hometown News Group Publications
23 N. Main St.
PO Box 27
Deerfield, WI 53531
Phone: (608)764-5515
Fax: (608)764-8214
**Subject(s):** Paid Community Newspapers
**Circ:** (Paid)‡2,745

**Springfield Advance-Press** (16654)
13 S Marshall Ave.
PO Box 78
Springfield, MN 56087
Phone: (507)723-4225
Fax: (507)723-4400
**Subject(s):** Paid Community Newspapers
**Circ:** (Paid)‡2,742

**Whitehall Times** (33658)
Whitehall Times Inc.
36435 Main St.
Whitehall, WI 54773
Phone: (715)538-4765
**Subject(s):** Paid Community Newspapers
**Circ:** (Free)70
(Paid)2,745

**The Hartville News** (24764)
The Knowles Press Inc.
316 E Maple St.
Box 428
Hartville, OH 44632
Phone: (330)877-9345
Fax: (330)877-1364
**Subject(s):** Paid Community Newspapers
**Circ:** (Free)⊕27
(Paid)⊕2,736

**Gillespie Area News** (8723)
112-16 W Chestnut St.
PO Box 209
Gillespie, IL 62033-0209
Phone: (217)839-2130
Fax: (217)839-2139
**Subject(s):** Paid Community Newspapers
**Circ:** ‡2,715

**Harlem-Irving Times** (8219)
Lerner Communications Inc.
1115 W. Belmont
Chicago, IL 60657
Phone: (312)281-7500
Fax: (312)281-0740

**Subject(s):** Free Newspapers
**Circ:** (Paid)2,715

**The Ada Herald  (24089)**
Brown Publishing Co.
309 S. Main
PO Box 117
Ada, OH 45810
Phone: (419)634-6055
Fax: (419)634-0912
**Subject(s):** Paid Community Newspapers
**Circ:** ‡2,700

**The Chisholm Tribune-Press  (16009)**
327 W Lake St.
Chisholm, MN 55719-1717
Phone: (218)254-4432
Fax: (218)254-7141
**Subject(s):** Paid Community Newspapers
**Circ:** ‡2,700

**The Citizen  (15076)**
112 S Park Street
P.O. Box A
Boyne City, MI 49712
Phone: (231)582-6761
Fax: (231)582-6762
**Subject(s):** Paid Community Newspapers
**Circ:** (Paid)‡2,700

**The Germantown Press  (24748)**
PO Box 159
Germantown, OH 45327
Phone: (937)855-2300
Fax: (937)855-3860
**Subject(s):** Paid Community Newspapers
**Circ:** 2,700

**Independent News Herald  (16011)**
PO Box 188
Clarissa, MN 56440
Phone: (218)756-2131
Fax: (218)756-2126
**Subject(s):** Paid Community Newspapers
**Circ:** 2,700

**Iroquois County's Times-Republic  (9507)**
Twin States Publishing
1492 E Walnut St.
PO Box 250
Watseka, IL 60970
Phone: (815)432-5227
Fax: (815)432-5159
**Subject(s):** Daily Newspapers
**Circ:** 2,700

**Marion Advertiser  (33256)**
PO Box 268
109 North Main
Marion, WI 54950-0268
Phone: (715)754-5444
**Subject(s):** Paid Community Newspapers
**Circ:** 2,700

**New Carlisle Sun  (24931)**
Brown Publications
255 S Main St.
New Carlisle, OH 45344
Phone: (937)845-3861
Fax: (937)845-3577
**Subject(s):** Paid Community Newspapers
**Circ:** (Paid)2,700

**Hoffman Estates Review  (8796)**
Pioneer Press Newspapers
c/o Marc Alberts
291 N. Dunton Ave.
Arlington Heights, IL 60004
Phone: (847)797-5100
Fax: (847)797-5151
**Subject(s):** Paid Community Newspapers
**Circ:** (Thurs.)2,682

**News-Tribune  (24965)**
Gazette Publishing Company Inc.
42 S. Main St.
Oberlin, OH 44074
Phone: (440)775-1611
Fax: (440)774-2167
**Subject(s):** Paid Community Newspapers
**Circ:** ‡2,680

**The Courier  (33595)**
Hometown News Group Publications
114 N. Monroe St.
PO Box 6
Waterloo, WI 53594
Phone: (920)478-2188
Fax: (920)478-3618
**Subject(s):** Paid Community Newspapers
**Circ:** ‡2,665

**Libertyville News  (8872)**
Lakeland Media Inc.
30 S Whitney St.
PO Box 268
Grayslake, IL 60030-0268
Phone: (847)223-8161
Fax: (847)223-8810
**Subject(s):** Paid Community Newspapers
**Circ:** 2,652

**South Gibson Star-Times  (9711)**
PO Box 70
Fort Branch, IN 47648
Phone: (812)753-3553
Fax: (812)753-4251
**Subject(s):** Paid Community Newspapers
**Circ:** (Paid)⊕2,650

**Newburgh Chandler Register  (10069)**
Warrick Publishing Co.
PO Box 535
Newburgh, IN 47629
Phone: (812)853-3366
Fax: (812)853-8685
**Subject(s):** Paid Community Newspapers
**Circ:** ‡2,638

**Harlem-Foster Times  (8888)**
Pioneer Press Newspapers
7331 N Lincoln Ave.
Lincolnwood, IL 60712
Phone: (847)329-2000
Fax: (847)696-3229
**Subject(s):** Free Newspapers
**Circ:** (Paid)♦2,627

**Bridgeview Independent  (8966)**
Southwest Messenger Press Inc.
3840 W 147th St.
PO Box 548
Midlothian, IL 60445
Phone: (708)388-2425
Fax: (708)385-7811
**Subject(s):** Paid Community Newspapers
**Circ:** (Free)‡800
(Paid)‡2,600

**The Denmark Press  (32911)**
Brown County Publishing Co.
138 Main St.
PO Box 610
Denmark, WI 54208
Phone: (920)863-2154
Fax: (920)863-8652
**Subject(s):** Paid Community Newspapers
**Circ:** ‡2,600

**Farmers Independent  (15939)**
PO Box 130
Bagley, MN 56621
Phone: (218)694-6265
Fax: (218)694-6015
**Subject(s):** Paid Community Newspapers
**Circ:** ‡2,600

**Journal-Messenger  (9051)**
QUAD County Printing
113 North Van Buren St
New Athens, IL 62264
Phone: (618)295-2812
Fax: (618)475-2709
**Subject(s):** Paid Community Newspapers
**Circ:** 2,600

**Le Sueur News-Herald  (16212)**
Le Sueur Publishing
101 Bridge St.
Le Sueur, MN 56058
Phone: (507)665-3334
**Subject(s):** Paid Community Newspapers
**Circ:** ‡2,600

**The Lodi Enterprise  (33145)**
Hometown News Group Publications
146 S. Main St.
PO Box 16
Lodi, WI 53555
Phone: (608)592-3261
Fax: (608)592-3866
**Subject(s):** Paid Community Newspapers
**Circ:** ‡2,600

**Morton Times News  (9215)**
Times Newspapers
1616 W Pioneer Pkwy.
Peoria, IL 61615
Phone: (309)692-6600
Fax: (309)690-3399
**Subject(s):** Paid Community Newspapers
**Circ:** (Paid)2,600

**Record-Review  (32789)**
TP Printing Co.
PO Box 677
Abbotsford, WI 54405
Phone: (715)223-2342
Fax: (715)223-3505
**Subject(s):** Paid Community Newspapers
**Circ:** 2,600

**Tribune-Phonograph  (32790)**
T P Printing Co.
103 W Spruce St.
PO Box 667
Abbotsford, WI 54405
Phone: (715)223-2342
Fax: (715)223-3505
**Subject(s):** Paid Community Newspapers
**Circ:** 2,600

**The Vienna Times  (9495)**
PO Box 457
Vienna, IL 62995
Phone: (618)658-4321
Fax: (618)658-4322
**Subject(s):** Paid Community Newspapers
**Circ:** ‡2,600

**Worth Citizen  (8977)**
Southwest Messenger Press Inc.
3840 W 147th St.
PO Box 548
Midlothian, IL 60445
Phone: (708)388-2425
Fax: (708)385-7811
**Subject(s):** Free Newspapers
**Circ:** (Free)‡300
(Paid)‡2,600

**The Mosinee Times  (33384)**
407 3rd St.
Mosinee, WI 54455-1495
Phone: (715)693-2300
Fax: (715)693-1574
**Subject(s):** Paid Community Newspapers
**Circ:** ‡2,575

**Staples World  (16655)**
224 4th St. NE
PO Box 100
Staples, MN 56479
Phone: (218)894-1112
Fax: (218)894-3570
**Subject(s):** Paid Community Newspapers
**Circ:** ⊕2,569

**Charlevoix Courier  (15105)**
112 Mason St.
PO Box 117
Charlevoix, MI 49720-0117
Phone: (231)547-6558
Fax: (231)547-4992
**Subject(s):** Paid Community Newspapers
**Circ:** 2,513

**Lake Villa Record  (8855)**
Lakeland Media Inc.
30 S Whitney St.
PO Box 268
Grayslake, IL 60030-0268
Phone: (847)223-8161
Fax: (847)223-8810
**Subject(s):** Paid Community Newspapers
**Circ:** 2,513

Circulation: ★ = ABC; △ = BPA; ♦ = CAC; ● = CCAB; ❑ = VAC; ⊕ = PO Statement; ‡ = Publisher's Report; Boldface figures = sworn; Light figures = estimated.

# Great Lakes States

**Algoma Record-Herald** (32793)
Tri-County Publishing
203 Ellis St.
PO Box 68
Algoma, WI 54201
Phone: (920)487-2222
Fax: (920)487-3194
**Subject(s):** Paid Community Newspapers
**Circ:** 2,500

**The Arcadia News-Leader** (32821)
625 Dettloff Dr.
PO Box 220
Arcadia, WI 54612
Phone: (608)323-3366
Fax: (608)323-2185
**Subject(s):** Paid Community Newspapers
**Circ:** ‡2,500

**Armada Times** (15034)
PO Box 915
23061 Main St.
Armada, MI 48005-0915
Phone: (586)784-5551
Fax: (586)784-8710
**Subject(s):** Paid Community Newspapers
**Circ:** 2,500

**Berne Tri-Weekly News** (9567)
PO Box 324
153 S. Jefferson St.
Berne, IN 46711
Phone: (219)589-2101
Fax: (219)589-8614
**Subject(s):** Farm Newspapers
**Circ:** ‡2,500

**The Carletonian** (16439)
Carleton College
1 N. College St.
Northfield, MN 55057
Phone: (507)646-4000
Fax: (507)646-7900
**Subject(s):** College Publications
**Circ:** (Paid)500
(Non-paid)2,500

**The Clarion** (16574)
Bethel College
3900 Bethel Dr. No. 2381
Saint Paul, MN 55112
**Subject(s):** College Publications
**Circ:** (Controlled)‡2,500

**The Gustavian Weekly** (16631)
Gustavus Adolphus College
800 W. College Ave.
PO Box A-6
Saint Peter, MN 56082-1498
Phone: (507)933-8000
Fax: (507)933-7633
**Subject(s):** College Publications
**Circ:** (Free)‡2,500

**The Hagerstown Exponent** (9787)
35 W Main St.
Hagerstown, IN 47346
Phone: (765)489-4035
Fax: (765)489-5323
**Subject(s):** Paid Community Newspapers
**Circ:** ‡2,500

**Journal** (9688)
The Journal Publishing Co.
211 N Sale St.
PO Box 98
Ellettsville, IN 47429
Phone: (812)876-2254
Fax: (812)876-2853
**Subject(s):** Paid Community Newspapers
**Circ:** 2,500

**Kewaunee Enterprise** (33119)
Tri-County Publishing
206 Ellis St.
PO Box 86
Kewaunee, WI 54216
Phone: (920)388-3175
Fax: (920)388-0609
**Subject(s):** Paid Community Newspapers
**Circ:** 2,500

**The McDonough Democrates** (7937)
Spoon River Press
358 E Main St.
PO Box 269
Bushnell, IL 61422-0269
Phone: (309)772-2129
Fax: (309)772-3994
**Subject(s):** Paid Community Newspapers
**Circ:** ‡2,500

**Milford Spinal Column Newsweekly** (15593)
Spinal Column Publications
7196 Cooley Lake Rd.
PO Box 14
Union Lake, MI 48387-0014
Phone: (248)360-7355
Fax: (248)360-4711
**Subject(s):** Free Newspapers
**Circ:** (Free)‡2,500

**Montgomery Messenger** (16395)
Suel Printing Company Inc.
310 1st St. S
PO Box 49
Montgomery, MN 56069
Phone: (507)364-8601
Fax: (507)364-8602
**Subject(s):** Paid Community Newspapers
**Circ:** ‡2,500

**New Palestine Press** (10066)
PO Box 407
New Palestine, IN 46163-0407
Phone: (317)861-4242
Fax: (317)861-4201
**Subject(s):** Paid Community Newspapers
**Circ:** (Paid)2,500

**News Mirror** (16166)
PO Box 278
Hector, MN 55342
Phone: (320)848-2248
Fax: (320)848-2249
**Subject(s):** Paid Community Newspapers
**Circ:** (Free)200
(Paid)2,500

**The Northwest Phoenix** (9759)
Indiana University Northwest
3400 Broadway, Moraine Rm. 110,
Gary, IN 46408
Phone: (219)980-6795
Fax: (219)981-4233
**Subject(s):** College Publications
**Circ:** (Free)‡2,500

**Oregon Observer** (33446)
Unified Newspaper Group
845 Market St.
Box 26
Oregon, WI 53575
Phone: (608)270-7022
Fax: (608)835-0130
**Subject(s):** Paid Community Newspapers
**Circ:** (Paid)‡2,500

**Reporter** (7999)
Lincoln Trail Publishing
PO Box 158
Casey, IL 62420
Phone: (217)932-5211
Fax: (217)932-5214
**Subject(s):** Paid Community Newspapers
**Circ:** (Paid)‡2,500

**The Stanley Republican** (33554)
Inter County Publishing Co.
131 E 1st Ave.
PO Box 185
Stanley, WI 54768-0185
Phone: (715)644-3319
Fax: (715)644-5452
**Subject(s):** Paid Community Newspapers
**Circ:** 2,500

**ECM Post-Review** (16428)
ECM Publishers Inc. - North Branch
6448 Main St.
North Branch, MN 55056
Phone: (651)674-7025
Fax: (651)674-7026
**Subject(s):** Paid Community Newspapers
**Circ:** (Paid)‡2,495

**North Star News** (16194)
PO Box 158
204 S. Main St.
Karlstad, MN 56732
Phone: (218)436-2157
Fax: (218)436-3271
**Subject(s):** Paid Community Newspapers
**Circ:** (Free)‡75
(Paid)‡2,487

**Thorp Courier** (33576)
Box 487
Thorp, WI 54771
Phone: (715)669-5525
Fax: (715)669-5596
**Subject(s):** Paid Community Newspapers
**Circ:** ‡2,464

**Advertiser** (32940)
The Reporter Company Inc.
21 N Henry St.
Edgerton, WI 53534
Phone: (608)884-3367
Fax: (608)884-8187
**Subject(s):** Shopping Guides
**Circ:** (Free)‡2,450

**The News Tribune** (24765)
Tribune Printing Inc.
147 E. High St.
PO BOX 303
Hicksville, OH 43526
Phone: (419)542-7764
Fax: (419)542-7370
**Subject(s):** Paid Community Newspapers
**Circ:** (Non-paid)50
(Paid)2,450

**Tribune** (15870)
15 West Pearl
Union City, MI 49094
Phone: (517)278-2318
Fax: (517)278-6041
**Subject(s):** Free Newspapers
**Circ:** (Free)2,456

**Jackson County Pilot** (16187)
Livewire Printing Co.
310 2nd St.
PO Box 208
Jackson, MN 56143
Phone: (507)847-3771
Fax: (507)847-5822
**Subject(s):** Paid Community Newspapers
**Circ:** (Free)‡100
(Paid)‡2,426

**East Peoria Times-Courier** (8616)
Times Newspapers
1616 W Pioneer Pkwy.
Peoria, IL 61615
Phone: (309)692-6600
Fax: (309)690-3399
**Subject(s):** Free Newspapers
**Circ:** (Paid)2,415

**Alexandria Times-Tribune** (9549)
Elwood Publishing Co.
One Harrison Sq.
PO Box 330
Alexandria, IN 46001
Phone: (765)724-4469
Fax: (765)724-4460
**Subject(s):** Paid Community Newspapers
**Circ:** (Paid)2,400

**The Amboy News** (7837)
219 E Main St.
PO Box 162
Amboy, IL 61310-0162
Phone: (815)857-2311
Fax: (815)857-2517
**Subject(s):** Paid Community Newspapers
**Circ:** 2,400

**Hawley Herald** (16163)
608 Main St.
PO Box 709
Hawley, MN 56549
Phone: (218)483-3306
Fax: (218)483-4457
**Subject(s):** Paid Community Newspapers
**Circ:** (Free)‡50
(Paid)‡2,400

**Houston County News (16200)**
316 S 2nd St., Ste. 2
PO Box 205
La Crescent, MN 55947
Phone: (507)895-2940
Fax: (507)895-2942
**Subject(s):** Paid Community Newspapers
**Circ:** 2,400

**Liberty Herald (9998)**
PO Box 10
10-12 North Market Street
Liberty, IN 47353-0010
Phone: (765)458-5114
Fax: (765)458-5115
**Subject(s):** Paid Community Newspapers
**Circ:** ‡2,400

**Mercer County Chronicle (24525)**
Delphos Herald Inc.
PO Box 105
116 W. Main
Coldwater, OH 45828
Phone: (419)678-2324
Fax: (419)678-4659
**Subject(s):** Paid Community Newspapers
**Circ:** (Paid)‡2,400

**The Onaway Outlook (15655)**
Presque Newspaper
PO Box 176
Onaway, MI 49765-0176
Phone: (989)733-6543
Fax: (989)733-6572
**Subject(s):** Paid Community Newspapers
**Circ:** ‡2,400

**The Warroad Pioneer (16690)**
Warroad Pioneer
109 E. Lake St.
PO Box E.
Warroad, MN 56763
Phone: (218)386-1594
Fax: (218)386-1072
**Subject(s):** Paid Community Newspapers
**Circ:** ‡2,400

**Williamston Enterprise (15117)**
Community Newspapers
239 S Cochran
Charlotte, MI 48813
Phone: (517)543-9913
Fax: (517)543-3677
**Subject(s):** Paid Community Newspapers
**Circ:** ‡2,400

**Wayne Eagle (15888)**
The Journal Newspapers
35540 Michigan Ave.
PO Box 578
Wayne, MI 48184
Phone: (734)467-1900
Fax: (734)729-1840
**Subject(s):** Paid Community Newspapers
**Circ:** (Combined)2,396

**The Morenci Observer (15604)**
120 N St.
Morenci, MI 49256
Phone: (517)458-6811
Fax: (517)458-6811
**Subject(s):** Paid Community Newspapers
**Circ:** (Paid)‡2,370

**Free Press-Progress (9065)**
Free Press Inc.
112 W State St
PO Box 130
Nokomis, IL 62075-0130
Phone: (217)563-2115
Fax: (217)563-7464
**Subject(s):** Paid Community Newspapers
**Circ:** ‡2,350

**Norman County Index (15911)**
307 W Main St.
PO Box 148
Ada, MN 56510-0148
Phone: (218)784-2541
Fax: (218)784-2551
**Subject(s):** Paid Community Newspapers
**Circ:** ‡2,350

**Cheese Market News (33284)**
PO Box 620244
Middleton, WI 53562-0244
Phone: (608)831-6002
Fax: (608)831-1004
**Subject(s):** Milk and Dairy Products
**Circ:** (Paid)‡2,325

**Galva News-Register Press (8717)**
Galesburg Printing and Publishing Co.
210 S. Exchange St.
Galva, IL 61434
Phone: (309)923-2103
Fax: (309)932-3282
**Subject(s):** Paid Community Newspapers
**Circ:** 2,314

**Germantown Banner Press (33403)**
Community Newspapers
15700 W Cleveland Ave.
New Berlin, WI 53151
Phone: (262)938-5000
Fax: (262)938-5001
**Subject(s):** Paid Community Newspapers
**Circ:** 2,310

**Carlinville Democrat (7958)**
Macoupin County Enquirer Inc.
PO Box 200
Carlinville, IL 62626-0200
Phone: (217)854-2534
Fax: (217)854-2535
**Subject(s):** Paid Community Newspapers
**Circ:** ‡2,300

**Dodge County Independent (16195)**
105 1st Ave. NW
PO Box 367
Kasson, MN 55944
Phone: (507)634-7503
Fax: (507)634-4446
**Subject(s):** Paid Community Newspapers
**Circ:** ‡2,300

**Exponent (16086)**
PO Box 285
East Grand Forks, MN 56721-0285
Phone: (218)773-2808
Fax: (218)773-9212
**Subject(s):** Paid Community Newspapers
**Circ:** ‡2,300

**Limestone Independent News (7883)**
114 Roosevelt St.
Bartonville, IL 61607
Phone: (309)697-1851
Fax: (309)697-1851
**Subject(s):** Paid Community Newspapers
**Circ:** (Free)200
   (Paid)2,300

**The Valders Journal (33587)**
204 N Liberty St.
PO Box 400
Valders, WI 54245-0400
Phone: (920)775-4431
**Subject(s):** Paid Community Newspapers
**Circ:** ‡2,301

**The Walnut Leader (9498)**
110 Jackson St.
PO Box 280
Walnut, IL 61376-0280
Phone: (815)379-9290
Fax: (815)379-2659
**Subject(s):** Paid Community Newspapers
**Circ:** ‡2,300

**Wittenberg Torch (25056)**
PO Box 720
Springfield, OH 45501-0720
Phone: (937)327-6151
Fax: (937)327-6152
**Subject(s):** College Publications
**Circ:** (Controlled)‡2,300

**Hub (16138)**
PO Box 208
234 4th St.
Gaylord, MN 55334
Phone: (507)237-2476
Fax: (507)237-2476
**Subject(s):** Paid Community Newspapers
**Circ:** ‡2,260

**The Bronson Journal (15081)**
Patriot Publications
PO Box 38
113 W Chicago St
Bronson, MI 49028
Phone: (517)369-5085
Fax: (517)369-2225
**Subject(s):** Paid Community Newspapers
**Circ:** ‡2,250

**Community Post (24918)**
PO Box 155
Minster, OH 45865-0155
Phone: (419)628-2369
Fax: (419)628-4712
**Subject(s):** Paid Community Newspapers
**Circ:** (Paid)2,250

**Crawford County Independent Scout (32998)**
Southwest Publisher L.L.C.
PO Box 188
Gays Mills, WI 54631
Phone: (608)375-4458
Fax: (608)375-2369
**Subject(s):** Paid Community Newspapers
**Circ:** ‡2,250

**The Farmside: Huntley, Marengo (8803)**
Liberty Suburban Chicago Newspapers
7222 W. Cermak Rd., Ste. 505
PO Box 127
Huntley, IL 60142
Phone: (847)669-5621
Fax: (847)669-5623
**Subject(s):** Paid Community Newspapers
**Circ:** (Combined)2,250

**Louisville Clay County Republican (8912)**
Clay County Republican
124 S Church St.
PO Drawer B
Louisville, IL 62858
Phone: (618)665-3135
Fax: (618)665-3135
**Subject(s):** Paid Community Newspapers
**Circ:** ‡2,250

**Hardin County Independent (8637)**
PO Box 328
Elizabethtown, IL 62931
Phone: (618)287-2361
**Subject(s):** Paid Community Newspapers
**Circ:** (Paid)⊕2,240

**Lindenhurst News (8899)**
Lakeland Media Inc.
30 S Whitney St.
PO Box 268
Grayslake, IL 60030-0268
Phone: (847)223-8161
Fax: (847)223-8810
**Subject(s):** Paid Community Newspapers
**Circ:** 2,231

**Crown Point Star (9674)**
112 W Clark St.
PO Box 419
Crown Point, IN 46308
Phone: (219)663-4212
Fax: (219)663-0137
**Subject(s):** Paid Community Newspapers
**Circ:** ⊕2,224

**Herald-Independent (32902)**
Hometown News Group Publications
202 Cottage Grove Rd.
Ste. D
Cottage Grove, WI 53527
**Subject(s):** Paid Community Newspapers
**Circ:** ‡2,220

**Battle Lake Review (15942)**
Review Enterprises Inc.
114 Lake Ave.
PO Box 99
Battle Lake, MN 56515
Phone: (218)864-5952
Fax: (218)864-5212
**Subject(s):** Paid Community Newspapers
**Circ:** (Free)‡70
   (Paid)‡2,215

# Great Lakes States

**Albion New Era (9548)**
All Printing & Publications Inc.
407 S Orange St.
PO Box 25
Albion, IN 46701
Phone: (260)636-2727
Fax: (260)636-2042
**Subject(s):** Paid Community Newspapers
**Circ:** ‡2,200

**The Crestline Advocate (24639)**
Crestline Advocate Inc.
312 N Seltzer
PO Box 226
Crestline, OH 44827
Phone: (419)683-3355
Fax: (419)683-0175
**Subject(s):** Paid Community Newspapers
**Circ:** (Paid)‡2,200

**The Denisonian (24751)**
Denison University
Slayter Hall
Granville, OH 43023
Phone: (740)587-6378
Fax: (740)587-6767
**Subject(s):** College Publications
**Circ:** ‡2,200

**Golden Prairie News (7862)**
301 S Chestnut St.
Assumption, IL 62510-1229
Phone: (217)226-3721
Fax: (217)226-3579
**Subject(s):** Paid Community Newspapers
**Circ:** ‡2,200

**Granville Sentinel (24752)**
Gannett Co.
PO Box 357
Granville, OH 43023-0357
Phone: (740)587-3397
Fax: (740)587-3398
**Subject(s):** Paid Community Newspapers
**Circ:** (Controlled)2,200

**Lowell Ledger (15557)**
PO Box 128
105 North Broadway
Lowell, MI 49331-0128
Phone: (616)897-9261
Fax: (616)897-4809
**Subject(s):** Paid Community Newspapers
**Circ:** 2,200

**Tri-County News (16032)**
74 W Main
PO Box 76
Cottonwood, MN 56229
Phone: (507)423-6239
Fax: (507)423-6230
**Subject(s):** Paid Community Newspapers
**Circ:** 2,200

**The Versailles Policy (25133)**
Langston Graphics Inc.
PO Box 74
Versailles, OH 45380
**Subject(s):** Paid Community Newspapers
**Circ:** ‡2,200

**The Deckerville Recorder (15161)**
Regentin Publishing
3520 Main
PO Box 519
Deckerville, MI 48427
Phone: (810)376-3805
Fax: (810)376-4058
**Subject(s):** Paid Community Newspapers
**Circ:** ‡2,189

**The Scioto Voice (25166)**
Scioto Voice
PO Box 400
Wheelersburg, OH 45694
Phone: (740)574-8494
Fax: (740)574-2329
**Subject(s):** Paid Community Newspapers
**Circ:** (Free)⊕165
(Paid)⊕2,168

**Momence Progress-Reporter (8987)**
110 W River St.
Momence, IL 60954
Phone: (815)472-2000
Fax: (815)472-3877
**Subject(s):** Paid Community Newspapers
**Circ:** ‡2,150

**Dawson Sentinel (16037)**
Sentinel
PO Box 1015
Dawson, MN 56232
**Subject(s):** Paid Community Newspapers
**Circ:** (Free)‡15
(Paid)‡2,150

**The Sumner Press (9440)**
The Sumner Press Inc.
216 S Christy
PO Box 126
Sumner, IL 62466
Phone: (618)936-2212
Fax: (618)936-2858
**Subject(s):** Paid Community Newspapers
**Circ:** ‡2,150

**Twin City Journal-Reporter (9762)**
Community Publishing Co.
238 E Main St.
Gas City, IN 46933
Phone: (765)674-0070
**Subject(s):** Paid Community Newspapers
**Circ:** ‡2,150

**Tribune News (10172)**
Tranter Publishing Co.
113 S State St.
South Whitley, IN 46787
Phone: (260)723-5085
Fax: (260)723-4771
**Subject(s):** Paid Community Newspapers
**Circ:** ‡2,145

**Johnstown Independent (24804)**
CNS This Week
55 S. Main St., Ste. E
Johnstown, OH 43031-2201
Phone: (614)967-2045
Fax: (614)855-2857
**Subject(s):** Paid Community Newspapers
**Circ:** (Paid)2,128

**Times Reporter (32792)**
Richard Hannagan
116 Main St.
PO Box 99
Adams, WI 53910
Phone: (608)339-7844
Fax: (608)339-3903
**Subject(s):** Paid Community Newspapers
**Circ:** 2,124

**Arcola Record Herald (7843)**
Rankin Publishing
204 E. Main St.
PO Box 130
Arcola, IL 61910
Phone: (217)268-4959
Fax: (217)268-4815
**Subject(s):** Paid Community Newspapers
**Circ:** 2,100

**Crete Record (8521)**
Russell Publications
484 Cass St.
Crete, IL 60417
Phone: (708)672-8843
**Subject(s):** Paid Community Newspapers
**Circ:** 2,100

**Foxxy Shopper (33651)**
Coulee News
103 S Leonard St.
West Salem, WI 54669
Phone: (608)786-1950
Fax: (608)786-1670
**Subject(s):** Paid Community Newspapers
**Circ:** 2,100

**Herald-Enterprise (8747)**
PO Box 400
Golconda, IL 62938
Phone: (618)683-3531
Fax: (618)683-3831
**Subject(s):** Paid Community Newspapers
**Circ:** ‡2,100

**Pymatuning Area News (24125)**
Gazette Printing Company Inc.
PO Box 458
Andover, OH 44003-0458
Phone: (216)293-6097
Fax: (216)293-7374
**Subject(s):** Paid Community Newspapers
**Circ:** (Paid)‡2,100

**Times-Messenger (16231)**
Madelia Media Inc.
112 W Main St.
Madelia, MN 56062-1440
Phone: (507)642-3636
Fax: (507)642-3535
**Subject(s):** Paid Community Newspapers
**Circ:** (Paid)‡2,100

**Sheboygan Falls News (33475)**
113 E. Mill St.
PO Box 317
Plymouth, WI 53073
Phone: (920)980-5997
Fax: (920)893-5505
**Subject(s):** Paid Community Newspapers
**Circ:** ‡2,083

**The Belleville Enterprise (15056)**
The Journal Newspapers
35540 Michigan Ave.
PO Box 578
Wayne, MI 48184
Phone: (734)467-1900
Fax: (734)729-1840
**Subject(s):** Paid Community Newspapers
**Circ:** (Combined)2,068

**The Commercial Record (15757)**
Kaechele Publications Inc.
790 Lake St.
PO Box 246
Saugatuck, MI 49453
Phone: (616)857-2570
Fax: (616)857-4637
**Subject(s):** Paid Community Newspapers
**Circ:** (Free)33
(Paid)2,068

**The Daily Reporter (9110)**
Liberty Group Publishing Co.
3000 Dundee Rd., Ste. 202
Northbrook, IL 60062
Phone: (847)272-2244
Fax: (847)272-6244
**Subject(s):** Daily Newspapers
**Circ:** (Paid)‡2,050

**The Wells Mirror (16698)**
40 W Franklin
Wells, MN 56097
Phone: (507)553-3131
Fax: (507)553-3132
**Subject(s):** Paid Community Newspapers
**Circ:** 2,050

**Tower News (16667)**
News
Box 447
Tower, MN 55790
Phone: (218)753-3170
**Subject(s):** Paid Community Newspapers
**Circ:** 2,041

**The Journal-News (25053)**
PO Box 8
Spencerville, OH 45887
Phone: (419)647-4981
**Subject(s):** Paid Community Newspapers
**Circ:** ‡2,035

**Chillicothe Times-Bulletin (8502)**
Times Newspapers
1616 W Pioneer Pkwy.
Peoria, IL 61615
Phone: (309)692-6600
Fax: (309)690-3399
**Subject(s):** Paid Community Newspapers
**Circ:** (Paid)2,025

**The Florence Mining News (32948)**
Up North Publishing Inc.
PO Box 79
162 Florence Ave.
Florence, WI 54121
Phone: (715)696-3400

Fax: (715)528-5976
**Subject(s):** Paid Community Newspapers
**Circ:** (Combined)2,021

**Advocate (8509)**
487 S Main
Clifton, IL 60927
Phone: (815)694-2122
Fax: (815)694-3770
**Subject(s):** Paid Community Newspapers
**Circ:** (Paid)‡2,000

**Askov American (15936)**
PO Box 275
Askov, MN 55704
Phone: (320)838-3151
Fax: (320)838-3152
**Subject(s):** Paid Community Newspapers
**Circ:** ‡2,000

**Aurora Borealis (7871)**
Aurora University
347 S Gladstone Ave.
Aurora, IL 60506
Phone: (630)892-6431
Fax: (630)844-5463
**Subject(s):** College Publications
**Circ:** (Free)‡2,000

**The Bellville Star & Tri Forks Press (24184)**
Hirt Publishing Co.
107 Main St.
Bellville, OH 44813-1020
Phone: (419)886-2291
Fax: (419)886-2704
**Subject(s):** Paid Community Newspapers
**Circ:** 2,000

**Buffalo County Journal (32895)**
PO Box 40
104 East 5th Street
Cochrane, WI 54622-0040
Phone: (608)248-2451
Fax: (608)248-2422
**Subject(s):** Paid Community Newspapers
**Circ:** 2,000

**Campbellsport News (32880)**
101 N Fond du Lac Ave.
PO Box 138
Campbellsport, WI 53010
Phone: (920)533-8338
Fax: (920)533-5579
**Subject(s):** Paid Community Newspapers
**Circ:** 2,000

**Carroll County Mirror-Democrat (9005)**
Mirror-Democrat Publishing Co.
308 N Main St.
PO Box 191
Mount Carroll, IL 61053
Phone: (815)244-2411
Fax: (815)244-2965
**Subject(s):** Paid Community Newspapers
**Circ:** (Paid)‡2,000

**The Chieftain (8982)**
Black Hawk College
6600 34th Ave.
Moline, IL 61265
Phone: (309)796-5000
Fax: (309)792-5976
**Subject(s):** College Publications
**Circ:** (Free)‡2,000

**The Chimes (24538)**
Capital University
2199 E Main St.
Columbus, OH 43209
Phone: (614)236-6614
Fax: (614)236-6916
**Subject(s):** College Publications
**Circ:** (Free)2,000

**The Delta Atlas (24698)**
212 Main St.
Delta, OH 43515-1312
Phone: (419)822-3231
Fax: (419)822-3289
**Subject(s):** Free Newspapers; Paid Community Newspapers
**Circ:** (Non-paid)‡200
(Paid)‡2,000

**Fennimore Times (33140)**
208 W. Cherry St.
Lancaster, WI 53813
Phone: (608)723-2151
**Subject(s):** Paid Community Newspapers
**Circ:** 2,000

**Genesee County Herald (15133)**
PO Box 127
G10098 North Dort Hwy
Clio, MI 48420
Phone: (810)686-3840
Fax: (810)686-9181
**Subject(s):** Paid Community Newspapers
**Circ:** 2,000

**Harbor Springs Harbor Light (15388)**
North Country Publishing Corp.
211 E 3rd St.
Harbor Springs, MI 49740
Phone: (231)526-2191
Fax: (231)526-7634
**Subject(s):** Paid Community Newspapers
**Circ:** ‡2,000

**Herald (16427)**
PO Box 158
108 S Main St.
New York Mills, MN 56567
Phone: (218)385-2275
Fax: (218)385-3626
**Subject(s):** Paid Community Newspapers
**Circ:** ‡2,000

**The High Point (24766)**
Cuyahoga Community College
4250 Richmond Rd.
Highland Hills, OH 44122
Phone: (216)987-2344
Fax: (216)987-2104
**Subject(s):** College Publications
**Circ:** (Free)2,000

**The Hinckley News (16178)**
The Hinckley News Inc.
115 Main St.
PO Box 310
Hinckley, MN 55037
Phone: (320)384-6188
Fax: (320)384-7844
**Subject(s):** Paid Community Newspapers
**Circ:** ‡2,000

**Hudson Post Gazette (15438)**
113 S Market St.
PO Box 70
Hudson, MI 49247
Phone: (517)448-2611
**Subject(s):** Paid Community Newspapers
**Circ:** 2,000

**The Journal Era (15060)**
Pullano Publications Inc.
PO Box 98
Berrien Springs, MI 49103-0098
Phone: (269)473-5421
Fax: (269)471-1362
**Subject(s):** Paid Community Newspapers
**Circ:** ‡2,000

**Kettle Moraine Index (33041)**
Lake Country Publications
440 Cardinal Ln.
PO Box 200
Hartland, WI 53029-0200
Phone: (262)367-3272
Fax: (262)367-7414
**Subject(s):** Paid Community Newspapers
**Circ:** 2,004

**Knightstown Banner (9965)**
Eric M. Cox
24 N Washington St.
PO Box 116
Knightstown, IN 46148
Phone: (765)345-2292
Fax: (765)345-2113
**Subject(s):** Paid Community Newspapers
**Circ:** ‡2,000

**Le Center Leader (16210)**
Minnesota Valley News Publishing L.L.C.
PO Box 68
622 East Minnesota St
Le Center, MN 56057-1502
Phone: (507)357-2233
Fax: (507)357-6656
**Subject(s):** Paid Community Newspapers
**Circ:** (Free)20
(Paid)2,000

**Leader-Record (16145)**
Richards Publishing Company Inc.
PO Box 159
Gonvick, MN 56644
Phone: (218)487-5225
Fax: (218)487-5251
**Subject(s):** Paid Community Newspapers
**Circ:** (Paid)2,000

**Luxemburg News (33147)**
Tri-County Publishing
406 Elm St.
PO Box 130
Luxemburg, WI 54217
**Subject(s):** Paid Community Newspapers
**Circ:** 2,000

**The Manteno News (8929)**
PO Box 578
Manteno, IL 60950-0578
Phone: (815)468-6397
Fax: (815)468-7577
**Subject(s):** Paid Community Newspapers
**Circ:** ‡2,000

**The News (9651)**
Spencer Evening World
717 Main St.
Clay City, IN 47841
Phone: (812)939-2163
Fax: (812)939-2286
**Subject(s):** Paid Community Newspapers
**Circ:** 2,000

**The Paper (7880)**
725 Bainbridge St.
Barry, IL 62312
Phone: (217)335-2112
Fax: (217)335-2112
**Subject(s):** Paid Community Newspapers
**Circ:** ‡2,000

**Pine County Courier (16634)**
PO Box 230
Sandstone, MN 55072
Phone: (320)245-2368
Fax: (320)245-2438
**Subject(s):** Paid Community Newspapers
**Circ:** ‡2,000

**Press (16544)**
St. Charles Press
924 Whitewater Ave.
Saint Charles, MN 55972
Phone: (507)932-3663
Fax: (507)932-5337
**Subject(s):** Paid Community Newspapers
**Circ:** 2,000

**Progress-Examiner (10098)**
233 S 2nd St.
PO Box 225
Orleans, IN 47452
Phone: (812)865-3242
Fax: (812)865-3242
**Subject(s):** Paid Community Newspapers
**Circ:** ‡2,000

**Republican-Reporter (9184)**
121A S 4th
PO Box 8
Oregon, IL 61061
Phone: (815)732-6166
Fax: (815)732-4238
**Subject(s):** Paid Community Newspapers
**Circ:** (Paid)1,300
(Free)2,000

**The Review (8655)**
WNS Publications
914 Albany St.
Erie, IL 61250
Phone: (309)659-2761
Fax: (815)772-4105

**Subject(s):** Paid Community Newspapers

**Circ:** 2,000

**The Round Table (32844)**
Beloit College
700 College St.
Box 109
Beloit, WI 53511
Phone: (608)363-2000
**Subject(s):** College Publications
**Circ:** (Free)2,000

**Sawyer County Gazette (33665)**
PO Box 99
Winter, WI 54896
Phone: (715)266-2511
Fax: (715)266-2511
**Subject(s):** Paid Community Newspapers
**Circ:** 2,000

**Shepherd Argus (15769)**
PO Box 459
Shepherd, MI 48883
Phone: (989)828-6360
Fax: (989)828-5361
**Subject(s):** Paid Community Newspapers
**Circ:** 2,000

**Spencer County Leader (9676)**
Dubois Spencer Counties Publishing Company Inc.
PO Box 38
Ferdinand, IN 47532
Phone: (812)367-2041
Fax: (812)367-2371
**Subject(s):** Paid Community Newspapers
**Circ:** ‡2,000

**The Spokesman (8777)**
1 South Park Ave.
PO Box 128
Herrin, IL 62948
Phone: (618)942-5000
Fax: (618)942-4630
**Subject(s):** Paid Community Newspapers
**Circ:** (Paid)2,000

**Stark Jewish News (24242)**
Canton Jewish Community Federation
2631 Harvard Ave. NW
Canton, OH 44709
Phone: (330)453-0132
Fax: (330)452-4487
**Subject(s):** Jewish Publications; Paid Community Newspapers
**Circ:** (Controlled)2,000

**Tartan (8524)**
McHenry County College
8900 U.S Hwy. 14
Crystal Lake, IL 60012-2761
Phone: (815)455-3700
Fax: (815)479-7784
**Subject(s):** College Publications
**Circ:** (Free)‡2,000

**The Times (33656)**
111 East State St.
Westby, WI 54667-1301
Phone: (608)634-4317
Fax: (608)634-6499
**Subject(s):** Paid Community Newspapers
**Circ:** 2,000

**The Town Meeting (15259)**
Up North Publications Inc.
PO Box 335
Elk Rapids, MI 49629
Phone: (231)264-9711
Fax: (231)264-5191
**Subject(s):** Paid Community Newspapers
**Circ:** (Paid)2,000

**Waunakee Tribune (33622)**
PO Box 128
Waunakee, WI 53597
Phone: (608)849-5227
Fax: (608)849-4225
**Subject(s):** Paid Community Newspapers
**Circ:** 2,000

**The Weekly Home News (33553)**
PO Box 39
120 N. Worcester
Spring Green, WI 53588
Phone: (608)588-2508
Fax: (608)588-2509
**Subject(s):** Paid Community Newspapers
**Circ:** 2,000

**The Zephyr (8713)**
Norm Winick
251 E Main St.
PO Box 1
Galesburg, IL 61402
Phone: (309)342-2010
Fax: (309)342-2728
**Subject(s):** Paid Community Newspapers
**Circ:** (Paid)2,000

**News/Independent (8508)**
PO Box 8
Cissna Park, IL 60924-0008
Phone: (815)457-2245
Fax: (815)437-3245
**Subject(s):** Paid Community Newspapers
**Circ:** ‡1,992

**Northern Star (16012)**
Box 368
Clinton, MN 56225
Phone: (320)325-5152
Fax: (320)325-5280
**Subject(s):** Paid Community Newspapers
**Circ:** (Non-paid)20
(Paid)1,990

**West Salem Coulee News (33655)**
Capital Newspapers
PO Box 140
West Salem, WI 54669
Phone: (608)786-1950
Fax: (608)786-1670
**Subject(s):** Paid Community Newspapers
**Circ:** (Combined)1,998

**The Altamont News (7832)**
Altamont News Banner
118 N Main St.
Altamont, IL 62411
Phone: (618)483-6176
Fax: (618)483-5177
**Subject(s):** Paid Community Newspapers
**Circ:** ‡1,972

**Fox Point-Bayside-River Hills Herald (33401)**
Community Newspapers
15700 W Cleveland Ave.
New Berlin, WI 53151
Phone: (262)938-5000
Fax: (262)938-5001
**Subject(s):** Paid Community Newspapers
**Circ:** 1,966

**Tribune-Courier (24970)**
Stumbo Publishing Company Inc.
PO Box 127
Ontario, OH 44862
Phone: (419)529-2847
Fax: (419)529-2847
**Subject(s):** Paid Community Newspapers
**Circ:** (Free)⊕290
(Paid)⊕1,968

**Lakefield Standard (16206)**
403 Main St.
PO Box 249
Lakefield, MN 56150
Phone: (507)662-5555
Fax: (507)662-6770
**Subject(s):** Paid Community Newspapers
**Circ:** (Free)‡12
(Paid)‡1,950

**Middletown News (10026)**
106 N Fifth
Middletown, IN 47356
Phone: (765)354-2221
Fax: (765)354-2221
**Subject(s):** Paid Community Newspapers
**Circ:** ‡1,950

**Oquawka Current (9182)**
American Publish Co.
PO Box 606
Oquawka, IL 61469
Phone: (309)867-2515
Fax: (309)867-6215
**Subject(s):** Paid Community Newspapers
**Circ:** (Free)24
(Paid)1,957

**Pinconning Journal (15679)**
110 3rd St.
PO Box 626
Pinconning, MI 48650
Phone: (989)879-3811
Fax: (989)879-5529
**Subject(s):** Paid Community Newspapers
**Circ:** 1,950

**Proctor Journal (16494)**
215 5th St.
Proctor, MN 55810
Phone: (218)624-3344
Fax: (218)624-7037
**Subject(s):** Paid Community Newspapers
**Circ:** (Free)50
(Paid)1,950

**The Brillion News (32865)**
Zander Press Inc.
425 W. Ryan St.
Brillion, WI 54110
Phone: (920)756-2222
Fax: (920)756-2701
**Subject(s):** Paid Community Newspapers
**Circ:** ‡1,948

**Mt. Morris Times (9013)**
Ogle County Newspapers
121A S 4th St.
PO Box 8
Oregon, IL 61061
Phone: (815)732-6166
Fax: (815)946-2501
**Subject(s):** Paid Community Newspapers
**Circ:** ‡1,945

**Carver County News (16696)**
Box 188
130 Lewis Ave. N
Watertown, MN 55388
Phone: (952)955-1111
Fax: (952)955-2241
**Subject(s):** Paid Community Newspapers
**Circ:** (Non-paid)50
(Paid)1,920

**Black and Magenta (24932)**
Muskingum College
163 Stormont St.
New Concord, OH 43762
Phone: (740)826-8211
Fax: (740)826-8404
**Subject(s):** College Publications
**Circ:** (Paid)1,500
(Free)1,900

**Brown Publishing Company (25002)**
Central Ohio Printing
30 S Oak St.
PO Box 390
London, OH 43140-1079
Phone: (740)852-1616
Fax: (740)852-1620
**Subject(s):** Paid Community Newspapers
**Circ:** (Paid)‡1,900

**The Homer Index (15421)**
122 E Main St.
PO Box 236
Homer, MI 49245
Phone: (517)568-4646
Fax: (517)568-4346
**Subject(s):** Paid Community Newspapers
**Circ:** 1,900

**Jackson County Legal News (15455)**
Detroit Legal News Co.
304 Francis St.
Jackson, MI 49204
Phone: (517)782-0825
Fax: (517)782-4996
**Subject(s):** Law
**Circ:** 1,900

**News-Record (16229)**
Phillips Publishing Inc.
102 Fillmore
PO Box 307
Mabel, MN 55954
Phone: (507)495-5204
Fax: (507)495-5204
**Subject(s):** Paid Community Newspapers
**Circ:** ‡1,900

**Spring Valley Tribune (16653)**
Phillips Publishing Inc.
141 S Broadway
PO Box 112
Spring Valley, MN 55975
Phone: (507)346-7365
Fax: (507)346-7366
**Subject(s):** Paid Community Newspapers
**Circ:** ‡1,900

**The Kenyon Leader (16196)**
638 2nd St.
Kenyon, MN 55946
Phone: (507)789-6161
Fax: (507)789-5040
**Subject(s):** Paid Community Newspapers
**Circ:** (Free)49
(Paid)1,887

**Kittson County Enterprise (16158)**
Kittson County Enterprise Co.
109 S. 3rd St.
Hallock, MN 56728
Phone: (218)843-2312
Fax: (218)843-2312
**Subject(s):** Paid Community Newspapers
**Circ:** (Paid)‡1,885

**Carroll County Review (9447)**
Box 369
Thomson, IL 61285
Phone: (815)259-2131
Fax: (815)259-3226
**Subject(s):** Paid Community Newspapers
**Circ:** ‡1,878

**Wadsworth News (9499)**
Lakeland Media Inc.
30 S Whitney St.
PO Box 268
Grayslake, IL 60030-0268
Phone: (847)223-8161
Fax: (847)223-8810
**Subject(s):** Paid Community Newspapers
**Circ:** 1,862

**Chatham Clarion (7865)**
South County Publications
110 N 5th St.
PO Box 50
Auburn, IL 62615
Phone: (217)438-6155
Fax: (217)438-6156
**Subject(s):** Paid Community Newspapers
**Circ:** 1,850

**County Star (9456)**
News-Gazette Inc.
Drawer N
Tolono, IL 61880
Phone: (217)351-5631
Fax: (217)351-5259
**Subject(s):** Paid Community Newspapers
**Circ:** (Paid)⊕1,850

**Detroit Legal News (15847)**
Detroit Legal News Co.
1409 Allen Dr., Ste. B
Troy, MI 48083
Phone: (248)577-6100
Fax: (248)577-6111
**Subject(s):** Daily Periodicals; Banking, Finance, and Investments; Law
**Circ:** ⊕1,850

**Galesville Republican (32997)**
Republican
19852 Court Ave.
PO Box 695
Galesville, WI 54630-0695
Phone: (608)582-2330
Fax: (608)582-2455
**Subject(s):** Paid Community Newspapers
**Circ:** (Non-paid)‡25
(Paid)‡1,850

**Mountain Lake/Butterfield Observer/Advocate (16413)**
Central Publications
237 11th St. N.
Mountain Lake, MN 56159
Phone: (507)427-2725
Fax: (507)427-2724
**Subject(s):** Paid Community Newspapers
**Circ:** ‡1,856

**Glendale Herald (33404)**
Community Newspapers
15700 W Cleveland Ave.
New Berlin, WI 53151
Phone: (262)938-5000
Fax: (262)938-5001
**Subject(s):** Paid Community Newspapers
**Circ:** 1,840

**Ramsey News-Journal (9269)**
217 S Superior St.
PO Box 218
Ramsey, IL 62080-0218
Phone: (618)423-2411
Fax: (618)423-2514
**Subject(s):** Paid Community Newspapers
**Circ:** 1,847

**Oakland City Journal (10095)**
Princeton Publishing Inc.
222 N. Main St.
PO Box 187
Oakland City, IN 47660
Phone: (812)749-3913
**Subject(s):** Paid Community Newspapers
**Circ:** (Wed.)‡1,823

**The Transcript (24696)**
Ohio Wesleyan University
Phillips Hall 106
Delaware, OH 43015
Phone: (740)368-2911
Fax: (740)368-3649
**Subject(s):** College Publications
**Circ:** (Paid)‡175
(Free)‡1,825

**Normal Normalite (9072)**
Normalite
405 Pine Street Ste.A
P.O Box 67
Normal, IL 61761-0067
Phone: (309)454-5476
Fax: (309)454-5476
**Subject(s):** Paid Community Newspapers
**Circ:** ‡1,817

**Shorewood Herald (33415)**
Community Newspapers
15700 W Cleveland Ave.
New Berlin, WI 53151
Phone: (262)938-5000
Fax: (262)938-5001
**Subject(s):** Paid Community Newspapers
**Circ:** 1,811

**Argus (15258)**
217 N. 4th St.
Niles, MI 49120
**Subject(s):** Paid Community Newspapers
**Circ:** 1,800

**Epitaph News (33131)**
PO Box 8
La Farge, WI 54639
**Subject(s):** Paid Community Newspapers
**Circ:** 1,800

**The Garrett Clipper (9757)**
PO Box 59
Garrett, IN 46738
Phone: (260)357-4123
Fax: (260)925-2625
**Subject(s):** Paid Community Newspapers
**Circ:** ‡1,800

**Hillsboro Sentry-Enterprise (33052)**
Knowles Publications Inc.
839 Water Ave.
PO Box 469
Hillsboro, WI 54634
Phone: (608)489-2264
Fax: (608)489-2348
**Subject(s):** Paid Community Newspapers
**Circ:** ‡1,800

**The Independent (16463)**
Parkers Prairie Independent
117 N Otter Ave.
Parkers Prairie, MN 56361
Phone: (218)338-2741
Fax: (218)338-2745
**Subject(s):** Paid Community Newspapers
**Circ:** 1,800

**Knox Student (8711)**
Knox College
2 E S St.
Galesburg, IL 61401-4999
Phone: (309)341-7000
**Subject(s):** College Publications
**Circ:** ‡1,800

**The Leader-Enterprise (24919)**
Bryan Publishing Co.
319 W. Main
PO Box 149
Montpelier, OH 43543
Phone: (419)485-3113
Fax: (419)485-3114
**Subject(s):** Paid Community Newspapers
**Circ:** ‡1,800

**Rossford Record Journal (25027)**
Welch Publishing Co.
215 Osborn St.
PO Box 145
Rossford, OH 43460
Phone: (419)666-5344
**Subject(s):** Paid Community Newspapers
**Circ:** ‡1,800

**Skokie Life (9378)**
Lerner Communications Inc.
7331 N Lincoln Ave.
Lincolnwood, IL 60712
Phone: (847)329-2000
Fax: (847)329-2060
**Subject(s):** Paid Community Newspapers
**Circ:** (Paid)1,807

**Starbuck Times (16657)**
PO Box 457
508 Main St.
Starbuck, MN 56381
Phone: (320)239-2244
Fax: (320)239-2254
**Subject(s):** Paid Community Newspapers
**Circ:** (Free)‡25
(Paid)‡1,800

**Windy City Times (8447)**
1940 W. Irving Park Rd.
Chicago, IL 60657
Phone: (773)871-7610
Fax: (773)871-7609
**Subject(s):** Paid Community Newspapers
**Circ:** (Non-paid)1,800

**Yellow Springs News (25205)**
PO Box 187
Yellow Springs, OH 45387
Phone: (937)767-7373
**Subject(s):** Paid Community Newspapers
**Circ:** (Free)‡50
(Paid)‡1,800

**Rising Sun Recorder (10136)**
Register Publications
235 Main St.
PO Box 128
Rising Sun, IN 47040-0128
Phone: (812)438-2011
Fax: (812)438-3228
**Subject(s):** Paid Community Newspapers
**Circ:** (Free)15
(Paid)1,785

**The Courier-Sentinel (16198)**
405 W Center St.
Kiester, MN 56051
Phone: (507)294-3400
Fax: (507)294-3400
**Subject(s):** Paid Community Newspapers
**Circ:** 1,778

# Great Lakes States

**Manchester Enterprise  (15564)**
Heritage Newspapers Inc.
109 E. Main St.
PO Box 37
Manchester, MI 48158
Phone: (734)428-8173
**Subject(s):** Paid Community Newspapers
**Circ:** (Non-paid)23
   (Paid)1,775

**The Cheese Reporter  (33162)**
The Cheese Reporter Publishing Company Inc.
2810 Crossroads Dr., Ste. 3000
Madison, WI 53718-7972
Phone: (608)246-8430
Fax: (608)246-8431
**Subject(s):** Dairying; Food and Grocery Trade
**Circ:** (Free)170
   (Paid)1,760

**Churubusco News  (9650)**
Churubusco News and Printing
123 N Main St.
PO Box 8
Churubusco, IN 46723
Phone: (260)693-3949
Fax: (260)693-6545
**Subject(s):** Paid Community Newspapers
**Circ:** (Paid)⊕1,766

**Fairfax Standard  (16113)**
Fairfax Standard - Gazette
102 SE 1st
PO Box 589
Fairfax, MN 55332
Phone: (507)426-7235
Fax: (507)426-7264
**Subject(s):** Paid Community Newspapers
**Circ:** ‡1,760

**Hermantown Star  (16170)**
4850 Miller Trunk, Ste. 4B
Hermantown, MN 55811
Phone: (218)727-0419
Fax: (218)722-5821
**Subject(s):** Paid Community Newspapers
**Circ:** (Free)97
   (Paid)1,767

**Abingdon Argus  (8919)**
Eagle Publications of Western Illinois Inc.
210 S. Randolph St.
Macomb, IL 61455
Phone: (309)837-4428
Fax: (309)837-7188
**Subject(s):** Paid Community Newspapers
**Circ:** (Free)15
   (Paid)1,750

**Advertiser  (8863)**
Lebanon Advertiser
309 W St. Louis St.
PO Box 126
Lebanon, IL 62254-0126
Phone: (618)537-4498
**Subject(s):** Paid Community Newspapers
**Circ:** 1,750

**Hayfield Herald  (16164)**
108 E Main
PO Box 85
Hayfield, MN 55940-0085
Phone: (507)477-2232
Fax: (507)374-9327
**Subject(s):** Paid Community Newspapers
**Circ:** ‡1,750

**The Horicon Reporter  (33054)**
Wisconsin Free Press
319 E. Lake St.
PO Box 164
Horicon, WI 53032-0148
Phone: (414)485-2016
**Subject(s):** Paid Community Newspapers
**Circ:** ‡1,750

**Maple Lake Messenger  (16257)**
PO Box 817, 218 Division St., W.
Maple Lake, MN 55358
Phone: (320)963-3813
Fax: (320)963-6114
**Subject(s):** Paid Community Newspapers
**Circ:** ‡1,750

**Rinksider  (24601)**
Target Publishing Company Inc.
2470 E Main St.
Columbus, OH 43209
Phone: (614)235-1022
Fax: (614)235-3584
**Subject(s):** Management and Administration; Business; (Skating)
**Circ:** (Paid)‡750
   (Non-paid)‡1,750

**Steeleville Ledger  (9427)**
Webster Printing Co.
108 N Sparta St.
Steeleville, IL 62288
Phone: (618)965-3417
Fax: (618)965-3548
**Subject(s):** Paid Community Newspapers
**Circ:** (Non-paid)‡202
   (Paid)‡1,758

**Newton County Enterprise  (9960)**
Twin States Publishing
PO Box 107
Kentland, IN 47951
Phone: (219)474-5532
Fax: (219)474-5354
**Subject(s):** Paid Community Newspapers
**Circ:** (Paid)1,730

**Pine River Journal  (16478)**
Morris Communications Corp.
215 Norway Ave.
Pine River, MN 56474
**Subject(s):** Paid Community Newspapers
**Circ:** ‡1,725

**West Milton Record  (25084)**
Times Community Newspapers
1455 W Main St.
Tipp City, OH 45371-2803
Phone: (937)667-2214
Fax: (937)667-8987
**Subject(s):** Paid Community Newspapers
**Circ:** (Free)‡150
   (Paid)‡1,716

**The Clinton Local  (15131)**
108 Tecumseh St.
PO Box B
Clinton, MI 49236
Phone: (517)456-4100
Fax: (517)456-6372
**Subject(s):** Paid Community Newspapers
**Circ:** ‡1,700

**The Clyde Enterprise  (24524)**
Gazette Publishing Company Inc.
107 S. Main St.
PO Box 29
Clyde, OH 43410
Phone: (419)547-9726
Fax: (419)547-9726
**Subject(s):** Paid Community Newspapers
**Circ:** 1,700

**Farmer City Journal  (8693)**
Woodford County Journal
221 S. Main
PO Box 80
Farmer City, IL 61842
Phone: (309)928-2193
Fax: (309)928-0360
**Subject(s):** Paid Community Newspapers
**Circ:** (Combined)‡1,700

**Greenup Press  (8756)**
104 E. Cumberland
Box 127
Greenup, IL 62428
Phone: (217)923-3704
Fax: (217)923-3704
**Subject(s):** Paid Community Newspapers
**Circ:** (Paid)57
   (Paid)1,703

**The Henderson County Quill  (9436)**
Hancock-Henderson Quill Inc.
PO Box 149
Stronghurst, IL 61480-0149
Phone: (309)924-1871
Fax: (309)924-1212
**Subject(s):** Paid Community Newspapers
**Circ:** ‡1,700

**Lamberton News  (16209)**
218 E. Main St.
PO Box 308
Lamberton, MN 56152
Phone: (507)752-7181
Fax: (507)752-7181
**Subject(s):** Paid Community Newspapers
**Circ:** (Free)50
   (Paid)1,703

**Tri-County Record  (16540)**
Tri-County Publishing Inc.
PO Box 429
Rushford, MN 55971
Phone: (507)864-7700
Fax: (507)864-2356
**Subject(s):** Paid Community Newspapers
**Circ:** 1,700

**Tri-County Record Special Edition  (16541)**
Tri-County Publishing Inc.
PO Box 429
Rushford, MN 55971
Phone: (507)864-7700
Fax: (507)864-2356
**Subject(s):** Shopping Guides
**Circ:** (Paid)1,700

**Westbrook Sentinel & Tribune  (16700)**
621 1st Ave.
PO Box 98
Westbrook, MN 56183
Phone: (507)274-6136
Fax: (507)274-6137
**Subject(s):** Paid Community Newspapers
**Circ:** 1,700

**Wittenberg Enterprise and Birnamwood News  (33674)**
Wittenberg Press Inc.
PO Box 190
Wittenberg, WI 54499-0190
Phone: (715)253-2737
Fax: (715)253-2700
**Subject(s):** Paid Community Newspapers
**Circ:** (Free)300
   (Paid)1,700

**Woodford County Journal-Eureka Edition  (8657)**
Woodford County Journal
1926 S Main St.
PO Box 36
Eureka, IL 61530
Phone: (309)467-3314
Fax: (309)467-4563
**Subject(s):** Paid Community Newspapers
**Circ:** ‡1,700

**Inkster Ledger Star  (15440)**
The Journal Newspapers
35540 Michigan Ave.
PO Box 578
Wayne, MI 48184
Phone: (734)467-1900
Fax: (734)729-1840
**Subject(s):** Paid Community Newspapers
**Circ:** (Non-paid)889
   (Paid)1,695

**Lakeview Enterprise  (15506)**
The Pioneer Group
327 Lincoln Ave.
PO Box 500
Lakeview, MI 48850
Phone: (517)352-8210
Fax: (517)352-8210
**Subject(s):** Paid Community Newspapers
**Circ:** ‡1,685

**Villa Grove News  (9496)**
Holmes Publications
PO Box 20
Villa Grove, IL 61956
Phone: (217)832-4201
Fax: (217)834-4001
**Subject(s):** Paid Community Newspapers
**Circ:** ‡1,675

**The Bunker Hill Gazette-News  (7934)**
Bunker Hill Publications
PO Box Z
Bunker Hill, IL 62014
Phone: (618)585-4411
Fax: (618)585-3354
**Subject(s):** Paid Community Newspapers
**Circ:** ‡1,650

**Hampshire Register News (8764)**
Kane/DeKalb News Weeklies
PO Box 337
Hampshire, IL 60140
Phone: (847)683-2627
Fax: (815)899-4329
**Subject(s):** Paid Community Newspapers

**Circ:** (Free)23
(Paid)1,654

**Mt. Pulaski Weekly News (9022)**
311 S Washington St.
PO Box 114
Mount Pulaski, IL 62548
Phone: (217)792-5557
Fax: (217)792-5482
**Subject(s):** Paid Community Newspapers

**Circ:** 1,650

**Region News (9025)**
433 Hwy. 121
Box 79
Mount Zion, IL 62549
Phone: (217)864-4212
Fax: (217)864-4711
**Subject(s):** Paid Community Newspapers

**Circ:** ‡1,650

**The Mishawaka Enterprise (10033)**
PO Box 584
Mishawaka, IN 46546-0584
Phone: (574)255-4789
Fax: (574)255-4789
**Subject(s):** Law

**Circ:** (Controlled)1,625

**Northwoods Press (16414)**
PO Box 28
Nevis, MN 56467
Phone: (218)652-3475
**Subject(s):** Paid Community Newspapers

**Circ:** (Free)40
(Paid)1,620

**Western Itasca Review (16039)**
Deer River Publishing
PO Box 427
15 1st Street NE
Deer River, MN 56636
Phone: (218)246-8533
Fax: (218)246-8540
**Subject(s):** Paid Community Newspapers

**Circ:** (Free)27
(Paid)1,622

**Auburn Citizen (7864)**
110 N 5th St.
Auburn, IL 62615
Phone: (217)438-6155
Fax: (217)438-6156
**Subject(s):** Paid Community Newspapers

**Circ:** ‡1,600

**Bargain Searchlight (16265)**
Melrose Beacon
PO Box 186
Melrose, MN 56352-0186
Phone: (320)256-3240
Fax: (320)256-3363
**Subject(s):** Shopping Guides

**Circ:** (Free)1,600

**Beecher City Journal (7889)**
PO Box 38
Beecher City, IL 62414
Phone: (618)487-5634
Fax: (618)487-5180
**Subject(s):** Paid Community Newspapers

**Circ:** 1,600

**Blooming Prairie Times (15969)**
411 E Main St.
PO Box 247
Blooming Prairie, MN 55917
Phone: (507)583-4431
Fax: (507)583-4445
**Subject(s):** Paid Community Newspapers

**Circ:** ‡1,600

**Decatur Republican (15160)**
P O Box 36
120 South Phelps Street
Decatur, MI 49045-0036
Phone: (269)423-2411
Fax: (269)423-2411

**Subject(s):** Paid Community Newspapers

**Circ:** 1,600

**The East Troy News (32873)**
Southern Lakes Newspapers
140 Commerce St.
Burlington, WI 53105-0437
Phone: (262)763-3511
Fax: (262)763-2238
**Subject(s):** Paid Community Newspapers

**Circ:** ‡1,600

**Lake Region Life (16697)**
115 S 3rd St.
Waterville, MN 56096
Phone: (507)362-4495
Fax: (507)362-4458
**Subject(s):** Paid Community Newspapers

**Circ:** ‡1,603

**The Mac Weekly (16591)**
Macalester College
1600 Grand Ave.
Saint Paul, MN 55105
Phone: (651)696-6000
Fax: (651)696-6685
**Subject(s):** College Publications

**Circ:** ‡1,600

**Macedonian Tribune (9721)**
Macedonian Patriotic Organization
124 W Wayne St.
Fort Wayne, IN 46802
Phone: (260)422-5900
Fax: (260)422-1348
**Subject(s):** Bulgarian; Ethnic Publications

**Circ:** ‡1,600

**The Oracle (16605)**
Hamline University
1536 Hewitt Ave.
Saint Paul, MN 55104-1284
Phone: (651)523-2800
**Subject(s):** College Publications

**Circ:** ‡1,600

**Brown Deer Herald (33398)**
Community Newspapers
15700 W Cleveland Ave.
New Berlin, WI 53151
Phone: (262)938-5000
Fax: (262)938-5001
**Subject(s):** Paid Community Newspapers

**Circ:** 1,596

**Elm Grove Elm Leaves (33400)**
Community Newspapers
15700 W Cleveland Ave.
New Berlin, WI 53151
Phone: (262)938-5000
Fax: (262)938-5001
**Subject(s):** Paid Community Newspapers

**Circ:** 1,596

**Gazette (16496)**
PO Box 370
Red Lake Falls, MN 56750
Phone: (218)253-2594
Fax: (218)253-4114
**Subject(s):** Paid Community Newspapers

**Circ:** ‡1,599

**Gibson City Courier (9271)**
East Central Communications Inc.
1332 Harmon Dr. E
PO Box 5110
Rantoul, IL 61866
Phone: (217)892-9613
Fax: (217)892-9451
**Subject(s):** Paid Community Newspapers

**Circ:** (Non-paid)♦40
(Paid)♦1,587

**Reedsburg Times-Press (33498)**
South Central Wisconsin Newspapers Inc.
PO Box 269
Reedsburg, WI 53959-0269
Phone: (608)524-4336
Fax: (608)524-4337
**Subject(s):** Paid Community Newspapers

**Circ:** (Combined)1,582

**Washburn County Register (33542)**
PO Box 455
11 W. 5th Ave.
Shell Lake, WI 54871
Phone: (715)468-2314
Fax: (715)468-4900
**Subject(s):** Paid Community Newspapers

**Circ:** (Free)‡20
(Paid)‡1,566

**Arlington Enterprise (15935)**
402 W Alden St.
Arlington, MN 55307
**Subject(s):** Paid Community Newspapers

**Circ:** 1,550

**Cedar Lake Journal (10005)**
Pilcher Publishing Company Inc.
116-18 Clark St.
PO Box 248
Lowell, IN 46356
Phone: (219)696-7711
Fax: (219)696-7713
**Subject(s):** Free Newspapers

**Circ:** (Paid)‡1,550

**Dunkirk News & Sun (10115)**
The Graphic Printing Company Inc.
PO Box 1049
Portland, IN 47371
Phone: (260)726-8141
Fax: (260)726-8143
**Subject(s):** Paid Community Newspapers

**Circ:** ‡1,547

**Gazette-Patriot (7985)**
428 N Main St.
PO Box 231
Carrollton, IL 62016-0231
Phone: (217)942-3626
Fax: (217)942-3699
**Subject(s):** Paid Community Newspapers

**Circ:** (Free)⊕**60**
(Paid)⊕**1,546**

**Culver Citizen (9675)**
Citizen Publications
107 S Main St.
PO Box 90
Culver, IN 46511-0090
Phone: (219)842-3229
Fax: (219)935-0083
**Subject(s):** Paid Community Newspapers

**Circ:** (Non-paid)⊕30
(Paid)⊕**1,538**

**The Bay Viewer (33396)**
Community Newspapers
15700 W Cleveland Ave.
New Berlin, WI 53151
Phone: (262)938-5000
Fax: (262)938-5001
**Subject(s):** Paid Community Newspapers

**Circ:** 1,529

**The Henning Advocate (16168)**
803 Inman St.
PO Box 175
Henning, MN 56551
Phone: (218)548-5585
Fax: (218)548-5585
**Subject(s):** Paid Community Newspapers

**Circ:** ‡1,511

**New Washington Herald (24941)**
The Herald Printing Co.
625 S Kibler St.
PO Box 367
New Washington, OH 44854-0367
Phone: (419)492-2133
Fax: (419)492-2128
**Subject(s):** Paid Community Newspapers

**Circ:** ‡1,516

**Twin Valley Times/Gary Graphic (16671)**
Times Publishing Co.
PO Box 478
Twin Valley, MN 56584
Phone: (218)584-5195
Fax: (218)584-5196
**Subject(s):** Paid Community Newspapers

**Circ:** ‡1,515

Circulation: ★ = ABC; △ = BPA; ♦ = CAC; ● = CCAB; ▫ = VAC; ⊕ = PO Statement; ‡ = Publisher's Report; Boldface figures = sworn; Light figures = estimated.

# Great Lakes States

**Antwerp Bee-Argus (24126)**
113 N Main
PO Box 1065
Antwerp, OH 45813
Phone: (419)258-8161
Fax: (419)258-9365
**Subject(s):** Paid Community Newspapers
**Circ:** (Paid)1,500

**Aquinas Times (15331)**
Aquinas College Publications Board
1607 Robinson Rd. SE
Grand Rapids, MI 49506-1799
Phone: (616)459-8281
Fax: (616)732-4487
**Subject(s):** College Publications
**Circ:** (Non-paid)‡1,500

**Augusta Area Times (32827)**
PO Box 465
Augusta, WI 54722
Phone: (715)286-2655
Fax: (715)597-2705
**Subject(s):** Paid Community Newspapers
**Circ:** ‡1,500

**The Blair Press (32860)**
109 N Gilbert St.
Box 187
Blair, WI 54616
Phone: (608)989-2531
Fax: (608)989-9615
**Subject(s):** Paid Community Newspapers
**Circ:** ‡1,500

**Clinton County News (8940)**
Herald Publications
314 East Church St.
Drawer C
Mascoutah, IL 62258
Phone: (618)566-8282
Fax: (618)566-8283
**Subject(s):** Paid Community Newspapers
**Circ:** ‡1,500

**The Delavan Times (8569)**
314 Locust St.
PO Box 199
Delavan, IL 61734-0199
Phone: (309)244-7111
**Subject(s):** Paid Community Newspapers
**Circ:** ‡1,500

**Finance and Commerce (16298)**
Finance & Commerce Inc.
730 2nd Ave., No. 100
Minneapolis, MN 55402-3400
Phone: (612)333-4244
Fax: (612)333-3243
**Subject(s):** Business; Daily Periodicals
**Circ:** ‡1,500

**Herald (16651)**
115 W. Main Street
PO Box 68
Spring Grove, MN 55974
Phone: (507)498-3868
Fax: (507)498-6397
**Subject(s):** Paid Community Newspapers
**Circ:** ‡1,500

**Jordan Independent (16193)**
Southwest Suburban Publishing
c/o Mathias Baden
109 Rice St. S.
Jordan, MN 55352
Phone: (952)492-2224
Fax: (952)492-2231
**Subject(s):** Paid Community Newspapers
**Circ:** (Free)67
(Paid)⊕1,500

**The Kerkhoven Banner (16197)**
1003 Atlantic Ave.
PO Box 148
Kerkhoven, MN 56252
Phone: (320)264-3071
Fax: (320)264-3070
**Subject(s):** Paid Community Newspapers
**Circ:** 1,500

**The Mt. Olive Herald (9019)**
John & Suzie Galer
102 E Main St.
PO Box 300
Mount Olive, IL 62069
Phone: (217)999-3941
Fax: (217)999-5105
**Subject(s):** Paid Community Newspapers
**Circ:** 1,500

**Olivia Times-Journal (16447)**
Renco Publishing Inc.
816 E Lincoln
Olivia, MN 56277
Phone: (320)523-2032
Fax: (320)523-2033
**Subject(s):** Paid Community Newspapers
**Circ:** (Non-paid)‡445
(Paid)‡1,507

**Promethean (33571)**
University of Wisconsin
1800 Grand Ave.
Superior, WI 54880
Phone: (715)394-8335
Fax: (715)394-8454
**Subject(s):** College Publications
**Circ:** (Paid)‡1,500
(Non-paid)‡1,500

**The Rose Thorn (10192)**
Rose-Hulman Institute of Technology
5500 Wabash Ave.
Terre Haute, IN 47803
Phone: (812)877-8258
Fax: (812)877-8362
**Subject(s):** College Publications
**Circ:** (Free)‡1,500

**The Tyler Tribute (16674)**
151 N Tyler St.
Box Q
Tyler, MN 56178-0466
Phone: (507)247-5502
Fax: (507)247-5502
**Subject(s):** Paid Community Newspapers
**Circ:** ‡1,500

**Vassar Pioneer Times (15874)**
Hearst Corp.
113 S Main
Box 69
Vassar, MI 48768
Phone: (989)823-8579
Fax: (989)823-8778
**Subject(s):** Paid Community Newspapers
**Circ:** 1,500

**Clara City Herald (16010)**
Box 458
Clara City, MN 56222
Phone: (320)847-3130
Fax: (320)847-2630
**Subject(s):** Paid Community Newspapers
**Circ:** ‡1,490

**The Dalton Gazette & Kidron News (24641)**
PO Box 495
41 W Main St.
Dalton, OH 44618
Phone: (330)828-8401
Fax: (330)828-8401
**Subject(s):** Paid Community Newspapers
**Circ:** ‡1,385
1,495

**Enterprise (33002)**
Hart Publishing Co.
PO Box 128
Glidden, WI 54527
Phone: (715)264-3481
Fax: (715)264-3481
**Subject(s):** Paid Community Newspapers
**Circ:** 1,480

**The Edgerton Earth (24707)**
S.W.W. Publications L.L.C.
114 S Michigan St.
Edgerton, OH 43517
Phone: (419)298-2369
Fax: (419)298-2360
**Subject(s):** Paid Community Newspapers
**Circ:** ‡1,475

**Menomonee Falls News (33407)**
Community Newspapers
15700 W Cleveland Ave.
New Berlin, WI 53151
Phone: (262)938-5000
Fax: (262)938-5001
**Subject(s):** Paid Community Newspapers
**Circ:** 1,468

**Mequon-Thiensville Courant (33408)**
Community Newspapers
15700 W Cleveland Ave.
New Berlin, WI 53151
Phone: (262)938-5000
Fax: (262)938-5001
**Subject(s):** Paid Community Newspapers
**Circ:** 1,468

**Central St. Croix News (33036)**
815 Davis
Box 208
Hammond, WI 54015
Phone: (715)796-2356
Fax: (715)796-2355
**Subject(s):** Paid Community Newspapers
**Circ:** 1,450

**Dodge Center Star-Record (16046)**
Community News Corp.
PO Box 279
Box 279
Dodge Center, MN 55927
Phone: (507)374-6531
Fax: (507)374-9327
**Subject(s):** Paid Community Newspapers
**Circ:** (Free)50
(Paid)1,450

**Minden City Herald (15596)**
1524 Main Street
Minden City, MI 48456
Phone: (989)864-3630
Fax: (989)864-5363
**Subject(s):** Paid Community Newspapers
**Circ:** (Free)100
(Paid)1450

**Sun (9458)**
Sun Trenton Publishing
PO Box 118
Trenton, IL 62293
Phone: (618)224-9422
Fax: (618)224-9422
**Subject(s):** Paid Community Newspapers
**Circ:** (Free)‡50
(Paid)‡1,450

**The Ripley Bee (25022)**
Box 97
Ripley, OH 45167
Phone: (937)392-4321
Fax: (937)392-0317
**Subject(s):** Paid Community Newspapers
**Circ:** ‡1,425

**Messenger (32896)**
PO Box 517
Colfax, WI 54730
Phone: (715)962-3535
Fax: (715)962-3413
**Subject(s):** Paid Community Newspapers
**Circ:** 1410

**Fulda Free Press (16137)**
PO Box 439
118 North Saint Paul
Fulda, MN 56131
Phone: (507)425-2303
Fax: (507)425-2501
**Subject(s):** Paid Community Newspapers
**Circ:** ‡1,400

**The Knox County Citizen (24732)**
Knox County Printing Co.
PO Box 240
Fredericktown, OH 43019
Phone: (740)694-4016
Fax: (740)694-4555
**Subject(s):** Paid Community Newspapers
**Circ:** 1,400

**Liberty Bee-Times (8867)**
Elliott Publishing Inc.
PO Box 198
Liberty, IL 62347
Phone: (217)645-3033
Fax: (217)645-3083
**Subject(s):** Paid Community Newspapers
**Circ:** ‡1,400

**Marcellus News (15571)**
PO Box 277
Marcellus, MI 49067
Phone: (269)646-2101
Fax: (269)646-2101
**Subject(s):** Paid Community Newspapers
**Circ:** 1,400

**Minneota Mascot (16376)**
201 N Jefferson
PO Box 8
Minneota, MN 56264
Phone: (507)872-6492
Fax: (507)872-6492
**Subject(s):** Paid Community Newspapers
**Circ:** 1,400

**Nobles County Review (15913)**
PO Box 160
108 Main Ave
Adrian, MN 56110
Phone: (507)483-2213
Fax: (507)483-2219
**Subject(s):** Paid Community Newspapers
**Circ:** ‡1,400

**Princeton Times-Republic (32853)**
Berlin Journal Newspapers
PO Box 10
Berlin, WI 54923-0010
Phone: (920)361-1515
Fax: (920)361-1518
**Subject(s):** Paid Community Newspapers
**Circ:** ‡1,400

**Putnam County Vidette/Pandora Times (24629)**
Hirt Publishing Co.
109 W Sycamore St.
PO Box 127
Columbus Grove, OH 45830-0127
Phone: (419)659-2173
Fax: (419)659-2760
**Subject(s):** Paid Community Newspapers
**Circ:** ‡1,400

**Wabasso Standard (16680)**
PO Box 70
Wabasso, MN 56293
Phone: (507)342-5143
Fax: (507)342-5144
**Subject(s):** Paid Community Newspapers
**Circ:** 1,400

**Wakarusa Tribune (10232)**
Ecom Publishing
PO Box 507
Wakarusa, IN 46573
Fax: (219)293-3705
**Subject(s):** Paid Community Newspapers
**Circ:** (Free)‡90
      (Paid)‡1,400

**Tri-County News (16199)**
Box 220
Kimball, MN 55353
Phone: (320)398-5000
Fax: (320)398-5000
**Subject(s):** Paid Community Newspapers
**Circ:** (Free)25
      (Paid)1,375

**The Valley News (24801)**
Gazette Printing Company Inc.
34 S. Chestnut St.
Jefferson, OH 44047
Phone: (440)576-9155
Fax: (440)576-4337
**Subject(s):** Paid Community Newspapers
**Circ:** (Free)‡35
      (Paid)‡1,365

**Blaine Spring Lake Park Life (16027)**
Anoka County Shopper
4101 Coon Rapids Blvd.
PO Box 99
Coon Rapids, MN 55433
Phone: (763)421-4444
Fax: (763)421-4315
**Subject(s):** Paid Community Newspapers
**Circ:** (Paid)‡1,350

**The Le Roy Journal (8862)**
Woodford County Journal
1926 S Main St.
PO Box 36
Eureka, IL 61530
Phone: (309)467-3314
Fax: (309)467-4563
**Subject(s):** Paid Community Newspapers
**Circ:** (Paid)‡1,350

**The Republican (9678)**
Hendricks County Republican Inc.
6 E Main St.
PO Box 149
Danville, IN 46122
Phone: (317)745-2777
Fax: (317)745-2777
**Subject(s):** Paid Community Newspapers
**Circ:** ‡1,350

**Waverly Journal (9516)**
130 S Pearl
PO Box 78
Waverly, IL 62692
Phone: (217)435-9221
Fax: (217)435-4511
**Subject(s):** Paid Community Newspapers
**Circ:** ‡1,350

**Cass Lake Times (16004)**
Olson Communications Inc.
PO Box 398
Cass Lake, MN 56633
Phone: (218)335-2290
**Subject(s):** Paid Community Newspapers
**Circ:** (Paid)1,340

**Frost Illustrated (9716)**
Frost Inc.
3121 S Calhoun St.
Fort Wayne, IN 46807
Phone: (260)745-0552
Fax: (260)745-9503
**Subject(s):** Paid Community Newspapers; Black Publications
**Circ:** (Free)‡32
      (Paid)‡1,342

**The Hope Star-Journal (9803)**
611 Harrison St.
Hope, IN 47246
Phone: (812)546-4940
Fax: (812)546-4944
**Subject(s):** Paid Community Newspapers
**Circ:** (Free)102
      (Paid)1,312

**Banner (9341)**
407N. Main St.
PO Box 10
Saint Elmo, IL 62458
Phone: (618)829-3246
Fax: (618)483-6176
**Subject(s):** Paid Community Newspapers
**Circ:** ‡1,300

**The Clinton Topper (32893)**
242 Allen St.
Box 569
Clinton, WI 53525-0569
Phone: (608)676-4111
Fax: (608)676-4664
**Subject(s):** Paid Community Newspapers
**Circ:** (Free)‡50
      (Paid)‡1,300

**Daily Legal News (24395)**
Legal News Publishing Co.
2935 Prospect Ave.
Cleveland, OH 44115
Phone: (216)696-3322
Fax: (216)696-6329
**Subject(s):** Daily Periodicals; Law
**Circ:** ‡1,300

**Janesville Argus (16191)**
P.O.Box 220
Janesville, MN 56048
Phone: (507)234-6651
Fax: (507)234-6390
**Subject(s):** Paid Community Newspapers
**Circ:** 1,300

**Le Roy Independent (16211)**
Evans Printing & Publishing
135 E main St.
PO Box 89
Le Roy, MN 55951-0089
Phone: (507)324-5325
Fax: (507)324-5267
**Subject(s):** Paid Community Newspapers
**Circ:** ‡1,300

**The Liberty Press (24828)**
Mickens Inc.
PO Box 6
Liberty Center, OH 43532
Phone: (419)533-2401
Fax: (419)533-2401
**Subject(s):** Paid Community Newspapers
**Circ:** (Free)‡173
      (Paid)‡1,300

**The North Baltimore News (24948)**
Bluffton Printing & Publishing Co.
114 N Main St.
PO Box 67
North Baltimore, OH 45872
Phone: (419)257-2771
Fax: (419)257-3058
**Subject(s):** Paid Community Newspapers
**Circ:** ‡1,300

**Register (8612)**
East Dubuque Register
141 Sinsinawa Ave.
East Dubuque, IL 61025
Phone: (815)747-3171
**Subject(s):** Paid Community Newspapers
**Circ:** ‡1,300

**Herman Review (16169)**
Box E
Herman, MN 56248-0304
Phone: (320)677-2229
Fax: (320)677-2229
**Subject(s):** Paid Community Newspapers
**Circ:** ‡1,275

**Macomb County Legal News (15767)**
Advisor & Source Newspapers
48075 Van Dyke Ave.
Shelby Township, MI 48317
Phone: (586)731-1000
Fax: (586)731-8172
**Subject(s):** Paid Community Newspapers; Law
**Circ:** 1,279

**Chronicle (7940)**
119 W. Exchange
Cambridge, IL 61238
Phone: (309)937-3303
Fax: (309)944-5615
**Subject(s):** Paid Community Newspapers
**Circ:** (Paid)‡1,264

**Cadott Sentinel (32877)**
Box 70
Cadott, WI 54727
Phone: (715)289-4978
Fax: (715)239-6200
**Subject(s):** Paid Community Newspapers
**Circ:** (Paid)‡1,250

**Democrat-Tribune (33375)**
334 High St.
Mineral Point, WI 53565
Phone: (608)987-2141
Fax: (608)935-9531
**Subject(s):** Paid Community Newspapers
**Circ:** 1,259

**Hancock County Quill (9435)**
Hancock-Henderson Quill Inc.
PO Box 149
Stronghurst, IL 61480-0149
Phone: (309)924-1871
Fax: (309)924-1212

**IHM Connections** (15597)
IHM Sisters
610 W. Elm St.
Monroe, MI 48162
Phone: (734)240-9838
Fax: (734)240-9801
**Subject(s):** Religious Publications
Circ: (Paid)1,250

**The New Concord Area Leader** (24236)
The Jeffersonian Company Inc.
831 Wheeling Ave.
PO Box 10
Cambridge, OH 43725
Phone: (740)439-3531
Fax: (740)432-6219
**Subject(s):** Paid Community Newspapers
Circ: ‡1,250

**Register-Tribune** (15136)
15 W. Pearl St
PO Box 8
Coldwater, MI 49036
Phone: (517)741-8451
Fax: (517)278-6041
**Subject(s):** Paid Community Newspapers
Circ: (Free)‡20
 (Paid)‡1,256

**Toledo Democrat** (9455)
116 Courthouse Sq.
PO Box 7
Toledo, IL 62468
Phone: (217)849-2000
Fax: (217)849-3237
**Subject(s):** Paid Community Newspapers
Circ: 1,250

**The Ulen Union** (16675)
Box 248
Ulen, MN 56585
Phone: (218)596-8813
Fax: (218)861-6708
**Subject(s):** Paid Community Newspapers
Circ: (Free)25
 (Paid)1,250

**Lafayette-Nicollet Ledger** (16202)
Ledger Publishing Co.
Box 212
Lafayette, MN 56054
**Subject(s):** Paid Community Newspapers
Circ: 1,240

**Onalaska Community Life** (33653)
Lodestar Publications Inc.
Onalaska Community Life
PO Box 140
West Salem, WI 54669
Phone: (608)786-1950
Fax: (608)786-1670
**Subject(s):** Paid Community Newspapers
Circ: (Paid)⊕1,243

**Holmen Courier** (33652)
Lodestar Publications Inc.
Onalaska Community Life
PO Box 140
West Salem, WI 54669
Phone: (608)786-1950
Fax: (608)786-1670
**Subject(s):** Paid Community Newspapers
Circ: (Paid)⊕1,225

**Belgrade Observer** (15950)
PO Box 279
Belgrade, MN 56312
Phone: (320)254-8250
Fax: (320)254-3215
**Subject(s):** Paid Community Newspapers
Circ: 1,200

**Dodge County Independent News** (33112)
122 S Main St
PO Box 167
Juneau, WI 53039
Phone: (920)386-2421
Fax: (920)386-2422
**Subject(s):** Paid Community Newspapers
Circ: 1,200

**The Dynamo** (24118)
Mt. Union College
1972 Clark Ave.
PO Box 1283
Alliance, OH 44601
Phone: (330)823-2884
**Subject(s):** College Publications
Circ: 1,200

**The Encounter** (8826)
College of St. Francis
500 Wilcox
Joliet, IL 60435
Phone: (815)740-3360
Fax: (815)740-4285
**Subject(s):** College Publications
Circ: (Free)‡1,200

**Jonesville Independent** (15135)
Independent Newspapers
15 W. Pearl
Coldwater, MI 49036
Phone: (517)849-9880
Fax: (517)278-6041
**Subject(s):** Paid Community Newspapers
Circ: 1,200

**Mayville Monitor** (15589)
PO Box 299
Mayville, MI 48744-0299
**Subject(s):** Paid Community Newspapers
Circ: (Paid)1,200

**Monee Monitor** (8988)
Russell Publications
PO Box 429
Peotone, IL 60468
Phone: (708)258-3473
Fax: (708)258-6295
**Subject(s):** Paid Community Newspapers
Circ: 1,200

**Omro Herald** (32852)
Berlin Journal Newspapers
PO Box 10
Berlin, WI 54923-0010
Phone: (920)361-1515
Fax: (920)361-1518
**Subject(s):** Paid Community Newspapers
Circ: ‡1,200

**The Panhandle Press** (9273)
Gold Nugget Publications Inc.
PO Box 15
Raymond, IL 62560-0015
Phone: (217)229-4412
**Subject(s):** Paid Community Newspapers
Circ: ‡1,200

**The Progress** (8503)
PO Box A
Christopher, IL 62822
Phone: (618)724-9423
Fax: (618)724-9510
**Subject(s):** Paid Community Newspapers
Circ: ‡1,200

**Royal Center Record** (10142)
PO Box 638
111 South Chicago
Royal Center, IN 46978-0638
Phone: (574)643-3165
Fax: (574)643-9440
**Subject(s):** Paid Community Newspapers
Circ: ‡1,200

**Valley Farmer** (15053)
905 S Henry
Bay City, MI 48706
Phone: (989)893-6507
**Subject(s):** Farm Newspapers
Circ: ‡1,200

**Zeeland Record** (15908)
The Zeeland Record Co.
1622 S Elm St.
Zeeland, MI 49464
Phone: (616)772-2131
**Subject(s):** Paid Community Newspapers
Circ: ‡1,200

**Paxton Daily Record** (9207)
Paxton Printing Inc.
218 N Market
PO Box 73
Paxton, IL 60957
Phone: (217)379-2356
Fax: (217)379-3104
**Subject(s):** Daily Newspapers
Circ: ‡1,194

**Lincoln-Belmont Booster** (8890)
Chicago Lerner Newspapers
7331 N Lincoln Ave.
Lincolnwood, IL 60646
Phone: (847)329-2000
Fax: (847)329-2060
**Subject(s):** Free Newspapers
Circ: (Paid)1,188

**American** (9633)
Whitewater Publications Inc.
PO Box 38
Brookville, IN 47012
Phone: (317)647-4221
Fax: (317)647-4811
**Subject(s):** Free Newspapers
Circ: (Paid)1175

**Journal** (8701)
313 E. Main
Forreston, IL 61030
**Subject(s):** Paid Community Newspapers
Circ: 1,175

**Atwood Herald** (7863)
Tri-Village Publications
107 N Main St.
PO Box 589
Atwood, IL 61913
Phone: (217)578-3213
Fax: (217)578-2833
**Subject(s):** Paid Community Newspapers
Circ: ‡1,150

**Daily Journal** (8990)
Liberty Group
PO Box 650
Monmouth, IL 61462
Phone: (309)734-3176
Fax: (309)734-4649
**Subject(s):** Daily Newspapers
Circ: (Combined)1,159

**Fisher Reporter** (8696)
114 S 3rd St.
PO Box 400
Fisher, IL 61843
Phone: (217)897-1525
Fax: (217)897-1525
**Subject(s):** Paid Community Newspapers
Circ: ‡1,150

**Prairie Times** (8842)
McKirgan Productions
101 Jefferson
PO Box 27
La Fayette, IL 61449
Phone: (309)995-3877
**Subject(s):** Paid Community Newspapers
Circ: (Paid)‡1140

**The Braidwood Journal** (8514)
The Free Press Newspapers
273 South Broadway
PO Box 99
Coal City, IL 60416
Phone: (815)458-6246
Fax: (815)634-2815
**Subject(s):** Paid Community Newspapers
Circ: 1,125

**Court & Commercial Record** (9842)
41 E Washington St., Ste. 200
Indianapolis, IN 46204
Phone: (317)636-0200
Fax: (317)263-5259
**Subject(s):** Paid Community Newspapers; Law
Circ: (Controlled)⊕1,127

**Iola Herald** (33083)
Trey Foerster Ink Inc.
165 N. Main St.
PO Box 235
Iola, WI 54945
Phone: (715)445-3415

Fax: (715)445-3988
**Subject(s):** Paid Community Newspapers

Circ: 1,120

**Shores News (25024)**
Gazette Printing Company Inc.
34 S. Chestnut St.
Jefferson, OH 44047
Phone: (440)576-9115
Fax: (440)576-4337
**Subject(s):** Paid Community Newspapers

Circ: (Non-paid)‡200
(Paid)‡1,129

**Bird Island Union (16165)**
Hubin Publishing Company Inc.
Box 278
Hector, MN 55342
Phone: (320)365-3266
Fax: (320)365-4506
**Subject(s):** Paid Community Newspapers

Circ: ‡1,100

**The Glasford Gazette (8725)**
309 E Main St.
Glasford, IL 61533
Phone: (309)389-2811
Fax: (309)389-4949
**Subject(s):** Paid Community Newspapers

Circ: ‡1,100

**Green Lake County Reporter (32851)**
Berlin Journal Newspapers
PO Box 10
Berlin, WI 54923-0010
Phone: (920)361-1515
Fax: (920)361-1518
**Subject(s):** Paid Community Newspapers

Circ: ‡1,100

**Ivanhoe Times (16186)**
PO Box 100
315 North Norman St.
Ivanhoe, MN 56142-0100
Phone: (507)694-1246
Fax: (507)694-1246
**Subject(s):** Paid Community Newspapers

Circ: (Non-paid)55
(Paid)1,100

**Madison County Chronicle (9539)**
Bunker Hill Publications
PO Box 490
Worden, IL 62097-0490
Phone: (618)459-3655
Fax: (618)459-3655
**Subject(s):** Paid Community Newspapers

Circ: ‡1,100

**Sauk Rapids Herald (16636)**
Sauk Centre Publishers Inc.
522 Sinclair Lewis Ave.
Sauk Centre, MN 56378
Phone: (320)352-6577
Fax: (320)352-5647
**Subject(s):** Paid Community Newspapers

Circ: 1,100

**The Truman Tribune (16670)**
118 E Ciro St.
PO Box 98
Truman, MN 56088
Phone: (507)776-2751
Fax: (507)776-2751
**Subject(s):** Paid Community Newspapers

Circ: ‡1,100

**Advance Leader (9999)**
Advance News
121 S. Cavin Street
PO Box 30
Ligonier, IN 46767
Phone: (260)894-3102
Fax: (260)894-3104
**Subject(s):** Paid Community Newspapers

Circ: ‡1,081

**The Alden Advance (15925)**
150 E Main
Box 485
Alden, MN 56009
Phone: (507)874-3440
Fax: (507)874-3440

**Subject(s):** Paid Community Newspapers
Circ: ‡1,080

**Dakota County Tribune (15994)**
Dakota County Tribune Inc.
12190 County Rd. 11
Burnsville, MN 55337
Phone: (952)894-1111
Fax: (952)846-2010
**Subject(s):** Paid Community Newspapers

Circ: ‡1,084

**Maplewood Review (16434)**
Lillie Suburban Newspapers
2515 E 7th Ave.
North Saint Paul, MN 55109
Phone: (651)777-8800
Fax: (651)777-8288
**Subject(s):** Paid Community Newspapers

Circ: (Free)192
(Paid)1,077

**Teutopolis Press and Dieterich Special Gazette (9446)**
Liberty Group Publishing
PO Box 667
Teutopolis, IL 62467
Phone: (217)857-3116
Fax: (217)857-3623
**Subject(s):** Paid Community Newspapers

Circ: (Paid)1,070

**The Flanagan Home Times (9254)**
Liberty Group Publishing
318 N Main St.
Pontiac, IL 61764
Phone: (815)842-1153
Fax: (815)842-4388
**Subject(s):** Paid Community Newspapers

Circ: (Free)‡50
(Paid)‡1,050

**The Hamilton News (9788)**
Hamilton News Inc.
PO Box 326
Hamilton, IN 46742-0326
Phone: (260)488-3780
Fax: (260)488-4326
**Subject(s):** Paid Community Newspapers

Circ: ‡1,050

**News-Review (24632)**
201 N Main St.
PO Box 995
Continental, OH 45831-0995
Phone: (419)596-3897
**Subject(s):** Paid Community Newspapers

Circ: 1,050

**The Post-Abortion Review (9407)**
Elliot Institute
PO Box 7348
Springfield, IL 62791-7348
Phone: (217)525-8202
Fax: (217)525-8212
**Subject(s):** Abortion; Medicine and Surgery

Circ: (Controlled)1050

**Erskine Echo (16109)**
309 1st St.
P O Box A
Erskine, MN 56535
Phone: (218)687-3775
Fax: (218)687-3744
**Subject(s):** Paid Community Newspapers

Circ: ‡1,030

**The American (15966)**
25 Main St. NW
PO Box 100
Blackduck, MN 56630
Phone: (218)835-4211
Fax: (218)835-6992
**Subject(s):** Paid Community Newspapers

Circ: 1,021

**The Bulletin (15988)**
McLeod Publishing Inc.
134 4th Ave. N.
PO Box 309
Brownton, MN 55312
Phone: (320)328-4444
Fax: (320)328-4444
**Subject(s):** Paid Community Newspapers

Circ: ‡1,026

**The Heyworth Star (8779)**
Heyworth Star Inc.
101 W Main St., Ste. A
PO Box 318
Heyworth, IL 61745
Phone: (309)473-2840
Fax: (309)473-2840
**Subject(s):** Paid Community Newspapers

Circ: ‡1,025

**Jasper Journal (16192)**
PO Box 189
Jasper, MN 56144-0188
Phone: (507)348-4176
Fax: (507)348-4176
**Subject(s):** Paid Community Newspapers

Circ: ‡1,010

**Balaton-Press-Tribune (15941)**
Balaton Publishing
PO Box 310
Balaton, MN 56115
Phone: (507)734-5421
Fax: (507)734-2316
**Subject(s):** Paid Community Newspapers

Circ: ‡1,000

**The Butler Bulletin (9636)**
108 E Main St.
Butler, IN 46721
Phone: (260)868-5501
Fax: (260)868-5501
**Subject(s):** Paid Community Newspapers

Circ: (Paid)1000

**The Courier (8989)**
Monmouth College
700 E Broadway
Monmouth, IL 61462
Phone: (309)457-3456
Fax: (309)457-2363
**Subject(s):** College Publications

Circ: (Free)1,000

**The Forum (16128)**
Broadaxe Publishers
PO Box 286
120 W 7th Ave.
Floodwood, MN 55736
Phone: (218)476-2232
Fax: (218)476-2782
**Subject(s):** Paid Community Newspapers

Circ: (Free)‡60
(Paid)‡1,000

**Journal (8253)**
NADIG Newspapers Inc.
4937 N Milwaukee Ave.
Chicago, IL 60630
Phone: (773)286-6100
Fax: (773)286-8151
**Subject(s):** Free Newspapers

Circ: (Free)‡1,000

**Leader (9501)**
PO Box 490
Washburn, IL 61570
Phone: (309)248-7413
Fax: (309)367-4277
**Subject(s):** Paid Community Newspapers

Circ: 1,000

**The Legal Reporter (9136)**
O'Fallon Progress
PO Box 970
1840 Greenmount Rd., Ste. 200
O Fallon, IL 62269-0970
Phone: (618)632-3643
Fax: (618)632-6438
**Subject(s):** Law

Circ: (Free)10
(Paid)1,000

**Mendon Dispatch-Times (8956)**
Elliott Publishing Inc.
202 E State
PO Box 200
Camp Point, IL 62320
Phone: (217)593-6515
Fax: (217)593-7720
**Subject(s):** Paid Community Newspapers

Circ: 1,000

Circulation: ★ = ABC; △ = BPA; ♦ = CAC; • = CCAB; ▫ = VAC; ⊕ = PO Statement; ‡ = Publisher's Report; Boldface figures = sworn; Light figures = estimated.

**Meridosia Budget (7923)**
Beardstown Newspapers
PO Box 320
Bluffs, IL 62621-0320
Phone: (217)323-1010
Fax: (217)754-3369
**Subject(s):** Paid Community Newspapers
**Circ:** ‡1,000

**Morrisonville Times (8999)**
511 Carlin St.
PO Box 16
Morrisonville, IL 62546
Phone: (217)526-3323
Fax: (217)526-3323
**Subject(s):** Paid Community Newspapers
**Circ:** 1,000

**Morrow County Independent (24250)**
Hirt Publishing Co.
114 W Main St.
PO Box 66
Cardington, OH 43315
Phone: (419)864-6046
Fax: (419)864-2369
**Subject(s):** Free Newspapers
**Circ:** (Free)‡100
(Paid)‡1,000

**Papyrus (8757)**
Greenville College
315 E College Ave.
PO Box 159
Greenville, IL 62246-1199
Phone: (618)664-2800
Fax: (618)664-1373
**Subject(s):** College Publications
**Circ:** 1,000

**Rancho Santa Fe Sun (9157)**
Liberty Suburban Chicago Newspapers
709 Enterprise Dr.
Oak Brook, IL 60523
Phone: (630)368-1100
Fax: (630)368-1188
**Subject(s):** Paid Community Newspapers
**Circ:** ‡1,000

**The Tonica News (9457)**
Arnold Press
242 South Lasalle St.
PO Box 67
Tonica, IL 61370-0067
Phone: (815)442-8419
Fax: (815)339-7627
**Subject(s):** Paid Community Newspapers
**Circ:** ‡1,000

**Tri County News (16171)**
931 2nd Ave.
PO Box 227
Heron Lake, MN 56137
Phone: (507)793-2327
Fax: (507)793-2327
**Subject(s):** Paid Community Newspapers
**Circ:** (Free)‡25
(Paid)‡1,000

**Tri-County Times (7924)**
Beardstown Newspapers
PO Box 320
Bluffs, IL 62621-0320
Phone: (217)323-1010
Fax: (217)754-3369
**Subject(s):** Paid Community Newspapers
**Circ:** ‡1,000

**The Verndale Sun (16676)**
121 South Farwell
P.O Box E
Verndale, MN 56481
Phone: (218)445-5779
Fax: (218)445-5779
**Subject(s):** Paid Community Newspapers
**Circ:** (Free)‡26
(Paid)‡1,000

**Wenona Index (8776)**
PO Box 190
Henry, IL 61537
Phone: (309)364-3250
Fax: (309)364-3858
**Subject(s):** Paid Community Newspapers
**Circ:** 1,000

**Ford County Press (8954)**
115 W Main
PO Box 198
Melvin, IL 60952
Phone: (217)388-7721
Fax: (217)388-2864
**Subject(s):** Paid Community Newspapers
**Circ:** (Free)29
(Paid)983

**Woodford County Journal-Roanoke Edition (9287)**
Woodford County Journal
105 E. Broad
PO Box 200
Roanoke, IL 61561
Phone: (309)923-5841
**Subject(s):** Paid Community Newspapers
**Circ:** (Paid)‡988

**Eagle-Scribe (7867)**
Box 257
Augusta, IL 62311
**Subject(s):** Paid Community Newspapers
**Circ:** (Paid)‡960

**Lake Benton Valley Journal (16203)**
Valley Journal
115 S. Center St.
PO Box 116
Lake Benton, MN 56149-0116
Phone: (507)368-4275
Fax: (507)368-4276
**Subject(s):** Paid Community Newspapers
**Circ:** 960

**Orfordville Journal and Footville News (33448)**
124 E Spring St.
PO Box 248
Orfordville, WI 53576-0248
Phone: (608)879-2211
Fax: (608)879-2211
**Subject(s):** Paid Community Newspapers
**Circ:** 966

**The Comfrey Times (16022)**
Central Publications
Box 122
Comfrey, MN 56019
Phone: (507)877-2281
Fax: (507)897-2251
**Subject(s):** Paid Community Newspapers
**Circ:** ‡950

**The Gibbon Gazette (16139)**
Gibbon Gazette
PO Box 456 Gibbone
Gibbon, MN 55335
Phone: (507)834-6966
Fax: (507)834-6966
**Subject(s):** Paid Community Newspapers
**Circ:** (Free)20
(Paid)950

**Milan Standard-Watson Journal (16269)**
Box 190
Milan, MN 56262-0190
Phone: (320)734-4458
Fax: (320)289-2702
**Subject(s):** Paid Community Newspapers
**Circ:** ‡950

**New Lenox Community Reporter (9053)**
Russell Publications
PO Box 429
Peotone, IL 60468
Phone: (708)258-3473
Fax: (708)258-6295
**Subject(s):** Paid Community Newspapers
**Circ:** 950

**The Raymond-Prinsburg News (16495)**
204 Spicer Ave.
PO Box 157
Raymond, MN 56282
Phone: (320)967-4244
Fax: (320)967-4244
**Subject(s):** Paid Community Newspapers
**Circ:** ‡943

**The View (15057)**
Heritage Newspapers Inc.
159 Main St.
Belleville, MI 48111
Phone: (734)697-8255
Fax: (734)697-4610

**Subject(s):** Paid Community Newspapers
**Circ:** (Non-paid)♦234
(Paid)♦934

**Lincolnwood Life (8891)**
Lerner Communications Inc.
7331 N Lincoln Ave.
Lincolnwood, IL 60712
Phone: (847)329-2000
Fax: (847)329-2060
**Subject(s):** Paid Community Newspapers
**Circ:** (Paid)♦912

**Oakdale-Lake Elmo Review (16435)**
Lillie Suburban Newspapers
2515 E 7th Ave.
North Saint Paul, MN 55109
Phone: (651)777-8800
Fax: (651)777-8288
**Subject(s):** Paid Community Newspapers
**Circ:** (Free)128
(Paid)910

**The Ashton Gazette (7861)**
PO Box 287
Ashton, IL 61006
Phone: (815)453-2551
Fax: (815)453-2422
**Subject(s):** Paid Community Newspapers
**Circ:** (Free)‡10
(Paid)‡900

**Dongola Tri-County Record (8599)**
130 NE Front St.
Box 189
Dongola, IL 62926
Phone: (618)827-4353
Fax: (618)827-4193
**Subject(s):** Paid Community Newspapers
**Circ:** ‡909

**The Oklee Herald (16446)**
PO Box 9
Oklee, MN 56742
Phone: (218)796-5181
Fax: (218)487-5251
**Subject(s):** Paid Community Newspapers
**Circ:** 906

**The Sunfield Sentinel (15814)**
Sunfield Sentinel Publishing
PO Box 8
Sunfield, MI 48890
Phone: (517)566-8500
**Subject(s):** Paid Community Newspapers
**Circ:** ‡900

**Tribune (16377)**
PO Box 308
Minnesota Lake, MN 56068
Phone: (507)462-3575
**Subject(s):** Paid Community Newspapers
**Circ:** ‡900

**The New Wolcott Enterprise (10267)**
125 W Market St.
PO Box 78
Wolcott, IN 47995
Phone: (219)279-2167
Fax: (219)279-2167
**Subject(s):** Paid Community Newspapers
**Circ:** (Free)‡37
(Paid)‡896

**Ashland Sentinel (7860)**
Petersburg Observer
116 N. Hardin
PO Box 418
Ashland, IL 62612-0418
**Subject(s):** Paid Community Newspapers
**Circ:** ‡850

**Blue Mound Leader (7922)**
PO Box 318
Blue Mound, IL 62513-0318
Phone: (217)692-2323
Fax: (217)692-2323
**Subject(s):** Paid Community Newspapers
**Circ:** (Free)50
(Paid)850

**Crescent (15130)**
150 North Main St.
Climax, MI 49034
Phone: (269)746-4331
**Subject(s):** Paid Community Newspapers
**Circ:** ‡850

**The Edon Commercial (24708)**
PO Box 218
Edon, OH 43518
Phone: (419)272-2413
Fax: (419)924-5240
**Subject(s):** Paid Community Newspapers
**Circ:** (Free)150
(Paid)850

**Francesville Tribune (9743)**
PO Box 458
111 East Montgomery Street
Francesville, IN 47946-0458
Phone: (219)567-2221
**Subject(s):** Paid Community Newspapers
**Circ:** 850

**Herald News (9644)**
PO Box 158
Cayuga, IN 47928
Phone: (765)492-4401
Fax: (765)492-4401
**Subject(s):** Paid Community Newspapers
**Circ:** ‡850

**Lake Region Times (16234)**
513 Main
PO Box 128
Madison Lake, MN 56063-0128
Phone: (507)243-3031
Fax: (507)243-3122
**Subject(s):** Paid Community Newspapers
**Circ:** (Free)30
100
(Paid)855

**Woodville Leader (33675)**
Best Press
102 Trient Dr.
Woodville, WI 54028
Phone: (715)698-2401
Fax: (715)698-2952
**Subject(s):** Paid Community Newspapers
**Circ:** ‡850

**Sidell Reporter (9368)**
116 E Market St.
PO Box 475
Sidell, IL 61876
Phone: (217)288-9365
**Subject(s):** Paid Community Newspapers
**Circ:** ‡817

**The Forum (33632)**
University of Wisconsin
518 S 7th Ave.
Wausau, WI 54401-5362
Phone: (715)261-6100
Fax: (715)261-6333
**Subject(s):** College Publications
**Circ:** (Non-paid)800

**Goreville Gazette (8749)**
Hwy. 37
PO Box 70
Goreville, IL 62939
Phone: (618)995-9445
Fax: (618)995-9445
**Subject(s):** Paid Community Newspapers
**Circ:** (Free)100
(Paid)800

**Pawnee Post (7866)**
South County Publications
110 N 5th St.
PO Box 50
Auburn, IL 62615
Phone: (217)438-6155
Fax: (217)438-6156
**Subject(s):** Paid Community Newspapers
**Circ:** ‡800

**White River News (7931)**
Hometown Publications Inc.
PO Box 317
Bridgeport, IL 62417
Phone: (618)945-2111
Fax: (618)945-2131
**Subject(s):** Paid Community Newspapers
**Circ:** ‡800

**Middlebury Independent (10025)**
Largrange Publishing Company Inc.
PO Box 68
100 South State Road 9
Middlebury, IN 46540-0068
Phone: (574)825-9112
Fax: (574)463-2734
**Subject(s):** Paid Community Newspapers
**Circ:** 780

**Morton Grove-Niles Life (8892)**
Lerner Communications Inc.
7331 N Lincoln Ave.
Lincolnwood, IL 60712
Phone: (847)329-2000
Fax: (847)329-2060
**Subject(s):** Free Newspapers
**Circ:** (Paid)♦780

**The Grygla Eagle (16157)**
Richards Publishing Company Inc.
PO Box 17
Grygla, MN 56727
Phone: (218)294-6220
**Subject(s):** Paid Community Newspapers
**Circ:** ‡750

**Mechanicsburg Telegram (24893)**
Central Ohio Printing
30 S Oak St.
PO Box 390
London, OH 43140-1079
Phone: (740)852-1616
Fax: (740)852-1620
**Subject(s):** Paid Community Newspapers
**Circ:** (Paid)‡750

**Roseville Independent (8922)**
Eagle Publications of Western Illinois Inc.
210 S. Randolph St.
Macomb, IL 61455
Phone: (309)837-4428
Fax: (309)837-7188
**Subject(s):** Paid Community Newspapers
**Circ:** (Free)‡25
(Paid)‡750

**Wisconsin Law Journal (33344)**
Daily Reporter Publishing Co.
225 E Michigan St., Ste. 540
Milwaukee, WI 53202
Phone: (414)276-0273
Fax: (414)276-8057
**Subject(s):** Law
**Circ:** (Paid)747

**The Daily Other (8818)**
MacMurray College
447 E College Ave.
Box 1140
Jacksonville, IL 62650
Phone: (217)479-7000
Fax: (217)245-0405
**Subject(s):** College Publications
**Circ:** (Non-paid)‡700

**Illiopolis Sentinel (8804)**
Wilson Publications
PO Box 300
Illiopolis, IL 62539
Phone: (217)486-6496
**Subject(s):** Paid Community Newspapers
**Circ:** (Free)‡50
(Paid)‡675

**The Observer (9961)**
Box 307
Kewanna, IN 46939
Phone: (219)653-2101
Fax: (574)653-3418
**Subject(s):** Paid Community Newspapers
**Circ:** ‡650

**Ohio County News (10135)**
Register Publications
235 Main St.
PO Box 128
Rising Sun, IN 47040-0128
Phone: (812)438-2011
Fax: (812)438-3228
**Subject(s):** Paid Community Newspapers
**Circ:** (Free)‡8
(Paid)‡647

**The Herald-Star (8621)**
Herald-Star
PO Box 50
103 South Eaton St.
Edinburg, IL 62531-0050
Phone: (217)623-5523
Fax: (217)623-5523
**Subject(s):** Paid Community Newspapers
**Circ:** (Free)‡20
(Paid)‡630

**Williamsfield Times (9532)**
Tri-County News Edition
116 S Magnolia
PO Box 289
Elmwood, IL 61529
Phone: (309)742-2521
Fax: (309)742-2511
**Subject(s):** Paid Community Newspapers
**Circ:** ‡625

**The Franklin Times (8702)**
Franklin Times Publishing
208 Main
Franklin, IL 62638
Phone: (217)675-2461
Fax: (217)675-2470
**Subject(s):** Paid Community Newspapers
**Circ:** ‡600

**Murrayville Gazette (8819)**
356 E. Court St.
Jacksonville, IL 62650-2006
Phone: (217)675-2461
Fax: (217)675-2470
**Subject(s):** Free Newspapers
**Circ:** (Free)600

**The Ossian Journal (10099)**
News Banner Publications Inc.
105 N. Jefferson
PO Box 365
Ossian, IN 46777
Phone: (219)622-4108
Fax: (219)622-4108
**Subject(s):** Paid Community Newspapers
**Circ:** (Paid)‡600

**The Raymond News (9274)**
PO Box 200
Raymond, IL 62560
Phone: (217)229-3421
Fax: (217)532-3632
**Subject(s):** Paid Community Newspapers
**Circ:** (Non-paid)25
(Paid)600

**Record (15308)**
Freeport News
129 Division St.
Freeport, MI 49325
Phone: (616)765-8511
**Subject(s):** Paid Community Newspapers
**Circ:** 600

**The Niles Life (8893)**
Lerner Communications Inc.
7331 N Lincoln Ave.
Lincolnwood, IL 60712
Phone: (847)329-2000
Fax: (847)329-2060
**Subject(s):** Free Newspapers
**Circ:** (Paid)♦593

**Sussex-Lannon-Lisbon News (33417)**
Community Newspapers
15700 W Cleveland Ave.
New Berlin, WI 53151
Phone: (262)938-5000
Fax: (262)938-5001
**Subject(s):** Paid Community Newspapers
**Circ:** 596

**Chariton Courier (8930)**
American Publishing Co.
1120 N Carbon, Ste. 100
Marion, IL 62959
Phone: (618)993-1711
Fax: (618)997-5209

---

**Circulation:** ★ = ABC; △ = BPA; ♦ = CAC; • = CCAB; ▫ = VAC; ⊕ = PO Statement; ‡ = Publisher's Report; Boldface figures = sworn; Light figures = estimated.

# Great Plains States

**Subject(s):** Paid Community Newspapers
**Circ:** ‡550

**Eagles Scribe** (7868)
Eagle Pub.
PO Box 257
Augusta, IL 62311
Phone: (217)392-2715
Fax: (217)392-2715
**Subject(s):** Paid Community Newspapers
**Circ:** ‡552

**Elmwood Gazette** (8652)
Tri-County News Edition
116 S Magnolia
PO Box 289
Elmwood, IL 61529
Phone: (309)742-2521
Fax: (309)742-2511
**Subject(s):** Paid Community Newspapers
**Circ:** ‡550

**The Manawa Advocate** (33084)
Trey Foerster Ink Inc.
165 N. Main St.
Iola, WI 54945
Phone: (715)445-3415
Fax: (715)445-3988
**Subject(s):** Paid Community Newspapers
**Circ:** (Controlled)550

**Regional News** (9992)
PO Box 828
9852 W State Rd 2
Laporte, IN 46352-0828
Phone: (219)785-2234
Fax: (219)785-2442
**Subject(s):** Paid Community Newspapers
**Circ:** (Paid)‡550

**New River Record** (16156)
PO Box F
Greenbush, MN 56726
Phone: (218)782-2275
Fax: (218)782-2277
**Subject(s):** Free Newspapers
**Circ:** (Free)‡25
(Paid)‡540

**Spencer Owen Leader** (10173)
114 E Franklin St.
PO Box 22
Spencer, IN 47460
Phone: (812)829-3936
Fax: (812)829-4666
**Subject(s):** Paid Community Newspapers
**Circ:** (Free)25
(Paid)549

**Cedar Lake-Lowell Star** (9673)
112 W Clark St.
PO Box 419
Crown Point, IN 46308-0419
Phone: (219)663-4212
Fax: (219)663-0137
**Subject(s):** Paid Community Newspapers
**Circ:** ⊕520

**Elmwood Argus** (32945)
PO Box 69
Spring Valley, WI 54767
Phone: (715)778-4395
**Subject(s):** Paid Community Newspapers
**Circ:** ‡500

**Buffalo Ridge Gazette** (16542)
Hunt and Hunt Newspapers
320 Aetna St.
PO Box 70
Ruthton, MN 56170-0070
Phone: (507)658-3919
Fax: (507)658-3404
**Subject(s):** Paid Community Newspapers
**Circ:** (Free)20
(Paid)481

**The Elysian Enterprise** (16108)
PO Box 119
Elysian, MN 56028-0028
Phone: (507)267-4323
Fax: (507)362-4458
**Subject(s):** Paid Community Newspapers
**Circ:** (Free)‡27
(Paid)‡480

**The Saginaw Press** (15724)
410 Hancock St.
PO Box 1836
Saginaw, MI 48605-1836
Phone: (989)793-8070
**Subject(s):** Paid Community Newspapers
**Circ:** (Free)⊕6
(Paid)⊕462

**The Fox Lake Representative** (32850)
Berlin Journal Newspapers
PO Box 10
Berlin, WI 54923-0010
Phone: (920)361-1515
Fax: (920)361-1518
**Subject(s):** Paid Community Newspapers
**Circ:** ‡450

**Amherst Tomorrow River Times** (33059)
Trey Foerster Ink Inc.
PO Box 235
Iola, WI 54945
Phone: (715)445-6397
Fax: (715)445-3988
**Subject(s):** Paid Community Newspapers
**Circ:** (Controlled)⊕400

**Divernon News** (8596)
South County Publications
110 N 5th St.
PO Box 50
Auburn, IL 62615
Phone: (217)438-6155
Fax: (217)438-6156
**Subject(s):** Paid Community Newspapers
**Circ:** 400

**Lawrence County News** (8859)
Daily Record
1209 State St.
PO Box 559
Lawrenceville, IL 62439
Phone: (618)943-2331
Fax: (618)943-3976
**Subject(s):** Paid Community Newspapers
**Circ:** (Paid)401

**The Montpelier Herald** (10039)
Laymon Publishing Corp.
107 E High St.
Montpelier, IN 47359
Phone: (765)728-5322
Fax: (765)728-5322
**Subject(s):** Paid Community Newspapers
**Circ:** (Free)6
(Paid)406

**Newman Independent** (9055)
120 S Broadway
PO Box 417
Newman, IL 61942
Phone: (217)837-2414
Fax: (217)837-2071
**Subject(s):** Paid Community Newspapers
**Circ:** 400

**Record** (9333)
Record Press Inc.
6980 S Rt.1
Saint Anne, IL 60964
Phone: (815)427-6734
Fax: (815)427-6751
**Subject(s):** Paid Community Newspapers
**Circ:** ‡400

**The Weekly Herald** (10007)
The Madison Courier
310 Courier Sq.
Madison, IN 47250
Phone: (812)265-3641
Fax: (812)273-6903
**Subject(s):** Shopping Guides
**Circ:** ‡386

**Farmington Bugle** (8695)
Tri-County News Edition
116 S Magnolia
PO Box 289
Elmwood, IL 61529
Phone: (309)742-2521
Fax: (309)742-2511
**Subject(s):** Paid Community Newspapers
**Circ:** ‡375

**The Record/Journal** (9120)
Liberty Group Publishing Co.
3000 Dundee Rd., Ste. 202
Northbrook, IL 60062
Phone: (847)272-2244
Fax: (847)272-6244
**Subject(s):** Paid Community Newspapers
**Circ:** 375

**Noblesville Times** (10074)
PO Box 100
Noblesville, IN 46060
Phone: (317)773-3971
Fax: (317)773-3970
**Subject(s):** Paid Community Newspapers
**Circ:** 350

**Yates City Banner** (9540)
Tri-County News Edition
116 S Magnolia
PO Box 289
Elmwood, IL 61529
Phone: (309)742-2521
Fax: (309)742-2511
**Subject(s):** Paid Community Newspapers
**Circ:** ‡350

**Loda Times** (9206)
Paxton Printing Inc.
218 N Market
PO Box 73
Paxton, IL 60957
Phone: (217)379-2356
Fax: (217)379-3104
**Subject(s):** Paid Community Newspapers
**Circ:** ‡319

# Great Plains States

**St. Louis Post-Dispatch** (17817)
Lee Enterprises Inc.
900 N. Tucker Blvd.
Saint Louis, MO 63101
Phone: (314)340-8000
**Subject(s):** Daily Newspapers
**Circ:** (Mon.-Sat.)★286,310
(Sun.)★449,845

**The Kansas City Star** (17334)
Kansas City Star Co.
1729 Grand Blvd.
Kansas City, MO 64108
Phone: (816)234-4636
**Subject(s):** Daily Newspapers
**Circ:** (Mon.-Sat.)269,188
(Sun.)379,971

**Omaha World-Herald** (18537)
Omaha World-Herald Co.
1334 Dodge St.
Omaha, NE 68102-1122
Phone: (402)444-1000
Fax: (402)345-0183
**Subject(s):** Daily Newspapers
**Circ:** (Sat.)206,764
(Mon.-Fri.)214,651
(Sun.)261,036

**The Des Moines Register** (10466)
Gannett Company Inc.
715 Locust St.
PO Box 957
Des Moines, IA 50304
Phone: (515)284-8000
Fax: (800)247-5346
**Subject(s):** Daily Newspapers
**Circ:** (Mon.-Sat.)152,567
(Sun.)244,395

**AAA Southern Traveler** (17539)
12901 N. 40th Dr.
Saint Louis, MO 63141
Phone: (314)523-7350
Fax: (314)523-6982
**Subject(s):** Travel and Tourism; Automotive (Consumer); Clubs and Societies
**Circ:** (Non-paid)‡939
(Paid)‡172,971

**Midwest Messenger (18626)**
Plaindealer Publishing Co.
Box 239
Tekamah, NE 68061
Phone: (402)374-2226
Fax: (402)374-2739
**Subject(s):** General Agriculture; Shopping Guides
**Circ:** (Free)‡154,380

**Pennypower Shopping News (17970)**
Pennypower Shopping News Inc.
PO Box 798
Springfield, MO 65801
Phone: (417)887-9000
Fax: (417)862-1896
**Subject(s):** Shopping Guides
**Circ:** (Wed.)147,400

**Wichita Eagle (11493)**
Knight-Ridder Inc.
PO Box 820
Wichita, KS 67201
Phone: (316)268-6351
Fax: (316)268-6627
**Subject(s):** Daily Newspapers
**Circ:** (Mon.-Thurs.)★87,063
(Sat.)★92,678
(Fri.)★96,506
(Sun.)★146,727

**Shopper-News Network (10495)**
PO Box 4826
Des Moines, IA 50306
Phone: (515)262-2165
**Subject(s):** Shopping Guides
**Circ:** (Non-paid)145,764

**Mission Sun (11257)**
Sun Publications Inc.
7373 W 107th St.
Overland Park, KS 66212
Phone: (913)381-1010
Fax: (913)381-9889
**Subject(s):** Free Newspapers
**Circ:** (Combined)137,000

**Johnson County Sun (11315)**
Sun Publications Inc.
7373 W 107th St.
Overland Park, KS 66212
Phone: (913)381-1010
Fax: (913)381-9889
**Subject(s):** Free Newspapers
**Circ:** (Combined)112,441

**Leawood Sun (11196)**
Sun Publications Inc.
7373 W 107th St.
Overland Park, KS 66212
Phone: (913)381-1010
Fax: (913)381-9889
**Subject(s):** Free Newspapers
**Circ:** (Combined)112,441

**Leawood Sun, Blue Valley Edition (11160)**
Sun Publications Inc.
7373 W 107th St.
Overland Park, KS 66212
Phone: (913)381-1010
Fax: (913)381-9889
**Subject(s):** Free Newspapers
**Circ:** (Combined)‡112,441

**Lenexa Sun (11319)**
Sun Publications Inc.
7373 W 107th St.
Overland Park, KS 66212
Phone: (913)381-1010
Fax: (913)381-9889
**Subject(s):** Free Newspapers
**Circ:** (Combined)112,441

**Northeast Johnson County Sun (11254)**
Sun Publications Inc.
7373 W 107th St.
Overland Park, KS 66212
Phone: (913)381-1010
Fax: (913)381-9889
**Subject(s):** Free Newspapers
**Circ:** (Combined)‡112,441

**Olathe Sun (11282)**
Sun Publications Inc.
7373 W 107th St.
Overland Park, KS 66212
Phone: (913)381-1010
Fax: (913)381-9889
**Subject(s):** Free Newspapers
**Circ:** (Combined)112,441

**Overland Park Sun (11328)**
Sun Publications Inc.
7373 W 107th St.
Overland Park, KS 66212
Phone: (913)381-1010
Fax: (913)381-9889
**Subject(s):** Free Newspapers
**Circ:** (Combined)112,441

**Overland Park Sun, Blue Valley Edition (11329)**
Sun Publications Inc.
7373 W 107th St.
Overland Park, KS 66212
Phone: (913)381-1010
Fax: (913)381-9889
**Subject(s):** Free Newspapers
**Circ:** (Combined)112,441

**Prairie Village Sun (11381)**
Sun Publications Inc.
7373 W 107th St.
Overland Park, KS 66212
Phone: (913)381-1010
Fax: (913)381-9889
**Subject(s):** Free Newspapers
**Circ:** (Combined)112,441

**Shawnee-Merriam Sun (11411)**
Sun Publications Inc.
7373 W 107th St.
Overland Park, KS 66212
Phone: (913)381-1010
Fax: (913)381-9889
**Subject(s):** Free Newspapers
**Circ:** (Combined)‡112,441

**Spokesman (10970)**
Iowa Farm Bureau Federation
5400 University Ave.
West Des Moines, IA 50266
Phone: (515)225-4800
Fax: (515)225-5419
**Subject(s):** Farm Bureau, Grange, and Cooperative Associations; Farm Newspapers
**Circ:** (Paid)105,294

**Roeland Park Sun (11387)**
Sun Publications Inc.
7373 W 107th St.
Overland Park, KS 66212
Phone: (913)381-1010
Fax: (913)381-9889
**Subject(s):** Free Newspapers
**Circ:** (Combined)103,679

**Sun Newspaper (11418)**
Sun Publications Inc.
7373 W 107th St.
Overland Park, KS 66212
Phone: (913)381-1010
Fax: (913)381-9889
**Subject(s):** Free Newspapers
**Circ:** (Combined)103,679

**The Riverfront Times (17802)**
Riverfront Times L.L.C.
6358 Delmar Blvd., Ste. 200
Saint Louis, MO 63130-4719
Phone: (314)754-5966
Fax: (314)754-5955
**Subject(s):** Free Newspapers
**Circ:** (Paid)219
(Free)101,914

**St. Louis Review (17818)**
20 Archbishop May Dr.
Saint Louis, MO 63119-5738
Phone: (314)792-7500
Fax: (314)792-7534
**Subject(s):** Religious Publications
**Circ:** ‡90,000

**Boilermaker Reporter (11142)**
International Brotherhood of Boilermakers, Iron Shipbuilders, Blacksmiths, Forgers, and Helpers
753 State Ave., Ste. 570
Kansas City, KS 66101
Phone: (913)371-2640
Fax: (913)281-8104
**Subject(s):** Labor; Metal, Metallurgy, and Metal Trade
**Circ:** (Non-paid)85,000

**Sioux Falls Shopping News (28409)**
Sioux Falls Shopping News Inc.
4005 S. Western Ave.
PO Box 5184
Sioux Falls, SD 57117-5184
Phone: (605)339-3633
Fax: (605)335-6873
**Subject(s):** Shopping Guides
**Circ:** (Non-paid)85,000

**Sioux Falls Shopping News Informer (28410)**
Sioux Falls Shopping News Inc.
4005 S. Western Ave.
PO Box 5184
Sioux Falls, SD 57117-5184
Phone: (605)339-3633
Fax: (605)335-6873
**Subject(s):** Entertainment
**Circ:** (Free)‡85,000

**University of North Dakota Alumni Review (23989)**
University of North Dakota Alumni Association & the UND Foundation
PO Box 8157
Grand Forks, ND 58202-8157
Phone: (701)777-2611
Fax: (701)777-4054
**Subject(s):** College Publications
**Circ:** (Free)‡85,000

**Lincoln Journal Star (18417)**
Lee Enterprises Inc.
928 P St.
Lincoln, NE 68508
Phone: (402)475-4200
**Subject(s):** Daily Newspapers
**Circ:** (Mon.-Sat.)★74,893
(Sun.)★84,149

**Cedar Rapids Gazette (10365)**
500 3rd Ave. SE
PO Box 511
Cedar Rapids, IA 52406
Phone: (319)398-8211
Fax: (319)398-5846
**Subject(s):** Daily Newspapers
**Circ:** (Mon.-Sat.)★65,693
(Sun.)★80,229

**The Pitch (17346)**
Kansas City Pitch L.L.C.
1701 Main St.
Kansas City, MO 64108
Phone: (816)561-6061
Fax: (816)756-0502
**Subject(s):** Paid Community Newspapers
**Circ:** (Free)80,000

**Penny Saver (10369)**
Publications Inc.
500 3rd Ave. SE
Cedar Rapids, IA 52401
Phone: (319)399-5900
Fax: (319)399-5918
**Subject(s):** Shopping Guides
**Circ:** (Free)78,081

**St. Louis/Southern Illinois Labor Tribune (17819)**
St. Louis/Southern Illinois Tribune
505 S Ewing Ave.
Saint Louis, MO 63103
Phone: (314)535-9660
Fax: (314)531-6131
**Subject(s):** Labor
**Circ:** ‡78,000

**Wichita Pennypower News (11494)**
Wichita Pennypower News Inc.
650 N Carraige Pkwy., No. 60
Wichita, KS 67208
Phone: (316)688-6051
Fax: (316)688-6034
**Subject(s):** Shopping Guides
**Circ:** (Combined)76,687

---

Circulation: ★ = ABC; △ = BPA; ♦ = CAC; • = CCAB; □ = VAC; ⊕ = PO Statement; ‡ = Publisher's Report; Boldface figures = sworn; Light figures = estimated.

**Quad-City Times (10422)**
500 E 3rd St.
PO Box 3828
Davenport, IA 52801
Phone: (563)383-2200
Fax: (563)383-2370
**Subject(s):** Daily Newspapers
Circ: (Mon.-Fri.)★51,892
(Sat.)★58,941
(Sun.)★72,168

**Iowa Farmer Today (10368)**
1065 Sierra Ct. NE, Ste. E
Cedar Rapids, IA 52402
Phone: (319)398-2640
Fax: (319)398-2696
**Subject(s):** Farm Newspapers; Free Newspapers
Circ: (Controlled)‡71,228

**Blue Springs & Independence Examiner Suburban Life (Wednesday Edition) (17264)**
The Examiner
410 S Liberty St.
Independence, MO 64050-3805
Phone: (816)254-8600
Fax: (816)836-3805
**Subject(s):** Paid Community Newspapers
Circ: (Combined)67,135

**Blue Springs & Independence Examiner Extra (Daily Edition) (17263)**
The Examiner
410 S Liberty St.
Independence, MO 64050-3805
Phone: (816)254-8600
Fax: (816)836-3805
**Subject(s):** Daily Newspapers
Circ: (Paid)15,500
(Wed.)67,000

**The Topeka Capital-Journal (11445)**
616 SE Jefferson
Topeka, KS 66607
Phone: (785)295-1111
Fax: (913)295-1230
**Subject(s):** Daily Newspapers
Circ: (Mon.-Sat.)57,474
(Sun.)65,020

**The Forum (23951)**
Forum Communications Co.
301 8th St. S.
PO Box 2466
Fargo, ND 58103-1826
Phone: (701)237-6500
Fax: (701)241-5368
**Subject(s):** Daily Newspapers
Circ: (Mon.-Sat.)51,312
(Sun.)64,010

**St. Louis American (17805)**
American Publishing Co.
4242 Lindell Blvd.
Saint Louis, MO 63108-2916
Phone: (314)533-8000
Fax: (314)533-0038
**Subject(s):** Paid Community Newspapers; Black Publications
Circ: (Paid)393
(Non-paid)62,880

**Hometowner, Inc. (10353)**
Lee Enterprises Inc.
1904 Main St.
Cedar Falls, IA 50613
Phone: (319)277-3300
Fax: (319)277-3308
**Subject(s):** Shopping Guides
Circ: (Free)‡61,650

**Gladstone News (17240)**
Sun Publications Inc.
7373 W 107th St.
Overland Park, KS 66212
Phone: (913)381-1010
Fax: (913)381-9889
**Subject(s):** Shopping Guides
Circ: (Free)‡60,210

**Conservative Chronicle (10616)**
Hampton Publishing Co.
PO Box 317
Hampton, IA 50441
Phone: (641)456-2585
Fax: (641)456-2587

**Subject(s):** Social and Political Issues
Circ: (Free)30
(Paid)⊕57,960

**The Midweek (24077)**
Davon Press Inc.
Box 457
West Fargo, ND 58078
Phone: (701)282-2443
Fax: (701)282-9248
**Subject(s):** Shopping Guides
Circ: (Free)55,000

**The St. Louis Metro Evening Whirl (17815)**
Thomas Publication Company Inc.
PO Box 5088
Saint Louis, MO 63115
Phone: (314)535-4033
**Subject(s):** Black Publications; Paid Community Newspapers
Circ: ‡52,500

**Drake Blue (10467)**
Drake University
316 Old Main
Des Moines, IA 50311
Phone: (515)271-2169
Fax: (515)271-3798
**Subject(s):** College Publications
Circ: (Controlled)52,000

**Waterloo-Cedar Falls Courier (10941)**
Howard Publications
501 Commercial St.
PO Box 540
Waterloo, IA 50704
Phone: (319)291-1400
Fax: (319)291-2069
**Subject(s):** Daily Newspapers
Circ: (Mon.-Fri.)44,948
(Sun.)51,795

**The Leaven (11145)**
12615 Parallel Pkwy.
Kansas City, KS 66109
Phone: (913)721-1570
Fax: (913)721-5276
**Subject(s):** Religious Publications
Circ: (Non-paid)‡384
(Paid)‡47,453

**Warrenton Journal (17229)**
Pulitzer Publishing
998 E. Gannon Dr.
PO Box 309
Festus, MO 63028
Phone: (314)296-1800
Fax: (314)937-9811
**Subject(s):** Free Newspapers
Circ: (Free)46,438

**Wyandotte County Shopper (11152)**
Kansas City Kansan
8200 State Ave.
Kansas City, KS 66112
Phone: (913)371-4300
Fax: (913)342-8620
**Subject(s):** Shopping Guides
Circ: (Free)‡46,000

**Active Aging Publishing, Inc. (11479)**
Active Aging
125 S W St., Ste. 105
Wichita, KS 67213
Phone: (316)942-5385
Fax: (316)946-9180
**Subject(s):** Senior Citizens' Interests; Free Newspapers
Circ: (Free)‡45,500

**Nebraska Farm Bureau News (18425)**
Nebraska Farm Bureau Federation
PO Box 80299
5225 South 16th Street
Lincoln, NE 68502
Phone: (402)421-4446
Fax: (402)421-4432
**Subject(s):** Farm Bureau, Grange, and Cooperative Associations
Circ: (Non-paid)‡500
(Paid)‡45,000

**Independence Examiner (Wednesday Edition) (17270)**
The Examiner
410 S Liberty St.
Independence, MO 64050-3805
Phone: (816)254-8600

Fax: (816)836-3805
**Subject(s):** Paid Community Newspapers
Circ: (Combined)43,634

**Good News (11015)**
Kirk Clinkscales Sr.
PO Box 96
Caney, KS 67333
Phone: (620)879-5460
Fax: (620)879-2264
**Subject(s):** Free Newspapers
Circ: (Free)‡42,578

**Sioux City Journal (10873)**
Lee Enterprises Inc.
515 Pavonia St.
Sioux City, IA 51102
**Subject(s):** Daily Newspapers
Circ: (Mon.-Sat.)★41,182
(Sun.)★42,268

**North County Journal (17774)**
Pulitzer Publishing
7751 N. Lindbergh
Saint Louis, MO 63042
Phone: (314)972-1111
**Subject(s):** Paid Community Newspapers
Circ: (Sun.)40,072
(Wed.)41,025

**The Bishop's Bulletin (28406)**
Catholic Pastoral Center
523 N. Duluth Ave.
Sioux Falls, SD 57104
Phone: (605)334-9861
**Subject(s):** Religious Publications
Circ: ‡40,000

**St. Louis Watchman Advocate (17820)**
St. Louis County Printing & Pub. Co.
2111 S. Brentwood Blvd.
Saint Louis, MO 63114
Phone: (636)925-2045
Fax: (314)918-1311
**Subject(s):** Daily Periodicals; Banking, Finance, and Investments; Law
Circ: (Combined)‡40,000

**The Joplin Globe (17300)**
The Joplin Globe Publishing Co.
117 E. 4th St.
Joplin, MO 64801
Phone: (417)623-3480
Fax: (417)623-8450
**Subject(s):** Daily Newspapers
Circ: (Mon.-Sat.)30,903
(Sun.)39,793

**St. Joseph News-Press (17531)**
News-Press & Gazette Co.
825 Edmond St.
Saint Joseph, MO 64501
Phone: (816)271-8500
Fax: (816)271-8692
**Subject(s):** Daily Newspapers
Circ: (Mon.-Sat.)★36,578
(Sun.)★38,623

**The Finder (Mandan) (24026)**
North Dakota Printing Publishing
303 NE 1st St.
PO Box 908
Mandan, ND 58554
Phone: (701)663-6823
Fax: (701)663-2442
**Subject(s):** Shopping Guides
Circ: (Free)37,800

**The Dubuque Advertiser (10530)**
The Dubuque Advertiser Inc.
2966 John F. Kennedy Rd.
Dubuque, IA 52002
Phone: (563)588-0162
Fax: (563)582-0335
**Subject(s):** Shopping Guides
Circ: (Free)‡36,500

**The Hutchinson News (11121)**
Hutchinson Publishing Co.
300 W. 2nd St.
PO Box 190
Hutchinson, KS 67504-0190
Phone: (620)694-5700
Fax: (620)662-4186

**Subject(s):** Daily Newspapers
**Circ:** (Mon.-Sat.)★30,685
(Sun.)★36,034

**Press Journal (18037)**
Pulitzer Publishing
220 E Main
Warrenton, MO 63383
Phone: (636)456-3481
Fax: (636)456-3020
**Subject(s):** Free Newspapers
**Circ:** (Fri.)34,048
(Sun.)35,048
(Wed.)35,954

**The Community News Advertisers (10645)**
Publications Inc.
PO Box 2597
Iowa City, IA 52244
Phone: (319)339-3114
**Subject(s):** Shopping Guides
**Circ:** (Free)35,638

**Clay & Platte Dispatch-Tribune (17320)**
Townsend Communications Inc.
7007 NE Parvin Rd.
Kansas City, MO 64117
Phone: (816)454-9660
Fax: (816)452-5889
**Subject(s):** Free Newspapers
**Circ:** (Paid)7,229
(Free)35,221

**South County Times (17846)**
Webster-Kirkwood Times Inc.
122 W. Lockwood Ave., 2nd Fl.
Saint Louis, MO 63119
Phone: (314)968-2699
Fax: (314)968-2961
**Subject(s):** Free Newspapers
**Circ:** (Free)35,210

**Telegraph Herald (10532)**
Woodward Communications
Box 688
Dubuque, IA 52004-0668
Phone: (563)588-5611
Fax: (563)588-5739
**Subject(s):** Daily Newspapers
**Circ:** (Mon.-Sat.)29,206
(Sun.)34,787

**Rocket Common Supplement Shopper (10621)**
Tribune Newspapers Inc.
1114 7th St.
PO Box 721
Harlan, IA 51537-0721
Phone: (712)755-3111
Fax: (712)755-3324
**Subject(s):** Shopping Guides
**Circ:** (Free)34,559

**Rapid City Journal (28378)**
507 Main St.
PO Box 450
Rapid City, SD 57701
Phone: (605)394-8383
Fax: (605)394-8463
**Subject(s):** Daily Newspapers
**Circ:** (Mon.-Sat.)★29,696
(Sun.)★34,222

**St. Peters Journal (17934)**
Pulitzer Publishing
4212 N. Service Road
Saint Peters, MO 63376
Phone: (636)946-6111
**Subject(s):** Paid Community Newspapers
**Circ:** (Fri.)33,246
(Sun.)33,296
(Wed.)34,159

**St. Louis Argus (17806)**
4595 Martin Luther King Dr.
Saint Louis, MO 63113
Phone: (314)531-1323
Fax: (314)531-1324
**Subject(s):** Paid Community Newspapers; Black Publications
**Circ:** 33,000

**The New Earth (23954)**
1310 N. Broadway
Fargo, ND 58102
Phone: (701)235-0296
Fax: (701)235-0296

**Subject(s):** Religious Publications
**Circ:** 32,000

**North Side Journal (18036)**
Pulitzer Publishing
220 E Main
Warrenton, MO 63383
Phone: (636)456-3481
Fax: (636)456-3020
**Subject(s):** Free Newspapers
**Circ:** (Wed.)31,605

**The Bismarck Tribune (23896)**
Lee Enterprises
PO Box 5516
Bismarck, ND 58506
Phone: (701)223-2500
Fax: (701)223-4240
**Subject(s):** Daily Newspapers
**Circ:** (Mon.-Sat.)★27,620
(Sun.)★31,081

**The Catholic Mirror (10458)**
601 Grand Ave.
Des Moines, IA 50309
Phone: (515)237-5057
Fax: (515)244-3761
**Subject(s):** Religious Publications
**Circ:** ‡31,000

**The Salina Journal (11399)**
333 S 4th St.
PO Box 740
Salina, KS 67402-0740
Phone: (785)823-6363
Fax: (785)823-3207
**Subject(s):** Daily Newspapers
**Circ:** (Mon.-Sat.)29,123
(Sun.)30,688

**Webster-Kirkwood Times (18054)**
Webster-Kirkwood Times Inc.
122 W. Lockwood Ave., 2nd Fl.
Saint Louis, MO 63119
Phone: (314)968-2699
Fax: (314)968-2961
**Subject(s):** Free Newspapers
**Circ:** (Free)30,484

**Southeast Missourian (17113)**
Southeast Missourian Plus
301 Broadway
PO Box 699
Cape Girardeau, MO 63701
Phone: (573)335-6611
Fax: (573)334-7288
**Subject(s):** Daily Newspapers
**Circ:** (Sat.)16,110
(Mon.-Fri.)16,476
(Sun.)28,374
(Wed.)30,168

**College Boulevard News (11300)**
Sun Publications Inc.
7373 W 107th St.
Overland Park, KS 66212
Phone: (913)381-1010
Fax: (913)381-9889
**Subject(s):** Free Newspapers
**Circ:** (Paid)‡100
(Free)‡30,000

**Community News (17626)**
5748 Helen Ave.
Saint Louis, MO 63136
Phone: (314)261-5555
Fax: (314)261-2776
**Subject(s):** Free Newspapers
**Circ:** (Free)‡30,000

**Southwest County Journal (18041)**
Pulitzer Publishing
220 E Main
Warrenton, MO 63383
Phone: (636)456-3481
Fax: (636)456-3020
**Subject(s):** Free Newspapers
**Circ:** (Sun.)28,959
(Fri.)28,959
(Wed.)29,952

**Tri-State Neighbor (28413)**
309 W 43rd St.
Sioux Falls, SD 57105
Phone: (605)335-7300

Fax: (605)335-8141
**Subject(s):** Farm Newspapers
**Circ:** (Controlled)29,500

**South Side Journal (18040)**
Pulitzer Publishing
220 E Main
Warrenton, MO 63383
Phone: (636)456-3481
Fax: (636)456-3020
**Subject(s):** Free Newspapers
**Circ:** (Sun.)28,665
(Wed.)29,425

**Belleville Journal (18025)**
Pulitzer Publishing
220 E Main
Warrenton, MO 63383
Phone: (636)456-3481
Fax: (636)456-3020
**Subject(s):** Free Newspapers
**Circ:** (Sun.)27,301
(Wed.)28,310

**The Mason City Shopper (10742)**
Lee Enterprises Inc.
PO Box 271
Mason City, IA 50402-0271
Phone: (641)424-3044
Fax: (641)424-6786
**Subject(s):** Shopping Guides
**Circ:** (Free)28,204

**South Dakota Legion News (28456)**
The American Legion/South Dakota Department
PO Box 67
Watertown, SD 57201
Phone: (605)886-3604
Fax: (605)886-2870
**Subject(s):** Veterans
**Circ:** ‡27,815

**Cityview (10461)**
Business Publications Corp.
The Depot at Fourth
100 4th St.
Des Moines, IA 50309
Phone: (515)288-3336
Fax: (515)288-0309
**Subject(s):** Paid Community Newspapers
**Circ:** (Free)❑26,524

**Iowa Parent & Family (10482)**
PO Box 957
Des Moines, IA 50304
Phone: (515)284-8173
Fax: (515)286-2597
**Subject(s):** Free Newspapers; Parenting
**Circ:** (Non-paid)25,680
(Controlled)26,000

**Mighty Nickel (18356)**
Maverick Media Inc.
2538 N. St. Patrick Ave.
PO Box 850
Grand Island, NE 68802
Phone: (308)382-9303
**Subject(s):** Shopping Guides
**Circ:** (Free)‡25,950

**The Buyer's Guide (11396)**
1118 W. Cloud
PO Box 6134
Salina, KS 67401-0134
Phone: (785)823-3209
Fax: (785)823-3176
**Subject(s):** Shopping Guides
**Circ:** (Free)25,800

**Grand Island Independent (18355)**
422 W 1st St.
PO Box 1208
Grand Island, NE 68802-1208
Phone: (308)382-1000
Fax: (308)382-8129
**Subject(s):** Daily Newspapers
**Circ:** (Mon.-Sat.)23,842
(Sun.)25,673

**The Advertiser (10286)**
Iowa Community Publications
301 Fifth St.
PO Box 904
Ames, IA 50010
Phone: (515)233-1251

Circulation: ★ = ABC; △ = BPA; ♦ = CAC; • = CCAB; ❑ = VAC; ⊖ = PO Statement; ‡ = Publisher's Report; Boldface figures = sworn; Light figures = estimated.

Fax: (515)233-1244
**Subject(s):** Shopping Guides
**Circ:** (Free)‡25,623

**Bellevue Leader** (18281)
604 Fort Crook Rd. N.
Bellevue, NE 68005
Phone: (402)733-7300
Fax: (402)733-9116
**Subject(s):** Paid Community Newspapers
**Circ:** (Combined)‡25,629

**West County Journal** (18043)
Pulitzer Publishing
220 E Main
Warrenton, MO 63383
Phone: (636)456-3481
Fax: (636)456-3020
**Subject(s):** Free Newspapers
**Circ:** (Fri.)23,914
(Sun.)24,921
(Wed.)25,600

**Coteau Shopper** (28455)
Coteau Shopper Inc.
Box 1176
Watertown, SD 57201
Phone: (605)882-1152
Fax: (605)882-1158
**Subject(s):** Shopping Guides
**Circ:** (Free)‡25500

**The Examiner** (17266)
Morris Communications
410 S. Liberty St.
Independence, MO 64050
Phone: (816)254-8600
**Subject(s):** Daily Newspapers
**Circ:** (Mon.-Fri.)☐**13,808**
(Sat.)☐**14,924**
(Wed.)☐**25,450**

**St. Charles Journal** (18038)
Pulitzer Publishing
220 E Main
Warrenton, MO 63383
Phone: (636)456-3481
Fax: (636)456-3020
**Subject(s):** Free Newspapers
**Circ:** (Fri.)24,247
(Sun.)24,347
(Wed.)25,092

**Adoremus Bulletin** (17546)
Adoremus: Society for the Renewal of the Sacred Liturgy
PO Box 300561
Saint Louis, MO 63130
Phone: (314)863-8385
Fax: (314)863-5858
**Subject(s):** Religious Publications
**Circ:** (Non-paid)25,000

**Ozarks Senior Living** (17969)
Metropolitan Radio Group Inc.
318 E Pershing
Springfield, MO 65806
Phone: (417)862-0852
Fax: (417)862-0852
**Subject(s):** Free Newspapers; Senior Citizens' Interests
**Circ:** (Combined)25,000

**Southwest City Journal** (17847)
Pulitzer Publishing
4210 Chippewa
Saint Louis, MO 63116
Phone: (314)664-2700
**Subject(s):** Paid Community Newspapers
**Circ:** (Sun.)24,346
(Wed.)24,960

**Columbus Area Choice** (18314)
Morris/Stauffer Communications Inc.
1367 33rd Ave.
PO Box 1397
Columbus, NE 68602-1397
Phone: (402)564-1025
Fax: (402)564-1403
**Subject(s):** Shopping Guides
**Circ:** (Non-paid)24,940

**NSEA Voice** (18438)
Nebraska State Education Association
605 S. 14th St.
Lincoln, NE 68508
Phone: (402)475-7611

Fax: (402)475-2630
**Subject(s):** Education
**Circ:** ‡24,350

**Trade & Transactions** (18645)
Trade & Transactions Inc.
400 Lincoln Ave
York, NE 68467
Phone: (402)362-5561
Fax: (402)362-3697
**Subject(s):** Shopping Guides
**Circ:** (Paid)46
(Free)24,094

**Jefferson City News Tribune** (17279)
News Tribune Co.
210 Monroe St.
PO Box 420
Jefferson City, MO 65101-0420
Phone: (573)636-3131
**Subject(s):** Daily Newspapers
**Circ:** (Mon.-Sat.)17,377
(Sun.)23,959

**News Democrat Journal** (18035)
Pulitzer Publishing
220 E Main
Warrenton, MO 63383
Phone: (636)456-3481
Fax: (636)456-3020
**Subject(s):** Daily Newspapers
**Circ:** (Sun.)22,769
(Fri.)22,769
(Wed.)23,372

**Globe-Gazette** (10740)
Howard Query
300 N Washington Ave.
PO Box 271
Mason City, IA 50401-3222
Phone: (515)421-0500
Fax: (515)421-0516
**Subject(s):** Daily Newspapers
**Circ:** (Mon.-Sat.)★**18,963**
(Sun.)★**23,311**

**Daily Gate City** (10690)
Brehm Communications Inc.
c/o Daily Gate City
1016 Main St., PO Box 430
PO Box 430
Keokuk, IA 52632
Phone: (319)524-8300
Fax: (319)524-4363
**Subject(s):** Daily Newspapers
**Circ:** (Combined)23,300

**Columbia Daily Tribune** (17151)
Tribune Publishing Co.
101 N Fourth St.
PO Box 798
Columbia, MO 65205-0798
Phone: (573)815-1680
Fax: (573)815-1698
**Subject(s):** Daily Newspapers
**Circ:** (Mon.-Sat.)★**18,447**
(Sun.)★**23,250**

**Jefferson County Journal** (18033)
Pulitzer Publishing
220 E Main
Warrenton, MO 63383
Phone: (636)456-3481
Fax: (636)456-3020
**Subject(s):** Free Newspapers
**Circ:** (Sun.)22,745
(Fri.)22,745
(Wed.)23,234

**Missouri Valley Shopper** (28473)
329 Broadway St.
PO Box 773
Yankton, SD 57078-0773
Phone: (605)665-5884
Fax: (605)665-5882
**Subject(s):** Shopping Guides
**Circ:** (Free)‡23,220

**The Minot Daily News** (24033)
Minot Daily News
PO Box 1150
Minot, ND 58702
Phone: (701)857-1900
Fax: (701)857-1907

**Subject(s):** Daily Newspapers
**Circ:** (Mon.-Sat.)★**22,136**
(Sun.)★**22,975**

**Blue Springs Examiner (Wednesday Edition)** (17080)
The Blue Springs Examiner
500 W. R.D. Mize Rd.
Blue Springs, MO 64015
Phone: (816)229-9161
**Subject(s):** Paid Community Newspapers
**Circ:** (Combined)22,724

**South County Journal** (18039)
Pulitzer Publishing
220 E Main
Warrenton, MO 63383
Phone: (636)456-3481
Fax: (636)456-3020
**Subject(s):** Free Newspapers
**Circ:** (Sun.)22,011
(Fri.)22,011
(Wed.)22,586

**West End-Clayton Word** (17876)
Virginia Publishing Co.
625 N Euclid, Ste. 330
PO Box 4538
Saint Louis, MO 63108
Phone: (314)367-6612
Fax: (314)367-0727
**Subject(s):** Paid Community Newspapers
**Circ:** (Non-paid)22,500

**The Times Herald** (10347)
Herald Publishing
508 N Court St.
Carroll, IA 51401
Phone: (712)792-3573
Fax: (712)792-5218
**Subject(s):** Daily Newspapers
**Circ:** (Paid)6,051
(Free)‡22,320

**Fremont Area Shopper** (18343)
Fremont-Tribune Newspapers Inc.
135 N Main St.
PO Box 9
Fremont, NE 68025
Phone: (402)721-5000
Fax: (402)721-8047
**Subject(s):** Shopping Guides
**Circ:** (Non-paid)22,300

**St. Louis Business Journal** (17808)
American City Business Journals Inc.
1 Metropolitan Sq., Ste. 2170
PO Box 647
Saint Louis, MO 63102
Phone: (314)421-6200
Fax: (314)621-5031
**Subject(s):** Business; Local, State, and Regional Publications
**Circ:** (Paid)22,246

**Pennysaver** (10734)
507 East Anson
Box 246
Marshalltown, IA 50158
Phone: (641)752-6630
Fax: (641)752-7073
**Subject(s):** Shopping Guides
**Circ:** (Free)‡22,213

**AOA News** (17576)
American Optometric Association
243 N. Lindbergh Blvd.
Saint Louis, MO 63141
Phone: (314)991-4100
Fax: (314)991-4101
**Subject(s):** Ophthalmology, Optometry, and Optics
**Circ:** (Free)‡7,823
(Paid)‡22,189

**The Chronicle Shopper** (11189)
Chronicle Shopper
505 Cherokee
Leavenworth, KS 66048
Phone: (913)682-1334
Fax: (913)682-1089
**Subject(s):** Shopping Guides
**Circ:** (Non-paid)22,000

**Gale Directory of Publications & Broadcast Media/140th Ed.**  **Great Plains States**

**Granite City Journal** (18032)
Pulitzer Publishing
220 E Main
Warrenton, MO 63383
Phone: (636)456-3481
Fax: (636)456-3020
**Subject(s):** Free Newspapers
**Circ:** (Sun.)21,201
(Wed.)21,760

**Southern Nebraska Register** (18450)
PO Box 80329
Lincoln, NE 68501
Phone: (402)488-0090
Fax: (402)488-3569
**Subject(s):** Religious Publications
**Circ:** ‡21,500

**The Messenger** (10582)
Odgen Newspaper
713 Central Ave
PO Box 659
Fort Dodge, IA 50501
Phone: (515)573-2141
Fax: (515)573-2148
**Subject(s):** Daily Newspapers
**Circ:** (Mon.-Sat.)19,162
(Sun.)21,483

**Valley Shopper** (10499)
Gannett Company Inc.
Press Citizen Shopper Newspaper
525 SW 5th St., Ste. E
Des Moines, IA 50309
**Subject(s):** Shopping Guides
**Circ:** (Free)21,380

**Golden Shopper** (10853)
Iowa Information Inc.
227 9th St.
PO Box 160
Sheldon, IA 51201
Phone: (712)324-5347
Fax: (712)324-2345
**Subject(s):** Shopping Guides
**Circ:** (Free)‡21,242

**The Journal** (17495)
Butler County Publishing
208 Poplar St.
PO Box 7
Poplar Bluff, MO 63901
Phone: (573)785-1414
Fax: (573)785-2706
**Subject(s):** Free Newspapers
**Circ:** (Free)‡21,105

**Penny Press 1** (18496)
Nebraska City News Press Inc.
807 Central Ave.
Nebraska City, NE 68410
Phone: (402)873-3334
Fax: (402)873-5436
**Subject(s):** Shopping Guides
**Circ:** (Free)‡20,850

**The Post** (10771)
Lee Enterprises Inc.
301 E 3rd St.
Muscatine, IA 52761-4116
**Subject(s):** Shopping Guides
**Circ:** (Free)20,850

**Hawk Eye** (10335)
Harris Enterprizes
PO Box 10
Burlington, IA 52601
Phone: (319)754-6824
Fax: (319)754-6824
**Subject(s):** Daily Newspapers
**Circ:** (Mon.-Sat.)★18,775
(Sun.)★20,726

**The Daily Iowan** (10646)
Student Publications Inc.
111 Communications Dept.
Iowa City, IA 52242
Phone: (319)335-6063
Fax: (319)335-6297
**Subject(s):** Paid Community Newspapers
**Circ:** ‡20,500

**Oskaloosa Shopper** (10802)
1901 A Ave. W
Box 530
Oskaloosa, IA 52577-0530
Phone: (641)672-2581
Fax: (641)672-2294
**Subject(s):** Shopping Guides
**Circ:** (Free)20,500

**The Crier** (17372)
American Publishing Co.
110 E MCPherson St.
PO Box 809
Kirksville, MO 63501
Phone: (660)665-4663
Fax: (660)665-3048
**Subject(s):** Free Newspapers
**Circ:** (Paid)105
(Free)20,455

**The Standard Democrat** (17953)
205 S New Madrid St.
Sikeston, MO 63801
Phone: (314)471-1137
Fax: (314)471-6277
**Subject(s):** Daily Newspapers
**Circ:** (Mon.-Sat.)♦6,116
(Sun.)♦8,793
(Wed.)♦20,331

**Journal-World** (11176)
609 New Hampshire St.
PO Box 888
Lawrence, KS 66044
Phone: (785)843-1000
**Subject(s):** Daily Newspapers
**Circ:** (Mon.-Sat.)19,202
(Sun.)20,307

**The Catholic Missourian** (17276)
Diocese of Jefferson City
609 Clark Ave.
PO Box 104900
Jefferson City, MO 65110
Phone: (573)635-9127
Fax: (573)635-2286
**Subject(s):** Religious Publications
**Circ:** (Paid)‡20,211

**Town & Country Leader** (17216)
Excelsior Publishing Company Inc.
417 Thompson Ave.
PO Box 70
Excelsior Springs, MO 64024
Phone: (816)637-3147
Fax: (816)637-8411
**Subject(s):** Shopping Guides
**Circ:** (Paid)‡245
(Free)‡20,100

**Lees Summit Journal-Extra** (17391)
Lees Summit Journal Inc.
415 SE Douglas St.
PO Box 387
Lees Summit, MO 64063
Phone: (816)524-2345
Fax: (816)524-5136
**Subject(s):** Shopping Guides
**Circ:** (Paid)4,308
(Free)20,026

**Dos Mundos Bilingual Newspaper** (17324)
Dos Mondos Bilingual Newspaper
902-A SW Blvd.
Kansas City, MO 64108
Phone: (816)221-4747
Fax: (816)221-4894
**Subject(s):** Paid Community Newspapers; Hispanic Publications; Spanish
**Circ:** 20,000

**Franklin County Watchman** (17683)
St. Louis County Printing & Pub. Co.
2111 S. Brentwood Blvd.
Saint Louis, MO 63114
Phone: (636)925-2045
Fax: (314)918-1311
**Subject(s):** Paid Community Newspapers
**Circ:** (Combined)‡20,000

**Saint Charles Watchman** (17804)
St. Louis County Printing & Pub. Co.
2111 S. Brentwood Blvd.
Saint Louis, MO 63114
Phone: (636)925-2045
Fax: (314)918-1311
**Subject(s):** Daily Newspapers
**Circ:** (Combined)‡20,000

**The Catholic Messenger** (10419)
736 Federal St.
PO Box 460
Davenport, IA 52805-0460
Phone: (563)323-9959
Fax: (563)323-6612
**Subject(s):** Religious Publications
**Circ:** (Free)33
(Paid)19,962

**The Reminder Plus** (28366)
Hipple Publishing Company Inc.
333 W Dakota
PO Box 669
Pierre, SD 57501-0669
Phone: (605)224-7301
Fax: (605)224-9210
**Subject(s):** Shopping Guides
**Circ:** (Free)‡19,800

**Southside Shopper** (10496)
Gannett Company Inc.
Des Moines Press Citizen
525 SW 5th St., Ste. E
Des Moines, IA 50309
**Subject(s):** Shopping Guides
**Circ:** (Free)19,635

**Collinsville Herald-Journal** (18027)
Pulitzer Publishing
220 E Main
Warrenton, MO 63383
Phone: (636)456-3481
Fax: (636)456-3020
**Subject(s):** Free Newspapers
**Circ:** (Sun.)18,923
(Wed.)19,598

**Northland News** (17342)
Sun Publications Inc.
7373 W 107th St.
Overland Park, KS 66212
Phone: (913)381-1010
Fax: (913)381-9889
**Subject(s):** Free Newspapers
**Circ:** (Free)19,270

**The Lawrence Journal-World** (11179)
609 New Hampshire
PO Box 888
Lawrence, KS 66044
Phone: (785)832-1000
**Subject(s):** Daily Newspapers
**Circ:** (Mon.-Sat.)★19,203
(Sun.)★19,252

**Penny Press 2** (17418)
Maverick Media Inc.
PO Box 188
Maryville, MO 64468
**Subject(s):** Shopping Guides
**Circ:** ‡19,100

**Cass County Shopper** (17252)
Cass County Publishing Co.
PO Box 329
Harrisonville, MO 64701
Fax: (816)380-7650
**Subject(s):** Shopping Guides
**Circ:** (Free)19,032

**Aberdeen American News** (28261)
Knight-Ridder Inc.
124 S. Second St.
PO Box 4430
Aberdeen, SD 57402
Phone: (605)225-4100
**Subject(s):** Daily Newspapers
**Circ:** (Mon.-Sat.)17,160
(Sun.)19,006

**Eastern Iowa Shopping News** (10545)
Woodward Communications
PO Box 350
Dyersville, IA 52040
Phone: (319)875-7131
Fax: (319)875-2279
**Subject(s):** Shopping Guides
**Circ:** 19,000

---
Circulation: ★ = ABC; △ = BPA; ♦ = CAC; ◆ = CCAB; ❑ = VAC; ⊕ = PO Statement; ‡ = Publisher's Report; Boldface figures = sworn; Light figures = estimated.

**The Witness** (10533)
Witness Publishing Co.
1229 Mt. Loretta Ave.
PO Box 917
Dubuque, IA 52004
Phone: (563)588-0556
Fax: (563)556-5464
**Subject(s):** Religious Publications
**Circ:** (Free)100
(Paid)‡18,880

**Atlantic News-Telegraph** (10314)
410 Walnut St.
PO Box 230
Atlantic, IA 50022-0230
Phone: (712)243-2624
Fax: (712)243-4988
**Subject(s):** Daily Newspapers
**Circ:** (Paid)6,154
(Free)18,800

**The Daily Nonpareil** (10411)
535 W Broadway, No. 300
Council Bluffs, IA 51503-0631
Phone: (712)328-1811
Fax: (712)328-1597
**Subject(s):** Daily Newspapers
**Circ:** (Mon.-Sat.)17,012
(Sun.)18,704

**The Prairie Post** (24006)
PO Box 1760
Jamestown, ND 58402-1760
Phone: (701)952-2796
Fax: (701)952-0025
**Subject(s):** Shopping Guides
**Circ:** (Free)18,639

**The Christian News** (10460)
Christian Church in the Upper Midwest
3300 University Ave.
PO Box 41217
Des Moines, IA 50311
Phone: (515)255-3168
Fax: (515)255-2625
**Subject(s):** Religious Publications
**Circ:** ‡18,000

**DeKalb County Record-Herald** (17422)
Rebel Publishing Co.
PO Box 98
Maysville, MO 64469
Phone: (816)449-2121
Fax: (816)449-2808
**Subject(s):** Paid Community Newspapers
**Circ:** (Paid)18,000

**Raytown Post** (17508)
Gray Union Publishing Inc.
PO Box 9338
Raytown, MO 64133
Phone: (816)353-5545
Fax: (816)353-5589
**Subject(s):** Free Newspapers
**Circ:** (Free)‡18,000

**The Mirror** (17966)
Diocese of Springfield-Cape Girardeau
601 S Jefferson Ave.
Springfield, MO 65806-3143
Phone: (417)866-0841
Fax: (417)866-1140
**Subject(s):** Religious Publications
**Circ:** ‡17,500

**Chiefland Shopper** (10819)
Chief Printing Co.
1323 2nd St.
PO Box 98
Perry, IA 50220
Phone: (515)465-4666
Fax: (515)465-3087
**Subject(s):** Shopping Guides
**Circ:** (Free)17,400

**Call** (17317)
Kansas City Call Inc.
PO Box 410-477
1715 East 18 Street
Kansas City, MO 64108
Phone: (816)842-3804
Fax: (816)842-4420
**Subject(s):** Paid Community Newspapers; Black Publications
**Circ:** (Fri.)17,310

**Southeast Missourian Plus** (17114)
301 Broadway
PO Box 699
Cape Girardeau, MO 63701
Phone: (573)335-6611
Fax: (573)334-7288
**Subject(s):** Daily Newspapers
**Circ:** (Combined)17,215

**Norfolk Daily News** (18499)
Huse Publishing Co.
525 Norfolk Ave.
Box 977
Norfolk, NE 68702-0977
Phone: (402)371-1020
Fax: (402)371-5802
**Subject(s):** Daily Newspapers
**Circ:** (Mon.-Sat.)★17,125

**Northcentral Shopper** (10491)
Gannett Company Inc.
Des Moines Press Citizen
525 SW 5th St., Ste. E
Des Moines, IA 50309
**Subject(s):** Shopping Guides
**Circ:** (Free)17,045

**Daily American Republic** (17494)
Butler County Publishing
208 Poplar St.
PO Box 7
Poplar Bluff, MO 63901
Phone: (573)785-1414
Fax: (573)785-2706
**Subject(s):** Daily Newspapers
**Circ:** (Mon.-Fri.)13,138
(Sun.)13,988
(Wed.)17,034

**Dakota Catholic Action** (23898)
Diocese of Bismack
520 N Washington St.
PO Box 1137
Bismarck, ND 58502-1137
Phone: (701)222-3035
Fax: (701)222-0269
**Subject(s):** Religious Publications; Free Newspapers
**Circ:** (Non-paid)16,800

**The Iowa City Press-Citizen** (10649)
Gannett Company Inc.
1725 N. Dodge St.
Iowa City, IA 52245
Phone: (319)337-3181
Fax: (319)339-7342
**Subject(s):** Daily Newspapers
**Circ:** (Mon.-Fri.)★14,287
(Sat.)★16,640

**Star-Herald** (18595)
1405 Broadway
PO Box 1709
Scottsbluff, NE 69363-1709
Phone: (308)632-9000
Fax: (308)635-9001
**Subject(s):** Daily Newspapers
**Circ:** (Tues.-Fri.)15,765
(Sat.)15,765
(Sun.)16,539

**El Dorado Springs Sun** (17205)
PO Box 71
El Dorado Springs, MO 64744
Phone: (417)876-3841
Fax: (417)876-3848
**Subject(s):** Paid Community Newspapers
**Circ:** (Mon.-Sat.)9,904
(Sun.)16,420

**Meramec Journal** (18034)
Pulitzer Publishing
220 E Main
Warrenton, MO 63383
Phone: (636)456-3481
Fax: (636)456-3020
**Subject(s):** Free Newspapers
**Circ:** (Sun.)15,514
(Fri.)15,514
(Wed.)16,051

**Country Advocate** (11088)
NorWest Newspapers
1205 Main Ave.
Goodland, KS 67735
Phone: (785)899-2338

Fax: (785)899-6186
**Subject(s):** Shopping Guides
**Circ:** (Free)‡16,000

**The Ottumwa Courier** (10806)
Community Newspaper Holdings Inc.
213 E. 2nd St.
Ottumwa, IA 52501
Phone: (641)684-4611
Fax: (641)684-7834
**Subject(s):** Daily Newspapers
**Circ:** (Mon.-Sat.)16,000

**Pony Express** (17074)
Bethany Printing Co.
PO Box 351
Bethany, MO 64424
Phone: (660)425-6325
Fax: (660)425-3441
**Subject(s):** Shopping Guides
**Circ:** (Free)16,000

**East St. Louis Journal** (18029)
Pulitzer Publishing
220 E Main
Warrenton, MO 63383
Phone: (636)456-3481
Fax: (636)456-3020
**Subject(s):** Free Newspapers
**Circ:** (Wed.)15,855

**The Cameron Shopper** (17107)
Cameron Newspapers Inc.
402 E. Evergreen (BB Hwy.)
PO Box 498
Cameron, MO 64429
Phone: (816)632-6543
Fax: (816)632-4508
**Subject(s):** Shopping Guides
**Circ:** (Free)15,600

**Washington Missourian** (18047)
Missourian Publishing Co.
14 W. Main
Washington, MO 63090
**Subject(s):** Paid Community Newspapers
**Circ:** (Sat.)13,771
(Wed.)15,494

**St. Louis Jewish Light** (17812)
12 Millstone Campus Dr.
Saint Louis, MO 63146-5776
Phone: (314)432-3353
Fax: (314)432-0515
**Subject(s):** Jewish Publications
**Circ:** ‡14,800

**The Kayo** (17145)
Democrat Publishing Company Inc.
212 S Washington
PO Box 586
Clinton, MO 64735
Phone: (816)885-2281
Fax: (816)885-2265
**Subject(s):** Paid Community Newspapers
**Circ:** ‡14,700

**Ottawa Times Shopper** (11289)
The Ottawa Times
101 South Cedar St.
PO Box 246
Ottawa, KS 66067
Phone: (785)242-9200
Fax: (785)242-9595
**Subject(s):** Paid Community Newspapers
**Circ:** (Paid)1,200
(Free)14,475

**Northeast Shopper** (10492)
Gannett Company Inc.
Press Citizen Shopper Newspaper
525 SW 5th St., Ste. E
Des Moines, IA 50309
**Subject(s):** Shopping Guides
**Circ:** (Free)14,440

**Kansas State Collegian** (11231)
Kansas State University Student Publications Inc.
118 Kedzie Hall
Manhattan, KS 66506
Phone: (785)532-6560
**Subject(s):** College Publications
**Circ:** (Paid)‡312
(Free)‡14,260

**Leetown Shopper (10488)**
Gannett Company Inc.
Des Moines Press Citizen
525 SW 5th St., Ste. E
Des Moines, IA 50309
**Subject(s):** Shopping Guides
**Circ:** (Free)14,045

**Iowa State Daily (10289)**
Iowa State Daily Publication Board
Iowa State University
Rm. 108 Hamilton Hall
Ames, IA 50011
**Subject(s):** College Publications
**Circ:** 14,000

**McCook Daily Gazette (18482)**
Rest Communicatoion
W 1st & E St
PO Box 1268
McCook, NE 69001-1268
Phone: (308)345-4500
Fax: (308)345-7881
**Subject(s):** Daily Newspapers
**Circ:** (Paid)10,061
   (Free)14,000

**The Packer (11203)**
Vance Publishing Corp.
c/o Lance Jungmeyer, Managing Editor
10901 W. 84th Terrace
Lenexa, KS
Phone: (913)438-0768
Fax: (913)438-0691
**Subject(s):** Fruit, Fruit Products, and Produce Trade
**Circ:** (Paid)14,000

**Tri-State Livestock News (28440)**
Country Media
PO Box 69, 1022 Main St.
Sturgis, SD 57785
Phone: (605)347-2503
Fax: (605)347-2321
**Subject(s):** Farm Newspapers; Livestock
**Circ:** (Free)‡500
   (Paid)‡14,000

**Kearney Hub (18387)**
Kearney Hub Publishing Co.
13 E. 22 St.
PO Box 1988
Kearney, NE 68848
Phone: (308)237-2152
Fax: (308)233-9736
**Subject(s):** Daily Newspapers
**Circ:** (Mon.-Fri.)★12,654
   (Sat.)★13,804

**Edwardsville Journal (18030)**
Pulitzer Publishing
220 E Main
Warrenton, MO 63383
Phone: (636)456-3481
Fax: (636)456-3020
**Subject(s):** Free Newspapers
**Circ:** (Wed.)13,782

**Warrenton Journal (18042)**
Pulitzer Publishing
220 E Main
Warrenton, MO 63383
Phone: (636)456-3481
Fax: (636)456-3020
**Subject(s):** Free Newspapers
**Circ:** (Wed.)13,736

**Watertown Public Opinion (28457)**
120 3rd Ave. NW
Box 10
Watertown, SD 57201
Phone: (605)886-6901
Fax: (605)886-4280
**Subject(s):** Daily Newspapers
**Circ:** (Mon.-Sat.)13,558

**Tama County Shopper-Advisor (10916)**
Tama County Publishing Inc.
220 W 3rd St.
PO Box 118
Tama, IA 52339
Phone: (641)484-2841
Fax: (641)484-5705
**Subject(s):** Shopping Guides
**Circ:** (Free)‡13,500

**Daily Nebraskan (18408)**
University of Nebraska at Lincoln
PO Box 880448
Lincoln, NE 68588-0448
**Subject(s):** College Publications; Daily Newspapers
**Circ:** 13,400

**The Hays Daily News (11102)**
News Publishing Co.
507 Main St.
Hays, KS 67601
Phone: (785)628-1081
Fax: (785)628-8186
**Subject(s):** Daily Newspapers
**Circ:** (Mon.-Fri.)12,249
   (Sun.)13,255

**North Platte Telegraph (18505)**
Western Publishing Co.
621 N. Chestnut
PO Box 370
North Platte, NE 69101
Phone: (308)532-6000
Fax: (308)532-9268
**Subject(s):** Daily Newspapers
**Circ:** (Mon.-Sat.)★13,180
   (Sun.)★13,215

**The Reminder (10279)**
Algona Publishing Co.
14 E Nebraska
PO Box 400
Algona, IA 50511
Phone: (515)295-3535
Fax: (515)295-7217
**Subject(s):** Shopping Guides
**Circ:** (Free)‡13,100

**The Weekend Express (10280)**
Algona Publishing Co.
14 E Nebraska
PO Box 400
Algona, IA 50511
Phone: (515)295-3535
Fax: (515)295-7217
**Subject(s):** Shopping Guides
**Circ:** (Non-paid)‡13,100

**Platte County Sun Gazette (17393)**
Sun News
963 W Liberty Dr.
Liberty, MO 64068-2104
**Subject(s):** Free Newspapers
**Circ:** (Paid)158
   (Free)13,055

**Humboldt Reminder (10631)**
Humboldt Reminder Inc.
512 Sumner Ave.
PO Box 549
Humboldt, IA 50548
Phone: (515)332-3425
**Subject(s):** Shopping Guides
**Circ:** (Free)13,017

**The Air Pulse (18516)**
906 SAC Blvd., Ste. 1
Offutt AFB, NE 68113
Phone: (402)294-3663
Fax: (402)294-7172
**Subject(s):** Free Newspapers; Military and Navy
**Circ:** (Free)‡13,000

**West River Catholic (28382)**
606 Cathedral Dr.
PO Box 678
Rapid City, SD 57709
Phone: (605)343-3541
Fax: (605)348-7985
**Subject(s):** Religious Publications
**Circ:** (Paid)12,838

**The Reminder (10697)**
Journal/Express Inc.
122 E Robinson
PO Box 458
Knoxville, IA 50138
Phone: (641)842-2155
Fax: (641)842-2929
**Subject(s):** Shopping Guides
**Circ:** (Free)12,600

**Telegraph Happenings (18506)**
The North Platte Telegraph
621 N Chestnut St.
North Platte, NE 69101
Phone: (308)532-6000
Fax: (308)532-9268
**Subject(s):** Free Newspapers
**Circ:** (Free)‡12,554

**Sioux Center Shopper (10868)**
67 3rd St. NE
Sioux Center, IA 51250
Phone: (712)722-0511
Fax: (712)722-0507
**Subject(s):** Shopping Guides
**Circ:** (Free)‡12,500

**The Daily Republic (28348)**
Forum Communications Co.
120 S. Lawler
PO Box 1288
Mitchell, SD 57301
Phone: (605)996-7793
Fax: (605)996-7793
**Subject(s):** Daily Newspapers
**Circ:** (Mon.-Fri.)◻12,243
   (Sat.)◻12,485

**The Sedalia Democrat (17943)**
700 South Massachusetts Ave.
PO Box 848
Sedalia, MO 65302-0848
Phone: (660)826-1000
Fax: (660)826-2413
**Subject(s):** Daily Newspapers
**Circ:** (Mon.-Sat.)11,911
   (Sun.)12,425

**The Cash-Book Journal (17274)**
210 W Main St.
PO Box 369
Jackson, MO 63755-0369
Phone: (573)243-3515
Fax: (573)243-3517
**Subject(s):** Law
**Circ:** 5,325
   7,000
   12,325

**Kansas City Kansan (11144)**
8200 State Ave.
Kansas City, KS 66112
Phone: (913)371-4300
Fax: (913)342-8620
**Subject(s):** Daily Newspapers
**Circ:** (Mon.-Fri.)‡11,027
   (Sun.)‡12,100

**The Hastings Tribune (18366)**
Seaton Publications
912 W. 2nd St.
Hastings, NE 68901
Phone: (402)462-2131
Fax: (402)461-4657
**Subject(s):** Daily Newspapers
**Circ:** (Mon.-Sat.)12,002
   12,032

**Cahokia-Dupo Journal (18026)**
Pulitzer Publishing
220 E Main
Warrenton, MO 63383
Phone: (636)456-3481
Fax: (636)456-3020
**Subject(s):** Free Newspapers
**Circ:** (Sun.)11,125
   (Wed.)11,515

**EXTRA (10636)**
Record-Herald
1801 W 2nd Ave., Ste. 2
PO Box 259
Indianola, IA 50125-0259
Phone: (515)961-2511
Fax: (515)961-4833
**Subject(s):** Shopping Guides
**Circ:** (Free)11,500

**Weekly Bargain Shopper (17419)**
Maryville Daily Forum
111 E Jenkins
PO Box 188
Maryville, MO 64468
Phone: (660)582-3106
Fax: (660)562-2823

## Great Plains States

**Subject(s):** Shopping Guides
**Circ:** (Free)‡11,500

**Mercury (11234)**
Mercury Inc.
PO Box 787
Manhattan, KS 66502
Phone: (785)776-8805
Fax: (785)776-8807
**Subject(s):** Daily Newspapers

**Circ:** (Mon.-Fri.)10,125
(Sun.)11,450

**Raytown Dispatch-Tribune (17507)**
Townsend Communications Inc.
7007 NE Parvin Rd.
Kansas City, MO 64117
Phone: (816)454-9660
Fax: (816)452-5889
**Subject(s):** Free Newspapers

**Circ:** (Combined)11,442

**Boone County Shopping News (10325)**
Partnership Press Inc.
2136 E.Mamie Eisenhower
Boone, IA 50036
Phone: (515)432-6153
Fax: (515)432-7811
**Subject(s):** Free Newspapers

**Circ:** (Free)11,408

**The University Daily Kansan (11181)**
University of Kansas
111 Stauffer-Flint Hall
Lawrence, KS 66045
Phone: (785)864-4810
Fax: (785)864-0391
**Subject(s):** College Publications

**Circ:** (Free)200
(Paid)11,300

**Boone Today (10327)**
2136 Mamie Eisenhower
PO Box 375
Boone, IA 50036
Phone: (515)432-6694
Fax: (515)232-8395

**Circ:** (Free)11,238

**Central Shopper (10459)**
Gannett Company Inc.
525 SW 5th St., Ste. E
Des Moines, IA 50309
**Subject(s):** Shopping Guides

**Circ:** (Free)11,137

**The Finder - Bowman Edition (23925)**
Country Media Inc.
18 S Main
PO Drawer F
Bowman, ND 58623
Phone: (701)523-5263
Fax: (701)523-3441
**Subject(s):** Shopping Guides

**Circ:** (Free)11,000

**The Journal (17402)**
Liberty Publishing Co.
204 W Bourke St.
PO Box 7
Macon, MO 63552-1503
Phone: (660)385-3121
Fax: (660)385-3082
**Subject(s):** Free Newspapers

**Circ:** (Free)11,000

**Prairie Profile (28280)**
Brookings Register
312 5th St.
PO Box 177
Brookings, SD 57006
Phone: (605)692-6271
Fax: (605)692-2979
**Subject(s):** Shopping Guides

**Circ:** (Free)11,000

**Columbus Telegram (18315)**
The People Speak
Columbus Telegram
PO Box 648
Columbus, NE 68602-0648
Fax: (402)563-7500

**Subject(s):** Daily Newspapers
**Circ:** (Mon.-Fri.)10,100
(Sun.)10,970

**Kansas City Business Journal (17333)**
American City Business Journals Inc.
1101 Walnut, Ste. 800
Kansas City, MO 64106
Phone: (816)472-4010
Fax: (816)472-4010
**Subject(s):** Business; Local, State, and Regional Publications

**Circ:** (Paid)10,941

**Times-Republican (10735)**
Marshalltown Newspaper Inc.
135 W. Main St.
Marshalltown, IA 50158
Phone: (641)753-6611
Fax: (641)753-7221
**Subject(s):** Daily Newspapers

**Circ:** (Mon.-Sat.)★10,448
(Sun.)★10,797

**The Smoke Signal (11463)**
Montgomery Communications Inc.
PO Box 267
Wamego, KS 66547
Phone: (913)456-2602
Fax: (913)456-8400
**Subject(s):** Free Newspapers

**Circ:** (Free)‡10,700

**Independence Examiner (Daily Edition) (17269)**
The Examiner
410 S Liberty St.
Independence, MO 64050-3805
Phone: (816)254-8600
Fax: (816)836-3805
**Subject(s):** Daily Newspapers

**Circ:** (Free)146
(Paid)10,621

**The Country Mailbox (17413)**
Missouri Color Web Inc.
225 N Clay
PO Box A
Marshfield, MO 65706
Phone: (417)468-2013
Fax: (417)859-7930
**Subject(s):** Shopping Guides

**Circ:** 5,500
‡10,612

**Douglas County Post-Gazette (18336)**
Enterprise Publishing Company Inc.
117 Hillrise Center
PO Box 677
Elkhorn, NE 68022
Phone: (402)289-2329
Fax: (402)289-0861
**Subject(s):** Paid Community Newspapers

**Circ:** ‡10,600

**Twin Cities Weekly (18596)**
Star-Herald
1405 Broadway
PO Box 1709
Scottsbluff, NE 69363-1709
Phone: (308)632-9000
Fax: (308)635-9001
**Subject(s):** Shopping Guides

**Circ:** (Free)10,500

**Vinton Livewire (10934)**
110 E 5th Street
PO Box 468
Vinton, IA 52349
Phone: (319)472-3303
Fax: (319)472-4811
**Subject(s):** Shopping Guides

**Circ:** (Free)‡10,350

**Liberty Tribune (17392)**
Townsend Communications Inc.
7007 NE Parvin Rd.
Kansas City, MO 64117
Phone: (816)454-9660
Fax: (816)452-5889
**Subject(s):** Free Newspapers

**Circ:** (Combined)2,659
(Free)10,306

**Ad Express (10380)**
105 N. Main St
Centerville, IA 52544
Phone: (641)856-6336
Fax: (641)856-8118
**Subject(s):** Shopping Guides

**Circ:** (Free)10,200

**Mennonite Weekly Review (11267)**
Mennonite Weekly Review Inc.
Box 568
Newton, KS 67114
Phone: (316)283-3670
Fax: (316)283-6502
**Subject(s):** Religious Publications

**Circ:** (Free)‡840
(Paid)‡10,200

**Yankton Press & Dakotan (28476)**
Morris Communications Corp.
319 Walnut St.
PO Box 56
Yankton, SD 57078
Phone: (605)665-7811
Fax: (605)665-1721
**Subject(s):** Daily Newspapers

**Circ:** ‡10,180

**The Daily Dunklin Democrat (17366)**
203 1st St.
Kennett, MO 63857
Phone: (573)888-4505
Fax: (573)888-5114
**Subject(s):** Daily Newspapers

**Circ:** (Tues.-Fri.)3,224
(Sun.)3,316
(Wed.)10,078

**Elkhorn Valley Shopper (18638)**
West Point News
134 E. Grove St.
West Point, NE 68788
Phone: (402)372-2461
Fax: (402)372-3530
**Subject(s):** Shopping Guides

**Circ:** (Free)‡10,010

**Branson Daily News (17088)**
Branson TriLakes Daily News
P.O. Box 1900
Branson, MO 65615
Phone: (417)334-3161
Fax: (417)334-4299
**Subject(s):** Paid Community Newspapers

**Circ:** 10,000

**Shawnee Journal Herald (11410)**
Liberty Group Publishing
11004 Johnson Dr.
Shawnee, KS 66203-2869
Phone: (913)631-2550
Fax: (913)631-6552
**Subject(s):** Paid Community Newspapers

**Circ:** (Paid)350
(Non-paid)10,000

**The Tribune (10298)**
317 5th St.
PO Box 380
Ames, IA 50010
Phone: (515)232-2160
Fax: (515)232-2364
**Subject(s):** Daily Newspapers

**Circ:** ‡9,851

**The Daily Statesman (17195)**
Delta Publishing Co.
133 S. Walnut
Dexter, MO 63841
Fax: (573)722-5322
**Subject(s):** Daily Newspapers

**Circ:** (Sun.)3,656
(Tues.)9,747

**Clipper (18291)**
Enterprise Publishing Company Inc.
138 No. 16th St.
Blair, NE 68008
Phone: (402)332-3232
Fax: (402)332-4733
**Subject(s):** Shopping Guides

**Circ:** (Paid)4,366
(Free)9,483

**Great Plains States**

**West Plains Daily Quill (18056)**
125 N Jefferson St.
PO Box 110
West Plains, MO 65775-0110
Phone: (417)256-9191
Fax: (417)256-9196
**Subject(s):** Daily Newspapers
Circ: (Free)6
(Paid)9,484

**The Wayne Herald (18633)**
114 Main St.
Box 70
Wayne, NE 68787
Phone: (402)375-2600
Fax: (402)375-1888
**Subject(s):** Paid Community Newspapers
Circ: (Paid)2,600
(Free)9,300

**The Round-up (10271)**
Dallas County News Inc.
705 Main St.
PO Box 190
Adel, IA 50003
**Subject(s):** Shopping Guides
Circ: (Free)9,200

**Dodge City Daily Globe (11046)**
Morris Communications Inc.
705 2nd Ave.
Dodge City, KS 67801
Phone: (620)225-4151
Fax: (620)225-4154
**Subject(s):** Daily Newspapers
Circ: ‡9,185

**The 5 x 80 Bulletin (10908)**
The Stuart Herald
Box 608
Stuart, IA 50250
Phone: (515)523-1010
Fax: (515)523-2825
**Subject(s):** Shopping Guides
Circ: (Free)‡9,023

**The Advantage (17513)**
The Daily News
204 W N Main St.
PO Box 100
Richmond, MO 64085-0100
Phone: (816)776-5454
Fax: (816)470-6397
**Subject(s):** Shopping Guides
Circ: (Free)9,000

**The Advertiser (10679)**
406 Stevens St.
PO Box 640
Iowa Falls, IA 50126
Phone: (641)648-2521
Fax: (641)648-4765
**Subject(s):** Shopping Guides
Circ: (Free)9,000

**Northern Iowan (10357)**
University of Northern Iowa
L011 Maucker Union
Cedar Falls, IA 50614
Phone: (319)273-2157
**Subject(s):** College Publications
Circ: ‡9,000

**Times-Citizen (10680)**
Times-Citizen Co.
406 Stevens St.
PO Box 640
Iowa Falls, IA 50126-0640
Phone: (641)648-2521
Fax: (641)648-4765
**Subject(s):** Paid Community Newspapers
Circ: (Paid)‡4,200
(Free)‡9,000

**PennySaver (10620)**
Tribune Newspapers Inc.
1114 7th St.
PO Box 721
Harlan, IA 51537-0721
Phone: (712)755-3211
Fax: (712)755-3324
**Subject(s):** Shopping Guides
Circ: (Free)‡8,921

**The Garden City Telegram (11079)**
Telegram Publishing Co.
PO Box 958
Garden City, KS 67846
Phone: (316)275-8500
Fax: (316)275-5165
**Subject(s):** Daily Newspapers
Circ: (Mon.-Sat.)★8,912

**The Daily Journal (17473)**
Eastern Missouri Publishing Co.
1513 St. Joe Dr.
Park Hills, MO 63601
Phone: (573)431-2010
Fax: (573)431-7640
**Subject(s):** Daily Newspapers
Circ: (Mon.-Fri.)8,792
(Sun.)8,851

**Clipper Shopper (18292)**
Enterprise Publishing Company Inc.
138 No. 16th St.
Blair, NE 68008
Phone: (402)332-3232
Fax: (402)332-4733
**Subject(s):** Shopping Guides
Circ: (Combined)‡8,750

**Independence Daily Reporter (11127)**
320 N 6th St.
PO Box 869
Independence, KS 67301
Phone: (620)331-3550
Fax: (620)331-3550
**Subject(s):** Daily Newspapers
Circ: (Mon.-Fri.)7,992
(Sun.)8,547

**Ad-Visor (10448)**
The Denison Bulletin/Review
PO Box 550
Denison, IA 51442
Phone: (712)263-2122
**Subject(s):** Shopping Guides
Circ: (Free)‡8,500

**North Dakota Education News (23900)**
North Dakota Education Association
PO Box 5005
1410 E Thayer St
Bismarck, ND 58502
Phone: (701)223-0450
Fax: (701)224-8535
**Subject(s):** Education
Circ: (Non-paid)‡8,500

**Hannibal Courier-Post (17247)**
PO Box A
Hannibal, MO 63401
Phone: (573)221-1568
Fax: (573)221-1568
**Subject(s):** Daily Newspapers
Circ: (Sat.)★7,868
(Mon.-Fri.)★8,450

**The Republic-Monitor Shopping Guide (17478)**
Perryville Newspapers Inc.
10 W Ste., Maries St.
PO Drawer 367
Perryville, MO 63775
Phone: (573)547-4567
Fax: (573)547-1643
**Subject(s):** Shopping Guides
Circ: (Free)‡8,400

**The Marshall Democrat-News (17408)**
121 N Lafayette St
PO Box 100
Marshall, MO 65340
Phone: (660)886-2233
Fax: (660)886-8544
**Subject(s):** Daily Newspapers
Circ: (Paid)3,980
(Free)8,370

**The Salem News (17937)**
500 N Washington
PO Box 798
Salem, MO 65560
Phone: (573)729-4126
Fax: (573)729-4920
**Subject(s):** Paid Community Newspapers
Circ: (Combined)‡8,300

**Beatrice Daily Sun (18275)**
200 N 7th St.
PO Box 847
Beatrice, NE 68310-3916
Phone: (402)223-5233
Fax: (402)228-3571
**Subject(s):** Daily Newspapers
Circ: (Mon.-Sat.)★8,065

**Ad-Visor (10796)**
Pluim Publishing Inc.
113 Central Ave. SE
Orange City, IA 51041-1738
Phone: (712)737-4266
Fax: (712)737-3896
**Subject(s):** Shopping Guides
Circ: (Free)8,000

**Cadenza (17594)**
Washington University
Campus Box 1039
Saint Louis, MO 63130
Phone: (314)935-5941
Fax: (314)935-5938
**Subject(s):** Free Newspapers
Circ: (Non-paid)‡8,000

**Kirksville Daily Express and News (17375)**
Kirksville Daily Express
110 E McPherson
PO Box 809
Kirksville, MO 63501
Phone: (660)665-4663
Fax: (660)665-2608
**Subject(s):** Daily Newspapers
Circ: (Mon.-Fri.)‡7,600
(Sun.)‡8,000

**The Marketplace (17376)**
Kirksville Daily Express
110 E McPherson
PO Box 809
Kirksville, MO 63501
Phone: (660)665-4663
Fax: (660)665-2608
**Subject(s):** Shopping Guides
Circ: (Free)‡6,000
(Paid)‡8,000

**Northwest Missourian (17417)**
Northwest Missouri State University
6 Wells Hall
800 University Dr.
Maryville, MO 64468
Phone: (660)562-1521
Fax: (660)562-1521
**Subject(s):** College Publications
Circ: 8,000

**Prairie Advisor (11269)**
Kansan
121 W 6th St.
Newton, KS 67114
Phone: (316)283-1500
Fax: (316)283-2471
**Subject(s):** Shopping Guides
Circ: (Free)8,000

**The Sunflower (11490)**
Wichita State University
1845 Fairmount
Campus Box 134
Wichita, KS 67260-0134
Phone: (316)978-3640
Fax: (316)978-3778
**Subject(s):** College Publications
Circ: (Mon.)8,000
(Wed.)8,000
(Fri.)8,000

**University News (17353)**
University of Missouri-Kansas City
5327 Holmes St.
Kansas City, MO 64110
Phone: (816)235-1393
**Subject(s):** College Publications
Circ: (Controlled)8,000

**Muscatine Journal (10770)**
301 E. 3rd St.
Muscatine, IA 52761
Phone: (563)263-2331
Fax: (563)262-8042
**Subject(s):** Daily Newspapers
Circ: (Mon.-Sat.)★7,998

Circulation: ★ = ABC; △ = BPA; ♦ = CAC; • = CCAB; ❑ = VAC; ⊖ = PO Statement; ‡ = Publisher's Report; Boldface figures = sworn; Light figures = estimated.

# Great Plains States

**The Emporia Gazette** (11061)
Emporia Gazette
517 Merchant St.
Emporia, KS 66801
Phone: (316)342-4800
Fax: (316)342-8108
**Subject(s):** Daily Newspapers
Circ: (Mon.-Sat.)★7,943

**Chieftain** (11007)
Chieftain
PO Box 256
128 Oak
Bonner Springs, KS 66012
Phone: (913)724-1887
Fax: (913)422-4233
**Subject(s):** Paid Community Newspapers
Circ: (Paid)‡5,200
(Non-paid)‡7,800

**Chieftain Shopper** (11008)
Chieftain
PO Box 256
128 Oak
Bonner Springs, KS 66012
Phone: (913)724-1887
Fax: (913)422-4233
**Subject(s):** Shopping Guides
Circ: (Paid)‡5,200
(Non-paid)‡7,800

**Neosho Daily News** (17443)
1006 W Harmony St
PO Box 848
Neosho, MO 64850
Phone: (417)451-1520
Fax: (417)451-6408
**Subject(s):** Daily Newspapers
Circ: (Paid)5,100
(Wed.)7,800

**Sentinel** (11009)
Chieftan
PO Box 256
128 Oak
Bonner Springs, KS 66012
Phone: (913)724-1887
Fax: (913)422-4233
**Subject(s):** Paid Community Newspapers
Circ: (Paid)‡5,200
(Non-paid)‡7,800

**Tri-County Special** (10317)
PO Box E
117 Pine St
Auburn, IA 51433
Phone: (712)688-2216
Fax: (712)688-2216
**Subject(s):** Shopping Guides
Circ: (Free)7,800

**Newton Kansan** (11268)
Morris Communications Corp.
121 W. 6th St.
PO Box 268
Newton, KS 67114
Phone: (316)283-1500
Fax: (316)283-2471
**Subject(s):** Daily Newspapers
Circ: (Paid)7,750

**Chadron Record** (18307)
PO Box 1141
Chadron, NE 69337-1141
Phone: (308)432-5511
Fax: (308)432-2385
**Subject(s):** Paid Community Newspapers
Circ: (Paid)‡2,100
(Free)‡7,700

**Times-Plain Dealer** (10414)
Liberty Group Publishing
101 N Elm
PO Box 350
Cresco, IA 52136
Phone: (319)547-3601
Fax: (319)547-4602
**Subject(s):** Farm Newspapers; Free Newspapers
Circ: (Paid)‡3,450
(Free)‡7,650

**The Mexico Ledger** (17425)
PO Box 8
Mexico, MO 65265-0008
**Subject(s):** Daily Newspapers
Circ: (Mon.-Sat.)7,615

**Forest City Summit** (10570)
Forest City Publishing Co.
PO Box 350
Forest City, IA 50436-0350
Phone: (641)585-2112
Fax: (641)585-4442
**Subject(s):** Paid Community Newspapers
Circ: (Paid)‡3,573
(Free)‡7,564

**Fort Leavenworth Lamp** (11071)
Chronicle Shopper
600 Thomas Ave.
Fort Leavenworth, KS 66027
Phone: (913)684-5267
Fax: (913)680-1996
**Subject(s):** Free Newspapers
Circ: (Non-paid)7,500

**The 4-County Market** (10729)
Pioneer Republican
PO Box 208
Marengo, IA 52301
Phone: (319)642-5506
Fax: (319)642-5509
**Subject(s):** Shopping Guides
Circ: (Free)‡7450

**Bolivar Herald-Free Press** (17081)
Community Publishers Inc./Missouri
335 S. Springfield Ave.
PO Box 330
Bolivar, MO 65613
Phone: (417)326-7636
Fax: (417)326-7643
**Subject(s):** Paid Community Newspapers
Circ: ‡7,400

**Fort Riley Post** (11073)
Montgomery Communications Inc.
Bldg. 405
Fort Riley, KS 66442
Phone: (785)239-8851
Fax: (785)239-2592
**Subject(s):** Free Newspapers; Military and Navy
Circ: (Paid)‡250
(Free)‡7,391

**Great Bend Tribune** (11092)
Tribune
2012 Forest Ave.
Box 228
Great Bend, KS 67530
Phone: (620)792-1211
Fax: (620)792-3441
**Subject(s):** Daily Newspapers
Circ: (Mon.-Fri.)7,048
(Sun.)7,362

**Daily Union Extra** (11137)
Montgomery Communications Inc.
PO Box 129
Junction City, KS 66441
**Subject(s):** Shopping Guides
Circ: (Free)‡7,300

**Leavenworth Times** (11190)
PO Box 144
Leavenworth, KS 66048
Phone: (913)682-0305
**Subject(s):** Daily Newspapers
Circ: (Mon.-Fri.)6,300
(Sun.)7,294

**Parsons Sun** (11363)
Parsons Publishing Co.
220 S 18th
PO Box 836
Parsons, KS 67357
Phone: (620)421-2000
Fax: (620)421-2217
**Subject(s):** Daily Newspapers
Circ: 7,189

**Ft. Madison Daily Democrat** (10594)
Brehm Communication
1226 Ave. H
PO Box 160
Fort Madison, IA 52627-4544
Phone: (319)372-6421
Fax: (319)372-3867
**Subject(s):** Daily Newspapers
Circ: ‡7,148

**Ottawa Herald** (11287)
104 S Cedar
Ottawa, KS 66067
Phone: (785)242-4700
Fax: (785)242-9420
**Subject(s):** Daily Newspapers
Circ: (Paid)‡6,098
(Non-paid)‡7,123

**Daily Union** (11136)
Montgomery Communications Inc.
222 W 6th St.
Junction City, KS 66441
Phone: (785)762-5000
Fax: (785)762-4584
**Subject(s):** Daily Newspapers
Circ: (Mon.-Fri.)6,455
(Sun.)7,099

**Scott County Signal** (17136)
113 S Main St.
PO Box 97
Chaffee, MO 63740
Phone: (573)887-3636
Fax: (573)887-3637
**Subject(s):** Paid Community Newspapers
Circ: ‡7,000

**The Spectrum** (23955)
North Dakota State University
356 Memorial Union
Fargo, ND 58105
Phone: (701)231-8929
Fax: (701)231-9402
**Subject(s):** College Publications
Circ: ‡7,000

**The Standard** (17973)
Southwest Missouri State University
901 S. National Ave.
Springfield, MO 65804-0094
Phone: (417)836-5000
Fax: (417)836-6738
**Subject(s):** College Publications
Circ: (Free)‡7,000

**The Sullivan Independent News** (17999)
Sullivan Independent News
Sullivan Ind. News
Box 268
Sullivan, MO 63080
Phone: (573)468-6511
Fax: (573)468-4046
**Subject(s):** Paid Community Newspapers
Circ: ‡7,000

**East Central Ad Mart** (17467)
Warden Publishing Co.
106 E Washington
PO Box 540
Owensville, MO 65066-0540
Phone: (314)437-2323
Fax: (314)437-3033
**Subject(s):** Free Newspapers; Shopping Guides
Circ: (Free)‡6,934

**Fairbury Journal-News** (18338)
516 5th St.
PO Box 415
Fairbury, NE 68352
Phone: (402)729-6141
Fax: (402)729-5652
**Subject(s):** Paid Community Newspapers
Circ: ‡6,881

**Southwest Daily Times** (11214)
Liberal Newspapers Inc.
16 S. Kansas Ave.
Liberal, KS 67901-3732
**Subject(s):** Daily Newspapers
Circ: (Non-paid)328
(Paid)6,829

# Great Plains States

**Impact Advertiser Shopper** (10776)
New Hampton Publishing Co.
10 N Chestnut Ave.
PO Box 380
New Hampton, IA 50659
Phone: (641)394-2111
Fax: (641)394-2113
**Subject(s):** Shopping Guides

Circ: (Non-paid)6,800

**Northwestern Kansas Register** (11398)
Abilene Reflector-Chronicle
PO Box 1038
Salina, KS 67402-1038
Phone: (785)827-8746
Fax: (785)827-6133
**Subject(s):** Religious Publications

Circ: (Non-paid)97
  (Paid)6,803

**County Journal** (18028)
Pulitzer Publishing
220 E Main
Warrenton, MO 63383
Phone: (636)456-3481
Fax: (636)456-3020
**Subject(s):** Free Newspapers

Circ: (Wed.)6,790

**Dakota Student** (23985)
University of North Dakota
PO Box 7209
University Station
Grand Forks, ND 58202
Phone: (701)777-2011
**Subject(s):** College Publications

Circ: ‡6,500

**Sac City Reminder** (10846)
S.A.C. Sun
406 William St.
PO Box 426
Sac City, IA 50583-0426
Phone: (712)662-7161
Fax: (712)662-4198
**Subject(s):** Shopping Guides

Circ: (Free)6,500

**Student Life** (17849)
Washington University
One Brookings Dr.
Campus Box 1039
Washington University
Saint Louis, MO 63130
Phone: (314)935-5995
**Subject(s):** College Publications

Circ: (Paid)‡500
  (Free)‡6,500

**Volante** (28446)
University of South Dakota
Student Publications Board
414 E. Clark St.
Vermillion, SD 57069
Phone: (605)677-5494
Fax: (605)677-5105
**Subject(s):** College Publications

Circ: (Paid)‡200
  (Free)‡6,500

**The Olathe Daily News** (11281)
Keltatim Publishing Company Inc.
514 S. Kansas Ave.
Olathe, KS 66061
Phone: (913)764-2211
Fax: (913)764-3672
**Subject(s):** Daily Newspapers

Circ: (Sat.)6,450
  (Mon.-Fri.)6,477

**Journal** (10441)
Decorah Newspapers
107 E. Water St.
Box 350
Decorah, IA 52101
Phone: (563)382-4221
Fax: (563)382-5949
**Subject(s):** Paid Community Newspapers

Circ: ‡6,400

**Public Opinion** (10443)
Decorah Newspapers
107 E. Water St.
Box 350
Decorah, IA 52101
Phone: (563)382-4221
Fax: (563)382-5949
**Subject(s):** Paid Community Newspapers

Circ: (Paid)‡6,400

**Bremer County Independent** (10956)
Waverly Newspapers
PO Box 858
Waverly, IA 50677-0858
Phone: (319)352-3334
Fax: (319)352-5135
**Subject(s):** Paid Community Newspapers

Circ: 6,350

**The Dickinson Press** (23937)
1815 W 1st St.
PO Box 1367
Dickinson, ND 58601-1367
Phone: (701)225-8111
Fax: (701)225-4205
**Subject(s):** Daily Newspapers

Circ: (Free)❏184
  (Paid)❏6,349

**Waverly Democrat** (10959)
Waverly Newspapers
PO Box 858
Waverly, IA 50677-0858
Phone: (319)352-3334
Fax: (319)352-5135
**Subject(s):** Paid Community Newspapers

Circ: 6,326

**Calhoun County Reminder** (10845)
Dudley Printing Inc.
515 4th St.
Rockwell City, IA 50579-0106
Phone: (712)297-8931
Fax: (712)297-7193
**Subject(s):** Shopping Guides

Circ: (Free)‡6,200

**Jackson County Advocate** (17243)
502 Main St.
PO Box 620
Grandview, MO 64030
Phone: (816)761-6200
Fax: (816)761-8215
**Subject(s):** Paid Community Newspapers

Circ: 6,200

**Springfield Business Journal** (17971)
313 Park Central W
Springfield, MO 65806
Phone: (417)831-3238
Fax: (417)831-5478
**Subject(s):** Business

Circ: (Non-paid)800
  (Paid)6,200

**Columbia Missourian** (17152)
Missourian Publishing Association Inc.
221 S. 8th St.
Columbia, MO 65201
Phone: (573)882-5700
Fax: (573)882-5702
**Subject(s):** Daily Newspapers

Circ: (Sun.)5,065
  (Mon.-Fri.)6,188

**Cass County Democrat-Missourian** (17251)
Democrat-Missourian
301 S. Lexington
PO Box 329
Harrisonville, MO 64701
Phone: (816)380-3228
Fax: (816)380-7650
**Subject(s):** Paid Community Newspapers

Circ: (Paid)6,165

**McDonald County Press** (17484)
McDonald County Press Inc.
PO Box 266
Pineville, MO 64856
Phone: (417)223-4675
Fax: (417)223-4049
**Subject(s):** Paid Community Newspapers

Circ: 6,127

**The Monday Reminder** (28354)
Bridge City Publishing Inc.
111 W. 3rd St.
PO Box 250
Mobridge, SD 57601-0250
Phone: (605)845-3646
Fax: (605)845-7659
**Subject(s):** Shopping Guides

Circ: (Free)‡6,095

**Register** (10790)
Oelwein Publishing Co.
PO Box 511
25 1st St. SE
Oelwein, IA 50662-2306
Phone: (319)283-2144
Fax: (319)283-3268
**Subject(s):** Daily Newspapers

Circ: 6,067

**The Capaha Arrow** (17112)
Southeast Missouri State University
One University Plaza
MS 2225
Southeast Missouri State University
Cape Girardeau, MO 63701
Phone: (573)651-2549
**Subject(s):** College Publications

Circ: ‡6,000

**The Drury Mirror** (17960)
Drury University
900 N Benton Ave.
Springfield, MO 65802
Phone: (417)873-7318
Fax: (417)873-7533
**Subject(s):** College Publications

Circ: (Paid)4,177
  (Controlled)6,000

**The Gateway** (18525)
University of Nebraska at Omaha
6001 Dodge St.
Omaha, NE 68182
Phone: (402)554-2470
**Subject(s):** College Publications

Circ: (Free)6,000

**Index - Chappell** (17373)
Truman University
SUB Media Ctr.
Kirksville, MO 63501
Phone: (660)785-4449
Fax: (660)785-7601
**Subject(s):** College Publications

Circ: (Free)6,000

**Muleskinner** (18021)
Central Missouri State University
PO Box 800
Warrensburg, MO 64093
Phone: (660)543-4111
Fax: (660)543-8663
**Subject(s):** College Publications

Circ: 6,000

**Pleasant Hill Times** (17489)
Pleasant Hill Times Inc.
126 1st St.
Box 8
Pleasant Hill, MO 64080
Phone: (816)540-3500
Fax: (816)987-5699
**Subject(s):** Paid Community Newspapers

Circ: ‡6,000

**The North Scott Press** (10553)
214 N Second St.
PO Box 200
Eldridge, IA 52748
Phone: (563)285-8111
Fax: (563)285-8114
**Subject(s):** Paid Community Newspapers

Circ: (Paid)‡5,800

**The Perry County Republic-Monitor** (17476)
Perryville Newspapers Inc.
10 W Ste., Maries St.
PO Drawer 367
Perryville, MO 63775
Phone: (573)547-4567
Fax: (573)547-1643
**Subject(s):** Paid Community Newspapers

Circ: (Paid)5,800

Circulation: ★ = ABC; △ = BPA; ♦ = CAC; ● = CCAB; ❏ = VAC; ⊖ = PO Statement; ‡ = Publisher's Report; Boldface figures = sworn; Light figures = estimated.

# Great Plains States

**Rolla Daily News** (17520)
101 W 7th St.
PO Box 808
Rolla, MO 65401-0808
Phone: (573)364-2468
Fax: (573)341-5847
**Subject(s):** Daily Newspapers
**Circ:** 5,800

**The Waterways Journal** (17875)
Waterways Journal Inc.
319 N. 4th St., Ste. 650
Saint Louis, MO 63102
Phone: (314)241-7354
Fax: (314)241-4207
**Subject(s):** Ships and Shipping
**Circ:** ‡5,728

**The Brookings Register** (28278)
Brookings Publishing Co.
312 5th St.
PO Box 177
Brookings, SD 57006-0177
Phone: (605)692-6271
Fax: (605)692-2979
**Subject(s):** Daily Newspapers
**Circ:** (Mon.-Fri.)5,483
(Sat.)5,678

**Wichita Business Journal** (11492)
American City Business Journals Inc.
110 S. Main St., Ste. 200
Wichita, KS 67202
Phone: (316)267-8570
Fax: (316)267-8570
**Subject(s):** Local, State, and Regional Publications
**Circ:** (Paid)5,666

**Campus Ledger** (11297)
Johnson Co.
Johnson Community College
12345 College Blvd.
Overland Park, KS 66210
Phone: (913)469-8500
Fax: (913)469-2302
**Subject(s):** College Publications
**Circ:** (Free)5,600

**The Carthage Press** (17127)
527 S Main St.
PO Box 678
Carthage, MO 64836
Phone: (417)358-2191
Fax: (417)358-7428
**Subject(s):** Daily Newspapers
**Circ:** (Paid)‡5,600

**Garner Leader and Signal** (10596)
365 State St.
Garner, IA 50438
Phone: (641)923-2684
Fax: (641)923-2685
**Subject(s):** Free Newspapers
**Circ:** (Paid)‡2,250
(Free)‡5,600

**The Holden Image-Progress** (17254)
PO Box 8
117 E 2nd St.
Holden, MO 64040
Phone: (816)732-5552
Fax: (816)732-4696
**Subject(s):** Paid Community Newspapers
**Circ:** (Paid)‡2,150
(Free)‡5,600

**The Independent-Journal** (17502)
119 E High St.
PO Box 340
Potosi, MO 63664
Phone: (573)438-5141
Fax: (573)438-4472
**Subject(s):** Paid Community Newspapers
**Circ:** ‡5,600

**Creston News Advertiser** (10416)
Creston Publishing Co.
503 W. Adams St.
PO Box 126
Creston, IA 50801
Phone: (641)782-2141
Fax: (641)782-6628
**Subject(s):** Daily Newspapers
**Circ:** ‡5,590

**The Marysville Advocate** (11242)
107 S 9th St.
Po Box 271
Marysville, KS 66508-0271
Phone: (785)562-2317
Fax: (785)562-5589
**Subject(s):** Paid Community Newspapers
**Circ:** (Free)61
(Paid)5,534

**Barr's Post Card News** (10932)
1800 W. D St.
PO Box 601
Vinton, IA 52349-0601
Phone: (319)472-4763
Fax: (319)472-3117
**Subject(s):** Collecting; Crafts, Models, Hobbies, and Contests
**Circ:** (Non-paid)‡550
(Paid)‡5,500

**The Marshfield Mail** (17414)
225 N Clay St.
PO Box A
Marshfield, MO 65706
Phone: (417)859-2013
Fax: (417)859-7930
**Subject(s):** Paid Community Newspapers
**Circ:** (Paid)5,500

**The Newton Daily News** (10781)
Newton Printing Co.
200 1st Ave. E
P O Box 967
Newton, IA 50208-0967
Phone: (641)792-3121
Fax: (641)792-5505
**Subject(s):** Daily Newspapers
**Circ:** 5,500

**Prospect-News** (17199)
Box 367
110 Washington St
Doniphan, MO 63935-0367
Phone: (573)996-2103
Fax: (573)996-2217
**Subject(s):** Paid Community Newspapers
**Circ:** 5,500

**The Suburban Advertiser** (11150)
Wyandotte West Communications Inc.
7735 Washington Ave.
PO Box 12003
Kansas City, KS 66112
Phone: (913)788-5565
Fax: (913)788-9812
**Subject(s):** Shopping Guides
**Circ:** (Free)5,500

**Winfield Daily Courier** (11511)
201 E 9th Ave.
Winfield, KS 67156
Phone: (620)221-1050
Fax: (620)221-1101
**Subject(s):** Daily Newspapers
**Circ:** (Mon.-Sat.)5,445

**Atchison Daily Globe** (10991)
1015-25 Main St.
PO Box 247
Atchison, KS 66002
Phone: (913)367-0583
Fax: (913)367-7531
**Subject(s):** Daily Newspapers
**Circ:** (Mon.-Fri.)5,126
(Sun.)5,282

**Miami County Republic** (11360)
Miami County Publishing Co.
121 S Pearl St.
PO Box 389
Paola, KS 66071
Phone: (913)294-2311
Fax: (913)294-5318
**Subject(s):** Paid Community Newspapers
**Circ:** (Paid)5,277

**The Milford Times** (18491)
PO Box 723
Milford, NE 68405-0723
Phone: (402)761-2911
Fax: (402)761-2914
**Subject(s):** Paid Community Newspapers
**Circ:** (Non-paid)8
(Paid)5,259

**Plattsmouth Journal** (18582)
Lincoln Journal Star
410 Main St.
PO Box 250
Plattsmouth, NE 68048
Phone: (402)296-2141
Fax: (402)296-3401
**Subject(s):** Paid Community Newspapers
**Circ:** ‡5,234

**Frontier and Holt County Independent** (18563)
Miles Publishing Company Inc.
PO Box 360
114 North 4th Street
Oneill, NE 68763-0360
Phone: (402)336-1220
Fax: (402)336-1222
**Subject(s):** Paid Community Newspapers
**Circ:** 5,225

**The Fulton Sun** (17236)
The Fulton Sun Gazette
115 E. 5th St.
Fulton, MO 65251
Phone: (573)642-7272
Fax: (573)642-0656
**Subject(s):** Daily Newspapers
**Circ:** ‡5,200

**Maquoketa Sentinel-Press** (10724)
108 W Quarry
Maquoketa, IA 52060-1150
Phone: (563)652-2441
Fax: (563)652-6094
**Subject(s):** Paid Community Newspapers
**Circ:** ‡5,200

**The Manchester Press** (10716)
Manchester Publishing Co.
109 E Delaware St.
PO Box C
Manchester, IA 52057-0703
Phone: (563)927-2020
Fax: (563)927-4945
**Subject(s):** Paid Community Newspapers
**Circ:** ‡5,188

**Missouri Valley Merchandiser** (10752)
Missouri Valley Merchandiser/Missouri Valley Times-News
501 E Erie
PO Box 159
Missouri Valley, IA 51555
Phone: (712)642-2791
Fax: (712)642-2595
**Subject(s):** Shopping Guides
**Circ:** (Paid)⊕2,100
(Non-paid)⊕5,085

**Record-Herald and Indianola Tribune** (10637)
Record-Herald
1801 W 2nd Ave., Ste. 2
PO Box 259
Indianola, IA 50125-0259
Phone: (515)961-2511
Fax: (515)961-4833
**Subject(s):** Paid Community Newspapers
**Circ:** (Free)‡154
(Paid)‡5,056

**Osage County Chronicle** (11011)
107 E Santa Fe
Burlingame, KS 66413
Phone: (785)654-3621
Fax: (785)654-3438
**Subject(s):** Paid Community Newspapers
**Circ:** ⊕5,029

**Black Hills Pioneer** (28434)
Seaton Publishing Co.
315 Seaton Cir.
PO Box 7
Spearfish, SD 57783
Phone: (605)642-2761
Fax: (605)642-9060
**Subject(s):** Daily Newspapers
**Circ:** ‡5,000

**Cassville Democrat** (17132)
600 Main
PO Box 486
Cassville, MO 65625
Phone: (417)847-2610
Fax: (417)847-3092
**Subject(s):** Paid Community Newspapers
**Circ:** 5,000

**Christian County Headliners News (17469)**
Ozark Publications Inc.
PO Box 490
Ozark, MO 65721
Phone: (417)581-3541
Fax: (417)581-3577
**Subject(s):** Paid Community Newspapers
**Circ:** ‡5,000

**Collegio (11369)**
Pittsburg State University
1701 S Broadway
Pittsburg, KS 66762
Phone: (620)235-4251
Fax: (620)235-4817
**Subject(s):** College Publications
**Circ:** (Free)‡5,000

**Humboldt Independent (10630)**
Gargano Communications Inc.
PO Box 157
Humboldt, IA 50548
Phone: (515)332-2514
**Subject(s):** Paid Community Newspapers
**Circ:** ‡5,000

**York News-Times (18646)**
327 Platte Ave.
PO Box 279
York, NE 68467-3547
Phone: (402)362-4478
Fax: (402)362-6748
**Subject(s):** Daily Newspapers
**Circ:** 5,000

**The Algona Upper Des Moines (10278)**
Algona Publishing Co.
14 E Nebraska
PO Box 400
Algona, IA 50511
Phone: (515)295-3535
Fax: (515)295-7217
**Subject(s):** Paid Community Newspapers
**Circ:** ‡4,950

**The Red Oak Express (10831)**
2012 Commerce Dr.
Red Oak, IA 51566-1010
Phone: (712)623-2566
Fax: (712)623-2568
**Subject(s):** Paid Community Newspapers
**Circ:** 4,950

**Daily News (24070)**
PO Box 760
601 Dakato Ave
Wahpeton, ND 58074-0760
Phone: (701)642-8585
Fax: (701)642-1501
**Subject(s):** Daily Newspapers
**Circ:** (Paid)4,927

**The Fairfield Ledger (10561)**
112 E Broadway Ave.
Box 171
Fairfield, IA 52556-3202
Phone: (641)472-4129
Fax: (641)472-1916
**Subject(s):** Daily Newspapers
**Circ:** ‡4,910

**The Holton Recorder (11116)**
109 W. 4th St.
PO Box 311
Holton, KS 66436
Phone: (785)364-3141
Fax: (785)364-3422
**Subject(s):** Paid Community Newspapers
**Circ:** ‡4,900

**Blue Springs Examiner (Daily Edition) (17079)**
The Blue Springs Examiner
500 W. R.D. Mize Rd.
Blue Springs, MO 64015
Phone: (816)229-9161
**Subject(s):** Daily Newspapers
**Circ:** (Combined)4,868

**Black Hills Press (28438)**
Country Media
PO Box 69, 1022 Main St.
Sturgis, SD 57785
Phone: (605)347-2503
Fax: (605)347-2321
**Subject(s):** Paid Community Newspapers
**Circ:** ‡4,800

**Douglas County Herald (17067)**
Herald Publishing Co.
PO Box 577
Ava, MO 65608
Phone: (417)683-4181
Fax: (417)683-4102
**Subject(s):** Paid Community Newspapers
**Circ:** ‡4,800

**Farmer's Cattle-log (10797)**
Pluim Publishing Inc.
113 Central Ave. SE
Orange City, IA 51041-1738
Phone: (712)737-4266
Fax: (712)737-3896
**Subject(s):** Farm Newspapers
**Circ:** (Free)4,800

**Journal-Tribune (10731)**
PO Box 208
Marengo, IA 52301
Phone: (319)642-5506
Fax: (319)642-5509
**Subject(s):** Paid Community Newspapers
**Circ:** 4,800

**Meade County Times-Tribune (28439)**
Country Media
PO Box 69, 1022 Main St.
Sturgis, SD 57785
Phone: (605)347-2503
Fax: (605)347-2321
**Subject(s):** Paid Community Newspapers
**Circ:** ‡4,800

**Unterrified Democrat (17399)**
300 E Main St
PO Box 109
Linn, MO 65051-0109
Phone: (573)897-3150
Fax: (573)897-0076
**Subject(s):** Paid Community Newspapers
**Circ:** 4,800

**El Dorado Times (11053)**
Liberty Group
PO Box 694
114 North Vine St
El Dorado, KS 67042
Phone: (316)321-1120
Fax: (316)321-7722
**Subject(s):** Daily Newspapers
**Circ:** ‡4,768

**The Rock Valley Bee (10842)**
1442 Main St.
Rock Valley, IA 51247
Phone: (712)476-2795
Fax: (712)476-2796
**Subject(s):** Free Newspapers
**Circ:** (Paid)‡1,600
(Free)‡4,750

**News-Advertiser (10619)**
Tribune Newspapers Inc.
1114 7th St.
PO Box 721
Harlan, IA 51537-0721
Phone: (712)755-3111
Fax: (712)755-3324
**Subject(s):** Paid Community Newspapers
**Circ:** ‡4,725

**Tribune (10622)**
Tribune Newspapers Inc.
1114 7th St.
PO Box 721
Harlan, IA 51537-0721
Phone: (712)755-3111
Fax: (712)755-3324
**Subject(s):** Paid Community Newspapers
**Circ:** ‡4,725

**Williston Daily Herald (24080)**
PO Box 1447
Williston, ND 58801
Phone: (701)572-2165
Fax: (701)572-1965
**Subject(s):** Daily Newspapers
**Circ:** (Free)❑22
(Paid)❑4,728

**Buffalo Reflex (17097)**
P.O. Box 770
Buffalo, MO 65622
Phone: (417)345-2224
Fax: (417)345-2235
**Subject(s):** Paid Community Newspapers
**Circ:** ‡4,700

**The Odessan (17458)**
PO Box 80
204 W Mason
Odessa, MO 64076
Phone: (816)230-5311
Fax: (816)230-5313
**Subject(s):** Paid Community Newspapers
**Circ:** 4,700

**Ste. Genevieve Herald (17936)**
Ste. Genevieve Newspapers Inc.
PO Box 447
Sainte Genevieve, MO 63670
Phone: (573)883-2222
Fax: (573)883-2833
**Subject(s):** Paid Community Newspapers
**Circ:** ‡4,700

**The Tipton Conservative and Advertiser (10923)**
Conservative Publishing Co.
Box 271
Tipton, IA 52772
Phone: (563)886-2131
Fax: (563)886-6466
**Subject(s):** Farm Newspapers
**Circ:** ‡4,700

**Lees Summit Journal (17390)**
Lees Summit Journal Inc.
415 SE Douglas St.
PO Box 387
Lees Summit, MO 64063
Phone: (816)524-2345
Fax: (816)524-5136
**Subject(s):** Paid Community Newspapers
**Circ:** (Non-paid)224
(Paid)4,679

**Belleville Telescope (11000)**
Telescope Pub. Co.
1817 E U S 81, Frontage Rd.
Belleville, KS 66935
Phone: (785)527-2224
Fax: (785)527-2225
**Subject(s):** Paid Community Newspapers
**Circ:** ‡4,669

**Bandwagon (11262)**
Mulvane News
204 W Main St.
PO Box 157
Mulvane, KS 67110
Phone: (316)777-4233
**Subject(s):** Shopping Guides
**Circ:** (Free)4,650

**Wagner Announcer (28452)**
209 S Main
PO Box 187
Wagner, SD 57380
Phone: (605)384-5616
Fax: (605)384-5955
**Subject(s):** Shopping Guides
**Circ:** (Free)‡4,650

**The Chanute Tribune (11019)**
Chanute Publishing Co.
15 N Evergreen
PO Box 559
Chanute, KS 66720
Phone: (620)431-4100
Fax: (620)431-2635
**Subject(s):** Daily Newspapers
**Circ:** (Free)26
(Paid)4,644

**The Observer (10440)**
The DeWitt Observer Publishing Company Inc.
512 7th St.
PO Box 49
De Witt, IA 52742-0049
Phone: (563)659-3121
Fax: (563)659-3778
**Subject(s):** Paid Community Newspapers
**Circ:** (Free)‡2,387
(Paid)‡4,622

Circulation: ★ = ABC; △ = BPA; ♦ = CAC; • = CCAB; ❑ = VAC; ⊕ = PO Statement; ‡ = Publisher's Report; Boldface figures = sworn; Light figures = estimated.

**Antelope Newspaper (18386)**
University of Nebraska at Kearney
103 Thomas Hall
Kearney, NE 68849
Phone: (308)865-8488
Fax: (308)865-8157
**Subject(s):** College Publications

**Circ:** ‡4,600

**The Banner-Press (17406)**
103 Walnut St.
PO Box 109
Marble Hill, MO 63764
Phone: (573)238-2821
Fax: (573)238-0020
**Subject(s):** Paid Community Newspapers

**Circ:** (Free)16
(Paid)4,600

**Brandon Valley Challenger (28276)**
Prairie Publications
1400 East Cedar St.
PO Box 257
Brandon, SD 57005
Phone: (605)582-6025
Fax: (605)582-7184
**Subject(s):** Free Newspapers

**Circ:** (Paid)1,100
(Free)4,600

**Creightonian (18524)**
Creighton University
Dept. of Journalism & Mass Communication
2500 California Plz.
Omaha, NE 68178-0100
Phone: (402)280-2700
**Subject(s):** College Publications

**Circ:** (Free)‡200
(Paid)‡4,600

**Farmington Press (17218)**
218 N. Washington
Farmington, MO 63640
Phone: (573)756-8927
Fax: (573)756-9160
**Subject(s):** Free Newspapers

**Circ:** (Combined)‡4,600

**The Selma Enterprise (10423)**
Lee Enterprises Inc.
201 N. Harrison
Davenport, IA 52801
Phone: (563)383-2100
**Subject(s):** Paid Community Newspapers

**Circ:** ‡4,603

**Star Lite Shoppers Guide (17060)**
The Adrian Journal Inc.
39 E Main
Box 128
Adrian, MO 64720
Phone: (816)297-2100
Fax: (816)297-2149
**Subject(s):** Shopping Guides

**Circ:** (Free)‡4600

**The Lebanon Daily Record (17385)**
Lebanon Publishing Co.
100 E. Commercial St.
PO Box 192
Lebanon, MO 65536
Phone: (417)532-9131
Fax: (417)532-8140
**Subject(s):** Daily Newspapers

**Circ:** (Free)285
(Paid)4,528

**Benton County Enterprise (18045)**
Benton County Enterprise Inc.
PO Box 128
107 Main Street
Warsaw, MO 65355
Phone: (660)438-6312
Fax: (660)438-3464
**Subject(s):** Paid Community Newspapers

**Circ:** (Free)200
(Paid)4,500

**The SDSU Collegian (28281)**
South Dakota State University
Administration 200
PO Box 2201
Brookings, SD 57007
Phone: (605)688-6164
Fax: (605)688-6165

**Subject(s):** College Publications

**Circ:** (Free)‡4,500

**The Star Herald (17072)**
Belton Publishing Company Inc.
419 Main St.
Belton, MO 64012
Phone: (816)331-5353
Fax: (816)322-2943
**Subject(s):** Paid Community Newspapers

**Circ:** (Paid)4,500

**N'West Iowa Review (10854)**
Iowa Information Inc.
227 9th St.
PO Box 160
Sheldon, IA 51201
Phone: (712)324-5347
Fax: (712)324-2345
**Subject(s):** Paid Community Newspapers

**Circ:** (Non-paid)⊕100
(Paid)⊕4,491

**Bulletin (10449)**
The Denison Bulletin/Review
PO Box 550
Denison, IA 51442
Phone: (712)263-2122
Fax: (712)263-2125
**Subject(s):** Paid Community Newspapers

**Circ:** (Free)‡4,352
(Paid)‡4,383

**Wahoo Newspaper (18630)**
Saunders County Publishing Inc.
564 N Broadway
Wahoo, NE 68066
Phone: (402)443-4162
Fax: (402)443-4459
**Subject(s):** Paid Community Newspapers

**Circ:** ⊕4,329

**The Eldon Advertiser (17208)**
Vernon Publishing Inc.
409-15 S Maple
Eldon, MO 65026
Phone: (573)392-5658
Fax: (573)392-7755
**Subject(s):** Paid Community Newspapers

**Circ:** ‡4,300

**Wayne County Journal-Banner (17480)**
Ellinghouse Publishing Company Inc.
PO Box 97
Piedmont, MO 63957
Phone: (573)223-7122
Fax: (573)223-7871
**Subject(s):** Paid Community Newspapers

**Circ:** ‡4,300

**Review (10450)**
The Denison Bulletin/Review
PO Box 550
Denison, IA 51442
Phone: (712)263-2122
Fax: (712)263-2125
**Subject(s):** Free Newspapers; Free Newspapers

**Circ:** (Free)‡4,261
(Paid)‡4,286

**Houston Herald (17256)**
Houston Newspapers Inc.
PO Box 170
Houston, MO 65483
Phone: (417)967-2000
Fax: (417)967-2096
**Subject(s):** Paid Community Newspapers

**Circ:** ‡4,200

**The Iola Register (11131)**
The Iola Register Inc.
302 S Washington Ave.
PO Box 767
Iola, KS 66749
Phone: (620)365-2111
**Subject(s):** Daily Newspapers

**Circ:** (Free)85
(Paid)4,200

**The Crete News (18327)**
1201 Linden
PO Box 40
Crete, NE 68333
Phone: (402)826-2147
Fax: (402)826-5072
**Subject(s):** Paid Community Newspapers

**Circ:** ‡4,167

**McPherson Sentinel (11245)**
301 S Main
McPherson, KS 67460
Phone: (620)241-2422
Fax: (620)241-2425
**Subject(s):** Daily Newspapers

**Circ:** (Free)‡3,998
(Paid)‡4,169

**West Point News (18639)**
134 E. Grove St.
West Point, NE 68788
Phone: (402)372-2461
Fax: (402)372-3530
**Subject(s):** Paid Community Newspapers

**Circ:** 4,150

**The Washington Evening Journal (10937)**
111 N. Marion Ave.
Washington, IA 52353
Phone: (319)653-2191
Fax: (319)653-7524
**Subject(s):** Daily Newspapers

**Circ:** ‡4,117

**Blair Enterprise (18290)**
Enterprise Publishing Company Inc.
138 No. 16th St.
Blair, NE 68008
Phone: (402)332-3232
Fax: (402)332-4733
**Subject(s):** Paid Community Newspapers

**Circ:** ‡4,100

**The Connection (18605)**
129 S 6th St.
Box 449
Seward, NE 68434
Phone: (402)643-3676
Fax: (402)643-6774
**Subject(s):** Shopping Guides

**Circ:** (Free)‡4,100

**Grant County Review (28342)**
PO Box 390
Milbank, SD 57252-0390
Phone: (605)432-4516
Fax: (605)432-5042
**Subject(s):** Paid Community Newspapers

**Circ:** ‡4,100

**Abilene Reflector Chronicle (10982)**
Reflector Chronicle Publishing Corp.
303 N Broadway
PO Box 8
Abilene, KS 67410
Phone: (785)263-1000
Fax: (785)263-1645
**Subject(s):** Daily Newspapers

**Circ:** (Free)175
(Paid)4,088

**Review (11087)**
Garnett Publishing Inc.
PO Box 409
Garnett, KS 66032
Phone: (785)448-3121
Fax: (785)448-6253
**Subject(s):** Paid Community Newspapers

**Circ:** 4,074

**Seward County Independent (18606)**
129 S 6th St.
Box 449
Seward, NE 68434-0449
Phone: (402)643-3676
Fax: (402)643-6774
**Subject(s):** Paid Community Newspapers

**Circ:** (Free)107
(Paid)4,048

**California Democrat (17103)**
319 S High St.
PO Box 126
California, MO 65018-0126
Phone: (573)796-2135
Fax: (573)796-4220
**Subject(s):** Paid Community Newspapers

**Circ:** ‡4,000

**Dyersville Commercial (10544)**
Woodward Communications
PO Box 350
Dyersville, IA 52040-0128
Phone: (319)875-7131
Fax: (319)875-2279
**Subject(s):** Paid Community Newspapers

**Circ:** (Combined)4,000

**Platte County Citizen (17487)**
PO Box 888
Platte City, MO 64079
Phone: (816)858-5154
Fax: (816)858-2154
**Subject(s):** Paid Community Newspapers

**Circ:** (Paid)‡3,800
(Free)‡4,000

**St. Clair County Buyer's Guide (17463)**
SAC-Osage Publishing
PO Box 580
Osceola, MO 64776
Phone: (417)646-2211
Fax: (417)646-8015
**Subject(s):** Shopping Guides

**Circ:** (Free)‡4,000

**St. Clair County Courier (17464)**
SAC-Osage Publishing
PO Box 580
Osceola, MO 64776
Phone: (417)646-2211
Fax: (417)646-8015
**Subject(s):** Paid Community Newspapers

**Circ:** (Paid)2,165
(Free)4,000

**The SUNlight (10766)**
Wedel Publishing L.L.C.
113 1st St. W
PO Box 129
Mount Vernon, IA 52314-0129
Phone: (319)895-6216
Fax: (319)895-6217
**Subject(s):** Shopping Guides

**Circ:** (Free)‡4,000

**Wayne Stater (18634)**
Wayne State College
1111 Main St.
Wayne, NE 68787
Phone: (402)375-7489
Fax: (402)375-7130
**Subject(s):** College Publications

**Circ:** (Paid)800
(Non-paid)4,000

**Wilson County Citizen (11077)**
Box 330
406 North 7th Street
Fredonia, KS 66736
Phone: (620)378-4415
Fax: (620)378-4688
**Subject(s):** Paid Community Newspapers

**Circ:** (Free)‡40
(Paid)‡3,990

**The Clinton Daily Democrat (17144)**
Democrat Publishing Company Inc.
212 S Washington
PO Box 586
Clinton, MO 64735
Phone: (816)885-2281
Fax: (816)885-2265
**Subject(s):** Daily Newspapers

**Circ:** ‡3,989

**Maryville Daily Forum (17416)**
111 E Jenkins
PO Box 188
Maryville, MO 64468
Phone: (660)582-3106
Fax: (660)562-2823
**Subject(s):** Daily Newspapers

**Circ:** ‡3,983

**Smith County Pioneer (11414)**
PO Box 266
201 South Main
Smith Center, KS 66967
Phone: (785)282-3371
Fax: (785)282-6383
**Subject(s):** Paid Community Newspapers

**Circ:** 3,989

**Courier (28433)**
PO Box 169
Sisseton, SD 57262
Phone: (605)698-7642
Fax: (605)698-3641
**Subject(s):** Paid Community Newspapers

**Circ:** 3,950

**Cuba Free Press (17192)**
PO Box 568
Cuba, MO 65453
Phone: (573)885-7460
Fax: (573)885-3803
**Subject(s):** Paid Community Newspapers

**Circ:** 3,950

**Keith County News (18517)**
116 W A St.
PO Box 359
Ogallala, NE 69153
Phone: (308)284-4046
Fax: (308)284-4048
**Subject(s):** Paid Community Newspapers

**Circ:** (Paid)⊖3,950

**The Kearney Courier (17365)**
Whipple Printing Company Ltd.
102 N Jefferson
PO Box 140
Kearney, MO 64060-0140
Phone: (816)628-6010
Fax: (816)628-4422
**Subject(s):** Paid Community Newspapers

**Circ:** ‡3,940

**Des Moines Business Record (10465)**
Business Publications Corp.
The Depot at Fourth
100 4th St.
Des Moines, IA 50309
Phone: (515)288-3336
Fax: (515)288-0309
**Subject(s):** Business; Local, State, and Regional Publications

**Circ:** (Paid)‡3,932

**Courant (23921)**
Hills & Plains Free Press Inc.
419 Main St.
Box 29
Bottineau, ND 58318
Phone: (701)228-2605
Fax: (701)228-5864
**Subject(s):** Paid Community Newspapers

**Circ:** ‡3,900

**Daily Freeman-Journal (10963)**
7 22nd St.
PO Box 490
Webster City, IA 50595
Phone: (515)832-4350
Fax: (515)832-2314
**Subject(s):** Daily Newspapers

**Circ:** 3,908

**The Herald-Journal (10393)**
Southwest Iowa Newsgroup
205 E Main
PO Box 278
Clarinda, IA 51632-0278
Phone: (712)542-2181
Fax: (712)542-5424
**Subject(s):** Paid Community Newspapers

**Circ:** (Free)‡250
(Paid)‡3,900

**Lawrence County Record (17438)**
Lawrence County Record Inc.
312 S Hickory
PO Box 348
Mount Vernon, MO 65712
Phone: (417)466-2185
Fax: (417)466-7865
**Subject(s):** Free Newspapers

**Circ:** (Free)‡3,511
(Paid)‡3,900

**Mountain Echo/X-Tra (17273)**
110 N Main St.
PO Box 25
Ironton, MO 63650-0025
Phone: (573)546-3917
Fax: (573)546-3919
**Subject(s):** Shopping Guides

**Circ:** (Paid)3,000
(Free)3,900

**Gretna Guide & News (18363)**
PO Box 240
Gretna, NE 68028
Phone: (402)332-3232
Fax: (402)332-4733
**Subject(s):** Paid Community Newspapers

**Circ:** ‡3,890

**Lamar Democrat (17382)**
900 N Gulf. St.
PO Box 458
Lamar, MO 64759
Phone: (417)682-5529
Fax: (417)682-5595
**Subject(s):** Paid Community Newspapers

**Circ:** (Free)‡600
(Paid)‡3,850

**Osceola Sentinel-Tribune (10800)**
Clarke County Publishing Inc.
115 E. Washington
PO Box 447
Osceola, IA 50213
Phone: (641)342-2131
Fax: (641)342-2060
**Subject(s):** Paid Community Newspapers

**Circ:** (Free)‡75
(Paid)‡3,843

**Reporter and Farmer (28464)**
Day County Printing Co.
PO Box 30
Webster, SD 57274
Phone: (605)345-3356
Fax: (605)345-3739
**Subject(s):** Paid Community Newspapers

**Circ:** ‡3,830

**Glenwood Opinion Tribune (10599)**
PO Box 191
Glenwood, IA 51534
Phone: (712)527-3191
Fax: (712)527-3193
**Subject(s):** Paid Community Newspapers

**Circ:** (Free)6500
(Paid)3,800

**Jewish Press (18530)**
Jewish Federation of Omaha
333 S 132nd St.
Omaha, NE 68154-2198
Phone: (402)334-6448
Fax: (402)334-5422
**Subject(s):** Paid Community Newspapers; Jewish Publications

**Circ:** 3,800

**News Journal (17439)**
Lebanon Publishing Co.
150 E. First St.
Mountain Grove, MO 65711
Phone: (417)926-6648
Fax: (417)926-6648
**Subject(s):** Paid Community Newspapers

**Circ:** 3,800

**Wellington Daily News (11466)**
113 W Harvey Ave.
PO Box 368
Wellington, KS 67152-3840
Phone: (620)326-3326
Fax: (620)326-3290
**Subject(s):** Daily Newspapers

**Circ:** (Paid)3,800

**Western Trader (28295)**
Southern Hills Publishing Inc.
PO Box 551
Custer, SD 57730
Phone: (605)673-2217
Fax: (605)574-3321
**Subject(s):** Shopping Guides

**Circ:** (Free)3,800

**Jewell County News (11240)**
Superior Publishing Co.
111 E. Main
PO Box 305
Mankato, KS 66956
Phone: (785)378-3705
Fax: (785)378-3782
**Subject(s):** Paid Community Newspapers

**Circ:** ‡3,700

## Great Plains States

**Kingman Leader-Courier** (11156)
Courier/Journal Inc.
140 N Main
PO Box 353
Kingman, KS 67068
Phone: (620)532-3151
Fax: (620)532-3152
**Subject(s):** Paid Community Newspapers
**Circ:** 3,700

**Leader Courier** (11157)
Courier/Journal Inc.
140 N Main
PO Box 353
Kingman, KS 67068
Phone: (620)532-3151
Fax: (620)532-3152
**Subject(s):** Paid Community Newspapers
**Circ:** 3,700

**Leader-Statesman** (18018)
PO Box 348
Versailles, MO 65084
Phone: (573)378-5441
Fax: (573)378-4292
**Subject(s):** Paid Community Newspapers
**Circ:** 3,700

**The Superior Express** (18619)
PO Box 408
Superior, NE 68978
Phone: (402)879-3291
Fax: (402)879-3463
**Subject(s):** Paid Community Newspapers
**Circ:** (Paid)⊕**3,700**

**The University Leader** (11104)
Fort Hays State University
Malloy Hall Rm. 106
600 Park St.
Hays, KS 67601
Phone: (785)628-5301
Fax: (785)628-4004
**Subject(s):** College Publications
**Circ:** (Free)‡3,700

**The Milan Standard** (17429)
PO Box 266
Milan, MO 63556-0266
Phone: (660)265-3322
Fax: (660)265-4744
**Subject(s):** Paid Community Newspapers
**Circ:** ‡3,699

**Herald-Patriot** (10386)
Chariton Newspapers
PO Box 651
Chariton, IA 50049
Phone: (641)774-2137
Fax: (641)774-2139
**Subject(s):** Paid Community Newspapers
**Circ:** ‡3,650

**McLean County Independent** (23980)
BHG Inc.
PO Box 309
Garrison, ND 58540
Phone: (701)463-2201
Fax: (701)463-7487
**Subject(s):** Paid Community Newspapers
**Circ:** (Free)59
(Paid)3,616

**Eureka Herald** (11068)
Greenwood County Publishing Co.
106 W 2nd St.
PO Box 590
Eureka, KS 67045
Phone: (620)583-5721
Fax: (620)583-5922
**Subject(s):** Paid Community Newspapers
**Circ:** 3,600

**Valley News Today** (10859)
Valley Publications
702 W. Sheridan Ave.
Shenandoah, IA 51601
**Subject(s):** Daily Newspapers
**Circ:** ‡3,598

**Madison Daily Leader** (28336)
214 S. Egan Ave.
PO Box 348
Madison, SD 57042
Phone: (605)256-4555

Fax: (605)256-6190
**Subject(s):** Daily Newspapers
**Circ:** ‡3,551

**Bethany Republican-Clipper** (17073)
Bethany Printing Co.
PO Box 351
Bethany, MO 64424
Phone: (660)425-6325
Fax: (660)425-3441
**Subject(s):** Paid Community Newspapers
**Circ:** ‡3,500

**The Excelsior Springs Standard** (17215)
Excelsior Publishing Company Inc.
417 Thompson Ave.
PO Box 70
Excelsior Springs, MO 64024
Phone: (816)637-3147
Fax: (816)637-8411
**Subject(s):** Daily Newspapers
**Circ:** ‡3,500

**The Griffon News** (17529)
Missouri Western State College
4525 Downs Dr. SS/C 204
Saint Joseph, MO 64507
Phone: (816)271-4200
Fax: (816)271-4543
**Subject(s):** College Publications
**Circ:** (Free)‡3,500

**Journal-Express** (10696)
Journal/Express Inc.
122 E Robinson
PO Box 458
Knoxville, IA 50138
Phone: (641)842-2155
Fax: (641)842-2929
**Subject(s):** Paid Community Newspapers
**Circ:** 3500

**Monroe County News** (10274)
Albia Newspapers Inc.
PO Box 338
Albia, IA 52531
Phone: (641)932-7121
Fax: (641)932-2822
**Subject(s):** Paid Community Newspapers
**Circ:** (Free)300
(Paid)3,500

**New Hampton Tribune** (10777)
New Hampton Publishing Co.
10 N Chestnut Ave.
PO Box 380
New Hampton, IA 50659
Phone: (641)394-2111
Fax: (641)394-2113
**Subject(s):** Paid Community Newspapers
**Circ:** (Paid)3,500

**Press-News Journal** (17110)
130 N 4th St.
PO Box 227
Canton, MO 63435
Phone: (573)288-5668
Fax: (573)288-0000
**Subject(s):** Paid Community Newspapers
**Circ:** ‡3,500

**Republic Monitor** (17510)
Community Publishers
249 Hwy. 60 W.
Republic, MO 65738
Phone: (417)732-2525
Fax: (417)732-2980
**Subject(s):** Paid Community Newspapers
**Circ:** 3,500

**Union Republican** (10275)
Albia Newspapers Inc.
PO Box 338
Albia, IA 52531
Phone: (641)932-7121
Fax: (641)932-2822
**Subject(s):** Paid Community Newspapers
**Circ:** (Free)300
(Paid)3,500

**Mitchell County Press-News** (10799)
PO Box 60
112 N 6th St.
Osage, IA 50461
Phone: (641)732-3721

Fax: (641)732-5689
**Subject(s):** Paid Community Newspapers
**Circ:** (Free)61
(Paid)3,496

**Osawatomie Graphic** (11361)
Miami County Publishing Co.
121 S Pearl St.
PO Box 389
Paola, KS 66071
Phone: (913)294-2311
Fax: (913)294-5318
**Subject(s):** Paid Community Newspapers
**Circ:** (Combined)7000
3,490

**The Belle Plaine Union** (10728)
MPC Publishing Co.
100 W Main St.
Marengo, IA 52301-1412
Phone: (319)444-2520
Fax: (319)642-5509
**Subject(s):** Paid Community Newspapers
**Circ:** 3,465

**Grinnell Herald-Register** (10607)
Herald-Register Publishing Co.
813 5th Ave.
PO Box 360
Grinnell, IA 50112-1653
Phone: (641)236-3113
Fax: (641)236-5135
**Subject(s):** Paid Community Newspapers
**Circ:** (Free)355
(Paid)3,450

**Steelville Star/Crawford Mirror** (17193)
PO Box 568
Cuba, MO 65453
Phone: (573)885-3803
Fax: (573)885-3803
**Subject(s):** Paid Community Newspapers
**Circ:** ‡3,450

**Republican-Times** (18008)
W.B. Rogers Printing Company Inc.
122 E 8th St.
PO Box 548
Trenton, MO 64683-0548
Phone: (660)359-2212
Fax: (660)359-4414
**Subject(s):** Daily Newspapers
**Circ:** (Non-paid)‡72
(Paid)‡3,435

**Dakota County Star** (18610)
Star Printing & Publishing
1100 W. 29th Street, Ste. 116
PO Box 159
South Sioux City, NE 68776
Phone: (402)494-4264
Fax: (402)494-2414
**Subject(s):** Paid Community Newspapers
**Circ:** ‡3,400

**The Enterprise-Courier** (17137)
206 S Main St.
PO Box 69
Charleston, MO 63834-0069
Phone: (573)683-3351
Fax: (573)683-2217
**Subject(s):** Paid Community Newspapers
**Circ:** ‡3,400

**The Fort Scott Tribune** (11074)
Tribune-Monitor Co.
6 E Wall St.
PO Box 150
Fort Scott, KS 66701
Phone: (620)223-1460
Fax: (620)223-1469
**Subject(s):** Daily Newspapers
**Circ:** (Free)⊕**153**
(Paid)⊕**3,406**

**Gasconade County Republican** (17468)
Warden Publishing Co.
106 E Washington
PO Box 540
Owensville, MO 65066-0540
Phone: (314)437-2323
Fax: (314)437-3033
**Subject(s):** Paid Community Newspapers
**Circ:** ‡3,408

**Hebron Journal Register (18375)**
318 Lincoln Ave.
PO Box 210
Hebron, NE 68370
Phone: (402)768-6602
Fax: (402)768-7354
Subject(s): Paid Community Newspapers
Circ: 3,400

**The Monticello Express (10757)**
111 E Grand St.
PO Box 191
Monticello, IA 52310-0191
Phone: (319)465-3555
Fax: (319)465-4611
Subject(s): Paid Community Newspapers
Circ: ‡3,400

**Ozark County Times (17238)**
PO Box 188
Gainesville, MO 65655-0188
Phone: (417)679-4641
Fax: (417)679-3423
Subject(s): Paid Community Newspapers
Circ: (Paid)3,400

**Turtle Mountain Star (24054)**
PO Box 849
11 1st Ave NE
Rolla, ND 58367-0849
Phone: (701)477-6495
Fax: (701)477-3182
Subject(s): Paid Community Newspapers
Circ: (Paid)3,400

**The Bowling Green Times (17211)**
Lakeway Publishing of Missouri
106 A. North 3rd
PO Box 105
Elsberry, MO 63343
Phone: (573)898-2318
Fax: (573)898-2173
Subject(s): Paid Community Newspapers
Circ: 3,352

**The Herald-Press (23999)**
Eldredge Publishing Co.
913 Lincoln Ave.
Harvey, ND 58341
Phone: (701)324-4646
Fax: (701)324-4647
Subject(s): Paid Community Newspapers
Circ: 3,350

**The Pella Chronicle (10817)**
Community Newspaper Holdings Inc.
812 Main
PO Box 126
Pella, IA 50219
Phone: (641)628-3882
Fax: (641)628-3905
Subject(s): Paid Community Newspapers
Circ: ‡3,350

**Tri-City Trib (18320)**
617 CMR
Drawer A, Box A
Cozad, NE 69130-0006
Phone: (308)229-3644
Fax: (308)229-3647
Subject(s): Paid Community Newspapers
Circ: 3,350

**Times-Republican (10409)**
PO Box 258
205 West Jackson
Corydon, IA 50060-0258
Phone: (641)872-1234
Fax: (641)872-1965
Subject(s): Paid Community Newspapers
Circ: ‡3,320

**Coffey County Republican (11012)**
Faimon Publications L.L.C.
324 Hudson
PO Box A
Burlington, KS 66839-0218
Phone: (620)364-5325
Fax: (620)364-2607
Subject(s): Paid Community Newspapers
Circ: (Free)41
(Paid)3,318

**Cedar County Republican (17997)**
PO Box 1018
Stockton, MO 65785
Phone: (417)276-4211
Fax: (417)276-5760
Subject(s): Paid Community Newspapers
Circ: ‡3,300

**Colby Free Press (11027)**
155 W 5th St.
Colby, KS 67701-2312
Phone: (785)462-3963
Fax: (785)462-7749
Subject(s): Daily Newspapers
Circ: 3,300

**Doon Press (10527)**
209 Hubbard Ave.
Doon, IA 51235
Phone: (712)726-3313
Fax: (712)726-3334
Subject(s): Paid Community Newspapers
Circ: ‡3,300

**Valley City Times-Record (24064)**
146 3rd St. NE
PO Box 697
Valley City, ND 58072
Phone: (701)845-0463
Fax: (701)845-0175
Subject(s): Daily Newspapers
Circ: (Paid)‡3,300

**Nemaha County Herald (18268)**
Auburn Newspapers
PO Box 250
Auburn, NE 68305
Phone: (402)274-3185
Fax: (402)274-3273
Subject(s): Paid Community Newspapers
Circ: (Free)‡87
(Paid)‡3,275

**Auburn Press-Tribune (18267)**
Auburn Newspapers
PO Box 250
Auburn, NE 68305
Phone: (402)274-3185
Fax: (402)274-3273
Subject(s): Paid Community Newspapers
Circ: (Free)‡95
(Paid)‡3,267

**The Louisiana Press-Journal (17400)**
Press Journal Printing Corp.
3408 W Georgia
Louisiana, MO 63353-0466
Phone: (573)754-5566
Fax: (573)754-4749
Subject(s): Paid Community Newspapers
Circ: 3,263

**Macon Chronicle-Herald (17403)**
Liberty Publishing Co.
204 W Bourke St.
PO Box 7
Macon, MO 63552-1503
Phone: (660)385-3121
Fax: (660)385-3082
Subject(s): Daily Newspapers
Circ: ‡3,218

**Albion News (18255)**
328 W Church
Box 431
Albion, NE 68620
Phone: (402)395-2115
Fax: (402)395-2772
Subject(s): Paid Community Newspapers
Circ: ‡3,200

**Courier Tribune (11407)**
512 Main
Seneca, KS 66538
Phone: (785)336-2175
Fax: (785)336-3475
Subject(s): Paid Community Newspapers
Circ: ‡3,200

**Custer County Chief (18299)**
305 S 10th
PO Box 190
Broken Bow, NE 68822-0190
Phone: (308)872-2471
Fax: (308)872-2415
Subject(s): Paid Community Newspapers
Circ: 3,200

**The Grundy Register (10612)**
Register Printing Co.
601 G Ave.
Grundy Center, IA 50638-1549
Phone: (319)824-6958
Fax: (319)824-6288
Subject(s): Paid Community Newspapers
Circ: 3,200

**Nevada Journal (10775)**
1210 6th St.
PO Box 89
Nevada, IA 50201
Phone: (515)382-2161
Fax: (515)382-4299
Subject(s): Paid Community Newspapers
Circ: ‡3,200

**The North Stoddard Countian (17078)**
Delta Publishing Co.
615 No. Prairie
PO Box 680
Bloomfield, MO 63825
Phone: (573)568-3310
Fax: (573)568-3310
Subject(s): Paid Community Newspapers
Circ: ‡3,200

**The Pilot-Tribune (10899)**
Pilot-Tribune
PO Box 1187
111 W 7th St.
Storm Lake, IA 50588-1824
Phone: (712)732-3130
Fax: (712)732-3152
Subject(s): Paid Community Newspapers
Circ: ‡3,200

**Savannah Reporter (17941)**
115 S 4th St.
PO Box 299
Savannah, MO 64485
Phone: (816)324-3149
Fax: (816)324-3632
Subject(s): Paid Community Newspapers
Circ: ‡3,200

**The Tama News-Herald (10917)**
Tama County Publishing Inc.
220 W 3rd St.
PO Box 118
Tama, IA 52339
Phone: (641)484-2841
Fax: (641)484-5705
Subject(s): Paid Community Newspapers
Circ: (Paid)3,200

**Toledo Chronicle (10925)**
Tama County Publishing Inc.
220 W 3rd St.
PO Box 118
Tama, IA 52339
Phone: (641)484-2841
Fax: (641)484-5705
Subject(s): Paid Community Newspapers
Circ: ‡3200

**Holdrege Daily Citizen (18378)**
PO Box 344
Holdrege, NE 68949
Phone: (308)995-4441
Fax: (308)995-5992
Subject(s): Daily Newspapers
Circ: (Mon.-Fri.)3,199

**Boone News-Republican (10326)**
Boone Publishing Inc.
Box 100
Boone, IA 50036
Phone: (515)432-1234
Fax: (515)432-7811
Subject(s): Daily Newspapers
Circ: ‡3,149

**Alliance Times-Herald (18256)**
114 E. 4th St.
PO Box G
Alliance, NE 69301
Phone: (308)762-3060
Fax: (308)762-3063

**Subject(s):** Daily Newspapers
**Circ:** (Combined)⊕**3,117**

**Cass County Reporter  (23929)**
PO Box 190
Casselton, ND 58012
Phone: (701)347-4493
Fax: (701)347-4495
**Subject(s):** Paid Community Newspapers
**Circ:** (Free)⊕**50**
   (Paid)⊕**3,106**

**The Cavalier Chronicle  (23930)**
Cavalier Chronicle
PO Boc 520
Cavalier, ND 58220
Phone: (701)265-8844
Fax: (701)265-8089
**Subject(s):** Paid Community Newspapers
**Circ:** ‡3,100

**Lindsborg News-Record  (11219)**
Montgomery Communications Inc.
114 S. Main St.
PO Box 31
Lindsborg, KS 67456
Phone: (913)227-3348
Fax: (913)227-3740
**Subject(s):** Paid Community Newspapers
**Circ:** ‡3,100

**Montgomery County Chronicle  (11016)**
202 W 4th St.
PO Box 186
Caney, KS 67333
Phone: (620)879-2156
Fax: (620)879-2899
**Subject(s):** Paid Community Newspapers
**Circ:** 3,100

**The Story City Reminder  (10906)**
The Story City Herald
511 Broad St.
Story City, IA 50248
Phone: (515)733-4318
Fax: (515)733-4319
**Subject(s):** Shopping Guides
**Circ:** (Free)‡3,100

**Winner Advocate  (28468)**
125 W. 3rd St.
Winner, SD 57580
Phone: (605)842-1481
Fax: (605)842-1979
**Subject(s):** Paid Community Newspapers
**Circ:** ‡3,080

**The Ellsworth Reporter  (11058)**
220 N Douglas Ave.
Ellsworth, KS 67439-3216
Phone: (785)472-5085
Fax: (785)472-5087
**Subject(s):** Paid Community Newspapers
**Circ:** ‡3,050

**Star-Journal  (18252)**
PO Box 145
Ainsworth, NE 69210
Phone: (402)387-2844
Fax: (402)387-1234
**Subject(s):** Paid Community Newspapers
**Circ:** 3,056

**Washington County News  (11465)**
211 C. St., Box 316
Washington, KS 66968
Fax: (785)325-3255
**Subject(s):** Paid Community Newspapers
**Circ:** (Paid)‡3,050

**Hampton Chronicle  (10617)**
Hampton Publishing Co.
PO Box 317
Hampton, IA 50441
Phone: (641)456-2585
Fax: (641)456-2587
**Subject(s):** Paid Community Newspapers
**Circ:** (Free)2,400
   (Paid)3,049

**Hardin County Index  (10551)**
1513 Edgington Ave.
Eldora, IA 50627
Phone: (641)939-5051
Fax: (641)939-5541
**Subject(s):** Paid Community Newspapers
**Circ:** ‡3,020

**Herald-Ledger  (10552)**
1513 Edgington Ave.
Eldora, IA 50627
Phone: (641)939-5051
Fax: (641)939-5541
**Subject(s):** Paid Community Newspapers
**Circ:** ‡3,020

**The Mobridge Tribune  (28353)**
Bridge City Publishing Inc.
111 W. 3rd St.
PO Box 250
Mobridge, SD 57601-0250
Phone: (605)845-3646
Fax: (605)845-7659
**Subject(s):** Paid Community Newspapers
**Circ:** (Paid)‡3,021

**Altoona Herald-Mitchellville Index  (10285)**
100 8th South East Suite H
PO Box 427
Altoona, IA 50009
Phone: (515)967-4224
Fax: (515)967-0553
**Subject(s):** Paid Community Newspapers
**Circ:** ‡3,000

**The Chariton Leader  (10385)**
Chariton Newspapers
815 Braden Ave.
PO Box 651
Chariton, IA 50049
Phone: (641)774-2137
Fax: (641)774-2139
**Subject(s):** Paid Community Newspapers
**Circ:** ‡3,000

**The Chronicle  (10789)**
Community Publications
216 Main St.
PO Box 485
Odebolt, IA 51458
Phone: (712)668-2253
Fax: (712)668-4364
**Subject(s):** Paid Community Newspapers
**Circ:** ‡3,000

**Clipper-Herald  (18398)**
Western Publishing Co.
PO Box 599
Lexington, NE 68850-0599
Phone: (308)324-5511
Fax: (308)324-5240
**Subject(s):** Paid Community Newspapers
**Circ:** ‡3,000

**The Daily News  (17514)**
204 W N Main St.
PO Box 100
Richmond, MO 64085-0100
Phone: (816)776-5454
Fax: (816)470-6397
**Subject(s):** Daily Newspapers
**Circ:** ‡3,000

**Ida County Courier-Reminder  (10633)**
Ida County Courier-Reminder Inc.
210 Second St.
PO BOX 249
Ida Grove, IA 51445
Phone: (712)364-3131
Fax: (712)364-3010
**Subject(s):** Paid Community Newspapers
**Circ:** 3,000

**The Journal  (17714)**
Webster University
470 E. Lockwood Ave.
Saint Louis, MO 63119
Phone: (314)961-2660
Fax: (314)968-7059
**Subject(s):** College Publications
**Circ:** (Free)‡3,000

**The Kalona News  (10687)**
419 B Ave.
PO Box 430
Kalona, IA 52247-0430
Phone: (319)656-2273
Fax: (319)656-2299

**Subject(s):** Paid Community Newspapers
**Circ:** 3,000

**Logos  (10741)**
North Iowa Area Community College
500 College Dr.
Mason City, IA 50401-7213
Phone: (641)423-1264
Fax: (641)422-4304
**Subject(s):** College Publications
**Circ:** (Non-paid)3,000

**The Spring Hill New Era  (11086)**
Tri-County Newspapers
PO Box 303
Gardner, KS 66030
Phone: (913)856-7615
Fax: (913)856-6707
**Subject(s):** Free Newspapers
**Circ:** (Paid)1,000
   (Free)3,000

**West Fargo Pioneer  (24078)**
Davon Press Inc.
Box 457
West Fargo, ND 58078
Phone: (701)282-2443
Fax: (701)282-9248
**Subject(s):** Paid Community Newspapers
**Circ:** 3,000

**Van Buren County Register  (10693)**
Louisa Publishing Company Ltd.
106 Van Buren St.
PO Box 477
Keosauqua, IA 52565
Phone: (319)293-3197
**Subject(s):** Paid Community Newspapers
**Circ:** ‡2,987

**Augusta Daily Gazette  (10995)**
204 E 5th St.
PO Box 9
Augusta, KS 67010
Phone: (316)775-2218
Fax: (316)775-3220
**Subject(s):** Daily Newspapers
**Circ:** ‡2,972

**Missouri Lawyers Weekly  (17766)**
Lawyers Weekly Publications
c/o Kenneth C. Jones, Esq.
515 Olive St., Ste. 1606
Saint Louis, MO 63101
Phone: (314)621-1913
Fax: (314)621-1913
**Subject(s):** Paid Community Newspapers
**Circ:** (Non-paid)‡91
   (Paid)‡2,960

**Missouri Valley Observer  (28472)**
204 Walnut
PO Box 858
Yankton, SD 57078
Phone: (605)665-0484
**Subject(s):** Paid Community Newspapers
**Circ:** 2,950

**Ransom County Gazette  (24022)**
PO Box 473
Lisbon, ND 58054-0473
Phone: (701)683-4128
Fax: (701)683-4129
**Subject(s):** Paid Community Newspapers
**Circ:** 2,950

**Gypsum Advocate  (11099)**
Montgomery Communications Inc.
PO Box 31
Lindsborg, KS 67456
Phone: (913)227-3348
**Subject(s):** Paid Community Newspapers
**Circ:** (Non-paid)‡107
   (Paid)‡2,940

**Onawa Democrat  (10794)**
Wonder and Son Publishing
720 Iowa Ave.
PO Box 418
Onawa, IA 51040-0418
Phone: (712)423-2411
Fax: (712)423-2411
**Subject(s):** Paid Community Newspapers
**Circ:** (Paid)‡2,934

**Gale Directory of Publications & Broadcast Media/140th Ed.**  **Great Plains States**

**Emmons County Record (24021)**
201 N Broadway
PO Box 38
Linton, ND 58552
Phone: (701)254-4537
Fax: (701)254-4909
**Subject(s):** Paid Community Newspapers
**Circ:** ‡2,900

**Wright County Shopper's Guide (10549)**
Eagle Grove Eagle
314 W Broadway
PO Box 6
Eagle Grove, IA 50533-0006
Phone: (515)448-4745
Fax: (515)448-3182
**Subject(s):** Shopping Guides
**Circ:** (Free)‡2,900

**Towner County Record Herald (23927)**
423 Main
PO Box 519
Cando, ND 58324
Phone: (701)968-3223
Fax: (701)968-3345
**Subject(s):** Paid Community Newspapers
**Circ:** ‡2,840

**Charles City Press (10388)**
801 Riverside
PO Box 397
Charles City, IA 50616-0397
Phone: (641)228-3211
Fax: (641)228-2641
**Subject(s):** Daily Newspapers
**Circ:** ‡2,833

**The Jefferson Herald (10683)**
Bee and Herald Publishing Company Inc.
214 N Wilson Ave.
PO Box 440
Jefferson, IA 50129
Phone: (515)386-4161
Fax: (515)386-4162
**Subject(s):** Paid Community Newspapers
**Circ:** ⊕2,821

**Cavalier County Republican (24018)**
Country Media
618 3rd St.
Langdon, ND 58249
Phone: (701)256-5311
Fax: (701)256-5841
**Subject(s):** Paid Community Newspapers
**Circ:** ‡2,800

**Clay County News (18622)**
207 N Saunders
Box 405
Sutton, NE 68979-0405
Phone: (402)773-5576
Fax: (402)773-5577
**Subject(s):** Paid Community Newspapers
**Circ:** (Free)50
(Paid)2,805

**The Democrat-Argus (17131)**
Pemiscot Publishing
111 E 5th St.
PO Box 1059
Caruthersville, MO 63830-1059
Phone: (573)333-4336
Fax: (573)333-2307
**Subject(s):** Paid Community Newspapers
**Circ:** (Free)‡33
(Paid)‡2,802

**Gretna and Springfield Extra Connection (18293)**
Enterprise Publishing Company Inc.
138 No. 16th St.
Blair, NE 68008
Phone: (402)332-3232
Fax: (402)332-4733
**Subject(s):** Shopping Guides
**Circ:** (Free)‡2,800

**The Journal (23932)**
217 N Main
Crosby, ND 58730
Phone: (701)965-6088
**Subject(s):** Paid Community Newspapers
**Circ:** 2,800

**The Minden Courier (18492)**
Edgecombe Publishing Inc.
POB 379
Minden, NE 68959-0379
Fax: (308)832-2221
**Subject(s):** Paid Community Newspapers
**Circ:** ‡2,800

**Moody County Enterprise (28311)**
News Media Corp.
107 2nd Ave. W
PO Box 71
Flandreau, SD 57028-0071
Phone: (605)997-3725
Fax: (605)997-3194
**Subject(s):** Paid Community Newspapers
**Circ:** ‡2,800

**Palmyra Spectator (17470)**
304 S Main St.
PO Box 391
Palmyra, MO 63461
Phone: (573)769-3111
Fax: (573)769-3554
**Subject(s):** Paid Community Newspapers
**Circ:** 2,800

**Sigourney News-Review (10864)**
114 E. Washington
Sigourney, IA 52591
Phone: (515)622-3110
Fax: (515)622-2766
**Subject(s):** Paid Community Newspapers
**Circ:** (Free)‡48
(Paid)‡2,800

**Walsh County Press (24050)**
PO Box 49
Park River, ND 58270
Phone: (701)284-6333
Fax: (701)284-6091
**Subject(s):** Paid Community Newspapers
**Circ:** ‡2,800

**Mt. Pleasant News (10761)**
Mount Pleasant News
215 W Monroe St.
PO Box 240
Mount Pleasant, IA 52641-0240
Phone: (319)385-3131
**Subject(s):** Daily Newspapers
**Circ:** (Paid)‡2,795

**Business Farmer (18593)**
Business Farmer Inc.
22 W 17th
Box 2364
Scottsbluff, NE 69361
Phone: (308)635-3110
Fax: (308)635-7435
**Subject(s):** General Agriculture; Paid Community Newspapers
**Circ:** (Paid)2,750

**The Crane Chronicle/Stone County Republican (17189)**
Stone County Publishing Company Inc.
PO Box A
Crane, MO 65633
Phone: (417)723-8490
Fax: (417)723-8490
**Subject(s):** Paid Community Newspapers
**Circ:** (Non-paid)15
(Paid)2,750

**The Hillsboro Star-Journal (10764)**
Wedel Publishing L.L.C.
113 1st St. W
PO Box 129
Mount Vernon, IA 52314-0129
Phone: (319)895-6216
Fax: (319)895-6217
**Subject(s):** Paid Community Newspapers
**Circ:** (Free)‡150
(Paid)‡2,757

**Osborne County Farmer (11284)**
Osborne Publishing Company Inc.
PO Box 130
Osborne, KS 67473
Phone: (785)346-5424
Fax: (785)346-5400
**Subject(s):** Paid Community Newspapers
**Circ:** ‡2,755

**Perry Chief (10820)**
Chief Printing Co.
1323 2nd St.
PO Box 98
Perry, IA 50220
Phone: (515)465-4666
Fax: (515)465-3087
**Subject(s):** Paid Community Newspapers
**Circ:** (Free)36
(Paid)2,722

**Benson County Farmers Press (24032)**
120 B Ave. N
PO Box 98
Minnewaukan, ND 58351-0098
Phone: (701)473-5436
Fax: (701)473-5736
**Subject(s):** Farm Newspapers
**Circ:** ‡2,714

**The Anthony Republican (10987)**
L.D. Enterprises Inc.
121 E Main
Anthony, KS 67003-0031
Phone: (620)842-5129
Fax: (620)842-5117
**Subject(s):** Paid Community Newspapers
**Circ:** (Free)30
(Paid)2,700

**Business Farmer-Stockman (18594)**
Business Farmer Inc.
22 W 17th
Box 2364
Scottsbluff, NE 69361
Phone: (308)635-3110
Fax: (308)635-7435
**Subject(s):** Farm Newspapers
**Circ:** 2,700

**Carrollton Daily Democrat (17123)**
Hwy. 65 S
PO Box 69
Carrollton, MO 64633
Phone: (660)542-0881
Fax: (660)542-0889
**Subject(s):** Daily Newspapers
**Circ:** 2,700

**Pierce County Tribune (24055)**
Ogden Newspapers of North Dakota Inc.
PO Box 385
Rugby, ND 58368
Phone: (701)776-5252
Fax: (701)776-2159
**Subject(s):** Paid Community Newspapers
**Circ:** 2,700

**The Times-Delphic (10498)**
Drake University/Board of Student Communications
124 N Meredith Hall
2507 University Ave.
Des Moines, IA 50311-4505
Phone: (515)271-3181
Fax: (515)271-2798
**Subject(s):** College Publications
**Circ:** (Free)2,700

**The Concordian (17188)**
The Concordian Inc.
714 S Main St.
PO Box 999
Concordia, MO 64020-0999
Phone: (660)463-7522
Fax: (660)463-7942
**Subject(s):** Paid Community Newspapers
**Circ:** (Free)‡64
(Paid)‡2,695

**Syracuse Journal-Democrat (18623)**
Maverick Media Inc.
123 W 17th St.
PO Box O
Syracuse, NE 68446
Phone: (402)269-2135
Fax: (402)269-2392
**Subject(s):** Paid Community Newspapers
**Circ:** ‡2,694

**Gering Courier (18348)**
1428 10th St.
PO Box 70
Gering, NE 69341
Phone: (308)436-2222
Fax: (308)436-7127

---

Circulation: ★ = ABC; △ = BPA; ◆ = CAC; ● = CCAB; □ = VAC; ⊕ = PO Statement; ‡ = Publisher's Report; Boldface figures = sworn; Light figures = estimated.

# Great Plains States

**Subject(s):** Paid Community Newspapers
**Circ:** ‡2,681

**Pioneer Republican** (10732)
PO Box 208
Marengo, IA 52301
Phone: (319)642-5506
Fax: (319)642-5509
**Subject(s):** Paid Community Newspapers
**Circ:** ‡2,675

**Post-Telegraph** (17504)
Overland Courier
704 E Main St.
PO Box 286
Princeton, MO 64673
Phone: (660)748-3266
Fax: (660)748-3267
**Subject(s):** Paid Community Newspapers
**Circ:** ‡2,670

**Pilot** (17198)
302 Locust St.
PO Box Drawer V
Dixon, MO 65459
Phone: (573)759-2127
**Subject(s):** Paid Community Newspapers
**Circ:** ‡2,650

**Adams County Free Press** (10408)
J-D Publishing Co.
729 Davis Ave.
PO Box 46
Corning, IA 50841
Phone: (641)322-3161
Fax: (641)322-3461
**Subject(s):** Paid Community Newspapers
**Circ:** (Free)66
(Paid)2,645

**Wilton-Durant Advocate News** (10543)
North Scott Press Inc.
101 W 4th St.
PO Box 415
Wilton, IA 52778
Fax: (319)732-3144
**Subject(s):** Paid Community Newspapers
**Circ:** (Free)32
(Paid)2,628

**Clark County Courier** (28291)
Moritz Publishing Co.
117 1st Ave., E
PO Box 189
Clark, SD 57225
Phone: (605)532-5343
**Subject(s):** Paid Community Newspapers
**Circ:** ‡2,600

**Gordon Journal** (18352)
210 N Main
Gordon, NE 69343
Phone: (308)282-0118
Fax: (308)282-0119
**Subject(s):** Paid Community Newspapers
**Circ:** ‡2,600

**The Hill City Times** (11115)
110 N Pomeroy
PO Box 308
Hill City, KS 67642
Phone: (785)421-5700
Fax: (785)421-5712
**Subject(s):** Paid Community Newspapers
**Circ:** (Free)50
(Paid)2,600

**Media** (17310)
PO Box 230
Kahoka, MO 63445
Phone: (660)727-3395
Fax: (660)727-2475
**Subject(s):** Paid Community Newspapers
**Circ:** (Paid)‡2,600

**Mound City News** (17437)
511 State St.
PO Box 175
Mound City, MO 64470
Phone: (660)442-5423
Fax: (660)442-5423
**Subject(s):** Paid Community Newspapers
**Circ:** 2,600

**The Smithville Lake Herald** (17956)
110 N Bridge St.
PO Box 269
Smithville, MO 64089-0269
Phone: (816)532-4217
Fax: (816)532-4918
**Subject(s):** Paid Community Newspapers
**Circ:** (Free)⊕75
(Paid)⊕2,600

**North Missourian** (17239)
Gallatin Publishing Co.
203 N Main
PO Box 37
Gallatin, MO 64640
Phone: (660)663-2154
Fax: (660)663-2498
**Subject(s):** Paid Community Newspapers
**Circ:** ‡2,575

**World Journal** (10269)
Ackley World Journal
712 Main
Ackley, IA 50601
Phone: (641)847-2592
Fax: (641)847-3010
**Subject(s):** Free Newspapers
**Circ:** (Free)1,800
(Paid)2,570

**Neligh News and Leader** (18497)
News Publishing Co.
PO Box 46
Neligh, NE 68756
Phone: (402)887-4840
Fax: (402)887-4711
**Subject(s):** Paid Community Newspapers
**Circ:** ‡2,564

**The Atchison County Mail** (17517)
300 S Main St.
PO Box 40
Rock Port, MO 64482-0040
Phone: (660)744-6245
Fax: (660)744-2645
**Subject(s):** Paid Community Newspapers
**Circ:** (Free)‡23
(Paid)2,550

**The Guttenberg Press** (10615)
Guttenberg Publishing
Po Box 937
10 Schiller St.
Guttenberg, IA 52052
Phone: (563)252-2421
Fax: (563)252-1275
**Subject(s):** Paid Community Newspapers
**Circ:** (Non-paid)18
(Paid)2,543

**Lyon County Reporter** (10840)
Lyon-Sioux Newspaper Publishing
310 1st Ave. W
PO Box 28
Rock Rapids, IA 51246
Phone: (712)472-2525
Fax: (712)472-3414
**Subject(s):** Paid Community Newspapers
**Circ:** (Free)‡50
(Paid)‡2,542

**Sidney Sun Telegraph** (18608)
Robert D. Van Vleet, Sr.
1136 Illinois
PO Box 193
Sidney, NE 69162
Phone: (308)254-2818
Fax: (308)254-3925
**Subject(s):** Paid Community Newspapers; Daily Newspapers
**Circ:** (Paid)‡2518

**Cameron Citizen Observer** (17106)
Cameron Newspapers Inc.
402 E. Evergreen (BB Hwy.)
PO Box 498
Cameron, MO 64429
Phone: (816)632-6543
Fax: (816)632-4508
**Subject(s):** Paid Community Newspapers
**Circ:** (Free)58
(Paid)2,500

**The Clear Lake Mirror Reporter/Advertiser** (10398)
Prefin Inc.
12 N 4th St.
Clear Lake, IA 50428
Phone: (641)357-2131
Fax: (641)357-2133
**Subject(s):** Shopping Guides
**Circ:** (Free)2,500

**The Eagle** (18308)
Chadron State College
1000 Main St.
Chadron, NE 69337
Phone: (308)432-6303
Fax: (308)432-6464
**Subject(s):** College Publications
**Circ:** (Free)2,500

**Eagle Grove Eagle** (10548)
314 W Broadway
PO Box 6
Eagle Grove, IA 50533-0006
Phone: (515)448-4745
Fax: (515)448-3182
**Subject(s):** Paid Community Newspapers
**Circ:** ‡2,500

**East Prairie Eagle** (17203)
East Prairie Eagle News
PO Box 10
East Prairie, MO 63845
Phone: (573)649-3351
**Subject(s):** Paid Community Newspapers
**Circ:** ‡2,500

**The Gothenburg Times** (18354)
Box 385
Gothenburg, NE 69138
Phone: (308)537-3636
Fax: (308)537-7554
**Subject(s):** Paid Community Newspapers
**Circ:** ‡2,500

**Greenfield Vedette** (17245)
Liberty Group Pub.
PO Box 216
Greenfield, MO 65661
Phone: (417)637-2712
Fax: (417)637-2232
**Subject(s):** Paid Community Newspapers
**Circ:** 2,500

**Gregory Times Advocate** (28317)
623 Main St.
PO Box 378
Gregory, SD 57533
Phone: (605)835-8089
Fax: (605)835-8467
**Subject(s):** Paid Community Newspapers
**Circ:** 2,500

**The Hot Springs Star** (28322)
Country Media Inc.
107 N Chicago St.
PO Box 1000
Hot Springs, SD 57747
Phone: (605)745-4170
Fax: (605)745-3161
**Subject(s):** Paid Community Newspapers
**Circ:** 2,500

**The Landmark** (17486)
PO Box 410
Platte City, MO 64079
Phone: (816)858-0363
Fax: (816)858-2313
**Subject(s):** Paid Community Newspapers
**Circ:** ‡2,500

**The Leader-News** (24075)
BHG Inc.
PO Box 340
Washburn, ND 58577
Phone: (701)462-8126
Fax: (701)462-8128
**Subject(s):** Paid Community Newspapers
**Circ:** (Non-paid)50
(Paid)2,500

**Licking News** (17397)
Derrickson Printing Corp.
122 S Main St.
PO Box 297
Licking, MO 65542
Phone: (573)674-2412

Fax: (573)624-2412
**Subject(s):** Paid Community Newspapers
**Circ:** ‡2,500

**Plain Talk (28444)**
Bill Willroth
201 W. Cherry St.
PO Box 256
Vermillion, SD 57069-0256
Phone: (605)624-2695
Fax: (605)624-2696
**Subject(s):** Paid Community Newspapers
**Circ:** ‡2,500

**The Pratt Tribune (11382)**
320 S Main
PO Box 909
Pratt, KS 67124
Phone: (620)672-5511
Fax: (620)672-5514
**Subject(s):** Daily Newspapers
**Circ:** ‡2,500

**St. Paul Phonograph-Herald (18588)**
PO Box 27
406 Howard Ave
Saint Paul, NE 68873-0027
Phone: (308)754-4401
Fax: (308)754-4498
**Subject(s):** Paid Community Newspapers
**Circ:** ‡2,502

**South Benton Star-Press (10733)**
MPC Publishing Co.
100 W Main St.
Marengo, IA 52301-1412
Phone: (319)444-2520
Fax: (319)642-5509
**Subject(s):** Paid Community Newspapers
**Circ:** 2,500

**Tonganoxie Mirror (11420)**
WorldWest L.L.C.
520 E. 4th St.
PO Box 920
Tonganoxie, KS 66086
Phone: (913)845-2222
Fax: (913)845-5491
**Subject(s):** Paid Community Newspapers
**Circ:** 2,500

**The Sioux Center News (10867)**
PO Box 198
Sioux Center, IA 51250
Phone: (712)722-0741
Fax: (712)722-0744
**Subject(s):** Paid Community Newspapers
**Circ:** (Free)71
(Paid)2,473

**Linn News-Letter (10384)**
Fourth Publishing Co.
PO Box A
38 4th Street North
Central City, IA 52214
Phone: (319)438-1313
**Subject(s):** Paid Community Newspapers
**Circ:** ‡2,450

**Mt. Ayr Record-News (10760)**
Paragon Publications Inc.
122 W Madison
PO Box 346
Mount Ayr, IA 50854
Phone: (641)464-2440
Fax: (641)464-2229
**Subject(s):** Paid Community Newspapers
**Circ:** ‡2,450

**Plainville Times (11377)**
400 W Mill St.
Plainville, KS 67663
Phone: (785)434-4525
Fax: (785)434-2527
**Subject(s):** Paid Community Newspapers
**Circ:** (Free)‡40
(Paid)‡2,450

**The Wapello Republican (10936)**
Louisa Publishing Company Ltd.
301 James L. Hodges Ave. S
PO Box 306
Wapello, IA 52653-0306
Phone: (319)523-4631
Fax: (319)523-8167

**Subject(s):** Paid Community Newspapers
**Circ:** ‡2,450

**Valley Falls Vindicator (11460)**
Davis Publications Inc.
416 Broadway
PO Box 187
Valley Falls, KS 66088
Phone: (785)945-6170
Fax: (785)995-3444
**Subject(s):** Paid Community Newspapers
**Circ:** 2,435

**Adair County Free Press (10606)**
108 E Iowa St.
Box 148
Greenfield, IA 50849
Phone: (641)743-6121
Fax: (641)743-6378
**Subject(s):** Paid Community Newspapers
**Circ:** ‡2,426

**Ness County News (11266)**
P.O. Box C
Ness City, KS 67560
Phone: (785)798-2213
Fax: (785)798-2214
**Subject(s):** Paid Community Newspapers
**Circ:** ‡2,425

**The Democrat-Leader (17222)**
Wood Creek Media
202 E Morrison
PO Box 32
Fayette, MO 65248
Phone: (660)248-2235
Fax: (660)248-1200
**Subject(s):** Paid Community Newspapers
**Circ:** 2,410

**The Andover Journal Advocate (10986)**
The Andover Journal Publishing Inc.
202 E Rhondda Ave. Ste. C
Andover, KS 67002
Phone: (316)733-2002
Fax: (316)733-4221
**Subject(s):** Paid Community Newspapers
**Circ:** (Free)⊕47
(Paid)⊕**2,408**

**Courier (28313)**
PO Box 950
308 S Main St.
Freeman, SD 57029-0950
Phone: (605)925-7033
Fax: (605)925-4684
**Subject(s):** Paid Community Newspapers
**Circ:** ‡2,400

**Memphis Democrat (17423)**
Democrat
121 S Main St.
Memphis, MO 63555
Phone: (660)465-7016
Fax: (660)465-2803
**Subject(s):** Paid Community Newspapers
**Circ:** 2,400

**Mountrail County Promoter, Inc. (24057)**
Greater Northwest Printing Co.
117 Main St.,
P O Box 99
Stanley, ND 58784-0099
Phone: (701)628-2333
Fax: (701)628-2694
**Subject(s):** Paid Community Newspapers
**Circ:** ‡2,400

**Sentinel (10795)**
PO Box 208
1014 9th Street
Onawa, IA 51040-0208
Phone: (712)423-2021
Fax: (712)423-3038
**Subject(s):** Paid Community Newspapers
**Circ:** 2,400

**Vandalia Leader-Press (18017)**
108 W State
Box 239
Vandalia, MO 63382
Phone: (573)594-3322
Fax: (573)594-6741

**Subject(s):** Paid Community Newspapers
**Circ:** ‡2,400

**Webster County Citizen (17949)**
PO Box 190
Seymour, MO 65746-0190
Phone: (417)935-2257
Fax: (417)935-2487
**Subject(s):** Paid Community Newspapers
**Circ:** (Controlled)2,408

**Beulah Beacon (23894)**
BHG Inc.
324 2nd Ave. NE
Beulah, ND 58523
**Subject(s):** Paid Community Newspapers
**Circ:** (Free)39
(Paid)2,398

**Maries County Gazette (18020)**
Tri-County Newspapers
PO Box 202
Vienna, MO 65582
Phone: (573)422-3441
Fax: (573)859-6274
**Subject(s):** Paid Community Newspapers
**Circ:** 2,399

**Barber County Index (11252)**
PO Box 349
Medicine Lodge, KS 67104
Phone: (620)886-5617
Fax: (620)886-3457
**Subject(s):** Paid Community Newspapers
**Circ:** (Paid)2,350

**The Hugoton Hermes (11119)**
Goering Publishing Company Inc.
522 S Main
PO Box 849
Hugoton, KS 67951
Phone: (620)544-4321
Fax: (620)544-7321
**Subject(s):** Paid Community Newspapers
**Circ:** (Free)50
(Paid)2,350

**The Ord Quiz (18567)**
Quiz Graphic Arts Inc.
305 S 16th St.
Ord, NE 68862
Phone: (308)728-3262
Fax: (308)728-5715
**Subject(s):** Free Newspapers
**Circ:** (Free)‡85
(Paid)‡2,350

**Republican Nonpareil (18306)**
PO Box 26
Central City, NE 68826
Phone: (308)946-3081
Fax: (308)946-3082
**Subject(s):** Paid Community Newspapers
**Circ:** (Free)‡50
(Paid)‡2,350

**Eclipse-News-Review (10816)**
503 Coates St.
PO Box 340
Parkersburg, IA 50665
Phone: (319)346-1461
Fax: (319)346-1461
**Subject(s):** Paid Community Newspapers
**Circ:** (Free)‡52
(Paid)‡2,335

**Mapleton Press (10722)**
Lyon Publishing Inc.
PO Box 187
Mapleton, IA 51034-0187
Phone: (712)881-1101
Fax: (712)881-1330
**Subject(s):** Free Newspapers
**Circ:** (Free)75
(Paid)2,338

**The Fayette Advertiser (17223)**
Wood Creek Media
202 E Morrison
PO Box 32
Fayette, MO 65248
Phone: (660)248-2235
Fax: (660)248-1200

Circulation: ★ = ABC; △ = BPA; ◆ = CAC; ● = CCAB; ◻ = VAC; ⊕ = PO Statement; ‡ = Publisher's Report; Boldface figures = sworn; Light figures = estimated.

## Great Plains States

**Subject(s):** Paid Community Newspapers
**Circ:** (Free)92
(Paid)2,310

**Burt County Plaindealer** (18625)
Plaindealer Publishing Co.
Box 239
Tekamah, NE 68061
Phone: (402)374-2226
Fax: (402)374-2739
**Subject(s):** Paid Community Newspapers
**Circ:** ‡2,300

**The Marthasville Record** (17415)
Missourian Publishing Co.
PO Box 77
Marthasville, MO 63357
Phone: (636)433-2223
Fax: (636)433-5955
**Subject(s):** Paid Community Newspapers
**Circ:** (Combined)2,300

**McKenzie County Farmer** (24076)
McKenzie County Farmers Publishing Co.
PO Box 587
Watford City, ND 58854
Phone: (701)842-2351
Fax: (701)842-2352
**Subject(s):** Farm Newspapers; Paid Community Newspapers
**Circ:** ‡2,300

**Mirror-Republican** (17405)
Mansfield Mirror
300 E Commercial St.
Mansfield, MO 65704
Phone: (417)924-3226
Fax: (417)924-3227
**Subject(s):** Paid Community Newspapers
**Circ:** ‡2,300

**Puxico Weekly Press** (17505)
PO Box 277
Puxico, MO 63960
Phone: (573)222-3243
Fax: (573)222-6327
**Subject(s):** Paid Community Newspapers
**Circ:** 2,300

**Reynolds County Courier** (17210)
Ellinghouse Publishing Company Inc.
370 Main St.
Ellington, MO 63638
Phone: (573)663-2243
Fax: (573)663-2763
**Subject(s):** Paid Community Newspapers
**Circ:** ‡2,300

**Star-Clipper** (10926)
Ogden Publishing
625 2nd St.
PO Box 156
Traer, IA 50675
Phone: (319)478-2323
Fax: (319)478-2818
**Subject(s):** Paid Community Newspapers
**Circ:** 2,300

**The Goodland Daily News** (11089)
NorWest Newspapers
1205 Main Ave.
Goodland, KS 67735
Phone: (785)899-2338
Fax: (785)899-6186
**Subject(s):** Daily Newspapers
**Circ:** (Free)‡50
(Paid)2,297

**Cedar County News** (18364)
Cedar County
Box 977
Hartington, NE 68739
Phone: (402)254-3997
Fax: (402)254-3999
**Subject(s):** Paid Community Newspapers
**Circ:** (Paid)2,280

**The Leader** (17488)
Tin Publishing Co.
102 E Maple
Plattsburg, MO 64477
Phone: (816)539-2112
Fax: (816)539-3530
**Subject(s):** Paid Community Newspapers
**Circ:** ‡2,280

**The Oskaloosa Independent** (11285)
Davis Publications Inc.
607 Delaware
PO Box 278
Oskaloosa, KS 66066
Phone: (785)863-2520
Fax: (785)863-2730
**Subject(s):** Paid Community Newspapers
**Circ:** (Paid)2,281

**Reporter** (10558)
Emmetsburg Publishing Co.
Box 73
Emmetsburg, IA 50536
Phone: (712)852-2323
Fax: (712)852-3184
**Subject(s):** Paid Community Newspapers
**Circ:** ‡2,286

**Salisbury Press-Spectator** (17939)
111 S. Broadway
Salisbury, MO 65281
Phone: (816)388-6131
Fax: (816)388-6688
**Subject(s):** Paid Community Newspapers
**Circ:** ‡2,285

**The Belle Banner** (17070)
PO Box 711
Belle, MO 65013
Phone: (573)859-3328
Fax: (573)859-6274
**Subject(s):** Paid Community Newspapers
**Circ:** ‡2,278

**Democrat** (10557)
Emmetsburg Publishing Co.
Box 73
Emmetsburg, IA 50536
Phone: (712)852-2323
Fax: (712)852-3184
**Subject(s):** Paid Community Newspapers
**Circ:** ‡2,279

**Lyons Daily News** (11222)
Lyons Publishing Company Inc.
210 W Commercial
PO Box 768
Lyons, KS 67554-2716
Phone: (620)257-2368
Fax: (620)257-2369
**Subject(s):** Daily Newspapers
**Circ:** ‡2,278

**The Herington Times** (11111)
7 N Broadway
PO Box 310
Herington, KS 67449
Phone: (785)258-2211
Fax: (785)258-2400
**Subject(s):** Paid Community Newspapers
**Circ:** (Free)25
(Paid)2,250

**The Imperial Republican** (18383)
Johnson Publications Inc.
PO Box 727
Imperial, NE 69033
Phone: (308)882-4453
Fax: (308)882-5167
**Subject(s):** Paid Community Newspapers
**Circ:** (Free)‡50
(Paid)‡2,242

**Missouri Valley Times News** (10753)
501 E Erie St.
PO Box 159
Missouri Valley, IA 51555
Phone: (712)642-2791
Fax: (712)642-2595
**Subject(s):** Paid Community Newspapers
**Circ:** 2,229

**Clear Lake Reporter** (10399)
Prefin Inc.
12 N 4th St.
Clear Lake, IA 50428
Phone: (641)357-2131
Fax: (641)357-2133
**Subject(s):** Paid Community Newspapers
**Circ:** ‡2,200

**The Current Local** (18016)
PO Box 100
Van Buren, MO 63965
Phone: (573)323-4515
**Subject(s):** Paid Community Newspapers
**Circ:** ‡2,200

**Horton Headlight** (11117)
133 W 8th St.
PO Box 269
Horton, KS 66439
Phone: (913)486-2512
Fax: (913)486-2512
**Subject(s):** Paid Community Newspapers
**Circ:** 2,200

**Monroe County Appeal** (17471)
Appeal Publishing Co.
PO Box 207
Paris, MO 65275
Phone: (660)327-4192
Fax: (660)327-4847
**Subject(s):** Paid Community Newspapers
**Circ:** ‡2,200

**The Piper Advertiser** (11146)
Wyandotte West Communications Inc.
7735 Washington Ave.
PO Box 12003
Kansas City, KS 66112
Phone: (913)788-5565
Fax: (913)788-9812
**Subject(s):** Shopping Guides
**Circ:** 2,200

**The Story City Herald** (10905)
511 Broad St.
Story City, IA 50248
Phone: (515)733-4318
Fax: (515)733-4319
**Subject(s):** Paid Community Newspapers
**Circ:** (Paid)‡2,200

**The Sun** (10765)
Wedel Publishing L.L.C.
113 1st St. W
PO Box 129
Mount Vernon, IA 52314-0129
Phone: (319)895-6216
Fax: (319)895-6217
**Subject(s):** Paid Community Newspapers
**Circ:** ‡2,203

**Tioga Tribune** (24059)
PO Box 700
Tioga, ND 58852
Phone: (701)664-2222
Fax: (701)664-3333
**Subject(s):** Paid Community Newspapers
**Circ:** 2,200

**Unionville Republican & Putnam County Journal** (18012)
Black Bird Creek Printing Co.
PO Box 365
111 South 16th Street
Unionville, MO 63565-0365
Phone: (660)947-2222
Fax: (660)947-2223
**Subject(s):** Paid Community Newspapers
**Circ:** (Free)‡200
(Paid)‡2,200

**Wamego Times** (11464)
PO Box 247
Wamego, KS 66547
Phone: (785)456-7838
Fax: (785)456-6688
**Subject(s):** Paid Community Newspapers
**Circ:** 2,200

**Calhoun County Advocate** (10844)
Remma Inc.
328 Court St.
PO Box 31
Rockwell City, IA 50579-9998
Phone: (712)297-7544
Fax: (712)297-7544
**Subject(s):** Paid Community Newspapers
**Circ:** ‡2,187

**Graphic  (10701)**
Lake Mills Graphic
204 N Mill St.
Box 127
Lake Mills, IA 50450
Phone: (641)592-4222
Fax: (641)592-6397
**Subject(s):** Paid Community Newspapers
**Circ:**  2,187

**Audubon County Advocate Journal  (10318)**
Audubon County Newspapers
301 Broadway
PO Box 247
Audubon, IA 50025
Phone: (712)563-2661
Fax: (712)563-3118
**Subject(s):** Paid Community Newspapers
**Circ:** (Paid)2,172

**The Atkinson Graphic  (18266)**
207 E State St.
PO Box 159
Atkinson, NE 68713-0159
Phone: (402)925-5411
**Subject(s):** Paid Community Newspapers
**Circ:** 2,165

**Custer County Chronicle  (28293)**
Southern Hills Publishing Inc.
PO Box 551
Custer, SD 57730
Phone: (605)673-2217
Fax: (605)574-3321
**Subject(s):** Paid Community Newspapers
**Circ:** (Controlled)2,150

**Journal-Reporter  (10710)**
110 N Main St.
Leon, IA 50144
Phone: (641)446-4151
Fax: (641)446-7645
**Subject(s):** Paid Community Newspapers
**Circ:** ‡2,150

**The Wyandotte West  (11153)**
Wyandotte West Communications Inc.
7735 Washington Ave.
PO Box 12003
Kansas City, KS 66112
Phone: (913)788-5565
Fax: (913)788-9812
**Subject(s):** Paid Community Newspapers
**Circ:** 2,150

**Eagle Butte News  (28303)**
PO Box 210
Eagle Butte, SD 57625
Phone: (605)964-2100
Fax: (605)964-2100
**Subject(s):** Paid Community Newspapers
**Circ:** ‡2,139

**The Oberlin Herald  (11279)**
Nor'West Newspapers
170 S Penn Ave.
Oberlin, KS 67749
Phone: (785)475-2206
Fax: (785)475-2800
**Subject(s):** Paid Community Newspapers
**Circ:** (Paid)‡2,127

**Ark Valley News  (11459)**
236 E. Main
Valley Center, KS 67147
Phone: (316)755-0821
Fax: (316)755-0644
**Subject(s):** Paid Community Newspapers
**Circ:** ‡2,100

**Burwell Tribune  (18589)**
Burwell Tribune Newspapers
103 N 1st St.
PO Box 547
Sargent, NE 68874
Phone: (308)527-4210
Fax: (308)346-4018
**Subject(s):** Paid Community Newspapers
**Circ:** (Paid)‡2,100

**The Cabool Enterprise  (17102)**
Cabool Enterprise Inc.
525 Main St.
PO Box 40
Cabool, MO 65689-0040
Phone: (417)962-4411
Fax: (417)962-4455
**Subject(s):** Paid Community Newspapers
**Circ:** 2,100

**Council Grove Republican  (11039)**
208 W Main
PO Box 237
Council Grove, KS 66846
Phone: (620)767-5123
Fax: (620)767-5124
**Subject(s):** Daily Newspapers
**Circ:** (Free)37
(Paid)2,103

**Hazen Star  (24001)**
BHG Inc.
PO Box 508
Hazen, ND 58545
**Subject(s):** Paid Community Newspapers
**Circ:** (Free)49
(Paid)2,108

**Kenmare News  (24013)**
PO Box 896
20 N 2nd St.
Kenmare, ND 58746
Phone: (701)385-4275
Fax: (701)385-4395
**Subject(s):** Paid Community Newspapers
**Circ:** ‡2,100

**Nebraska City News-Press  (18495)**
American Publishing
806 Central Ave.
Nebraska City, NE 68410
**Subject(s):** Daily Newspapers
**Circ:** (Mon.-Fri.)‡2,100

**The Rush County News  (11159)**
112 W 8th
Box 60
La Crosse, KS 67548
Phone: (785)222-2555
Fax: (785)222-2557
**Subject(s):** Paid Community Newspapers
**Circ:** (Free)‡200
(Paid)‡2,100

**Sedan Times-Star  (11406)**
Prairie Media LLC
226 E Main
PO Box 417
Sedan, KS 67361
Phone: (620)725-3176
Fax: (620)725-3272
**Subject(s):** Paid Community Newspapers
**Circ:** (Paid)2,100

**Shelbina Democrat  (17950)**
115 S Center St.
PO Box 138
Shelbina, MO 63468
Phone: (573)588-2133
Fax: (573)588-2134
**Subject(s):** Paid Community Newspapers
**Circ:** 2,100

**Shelby County Herald  (17951)**
106 E Main St
PO Box 225
Shelbyville, MO 63469-0225
Phone: (573)633-2261
Fax: (573)633-2133
**Subject(s):** Paid Community Newspapers
**Circ:** (Free)40
(Paid)2,105

**Logan Herald-Observer  (10712)**
Bloom Publishing Co.
107 North 4th Ave.
PO Box 148
Logan, IA 51546
Phone: (712)644-2705
Fax: (712)644-2788
**Subject(s):** Paid Community Newspapers
**Circ:** (Free)35
(Paid)2,095

**Calhoun County Journal'herald  (10720)**
Dudley Printing
931 Main St.
PO Box 40
Manson, IA 50563
Phone: (712)469-3381
Fax: (712)469-2648
**Subject(s):** Paid Community Newspapers
**Circ:** 2,085

**The Miller Press  (28345)**
Miller Publishing Co.
114 W. 3rd St.
PO Box 196
Miller, SD 57362
Phone: (605)853-3575
Fax: (605)853-2478
**Subject(s):** Paid Community Newspapers
**Circ:** 2,081

**The Index  (18493)**
PO Box 158
1269 Center Ave.
Mitchell, NE 69357
Phone: (308)623-1322
Fax: (308)623-1322
**Subject(s):** Paid Community Newspapers
**Circ:** 2,075

**Pierce County Leader  (18580)**
109 E Main St.
Pierce, NE 68767-1343
Phone: (402)329-4665
Fax: (402)329-6337
**Subject(s):** Paid Community Newspapers
**Circ:** ‡2,075

**Western Kansas World  (11461)**
PO Box 218
205 Main St.
Wa Keeney, KS 67672
Phone: (785)743-2155
Fax: (785)743-5340
**Subject(s):** Paid Community Newspapers
**Circ:** 2,050

**Guthrie Center Times  (10614)**
PO Box 217
Guthrie Center, IA 50115
**Subject(s):** Paid Community Newspapers
**Circ:** (Non-paid)17
(Paid)2,022

**Enterprise  (28375)**
PO Box 546
Platte, SD 57369
Phone: (605)337-3101
Fax: (605)337-3433
**Subject(s):** Paid Community Newspapers
**Circ:** (Free)‡25
(Paid)‡2,014

**Sheldon Mail-Sun  (10855)**
Iowa Information Inc.
227 9th St.
PO Box 160
Sheldon, IA 51201
Phone: (712)324-5347
Fax: (712)324-2345
**Subject(s):** Paid Community Newspapers
**Circ:** (Free)⊕17
(Paid)⊕**2,011**

**Adams County Record  (24003)**
Country Media
PO Box 749
405 Adams Ave
Hettinger, ND 58639
Phone: (701)567-2424
Fax: (701)567-2425
**Subject(s):** Paid Community Newspapers
**Circ:** ‡2,000

**The Advocate  (11141)**
Kansas City Kansas Community College
7250 State Ave.
Kansas City, KS 66112
Phone: (913)334-1100
**Subject(s):** College Publications
**Circ:** (Free)‡2,000

Circulation: ★ = ABC; Δ = BPA; ♦ = CAC; • = CCAB; ❑ = VAC; ⊕ = PO Statement; ‡ = Publisher's Report; Boldface figures = sworn; Light figures = estimated.

**Belmond Independent (10321)**
215 E Main St.
Box 126
Belmond, IA 50421
Phone: (641)444-3333
**Subject(s):** Paid Community Newspapers
**Circ:** ‡2,000

**The Britt News-Tribune (10331)**
Delete Prefin Inc.
42 Center St. W.
P.O. Box 38
Britt, IA 50423-1655
Phone: (641)843-3851
Fax: (641)843-3307
**Subject(s):** Paid Community Newspapers
**Circ:** ‡2,000

**Calmar Courier (10342)**
PO Box 507
114 N Maryville
Calmar, IA 52132-0507
Phone: (563)562-3329
Fax: (563)562-3940
**Subject(s):** Paid Community Newspapers
**Circ:** 2,000

**Carroll Today (10346)**
Carroll Today Newspaper
102 W 6th St.
Carroll, IA 51401
Phone: (712)792-2179
Fax: (712)792-2309
**Subject(s):** Paid Community Newspapers
**Circ:** 2,000

**Cedar Valley Times (10933)**
Community Media Group
108 E 5th St.
PO Box 468
Vinton, IA 52349
Phone: (319)472-2311
Fax: (319)472-4811
**Subject(s):** Daily Newspapers
**Circ:** ‡2,000

**The Crusader (11212)**
Seward County Community College
Box 1137
Liberal, KS 67905-1137
Phone: (620)629-2669
Fax: (620)629-2725
**Subject(s):** College Publications
**Circ:** (Free)‡2,000

**The Current Wave (17214)**
Current Wave Newspaper
PO Box 728
Eminence, MO 65466-9998
Phone: (573)226-3335
Fax: (573)226-3335
**Subject(s):** Paid Community Newspapers
**Circ:** ‡2,000

**Fayette Leader (10568)**
PO Box 220
112 South Main
Fayette, IA 52142-0220
Phone: (563)425-4162
**Subject(s):** Paid Community Newspapers
**Circ:** ‡2,000

**Gardner News (11085)**
Tri-County Newspapers
PO Box 303
Gardner, KS 66030
Phone: (913)856-7615
Fax: (913)856-6707
**Subject(s):** Paid Community Newspapers
**Circ:** 2,000

**Grant Tribune Sentinel (18362)**
Johnson Publications Inc.
PO Box 67
327 Cnetral Avenue
Grant, NE 69140
Phone: (308)352-4311
Fax: (308)352-4101
**Subject(s):** Paid Community Newspapers
**Circ:** (Non-paid)100
(Paid)2,000

**Jasper County Tribune (10404)**
PO Box 7
Colfax, IA 50054
Phone: (515)674-3591
Fax: (515)674-3591
**Subject(s):** Paid Community Newspapers
**Circ:** 2,000

**Lennox Independent (28334)**
116 S Main St.
PO Box 76
Lennox, SD 57039
Phone: (605)647-2284
Fax: (605)647-2218
**Subject(s):** Paid Community Newspapers
**Circ:** 2,000

**Louisburg Herald (11221)**
15 S Broadway
Box 99
Louisburg, KS 66053-0099
Phone: (913)837-4321
Fax: (913)837-4322
**Subject(s):** Paid Community Newspapers
**Circ:** 2,000

**McDonald County News-Gazette (17483)**
McDonald County Press Inc.
PO Box 266
Pineville, MO 64856
Phone: (417)223-4675
Fax: (417)223-4049
**Subject(s):** Paid Community Newspapers
**Circ:** ‡2,000

**Mouse River Journal (24061)**
PO Box 268
215 Main St S
Towner, ND 58788-0328
Phone: (701)537-5610
Fax: (701)537-5493
**Subject(s):** Paid Community Newspapers
**Circ:** 2,000

**Ogden Reporter (10793)**
The Ogden
Po Box R
222 W. Walnut St.
Ogden, IA 50212
Phone: (515)275-4101
Fax: (515)275-2678
**Subject(s):** Paid Community Newspapers
**Circ:** 2,000

**Phillips County Review (11366)**
Box 446
Phillipsburg, KS 67661
Phone: (785)543-5242
Fax: (785)543-5243
**Subject(s):** Paid Community Newspapers
**Circ:** (Paid)‡2,000

**The Richland Mirror (17512)**
Box 757
115 Chestnut St
Richland, MO 65556
Phone: (573)765-3391
Fax: (573)765-3235
**Subject(s):** Paid Community Newspapers
**Circ:** (Paid)‡2,000

**Rustler Sentinel (18604)**
PO Box 370
Scribner, NE 68057
Phone: (402)664-3198
Fax: (402)664-3141
**Subject(s):** Paid Community Newspapers
**Circ:** (Free)13
(Paid)2,000

**Todd County Tribune (28347)**
PO Box 229
166 W 2nd
Mission, SD 57555-0229
Phone: (605)856-4469
Fax: (605)856-2428
**Subject(s):** Paid Community Newspapers
**Circ:** ‡2,000

**Transcript (24046)**
Transcript Publishing
632 1st Ave. N
PO Box 752
New Rockford, ND 58356
Phone: (701)947-2417

Fax: (701)947-2418
**Subject(s):** Free Newspapers; Free Newspapers
**Circ:** (Free)‡1,000
(Paid)‡2,000

**Turtle Mountain Times (23892)**
PO Box 1270
Bia House, No. 177
Belcourt, ND 58316
Phone: (701)477-6670
Fax: (701)477-6875
**Subject(s):** Paid Community Newspapers; Native American Interests
**Circ:** (Combined)2,000

**Webb City Sentinel (18053)**
Webb City Sentinel Inc.
8 S Main
PO Box 150
Webb City, MO 64870
Phone: (417)673-5308
**Subject(s):** Paid Community Newspapers
**Circ:** ‡2,000

**Wellsville Optic-News (18055)**
PO Box 73
Wellsville, MO 63384
Phone: (573)684-2929
**Subject(s):** Paid Community Newspapers
**Circ:** ‡2,000

**West Liberty Index (10973)**
Slechta Communications Inc.
PO Box 96
West Liberty, IA 52776-0096
Phone: (319)627-2814
Fax: (319)627-2110
**Subject(s):** Paid Community Newspapers
**Circ:** ‡2,000

**The Winthrop News (10980)**
Box 9
225 West Madison
Winthrop, IA 50682
Phone: (319)935-3027
Fax: (319)935-3082
**Subject(s):** Paid Community Newspapers
**Circ:** ‡2,000

**Wright County Monitor (10395)**
PO Box 153
107 Second Ave NorthEast
Clarion, IA 50525-0153
Phone: (515)532-2871
Fax: (515)532-2872
**Subject(s):** Paid Community Newspapers
**Circ:** ⊕2,000

**Sweet Springs Herald (18002)**
Heartland Publishing Inc.
238 Main St.
Sweet Springs, MO 65351
Phone: (660)335-6366
Fax: (660)335-6366
**Subject(s):** Paid Community Newspapers
**Circ:** ‡1,990

**The Yates Center News (11514)**
PO Box 285
Yates Center, KS 66783
Phone: (620)625-2181
Fax: (620)625-2081
**Subject(s):** Paid Community Newspapers
**Circ:** (Free)‡100
(Paid)‡1,998

**Oakland Independent (18515)**
Gahan Publishing Company Inc.
217 N Oakland Ave.
Oakland, NE 68045
Phone: (402)685-5624
Fax: (402)685-5625
**Subject(s):** Paid Community Newspapers
**Circ:** ‡1,980

**Hamilton Advocate (17246)**
L & L Publications Inc.
412 S Davis St.
Box 187
Hamilton, MO 64644
Phone: (816)583-2116
Fax: (816)583-2118
**Subject(s):** Paid Community Newspapers
**Circ:** 1,973

**The Edwards County Sentinel (11210)**
The Lewis Press Inc.
PO Box 68
Lewis, KS 67552
Phone: (620)659-2080
Fax: (620)324-5879
**Subject(s):** Paid Community Newspapers
**Circ:** ‡1,958

**Pocahontas Record Democrat (10824)**
Community Publications
218 N. Main
Pocahontas, IA 50574
Phone: (712)335-3553
Fax: (712)335-3856
**Subject(s):** Paid Community Newspapers
**Circ:** 1,950

**The Redfield Press (28397)**
Redfield Press Inc.
16 E 7th Ave.
PO Box 440
Redfield, SD 57469
Phone: (605)472-0822
Fax: (605)472-3634
**Subject(s):** Paid Community Newspapers
**Circ:** ‡1,950

**Wisner News-Chronicle (18642)**
1014 Ave. E
PO Box 460
Wisner, NE 68791
Phone: (402)529-3228
Fax: (402)529-3279
**Subject(s):** Paid Community Newspapers
**Circ:** (Free)‡38
  (Paid)‡1,957

**Journal (28277)**
Britton Journal Inc.
706 7th St.
PO Box 69
Britton, SD 57430
Phone: (605)448-2281
Fax: (605)448-2282
**Subject(s):** Paid Community Newspapers
**Circ:** (Paid)‡1,946

**The Tipton Times (18007)**
Vernon Publishing Inc.
PO Box U
123 W. Moniteau
Tipton, MO 65081
Phone: (660)433-5721
Fax: (660)433-2222
**Subject(s):** Paid Community Newspapers
**Circ:** ‡1,947

**Harper Advocate (11101)**
Advocate
PO Box 36
907 Central
Harper, KS 67058-0036
Phone: (620)896-7311
Fax: (620)896-2754
**Subject(s):** Paid Community Newspapers
**Circ:** 1,910

**Norton Daily Telegram (11276)**
215 S Kansas Ave.
Norton, KS 67654-0320
Phone: (785)877-3361
**Subject(s):** Daily Newspapers
**Circ:** (Free)1,915

**Brooklyn Chronicle (10332)**
PO Box 533
Brooklyn, IA 52211
Phone: (641)522-7155
Fax: (641)522-7909
**Subject(s):** Paid Community Newspapers
**Circ:** (Free)‡22
  (Paid)‡1,900

**Meade County News (11249)**
Meade News
PO Box 310
105 S. Fowler St.
Meade, KS 67864
Phone: (620)873-2118
Fax: (620)873-5456
**Subject(s):** Paid Community Newspapers
**Circ:** ‡1,900

**Montezuma Republican (10756)**
406 E Main St.
PO Box 100
Montezuma, IA 50171-0100
Phone: (641)623-5116
Fax: (641)623-5580
**Subject(s):** Paid Community Newspapers
**Circ:** 1,900

**Prairie Pioneer (28376)**
PO Box 218
Pollock, SD 57648
Phone: (605)889-2320
Fax: (605)889-2361
**Subject(s):** Paid Community Newspapers
**Circ:** 1,900

**The Rockhurst Sentinel (17349)**
Rockhurst University
1100 Rockhurst Rd.
Kansas City, MO 64110-2561
Phone: (816)501-4051
Fax: (816)501-4290
**Subject(s):** College Publications
**Circ:** (Free)1,900

**Sac Sun (10847)**
S.A.C. Sun
406 William St.
PO Box 426
Sac City, IA 50583-0426
Phone: (712)662-7161
Fax: (712)662-4198
**Subject(s):** Paid Community Newspapers
**Circ:** ‡1,900

**The Steele Enterprise (17996)**
Tennyson Publishing
225 W Main
Box 60
Steele, MO 63877
Phone: (573)695-3415
Fax: (573)695-2114
**Subject(s):** Paid Community Newspapers
**Circ:** (Free)‡383
  (Paid)‡1,894

**Western Nebraska Observer (18394)**
118 E 2nd St.
Kimball, NE 69145
Phone: (308)235-3631
Fax: (308)235-3632
**Subject(s):** Paid Community Newspapers
**Circ:** (Free)‡15
  (Paid)‡1,891

**Garden County News (18571)**
Oshkosh
204 Main St.
Box 290
Oshkosh, NE 69154-0290
Phone: (308)772-3555
Fax: (308)772-4475
**Subject(s):** Paid Community Newspapers
**Circ:** 1,884

**The Ashland Gazette (18265)**
The Gazette
1518 Silver St.
Box 127
Ashland, NE 68003-0127
Phone: (402)944-3397
Fax: (402)944-3398
**Subject(s):** Paid Community Newspapers
**Circ:** ⊕1,870

**Miller County Autogram-Sentinel (17209)**
Vernon Publishing Inc.
409-15 S Maple
Eldon, MO 65026
Phone: (573)392-5658
Fax: (573)392-7755
**Subject(s):** Paid Community Newspapers
**Circ:** (Paid)1,875

**Press Journal (10907)**
PO Box 70
Strawberry Point, IA 52076
Phone: (563)933-4370
Fax: (563)933-4370
**Subject(s):** Paid Community Newspapers
**Circ:** 1,876

**Diamond Trail News (10912)**
PO Box 267
Sully, IA 50251-0267
Phone: (641)594-4488
Fax: (641)594-4498
**Subject(s):** Paid Community Newspapers
**Circ:** (Free)18
  (Paid)1,850

**Gazette (10852)**
Box 7
Neola, IA 51559-0007
Phone: (712)485-2276
Fax: (712)485-2277
**Subject(s):** Paid Community Newspapers
**Circ:** ‡1,850

**Homestead (24044)**
PO Box 29
323 Main
Napoleon, ND 58561
Phone: (701)754-2212
Fax: (701)754-2212
**Subject(s):** Paid Community Newspapers
**Circ:** ‡1,850

**The Ralston Recorder (18575)**
Times Publishing
1413 Washington St
Papillion, NE 68046
Phone: (402)331-6300
Fax: (402)537-2997
**Subject(s):** Paid Community Newspapers
**Circ:** 1,850

**Red Cloud Chief (18585)**
322 N Webster
PO Box 484
Red Cloud, NE 68970
Phone: (402)746-3700
**Subject(s):** Paid Community Newspapers
**Circ:** 1,850

**Rich Hill Mining Review (17511)**
PO Box 29
602 East Park SAve
Rich Hill, MO 64779
Phone: (417)395-4131
Fax: (417)396-4366
**Subject(s):** Paid Community Newspapers
**Circ:** 1,850

**Stephens Life (17173)**
Stephens College
PO Box 2014
Columbia, MO 65215
Phone: (573)876-7254
Fax: (573)876-2318
**Subject(s):** College Publications
**Circ:** (Paid)150
  (Non-paid)1,850

**Tri-County News (17371)**
Pearl Publishing Co.
PO Box 428
King City, MO 64463
Phone: (816)535-4313
**Subject(s):** Paid Community Newspapers
**Circ:** 1,850

**Wartburg Trumpet (10958)**
Wartburg College
C/O McElroy Communication Arts Ctr.
Waverly, IA 50677
Phone: (319)352-8200
Fax: (319)352-8610
**Subject(s):** College Publications
**Circ:** (Free)350
  (Paid)1,850

**Winfield Beacon & Wayland News (10979)**
107 E Elm St
Box F
Winfield, IA 52659
Phone: (319)257-6813
Fax: (319)257-6902
**Subject(s):** Paid Community Newspapers
**Circ:** ‡1,850

**The Pawnee Republican (18576)**
PO Box 111
Pawnee City, NE 68420
Phone: (402)852-2575

Circulation: ★ = ABC; △ = BPA; ♦ = CAC; • = CCAB; ▫ = VAC; ⊕ = PO Statement; ‡ = Publisher's Report; Boldface figures = sworn; Light figures = estimated.

**Subject(s):** Paid Community Newspapers
**Circ:** (Free)52
(Paid)1,834

**The Herald (10787)**
PO Box 556
Oakland, IA 51560
**Subject(s):** Paid Community Newspapers
**Circ:** (Free)‡22
(Paid)‡1,814

**St. Marys Star (11395)**
517 W Bertrand
PO Box 190
Saint Marys, KS 66536-0190
Phone: (785)437-2935
Fax: (785)437-2095
**Subject(s):** Paid Community Newspapers
**Circ:** (Free)‡10
(Paid)‡1,815

**The Brunswicker (17096)**
118 E Broadway
PO Box 188
Brunswick, MO 65236-0188
Phone: (660)548-3171
Fax: (660)388-6688
**Subject(s):** Paid Community Newspapers
**Circ:** ‡1,800

**Des Moines County News (10968)**
Louisa Publishing Company Ltd.
204 Broadway
PO Box 177
West Burlington, IA 52655
Phone: (319)752-8328
Fax: (319)752-8328
**Subject(s):** Paid Community Newspapers
**Circ:** 1,800

**The Excelsior (17383)**
Excelsior Publishing Company Inc.
417 Thompson Ave.
PO Box 70
Excelsior Springs, MO 64024
Phone: (816)637-3147
Fax: (816)637-8411
**Subject(s):** Paid Community Newspapers
**Circ:** ‡1,800

**The Hoxie Sentinel (11118)**
Box 78
640 Main
Hoxie, KS 67740
Phone: (785)675-3321
Fax: (785)675-3421
**Subject(s):** Paid Community Newspapers
**Circ:** ‡1,800

**Lake City Graphic (10700)**
103 N Center St.
PO Box 121
Lake City, IA 51449
Phone: (712)464-3188
Fax: (712)464-3188
**Subject(s):** Paid Community Newspapers
**Circ:** ‡1,800

**The Leader-Courier (28306)**
Lead Courier
PO Box 310
Elk Point, SD 57025
Phone: (605)356-2632
Fax: (605)356-3626
**Subject(s):** Paid Community Newspapers
**Circ:** (Free)‡35
(Paid)‡1,807

**The Ledger (11260)**
Davies Communications Inc.
135 S Christian
PO Box 720
Moundridge, KS 67107
Phone: (620)345-6353
Fax: (620)345-2170
**Subject(s):** Paid Community Newspapers
**Circ:** 1,800

**Missourian News (17501)**
PO Box 456
413 EAst Main Street
Portageville, MO 63873-0456
Phone: (573)379-5355
Fax: (573)379-5488

**Subject(s):** Paid Community Newspapers
**Circ:** ‡1,800

**Neodesha Derrick (11265)**
502 Main St.
PO Box 356
Neodesha, KS 66757
Phone: (620)325-3000
Fax: (620)325-2880
**Subject(s):** Paid Community Newspapers
**Circ:** ‡1,800

**Osceola County Gazette-Tribune (10862)**
Sibley Printing and Publishing Co.
201 9th St.
Sibley, IA 51249
Phone: (712)754-3656
Fax: (712)754-2552
**Subject(s):** Paid Community Newspapers
**Circ:** ‡1,800

**Richland County News-Monitor (23998)**
Wick Communications
107 Main St.
P O Box 190
Hankinson, ND 58041-0190
Phone: (701)242-7696
Fax: (701)242-7406
**Subject(s):** Paid Community Newspapers
**Circ:** ‡1,800

**Sioux County Capital-Democrat (10798)**
Pluim Publishing Inc.
113 Central Ave. SE
Orange City, IA 51041-1738
Phone: (712)737-4266
Fax: (712)737-3896
**Subject(s):** Paid Community Newspapers
**Circ:** (Free)‡50
(Paid)‡1,800

**Sumner Gazette (10913)**
106 E 1st St.
Box 208
Sumner, IA 50674-0280
Phone: (563)578-3351
Fax: (563)578-3352
**Subject(s):** Paid Community Newspapers
**Circ:** (Free)65
(Paid)1808

**The Wagner Post and Announcer (28453)**
Printers Inc.
PO Box 187
Wagner, SD 57380
Phone: (605)384-5616
Fax: (605)384-5955
**Subject(s):** Paid Community Newspapers
**Circ:** 1800

**Weston Chronicle (18058)**
McPherson Pub. Co.
18275 Hwy. 45 N
PO Box 6
Weston, MO 64098
Phone: (816)640-2251
Fax: (816)386-2251
**Subject(s):** Paid Community Newspapers
**Circ:** (Free)‡50
(Paid)‡1,800

**Seneca News-Dispatch (17948)**
1103 Cherokee St.
PO Box 1110
Seneca, MO 64865
Phone: (417)776-2236
Fax: (417)776-2204
**Subject(s):** Paid Community Newspapers
**Circ:** 1,790

**Humansville Star-Leader (17462)**
PO Box 406
Osceola, MO 64776
Phone: (417)646-2211
Fax: (417)646-8015
**Subject(s):** Paid Community Newspapers
**Circ:** 1,785

**Siouxland Press (10628)**
PO Box 278
Hospers, IA 51238
Phone: (712)752-8401
Fax: (712)752-8405

**Subject(s):** Paid Community Newspapers
**Circ:** (Free)‡50
(Paid)‡1,785

**Van Buren County Leader-Record (10566)**
102 Elm St.
PO Box 155
Farmington, IA 52626
Phone: (319)878-4111
Fax: (319)878-4111
**Subject(s):** Paid Community Newspapers
**Circ:** ‡1,784

**Avoca Journal-Herald (10319)**
Nielson Publishing
PO Box 308
164 S. Elm St
Avoca, IA 51521
Phone: (712)343-2154
Fax: (712)343-2262
**Subject(s):** Paid Community Newspapers
**Circ:** 1,750

**Boone County Journal (17065)**
PO Box 197
209 East Johnson
Ashland, MO 65010
Phone: (573)657-2334
Fax: (573)657-2002
**Subject(s):** Paid Community Newspapers
**Circ:** ‡1,750

**Courier (10835)**
PO Box O
Reinbeck, IA 50669-0177
Phone: (319)345-2031
Fax: (319)345-6767
**Subject(s):** Paid Community Newspapers
**Circ:** (Paid)‡1,750

**The Herald (24045)**
Jeff Schumacher
PO Box 517
744 Main St.
New England, ND 58647
Phone: (701)579-4530
Fax: (701)579-4180
**Subject(s):** Paid Community Newspapers
**Circ:** ‡1,750

**The Mulvane News (11263)**
Mulvane News
204 W Main St.
PO Box 157
Mulvane, KS 67110
Phone: (316)777-4233
**Subject(s):** Paid Community Newspapers
**Circ:** 1,750

**Natoma-Luray Independent (11264)**
Natoma Publishing Co.
PO Box 126
Natoma, KS 67651-0160
Phone: (785)885-4582
Fax: (785)885-4582
**Subject(s):** Paid Community Newspapers
**Circ:** ‡1,750

**Plainview News (18581)**
Box 9
Plainview, NE 68769-0009
Phone: (402)582-4921
Fax: (402)582-4922
**Subject(s):** Paid Community Newspapers
**Circ:** ‡1757

**The Stafford Courier (11416)**
114 E Bdwy
PO Box 276
Stafford, KS 67578
Phone: (620)234-5241
**Subject(s):** Paid Community Newspapers
**Circ:** ‡1,750

**Nation's Center News (28288)**
PO Box 107
604 West 4th Street
Buffalo, SD 57720
Phone: (605)375-3228
Fax: (605)375-3615
**Subject(s):** Paid Community Newspapers
**Circ:** (Free)50
(Paid)1,744

**Pioneer Review** (28360)
Ravellette Publishing Inc.
Box 788
Philip, SD 57567-0788
Phone: (605)859-2516
Fax: (605)859-2410
**Subject(s):** Paid Community Newspapers
**Circ:** 1,740

**Griswold American** (10610)
PO Box 687
Griswold, IA 51535
Phone: (712)778-4337
Fax: (712)778-4350
**Subject(s):** Paid Community Newspapers
**Circ:** 1,722

**Augustana Mirror** (28405)
Augustana College
2201 South Summit
Sioux Falls, SD 57197
Phone: (605)274-0770
Fax: (605)274-4999
**Subject(s):** College Publications
**Circ:** 1700

**Chase County Leader-News** (11037)
PO Box K
306 Broadway
Cottonwood Falls, KS 66845-0436
Phone: (620)273-6391
Fax: (620)273-8674
**Subject(s):** Paid Community Newspapers
**Circ:** 1700

**The Deshler Rustler** (18332)
Struve Enterprises Inc.
PO Box 647
Deshler, NE 68340
Phone: (402)365-7575
Fax: (402)365-4439
**Subject(s):** Free Newspapers
**Circ:** (Paid)‡1,700

**Grant County News** (23948)
Box 100
Elgin, ND 58533-0100
Phone: (701)584-2900
**Subject(s):** Paid Community Newspapers
**Circ:** ⊕1,700

**Griggs County Sentinel-Courier** (23931)
Devlin Publications Inc.
Box 525
Cooperstown, ND 58425
Phone: (701)797-3331
**Subject(s):** Paid Community Newspapers
**Circ:** ‡1,700

**Independent** (11161)
PO Box 45
118 N.Main
Lakin, KS 67860-0045
Phone: (620)355-6162
**Subject(s):** Paid Community Newspapers
**Circ:** ‡1,705

**The Lawson Review** (17384)
405 N Pennsylvania Ave.
Box 125
Lawson, MO 64062-0125
Phone: (816)296-3412
**Subject(s):** Paid Community Newspapers
**Circ:** ‡1,700

**Miner County Pioneer** (28326)
PO Box 220
Howard, SD 57349
Phone: (605)772-5644
Fax: (605)772-5644
**Subject(s):** Paid Community Newspapers
**Circ:** ‡1,700

**Nance County Journal** (18347)
416 4th St.
PO Box 10
Fullerton, NE 68638
Phone: (308)536-3100
Fax: (308)536-3100
**Subject(s):** Paid Community Newspapers
**Circ:** 1,700

**The Ravenna News** (18584)
322 Grand Ave.
PO BOX 110
Ravenna, NE 68869
Phone: (308)452-3411
Fax: (308)452-3511
**Subject(s):** Paid Community Newspapers
**Circ:** ‡1,700

**Renville County Farmer** (24043)
Greater Northwest Publishing Inc.
PO Box 98
Mohall, ND 58761
Phone: (701)756-6363
Fax: (701)756-7136
**Subject(s):** Paid Community Newspapers
**Circ:** ‡1,700

**Wymore Arbor State** (18644)
PO Box 327
204 S.7th St.
Wymore, NE 68466
Phone: (402)645-3344
Fax: (402)645-3345
**Subject(s):** Paid Community Newspapers
**Circ:** 1,700

**Rock County Leader** (18271)
PO Box 488
118 Clark Street
Bassett, NE 68714
Phone: (402)684-3771
**Subject(s):** Paid Community Newspapers
**Circ:** ‡1,687

**The Beacon-Observer** (18573)
PO Box 330
Overton, NE 68863
Phone: (308)987-2451
Fax: (308)987-2452
**Subject(s):** Paid Community Newspapers
**Circ:** ‡1,650

**The Glasgow Missourian** (17241)
PO Box 248
Glasgow, MO 65254
Phone: (660)338-2195
Fax: (660)338-2494
**Subject(s):** Paid Community Newspapers
**Circ:** ‡1,650

**The Grant City Times-Tribune** (17244)
T.T. Publications
PO Box 130
Grant City, MO 64456
Phone: (660)564-3603
Fax: (660)564-3603
**Subject(s):** Paid Community Newspapers
**Circ:** 1,650

**Lake View Resort and Green Saver** (10703)
PO Box 470
Lake View, IA 51450
Phone: (712)657-8588
Fax: (712)657-2495
**Subject(s):** Paid Community Newspapers
**Circ:** ‡1,650

**Leoti Standard** (11209)
The Leoti
114 S 4th St.
PO Box N
Leoti, KS 67861
Phone: (620)375-2631
Fax: (620)375-2184
**Subject(s):** Paid Community Newspapers
**Circ:** ‡1,650

**News** (11158)
Kiowa News
614 Main St.
Kiowa, KS 67070
Phone: (620)825-4229
Fax: (620)825-4229
**Subject(s):** Paid Community Newspapers
**Circ:** 1,650

**Plainsman-Clarion** (10838)
Louisa Publishing Company Ltd.
PO Box 188
Richland, IA 52585
Phone: (319)456-6641
**Subject(s):** Paid Community Newspapers
**Circ:** ‡1,656

**Wabaunsee County Signal-Enterprise** (10985)
The Signal-Enterprise
PO Box 158
Alma, KS 66401-0158
Phone: (785)765-3327
Fax: (785)765-3384
**Subject(s):** Paid Community Newspapers
**Circ:** (Free)‡50
(Paid)‡1,650

**Bloomfield Monitor** (18297)
110 N Broadway
PO Box 367
Bloomfield, NE 68718
Phone: (402)373-2332
Fax: (402)373-2887
**Subject(s):** Paid Community Newspapers
**Circ:** ‡1,640

**Commonwealth** (17064)
PO Box 277
105 East Main Strret
Ash Grove, MO 65604-0277
Phone: (417)751-2322
Fax: (417)751-2322
**Subject(s):** Paid Community Newspapers
**Circ:** ‡1,645

**The South Missourian News** (18004)
Areawide Media Inc.
101 Chestnut St.
Thayer, MO 65791
Phone: (417)264-3085
Fax: (417)264-3814
**Subject(s):** Paid Community Newspapers
**Circ:** ‡1,632

**Faulk County Record** (28310)
Moritz Publishing Inc.
PO Box 68
Faulkton, SD 57438
Phone: (605)598-6525
Fax: (605)598-4355
**Subject(s):** Paid Community Newspapers
**Circ:** (Free)⊕5
(Paid)⊕**1,620**

**The Register** (18614)
Stanton Printing Co.
907 Ivy St.
PO Box 719
Stanton, NE 68779-0719
Phone: (402)439-2173
Fax: (402)439-2273
**Subject(s):** Paid Community Newspapers
**Circ:** ‡1,624

**Burke Gazette** (28289)
PO Box 359
Burke, SD 57523
Phone: (605)775-2612
Fax: (605)775-2612
**Subject(s):** Paid Community Newspapers
**Circ:** ‡1,613

**The Albany Ledger Headlight** (17061)
The Ledger
Smith & Clay Streets
PO Box 247
Albany, MO 64402
Phone: (660)726-3997
Fax: (660)726-3997
**Subject(s):** Paid Community Newspapers
**Circ:** ‡1,600

**Bowman County Pioneer** (23924)
Country Media Inc.
18 S Main
PO Drawer F
Bowman, ND 58623
Phone: (701)523-5623
Fax: (701)523-3441
**Subject(s):** Paid Community Newspapers
**Circ:** 1,600

**The Columbus Gazette** (10405)
209 Main St.
PO Box 267
Columbus Junction, IA 52738
Phone: (319)728-2413
Fax: (319)728-3272
**Subject(s):** Paid Community Newspapers; Hispanic Publications
**Circ:** ‡1,600

Circulation: ★ = ABC; △ = BPA; ♦ = CAC; • = CCAB; □ = VAC; ⊕ = PO Statement; ‡ = Publisher's Report; Boldface figures = sworn; Light figures = estimated.

**Gleaner** (24048)
Community News
22 N Main
PO Box C
Northwood, ND 58267
Phone: (701)587-6126
Fax: (701)587-5219
**Subject(s):** Paid Community Newspapers
**Circ:** 1,600

**Haskell County Monitor-Chief** (11023)
Golden Plains Publications
PO Box 528
Cimarron, KS 67835
Phone: (620)855-3902
Fax: (620)655-2489
**Subject(s):** Paid Community Newspapers
**Circ:** (Free)‡10
  (Paid)‡1,600

**Kiowa County Signal** (11098)
Tribune Newspaper Co.
120 N Main St.
PO Box 368
Greensburg, KS 67054
Phone: (620)723-2115
**Subject(s):** Paid Community Newspapers
**Circ:** (Free)50
  (Paid)1,600

**Lakota American** (24017)
PO Box 507
Lakota, ND 58344
Phone: (701)247-2482
Fax: (701)247-2482
**Subject(s):** Paid Community Newspapers
**Circ:** 1,600

**Marcus News** (10727)
PO Box 445
Marcus, IA 51035
Phone: (712)376-4712
Fax: (712)376-4605
**Subject(s):** Paid Community Newspapers
**Circ:** 1,600

**Mediapolis News** (10750)
Box 548
616 Main
Mediapolis, IA 52637
Phone: (319)394-3174
Fax: (319)394-3134
**Subject(s):** Paid Community Newspapers
**Circ:** 1,600

**The Seymour Herald** (10851)
116 North 4th St.
Seymour, IA 52590
Phone: (641)898-7554
Fax: (641)898-7554
**Subject(s):** Paid Community Newspapers
**Circ:** 1,600

**Syracuse Journal** (11419)
203 N Main
PO Box 1137
Syracuse, KS 67878-1137
Phone: (620)384-5640
Fax: (620)384-5228
**Subject(s):** Paid Community Newspapers
**Circ:** (Paid)1,600

**The Carlisle Citizen** (10343)
210 South 1st. St
Carlisle, IA 50047
Phone: (515)989-0525
Fax: (515)989-0743
**Subject(s):** Paid Community Newspapers
**Circ:** ‡1,550

**County Courier** (17098)
PO Box 440
206-208 W Main St.
Buffalo, MO 65622
Phone: (417)345-2323
Fax: (417)345-6800
**Subject(s):** Paid Community Newspapers
**Circ:** ‡1,550

**Butler County Tribune Journal** (10283)
The Star Co.
PO Box 8
Allison, IA 50602
Phone: (319)267-2731
Fax: (319)267-2731

**Subject(s):** Paid Community Newspapers
**Circ:** ‡1,545

**Sherman County Times** (18480)
Box 430
Loup City, NE 68853-0430
Phone: (308)745-1260
Fax: (308)745-0541
**Subject(s):** Paid Community Newspapers
**Circ:** ‡1,541

**What Cheer Paper** (10978)
What Cheer
PO Box 414
What Cheer, IA 50268
Phone: (641)634-2092
Fax: (641)634-2122
**Subject(s):** Paid Community Newspapers
**Circ:** ‡1,535

**Elkhart Tri-State News** (11054)
PO Box 777
Elkhart, KS 67950
Phone: (620)697-4716
Fax: (620)697-2411
**Subject(s):** Paid Community Newspapers
**Circ:** (Free)50
  (Paid)1,525

**Ocheyedan Press and Melvin News** (10788)
The Press Inc.
PO Box 456
Ocheyedan, IA 51354
Phone: (712)758-3140
Fax: (712)758-3186
**Subject(s):** Paid Community Newspapers
**Circ:** ‡1,524

**Tripoli Leader** (10927)
Leader
PO Box 39
204 South Main Street
Tripoli, IA 50676
Phone: (319)882-4207
Fax: (319)882-4200
**Subject(s):** Paid Community Newspapers
**Circ:** 1,512

**The Adrian Journal** (17058)
The Adrian Journal Inc.
39 E Main
Box 128
Adrian, MO 64720
Phone: (816)297-2100
Fax: (816)297-2149
**Subject(s):** Paid Community Newspapers
**Circ:** ‡1,500

**Anita Tribune** (10306)
850 Main St.
PO Box 216
Anita, IA 50020-0216
Phone: (712)762-4188
Fax: (712)762-4189
**Subject(s):** Paid Community Newspapers
**Circ:** ‡1,500

**Arlington Sun** (28272)
Community Webb Inc.
PO Box 370
Arlington, SD 57212
Phone: (605)983-5491
Fax: (605)983-5715
**Subject(s):** Paid Community Newspapers
**Circ:** 1,500

**Burke County Tribune** (23923)
Box 40
104 Railway Street SE
Bowbells, ND 58721
Phone: (701)377-2626
Fax: (701)377-2717
**Subject(s):** Paid Community Newspapers
**Circ:** ‡1,500

**The Creighton News** (18325)
New Publishing Co.
816 Main St.
PO Box 55
Creighton, NE 68729
Phone: (402)358-5220
Fax: (402)358-5132
**Subject(s):** Paid Community Newspapers
**Circ:** ‡1,500

**Elsberry Democrat** (17213)
Elsberry News Inc.
PO Box 105
Elsberry, MO 63343
Phone: (573)898-9814
Fax: (573)898-2173
**Subject(s):** Paid Community Newspapers
**Circ:** 1,500

**Greeley County Republican** (11453)
507 Broadway
Box 610
Tribune, KS 67879
Phone: (620)376-4264
Fax: (620)376-2433
**Subject(s):** Paid Community Newspapers
**Circ:** (Free)16
  (Paid)1,500

**Mid Iowa Enterprise** (10897)
Mid-Iowa Publishing Co.
130 W Main
PO Box 634
State Center, IA 50247
Phone: (641)483-2120
Fax: (641)483-2938
**Subject(s):** Paid Community Newspapers
**Circ:** ‡1,500

**The Midland** (18344)
Midland Lutheran College
Journalism Dept.
900 N Clarkson
Fremont, NE 68025
Phone: (402)721-5480
Fax: (402)721-0250
**Subject(s):** College Publications
**Circ:** (Free)‡1,500

**Morgan County Press** (17998)
Vernon Publishing Inc.
PO Box 130
Stover, MO 65078
Phone: (573)377-4616
Fax: (573)377-4512
**Subject(s):** Paid Community Newspapers
**Circ:** ‡1,500

**New Salem Journal** (24047)
PO Box 416
New Salem, ND 58563-0416
Phone: (701)843-7567
Fax: (701)843-7623
**Subject(s):** Paid Community Newspapers
**Circ:** ‡1,500

**North Bend Eagle** (18504)
PO Box 100
721 Main St.
North Bend, NE 68649
Phone: (402)652-8312
Fax: (402)652-8312
**Subject(s):** Paid Community Newspapers
**Circ:** ‡1,500

**Oakes Times** (23905)
Olson Press
2900 E Broadway
PO Box 1697
Bismarck, ND 58506-1697
Phone: (701)258-4970
Fax: (701)258-4258
**Subject(s):** Paid Community Newspapers
**Circ:** (Paid)1,500

**The Oakley Graphic** (11278)
118 Center St.
Oakley, KS 67748-0545
Phone: (785)672-3228
Fax: (785)672-3229
**Subject(s):** Paid Community Newspapers
**Circ:** (Free)‡30
  (Paid)‡1,500

**The Pender Times** (18577)
313 Main St.
PO Box 280
Pender, NE 68047
Phone: (402)385-3013
Fax: (402)385-3013
**Subject(s):** Paid Community Newspapers
**Circ:** ‡1,500

**Progress Review** (10699)
313 Main St.
La Porte City, IA 50651
Phone: (319)342-2429
Fax: (319)342-2433
**Subject(s):** Paid Community Newspapers
**Circ:** (Paid)1,400
1,500

**Steele County Press** (23978)
Steele County Press Inc.
215 4th St. W
PO Box 475
Finley, ND 58230
Phone: (701)524-1640
**Subject(s):** Paid Community Newspapers
**Circ:** ‡1,500

**Timber Lake Topic** (28442)
Timber Lake
PO Box 10
Timber Lake, SD 57656-0010
Phone: (605)865-3546
Fax: (605)865-3787
**Subject(s):** Paid Community Newspapers
**Circ:** 1,500

**Today** (28435)
Black Hills State University
PO Box 9003
1200 University
Spearfish, SD 57799-9003
Phone: (605)642-6011
Fax: (605)642-6762
**Subject(s):** College Publications
**Circ:** ‡1,500

**Tribune** (10334)
124 N Main St.
Box 367
Buffalo Center, IA 50424
Phone: (515)562-2606
Fax: (515)562-2636
**Subject(s):** Paid Community Newspapers
**Circ:** (Paid)‡1,500

**Tyndall Tribune & Register** (28443)
P. B & H Publishing Inc.
1614 Main St.
Tyndall, SD 57066
Phone: (605)589-3242
Fax: (605)589-3448
**Subject(s):** Paid Community Newspapers
**Circ:** 1,500

**Vantage** (11491)
Kansas Newman College
3100 McCormick St.
Wichita, KS 67213
Phone: (316)942-4291
Fax: (316)942-4483
**Subject(s):** College Publications
**Circ:** (Paid)20
(Free)‡1,500

**Verdigre Eagle** (18629)
202 Main St.
PO Box 309
Verdigre, NE 68783
Phone: (402)668-2242
Fax: (402)668-2242
**Subject(s):** Paid Community Newspapers
**Circ:** ‡1,500

**Wessington Springs True Dakotan** (28465)
113 E Main St.
PO Box T
Wessington Springs, SD 57382
Phone: (605)539-1281
Fax: (605)539-9315
**Subject(s):** Free Newspapers
**Circ:** (Free)50
(Paid)1,500

**Western Concept** (23938)
Dickinson State College
291 Campus Dr.
Dickinson, ND 58601
Phone: (701)483-2507
**Subject(s):** College Publications
**Circ:** ‡1,500

**The Caldwell Messenger** (11014)
PO Box 313
111 South Main
Caldwell, KS 67022
Phone: (620)845-2320
Fax: (620)845-6461
**Subject(s):** Paid Community Newspapers
**Circ:** (Free)‡30
(Paid)‡1,498

**The Monitor Review** (10896)
PO Box 276
117 South Broad Street
Stacyville, IA 50476
Phone: (641)710-2119
Fax: (641)710-3119
**Subject(s):** Paid Community Newspapers
**Circ:** ‡1,475

**Moville Record** (10768)
PO Box 546
Moville, IA 51039
Phone: (712)873-3141
Fax: (712)873-3142
**Subject(s):** Paid Community Newspapers
**Circ:** ‡1,475

**Akron Register-Tribune** (10273)
Good News Inc.
131 Reed St
PO Box 407
Akron, IA 51001
Phone: (712)568-2551
Fax: (712)568-3171
**Subject(s):** Paid Community Newspapers
**Circ:** (Paid)1,400
(Free)1,450

**The Highmore Herald** (28321)
PO Box 435
Highmore, SD 57345
Phone: (605)852-2927
Fax: (605)852-2927
**Subject(s):** Paid Community Newspapers
**Circ:** ‡1,450

**The Northwest-Blade** (28309)
PO Box 797
Eureka, SD 57437
Phone: (605)284-2631
Fax: (605)284-2632
**Subject(s):** Paid Community Newspapers
**Circ:** ‡1,456

**West Branch Times** (10967)
PO Box 368
West Branch, IA 52358
Phone: (319)643-2131
Fax: (319)643-5853
**Subject(s):** Paid Community Newspapers
**Circ:** ‡1,450

**The Wishek Star** (24087)
Redhead Publishing
511 Beaver Ave.
PO Box 275
Wishek, ND 58495
Phone: (701)452-2331
Fax: (701)452-2340
**Subject(s):** Paid Community Newspapers
**Circ:** ‡1,450

**Blue Hill Leader** (18298)
514 Gage St.
Box 38
Blue Hill, NE 68930
Phone: (402)756-2077
Fax: (402)756-2097
**Subject(s):** Paid Community Newspapers
**Circ:** ‡1,440

**North Warren Town and County News** (10786)
North Warren Town and Country News
PO Box 325
Norwalk, IA 50211
Phone: (515)981-0406
**Subject(s):** Paid Community Newspapers
**Circ:** (Combined)1,445

**Hartley Sentinel** (10625)
Hartley Sentinel Inc.
71 1st St. SE
Hartley, IA 51346
Phone: (712)928-2223
Fax: (712)928-2223

**Subject(s):** Paid Community Newspapers
**Circ:** (Free)45
(Paid)1,433

**Times Observer** (17459)
119 W Nodaway
PO Box 317
Oregon, MO 64473-0317
Phone: (660)446-3331
Fax: (660)446-3409
**Subject(s):** Paid Community Newspapers
**Circ:** ‡1,438

**The Adair News** (10270)
403 Audubon St.
PO Box 8
Adair, IA 50002-0008
Phone: (641)742-3241
Fax: (641)742-3489
**Subject(s):** Paid Community Newspapers
**Circ:** (Paid)‡1,427

**Steele Ozone-Press** (24058)
Steele Ozone-Press Inc.
PO Box 350
Steele, ND 58482-0350
Phone: (701)475-2513
**Subject(s):** Paid Community Newspapers
**Circ:** 1,425

**Courier-Times** (18621)
PO Box 367
Sutherland, NE 69165
Phone: (308)386-4617
Fax: (308)386-2437
**Subject(s):** Paid Community Newspapers
**Circ:** ‡1,400

**The De Smet News** (28298)
Blegen Publishing Inc.
220 Calumet Ave.
De Smet, SD 57231
Phone: (605)854-3331
Fax: (605)854-9977
**Subject(s):** Paid Community Newspapers
**Circ:** ‡1,405

**The Dunlap Reporter** (10542)
Dunlap Reporter
114 Iowa Avenue
Dunlap, IA 51529
Phone: (712)643-5380
Fax: (712)643-2173
**Subject(s):** Paid Community Newspapers
**Circ:** ‡1,400

**Dunn County Herald** (24014)
PO Box 609
26 Central Ave.
Killdeer, ND 58640-0609
Phone: (701)764-5312
Fax: (701)764-5049
**Subject(s):** Paid Community Newspapers
**Circ:** 1,400

**The Ellinwood Leader** (11056)
The Leader
PO Box 487
Ellinwood, KS 67526
Phone: (620)564-3116
Fax: (620)564-2550
**Subject(s):** Paid Community Newspapers
**Circ:** ‡1,400

**The Gowrie News** (10604)
Gowrie News
Po Box 473
Gowrie, IA 50543
Phone: (515)352-3325
Fax: (515)352-3309
**Subject(s):** Paid Community Newspapers; Farm Newspapers
**Circ:** ‡1,400

**Guthrie County Vedette** (10814)
111 E Main St.
PO Box 38
Panora, IA 50216
Phone: (641)755-2115
Fax: (641)755-2425
**Subject(s):** Paid Community Newspapers
**Circ:** 1,400

## Great Plains States

**Journal Herald (10825)**
Dudley Printing
104 S 1st St.
Pomeroy, IA 50575
Phone: (712)468-2266
**Subject(s):** Paid Community Newspapers
**Circ:** 1,400

**The Lance (17965)**
Evangel University
1111 N Glenstone Ave.
PO Box 728
Springfield, MO 65802-2191
Phone: (417)865-2815
Fax: (417)865-9599
**Subject(s):** College Publications
**Circ:** (Free)‡1,400

**Madrid Register-News (10714)**
Medrid Register
102 S Main
P O Box 177
Madrid, IA 50156-0177
Phone: (515)795-2730
Fax: (515)795-2012
**Subject(s):** Paid Community Newspapers
**Circ:** 1,400

**Omnibus (17082)**
Southwest Baptist University
1600 University Ave.
Bolivar, MO 65613
Phone: (417)328-1833
Fax: (417)328-1579
**Subject(s):** College Publications
**Circ:** (Free)‡1,400

**The Sarcoxie Record (17940)**
Sarcoxie Publishing Co.
101 N 6th
Box 400
Sarcoxie, MO 64862
Phone: (417)548-3311
Fax: (417)548-3312
**Subject(s):** Paid Community Newspapers
**Circ:** ‡1,400

**The Simpsonian (10638)**
Simpson College
8 McNeil Hall
Simpson College
Indianola, IA 50125
Phone: (515)961-1498
Fax: (515)961-1498
**Subject(s):** College Publications
**Circ:** ‡1,400

**Star-Mail (18481)**
PO Box 487
Madison, NE 68748-0487
Phone: (402)454-3818
Fax: (402)454-3818
**Subject(s):** Paid Community Newspapers
**Circ:** ‡1,400

**Walhalla Mountaineer (24073)**
PO Box 497
1001 Central Ave.
Walhalla, ND 58282
Phone: (701)549-2580
**Subject(s):** Paid Community Newspapers
**Circ:** 1,400

**Woonsocket News (28471)**
PO Box 218
Woonsocket, SD 57385-0218
Phone: (605)796-4221
Fax: (605)796-4221
**Subject(s):** Paid Community Newspapers
**Circ:** ‡1,370

**Corsica Globe (28292)**
Douglas County Publishing
PO Box 45
215 Main St.
Corsica, SD 57328
Phone: (605)946-5489
Fax: (605)946-5179
**Subject(s):** Free Newspapers
**Circ:** (Free)‡15
(Paid)‡1,365

**The Humboldt Standard (18382)**
PO Box 627
Humboldt, NE 68376-0627
Phone: (402)862-2200
Fax: (402)862-2209
**Subject(s):** Paid Community Newspapers
**Circ:** ‡1,363

**South Hardin Signal-Review (10828)**
Box 457
302 Eizabella
Radcliffe, IA 50230
Phone: (641)864-2288
Fax: (641)864-2288
**Subject(s):** Paid Community Newspapers
**Circ:** (Free)‡31
(Paid)‡1,361

**Galena Sentinel-Times (11078)**
Galena Times
511 Main St.
Galena, KS 66739
Phone: (620)783-5034
Fax: (620)783-1388
**Subject(s):** Paid Community Newspapers
**Circ:** 1,350

**The Keota Eagle (10694)**
Box 18
Keota, IA 52248
Phone: (641)636-2309
Fax: (641)636-2309
**Subject(s):** Paid Community Newspapers
**Circ:** ‡1,350

**La Moure Chronicle (24016)**
Box 196
La Moure, ND 58458
Phone: (701)883-5393
Fax: (701)883-5076
**Subject(s):** Paid Community Newspapers
**Circ:** 1,350

**The Laurens Sun (10706)**
119 S 3rd St.
PO Box 125
Laurens, IA 50554-0125
Phone: (712)841-4541
Fax: (712)841-4542
**Subject(s):** Paid Community Newspapers
**Circ:** ‡1,350

**Norborne Democrat-Leader (17456)**
106 S Pine St.
Box 195
Norborne, MO 64668-0195
Phone: (660)593-3712
Fax: (660)593-3712
**Subject(s):** Paid Community Newspapers
**Circ:** ‡1,350

**Riceville Recorder (10837)**
Lock Box A
Riceville, IA 50466
Phone: (641)985-2142
Fax: (641)985-4185
**Subject(s):** Paid Community Newspapers
**Circ:** ‡1,350

**St. John News (11394)**
The Pratt Tribune
PO Box 488
Saint John, KS 67576
Phone: (316)549-3201
**Subject(s):** Paid Community Newspapers
**Circ:** ‡1,350

**The Stuart Herald (10909)**
Box 608
Stuart, IA 50250
Phone: (515)523-1010
Fax: (515)523-2825
**Subject(s):** Paid Community Newspapers
**Circ:** (Free)‡50
(Paid)‡1,350

**Western Times (11408)**
J & D Publishing Inc.
126 Main
PO Box 279
Sharon Springs, KS 67758
Phone: (785)852-4900
Fax: (785)852-4804

**Subject(s):** Paid Community Newspapers
**Circ:** ‡1,353

**Clark County Clipper (10990)**
Box 457
705 Main Street
Ashland, KS 67831-0457
Phone: (620)635-2312
Fax: (620)635-2643
**Subject(s):** Paid Community Newspapers
**Circ:** 1,345

**The Elsberry (17212)**
Lakeway Publishing of Missouri
106 A. North 3rd
PO Box 105
Elsberry, MO 63343
Phone: (573)898-2318
Fax: (573)898-2173
**Subject(s):** Paid Community Newspapers
**Circ:** 1,337

**Golden Valley News (23891)**
Olson Press
97 E. Main
Box 156
Beach, ND 58621
Phone: (701)872-3755
Fax: (701)872-3756
**Subject(s):** Paid Community Newspapers
**Circ:** (Free)‡45
(Paid)‡1,317

**The Bayard Transcript (18274)**
336 Main
PO Box 626
Bayard, NE 69334
Phone: (308)586-1313
Fax: (308)586-2312
**Subject(s):** Paid Community Newspapers
**Circ:** ‡1,300

**Braymer Bee (17095)**
L & L Publications Inc.
PO Box 308
Braymer, MO 64624
Phone: (816)645-2217
Fax: (816)645-2217
**Subject(s):** Paid Community Newspapers
**Circ:** 1,300

**The Crawford Clipper/Harrison Sun (18323)**
435 2nd St.
Crawford, NE 69339
Phone: (308)665-2310
Fax: (308)665-2310
**Subject(s):** Paid Community Newspapers
**Circ:** (Non-paid)‡100
(Paid)‡1,300

**The Dighton Herald (11044)**
113 E Long
PO Box 637
Dighton, KS 67839-0637
Phone: (620)397-5347
Fax: (620)397-2618
**Subject(s):** Paid Community Newspapers
**Circ:** 1,303

**Hudson Herald (10629)**
Box 210
Hudson, IA 50643-0210
Phone: (319)988-3855
Fax: (319)988-3855
**Subject(s):** Paid Community Newspapers
**Circ:** ‡1,300

**Marion County News (10344)**
Photo Printing
210 S 1st St.
Carlisle, IA 50047
Phone: (515)989-3251
Fax: (515)989-0743
**Subject(s):** Paid Community Newspapers
**Circ:** 1,300

**Nebraska Journal-Leader (18583)**
110 E St.
PO Box 545
Ponca, NE 68770-0545
Phone: (402)755-2203
Fax: (402)755-2205
**Subject(s):** Paid Community Newspapers
**Circ:** 1,300

**Gale Directory of Publications & Broadcast Media/140th Ed.**  **Great Plains States**

**New Haven Leader** (17452)
Spirit Newspapers of Missouri Inc.
403 Charles Cook Plz.
PO Box 168
New Haven, MO 63068
Phone: (573)237-3222
Fax: (573)237-7222
**Subject(s):** Paid Community Newspapers
**Circ:** ‡1,300

**Ralls County Herald-Enterprise** (17453)
PO Box 426
608 S Main St.
New London, MO 63459
Phone: (573)985-5531
Fax: (573)985-5531
**Subject(s):** Paid Community Newspapers
**Circ:** ‡1,300

**St. Louis Countian** (17811)
Legal Communications Corp.
612 N 2nd St., 4th Fl.
PO Box 88910
Saint Louis, MO 63102
Phone: (314)421-1880
Fax: (314)421-0436
**Subject(s):** Daily Periodicals; Business; Local, State, and Regional Publications
**Circ:** 1,300

**Tilden Citizen** (18627)
PO Box 280
202 E.Second St.
Tilden, NE 68781
Phone: (402)368-5315
Fax: (402)368-5315
**Subject(s):** Paid Community Newspapers
**Circ:** 1,300

**Wellman Advance** (10966)
Louisa Publishing Company Ltd.
PO Box 1
Wellman, IA 52356
Phone: (319)646-2712
Fax: (319)646-5904
**Subject(s):** Paid Community Newspapers
**Circ:** 1,300

**The Polk County News** (18618)
P O Box 365
205 East 4th Street
Stromsburg, NE 68666-0365
Phone: (402)764-5341
Fax: (402)764-5341
**Subject(s):** Paid Community Newspapers
**Circ:** ‡1,281

**The Rosholt Review** (28402)
P.O. Box 136
Rosholt, SD 57260-0136
Phone: (605)537-4276
Fax: (605)537-4858
**Subject(s):** Paid Community Newspapers
**Circ:** (Free)‡32
(Paid)‡1,280

**Benkelman Post and News-Chronicle** (18288)
513 Chief St.
PO Box 800
Benkelman, NE 69021-0800
Phone: (308)423-2337
Fax: (308)423-5555
**Subject(s):** Paid Community Newspapers
**Circ:** (Non-paid)‡30
(Paid)‡1,276

**Delta News-Journal** (17404)
Delta Publishing
127 W Main
PO Box 701
Malden, MO 63863
Phone: (573)276-5148
Fax: (573)276-3687
**Subject(s):** Paid Community Newspapers
**Circ:** ‡1,262

**Arapahoe Public Mirror** (18262)
420 Nebraska Ave.
PO Box 660
Arapahoe, NE 68922-0348
Phone: (308)962-7261
Fax: (308)962-7865
**Subject(s):** Paid Community Newspapers
**Circ:** 1,250

**Clarence-Lowden Sun News** (10922)
Conservative Publishing Co.
Box 271
Tipton, IA 52772
Phone: (563)886-2131
Fax: (563)886-6466
**Subject(s):** Paid Community Newspapers
**Circ:** ‡1,250

**Downs News and Times** (11052)
717 E Railroad St.
Downs, KS 67437
Phone: (785)781-4831
Fax: (785)454-3866
**Subject(s):** Paid Community Newspapers
**Circ:** (Paid)‡1,250

**Howells Journal** (18381)
MEC Publishing Inc.
Box 335
137 South 3rd St.
Howells, NE 68641
Phone: (402)986-1777
**Subject(s):** Paid Community Newspapers
**Circ:** ‡1,250

**The Record** (10406)
PO Box 190
Conrad, IA 50621
Phone: (641)366-2020
Fax: (641)366-2020
**Subject(s):** Paid Community Newspapers
**Circ:** ‡1,250

**The Western Star** (11032)
113 S Central
PO Box 518
Coldwater, KS 67029
Phone: (620)582-2101
**Subject(s):** Paid Community Newspapers
**Circ:** ‡1,250

**Selby Record** (28404)
4411 Main St.
PO Box 421
Selby, SD 57472
Phone: (605)649-7866
Fax: (605)649-7054
**Subject(s):** Paid Community Newspapers
**Circ:** (Free)24
(Paid)1,243

**Hebron Herald** (24002)
102 S. Park Ave.
Hebron, ND 58638
Phone: (701)878-4494
Fax: (701)878-4494
**Subject(s):** Paid Community Newspapers
**Circ:** (Free)‡65
(Paid)‡1,225

**The Ledger** (18376)
714 Box Butte Ave.
Hemingford, NE 69348
Phone: (308)487-3334
Fax: (308)487-3347
**Subject(s):** Paid Community Newspapers
**Circ:** (Free)‡31
(Paid)‡1,214

**Bulletin** (24025)
PO Box 46
Litchville, ND 58461-0046
Phone: (701)762-4267
Fax: (701)762-4267
**Subject(s):** Paid Community Newspapers
**Circ:** ‡1,200

**Cawker City Ledger** (11017)
PO Box 7
Cawker City, KS 67430
Phone: (785)454-3866
Fax: (785)781-4831
**Subject(s):** Paid Community Newspapers
**Circ:** ‡1,200

**The Chappell Register** (18312)
273 Vincent Ave.
PO Box 528
Chappell, NE 69129
Phone: (308)874-2207
Fax: (308)874-2207
**Subject(s):** Paid Community Newspapers
**Circ:** ‡1,200

**Clarksville Star** (10396)
The Star Co.
PO Box 788
Clarksville, IA 50619
Phone: (319)278-4641
**Subject(s):** Paid Community Newspapers
**Circ:** 1,200

**Crofton Journal** (18329)
Kevin Hensleler
108 W Main.
PO Box 339
Crofton, NE 68730-0339
Phone: (402)388-4355
Fax: (402)388-4336
**Subject(s):** Paid Community Newspapers
**Circ:** ‡1,200

**Hutchinson Collegian** (11120)
Hutchinson Community College
1300 N Plum
Hutchinson, KS 67501
Phone: (620)665-3500
Fax: (620)665-3310
**Subject(s):** College Publications
**Circ:** (Free)‡1,200

**Knob Noster Item** (17380)
111 N Jackson
P O Box 188
Knob Noster, MO 65336-0188
Phone: (660)563-3606
**Subject(s):** Paid Community Newspapers
**Circ:** ‡1,200

**The Leader** (10715)
The Malvern Leader
PO Box 129
Malvern, IA 51551
Phone: (712)624-8512
Fax: (712)624-9041
**Subject(s):** Paid Community Newspapers
**Circ:** (Free)‡50
(Paid)‡1,200

**The Manilla Times** (10718)
Manilla Printing Co.
Box 365
Manilla, IA 51454
Phone: (712)654-2911
Fax: (712)654-2910
**Subject(s):** Paid Community Newspapers
**Circ:** ‡1,200

**The Onida Watchman** (28358)
116 S Main
PO Box 245
Onida, SD 57564
Phone: (605)258-2604
Fax: (605)258-2572
**Subject(s):** Paid Community Newspapers
**Circ:** 1,200

**The Press** (10988)
Cowley County Community College
125 S. 2nd St.
Arkansas City, KS 67005
Phone: (620)441-5287
**Subject(s):** College Publications
**Circ:** (Free)1,200
(Free)‡1,200

**Remsen Bell-Enterprise** (10836)
Box 10
246 S. Washington St.
Remsen, IA 51050
Phone: (712)786-1196
Fax: (712)786-1257
**Subject(s):** Paid Community Newspapers
**Circ:** ‡1,200

**The Riley Countian** (11386)
Countian
PO Box 333
Riley, KS 66531
Phone: (785)485-2290
**Subject(s):** Paid Community Newspapers
**Circ:** 1,200

**The Sidney Argus-Herald** (10863)
PO Box 190
Sidney, IA 51652
Phone: (712)374-2251

Circulation: ★ = ABC; △ = BPA; ♦ = CAC; • = CCAB; □ = VAC; ⊕ = PO Statement; ‡ = Publisher's Report; Boldface figures = sworn; Light figures = estimated.

3675

**Subject(s):** Paid Community Newspapers
**Circ:** (Paid)‡1,200

**Sterling Bulletin (11417)**
PO Box 97
Sterling, KS 67579
Phone: (620)278-2114
Fax: (620)278-2330
**Subject(s):** Paid Community Newspapers
**Circ:** (Paid)1,200

**The Tack (10900)**
Buena Vista University
610 W Fourth St.
Storm Lake, IA 50588
Phone: (712)749-2120
Fax: (712)749-2037
**Subject(s):** College Publications
**Circ:** (Non-paid)1,200

**The Wood River Sunbeam (18643)**
PO Box 356
Wood River, NE 68883-0356
Phone: (308)583-2241
Fax: (308)583-2543
**Subject(s):** Paid Community Newspapers
**Circ:** 1,200

**Citizen Herald (10684)**
Horizon Publishing Co.
930 6th St.
Po Box 545
Jesup, IA 50648-0545
Phone: (319)827-1128
Fax: (319)827-1125
**Subject(s):** Paid Community Newspapers
**Circ:** (Paid)‡1,192

**Afton Star-Enterprise (10272)**
Box 128
Afton, IA 50830
Phone: (641)347-8721
**Subject(s):** Paid Community Newspapers
**Circ:** ‡1185

**The Erie Record (11067)**
317 S Main
PO Box 159
Erie, KS 66733
Phone: (620)244-3371
Fax: (620)244-3371
**Subject(s):** Paid Community Newspapers
**Circ:** ‡1,189

**Schleswig Leader (10723)**
Lyon Publishing Inc.
PO Box 187
Mapleton, IA 51034-0187
Phone: (712)881-1101
Fax: (712)881-1330
**Subject(s):** Paid Community Newspapers
**Circ:** 1,175

**The Weekly Record (17454)**
218 Main St.
New Madrid, MO 63869-1997
Phone: (573)748-2120
Fax: (573)748-5435
**Subject(s):** Paid Community Newspapers
**Circ:** ‡1150

**Milford Mail and Terril Record (10892)**
Spirit Lake Publishing Co.
P.O. Box AE
Spirit Lake, IA 51360
Phone: (712)338-4712
**Subject(s):** Paid Community Newspapers
**Circ:** (Free)25
(Paid)1,148

**Butte County Valley Irrigator (28357)**
Country Media
PO Box 167
Newell, SD 57760
Phone: (605)456-2587
Fax: (605)456-2587
**Subject(s):** Paid Community Newspapers
**Circ:** (Paid)‡1,135

**The Gibbon Reporter (18351)**
PO Box 820
817 B Front Street
Gibbon, NE 68840-0820
Phone: (308)468-5393

Fax: (308)468-5222
**Subject(s):** Paid Community Newspapers
**Circ:** (Free)‡13
(Paid)‡1,121

**Times (28332)**
PO Box 368
Lake Preston, SD 57249
Phone: (605)847-4421
Fax: (605)847-4421
**Subject(s):** Paid Community Newspapers
**Circ:** (Non-paid)‡35
(Controlled)‡1,122

**The Wakefield Republican (18631)**
PO Box 110
Wakefield, NE 68784-0110
Phone: (402)287-2323
**Subject(s):** Paid Community Newspapers
**Circ:** ‡1,121

**Wauneta Breeze (18384)**
Johnson Publications Inc.
PO Box 727
Imperial, NE 69033
Phone: (308)882-4453
Fax: (308)882-5167
**Subject(s):** Paid Community Newspapers
**Circ:** ‡1,123

**The Jetmore Republican (11134)**
PO Box 337
Jetmore, KS 67854
Phone: (620)357-8316
Fax: (620)357-8464
**Subject(s):** Paid Community Newspapers
**Circ:** (Free)‡20
(Paid)‡1,110

**The Observer (10977)**
Kock Publishing Inc.
PO Box 156
Westside, IA 51467-0156
Phone: (712)663-4362
Fax: (712)663-4363
**Subject(s):** Paid Community Newspapers
**Circ:** ‡1,114

**Bucklin Banner (11022)**
Golden Plains Publications
PO Box 528
Cimarron, KS 67835
Phone: (620)855-3902
Fax: (620)655-2489
**Subject(s):** Paid Community Newspapers
**Circ:** 1,100

**The Cornellian (10763)**
Cornell College
810 Commons Cir.
Mount Vernon, IA 52314
Phone: (319)895-4499
Fax: (319)895-5264
**Subject(s):** College Publications
**Circ:** (Paid)200
(Free)1,100

**Diamond (10865)**
Dordt College
DC116
Sioux Center, IA 51250
Phone: (712)722-6431
**Subject(s):** College Publications
**Circ:** ‡1,100

**Doane Owl (18328)**
Doane College
1014 Boswell Ave.
Crete, NE 68333
Phone: (402)826-6731
Fax: (402)826-8278
**Subject(s):** College Publications
**Circ:** (Paid)1,100

**Fontanelle Observer (10569)**
PO Box 248
313 5th Street
Fontanelle, IA 50846-0248
Phone: (641)745-3161
Fax: (641)745-1201
**Subject(s):** Paid Community Newspapers
**Circ:** ‡1,100

**Hill City Prevailer-News (28294)**
Southern Hills Publishing Inc.
PO Box 551
Custer, SD 57730
Phone: (605)673-2217
Fax: (605)574-3321
**Subject(s):** Paid Community Newspapers
**Circ:** ‡1,100

**The Johnson Pioneer (11135)**
103 N Main
PO Box 10
Johnson, KS 67855
Phone: (620)492-6244
Fax: (620)492-6245
**Subject(s):** Paid Community Newspapers
**Circ:** ‡1,100

**Lone Tree Reporter (10713)**
PO Box 13
Lone Tree, IA 52755-0013
Phone: (319)629-5207
Fax: (319)629-4203
**Subject(s):** Paid Community Newspapers
**Circ:** ‡1,100

**Montezuma Press (11259)**
Jean Loewen
208 Aztec
PO Box 188
Montezuma, KS 67867
Phone: (316)846-2312
Fax: (316)846-2312
**Subject(s):** Paid Community Newspapers
**Circ:** 1,100

**Nashua Reporter and Weekly Post (10774)**
216 Main St.
PO Box 67
Nashua, IA 50658
Phone: (641)435-4151
**Subject(s):** Paid Community Newspapers
**Circ:** (Free)‡20
(Paid)‡1,100

**Onaga Herald (11283)**
PO Box 309
Onaga, KS 66521
Phone: (785)889-4681
Fax: (785)889-4610
**Subject(s):** Paid Community Newspapers
**Circ:** ‡1,100

**The Record (11149)**
The Record Publications
3414 Strong Ave.
Kansas City, KS 66106
Phone: (913)362-1988
Fax: (913)362-8406
**Subject(s):** Paid Community Newspapers
**Circ:** ‡1,100

**Scranton Journal (10320)**
Central Iowa Publishing Inc.
PO Box 130
Bayard, IA 50029
Phone: (712)651-2321
Fax: (712)651-2599
**Subject(s):** Paid Community Newspapers
**Circ:** ‡1,100

**Jewell County Record (11241)**
Superior Publishing Company Inc.
111 E Main
PO Box 305
Mankato, KS 66956
Phone: (785)378-3191
Fax: (785)378-5437
**Subject(s):** Paid Community Newspapers
**Circ:** (Free)‡50
(Paid)‡1,095

**Kadoka Press (28330)**
Ravellette Publications Inc.
PO Box 309
1915 Main Street
Kadoka, SD 57543-0309
Phone: (605)837-2259
Fax: (605)837-2312
**Subject(s):** Paid Community Newspapers
**Circ:** 1,091

**Gale Directory of Publications & Broadcast Media/140th Ed.**  **Great Plains States**

**The New London Journal (10778)**
Louisa Publishing Company Ltd.
138 W. Main
New London, IA 52645
Phone: (319)367-2366
**Subject(s):** Paid Community Newspapers

Circ: 1,092

**The Spencer Advocate (18612)**
100 S Thayer
Box 187
Spencer, NE 68777
Phone: (402)589-1010
Fax: (402)589-1010
**Subject(s):** Paid Community Newspapers

Circ: 1,082

**Buena Vista County Journal (10780)**
PO Box 666
Newell, IA 50568
Phone: (712)272-4417
Fax: (712)272-4417
**Subject(s):** Paid Community Newspapers

Circ: (Free)‡63
 (Paid)‡1,071

**The Times (28370)**
Hipple Publishing Company Inc.
333 W Dakota
PO Box 669
Pierre, SD 57501-0669
Phone: (605)224-7301
Fax: (605)224-9210
**Subject(s):** Paid Community Newspapers

Circ: (Non-paid)‡27
 (Paid)‡1069

**The Collegian (18365)**
Hastings College
710 Turner
Hastings, NE 68901-7621
Phone: (402)461-7399
Fax: (402)461-7442
**Subject(s):** College Publications

Circ: (Free)‡98
 (Paid)‡1,050

**Dodge Criterion (18333)**
140 Oak St.
PO Box 68
Dodge, NE 68633-0068
Phone: (402)693-2415
Fax: (402)693-2415
**Subject(s):** Paid Community Newspapers

Circ: ‡1,051

**The Ellis Review (11057)**
Box 227
1018 Washington
Ellis, KS 67637
Phone: (785)726-4583
Fax: (785)726-3821
**Subject(s):** Paid Community Newspapers

Circ: (Free)33
 (Paid)1,054

**Glidden Graphic (10601)**
PO Box 607
Glidden, IA 51443
Phone: (712)659-3144
Fax: (712)659-3143
**Subject(s):** Paid Community Newspapers

Circ: 1,054

**O'Brien County Bell (10827)**
O'Bren County Bell
Box 478
Primghar, IA 51245
Phone: (712)957-4055
Fax: (712)957-4055
**Subject(s):** Paid Community Newspapers

Circ: ‡1,042

**Leigh World (18397)**
PO Box 266
Clarkson, NE 68629
Phone: (402)892-2544
**Subject(s):** Paid Community Newspapers

Circ: ‡1,027

**The Marion Record (28339)**
P O Box 298
305 North Broadway Ave.
Marion, SD 57043
Phone: (605)648-3821

Fax: (605)648-3920
**Subject(s):** Paid Community Newspapers

Circ: ‡1025

**The Wausa Gazette (18632)**
PO Box G
Wausa, NE 68786-0318
Phone: (402)586-2661
**Subject(s):** Paid Community Newspapers

Circ: ‡1,025

**The Polk County News (18570)**
J & B Thompson
PO Box 258
Osceola, NE 68651
Phone: (402)747-2431
Fax: (402)764-5341
**Subject(s):** Paid Community Newspapers

Circ: ‡1,015

**Arnold Sentinel (18615)**
Creative Printers Inc.
238 Main St.
Stapleton, NE 69163
Phone: (308)636-2444
Fax: (308)636-2445
**Subject(s):** Paid Community Newspapers

Circ: ‡1,000

**Carson Press (23947)**
Grant County News
Box 100
Elgin, ND 58533-0100
Phone: (701)584-2900
**Subject(s):** Paid Community Newspapers

Circ: ‡1,000

**Clarke Courier (10529)**
Clarke College
1550 Clarke Dr.
Atten: Dianne Russo
Dubuque, IA 52001-3198
Phone: (563)588-6306
Fax: (563)588-6789
**Subject(s):** College Publications

Circ: (Free)1,000

**Clyde Republican (11025)**
305 Washington
PO Box 397
Clyde, KS 66938-0397
**Subject(s):** Paid Community Newspapers

Circ: ‡1,000

**Coleridge Blade (18313)**
PO Box 8
107 W. Broadway
Coleridge, NE 68727
Phone: (402)283-4267
Fax: (402)283-4267
**Subject(s):** Paid Community Newspapers

Circ: 1,000

**Collegian Reporter (10872)**
Morningside College
1501 Morningside Ave.
Sioux City, IA 51106
Phone: (712)274-5000
Fax: (712)274-5100
**Subject(s):** College Publications

Circ: (Free)‡1,000

**The Danish Villages Voice (10554)**
PO Box 469
Elk Horn, IA 51531-0469
Phone: (712)764-4800
Fax: (712)764-4801
**Subject(s):** Paid Community Newspapers

Circ: 1,000

**The Edgeley Mail (23946)**
PO Box 278
516 Main Street
Edgeley, ND 58433
Phone: (701)493-2261
Fax: (701)493-2261
**Subject(s):** Paid Community Newspapers

Circ: (Free)‡45
 (Paid)‡1,000

**Enderlin Independent (23950)**
209 4th Ave.
Enderlin, ND 58027
Phone: (701)437-3131
Fax: (701)437-3131

**Subject(s):** Paid Community Newspapers; Farm Newspapers

Circ: ‡1,000

**The Gallery (10400)**
Clinton Community College
1000 Lincoln Blvd.
Clinton, IA 52732
Phone: (563)244-7046
Fax: (563)244-7107
**Subject(s):** College Publications

Circ: (Paid)‡1,000
 (Controlled)‡1,000

**Garretson Weekly (28314)**
512 Main Ave.
PO Box 310
Garretson, SD 57030-0310
Phone: (605)594-6315
Fax: (605)594-3442
**Subject(s):** Paid Community Newspapers

Circ: ‡1,000

**Hamlin County Herald-Enterprise (28320)**
Hamlin County
Box 207
Hayti, SD 57241
Phone: (605)783-3636
Fax: (605)793-9140
**Subject(s):** Paid Community Newspapers

Circ: ‡1,000

**The Hesston Record (11113)**
105 N Main St.
PO Box 340
Hesston, KS 67062-0340
Phone: (620)327-4831
Fax: (620)327-4830
**Subject(s):** Paid Community Newspapers

Circ: (Paid)‡1,000

**The Ipswich Tribune (28328)**
Gibson Publishing Co.
Box 7
Ipswich, SD 57451
Phone: (605)426-6471
Fax: (605)426-6202
**Subject(s):** Paid Community Newspapers

Circ: 1,000

**The La Belle Star (17381)**
PO Box 66
La Belle, MO 63447
Phone: (816)462-3848
Fax: (816)727-2475
**Subject(s):** Paid Community Newspapers

Circ: ‡1,000

**Lyman County Herald (28377)**
121-1 Main, PO Box 518
Presho, SD 57568
Phone: (605)895-6397
Fax: (605)895-6377
**Subject(s):** Paid Community Newspapers

Circ: (Paid)1,000

**Megaphone (17109)**
Culver-Stockton College
Culver-Stockton College
Canton, MO 63435
**Subject(s):** College Publications

Circ: (Free)‡1,000

**Moderator (28474)**
Mount Marty College
1105 W 8th St.
PO Box 564
Yankton, SD 57078
Phone: (605)668-1011
**Subject(s):** College Publications

Circ: (Free)‡1,000

**Moravia Union (10758)**
PO Box 468
Moravia, IA 52571
Phone: (641)724-3224
Fax: (641)724-3224
**Subject(s):** Paid Community Newspapers

Circ: ‡1,000

**Oxford Standard (18574)**
Box 125
Oxford, NE 68967
Phone: (308)824-3582
Fax: (308)824-3582

Circulation: ★ = ABC; △ = BPA; ♦ = CAC; • = CCAB; ▫ = VAC; ⊕ = PO Statement; ‡ = Publisher's Report; Boldface figures = sworn; Light figures = estimated.

**Subject(s):** Paid Community Newspapers
**Circ:** ‡1,000

**The Raver (28379)**
South Dakota School of Mines & Technology
501 E St. Joseph
Surbeck Ctr.
Rapid City, SD 57701
Phone: (605)394-2653
**Subject(s):** College Publications
**Circ:** (Free)‡1,000

**The St. Joseph Telegraph (17532)**
PO Box 1087
Saint Joseph, MO 64502-1087
Phone: (816)364-1323
Fax: (816)364-3083
**Subject(s):** Paid Community Newspapers
**Circ:** 1,000

**Scotland Journal (28403)**
PO Box 388
Scotland, SD 57059
Phone: (605)583-4419
**Subject(s):** Paid Community Newspapers
**Circ:** 1,000

**The Shelton Clipper (18607)**
Clipper Publishing Co.
PO Box 640
113 C Street
Shelton, NE 68876
Phone: (308)647-5158
**Subject(s):** Paid Community Newspapers
**Circ:** (Free)‡8
(Paid)‡1,006

**Signal (10719)**
PO Box 250
Manly, IA 50456
Phone: (641)454-2216
Fax: (641)454-2216
**Subject(s):** Paid Community Newspapers
**Circ:** ‡1,000

**Southern County News (10921)**
PO Box 96
Thornton, IA 50479-0096
Phone: (641)998-2712
Fax: (641)998-2712
**Subject(s):** Paid Community Newspapers
**Circ:** (Paid)1,000

**Time Table (10709)**
Last Time Table
101 1/2 E Temple
Lenox, IA 50851
Phone: (641)333-2810
Fax: (641)333-2506
**Subject(s):** Paid Community Newspapers
**Circ:** (Free)15
(Paid)1,000

**Westmoreland Recorder (11470)**
PO Box 128
Westmoreland, KS 66549-0128
Phone: (785)457-3411
**Subject(s):** Paid Community Newspapers
**Circ:** ‡1,000

**The Kulm Messenger (24015)**
Box J
Kulm, ND 58456
Phone: (701)647-2411
Fax: (701)647-2411
**Subject(s):** Paid Community Newspapers
**Circ:** (Free)‡48
(Paid)‡992

**Alcester Union (28270)**
PO Box 227
110 E 1st Street
Alcester, SD 57001-0227
Phone: (605)934-2640
Fax: (605)934-2096
**Subject(s):** Paid Community Newspapers
**Circ:** ‡976

**The Spearville News (11415)**
Spearville News
400 Main St.
PO Box 127
Spearville, KS 67876
Phone: (620)385-2200

Fax: (620)385-2610
**Subject(s):** Paid Community Newspapers
**Circ:** (Paid)975

**Prairie City News (10826)**
Prairie City News Inc.
108 E Jefferson
Box 249
Prairie City, IA 50228
Phone: (515)994-2349
Fax: (515)994-3169
**Subject(s):** Paid Community Newspapers
**Circ:** (Free)48
(Paid)964

**Laurel Advocate (18395)**
PO Box 688
Laurel, NE 68745
Phone: (402)256-3200
Fax: (402)256-3200
**Subject(s):** Paid Community Newspapers
**Circ:** ‡950

**South Hamilton Record News (10685)**
PO Box 130
Jewell, IA 50130
Phone: (515)827-5931
Fax: (515)827-5760
**Subject(s):** Paid Community Newspapers; Farm Newspapers
**Circ:** 950

**Valley News & Views (23945)**
PO Box 309
104 North Main Street
Drayton, ND 58225-0309
Phone: (701)454-6333
Fax: (701)454-6333
**Subject(s):** Paid Community Newspapers
**Circ:** ‡945

**Times-Republican (18373)**
Box 7
Hayes Center, NE 69032
Phone: (308)286-3325
**Subject(s):** Paid Community Newspapers
**Circ:** ‡936

**Osmond Republican (18572)**
Northeast Nebraska News Co.
PO Box 428
Osmond, NE 68765
Phone: (402)748-3666
Fax: (402)748-3354
**Subject(s):** Paid Community Newspapers
**Circ:** ‡925

**The Armstrong Journal (10310)**
Community Publications
520 6th St.
PO Box 289
Armstrong, IA 50514
Phone: (712)868-3460
Fax: (712)335-3856
**Subject(s):** Paid Community Newspapers
**Circ:** 915

**The Logan Republican (11220)**
Logan Republican
101 East Main St.
Box 97
Logan, KS 67646-0097
Phone: (785)689-4339
Fax: (785)689-4338
**Subject(s):** Paid Community Newspapers
**Circ:** ‡912

**Alta Advertiser (10284)**
Edwards Publishing
212 1/2 Main St.
Alta, IA 51002
Phone: (712)284-2300
Fax: (712)732-3152
**Subject(s):** Paid Community Newspapers
**Circ:** ‡900

**Bland Courier (17071)**
Tri-County Newspapers L.L.C.
PO Box 711
Belle, MO 65013
Phone: (573)859-3328
Fax: (573)859-6274
**Subject(s):** Paid Community Newspapers
**Circ:** 900

**Glen Ullin Times (23981)**
Bittner Schatz Publishing Inc.
PO Box 668
Glen Ullin, ND 58631
Phone: (701)348-3325
Fax: (701)348-3325
**Subject(s):** Paid Community Newspapers
**Circ:** 900

**The Highland Vidette (11454)**
PO Box 369
Troy, KS 66087-0369
Phone: (913)442-3791
Fax: (913)442-3260
**Subject(s):** Paid Community Newspapers
**Circ:** ‡900

**The Hopkins Journal (17255)**
411 Barnard St.
PO Box 170
Hopkins, MO 64461-0170
Phone: (660)778-3205
Fax: (660)778-3205
**Subject(s):** Paid Community Newspapers
**Circ:** ‡900

**Lyon County News (10597)**
P.O Box 68
113 East Michigan
George, IA 51237-0068
Phone: (712)475-3351
Fax: (712)475-3353
**Subject(s):** Paid Community Newspapers
**Circ:** 900

**Moulton Tribune (10759)**
Moravia Union
PO Box 468
Moravia, IA 52571
Phone: (641)724-3224
Fax: (641)724-3224
**Subject(s):** Paid Community Newspapers
**Circ:** ‡900

**The North English Record (10784)**
Marengo Publishing Corp.
PO Box 160
North English, IA 52316
Phone: (319)664-3237
Fax: (319)664-3237
**Subject(s):** Paid Community Newspapers
**Circ:** ‡900

**The Santa Fe Times (17062)**
Standard-Herald Inc.
102 N County Rd.
PO Box 76
Alma, MO 64001
Phone: (660)674-2250
Fax: (660)674-2250
**Subject(s):** Paid Community Newspapers
**Circ:** (Paid)820
(Non-paid)900

**The Thompson Courier-Rake Register (10920)**
Courier Register Corp.
246 Harrison St.
Thompson, IA 50478-0350
Phone: (641)584-2770
Fax: (641)584-2802
**Subject(s):** Paid Community Newspapers
**Circ:** (Free)‡20
(Paid)‡900

**The Belle Plaine News (10998)**
431 N Merchant
PO Box 128
Belle Plaine, KS 67013
Phone: (316)488-2234
**Subject(s):** Paid Community Newspapers
**Circ:** (Free)⊕50
(Paid)⊕895

**Hooker County Tribune (18494)**
PO Box 125
Mullen, NE 69152
Phone: (308)546-2242
Fax: (308)546-2722
**Subject(s):** Paid Community Newspapers
**Circ:** 875

**Gale Directory of Publications & Broadcast Media/140th Ed.**  **Great Plains States**

**Locomotive (18396)**
Ostdiek Publishing Inc.
PO Box 188
100 S. Main St
Lawrence, NE 68957
Phone: (402)756-7284
Fax: (402)756-7285
**Subject(s):** Paid Community Newspapers
**Circ:** ‡871

**Elwood Bulletin (18337)**
308 Smith
PO Box 115
Elwood, NE 68937
Phone: (308)785-2251
Fax: (308)785-2251
**Subject(s):** Paid Community Newspapers
**Circ:** 850

**Lime Springs Herald (10711)**
PO Box 187
Lime Springs, IA 52155
Phone: (563)566-2687
**Subject(s):** Paid Community Newspapers
**Circ:** ‡850

**The St. Edward Advance (18587)**
PO Box 287
Saint Edward, NE 68660
Phone: (402)678-2771
Fax: (402)678-2556
**Subject(s):** Paid Community Newspapers
**Circ:** ‡855

**Schaller Herald (10849)**
203 S Main
PO Box 129
Schaller, IA 51053-0129
Phone: (712)275-4229
**Subject(s):** Paid Community Newspapers
**Circ:** 850

**Springview Herald (18613)**
Box 369
Springview, NE 68778
Phone: (402)497-3651
Fax: (402)497-2651
**Subject(s):** Paid Community Newspapers
**Circ:** ‡850

**Dayton Review (10439)**
24 E Skillet
Box 6
Dayton, IA 50530
Phone: (515)547-2811
Fax: (515)547-2337
**Subject(s):** Farm Newspapers; Paid Community Newspapers
**Circ:** ‡845

**McLean County Journal (24062)**
BHG Inc.
PO Box 220
Turtle Lake, ND 58575
Phone: (701)448-2649
**Subject(s):** Paid Community Newspapers
**Circ:** (Free)56
(Paid)846

**Monroe Legacy (10755)**
KAB Enterprises Inc.
PO Box 340
Monroe, IA 50170
Phone: (641)259-2708
**Subject(s):** Paid Community Newspapers
**Circ:** 840

**Prairie Post (11478)**
PO Box 326
108 East Mackenie
White City, KS 66872-0326
Phone: (785)349-5516
Fax: (785)349-5516
**Subject(s):** Paid Community Newspapers
**Circ:** (Controlled)21
(Paid)840

**Times-Tribune (18277)**
P O Box 258
903 O Street
Beaver City, NE 68926-0258
Phone: (308)268-2205
Fax: (308)268-4000

**Subject(s):** Paid Community Newspapers
**Circ:** (Free)‡13
(Paid)‡820

**Attica Independent (10993)**
115 N Main
Attica, KS 67009
Phone: (620)254-7660
**Subject(s):** Paid Community Newspapers
**Circ:** 800

**Courtland Journal-Empire (11040)**
Box 318
Courtland, KS 66939
Phone: (785)374-4428
Fax: (785)374-4209
**Subject(s):** Paid Community Newspapers
**Circ:** 800

**The Dysart Reporter (10547)**
PO Box 70
Dysart, IA 52224
Phone: (319)476-3550
Fax: (319)476-2813
**Subject(s):** Paid Community Newspapers
**Circ:** ‡800

**The Elkton Record (28307)**
RFD News Group Inc.
207 Kasan Ave.
PO Box 18
Volga, SD 57071
Phone: (605)627-9471
Fax: (605)627-9310
**Subject(s):** Paid Community Newspapers
**Circ:** ‡800

**Hamlin County Republican (28290)**
Box 50
Castlewood, SD 57223
Phone: (605)793-2293
Fax: (605)793-9140
**Subject(s):** Paid Community Newspapers
**Circ:** ‡800

**New Era (24052)**
News Press
PO Box 23
Pembina, ND 58271
Phone: (701)825-6937
Fax: (701)825-6937
**Subject(s):** Paid Community Newspapers
**Circ:** ‡800

**The Record (11455)**
Larry Green
PO Box 38
Turon, KS 67583-0038
Phone: (316)497-6448
**Subject(s):** Paid Community Newspapers
**Circ:** ‡800

**Sanborn Pioneer (10848)**
Sanborn Publishing Co.
Box 280
Sanborn, IA 51248
Phone: (712)729-3201
**Subject(s):** Paid Community Newspapers
**Circ:** (Paid)800

**Standard (24079)**
Standard Press
PO Box 267
Westhope, ND 58793
Phone: (701)245-6461
Fax: (701)245-6461
**Subject(s):** Paid Community Newspapers
**Circ:** ‡800

**Volga Tribune (28451)**
RFD News Group Inc.
207 Kasan Ave.
PO Box 18
Volga, SD 57071
Phone: (605)627-9471
Fax: (605)627-9310
**Subject(s):** Paid Community Newspapers
**Circ:** ‡800

**Meadow Grove News (18489)**
Meadow Grove
PO Box 5
Meadow Grove, NE 68752
Phone: (402)634-2332

Fax: (402)634-2332
**Subject(s):** Paid Community Newspapers
**Circ:** 790

**Courier (10914)**
PO Box 160
Sutherland, IA 51058
Phone: (712)446-3450
Fax: (712)446-3450
**Subject(s):** Paid Community Newspapers
**Circ:** (Free)‡30
(Paid)‡764

**Hoven Review (28325)**
Box 37
Hoven, SD 57450
Phone: (605)948-2578
Fax: (605)948-2110
**Subject(s):** Paid Community Newspapers
**Circ:** (Free)‡20
(Paid)‡760

**Cairo Record (18304)**
Box 540
Cairo, NE 68824
Phone: (308)485-4284
Fax: (308)485-4286
**Subject(s):** Paid Community Newspapers
**Circ:** ‡750

**Collegian (10567)**
Upper Iowa University
PO Box 1857
Fayette, IA 52142
Phone: (563)425-5200
Fax: (563)425-5749
**Subject(s):** College Publications
**Circ:** 750

**The Kanawha Reporter (10688)**
101 N Main St.
PO Box 190
Kanawha, IA 50447
Phone: (641)762-3994
Fax: (641)762-3994
**Subject(s):** Paid Community Newspapers
**Circ:** (Free)50
(Paid)750

**Ninnescah Valley News (11385)**
Valley News
201 Maple
PO Box 327
Pretty Prairie, KS 67570-0327
Phone: (620)459-6322
Fax: (620)459-6729
**Subject(s):** Paid Community Newspapers
**Circ:** ‡750

**Orchard News (18566)**
235 Windom St.
PO Box 130
Orchard, NE 68764
Phone: (402)893-2535
Fax: (402)893-2535
**Subject(s):** Paid Community Newspapers
**Circ:** ‡750

**Quad River News (17952)**
12634 Noble Rd.
Sheridan, MO 64486
Phone: (660)799-3735
Fax: (603)697-0370
**Subject(s):** Paid Community Newspapers
**Circ:** (Paid)750

**Sargent Leader (18590)**
Burwell Tribune Newspapers
103 N 1st St.
PO Box 547
Sargent, NE 68874
Phone: (308)527-4210
Fax: (308)346-4018
**Subject(s):** Paid Community Newspapers
**Circ:** (Free)‡50
(Paid)‡750

**The Doniphan Herald (18334)**
304 Campbell Ave.
Doniphan, NE 68832
Phone: (402)845-2728
Fax: (402)845-2220

---

**Circulation:** ★ = ABC; △ = BPA; ♦ = CAC; • = CCAB; ❑ = VAC; ⊕ = PO Statement; ‡ = Publisher's Report; Boldface figures = sworn; Light figures = estimated.

## Great Plains States

**Subject(s):** Paid Community Newspapers
**Circ:** (Free)26
(Paid)742

**The Graettinger Times** (10605)
102 E Robbins Ave.
PO Box 118
Graettinger, IA 51342
Phone: (712)859-3780
Fax: (712)859-3039
**Subject(s):** Paid Community Newspapers
**Circ:** (Free)‡100
(Paid)‡741

**Arlington Citizen** (18263)
Enterprise Publishing Company Inc.
PO Box 460
Arlington, NE 68002
Phone: (402)426-2121
Fax: (402)426-2227
**Subject(s):** Paid Community Newspapers
**Circ:** (Paid)‡726

**The Groton Independent** (28318)
PO Box 588
Groton, SD 57445-0588
Phone: (605)397-2676
Fax: (605)397-4553
**Subject(s):** Paid Community Newspapers
**Circ:** ‡720

**Spalding Enterprise** (18611)
140 S Cedar
PO Box D
Spalding, NE 68665
Phone: (308)497-2153
Fax: (308)497-2153
**Subject(s):** Paid Community Newspapers
**Circ:** ‡725

**The Stapleton Enterprise** (18617)
Creative Printers Inc.
238 Main St.
Stapleton, NE 69163
Phone: (308)636-2444
Fax: (308)636-2445
**Subject(s):** Paid Community Newspapers
**Circ:** ‡725

**The West River Progress** (28302)
Missouri Dakota Publishing Inc.
PO Box 158
Dupree, SD 57623-0158
Phone: (605)365-5145
Fax: (605)365-5145
**Subject(s):** Paid Community Newspapers
**Circ:** 721

**Battle Creek Enterprise** (18273)
PO Box 70
Battle Creek, NE 68715
Phone: (402)675-5333
Fax: (402)368-5315
**Subject(s):** Paid Community Newspapers
**Circ:** 700

**Bethany Messenger** (11218)
Bethany College Press
Student Publications
Union Box 181
421 N. 1st St.
Lindsborg, KS 67456-1897
Phone: (913)227-3311
Fax: (917)227-2004
**Subject(s):** College Publications
**Circ:** 700

**Charles Mix County News** (28316)
PO Box 257
Geddes, SD 57342
Phone: (605)337-2571
Fax: (605)337-2363
**Subject(s):** Paid Community Newspapers
**Circ:** ‡700

**Drexel Star** (17202)
Adrian Journal
130 Main St.
PO Box 378
Drexel, MO 64742-0378
Phone: (816)657-2222
Fax: (816)657-2045
**Subject(s):** Paid Community Newspapers
**Circ:** 700

**Frankfort Area News** (11076)
P.O. Box 156
116 East Second Street
Frankfort, KS 66427-0156
Phone: (785)292-4726
Fax: (785)292-4726
**Subject(s):** Paid Community Newspapers
**Circ:** (Paid)700

**The Henderson News** (18377)
1021 N Main St.
Henderson, NE 68371
Phone: (402)723-5861
Fax: (402)723-5863
**Subject(s):** Paid Community Newspapers
**Circ:** ‡700

**Nelson Gazette** (18498)
63 E 4th St.
PO Box 285
Nelson, NE 68961
Phone: (402)225-2301
Fax: (402)225-2301
**Subject(s):** Paid Community Newspapers
**Circ:** ‡700

**Tri-City Star** (28466)
RFD News Group Inc.
207 Kasan Ave.
PO Box 18
Volga, SD 57071
Phone: (605)627-9471
Fax: (605)627-9310
**Subject(s):** Paid Community Newspapers
**Circ:** ‡700

**The Wilmot Enterprise** (28467)
PO Box 6
Wilmot, SD 57279
Phone: (605)938-4651
Fax: (605)938-4683
**Subject(s):** Paid Community Newspapers
**Circ:** ‡700

**The Alexandria Herald** (28271)
531 Main St.
PO Box 450
Alexandria, SD 57311
Phone: (605)239-4521
Fax: (605)239-4521
**Subject(s):** Paid Community Newspapers
**Circ:** ‡685

**Center Republican** (24074)
BHG Inc.
PO Box 340
Washburn, ND 58577
**Subject(s):** Paid Community Newspapers
**Circ:** (Free)18
(Paid)680

**News** (10893)
Spirit Lake Publishing Co.
PO Box AE
Spirit Lake, IA 51360
**Subject(s):** Paid Community Newspapers
**Circ:** 660

**Underwood News** (24063)
BHG Inc.
216 Lincoln Ave.
Underwood, ND 58576
**Subject(s):** Paid Community Newspapers
**Circ:** (Free)19
(Paid)662

**The Bowdle Pioneer** (28275)
PO Box 368
Bowdle, SD 57428
Phone: (605)285-6101
Fax: (605)285-6520
**Subject(s):** Paid Community Newspapers
**Circ:** ‡650

**The Independence News** (11128)
210 W Main
Independence, KS 67301
Phone: (316)331-4711
Fax: (316)251-1905
**Subject(s):** Free Newspapers
**Circ:** (Free)‡350
(Paid)‡650

**The Lebanon Times** (11197)
PO Box 158
Lebanon, KS 66952-0158
Phone: (785)389-6631
Fax: (785)454-3866
**Subject(s):** Paid Community Newspapers
**Circ:** ‡650

**Marquette Tribune** (11060)
The Ellsworth Reporter
220 N Douglas Ave.
Ellsworth, KS 67439-3216
Phone: (785)472-5085
Fax: (785)472-5087
**Subject(s):** Paid Community Newspapers
**Circ:** ‡659

**Record** (11255)
12 Spruce
Miltonvale, KS 67466-0414
Phone: (785)427-2680
Fax: (785)427-2680
**Subject(s):** Paid Community Newspapers
**Circ:** (Free)10
(Paid)650

**Bird City Times** (11006)
PO Box 220
Bird City, KS 67731-0220
Phone: (785)332-3162
Fax: (785)332-3001
**Subject(s):** Paid Community Newspapers
**Circ:** 628

**The Butte Gazette** (18303)
Box 6
Butte, NE 68722-0006
Phone: (402)775-2431
Fax: (402)775-2431
**Subject(s):** Paid Community Newspapers
**Circ:** 622

**Riverside Current** (10839)
PO Box H
MF 8-5 CST
Riverside, IA 52327
Phone: (319)648-2542
Fax: (319)648-2542
**Subject(s):** Paid Community Newspapers
**Circ:** ‡620

**The Bertrand Herald** (18289)
PO Box 425
Bertrand, NE 68927
Phone: (308)472-3217
Fax: (308)472-5165
**Subject(s):** Paid Community Newspapers
**Circ:** (Paid)‡600

**Fairview Enterprise** (11070)
PO Box 98
Fairview, KS 66425
Phone: (785)467-3461
**Subject(s):** Paid Community Newspapers
**Circ:** 600

**Petersburg Press** (18578)
PO Box 177
Petersburg, NE 68652
Phone: (402)386-5384
Fax: (402)386-5384
**Subject(s):** Paid Community Newspapers
**Circ:** 600

**The Ringsted Dispatch** (10311)
Community Publications
520 6th St.
PO Box 289
Armstrong, IA 50514
Phone: (712)868-3460
Fax: (712)335-3856
**Subject(s):** Paid Community Newspapers
**Circ:** (Free)50
(Paid)600

**Titonka Topic** (10924)
Box 329
Titonka, IA 50480
Phone: (515)928-2723
Fax: (515)928-2506
**Subject(s):** Paid Community Newspapers
**Circ:** 50
(Paid)600

**Conde News (28300)**
Doland Times Record
PO Box 387
Doland, SD 57436-0387
Phone: (605)897-6636
Fax: (605)897-6636
**Subject(s):** Paid Community Newspapers

**Circ:** (Paid)570

**Doland Times Record (28301)**
PO Box 387
Doland, SD 57436-0387
Phone: (605)897-6636
Fax: (605)897-6636
**Subject(s):** Paid Community Newspapers

**Circ:** (Paid)570

**Scandia Journal (11002)**
1710 M St.
Belleville, KS 66935
Phone: (785)527-5182
Fax: (785)527-2159
**Subject(s):** Paid Community Newspapers

**Circ:** (Free)15
(Paid)550

**The Emery Enterprise (28308)**
143 N 3rd St.
PO Box 244
Emery, SD 57332
Phone: (605)449-4420
Fax: (605)449-4430
**Subject(s):** Paid Community Newspapers

**Circ:** ‡538

**The Isabel Dakotan (28329)**
The Isabel and Dakolan
PO Box 207
403 North Main
Isabel, SD 57633-0207
Phone: (605)466-2258
Fax: (605)466-2124
**Subject(s):** Paid Community Newspapers

**Circ:** (Free)‡79
(Paid)‡521

**The Miller Press (17430)**
PO Box 216
Greenfield, MO 65661-0216
Phone: (417)452-3792
Fax: (417)637-2232
**Subject(s):** Paid Community Newspapers

**Circ:** 525

**Arthur Enterprise (18264)**
PO Box 165
Arthur, NE 69121-0165
Phone: (308)764-2402
**Subject(s):** Paid Community Newspapers

**Circ:** ‡500

**The Business Daily (10457)**
Business Publications Corp.
The Depot at Fourth
100 4th St.
Des Moines, IA 50309
Phone: (515)288-3336
Fax: (515)288-0309
**Subject(s):** Business; Daily Newspapers

**Circ:** (Combined)500

**Edgemont Herald-Tribune (28305)**
Cassens Co.
410 2nd Ave.
PO Box 660
Edgemont, SD 57735
Phone: (605)662-7201
Fax: (605)662-7202
**Subject(s):** Paid Community Newspapers

**Circ:** (Paid)500

**The Indianola News (18385)**
PO Box 130
Indianola, NE 69034
Phone: (308)364-2130
Fax: (308)364-2316
**Subject(s):** Paid Community Newspapers

**Circ:** ‡500

**Mellette County News (28346)**
Hwy. 18
PO Box 229
Mission, SD 57555
Phone: (605)259-3642
Fax: (605)856-2428

**Subject(s):** Paid Community Newspapers

**Circ:** 500

**The South Haven New Era (11036)**
A.J.'s Printing
309 W Spring Ave.
Conway Springs, KS 67031
Phone: (620)456-2232
**Subject(s):** Paid Community Newspapers

**Circ:** ‡500

**New Sharon Sun (10779)**
Box 502
New Sharon, IA 50207
Phone: (641)637-1081
Fax: (641)637-1081
**Subject(s):** Paid Community Newspapers

**Circ:** ‡480

**The Piper Press (11147)**
Wyandotte West Communications Inc.
7735 Washington Ave.
PO Box 12003
Kansas City, KS 66112
Phone: (913)788-5565
Fax: (913)788-9812
**Subject(s):** Paid Community Newspapers

**Circ:** 488

**The Diagonal Progress (10526)**
PO Box 77
Diagonal, IA 50845-0077
**Subject(s):** Paid Community Newspapers

**Circ:** (Paid)465

**The Graphic (18616)**
Creative Printers Inc.
238 Main St.
Stapleton, NE 69163
Phone: (308)636-2444
Fax: (308)636-2445
**Subject(s):** Paid Community Newspapers

**Circ:** 467

**Billings County Pioneer (23890)**
Olson Press
Box 156
Beach, ND 58621
Phone: (701)872-3755
Fax: (701)872-3756
**Subject(s):** Paid Community Newspapers

**Circ:** ‡440

**Lewis Press (11211)**
The Lewis Press Inc.
PO Box 68
Lewis, KS 67552
Phone: (620)659-2080
Fax: (620)324-5879
**Subject(s):** Paid Community Newspapers

**Circ:** 400

**Wakonda Times (28454)**
Bill Willroth
201 W. Cherry St.
PO Box 256
Vermillion, SD 57069-0256
Phone: (605)624-2695
Fax: (605)624-2696
**Subject(s):** Paid Community Newspapers

**Circ:** ‡400

**The Oxford Register (10999)**
The Belle Plaine News
431 N Merchant
PO Box 128
Belle Plaine, KS 67013
Phone: (316)488-2234
**Subject(s):** Paid Community Newspapers

**Circ:** (Free)⊕24
(Paid)⊕371

**Taylor Clarion (18624)**
Burwell Tribune Newspapers
103 N 1st St.
PO Box 547
Sargent, NE 68874
Phone: (308)527-4210
Fax: (308)346-4018
**Subject(s):** Paid Community Newspapers

**Circ:** (Non-paid)25
(Paid)375

**Cedar Rapids Press (18305)**
PO Box D
140 South Cedar Street
Spalding, NE 68665-0157
Phone: (308)497-2153
Fax: (308)497-2153
**Subject(s):** Paid Community Newspapers

**Circ:** ‡350

**Wheeler County Independent (18591)**
Burwell Tribune Newspapers
103 N 1st St.
PO Box 547
Sargent, NE 68874
Phone: (308)527-4210
Fax: (308)346-4018
**Subject(s):** Paid Community Newspapers

**Circ:** 325

**The Archie News (17059)**
The Adrian Journal Inc.
39 E Main
Box 128
Adrian, MO 64720
Phone: (816)297-2100
Fax: (816)297-2149
**Subject(s):** Paid Community Newspapers

**Circ:** ‡300

**University News (17865)**
20 N. Grand, Ste. 301
Saint Louis, MO 63103
Phone: (314)977-2812
Fax: (314)977-1588
**Subject(s):** College Publications

**Circ:** (Paid)250

**Wichita Journal (11042)**
Liberty Group Publishing Co.
PO Box 190
Derby, KS 67037
**Subject(s):** Paid Community Newspapers

**Circ:** 202

## Middle Atlantic States

**USA TODAY (31595)**
Gannett Company Inc.
7950 Jones Branch Dr. 7th Fl.
Mc Lean, VA 22108
**Subject(s):** Daily Newspapers

**Circ:** (Mon.-Thurs.)★2,220,863
(Fri.)★2,665,815

**Pennysaver (13207)**
1342 Charwood Rd.
Hanover, MD 21076
Phone: (410)684-2600
Fax: (410)865-4510
**Subject(s):** Shopping Guides

**Circ:** (Free)‡1,200,000

**The Washington Post (5743)**
1150 15th St. NW
Washington, DC 20071-2400
Phone: (202)334-6000
Fax: (703)469-2995
**Subject(s):** Daily Newspapers

**Circ:** (Sat.)★697,437
(Mon.-Fri.)★772,553
(Sun.)★1,025,579

**American Teacher (5230)**
American Federation of Teachers
555 New Jersey Ave. NW
Washington, DC 20001-2079
Phone: (202)879-4430
Fax: (202)879-2014
**Subject(s):** Education; Labor

**Circ:** (Paid)850,000

**The Chronicle (5305)**
1255 23rd St. NW
Suite 700
Washington, DC 20037
Phone: (202)466-1000
Fax: (203)423-7641
**Subject(s):** Daily Newspapers

**Circ:** (Mon.-Sat.)500,000

**Preservation (5626)**
National Trust for Historic Preservation
1785 Massachusetts Ave. NW
Washington, DC 20036
Phone: (202)588-6000
Fax: (202)588-6223
**Subject(s):** Architecture; History and Genealogy

Circ: (Paid)500,000

**The Baltimore Sun (12674)**
501 N Calvert St.
Baltimore, MD 21278-0001
Phone: (410)332-6000
Fax: (410)752-6049
**Subject(s):** Daily Newspapers

Circ: (Mon.-Thurs.)★254,763
(Sat.)★280,717
(Fri.)★320,912
(Sun.)★454,045

**The Final Call (5388)**
FCN Publishing
236 Massachusetts Ave., NE, Ste. 610
Washington, DC 20002
Phone: (202)543-7796
Fax: (202)543-8074
**Subject(s):** Black Publications

Circ: (Free)2,000
400,000

**Asbury Park Press (31573)**
Gannett Company Inc.
7950 Jones Branch Dr.
Mc Lean, VA 22107
Phone: (703)854-6000
Fax: (732)937-6046
**Subject(s):** Daily Newspapers

Circ: (Mon.-Sat.)★232,086
(Sun.)★299,699

**The Home News & Tribune (31583)**
Gannett Company Inc.
7950 Jones Branch Dr.
Mc Lean, VA 22107
Phone: (703)854-6000
Fax: (732)937-6046
**Subject(s):** Daily Newspapers

Circ: (Mon.-Sat.)232,086
(Sun.)299,699

**The Virginian Pilot (31635)**
Landmark Communications Inc.
150 W. Brambleton Ave.
Box 449
Norfolk, VA 23501-0449
Phone: (757)446-2000
Fax: (757)446-2983
**Subject(s):** Daily Newspapers

Circ: (Mon.-Fri.)192,924
(Sat.)218,940
(Sun.)231,845

**Richmond Times-Dispatch (31794)**
Richmond Newspapers Inc.
300 E. Franklin St.
Richmond, VA 23219
Phone: (804)649-6000
**Subject(s):** Daily Newspapers

Circ: (Mon.-Sat.)★184,950
(Sun.)★225,293

**The American Nurse (13340)**
American Nurses Association
8515 Georgia Ave., Ste. 400
Silver Spring, MD 20910
Phone: (301)628-5000
Fax: (202)628-5001
**Subject(s):** Nursing

Circ: ‡210,000

**HR News (31008)**
Society for Human Resource Management
1800 Duke St.
Alexandria, VA 22314
Phone: (703)548-3440
Fax: (703)535-6490
**Subject(s):** Employment and Human Resources

Circ: (Paid)170,000

**America Work (5201)**
AFL-CIO
815 16th St. NW, 5th Fl.
Washington, DC 20006
Phone: (202)637-5000
Fax: (202)637-5058

**Subject(s):** Labor

Circ: ‡168,000

**The Journal Friday Home Report (31025)**
The Journal Newspapers
6408 Edsall Rd.
Alexandria, VA 22312
Phone: (703)846-8400
Fax: (703)846-8505
**Subject(s):** Paid Community Newspapers

Circ: (Free)50,000
(Paid)150,000

**The News Journal (5137)**
Gannett
950 W Basin Rd.
PO Box 15505
New Castle, DE 19720
Phone: (302)324-2898
Fax: (302)324-5518
**Subject(s):** Daily Newspapers

Circ: (Mon.-Sat.)121,298
(Sun.)142,858

**Graphic Communicator (5411)**
Graphic Communications International Union
1900 L St. NW
Washington, DC 20036
Phone: (202)462-1400
Fax: (202)721-0600
**Subject(s):** Labor

Circ: ‡140,000

**The Scene (31593)**
Gannett Company Inc.
7950 Jones Branch Dr.
Mc Lean, VA 22107
Phone: (703)854-6000
**Subject(s):** Free Newspapers

Circ: (Free)‡138,500

**Virginia Farm Bureau News (31804)**
Virginia Farm Bureau Federation
PO Box 27552
Richmond, VA 23261-7552
Phone: (804)290-1000
**Subject(s):** Farm Bureau, Grange, and Cooperative Associations; Paid Community Newspapers

Circ: ‡136,000

**Recreation News (12910)**
730 Heston Lane
Bel Air, MD 21014
Phone: (301)474-4600
Fax: (410)638-6902
**Subject(s):** Entertainment

Circ: (Non-paid)‡130,000

**Thrifty Nickel (31386)**
127 S. Washington St.
Falls Church, VA 22046
**Subject(s):** Shopping Guides

Circ: (Free)‡125,000

**The Roanoke Times (31838)**
201 W Campbell Ave.
PO Box 2491
Roanoke, VA 24010-2491
Phone: (540)981-3340
**Subject(s):** Daily Newspapers

Circ: (Mon.-Sat.)98,552
(Sun.)116,207

**The Daily Press (31616)**
Tribune Co.
7505 Warwick Blvd.
Newport News, VA 23607
**Subject(s):** Daily Newspapers

Circ: (Mon.-Sat.)★91,307
(Sun.)★112,955

**Sunday Gazette-Mail (32557)**
Charleston Newspapers
1001 Virginia St. E
Charleston, WV 25301
Phone: (304)348-5140
Fax: (304)348-1233
**Subject(s):** Paid Community Newspapers

Circ: (Sun.)102,089

**The Washington Times (5748)**
News World Communications
3600 New York Ave., NE
Washington, DC 20002
Phone: (202)636-4859
Fax: (202)526-6820
**Subject(s):** Daily Newspapers

Circ: (Sun.)★46,619
(Sat.)★84,250
(Mon.-Fri.)★101,038

**ASCE News (31694)**
American Society of Civil Engineers
1801 Alexander Bell Dr.
Reston, VA 20191-4400
Phone: (703)295-6300
Fax: (703)295-6222
**Subject(s):** Engineering (Various branches)

Circ: (Paid)‡100,000

**The New Federalist (31517)**
KMW Publishing Company Inc.
PO Box 889
Leesburg, VA 20178-0889
Phone: (703)777-9451
Fax: (703)771-3099
**Subject(s):** Paid Community Newspapers

Circ: (Non-paid)1,105
(Paid)93,000

**Baltimore City Paper (12671)**
Times-Shamrock Communications of Scranton
812 Park Ave.
Baltimore, MD 21201-4847
Phone: (410)889-6600
Fax: (410)523-2222
**Subject(s):** Entertainment; Lifestyle; Free Newspapers

Circ: (Non-paid)86,113

**Federal Computer Week (31379)**
101 Communications
3141 Fairview Park Dr., Ste. 777
Falls Church, VA 22042
Phone: (703)876-5100
Fax: (703)876-5126
**Subject(s):** Computers; State, Municipal, and County Administration

Circ: (Free)‡86,000

**Charleston Daily Mail (32551)**
1001 Virginia St. E.
Charleston, WV 25301-2835
Phone: (304)348-5140
Fax: (304)348-4847
**Subject(s):** Daily Newspapers

Circ: (Mon.-Sat.)★31,911
(Sun.)★84,676

**Charleston Gazette (32552)**
Gazette Daily Inc.
1001 Virginia St. E.
Charleston, WV 25301
Phone: (304)348-5100
Fax: (304)348-1233
**Subject(s):** Daily Newspapers

Circ: (Mon.-Sat.)★47,119
(Sun.)★84,676

**Reading Today (5152)**
International Reading Association
800 Barksdale Rd.
PO Box 8139
Newark, DE 19714-8139
Phone: (302)731-1600
Fax: (302)731-1057
**Subject(s):** Education

Circ: (Paid)80,000

**Jewish Woman (5454)**
Jewish Women International
2000 M St. NW, Ste 720
Washington, DC 20036
Phone: (202)857-1300
Fax: (202)857-1380
**Subject(s):** Women's Interests; Jewish Publications

Circ: (Combined)‡75,000

**Argus Leader (31572)**
Gannett Company Inc.
7950 Jones Branch Dr.
Mc Lean, VA 22107
Phone: (703)854-6000
**Subject(s):** Daily Newspapers

Circ: (Mon.-Sat.)52,531
(Sun.)74,519

## Middle Atlantic States

**Frederick Gazette (13126)**
The Gazette Newspapers
2A N. Market St., 4th Fl.
Frederick, MD 21701
Phone: (301)846-2100
Fax: (301)846-2114
**Subject(s):** Free Newspapers

**Circ:** (Combined)69,679

**Northern Virginia Sun (31606)**
Sun Newspapers
PO Box 2410
Merrifield, VA 22116-2410
Phone: (703)204-2800
Fax: (703)204-3455
**Subject(s):** Paid Community Newspapers

**Circ:** (Paid)245
(Non-paid)68,678

**The Catholic Review (12688)**
Cathedral Foundation Inc.
880 Park Ave
PO Box 777
Baltimore, MD 21203
Phone: (443)524-3150
Fax: (443)524-3155
**Subject(s):** Religious Publications

**Circ:** ‡68,000

**Air Force Times (31879)**
Army Times Publishing Co.
6883 Commercial Dr.
Springfield, VA 22159-0500
Phone: (703)750-9000
Fax: (703)750-8767
**Subject(s):** Paid Community Newspapers; Military and Navy

**Circ:** (Paid)61,846

**Youth Today (5767)**
American Youth Work Center
1200 17th Street North West 4th Floor
Washington, DC 20036-3006
Phone: (202)785-0764
Fax: (202)728-0657
**Subject(s):** Social Sciences; Substance Abuse and Treatment; Vocational Education; Health and Healthcare; Safety

**Circ:** (Combined)58,000

**Counseling Today (30993)**
American Counseling Association
5999 Stevenson Ave.
Alexandria, VA 22304
Phone: (703)823-6862
Fax: (703)823-0252
**Subject(s):** Employment and Human Resources; Psychology and Psychiatry; Education

**Circ:** (Free)‡59
(Paid)‡56,000

**White Plains Reporter Dispatch (31599)**
Gannett Company Inc.
7950 Jones Branch Dr.
Mc Lean, VA 22107
Phone: (703)854-6000
**Subject(s):** Daily Newspapers

**Circ:** (Mon.-Sat.)46,715
(Sun.)55,276

**NSTA Reports (31145)**
National Science Teachers Association
1840 Wilson Blvd.
Arlington, VA 22201-3000
Phone: (703)243-7100
Fax: (703)243-7177
**Subject(s):** Science (General); Education

**Circ:** (Paid)55,000

**Arlington Catholic Herald (31110)**
Arlington Herald
200 N Glebe Rd., Ste. 600
Arlington, VA 22203
Phone: (202)841-2590
Fax: (703)524-2782
**Subject(s):** Religious Publications

**Circ:** (Non-paid)369
(Paid)53,000

**Education Week (12961)**
Editorial Projects in Education Inc.
6935 Arlington Rd., Ste. 100
Bethesda, MD 20814-5233
Phone: (301)280-3100
Fax: (301)280-3200
**Subject(s):** Education

**Circ:** (Paid)52,997

**Fairfax Journal (30999)**
The Journal Newspapers
6408 Edsall Rd.
Alexandria, VA 22312
Phone: (703)846-8400
Fax: (703)846-8505
**Subject(s):** Daily Newspapers

**Circ:** (Mon.-Fri.)52,358

**The Free Lance-Star (31409)**
The Free Lance-Star Publishing Co.
616 Amelia St.
Fredericksburg, VA 22401
Phone: (540)720-5470
**Subject(s):** Daily Newspapers

**Circ:** (Mon.-Sat.)★47,065
(Sun.)★51,721

**Navy Times (31889)**
Army Times Publishing Co.
6883 Commercial Dr.
Springfield, VA 22159-0500
Phone: (703)750-9000
Fax: (703)750-8767
**Subject(s):** Military and Navy

**Circ:** (Paid)51,170

**Catholic Standard (12951)**
Carroll Publishing
4701 Sangamore Rd., Ste. S-155
Bethesda, MD 20816
Phone: (301)263-9800
Fax: (301)263-9801
**Subject(s):** Religious Publications

**Circ:** ‡51,000

**The Putnam Cabell Post (32581)**
P.C. Publishing
2085 U. S. Rte. 60
Culloden, WV 25510
Phone: (304)743-6731
Fax: (304)562-6214
**Subject(s):** Shopping Guides

**Circ:** (Free)⊕47,773

**The Capital (12628)**
The Capital-Gazette Newspapers
2000 Capital Dr.
Annapolis, MD 21401
Phone: (410)268-5000
Fax: (410)268-4643
**Subject(s):** Daily Newspapers

**Circ:** (Mon.-Sat.)★44,211
(Sun.)★46,655

**Loudoun Easterner (31178)**
Creative Publications of Virginia Inc.
20735 Ashburn Rd.
Ashburn, VA 20147
Phone: (703)858-5300
Fax: (703)723-4599
**Subject(s):** Paid Community Newspapers

**Circ:** (Non-paid)‡44,000

**Buyers Guide (32662)**
Panhandle Buyers Guide Publications Inc.
415 Wilson St.
PO Box 2118
Martinsburg, WV 25401
Phone: (304)267-9983
Fax: (304)263-7106
**Subject(s):** Shopping Guides

**Circ:** (Free)43,930

**The News & Daily Advance (31540)**
The News & Advance
101 Wyndale Dr.
PO Box 10129
Lynchburg, VA 24506-0129
Phone: (434)385-5440
Fax: (434)385-5472
**Subject(s):** Daily Newspapers

**Circ:** (Mon.-Sat.)37,245
(Sun.)42,879

**The News Advance (31539)**
Spectrum Publishing Inc.
101 Wyndale Dr.
PO Box 10129
Lynchburg, VA 24506
Phone: (804)385-5538
Fax: (804)385-5538
**Subject(s):** Paid Community Newspapers

**Circ:** (Mon.-Sat.)37,177
(Sun.)42,344

**Bristol Herald Courier (31220)**
Herald-Courier Virginia-Tennessean
320 Morrison Blvd.
Bristol, VA 24201
Phone: (540)669-2181
Fax: (540)669-3696
**Subject(s):** Daily Newspapers

**Circ:** (Mon.-Sat.)★39,109
(Sun.)★41,988

**Baltimore Times (12675)**
2513 N Charles St.
Baltimore, MD 21218
Phone: (410)366-3900
Fax: (410)243-1627
**Subject(s):** Free Newspapers

**Circ:** (Non-paid)♦41,922

**The Herald-Dispatch (32619)**
Gannett Company Inc.
The Herald-Dispatch
946 Fifth Ave.
Huntington, WV 25701
Phone: (304)526-4000
**Subject(s):** Daily Newspapers

**Circ:** (Mon.-Sat.)35,503
(Sun.)41,041

**EOS (5378)**
American Geophysical Union
2000 Florida Ave. NW
Washington, DC 20009
Phone: (202)462-6900
Fax: (202)328-0566
**Subject(s):** Geology

**Circ:** 41,000

**News-Register (32778)**
Ogden Newspapers Inc.
1500 Main St.
Wheeling, WV 26003
Phone: (304)233-0100
Fax: (304)233-9397
**Subject(s):** Daily Newspapers

**Circ:** (Mon.-Fri.)★15,802
(Sun.)★40,574

**The Georgetown Current (5401)**
The Current Newspapers Inc.
PO Box 40400
Washington, DC 20016-0400
Phone: (202)244-7223
Fax: (202)244-5924
**Subject(s):** Free Newspapers

**Circ:** (Combined)‡40,250

**The Frederick-News Post (13128)**
200 E. Patrick St.
PO Box 578
Frederick, MD 21705-0578
Phone: (301)662-1177
Fax: (301)662-8299
**Subject(s):** Daily Newspapers

**Circ:** (Sun.)★38,264
(Mon.-Sat.)★40,209

**U.S. Medicine (5728)**
U.S. Medicine Inc.
2021 L St. NW, Ste. 400
Washington, DC 20036-3362
Phone: (202)463-6000
Fax: (202)223-2849
**Subject(s):** Medicine and Surgery; Congressional and Federal Government Affairs

**Circ:** (Paid)70
(Free)40,192

**Air Jobs Digest (5195)**
World Air Data
P.O.Box 42724
Washington, DC 20015
Phone: (301)990-6800
Fax: (301)990-8484
**Subject(s):** Employment and Human Resources; Aviation; Astronautics

**Circ:** (Combined)40,000

**Soundings (31633)**
Military Newspapers of Virginia
2509 Walmer Ave.
Norfolk, VA 23513
Phone: (757)857-1212
Fax: (757)853-1634
**Subject(s):** Free Newspapers

**Circ:** (Free)‡40,000

Circulation: ★ = ABC; △ = BPA; ♦ = CAC; • = CCAB; ▫ = VAC; ⊕ = PO Statement; ‡ = Publisher's Report; Boldface figures = sworn; Light figures = estimated.

## Middle Atlantic States

**Avenue News (12667)**
The Avenue Inc.
442 Eastern Blvd.
Baltimore, MD 21221
Phone: (410)687-7775
Fax: (410)687-7881
**Subject(s):** Free Newspapers
**Circ:** (Wed.)33,663
(Thurs.)39,927

**The Morning Herald (13194)**
The Herald-Mail Co.
100 Summit Ave.
Hagerstown, MD 21741
Phone: (301)733-5131
Fax: (301)733-7264
**Subject(s):** Daily Newspapers
**Circ:** (Mon.-Fri.)21,348
(Sat.)35,725
(Sun.)39,849

**The Baltimore Guide (12672)**
R & B Publishing Co.
526 S Conkling St.
Baltimore, MD 21224
Phone: (410)732-6600
Fax: (410)732-6336
**Subject(s):** Free Newspapers
**Circ:** (Paid)159
(Non-paid)39,398

**The Daily-Mail (13189)**
The Herald-Mail Co.
100 Summit Ave.
Hagerstown, MD 21741
Phone: (301)733-5131
Fax: (301)733-7264
**Subject(s):** Daily Newspapers
**Circ:** (Mon.-Fri.)34,484
(Sat.)35,208
(Sun.)39,368

**Columbia Flier (13074)**
Patuxent Publishing Co.
10750 Little Patuxent Pkwy.
Columbia, MD 21044
Phone: (410)730-3990
Fax: (410)997-4564
**Subject(s):** Free Newspapers
**Circ:** (Non-paid)38,394

**Sun Gazette (31608)**
Sun Newspapers
PO Box 2410
Merrifield, VA 22116
**Subject(s):** Free Newspapers
**Circ:** (Paid)85
(Non-paid)37,738

**Towson Times (13380)**
Patuxent Publishing Co.
409 Washington Ave.
Towson, MD 21204
Phone: (410)337-2400
Fax: (410)337-2490
**Subject(s):** Paid Community Newspapers
**Circ:** (Paid)190
(Non-paid)37,724

**The Maryland Gazette (13180)**
Capital Gazette Printing
306 Crane Hwy.
Glen Burnie, MD 21061
Phone: (410)766-3700
Fax: (410)766-7031
**Subject(s):** Paid Community Newspapers
**Circ:** 36,573

**The Bargaineer (12622)**
Chesapeake Publishing Corp.
214 W Belair Ave.
Aberdeen, MD 21001
Phone: (410)398-3311
Fax: (410)398-4044
**Subject(s):** Shopping Guides
**Circ:** (Mon.)✦36,015

**Intelligencer (32777)**
Ogden Newspapers Inc.
1500 Main St.
Wheeling, WV 26003
Phone: (304)233-0100
**Subject(s):** Daily Newspapers
**Circ:** (Mon.-Fri.)★20,971
(Sat.)★35,657

**El Tiempo Latino (31120)**
Farragut Media Group
1916 Wilson Blvd., Ste. 204
Arlington, VA 22201
Phone: (703)527-7860
Fax: (703)527-0369
**Subject(s):** Free Newspapers
**Circ:** (Controlled)★35,320

**Today's Shopper (32639)**
Mineral Daily News-Tribune
24 Armstrong St.
PO Box 879
Keyser, WV 26726
Phone: (304)788-3333
Fax: (304)788-3398
**Subject(s):** Shopping Guides
**Circ:** (Free)35,000

**The Washington Diplomat (13394)**
The Washington Diplomat Inc.
PO Box 1345
Wheaton, MD 20915-1345
Phone: (301)933-3552
Fax: (301)949-0065
**Subject(s):** Paid Community Newspapers
**Circ:** (Combined)35,000

**Owings Mills Times (13375)**
Patuxent Publishing Co.
409 Washington Ave.
Towson, MD 21204
Phone: (410)337-2400
Fax: (410)337-2490
**Subject(s):** Free Newspapers
**Circ:** (Paid)133
(Non-paid)34,914

**The Parkersburg News (32701)**
PO Box 1787
519 Julaina
Parkersburg, WV 26101-1787
Phone: (304)485-1891
Fax: (304)485-2061
**Subject(s):** Daily Newspapers
**Circ:** (Mon.-Sat.)20,811
(Sun.)34,522

**The Daily Progress (31244)**
685 W. Rio Rd.
PO Box 9030
Charlottesville, VA 22901
Phone: (804)978-7200
Fax: (804)978-7223
**Subject(s):** Daily Newspapers
**Circ:** (Mon.-Sat.)30,189
(Sun.)34,328

**Leesburg Today (31514)**
1 E Market St.
Leesburg, VA 20176
Phone: (703)771-8800
Fax: (703)771-8833
**Subject(s):** Free Newspapers
**Circ:** (Free)34,100

**Potomac Children (13035)**
3908 Underwood St.
Chevy Chase, MD 20815
Phone: (301)656-2133
Fax: (301)656-7830
**Subject(s):** Free Newspapers
**Circ:** (Paid)72
(Free)33,988

**Cumberland Times News (13082)**
McLeansboro Times-Leader
19 Baltimore St.
PO Box 1662
Cumberland, MD 21502
Phone: (301)722-4600
Fax: (301)722-4870
**Subject(s):** Daily Newspapers
**Circ:** (Mon.-Sat.)31,026
(Sun.)33,553

**Nation's Cities Weekly (5577)**
National League of Cities
1301 Pennsylvania Ave. NW, Ste. 550
Washington, DC 20004
Phone: (202)626-3000
Fax: (202)626-3043
**Subject(s):** State, Municipal, and County Administration
**Circ:** ‡32,500

**Arlington Sun Gazette (30978)**
Sunburn Washington Newspapers, Inc.
6408 Edsall Rd.
Alexandria, VA 22312
Phone: (703)204-2800
Fax: (703)204-3455
**Subject(s):** Free Newspapers
**Circ:** (Combined)32,073

**The InTowner Newspaper (5450)**
1730-B Corcoran St. NW
Washington, DC 20009
Phone: (202)234-1717
**Subject(s):** Free Newspapers
**Circ:** (Paid)100
(Free)32,000

**Daily News-Record (31465)**
Rockingham Publishing Company Inc.
231 S Liberty St.
PO Box 193
Harrisonburg, VA 22803
Phone: (540)574-6200
Fax: (540)433-9112
**Subject(s):** Daily Newspapers
**Circ:** (Mon.-Sat.)★31,726

**The Gaithersburg Gazette (13165)**
The Gazette Newspapers
PO Box Caller No. 6006
Gaithersburg, MD 20884
Phone: (301)948-3120
**Subject(s):** Free Newspapers
**Circ:** (Combined)31,522

**The Observer (31494)**
Herndon Publishing Inc.
1043 Sterling Rd., Ste. 104
PO Box 109
Herndon, VA 20170
Phone: (703)437-5886
Fax: (703)834-3142
**Subject(s):** Free Newspapers
**Circ:** (Combined)31,492

**The Bellingham Herald (31577)**
Gannett Company Inc.
7950 Jones Branch Dr.
Mc Lean, VA 22107
Phone: (703)854-6000
**Subject(s):** Daily Newspapers
**Circ:** (Mon.-Sat.)24,710
(Sun.)31,478

**The Daily Times (13318)**
115 E. Carroll St.
Salisbury, MD 21801
Phone: (410)749-7171
Fax: (410)543-8736
**Subject(s):** Daily Newspapers
**Circ:** (Mon.-Sat.)27,263
(Sun.)30,894

**Laurel Leader (13237)**
Patuxent Publishing Co.
615 Main St.
Laurel, MD 20707
Phone: (301)725-2000
Fax: (301)317-8736
**Subject(s):** Paid Community Newspapers
**Circ:** (Paid)318
(Non-paid)30,771

**Wausau Daily Herald (31598)**
Gannett Company Inc.
7950 Jones Branch Dr.
Mc Lean, VA 22107
Phone: (703)854-6000
**Subject(s):** Daily Newspapers
**Circ:** (Mon.-Fri.)22,942
(Sat.)24,226
(Sun.)30,640

**Transport Topics (31080)**
American Trucking Associations Inc.
2200 Mill Rd.
Alexandria, VA 22314-4677
Phone: (703)838-1700
Fax: (703)683-2292
**Subject(s):** Trucks and Trucking
**Circ:** (Paid)30,592

# Middle Atlantic States

**Aegis (12908)**
Homestead Publishing Company Inc.
10 Hays St.
PO Box 189
Bel Air, MD 21014
Phone: (410)838-4400
Fax: (410)638-0357
**Subject(s):** Paid Community Newspapers
**Circ:** (Fri.)27,565
(Wed.)30,580

**The Washington Examiner (31084)**
The Journal Newspapers
6408 Edsall Rd.
Alexandria, VA 22312
Phone: (703)846-8400
Fax: (703)846-8505
**Subject(s):** Daily Newspapers
**Circ:** (Mon.-Fri.)30,184

**Shofar (5693)**
B'nai B'rith Youth Organization
1640 Rhode Island Ave. NW
Washington, DC 20036
Phone: (202)857-6600
Fax: (202)857-6568
**Subject(s):** Youths' Interests; Jewish Publications
**Circ:** ‡30,000

**Cecil Whig (13105)**
601 Bridge St.
PO Box 429
Elkton, MD 21922-0429
Phone: (410)398-3311
Fax: (410)398-4044
**Subject(s):** Daily Newspapers
**Circ:** (Mon.-Fri.)♦14,168
(Sun.)♦29,648

**Register-Herald (32527)**
PO Box 2594
Beckley, WV 25802
Phone: (304)255-4400
Fax: (304)255-4427
**Subject(s):** Daily Newspapers
**Circ:** (Mon.-Sat.)★28,567
(Sun.)★29,554

**Business Gazette (13119)**
The Gazette Newspapers
2A N. Market St., 4th Fl.
Frederick, MD 21701
Phone: (301)846-2100
Fax: (301)846-2114
**Subject(s):** Free Newspapers; Business
**Circ:** (Non-paid)28,191

**Greenbrier Valley Ranger (32649)**
Greenbrier Daily Newspapers Inc.
200 South Court Street
Lewisburg, WV 24901-0471
Phone: (304)645-1206
Fax: (304)645-7104
**Subject(s):** Paid Community Newspapers
**Circ:** (Non-paid)27,011

**The Washington Informer (5739)**
3117 Martin Luther King Jr. Ave. SE
Washington, DC 20032-1537
Phone: (202)561-4100
Fax: (202)574-3785
**Subject(s):** Paid Community Newspapers; Black Publications
**Circ:** ‡27,000

**Pentagram (31146)**
Comprint Military Publications
204 Lee Ave.
Arlington, VA 22211-1199
Phone: (703)696-2674
Fax: (703)696-2674
**Subject(s):** Free Newspapers; Military and Navy
**Circ:** (Free)26,000

**The Winchester Star (31962)**
Winchester Star
2 N Kent St.
Winchester, VA 22601
Phone: (540)667-3200
Fax: (540)667-1649
**Subject(s):** Daily Newspapers
**Circ:** (Mon.-Fri.)★21,253
(Sat.)★25,528

**Delaware State News (5117)**
Independent Newspapers Inc.
PO Box 737
PO Box 7001
Dover, DE 19903
Phone: (302)674-3600
Fax: (302)741-8261
**Subject(s):** Daily Newspapers
**Circ:** (Mon.-Sat.)17,693
(Sun.)25,316

**Yonkers Herald Statesman (31600)**
Gannett Company Inc.
7950 Jones Branch Dr.
Mc Lean, VA 22107
Phone: (703)854-6000
**Subject(s):** Daily Newspapers
**Circ:** (Mon.-Sat.)20,718
(Sun.)25,300

**Delaware Beachcomber (5157)**
Gannett Company Inc.
PO Box 309
Rehoboth Beach, DE 19971
Phone: (302)227-9466
Fax: (302)227-9469
**Subject(s):** Shopping Guides
**Circ:** (Free)‡25,000

**Maryland Coast Dispatch (12913)**
10012 Old Ocean City Blvd.
PO Box 467
Berlin, MD 21811
Phone: (410)641-4561
Fax: (410)641-0966
**Subject(s):** Paid Community Newspapers
**Circ:** (Paid)‡25,000

**New Journal & Guide (31630)**
362 Campostella Rd.
Norfolk, VA 23523
Phone: (757)543-6531
Fax: (757)543-7620
**Subject(s):** Black Publications; Paid Community Newspapers
**Circ:** (Combined)25,000
(Wed.)25,000

**Richmond Free Press (31792)**
Paradigm Communications Inc.
422 E Franklin St.
Richmond, VA 23219-2226
**Subject(s):** Free Newspapers
**Circ:** (Paid)167
(Free)24,903

**Dover Post (5118)**
Dover Post Co.
609 E. Division St.
Dover, DE 19901
Phone: (302)678-3616
Fax: (302)678-8291
**Subject(s):** Free Newspapers
**Circ:** (Paid)1,917
(Free)24,615

**Silver Spring Gazette (13143)**
The Gazette Newspapers
2A N. Market St., 4th Fl.
Frederick, MD 21701
Phone: (301)846-2100
Fax: (301)846-2114
**Subject(s):** Free Newspapers
**Circ:** (Combined)24,558

**Howard County Times (13078)**
Patuxent Publishing Co.
10750 Little Patuxent Pkwy.
Columbia, MD 21044
Phone: (410)730-3990
Fax: (410)997-4564
**Subject(s):** Paid Community Newspapers
**Circ:** (Paid)24,406

**Danville Register & Bee (31312)**
Register Publishing Company Inc.
PO Box 331
Danville, VA 24543
**Subject(s):** Daily Newspapers
**Circ:** (Mon.-Sat.)★21,139
(Sun.)★24,052

**Carroll County Times (13388)**
Landmark Community Newspapers Inc.
201 Railroad Ave.
PO Box 346
Westminster, MD 21157-4823
Phone: (410)857-8749
Fax: (410)857-8749
**Subject(s):** Daily Newspapers
**Circ:** (Mon.-Sat.)22,936
(Sun.)24,047

**Better Years (5115)**
Dover Post Co.
609 E. Division St.
Dover, DE 19901
Phone: (302)678-3616
Fax: (302)678-8291
**Subject(s):** Paid Community Newspapers; Senior Citizens' Interests
**Circ:** (Free)24,000

**The Catholic War Veteran (30986)**
Catholic War Veterans, U.S.A.
National Headquarters
441 N Lee St.
Alexandria, VA 22314-2301
Phone: (703)549-3622
Fax: (703)684-5196
**Subject(s):** Veterans; Religious Publications
**Circ:** (Free)‡1,000
(Paid)‡24,000

**Dominion Post (32676)**
Greer Bldg.
1251 Earl L Core Rd.
Morgantown, WV 26505
Phone: (304)292-6301
Fax: (304)291-2326
**Subject(s):** Daily Newspapers
**Circ:** (Mon.-Sat.)★19,681
(Sun.)★23,837

**Eastern Loudoun Times (31901)**
Arcom Publishing Inc.
10 E. Holly Ave.
Sterling, VA 20164
**Subject(s):** Free Newspapers
**Circ:** (Paid)35
(Non-paid)23,682

**Daily Telegraph (32541)**
PO Box 1599
Bluefield, WV 24701
Phone: (304)327-2811
**Subject(s):** Daily Newspapers
**Circ:** (Mon.-Sat.)21,573
(Sun.)23,402

**The Mechanicsville Local (31602)**
Richmond Suburban Newspapers
6400 Mechanicsville Turnpike
P.O.Box 1118
Mechanicsville, VA 23111
Phone: (804)746-1235
Fax: (804)730-0476
**Subject(s):** Free Newspapers
**Circ:** (Paid)143
(Non-paid)22,537

**The Hill (5418)**
733 15th St. NW, No. 1140
Washington, DC 20005
Phone: (202)628-8500
Fax: (202)628-8503
**Subject(s):** Politics; Congressional and Federal Government Affairs
**Circ:** 22,500

**Maryland Independent (13385)**
Chesapeake Publishing Corp.
7 Industrial Park
Waldorf, MD 20602
Phone: (301)645-9480
Fax: (301)884-9403
**Subject(s):** Paid Community Newspapers
**Circ:** (Non-paid)321
(Paid)21,677

**The News Leader (31894)**
Leader Publishing Company Inc.
11 N. Central Ave.
PO Box 59
Staunton, VA 24402
Phone: (540)885-7281

---

Circulation: ★ = ABC; △ = BPA; ♦ = CAC; • = CCAB; □ = VAC; ⊕ = PO Statement; ‡ = Publisher's Report; Boldface figures = sworn; Light figures = estimated.

# Middle Atlantic States

**Subject(s):** Daily Newspapers

**Circ:** (Mon.-Sat.)18,354
(Sun.)21,517

**Northeast Booster (13373)**
Patuxent Publishing Co.
409 Washington Ave.
Towson, MD 21204
Phone: (410)337-2400
Fax: (410)337-2490
**Subject(s):** Paid Community Newspapers

**Circ:** (Paid)11
(Non-paid)21,444

**The View from Ellicott City (13109)**
ZIP Publishing Inc.
800 Main St.
Ellicott City, MD 21043
Phone: (410)480-0816
Fax: (410)480-0834
**Subject(s):** Free Newspapers

**Circ:** (Non-paid)21,230

**Sun (31906)**
Virginian Pilot
157 N Main St., Ste. B
Suffolk, VA 23434-4507
Phone: (757)222-5550
Fax: (757)222-5515
**Subject(s):** Paid Community Newspapers

**Circ:** ‡21,204

**BaptistLIFE (13072)**
Baptist Convention of Maryland/Delaware
10255 Old Columbia Rd.
Columbia, MD 21046
Phone: (410)290-5290
Fax: (410)290-6627
**Subject(s):** Religious Publications

**Circ:** 21,000

**Clarksburg Exponent (32576)**
Clarksburg Publishing
PO Box 2000
Clarksburg, WV 26302
Phone: (304)626-1400
Fax: (304)622-3629
**Subject(s):** Daily Newspapers

**Circ:** (Mon.-Sat.)★16,216
(Sun.)★20,464

**Clarksburg Telegram (32577)**
Clarksburg Publishing
PO Box 2000
Clarksburg, WV 26302
Phone: (304)626-1400
Fax: (304)622-3629
**Subject(s):** Daily Newspapers

**Circ:** (Mon.-Sat.)★16,066
(Sun.)★20,262

**Washington Business Journal (5737)**
American City Business Journals Inc.
1555 Wilson Blvd., Ste. 400
Arlington, VA 22209-2405
Phone: (703)875-2231
Fax: (703)875-2231
**Subject(s):** Business; Local, State, and Regional Publications

**Circ:** (Paid)20,208

**The Germantown Gazette (13179)**
The Gazette Newspapers
2A N. Market St., 4th Fl.
Frederick, MD 21701
Phone: (301)846-2100
Fax: (301)846-2114
**Subject(s):** Free Newspapers

**Circ:** (Combined)20,099

**The Progress-Index Extra (31665)**
15 Franklin St.
Petersburg, VA 23803
Phone: (804)732-3456
Fax: (804)861-9452
**Subject(s):** Shopping Guides

**Circ:** (Free)‡20,040

**Dundalk Eagle (13091)**
Kimbel Publication Inc.
4 North Center Place
Dundalk, MD 21222
Phone: (410)288-6060
Fax: (410)288-2712

**Subject(s):** Paid Community Newspapers

**Circ:** (Free)‡1,030
(Paid)‡20,000

**Wetzel Green Tab (32693)**
Green Tab Publishing Co.
518 7th St.
P.O. Box 536
Moundsville, WV 26041
Phone: (304)845-4050
Fax: (304)845-4312
**Subject(s):** Shopping Guides

**Circ:** (Non-paid)19,923

**The Journal (32664)**
The Journal Publishing Company Inc.
207 W. King St.
PO Box 807
Martinsburg, WV 25402-0807
Phone: (304)263-8931
Fax: (304)263-8058
**Subject(s):** Daily Newspapers

**Circ:** (Mon.-Sat.)18,582
(Sun.)19,665

**CentreView (31230)**
Connection Newspapers L.L.C.
7913 Westpark Dr.
Mc Lean, VA 22102-4201
Phone: (703)821-5050
Fax: (703)917-0991
**Subject(s):** Free Newspapers

**Circ:** (Free)19,611

**Martinsville Bulletin (31565)**
204 Broad St.
Martinsville, VA 24115-3199
Phone: (276)638-8801
Fax: (276)638-4153
**Subject(s):** Daily Newspapers

**Circ:** (Mon.-Fri.)★17,269
(Sun.)★19,479

**Belvoir Eagle (31404)**
Media General Newspapers Inc.
9820 Flagler Rd., Bldg. 269
Fort Belvoir, VA 22060-5932
Phone: (703)805-3397
Fax: (703)780-6145
**Subject(s):** Free Newspapers; Military and Navy

**Circ:** (Free)19,000

**Diamondback (13043)**
Maryland Media Inc.
3150 S. Campus Dining Hall
University of Maryland
College Park, MD 20742
Phone: (301)314-8200
Fax: (301)314-8358
**Subject(s):** College Publications

**Circ:** ‡19,000

**Manassas Journal Messenger (31556)**
9009 Church St.
Manassas, VA 20110
Phone: (703)368-3101
Fax: (703)368-9017
**Subject(s):** Daily Newspapers

**Circ:** (Mon.-Fri.)5,600
(Sun.)18,602
(Sat.)18,820

**Potomac News (31968)**
14010 Smoketown Rd.
PO Box 2470
Woodbridge, VA 22192
Phone: (703)878-8000
Fax: (703)878-3993
**Subject(s):** Daily Newspapers

**Circ:** (Mon.-Fri.)15,086
(Sun.)18,602
(Sat.)18,820

**Star-Democrat & Sunday Star (13097)**
Chesapeake Publishing Corp.
PO Box 600
Easton, MD 21601
Phone: (410)822-1500
Fax: (410)770-4012
**Subject(s):** Daily Newspapers

**Circ:** (Mon.-Fri.)17,042
(Sun.)18,813

**Northeast Times Booster (13079)**
Patuxent Publishing Co.
10750 Little Patuxent Pkwy.
Columbia, MD 21044
Phone: (410)730-3990
Fax: (410)997-4564
**Subject(s):** Free Newspapers

**Circ:** (Paid)21
(Non-paid)18,793

**The Progress-Index (31664)**
McLeansboro Times-Leader
15 Franklin St.
Petersburg, VA 23803
Phone: (804)732-3456
Fax: (804)861-9452
**Subject(s):** Daily Newspapers

**Circ:** (Mon.-Sat.)17,878
(Sun.)18,406

**The Sussex Post (5126)**
Independent Newspapers Inc.
PO Box 1130
Dover, DE 19903
Phone: (302)934-9261
Fax: (302)629-6700
**Subject(s):** Free Newspapers

**Circ:** (Paid)❏39
(Free)❏18,056

**Community College Week (31339)**
Cox, Matthews, & Associates Inc.
10520 Warwick Ave., Ste. B-8
Fairfax, VA 22030-3136
Phone: (703)385-2981
Fax: (703)385-1839
**Subject(s):** College Publications

**Circ:** 18,000

**Green Tab-Northern Valley (32687)**
Green Tab Publishing Co.
518 7th St.
P.O. Box 536
Moundsville, WV 26041
Phone: (304)845-4050
Fax: (304)845-4312
**Subject(s):** Shopping Guides

**Circ:** (Combined)17,865

**Burtonsville Gazette (13118)**
The Gazette Newspapers
2A N. Market St., 4th Fl.
Frederick, MD 21701
Phone: (301)846-2100
Fax: (301)846-2114
**Subject(s):** Free Newspapers

**Circ:** (Paid)6
(Controlled)17,653

**North County News (13372)**
Patuxent Publishing Co.
409 Washington Ave.
Towson, MD 21204
Phone: (410)337-2400
Fax: (410)337-2490
**Subject(s):** Free Newspapers

**Circ:** (Paid)12
(Non-paid)17,525

**College Park Gazette (13122)**
The Gazette Newspapers
2A N. Market St., 4th Fl.
Frederick, MD 21701
Phone: (301)846-2100
Fax: (301)846-2114
**Subject(s):** Free Newspapers

**Circ:** (Combined)17,460

**Loudoun Times-Mirror (31532)**
9 E. Market St.
Leesburg, VA 20176-3013
Phone: (703)777-1111
Fax: (703)771-0036
**Subject(s):** Paid Community Newspapers

**Circ:** (Free)‡3,627
(Paid)‡17,173

**Vienna Times (31921)**
Arcom Publishing Inc.
1760 Reston Pkwy., Ste. 411
Reston, VA 20190
Phone: (703)437-5400
Fax: (703)437-6019

**Subject(s):** Free Newspapers
**Circ:** (Paid)180
(Non-paid)10,766
17,033

**The Breeze** (31464)
James Madison University
800 S. Main St.
Harrisonburg, VA 22807
Phone: (540)568-6211
**Subject(s):** College Publications
**Circ:** (Free)‡17,000

**The Mace and Crown** (31629)
Old Dominion University
2101 Webb University Ctr.
Hampton Blvd.
Norfolk, VA 23529
Phone: (757)683-4773
Fax: (757)683-3459
**Subject(s):** College Publications
**Circ:** (Free)‡17,000

**York Town Crier** (31974)
Spectrum Publishing Inc.
4824 George Washington Hwy.
PO Box 978
Yorktown, VA 23692
Phone: (757)898-7225
Fax: (757)890-0119
**Subject(s):** Paid Community Newspapers
**Circ:** (Combined)⊕17,000

**Northeast Reporter** (13374)
Patuxent Publishing Co.
409 Washington Ave.
Towson, MD 21204
Phone: (410)337-2400
Fax: (410)337-2490
**Subject(s):** Paid Community Newspapers
**Circ:** (Paid)14
(Non-paid)16,978

**The Virginia Gazette** (31952)
Virginia Gazette Companies L.L.C.
216 Ironbound Rd.
Williamsburg, VA 23188
Phone: (757)220-1736
Fax: (757)220-1390
**Subject(s):** Paid Community Newspapers
**Circ:** ‡16,500

**The Gazette** (12735)
Johns Hopkins University
901 S. Bond St., Ste. 540
Baltimore, MD 21231
Phone: (443)287-9900
Fax: (443)287-9898
**Subject(s):** College Publications
**Circ:** (Free)‡16,000

**Northern Virginia Daily** (31902)
152 N Holliday St.
PO Box 69
Strasburg, VA 22657-0069
Phone: (540)465-5137
Fax: (540)465-9388
**Subject(s):** Daily Newspapers
**Circ:** (Mon.-Sat.)15,772

**The Weekender** (31526)
News-Gazette Corp.
PO Box 1153
Lexington, VA 24450
Phone: (540)463-3113
Fax: (540)464-6197
**Subject(s):** Free Newspapers
**Circ:** (Controlled)15,500

**The Daily Athenaeum** (32675)
West Virginia University
284 Prospect St.
Morgantown, WV 26506
Phone: (304)293-4141
Fax: (304)293-6857
**Subject(s):** College Publications
**Circ:** (Free)‡15,000

**The Review** (5153)
University of Delaware
250 Perkins Student Ctr.
Newark, DE 19716
Phone: (302)831-1395
Fax: (302)831-1396
**Subject(s):** College Publications
**Circ:** (Paid)‡15,000

**Reston/Herndon Times-Mirror** (31752)
Arcom Publishing Inc.
1760 Reston Pkwy., Ste. 411
Reston, VA 20190
Phone: (703)437-5400
Fax: (703)437-6019
**Subject(s):** Free Newspapers
**Circ:** (Paid)499
(Non-paid)14,985

**Jefferson Buyers Guide** (32556)
Panhandle Buyers Guide Publications Inc.
415 Wilson St.
PO Box 2118
Martinsburg, WV 25401
Phone: (304)267-9983
Fax: (304)263-7106
**Subject(s):** Shopping Guides
**Circ:** (Free)14,964

**Fauquier Times-Democrat** (31937)
Arcom Publishing Inc.
39 Culpeper St.
Warrenton, VA 20186
Phone: (540)347-4222
Fax: (540)349-8676
**Subject(s):** Paid Community Newspapers
**Circ:** 14,924

**St. Mary's Enterprise** (13240)
Chesapeake Publishing Corp.
PO Box 700
Lexington Park, MD 20653
Phone: (301)862-2111
Fax: (301)737-1665
**Subject(s):** Paid Community Newspapers
**Circ:** (Non-paid)554
(Paid)14,776

**Hockessin Community News** (5120)
Dover Post Co.
609 E. Division St.
Dover, DE 19901
Phone: (302)678-3616
Fax: (302)678-8291
**Subject(s):** Paid Community Newspapers
**Circ:** (Combined)14,600

**Gazette Virginian.Com** (31875)
Gazette Virginian
3201-3209 Halifax Rd.
PO Box 524
South Boston, VA 24592
Phone: (434)572-3945
Fax: (434)572-1173
**Subject(s):** Paid Community Newspapers
**Circ:** ‡14,384

**The Mecklenberg Sun** (31296)
Sun Publishing Company Inc.
PO Box 997
Clarksville, VA 23927
Phone: (434)374-8152
Fax: (434)374-8153
**Subject(s):** Paid Community Newspapers
**Circ:** (Paid)4,000
(Free)14,333

**Delaware Coast Press** (13319)
Gannett Company Inc.
c/o Greg Bassett, Executive Editor
115 East Carroll St.
Salisbury, MD 21801
Phone: (877)335-6278
Fax: (410)341-6709
**Subject(s):** Free Newspapers
**Circ:** (Paid)342
(Non-paid)14,137

**The Baltimore Chronicle** (12670)
30 W. 25th St.
Baltimore, MD 21218
Phone: (410)243-4141
**Subject(s):** Free Newspapers
**Circ:** (Paid)‡450
(Free)‡14,000

**The Burke/Fairfax Station Connection** (31229)
Connection Newspapers L.L.C.
7913 Westpark Dr.
Mc Lean, VA 22102-4201
Phone: (703)821-5050

Fax: (703)917-0991
**Subject(s):** Free Newspapers
**Circ:** (Free)14,006

**Collegiate Times** (31194)
121 Squires Student Ctr.
Blacksburg, VA 24061
Phone: (540)231-9860
Fax: (540)231-5057
**Subject(s):** College Publications
**Circ:** (Free)‡14,000

**Radio World** (31385)
IMAS Publishing Inc.
5827 Columbia Pike
Falls Church, VA 22041
Phone: (703)998-7600
Fax: (703)671-7409
**Subject(s):** Radio, Television, Cable, and Video
**Circ:** (Controlled)‡14,000

**The Eastern Shore News** (31651)
Thomson Publishing Inc.
PO Box 249
Onley, VA 23418
Phone: (804)787-1200
**Subject(s):** Paid Community Newspapers
**Circ:** ‡13,800

**The Baltimore Messenger** (13367)
Patuxent Publishing Co.
409 Washington Ave.
Towson, MD 21204
Phone: (410)337-2400
Fax: (410)337-2490
**Subject(s):** Free Newspapers
**Circ:** (Paid)43
(Non-paid)13,793

**PA Times** (5608)
American Society for Public Administration
1120 G St. NW, Ste. 700
Washington, DC 20005
Phone: (202)393-7878
Fax: (202)638-4952
**Subject(s):** State, Municipal, and County Administration
**Circ:** 13,500

**Tazewell County Free Press** (31765)
1249 Front St.
PO Box 1205
Richlands, VA 24641-1049
Phone: (276)963-0127
Fax: (276)963-0127
**Subject(s):** Free Newspapers
**Circ:** (Free)13,500

**York Towncrier** (31457)
Spectrum Publishing Inc.
159 Sweeney Blvd.
Langley AFB
Hampton, VA 23665-2207
Phone: (804)764-2018
**Subject(s):** Free Newspapers; Military and Navy
**Circ:** (Controlled)‡13,500

**Blade-News** (13018)
Capital Publishing Co.
PO Box 790
Bowie, MD 20718
**Subject(s):** Paid Community Newspapers
**Circ:** (Thurs.)13,402

**Mt. Vernon Gazette** (31042)
Connection Publishing Inc.
1610 King St.
Alexandria, VA 22314
Phone: (703)549-7185
Fax: (703)549-9655
**Subject(s):** Free Newspapers
**Circ:** (Non-paid)13,100

**Washington Jewish Week** (13310)
1500 E Jefferson St.
Rockville, MD 20852
Phone: (301)230-2222
Fax: (301)881-1994
**Subject(s):** Jewish Publications
**Circ:** ‡13,000

**Brandywine Community News** (5116)
Dover Post Co.
609 E. Division St.
Dover, DE 19901
Phone: (302)678-3616
Fax: (302)678-8291
**Subject(s):** Paid Community Newspapers
**Circ:** (Paid)12,955

**Times-West Virginian** (32594)
PO Box 2530
Fairmont, WV 26555-2530
Phone: (304)363-5000
Fax: (304)366-9620
**Subject(s):** Daily Newspapers
**Circ:** (Mon.-Sat.)★**11,264**
 (Sun.)★**12,812**

**Herndon Times** (31492)
Arcom Publishing Inc.
13873 Park Center Rd., Ste. 301
Herndon, VA 20171-3285
Phone: (703)478-6666
Fax: (703)435-9754
**Subject(s):** Free Newspapers
**Circ:** (Paid)220
 (Free)12,525

**Alexandria Gazette Packet** (30970)
Connection Publishing Inc.
1610 King St.
Alexandria, VA 22314
Phone: (703)549-7185
Fax: (703)549-9655
**Subject(s):** Paid Community Newspapers
**Circ:** (Combined)12,508

**Star Herald** (32727)
Ripley Newspaper Inc.
PO Box 31
Ripley, WV 25271
Fax: (304)372-8240
**Subject(s):** Shopping Guides; Free Newspapers
**Circ:** (Non-paid)12,500

**Lincoln Journal** (32612)
The Lincoln Journal Inc.
328 Walnut St.
PO Box 308
Hamlin, WV 25523
Phone: (304)824-5101
Fax: (304)824-5210
**Subject(s):** Paid Community Newspapers
**Circ:** ‡12,433

**Potomac/Bethesda Almanac** (13269)
Connection Publishing Inc.
10220 River Rd., No. 303
Potomac, MD 20854
Phone: (301)983-3350
**Subject(s):** Free Newspapers
**Circ:** (Combined)12,400

**Roll Call** (5674)
Roll Call Inc.
50 F St. NW, Ste. 700
Washington, DC 20001-1572
Phone: (202)824-6800
Fax: (202)824-0475
**Subject(s):** Congressional and Federal Government Affairs
**Circ:** (Paid)5,161
 (Non-paid)12,244

**The Dorchester Star** (13094)
Chesapeake Publishing Corp.
PO Box 600
Easton, MD 21601
Phone: (410)822-1500
Fax: (410)770-4012
**Subject(s):** Free Newspapers
**Circ:** (Non-paid)♦**12,177**

**The GW Hatchet** (5414)
George Washington University
2140 G St. NW
Washington, DC 20052
Phone: (202)994-7079
Fax: (202)994-1309
**Subject(s):** College Publications
**Circ:** (Paid)‡150
 (Free)‡12,000

**Rural Virginian** (31263)
PO Box 9030
Charlottesville, VA 22906-9030
Phone: (434)978-7216
Fax: (434)978-7204
**Subject(s):** Paid Community Newspapers
**Circ:** (Non-paid)12,000

**Tribune** (31267)
Orange Review
PO Box 3428
Charlottesville, VA 22903
Phone: (434)979-0373
Fax: (434)971-5821
**Subject(s):** Paid Community Newspapers
**Circ:** (Free)‡125
 (Paid)‡12,000

**Soundoff** (13112)
Patuxent Publishing Co.
Post Public Affairs Office
Bldg. 2837, Ernie Pyle St.
Fort Meade, MD 20755-5025
Phone: (410)677-1388
Fax: (410)799-5911
**Subject(s):** Free Newspapers; Military and Navy
**Circ:** (Paid)8
 (Non-paid)11,841

**Gloucester-Mathews Gazette-Journal** (31441)
Tidewater Newspaper Inc.
PO Box 2060
Gloucester, VA 23061
Phone: (804)693-3101
Fax: (804)693-7844
**Subject(s):** Paid Community Newspapers
**Circ:** (Thurs.)11,463

**The Republican** (13253)
Sincell Publishing Company Inc.
PO Box 326
Oakland, MD 21550
Phone: (301)334-3963
Fax: (301)334-5904
**Subject(s):** Paid Community Newspapers
**Circ:** (Thurs.)11,425

**The Loudoun Connection** (31586)
Connection Newspapers L.L.C.
7913 Westpark Dr.
Mc Lean, VA 22102-4201
Phone: (703)821-5050
Fax: (703)917-0991
**Subject(s):** Free Newspapers
**Circ:** (Free)11,389

**The Presbyterian Outlook** (31788)
The Presbyterian Outlook Foundation Inc.
Box 85623
Richmond, VA 23227
Phone: (804)359-8442
Fax: (804)353-6369
**Subject(s):** Religious Publications
**Circ:** (Paid)11,020

**Quantico Sentry** (31675)
MCB Quantico
Commanding General, MCB Quantico
Attn: Public Affairs Office
3250 Catlin Ave.
Quantico, VA 22134
Phone: (703)784-2741
**Subject(s):** Military and Navy; Free Newspapers
**Circ:** (Free)‡11,000

**Centerville Times** (31490)
Arcom Publishing Inc.
13873 Park Center Rd., Ste. 301
Herndon, VA 20171-3285
Phone: (703)478-6666
Fax: (703)435-9754
**Subject(s):** Free Newspapers
**Circ:** (Paid)189
 (Free)10,929

**Greenbelt News Review** (13185)
Greenbelt Cooperative Publishing Association Inc.
15 Crescent Rd., Ste. 100
Greenbelt, MD 20770-1887
Phone: (301)474-4131
Fax: (301)474-5880
**Subject(s):** Free Newspapers
**Circ:** (Paid)‡100
 (Free)‡10,900

**Mill Creek Community News** (5122)
Dover Post Co.
609 E. Division St.
Dover, DE 19901
Phone: (302)678-3616
Fax: (302)678-8291
**Subject(s):** Paid Community Newspapers
**Circ:** (Paid)10,800

**The Reston Connection** (31591)
Connection Newspapers L.L.C.
7913 Westpark Dr.
Mc Lean, VA 22102-4201
Phone: (703)821-5050
Fax: (703)917-0991
**Subject(s):** Free Newspapers
**Circ:** (Free)10,709

**News** (32785)
Williamson Daily News
100 Block E. 3rd Ave.
PO Box 1660
Williamson, WV 25661
Phone: (304)235-4242
Fax: (304)235-0730
**Subject(s):** Daily Newspapers
**Circ:** 10,627

**The Wheel** (31618)
Military Newspapers of Virginia
213 Calhoun St.
Fort Eustis, VA 23604
**Subject(s):** Free Newspapers
**Circ:** (Free)‡10,500

**The Herndon Connection** (31582)
Connection Newspapers L.L.C.
7913 Westpark Dr.
Mc Lean, VA 22102-4201
Phone: (703)821-5050
Fax: (703)917-0991
**Subject(s):** Free Newspapers
**Circ:** (Free)10,123

**The Cavalier Daily** (31240)
University of Virginia
PO Box 400703
Charlottesville, VA 22904-4703
Phone: (434)924-1086
Fax: (434)924-7290
**Subject(s):** College Publications; Daily Newspapers
**Circ:** (Free)‡10,000

**Gay Life** (12734)
Gay and Lesbian Community Center of Baltimore
241 W. Chase St.
Baltimore, MD 21201
**Subject(s):** Gay and Lesbian Interests
**Circ:** (Paid)‡3,000
 (Free)‡10,000

**Prince George's Times** (12849)
Baltimore Times
2513 N Charles St.
Baltimore, MD 21218
Phone: (410)366-3900
Fax: (410)243-1627
**Subject(s):** Free Newspapers
**Circ:** (Non-paid)‡10,000

**The Towerlight** (13379)
Towson University
8000 York Rd.
Towson, MD 21252-0001
Phone: (410)704-2000
**Subject(s):** College Publications
**Circ:** ‡10,000

**Virginia Cattleman** (31311)
Virginia Cattleman's Association
PO Box 9
Daleville, VA 24083-0009
Phone: (540)992-1009
Fax: (540)992-4632
**Subject(s):** Livestock
**Circ:** ‡10,000

**The Weekender** (12911)
Homestead Publishing Company Inc.
10 Hays St.
PO Box 189
Bel Air, MD 21014
Phone: (410)838-4400
Fax: (410)638-0357

# Gale Directory of Publications & Broadcast Media/140th Ed.   Middle Atlantic States

**Subject(s):** Paid Community Newspapers
**Circ:** ‡10,000

**Walkersville/Thurmont Gazette** (13148)
The Gazette Newspapers
2A N. Market St., 4th Fl.
Frederick, MD 21701
Phone: (301)846-2100
Fax: (301)846-2114
**Subject(s):** Free Newspapers
**Circ:** (Combined)9,961

**Baltimore Afro-American** (12668)
The Afro-American Co.
2519 N. Charles St.
Baltimore, MD 21218
Phone: (410)554-8200
Fax: (410)554-8213
**Subject(s):** Paid Community Newspapers; Black Publications
**Circ:** (Sat.)9,947

**Montgomery Village Gazette** (13136)
The Gazette Newspapers
2A N. Market St., 4th Fl.
Frederick, MD 21701
Phone: (301)846-2100
Fax: (301)846-2114
**Subject(s):** Free Newspapers
**Circ:** (Combined)9,888

**The Springfield Connection** (31890)
Connection Newspapers L.L.C.
7913 Westpark Dr.
Mc Lean, VA 22102-4201
Phone: (703)821-5050
Fax: (703)917-0991
**Subject(s):** Free Newspapers
**Circ:** (Free)9,742

**The Fauquier Citizen** (31936)
17 S. 5th St.
Warrenton, VA 20186
Phone: (540)347-5522
Fax: (540)347-7363
**Subject(s):** Paid Community Newspapers
**Circ:** (Paid)9,545

**The Vienna/Oakton Connection** (31920)
Connection Newspapers L.L.C.
7913 Westpark Dr.
Mc Lean, VA 22102-4201
Phone: (703)821-5250
Fax: (703)917-0997
**Subject(s):** Free Newspapers
**Circ:** (Free)❑9,518

**Greenbrier Valley Trader** (32650)
Greenbrier Valley Advertiser
122 N Court St.
Lewisburg, WV 24901
Phone: (304)647-5724
Fax: (304)647-5767
**Subject(s):** Shopping Guides
**Circ:** 9,500

**Greenville Community News** (5119)
Dover Post Co.
609 E. Division St.
Dover, DE 19901
Phone: (302)678-3616
Fax: (302)678-8291
**Subject(s):** Paid Community Newspapers
**Circ:** (Combined)9,500

**The Calvert Independent** (13275)
PO Box 910
424 Solomons Island Rd.
Prince Frederick, MD 20678
Phone: (301)855-1000
Fax: (301)855-9070
**Circ:** (Paid)9,308

**Business Ledger** (5140)
153 E. Chestnut Hill Rd.
Ste. 104 Robscott Bldg.
Newark, DE 19713-4054
Phone: (302)737-0923
Fax: (302)737-9019
**Subject(s):** Business
**Circ:** (Paid)954
(Non-paid)9,126

**Baltimore Business Journal** (12669)
American City Business Journals Inc.
111 Market Pl., Ste. 720
Baltimore, MD 21202
Phone: (410)752-3112
Fax: (410)752-3112
**Subject(s):** Business; Local, State, and Regional Publications
**Circ:** (Paid)9,089

**New Market/Urbana Gazette** (13137)
The Gazette Newspapers
2A N. Market St., 4th Fl.
Frederick, MD 21701
Phone: (301)846-2100
Fax: (301)846-2114
**Subject(s):** Free Newspapers
**Circ:** (Combined)8,905

**The News-Gazette** (31523)
News-Gazette Corp.
PO Box 1153
Lexington, VA 24450
Phone: (540)463-3113
Fax: (540)464-6397
**Subject(s):** Paid Community Newspapers
**Circ:** (Wed.)8,861

**The Gazette** (31424)
Landmark Community Newspapers Inc.
108 W. Stuart Dr.
PO Box 68
Galax, VA 24333-0068
Phone: (540)236-0756
Fax: (540)236-0756
**Subject(s):** Paid Community Newspapers
**Circ:** ‡8,800

**The Mc Lean Connection** (31587)
Connection Newspapers L.L.C.
7913 Westpark Dr.
Mc Lean, VA 22102-4201
Phone: (703)821-5250
Fax: (703)917-0997
**Subject(s):** Free Newspapers
**Circ:** (Free)❑8,782

**The Farmville Herald** (31392)
114 N St.
PO Box 307
Farmville, VA 23901
Phone: (434)392-4151
Fax: (434)392-6298
**Subject(s):** Paid Community Newspapers
**Circ:** ‡8,600

**Star-Tribune** (31285)
Womack Publishing Co.
30 N. Main St.
Chatham, VA 24531
Phone: (434)432-1654
Fax: (434)432-1005
**Subject(s):** Paid Community Newspapers
**Circ:** ‡8,372
8,532

**Bedford Bulletin** (31185)
Landmark Community Newspapers Inc.
PO Box 331
Bedford, VA 24523
Phone: (540)586-8612
Fax: (540)586-0834
**Subject(s):** Paid Community Newspapers
**Circ:** ‡8,500

**The Georgetown Voice** (5404)
Georgetown University
PO Box 571066
Georgetown University
Washington, DC 20057-1066
Phone: (202)687-6780
Fax: (202)687-6763
**Subject(s):** College Publications
**Circ:** (Free)‡8,400

**The HOYA** (5425)
Georgetown University
Georgetown University Main Campus and Medical Center
37th and O Street, NW
Washington, DC 20057
Phone: (202)687-3415
Fax: (202)687-2741
**Subject(s):** College Publications
**Circ:** (Paid)‡500
(Free)‡8,400

**Aspen Hill Gazette** (13116)
The Gazette Newspapers
2A N. Market St., 4th Fl.
Frederick, MD 21701
Phone: (301)846-2100
Fax: (301)846-2114
**Subject(s):** Free Newspapers
**Circ:** (Combined)8,324

**Richlands News Press** (31655)
Central Virginia Weekly Group
110 Berry Hill Rd.
PO Box 589
Orange, VA 22960
Fax: (703)672-5831
**Subject(s):** Paid Community Newspapers
**Circ:** ‡8,300

**The Fairfax Connection** (31342)
Connection Newspapers L.L.C.
7913 Westpark Dr.
Mc Lean, VA 22102-4201
Phone: (703)821-5050
Fax: (703)917-0991
**Subject(s):** Free Newspapers
**Circ:** (Free)8,270

**The Virginia Mountaineer** (31446)
Mountaineer Publishing Co.
1200 Plaza Dr Ste. 2400
Grundy, VA 24614
Phone: (276)935-2123
Fax: (276)935-2125
**Subject(s):** Paid Community Newspapers
**Circ:** (Free)‡125
(Paid)‡8,270

**County News** (5340)
National Association of Counties
440 1st St. NW
Washington, DC 20001-2082
Phone: (202)942-2630
Fax: (202)393-2630
**Subject(s):** State, Municipal, and County Administration
**Circ:** (Free)2,500
(Paid)8,000

**The Delmarva Farmer** (13093)
American Farm Publications Inc.
505 Brookletts Ave.
PO Box 2026
Easton, MD 21601
Phone: (410)822-3965
Fax: (410)822-5068
**Subject(s):** Farm Newspapers
**Circ:** (Free)‡3,702
(Paid)‡8,000

**The Eagle-News** (5363)
American University Eagle
227 Mary Graydon
4400 Massachusetts Ave. NW
Washington, DC 20016
Phone: (202)885-1400
Fax: (202)885-1428
**Subject(s):** College Publications
**Circ:** (Paid)150
(Free)8,000

**Franklin News-Post** (31857)
Franklin County Newspapers Inc.
310 S Main St.
PO Box 250
Rocky Mount, VA 24151-0250
Phone: (540)483-5113
Fax: (540)483-8013
**Subject(s):** Paid Community Newspapers
**Circ:** ‡8,000

**Herald-Progress** (31181)
11293 Air Park Rd.
Ashland, VA 23005-3452
Phone: (804)798-9031
Fax: (804)798-9036
**Subject(s):** Paid Community Newspapers
**Circ:** (Mon.)8,000
(Thurs.)8,000

**The Central Virginian** (31533)
PO Box 464
Louisa, VA 23093
Phone: (540)967-0368
Fax: (540)967-0457

Circulation: ★ = ABC; △ = BPA; ♦ = CAC; • = CCAB; ❑ = VAC; ⊕ = PO Statement; ‡ = Publisher's Report; Boldface figures = sworn; Light figures = estimated.

## Middle Atlantic States

**Subject(s):** Paid Community Newspapers
**Circ:** (Free)‡100
(Paid)‡7,800

**Culpeper Star-Exponent (31308)**
Robin L. Quillon
122 W Spencer St.
PO Box 111
Culpeper, VA 22701
Phone: (540)825-0771
Fax: (540)825-0778
**Subject(s):** Daily Newspapers
**Circ:** 7,800

**Virginian Review (31303)**
Covington Virginian Inc.
128 N Maple Ave.
PO Box 271
Covington, VA 24426
Phone: (540)962-2121
Fax: (540)902-5072
**Subject(s):** Daily Newspapers
**Circ:** (Mon.-Sat.)7,808

**The Coalfield Progress (31646)**
The Norton Press Inc.
725 Park Ave.
PO Box 380
Norton, VA 24273
Phone: (276)679-1101
Fax: (276)679-5922
**Subject(s):** Paid Community Newspapers
**Circ:** (Tues.)7,373
(Thurs.)7,731

**Kent County News (13032)**
PO Box 30
Chestertown, MD 21620
Phone: (410)778-2011
Fax: (410)778-6522
**Subject(s):** Paid Community Newspapers
**Circ:** (Non-paid)55
(Paid)7,641

**Page News and Courier (31535)**
Page-Shenandoah Newspaper Corp.
17 S. Broad St.
Luray, VA 22835
Phone: (540)743-5123
**Subject(s):** Paid Community Newspapers
**Circ:** (Thurs.)7,646

**The Daily Record (12716)**
The Daily Record Co.
11 E. Saratoga St.
Baltimore, MD 21202
Phone: (410)752-3849
Fax: (410)752-2894
**Subject(s):** Daily Periodicals
**Circ:** (Free)‡1,747
‡7,597

**Southwest Virginia Enterprise (31972)**
460 W Main St.
Wytheville, VA 24382
Phone: (276)228-6611
Fax: (276)228-7260
**Subject(s):** Paid Community Newspapers
**Circ:** 7,500

**The News-Virginian (31945)**
Park Communications
544 W Main St.
PO Box 1027
Waynesboro, VA 22980
Phone: (540)949-8213
**Subject(s):** Daily Newspapers
**Circ:** (Sun.)★7,263
(Mon.-Sat.)★7,492

**Powell Valley News (31659)**
Powell Valley Printing Co.
Po Box 459
Pennington Gap, VA 24277-0459
Phone: (276)546-1210
Fax: (276)546-5468
**Subject(s):** Paid Community Newspapers
**Circ:** 7,471

**Orange County Review (31654)**
Central Virginia Weekly Group
110 Berry Hill Rd.
PO Box 589
Orange, VA 22960
Fax: (703)672-5831

**Subject(s):** Paid Community Newspapers
**Circ:** ‡7,400

**Damascus Courier-Gazette (13088)**
The Gazette Newspapers
2A N. Market St., 4th Fl.
Frederick, MD 21701
Phone: (301)846-2100
Fax: (301)846-2114
**Subject(s):** Free Newspapers
**Circ:** (Combined)7,392

**Enterprise Buyers' Catalogue (31971)**
Community Newspapers
460 W Main St.
Wytheville, VA 24382
Phone: (276)228-6611
Fax: (276)228-7260
**Subject(s):** Shopping Guides
**Circ:** (Free)7,350

**Cape Gazette (5130)**
17585 Nassau Commons Blvd. Ste.600
PO Box 213
Lewes, DE 19958
Phone: (302)645-7700
Fax: (302)645-1664
**Subject(s):** Paid Community Newspapers
**Circ:** (Combined)⊕7,300

**Northern Neck News (31942)**
Chesapeake Publishing Corp.
132 Court Cir.
PO Box 8
Warsaw, VA 22572-0008
Phone: (804)333-3655
Fax: (804)333-0033
**Subject(s):** Paid Community Newspapers
**Circ:** 7,286

**Courier-Record (31215)**
Nottoway Publishing Company Inc.
111 W Maple St.
PO Box 460
Blackstone, VA 23824
Phone: (434)292-3019
Fax: (434)292-5966
**Subject(s):** Paid Community Newspapers
**Circ:** (Free)‡200
(Paid)‡7,150

**Kensington Gazette (13135)**
The Gazette Newspapers
2A N. Market St., 4th Fl.
Frederick, MD 21701
Phone: (301)846-2100
Fax: (301)846-2114
**Subject(s):** Free Newspapers
**Circ:** (Combined)7,158

**The News Progress (31297)**
Mecklenburg News
329 Virginia Ave.
Box 1015
Clarksville, VA 23927
Phone: (434)374-2451
Fax: (434)374-2074
**Subject(s):** Paid Community Newspapers
**Circ:** ‡7,100

**The Airlifter (5114)**
Dover Post Co.
436 AW/PA
Dover AFB
Dover, DE 19902-5154
Phone: (302)677-3373
**Subject(s):** Free Newspapers; Military and Navy
**Circ:** (Free)7,000

**The Flat Hat (31948)**
The Campus Ctr.
College of William and Mary
Williamsburg, VA 23185
Phone: (757)221-3283
Fax: (757)221-3242
**Subject(s):** College Publications
**Circ:** (Paid)‡400
(Free)‡7,000

**NADmag (13352)**
National Association of the Deaf
814 Thayer Ave.
Silver Spring, MD 20910-4500
Phone: (301)587-1788
Fax: (301)587-1791

**Subject(s):** Hearing and Speech
**Circ:** 7,000

**The Welch Daily News (32767)**
Moffitt Newspapers
125 Wyoming St.
PO Box 569
Welch, WV 24801
Phone: (304)436-3144
Fax: (304)436-3146
**Subject(s):** Daily Newspapers
**Circ:** ‡7,000

**The Weston Democrat (32772)**
306 Main Ave.
Weston, WV 26452
**Subject(s):** Paid Community Newspapers
**Circ:** ‡7,000

**Catonsville Times (13029)**
Patuxent Publishing Co.
757 Frederick Rd.
Ste. 103
Catonsville, MD
Phone: (410)788-4500
Fax: (410)788-4103
**Subject(s):** Paid Community Newspapers
**Circ:** (Non-paid)4,108
(Paid)6,991

**Jeffersonian (13368)**
Patuxent Publishing Co.
409 Washington Ave.
Towson, MD 21204
Phone: (410)337-2400
Fax: (410)337-2490
**Subject(s):** Paid Community Newspapers
**Circ:** (Non-paid)869
(Paid)6,783

**Rockland Journal-News (31592)**
Gannett Company Inc.
7950 Jones Branch Dr.
Mc Lean, VA 22107
Phone: (703)854-6000
**Subject(s):** Daily Newspapers
**Circ:** (Mon.-Fri.)6,650
(Sun.)6,728

**The Carroll News (31498)**
PO Box 487
Hillsville, VA 24343
Phone: (276)728-7311
Fax: (276)728-4119
**Subject(s):** Paid Community Newspapers
**Circ:** ‡6,700

**Scott County Virginia Star (31433)**
Scott County Herald Virginian Inc.
PO Box 218
113 W. Jackson St.
Gate City, VA 24251
Phone: (276)386-7027
Fax: (276)386-2354
**Subject(s):** Paid Community Newspapers
**Circ:** (Paid)6,700

**Amelia Bulletin Monitor (31092)**
The Monitor
PO Box 123
Amelia Court House, VA 23002
Phone: (804)561-3655
Fax: (804)561-2065
**Subject(s):** Free Newspapers
**Circ:** (Free)‡2,798
(Paid)‡6,692

**Ossining Citizen Register (31590)**
Gannett Company Inc.
7950 Jones Branch Dr.
Mc Lean, VA 22107
Phone: (703)854-6000
**Subject(s):** Daily Newspapers
**Circ:** (Mon.-Sat.)5,876
(Sun.)6,675

**The Altavista Journal (31089)**
Womack Publishing Co.
PO Box 630
Altavista, VA 24517
Phone: (804)369-6688
Fax: (804)369-6689
**Subject(s):** Paid Community Newspapers
**Circ:** ‡6,600

**Smyth County News & Messenger (31559)**
Community Newspapers
119 S. Sheffey St.
PO Box 640
Marion, VA 24354
Phone: (276)783-5121
Fax: (276)783-9713
**Subject(s):** Paid Community Newspapers
**Circ:** (Wed.)6,600
(Sat.)6,600

**Independent-Messenger (31324)**
Byerly Publications
111 Baker St.
PO Box 786
Emporia, VA 23847
Phone: (434)634-4153
**Subject(s):** Paid Community Newspapers
**Circ:** ‡6,540

**Braxton Citizens' News (32752)**
Braxton Citizen's News
PO Box 516
Sutton, WV 26601
Phone: (304)765-5193
Fax: (304)765-2754
**Subject(s):** Paid Community Newspapers
**Circ:** ‡6,500

**The Jackson Herald (32725)**
Ripley Newspaper Inc.
PO Box 31
Ripley, WV 25271
Fax: (304)372-8240
**Subject(s):** Paid Community Newspapers
**Circ:** ‡6,500

**The Parkersburg Sentinel (32702)**
519 Juliana St.
PO Box 1788
Parkersburg, WV 26102
Phone: (304)485-1891
Fax: (304)485-1891
**Subject(s):** Daily Newspapers
**Circ:** (Mon.-Sat.)6,419

**The Pocahontas Times (32661)**
Pocahontas Times
810 2nd Ave.
Marlinton, WV 24954
**Subject(s):** Paid Community Newspapers
**Circ:** ‡6,325

**Hampshire Review (32729)**
New Hampshire Review
PO Box 1036
25 South Grafton Street
Romney, WV 26757
Phone: (304)822-3871
Fax: (304)822-4487
**Subject(s):** Paid Community Newspapers
**Circ:** ‡6100

**The Great Falls Connection (31581)**
Connection Newspapers L.L.C.
7913 Westpark Dr.
Mc Lean, VA 22102-4201
Phone: (703)821-5250
Fax: (703)917-0997
**Subject(s):** Free Newspapers
**Circ:** (Free)◻6,046

**Alleghany Highlander (31302)**
PO Box 271
Covington, VA 24426
Phone: (540)962-2121
Fax: (540)962-5072
**Subject(s):** Shopping Guides
**Circ:** (Free)‡6,000

**Hoa Thinh Don Viet Bao (31530)**
8394-C2 Terminal Rd.
Lorton, VA 22079
Phone: (703)339-9852
Fax: (703)339-9857
**Subject(s):** Free Newspapers; Vietnamese; Ethnic Publications
**Circ:** (Combined)6,000

**The Nicholas Chronicle (32750)**
Nicholas County Publishing Company Inc.
718 Broad Street
PO Box 503
Summersville, WV 26651-0503
Phone: (304)872-2251

Fax: (304)872-2254
**Subject(s):** Paid Community Newspapers
**Circ:** (Free)‡200
(Paid)‡6,000

**Brunswick Times-Gazette (31504)**
Byerly Publications
213 Main St.
PO Box 250
Lawrenceville, VA 23868
Phone: (804)848-2114
Fax: (804)848-2115
**Subject(s):** Paid Community Newspapers
**Circ:** ‡5,990

**Harford Business Ledger, Inc. (13206)**
Harford Business Ledger Inc.
316 Saint Johns St.
Hanover, MD 21098
Phone: (410)939-4040
Fax: (410)939-1390
**Subject(s):** Paid Community Newspapers
**Circ:** (Controlled)5,954

**Virginian-Leader (31658)**
511 Mountain Lake Ave.
Pearisburg, VA 24134-0702
Phone: (540)921-3434
Fax: (540)921-2563
**Subject(s):** Free Newspapers
**Circ:** (Free)20
(Paid)5,941

**The Fincastle Herald and Botetourt County News (31400)**
Salem Publishing
PO Box 127
276 Botetourt Road
Fincastle, VA 24090
Phone: (540)473-2741
Fax: (540)473-2741
**Subject(s):** Paid Community Newspapers
**Circ:** ‡5,900

**The News-Messenger (31294)**
Main Street Newspapers Inc.
PO Box 419
20 West Main Street
Christiansburg, VA 24068-0419
Phone: (540)382-6171
Fax: (540)382-3009
**Subject(s):** Daily Newspapers
**Circ:** (Free)‡4,200
(Paid)‡5,907

**Wayne County Publication Inc (32760)**
Wayne County Publications Inc.
310 Central Ave.
Wayne, WV 25570
Phone: (304)272-3433
Fax: (304)272-6516
**Subject(s):** Paid Community Newspapers
**Circ:** 5,860

**Culpeper News (31307)**
V.P. Culpeper Communications Corp.
605 S Main St.
Culpeper, VA 22701-3209
Phone: (540)825-3232
Fax: (540)825-5670
**Subject(s):** Paid Community Newspapers
**Circ:** (Free)300
(Paid)5,800

**The Daily Times (32764)**
114 Lee Ave.
Weirton, WV 26062-4619
Phone: (304)748-0606
Fax: (304)748-2202
**Subject(s):** Daily Newspapers
**Circ:** (Mon.-Sat.)★5,712
(Sun.)★5,752

**The Enterprise (31903)**
Enterprise Inc.
PO Box 348
Stuart, VA 24171-0348
Phone: (276)694-3101
Fax: (276)694-5110
**Subject(s):** Paid Community Newspapers
**Circ:** (Free)‡150
(Paid)‡5,750

**Takoma Park (13144)**
The Gazette Newspapers
2A N. Market St., 4th Fl.
Frederick, MD 21701
Phone: (301)846-2100
Fax: (301)846-2114
**Subject(s):** Free Newspapers
**Circ:** (Combined)5,720

**Hamlin Weekly News Sentinel (32611)**
The Lincoln Journal Inc.
328 Walnut St.
PO Box 308
Hamlin, WV 25523
Phone: (304)824-5101
Fax: (304)824-5210
**Subject(s):** Paid Community Newspapers
**Circ:** (Controlled)5,620

**Sussex-Surry Dispatch (31934)**
Virginia Gazette Companies L.L.C.
228 Fleetwood Ave.
PO Box 370
Wakefield, VA 23888
Phone: (757)899-3551
Fax: (757)899-7312
**Subject(s):** Paid Community Newspapers
**Circ:** (Paid)‡3,500
(Free)‡5,600

**The Shenandoah Valley-Herald (31970)**
Page-Shenandoah Newspaper Corp.
PO Box 507
Woodstock, VA 22664
Phone: (703)459-4078
Fax: (703)459-4077
**Subject(s):** Paid Community Newspapers
**Circ:** (Wed.)5,587

**Abingdon Virginian (30963)**
170 E Main St.
Abingdon, VA 24210
Phone: (540)628-2962
Fax: (540)676-6220
**Subject(s):** Paid Community Newspapers
**Circ:** (Free)‡1,000
(Paid)‡5,500

**Maryland Times-Press (13255)**
Gannett Company Inc.
214 16th St.
PO Box 479
Ocean City, MD 21842
Phone: (410)289-6834
Fax: (410)289-6838
**Subject(s):** Paid Community Newspapers
**Circ:** (Paid)5,500

**Middletown Transcript (5132)**
Dover Post Co.
24 W. Main St.
Middletown, DE 19709-1039
Phone: (302)378-0647
Fax: (302)378-0647
**Subject(s):** Paid Community Newspapers
**Circ:** (Paid)5,500

**The Morgan Messenger (32532)**
PO Box 567
Berkeley Springs, WV 25411
Phone: (304)258-1800
Fax: (304)258-8441
**Subject(s):** Paid Community Newspapers
**Circ:** ⊕5,500

**Preston County Journal (32644)**
PO Box 587
Kingwood, WV 26537
Phone: (304)329-0090
Fax: (304)329-2450
**Subject(s):** Paid Community Newspapers
**Circ:** 5,400

**Rappahannock Times (31907)**
W. A. Cleaton & Sons
PO Box 1025
Tappahannock, VA 22560
Phone: (804)443-2200
Fax: (804)443-9684
**Subject(s):** Paid Community Newspapers
**Circ:** ‡5,400

Circulation: ★ = ABC; △ = BPA; ♦ = CAC; • = CCAB; ◻ = VAC; ⊕ = PO Statement; ‡ = Publisher's Report; Boldface figures = sworn; Light figures = estimated.

## Middle Atlantic States

**Southside Sentinel  (31911)**
Rappahannock Press Inc.
PO Box 549
Urbanna, VA 23175
Phone: (804)758-2328
Fax: (804)758-5896
**Subject(s):** Paid Community Newspapers
**Circ:** (Free)75
(Paid)5,400

**Wetzel Chronicle  (32692)**
Wetzel Tyler Newspapers
PO Box 289
New Martinsville, WV 26155
Phone: (304)455-3300
Fax: (304)455-1275
**Subject(s):** Paid Community Newspapers
**Circ:** ‡5,400

**Grant County Press  (32709)**
Box 39
Petersburg, WV 26847
Phone: (304)257-1844
Fax: (304)257-1691
**Subject(s):** Paid Community Newspapers
**Circ:** ‡5,325

**Barbour Democrat  (32711)**
Barbour Publishing Co.
113 Church St.
Philippi, WV 26416
Phone: (304)457-2222
Fax: (304)457-2235
**Subject(s):** Paid Community Newspapers
**Circ:** ‡5,300

**Coal Valley News  (32659)**
PO Box 508
Madison, WV 25130
Phone: (304)369-1165
Fax: (304)369-1166
**Subject(s):** Paid Community Newspapers
**Circ:** ‡5,300

**The Pennsboro News  (32708)**
West Central Publishing Inc.
PO Box 368
Pennsboro, WV 26415
Phone: (304)684-2441
Fax: (304)659-3117
**Subject(s):** Paid Community Newspapers
**Circ:** ‡5,200

**The Recorder  (31611)**
Recorder Publishing of Virginia Inc.
PO Box 10
Monterey, VA 24465
Phone: (540)468-2147
Fax: (540)468-2048
**Subject(s):** Paid Community Newspapers
**Circ:** ‡5,200

**Roanoke Tribune  (31839)**
Roanoke Tribune Inc.
PO Box 6021
Roanoke, VA 24017
Phone: (540)343-0326
Fax: (540)343-7366
**Subject(s):** Black Publications; Paid Community Newspapers
**Circ:** 5,200

**The Montgomery Herald  (32670)**
406 Lee St.
PO Box 240
Montgomery, WV 25136
Phone: (304)442-4156
Fax: (304)442-8753
**Subject(s):** Paid Community Newspapers
**Circ:** 5,100

**The Smithfield Times  (31872)**
Times Publishing Co.
PO Box 366
Smithfield, VA 23431
Phone: (757)357-3288
**Subject(s):** Paid Community Newspapers
**Circ:** ‡5,100

**Broadside  (31338)**
George Mason Univ.
4400 University Dr.
Mail Stop 2C5
Fairfax, VA 22030-4444
Phone: (703)993-2950
Fax: (703)993-2948
**Subject(s):** Free Newspapers
**Circ:** (Free)‡5,000

**Casemate  (31452)**
Military Newspapers of Virginia
66 Ingalls Rd., Bldg. 27
Fort Monroe, VA 23651-1032
Phone: (757)788-3520
Fax: (757)788-2404
**Subject(s):** Free Newspapers
**Circ:** (Free)‡5,000

**The Declaration  (31245)**
University of Virginia
Newcomb Hall Sta.
PO Box 400418
Charlottesville, VA 22904
**Subject(s):** College Publications
**Circ:** (Free)‡5,000

**Hampton Script  (31453)**
Hampton University
PO Box 6237
Hampton, VA 23668
Phone: (757)727-5385
Fax: (757)727-5085
**Subject(s):** College Publications; Free Newspapers
**Circ:** (Combined)5,000

**Salem Times-Register  (31866)**
Salem Publishing Co.
PO Box 1125
Salem, VA 24153
Phone: (540)389-9355
Fax: (540)389-2930
**Subject(s):** Paid Community Newspapers
**Circ:** ‡5,000

**Spirit of Jefferson-Advocate  (32550)**
Jefferson Publishing Company Inc.
210 N George St.
PO Box 966
Charles Town, WV 25414-0966
Phone: (304)725-2046
**Subject(s):** Paid Community Newspapers
**Circ:** ‡5,000

**The Tartan  (31680)**
Radford University
PO Box 6985
Radford, VA 24142-5905
Phone: (540)831-5045
**Subject(s):** College Publications
**Circ:** (Free)‡5,000

**The Tower  (5721)**
127 Pryzbyla Center
Catholic University of America
Washington, DC 20064
Phone: (202)319-5778
Fax: (202)319-6675
**Subject(s):** College Publications
**Circ:** (Free)5,000

**Jackson Star News  (32726)**
305 N Church St.
PO Box 31
Ripley, WV 25271
Phone: (304)273-9333
Fax: (304)273-3401
**Subject(s):** Paid Community Newspapers
**Circ:** ‡4,884

**Mountain Messenger Newspaper  (32651)**
PO Box 429
Lewisburg, WV 24901
Phone: (304)647-5724
**Subject(s):** Paid Community Newspapers
**Circ:** (Non-paid)300
(Paid)4,776

**Sussex Countian  (5125)**
Dover Post Co.
115 N. Race St.
Georgetown, DE 19947
Phone: (302)856-0026
Fax: (302)856-0925
**Subject(s):** Paid Community Newspapers
**Circ:** ‡4,740

**Press  (31401)**
Box 155
Floyd, VA 24091-0155
Phone: (540)745-2127
Fax: (540)745-2126
**Subject(s):** Paid Community Newspapers
**Circ:** 4,700

**The Caroline Progress/Caroline Express  (31218)**
Chesapeake Publishing Corp.
PO Box 69
Bowling Green, VA 22427
Phone: (804)633-5005
Fax: (804)633-6740
**Subject(s):** Paid Community Newspapers
**Circ:** (Paid)‡4,595
(Free)‡4,650

**Mineral Daily News-Tribune  (32638)**
24 Armstrong St.
PO Box 879
Keyser, WV 26726
Phone: (304)788-3333
Fax: (304)788-3398
**Subject(s):** Daily Newspapers
**Circ:** ‡4,551

**Passenger Transport  (5614)**
American Public Transportation Association
1666 K St. NW, 11th Fl.
Washington, DC 20006
Phone: (202)496-4800
Fax: (202)496-4321
**Subject(s):** Transportation, Traffic, and Shipping
**Circ:** (Free)401
(Paid)4,535

**New Era-Progress  (31094)**
Amherst Publishing
113 2nd St.
PO Box 90
Amherst, VA 24521
Phone: (804)946-7195
Fax: (804)946-2684
**Subject(s):** Paid Community Newspapers
**Circ:** (Thurs.)4,414

**The Weekender Mountain Echo-News Tribune  (32640)**
PO Box 879
Keyser, WV 26726
Phone: (304)788-3333
Fax: (304)788-3398
**Subject(s):** Paid Community Newspapers
**Circ:** 4,400

**The Post  (31188)**
PO Box 250
215 Wood Ave.
Big Stone Gap, VA 24219
Phone: (276)523-1141
Fax: (276)523-1175
**Subject(s):** Paid Community Newspapers
**Circ:** ⊕4,394

**The Valley Banner  (31323)**
Rockingham Publishing Company Inc.
157 W. Spotswood Ave.
Elkton, VA 22827
Phone: (540)298-9444
Fax: (540)298-2560
**Subject(s):** Paid Community Newspapers
**Circ:** (Thurs.)4,372

**Suffolk News-Herald  (31905)**
PO Box 1220
130 South Saratoga Street
Suffolk, VA 23434-1220
Phone: (757)539-3437
**Subject(s):** Daily Newspapers
**Circ:** (Mon.-Fri.)4,240
(Sun.)4,318

**Madison County Eagle  (31552)**
Central Virginia Weekly Group
PO Box 325
201 N. Main St.
Madison, VA 22727-0325
Phone: (540)948-5121
Fax: (540)948-3045
**Subject(s):** Paid Community Newspapers
**Circ:** ‡4,300

**Gazette/Virginia Shopper  (31874)**
Halifax Gazette Publishing Co.
3201-3209 Halifax Rd.
South Boston, VA 24592
Phone: (434)572-3945
Fax: (434)572-1173

**Subject(s):** Shopping Guides
**Circ:** (Free)4,274

**Clay County Free Press (32580)**
Elk Printing Co.
PO Box 180
291 Main St
Clay, WV 25043
Phone: (304)587-4253
Fax: (304)587-7300
**Subject(s):** Paid Community Newspapers

**Circ:** ‡4,250

**Arbutus Times (13028)**
Patuxent Publishing Co.
757 Frederick Rd.
Ste. 103
Catonsville, MD
Phone: (410)788-4500
Fax: (410)788-4103
**Subject(s):** Paid Community Newspapers

**Circ:** (Non-paid)1,060
(Paid)4,207

**Braxton Democrat-Central (32753)**
205 Main St
Sutton, WV 26601
Phone: (304)765-5555
Fax: (304)765-5555
**Subject(s):** Paid Community Newspapers

**Circ:** ‡4,200

**Fayette Tribune (32697)**
417 Main St.
PO Box 139
Oak Hill, WV 25901
Phone: (304)469-3373
Fax: (304)469-4105
**Subject(s):** Paid Community Newspapers

**Circ:** (Paid)4,200

**Moundsville Daily Echo (32688)**
713 Lafayette Ave.
PO Box 369
Moundsville, WV 26041
Phone: (304)845-2660
Fax: (304)845-2661
**Subject(s):** Daily Newspapers

**Circ:** ‡4,200

**Association Trends (12945)**
Martineau Corp.
7910 Woodmont Ave., No. 1150
Bethesda, MD 20814-3062
Phone: (301)652-8666
Fax: (301)656-8654
**Subject(s):** Management and Administration

**Circ:** (Free)‡2,997
(Paid)‡4,154

**Westmoreland News (31612)**
Virginia Gazette Companies L.L.C.
PO Box 699
Montross, VA 22520
Phone: (804)493-8096
Fax: (804)493-8009
**Subject(s):** Paid Community Newspapers

**Circ:** (Free)‡118
(Paid)‡4,152

**Poolesville Gazette (13141)**
The Gazette Newspapers
2A N. Market St., 4th Fl.
Frederick, MD 21701
Phone: (301)846-2100
Fax: (301)846-2114
**Subject(s):** Free Newspapers

**Circ:** (Combined)4,144

**North Potomac Gazette (13138)**
The Gazette Newspapers
2A N. Market St., 4th Fl.
Frederick, MD 21701
Phone: (301)846-2100
Fax: (301)846-2114
**Subject(s):** Free Newspapers

**Circ:** (Combined)4,079

**The Collective (30988)**
North Virginia Community College
3001 N Beauregard
Alexandria, VA 22311
Phone: (703)845-6200

**Subject(s):** College Publications
**Circ:** 4,000

**The Shepherd College Picket (32743)**
Shepherd College
Miller Hall
PO Box 3210
Shepherdstown, WV 25443
Phone: (304)876-5377
**Subject(s):** College Publications

**Circ:** (Free)4,000

**The Shinnston News/The Harrison County Journal (32745)**
PO Box 187
Shinnston, WV 26431
Phone: (304)592-1030
Fax: (304)592-0603
**Subject(s):** Paid Community Newspapers

**Circ:** ‡4,000

**The Parsons Advocate (32707)**
The Parson Advocate
Po Box 345
Parsons, WV 26287
Phone: (304)478-3533
Fax: (304)478-1086
**Subject(s):** Free Newspapers

**Circ:** (Free)‡66
(Paid)‡3,900

**Smith Mountain Eagle (31610)**
Womack Publishing
14245 Moneta Rd.
PO Box 231
Moneta, VA 24121-0231
Phone: (540)297-1222
Fax: (540)297-1944
**Subject(s):** Paid Community Newspapers

**Circ:** ‡3,900

**Times-Virginian (31098)**
PO Box 2097
Appomattox, VA 24522-2097
Phone: (434)352-8215
Fax: (434)352-2216
**Subject(s):** Paid Community Newspapers

**Circ:** (Free)3,200
(Paid)3,900

**Nelson County Times (31093)**
Amherst Publishing
113 2nd St.
PO Box 90
Amherst, VA 24521
Phone: (804)946-7195
Fax: (804)946-2684
**Subject(s):** Paid Community Newspapers

**Circ:** (Thurs.)3,887

**Enquirer Gazette (13382)**
Washington Post Companies
PO Box 30
1481 Prat Street
Upper Marlboro, MD 20773-0030
Phone: (301)627-2833
Fax: (301)627-2835
**Subject(s):** Paid Community Newspapers

**Circ:** (Non-paid)1,002
(Paid)3,866

**West Virginia Daily News (32652)**
P.O. Box 471
Lewisburg, WV 24901
Phone: (304)645-1206
Fax: (304)645-7104
**Subject(s):** Daily Newspapers

**Circ:** (Free)⊕62
(Paid)⊕3,860

**Ritchie Gazette and The Cairo Standard (32614)**
200 E Main St.
PO Box 215
Harrisville, WV 26362-0215
Phone: (304)643-2221
Fax: (304)643-2156

**Circ:** (Free)‡44
(Paid)‡3,850

**Times Record (32748)**
Spencer Newspapers Inc.
210 E. Main St.
Spencer, WV 25276
Phone: (304)927-2360
Fax: (304)927-2361

**Subject(s):** Paid Community Newspapers
**Circ:** ‡3,776

**Smyrna/Clayton Sun-Times (5159)**
Dover Post Co.
25 W. Commerce St.
PO Box 327
Smyrna, DE 19977
Phone: (302)653-8821
Fax: (302)653-8821
**Subject(s):** Free Newspapers

**Circ:** (Paid)3,700

**Dinwiddie Monitor (31318)**
PO Box 66
Dinwiddie, VA 23841-0066
Phone: (804)733-8636
**Subject(s):** Paid Community Newspapers

**Circ:** (Non-paid)1,550
(Paid)3,690

**Tarrytown Daily News (31908)**
Gannett Company Inc.
7950 Jones Branch Dr.
Mc Lean, VA 22107
Phone: (703)854-6000
**Subject(s):** Daily Newspapers

**Circ:** (Mon.-Sat.)3,172
(Sun.)3,625

**The Brunswick Citizen (13022)**
Citizen Communications Inc.
101 W Potomac St.
Brunswick, MD 21716
Phone: (301)834-7722
**Subject(s):** Paid Community Newspapers

**Circ:** 3,500

**The Collegian (31774)**
University of Richmond
Tyler Haynes Commons, Rm. 327
University of Richmond
Richmond, VA 23173
Phone: (804)289-8483
Fax: (804)287-6092
**Subject(s):** College Publications

**Circ:** (Free)‡3,500

**Mountain Statesman (32606)**
914 W Main St.
PO Box 218
Grafton, WV 26354
Phone: (304)265-3333
Fax: (304)265-3342
**Subject(s):** Paid Community Newspapers

**Circ:** ‡3,500

**The St. Marys Oracle (32740)**
West Central Publishing Inc.
PO Box 27
Saint Marys, WV 26170
Phone: (304)684-2424
Fax: (304)684-2426
**Subject(s):** Paid Community Newspapers

**Circ:** ‡3,500

**Writer's Carousel (13015)**
The Writer's Center
4508 Walsh St.
Bethesda, MD 20815
Phone: (301)654-8664
Fax: (301)654-8667
**Subject(s):** Literature and Literary Reviews

**Circ:** (Paid)‡3,000
(Non-paid)‡3,500

**The Independent Herald (32716)**
Po Box 100
Pineville, WV 24874-0100
Phone: (304)732-6060
Fax: (304)732-8228
**Subject(s):** Free Newspapers

**Circ:** (Free)‡1,507
(Paid)‡3,484

**Clinch Valley News (31909)**
PO Box 977
119E. Fincastle
Tazewell, VA 24651
Phone: (276)988-4770
Fax: (276)963-0123
**Subject(s):** Paid Community Newspapers

**Circ:** (Free)36
(Paid)3,462

Circulation: ★ = ABC; ∆ = BPA; ♦ = CAC; • = CCAB; ❑ = VAC; ⊕ = PO Statement; ‡ = Publisher's Report; Boldface figures = sworn; Light figures = estimated.

## Middle Atlantic States

**Tyler Star-News  (32746)**
727 Wells St.
PO Box 191
Sistersville, WV 26175
Phone: (304)652-4141
Fax: (304)652-1454
**Subject(s):** Paid Community Newspapers
**Circ:** ‡3,400

**Calhoun Chronicle  (32609)**
Calhoun Publishing
PO Box 400
Grantsville, WV 26147
Phone: (304)354-6917
Fax: (304)354-7142
**Subject(s):** Paid Community Newspapers
**Circ:** 3,300

**Kenbridge-Victoria Dispatch  (31913)**
PO Box 40
Victoria, VA 23974-0040
Phone: (434)696-5550
Fax: (434)696-2958
**Subject(s):** Paid Community Newspapers
**Circ:** ‡3,300

**Charlotte Gazette  (31319)**
Charlotte Publishing
PO Box 214
Drakes Branch, VA 23937-0214
Phone: (434)568-3341
Fax: (434)568-3731
**Subject(s):** Paid Community Newspapers
**Circ:** 3,200

**Webster Echo  (32761)**
Echo Publishing Co.
219 Back Fork St.
Webster Springs, WV 26288
Phone: (304)847-5828
Fax: (304)847-5991
**Subject(s):** Paid Community Newspapers
**Circ:** 3,200

**Clarke Times-Courier  (31187)**
ARCOM Inc.
16 W Main
PO Box 32
Berryville, VA 22611
Phone: (540)955-1111
Fax: (540)955-1334
**Subject(s):** Paid Community Newspapers
**Circ:** ‡3,160

**The Northumberland Echo  (13096)**
Chesapeake Publishing Corp.
PO Box 600
Easton, MD 21601
Phone: (410)822-1500
Fax: (410)770-4012
**Subject(s):** Paid Community Newspapers
**Circ:** (Free)‡75
 (Paid)‡3,100

**Campus Crier  (12641)**
Anne Arundel Community College
101 College Pkwy.
Arnold, MD 21012-1857
Phone: (410)777-2803
Fax: (410)777-2201
**Subject(s):** College Publications
**Circ:** ‡3,000

**Commonwealth Times  (31775)**
T.Edward Temple Bldg., Rm. 1149, 901 W. Main St.
PO Box 842010
Richmond, VA 23284-2010
Phone: (804)828-1058
Fax: (804)828-9201
**Subject(s):** College Publications
**Circ:** 3,000

**Greene County Record  (31891)**
Central Virginia Weekly Group
PO Box 66
Main St.
Stanardsville, VA 22973
Phone: (434)985-2315
Fax: (434)985-8356
**Subject(s):** Paid Community Newspapers
**Circ:** ‡3,000

**The Greyhound  (12739)**
4501 N. Charles St.
Bellarmine Hall 01
Baltimore, MD 21210
Phone: (410)617-2282
Fax: (410)617-2982
**Subject(s):** College Publications
**Circ:** (Free)3,000

**Hinton News  (32617)**
210 2nd Ave.
PO Box 1000
Hinton, WV 25951
Phone: (304)466-0005
**Subject(s):** Paid Community Newspapers
**Circ:** 3,000

**The Moving World  (31043)**
American Moving & Storage Association
1611 Duke St.
Alexandria, VA 22314
Phone: (703)683-7410
Fax: (703)683-7527
**Subject(s):** Transportation, Traffic, and Shipping
**Circ:** ‡3,000

**The Rotunda  (31393)**
Longwood University
P O Box 2901
Farmville, VA 23909-2901
Phone: (434)395-2120
Fax: (434)395-2237
**Subject(s):** College Publications
**Circ:** (Free)‡3,000

**Somerset Herald  (13277)**
Gannett Company Inc.
PO Box 310
Princess Anne, MD 21853
Phone: (410)651-1600
Fax: (410)651-3785
**Subject(s):** Paid Community Newspapers
**Circ:** (Paid)3,000
 (Free)3,000

**The Union Star  (31226)**
Womack Publishing Co.
PO Box 180
Brookneal, VA 24528
Phone: (804)376-2795
Fax: (804)376-2676
**Subject(s):** Paid Community Newspapers
**Circ:** ‡3,000

**The Vinton Messenger  (31867)**
Robinson Community Newspaper
1633 W. Main St.
Salem, VA 24153
Phone: (540)343-0720
Fax: (540)389-2930
**Subject(s):** Paid Community Newspapers
**Circ:** 3,000

**Goochland Gazette  (31601)**
Richmond Suburban Newspapers
6400 Mechanicsville Turnpike
P.O.Box 1118
Mechanicsville, VA 23111
Phone: (804)746-1235
Fax: (804)730-0476
**Subject(s):** Paid Community Newspapers
**Circ:** (Non-paid)10
 (Paid)2,915

**The Herald Record  (32771)**
202 E Main St.
West Union, WV 26456
Phone: (304)873-1600
Fax: (304)873-1600
**Subject(s):** Paid Community Newspapers
**Circ:** ‡2,900

**Times/Record  (13089)**
Chesapeake Publishing Corp.
219 Market
Denton, MD 21629
Phone: (410)479-1800
Fax: (410)479-3174
**Subject(s):** Paid Community Newspapers
**Circ:** (Non-paid)139
 (Paid)2,882

**Record Observer  (13031)**
Chesapeake Publishing Corp.
114 Broadway
Centreville, MD 21617
Phone: (410)758-1400
Fax: (410)758-1701
**Subject(s):** Paid Community Newspapers
**Circ:** (Non-paid)76
 (Paid)2,829

**Rappahannock News  (31495)**
Arcom Publishing Inc.
13873 Park Center Rd., Ste. 301
Herndon, VA 20171-3285
Phone: (703)478-6666
Fax: (703)435-9754
**Subject(s):** Paid Community Newspapers
**Circ:** (Free)‡106
 (Paid)‡2,751

**The Piedmont Herald  (32715)**
33 E. Fairview
Piedmont, WV 26750
Phone: (304)355-2381
Fax: (304)355-2383
**Subject(s):** Paid Community Newspapers
**Circ:** ‡2,700

**The Hancock News  (13205)**
263 Pennsylvania Ave.
Hancock, MD 21750
Phone: (301)678-6255
Fax: (301)678-5520
**Subject(s):** Paid Community Newspapers
**Circ:** ‡2,600

**The Industrial News  (32636)**
Welch Daily News Inc.
100 Center St.
PO Box 180
Iaeger, WV 24844
Phone: (304)938-2142
Fax: (304)938-2142
**Subject(s):** Paid Community Newspapers
**Circ:** ‡2,510

**Clinch Valley Times  (31865)**
Clinch Valley Publishing Company Inc.
16541 Russell St.
PO Drawer 817
Saint Paul, VA 24283-0817
Phone: (276)762-7671
Fax: (276)762-0929
**Subject(s):** Paid Community Newspapers
**Circ:** ‡2,500

**The Flyer  (13320)**
Salisbury State University
P O Box 3183
Salisbury, MD 21801-6860
Phone: (410)543-6000
Fax: (410)548-2800
**Subject(s):** College Publications
**Circ:** (Free)‡2,500

**Tech Collegian  (32672)**
West Virginia University Institute of Technology
Box 1, Old Main
Montgomery, WV 25136
Phone: (304)442-3180
Fax: (304)442-3464
**Subject(s):** College Publications
**Circ:** (Free)‡2,500

**Roane County Reporter  (32747)**
Spencer Newspapers Inc.
210 E. Main St.
Spencer, WV 25276
Phone: (304)927-2360
Fax: (304)927-2361
**Subject(s):** Paid Community Newspapers
**Circ:** ‡2,321

**Wirt County Journal  (32587)**
The Little Kanawha Publishing Co.
PO Box 309
Elizabeth, WV 26143
Phone: (304)275-8981
Fax: (304)275-8981
**Subject(s):** Paid Community Newspapers
**Circ:** (Paid)2,300

**Hancock County Courier** (32691)
Hancock Courier Printing Co.
PO Box 547
New Cumberland, WV 26047
Phone: (304)564-3131
Fax: (304)564-3867
**Subject(s):** Paid Community Newspapers
**Circ:** (Free)‡30
(Paid)‡2,253

**Pleasants County Leader** (32739)
West Central Publishing Inc.
PO Box 27
Saint Marys, WV 26170
Phone: (304)684-2424
Fax: (304)684-2426
**Subject(s):** Paid Community Newspapers
**Circ:** ‡2,200

**Princeton Times** (32720)
McLeansboro Times-Leader
109 Thorn St.
PO Box 1199
Princeton, WV 24740-3561
Phone: (304)425-8191
Fax: (304)487-1632
**Subject(s):** Paid Community Newspapers
**Circ:** (Free)‡15
(Paid)‡2,175

**The Brooke County Review** (32769)
319 Charles St.
PO Box 591
Wellsburg, WV 26070
Phone: (304)737-0946
Fax: (304)737-0297
**Subject(s):** Paid Community Newspapers
**Circ:** ‡2,000

**The Glenville Democrat** (32603)
Democrat/Pathfinder
PO Box 458
Glenville, WV 26351
Phone: (304)462-7309
Fax: (304)462-7300
**Subject(s):** Paid Community Newspapers
**Circ:** (Free)100
(Paid)2,000

**Mercury** (32605)
Glenville State College
200 High St.
PO Box 207
Glenville, WV 26351-0207
Phone: (304)462-7361
**Subject(s):** College Publications
**Circ:** (Paid)200
(Free)2,000

**The Middletown Valley Citizen** (13246)
Citizen Communications Inc.
1220 Marker Rd.
Middletown, MD 21769
Phone: (301)371-9399
**Subject(s):** Paid Community Newspapers
**Circ:** (Non-paid)‡35
(Paid)‡2,000

**U.S.A.E.** (13013)
Custom News Inc.
4341 Montgomery Ave.
Bethesda, MD 20814
Phone: (301)951-1881
Fax: (301)656-2845
**Subject(s):** Management and Administration
**Circ:** 2,000

**The V.U.U. Informer** (31814)
Virginia Union University
1500 N Lombardy St.
Richmond, VA 23220
Phone: (804)257-5678
Fax: (804)257-5625
**Subject(s):** College Publications
**Circ:** (Free)‡2,000

**Crisfield Times** (13081)
Independent Newspapers Inc.
914 W. Main St.
Crisfield, MD 21817
Phone: (410)968-1188
Fax: (410)968-1197
**Subject(s):** Paid Community Newspapers
**Circ:** (Combined)1,884

**The New Castle Record** (31615)
Salem Publishing Co.
PO Box 1125
Salem, VA 24153
Phone: (540)389-9355
Fax: (540)389-2930
**Subject(s):** Paid Community Newspapers
**Circ:** ‡1,870

**Pendleton Times** (32601)
PO Box 906
Franklin, WV 26807
Phone: (304)358-2304
Fax: (304)358-2304
**Subject(s):** Paid Community Newspapers
**Circ:** 1,800

**Somerset/Crisfield Express** (13276)
Virginia Gazette Companies L.L.C.
PO Box 310
Princess Anne, MD 21853
Phone: (410)289-6834
Fax: (410)289-6838
**Subject(s):** Shopping Guides
**Circ:** (Free)‡1,700

**The Hurricane Breeze** (32634)
Hurricane Breeze
PO Box 310
488 Hurricane Creek Road
Hurricane, WV 25526-0310
Phone: (304)562-9881
Fax: (304)562-9881
**Subject(s):** Paid Community Newspapers
**Circ:** 1,675

**Webster Republican** (32762)
Webster Publishing Co.
PO Box 749
Webster Springs, WV 26288
Phone: (304)847-5828
Fax: (304)847-5991
**Subject(s):** Paid Community Newspapers
**Circ:** 1,515

**The Glenville Pathfinder** (32604)
Democrat/Pathfinder
108 N. Court St.
PO Box 458
Glenville, WV 26351
Phone: (304)462-7309
Fax: (304)462-7300
**Subject(s):** Paid Community Newspapers
**Circ:** (Non-paid)‡30
(Paid)‡1,500

**The Phoenix** (13390)
The Phoenix, WMC
2 College Hill
Westminster, MD 21157-4390
Phone: (410)751-8600
**Subject(s):** College Publications
**Circ:** ‡1,500

**The Trumpet** (32770)
West Liberty State College
PO Box 295
West Liberty, WV 26074-0295
Phone: (304)336-8360
Fax: (304)336-8323
**Subject(s):** College Publications
**Circ:** (Free)‡1,500

**The Hampden-Sydney Tiger** (31449)
PO Box 635
Hampden Sydney, VA 23943-0626
Phone: (434)223-6359
Fax: (434)223-6399
**Subject(s):** College Publications
**Circ:** (Paid)‡105
(Free)‡1,300

**Putnam Democrat** (32582)
P.C. Publishing
2085 U. S. Rte. 60
Culloden, WV 25510
Phone: (304)743-6731
Fax: (304)562-6214
**Subject(s):** Paid Community Newspapers
**Circ:** 1,300

**Hood Today** (13129)
401 Rosemont Ave.
Frederick, MD 21701-8575
Phone: (301)663-3131

**Subject(s):** College Publications
**Circ:** (Free)‡1,250

**New Castle Weekly** (5136)
203 Delaware St.
New Castle, DE 19720
Phone: (302)328-6005
**Subject(s):** Paid Community Newspapers
**Circ:** ‡1,200

**The Sundial** (31542)
Randolph-Macon Woman's College
2500 Rivermont Ave.
Lynchburg, VA 24503
Phone: (434)947-8000
Fax: (434)947-8148
**Subject(s):** College Publications
**Circ:** 1,200

**Bluefieldian** (32539)
Bluefield State College
219 Rock St.
Bluefield, WV 24701-2198
Phone: (304)327-4186
Fax: (304)327-4188
**Subject(s):** College Publications
**Circ:** 1,000

**Campus Comments** (31893)
Mary Baldwin College
12th N Naw & Fredricks
Staunton, VA 24401
Phone: (540)887-7112
Fax: (540)887-7040
**Subject(s):** College Publications
**Circ:** (Non-paid)1,000

**The Tower** (32535)
Bethany College
PO Box 209
Bethany, WV 26032
Phone: (304)829-7500
**Subject(s):** College Publications
**Circ:** (Paid)1,000

**Bon Homme Richard** (31662)
Richard Bland College
11301 Johnson
Petersburg, VA 23805
Phone: (804)862-6226
Fax: (804)862-6455
**Subject(s):** College Publications
**Circ:** (Free)600

**Montessori News** (13351)
International Montessori Society
8115 Fenton St., Ste. 304
Silver Spring, MD 20910
Phone: (301)589-1127
Fax: (301)589-0733
**Subject(s):** Education
**Circ:** (Paid)‡550

# Northeastern States

**AAA World—Keystone** (26794)
AAA World Publishing
2040 Market St.
Philadelphia, PA 19103
Phone: (215)851-0291
Fax: (215)851-0297
**Subject(s):** Travel and Tourism; Automotive (Consumer); Insurance
**Circ:** 2,300,000

**Wall Street Journal** (13736)
Dow Jones & Company Inc.
200 Burnett Rd.
Chicopee, MA
Phone: (800)568-7625
Fax: (800)975-8618
**Subject(s):** Daily Newspapers; Business
**Circ:** (Mon.-Fri.)★1,800,607

**The New York Times** (22167)
The New York Times Co.
229 W 43rd St.
New York, NY 10036-3913
Phone: (212)556-1234
Fax: (212)556-3535

Circulation: ★ = ABC; △ = BPA; ♦ = CAC; • = CCAB; ▫ = VAC; ⊕ = PO Statement; ‡ = Publisher's Report; Boldface figures = sworn; Light figures = estimated.

## Northeastern States

Subject(s): Daily Newspapers
Circ: (Sat.)★1,056,390
(Mon.-Fri.)★1,121,057
(Sun.)★1,680,583

**KIND News (4680)**
National Association for Humane and Environmental Education
67 Norwich Essex Tpke.
PO Box 362
East Haddam, CT 06423-1736
Phone: (860)434-8666
Fax: (860)434-9579
Subject(s): Children's Interests; Education; Environmental and Natural Resources Conservation
Circ: 1,222,800

**Pennsyavers Shoppers Guide (20899)**
Star Community Publishing
250 Miller Pl.
Hicksville, NY 11801
Phone: (516)393-9300
Fax: (516)393-9304
Subject(s): Shopping Guides
Circ: (Non-paid)966,536

**New York Daily News (22156)**
New York News Inc.
450 W 33rd St.
New York, NY 10001
Phone: (212)210-2100
Fax: (212)210-2049
Subject(s): Daily Newspapers
Circ: (Sat.)548,380
(Mon.-Fri.)716,095
(Sun.)821,080

**Philadelphia Inquirer (27222)**
Philadelphia Newspapers Inc.
PO Box 8263
Philadelphia, PA 19101
Phone: (215)854-2000
Fax: (215)854-4794
Subject(s): Daily Newspapers
Circ: (Sat.)★328,178
(Mon.-Sat.)★368,883
(Sun.)★750,780

**The Wall Street Journal—Classroom Edition (22526)**
Dow Jones & Company Inc.
200 Liberty St.
New York, NY 10281
Phone: (212)416-2000
Fax: (212)416-2658
Subject(s): Education
Circ: 750,000

**The Boston Globe (13482)**
New York Times Co./Globe Newspaper Co.
135 Morrissey Blvd.
PO Box 2378
Boston, MA 02107-3310
Phone: (617)929-2935
Fax: (617)929-3192
Subject(s): Daily Newspapers
Circ: (Sat.)★423,632
(Mon.-Fri.)★451,471
(Sun.)★707,813

**Newsday (21172)**
235 Pinelawn Rd.
Melville, NY 11747-4250
Phone: (516)843-2700
Fax: (516)843-2953
Subject(s): Daily Newspapers
Circ: (Sat.)417,949
(Mon.-Fri.)576,692
(Sun.)663,220

**This Week (20901)**
Star Community Publishing
250 Miller Pl.
Hicksville, NY 11801
Phone: (516)393-9300
Fax: (516)393-9344
Subject(s): Shopping Guides
Circ: (Paid)332,402
(Non-paid)637,286

**Star-Ledger (19622)**
Newark Morning Ledger Co.
1 Star-Ledger Plz.
Newark, NJ 07102-1200
Phone: (973)877-4141
Fax: (973)877-5845

Subject(s): Daily Newspapers
Circ: (Sat.)332,586
(Mon.-Fri.)407,592
(Sun.)606,462

**Phoenix Register (22700)**
Oswego County Weeklies
71 State St.
Phoenix, NY 13135
Phone: (315)695-4771
Subject(s): Paid Community Newspapers
Circ: (Mon.-Fri.)482,259
(Sat.)508,025
(Sun.)599,450

**Suffolk County Life (22800)**
Suffolk Life Newspapers
PO Box 9167
Riverhead, NY 11901
Phone: (631)369-0800
Fax: (631)369-5190
Subject(s): Paid Community Newspapers
Circ: (Wed.)516,251

**Weekly Reader (Pre-K edition) (5040)**
Weekly Reader Corp.
200 First Stamford Pl.
PO Box 120023
Stamford, CT 06912-0023
Phone: (203)705-3500
Fax: (203)705-1661
Subject(s): Education
Circ: (Paid)508,153

**New York Post (22163)**
New York Post Corp.
1211 6th Ave.
New York, NY 10036-8790
Phone: (212)930-8000
Subject(s): Daily Newspapers
Circ: (Sun.)368,636
(Sat.)376,871
(Mon.-Fri.)487,219

**South Jersey Shoppers Guide (19024)**
8 Ranoldo Ter.
P O Box 2855
Cherry Hill, NJ 08034-2132
Phone: (856)616-4900
Fax: (856)616-0299
Subject(s): Shopping Guides
Circ: (Free)416,200

**Pittsburgh Post-Gazette (27392)**
Post Gazette
34 Blvd. of the Allies
Pittsburgh, PA 15222
Phone: (412)263-1100
Fax: (412)391-8452
Subject(s): Daily Newspapers
Circ: (Sat.)★226,962
(Mon.-Fri.)★238,860
(Sun.)★402,981

**The Pennysaver (22694)**
Pennysaver Group Inc.
510 5TH. Ave
Pelham, NY 10803
Phone: (914)592-5222
Fax: (914)592-4570
Subject(s): Shopping Guides
Circ: (Non-paid)375,000

**Yorktown Pennysaver Corp. (23212)**
1520 Front St.
Yorktown Heights, NY 10598
Phone: (914)962-3871
Fax: (914)962-4820
Subject(s): Shopping Guides
Circ: (Combined)352,085

**The New York Teacher (21048)**
New York State United Teachers
800 Troy-Schenectady Rd.
Latham, NY 12110
Phone: (518)213-6000
Fax: (518)213-6415
Subject(s): Education
Circ: (Paid)337,000

**The Jewish Herald (20515)**
1689 46th St.
Brooklyn, NY 11204
Phone: (718)972-4000

Subject(s): Jewish Publications; Paid Community Newspapers
Circ: ‡312,000

**Metro Community News (20642)**
Metro Group Inc.
25 Boxwood Ln.
P O Box 211
Cheektowaga, NY 14227-0211
Phone: (716)668-5223
Fax: (716)668-4526
Subject(s): Free Newspapers
Circ: (Free)306,143

**The Buffalo News (20560)**
Stanford Lipsey Publishers
1 News Plz.
PO Box 100
Buffalo, NY 14240
Phone: (716)849-3434
Fax: (716)849-3409
Subject(s): Daily Newspapers
Circ: (Mon.-Sat.)★196,429
(Sun.)★282,618

**The Hartford Courant (4803)**
Tribune Co.
285 Broad St.
Hartford, CT 06115
Phone: (860)241-6200
Fax: (860)520-3176
Subject(s): Daily Newspapers
Circ: (Sat.)★204,664
(Mon.-Fri.)★238,965
(Sun.)★281,714

**Episcopal Life (21655)**
The Episcopal Church in the United States
815 2nd Ave.
New York, NY 10017
Phone: (212)716-6000
Subject(s): Religious Publications
Circ: (Paid)‡280,000

**Shopping Bag & Advertiser (20730)**
Greater Rochester Advertiser
201 Main St.
East Rochester, NY 14445
Phone: (585)385-1974
Fax: (585)385-3507
Subject(s): Shopping Guides
Circ: (Free)261,407

**Current Events (5029)**
Weekly Reader Corp.
200 First Stamford Pl.
PO Box 120023
Stamford, CT 06912-0023
Phone: (203)705-3500
Fax: (203)705-1661
Subject(s): Education; Youths' Interests
Circ: ‡257,402

**RWDSU Record (22332)**
Retail, Wholesale and Dept. Store Union-AFL-CIO
30 E 29th St.
New York, NY 10016
Phone: (212)684-5300
Fax: (212)779-2809
Subject(s): Labor
Circ: ‡250,000

**The Village Voice (22518)**
Village Voice Media
36 Cooper Sq.
New York, NY 10003-7149
Phone: (212)475-3300
Fax: (212)475-8944
Subject(s): General Editorial
Circ: (Paid)12,087
(Non-paid)241,874

**Boston Herald (13483)**
One Herald Sq.
PO Box 55843
Boston, MA 02205
Phone: (617)426-3000
Fax: (617)619-6461
Subject(s): Daily Newspapers
Circ: (Sun.)★152,813
(Sat.)★181,018
(Mon.-Fri.)★240,759

**The Providence Journal** (27913)
The Providence Journal Co.
75 Fountain St.
Providence, RI 02902-0050
Phone: (401)277-7000
Fax: (401)277-7889
**Subject(s):** Paid Community Newspapers

**Circ:** (Mon.-Sat.)160,610
(Sun.)229,271

**AAA Traveler** (19091)
AAA New Jersey Automobile Club
1 Hanover Rd.
Florham Park, NJ 07932
Phone: (973)377-7200
Fax: (973)377-2979
**Subject(s):** Automotive (Consumer); Travel and Tourism

**Circ:** (Free)225,000

**Democrat and Chronicle** (22815)
Gannett Company Inc.
55 Exchange Blvd.
Rochester, NY 14614-2001
Phone: (716)232-7100
Fax: (716)258-3027
**Subject(s):** Daily Newspapers

**Circ:** (Mon.-Sat.)★166,727
(Sun.)★224,408

**The Record** (19128)
North Jersey Media Group
150 River St.
Hackensack, NJ 07601-7172
Phone: (201)646-4000
Fax: (201)646-4310
**Subject(s):** Daily Newspapers

**Circ:** (Mon.-Sat.)★167,180
(Sun.)★212,333

**The Upper East Side Resident** (22507)
Resident Publications
28 East 28th St.
New York, NY 10016
Phone: (212)993-9410
**Subject(s):** Free Newspapers

**Circ:** (Non-paid)200,000

**SJ First** (19926)
AAA Auto Club of South Jersey
700 Laurel Oak Rd.
PO Box 1953
Voorhees, NJ 08043
Phone: (856)783-4222
Fax: (856)627-9100
**Subject(s):** Travel and Tourism

**Circ:** ‡180,000

**Tribune-Review** (26407)
Tribune Review Publishing Co.
622 Cabin Hill Dr.
Greensburg, PA 15601
Phone: (724)834-1151
Fax: (724)838-5171
**Subject(s):** Daily Newspapers

**Circ:** (Mon.)★107,395
(Tues.-Fri.)★119,338
(Sat.)★119,338
(Sun.)★179,567

**The Post-Standard** (23031)
The Syracuse Newspapers Inc.
PO Box 4915
Syracuse, NY 13221
Phone: (315)470-0011
Fax: (315)470-3081
**Subject(s):** Daily Newspapers

**Circ:** (Mon.-Sat.)★118,962
(Sun.)★175,020

**Know Your World Extra** (5034)
Weekly Reader Corp.
200 First Stamford Pl.
PO Box 120023
Stamford, CT 06912-0023
Phone: (203)705-3500
Fax: (203)705-1661
**Subject(s):** Education; Youths' Interests

**Circ:** ‡172,109

**The Morning Call** (26094)
101 N 6th St., No. 1260
Allentown, PA 18101-1403
Phone: (610)820-6500
Fax: (610)820-6617

**Subject(s):** Daily Newspapers
**Circ:** (Mon.-Sat.)127,175
(Sun.)170,744

**Computerworld** (13789)
101 Communications
500 Old Connecticut Path
Framingham, MA 01701
Phone: (508)875-8931
Fax: (508)875-8931
**Subject(s):** Computers

**Circ:** (Paid)170,031

**The Guide News** (26442)
Fry Communications Inc.
800 W Church St.
Mechanicsburg, PA 17055
Phone: (717)766-0211
Fax: (717)691-5796
**Subject(s):** Shopping Guides

**Circ:** (Free)‡161,543

**Queens Chronicle** (22778)
Mark I. Publications Inc.
62-33 Woodhaven Blvd.
PO Box 74-7769
Rego Park, NY 11374-7769
Phone: (718)205-8000
Fax: (718)205-0150
**Subject(s):** Free Newspapers

**Circ:** (Non-paid)160,000

**Electronic Engineering Times** (21103)
CMP Media L.L.C.
600 Community Dr.
Manhasset, NY 11030
Phone: (516)562-5000
Fax: (516)562-5995
**Subject(s):** Electronics Engineering

**Circ:** (Free)‡158,433

**Bay Shore Suffolk Life** (20352)
Suffolk Life Newspapers
PO Box 9167
Riverhead, NY 11901
Phone: (631)369-0800
Fax: (631)369-5190
**Subject(s):** Free Newspapers

**Circ:** (Free)154,464

**Philadelphia Daily News** (27220)
Knight-Ridder Inc.
400 N. Broad St.
Philadelphia, PA 19130-4015
Phone: (215)854-5900
Fax: (215)854-5910
**Subject(s):** Daily Newspapers

**Circ:** (Sat.)75,981
(Mon.-Fri.)152,037

**The Patriot-News** (26452)
812 Market St.
Harrisburg, PA 17105
Phone: (717)255-8100
Fax: (717)255-8456
**Subject(s):** Daily Newspapers

**Circ:** (Mon.-Sat.)★100,129
(Sun.)★150,061

**The Times Union** (20234)
News Plz.
Box 15000
Albany, NY 12212
Phone: (518)454-5420
Fax: (518)454-5514
**Subject(s):** Daily Newspapers

**Circ:** (Mon.-Sat.)★100,628
(Sun.)★146,464

**Bucks County Midweek** (27583)
Times Newspapers Inc.
2512 Metropolitan Dr.
Trevose, PA 19053
Phone: (215)355-9009
Fax: (215)355-4812
**Subject(s):** Shopping Guides

**Circ:** (Non-paid)145,598

**Maine Sunday Telegram** (12561)
Blethen Maine Newspapers
390 Congress St.
Portland, ME 04101-5009
Phone: (207)791-6650
Fax: (207)791-6925

**Subject(s):** Daily Newspapers
**Circ:** (Paid)145,000

**Queens Tribune** (20801)
Tribco Inc.
174-15 Horace Harding Expy.
Fresh Meadows, NY 11365
Phone: (718)357-7400
Fax: (718)357-9417
**Subject(s):** Paid Community Newspapers

**Circ:** (Paid)2,000
(Free)144,000

**Metropolitan News** (20526)
EWA Publications
2446 E 65th St.
Brooklyn, NY 11234
Phone: (718)763-7034
Fax: (718)763-7035
**Subject(s):** Paid Community Newspapers

**Circ:** 142,600

**The News Transcript** (19108)
Greater Media Newspapers
PO Box 5001
Freehold, NJ 07728-5001
Phone: (732)972-6740
Fax: (732)972-6746
**Subject(s):** Free Newspapers

**Circ:** (Combined)‡140,000

**Orthodox Observer** (22199)
Greek Orthodox Archdiocese Press
8 E. 79th St.
New York, NY 10021
Phone: (212)570-3500
Fax: (212)570-3569
**Subject(s):** Religious Publications; Greek

**Circ:** 140,000

**Genesee Valley** (20329)
Genesee Valley Publications Inc.
1471 Rte. 15
Avon, NY 14414
Phone: (585)226-8111
Fax: (585)226-3395
**Subject(s):** Shopping Guides

**Circ:** (Combined)131,888

**EDN Products and Careers** (14858)
Reed Business Information
225 Wyman St.
Waltham, MA 02451-1216
**Subject(s):** Electronics Engineering

**Circ:** (Controlled)‡131,000

**Caribbean Life** (20499)
Courier Life Publications
1733 Sheepshead Bay Rd.
Brooklyn, NY 11235-3606
Phone: (718)615-2500
Fax: (718)615-3835
**Subject(s):** Free Newspapers

**Circ:** (Non-paid)♦130,024

**Republican** (14806)
Union News & Sunday Republican
1860 Main St.
Springfield, MA 01101
Phone: (413)788-1000
Fax: (413)788-1301
**Subject(s):** Daily Newspapers

**Circ:** (Mon.-Sat.)★85,745
(Sun.)★128,627

**Impacto Latin News** (21811)
853 Broadway, Ste. 811
New York, NY 10003
Phone: (212)505-0288
Fax: (212)598-9414
**Subject(s):** Spanish; Hispanic Publications; Paid Community Newspapers

**Circ:** 128,000

**Hartford Inquirer** (4804)
Inquires Newspaper Group
PO Box 1260
3281 Main St.
Hartford, CT 06143
Phone: (860)522-1462
Fax: (860)522-3014
**Subject(s):** Paid Community Newspapers; Black Publications

**Circ:** 125,000

Circulation: ★ = ABC; △ = BPA; ♦ = CAC; ● = CCAB; ▢ = VAC; ⊕ = PO Statement; ‡ = Publisher's Report; Boldface figures = sworn; Light figures = estimated.

**Portland Press Herald (12566)**
Blethen Maine Newspapers
390 Congress St.
Portland, ME 04101-5009
Phone: (207)791-6650
Fax: (207)791-6925
**Subject(s):** Daily Newspapers
**Circ:** (Mon.-Sat.)★76,833
(Sun.)★124,060

**The Catholic Advocate (19613)**
171 Clifton Ave.
PO Box 9500
Newark, NJ 07104-9500
Phone: (973)497-4200
Fax: (973)497-4192
**Subject(s):** Religious Publications
**Circ:** (Free)‡4,800
(Paid)‡122,300

**Telegram & Gazette (14945)**
Worchester Telegram & Gazette Corp.
20 Franklin St.
PO Box 15012
Worcester, MA 01615-0012
Phone: (508)793-9100
Fax: (508)793-9313
**Subject(s):** Daily Newspapers
**Circ:** (Mon.-Sat.)★103,113
(Sun.)★121,437

**TeeVee Moneysaver (Edition 1) (19825)**
TeeVee Moneysaver Inc., Publications
52 W Main St.
PO Box 954
Somerville, NJ 08876
Phone: (908)722-6270
Fax: (908)722-7303
**Subject(s):** Local, State, and Regional Publications; Entertainment
**Circ:** (Non-paid)120,000

**Entertainment Lifestyles (20508)**
EWA Publications
2446 E 65th St.
Brooklyn, NY 11234
Phone: (718)763-7034
Fax: (718)763-7035
**Subject(s):** Paid Community Newspapers
**Circ:** 119,000

**CRN (21101)**
CMP Media L.L.C.
600 Community Dr.
Manhasset, NY 11030
Phone: (516)562-5000
Fax: (516)562-5995
**Subject(s):** Selling and Salesmanship; Computers
**Circ:** (Free)117,500

**New York Entertainment Scene (20528)**
EWA Publications
2446 E 65th St.
Brooklyn, NY 11234
Phone: (718)763-7034
Fax: (718)763-7035
**Subject(s):** Paid Community Newspapers
**Circ:** 116,000

**New York Press (22164)**
New York Press Inc.
333 7th Ave., 14th Fl.
New York, NY 10001
Phone: (212)244-2282
Fax: (212)941-7824
**Subject(s):** Free Newspapers
**Circ:** (Non-paid)★116,002

**Travel International (20543)**
EWA Publications
2446 E 65th St.
Brooklyn, NY 11234
Phone: (718)763-7034
Fax: (718)763-7035
**Subject(s):** Paid Community Newspapers
**Circ:** 116,000

**Northeast Times (27585)**
Times Newspapers Inc.
2512 Metropolitan Dr.
Trevose, PA 19053
Phone: (215)355-9009
Fax: (215)355-4812
**Subject(s):** Free Newspapers
**Circ:** (Combined)114,332

**The Marketplace Pennysaver (20877)**
Marketplace Publications
Box 953
Harriman, NY 10926
**Subject(s):** Shopping Guides
**Circ:** (Controlled)113,000

**Philadelphia Weekly (27229)**
Review Publishing Ltd.
1500 Sansom St., 3rd Fl.
Philadelphia, PA 19102
Phone: (215)563-7400
Fax: (215)563-6799
**Subject(s):** Free Newspapers; Alternative and Underground
**Circ:** (Free)111,613

**Ale Street News (19510)**
Tuscarora Inc.
PO Box 1125
Maywood, NJ 07607
Phone: (201)368-9100
Fax: (201)368-9101
**Subject(s):** Paid Community Newspapers; Beverages, Brewing, and Bottling
**Circ:** (Combined)110,000

**The Long Island Catholic (22881)**
200 W Centennial Ave., Ste. 201
Roosevelt, NY 11575
Phone: (516)594-1000
Fax: (516)594-1092
**Subject(s):** Religious Publications
**Circ:** (Paid)★108,507

**Herald/PrimeTime Online (21055)**
Richner Communications
P.O. Box 9001
Lawrence, NY 11559-1616
Phone: (516)569-4000
Fax: (516)569-4942
**Subject(s):** Shopping Guides
**Circ:** (Free)108,240

**Jewish Press (20516)**
Jewish Press Inc.
338 3rd Ave.
Brooklyn, NY 11215-1897
Phone: (718)330-1100
Fax: (718)330-1100
**Subject(s):** Paid Community Newspapers; Jewish Publications
**Circ:** (Free)⊕1,930
(Paid)⊕105,203

**South Bay's Shopping Newspaper (21067)**
Excel Promotions Corp.
150 W Hoffman Ave.
Lindenhurst, NY 11757
Phone: (631)226-2636
**Subject(s):** Free Newspapers
**Circ:** (Free)‡103,100

**Lancaster Sunday News (26603)**
Lancaster Newspapers Inc.
8 W. King St.
PO Box 1328
Lancaster, PA 17608-1328
Phone: (717)291-8811
Fax: (717)399-6513
**Subject(s):** Paid Community Newspapers
**Circ:** (Sun.)102,457

**Lancaster New Era (26602)**
Lancaster Newspapers Inc.
8 W. King St.
PO Box 1328
Lancaster, PA 17608-1328
Phone: (717)291-8811
Fax: (717)399-6513
**Subject(s):** Daily Newspapers
**Circ:** (Mon.-Sat.)★43,151
(Sun.)★101,694

**Restaurant/Food Review (20536)**
EWA Publications
2446 E 65th St.
Brooklyn, NY 11234
Phone: (718)763-7034
Fax: (718)763-7035
**Subject(s):** Paid Community Newspapers
**Circ:** 101,000

**New Haven Register (4900)**
Long Wharf, 40 Sargent Dr.
New Haven, CT 06511
Phone: (203)789-5200
Fax: (203)865-7894
**Subject(s):** Daily Newspapers
**Circ:** (Sat.)83,460
(Mon.-Fri.)100,048
(Sun.)100,438

**Out Magazine (22203)**
80 8th Ave., No. 315
New York, NY 10011-5126
**Subject(s):** Gay and Lesbian Interests; Lifestyle; Social and Political Issues
**Circ:** (Paid)100,126

**Counterpoint (26512)**
LRP Publications
747 Dresher Rd., Ste. 500
PO Box 980
Horsham, PA 19044
Phone: (215)784-0860
Fax: (215)784-9639
**Subject(s):** Education; Handicapped
**Circ:** (Paid)100,000

**Arts and Leisure Times (20488)**
EWA Publications
2446 E 65th St.
Brooklyn, NY 11234
Phone: (718)763-7034
Fax: (718)763-7035
**Subject(s):** Paid Community Newspapers
**Circ:** (Paid)98,000

**City Paper (26865)**
Montgomery Newspapers
123 Chestnut St., 3rd Fl.
Philadelphia, PA 19106
Phone: (215)735-8444
Fax: (215)735-8535
**Subject(s):** Free Newspapers
**Circ:** (Free)97,555

**Dauphin Schuylkill Area Merchandiser (26622)**
Kapp Advertising Service Inc.
100 E. Cumberland St.
Lebanon, PA 17042
Phone: (717)273-8127
Fax: (717)273-0420
**Subject(s):** Shopping Guides
**Circ:** (Combined)97,201

**Hershey Area Merchandiser (26624)**
Kapp Advertising Service Inc.
100 E. Cumberland St.
Lebanon, PA 17042
Phone: (717)273-8127
Fax: (717)273-0420
**Subject(s):** Shopping Guides
**Circ:** (Combined)97,201

**Lebanon Valley Area Merchandiser (26626)**
Kapp Advertising Service Inc.
100 E. Cumberland St.
Lebanon, PA 17042
Phone: (717)273-8127
Fax: (717)273-0420
**Subject(s):** Shopping Guides
**Circ:** (Combined)97,201

**Myerstown Area Merchandiser (26627)**
Kapp Advertising Service Inc.
100 E. Cumberland St.
Lebanon, PA 17042
Phone: (717)273-8127
Fax: (717)273-0420
**Subject(s):** Shopping Guides
**Circ:** (Combined)97,201

**Ocean County Reporter (19880)**
Ocean County Newspapers Inc.
PO Box 2449
Toms River, NJ 08754
**Subject(s):** Free Newspapers
**Circ:** (Combined)97,113

**Greater Reading Area Merchandiser (27468)**
Kapp Advertising Service Inc.
100 E. Cumberland St.
Lebanon, PA 17042
Phone: (717)273-8127
Fax: (717)273-0420

**Subject(s):** Shopping Guides
**Circ:** (Free)96,825

**York County Coast Star  (12526)**
York County Coast Star Inc.
PO Box 979
Kennebunk, ME 04043-0979
Phone: (207)985-2961
Fax: (207)985-9050
**Subject(s):** Paid Community Newspapers
**Circ:** (Non-paid)100
(Paid)9,5827

**News Gleaner (Bustleton-Somerton Edition)  (27168)**
News Gleaner Publications
9999 Gantry Rd.
Philadelphia, PA 19149
Phone: (215)969-5100
Fax: (215)969-5400
**Subject(s):** Free Newspapers
**Circ:** (Combined)93,923

**News Gleaner (Far Northeast Edition)  (27169)**
News Gleaner Publications
9999 Gantry Rd.
Philadelphia, PA 19149
Phone: (215)969-5100
Fax: (215)969-5400
**Subject(s):** Free Newspapers
**Circ:** (Combined)93,923

**News Gleaner (Frankford Juniata Edition)  (27170)**
News Gleaner Publications
9999 Gantry Rd.
Philadelphia, PA 19149
Phone: (215)969-5100
Fax: (215)969-5400
**Subject(s):** Free Newspapers
**Circ:** (Combined)93,923

**News Gleaner (Mayfair-Northeast Edition)  (27171)**
News Gleaner Publications
9999 Gantry Rd.
Philadelphia, PA 19149
Phone: (215)969-5100
Fax: (215)969-5400
**Subject(s):** Free Newspapers
**Circ:** (Combined)93,923

**Elizabeth City News  (19030)**
North Jersey Newspapers
301 Central Ave.
Clark, NJ 07066
Phone: (732)396-4404
Fax: (732)396-4770
**Subject(s):** Free Newspapers
**Circ:** (Non-paid)93,757

**Morning News  (26351)**
Erie Times News
205 W. 12th St.
Erie, PA 16534
Phone: (814)870-1600
**Subject(s):** Daily Newspapers
**Circ:** (Mon.-Fri.)35,912
(Sat.)61,625
(Sun.)93,645

**The Press of Atlantic City  (18966)**
South Jersey Publishing Co.
11 Devins Ln.
Pleasantville, NJ 08232
Phone: (609)272-7266
**Subject(s):** Daily Newspapers
**Circ:** (Mon.-Sat.)★74,655
(Sun.)★93,129

**Times Herald-Record  (21209)**
Ottaway News Service
40 Mulberry St.
Middletown, NY 10940
Phone: (914)343-2181
Fax: (914)343-2170
**Subject(s):** Daily Newspapers
**Circ:** (Mon.-Sat.)★80,385
(Sun.)★91,601

**The Step Saver  (5020)**
The Step Saver Inc.
PO Box 548
Southington, CT 06489-0548
Phone: (860)628-9645
Fax: (860)621-1841

**Subject(s):** Shopping Guides
**Circ:** (Non-paid)‡90,330

**Connecticut Post  (4636)**
410 State St.
Bridgeport, CT 06604-4501
Phone: (203)333-0161
Fax: (203)367-8158
**Subject(s):** Daily Newspapers
**Circ:** (Mon.-Sat.)78,455
(Sun.)90,217

**New Canaan Lifestyles  (4958)**
Brooks Community Newspapers Inc.
542 Westport Ave.
Norwalk, CT 06851
Phone: (203)849-1600
Fax: (203)840-4844
**Subject(s):** Paid Community Newspapers
**Circ:** 90,177

**Wilton Lifestyles  (4969)**
Brooks Community Newspapers Inc.
542 Westport Ave.
Norwalk, CT 06851
Phone: (203)849-1600
Fax: (203)840-4844
**Subject(s):** Paid Community Newspapers
**Circ:** (Combined)90,177

**Digital News & Review  (14856)**
Reed Business Information
225 Wyman St.
Waltham, MA 02451-1216
**Subject(s):** Computers
**Circ:** (Controlled)‡90,000

**Fairfield County Catholic  (4637)**
238 Jewett Ave.
Bridgeport, CT 06606
Phone: (203)372-4301
Fax: (203)374-2044
**Subject(s):** Religious Publications
**Circ:** ‡90,000

**Town Talk  (26690)**
P.O. Box 110
Media, PA 19063
Phone: (610)566-6755
Fax: (610)566-1261
**Subject(s):** Free Newspapers
**Circ:** (Free)‡90,000

**Courier-Post  (19019)**
Gannett Company Inc.
301 Cuthbert Blvd.
Cherry Hill, NJ 08002
Phone: (609)486-2411
Fax: (609)663-2831
**Subject(s):** Daily Newspapers
**Circ:** (Mon.-Sat.)★75,408
(Sun.)★89,922

**Exercise For Men Only  (21672)**
Chelo Publishing Incorporated and Pumpkin Press Inc.
The Empire State Bldg.
350 Fifth Ave., Ste. 3323
New York, NY 10118
Phone: (212)947-4322
Fax: (212)563-4774
**Subject(s):** (Physical Fitness); Men's Interests
**Circ:** (Paid)89,163

**Reading Eagle  (27469)**
Eagle Times
345 Penn St.
PO Box 582
Reading, PA 19603-0582
Phone: (610)376-0303
Fax: (610)478-4811
**Subject(s):** Daily Newspapers
**Circ:** (Mon.-Sat.)★61,897
(Sun.)★88,603

**Erie Times-News  (26348)**
205 W. 12th St.
Erie, PA 16534
Phone: (814)870-1600
**Subject(s):** Daily Newspapers
**Circ:** (Mon.-Fri.)★58,101
(Sat.)★59,928
(Sun.)★87,913

**The Times  (19896)**
Times of Trenton Publishing Corp.
500 Perry St.
Trenton, NJ 08605
Phone: (609)989-5454
Fax: (609)396-3633
**Subject(s):** Daily Newspapers
**Circ:** (Mon.-Sat.)78,202
(Sun.)87,471

**Western Itasca Review & Deerpath Shopper  (22533)**
Lebhar-Friedman Inc.
425 Park Ave.
New York, NY 10022
Phone: (212)756-5000
Fax: (212)756-5295
**Subject(s):** Hotels, Motels, Restaurants, and Clubs
**Circ:** (Free)‡4,307
(Paid)‡86,801

**Sunday Dispatch  (27440)**
109 New St.
Pittston, PA 18640
Phone: (570)655-1418
Fax: (570)883-1266
**Subject(s):** Paid Community Newspapers
**Circ:** 8,5000

**News Gleaner (Six Editions)  (27172)**
News Gleaner Publications
9999 Gantry Rd.
Philadelphia, PA 19149
Phone: (215)969-5100
Fax: (215)969-5400
**Subject(s):** Free Newspapers
**Circ:** (Paid)♦31
(Non-paid)♦82,229

**Nation's Restaurant News  (22131)**
425 Park Ave., 6th Fl.
New York, NY 10022
Phone: (212)756-5000
Fax: (212)756-5215
**Subject(s):** Hotels, Motels, Restaurants, and Clubs
**Circ:** (Paid)81,202

**The Union Leader  (18876)**
Union Leader Corp.
100 William Loeb Dr.
PO Box 9555
Manchester, NH 03109-5309
Phone: (603)668-4321
Fax: (603)668-0382
**Subject(s):** Daily Newspapers
**Circ:** (Sat.)★57,754
(Mon.-Fri.)★59,384
(Sun.)★81,144

**The Brooklyn Paper/Brooklyn's Weekly Newspaper  (20495)**
Brooklyn Paper Publications
55 Washington St.
Ste. 624
Brooklyn, NY 11201
Phone: (718)834-9350
Fax: (718)834-9278
**Subject(s):** Paid Community Newspapers
**Circ:** (Combined)‡81,000

**Downtown News  (20506)**
Brooklyn Paper Publications
55 Washington St.
Ste. 624
Brooklyn, NY 11201
Phone: (718)834-9350
Fax: (718)834-9278
**Subject(s):** Paid Community Newspapers
**Circ:** (Combined)81,000

**Park Slope Paper  (20530)**
Brooklyn Paper Publications
55 Washington St.
Ste. 624
Brooklyn, NY 11201
Phone: (718)834-9350
Fax: (718)834-9278
**Subject(s):** Paid Community Newspapers
**Circ:** (Combined)‡81,000

**The Asian Wall Street Journal Weekly Edition  (21369)**
Dow Jones & Company Inc.
200 Liberty St.
New York, NY 10281
Phone: (212)416-2000
Fax: (212)416-2658

---

Circulation:  ★ = ABC;  △ = BPA;  ♦ = CAC;  ● = CCAB;  ❏ = VAC;  ⊕ = PO Statement;  ‡ = Publisher's Report;  Boldface figures = sworn;  Light figures = estimated.

## Northeastern States

**Subject(s):** Paid Community Newspapers; Business

**Circ:** (Paid)‡80,141

**The Fifty Plus Advocate (14936)**
Mar-Len Publications
131 Lincoln St.
Worcester, MA 01605
Phone: (508)752-2512
Fax: (508)752-9057
**Subject(s):** Senior Citizens' Interests; Free Newspapers

**Circ:** (Paid)1,303
(Free)80,000

**Daily Challenge (20502)**
1360 Fulton St.
Brooklyn, NY 11216
Phone: (718)636-9500
Fax: (718)857-9115
**Subject(s):** Daily Newspapers; Black Publications

**Circ:** 79,000

**Staten Island Advance (22965)**
Advance Publications Inc.
950 Fingerboard Rd.
Staten Island, NY 10305
Fax: (718)981-5679
**Subject(s):** Daily Newspapers

**Circ:** (Mon.-Sat.)★61,443
(Sun.)★78,517

**This Week in Jersey City (19436)**
Evening Journal Association
30 Journal Sq.
Jersey City, NJ 07306
Phone: (201)653-1000
Fax: (201)653-1414
**Subject(s):** Free Newspapers

**Circ:** (Non-paid)77,880

**The Quad (27673)**
West Chester State University
253 Sykes Union Bldg.
West Chester, PA 19383-0001
Phone: (610)436-2793
Fax: (215)436-2287
**Subject(s):** College Publications

**Circ:** (Combined)‡77,500

**Salon News (22336)**
Fairchild Publications Inc.
7 W 34th St.
New York, NY 10001
Phone: (212)630-4000
Fax: (212)630-3555
**Subject(s):** Hairstyling

**Circ:** (Combined)77,000

**Hanover Area Merchandiser (26428)**
Kapp Advertising Service Inc.
100 E. Cumberland St.
Lebanon, PA 17042
Phone: (717)273-8127
Fax: (717)273-0420
**Subject(s):** Shopping Guides

**Circ:** (Combined)76,590

**Northern Adams-York Area Merchandiser (26628)**
Kapp Advertising Service Inc.
100 E. Cumberland St.
Lebanon, PA 17042
Phone: (717)273-8127
Fax: (717)273-0420
**Subject(s):** Shopping Guides

**Circ:** (Combined)76,590

**Manhattan Spirit (22054)**
New York Press Inc.
333 7th Ave., 14th Fl.
New York, NY 10001
Phone: (212)244-2282
Fax: (212)941-7824
**Subject(s):** Free Newspapers

**Circ:** (Free)‡76,000

**News for You (23025)**
New Readers Press
1320 Jamesville Ave.
Syracuse, NY 13210
Phone: (315)422-9121
Fax: (866)894-2100
**Subject(s):** Education; Paid Community Newspapers

**Circ:** ‡75,700

**The Scranton Times (27507)**
149 Penn Ave.
PO Box 3311
Scranton, PA 18505-3311
Phone: (570)348-9100
Fax: (570)348-9135
**Subject(s):** Daily Newspapers

**Circ:** (Mon.-Fri.)★33,226
(Sat.)★58,702
(Sun.)★75,675

**The Jewish Week (21863)**
1501 Broadway
New York, NY 10036
Phone: (212)921-7822
Fax: (212)921-8420
**Subject(s):** Paid Community Newspapers; Jewish Publications

**Circ:** (Paid)★75,227

**Staten Island Pennysaver (22966)**
Staten Island Register
101 Tyrellan Ave., Ste.420
Staten Island, NY 10309
Phone: (718)966-1200
Fax: (718)966-7775
**Subject(s):** Shopping Guides

**Circ:** (Free)‡75,000

**Bangor Daily News (12457)**
491 Main St.
PO Box 1329
Bangor, ME 04402-1329
Phone: (207)990-8000
Fax: (207)941-0885
**Subject(s):** Daily Newspapers

**Circ:** (Mon.-Fri.)★62,642
(Sun.)★74,754

**Metro West Daily News (14266)**
Community Newspaper Co.
254 2nd Ave.
Needham, MA 02494
Phone: (781)433-6700
**Subject(s):** Paid Community Newspapers

**Circ:** (Non-paid)‡73,928

**Soundings (4685)**
Trader Publishing Co.
10 Bokum Rd.
Essex, CT 06426
Phone: (860)767-3200
Fax: (860)767-0642
**Subject(s):** (Boating and Yachting)

**Circ:** (Paid)‡73,487

**The Shopper News (19080)**
North Jersey Community Newspapers
12-38 River Rd.
Fair Lawn, NJ 07410-1802
Phone: (201)791-8994
Fax: (201)791-3259
**Subject(s):** Free Newspapers

**Circ:** (Non-paid)♦72,344

**Woodshop News (4687)**
Trader Publishing Co.
10 Bokum Rd.
Essex, CT 06426
Phone: (860)767-3200
Fax: (860)767-1048
**Subject(s):** Wood and Woodworking

**Circ:** (Free)⊕21,500
(Paid)⊕72,176

**About Action Unlimited (13742)**
Action Unlimited
100-1 Domino Dr.
Concord, MA 01742
Phone: (978)371-2442
**Subject(s):** Free Newspapers

**Circ:** (Combined)72,011

**The New York Beacon (22152)**
Smith Haj Group Inc.
12 E. 33 St., 6th Fl.
New York, NY 10016
Phone: (212)213-8585
Fax: (212)213-6291
**Subject(s):** Paid Community Newspapers; Black Publications

**Circ:** 71,750

**El Especial (19913)**
3510 Bergenline Ave.
Union City, NJ 07087-4751
Phone: (201)348-1959
Fax: (201)348-3385
**Subject(s):** Hispanic Publications; Spanish; Paid Community Newspapers

**Circ:** (Free)1,400
(Paid)71,250

**York Daily Record (27730)**
122 S George St.
PO Box 15122
York, PA 17405-7122
Phone: (717)771-2000
Fax: (717)771-2009
**Subject(s):** Daily Newspapers

**Circ:** (Mon.-Fri.)★46,240
(Sat.)★71,006

**The Patriot Ledger (14758)**
PO Box 699159
Quincy, MA 02269-9159
Phone: (617)786-7000
Fax: (617)786-7298
**Subject(s):** Daily Newspapers

**Circ:** (Mon.-Fri.)★57,676
(Sat.)★70,703

**Philadelphia New Observer (27225)**
1930 Chestnut St., Ste. 900
PO Box 30092
Philadelphia, PA 19103-0092
Phone: (215)545-7500
Fax: (215)665-8914
**Subject(s):** Free Newspapers; Black Publications

**Circ:** (Paid)‡10,303
(Free)‡70,697

**Pittsburgh City Paper (27388)**
Steel City Media
650 Smithfield St., Ste. 2200
Pittsburgh, PA 15222
Phone: (412)316-3342
Fax: (412)316-3388
**Subject(s):** Free Newspapers

**Circ:** (Free)□70,682

**Our Town (22202)**
News Communications
63 W 38th St., Ste. 206
New York, NY 10018-3818
Phone: (212)268-8600
**Subject(s):** Paid Community Newspapers

**Circ:** ‡70,000

**Rochester Business Journal (22839)**
45 E. Ave., Ste. 500
Rochester, NY 14604
Phone: (585)546-8303
Fax: (585)546-3398
**Subject(s):** Business; Business

**Circ:** (Combined)70,000

**Bucks County Courier Times (26639)**
Greater Philadelphia Newspapers
8400 Rte. 13
Levittown, PA 19057
Phone: (215)949-4000
Fax: (215)949-4114
**Subject(s):** Daily Newspapers

**Circ:** (Mon.-Fri.)★63,408
(Sun.)★69,151

**Arlington Advocate (13433)**
Community Newspaper Co.
254 2nd Ave.
Needham, MA 02494
Phone: (781)433-6700
**Subject(s):** Paid Community Newspapers

**Circ:** (Combined)69,131

**Bedford Minuteman (13448)**
Community Newspaper Co.
254 2nd Ave.
Needham, MA 02494
Phone: (781)433-6700
**Subject(s):** Paid Community Newspapers

**Circ:** (Combined)69,131

**Belmont Citizen—Herald (13453)**
Community Newspaper Co.
254 2nd Ave.
Needham, MA 02494
Phone: (781)433-6700

Subject(s): Paid Community Newspapers
Circ: (Combined)69,131

**Billerica Minuteman (14255)**
Community Newspaper Co.
254 2nd Ave.
Needham, MA 02494
Phone: (781)433-6700
Subject(s): Paid Community Newspapers
Circ: (Combined)69,131

**Burlington Union (14257)**
Community Newspaper Co.
254 2nd Ave.
Needham, MA 02494
Phone: (781)433-6700
Subject(s): Paid Community Newspapers
Circ: (Combined)69,131

**Chelmsford Independent (13745)**
Community Newspaper Co.
PO Box 9191
Concord, MA 01742-9191
Phone: (508)256-6111
Fax: (508)256-6111
Subject(s): Paid Community Newspapers
Circ: (Combined)69,131

**Lexington Minuteman (13746)**
Community Newspaper Co.
PO Box 9191
Concord, MA 01742-9191
Phone: (617)861-9110
Fax: (617)863-8662
Subject(s): Paid Community Newspapers
Circ: (Combined)69,131

**Lincoln Journal (14264)**
Community Newspaper Co.
254 2nd Ave.
Needham, MA 02494
Phone: (781)433-6700
Subject(s): Paid Community Newspapers
Circ: (Combined)69,131

**Littleton Independent (13860)**
Community Newspaper Co.
254 2nd Ave.
Needham, MA 02494
Phone: (781)433-6700
Subject(s): Paid Community Newspapers
Circ: (Combined)69,131

**Maynard Beacon (14230)**
Community Newspaper Co.
254 2nd Ave.
Needham, MA 02494
Phone: (781)433-6700
Subject(s): Paid Community Newspapers
Circ: (Combined)69,131

**Tewksbury Advertiser (14840)**
Community Newspaper Co.
Box 9191
Concord, MA 01742-9191
Phone: (508)667-2156
Fax: (508)262-9947
Subject(s): Free Newspapers
Circ: (Combined)69,131

**Winchester Star (13858)**
Community Newspaper Co.
9 Meriam St.
Lexington, MA 02420-5300
Subject(s): Paid Community Newspapers
Circ: (Combined)69,131

**The Sun-Bulletin (20403)**
Gannett Company Inc.
Press & Sun-Bulletin
Vestal Pkwy. E.
PO Box 1270
Binghamton, NY 13902
Phone: (607)798-1151
Fax: (607)798-1113
Subject(s): Daily Newspapers
Circ: (Mon.-Sat.)★54,761
 (Sun.)★68,678

**Strictly Somerset (19817)**
Courier News
1201 Rte. 22 W
Bridgewater, NJ 08807
Phone: (908)722-8800

Fax: (908)707-3205
Subject(s): Entertainment
Circ: (Non-paid)68,283

**The Boston Phoenix (13487)**
Phoenix Media Group
126 Brookline Ave.
Boston, MA 02215
Phone: (617)536-5390
Fax: (617)536-1463
Subject(s): Paid Community Newspapers
Circ: (Free)50,000
 (Paid)68,000

**The Catholic Transcript (4625)**
The Catholic Transcript Inc.
467 Bloomfield Ave.
Bloomfield, CT 06002
Phone: (860)286-2828
Fax: (860)726-0000
Subject(s): Religious Publications
Circ: (Non-paid)⊕456
 (Paid)⊕67,000

**NY Carib News (22185)**
Carib News
7 W 39th St.
8th Floor
New York, NY 10018
Phone: (212)944-1991
Fax: (212)944-2089
Subject(s): Black Publications; Paid Community Newspapers
Circ: (Free)‡4,500
 (Paid)‡67,000

**The Christian Science Monitor (13498)**
The Christian Science Publishing Society
One Norway St.
Boston, MA 02115
Phone: (617)450-2000
Fax: (617)450-2930
Subject(s): Daily Newspapers
Circ: (Mon.-Fri.)65,277

**Courier News Weekly (26615)**
1570 A Sumneytown Pke.
Lansdale, PA 19446
Subject(s): Free Newspapers
Circ: (Free)‡65,000

**Irish Voice Newspaper (21851)**
875 Ave. of the Americas, Ste. 2100
New York, NY 10001
Phone: (212)684-3366
Fax: (212)244-3344
Subject(s): Ethnic Publications
Circ: 65,000

**Republican-American (5070)**
American-Republican Inc.
389 Meadow St.
Waterbury, CT 06722
Phone: (203)574-3636
Fax: (203)596-9277
Subject(s): Daily Newspapers
Circ: (Mon.-Sat.)★54,584
 (Sun.)★64,784

**Advertising Age (21270)**
Crain Communications Inc.
711 3rd Ave., 3rd Fl.
New York, NY 10017-4036
Phone: (212)210-0100
Fax: (212)210-0244
Subject(s): Advertising and Marketing
Circ: (Paid)★64,018

**The Philadelphia Tribune Metro Edition (27228)**
Philadelphia Tribune Co.
522 S 16th St.
Philadelphia, PA 19146
Phone: (215)893-4097
Fax: (215)735-3612
Subject(s): Free Newspapers; Black Publications; Free Newspapers
Circ: (Fri.)10,643
 (Tues.)20,250
 (Wed.)34,000
 (Sun.)47,408
 (Thurs.)64,000

**Providence Phoenix (27914)**
ProvPhoenix
150 Chestnut St.
Providence, RI 02903
Phone: (401)273-6397
Fax: (401)273-0920
Subject(s): Free Newspapers
Circ: (Free)‡64,000

**Daily Racing Form (21584)**
100 Broadway, 7th Fl.
New York, NY 10005-1902
Phone: (212)366-7600
Fax: (212)366-7738
Subject(s): Daily Periodicals; (Horses and Horse Racing)
Circ: (Tues.)10,481
 (Mon.)18,467
 (Fri.)40,319
 (Sun.)46,672
 (Sat.)63,430

**Penny Power (26265)**
Penny Power Ltd.
202-212 S 3rd St.
PO Box 250
Coopersburg, PA 18036
Phone: (610)282-4808
Fax: (610)282-1932
Subject(s): Shopping Guides
Circ: (Paid)9
 (Non-paid)63,337

**The Times Leader (27692)**
15 N Main St.
Wilkes Barre, PA 18711
Phone: (570)829-7100
Fax: (570)829-2002
Subject(s): Daily Newspapers
Circ: (Mon.-Sat.)44,131
 (Sun.)62,738

**Catholic Standard (26859)**
Catholic Standard and Times Publishing Co.
222 N 17th St.
Philadelphia, PA 19103-1202
Phone: (215)587-3660
Fax: (215)587-3979
Subject(s): Religious Publications
Circ: ‡62,500

**Orchard Park Pennysaver (22667)**
RW Publications
3770 Transit Rd.
Orchard Park, NY 14127
Phone: (716)662-4200
Fax: (716)662-0740
Subject(s): Shopping Guides
Circ: (Non-paid)61,717

**The Burlington Free Press (30855)**
Burlington Free Press
191 College St.
PO Box 10
Burlington, VT 05402
Phone: (802)863-3441
Fax: (802)660-1802
Subject(s): Daily Newspapers
Circ: (Mon.-Sat.)49,559
 (Sun.)60,265

**Danvers Herald (14260)**
Community Newspaper Co.
254 2nd Ave.
Needham, MA 02494
Phone: (781)433-6700
Subject(s): Paid Community Newspapers
Circ: (Combined)60,253

**Hamilton—Wenham Chronicle (13814)**
Community Newspaper Co.
152 Sylvan St.
Danvers, MA 01923
Phone: (978)739-8513
Fax: (978)739-8501
Subject(s): Paid Community Newspapers
Circ: (Combined)60,253

**Ipswich Chronicle (14262)**
Community Newspaper Co.
254 2nd Ave.
Needham, MA 02494
Phone: (781)433-6700
Subject(s): Paid Community Newspapers
Circ: (Combined)60,253

## Northeastern States

**Malden Observer (14237)**
Community Newspaper Co.
57 High St.
Medford, MA 02155-3808
Phone: (617)655-4001
Fax: (617)655-2195
**Subject(s):** Free Newspapers
**Circ:** (Combined)60,253

**Marblehead Reporter (14222)**
Community Newspaper Co.
PO Box 468
Marblehead, MA 01945
Phone: (617)631-7700
Fax: (617)639-2830
**Subject(s):** Free Newspapers
**Circ:** (Combined)60,253

**Melrose Free Press (14244)**
Community Newspaper Co.
152 Sylvan Way
Danvers, MA 01923-3568
Phone: (617)665-4001
Fax: (617)665-2195
**Subject(s):** Paid Community Newspapers
**Circ:** (Combined)60,253

**North Andover Citizen (14273)**
Community Newspaper Co.
254 2nd Ave.
Needham, MA 02494
Phone: (781)433-6700
**Subject(s):** Paid Community Newspapers
**Circ:** (Combined)60,253

**North Shore Sunday (13750)**
Community Newspaper Co.
152 Sylvan St.
Danvers, MA 01923
Phone: (508)774-0505
Fax: (508)762-0450
**Subject(s):** Free Newspapers
**Circ:** (Combined)60,253

**Saugus Advertiser (14238)**
Community Newspaper Co.
57 High St.
Medford, MA 02155-3808
Phone: (617)665-4001
Fax: (617)665-2195
**Subject(s):** Paid Community Newspapers
**Circ:** (Combined)60,253

**Swampscott Reporter (14836)**
Community Newspaper Co.
122 Washington St.
Marblehead, MA 01945-3590
Phone: (781)639-4800
Fax: (781)639-4801
**Subject(s):** Paid Community Newspapers
**Circ:** (Combined)60,253

**Weekend Reporter (19883)**
Ocean County Newspapers Inc.
8 Robbins St.
Toms River, NJ 08753
Phone: (732)349-3000
Fax: (732)557-5658
**Subject(s):** Paid Community Newspapers
**Circ:** (Non-paid)60,124

**La Voz Hispana (22018)**
159 E 116th St.
New York, NY 10029
Phone: (212)348-2100
**Subject(s):** Paid Community Newspapers; Hispanic Publications; Spanish
**Circ:** 60,082

**Big Saver (21207)**
Adwise
PO Box 2181
Middletown, NY 10940
Phone: (845)342-9090
**Subject(s):** Shopping Guides
**Circ:** (Free)‡60,000

**Cape Cod Times (13834)**
319 Main St.
Hyannis, MA 02601
Phone: (508)775-1200
**Subject(s):** Daily Newspapers
**Circ:** (Mon.-Sat.)★50,896
(Sun.)★60,004

**Education Update (21634)**
Education Update Inc.
17 Lexington Ave., A1207
New York, NY 10010-5520
Phone: (212)477-5600
Fax: (212)477-5893
**Subject(s):** Education
**Circ:** (Free)60,000

**The A.D. Times (26090)**
PO Box F
1101 Hamilton Street 7
Allentown, PA 18105-1538
Phone: (610)871-5200
Fax: (610)439-7694
**Subject(s):** Religious Publications
**Circ:** 59,350

**Journal of Counseling and Development (20550)**
American Counseling Association
c/o A. Scott McGowan, JCD Editor
Department of Counseling and Development
Long Island University, C. W. Post Campus
720 Northern Blvd.
Brookville, NY 11548-1300
Phone: (516)299-2815
Fax: (516)299-3312
**Subject(s):** Paid Community Newspapers; Education; Psychology and Psychiatry
**Circ:** (Paid)59,000

**Irish Echo (21850)**
Irish Echo Newspaper Corp.
14 E. 47th St.
New York, NY 10017
Phone: (212)686-1266
Fax: (212)683-6455
**Subject(s):** Ethnic Publications; Paid Community Newspapers
**Circ:** 58,000

**La Tribuna Hispana-USA (20886)**
PO Box 186
Hempstead, NY 11550
Phone: (516)486-6457
Fax: (516)292-3972
**Subject(s):** Paid Community Newspapers
**Circ:** (Paid)2,000
(Non-paid)58,000

**The Eagle-Tribune (14312)**
Eagle-Tribune Publishing
100 Turnpike St.
North Andover, MA 01845
Phone: (978)946-2000
Fax: (978)685-1588
**Subject(s):** Daily Newspapers
**Circ:** (Mon.-Sat.)51,940
(Sun.)57,731

**The Evangelist (20213)**
Albany Catholic Press Association Inc.
40 N. Main Ave.
Albany, NY 12203
Phone: (518)453-6688
Fax: (518)453-8448
**Subject(s):** Religious Publications
**Circ:** 57,300

**Valley Advocate (13768)**
New Mass Media Inc.
116 Pleasant St., 3rd Fl.
Easthampton, MA 01027
Phone: (413)529-2840
Fax: (413)529-2844
**Subject(s):** Paid Community Newspapers
**Circ:** 57,307

**Downtown Express (21617)**
Community Media L.L.C.
487 Greenwich St., Ste. 6A
New York, NY 10013
Phone: (212)242-6162
Fax: (212)229-2790
**Subject(s):** Free Newspapers
**Circ:** (Free)‡56,897

**The Almanac (26678)**
Observer Publishing Co.
395 Valley Brook Rd.
McMurray, PA 15317
Phone: (724)941-7725
Fax: (724)942-3923
**Subject(s):** Free Newspapers
**Circ:** (Paid)♦279
(Non-paid)♦56,623

**Artvoice (20555)**
810-812 Main St.
Buffalo, NY 14202
Phone: (716)881-6604
Fax: (716)881-6682
**Subject(s):** Free Newspapers
**Circ:** (Free)☐55,421

**El Nuevo Hudson (19424)**
The Jersey Journal
30 Journal Sq.
Jersey City, NJ 07306
Phone: (201)217-2524
Fax: (201)653-3125
**Subject(s):** Free Newspapers; Ethnic Publications; Hispanic Publications
**Circ:** (Non-paid)♦55,425

**Afro-American Times (20486)**
The Challenge Group
1195 Alantic Ave.
Brooklyn, NY 11216
Phone: (718)636-9500
Fax: (718)857-9115
**Subject(s):** Paid Community Newspapers; Black Publications
**Circ:** 55,000

**Hartford Advocate (4802)**
New Mass Media Inc.
100 Constitution Plaza
Hartford, CT 06103-1721
Phone: (860)548-9300
**Subject(s):** Paid Community Newspapers; Alternative and Underground
**Circ:** (Paid)55,000

**New Haven Advocate (4899)**
900 Chapel St., Ste. 1100
New Haven, CT 06510
Phone: (203)789-0010
Fax: (203)787-1418
**Subject(s):** Free Newspapers
**Circ:** (Free)55,000

**Business Travel News (21441)**
VNU Business Media USA
770 Broadway
New York, NY 10003
Phone: (646)654-5000
**Subject(s):** Travel and Tourism
**Circ:** (Non-paid)‡54,795

**The Daily Gazette (22919)**
Daily Gazette Co.
2345 Maxon Rd. Ext.
PO Box 1090
Schenectady, NY 12301-1090
Phone: (518)374-4141
Fax: (518)395-3089
**Subject(s):** Daily Newspapers
**Circ:** (Mon.-Sat.)53,787
(Sun.)54,764

**The Catholic Accent (26405)**
Greensburg Catholic Accent and Communications Inc.
725 E. Pittsburgh St.
Greensburg, PA 15601
Phone: (724)834-4010
Fax: (724)836-5650
**Subject(s):** Religious Publications
**Circ:** ‡54,000

**South Look (14276)**
Mariner Newspapers
254 2nd Ave
PO Box 9113
Needham, MA 02494
Phone: (781)837-3500
Fax: (781)837-4540
**Subject(s):** Paid Community Newspapers
**Circ:** (Free)2,500
(Paid)54,000

**India Abroad (21817)**
India Abroad Publications Inc.
43 W. 24th St.
New York, NY 10010
Phone: (212)929-1727
Fax: (212)627-9503
**Subject(s):** Intercultural Interests; Politics; Economics; (General Sports)
**Circ:** (Fri.)53,851

**El Diario/La Prensa** (21635)
345 Hudson St.
New York, NY 10014
Phone: (212)807-4600
Fax: (212)807-4617
Subject(s): Spanish; Daily Newspapers; Hispanic Publications

Circ: (Sun.)36,152
(Sat.)46,090
(Mon.-Fri.)53,843

**Fairfield County Weekly** (4946)
New Mass Media Inc.
3 Quincy St.
Norwalk, CT 06850
Phone: (203)838-1825
Fax: (203)838-1872
Subject(s): Gay and Lesbian Interests; Paid Community Newspapers

Circ: 52,769

**The Intelligencer Record** (26286)
Calkins Media Inc.
333 N Broad St.
P.O. Box 858
Doylestown, PA 18901-0858
Phone: (215)345-3000
Fax: (215)345-3150
Subject(s): Daily Newspapers

Circ: (Mon.-Thurs.)★43,819
(Sat.)★47,944
(Fri.)★51,384
(Sun.)★52,197

**The Intelligencer** (26516)
Calkins Media Inc.
145 N. Easton Rd.
Horsham, PA 19044
Phone: (215)957-8100
Fax: (215)957-6375
Subject(s): Daily Newspapers

Circ: (Mon.-Fri.)‡44,729
(Sun.)‡52,143

**The Chief Civil Service Leader** (21482)
The New York Civil Service Employees Publishing Company Inc.
277 Broadway, Ste. 1506
New York, NY 10007-2008
Phone: (212)962-2690
Fax: (212)962-2556
Subject(s): State, Municipal, and County Administration

Circ: (Fri.)52,087

**Mensaje** (19067)
Latin American News and Book Inc.
PO Box 2109
Elizabeth, NJ 07207-2109
Phone: (908)355-8835
Fax: (908)527-9160
Subject(s): Free Newspapers; Hispanic Publications; Spanish

Circ: (Paid)52,000

**Beacon Mailbag** (19503)
Manahawkin Newspapers Inc.
345 E Bay Ave.
Manahawkin, NJ 08050-3320
Phone: (609)597-3211
Fax: (609)978-4592
Subject(s): Free Newspapers

Circ: (Fri.)51,593

**Intelligencer Journal** (26598)
Lancaster Newspapers Inc.
8 W. King St.
PO Box 1328
Lancaster, PA 17608-1328
Phone: (717)291-8811
Fax: (717)399-6513
Subject(s): Daily Newspapers

Circ: (Mon.-Sat.)★45,424
(Fri.)★51,066
(Sun.)★51,576

**Amsterdam News** (21331)
2340 Frederick Douglass Blvd.
New York, NY 10027
Phone: (212)932-7440
Fax: (212)222-3842
Subject(s): Paid Community Newspapers; Black Publications

Circ: (Wed.)51,133

**The Daily Times** (27459)
Journal Register Co.
500 Mildred Ave.
Primos, PA 19018
Phone: (610)622-8887
Fax: (800)258-9258
Subject(s): Daily Newspapers

Circ: (Sat.)42,431
(Sun.)49,218
(Mon.-Fri.)51,098

**Lancaster Farming** (26338)
Lancaster Newspapers Inc.
1 E. Main St.
PO Box 609
Ephrata, PA 17522
Phone: (717)626-1164
Fax: (717)733-6058
Subject(s): Paid Community Newspapers; Farm Newspapers

Circ: (Free)⊕1,000
(Paid)⊕51,000

**The Trentonian** (19897)
Capitol City Publishing Company Inc.
600 Perry St.
Trenton, NJ 08618
Phone: (609)989-7800
Fax: (609)989-9252
Subject(s): Daily Newspapers

Circ: (Sun.)40,527
(Sat.)45,698
(Mon.-Fri.)50,980

**Delaware County Times** (20700)
Delaware County Times Inc.
56 Main St.
Delhi, NY 13753
Phone: (607)746-2176
Fax: (607)746-3135
Subject(s): Paid Community Newspapers

Circ: (Sat.)42,355
(Sun.)48,178
(Mon.-Fri.)50,746

**Lowell Sun** (13862)
Lowell Sun Publishing Co.
15 Kearney Sq.
Lowell, MA 01852
Phone: (978)458-7100
Subject(s): Daily Newspapers

Circ: (Sat.)★42,065
(Mon.-Fri.)★48,584
(Sun.)★50,660

**Manahawkin Newspaper** (19504)
The Times Beacon Publishing
345 E Bay Ave.
Manahawkin, NJ 08050
Phone: (609)597-3211
Fax: (609)978-4592
Subject(s): Paid Community Newspapers

Circ: (Paid)22,000
(Free)50,400

**The Parent Paper** (19956)
Parent Paper Inc.
1 Garrett Mountain Plaza
PO Box 471
West Paterson, NJ 07424
Phone: (973)569-7720
Fax: (973)569-7725
Subject(s): Parenting; Free Newspapers

Circ: (Combined)50,409

**Jersey Journal** (19429)
Evening Journal Association
30 Journal Sq.
Jersey City, NJ 07306
Phone: (201)653-1000
Fax: (201)653-1414
Subject(s): Daily Newspapers

Circ: (Mon.-Sat.)50,386

**Observer-Dispatch** (23087)
221 Oriskany Plz.
Utica, NY 13501
Phone: (315)792-5000
Fax: (315)792-5033
Subject(s): Daily Newspapers

Circ: (Mon.-Sat.)★43,421
(Sun.)★50,274

**The Scientist** (27251)
The Scientist Inc.
3535 Market St., Ste. 200
Philadelphia, PA 19104
Phone: (215)387-7542
Subject(s): Science (General)

Circ: (Paid)1,240
4,419
50,041

**Bronx Press-Review** (20448)
Metro North Media
6050 Riverdale Ave.
Bronx, NY 10471
Phone: (718)543-5200
Fax: (718)543-4206
Subject(s): Paid Community Newspapers

Circ: ‡30,000
(Combined)50,000

**1590 Broadcaster** (18910)
255 Main St.
Nashua, NH 03060
Phone: (603)886-6075
Fax: (603)866-8180
Subject(s): Free Newspapers

Circ: (Free)‡50,000

**Poughkeepsie Journal** (22744)
Gannett Company Inc.
85 Civic Center Plaza
Poughkeepsie, NY 12601
Phone: (845)454-2000
Fax: (800)876-6397
Subject(s): Daily Newspapers

Circ: (Mon.-Sat.)★39,707
(Sun.)★48,948

**The Express-Times** (26301)
30 N 4th S
PO Box 391
Easton, PA 18044
Phone: (610)258-7171
Fax: (610)258-2130
Subject(s): Daily Newspapers

Circ: (Sat.)★44,390
(Mon.-Fri.)★48,088
(Sun.)★48,419

**Gambit Weekly** (18900)
Gambit Communications
76 Northeastern Blvd., Ste. 30B
Nashua, NH 03062
Phone: (603)881-3500
Subject(s): Free Newspapers

Circ: (Paid)❏53
(Free)❏48,036

**Catholic Light** (27503)
Catholic Light Publishing Co.
300 Wyoming Ave.
PO Box 708
Scranton, PA 18501-0708
Phone: (570)207-2229
Fax: (570)207-2271
Subject(s): Religious Publications

Circ: ‡48,000

**El Tiempo de New York** (20983)
37-37-88 St., Ste. A
Jackson Heights, NY 11372
Phone: (718)507-0832
Fax: (718)507-2105
Subject(s): Paid Community Newspapers; Hispanic Publications; Spanish

Circ: (Free)‡500
(Paid)‡48,000

**North Jersey Prospector** (19037)
North Jersey Prospector Inc.
479 Grove
Clifton, NJ 07013
Phone: (973)773-8300
Subject(s): Paid Community Newspapers

Circ: (Paid)‡42,010
(Free)‡48,000

**Vista** (27532)
Shippensburg University
Office of University Publications
1871 Old Main Dr.
Shippensburg, PA 17257
Phone: (717)477-7447
Fax: (717)477-1253

---

Circulation: ★ = ABC; △ = BPA; ♦ = CAC; ● = CCAB; ❏ = VAC; ⊕ = PO Statement; ‡ = Publisher's Report; Boldface figures = sworn; Light figures = estimated.

Subject(s): College Publications
Circ: 47,500

**Beaver County Times  (26144)**
400 Fair Ave.
PO Box 400
Beaver, PA 15009-0400
Phone: (412)775-3200
Fax: (412)775-7212
Subject(s): Daily Newspapers
Circ: (Mon.-Sat.)★41,765
(Sun.)★47,201

**El Hispano  (27618)**
8605 W Chester Pke.
Upper Darby, PA 19082
Phone: (610)789-5512
Fax: (610)789-5524
Subject(s): Free Newspapers
Circ: (Paid)1,000
(Non-paid)47,000

**Caring for the Ages  (21459)**
Lippincott Williams & Wilkins
c/o Lisa Dionne
333 7th Av., 20th Fl.
New York, NY 10001
Subject(s): Medicine and Surgery; Health and Healthcare; Nursing; Gerontology
Circ: (Paid)46,983

**Syracuse New Times  (23042)**
A.Z. Limited Inc.
1415 W. Genessee St.
Syracuse, NY 13204-2156
Phone: (315)422-7011
Fax: (315)422-1721
Subject(s): Paid Community Newspapers
Circ: (Paid)400
(Controlled)46,200

**The Day  (4914)**
Day Publishing Co.
47 Eugene O'Neill Dr.
New London, CT 06320-1231
Phone: (860)442-2200
Fax: (860)442-5599
Subject(s): Daily Newspapers
Circ: (Mon.-Sat.)★39,472
(Sun.)★45,848

**Belleville Times  (18974)**
North Jersey Community Newspapers
90 Centre St.
Nutley, NJ 07110-3270
Phone: (973)667-2100
Fax: (973)667-3904
Subject(s): Paid Community Newspapers
Circ: (Wed.)3,250
(Paid)45,524

**Glen Ridge Voice  (19115)**
North Jersey Community Newspapers
90 Centre St.
Nutley, NJ 07110-3270
Phone: (973)667-2100
Fax: (973)667-3904
Subject(s): Paid Community Newspapers
Circ: (Thurs.)45,524

**The Item of Millburn and Short Hills  (19524)**
North Jersey Community Newspapers
343 Millburn Ave., Ste. 100
Millburn, NJ 07041-1940
Phone: (973)376-1200
Fax: (973)376-8556
Subject(s): Paid Community Newspapers
Circ: (Wed.)4,701
(Paid)45,524

**The Montclair Times  (19528)**
North Jersey Community Newspapers
114 Valley Rd.
Montclair, NJ 07042
Phone: (973)233-5000
Fax: (973)233-5031
Subject(s): Paid Community Newspapers
Circ: (Thurs.)45,524

**Northern Valley Suburbanite  (19051)**
North Jersey Community Newspapers
300 Knickerbocker Rd.
Cresskill, NJ 07626-1343
Phone: (201)568-6090
Fax: (201)568-4360

Subject(s): Free Newspapers
Circ: (Non-paid)45,524

**The Nutley Sun  (19639)**
North Jersey Community Newspapers
90 Centre St.
Nutley, NJ 07110-3270
Phone: (973)667-2100
Fax: (973)667-3904
Subject(s): Paid Community Newspapers
Circ: (Wed.)5,000
(Paid)45,524

**Pascack Valley Community Life  (19970)**
North Jersey Community Newspapers
372 Kinderkamack Rd.
Westwood, NJ 07675-1600
Phone: (201)664-2501
Fax: (201)664-1332
Subject(s): Free Newspapers
Circ: (Non-paid)45,524

**The Ridgewood News  (19763)**
North Jersey Community Newspapers
41 Oak St.
Ridgewood, NJ 07450-3805
Phone: (201)612-5400
Fax: (201)612-5410
Subject(s): Paid Community Newspapers
Circ: (Wed.)6,873
(Sun.)7,115
(Fri.)45,524

**South Bergenite  (19774)**
North Jersey Community Newspapers
33 Lincoln Ave.
Rutherford, NJ 07070-2112
Phone: (201)933-1166
Fax: (201)933-5496
Subject(s): Free Newspapers
Circ: (Non-paid)45,524

**Suburban Trends  (19444)**
North Jersey Community Newspapers
300 Kakeout Rd.
Kinnelon, NJ 07405-2548
Phone: (973)283-5600
Fax: (973)283-5623
Subject(s): Paid Community Newspapers
Circ: (Sun.)11,029
(Wed.)45,524

**Wayne Today  (19934)**
North Jersey Community Newspapers
1 Garrett Mountain Plz.
PO Box 471
West Paterson, NJ 07424-0471
Subject(s): Free Newspapers
Circ: (Combined)45,524

**Tribune-Democrat  (26548)**
The Tribune
425 Locust St.
Johnstown, PA 15907
Phone: (814)532-5199
Fax: (814)539-1409
Subject(s): Daily Newspapers
Circ: (Mon.-Sat.)★40,943
(Sun.)★45,142

**FoodService Director  (21703)**
VNU Business Publications
770 Broadway
New York, NY 10003-9595
Phone: (646)654-5000
Fax: (646)654-7265
Circ: (Controlled)45,100

**Italian Tribune  (19615)**
427 Bloomfield Ave.
Newark, NJ 07107
Phone: (973)485-6000
Fax: (973)485-8967
Subject(s): Paid Community Newspapers; Ethnic Publications
Circ: ‡45,000

**Sentinel  (19109)**
Greater Media Newspapers
PO Box 5001
Freehold, NJ 07728-5001
Phone: (732)358-5200
Subject(s): Paid Community Newspapers
Circ: ‡45,000

**Suburban  (19110)**
Greater Media Newspapers
PO Box 5001
Freehold, NJ 07728-5001
Phone: (732)358-5200
Subject(s): Paid Community Newspapers
Circ: ‡45,000

**Today Newspapers  (19961)**
North Jersey Community Newspapers
The Weekly Division of N Jersey Media Group
1 Garret Mountain Plz.
PO Box 471
West Paterson, NJ 07424-0471
Phone: (973)569-7000
Fax: (973)569-7310
Subject(s): Free Newspapers
Circ: (Paid)♦34
(Non-paid)♦44,507

**Burlington County Times  (19975)**
4284 Rte. 130
Willingboro, NJ 08046
Phone: (609)871-8000
Fax: (609)877-2706
Subject(s): Daily Newspapers
Circ: (Mon.-Fri.)40,608
(Sun.)44,353

**Catholic Courier  (22872)**
Rochester Catholic Press Association
3555 Veterans Memorial Hwy., Unit O
Ronkonkoma, NY 11779
Phone: (631)471-4730
Fax: (631)471-4804
Subject(s): Religious Publications
Circ: (Paid)⊕44,299

**Women's Wear Daily  (22555)**
Fairchild Publications Inc.
7 W 34th St.
New York, NY 10001
Phone: (212)630-4000
Fax: (212)630-3555
Subject(s): Daily Newspapers; Clothing; Women's Interests
Circ: (Mon.-Fri.)44,015

**The Herald  (4871)**
1 Herald Sq.
PO Box 2050
New Britain, CT 06050
Phone: (860)225-4601
Fax: (860)225-2601
Subject(s): Daily Newspapers
Circ: (Mon.-Sat.)22,756
(Sun.)43,948

**Senior Scoop  (19881)**
Ocean County Newspapers Inc.
8 Robbins St.
Toms River, NJ 08753
Phone: (732)349-3000
Fax: (732)557-5658
Subject(s): Senior Citizens' Interests
Circ: (Combined)42,851

**Hudson Valley Black Press  (22609)**
PO Box 2160
343 Broadway
Newburgh, NY 12550
Phone: (845)562-1313
Fax: (845)562-1348
Subject(s): Paid Community Newspapers; Black Publications
Circ: ‡42,500

**Foothills Trader  (5057)**
190 Water St.
Torrington, CT 06790
Phone: (860)489-3121
Subject(s): Shopping Guides
Circ: (Paid)‡25
(Free)‡42,000

**The Weekender  (27693)**
Weekender
15 N. Main St.
Wilkes Barre, PA 18711
Phone: (570)829-7101
Subject(s): Free Newspapers; Entertainment; Alternative and Underground
Circ: (Non-paid)‡42,000

**The Enterprise (13626)**
Enterprise
60 Main St.
PO Box 1450
Brockton, MA 02303
Phone: (508)586-6200
Fax: (508)427-4949
**Subject(s):** Daily Newspapers

**Circ:** (Sun.)40,212
(Sat.)40,762
(Mon.-Fri.)41,197

**Der Yid (20504)**
Der Yid Publication Association
84 Broadway St.
Brooklyn, NY 11211
Phone: (718)797-3900
Fax: (718)797-1985
**Subject(s):** Yiddish; Jewish Publications; Religious Publications

**Circ:** (Free)‡2,500
(Paid)‡41,000

**The Monadnock Shopper News (18843)**
Shakour Publishers
445 West St.
PO Box 487
Keene, NH 03431-0487
Phone: (603)352-5250
Fax: (603)357-9351
**Subject(s):** Shopping Guides

**Circ:** (Free)‡41,000

**The Franklin Shopper (26230)**
25 Penncraft Ave.
Chambersburg, PA 17201
Phone: (717)263-0359
Fax: (717)263-1314
**Subject(s):** Shopping Guides

**Circ:** (Non-paid)40,517

**The Courier-News (19822)**
Gannett Company Inc.
1201 Rte. 22 W
PO Box 6600
Bridgewater, NJ 08807
Phone: (908)722-8800
Fax: (908)707-3252
**Subject(s):** Daily Newspapers

**Circ:** (Sat.)★35,788
(Sun.)★39,781
(Mon.-Fri.)★40,098

**Bargain Sheet (26155)**
111 Boal Ave.
Boalsburg, PA 16827
Phone: (814)466-2200
Fax: (814)466-2191
**Subject(s):** Shopping Guides

**Circ:** (Free)‡40,000

**DM News (21613)**
100 Ave.of the Americas
New York, NY 10013
Phone: (212)925-7300
Fax: (212)925-8752
**Subject(s):** Advertising and Marketing

**Circ:** (Controlled)‡40,000

**The Episcopal Times (13513)**
Episcopal Diocese of Massachusetts
138 Tremont St.
Boston, MA 02111
Phone: (617)482-5800
Fax: (617)482-8431
**Subject(s):** Religious Publications

**Circ:** (Free)‡40,000

**New York Blade News (22153)**
333 7th Ave., 14th Fl.
New York, NY 10011
Phone: (212)268-2701
Fax: (212)268-2069
**Subject(s):** Gay and Lesbian Interests; Paid Community Newspapers

**Circ:** (Paid)83
(Free)40,000

**The Sae Gae Times (21078)**
The S.A.E. Gae Times
38-42 9th St.
Long Island City, NY 11101
Phone: (718)361-2600
Fax: (718)361-2368
**Subject(s):** Daily Newspapers; Korean; Ethnic Publications

**Circ:** (Combined)40,000

**A Shopper's Guide (19633)**
New Jersey Herald
2 Spring St.
PO Box 10
Newton, NJ 07860-0010
Phone: (973)383-1500
Fax: (973)383-8477
**Subject(s):** Free Newspapers

**Circ:** (Non-paid)39,708

**The Advocate (5024)**
Southern Connecticut Newspapers Inc.
75 Tresser Blvd.
PO Box 9307
Stamford, CT 06904-3304
Phone: (203)964-2200
Fax: (203)964-2345
**Subject(s):** Daily Newspapers

**Circ:** (Sat.)26,817
(Mon.-Fri.)28,514
(Sun.)39,448

**Star-Gazette (20745)**
PO Box 285
Elmira, NY 14902
Phone: (607)734-5151
Fax: (607)734-4408
**Subject(s):** Daily Newspapers

**Circ:** (Mon.-Sat.)★28,256
(Sun.)★39,227

**News-Times (4661)**
Ottaway Newspapers Inc.
333 Main St.
Danbury, CT 06810
Phone: (203)744-5100
Fax: (203)792-8730
**Subject(s):** Daily Newspapers

**Circ:** (Mon.-Sat.)33,743
(Sun.)39,024

**Colgate Scene (20874)**
Colgate University
13 Oak Dr.
Hamilton, NY 13346
Phone: (315)228-7417
Fax: (315)228-7798
**Subject(s):** College Publications

**Circ:** (Free)‡39,000

**Polish Daily News (22245)**
Bicentennial Publishing Corp.
333 W 38th St.
New York, NY 10018
Phone: (212)594-2266
Fax: (212)594-2383
**Subject(s):** Daily Newspapers; Polish

**Circ:** (Free)450
(Paid)39,000

**Observer-Reporter (27647)**
Observer Publishing Co.
122 S. Main St.
Washington, PA 15301
Phone: (724)222-2200
Fax: (724)225-2077
**Subject(s):** Daily Newspapers

**Circ:** (Mon.-Sat.)★36,399
(Sun.)★38,817

**Weekly Record (27729)**
York Newspaper Co.
PO Box 15122
York, PA 17405-7122
Phone: (717)771-2021
Fax: (717)771-2009
**Subject(s):** Free Newspapers

**Circ:** (Free)38,400

**Altoona Mirror (26101)**
Thomson Newspapers
PO Box 2008
Altoona, PA 16603-2008
Phone: (814)946-7411
Fax: (814)946-7547
**Subject(s):** Daily Newspapers

**Circ:** (Mon.-Sat.)★31,805
(Sun.)★38,023

**Jewish Exponent Inside (27004)**
Jewish Exponent
2100 Arch St.
Philadelphia, PA 19103
Phone: (215)832-0700
**Subject(s):** Jewish Publications; Religious Publications

**Circ:** (Non-paid)3,206
(Paid)38,007

**La Salle Collegian (27114)**
La Salle University
1900 W. Olney Ave.
Campus Box 417
Philadelphia, PA 19141
Phone: (215)951-1398
Fax: (215)951-1399
**Subject(s):** College Publications

**Circ:** (Non-paid)38,000

**La Voz (19066)**
1020 Kipling Road
PO Box 899
Elizabeth, NJ 07208
Phone: (908)352-6654
Fax: (908)352-9735
**Subject(s):** Hispanic Publications; Spanish; Paid Community Newspapers

**Circ:** ⊕38,000

**The Week Ahead (19081)**
North Jersey Community Newspapers
12-38 River Rd.
Fair Lawn, NJ 07410-1897
Phone: (201)791-8400
Fax: (201)794-3259
**Subject(s):** Free Newspapers

**Circ:** (Free)‡37,949

**The Post-Star (20840)**
Lawrence & Cooper St.
Glens Falls, NY 12801
Phone: (518)792-3131
Fax: (518)792-6867
**Subject(s):** Daily Newspapers

**Circ:** (Mon.-Sat.)★34,447
(Sun.)★37,550

**The Standard-Times (14280)**
Standard-Times Publishing Co.
25 Elm St.
New Bedford, MA 02740
Phone: (508)997-7411
**Subject(s):** Daily Newspapers

**Circ:** (Mon.-Sat.)★34,417
(Sun.)★37,416

**New York Trend (20861)**
T.T.W. Associates Inc.
11 Middleneck Rd., Ste. 208
Great Neck, NY 11021
Phone: (516)466-0028
Fax: (516)466-0062
**Subject(s):** Ethnic Publications

**Circ:** (Non-paid)24,800
(Paid)37,200

**Daily Transcript (13751)**
Community Newspaper Co.
254 2nd Ave.
Needham, MA 02494
Phone: (781)433-6700
**Subject(s):** Daily Newspapers

**Circ:** (Combined)36,984

**Marlborough Enterprise (14224)**
Community Newspaper Co.
40 Mechanic St.
Marlborough, MA 01752-4425
**Subject(s):** Daily Newspapers

**Circ:** (Combined)36,984

**Sharon Advocate (14275)**
Community Newspaper Co.
254 2nd Ave.
Needham, MA 02494
Phone: (781)433-6700
**Subject(s):** Paid Community Newspapers

**Circ:** (Combined)36,984

**Stoughton Journal (14277)**
Community Newspaper Co.
254 2nd Ave.
Needham, MA 02494
Phone: (781)433-6700

Circulation: ★ = ABC; △ = BPA; ♦ = CAC; • = CCAB; ▢ = VAC; ⊕ = PO Statement; ‡ = Publisher's Report; Boldface figures = sworn; Light figures = estimated.

**The Sudbury Town Crier** (14832)
Community Newspaper Co.
33 New York Ave.
Framingham, MA 01701
Phone: (508)626-4444
Fax: (508)626-4444
**Subject(s):** Paid Community Newspapers
**Circ:** (Combined)36,984

**THE DAILYNEWSTRIBUNE** (14866)
Community Newspaper Co.
254 2nd Ave.
Needham, MA 02494
Phone: (781)433-6700
**Subject(s):** Daily Newspapers
**Circ:** (Combined)36,984

**Wayland Town Crier & TAB** (14874)
Community Newspaper Co.
254 2nd Ave.
Needham, MA 02494
Phone: (781)433-6700
**Subject(s):** Free Newspapers
**Circ:** (Combined)36,984

**The Providence Visitor** (27915)
184 Broad Street
Providence, RI 02903
Phone: (401)272-1010
Fax: (401)421-8418
**Subject(s):** Religious Publications
**Circ:** 36,674

**City Newspaper** (22812)
W.M.T. Publications Inc.
250 N. Goodman St.
Rochester, NY 14607-1199
Phone: (585)244-3329
Fax: (585)244-1126
**Subject(s):** Free Newspapers
**Circ:** (Paid)❏104
 (Free)❏36,344

**Shopping News of Lancaster County** (26339)
Hocking Printing Company Inc.
615 E. Main St.
PO Box 456
Ephrata, PA 17522
Phone: (717)738-1151
Fax: (717)733-3900
**Subject(s):** Shopping Guides
**Circ:** (Paid)43
 (Non-paid)35,785

**Watertown Daily Times** (23128)
Johnson Newspaper Corp.
260 Washington St.
Times Bldg.
Watertown, NY 13601-3301
Phone: (315)782-1000
Fax: (315)782-2337
**Subject(s):** Daily Newspapers
**Circ:** (Mon.-Sat.)★31,507
 (Sun.)★35,507

**Atlantic City Weekly** (19938)
Whoot Newspaper
Ste. 350, 8025 Black Horse Pike
West Atlantic City, NJ 08232-2965
Phone: (609)646-4848
Fax: (609)646-7338
**Subject(s):** Free Newspapers; Entertainment; Travel and Tourism
**Circ:** (Paid)❏219
 (Free)❏35,232

**The Berkshire Eagle** (14736)
New England Newspapers Inc.
Clocktower Business Park
75 S Church St.
Pittsfield, MA 01201
Phone: (413)496-6355
Fax: (413)499-3419
**Subject(s):** Daily Newspapers
**Circ:** (Mon.-Sat.)31,363
 (Sun.)35,146

**Jednota (Union)** (26699)
First Catholic Slovak Union
1011 Rosedale Ave.
Middletown, PA 17057
Phone: (717)944-0461

Fax: (717)944-3107
**Subject(s):** Religious Publications; Slovak; Unclassified Fraternal
**Circ:** (Paid)‡535
 (Free)‡35,105

**Able Newspaper** (22644)
Able
PO Box 395
Old Bethpage, NY 11804
Phone: (516)939-2253
Fax: (516)939-0540
**Subject(s):** Paid Community Newspapers
**Circ:** 35,000

**Catholic Star Herald** (19004)
15 N. 7th St.
Camden, NJ 08102
Phone: (856)756-7900
Fax: (856)756-7938
**Subject(s):** Religious Publications
**Circ:** ‡35,000

**The Inner City Newspaper** (4889)
Penfield Communications Inc.
50 Fitch St.
P O Box 9431
New Haven, CT 06515-9431
Phone: (203)387-0354
Fax: (203)387-2684
**Subject(s):** Free Newspapers; Hispanic Publications; Black Publications
**Circ:** (Free)‡35,000

**Middlebury College Magazine** (30899)
Middlebury College Publications
Middlebury College
Middlebury, VT 05753
Phone: (802)443-5000
Fax: (802)443-2088
**Subject(s):** College Publications
**Circ:** 35,000

**The Sandpaper** (19846)
SandPaper Inc.
1816 Long Beach Blvd.
Surf City, NJ 08008
Phone: (609)494-5900
Fax: (609)494-1437
**Subject(s):** Free Newspapers
**Circ:** (Non-paid)35,000

**Independent Press** (19609)
80 S St.
New Providence, NJ 07974-1991
Phone: (908)464-1025
Fax: (908)464-9085
**Subject(s):** Free Newspapers
**Circ:** (Paid)196
 (Free)34,813

**Lewiston Sun-Journal** (12528)
Sun-Journal
104 Park St.
Lewiston, ME 04240
Phone: (207)784-5411
Fax: (207)786-3940
**Subject(s):** Daily Newspapers
**Circ:** (Mon.-Sat.)★34,035
 (Sun.)★34,808

**East Penn Valley Merchandiser** (26421)
Windsor Press Inc.
6 N. 3rd St.
PO Box 465
Hamburg, PA 19526
Phone: (610)562-2267
Fax: (610)562-2770
**Subject(s):** Shopping Guides
**Circ:** (Paid)24
 (Non-paid)34,757

**Northern Light** (18796)
PO Box 2230
Conway, NH 03818
Phone: (603)447-3824
Fax: (603)447-3825
**Subject(s):** Free Newspapers
**Circ:** (Non-paid)34,759

**Go Out** (19425)
The Jersey Journal
30 Journal Sq.
Jersey City, NJ 07306
Phone: (201)217-2524

Fax: (201)653-3125
**Subject(s):** Free Newspapers; Entertainment
**Circ:** (Non-paid)34,433

**Salem Evening News** (13459)
32 Dunham Rd.
Beverly, MA 01915
Phone: (978)922-1234
Fax: (978)922-4330
**Subject(s):** Daily Newspapers
**Circ:** (Mon.-Sat.)34,413

**Ocular Surgery News Europe/Asia-Pacific Edition** (19865)
SLACK Inc.
6900 Grove Rd.
Thorofare, NJ 08086-9447
Phone: (856)848-1000
Fax: (856)848-6091
**Subject(s):** Medicine and Surgery
**Circ:** (Controlled)‡34,244

**Today in Cardiology** (19875)
SLACK Inc.
6900 Grove Rd.
Thorofare, NJ 08086-9447
Phone: (856)848-1000
Fax: (856)848-6091
**Subject(s):** Medicine and Surgery; Health and Healthcare
**Circ:** (Paid)34,149

**Salem News** (14314)
Eagle-Tribune Publishing
100 Turnpike St.
North Andover, MA 01845
Phone: (978)946-2000
Fax: (978)685-1588
**Subject(s):** Daily Newspapers
**Circ:** (Mon.-Sat.)34,133

**Williamsport Sun-Gazette** (27703)
Sun-Gazette
252 W 4th St.
Williamsport, PA 17701
Phone: (717)326-1551
Fax: (717)323-0948
**Subject(s):** Paid Community Newspapers
**Circ:** (Mon.-Sat.)★26,805
 (Sun.)★34,115

**The Sunday Shopper** (27542)
Daily American
334 W Main St.
PO Box 638
Somerset, PA 15501
Phone: (814)444-5900
Fax: (814)444-5966
**Subject(s):** Shopping Guides
**Circ:** (Free)‡34,100

**Lincoln County Weekly** (12591)
Courier Publications
PO Box 249
Rockland, ME 04841
Phone: (207)594-4401
Fax: (207)596-6981
**Subject(s):** Paid Community Newspapers
**Circ:** (Free)34,054

**Valley Breeze** (27841)
2190 Mendon Rd., Ste. 1
Cumberland, RI 02864-3830
Phone: (401)334-9555
Fax: (401)334-9994
**Subject(s):** Free Newspapers; Youths' Interests
**Circ:** (Non-paid)‡34,000

**Brookfield Journal** (4650)
Housatonic Publications
65 Bank St.
New Milford, CT 06776
Fax: (860)354-2645
**Subject(s):** Paid Community Newspapers
**Circ:** (Paid)9,704
 (Non-paid)33,884

**The York Dispatch** (27731)
1517 E Philadelphia, Ste. 2807
York, PA 17403-1234
Phone: (717)854-1575
Fax: (717)843-2958
**Subject(s):** Daily Newspapers
**Circ:** (Mon.-Fri.)★33,784

**Metro Retailer (21072)**
Metro Reatiler
8 S St.
Lockport, NY 14094
Phone: (716)434-4055
Fax: (716)434-6022
**Subject(s):** Shopping Guides

Circ: (Non-paid)33,576

**Mercury Tri-County Market Place (27453)**
24 N Hanover St.
Pottstown, PA 19464-5480
Phone: (610)323-3000
Fax: (610)323-0682
**Subject(s):** Shopping Guides

Circ: (Free)‡33,500

**The Home and Store News (19749)**
Aldrich Publishing Company Inc.
6A Main St.
PO Box 329
Ramsey, NJ 07446-0329
Phone: (201)327-1212
Fax: (201)327-3684
**Subject(s):** Free Newspapers

Circ: (Free)33,316

**Neighbor News (19770)**
North Jersey Community Newspapers
100 Commons Way
Rockaway, NJ 07866
Phone: (973)586-8190
Fax: (973)586-8199
**Subject(s):** Free Newspapers

Circ: (Non-paid)33,207

**The Telegraph (18916)**
17 Executive Dr.
PO Box 1008
Nashua, NH 03061
Phone: (603)882-2741
Fax: (603)882-2681
**Subject(s):** Daily Newspapers

Circ: (Mon.-Sat.)26,890
(Sun.)33,183

**Rhode Island Senior Times (27856)**
89 Neptune St.
Jamestown, RI 02835
Phone: (401)423-3900
Fax: (401)423-3805
**Subject(s):** Paid Community Newspapers

Circ: (Paid)2,100
(Non-paid)32,900

**The Hollywood Reporter (21771)**
VNU Business Media
770 Broadway
New York, NY 10003-9522
Phone: (646)654-5000
Fax: (646)654-5487
**Subject(s):** Daily Periodicals; Entertainment

Circ: (Mon.-Fri.)24,608
(Tues.)32,799

**The Beacon (19032)**
The Beacon Publishing Co.
597 Valley Rd.
PO Box 1887
Clifton, NJ 07015-1887
Phone: (973)279-8845
Fax: (973)279-2265
**Subject(s):** Religious Publications

Circ: (Paid)‡32,761

**Centre Daily Times (27549)**
Knight-Ridder Inc.
3400 E. College Ave.
State College, PA 16801-7528
Phone: (814)238-5000
**Subject(s):** Daily Newspapers

Circ: (Mon.-Fri.)25,503
(Sat.)26,447
(Sun.)32,633

**Record Advertiser (22624)**
Tonawanda News
435 River Rd.
North Tonawanda, NY 14120-6809
Phone: (716)693-1000
Fax: (716)693-0124
**Subject(s):** Free Newspapers

Circ: (Paid)14
(Non-paid)32,635

**The Telegraph (18840)**
17 Executive Dr.
Hudson, NH 03051
Phone: (603)882-2741
Fax: (603)882-5138
**Subject(s):** Daily Newspapers

Circ: (Mon.-Sat.)26,442
(Sun.)32,529

**Shop-Right 1 & 2 (27482)**
Shop Right
PO Box T
Ridgway, PA 15853
Phone: (814)776-2121
Fax: (814)776-1086
**Subject(s):** Shopping Guides

Circ: (Free)‡32,492

**Ashland TAB (13438)**
Community Newspaper Co.
254 2nd Ave.
Needham, MA 02494
Phone: (781)433-6700
**Subject(s):** Free Newspapers

Circ: (Combined)32,287

**Holliston TAB (13824)**
Community Newspaper Co.
254 2nd Ave.
Needham, MA 02494
Phone: (781)433-6700
**Subject(s):** Free Newspapers

Circ: (Combined)32,287

**Parkway Transcript (14274)**
Community Newspaper Co.
254 2nd Ave.
Needham, MA 02494
Phone: (781)433-6700
**Subject(s):** Free Newspapers

Circ: (Combined)32,287

**The Wellesley Townsman (14278)**
Community Newspaper Co.
254 2nd Ave.
Needham, MA 02494
Phone: (781)433-6700
**Subject(s):** Paid Community Newspapers

Circ: (Combined)32,287

**The Catholic Sun (22999)**
Syracuse Catholic Press Association Inc.
240 E Onondaga St.
Syracuse, NY 13201
Phone: (315)422-8153
Fax: (315)422-7549
**Subject(s):** Religious Publications

Circ: ‡32,000

**The National Clothesline (27713)**
BPS Communications
PO Box 340
Willow Grove, PA 19090
Phone: (215)830-8467
Fax: (215)830-8490
**Subject(s):** Laundry and Dry Cleaning

Circ: (Controlled)‡32,000

**The Citizens' Voice (27688)**
Times-Shamrock
75 N. Washington St.
Wilkes Barre, PA 18711
Phone: (570)821-2000
Fax: (570)821-2247
**Subject(s):** Daily Newspapers

Circ: (Sun.)★30,664
(Mon.-Sat.)★31,606

**Clinton County Free Trader Today (20740)**
Denton Publications
14 Hand Ave.
Elizabethtown, NY 12932
Phone: (518)873-6368
Fax: (518)873-6360
**Subject(s):** Free Newspapers

Circ: (Free)‡31,591

**Argus (19949)**
North Jersey Community Newspapers
The Weekly Division of N Jersey Media Group
1 Garret Mountain Plz.
PO Box 471
West Paterson, NJ 07424-0471
Phone: (973)569-7000
Fax: (973)569-7310

**Subject(s):** Free Newspapers

Circ: (Thurs.)14,842
(Sun.)31,510

**The Advisor (4936)**
83 State St.
Box 460
North Haven, CT 06473-0071
Phone: (203)239-5404
Fax: (203)239-7097
**Subject(s):** Free Newspapers

Circ: (Free)‡31,500

**The East Hampton Star (20721)**
PO Box 5002
East Hampton, NY 11937
Phone: (631)324-0002
Fax: (631)324-7943
**Subject(s):** Paid Community Newspapers

Circ: (Thurs.)31,237

**The Pilot (13576)**
Catholic Diocese of Boston
141 Tremont St.
Boston, MA 02111-1209
Phone: (617)482-5647
**Subject(s):** Religious Publications

Circ: 31,000

**Valley News Dispatch (27577)**
Tribune Review Publishing Co.
210 4th Ave.
Tarentum, PA 15084
Phone: (724)226-4666
Fax: (724)226-4677
**Subject(s):** Daily Newspapers

Circ: (Mon.-Sat.)★30,572
(Sun.)★30,604

**Daily Local News (27667)**
Journal Register Co.
250 N Bradford Ave.
West Chester, PA 19382-2800
Phone: (610)696-1776
Fax: (610)430-1180
**Subject(s):** Daily Newspapers

Circ: (Sat.)27,275
(Sun.)30,022
(Mon.-Fri.)30,451

**County Pennysaver (21135)**
305 Main St.
Massena, NY 13662
Phone: (315)764-1555
Fax: (315)764-0782
**Subject(s):** Shopping Guides

Circ: (Paid)89
(Non-paid)30,420

**Daily Variety (21585)**
Reed Business Information
249 W. 17th St.
New York, NY 10011-5322
Phone: (212)337-6900
Fax: (212)337-6977
**Subject(s):** Entertainment; Daily Newspapers

Circ: (Mon.-Fri.)30,406

**Butler Eagle (26209)**
Eagle Printing Company Inc.
PO Box 271
Butler, PA 16003
**Subject(s):** Daily Newspapers

Circ: (Mon.-Fri.)★28,394
(Sun.)★30,341

**Northern Berks Merchandiser (26423)**
Windsor Press Inc.
6 N. 3rd St.
PO Box 465
Hamburg, PA 19526
Phone: (610)562-2267
Fax: (610)562-2770
**Subject(s):** Shopping Guides

Circ: (Paid)30
(Non-paid)30,201

**Dateline Journal (19034)**
North Jersey Community Newspapers
1187 Main Ave., Ste. 2D
Clifton, NJ 07011-2252
Phone: (973)478-7958
Fax: (973)478-9754

Circulation: ★ = ABC; △ = BPA; ♦ = CAC; ● = CCAB; ▫ = VAC; ⊖ = PO Statement; ‡ = Publisher's Report; Boldface figures = sworn; Light figures = estimated.

3707

## Northeastern States

**Subject(s):** Free Newspapers
**Circ:** (Thurs.)30,175

**Harvard University Gazette (13678)**
Holyoke Ctr. 1060
1350 Massachusetts Ave.
Cambridge, MA 02138
Phone: (617)496-2651
Fax: (617)496-9351
**Subject(s):** Paid Community Newspapers
**Circ:** 30,150

**The Hudson Dispatch (19427)**
Evening Journal Association
30 Journal Sq.
Jersey City, NJ 07306
Phone: (201)653-1000
Fax: (201)653-1414
**Subject(s):** Daily Newspapers
**Circ:** ‡30,077

**Connecticut Jewish Ledger (5079)**
740 N Main St.
West Hartford, CT 06117
Phone: (860)231-2424
Fax: (860)231-2428
**Subject(s):** Paid Community Newspapers; Jewish Publications
**Circ:** ‡30,000

**Greece Pennysaver (22821)**
Suburban Circle Publications Inc.
2808 Dewey Ave.
Rochester, NY 14616-4628
Phone: (716)663-0068
Fax: (716)663-0146
**Subject(s):** Shopping Guides
**Circ:** (Free)‡30,000

**New Pittsburgh Courier (27378)**
315 E Carson St.
Pittsburgh, PA 15219
Phone: (412)481-8302
Fax: (412)481-1360
**Subject(s):** Paid Community Newspapers; Black Publications
**Circ:** ‡30,000

**The Observer (19441)**
531 Kearny Ave.
Kearny, NJ 07032
Phone: (201)991-1600
Fax: (201)991-8049
**Subject(s):** Free Newspapers
**Circ:** (Free)30,000

**Pennsylvania Bar News (26455)**
The Pennsylvania Bar Association
100 S.St.
PO Box 186
Harrisburg, PA 17108-0186
Phone: (717)238-6715
Fax: (717)238-1204
**Subject(s):** Law
**Circ:** (Controlled)750
(Paid)30,000

**Pittsburgh Hospital News (27389)**
Medical Publications Inc.
2020 Ardmore Blvd., Ste. 160
Pittsburgh, PA 15221
Phone: (412)273-1775
Fax: (412)273-1776
**Subject(s):** Medicine and Surgery; Health and Healthcare
**Circ:** 30,000

**Pittsburgh Renaissance News (27393)**
Renaissance Publications
1516 5th Ave.
Pittsburgh, PA 15219-5198
Phone: (412)391-8208
Fax: (412)391-8006
**Subject(s):** Free Newspapers
**Circ:** (Free)‡30,000

**The Recorder (22299)**
American Lawyer Media L.P.
105 Madison Ave., 7th Fl.
New York, NY 10016
Phone: (415)749-5500
Fax: (212)481-8255
**Subject(s):** Law; Daily Periodicals
**Circ:** ‡6,600
(Paid)30,000

**The Reminder (27833)**
Stevens Publishing Inc.
1049 Main St.
PO Box 33
Coventry, RI 02816
Phone: (401)821-2216
Fax: (401)821-0397
**Subject(s):** Shopping Guides
**Circ:** (Free)‡30,000

**The Reminder (13762)**
Reminder Publications Inc.
280 N. Main St.
East Longmeadow, MA 01028
Phone: (413)525-6661
Fax: (413)525-5882
**Subject(s):** Free Newspapers
**Circ:** (Free)‡30,000

**Citizen (18847)**
Citizen Publishing Co.
171 Fair St.
Laconia, NH 03246
Phone: (603)524-3800
Fax: (603)524-6702
**Subject(s):** Daily Newspapers
**Circ:** (Mon.-Sat.)10,000
(Sun.)29,976

**Bergen News (19647)**
Bergen News Publishing Co.
111 Grand Ave.
Palisades Park, NJ 07650
Phone: (201)947-5000
Fax: (201)947-6968
**Subject(s):** Paid Community Newspapers
**Circ:** (Non-paid)29,939

**The Anchor (13776)**
887 Highland Ave.
PO Box 7
Fall River, MA 02720
Phone: (508)675-7151
Fax: (508)675-7048
**Subject(s):** Religious Publications
**Circ:** ‡29,890

**Newton TAB (14272)**
Community Newspaper Co.
254 2nd Ave.
Needham, MA 02494
Phone: (781)433-6700
**Subject(s):** Free Newspapers
**Circ:** (Free)29,853

**Norwich Bulletin (4971)**
66 Franklin St.
Norwich, CT 06360
Phone: (860)887-9211
Fax: (860)887-9666
**Subject(s):** Daily Newspapers
**Circ:** (Mon.-Sat.)★26,583
(Sun.)★29,371

**Times-News (26635)**
594 Blakeslee Blvd. Dr. W.
Lehighton, PA 18235
Phone: (610)377-2051
Fax: (610)826-9607
**Subject(s):** Daily Newspapers
**Circ:** (Mon.-Sat.)27,418
(Sun.)29,203

**Herald-Standard (27595)**
8-18 E Church St.
PO Box 848
Uniontown, PA 15401-3563
Phone: (412)439-7500
Fax: (412)439-7528
**Subject(s):** Daily Newspapers
**Circ:** (Mon.-Sat.)★26,865
(Sun.)★29,026

**The World (Vermont) (30831)**
The World
403 US Rte. 302 Berlin
Barre, VT 05641
Phone: (802)479-2582
**Subject(s):** Free Newspapers
**Circ:** (Combined)28,941

**Daily Freeman, Sunday Freeman (21006)**
Daily Freeman
79 Hurley Ave.
Kingston, NY 12401
Phone: (845)331-5000
Fax: (845)331-3557
**Subject(s):** Daily Newspapers
**Circ:** (Mon.-Fri.)21,662
(Sun.)28,564
(Sun.)28,684

**Bayonne Community News (18972)**
13 E 21st St.
Bayonne, NJ 07002
Phone: (201)437-2460
Fax: (201)437-7127
**Subject(s):** Free Newspapers
**Circ:** (Free)28,525

**The Community Sun (26426)**
The Evening Sun
135 Baltimore St.
Hanover, PA 17331
Phone: (717)637-3736
Fax: (717)637-7730
**Subject(s):** Free Newspapers
**Circ:** (Non-paid)28,529

**Sun Marketplace (26429)**
The Evening Sun
135 Baltimore St.
Hanover, PA 17331
Phone: (717)637-3736
Fax: (717)637-7730
**Subject(s):** Free Newspapers
**Circ:** (Non-paid)♦28,469

**Fair Lawn-Elmwood Park-Saddle Brook Shopper (19078)**
North Jersey Community Newspapers
12-38 River Rd.
Fair Lawn, NJ 07410-1897
Phone: (201)791-8400
Fax: (201)794-3259
**Subject(s):** Shopping Guides
**Circ:** (Free)‡28,195

**New Jersey Jewish News—Metrowest Edition (19973)**
New Jersey Jewish News
901 Rte. 10
Whippany, NJ 07981-1157
Phone: (973)887-8500
Fax: (973)887-5999
**Subject(s):** Paid Community Newspapers; Jewish Publications
**Circ:** (Paid)28,186

**Voices (5109)**
Prime Publishers Inc.
90 Middle Quarter Mall
Woodbury, CT 06798
Phone: (203)263-2116
Fax: (203)266-0199
**Subject(s):** Free Newspapers
**Circ:** (Paid)365
(Non-paid)28,096

**Newton Graphic (14292)**
Community Newspaper Co.
254 2nd Ave.
Needham, MA 02494
Phone: (781)433-6700
**Subject(s):** Free Newspapers
**Circ:** (Paid)323
(Free)28,018

**Orthopedics Today (19870)**
SLACK Inc.
6900 Grove Rd.
Thorofare, NJ 08086-9447
Phone: (856)848-1000
Fax: (856)848-6091
**Subject(s):** Medicine and Surgery
**Circ:** (Free)‡27,800

**Foster's Democrat (18803)**
333 Central Ave.
Dover, NH 03820-4127
Phone: (603)742-4455
Fax: (603)742-4455
**Subject(s):** Daily Newspapers
**Circ:** (Mon.-Sat.)★22,720
(Sun.)★27,728

**Resumen Newspaper** (23199)
6908 Roosevelt Ave.
Woodside, NY 11377
Phone: (718)899-8603
Fax: (718)899-7616
**Subject(s):** Paid Community Newspapers; Hispanic Publications; Spanish

**Circ:** ‡27,500

**Voices** (5018)
Prime Publishers Inc.
PO Box 383
Southbury, CT 06488
Phone: (203)263-2116
Fax: (203)266-0199
**Subject(s):** Free Newspapers

**Circ:** (Sun.)22,048
(Wed.)27,233

**Pennysaver Press** (30841)
ADD Inc.
109 S St.
Bennington, VT 05201
Phone: (802)447-3381
Fax: (802)447-3270
**Subject(s):** Shopping Guides

**Circ:** (Non-paid)27,212

**El Mundo** (13512)
Caribe Communication
408 S Huntington Ave.
Boston, MA 02130
Phone: (617)522-5060
Fax: (617)524-5886
**Subject(s):** Paid Community Newspapers; Hispanic Publications; Spanish

**Circ:** 27,000

**The Shopper** (20916)
E-Z Shopper Inc.
57 S. Carroll St.
Horseheads, NY 14845
Phone: (607)796-2800
Fax: (607)796-0319
**Subject(s):** Shopping Guides

**Circ:** (Free)27,000

**The Wallace Pennysaver** (14897)
Westfield News Advertiser Inc.
62 School St., No. 64
Westfield, MA 01085-2835
Phone: (413)568-4921
Fax: (413)562-4185
**Subject(s):** Shopping Guides

**Circ:** (Free)‡26,837

**Item** (26422)
3rd & State Sts.
Hamburg, PA 19526
Phone: (610)562-7515
Fax: (610)562-4644
**Subject(s):** Paid Community Newspapers

**Circ:** (Mon.-Sat.)24,518
(Sun.)26,621

**Record-Journal** (4840)
The Record-Journal Publishing Co.
11 Crown St.
PO Box 915
Meriden, CT 06450
Phone: (203)235-1661
Fax: (203)639-0210
**Subject(s):** Daily Newspapers

**Circ:** (Mon.-Sat.)26,070
(Sun.)26,287

**Herald News** (13777)
Northeast Publishing Inc.
207 Pocasset St.
Box 2410
Fall River, MA 02722
Phone: (508)676-8211
Fax: (508)676-2566
**Subject(s):** Daily Newspapers

**Circ:** (Mon.-Sat.)23,854
(Sun.)26,211

**The Mercury** (27452)
Goodson Newspaper Group
24 N. Hanover St.
Pottstown, PA 19464
Phone: (215)323-3000
Fax: (610)970-4492

**Subject(s):** Daily Newspapers
**Circ:** (Mon.-Sat.)25,350
(Sun.)26,173

**Rivereast News Bulletin** (4772)
The Glastonbury Citizen Inc.
PO Box 373
87 Nutmeg Ln.
Glastonbury, CT 06033
Phone: (860)633-4691
Fax: (860)657-3258
**Subject(s):** Free Newspapers

**Circ:** (Combined)26,060

**Pocono Record** (27566)
Ottaway Newspapers Inc.
511 Lenox St.
Stroudsburg, PA 18360
Phone: (570)421-3000
Fax: (570)424-2625
**Subject(s):** Daily Newspapers

**Circ:** (Mon.-Sat.)20,447
(Sun.)26,023

**The Shoppers Guide** (26361)
Gazette Publishing Co.
6 E. Main St.
PO Box 328
Everett, PA 15537
Phone: (814)652-5191
Fax: (814)652-9544
**Subject(s):** Free Newspapers

**Circ:** (Paid)56
(Free)26,027

**Community News** (20648)
Gannett Company Inc.
Clifton Corporate Park
Bldg. 400, Ste. 482
STE. 429
Clifton Park, NY 12065
Phone: (518)371-7108
Fax: (518)371-0933
**Subject(s):** Free Newspapers

**Circ:** (Free)‡26,000

**Country Focus** (26214)
Pennsylvania Farm Bureau
P.O. Box 8736
510 South 31st Street
Camp Hill, PA 17001-8736
Phone: (717)761-2740
Fax: (717)731-3506
**Subject(s):** Farm Newspapers

**Circ:** (Controlled)26,000

**Rochester Golf Week Newspaper** (22840)
2535 Brighton Henrietta Townline Rd.
Rochester, NY 14623-2711
Phone: (585)427-2160
**Subject(s):** (Golf)

**Circ:** ‡26,000

**Gloucester County Times** (19978)
South Jersey Newspaper
309 S Broad St.
Woodbury, NJ 08096
Phone: (609)845-3300
Fax: (609)845-5480
**Subject(s):** Daily Newspapers

**Circ:** (Sat.)★20,920
(Mon.-Fri.)★23,249
(Sun.)★25,958

**Public Relations Tactics** (22280)
Public Relations Society of America (PRSA)
33 Maiden Ln.
11th Fl.
New York, NY 10038-5150
Phone: (212)460-1400
Fax: (212)995-0757
**Subject(s):** Public Relations

**Circ:** (Paid)25,900

**Times Newsweekly** (22794)
PO Box 299
Ridgewood, NY 11386
Phone: (718)821-7500
Fax: (718)456-0120
**Subject(s):** Paid Community Newspapers

**Circ:** (Free)325
(Paid)25,627

**Hamburg Pennysaver** (20870)
H & K Publications Inc.
50 Buffalo St.
Hamburg, NY 14075-5002
Phone: (716)649-4413
Fax: (716)649-6374
**Subject(s):** Shopping Guides

**Circ:** (Non-paid)25,100

**The Allegany County Pennysaver** (23145)
Wellsville Daily Reporter
159 N Main St.
Wellsville, NY 14895-1149
Phone: (585)593-5300
Fax: (585)593-5303
**Subject(s):** Shopping Guides

**Circ:** (Free)25,000

**Country Folks Grower** (22680)
Lee Publications Inc.
6113 State Hwy. 5
PO Box 121
Palatine Bridge, NY 13428
Phone: (518)673-3237
Fax: (518)673-2381
**Subject(s):** Farm Newspapers

**Circ:** (Combined)25,000

**The Island-Ear** (20810)
The Island-Ear Inc.
1103 Stewart Ave.
Garden City, NY 11530
Phone: (516)889-6045
Fax: (516)889-6983
**Subject(s):** Free Newspapers; Entertainment

**Circ:** 25,000

**Jewish Forward** (21860)
Forward Association Inc.
45 E 33rd St.
New York, NY 10016
Phone: (212)889-8200
Fax: (212)684-3949
**Subject(s):** Yiddish; Paid Community Newspapers; Jewish Publications

**Circ:** 25,000

**Men of Malvern** (26661)
Laymen's Retreat League
Malvern Retreat House
315 Warren Ave.
Malvern, PA 19355-0315
Phone: (610)644-0400
Fax: (610)644-4363
**Subject(s):** Religious Publications

**Circ:** (Non-paid)‡25,000

**Snyder County Times** (26695)
Snyder County Times & Union County Times
405 E Main St.
PO Box 356
Middleburg, PA 17842-0356
Phone: (570)837-6065
Fax: (570)837-0776
**Subject(s):** Paid Community Newspapers

**Circ:** (Combined)‡25,000

**Sokol Polski (Polish Falcon)** (27402)
Polish Falcons of America
615 Iron City Dr.
Pittsburgh, PA 15205-4397
Phone: (412)922-2244
Fax: (412)922-5029
**Subject(s):** Unclassified Fraternal; Polish; Ethnic Publications

**Circ:** (Free)‡25,000

**Southwest Globe Times** (27274)
Southwest Globe Times Inc.
2821 Island Ave.
Philadelphia, PA 19153-2314
Phone: (215)727-7777
Fax: (215)727-5116
**Subject(s):** Free Newspapers

**Circ:** (Free)‡25,000

**Union County Times** (26696)
Snyder County Times & Union County Times
405 E Main St.
PO Box 356
Middleburg, PA 17842-0356
Phone: (570)837-6065
Fax: (570)837-0776
**Subject(s):** Free Newspapers

**Circ:** ‡25,000

Circulation: ★ = ABC; △ = BPA; ◆ = CAC; • = CCAB; ❑ = VAC; ⊕ = PO Statement; ‡ = Publisher's Report; Boldface figures = sworn; Light figures = estimated.

# Northeastern States

**Discount Store News (21604)**
Lebhar-Friedman Inc.
425 Park Ave.
New York, NY 10022-3556
Phone: (212)756-5125
Fax: (212)756-5125
**Subject(s):** Retail
**Circ:** (Paid)7,904
(Non-paid)24,957

**The Catholic Free Press (14932)**
The Roman Catholic Diocese of Worcester
51 Elm St.
Worcester, MA 01609
Phone: (508)757-6387
Fax: (508)756-8315
**Subject(s):** Religious Publications
**Circ:** ‡24,500

**Orthopaedics Today International (19868)**
SLACK Inc.
6900 Grove Rd.
Thorofare, NJ 08086-9447
Phone: (856)848-1000
Fax: (856)848-6091
**Subject(s):** Medicine and Surgery
**Circ:** (Combined)24,461

**Gourmet News (12618)**
United Publications Inc.
106 Lafayette St.
Yarmouth, ME 04096
Phone: (207)846-0600
Fax: (207)846-0657
**Subject(s):** Food and Grocery Trade; Food Production
**Circ:** (Non-paid)24,433

**Su Guia (19959)**
North Jersey Community Newspapers
The Weekly Division of N Jersey Media Group
1 Garret Mountain Plz.
PO Box 471
West Paterson, NJ 07424-0471
Phone: (973)569-7000
Fax: (973)569-7310
**Subject(s):** Free Newspapers
**Circ:** (Fri.)24,385

**Tri-County Times (20720)**
PowerOne Media Inc.
99 Troy Rd.
East Greenbush, NY 12061
Phone: (518)687-6000
Fax: (518)687-6060
**Subject(s):** Paid Community Newspapers
**Circ:** (Wed.)13,582
(Sun.)24,285

**Portsmouth Herald (18950)**
111 Maplewood Ave.
Portsmouth, NH 03801
Phone: (603)436-1800
Fax: (603)427-0550
**Subject(s):** Daily Newspapers
**Circ:** (Mon.-Sat.)15,109
(Sun.)24,136

**The Clark/Cranford Eagle (19029)**
Worrall Community Newspapers
1291 Stuyvesant Ave.
PO Box 3109
Union, NJ 07083
Phone: (908)686-7700
Fax: (908)686-4169
**Subject(s):** Paid Community Newspapers
**Circ:** (Non-paid)♦333
(Paid)♦24,055

**Stony Brook Statesman (22986)**
State University of New York at Stony Brook
PO Box 1530
Stony Brook, NY 11790
Phone: (631)632-6479
Fax: (516)632-9128
**Subject(s):** College Publications
**Circ:** ‡24,000

**The Record (23075)**
Troy Publishing Company Inc.
501 Broadway
Troy, NY 12181
Phone: (518)270-1200
Fax: (518)270-1202

**Subject(s):** Daily Newspapers
**Circ:** (Mon.-Sat.)22,291
(Sun.)23,908

**New Jersey Herald (19628)**
2 Spring St.
PO Box 10
Newton, NJ 07860-0010
Phone: (973)383-1500
Fax: (973)383-8477
**Subject(s):** Daily Newspapers
**Circ:** (Mon.-Fri.)16,999
(Sun.)23,643

**Press-Republican (22708)**
Ottaway Newspaper
170 Margaret St.
PO Box 459
Plattsburgh, NY 12901
Phone: (518)561-2300
**Subject(s):** Daily Newspapers
**Circ:** (Mon.-Sat.)22,685
(Sun.)23,584

**Lindenhurst/South Bay's Shopping Newspaper (21065)**
Excel Promotions Corp.
150 W Hoffman Ave.
Lindenhurst, NY 11757
Phone: (631)226-2636
**Subject(s):** Shopping Guides
**Circ:** (Free)‡23,498

**Hunterdon County Democrat (19089)**
8 Minneakoning Rd.
PO Box 32
Flemington, NJ 08822-0032
Phone: (908)782-4747
Fax: (908)782-6572
**Subject(s):** Paid Community Newspapers
**Circ:** (Thurs.)23,355

**Suburban Cortland-Ithaca Shopper (20799)**
Freeville Publishing Company Inc.
9 Main St.
PO Box 210
Freeville, NY 13068
Phone: (607)844-9119
Fax: (607)844-3381
**Subject(s):** Shopping Guides
**Circ:** (Free)23,225

**The Drummer Pennysaver (20337)**
Batavia Newspapers Corp.
2 Apollo Dr.
Batavia, NY 14021
Phone: (716)343-8000
Fax: (716)343-2623
**Subject(s):** Shopping Guides
**Circ:** (Non-paid)23,015

**The Herald (27527)**
Ottaway Newspapers Inc.
PO Box 51
Sharon, PA 16146
Phone: (412)981-6100
Fax: (412)981-5116
**Subject(s):** Daily Newspapers
**Circ:** (Mon.-Sat.)21,603
(Sun.)23,019

**The Dong-A Daily News (26320)**
Korean Daily Tribune Inc.
1330 Willow Ave. Ste.101
Elkins Park, PA 19027
Phone: (215)935-5000
Fax: (215)935-8888
**Subject(s):** Daily Newspapers; Korean; Ethnic Publications
**Circ:** (Combined)23,000

**The Forecaster—Northern Edition (12514)**
The Forecaster
8 Fundy Rd.
PO Box 66797
Falmouth, ME 04105-6797
Phone: (207)781-3661
Fax: (207)781-2060
**Subject(s):** Paid Community Newspapers
**Circ:** (Non-paid)23,000

**VOICES Sunday-The Weekly Star (5110)**
Prime Publishers Inc.
90 Middle Quarter Mall
Woodbury, CT 06798
Phone: (203)263-2116
Fax: (203)266-0199

**Subject(s):** Free Newspapers
**Circ:** (Paid)70
(Non-paid)22,914

**Concord Monitor (18782)**
1 Monitor Dr.
PO Box 1177
Concord, NH 03302-1177
Phone: (603)224-5301
Fax: (603)224-8120
**Subject(s):** Daily Newspapers
**Circ:** (Mon.-Sat.)★20,107
(Sun.)★22,747

**The Times Herald (26780)**
Times Herald Publishing Company Inc./Journal Register Co.
410 Markley St.
PO Box 591
Norristown, PA 19404
Phone: (610)272-2500
Fax: (610)272-4003
**Subject(s):** Daily Newspapers
**Circ:** (Sun.)19,050
(Mon.-Sat.)22,601

**The Messenger (18838)**
Granite Quill
PO Box 1190
Hillsboro, NH 03244-1190
Phone: (603)464-3388
Fax: (603)464-4106
**Subject(s):** Paid Community Newspapers
**Circ:** (Free)‡22,506

**The Ithaca Journal (20956)**
123-127 W. State St.
Ithaca, NY 14850
Phone: (607)272-2321
Fax: (607)272-9290
**Subject(s):** Daily Newspapers
**Circ:** (Mon.-Fri.)★17,748
(Sat.)★22,249

**The Daily News (26674)**
The Daily News Publishing Co.
409 Walnut St.
Mc Keesport, PA 15132
Phone: (412)664-9161
Fax: (412)664-3972
**Subject(s):** Daily Newspapers
**Circ:** (Mon.-Sat.)22,079

**Advance News (19445)**
Advance Nickel & Dime News Inc.
2048 Rte. 37
Lakehurst, NJ 08733-5645
Phone: (732)657-8936
Fax: (732)657-2970
**Subject(s):** Paid Community Newspapers
**Circ:** (Paid)⊕22,000

**Brand Marketing (21422)**
Fairchild Publications Inc.
7 W. 34th St.
New York, NY 10001
**Subject(s):** Business; Advertising and Marketing
**Circ:** △22,000

**Farm Chronicle (22681)**
Lee Newspapers Inc.
PO Box 121
6113 State Hwy. 5
Palatine Bridge, NY 13428
Phone: (518)673-3237
Fax: (518)673-2381
**Subject(s):** Farm Newspapers; Paid Community Newspapers
**Circ:** (Paid)22,000

**Forum of Queens (22679)**
Queens Herald Corp.
132-43 87th Street
Ozone Park, NY 11417
Phone: (718)845-3221
Fax: (718)738-7645
**Subject(s):** Free Newspapers
**Circ:** (Free)22,000

**The Jewish Advocate (13532)**
15 School St.
Boston, MA 02108
Phone: (617)367-9100
Fax: (617)367-9310

**Subject(s):** Jewish Publications; Paid Community Newspapers
**Circ:** 22,000

**Mattydale-North Syracuse Pennysaver (23022)**
Scotsman Community Publications
750 W. Genesee St.
PO Box 4970
Syracuse, NY 13221
Phone: (315)472-7825
Fax: (315)478-1434
**Subject(s):** Shopping Guides
**Circ:** (Non-paid)‡21,791

**Fairfield Minuteman (4922)**
Housatonic Publications
65 Bank St.
New Milford, CT 06776
Fax: (860)354-2645
**Subject(s):** Free Newspapers
**Circ:** (Non-paid)21,652

**Public Opinion (26231)**
Gannett Company Inc.
77 N. 3rd St.
PO Box 499
Chambersburg, PA 17201
Phone: (717)264-6161
Fax: (717)264-0377
**Subject(s):** Daily Newspapers
**Circ:** (Mon.-Sat.)21,448

**Lodi-Hasbrouck Heights-Woodridge-Maywood-Rochelle Park Shopper (19465)**
North Jersey Community Newspapers
12-38 River Rd.
Fair Lawn, NJ 07410-1897
Phone: (201)791-8400
Fax: (201)794-3259
**Subject(s):** Shopping Guides
**Circ:** (Free)‡21,434

**Bay News (20491)**
Courier Life Publications
1733 Sheepshead Bay Rd.
Brooklyn, NY 11235-3606
Phone: (718)615-2500
Fax: (718)615-3835
**Subject(s):** Paid Community Newspapers
**Circ:** (Mon.)21,420

**Tri-County News (27539)**
Pollock Advertising Inc.
PO Box 777
Slippery Rock, PA 16057
Phone: (724)794-6857
Fax: (724)794-1314
**Subject(s):** Free Newspapers
**Circ:** (Paid)20
 (Free)‡21,147

**Rutland Herald (30926)**
Herald Association Inc.
27 Wales St.
PO Box 668
Rutland, VT 05702-0668
Phone: (802)747-6121
Fax: (802)775-2423
**Subject(s):** Daily Newspapers
**Circ:** (Sun.)20,928
 (Mon.-Sat.)21,125

**Prosveta (26525)**
Slovene National Benefit Society (SNPJ)
247 W. Allegheny Rd.
Imperial, PA 15126-9774
Phone: (724)695-1100
Fax: (724)695-1555
**Subject(s):** Slovene; Unclassified Fraternal; Ethnic Publications
**Circ:** ‡21,000

**The Vermont Catholic Tribune (30861)**
Roman Catholic Diocese of Burlington
PO Box 489
Burlington, VT 05402
Phone: (802)658-6110
Fax: (802)863-3866
**Subject(s):** Religious Publications
**Circ:** (Paid)21,000

**Press Enterprise (26183)**
Press Enterprise Inc.
3185 Lackawanna Ave.
Bloomsburg, PA 17815-3398
Phone: (717)784-2121
Fax: (717)784-9226
**Subject(s):** Daily Newspapers
**Circ:** (Sun.)20,347
 (Mon.-Sat.)20,990

**Standard-Speaker (26480)**
Hazleton Standard-Speaker Inc.
PO Box 578
Hazleton, PA 18201
Phone: (717)455-3636
Fax: (717)455-4244
**Subject(s):** Daily Newspapers
**Circ:** (Mon.-Sat.)★20,821
 (Sun.)★20,981

**Lebanon Daily News (26625)**
718 Poplar St.
PO Box 600
Lebanon, PA 17042-0600
Phone: (717)272-5611
Fax: (717)274-1608
**Subject(s):** Daily Newspapers
**Circ:** (Mon.-Sat.)20,484
 (Sun.)20,801

**Liverpool-Phoenix Pennysaver (23020)**
Scotsman Community Publications
750 W. Genesee St.
PO Box 4970
Syracuse, NY 13221
Phone: (315)472-7825
Fax: (315)478-1434
**Subject(s):** Shopping Guides
**Circ:** (Non-paid)‡20,688

**Mountain Pennysaver (20625)**
Country Folks of Pennsylvania
1131 SR 23
Catskill, NY 12414
Phone: (518)943-9250
Fax: (518)943-6918
**Subject(s):** Shopping Guides
**Circ:** (Free)20,669

**The Advocate (14307)**
124 Amaerican Legion Dr.
North Adams, MA 01247
Phone: (413)664-6900
Fax: (413)664-7900
**Subject(s):** Free Newspapers
**Circ:** (Paid)‡62
 (Free)‡20,500

**The Traveler-Watchman (22952)**
Traveler St.
PO Box 725
Southold, NY 11971
Phone: (631)765-3425
Fax: (631)765-1756
**Subject(s):** Paid Community Newspapers
**Circ:** (Free)‡500
 (Paid)‡20,500

**Webster-Ontario-Walworth Pennysaver (23142)**
164 E Main St.
Webster, NY 14580
Phone: (585)265-3620
Fax: (585)265-3882
**Subject(s):** Shopping Guides
**Circ:** (Free)20,349

**The Daily Collegian (27550)**
Penn State University
123 S. Burrowes St.
James Bldg.
State College, PA 16801-3882
Phone: (814)865-1828
Fax: (814)865-3848
**Subject(s):** College Publications
**Circ:** (Free)‡20,300

**Staten Island Register (22967)**
101 Tyrellan Ave., Ste.420
Staten Island, NY 10309
Phone: (718)966-1200
Fax: (718)966-7775
**Subject(s):** Paid Community Newspapers
**Circ:** 20,300

**The Evening Sun (26427)**
135 Baltimore St.
Hanover, PA 17331
Phone: (717)637-3736
Fax: (717)637-7730
**Subject(s):** Daily Newspapers
**Circ:** (Mon.-Sat.)19,348
 (Sun.)20,242

**Ithaca Times (20957)**
109 N Cayuga St.
PO Box 27
Ithaca, NY 14851
Phone: (607)277-7000
Fax: (607)277-1012
**Subject(s):** College Publications
**Circ:** (Paid)‡274
 (Free)‡20,159

**The Post-Journal (20990)**
15 W. 2nd St.
Jamestown, NY 14701
Phone: (716)487-1111
Fax: (716)664-3119
**Subject(s):** Daily Newspapers
**Circ:** (Mon.-Sat.)★19,750
 (Sun.)★20,121

**North Shore Today's (22989)**
The Sale Line Inc.
6851 Jericho Tpke.
Syosset, NY 11791
Phone: (516)496-4300
Fax: (516)496-9898
**Subject(s):** Shopping Guides
**Circ:** (Free)20,108

**The Yonkers Home News & Times (23207)**
Martinelli Publications
40 Larkin Plz.
Yonkers, NY 10701
Phone: (914)965-4000
Fax: (914)965-2892
**Subject(s):** Paid Community Newspapers
**Circ:** (Combined)20,100

**Twin-Boro News (19052)**
North Jersey Community Newspapers
300 Knickerbocker Rd.
Cresskill, NJ 07626-1343
Phone: (201)568-6272
Fax: (201)568-2609
**Subject(s):** Free Newspapers
**Circ:** (Free)♦20,072

**This Week in Bayonne (19435)**
Evening Journal Association
30 Journal Sq.
Jersey City, NJ 07306
Phone: (201)653-1000
Fax: (201)653-1414
**Subject(s):** Free Newspapers
**Circ:** (Non-paid)20,061

**The Jersey City Reporter (19428)**
Hudson Reporter Associates
1400 Washington St.
PO Box 3069
Hoboken, NJ 07030-1601
Phone: (201)798-7800
Fax: (201)798-0018
**Subject(s):** Free Newspapers
**Circ:** (Non-paid)20,050

**Deerfield Valley News (30954)**
Vermont Media Publishing Co.
Rte. 100, W. Dover
PO Box 310
West Dover, VT 05356
Phone: (802)464-3388
Fax: (802)464-7255
**Subject(s):** Paid Community Newspapers
**Circ:** ‡20,000

**Edward A. Heffernan (19890)**
The Monitor
PO Box 5147
Trenton, NJ 08638-0147
Phone: (609)406-7404
Fax: (609)406-7423
**Subject(s):** Religious Publications
**Circ:** ‡20,000

Circulation: ★ = ABC; △ = BPA; ♦ = CAC; ● = CCAB; ▫ = VAC; ⊕ = PO Statement; ‡ = Publisher's Report; Boldface figures = sworn; Light figures = estimated.

## Northeastern States

**Golden Times (20728)**
Piano Works Mall, Ste. 1025
349 W Commerical St.
East Rochester, NY 14445
Phone: (585)586-1445
Fax: (585)586-2093
**Subject(s):** Paid Community Newspapers; Senior Citizens' Interests
**Circ:** (Paid)20,000

**Jewish Voice and Herald (27904)**
130 Sessions St.
Providence, RI 02906
Phone: (401)421-4111
Fax: (401)331-7961
**Subject(s):** Paid Community Newspapers; Jewish Publications
**Circ:** (Paid)‡5,600
(Non-paid)‡20,000

**The Philadelphia Sunday Sun (27227)**
6661 Germantown Ave.
Philadelphia, PA 19119-2251
Phone: (215)848-7864
Fax: (215)848-7893
**Subject(s):** Ethnic Publications
**Circ:** (Paid)20,000

**Riverdale Review (20476)**
Metro North Media
6050 Riverdale Ave.
Bronx, NY 10471
Phone: (718)543-5200
Fax: (718)543-4206
**Subject(s):** Free Newspapers
**Circ:** (Combined)20,000

**The Sound (4837)**
Shore Publishing
724 Boston Post Rd., Ste. 202
PO Box 1010
Madison, CT 06443
Phone: (203)245-1877
Fax: (203)245-9773
**Subject(s):** Paid Community Newspapers
**Circ:** (Combined)20,000

**Southern Berkshire Shopper's Guide (13806)**
141 West Ave.
PO Box 89
Great Barrington, MA 01230
Phone: (413)528-0095
Fax: (413)528-4805
**Subject(s):** Shopping Guides
**Circ:** (Free)‡5,000
(Controlled)‡20,000

**The Villager (22519)**
487 Greenwich St., Ste. 6A
New York, NY 10013
Phone: (212)229-1890
Fax: (212)229-2790
**Subject(s):** Paid Community Newspapers
**Circ:** (Paid)20,000

**Weekly Bargain Bulletin (26758)**
1576 Sunrise Dr.
New Castle, PA 16105
Phone: (724)654-5529
**Subject(s):** Free Newspapers
**Circ:** (Free)‡20,000

**Deer Park Suffolk Life (22795)**
Suffolk Life Newspapers
PO Box 9167
Riverhead, NY 11901
Phone: (631)369-0800
Fax: (631)369-5190
**Subject(s):** Free Newspapers
**Circ:** (Wed.)19,889

**Daily Hampshire Gazette (14321)**
H.S. Gere & Sons Inc.
PO Box 299
Northampton, MA 01061
**Subject(s):** Daily Newspapers
**Circ:** (Mon.-Sat.)19,851

**Auburn Pennysaver (22995)**
Scotsman Community Publications
750 W. Genesee St.
PO Box 4970
Syracuse, NY 13221
Phone: (315)472-7825
Fax: (315)478-1434
**Subject(s):** Shopping Guides
**Circ:** (Non-paid)‡19,731

**The Sun Chronicle (13441)**
PO Box 600
Attleboro, MA 02703-0600
Phone: (508)222-7000
Fax: (508)236-0462
**Subject(s):** Daily Newspapers
**Circ:** (Mon.-Sat.)★19,246
(Sun.)★19,729

**Lake Country Pennysaver (20245)**
170 N Main St.
PO Box 231
Albion, NY 14411
Phone: (585)589-5641
Fax: (585)589-1239
**Subject(s):** Shopping Guides
**Circ:** (Paid)9
(Non-paid)19,643

**Finger Lakes Times (20821)**
Finger Lakes Printing Co.
218 Genesee St.
PO Box 393
Geneva, NY 14456
Phone: (315)789-3376
Fax: (315)789-4077
**Subject(s):** Daily Newspapers
**Circ:** (Mon.-Fri.)★16,724
(Sun.)★19,598

**The Gazette (4681)**
1171 Main St.
East Hartford, CT 06108
Phone: (860)289-6468
Fax: (860)289-6469
**Subject(s):** Paid Community Newspapers
**Circ:** (Paid)‡209
(Free)‡19,497

**Dispatch (26179)**
Tribune Review Publishing Co.
PO Box 37
Blairsville, PA 15717
Phone: (412)459-6100
Fax: (412)459-7366
**Subject(s):** Paid Community Newspapers
**Circ:** (Paid)♦1,726
(Non-paid)♦19,478

**Solvay-Camillus Pennysaver (23036)**
Scotsman Community Publications
750 W. Genesee St.
PO Box 4970
Syracuse, NY 13221
Phone: (315)472-7825
Fax: (315)478-1434
**Subject(s):** Shopping Guides
**Circ:** (Non-paid)‡19,475

**Kings Courier (20522)**
Courier Life Publications
1733 Sheepshead Bay Rd.
Brooklyn, NY 11235-3606
Phone: (718)615-2500
Fax: (718)615-3835
**Subject(s):** Paid Community Newspapers
**Circ:** 19,430

**West Babylon Suffolk Life (20331)**
Suffolk Life Newspapers
PO Box 9167
Riverhead, NY 11901
Phone: (631)369-0800
Fax: (631)369-5190
**Subject(s):** Free Newspapers
**Circ:** (Wed.)19,349

**Peabody-Lynnfield Edition (14732)**
Suburban Publishing Corp.
PO Box 6039
Peabody, MA 01961-6039
Phone: (978)532-5880
Fax: (978)532-4250
**Subject(s):** Free Newspapers
**Circ:** (Non-paid)19,330

**Upper Perk Shoppers Guide (27475)**
Shoppers Guide
PO Box 443
878 Main St.
Red Hill, PA 18076
Phone: (215)679-4133

Fax: (215)679-5490
**Subject(s):** Shopping Guides
**Circ:** (Free)19,220

**Brooklyn Heights Press (20494)**
Brooklyn Eagle Publications
30 Henry St.
Brooklyn, NY 11201-3504
Phone: (718)858-2300
Fax: (718)858-4483
**Subject(s):** Paid Community Newspapers
**Circ:** 19,200

**West Seneca Pennysaver (23159)**
RW Publications
3770 Transit Rd.
Orchard Park, NY 14127
Phone: (716)662-4200
Fax: (716)662-0740
**Subject(s):** Shopping Guides
**Circ:** (Non-paid)19,200

**Germantown Courier (26122)**
Acme Newspapers Inc.
311 E. Lancaster Ave.
Ardmore, PA 19003
Phone: (610)642-4300
Fax: (610)642-6911
**Subject(s):** Free Newspapers
**Circ:** (Paid)♦12
(Non-paid)♦19,192

**The Greenfield Town Crier (13810)**
The Town Crier Community Newspapers
PO Box 1435
393 Main Street
Greenfield, MA 01302
Phone: (413)774-7226
Fax: (413)774-6809
**Subject(s):** Free Newspapers
**Circ:** (Free)19,119

**Hawthorne-Glen Rock-Haledon-North Haledon-Prospect Park Shopper (19145)**
North Jersey Community Newspapers
12-38 River Rd.
Fair Lawn, NJ 07410-1897
Phone: (201)791-8400
Fax: (201)794-3259
**Subject(s):** Shopping Guides
**Circ:** (Free)‡19,086

**Shop-Right 1 (27481)**
Shop Right
PO Box T
Ridgway, PA 15853
Phone: (814)776-2121
Fax: (814)776-1086
**Subject(s):** Shopping Guides
**Circ:** (Free)‡19,086

**The North Bergen/Reporter (18977)**
Hudson Reporter Associates
1400 Washington St.
PO Box 3069
Hoboken, NJ 07030-1601
Phone: (201)798-7800
Fax: (201)798-0018
**Subject(s):** Free Newspapers
**Circ:** (Non-paid)19,050

**Coastal Journal (12468)**
PO Box 705
99 Commercial St
Bath, ME 04530
Phone: (207)443-6241
Fax: (207)443-5605
**Subject(s):** Free Newspapers
**Circ:** (Free)19,000

**The Dispatch News (13861)**
15 Kearney Sq.
Lowell, MA 01852
Phone: (978)458-7100
**Subject(s):** Paid Community Newspapers
**Circ:** (Paid)‡1,000
(Free)‡19,000

**Philadelphia Gay News (27221)**
PGN
505 S. 4th St.
Philadelphia, PA 19147-1506
Phone: (215)625-8501
Fax: (215)925-6437

**Subject(s):** Gay and Lesbian Interests
**Circ:** 19,000

**U.S. 1 Newspaper** (19740)
U.S. 1 Publishing Co.
12 Roszel Rd.
Princeton, NJ 08540
Phone: (609)452-7000
Fax: (609)452-0033
**Subject(s):** Free Newspapers
**Circ:** (Free)‡19,000

**Long Beach Pennysaver** (21075)
Star Community Publishing
250 Miller Pl.
Hicksville, NY 11801
Phone: (516)393-9300
Fax: (516)393-9344
**Subject(s):** Shopping Guides
**Circ:** (Free)18,966

**Dunkirk-Fredonia-Westfield Pennysaver** (20795)
Fredonia Pennysaver Inc.
276 West Main
PO Box 493
Fredonia, NY 14063
Phone: (716)679-1509
Fax: (716)672-2626
**Subject(s):** Shopping Guides
**Circ:** (Non-paid)18,880

**Daily Item** (13866)
Hastings & Sons
38 Exchange St.
PO Box 951
Lynn, MA 01903
Phone: (617)593-7700
Fax: (617)581-3178
**Subject(s):** Daily Newspapers
**Circ:** (Sat.)17,652
(Mon.-Fri.)18,816

**East Lycoming Shopper and News** (26518)
Sun-Gazette Newspapers
PO Box 266
Hughesville, PA 17737
Phone: (570)584-2134
Fax: (570)584-5399
**Subject(s):** Shopping Guides
**Circ:** (Free)18,800

**Olney Times** (27191)
News Gleaner Publications
9999 Gantry Rd.
Philadelphia, PA 19149
Phone: (215)969-5100
Fax: (215)969-5400
**Subject(s):** Free Newspapers
**Circ:** (Free)♦18,800

**The Penny Saver** (18946)
The Pennysaver Inc.
607 Tenney Mtn. Hwy.
Village Sq., Ste. 137
Plymouth, NH 03264
Phone: (603)536-3160
Fax: (603)536-8150
**Subject(s):** Shopping Guides
**Circ:** (Free)‡18,748

**The Reporter** (26616)
Journal Register Co.
The Reporter
307 Derstine Ave.
Lansdale, PA 19446-3532
Phone: (215)855-8440
Fax: (215)855-3432
**Subject(s):** Daily Newspapers
**Circ:** 18,602

**Coram/Middle Island Suffolk Life** (20677)
Suffolk Life Newspapers
PO Box 9167
Riverhead, NY 11901
Phone: (631)369-0800
Fax: (631)369-5190
**Subject(s):** Free Newspapers
**Circ:** (Wed.)18,554

**Babylon South Bay's Shopper** (21063)
Excel Promotions Corp.
150 W Hoffman Ave.
Lindenhurst, NY 11757
Phone: (631)226-2636

**Subject(s):** Shopping Guides
**Circ:** (Free)18,511

**Columbia University Record** (21518)
Columbia University
2960 Broadway
New York, NY 10027-6902
Phone: (212)854-1754
Fax: (212)678-4817
**Subject(s):** College Publications
**Circ:** (Controlled)⊕18,500

**Moneysaver** (14762)
41 Highland Ave., Ste 1
Randolph, MA 02368
Phone: (781)963-8267
**Subject(s):** Shopping Guides
**Circ:** (Free)‡18,500

**The South End News** (13588)
637 Tremont Street
Boston, MA 02118
Phone: (617)266-6670
Fax: (617)266-5973
**Subject(s):** Free Newspapers; Free Newspapers
**Circ:** (Paid)300
(Free)18,500

**News of Delaware County** (26476)
Acme Newspapers Inc.
Manoa Shopping Ctr.
Havertown, PA 19083
Phone: (610)446-8700
Fax: (610)449-0419
**Subject(s):** Free Newspapers
**Circ:** (Paid)13,817
(Non-paid)18,212

**The Daily Star** (20609)
Ottaway Newspaper
PO Box 401
PO Box 250
Campbell Hall, NY 10916
Fax: (607)432-5847
**Subject(s):** Daily Newspapers
**Circ:** (Mon.-Sat.)18,181

**Shopping News** (4678)
Valley Publishing Co.
7 Francis St.
Derby, CT 06418
Phone: (203)735-6696
Fax: (203)735-0334
**Subject(s):** Shopping Guides
**Circ:** (Non-paid)18,189

**Deer Park South Bay's Shopper** (21064)
Excel Promotions Corp.
150 W Hoffman Ave.
Lindenhurst, NY 11757
Phone: (631)226-2636
**Subject(s):** Shopping Guides
**Circ:** (Free)18,156

**Riverhead Suffolk Life** (22798)
Suffolk Life Newspapers
PO Box 9167
Riverhead, NY 11901
Phone: (631)369-0800
Fax: (631)369-5190
**Subject(s):** Free Newspapers
**Circ:** (Wed.)18,153

**Moneysaver** (20650)
Capital Region Weekly Newspaper Group
P.O. Box 1450
Clifton Park, NY 12065
Phone: (518)877-7160
Fax: (518)877-7824
**Subject(s):** Shopping Guides
**Circ:** (Free)‡18,103

**The Derrick** (26788)
PO Box 928
Oil City, PA 16301
Phone: (814)676-7444
Fax: (814)677-8347
**Subject(s):** Daily Newspapers
**Circ:** ‡18,096

**Airport Press** (20986)
P.A.T.I. Inc.
PO Box 879, JFK Sta.
Jamaica, NY 11430-0879
Phone: (718)244-6788
Fax: (718)995-3432
**Subject(s):** Aviation; Transportation, Traffic, and Shipping
**Circ:** (Free)18,000

**Jewish Post of New York** (21862)
260 W. 35th St., Ste. 300
New York, NY 10001
Phone: (212)563-9219
Fax: (212)594-1297
**Subject(s):** Paid Community Newspapers; Jewish Publications
**Circ:** (Controlled)18,000

**Massachusetts Bar Association Lawyers Journal** (13546)
Massachusetts Bar Association
20 W St.
Boston, MA 02111-1204
Phone: (617)338-0500
Fax: (617)338-0650
**Subject(s):** Law
**Circ:** (Controlled)18,000

**Queens Ledger** (22767)
Midnight Publishing Corp.
55-51 69th St.
PO Box 780376
Maspeth, NY 11378
Phone: (718)639-7000
Fax: (718)429-1234
**Subject(s):** Paid Community Newspapers
**Circ:** (Paid)18,000

**Middletown Independent** (19521)
Greater Media Newspapers
PO Box 5001
Freehold, NJ 07728
Phone: (732)358-5200
**Subject(s):** Free Newspapers
**Circ:** (Non-paid)17,985

**Clifton Park South Pennysaver** (20647)
Capital Region Weekly Newspaper Group
P.O. Box 1450
Clifton Park, NY 12065
Phone: (518)877-7160
Fax: (518)877-7824
**Subject(s):** Shopping Guides
**Circ:** (Non-paid)17,955

**Huntington Station Suffolk Life** (20932)
Suffolk Life Newspapers
PO Box 9167
Riverhead, NY 11901
Phone: (631)369-0800
Fax: (631)369-5190
**Subject(s):** Free Newspapers
**Circ:** (Wed.)17,890

**Workers Vanguard** (22556)
Spartacist Publishing Co.
PO Box 1377 GPO
New York, NY 10116
Phone: (212)732-7861
Fax: (212)406-2210
**Subject(s):** Politics
**Circ:** ‡17,895

**Northeast Breeze Edition** (27178)
News Gleaner Publications
9999 Gantry Rd.
Philadelphia, PA 19149
Phone: (215)969-5100
Fax: (215)969-5400
**Subject(s):** Free Newspapers
**Circ:** (Paid)18
(Non-paid)17,800

**Owego Pennysaver** (22674)
181-183 Front St.
Owego, NY 13827
Phone: (607)687-2434
**Subject(s):** Paid Community Newspapers
**Circ:** (Paid)6
(Non-paid)17,787

# Northeastern States

**Clifton Park North Pennysaver (20646)**
Capital Region Weekly Newspaper Group
P.O. Box 1450
Clifton Park, NY 12065
Phone: (518)877-7160
Fax: (518)877-7824
**Subject(s):** Shopping Guides
**Circ:** (Non-paid)17,669

**The Call (27956)**
75 Main St.
Woonsocket, RI 02895
Phone: (401)762-3000
Fax: (401)765-2834
**Subject(s):** Daily Newspapers
**Circ:** (Mon.-Sat.)★11,984
(Sun.)★17,638

**The Hoboken Reporter (19243)**
Hudson Reporter Associates
1400 Washington St.
PO Box 3069
Hoboken, NJ 07030-1601
Phone: (201)798-7800
Fax: (201)798-0018
**Subject(s):** Free Newspapers
**Circ:** (Non-paid)17,600

**Commack/Kings Park Suffolk Life (20666)**
Suffolk Life Newspapers
PO Box 9167
Riverhead, NY 11901
Phone: (631)369-0800
Fax: (631)369-5190
**Subject(s):** Free Newspapers
**Circ:** (Wed.)17,559

**Valley News (18961)**
24 Interchange Dr.
West Lebanon, NH 03784
Phone: (603)298-8711
Fax: (603)298-0212
**Subject(s):** Daily Newspapers
**Circ:** (Sun.)17,534
(Mon.-Sat.)17,544

**Jamesville/Dewitt/Fayetteville/Manlius Pennysaver (21126)**
Scotsman Community Publications
750 W. Genesee St.
PO Box 4970
Syracuse, NY 13221
Phone: (315)472-7825
Fax: (315)478-1434
**Subject(s):** Shopping Guides
**Circ:** (Non-paid)‡17,536

**The Advertiser (4850)**
The Eln City Newspapers
349 New Haven Ave.
PO Box 5339
Milford, CT 06460
Phone: (203)876-6800
Fax: (203)877-4772
**Subject(s):** Paid Community Newspapers
**Circ:** ‡17,500

**Face Magazine (12557)**
About Face Inc.
16 York St., Ste. 102
Portland, ME 04101
**Subject(s):** Entertainment
**Circ:** (Free)17,500

**Hatboro Progress (26473)**
Progress Newspapers Inc.
390 Easton Rd.
Horsham, PA 19044-2532
Phone: (215)368-8600
Fax: (215)836-5398
**Subject(s):** Paid Community Newspapers
**Circ:** 17,500

**Sentinel & Enterprise (13781)**
808 Main St.
Fitchburg, MA 01420
Phone: (978)343-6911
Fax: (978)342-1158
**Subject(s):** Daily Newspapers
**Circ:** (Mon.-Sat.)★16,782
(Sun.)★17,494

**Norwich Pennysaver (22629)**
The Norwich and Sidney Pennysavers Inc.
18-20 Mechanic St.
PO BOX 111
Norwich, NY 13815
Phone: (607)334-4714
Fax: (607)336-7318
**Subject(s):** Shopping Guides
**Circ:** (Non-paid)17,418

**Huntington Suffolk Life (20927)**
Suffolk Life Newspapers
PO Box 9167
Riverhead, NY 11901
Phone: (631)369-0800
Fax: (631)369-5190
**Subject(s):** Free Newspapers
**Circ:** (Wed.)17,315

**Northport Suffolk Life (22627)**
Suffolk Life Newspapers
PO Box 9167
Riverhead, NY 11901
Phone: (631)369-0800
Fax: (631)369-5190
**Subject(s):** Free Newspapers
**Circ:** (Wed.)17,262

**The Eastern Gazette (12504)**
PO Box 306
Dexter, ME 04930
Phone: (207)924-7402
Fax: (207)924-6215
**Subject(s):** Paid Community Newspapers
**Circ:** ‡17,250

**DNR (21614)**
Fairchild Publications Inc.
7 W. 34th St.
New York, NY 10001
Phone: (212)630-3602
Fax: (212)630-3602
**Subject(s):** Daily Periodicals; Textiles; Clothing
**Circ:** (Paid)17,069

**Gazette (26531)**
Indiana Gazette
899 Water St.
PO Box 10
Indiana, PA 15701-1705
Phone: (724)465-5555
Fax: (724)349-4550
**Subject(s):** Daily Newspapers
**Circ:** (Sun.)9,068
(Mon.-Sat.)17,012

**Hampton East Suffolk Life (20722)**
Suffolk Life Newspapers
PO Box 9167
Riverhead, NY 11901
Phone: (631)369-0800
Fax: (631)369-5190
**Subject(s):** Free Newspapers
**Circ:** (Wed.)17,019

**The Daily Targum (19588)**
126 College Ave., Ste. 431
New Brunswick, NJ 08901
Phone: (732)932-7051
Fax: (732)246-7299
**Subject(s):** College Publications
**Circ:** ‡17,000

**The Forecaster—Southern Edition (12515)**
The Forecaster
8 Fundy Rd.
PO Box 66797
Falmouth, ME 04105-6797
Phone: (207)781-3661
Fax: (207)781-2060
**Subject(s):** Paid Community Newspapers
**Circ:** (Non-paid)17,000

**Massachusetts Daily Collegian (13417)**
University of Massachusetts
113 Campus Ctr.
Amherst, MA 01003
Phone: (413)577-5000
Fax: (413)545-1592
**Subject(s):** College Publications
**Circ:** (Free)‡17,000

**Ocular Surgery News (19864)**
SLACK Inc.
6900 Grove Rd.
Thorofare, NJ 08086-9447
Phone: (856)848-1000
Fax: (856)848-6091
**Subject(s):** Medicine and Surgery; Ophthalmology, Optometry, and Optics
**Circ:** (Controlled)‡17,000

**Stratford Bard (4855)**
Elm City Newspapers
349 New Haven Ave.
Milford, CT 06460
Phone: (203)876-6800
Fax: (203)877-4772
**Subject(s):** Free Newspapers
**Circ:** (Free)‡17,000

**Amityville Suffolk Life (20261)**
Suffolk Life Newspapers
PO Box 9167
Riverhead, NY 11901
Phone: (631)369-0800
Fax: (631)369-5190
**Subject(s):** Free Newspapers
**Circ:** (Wed.)16,921

**Pennysaver Town Crier (20770)**
Guinan Publishing Corp.
1538 Old Country Rd.
Plainview, NY 11803
Phone: (516)249-0750
Fax: (516)249-0789
**Subject(s):** Shopping Guides
**Circ:** (Free)16,889

**Albion Advertiser (21145)**
Medina Daily Journal-Register Inc.
409-13 Main St.
Medina, NY 14103-1416
Phone: (585)798-1400
Fax: (585)798-0290
**Subject(s):** Shopping Guides
**Circ:** (Free)16,800

**Chemical Market Reporter (21479)**
Schnell Publishing Company Inc.
2 Rector St., 26th Fl.
New York, NY 10006-1819
Phone: (212)791-4267
Fax: (212)791-4313
**Subject(s):** Chemistry, Chemicals, and Chemical Engineering
**Circ:** ‡16,801

**Pittsburgh Business Times (27386)**
American City Business Journals Inc.
2313 E. Carson St., Ste. 200
Pittsburgh, PA 15203
Phone: (412)481-9956
Fax: (412)481-6397
**Subject(s):** Business; Local, State, and Regional Publications
**Circ:** (Paid)16,731

**Daily Sentinel (22870)**
Rome Sentinel Co.
333 W. Dominick St.
PO Box 471
Rome, NY 13442-0471
Phone: (315)337-4000
Fax: (315)339-6281
**Subject(s):** Daily Newspapers
**Circ:** (Mon.-Sat.)15,030
16,500

**Suburban Advertiser (26792)**
Suburban Publications Inc.
315 Lancaster Ave.
PO Box 292
Exeter, PA 18643
Phone: (610)363-2815
Fax: (610)524-1997
**Subject(s):** Paid Community Newspapers
**Circ:** (Paid)♦6
(Non-paid)♦16,445

**Olean Times-Herald (22648)**
639 Norton Dr.
Olean, NY 14760
Phone: (716)372-3121
Fax: (716)372-0740
**Subject(s):** Daily Newspapers
**Circ:** (Mon.-Sat.)★16,092
(Sun.)★16,430

**Suburban Life (19771)**
North Jersey Community Newspapers
100 Common Way
Rockaway, NJ 07866
Phone: (973)586-8190
**Subject(s):** Free Newspapers

Circ: (Non-paid)16,430

**Hampton West Suffolk Life (23176)**
Suffolk Life Newspapers
PO Box 9167
Riverhead, NY 11901
Phone: (631)369-0800
Fax: (631)369-5190
**Subject(s):** Free Newspapers

Circ: (Wed.)16,408

**Fulton Pennysaver (23016)**
Scotsman Community Publications
750 W. Genesee St.
PO Box 4970
Syracuse, NY 13221
Phone: (315)472-7825
Fax: (315)478-1434
**Subject(s):** Shopping Guides

Circ: (Non-paid)‡16,335

**Lynbrook Pennysaver (21085)**
Star Community Publishing
250 Miller Pl.
Hicksville, NY 11801
Phone: (516)393-9300
Fax: (516)393-9344
**Subject(s):** Shopping Guides

Circ: (Free)16,288

**Mid-Hampton Suffolk Life (22796)**
Suffolk Life Newspapers
PO Box 9167
Riverhead, NY 11901
Phone: (631)369-0800
Fax: (631)369-5190
**Subject(s):** Free Newspapers

Circ: (Wed.)16,132

**Mohawk Valley Pennysaver (21235)**
Country Folks of Pennsylvania
55 E. Main St. (Rte.5)
Nelliston, NY 13410
Phone: (518)993-2772
Fax: (518)993-2726
**Subject(s):** Shopping Guides

Circ: (Free)‡16,108

**The Hour (4952)**
The Hour Publishing Co.
346 Main Ave.
Norwalk, CT 06851
Phone: (203)846-3281
Fax: (203)846-9897
**Subject(s):** Daily Newspapers

Circ: (Sun.)★15,590
(Mon.-Sat.)★16,070

**Mastic/Shirley Suffolk Life (21139)**
Suffolk Life Newspapers
PO Box 9167
Riverhead, NY 11901
Phone: (631)369-0800
Fax: (631)369-5190
**Subject(s):** Free Newspapers

Circ: (Wed.)16,048

**Boston University Bridge (13490)**
Boston University
1 Sherborn St.
Boston, MA 02215
Phone: (617)353-2000
Fax: (617)353-6480
**Subject(s):** College Publications

Circ: (Paid)‡500
(Free)‡16,000

**Massachusetts Lawyers Weekly (13549)**
Lawyers Weekly Publications
41 W. St.
Boston, MA 02111
Phone: (617)451-7300
Fax: (617)451-7323
**Subject(s):** Law; Local, State, and Regional Publications

Circ: ‡16,000

**The Spotlight (20702)**
Spotlight Newspapers
125 Adams St.
PO Box 100
Delmar, NY 12054-0100
Phone: (518)439-4949
Fax: (518)439-0609
**Subject(s):** Paid Community Newspapers

Circ: ‡16,000

**East Aurora/Elma Pennysaver (20716)**
RW Publications
3770 Transit Rd.
Orchard Park, NY 14127
Phone: (716)662-4200
Fax: (716)662-0740
**Subject(s):** Shopping Guides

Circ: (Non-paid)15,928

**Tri-County Advertiser (20431)**
Rheinwald Printing Company Inc.
15 Main St.
PO Box 378
Brockport, NY 14420
Phone: (585)637-5100
Fax: (585)637-0111
**Subject(s):** Shopping Guides

Circ: (Non-paid)15,924

**Boston Business Journal (13481)**
MCP Inc.
200 High St.
Boston, MA 02110
Phone: (617)330-1000
Fax: (617)330-1016
**Subject(s):** Business

Circ: (Paid)★15,918

**Post-Gazette (13578)**
5 Prince St.
PO Box 135
Boston, MA 02113
Phone: (617)227-8929
Fax: (617)227-5307
**Subject(s):** Paid Community Newspapers

Circ: (Paid)15,900

**Rocky Point Suffolk Life (22868)**
Suffolk Life Newspapers
PO Box 9167
Riverhead, NY 11901
Phone: (631)369-0800
Fax: (631)369-5190
**Subject(s):** Free Newspapers

Circ: (Wed.)15,770

**Bayshore Independent (19107)**
Greater Media Newspapers
PO Box 5001
Freehold, NJ 07728
Phone: (732)358-5200
**Subject(s):** Free Newspapers

Circ: (Non-paid)15,715

**Vermont News Guide (30897)**
PO Box 1265, Rte. 7A Main St.
Manchester Center, VT 05255
Phone: (802)362-3535
Fax: (802)362-5368
**Subject(s):** Shopping Guides

Circ: (Paid)400
(Free)15,600

**Focus on Farming (21221)**
6 Central St.
PO Box 591
Moravia, NY 13118
Phone: (315)497-1551
**Subject(s):** Farm Newspapers

Circ: ‡15,500

**Sentinel (26224)**
Cumberland Publishers Inc.
457 E North St.
PO Box 130
Carlisle, PA 17013
Phone: (717)243-2611
Fax: (717)243-2131
**Subject(s):** Daily Newspapers

Circ: (Mon.-Sat.)15,287
(Sun.)15,497

**Courier Express (26292)**
500 Jeffers St.
PO Box 407
Du Bois, PA 15801
Phone: (814)371-4200
Fax: (814)371-3241
**Subject(s):** Paid Community Newspapers

Circ: (Mon.-Fri.)★10,198
(Sun.)★15,486

**Garfield-Wallington-South Hackensack Shopper (19111)**
North Jersey Community Newspapers
12-38 River Rd.
Fair Lawn, NJ 07410-1897
Phone: (201)791-8400
Fax: (201)794-3259
**Subject(s):** Shopping Guides

Circ: (Free)‡15,473

**Town & Country Pennysaver (23045)**
Scotsman Community Publications
750 W. Genesee St.
PO Box 4970
Syracuse, NY 13221
Phone: (315)472-7825
Fax: (315)478-1434
**Subject(s):** Shopping Guides

Circ: (Non-paid)‡15,442

**Chester County Press (26790)**
Ad Pro Inc.
309 limestone Rd.
PO Box 520
Oxford, PA 19363
Phone: (610)932-2444
Fax: (610)932-2246
**Subject(s):** Paid Community Newspapers

Circ: ‡15,438

**News (20338)**
Batavia Newspapers Corp.
2 Apollo Dr.
Batavia, NY 14021
Phone: (716)343-8000
Fax: (716)343-2623
**Subject(s):** Daily Newspapers

Circ: (Mon.-Sat.)15,427

**Lakeland Today (19953)**
North Jersey Community Newspapers
The Weekly Division of N Jersey Media Group
1 Garret Mountain Plz.
PO Box 471
West Paterson, NJ 07424-0471
Phone: (973)569-7000
Fax: (973)569-7310
**Subject(s):** Free Newspapers

Circ: (Non-paid)15,387

**Latham Pennysaver (20649)**
Capital Region Weekly Newspaper Group
P.O. Box 1450
Clifton Park, NY 12065
Phone: (518)877-7160
Fax: (518)877-7824
**Subject(s):** Shopping Guides

Circ: (Non-paid)15,309

**Town News (19765)**
North Jersey Community Newspapers
41 Oak St.
Ridgewood, NJ 07450-3805
Phone: (201)612-5425
Fax: (201)612-5421
**Subject(s):** Free Newspapers

Circ: (Non-paid)♦15,304

**Westport Minuteman (4925)**
Housatonic Publications
65 Bank St.
New Milford, CT 06776
Fax: (860)354-2645
**Subject(s):** Free Newspapers

Circ: (Non-paid)15,217

**Kennebec Journal (12446)**
274 Western Ave.
PO Box 1052
Augusta, ME 04330-4976
Phone: (207)623-3811
Fax: (207)623-3811
**Subject(s):** Daily Newspapers

Circ: (Sun.)★14,422
(Mon.-Sat.)★15,167

## Northeastern States

**Stratford Star** (5054)
Hometown Publications Inc.
1000 Bridgeport Ave.
Shelton, CT 06484
Phone: (203)926-2080
Fax: (203)926-2091
**Subject(s):** Paid Community Newspapers
**Circ:** (Non-paid)♦15,065

**Norwalk Lifestyles** (4960)
Brooks Community Newspapers Inc.
542 Westport Ave.
Norwalk, CT 06851
Phone: (203)849-1600
Fax: (203)840-4844
**Subject(s):** Free Newspapers
**Circ:** (Free)15,059

**Griffin's Tri-State Food News** (27355)
Tri State Food News
PO Box 16261
Pittsburgh, PA 15220
Phone: (412)937-1000
Fax: (412)531-7900
**Subject(s):** Free Newspapers
**Circ:** (Paid)‡15,000

**Leader-Herald and News Gazette** (13772)
Leader Publishing Company Inc.
28 Church St.
Everett, MA 02149
Phone: (617)387-4570
Fax: (617)387-0409
**Subject(s):** Free Newspapers
**Circ:** (Free)‡15,000

**Malden Evening News** (14214)
Eastern Middlesex Press Publications Inc.
277 Commercial St.
Malden, MA 02148
Phone: (617)321-8000
Fax: (617)321-8008
**Subject(s):** Daily Newspapers
**Circ:** ‡15,000

**The Manchester Journal** (30896)
New England Newspapers Inc.
PO Box 569
Manchester Center, VT 05255
Phone: (802)362-2222
Fax: (802)362-5327
**Subject(s):** Free Newspapers
**Circ:** 15,000

**The Mount Washington Valley Mountain Ear** (18795)
PO Box 530
Conway, NH 03818
Phone: (603)447-6336
Fax: (603)447-5474
**Subject(s):** Free Newspapers
**Circ:** ‡15,000

**New Hampshire Business Review** (18871)
Business Publications Inc.
150 Dow St.
Manchester, NH 03101
Phone: (603)624-1442
Fax: (603)624-1310
**Subject(s):** Business; Local, State, and Regional Publications
**Circ:** 15,000

**The New York Times Large Type Weekly** (22169)
The New York Times Co.
229 W 43rd St.
New York, NY 10036-3913
Phone: (212)556-1234
Fax: (212)556-3535
**Subject(s):** Paid Community Newspapers; Blind and Visually Challenged
**Circ:** (Paid)15,000

**Pennysaver** (26310)
Traders Guide Inc.
118 Ebony Rd., Ste. 102
PO Box 30
Ebensburg, PA 15931-0030
Phone: (814)472-8600
Fax: (814)472-9292
**Subject(s):** Shopping Guides
**Circ:** (Free)‡15,000

**Pennysaver/News** (20678)
217 Maple St.
PO Box 130
Corinth, NY 12822-0130
Phone: (518)654-9331
Fax: (518)654-2935
**Subject(s):** Shopping Guides
**Circ:** (Free)‡15,000

**The Progress News** (26322)
Staab Typographic
Box A
408 Main St.
Emlenton, PA 16373
Phone: (724)867-2435
Fax: (724)867-5933
**Subject(s):** Shopping Guides; Free Newspapers
**Circ:** (Free)‡15,000

**Record** (20577)
State University College at Buffalo
109 Cassety Hall
1300 Elmwood Ave.
Buffalo, NY 14222
Phone: (716)878-4000
Fax: (716)878-4539
**Subject(s):** College Publications
**Circ:** (Free)‡15,000

**Suffolk County News** (22915)
John Lor Publishing
PO Box 367
Sayville, NY 11782
Phone: (631)589-6200
Fax: (631)589-3246
**Subject(s):** Paid Community Newspapers
**Circ:** (Paid)15,000

**Temple Times** (27284)
Temple University
302 University Services Bldg.
1601 N Broad St., Temple Zip: No. 083-43
Philadelphia, PA 19122-6099
Phone: (215)204-8963
Fax: (215)204-3753
**Subject(s):** College Publications
**Circ:** (Free)‡15,000

**Cape Codder** (14259)
Community Newspaper Co.
254 2nd Ave.
Needham, MA 02494
Phone: (781)433-6700
**Subject(s):** Paid Community Newspapers
**Circ:** (Paid)14,988

**Elmont Pennysaver** (20752)
Star Community Publishing
250 Miller Pl.
Hicksville, NY 11801
Phone: (516)393-9300
Fax: (516)393-9344
**Subject(s):** Shopping Guides
**Circ:** (Free)14,988

**Westfield Quality Guide** (23174)
Ogden Newspapers Inc.
PO Box 38
Westfield, NY 14787
Phone: (716)326-3163
Fax: (716)326-3165
**Subject(s):** Shopping Guides
**Circ:** (Free)‡14,893

**The Warrensburg-Lake George News** (23120)
Denton Publications
PO Box 410
Warrensburg, NY 12885
Phone: (518)623-3187
Fax: (518)623-3411
**Subject(s):** Paid Community Newspapers
**Circ:** (Combined)‡14,800

**The Meadville Tribune** (26682)
947 Federal Ct.
Meadville, PA 16335
Phone: (814)724-6370
Fax: (814)724-8755
**Subject(s):** Daily Newspapers
**Circ:** (Sun.)★14,636
(Mon.-Sat.)★14,746

**The Daily Messenger** (20612)
Messenger Post Newspapers
73 Buffalo St.
Canandaigua, NY 14424
Phone: (585)394-0770
Fax: (585)394-1675
**Subject(s):** Daily Newspapers
**Circ:** (Mon.-Fri.)13,686
(Sun.)14,647

**Smithtown Suffolk Life** (22799)
Suffolk Life Newspapers
PO Box 9167
Riverhead, NY 11901
Phone: (631)369-0800
Fax: (631)369-5190
**Subject(s):** Free Newspapers
**Circ:** (Wed.)14,629

**Leader** (20679)
The Leader
34 W. Pulteney St.
Corning, NY 14830
Phone: (607)936-4651
Fax: (607)936-9939
**Subject(s):** Daily Newspapers
**Circ:** (Sun.)14,286
(Mon.-Sat.)14,594

**Valley Stream Pennysaver** (23104)
Star Community Publishing
250 Miller Pl.
Hicksville, NY 11801
Phone: (516)393-9300
Fax: (516)393-9344
**Subject(s):** Shopping Guides
**Circ:** (Free)14,591

**Lindenhurst Suffolk Life** (21066)
Suffolk Life Newspapers
PO Box 9167
Riverhead, NY 11901
Phone: (631)369-0800
Fax: (631)369-5190
**Subject(s):** Free Newspapers
**Circ:** (Wed.)14,538

**Port Jefferson Suffolk Life** (22719)
Suffolk Life Newspapers
PO Box 9167
Riverhead, NY 11901
Phone: (631)369-0800
Fax: (631)369-5190
**Subject(s):** Free Newspapers
**Circ:** (Wed.)14,538

**The Berkshire Penny Saver** (13851)
Add Inc.
14 Park Pl.
PO Box 300
Lee, MA 01238-0300
Phone: (413)243-2341
Fax: (413)243-4662
**Subject(s):** Shopping Guides
**Circ:** (Free)‡14,500

**Polish-American Journal** (20419)
Panagraphics Inc.
PO Box 328
Boston, NY 14025-0328
Phone: (716)312-8088
**Subject(s):** Ethnic Publications; Polish
**Circ:** ‡14,500

**Brookline TAB** (13631)
Community Newspaper Co.
254 2nd Ave.
Needham, MA 02494
Phone: (781)433-6700
**Subject(s):** Free Newspapers
**Circ:** (Free)14,391

**Cranberry Eagle/The News Weekly** (26273)
Eagle Printing Company Inc.
114 W Diamond St.
Butler, PA 16001-5747
Phone: (724)282-7209
Fax: (724)282-1780
**Subject(s):** Free Newspapers
**Circ:** (Wed.)12,108
(Sun.)14,392

**Bellmore South This Week/Pennysaver** (20363)
Star Community Publishing
250 Miller Pl.
Hicksville, NY 11801
Phone: (516)393-9300
Fax: (516)393-9344
**Subject(s):** Shopping Guides
**Circ:** (Free)‡14,348

**Herkimer Pennysaver** (20891)
Mid York Weekly Pennysaver Inc.
55 Oriskany Blvd
PO Box 203
Yorkville, NY 13495
Phone: (315)736-1494
Fax: (315)736-1496
**Subject(s):** Shopping Guides
**Circ:** (Combined)14,341

**Holbrook/Bohemia Suffolk Life** (21142)
Suffolk Life Newspapers
PO Box 9167
Riverhead, NY 11901
Phone: (631)369-0800
Fax: (631)369-5190
**Subject(s):** Free Newspapers
**Circ:** (Wed.)14,337

**Brentwood Suffolk Life** (20420)
Suffolk Life Newspapers
PO Box 9167
Riverhead, NY 11901
Phone: (631)369-0800
Fax: (631)369-5190
**Subject(s):** Free Newspapers
**Circ:** (Wed.)14,324

**Riverside Review** (20578)
Worral Publishing Inc.
215 Military Rd.
Buffalo, NY 14207-2631
Phone: (716)877-8400
Fax: (716)877-8742
**Subject(s):** Free Newspapers
**Circ:** (Free)‡14,300

**The Milford Mirror** (5010)
Hometown Publications Inc.
1000 Bridgeport Ave.
Shelton, CT 06484
Phone: (203)926-2080
Fax: (203)926-2091
**Subject(s):** Free Newspapers
**Circ:** (Non-paid)♦14,249

**Daily Chronicle** (14764)
531 Main St
Reading, MA 01867-0240
Phone: (781)944-2200
Fax: (781)942-0884
**Subject(s):** Daily Newspapers
**Circ:** (Controlled)2,092
(Paid)‡14,215

**The Coast Star** (19506)
13 Broad St.
Manasquan, NJ 08736
Phone: (732)223-0076
Fax: (732)223-8212
**Subject(s):** Paid Community Newspapers
**Circ:** 14,200

**The Valley Independent** (26718)
Eastgate 19
Monessen, PA 15062
Phone: (724)684-5200
Fax: (724)684-2602
**Subject(s):** Daily Newspapers
**Circ:** (Mon.-Sat.)★14,202

**The Citizen** (20326)
Auburn Publishers Inc.
25 Dill St.
Auburn, NY 13021
Phone: (315)253-5311
Fax: (315)253-5311
**Subject(s):** Daily Newspapers
**Circ:** (Sat.)11,823
(Mon.-Fri.)12,540
(Sun.)14,171

**Suburban Pennysaver** (23186)
Mid York Weekly Pennysaver Inc.
55 Oriskany Blvd
PO Box 203
Yorkville, NY 13495
Phone: (315)736-1494
Fax: (315)736-1496
**Subject(s):** Shopping Guides
**Circ:** (Combined)14,019

**The Beacon Hill Times** (13478)
25 Myrtle St.
Boston, MA 02114
Phone: (617)523-9490
Fax: (617)523-8668
**Subject(s):** Free Newspapers
**Circ:** (Paid)100
(Non-paid)14,000

**Bradford Journal/Miner** (26744)
Bradford Journal
265 S Ave.
PO Box 17
Bradford, PA 16701-0017
Phone: (814)362-6563
Fax: (413)403-7272
**Subject(s):** Paid Community Newspapers
**Circ:** (Combined)14,000

**The Buffalo Rocket** (20561)
2507 Delaware Ave.
Buffalo, NY 14216
Phone: (716)873-2594
Fax: (716)873-0809
**Subject(s):** Free Newspapers
**Circ:** (Free)‡14,000

**The Daily Pennsylvanian** (26915)
The Daily Pennsylvanian Inc.
4015 Walnut St.
Philadelphia, PA 19104
Phone: (215)898-6581
Fax: (215)898-2050
**Subject(s):** College Publications
**Circ:** (Free)‡14,000

**Darbininkas (The Worker)** (20503)
Franciscan Fathers-Publishers
361 Highland Blvd.
Brooklyn, NY 11207
Phone: (718)235-5962
**Subject(s):** Religious Publications; Labor
**Circ:** ‡14,000

**Journal of the Pocono Plateau** (27681)
Journal Newspapers of P.A. Inc.
211 Main St.
White Haven, PA 18661
Phone: (570)443-8321
Fax: (570)443-8142
**Subject(s):** Paid Community Newspapers
**Circ:** (Controlled)14,000

**Mid York Weekly Pennysaver** (23214)
Mid York Weekly Pennysaver Inc.
55 Oriskany Blvd
PO Box 203
Yorkville, NY 13495
Phone: (315)736-1494
Fax: (315)736-1496
**Subject(s):** Shopping Guides
**Circ:** (Free)14,000

**Newport This Week** (27872)
Community Communications Corp.
38 Bellevue Ave.
Newport, RI 02840
Phone: (401)847-7766
Fax: (401)846-4974
**Subject(s):** Free Newspapers
**Circ:** (Paid)600
(Free)14,000

**The Pitt News** (27385)
University of Pittsburgh
434 William Pitt Union
Pittsburgh, PA 15260
Phone: (412)648-7980
Fax: (412)648-7978
**Subject(s):** College Publications
**Circ:** (Free)‡14,000

**Post Eagle** (19038)
Post Publishing Company Inc.
800 Van Houten Ave.
PO Box 2127
Clifton, NJ 07015
Phone: (973)473-5414
Fax: (973)473-3211
**Subject(s):** Paid Community Newspapers
**Circ:** ‡14,000

**The Somerville News** (14793)
21 A College Ave.
Somerville, MA 02144-2917
Phone: (617)666-4010
Fax: (617)591-0362
**Subject(s):** Free Newspapers
**Circ:** (Combined)‡14,000

**Tempo-Mercer** (19136)
The Princeton Packet Inc.
300 Witherspoon St.
Princeton, NJ 08542
Phone: (609)924-3244
Fax: (609)924-3842
**Subject(s):** Free Newspapers
**Circ:** (Free)14,000

**TIE (The International Educator)** (13749)
TIE - The International Educator
PO Box 513
Cummaquid, MA 02637
Phone: (508)362-1414
Fax: (508)362-1411
**Subject(s):** Education; Employment and Human Resources
**Circ:** 14,000

**Norwin Star** (26727)
Gateway Publications
610 Beatty Rd.
Monroeville, PA 15146
Phone: (412)856-7400
Fax: (412)856-7954
**Subject(s):** Free Newspapers
**Circ:** (Paid)12,000
(Non-paid)13,983

**The Central Record** (19513)
Central Record Inc.
PO Box 1027
Medford, NJ 08055-0127
Phone: (609)654-5000
Fax: (609)654-8237
**Subject(s):** Paid Community Newspapers
**Circ:** (Non-paid)74
(Paid)13,912

**The Progress** (26249)
Progress
206 E Locust St.
PO Box 291
Clearfield, PA 16830
Phone: (814)765-5581
Fax: (814)765-5165
**Subject(s):** Daily Newspapers
**Circ:** (Mon.-Sat.)13,911

**East Islip Suffolk Life** (20724)
Suffolk Life Newspapers
PO Box 9167
Riverhead, NY 11901
Phone: (631)369-0800
Fax: (631)369-5190
**Subject(s):** Free Newspapers
**Circ:** (Wed.)13,908

**Central Islip/Hauppauge Suffolk Life** (20634)
Suffolk Life Newspapers
PO Box 9167
Riverhead, NY 11901
Phone: (631)369-0800
Fax: (631)369-5190
**Subject(s):** Free Newspapers
**Circ:** (Wed.)13,860

**Blasdell Lackawanna Pennysaver** (20416)
H & K Publications Inc.
50 Buffalo St.
Hamburg, NY 14075-5002
Phone: (716)649-4413
Fax: (716)649-6374
**Subject(s):** Shopping Guides
**Circ:** (Non-paid)13,808

Circulation: ★ = ABC; △ = BPA; ♦ = CAC; • = CCAB; ❏ = VAC; ⊕ = PO Statement; ‡ = Publisher's Report; Boldface figures = sworn; Light figures = estimated.

## Northeastern States

**New England Wine Gazette (27882)**
Recorder Publishing Company Inc.
Editorial and Advertising Dept.
582 Wapping Rd.
Portsmouth, RI 02871
**Subject(s):** Free Newspapers; Food and Cooking
**Circ:** (Non-paid)♦13,793

**The Times (27880)**
23 Exchange St.
PO Box 307
Pawtucket, RI 02860
Phone: (401)722-4000
Fax: (401)727-9252
**Subject(s):** Daily Newspapers
**Circ:** (Mon.-Sat.)13,763

**The New York Law Journal (22160)**
345 Park Ave. S.
New York, NY 10010
Phone: (212)779-9200
Fax: (212)481-8110
**Subject(s):** Daily Newspapers; Law
**Circ:** (Mon.-Fri.)13,745

**Daily American (27541)**
334 W Main St.
PO Box 638
Somerset, PA 15501
Phone: (814)444-5900
Fax: (814)444-5966
**Subject(s):** Daily Newspapers
**Circ:** (Mon.-Sat.)13,676

**Ambler Gazette (26369)**
Journal Register Co.
Montgomery Newspapers
290 Commerce Dr.
Fort Washington, PA 19034
Phone: (215)542-0200
Fax: (215)643-9475
**Subject(s):** Paid Community Newspapers
**Circ:** (Combined)13,580

**The Keene Sentinel (18842)**
Keene Publishing Corp.
60 W St.
PO Box 546
Keene, NH 03431-0546
Phone: (603)352-1234
Fax: (603)352-0437
**Subject(s):** Daily Newspapers
**Circ:** (Sun.)★13,100
(Mon.-Sat.)★13,544

**Hornell-Canisteo Penn-E-Saver (20909)**
112 Main St
Hornell, NY 14843
Phone: (607)324-1010
Fax: (607)324-2637
**Subject(s):** Shopping Guides
**Circ:** (Paid)16
(Non-paid)13,518

**The Jewish Journal/North of Boston (14775)**
North Shore Jewish Press
201 Washington St., Ste. 14
Salem, MA 01970
Phone: (978)745-4111
Fax: (978)745-5333
**Subject(s):** Jewish Publications
**Circ:** 13,500

**Mt. Airy Times Express (27156)**
Acme Newspapers Inc.
6622 Germantown Ave.
Philadelphia, PA 19119
Phone: (215)848-4300
Fax: (215)848-9160
**Subject(s):** Free Newspapers
**Circ:** (Paid)♦12
(Non-paid)♦13,507

**The Syracuse Record (23044)**
Syracuse University
820 Comstock Ave., Rm. 014
Syracuse, NY 13244-5040
Phone: (315)443-3784
Fax: (315)443-3786
**Subject(s):** College Publications
**Circ:** (Free)13,500

**The Transcript (30911)**
PO Box 369
Morrisville, VT 05661
Phone: (802)888-2212
Fax: (802)888-2173
**Subject(s):** Free Newspapers
**Circ:** (Free)‡13,500

**Vineyard Gazette (13771)**
Vineyard Gazette Inc.
34 S Summer St.
PO Box 66
Edgartown, MA 02539
Phone: (508)627-4311
Fax: (508)627-7444
**Subject(s):** Paid Community Newspapers
**Circ:** 13,500

**Ronkonkoma Suffolk Life (22880)**
Suffolk Life Newspapers
PO Box 9167
Riverhead, NY 11901
Phone: (631)369-0800
Fax: (631)369-5190
**Subject(s):** Free Newspapers
**Circ:** (Wed.)13,496

**Newburyport Daily News (14283)**
Eagle-Tribune Publishing
23 Liberty St.
Newburyport, MA 01950-2750
Phone: (978)462-6666
Fax: (978)463-9612
**Subject(s):** Daily Newspapers
**Circ:** (Mon.-Sat.)★13,445

**Northfolk Suffolk Life (22797)**
Suffolk Life Newspapers
PO Box 9167
Riverhead, NY 11901
Phone: (631)369-0800
Fax: (631)369-5190
**Subject(s):** Free Newspapers
**Circ:** (Wed.)13,441

**Dix Hills/Melville Suffolk Life (21155)**
Suffolk Life Newspapers
PO Box 9167
Riverhead, NY 11901
Phone: (631)369-0800
Fax: (631)369-5190
**Subject(s):** Free Newspapers
**Circ:** (Wed.)13,429

**Medford/Holtsville Suffolk Life (21143)**
Suffolk Life Newspapers
PO Box 9167
Riverhead, NY 11901
Phone: (631)369-0800
Fax: (631)369-5190
**Subject(s):** Free Newspapers
**Circ:** (Wed.)13,269

**The Hamden Journal (5006)**
Hometown Publications Inc.
1000 Bridgeport Ave.
Shelton, CT 06484
Phone: (203)926-2080
Fax: (203)926-2091
**Subject(s):** Free Newspapers
**Circ:** (Non-paid)♦13,192

**Westfield/Corry Quality Guide (23173)**
Ogden Newspapers Inc.
PO Box 38
Westfield, NY 14787
Phone: (716)326-3163
Fax: (716)326-3165
**Subject(s):** Shopping Guides
**Circ:** (Free)‡13,186

**Arcade Pennysaver (20286)**
H & K Publications Inc.
318 Main St.
Arcade, NY 14009
Phone: (716)496-7291
Fax: (716)492-5474
**Subject(s):** Shopping Guides
**Circ:** (Non-paid)13,102

**The Princeton Packet (19734)**
The Princeton Packet Inc.
300 Witherspoon St.
Princeton, NJ 08542
Phone: (609)924-3244
Fax: (609)924-3842
**Subject(s):** Paid Community Newspapers
**Circ:** 13,087

**American Banker (21299)**
American Banker/Bond Buyer Inc.
1 State St. Plz. 27 Fl.
New York, NY 10004
Phone: (212)803-8200
Fax: (212)843-9600
**Subject(s):** Daily Newspapers; Banking, Finance, and Investments
**Circ:** (Mon.-Fri.)★13,074

**Stony Brook/Setauket Suffolk Life (22985)**
Suffolk Life Newspapers
PO Box 9167
Riverhead, NY 11901
Phone: (631)369-0800
Fax: (631)369-5190
**Subject(s):** Free Newspapers
**Circ:** (Wed.)13,014

**Taunton Daily Gazette (14837)**
5 Cohannet St.
Taunton, MA 02780-3903
Phone: (508)880-9000
Fax: (508)824-3487
**Subject(s):** Daily Newspapers
**Circ:** (Sun.)12,486
(Mon.-Sat.)13,013

**Amherst Bulletin (13402)**
H.S. Gere & Sons Inc.
55 University Dr.
Amherst, MA 01002
Phone: (413)549-2000
Fax: (413)549-8181
**Subject(s):** Paid Community Newspapers
**Circ:** (Controlled)13,000

**AUFBAU - The Transatlantic Jewish Paper (21375)**
Aufbau Trust
2121 Broadway
New York, NY 10023
Phone: (212)873-7400
Fax: (212)496-5736
**Subject(s):** German; Ethnic Publications; Jewish Publications
**Circ:** ‡13,000

**County Transcript (27572)**
212-216 Exchange St.
Susquehanna, PA 18847
Phone: (717)853-3134
Fax: (717)853-4707
**Subject(s):** Paid Community Newspapers
**Circ:** ‡13,000

**The Riverdale Press (20475)**
6155 Broadway
Bronx, NY 10471
Phone: (718)543-6065
Fax: (718)548-4038
**Subject(s):** Paid Community Newspapers
**Circ:** (Free)2,000
(Paid)13,000

**West Side Times (20583)**
The Buffalo Rocket
2507 Delaware Ave.
Buffalo, NY 14216
Phone: (716)873-2594
Fax: (716)873-0809
**Subject(s):** Free Newspapers
**Circ:** (Free)‡13,000

**Blackstone Valley Tribune (14910)**
Stonebridge Press
PO Box 210
Whitinsville, MA 01588
**Subject(s):** Paid Community Newspapers
**Circ:** (Wed.)‡5,300
(Fri.)‡12,996

**Baldwinsville Pennysaver (22996)**
Scotsman Community Publications
750 W. Genesee St.
PO Box 4970
Syracuse, NY 13221
Phone: (315)472-7825
Fax: (315)478-1434
**Subject(s):** Shopping Guides
**Circ:** (Non-paid)‡12,960

# Gale Directory of Publications & Broadcast Media/140th Ed.

## Northeastern States

**The Saratogian (22908)**
The Saratogian L.L.C.
20 Lake Ave.
Saratoga Springs, NY 12866
Phone: (518)584-4242
Fax: (518)587-7750
**Subject(s):** Daily Newspapers
**Circ:** (Mon.-Sat.)11,461
(Sun.)12,932

**Chronicle Ad-Viser (22695)**
Chronicle Adviser
138 Main St.
Penn Yan, NY 14527-1219
Phone: (315)536-4422
Fax: (315)536-0682
**Subject(s):** Shopping Guides
**Circ:** (Free)‡12,925

**The Newport Daily News (27868)**
Edward A. Sherman Publishing Co.
PO Box 420
101 Malbone Rd.
Newport, RI 02840
Phone: (401)849-3300
Fax: (401)849-3306
**Subject(s):** Daily Newspapers
**Circ:** (Mon.-Sat.)12,680

**Milford Daily News (14267)**
Community Newspaper Co.
254 2nd Ave.
Needham, MA 02494
Phone: (781)433-6700
**Subject(s):** Daily Newspapers
**Circ:** (Mon.-Sat.)12,679

**Observer (20712)**
The Observer
10 E. 2nd St.
Dunkirk, NY 14048-0391
Phone: (716)366-3000
Fax: (716)366-3005
**Subject(s):** Daily Newspapers
**Circ:** (Mon.-Sat.)12,483
(Sun.)12,670

**Cranberry Star (26724)**
Gateway Publications
610 Beatty Rd.
Monroeville, PA 15146
Phone: (412)856-7400
Fax: (412)856-7954
**Subject(s):** Paid Community Newspapers
**Circ:** (Paid)322
(Non-paid)12,555

**Brunswick Times Record (12485)**
Times Record
6 Industry Rd.
PO Box 10
Brunswick, ME 04011
Phone: (207)729-3311
Fax: (207)729-5728
**Subject(s):** Daily Newspapers
**Circ:** (Mon.-Thurs.)★10,531
(Fri.)★12,528

**Parkchester News (21243)**
Hagedorn Communications
662 Main St.
New Rochelle, NY 10801
Phone: (914)636-7400
Fax: (914)636-2957
**Subject(s):** Paid Community Newspapers
**Circ:** (Free)‡12,500

**The Review (27249)**
The New Hope Gazette
6220 Ridge Ave.
Philadelphia, PA 19128
**Subject(s):** Free Newspapers
**Circ:** (Free)‡11,000
(Paid)‡12,500

**SVOBODA (19668)**
Ukrainian National Association Inc.
2200 Rte. 10
PO Box 280
Parsippany, NJ 07054
Phone: (973)292-9800
Fax: (973)292-0900
**Subject(s):** Daily Newspapers; Ukrainian
**Circ:** (Free)‡300
(Paid)‡12,500

**Greenwich Time (4776)**
20 E Elm St.
Greenwich, CT 06830-6529
Phone: (203)625-4400
Fax: (203)625-4419
**Subject(s):** Daily Newspapers
**Circ:** (Sat.)★10,712
(Mon.-Fri.)★11,672
(Sun.)★12,452

**Old Colony Memorial (14747)**
MPG Newspapers
9 Long Pond Rd.
PO Box 959
Plymouth, MA 02362-0959
Phone: (508)746-5555
Fax: (508)747-2148
**Subject(s):** Paid Community Newspapers
**Circ:** (Combined)12,437

**Flatbush Life (20509)**
Courier Life Publications
1733 Sheepshead Bay Rd.
Brooklyn, NY 11235-3606
Phone: (718)615-2500
Fax: (718)615-3835
**Subject(s):** Paid Community Newspapers
**Circ:** 12,350

**Sayville/Oakdale Suffolk Life (22914)**
Suffolk Life Newspapers
PO Box 9167
Riverhead, NY 11901
Phone: (631)369-0800
Fax: (631)369-5190
**Subject(s):** Free Newspapers
**Circ:** (Wed.)12,320

**Selden/Farmingville Suffolk Life (22932)**
Suffolk Life Newspapers
PO Box 9167
Riverhead, NY 11901
Phone: (631)369-0800
Fax: (631)369-5190
**Subject(s):** Free Newspapers
**Circ:** (Wed.)12,301

**The Valley Gazette (5013)**
Hometown Publications Inc.
1000 Bridgeport Ave.
Shelton, CT 06484
Phone: (203)926-2080
Fax: (203)926-2091
**Subject(s):** Free Newspapers
**Circ:** (Non-paid)♦12,301

**The Wave (20767)**
Wave Publishing Co.
8808 Rockaway Beach Blvd.
PO Box 97
Rockaway Beach, NY 11693
Phone: (718)634-4000
Fax: (718)945-0913
**Subject(s):** Paid Community Newspapers
**Circ:** ‡12,300

**Patchogue Suffolk Life (22684)**
Suffolk Life Newspapers
PO Box 9167
Riverhead, NY 11901
Phone: (631)369-0800
Fax: (631)369-5190
**Subject(s):** Free Newspapers
**Circ:** (Wed.)12,212

**Main Line Life (27719)**
311 E. Lancaster Ave.
Wynnewood, PA 19096
Phone: (610)896-9555
Fax: (610)896-9560
**Subject(s):** Paid Community Newspapers
**Circ:** (Combined)12,158

**County Shopper—Delaware Edition (20699)**
Decker Advertising Inc.
97 Main St., No. 5
Delhi, NY 13753-1234
Phone: (607)746-2178
Fax: (607)746-6272
**Subject(s):** Shopping Guides
**Circ:** (Non-paid)12,041

**American Srbobran (27324)**
Serb National Federation
1 5th Ave.
Pittsburgh, PA 15222
Phone: (412)642-7372
Fax: (412)642-1372
**Subject(s):** Serbian; Unclassified Fraternal; Ethnic Publications
**Circ:** ‡12,000

**Asahi Shimbun (21366)**
845 3rd Ave.
New York, NY 10022
Phone: (212)755-3900
Fax: (212)317-3025
**Subject(s):** Daily Newspapers; Japanese; Ethnic Publications
**Circ:** (Combined)12,000

**Carmel Times (20622)**
Putnam County Press
PO Box 608
Mahopac, NY 10541
Phone: (845)628-8400
Fax: (845)628-8400
**Subject(s):** Paid Community Newspapers
**Circ:** 12,000

**The Catholic Observer (14803)**
Catholic Communications Corp.
65 Elliot St.
PO Box 1730
Springfield, MA 01102-1730
Phone: (413)732-3175
Fax: (413)747-0273
**Subject(s):** Religious Publications
**Circ:** 12,000

**The Gateway (20781)**
Nassau Border Papers Inc.
PO Box 227
Floral Park, NY 11002
Phone: (516)775-7700
**Subject(s):** Paid Community Newspapers
**Circ:** (Free)‡200
(Paid)‡12,000

**The Public Spirit (13757)**
Nashoba Publications Inc.
78 Barnum Rd.
Devens, MA 01434
Phone: (978)772-0777
Fax: (978)772-4012
**Subject(s):** Paid Community Newspapers
**Circ:** 12,000

**Slippery Rock Eagle (27538)**
Eagle Printing Co.
120 Franklin St., No. 1B
Slippery Rock, PA 16057-1101
Phone: (724)794-6797
Fax: (724)794-5694
**Subject(s):** Free Newspapers
**Circ:** (Combined)12,000

**South Pittsburgh Reporter (27404)**
Neighborhood Publications Inc.
PO Box 4285
Pittsburgh, PA 15203-0285
Phone: (412)481-0266
Fax: (412)488-8011
**Subject(s):** Free Newspapers
**Circ:** (Free)12,000

**Town and Village (21244)**
Hagedorn Communications
662 Main St.
New Rochelle, NY 10801
Phone: (914)636-7400
Fax: (914)636-2957
**Subject(s):** Paid Community Newspapers
**Circ:** ‡12,000

**The Independent Olean Press (22897)**
Olean Independent Press
36 River St.
Salamanca, NY 14779-1474
Phone: (716)945-1644
**Subject(s):** Free Newspapers
**Circ:** (Free)‡11,900

---

Circulation: ★ = ABC; △ = BPA; ♦ = CAC; ● = CCAB; ▫ = VAC; ⓟ = PO Statement; ‡ = Publisher's Report; Boldface figures = sworn; Light figures = estimated.

# Northeastern States

**Sidney Pennysaver** (22630)
The Norwich and Sidney Pennysavers Inc.
18-20 Mechanic St.
PO BOX 111
Norwich, NY 13815
Phone: (607)334-4714
Fax: (607)336-7318
**Subject(s):** Shopping Guides
**Circ:** (Non-paid)11,897

**Seneca Falls Pennysaver** (23034)
Scotsman Community Publications
750 W. Genesee St.
PO Box 4970
Syracuse, NY 13221
Phone: (315)472-7825
Fax: (315)478-1434
**Subject(s):** Shopping Guides
**Circ:** (Non-paid)‡11,822

**Footwear News (FN)** (21705)
Fairchild Publications Inc.
7 W 34th St.
New York, NY 10001
Phone: (212)630-4000
Fax: (212)630-3555
**Subject(s):** Shoes, Leather, and Luggage
**Circ:** (Non-paid)3,311
(Paid)11,725

**Geneseeway Shopper** (20694)
113 Main St.
Dansville, NY 14437
Phone: (585)335-2271
Fax: (585)335-6957
**Subject(s):** Shopping Guides
**Circ:** (Free)‡11,700

**Needham Times** (14271)
Suburban World Inc.
992 Great Plain Ave.
PO Box 358
Needham, MA 02492
Fax: (781)444-1795
**Subject(s):** Free Newspapers
**Circ:** (Free)11,700

**Framingham TAB** (13791)
Community Newspaper Co.
254 2nd Ave.
Needham, MA 02494
Phone: (781)433-6700
**Subject(s):** Free Newspapers
**Circ:** (Free)11,680

**The Leader-Herald** (20842)
William B. Collins Co.
8-10 E Fulton St.
Gloversville, NY 12078-3283
Phone: (518)725-8616
Fax: (518)725-8616
**Subject(s):** Daily Newspapers
**Circ:** (Mon.-Sat.)★10,447
(Sun.)★11,632

**Hudson Litchfield News** (18839)
The Bell Twr.
43 Lowell Rd.
Hudson, NH 03051-2480
Phone: (603)880-1516
Fax: (603)879-9707
**Subject(s):** Free Newspapers
**Circ:** (Free)⊕11,600

**The Daily Courier Observer** (21136)
St. Lawrence County Newspapers
PO Box 300
1 Herald Gate Common
Massena, NY 13662
Phone: (315)393-1002
Fax: (315)764-0337
**Subject(s):** Daily Newspapers
**Circ:** ‡11,500

**Bellevue-Geddes Pennysaver** (22997)
Scotsman Community Publications
750 W. Genesee St.
PO Box 4970
Syracuse, NY 13221
Phone: (315)472-7825
Fax: (315)478-1434
**Subject(s):** Shopping Guides
**Circ:** (Non-paid)‡11,487

**Brattleboro Reformer** (30849)
Eagle Publishing
Black Mountain Rd.
PO Box 802
Brattleboro, VT 05301-0802
Phone: (802)254-2311
Fax: (802)257-1305
**Subject(s):** Daily Newspapers
**Circ:** (Mon.-Fri.)★10,003
(Sat.)★11,453

**The Adirondack Journal** (20739)
Denton Publications
14 Hand Ave.
Elizabethtown, NY 12932
Phone: (518)873-6368
Fax: (518)873-6360
**Subject(s):** Paid Community Newspapers
**Circ:** (Paid)168
(Non-paid)11,447

**The Brattleboro Town Crier** (30850)
Brattleboro Town Crier
62 Black Mountain Rd.
Brattleboro, VT 05302-0537
Phone: (802)257-7771
Fax: (802)257-2211
**Subject(s):** Free Newspapers
**Circ:** (Free)11,443

**Far Rockaway Pennysaver** (20765)
Star Community Publishing
250 Miller Pl.
Hicksville, NY 11801
Phone: (516)393-9300
Fax: (516)393-9344
**Subject(s):** Shopping Guides
**Circ:** (Free)11,440

**Main Line Times** (26124)
Acme Newspapers Inc.
311 E. Lancaster Ave.
Ardmore, PA 19003
Phone: (610)642-4300
Fax: (610)642-6911
**Subject(s):** Paid Community Newspapers
**Circ:** (Thurs.)11,433

**Eastern Catholic Life** (19950)
The Byzantine Catholic Diocese
445 Lackawanna Ave.
West Paterson, NJ 07424
Phone: (973)890-7777
Fax: (973)890-7175
**Subject(s):** Religious Publications
**Circ:** (Controlled)‡718
(Paid)‡11,400

**Consumer News** (20687)
PO Box 5548
Cortland, NY 13045
Phone: (607)756-5665
Fax: (607)756-5665
**Subject(s):** Free Newspapers
**Circ:** (Free)‡11,337

**Oceanside Pennysaver** (22639)
Star Community Publishing
250 Miller Pl.
Hicksville, NY 11801
Phone: (516)393-9300
Fax: (516)393-9344
**Subject(s):** Shopping Guides
**Circ:** (Free)11,326

**Milford Reporter** (4854)
Elm City Newspapers
349 New Haven Ave.
PO Box 5339
Milford, CT 06460-6647
Phone: (203)876-6800
Fax: (203)877-4772
**Subject(s):** Free Newspapers
**Circ:** (Free)‡11,300

**Suburban News (South Edition)** (22958)
Westside News
1835 N Union St.
PO Box 106
Spencerport, NY 14559
Phone: (585)352-3411
Fax: (585)352-4811
**Subject(s):** Free Newspapers
**Circ:** (Paid)80
(Non-paid)11,274

**Tri Lakes Free Trader** (20742)
Denton Publications
14 Hand Ave.
Elizabethtown, NY 12932
Phone: (518)873-6368
Fax: (518)873-6360
**Subject(s):** Shopping Guides
**Circ:** (Non-paid)11,267

**The Suffolk Times** (21141)
7785 Main Rd.
PO Box 1500
Mattituck, NY 11952
Phone: (631)298-3200
Fax: (631)298-3287
**Subject(s):** Paid Community Newspapers
**Circ:** (Free)‡441
(Paid)11,236

**The Times-Argus** (30829)
540 N Main St.
PO Box 707
Barre, VT 05641
Phone: (802)479-0191
Fax: (802)479-4032
**Subject(s):** Daily Newspapers
**Circ:** (Mon.-Sat.)★10,343
(Sun.)★11,228

**Cortland Standard** (20688)
Cortland Standard Printing Company Inc.
PO Box 5548
Cortland, NY 13045
Phone: (607)756-5665
Fax: (607)756-5665
**Subject(s):** Daily Newspapers
**Circ:** (Paid)‡11,202

**The Athol/Orange Town Crier** (13809)
The Town Crier Community Newspapers
PO Box 1435
393 Main Street
Greenfield, MA 01302
Phone: (413)774-7226
Fax: (413)774-6809
**Subject(s):** Free Newspapers
**Circ:** (Free)11,166

**Geneva Pennysaver** (23017)
Scotsman Community Publications
750 W. Genesee St.
PO Box 4970
Syracuse, NY 13221
Phone: (315)472-7825
Fax: (315)478-1434
**Subject(s):** Shopping Guides
**Circ:** (Non-paid)‡11,112

**Moriches Suffolk Life** (21223)
Suffolk Life Newspapers
PO Box 9167
Riverhead, NY 11901
Phone: (631)369-0800
Fax: (631)369-5190
**Subject(s):** Free Newspapers
**Circ:** (Wed.)11,100

**The Bayside Times** (20354)
Queens Publishing Corp.
41-02 Bell Blvd., 2nd Fl.
Bayside, NY 11361
Phone: (718)229-0300
Fax: (718)225-7117
**Subject(s):** Paid Community Newspapers
**Circ:** (Paid)11,088

**Bellport/East Patchogue Suffolk Life** (20365)
Suffolk Life Newspapers
PO Box 9167
Riverhead, NY 11901
Phone: (631)369-0800
Fax: (631)369-5190
**Subject(s):** Free Newspapers
**Circ:** (Wed.)11,078

**Teaneck Suburbanite** (19849)
North Jersey Newspapers Co.
50 Piermont Rd., No. J
Cresskill, NJ 07626-2121
Phone: (201)568-6600
Fax: (201)784-0561
**Subject(s):** Free Newspapers
**Circ:** (Non-paid)♦11,069

**East Syracuse/Minoa/Kirkville/Bridgeport Pennysaver  (23012)**
Scotsman Community Publications
750 W. Genesee St.
PO Box 4970
Syracuse, NY 13221
Phone: (315)472-7825
Fax: (315)478-1434
**Subject(s):** Shopping Guides
**Circ:** (Non-paid)‡11,024

**The Boston Jewish Times  (13484)**
15 School St.
Boston, MA 02108-4307
Phone: (617)227-7979
Fax: (617)367-9310
**Subject(s):** Paid Community Newspapers; Jewish Publications
**Circ:** ‡11,000

**Derry News  (18800)**
Derry Publishing Co.
46 W Broadway
PO Box 307
Derry, NH 03038-2329
Phone: (603)437-7000
Fax: (603)432-4510
**Subject(s):** Paid Community Newspapers
**Circ:** ‡11,000

**Home Textiles Today  (21777)**
Reed Business Information
360 Park Ave. S.
New York, NY 10010
Phone: (646)746-6400
Fax: (646)746-6734
**Subject(s):** Textiles
**Circ:** (Controlled)‡11,000

**Warren Times Observer  (27637)**
Central Publishing Co.
205 Pennsylvania Ave. W
PO Box 188
Warren, PA 16365-2412
Phone: (814)723-8200
Fax: (814)723-6922
**Subject(s):** Daily Newspapers
**Circ:** (Mon.-Sat.)★**10,959**

**The Bradford Era  (26194)**
43 Main St.
PO Box 365
Bradford, PA 16701-0365
Phone: (814)368-3173
Fax: (814)362-6510
**Subject(s):** Daily Newspapers
**Circ:** (Mon.-Sat.)10,937

**Allied News  (26415)**
Ottaway Newspapers Inc.
201 Erie St.
Grove City, PA 16127
**Subject(s):** Free Newspapers
**Circ:** (Paid)‡4,152
  (Free)‡10,927

**The Ellsworth American  (12510)**
Ellsworth American Inc.
30 Water St.
PO Box 509
Ellsworth, ME 04605-0509
Phone: (207)667-2576
Fax: (207)667-7656
**Subject(s):** Paid Community Newspapers
**Circ:** (Free)⊕97
  (Paid)⊕**10,884**

**Ocean City Sentinel  (19642)**
112 E 8th St.
PO Box 238
Ocean City, NJ 08226-0238
Phone: (609)399-5411
Fax: (609)399-0416
**Subject(s):** Paid Community Newspapers
**Circ:** 10,888

**Tonawanda News  (22625)**
435 River Rd.
North Tonawanda, NY 14120-6809
Phone: (716)693-1000
Fax: (716)693-0124
**Subject(s):** Daily Newspapers
**Circ:** (Mon.-Sat.)★**10,862**

**The Bristol Press  (4645)**
99 Main St.
Bristol, CT 06010-6579
Phone: (203)584-0501
Fax: (203)584-2192
**Subject(s):** Daily Newspapers
**Circ:** (Mon.-Sat.)★**10,852**

**Journal Tribune  (12473)**
Journal Publishing Corp.
PO Box 627
Biddeford, ME 04005
Phone: (207)282-1535
Fax: (207)282-3138
**Subject(s):** Daily Newspapers
**Circ:** (Mon.-Fri.)9,148
  (Sat.)10,827

**Needham TAB  (14270)**
Community Newspaper Co.
254 2nd Ave.
Needham, MA 02494
Phone: (781)433-6700
**Subject(s):** Free Newspapers
**Circ:** (Free)10,811

**The Spirit Extra  (27462)**
Spirit Publishing Co.
510 Pine St.
PO Box 444
Punxsutawney, PA 15767-0444
Phone: (814)938-8740
Fax: (814)938-3794
**Subject(s):** Free Newspapers
**Circ:** (Paid)3,188
  (Free)10,769

**Steuben Courier-Advocate  (20342)**
10 W Stueben St.
Bath, NY 14810
Phone: (607)776-2121
Fax: (607)776-3967
**Subject(s):** Free Newspapers
**Circ:** (Free)10,760

**Court-Butternut Pennysaver  (23009)**
Scotsman Community Publications
750 W. Genesee St.
PO Box 4970
Syracuse, NY 13221
Phone: (315)472-7825
Fax: (315)478-1434
**Subject(s):** Shopping Guides
**Circ:** (Non-paid)‡10,705

**The Inquirer and Mirror  (14252)**
The Inquirer and Mirror Inc.
1 Old S. Rd.
PO Box 1198
Nantucket, MA 02554-1198
Phone: (508)228-0001
Fax: (508)325-5089
**Subject(s):** Paid Community Newspapers
**Circ:** (Non-paid)187
  (Paid)10,609

**Lewiston-Porter Sentinel  (20849)**
Niagara Frontier Publications
1859 Whitehaven Rd.
PO Box 130
Grand Island, NY 14072-0130
Phone: (716)773-7676
Fax: (716)773-7190
**Subject(s):** Free Newspapers
**Circ:** (Free)10,600

**The Register Citizen  (5058)**
Journal Register Inc.
190 Water St.
PO Box 58
Torrington, CT 06790
Phone: (860)489-3121
Fax: (860)489-6790
**Subject(s):** Daily Newspapers
**Circ:** (Sun.)9,820
  (Mon.-Sat.)10,581

**News-Item  (27525)**
The News-Item
707 N. Rock St.
Shamokin, PA 17872
Phone: (570)644-6397
Fax: (570)644-0892
**Subject(s):** Daily Newspapers
**Circ:** (Mon.-Sat.)★**10,569**

**East Aurora Bee  (23189)**
Bee Group Newspapers
5564 Main St.
PO Box 150
Williamsville, NY 14231-0150
Phone: (716)632-4700
Fax: (716)633-8601
**Subject(s):** Free Newspapers
**Circ:** (Non-paid)5
  (Paid)10,530

**Hewlett/Woodmere Pennysaver  (20893)**
Star Community Publishing
250 Miller Pl.
Hicksville, NY 11801
Phone: (516)393-9300
Fax: (516)393-9344
**Subject(s):** Shopping Guides
**Circ:** (Free)10,536

**Port Byron Shopping Guide  (22717)**
Port Byron Shopping Press Inc.
97 Main St.
Port Byron, NY 13140
Phone: (315)776-5512
**Subject(s):** Shopping Guides
**Circ:** (Free)‡10,523

**Long Island Advance  (22683)**
20 Medford Ave.
Patchogue, NY 11772
Phone: (631)475-1000
Fax: (631)475-1565
**Subject(s):** Paid Community Newspapers
**Circ:** 10,500

**Floor Covering Weekly  (23085)**
FCW Div.
50 Charles Lindbergh Blvd.
Ste. 100
Uniondale, NY 11553
Phone: (516)229-3600
Fax: (516)227-1342
**Subject(s):** Flooring and Floor Covering
**Circ:** (Non-paid)8,304
  (Paid)10,470

**The Recorder  (20281)**
PO Box 640
1 Venner Rd
Amsterdam, NY 12010-0640
Phone: (518)843-1100
Fax: (518)843-1338
**Subject(s):** Daily Newspapers
**Circ:** (Mon.-Sat.)10,124
  (Sun.)10,369

**Sun & Erie County Independent  (20871)**
H & K Publications Inc.
50 Buffalo St.
Hamburg, NY 14075-5002
Phone: (716)649-4413
Fax: (716)649-6374
**Subject(s):** Paid Community Newspapers
**Circ:** ‡10,349

**East Boston Sun Transcript  (14766)**
Independent Newspaper Group
385 Broadway, Ste. 105
Revere, MA 02151
Phone: (781)284-2400
Fax: (781)485-1403
**Subject(s):** Free Newspapers
**Circ:** (Non-paid)10,300

**The Mountain Times  (30891)**
BRD Corp.
PO Box 183
Killington, VT 05751
Phone: (802)422-2399
Fax: (802)422-2395
**Subject(s):** Travel and Tourism; Local, State, and Regional Publications; Free Newspapers; Free Newspapers
**Circ:** (Paid)‡300
  (Free)‡10,300

**Rockville Centre Pennysaver  (22867)**
Star Community Publishing
250 Miller Pl.
Hicksville, NY 11801
Phone: (516)393-9300
Fax: (516)393-9344
**Subject(s):** Shopping Guides
**Circ:** (Free)10,280

Circulation: ★ = ABC; △ = BPA; ♦ = CAC; ♦ = CCAB; ▫ = VAC; ⊕ = PO Statement; ‡ = Publisher's Report; Boldface figures = sworn; Light figures = estimated.

**Northeastern States**

**North Country This Week (22734)**
PO Box 975
Potsdam, NY 13676
Phone: (315)265-1000
Fax: (315)268-8701
**Subject(s):** Free Newspapers
**Circ:** (Paid)12
(Non-paid)10,277

**Passaic Valley Today (19957)**
North Jersey Community Newspapers
1 Garret Mountain Plaza
PO Box 471
West Paterson, NJ 07424-0471
Phone: (973)569-7393
Fax: (973)569-7377
**Subject(s):** Free Newspapers
**Circ:** (Non-paid)10,263

**The Daily Review (27581)**
Towanda Printing Co.
116 Main St.
Towanda, PA 18848
Phone: (570)265-2151
Fax: (570)265-0613
**Subject(s):** Daily Newspapers
**Circ:** (Mon.-Sat.)♦9,127
(Sun.)♦10,241

**Bay Ridge Courier (20492)**
Courier Life Publications
1733 Sheepshead Bay Rd.
Brooklyn, NY 11235-3606
Phone: (718)615-2500
Fax: (718)615-3835
**Subject(s):** Paid Community Newspapers
**Circ:** 10,225

**The Daily News (26520)**
Joseph F. Biddle Publishing Co.
325 Penn St.
Huntingdon, PA 16652
Phone: (814)643-4040
Fax: (814)643-0376
**Subject(s):** Daily Newspapers
**Circ:** ‡10,227

**Bedford Daily Gazette (26148)**
Bedford Gazette
424 W. Penn St.
Bedford, PA 15522
Phone: (814)623-1151
Fax: (814)623-5055
**Subject(s):** Daily Newspapers
**Circ:** ‡10,200

**Press Journal/Valley Star (19072)**
Bergen News Publishing Co.
PO Box 631
Englewood, NJ 07631
Phone: (201)871-6900
Fax: (201)947-5055
**Subject(s):** Paid Community Newspapers
**Circ:** ‡10,160

**Canarsie Digest (20498)**
Courier Life Publications
1733 Sheepshead Bay Rd.
Brooklyn, NY 11235-3606
Phone: (718)615-2500
Fax: (718)615-3835
**Subject(s):** Paid Community Newspapers
**Circ:** 10,135

**Niagara-Wheatfield Tribune (20850)**
Niagara Frontier Publications
1859 Whitehaven Rd.
PO Box 130
Grand Island, NY 14072-0130
Phone: (716)773-7676
Fax: (716)773-7190
**Subject(s):** Free Newspapers
**Circ:** (Paid)10,100

**Caledonian-Record (30935)**
Caledonian-Record Publishing Company Inc.
25 Federal St.
Saint Johnsbury, VT 05819
**Subject(s):** Daily Newspapers
**Circ:** (Mon.-Sat.)★10,094

**National Mortgage News (22128)**
Thomson Financial
195 Broadway
New York, NY 10007
Phone: (646)822-2000
Fax: (646)822-3230
**Subject(s):** Banking, Finance, and Investments
**Circ:** (Paid)10,097

**The Bourne Enterprise (13622)**
Falmouth Publishing Co.
50 Depot Ave.
Falmouth, MA 02540
Phone: (508)548-4700
Fax: (508)540-8407
**Subject(s):** Free Newspapers
**Circ:** (Paid)10,087

**North County News (23211)**
Northern Tier Publishing Corp.
1520 Front St.
Yorktown Heights, NY 10598
Phone: (914)962-4748
Fax: (914)962-6763
**Subject(s):** Paid Community Newspapers
**Circ:** 10,086

**Daily Times Chronicle (14921)**
Woburn Daily Times Inc.
1 Arrow Dr.
Woburn, MA 01801
Phone: (781)933-3700
Fax: (781)932-3321
**Subject(s):** Daily Newspapers
**Circ:** (Non-paid)354
(Paid)10,077

**The Motorcyclist's Post (4828)**
11 Haven Ln.
Huntington, CT 06484
Phone: (203)929-9409
Fax: (203)926-9347
**Subject(s):** Motorbikes and Motorcycles
**Circ:** ‡10,060

**Moravia Pennysaver (23024)**
Scotsman Community Publications
750 W. Genesee St.
PO Box 4970
Syracuse, NY 13221
Phone: (315)472-7825
Fax: (315)478-1434
**Subject(s):** Shopping Guides
**Circ:** (Non-paid)‡10,053

**Today's Sunbeam (19780)**
Salem Newspapers Inc.
93 5th St.
Salem, NJ 08079
Phone: (609)935-1500
Fax: (609)845-3139
**Subject(s):** Daily Newspapers
**Circ:** (Sat.)★8,718
(Sun.)★9,677
(Mon.-Fri.)★10,011

**Bronx Press Blue (20445)**
Metro North Media
6050 Riverdale Ave.
Bronx, NY 10471
Phone: (718)543-5200
Fax: (718)543-4206
**Subject(s):** Paid Community Newspapers
**Circ:** (Non-paid)10,000

**Bronx Press Gold (20446)**
Metro North Media
6050 Riverdale Ave.
Bronx, NY 10471
Phone: (718)543-5200
Fax: (718)543-4206
**Subject(s):** Paid Community Newspapers
**Circ:** (Non-paid)10,000

**Bronx Press Red (20447)**
Metro North Media
6050 Riverdale Ave.
Bronx, NY 10471
Phone: (718)543-5200
Fax: (718)543-4206
**Subject(s):** Paid Community Newspapers
**Circ:** (Non-paid)10,000

**Business Strategies (22809)**
Business Strategies Inc.
1240 Jefferson Rd.
Rochester, NY 14623-3104
Phone: (585)292-0171
Fax: (585)292-0389
**Subject(s):** Business
**Circ:** (Paid)‡10,000

**Cedarhurst Pennysaver (20630)**
Star Community Publishing
250 Miller Pl.
Hicksville, NY 11801
Phone: (516)393-9300
Fax: (516)393-9344
**Subject(s):** Shopping Guides
**Circ:** (Free)10,000

**The Challenger (20563)**
Challenger Publishing Inc.
108 Sycamore St.
Buffalo, NY 14204-1414
Phone: (716)897-0442
Fax: (716)897-3307
**Subject(s):** Black Publications; Paid Community Newspapers
**Circ:** ‡10,000

**Columbia Daily Spectator (21511)**
Columbia University/Spectator Publishing Co.
2875 Broadway, 3rd Fl.
New York, NY 10025
Phone: (212)854-9555
Fax: (212)854-9553
**Subject(s):** College Publications
**Circ:** (Paid)‡250
(Free)‡9,750
(Combined)10,000

**The Cornell Daily Sun (20945)**
The Cornell Daily Sun Inc.
139 W. State St.
Ithaca, NY 14850
Phone: (607)273-3606
Fax: (607)273-0746
**Subject(s):** College Publications
**Circ:** ‡10,000

**The Daily Campus (5044)**
University of Connecticut
11 Dog Ln.
Storrs, CT 06268
Phone: (860)486-3407
Fax: (860)486-4388
**Subject(s):** College Publications
**Circ:** (Combined)‡10,000

**East Providence Post (27845)**
Post and Star Publishing Co.
1027 Waterman Ave.
East Providence, RI 02914
Phone: (401)434-7210
Fax: (401)434-9469
**Subject(s):** Paid Community Newspapers
**Circ:** 10,000

**The Food Industry Advisor (26216)**
Pennsylvania Food Merchants Association
1029 Mumma Rd.
PO Box 870
Camp Hill, PA 17001-0870
Phone: (717)731-0600
Fax: (717)703-3140
**Subject(s):** Food and Grocery Trade
**Circ:** (Non-paid)1,000
(Paid)10,000

**Glendale Register (20838)**
Midnight Publishing Corp.
55-51 69th St.
PO Box 780376
Maspeth, NY 11378
Phone: (718)639-7000
Fax: (718)429-1234
**Subject(s):** Paid Community Newspapers
**Circ:** 10,000

**Harvard Crimson (13666)**
Harvard Crimson Inc.
14 Plympton St.
Cambridge, MA 02138
Phone: (617)576-6565
Fax: (617)576-7860
**Subject(s):** College Publications
**Circ:** ‡10,000

**The Heights  (13728)**
Boston College
McElroy Commons, No. 113
140 Commonwealth Ave.
Chestnut Hill, MA 02467
Phone: (617)552-2221
Fax: (617)552-4823
**Subject(s):** College Publications

**Circ:** (Free)10,000

**Illinois Valley Peach  (23064)**
Marshall County Publishing Co.
PO Box 2001
Tarrytown, NY 10591
Phone: (914)332-8888
Fax: (914)332-1082
**Subject(s):** Shopping Guides

**Circ:** (Free)⊕**10,000**

**Juniata News  (27113)**
2241 N 5th St.
Philadelphia, PA 19133
Phone: (215)739-8197
Fax: (215)739-9290
**Subject(s):** Free Newspapers

**Circ:** (Free)‡10,000

**Kingsman  (20523)**
Brooklyn College
2900 Bedford Ave.
Brooklyn, NY 11210
Phone: (718)951-5001
**Subject(s):** College Publications

**Circ:** 10,000

**Merrimack Journal  (18890)**
The Cabinet Press Inc.
54 School St.
PO Box 180
Milford, NH 03055-0180
Phone: (603)673-3100
Fax: (603)673-8250
**Subject(s):** Paid Community Newspapers

**Circ:** (Non-paid)10,000

**Newbury Street and Back Bay Guide  (13563)**
Jacaranda Publishing Inc.
143 Newbury St., 6th Fl.
Boston, MA 02116-2925
Phone: (617)424-9005
Fax: (617)262-5333
**Subject(s):** Paid Community Newspapers; Travel and Tourism

**Circ:** (Combined)10,000

**Night Call  (20529)**
Brooklyn College
2900 Bedford Ave.
Brooklyn, NY 11210
Phone: (718)951-5001
**Subject(s):** College Publications

**Circ:** (Free)‡10,000

**The Northeastern News  (13565)**
Northeastern University
360 Huntington Ave.
Boston, MA 02115
Phone: (617)373-2000
Fax: (617)373-3768
**Subject(s):** College Publications

**Circ:** (Free)‡10,000

**Polish American World  (20332)**
3100 Grand Blvd.
Baldwin, NY 11510
Phone: (516)223-6514
Fax: (516)868-6618
**Subject(s):** Ethnic Publications

**Circ:** (Free)‡5,550
       (Paid)‡10,000

**The Spectrum  (20580)**
Spectrum Student Periodical Inc.
State University of New York at Buffalo
Student Union, Ste. 132
Buffalo, NY 14260
Phone: (716)645-2468
Fax: (716)645-2766
**Subject(s):** College Publications

**Circ:** (Free)‡10,000

**Spring Creek Sun  (20541)**
1540 Van Siclen Ave.
Brooklyn, NY 11239
Phone: (718)642-2718

Fax: (718)240-4599
**Subject(s):** Free Newspapers

**Circ:** (Non-paid)10,000

**The Steuben News  (22793)**
National Council of the Steuben Society of America
67-05 Fresh Pond Rd.
Ridgewood, NY 11385
Phone: (718)381-0900
Fax: (718)628-4874
**Subject(s):** Paid Community Newspapers

**Circ:** (Controlled)‡10,000

**Voices of Central Pennsylvania  (27554)**
103 E.Beaver Ave., Ste. 11
State College, PA 16801
Phone: (814)234-1699
**Subject(s):** Paid Community Newspapers

**Circ:** (Non-paid)‡10,000

**The Washington Square News  (22529)**
New York University
7 E 12th St., Ste. 800
New York, NY 10003
Phone: (212)998-4300
Fax: (212)995-3790
**Subject(s):** College Publications

**Circ:** (Free)‡10,000

**Putnam Courier Trader  (4981)**
Housatonic Publications
65 Bank St.
New Milford, CT 06776
Fax: (860)354-2645
**Subject(s):** Free Newspapers

**Circ:** (Paid)1,326
       (Non-paid)9,994

**Traders Guide  (26311)**
Traders Guide Inc.
118 Ebony Rd., Ste. 102
PO Box 30
Ebensburg, PA 15931-0030
Phone: (814)472-8600
Fax: (814)472-9292
**Subject(s):** Shopping Guides

**Circ:** (Paid)9,980

**The Westerly Sun  (27954)**
The Utter Co.
PO Box 520
Westerly, RI 02891-0520
Phone: (401)596-7791
Fax: (401)348-5080
**Subject(s):** Daily Newspapers

**Circ:** (Mon.-Sat.)★**9,421**
       (Sun.)★**9,978**

**Cortland Sunday /Democrat  (23007)**
Scotsman Community Publications
750 W. Genesee St.
PO Box 4970
Syracuse, NY 13221
Phone: (315)472-7825
Fax: (315)478-1434
**Subject(s):** Paid Community Newspapers

**Circ:** ‡9,965

**Press & Journal  (26706)**
Press & Journal Publication
20 S. Union St.
PO Box 310
Middletown, PA 17057
Phone: (717)944-4628
Fax: (717)944-2083
**Subject(s):** Paid Community Newspapers

**Circ:** ‡9,900

**Springville PennySaver  (22961)**
H & K Publications Inc.
49 E. Main St.
Springville, NY 14141
Phone: (716)592-2818
Fax: (716)592-3948
**Subject(s):** Shopping Guides

**Circ:** (Non-paid)9,900

**The Potter Leader Enterprise  (26269)**
Leader Publishing Company Inc.
6 W 2nd St.
PO Box 29
Coudersport, PA 16915
Phone: (814)274-8044
Fax: (814)274-8120

**Subject(s):** Paid Community Newspapers

**Circ:** (Free)‡225
       (Paid)‡9,800

**Princeton Weekly Bulletin  (19735)**
Princeton University
22 Chambers St., Ste. 201
Princeton, NJ 08542
Phone: (609)258-3601
Fax: (609)258-1301
**Subject(s):** College Publications

**Circ:** (Paid)4,403
       (Non-paid)9,800

**Gettysburg Times  (26391)**
Times & News Publishing Co.
1570 Fairfield Rd.
PO Box 3669
Gettysburg, PA 17325
Phone: (717)334-1131
Fax: (717)334-4243
**Subject(s):** Daily Newspapers

**Circ:** (Mon.-Sat.)9,775

**Ocean County Observer  (19879)**
Ocean County Newspapers Inc.
8 Robbins St.
Toms River, NJ 08753
Phone: (732)349-3000
Fax: (732)557-5658
**Subject(s):** Daily Newspapers

**Circ:** (Sun.)9,405
       (Mon.-Fri.)9,757

**Bridgeport News  (4635)**
Hometown Publications Inc.
1000 Bridgeport Ave.
Shelton, CT 06484
Phone: (203)926-2080
Fax: (203)926-2091
**Subject(s):** Paid Community Newspapers

**Circ:** (Non-paid)♦**9,718**

**Times-Free Press  (14735)**
Nashoba Publications Inc.
78 Barnum Rd.
Devens, MA 01434
Phone: (978)772-0777
Fax: (978)772-4012
**Subject(s):** Paid Community Newspapers

**Circ:** 9,700

**Business First of Buffalo  (20562)**
American City Business Journals Inc.
c/o Jeff Wright
465 Main St.
Buffalo, NY 14203-1793
Phone: (716)854-3394
Fax: (716)854-3394
**Subject(s):** Local, State, and Regional Publications; Business

**Circ:** (Paid)9,696

**St. James/Nesconset Suffolk Life  (22896)**
Suffolk Life Newspapers
PO Box 9167
Riverhead, NY 11901
Phone: (631)369-0800
Fax: (631)369-5190
**Subject(s):** Free Newspapers

**Circ:** (Wed.)9,694

**The Daily Courier  (26258)**
127 N Apple St.
Connellsville, PA 15425-3196
Phone: (724)628-2000
Fax: (724)626-3568
**Subject(s):** Daily Newspapers

**Circ:** (Mon.-Sat.)9,686

**Times Chronicle  (26384)**
Journal Register Co.
c/o Sean Smith
290 Commerce Dr.
Fort Washington, PA 19034
Phone: (215)542-0200
**Subject(s):** Paid Community Newspapers

**Circ:** (Combined)9,645

**Woburn Advocate  (13747)**
Community Newspaper Co./Northwest
150 Baker Ave., Ste. 305
PO Box 9191
Concord, MA 01742-9191
Phone: (978)371-5754
Fax: (978)371-5220

Circulation: ★ = ABC; △ = BPA; ♦ = CAC; ● = CCAB; ❑ = VAC; ⊕ = PO Statement; ‡ = Publisher's Report; Boldface figures = sworn; Light figures = estimated.

## Northeastern States

**Subject(s):** Paid Community Newspapers

**Circ:** (Paid)75
(Non-paid)9,624

**The Bulletin** (4851)
Elm City Newspapers
349 New Haven Ave.
PO Box 5339
Milford, CT 06460-6647
Phone: (203)876-6800
Fax: (203)877-4772
**Subject(s):** Free Newspapers

**Circ:** (Free)‡9,600

**Syracuse East Pennysaver** (23040)
Scotsman Community Publications
750 W. Genesee St.
PO Box 4970
Syracuse, NY 13221
Phone: (315)472-7825
Fax: (315)478-1434
**Subject(s):** Shopping Guides

**Circ:** (Non-paid)‡9,595

**Shore Line Times** (4787)
Shore Line Newspapers
1100 Boston Post Rd.
PO Box 349
Guilford, CT 06437
Phone: (203)453-2711
Fax: (203)453-4152
**Subject(s):** Paid Community Newspapers

**Circ:** (Wed.)‡9,548
(Fri.)‡9,548

**The Evening Tribune** (20908)
American Publishing Co.
85 Canisteo St.
Hornell, NY 14843
Phone: (607)324-1425
Fax: (607)324-9485
**Subject(s):** Daily Newspapers

**Circ:** (Paid)‡9,500

**The Front Page** (21012)
Front Page Group Inc.
2703 S Park Ave.
Lackawanna, NY 14218
Phone: (716)823-8222
Fax: (716)821-0550
**Subject(s):** Paid Community Newspapers

**Circ:** (Combined)‡9,500

**Jersey Journeys** (19616)
The New Jersey Historical Society
52 Park Pl.
Newark, NJ 07102
Phone: (973)596-8500
Fax: (973)596-6957
**Subject(s):** Children's Interests; History and Genealogy

**Circ:** 9,500

**Nassau Herald** (21057)
Richner Communications
P.O. Box 9001
Lawrence, NY 11559-1616
Phone: (516)569-4000
Fax: (516)569-4942
**Subject(s):** Paid Community Newspapers

**Circ:** (Free)‡1,144
(Paid)‡9,505

**The Post** (19976)
Burlington County Times
4284 Rte. 130
Willingboro, NJ 08046
Phone: (609)871-8000
Fax: (609)877-2706
**Subject(s):** Free Newspapers; Military and Navy

**Circ:** (Non-paid)♦9,455

**Pennywise/Villager** (23030)
Scotsman Community Publications
750 W. Genesee St.
PO Box 4970
Syracuse, NY 13221
Phone: (315)472-7825
Fax: (315)478-1434
**Subject(s):** Free Newspapers

**Circ:** (Non-paid)‡9,311

**The Bellows Falls Town Crier** (30835)
Bellows Falls Town Crier
4 Atkinson St.
Bellows Falls, VT 05101
Phone: (802)463-9591
Fax: (802)463-9818
**Subject(s):** Free Newspapers

**Circ:** (Free)9,301

**Mid-York Weekly** (20875)
Mid York Weekly Pennysaver Inc.
55 Utica St.
Hamilton, NY 13346
Phone: (315)824-4220
Fax: (315)824-4220
**Subject(s):** Paid Community Newspapers

**Circ:** (Combined)9,300

**Warsaw Penny Saver** (23121)
72 N Main St.
Warsaw, NY 14569
Phone: (585)786-8161
Fax: (585)786-5159
**Subject(s):** Free Newspapers; Shopping Guides

**Circ:** (Non-paid)9,301

**Airtides** (19974)
Burlington County Times
4284 Rte. 130
Willingboro, NJ 08046
Phone: (609)871-8000
Fax: (609)877-2706
**Subject(s):** Free Newspapers; Military and Navy

**Circ:** (Non-paid)♦9,267

**The Fort Dix Post** (19097)
Fort Dix Public Affairs Office
AFRC-FA-PA-CI
Bldg. 5407 Pennsylvania Ave.
Fort Dix, NJ 08640-5075
Phone: (609)562-5037
Fax: (609)562-3337
**Subject(s):** Free Newspapers

**Circ:** (Free)9,263

**The Ephrata Review** (26337)
Lancaster County Weeklies Inc.
1 E Main St.
PO Box 527
Ephrata, PA 17522-0527
Phone: (717)733-6397
Fax: (717)733-6058
**Subject(s):** Paid Community Newspapers

**Circ:** ‡9,246

**The Landmark** (13823)
PO Box 546
Holden, MA 01520
Phone: (508)829-5981
Fax: (508)829-5984
**Subject(s):** Paid Community Newspapers

**Circ:** ⊕9,244

**The Record Northport** (20929)
Long Islander Newspapers Inc.
322 Main St.
Huntington, NY 11743
Phone: (631)427-7000
Fax: (631)427-5820
**Subject(s):** Paid Community Newspapers

**Circ:** ‡9,222

**The Glastonbury Citizen** (4771)
The Glastonbury Citizen Inc.
PO Box 373
87 Nutmeg Ln.
Glastonbury, CT 06033
Phone: (860)633-4691
Fax: (860)657-3258
**Subject(s):** Paid Community Newspapers

**Circ:** (Combined)‡9,200

**The Village Times** (20732)
Times Beacon Record Newspapers
Box 707
Setauket, NY 11733
Phone: (631)751-7744
Fax: (631)751-4165
**Subject(s):** Paid Community Newspapers

**Circ:** ‡9,188

**Chelsea Clinton News** (21476)
News Communications
63 W 38th St., Ste. 206
New York, NY 10018-3818
Phone: (212)268-8600
**Subject(s):** Paid Community Newspapers

**Circ:** ‡9,162

**The Courier-Publications** (12590)
Courier-Gazette Inc.
301 Park St.
PO Box 249
Rockland, ME 04841-0249
Phone: (207)594-4401
Fax: (207)596-6981
**Subject(s):** Paid Community Newspapers

**Circ:** 9,129

**Upper Dauphin Sentinel** (26711)
510 Union St.
Millersburg, PA 17061
Phone: (717)692-4737
Fax: (717)692-2420
**Subject(s):** Paid Community Newspapers

**Circ:** (Free)2,000
(Paid)9,129

**West Hartford News** (4648)
Imprint Newspapers
99 Main St.
Bristol, CT 06010
Phone: (860)236-3571
Fax: (860)233-2080
**Subject(s):** Paid Community Newspapers

**Circ:** (Non-paid)270
(Paid)9,122

**Town Times** (5077)
Prime Publishers Inc.
Heminway Center
469 Main St.
PO Box 1
Watertown, CT 06795
Phone: (860)274-8851
Fax: (860)945-3116
**Subject(s):** Paid Community Newspapers

**Circ:** (Paid)260
(Non-paid)9,119

**Eagle Times** (18776)
Eagle Publications Inc.
401 River Rd.
Claremont, NH 03743-9308
Phone: (603)543-3100
Fax: (603)542-9705
**Subject(s):** Daily Newspapers

**Circ:** (Mon.-Fri.)8,691
(Sun.)9,096

**The Palladium-Times** (22670)
140 W. 1st St.
Oswego, NY 13126
Phone: (315)343-3800
Fax: (315)343-0273
**Subject(s):** Daily Newspapers

**Circ:** (Mon.-Sat.)9,049

**The Chronicle** (21217)
Straus Newspapers
45 Gilbert St.
Monroe, NY 10950
Phone: (845)782-4000
Fax: (845)782-1711
**Subject(s):** Free Newspapers

**Circ:** (Non-paid)9,000

**The Civil War News** (30947)
Historical Publications Inc.
234 Monarch Hill Rd.
Tunbridge, VT 05077
Phone: (802)889-3500
Fax: (802)889-5627
**Subject(s):** History and Genealogy; Military and Navy

**Circ:** (Free)400
(Paid)9,000

**Country Folks** (22912)
Country Folks of Pennsylvania
141 Ulster Ave.
Saugerties, NY 12477
Fax: (914)246-5108
**Subject(s):** Farm Newspapers

**Circ:** (Combined)9,000

**The Daily Orange** (23010)
The Daily Orange Corp.
744 Ostrom Ave.
Syracuse, NY 13210
Phone: (315)443-2314
Fax: (315)443-3689
**Subject(s):** College Publications
**Circ:** (Free)9,000

**The Independent** (20904)
PO Box 360
Hillsdale, NY 12529
Phone: (518)325-4400
Fax: (518)325-4497
**Subject(s):** Paid Community Newspapers
**Circ:** (Tues.)8,500
(Fri.)9,000

**The MAILeader** (21086)
Nassau Community Newspaper Group
42 Broadway, Ste. 202
Lynbrook, NY 11563
Fax: (516)599-3535
**Subject(s):** Paid Community Newspapers
**Circ:** ‡9,000

**Monroe Woodbury Photo News** (23198)
Straus Newspapers
45 Gilbert St.
Monroe, NY 10950
Phone: (845)782-4000
Fax: (845)782-1711
**Subject(s):** Paid Community Newspapers
**Circ:** (Free)9,000

**The Older American** (13568)
Massachusetts Association of Older Americans
105 Chauncy St.
Boston, MA 02111
Phone: (617)426-0804
Fax: (617)426-0070
**Subject(s):** Senior Citizens' Interests
**Circ:** (Controlled)‡3,000
(Paid)‡9,000

**The Warwick Advertiser** (21218)
Straus Newspapers
45 Gilbert St.
Monroe, NY 10950
Phone: (845)782-4000
Fax: (845)782-1711
**Subject(s):** Paid Community Newspapers
**Circ:** (Free)⊕**9,000**

**The Westsider** (22534)
News Communications
63 W 38th St., Ste. 206
New York, NY 10018-3818
Phone: (212)268-8600
**Subject(s):** Paid Community Newspapers
**Circ:** (Free)3,000
(Paid)8,983

**Westport News** (4968)
Brooks Community Newspapers Inc.
542 Westport Ave.
Norwalk, CT 06851
Phone: (203)849-1600
Fax: (203)840-4844
**Subject(s):** Paid Community Newspapers
**Circ:** (Paid)8,953

**Home Reporter & Sunset News** (20512)
Home Reporter Inc.
8723 3rd Ave.
Brooklyn, NY 11209
Phone: (718)238-6600
Fax: (718)238-6630
**Subject(s):** Paid Community Newspapers
**Circ:** ‡8,941

**The Bernardsville News** (18980)
Recorder Publishing Company Inc.
17-19 Morristown Rd.
Bernardsville, NJ 07924-2312
**Subject(s):** Paid Community Newspapers
**Circ:** (Combined)8,880

**Hall of Fame Pennysaver** (20674)
Snyder Communications Corp.
42 Lake St.
PO Box 671
Richfield Springs, NY 13439
Phone: (315)858-1730
Fax: (607)431-2519

**Subject(s):** Shopping Guides
**Circ:** (Paid)7
(Non-paid)8,848

**Kampana–Campana** (21077)
30-96 42nd St.
Long Island City, NY 11103-3031
Phone: (718)278-3014
Fax: (718)278-3023
**Subject(s):** Greek; Paid Community Newspapers; Ethnic Publications
**Circ:** ‡8,800

**Vermont-NEA Today** (30907)
Vermont National Education Association
10 Wheelock St.
Montpelier, VT 05602
Phone: (802)223-6375
Fax: (802)223-1253
**Subject(s):** Education
**Circ:** ‡8,800

**Record Herald** (27658)
PO Box 271
30 Walnut St.
Waynesboro, PA 17268-2156
Phone: (717)762-2151
Fax: (717)762-3824
**Subject(s):** Daily Newspapers
**Circ:** (Mon.-Sat.)8,789

**Church Acts of Western New York** (20565)
Episcopal Diocese of Western N.Y.
1114 Delaware Ave.
Buffalo, NY 14209-1604
Phone: (716)881-0660
Fax: (716)881-1724
**Subject(s):** Religious Publications
**Circ:** (Free)‡8,750

**Observer** (22947)
The Smithtown News Inc.
1 Brooksite Dr.
Smithtown, NY 11787-3454
Phone: (631)265-2100
Fax: (631)265-6237
**Subject(s):** Paid Community Newspapers
**Circ:** 8,750

**The Current** (19206)
Hudson Reporter Associates
1400 Washington St.
PO Box 3069
Hoboken, NJ 07030-1601
Phone: (201)798-7800
Fax: (201)798-0018
**Subject(s):** Free Newspapers
**Circ:** (Free)8,700

**The Franklin Square Bulletin** (20792)
Nassau Border Papers Inc.
PO Box 155
Franklin Square, NY 11010
Phone: (516)775-7700
**Subject(s):** Paid Community Newspapers
**Circ:** (Free)‡200
(Paid)‡8,700

**Chestnut Hill Local** (26862)
Chestnut Hill Community Association
8434 Germantown Ave.
Philadelphia, PA 19118
Phone: (215)248-8800
Fax: (215)248-8814
**Circ:** (Free)‡402
(Paid)‡8,698

**Eastwood Pennysaver** (23013)
Scotsman Community Publications
750 W. Genesee St.
PO Box 4970
Syracuse, NY 13221
Phone: (315)472-7825
Fax: (315)478-1434
**Subject(s):** Shopping Guides
**Circ:** (Non-paid)‡8,655

**West Haven News** (4856)
Elm City Newspapers
349 New Haven Ave.
PO Box 5339
Milford, CT 06460-6647
Phone: (203)876-6800
Fax: (203)877-4772

**Subject(s):** Paid Community Newspapers
**Circ:** (Paid)‡550
(Free)‡8,600

**Souderton Independent** (27543)
Journal Register Co.
673 E. Broad St.
PO Box 64459
Souderton, PA 18964
Phone: (215)723-4801
Fax: (215)723-8779
**Subject(s):** Paid Community Newspapers
**Circ:** (Combined)8,592

**Suburban News West** (22959)
Westside News
1835 N Union St.
PO Box 106
Spencerport, NY 14559
Phone: (585)352-3411
Fax: (585)352-4811
**Subject(s):** Free Newspapers
**Circ:** (Non-paid)8,590

**North Area Pennysaver** (23026)
Scotsman Community Publications
750 W. Genesee St.
PO Box 4970
Syracuse, NY 13221
Phone: (315)472-7825
Fax: (315)478-1434
**Subject(s):** Shopping Guides
**Circ:** (Non-paid)‡8,583

**Beacon Free Press** (23118)
84 E Main St.
Wappingers Falls, NY 12590
Phone: (845)297-3723
Fax: (845)297-6810
**Subject(s):** Free Newspapers
**Circ:** (Paid)‡247
(Free)‡8,550

**Erie Daily Times** (26347)
Erie Times News
205 W. 12th St.
Erie, PA 16534
Phone: (814)870-1600
**Subject(s):** Daily Newspapers
**Circ:** (Mon.-Fri.)8,513

**Brooklyn Record** (20496)
Brooklyn Eagle Publications
30 Henry St.
Brooklyn, NY 11201-3504
Phone: (718)858-2300
Fax: (718)858-4483
**Subject(s):** Paid Community Newspapers
**Circ:** ‡8,500

**Canarsie Courier** (20497)
Canarsie Publications Courier Inc.
1142 E 92 St.
Brooklyn, NY 11236
Phone: (718)257-0600
Fax: (718)272-0870
**Subject(s):** Paid Community Newspapers
**Circ:** 8,500

**Fish Farming News** (12607)
Compass Publications Inc. Fisheries Div.
PO Box 37
Stonington, ME 04681
Phone: (207)367-2396
Fax: (207)367-2490
**Subject(s):** Fish and Commercial Fisheries
**Circ:** (Controlled)8,500

**Pictorial-Gazette** (4976)
Shore Line Newspapers
PO Box 813
Old Saybrook, CT 06475
Phone: (860)388-3441
Fax: (860)388-5613
**Subject(s):** Paid Community Newspapers
**Circ:** (Paid)‡8,500

**The Tech** (13712)
Rm. W20-483
PO Box 397029
Cambridge, MA 02139-7029
Phone: (617)253-1541
Fax: (617)258-8226

**Subject(s):** College Publications
**Circ:** (Paid)‡500
(Free)‡8,500

**The Wayne Independent (26506)**
220 8th St., No. 122
Honesdale, PA 18431-1854
Phone: (570)253-3055
Fax: (570)253-5387
**Subject(s):** Daily Newspapers
**Circ:** 8,500

**The Long Islander (20928)**
Long Islander Newspapers Inc.
322 Main St.
Huntington, NY 11743
Phone: (631)427-7000
Fax: (631)427-5820
**Subject(s):** Paid Community Newspapers
**Circ:** ‡8,473

**The Suburban (27657)**
Suburban Publications Inc.
134 N Wayne Ave.
Wayne, PA 19087
Phone: (610)688-3000
Fax: (610)964-1346
**Subject(s):** Paid Community Newspapers
**Circ:** (Thurs.)8,463

**Real Estate Weekly (22295)**
Hagedorn Communications
662 Main St.
New Rochelle, NY 10801
Phone: (914)636-7400
Fax: (914)636-2957
**Subject(s):** Real Estate
**Circ:** (Free)512
(Paid)8,453

**Sodus Pennysaver (22605)**
AD Group WC Inc.
613 S Main St.
Newark, NY 14513
Phone: (315)331-6956
**Subject(s):** Shopping Guides
**Circ:** (Non-paid)8,440

**The Andover Townsman (13428)**
33 Chestnut St.
P O Box 1986
Andover, MA 01810-1986
Phone: (978)475-7000
Fax: (978)475-5731
**Subject(s):** Paid Community Newspapers
**Circ:** ⊕8,401

**Fairfield Citizen-News (4688)**
Brooks Community Newspapers Inc.
220 Carter Henry Dr.
Fairfield, CT 06824-5701
Phone: (203)255-0456
Fax: (203)255-0456
**Subject(s):** Paid Community Newspapers
**Circ:** (Paid)8,409

**The Amity Observer (5004)**
Hometown Publications Inc.
1000 Bridgeport Ave.
Shelton, CT 06484
Phone: (203)926-2080
Fax: (203)926-2091
**Subject(s):** Free Newspapers
**Circ:** (Non-paid)♦8,387

**Warwick Beacon (27950)**
Beacon Communications of Rhode Island
1944 Warwick Ave.
Warwick, RI 02889-5000
Phone: (401)732-3100
Fax: (401)732-3110
**Subject(s):** Paid Community Newspapers
**Circ:** (Non-paid)♦177
(Paid)♦8,341

**The Wilton Villager (5104)**
The Hour Publishing Co.
79 Old Ridgefield Rd.
Wilton, CT 06897-3018
Phone: (203)762-0400
Fax: (203)761-0634
**Subject(s):** Free Newspapers
**Circ:** (Paid)35
(Non-paid)8,338

**Franklin Square Pennysaver (20793)**
Star Community Publishing
250 Miller Pl.
Hicksville, NY 11801
Phone: (516)393-9300
Fax: (516)393-9344
**Subject(s):** Shopping Guides
**Circ:** (Free)8,321

**Suburban Gazette (26673)**
421 Locust St.
Mc Kees Rocks, PA 15136
Phone: (412)331-2645
**Subject(s):** Paid Community Newspapers
**Circ:** ‡8,300

**The Bar Harbor Times (12467)**
Courier Publications
PO Box 68
Bar Harbor, ME 04609-0068
Phone: (207)288-3311
Fax: (207)288-5813
**Subject(s):** Paid Community Newspapers
**Circ:** (Free)‡121
(Paid)‡8,266

**The Monadnock Ledger (18939)**
20 Grove St.
PO Box 36
Peterborough, NH 03458
Phone: (603)924-7172
Fax: (603)924-3681
**Subject(s):** Paid Community Newspapers
**Circ:** (Free)49
(Paid)8,265

**News-Herald (26378)**
Journal Register Co.
290 Commerce Dr.
PO Box 64459
Fort Washington, PA 19034
Phone: (215)542-0200
Fax: (215)723-8779
**Subject(s):** Paid Community Newspapers
**Circ:** (Combined)8,263

**The Sower (5039)**
The Ukrainian Catholic Diocese of Stamford
14 Peveril Rd.
Stamford, CT 06902-3019
Phone: (203)324-7698
Fax: (203)967-9905
**Subject(s):** Religious Publications; Ukrainian
**Circ:** (Non-paid)‡140
(Paid)‡8,220

**Brewster Times (20422)**
Putnam County Press
PO Box 608
Mahopac, NY 10541
Phone: (845)628-8400
Fax: (845)628-8400
**Subject(s):** Paid Community Newspapers
**Circ:** 8,200

**Onondaga Valley News (23028)**
Scotsman Community Publications
750 W. Genesee St.
PO Box 4970
Syracuse, NY 13221
Phone: (315)472-7825
Fax: (315)478-1434
**Subject(s):** Free Newspapers
**Circ:** (Non-paid)‡8,154

**Cambridge Chronicle (14258)**
Community Newspaper Co.
254 2nd Ave.
Needham, MA 02494
Phone: (781)433-6700
**Subject(s):** Paid Community Newspapers
**Circ:** (Non-paid)1,589
(Paid)8,106

**Sullivan County Democrat (20607)**
5 Lower Main St.
PO Box 308
Callicoon, NY 12723
Phone: (914)887-5200
Fax: (914)887-5386
**Subject(s):** Paid Community Newspapers
**Circ:** (Free)‡225
(Paid)‡8,050

**Albany Student Press (20206)**
Albany Student Press Corp.
State University Of New York
1400 Washington Ave.
CC 329
Albany, NY 12222
Phone: (518)442-5665
Fax: (518)442-5664
**Subject(s):** College Publications
**Circ:** (Free)‡8,000

**The Bennington Banner (30837)**
Banner Publishing Inc.
425 Main St.
Bennington, VT 05201
Phone: (802)447-7567
Fax: (802)442-3413
**Subject(s):** Daily Newspapers
**Circ:** (Mon.-Fri.)★7,500
(Sat.)★8,007

**The Cabinet (18888)**
The Cabinet Press Inc.
54 School St.
PO Box 180
Milford, NH 03055-0180
Phone: (603)673-3100
Fax: (603)673-8250
**Subject(s):** Paid Community Newspapers
**Circ:** 8,000

**The Coshohocken Recorder (26260)**
Skip Henry Inc.
700 W. Fayette
Conshohocken, PA 19428
Phone: (610)828-4600
Fax: (610)941-0547
**Subject(s):** Paid Community Newspapers
**Circ:** (Free)‡300
(Paid)‡8,000

**The Floral Park Bulletin (20779)**
Nassau Border Papers Inc.
PO Box 227
Floral Park, NY 11002
Phone: (516)775-7700
**Subject(s):** Paid Community Newspapers
**Circ:** (Free)100
(Paid)8,000

**Lakes Region Suburban Weekly (12617)**
76 Tandberg Trail
P.O. Box 790
Windham, ME 04062
Phone: (207)892-1166
Fax: (207)892-1171
**Subject(s):** Paid Community Newspapers
**Circ:** (Combined)8000

**New England Real Estate Journal (14643)**
East Coast Publications
57 Washington St.
Norwell, MA 02061
**Subject(s):** Real Estate; Business
**Circ:** (Free)‡1,200
(Paid)‡8,000

**The Polytechnic (23073)**
Rensselaer Polytechnic Institute
Rensselaer Union, 110 8th St.
Box 35
Troy, NY 12180
Phone: (518)276-6770
Fax: (518)276-8728
**Subject(s):** College Publications
**Circ:** (Paid)50
(Free)8,000

**South Boston Tribune (14794)**
PO Box 6
South Boston, MA 02127
Phone: (617)268-3440
Fax: (617)268-6420
**Subject(s):** Paid Community Newspapers
**Circ:** ‡8,000

**Southern Dutchess News (23119)**
84 E Main St.
Wappingers Falls, NY 12590
Phone: (845)297-3723
Fax: (845)297-6810
**Subject(s):** Paid Community Newspapers
**Circ:** (Free)‡200
(Paid)‡8,000

**Gale Directory of Publications & Broadcast Media/140th Ed.**  Northeastern States

**The Times of Scotch Plains-Fanwood** (19967)
Westfield Leader
50 Elm St.
PO BOX 250
Westfield, NJ 07091
Phone: (908)232-4407
Fax: (908)232-0473
**Subject(s):** Paid Community Newspapers
**Circ:** ‡8,000

**The Villanovan** (27631)
Villanova University
201 Dougherty Hall
Villanova, PA 19085
Phone: (610)519-7207
Fax: (610)519-5666
**Subject(s):** College Publications
**Circ:** ‡8,000

**The Westfield Leader** (19968)
Westfield Leader
50 Elm St.
PO BOX 250
Westfield, NJ 07091
Phone: (908)232-4407
Fax: (908)232-0473
**Subject(s):** Paid Community Newspapers
**Circ:** (Paid)8,000

**Juniata Sentinel** (26709)
PO Box 127
Mifflintown, PA 17059
Phone: (717)436-8206
Fax: (717)436-5174
**Subject(s):** Paid Community Newspapers
**Circ:** ‡7,900

**The Latrobe Bulletin** (26619)
The Latrobe Printing & Publishing Company Inc.
1211 Ligonier St.
PO Box 111
Latrobe, PA 15650-0111
Phone: (724)537-3351
Fax: (724)537-0489
**Subject(s):** Daily Newspapers
**Circ:** (Mon.-Sat.)7,900

**The Valley News** (20803)
Valley Newspapers Inc.
117 Oneida St.
Fulton, NY 13069
Phone: (315)598-6397
**Subject(s):** Paid Community Newspapers
**Circ:** (Paid)‡7,870

**Brighton Pittsford Post** (20611)
Messenger-Post Newspapers
73 Buffalo St.
Canandaigua, NY 14424
Phone: (800)724-2099
Fax: (585)394-1675
**Subject(s):** Paid Community Newspapers
**Circ:** (Non-paid)♦482
(Paid)♦7,860

**the Chronicle** (30834)
The Chronicle
PO Box 660
Barton, VT 05822
Fax: (800)564-3521
**Subject(s):** Paid Community Newspapers
**Circ:** (Free)215
(Paid)⊕7,863

**The Morning Times** (27490)
Liberty Group Publishing
201 N Lehigh Ave.
Sayre, PA 18840
Phone: (570)888-9643
Fax: (570)888-6463
**Subject(s):** Daily Newspapers
**Circ:** (Free)42
7,841

**Smithtown Messenger** (22948)
ESP Publications
127 E. Main St.
Smithtown, NY 11787
Phone: (516)265-3500
Fax: (516)265-3504
**Subject(s):** Paid Community Newspapers
**Circ:** 7,820

**The Gardner News** (13801)
The Gardner News Inc.
309 Central St.
Gardner, MA 01440
Phone: (978)632-8000
Fax: (978)630-2231
**Subject(s):** Daily Newspapers
**Circ:** (Mon.-Sat.)7,818

**Lincoln County News** (12503)
PO Box 36
Damariscotta, ME 04543
Phone: (207)563-3171
Fax: (207)563-3127
**Subject(s):** Paid Community Newspapers
**Circ:** (Non-paid)58
(Paid)7,800

**Bergen News Sun Bulletin** (19648)
Bergen News Publishing Co.
111 Grand Ave.
Palisades Park, NJ 07650
Phone: (201)947-5000
Fax: (201)947-6968
**Subject(s):** Free Newspapers
**Circ:** (Paid)1,558
(Free)7,783

**The Merchandiser** (20651)
Cheryl Tears
70 Stevens St.
Clifton Springs, NY 14432
Phone: (315)462-6411
Fax: (315)462-7627
**Subject(s):** Shopping Guides
**Circ:** (Combined)7,770

**Franklin Lakes/Oakland Suburban News** (19951)
North Jersey Community Newspapers
The Weekly Division of N Jersey Media Group
1 Garret Mountain Plz.
PO Box 471
West Paterson, NJ 07424-0471
Phone: (973)569-7000
Fax: (973)569-7310
**Subject(s):** Free Newspapers
**Circ:** (Wed.)7,747

**Hershey Chronicle** (26486)
513 W Chocolate Ave.
Hershey, PA 17033-1632
Phone: (717)533-2900
Fax: (717)531-2561
**Subject(s):** Paid Community Newspapers
**Circ:** 7,700

**Bridgeton Evening News** (18993)
100 Commerce
PO Box 596
Bridgeton, NJ 08302-2602
Phone: (609)451-1000
Fax: (609)451-7214
**Subject(s):** Daily Newspapers
**Circ:** (Mon.-Sat.)★7,684

**The Progress** (18982)
Recorder Publishing Company Inc.
17-19 Morristown Rd.
PO Box 687
Bernardsville, NJ 07924
Phone: (908)766-3900
Fax: (908)766-6365
**Subject(s):** Paid Community Newspapers
**Circ:** (Paid)274
(Non-paid)7,685

**Port Washington News** (22731)
Anton Community Newspapers
132 E. 2nd St.
Mineola, NY 11501
Phone: (516)747-8282
Fax: (516)742-5867
**Subject(s):** Paid Community Newspapers
**Circ:** (Free)‡500
(Paid)‡7,668

**Natick TAB** (14254)
Community Newspaper Co.
254 2nd Ave.
Needham, MA 02494
Phone: (781)433-6700
**Subject(s):** Free Newspapers
**Circ:** (Free)7,647

**Suburban News/Village Gazette** (19960)
North Jersey Community Newspapers
The Weekly Division of N Jersey Media Group
1 Garret Mountain Plz.
PO Box 471
West Paterson, NJ 07424-0471
Phone: (973)569-7000
Fax: (973)569-7310
**Subject(s):** Free Newspapers
**Circ:** (Wed.)7,623

**Transcript** (14308)
North Adams Publishing Co.
Box 473
North Adams, MA 01247
Phone: (413)663-3741
Fax: (413)662-2792
**Subject(s):** Daily Newspapers
**Circ:** (Mon.-Fri.)★6,553
(Sat.)★7,589

**Elm City Citizen Newspaper** (4852)
ABC Capital City
349 New Haven Ave.
PO Box 5339
Milford, CT 06460
Phone: (203)876-6800
Fax: (203)877-4772
**Subject(s):** Daily Newspapers
**Circ:** (Mon.-Fri.)6,496
(Sun.)7,530

**Addison County Independent** (30898)
58 Maple St.
PO Box 31
Middlebury, VT 05753
Phone: (802)388-4944
Fax: (802)388-3100
**Subject(s):** Paid Community Newspapers
**Circ:** (Paid)7,500

**Advertiser-Democrat** (12544)
James Newspaper Inc.
PO Box 269
Norway, ME 04268
Phone: (207)743-7011
**Subject(s):** Paid Community Newspapers
**Circ:** ‡7,500

**Bedford Journal** (18887)
The Cabinet Press Inc.
54 School St.
PO Box 180
Milford, NH 03055-0180
Phone: (603)673-3100
Fax: (603)673-8250
**Subject(s):** Paid Community Newspapers
**Circ:** (Combined)7,500

**The Everett Independent** (14767)
The Independent Newspapers
385 Broadway, Ste. 105, Citizens Bank Bldg.
Revere, MA 02151
Phone: (781)485-0588
Fax: (781)485-1403
**Subject(s):** Free Newspapers
**Circ:** (Non-paid)‡7,500

**The Haverhill Gazette** (14313)
Havenhill Gazette
Eagle-Tribune, 100 Turnpike St. N.
PO Box 991
North Andover, MA 01845
Phone: (978)946-2000
Fax: (978)685-1588
**Subject(s):** Daily Newspapers
**Circ:** 7,500

**Leader Observer** (20988)
Leader-Observer Inc.
PO Box 780376
Maspeth, NY 11378-0376
**Subject(s):** Paid Community Newspapers
**Circ:** ‡7,500

**Salmon River News** (22763)
Oswego County Weeklies
1 Broad St.
Pulaski, NY 13142
Phone: (315)298-6517
**Subject(s):** Paid Community Newspapers
**Circ:** 7,500

Circulation: ★ = ABC; Δ = BPA; ♦ = CAC; • = CCAB; □ = VAC; ⊕ = PO Statement; ‡ = Publisher's Report; Boldface figures = sworn; Light figures = estimated.

## Northeastern States

**The Tartan (27407)**
Carnegie Mellon University
143 N. Craig St. Whitfield Hall
Pittsburgh, PA 15213-3890
Phone: (412)268-4747
**Subject(s):** College Publications
**Circ:** ‡7,500

**The Ukrainian Weekly (19669)**
Ukrainian National Association Inc.
2200 Rte. 10
PO Box 280
Parsippany, NJ 07054
Phone: (973)292-9800
Fax: (973)292-0900
**Subject(s):** Ethnic Publications; Paid Community Newspapers
**Circ:** (Free)‡500
(Paid)‡7,500

**Yale Daily News (4903)**
Yale Daily News Publishing Company Inc.
PO Box 209007
Yale Sta.
New Haven, CT 06520-9007
Phone: (203)432-7425
Fax: (203)432-7425
**Subject(s):** College Publications
**Circ:** (Paid)‡200
(Free)‡7,500

**Garden City News (20809)**
Litmor Publications Inc.
81 E Barclay St.
Hicksville, NY 11801
Phone: (516)931-0012
Fax: (516)931-0027
**Subject(s):** Paid Community Newspapers
**Circ:** (Non-paid)100
(Paid)7,490

**Revere Journal (14768)**
Independent Newspaper Group
385 Broadway, Ste. 105
Revere, MA 02151
Phone: (781)284-2400
Fax: (781)485-1403
**Subject(s):** Paid Community Newspapers
**Circ:** (Non-paid)75
(Paid)7,494

**The Republican Journal (12470)**
Courier Publications
71 High St.
PO Box 327
Belfast, ME 04915-0327
Phone: (207)338-3333
Fax: (207)338-5498
**Subject(s):** Paid Community Newspapers
**Circ:** (Paid)7,450

**Standard-Observer (26406)**
Tribune Review Publishing Co.
622 Cabin Hill Dr.
Greensburg, PA 15601
Phone: (724)834-1151
Fax: (724)838-5171
**Subject(s):** Daily Newspapers
**Circ:** (Mon.-Sat.)7,428

**Fairfield County Business Times (4886)**
Choice Media L.L.C.
PO Box 580
New Haven, CT 06513-0580
Phone: (203)782-1420
**Subject(s):** Business; Local, State, and Regional Publications
**Circ:** ‡7,400

**Skaneateles-Marcellus Pennysaver (23035)**
Scotsman Community Publications
750 W. Genesee St.
PO Box 4970
Syracuse, NY 13221
Phone: (315)472-7825
Fax: (315)478-1434
**Subject(s):** Shopping Guides
**Circ:** (Non-paid)‡7,404

**Times-Journal (20659)**
Division Street News
PO Box 339
108 Division St.
Cobleskill, NY 12043
Phone: (518)234-2515
Fax: (518)234-7898

**Akron-Corfu Pennysaver (20203)**
RW Publications
3770 Transit Rd.
Orchard Park, NY 14127
Phone: (716)662-4200
Fax: (716)662-0740
**Subject(s):** Shopping Guides
**Circ:** (Non-paid)7,394

**Dorchester Argus-Citizen (13758)**
South Boston Tribune
PO Box 6
South Boston, MA 02127
Phone: (617)268-3440
Fax: (617)268-6420
**Subject(s):** Paid Community Newspapers
**Circ:** ‡7,350

**Perry Shopper (22699)**
12 Borden Ave.
PO Box 219
Perry, NY 14530
Phone: (585)237-2212
**Subject(s):** Shopping Guides
**Circ:** (Combined)7,350

**Times of Ticonderoga (20741)**
Denton Publications
14 Hand Ave.
Elizabethtown, NY 12932
Phone: (518)873-6368
Fax: (518)873-6360
**Subject(s):** Free Newspapers
**Circ:** (Paid)456
(Non-paid)7,317

**Sakonnet Times (27831)**
East Bay Newspapers
1 Bradford St.
PO Box 90
Bristol, RI 02809-0900
Phone: (401)253-6000
Fax: (401)253-6055
**Subject(s):** Paid Community Newspapers
**Circ:** (Non-paid)♦59
(Paid)♦7,267

**The Cheshire Herald (4658)**
The True Publishing Co.
PO Box 247
Cheshire, CT 06410
Phone: (203)272-5316
Fax: (203)250-7145
**Subject(s):** Paid Community Newspapers
**Circ:** ‡7,200

**The News Eagle (26478)**
News Eagle Inc.
522-524 Spring St.
Hawley, PA 18428-1499
Phone: (717)226-4547
Fax: (717)226-4548
**Subject(s):** Paid Community Newspapers
**Circ:** (Free)⊕203
(Paid)⊕7,169

**Observer-Tribune (19027)**
Recorder Publishing Company Inc.
PO Box 600
Chester, NJ 07930-0600
Phone: (908)879-4100
Fax: (908)647-5952
**Subject(s):** Paid Community Newspapers
**Circ:** (Combined)7,115

**Altamont Enterprise and Albany County Post (20253)**
123 Maple Ave.
PO Box 654
Altamont, NY 12009
Phone: (518)861-6641
Fax: (518)861-5105
**Subject(s):** Paid Community Newspapers
**Circ:** ‡7,100

**Great Neck Record (20856)**
Anton Community Newspapers
132 E. 2nd St.
Mineola, NY 11501
Phone: (516)747-8282
Fax: (516)742-5867

**Subject(s):** Paid Community Newspapers
**Circ:** (Paid)7,109

**Somerset Spectator (19816)**
PO Box 985
Belle Mead, NJ 08502-0985
Phone: (908)359-2828
Fax: (908)428-4459
**Subject(s):** Free Newspapers
**Circ:** (Free)‡500
(Paid)‡7,100

**The Walton Reporter (23114)**
The Reporter Co.
181 Delaware St.
Walton, NY 13856
Phone: (607)865-4132
Fax: (607)865-8983
**Subject(s):** Paid Community Newspapers
**Circ:** (Free)‡175
(Paid)‡7,100

**Irondequoit Post (20937)**
Messenger-Post Newspapers
440 Titus Ave.
Irondequoit, NY 14617-3517
Phone: (716)342-9450
**Subject(s):** Paid Community Newspapers
**Circ:** (Non-paid)♦306
(Paid)♦7,011

**Branford Review (4632)**
Shore Line Newspapers
POB 829
230 E. Main St.
Branford, CT 06405
Phone: (203)488-2535
Fax: (203)481-4125
**Subject(s):** Paid Community Newspapers
**Circ:** (Sat.)‡6,000
(Wed.)‡7,000

**Brown and White (26162)**
Lehigh University
Dept. of Journalism, Lehigh University
33 Coppee Dr.
Lehigh University
Bethlehem, PA 18015-3065
**Subject(s):** College Publications
**Circ:** 7,000

**Community Journal (23112)**
Box 619
Wading River, NY 11792
Phone: (631)929-8882
**Subject(s):** Free Newspapers; Free Newspapers
**Circ:** (Free)‡7,000

**The Daily Herald (27593)**
Joseph F. Biddle Publishing Co.
1067 Pennsylvania Ave.
Tyrone, PA 16686
Phone: (814)684-4000
Fax: (814)684-4238
**Subject(s):** Daily Newspapers
**Circ:** ‡2,300
(Sat.)7,000

**Item Extra (13740)**
The Coulter Press
156 Church St.
Clinton, MA 01510
Phone: (978)368-0176
Fax: (978)368-1151
**Subject(s):** Shopping Guides
**Circ:** (Free)‡7,000

**Jewish Ledger (22826)**
2535 Brighton Henrietta Town Line Rd.
Rochester, NY 14623-2711
Phone: (585)427-2434
**Subject(s):** Jewish Publications
**Circ:** (Free)‡1,000
(Paid)‡7,000

**Printing News/East (21181)**
Cygnus Business Media Inc.
3 Huntington Quadrangle, Ste. 301 N.
Melville, NY 11747
Phone: (631)845-2700
Fax: (631)845-2798
**Subject(s):** Printing and Typography
**Circ:** (Free)‡500
(Paid)‡7,000

**The RAM** (20473)
Fordham University
PO Box B
Bronx, NY 10458
Phone: (718)817-1000
Fax: (718)817-4319
**Subject(s):** College Publications
**Circ:** (Free)‡7,000

**Ridley Press** (26366)
Press Publishing Co.
3245 Garrett Rd.
Drexel Hill, PA 19026
Phone: (610)259-4141
**Subject(s):** Paid Community Newspapers
**Circ:** ⊕7,000

**The Rocket** (27537)
Slippery Rock University
220 Eisenberg Classroom Bldg.
Slippery Rock, PA 16057
Phone: (724)738-4438
Fax: (724)738-4896
**Subject(s):** College Publications
**Circ:** (Free)7,000

**The Triangle** (27292)
Drexel University
3141 Chestnut St.
Philadelphia, PA 19104
Phone: (215)895-2585
Fax: (215)895-5935
**Subject(s):** College Publications
**Circ:** (Free)‡7,000

**The Valley Mirror** (27412)
Woodland Publishing Co.
3910 Main St.
Munhall, PA 15120-3299
Phone: (412)462-0626
Fax: (412)462-1847
**Subject(s):** Free Newspapers
**Circ:** (Paid)‡7,000

**The Village Beacon Record** (22720)
Times Beacon Record Newspapers
Box 707
Setauket, NY 11733
Phone: (631)751-7744
Fax: (631)751-4165
**Subject(s):** Paid Community Newspapers
**Circ:** ‡7,000

**Ellwood City Ledger** (26321)
Citizens Publishing & Printing Co.
835 Lawrence Ave.
PO Box 471
Ellwood City, PA 16117-0471
Phone: (724)758-5573
Fax: (724)758-2410
**Subject(s):** Daily Newspapers
**Circ:** ‡6,991

**The Greece Post** (20864)
Messenger-Post Newspapers
1110 Long Pond Rd. Ste. 104
Rochester, NY 14626
Phone: (716)227-6900
Fax: (716)227-9728
**Subject(s):** Paid Community Newspapers
**Circ:** (Non-paid)♦2,903
  (Paid)♦6,984

**Sullivan Review** (26297)
Shoemaker Publications
PO Box 305
Dushore, PA 18614-0305
Phone: (570)928-8403
Fax: (570)928-8006
**Subject(s):** Paid Community Newspapers
**Circ:** (Free)61
  (Paid)6,974

**The Newtown Bee** (4934)
Bee Publishing Company Inc.
5 Church Hill Rd.
PO Box 5503
Newtown, CT 06470-5503
Phone: (203)426-8036
Fax: (203)426-1394
**Subject(s):** Paid Community Newspapers
**Circ:** (Non-paid)♦61
  (Paid)♦6,936

**The Courier** (18883)
Salmon Press
5 Water St.
PO Box 729
Meredith, NH 03253
Phone: (603)279-4516
**Subject(s):** Paid Community Newspapers
**Circ:** ‡6,925

**Lititz Record-Express** (26654)
Lancaster County Weeklies Inc.
22 E. Main St.
PO Box 366
Lititz, PA 17543
Phone: (717)626-2191
Fax: (717)626-1210
**Subject(s):** Paid Community Newspapers
**Circ:** (Free)‡190
  (Paid)‡6,910

**Clarion News** (26241)
Western Pennsylvania Newspaper Co.
PO Box 647
Clarion, PA 16214
Phone: (814)226-7000
Fax: (814)226-7518
**Subject(s):** Paid Community Newspapers
**Circ:** (Free)200
  (Paid)6,900

**The Evening Telegram** (20890)
111 Green St.
Herkimer, NY 13350
Phone: (315)866-2220
Fax: (315)866-5913
**Subject(s):** Daily Newspapers
**Circ:** (Mon.-Sat.)6,900

**Johnston Sunrise** (27853)
Observer Publications Inc.
1 Whipple Ln.
Box 950
Greenville, RI 02828
Phone: (401)949-2700
Fax: (401)333-4600
**Subject(s):** Free Newspapers
**Circ:** (Non-paid)♦6,892

**The Ridgefield Press** (4994)
Hersam Acorn Newspapers L.L.C.
c/o Jack Sanders
PO Box 1019
Ridgefield, CT 06877
Phone: (203)438-6544
**Subject(s):** Paid Community Newspapers
**Circ:** (Non-paid)163
  (Paid)6,892

**West Essex Tribune** (19464)
West Essex Tribune Inc.
495 S Livingston Ave.
PO Box 65
Livingston, NJ 07039-0065
Phone: (973)992-1771
Fax: (972)992-7015
**Subject(s):** Paid Community Newspapers
**Circ:** (Thurs.)6,860

**Fulton County News** (26676)
Box 635
McConnellsburg, PA 17233
Phone: (717)485-3811
Fax: (717)485-5187
**Subject(s):** Paid Community Newspapers
**Circ:** ‡6,820

**The Town Journal** (19764)
North Jersey Community Newspapers
41 Oak St.
Ridgewood, NJ 07450-3805
Phone: (201)612-5434
Fax: (201)612-5436
**Subject(s):** Paid Community Newspapers
**Circ:** (Non-paid)♦6,821

**Grand Island PennySaver** (20847)
Niagara Frontier Publications
1859 Whitehaven Rd.
PO Box 130
Grand Island, NY 14072-0130
Phone: (716)773-7676
Fax: (716)773-7190
**Subject(s):** Shopping Guides
**Circ:** (Free)6,800

**The Bridgton News** (12481)
Bridgton News Corp.
118 Main St.
PO Box 244
Bridgton, ME 04009
Phone: (207)647-2851
Fax: (207)647-5001
**Subject(s):** Paid Community Newspapers
**Circ:** ⊕6,783

**Attica Pennysaver** (20325)
RW Publications
3770 Transit Rd.
Orchard Park, NY 14127
Phone: (716)662-4200
Fax: (716)662-0740
**Subject(s):** Shopping Guides
**Circ:** (Non-paid)6,764

**Mount Vernon Daily Argus** (21229)
Gannett Company Inc.
1 Gannett Dr.
White Plains, NY 10604-3406
Phone: (914)694-9300
Fax: (914)694-5018
**Subject(s):** Daily Newspapers
**Circ:** (Mon.-Sat.)6,020
  (Sun.)6,740

**The Oneida Daily Dispatch** (22653)
Goodson Newspaper Group
130 Broad St.
PO Box 120
Oneida, NY 13421
Phone: (315)363-5100
Fax: (315)363-9832
**Subject(s):** Daily Newspapers
**Circ:** (Mon.-Sat.)★6,729

**American Journal** (12616)
910 Main St.
Westbrook, ME 04092
Phone: (207)854-2577
Fax: (207)854-0018
**Subject(s):** Paid Community Newspapers
**Circ:** (Free)122
  (Paid)6,700

**Suburban News (North Edition)** (22957)
Westside News
1835 N Union St.
PO Box 106
Spencerport, NY 14559
Phone: (585)352-3411
Fax: (585)352-4811
**Subject(s):** Free Newspapers
**Circ:** (Paid)7
  (Non-paid)6,705

**Register-Star** (20922)
Record Printing & Publishing Co.
364 Warren St.
Hudson, NY 12534
Phone: (518)828-1616
Fax: (518)828-9437
**Subject(s):** Daily Newspapers
**Circ:** (Mon.-Fri.)6,444
  (Sun.)6,688

**Valley Stream Herald** (21058)
Richner Communications
P.O. Box 9001
Lawrence, NY 11559-1616
Phone: (516)569-4000
Fax: (516)569-4942
**Subject(s):** Paid Community Newspapers
**Circ:** (Free)‡1,399
  (Paid)‡6,671

**County Shopper—Catskill Park Edition** (20698)
Decker Advertising Inc.
97 Main St., No. 5
Delhi, NY 13753-1234
Phone: (607)746-2178
Fax: (607)746-6272
**Subject(s):** Shopping Guides
**Circ:** (Non-paid)6,665

**Port Times Record** (22721)
Times Beacon Record Newspapers
Box 707
Setauket, NY 11733
Phone: (631)751-7744
Fax: (631)751-4165

Circulation: ★ = ABC; △ = BPA; ♦ = CAC; ● = CCAB; ❏ = VAC; ⊕ = PO Statement; ‡ = Publisher's Report; Boldface figures = sworn; Light figures = estimated.

## Northeastern States

**Subject(s):** Paid Community Newspapers

Circ: ‡6,659

**Southampton Press-Western Edition (23177)**
12 Mitchell Rd.
PO Box 1071
Westhampton Beach, NY 11978
Phone: (516)288-1100
Fax: (516)288-4965
**Subject(s):** Paid Community Newspapers

Circ: (Thurs.)6,556

**Lyncourt Pennysaver (23021)**
Scotsman Community Publications
750 W. Genesee St.
PO Box 4970
Syracuse, NY 13221
Phone: (315)472-7825
Fax: (315)478-1434
**Subject(s):** Shopping Guides

Circ: (Non-paid)‡6,535

**Glen Cove Record Pilot (20828)**
Anton Community Newspapers
132 E. 2nd St.
Mineola, NY 11501
Phone: (516)747-8282
Fax: (516)742-5867
**Subject(s):** Paid Community Newspapers

Circ: (Paid)‡6,520

**The Chronicle (20884)**
200 Hofstra Univ.
Rm. 203 Student Center
Hempstead, NY 11549
Phone: (516)463-6966
**Subject(s):** College Publications

Circ: (Free)‡6,500

**Coos County Democrat (18852)**
North Country Publishing Co.
79 Main St.
Box 29
Lancaster, NH 03584
Phone: (603)788-4939
Fax: (603)788-3022
**Subject(s):** Paid Community Newspapers

Circ: ‡6,500

**Morrisons Cove Herald (26668)**
113 N Market St.
Martinsburg, PA 16662-0165
Phone: (814)793-2144
Fax: (814)793-4882
**Subject(s):** Paid Community Newspapers

Circ: (Free)125
 (Paid)6,500

**Penn Franklin News (26750)**
Penn News
PO Box 73
4021 Old William Penn Hwy
Murrysville, PA 15668
Phone: (724)327-3471
Fax: (724)325-4591
**Subject(s):** Paid Community Newspapers

Circ: 6,500

**The Sanford News (12593)**
George J. Foster Co.
PO Box D
Sanford, ME 04073
Phone: (207)324-5986
Fax: (207)490-1431
**Subject(s):** Paid Community Newspapers

Circ: (Paid)‡6,500

**The Torch (22768)**
St. John's University
8000 Utopia Pkwy.
Queens, NY 11439
**Subject(s):** College Publications

Circ: (Free)‡6,500

**Ballston-Malta Pennysaver (20336)**
Capital Region Weekly Newspaper Group
P.O. Box 1450
Clifton Park, NY 12065
Phone: (518)877-7160
Fax: (518)877-7824
**Subject(s):** Shopping Guides

Circ: (Free)6,485

**King of Prussia Courier (26588)**
Suburban Publications Inc.
134 N Wayne Ave.
Wayne, PA 19087
Phone: (610)688-3000
Fax: (610)964-1346
**Subject(s):** Free Newspapers

Circ: (Non-paid)♦6,486

**New Canaan Advertiser (4875)**
Hersam Publishing Co.
42 Vitti St.
PO Box 605
New Canaan, CT 06840
Phone: (203)966-9541
Fax: (203)966-8006
**Subject(s):** Paid Community Newspapers

Circ: (Thurs.)6,462

**The Scarsdale Inquirer (22918)**
S.I. Communications Inc.
PO Box 418
Scarsdale, NY 10583-0418
Phone: (914)725-2500
Fax: (914)725-1552
**Subject(s):** Paid Community Newspapers

Circ: (Free)425
 (Paid)6,410

**Trumbull Times (5012)**
Hometown Publications Inc.
1000 Bridgeport Ave.
Shelton, CT 06484
Phone: (203)926-2080
Fax: (203)926-2091
**Subject(s):** Paid Community Newspapers

Circ: (Non-paid)♦639
 (Paid)♦6,403

**Thousand Islands Sun (20247)**
Thousand Islands Printing Company Inc.
PO Box 277
Alexandria Bay, NY 13607-0277
Phone: (315)482-2581
Fax: (315)482-6315
**Subject(s):** Paid Community Newspapers

Circ: (Paid)‡6,397

**Springfield Press (27546)**
Press Newspapers
PO Box 291
Springfield, PA 19064
Phone: (610)522-9350
Fax: (610)522-9350
**Subject(s):** Paid Community Newspapers

Circ: ‡6,360

**The Sun (26519)**
115-117 S Water St.
PO Box C
Hummelstown, PA 17036
Phone: (717)566-3251
Fax: (717)566-6196
**Subject(s):** Paid Community Newspapers

Circ: (Free)722
 (Paid)6,352

**Tri-Town News (22940)**
Tri-Town News Inc.
PO Box 208
Sidney, NY 13838-0208
Phone: (607)563-3526
Fax: (607)563-8999
**Subject(s):** Paid Community Newspapers

Circ: ‡6,300

**Church World (12555)**
Brunswick Publishing Co.
PO Box 11559
Portland, ME 04104-7559
Phone: (207)773-6471
Fax: (207)773-0182
**Subject(s):** Religious Publications

Circ: ‡6,271

**The Herald of Randolph (30922)**
The Herald
30 Pleasant St.
PO Box 309
Randolph, VT 05060-0309
Phone: (802)728-3232
Fax: (802)728-9275
**Subject(s):** Paid Community Newspapers

Circ: 6,278

**The Boyertown Area Times (26193)**
Berks-Mont Newspapers Inc.
124 N Chestnut St.
PO Box 565
Boyertown, PA 19512
Phone: (610)367-6041
Fax: (610)369-0233
**Subject(s):** Paid Community Newspapers

Circ: (Free)315
 (Paid)6,268

**The Hampton Union (18819)**
Seacoast Newspapers Inc.
PO Box 250
Exeter, NH 03833-0250
Phone: (603)772-6000
Fax: (603)772-3830
**Subject(s):** Paid Community Newspapers

Circ: (Combined)6,252

**Maine Potato News (12582)**
NE Publishing
PO Box 510
Presque Isle, ME 04769
Phone: (207)764-4471
Fax: (207)764-4499
**Subject(s):** Socialized Farming

Circ: (Free)‡6,250

**The Rockingham News (18820)**
Seacoast Newspapers Inc.
PO Box 250
Exeter, NH 03833-0250
Phone: (603)772-6000
Fax: (603)772-3830
**Subject(s):** Paid Community Newspapers

Circ: (Paid)6,235

**Hudson Daily Sun (14223)**
Marlboro Enterprise
40 Mechanic St.
Marlborough, MA 01752-4425
Phone: (508)490-7450
Fax: (508)490-7471
**Subject(s):** Daily Newspapers

Circ: (Combined)6,227

**Fishkill Standard (20776)**
Putnam County Press
PO Box 608
Mahopac, NY 10541
Phone: (845)628-8400
Fax: (845)628-8400
**Subject(s):** Paid Community Newspapers

Circ: 6,200

**Gates Chili Post (22819)**
Messenger-Post Newspapers
2968 Chili Ave.
Rochester, NY 14624
Phone: (585)247-9200
Fax: (585)247-9210
**Subject(s):** Free Newspapers

Circ: (Non-paid)♦590
 (Paid)♦6,203

**Sun (14760)**
The Quincy Sun Publishing Company Inc.
1372 Hancock St.
Quincy, MA 02169
Phone: (617)471-3100
Fax: (617)472-3963
**Subject(s):** Paid Community Newspapers

Circ: (Free)‡440
 (Paid)‡6,150

**New York Construction News (22155)**
McGraw-Hill Inc.
New York Construction
2 Penn Plaza 9th Fl.
New York, NY 10121
Fax: (212)904-2335
**Subject(s):** Building Materials, Concrete, Brick, and Tile; Construction, Contracting, Building, and Excavating

Circ: (Paid)‡6,100

**The News-Review (21140)**
Times Review Newspapers
7785 Main Rd.
PO Box 1500
Mattituck, NY 11952
Phone: (631)298-3200
Fax: (631)298-3287
**Subject(s):** Paid Community Newspapers

Circ: (Paid)‡6,105

**Gale Directory of Publications & Broadcast Media/140th Ed.**      **Northeastern States**

**The Rivertowns Enterprise (20706)**
W.H. White Publications
Box 330
Dobbs Ferry, NY 10522
Phone: (914)478-2787
Fax: (914)478-2863
**Subject(s):** Paid Community Newspapers

**Circ:** (Free)‡250
    (Paid)‡6,100

**Hamlin Clarkson Herald (22956)**
Westside News
1835 N Union St.
PO Box 106
Spencerport, NY 14559
Phone: (585)352-3411
Fax: (585)352-4811
**Subject(s):** Free Newspapers

**Circ:** (Paid)11
    (Non-paid)6,094

**The Secaucus Reporter (19786)**
Hudson Reporter Associates
1400 Washington St.
PO Box 3069
Hoboken, NJ 07030-1601
Phone: (201)798-7800
Fax: (201)798-0018
**Subject(s):** Free Newspapers

**Circ:** (Non-paid)6,050

**The Exeter News-Letter (18818)**
Seacoast Newspapers Inc.
PO Box 250
Exeter, NH 03833-0250
Phone: (603)772-6000
Fax: (603)772-3830
**Subject(s):** Free Newspapers

**Circ:** (Combined)6,010

**The Advance of Bucks County (26771)**
The New Hope Gazette
PO Box 910
Newtown, PA 18940
Phone: (215)862-9435
Fax: (215)968-2244
**Subject(s):** Paid Community Newspapers

**Circ:** ‡6,000

**The Advantage (26186)**
Montgomery County Community College
340 DeKalb Pike
Blue Bell, PA 19422
Phone: (215)641-6300
**Subject(s):** College Publications

**Circ:** (Free)6,000

**Binnewater Tides (22884)**
Women's Studio Workshop
PO Box 489
Rosendale, NY 12472
Phone: (845)658-9133
Fax: (845)658-9031
**Subject(s):** Women's Interests; Art and Art History

**Circ:** (Paid)‡1,000
    (Non-paid)‡6,000

**Boston Seaport Journal (13488)**
Boston Airport Journal
256 Marginal St.
East Boston, MA 02128-2823
Phone: (617)561-4000
Fax: (617)561-2821
**Subject(s):** Travel and Tourism; Local, State, and Regional Publications

**Circ:** (Non-paid)6,000

**Colonie Spotlight (20665)**
Spotlight Newspapers
125 Adams St.
PO Box 100
Delmar, NY 12054-0100
Phone: (518)439-4949
Fax: (518)439-0609
**Subject(s):** Paid Community Newspapers

**Circ:** ‡6,000

**The Empire State Farmer (20201)**
Journal Publishing Co.
7 Main St.
PO Box 68
Adams, NY 13605
Phone: (315)232-2141
Fax: (315)232-4586
**Subject(s):** Free Newspapers; Farm Newspapers

**Circ:** (Free)‡6,000

**The Ionian (21240)**
Iona College
715 N. Ave.
New Rochelle, NY 10801
Phone: (914)633-2370
Fax: (914)633-2404
**Subject(s):** College Publications

**Circ:** (Free)6,000

**Law Enforcement News (22027)**
John Jay College of Criminal Justice
555 W. 57th St.
New York, NY 10019
Phone: (212)237-8442
Fax: (212)237-8486
**Subject(s):** Law; Police, Penology, and Penal Institutions

**Circ:** (Paid)‡6,000

**The Mt. Vernon Independent (21230)**
Martinelli Publications
40 Larkin Plz.
Yonkers, NY 10701
Phone: (914)965-4000
Fax: (914)965-2892
**Subject(s):** Paid Community Newspapers

**Circ:** (Combined)6,000

**The Newport Navalog (27871)**
Edward A. Sherman Publishing Co.
PO Box 420
101 Malbone Rd.
Newport, RI 02840
Phone: (401)849-3300
Fax: (401)849-3306
**Subject(s):** Military and Navy; Free Newspapers

**Circ:** (Free)‡6,000

**Newsweekly (19768)**
PO Box 405
301 Mill St
Moorestown, NJ 08057
Phone: (856)231-7600
Fax: (856)231-4333
**Subject(s):** Paid Community Newspapers

**Circ:** (Paid)6,000

**Sampan (13585)**
Asian-American Civic Association
200 Tremont St.
Boston, MA 02116-4705
Phone: (617)426-9492
Fax: (617)482-2316
**Subject(s):** Free Newspapers; Ethnic Publications

**Circ:** (Controlled)6,000

**The Sound View News (23206)**
Martinelli Publications
40 Larkin Plz.
Yonkers, NY 10701
Phone: (914)965-4000
Fax: (914)965-2892
**Subject(s):** Paid Community Newspapers

**Circ:** (Combined)6,000

**Star and Wave (19010)**
600 Park Blvd., Ste. 5
Cape May, NJ 08204-1265
Phone: (609)884-3465
Fax: (609)884-2893
**Subject(s):** Paid Community Newspapers

**Circ:** ‡6,000

**Tri-Village Pennysaver (20936)**
Tri-Village Pennysaver Inc.
15 Geneva St.
PO Box 416
Interlaken, NY 14847
Phone: (607)532-4320
Fax: (607)273-9557
**Subject(s):** Shopping Guides

**Circ:** (Paid)200
    (Non-paid)6,000

**The Herald (26128)**
Tribune Review Publishing
101 Emerson Ave.
Aspinwall, PA 15215
Phone: (412)782-2121
Fax: (412)782-1195
**Subject(s):** Paid Community Newspapers

**Circ:** (Free)50
    (Paid)5,944

**The Record Enterprise (18947)**
Salmon Press
PO Box 148
Plymouth, NH 03264-0148
Phone: (603)536-1311
Fax: (603)536-8940
**Subject(s):** Paid Community Newspapers

**Circ:** (Paid)⊕5,942

**The Independent-Enterprise (26312)**
Brown Thompson Newspapers Inc.
109 Erie St., Ste. 5
Edinboro, PA 16412
Phone: (814)734-1234
Fax: (814)734-8973
**Subject(s):** Paid Community Newspapers; Shopping Guides

**Circ:** (Paid)2,311
    (Free)5,934

**The Clarion Call (26240)**
Clarion University of Pennsylvania
270 Gemmell Complex
Clarion, PA 16214
Phone: (814)226-2380
Fax: (814)226-2557
**Subject(s):** College Publications

**Circ:** (Paid)‡100
    (Free)‡5,900

**Infectious Disease News (19856)**
SLACK Inc.
6900 Grove Rd.
Thorofare, NJ 08086-9447
Phone: (856)848-1000
Fax: (856)848-6091
**Subject(s):** Medicine and Surgery

**Circ:** (Controlled)‡5,900

**Milton Record Transcript (14250)**
Tribune Publishing Co.
1261 Hyde Park Ave.
Hyde Park, MA 02136
Phone: (617)361-6500
Fax: (617)361-6503
**Subject(s):** Paid Community Newspapers

**Circ:** ‡5,900

**The Peterborough Transcript (18941)**
One Phoenix Mill Ln., Ste. 100
PO Box 419
Peterborough, NH 03458-0419
Phone: (603)924-3333
Fax: (603)924-7946
**Subject(s):** Paid Community Newspapers

**Circ:** 5,900

**Turnpike Pennysaver (22783)**
Snyder Communications Corp.
PO Box 671
Richfield Springs, NY 13439
Phone: (315)858-1730
Fax: (315)858-2988
**Subject(s):** Shopping Guides

**Circ:** (Paid)11
    (Non-paid)5,883

**Middleboro Gazette (14247)**
Hathaway Publishing
148 W. Grove St.
PO Box 551
Middleboro, MA 02346
Phone: (617)947-1760
Fax: (617)942-9426
**Subject(s):** Paid Community Newspapers

**Circ:** 5,860

**The Spirit (27461)**
Spirit Publishing Co.
510 Pine St.
PO Box 444
Punxsutawney, PA 15767-0444
Phone: (814)938-8740
Fax: (814)938-3794
**Subject(s):** Daily Newspapers

**Circ:** (Free)44
    (Paid)5,862

---

Circulation: ★ = ABC; △ = BPA; ◆ = CAC; ● = CCAB; ▫ = VAC; ⊕ = PO Statement; ‡ = Publisher's Report; Boldface figures = sworn; Light figures = estimated.

## Northeastern States

**Bristol Phoenix (27830)**
East Bay Newspapers
1 Bradford St.
PO Box 90
Bristol, RI 02809-0900
Phone: (401)253-6000
Fax: (401)253-6055
Subject(s): Paid Community Newspapers
Circ: (Non-paid)♦150
(Paid)♦5,828

**Somerset Messenger Gazette (19815)**
NJN Publishing
44 Veterans Memorial Dr. E.
PO Box 699
Somerville, NJ 08876
Phone: (908)575-6660
Fax: (908)575-6683
Subject(s): Paid Community Newspapers
Circ: (Paid)5,807

**Providence Business News (27912)**
300 Richmond St. Ste. 202
Providence, RI 02903
Phone: (401)273-2201
Fax: (401)274-0270
Subject(s): Business; Local, State, and Regional Publications
Circ: (Paid)5,785

**Star-Herald (12583)**
Northeast Publishing Co.
40 North St., Ste. B
PO Box 510
Presque Isle, ME 04769
Phone: (207)764-4471
Fax: (207)764-7585
Subject(s): Paid Community Newspapers
Circ: ‡5775

**The Narragansett Times (27942)**
Southern Rhode Island Newspapers
187 Main St.
PO Box 232
Wakefield, RI 02880
Phone: (401)789-9744
Fax: (401)783-1550
Subject(s): Paid Community Newspapers
Circ: (Non-paid)♦120
(Paid)♦5,761

**The Observer (5019)**
The Step Saver Inc.
PO Box 648
Southington, CT 06489-0648
Phone: (860)621-6751
Fax: (860)621-1841
Subject(s): Paid Community Newspapers
Circ: (Non-paid)42
(Paid)5,755

**Cosmopolite Herald (26396)**
Brown Thompson Newspapers Inc.
225 Main St., E
PO Box 403
Girard, PA 16417-0403
Phone: (814)774-9648
Fax: (814)774-0328
Subject(s): Paid Community Newspapers
Circ: (Paid)‡2,589
(Free)‡5,722

**Houlton Pioneer Times (12523)**
Northeast Publishing Co.
PO Box 456
Houlton, ME 04730
Phone: (207)532-2281
Subject(s): Paid Community Newspapers
Circ: ‡5,700

**The Item (13739)**
The Coulter Press
156 Church St.
Clinton, MA 01510
Phone: (978)368-0176
Fax: (978)368-1151
Subject(s): Paid Community Newspapers
Circ: ‡5,700

**The Walpole Times (14848)**
7 W St.
Walpole, MA 02081
Phone: (508)668-0243
Fax: (508)668-5174

Subject(s): Paid Community Newspapers
Circ: (Free)121
(Paid)5,700

**The Wyckoff Suburban News (19766)**
North Jersey Community Newspapers
41 Oak St.
Ridgewood, NJ 07450-3805
Phone: (201)612-5415
Fax: (201)612-5421
Subject(s): Paid Community Newspapers
Circ: (Wed.)5,702

**Huntington Herald (5007)**
Hometown Publications Inc.
1000 Bridgeport Ave.
Shelton, CT 06484
Phone: (203)926-2080
Fax: (203)926-2091
Subject(s): (Non-paid)♦597
(Paid)♦5,698

**Athol Daily News (13440)**
Athol Press
225 Exchange St.
PO Box 1000
Athol, MA 01331
Phone: (978)249-3535
Fax: (978)249-9630
Subject(s): Daily Newspapers
Circ: ‡5,684

**Boothbay Register (12476)**
Maine-OK Enterprises
PO Box 357
Boothbay Harbor, ME 04538-0357
Subject(s): Paid Community Newspapers
Circ: 5,684

**The Beacon (13744)**
Community Newspaper Co./Northwest
150 Baker Ave., Ste. 305
PO Box 9191
Concord, MA 01742-9191
Phone: (978)371-5754
Fax: (978)371-5220
Subject(s): Paid Community Newspapers
Circ: (Non-paid)44
(Paid)5,669

**The Standard Times (27877)**
SRI Newspapers Inc.
13 W. Main St.
North Kingstown, RI 02852
Phone: (401)299-4576
Fax: (401)294-9736
Subject(s): Paid Community Newspapers
Circ: (Combined)5,657

**Wellesley Townsman (14879)**
Community Newspaper Co.
254 2nd Ave.
Needham, MA 02494
Phone: (781)433-6700
Subject(s): Free Newspapers
Circ: (Non-paid)5,622

**Central Square Citizen Outlet (20635)**
Oswego County Weeklies
Rte. 49
Central Square, NY 13036
Phone: (315)668-2695
Subject(s): Paid Community Newspapers
Circ: 5,600

**West Springfield Record (14883)**
West Springfield Record Inc.
516 Main St.
PO Box 357
West Springfield, MA 01089
Phone: (413)736-1587
Fax: (413)739-2477
Subject(s): Paid Community Newspapers
Circ: 5,600

**Capital Weekly (12443)**
Courier Publications
PO Box 2788
Augusta, ME 04338
Phone: (207)621-6000
Fax: (207)621-6006
Subject(s): Paid Community Newspapers
Circ: (Non-paid)‡260
(Paid)‡5,573

**Mahwah Suburban News (19954)**
North Jersey Community Newspapers
The Weekly Division of N Jersey Media Group
1 Garret Mountain Plz.
PO Box 471
West Paterson, NJ 07424-0471
Phone: (973)569-7000
Fax: (973)569-7310
Subject(s): Free Newspapers
Circ: (Wed.)5,521

**Brown Daily Herald (27892)**
The Brown Daily Herald Inc.
PO Box 2538
Providence, RI 02906
Phone: (401)351-3372
Fax: (401)351-9297
Subject(s): College Publications
Circ: ‡5,500

**The Dragon Chronicle (20689)**
State University of New York College at Cortland
111 Corey Union
Cortland, NY 13045
Phone: (607)753-2526
Fax: (607)753-2807
Subject(s): College Publications
Circ: (Free)‡5,500

**The Fulton Patriot (20802)**
PO Box 299
Fulton, NY 13069
Phone: (315)592-2459
Subject(s): Paid Community Newspapers
Circ: 5,500

**Granite State News (18963)**
Salmon Press
PO Box 879
Wolfeboro, NH 03894
Phone: (603)569-4743
Fax: (603)569-4743
Subject(s): Paid Community Newspapers
Circ: ‡5,500

**The Piscataquis Observer (12505)**
Northeast Publishing Co.
PO Box 30
12 East Main St
Dover Foxcroft, ME 04426-0030
Phone: (207)564-8355
Fax: (207)564-7056
Subject(s): Paid Community Newspapers
Circ: ‡5,500

**Republican-Register (21222)**
6 Central St.
PO Box 591
Moravia, NY 13118
Phone: (315)497-1551
Subject(s): Paid Community Newspapers
Circ: ‡5,500

**Triboro Banner (27508)**
Triboro Banner Newspaper
149 Penn Ave.
Scranton, PA 18503
Phone: (570)207-9001
Fax: (570)207-3448
Subject(s): Paid Community Newspapers
Circ: ‡5,500

**Yardley News (27724)**
The New Hope Gazette
PO Box 334
Yardley, PA 19067
Subject(s): Paid Community Newspapers
Circ: ‡5,500

**The Mount Pleasant Journal (26747)**
Mount Pleasant Publishing Corp.
23-33 S. Church St.
Mount Pleasant, PA 15666
Phone: (412)547-5722
Fax: (412)887-5115
Subject(s): Paid Community Newspapers
Circ: ⊕5,492

**The Daily Press (27487)**
245 Brussels St.
PO Box 353
Saint Marys, PA 15857-0353
Phone: (814)781-1596
Fax: (814)834-7473

**Subject(s):** Daily Newspapers
**Circ:** ‡5,489

**The Stowe Reporter** (30944)
School St.
PO Box 489
Stowe, VT 05672-0489
Phone: (802)253-2101
Fax: (802)253-8332
**Subject(s):** Paid Community Newspapers
**Circ:** (Free)‡50
(Paid)‡5,485

**Wilmington-Tewksbury Town Crier** (14841)
Daily Times
104 Lowell Street
Wilmington, MA 01887
**Subject(s):** Paid Community Newspapers
**Circ:** (Non-paid)343
(Paid)5,486

**Franklinville Pennysaver** (20794)
H & K Publications Inc.
4 Genesee St.
Cuba, NY 14727
Phone: (716)968-3880
Fax: (716)968-3881
**Subject(s):** Shopping Guides
**Circ:** (Non-paid)5,460

**North Penn Life** (26379)
Journal Register Co.
North Penn Life
PO Box 1628
Fort Washington, PA 19034
Phone: (215)542-0200
Fax: (215)643-9475
**Subject(s):** Free Newspapers
**Circ:** (Combined)5,456

**Record-Argus** (26410)
10 Penn Ave.
PO Box 711
Greenville, PA 16125-0711
Phone: (724)588-5000
Fax: (724)588-4691
**Subject(s):** Daily Newspapers
**Circ:** (Mon.-Sat.)5,443

**The Darien Times** (4673)
Hersam Acorn Newspapers L.L.C.
4 Corbin Dr.
Darien, CT 06820
Phone: (203)656-4230
**Subject(s):** Free Newspapers
**Circ:** (Paid)♦1,010
(Non-paid)♦5,432

**Hicksville Illustrated News** (20895)
Anton Community Newspapers
132 E. 2nd St.
Mineola, NY 11501
Phone: (516)747-8282
Fax: (516)742-5867
**Subject(s):** Paid Community Newspapers
**Circ:** (Paid)‡5,434

**Lincoln News** (12533)
PO Box 35
Lincoln, ME 04457
Phone: (207)794-6532
Fax: (207)794-2004
**Subject(s):** Paid Community Newspapers
**Circ:** (Free)‡20
(Paid)‡5,439

**East Meadow Beacon** (20725)
Beacon Newspapers
5 Centre St.
Hempstead, NY 11550-2422
Phone: (516)481-5400
**Subject(s):** Paid Community Newspapers
**Circ:** 5,400

**Finger Lake Community Newspaper** (23078)
PO Box 714
Trumansburg, NY 14886
Phone: (607)387-3181
Fax: (607)387-9421
**Subject(s):** Paid Community Newspapers
**Circ:** 5,400

**Hammonton News** (19139)
PO Box 596
Hammonton, NJ 08037
Phone: (609)561-2300
Fax: (609)567-2249
**Subject(s):** Paid Community Newspapers
**Circ:** ‡5,400

**Hempstead Beacon** (20885)
Beacon Newspapers
5 Centre St.
Hempstead, NY 11550-2422
Phone: (516)481-5400
**Subject(s):** Paid Community Newspapers
**Circ:** ‡5,400

**The Leader-Vindicator** (26755)
435 Broad St.
PO Box 158
New Bethlehem, PA 16242-1102
Phone: (814)275-3131
Fax: (814)275-3531
**Subject(s):** Paid Community Newspapers
**Circ:** 5,400

**The Rocket-Courier** (27716)
302 State St.
PO Box 187
Wyalusing, PA 18853
Phone: (570)746-1217
Fax: (570)746-7737
**Subject(s):** Free Newspapers
**Circ:** (Controlled)‡5,400

**The Southbridge Evening News** (14801)
Stonebridge Press Inc.
25 Elm St.
Southbridge, MA 01550
Phone: (508)764-6102
Fax: (508)764-8015
**Subject(s):** Daily Newspapers
**Circ:** (Paid)‡5,400

**Trumansburg Free Press** (23080)
Finger Lake Community Newspaper
PO Box 714
Trumansburg, NY 14886
Phone: (607)387-3181
Fax: (607)387-9421
**Subject(s):** Paid Community Newspapers
**Circ:** ‡5,400

**West Hempstead Beacon** (20887)
Beacon Newspapers
5 Centre St.
Hempstead, NY 11550-2422
Phone: (516)481-5400
**Subject(s):** Paid Community Newspapers
**Circ:** ‡5,400

**The Progress Star** (26731)
Gateway Press
610 Beatty Rd.
PO Box 6429
Monroeville, PA 15146-1502
Phone: (412)856-7400
Fax: (412)856-7954
**Subject(s):** Paid Community Newspapers
**Circ:** (Free)‡325
(Paid)‡5,367

**Merrick Life** (21203)
L & M Publications Inc.
1840 Merrick Ave.
Merrick, NY 11566-2730
Phone: (516)378-5320
Fax: (516)378-0287
**Subject(s):** Paid Community Newspapers
**Circ:** (Thurs.)5,344

**Hyde Park Mattapan Tribune** (13840)
Tribune Publishing Co.
1261 Hyde Park Ave.
Hyde Park, MA 02136
Phone: (617)361-6500
Fax: (617)361-6503
**Subject(s):** Paid Community Newspapers
**Circ:** (Free)‡539
(Paid)‡5,330

**The Glen Rock Gazette** (19952)
North Jersey Community Newspapers
The Weekly Division of N Jersey Media Group
1 Garret Mountain Plz.
PO Box 471
West Paterson, NJ 07424-0471
Phone: (973)569-7000
Fax: (973)569-7310
**Subject(s):** Free Newspapers
**Circ:** (Fri.)5,320

**Berlin Reporter** (18770)
Salmon Press
151 Main St.
PO Box 38
Berlin, NH 03570-0038
Phone: (603)752-1200
Fax: (603)752-2339
**Subject(s):** Paid Community Newspapers
**Circ:** 5,300

**The Chatham Courier-Rough Notes** (20636)
Park Communications
PO Box 355
Chatham, NY 12037
Phone: (518)392-4141
Fax: (518)392-7322
**Subject(s):** Paid Community Newspapers
**Circ:** (Free)‡500
(Paid)‡5,306

**Perry County Times** (26756)
Advance Publications of Perry & Juniata Counties Inc.
PO Box 130
New Bloomfield, PA 17068
Phone: (717)582-4305
Fax: (717)582-7933
**Subject(s):** Paid Community Newspapers
**Circ:** ‡5,300

**South Buffalo News** (21013)
Front Page Group Inc.
2703 S Park Ave.
Lackawanna, NY 14218
Phone: (716)823-8222
Fax: (716)821-0550
**Subject(s):** Paid Community Newspapers
**Circ:** ‡5,300

**City Edition Pennysaver** (23002)
Scotsman Community Publications
750 W. Genesee St.
PO Box 4970
Syracuse, NY 13221
Phone: (315)472-7825
Fax: (315)478-1434
**Subject(s):** Shopping Guides
**Circ:** (Non-paid)‡5,290

**Mercersburg Journal/Ad Journal** (26692)
11 S Main St.
PO Box 239
Mercersburg, PA 17236-0239
Phone: (717)328-3223
**Subject(s):** Free Newspapers; Shopping Guides
**Circ:** (Paid)2,700
(Free)5,295

**North Country Pennysaver** (20418)
Mid York Weekly Pennysaver Inc.
55 Oriskany Blvd
PO Box 203
Yorkville, NY 13495
Phone: (315)736-1494
Fax: (315)736-1496
**Subject(s):** Shopping Guides
**Circ:** (Combined)5,280

**The Portage Dispatch** (27451)
Mainline Newspapers
PO Box 777
Ebensburg, PA 15931-0777
Phone: (814)472-4110
Fax: (814)472-2275
**Subject(s):** Paid Community Newspapers
**Circ:** 5,272

**Echoes-Sentinel** (19841)
254 Mercer St.
PO Box 157
Stirling, NJ 07980
Phone: (908)647-1187
Fax: (908)647-5952
**Subject(s):** Paid Community Newspapers
**Circ:** (Combined)5,264

## Northeastern States

**The Weekly Collegian (27555)**
Penn State University
123 S. Burrowes St.
James Bldg.
State College, PA 16801-3882
Phone: (814)865-1828
Fax: (814)865-3848
**Subject(s):** College Publications
**Circ:** (Free)13
(Paid)5,250

**Daily Bulletin (20501)**
Brooklyn Eagle Publications
30 Henry St.
Brooklyn, NY 11201-3504
Phone: (718)858-2300
Fax: (718)858-4483
**Subject(s):** Business; Law; Daily Periodicals
**Circ:** ‡5,200

**Empty Closet (22817)**
Gay Alliance of Genesee Valley Inc.
875 E Main St., Ste 500
Rochester, NY 14605
Phone: (585)244-8640
Fax: (585)244-8246
**Subject(s):** Free Newspapers; Gay and Lesbian Interests
**Circ:** (Non-paid)⊕5,200

**The Foxboro Reporter (13784)**
The Sun Chronicle
36 Mechanic St.
PO Box 289
Foxboro, MA 02035
**Subject(s):** Paid Community Newspapers
**Circ:** ‡5,200

**Journal Register (14724)**
Turley Publications
24 Water St.
Palmer, MA 01069
Phone: (413)283-8393
Fax: (413)289-1977
**Subject(s):** Paid Community Newspapers
**Circ:** 5,200

**Uniondale Beacon (23086)**
Beacon Newspapers
5 Centre St.
Hempstead, NY 11550-2422
Phone: (516)481-5400
**Subject(s):** Paid Community Newspapers
**Circ:** ‡5,200

**The Spectator (14786)**
Hathaway Publishing
780 County St.
Somerset, MA 02726
Phone: (508)674-4656
Fax: (508)677-1210
**Subject(s):** Paid Community Newspapers
**Circ:** (Non-paid)♦377
(Paid)♦5,194

**The Hearthstone Town and Country (27474)**
PO Box 446
Red Hill, PA 18076
Phone: (215)679-5060
Fax: (215)679-5077
**Subject(s):** Paid Community Newspapers
**Circ:** (Paid)5,175

**Franklin News Record (19718)**
The Princeton Packet Inc.
300 Witherspoon St.
Princeton, NJ 08542
Phone: (609)924-3244
Fax: (609)924-3842
**Subject(s):** Paid Community Newspapers
**Circ:** (Paid)5,148

**News-Record of Maplewood and South Orange (19910)**
Worrall Community Newspapers
1291 Stuyvesant Ave.
PO Box 3109
Union, NJ 07083
Phone: (908)686-7700
Fax: (908)686-4169
**Subject(s):** Paid Community Newspapers
**Circ:** (Non-paid)78
(Paid)5,127

**The Standard (13589)**
Standard Publishing Corp.
155 Federal St., 13th Fl.
Boston, MA 02110
Phone: (617)457-0600
Fax: (617)482-7820
**Subject(s):** Insurance
**Circ:** 5,123

**Adirondack Daily Enterprise (22901)**
Adirondack Publishing Co.
POB 318
54 Broadway
Saranac Lake, NY 12983
Phone: (518)891-2600
Fax: (518)891-2756
**Subject(s):** Daily Newspapers
**Circ:** (Paid)5,100

**The Weehawken Reporter (19937)**
Hudson Reporter Associates
1400 Washington St.
PO Box 3069
Hoboken, NJ 07030-1601
Phone: (201)798-7800
Fax: (201)798-0018
**Subject(s):** Free Newspapers
**Circ:** (Non-paid)5,100

**Aroostook Republican & News (12498)**
Northeast Publishing Co.
PO Box 608
Caribou, ME 04736
Phone: (207)496-3251
Fax: (207)492-4351
**Subject(s):** Paid Community Newspapers
**Circ:** (Paid)5,075

**News-Record (19909)**
Worrall Community Newspapers
1291 Stuyvesant Ave.
PO Box 3109
Union, NJ 07083
Phone: (908)686-7700
Fax: (908)686-4169
**Subject(s):** Paid Community Newspapers
**Circ:** (Combined)5,078

**County Press (26772)**
3732 W Chester Pke.
PO Box 249
Newtown Square, PA 19073
Phone: (610)356-3820
Fax: (610)353-5321
**Subject(s):** Paid Community Newspapers
**Circ:** (Free)‡533
(Paid)‡5,031

**East Penn Press (26091)**
East Penn Publishing
1633 N 26th St.
Allentown, PA 18104
Phone: (610)740-0944
Fax: (610)740-0947
**Subject(s):** Paid Community Newspapers
**Circ:** (Free)‡815
(Paid)‡5,023

**Middlesex East Update (14923)**
Woburn Daily Times Inc.
1 Arrow Dr.
Woburn, MA 01801
Phone: (781)933-3700
Fax: (781)932-3321
**Subject(s):** Free Newspapers
**Circ:** (Non-paid)5,011

**Tri-County Sunday (26201)**
McLean Publishing Co.
301 Main St.
PO Box 498
Brookville, PA 15825-0498
Phone: (814)849-5339
Fax: (814)849-4333
**Subject(s):** Paid Community Newspapers
**Circ:** (Paid)‡5,011

**The Anchor (27887)**
Rhode Island College
Student Union, Rm. 308
600 Mt. Pleasant Ave.
Providence, RI 02908
Phone: (401)456-8000
Fax: (401)456-8379

**Subject(s):** College Publications
**Circ:** ‡5,000

**Bellmore/Merrick Observer (20362)**
The Observer Newspapers
PO Box 407
Bellmore, NY 11710-0407
Phone: (516)679-9888
Fax: (516)731-0338
**Subject(s):** Paid Community Newspapers
**Circ:** ‡5,000

**Brookhaven Review (22944)**
ESP Publications
127 E. Main St.
Smithtown, NY 11787
**Subject(s):** Paid Community Newspapers
**Circ:** (Paid)5,000

**The Camden Herald (12492)**
Courier Publications
PO Box 248
Camden, ME 04843
Phone: (207)236-8511
**Subject(s):** Paid Community Newspapers
**Circ:** 5,000

**Campus Times (22810)**
University of Rochester Students Association
Wilson Commons 102
CPU 277086
Rochester, NY 14627-7086
Phone: (585)275-5942
Fax: (585)273-5303
**Subject(s):** College Publications; Paid Community Newspapers
**Circ:** (Controlled)5,000

**County Neighbors (27460)**
Spirit Publishing Co.
510 Pine St.
PO Box 444
Punxsutawney, PA 15767-0444
Phone: (814)938-8740
Fax: (814)938-3794
**Subject(s):** Paid Community Newspapers
**Circ:** ‡5,000

**Gloucester City News (19119)**
34 S Broadway
PO Box 151
Gloucester City, NJ 08030
Phone: (856)456-1199
Fax: (856)456-1330
**Subject(s):** Paid Community Newspapers
**Circ:** (Free)‡100
(Paid)‡5,000

**Greenpoint Gazette (20510)**
Community Gazette Inc.
597 Manhattan Ave.
Brooklyn, NY 11222
Phone: (718)389-6067
Fax: (718)349-3471
**Subject(s):** Paid Community Newspapers; Ethnic Publications
**Circ:** 5,000

**Hollis Brookline Journal (18889)**
The Cabinet Press Inc.
54 School St.
PO Box 180
Milford, NH 03055-0180
Phone: (603)673-3100
Fax: (603)673-8250
**Subject(s):** Paid Community Newspapers
**Circ:** (Non-paid)5,000

**The L (22017)**
New York Law School
57 Worth St.
New York, NY 10013
Phone: (212)431-2100
Fax: (212)966-1522
**Subject(s):** College Publications
**Circ:** ‡5,000

**The Long Term View (13431)**
Massachusetts School of Law
Woodland Park
500 Federal St.
Andover, MA 01810
Phone: (978)681-0800
Fax: (978)681-6330

**Subject(s):** College Publications; Law
**Circ:** (Non-paid)5,000

**Maine Organic Farmer and Gardener (12534)**
Maine Organic Farmers and Gardeners Association
RR2, Box 594
Lincolnville, ME 04849
Phone: (207)763-3043
**Subject(s):** Farm Newspapers

**Circ:** (Non-paid)‡100
(Paid)‡5,000

**The Montclarion (19917)**
Montclair State University
Student Center Annex, Rm. 113
Upper Montclair, NJ 07043
Phone: (973)655-5241
Fax: (973)655-7804
**Subject(s):** College Publications

**Circ:** 5,000

**The New Republic (26694)**
PO Box 239
145 Center St.
Meyersdale, PA 15552
Phone: (814)634-8321
Fax: (814)634-5556
**Subject(s):** Paid Community Newspapers

**Circ:** ‡5,000

**The Newport Daily Express (30914)**
PO Box 347
Newport, VT 05855
Phone: (802)334-6568
Fax: (802)334-6891
**Subject(s):** Daily Newspapers

**Circ:** (Paid)‡4,600
(Free)‡5,001

**News Report (18984)**
Cam-Glo Newspapers
PO Box 67
Blackwood, NJ 08012-0067
Phone: (856)228-7300
Fax: (856)232-0213
**Subject(s):** Paid Community Newspapers

**Circ:** (Paid)‡3,854
(Free)‡5,000

**The News and Sentinel (18779)**
6 Bridge St.
Box 39
Colebrook, NH 03576
Phone: (603)237-5501
Fax: (603)237-5060
**Subject(s):** Paid Community Newspapers

**Circ:** 5,000

**Nordstjernan (Swedish News) (22179)**
PO Box 4587
New York, NY 10163-4587
Phone: (212)490-3900
Fax: (212)490-5979
**Subject(s):** Paid Community Newspapers; Swedish

**Circ:** (Free)‡100
(Paid)‡5,000

**NY-PA Collector (20613)**
Messenger-Post Newspapers
73 Buffalo St.
Canandaigua, NY 14424
Phone: (585)394-0770
Fax: (585)394-1675
**Subject(s):** Antiques; Collecting; Paid Community Newspapers

**Circ:** (Non-paid)2,500
(Paid)5,000

**Salem Observer (18957)**
88 Stiles Rd., No. 103
PO Box 720
Salem, NH 03079
Phone: (603)893-4356
Fax: (603)893-0721
**Subject(s):** Paid Community Newspapers

**Circ:** ‡5,000

**State Times (22659)**
State University of New York College at Oneonta
Ravine Pkwy.
Oneonta, NY 13820
Phone: (607)436-3500
Fax: (607)436-2415

**Subject(s):** College Publications
**Circ:** (Free)‡5,000

**The Stylus (20430)**
State University of New York College at Brockport
B30 Seymour Union
Brockport, NY 14420-2948
Phone: (585)395-5623
Fax: (585)395-2609
**Subject(s):** College Publications

**Circ:** (Free)‡5,000

**The Ticker (22453)**
1 Bernard Baruch Way
New York, NY 10010
Phone: (646)312-1000
**Subject(s):** College Publications

**Circ:** (Free)‡5,000

**Viking News (19882)**
Ocean County College
College Dr.
PO Box 2001
Toms River, NJ 08754-2001
Phone: (732)255-0481
Fax: (732)255-0444
**Subject(s):** College Publications

**Circ:** (Free)‡5,000

**The Voice (26184)**
Bloomsburg University
The Voice
400 E. 2ND St.
Bloomsburg, PA 17815-1301
Phone: (570)389-4000
**Subject(s):** College Publications

**Circ:** (Free)‡5,000

**The Wharton Journal (27297)**
University of Pennsylvania Wharton School
330 Jon M. Huntsman Hall
3730 Walnut St.
Philadelphia, PA 19104
Phone: (215)898-3200
Fax: (215)898-1200
**Subject(s):** College Publications

**Circ:** 5,000

**Daily Mercury (14235)**
Associated Newspapers
800 Hingham St.
PO Box 309
Rockland, MA 02370
Phone: (781)878-1111
Fax: (781)878-3333
**Subject(s):** Daily Newspapers

**Circ:** ‡4,995

**Barrington Times (27945)**
East Bay Newspapers
Barrington Times
139 Main St
Warren, RI 02885-4302
Phone: (401)245-6000
Fax: (401)245-3640
**Subject(s):** Paid Community Newspapers

**Circ:** (Non-paid)♦110
(Paid)♦4,988

**Pawling News Chronicle (22689)**
Taconic Press
3 Memorial Ave.
Pawling, NY 12564
Phone: (914)855-1100
Fax: (914)855-1106
**Subject(s):** Paid Community Newspapers

**Circ:** (Free)312
(Paid)4,984

**The St. Albans Messenger (30932)**
Vermont Publishing Inc.
281 N Main St.
PO Box 1250
Saint Albans, VT 05478-1250
Phone: (802)524-9771
Fax: (802)527-1948
**Subject(s):** Daily Newspapers

**Circ:** (Free)140
(Paid)4,989

**North East Breeze (26783)**
Brown Thompson Newspapers Inc.
39 S. Lake St.
North East, PA 16428
Phone: (814)725-4557

Fax: (814)725-1981
**Subject(s):** Paid Community Newspapers

**Circ:** (Paid)‡2,628
(Free)‡4,977

**Manhasset Press (21111)**
Anton Community Newspapers
132 E. 2nd St.
Mineola, NY 11501
Phone: (516)747-8282
Fax: (516)742-5867
**Subject(s):** Paid Community Newspapers

**Circ:** (Paid)‡4,961

**The Flushing Times (20783)**
Queens Publishing Corp.
41-02 Bell Blvd., 2nd Fl.
Bayside, NY 11361
Phone: (718)229-0300
Fax: (718)225-7117
**Subject(s):** Paid Community Newspapers

**Circ:** (Paid)4,959

**The York Weekly (12621)**
James Carter Publications Inc.
15A Woodbridge Rd.
PO Box 7
York, ME 03909
Phone: (207)363-4343
Fax: (207)351-2849
**Subject(s):** Paid Community Newspapers

**Circ:** (Free)‡175
(Paid)‡4,918

**Pennysaver (Chittenango Edition) (22654)**
Oneida-Chittenango Pennysaver Inc.
208 Lenox Ave.
PO Box 297
Oneida, NY 13421
Phone: (315)697-2969
Fax: (315)363-3119
**Subject(s):** Shopping Guides

**Circ:** (Free)4,870

**The Putnam County Courier (4924)**
Housatonic Publications
65 Bank St.
New Milford, CT 06776
Fax: (860)354-2645
**Subject(s):** Paid Community Newspapers

**Circ:** (Free)207
(Paid)4,875

**Ulster County Townsman (23201)**
18 Rock City Rd.
Woodstock, NY 12498
**Subject(s):** Paid Community Newspapers

**Circ:** (Free)‡32
(Paid)‡4,870

**The Titusville Herald (27579)**
Titusville Herald
209 W Spring St.
PO Box 328
Titusville, PA 16354
Phone: (814)827-3634
Fax: (814)827-2512
**Subject(s):** Daily Newspapers

**Circ:** 4,833

**Strathmore-Onondaga Hill Pennysaver (23039)**
Scotsman Community Publications
750 W. Genesee St.
PO Box 4970
Syracuse, NY 13221
Phone: (315)472-7825
Fax: (315)478-1434
**Subject(s):** Shopping Guides

**Circ:** (Non-paid)‡4,822

**Wayne County Star (21088)**
36 B Canal St.
PO Box 430
Lyons, NY 14489
Phone: (315)946-9701
Fax: (315)946-4382
**Subject(s):** Paid Community Newspapers

**Circ:** 4,819

# Northeastern States

**County Wide Newspaper** (12537)
County Wide Communications Inc.
26 Main St.
PO Box 497
Machias, ME 04654
**Subject(s):** Paid Community Newspapers
**Circ:** (Free)300
(Paid)4,800

**The Forest Press** (27578)
Forest Press
PO Box 366
Tionesta, PA 16353
Phone: (814)755-4900
Fax: (814)755-4429
**Subject(s):** Paid Community Newspapers
**Circ:** ‡4,800

**The Quoddy Tides** (12507)
123 Water St.
PO Box 213
Eastport, ME 04631
Phone: (207)853-4806
Fax: (207)853-4095
**Subject(s):** Paid Community Newspapers
**Circ:** ‡4,805

**Ronkonkoma Review** (22879)
ESP Publications
127 E. Main St.
Smithtown, NY 11787
**Subject(s):** Paid Community Newspapers
**Circ:** (Free)600
(Paid)4,800

**The Roslyn News** (22885)
Anton Community Newspapers
132 E. 2nd St.
Mineola, NY 11501
Phone: (516)747-8282
Fax: (516)742-5867
**Subject(s):** Paid Community Newspapers
**Circ:** (Free)‡500
(Paid)‡4,788

**Webster Herald** (23141)
Empire State Weeklies Inc.
2010 Empire Blvd.
Webster, NY 14580
Phone: (585)671-1533
Fax: (585)671-7067
**Subject(s):** Paid Community Newspapers
**Circ:** (Paid)‡4,782

**Courier-Standard-Enterprise** (20791)
The Kline
81 Canal St.
PO Box 351
Fort Plain, NY 13339
Phone: (518)993-2321
Fax: (518)993-4919
**Subject(s):** Paid Community Newspapers
**Circ:** ‡4,778

**South County Independent** (27944)
South County Newspapers Inc.
203 Main St.
PO BOX 5679
Wakefield, RI 02879-5679
Phone: (401)789-6000
Fax: (401)792-9176
**Subject(s):** Paid Community Newspapers
**Circ:** (Paid)♦4,752

**Wareham Courier** (14750)
MPG Newspapers
9 Long Pond Rd.
PO Box 959
Plymouth, MA 02362-0959
Phone: (508)746-5555
Fax: (508)747-2148
**Subject(s):** Paid Community Newspapers
**Circ:** (Combined)4,717

**Advance Leader Star** (26719)
Gateway Press
610 Beatty Rd.
PO Box 6429
Monroeville, PA 15146-1502
Phone: (412)856-7400
Fax: (412)856-7954
**Subject(s):** Paid Community Newspapers
**Circ:** (Free)‡170
(Paid)‡4,708

**Journal Opinion** (30848)
The Mill
PO Box 378
Bradford, VT 05033
Phone: (802)222-5281
Fax: (802)222-5438
**Subject(s):** Paid Community Newspapers
**Circ:** (Paid)‡4,700

**The Ligonier Echo** (27499)
229 Pittsburgh St.
Scottdale, PA 15683
Phone: (724)887-7400
Fax: (724)887-5115
**Subject(s):** Paid Community Newspapers
**Circ:** ‡4,692

**Weymouth News** (14909)
Community Newspaper Co.
91 Washington St.
Weymouth, MA 02188
Phone: (781)843-2937
Fax: (781)682-4851
**Subject(s):** Paid Community Newspapers
**Circ:** (Non-paid)208
(Paid)4,692

**Gouverneur Tribune-Press** (20844)
Gouverneur Tribune-Press Inc.
74 Trinty Ave.
Gouverneur, NY 13642
Phone: (315)287-2100
**Subject(s):** Paid Community Newspapers
**Circ:** ‡4,680

**The Messenger-Press** (19727)
Princeton Packet Inc.
300 Witherspoon St.
P.O. Box 350
Princeton, NJ 08542
Phone: (609)924-3244
Fax: (609)924-3842
**Subject(s):** Paid Community Newspapers
**Circ:** (Paid)4,650

**The Barnstable Patriot** (13833)
The Barnstable Patriot Newspaper Inc.
396 Main St., Ste. 15
PO Box 1208
Hyannis, MA 02601
Phone: (508)771-1427
Fax: (508)790-3997
**Subject(s):** Paid Community Newspapers
**Circ:** ‡4,614

**Cranbury Press** (19714)
The Princeton Packet Inc.
300 Witherspoon St.
Princeton, NJ 08542
Phone: (609)924-3244
Fax: (609)924-3842
**Subject(s):** Paid Community Newspapers
**Circ:** ‡4,616

**Pennysaver** (27948)
Beacon Communications of Rhode Island
1944 Warwick Ave.
Warwick, RI 02889-5000
Phone: (401)732-3100
Fax: (401)732-3110
**Subject(s):** Shopping Guides
**Circ:** (Free)♦4,615

**Plum Advance Leader Star** (26730)
Gateway Publications
610 Beatty Rd.
Monroeville, PA 15146
Phone: (412)856-7400
Fax: (412)856-7954
**Subject(s):** Paid Community Newspapers
**Circ:** (Combined)4,612

**Ware River News** (14726)
Turley Publications
24 Water St.
Palmer, MA 01069
Phone: (413)283-8393
Fax: (413)283-7107
**Subject(s):** Paid Community Newspapers
**Circ:** ‡4,600

**New Milford Times** (4923)
Housatonic Publications
65 Bank St.
New Milford, CT 06776
Fax: (860)354-2645
**Subject(s):** Paid Community Newspapers
**Circ:** (Non-paid)5
(Paid)4,575

**The Eagle** (20608)
14 S Park St.
PO Box 36
Cambridge, NY 12816
Phone: (518)677-5158
Fax: (518)677-8323
**Subject(s):** Paid Community Newspapers
**Circ:** (Free)35
(Paid)4,550

**Berkshire Record** (13804)
21 Elm St.
Great Barrington, MA 01230
Phone: (413)528-5380
**Subject(s):** Paid Community Newspapers
**Circ:** ‡4,500

**Braintree Forum** (14256)
Community Newspaper Co.
254 2nd Ave.
Needham, MA 02494
Phone: (781)433-6700
**Subject(s):** Paid Community Newspapers
**Circ:** (Non-paid)189
(Paid)4,508

**Charlestown Patriot & Somerville Chronicle** (13725)
Charlestown Patriot Publications Inc.
1 Thompson Sq.
P O Box 54
Charlestown, MA 02129-0054
Phone: (617)241-9511
**Subject(s):** Paid Community Newspapers
**Circ:** ‡4,500

**Citizen-Standard** (27623)
104 W. Main St.
PO Box 147
Valley View, PA 17983
Phone: (570)682-9081
Fax: (570)682-8734
**Subject(s):** Paid Community Newspapers
**Circ:** 4,500

**The Colgate Maroon-News** (20873)
Student Union
13 Oak Dr.
Hamilton, NY 13346
Phone: (315)228-7744
Fax: (315)228-7745
**Subject(s):** College Publications
**Circ:** (Free)‡4,500

**Duxbury Clipper** (13760)
PO Box 1656
Duxbury, MA 02331
Phone: (781)934-2811
Fax: (781)934-5917
**Subject(s):** Paid Community Newspapers
**Circ:** (Free)‡150
(Paid)‡4,500

**Frontpage** (21719)
Newspaper Guild of New York
1501 Broadway, 7th Fl., Ste. 708
New York, NY 10036
Phone: (212)575-1580
**Subject(s):** Labor
**Circ:** ‡4,500

**The Gazette** (19790)
Gloucester County College
1400 Tanyard Rd.
College, Ctr., Ste. 100
Sewell, NJ 08080
Phone: (856)468-5000
Fax: (856)464-9153
**Subject(s):** College Publications
**Circ:** (Free)4,500

**Home News** (26143)
Home News Inc.
120 S Walnut St.
PO Box 39
Bath, PA 18014
Phone: (610)837-0107

Fax: (610)837-0482
**Subject(s):** Paid Community Newspapers

Circ: (Free)‡85
(Paid)‡4,500

**Jewish Observer** (20705)
The Syracuse Jewish Federation Inc.
5655 Thompson Rd.
DeWitt, NY 13214
Phone: (315)445-2040
Fax: (315)445-1559
**Subject(s):** Jewish Publications; Religious Publications

Circ: 4,500

**The Lake Placid News** (21019)
Ogden Newspapers Inc.
412 S Main St.
Lake Placid, NY 12946
Phone: (518)523-4401
Fax: (518)891-1351
**Subject(s):** Paid Community Newspapers

Circ: (Paid)‡4,500

**Merrick Beacon** (21202)
Beacon Newspapers
5 Centre St.
Hempstead, NY 11550-2422
Phone: (516)481-5400
**Subject(s):** Paid Community Newspapers

Circ: ‡4,500

**Putnam County News & Recorder** (20663)
86 Main St.
PO Box 185
Cold Spring, NY 10516
Phone: (845)265-2468
Fax: (845)265-2144
**Subject(s):** Paid Community Newspapers

Circ: ‡4,500

**Lakeville Journal** (4831)
The Lakeville Journal Company L.L.C.
PO Box 1688
Lakeville, CT 06039-1688
Phone: (860)435-9873
Fax: (860)435-0146
**Subject(s):** Paid Community Newspapers

Circ: (Non-paid)47
(Paid)4,493

**Levittown Tribune** (21059)
Anton Community Newspapers
132 E. 2nd St.
Mineola, NY 11501
Phone: (516)747-8282
Fax: (516)742-5867
**Subject(s):** Paid Community Newspapers

Circ: ‡4,457

**Long Beach Herald** (21056)
Richner Communications
P.O. Box 9001
Lawrence, NY 11559-1616
Phone: (516)569-4000
Fax: (516)569-4942
**Subject(s):** Paid Community Newspapers

Circ: (Free)‡1,883
(Paid)‡4,451

**Ramsey Suburban News** (19958)
North Jersey Community Newspapers
The Weekly Division of N Jersey Media Group
1 Garret Mountain Plz.
PO Box 471
West Paterson, NJ 07424-0471
Phone: (973)569-7000
Fax: (973)569-7310
**Subject(s):** Free Newspapers

Circ: (Wed.)4,458

**East Aurora Advertiser** (20714)
710 Main St.
East Aurora, NY 14052-2486
Phone: (716)652-0320
Fax: (716)652-8383
**Subject(s):** Paid Community Newspapers

Circ: ‡4,400

**Patriot & Free Press** (20693)
Patriot Newspapers
34 Water St.
Cuba, NY 14727-1490
Phone: (585)968-2580
Fax: (585)968-2622

**Subject(s):** Paid Community Newspapers

Circ: ‡4,400

**The Valley Shopper** (20804)
Valley Newspapers Inc.
117 Oneida St.
Fulton, NY 13069
Phone: (315)598-6397
**Subject(s):** Shopping Guides

Circ: (Non-paid)4,400

**Marshfield Mariner** (14265)
Community Newspaper Co.
254 2nd Ave.
Needham, MA 02494
Phone: (781)433-6700
**Subject(s):** Paid Community Newspapers

Circ: (Non-paid)175
(Paid)4,399

**South Hills Record** (27403)
Gateway Publications
3623 Brownsville Rd.
Pittsburgh, PA 15227
**Subject(s):** Paid Community Newspapers

Circ: (Non-paid)354
(Paid)4,394

**Times-Express Star** (26734)
Gateway Publications
610 Beatty Rd.
Monroeville, PA 15146
Phone: (412)856-7400
Fax: (412)856-7954
**Subject(s):** Paid Community Newspapers

Circ: (Non-paid)221
(Paid)4,370

**The Calais Advertiser** (12489)
Advertiser Publishing Co.
23 Church St.
PO Box 660
Calais, ME 04619-0660
Phone: (207)454-3561
Fax: (207)454-3458
**Subject(s):** Paid Community Newspapers

Circ: 4,350

**The Evening Times** (21068)
Liberty Group Publishing
PO Box 1007
Little Falls, NY 13365
Phone: (315)823-3680
Fax: (315)823-4086
**Subject(s):** Daily Newspapers

Circ: ‡4,350

**Wallkill Valley Times** (23113)
23 E Main St.
PO Box 446
Walden, NY 12586
Phone: (845)778-2181
Fax: (845)778-1196
**Subject(s):** Paid Community Newspapers

Circ: (Free)‡100
(Paid)‡4,352

**North Reading Transcript** (14320)
Great Oak Publications Inc.
7 Bow St.
North Reading, MA 01864
Phone: (978)664-4761
Fax: (978)664-4954
**Subject(s):** Paid Community Newspapers

Circ: (Non-paid)193
(Paid)4,345

**Cranford Chronicle** (19049)
The Chronicle
102 Walnut Ave.
Cranford, NJ 07016
Phone: (908)276-6000
Fax: (908)276-6220
**Subject(s):** Paid Community Newspapers

Circ: (Paid)4,320

**South Brunswick Post** (19054)
The Princeton Packet Inc.
PO Box 309
Dayton, NJ 08810
Phone: (908)529-9214
Fax: (908)529-9286
**Subject(s):** Paid Community Newspapers

Circ: (Paid)4,316

**The Harrison Independent** (20878)
Martinelli Publications
40 Larkin Plz.
Yonkers, NY 10701
Phone: (914)965-4000
Fax: (914)965-2892
**Subject(s):** Paid Community Newspapers

Circ: (Combined)⊕4,300

**Medina Daily Journal-Register–Eastern Niagara Edition** (21147)
Medina Daily Journal-Register Inc.
409-13 Main St.
Medina, NY 14103-1416
Phone: (585)798-1400
Fax: (585)798-0290
**Subject(s):** Free Newspapers

Circ: (Mon.-Fri.)★4,301

**Tuckerton Beacon** (19906)
Manahawkin Newspapers Inc.
345 E Bay Ave.
Manahawkin, NJ 08050-3320
Phone: (609)597-3211
Fax: (609)978-4592
**Subject(s):** Paid Community Newspapers

Circ: (Thurs.)4,305

**The Westborough News** (14894)
10 E Main St.
Westborough, MA 01581
Phone: (508)366-1511
Fax: (508)366-5265
**Subject(s):** Paid Community Newspapers

Circ: (Paid)4,300

**Hamilton County News** (22954)
William J. Kline and Son Inc.
Rte. 30
Speculator, NY 12164
**Subject(s):** Paid Community Newspapers

Circ: ‡4,285

**Mineola American** (21214)
Anton Community Newspapers
132 E. 2nd St.
Mineola, NY 11501
Phone: (516)747-8282
Fax: (516)742-5867
**Subject(s):** Paid Community Newspapers

Circ: (Paid)‡4,280

**The Webster Post** (23143)
Messenger-Post Newspapers
40 North Ave.
Webster, NY 14580
Phone: (716)872-2221
Fax: (716)872-0494
**Subject(s):** Paid Community Newspapers

Circ: (Non-paid)♦528
(Paid)♦4,288

**The Observer** (27855)
Observer Publications Inc.
1 Whipple Ln.
Box 950
Greenville, RI 02828
Phone: (401)949-2700
Fax: (401)333-4600
**Subject(s):** Paid Community Newspapers

Circ: (Non-paid)♦351
(Paid)♦4,271

**The Jerusalem Post, International Edition** (21856)
80 Wall St Ste. 715
New York, NY 10005
Phone: (212)226-0955
Fax: (212)742-0880
**Subject(s):** Paid Community Newspapers; Jewish Publications

Circ: 4,200

**The Justice** (14862)
Brandeis University
Usdan Student Center 7
Waltham, MA 02453
**Subject(s):** College Publications

Circ: (Paid)300
(Free)4,200

---

Circulation: ★ = ABC; △ = BPA; ♦ = CAC; • = CCAB; ❑ = VAC; ⊕ = PO Statement; ‡ = Publisher's Report; Boldface figures = sworn; Light figures = estimated.

# Northeastern States

**The Katahdin Times (12541)**
Eastern Publishing Ltd.
202 Penobscot Ave.
PO Box 330
Millinocket, ME 04462
Phone: (207)723-8118
Fax: (207)723-4434
**Subject(s):** Paid Community Newspapers
**Circ:** (Free)160
(Paid)4,200

**Massapequa Post (20276)**
ACJ Communication Inc.
85 Broadway
Amityville, NY 11701
Phone: (631)264-0077
Fax: (631)264-5310
**Subject(s):** Free Newspapers
**Circ:** (Free)100
(Paid)4,200

**The Vermont Standard (30962)**
PO Box 88
Woodstock, VT 05091
Phone: (802)457-1313
Fax: (802)457-3639
**Subject(s):** Paid Community Newspapers
**Circ:** ‡4,200

**Perinton-Fairport Post (20763)**
Messenger-Post Newspapers
1 Grove St., Ste. 101
Pittsford, NY 14534
Phone: (585)381-3300
Fax: (585)381-5325
**Subject(s):** Paid Community Newspapers
**Circ:** (Non-paid)♦170
(Paid)♦4,190

**Corry Journal (26267)**
28 W South St.
Corry, PA 16407-0709
Phone: (814)665-8291
Fax: (814)664-2288
**Subject(s):** Daily Newspapers
**Circ:** (Free)200
(Paid)4,184

**Farmingdale Observer (20769)**
Anton Community Newspapers
132 E. 2nd St.
Mineola, NY 11501
Phone: (516)747-8282
Fax: (516)742-5867
**Subject(s):** Paid Community Newspapers
**Circ:** ‡4,174

**Oceanside-Island Park Herald (22638)**
Richner Communications
143 E. Park Ave.
Long Beach, NY 11561
Phone: (516)431-3400
Fax: (516)889-4419
**Subject(s):** Paid Community Newspapers
**Circ:** (Free)‡1,105
(Paid)‡4,163

**Syosset/Jericho Tribune (20998)**
Anton Community Newspapers
132 E. 2nd St.
Mineola, NY 11501
Phone: (516)747-8282
Fax: (516)742-5867
**Subject(s):** Paid Community Newspapers
**Circ:** (Paid)‡4,114

**Buffalo Jewish Review (20558)**
15 E Mohawk St.
Buffalo, NY 14203
Phone: (716)854-2192
Fax: (716)854-2198
**Subject(s):** Jewish Publications; Paid Community Newspapers
**Circ:** ‡4,100

**Upper Darby Press (26291)**
Press Publishing Co.
3245 Garrett Rd.
Drexel Hill, PA 19026
Phone: (610)259-4141
**Subject(s):** Paid Community Newspapers
**Circ:** ‡4,100

**Dover-Sherborn TAB (13759)**
Community Newspaper Co.
254 2nd Ave.
Needham, MA 02494
Phone: (781)433-6700
**Subject(s):** Free Newspapers
**Circ:** (Free)4,094

**The Illustrated News (21236)**
Anton Community Newspapers
132 E. 2nd St.
Mineola, NY 11501
Phone: (516)747-8282
Fax: (516)742-5867
**Subject(s):** Paid Community Newspapers
**Circ:** ‡4,098

**Clarence Bee (20645)**
Bee Publications Inc.
5564 Main St.
PO Box 150
Buffalo, NY 14231-0150
Phone: (716)632-4700
Fax: (716)633-8601
**Subject(s):** Paid Community Newspapers
**Circ:** (Free)⊕54
(Paid)⊕4,067

**The Eastchester Record (20738)**
Martinelli Publications
40 Larkin Plz.
Yonkers, NY 10701
Phone: (914)965-4000
Fax: (914)965-2892
**Subject(s):** Paid Community Newspapers
**Circ:** (Combined)⊕4,058

**The Call (27496)**
South Schuylkill Printing & Publishing
PO Box 178
Schuylkill Haven, PA 17972
Phone: (570)385-3120
Fax: (570)385-0725
**Subject(s):** Paid Community Newspapers
**Circ:** (Paid)4,047

**The Record Star (26742)**
Gateway Press
5500 Steubenville Pike
Mc Kees Rocks, PA 15136-1401
Phone: (412)494-9017
Fax: (412)494-9080
**Subject(s):** Paid Community Newspapers
**Circ:** (Non-paid)401
(Paid)4,047

**Hingham Mariner (13820)**
Mariner Newspapers
254 2nd Ave
PO Box 9113
Needham, MA 02494
Phone: (781)837-3500
Fax: (781)837-4540
**Subject(s):** Paid Community Newspapers
**Circ:** (Non-paid)166
(Paid)4,038

**West Roxbury Transcript (14279)**
Community Newspaper Co.
254 2nd Ave.
Needham, MA 02494
Phone: (781)433-6700
**Subject(s):** Free Newspapers
**Circ:** (Free)190
(Paid)4,032

**Randolph Reporter (19758)**
Recorder Publishing Company Inc.
530 E. Main St.
Chester, NJ 07930
**Subject(s):** Free Newspapers
**Circ:** (Combined)4,029

**The Cape Courier (12497)**
PO Box 6242
Cape Elizabeth, ME 04107
Phone: (207)767-5023
**Subject(s):** Paid Community Newspapers
**Circ:** (Combined)4,000

**Catskill Mountain News (20287)**
PO Box 515
Arkville, NY 12406-0515
Phone: (845)586-2601
Fax: (845)586-2366
**Subject(s):** Paid Community Newspapers
**Circ:** ‡4,000

**Cheektowaga Times (20641)**
Cheektowaga Times Inc.
343 Maryvale Dr.
Cheektowaga, NY 14225
Phone: (716)892-5323
Fax: (716)892-4925
**Subject(s):** Paid Community Newspapers
**Circ:** (Paid)‡4,000

**Colby Echo (12614)**
The Colby Echo
4000 Mayflower Hill
Waterville, ME 04901-8440
Phone: (207)872-3000
Fax: (207)872-3555
**Subject(s):** College Publications
**Circ:** 4,000

**The Cowl (27895)**
Providence College
549 River Ave.
Providence, RI 02918-0001
Phone: (401)865-1000
Fax: (401)865-2822
**Subject(s):** College Publications
**Circ:** 4,000

**The Crusader (14933)**
College of the Holy Cross
PO Box 32-A
Worcester, MA 01610
Phone: (508)793-2668
Fax: (508)793-3020
**Subject(s):** College Publications
**Circ:** ‡4,000

**Development Business (21597)**
United Nations
Grand Central Sta.
PO Box 5850
New York, NY 10163
Phone: (212)963-1516
Fax: (212)963-1381
**Subject(s):** Business; International Business and Economics
**Circ:** (Paid)4,000

**The Duquesne Duke (27343)**
Duquesne University
600 Forbes Ave.
Pittsburgh, PA 15282
Phone: (412)396-6610
Fax: (412)396-5984
**Subject(s):** College Publications
**Circ:** (Paid)‡300
(Free)‡4000

**Greenwood Lake and West Milford News (20869)**
Greenwood Lake News Inc.
POB 1117
Greenwood Lake, NY 10925
**Subject(s):** Paid Community Newspapers
**Circ:** ‡4,000

**Jewish Chronicle (14940)**
Mar-Len Publications
131 Lincoln St.
Worcester, MA 01605
Phone: (508)752-2512
Fax: (508)752-9057
**Subject(s):** Paid Community Newspapers; Jewish Publications
**Circ:** ‡4000

**LehighNow (26167)**
Lehigh University
436 Brodhead Ave.
Bethlehem, PA 18015-1690
Phone: (610)758-4180
**Subject(s):** College Publications
**Circ:** (Free)‡4,000

**The Meredith News (18885)**
Salmon Press
PO Box 729
Meredith, NH 03253-0729
Phone: (603)279-4516
Fax: (603)279-3331
**Subject(s):** Paid Community Newspapers
**Circ:** (Free)21
(Paid)4,000

**New Hope Gazette (26764)**
InterCounty Newspaper Group
142 S. Main St.
PO Box 180
New Hope, PA 18938
Phone: (215)862-9435
Fax: (215)862-2160
Subject(s): Paid Community Newspapers

Circ: ‡4,000

**The New Leader (14802)**
Stonebridge Press Inc.
369 Main St.
PO Box 911
Spencer, MA 01562
Phone: (508)885-9402
Fax: (508)885-4213
Subject(s): Paid Community Newspapers

Circ: 4,000

**The News Beacon (19079)**
North Jersey Community Newspapers
12-38 River Rd.
Fair Lawn, NJ 07410-1897
Phone: (201)791-8400
Fax: (201)794-3259
Subject(s): Paid Community Newspapers

Circ: 4,000

**The Salem State Log (14777)**
Salem College
352 Lafayette
Salem, MA 01970
Phone: (978)542-6448
Fax: (978)542-8126
Subject(s): College Publications

Circ: (Free)‡4,000

**The Setonian (19832)**
Seton Hall University
400 S. Orange Ave.
South Orange, NJ 07079
Phone: (973)761-9083
Fax: (973)761-7943
Subject(s): College Publications

Circ: (Non-paid)4,000

**The Slate (27530)**
Shippensburg University
3rd Fl., Cumberland Union Bldg.
Shippensburg University
Shippensburg, PA 17257
Phone: (717)477-1778
Fax: (717)532-2900
Subject(s): Free Newspapers; College Publications

Circ: (Non-paid)4,000

**Susquehanna County Independent (26739)**
County Publishers Corp.
24 S Main St.
Montrose, PA 18801
Phone: (570)278-6397
Fax: (570)278-4305
Subject(s): Paid Community Newspapers

Circ: (Free)300
(Paid)4,000

**The Vanguard (14868)**
Bentley College
310M Student Ctr.
385 Beaver St.
Waltham, MA 02452
Phone: (781)891-2912
Fax: (781)891-2574
Subject(s): College Publications

Circ: (Free)‡4,000

**The Wellsville Daily Reporter (23146)**
Wellsville Daily Reporter
159 N Main St.
Wellsville, NY 14895-1149
Phone: (585)593-5300
Fax: (585)593-5303
Subject(s): Daily Newspapers

Circ: (Paid)‡4,000

**Springville Journal (22960)**
H & K Publications Inc.
PO Box 99
Springville, NY 14141
Phone: (716)592-4550
Fax: (716)592-4663
Subject(s): Paid Community Newspapers

Circ: (Free)1,004
(Paid)3,999

**Star (26278)**
Star Printing Co.
811 Main St.
PO Box 47
Delta, PA 17314
Phone: (717)456-5692
Fax: (717)456-5692
Subject(s): Paid Community Newspapers

Circ: ‡3,995

**The Westbury Times (23170)**
Anton Community Newspapers
132 E. 2nd St.
Mineola, NY 11501
Phone: (516)747-8282
Fax: (516)742-5867
Subject(s): Paid Community Newspapers

Circ: (Free)‡500
(Paid)‡3,975

**The Chronicle (19821)**
44 Veterans Memorial Pkwy. E
PO Box 699
Somerville, NJ 08876
Phone: (908)722-3000
Fax: (908)526-2509
Subject(s): Paid Community Newspapers

Circ: (Paid)3,960

**Rye Chronicle (22886)**
Martinelli Publications
40 Larkin Plz.
Yonkers, NY 10701
Phone: (914)965-4000
Fax: (914)965-2892
Subject(s): Paid Community Newspapers

Circ: ⊕3,966

**Kingston Reporter (13849)**
MPG Newspapers
9 Long Pond Rd.
PO Box 959
Plymouth, MA 02362-0959
Phone: (508)746-5555
Fax: (508)747-2148
Subject(s): Free Newspapers

Circ: (Combined)3,953

**The Whitestone Times (23187)**
Queens Publishing Corp.
41-02 Bell Blvd., 2nd Fl.
Bayside, NY 11361
Phone: (718)229-0300
Fax: (718)225-7117
Subject(s): Paid Community Newspapers

Circ: (Paid)3,908

**Winthrop Sun Transcript (14769)**
Independent Newspaper Group
385 Broadway, Ste. 105
Revere, MA 02151
Phone: (781)284-2400
Fax: (781)485-1403
Subject(s): Paid Community Newspapers

Circ: (Non-paid)66
(Paid)3,902

**Jeffersonian Democrat (26200)**
McLean Publishing Co.
301 Main St.
PO Box 498
Brookville, PA 15825-0498
Phone: (814)849-5339
Fax: (814)849-4333
Subject(s): Free Newspapers

Circ: (Wed.)3,894

**Leader (21074)**
Lally Communications Inc.
160 Birch Hill Rd.
PO Box 468
Locust Valley, NY 11560
Phone: (516)759-2639
Fax: (516)671-7442
Subject(s): Paid Community Newspapers

Circ: ‡3,875

**The Chronicle-Express (22696)**
Community Newspaper Holdings Inc.
138 Main St.
Penn Yan, NY 14527-1219
Phone: (315)536-4422
Fax: (315)536-0682

**Subject(s):** Paid Community Newspapers

Circ: (Free)31
(Paid)3,860

**The Colonial (26370)**
Journal Register Co.
Montgomery Newspapers
290 Commerce Dr.
Fort Washington, PA 19034
Phone: (215)542-0200
Subject(s): Paid Community Newspapers

Circ: (Combined)3,862

**Carroll County Independent and Pioneer (18775)**
Salmon Press
PO Box 38
Center Ossipee, NH 03814
Phone: (603)539-4111
Fax: (603)539-5564
Subject(s): Paid Community Newspapers

Circ: ‡3859

**The Kent County Daily Times (27951)**
1353 Main St.
West Warwick, RI 02893
Phone: (401)821-7400
Fax: (401)828-0810
Subject(s): Daily Newspapers

Circ: (Mon.-Sat.)★3,830

**Abington Journal (26246)**
Cypress Media Inc.
211 State St.
PO Box 277
Clarks Summit, PA 18411
Phone: (571)587-1148
Fax: (570)586-3980
Subject(s): Paid Community Newspapers

Circ: (Free)178
(Paid)3,820

**Hopewell Valley News (19409)**
The Princeton Packet Inc.
PO Box 8
Hopewell, NJ 08525
Phone: (609)466-2133
Fax: (609)466-2133
Subject(s): Paid Community Newspapers

Circ: 3829

**Glenside News (26376)**
Journal Register Co.
c/o Sean Smith
290 Commerce Dr.
Fort Washington, PA 19034
Phone: (215)542-0200
Subject(s): Paid Community Newspapers

Circ: (Combined)3,817

**Wethersfield Post (4649)**
Imprint Newspapers
99 Main St.
Bristol, CT 06010
Phone: (860)236-3571
Fax: (860)233-2080
Subject(s): Paid Community Newspapers

Circ: (Non-paid)188
(Paid)3,817

**News and Citizen (30910)**
News & Citizen
PO Box 369
Morrisville, VT 05661
Phone: (802)888-2212
Fax: (802)888-2173
Subject(s): Paid Community Newspapers

Circ: (Paid)‡3,800

**The Stoneham Independent (14823)**
Woburn Daily Times Inc.
377 Main St.
Stoneham, MA 02180
Phone: (781)438-1660
Fax: (781)436-6762
Subject(s): Paid Community Newspapers

Circ: (Non-paid)14
(Paid)3,800

**Journal and Republican (21080)**
7567 State St.
Lowville, NY 13367-0033
Phone: (315)376-3525
Fax: (315)376-4136

Circulation: ★ = ABC; △ = BPA; ♦ = CAC; • = CCAB; ☐ = VAC; ⊕ = PO Statement; ‡ = Publisher's Report; Boldface figures = sworn; Light figures = estimated.

## Northeastern States

**Subject(s):** Paid Community Newspapers
**Circ:** (Paid)‡3,798

**The Press Herald (27497)**
South Schuylkill Printing and Publishing
960 E Main St.
PO Box 178
Schuylkill Haven, PA 17972
Phone: (570)385-3120
Fax: (570)385-0725
**Subject(s):** Paid Community Newspapers
**Circ:** ‡3,795

**Lancaster Bee (21026)**
Bee Publications Inc.
5564 Main St.
PO Box 150
Buffalo, NY 14231-0150
Phone: (716)632-4700
Fax: (716)633-8601
**Subject(s):** Paid Community Newspapers
**Circ:** (Free)⊕39
(Paid)⊕3,775

**Monroe Courier (5011)**
Hometown Publications Inc.
1000 Bridgeport Ave.
Shelton, CT 06484
Phone: (203)926-2080
Fax: (203)926-2091
**Subject(s):** Paid Community Newspapers
**Circ:** (Non-paid)♦500
(Paid)♦3,773

**Scituate Mariner (14780)**
Community Newspaper Co.
254 2nd Ave.
Needham, MA 02494
Phone: (781)433-6700
**Subject(s):** Paid Community Newspapers
**Circ:** (Non-paid)130
(Paid)3,777

**West Orange Chronicle (19646)**
Worrall Community Newspapers
170 Scotland Rd.
Orange, NJ 07051
Phone: (973)674-8000
Fax: (973)674-2038
**Subject(s):** Paid Community Newspapers
**Circ:** (Paid)3,771

**Berger County Newspapers, Inc. (19762)**
North Jersey Media Group
41 Oak St.
Ridgewood, NJ 07450
Phone: (201)599-6090
Fax: (201)847-1144
**Subject(s):** Paid Community Newspapers
**Circ:** (Free)‡2,500
(Paid)‡3,751

**Bellmore Life (21200)**
L & M Publications Inc.
1840 Merrick Ave.
Merrick, NY 11566-2730
Phone: (516)378-5320
Fax: (516)378-0287
**Subject(s):** Paid Community Newspapers
**Circ:** 3,728

**The New Age-Examiner (27591)**
PO Box 59
Tunkhannock, PA 18657
Phone: (570)836-2123
Fax: (570)836-3378
**Subject(s):** Paid Community Newspapers
**Circ:** (Free)35
(Paid)3,720

**Springfield Sun (26383)**
Journal Register Co.
Montgomery Newspapers
290 Commerce Dr.
Fort Washington, PA 19034
Phone: (215)542-0200
**Subject(s):** Paid Community Newspapers
**Circ:** (Combined)3,712

**Gazette-Advertiser (22781)**
Taconic Press
Box 227
Rhinebeck, NY 12572-0227
Phone: (914)876-3033
Fax: (914)876-2361

**Subject(s):** Paid Community Newspapers
**Circ:** ‡3,700

**Jamaica Plain/Roxbury Citizen (13847)**
Tribune Publishing Co.
1261 Hyde Park Ave.
Hyde Park, MA 02136
Phone: (617)361-6500
Fax: (617)361-6503
**Subject(s):** Paid Community Newspapers
**Circ:** ‡3,700

**The Weston Forum (5088)**
Hersam Acorn Newspapers L.L.C.
PO Box 1185
Weston, CT 06883
Phone: (203)544-9990
**Subject(s):** Paid Community Newspapers
**Circ:** (Paid)♦232
(Non-paid)♦3,707

**Record Breeze (18986)**
Cam-Glo Newspapers
PO Box 67
Blackwood, NJ 08012-0067
Phone: (856)228-7300
Fax: (856)232-0213
**Subject(s):** Paid Community Newspapers
**Circ:** ‡3,667

**Our Town (19511)**
58 W Pleasant Ave.
Maywood, NJ 07607
Phone: (201)843-5700
Fax: (201)843-5781
**Subject(s):** Paid Community Newspapers
**Circ:** ‡3,650

**Delaware Valley News (19088)**
Hunterdon County Democrat
8 Minneakoning Rd.
PO Box 32
Flemington, NJ 08822-0032
Phone: (908)782-4747
Fax: (908)782-6572
**Subject(s):** Paid Community Newspapers
**Circ:** (Thurs.)3,622

**Independent Mirror (21205)**
Oswego County Weeklies
N Jefferson 80
PO Box 129
Mexico, NY 13114
Phone: (315)963-7813
Fax: (315)963-4087
**Subject(s):** Paid Community Newspapers
**Circ:** 3,600

**Union Leader (19912)**
Worrall Community Newspapers
1291 Stuyvesant Ave.
PO Box 3109
Union, NJ 07083
Phone: (908)686-7700
Fax: (908)686-4169
**Subject(s):** Paid Community Newspapers
**Circ:** (Paid)3,607

**West Seneca Bee (23158)**
Bee Publications Inc.
5564 Main St.
PO Box 150
Buffalo, NY 14231-0150
Phone: (716)632-4700
Fax: (716)633-8601
**Subject(s):** Paid Community Newspapers
**Circ:** (Free)⊕25
(Paid)⊕3,608

**Daily Mail (20624)**
PO Box 484
Catskill, NY 12414-0484
Phone: (518)943-2100
Fax: (518)943-2063
**Subject(s):** Daily Newspapers
**Circ:** 3,579

**The Outlook (19944)**
Monmouth University
400 Cedar Ave.
West Long Branch, NJ 07764-1898
Phone: (732)571-3481
Fax: (732)263-5151

**Subject(s):** College Publications
**Circ:** (Paid)‡25
(Free)‡3,575

**Chatham Courier (19840)**
Recorder Publishing Company Inc.
254 Mercer St.
Stirling, NJ 07980
Phone: (908)647-1180
**Subject(s):** Paid Community Newspapers
**Circ:** (Combined)3,532

**Murrysville Star (26726)**
Gateway Publications
610 Beatty Rd.
Monroeville, PA 15146
Phone: (412)856-7400
Fax: (412)856-7954
**Subject(s):** Paid Community Newspapers
**Circ:** (Paid)774
(Non-paid)3,539

**The Bona Venture (22893)**
St. Bonaventure University
3261 W. State Rd.
Saint Bonaventure, NY 14778
Phone: (716)375-2000
**Subject(s):** College Publications
**Circ:** ‡3,500

**Chenango American, Whitney Point Reporter, and Oxford Review Times (20865)**
PO Box 566
Greene, NY 13778
Phone: (607)656-4511
Fax: (607)656-8544
**Subject(s):** Paid Community Newspapers
**Circ:** ‡3,500

**Courier-Gazette (22604)**
613 S Main St.
Newark, NY 14513
Phone: (315)331-1000
Fax: (315)331-1053
**Subject(s):** Paid Community Newspapers
**Circ:** ‡3,500

**Dillsburg Banner (26282)**
31 S Baltimore St.
Dillsburg, PA 17019
Phone: (717)432-3456
Fax: (717)432-1518
**Subject(s):** Paid Community Newspapers
**Circ:** (Non-paid)500
(Paid)3,500

**The Hill News (20617)**
St. Lawrence University
617 CMR
Saint Lawrence University
Canton, NY 13617
Phone: (315)229-5944
Fax: (315)229-5944
**Subject(s):** College Publications
**Circ:** (Free)‡3,500

**Home News (19783)**
766 Irving Pl.
PO Box 1100
Secaucus, NJ 07096
Phone: (201)867-2071
Fax: (201)865-3806
**Subject(s):** Paid Community Newspapers
**Circ:** ‡3,500

**Marcus Hook Press (26290)**
Press Publishing Co.
3245 Garrett Rd.
Drexel Hill, PA 19026
Phone: (610)259-4141
**Subject(s):** Paid Community Newspapers
**Circ:** ‡3,500

**New Morning (22714)**
Pace University
861 Bedford Rd.
Pleasantville, NY 10570
Phone: (914)773-3401
Fax: (914)773-3402
**Subject(s):** College Publications
**Circ:** (Free)‡3,500

**Seawanhaka (20539)**
Long Island University Press
1 University Plz., Rm. 5219
Brooklyn, NY 11201
Phone: (718)488-1591
Fax: (718)780-4182
**Subject(s):** College Publications
**Circ:** (Free)‡3,500

**The Sophian (14326)**
Smith College
Capen Annex
Northampton, MA 01063
Phone: (413)585-4971
Fax: (413)585-2075
**Subject(s):** College Publications
**Circ:** ‡3,500

**The Stanstead Journal (30882)**
515 A Dufferin Stanstead
PO Box 491
Derby Line, VT 05830
Phone: (819)876-7514
Fax: (819)876-7515
**Subject(s):** Paid Community Newspapers
**Circ:** ‡3,500

**The Suffolk Lawyer (20930)**
Long Islander Newspapers Inc.
322 Main St.
Huntington, NY 11743
Phone: (631)427-7000
Fax: (631)427-5820
**Subject(s):** Law
**Circ:** (Controlled)‡3,500

**Tevyne (22448)**
Lithuanian Alliance of America
307 W 30th St.
New York, NY 10001
Phone: (212)563-2210
Fax: (212)563-2210
**Subject(s):** Lithuanian; Paid Community Newspapers
**Circ:** ‡3,500

**UMASS Lowell Connector (13863)**
University of Massachusetts at Lowell
McGauvran Student Center, Ste. 347
Connector at Umass, 71 Wilder St.
71 Wilder St.
Lowell, MA 01854
Phone: (978)934-5009
Fax: (978)934-3031
**Subject(s):** College Publications
**Circ:** (Free)‡3,500

**The Valley Reporter (30949)**
The Valley Reporter Inc.
Mad River Green Rte. 100
PO Box 119
Waitsfield, VT 05673
Phone: (802)496-3607
Fax: (802)496-4703
**Subject(s):** Paid Community Newspapers
**Circ:** (Free)78
(Paid)3,500

**Valley Times-Star (27531)**
News-Chronicle Co.
PO Box 100
Shippensburg, PA 17257-0100
Phone: (717)776-3197
Fax: (717)776-9290
**Subject(s):** Paid Community Newspapers
**Circ:** ‡3,500

**Weekly Recorder (26248)**
256 Main St.
PO Drawer F
Claysville, PA 15323-0506
Phone: (724)663-7742
Fax: (724)663-3698
**Subject(s):** Paid Community Newspapers
**Circ:** 3,500

**The Spring-Ford Reporter (27486)**
Journal Register Co.
c/o Melissa Finley
265 Main St.
Royersford, PA 19468
Phone: (610)948-4850
Fax: (610)948-5914
**Subject(s):** Paid Community Newspapers
**Circ:** (Combined)3,490

**Harlem Valley Times (20255)**
Taconic Press
PO Box H
Amenia, NY 12501
Phone: (914)373-8800
Fax: (914)373-8938
**Subject(s):** Paid Community Newspapers
**Circ:** ‡3,476

**The Independent-Observer (27498)**
Laurel Group Press
229 Pittsburgh St.
PO Box 222
Scottdale, PA 15683
Phone: (724)887-7400
Fax: (724)887-5115
**Subject(s):** Paid Community Newspapers
**Circ:** ⊕3,470

**The Review (19824)**
The Chronicle
44 Veterans Memorial Pkwy. E
PO Box 699
Somerville, NJ 08876
Phone: (908)722-3000
Fax: (908)526-2509
**Subject(s):** Paid Community Newspapers
**Circ:** (Paid)3,478

**The Advisor - Youngwood (26746)**
Laurel Group Press
23 S. Church St.
Mount Pleasant, PA 15666
Phone: (412)547-5722
**Subject(s):** Free Newspapers
**Circ:** (Free)⊕3,426

**The Cresson/Gallitzin Mainliner (26306)**
Mainline Newspapers
PO Box 777
Ebensburg, PA 15931-0777
Phone: (814)472-4110
Fax: (814)472-2275
**Subject(s):** Paid Community Newspapers
**Circ:** 3,425

**Harwich Oracle (13817)**
Community Newspaper Co.
254 2nd Ave.
Needham, MA 02494
Phone: (781)433-6700
**Subject(s):** Free Newspapers
**Circ:** (Non-paid)3,425

**Wantagh-Seaford Citizen (21204)**
L & M Publications Inc.
1840 Merrick Ave.
Merrick, NY 11566-2730
Phone: (516)378-5320
Fax: (516)378-0287
**Subject(s):** Paid Community Newspapers
**Circ:** (Thurs.)3,398

**Village Herald (21087)**
Richner Communications
P.O. Box 9001
Lawrence, NY 11559-1616
Phone: (516)569-4000
Fax: (516)569-4942
**Subject(s):** Paid Community Newspapers
**Circ:** (Free)‡1,902
(Paid)‡3,369

**Oyster Bay Enterprise Pilot (22676)**
Anton Community Newspapers
132 E. 2nd St.
Mineola, NY 11501
Phone: (516)747-8282
Fax: (516)742-5867
**Subject(s):** Paid Community Newspapers
**Circ:** (Paid)‡3,358

**Alden Advertiser (20246)**
Weisbeck Publishing & Printing Inc.
13200 Broadway
Alden, NY 14004
Phone: (716)937-9226
**Subject(s):** Paid Community Newspapers
**Circ:** (Free)‡108
(Paid)‡3,345

**The River Reporter (21233)**
93 Erie Ave.
PO Box 150
Narrowsburg, NY 12764
Phone: (845)252-7414
Fax: (845)252-3298
**Subject(s):** Paid Community Newspapers
**Circ:** (Non-paid)⊕**330**
(Paid)⊕**3,332**

**The Jewish World (20216)**
The Jewish World Inc.
3 Vatrano Rd.
Albany, NY 12205-3403
Phone: (518)459-8455
Fax: (518)459-5289
**Subject(s):** Paid Community Newspapers; Jewish Publications
**Circ:** (Paid)‡3,311

**Cornwall Local (20686)**
News of the Highlands Inc.
PO Box 518
Cornwall, NY 12518
Phone: (845)446-4519
Fax: (845)534-3855
**Subject(s):** Shopping Guides
**Circ:** ‡3,300

**New Gloucester News (12542)**
PO Box 102
New Gloucester, ME 04260
Phone: (207)926-4036
Fax: (207)926-4034
**Subject(s):** Paid Community Newspapers
**Circ:** 3,300

**The North Castle News (22620)**
Martinelli Publications
40 Larkin Plz.
Yonkers, NY 10701
Phone: (914)965-4000
Fax: (914)965-2892
**Subject(s):** Paid Community Newspapers
**Circ:** (Combined)⊕**3,300**

**Waldwick Suburban News (19962)**
North Jersey Community Newspapers
The Weekly Division of N Jersey Media Group
1 Garret Mountain Plz.
PO Box 471
West Paterson, NJ 07424-0471
Phone: (973)569-7000
Fax: (973)569-7310
**Subject(s):** Free Newspapers
**Circ:** (Wed.)3,297

**Hunterdon Review (19842)**
Recorder Publishing Company Inc.
254 Mercer St.
Stirling, NJ 07980
Phone: (908)647-1180
**Subject(s):** Paid Community Newspapers
**Circ:** (Combined)3,288

**The Lawrence Ledger (19449)**
The Princeton Packet Inc.
PO Box 8
Hopewell, NJ 08525
Phone: (609)466-2123
Fax: (609)466-2123
**Subject(s):** Paid Community Newspapers
**Circ:** 3,283

**Garden City Life (20808)**
Anton Community Newspapers
132 E. 2nd St.
Mineola, NY 11501
Phone: (516)747-8282
Fax: (516)742-5867
**Subject(s):** Paid Community Newspapers
**Circ:** (Free)‡500
(Paid)‡3,261

**The Times Sun (27675)**
Laurel Group Press
205 E. Main St.
West Newton, PA 15089
Phone: (724)872-6800
Fax: (724)887-5115
**Subject(s):** Paid Community Newspapers
**Circ:** 3,268

## Northeastern States

**Broad Top Bulletin (27489)**
PO Box 188
900 6th St.
Saxton, PA 16678-0188
Phone: (814)635-2851
**Subject(s):** Paid Community Newspapers
**Circ:** ‡3,250

**Penfield Post Republican (23139)**
Messenger-Post Newspapers
40 North Ave.
Webster, NY 14580
Phone: (585)872-2221
Fax: (585)872-0494
**Subject(s):** Paid Community Newspapers
**Circ:** (Non-paid)♦291
 (Paid)♦3,253

**Verona-Cedar Grove Times (19014)**
North Jersey Community Newspapers
433 Pompton Ave.
Cedar Grove, NJ 07009-1802
Phone: (973)239-0900
Fax: (973)239-7739
**Subject(s):** Paid Community Newspapers
**Circ:** (Paid)3,250

**Weston Voice (4623)**
Hometown Publications Inc.
1000 Bridgeport Ave.
Shelton, CT 06484
Phone: (203)926-2080
Fax: (203)926-2091
**Subject(s):** Free Newspapers
**Circ:** (Free)3,250

**Am-Pol Eagle (20639)**
3620 Harlem Rd.
Cheektowaga, NY 14215
Phone: (716)835-9454
Fax: (716)835-9457
**Subject(s):** Ethnic Publications; Paid Community Newspapers
**Circ:** (Paid)3,200

**The Dundee Observer (20709)**
PO Box 127
Dundee, NY 14837
Phone: (607)243-7600
Fax: (607)243-5833
**Subject(s):** Paid Community Newspapers
**Circ:** 3,200

**Elizabethtown Chronicle (26316)**
Journal Register Co.
25 Center Sq.
Elizabethtown, PA 17022
Phone: (717)367-7152
Fax: (717)367-3655
**Subject(s):** Paid Community Newspapers
**Circ:** (Paid)‡3,200

**Machias Valley News Observer (12538)**
Machias Valley Publishing Company Inc.
PO Box 357
Machias, ME 04654-0357
Phone: (207)255-6561
Fax: (207)255-4058
**Subject(s):** Paid Community Newspapers
**Circ:** (Non-paid)100
 (Paid)3,200

**The Mountaineer-Herald (26308)**
975 Rowena Drive
PO Box 777
Ebensburg, PA 15931
Phone: (814)472-4110
Fax: (814)472-2275
**Subject(s):** Paid Community Newspapers
**Circ:** 3,200

**Oyster Bay-Syosset Guardian (22677)**
Oyster Bay Guardian
32 E Main St
PO Box 28
Oyster Bay, NY 11771
Phone: (516)922-4215
Fax: (516)922-4227
**Subject(s):** Paid Community Newspapers
**Circ:** ‡3,200

**The Rider News (19451)**
Rider University
2083 Lawrenceville Rd.
Lawrenceville, NJ 08648
Phone: (609)896-5000

Fax: (609)895-5440
**Subject(s):** College Publications
**Circ:** ‡3,200

**Sentinel (20852)**
Manchester Newspapers
PO Box 330
Granville, NY 12832
**Subject(s):** Paid Community Newspapers
**Circ:** ‡3,200

**The Spectator (20656)**
Hamilton College
College Publications
198 College Hill Rd.
Clinton, NY 13323
Phone: (315)859-4421
Fax: (315)859-4457
**Subject(s):** College Publications
**Circ:** (Combined)‡3,200

**Watkins Review & Express (23137)**
Finger Lakes Media
210 N Franklin St.
Watkins Glen, NY 14891
Phone: (607)535-2711
Fax: (607)535-2500
**Subject(s):** Paid Community Newspapers
**Circ:** ‡3,200

**The Wesleyan Argus (4847)**
The Argus
45 Broad St.
Wesleyan Sta.
Middletown, CT
**Subject(s):** College Publications
**Circ:** 3,200

**The Madison Eagle (19843)**
Recorder Publishing Company Inc.
254 Mercer St.
Stirling, NJ 07980
Phone: (908)647-1180
**Subject(s):** Paid Community Newspapers
**Circ:** (Combined)3,175

**Rockville Centre Herald (22864)**
Richner Communications
143 E. Park Ave.
Long Beach, NY 11561-3522
Phone: (516)431-3400
Fax: (516)889-4419
**Subject(s):** Paid Community Newspapers
**Circ:** (Non-paid)‡2,011
 (Paid)‡3,160

**Wilton Bulletin (5103)**
Hersam Acorn Newspapers L.L.C.
PO Box 367
Wilton, CT 06897
Phone: (203)762-3866
Fax: (203)762-3120
**Subject(s):** Paid Community Newspapers
**Circ:** (Non-paid)♦142
 (Paid)♦3,154

**The Little Neck Ledger (21069)**
Queens Publishing Corp.
41-02 Bell Blvd., 2nd Fl.
Bayside, NY 11361
Phone: (718)229-0300
Fax: (718)225-7117
**Subject(s):** Paid Community Newspapers
**Circ:** (Paid)3,113

**Bethel Citizen (12471)**
Box 109
Bethel, ME 04217
Phone: (207)824-2444
Fax: (207)824-2426
**Subject(s):** Paid Community Newspapers
**Circ:** 3,100

**The Circle (22739)**
Marist College
3399 North Rd.
Poughkeepsie, NY 12601-1387
Phone: (845)575-3000
**Subject(s):** College Publications
**Circ:** (Non-paid)3,100

**East Fishkill Record (20718)**
Putnam County Press
PO Box 608
Mahopac, NY 10541
Phone: (845)628-8400
Fax: (845)628-8400
**Subject(s):** Paid Community Newspapers
**Circ:** 3,100

**The Nanty Glo Journal (26309)**
Mainline Newspapers
PO Box 777
Ebensburg, PA 15931-0777
Phone: (814)472-4110
Fax: (814)472-2275
**Subject(s):** Paid Community Newspapers
**Circ:** 3,088

**Livermore Falls Advertiser (12536)**
Kirkland Newspapers Inc.
PO Box B.
Livermore Falls, ME 04254
Phone: (207)897-4321
Fax: (207)897-4322
**Subject(s):** Paid Community Newspapers
**Circ:** (Non-paid)⊕10
 (Paid)⊕3,060

**Plain Dealer (18985)**
Cam-Glo Newspapers
PO Box 67
Blackwood, NJ 08012-0067
Phone: (856)228-7300
Fax: (856)232-0213
**Subject(s):** Paid Community Newspapers
**Circ:** ‡3,040

**The Forest City News (26368)**
John P. Kameen
636 Main St.
Forest City, PA 18421
Phone: (717)785-3800
Fax: (717)785-9840
**Subject(s):** Paid Community Newspapers
**Circ:** (Free)‡166
 (Paid)‡3,021

**The Valley Trader (26645)**
Oberdorf Publishing
PO Box 392
Lewisburg, PA 17837
Phone: (570)524-9850
Fax: (570)524-4048
**Subject(s):** College Publications
**Circ:** (Controlled)‡3,029

**The Archway (27939)**
Bryant College
1150 Douglas Pike.
PO Box 7
Smithfield, RI 02917
Phone: (401)232-6488
Fax: (401)232-6710
**Subject(s):** College Publications
**Circ:** (Free)3,000

**Bloomfield Life (18989)**
North Jersey Community Newspapers
90 Centre St.
Nutley, NJ 07110-3270
Phone: (973)667-2100
Fax: (973)667-3904
**Subject(s):** Paid Community Newspapers
**Circ:** (Thurs.)3,000

**The College Reporter (26597)**
Franklin and Marshall College
PO Box 3003
Lancaster, PA 17604-3003
Phone: (717)291-3911
Fax: (717)291-3886
**Subject(s):** College Publications
**Circ:** (Free)3,000

**The Collegian (26888)**
La Salle University
1900 W. Olney Ave.
Campus Box 417
Philadelphia, PA 19141
Phone: (215)951-1398
Fax: (215)951-1399
**Subject(s):** College Publications
**Circ:** (Free)‡3,000

**Courier Journal (22813)**
Suburban Circle Publications Inc.
2808 Dewey Ave.
Rochester, NY 14616
Phone: (585)663-0068
Fax: (585)663-0146
**Subject(s):** Paid Community Newspapers

**Circ:** 3,000

**The Dartmouth (18829)**
6175 Robinson Hall
Hanover, NH 03755
Phone: (603)646-2600
Fax: (603)646-3443
**Subject(s):** College Publications

**Circ:** ‡3,000

**The Defender (30871)**
SMS Students Publishing Association
St. Michael's College
PO Box 275
Colchester, VT 05439
Phone: (802)654-2442
Fax: (802)654-2560
**Subject(s):** College Publications

**Circ:** (Paid)75
(Free)3,000

**Free Press (19675)**
198 Chambers St.
Phillipsburg, NJ 08865
Phone: (908)859-6000
Fax: (908)859-3084
**Subject(s):** Paid Community Newspapers

**Circ:** ‡3,000

**Jefferson County Journal (20202)**
Journal Publishing Co.
7 Main St.
PO Box 68
Adams, NY 13605
Phone: (315)232-2141
Fax: (315)232-4586
**Subject(s):** Paid Community Newspapers

**Circ:** 3,000

**Kingston Independent Voice (13848)**
Mariner Newspapers
254 2nd Ave
PO Box 9113
Needham, MA 02494
Phone: (781)837-3500
Fax: (781)837-4540
**Subject(s):** Paid Community Newspapers

**Circ:** ‡3,000

**Narodna Volya Ukrainian (27505)**
Ukrainian Fraternal Association
1327 Wyoming Ave.
Scranton, PA 18509
Phone: (570)342-0937
Fax: (570)347-5649
**Subject(s):** Paid Community Newspapers; Ukrainian

**Circ:** (Free)‡200
(Paid)‡3,000

**The Observer (22189)**
Fordham University
Fordham College at Lincoln Center
113 W. 60th St., Rm. 408
New York, NY 10023
Phone: (212)636-6000
**Subject(s):** College Publications

**Circ:** (Free)‡3,000

**Pioneer (22835)**
St. John Fisher College
3690 E Ave.
Rochester, NY 14618
Phone: (585)385-8000
Fax: (585)385-8129
**Subject(s):** College Publications

**Circ:** (Free)‡3,000

**The Polytechnic Reporter (20535)**
Polytechnic University
6 Metrotech Center
Box 625
Brooklyn, NY 11201
Phone: (718)637-5959
Fax: (718)637-5959
**Subject(s):** College Publications

**Circ:** (Free)‡3,000

**The Trinity Tripod (4810)**
Rare Reminders
Trinity College 702582, 300 Summit St.
Hartford, CT 06106-3100
Phone: (860)297-2584
Fax: (860)563-4688
**Subject(s):** College Publications

**Circ:** (Paid)500
(Free)3,000

**The Williams Record (14914)**
Williams College
SU Box 1018
Williamstown, MA 01267
Phone: (413)597-2289
Fax: (413)597-2450
**Subject(s):** College Publications

**Circ:** (Paid)‡500
(Free)‡3,000

**Workers World (22557)**
WW Publishers Inc.
55 W 17th St., 5th Fl.
New York, NY 10011
Phone: (212)255-0352
**Subject(s):** Paid Community Newspapers; Labor

**Circ:** (Paid)3,000

**The Newington Town Crier (4646)**
Imprint Newspapers
99 Main St.
Bristol, CT 06010
Phone: (860)236-3571
Fax: (860)233-2080
**Subject(s):** Paid Community Newspapers

**Circ:** (Non-paid)32
(Paid)2,993

**Shelter Island Reporter (22936)**
PO Box 756
Shelter Island, NY 11964
Phone: (631)749-1000
Fax: (631)749-0144
**Subject(s):** Paid Community Newspapers

**Circ:** (Free)‡200
(Paid)‡2,995

**Cranston Herald (27835)**
Beacon Communications of Rhode Island
789 Park Ave.
Cranston, RI 02910
Phone: (401)732-3100
Fax: (401)732-3110
**Subject(s):** Paid Community Newspapers

**Circ:** (Non-paid)♦101
(Paid)♦2,956

**Montgomery Life (26377)**
Journal Register Co.
Montgomery Newspapers
290 Commerce Dr.
Fort Washington, PA 19034
Phone: (215)542-0200
**Subject(s):** Paid Community Newspapers

**Circ:** (Combined)2,952

**Boonville Herald & Adirondack Tourist (20417)**
Black River Publishing Company Inc.
E Schuyler St.
PO Box 372
Boonville, NY 13309
Phone: (315)942-4449
Fax: (315)942-4440
**Subject(s):** Paid Community Newspapers

**Circ:** (Free)233
(Paid)2,937

**The Dallas Post (27690)**
15 North Main St.
Wilkes Barre, PA 18711
Phone: (570)675-5211
**Subject(s):** Paid Community Newspapers

**Circ:** ⊕2,917

**Campus Lantern (5093)**
Eastern Connecticut State College
110 Student Ctr.
83 Windham St.
Willimantic, CT 06226-2308
Phone: (860)465-4445
Fax: (860)465-4685
**Subject(s):** College Publications

**Circ:** (Controlled)2,900

**Island Dispatch (20848)**
Niagara Frontier Publications
1859 Whitehaven Rd.
PO Box 130
Grand Island, NY 14072-0130
Phone: (716)773-7676
Fax: (716)773-7190
**Subject(s):** Paid Community Newspapers

**Circ:** (Paid)2,900

**The Miscellany News (22743)**
Vassar College
124 Raymond Ave.
PO Box 149
Poughkeepsie, NY 12604
Phone: (845)437-7000
**Subject(s):** College Publications

**Circ:** (Paid)100
(Free)2,900

**Massapequan Observer (21134)**
Anton Community Newspapers
132 E. 2nd St.
Mineola, NY 11501
Phone: (516)747-8282
Fax: (516)742-5867
**Subject(s):** Paid Community Newspapers

**Circ:** (Paid)‡2,898

**The Daily Record (19661)**
The Daily Record Corp.
800 Jefferson Rd.
Parsippany, NJ 07054
Phone: (973)428-6200
Fax: (973)428-6720
**Subject(s):** Daily Newspapers; Business

**Circ:** (Free)‡150
(Paid)‡2,860

**Warren Times-Gazette (27946)**
East Bay Newspapers
PO Box 50
Warren, RI 02885-0050
Phone: (401)245-6000
Fax: (401)245-3640
**Subject(s):** Paid Community Newspapers

**Circ:** (Non-paid)♦121
(Paid)♦2,861

**Amityville Record (20260)**
ACJ Communication Inc.
85 Broadway
Amityville, NY 11701
Phone: (631)264-0077
Fax: (631)264-5310
**Subject(s):** Paid Community Newspapers

**Circ:** (Free)150
(Paid)2,850

**Chelsea Record (14765)**
Independent Newspaper Group
385 Broadway, Ste. 105
Revere, MA 02151
Phone: (781)284-2400
Fax: (781)485-1403
**Subject(s):** Paid Community Newspapers

**Circ:** (Non-paid)300
(Paid)2,852

**Kane Republican (26561)**
200 N Fraley St.
Kane, PA 16735
Phone: (814)837-6000
Fax: (814)837-2227
**Subject(s):** Daily Newspapers

**Circ:** (Combined)⊕2,850

**Orange County Post (23127)**
15 Goshen Ave.
Washingtonville, NY 10992
Phone: (914)496-3611
Fax: (914)496-1715
**Subject(s):** Paid Community Newspapers

**Circ:** ‡2,842

**The Gazette (20691)**
160 Cleveland Dr.
PO Box 810
Croton On Hudson, NY 10520
Phone: (914)271-2088
Fax: (914)271-4219
**Subject(s):** Paid Community Newspapers

**Circ:** (Controlled)‡2,825

Circulation: ★ = ABC; △ = BPA; ♦ = CAC; ● = CCAB; ▢ = VAC; ⊕ = PO Statement; ‡ = Publisher's Report; Boldface figures = sworn; Light figures = estimated.

## Northeastern States

**News of the Highlands (20903)**
News of the Highlands Inc.
PO Box 278
Highland Falls, NY 10928
Phone: (914)446-4519
**Subject(s):** Paid Community Newspapers
**Circ:** 2,800

**West County News (14782)**
45 Conway St.
PO Box 218
Shelburne Falls, MA 01370
Phone: (413)625-4660
Fax: (413)625-4661
**Subject(s):** Paid Community Newspapers
**Circ:** ‡2,800

**The Blairstown Press (19129)**
NJN Publishing
PO Box 425
Hackettstown, NJ 07840
Phone: (908)362-6161
Fax: (908)852-9320
**Subject(s):** Paid Community Newspapers
**Circ:** (Paid)♦2,774

**Penn Hills Progress Star (26729)**
Gateway Publications
610 Beatty Rd.
Monroeville, PA 15146
Phone: (412)856-7400
Fax: (412)856-7954
**Subject(s):** Paid Community Newspapers
**Circ:** (Non-paid)166
(Paid)2,777

**The Evening Sun (22628)**
The Gazette
PO Box 151
29 Lackawanna Ave.
Norwich, NY 13815
Phone: (607)334-3276
Fax: (607)334-8273
**Subject(s):** Paid Community Newspapers
**Circ:** 2,750

**Vaba Eesti Sona (Free Estonian Word) (22512)**
The Nordic Press Inc.
243 E 34th St.
New York, NY 10016
Phone: (212)686-3356
Fax: (212)689-2939
**Subject(s):** Estonian; Paid Community Newspapers
**Circ:** ‡2,750

**Bethpage Newsgram (20366)**
Litmor Publications Inc.
81 E Barclay St.
Hicksville, NY 11801
Phone: (516)931-0012
Fax: (516)931-0027
**Subject(s):** Paid Community Newspapers
**Circ:** (Paid)‡2,740

**Baldwin Herald (21054)**
Richner Communications
P.O. Box 9001
Lawrence, NY 11559-1616
Phone: (516)569-4000
Fax: (516)569-4942
**Subject(s):** Paid Community Newspapers
**Circ:** (Free)‡1,704
(Paid)‡2,738

**Beacon Light (20355)**
Putnam County Press
PO Box 608
Mahopac, NY 10541
Phone: (845)628-8400
Fax: (845)628-8400
**Subject(s):** Paid Community Newspapers
**Circ:** 2,700

**The Hardwick Gazette (30887)**
Hardwick Publishing Company Inc.
42 S Main St.
Box 367
Hardwick, VT 05843
Phone: (802)472-6521
**Subject(s):** Paid Community Newspapers
**Circ:** (Free)20
(Paid)2,700

**Mountaintop Eagle (26748)**
85 S Main Rd.
PO Box 10
Mountain Top, PA 18707
Phone: (570)474-6397
Fax: (570)474-9272
**Subject(s):** Paid Community Newspapers
**Circ:** (Free)⊕33
(Paid)⊕2,708

**Mount Olive Chronicle (19026)**
Recorder Publishing Company Inc.
PO Box 600
Chester, NJ 07930-0600
Phone: (908)879-4100
**Subject(s):** Free Newspapers
**Circ:** (Combined)2,683

**The East Greenwich Pendulum Times (27843)**
Southern Rhode Island Newspapers
PO Box 350
East Greenwich, RI 02818
Phone: (401)884-4662
Fax: (401)884-9819
**Subject(s):** Paid Community Newspapers
**Circ:** (Non-paid)♦27
(Paid)♦2,675

**The Waterville Times (23136)**
128 Main St.
Box C
Waterville, NY 13480
Phone: (315)841-4105
Fax: (315)841-4104
**Subject(s):** Paid Community Newspapers
**Circ:** ‡2,670

**The Forest Hills Ledger (20789)**
Queens Publishing Corp.
41-02 Bell Blvd., 2nd Fl.
Bayside, NY 11361
Phone: (718)229-0300
Fax: (718)225-7117
**Subject(s):** Paid Community Newspapers
**Circ:** (Paid)2,659

**Midland Park Suburban News (19955)**
North Jersey Community Newspapers
The Weekly Division of N Jersey Media Group
1 Garret Mountain Plz.
PO Box 471
West Paterson, NJ 07424-0471
Phone: (973)569-7000
Fax: (973)569-7310
**Subject(s):** Free Newspapers
**Circ:** (Wed.)2,653

**Tech News (14944)**
Worcester Polytechnic Institute
100 Institute Rd.
Worcester, MA 01609
Phone: (508)831-5464
Fax: (508)831-5721
**Subject(s):** College Publications
**Circ:** (Paid)‡100
(Free)‡2,650

**Warwick Valley Dispatch (23123)**
PO Box 594
Warwick, NY 10990-0594
Phone: (845)986-2216
Fax: (845)987-1180
**Subject(s):** Paid Community Newspapers
**Circ:** ‡2,650

**Hanover Eagle & Weekly Regional News (19468)**
Parker Publishing Inc.
155 Main St.
Madison, NJ 07940
Phone: (908)766-3900
Fax: (908)766-6365
**Subject(s):** Paid Community Newspapers
**Circ:** (Non-paid)32
(Paid)2,626

**Apollo News-Record (27624)**
Buttermilk Falls Co.
143 Washington Ave
Vandergrift, PA 15690
Phone: (724)567-5656
Fax: (724)568-3818
**Subject(s):** Paid Community Newspapers
**Circ:** ‡2,600

**Duncannon Record (26296)**
Advance Publications of Perry & Juniata Counties Inc.
Box A
Duncannon, PA 17020
Phone: (717)834-4616
**Subject(s):** Paid Community Newspapers
**Circ:** ‡2,600

**The Gettysburgian (26392)**
Gettysburg College
300 N. Washington St.
Gettysburg, PA 17325-1491
Phone: (717)337-6770
Fax: (717)337-6775
**Subject(s):** College Publications
**Circ:** (Paid)‡800
(Free)‡2,600

**The Globe (27354)**
Point Park College
201 Wood St.
Box 627
Pittsburgh, PA 15222
Phone: (412)391-4100
Fax: (412)391-1980
**Subject(s):** College Publications
**Circ:** (Free)2,600

**La Grange Independent (21011)**
Putnam County Press
PO Box 608
Mahopac, NY 10541
Phone: (845)628-8400
Fax: (845)628-8400
**Subject(s):** Paid Community Newspapers
**Circ:** 2,600

**The New Egypt Press (19608)**
The New Hope Gazette
PO Box 188
New Egypt, NJ 08533
Phone: (609)758-2112
Fax: (609)758-1816
**Subject(s):** Paid Community Newspapers
**Circ:** ‡2,600

**Voice Ledger (22713)**
Taconic Press
PO Box 316
Millbrook, NY 12545-0316
Phone: (845)677-8241
Fax: (845)677-6337
**Subject(s):** Paid Community Newspapers
**Circ:** 2,600

**Westmore News (22718)**
38 Broad St.
Port Chester, NY 10573-4197
Phone: (914)939-6864
Fax: (914)939-6877
**Subject(s):** Paid Community Newspapers
**Circ:** (Free)700
(Paid)2,600

**Williston Times (23191)**
Litmor Publications Inc.
99 Hillside Ave.
Williston Park, NY 11596
Phone: (516)746-0240
**Subject(s):** Paid Community Newspapers
**Circ:** 2,600

**Carthage Republican Tribune (20623)**
Johnson Newspaper Corp.
PO Box 549
Carthage, NY 13619
Phone: (315)493-1270
Fax: (315)493-1271
**Subject(s):** Paid Community Newspapers
**Circ:** (Free)‡39
(Paid)‡2,584

**Carver Reporter (13724)**
MPG Newspapers
9 Long Pond Rd.
PO Box 959
Plymouth, MA 02362-0959
Phone: (508)746-5555
Fax: (508)747-2148
**Subject(s):** Paid Community Newspapers
**Circ:** (Combined)2,559

**The Sentinel (14749)**
MPG Newspapers
9 Long Pond Rd.
PO Box 959
Plymouth, MA 02362-0959
Phone: (508)746-5555
Fax: (508)747-2148
**Subject(s):** Paid Community Newspapers
**Circ:** (Combined)2,551

**Duxbury Reporter (13761)**
MPG Newspapers
9 Long Pond Rd.
PO Box 959
Plymouth, MA 02362-0959
Phone: (508)747-2148
Fax: (800)242-0264
**Subject(s):** Free Newspapers
**Circ:** (Combined)2,540

**North-East Independent (27943)**
South County Newspapers Inc.
203 Main St.
PO BOX 5679
Wakefield, RI 02879-5679
Phone: (401)789-6000
Fax: (401)792-9176
**Subject(s):** Paid Community Newspapers
**Circ:** (Paid)♦2,537

**Amherst Student (13403)**
Amherst College
PO Box 1912
Amherst, MA 01002
Phone: (413)542-2304
Fax: (413)542-2305
**Subject(s):** College Publications; Paid Community Newspapers
**Circ:** (Controlled)2,500

**Barre Gazette (13445)**
5 Exchange St.
PO Box 448
Barre, MA 01005
Phone: (978)355-4000
Fax: (978)355-6274
**Subject(s):** Paid Community Newspapers
**Circ:** ‡2,500

**Chautauquan Daily (20637)**
Chautauqua Institution
Box 1095
Chautauqua, NY 14722-1095
Phone: (716)357-2000
Fax: (716)357-6369
**Subject(s):** Daily Periodicals; Education; Art; Performing Arts
**Circ:** ‡2,500

**The Dolphin (23011)**
LeMoyne College
16 Loyola Hall
Syracuse, NY 13214
Phone: (315)445-4100
**Subject(s):** College Publications
**Circ:** 2,500

**Echo-Pilot (26401)**
Echo-Pilot Newspaper
Box 159
Greencastle, PA 17225
Phone: (717)597-2164
Fax: (717)597-3754
**Subject(s):** Paid Community Newspapers
**Circ:** 2,500

**Garnet Valley Press (26398)**
PO Box 1001
Glen Mills, PA 19342-1001
Phone: (610)358-1516
Fax: (610)558-3406
**Subject(s):** Paid Community Newspapers
**Circ:** (Controlled)2,500

**The Gothic Times (19426)**
Jersey City State College
2039 Kennedy Blvd.
Jersey City, NJ 07305
Phone: (201)200-3575
Fax: (201)200-2329
**Subject(s):** College Publications
**Circ:** (Free)‡2500

**Hyde Park Townsman (20933)**
Taconic Press
PO Box 316
Millbrook, NY 12545-0316
Phone: (845)677-8241
Fax: (845)677-6337
**Subject(s):** Paid Community Newspapers
**Circ:** 2,500

**Manhattan College Quadrangle (20467)**
Manhattan College
4513 Manhattan College Pkwy.
Bronx, NY 10471-4098
Phone: (718)862-8000
Fax: (718)862-8043
**Subject(s):** College Publications
**Circ:** 2,500

**The Phoenix (27573)**
Swarthmore College
500 College Ave.
Swarthmore, PA 19081-1390
Phone: (610)328-8000
**Subject(s):** College Publications
**Circ:** (Free)‡2,500

**The Quill (23074)**
Russell Sage College
45 Ferry St.
Troy, NY 12180
Phone: (518)244-2000
**Subject(s):** College Publications
**Circ:** (Free)‡2,500

**Simsbury News (5014)**
Imprint Newspapers
99 Main St.
Bristol, CT 06010
Phone: (860)236-3571
Fax: (860)233-2080
**Subject(s):** Paid Community Newspapers
**Circ:** (Non-paid)46
 (Paid)2,506

**The Stute (19394)**
Stevens Institute of Technology
Castle Point on Hudson
Hoboken, NJ 07030
Phone: (201)216-5263
Fax: (201)216-8909
**Subject(s):** College Publications
**Circ:** (Free)2,500

**Tangerine (23088)**
Utica College of Syracuse University
Burrstone Rd.
Utica, NY 13502
Phone: (315)792-3111
Fax: (315)792-3073
**Subject(s):** College Publications
**Circ:** (Free)‡2,500

**Y Drych (The Mirror) (23089)**
Box 8337
Utica, NY 13505-8337
**Subject(s):** Ethnic Publications; Welsh
**Circ:** (Non-paid)‡500
 (Paid)‡2,500

**Yeadon Times (27725)**
Press Publishing Co.
3245 Garrett Rd.
Drexel Hill, PA 19026
Phone: (610)259-4141
**Subject(s):** Paid Community Newspapers
**Circ:** ‡2,500

**Island Ad-Vantages (12608)**
Penobscot Bay Press Inc.
PO Box 36
Stonington, ME 04681
Phone: (207)367-2200
Fax: (207)367-6397
**Subject(s):** Paid Community Newspapers
**Circ:** 2,491

**The Dome (26234)**
Widener University
1 University Pl.
PO Box 1175
Chester, PA 19013
Phone: (610)499-4000
Fax: (610)499-4531
**Subject(s):** College Publications
**Circ:** (Paid)‡25
 (Free)‡2,475

**Signal Item Star (26733)**
Gateway Publications
610 Beatty Rd.
Monroeville, PA 15146
Phone: (412)856-7400
Fax: (412)856-7954
**Subject(s):** Paid Community Newspapers
**Circ:** (Combined)2,471

**Abington/Rockland Mariner (13397)**
Community Newspaper Co.
254 2nd Ave.
Needham, MA 02494
Phone: (781)433-6700
**Subject(s):** Paid Community Newspapers
**Circ:** (Non-paid)86
 (Paid)2,461

**Henrietta Post (20889)**
Messenger-Post Newspapers
1 Grove St., Ste. 101
Pittsford, NY 14534
Phone: (585)381-3300
Fax: (585)381-5325
**Subject(s):** Paid Community Newspapers
**Circ:** (Non-paid)♦180
 (Paid)♦2,441

**Weston Town Crier & TAB (14908)**
Community Newspaper Co.
254 2nd Ave.
Needham, MA 02494
Phone: (781)433-6700
**Subject(s):** Free Newspapers
**Circ:** (Non-paid)2,424

**The College Voice (4912)**
Connecticut College
270 Mohegan Ave.
New London, CT 06320
Phone: (860)439-2812
**Subject(s):** College Publications
**Circ:** (Paid)300
 (Free)2,400

**The Dedham Times (13752)**
395 Washington St.
Dedham, MA 02026
Phone: (781)329-5553
Fax: (781)329-8291
**Subject(s):** Paid Community Newspapers
**Circ:** (Paid)⊕2,400

**Lafayette News (23071)**
PowerOne Media Inc.
400 Jordan Rd.
Troy, NY 12180
**Subject(s):** Paid Community Newspapers
**Circ:** ‡2,400

**Millbrook Round Table (21210)**
Taconic Press
PO Box 316
Millbrook, NY 12545-0316
Phone: (845)677-8241
Fax: (845)677-6337
**Subject(s):** Paid Community Newspapers
**Circ:** ‡2,400

**Hanover Mariner (13816)**
Community Newspaper Co.
254 2nd Ave.
Needham, MA 02494
Phone: (781)433-6700
**Subject(s):** Paid Community Newspapers
**Circ:** (Non-paid)124
 (Paid)2,381

**The Manchester Cricket (14221)**
Cricket Press Inc.
PO Box 357
Manchester, MA 01944-0357
Phone: (978)526-7131
Fax: (978)526-8193
**Subject(s):** Paid Community Newspapers
**Circ:** ‡2,376

**The Pelham Sun (22693)**
Martinelli Publications
40 Larkin Plz.
Yonkers, NY 10701
Phone: (914)965-4000
Fax: (914)965-2892
**Subject(s):** Paid Community Newspapers
**Circ:** ‡2,360

**Lacey Beacon (19096)**
Manahawkin Newspapers Inc.
345 E Bay Ave.
Manahawkin, NJ 08050-3320
Phone: (609)597-3211
Fax: (609)978-4592
**Subject(s):** Paid Community Newspapers
**Circ:** (Thurs.)2,359

**Haverford Press (26773)**
County Press
3732 W Chester Pke.
PO Box 249
Newtown Square, PA 19073
Phone: (610)356-3820
Fax: (610)353-5321
**Subject(s):** Paid Community Newspapers
**Circ:** (Non-paid)‡206
       (Paid)‡2,340

**The Observer (19143)**
Hasbrouck Heights Publishing Company Inc.
194 Blvd.
Hasbrouck Heights, NJ 07604
Phone: (201)288-0333
Fax: (201)288-1847
**Subject(s):** Paid Community Newspapers
**Circ:** ‡2,322

**The Clinton Courier (20653)**
Courier Enterprises Inc.
4 Meadow St.
PO Box 294
Clinton, NY 13323-0294
Phone: (315)853-3490
Fax: (315)853-3522
**Subject(s):** Paid Community Newspapers
**Circ:** ‡2,300

**Independent-Sentinel (26219)**
PO Box 128
Canton, PA 17724-0128
Phone: (570)673-5151
Fax: (570)673-5152
**Subject(s):** Paid Community Newspapers
**Circ:** ‡2,300

**The Redding Pilot (4993)**
Hersam Acorn Newspapers L.L.C.
16 Bailey Ave.
PO Box 1019
Ridgefield, CT 06877
Phone: (203)438-6544
**Subject(s):** Paid Community Newspapers
**Circ:** (Non-paid)♦62
       (Paid)♦2,290

**The Register (14227)**
Community Newspaper
923 G Rte. 6A
Yarmouth Port, MA 02675
Phone: (508)375-4945
Fax: (508)375-4903
**Subject(s):** Free Newspapers
**Circ:** (Non-paid)2,290

**The Independent Press (18991)**
Worrall Community Newspapers
266 Liberty St.
Bloomfield, NJ 07003
Phone: (973)743-4040
Fax: (973)680-8848
**Subject(s):** Paid Community Newspapers
**Circ:** (Non-paid)670
       (Paid)2,284

**New Hyde Park Herald Courier (21237)**
Litmor Publications Inc.
81 E Barclay St.
Hicksville, NY 11801
Phone: (516)931-0012
Fax: (516)931-0027
**Subject(s):** Paid Community Newspapers
**Circ:** (Non-paid)120
       (Paid)2,258

**Cazenovia Republican (20627)**
Eagle Newspapers
c/o Kim Dam, Editor
PO Box 301
Cazenovia, NY 13035
Phone: (315)655-3415
Fax: (315)655-3813
**Subject(s):** Paid Community Newspapers
**Circ:** (Free)279
       (Paid)2,245

**The Freeport-Baldwin Leader (21201)**
L & M Publications Inc.
1840 Merrick Ave.
Merrick, NY 11566-2730
Phone: (516)378-5320
Fax: (516)378-0287
**Subject(s):** Paid Community Newspapers
**Circ:** (Thurs.)2,232

**The Queens Village Times (22769)**
Queens Publishing Corp.
41-02 Bell Blvd., 2nd Fl.
Bayside, NY 11361
Phone: (718)229-0300
Fax: (718)225-7117
**Subject(s):** Paid Community Newspapers
**Circ:** (Paid)2,211

**The Dickinsonian (26222)**
Dickinson College
PO Box 4888
Carlisle, PA 17013
Phone: (717)243-5121
**Subject(s):** College Publications
**Circ:** (Paid)250
       (Non-paid)2200

**The Herald (20822)**
Hobart and William Smith Colleges
Box SF-92
Geneva, NY 14456-3397
Phone: (315)789-5500
Fax: (315)781-0643
**Subject(s):** College Publications
**Circ:** (Free)2,200

**The Johnsonburg Press (26544)**
The Johnsonburg Press Inc.
517 Market St.
Johnsonburg, PA 15845
Phone: (814)965-2503
Fax: (814)965-2504
**Subject(s):** Paid Community Newspapers
**Circ:** (Paid)‡2,200

**Norwell Mariner (14646)**
Community Newspaper Co.
254 2nd Ave.
Needham, MA 02494
Phone: (781)433-6700
**Subject(s):** Paid Community Newspapers
**Circ:** (Non-paid)104
       (Paid)2,188

**Plainview Herald (22703)**
Anton Community Newspapers
132 E. 2nd St.
Mineola, NY 11501
Phone: (516)747-8282
Fax: (516)742-5867
**Subject(s):** Paid Community Newspapers
**Circ:** ‡2,178

**The Valley News (20743)**
Denton Publications
14 Hand Ave.
Elizabethtown, NY 12932
Phone: (518)873-6368
Fax: (518)873-6360
**Subject(s):** Paid Community Newspapers
**Circ:** (Non-paid)101
       (Paid)2,171

**Mid Island News (22945)**
PO Box 805
Smithtown, NY 11787
**Subject(s):** Paid Community Newspapers
**Circ:** (Paid)⊕2,149

**The Lewisboro Ledger (4986)**
Hersam Acorn Newspapers L.L.C.
16 Bailey Ave.
PO Box 1019
Ridgefield, CT 06877
Phone: (203)438-6544
**Subject(s):** Paid Community Newspapers
**Circ:** (Non-paid)♦52
       (Paid)♦2,137

**The Chariho Times (27959)**
Southern Rhode Island Newspapers
1171 Main St.
PO Box 620
Wyoming, RI 02898
Phone: (401)539-0100
Fax: (401)539-2330
**Subject(s):** Paid Community Newspapers
**Circ:** (Non-paid)♦57
       (Paid)♦2,124

**The Ebensburg News Leader (26307)**
Mainline Newspapers
PO Box 777
Ebensburg, PA 15931-0777
Phone: (814)472-4110
Fax: (814)472-2275
**Subject(s):** Paid Community Newspapers
**Circ:** 2,110

**Deposit Courier (20703)**
Evans Communications Inc.
24 Laurel Bank Ave.
Deposit, NY 13754
Phone: (607)467-3600
Fax: (607)467-5330
**Subject(s):** Paid Community Newspapers
**Circ:** (Paid)‡2,100

**The North Creek News-Enterprise (22622)**
Sawyer Press
PO Box 85
34 E. holcomb St.
North Creek, NY 12853
Phone: (518)251-3012
Fax: (518)251-4147
**Subject(s):** Paid Community Newspapers
**Circ:** ‡2,100

**Orchard Park Bee (22666)**
Bee Publications Inc.
5564 Main St.
PO Box 150
Buffalo, NY 14231-0150
Phone: (716)632-4700
Fax: (716)633-8601
**Subject(s):** Free Newspapers
**Circ:** (Free)42
       (Paid)2,100

**Post Herald (22776)**
Wayuga Community Newspapers Inc.
PO Box 199
Red Creek, NY 13143
Phone: (315)754-6229
Fax: (315)754-6431
**Subject(s):** Paid Community Newspapers
**Circ:** ‡2,100

**Syosset Advance (22990)**
Litmor Publications Inc.
81 E Barclay St.
Hicksville, NY 11801
Phone: (516)931-0012
Fax: (516)931-0027
**Subject(s):** Paid Community Newspapers
**Circ:** (Non-paid)150
       (Paid)2,100

**The Windham Journal (23193)**
The Daily Mail
PO Box 128
Windham, NY 12496
Phone: (518)943-2100
Fax: (518)734-5179
**Subject(s):** Paid Community Newspapers
**Circ:** ‡2,100

**Scotch Plains-Fanwood Press (19781)**
The Chronicle
44 Veterans Memorial Pkwy. E
PO Box 699
Somerville, NJ 08876
Phone: (908)722-3000
Fax: (908)526-2509

Subject(s): Paid Community Newspapers

Circ: (Non-paid)5
(Paid)2,084

**The Bernards Township Community News (18979)**
Recorder Publishing Company Inc.
17-19 Morristown Rd.
PO Box 687
Bernardsville, NJ 07924
Phone: (908)766-3900
Fax: (908)766-6365
Subject(s): Paid Community Newspapers

Circ: (Non-paid)♦2,023

**Elmer Times (19069)**
Elmer Times Co.
PO Box 1160
Elmer, NJ 08318
Phone: (856)358-6171
Fax: (856)358-7951
Subject(s): Paid Community Newspapers

Circ: 2,021

**Roxbury Register (19773)**
Recorder Publishing Company Inc.
530 E. Main St.
Chester, NJ 07930
Phone: (908)766-6365
Fax: (908)766-6365
Subject(s): Paid Community Newspapers

Circ: (Non-paid)362
(Paid)2,012

**The Swarthmorean (27575)**
Swarthmorean
107 Rutgers
Box 59
Swarthmore, PA 19081
Phone: (610)543-0900
Fax: (610)543-3790
Subject(s): Paid Community Newspapers

Circ: ‡2,010

**Bloomfield Journal (4644)**
Imprint Newspapers
99 Main St.
Bristol, CT 06010
Phone: (860)236-3571
Fax: (860)233-2080
Subject(s): Paid Community Newspapers

Circ: (Non-paid)414
(Paid)2,008

**The Bryn Mawr & Haverford News (26474)**
Haverford College
370 W Lancaster Ave.
Box 132
Haverford, PA 19041
Phone: (610)649-9712
Subject(s): College Publications

Circ: (Free)‡2,000

**The Crown (27689)**
King's College
133 N Franklin St.
Box SA18
Wilkes Barre, PA 18711
Phone: (570)208-5900
Fax: (570)825-9049
Subject(s): College Publications

Circ: (Free)‡2,000

**East Aurora Bee (20715)**
Bee Publications Inc.
5564 Main St.
PO Box 150
Buffalo, NY 14231-0150
Phone: (716)632-4700
Fax: (716)633-8601
Subject(s): Paid Community Newspapers

Circ: (Free)⊕163
(Paid)⊕2,000

**The Equinox (19848)**
Fairleigh Dickinson Univ.
1000 River Rd., T-SU2-01
Teaneck, NJ 07666
Phone: (201)692-2046
Fax: (201)692-2376
Subject(s): College Publications

Circ: (Free)2,000

**The Griffin (20571)**
Canisius College
2001 Main St.
Buffalo, NY 14215
Phone: (716)888-7000
Fax: (716)888-2525
Subject(s): College Publications

Circ: (Free)‡2,000

**The Grizzly (26254)**
Ursinus College
PO Box 1000
Collegeville, PA 19426
Phone: (610)409-3586
Subject(s): College Publications

Circ: (Free)‡2,000

**Mainland Journal (19140)**
Atlantic County Newspaper Group
115 12th St.
PO Box 596
Hammonton, NJ 08037
Phone: (609)561-2300
Fax: (609)567-2249
Subject(s): Paid Community Newspapers

Circ: ‡2,000

**The Norwich Guidon (30917)**
Norwich University
158 Harmon Dr.
Northfield, VT 05663
Phone: (802)485-2000
Fax: (802)485-2580
Subject(s): College Publications

Circ: (Free)‡2,000

**Pioneer (13780)**
Raivaaja Publishing Co.
164 Elm St.
Fitchburg, MA 01420
Subject(s): Finnish; Paid Community Newspapers

Circ: ‡2,000

**The Scarlet (14943)**
Clark University
950 Main St.
Worcester, MA 01610
Phone: (508)793-7711
Subject(s): College Publications

Circ: (Free)2,000

**The Skidmore News (22909)**
Skidmore College
815 N. Broadway
Saratoga Springs, NY 12866
Phone: (518)580-5186
Fax: (518)580-5188
Subject(s): College Publications

Circ: 2,000

**West Schuylkill Herald (27582)**
South Schuylkill Printing & Publishing
613 E. Grand Ave.
Tower City, PA 17980
Subject(s): Paid Community Newspapers

Circ: ‡2,000

**The Winchendon Courier (14917)**
Stonebridge Press Inc.
110 Front St.
Winchendon, MA 01475-1749
Phone: (978)297-0050
Fax: (978)297-2177
Subject(s): Paid Community Newspapers

Circ: 2,000

**The Weekly Packet (12475)**
Penobscot Bay Press Inc.
PO Box 646
Blue Hill, ME 04614
Phone: (207)374-2341
Fax: (207)374-2343
Subject(s): Paid Community Newspapers

Circ: (Free)53
(Paid)1,984

**Brockport Post (22807)**
Messenger-Post Newspapers
2968 Chili Ave.
Rochester, NY 14624
Phone: (585)247-9200
Fax: (585)247-9210

Subject(s): Paid Community Newspapers

Circ: (Non-paid)♦181
(Paid)♦1,970

**The Bethel Home News (4985)**
Hersam Acorn Newspapers L.L.C.
PO Box 1019
Ridgefield, CT 06877
Phone: (203)743-5517
Fax: (203)438-3395
Subject(s): Paid Community Newspapers

Circ: (Free)33
(Paid)1,958

**Morris News Bee (19844)**
Recorder Publishing Company Inc.
254 Mercer St.
Stirling, NJ 07980
Phone: (908)647-1180
Subject(s): Paid Community Newspapers

Circ: (Combined)1,946

**The Longmeadow News (14896)**
Westfield News Advertiser Inc.
62 School St., No. 64
Westfield, MA 01085-2835
Phone: (413)568-4921
Fax: (413)562-4185
Subject(s): Paid Community Newspapers

Circ: ‡1,930

**Reveille/Between the Lakes (22933)**
Reveille Publishing Company Inc.
PO Box 557
Seneca Falls, NY 13148
Phone: (607)869-5344
Fax: (607)869-9208
Subject(s): Paid Community Newspapers

Circ: (Free)‡305
(Paid)‡1,925

**East Orange Record (19059)**
Worrall Community Newspapers
170 Scotland Rd.
Orange, NJ 07051
Phone: (973)674-8000
Fax: (973)674-2038
Subject(s): Paid Community Newspapers

Circ: (Combined)1,903

**Thomaston Express (5055)**
Bristol Acquisition Corp.
PO Box 250
Thomaston, CT 06787
Phone: (860)283-4356
Fax: (860)283-4356
Subject(s): Paid Community Newspapers

Circ: ‡1,900

**Avon News (4643)**
Imprint Newspapers
99 Main St.
Bristol, CT 06010
Phone: (860)236-3571
Fax: (860)233-2080
Subject(s): Paid Community Newspapers

Circ: (Non-paid)160
(Paid)1,883

**Holbrook Sun (13822)**
Community Newspaper Co.
PO Box 355
Holbrook, MA 02343
Phone: (617)767-4000
Fax: (617)849-3319
Subject(s): Paid Community Newspapers

Circ: (Non-paid)173
(Paid)1,871

**Litchfield Enquirer (4834)**
Housatonic Publications
43 West St.
PO Box 547
Litchfield, CT 06759
Subject(s): Free Newspapers

Circ: (Non-paid)2
(Paid)1,875

**Carlisle Mosquito (13723)**
Carlisle Communications Inc.
PO Box 616
872 Westford St
Carlisle, MA 01741-0616
Phone: (978)369-8313
Fax: (978)369-3569

Circulation: ★ = ABC; △ = BPA; ♦ = CAC; • = CCAB; ▫ = VAC; ⊕ = PO Statement; ‡ = Publisher's Report; Boldface figures = sworn; Light figures = estimated.

**Subject(s):** Free Newspapers
**Circ:** (Free)‡1,850

**Pravoslavnaya Rus (21003)**
Holy Trinity Monastery
PO Box 36
Jordanville, NY 13361-0036
Phone: (315)858-0940
Fax: (315)858-0505
**Subject(s):** Russian; Religious Publications
**Circ:** ‡1,850

**Sherburne News (22937)**
17 E State St.
Sherburne, NY 13460
Phone: (607)674-6071
Fax: (607)674-6071
**Subject(s):** Paid Community Newspapers
**Circ:** ‡1,850

**Mid-Island Times (20897)**
Litmor Publications Inc.
81 E Barclay St.
Hicksville, NY 11801
Phone: (516)931-0012
Fax: (516)931-0027
**Subject(s):** Paid Community Newspapers
**Circ:** (Non-paid)150
(Paid)1,840

**The Three Village Times (20753)**
Anton Community Newspapers
132 E. 2nd St.
Mineola, NY 11501
Phone: (516)747-8282
Fax: (516)742-5867
**Subject(s):** Paid Community Newspapers
**Circ:** ‡1,849

**Wayne County Mail (23140)**
Empire State Weeklies Inc.
2010 Empire Blvd.
Webster, NY 14580
Phone: (585)671-1533
Fax: (585)671-7067
**Subject(s):** Paid Community Newspapers
**Circ:** ‡1,837

**Florham Park Eagle (19093)**
Recorder Publishing Company Inc.
254 Mercer St.
Stirling, NJ 07980
Phone: (908)647-1180
**Subject(s):** Paid Community Newspapers
**Circ:** (Combined)1,828

**The Northport Journal (22626)**
Long Islander Newspapers Inc.
322 Main St.
Huntington, NY 11743
Phone: (631)427-7000
Fax: (631)427-5820
**Subject(s):** Paid Community Newspapers
**Circ:** ‡1,820

**Woodland Hills Progress (26736)**
Gateway Publications
610 Beatty Rd.
Monroeville, PA 15146
Phone: (412)856-7400
Fax: (412)856-7954
**Subject(s):** Free Newspapers
**Circ:** (Non-paid)147
(Paid)1,811

**The Laurelton Times (21053)**
Queens Publishing Corp.
41-02 Bell Blvd., 2nd Fl.
Bayside, NY 11361
Phone: (718)229-0300
Fax: (718)225-7117
**Subject(s):** Paid Community Newspapers
**Circ:** (Paid)1,808

**Pine Plains Register Herald (21211)**
Taconic Press
PO Box 316
Millbrook, NY 12545-0316
Phone: (845)677-8241
Fax: (845)677-6337
**Subject(s):** Paid Community Newspapers
**Circ:** ‡1,800

**Star Gazette (19130)**
NJN Publishing
106 E. Moore St.
Hackettstown, NJ 07840
Phone: (908)852-1212
Fax: (908)852-9320
**Subject(s):** Paid Community Newspapers
**Circ:** (Paid)♦1,805

**Moon Record Star (26725)**
Gateway Publications
610 Beatty Rd.
Monroeville, PA 15146
Phone: (412)856-7400
Fax: (412)856-7954
**Subject(s):** Paid Community Newspapers
**Circ:** (Non-paid)98
(Paid)1,790

**The Richmond Hill Times (22784)**
Queens Publishing Corp.
41-02 Bell Blvd., 2nd Fl.
Bayside, NY 11361
Phone: (718)229-0300
Fax: (718)225-7117
**Subject(s):** Paid Community Newspapers
**Circ:** (Paid)1,792

**Cohasset Mariner (13741)**
Community Newspaper Co.
254 2nd Ave.
Needham, MA 02494
Phone: (781)433-6700
**Subject(s):** Paid Community Newspapers
**Circ:** (Non-paid)86
(Paid)1,756

**The Fresh Meadows Times (20800)**
Queens Publishing Corp.
41-02 Bell Blvd., 2nd Fl.
Bayside, NY 11361
Phone: (718)229-0300
Fax: (718)225-7117
**Subject(s):** Paid Community Newspapers
**Circ:** (Paid)1,758

**Hilltops (22657)**
Hartwick College
One Hartwick Dr.
Oneonta, NY 13820
Phone: (607)431-4000
**Subject(s):** College Publications
**Circ:** (Free)‡1,750

**Northfield News (30916)**
Celia Barnes
40 Central St.
Northfield, VT 05663
Phone: (802)485-6397
**Subject(s):** Paid Community Newspapers
**Circ:** (Paid)‡1,750

**Summit Herald (19611)**
80 South St.
New Providence, NJ 07974
Phone: (908)464-1025
Fax: (908)464-9085
**Subject(s):** Paid Community Newspapers
**Circ:** (Non-paid)158
(Paid)1,751

**Ken-Ton Bee (20574)**
Bee Publications Inc.
5564 Main St.
PO Box 150
Buffalo, NY 14231-0150
Phone: (716)632-4700
Fax: (716)633-8601
**Subject(s):** Paid Community Newspapers
**Circ:** (Free)⊕42
(Paid)⊕1,731

**Whitman/Hanson Mariner (14911)**
Mariner Newspapers
254 2nd Ave
PO Box 9113
Needham, MA 02494
Phone: (781)837-3500
Fax: (781)837-4540
**Subject(s):** Paid Community Newspapers
**Circ:** (Non-paid)39
(Paid)1,730

**South Plainfield Reporter (19835)**
NJN Publishing
44 Veterans Memorial Dr. E.
PO Box 699
Somerville, NJ 08876
Phone: (908)575-6660
Fax: (908)575-6683
**Subject(s):** Paid Community Newspapers
**Circ:** (Paid)1,729

**Echo Leader (19838)**
Worrall Community Newspapers
1291 Stuyvesant Ave.
PO Box 3109
Union, NJ 07083
Phone: (908)686-7700
Fax: (908)686-4169
**Subject(s):** Paid Community Newspapers
**Circ:** (Non-paid)53
(Paid)1,717

**The Boyce Collegian (26721)**
Community College of Allegheny County
Boyce Campus
595 Beatty Rd.
Monroeville, PA 15146
Phone: (412)371-8651
Fax: (412)325-6859
**Subject(s):** College Publications
**Circ:** (Free)‡1,700

**Springfield Reporter (30943)**
151 Summer St.
Springfield, VT 05156-3503
Phone: (802)885-2246
Fax: (802)885-9821
**Subject(s):** Paid Community Newspapers
**Circ:** (Non-paid)100
(Paid)1,700

**The Summit (14317)**
Stonehill College
320 Washington St. No. 1974
North Easton, MA 02357
Phone: (508)565-1838
Fax: (508)565-1794
**Subject(s):** College Publications
**Circ:** (Free)1,700

**Westfield Republican (23175)**
Ogden Newspapers Inc.
PO Box 38
Westfield, NY 14787
Phone: (716)326-3163
Fax: (716)326-3165
**Subject(s):** Paid Community Newspapers
**Circ:** ‡1,690

**The North Countryman (22707)**
Denton Publications
21 McKinley Ave., Ste. 2
Plattsburgh, NY 12901
Phone: (518)561-1198
Fax: (518)561-1198
**Subject(s):** Paid Community Newspapers
**Circ:** (Paid)17
(Non-paid)1,675

**The Glen Oaks Ledger (20837)**
Queens Publishing Corp.
41-02 Bell Blvd., 2nd Fl.
Bayside, NY 11361
Phone: (718)229-0300
Fax: (718)225-7117
**Subject(s):** Paid Community Newspapers
**Circ:** (Paid)1,640

**Canastota Bee-Journal (20614)**
Eagle Newspapers
c/o Martha Rush Conway, Editor
PO Box 228
Canastota, NY 13032
Phone: (315)697-7142
Fax: (315)697-6283
**Subject(s):** Paid Community Newspapers
**Circ:** (Free)171
(Paid)1,632

**Halifax Reporter (13813)**
MPG Newspapers
9 Long Pond Rd.
PO Box 959
Plymouth, MA 02362-0959
Phone: (508)746-5555
Fax: (508)747-2148

**Subject(s):** Paid Community Newspapers

**Circ:** (Combined)1,616

**Greenville Local (20867)**
The News-Herald Inc.
164 Main St.
Ravena, NY 12143
Phone: (518)756-2030
Fax: (518)756-8555
**Subject(s):** Paid Community Newspapers

**Circ:** ‡1,600

**Journal of Commerce Import Bulletin (19617)**
The Journal of Commerce
33 Washington St.
Newark, NJ 07102
Phone: (973)848-7000
Fax: (973)454-6507
**Subject(s):** International Business and Economics

**Circ:** ‡1,608

**The Journal-Press (20868)**
Tefft Publishers Inc.
35 Salem St.
PO Box 185
Greenwich, NY 12834-0185
Phone: (518)692-2266
Fax: (518)692-2589
**Subject(s):** Paid Community Newspapers

**Circ:** (Non-paid)⊕71
(Paid)⊕**1,606**

**Windsor Locks Journal (5106)**
Imprint Newspapers
99 Main St.
Bristol, CT 06010
Phone: (860)236-3571
Fax: (860)233-2080
**Subject(s):** Paid Community Newspapers

**Circ:** (Non-paid)32
(Paid)1,594

**Rocky Hill Post (4647)**
Imprint Newspapers
99 Main St.
Bristol, CT 06010
Phone: (860)236-3571
Fax: (860)233-2080
**Subject(s):** Paid Community Newspapers

**Circ:** (Non-paid)34
(Paid)1,585

**Cheektowaga Bee (20640)**
Bee Group Newspapers
5564 Main St.
PO Box 150
Williamsville, NY 14231-0150
Phone: (716)632-4700
Fax: (716)633-8601
**Subject(s):** Paid Community Newspapers

**Circ:** (Free)⊕23
(Paid)⊕**1,572**

**Depew Bee (20567)**
Bee Publications Inc.
5564 Main St.
PO Box 150
Buffalo, NY 14231-0150
Phone: (716)632-4700
Fax: (716)633-8601
**Subject(s):** Free Newspapers

**Circ:** (Free)22
(Paid)1,572

**Oakmont Advance Leader (26728)**
Gateway Publications
610 Beatty Rd.
Monroeville, PA 15146
Phone: (412)856-7400
Fax: (412)856-7954
**Subject(s):** Paid Community Newspapers

**Circ:** (Combined)1,578

**Randolph Mariner (14763)**
Mariner Newspapers
254 2nd Ave
PO Box 9113
Needham, MA 02494
Phone: (781)837-3500
Fax: (781)837-4540
**Subject(s):** Paid Community Newspapers

**Circ:** (Non-paid)88
(Paid)1,565

**Chittenango-Bridgeport Times (20615)**
Eagle Newspapers
c/o Martha Rush Conway, Editor
114 Canal St.
PO Box 228
Canastota, NY 13032
Phone: (315)697-7142
Fax: (315)697-6283
**Subject(s):** Paid Community Newspapers

**Circ:** (Free)239
(Paid)1,551

**Pembroke Mariner (14733)**
Community Newspaper Co.
165 Enterprise Dr.
Marshfield, MA 02050
Phone: (781)293-6980
Fax: (781)837-4540
**Subject(s):** Paid Community Newspapers

**Circ:** (Non-paid)178
(Paid)1,531

**Upper Darby and Drexel Hill Press (26778)**
County Press
3732 W Chester Pke.
PO Box 249
Newtown Square, PA 19073
Phone: (610)356-3820
Fax: (610)353-5321
**Subject(s):** Paid Community Newspapers

**Circ:** (Non-paid)‡113
(Paid)‡1,516

**Beacon (27687)**
Wilkes University
PO Box 111
Wilkes Barre, PA 18766
Phone: (570)408-4000
Fax: (570)408-7800
**Subject(s):** College Publications

**Circ:** (Paid)100
(Non-paid)1,500

**The Country Courier (20670)**
Masthead Publications Inc.
1035 Conklin Rd.
Conklin, NY 13748
Phone: (607)775-0472
Fax: (607)775-5863
**Subject(s):** Paid Community Newspapers

**Circ:** (Paid)1,500

**The Lincolnian (26652)**
Lincoln University
Office of Communications
PO Box 179
Lincoln University, PA 19352
Phone: (610)932-8300
Fax: (610)932-0195
**Subject(s):** College Publications; Black Publications

**Circ:** (Free)1,500

**The Luminary (26749)**
Sun-Gazette Co.
41 S. Main St.
Muncy, PA 17756
Phone: (570)546-8555
Fax: (570)546-8974
**Subject(s):** Paid Community Newspapers

**Circ:** 1,500

**The New Englander (18836)**
New England College
24 Bridge St.
Henniker, NH 03242
Phone: (603)428-2211
Fax: (603)428-7230
**Subject(s):** College Publications

**Circ:** (Free)‡1,500

**The Promethean (21079)**
Siena College
515 Loudon Rd.
Loudonville, NY 12211
Phone: (518)783-2300
Fax: (518)783-2493
**Subject(s):** College Publications

**Circ:** (Free)‡1,500

**Syndicated Columnists Weekly (13594)**
National Braille Press Inc.
88 Saint Stephen St.
Boston, MA 02115-4302
Phone: (617)266-6160
Fax: (617)437-0456

**Subject(s):** Paid Community Newspapers

**Circ:** (Combined)1,500

**Newport Mercury (27870)**
Edward A. Sherman Publishing Co.
PO Box 420
101 Malbone Rd.
Newport, RI 02840
Phone: (401)849-3300
Fax: (401)849-3306
**Subject(s):** Paid Community Newspapers

**Circ:** ‡1,471

**Easton Courier (4682)**
Hometown Publications Inc.
1000 Bridgeport Ave.
Shelton, CT 06484
Phone: (203)926-2080
Fax: (203)926-2091
**Subject(s):** Free Newspapers

**Circ:** (Non-paid)♦155
(Paid)♦**1,466**

**The Lynnfield Villager (13868)**
Great Oak Publications Inc.
55 Salem St.
Lynnfield, MA 01940
Phone: (781)334-6319
Fax: (978)664-4954
**Subject(s):** Paid Community Newspapers

**Circ:** (Non-paid)151
(Paid)1,467

**Floral Park Dispatch (20780)**
Anton Community Newspapers
132 E. 2nd St.
Mineola, NY 11501
Phone: (516)747-8282
Fax: (516)742-5867
**Subject(s):** Paid Community Newspapers

**Circ:** ‡1,452

**The Windsor Standard (20672)**
Masthead Publications Inc.
1035 Conklin Rd.
Conklin, NY 13748
Phone: (607)775-0472
Fax: (607)775-5863
**Subject(s):** Paid Community Newspapers

**Circ:** 1,450

**Pembroke Reporter (14734)**
MPG Newspapers
9 Long Pond Rd.
PO Box 959
Plymouth, MA 02362-0959
Phone: (508)746-5555
Fax: (508)747-2148
**Subject(s):** Paid Community Newspapers

**Circ:** (Paid)1,441

**The Messenger (19112)**
Bergen Gazette
48 Harrison Ave.
Garfield, NJ 07026
Phone: (973)473-1927
Fax: (973)546-4233
**Subject(s):** Paid Community Newspapers

**Circ:** ‡1,430

**East Meadow Herald (20726)**
Richner Communications
P.O. Box 9001
Lawrence, NY 11559-1616
Phone: (516)569-4000
Fax: (516)569-4942
**Subject(s):** Paid Community Newspapers

**Circ:** (Free)‡225
(Paid)‡1,422

**Rockaway Journal (20766)**
Richner Communications
P.O. Box 9001
Lawrence, NY 11559-1616
Phone: (516)569-4000
Fax: (516)569-4942
**Subject(s):** Paid Community Newspapers

**Circ:** (Free)‡318
(Paid)‡1,410

**The Randolph Register (22775)**
220 Main St.
PO Box 98
Randolph, NY 14772
Phone: (716)358-2921

# Northeastern States

Fax: (716)358-5695
**Subject(s):** Paid Community Newspapers
**Circ:** (Paid)1,400

**Willow Grove Guide (26385)**
Journal Register Co.
Montgomery Newspapers
290 Commerce Dr.
Fort Washington, PA 19034
Phone: (215)542-0200
**Subject(s):** Paid Community Newspapers
**Circ:** (Combined)1,373

**The Catholic Journalist (22873)**
Catholic Press Association
3555 Veterans Memorial Hwy.
Unit O
Ronkonkoma, NY 11779
Phone: (631)471-4730
Fax: (631)471-4804
**Subject(s):** Religious Publications; Journalism and Publishing
**Circ:** ‡1357

**Spectator Leader (19457)**
Worrall Community Newspapers
1291 Stuyvesant Ave.
PO Box 3109
Union, NJ 07083
Phone: (908)686-7700
Fax: (908)686-4169
**Subject(s):** Paid Community Newspapers
**Circ:** (Paid)1,339

**Leechburg Advance (27626)**
Buttermilk Falls Co.
143 Washington Ave
Vandergrift, PA 15690
Phone: (724)567-5656
Fax: (724)568-3818
**Subject(s):** Paid Community Newspapers
**Circ:** (Non-paid)‡15
(Paid)‡1,313

**The Bengal Review (12518)**
University of Maine-Fort Kent
25 Pleasent
Fort Kent, ME 04743-1222
Phone: (207)834-7500
**Subject(s):** College Publications
**Circ:** (Free)‡1,300

**The Leader (19442)**
Worrall Community Newspapers
1291 Stuyvesant Ave.
PO Box 3109
Union, NJ 07083
Phone: (908)686-7700
Fax: (908)686-4169
**Subject(s):** Free Newspapers
**Circ:** (Non-paid)21
(Paid)1,299

**Marcellus Observer (21127)**
Eagle Newspapers
c/o Ellen Leahy, Editor
2 Fennell St.
Skaneateles, NY 13152-1138
Phone: (315)685-8338
Fax: (315)685-8338
**Subject(s):** Paid Community Newspapers
**Circ:** (Free)‡98
(Paid)‡1,288

**Bethel Beacon (4921)**
Housatonic Publications
65 Bank St.
New Milford, CT 06776
Fax: (860)354-2645
**Subject(s):** Paid Community Newspapers
**Circ:** (Non-paid)1
(Paid)1,278

**The Manville News (19726)**
The Princeton Packet Inc.
300 Witherspoon St.
Princeton, NJ 08542-3477
Phone: (609)924-3244
Fax: (609)924-8492
**Subject(s):** Paid Community Newspapers
**Circ:** ‡1,261

**Troy Gazette Register (27586)**
Troy Gazette-Register Inc.
11 Canton St.
Troy, PA 16947
Phone: (570)297-3024
Fax: (570)297-2954
**Subject(s):** Paid Community Newspapers
**Circ:** ‡1,250

**Bridgeville Area News (26722)**
Gateway Publications
610 Beatty Rd.
Monroeville, PA 15146
Phone: (412)856-7400
Fax: (412)856-7954
**Subject(s):** Paid Community Newspapers
**Circ:** (Non-paid)131
(Paid)1,248

**Canton News (4657)**
Imprint Newspapers
99 Main St.
Bristol, CT 06010
Phone: (860)236-3571
Fax: (860)233-2080
**Subject(s):** Paid Community Newspapers
**Circ:** (Non-paid)169
(Paid)1,246

**The Glen Ridge Paper (18990)**
Worrall Community Newspapers
266 Liberty St.
Bloomfield, NJ 07003
Phone: (973)743-4040
Fax: (973)680-8848
**Subject(s):** Paid Community Newspapers
**Circ:** (Combined)1,211

**The Comenian (26163)**
Moravian College
1200 Main St.
Bethlehem, PA 18018
Phone: (610)861-1320
**Subject(s):** College Publications
**Circ:** (Free)1200

**Egg Harbor News (19138)**
Atlantic County Newspaper Group
115 12th St.
PO Box 596
Hammonton, NJ 08037
Phone: (609)561-2300
Fax: (609)567-2249
**Subject(s):** Paid Community Newspapers
**Circ:** ‡1,200

**Hamilton/Morrisville Tribune (20628)**
Eagle Newspapers
c/o Kim Dam, Editor
PO Box 301
Cazenovia, NY 13035-0301
Phone: (315)655-3415
Fax: (315)655-3813
**Subject(s):** Paid Community Newspapers
**Circ:** (Free)160
(Paid)1,202

**The FORUM (30942)**
Vermont Law School
Chelsea St.
PO Box 96
South Royalton, VT 05068
Phone: (802)763-8303
Fax: (802)763-2663
**Subject(s):** Law
**Circ:** (Free)‡1,100

**The Coventry Courier (27941)**
Southern Rhode Island Newspapers
187 Main St.
PO Box 232
Wakefield, RI 02880
Phone: (401)789-9744
Fax: (401)783-1550
**Subject(s):** Paid Community Newspapers
**Circ:** (Non-paid)♦28
(Paid)♦1,077

**The Vestal Town Crier (20671)**
Masthead Publications Inc.
1035 Conklin Rd.
Conklin, NY 13748
Phone: (607)775-0472
Fax: (607)775-5863

**Subject(s):** Paid Community Newspapers
**Circ:** 1,050

**Nutley Journal (19638)**
Worrall Community Newspapers
170 Scotland Rd.
Orange, NJ 07051
Phone: (973)674-8000
Fax: (973)674-2038
**Subject(s):** Paid Community Newspapers
**Circ:** (Paid)1,040

**Orange Transcript (19645)**
Worrall Community Newspapers
170 Scotland Rd.
Orange, NJ 07051
Phone: (973)674-8000
Fax: (973)674-2038
**Subject(s):** Paid Community Newspapers
**Circ:** (Paid)1,046

**Castine Patriot (12501)**
Penobscot Bay Press
PO Box 205
Castine, ME 04421-0205
Phone: (207)326-9300
Fax: (207)326-4383
**Subject(s):** Paid Community Newspapers
**Circ:** 1,000

**The Gwynmercian (26419)**
Gwynedd Mercy College
1325 Sumney Town Pke.
Gwynedd Valley, PA 19437
Phone: (215)646-7300
**Subject(s):** College Publications
**Circ:** (Free)‡1,000

**Hanover News (14938)**
440 Lincoln St.
Worcester, MA 01653-0002
**Subject(s):** Paid Community Newspapers
**Circ:** 1,000

**Houghton Star (22647)**
Olean Times-Herald
639 Norton Dr.
Olean, NY 14760
Phone: (716)372-3121
Fax: (716)372-0740
**Subject(s):** College Publications
**Circ:** ‡1,000

**Red and Black (27648)**
Washington and Jefferson College
60 S Lincoln St.
Washington, PA 15301
Phone: (724)222-4400
Fax: (724)223-5267
**Subject(s):** College Publications
**Circ:** (Non-paid)1,000

**Warner's New Paper (18959)**
PO Box 92
Warner, NH 03278
Phone: (603)456-1423
Fax: (603)456-3087
**Subject(s):** Paid Community Newspapers
**Circ:** 1,000

**The Alfred Sun (20248)**
Twin Creek Publishing
PO Box 811
Alfred, NY 14802-0811
Phone: (607)587-8110
Fax: (607)587-8113
**Subject(s):** Paid Community Newspapers
**Circ:** (Free)‡50
(Paid)‡950

**Atlantic County Record (19137)**
Atlantic County Weekly Newspaper Group
115 12th St.
PO Box 596
Hammonton, NJ 08037
Phone: (609)641-3100
Fax: (609)646-0561
**Subject(s):** Paid Community Newspapers
**Circ:** ‡928

**Perry Herald (22698)**
12 Borden Ave.
PO Box 219
Perry, NY 14530
Phone: (585)237-2212
Fax: (585)237-2211
**Subject(s):** Paid Community Newspapers

**Circ:** (Free)36
(Paid)920

**Summit Observer (19911)**
Worrall Community Newspapers
1291 Stuyvesant Ave.
PO Box 3109
Union, NJ 07083
Phone: (908)686-7700
Fax: (908)686-4169
**Subject(s):** Paid Community Newspapers

**Circ:** (Combined)917

**Irvington Herald (19410)**
Worrall Community Newspapers
PO Box 158ey St.
Maplewood, NJ 07040
Phone: (201)763-0700
Fax: (201)763-2557
**Subject(s):** Paid Community Newspapers

**Circ:** (Combined)904

**Drug Metabolism and Disposition (26925)**
Lippincott Williams & Wilkins
530 Walnut St.
Philadelphia, PA 19106-3261
Phone: (215)521-8300
Fax: (215)521-8902
**Subject(s):** Drugs and Pharmaceuticals

**Circ:** (Non-paid)‡93
(Paid)‡875

**The Pound Ridge Review (4989)**
Hersam Acorn Newspapers L.L.C.
16 Bailey Ave.
PO Box 1019
Ridgefield, CT 06877
Phone: (203)438-6544
**Subject(s):** Paid Community Newspapers

**Circ:** (Paid)870

**News (18976)**
Press Publications Inc.
PO Box 265
Belvidere, NJ 07823
**Subject(s):** Paid Community Newspapers

**Circ:** (Paid)♦848

**Long Island Graphic (20798)**
Richner Communications
P.O. Box 9001
Lawrence, NY 11559-1616
Phone: (516)569-4000
Fax: (516)569-4942
**Subject(s):** Paid Community Newspapers

**Circ:** (Free)‡192
(Paid)‡820

**Bucks County Law Reporter (26285)**
Bucks County Bar Association
135 E State St.
PO Box 300
Doylestown, PA 18901-0300
Phone: (215)348-9413
Fax: (215)348-3277
**Subject(s):** Law

**Circ:** (Free)‡50
(Paid)‡810

**Thielensian (26411)**
Thiel College
Box 1654
Thiel College 75 College Ave
Greenville, PA 16125
Phone: (724)589-2000
Fax: (724)589-2010
**Subject(s):** College Publications

**Circ:** (Free)800

**Yellow Jacket (14807)**
American International College
1000 State St.
Springfield, MA 01109-3189
Phone: (413)205-3201
Fax: (413)205-3405
**Subject(s):** College Publications

**Circ:** 800

**Kent Good Times Dispatch (4830)**
Housatonic Publications
14 Main St.
PO Box 430
Kent, CT 06757
Phone: (860)927-4621
Fax: (860)927-4622
**Subject(s):** Paid Community Newspapers

**Circ:** (Non-paid)1
(Paid)793

**Random Harvest Weekly (22955)**
Finger Lake Community Newspaper
PO Box 714
Trumansburg, NY 14886
Phone: (607)387-3181
Fax: (607)387-9421
**Subject(s):** Paid Community Newspapers

**Circ:** (Free)29
(Paid)789

**Strasburg Weekly News (27565)**
140 W Main St.
Box 160
Strasburg, PA 17579
Phone: (717)687-7721
Fax: (717)687-6551
**Subject(s):** Paid Community Newspapers

**Circ:** (Free)‡84
(Paid)‡782

**North Providence North Star (27854)**
Observer Publications Inc.
1 Whipple Ln.
Box 950
Greenville, RI 02828
Phone: (401)949-2700
Fax: (401)333-4600
**Subject(s):** Paid Community Newspapers

**Circ:** (Non-paid)♦192
(Paid)♦743

**Chautauqua News (23171)**
Ogden Newspapers Inc.
PO Box 38
Westfield, NY 14787
Phone: (716)326-3163
Fax: (716)326-3165
**Subject(s):** Paid Community Newspapers

**Circ:** (Free)‡93
(Paid)‡702

**Jericho News Journal (20997)**
Litmor Publications Inc.
81 E Barclay St.
Hicksville, NY 11801
Phone: (516)931-0012
Fax: (516)931-0027
**Subject(s):** Paid Community Newspapers

**Circ:** (Non-paid)50
(Paid)690

**Mayville Sentinel (23172)**
Ogden Newspapers Inc.
PO Box 38
Westfield, NY 14787
Phone: (716)326-3163
Fax: (716)326-3165
**Subject(s):** Paid Community Newspapers

**Circ:** (Free)‡63
(Paid)‡687

**Mifflinburg Telegraph (26708)**
PO Box 189
Mifflinburg, PA 17844
Phone: (570)966-2255
Fax: (570)966-0062
**Subject(s):** Paid Community Newspapers

**Circ:** (Paid)650

**Rahway Progress (19746)**
Worrall Community Newspapers
1291 Stuyvesant Ave.
PO Box 3109
Union, NJ 07083
Phone: (908)686-7700
Fax: (908)686-4169
**Subject(s):** Paid Community Newspapers

**Circ:** (Combined)633

**Afro-Americans in New York Life and History (20554)**
Afro-American Historical Association of the Niagara Frontier Inc.
PO Box 63
Buffalo, NY 14216
Phone: (716)633-7058
**Subject(s):** Black Publications; Local, State, and Regional Publications

**Circ:** (Paid)600

**Inquirer (26149)**
Bedford Gazette
424 W. Penn St.
Bedford, PA 15522
Phone: (814)623-1151
Fax: (814)623-5055
**Subject(s):** Paid Community Newspapers

**Circ:** ‡585

**Belleville Post (18988)**
Worrall Community Newspapers
266 Liberty St.
Bloomfield, NJ 07003
Phone: (973)743-4040
Fax: (973)680-8848
**Subject(s):** Paid Community Newspapers

**Circ:** (Combined)572

**Chester County Law Reporter (27664)**
Chester County Bar Association
15 W Gay Street 2nd Floor
West Chester, PA 19381-3191
Phone: (610)692-1889
Fax: (610)692-9546
**Subject(s):** Law

**Circ:** 420

**News-Leader (19584)**
Press Publications
26 Main St.
PO Box 637
Netcong, NJ 07857-1111
Fax: (908)362-9223
**Subject(s):** Paid Community Newspapers

**Circ:** (Combined)397

**Boston Seniority (13489)**
Mayor's Commission on Affairs of the Elderly
One City Hall Pl., Rm. 271
Boston, MA 02201
Phone: (617)635-2712
Fax: (617)635-3213
**Subject(s):** Senior Citizens' Interests; Free Newspapers

**Circ:** (Free)‡20

## Southern Central States

**The Dallas Morning News (29528)**
Dallas Tribune
508 Young St.
PO Box 655237
Dallas, TX 75202
Phone: (214)977-8222
Fax: (214)977-8638
**Subject(s):** Daily Newspapers

**Circ:** (Mon.-Thurs.)505,724
515,000
(Sat.)543,411
(Fri.)586,886
(Sun.)784,905

**Houston Chronicle (29851)**
801 Texas Ave.
Houston, TX 77002
Phone: (713)220-7171
Fax: (713)220-6677
**Subject(s):** Daily Newspapers

**Circ:** (Mon.-Sat.)★554,783
(Sun.)★737,580

**Houston Greensheet (29855)**
Greensheet Inc.
2601 Main St., 4th Fl.
Houston, TX 77002
Phone: (713)371-3500
Fax: (713)371-3702
**Subject(s):** Shopping Guides

**Circ:** (Free)❑369,726

**Express-News (30359)**
PO Box 2171
San Antonio, TX 78297-2171
Phone: (210)250-3000

## Southern Central States

**Subject(s):** Daily Newspapers
**Circ:** (Mon.-Thurs.)★226,109
(Sat.)★255,167
(Fri.)★270,067
(Sun.)★356,680

**African-American News & Issues** (29823)
Malonson Company Inc.
6130 Wheatley St.
Houston, TX 77091-3947
Phone: (713)692-1892
Fax: (713)692-1183
**Subject(s):** Black Publications; Free Newspapers
**Circ:** (Combined)350,000

**Star-Telegram Newspaper** (29728)
Knight-Ridder Inc.
400 W. 7th
Fort Worth, TX 76102
Phone: (817)335-4837
Fax: (817)390-7831
**Subject(s):** Daily Newspapers
**Circ:** (Mon.-Thurs.)★223,098
(Sat.)★249,562
(Fri.)★258,489
(Sun.)★326,803

**Oklahoman** (25479)
Oklahoma Publishing Co.
9000 N Broadway
PO Box 25125
Oklahoma City, OK 73125-0125
Phone: (405)475-3311
Fax: (405)475-3970
**Subject(s):** Daily Newspapers
**Circ:** (Mon.-Sat.)★197,507
(Wed.)★250,496
(Sun.)★288,948

**Arkansas Democrat-Gazette** (1163)
Arkansas Democrat-Gazette Inc.
Capitol Ave. & Scott St.
PO Box 2221
Little Rock, AR 72203
Phone: (501)378-3400
Fax: (501)372-3908
**Subject(s):** Daily Newspapers
**Circ:** (Mon.-Sat.)183,343
(Sun.)283,538

**The Times-Picayune** (12324)
Times-Picayune Publishing Corp.
3800 Howard Ave.
New Orleans, LA 70125-1429
Phone: (504)826-3729
Fax: (504)826-3007
**Subject(s):** Daily Newspapers
**Circ:** (Mon.-Sat.)★252,799
(Sun.)★281,374

**United Methodist Reporter** (29575)
Newspaper Division United Methodist Communications Council
Dallas, TX 75266-0275
Phone: (214)630-6495
Fax: (214)630-0079
**Subject(s):** Religious Publications
**Circ:** (Paid)⊕130,000
260,000

**Front Porch** (1176)
Arkansas Farm Bureau Federation
Box 31
Little Rock, AR 72203-0031
Phone: (501)228-1307
Fax: (501)228-1557
**Subject(s):** Farm Bureau, Grange, and Cooperative Associations
**Circ:** ‡231,000

**Austin American-Statesman** (29131)
Cox Texas Publications Inc.
305 S Congress Ave.
Austin, TX 78704
Phone: (512)445-4000
Fax: (512)445-3503
**Subject(s):** Daily Newspapers
**Circ:** (Mon.-Sat.)★177,926
(Sun.)★226,766

**Tulsa World** (25630)
World Publishing Co.
315 S. Boulder Ave.
PO Box 1770
Tulsa, OK 74103
Phone: (918)583-2161
**Subject(s):** Daily Newspapers
**Circ:** (Mon.-Sat.)143,582
(Sun.)206,801

**Dallas Greensheet** (29526)
Greensheet Inc.
2601 Main St., 4th Fl.
Houston, TX 77002
Phone: (713)371-3500
Fax: (713)371-3702
**Subject(s):** Shopping Guides
**Circ:** (Free)❏192,881

**The Texas Catholic Herald** (29911)
1700 San Jacinto St.
Houston, TX 77002
Phone: (713)659-5461
Fax: (713)659-3444
**Subject(s):** Religious Publications
**Circ:** (Paid)‡158,500
(Controlled)‡192,500

**Albuquerque Journal** (19984)
Albuquerque Publishing Co.
7777 Jefferson St. NE
Albuquerque, NM 87109-4360
Phone: (505)823-3800
Fax: (505)823-3369
**Subject(s):** Daily Newspapers
**Circ:** (Mon.-Sat.)108,931
(Sun.)153,560

**The Advocate** (12060)
Capital City Press
525 Lafayette St.
Baton Rouge, LA 70802-5410
Phone: (225)388-0216
Fax: (225)388-0348
**Subject(s):** Daily Newspapers
**Circ:** (Mon.-Fri.)96,239
(Sat.)109,897
(Sun.)129,706

**Texas Agriculture** (30598)
Texas Farm Bureau
PO Box 2689
1520 Fish Pond Rd.
Waco, TX 76702
Phone: (254)772-3030
Fax: (254)772-1766
**Subject(s):** Farm Newspapers
**Circ:** (Free)1,009
(Paid)125,065

**The Presbyterian Sun** (29387)
Synod of the Sun
1925 E Belt Line Rd., Ste. 220
Carrollton, TX 75006-5826
Phone: (817)382-9656
Fax: (817)383-8253
**Subject(s):** Religious Publications
**Circ:** (Non-paid)‡118,089

**Houston Press** (29858)
New Times Inc.
1621 Milam, Ste. 100
Houston, TX 77002
Phone: (713)280-2400
Fax: (713)280-2444
**Subject(s):** Free Newspapers; Entertainment; Local, State, and Regional Publications
**Circ:** (Non-paid)115,123

**Dallas Observer** (29529)
New Times Inc.
2130 Commerce St.
Dallas, TX 75201
Phone: (713)757-9000
**Subject(s):** Free Newspapers
**Circ:** (Non-paid)110,684

**TEXAS LEGION TIMES** (29228)
American Legion—Dept. of Texas
3401 Ed Bluestein Blvd.
Austin, TX 78721-2902
Phone: (512)472-4138
Fax: (512)472-0603
**Subject(s):** Veterans
**Circ:** ‡110,000

**La Subasta** (29878)
6120 Tarnef, Ste. 110
Houston, TX 77074
Phone: (214)951-9500
**Subject(s):** Hispanic Publications
**Circ:** (Free)101,168

**The Christian Chronicle** (25456)
Oklahoma Christian University
PO Box 11000
Oklahoma City, OK 73136-1100
Phone: (405)425-5070
Fax: (405)425-5076
**Subject(s):** Religious Publications
**Circ:** 100,000

**Valley Town Crier** (30147)
Valley Media Inc.
1811 N. 23rd St.
McAllen, TX 78501
Phone: (956)682-2423
Fax: (956)630-6371
**Subject(s):** Free Newspapers
**Circ:** (Free)❏99,405

**La Voz de Houston Newspaper** (29879)
La Voz Publishing Corp.
6101 SW Fwy., Ste. 127
Houston, TX 77057
Phone: (713)664-4404
Fax: (713)664-4414
**Subject(s):** Paid Community Newspapers; Spanish
**Circ:** (Non-paid)96,780

**The Times** (12386)
222 Lake St.
Shreveport, LA 71101
Phone: (318)459-3200
Fax: (318)459-3301
**Subject(s):** Daily Newspapers
**Circ:** (Mon.-Sat.)77,323
(Sun.)95,275

**Baptist Messenger** (25450)
Baptist General Convention of Oklahoma
PO Box 12130
Oklahoma City, OK 73157-2130
**Subject(s):** Religious Publications
**Circ:** (Non-paid)‡1,500
(Paid)‡92,000

**Austin Chronicle** (29133)
PO Box 49066
Austin, TX 78765
Phone: (512)454-5766
Fax: (512)458-6910
**Subject(s):** Entertainment
**Circ:** (Paid)267
(Free)90,000

**El Paso Times** (29659)
Times Plz.
El Paso, TX 79901-1470
Phone: (915)546-6104
Fax: (915)546-6496
**Subject(s):** Daily Newspapers
**Circ:** (Mon.-Sat.)★72,132
(Sun.)★87,581

**The North Freeway Leader** (29887)
The Leader
3500 A E TC Jester Blvd.
Houston, TX 77018
Phone: (713)686-8494
Fax: (713)686-0970
**Subject(s):** Free Newspapers
**Circ:** (Free)84,459

**La Informacion** (29877)
La Informacion Publishing Company Inc.
6065 Hillcroft, Ste. 400
PO Box 207255
Houston, TX 77225
Phone: (713)272-0100
Fax: (713)272-0011
**Subject(s):** Spanish; Hispanic Publications; Paid Community Newspapers
**Circ:** 84,000

**San Angelo Standard-Times** (30337)
San Angelo Standard Inc.
PO Box 5111
San Angelo, TX 76902
Phone: (915)658-7341
Fax: (800)588-1884

**Subject(s):** Daily Newspapers

**Circ:** (Mon.-Sat.)★27,933
(Sun.)★33,219
(Mon.-Sat.)65,000
(Sun.)78,000

**Corpus Christi Caller-Times (29461)**
Caller-Times
820 N. Lower Broadway
Corpus Christi, TX 78401
Phone: (361)884-2011
**Subject(s):** Daily Newspapers

**Circ:** (Mon.-Sat.)★57,591
(Sun.)★75,869

**The 1960 Sun (29895)**
Sun Newspapers Inc.
3730 FM 1960 W, Ste. 108
Houston, TX 77068
Phone: (281)537-7528
Fax: (281)537-7528
**Subject(s):** Free Newspapers

**Circ:** (Paid)33
(Non-paid)75,584

**Clarion Herald (12295)**
Clarion Herald Publishing Company Inc.
1000 Howard Ave., Ste. 400
PO Box 53247
New Orleans, LA 70113
Phone: (504)524-1618
Fax: (504)596-3039
**Subject(s):** Religious Publications

**Circ:** (Paid)‡75,000

**Fort Bend/Southwest Sun (30257)**
Sun Newspapers Inc.
PO Box 6192
Pasadena, TX 77506-0192
**Subject(s):** Free Newspapers

**Circ:** (Combined)69,535

**Houston Forward Times (29854)**
Forward Times Publishing Co.
4411 Almeda
PO Box 8346
Houston, TX 77004
Phone: (713)526-4727
Fax: (713)526-3170
**Subject(s):** Paid Community Newspapers; Black Publications

**Circ:** ‡64,580

**Lubbock Avalanche-Journal (30084)**
710 Ave. J, No. 491
Lubbock, TX 79401-1808
Phone: (806)762-8844
Fax: (806)744-9603
**Subject(s):** Daily Newspapers

**Circ:** (Mon.-Sat.)★52,976
(Sun.)★62,710

**Amarillo Globe-News (29077)**
PO Box 2091
Amarillo, TX 79166
Phone: (806)376-4488
Fax: (806)376-9217
**Subject(s):** Daily Newspapers

**Circ:** (Mon.-Sat.)★49,190
(Sun.)★61,304

**Beaumont Enterprise (29289)**
Hearst Publishing Co.
380 Main St.
Beaumont, TX 77701
Phone: (409)833-3311
Fax: (409)838-2845
**Subject(s):** Daily Newspapers

**Circ:** (Mon.-Sat.)★51,296
(Sun.)★58,692

**Oklahoma Gazette (25471)**
PO Box 54649
Oklahoma City, OK 73154-1649
Phone: (405)528-6046
Fax: (405)528-4949
**Subject(s):** Free Newspapers

**Circ:** (Non-paid)54,709

**Northwest Arkansas Times (1074)**
PO Box 1607
Fayetteville, AR 72702
Fax: (479)442-1714

**Subject(s):** Daily Newspapers

**Circ:** (Mon.-Sat.)‡38,000
(Sun.)‡53,000

**Waco Tribune-Herald (30602)**
900 Franklin Ave.
Waco, TX 76701-1906
Phone: (254)757-5757
Fax: (254)757-0302
**Subject(s):** Daily Newspapers

**Circ:** (Mon.-Sat.)40,863
(Sun.)51,519

**The Texas Catholic (29571)**
3725 Blackburn
PO Box 190347
Dallas, TX 75219
Phone: (214)528-8792
Fax: (214)528-3411
**Subject(s):** Religious Publications

**Circ:** (Free)⊕900
(Paid)⊕51,000

**Capitol Hill Beacon (25453)**
124 W Commerce
Oklahoma City, OK 73109
Phone: (405)232-4151
Fax: (405)235-0818
**Subject(s):** Free Newspapers

**Circ:** (Paid)921
(Free)50,845

**Tyler Courier-Times-Telegraph (30548)**
T.B. Butler Publishing Co.
410 W. Erwin St.
PO Box 2030
Tyler, TX 75702
Phone: (903)597-8111
Fax: (903)595-0335
**Subject(s):** Paid Community Newspapers

**Circ:** (Sun.)50,418

**Ad Sack (29459)**
PO Box 8729
Corpus Christi, TX 78468-8729
Phone: (361)854-0137
Fax: (361)854-2439
**Subject(s):** Shopping Guides

**Circ:** (Free)‡50,000

**The Catholic Commentator (12062)**
Diocese of Baton Rouge
1800 S Acadian Thruway
PO Box 14746
Baton Rouge, LA 70808-1663
Phone: (225)387-0983
Fax: (225)336-8710
**Subject(s):** Religious Publications

**Circ:** ‡50,000

**Tyler Morning Telegraph (30549)**
T.B. Butler Publishing Co.
410 W. Erwin St.
PO Box 2030
Tyler, TX 75702
Phone: (903)597-8111
Fax: (903)595-0335
**Subject(s):** Daily Newspapers

**Circ:** (Mon.-Sat.)★41,476
(Sun.)★48,671

**Observer Newspapers (30023)**
Westward Communications L.L.C.
1129 Kingwood Dr.
Kingwood, TX 77339
Phone: (281)359-2799
Fax: (281)359-0017
**Subject(s):** Free Newspapers

**Circ:** (Free)47,415

**Sunday News (29642)**
New Guide
1342 Main St.
PO Box 764
Eagle Pass, TX 78852
Phone: (830)773-2309
Fax: (830)773-3398
**Subject(s):** Free Newspapers

**Circ:** (Free)‡47,413

**Bargain Book (South) (29341)**
Valley Media Inc.
1300 Wild Rose Ln. Rd.
Brownsville, TX 78520
Phone: (956)546-5113

Fax: (956)546-0903
**Subject(s):** Shopping Guides

**Circ:** (Free)47,072

**Southwest Times Record (1096)**
Community Newspaper Holdings Inc.
3600 Wheeler Ave.
Fort Smith, AR 72901
Phone: (479)784-0413
Fax: (888)274-4049
**Subject(s):** Daily Newspapers

**Circ:** (Mon.-Sat.)44,554
(Sun.)46,300

**Louisiana Baptist Message (LBM) (12042)**
The Baptist Message
1226 MacArthur Dr.
Alexandria, LA 71301
**Subject(s):** Religious Publications

**Circ:** (Paid)45,000

**Thrifty Nickel Want Ads (30087)**
PO Box 6637
Lubbock, TX 79493-6637
Phone: (806)793-9990
Fax: (806)793-9922
**Subject(s):** Shopping Guides

**Circ:** (Free)‡45,000

**The Monitor (30146)**
Freedom Communications Inc.
PO Box 3267
McAllen, TX 78502-3267
Phone: (956)686-4000
Fax: (956)683-4201
**Subject(s):** Daily Newspapers

**Circ:** (Mon.-Sat.)36,796
(Sun.)43,623

**The News-Star (12260)**
411 N. 4th St.
Monroe, LA 71201
Phone: (318)322-5161
Fax: (318)362-0357
**Subject(s):** Daily Newspapers

**Circ:** (Mon.-Sat.)37,180
(Sun.)42,163

**Abilene Reporter-News (29036)**
101 Cypress St.
Abilene, TX 79601
Phone: (325)673-4271
**Subject(s):** Daily Newspapers

**Circ:** (Mon.-Sat.)★32,627
(Sun.)★41,621

**Weekly Alibi (20015)**
2118 Central Ave. SE, Ste. 151
Albuquerque, NM 87106-4004
Phone: (505)346-0660
Fax: (505)256-9651
**Subject(s):** Paid Community Newspapers

**Circ:** (Paid)16
(Free)41,276

**Austin Greensheet (29135)**
Greensheet Inc.
2601 Main St., 4th Fl.
Houston, TX 77002
Phone: (713)371-3500
Fax: (713)371-3702
**Subject(s):** Shopping Guides

**Circ:** (Free)❑41,236

**Alexandria Daily Town Talk (12039)**
Central Newspapers Inc.
1201 3rd St.
PO Box 7558
Alexandria, LA 71306
Phone: (318)487-6397
Fax: (318)487-6315
**Subject(s):** Daily Newspapers

**Circ:** (Mon.-Sat.)35,314
(Sun.)41,167

**Auto Revista (29505)**
14330 Midway Rd., Ste. 202
Dallas, TX 75244
Phone: (214)386-4255
Fax: (214)386-4255
**Subject(s):** Hispanic Publications; Free Newspapers; Automotive (Trade)

**Circ:** (Free)41,000

Circulation: ★ = ABC; △ = BPA; ♦ = CAC; • = CCAB; ❑ = VAC; ⊕ = PO Statement; ‡ = Publisher's Report; Boldface figures = sworn; Light figures = estimated.

**Denton Record Chronicle (29619)**
Denton Publishing Co.
314 E Hickory
PO Box 369
Denton, TX 76201
Phone: (940)387-3811
Fax: (940)566-6818
**Subject(s):** Daily Newspapers

Circ: (Mon.-Fri.)16,272
(Sun.)19,403
(Wed.)40,428

**Times Record News (30638)**
1301 Lamar
Wichita Falls, TX 76301
Phone: (940)767-5201
Fax: (800)627-1646
**Subject(s):** Daily Newspapers

Circ: (Mon.-Sat.)35,505
(Sun.)40,141

**Christian Ranchman (29710)**
Cowboys for Christ
7022 A Lake County Dr.
Fort Worth, TX 76179
Phone: (817)236-0023
Fax: (817)236-2934
**Subject(s):** Religious Publications; Livestock

Circ: (Free)39,470

**Lake Charles American Press (12210)**
PO Box 2893
Lake Charles, LA 70602
Phone: (318)433-3000
Fax: (318)494-4008
**Subject(s):** Daily Newspapers

Circ: (Mon.-Sat.)★35,410
(Sun.)★39,193

**People of God (20010)**
4000 St. Joseph Pl. NW
Albuquerque, NM 87120
Phone: (505)831-8188
Fax: (505)831-8225
**Subject(s):** Religious Publications

Circ: (Non-paid)‡39,000

**Bargain Book (North) (29340)**
Valley Media Inc.
1300 Wild Rose Ln. Rd.
Brownsville, TX 78520
Phone: (956)546-5113
Fax: (956)546-0903
**Subject(s):** Shopping Guides

Circ: (Free)37,120

**The Morning News of Northwest Arkansas (1271)**
Community Newspaper Holdings Inc.
313 S. 2nd St.
PO Box 718
Rogers, AR 72757
Phone: (501)636-6270
Fax: (479)619-2507
**Subject(s):** Daily Newspapers

Circ: (Mon.-Sat.)35,035
(Sun.)36,443

**The Victoria Advocate (30581)**
311 E. Constitution
PO Box 1518
Victoria, TX 77901-1518
Phone: (361)575-1451
Fax: (361)574-1225
**Subject(s):** Daily Newspapers

Circ: (Mon.-Sat.)★34,747
(Sun.)★36,264

**Longview News-Journal (30072)**
Longview Newspapers Inc.
320 Methvin St.
Longview, TX 75601
Phone: (903)757-3311
Fax: (903)757-3742
**Subject(s):** Daily Newspapers

Circ: (Mon.-Sat.)★28,848
(Sun.)★35,313

**Aging Arkansas (1158)**
Arkansas Aging Foundation
706 S Pulaski St.
Little Rock, AR 72201
Phone: (501)376-6083
Fax: (501)376-6084

**Subject(s):** Senior Citizens' Interests; Paid Community Newspapers

Circ: (Paid)35,000

**El Periodico, U.S.A. (30145)**
1016 Ivy Ave.
McAllen, TX 78501-4309
Phone: (956)631-5628
Fax: (956)631-0832
**Subject(s):** Free Newspapers

Circ: (Free)‡35,000

**Urban Tulsa (25631)**
Renegade Publishing Inc.
710 S. Kenosha
PO Box 50499
Tulsa, OK 74110
Phone: (918)592-5550
Fax: (918)592-5970
**Subject(s):** Paid Community Newspapers

Circ: (Free)35,000

**Zanesville Muskingum Advertiser (25274)**
Add Inc.—Ohio Group
PO Box 840
Bristow, OK 74010
Phone: (918)367-2282
Fax: (918)367-2724
**Subject(s):** Shopping Guides

Circ: (Non-paid)♦34,825

**Texarkana Gazette (30537)**
WEHCO Media Group
315 Pine St.
Texarkana, TX 75501
Phone: (903)794-3311
Fax: (903)794-3315
**Subject(s):** Daily Newspapers

Circ: (Mon.-Sat.)★30,508
(Sun.)★33,278

**The Keller Citizen (30010)**
PO Box 615
Keller, TX 76244-0615
Phone: (817)431-2231
Fax: (817)431-5534
**Subject(s):** Free Newspapers

Circ: (Paid)252
(Free)33,242

**The Bayou Catholic (12380)**
H.T. Publishing Co.
PO Box 505
Schriever, LA 70395
Phone: (985)850-3132
Fax: (985)850-3215
**Subject(s):** Religious Publications

Circ: (Paid)‡33,000

**The Times of Acadiana (12192)**
South Louisiana Publishing
221 Jefferson St.
Lafayette, LA 70501
Phone: (337)289-6300
Fax: (337)289-6496
**Subject(s):** Free Newspapers

Circ: (Non-paid)32,785

**Northeast News (29888)**
Grafikpress Corp.
PO Box 11555
Houston, TX 77293-1555
Phone: (281)449-9945
Fax: (281)987-8522
**Subject(s):** Free Newspapers

Circ: (Free)32,500

**The Ledger (25276)**
110 Kenosha St.
Broken Arrow, OK 74012
Phone: (918)258-7171
Fax: (918)258-9908
**Subject(s):** Paid Community Newspapers

Circ: (Paid)‡3,812
(Free)30,500

**The Mesquite News (30165)**
DFW Community Newspapers
303 N. Galloway St.
Mesquite, TX 75149-4325
Phone: (972)285-6301
Fax: (972)288-9383
**Subject(s):** Paid Community Newspapers

Circ: (Combined)30,247

**Arkansas Times (1167)**
PO Box 34010
Little Rock, AR 72203
Phone: (501)375-2985
Fax: (501)375-3623
**Subject(s):** Local, State, and Regional Publications; Paid Community Newspapers

Circ: (Paid)6,000
(Non-paid)30,000

**The Daily Texan (29152)**
University of Texas Student Publications
2500 Whitis Ave.
Austin, TX 78713
Phone: (512)471-1576
Fax: (512)471-1576
**Subject(s):** College Publications

Circ: ‡30,000

**The Informer & Texas Freeman (29862)**
PO Box 3086
2646 West Loop S Suite 375
Houston, TX 77054
Phone: (713)218-7400
Fax: (713)218-7077
**Subject(s):** Paid Community Newspapers; Black Publications

Circ: 30,000

**The Round Top Register (30323)**
PO Box 225
Round Top, TX 78954
Phone: (979)249-5550
**Subject(s):** Free Newspapers

Circ: (Combined)‡30,000

**Lewisville Leader (30058)**
DFW Community Newspapers
405A SH121 Bypass, Ste. 110
Lewisville, TX 75067
Phone: (972)436-3566
Fax: (972)436-7432
**Subject(s):** Paid Community Newspapers

Circ: (Sat.)28,034
(Wed.)29,372

**The Black Chronicle (25451)**
PO Box 17498
Oklahoma City, OK 73136
Phone: (405)424-4695
Fax: (405)424-6708
**Subject(s):** Black Publications; Paid Community Newspapers

Circ: (Paid)‡28,927

**Herald (30362)**
Prime Time Publishing Co.
17400 Judson Rd.
San Antonio, TX 78247
Phone: (210)658-7424
Fax: (210)658-0390
**Subject(s):** Free Newspapers

Circ: (Paid)143
(Free)27,657

**El Extra (29536)**
PO Box 270432
Dallas, TX 75227
Phone: (214)309-0990
Fax: (214)309-0204
**Subject(s):** Shopping Guides; Hispanic Publications; Spanish

Circ: (Free)❏27,578

**But Viet Weekly News (29516)**
9780 Walnut St., Ste. 180
Dallas, TX 75243-2396
Phone: (972)808-9700
Fax: (972)808-9701
**Subject(s):** Vietnamese; Free Newspapers; Ethnic Publications

Circ: (Combined)27,500

**North Texas Catholic (29723)**
800 W Loop 820 S
Fort Worth, TX 76108
Phone: (817)560-3300
Fax: (817)244-8839
**Subject(s):** Religious Publications

Circ: (Non-paid)700
(Paid)27,500

**Mid-Valley Town Crier (30622)**
Mid-Valley Newspaper Inc.
401 S Iowa
Weslaco, TX 78596
Phone: (210)969-2543
Fax: (210)968-0855

## Southern Central States

**Subject(s):** Free Newspapers
**Circ:** (Fri.)♦11,960
(Sun.)♦17,960
(Wed.)♦27,498

**Bryan-College Station Eagle (29358)**
1729 Briarcrest Dr.
PO Box 3000
Bryan, TX 77802
Phone: (979)776-4444
Fax: (979)774-0496
**Subject(s):** Daily Newspapers
**Circ:** (Mon.-Sat.)★24,441
(Sun.)★27,279

**Odessa American (30220)**
222 E. 4th St.
PO Box 2952
Odessa, TX 79760
Phone: (915)337-6262
Fax: (915)334-8641
**Subject(s):** Daily Newspapers
**Circ:** (Mon.-Sat.)★24,139
(Sun.)★26,886

**The Santa Fe New Mexican (20168)**
202 E Marcy St.
Santa Fe, NM 87501-2021
Phone: (505)986-3075
Fax: (505)984-1785
**Subject(s):** Daily Newspapers
**Circ:** (Mon.-Sat.)★24,667
(Sun.)★26,812

**Herald Democrat (30431)**
Donrey Media Group
603 Sam Rayburn Fwy. S.
Sherman, TX 75090
Phone: (903)893-8181
Fax: (903)868-1930
**Subject(s):** Daily Newspapers
**Circ:** (Mon.-Fri.)23,866
(Sun.)26,745

**Clear Lake Citizen & Exchange News (29830)**
Houston Community Newspapers
17511 El Camino
Houston, TX 77058-3049
Phone: (281)488-1108
Fax: (281)286-0750
**Subject(s):** Shopping Guides
**Circ:** 26,700

**The Jonesboro Sun (1147)**
PO Box 1249
Jonesboro, AR 72403
Phone: (501)935-5525
Fax: (501)935-1674
**Subject(s):** Daily Newspapers
**Circ:** (Mon.-Sat.)★23,156
(Sun.)★26,481

**Valley Star (29792)**
Freedom Communication Inc.
1310 S. Commerce
PO Box 511
Harlingen, TX 78551
Phone: (956)430-6200
Fax: (956)430-6231
**Subject(s):** Daily Newspapers
**Circ:** (Mon.-Sat.)23,492
(Sun.)25,577

**Navarro County Sun Extra (29485)**
Corsicana Daily
PO Box 622
Corsicana, TX 75110
Phone: (903)874-7355
Fax: (903)872-6878
**Subject(s):** Shopping Guides
**Circ:** (Free)‡25,250

**Sun-News (20106)**
Las Cruces Sun-News
256 W. Las Cruces
Las Cruces, NM 88005
**Subject(s):** Daily Newspapers
**Circ:** (Sat.)21,803
(Mon.-Fri.)22,432
(Sun.)25,164

**Hunt County Shopper (29782)**
Hunt County Shopper Inc.
3617 Wesley
PO Box 906
Greenville, TX 75401
Phone: (903)455-5254
Fax: (903)455-3297
**Subject(s):** Shopping Guides
**Circ:** (Free)‡25,020

**Kingwood Observer (30022)**
1129 Kingwood Dr.
Kingwood, TX 77339-3033
Phone: (281)359-2799
Fax: (281)359-0017
**Subject(s):** Free Newspapers
**Circ:** (Non-paid)❑25,000

**Shopper's Edge (25324)**
PO Box 3511
Enid, OK 73702
Phone: (580)233-1722
Fax: (580)233-3764
**Subject(s):** Shopping Guides
**Circ:** (Non-paid)25,000

**The Galveston County Daily News (29752)**
Southern Newspaper Inc.
8522 Teichman Rd.
PO Box 628
Galveston, TX 77553
Phone: (409)683-5200
Fax: (409)744-6268
**Subject(s):** Daily Newspapers
**Circ:** (Mon.-Sat.)24,025
(Sun.)24,875

**Temple Daily Telegram (30532)**
PO Box 6114
Temple, TX 76503-6114
**Subject(s):** Daily Newspapers
**Circ:** (Mon.-Fri.)21,749
(Sun.)24,772

**The Lawton Constitution (25385)**
Lawton Publishing Co.
102 SW 3rd St.
PO Box 2069
Lawton, OK 73502-0848
Phone: (580)335-3062
Fax: (800)385-5140
**Subject(s):** Daily Newspapers
**Circ:** (Mon.-Sat.)★20,953
(Sun.)★24,567

**Today's Catholic (30380)**
2718 W Woodlawn
San Antonio, TX 78228-0410
Phone: (210)734-2620
Fax: (210)734-2939
**Subject(s):** Religious Publications
**Circ:** ‡24,000

**The Sooner Catholic (25485)**
7501 NW Expwy.
PO Box 32180
Oklahoma City, OK 73123
Phone: (405)721-1810
Fax: (405)721-5210
**Subject(s):** Religious Publications
**Circ:** (Paid)8,108
(Free)23,987

**Killeen Daily Herald (30018)**
1809 Florence Rd.
PO Box 1300
Killeen, TX 76540
Phone: (254)634-2125
Fax: (254)634-3293
**Subject(s):** Paid Community Newspapers
**Circ:** (Mon.-Sat.)★18,530
(Sun.)★23,937

**Laredo Morning Times (30045)**
111 Esperanza Dr.
Laredo, TX 78041-2607
Phone: (956)728-2500
Fax: (956)723-1227
**Subject(s):** Daily Newspapers
**Circ:** (Mon.-Sat.)21,256
(Sun.)23,593

**The Las Cruces Sun-News (20103)**
Mid-States Newspapers Inc.
256 W Las Cruces Ave.
Las Cruces, NM 88004
Phone: (505)541-5400
Fax: (505)541-5498
**Subject(s):** Daily Newspapers
**Circ:** (Sat.)★21,166
(Mon.-Fri.)★21,190
(Sun.)★23,597

**Midland Reporter-Telegram (30171)**
201 E Illinois St.
PO Box 1650
Midland, TX 79701-4852
Phone: (915)682-5311
Fax: (915)682-6173
**Subject(s):** Daily Newspapers
**Circ:** (Mon.-Sat.)★19,785
(Sun.)★23,564

**Mid County Chronicle (30209)**
Beaumont Printing Co.
PO Box 2140
Nederland, TX 77627
Phone: (409)722-0479
Fax: (409)729-7626
**Subject(s):** Free Newspapers
**Circ:** (Free)‡23,500

**Houston Defender (29852)**
PO Box 8005
3003 S.loop W Ste.320
Houston, TX 77054
Phone: (713)663-6996
Fax: (713)663-7116
**Subject(s):** Paid Community Newspapers; Black Publications
**Circ:** (Free)‡4,000
(Paid)‡23,000

**Fort Hood Sentinel (30530)**
PO Box 6114
Temple, TX 76503-6114
Phone: (817)778-4444
Fax: (817)771-3516
**Subject(s):** Free Newspapers
**Circ:** ‡22,500

**Houston Tribune (29859)**
Tribune Publishing
373 1/2 West 19th St.
Houston, TX 77008
Phone: (713)862-9603
**Subject(s):** Paid Community Newspapers
**Circ:** (Controlled)22,500

**The News Banner (12135)**
PO Drawer 90
Covington, LA 70433
Phone: (985)892-7980
Fax: (985)867-8572
**Subject(s):** Paid Community Newspapers
**Circ:** (Controlled)22,500

**The Picayune (30131)**
Victory Publishing Ltd.
PO Box 10
Marble Falls, TX 78654
Phone: (830)693-7152
Fax: (830)693-3085
**Subject(s):** Free Newspapers
**Circ:** (Controlled)22,250

**The Battalion (29419)**
Texas A & M University
015 Reed McDonald Bldg.
College Station, TX 77843-1111
Phone: (979)845-2611
Fax: (979)845-2678
**Subject(s):** College Publications
**Circ:** (Paid)‡22,000

**The Catholic Lighthouse (30579)**
Catholic Diocese of Victoria in Texas
1505 E Mesquite Ln.
Victoria, TX 77901
Phone: (361)573-0828
Fax: (361)573-5725
**Subject(s):** Religious Publications
**Circ:** (Non-paid)22,000

---

Circulation: ★ = ABC; △ = BPA; ♦ = CAC; • = CCAB; ❑ = VAC; ⊕ = PO Statement; ‡ = Publisher's Report; Boldface figures = sworn; Light figures = estimated.

## Southern Central States

**L'Observateur** (12226)
L'Observateur
PO Box 1010
LaPlace, LA 70069
Phone: (985)652-9545
Fax: (985)652-3885
Subject(s): Paid Community Newspapers
Circ: (Paid)5,000
(Non-paid)21,580

**East Arkansas News Leader** (1315)
Wynne Progress Inc.
702 N Falls Blvd.
PO Box 308
Wynne, AR 72396
Phone: (870)238-2375
Fax: (870)238-4655
Subject(s): Shopping Guides
Circ: 21,340

**The Jasper News Boy** (29994)
PO Box 1419
Jasper, TX 75951-1419
Phone: (409)384-3441
Fax: (409)384-8803
Subject(s): Paid Community Newspapers
Circ: 21,160

**Las Cruces Bulletin** (20102)
FIG Publications L.L.C.
840 N. Telshor, Ste. E
Las Cruces, NM 88011
Phone: (505)524-8061
Fax: (505)526-4621
Subject(s): Free Newspapers
Circ: (Paid)500
(Free)21,000

**Phoenix & Times-Democrat** (25417)
Gannet Publishing Co.
214 Wall St.
Muskogee, OK 74401
Phone: (918)684-2900
Fax: (918)684-2865
Subject(s): Daily Newspapers
Circ: (Mon.-Sat.)19,660
(Sun.)20,656

**Valencia County News-Bulletin** (20048)
WorldWest L.L.C.
1837 Sosimo Padilla Blvd.
Belen, NM 87002
Phone: (505)864-4472
Fax: (505)864-3549
Subject(s): Paid Community Newspapers
Circ: (Paid)⊐2,580
(Free)⊐20,195

**The Grapevine Sun** (29779)
Denton Publishing Co.
332 S. Main
PO Box 400
Grapevine, TX 76051
Phone: (817)488-8561
Fax: (817)488-5339
Subject(s): Free Newspapers
Circ: (Combined)20,127

**Bargain Book (Central)** (29339)
Valley Media Inc.
1300 Wild Rose Ln. Rd.
Brownsville, TX 78520
Phone: (956)546-5113
Fax: (956)546-0903
Subject(s): Shopping Guides
Circ: (Free)20,109

**Buzz'n** (20160)
New Mexican Inc.
202 E Marcy St.
Santa Fe, NM 87501
Phone: (505)983-3303
Fax: (505)984-1785
Subject(s): Free Newspapers
Circ: (Non-paid)20,000

**Dallas Post Tribune** (29530)
Dallas Tribune
2726 S Beckley
Dallas, TX 75224
Phone: (214)946-7678
Fax: (214)946-6823
Subject(s): Paid Community Newspapers; Black Publications
Circ: ‡20,000

**Louisiana Weekly** (12306)
PO Box 53008
New Orleans, LA 70113
Subject(s): Paid Community Newspapers; Black Publications
Circ: 20,000

**New Mexico Jewish Link** (20005)
5520 Wyoming Blvd. NE
Albuquerque, NM 87109
Phone: (505)821-3214
Fax: (505)821-3351
Subject(s): Paid Community Newspapers; Jewish Publications
Circ: (Combined)20,000

**New Orleans Data News Weekly** (12311)
Data Enterprises Inc.
3501 Napolean Ave.
New Orleans, LA 70125
Phone: (504)822-4433
Fax: (504)821-0320
Subject(s): Paid Community Newspapers; Black Publications
Circ: (Paid)‡380
(Free)‡20,000

**Santa Fe Reporter** (20169)
132 E. Marcy St.
Santa Fe, NM 87501
Phone: (505)988-5541
Fax: (505)988-5348
Subject(s): Free Newspapers
Circ: (Paid)105
(Free)20,000

**The University Star** (30418)
Southwest Texas State University
601 Univ. Dr.
102 Old Main
San Marcos, TX 78666-4615
Phone: (512)245-2533
Fax: (512)245-3620
Subject(s): College Publications
Circ: (Free)20,000

**News and Eagle** (25323)
227 W Broadway
PO Box 1192
Enid, OK 73702
Phone: (405)233-6600
Fax: (405)233-7645
Subject(s): Daily Newspapers
Circ: (Mon.-Sat.)★18,611
(Sun.)★19,787

**Pine Bluff Commercial** (1258)
Community Newspaper Holdings Inc.
300 Beech St.
Pine Bluff, AR 71601
Phone: (501)534-3400
Fax: (501)543-1455
Subject(s): Daily Newspapers
Circ: (Mon.-Sat.)19,051
(Sun.)19,749

**The Independent** (20086)
Gallup Independent Co.
500 N 9th St.
PO Box 1210
Gallup, NM 87305
Phone: (505)863-6811
Fax: (505)722-5750
Subject(s): Daily Newspapers
Circ: (Mon.-Fri.)16,998
(Sat.)19,450

**Port Arthur News** (30290)
CNHI
PO Box 789
Port Arthur, TX 77640
Phone: (409)729-6397
Subject(s): Daily Newspapers
Circ: (Mon.-Sat.)18,726
(Sun.)19,299

**The Shawnee News-Star** (25551)
Stauffer Communications Inc.
215 N. Bell
PO Box 1688
Shawnee, OK 74801
Phone: (405)273-4200
Fax: (405)273-4207
Subject(s): Daily Newspapers
Circ: (Tues.-Fri.)10,288
(Sun.)11,396
(Sat.)19,288

**The Edmond Sun** (25314)
The Edmond Evening Sun
123 S. Broadway
Edmond, OK 73083
Phone: (405)341-2121
Fax: (405)340-7363
Subject(s): Daily Newspapers
Circ: (Mon.-Fri.)⊐6,907
(Sun.)⊐12,341
(Combined)⊐19,248

**The Sentinel-Record** (1133)
PO Box 580
Hot Springs, AR 71902
Phone: (501)623-7711
Fax: (501)623-2984
Subject(s): Daily Newspapers
Circ: (Mon.-Sat.)17,774
(Sun.)19,216

**The Daily Times** (20074)
201 N Allen Ave.
PO Box 450
Farmington, NM 87401-6212
Phone: (505)325-4545
Fax: (505)564-4630
Subject(s): Daily Newspapers
Circ: (Mon.-Sat.)17,440
(Sun.)19,102

**Eastern Oklahoma Catholic** (25599)
PO Box 690240
Tulsa, OK 74169-0240
Phone: (918)294-1904
Fax: (918)294-0920
Subject(s): Religious Publications
Circ: (Combined)19,000

**The Albuquerque Tribune** (19985)
Scripps Howard Inc.
7777 Jefferson NE
Albuquerque, NM 87109
Phone: (505)823-7777
Fax: (505)823-3689
Subject(s): Daily Newspapers
Circ: (Mon.-Sat.)18,919

**Livestock Weekly** (30332)
Southwest Publishers Inc.
PO Box 3306
San Angelo, TX 76902
Phone: (915)949-4611
Fax: (915)949-4614
Subject(s): Livestock
Circ: (Paid)⊕18,211
18,761

**Kelly Observer** (30368)
Prime Time Incorporated Newspapers
17400 Judson Rd.
San Antonio, TX 78247
Phone: (210)453-3300
Fax: (210)736-5506
Subject(s): Paid Community Newspapers; Military and Navy
Circ: (Combined)18,500

**Brazosport Facts** (29413)
Southern Newspapers Inc.
PO Box 549
720 S Main
PO Box 549
Clute, TX 77531
Phone: (979)265-7411
Fax: (979)265-9052
Subject(s): Daily Newspapers
Circ: (Mon.-Sat.)16,727
(Sun.)17,861

**Avoyelles Journal** (12125)
Avoyelles Publishing Co.
637 Evergreen Hwy.
PO Box 179
Bunkie, LA 71322
Phone: (318)346-7253
Fax: (318)253-7223
Subject(s): Free Newspapers
Circ: (Free)17,600

**St. Tammany News-Banner** (12137)
Pontchartrain Newspapers
PO Drawer 90
Covington, LA 70434
Phone: (985)892-7980
Fax: (985)867-8572

**Subject(s):** Free Newspapers
**Circ:** (Paid)5,000
(Non-paid)17,500

**Direct Mail Rocket (1146)**
Corning Publishing
2919 E. Matthews St., Ste B
Jonesboro, AR 72401
Phone: (870)239-5000
Fax: (870)239-3403
**Subject(s):** Free Newspapers
**Circ:** (Non-paid)17,412

**The Norman Transcript (25430)**
Community Newspaper Holdings Inc.
PO Drawer 1058
Norman, OK 73070-1058
Phone: (405)321-1800
Fax: (405)366-3516
**Subject(s):** Daily Newspapers
**Circ:** (Mon.-Sat.)15,475
(Sun.)17,241

**The HP Chronicle (30591)**
Publications and Communications LP
579 N. Valley Milss, Ste. 3
Waco, TX 76710
Phone: (254)399-6051
Fax: (254)399-6051
**Subject(s):** Computers
**Circ:** (Combined)‡17,000

**National Christian Reporter (29558)**
United Methodist Communications Council Inc.
2400 Lone Star Dr.
Dallas, TX 75212
Phone: (214)630-6495
Fax: (214)630-0079
**Subject(s):** Religious Publications
**Circ:** 17,000

**The University Daily (30088)**
Texas Tech University
PO Box 43081
Lubbock, TX 79409
Phone: (806)742-3603
Fax: (806)742-2434
**Subject(s):** College Publications
**Circ:** ‡17,000

**Louisiana Market Bulletin (12083)**
Louisiana Dept. of Agriculture
PO Box 631
Baton Rouge, LA 70821
Phone: (225)922-1284
Fax: (225)922-1253
**Subject(s):** Farm Newspapers; Paid Community Newspapers
**Circ:** ‡16,800

**Star Shopping Guide (12170)**
Daily Star Publishing Co.
PO Box 1149
Hammond, LA 70404-1149
Phone: (985)254-7827
Fax: (985)542-0242
**Subject(s):** Shopping Guides
**Circ:** (Sun.)‡15,900
(Wed.)‡16,800

**The Alvin Advertiser (29072)**
Henderson Newspapers Inc.
570 Dula St.
Alvin, TX 77511-2942
Phone: (281)331-4421
Fax: (281)331-4424
**Subject(s):** Shopping Guides
**Circ:** (Free)16,794

**The Lufkin Daily News (30109)**
Cox Newspapers
300 Ellis at Herndon
Lufkin, TX 75902-1089
Phone: (936)632-6631
**Subject(s):** Daily Newspapers
**Circ:** (Mon.-Fri.)14,608
(Sat.)14,852
(Sun.)16,600

**Daily Iberian (12290)**
Wick Communications
PO Box 9290
New Iberia, LA 70562-9290
Phone: (337)365-6773
Fax: (337)367-9640

**Subject(s):** Daily Newspapers
**Circ:** (Mon.-Sat.)15,000
(Sun.)16,000

**Footprints (30276)**
Wayland Baptist University, No. 437
Plainview, TX 79072
Phone: (806)291-3600
Fax: (806)291-1966
**Subject(s):** College Publications
**Circ:** (Free)‡16,000

**Southwest Daily News (12410)**
News Leader Inc.
716 E Napoleon
PO Box 1999
Sulphur, LA 70664-1999
Phone: (337)462-1186
Fax: (318)528-9557
**Subject(s):** Daily Newspapers
**Circ:** (Combined)‡16,000

**The Dallas Weekly Newspaper (29531)**
Dallas Weekly Newspaper
Anthony T. Davis Bldg.
3101 Martin Luther King, Jr. Blvd.
Dallas, TX 75215
Phone: (214)428-8958
Fax: (214)428-2807
**Subject(s):** Free Newspapers; Black Publications
**Circ:** (Paid)78
(Free)15,258

**Fannin County Special (29320)**
Fannin County
2501 N Ctr., Ste. A
Bonham, TX 75418
Phone: (903)583-3556
Fax: (903)583-9459
**Subject(s):** Shopping Guides
**Circ:** (Free)‡15,106

**El Editor (30078)**
Amigo Publications
PO Box 11250
Lubbock, TX 79408
Phone: (806)763-3841
Fax: (806)741-1110
**Subject(s):** Hispanic Publications
**Circ:** (Controlled)‡15,000

**Focus KAFB Newspaper (19994)**
377 ABW/PA 2000 Wyoming SE
Albuquerque, NM 87117
Phone: (505)846-5991
Fax: (505)846-4897
**Subject(s):** Free Newspapers; Military and Navy
**Circ:** (Free)‡15,000

**Guardian (12143)**
News Leader Inc.
PO Box 846
Deridder, LA 70634
Phone: (318)463-6204
Fax: (318)463-5347
**Subject(s):** Free Newspapers; Military and Navy
**Circ:** (Free)‡15,000

**The Piney Woods Journal (12145)**
Cheallaigh Shamrock
104 North 3rd St.
PO Box 190
Dodson, LA 71422
Phone: (318)628-8671
Fax: (318)628-8673
**Subject(s):** Paid Community Newspapers; Forestry
**Circ:** (Combined)15,000

**Press (25386)**
Lawton Publishing Co.
102 SW 3rd St.
PO Box 2069
Lawton, OK 73502-0848
Phone: (580)335-3062
Fax: (800)385-5140
**Subject(s):** Daily Newspapers
**Circ:** (Free)‡164
(Paid)‡14,818

**The Cannoneer (25337)**
Lawton Publishing Co.
ATZR-A Cannoneer
USAFACFS
Public Affairs Office
Fort Sill, OK 73503-5100
Phone: (405)442-8111
**Subject(s):** Free Newspapers; Military and Navy
**Circ:** (Free)‡14,500

**Citizens Journal (29124)**
The Atlanta Citizens Journal
PO Box 1188
306 West Main
Atlanta, TX 75551
Phone: (903)796-3655
Fax: (903)796-3294
**Subject(s):** Free Newspapers
**Circ:** (Paid)‡6,200
(Free)‡14,500

**El Mensajero (29080)**
PO Box 895
Amarillo, TX 79105
Phone: (806)371-7084
Fax: (806)371-7090
**Subject(s):** Hispanic Publications; Paid Community Newspapers
**Circ:** (Paid)500
(Non-paid)14,500

**New Mexico Daily Lobo (20003)**
University of New Mexico
Marrow Hall, Rm. 131
Albuquerque, NM 87131-0001
Phone: (505)277-5656
Fax: (505)277-7530
**Subject(s):** College Publications
**Circ:** ‡14,500

**Hammond Daily Star (12168)**
Daily Star Publishing Co.
725 S. Morrison Blvd.
Hammond, LA 70404
**Subject(s):** Daily Newspapers
**Circ:** (Mon.-Fri.)12,172
(Sun.)14,325

**Pearland Reporter News (30261)**
Texas City Sun
2404 S Park
Pearland, TX 77581
Phone: (409)945-3441
Fax: (409)935-0428
**Subject(s):** Free Newspapers
**Circ:** (Paid)‡892
(Free)‡14,108

**Daily World (12359)**
2781 F49 S Service Rd.
PO Box 1179
Opelousas, LA 70571-1179
Phone: (337)942-4971
Fax: (337)948-6572
**Subject(s):** Daily Newspapers
**Circ:** (Mon.-Fri.)12,558
(Sun.)14,000

**The Lafourche Gazette (12227)**
Lafourche Gazette News
PO Box 1450
Larose, LA 70373
Phone: (985)693-7229
Fax: (985)693-8282
**Subject(s):** Free Newspapers
**Circ:** (Free)‡14,000

**Roswell Daily Record (20140)**
2301 N Main St.
PO Box 1897
Roswell, NM 88201-6452
Phone: (505)622-7710
Fax: (505)625-0421
**Subject(s):** Daily Newspapers
**Circ:** (Mon.-Fri.)‡13,864
(Sun.)‡13,864

**The Alexandria News Weekly (12040)**
PO Box 608
Alexandria, LA 71309
Phone: (318)443-7664
Fax: (318)487-1827
**Subject(s):** Paid Community Newspapers; Black Publications
**Circ:** ‡13,750

**Herald Coaster Extra** (30320)
Hartman Newspapers Inc.
1902 S. Fourth St.
Rosenberg, TX 77471-4998
Phone: (281)342-4474
Fax: (281)342-3219
**Subject(s):** Shopping Guides
**Circ:** (Free)13,435

**North Texas Life** (30160)
Hartman Newspapers Inc.
PO Box 400
McKinney, TX 75071
Phone: (972)542-2631
Fax: (972)529-1684
**Subject(s):** Free Newspapers
**Circ:** (Non-paid)13,200

**The Daily Ardmoreite** (25251)
117 W. Broadway
Ardmore, OK 73401
Phone: (580)223-2200
Fax: (580)226-0050
**Subject(s):** Daily Newspapers
**Circ:** (Mon.-Fri.)10,995
(Sun.)13,087

**The Daily Cougar** (29837)
University of Houston
Student Publications Dept.
Communications Bldg.
Houston, TX 77204-4015
Phone: (713)743-5350
Fax: (713)743-5384
**Subject(s):** College Publications
**Circ:** (Free)‡13,000

**DFW People** (29686)
Wood Publications Inc.
400 Fuller-Wiser, Ste. 125
Euless, TX 76039
Phone: (817)540-4666
Fax: (817)685-7562
**Subject(s):** Local, State, and Regional Publications
**Circ:** (Controlled)‡13,000

**Round Up** (20105)
New Mexico State University
PO Box 30004
Dept. CC
Las Cruces, NM 88003
Phone: (505)646-NEWS
Fax: (505)646-7905
**Subject(s):** College Publications
**Circ:** (Paid)15
(Free)13,000

**New Orleans CityBusiness** (12247)
1111 Veterans Blvd., Ste. 1440
Metairie, LA 70005
Phone: (504)834-9292
Fax: (504)832-3550
**Subject(s):** Paid Community Newspapers; Business
**Circ:** (Combined)12,800

**The Oklahoma Eagle** (25614)
PO Box 3267
Tulsa, OK 74101-3267
Phone: (918)582-7124
Fax: (918)582-8905
**Subject(s):** Paid Community Newspapers; Black Publications
**Circ:** ‡12,800

**Winter Texan** (30148)
Valley Media Inc.
1811 N 23rd St.
McAllen, TX 78501
Phone: (956)682-2423
Fax: (936)630-6371
**Subject(s):** Free Newspapers
**Circ:** (Free)12,572

**The Oklahoma Daily** (25434)
University of Oklahoma
860 Van Vleet, Rm. 149A
Copend Hall
Norman, OK 73019
Phone: (405)325-2521
Fax: (405)325-7517
**Subject(s):** College Publications
**Circ:** 12,500

**UNISYS World** (30600)
Publications and Communications LP
579 N. Valley Mills Dr.
Waco, TX 76710
Phone: (254)399-6651
Fax: (254)399-6651
**Subject(s):** Computers
**Circ:** ‡12,500

**Catholic East Texas** (30545)
1015 E SE Loop 323
Tyler, TX 75701-9663
Phone: (903)534-1077
Fax: (903)534-1370
**Subject(s):** Religious Publications
**Circ:** 12,450

**Banner Extra** (29332)
Hartman Newspapers Inc.
PO Box 585
2430 Stringer St.
Brenham, TX 77834
Phone: (979)836-7956
Fax: (979)830-8577
**Subject(s):** Shopping Guides
**Circ:** (Free)12,394

**Eastex News-Shopper** (29410)
Westward Communications
PO Box 1628
Cleveland, TX 77327
Phone: (281)592-2626
Fax: (281)592-2629
**Subject(s):** Shopping Guides
**Circ:** (Free)‡12,275

**Conroe Courier** (29454)
Gulf Coast Newspapers North
100 Ave. A
PO Box 609
Conroe, TX 77301
Phone: (936)756-6671
Fax: (936)756-6676
**Subject(s):** Daily Newspapers
**Circ:** (Mon.-Sat.)11,031
(Sun.)12,179

**Neighbor Shopper** (1016)
Community Publishers Inc.
PO Box 1049
Bentonville, AR 72712
Phone: (479)271-3726
Fax: (479)273-7777
**Subject(s):** Shopping Guides
**Circ:** (Free)12,059

**Vietnam Weekly News** (29757)
3250 W Walnut St.
Garland, TX 75042
Phone: (972)272-4898
Fax: (972)272-4657
**Subject(s):** Vietnamese; Paid Community Newspapers
**Circ:** (Combined)12,000

**Daily Comet** (12416)
The Daily Comet
705 W. 5th St.
PO Box 5238
Thibodaux, LA 70302
Phone: (985)448-7600
**Subject(s):** Daily Newspapers
**Circ:** (Mon.-Fri.)11,971

**The Daily Sentinel** (30200)
4920 Colonial Dr.
Nacogdoches, TX 75963
Phone: (936)564-8361
Fax: (936)560-4267
**Subject(s):** Daily Newspapers
**Circ:** (Mon.-Fri.)‡9,000
(Sun.)‡11,950

**San Antonio Business Journal** (30378)
American City Business Journals Inc.
70 NE Loop 410, Ste. 350
San Antonio, TX 78216
Phone: (210)341-3031
Fax: (210)341-3031
**Subject(s):** Business; Local, State, and Regional Publications
**Circ:** (Paid)11,932

**Weekly Livestock Reporter** (29731)
Live Stock News Service
120 N Rayner St.
PO Box 7655
Fort Worth, TX 76111
Phone: (817)831-3147
Fax: (817)831-3117
**Subject(s):** Livestock
**Circ:** (Free)‡662
(Paid)‡11,903

**Review-Appeal** (29735)
Franklin Publishing Company Inc.
PO Box 681988
Franklin, TN 37068-1988
**Subject(s):** Paid Community Newspapers
**Circ:** (Paid)8,883
(Free)11,870

**The Ponca City News** (25521)
Ponca City Publishing Company Inc.
300 N. 3rd St.
PO Box 191
Ponca City, OK 74601
Phone: (580)765-3311
Fax: (580)762-6397
**Subject(s):** Daily Newspapers
**Circ:** (Mon.-Fri.)10,201
(Sun.)11,585

**The McAlester NEWS-CAPITAL & Democrat** (25405)
New Capital & Democrat
PO Box 987
McAlester, OK 74502
Phone: (918)423-1700
Fax: (918)426-3081
**Subject(s):** Daily Newspapers
**Circ:** (Mon.-Fri.)11,380
(Sun.)11,502

**The Baxter Bulletin** (1229)
PO Drawer A
Mountain Home, AR 72653
Phone: (870)425-3133
Fax: (870)425-5091
**Subject(s):** Daily Newspapers
**Circ:** (Mon.-Sat.)★11,410

**The Daily O'Collegian** (25563)
Oklahoma State University
School of Journalism & Broadcasting
206 Paul Miller Bldg.
Stillwater, OK 74078-4053
Phone: (405)744-6354
Fax: (405)744-7104
**Subject(s):** College Publications
**Circ:** (Paid)‡11,400

**The Paris News** (30252)
PO Box 1078
Paris, TX 75461
Phone: (903)785-8744
Fax: (903)785-1263
**Subject(s):** Daily Newspapers
**Circ:** (Mon.-Fri.)10,314
(Sun.)11,318

**The Raton Range** (20137)
208 S 3rd St.
PO Box 1068
Raton, NM 87740
Phone: (505)445-2721
Fax: (505)445-2723
**Subject(s):** Free Newspapers
**Circ:** (Paid)‡2,700
(Free)‡11,300

**Pasadena Citizen** (30258)
P.L.C. Publishing Co.
PO Box 6192
Pasadena, TX 77506
Phone: (713)477-0221
Fax: (713)477-9090
**Subject(s):** Daily Newspapers
**Circ:** (Combined)6,174
(Sun.)11,111

**Rio Grande Sun** (20072)
PO Box 790
Espanola, NM 87532
Phone: (505)753-2126
Fax: (505)753-2140
**Subject(s):** Paid Community Newspapers
**Circ:** ‡11,079

**Gale Directory of Publications & Broadcast Media/140th Ed.**  **Southern Central States**

**Log Cabin Democrat** (1043)
1058 Front St.
PO Box 969
Conway, AR 72032
Phone: (501)327-6621
Fax: (501)327-6787
**Subject(s):** Daily Newspapers
Circ: (Mon.-Fri.)10,004
  (Sun.)11,019

**The Brazoria County News** (30629)
PO Box 488
West Columbia, TX 77486
Phone: (979)345-3127
Fax: (979)345-5308
**Subject(s):** Free Newspapers
Circ: ‡10,300
  ‡11,000

**Brownwood Bulletin** (29349)
Brownwood Newspapers Inc.
700 Carnegie St.
PO Box 1189
Brownwood, TX 76801
Phone: (325)646-2541
Fax: (325)646-6835
**Subject(s):** Daily Newspapers
Circ: (Mon.-Fri.)‡9,000
  (Sun.)‡11,000

**Deer Park Broadcaster/Progress** (29606)
Broadcaster Publications Inc.
PO Box 369
Deer Park, TX 77536
Phone: (281)479-5263
Fax: (281)479-3415
**Subject(s):** Free Newspapers
Circ: (Paid)200
  (Free)11,000

**The Shorthorn** (29110)
University of Texas at Arlington
Box 19038
UTA Student Publications
Arlington, TX 76019
Phone: (817)272-3188
Fax: (817)272-5009
**Subject(s):** College Publications
Circ: ‡11,000

**Vidorian Shopper** (30589)
Orange County Publishing Co.
450 W Bolivar
PO Box 1236
Vidor, TX 77670-1236
Phone: (409)769-5428
Fax: (409)769-2600
**Subject(s):** Shopping Guides
Circ: (Free)‡11,000

**Wilson County News** (29695)
1012 C St.
Floresville, TX 78114
Phone: (830)216-4519
Fax: (830)393-3219
**Subject(s):** Paid Community Newspapers
Circ: (Combined)11,000

**Corsicana Daily Sun** (29484)
American Publishing
405 E. Collin St.
Corsicana, TX 75110
Phone: (903)872-3931
Fax: (903)872-6878
**Subject(s):** Daily Newspapers
Circ: (Mon.-Sat.)‡10,444
  (Sun.)‡10,996

**The Baytown Sun** (29285)
Southern Newspapers
1301 Memorial Dr.
PO Box 90
Baytown, TX 77522
Phone: (281)422-8302
Fax: (281)427-5252
**Subject(s):** Daily Newspapers
Circ: (Mon.-Fri.)9,976
  (Sun.)10,954

**Hood County News** (29772)
PO Box 879
1501 South Morgan Street
Granbury, TX 76048-0879
Phone: (817)573-7066
Fax: (817)279-8371

**Subject(s):** Paid Community Newspapers
Circ: 10,953

**Nacogdoches Daily Sentinel** (30202)
Cox Newspapers
4920 Colonial Drive
Nacogdoches, TX 75963-0068
Phone: (936)564-8361
**Subject(s):** Daily Newspapers
Circ: (Mon.-Fri.)8,825
  (Sat.)9,146
  (Sun.)10,904

**News Examiner** (12235)
Ruhr Valley Publishing Inc.
2290 Texas St.
PO Drawer 460
Lutcher, LA 70071
Phone: (225)869-5784
Fax: (225)869-4386
**Subject(s):** Paid Community Newspapers
Circ: (Combined)10,703

**Blytheville Courier News** (1021)
Village News Inc.
PO Box 1108
Blytheville, AR 72316-1108
Phone: (870)763-4461
Fax: (870)763-6874
**Subject(s):** Paid Community Newspapers
Circ: (Sun.)♦3,228
  (Mon.-Fri.)♦3,361
  (Wed.)♦10,652

**The Taos News** (20190)
226 Albright St.
PO Box U
Taos, NM 87571
Phone: (505)758-2241
Fax: (505)758-9647
**Subject(s):** Paid Community Newspapers
Circ: (Thurs.)10,553

**The Booster** (30654)
Woodsman Publishing Company Inc.
PO Box 339
205 West Bluff St
Woodville, TX 75979
Phone: (409)283-2516
Fax: (409)283-2560
**Subject(s):** History and Genealogy
Circ: (Paid)‡4,500
  (Non-paid)‡10,500

**St. Mary Journal** (12277)
1014 Front St.
PO Box 31
Morgan City, LA 70381
Phone: (985)384-1350
Fax: (985)384-4255
**Subject(s):** Free Newspapers
Circ: (Free)‡10,500

**Kerrville Daily Times** (30013)
429 Jefferson St.
Kerrville, TX 78028
Phone: (830)896-7000
Fax: (830)896-1150
**Subject(s):** Daily Newspapers
Circ: (Mon.-Fri.)8,627
  (Sun.)10,437

**The Duncan Banner** (25301)
1001 Elm St.
PO Box 1268
Duncan, OK 73534-1268
Phone: (580)255-5354
Fax: (580)255-8889
**Subject(s):** Daily Newspapers
Circ: (Mon.-Fri.)8,996
  (Sun.)10,300

**Sapulpa Herald Extra** (25541)
Sapulpa Daily Herald
PO Box 1370
Sapulpa, OK 74067-1370
Phone: (918)224-5185
Fax: (918)224-5196
**Subject(s):** Shopping Guides
Circ: (Free)‡10,294

**Greenville Herald Banner** (29781)
2305 King St.
PO Box 6000
Greenville, TX 75403-1047
Phone: (903)455-4220
Fax: (903)455-6281
**Subject(s):** Daily Newspapers
Circ: (Mon.-Sat.)8,935
  (Sun.)10,138

**Plano Star Courier** (30285)
DFW Community Newspapers
801 E. Plano Pkwy., Ste. 100
Plano, TX 75074
Phone: (972)424-6565
Fax: (972)424-4388
**Subject(s):** Paid Community Newspapers
Circ: 8,312
  (Sun.)10,049

**El Dorado News-Times** (1063)
111 N Madison
PO Box 912
El Dorado, AR 71731-0912
Phone: (870)862-6611
Fax: (870)862-5226
**Subject(s):** Daily Newspapers
Circ: (Mon.-Sat.)10,020

**Woodward News** (25680)
Woodward Publishing Inc.
904 Oklahoma Ave.
PO Box 928
Woodward, OK 73801-0928
Phone: (580)256-2200
Fax: (580)254-2159
**Subject(s):** Daily Newspapers; Free Newspapers
Circ: (Paid)6,411
  (Free)10,019

**Acres U.S.A.** (29125)
PO Box 91299
Austin, TX 78709-1299
Phone: (512)892-4400
Fax: (512)892-4448
**Subject(s):** General Agriculture
Circ: 10,000

**The Progressive Populist** (29195)
PO Box 150517
Austin, TX 78715-0517
Phone: (512)447-0455
**Subject(s):** Paid Community Newspapers; Social and Political Issues
Circ: (Paid)‡7,500
  (Non-paid)‡10,000

**The TSU Herald** (29916)
Texas Southern University
3100 Cleburne Ave.
Houston, TX 77004-4583
Phone: (713)313-7011
Fax: (713)313-7188
**Subject(s):** College Publications
Circ: (Non-paid)10,000

**The Vermilion** (12193)
University of Southwestern Louisiana
PO Box 44813
Lafayette, LA 70504
Phone: (337)482-6960
Fax: (337)482-6959
**Subject(s):** College Publications
Circ: (Free)‡10,000

**West Texas County Courier** (29820)
Homesteader News Inc.
15344 Werling Ct.
Horizon City, TX 79928-7012
**Subject(s):** Free Newspapers
Circ: (Paid)‡150
  (Free)‡10,000

**Williamson County Sun** (29762)
Williamson County Sun Inc.
Box 39
Georgetown, TX 78627-0039
Phone: (512)863-2474
**Subject(s):** Paid Community Newspapers
Circ: ‡9,975

Circulation: ★ = ABC; △ = BPA; ♦ = CAC; • = CCAB; ▢ = VAC; ⊕ = PO Statement; ‡ = Publisher's Report; Boldface figures = sworn; Light figures = estimated.

## Southern Central States

**Drew County Shopper's Guide (1224)**
Tom White
314 N Main St.
PO Box 486
Monticello, AR 71655
Phone: (501)367-5325
Fax: (501)367-6612
**Subject(s):** Shopping Guides
**Circ:** 9,800

**Hobbs News-Sun (20095)**
PO Box 850
Hobbs, NM 88241
Phone: (505)391-5402
Fax: (505)393-5724
**Subject(s):** Daily Newspapers
**Circ:** (Mon.-Fri.)9,218
(Sun.)9,801

**Pony Express Mail (30061)**
Aldebaran
PO Box 1908
Liberty, TX 77575
Phone: (936)336-6416
Fax: (936)336-9400
**Subject(s):** Free Newspapers
**Circ:** (Free)⊕9,682

**The Orange Leader (30234)**
Community Newspaper Holdings Inc.
200 W Front Ave.
PO Box 1028
Orange, TX 77630-0128
Phone: (409)883-3571
Fax: (409)883-6342
**Subject(s):** Daily Newspapers
**Circ:** (Mon.-Fri.)8,616
(Sat.)8,616
(Sun.)9,620

**The Colony Courier-Leader (30057)**
DFW Community Newspapers
405A SH121 Bypass, Ste. 110
Lewisville, TX 75067
Phone: (972)436-3566
Fax: (972)436-7432
**Subject(s):** Free Newspapers
**Circ:** (Paid)2,915
(Free)9,500

**Ada Evening News (25234)**
116 N Broadway
PO Box 489
Ada, OK 74820
Phone: (580)332-4433
Fax: (580)332-8734
**Subject(s):** Daily Newspapers
**Circ:** (Mon.-Fri.)9,375
(Sun.)9,483

**Standard-Radio Post (29737)**
PO Box 1639
Fredericksburg, TX 78624
Phone: (830)997-2155
Fax: (830)990-0036
**Subject(s):** Paid Community Newspapers
**Circ:** (Free)‡60
(Paid)‡9,485

**The News Press (25566)**
Stillwater Publishing Co.
PO Box 2288
Stillwater, OK 74076
Phone: (405)372-5000
Fax: (405)372-3112
**Subject(s):** Daily Newspapers
**Circ:** (Mon.-Sat.)★8,600
(Sun.)★9,424

**Village News (1023)**
Tennyson Publishing
PO Box 13
Blytheville, AR 72315
Phone: (870)763-4461
Fax: (870)763-6874
**Subject(s):** Free Newspapers
**Circ:** (Free)9,348

**Cleburne Times-Review (29405)**
Community Newspaper Holdings Inc.
c/o Dale Gosser, Editor
PO Box 1569
108 S.Anglin St.
Cleburne, TX 76031
Phone: (817)645-2441
Fax: (817)645-4020
**Subject(s):** Daily Newspapers
**Circ:** (Mon.-Fri.)‡7,850
(Sun.)‡9,200

**The Liberty Gazette (30060)**
Aldebaran
PO Box 1908
Liberty, TX 77575
Phone: (936)336-6416
Fax: (936)336-9400
**Subject(s):** Free Newspapers
**Circ:** (Free)‡9,200

**The Shopper (Zone II) (25308)**
Cox Publishing Co.
120 N 12th Ave.
Durant, OK 74701-4718
Phone: (405)924-1770
Fax: (405)924-1792
**Subject(s):** Shopping Guides
**Circ:** (Free)‡9,191

**Leesville Daily Leader (12229)**
News Leader Inc.
206 E Texas
PO Box 619
Leesville, LA 71446
Phone: (337)239-3444
Fax: (337)238-1152
**Subject(s):** Daily Newspapers
**Circ:** (Paid)‡6,460
(Free)‡9,153

**The Advertiser (12406)**
Springhill Press & News Journal
PO Box 669
Springhill, LA 71075
Phone: (318)539-3511
Fax: (318)539-3512
**Subject(s):** Free Newspapers
**Circ:** (Free)9,100

**The Merchandiser (29394)**
Light & Champion Newspaper
Box 1989
Center, TX 75935
Phone: (936)598-3377
Fax: (936)598-6394
**Subject(s):** Shopping Guides
**Circ:** (Free)‡9,000

**Batesville Guard (1007)**
Batesville Guard-Record Company Inc.
258 W Main St.
Box 2036
Batesville, AR 72501
Phone: (870)793-2383
Fax: (870)793-9268
**Subject(s):** Daily Newspapers
**Circ:** (Non-paid)⊕121
(Paid)8,973

**Palestine Herald-Press (30243)**
Herald Press
519 N Elm St.
PO Box 379
Palestine, TX 75802-0379
Phone: (903)729-0281
Fax: (903)729-0284
**Subject(s):** Daily Newspapers
**Circ:** (Mon.-Sat.)8,505
(Sun.)8,930

**Clovis News Journal (20058)**
PO Box 1689
Clovis, NM 88102
Phone: (505)763-3431
Fax: (505)762-3879
**Subject(s):** Daily Newspapers
**Circ:** (Mon.-Thurs.)★7,576
(Fri.)★8,367
(Sun.)★8,775

**Gonzales Weekly (12163)**
PO Box 38
Gonzales, LA 70707-0038
Phone: (225)647-4569
Fax: (225)644-8238
**Subject(s):** Paid Community Newspapers
**Circ:** ‡8,700

**Sun Advertiser (29761)**
Williamson County Sun Inc.
Box 39
Georgetown, TX 78627-0039
Phone: (512)863-2474
**Subject(s):** Shopping Guides
**Circ:** (Free)‡8,650

**Early Bird Express (25420)**
Chickasaw Enterprises
PO Box 429
Newcastle, OK 73065
Phone: (405)387-5277
Fax: (405)387-9863
**Subject(s):** Shopping Guides
**Circ:** ‡8,500

**Beauregard Daily News (12142)**
News Leader Inc.
PO Box 698
Deridder, LA 70634-0698
Phone: (318)462-0616
Fax: (318)463-5347
**Subject(s):** Free Newspapers
**Circ:** (Free)‡5,400
(Paid)‡8,400

**McCurtain Daily Gazette (25374)**
PO Box 179
Idabel, OK 74745
Phone: (580)286-3321
Fax: (580)286-2208
**Subject(s):** Daily Newspapers
**Circ:** (Tues.-Fri.)‡6,400
(Sun.)‡8,400

**Polk County Enterprise (30068)**
Polk County Publishing Company Inc.
PO Box 1276
Livingston, TX 77351
Phone: (936)327-4357
Fax: (936)327-7156
**Subject(s):** Paid Community Newspapers
**Circ:** (Combined)8,400

**Friday (25423)**
Nichols Hills Publishing Company Inc.
Box 20340
10801 N Quail Plaza Dr.
Oklahoma City, OK 73156
Phone: (405)755-3311
Fax: (405)753-3315
**Subject(s):** Paid Community Newspapers
**Circ:** (Paid)8,290

**Johnson County Graphic (1040)**
Johnson County Graphic Inc.
203 E. Cherry St.
PO Box 289
Clarksville, AR 72830-0289
Phone: (479)754-2005
Fax: (479)754-2098
**Subject(s):** Paid Community Newspapers
**Circ:** ‡8,200

**The Advertiser (29121)**
Athen Review
PO Box 32
Athens, TX 75751
Phone: (903)675-5626
Fax: (903)675-9450
**Subject(s):** Shopping Guides
**Circ:** (Free)‡8,150

**Alamogordo Daily News (19980)**
Community Newspaper Holdings Inc.
518 24th St.
Alamogordo, NM 88310
Phone: (505)437-7120
Fax: (505)437-7795
**Subject(s):** Daily Newspapers
**Circ:** (Mon.-Fri.)★7,025
(Sun.)★8,120

**The Times (1245)**
KDC Communications Inc.
26th & Willow St.
PO Box 428
North Little Rock, AR 72115
Phone: (501)758-2571
Fax: (501)758-2597
**Subject(s):** Paid Community Newspapers
**Circ:** ‡8,091

**Silver City Daily Press (20180)**
Silver City Daily Press and Independent Publishing Company Inc.
300 W Market St.
PO Box 740
Silver City, NM 88062
Phone: (505)388-1576
Fax: (505)388-1196
**Subject(s):** Daily Newspapers

**Circ:** (Free)150
(Paid)8,025

**Wise County Messenger (29605)**
115 S Trinty
PO Box 149
Decatur, TX 76234
Phone: (940)627-5987
Fax: (940)627-1004
**Subject(s):** Paid Community Newspapers

**Circ:** (Sun.)5,900
(Mon.-Fri.)8,026

**Friendswood Reporter News & Pearland Reporter News (29740)**
Texas City Sun
PO Box 954
Friendswood, TX 77549-0954
Phone: (281)485-7501
Fax: (281)485-6397
**Subject(s):** Free Newspapers

**Circ:** (Paid)2,500
(Free)8,000

**The Herald of Arkansas State University (1292)**
Arkansas State University
104 Cooley Drive
P.O. Box 1930
State University, AR 72467
Phone: (870)972-3075
Fax: (870)972-3329
**Subject(s):** College Publications

**Circ:** ‡8,000

**The Natchitoches Times (12286)**
Natchitoches Times Publications
PO Box 448
Natchitoches, LA 71458
Phone: (318)352-3618
Fax: (318)352-7842
**Subject(s):** Paid Community Newspapers

**Circ:** 8,000

**The Pan American (29650)**
The University of Texas—Pan American
1201 W. University Dr.
Edinburg, TX 78539-2999
**Subject(s):** College Publications

**Circ:** 8,000

**Randco Trading Post (1261)**
Rockwell Publishing Co.
109 N VanBibber
PO Box 608
Pocahontas, AR 72455
Phone: (870)892-4451
Fax: (870)892-4453
**Subject(s):** Shopping Guides

**Circ:** (Free)‡8,000

**Speedhorse Racing Report (25438)**
Speedhorse Inc.
1903 48th St. N.W.
Norman, OK 73072
Phone: (405)573-1050
Fax: (405)573-1059
**Subject(s):** Livestock; (Horses and Horse Racing)

**Circ:** ‡8,000

**The Tech Talk (12373)**
Louisiana Tech University
PO Box 10258
Ruston, LA 71272-0045
Phone: (318)257-4427
Fax: (318)257-4558
**Subject(s):** College Publications

**Circ:** (Paid)‡8,000

**Carlsbad Current-Argus (20050)**
PO Box 1629
Carlsbad, NM 88220
Phone: (505)887-5501
Fax: (505)885-1066
**Subject(s):** Daily Newspapers

**Circ:** (Tues.-Fri.)★7,857
(Sun.)★7,999

**The Herald Coaster (30319)**
Hartman Newspapers Inc.
1902 S. Fourth St.
Rosenberg, TX 77471-4998
Phone: (281)342-4474
Fax: (281)342-3219
**Subject(s):** Daily Newspapers

**Circ:** (Mon.-Fri.)7,724
(Sun.)7,967

**The Daily Citizen (1281)**
Paxton Media Group
3000 E. Race Ave.
Searcy, AR 72143
Phone: (501)268-8621
Fax: (501)268-6277
**Subject(s):** Daily Newspapers

**Circ:** ‡7,251
(Sun.)‡7,833

**The Benton Courier (1013)**
Benton Publishing Company Inc.
321 N. Market St.
Benton, AR 72015
Phone: (501)315-8228
Fax: (501)315-1920
**Subject(s):** Daily Newspapers

**Circ:** (Sun.)7,367
(Mon.-Fri.)7,788

**McKinney Courier Gazette (30157)**
Hartman Newspapers Inc.
PO Box 400
McKinney, TX 75071
Phone: (972)542-2631
Fax: (972)529-1684
**Subject(s):** Daily Newspapers

**Circ:** (Mon.-Fri.)6,802
(Sun.)7,530

**Baton Rouge Weekly Press (12061)**
1283 Rosenwald Rd., Ste. 1
Baton Rouge, LA 70807-4173
Phone: (225)775-2002
Fax: (225)775-4216
**Subject(s):** Paid Community Newspapers; Black Publications

**Circ:** (Paid)7,500

**Benbrook News (29306)**
Suburban Newspapers Inc.
7820 Wyatt Dr.
Fort Worth, TX 76108-2595
Phone: (817)246-2473
Fax: (817)246-2474
**Subject(s):** Free Newspapers

**Circ:** (Free)‡7,500

**Gainesville Daily Register (29747)**
Community Newspaper Holdings Inc.
306 E. California St.
PO Box 309
Gainesville, TX 76241
Phone: (817)665-5511
Fax: (817)665-0920
**Subject(s):** Daily Newspapers

**Circ:** (Free)45
(Paid)7,500

**Highland Star/Crosby Courier (29815)**
Highlands Star/Crosby Courier
PO Box 405
Highlands, TX 77562
Phone: (281)328-9605
Fax: (281)328-9605
**Subject(s):** Paid Community Newspapers

**Circ:** (Paid)‡7,500

**The Oklahoma Observer (25473)**
PO BOX 53371
Oklahoma City, OK 73152
Phone: (405)525-5582
**Subject(s):** Paid Community Newspapers

**Circ:** ‡7,500

**Owasso Reporter (25513)**
Neighbor Newspapers Inc.
202 E. 2nd Ave.
Owasso, OK 74055
Phone: (918)272-1155
Fax: (918)664-8161
**Subject(s):** Paid Community Newspapers

**Circ:** ‡7,500

**Weatherford Democrat (30617)**
Community Newspaper Holdings Inc.
512 Palo Pinto St.
Weatherford, TX 76086
Phone: (817)594-9734
Fax: (817)594-9734
**Subject(s):** Daily Newspapers

**Circ:** 5,935
7,473

**Marshall News Messenger (30135)**
Thomson Newspaper
PO Box 730
Marshall, TX 75671-0730
Phone: (903)935-7914
Fax: (903)935-6242
**Subject(s):** Daily Newspapers

**Circ:** (Mon.-Sat.)★6,871
(Sun.)★7,385

**The Pampa News (30246)**
Gray County Newspapers L.L.C.
403 W Atchison St.
PO Box 2198
Pampa, TX 79066
Phone: (806)669-2525
Fax: (806)669-2520
**Subject(s):** Daily Newspapers

**Circ:** (Mon.-Fri.)6,614
(Sun.)7,358

**Chaparral Guide (20194)**
Herald Publishing Company Inc.
1204 N. Date St.
PO Box 752
Truth or Consequences, NM 87901
Phone: (505)894-2143
Fax: (505)894-7824
**Subject(s):** Travel and Tourism; History and Genealogy

**Circ:** (Free)7,300

**Athens Daily Review (29122)**
Community Newspaper Holdings Inc.
201 S. Prairieville St.
PO Box 32
Athens, TX 75751-0032
Phone: (903)675-5626
Fax: (903)675-9450
**Subject(s):** Daily Newspapers

**Circ:** ‡7,250

**Burleson Star (29370)**
The Star Group
PO Drawer 909
Burleson, TX 76097-0909
Phone: (817)295-0486
Fax: (817)295-5278
**Subject(s):** Paid Community Newspapers

**Circ:** ‡7,211

**Cibola County Beacon (20094)**
523 W Santa Fe Ave.
PO Box 579
Grants, NM 87020
Phone: (505)287-4411
Fax: (505)287-7822
**Subject(s):** Daily Newspapers

**Circ:** (Fri.)3,200
(Tues.)‡7,200

**Express (30289)**
Pleasanton Express
PO Box 880
114 Goodwin Street
Pleasanton, TX 78064-0880
Phone: (830)569-4967
Fax: (830)569-6100
**Subject(s):** Paid Community Newspapers

**Circ:** ‡7,200

**The Ponchatoula Times (12365)**
170 N. 7th St.
Ponchatoula, LA 70454
Phone: (985)386-2877
Fax: (985)386-0458
**Subject(s):** Paid Community Newspapers

**Circ:** (Paid)‡7,100

**Sapulpa Daily Herald (25540)**
PO Box 1370
Sapulpa, OK 74067-1370
Phone: (918)224-5185
Fax: (918)224-5196

## Southern Central States

**Subject(s):** Daily Newspapers

**Circ:** (Free)⊕25
(Paid)⊕**7,075**

**Deming Headlight (20069)**
Las Cruces Publishing Co.
219 E Maple St
PO Box 881
Deming, NM 88031
**Phone:** (505)546-2611
**Fax:** (505)546-8116
**Subject(s):** Daily Newspapers

**Circ:** (Paid)3650
(Free)‡7000

**Jewish Herald-Voice (29869)**
3403 Audley St.
PO Box 153
Houston, TX 77098-1923
**Phone:** (713)630-0391
**Fax:** (713)630-0404
**Subject(s):** Jewish Publications; Paid Community Newspapers

**Circ:** (Free)‡53
(Paid)‡7,000

**The Lariat (30595)**
Baylor University
One Bear Place
Waco, TX 76798-7330
**Phone:** (254)710-1711
**Fax:** (254)710-1714
**Subject(s):** College Publications; Free Newspapers

**Circ:** (Paid)500
(Non-paid)7,000

**The Pine Log (30203)**
Stephen F. Austin State University
13049 SFA Sta.
Nacogdoches, TX 75962
**Phone:** (936)468-4703
**Fax:** (936)468-1016
**Subject(s):** College Publications

**Circ:** (Free)‡6,500
7,000

**The Pow Wow (12261)**
Northeast Louisiana University
700 University Ave.
Monroe, LA 71209
**Phone:** (318)342-1000
**Fax:** (318)342-5452
**Subject(s):** College Publications

**Circ:** ‡7,000

**The Prospector (29661)**
University of Texas at El Paso Student Publications
University of Texas El Paso
500 University Ave. W
El Paso, TX 79968-0622
**Phone:** (915)747-5161
**Fax:** (915)747-8031
**Subject(s):** College Publications

**Circ:** ‡7,000

**Ruston Daily Leader (12372)**
212 W Park Ave.,
PO Box 520
Ruston, LA 71270-4314
**Phone:** (318)255-4353
**Fax:** (318)255-4006
**Subject(s):** Daily Newspapers

**Circ:** (Paid)‡6,990
(Non-paid)‡7,000

**University Press (29291)**
Lamar University
PO Box 10055, University Sta.
Beaumont, TX 77710
**Phone:** (409)880-8102
**Fax:** (409)880-8735
**Subject(s):** College Publications

**Circ:** (Free)7,000

**Van Zandt News (30647)**
Van Zandt Newpapers L.L.C.
PO Box 60
Wills Point, TX 75169
**Phone:** (903)873-2525
**Fax:** (903)873-4321
**Subject(s):** Paid Community Newspapers

**Circ:** (Paid)‡7,000

**White Settlement Bomber News (30635)**
Suburban Newspapers Inc.
7820 Wyatt Dr.
Fort Worth, TX 76108-2595
**Phone:** (817)246-2473
**Fax:** (817)246-2474
**Subject(s):** Free Newspapers

**Circ:** (Free)‡7,000

**San Marcos Daily Record (30416)**
American Publishing Co.
1910 S Interstate Hwy. 35
PO Box 1109
San Marcos, TX 78666-5901
**Phone:** (512)392-2458
**Fax:** (512)392-1514
**Subject(s):** Daily Newspapers

**Circ:** (Tues.-Fri.)4,856
(Sun.)6,982

**Claremore Daily Progress (25290)**
Claremore Progress
315 W. Will Rogers Blvd.
Claremore, OK 74017
**Phone:** (918)341-1101
**Fax:** (918)341-1131
**Subject(s):** Daily Newspapers

**Circ:** (Tues.-Fri.)6,018
(Sun.)6,881

**News-Telegram (30518)**
FO Publishers.
PO Box 598
Sulphur Springs, TX 75483
**Phone:** (903)885-8663
**Fax:** (903)885-8768
**Subject(s):** Daily Newspapers

**Circ:** (Paid)6,879

**Coppell Gazette (29456)**
DFW Community Newspapers
405A SH121 Bypass, Ste. 110
Lewisville, TX 75067-0539
**Phone:** (972)436-3566
**Fax:** (972)436-7432
**Subject(s):** Free Newspapers

**Circ:** (Paid)1,091
(Free)6,852

**Canton Herald (29378)**
Van Zandt Newspapers
103 Tyler St.
Canton, TX 75103
**Phone:** (903)567-4000
**Fax:** (903)567-6076
**Subject(s):** Paid Community Newspapers

**Circ:** 6,800

**Austin Business Journal (29132)**
Austin Business Journal Inc.
111 Congress Ave., Ste. 750
Austin, TX 78701
**Phone:** (512)494-2500
**Fax:** (512)494-2525
**Subject(s):** Local, State, and Regional Publications; Business

**Circ:** (Paid)★**6,765**

**Henderson Daily News (29807)**
1711 S Hwy. 79
PO Box 30
Henderson, TX 75653-0030
**Phone:** (903)657-2501
**Fax:** (903)657-2452
**Subject(s):** Daily Newspapers

**Circ:** (Paid)⊕**6,600**

**The Huntsville Item (29969)**
PO Box 539
Huntsville, TX 77342-0534
**Fax:** (409)293-3909
**Subject(s):** Daily Newspapers

**Circ:** (Mon.-Fri.)6,276
(Sun.)6,588

**The Seguin Gazette-Enterprise (30424)**
Southern Newspapers Inc.
1012 Schriewer Rd.
PO Box 1200
Seguin, TX 78155
**Phone:** (830)379-5404
**Fax:** (830)372-4191
**Subject(s):** Daily Newspapers

**Circ:** (Tues.-Fri.)4,790
(Sun.)6,526

**Democrat-Journal (25578)**
PO Box 508
118 South 2nd
Stilwell, OK 74960
**Phone:** (918)696-2228
**Fax:** (918)696-7066
**Subject(s):** Paid Community Newspapers

**Circ:** ‡6,500

**Osceola Times (1247)**
Rust Communications
112 N Poplar
Po Box 408
Osceola, AR 72370-2665
**Phone:** (870)563-2615
**Fax:** (501)563-2616
**Subject(s):** Paid Community Newspapers

**Circ:** 6,500

**Plainview Daily Herald (30277)**
820 Broadway
Plainview, TX 79072
**Phone:** (806)296-1300
**Fax:** (806)296-1315
**Subject(s):** Daily Newspapers

**Circ:** (Mon.-Fri.)6,000
(Sun.)6,500

**Progress-Times (30187)**
Mission Publishing Company Inc.
1217 N. Conway
Mission, TX 78572
**Phone:** (956)585-4893
**Fax:** (512)585-2304
**Subject(s):** Paid Community Newspapers

**Circ:** ‡6,500

**Shoppers Guide Weekly (1309)**
Warren Eagle Democrat
200 W Cypress St.
Warren, AR 71671
**Phone:** (870)226-5831
**Fax:** (870)226-6601
**Subject(s):** Shopping Guides

**Circ:** (Free)6,500

**Durant Daily Democrat (25305)**
Community Newspaper Holdings Inc.
200 W. Beech
PO Box 250
Durant, OK 74701
**Phone:** (405)924-6026
**Fax:** (405)924-6026
**Subject(s):** Daily Newspapers

**Circ:** (Free)604
(Paid)6,440

**Uvalde Leader-News (30570)**
Leader-News Inc.
110 N E St.
PO Box 740
Uvalde, TX 78801-5312
**Phone:** (830)278-3335
**Fax:** (830)278-9191
**Subject(s):** Paid Community Newspapers

**Circ:** 6,410

**The Daily Review (12276)**
1014 Front St.
PO Box 948
Morgan City, LA 70381
**Phone:** (985)384-8370
**Fax:** (985)384-4255
**Subject(s):** Daily Newspapers

**Circ:** ‡6,374

**Grove Sun (25346)**
The Grove Sun Daily
14 W 3rd St.
Grove, OK 74344
**Phone:** (918)786-2228
**Fax:** (918)786-2156
**Subject(s):** Paid Community Newspapers

**Circ:** (Paid)6,271

**Cabot Star-Herald (1029)**
Magie Enterprises Inc.
9035 S. Pine
PO Box 1058
Cabot, AR 72023
**Phone:** (501)843-3534
**Fax:** (501)843-6447
**Subject(s):** Paid Community Newspapers

**Circ:** (Free)250
(Paid)6,250

**The Seminole Producer (25542)**
121 N Main St.
PO Box 431
Seminole, OK 74868
Phone: (405)382-1100
Fax: (405)382-1104
**Subject(s):** Daily Newspapers
**Circ:** (Tues.-Fri.)‡5,626
(Sun.)‡6,250

**The Bogalusa Daily News (12134)**
Pontchartrain Newspapers
PO Drawer 90
Covington, LA 70434
Phone: (985)892-7980
Fax: (985)867-8572
**Subject(s):** Daily Newspapers
**Circ:** (Paid)6,237

**Shopper News Note (25397)**
PO Box 8
Lindsay, OK 73052-0008
Phone: (405)756-3169
Fax: (405)756-8609
**Subject(s):** Shopping Guides
**Circ:** (Paid)⊕**219**
(Free)⊕**6,213**

**The Fayette County Record (30031)**
Fayette County Record
127 S Washington St.
P O Box 400
La Grange, TX 78945-0400
Phone: (979)968-3155
Fax: (979)968-6767
**Subject(s):** Paid Community Newspapers
**Circ:** ‡6,200

**The Franklin Sun (12437)**
Hanna Publications
514 Prairie St.
PO Box 550
Winnsboro, LA 71295-0550
Phone: (318)435-4521
Fax: (318)435-9220
**Subject(s):** Paid Community Newspapers
**Circ:** ‡6,200

**Panola Watchman (30250)**
109 W Panola St
PO Box 518
Carthage, TX 75633
Phone: (903)693-7888
Fax: (903)693-5857
**Subject(s):** Paid Community Newspapers
**Circ:** (Paid)4,500
(Non-paid)6,200

**Sequoyah County Times (25537)**
Cookson Hills Publishers Inc.
111 N Oak St.
Sallisaw, OK 74955
Phone: (918)775-4433
Fax: (918)775-3023
**Subject(s):** Paid Community Newspapers
**Circ:** ‡6,171

**Spring Observer (29411)**
Westward Communications
PO Box 1628
Cleveland, TX 77327
Phone: (281)592-2626
Fax: (281)592-2629
**Subject(s):** Paid Community Newspapers
**Circ:** (Free)62
(Paid)6,173

**El Campo Leader-News (29654)**
El Campo Newspapers Inc.
203 E. Jackson St.
PO Box 1180
El Campo, TX 77437-1180
Phone: (979)543-3363
Fax: (979)543-0097
**Subject(s):** Paid Community Newspapers
**Circ:** ‡6,100

**Hill Country Recorder (29316)**
PO Box 820
Boerne, TX 78006
Phone: (830)249-9524
Fax: (830)249-4607
**Subject(s):** Paid Community Newspapers
**Circ:** (Paid)‡6,100

**Pocahontas Star Herald (1260)**
Rockwell Publishing Co.
109 N VanBibber
PO Box 608
Pocahontas, AR 72455
Phone: (870)892-4451
Fax: (870)892-4453
**Subject(s):** Paid Community Newspapers
**Circ:** ‡6,100

**Sabine Index (12238)**
Box 850
Many, LA 71449
Phone: (318)256-3495
Fax: (318)256-9151
**Subject(s):** Paid Community Newspapers
**Circ:** ‡6,100

**Snyder Daily News (30441)**
Roberts Publishing
3600 College Ave.
PO Box 949
Snyder, TX 79549
Phone: (325)573-5486
Fax: (325)573-0044
**Subject(s):** Daily Newspapers
**Circ:** (Mon.-Fri.)‡5,050
(Sun.)‡6,100

**The Round Rock Leader (30322)**
Todd Publications Inc.
PO Box 459
Round Rock, TX 78680-0459
Phone: (512)255-3733
Fax: (512)255-3733
**Subject(s):** Paid Community Newspapers
**Circ:** (Free)⊕**450**
(Paid)⊕**6,093**

**The Silsbee Bee (30434)**
Drawer 547
Silsbee, TX 77656
Phone: (409)385-5278
Fax: (409)385-5270
**Subject(s):** Paid Community Newspapers
**Circ:** (Paid)6,014

**The Arkansas Traveler (1072)**
University of Arkansas
119 Kimpel Hall
Fayetteville, AR 72701
Phone: (501)575-3406
Fax: (501)575-3306
**Subject(s):** Education
**Circ:** (Non-paid)‡6,000

**The Bulletin (29101)**
PO Box 2426
Angleton, TX 77516
Phone: (979)849-5407
Fax: (979)849-5107
**Subject(s):** Free Newspapers
**Circ:** (Combined)6000

**Nolan County Shopper (30521)**
Sweetwater Reporter
112 W. Third St.
PO Box 750
Sweetwater, TX 79556
Phone: (325)236-6677
Fax: (325)235-4967
**Subject(s):** Paid Community Newspapers
**Circ:** ‡6,000

**The Ouachita Citizen (12431)**
PO Box 758
807 Drago Street
West Monroe, LA 71294-0758
Phone: (318)322-3161
Fax: (318)325-2285
**Subject(s):** Paid Community Newspapers
**Circ:** ‡6,000

**Rice Thresher (29903)**
Rice University
6100 Main St.
2nd Fl., Ley Student Center
Houston, TX 77005-1892
Phone: (713)348-4801
Fax: (713)348-5238
**Subject(s):** College Publications
**Circ:** (Free)‡6,000
6,000

**The Stuttgart Daily Leader (1295)**
Liberty Group Publishing
111 W. 6th St.
Stuttgart, AR 72160
Phone: (870)673-8533
Fax: (870)673-3671
**Subject(s):** Daily Newspapers
**Circ:** (Paid)3,600
(Non-paid)6,000

**Texas Observer (29232)**
The Texas Democracy Foundation
307 W. 7th St.
Austin, TX 78701
Phone: (512)477-0746
Fax: (512)474-1175
**Subject(s):** Paid Community Newspapers
**Circ:** 6,000

**United Caprine News (29493)**
PO Box 328
Crowley, TX 76036-0328
Phone: (817)297-3411
Fax: (817)297-4101
**Subject(s):** Livestock; Dairying
**Circ:** ‡6,000

**The Villager (29252)**
1223-A Rosewood Ave.
Austin, TX 78702
Phone: (512)476-0082
Fax: (512)476-0179
**Subject(s):** Free Newspapers; Black Publications
**Circ:** (Free)‡6,000

**The Vinita Daily Journal (25663)**
Vinita Printing Company Inc.
138 S Wilson
PO Box 328
Vinita, OK 74301-0328
Phone: (918)256-6422
Fax: (918)256-7100
**Subject(s):** Daily Newspapers
**Circ:** (Paid)4,150
(Free)6,000

**White Sands Missile Ranger (20200)**
Sun News
Stews-Pa, Bldg. 122
White Sands Missile Range, NM 88002-5047
Phone: (505)678-2716
Fax: (505)678-7174
**Subject(s):** Free Newspapers
**Circ:** (Free)‡6,000

**Las Vegas Optic (20118)**
Landmark Communications
PO Box 2670
Las Vegas, NM 87701
**Subject(s):** Daily Newspapers
**Circ:** ‡5,986

**Lake Livingston Progress (30067)**
Polk County Publishing Company Inc.
PO Box 1276
Livingston, TX 77351
Phone: (936)327-4357
Fax: (936)327-7156
**Subject(s):** Paid Community Newspapers
**Circ:** ⊕**5,898**

**Abbeville Meridional (12038)**
318 North Main St.
PO Box 400
Abbeville, LA 70510
Phone: (337)893-4223
Fax: (337)898-9022
**Subject(s):** Daily Newspapers
**Circ:** (Mon.-Fri.)5,457
(Sun.)5,860

**Bulverde Community News (30356)**
Prime Time Incorporated Newspapers
17400 Judson Rd.
San Antonio, TX 78247
Phone: (210)453-3300
Fax: (210)736-5506
**Subject(s):** Paid Community Newspapers
**Circ:** (Combined)5,865

**Ozark Spectator (1248)**
Ozark Spectator Corp.
207 W Main
Ozark, AR 72949
Fax: (501)667-4365

Circulation: ★ = ABC; △ = BPA; ♦ = CAC; • = CCAB; □ = VAC; ⊕ = PO Statement; ‡ = Publisher's Report; Boldface figures = sworn; Light figures = estimated.

**Subject(s):** Paid Community Newspapers
**Circ:** 5,800

**Stephenville Empire-Tribune (30458)**
590 S Loop
PO Box 958
Stephenville, TX 76401-4224
Phone: (254)965-3124
Fax: (254)965-4269
**Subject(s):** Daily Newspapers
**Circ:** 5,800

**The Daily Tribune (29282)**
Bay City Newspapers Inc.
PO Box 2450
Bay City, TX 77414
Phone: (979)245-5555
Fax: (979)244-5908
**Subject(s):** Daily Newspapers
**Circ:** (Free)1,413
(Paid)5,739

**Teche News (12379)**
Louisiana Suburban Press Inc.
214 N Main
PO Box 69
Saint Martinville, LA 70582
Phone: (337)394-6232
Fax: (337)394-7511
**Subject(s):** Paid Community Newspapers
**Circ:** (Non-paid)⊕38
(Paid)⊕**5,721**

**Kerrville Mountain Sun (30014)**
The Mountain Sun
429 Jefferson St.
Kerrville, TX 78028
Phone: (830)896-7000
**Subject(s):** Paid Community Newspapers
**Circ:** (Free)‡20
(Paid)‡5,700

**The Times Dispatch (1308)**
225 W. Main St.
PO Box 389
Walnut Ridge, AR 72476-0389
Phone: (870)886-2464
Fax: (870)886-9369
**Subject(s):** Paid Community Newspapers
**Circ:** (Free)‡39
(Paid)‡5,700

**Brenham Banner Press (29333)**
Fredhartman Interprise
PO Box 585
Brenham, TX 77834
Fax: (409)830-8577
**Subject(s):** Daily Newspapers
**Circ:** (Sun.)5,587
(Mon.-Fri.)5,627

**Poteau Daily News & Sun (25528)**
804 N. Broadway
PO Box 1237
Poteau, OK 74953
Phone: (918)647-3188
Fax: (918)647-8198
**Subject(s):** Daily Newspapers
**Circ:** ‡5,550

**Navasota Examiner (30208)**
115 Railroad St.
PO Box 751
Navasota, TX 77868
Phone: (936)825-6484
Fax: (936)825-2230
**Subject(s):** Paid Community Newspapers
**Circ:** (Free)73
(Paid)5,535

**Bulletin (29279)**
Bandera Bulletin
Box 697
1110 Main Street
Bandera, TX 78003
Phone: (830)796-3718
Fax: (830)796-4885
**Subject(s):** Paid Community Newspapers
**Circ:** (Paid)‡5,400

**The Concordia Sentinel (12158)**
PO Box 1485
Ferriday, LA 71334
Phone: (318)757-3646
Fax: (318)757-3001
**Subject(s):** Paid Community Newspapers
**Circ:** ‡5,500

**The Houstonian (29968)**
Sam Houston State University
PO Box 2178
Huntsville, TX 77341
Phone: (936)294-1503
Fax: (936)294-1503
**Subject(s):** College Publications
**Circ:** (Free)‡5,500

**Light & Champion (29393)**
Light & Champion Newspaper
Box 1989
Center, TX 75935
Phone: (936)598-3377
Fax: (936)598-6394
**Subject(s):** Paid Community Newspapers
**Circ:** ‡5,500

**The Lion's Roar (12169)**
Southeastern Louisiana University
SLU 10877
Hammond, LA 70402
Phone: (985)549-3731
Fax: (985)549-3842
**Subject(s):** College Publications
**Circ:** (Free)‡5,500

**Mount Pleasant Daily Tribune (30192)**
Tribune
1705 Industrial
PO Box 1177
Mount Pleasant, TX 75456-1177
Phone: (903)572-1705
Fax: (903)572-6026
**Subject(s):** Daily Newspapers
**Circ:** (Non-paid)⊕175
(Paid)⊕**5,500**

**The Nicholls Worth (12418)**
Nicholls State University
PO Box 2010
906 E 1st.St
Thibodaux, LA 70310-2010
Phone: (985)448-4259
Fax: (985)448-4267
**Subject(s):** College Publications
**Circ:** ‡5,500

**Plaquemine Post-South (12363)**
Plaquemine Publishing Inc.
58650 Belleview Dr.
PO Box 589
Plaquemine, LA 70764
Phone: (225)687-3288
Fax: (225)687-1814
**Subject(s):** Paid Community Newspapers
**Circ:** (Non-paid)146
(Paid)5,500

**Sand Springs Leader (25538)**
303 N McKinley
Sand Springs, OK 74063
Phone: (918)245-6634
Fax: (918)241-3610
**Subject(s):** Paid Community Newspapers
**Circ:** (Paid)4,500
(Non-paid)5,500

**Houston County Courier (29487)**
Polk County Publishing
PO Box 551
Crockett, TX 75835
Phone: (936)544-2238
Fax: (936)544-4088
**Subject(s):** Paid Community Newspapers
**Circ:** ‡5,435

**The Port Lavaca Wave & Calhoun County WAVE EXTRA (30293)**
The Wave
107 E Austin
PO Box 88
Port Lavaca, TX 77979
Phone: (361)552-9788
Fax: (361)552-3108
**Subject(s):** Paid Community Newspapers
**Circ:** ‡5,392

**Big Spring Herald (29310)**
710 Scurry
PO Box 1431
Big Spring, TX 79720
Phone: (915)263-7331
Fax: (915)264-7205
**Subject(s):** Daily Newspapers
**Circ:** (Mon.-Fri.)4,337
(Sun.)5,364

**The Allen American (29063)**
DFW Community Newspapers
705 N.Greenville Ave. No. 100
Allen, TX 75002
Phone: (972)727-3352
Fax: (972)727-8215
**Circ:** (Sat.)4,814
(Wed.)5,342

**Waxahachie Daily Light (30616)**
Boone Newspapers Inc.
200 W. Marvin
PO Box 877
Waxahachie, TX 75168
Phone: (972)937-3310
Fax: (214)937-1139
**Subject(s):** Daily Newspapers
**Circ:** (Mon.-Fri.)‡5,313
(Sun.)‡5,313

**Malvern Daily Record (1209)**
Horizon Publishing Co.
219 Locust St.
PO Box 70
Malvern, AR 72104-3721
Phone: (501)337-7523
Fax: (501)337-1226
**Subject(s):** Daily Newspapers
**Circ:** (Free)‡3,100
(Paid)‡5,300

**The Rockport Pilot (30315)**
PO Box 730
1002 E.Wharf St.
Rockport, TX 78381
Phone: (361)729-9900
Fax: (361)729-8903
**Subject(s):** Paid Community Newspapers
**Circ:** (Paid)⊕**5,300**

**The Clinton Daily News (25293)**
Clinton Daily News Co.
522 Avant Ave.
Clinton, OK 73601-3431
Phone: (580)323-5151
Fax: (580)323-5154
**Subject(s):** Daily Newspapers
**Circ:** (Free)‡21
(Paid)‡5,243

**The Free Press (29368)**
PO Box 339
Buda, TX 78610
Phone: (512)268-7862
Fax: (512)268-0262
**Subject(s):** Paid Community Newspapers
**Circ:** (Paid)⊕**5,203**

**Madison County Record (1142)**
PO Drawer A
Huntsville, AR 72740
Phone: (479)738-2141
Fax: (479)738-1250
**Subject(s):** Paid Community Newspapers
**Circ:** 5,200

**The Pointe Coupee Banner (12355)**
Pointe Coupee Printing & Publishing Inc.
123 St. Mary St.
PO Box 400
New Roads, LA 70760-0400
Phone: (225)638-7155
Fax: (225)638-8442
**Subject(s):** Paid Community Newspapers
**Circ:** 5,200

**The Sealy News (30423)**
193 Schmidt Road
PO Box 480
Sealy, TX 77474
Phone: (979)885-3562
Fax: (979)885-3564
**Subject(s):** Paid Community Newspapers
**Circ:** ‡5,195

**Sun Times (1124)**
Liberty Group Publishing
107 N. 4th St.
PO Box 669
Heber Springs, AR 72543
Phone: (501)362-2425
Fax: (501)362-5877
Subject(s): Paid Community Newspapers

Circ: (Wed.)4,962
(Fri.)5,140

**Kingsville Record (30021)**
PO Box 951
105 S. 5th St.
Kingsville, TX 78364-0951
Phone: (361)592-6397
Fax: (361)592-1015
Subject(s): Paid Community Newspapers

Circ: (Sun.)4,848
(Wed.)5,125

**Latimer County Today (25678)**
Talihina America
116 W. Main
Box 606
Wilburton, OK 74578
Phone: (918)465-3851
Fax: (918)465-2170
Subject(s): Paid Community Newspapers

Circ: ‡5,026

**The Banner Press Newspaper (29448)**
1217 Bowie
PO Box 490
Columbus, TX 78934
Phone: (979)732-6243
Fax: (979)732-6245
Subject(s): Paid Community Newspapers

Circ: (Paid)‡5,000

**The Bastrop Advertiser (29281)**
Cox Enterprises
908 Water St.
PO Box 459
Bastrop, TX 78602-0459
Phone: (512)321-2557
Fax: (512)321-1680
Subject(s): Paid Community Newspapers

Circ: ‡5,000

**The Daily Campus (29524)**
Student Media Co.
Southern Methodist Univ.
PO Box 456
Dallas, TX 75275
Phone: (214)768-4555
Fax: (214)768-8787
Subject(s): College Publications

Circ: (Free)‡5,000

**Ellis County News (29684)**
Ellis County Newspapers Inc.
213 N Dallas St.
PO Box 100
Ennis, TX 75120
Phone: (972)875-3801
Fax: (972)875-9747
Subject(s): Paid Community Newspapers

Circ: ‡5,000

**The Foghorn (29462)**
Del Mar College
101 Baldwin Blvd., HC 212
Corpus Christi, TX 78404
Phone: (361)698-1390
Fax: (361)698-1599
Subject(s): College Publications

Circ: (Free)‡5,000

**Goodfellow Monitor (30331)**
San Angelo Standard Inc.
34 W Harris Ave.
San Angelo, TX 76903
Phone: (325)653-1221
Fax: (325)658-6192
Subject(s): Free Newspapers; Military and Navy

Circ: (Controlled)5,000

**La Feria News (30030)**
102 S Main
PO Box 999
La Feria, TX 78559
Phone: (956)797-9920
Fax: (956)797-9921
Subject(s): Paid Community Newspapers

Circ: (Paid)5,000

**Patriot (25240)**
Altus Times
218-20 W Commerce St.
PO Box 578
Altus, OK 73521-0578
Phone: (580)482-1221
Fax: (580)482-5709
Subject(s): Military and Navy; Free Newspapers

Circ: (Free)5,000

**Port Isabel/South Padre Press (30291)**
New Horizon Publishers Inc.
PO Box 308
Port Isabel, TX 78578
Phone: (210)943-5545
Fax: (210)943-4782
Subject(s): Paid Community Newspapers

Circ: (Non-paid)150
(Paid)5,000

**Reporter (29816)**
Hillsboro Reporter
PO Box 569
Hillsboro, TX 76645
Phone: (254)582-3431
Fax: (254)582-3800
Subject(s): Paid Community Newspapers

Circ: (Free)‡2,500
(Paid)‡5,000

**San Augustine Tribune (30411)**
807 E. Columbia St.
PO Box 539
San Augustine, TX 75972
Phone: (936)275-2181
Fax: (936)275-0572
Subject(s): Paid Community Newspapers

Circ: (Paid)‡5,000

**The Southwestern (25667)**
Southwestern Oklahoma State University
100 Campus Dr.
Journalism Dept.
Weatherford, OK 73096
Phone: (580)772-6611
Fax: (580)774-7111
Subject(s): College Publications

Circ: ‡5,000

**The Vista (25315)**
The Vista Advertising
100 N. University Dr.
Edmond, OK 73034
Phone: (405)974-2000
Subject(s): College Publications

Circ: ‡5,000

**The Weekly Vista (1012)**
Community Publishers Inc.
313 Town Center West
Bella Vista, AR 72714
Phone: (479)855-3724
Fax: (479)855-6992
Subject(s): Paid Community Newspapers

Circ: (Paid)‡5,000

**Hondo Anvil Herald (29818)**
Associated Texas Newspapers Inc.
1601 Ave. K
PO Box 400
Hondo, TX 78861-0400
Phone: (830)426-3346
Fax: (830)426-3348
Subject(s): Paid Community Newspapers

Circ: ‡4,964

**Los Alamos Monitor (20122)**
Landmark Community Newspapers Inc.
256 O.P. Rd.
PO Box 1268
Los Alamos, NM 87544
Phone: (505)662-4185
Fax: (505)662-4334
Subject(s): Daily Newspapers

Circ: (Free)12
(Paid)4,966

**The Shreveport Sun (12385)**
The Shreveport Sun Inc.
PO Box 38357
Shreveport, LA 71133
Phone: (318)631-6222
Fax: (318)635-2822
Subject(s): Paid Community Newspapers; Black Publications

Circ: (Free)102
(Paid)4,968

**Ashley News Observer (1052)**
Ashley County Publishing Company Inc.
102 Pine St.
PO Box 798
Crossett, AR 71635
Phone: (870)364-5186
Fax: (870)364-2116
Subject(s): Paid Community Newspapers

Circ: 4,950

**The Crowley Post-Signal (12138)**
Crowley Post-Signal
602 N Parkerson Ave.
Box 1589
Crowley, LA 70526
Phone: (337)783-3450
Fax: (337)788-0949
Subject(s): Daily Newspapers

Circ: 4,950

**Levelland & Hockley County News Press (30054)**
Hockley County Publishing
Drawer 1628
Levelland, TX 79336
Phone: (806)894-3121
Fax: (806)894-7957
Subject(s): Paid Community Newspapers

Circ: ‡4,875

**The Rockdale Reporter & Messenger (30314)**
221-225 E Cameron Ave.
PO Box 552
Rockdale, TX 76567
Phone: (512)446-5838
Fax: (512)446-5317
Subject(s): Paid Community Newspapers

Circ: (Free)⊕130
(Paid)⊕4,867

**The Ruidoso News (20155)**
WorldWest L.L.C.
104 Park Ave.
PO Box 128
Ruidoso, NM 88345
Phone: (505)257-4001
Subject(s): Paid Community Newspapers

Circ: (Non-paid)⊕154
(Paid)⊕4,854

**Minden Press-Herald (12254)**
203 Gleason St.
PO Box 1339
Minden, LA 71058-1339
Phone: (318)377-1866
Fax: (318)377-1895
Subject(s): Daily Newspapers

Circ: (Free)275
(Paid)4,844

**Pauls Valley Daily Democrat (25514)**
Community Newspaper Holdings Inc.
108 S. Willow
PO Box 790
Pauls Valley, OK 73075
Phone: (405)238-6464
Fax: (405)238-3042
Subject(s): Daily Newspapers

Circ: (Tues.-Fri.)‡3,800
(Sun.)‡4,800

**Times Herald (1091)**
703 Garland St.
Forrest City, AR 72335
Phone: (870)633-3130
Fax: (870)633-0599
Subject(s): Daily Newspapers

Circ: (Paid)4,800

**Slidell Sentry-News (12404)**
Pontchartrain Newspapers
3648 Pontchartrain Dr.
PO Box 910
Slidell, LA 70459
Phone: (504)643-4918
Fax: (504)643-4966
Subject(s): Free Newspapers

Circ: (Free)247
(Paid)4,797

Circulation: ★ = ABC; △ = BPA; ♦ = CAC; • = CCAB; ❏ = VAC; ⊕ = PO Statement; ‡ = Publisher's Report; Boldface figures = sworn; Light figures = estimated.

## Southern Central States

**The Gilmer Mirror (29764)**
Greeneway Enterprises
PO Box 250
Gilmer, TX 75644-0250
Phone: (903)843-2503
Fax: (903)843-5123
**Subject(s):** Paid Community Newspapers
**Circ:** (Free)25
(Paid)4,777

**Wharton Journal-Spectator (30630)**
River Publishers
115 W Burleson
PO Box 111
Wharton, TX 77488
Phone: (979)532-8840
Fax: (979)532-8845
**Subject(s):** Paid Community Newspapers
**Circ:** (Free)‡40
(Paid)‡4,773

**Purcell Register (25534)**
McClain County Publishing Co.
225 W Main St.
PO Box 191
Purcell, OK 73080
Phone: (405)527-2126
Fax: (405)527-3299
**Subject(s):** Paid Community Newspapers
**Circ:** (Free)25
(Paid)4,746

**Van Buren County Democrat (1042)**
114 S Court St.
PO Box 119
Clinton, AR 72031-0119
Phone: (501)745-5175
Fax: (501)745-8865
**Subject(s):** Paid Community Newspapers
**Circ:** (Paid)‡4,700

**River Cities Tribune (30132)**
Victory Publishing Ltd.
PO Box 10
Marble Falls, TX 78654
Phone: (830)693-7152
Fax: (830)693-3085
**Subject(s):** Paid Community Newspapers
**Circ:** (Combined)⊕4,650

**San Benito News (30412)**
New Horizon Publishers Inc.
PO Box 1791
San Benito, TX 78586
Phone: (956)399-2436
Fax: (956)399-2430
**Subject(s):** Paid Community Newspapers
**Circ:** (Free)125
(Paid)4,612

**Wills Point Chronicle (30648)**
The Chronicle
109 N. 5th St.
PO Box 60
Wills Point, TX 75169
Phone: (903)873-2525
Fax: (903)873-4321
**Subject(s):** Paid Community Newspapers
**Circ:** 4,600

**Tribune Plus (12370)**
Rayne Acadian Tribune
108 N Adams Ave.
PO Box 260
Rayne, LA 70578-0260
Phone: (337)334-3186
Fax: (337)334-8474
**Subject(s):** Shopping Guides
**Circ:** (Free)4,572

**Alpine Avalanche (29065)**
Box 719
Alpine, TX 79831
Phone: (423)837-3334
Fax: (423)837-7181
**Subject(s):** Paid Community Newspapers
**Circ:** 4,500

**The Bowie News (29325)**
218 W Tarrant St.
Box 831
Bowie, TX 76230
Phone: (940)872-2247
Fax: (940)872-4812

**Subject(s):** Paid Community Newspapers
**Circ:** ‡4,500

**Contraband (12208)**
McNeese State University
4205 Ryan St.
PO Box 93465
Lake Charles, LA 70609
Phone: (337)475-5000
Fax: (337)475-5637
**Subject(s):** College Publications
**Circ:** ‡4,500

**The East Texan (29451)**
Texas A & M University-Commerce
PO Box 4104, ET Sta.
Commerce, TX 75429
Phone: (903)450-4351
Fax: (903)886-5230
**Subject(s):** College Publications
**Circ:** 4,500

**Messenger and Star-Forum (29759)**
Messenger Publishing Co.
PO Box 799
Gatesville, TX 76528
Phone: (254)865-5212
Fax: (254)865-2361
**Subject(s):** Paid Community Newspapers
**Circ:** 4,500

**The Ram Page (30334)**
Angelo State University
PO Box 10899
San Angelo, TX 76909
Phone: (915)942-2078
Fax: (915)942-2078
**Subject(s):** College Publications
**Circ:** (Free)‡4,500

**River Oaks News (30311)**
Suburban Newspapers Inc.
7820 Wyatt Dr.
Fort Worth, TX 76108-2595
Phone: (817)246-2473
Fax: (817)246-2474
**Subject(s):** Free Newspapers
**Circ:** (Free)‡4,500

**The White Rocker (29577)**
White Rocker
10809 Garland Rd.
PO Box 180698
Dallas, TX 75218
Phone: (214)327-9335
**Subject(s):** Paid Community Newspapers
**Circ:** ‡4,500

**Mountain Wave (1215)**
103 E Main
PO Box 220
Marshall, AR 72650
Phone: (870)448-3321
Fax: (870)448-5659
**Subject(s):** Paid Community Newspapers
**Circ:** ‡4,450

**The Madill Record (25399)**
211 Plz.
PO Box 529
Madill, OK 73446-0529
Phone: (580)795-3355
Fax: (580)795-3530
**Subject(s):** Paid Community Newspapers
**Circ:** (Free)100
(Paid)4,448

**Oklahoma Retailer (25477)**
Oklahoma Retailer Publishing Company Inc.
4405 NW 4th St., Ste. 135
Oklahoma City, OK 73107-6541
Phone: (405)942-0091
Fax: (405)942-0091
**Subject(s):** General Merchandise
**Circ:** (Controlled)‡4,400

**St. Charles Herald-Guide (12124)**
PO Box 1199
Boutte, LA 70039
Phone: (504)758-2795
Fax: (504)758-7000
**Subject(s):** Paid Community Newspapers
**Circ:** ‡4,400

**The Town Crier (1212)**
PO Box 1326
Manila, AR 72442-1326
Phone: (870)561-4634
Fax: (870)561-3602
**Subject(s):** Paid Community Newspapers
**Circ:** (Paid)3,000
(Free)4,400

**Duncanville Today (29638)**
Today Newspapers Inc.
1701 N. Hampton Rd., Ste. A
DeSoto, TX 75115
Phone: (972)298-4211
Fax: (972)298-6369
**Subject(s):** Paid Community Newspapers
**Circ:** (Free)❑100
(Paid)❑4,387

**The Herald-Leader (1015)**
Community Publishers Inc.
PO Box 1049
Bentonville, AR 72712
Phone: (479)271-3726
Fax: (479)273-7777
**Subject(s):** Paid Community Newspapers
**Circ:** (Non-paid)60
(Paid)4,358

**The Graham Leader (29770)**
Graham Newspapers Inc.
PO Box 600
Graham, TX 76450
Phone: (940)549-7800
Fax: (940)549-4364
**Subject(s):** Paid Community Newspapers
**Circ:** (Paid)⊕4,342

**Stone County Leader (1235)**
Stone County Publishing Co.
PO Box 509
401 W Main ST.
Mountain View, AR 72560-0509
Phone: (870)269-3841
Fax: (870)269-2171
**Subject(s):** Paid Community Newspapers
**Circ:** ‡4,339

**Commerce Journal (29780)**
Herald Banner
PO Box 6000
Greenville, TX 75403
Phone: (903)886-3196
Fax: (903)455-6281
**Subject(s):** Paid Community Newspapers
**Circ:** (Paid)‡2,740
(Free)‡4,300

**Courier News (1022)**
Blytheville Courier News
PO Box 1108
Blytheville, AR 72316
Phone: (870)763-4461
Fax: (870)763-6874
**Subject(s):** Daily Newspapers
**Circ:** (Mon.-Fri.)4,308

**The Herald (20195)**
Herald Publishing Company Inc.
1204 N. Date St.
PO Box 752
Truth or Consequences, NM 87901
Phone: (505)894-2143
Fax: (505)894-7824
**Subject(s):** Paid Community Newspapers
**Circ:** ‡4,300

**The Hereford Brand (29810)**
Heneford Brand
PO Box 673
313 North Lee
Hereford, TX 79045
Phone: (806)364-2030
Fax: (806)364-8364
**Subject(s):** Daily Newspapers
**Circ:** ‡4,300

**Journal (29785)**
Groesbeck Journal Inc.
PO Box 440
Groesbeck, TX 76642
Phone: (254)729-5103
Fax: (254)729-8310
**Subject(s):** Paid Community Newspapers
**Circ:** ‡4,300

**Weatherford Daily News** (25668)
118, S.Broadway
Weatherford, OK 73096-0919
Phone: (580)772-3301
Fax: (580)772-7329
**Subject(s):** Daily Newspapers
**Circ:** ‡4,300

**The Wylie News** (30655)
110 N. Ballard St.
PO Box 369
Wylie, TX 75098
Phone: (214)442-5515
Fax: (214)442-4318
**Subject(s):** Paid Community Newspapers
**Circ:** (Combined)‡4,302

**Advance-Monticellonian** (1223)
Tom White
314 N Main St.
PO Box 486
Monticello, AR 71655
Phone: (501)367-5325
Fax: (501)367-6612
**Subject(s):** Paid Community Newspapers
**Circ:** ‡4,250

**Lampasas Dispatch Record** (30038)
416 S Live Oak
PO Box 631
Lampasas, TX 76550
Phone: (512)556-6262
Fax: (512)556-3278
**Subject(s):** Paid Community Newspapers
**Circ:** ‡4,238

**Banner-News** (1205)
Banner-News Publishing Co.
134 S Washington
Box 100
Magnolia, AR 71753
Phone: (870)234-5130
Fax: (870)234-2551
**Subject(s):** Daily Newspapers
**Circ:** (Paid)‡4,200

**The Belton Journal** (29304)
210 N Penelope
PO Box 180
Belton, TX 76513
Phone: (254)939-5754
Fax: (254)939-2333
**Subject(s):** Paid Community Newspapers
**Circ:** ‡4,200

**Burleson County Citizen-Tribune** (29374)
Burleson Publishing Company Inc.
306 W. Hwy. 21
Caldwell, TX 77836
Phone: (979)567-3286
Fax: (979)567-7898
**Subject(s):** Paid Community Newspapers
**Circ:** ‡4,200

**Burnet Bulletin** (29372)
American Consolidated Media
1001 Buchanan Ste.2
PO Box 160
Burnet, TX 78611
Phone: (512)756-6136
Fax: (512)756-8911
**Subject(s):** Paid Community Newspapers
**Circ:** ‡4,200

**The Gazette** (12156)
Union Publishing Co.
104 N Washington
PO Box 722
Farmerville, LA 71241
Phone: (318)368-9732
Fax: (318)368-7331
**Subject(s):** Paid Community Newspapers
**Circ:** ‡4,200

**Mansfield Enterprise-Progress** (12237)
The Enterprise
202 Adams St.
PO Box 840
Mansfield, LA 71052
Phone: (318)872-4120
Fax: (318)872-6038
**Subject(s):** Paid Community Newspapers
**Circ:** ‡4,200

**The Perryton Herald** (30269)
401 S Amherst
PO Box 989
Perryton, TX 79070
Phone: (806)435-3631
Fax: (806)435-2420
**Subject(s):** Paid Community Newspapers
**Circ:** 4,200

**Winn Parish Enterprise** (12434)
Pineland Publishing Co.
PO Box 750
Winnfield, LA 71483
Phone: (318)628-2712
Fax: (318)628-6196
**Subject(s):** Paid Community Newspapers
**Circ:** ‡4,200

**Wood County Democrat** (30300)
Westwood Publishing
P.O. Box 308
Quitman, TX 75783
Phone: (903)763-4522
Fax: (903)763-2313
**Subject(s):** Paid Community Newspapers
**Circ:** ‡4,200

**Oak Cliff Tribune** (29559)
Oak Cliff Tribune Ltd.
PO Box 4650
Dallas, TX 75208
Phone: (214)943-7755
Fax: (214)943-7775
**Subject(s):** Paid Community Newspapers
**Circ:** (Paid)‡4,100

**Ennis Daily News** (29685)
Ellis County Newspapers Inc.
213 N Dallas St.
PO Box 100
Ennis, TX 75120
Phone: (972)875-3801
Fax: (972)875-9747
**Subject(s):** Daily Newspapers
**Circ:** (Mon.-Fri.)‡4,050
(Sun.)‡4,050

**Sheridan Headlight** (1286)
Sheridan Headlights
211 W. High St.
PO Box 539
Sheridan, AR 72150
Phone: (870)942-2142
Fax: (870)942-8823
**Subject(s):** Paid Community Newspapers
**Circ:** ‡4,050

**Carroll County News** (1018)
Carroll County Newspapers
PO Box 232
Berryville, AR 72616
Phone: (870)423-6636
Fax: (870)423-6640
**Subject(s):** Paid Community Newspapers
**Circ:** ‡4,007

**Collegian Newspaper** (25594)
University of Tulsa
600 S College Ave.
Tulsa, OK 74104-3189
Phone: (918)631-3080
Fax: (918)631-3033
**Subject(s):** College Publications
**Circ:** ‡4,000

**Denton County Express** (30034)
Sun Newspapers
275 Market St.
PO Box 879
Lake Dallas, TX 75065
Phone: (940)497-4141
**Subject(s):** Paid Community Newspapers
**Circ:** 4,000

**Floresville Chronicle-Journal** (29694)
1433 3rd St.
PO Box 820
Floresville, TX 78114
Phone: (830)393-2111
Fax: (830)393-9012
**Subject(s):** Paid Community Newspapers
**Circ:** ‡4,000

**The J-TAC** (30457)
T-0440
Stephenville, TX 76402
Phone: (254)968-9056
Fax: (254)968-9709
**Subject(s):** College Publications
**Circ:** ‡4,000

**Pecos Free Press** (30266)
324 S Cedar
Pecos, TX 79772
Phone: (432)445-5475
Fax: (432)445-4321
**Subject(s):** Shopping Guides
**Circ:** (Free)4,000

**Springhill Press & News Journal** (12407)
PO Box 669
Springhill, LA 71075
Phone: (318)539-3511
Fax: (318)539-3512
**Subject(s):** Paid Community Newspapers
**Circ:** ‡4,000

**News-Mirror** (30127)
Mansfield News-Mirror
PO Box 337
Mansfield, TX 76063
Phone: (817)473-4451
Fax: (817)473-0730
**Subject(s):** Paid Community Newspapers
**Circ:** (Non-paid)29
(Paid)3,968

**The Canyon News** (29380)
1500 5th Ave.
Canyon, TX 79015
Phone: (806)655-7121
Fax: (806)655-0823
**Subject(s):** Paid Community Newspapers
**Circ:** (Free)‡300
(Paid)‡3,950

**Lockhart Post-Register** (30071)
Garrett Publishing Company Inc.
111 S Church St.
PO Box 929
Lockhart, TX 78644-0360
Phone: (512)398-4886
Fax: (512)398-6144
**Subject(s):** Paid Community Newspapers
**Circ:** (Free)28
(Paid)3,908

**News-Sentinel** (25561)
204 S Broadway
PO Box 549
Stigler, OK 74462-0549
Phone: (918)967-4655
Fax: (918)967-4289
**Subject(s):** Paid Community Newspapers
**Circ:** ‡3,906

**Times-Democrat** (25580)
115 W Muskogee
P O Box 131
Sulphur, OK 73086
Phone: (580)622-2102
Fax: (580)622-2937
**Subject(s):** Paid Community Newspapers
**Circ:** 3,900

**The Lincoln County News** (25283)
Lincoln County Publishing Company Inc.
718 Manvel
Box 248
Chandler, OK 74834-0248
Phone: (405)258-1818
Fax: (405)258-1824
**Subject(s):** Paid Community Newspapers
**Circ:** (Free)‡134
(Paid)‡3,899

**Cherokeean/Herald** (30325)
Whitehead Enterprises Inc.
618 N Main
PO Box 475
Rusk, TX 75785
Phone: (903)683-2257
Fax: (903)683-5104
**Subject(s):** Paid Community Newspapers
**Circ:** (Paid)3,809

Circulation: ★ = ABC; △ = BPA; ♦ = CAC; ● = CCAB; ☐ = VAC; ⊕ = PO Statement; ‡ = Publisher's Report; Boldface figures = sworn; Light figures = estimated.

## Southern Central States

**The Fairfield Recorder (29687)**
101 E Commerce
Fairfield, TX 75840
Phone: (903)389-3334
Fax: (903)389-8255
**Subject(s):** Paid Community Newspapers
**Circ:** 3,800

**Kingfisher Times and Free Press (25379)**
PO Box 209
Kingfisher, OK 73750-0209
Phone: (405)375-3220
Fax: (405)375-3222
**Subject(s):** Paid Community Newspapers
**Circ:** ‡3,800

**Medina Valley Times (29390)**
Medina Times
501 Madrid St., No. 1
Castroville, TX 78009-4528
Phone: (830)931-0983
Fax: (830)931-3450
**Subject(s):** Paid Community Newspapers
**Circ:** (Paid)3,800

**Moore County News-Press (29635)**
Moore County Publishing Company L.L.C.
Seventh and Meredith
PO Box 757
Dumas, TX 79029
Phone: (806)935-4111
Fax: (806)935-2348
**Subject(s):** Paid Community Newspapers
**Circ:** ⊕3,800

**Optimist (29039)**
Abilene Christian University
ACU Box 27892
Abilene, TX 79699-7892
Phone: (325)674-2439
Fax: (325)674-2139
**Subject(s):** College Publications
**Circ:** (Free)‡3,800

**Paris Express (1254)**
PO Box 551
Paris, AR 72855
Phone: (479)963-2901
Fax: (479)963-3062
**Subject(s):** Paid Community Newspapers
**Circ:** 3,800

**The Rayne Independent (12369)**
The Rayne Independent Newspaper
201 E S 1st St.
PO Box 428
Rayne, LA 70578
Phone: (337)334-2128
Fax: (337)334-2120
**Subject(s):** Paid Community Newspapers
**Circ:** ‡3,800

**Lamesa Press-Reporter (30036)**
523 N 1st St.
PO Box 710
Lamesa, TX 79331-0710
Phone: (806)872-2177
Fax: (806)872-2623
**Subject(s):** Paid Community Newspapers
**Circ:** (Paid)‡3,779

**The Cameron Herald (29375)**
Milam County Newpaper L.L.C.
108 E 1st St.
PO Drawer 1230
Cameron, TX 76520
Phone: (254)697-6672
Fax: (254)697-4902
**Subject(s):** Free Newspapers; Free Newspapers
**Circ:** (Free)‡3,000
(Paid)‡3,763

**The Hearne Democrat (29801)**
Community Media Newspapers Inc.
120 West 3rd Street
Hearne, TX 77859
Phone: (979)279-3411
Fax: (979)279-5401
**Subject(s):** Paid Community Newspapers
**Circ:** ‡3,750

**Breckenridge American (29330)**
114 E. Elm St.
Breckenridge, TX 76424
Phone: (254)559-5412

Fax: (254)559-3491
**Subject(s):** Paid Community Newspapers
**Circ:** (Free)‡42
(Paid)‡3,702

**The Hamilton Herald-News (29788)**
112 E Main St.
PO Box 833
Hamilton, TX 76531-0833
Phone: (254)386-3145
Fax: (254)386-3001
**Subject(s):** Paid Community Newspapers
**Circ:** 3,700

**Little River News (1004)**
45 E Commence
PO Box 608
Ashdown, AR 71822
Phone: (870)898-3462
Fax: (870)898-6213
**Subject(s):** Paid Community Newspapers
**Circ:** 3,700

**The Winkler County News (30012)**
Golden West Free Press Inc.
Drawer A
109 S Poplar St.
Kermit, TX 79745-0769
Phone: (432)586-2561
Fax: (432)586-2562
**Subject(s):** Paid Community Newspapers
**Circ:** (Paid)3,700

**Caddo Citizen (12428)**
Po Box 312
203 S. Spruce St
Vivian, LA 71082-0312
Phone: (318)375-3294
Fax: (318)375-4578
**Subject(s):** Paid Community Newspapers
**Circ:** ‡3,600

**Catahoula News-Booster (12184)**
103 3rd St.
PO Box 188
Jonesville, LA 71343
Phone: (318)339-7242
Fax: (318)339-7243
**Subject(s):** Paid Community Newspapers
**Circ:** ‡3,600

**Colorado City Record (29447)**
Colorado Record
PO Box 92
Colorado City, TX 79512
Phone: (325)728-3413
Fax: (325)728-3414
**Subject(s):** Paid Community Newspapers
**Circ:** ‡3,600

**Guymon Daily Herald (25354)**
Community Newspaper Holdings Inc.
PO Box 19
Guymon, OK 73942
Phone: (405)338-3355
Fax: (405)338-5000
**Subject(s):** Daily Newspapers
**Circ:** (Non-paid)150
(Paid)3,600

**The Heavener Ledger (25360)**
507 E 1st St.
PO Box 38
Heavener, OK 74937
Phone: (918)653-2425
Fax: (918)653-7305
**Subject(s):** Paid Community Newspapers
**Circ:** ‡3,600

**Indian Journal (25330)**
Lake Eusaula Pub
PO Box 689
109 South Main St.
Eufaula, OK 74432
Phone: (918)689-2191
Fax: (918)689-2377
**Subject(s):** Paid Community Newspapers
**Circ:** ⊕503
‡3,600

**Llano News (30070)**
813 Berry St.
PO Box 187
Llano, TX 78643-1907
Phone: (325)247-4433

Fax: (325)247-3338
**Subject(s):** Paid Community Newspapers
**Circ:** ‡3,600

**Rogers Hometown News (1272)**
Community Publishers Inc.
1400 W. Walnut, No. 123
Rogers, AR 72756
Phone: (501)621-6399
Fax: (501)621-6399
**Subject(s):** Paid Community Newspapers
**Circ:** (Wed.)3,600

**Sweetwater Reporter (30522)**
112 W. Third St.
PO Box 750
Sweetwater, TX 79556
Phone: (325)236-6677
Fax: (325)235-4967
**Subject(s):** Daily Newspapers
**Circ:** (Non-paid)115
(Paid)3,600

**The Cuero Record (29494)**
119 E Main St.
Box 351
Cuero, TX 77954
Phone: (361)275-3464
Fax: (361)275-3131
**Subject(s):** Paid Community Newspapers
**Circ:** ‡3,550

**The News (1279)**
Area Wide Media
PO Box 248
Salem, AR 72576
Phone: (870)895-3207
Fax: (870)895-4277
**Subject(s):** Paid Community Newspapers
**Circ:** 3,550

**Moore American (25416)**
South Metro Publications
P.O. Box 6739
Moore, OK 73153
Phone: (405)794-5555
Fax: (405)799-8046
**Subject(s):** Free Newspapers
**Circ:** (Combined)3530

**The Journal Record (25463)**
Journal Publishing Co.
222 N. Robinson
Oklahoma City, OK 73102
Phone: (405)235-3100
Fax: (405)278-2890
**Subject(s):** Daily Periodicals
**Circ:** (Mon.-Fri.)★3,511

**The Clarksville Times (29402)**
106 E Main St.
PO Box 1018
Clarksville, TX 75426
Phone: (903)427-5616
Fax: (903)427-3068
**Subject(s):** Paid Community Newspapers
**Circ:** 3,500

**Current Sauce (12284)**
Northwestern State University
Box 5306
Natchitoches, LA 71497
Phone: (318)357-4439
Fax: (318)357-6564
**Subject(s):** College Publications
**Circ:** ‡3,500

**The DeQuincy News (12141)**
203 E Harrsion
PO Box 995
DeQuincy, LA 70633
Phone: (318)786-8004
Fax: (318)786-8131
**Subject(s):** Paid Community Newspapers
**Circ:** ‡3,500

**Free Press (29632)**
Angelina Free Press Inc.
201 N Temple
Diboll, TX 75941-1701
Phone: (936)829-1806
Fax: (936)829-1811
**Subject(s):** Paid Community Newspapers
**Circ:** 3,500

**Jackson Independent (12182)**
624 Hudson Ave.
PO Box 520
Jonesboro, LA 71251
Phone: (318)259-2551
Fax: (318)259-8537
**Subject(s):** Paid Community Newspapers
**Circ:** 3,500

**Kaplan Herald (12185)**
219 N Cushing Ave.
PO Box 236
Kaplan, LA 70548
Phone: (337)643-8002
Fax: (337)643-1382
**Subject(s):** Paid Community Newspapers
**Circ:** ‡3,500

**Pearland Journal (30260)**
Houston Community Newspapers
2206 E. Broadway
Pearland, TX 77581
Phone: (281)485-2785
Fax: (281)485-4464
**Subject(s):** Paid Community Newspapers
**Circ:** ‡3500

**The Tribune (25265)**
7300 N.W. 23rd St., Ste 400
Bethany, OK 73008
Phone: (405)789-1962
Fax: (405)789-4253
**Subject(s):** Paid Community Newspapers
**Circ:** 3,500

**Wynne Progress (1316)**
Wynne Progress Inc.
702 N Falls Blvd.
PO Box 308
Wynne, AR 72396
Phone: (870)238-2375
Fax: (870)238-4655
**Subject(s):** Paid Community Newspapers
**Circ:** ‡3,500

**Franklinton Era-Leader (12162)**
The Leader
1137 Main St.
PO Drawer F
Franklinton, LA 70438
Phone: (985)839-9077
Fax: (985)839-9077
**Subject(s):** Paid Community Newspapers
**Circ:** 3,485

**Artesia Daily Press (20045)**
PO Box 190
Artesia, NM 88211-0190
**Subject(s):** Daily Newspapers
**Circ:** 3,446

**Clay County Courier (1050)**
PO Box 85, Hwy. 67 N
Corning, AR 72422
Phone: (870)857-6397
Fax: (870)857-5204
**Subject(s):** Paid Community Newspapers
**Circ:** 3,400

**Dumas Clarion (1062)**
Clarion Publishing Co.
136 E Waterman St.
PO Box 220
Dumas, AR 71639
Phone: (870)382-4925
Fax: (870)382-6421
**Subject(s):** Paid Community Newspapers
**Circ:** ‡3,400

**Latimer County News-Tribune (25677)**
111 W Ada
PO Drawer 10
Wilburton, OK 74578
Phone: (918)465-2321
Fax: (918)465-3011
**Subject(s):** Paid Community Newspapers
**Circ:** ‡3,400

**The Madison Journal (12413)**
300 S Chestnut St.
PO Box 791
Tallulah, LA 71284
Phone: (318)574-1404
Fax: (318)574-4219

**Subject(s):** Paid Community Newspapers
**Circ:** ‡3,400

**The Madisonville Meteor and Times (30120)**
Madisonville Newspapers Inc.
PO Drawer 999
205 North Madison
Madisonville, TX 77864-0999
Phone: (936)348-3505
Fax: (936)348-3338
**Subject(s):** Paid Community Newspapers
**Circ:** (Non-paid)25
(Paid)3,400

**Times-News (1218)**
McGehee Publishing Co.
PO Box 290
McGehee, AR 71654
Phone: (870)222-3922
Fax: (870)222-3726
**Subject(s):** Paid Community Newspapers
**Circ:** ‡3,400

**Villager Journal (1038)**
PO Box 480
Cherokee Village, AR 72525
Phone: (870)856-2582
Fax: (870)895-4277
**Subject(s):** Paid Community Newspapers
**Circ:** (Paid)3,373

**Fairview Republican (25334)**
112 N Main St.
PO Box 497
Fairview, OK 73737
Phone: (580)227-4439
Fax: (580)227-4430
**Subject(s):** Paid Community Newspapers
**Circ:** ‡3,341

**St. Tammany Farmer (12136)**
St. Tammany Farmer Inc.
PO Box 269
321 N New Hampshire St.
Covington, LA 70434
Phone: (985)892-2323
Fax: (985)892-2325
**Subject(s):** Paid Community Newspapers
**Circ:** (Free)⊕350
(Paid)⊕3,330

**Weimar Mercury (30620)**
Weimar Merway
200 W Main
Weimar, TX 78962
Phone: (979)725-8444
Fax: (979)725-9051
**Subject(s):** Paid Community Newspapers
**Circ:** (Free)‡234
(Paid)‡3,328

**De Witt Era-Enterprise (1061)**
De Witt Publishing Co.
PO Box 431
De Witt, AR 72042
Phone: (870)946-3241
Fax: (870)946-1888
**Subject(s):** Paid Community Newspapers
**Circ:** 3,300

**The Wimberley View (30651)**
Holly Media Group
PO Box 393
Wimberley, TX 78676
Phone: (512)847-2202
Fax: (512)847-9054
**Subject(s):** Paid Community Newspapers
**Circ:** (Sat.)1,500
(Wed.)3,300

**Franklin Banner-Tribune (12161)**
115 Wilson St.
PO Box 566
Franklin, LA 70538-6150
Phone: (337)828-3706
Fax: (337)828-2874
**Subject(s):** Daily Newspapers
**Circ:** (Non-paid)1,720
(Paid)3,280

**Holdenville Daily News (25368)**
1112 S Creek
PO Box 751
Holdenville, OK 74848
Phone: (405)379-5411

Fax: (405)379-5413
**Subject(s):** Daily Newspapers
**Circ:** (Free)‡410
(Paid)‡3,270

**The Perry Daily Journal (25517)**
Perry Journal Co.
714 Delaware St.
PO Box 311
Perry, OK 73077-0311
Phone: (405)336-2222
Fax: (405)336-3222
**Subject(s):** Daily Newspapers
**Circ:** ‡3,260

**News-Guide (29641)**
New Guide
1342 Main St.
PO Box 764
Eagle Pass, TX 78852
Phone: (830)773-2309
Fax: (830)773-3398
**Subject(s):** Paid Community Newspapers
**Circ:** ‡3,250

**The Bristow News (25272)**
East Central Oklahoma Publishers Inc.
PO Box 840
Bristow, OK 74010-0840
Phone: (918)367-2282
Fax: (918)367-2724
**Subject(s):** Paid Community Newspapers
**Circ:** ‡3,225

**The Brady Herald (29327)**
Brady Standard-Herald
PO Box 1151
Brady, TX 76825
Phone: (915)597-2959
Fax: (915)597-1434
**Subject(s):** Paid Community Newspapers
**Circ:** (Free)62
(Paid)3,219

**The Bee (29497)**
Asp Westward L.P.
201 1/2 William Watson Blvd.
Daingerfield, TX 75638
Phone: (903)645-3948
Fax: (903)645-3731
**Subject(s):** Paid Community Newspapers
**Circ:** 3,200

**Copperas Cove Leader-Press (29458)**
Leader-Press
PO Box 370
115 West Ave D
Copperas Cove, TX 76522
Phone: (254)547-4207
Fax: (254)542-3299
**Subject(s):** Paid Community Newspapers
**Circ:** ‡3,200

**Friendswood Journal (30259)**
Houston Community Newspapers
2206 E. Broadway
Pearland, TX 77588
Phone: (281)485-2785
Fax: (281)485-4464
**Subject(s):** Paid Community Newspapers
**Circ:** 3,200

**Hobart Democrat-Chief (25364)**
407 S Main
PO Box 432
Hobart, OK 73651
Phone: (580)726-3333
Fax: (580)726-3431
**Subject(s):** Paid Community Newspapers
**Circ:** ‡3,200

**The Monahans News (30189)**
Monahans News
Box 767
Monahans, TX 79756
Phone: (432)943-4313
Fax: (432)943-4314
**Subject(s):** Paid Community Newspapers
**Circ:** ‡3,200

# Southern Central States

**Quay County Sun** (20197)
Freedom Newspapers of New Mexico
902 S 1st St.
PO Drawer 1408
Tucumcari, NM 88401
Phone: (505)461-1952
Fax: (505)461-1965
**Subject(s):** Paid Community Newspapers
**Circ:** (Paid)‡3,200

**The Childress Index** (29397)
224 Main St.
PO Box 1210
Childress, TX 79201-1210
Phone: (940)937-2525
Fax: (940)937-2239
**Subject(s):** Paid Community Newspapers
**Circ:** (Paid)‡3,047
(Sun.)‡3,181

**The Progress** (30542)
109 W. Alexander
PO Box 848
Three Rivers, TX 78071
Phone: (361)786-3022
Fax: (361)786-3671
**Subject(s):** Paid Community Newspapers
**Circ:** (Free)‡13
(Paid)‡3,173

**Johnston County Capital Democrat** (25586)
Johnston Democrat
103 N Neshoba St.
PO Box 520
Tishomingo, OK 73460
Phone: (580)371-2356
Fax: (580)371-9648
**Subject(s):** Paid Community Newspapers
**Circ:** ‡3,150

**Walters Herald** (25666)
112 E Colorado St.
PO Box 247
Walters, OK 73572
Phone: (580)875-3326
Fax: (580)875-3150
**Subject(s):** Paid Community Newspapers
**Circ:** ‡3,150

**Lubbock Southwest Digest** (30085)
1302 Ave Q
Lubbock, TX 79401
Phone: (806)762-3612
Fax: (806)741-0000
**Subject(s):** Free Newspapers; Black Publications
**Circ:** (Free)‡1,243
(Paid)‡3,137

**Sabine County Reporter** (29803)
Box 700
Hemphill, TX 75948
Phone: (409)787-2172
Fax: (409)787-4300
**Subject(s):** Paid Community Newspapers
**Circ:** (Non-paid)59
(Paid)3,132

**The Record-Citizen** (25273)
East Central Oklahoma Publishers Inc.
PO Box 840
Bristow, OK 74010-0840
Phone: (918)367-2282
Fax: (918)367-2724
**Subject(s):** Paid Community Newspapers
**Circ:** ‡3,125

**EL Defensor Chieftain** (20184)
WorldWest L.L.C.
200 Winkler SW
Socorro, NM 87801-4200
Phone: (505)835-0520
**Subject(s):** Paid Community Newspapers
**Circ:** ‡3,117

**Brownfield News** (29336)
Brownfield News Inc.
409 W. Hill St.
PO Box 1272
Brownfield, TX 79316
Phone: (806)637-4535
Fax: (806)637-3795
**Subject(s):** Paid Community Newspapers
**Circ:** (Paid)‡3,100

**Daily Siftings Herald** (998)
Community Newspaper Holdings Inc.
205 S. 26th St.
PO Box 10
Arkadelphia, AR 71923
Phone: (501)246-5525
Fax: (501)246-6556
**Subject(s):** Daily Newspapers
**Circ:** (Non-paid)‡125
(Paid)‡3,100

**Mineola Monitor** (30184)
Westward Publications
PO Box 210
715 Mimosa Street
Mineola, TX 75773
Phone: (903)569-2047
Fax: (903)569-6863
**Subject(s):** Paid Community Newspapers
**Circ:** ‡3,100

**Optic-Herald** (30195)
Four Corners Pub. Inc.
108 S. Kaufman St.
Mount Vernon, TX 75457
Phone: (903)537-2228
Fax: (903)537-2227
**Subject(s):** Paid Community Newspapers
**Circ:** ‡3,100

**The Piggott Times** (1257)
Delta Publishing Co.
209 W. Main St.
PO Box 59
Piggott, AR 72454-0059
Phone: (870)598-2201
Fax: (870)598-5189
**Subject(s):** Paid Community Newspapers
**Circ:** (Paid)3,100

**The West News** (30628)
214 W Oak
PO Box 38
West, TX 76691
Phone: (817)826-3718
**Subject(s):** Paid Community Newspapers
**Circ:** (Paid)‡3,100

**The Mexia Daily News** (30168)
Mexia News
214 N Railroad St.
PO Box 431
Mexia, TX 76667
Phone: (254)562-2868
Fax: (254)562-3121
**Subject(s):** Daily Newspapers
**Circ:** (Paid)‡3,051

**The Clifton Record** (29412)
310 W. 5th St.
Clifton, TX 76634
Phone: (254)675-3336
**Subject(s):** Paid Community Newspapers
**Circ:** ‡3,010

**The Countywide** (30008)
Karnes Multi Media Inc.
110 S Market
PO Box 129
Karnes City, TX 78118-0129
Phone: (830)780-3924
Fax: (830)780-3711
**Subject(s):** Paid Community Newspapers
**Circ:** ‡3,016

**Antlers American** (25249)
PO Box 578
Antlers, OK 74523
Phone: (580)298-3314
Fax: (580)298-3316
**Subject(s):** Paid Community Newspapers
**Circ:** 3,000

**Ashley County Ledger** (1116)
Ashley Publishing Company Inc.
107 Main St.
PO Box 471
Hamburg, AR 71646
Phone: (501)853-2424
Fax: (501)853-8203
**Subject(s):** Paid Community Newspapers
**Circ:** ‡3,000

**The Chronicle** (12129)
305 Main St.
Colfax, LA 71417
Phone: (318)627-3737
Fax: (318)627-3019
**Subject(s):** Paid Community Newspapers
**Circ:** ‡3,000

**Chronicle & Democrat-Voice** (29415)
PO Box 840
Coleman, TX 76834
Phone: (915)625-4128
Fax: (915)625-4129
**Subject(s):** Paid Community Newspapers
**Circ:** 3,000

**Clay County Leader** (29809)
Drawer 10
Henrietta, TX 76365-0010
Phone: (817)538-4333
Fax: (817)538-4542
**Subject(s):** Paid Community Newspapers
**Circ:** (Paid)3,000

**Collegian** (25384)
Cameron University
Dept. of English, Foreign Languages, and Journalism
2800 W. Gore Blvd.
Lawton, OK 73505-6377
Phone: (580)581-2260
Fax: (580)581-2261
**Subject(s):** College Publications
**Circ:** ‡3,000

**Crowley Review** (29492)
Crowley Publishing Inc.
PO Box 300
Crowley, TX 76036
Phone: (817)297-6707
Fax: (817)295-0486
**Subject(s):** Paid Community Newspapers
**Circ:** (Paid)⊕3,000

**Delaware County Journal** (25377)
Box 1050
Jay, OK 74346
Phone: (918)253-4322
Fax: (918)253-4380
**Subject(s):** Paid Community Newspapers
**Circ:** (Paid)1,800
3,000

**Donaldsonville Chief** (12148)
120 Railroad Ave
PO Box 309
Donaldsonville, LA 70346
Phone: (225)473-3101
Fax: (225)473-4060
**Subject(s):** Paid Community Newspapers
**Circ:** (Paid)‡3,000
(Non-paid)‡3,000

**The Frederick Press** (25339)
117 N 9th
Frederick, OK 73542
Phone: (580)335-3893
Fax: (580)335-5400
**Subject(s):** Paid Community Newspapers
**Circ:** ‡3,000

**Hilltop Views** (29161)
St. Edward's University
3001 S Congress
PO Box 1029
Austin, TX 78704
Phone: (512)448-8400
Fax: (512)448-8492
**Subject(s):** College Publications
**Circ:** (Free)3,000

**The Lasso** (29624)
Texas Woman's University
PO Box 425828
Denton, TX 76204-5828
Phone: (940)898-2185
Fax: (940)898-2188
**Subject(s):** College Publications; Women's Interests
**Circ:** 3,000

**Logos** (30369)
Incarnate Word College
4301 Broadway
San Antonio, TX 78209-6397
Phone: (210)829-6005

**Subject(s):** College Publications
**Circ:** ‡3,000

**Marlin Democrat (30134)**
211 Fortune Street
PO Box 112
Marlin, TX 76661-0112
Phone: (254)883-2554
Fax: (254)883-6553
**Subject(s):** Paid Community Newspapers
**Circ:** ‡3,000

**Newton County Times (1145)**
Box 453
Jasper, AR 72641
Phone: (870)446-2645
Fax: (870)446-6286
**Subject(s):** Paid Community Newspapers
**Circ:** ‡3,000

**Oakdale Journal (12358)**
PO Box 668
Oakdale, LA 71463-0668
Phone: (318)335-0635
Fax: (318)335-0431
**Subject(s):** Paid Community Newspapers
**Circ:** 3,000

**Okemah News Leader (25446)**
602 W Broadway
PO Box 191
Okemah, OK 74859
Phone: (918)623-0123
Fax: (918)623-0124
**Subject(s):** Paid Community Newspapers
**Circ:** ‡3,000

**The Pawnee Chief (Division of American-Chief Co.) (25516)**
The Pawnee Chief
PO Drawer 370
558 Illinois St.
Pawnee, OK 74058
Phone: (918)762-2552
Fax: (918)762-2554
**Subject(s):** Paid Community Newspapers
**Circ:** ‡3,001

**The Plaquemines Gazette (12111)**
Plaquemines Newspaper Publishing Inc.
PO Box 700
Belle Chasse, LA 70037
**Subject(s):** Paid Community Newspapers
**Circ:** ‡3,000

**The Plaquemines Watchman (12112)**
Plaquemines Newspaper Publishing Inc.
7952 HWY 23
Belle Chasse, LA 70037
Phone: (504)392-1619
Fax: (504)393-9327
**Subject(s):** Paid Community Newspapers
**Circ:** ‡3,000

**The Southwest Catholic (12217)**
Diocese of Lake Charles
PO Box 3223
Lake Charles, LA 70602-3223
Phone: (337)439-7426
Fax: (337)439-7428
**Subject(s):** Religious Publications
**Circ:** (Non-paid)1,000
(Paid)3,000

**Spiro Graphic (25560)**
PO Box 190
212 S Main St.
Spiro, OK 74959
Phone: (918)962-2075
Fax: (918)962-3531
**Subject(s):** Free Newspapers
**Circ:** (Free)‡50
(Paid)‡3,000

**Waco Citizen Newspaper (30601)**
1020 N. 25th St.
Waco, TX 76707
Phone: (254)754-3511
Fax: (254)754-3541
**Subject(s):** Paid Community Newspapers
**Circ:** (Free)600
(Paid)3,000

**West Side Journal (12367)**
PO Box 260
Port Allen, LA 70767
Phone: (225)343-2540
Fax: (225)344-0923
**Subject(s):** Paid Community Newspapers
**Circ:** 3,000

**Westlake Picayune (29253)**
Cox Enterprises
3103 Bee Cave Rd., Ste. 102
Austin, TX 78746
Phone: (512)327-2990
Fax: (512)328-6470
**Subject(s):** Paid Community Newspapers
**Circ:** ‡3,000

**Yoakum Herald-Times (30656)**
PO Box 798
Yoakum, TX 77995
**Subject(s):** Paid Community Newspapers
**Circ:** (Paid)3,000

**Oologah Lake Leader (25512)**
109 S Maple
PO Box 1175
Oologah, OK 74053-1175
Phone: (918)443-2428
**Subject(s):** Paid Community Newspapers
**Circ:** (Paid)‡2,998

**Zapata County News (30658)**
PO Box 216
Hwy 83
Zapata, TX 78076
Phone: (956)765-6931
Fax: (956)765-9058
**Subject(s):** Paid Community Newspapers
**Circ:** (Combined)⊕2,992

**The Mena Star (1220)**
Mena Star Company Inc.
501 Mena St.
PO Box 1307
Mena, AR 71953
Phone: (479)394-1900
Fax: (479)394-1908
**Subject(s):** Daily Newspapers
**Circ:** (Free)80
(Paid)2,958

**Glen Rose Reporter (29767)**
Glen Rose Inc.
PO Box 2009
100 Vernon
Glen Rose, TX 76043-2009
Phone: (254)897-2282
Fax: (254)897-9423
**Subject(s):** Paid Community Newspapers
**Circ:** 2,938

**Blanco County News (29313)**
PO Box 429
310 Peacon Street
Blanco, TX 78606-0429
Phone: (830)833-4812
Fax: (830)833-4246
**Subject(s):** Paid Community Newspapers
**Circ:** 2,900

**Cleveland Advocate (29409)**
Westward Communications
PO Box 1628
Cleveland, TX 77327
Phone: (281)592-2626
Fax: (281)592-2629
**Subject(s):** Paid Community Newspapers
**Circ:** ‡2,900

**The Coushatta Citizen (12132)**
The Coushatta Citizen Shopper
1904 Ringgold Ave.
PO Drawer 1365
Coushatta, LA 71019-2006
Phone: (318)932-4201
Fax: (318)932-4285
**Subject(s):** Paid Community Newspapers
**Circ:** ‡2,900

**Grand Saline Sun (29776)**
Cox Enterprises
116 N. Main St.
PO Drawer G
Grand Saline, TX 75140
Phone: (903)962-4275

Fax: (903)962-3660
**Subject(s):** Paid Community Newspapers
**Circ:** ‡2,900

**The Smithville Times (30440)**
Greater Austin Community Newspapers
PO Box 659
Smithville, TX 78957
Phone: (512)237-4655
Fax: (512)237-5443
**Subject(s):** Paid Community Newspapers
**Circ:** (Free)100
(Paid)2,900

**Whitesboro News-Record (30636)**
130 E Main
PO Box 68
Whitesboro, TX 76273
Phone: (903)564-3565
Fax: (903)564-9655
**Subject(s):** Paid Community Newspapers
**Circ:** 2,900

**Aransas Pass Progress (29102)**
The Aransas Pass Progress/Ingleside Index
PO Box 2100
Aransas Pass, TX 78335
Phone: (361)758-5391
Fax: (361)758-5393
**Subject(s):** Paid Community Newspapers
**Circ:** (Paid)⊕2,876

**DeSoto Today (29630)**
Today Newspapers Inc.
1701 N. Hampton Rd., Ste. A
DeSoto, TX 75115
Phone: (972)298-4211
Fax: (972)298-6369
**Subject(s):** Paid Community Newspapers
**Circ:** (Free)☐100
(Paid)☐2,878

**Canyon Lake Times Guardian (29382)**
Times Guardian/Chronicle
PO Box 1940
1151 FM 2673
Canyon Lake, TX 78133
Phone: (830)907-3882
Fax: (830)964-2771
**Subject(s):** Paid Community Newspapers
**Circ:** (Free)‡140
(Paid)‡2,860

**Stamford American (30456)**
112 E. McHarg St.
Stamford, TX 79553-4603
Phone: (325)773-3621
Fax: (325)773-3622
**Subject(s):** Paid Community Newspapers
**Circ:** ‡2,845

**Angleton Times (29100)**
700 Western Ave.
Angleton, TX 77515
Phone: (979)849-8581
Fax: (979)849-0230
**Subject(s):** Daily Newspapers
**Circ:** (Non-paid)♦78
(Paid)♦2,835

**Cleveland County Herald (1269)**
Talent Publishing L.L.C.
PO Box 657
Rison, AR 71665
Phone: (870)325-6412
Fax: (870)325-6127
**Subject(s):** Paid Community Newspapers
**Circ:** 2,800

**Sangre de Cristo Chronicle (20044)**
Centro Plz.
Drawer I
Angel Fire, NM 87710
Phone: (505)377-2358
Fax: (505)377-2679
**Subject(s):** Paid Community Newspapers
**Circ:** ‡2,800

**The Tulia Herald (30543)**
115 S Austin
PO Drawer 87
Tulia, TX 79088-0087
Phone: (806)995-3535
Fax: (806)995-3536

## Southern Central States

**Subject(s):** Paid Community Newspapers
**Circ:** (Paid)2,776

**Informer Star** (29369)
417 Ave. C
Burkburnett, TX 76354-3424
Phone: (940)569-2191
Fax: (940)569-0704
**Subject(s):** Paid Community Newspapers
**Circ:** ‡2,750

**The Shiner Gazette** (30433)
Shiner Gazette Inc.
713 N Ave. D.
PO Box 727
Shiner, TX 77984
Phone: (361)594-3346
Fax: (361)594-2655
**Subject(s):** Paid Community Newspapers
**Circ:** (Free)98
(Paid)2,748

**Frio-Nueces Current** (30262)
Frio-Nueces Publications Ltd.
PO Box 1208
321 East San Mararas
Pearsall, TX 78061-1208
Phone: (830)334-3643
Fax: (830)334-3647
**Subject(s):** Paid Community Newspapers
**Circ:** 2,700

**Jefferson Jimplecute** (30000)
205 W. Austin
PO Box 1007
Jefferson, TX 75657
Phone: (903)665-2462
Fax: (903)665-3802
**Subject(s):** Paid Community Newspapers
**Circ:** 2,700

**Nowata Star** (25443)
Vinita Printing Company Inc.
126 E. Cherokee
PO Box 429
Nowata, OK 74048
Phone: (918)273-2446
**Subject(s):** Paid Community Newspapers
**Circ:** ‡2,700

**The Schulenburg Sticker** (30422)
Schulenburg Sticker Inc.
PO Box 160
Schulenburg, TX 78956-0160
**Subject(s):** Paid Community Newspapers
**Circ:** (Free)⊕134
(Paid)⊕**2,709**

**Blackwell Journal-Tribune** (25269)
PO Box 760
Blackwell, OK 74631-0760
Phone: (405)363-3370
Fax: (405)363-4415
**Subject(s):** Daily Newspapers
**Circ:** (Mon.-Fri.)‡2,540
(Sun.)‡2,690

**Greenwood Democrat** (1114)
PO Box 398
38 Town Square
Greenwood, AR 72936-0398
Phone: (479)996-4494
Fax: (479)996-4122
**Subject(s):** Paid Community Newspapers
**Circ:** (Non-paid)12
(Paid)2,680

**Hughes County Times** (25675)
Box 38
120 S Main
Wetumka, OK 74883
Phone: (405)452-3294
Fax: (405)452-3329
**Subject(s):** Paid Community Newspapers
**Circ:** 2,650

**The Teague Chronicle** (30529)
319 Main
Box 631
Teague, TX 75860
Phone: (254)739-2141
Fax: (254)739-2144
**Subject(s):** Paid Community Newspapers
**Circ:** ‡2,650

**Dalhart Daily Texan** (29498)
Dalhart Publishing Co.
410 Denrock Ave.
Dalhart, TX 79022
Phone: (806)244-4511
Fax: (806)244-2395
**Subject(s):** Daily Newspapers
**Circ:** (Tues.-Fri.)‡2,600
(Sun.)‡2,600

**De Queen Daily Citizen** (1058)
404 De Queen Ave.
PO Box 1000
De Queen, AR 71832
Phone: (870)642-2111
**Subject(s):** Daily Newspapers
**Circ:** ‡2,601

**Lonoke Democrat** (1204)
Magie Enterprises Inc.
402 N Center
PO Box 747
Lonoke, AR 72086
**Subject(s):** Paid Community Newspapers
**Circ:** (Free)100
(Paid)2,600

**Saint Bernard Voice** (12054)
234 Mehle Ave.
Arabi, LA 70032-1054
**Subject(s):** Paid Community Newspapers
**Circ:** (Paid)⊕**2,600**

**Union County Leader** (20056)
15 N. 1st St.
Clayton, NM 88415
Phone: (505)374-2587
Fax: (505)374-8117
**Subject(s):** Paid Community Newspapers
**Circ:** (Free)⊕31
(Paid)⊕**2,602**

**The Westville Reporter** (25674)
Community First Holdings Inc.
122 S. William
PO Box 550
Westville, OK 74965-0550
Phone: (918)723-5445
Fax: (918)723-5511
**Subject(s):** Paid Community Newspapers
**Circ:** (Paid)2,600

**The Waller County News-Citizen** (29806)
ASP Westward L.P.
PO Box 556
Hempstead, TX 77445
Phone: (979)826-3361
Fax: (979)826-3360
**Subject(s):** Paid Community Newspapers
**Circ:** (Paid)‡2,551

**The Olney Enterprise** (30233)
Enterprise Publishing Company Inc.
213 E Main
PO Box 577
Olney, TX 76374
Phone: (940)564-5558
**Subject(s):** Paid Community Newspapers
**Circ:** ‡2,528

**The Baylor County Banner** (30430)
Banner Publishing Co.
109 E Morris St.
PO Box 912
Seymour, TX 76380
Phone: (940)889-2616
Fax: (940)889-3610
**Subject(s):** Paid Community Newspapers
**Circ:** (Free)45
(Paid)2,518

**Amite Tangi-Digest** (12052)
120 NE Central
PO Box 698
Amite, LA 70422
Phone: (985)748-7156
Fax: (985)748-7104
**Subject(s):** Paid Community Newspapers
**Circ:** ‡2,500

**Arka Tech** (1274)
Arkansas Tech University
Bryan Hall, Rm. 102
Russellville, AR 72801-2222
Phone: (479)968-0343

Fax: (479)890-8074
**Subject(s):** College Publications
**Circ:** (Free)‡2,500

**Beebe News** (1011)
107 E. Center St.,
PO Box 910
Beebe, AR 72012-0910
Phone: (501)882-5414
Fax: (501)882-3576
**Subject(s):** Paid Community Newspapers
**Circ:** ‡2,500

**The Business Journal** (30437)
San Patricio Publishing Company Inc.
PO Drawer B
Sinton, TX 78387
Phone: (361)364-1270
Fax: (361)364-3833
**Subject(s):** Paid Community Newspapers
**Circ:** ‡2,500

**The Courier** (29690)
Brookhaven College
3939 Valley View Ln.
Farmers Branch, TX 75244
Phone: (972)860-4787
Fax: (972)860-4142
**Subject(s):** College Publications
**Circ:** (Free)2,500

**Courier-Index** (1213)
PO Box 569
Marianna, AR 72360-0569
Phone: (870)295-2521
Fax: (870)295-9662
**Subject(s):** Paid Community Newspapers
**Circ:** ‡2,500

**Falfurrias Facts** (29689)
Falfurrias Publishing Company Inc.
219 E Rice St.
PO Box 619
Falfurrias, TX 78355
Phone: (512)325-2200
Fax: (512)325-2200
**Subject(s):** Paid Community Newspapers
**Circ:** (Paid)⊕**2,500**

**Journal** (29414)
The Clyde Journal
PO Box 979
Clyde, TX 79510
Phone: (325)893-4244
Fax: (325)893-2780
**Subject(s):** Paid Community Newspapers
**Circ:** 2,500

**Lindsay News** (25396)
Cable Printing Co.
117 S Main St.
PO Box 768
Lindsay, OK 73052
Phone: (405)756-4045
Fax: (405)756-2729
**Subject(s):** Paid Community Newspapers
**Circ:** (Paid)⊕**2,500**

**Mamou Acadian Press** (12422)
PO Box 220
Ville Platte, LA 70586
Phone: (337)363-2103
Fax: (337)363-2841
**Subject(s):** Free Newspapers
**Circ:** (Paid)64
(Free)2,500

**Oklahoma Banker** (25466)
Oklahoma Bankers Association
643 NE 41st St.
PO Box 18246
Oklahoma City, OK 73154-0246
Phone: (405)424-5252
Fax: (405)424-4518
**Subject(s):** Banking, Finance, and Investments
**Circ:** ‡2,500

**The Pacer** (30110)
Angelina College
PO Box 1768
Lufkin, TX 75902-1768
Phone: (936)633-5288
Fax: (936)633-5247

**Gale Directory of Publications & Broadcast Media/140th Ed.**         **Southern Central States**

**Subject(s):** College Publications
**Circ:** (Free)‡2,500

**The Ranger (29082)**
Amarillo College
PO Box 447
Amarillo, TX 79178-0001
Phone: (806)371-5290
Fax: (806)371-5398
**Subject(s):** College Publications
**Circ:** (Free)‡2,500

**San Patricio County News (30438)**
San Patricio Publishing Company Inc.
PO Drawer B
Sinton, TX 78387
Phone: (361)364-1270
Fax: (361)364-3833
**Subject(s):** Paid Community Newspapers
**Circ:** ‡2,500

**Stroud American (25579)**
Stroud American Inc.
PO Box 400
315 W Main St
Stroud, OK 74079
Phone: (918)968-2581
Fax: (918)968-3864
**Subject(s):** Paid Community Newspapers
**Circ:** ‡2,500

**Tri-City Tribune (1214)**
PO Box 490
Marked Tree, AR 72365
Phone: (870)358-2993
Fax: (870)358-4538
**Subject(s):** Paid Community Newspapers
**Circ:** ‡2,500

**The Wichitan (30639)**
Midwestern State University
3410 Taft Blvd.
Box 14
Wichita Falls, TX 76308-2099
Phone: (940)397-4000
**Subject(s):** College Publications
**Circ:** (Paid)‡50
     (Free)‡2,500

**Floyd County Hesperian-Beacon (29699)**
Hesperian
111 E Missouri St.
Floydada, TX 79235
Phone: (806)983-3737
Fax: (806)983-3141
**Subject(s):** Paid Community Newspapers
**Circ:** (Free)31
     (Paid)2,485

**San Jacinto News Times (30413)**
Polk County Publishing Company Inc.
PO Box 1276
Livingston, TX 77351
Phone: (936)327-4357
Fax: (936)327-7156
**Subject(s):** Paid Community Newspapers
**Circ:** 2,486

**Post Dispatch (1056)**
Russellville Newspapers
107 Harrison St.
PO Box 270
Dardanelle, AR 72834-0270
Phone: (479)229-2250
Fax: (479)229-1159
**Subject(s):** Paid Community Newspapers
**Circ:** (Free)‡96
     (Paid)‡2,462

**Rains County Leader (29683)**
PO Box 127
239 North Texes
Emory, TX 75440
Phone: (903)473-2653
Fax: (903)473-0050
**Subject(s):** Paid Community Newspapers
**Circ:** ‡2,467

**Refugio County Press (30304)**
PO Drawer 200
Refugio, TX 78377
Phone: (361)526-2397
Fax: (361)526-2398

**Subject(s):** Paid Community Newspapers
**Circ:** (Free)‡34
     (Paid)‡2,461

**The Alvin Sun (29073)**
Henderson Newspapers Inc.
570 Dula St.
Alvin, TX 77511-2942
Phone: (281)331-4421
Fax: (281)331-4424
**Subject(s):** Paid Community Newspapers
**Circ:** (Free)20
     (Paid)2,450

**Cherokee Messenger & Republican (25285)**
216 S Grand Ave.
PO Box 245
Cherokee, OK 73728
Phone: (580)596-3344
Fax: (580)596-2959
**Subject(s):** Paid Community Newspapers
**Circ:** ‡2,450

**Eagle Lake Headlight (29640)**
Eagle Publishing Inc.
220 E Main
PO Box 67
Eagle Lake, TX 77434-0067
Phone: (979)234-5521
Fax: (979)234-5522
**Subject(s):** Paid Community Newspapers
**Circ:** (Free)‡46
     (Paid)‡2,450

**The Prague Times-Herald (25531)**
N Jim Thrope Blvd
PO Box U
Prague, OK 74864
Phone: (405)567-3933
Fax: (405)567-3934
**Subject(s):** Paid Community Newspapers
**Circ:** ‡2,450

**The Slatonite (30439)**
Slaton Publishing Co.
139 S 9th St.
P O Box 667
Slaton, TX 79364-0667
Phone: (806)828-6201
Fax: (806)828-6202
**Subject(s):** Paid Community Newspapers
**Circ:** ‡2,450

**Lamb County Leader-News (30065)**
Lamb County Publishing Company Inc.
PO Box 310
313 West 4th Street
Littlefield, TX 79339-0310
Phone: (806)385-4481
Fax: (806)385-4640
**Subject(s):** Paid Community Newspapers
**Circ:** (Combined)‡2,425

**Chronicle (1005)**
The Atkins Chronicle
204 Ave. One NE
PO Box 188
Atkins, AR 72823
Phone: (479)641-7161
Fax: (479)641-1604
**Subject(s):** Paid Community Newspapers
**Circ:** 2,400

**The Guardian-Journal (12177)**
PO Box 119
620 North Main St.
Homer, LA 71040-0119
Phone: (318)927-3541
Fax: (318)927-3542
**Subject(s):** Paid Community Newspapers
**Circ:** (Free)1,100
     (Paid)2,400

**The Junction Eagle (30006)**
215 N. 6th St.
PO Box 226
Junction, TX 76849
Phone: (915)446-4025
Fax: (915)446-4025
**Subject(s):** Paid Community Newspapers
**Circ:** (Paid)2,400

**The Lovington Daily Leader (20126)**
14 W Ave. B
PO Box 1717
Lovington, NM 88260
Phone: (505)396-2844
Fax: (505)396-5775
**Subject(s):** Daily Newspapers
**Circ:** (Free)50
     (Paid)2,390

**Skiatook Journal (25558)**
500 W Rogers Blvd.
Skiatook, OK 74070
Phone: (918)396-1616
Fax: (918)396-1618
**Subject(s):** Paid Community Newspapers
**Circ:** (Paid)‡2,373

**Wellington Leader (30621)**
913 W Ave.
Box 992
Wellington, TX 79095
Phone: (806)447-2559
Fax: (806)447-2463
**Subject(s):** Paid Community Newspapers
**Circ:** (Free)95
     (Paid)2,350

**The Community News (29059)**
PO Box 1031
Aledo, TX 76008
Phone: (817)441-7661
Fax: (817)441-7881
**Subject(s):** Paid Community Newspapers
**Circ:** (Paid)⊕**2,328**

**The Ballinger Ledger (29278)**
810 Hutchins
Ballinger, TX 76821
Phone: (325)365-3501
Fax: (325)365-5389
**Subject(s):** Paid Community Newspapers
**Circ:** (Thurs.)‡2,300

**Cameron Parish Pilot (12127)**
PO Box 995
DeQuincy, LA 70633
Phone: (318)786-8004
Fax: (318)786-8131
**Subject(s):** Paid Community Newspapers
**Circ:** ‡2,300

**The Cauldron (29827)**
University of St. Thomas
3800 Montrose Blvd.
Houston, TX 77006
Phone: (713)525-3579
Fax: (713)525-2159
**Subject(s):** College Publications
**Circ:** (Free)‡2,300

**Forney Messenger (29702)**
Forney Messenger Inc.
201 W Broad St.
PO Box 936
Forney, TX 75126-0936
Phone: (972)564-3121
Fax: (972)552-3599
**Subject(s):** Paid Community Newspapers
**Circ:** ‡2,300

**The Seminole Sentinel (30426)**
406 S Main St.
PO Drawer 1200
Seminole, TX 79360
Phone: (432)758-3667
Fax: (432)758-2136
**Subject(s):** Paid Community Newspapers
**Circ:** ‡2,300

**West Carroll Gazette (12356)**
North Louisiana Publishing Inc.
PO Box 1007
Oak Grove, LA 71263
Phone: (318)428-3207
Fax: (318)428-2747
**Subject(s):** Paid Community Newspapers
**Circ:** ‡2,300

**Cedar Hill Today (29392)**
Today Newspapers Inc.
1701 N. Hampton Rd., Ste. A
DeSoto, TX 75115
Phone: (972)298-4211
Fax: (972)298-6369

---

Circulation: ★ = ABC; △ = BPA; ♦ = CAC; ● = CCAB; ❑ = VAC; ⊕ = PO Statement; ‡ = Publisher's Report; Boldface figures = sworn; Light figures = estimated.

## Southern Central States

**Subject(s):** Paid Community Newspapers
**Circ:** (Free)☐100
(Paid)☐2,269

**The South Grand Laker  (25348)**
The Grove Sun Daily
14 W 3rd St.
Grove, OK 74344
Phone: (918)786-2228
Fax: (918)786-2156
**Subject(s):** Paid Community Newspapers
**Circ:** (Combined)2,260

**The Vinton News  (12426)**
News Leader Inc.
716 E Napoleon
PO Box 1999
Sulphur, LA 70664-1999
Phone: (337)462-1186
Fax: (318)528-9557
**Subject(s):** Paid Community Newspapers
**Circ:** ‡2,260

**Charleston Express  (1037)**
PO Box 39
511 Main St.
Charleston, AR 72933
Phone: (479)965-7368
Fax: (479)965-7206
**Subject(s):** Paid Community Newspapers
**Circ:** (Free)25
(Paid)2,250

**The Friona Star  (29741)**
Friona Stan
916 Main
Po Box 789
Friona, TX 79035
Phone: (806)250-2211
Fax: (806)250-5127
**Subject(s):** Paid Community Newspapers
**Circ:** ‡2,250

**Real American  (30052)**
Real American Newspaper Corp.
PO Box 840
Leakey, TX 78873-0840
Phone: (830)232-5204
Fax: (830)232-5630
**Subject(s):** Paid Community Newspapers
**Circ:** ‡2,250

**Waldron News  (1307)**
PO Box 745
Waldron, AR 72958
Phone: (479)637-4161
Fax: (479)637-4162
**Subject(s):** Paid Community Newspapers
**Circ:** 2,250

**Lincoln Ledger  (1290)**
Lincoln County Publishing Company Inc.
216 W Bradley
Star City, AR 71667
Phone: (870)628-4161
Fax: (870)628-3802
**Subject(s):** Paid Community Newspapers
**Circ:** (Free)‡75
(Paid)‡2,225

**The Mc Gregor Mirror and Crawford Sun  (30142)**
311 S Main
Mc Gregor, TX 76657-0415
Phone: (254)840-2091
Fax: (254)840-2091
**Subject(s):** Paid Community Newspapers
**Circ:** 2,229

**Henryetta Daily Free-Lance  (25362)**
Community Newspaper Holdings Inc.
PO Box 848
812 W. Main
Henryetta, OK 74437
Phone: (918)652-3311
Fax: (918)652-7407
**Subject(s):** Paid Community Newspapers
**Circ:** (Controlled)‡2,212

**Banner-Democrat  (12224)**
313 Lake St.
Lake Providence, LA 71254-2688
Phone: (318)559-2750
Fax: (318)559-2750

**Subject(s):** Paid Community Newspapers; Farm Newspapers
**Circ:** ‡2,200

**Cass County Sun  (30063)**
103 E Houston
PO Box 779
Linden, TX 75563
Phone: (903)756-7396
Fax: (214)796-3294
**Subject(s):** Paid Community Newspapers
**Circ:** ‡2,200

**The Lake Cities Sun  (30035)**
Sun Newspapers
275 Market St.
PO Box 879
Lake Dallas, TX 75065
Phone: (940)497-4141
**Subject(s):** Paid Community Newspapers
**Circ:** (Free)‡200
(Paid)‡2,200

**Leonard Graphic  (30053)**
PO Box 1108
Leonard, TX 75452-1108
Phone: (903)587-3303
Fax: (903)587-9893
**Subject(s):** Paid Community Newspapers
**Circ:** ‡2,200

**The Midlothian Mirror  (30181)**
110 N 8th St.
PO Box 70
Midlothian, TX 76065
Phone: (972)775-4669
Fax: (972)723-0167
**Subject(s):** Paid Community Newspapers
**Circ:** ‡2,200

**Prairie Grove Enterprise  (1266)**
PO Box 650
Prairie Grove, AR 72753
Phone: (501)846-2191
Fax: (479)824-2192
**Subject(s):** Paid Community Newspapers
**Circ:** (Free)‡100
(Paid)‡2,200

**Santa Rosa News  (20177)**
PO Box 511
Santa Rosa, NM 88435
Phone: (505)472-5454
Fax: (505)472-5453
**Subject(s):** Paid Community Newspapers; Spanish
**Circ:** ‡2,200

**Bixby Bulletin  (25267)**
8545 E 41st. St.
Tulsa, OK 74145
Phone: (918)663-1414
Fax: (918)664-8161
**Subject(s):** Paid Community Newspapers
**Circ:** (Paid)‡2,197

**The Texan Express  (29768)**
202 S Commercial
PO Box 1
Goliad, TX 77963
Phone: (361)645-2330
Fax: (361)645-2812
**Subject(s):** Paid Community Newspapers
**Circ:** (Free)‡26
(Paid)‡2,196

**Bogata News  (29318)**
Thunder Prairie Publishing Co.
Box 310
Bogata, TX 75417
Phone: (903)632-5322
Fax: (903)652-6041
**Subject(s):** Farm Newspapers
**Circ:** ‡2,184

**The Monitor  (30207)**
PO Box 39
101 W L Dodson Blvd.
Naples, TX 75568-0039
Phone: (903)897-2281
Fax: (903)897-2095
**Subject(s):** Paid Community Newspapers
**Circ:** (Free)49
(Paid)2,188

**Zachary Plainsman-News  (12438)**
Louisiana Suburban Press
5145 Main St.
Suite C
Zachary, LA 70791
Phone: (504)654-6841
Fax: (504)654-8271
**Subject(s):** Paid Community Newspapers
**Circ:** 2,163

**The Gurdon Times  (1115)**
PO Box 250
Gurdon, AR 71743-0250
Phone: (870)353-4482
**Subject(s):** Paid Community Newspapers
**Circ:** ‡2,132

**Castro County News  (29633)**
PO Box 67
Dimmitt, TX 79027-0067
Phone: (806)647-3123
**Subject(s):** Paid Community Newspapers
**Circ:** (Free)‡42
(Paid)‡2,127

**Daily Court Review  (29838)**
6807 Wynnwood
PO Box 1889
Houston, TX 77008
Phone: (713)869-5434
Fax: (713)869-8887
**Subject(s):** Daily Periodicals; Law; Real Estate
**Circ:** 2,120

**Lancaster Today  (30041)**
Today Newspapers Inc.
1701 N. Hampton Rd., Ste. A
DeSoto, TX 75115
Phone: (972)298-4211
Fax: (972)298-6369
**Subject(s):** Paid Community Newspapers
**Circ:** (Free)☐100
(Paid)☐2,126

**Jack County Herald  (29988)**
Jacksboro Newspapers
212 N Church
PO Drawer 70
Jacksboro, TX 76458
Phone: (940)567-2616
Fax: (940)567-2071
**Subject(s):** Paid Community Newspapers
**Circ:** (Paid)⊕2,111

**Jacksboro Gazette-News  (29989)**
Jacksboro Newspapers
212 N Church
PO Drawer 70
Jacksboro, TX 76458
Phone: (940)567-2616
Fax: (940)567-2071
**Subject(s):** Paid Community Newspapers
**Circ:** (Paid)⊕2,111

**The Big Bend Sentinel  (30133)**
LaFrontera Publications Inc.
110 N Highland Ave.
PO Drawer P
Marfa, TX 79843-0459
Fax: (915)729-4601
**Subject(s):** Paid Community Newspapers
**Circ:** (Free)54
(Paid)2,106

**Cheyenne Star  (25286)**
PO Box 250
Cheyenne, OK 73628
Phone: (580)497-3324
Fax: (580)497-3516
**Subject(s):** Paid Community Newspapers
**Circ:** ‡2,100

**The Enterprise  (12364)**
PO Box 218
Ponchatoula, LA 70454
Phone: (985)386-6537
Fax: (985)386-6537
**Subject(s):** Paid Community Newspapers
**Circ:** (Free)‡250
(Paid)‡2,100

**The Haskell Free Press (29799)**
The Haskell Press
PO Box 555
Haskell, TX 79521-0555
Phone: (940)864-2686
Fax: (940)864-2687
Subject(s): Paid Community Newspapers
Circ: ‡2,100

**Haskell News (25358)**
PO Box 158
108 E. Main
Haskell, OK 74436
Phone: (918)482-5619
Fax: (918)482-5619
Subject(s): Paid Community Newspapers
Circ: ‡2,100

**The Modern News (1117)**
PO Box 400
Harrisburg, AR 72432
Phone: (870)578-2121
Fax: (870)578-9415
Subject(s): Paid Community Newspapers
Circ: (Free)30
(Paid)2,100

**Westlake/Moss Bluff News (12433)**
News Leader Inc.
PO Box 127
Westlake, LA 70669
Phone: (318)436-0583
Fax: (318)436-0584
Subject(s): Paid Community Newspapers
Circ: ‡2,091

**The Mathis News (30140)**
San Patricio Publishing Company Inc.
620 E. San Patricio
Mathis, TX 78368
Phone: (512)547-3274
Fax: (512)547-3275
Subject(s): Paid Community Newspapers
Circ: (Free)‡50
(Paid)‡2,071

**The Rosebud News (30317)**
PO Box 516
Rosebud, TX 76570
Phone: (254)583-2493
Fax: (254)583-4000
Subject(s): Paid Community Newspapers
Circ: 2,074

**The Cisco Press (29400)**
Po Box 29 Iseland
Cisco, TX 76437-0470
Phone: (254)442-2244
Fax: (254)629-2092
Subject(s): Paid Community Newspapers
Circ: ‡2,050

**Springtown Epigraph (30452)**
109 First St.
Springtown, TX 76082
Phone: (817)220-7217
Fax: (817)523-4457
Subject(s): Paid Community Newspapers
Circ: (Paid)⊕2,015

**Bossier Press Tribune (12119)**
Bossier Newspapers
PO Box 6267
Bossier City, LA 71171
Phone: (318)747-7900
Fax: (318)747-5298
Subject(s): Paid Community Newspapers
Circ: (Free)300
(Paid)2,000

**The Canadian Record (29377)**
211 Main St.
PO Box 898
Canadian, TX 79014
Phone: (806)323-6461
Fax: (806)323-5738
Subject(s): Paid Community Newspapers
Circ: ‡2,000

**Chicot County Spectator (1157)**
105 N Court St.
PO Box 552
Lake Village, AR 71653
Phone: (870)265-2071
Fax: (870)265-2807

Subject(s): Paid Community Newspapers
Circ: ‡2,000

**Choctaw County Times (25370)**
128 E.Jackson
Hugo, OK 74743
Phone: (580)326-8353
Fax: (580)326-6397
Circ: (Free)100
(Paid)2,000

**Clay County Democrat (1268)**
Delta Publishing Co.
P.O. Box 366
Rector, AR 72461
Phone: (870)595-3549
Fax: (870)595-3611
Subject(s): Paid Community Newspapers
Circ: 2,000

**Electra Star-News (29682)**
PO Box 1192
Electra, TX 76360
Phone: (940)495-2149
Fax: (940)495-2627
Subject(s): Paid Community Newspapers
Circ: (Free)‡100
(Paid)‡2,000

**The Grapeland Messenger (29777)**
Grapeland Printing
Box 99
Grapeland, TX 75844
Phone: (936)687-2424
Fax: (936)544-9695
Subject(s): Paid Community Newspapers
Circ: (Free)‡300
(Paid)‡2,000

**The Herald-Democrat (25262)**
108 S Douglas
PO Box 490
Beaver, OK 73932
Phone: (580)625-3241
Fax: (580)625-4269
Subject(s): Paid Community Newspapers
Circ: ‡2,000

**Jacksonville Patriot (1030)**
Magie Enterprises Inc.
9035 S. Pine
PO Box 1058
Cabot, AR 72023
Phone: (501)843-3534
Fax: (501)843-6447
Subject(s): Daily Newspapers
Circ: (Non-paid)‡131
(Paid)‡2,000

**The Luling Newsboy & Signal (30118)**
Luling Publishing Company Inc.
415 E Davis St.
Luling, TX 78648
Phone: (830)875-2116
Fax: (830)875-2124
Subject(s): Paid Community Newspapers
Circ: ‡2,009

**Nevada County Picayune (1267)**
Nevada County
PO Box 60
Prescott, AR 71857
Phone: (501)887-2002
Fax: (501)887-2949
Subject(s): Paid Community Newspapers
Circ: 2,000

**News (30217)**
Nocona News
PO Box 539
Nocona, TX 76255
Phone: (940)825-3201
Subject(s): Paid Community Newspapers
Circ: 2,000

**Northwestern News (25245)**
Northwestern Oklahoma State University
Jesse Dunn Annex, Rm. 232
709 Oklahoma Blvd.
Alva, OK 73717
Phone: (580)327-8479
Fax: (580)327-8660
Subject(s): College Publications
Circ: 2,000

**Observer/Enterprise (30312)**
PO Box 1329
Robert Lee, TX 76945
Phone: (325)453-2433
Fax: (325)453-4643
Subject(s): Paid Community Newspapers
Circ: 2,000

**The OBU Bison (25550)**
Oklahoma Baptist University
Journalism Dept., Box 61704
500 W. University Blvd.
Shawnee, OK 74804
Phone: (405)275-2850
Fax: (405)878-2113
Subject(s): College Publications
Circ: (Free)‡2,000

**Palacios Beacon (30240)**
Toney Publishing
PO Box 817
Palacios, TX 77465
Phone: (361)972-3009
Fax: (361)972-2610
Subject(s): Paid Community Newspapers
Circ: (Paid)‡2,000

**Pawhuska Journal-Capital (25515)**
Community Newspaper Holdings Inc.
PO Box 238
Pawhuska, OK 74056
Phone: (918)287-1590
Fax: (918)287-1804
Subject(s): Paid Community Newspapers
Circ: 2,000

**Pecos Enterprise (30265)**
324 S Cedar St.
PO Box 2057
Pecos, TX 79772
Phone: (432)445-5475
Fax: (432)445-4321
Subject(s): Daily Newspapers
Circ: 2,000

**Post Signal (30274)**
Lewis Newspapers Inc.
111 E Main
PO Box 249
Pilot Point, TX 76258
Phone: (940)686-2169
Fax: (940)686-2437
Subject(s): Paid Community Newspapers
Circ: 2,000

**The Texas Spur (30453)**
121 E. Third
Spur, TX 79370
Phone: (806)271-3336
Fax: (806)271-3966
Subject(s): Paid Community Newspapers
Circ: 2,000

**University News (29983)**
University of Dallas
1845 E. Northgate Dr.
U.D. Box 732
Irving, TX 75062-4736
Phone: (972)721-5000
Subject(s): College Publications
Circ: (Free)‡2,000

**Viking Banner (25529)**
Carl Albert State College
1507 S McKenna St.
Poteau, OK 74953-5208
Phone: (918)647-1200
Fax: (918)647-1266
Subject(s): College Publications
Circ: ‡2,000

**Montgomery County News (1228)**
Graves Publishing Co.
PO Box 195
Mount Ida, AR 71957
Phone: (501)867-2821
Fax: (501)356-4400
Subject(s): Paid Community Newspapers
Circ: ‡1,950

Circulation: ★ = ABC; △ = BPA; ♦ = CAC; • = CCAB; □ = VAC; ⊕ = PO Statement; ‡ = Publisher's Report; Boldface figures = sworn; Light figures = estimated.

## Southern Central States

**Centerville News (29395)**
Centerville News Inc.
204 E Main St.
PO Box 97
Centerville, TX 75833-0097
Phone: (903)536-2015
Fax: (903)536-2329
**Subject(s):** Paid Community Newspapers
**Circ:** (Free)‡394
(Paid)‡1,906

**The Gladewater Mirror (29766)**
Cox Enterprises
PO Box 1352
Gladewater, TX 75647-1352
Phone: (903)845-2235
Fax: (903)845-2257
**Subject(s):** Paid Community Newspapers
**Circ:** ‡1,900

**St. Francisville Democrat (12378)**
Louisiana Suburban Press
4749 Johnson St.
PO Drawer 1876
Saint Francisville, LA 70775-1876
Phone: (504)635-3366
Fax: (504)635-3398
**Subject(s):** Paid Community Newspapers
**Circ:** ‡1,900

**St. Helena Echo (12165)**
PO Box 190
Greensburg, LA 70441
Phone: (225)222-4541
Fax: (225)222-4542
**Subject(s):** Paid Community Newspapers
**Circ:** ‡1,900

**White Deer News (30634)**
The White Deer News
206 S Main St.
PO Box 728
White Deer, TX 79097
Phone: (806)883-4881
Fax: (806)883-4881
**Subject(s):** Paid Community Newspapers
**Circ:** 1,900

**Chelsea Reporter (25284)**
Chelsea Reporter
Box 6
Chelsea, OK 74016
Phone: (918)789-2331
Fax: (918)789-2333
**Subject(s):** Paid Community Newspapers
**Circ:** ‡1,889

**Lincoln County News (20055)**
309 Central Ave.
PO Box 459
Carrizozo, NM 88301-0459
Phone: (505)648-2333
Fax: (505)648-2333
**Subject(s):** Paid Community Newspapers
**Circ:** (Free)93
(Paid)1,823

**The Albany News (29058)**
Lucas Publications Inc.
49 S. Main St.
PO Box 278
Albany, TX 76430
Phone: (915)762-2201
Fax: (915)762-3201
**Subject(s):** Paid Community Newspapers
**Circ:** 1,800

**The Boise City News (25271)**
105 W Main
PO Box 278
Boise City, OK 73933-0278
Phone: (580)544-2222
Fax: (580)544-3281
**Subject(s):** Paid Community Newspapers; Farm Newspapers
**Circ:** (Free)60
(Paid)1,800

**The Davis News (25300)**
400 E Main St.
PO Box 98
Davis, OK 73030-0098
Phone: (580)369-2807
Fax: (580)369-2574
**Subject(s):** Free Newspapers
**Circ:** (Paid)‡1,800

**The Interstate Progress (12236)**
Natchitoches Times Publications
PO Box 840
Mansfield, LA 71052-0840
**Subject(s):** Paid Community Newspapers
**Circ:** ‡1,800

**The Jewett Messenger (30001)**
Jewett Messenger Inc.
Hwy. 79 & Division
104 N Main
PO Box 155
Jewett, TX 75846
Phone: (903)626-4296
Fax: (903)626-5248
**Subject(s):** Paid Community Newspapers
**Circ:** 1,800

**McCrory Monitor-Leader-Advocate (1217)**
Gladys Price Press
PO Box 898
McCrory, AR 72101
Phone: (870)731-2263
Fax: (870)731-5899
**Subject(s):** Paid Community Newspapers
**Circ:** ‡1,800

**Muenster Enterprise (30196)**
PO Box 190
Muenster, TX 76252-0190
Phone: (940)759-4311
Fax: (940)759-4110
**Subject(s):** Paid Community Newspapers
**Circ:** (Free)20
(Paid)1,800

**Muleshoe and Baily County Journal (30197)**
Muleshoe Journal
201 W. Avenue C
PO Box 449
Muleshoe, TX 79347
Phone: (806)272-4536
Fax: (806)272-3567
**Subject(s):** Paid Community Newspapers
**Circ:** ‡1,800

**Murfreesboro Diamond (1237)**
Graves Publishing Co.
PO Box 297
Nashville, AR 71852
Phone: (870)845-2010
Fax: (870)845-5091
**Subject(s):** Paid Community Newspapers
**Circ:** ‡1,800

**The Post Dispatch (30295)**
123 E Main
PO Box 426
Post, TX 79356-0426
Phone: (806)495-2816
Fax: (806)495-2059
**Subject(s):** Paid Community Newspapers
**Circ:** 1,800

**Carnegie Herald (25282)**
Carnegie Herald Publishing Co.
14 W Main
PO Box 129
Carnegie, OK 73015-0129
Phone: (580)654-1443
Fax: (580)654-1608
**Subject(s):** Paid Community Newspapers
**Circ:** ‡1,795

**The Ozona Stockman (30237)**
1000 Ave. E.
PO Box 370
Ozona, TX 76943-2551
Phone: (915)392-2551
Fax: (915)392-2439
**Subject(s):** Paid Community Newspapers
**Circ:** (Paid)1,755

**The Hansford County Reporter-Statesman (30450)**
213 Main St.
Spearman, TX 79081
Phone: (806)659-3434
Fax: (806)659-3368
**Subject(s):** Paid Community Newspapers
**Circ:** ‡1,700

**Panhandle Herald (30249)**
Box 429
Panhandle, TX 79068-0429
Phone: (806)537-3634

Fax: (806)537-3634
**Subject(s):** Paid Community Newspapers
**Circ:** (Free)‡42
(Paid)‡1,700

**Wynnewood Gazette (25684)**
PO Box 309
210 South Dean A McGee
Wynnewood, OK 73098-0309
Phone: (405)665-4333
Fax: (405)665-4334
**Subject(s):** Paid Community Newspapers
**Circ:** 1,700

**The Times of Northeast Benton County (1256)**
PO Box 25
Pea Ridge, AR 72751
Phone: (479)451-1196
Fax: (479)451-9456
**Subject(s):** Paid Community Newspapers
**Circ:** ‡1,690

**De Queen Bee (1057)**
De Queen Bee Co.
404 De Queen Ave.
PO Box 1000
De Queen, AR 71832
Phone: (870)642-2111
Fax: (870)642-3138
**Subject(s):** Paid Community Newspapers
**Circ:** ‡1,677

**Deport Times (29629)**
Thunder Prairie Publishing Co.
PO Box 98
Deport, TX 75435
Phone: (903)652-4205
Fax: (903)652-6041
**Subject(s):** Paid Community Newspapers
**Circ:** ‡1,675

**Hartshorne Sun (25357)**
PO Box 330
1005 Penn Ave
Hartshorne, OK 74547
Phone: (918)297-2577
Fax: (918)297-2577
**Subject(s):** Paid Community Newspapers
**Circ:** ‡1,671

**Grand Prairie Herald (1123)**
Herald Publishing Company Inc.
77 Highway 70 W.
PO Box 370
Hazen, AR 72064
Phone: (870)255-4538
Fax: (870)255-4539
**Subject(s):** Paid Community Newspapers
**Circ:** (Free)50
(Paid)1,650

**Leader Tribune (25382)**
205 S Broadway
PO Box 370
Laverne, OK 73848
Phone: (580)921-3391
Fax: (580)921-3392
**Subject(s):** Paid Community Newspapers
**Circ:** ‡1,650

**The Paducah Post (30239)**
PO Box E
Paducah, TX 79248
Phone: (806)492-3585
**Subject(s):** Paid Community Newspapers
**Circ:** ‡1,645

**The Honey Grove Signal-Citizen (25306)**
The Bonham Daily Favorite
200 Beech St.
Durant, OK 74701
**Subject(s):** Paid Community Newspapers
**Circ:** (Free)45
(Paid)1,637

**Church Point News (12128)**
315 North Main Street
Drawer 319
Church Point, LA 70525
Phone: (337)684-5711
Fax: (337)684-5793
**Subject(s):** Paid Community Newspapers
**Circ:** 1,600

**The Clarendon Enterprise  (29401)**
105 S. Kearney St.
PO Box 1110
Clarendon, TX 79226-1110
Phone: (806)874-2259
Fax: (806)874-2423
**Subject(s):** Paid Community Newspapers

**Circ:** ‡1,600

**Kinder Courier-News  (12187)**
PO Drawer A K
Kinder, LA 70648
Phone: (337)738-5642
Fax: (337)738-5630
**Subject(s):** Paid Community Newspapers

**Circ:**  1,600

**Groveton News  (29786)**
Polk County Publishing
PO Box 730
Groveton, TX 75845
Phone: (409)642-1891
**Subject(s):** Paid Community Newspapers

**Circ:**  (Free)40
            (Paid)1,583

**Advance Star Record  (30321)**
PO Drawer A
Rotan, TX 79546
Phone: (325)735-2562
Fax: (325)735-2230
**Subject(s):** Paid Community Newspapers

**Circ:** ‡1,550

**Fairfax Chief  (25332)**
153 E Elm
Fairfax, OK 74637
Phone: (918)642-3814
Fax: (918)642-1376
**Subject(s):** Paid Community Newspapers

**Circ:**  (Free)50
            (Paid)1,550

**Tribune-Progress  (29280)**
Tribune Progress News
108 W Clark
PO Box 50
Bartlett, TX 76511-0050
Phone: (254)527-4333
Fax: (254)527-4333
**Subject(s):** Paid Community Newspapers

**Circ:**  (Paid)1,550

**The Merkel Mail  (30163)**
PO Box 428
Merkel, TX 79536
Phone: (325)928-5712
Fax: (325)928-5899
**Subject(s):** Paid Community Newspapers

**Circ:** ‡1,538

**Carlisle Independent  (1035)**
Magie Enterprises Inc.
PO Box 47
Carlisle, AR 72024
Phone: (501)552-3111
**Subject(s):** Paid Community Newspapers

**Circ:**  (Free)109
            (Paid)1,515

**Newkirk Herald-Journal  (25422)**
121 N Main St.
PO Box 131
Newkirk, OK 74647-0131
Phone: (580)362-2140
Fax: (580)362-2348
**Subject(s):** Paid Community Newspapers

**Circ:**  (Free)‡200
            (Paid)‡1,510

**Catoosa Times  (25593)**
Retherford Publications Inc.
8545 E. 41st St.
Tulsa, OK 74145-3305
Phone: (918)663-1414
**Subject(s):** Free Newspapers

**Circ:**  (Paid)‡1,500

**Chandler & Brownsboro Statesman  (29338)**
Chandler & Brownsboro
PO Box 168
14631 State Highway 31 East
Brownsboro, TX 75756-0168
Phone: (903)852-7641
Fax: (903)852-7631

**Subject(s):** Paid Community Newspapers
**Circ:**  (Paid)‡1,500

**Health City Sun  (19995)**
900 Park Ave. SW
PO Box 1517
Albuquerque, NM 87103
Phone: (505)242-3010
Fax: (505)842-5464
**Subject(s):** Paid Community Newspapers

**Circ:**  (Free)⊕500
            (Paid)⊕**1,500**

**Johnson City Record Courier  (30002)**
Hill Country Community Press
PO Box 205
Johnson City, TX 78636
Phone: (830)868-7181
Fax: (830)868-7182
**Subject(s):** Paid Community Newspapers

**Circ:**  1,500

**The Maverick  (25587)**
Northern Oklahoma College
1220 E. Grand
PO Box 310
Tonkawa, OK 74653
Phone: (580)628-6200
Fax: (580)628-6371
**Subject(s):** College Publications

**Circ:**  (Free)1,500

**Medford Patriot-Star and Grant County Journal  (25411)**
Grant County News
PO Box 49
Medford, OK 73759-0049
Phone: (580)395-2212
Fax: (580)395-2907
**Subject(s):** Paid Community Newspapers

**Circ:**  (Paid)⊕**1,500**

**Quanah Tribune-Chief  (30297)**
310 Mercer St.
Quanah, TX 79252
Phone: (940)663-5333
Fax: (940)663-5073
**Subject(s):** Paid Community Newspapers

**Circ:**  1500

**Van Alstyne Leader  (30574)**
209 N. Dallas
PO Box 578
Van Alstyne, TX 75495
Phone: (903)482-5253
Fax: (903)482-5656
**Subject(s):** Paid Community Newspapers

**Circ:**  1,500

**Yellow Jacket  (29350)**
Howard Payne University
1000 Fisk
Brownwood, TX 76801
Phone: (325)649-8514
Fax: (325)649-8902
**Subject(s):** College Publications

**Circ:**  (Free)‡1,500

**Northwest Oklahoman and Ellis County News  (25545)**
Northwest Oklahoman
PO Box 460
Shattuck, OK 73858
Phone: (580)938-2533
Fax: (580)938-5240
**Subject(s):** Paid Community Newspapers

**Circ:** ‡1,491

**Enterprise  (30216)**
New Ulm Enterprise
PO Box 128
New Ulm, TX 78950
Phone: (979)992-3352
**Subject(s):** Paid Community Newspapers

**Circ:** ‡1,486

**The Ozark Journal  (1144)**
PO Box 598
Imboden, AR 72434
Phone: (870)869-2220
**Subject(s):** Paid Community Newspapers

**Circ:** ‡1,483

**Kiowa County Democrat  (25559)**
610 E St.
PO Box 305
Snyder, OK 73566
Phone: (580)569-2684
Fax: (580)569-2640
**Subject(s):** Paid Community Newspapers

**Circ:** ‡1,475

**The Healdton Herald  (25359)**
Herald Company of Oklahoma Inc.
PO Box 250
Healdton, OK 73438
Phone: (580)229-0132
Fax: (580)229-0132
**Subject(s):** Paid Community Newspapers

**Circ:**  (Free)‡12
            (Paid)‡1,461

**News Progress  (25369)**
Ferguson & Ferguson
PO Box 38
115 West Main
Hominy, OK 74035-0038
Phone: (918)885-2101
Fax: (918)885-4596
**Subject(s):** Paid Community Newspapers

**Circ:**  (Non-paid)35
            (Paid)1,445

**Midlothian Today  (30182)**
Today Newspapers Inc.
PO Box 381029
Duncanville, TX 75138
**Subject(s):** Free Newspapers; Free Newspapers

**Circ:**  (Free)❏100
            (Paid)❏**1,437**

**The England Democrat  (1067)**
PO Drawer 250
121 E Haywood
England, AR 72046
Phone: (501)842-3111
Fax: (501)842-3081
**Subject(s):** Paid Community Newspapers

**Circ:** ‡1,426

**Barnsdall Times  (25259)**
Box 469
Barnsdall, OK 74002
Phone: (918)847-2916
Fax: (918)847-2115
**Subject(s):** Paid Community Newspapers

**Circ:**  1,400

**The Corrigan Times  (29483)**
PO Box 115-V
Corrigan, TX 75939
Phone: (936)398-2535
Fax: (936)327-7156
**Subject(s):** Paid Community Newspapers

**Circ:** ‡1,400

**De Baca County News  (20085)**
PO Box 448
503 East Summer
Fort Sumner, NM 88119-0448
Phone: (505)355-2462
Fax: (505)355-7253
**Subject(s):** Paid Community Newspapers

**Circ:** ‡1,400

**Devil's River News  (30446)**
228 E Main
Sonora, TX 76950
Phone: (325)387-2507
Fax: (325)387-5691
**Subject(s):** Paid Community Newspapers

**Circ:** ‡1,400

**The Foard County News  (29491)**
Po Box 489
108 S. First St.
Crowell, TX 79227-0489
Phone: (940)684-1355
Fax: (940)684-1700
**Subject(s):** Paid Community Newspapers

**Circ:** ‡1,400

**Gulf Coast Tribune  (30211)**
Toney Publishing
PO Box 488
Needville, TX 77461
Phone: (979)793-6560
Fax: (979)793-4260

## Southern Central States

**Subject(s):** Paid Community Newspapers
**Circ:** ‡1,400

**Joshua Tribune** (30005)
The Star Group
PO Drawer 909
Burleson, TX 76097-0909
Phone: (817)295-0486
Fax: (817)295-5278
**Subject(s):** Paid Community Newspapers
**Circ:** ‡1,400

**La Vernia News** (30033)
PO Box 129
La Vernia, TX 78121-0129
Phone: (830)779-3751
Fax: (830)779-3751
**Subject(s):** Paid Community Newspapers
**Circ:** (Free)‡30
(Paid)‡1,400

**Lynn County News** (30526)
Box 1170
Tahoka, TX 79373
Phone: (806)561-4888
Fax: (806)561-6308
**Subject(s):** Paid Community Newspapers
**Circ:** (Free)40
(Paid)1,400

**The Meeker News** (25412)
Box 686
620 W Carl Hubbell Blvd
Meeker, OK 74855-0686
Phone: (405)279-2363
Fax: (405)279-3850
**Subject(s):** Paid Community Newspapers
**Circ:** ‡1,400

**The Munday Courier** (30199)
111 E. B St.
PO Box 130
Munday, TX 76371
Phone: (940)422-4314
Fax: (940)422-4333
**Subject(s):** Paid Community Newspapers
**Circ:** (Free)41
(Paid)1,403

**The Newcastle Pacer** (25421)
Chickasaw Enterprises
PO Box 429
Newcastle, OK 73065
Phone: (405)387-5277
Fax: (405)387-9863
**Subject(s):** Paid Community Newspapers
**Circ:** ‡1,400

**The Normangee Star** (30218)
PO Box 97
Normangee, TX 77871
Phone: (936)396-3391
Fax: (936)396-2478
**Subject(s):** Paid Community Newspapers
**Circ:** ‡1,400

**Richland Beacons News** (12371)
The Delhi Dispatch
603 Louisa
PO Box 209
Rayville, LA 71269
Phone: (318)878-2444
Fax: (318)728-5991
**Subject(s):** Paid Community Newspapers
**Circ:** ‡1,400

**The McLoud News** (25410)
The McLoud News Inc.
109 N Main
PO Box 517
McLoud, OK 74851-0517
Phone: (405)964-6566
Fax: (405)946-2930
**Subject(s):** Paid Community Newspapers
**Circ:** (Combined)1,374

**Sentinel Leader** (25544)
Sentinel
PO Box 69
Sentinel, OK 73664
Phone: (580)393-4348
Fax: (580)393-4349
**Subject(s):** Paid Community Newspapers
**Circ:** 1,350

**The Basile Weekly** (12058)
PO Box 578
Basile, LA 70515
Phone: (337)432-6807
Fax: (337)432-6807
**Subject(s):** Paid Community Newspapers
**Circ:** (Free)‡36
(Paid)‡1,300

**The Big Lake Wildcat** (29307)
The Big Lake Wildcat Inc.
707 Florida Ave.
PO Box 946
Big Lake, TX 76932-0946
Phone: (325)884-2215
Fax: (325)884-5771
**Subject(s):** Paid Community Newspapers
**Circ:** ‡1,300

**The Bunkie Record** (12126)
Avoyelles Publishing Co.
637 Evergreen Hwy.
PO Box 179
Bunkie, LA 71322
Phone: (318)346-7253
Fax: (318)253-7223
**Subject(s):** Paid Community Newspapers
**Circ:** 1,300

**The Okeene Record** (25445)
211 N Main St.
PO Box 664
Okeene, OK 73763
Phone: (580)822-4401
Fax: (580)822-3051
**Subject(s):** Paid Community Newspapers
**Circ:** ‡1,300

**Bremond Press** (29331)
PO Box 490
301 South Main Street
Bremond, TX 76629
Phone: (254)746-7033
Fax: (254)746-7089
**Subject(s):** Paid Community Newspapers
**Circ:** ‡1,250

**The Malakoff News** (30123)
Loretta Humble
PO Box 509
103 South Perry
Malakoff, TX 75148-0509
Phone: (903)489-0531
Fax: (903)489-2543
**Subject(s):** Paid Community Newspapers
**Circ:** (Free)‡246
(Paid)‡1,254

**Wewoka Daily Times** (25676)
210 S Wewoka
PO Box 61
Wewoka, OK 74884
Phone: (405)257-3341
Fax: (405)257-3342
**Subject(s):** Daily Newspapers
**Circ:** ‡1,250

**State Line Tribune** (29691)
Box 255
Farwell, TX 79325
Phone: (806)481-3681
**Subject(s):** Paid Community Newspapers
**Circ:** ‡1,228

**The Afton-Fairland American** (25333)
PO Box 339
Fairland, OK 74343
Phone: (918)676-3484
Fax: (918)256-7100
**Subject(s):** Free Newspapers
**Circ:** (Free)37
(Paid)1,200

**Apache News** (25250)
Box 778
Apache, OK 73006
Phone: (580)588-3862
Fax: (580)588-3862
**Subject(s):** Paid Community Newspapers
**Circ:** (Free)‡20
(Paid)‡1,200

**Caldwell Watchman Progress** (12130)
PO Box 1269
Columbia, LA 71418
Phone: (318)649-6411
Fax: (318)649-7776
**Subject(s):** Paid Community Newspapers
**Circ:** (Wed.)1,200

**The Campus** (25452)
Oklahoma City University
2501 N Blackwelder Ave.
Oklahoma City, OK 73106-1402
Phone: (405)208-6068
Fax: (405)208-6069
**Subject(s):** College Publications
**Circ:** (Non-paid)1,200

**East Bernard Express** (29644)
East Bernard Tribune
PO Box 1210
East Bernard, TX 77435-1210
Phone: (979)532-0095
Fax: (979)532-8845
**Subject(s):** Paid Community Newspapers
**Circ:** ‡1,200

**The Echo** (25263)
Southern Nazarene University
6729 NW 39th Expy.
Bethany, OK 73008-2605
Phone: (405)789-6400
Fax: (405)491-6381
**Subject(s):** College Publications
**Circ:** 1,200

**The Eden Echo** (29648)
Eden Echo
135 Market
PO Box 1069
Eden, TX 76837
Phone: (325)869-3561
**Subject(s):** Paid Community Newspapers
**Circ:** ‡1,200

**Harper County Journal** (25280)
Golden Plains Publications
POB 240
Buffalo, OK 73834
Phone: (580)735-2526
Fax: (580)735-2527
**Subject(s):** Paid Community Newspapers
**Circ:** (Free)400
(Paid)1,200

**Morton Tribune** (30191)
PO Box 1016
101 North West 1st Street
Morton, TX 79346-1016
Phone: (806)266-5576
Fax: (806)266-8841
**Subject(s):** Paid Community Newspapers
**Circ:** ‡1,200

**Motley County Tribune** (30139)
724 Dundee
PO Box 490
Matador, TX 79244
Phone: (806)347-2400
Fax: (806)347-2774
**Subject(s):** Paid Community Newspapers
**Circ:** ‡1,200

**News and Messenger** (30162)
200 Mission St.
PO Box 248
Menard, TX 76859
Phone: (915)396-2243
Fax: (915)396-2739
**Subject(s):** Paid Community Newspapers
**Circ:** ‡1,205

**Oklahoma Publisher** (25476)
Oklahoma Press Association
3601 N. Lincoln Blvd.
Oklahoma City, OK 73105
Phone: (405)524-4421
Fax: (405)524-2201
**Subject(s):** Journalism and Publishing
**Circ:** ‡1,200

**Piedmont-Surrey Gazette  (25518)**
Hometown News Inc.
109 Monroe NW
PO Box 146
Piedmont, OK 73078
Phone: (405)373-1616
Fax: (405)373-1636
**Subject(s):** Paid Community Newspapers
**Circ:** 1,200

**Smackover Journal  (1289)**
PO Box 147
Smackover, AR 71762
Phone: (870)725-3131
Fax: (870)725-3131
**Subject(s):** Paid Community Newspapers
**Circ:** 1,200

**The Taft Tribune  (30525)**
San Patricio Publishing Company Inc.
325 Green Ave.
Taft, TX 78390
Phone: (361)364-1270
Fax: (361)364-3833
**Subject(s):** Paid Community Newspapers
**Circ:** ‡1,200

**The Texas Mohair Weekly  (30316)**
PO Box 287
Rocksprings, TX 78880
Phone: (830)683-3130
**Subject(s):** Paid Community Newspapers
**Circ:** 1,200

**The Times  (1219)**
PO Box 308
Melbourne, AR 72556
Phone: (870)368-4421
Fax: (870)368-4721
**Subject(s):** Paid Community Newspapers
**Circ:** 1,200

**The Western Texan  (30442)**
Western Texas College
6200 College Ave.
Snyder, TX 79549
Phone: (325)573-8511
Fax: (325)573-9321
**Subject(s):** College Publications
**Circ:** (Free)1,200

**The Frankston Citizen  (29736)**
PO Box 188
Frankston, TX 75763
Phone: (903)876-2218
Fax: (903)876-4974
**Subject(s):** Paid Community Newspapers
**Circ:** ‡1,184

**The Ringling Eagle  (25535)**
103 E Main
PO Box 626
Ringling, OK 73456-0626
Phone: (405)662-2221
**Subject(s):** Paid Community Newspapers
**Circ:** ‡1171

**Tulsa County News  (25626)**
Retherford Publications Inc.
8545 E 41st St.
Tulsa, OK 74145-3305
Phone: (918)663-1414
**Subject(s):** Paid Community Newspapers
**Circ:** (Paid)‡1,177

**The Banner  (12115)**
Jessie M. Boyett
PO Box 568
Bernice, LA 71222
Phone: (318)285-7424
Fax: (318)285-7420
**Subject(s):** Paid Community Newspapers
**Circ:** (Combined)⊕1,139

**Edgewood Enterprise  (29649)**
Asp Westward
PO Box 7
101 East Houston
Edgewood, TX 75117-0007
Phone: (903)896-4401
Fax: (903)962-3660
**Subject(s):** Paid Community Newspapers
**Circ:** ‡1,120

**The Ingleside Index  (29104)**
The Aransas Pass Progress/Ingleside Index
PO Box 2100
Aransas Pass, TX 78335
Phone: (361)758-5391
Fax: (361)758-5393
**Subject(s):** Paid Community Newspapers
**Circ:** (Paid)⊕1,111

**Cache Times Weekly  (25383)**
2101 N Sheridan
PO Box 1283
Lawton, OK 73502
Phone: (580)357-8200
Fax: (580)353-6646
**Subject(s):** Paid Community Newspapers
**Circ:** ‡1,108

**Ellis County Capital  (25256)**
PO Box 236
323 East Renford
Arnett, OK 73832-0236
Phone: (580)885-7788
Fax: (580)885-7296
**Subject(s):** Paid Community Newspapers
**Circ:** (Free)⊕35
  (Paid)⊕1,100

**The Maysville News  (25403)**
Maysville News
Box 617
Maysville, OK 73057-0617
Phone: (405)867-4457
Fax: (405)867-5115
**Subject(s):** Paid Community Newspapers
**Circ:** (Free)25
  (Paid)1,100

**The Review  (25557)**
PO Box 6
Shidler, OK 74652
Phone: (918)793-3841
Fax: (918)793-3842
**Subject(s):** Paid Community Newspapers
**Circ:** ‡1,100

**Wallis News-Review  (30614)**
The Wallis-News Review
PO Box 668
Wallis, TX 77485-0668
Phone: (979)478-6412
Fax: (979)478-2198
**Subject(s):** Paid Community Newspapers
**Circ:** ‡1,100

**The Whitewright Sun  (30637)**
The Whitewright Sun Inc.
PO Box 218
Whitewright, TX 75491-0218
Phone: (903)364-2276
Fax: (903)364-2276
**Subject(s):** Paid Community Newspapers
**Circ:** ‡1,100

**Bayou Bengal  (12152)**
Louisiana State University at Eunice
Box 1129
Eunice, LA 70535
Phone: (337)550-1211
Fax: (337)546-6620
**Subject(s):** College Publications
**Circ:** (Non-paid)1,000

**The Clarion  (30241)**
Meaux Walsh Publishing Inc.
309 W. Oak
Palestine, TX 75801
Phone: (903)727-0316
Fax: (903)727-0317
**Subject(s):** Paid Community Newspapers
**Circ:** (Paid)1,000

**The Duster  (30076)**
Lubbock Christian University
5601 19th St.
Lubbock, TX 79407
Phone: (806)796-8800
Fax: (806)796-8917
**Subject(s):** College Publications
**Circ:** 1,000

**Fletcher Herald  (25336)**
Fletcher Herald Publishing Co.
Box 469
Fletcher, OK 73541
Phone: (580)549-6045
Fax: (580)549-6107
**Subject(s):** Paid Community Newspapers
**Circ:** 1,000

**The Gorman Progress  (29769)**
106 S Kent
PO Box 68
Gorman, TX 76454-0068
Phone: (254)734-2410
Fax: (254)734-2799
**Subject(s):** Paid Community Newspapers
**Circ:** ‡1,005

**The Rising Star  (29645)**
Eastland County Newspaper Inc.
PO Box 29
Eastland, TX 76448
Phone: (254)629-1707
Fax: (254)629-2092
**Subject(s):** Paid Community Newspapers
**Circ:** (Combined)1,000

**Valley Tribune  (30299)**
PO Box 478
Quitaque, TX 79255
Phone: (806)455-1101
Fax: (806)455-1101
**Subject(s):** Paid Community Newspapers
**Circ:** ‡1,000

**The Van Horn Advocate  (30575)**
701B W Broadway
PO Box 8
Van Horn, TX 79855
Phone: (915)283-2003
Fax: (915)283-7334
**Subject(s):** Paid Community Newspapers
**Circ:** 1,000

**Washita County Enterprise  (25296)**
PO Box 68
Corn, OK 73024
Phone: (580)343-2513
Fax: (580)343-2513
**Subject(s):** Paid Community Newspapers
**Circ:** ‡1,000

**The Weleetkan  (25672)**
P O Box 427
Weleetka, OK 74880-0427
Phone: (405)786-2224
Fax: (405)452-3329
**Subject(s):** Paid Community Newspapers
**Circ:** 1,000

**Wildcat  (12362)**
Louisiana College
1140 College Dr.
Pineville, LA 71360
Phone: (318)487-7011
Fax: (318)487-7310
**Subject(s):** College Publications
**Circ:** (Free)1,000

**The Saint Jo Tribune  (30329)**
Drawer 160
Saint Jo, TX 76265
Phone: (940)995-2586
Fax: (940)995-2586
**Subject(s):** Paid Community Newspapers
**Circ:** ‡991

**Index  (29103)**
PO Box 2100
Aransas Pass, TX 78335
Phone: (361)758-5391
Fax: (361)758-5393
**Subject(s):** Paid Community Newspapers
**Circ:** ‡972

**Crosby County News & Chronicle  (29490)**
109 W Aspen
Crosbyton, TX 79322
Phone: (806)675-2881
Fax: (806)675-2855
**Subject(s):** Paid Community Newspapers
**Circ:** ‡950

Circulation: ★ = ABC; △ = BPA; ◆ = CAC; • = CCAB; ▫ = VAC; ⊕ = PO Statement; ‡ = Publisher's Report; Boldface figures = sworn; Light figures = estimated.

## Southern Central States

**Hinton Record** (25363)
PO Box 959
Hinton, OK 73047
Phone: (405)542-6644
Fax: (405)542-3120
**Subject(s):** Paid Community Newspapers
**Circ:** (Paid)950

**Hopkins County Echo** (30517)
Echo Publishing Co.
401 Church St.
P O Box 598
Sulphur Springs, TX 75482-0598
Phone: (903)885-8663
Fax: (903)885-8768
**Subject(s):** Paid Community Newspapers
**Circ:** ‡930

**Star** (25342)
Geary Star
114 W Main Street
Geary, OK 73040
Phone: (405)884-2424
Fax: (405)884-2424
**Subject(s):** Paid Community Newspapers
**Circ:** (Free)‡150
(Paid)‡865

**Abernathy Weekly Review** (29035)
916 Ave. D
PO Box 160
Abernathy, TX 79311-0160
Phone: (806)298-2033
Fax: (806)298-2033
**Subject(s):** Paid Community Newspapers
**Circ:** (Free)‡11
(Paid)‡850

**The Canton Times** (25281)
Blaine County Publishing
PO Box 579
Canton, OK 73724-0579
Phone: (580)822-4401
Fax: (580)886-3320
**Subject(s):** Paid Community Newspapers
**Circ:** 800

**Clipper** (25361)
The Hennessey Clipper
117 S Main
Box 338
Hennessey, OK 73742
Phone: (405)853-4888
Fax: (405)853-4890
**Subject(s):** Paid Community Newspapers
**Circ:** 800

**Kerens Tribune** (30011)
Kerens Tribune Inc.
1001 Nw. Secound St. Ste.100
Kerens, TX 75144
Phone: (903)396-2261
Fax: (903)396-2728
**Subject(s):** Paid Community Newspapers
**Circ:** 800

**The Moody Courier** (30596)
Bill Foster Pub.
1020 N 25th St.
Waco, TX 76707
Phone: (254)754-3511
Fax: (254)754-3541
**Subject(s):** Paid Community Newspapers
**Circ:** (Free)200
(Paid)800

**Baker Observer** (12055)
5240 Groom Rd.
Baker, LA 70714
Phone: (225)775-2315
Fax: (225)774-9212
**Subject(s):** Paid Community Newspapers
**Circ:** ‡779

**Hudspeth County Herald-Dell Valley Review** (29612)
Hudspeth Herald
290 Trl. W Park
PO Box 659
Dell City, TX 79837-0659
Phone: (915)964-2426
Fax: (915)964-2426
**Subject(s):** Paid Community Newspapers
**Circ:** (Free)‡10
(Paid)‡738

**Big Pasture News** (25344)
PO Box 508
Grandfield, OK 73546-0608
Phone: (580)479-5757
Fax: (580)479-5232
**Subject(s):** Paid Community Newspapers
**Circ:** (Paid)‡700

**Okarche Chieftain** (25444)
PO Box 468
Okarche, OK 73762
Phone: (405)373-1616
Fax: (405)373-1636
**Subject(s):** Paid Community Newspapers
**Circ:** 700

**Chico Texan** (29396)
Bridwell Publishing
PO Box 1150
Bridgeport, TX 76426
Phone: (940)683-4412
Fax: (940)683-3841
**Subject(s):** Paid Community Newspapers
**Circ:** 680

**Garber-Billings News** (25341)
Garber-Billing News
516 Main St.
Box 9
Garber, OK 73738
Phone: (580)863-2240
**Subject(s):** Paid Community Newspapers
**Circ:** (Free)‡177
(Paid)‡678

**The Wakita Herald** (25665)
Ken Kiser
104 W Main
PO Box 46
Wakita, OK 73771
Phone: (580)594-2440
**Subject(s):** Paid Community Newspapers
**Circ:** ‡650

**The Miami Chief** (30170)
PO Box 396
Miami, TX 79059-0396
Phone: (806)868-2521
Fax: (806)868-6051
**Subject(s):** Paid Community Newspapers
**Circ:** ‡630

**Texoma Enterprise** (29965)
805 N Hughes
Howe, TX 75459-3587
Phone: (903)532-6012
Fax: (903)532-6012
**Subject(s):** Paid Community Newspapers
**Circ:** (Free)⊕53
(Paid)⊕638

**The Wilson Post-Democrat** (25679)
Herald Company of Oklahoma Inc.
PO Box 250
Healdton, OK 73438
Phone: (580)229-0132
Fax: (580)229-0132
**Subject(s):** Paid Community Newspapers
**Circ:** ‡617

**Messenger** (30183)
Box 307
Miles, TX 76861
Phone: (325)468-3611
**Subject(s):** Paid Community Newspapers
**Circ:** ‡600

**The Odem-Edroy Times** (30219)
San Patricio Publishing Company Inc.
PO Drawer B
Sinton, TX 78387
Phone: (361)364-1270
Fax: (361)364-3833
**Subject(s):** Paid Community Newspapers
**Circ:** ‡600

**Sabinal Sampler** (30328)
Associated Texas Newspapers Inc.
1601 Ave. K
PO Box 400
Hondo, TX 78861-0400
Phone: (830)426-3346
Fax: (830)426-3348
**Subject(s):** Free Newspapers
**Circ:** (Free)‡600

**The Vega Enterprise** (30576)
116 S Main St.
PO Box 130
Vega, TX 79092
Phone: (806)267-2230
Fax: (806)267-2889
**Subject(s):** Paid Community Newspapers
**Circ:** ‡600

**The Ryan Leader** (25536)
Ryan Leader
606 Washington
PO Box 220
Ryan, OK 73565-0220
Phone: (580)757-2281
**Subject(s):** Paid Community Newspapers
**Circ:** (Free)‡20
(Paid)‡560

**The Borden Star** (29746)
PO Box 137
Gail, TX 79738-0137
Phone: (806)756-4402
Fax: (806)756-4310
**Subject(s):** Paid Community Newspapers
**Circ:** (Free)10
(Paid)500

**Bossier Banner-Progress** (12118)
Bossier Newspapers
PO Box 6267
Bossier City, LA 71171
Phone: (318)747-7900
Fax: (318)747-5298
**Subject(s):** Paid Community Newspapers
**Circ:** ‡500

**Eldorado Courier** (25318)
507 W Main St.
PO Box 160
Eldorado, OK 73537
Phone: (580)633-2643
Fax: (580)633-2643
**Subject(s):** Free Newspapers
**Circ:** (Free)‡19
(Paid)‡500

**O'Donnell Index-Press** (30232)
PO Box 457
Odonnell, TX 79351
Phone: (806)428-3591
Fax: (806)428-3360
**Subject(s):** Paid Community Newspapers; Farm Newspapers; General Agriculture
**Circ:** (Combined)495

**The DeValls Bluff Times** (1122)
Herald Publishing Company Inc.
77 Highway 70 W.
PO Box 370
Hazen, AR 72064
Phone: (870)255-4538
Fax: (870)255-4539
**Subject(s):** Paid Community Newspapers
**Circ:** (Free)14
(Paid)486

**Kress Chronicle** (30027)
7580 Fm. 145
Kress, TX 79052
Phone: (806)684-2586
Fax: (806)684-2456
**Subject(s):** Paid Community Newspapers
**Circ:** (Combined)⊕480

**Tulsa Daily Commerce & Legal News** (25627)
Retherford Publications Inc.
8545 E. 41st St.
Tulsa, OK 74145-3305
Phone: (918)663-1414
**Subject(s):** Daily Periodicals; Business; Law
**Circ:** ‡450

**The Hart Beat** (29798)
PO Box 350
407 Broadway
Hart, TX 79043-0350
Phone: (806)938-2640
Fax: (806)938-2216

**Subject(s):** Paid Community Newspapers
**Circ:** (Non-paid)‡50
(Paid)‡400

**Talco Times (30527)**
Thunder Prairie Publishing Co.
PO Box 98
Deport, TX 75435
Phone: (903)379-4445
Fax: (903)652-4205
**Subject(s):** Paid Community Newspapers
**Circ:** ‡400

**The Gage Record (25257)**
PO Box 236
Arnett, OK 73832-0236
Phone: (580)885-7788
**Subject(s):** Paid Community Newspapers
**Circ:** (Free)⊕15
(Paid)⊕390

**Blossom Times (29314)**
Thunder Prairie Publishing Co.
PO Box 5
Blossom, TX 75416
Fax: (903)652-6041
**Subject(s):** Paid Community Newspapers
**Circ:** 375

**The County Democrat Publishing Co. (25546)**
226 N Broadway
PO Box 367
Shawnee, OK 74802-0367
Phone: (405)273-8888
Fax: (405)275-6473
**Subject(s):** Paid Community Newspapers
**Circ:** ‡230

## Southern States

**National Enquirer (6420)**
PO Box 420235
Palm Coast, FL 32142
**Subject(s):** Paid Community Newspapers
**Circ:** (Paid)2,075,063

**Habitat World (6781)**
Habitat for Humanity International Inc.
121 Habitat St.
Americus, GA 31709-3498
Phone: (229)924-6935
Fax: (229)924-6541
**Subject(s):** Religious Publications; Social and Political Issues
**Circ:** (Free)1,050,000

**The Flyer (6632)**
201 Kelsey Ln.
Tampa, FL 33619
Phone: (813)626-9430
Fax: (813)626-8923
**Subject(s):** Shopping Guides
**Circ:** (Free)815,000

**Herald Values (6237)**
The Miami Herald Publishing Co.
One Herald Plz.
Miami, FL 33132
Phone: (305)350-2222
Fax: (305)376-3201
**Subject(s):** Shopping Guides
**Circ:** (Combined)729,186

**The Atlanta Journal and Constitution (6838)**
PO Box 4689
Atlanta, GA 30302
Phone: (404)526-5151
Fax: (404)526-5610
**Subject(s):** Daily Newspapers
**Circ:** (Mon.-Thurs.)★371,161
(Fri.)★424,521
(Sat.)★460,672
(Sun.)★620,782

**Layman (23615)**
The Presbyterian Lay Committee
PO Box 2210
Lenoir, NC 28645
Phone: (828)758-8716
Fax: (828)758-0920
**Subject(s):** Religious Publications
**Circ:** (Free)‡580,000

**National Examiner (5824)**
American Media
5401 NW Broken Sound Blvd.
Boca Raton, FL 33487-3587
Phone: (561)994-7210
Fax: (561)241-5689
**Subject(s):** Paid Community Newspapers
**Circ:** (Paid)432,886

**The Miami Herald (6250)**
Knight-Ridder Inc.
The Miami Herald
One Herald Plaza
Miami, FL 33132-1693
Phone: (305)350-2111
**Subject(s):** Daily Newspapers
**Circ:** (Mon.-Sat.)312,109
(Sun.)429,221

**St. Petersburg Times (6507)**
Times Publishing Co.
490 1st Ave. S.
PO Box 1121
Saint Petersburg, FL 33701-1121
Phone: (727)893-8111
Fax: (727)893-8675
**Subject(s):** Daily Newspapers
**Circ:** (Mon.-Sat.)★314,337
(Sun.)★396,638

**Sun-Sentinel (5968)**
Sun-Sentinel Co.
200 E. Las Olas Blvd.
Fort Lauderdale, FL 33301
Phone: (954)356-4000
Fax: (954)356-4093
**Subject(s):** Daily Newspapers
**Circ:** (Mon.-Sat.)267,677
(Sun.)381,838

**The Orlando Sentinel (6377)**
Orlando Sentinel Communications
633 N. Orange Ave.
Orlando, FL 32801
Phone: (407)420-5000
Fax: (407)420-5661
**Subject(s):** Daily Newspapers
**Circ:** (Mon.-Sat.)★247,674
(Sun.)★366,028

**Le Soleil de la Floride (6076)**
Worldwide Publications No. 1 Inc.
2117 Hollywood Blvd.
Hollywood, FL 33020
Phone: (954)922-1800
Fax: (954)922-8965
**Subject(s):** Travel and Tourism; French
**Circ:** (Controlled)150,000
(Free)350,000

**The PACEsetter (28873)**
PACE International Union
3340 Perimeter Hill Dr.
PO Box 1475
Nashville, TN 37202
Phone: (615)834-8590
Fax: (615)831-6791
**Subject(s):** Labor; Paper
**Circ:** (Free)‡320,000

**The Tampa Tribune (6655)**
The Tampa Bay Online
200 S. Parker St.
Tampa, FL 33606
Phone: (813)259-8225
**Subject(s):** Daily Newspapers
**Circ:** (Mon.-Sat.)211,055
(Sun.)300,738

**The Courier-Journal (11807)**
Courier-Journal Co.
525 W Broadway
PO Box 740031
Louisville, KY 40201-7431
Phone: (502)582-4011
Fax: (502)582-4075
**Subject(s):** Daily Newspapers
**Circ:** (Mon.-Sat.)★207,665
(Sun.)★273,891

**The Tennessean (28883)**
Gannett Company Inc.
The Tennessean
1100 Broadway
Nashville, TN 37203
Phone: (615)259-8300
**Subject(s):** Daily Newspapers
**Circ:** (Mon.-Fri.)181,702
(Sat.)213,019
(Sun.)260,992

**The Florida Times-Union (6094)**
Morris Communications Corp.
1 Riverside Ave.
Jacksonville, FL 32202-4904
Phone: (904)359-4478
Fax: (800)472-6397
**Subject(s):** Daily Newspapers
**Circ:** (Mon.-Fri.)182,136
(Sat.)208,916
(Sun.)256,710

**El Nuevo Dia (27799)**
El Dia Inc.
PO Box 9067512
San Juan, PR 00906-7512
Phone: (787)641-8000
**Subject(s):** Spanish; Daily Newspapers; Hispanic Publications
**Circ:** (Mon.-Sat.)200,484
(Sun.)239,494

**The Palm Beach Post (6719)**
2751 S Dixie Hwy.
West Palm Beach, FL 33405
Phone: (561)820-4401
Fax: (561)820-4407
**Subject(s):** Daily Newspapers
**Circ:** (Mon.-Sat.)187,943
(Sun.)238,334

**Pasco Shopper (5912)**
Sunpress Publications Inc.
13032 U.S Hwy. 301
PO Box 187
Dade City, FL 33525
Phone: (352)567-5639
Fax: (352)567-5640
**Subject(s):** Shopping Guides
**Circ:** (Free)‡223,167

**The News and Observer (23704)**
The News & Observer Publishing Co.
215 S McDowell St.
PO Box 191
Raleigh, NC 27602
Phone: (919)829-4500
**Subject(s):** Daily Newspapers
**Circ:** (Mon.-Fri.)★166,098
(Sat.)★182,783
(Sun.)★210,287

**Farmers & Consumers Market Bulletin (6872)**
Georgia Dept. of Agriculture
Agriculture Bldg.
Capitol Sq., Rm. 226
19 Martin Luther King Jr. Dr., SW
Atlanta, GA 30334
Phone: (404)656-3685
Fax: (404)651-7957
**Subject(s):** Farm Newspapers; General Agriculture
**Circ:** (Free)205,428

**The Birmingham News (58)**
PO Box 2553
Birmingham, AL 35202
Phone: (205)325-2444
Fax: (205)325-2283
**Subject(s):** Daily Newspapers
**Circ:** (Mon.-Thurs.)★145,506
(Sat.)★150,353
(Fri.)★167,889
(Sun.)★184,036

**El Vocero de Puerto Rico (27801)**
Gastar Roca Inc.
Apartado 7515
San Juan, PR 00906-7515
Phone: (787)721-2300
Fax: (787)725-8422
**Subject(s):** Spanish; Daily Newspapers; Hispanic Publications
**Circ:** (Sat.)156,051
(Mon.-Fri.)181,168

Circulation: ★ = ABC; △ = BPA; ◆ = CAC; • = CCAB; ▫ = VAC; ⊕ = PO Statement; ‡ = Publisher's Report; Boldface figures = sworn; Light figures = estimated.

# Southern States

**The Knoxville News-Sentinel  (28684)**
Knoxville News Sentinel Co.
2332 News Sentinel Dr.
Knoxville, TN 37921-5761
Phone: (865)523-3131
Fax: (865)342-6400
**Subject(s):** Daily Newspapers

**Circ:**  (Mon.-Thurs.)119,901
     (Sat.)130,890
     (Fri.)133,856
     (Sun.)159,109

**The State  (28067)**
Knight-Ridder Inc.
C/O Mark Lett
PO Box 1333
Columbia, SC 29202
Phone: (803)771-8380
Fax: (803)771-8430
**Subject(s):** Daily Newspapers

**Circ:**  (Mon.-Sat.)118,783
     (Sun.)156,165

**GOLFWEEK  (6366)**
Golfweek
1500 Park Center Dr.
Orlando, FL 32835
Phone: (407)563-7000
Fax: (407)563-7076
**Subject(s):** (Golf)

**Circ:** 155,000

**Birmingham Post-Herald  (60)**
Birmingham Post Co.
2200 4th Ave. N.
Birmingham, AL 35203
Phone: (205)325-2344
Fax: (205)325-2410
**Subject(s):** Daily Newspapers

**Circ:**  (Combined)★153,525

**The Florida Catholic  (6361)**
The Florida Catholic Newspaper
498 S. Lake Destiny Rd.
Orlando, FL 32810
Phone: (407)660-9141
Fax: (407)660-2977
**Subject(s):** Religious Publications

**Circ:**  ⊕142,000

**Creative Loafing  (6862)**
750 Willoughby Way
Atlanta, GA 30312
Phone: (404)688-5623
Fax: (404)614-3599
**Subject(s):** Free Newspapers

**Circ:**  (Paid)124
     (Free)140,000

**Rock and Dirt  (28576)**
TAP Publishing Co.
174 Fourth St.
PO Box 3079
Crossville, TN 38555
Phone: (931)484-5137
Fax: (931)484-2532
**Subject(s):** Machinery and Equipment

**Circ:**  (Paid)36,000
     (Free)137,000

**Suncoast News  (6322)**
6214 U.S Hwy. 19
New Port Richey, FL 34652
Phone: (727)815-1000
Fax: (727)815-1025
**Subject(s):** Paid Community Newspapers

**Circ:**  (Sat.)127,730
     (Wed.)134,488

**The Advertiser  (6701)**
Sun Coast Media
200 E Venice Ave.
Venice, FL 34285
Phone: (941)484-2611
Fax: (941)484-8460
**Subject(s):** Shopping Guides

**Circ:**  (Free)131,900

**FloridAgriculture  (6024)**
Florida Farm Bureau Federation
PO Box 147030
Gainesville, FL 32614-7030
Phone: (352)378-1321
Fax: (352)374-1530

**Subject(s):** Farm Bureau, Grange, and Cooperative Associations

**Circ:**  (Free)‡800
     (Paid)‡127,000

**Entertainment News & Views  (6232)**
PO Box 38-1817
Miami, FL 33238
**Subject(s):** Entertainment; Local, State, and Regional Publications

**Circ:**  (Free)125,000

**La Estrella De Puerto Rico  (27764)**
Paris St., No. 165
Floral Park
Hato Rey, PR 00917
Fax: (809)754-4457
**Subject(s):** Paid Community Newspapers

**Circ:**  (Combined)123,300

**The News-Journal  (5918)**
News-Journal Corp.
901 6th St.
Daytona Beach, FL 32117
Phone: (386)252-1511
Fax: (386)258-8465
**Subject(s):** Daily Newspapers

**Circ:**  (Mon.-Sat.)★101,226
     (Sun.)★119,498

**The Greenville News  (28111)**
Greenville News
305 S. Main St.
P.O. Box 1688
Greenville, SC 29602
Phone: (864)298-4831
Fax: (864)298-4395
**Subject(s):** Daily Newspapers

**Circ:**  (Mon.-Fri.)★88,870
     (Sat.)★97,274
     (Sun.)★119,410

**Sarasota Herald-Tribune  (6535)**
The New York Times Co.
801 S. Tamiami Trail
Sarasota, FL 34236
Phone: (941)953-7755
Fax: (941)957-5276
**Subject(s):** Daily Newspapers

**Circ:**  (Mon.-Sat.)94,912
     (Sun.)118,785

**Florida Today  (6214)**
Cape Publications Inc.
Gannett Plz.
PO Box 419000
Melbourne, FL 32941-9000
Phone: (321)242-3500
Fax: (321)242-6620
**Subject(s):** Daily Newspapers

**Circ:**  (Mon.-Fri.)96,626
     (Sun.)117,981

**Tennessee Farm Bureau News  (28559)**
Tennessee Farm Bureau Federation
147 Bear Creek Pke.
PO Box 313
Columbia, TN 38402
Phone: (931)388-7872
Fax: (931)388-5818
**Subject(s):** Farm Bureau, Grange, and Cooperative Associations; Farm Newspapers

**Circ:**  ‡117,000

**The Post and Courier  (28011)**
Evening Post Publishing Co.
134 Columbus St.
Charleston, SC 29403
Phone: (843)577-7111
Fax: (843)937-5579
**Subject(s):** Daily Newspapers

**Circ:**  (Mon.-Sat.)★101,288
     (Sun.)★113,999

**News & Record  (23524)**
Landmark Communications Inc.
200 E. Market St.
PO Box 20848
Greensboro, NC 27420-0848
Phone: (336)373-7000
Fax: (336)373-7183
**Subject(s):** Daily Newspapers

**Circ:**  (Mon.-Fri.)86,241
     (Sat.)101,618
     (Sun.)112,259

**The Mobile Register  (317)**
PO Box 2488
Mobile, AL 36652-2488
Phone: (251)219-5454
**Subject(s):** Daily Newspapers

**Circ:**  (Sat.)★88,253
     (Mon.-Fri.)★94,045
     (Sun.)★111,778

**The Stuart News  (6564)**
PO Box 9009
Stuart, FL 34995-9009
Phone: (561)287-1550
Fax: (561)221-4250
**Subject(s):** Daily Newspapers

**Circ:**  (Mon.-Sat.)★94,805
     (Sun.)★108,014

**The Clarion Ledger  (16878)**
Gannett Company Inc.
201 S. Congress
PO Box 40
Jackson, MS 39205
Phone: (601)961-7000
Fax: (601)961-7211
**Subject(s):** Daily Newspapers

**Circ:**  (Mon.-Sat.)★94,938
     (Sun.)★107,865

**Flagler/Palm Coast News-Tribune  (5917)**
News-Journal Corp.
901 6th St.
Daytona Beach, FL 32117
Phone: (386)252-1511
Fax: (386)258-8465
**Subject(s):** Paid Community Newspapers

**Circ:** 10,500.

**Lee County Shopper  (5860)**
Breeze Publishing Co.
PO Box 151306
2510 Del Prado Blvd.
Cape Coral, FL 33904
Phone: (941)574-1110
Fax: (941)574-3403
**Subject(s):** Shopping Guides

**Circ:**  (Free)105,000

**Chattanooga Times & Free Press  (28518)**
Chattanooga Publishing Co.
400 E. 11th St.
Chattanooga, TN 37403
Phone: (423)756-6900
Fax: (423)752-3388
**Subject(s):** Daily Newspapers

**Circ:**  (Mon.-Sat.)72,449
     (Sun.)100,997

**Elder Update  (6571)**
Department of Elder Affairs
4040 Esplanade Way
Tallahassee, FL 32399-7000
Phone: (850)414-2000
Fax: (850)414-2004
**Subject(s):** Senior Citizens' Interests

**Circ:**  (Free)‡100,000

**Tech Topics  (6923)**
Georgia Tech Alumni Association
190 N. Ave. NW
Atlanta, GA 30313
Phone: (404)894-2391
Fax: (404)894-5113
**Subject(s):** College Publications

**Circ:**  (Controlled)100,000

**Korean Journal  (7117)**
5455 Buford Hwy., No. 207-A
Doraville, GA 30340
Phone: (770)451-6946
Fax: (770)451-6955
**Subject(s):** Free Newspapers; Korean; Ethnic Publications

**Circ:**  (Paid)2,389
     (Non-paid)97,811

**El Nuevo Herald  (6229)**
Hometown Herald
1 Herald Plaza
Miami, FL 33132
Phone: (954)462-3000
Fax: (305)376-2378
**Subject(s):** Daily Newspapers; Hispanic Publications; Spanish

**Circ:**  (Mon.-Sat.)90,543
     (Sun.)97,705

**The Augusta Chronicle (6967)**
PO Box 1928
PO Box 1928
Augusta, GA 30903-1928
Phone: (706)823-3255
Fax: (706)823-3795
**Subject(s):** Daily Newspapers

Circ: (Mon.-Thurs.)72,726
(Sat.)85,652
(Fri.)88,199
(Sun.)97,488

**Fifty Plus (23415)**
109 Montrose Dr.
Durham, NC 27707-3900
Phone: (919)493-5900
Fax: (919)490-1925
**Subject(s):** Lifestyle

Circ: (Paid)1,500
(Non-paid)97,200

**Winston-Salem Journal (23876)**
Piedmont Publishing Co.
PO Box 3159
Winston-Salem, NC 27102-3159
Phone: (336)727-7211
Fax: (336)727-7315
**Subject(s):** Daily Newspapers

Circ: (Mon.-Sat.)★84,459
(Sun.)★95,179

**Comic Shop News (7278)**
c/o Cliff Biggers, 2770 Carillon Crossing
Marietta, GA 30066
Phone: (770)973-6949
Fax: (770)973-6949
**Subject(s):** Comics and Comic Technique

Circ: (Combined)94,400

**The Macon Telegraph (7247)**
Knight-Ridder Inc.
The Macon Telegraph
120 Broadway
Macon, GA 31201-3444
Phone: (478)744-4200
**Subject(s):** Daily Newspapers

Circ: (Mon.-Thurs.)68,191
(Sat.)70,920
(Fri.)74,140
(Sun.)87,878

**The Ledger (6169)**
300 W. Lime St.
Lakeland, FL 33815
Phone: (863)802-7323
**Subject(s):** Daily Newspapers

Circ: (Mon.-Sat.)★65,987
(Sun.)★81,366

**The Broward Informer (6565)**
PO Box 130207
Sunrise, FL 33313
Phone: (954)370-6009
**Subject(s):** Free Newspapers

Circ: (Paid)‡2,000
(Free)‡80,000

**The News Herald (28870)**
PO Box 140628
Nashville, TN 37214
Phone: (615)889-1860
**Subject(s):** Paid Community Newspapers

Circ: (Sun.)♦70,450
(Wed.)♦80,000

**Pensacola News Journal (6442)**
1 News-Journal Plz.
Pensacola, FL 32501-5670
Phone: (904)435-8500
Fax: (904)435-8633
**Subject(s):** Daily Newspapers

Circ: (Mon.-Sat.)★61,452
(Sun.)★79,513

**Savannah Pennysaver (7399)**
Wilmington Media Co.
PO Box 5100
Savannah, GA 31414-5100
Phone: (912)238-2040
Fax: (912)238-2041
**Subject(s):** Shopping Guides

Circ: (Free)‡79,500

**Naples Daily News (6314)**
Collier County Publishing Co.
1075 Central Ave.
Naples, FL 34102
Phone: (239)262-3161
Fax: (239)435-3451
**Subject(s):** Daily Newspapers

Circ: (Mon.-Sat.)64,321
(Sun.)77,198

**The Georgia Bulletin (6878)**
680 W Peachtree St. NW
Atlanta, GA 30308-1984
Phone: (404)877-5500
Fax: (404)877-5505
**Subject(s):** Religious Publications

Circ: 77,000

**La Perla Del Sur (27784)**
Juno Commercial Printing
Sabanetas Industrial Park Ast 22
Mercedita, PR 00715
Phone: (787)842-5866
Fax: (787)842-5823
**Subject(s):** Free Newspapers

Circ: (Non-paid)76,650

**Savannah Morning News (7398)**
PO Box 1088
Savannah, GA 31402-1088
Phone: (912)236-0271
Fax: (912)234-6522
**Subject(s):** Daily Newspapers

Circ: (Mon.-Sat.)62,715
(Sun.)75,960

**The International American Sunbeam (28951)**
Gerald L. Sprouse Publishing Co.
PO Drawer 830
Ooltewah, TN 37363
**Subject(s):** Alternative and Underground

Circ: ‡75,000

**Save Our World (28548)**
Church of God World Missions
2490 Keith St. NW
Cleveland, TN 37311
Phone: (423)478-7190
**Subject(s):** Religious Publications

Circ: (Free)‡75,000

**The Huntsville Times (268)**
PO Box 1487, W Sta.
Huntsville, AL 35807-0487
Phone: (205)532-4000
Fax: (205)532-4420
**Subject(s):** Daily Newspapers

Circ: (Mon.-Sat.)★53,145
(Sun.)★74,401

**The Fayetteville Observer (23470)**
Fayetteville Publishing Co.
PO Box 849
458 Whitfield St.
Fayetteville, NC 28302
Phone: (910)323-4848
Fax: (910)486-3531
**Subject(s):** Daily Newspapers

Circ: (Mon.-Fri.)★66,245
(Sat.)★68,860
(Sun.)★71,765

**Asheville Citizen-Times (23229)**
Asheville Citizen-Times Publishing Co.
14 O. Henry Ave.
Asheville, NC 28801
Phone: (828)252-5611
Fax: (828)251-2659
**Subject(s):** Daily Newspapers

Circ: (Mon.-Sat.)56,683
(Sun.)71,502

**Diario las Americas (6227)**
The Americas Publishing Co.
2900 NW 39th Street
Miami, FL 33142
Phone: (305)633-3341
Fax: (305)635-4002
**Subject(s):** Daily Newspapers; Spanish; Hispanic Publications

Circ: (Mon.-Fri.)‡65,670
(Sun.)‡69,580

**Tallahassee Democrat (6603)**
Knight-Ridder Inc.
Tallahassee Democrat
277 N. Magnolia Dr.
Tallahassee, FL 32301-2695
Phone: (850)599-2100
**Subject(s):** Daily Newspapers

Circ: (Mon.-Sat.)49,142
(Sun.)66,199

**El Visitante de Puerto Rico (27800)**
Puerto Rican Catholic Conference
Apartado 41305 Est Minillas Sta.
San Juan, PR 00940-1305
Phone: (787)728-3710
Fax: (787)286-1748
**Subject(s):** Religious Publications; Spanish; Hispanic Publications

Circ: (Free)400
(Paid)65,000

**Bradenton Shopping Guide (5843)**
Florida Sun Publications
116 6th Ave. E.
Bradenton, FL 34208
Phone: (941)747-3699
Fax: (941)747-3699
**Subject(s):** Shopping Guides

Circ: (Non-paid)63,960

**The Scottish Banner (5940)**
249 Main St.
Dunedin, FL 34698
Phone: (727)738-9590
Fax: (727)738-9592
**Subject(s):** Unclassified Fraternal; Ethnic Publications

Circ: ‡62,708

**Gwinnett Daily Post (7231)**
Gray Communications Systems
725 Old Norcross Road
Lawrenceville, GA 30045
Phone: (770)963-9205
Fax: (770)338-7353
**Subject(s):** Paid Community Newspapers

Circ: (Non-paid)126
(Paid)61,738

**Impact of Hattiesburg (16922)**
Buckley Newspapers Inc.
PO Box 4406
Laurel, MS 39441
Phone: (601)649-1129
Fax: (601)649-0424
**Subject(s):** Shopping Guides

Circ: (Non-paid)61,402

**Flashes Shopping Guide (6562)**
Flashes Inc.
742 Colorado Ave.
Stuart, FL 34994-3005
Phone: (772)287-0650
Fax: (772)283-5090
**Subject(s):** Shopping Guides

Circ: (Free)61,300

**Wilmington Morning Star (23847)**
Wilmington Star-News
PO Box 840
Wilmington, NC 28402
Phone: (910)343-2391
**Subject(s):** Daily Newspapers

Circ: (Mon.-Sat.)★53,571
(Sun.)★61,219

**The Atlanta Inquirer (6837)**
947 Martin Luther King Jr. Dr. NW
Atlanta, GA 30314-0367
Phone: (404)523-6086
Fax: (404)523-6088
**Subject(s):** Paid Community Newspapers; Black Publications

Circ: (Paid)61,000

**Columbus Ledger-Enquirer (7063)**
Knight-Ridder Inc.
PO Box 711
Columbus, GA
Phone: (706)571-8565
**Subject(s):** Daily Newspapers

Circ: (Mon.-Thurs.)47,763
(Sat.)55,506
(Fri.)56,858
(Sun.)60,172

Circulation: ★ = ABC; △ = BPA; ♦ = CAC; ♦ = CCAB; ▫ = VAC; ⊖ = PO Statement; ‡ = Publisher's Report; Boldface figures = sworn; Light figures = estimated.

# Southern States

**Civil Air Patrol News** (348)
Civil Air Patrol Inc.
105, S. Hansell St. Bldg. 714
Maxwell AFB
Montgomery, AL 36112-6332
**Subject(s):** Aviation
**Circ:** ‡60,000

**Pulpit Helps** (28523)
AMG Publishers
6815 Shallowford Rd.
Chattanooga, TN 37421
Phone: (423)894-6060
Fax: (423)894-9511
**Subject(s):** Religious Publications
**Circ:** (Paid)‡16,000
    (Free)‡60,000

**Periodico El Oriental** (27765)
Periodico El Oriental Inc.
Ave. Cruz Ortiz Stella 36
Humacao, PR 00791
Phone: (787)852-1496
Fax: (787)852-3405
**Subject(s):** Free Newspapers
**Circ:** (Combined)59,500

**The Montgomery Advertiser** (355)
MultiMedia Inc.
200 Washington Ave.
PO Box 1000
Montgomery, AL 36101-1000
Phone: (334)262-1611
Fax: (334)261-1591
**Subject(s):** Daily Newspapers
**Circ:** (Mon.-Sat.)★48,389
    (Sun.)★58,429

**The Gainesville Sun** (6025)
2700 SW 13th St.
Gainesville, FL 32608
Phone: (352)378-1411
Fax: (352)338-3128
**Subject(s):** Daily Newspapers
**Circ:** (Mon.-Sat.)51,407
    (Sun.)58,238

**La Voz Catolica** (6247)
Arquidiocesis de Miami
9401 Biscayne Blvd.
Miami, FL 33138-2970
Phone: (305)757-6241
Fax: (305)762-1223
**Subject(s):** Paid Community Newspapers; Hispanic Publications; Spanish
**Circ:** (Free)58,025

**Daytona Pennysaver** (6404)
Volusia Pennysaver Inc.
454 S Young St.
PO Box 67
Ormond Beach, FL 32174
Phone: (386)677-4262
Fax: (386)672-7453
**Subject(s):** Shopping Guides
**Circ:** (Free)‡57,660

**Mundo Hispanico** (6903)
PO Box 13808
1927 Piebmont Cir.
Atlanta, GA 30324-0808
Phone: (404)881-0441
Fax: (404)881-6085
**Subject(s):** Free Newspapers; Hispanic Publications; Spanish
**Circ:** (Combined)57,500

**The Lipscomb News** (28862)
Lipscomb University
3901 Granny White Pke.
LU Box 4236
Nashville, TN 37204-3951
Phone: (615)279-6604
**Subject(s):** College Publications
**Circ:** (Free)‡57,000

**Herald-Journal** (28229)
PO Box 1657
Spartanburg, SC 29304-1657
Phone: (864)582-4511
Fax: (864)594-6350
**Subject(s):** Daily Newspapers
**Circ:** (Mon.-Sat.)★48,798
    (Sun.)★56,981

**Ocala Star-Banner** (6342)
Star Banner
2121 SW 19th Ave.
PO Box 490
Ocala, FL 34474
Phone: (352)867-4010
Fax: (352)867-4018
**Subject(s):** Daily Newspapers
**Circ:** (Mon.-Sat.)51,358
    (Sun.)55,234

**The Herald-Sun** (23417)
Herald-Sun Papers
2828 Picket Rd.
Durham, NC 27705
Phone: (919)419-6500
**Subject(s):** Daily Newspapers
**Circ:** (Mon.-Sat.)★50,379
    (Sun.)★54,107

**Impact of Laurel** (16923)
Buckley Newspapers Inc.
PO Box 4406
Laurel, MS 39441
Phone: (601)649-1129
Fax: (601)649-0424
**Subject(s):** Shopping Guides
**Circ:** (Wed.)46,695
    (Sun.)53,854

**Southeast Farm Press** (16780)
Southwest Farm Press
Southeast Farm Press
14920 US Hwy. 61
Clarksdale, MS 38614
Phone: (662)624-8503
Fax: (662)627-1137
**Subject(s):** General Agriculture
**Circ:** (Combined)53,000

**Spectator Magazine** (6651)
Spectator Publications Inc.
1310 E 9th Ave.
Tampa, FL 33605-3616
**Subject(s):** Free Newspapers
**Circ:** (Non-paid)52,740

**Nashville Scene** (28867)
City Press Publishing Inc.
2120 Eighth Ave. S
Nashville, TN 37204
Phone: (615)244-7989
Fax: (615)244-8578
**Subject(s):** Local, State, and Regional Publications; Entertainment
**Circ:** (Non-paid)52,500

**City Link** (5955)
Sun Sentinel
Attn: City Link
PO Box 14426
Fort Lauderdale, FL 33302
Phone: (954)356-4943
Fax: (954)356-4949
**Subject(s):** Free Newspapers; Alternative and Underground
**Circ:** (Non-paid)51,798

**Northwest Florida Daily News** (6005)
Freedom Communications Inc.
200 Racetrack Rd. NW
Fort Walton Beach, FL 32547
Phone: (850)863-1111
Fax: (850)863-9348
**Subject(s):** Daily Newspapers
**Circ:** (Mon.-Sat.)39,195
    (Sun.)51,226

**National Speed Sport News** (23568)
PO Box 1210
Harrisburg, NC 28075
Phone: (704)455-2531
Fax: (704)455-2605
**Subject(s):** (Auto Racing)
**Circ:** ‡50,500

**The Atlanta Voice** (6840)
633 Pryor St. SW
Box 92405
Atlanta, GA 30312
Phone: (404)524-6426
Fax: (404)523-7853
**Subject(s):** Paid Community Newspapers; Black Publications
**Circ:** 50,000

**The Beach Weekly** (6523)
Florida Sun Publications
3755 S. Tuttle Ave.
Sarasota, FL 34239
Phone: (813)923-2544
Fax: (813)924-1866
**Circ:** (Free)50,000

**Bull & Bear Financial Report** (6191)
Bull & Bear Financial Newspaper
PO Box 917179
Longwood, FL 32791
Phone: (407)682-6170
Fax: (407)682-6170
**Subject(s):** Banking, Finance, and Investments
**Circ:** (Non-paid)17,000
    (Paid)50,000

**Carolina Parent** (23405)
Carolina Parenting Inc.
5716 Fayetteville Rd., Ste. 201
Durham, NC 27713
Phone: (919)956-2430
Fax: (919)956-2427
**Subject(s):** Paid Community Newspapers; Parenting
**Circ:** (Combined)50,000

**Creations** (23246)
Creations Magazine
PO Box 970
Black Mountain, NC 28711
Fax: (888)669-2050
**Subject(s):** Free Newspapers
**Circ:** (Combined)50,000

**El Norte** (27744)
El Norte, Acquisitions Inc.
PO Box 140995
Arecibo, PR 00614
Phone: (787)262-0130
Fax: (787)262-0160
**Subject(s):** Free Newspapers
**Circ:** (Combined)50,000

**West Volusia Pennysaver** (5935)
Volusia Pennysaver Inc.
PO Box 3536
DeLand, FL 32721-3536
**Subject(s):** Shopping Guides
**Circ:** (Non-paid)50,000

**Periodico La Opinion Del Sur** (27767)
Periodico El Oriental Inc.
Ave. Cruz Ortiz Stella 36
Humacao, PR 00791
Phone: (787)852-1496
Fax: (787)852-3405
**Subject(s):** Free Newspapers
**Circ:** (Paid)49,500

**The Catholic News & Herald** (23336)
Cathedral Publishing Corp.
1123 S. Church St.
Charlotte, NC 28203
Phone: (704)370-6299
Fax: (704)370-3378
**Subject(s):** Religious Publications
**Circ:** (Paid)⊕49,000

**Gwinnett Extra** (7333)
The Atlanta Journal and Constitution
6455 Best Friend Rd.
Norcross, GA 30071
Phone: (404)263-3858
Fax: (404)263-3011
**Subject(s):** Free Newspapers
**Circ:** (Sun.)41,230
    (Wed.)48,758

**Western Recorder** (11894)
Western Recorder Inc.
PO Box 43969
10605 Shelbyville Road( ZipC 40223)
Louisville, KY 40253
Phone: (502)244-6470
Fax: (502)244-6474
**Subject(s):** Religious Publications
**Circ:** (Free)1,120
    (Paid)48,500

**The Digest** (6068)
Box 785
Hallandale, FL 33009-0785
Phone: (305)457-8029
Fax: (305)457-1284

Subject(s): Free Newspapers
Circ: (Free)‡48,000

**The Kentucky Post** (11629)
Scripps Howard Inc.
421 Madison Ave.
PO Box 2678
Covington, KY 41011
Phone: (606)292-2600
Fax: (606)291-2525
Subject(s): Daily Newspapers
Circ: ‡47,742

**The AD-PAK (Wilmington Edition)** (23842)
Wilmington Media Co.
25 N Kerr Ave.
Wilmington, NC 28405
Phone: (910)791-0688
Fax: (910)791-9534
Subject(s): Shopping Guides
Circ: (Free)‡47,400

**Bright Side** (7218)
PO Box 935
Kennesaw, GA 30144
Phone: (770)423-9555
Subject(s): Paid Community Newspapers
Circ: (Combined)47,000

**Decatur De Kalb Neighbor** (7111)
Neighbor Newspapers Inc.
580 Fairground St.
PO Box 449
Marietta, GA 30060
Phone: (770)795-3000
Fax: (770)428-7945
Subject(s): Free Newspapers
Circ: (Combined)45,551

**The Stone Mountain De Kalb Neighbor** (7294)
Neighbor Newspapers Inc.
580 Fairground St.
PO Box 449
Marietta, GA 30060
Phone: (770)795-3000
Fax: (770)428-7945
Subject(s): Free Newspapers
Circ: (Combined)45,551

**Tucker De Kalb Neighbor** (7296)
Neighbor Newspapers Inc.
580 Fairground St.
PO Box 449
Marietta, GA 30060
Phone: (770)795-3000
Fax: (770)428-7945
Subject(s): Free Newspapers
Circ: (Combined)45,551

**The Free Press** (23609)
2103 N. Queen St.
Kinston, NC 28501
Phone: (252)527-3191
Fax: (252)527-8238
Subject(s): Daily Newspapers
Circ: (Mon.-Fri.)36,947
(Sun.)45,149

**Louisville Eccentric Observer (LEO)** (11832)
Louisville Eccentric Observer
600 E. Main St., Ste. 102
Louisville, KY 40202
Phone: (502)895-9770
Fax: (502)895-9779
Subject(s): Free Newspapers
Circ: (Combined)45,000

**The Sun Post** (6288)
Post Newspaper Group Inc.
1688 Meridian Ave. No. 404
PO Box 19-1870
Miami Beach, FL 33139
Phone: (305)538-9700
Fax: (305)538-6077
Subject(s): Free Newspapers
Circ: (Paid)‡2,000
(Free)‡45,000

**The Weekly Challenger** (6509)
2500 9th St. S
Saint Petersburg, FL 33705
Phone: (727)896-2922
Fax: (727)823-2568
Subject(s): Paid Community Newspapers; Black Publications
Circ: 45,000

**Southside Shopper** (23496)
2339 Timber Dr.
PO Box 449
Garner, NC 27529
Phone: (919)772-9002
Fax: (919)772-4172
Subject(s): Shopping Guides
Circ: (Free)‡44,000

**Kingsport Times News** (28666)
701 Lynn Garden Dr.
PO Box 479
Kingsport, TN 37660
Phone: (423)246-8121
Fax: (423)392-1390
Subject(s): Daily Newspapers
Circ: (Sat.)★40,434
(Mon.-Fri.)★41,484
(Sun.)★43,905

**Anderson Independent-Mail** (27968)
PO Box 2507
Anderson, SC 29622
Phone: (864)224-4321
Fax: (864)260-1276
Subject(s): Daily Newspapers
Circ: (Mon.-Sat.)★36,871
(Sun.)★42,681

**The Clayton Neighbor** (7149)
Neighbor Newspapers Inc.
5300 Frontage Rd., Ste. B
Forest Park, GA 30297
Phone: (404)363-8484
Fax: (404)363-0212
Subject(s): Free Newspapers
Circ: (Paid)11
(Non-paid)42,683

**Hometown Herald** (5958)
1520 E. Sunrise Blvd.
Fort Lauderdale, FL 33304
Phone: (954)985-4595
Fax: (954)985-4687
Subject(s): Free Newspapers
Circ: (Paid)‡42,200

**Florida Baptist Witness** (6092)
1230 Hendricks Ave.
Jacksonville, FL 32207
Phone: (904)596-3165
Fax: (904)346-0696
Subject(s): Religious Publications
Circ: (Free)‡1,500
(Paid)‡42,000

**Louisville Snitch** (11833)
Snitch, LLC
161 Chenoweth Ln.
Louisville, KY 40207
Phone: (502)893-3005
Fax: (502)896-4824
Subject(s): Free Newspapers
Circ: (Free)❏41,316

**Independent Weekly** (23421)
The Independent Weekly
2810 Hillsborough Rd.
PO Box 2690
Durham, NC 27715
Phone: (919)286-1972
Fax: (919)286-4274
Subject(s): Free Newspapers
Circ: (Paid)81
(Free)40,184

**Buyers' Guide** (6015)
Buyers Guide
2251 NW 41st St., Ste. B
Gainesville, FL 32607
Phone: (352)372-5468
Fax: (352)373-9178
Subject(s): Shopping Guides
Circ: (Free)‡40,000

**The Jackson Sun** (28639)
Gannett Company Inc.
The Jackson Sun
245 W. Lafayette
Jackson, TN 38302
Phone: (731)427-3333

Subject(s): Daily Newspapers
Circ: (Mon.-Sat.)37,311
(Sun.)40,000

**Periodico El Regional de Guayama** (27766)
Periodico El Oriental Inc.
Ave. Cruz Ortiz Stella 36
Humacao, PR 00791
Phone: (787)852-1496
Fax: (787)852-3405
Subject(s): Free Newspapers; Spanish
Circ: (Non-paid)39,800

**Caribbean Business** (27797)
Casiano Communications Inc.
1700 Fernandez Juncos Ave.
San Juan, PR 00909
Phone: (787)728-3000
Fax: (787)268-1001
Subject(s): International Business and Economics
Circ: (Free)4,500
(Paid)39,500

**Atlanta Business Chronicle** (6834)
American City Business Journals Inc.
1801 Peachtree St., Ste. 150
Atlanta, GA 30309
Phone: (404)249-1048
Fax: (404)249-1048
Subject(s): Business
Circ: (Paid)39,462

**Press-Journal** (6707)
PO Box 1268
Vero Beach, FL 32961
Phone: (561)562-2315
Fax: (561)978-2365
Subject(s): Daily Newspapers
Circ: (Mon.-Sat.)35,848
(Sun.)39,046

**KEA News** (11668)
Kentucky Education Association
401 Capital Ave.
Frankfort, KY 40601
Phone: (502)875-2889
Fax: (502)227-8062
Subject(s): Education
Circ: (Free)39,000

**Waterfront News** (5971)
Ziegler Publishing Company Inc.
1515 SW 1 Ave.
Fort Lauderdale, FL 33315
Phone: (954)524-9450
Fax: (954)524-9464
Subject(s): Boats and Marine; Free Newspapers
Circ: (Paid)‡750
(Free)‡39,000

**Albany Area Advertiser** (6764)
132 Pine Ave.
Albany, GA 31701
Phone: (229)888-7653
Fax: (229)438-7593
Subject(s): Shopping Guides
Circ: (Free)38,000

**Charlotte Shopping Guide** (6478)
Cape Coral Daily Breeze
128 W Charlotte Ave.
Punta Gorda, FL 33950
Phone: (941)639-1136
Fax: (941)639-4832
Subject(s): Shopping Guides
Circ: (Free)‡38,000

**News Herald** (6428)
Freedom Communications Inc.
501 W 11th St.
Panama City, FL 32402
Phone: (850)747-5000
Fax: (850)763-4636
Subject(s): Daily Newspapers
Circ: (Mon.-Sat.)32,593
(Sun.)37,399

**The Tuscaloosa News** (470)
6th St. & 20th Ave.
PO Box 20587
Tuscaloosa, AL 35401
Phone: (205)345-0505
Fax: (205)349-0845

## Southern States

Subject(s): Daily Newspapers
Circ: (Mon.-Sat.)★34,332
(Sun.)★36,205

**Northeast Mississippi Daily Journal (17020)**
Journal Publishing Co.
PO Box 909
Tupelo, MS 38802-0909
Phone: (662)842-2611
Fax: (662)620-8301
Subject(s): Daily Newspapers
Circ: (Mon.-Sat.)36,032
(Sun.)36,052

**Lake Worth Herald (6166)**
Lake Worth Herald Press
130 S H St.
Lake Worth, FL 33460
Phone: (561)585-9387
Fax: (561)585-5434
Subject(s): Free Newspapers
Circ: (Paid)2,000
(Free)36,000

**Pensacola Voice (6443)**
213 E Yonge St.
Pensacola, FL 32503-3766
Phone: (850)434-6963
Fax: (850)469-8745
Subject(s): Paid Community Newspapers; Black Publications
Circ: ‡35,896

**Florence Morning News (28094)**
Thomson Newspapers
PO Box 100528
Florence, SC 29501-0528
Phone: (803)317-6397
Fax: (803)661-6558
Subject(s): Daily Newspapers
Circ: (Mon.-Sat.)★32,664
(Sun.)★35,708

**Osceola Shopper (6142)**
Florida Sun Publications
108 Church St.
Kissimmee, FL 34741
Phone: (407)846-7600
Fax: (407)846-8516
Subject(s): Free Newspapers
Circ: (Non-paid)35,500

**The News Journal (28095)**
1460 W Evans St.
Florence, SC 29501
Phone: (843)667-9656
Fax: (843)661-7102
Subject(s): Free Newspapers
Circ: (Free)‡35,053

**Shelby Sun Times (28618)**
7508 Captial Dr.
Germantown, TN 38138-0801
Phone: (901)755-7386
Fax: (901)755-0827
Subject(s): Free Newspapers
Circ: (Non-paid)35,000

**The Dothan Eagle (190)**
Eagle
227 N Oates St.
PO Box 1968
Dothan, AL 36302
Phone: (334)792-3141
Fax: (334)712-7979
Subject(s): Daily Newspapers
Circ: (Mon.-Sat.)★32,891
(Sun.)★34,776

**Johnson City Press (28658)**
Carl A. Jones Newspapers
204 W Main St.
PO Box 1717
Johnson City, TN 37605
Phone: (423)929-3111
Fax: (423)461-9558
Subject(s): Daily Newspapers
Circ: (Mon.-Sat.)30,365
(Sun.)34,413

**TimesDaily (5949)**
PO Box 797
Florence, FL
Phone: (256)740-4717
Fax: (205)740-4717

Subject(s): Daily Newspapers
Circ: (Mon.-Sat.)31,639
(Sun.)34,267

**Gaston Gazette (23497)**
Freedom Communications Inc.
2500 E Franklin Blvd.
PO Box 1538
Gastonia, NC 28053
Phone: (704)864-3291
Fax: (704)867-6988
Subject(s): Daily Newspapers
Circ: (Mon.-Sat.)★31,349
(Sun.)★34,110

**Country Peddler (11553)**
PO Box 492
Bowling Green, KY 42102
Phone: (270)842-3314
Fax: (270)842-4220
Subject(s): Shopping Guides
Circ: (Free)‡33,700

**The Charlotte Sun Herald (6465)**
Sun Coast Media Group Inc.
23170 Harborview Rd.
Port Charlotte, FL 33980
Phone: (941)206-1000
Fax: (206)629-2085
Subject(s): Daily Newspapers
Circ: (Mon.-Sat.)30,359
(Sun.)33,225

**Bonita Banner (5832)**
Scripps Howard Inc.
PO Box 40
Bonita Springs, FL 34133
Phone: (941)992-2110
Fax: (941)992-7819
Subject(s): Free Newspapers
Circ: (Free)33,000

**Winter Haven Shopper (6739)**
News Chief Publishing Group
650 Sixth St. SW
Winter Haven, FL 33882
Phone: (863)294-1100
Fax: (863)294-2008
Subject(s): Shopping Guides
Circ: (Free)‡33,000

**The Herald (28214)**
132 W Main St.
PO Box 11707
Rock Hill, SC 29731
Phone: (803)329-4000
Fax: (803)329-4028
Subject(s): Daily Newspapers
Circ: (Mon.-Sat.)31,050
(Sun.)32,918

**Busy Shopper (7156)**
Busy Shopper Inc.
2712 Lafayette Rd
Fort Oglethorpe, GA 30742
Phone: (706)866-1020
Fax: (706)866-1128
Subject(s): Shopping Guides
Circ: (Non-paid)32,900

**Athens Banner Herald (6788)**
Morris Communications Corp.
One Press Pl.
Athens, GA 30601
Phone: (706)549-0123
Fax: (706)543-5234
Subject(s): Daily Newspapers
Circ: (Mon.-Thurs.)★26,606
(Sat.)★27,001
(Fri.)★29,055
(Sun.)★32,335

**Miami Today (6253)**
Today Enterprises Inc.
710 Breickell Ave.
Miami, FL 33131
Phone: (305)358-2663
Subject(s): Business; Local, State, and Regional Publications; Paid Community Newspapers
Circ: (Paid)△601
(Controlled)△32,146

**Iwanna (23231)**
Iwanna Inc.
991 Sweeten Creek Rd.
PO Box 15228
Asheville, NC 28813-5228
Phone: (828)274-8888
Fax: (828)258-9781
Subject(s): Shopping Guides
Circ: (Free)3,000
(Paid)32,000

**The Weekly News (6266)**
The Weekly News Inc.
901 NE 79th St.
Miami, FL 33138
Phone: (305)757-6333
Fax: (305)756-6488
Subject(s): Gay and Lesbian Interests; Free Newspapers
Circ: (Free)‡32,000

**Carrollwood News (5863)**
Sunbelt Newspapers Inc.
5501 W. Waters Ave., Ste. 404
Tampa, FL 33634-1229
Subject(s): Free Newspapers
Circ: (Free)31,951

**The Independent Florida Alligator (6028)**
Campus Communications Inc.
PO Box 14257
Gainesville, FL 32604-2257
Phone: (352)376-4446
Fax: (352)376-4556
Subject(s): College Publications
Circ: (Paid)‡93
(Free)‡31,907

**Messenger-Inquirer (11924)**
Owensboro Messenger-Inquirer
1401 Frederica St.
PO Box 1480
Owensboro, KY 42301-1480
Phone: (270)926-0123
Fax: (270)691-7244
Subject(s): Daily Newspapers
Circ: (Mon.-Sat.)★27,960
(Sun.)★30,973

**The Mountain Times (23251)**
Sundown Times
PO Box 1815
Boone, NC 28607
Phone: (828)264-6397
Fax: (828)262-0282
Subject(s): Free Newspapers
Circ: (Combined)30,842

**Sunbelt Foodservice (7167)**
Shelby Publishing Company Inc.
517 Green St.
Gainesville, GA 30501
Phone: (770)534-8380
Fax: (770)535-0110
Subject(s): Food and Grocery Trade; Hotels, Motels, Restaurants, and Clubs
Circ: (Paid)1,533
(Controlled)30,090

**Carolina Farmer (23858)**
Farm Progress Cos.
700 Privette St.
Wilson, NC 27893
Phone: (252)237-8999
Fax: (252)237-8999
Subject(s): Farm Newspapers
Circ: ‡30,000

**Free Times (28045)**
Free Times Inc.
6904 N. Main St.
Columbia, SC 29203
Phone: (803)765-0707
Fax: (803)765-0727
Subject(s): Free Newspapers
Circ: (Combined)⊕30,000

**Lake Cumberland Shopper (11993)**
CNHI
110-112 E Mount Vernon St.
PO Box 859
Somerset, KY 42502
Phone: (606)678-8191
Fax: (606)679-9225
Subject(s): Shopping Guides
Circ: (Free)30,000

**Gale Directory of Publications & Broadcast Media/140th Ed.**  **Southern States**

**The Observer News** (6485)
210 Woodland Estates Ave. SW
Ruskin, FL 33570
Phone: (813)645-3111
Fax: (813)645-4118
**Subject(s):** Paid Community Newspapers
**Circ:** (Free)30,000

**The Truth at Last** (7295)
The Thunderbolt Inc.
PO Box 1211
Marietta, GA 30061
**Subject(s):** Alternative and Underground; Politics; Paid Community Newspapers
**Circ:** (Free)‡12,000
(Paid)‡30,000

**The Henry Neighbor** (7282)
Neighbor Newspapers Inc.
580 Fairground St.
PO Box 449
Marietta, GA 30060
Phone: (770)795-3000
Fax: (770)428-7945
**Subject(s):** Free Newspapers
**Circ:** (Paid)7
(Non-paid)29,909

**Daily Commercial** (6180)
PO Box 490007
Leesburg, FL 34749-0007
Phone: (352)365-8200
Fax: (352)365-1951
**Subject(s):** Daily Newspapers
**Circ:** (Sun.)29,423
(Mon.-Sat.)29,764

**High Point Enterprise** (23586)
H.P. Enterprise Inc.
210 Church Ave.
PO Box 1009
High Point, NC 27261
Phone: (336)888-3500
Fax: (336)841-5165
**Subject(s):** Daily Newspapers
**Circ:** (Mon.-Sat.)★27,917
(Sun.)★29,544

**Venice Weekly** (6540)
Florida Sun Publications
3755 S. Tuttle Ave.
Sarasota, FL 34239
Phone: (914)923-2544
Fax: (914)924-1866
**Subject(s):** Shopping Guides
**Circ:** (Non-paid)29,349

**Southern Voice** (6919)
The Atlanta Pride Committee
1075 Zonolite Rd., Ste. 1-D
Atlanta, GA 30306
Phone: (404)876-1819
Fax: (404)876-2709
**Subject(s):** Gay and Lesbian Interests
**Circ:** (Paid)◻21
(Non-paid)◻29,047

**Citrus County Chronicle** (5910)
Landmark Community Newspapers Inc.
1624 N. Meadowcrest Blvd.
Crystal River, FL 34429
Phone: (904)563-6363
**Subject(s):** Daily Newspapers
**Circ:** (Mon.-Sat.)★25,736
(Sun.)★28,978

**Harbor Sound** (7022)
1326 Newcastle St.
PO Box 606
Brunswick, GA 31521
Phone: (912)264-4521
Fax: (912)264-4531
**Subject(s):** Free Newspapers
**Circ:** (Free)‡28,000

**Decatur Daily** (177)
Tennessee Valley Printing
PO Box 2213
Decatur, AL 35609-2213
**Subject(s):** Daily Newspapers
**Circ:** (Mon.-Fri.)25,459
(Sat.)25,750
(Sun.)27,950

**The Paducah Sun** (11932)
PO Box 2300
Paducah, KY 42002-2300
Phone: (502)443-1771
Fax: (502)442-7859
**Subject(s):** Daily Newspapers
**Circ:** (Mon.-Sat.)25,165
(Sun.)27,900

**Osceola News-Gazette** (6141)
Florida Sun Publications
108 Church St.
Kissimmee, FL 34741
Phone: (407)846-7600
Fax: (407)846-8516
**Subject(s):** Paid Community Newspapers
**Circ:** (Paid)990
(Non-paid)27,568

**The South Fulton Neighbor** (7292)
Neighbor Newspapers Inc.
580 Fairground St.
PO Box 449
Marietta, GA 30060
Phone: (770)795-3000
Fax: (770)428-7945
**Subject(s):** Free Newspapers
**Circ:** (Paid)11
(Non-paid)27,489

**Sandy Springs Neighbor** (7290)
Neighbor Newspapers Inc.
580 Fairground St.
PO Box 449
Marietta, GA 30060
Phone: (770)795-3000
Fax: (770)428-7945
**Subject(s):** Free Newspapers
**Circ:** (Paid)215
(Free)27,259

**The Anniston Star** (14)
PO Box 189
Anniston, AL 36202
Phone: (256)236-1551
Fax: (256)241-1991
**Subject(s):** Daily Newspapers
**Circ:** (Mon.-Sat.)25,668
(Sun.)27,019

**The Catholic Miscellany** (28001)
New Catholic Miscellany
PO Box 818
Charleston, SC 29402-0818
Phone: (843)724-8375
Fax: (843)724-8368
**Subject(s):** Religious Publications
**Circ:** ‡27,000

**The Peddler** (28544)
Peddler
1860 Wilma Rudolph Blvd., Ste. 101
Clarksville, TN 37040
Phone: (931)552-1160
Fax: (931)552-1777
**Subject(s):** Shopping Guides
**Circ:** (Free)‡27,000

**The Hattiesburg American** (16846)
Gannett Company Inc.
825 N. Main St.
PO Box 1111
Hattiesburg, MS 39401
Phone: (601)583-4321
Fax: (601)583-8244
**Subject(s):** Daily Newspapers
**Circ:** (Mon.-Sat.)22,741
(Sun.)26,958

**Daily News Shopping Guide** (11556)
Daily News Publishing Inc.
813 College St.
PO Box 90012
Bowling Green, KY 42102
Phone: (270)781-1700
Fax: (270)781-0726
**Subject(s):** Shopping Guides
**Circ:** (Mon.-Sun.)21,000
(Sun.)26,800

**Plant City Shopper** (6458)
Sunbelt Newspapers Inc.
101 N. Wheeler St.
Plant City, FL 33566
Phone: (813)752-3113

Fax: (813)865-4449
**Subject(s):** Shopping Guides
**Circ:** (Free)26,800

**The Albany Herald** (6765)
PO Box 48
Albany, GA 31702
**Subject(s):** Daily Newspapers
**Circ:** (Mon.-Sat.)★24,831
(Sun.)★26,796

**Daily News** (11554)
813 College St.
PO Box 90012
Bowling Green, KY 42102
Phone: (270)781-1700
Fax: (502)781-0726
**Subject(s):** Daily Newspapers
**Circ:** (Mon.-Sat.)21,884
(Sun.)26,449

**Putnam Pennysaver** (6409)
Volusia Pennysaver Inc.
PO Box 220
1095 Hwy 19 North
Palatka, FL 32178
Phone: (386)328-4649
Fax: (386)325-4617
**Subject(s):** Shopping Guides
**Circ:** (Free)‡26,015

**Columbia County News Times** (7144)
4272 Washington Rd. 3-B
Evans, GA 30809
Phone: (706)863-6165
Fax: (706)868-9824
**Subject(s):** Paid Community Newspapers
**Circ:** (Wed.)18,000
(Sun.)26,000

**La Noticia** (23348)
5936 Monroe Rd.
Charlotte, NC 28212
Phone: (704)568-6966
Fax: (704)568-8936
**Subject(s):** Paid Community Newspapers; Spanish; Ethnic Publications
**Circ:** ⊕26,000

**Mississippi Legionnaire** (16888)
The American Legion Mississippi Dept.
PO Box 688
120 N State St 1st Floor
Jackson, MS 39202
Phone: (601)353-3681
Fax: (601)352-7181
**Subject(s):** Veterans
**Circ:** 26,000

**New Smyrna Pennysaver** (6324)
Volusia Pennysaver Inc.
237 Canal St.
Box 767
New Smyrna Beach, FL 32168
Phone: (386)423-2300
Fax: (386)426-2807
**Subject(s):** Shopping Guides
**Circ:** (Free)‡26,000

**Wilson Post** (28721)
Wilson Post, LLC
216 Hartmann Dr.
PO Box 857
Lebanon, TN 37088
Phone: (615)444-6008
Fax: (615)444-6018
**Subject(s):** Paid Community Newspapers
**Circ:** (Fri.)9,500
(Wed.)26,000

**The Daily Independent** (11518)
Ashland Publishing Co.
224 17th St.
Ashland, KY 41101
Fax: (606)326-2600
**Subject(s):** Daily Newspapers
**Circ:** (Mon.-Sat.)22,532
(Sun.)25,888

**The Salisbury Post** (23768)
Post Publishing Co.
131 W. Innes St.
Salisbury, NC 28144
Phone: (704)633-8950
Fax: (704)639-0003

---

Circulation: ★ = ABC; △ = BPA; ◆ = CAC; ● = CCAB; ◻ = VAC; ⊕ = PO Statement; ‡ = Publisher's Report; Boldface figures = sworn; Light figures = estimated.

3787

**Subject(s):** Daily Newspapers
**Circ:** (Mon.-Sat.)24,178
(Sun.)25,874

**St. John's Pennysaver** (6490)
Volusia Pennysaver Inc.
1740 A1A S.
PO Box 500
Saint Augustine, FL 32085
Phone: (904)471-8488
Fax: (904)471-4519
**Subject(s):** Shopping Guides
**Circ:** (Free)25,222

**The Times** (7168)
345 Green St., NW
PO Box 838
Gainesville, GA 30503
Phone: (770)532-1234
Fax: (770)532-7085
**Subject(s):** Daily Newspapers
**Circ:** (Mon.-Sat.)21,153
(Sun.)25,200

**The News Beacon** (28869)
The News Herald
PO Box 140628
Nashville, TN 37214
Phone: (615)889-1860
**Subject(s):** Free Newspapers
**Circ:** (Free)‡25,000

**Observer Community Newspaper** (5928)
Deerfield Publishers
43 NE 2nd St.
Deerfield Beach, FL 33441
Phone: (954)428-9045
Fax: (954)428-9096
**Subject(s):** Paid Community Newspapers
**Circ:** 25,000

**Simple Pleasures** (23656)
Mount Airy Newspapers Inc.
319 N Renfro St.
PO Box 808
Mount Airy, NC 27030-0808
Phone: (336)786-4141
Fax: (336)789-2816
**Subject(s):** Travel and Tourism; Local, State, and Regional Publications
**Circ:** (Paid)‡10,000
(Non-paid)‡25,000

**The Tennessee Tribune** (28892)
Perry & Perry & Associates
Tennessee Tribune Bldg.
1501 Jefferson St.
Nashville, TN 37208
Phone: (615)321-3268
Fax: (615)321-0409
**Subject(s):** Paid Community Newspapers; Black Publications
**Circ:** (Paid)‡25,000

**Mountain Xpress** (23232)
Green Line Media Inc.
PO Box 144
Asheville, NC 28802
Phone: (828)251-1333
Fax: (828)251-1311
**Subject(s):** Free Newspapers
**Circ:** (Combined)24,877

**Citizen Tribune** (28813)
Lakeway Publishers Inc.
PO Box 625
Morristown, TN 37815-0625
Phone: (423)581-5630
Fax: (423)581-3061
**Subject(s):** Daily Newspapers
**Circ:** (Mon.-Fri.)★18,236
(Sun.)★24,441

**Speakin' Out News** (271)
115 Wholesale Ave.
Huntsville, AL 35811
Phone: (226)551-1020
Fax: (256)551-0607
**Subject(s):** Paid Community Newspapers; Black Publications
**Circ:** ‡24,000

**Western Farm Press** (16781)
Southwest Farm Press
Western Farm Press
14920 US Hwy. 61
Clarksdale, MS 38614
Phone: (662)624-8503
Fax: (662)627-1137
**Subject(s):** General Agriculture
**Circ:** (Combined)24,000

**Alpharetta Neighbor** (6777)
Neighbor Newspapers Inc.
10930 Crabapple Rd., Ste. 9
Roswell, GA 30075-5812
**Subject(s):** Free Newspapers
**Circ:** (Combined)23,943

**Gadsden Times** (234)
The Gadsden Times Inc.
401 Locust St.
PO Box 188
Gadsden, AL 35901-3737
Phone: (205)549-2000
Fax: (205)549-2105
**Subject(s):** Daily Newspapers
**Circ:** (Mon.-Sat.)★22,014
(Sun.)★23,939

**Goldsboro News-Argus** (23500)
News-Argus
310 N Berkeley Blvd.
Goldsboro, NC 27534
Phone: (919)778-2211
Fax: (919)778-9891
**Subject(s):** Daily Newspapers
**Circ:** (Mon.-Fri.)★20,692
(Sun.)★23,578

**The Daily Reflector** (23551)
Cox North Carolina Publications Inc.
PO Box 1967
1150 Sugg Parkway
Greenville, NC 27835
Phone: (252)329-9500
Fax: (252)752-9583
**Subject(s):** Daily Newspapers
**Circ:** (Mon.-Sat.)20,359
(Sun.)23,550

**Pelican Press** (6534)
Journal Communications
5011 Ocean Blvd
Sarasota, FL 34242
Phone: (941)349-4949
Fax: (941)346-7118
**Subject(s):** Free Newspapers; Free Newspapers
**Circ:** (Paid)‡800
(Free)‡23,500

**Sun-Times** (6126)
The Leader Group
1114 Beach Blvd.
Jacksonville Beach, FL 32250
Phone: (904)249-9033
Fax: (904)249-1501
**Subject(s):** Free Newspapers
**Circ:** (Free)‡23,500

**Florida Sentinel-Bulletin** (6631)
2207-21st Ave.
PO Box 3363
Tampa, FL 33601
Phone: (813)248-1921
Fax: (813)248-4507
**Subject(s):** Paid Community Newspapers; Black Publications
**Circ:** ‡23,345

**Delta Farm Press** (16779)
Southwest Farm Press
Delta Farm Press
14920 US Hwy. 61
Clarksdale, MS 38614
Phone: (662)624-8503
Fax: (662)627-1137
**Subject(s):** Farm Newspapers
**Circ:** (Non-paid)7,977
(Paid)23,224

**Daily News** (23598)
Freedom Communications Inc.
724 Bell Fork Rd.
Jacksonville, NC 28546
Phone: (910)353-1171
Fax: (910)353-7316

**Subject(s):** Daily Newspapers
**Circ:** (Mon.-Sat.)21,101
(Sun.)23,217

**Shelby Report of the Southeast** (7165)
Shelby Publishing Company Inc.
517 Green St.
Gainesville, GA 30501
Phone: (770)534-8380
Fax: (770)535-0110
**Subject(s):** Food and Grocery Trade
**Circ:** (Paid)2,059
(Controlled)23,077

**Ft. Campbell Courier** (11660)
Kentucky New Era
Public Affairs Office
2334 19th St.
Fort Campbell, KY 42223
Phone: (502)798-6759
Fax: (502)798-6247
**Subject(s):** Free Newspapers; Military and Navy
**Circ:** (Free)23,000

**Georgia College & State University Connection** (7307)
Georgia College Alumni Association Inc.
CBX 097
Milledgeville, GA 31061
Phone: (478)445-6804
Fax: (478)445-6795
**Subject(s):** College Publications
**Circ:** (Free)‡23,000

**The Independent Tribune** (23602)
924 Cloverleaf Plz.
Kannapolis, NC 28083
Phone: (704)782-3155
Fax: (704)786-0645
**Subject(s):** Daily Newspapers
**Circ:** (Mon.-Fri.)20,538
(Sun.)22,887

**The Fayette Neighbor** (7177)
Neighbor Newspapers Inc.
323 E. Solomon St.
P.O. Box M
Griffin, GA 30224
Phone: (770)227-3276
Fax: (404)412-1678
**Subject(s):** Free Newspapers
**Circ:** (Paid)7
(Non-paid)22,701

**Vallejo Times-Herald** (107)
Community Newspaper Holdings Inc.
3500 Colonnade Pkwy., Ste. 600
Birmingham, AL 35243
Phone: (205)298-7100
Fax: (205)298-7101
**Subject(s):** Daily Newspapers
**Circ:** (Sat.)★18,920
(Mon.-Fri.)★20,927
(Sun.)★22,464

**Jewish Journal Dade** (5927)
Forum Publishing Group Inc.
1701 Green Rd., Ste. B
Deerfield Beach, FL 33064
Phone: (954)698-6397
Fax: (954)429-1207
**Subject(s):** Free Newspapers
**Circ:** (Combined)22,315

**The Miami Times** (6252)
900 NW 54th St.
Miami, FL 33127
Phone: (305)757-1147
Fax: (305)757-5770
**Subject(s):** Paid Community Newspapers; Black Publications
**Circ:** (Wed.)22,050

**The Auburn Plainsman** (35)
Auburn University
B-100 Foy Union Bldg.
Foy Student Union
Auburn, AL 36849-5542
Phone: (334)844-4130
Fax: (334)844-9114
**Subject(s):** College Publications
**Circ:** 22,000

**Town'n Country News** (6656)
Sunbelt Newspapers Inc.
5501 W. Waters Ave., Ste. 404
Tampa, FL 33634-1229
**Subject(s):** Free Newspapers

**Circ:** (Free)22,000

**South Orange News** (6143)
Florida Sun Publications
108 Church St.
Kissimmee, FL 34741
Phone: (407)846-7600
Fax: (407)846-8516
**Subject(s):** Free Newspapers

**Circ:** (Non-paid)21,900

**Dunwoody De Kalb Neighbor** (7132)
Neighbor Newspapers Inc.
580 Fairground St.
PO Box 449
Marietta, GA 30060
Phone: (770)795-3000
Fax: (770)428-7945
**Subject(s):** Free Newspapers

**Circ:** (Paid)♦5
(Non-paid)♦**21,772**

**Clayton News/Daily** (7215)
News Daily
138 Church St.
Jonesboro, GA 30236
Phone: (770)478-5753
Fax: (770)473-9032
**Subject(s):** Daily Newspapers

**Circ:** (Wed.)21,625

**Northside Neighbor/Sandy Springs Neighbor** (6906)
Neighbor Newspapers Inc.
5290 Roswell Rd. NW, Ste. M
Atlanta, GA 30342
Phone: (404)256-3100
Fax: (404)256-3292
**Subject(s):** Free Newspapers

**Circ:** (Paid)37
(Non-paid)21,519

**Santa Rosa Free Press** (6294)
Press Gazette
6629 SW Elva St.
Milton, FL 32570
Phone: (850)623-2120
Fax: (850)623-2007
**Subject(s):** Free Newspapers

**Circ:** (Free)‡21,500

**Surry Scene** (23657)
Mount Airy Newspapers Inc.
319 N Renfro St.
PO Box 808
Mount Airy, NC 27030-0808
Phone: (336)786-4141
Fax: (336)789-2816
**Subject(s):** Free Newspapers

**Circ:** (Free)‡21,500

**Tri-County Penny Saver** (7196)
PO Box 498
Hinesville, GA 31313
Phone: (912)876-0156
Fax: (912)368-6329
**Subject(s):** Shopping Guides

**Circ:** (Free)21,500

**The Item** (28237)
Osteen Publishing Company Inc.
20 N. Magnolia St.
PO Box 1677
Sumter, SC 29151
Phone: (803)774-1200
Fax: (803)775-1024
**Subject(s):** Daily Newspapers

**Circ:** (Sun.)★**20,745**
(Mon.-Sat.)★**21,389**

**Chamblee De Kalb Neighbor** (7276)
Neighbor Newspapers Inc.
580 Fairground St.
PO Box 449
Marietta, GA 30060
Phone: (770)795-3000
Fax: (770)428-7945
**Subject(s):** Free Newspapers

**Circ:** (Combined)21,344

**The Douglas Neighbor** (7279)
Neighbor Newspapers Inc.
580 Fairground St.
PO Box 449
Marietta, GA 30060
Phone: (770)795-3000
Fax: (770)428-7945
**Subject(s):** Free Newspapers

**Circ:** (Paid)13
(Non-paid)21,115

**Margate/Coconut Creek Forum** (6206)
Tribune Co.
9660 W. Sample Rd., Ste. 203
Coral Springs, FL 33065
Phone: (954)752-7474
Fax: (954)752-7855
**Subject(s):** Paid Community Newspapers

**Circ:** (Combined)21,070

**Mississippi Press** (16987)
Newhouse Newspapers
PO Box 849
Pascagoula, MS 39568
Phone: (228)762-1111
Fax: (228)934-1454
**Subject(s):** Daily Newspapers

**Circ:** (Mon.-Fri.)20,108
(Sun.)21,038

**Moultrie News** (28173)
Island Publications
PO Box 2014
Mount Pleasant, SC 29465
Phone: (843)849-1778
Fax: (843)849-0214
**Subject(s):** Free Newspapers

**Circ:** (Free)‡21,000

**Wesleyan Christian Advocate** (7432)
Wesleyan Christian Advocate Inc.
PO Box 427
Stone Mountain, GA 30086-0427
Phone: (770)465-1685
Fax: (770)465-0685
**Subject(s):** Religious Publications

**Circ:** ‡21,000

**Exchange** (28599)
404 S Main St.
PO Box 490
Fayetteville, TN 37334
Phone: (931)433-9737
Fax: (931)433-0053
**Subject(s):** Shopping Guides

**Circ:** (Free)‡20,850

**The Daily Times** (28745)
307 E Harper St.
PO Box 9740
Maryville, TN 37802
Phone: (865)981-1100
Fax: (865)681-1175
**Subject(s):** Daily Newspapers

**Circ:** (Sun.)19,963
(Mon.-Sat.)20,811

**Chapel Hill News** (23295)
505 W. Franklin St.
PO Box 870
Chapel Hill, NC 27516
Phone: (919)932-2000
Fax: (919)968-4953
**Subject(s):** Paid Community Newspapers

**Circ:** (Wed.)20,538
(Sun.)20,608

**The Advantage** (7486)
Advance Publishing Company Inc.
PO Box 669
Vidalia, GA 30474
Phone: (912)537-3131
Fax: (912)537-4899
**Subject(s):** Shopping Guides

**Circ:** (Free)20,400

**The Charlotte Post** (23338)
Charlotte Post Pub.
1531 Camden Rd.
PO Box 30144
Charlotte, NC 28230
Phone: (704)376-0496
Fax: (704)342-2160
**Subject(s):** Paid Community Newspapers; Black Publications

**Circ:** ‡20,378

**Shelby Report of the Southwest** (7166)
Shelby Publishing Company Inc.
517 Green St.
Gainesville, GA 30501
Phone: (770)534-8380
Fax: (770)535-0110
**Subject(s):** Food and Grocery Trade

**Circ:** (Paid)‡1,846
(Non-paid)‡3,638
(Controlled)‡20,357

**The Kershaw County Current** (27992)
PO Box 9
Camden, SC 29020
Phone: (803)432-8439
Fax: (803)432-5881
**Subject(s):** Free Newspapers

**Circ:** ⊕**20,200**

**Daytona Times** (5916)
Daytona Times Inc.
427 S Dr. M.L. King Jr. Blvd.
Daytona Beach, FL 32114
Phone: (386)253-0321
Fax: (386)254-7510
**Subject(s):** Paid Community Newspapers; Black Publications

**Circ:** ‡20,150

**Advertiser** (11884)
PO Box 518
Maysville, KY 41056
Phone: (606)564-9091
Fax: (606)564-6893
**Subject(s):** Shopping Guides

**Circ:** (Free)‡20,133

**Bargain Browser** (29029)
101 Highland Dr.& Hwy. 31
PO Box 347
White House, TN 37188
Phone: (615)672-3555
Fax: (615)672-5971
**Subject(s):** Shopping Guides

**Circ:** (Free)20,136

**AUC Digest** (6841)
Atlanta University Center
PO Box 3191
Atlanta, GA 30302
Phone: (404)523-6136
Fax: (404)523-5467
**Subject(s):** Black Publications; College Publications

**Circ:** (Paid)‡100
(Non-paid)‡20,000

**The Business Report & Journal** (7393)
Coastal Empire Media Inc.
5 Oglethorpe Professional Blvd., Ste. 100
Savannah, GA 31406
Phone: (912)351-9122
Fax: (912)351-9045
**Subject(s):** Business

**Circ:** (Mon.)20,000

**The Columbus Times** (7064)
Columbus Times
2230 Buena Vista Rd.
Columbus, GA 31906
Phone: (706)324-2404
Fax: (706)596-0657
**Subject(s):** Paid Community Newspapers; Black Publications

**Circ:** ‡20,000

**Daily News Express** (11555)
Daily News Publishing Inc.
813 College St.
PO Box 90012
Bowling Green, KY 42102
Phone: (502)781-1700
Fax: (502)781-0726
**Subject(s):** Shopping Guides

**Circ:** (Wed.)†1,500
(Sun.)20,000

**The Daily Tar Heel** (23297)
DTH Publishing Corp.
104 Carolina Union
CB 5210
Chapel Hill, NC 27514
Phone: (919)962-5387
Fax: (919)962-5387
**Subject(s):** College Publications

**Circ:** (Free)‡20,000

## Southern States

**Inside the Turret** (11663)
News-Enterprise
PO Box 995
Fort Knox, KY 40121-0995
Phone: (502)624-1211
Fax: (502)624-6074
**Subject(s):** Free Newspapers; Military and Navy
**Circ:** (Free)‡20,000

**Jackson Advocate** (16880)
Natchez Democrate Inc.
300 N Fanisha
PO Box 3708
Jackson, MS 39207
Phone: (601)948-4122
Fax: (601)948-4125
**Subject(s):** Black Publications; Paid Community Newspapers
**Circ:** (Free)‡3,000
 (Paid)‡20,000

**Robins Rev-Up** (7492)
The Daily Sun
WR-ALC Office of Public Affairs
215 Page Rd., Ste. 106
Warner Robins, GA 31098-1662
Phone: (912)926-2137
Fax: (912)926-9597
**Subject(s):** Free Newspapers; Military and Navy
**Circ:** (Free)‡20,000

**Southern Festivals** (7014)
PO Box 390
Blakely, GA 39823
Phone: (912)723-2778
Fax: (912)723-2779
**Subject(s):** Local, State, and Regional Publications; Travel and Tourism
**Circ:** (Paid)3,000
 (Non-paid)20,000

**The Swap Shop** (16995)
PO Box 907
Picayune, MS 39466
Phone: (601)798-4835
Fax: (601)798-9755
**Subject(s):** Paid Community Newspapers
**Circ:** 20,000

**The Island Packet** (28143)
PO Box 5727
Hilton Head Island, SC 29938
Phone: (843)706-8100
Fax: (843)706-3070
**Subject(s):** Daily Newspapers
**Circ:** (Mon.-Sat.)★18,416
 (Sun.)★19,972

**The Hanahan News** (28140)
Hanahan Publications
PO Box 60580
1928 East Montague
Charleston, SC 29405
Phone: (843)744-8000
Fax: (843)744-5505
**Subject(s):** Free Newspapers
**Circ:** (Paid)1,225
 (Free)19,925

**La Prensa Newspaper** (6734)
News Chief Publishing Group
650 Sixth St. SW
Winter Haven, FL 33882
Phone: (863)294-1100
Fax: (863)294-2008
**Subject(s):** Free Newspapers; Spanish; Hispanic Publications
**Circ:** (Free)‡19,828

**The Times-News** (23573)
Hendersonville Newspaper Co.
PO Box 490
Hendersonville, NC 28793-0490
Phone: (704)692-0505
Fax: (704)692-2319
**Subject(s):** Daily Newspapers
**Circ:** (Mon.-Sat.)★19,487
 (Sun.)★19,604

**Meridian Star** (16945)
Meridian Star Inc.
814 22nd Ave.
Box 1591
Meridian, MS 39301
Phone: (601)693-1551
Fax: (601)485-1275

**Subject(s):** Daily Newspapers
**Circ:** (Mon.-Sat.)17,701
 (Sun.)19,532

**Cherokee Plus** (7050)
Neighbor Newspapers Inc.
Location Cherokee Tribune
521 E. Main St.
Canton, GA 30114
Phone: (770)479-1441
**Subject(s):** Free Newspapers
**Circ:** (Non-paid)♦19,500

**The Democrat-Observer** (28738)
The Advocate-Democrat
509 Cook St.
PO Box 8
Madisonville, TN 37354
Phone: (423)442-4575
Fax: (423)442-1416
**Subject(s):** Paid Community Newspapers
**Circ:** ‡19,500

**Rome News-Tribune** (7368)
News Publishing Co.
PO Box 1633
Rome, GA 30162-1633
Phone: (706)291-6397
Fax: (706)232-9632
**Subject(s):** Daily Newspapers
**Circ:** (Mon.-Fri.)16,118
 (Sun.)19,472

**The Herald-News** (28579)
Rhea County Publishing Co.
PO Box 286
Dayton, TN 37321
Phone: (423)775-6111
Fax: (423)775-8218
**Subject(s):** Paid Community Newspapers
**Circ:** (Combined)‡19,400

**News Shopper** (7510)
News Shopper Inc.
8608 Main St.
Woodstock, GA 30188
Phone: (770)926-4467
Fax: (770)591-8478
**Subject(s):** Shopping Guides
**Circ:** (Non-paid)19,190

**Roswell Neighbor** (7289)
Neighbor Newspapers Inc.
580 Fairground St.
PO Box 449
Marietta, GA 30060
Phone: (770)795-3000
Fax: (770)428-7945
**Subject(s):** Free Newspapers
**Circ:** (Paid)♦15
 (Non-paid)♦19,023

**The Douglas Shopper** (7120)
Coffee County News & Shopper Inc.
213 N. Peterson Ave
Douglas, GA 31533
**Subject(s):** Shopping Guides
**Circ:** (Free)‡18,700

**Hi-Riser** (5957)
Tribune Co.
Forum Community News Group
3115 NW 10th Ter., Ste. 106
Fort Lauderdale, FL
Phone: (954)563-3311
Fax: (954)563-4230
**Subject(s):** Paid Community Newspapers
**Circ:** (Combined)18,575

**The Valdosta Daily Times** (7476)
Thomson Newspapers
PO Box 968
Valdosta, GA 31603
Phone: (912)244-1880
Fax: (912)244-2560
**Subject(s):** Daily Newspapers
**Circ:** (Mon.-Sat.)★16,378
 (Sun.)★18,472

**Daily News-Journal** (28826)
224 N Walnut St.
PO Box 68
Murfreesboro, TN 37133-0068
Phone: (615)893-5860
Fax: (615)896-8702

**Subject(s):** Daily Newspapers
**Circ:** (Mon.-Sat.)15,465
 (Sun.)18,235

**The Yadkin Valley Advertiser** (23461)
PO Box 1009
Elkin, NC 28621-1009
Phone: (336)835-1513
Fax: (336)835-8742
**Subject(s):** Shopping Guides
**Circ:** (Non-paid)⊕18,225

**Tamarac/North Lauderdale Forum** (5899)
Tribune Co.
9660 W. Sample Rd., Ste. 203
Coral Springs, FL 33065
Phone: (954)752-7474
Fax: (954)752-7855
**Subject(s):** Free Newspapers
**Circ:** (Non-paid)18,165

**La Gaceta** (6643)
La Gaceta Publishing Inc.
PO Box 5536
Tampa, FL 33675
**Subject(s):** Paid Community Newspapers; Italian; Spanish; Hispanic Publications
**Circ:** ‡18,079

**Technician** (23716)
North Carolina State University
323 Witherspoon Student Ctr.
NCSU Campus
Raleigh, NC 27695
Phone: (919)515-2411
Fax: (919)515-5133
**Subject(s):** College Publications
**Circ:** (Free)18,000

**Statesville Record and Landmark** (23799)
Park Newspapers of Statesville Inc.
222 E Broad St.
PO Box 1071
Statesville, NC 28677-5325
Phone: (704)873-1451
Fax: (704)872-3150
**Subject(s):** Daily Newspapers
**Circ:** (Mon.-Sat.)★14,685
 (Sun.)★17,973

**The Times & Democrat** (28204)
Times & Democrat
1010 Broughton
PO Drawer 1766
Orangeburg, SC 29115
Phone: (803)534-3352
Fax: (803)533-5526
**Subject(s):** Daily Newspapers
**Circ:** (Sun.)★17,712
 (Mon.-Sat.)★17,947

**The South De Kalb Neighbor** (7291)
Neighbor Newspapers Inc.
580 Fairground St.
PO Box 449
Marietta, GA 30060
Phone: (770)795-3000
Fax: (770)428-7945
**Subject(s):** Free Newspapers
**Circ:** (Non-paid)17,575

**The Courier-Tribune** (23223)
Stephens Media Group
500 Sunset Ave.
PO Box 340
Asheboro, NC 27204-0340
Phone: (336)625-2101
Fax: (336)626-7074
**Subject(s):** Daily Newspapers
**Circ:** (Mon.-Sat.)16,327
 (Sun.)17,500

**Mt. Sterling Advocate-Advertiser** (11908)
Mt. Sterling Advocate
219 Midland Trail
PO Box 406
Mount Sterling, KY 40353
Phone: (859)498-2222
Fax: (859)498-2228
**Subject(s):** Shopping Guides
**Circ:** (Free)17,400

**Gale Directory of Publications & Broadcast Media/140th Ed.**  **Southern States**

**The St. Augustine Record (6489)**
Morris Communications Corp.
PO Box 1630
Saint Augustine, FL 32085-1630
Phone: (904)819-3558
Fax: (904)819-3558
**Subject(s):** Daily Newspapers
**Circ:** (Mon.-Fri.)★15,572
(Sat.)★15,842
(Sun.)★17,281

**El Nuevo Patria (6230)**
El Nuevo Patria Publishing Co.
PO Box 2, Jose Marti Sta.
Miami, FL 33135-0002
Phone: (305)530-8787
**Subject(s):** Paid Community Newspapers; Hispanic Publications; Spanish
**Circ:** (Paid)‡12,910
(Free)‡17,090

**The Sampson Independent (23385)**
Community Newspaper Holdings Inc.
303 Elizabeth St.
PO Box 110
Clinton, NC 28328
Phone: (910)592-8137
Fax: (910)592-8756
**Subject(s):** Daily Newspapers
**Circ:** (Combined)17,048

**Brunswick Beacon (23776)**
PO Box 2558
Shallotte, NC 28459-2558
**Subject(s):** Paid Community Newspapers
**Circ:** ‡17,000

**County News-Enterprise (23483)**
Forest City Publishing Company Inc.
601 Oak St.
PO Box 1149
Forest City, NC 28043-1149
Phone: (828)245-6431
Fax: (828)248-2790
**Subject(s):** Free Newspapers
**Circ:** (Free)‡17,000

**East Bay Breeze (5798)**
Sunbelt Newspapers Inc.
3036 College Ave. E
Ruskin, FL 33570-5220
**Subject(s):** Free Newspapers
**Circ:** (Free)17,000

**The Jupiter Courier (6130)**
Scripps Howard Inc.
PO Box 1486
Jupiter, FL 33468-1486
Phone: (407)746-5111
Fax: (407)743-0673
**Subject(s):** Paid Community Newspapers
**Circ:** (Paid)‡8,000
(Free)‡17,000

**Kentucky Kernel (11769)**
Kernel Press Inc.
University of Kentucky
026 Grehan Journalism Bldg.
Lexington, KY 40506-0042
Phone: (606)257-2871
Fax: (606)323-1906
**Subject(s):** College Publications
**Circ:** 17,000

**The Louisville Cardinal (11830)**
University of Louisville
Old Student Ctr., Ste. 305
Louisville, KY 40292-0001
Phone: (502)852-0701
Fax: (502)588-0700
**Subject(s):** College Publications
**Circ:** (Free)17,000

**Pioneer News (11989)**
Landmark Community Newspapers Inc.
PO Box 98
Shepherdsville, KY 40165
Phone: (502)955-9701
Fax: (502)955-9704
**Subject(s):** Free Newspapers; Free Newspapers
**Circ:** (Paid)7,500
(Free)17,000

**Rocky Mount Telegram (23758)**
Cox Newspapers
Tiffany Office Plaza Bldg.
800 Tiffany Blvd.
Rocky Mount, NC 27802
Phone: (252)446-5161
**Subject(s):** Daily Newspapers
**Circ:** (Mon.-Sat.)★14,210
(Mon.-Fri.)15,000
(Sun.)★16,633
(Sun.)17,000

**The Tennessee Register (28890)**
Diocese of Nashville
2400 21st Ave. S
Nashville, TN 37212
Phone: (615)383-6393
Fax: (615)783-0285
**Subject(s):** Religious Publications
**Circ:** (Free)‡330
(Paid)‡17,000

**The West Tennessee Catholic (28782)**
Diocese of Memphis
5825 Shelby Oaks Dr.
Memphis, TN 38134-7389
Phone: (901)373-1213
Fax: (901)373-1269
**Subject(s):** Religious Publications
**Circ:** (Paid)17,000

**Oracle (6646)**
University of South Florida
4202 E. Fowler Ave.
Tampa, FL 33620
Phone: (813)974-2011
**Subject(s):** College Publications
**Circ:** (Paid)‡150
(Free)‡16,850

**Tiftarea Shopper (7458)**
147 Love Ave.
Tifton, GA 31793
Phone: (229)386-0472
Fax: (229)386-0478
**Subject(s):** Shopping Guides
**Circ:** (Free)16,500

**Wilson Daily Times (23861)**
Wilson Daily Times Inc.
2001 Downing St.
PO Box 2447
Wilson, NC 27894-2447
Fax: (252)243-2999
**Subject(s):** Daily Newspapers
**Circ:** (Mon.-Sat.)16,400

**The Brunswick News (7021)**
Brunswick News Publishing Co.
3011 Altama Ave.
PO Box 1557
Brunswick, GA 31521
Phone: (912)265-8320
Fax: (912)264-4973
**Subject(s):** Daily Newspapers
**Circ:** ‡16,284

**Index Journal (28131)**
PO Box 1018
Greenwood, SC 29648
**Subject(s):** Daily Newspapers
**Circ:** (Mon.-Sat.)14,575
(Sun.)16,172

**Rockdale Neighbor (7288)**
Neighbor Newspapers Inc.
580 Fairground St.
PO Box 449
Marietta, GA 30060
Phone: (770)795-3000
Fax: (770)428-7945
**Subject(s):** Free Newspapers
**Circ:** (Paid)5
(Non-paid)16,096

**Florida Medical Association (6580)**
Florida Medical Association Inc.
123 Adams St.
Tallahassee, FL 32301
Phone: (850)224-6496
Fax: (850)222-8030
**Subject(s):** Medicine and Surgery; Paid Community Newspapers
**Circ:** 16,000

**Fort Myers Beach Bulletin (6000)**
Breeze Newspapers
19260 San Carlos Blvd.
Fort Myers Beach, FL 33931
Phone: (239)463-4421
Fax: (239)463-1402
**Subject(s):** Paid Community Newspapers
**Circ:** (Free)‡14,500
(Paid)‡16,000

**Journal-Patriot (23681)**
Carter-Hubbard Publishing Company Inc.
711 Main St.
Box 70
North Wilkesboro, NC 28659
Phone: (336)838-4117
Fax: (336)838-9864
**Subject(s):** Paid Community Newspapers
**Circ:** ‡16,000

**Lawrence County Advocate (28717)**
Lawrence County Advocate Inc.
121 N. Military Ave.
Lawrenceburg, TN 38464
Phone: (931)762-1726
**Subject(s):** Free Newspapers
**Circ:** (Paid)267
(Sun.)14,500
(Wed.)16,000

**The 'M' Voice Newspaper (23555)**
PO Box 8361
Greenville, NC 27834
Phone: (252)757-0365
Fax: (252)757-1793
**Subject(s):** Black Publications
**Circ:** (Non-paid)‡12,000
(Paid)‡16,000

**The Red and Black (6813)**
The Red and Black Publishing Co.
540 Baxter St
Athens, GA 30605
Phone: (706)543-1791
Fax: (706)433-3033
**Subject(s):** College Publications
**Circ:** (Free)16,000

**Shopper (6737)**
Polk Shopper
650 Sixth St. SW
Winter Haven, FL 33882-1440
Phone: (863)294-1100
Fax: (863)294-2008
**Subject(s):** Shopping Guides
**Circ:** (Free)16,000

**The Signal (7155)**
Citizen Newspapers
Bldg. 29801
Rm. 209
520 Chamberlain Ave.
Fort Gordon, GA 30905-5735
Phone: (706)791-7069
**Subject(s):** Paid Community Newspapers; Military and Navy
**Circ:** ‡16,000

**Southaven Press (28779)**
Memphis Offset Printing Inc.
Memphis, TN 38111
Phone: (901)458-8030
Fax: (901)458-3104
**Subject(s):** Free Newspapers
**Circ:** (Free)16,000

**UT Daily Beacon (28689)**
University of Tennessee
5 Communications Bldg.
Knoxville, TN 37996
Phone: (865)974-3231
**Subject(s):** College Publications
**Circ:** (Free)‡16,000

**Walton Tribune/Advertiser (7314)**
PO Box 808
Monroe, GA 30655-0808
Phone: (770)267-8371
Fax: (770)267-7780
**Subject(s):** Paid Community Newspapers
**Circ:** (Paid)6,122
(Non-paid)16,000

Circulation: ★ = ABC; △ = BPA; ♦ = CAC; • = CCAB; ❏ = VAC; ⊕ = PO Statement; ‡ = Publisher's Report; Boldface figures = sworn; Light figures = estimated.

## Southern States

**Sacramento Business Journal** (23352)
American City Business Journals Inc.
120 W Morehead St., Ste. 200
Charlotte, NC 28202
Phone: (704)973-1000
Fax: (704)973-1001
**Subject(s):** Business
**Circ:** (Paid)15,979

**The Smithfield Herald** (23784)
PO Box 1417
Smithfield, NC 27577-1417
Phone: (919)934-2176
Fax: (919)989-7093
**Subject(s):** Paid Community Newspapers
**Circ:** (Tues.)15,850
(Fri.)15,850

**North Carolina Christian Advocate** (23525)
Methodist Board of Publication Inc.
PO Box 508
815 West Market St
Greensboro, NC 27402-0508
Phone: (336)272-1196
Fax: (336)271-6634
**Subject(s):** Religious Publications
**Circ:** ‡15,577

**Bay Beacon and Beacon Express** (6328)
Beacon Newspapers
1181 E John Sims Pkwy.
Niceville, FL 32578
Phone: (850)678-1080
Fax: (850)729-3225
**Subject(s):** Paid Community Newspapers
**Circ:** ‡15,500

**Dollar Saver** (7452)
McDuffie Progress
101 Church St.
PO Box 1090
Thomson, GA 30824
Phone: (706)595-1601
Fax: (706)597-8974
**Subject(s):** Shopping Guides
**Circ:** (Free)15,500

**The Post-Searchlight Extra** (7001)
The Bainbridge Post-Searchlight Inc.
301 N Crawford St.
PO Box 277
Bainbridge, GA 39817-3612
Phone: (229)246-2827
Fax: (229)246-7665
**Subject(s):** Shopping Guides
**Circ:** (Paid)‡6,000
(Free)‡15,500

**Aiken Standard** (27963)
Evening Post Publishing Co.
326 Rutland Dr.
PO Box 456
Aiken, SC 29801-4006
Phone: (803)648-2311
Fax: (803)648-6052
**Subject(s):** Daily Newspapers
**Circ:** (Mon.-Sat.)★15,451
(Sun.)★15,472

**The Robesonian** (23629)
Community Newspaper Holdings Inc.
121 W. 5th St.
PO Box 1028
Lumberton, NC 28359
Phone: (910)739-4322
Fax: (910)739-6553
**Subject(s):** Daily Newspapers
**Circ:** (Mon.-Sat.)★12,689
(Sun.)★15,457

**Sun Journal** (23671)
Freedom Communications Inc.
3200 Wellons Blvd.
New Bern, NC 28562
Phone: (252)638-8101
Fax: (252)638-4664
**Subject(s):** Daily Newspapers
**Circ:** (Mon.-Sat.)★15,402

**The Villages Daily Sun** (6711)
1100 Main St.
The Villages, FL 32159
Phone: (352)753-1119
Fax: (352)753-2380

**Subject(s):** Daily Newspapers
**Circ:** (Paid)15,236

**Carolina/Virginia Farmer** (23859)
Farm Progress Cos.
c/o Richard Davis,Editor, Carolina-Virginia Farmer
700 Privette St.
Wilson, NC 27893
Phone: (252)237-4422
Fax: (252)237-8999
**Subject(s):** Farm Newspapers
**Circ:** ‡15,177

**Monroe County Advocate/Democrat** (29010)
PO Box 389
Sweetwater, TN 37874
Phone: (423)337-7101
Fax: (423)337-5932
**Subject(s):** Paid Community Newspapers
**Circ:** (Non-paid)1
(Paid)15,100

**Buyers Guide** (16767)
Ole Brook Broadcasting Inc.
Hwy. 550 & 51
PO Box 711
Brookhaven, MS 39601
Phone: (601)833-7149
Fax: (601)833-9683
**Subject(s):** Shopping Guides
**Circ:** (Free)‡15,000

**Cattle Today** (214)
Cattle Today Inc.
204 Temple Ave. S
Fayette, AL 35555
Phone: (205)932-8000
Fax: (205)932-4000
**Subject(s):** Livestock
**Circ:** ‡15,000

**The Chronicle** (23407)
Duke University
PO Box 90858, Duke Sta.
101 West Union Building
Durham, NC 27706-0858
Phone: (919)684-3811
Fax: (919)684-8295
**Subject(s):** College Publications
**Circ:** ‡15,000

**The Cullman Tribune** (169)
219 2nd Ave. SE
Cullman, AL 35055
Phone: (256)739-1351
Fax: (256)739-4422
**Subject(s):** Paid Community Newspapers
**Circ:** ‡15,000

**The Goose Creek Gazette** (28109)
PO Box 304
Goose Creek, SC 29445
Phone: (843)572-0511
Fax: (843)572-0312
**Subject(s):** Paid Community Newspapers
**Circ:** ‡15,000

**Hernando Today** (5851)
15299 Cortez Blvd.
Brooksville, FL 34613
Phone: (352)796-1949
Fax: (352)544-5249
**Subject(s):** Paid Community Newspapers
**Circ:** (Free)‡12,000
(Paid)‡15,000

**Kendall gazette** (6246)
Community Newspapers
6796 S.W. 62 Ave.
Miami, FL 33143
Phone: (305)669-7355
Fax: (305)661-0954
**Subject(s):** Free Newspapers
**Circ:** (Free)‡15,000

**Kings Mountain Herald** (23607)
Republic Newspaper
PO Box 769
824-1 East King St
Kings Mountain, NC 28086
Phone: (704)739-7496
Fax: (704)739-0611
**Subject(s):** Paid Community Newspapers
**Circ:** (Combined)15,000

**The Peddler** (28565)
The Peddler of Tennessee
PO Box 701
420 N Washington Ave
Cookeville, TN 38503-0701
Phone: (931)526-5910
Fax: (931)528-9735
**Subject(s):** Shopping Guides
**Circ:** (Free)‡15,000

**The Roane County News/Record** (28675)
The Roane County News-Record
204 Franklin St.
Kingston, TN 37763
Phone: (865)376-3481
Fax: (865)376-1945
**Subject(s):** Shopping Guides
**Circ:** (Free)‡15,000

**Tri-State Defender** (28781)
124 E Calhoun Ave.
PO Box 2065
Memphis, TN 38103
Phone: (901)523-1818
Fax: (901)523-1820
**Subject(s):** Paid Community Newspapers; Black Publications
**Circ:** ‡15,000

**The Weekly Leader** (16990)
PO Box 54241
Pearl, MS 39208
Phone: (601)825-8333
Fax: (601)825-8334
**Subject(s):** Free Newspapers
**Circ:** (Free)‡14,800

**The Commercial Dispatch** (16794)
The Commercial Dispatch Publishing Inc.
PO Box 511
Columbus, MS 39703-0511
Phone: (601)328-2424
Fax: (601)329-8937
**Subject(s):** Daily Newspapers
**Circ:** (Mon.-Fri.)❏13,834
(Sun.)❏14,745

**West Hawaii Today** (109)
Community Newspaper Holdings Inc.
3500 Colonnade Pkwy., Ste. 600
Birmingham, AL 35243
Phone: (205)298-7100
Fax: (205)298-7101
**Subject(s):** Daily Newspapers
**Circ:** (Mon.-Thurs.)10,810
(Fri.)12,450
(Sun.)14,636

**The Pilot** (23787)
145 W. Pennsylvania Ave.
PO Box 58
Southern Pines, NC 28387
Phone: (910)692-7271
Fax: (910)692-9382
**Subject(s):** Paid Community Newspapers
**Circ:** (Paid)⊕14,500

**Westside Gazette** (5972)
PO Box 5304
Fort Lauderdale, FL 33310
Phone: (954)525-1489
Fax: (954)522-2553
**Subject(s):** Black Publications; Free Newspapers
**Circ:** (Paid)‡7,000
(Free)‡14,500

**The Greeneville Sun** (28623)
Greeneville Sun
121 W Summer St.
PO Box 1630
Greeneville, TN 37743-4923
Phone: (615)638-4181
Fax: (615)638-3645
**Subject(s):** Daily Newspapers
**Circ:** (Mon.-Sat.)★14,474

**The Shelby Star** (23780)
315 E Graham St.
PO Box 48
Shelby, NC 28150
Phone: (704)484-7000
Fax: (704)484-0805
**Subject(s):** Daily Newspapers
**Circ:** (Mon.-Sat.)★14,364
(Sun.)★14,366

**Vicksburg Evening Post** (17042)
Vicksburg Printing & Publishing Company Inc.
PO Box 821668
Vicksburg, MS 39182-1668
**Subject(s):** Daily Newspapers
**Circ:** (Mon.-Sat.)14,070
(Sun.)14,350

**Forsyth County News** (7094)
PO Box 210
Cumming, GA 30028-0210
Phone: (770)887-3126
Fax: (770)889-6017
**Subject(s):** Free Newspapers
**Circ:** (Mon.-Fri.)12,701
(Sun.)14,202

**Opelika-Auburn News** (390)
3505 Pepperell Pkwy.
PO Box 2208
Opelika, AL 36803
Phone: (334)749-6271
Fax: (334)749-1228
**Subject(s):** Daily Newspapers
**Circ:** (Mon.-Sat.)13,438
(Sun.)14,068

**Messenger** (448)
Troy Publishing Corp.
918 S Brundidge St.
PO Box 727
Troy, AL 36081-0727
Phone: (334)566-4270
Fax: (334)566-4281
**Subject(s):** Daily Newspapers
**Circ:** (Paid)4,000
(Non-paid)14,000

**The Newnan Times-Herald** (7324)
16 Jefferson St.
PO Box 1052
Newnan, GA 30264
**Subject(s):** Paid Community Newspapers
**Circ:** 14,000

**Openings** (6907)
American Academy of Religion
825 Houston Mill Rd., NE, Ste. 300
Atlanta, GA 30329-4205
Phone: (404)727-3049
Fax: (404)727-7959
**Circ:** 14,000

**The Business Journal of Charlotte** (23332)
American City Business Journals Inc.
120 W Morehead St., Ste. 200
Charlotte, NC 28202
Phone: (704)973-1000
Fax: (704)973-1001
**Subject(s):** Business; Local, State, and Regional Publications
**Circ:** (Paid)13,922

**The Robins Review** (7061)
RR 4
Box 275
Cochran, GA 31014-9252
Phone: (478)922-5758
Fax: (478)922-4559
**Subject(s):** Labor
**Circ:** (Free)‡13,800

**Herald-Citizen Plus** (28564)
Herald-Citizen
555 S Old Kentucky Rd.
PO Box 2729
Cookeville, TN 38502
Phone: (931)526-9715
Fax: (931)526-1209
**Subject(s):** Daily Newspapers
**Circ:** (Mon.-Fri.)★11,241
(Sun.)★13,723

**Picayune Item** (16994)
Community Newspaper Holdings Inc.
PO Box 580
Picayune, MS 39466-0580
Phone: (601)798-4766
Fax: (601)798-8602
**Subject(s):** Daily Newspapers
**Circ:** ‡13,585

**Delta Democrat Times** (16819)
Freedom Communications Inc.
988 N. Broadway
PO Box 1618
Greenville, MS 38702
Phone: (662)335-1155
Fax: (662)335-2860
**Subject(s):** Daily Newspapers
**Circ:** (Mon.-Fri.)12,346
(Sun.)13,521

**Mississippi Today** (16893)
Catholic Diocese of Jackson
237 E Amite
PO Box 2130
Jackson, MS 39201
Phone: (601)969-1880
Fax: (601)960-8455
**Subject(s):** Religious Publications
**Circ:** 13,500

**The Daily Herald** (72)
Community Newspaper Holdings Inc.
3500 Colonnade Pkwy., Ste. 600
Birmingham, AL 35243
Phone: (205)298-7100
Fax: (205)298-7101
**Subject(s):** Daily Newspapers
**Circ:** (Mon.-Fri.)11,769
(Sun.)13,452

**North Myrtle Beach Times** (28201)
203 N Kings Hwy.
PO Box 725
North Myrtle Beach, SC 29597
Phone: (843)249-3525
Fax: (843)249-7012
**Subject(s):** Paid Community Newspapers
**Circ:** ‡13,400

**Sequatchie Valley Purchase** (28998)
Marion County Newspapers Inc.
307 1/2 Elm. Ave.
PO Box 765
South Pittsburg, TN 37380-1337
Phone: (423)837-6312
Fax: (423)837-8715
**Subject(s):** Shopping Guides
**Circ:** (Free)‡13,300

**The Apostle** (51)
The Episcopal Diocese of Alabama
521 N. 20th St.
Birmingham, AL 35203
Phone: (205)715-2060
Fax: (205)715-2066
**Subject(s):** Religious Publications
**Circ:** (Non-paid)‡13,000

**Duplin Times Progress** (23605)
Cox Publications (North Carolina) Inc.
102 Front St.
PO Box 69
Kenansville, NC 28349
Phone: (910)296-0239
Fax: (910)296-9545
**Subject(s):** Paid Community Newspapers
**Circ:** 13,000

**The Enterprise Mountaineer** (23827)
The Mountaineer Publishing Company Inc.
PO Box 129
Waynesville, NC 28786
Phone: (828)452-0661
Fax: (828)452-0665
**Subject(s):** Paid Community Newspapers
**Circ:** (Free)12,000
(Paid)13,000

**Free Press** (6087)
81549 Old Highway
Islamorada, FL 33036
Phone: (305)664-2266
Fax: (305)664-8411
**Subject(s):** Free Newspapers
**Circ:** 12,000
(Free)‡13,000

**Georgetown Time** (28107)
PO Box 2778
Georgetown, SC 29442-0546
Phone: (803)546-4148
Fax: (803)546-2395
**Subject(s):** Free Newspapers
**Circ:** (Free)13,000

**Herald-News Sunrise Edition** (28580)
Rhea County Publishing Co.
PO Box 286
Dayton, TN 37321
Phone: (423)775-6111
Fax: (423)775-8218
**Subject(s):** Shopping Guides
**Circ:** (Free)‡13,000

**The Oxford Eagle** (16983)
PO Box 866
916 Jackson Ave
Oxford, MS 38655
Phone: (662)234-4331
Fax: (662)234-4351
**Subject(s):** Daily Newspapers
**Circ:** (Paid)‡4,982
(Free)11,000
(Free)‡13,000

**Star News** (28630)
Gallatin News Examiner
105 Maple Row Blvd.
Hendersonville, TN 37075-3853
Phone: (615)824-8480
Fax: (615)824-3126
**Subject(s):** Free Newspapers
**Circ:** 13,000

**The Sun** (6486)
Sunbelt Newspapers Inc.
3036 College Ave.
Ruskin, FL 33570
Phone: (813)645-6858
Fax: (813)645-1297
**Subject(s):** Free Newspapers
**Circ:** (Combined)13,000

**Chesterfield County Shopper** (28020)
Titan Publishers Inc.
25 Chesterfield Hwy.
Cheraw, SC 29520
Phone: (843)537-2791
Fax: (843)537-1912
**Subject(s):** Shopping Guides
**Circ:** (Free)‡12,976

**The Southeast Sun** (205)
QST Publications Inc.
P O Box 311546
Enterprise, AL 36331
Phone: (334)393-2969
Fax: (334)393-2987
**Subject(s):** Free Newspapers
**Circ:** (Paid)66
(Free)12,905

**Miss-Lou Guide** (16967)
Natchez Newspapers Inc.
PO Box 1447
Natchez, MS 39121
Phone: (601)442-9101
Fax: (601)442-7315
**Subject(s):** Shopping Guides
**Circ:** (Free)□12,880

**The Dispatch** (23620)
PO Box 908
PO Box 908
Lexington, NC 27293
Phone: (336)249-3981
**Subject(s):** Daily Newspapers
**Circ:** (Mon.-Sat.)12,864

**The News-Sun** (6548)
2227 U.S. Hwy. 27 S.
Sebring, FL 33870
Phone: (863)385-6155
Fax: (863)385-1954
**Subject(s):** Paid Community Newspapers
**Circ:** (Fri.)11,200
(Wed.)11,625
(Sun.)12,685

**The Lancaster News** (28160)
Landmark Community Newspapers Inc.
701 N. White St.
PO Box 640
Lancaster, SC 29720
Phone: (803)283-1133
Fax: (803)283-8969
**Subject(s):** Paid Community Newspapers
**Circ:** ‡12,606

Circulation: ★ = ABC; △ = BPA; ♦ = CAC; ● = CCAB; □ = VAC; ⊕ = PO Statement; ‡ = Publisher's Report; Boldface figures = sworn; Light figures = estimated.

# Southern States

**The News Herald (23649)**
301 Collett St.
PO Box 280
Morganton, NC 28655-3322
Phone: (828)328-8725
Fax: (828)437-5372
**Subject(s):** Daily Newspapers

Circ: (Mon.-Fri.)11,918
(Sun.)12,523

**South Dade News Leader (6083)**
Calkins Inc.
15 North East 1st Rd.
Homestead, FL 33030
Phone: (305)245-2311
Fax: (305)248-0596
**Subject(s):** Daily Newspapers

Circ: (Combined)‡12,514

**The Columbia Star (28040)**
PO Box 5955
Columbia, SC 29250-5955
Phone: (803)771-0219

Circ: (Paid)‡1,500
(Free)‡12,500

**Lincoln Times (23624)**
The Lincoln Journal Inc.
117-120 W. Water St.
PO Box 40
Lincolnton, NC 28093-0094
Phone: (704)735-3031
Fax: (704)735-3037
**Subject(s):** Shopping Guides

Circ: (Non-paid)⊕12,400

**Clinton Herald (68)**
Community Newspaper Holdings Inc.
3500 Colonnade Pkwy., Ste. 600
Birmingham, AL 35243
Phone: (205)298-7100
Fax: (205)298-7101
**Subject(s):** Daily Newspapers

Circ: (Mon.-Sat.)★12,371

**The Cary News (23280)**
McClatchy
212 E. Chatham St.
PO Box 4949
Cary, NC 27519
Phone: (919)460-2600
Fax: (919)460-6034
**Subject(s):** Paid Community Newspapers

Circ: ‡12,347

**The Mountaineer (23829)**
The Mountaineer Publishing Company Inc.
PO Box 129
Waynesville, NC 28786
Phone: (828)452-0661
Fax: (828)452-0665
**Subject(s):** Paid Community Newspapers

Circ: (Combined)12,231

**The Sanford Herald (23772)**
PO Box 100
208 Saint Clair Court
Sanford, NC 27331-0100
Phone: (919)708-9000
Fax: (919)708-9001
**Subject(s):** Daily Newspapers

Circ: (Sun.)12,047
(Sat.)12,220
(Tues.-Fri.)12,220

**Columbian-Progress/Marion County Advertiser (16790)**
Emmerich Enterprises Inc.
PO Box 1171
Columbia, MS 39429-1171
Phone: (601)736-2611
Fax: (601)736-4507
**Subject(s):** Paid Community Newspapers

Circ: (Sun.)‡11,636
(Thurs.)‡12,200

**Business First of Columbus (23331)**
American City Business Journals Inc.
120 W Morehead St., Ste. 200
Charlotte, NC 28202
Phone: (704)973-1000
Fax: (704)973-1001
**Subject(s):** Business

Circ: (Paid)12,133

**New Albany Gazette (16973)**
713 Carter Ave.
PO Box 300
New Albany, MS 38652
Phone: (662)534-6321
Fax: (662)534-6355
**Subject(s):** Paid Community Newspapers

Circ: (Paid)‡6,095
(Free)‡12,112

**Enterprise-Journal (16941)**
J.O. Emmerich & Associates Inc.
112 Oliver Emmerich Dr.
McComb, MS 39648
Phone: (601)684-2421
Fax: (601)684-0836
**Subject(s):** Daily Newspapers

Circ: (Mon.-Fri.)★11,492
(Sun.)★12,083

**Advocate-Messenger (11638)**
Advocate-Messenger Co.
330 S 4th St.
Danville, KY 40422-2033
Phone: (606)236-2551
Fax: (606)236-9566
**Subject(s):** Daily Newspapers

Circ: (Mon.-Fri.)★10,795
(Sun.)★12,049

**The Albany Journal (6766)**
PO Box 1628
Albany, GA 31702-1628
Phone: (229)435-6222
Fax: (229)435-0557
**Subject(s):** Paid Community Newspapers

Circ: (Fri.)12,000

**Beaches Leader/Ponte Vedra Leader (6125)**
The Leader Group
1114 Beach Blvd.
Jacksonville Beach, FL 32250
Phone: (904)249-9033
Fax: (904)249-1501
**Subject(s):** Paid Community Newspapers

Circ: ‡12,000

**Coral Gables News (6224)**
Community Newspapers
6796 S.W. 62 Ave.
Miami, FL 33143
Phone: (305)669-7355
Fax: (305)661-0954
**Subject(s):** Free Newspapers

Circ: (Free)‡12,000

**Key West Citizen (6133)**
Cooke Communications L.L.C.
3420 Northside Dr.
Key West, FL 33040
Phone: (305)292-7777
Fax: (305)294-0768
**Subject(s):** Daily Newspapers

Circ: (Mon.-Fri.)10,500
(Sun.)12,000

**The Reflector (16960)**
Mississippi State University
Student Media Center
Mississippi State, MS 39762
Phone: (662)325-7905
**Subject(s):** College Publications

Circ: (Free)‡12,000

**Rogersville Review (28971)**
PO Box 100
Rogersville, TN 37857
Phone: (423)272-7422
Fax: (423)272-7889
**Subject(s):** Paid Community Newspapers

Circ: (Wed.)‡5,600
(Paid)‡6,000
(Sat.)‡12,000

**The Tiger (28028)**
Clemson University
PO Box 1586
Clemson, SC 29633-1586
Phone: (864)656-2150
Fax: (864)656-4772
**Subject(s):** College Publications

Circ: (Free)12,000

**Voyager (6444)**
University of West Florida
11000 Univ. Pkwy.
Pensacola, FL 32514-5751
Phone: (850)474-2191
**Subject(s):** College Publications

Circ: (Free)‡12,000

**Waycross Journal Herald (7499)**
400 Isabella St.
PO Box 219
Waycross, GA 31502
Phone: (912)283-2244
Fax: (912)285-5255
**Subject(s):** Daily Newspapers

Circ: (Paid)‡12,000

**The Beaufort Gazette (27981)**
1556 Salem Rd.
PO Box 399
Beaufort, SC 29901
Phone: (843)524-3183
Fax: (843)524-8728
**Subject(s):** Daily Newspapers

Circ: (Sun.)★11,246
(Mon.-Sat.)★11,985

**Kentucky New Era (11727)**
1618 E. 9th St.
Hopkinsville, KY 42240
Phone: (270)886-4444
Fax: (270)887-3222
**Subject(s):** Daily Newspapers

Circ: (Mon.-Sat.)★11,967

**Daily Post-Athenian (28488)**
PO Box 340
Athens, TN 37371-0340
Phone: (423)745-5664
Fax: (423)745-8259
**Subject(s):** Daily Newspapers

Circ: (Mon.-Fri.)10,807
(Sat.)11,958
(Sun.)11,958

**The Daily Courier (23484)**
Forest City Publishing Company Inc.
601 Oak St.
PO Box 1149
Forest City, NC 28043-1149
Phone: (828)245-6431
Fax: (828)248-2790
**Subject(s):** Free Newspapers

Circ: (Free)129
(Paid)11,937

**The Voice-Tribune (11846)**
Southern Publishing Inc.
3818 Shelbyville Rd.
P.O. Box 7129
Louisville, KY 40257-0129
Phone: (502)897-8900
Fax: (502)897-8915
**Subject(s):** Paid Community Newspapers

Circ: (Free)‡1,571
(Paid)‡11,859

**The Daily Advance (23453)**
215 S Water St.
Elizabeth City, NC 27909-4835
Phone: (252)335-0841
Fax: (252)335-4415
**Subject(s):** Daily Newspapers

Circ: (Mon.-Fri.)11,193
(Sun.)11,792

**Carteret County News-Times (23647)**
Carteret Publishing Co.
PO Box 1679
Morehead City, NC 28557
Phone: (252)726-7081
Fax: (252)726-6016
**Subject(s):** Paid Community Newspapers

Circ: (Wed.)10,218
(Fri.)10,218
(Sun.)11,702

**The Chronicle of Mt. Juliet (28820)**
11509 Lebanon Rd.
PO Box 647
Mount Juliet, TN 37122
Phone: (615)754-6111
Fax: (615)754-8203

# Gale Directory of Publications & Broadcast Media/140th Ed.  Southern States

**Subject(s):** Free Newspapers
**Circ:** (Paid)150
 (Free)11,600

**Orlando Business Journal (6376)**
American City Business Journals Inc.
315 E. Robinson St., Ste. 250
Orlando, FL 32801
Phone: (407)420-1625
Fax: (407)420-1625
**Subject(s):** Business; Local, State, and Regional Publications
**Circ:** (Paid)11,536

**The Daily Mississippian (17033)**
University of Mississippi Student Media Center
University, MS 38677
Phone: (662)915-5503
Fax: (662)915-5703
**Subject(s):** College Publications
**Circ:** ‡11,500

**The Barrow County Shopper (7508)**
Swartz-Morris Media Inc.
189 W Athens St.
PO Drawer C
Winder, GA 30680
Phone: (770)867-7557
Fax: (770)867-1034
**Subject(s):** Shopping Guides
**Circ:** (Free)11,421

**The Advertiser-Gleam (254)**
2218 Taylor St.
PO Box 190
Guntersville, AL 35976
Phone: (256)582-3232
Fax: (256)582-3231
**Subject(s):** Paid Community Newspapers
**Circ:** (Paid)11,401

**The Cullman Times (168)**
Cullman Times
300 4th Ave. SE
Cullman, AL 35055
Phone: (256)734-2131
Fax: (256)734-7310
**Subject(s):** Daily Newspapers
**Circ:** (Mon.-Sat.)10,759
 (Sun.)11,387

**Palatka Daily News (6408)**
1825 St. Johns Ave.
PO Box 777
Palatka, FL 32177
Phone: (386)312-5200
**Subject(s):** Daily Newspapers
**Circ:** (Mon.-Fri.)11,372

**Capital Outlook (6570)**
Capitol Outlook
225 E. Jennings St.
Tallahassee, FL 32301-1114
Phone: (850)681-1852
Fax: (850)681-1093
**Subject(s):** Paid Community Newspapers; Black Publications
**Circ:** 11,333

**Marathon/Big Pine Key Free Press (6202)**
6363 Overseas Hwy.
Marathon, FL 33050
Phone: (305)743-8766
Fax: (305)743-9977
**Subject(s):** Free Newspapers
**Circ:** (Free)11,300

**The Venice Gondolier (6704)**
Sun Coast Media
200 E Venice Ave.
Venice, FL 34285
Phone: (941)484-2611
Fax: (941)484-8460
**Subject(s):** Paid Community Newspapers
**Circ:** (Wed.)10,603
 (Sat.)11,189

**Pioneer News Extra (11990)**
Landmark Community Newspapers Inc.
PO Box 98
Shepherdsville, KY 40165
Phone: (502)543-2288
Fax: (502)955-9704
**Subject(s):** Paid Community Newspapers
**Circ:** (Paid)⊕6,324
 (Controlled)⊕11,132

**Chattooga Press (7433)**
News Publishing Co.
PO Box 485
Summerville, GA 30747
Phone: (706)857-5433
**Subject(s):** Free Newspapers
**Circ:** (Free)11,100

**Golden Corner Shopper (28224)**
Oconee Publishing
PO Box 547
Seneca, SC 29679
Phone: (864)882-2375
Fax: (864)882-2381
**Subject(s):** Shopping Guides
**Circ:** (Non-paid)11,067

**The Courier Herald (7124)**
Courier Herald
115 S. Jefferson St.
Dublin, GA 31040
Phone: (478)272-5522
Fax: (478)272-2189
**Subject(s):** Daily Newspapers
**Circ:** (Mon.-Sat.)11,056

**Jasper Mountain Eagle (293)**
Daily Mountain Eagle
1301 Viking Dr.
PO Box 1469
Jasper, AL 35501
Phone: (205)221-2840
Fax: (205)221-2421
**Subject(s):** Daily Newspapers
**Circ:** (Sun.)★10,835
 (Mon.-Sat.)★11,026

**Winter Haven News Chief (6738)**
Stauffer Communications
PO Box 1440
Winter Haven, FL 33882
**Subject(s):** Daily Newspapers
**Circ:** (Combined)11,026

**Bulletin Times (28492)**
Box 152
Bolivar, TN 38008
Phone: (731)658-3691
Fax: (731)658-7222
**Subject(s):** Paid Community Newspapers
**Circ:** (Paid)4,800
 (Free)11,000

**Journal-Scene (28234)**
Summerville Journal Inc.
PO Drawer 715
Summerville, SC 29484
Phone: (843)873-9424
Fax: (843)873-9432
**Subject(s):** Paid Community Newspapers
**Circ:** 11,000

**The Orlando Times (6378)**
4403 Vineland Rd., Ste. B-5
PO Box 555339
Orlando, FL 32855-5339
Phone: (407)841-3052
Fax: (407)849-0434
**Subject(s):** Paid Community Newspapers; Black Publications
**Circ:** 11,000

**Lincoln Times-News (23625)**
Western Carolina Publishing Company Inc.
119 W. Water St.
PO Box 40
Lincolnton, NC 28092
Phone: (704)735-3031
Fax: (704)735-3037
**Subject(s):** Paid Community Newspapers
**Circ:** 10,903

**Appalachian News Express (11947)**
Lancaster Management
129 Caroline Ave.
PO Box 802
Pikeville, KY 41501
Phone: (606)437-4054
Fax: (606)437-4246
**Subject(s):** Paid Community Newspapers
**Circ:** ‡10,800

**The News-Examiner (28613)**
Gannett Company Inc.
1 Examiner Court
PO Box 1387
Gallatin, TN 37066
Phone: (615)452-2561
Fax: (615)452-9110
**Subject(s):** Paid Community Newspapers
**Circ:** (Free)169
 (Paid)10,800

**The Technique (6925)**
Georgia Institute of Technology
353 Ferst Dr., Rm. 137
Atlanta, GA 30332-0290
Phone: (404)894-2830
Fax: (404)894-1650
**Subject(s):** College Publications
**Circ:** (Paid)‡300
 (Non-paid)‡10,700

**Crossville Chronicle (28574)**
125 West Ave.
Crossville, TN 38555-4478
Phone: (931)484-5145
Fax: (931)456-7683
**Subject(s):** Paid Community Newspapers
**Circ:** ‡7,000
 ‡10,600

**Florida Keys Keynoter (6201)**
3015 Overseas Hwy.
PO Box 158
Marathon, FL 33050
Phone: (305)743-5551
Fax: (305)743-6397
**Subject(s):** Paid Community Newspapers
**Circ:** (Wed.)9,730
 (Sat.)10,539

**The Greer Citizen (28136)**
PO Box 70
Greer, SC 29652
Phone: (864)877-2076
Fax: (864)877-3563
**Subject(s):** Paid Community Newspapers
**Circ:** (Paid)‡10,500

**GSA Business (28112)**
1204-B E Washington St.
Greenville, SC 29601
Phone: (864)235-5677
Fax: (864)235-4868
**Subject(s):** Business; Paid Community Newspapers
**Circ:** (Controlled)10,500

**State Journal (11679)**
Frankfort Publishing Co.
1216 Wilkinson Blvd.
Frankfort, KY 40601-1200
**Subject(s):** Daily Newspapers
**Circ:** (Mon.-Fri.)8,944
 (Sun.)10,505

**The Sand Mountain Reporter (2)**
Sand Mountain Reporter
PO Box 1729
Albertville, AL 35950
**Subject(s):** Paid Community Newspapers
**Circ:** (Paid)10,492

**Mount Airy News (23654)**
Mount Airy Newspapers Inc.
319 N Renfro St.
PO Box 808
Mount Airy, NC 27030-0808
Phone: (336)786-4141
Fax: (336)789-2816
**Subject(s):** Daily Newspapers
**Circ:** (Mon.-Fri.)9,556
 (Sun.)10,285

**Rockdale Citizen (7082)**
969 Main St.
PO Box 136
Conyers, GA 30012
Phone: (770)483-7108
Fax: (770)483-5797
**Subject(s):** Daily Newspapers
**Circ:** (Non-paid)1,093
 (Paid)10,232

Circulation: ★ = ABC; △ = BPA; ♦ = CAC; ● = CCAB; ▫ = VAC; ⊕ = PO Statement; ‡ = Publisher's Report; Boldface figures = sworn; Light figures = estimated.

## Southern States

**The News Observer** (7015)
PO Box 989
5748 Appalachian Hwy.
Blue Ridge, GA 30513
Phone: (706)632-2019
Fax: (706)632-2577
**Subject(s):** Paid Community Newspapers
**Circ:** 10,200

**Washington Daily News** (23823)
Washington News Publishing Co.
217 N Market St.
PO Box 1788
Washington, NC 27889-1788
Phone: (252)946-2144
Fax: (252)946-9797
**Subject(s):** Daily Newspapers
**Circ:** (Mon.-Sat.)10,019
(Sun.)10,200

**Daily Business Review** (6226)
American Lawyer Media L.P.
1 SE 3rd Ave., Ste. 900
Miami, FL 33131
Phone: (305)377-3721
Fax: (305)374-8474
**Subject(s):** Daily Periodicals; Law; Business; Real Estate; Local, State, and Regional Publications
**Circ:** (Controlled)286
(Paid)10,184

**Griffin Daily News** (7178)
323 E Solomon St.
PO Box M
Griffin, GA 30224
Phone: (770)227-3276
Fax: (770)412-1678
**Subject(s):** Daily Newspapers
**Circ:** (Sun.)9,980
(Mon.-Fri.)10,090

**News-Leader** (5948)
511 Ash St.
Fernandina Beach, FL 32034
Phone: (904)261-3696
Fax: (904)261-3698
**Subject(s):** Paid Community Newspapers
**Circ:** (Wed.)10,068

**The Natchez Democrat** (16968)
Natchez Newspapers Inc.
PO Box 1447
Natchez, MS 39121
Phone: (601)442-9101
Fax: (601)442-7315
**Subject(s):** Daily Newspapers
**Circ:** (Sun.)▫9,912
(Mon.-Sat.)▫10,026

**Atlanta Daily World** (6835)
145 Auburn Ave. NE
Atlanta, GA 30303
Phone: (404)659-1110
Fax: (404)659-4988
**Subject(s):** Black Publications; Paid Community Newspapers
**Circ:** ‡10,000

**Birmingham Times** (61)
The Birmingham Times Publishing Co.
115 3rd Ave. W.
Birmingham, AL 35204
Phone: (205)251-5158
Fax: (205)323-2294
**Subject(s):** Paid Community Newspapers; Black Publications
**Circ:** (Free)‡350
(Paid)‡10,000

**College Heights Herald** (11552)
Western Kentucky University
122 Garrett Ctr.
Bowling Green, KY 42101
Phone: (270)745-6291
Fax: (270)745-2697
**Subject(s):** College Publications
**Circ:** (Free)10,000

**Community Voice** (5979)
3046 Lafayette St.
Fort Myers, FL 33916-4324
Phone: (239)337-4444
**Subject(s):** Free Newspapers
**Circ:** (Non-paid)10,000

**Cow Country News** (11760)
Kentucky Cattlemen's Association
176 Pasadena Dr.
Lexington, KY 40503
Phone: (859)278-0899
Fax: (859)260-2060
**Subject(s):** Livestock
**Circ:** 10,000

**The Easley Progress** (28090)
Easley Publications L.L.C.
PO Box 709
Easley, SC 29641
Phone: (864)855-0355
Fax: (864)855-6825
**Subject(s):** Paid Community Newspapers
**Circ:** (Controlled)⊕10,000

**The Eastern Progress** (11967)
117 Donovan Annex
Richmond, KY 40475
Phone: (859)622-1881
Fax: (859)622-2354
**Subject(s):** College Publications
**Circ:** (Free)‡10,000

**Independent** (28558)
Southern Media Properties Inc.
151 N Main St.
Collierville, TN 38017-2670
Phone: (901)853-7060
Fax: (901)854-0727
**Subject(s):** Paid Community Newspapers
**Circ:** (Free)10,000

**The Miami Hurricane** (5893)
University of Miami
PO Box 248132
Coral Gables, FL 33124
Phone: (305)284-4401
Fax: (305)284-4404
**Subject(s):** College Publications
**Circ:** (Free)‡10,000

**The Northeast Georgian** (7088)
Community Newspapers Inc.
2440 Old Athens Hwy.
PO Box 1555
Cornelia, GA 30531
Phone: (706)778-4215
Fax: (706)778-4114
**Subject(s):** Paid Community Newspapers
**Circ:** 10,000

**The Observer** (5914)
Broward Community College
3501 S.W. Davie Rd.
Davie, FL 33314
Phone: (954)475-6700
Fax: (954)423-6405
**Subject(s):** College Publications
**Circ:** (Free)10,000

**The Planter Newspaper** (5801)
439 W. Main St.
Apopka, FL 32712
Phone: (407)886-2777
Fax: (407)889-4121
**Subject(s):** Free Newspapers
**Circ:** (Free)10,000

**Q-Notes** (23351)
PO Box 221841
Charlotte, NC 28222
**Subject(s):** Paid Community Newspapers; Gay and Lesbian Interests
**Circ:** (Non-paid)‡10,000

**The Selma Times-Journal** (431)
Selma Newspapers Inc.
1018 Water Ave.
PO Box 611
Selma, AL 36701
Phone: (334)875-2110
Fax: (334)875-5896
**Subject(s):** Daily Newspapers
**Circ:** (Paid)10,000

**Senior Observer** (6751)
Winter Park Publishing Company Inc.
PO Box 2426
Winter Park, FL 32790-2426
Phone: (407)628-8500

**Subject(s):** Paid Community Newspapers
**Circ:** (Free)10,000

**The University Times** (23358)
University of North Carolina at Charlotte
9201 University City Blvd.
Charlotte, NC 29223-0001
Phone: (704)547-2324
Fax: (704)547-2663
**Subject(s):** College Publications
**Circ:** (Paid)‡193
(Free)‡10,000

**The Western Star** (48)
Trib Publications
1709 3rd Ave. N
PO Box 1900
Bessemer, AL 35020
Phone: (205)424-7827
Fax: (205)424-8118
**Subject(s):** Law
**Circ:** ⊕10,000

**Winter Park/Maitland Observer** (6757)
Winter Park Publishing Company Inc.
PO Box 2426
Winter Park, FL 32790-2426
Phone: (407)628-8500
**Subject(s):** Paid Community Newspapers
**Circ:** (Thurs.)10,000

**Elizabethton Star** (28592)
300 Sycamore St.
PO Box 1960
Elizabethton, TN 37644-1960
Phone: (423)542-4151
Fax: (423)542-2004
**Subject(s):** Daily Newspapers
**Circ:** (Mon.-Fri.)8,315
(Sun.)9,963

**Glasgow Daily Times** (11690)
Community Newspaper Holdings Inc.
100 Commerce Dr.
Glasgow, KY 42141
Phone: (502)678-5171
Fax: (502)678-5052
**Subject(s):** Daily Newspapers
**Circ:** (Mon.-Fri.)★9,350
(Sun.)★9,941

**Village Advocate** (23325)
The Village Publishing Corp.
505 W Franklin St.
Chapel Hill, NC 27516
Phone: (919)932-2000
Fax: (919)932-2027
**Subject(s):** Shopping Guides
**Circ:** (Sun.)♦9,885
(Wed.)♦9,908

**DeSoto County Tribune** (16979)
8885 Goodman
PO Box 1486
Olive Branch, MS 38654
Phone: (662)895-6220
Fax: (662)895-4377
**Subject(s):** Free Newspapers
**Circ:** (Free)‡8,100
(Paid)‡9,897

**The Tifton Gazette** (7459)
211 N. Tift Ave.
PO Box 708
Tifton, GA 31793
Phone: (229)382-4321
Fax: (229)387-7322
**Subject(s):** Daily Newspapers
**Circ:** 9,880

**The Daily Record** (23397)
Record Publishing Company Inc.
99 W. Broad St.
PO Box 1448
Dunn, NC 28335
Phone: (910)891-1234
Fax: (910)891-4445
**Subject(s):** Daily Newspapers
**Circ:** (Mon.-Fri.)9,870

**Mountain Press** (28979)
Mountain Press Inc.
119 Riverbend Dr.
Sevierville, TN 37876
Phone: (865)428-0746

# Gale Directory of Publications & Broadcast Media/140th Ed.  Southern States

**Newspaper Index**

Fax: (865)453-4913
**Subject(s):** Daily Newspapers
**Circ:** ‡9,787

**Citizen Voice & Times  (11736)**
Citizen Voice Inc.
108 Court St.
PO Box 660
Irvine, KY 40336
Phone: (606)723-5161
Fax: (606)723-5509
**Subject(s):** Paid Community Newspapers
**Circ:**  (Paid)‡4,750
        (Free)‡9,700

**Community Times  (11985)**
Landmark Community Newspapers Inc.
PO Box 549
Shelbyville, KY 40065-0549
Phone: (502)633-4334
Fax: (502)732-0453
**Subject(s):** Paid Community Newspapers
**Circ:**  (Paid)1,294
        (Free)9,706

**North Georgia News  (7012)**
PO Box 2029
Blairsville, GA 30514
Phone: (706)745-6343
Fax: (706)745-1830
**Subject(s):** Free Newspapers
**Circ:**  (Free)‡5,000
        (Paid)‡9,700

**The Panolian  (16742)**
Panolian Inc.
363 Highway 51 N
Batesville, MS 38606-0393
Phone: (662)563-4591
Fax: (662)563-5610
**Subject(s):** Paid Community Newspapers
**Circ:** ‡9,675

**Stanly News and Press  (23219)**
Community Newspaper Holdings Inc.
237 W. North St.
PO Box 488
Albemarle, NC 28002-0488
Phone: (704)983-7999
Fax: (704)983-7999
**Subject(s):** Paid Community Newspapers
**Circ:**  (Thurs.)9,268
        (Tues.)9,268
        (Sun.)9,664

**Kentucky Standard  (11526)**
Landmark Community Newspapers Inc.
PO Box 639
Bardstown, KY 40004
Phone: (502)348-9003
Fax: (502)349-3005
**Subject(s):** Paid Community Newspapers
**Circ:** 9,650

**Shelby County Reporter  (167)**
Shelby County Newspapers Inc.
115 Main St.
Columbiana, AL 35051
Phone: (205)669-3131
Fax: (205)669-4217
**Subject(s):** Paid Community Newspapers
**Circ:**  (Paid)9,588

**The Shopper's Guide  (29027)**
Kennedy Newspapers Inc.
302-A W Main
PO Box 626
Waverly, TN 37185-0626
Phone: (931)296-7705
Fax: (931)296-5156
**Subject(s):** Shopping Guides
**Circ:**  (Free)9,500

**The Tullahoma News and Guardian  (29018)**
Lakeway Publishers Inc.
505 Lakeway Pl.
PO Box 400
Tullahoma, TN 37388
**Subject(s):** Paid Community Newspapers
**Circ:** ‡9,500

**The Mobile Press  (316)**
304 Government St.
PO Box 2488
Mobile, AL 36630
Phone: (334)433-1551
Fax: (334)434-8662
**Subject(s):** Daily Newspapers
**Circ:**  (Mon.-Fri.)9,471

**The State Port Pilot  (23791)**
114 E. Moore St.
PO Box 10548
Southport, NC 28461
Phone: (910)457-4568
Fax: (910)457-9427
**Subject(s):** Paid Community Newspapers
**Circ:**  (Paid)9,450

**Samson Ledger  (241)**
803 East Town Ave.
Geneva, AL 36340
Phone: (334)684-2280
Fax: (334)684-3099
**Subject(s):** Free Newspapers
**Circ:**  (Paid)‡5,700
        (Free)‡9,400

**Roane County News  (28674)**
204 Franklin St.
PO Box 610
Kingston, TN 37763
Phone: (423)376-3481
Fax: (423)376-1945
**Subject(s):** Paid Community Newspapers
**Circ:** 9,369

**Times-Enterprise  (7448)**
PO Box 650
Thomasville, GA 31792
Phone: (912)226-2400
Fax: (912)228-5863
**Subject(s):** Daily Newspapers
**Circ:**  (Sun.)★9,287
        (Tues.-Fri.)★9,347

**Newport Plain Talk  (28939)**
145 East Broadway
Newport, TN 37821
Phone: (423)623-6171
Fax: (423)625-1995
**Subject(s):** Paid Community Newspapers
**Circ:** ‡9250

**The Calhoun Times  (7030)**
News Publishing Co.
PO Box 8
Calhoun, GA 30703
Phone: (706)629-2231
Fax: (706)625-0899
**Subject(s):** Paid Community Newspapers
**Circ:**  (Paid)9,200

**The Franklin Press  (23488)**
Community Newspapers Inc.
PO Box 350
Franklin, NC 28744
Phone: (828)524-2010
Fax: (828)524-8821
**Subject(s):** Paid Community Newspapers
**Circ:** ‡9,200

**Lenoir News-Topic  (23616)**
The New York Times Co.
PO Box 1110
Lenoir, NC 28645
Phone: (704)758-7381
Fax: (704)754-0110
**Subject(s):** Daily Newspapers
**Circ:**  (Sun.)★8,832
        (Mon.-Fri.)★9,195

**The Times-Record  (258)**
Northwest Alabamian
PO Box 430
Haleyville, AL 35565
Phone: (205)486-9461
Fax: (205)486-4849
**Subject(s):** Free Newspapers
**Circ:**  (Paid)‡4,600
        (Free)‡9,196

**The Destin Log  (5939)**
PO Box 957
Destin, FL 32540
Phone: (850)837-2828

Fax: (850)654-8427
**Subject(s):** Paid Community Newspapers
**Circ:**  (Non-paid)285
        (Paid)9,181

**The Messenger  (11868)**
The Messenger Newspaper
221 S. Main St.
Madisonville, KY 42431
Phone: (270)824-3300
Fax: (270)821-6855
**Subject(s):** Daily Newspapers
**Circ:**  (Sun.)8,905
        (Sat.)9,162
        (Tues.-Fri.)9,162

**Fayette Daily News  (7145)**
Fayette Newspapers Inc.
210 Jeff Davis Place
PO Box 96
Fayetteville, GA 30214
Phone: (770)461-6317
Fax: (770)460-8172
**Subject(s):** Paid Community Newspapers
**Circ:** ‡9,100

**Herald-Chronicle  (29030)**
906 Dinah Shore Blvd.
Winchester, TN 37398
Fax: (615)967-2299
**Subject(s):** Paid Community Newspapers
**Circ:**  (Free)‡43
        (Paid)‡9100

**Henderson Daily Dispatch  (23570)**
Henderson Dispatch Company Inc.
PO Box 908
Henderson, NC 27536-0908
Phone: (252)436-2700
**Subject(s):** Daily Newspapers
**Circ:**  (Tues.-Fri.)8,562
        (Sat.)8,562
        (Sun.)9,099

**The Shopper's Outlook  (11946)**
Cynthiana Democrat
PO Box 111
Falmouth, KY 41040-0111
Phone: (606)654-3332
Fax: (606)654-4365
**Subject(s):** Shopping Guides
**Circ:**  (Free)‡9,080

**The East Carolinian  (23552)**
East Carolina University
Student Publications Bldg., 2nd Fl.
Greenville, NC 27858-4353
Phone: (252)328-6366
Fax: (252)328-6558
**Subject(s):** College Publications
**Circ:**  (Free)‡9,000

**Mid-Week Messenger  (23828)**
The Mountaineer Publishing Company Inc.
PO Box 129
Waynesville, NC 28786
Phone: (828)452-0661
Fax: (828)452-0665
**Subject(s):** Shopping Guides
**Circ:**  (Free)9,000

**The Wilmington Journal  (23846)**
412 S. 7th St.
PO Box 1020
Wilmington, NC 28402
Phone: (910)762-5502
Fax: (910)343-1334
**Subject(s):** Paid Community Newspapers; Black Publications
**Circ:** 9,000

**Amusement Business  (28840)**
VNU Business Publications
PO Box 24970
Nashville, TN 37202
Phone: (615)321-4250
Fax: (615)327-1575
**Subject(s):** Business
**Circ:**  (Paid)8,981

**Daily Journal Messenger  (28223)**
Box 547
Seneca, SC 29679
Phone: (864)882-2375
Fax: (864)882-2381

---

Circulation: ★ = ABC;  △ = BPA;  ♦ = CAC;  • = CCAB;  ❑ = VAC;  ⊕ = PO Statement;  ‡ = Publisher's Report;  Boldface figures = sworn;  Light figures = estimated.

3797

## Southern States

**Subject(s):** Paid Community Newspapers
**Circ:** (Combined)8,943

**Commonwealth-Journal** (11992)
CNHI
110-112 E Mount Vernon St.
PO Box 859
Somerset, KY 42502
Phone: (606)678-8191
Fax: (606)679-9225
**Subject(s):** Daily Newspapers
**Circ:** 8,663
(Sun.)8,904

**Courier-Times** (23762)
109 Clayton Ave.
PO Box 311
Roxboro, NC 27573
Phone: (336)599-0162
Fax: (336)597-2773
**Subject(s):** Paid Community Newspapers
**Circ:** ‡8,900

**The Houston Home Journal** (7354)
1210 Washington St.
PO Box 1910
Perry, GA 31069
Phone: (478)987-1823
Fax: (478)988-1181
**Subject(s):** Paid Community Newspapers
**Circ:** 8,900

**Marco Island Eagle** (6313)
1075 Central Ave.
Naples, FL 34102
Phone: (239)262-3161
Fax: (239)435-3451
**Subject(s):** Paid Community Newspapers
**Circ:** (Wed.)8,838

**Roanoke Chowen News-Herald** (23216)
Boone Newspapers
801 Parker Ave.
PO Box 1325
Ahoskie, NC 27910
Phone: (252)332-2123
**Subject(s):** Paid Community Newspapers
**Circ:** ‡8,800

**The Times-Georgian** (7038)
PO Box 460
Carrollton, GA 30117-0460
Phone: (404)834-6631
Fax: (404)834-9991
**Subject(s):** Daily Newspapers
**Circ:** (Tues.-Fri.)★8,604
(Sun.)★8,724

**Union City Daily Messenger** (29020)
613 E Jackson St.
PO Box 430
Union City, TN 38261
Phone: (731)885-0744
Fax: (731)885-0782
**Subject(s):** Daily Newspapers
**Circ:** ‡8,700

**News-Times** (23288)
News Reporter
114 E. 1st Ave.
Chadbourn, NC 28431
Phone: (910)654-3762
Fax: (910)642-1856
**Subject(s):** Free Newspapers
**Circ:** (Free)8,656

**Franklin Times** (23628)
Franklin County Newspapers Inc.
109 S Bickett Blvd.
Box 119
Louisburg, NC 27549-0119
Phone: (919)496-6503
Fax: (919)496-1689
**Subject(s):** Paid Community Newspapers
**Circ:** ‡8,569

**Pulaski Citizen** (28965)
308 W College St.
PO Box 905
Pulaski, TN 38478
Phone: (931)363-3544
Fax: (615)363-4312
**Subject(s):** Paid Community Newspapers
**Circ:** ‡8,561

**The Clanton Advertiser** (163)
Selma Times Journal
PO Box 1379
1109 7th St.N.
Clanton, AL 35045
Phone: (205)755-5747
Fax: (205)755-5857
**Subject(s):** Free Newspapers
**Circ:** (Paid)‡4,000
(Free)‡8,500

**The Douglas Enterprise & Bonus** (7119)
1823 S Peterson Ave.
PO Box 750
Douglas, GA 31533
Phone: (912)384-2323
Fax: (912)283-0218
**Subject(s):** Paid Community Newspapers
**Circ:** ‡8,500

**The Gaffney Ledger** (28104)
1604 Baker Blvd.
PO Box 670
Gaffney, SC 29342
Phone: (864)489-1131
Fax: (864)487-7667
**Subject(s):** Paid Community Newspapers
**Circ:** (Free)116
(Paid)8,500

**The Herald-Gazette** (29015)
111 E 1st St.
PO Box 7
Trenton, TN 38382
Phone: (731)855-1711
Fax: (731)855-9587
**Subject(s):** Paid Community Newspapers
**Circ:** (Paid)3,500
(Free)8,500

**Island Reporter** (6521)
PO Box 809
2340 Perry Winkle Way
Sanibel, FL 33957
Phone: (239)472-1587
Fax: (239)472-8398
**Subject(s):** Paid Community Newspapers
**Circ:** 8,500

**The Pine Island Eagle** (5861)
Breeze Publishing Co.
2510 Del Prado Blvd.
Cape Coral, FL
Phone: (239)574-1110
Fax: (239)574-3403
**Subject(s):** Free Newspapers
**Circ:** (Free)‡8,500

**The Savannah Herald** (7396)
1803 Barnard St.
PO Box 486
Savannah, GA 31402
Phone: (912)232-4505
Fax: (912)231-0018
**Subject(s):** Paid Community Newspapers; Black Publications
**Circ:** (Paid)8,500

**Sentinel—News** (11987)
Landmark Community Newspapers Inc.
PO Box 549
Shelbyville, KY 40065-0549
Phone: (502)633-4334
Fax: (502)732-0453
**Subject(s):** Paid Community Newspapers
**Circ:** (Paid)‡8,500

**Southeastern Peanut Farmer** (7457)
PO Box 706
Tifton, GA 31793
**Subject(s):** Socialized Farming
**Circ:** ‡8,500

**Spring Lake News** (23472)
Dickson Press
PO Box 35395
Fayetteville, NC 28303-0395
Phone: (910)864-9207
Fax: (910)864-8911
**Subject(s):** Free Newspapers
**Circ:** (Free)‡8,500

**Times-Tribune** (11624)
APMS
201 N. Kentucky Ave.
PO Box 516
Corbin, KY 40701-1529
Phone: (606)528-2464
Fax: (606)528-9850
**Subject(s):** Daily Newspapers
**Circ:** 8,500

**The Union-Recorder** (7308)
Community Newspaper Holdings Inc.
1 U-Recorder Plz.
PO Box 520
Milledgeville, GA 31061
Phone: (912)453-1450
Fax: (912)453-1449
**Subject(s):** Daily Newspapers
**Circ:** 8,500

**Wake Weekly** (23816)
229 E. Owen Ave.
PO Box 1919
Wake Forest, NC 27588
Phone: (919)556-3182
Fax: (919)556-2233
**Subject(s):** Paid Community Newspapers
**Circ:** 8,500

**Robertson County Times** (29006)
PO Box 637
505 W Ct. Sq.
Springfield, TN 37172
Phone: (615)384-3567
Fax: (615)384-1221
**Subject(s):** Paid Community Newspapers
**Circ:** (Combined)8,470

**Shelbyville Times-Gazette** (28989)
323 E Depot St.
PO Box 380
Shelbyville, TN 37162
Phone: (931)684-1200
Fax: (931)684-3228
**Subject(s):** Daily Newspapers
**Circ:** ‡8,458

**Chronicle-Independent** (27991)
909 W DeKalb St.
PO Box 1137
Camden, SC 29020
Phone: (803)432-6157
Fax: (803)432-7609
**Subject(s):** Paid Community Newspapers
**Circ:** (Non-paid)⊕87
(Paid)⊕8,436

**Northside Sun** (16895)
Sunland Publishing Co.
PO Box 16709
246 Briarwood Dr.
Jackson, MS 39236
Phone: (601)957-1122
Fax: (601)957-1533
**Subject(s):** Free Newspapers
**Circ:** (Free)‡595
(Paid)‡8,430

**Elk Valley Times** (28598)
Lakeway Publishers Inc.
PO Box 9
Fayetteville, TN 37334
Phone: (615)433-6151
Fax: (615)433-6151
**Subject(s):** Paid Community Newspapers
**Circ:** 8,400

**Athens News Courier** (24)
410 W Green St.
PO Box 670
Athens, AL 35611-2518
Phone: (256)232-2720
Fax: (256)233-7753
**Subject(s):** Daily Newspapers
**Circ:** (Tues.-Fri.)7,549
(Sun.)8,393

**Lehigh Acres News Star** (5981)
News-Press Publications Inc.
2442 Dr. Martin Luther King Jr.Blvd.
Fort Myers, FL 33901
Phone: (239)335-0200
Fax: (239)369-1396

**Subject(s):** Free Newspapers

**Circ:** (Free)6,889
(Paid)8,393

**The Blade (7438)**
Forest-Blade Publishing Inc.
Box 938
Swainsboro, GA 30401
Phone: (478)237-9971
Fax: (478)237-9451
**Subject(s):** Paid Community Newspapers

**Circ:** (Paid)6,000
(Free)8,388

**The Express (23632)**
McDowell Newspapers
136 Logan St.
PO Box 610
Marion, NC 28752-0610
Phone: (828)652-3313
Fax: (478)374-3585
**Subject(s):** Free Newspapers

**Circ:** (Free)‡8,350

**Messenger Plus (7138)**
Putnam Printing Company Inc.
PO Box 4027
Eatonton, GA 31024
Phone: (706)485-3501
Fax: (706)485-4166
**Subject(s):** Shopping Guides

**Circ:** (Non-paid)‡8,300

**Southern Standard (28751)**
105 College St.
PO Box 150
Mc Minnville, TN 37110
Phone: (931)473-2191
Fax: (931)473-6823
**Subject(s):** Paid Community Newspapers

**Circ:** ‡8,300

**Valdese News (23650)**
PO Box 280
Morganton, NC 28680-0280
Phone: (704)437-2161
Fax: (704)437-5372
**Subject(s):** Paid Community Newspapers

**Circ:** (Paid)555
(Free)8,300

**Richmond County Daily Journal (23755)**
Community Newspapers Inc.
105 E Washington St.
Rockingham, NC 28379
Phone: (919)997-3111
Fax: (919)997-4321
**Subject(s):** Daily Newspapers

**Circ:** (Mon.-Fri.)★8,184
(Sun.)★8,288

**Greenwood Commonwealth (16830)**
329 Hwy., 82 W.
PO Box 8050
Greenwood, MS 38935-8050
Phone: (662)453-5312
Fax: (601)453-2908
**Subject(s):** Daily Newspapers

**Circ:** (Mon.-Fri.)7,915
(Sun.)8,259

**Giles Free Press (28964)**
Pulaski Publishing
PO Box 905
Pulaski, TN 38478
Phone: (931)363-3544
Fax: (931)363-4312
**Subject(s):** Paid Community Newspapers

**Circ:** ‡8,247

**Charleston Regional Business Journal (28171)**
Setcom Inc.
389 Johnnie Dodds Blvd., Ste. 200
Mount Pleasant, SC 29464
Phone: (843)849-3100
Fax: (843)849-3122
**Subject(s):** Business; Paid Community Newspapers

**Circ:** (Combined)8,200

**The Charlotte World (23339)**
8701 Mallard Creek Rd.
Charlotte, NC 28262
Phone: (704)548-1737
Fax: (704)503-6691

**Subject(s):** Paid Community Newspapers; Religious Publications

**Circ:** (Paid)‡1,800
(Non-paid)‡8,200

**The Ledger-Independent (11885)**
Lee Enterprises Inc.
41-42 W. Second St.
PO Box 518
Maysville, KY 41056
Phone: (606)564-9091
Fax: (606)564-6893
**Subject(s):** Daily Newspapers

**Circ:** ‡8,200

**DeSoto Times Today (16863)**
P.H. Publishing
295 Losher St.
PO Box 100
Hernando, MS 38632
Phone: (662)429-6397
Fax: (662)429-5229
**Subject(s):** Paid Community Newspapers

**Circ:** (Paid)‡8,138

**Franklin County Times (422)**
Franklin County Times Inc.
PO Box 1088
Russellville, AL 35653
Phone: (256)332-1881
Fax: (256)332-1883
**Subject(s):** Paid Community Newspapers

**Circ:** (Paid)4,200
(Free)8,125

**The Tallahassee Advertiser (6602)**
PO Box 2213
Tallahassee, FL 32316
Phone: (850)574-0520
Fax: (850)574-0457
**Subject(s):** Paid Community Newspapers

**Circ:** (Free)1,880
(Paid)8,120

**Lake City Reporter (6148)**
Community Newspapers Inc.
126 E Duval St.
PO Box 1709
Lake City, FL 32055
Phone: (386)752-9400
Fax: (386)752-9400
**Subject(s):** Daily Newspapers

**Circ:** (Mon.-Sat.)★8,106
(Sun.)★8,110

**The Cheraw Chronicle (28019)**
Community Newspapers Inc.
c/o Wylie Cox
114 Front St.
PO Box 1389
Cheraw, SC 29520
Phone: (843)537-5261
Fax: (843)537-4518
**Subject(s):** Paid Community Newspapers

**Circ:** ‡8,050

**Grenada Lake Herald (16839)**
PO Box 907
50 Corporate Row
Grenada, MS 38902-0907
Phone: (662)226-4321
Fax: (662)226-8310
**Subject(s):** Paid Community Newspapers

**Circ:** 8,050

**Cherokee Scout (23662)**
Community Newspapers Inc.
110 S. Church St.
Murphy, NC 28906
Phone: (828)837-5122
Fax: (828)837-5832
**Subject(s):** Paid Community Newspapers

**Circ:** ‡8,000

**The Florida Newspaper (6233)**
PO Box 97-1490
Miami, FL 33197
Phone: (305)254-3400
Fax: (305)254-6007
**Subject(s):** Paid Community Newspapers

**Circ:** (Free)‡200
(Paid)‡8,000

**Hare Krishna World (5788)**
PO Box 238
Alachua, FL 32616
Phone: (386)462-5054
Fax: (386)462-5056
**Subject(s):** Free Newspapers; Religious Publications

**Circ:** (Paid)⊕8,000

**The Jewish Star (83)**
PO Box 130603
Birmingham, AL 35213
Phone: (205)956-3929
Fax: (205)967-1417
**Subject(s):** Jewish Publications

**Circ:** ‡8,000

**Kaleidoscope (87)**
University of Alabama at Birmingham
Hill University Ctr.
HUC 135, 1400 Univ. Blvd.
Birmingham, AL 35294-1150
Phone: (205)934-3354
Fax: (205)934-8050
**Subject(s):** College Publications

**Circ:** (Paid)300
(Free)8,000

**Libre (6248)**
LIBRE
904 SW 23rd Ave.
Miami, FL 33135
Phone: (305)643-4888
Fax: (305)643-1226
**Subject(s):** Free Newspapers; Hispanic Publications; Spanish

**Circ:** (Paid)2,000
(Free)8,000

**Perido Pelican (6063)**
Gulf Breeze Publishing Co.
1200 Gulf Breeze Pkwy.
Gulf Breeze, FL 32561
Phone: (850)934-5108
Fax: (850)932-8765
**Subject(s):** Free Newspapers

**Circ:** (Non-paid)‡8,000

**The Savannah Tribune (7401)**
Savannah Tribune Inc.
916 Montgomery St.
PO Box 2066
Savannah, GA 31402
Phone: (912)233-6128
Fax: (912)233-6140
**Subject(s):** Paid Community Newspapers; Black Publications

**Circ:** (Paid)‡8,000
(Free)‡8,000

**Sidelines (28828)**
Middle Tennessee State University
1301 E. Main St.
Murfreesboro, TN 37132
Phone: (615)898-2300
Fax: (615)904-8487
**Subject(s):** College Publications

**Circ:** (Free)‡8,000

**South Miami News (6259)**
Community Newspapers
6796 S.W. 62 Ave.
Miami, FL 33143
Phone: (305)669-7355
Fax: (305)661-0954
**Subject(s):** Paid Community Newspapers

**Circ:** ‡8,000

**Southwest Sun (16942)**
J.O. Emmerich & Associates Inc.
112 Oliver Emmerich Dr.
McComb, MS 39648
Phone: (601)684-2421
Fax: (601)684-0836
**Subject(s):** Shopping Guides

**Circ:** (Free)8,000

**Statesboro Herald (7426)**
Statesboro Publishing Company Inc.
1 Herald Sq.
PO Box 888
Statesboro, GA 30458
Phone: (912)764-9031
Fax: (912)489-8181
**Subject(s):** Daily Newspapers

**Circ:** 8,000

Circulation: ★ = ABC; △ = BPA; ♦ = CAC; • = CCAB; ▫ = VAC; ⊕ = PO Statement; ‡ = Publisher's Report; Boldface figures = sworn; Light figures = estimated.

**The Vanguard** (321)
University of South Alabama
The Vanguard
PO Drawer U-25100
Mobile, AL 36688
Phone: (251)460-6442
Fax: (251)414-8293
**Subject(s):** College Publications

Circ: (Combined)‡8,000

**Hartselle Enquirer** (262)
Hartselle Newspapers L.L.C.
407 W Chestnut St.
PO Box 929
Hartselle, AL 35640
Phone: (256)773-6566
Fax: (256)773-1953
**Subject(s):** Paid Community Newspapers

Circ: (Paid)7,650
(Free)7,980

**Hartselle Shopping Guide** (263)
Hartselle Newspapers L.L.C.
407 W Chestnut St.
PO Box 929
Hartselle, AL 35640
Phone: (256)773-6566
Fax: (256)773-1953
**Subject(s):** Shopping Guides

Circ: (Paid)‡7,019
(Free)‡7,980

**The Paris Post-Intelligencer** (28952)
Paris Publishing Company Inc.
208 E Wood St.
PO Box 310
Paris, TN 38242-0310
Phone: (731)642-1162
Fax: (731)642-1165
**Subject(s):** Daily Newspapers

Circ: (Non-paid)105
(Paid)7,900

**The Summerville News** (7434)
ESPY Pub. Co.
PO Box 310
20 Wildlife Lake Rd
Summerville, GA 30747
Phone: (706)857-2494
Fax: (706)857-2393
**Subject(s):** Paid Community Newspapers

Circ: ‡7,850

**News-Herald** (28723)
Box 310
508 E. Broadway
Lenoir City, TN 37771
Phone: (423)986-6581
Fax: (423)988-3261
**Subject(s):** Paid Community Newspapers

Circ: ‡7,823

**Avery Journal** (23676)
High Country Media L.L.C.
PO Box 1330
335 Linville Street
Newland, NC 28657-1330
Phone: (828)733-2448
Fax: (828)733-0639
**Subject(s):** Paid Community Newspapers

Circ: (Free)250
(Paid)7,800

**Douglas Daily News** (7118)
Coffee County News & Shopper Inc.
213 N Peterson Ave.
Douglas, GA 31533
Phone: (912)384-9112
Fax: (912)384-4220
**Subject(s):** Jewish Publications

Circ: (Paid)‡7,800

**The Jackson Herald** (7209)
MainStreet Newspapers Inc.
PO Box 908
33 Lee St.
Jefferson, GA 30549
Phone: (706)367-5233
Fax: (706)367-8056
**Subject(s):** Paid Community Newspapers

Circ: ‡7,800

**Laurel Leader Call** (16924)
PO Box 728
Laurel, MS 39441-0728
Phone: (601)428-0551
Fax: (601)426-3550
**Subject(s):** Daily Newspapers

Circ: (Sun.)★7,479
(Mon.-Sat.)★7,808

**Tribune & Georgian** (6816)
Community Newspapers Inc.
297 Prince Ave., No. 14
Athens, GA 30601
Phone: (706)548-0010
Fax: (706)548-0808
**Subject(s):** Paid Community Newspapers

Circ: ‡7,800

**Eastern Wake News** (23888)
The News & Observer Publishing Co.
110 Arendell Ave.
PO Box 1167
Zebulon, NC 27597
Phone: (919)269-6101
Fax: (919)269-8383
**Subject(s):** Paid Community Newspapers

Circ: 7,700

**Mooresville Tribune** (23645)
147 E Center Ave.
PO Box 300
Mooresville, NC 28115
Phone: (704)664-5554
Fax: (704)664-3614
**Subject(s):** Paid Community Newspapers

Circ: 7,650

**The Daily Corinthian** (16805)
1607 S Harper Rd.
PO Box 1800
Corinth, MS 38834
Phone: (662)287-6111
Fax: (662)287-3525
**Subject(s):** Daily Newspapers

Circ: (Tues.-Fri.)7,500
(Sat.)7,500
(Sun.)7,610

**Outer Banks Sentinel** (23666)
Womack Publishing Co.
PO Box 546
Nags Head, NC 27959
Phone: (252)480-2234
Fax: (252)480-1146
**Subject(s):** Paid Community Newspapers

Circ: (Paid)⊕7,610

**Laurens County Advertiser** (28162)
226 W Laurens St.
PO Box 490
Laurens, SC 29360-0490
Phone: (864)984-2586
Fax: (864)984-4039
**Subject(s):** Paid Community Newspapers

Circ: (Free)‡200
(Paid)‡7,600

**Caloosa Belle** (6145)
The Caloose Belle
PO Box 518
22 Ft. Thompson Ave.
Labelle, FL 33975
Phone: (863)675-2541
Fax: (863)675-1449
**Subject(s):** Free Newspapers

Circ: (Free)7,500

**DeFuniak Herald** (5929)
Woodham Family Publications
14-16 Baldwin Ave.
PO Box 1546
DeFuniak Springs, FL 32433
Phone: (904)892-3232
Fax: (904)894-2270
**Subject(s):** Paid Community Newspapers

Circ: 7,500

**The Emory Wheel** (6870)
Emory University
1380 Oxford Rd.
Atlanta, GA 30322
Phone: (404)727-6178
Fax: (404)727-3613
**Subject(s):** College Publications

Circ: (Combined)7,500

**Murray Ledger and Times** (11913)
1001 Whitnell Ave.
Box 1040
Murray, KY 42071
Phone: (270)753-1916
Fax: (270)753-1927
**Subject(s):** Daily Newspapers

Circ: (Paid)‡7,500
(Free)‡7,500

**Santa Rosa Press Gazette** (6295)
Press Gazette
6629 SW Elva St.
Milton, FL 32570
Phone: (850)623-2120
Fax: (850)623-2007
**Subject(s):** Paid Community Newspapers

Circ: ‡7,500

**Times-Courier** (7143)
Times-Courier Pub.
PO Box 1076
Ellijay, GA 30540
Phone: (706)635-4313
Fax: (706)635-7006
**Subject(s):** Paid Community Newspapers

Circ: (Non-paid)35
(Paid)7,500

**Wallace Enterprise** (23818)
PO Box 699
Wallace, NC 28466-0699
Phone: (910)285-2178
Fax: (910)285-3179
**Subject(s):** Paid Community Newspapers

Circ: 7,500

**Flagler Pennysaver** (5854)
Volusia Pennysaver Inc.
2A McCormick Dr.
Bunnell, FL 32110
Phone: (386)437-5971
Fax: (386)437-9524
**Subject(s):** Shopping Guides

Circ: (Free)‡7,480

**Covington News** (7091)
Covington Newspaper Company Inc.
1166 Usher St.
PO Box 1249
Covington, GA 30014
Phone: (770)787-6397
Fax: (770)786-6451
**Subject(s):** Paid Community Newspapers

Circ: ‡7,450

**Chester News and Reporter** (11984)
Landmark Community Newspapers Inc.
PO Box 549
Shelbyville, KY 40065-0549
Phone: (502)633-4334
Fax: (502)732-0453
**Subject(s):** Paid Community Newspapers

Circ: (Free)80
(Paid)7,400

**Tribune Courier** (11533)
100 West 11th St.
PO Box 410
Benton, KY 42025
Phone: (270)527-3162
Fax: (270)527-4567
**Subject(s):** Paid Community Newspapers

Circ: (Free)200
(Paid)7,400

**Union Daily Times** (28248)
Union Times Company Inc.
PO Box 749
100 Times Blvd.
Union, SC 29379-0749
Phone: (864)427-1234
Fax: (864)427-1237
**Subject(s):** Daily Newspapers

Circ: (Paid)‡7,400

**Borger News-Herald** (64)
Community Newspaper Holdings Inc.
3500 Colonnade Pkwy., Ste. 600
Birmingham, AL 35243
Phone: (205)298-7100
Fax: (205)298-7101
**Subject(s):** Daily Newspapers

Circ: (Mon.-Fri.)6,448
(Sun.)7,321

**The Jessamine Journal** (11922)
507 N Main St.
PO Box 8
Nicholasville, KY 40340-0008
Phone: (859)885-5381
Fax: (859)887-2966
**Subject(s):** Paid Community Newspapers
**Circ:** 7,329

**The Messenger** (23630)
Media General Newspapers Inc.
208 W Murphy St.
PO Box 508
Madison, NC 27025
Phone: (336)548-6047
Fax: (336)548-2853
**Subject(s):** Paid Community Newspapers
**Circ:** 7,310

**The Blount County Shopping Guide** (387)
Arab Tribune
PO Box 310
217 3rd Street South
Oneonta, AL 35121
Phone: (205)625-3231
Fax: (205)625-3239
**Subject(s):** Shopping Guides
**Circ:** (Free)‡7,300

**Moultrie Observer** (7318)
PO Box 2349
Moultrie, GA 31776-0889
Phone: (229)985-4545
Fax: (229)985-3569
**Subject(s):** Daily Newspapers
**Circ:** 7,306

**The Toccoa Record** (7465)
The Toccoa Record Co.
151 W. Doyle St.
PO Drawer 1069
Toccoa, GA 30577
Phone: (706)886-9476
Fax: (706)886-2161
**Subject(s):** Paid Community Newspapers
**Circ:** (Free)125
(Paid)7,300

**The Winchester Sun** (12037)
20 Wall St.
PO Box 4300
Winchester, KY 40392-4300
Phone: (859)744-3123
Fax: (859)745-0638
**Subject(s):** Daily Newspapers
**Circ:** 7,300

**The Dickson Herald** (28581)
104 Church St.
Dickson, TN 37055
Phone: (615)446-2811
Fax: (615)446-5560
**Subject(s):** Paid Community Newspapers
**Circ:** (Non-paid)271
(Paid)7,236

**Daily News** (11890)
American Publishing Co.
PO Box 579
Middlesboro, KY 40965
Phone: (606)248-1010
Fax: (606)248-7614
**Subject(s):** Daily Newspapers
**Circ:** (Mon.-Fri.)7,200

**Enterprise** (11874)
PO Box 449
Manchester, KY 40962
Phone: (606)598-6174
Fax: (606)598-2330
**Subject(s):** Paid Community Newspapers
**Circ:** 7,200

**Northwest Alabamian** (257)
PO Box 430
Haleyville, AL 35565
Phone: (205)486-9461
Fax: (205)486-4849
**Subject(s):** Paid Community Newspapers
**Circ:** ‡7,200

**The Press-Sentinel** (7211)
252 W Walnut St.
Jesup, GA 31545
Phone: (912)427-3757

Fax: (912)427-4092
**Subject(s):** Paid Community Newspapers
**Circ:** 7,200

**The Trail Blazer** (11901)
Morehead State University Board of Student Publications
317 Breckenridge Hall
Morehead, KY 40351
Phone: (606)783-2697
Fax: (606)783-9113
**Subject(s):** College Publications
**Circ:** (Paid)523
(Free)7,200

**Tribune-Times** (28227)
Greenville News
PO Box 1179
Simpsonville, SC 29681
Phone: (864)967-9580
Fax: (864)967-9585
**Subject(s):** Paid Community Newspapers
**Circ:** ‡7,200

**The Sylva Herald & Ruralite** (23806)
The Sylva Herald Publishing Company Inc.
539 W. Main St.
PO Box 307
Sylva, NC 28779
Phone: (828)586-2611
Fax: (828)586-2637
**Subject(s):** Paid Community Newspapers
**Circ:** 7,195

**The Democrat-Reporter** (300)
PO Box 480040
Linden, AL 36748
Phone: (334)295-5224
**Subject(s):** Paid Community Newspapers
**Circ:** ‡7,125

**Central Kentucky News-Journal** (11613)
Landmark Community Newspapers Inc.
428 Woodlawn Ave.
Campbellsville, KY 42718
Phone: (270)465-2500
Fax: (270)465-2500
**Subject(s):** Paid Community Newspapers
**Circ:** (Free)‡20
(Paid)‡7,115

**The Blount Countian** (386)
The Southern Democrat Inc.
PO Box 310
Oneonta, AL 35121
Phone: (205)625-3231
Fax: (205)625-3239
**Subject(s):** Paid Community Newspapers
**Circ:** 7,100

**The Times-Journal Midweek** (232)
Fort Payne Newspapers Inc.
PO Box 680349
Fort Payne, AL 35968-1604
Phone: (256)845-2550
Fax: (256)845-7459
**Subject(s):** Daily Newspapers
**Circ:** ‡7,100

**The Hartwell Sun** (7188)
Community Newspapers Inc.
c/o Judy Salter
8 Benson St.
PO Box 700
Hartwell, GA 30643
Phone: (706)376-8025
Fax: (706)376-3016
**Subject(s):** Paid Community Newspapers
**Circ:** ‡7,085

**Claiborne Progress** (29011)
PO Box 40
Tazewell, TN 37879
Phone: (423)626-3222
Fax: (423)626-6868
**Subject(s):** Paid Community Newspapers
**Circ:** ‡7,076

**Aberdeen Examiner** (16735)
North Mississippi Community Newspaper
209 E. Commerce St.
PO Box 279
Aberdeen, MS 39730
Phone: (662)369-4507
Fax: (662)369-4508

**Subject(s):** Paid Community Newspapers
**Circ:** ‡7,000

**Americus Times-Recorder** (6780)
South Georgia Media Group
101 Hwy. 27th E.
Americus, GA 31709
Phone: (229)924-2751
Fax: (229)928-6344
**Subject(s):** Daily Newspapers
**Circ:** (Combined)7,000

**The Amory Advertiser** (16737)
PO Box 519
Amory, MS 38821
Phone: (662)256-5647
Fax: (662)256-5701
**Subject(s):** Paid Community Newspapers
**Circ:** ‡7,000

**The Auburn Bulletin** (33)
Auburn Bulletin
PO Box 3240
Auburn, AL 36831-3240
Phone: (334)821-7150
Fax: (334)887-0037
**Subject(s):** Free Newspapers
**Circ:** (Paid)3,200
(Free)7,000

**Carolina Cattle Connection** (23493)
N.C. Cattlemen's Association
2228 N Main St.
Fuquay Varina, NC 27526
Phone: (919)552-9111
Fax: (919)552-9216
**Subject(s):** Livestock
**Circ:** ‡7,000

**The Catalyst** (28000)
Island Publications
Office of Public Relations, MUSC
171 Ashley Ave.
Charleston, SC 29425
Phone: (843)792-3622
Fax: (843)792-6723
**Subject(s):** College Publications
**Circ:** (Free)‡7,000

**The Collierville Herald** (28555)
Pritchartt Publishing Co.
PO Box 427
148 North Main
Collierville, TN 38017
Phone: (901)853-2241
Fax: (901)853-8507
**Subject(s):** Paid Community Newspapers
**Circ:** ‡7,000

**The Covington Leader** (28571)
2001 Hwy. 51 S
PO Box 529
Covington, TN 38019-0529
Phone: (901)476-7116
Fax: (901)476-0373
**Subject(s):** Paid Community Newspapers
**Circ:** (Paid)‡7,000

**The Daily Herald** (7300)
Community Newspaper Holdings Inc.
138 Sloan St.
PO Box 278
McDonough, GA 30253
Phone: (770)957-9161
Fax: (770)954-0282
**Subject(s):** Paid Community Newspapers
**Circ:** ‡7,000

**The George-Anne** (7420)
Georgia Southern University
Rm. 2023
Georgia Southern Univ.
Statesboro, GA 30460
Phone: (912)681-5418
Fax: (912)486-7113
**Subject(s):** College Publications
**Circ:** (Free)‡7,000

**Hialea-Opa Locka News** (6238)
Community Newspapers
6796 S.W. 62 Ave.
Miami, FL 33143
Phone: (305)669-7355
Fax: (305)661-0954

Circulation: ★ = ABC; △ = BPA; ♦ = CAC; ● = CCAB; ▣ = VAC; ⊕ = PO Statement; ‡ = Publisher's Report; Boldface figures = sworn; Light figures = estimated.

# Southern States

**Subject(s):** Free Newspapers
**Circ:** (Free)‡7,000

**Marion Star and Mullins Enterprise (28169)**
211 Bobby Gerald Pkwy.
PO Box 880
Marion, SC 29571
Phone: (843)423-2050
Fax: (843)423-2542
**Subject(s):** Paid Community Newspapers
**Circ:** (Paid)‡7,000

**The Murray State News (11914)**
Murray State University
PO Box 9
Murray, KY 42071
Phone: (502)762-2998
Fax: (502)762-3175
**Subject(s):** College Publications
**Circ:** (Paid)‡250
(Free)‡7,000

**North Bartow News (6760)**
321B N Main St.
PO Box 374
Adairsville, GA 30103
Phone: (770)773-3754
Fax: (770)773-3754
**Subject(s):** Free Newspapers
**Circ:** (Free)‡7,000

**Pickens County Progress (7204)**
PO Box 67
Jasper, GA 30143
Phone: (706)253-2457
Fax: (706)253-9738
**Subject(s):** Paid Community Newspapers
**Circ:** ‡7,000

**The Pickens Sentinel (28213)**
PO Box 95
Pickens, SC 29671
Phone: (864)878-2453
Fax: (864)878-2454
**Subject(s):** Paid Community Newspapers
**Circ:** ‡7,000

**The Post-Searchlight (7000)**
The Bainbridge Post-Searchlight Inc.
301 N Crawford St.
PO Box 277
Bainbridge, GA 39817-3612
Phone: (229)246-2827
Fax: (229)246-7665
**Subject(s):** Paid Community Newspapers
**Circ:** ‡7,000

**The Press and Standard (28252)**
The Press & Standard
113 Washington St.
Walterboro, SC 29488
Phone: (843)549-2586
Fax: (843)549-2446
**Subject(s):** Paid Community Newspapers
**Circ:** ‡7,000

**Rankin County News (16766)**
207 E. Government St.
Town Square
Brandon, MS 39042
Phone: (601)825-8333
Fax: (601)825-8334
**Subject(s):** Paid Community Newspapers
**Circ:** ‡7,000

**Scott County News (28948)**
The Bell Press Inc.
18289 Alberta St.
PO Box 4399
Oneida, TN 37841-4399
Phone: (423)569-8351
Fax: (423)569-4500
**Subject(s):** Paid Community Newspapers
**Circ:** 7,000

**Vanderbilt Hustler (28895)**
Vanderbilt Student Communications
Box 1504 - Sta. B
Nashville, TN 37235
Phone: (615)322-2424
Fax: (615)322-3762
**Subject(s):** College Publications
**Circ:** 7,000

**The Western Carolinian (23389)**
Western Carolina University
PO Box 66
Western Carolina University
Cullowhee, NC 28723-0066
Phone: (828)227-7211
Fax: (828)227-7043
**Subject(s):** College Publications
**Circ:** (Free)7,000

**Jewish Press of Tampa (5875)**
Jewish Press Group of Tampa Bay (FL) Inc.
PO Box 6970
Clearwater, FL 33758-6970
Phone: (727)535-4400
Fax: (727)530-3039
**Subject(s):** Paid Community Newspapers; Jewish Publications
**Circ:** (Controlled)6,984

**Dallas New Era (7100)**
121 W Spring St.
PO Box 530
Dallas, GA 30132
Phone: (770)445-3379
Fax: (770)445-5726
**Subject(s):** Paid Community Newspapers
**Circ:** (Free)125
(Paid)6,900

**The Oldham Era (11986)**
Landmark Community Newspapers Inc.
PO Box 549
Shelbyville, KY 40065-0549
Phone: (502)633-4334
Fax: (502)732-0453
**Subject(s):** Paid Community Newspapers
**Circ:** ‡6,900

**Charleston Black Times (28002)**
S. Carolina Black Media Group
1310 Harden
PO Box 11128
Columbia, SC 29211
Phone: (803)799-5252
Fax: (803)799-7709
**Subject(s):** Paid Community Newspapers; Black Publications
**Circ:** 6,883

**The Barefoot Tattler (5804)**
222 Kiwi Dr.
Barefoot Bay, FL 32976
Phone: (772)664-9381
Fax: (772)664-6236
**Subject(s):** Paid Community Newspapers; Senior Citizens' Interests
**Circ:** (Combined)⊕6,850

**Watauga Democrat (23255)**
Watauga Newspapers Inc.
474 Industrial Park Dr.
Boone, NC 28607
Phone: (828)264-3612
Fax: (828)262-0282
**Subject(s):** Paid Community Newspapers
**Circ:** (Paid)6,848

**Independent-Appeal (28978)**
McNary County Publishing Co.
111 North 2nd Street
PO Box 220
Selmer, TN 38375-0220
Phone: (731)645-5346
Fax: (731)645-3591
**Subject(s):** Paid Community Newspapers
**Circ:** ‡6,800

**Malboro Herald-Advocate (27987)**
Marlboro Publishing Company Inc.
PO Box 656
Bennettsville, SC 29512
Phone: (803)479-3815
Fax: (803)479-7671
**Subject(s):** Paid Community Newspapers
**Circ:** ‡6,800

**The Bartlett Express (28757)**
Bartlett Newspapers Inc.
PO Box 34967
Memphis, TN 38184-0967
Phone: (901)388-1500
Fax: (901)386-3157
**Subject(s):** Paid Community Newspapers
**Circ:** ‡6,790

**Washington County News (160)**
Washington County Publications Inc.
305 Jordan St.
PO Box 510
Chatom, AL 36518
Phone: (251)847-2599
Fax: (251)847-3847
**Subject(s):** Paid Community Newspapers
**Circ:** ‡4,000
6,780

**The Harlan Daily Enterprise (11700)**
1548 S U.S. Hwy. 421
PO Box E
Harlan, KY 40831
Phone: (606)573-4510
Fax: (606)573-0042
**Subject(s):** Daily Newspapers
**Circ:** 6,766

**McDowell News (23633)**
McDowell Newspapers
136 Logan St.
PO Box 610
Marion, NC 28752-0610
Phone: (828)652-3313
Fax: (478)374-3585
**Subject(s):** Daily Newspapers
**Circ:** (Non-paid)‡254
(Paid)‡6,769

**The Daily Sentinel (424)**
Scottsboro Newspapers Inc.
701 Veterans Dr.
Scottsboro, AL 35768-2132
Phone: (205)259-1020
Fax: (205)259-2709
**Subject(s):** Daily Newspapers
**Circ:** (Tues.-Fri.)6,056
(Sun.)6,741

**The Dillon Herald (28088)**
The Herald Publishing Co.
PO Box 1288
Dillon, SC 29536
Phone: (843)774-3311
Fax: (843)841-1930
**Subject(s):** Paid Community Newspapers
**Circ:** (Free)‡563
(Paid)‡6,742

**Messenger (28141)**
Hartsville Messenger
207 E Carolina Ave.
Box 1865
Hartsville, SC 29551-1865
Phone: (843)332-6545
Fax: (843)332-1341
**Subject(s):** Paid Community Newspapers
**Circ:** (Mon.)4,986
(Wed.)6,719

**Anson Record (23814)**
Community Newspapers Inc.
PO Box 959
Wadesboro, NC 28170
Phone: (704)694-2161
Fax: (704)694-7060
**Subject(s):** Paid Community Newspapers
**Circ:** ‡6,700

**Banks County News (7208)**
MainStreet Newspapers Inc.
PO Box 908
33 Lee St.
Jefferson, GA 30549
Phone: (706)367-5233
Fax: (706)367-8056
**Subject(s):** Paid Community Newspapers
**Circ:** 6,700

**The Clayton Tribune (7054)**
Community Newspapers Inc.
c/o Blake Spurney
104 N. Main St.
PO Box 425
Clayton, GA 30525
Phone: (706)782-3312
Fax: (706)782-4230
**Subject(s):** Paid Community Newspapers
**Circ:** 6,700

**Moberly Monitor-Index & Evening Democrat (90)**
3800 Colonnade Pkwy., Ste. 450
Birmingham, AL 35243
Phone: (205)298-7101
Fax: (205)298-7101
Subject(s): Daily Newspapers

Circ: (Mon.-Fri.)6,395
(Sun.)6,700

**The Monroe Journal (335)**
Bolton Newspapers Inc.
49 Hines St.
Monroeville, AL 36461
Phone: (251)575-3282
Fax: (251)575-3284
Subject(s): Paid Community Newspapers

Circ: ‡6,700

**Montgomery Herald (23811)**
Womack Publishing Company Inc.
139 Bruton St.
PO Box 466
Troy, NC 27371
Phone: (910)576-6051
Fax: (910)576-1050
Subject(s): Paid Community Newspapers

Circ: ‡6,700

**Ohio County Times-News (11707)**
Andy Anderson Inc.
314 Main St.
PO Box 226
Hartford, KY 42347
Phone: (270)298-7100
Fax: (270)298-9572
Subject(s): Paid Community Newspapers

Circ: ‡6,700

**Carroll County News (28638)**
163 Court Sq.
Huntingdon, TN 38344
Subject(s): Free Newspapers

Circ: (Free)‡4,850
(Paid)‡6,650

**The Sea Coast Echo (16744)**
Bay Saint Louis Newspapers
124 Court St.
PO Box 2009
Bay Saint Louis, MS 39521
Phone: (228)467-5474
Fax: (228)467-0333
Subject(s): Paid Community Newspapers

Circ: ‡6,630

**News-Democrat & Leader (11975)**
120 Public Sq.
PO Box 270
Russellville, KY 42276
Phone: (270)726-8394
Fax: (270)726-8398
Subject(s): Paid Community Newspapers

Circ: (Paid)‡6,621

**Altus Times (50)**
Community Newspaper Holdings Inc.
3500 Colonnade Pkwy., Ste. 600
Birmingham, AL 35243
Phone: (205)298-7100
Fax: (205)298-7101
Subject(s): Daily Newspapers

Circ: ‡6,600

**Mebane Enterprise (23640)**
Womack Publishing Co.
106 N. 4th St.
Mebane, NC 27302
Phone: (919)563-3555
Fax: (919)563-9242
Subject(s): Paid Community Newspapers

Circ: 6,600

**Marianna Jackson County Floridan (6207)**
Thomson Newspapers
4403 Constitution Ln.
Marianna, FL 32446
Phone: (904)526-3614
Fax: (904)482-4470
Subject(s): Daily Newspapers

Circ: (Tues.-Fri.)5,968
(Sun.)6,576

**The Taylorsville Times (23810)**
PO Box 279
24 E Main Ave
Taylorsville, NC 28681
Phone: (828)632-2532
Fax: (828)632-8233
Subject(s): Paid Community Newspapers

Circ: (Free)‡105
(Paid)‡6,570

**The Dahlonega Nugget (7098)**
Community Newspapers Inc.
1074 Morrison Moor Pkwy.
PO Box 36
Dahlonega, GA 30533
Phone: (706)864-3613
Fax: (706)864-4360
Subject(s): Paid Community Newspapers

Circ: ‡6,550

**Fort Mill Times (28101)**
East Coast Newspapers
124 Main St.
Fort Mill, SC 29715
Phone: (803)547-2353
Fax: (803)547-2321
Subject(s): Paid Community Newspapers

Circ: ‡6,500

**The Haralson Gateway Beacon (7019)**
Paxton Media Group
222 Tallapoosa
PO Box 685
Bremen, GA 30110
Phone: (770)537-2434
Fax: (770)537-0826
Subject(s): Paid Community Newspapers

Circ: ‡6,500

**The Jefferson Post (23833)**
PO Box 808
West Jefferson, NC 28694
Phone: (336)846-7164
Fax: (336)846-7165
Subject(s): Paid Community Newspapers

Circ: (Free)‡5,000
(Paid)‡6,500

**Mitchell News Journal (23797)**
Community Newspapers Inc.
c/o Andy Ashurst
261 Locust Ave.
PO Box 339
Spruce Pine, NC 28777
Phone: (828)765-2071
Fax: (828)765-1616
Subject(s): Paid Community Newspapers

Circ: ‡6,500

**Oxford Public Ledger (23683)**
PO Box 643
Oxford, NC 27565
Phone: (919)693-2646
Fax: (919)693-3704
Subject(s): Paid Community Newspapers

Circ: ‡6,500

**Pigeon Roost News (16864)**
The South Reporter
PO Box 278
Holly Springs, MS 38635
Phone: (662)252-4261
Fax: (662)252-3388
Subject(s): Free Newspapers

Circ: (Free)6,500

**Bolivar Commercial (16783)**
Division of Cleveland Newspapers Inc.
821 N. Chrisman Ave.
PO Box 1050
Cleveland, MS 38732
Phone: (662)843-4241
Fax: (662)843-1830
Subject(s): Daily Newspapers

Circ: (Mon.-Fri.)★6,484

**Carolina Peacemaker (23511)**
400 Summit Ave.
PO Box 20853
Greensboro, NC 27420-0853
Phone: (336)274-6210
Fax: (336)273-5103
Subject(s): Paid Community Newspapers; Black Publications

Circ: ‡6,400

**Express-Star (77)**
Community Newspaper Holdings Inc.
3500 Colonnade Pkwy., Ste. 600
Birmingham, AL 35243
Phone: (205)298-7100
Fax: (205)298-7101
Subject(s): Daily Newspapers

Circ: (Mon.-Fri.)‡5,500
(Sun.)‡6,400

**The Eufaula Tribune (207)**
Tribune Publishing Co.
514 E Barbour St.
PO Box 628
Eufaula, AL 36072-0628
Phone: (334)687-3506
Fax: (334)687-3229
Subject(s): Paid Community Newspapers

Circ: 6,350

**Mt. Sterling Advocate (11907)**
219 Midland Trail
PO Box 406
Mount Sterling, KY 40353
Phone: (859)498-2222
Fax: (859)498-2228
Subject(s): Paid Community Newspapers

Circ: 6,350

**The Clarksdale Press Register (16778)**
Delta Press Publishing Co.
123 2nd St.
PO Box 1119
Clarksdale, MS 38614-1119
Phone: (662)627-2201
Fax: (662)624-5125
Subject(s): Daily Newspapers

Circ: (Mon.-Sat.)6,307

**Grayson County News-Gazette (11752)**
Park Newspapers of Kentucky Inc.
PO Box 305
Leitchfield, KY 42755
Phone: (502)259-9622
Fax: (502)259-5537
Subject(s): Paid Community Newspapers

Circ: ‡6,220

**Cairo Messenger (7029)**
Cairo Messenger Inc.
31-35 1st Ave. NE
PO Box 30
Cairo, GA 39828-0030
Phone: (229)377-2032
Fax: (229)377-4640
Subject(s): Paid Community Newspapers

Circ: 6,200

**Hickory News (23576)**
Catawba Valley Publishing Company Inc.
PO Box 2650
Hickory, NC 28603-2650
Phone: (828)328-6164
Fax: (828)322-6398
Subject(s): Paid Community Newspapers

Circ: ‡6,200

**The Loris Scene (28083)**
Waccamaw Publishing Co.
2510 Main St.
Conway, SC 29528
Phone: (843)248-6671
Fax: (843)248-6024
Subject(s): Paid Community Newspapers

Circ: (Free)‡6,200

**Nashville Business Journal (28866)**
PO Box 23229
Nashville, TN 37202-3229
Phone: (615)248-2222
Fax: (615)248-6248
Subject(s): Local, State, and Regional Publications; Business

Circ: (Paid)6,200

**Plain Dealer (10229)**
Paxton Media Group
201 S. 4th St.
Paducah, KY 42003
Phone: (270)575-8630
Subject(s): Daily Newspapers

Circ: (Non-paid)51
(Paid)6,204

Circulation: ★ = ABC; △ = BPA; ♦ = CAC; • = CCAB; ▫ = VAC; ⊕ = PO Statement; ‡ = Publisher's Report; Boldface figures = sworn; Light figures = estimated

# Southern States

**The South Reporter** (16865)
PO Box 278
Holly Springs, MS 38635
Phone: (662)252-4261
Fax: (662)252-3388
**Subject(s):** Paid Community Newspapers
**Circ:** ‡6,200

**Dekalb Advertiser** (230)
PO Box 680559
Fort Payne, AL 35968-1606
Phone: (256)845-6156
Fax: (256)845-1105
**Subject(s):** Paid Community Newspapers
**Circ:** (Non-paid)⊕60
(Paid)⊕**6,172**

**Belmont Banner** (23241)
PO Box 589
Belmont, NC 28012
Phone: (704)825-0104
Fax: (704)825-0894
**Subject(s):** Paid Community Newspapers
**Circ:** (Combined)6,150

**Simpson County News** (16938)
206 N. Main
Magee, MS 39111
Phone: (601)849-3434
Fax: (601)849-6828
**Subject(s):** Paid Community Newspapers
**Circ:** ‡6108

**Alamance News** (23504)
Boney Publishers Inc.
Box 431
Graham, NC 27253
Phone: (336)228-7851
Fax: (336)229-9602
**Subject(s):** Paid Community Newspapers
**Circ:** (Thurs.)6,065

**Bradford County Telegraph** (6558)
Bradford Telegraph
131 W. Call St.
PO Drawer A
Starke, FL 32091
Phone: (904)964-6305
Fax: (904)964-8628
**Subject(s):** Paid Community Newspapers
**Circ:** 6,000

**The Carolinian** (23512)
University of North Carolina at Greensboro
Box 10
Elliott University Center, UNCG
Greensboro, NC 27413
**Subject(s):** College Publications
**Circ:** (Free)6,000

**Cordele Dispatch** (7084)
McLeansboro Times-Leader
306 13th Ave. W.
PO Box 1058
Cordele, GA 31015-1058
Phone: (912)273-2277
Fax: (912)273-7239
**Subject(s):** Daily Newspapers
**Circ:** ‡6,000

**The Horry Independent** (28081)
Waccamaw Publishing Co.
2510 Main St.
Conway, SC 29528
Phone: (843)248-6671
**Subject(s):** Paid Community Newspapers
**Circ:** (Non-paid)‡400
(Paid)‡6,000

**Jackson Times** (11739)
Intermountain Publishing Co.
PO Box 999
Jackson, KY 41339-0999
Phone: (606)666-2451
Fax: (606)666-5757
**Subject(s):** Paid Community Newspapers
**Circ:** 6,000

**Macon County Times** (28714)
PO Box 129
200 Times Ave.
Lafayette, TN 37083
Phone: (615)666-2440
Fax: (615)666-4909

**News and Press** (28087)
117 S Main St.
Box 513
Darlington, SC 29532
Phone: (843)393-3811
Fax: (843)393-6811
**Subject(s):** Paid Community Newspapers
**Circ:** ‡6,000

**Palmetto Bay News** (6254)
Community Newspapers
6796 S.W. 62 Ave.
Miami, FL 33143
Phone: (305)669-7355
Fax: (305)661-0954
**Subject(s):** Free Newspapers
**Circ:** (Free)6,000

**The Paper** (6380)
Valencia Community College
1800 S Kirkman Rd.
PO Box 3028
Orlando, FL 32811
Phone: (407)299-5000
Fax: (407)582-1286
**Subject(s):** College Publications
**Circ:** (Free)‡6,000

**People-Sentinel** (27977)
PO Box 1255
9988 Dunbarton Blvd.
Barnwell, SC 29812
Phone: (803)259-3501
Fax: (803)259-2703
**Subject(s):** Paid Community Newspapers
**Circ:** ‡6,000

**Tishomingo County News** (16875)
County News
PO Box 70
123 Front St.
Iuka, MS 38852
Phone: (662)423-2211
Fax: (662)423-2214
**Subject(s):** Paid Community Newspapers
**Circ:** ‡6,000

**Wayne County Outlook** (11895)
Wayne County Newspaper Inc.
PO Box 432
109 E Columiba Ave.
Monticello, KY 42633
Phone: (606)348-3338
Fax: (606)348-8848
**Subject(s):** Paid Community Newspapers
**Circ:** 6,000

**Woodford Sun** (12014)
PO Box 29
Versailles, KY 40383-0029
Phone: (859)873-4131
Fax: (859)873-0300
**Subject(s):** Paid Community Newspapers
**Circ:** 6,000

**The Yancey Journal** (23271)
Times Journal
PO Drawer 280
Burnsville, NC 28714
Phone: (828)682-2120
Fax: (828)682-3701
**Subject(s):** Paid Community Newspapers
**Circ:** (Free)‡360
(Paid)‡6,000

**The Observer** (6325)
823 S Dixie Fwy.
PO Box 10
New Smyrna Beach, FL 32170
Phone: (386)427-1000
Fax: (386)428-1265
**Subject(s):** Daily Newspapers
**Circ:** (Paid)5,992

**Daleville Sun Courier** (203)
QST Publications Inc.
PO Box 311546
Enterprise, AL 36331-1546
Phone: (334)598-3891
Fax: (334)393-2987

**Subject(s):** Free Newspapers
**Circ:** (Paid)67
(Free)5,960

**Grant County News** (12031)
151 N Main
PO Box 247
Williamstown, KY 41097
Phone: (859)824-3343
Fax: (859)824-5888
**Subject(s):** Paid Community Newspapers
**Circ:** (Non-paid)⊕12
(Paid)⊕**5,958**

**The Citizen-Times** (11980)
PO Box 310
Scottsville, KY 42164
Phone: (270)237-3441
Fax: (270)237-4943
**Subject(s):** Paid Community Newspapers
**Circ:** ‡5,900

**The Barrow County News** (7507)
Swartz-Morris Media Inc.
189 W Athens St.
PO Drawer C
Winder, GA 30680
Phone: (770)867-7557
Fax: (770)867-1034
**Subject(s):** Paid Community Newspapers
**Circ:** (Sun.)5,713
(Wed.)5,883

**The Carolina Times** (23406)
PO Box 3825
923 Old Sayette St
Durham, NC 27701
Phone: (919)682-2913
Fax: (919)688-8434
**Subject(s):** Black Publications; Paid Community Newspapers
**Circ:** ‡5,800

**The Mountain Citizen** (11735)
New Wave Communications Inc.
Box 1029
Inez, KY 41224
Phone: (606)298-7570
Fax: (606)298-3711
**Subject(s):** Paid Community Newspapers
**Circ:** ‡5,800

**The Stewart-Houston Times** (28595)
The Leaf-Chronicle
105 Court St.
PO Box 250
Erin, TN 37061
**Subject(s):** Paid Community Newspapers
**Circ:** ‡5,800

**Yadkin Ripple** (23886)
Yadkin Ripple Inc.
PO Box 7
Yadkinville, NC 27055
Phone: (336)679-2341
Fax: (336)679-2340
**Subject(s):** Paid Community Newspapers
**Circ:** 5,800

**The Anderson News** (11748)
Landmark Community Newspapers Inc.
PO Box 410
Lawrenceburg, KY 40342-0410
Phone: (502)839-6906
**Subject(s):** Paid Community Newspapers
**Circ:** ‡5,755

**Garner News** (23495)
Garner Inc.
905c 5th Ave.
PO Box 466
Garner, NC 27529
Phone: (919)772-7751
Fax: (919)779-7824
**Subject(s):** Paid Community Newspapers
**Circ:** ‡5,750

**Standard Banner** (28654)
Jefferson County Standard Publishing Co.
122 Andrew Johnson Hwy.
PO Box 310
Jefferson City, TN 37760
Phone: (865)475-2081
Fax: (865)475-8539

**Subject(s):** Paid Community Newspapers
**Circ:** (Non-paid)109
     (Paid)5,746

**The Camden Chronicle (28508)**
Magic Valley Publishing Company Inc.
144 W Main Street
PO Box 899
Camden, TN 38320-0899
Phone: (731)584-7200
Fax: (731)584-4943
**Subject(s):** Paid Community Newspapers
**Circ:** 5700

**The Elberton Star & Examiner (7140)**
Community Newspapers Inc.
25 N. Public Sq.
PO Box 280
Elberton, GA 30635-0280
Phone: (706)283-8500
Fax: (706)283-9700
**Subject(s):** Paid Community Newspapers
**Circ:** (Free)‡140
     (Paid)‡5,700

**Times Leader (11961)**
607 W. Washington St.
PO Box 439
Princeton, KY 42445
Phone: (270)365-5588
Fax: (270)365-7299
**Subject(s):** Paid Community Newspapers
**Circ:** ‡5,700

**The Meade County Messenger (11570)**
235 Main St.
PO Box 678
Brandenburg, KY 40108-0678
Phone: (270)422-2155
Fax: (270)422-2110
**Subject(s):** Paid Community Newspapers
**Circ:** 5,686

**The Morehead News (11900)**
722 West 1st St.
Morehead, KY 40351
Phone: (606)784-4116
Fax: (606)784-7337
**Subject(s):** Paid Community Newspapers
**Circ:** (Paid)⊕5,629

**Ashland City Times (28487)**
Gannett Company Inc.
202A Main St.
Ashland City, TN 37015
Phone: (615)792-4230
Fax: (615)792-3671
**Subject(s):** Paid Community Newspapers
**Circ:** (Combined)5,601

**Birmingham Business Journal (56)**
American City Business Journals Inc.
2140 11th Ave. S., Ste. 205
Birmingham, AL 35205
Phone: (205)322-0040
Fax: (205)322-0040
**Subject(s):** Business
**Circ:** (Paid)5,600

**Breckinridge County Herald-News (11699)**
US 60 E
PO Box 6
Hardinsburg, KY 40143
Phone: (270)756-2109
Fax: (270)756-1003
**Subject(s):** Paid Community Newspapers
**Circ:** (Paid)‡5,600

**The Leslie County News (11733)**
Thousand Sticks News
Box 967
Hyden, KY 41749
Phone: (606)672-2841
Fax: (606)672-7409
**Subject(s):** Paid Community Newspapers
**Circ:** 5,600

**Stokes News (23819)**
PO Box 647
1072 N Main St.
Walnut Cove, NC 27052
Phone: (336)591-8191
Fax: (336)591-4379

**Subject(s):** Paid Community Newspapers
**Circ:** 5,600

**Tennessee Town & City (28891)**
Tennessee Municipal League
226 Capitol Blvd., Ste. 710
Nashville, TN 37219
Phone: (615)255-6416
Fax: (615)255-4752
**Subject(s):** State, Municipal, and County Administration; Politics
**Circ:** (Non-paid)‡300
     (Paid)‡5,600

**The Tomahawk (28822)**
Sandusky Newspapers
116 S Church St.
PO Box 90
Mountain City, TN 37683
Phone: (423)727-6121
Fax: (423)727-4833
**Subject(s):** Paid Community Newspapers
**Circ:** ‡5,600

**Daily Report (6864)**
American Lawyer Media L.P.
190 Pryor St. SW
Atlanta, GA 30303
Phone: (404)521-1227
Fax: (404)659-4739
**Subject(s):** Paid Community Newspapers; Law
**Circ:** (Non-paid)♦336
     (Paid)♦5,512

**The Cape Coral Daily Breeze (5858)**
Breeze Publishing Co.
PO Box 151306
2510 Del Prado Blvd.
Cape Coral, FL 33904
Phone: (941)574-1110
Fax: (941)574-3403
**Subject(s):** Daily Newspapers
**Circ:** ‡5,500

**The Coastal Courier (7195)**
PO Box 498
Hinesville, GA 31310
Phone: (912)876-0156
Fax: (912)368-6329
**Subject(s):** Paid Community Newspapers
**Circ:** 5,500

**The Courier-News (28554)**
233 N Hicks St.
PO Box 270
Clinton, TN 37716
Phone: (865)457-2515
Fax: (865)457-1586
**Subject(s):** Paid Community Newspapers
**Circ:** ‡5,500

**Dawson News & Advertiser (7109)**
Community Newspapers Inc.
c/o Brian Blackley
40 N. Hwy. 9 in downtown Dawsonville
PO Box 225
Dawsonville, GA 30534
Phone: (706)265-2345
Fax: (706)265-7842
**Subject(s):** Paid Community Newspapers
**Circ:** ‡5,500

**The Expositor (29001)**
Sparta Newspapers Inc.
PO Box 179
Sparta, TN 38583
Phone: (931)836-3284
Fax: (931)836-6273
**Subject(s):** Paid Community Newspapers
**Circ:** (Non-paid)5,000
     (Paid)5,500

**Itawamba County Times (16817)**
106 W Main
Fulton, MS 38843
Phone: (662)862-3141
Fax: (662)862-7804
**Subject(s):** Paid Community Newspapers
**Circ:** ‡5,500

**The Jones County News (7175)**
PO Box 1538
Gray, GA 31032
Phone: (478)986-3929
Fax: (478)986-1935

**Subject(s):** Paid Community Newspapers
**Circ:** 5,500

**Live Oak Suwannee Democrat (6185)**
Live Oak Publications
211 Howard St. E
PO Box 370
Live Oak, FL 32060
Phone: (386)362-1734
Fax: (386)364-5578
**Subject(s):** Paid Community Newspapers
**Circ:** 5,500

**The Moulton Advertiser (380)**
Slaton Newspapers Inc.
PO Box 517
Moulton, AL 35650
Phone: (256)974-1114
Fax: (256)974-3097
**Subject(s):** Paid Community Newspapers
**Circ:** 5,500

**Sumter County Times (5855)**
Landmark Community Newspapers Inc.
204 E. McCollum Ave.
Bushnell, FL 33513
Phone: (352)793-2161
Fax: (352)793-1486
**Subject(s):** Paid Community Newspapers
**Circ:** ‡5,500

**The Tribune (23460)**
214 E Main St.
PO Drawer 1009
Elkin, NC 28621
Phone: (336)835-1513
Fax: (336)835-8742
**Subject(s):** Paid Community Newspapers
**Circ:** (Paid)‡5,500

**The Prentiss Headlight (17000)**
Prentiss Publishers Inc.
PO Box 1257
10 23rd Street
Prentiss, MS 39474-1257
Phone: (601)792-4221
Fax: (601)792-4222
**Subject(s):** Free Newspapers
**Circ:** (Paid)2,366
     (Free)5,482

**Palm Beach Daily News (6412)**
Palm Beach Newspapers Inc.
265 Royal Poinciana Way
Palm Beach, FL 33480-4007
Phone: (561)820-3800
Fax: (561)655-4594
**Subject(s):** Daily Newspapers
**Circ:** (Free)‡2,101
     (Paid)‡5,458

**Cedar Creek Pilot (66)**
Community Newspaper Holdings Inc.
3500 Colonnade Pkwy., Ste. 600
Birmingham, AL 35243
Phone: (205)298-7100
Fax: (205)298-7101
**Subject(s):** Paid Community Newspapers
**Circ:** ‡5,444

**Times-Journal (231)**
Fort Payne Newspapers Inc.
PO Box 680349
Fort Payne, AL 35968-1604
Phone: (256)845-2550
Fax: (256)845-7459
**Subject(s):** Shopping Guides
**Circ:** (Mon.-Fri.)4,648
     (Sun.)5,442

**Carthaginian (16776)**
PO Box 457
111 Franklin Street
Carthage, MS 39051-0457
Phone: (601)267-4501
Fax: (601)267-5290
**Subject(s):** Paid Community Newspapers
**Circ:** ‡5,400

**Chatsworth Times (7048)**
Walls Newspapers
224 North 3rd Ave.
PO Box 130
Chatsworth, GA 30705
Phone: (706)695-4646

Fax: (706)695-7181
**Subject(s):** Paid Community Newspapers
**Circ:** (Paid)5,400

**Milan Mirror-Exchange (28808)**
Box 549
Milan, TN 38358
Phone: (901)686-1632
Fax: (901)686-9005
**Subject(s):** Paid Community Newspapers
**Circ:** ‡5,400

**Mt. Vernon Signal (11910)**
PO Box 185
Mount Vernon, KY 40456-0185
Phone: (606)256-2244
Fax: (606)256-9526
**Subject(s):** Paid Community Newspapers
**Circ:** ‡5,400

**The Press and Banner (27960)**
Banner Corp.
PO Box 769
107 West Pickens Street
Abbeville, SC 29620-0769
Phone: (864)366-5461
Fax: (864)366-5463
**Subject(s):** Paid Community Newspapers
**Circ:** ‡5,400

**The Wakulla News (5902)**
Wakulla Publishing Co.
PO Box 307
Crawfordville, FL 32326
Phone: (850)926-7102
Fax: (850)926-3815
**Subject(s):** Paid Community Newspapers
**Circ:** ‡5,400

**Orangeburg Black Voice (28202)**
PO Box 11128
Columbia, SC 29211
Phone: (803)799-5252
Fax: (803)799-7709
**Subject(s):** Paid Community Newspapers; Black Publications
**Circ:** 5,365

**The Herald-Leader (7146)**
Pryor Publications Inc.
Drawer 40
202 E. Central Ave
Fitzgerald, GA 31750
Phone: (229)423-9331
Fax: (229)423-6533
**Subject(s):** Paid Community Newspapers
**Circ:** ‡5,341

**Banner Independent (16762)**
PO Box 10
208 North Main Street
Booneville, MS 38829
Phone: (662)728-6214
Fax: (662)728-1636
**Subject(s):** Paid Community Newspapers
**Circ:** 5,304

**The Butler County and Green River Republican Banner (11906)**
P.O.Box 219
Morgantown, KY 42261
Phone: (270)526-4151
Fax: (270)526-3111
**Subject(s):** Paid Community Newspapers
**Circ:** ‡5,300

**Effingham Herald (7362)**
586 S. Columbia Ave
PO Box 799
Rincon, GA 31326
Phone: (912)826-5012
Fax: (912)826-0381
**Subject(s):** Paid Community Newspapers
**Circ:** 5,300

**The Red Bay News (412)**
120 4th Ave. South East
PO Box 1339
Red Bay, AL 35582-1339
Phone: (256)356-2148
Fax: (256)356-2787
**Subject(s):** Paid Community Newspapers
**Circ:** 5,300

**Sandersville Progress (7388)**
The Sandersville Georgian Inc.
PO Box 431
Sandersville, GA 31082
Phone: (478)552-3161
Fax: (478)552-5177
**Subject(s):** Paid Community Newspapers
**Circ:** 5,300

**The Union County Advocate (11903)**
The Cadiz Record
214 W. Main
PO Box 370
Morganfield, KY 42437
Phone: (270)389-1833
Fax: (502)522-3001
**Subject(s):** Paid Community Newspapers
**Circ:** (Free)200
(Paid)5,300

**The Wetumpka Herald (490)**
The Wetumpka Herald Inc.
300 Green St.
PO Box 99
Wetumpka, AL 36092-0099
Phone: (334)567-7811
Fax: (334)567-3284
**Subject(s):** Paid Community Newspapers
**Circ:** ‡5,300

**Herald-Independent (28257)**
The Herald Independent
PO Box 90
Winnsboro, SC 29180
Phone: (803)635-4016
Fax: (803)635-2948
**Subject(s):** Paid Community Newspapers
**Circ:** (Free)‡145
(Paid)‡5,295

**Winston-Salem Chronicle (23875)**
617 N Liberty St.
PO Box 1636
Winston-Salem, NC 27101-2912
Phone: (336)723-8428
Fax: (336)723-9173
**Subject(s):** Paid Community Newspapers; Black Publications
**Circ:** (Non-paid)497
(Paid)5,292

**Fulton County Daily Report (6876)**
Daily Report Co.
190 Pryor St. SW
Atlanta, GA 30303
Phone: (404)521-1227
Fax: (404)523-5924
**Subject(s):** Law; Daily Periodicals
**Circ:** (Non-paid)552
(Paid)5,270

**The Democrat (17012)**
219 E. Main St.
PO Box 369
Senatobia, MS 38668
Phone: (662)562-4414
Fax: (662)562-8866
**Subject(s):** Paid Community Newspapers
**Circ:** ‡5,200

**Dresden Enterprise (28586)**
Tri-County Publishing Company Inc.
113 Wilson St.
PO Box 139
Dresden, TN 38225-0139
Phone: (731)364-2234
Fax: (731)364-5774
**Subject(s):** Paid Community Newspapers; Farm Newspapers
**Circ:** ‡5,200

**The Paintsville Herald (11940)**
PO Box 1547
Paintsville, KY 41240
Phone: (606)789-5315
Fax: (606)789-9717
**Subject(s):** Paid Community Newspapers
**Circ:** ‡5,200

**The True Citizen (7504)**
Citizen Newspapers
601 E 6th St.
PO Box 948
Waynesboro, GA 30830
Phone: (706)554-2111
Fax: (706)554-2437

**Subject(s):** Paid Community Newspapers
**Circ:** ‡5,200

**The Tryon Daily Bulletin (23813)**
Tryon Daily Bulletin Inc.
16 N Trade St.
Tryon, NC 28782
Phone: (828)859-9151
Fax: (828)859-5575
**Subject(s):** Daily Newspapers
**Circ:** ‡5,200

**The Wayne County News (17044)**
News Publishing Company of Mississippi
713 Lomax Dr.
Po Box 509
Waynesboro, MS 39367
Phone: (601)735-4341
Fax: (601)735-1111
**Subject(s):** Paid Community Newspapers
**Circ:** ‡5,202

**Monroe County Citizen (12005)**
301 N Main
Tompkinsville, KY 42167
Phone: (270)487-8666
Fax: (270)487-8666
**Subject(s):** Free Newspapers
**Circ:** (Non-paid)‡5,169

**Gadsden County Times (6484)**
PO Box 790
Quincy, FL 32353-0790
Phone: (850)627-7649
Fax: (850)627-7191
**Subject(s):** Paid Community Newspapers
**Circ:** (Free)⊕380
(Paid)⊕**5,120**

**Hazard Herald (11710)**
439 High St.
PO Box 869
Hazard, KY 41702-0869
Phone: (606)436-5771
Fax: (606)436-3140
**Subject(s):** Paid Community Newspapers
**Circ:** ‡5,126

**Sumter County Record-Journal (302)**
210 S. Washington St.
PO Drawer B
Livingston, AL 35470
Phone: (205)652-6100
Fax: (205)652-4466
**Subject(s):** Paid Community Newspapers
**Circ:** 5,125

**The Growl (16818)**
Holmes Community College
PO Box 367
9216 Hwy 14
Goodman, MS 39079
Phone: (662)472-9062
Fax: (662)472-9156
**Subject(s):** College Publications
**Circ:** (Paid)3,750
(Free)5,100

**Gulf Pine Catholic (16754)**
1790 Popps Ferry Rd.
PO Box 1189
Biloxi, MS 39533-1189
Phone: (228)702-2127
Fax: (228)702-2128
**Subject(s):** Religious Publications
**Circ:** ‡5,100

**Sylvania Telephone (7441)**
PO Box 10
Sylvania, GA 30467-0010
Phone: (912)564-2045
Fax: (912)564-7085
**Subject(s):** Paid Community Newspapers
**Circ:** 5,061

**The Calhoun-Liberty Journal (5849)**
Summers Road
PO Box 536
Bristol, FL 32321
Phone: (850)643-3333
Fax: (850)643-3334
**Subject(s):** Paid Community Newspapers
**Circ:** 5,050

**Augusta Focus** (6968)
1143 Laney-Walker Blvd.
Augusta, GA 30901
Phone: (706)722-4222
Fax: (706)724-8432
**Subject(s):** Paid Community Newspapers
**Circ:** (Paid)‡5,000

**The Baker County Press** (6193)
104 S 5th St.
PO Box 598
Macclenny, FL 32063-0598
Phone: (904)259-2400
Fax: (904)259-6502
**Subject(s):** Paid Community Newspapers
**Circ:** ‡5,000

**Brownsville States-Graphic** (28502)
Haywood County Newspapers L.L.C.
42 S Washington
Brownsville, TN 38012
Phone: (731)772-1172
Fax: (731)772-5451
**Subject(s):** Paid Community Newspapers
**Circ:** (Paid)‡5,000

**Cherokee County Herald** (156)
News Publishing Co.
107 W. 1st Ave.
Centre, AL 35960
Phone: (205)927-5236
Fax: (205)927-4853
**Subject(s):** Paid Community Newspapers
**Circ:** (Paid)5,000

**Clarke County Democrat** (248)
PO Box 39
261 N.Jackson St
Grove Hill, AL 36451-0039
Phone: (251)275-3375
Fax: (251)275-3060
**Subject(s):** Paid Community Newspapers
**Circ:** ‡5,000

**Fuquay Varina Independent** (23494)
Crooklyn Publishers
209 E Vance
PO Box 669
Fuquay Varina, NC 27526
Phone: (919)552-4112
Fax: (919)552-7564
**Subject(s):** Paid Community Newspapers
**Circ:** (Free)‡125
(Paid)‡5,000

**The Georgetown-News Graphic** (11689)
Georgetown Newspapers Inc.
1481 Cherry Blossom Way
Georgetown, KY 40324
Phone: (502)863-1111
Fax: (502)863-6296
**Subject(s):** Paid Community Newspapers
**Circ:** 5,000

**Grundy County Herald** (29014)
Lakeway Publishers Inc.
PO Box 189
Tracy City, TN 37387
Phone: (615)592-2781
Fax: (615)598-5812
**Subject(s):** Paid Community Newspapers
**Circ:** ‡5,000

**HAWKEYE** (6634)
Hillsborough Community College
PO Box 31127
Tampa, FL 33631-3127
Phone: (813)253-7000
**Subject(s):** College Publications
**Circ:** (Free)‡5,000

**The Herald-Gazette** (7005)
509 Greenwood St.
PO Box 220
Barnesville, GA 30204
Phone: (770)358-6397
Fax: (770)358-0756
**Subject(s):** Paid Community Newspapers
**Circ:** ‡5,000

**The Herald-Journal** (7176)
PO Box 149
Greensboro, GA 30642
Phone: (706)453-7988
Fax: (706)453-2311

**Subject(s):** Paid Community Newspapers
**Circ:** ‡5,000

**The High Springs Herald** (6071)
The Herald Publishing Company Inc.
5 NW 1st St.
High Springs, FL 32643
**Subject(s):** Paid Community Newspapers
**Circ:** (Paid)‡5,000

**Meteor** (16809)
Meteor Newspaper Inc.
201 E Georgetown St.
PO Box 353
Crystal Springs, MS 39059-0353
Phone: (601)892-2581
Fax: (601)892-2249
**Subject(s):** Paid Community Newspapers
**Circ:** ‡5,000

**Nassau County Record** (5857)
PO Box 609
Callahan, FL 32011
Phone: (904)879-2727
Fax: (904)879-5155
**Subject(s):** Paid Community Newspapers
**Circ:** ‡5,000

**North Port Sun Herald** (6339)
Sun Coast Media Group
13644 S Tamiami Trl.
North Port, FL 34287
Phone: (941)426-9544
Fax: (941)423-2318
**Subject(s):** Paid Community Newspapers
**Circ:** (Paid)3,200
(Free)5,000

**Pasco News** (5911)
Sunpress Publications Inc.
13032 U.S Hwy. 301
PO Box 187
Dade City, FL 33525
Phone: (352)567-5639
Fax: (352)567-5640
**Subject(s):** Paid Community Newspapers
**Circ:** ‡5,000

**Perry Taco Times** (6453)
Perry Newspapers Inc.
PO Box 888
Perry, FL 32347
Phone: (850)584-5513
Fax: (850)838-1566
**Subject(s):** Paid Community Newspapers
**Circ:** ‡5,000

**The Phenix Citizen** (404)
Chicken Dinner News
PO Box 1267
Phenix City, AL 36868
Phone: (205)298-0679
Fax: (205)298-0690
**Subject(s):** Paid Community Newspapers
**Circ:** ‡5,000

**The Record** (6042)
Sante Fe Publishing Company Inc.
PO Box 806
620 North Main St.
Gainesville, FL 32602
Phone: (352)377-2444
Fax: (352)338-1986
**Subject(s):** Farm Newspapers; Paid Community Newspapers
**Circ:** ‡5,000

**The Record-Local** (6043)
The Record Farmer and Ranch-Statewide
PO Box 806
620 N Main St.
Gainesville, FL 32602
Phone: (352)377-2444
Fax: (352)338-1986
**Subject(s):** Paid Community Newspapers
**Circ:** ‡5,000

**The Rutherford Courier** (28994)
Wilmington Media Co.
PO Box 127
Smyrna, TN 37167
Phone: (615)459-3868
Fax: (615)459-3878
**Subject(s):** Paid Community Newspapers
**Circ:** (Paid)‡5,000

**Scott County Times** (16814)
Scott Publishing Inc.
PO Box 89
Forest, MS 39074
Phone: (601)469-2561
Fax: (601)469-2004
**Subject(s):** Paid Community Newspapers
**Circ:** 5,000

**The Southeast Georgian** (7386)
The Tribune/Georgian
PO Box 470
Saint Marys, GA 31558-0470
Phone: (912)729-5231
Fax: (912)729-1589
**Subject(s):** Paid Community Newspapers
**Circ:** ‡5,000

**The Southern Star** (399)
373 Ed Lisenby Rd.
PO Box 1729
Ozark, AL 36361
Phone: (334)774-2715
Fax: (334)774-9619
**Subject(s):** Paid Community Newspapers
**Circ:** 5,000

**The Spectator** (7475)
Valdosta State University
1500 N. Patterson St.
PO Box 7052
Valdosta, GA 31698
Phone: (229)333-5800
Fax: (229)249-2618
**Subject(s):** College Publications
**Circ:** (Combined)5,000

**The Weekly Star** (28959)
PO Box 898
2713 Parkway
Pigeon Forge, TN 37868
Phone: (865)453-0626
Fax: (865)453-4888
**Subject(s):** Paid Community Newspapers
**Circ:** (Paid)‡3,500
(Free)‡5,000

**WESTVIEW** (28899)
8120 Sawyer Brown Rd., Ste.107
PO Box 210183
Nashville, TN 37221
Phone: (615)646-6131
Fax: (615)662-0946
**Subject(s):** Paid Community Newspapers
**Circ:** ‡5,000

**The Herald-Advocate** (6712)
The Herald-Advocate Publishing Company Inc.
115 S 7th Ave.
PO Box 338
Wauchula, FL 33873
Phone: (863)773-3255
Fax: (863)773-0657
**Subject(s):** Paid Community Newspapers
**Circ:** (Free)⊕75
(Paid)⊕4,990

**Jewish Press of Pinellas County** (5874)
Jewish Press Group of Tampa Bay (FL) Inc.
PO Box 6970
Clearwater, FL 33758-6970
Phone: (727)535-4400
Fax: (727)530-3039
**Subject(s):** Paid Community Newspapers; Jewish Publications
**Circ:** (Controlled)4,967

**Mount Olive Tribune** (23660)
Hwy. 55 West
PO Box 1039
Mount Olive, NC 28365-1039
Phone: (919)658-9456
Fax: (919)658-9559
**Subject(s):** Paid Community Newspapers
**Circ:** ‡4,965

**Mobile Beacon** (315)
2311 Costarides St.
PO Box 1407
Mobile, AL 36633
Phone: (251)479-0629
Fax: (251)479-0610
**Subject(s):** Paid Community Newspapers; Black Publications
**Circ:** ‡4,952

---

Circulation: ★ = ABC; △ = BPA; ♦ = CAC; ● = CCAB; □ = VAC; ⊕ = PO Statement; ‡ = Publisher's Report; Boldface figures = sworn; Light figures = estimated.

# Southern States

**The Star (6470)**
PO Box 308
Port Saint Joe, FL 32457
Phone: (850)227-1278
Fax: (850)227-7212
**Subject(s):** Paid Community Newspapers
**Circ:** ‡4,950

**Times Journal Spotlight (7134)**
The Time Journal & Spotlight
PO Drawer 4189
Eastman, GA 31023
Phone: (478)374-5562
Fax: (478)374-3464
**Subject(s):** Paid Community Newspapers
**Circ:** ‡4,950

**The Erwin Record (28596)**
Erwin Record
PO Box 700
Erwin, TN 37650
Phone: (423)743-4112
Fax: (423)743-6125
**Subject(s):** Paid Community Newspapers
**Circ:** 4,920

**The Caswell Messenger (23887)**
Womack Publishing Co.
PO Box 100
Yanceyville, NC 27379-0100
Phone: (919)694-4145
Fax: (919)694-5637
**Subject(s):** Paid Community Newspapers
**Circ:** ‡4,900

**The Citizen-News (28092)**
PO Box 448
Edgefield, SC 29824
Phone: (803)637-5306
Fax: (803)637-5661
**Subject(s):** Paid Community Newspapers
**Circ:** ‡4,900

**News-Reporter (7494)**
116 W Robert Toombs Ave.
PO Box 340
Washington, GA 30673
Phone: (706)678-2636
Fax: (706)678-3857
**Subject(s):** Paid Community Newspapers
**Circ:** 4,900

**The South Alabamian (288)**
PO Box 68
1064 Coffeeville Rd.
Jackson, AL 36545
Phone: (251)246-4494
Fax: (251)246-7486
**Subject(s):** Paid Community Newspapers
**Circ:** ‡4,900

**Baldwin Times (47)**
Gulf Coast Newspapers
PO Box 519
Bay Minette, AL 36507
Phone: (334)937-2511
Fax: (334)937-1637
**Subject(s):** Paid Community Newspapers
**Circ:** ‡4,800

**The Cadiz Record (11609)**
Jim Ward
PO Box 747
Eddyville, KY 42038
Phone: (270)388-2269
Fax: (270)388-5540
**Subject(s):** Paid Community Newspapers
**Circ:** ‡4,800

**Carthage Courier (28511)**
509 N Main St.
PO Box 239
Carthage, TN 37030
Phone: (615)735-1110
Fax: (615)735-0635
**Subject(s):** Paid Community Newspapers
**Circ:** ‡4,800

**Hampton County Guardian (28139)**
Community Newspapers Inc.
200 Lee Ave.
PO Box 625
Hampton, SC 29924
Phone: (803)943-4645
Fax: (803)943-9365

**Subject(s):** Paid Community Newspapers
**Circ:** 4,800

**The News (28158)**
Evening Post Publishing Co.
107 E. Mill St.
Kingstree, SC 29556
Phone: (843)355-6397
Fax: (843)355-6530
**Subject(s):** Paid Community Newspapers
**Circ:** 4,800

**News & Farmer & Wadley Herald/The Jefferson Reporter (7240)**
Fall Line Publishing Inc.
PO Box 487
Louisville, GA 30434
Phone: (478)625-7722
Fax: (478)625-8816
**Subject(s):** Paid Community Newspapers
**Circ:** (Free)‡65
(Paid)‡4,800

**The Tuskegee News (484)**
Tuskegee Newspapers Inc.
120 Eastside St
Tuskegee, AL 36083
**Subject(s):** Paid Community Newspapers
**Circ:** (Paid)4,800

**The Twin-City News (27979)**
PO Box 2529
Batesburg-Leesville, SC 29070-2529
Phone: (803)532-6203
Fax: (803)532-6204
**Subject(s):** Paid Community Newspapers
**Circ:** ‡4,800

**Henry County Local (11918)**
Landmark Community Newspapers Inc.
PO Box 209
New Castle, KY 40050
Phone: (502)845-2921
Fax: (502)845-2921
**Subject(s):** Paid Community Newspapers
**Circ:** ‡4,770

**The Chatham News (23782)**
The Chatham News Publishing Co.
PO Box 290
Siler City, NC 27344
Phone: (919)663-3232
Fax: (919)663-4042
**Subject(s):** Free Newspapers
**Circ:** (Free)‡191
(Paid)‡4,733

**Catoosa County News (7363)**
7513 Nashville St.
PO Box 40
Ringgold, GA 30736
Phone: (706)935-2621
Fax: (706)965-5934
**Subject(s):** Paid Community Newspapers
**Circ:** 4,700

**Central Record (11746)**
106 Richmond St.
PO Box 800
Lancaster, KY 40444-0492
Phone: (859)792-2831
Fax: (859)792-3448
**Subject(s):** Paid Community Newspapers
**Circ:** ‡4,700

**Coastal Observer (28212)**
97 Commerce Dr.
PO Box 1170
Pawleys Island, SC 29585
Phone: (843)237-8438
Fax: (843)235-0084
**Subject(s):** Paid Community Newspapers
**Circ:** (Combined)4,700

**The Flor-Ala (220)**
University of North Alabama
UNA Box 5300
Florence, AL 35630-0001
Phone: (256)765-4364
Fax: (256)765-4275
**Subject(s):** College Publications
**Circ:** (Paid)300
(Non-paid)4,700

**Montgomery Independent (356)**
RAM Publications Inc.
1810 W. Fifth St.
Montgomery, AL 36106-1516
Phone: (334)265-7323
Fax: (334)265-7320
**Subject(s):** Paid Community Newspapers
**Circ:** (Free)‡2,300
(Paid)‡4,700

**Walking Horse Report (28990)**
Saddle Horse Report
730 Madison St.
Shelbyville, TN 37162-1007
Phone: (931)684-8123
Fax: (931)684-8196
**Subject(s):** (Horses and Horse Racing)
**Circ:** (Paid)‡4,700

**Roanoke Beacon (23688)**
Roanoke
PO Box 726
Plymouth, NC 27962
Phone: (252)793-2123
Fax: (252)793-5365
**Subject(s):** Paid Community Newspapers
**Circ:** ‡4,691

**The Baxley News-Banner (7007)**
PO Box 410
Baxley, GA 31515
Phone: (912)367-2468
Fax: (912)367-0277
**Subject(s):** Paid Community Newspapers
**Circ:** ‡4,600

**Clay Today (6355)**
ADD Inc.
1564 Kingsley Ave.
Orange Park, FL 32073-4594
Phone: (904)264-3200
Fax: (904)269-6958
**Circ:** (Non-paid)‡1,400
(Paid)‡4,600

**The Commerce News (7080)**
Jackson Herald Inc.
1672 S. Broad St.
PO Box 459
Commerce, GA 30529
Phone: (706)335-2927
**Subject(s):** Paid Community Newspapers
**Circ:** ‡4,600

**Independent Herald (28947)**
Liberty Press Inc.
19391 N Alberta St.
Oneida, TN 37841-3359
Phone: (423)569-6343
Fax: (423)569-9566
**Subject(s):** Paid Community Newspapers
**Circ:** ‡4,600

**LaRue County Herald News (11725)**
Landmark Community Newspapers Inc.
40 Shawnee Dr.
Hodgenville, KY 42748
Phone: (270)358-3118
Fax: (270)358-4852
**Subject(s):** Paid Community Newspapers
**Circ:** ‡4,600

**Loris Times (28167)**
4111 Walnut St.
PO Box 796
Loris, SC 29569-0796
Phone: (843)756-7224
Fax: (843)756-7812
**Subject(s):** Local, State, and Regional Publications
**Circ:** (Combined)4,600

**The Enterprise (23838)**
106 W Main St.
PO Box 387
Williamston, NC 27892-0387
Phone: (252)792-1181
Fax: (252)792-1921
**Subject(s):** Paid Community Newspapers
**Circ:** (Free)⊕62
(Paid)⊕4,597

**Record-Herald (11695)**
PO Box 130
Greensburg, KY 42743
Phone: (270)932-4381

Fax: (270)932-4441
**Subject(s):** Paid Community Newspapers
**Circ:** 4,587

**Morgan County News (29023)**
Roane Newspapers
PO Box 346
Wartburg, TN 37887
Phone: (423)346-6225
Fax: (423)346-5788
**Subject(s):** Paid Community Newspapers
**Circ:** ‡4,574

**The Alleghany News (23792)**
Alleghany News Publishing Company Inc.
PO Box 8
Sparta, NC 28675
Phone: (336)372-8999
Fax: (336)372-5707
**Subject(s):** Paid Community Newspapers
**Circ:** (Free)‡100
(Paid)‡4,540

**Englewood Sun Herald (6702)**
200 E Venice Ave.
Venice, FL 34285
Phone: (941)484-2611
Fax: (941)485-3036
**Subject(s):** Paid Community Newspapers
**Circ:** ‡4,500

**Four Oaks-Benson News in Review (23244)**
The County Press
PO Box 9
Benson, NC 27504
Phone: (919)894-3331
Fax: (919)894-1069
**Subject(s):** Paid Community Newspapers
**Circ:** ‡4,500

**Henry County Local & Shopper (11919)**
Landmark Community Newspapers Inc.
1378 Eminence Rd.
PO Box 209
New Castle, KY 40050
Phone: (502)845-2858
Fax: (502)845-2921
**Subject(s):** Paid Community Newspapers
**Circ:** (Controlled)⊕35
(Paid)⊕**4,500**

**Herald and Tribune (28664)**
PO Box 277
Jonesborough, TN 37659
Phone: (423)753-3136
Fax: (423)753-6528
**Subject(s):** Paid Community Newspapers
**Circ:** ‡4,500

**The Independent (418)**
Gulf Coast Newspapers
PO Box 509
Robertsdale, AL 36567
Phone: (251)947-7712
Fax: (251)947-7652
**Subject(s):** Paid Community Newspapers
**Circ:** 4,500

**The Journal-Enterprise (11963)**
PO Box 190
100 Walnut
Providence, KY 42450-0190
Phone: (270)667-2068
Fax: (270)667-9160
**Subject(s):** Paid Community Newspapers
**Circ:** ‡4,500

**Lewis County Herald (12007)**
Lewis County Herald Publishing Co.
206 Main St.
Vanceburg, KY 41179
Phone: (606)796-2331
Fax: (606)796-3110
**Subject(s):** Paid Community Newspapers
**Circ:** ‡4,500

**Macon Beacon (16937)**
PO Box 32
Macon, MS 39341
Phone: (662)726-4747
Fax: (662)726-4742
**Subject(s):** Paid Community Newspapers
**Circ:** 4,500

**Madison County Herald (16773)**
Gannett Company Inc.
PO Box 119
Canton, MS 39046
Phone: (601)859-1221
Fax: (601)859-9409
**Subject(s):** Paid Community Newspapers
**Circ:** ‡4,500

**The Manning Times (28168)**
Times Publishing Co.
4 S Brooks St.
PO Box 576
Manning, SC 29102
Phone: (803)435-8422
Fax: (803)435-4189
**Subject(s):** Paid Community Newspapers
**Circ:** ‡4,500

**McDuffie Progress (7453)**
101 Church St.
PO Box 1090
Thomson, GA 30824
Phone: (706)595-1601
Fax: (706)597-8974
**Subject(s):** Paid Community Newspapers
**Circ:** 4,500

**The New Volusian (5933)**
News-Journal Corp.
111 S. Alabama Ave.
Box 1119
DeLand, FL 32721
Phone: (904)736-8972
Fax: (904)736-8972
**Subject(s):** Paid Community Newspapers
**Circ:** ‡4,500

**News-Journal (23689)**
Dickson Press
119 W Elwood Ave.
Box 550
Raeford, NC 28376
Phone: (910)875-2121
Fax: (910)875-7256
**Subject(s):** Paid Community Newspapers
**Circ:** ‡4,500

**The News Record (23636)**
The News Record Inc.
PO Box 369
Marshall, NC 28753
Phone: (828)649-1075
Fax: (828)649-3722
**Subject(s):** Paid Community Newspapers
**Circ:** (Free)100
(Paid)4,500

**Old Gold and Black (23873)**
Wake Forest University
518 Benson University Center
PO Box 7569
Winston-Salem, NC 27109
Phone: (336)758-5279
Fax: (336)758-4561
**Subject(s):** College Publications
**Circ:** (Paid)‡1,000
(Free)‡4,500

**Pickens County Herald (154)**
PO Box 390
215 North Reform Street
Carrollton, AL 35447-0390
Phone: (205)367-2217
Fax: (205)367-2217
**Subject(s):** Paid Community Newspapers
**Circ:** (Paid)‡4,500

**Saluda Standard Sentinel (28221)**
Saluda Standard
PO Box 668
Saluda, SC 29138
Phone: (864)445-2527
Fax: (864)445-8679
**Subject(s):** Paid Community Newspapers
**Circ:** ‡4,500

**The Times Post (16869)**
219 N Jackson St.
PO Box 629
Houston, MS 38851
Phone: (662)456-3771
Fax: (662)456-3772
**Subject(s):** Paid Community Newspapers
**Circ:** 4,500

**Copiah County Courier (16862)**
Courier
103 S Ragsdale St.
PO Box 351
Hazlehurst, MS 39083
Phone: (601)894-3141
Fax: (601)894-3144
**Subject(s):** Paid Community Newspapers
**Circ:** (Free)‡2,500
(Paid)‡4,450

**Lauderdale County Enterprise (28968)**
145 E Jackson St.
PO Drawer 289
Ripley, TN 38063
Phone: (731)635-1771
Fax: (731)635-2111
**Subject(s):** Free Newspapers
**Circ:** (Free)‡22
(Paid)‡4,427

**Choctaw Advocate (148)**
PO Box 475
210 North Mulberry
Butler, AL 36904
Phone: (205)459-2858
Fax: (205)459-3000
**Subject(s):** Paid Community Newspapers
**Circ:** ‡4,400

**East Lauderdale News (421)**
PO Box 479
1617 Lee St.
Rogersville, AL 35652
Phone: (256)247-5565
Fax: (256)247-1902
**Subject(s):** Paid Community Newspapers
**Circ:** ‡4,400

**Fairhope Courier (417)**
Gulf Coast Newspapers
PO Box 509
Robertsdale, AL 36567
Phone: (334)947-7712
Fax: (334)947-2062
**Subject(s):** Paid Community Newspapers
**Circ:** ‡4,400

**The News Chronicle (27986)**
PO Box 606
Belton, SC 29627
Phone: (864)338-6124
Fax: (864)338-1109
**Subject(s):** Paid Community Newspapers
**Circ:** ‡4400

**The Pageland Progressive-Journal (28209)**
Progressive Publishers
PO Box 218
Pageland, SC 29728
Phone: (843)672-2358
Fax: (843)672-5593
**Subject(s):** Paid Community Newspapers
**Circ:** ‡4,400

**The Polk County Democrat (5805)**
Frisbie Publishing
Box 120
Bartow, FL 33831
Phone: (863)533-4183
Fax: (863)533-0402
**Subject(s):** Paid Community Newspapers
**Circ:** (Combined)⊕**4,393**

**Bertie Ledger-Advance (23865)**
Cox North Carolina Publications Inc.
PO Drawer 69
Windsor, NC 27983
Phone: (252)794-3185
Fax: (252)794-2835
**Subject(s):** Paid Community Newspapers
**Circ:** 4,150
4,175
‡4,375

**Tompkinsville News (12006)**
Monroe County Press Inc.
105 N. Main St.
Tompkinsville, KY 42167-1599
Phone: (502)487-5576
Fax: (502)487-8839
**Subject(s):** Paid Community Newspapers
**Circ:** (Free)‡216
(Paid)‡4,365

## Southern States

**The Springfield Sun (11999)**
Landmark Community Newspapers Inc.
PO Box 31
Springfield, KY 40069
Phone: (859)336-3716
Fax: (859)336-7718
**Subject(s):** Paid Community Newspapers
Circ: (Free)‡16
      (Paid)‡4,350

**The Interior Journal (12000)**
111 E Main St.
Stanford, KY 40484
Phone: (606)365-2104
Fax: (606)365-2105
**Subject(s):** Paid Community Newspapers
Circ: 4,314

**Kilgore News Herald (88)**
Community Newspaper Holdings Inc.
3500 Colonnade Pkwy., Ste. 600
Birmingham, AL 35243
Phone: (205)298-7100
Fax: (205)298-7101
**Subject(s):** Daily Newspapers
Circ: (Mon.-Fri.)‡3,737
      (Sun.)‡4,316

**Glennville Sentinel (7174)**
105 Barnard St.
PO Box 218
Glennville, GA 30427
Phone: (912)654-2515
Fax: (912)654-2527
**Subject(s):** Paid Community Newspapers
Circ: (Paid)⊕4,300

**The Crittenden Press (11877)**
The Crittenden Press Inc.
125 E. Bellville St.
PO Box 191
Marion, KY 42064-0191
Phone: (270)965-3191
Fax: (270)965-2516
**Subject(s):** Paid Community Newspapers
Circ: ‡4,250

**Atmore Advance (30)**
Boone Newspapers Inc.
PO Box 28
301 S Main St.
Atmore, AL 36504
Phone: (251)368-2123
Fax: (251)368-2124
**Subject(s):** Paid Community Newspapers
Circ: 4,213

**The Berrien Press (7323)**
P.O.Box 455
Nashville, GA 31639
Phone: (229)686-3523
Fax: (229)686-7771
**Subject(s):** Paid Community Newspapers
Circ: ‡4,200

**The Big Sandy News (11802)**
115 Louisa Plaza. Suite 4
PO Box 766
Louisa, KY 41230
Phone: (606)638-4581
Fax: (606)638-9949
**Subject(s):** Paid Community Newspapers
Circ: ‡4,200

**Centreville Press (159)**
Bibb Publications
32 Court Sq. W
PO Box 127
Centreville, AL 35042
Phone: (205)926-9769
Fax: (205)926-9760
**Subject(s):** Paid Community Newspapers
Circ: 4,200

**Chiefland Citizen (5868)**
PO Box 980
Chiefland, FL 32644
Phone: (904)493-4796
Fax: (904)493-9336
**Subject(s):** Paid Community Newspapers
Circ: 4,200

**Holmes County Advertiser (5831)**
Woodham Family Publications
112 E. Virginia Ave.
Bonifay, FL 32425
Phone: (850)547-2270
Fax: (850)547-9200
**Subject(s):** Free Newspapers
Circ: (Free)‡4,200

**Leader-Tribune (7159)**
Leader-Tribune Inc.
PO Box 1060
109 Anderson Ave
Fort Valley, GA 31030-1060
Phone: (478)825-2432
Fax: (478)825-4130
**Subject(s):** Paid Community Newspapers
Circ: 4,200

**The Nashville Graphic (23668)**
203 W Washington St.
Nashville, NC 27856
Phone: (252)459-7101
Fax: (252)459-3052
**Subject(s):** Paid Community Newspapers
Circ: (Paid)‡4,200

**Salyersville Independent (11976)**
102 E Maple Street
PO Box 29
Salyersville, KY 41465-9466
Phone: (606)349-2915
Fax: (606)349-8609
**Subject(s):** Paid Community Newspapers
Circ: ‡4,200

**The Tallassee Tribune (442)**
301 Gilmer
PO Drawer 780730
Tallassee, AL 36078-0730
Phone: (334)283-6568
Fax: (334)283-6569
**Subject(s):** Paid Community Newspapers
Circ: 4,200

**Troublesome Creek Times (11722)**
Knott County Publishing Company Inc.
PO Box 1500
Hindman, KY 41822-1500
Phone: (606)785-5134
Fax: (606)785-0105
**Subject(s):** Paid Community Newspapers
Circ: (Free)⊕207
      (Paid)⊕4,185

**Walker County Messenger (7224)**
News Publishing Co.
120 E. Patton St.
La Fayette, GA 30728
Phone: (706)638-1859
Fax: (706)638-7045
**Subject(s):** Paid Community Newspapers
Circ: (Paid)‡4,170

**Smithville Review (28993)**
106 S 1st Ave.
PO Box 247
Smithville, TN 37166
Phone: (615)597-5485
Fax: (615)597-5489
**Subject(s):** Paid Community Newspapers
Circ: (Free)406
      (Paid)4,114

**Bladen Journal (23457)**
Park Newspapers
PO Box 67
Elizabethtown, NC 28337
Phone: (919)862-4163
Fax: (919)862-6602
**Subject(s):** Daily Newspapers
Circ: 4,100

**Bourbon County Citizen (11944)**
Advertiser
PO Box 158
Paris, KY 40362-0158
Fax: (606)987-3729
**Subject(s):** Paid Community Newspapers
Circ: ‡4,100

**The Brewton Standard (145)**
Brewton Newspapers Inc.
407 St. Nicholas
P O Box 887
Brewton, AL 36427-0887
Phone: (251)867-4876
Fax: (251)867-4877
**Subject(s):** Paid Community Newspapers
Circ: ‡4,100

**The Chronicle (28633)**
PO Box 448
Humboldt, TN 38343
Phone: (731)784-2531
Fax: (731)784-2533
**Subject(s):** Paid Community Newspapers
Circ: ‡4,100

**Clinton Chronicle (28031)**
513 N Broad St.
PO Box 180
Clinton, SC 29325
Phone: (864)833-1900
Fax: (864)833-1902
**Subject(s):** Paid Community Newspapers
Circ: ‡4,100

**Hancock Clarion (11709)**
230 Main St.
Hawesville, KY 42348
Phone: (270)927-6945
Fax: (270)927-6947
**Subject(s):** Paid Community Newspapers
Circ: ‡4,100

**Jackson Progress-Argus (7202)**
PO Box 249
129 South Mulberry St
Jackson, GA 30233
Phone: (770)775-3107
Fax: (770)775-3855
**Subject(s):** Paid Community Newspapers
Circ: ‡4,100

**Madison County Carrier (6194)**
Tommy Greene Publishing Company Inc.
PO Drawer 772
Madison, FL 32341
Phone: (850)973-4141
Fax: (850)973-4121
**Subject(s):** Paid Community Newspapers
Circ: ‡4,100

**The Oskaloosa Herald (93)**
Community Newspaper Holdings Inc.
3500 Colonnade Pkwy., Ste. 600
Birmingham, AL 35243
Phone: (205)298-7100
Fax: (205)298-7101
**Subject(s):** Daily Newspapers
Circ: ‡4,100

**Observer-News-Enterprise (23679)**
309 N College Ave.
PO Box 48
Newton, NC 28658-0048
Phone: (828)464-0221
Fax: (828)464-1267
**Subject(s):** Daily Newspapers
Circ: ‡4,031

**Oconee Enterprise (7497)**
PO Box 535
Watkinsville, GA 30677-0535
Phone: (706)769-5175
Fax: (706)769-8532
**Subject(s):** Paid Community Newspapers
Circ: (Thurs.)4,031

**The Times Journal (11974)**
Community Newspaper Holdings Inc.
120 Wilson St.
PO Box 190
Russell Springs, KY 42642
Phone: (270)866-3191
Fax: (270)866-3198
**Subject(s):** Paid Community Newspapers
Circ: (Free)‡235
      (Paid)‡4,015

**The Camilla Enterprise & The Pelham Journal (7033)**
The Camilla Enterprise
PO Box 365
Camilla, GA 31730-0365
Phone: (229)336-5265

Fax: (229)336-8476
**Subject(s):** Paid Community Newspapers
**Circ:** ‡4,000

**East Tennessean (28657)**
East Tennessee State University
Box 70688
Johnson City, TN 37614
Phone: (423)439-5363
**Subject(s):** College Publications
**Circ:** (Free)‡4,000

**The Eatonton Messenger (7137)**
Putnam Printing Company Inc.
PO Box 4027
Eatonton, GA 31024
Phone: (706)485-3501
Fax: (706)485-4166
**Subject(s):** Paid Community Newspapers
**Circ:** (Paid)‡4,000

**Gilchrist County Journal (6699)**
207 N Main St.
Trenton, FL 32693
Phone: (352)463-7135
Fax: (352)463-7393
**Subject(s):** Paid Community Newspapers
**Circ:** 4,000

**The Islander (7387)**
PO Box 20539
Saint Simons Island, GA 31522
Phone: (912)265-9654
Fax: (912)265-3699
**Subject(s):** Paid Community Newspapers
**Circ:** 4,000

**Jamestown News (23601)**
Womack Publishing Co.
PO Box 307
Jamestown, NC 27282
Phone: (336)841-4933
Fax: (336)841-4953
**Subject(s):** Paid Community Newspapers
**Circ:** 4,000

**Journal (28172)**
Island Publications
PO Box 2014
Mount Pleasant, SC 29465
Phone: (843)849-1778
Fax: (843)849-0214
**Subject(s):** Paid Community Newspapers
**Circ:** (Combined)‡4,000

**Lee County Observer (27988)**
Lee County Observer Inc.
218 Main St.
PO Box 567
Bishopville, SC 29010
Phone: (803)484-9431
Fax: (803)484-5055
**Subject(s):** Paid Community Newspapers
**Circ:** ‡4,000

**Madison County Record (305)**
PO Box 858
Madison, AL 35758
Phone: (256)772-6677
Fax: (256)773-1953
**Subject(s):** Free Newspapers
**Circ:** (Paid)‡4,000

**Miami Shores News (6251)**
Community Newspapers
6796 S.W. 62 Ave.
Miami, FL 33143
Phone: (305)669-7355
Fax: (305)661-0954
**Subject(s):** Free Newspapers
**Circ:** (Free)‡4,000

**The Millington Star (28809)**
PO Box 305
Millington, TN 38083
Phone: (901)872-2286
Fax: (901)872-2965
**Subject(s):** Paid Community Newspapers
**Circ:** ‡4,000

**The Monitor-Herald (16772)**
PO Box 69
135 Public Square
Calhoun City, MS 38916-0069
Phone: (662)628-5241
Fax: (662)628-4651
**Subject(s):** Paid Community Newspapers
**Circ:** ‡4,000

**Monroe County Reporter (7151)**
PO Box 795
Forsyth, GA 31029
Phone: (478)994-2358
Fax: (478)994-2359
**Subject(s):** Paid Community Newspapers
**Circ:** 4,000

**The News Leader (28161)**
PO Box 9
Landrum, SC 29356-0009
Phone: (864)457-3337
Fax: (864)472-6900
**Subject(s):** Paid Community Newspapers
**Circ:** 4,000

**Okeechobee News (6351)**
Independent Newspapers Inc.
PO Box 639
Okeechobee, FL 34973
Phone: (863)763-5901
Fax: (863)763-5901
**Subject(s):** Paid Community Newspapers
**Circ:** (Sun.)‡4,000

**The Thomasville Times (444)**
PO Box 367
Thomasville, AL 36784
**Subject(s):** Paid Community Newspapers
**Circ:** (Paid)4,000

**The University Echo (28526)**
University of Tennessee at Chattanooga
615 McCallie
Chattanooga, TN 37403
Phone: (423)425-4111
Fax: (423)755-5357
**Subject(s):** College Publications
**Circ:** ‡4,000

**The Voice (108)**
North Alabama Conference of the United Methodist Church
898 Arkadelphia Rd.
Birmingham, AL 35204
Phone: (205)226-7950
Fax: (205)226-7975
**Subject(s):** Religious Publications
**Circ:** (Paid)4,000

**The Yazoo Herald (17055)**
Yazoo Newspaper Inc.
1035 Grand Ave.
PO Box 720
Yazoo City, MS 39194-0720
Phone: (662)746-4911
Fax: (662)746-4915
**Subject(s):** Paid Community Newspapers
**Circ:** ‡4,000

**Tabor-Loris Tribune (23808)**
U.S 701 N
PO Box 67
Tabor City, NC 28463
Phone: (910)653-3153
Fax: (910)653-9440
**Subject(s):** Paid Community Newspapers
**Circ:** ‡3,972

**Early County News (7013)**
The Early County News
PO Box 748
Blakely, GA 39823-0748
Phone: (229)723-4376
Fax: (229)723-6097
**Subject(s):** Paid Community Newspapers
**Circ:** ‡3,900

**Graham Star (23753)**
Community Newspapers Inc.
c/o Matthew Osborne
62 Rodney Orr Bypass
PO Box 69
Robbinsville, NC 28771-0068
Phone: (828)479-3383
Fax: (828)479-1044

**Subject(s):** Paid Community Newspapers
**Circ:** (Free)‡50
(Paid)‡3,900

**Wendell Clarion (23831)**
PO Box 400
Wendell, NC 27591
Phone: (919)365-6262
Fax: (919)269-8383
**Subject(s):** Paid Community Newspapers
**Circ:** ‡3,880

**The Falmouth Outlook (11945)**
Cynthiana Democrat
PO Box 111
Falmouth, KY 41040-0111
Phone: (859)654-3332
**Subject(s):** Free Newspapers
**Circ:** (Free)⊕10
(Paid)⊕**3,875**

**The Black Mountain News (23245)**
Black Mountain News Inc.
PO Box 9
Black Mountain, NC 28711
Phone: (828)669-8727
Fax: (828)669-8619
**Subject(s):** Paid Community Newspapers
**Circ:** 3,850

**The Clay County Progress (23569)**
Community Newspapers Inc.
c/o Becky Long
PO Box 483
Hayesville, NC 28904
Phone: (828)389-8431
Fax: (828)389-9997
**Subject(s):** Paid Community Newspapers
**Circ:** ‡3,850

**The Dade County Sentinel (7468)**
The Sentinel
385 W Church St.
PO Box 277
Trenton, GA 30752
Phone: (706)657-6182
Fax: (706)657-4970
**Subject(s):** Paid Community Newspapers
**Circ:** ‡3,850

**Smith County Reformer (17003)**
PO Box 187
Raleigh, MS 39153
Phone: (601)782-4358
Fax: (601)782-9081
**Subject(s):** Paid Community Newspapers
**Circ:** 3,859

**Holmes County Herald (16928)**
East Holmes Publishing Enterprises Inc.
308 Ct. Sq.
PO Box 60
Lexington, MS 39095
Phone: (662)834-1151
Fax: (662)834-1074
**Subject(s):** Paid Community Newspapers
**Circ:** (Paid)⊕**3,813**

**Cherryville Eagle (23381)**
Republic Newspaper Inc.
107 1/2 E Main St.
PO Box 699
Cherryville, NC 28021-0699
Phone: (704)435-6752
Fax: (704)435-8293
**Subject(s):** Paid Community Newspapers
**Circ:** 3,800

**Jeff Davis Ledger (7191)**
12 Latimer St.
PO Box 460
Hazlehurst, GA 31539
Phone: (912)375-4225
Fax: (912)375-3704
**Subject(s):** Paid Community Newspapers
**Circ:** ‡3,800

**The Sebree Banner (11983)**
Box 36
Sebree, KY 42455
Phone: (270)835-7521
Fax: (270)835-9521
**Subject(s):** Paid Community Newspapers
**Circ:** ‡3,800

Circulation: ★ = ABC; △ = BPA; ♦ = CAC; • = CCAB; ▫ = VAC; ⊕ = PO Statement; ‡ = Publisher's Report; Boldface figures = sworn; Light figures = estimated.

# Southern States

**The Sylvester Local News (7442)**
103 E Kelly
PO Box 387
Sylvester, GA 31791
Phone: (229)776-7713
**Subject(s):** Paid Community Newspapers
**Circ:** ‡3,800

**The Greenup News (11696)**
Morehead News
PO Box 724
Greenup, KY 41144
Phone: (606)473-9851
Fax: (606)473-7591
**Subject(s):** Paid Community Newspapers
**Circ:** ‡3,768

**The Highlander (23595)**
Community Newspapers Inc.
c/o Debbie Putney
134 N Fifth St.
PO Box 249
Highlands, NC 28741
Phone: (828)526-4114
Fax: (828)526-3658
**Subject(s):** Paid Community Newspapers
**Circ:** ‡3,750

**The Apopka Chief (5799)**
439 W Main St.
Apopka, FL 32712
Phone: (407)886-2777
Fax: (407)889-4121
**Subject(s):** Paid Community Newspapers
**Circ:** (Paid)3,700

**Yorkville Enquirer (28260)**
Carolina Newspapers
PO Box 30
128 North Congress Street
York, SC 29745-0030
Phone: (803)684-9903
Fax: (803)628-0300
**Subject(s):** Paid Community Newspapers
**Circ:** ⊖3,700

**Clinton County News (11515)**
Gibson Printing Company Inc.
116 Washington St.
PO Box 360
Albany, KY 42602
Phone: (606)387-5144
Fax: (606)387-7949
**Subject(s):** Paid Community Newspapers
**Circ:** ‡3,650

**The Jackson County Sun (11888)**
PO Box 130
Mc Kee, KY 40447
Phone: (606)287-7197
Fax: (606)287-7196
**Subject(s):** Paid Community Newspapers
**Circ:** (Free)12
(Paid)3,650

**Manchester Star-Mercury (7273)**
Star Mercury Publishing Co.
PO Box 426
Manchester, GA 31816
Phone: (706)846-3188
Fax: (706)846-2206
**Subject(s):** Paid Community Newspapers
**Circ:** (Free)‡26
(Paid)‡3,650

**The News-Democrat (11618)**
Landmark Community Newspapers Inc.
PO Box 60
Carrollton, KY 41008
Phone: (502)732-4261
Fax: (502)732-0453
**Subject(s):** Paid Community Newspapers
**Circ:** 3,615

**Berea Citizen (11538)**
PO Box 207
Berea, KY 40403
Phone: (859)986-0959
Fax: (859)986-0960
**Subject(s):** Paid Community Newspapers
**Circ:** ‡3,600

**The Cochran Journal (7060)**
The Cochran Journal Inc.
PO Box 856
Cochran, GA 31014-0856
Phone: (478)934-6303
Fax: (478)934-6800
**Subject(s):** Paid Community Newspapers
**Circ:** ‡3,600

**Fayette County Review (28996)**
Color Printing
PO Box 519
Somerville, TN 38068
Phone: (901)465-4042
Fax: (800)869-7941
**Subject(s):** Paid Community Newspapers
**Circ:** (Paid)‡3,600

**The Fleming Gazette (11658)**
PO Box 32
Flemingsburg, KY 41041
Phone: (606)845-9211
Fax: (606)845-3299
**Subject(s):** Paid Community Newspapers
**Circ:** 3,600

**The News-Herald (11928)**
PO Box 219
Owenton, KY 40359
Phone: (502)484-3431
Fax: (502)484-3221
**Subject(s):** Paid Community Newspapers
**Circ:** ‡3,600

**Stone County Enterprise (17050)**
PO Box 157
Wiggins, MS 39577
Phone: (601)928-4802
Fax: (601)928-2191
**Subject(s):** Paid Community Newspapers
**Circ:** 3,600

**Saddle Horse Report (28988)**
730 Madison St.
Shelbyville, TN 37162-1007
Phone: (931)684-8123
Fax: (931)684-8196
**Subject(s):** (Horses and Horse Racing)
**Circ:** (Paid)‡3,555

**News-Democrat (29026)**
Kennedy Newspapers Inc.
302-A W Main
PO Box 626
Waverly, TN 37185-0626
Phone: (931)296-7705
Fax: (931)296-5156
**Subject(s):** Paid Community Newspapers
**Circ:** (Free)110
(Paid)3,530

**The Blowing Rocket (23248)**
High Country Media Inc.
PO Box 1026
Blowing Rock, NC 28605
Phone: (828)295-7522
Fax: (828)295-7507
**Subject(s):** Paid Community Newspapers
**Circ:** (Free)‡200
(Paid)‡3,500

**Carlisle County News (11931)**
Kentucky Publishing Inc.
701 Jefferson
Paducah, KY 42001
Phone: (270)443-5635
Fax: (270)442-5220
**Subject(s):** Paid Community Newspapers
**Circ:** ‡3,500

**The Cleburne News (264)**
Consolidated Publishing
926 Ross St.
PO Box 67
Heflin, AL 36264
Phone: (256)463-2872
Fax: (256)463-7127
**Subject(s):** Paid Community Newspapers
**Circ:** (Paid)‡3,500

**Clewiston News (5882)**
Independent Newspapers Inc.
PO Box 1236
Clewiston, FL 33440
Phone: (941)983-9148

Fax: (941)983-7537
**Subject(s):** Paid Community Newspapers
**Circ:** ‡3,500

**Dixie County Advocate (5909)**
PO Box 5030
Cross City, FL 32628
Phone: (904)498-3312
Fax: (904)498-0420
**Subject(s):** Paid Community Newspapers
**Circ:** ‡3,500

**Donalsonville News (7116)**
PO Box 338
Donalsonville, GA 39845-0338
Phone: (229)524-2343
Fax: (229)524-2343
**Subject(s):** Paid Community Newspapers
**Circ:** ‡3,500

**The Enterprise (7052)**
PO Box 218
Claxton, GA 30417
Phone: (912)739-2132
Fax: (912)739-2140
**Subject(s):** Paid Community Newspapers
**Circ:** ‡3,500

**The Escambia Sun-Press (6440)**
Escambia Sun-Press Inc.
3610 Barrancas Ave
PO Box 4625
Pensacola, FL 32507
Phone: (850)456-3121
Fax: (850)456-0103
**Subject(s):** Paid Community Newspapers
**Circ:** 3,500

**Greene County Democrat (210)**
Greene County Newspaper Co.
265 Prarie Ave.
PO Box 598
Eutaw, AL 35462
Phone: (205)372-3373
Fax: (205)372-2243
**Subject(s):** Paid Community Newspapers; Black Publications
**Circ:** ‡3,500

**The Herald Breeze (5930)**
PO Box 1546
DeFuniak Springs, FL 32435
Phone: (850)892-3232
Fax: (850)892-2270
**Subject(s):** Paid Community Newspapers
**Circ:** (Paid)877
(Free)3,500

**Immokalee Bulletin (6146)**
The Caloose Belle
PO Box 518
22 Ft. Thompson Ave.
Labelle, FL 33975
Phone: (863)675-2541
Fax: (863)675-1449
**Subject(s):** Free Newspapers
**Circ:** (Free)‡3,500

**Lamar Leader (438)**
55071 Hwy. 17
PO Box 988
Sulligent, AL 35586
Phone: (205)698-8148
Fax: (205)698-8146
**Subject(s):** Paid Community Newspapers
**Circ:** ‡3,500

**North Jackson Progress (287)**
P.O. Drawer 625
Stevenson, AL 35772
Phone: (256)437-2395
Fax: (256)437-2592
**Subject(s):** Paid Community Newspapers
**Circ:** 3,500

**The Samford Crimson (98)**
Samford University
PO Box 292269
Birmingham, AL 35229
Phone: (205)726-2998
**Subject(s):** College Publications
**Circ:** (Non-paid)‡3,500

**The Star** (28192)
106 E Buena Vista Ave.
North Augusta, SC 29841-3821
Phone: (803)279-2793
Fax: (803)278-4070
**Subject(s):** Paid Community Newspapers
**Circ:** (Combined)⊕**3,500**

**Towns County Herald** (7194)
Box 365
Hiawassee, GA 30546
Phone: (706)896-4454
Fax: (706)745-1830
**Subject(s):** Paid Community Newspapers
**Circ:** ‡3,500

**Calhoun County Journal** (16770)
PO Box 278
Bruce, MS 38915
Phone: (662)983-2570
Fax: (662)983-7667
**Subject(s):** Paid Community Newspapers
**Circ:** 3,450

**The Darien News** (7106)
PO Box 496
Darien, GA 31305
Phone: (912)437-4251
Fax: (912)437-2299
**Subject(s):** Paid Community Newspapers
**Circ:** ‡3,451

**The Journal Independent** (408)
115 N Center Ave.
Piedmont, AL 36272
Phone: (205)447-2837
Fax: (205)447-2837
**Subject(s):** Paid Community Newspapers
**Circ:** ‡3,450

**Lawrence County Press** (16964)
534 Broad St.
PO Box 549
Monticello, MS 39654
Phone: (601)587-2781
Fax: (601)587-2794
**Subject(s):** Paid Community Newspapers
**Circ:** (Paid)‡3,450

**The Cedartown Standard** (7046)
News Publishing Co.
PO Box 308
Cedartown, GA 30125
Phone: (770)748-1520
Fax: (770)748-1524
**Subject(s):** Paid Community Newspapers
**Circ:** (Paid)‡3,400

**The Famuan** (6572)
Florida A&M University
309 Tucker Hall
Tallahassee, FL 32307
Phone: (850)599-3000
**Subject(s):** College Publications; Black Publications
**Circ:** (Free)‡3,400

**The Lamar Democrat** (487)
PO Box 587
Vernon, AL 35592
Phone: (205)695-7029
Fax: (205)695-9501
**Subject(s):** Paid Community Newspapers
**Circ:** ‡3,400

**Quitman Free Press** (6762)
Quitman
PO Box 312
Adel, GA 31620
Phone: (229)896-2233
Fax: (229)896-7237
**Subject(s):** Paid Community Newspapers
**Circ:** 3,400

**Telfair Enterprise** (7302)
237 W Oak St.
PO Box 269
McRae, GA 31055
Phone: (229)868-6015
Fax: (229)868-5486
**Subject(s):** Paid Community Newspapers
**Circ:** ‡3,400

**The Dunlap Tribune** (28587)
Valley Publishing Company Inc.
PO Box 487
Dunlap, TN 37327-0487
Phone: (423)949-2505
Fax: (423)949-5297
**Subject(s):** Paid Community Newspapers
**Circ:** (Free)15
   (Paid)3,335

**Fayette Falcon** (28997)
PO Box 39
Somerville, TN 38068-0039
Phone: (901)465-3567
Fax: (901)465-3568
**Subject(s):** Paid Community Newspapers
**Circ:** ‡3,310

**Geneva County Reaper** (240)
Geneva Publications Inc.
PO Box 160
Geneva, AL 36340
Phone: (334)684-2280
Fax: (334)684-3099
**Subject(s):** Paid Community Newspapers
**Circ:** 3,300

**The Jacksonville News** (291)
Consolidating Publishing
203 Pelham Rd. S
Jacksonville, AL 36265
Phone: (256)435-5021
Fax: (256)435-1028
**Subject(s):** Paid Community Newspapers
**Circ:** (Combined)‡3,300

**Lake County Banner** (29013)
315 Church St.
Tiptonville, TN 38079
Phone: (731)253-6666
Fax: (731)253-6667
**Subject(s):** Paid Community Newspapers
**Circ:** ‡3,300

**The Lake Wales News** (6163)
The Lake Wales News Inc.
140 E. Stuart Ave.
Lake Wales, FL 33853
Phone: (863)676-3467
Fax: (863)676-3468
**Subject(s):** Paid Community Newspapers
**Circ:** (Free)‡25
   (Paid)‡3,300

**The News Leader** (7383)
PO Box 26
Royston, GA 30662-0006
Phone: (706)245-7351
Fax: (706)245-5991
**Subject(s):** Paid Community Newspapers
**Circ:** ‡3,300

**The Warrenton Clipper** (7493)
407 Norwood St.
PO Box 306
Warrenton, GA 30828-0306
Phone: (706)465-3395
Fax: (706)465-3396
**Subject(s):** Paid Community Newspapers
**Circ:** 3,300

**The Tylertown Times** (17032)
727 Beulah Ave.
PO Box 72
Tylertown, MS 39667
Phone: (601)876-5111
Fax: (601)876-5280
**Subject(s):** Paid Community Newspapers
**Circ:** ‡3,294

**The Clayton News-Star** (23243)
The County Press
PO Box 9
Benson, NC 27504
Phone: (919)894-3331
Fax: (919)894-1069
**Subject(s):** Paid Community Newspapers
**Circ:** (Combined)3,250

**Tri-City Reporter** (28589)
121 South Main
PO Box 266
Dyer, TN 38330
Phone: (731)692-3506
Fax: (731)692-4844

**Subject(s):** Paid Community Newspapers
**Circ:** ‡3,250

**Adel News-Tribune** (6761)
Quitman
PO Box 312
Adel, GA 31620
Phone: (229)896-2233
Fax: (229)896-7237
**Subject(s):** Paid Community Newspapers
**Circ:** 3,200

**Clemmons Courier** (23383)
PO Drawer 765
Clemmons, NC 27012
Phone: (336)766-4126
Fax: (336)766-7350
**Subject(s):** Paid Community Newspapers
**Circ:** ‡3,200

**Deep South Jewish Voice** (73)
Lawrence Brook
PO Box 130052
Birmingham, AL 35213
Phone: (205)322-9002
Fax: (205)322-9004
**Subject(s):** Paid Community Newspapers; Jewish Publications
**Circ:** (Combined)3,200

**The Eagle-Record** (28219)
5549 Memorial Blvd.
PO Drawer 278
Saint George, SC 29477
Phone: (843)563-3121
Fax: (843)563-5355
**Subject(s):** Paid Community Newspapers
**Circ:** 3,200

**The Elba Clipper** (200)
PO Drawer A
Elba, AL 36323
Phone: (334)897-2823
Fax: (334)897-3434
**Subject(s):** Paid Community Newspapers
**Circ:** 3,200

**The St. Pauls Review** (23766)
PO Box 265
Saint Pauls, NC 28384
Phone: (910)865-4179
Fax: (910)865-4995
**Subject(s):** Paid Community Newspapers
**Circ:** ‡3,200

**The Sturgis News** (12003)
News
617 N Adams St.
PO Box 218
Sturgis, KY 42459
Phone: (270)333-5545
Fax: (270)333-9943
**Subject(s):** Paid Community Newspapers
**Circ:** 3,200

**Herald-News** (11648)
116 S Main
PO Box 87
Edmonton, KY 42129
Phone: (270)432-3291
Fax: (270)432-4414
**Subject(s):** Paid Community Newspapers
**Circ:** (Paid)3,167

**The Fulton Leader** (11686)
Fulton Publishing Co.
Box 1200
Fulton, KY 42041
Phone: (270)472-1121
Fax: (270)472-1129
**Subject(s):** Paid Community Newspapers
**Circ:** ‡3,150

**The Sentinel** (11964)
Royalty Printing Inc.
1558 Hill St.
Radcliff, KY 40160
Phone: (270)351-4407
Fax: (270)351-4407
**Subject(s):** Paid Community Newspapers
**Circ:** (Non-paid)⊕**305**
   (Paid)⊕**3,133**

# Southern States

**The Ridgway Record (97)**
Community Newspaper Holdings Inc.
3500 Colonnade Pkwy., Ste. 600
Birmingham, AL 35243
Phone: (205)298-7100
Fax: (205)298-7101
**Subject(s):** Daily Newspapers
**Circ:** ‡3,112

**Alma Times (6776)**
South Fire News
PO Box 428
402 W 12th St.
Alma, GA 31510-0428
Phone: (912)632-7201
Fax: (912)632-4156
**Subject(s):** Paid Community Newspapers
**Circ:** ‡3,100

**Chatham Record (23687)**
Chatham News Publishing Co.
PO Box 459
19 Hillsboro St.
Pittsboro, NC 27312
Phone: (919)542-3013
Fax: (919)542-2590
**Subject(s):** Paid Community Newspapers
**Circ:** 3,100

**Harnett County News (23623)**
PO Box 939
407 North Main
Lillington, NC 27546
Phone: (910)893-5121
Fax: (910)893-6128
**Subject(s):** Paid Community Newspapers
**Circ:** ‡3,100

**The Islander News (6131)**
104 Crandon Blvd., No. 301
Key Biscayne, FL 33149
Phone: (305)361-3333
Fax: (305)361-5051
**Subject(s):** Paid Community Newspapers
**Circ:** (Free)‡600
(Paid)‡3,100

**Farmville Enterprise (23468)**
PO Box 247
Farmville, NC 27828
Phone: (919)753-4126
Fax: (919)753-4127
**Subject(s):** Paid Community Newspapers
**Circ:** ‡3,050

**The Greensboro Watchman (243)**
The Greensboro Watchman Inc.
1005 Market St.
PO Drawer 550
Greensboro, AL 36744
Phone: (334)624-8323
Fax: (334)624-8327
**Subject(s):** Paid Community Newspapers
**Circ:** 3,050

**Jasper County News (16746)**
Buckley Newspapers Inc.
3362 Hwy. 15
PO Box 449
Bay Springs, MS 39422-0449
Phone: (601)764-3104
Fax: (601)764-3106
**Subject(s):** Paid Community Newspapers
**Circ:** (Free)‡350
(Paid)‡3,046

**Crestview News Bulletin (5904)**
Okaloosa Publishing Co.
295 W. James Lee Blvd
PO Box 447
Crestview, FL 32536
Phone: (850)682-6524
Fax: (850)682-2246
**Subject(s):** Paid Community Newspapers
**Circ:** (Combined)3,014

**The All State (28543)**
Austin Peay State University
PO Box 4634
Clarksville, TN 37044-0001
Phone: (931)221-7376
Fax: (931)221-7377
**Subject(s):** College Publications
**Circ:** ‡3,000

**Beattyville Enterprise (11738)**
Intermountain Publishing Co.
PO Box 999
Jackson, KY 41339-0999
Phone: (606)666-2451
Fax: (606)666-5757
**Subject(s):** Paid Community Newspapers
**Circ:** 3,000

**Bracken County News (11573)**
Bay Publishing
216 Frankfort St.
PO Box 68
Brooksville, KY 41004
Phone: (606)735-2198
Fax: (606)735-2199
**Subject(s):** Paid Community Newspapers
**Circ:** ‡3,000

**Cannon Courier (29033)**
Andy Bryson
210 Water St.
Woodbury, TN 37190
Phone: (615)563-2512
Fax: (615)563-2519
**Subject(s):** Paid Community Newspapers
**Circ:** 3,000

**The Charleston Chronicle (28003)**
Chronicle Communications Corp.
1109 King St.
PO Box 20548
Charleston, SC 29413-0548
Phone: (803)723-2785
Fax: (803)577-6099
**Subject(s):** Paid Community Newspapers; Black Publications
**Circ:** (Paid)3,000
(Free)3,000

**Charlton County Herald (7148)**
Thompson Publishing Inc.
204 S First St.
PO Box 398
Folkston, GA 31537-3062
Phone: (912)496-3585
Fax: (912)496-4585
**Subject(s):** Paid Community Newspapers
**Circ:** 3,000

**Clover Herald (28259)**
Carolina Newspapers
PO Box 38
128 North Congress Street Ste C
York, SC 29745
Phone: (803)684-9903
Fax: (803)628-0300
**Subject(s):** Paid Community Newspapers
**Circ:** ‡3,000

**Construction Market Data Inc. (7330)**
Reed construction Data
30 Technology Pkwy. S., Ste. 100
Norcross, GA 30092
Phone: (770)417-4122
Fax: (800)930-3003
**Subject(s):** Daily Periodicals; Construction, Contracting, Building, and Excavating
**Circ:** (Combined)‡3,000

**The County Record (5813)**
PO Box 366
20311 Central Ave West
Blountstown, FL 32424
Phone: (850)674-5041
Fax: (850)674-5008
**Subject(s):** Paid Community Newspapers
**Circ:** 3,000

**Cover Story (7085)**
Cordele Dispatch
306 13th Ave. W
Cordele, GA 31015
**Subject(s):** Shopping Guides
**Circ:** (Free)‡3,000

**Greene County Herald (16926)**
PO Box 220
Leakesville, MS 39451
Phone: (601)394-5070
Fax: (601)394-5070
**Subject(s):** Paid Community Newspapers
**Circ:** 3,000

**Herald Ledger (11647)**
Jim Ward
PO Box 747
Eddyville, KY 42038
Phone: (270)388-2269
Fax: (270)388-5540
**Subject(s):** Paid Community Newspapers
**Circ:** ‡3,000

**Inman Times (28150)**
PO Drawer 7
8th South Main Street
Inman, SC 29349
Phone: (864)472-9548
Fax: (864)476-5398
**Subject(s):** Paid Community Newspapers
**Circ:** ‡3,000

**Lafayette Sun (297)**
The Lafayette Sun
PO Box 378
Lafayette, AL 36862
Phone: (334)864-8885
Fax: (334)864-8310
**Subject(s):** Paid Community Newspapers
**Circ:** 3,000

**The Monticello News (7316)**
237 Washington St.
PO Box 30
Monticello, GA 31064-0030
Phone: (706)468-6511
Fax: (706)468-6576
**Subject(s):** Paid Community Newspapers
**Circ:** ‡3,000

**Monticello News (6307)**
100 W Dogwood St.
PO Box 428
Monticello, FL 32344
Phone: (850)997-3568
Fax: (850)997-3774
**Subject(s):** Paid Community Newspapers
**Circ:** ‡3,000

**The News Leader (28749)**
The Union County News Leader Inc.
PO Box 866
37755 Maynardville Highway
Maynardville, TN 37807
Phone: (865)992-3392
Fax: (865)992-6861
**Subject(s):** Paid Community Newspapers
**Circ:** ‡3,000

**Pacer (28741)**
University of Tennessee at Martin
314 Gooch Hall
Martin, TN 38238
Phone: (731)587-7780
Fax: (731)587-7791
**Subject(s):** College Publications
**Circ:** (Free)3,000

**The Paladin (28113)**
Furman University
3300 Poinsett Hwy.
PO Box 28584
Greenville, SC 29613
Phone: (864)294-2077
Fax: (864)294-3339
**Subject(s):** College Publications
**Circ:** (Combined)‡3,000

**Pike County Journal-Reporter (7512)**
Hometown News Corp.
PO Box 789
Zebulon, GA 30295
Phone: (770)567-3446
Fax: (770)567-8814
**Subject(s):** Paid Community Newspapers
**Circ:** ‡3,000

**The Pineville Sun (11955)**
Associated Publications Inc.
PO Box 250
Pineville, KY 40977
Phone: (606)337-2333
Fax: (606)337-2360
**Subject(s):** Paid Community Newspapers
**Circ:** 3,000

**Silver Wings (16796)**
Service Publications
14 FTW Public Affairs
Columbus, MS 39710-1009
Phone: (662)742-7066
Fax: (662)434-7009
**Subject(s):** Free Newspapers; Military and Navy
**Circ:** (Free)3,000

**Smoky Mountain Times (23263)**
Community News Inc.
PO Box 730
Bryson City, NC 28713
Phone: (828)667-2727
Fax: (828)488-0315
**Subject(s):** Paid Community Newspapers
**Circ:** (Free)‡25
(Paid)‡3,000

**Spring Hope Enterprise/Bailey News (23796)**
Box 399
Spring Hope, NC 27882
Phone: (252)478-3651
Fax: (252)478-3075
**Subject(s):** Paid Community Newspapers
**Circ:** 3,000

**Times (7011)**
113 S Central Ave.
PO Box 410
Blackshear, GA 31516
Phone: (912)449-6693
Fax: (912)449-1719
**Subject(s):** Paid Community Newspapers
**Circ:** 3,000

**Tropolitan (449)**
Troy State University
Wallace Hall
Troy, AL 36082
Phone: (334)670-3327
Fax: (334)670-3707
**Subject(s):** College Publications
**Circ:** (Free)3,000

**Union Springs Herald (486)**
PO Box 600
Union Springs, AL 36089
Phone: (334)738-2360
Fax: (334)738-2342
**Subject(s):** Paid Community Newspapers
**Circ:** 3,000

**Voice (5921)**
Bethune-Cookman College
640 Mary McLeod Bethune Blvd.
Daytona Beach, FL 32114
Phone: (386)481-2707
Fax: (386)481-2701
**Subject(s):** Black Publications; College Publications
**Circ:** ‡3,000

**The Wiregrass Farmer (6786)**
Ashburn Newspapers
109 Gordon St.
Ashburn, GA 31714
Phone: (229)567-3655
Fax: (229)567-4402
**Subject(s):** Paid Community Newspapers
**Circ:** 3,000

**The Winona Times (17053)**
Montgomery Publishing Inc.
PO Box 151
Winona, MS 38967
Phone: (662)283-1131
Fax: (662)283-5374
**Subject(s):** Paid Community Newspapers
**Circ:** (Paid)‡2,979

**The Metter Advertiser (7304)**
Snell Publications Inc.
15 S Rountree
Metter, GA 30439
Phone: (912)685-6566
Fax: (912)685-4901
**Subject(s):** Paid Community Newspapers
**Circ:** ‡2,966

**The Home News (23637)**
PO Box 100
Marshville, NC 28103
Phone: (704)624-5068
Fax: (704)624-2371

**Subject(s):** Paid Community Newspapers
**Circ:** 2,950

**Cumberland County News (11607)**
PO Box 307
Burkesville, KY 42717
Phone: (270)864-3891
Fax: (270)864-3497
**Subject(s):** Paid Community Newspapers
**Circ:** 2,900

**Miller County Liberal (7062)**
157 E Main St.
PO Box 37
Colquitt, GA 39837-0037
Phone: (229)758-5549
Fax: (229)758-5540
**Subject(s):** Paid Community Newspapers
**Circ:** ‡2,900

**Olive Hill Times (11923)**
Post Office Bldg.
215 W.Tom T.Hall Blvd
Olive Hill, KY 41164
Phone: (606)286-4201
Fax: (606)286-4201
**Subject(s):** Paid Community Newspapers
**Circ:** (Paid)‡2,905

**The Dawson News (7107)**
139 W Lee St.
PO Box 350
Dawson, GA 39842-9842
Phone: (229)995-2175
Fax: (229)995-2176
**Subject(s):** Paid Community Newspapers
**Circ:** ‡2,800

**South Lake Press (5881)**
Republic Newspapers Inc.
732 W Montrose St.
Clermont, FL 34711
Phone: (352)394-2183
Fax: (352)394-8001
**Subject(s):** Paid Community Newspapers
**Circ:** (Free)300
(Paid)2,800

**Voice of South Marion (5810)**
PO Box 700
Belleview, FL 34421
Phone: (352)245-3161
Fax: (352)347-7444
**Subject(s):** Paid Community Newspapers
**Circ:** 2,800

**Wolfe County News (11617)**
Courier Publishing
PO Box 129
Campton, KY 41301
Phone: (606)668-3595
Fax: (606)662-4010
**Subject(s):** Paid Community Newspapers
**Circ:** (Paid)2,800

**Lake Wales Highlander (6735)**
Polk Shopper
650 Sixth St. SW
Winter Haven, FL 33882-1440
Phone: (863)294-1100
Fax: (863)294-2008
**Subject(s):** Daily Newspapers
**Circ:** (Paid)2,798

**The Cherokee One Feather (23380)**
Eastern Band of Cherokee Indians
PO Box 501
Cherokee, NC 28719
**Subject(s):** Paid Community Newspapers; Native American Interests
**Circ:** (Free)‡15
(Paid)‡2,750

**The Demopolis Times (185)**
Boone Newspapers Inc.
315 E. Jefferson Street
PO Box 860
Demopolis, AL 36732
Phone: (334)289-4017
Fax: (334)289-4019
**Subject(s):** Paid Community Newspapers
**Circ:** ‡2,750

**Broward Daily Business Review (5953)**
American Lawyer Media L.P.
633 S. Andrews Ave.
Fort Lauderdale, FL 33301
Phone: (954)468-2630
Fax: (800)777-7300
**Subject(s):** Business; Law
**Circ:** (Non-paid)154
(Paid)2,736

**Choctaw Plaindealer (16736)**
The Plaindealer Publishing Company Inc.
PO Box 910
Ackerman, MS 39735-0910
Phone: (662)773-6241
Fax: (662)285-6695
**Subject(s):** Paid Community Newspapers
**Circ:** (Free)‡89
(Paid)‡2,700

**Courier Journal (5903)**
Lake Street Publishing Co.
330 N Summit St.
Crescent City, FL 32112
Phone: (386)698-1644
Fax: (386)698-1994
**Subject(s):** Paid Community Newspapers
**Circ:** (Paid)2,700

**Gates County Index (23499)**
Boone Newspapers
715 Main St.
PO Box 148
Gatesville, NC 27938-0148
Phone: (252)357-0973
**Subject(s):** Paid Community Newspapers
**Circ:** 2,700

**The Newton Record (16975)**
120 S Main St.
PO Box 60
Newton, MS 39345
Phone: (601)683-2001
Fax: (601)683-2360
**Subject(s):** Paid Community Newspapers
**Circ:** ‡2,700

**The Baldwyn News (16741)**
Baldwyn News
102 W Main
PO Drawer 130
Baldwyn, MS 38824
Phone: (662)365-3232
Fax: (662)365-7989
**Subject(s):** Paid Community Newspapers
**Circ:** (Paid)2,650

**Lee County Ledger (7233)**
126 4th St.
PO Box 715
Leesburg, GA 31763
Phone: (912)759-2413
Fax: (912)759-6599
**Subject(s):** Paid Community Newspapers
**Circ:** (Free)‡25
(Paid)‡2,650

**Wilkinson County News (7200)**
Box 205
100 High Hill Street
Irwinton, GA 31042
Phone: (478)946-2218
Fax: (478)946-7226
**Subject(s):** Paid Community Newspapers
**Circ:** (Paid)‡2,650

**Webster Progress-Times (16812)**
Webster Progress
PO Drawer D
122 N. Dunn St
Eupora, MS 39744
Phone: (662)258-7532
Fax: (662)258-6474
**Subject(s):** Paid Community Newspapers
**Circ:** (Free)‡90
(Paid)‡2638

**The Andrews Journal (23220)**
Community Newspapers
PO Box 250
36 Laurel Street
Andrews, NC 28901
Phone: (828)321-4271
Fax: (828)321-5890

**Subject(s):** Paid Community Newspapers
**Circ:** 2,600

**Citizen-Statesman (28514)**
Citizen-Statesman Corp.
801 E Lake Ave.
PO Box 670
Celina, TN 38551
Phone: (931)243-2235
Fax: (931)243-2232
**Subject(s):** Paid Community Newspapers
**Circ:** (Paid)2,600

**The Woodville Republican (17054)**
The Woodville Republican Inc.
425 Depot St.
PO Box 696
Woodville, MS 39669
Phone: (601)888-4293
Fax: (601)888-6156
**Subject(s):** Paid Community Newspapers
**Circ:** 2,551

**Advertizer-Herald (27974)**
Kilgus Publishing Co.
369 McGee St.
PO Box 929
Bamberg, SC 29003
Phone: (803)245-5204
Fax: (803)245-3900
**Subject(s):** Paid Community Newspapers
**Circ:** (Non-paid)⊕496
(Paid)⊕2,504

**The Alabamian (338)**
University of Montevallo
Sta. 6222
Montevallo, AL 35115
Phone: (205)665-6222
Fax: (205)665-6232
**Subject(s):** College Publications
**Circ:** (Paid)40
(Non-paid)2,500

**Belmont Vision (28844)**
Belmont University
1900 Belmont Blvd.
Nashville, TN 37212
Phone: (615)460-6433
Fax: (615)460-5532
**Subject(s):** College Publications
**Circ:** (Free)‡2,500

**The Chanticleer (28080)**
Coastal Carolina University
PO Box 261954
Conway, SC 29528-6054
Phone: (843)347-3161
Fax: (843)349-2317
**Subject(s):** College Publications
**Circ:** (Free)‡2,500

**The Clayton Record (166)**
PO Box 69
Clayton, AL 36016
Phone: (334)775-3254
Fax: (334)775-8554
**Subject(s):** Paid Community Newspapers
**Circ:** ‡2,500

**County News (23798)**
PO Box 407
505 South Center St
Statesville, NC 28687-0407
Phone: (704)873-1054
Fax: (704)873-1054
**Subject(s):** Paid Community Newspapers; Black Publications
**Circ:** (Paid)‡2,500
(Free)‡2,500

**The Fayette Chronicle (16813)**
PO Box 536
Fayette, MS 39069
Phone: (601)786-3661
Fax: (601)786-3661
**Subject(s):** Paid Community Newspapers
**Circ:** (Free)‡100
(Paid)‡2,500

**Gallatin County News (12016)**
211 3rd St.
Box 435
Warsaw, KY 41095
Phone: (859)567-5051
Fax: (859)567-6397

**Subject(s):** Paid Community Newspapers
**Circ:** (Paid)2,500

**The Livingston Ledger (11991)**
Kentucky Publishing Inc.
PO Box 129
Smithland, KY 42081
Phone: (502)928-2182
Fax: (502)442-5220
**Subject(s):** Paid Community Newspapers
**Circ:** ‡2,500

**SCTA Hi-Lights (28059)**
South Carolina Trucking Association
2425 Devine St.
PO Box 50166
Columbia, SC 29250-0166
Phone: (803)256-4290
Fax: (803)254-7148
**Subject(s):** Trucks and Trucking; Transportation, Traffic, and Shipping
**Circ:** ‡2,500

**South Pittsburg Hustler (28999)**
Marion County Newspapers Inc.
307 1/2 Elm. Ave.
PO Box 765
South Pittsburg, TN 37380-1337
Phone: (423)837-6312
Fax: (423)837-8715
**Subject(s):** Paid Community Newspapers
**Circ:** 2,500

**The Southern (6173)**
Florida Southern College
111 Lake Hollingsworth Dr.
Lakeland, FL 33801-5698
Phone: (941)680-4170
Fax: (941)680-6244
**Subject(s):** College Publications
**Circ:** (Free)‡2,500

**The Speedy Bee (7212)**
PO Box 1317
Jesup, GA 31598
Phone: (912)427-4018
Fax: (912)427-8447
**Subject(s):** Beekeeping
**Circ:** ‡2,500

**The Sting (7293)**
Southern Polytechnic State University
1110 S. Marietta Pkwy.
Marietta, GA 30060-2896
Phone: (770)528-7200
**Subject(s):** College Publications
**Circ:** (Free)‡2,500

**Taylor County News (7028)**
Taylor News
PO Box 550
Butler, GA 31006
Phone: (478)862-5101
Fax: (478)862-9668
**Subject(s):** Paid Community Newspapers
**Circ:** 2,500

**Tideland News (23803)**
Carteret Publishing Co.
PO Box 1000
Swansboro, NC 28584
Phone: (910)326-5066
Fax: (910)326-1165
**Subject(s):** Paid Community Newspapers
**Circ:** (Free)400
(Paid)2,500

**Tri-County News (28987)**
PO Box 130
Seymour, TN 37865
**Subject(s):** Paid Community Newspapers
**Circ:** (Paid)‡2,500

**The Westminster News (28255)**
Keowee Publications Inc.
100 Main St.
PO Box 278
Westminster, SC 29693
Phone: (864)647-5404
Fax: (864)647-5405
**Subject(s):** Paid Community Newspapers
**Circ:** ‡2,500

**Charleston Sun-Sentinel (16777)**
PO Box 250
Charleston, MS 38921
Phone: (662)647-8462
Fax: (662)647-3830
**Subject(s):** Paid Community Newspapers
**Circ:** (Free)‡105
(Paid)‡2,479

**Crossroads Chronicle (23287)**
Community Newspapers Inc.
PO Box 1040
Cashiers, NC 28717
Phone: (828)743-5101
Fax: (828)743-4173
**Subject(s):** Paid Community Newspapers
**Circ:** ‡2,400

**The Dawson Springs Progress (11645)**
Progress Publishing Company Inc.
131 S Main St.
PO Box 460
Dawson Springs, KY 42408
Phone: (502)797-3271
Fax: (502)797-3273
**Subject(s):** Paid Community Newspapers
**Circ:** 2,400

**Kemper County Messenger (16810)**
Messenger
PO Box 546
102 Main Street
De Kalb, MS 39328
Phone: (601)743-5760
Fax: (601)743-4430
**Subject(s):** Paid Community Newspapers
**Circ:** ‡2,400

**Keowee Courier (28250)**
Keowee Publications Inc.
50 Short St.
PO Box 528
Walhalla, SC 29691-0538
Phone: (864)638-5856
Fax: (864)638-5857
**Subject(s):** Paid Community Newspapers
**Circ:** ‡2,400

**Okolona Messenger (16978)**
Messenger
249 Main St.
Okolona, MS 38860
Phone: (662)447-5501
Fax: (662)447-5571
**Subject(s):** Paid Community Newspapers
**Circ:** 2,400

**Poplarville Democrat (16997)**
Donrey Media Group
109 W Pearl St.
PO Box 549
Poplarville, MS 39470
Phone: (601)795-2247
Fax: (601)795-2232
**Subject(s):** Paid Community Newspapers
**Circ:** ‡2,400

**The Red Springs Citizen (23735)**
131 S Main St.
Red Springs, NC 28377
Phone: (910)843-4631
Fax: (910)843-8171
**Subject(s):** Paid Community Newspapers
**Circ:** 2,400

**The Randolph Guide (23225)**
431 S Fayetteville St.
PO Box 1044
Asheboro, NC 27204-1044
Phone: (336)625-5576
Fax: (336)625-1228
**Subject(s):** Paid Community Newspapers
**Circ:** (Paid)‡2,332

**The Southern Reporter (17011)**
TSR Publications Inc.
PO Box 157
206 S. Main St.
Sardis, MS 38666-0157
Phone: (662)487-1593
Fax: (662)487-1552
**Subject(s):** Paid Community Newspapers
**Circ:** ‡2,311

**Lincolnton Journal** (7239)
PO Box 399
157 N Peach St.
Lincolnton, GA 30817
Phone: (706)359-3229
Fax: (706)359-2884
**Subject(s):** Paid Community Newspapers
**Circ:** 2,300

**Star** (7347)
102 East 4th St.
PO Box 25
Ocilla, GA 31774
Phone: (229)468-5433
Fax: (229)468-5045
**Subject(s):** Paid Community Newspapers
**Circ:** 2,300

**Todd County Standard** (11655)
PO Box 308
Public Sq.
Elkton, KY 42220
Phone: (270)265-2439
Fax: (270)265-2571
**Subject(s):** Paid Community Newspapers
**Circ:** ‡2,300

**The Hickman Courier** (11720)
Box 70
Hickman, KY 42050-0070
Phone: (270)236-2726
Fax: (270)236-2726
**Subject(s):** Paid Community Newspapers
**Circ:** ‡2,250

**Lake Region Monitor** (6560)
Bradford Telegraph
131 W. Call St.
PO Drawer A
Starke, FL 32091
Phone: (904)964-6305
Fax: (904)964-8628
**Subject(s):** Paid Community Newspapers
**Circ:** 2,250

**The Times-Leader** (23567)
Cox North Carolina Publications
209 S Highland Ave.
PO Box 369
Grifton, NC 28530
Phone: (252)524-4376
Fax: (252)524-3312
**Subject(s):** Paid Community Newspapers
**Circ:** (Paid)2,250

**Union County Times** (6561)
PO Drawer A
Starke, FL 32091
Phone: (904)496-2261
Fax: (904)964-8268
**Subject(s):** Paid Community Newspapers
**Circ:** (Free)300
(Paid)2,250

**The Weekly Post** (410)
PO Box 849
Rainsville, AL 35986
Phone: (256)638-4027
Fax: (256)638-2329
**Subject(s):** Paid Community Newspapers
**Circ:** (Free)‡200
(Paid)‡2,250

**The Port Gibson Reveille** (16999)
Claiborne Publishing Company Inc.
708 Market St.
PO Box 1002
Port Gibson, MS 39150-1002
Phone: (601)437-5103
Fax: (601)437-4410
**Subject(s):** Paid Community Newspapers
**Circ:** (Free)‡49
(Paid)2,222

**Bay Beacon** (6327)
Beacon Newspapers
1181 E John Sims Pkwy.
Niceville, FL 32578
Phone: (850)678-1080
Fax: (850)729-3225
**Subject(s):** Paid Community Newspapers
**Circ:** (Paid)2,200

**The Butler County News** (11)
Andalusia Star
PO Drawer 430
Andalusia, AL 36420
Phone: (334)222-2402
Fax: (334)222-6597
**Subject(s):** Paid Community Newspapers
**Circ:** 2,200

**Tri-City News** (11632)
805 E Main St.
Cumberland, KY 40823-1711
Phone: (606)589-2588
Fax: (606)589-2589
**Subject(s):** Paid Community Newspapers
**Circ:** ‡2,200

**The Wrightsville Headlight** (7389)
The Sandersville Georgian Inc.
PO Box 431
Sandersville, GA 31082
Phone: (478)552-3161
Fax: (478)552-5177
**Subject(s):** Paid Community Newspapers
**Circ:** ‡2,200

**The Hartsville Vidette** (28628)
111 Marlene St.
PO Box 47
Hartsville, TN 37074
Phone: (615)374-3556
Fax: (615)374-4002
**Subject(s):** Paid Community Newspapers
**Circ:** ‡2,152

**Belmont-Tishomingo Journal** (16749)
The Belmont and Tishomongo Journal Inc.
PO Box 70
430 North 2nd Street
Belmont, MS 38827
Phone: (662)454-7196
Fax: (662)454-0055
**Subject(s):** Paid Community Newspapers
**Circ:** ‡2,100

**Booneville Sentinel** (11550)
Southfork Publishing Co.
PO Box 129
Booneville, KY 41314
Phone: (606)593-6627
Fax: (606)598-2330
**Subject(s):** Paid Community Newspapers
**Circ:** ‡2,100

**The Calhoun Times** (28220)
PO Box 176
Saint Matthews, SC 29135
Phone: (803)874-3137
Fax: (803)874-1588
**Subject(s):** Paid Community Newspapers
**Circ:** (Paid)2,100

**The Jasper News** (6184)
Live Oak Publications
211 Howard St. E
PO Box 370
Live Oak, FL 32060
Phone: (386)362-1734
Fax: (386)364-5578
**Subject(s):** Paid Community Newspapers
**Circ:** (Free)300
(Paid)2,100

**Marion Times-Standard** (307)
PO Box 418
Marion, AL 36756
Phone: (334)683-6318
Fax: (334)683-4616
**Subject(s):** Paid Community Newspapers
**Circ:** 2,100

**Newschief** (6736)
Morris Communication Corp.
PO Box 1440
Winter Haven, FL 33882-1440
Fax: (941)294-2008
**Subject(s):** Paid Community Newspapers
**Circ:** (Combined)2,104

**The Abbeville Herald** (1)
PO Box 609
Abbeville, AL 36310
Phone: (334)585-2331
Fax: (334)585-6835
**Subject(s):** Paid Community Newspapers
**Circ:** 2,080

**The Georgia Post** (7364)
PO Box 860
Roberta, GA 31078
Phone: (478)836-3195
Fax: (478)836-9634
**Subject(s):** Free Newspapers
**Circ:** (Free)3
(Paid)2,050

**The Soperton News** (7419)
Soperton News Building
PO Box 527
2nd Main St.
Soperton, GA 30457
Phone: (912)529-6624
Fax: (912)529-5399
**Subject(s):** Paid Community Newspapers
**Circ:** 2,050

**Aynor Journal** (27973)
PO Box 665
Aynor, SC 29511
Phone: (843)358-2010
Fax: (843)358-0250
**Subject(s):** Paid Community Newspapers
**Circ:** (Combined)2,000

**The Babbler** (28843)
Lipscomb University
Box 4236
Nashville, TN 37204-3951
Phone: (615)279-6601
Fax: (800)333-4358
**Subject(s):** College Publications
**Circ:** (Free)‡2,000

**The Branford News** (5847)
Branford News Inc.
PO Box 148
Branford, FL 32008
Phone: (386)935-1427
Fax: (386)935-3043
**Subject(s):** Paid Community Newspapers
**Circ:** (Paid)‡2,000

**Buc In Print** (27999)
Charleston Southern University
PO Box 118087
Charleston, SC 29423-8087
Phone: (843)863-8042
Fax: (843)863-7021
**Subject(s):** College Publications
**Circ:** (Free)‡2,000

**The Campbell Times** (23265)
Campbell University
PO Box 567
143 Main St.
J. A. Campbell Administration Bldg., Rm. 227, 2nd Fl.
Buies Creek, NC 27506
Phone: (910)893-1224
Fax: (910)893-1922
**Subject(s):** College Publications
**Circ:** (Free)2,000

**Campus Digest** (483)
Tuskegee University
Tuskegee, AL 36083
Phone: (334)727-8710
**Subject(s):** College Publications; Black Publications
**Circ:** (Non-paid)2,000

**Catamaran Sailor** (6132)
Ram Press
PO Box 2060
Key Largo, FL 33037
Phone: (305)451-3287
Fax: (305)453-0255
**Subject(s):** (Boating and Yachting)
**Circ:** (Paid)2,000
(Non-paid)2,000

**Chieftain** (16816)
Itawamba Community College
602 W Hill St.
Fulton, MS 38843
Phone: (662)862-8000
Fax: (662)862-8245
**Subject(s):** College Publications
**Circ:** (Free)‡2,000

**Chilton County News (162)**
PO Box 189
Clanton, AL 35046-0189
Phone: (205)755-0110
Fax: (205)755-6227
**Subject(s):** Paid Community Newspapers
**Circ:** (Paid)2,000

**The Daily News (28765)**
The Daily News Publishing Co.
193 Jefferson Ave.
Memphis, TN 38103
Phone: (901)523-1561
Fax: (901)526-5813
**Subject(s):** Daily Newspapers
**Circ:** ‡2,000

**Frostproof News (6010)**
Sunshine Printing
19 S. Scenic Hwy.
PO Box 67
Frostproof, FL 33843
Phone: (941)635-2171
Fax: (941)635-4265
**Subject(s):** Paid Community Newspapers
**Circ:** ‡2,000

**The Georgetonian (11688)**
Georgetown College
400 E College St.
PO Box 334
Georgetown, KY 40324
Phone: (502)863-8009
Fax: (502)868-8888
**Subject(s):** College Publications
**Circ:** (Free)‡2,000

**The Lenoir Rhynean (23577)**
Lenior-Rhyne College
625, 7th Ave. NE
Hickory, NC 28603-7229
Phone: (828)328-1741
**Subject(s):** College Publications
**Circ:** (Paid)100
(Non-paid)2,000

**Letcher County Community News-Press (11744)**
Superior Printing and Publishing
PO Box 217, Rte. 805
10001 Community Drive
Cromona, KY 41810
Phone: (606)855-4541
Fax: (606)855-9290
**Subject(s):** Paid Community Newspapers
**Circ:** ‡2,000

**Millen News (7313)**
The Millen News
PO Box 909
Millen, GA 30442
Phone: (478)982-5460
Fax: (478)982-1785
**Subject(s):** Paid Community Newspapers
**Circ:** 2,000

**Pacer Times (27964)**
University of South Carolina
471 University Pkwy.
Aiken, SC 29801
Phone: (803)648-6851
Fax: (803)641-3461
**Subject(s):** College Publications
**Circ:** (Free)2,000

**Perquimans Weekly (23575)**
Cox North Carolina Publications
119 W Grubb St.
PO Box 277
Hertford, NC 27944
Phone: (919)426-5728
Fax: (919)426-4625
**Subject(s):** Paid Community Newspapers
**Circ:** 2,000

**Res Ipsa Loquitur (5894)**
University of Miami School of Law
PO Box 248087
1311 Miller Dr.
Coral Gables, FL 33146
Phone: (305)284-2339
Fax: (305)284-2861
**Subject(s):** College Publications
**Circ:** (Free)2,000

**South Tipton Star (28810)**
The Millington Star
PO Box 305
Millington, TN 38083
Phone: (901)872-2286
Fax: (901)872-2965
**Subject(s):** Shopping Guides
**Circ:** (Free)‡2,000

**The Springhillian (319)**
Spring Hill College
4000 Dauphin St.
Mobile, AL 36608
Phone: (251)380-3030
**Subject(s):** College Publications
**Circ:** (Free)‡2,000

**Twiggs County New Era (7210)**
The Twiggs Times New Era
PO Box 800
Jeffersonville, GA 31044
Phone: (478)945-6037
Fax: (478)945-6014
**Subject(s):** Paid Community Newspapers
**Circ:** (Free)50
(Paid)2,009

**Wolf Tales (17046)**
Copiah-Lincoln Community College
PO Box 649
Wesson, MS 39191
Phone: (601)643-8354
Fax: (601)643-8226
**Subject(s):** College Publications
**Circ:** (Free)‡2,000

**Blacksburg Times (27990)**
PO Box 155
Blacksburg, SC 29702
Phone: (864)839-2621
Fax: (864)839-5710
**Subject(s):** Paid Community Newspapers
**Circ:** ‡1,990

**The Dadeville Record (6)**
Tallapoosa Publishers
PO Box 999
Alexander City, AL 35011
Phone: (256)234-4281
Fax: (256)234-6550
**Subject(s):** Paid Community Newspapers
**Circ:** 1,988

**Louisville Defender (11831)**
Consumer Communications Industries
1720 Dixie Hwy.
Louisville, KY 40210
Phone: (502)772-2591
Fax: (502)775-8655
**Subject(s):** Paid Community Newspapers; Black Publications
**Circ:** (Non-paid)♦748
(Paid)♦1,987

**The Tunica Times (17018)**
Tunica Publishing Co.
986 Magnolia St.
PO Box 308
Tunica, MS 38676
Phone: (662)363-1511
Fax: (662)363-9969
**Subject(s):** Paid Community Newspapers
**Circ:** (Paid)‡1,907

**Chesnee Tribune (28022)**
Hometown News
PO Box 158
Chesnee, SC 29323
Phone: (864)461-2815
Fax: (864)476-3513
**Subject(s):** Paid Community Newspapers
**Circ:** (Free)‡100
(Paid)‡1,850

**Palm Beach Daily Business Review (6718)**
American Lawyer Media L.P.
324 Datura St., Ste 140
West Palm Beach, FL 33401
Phone: (561)820-2060
Fax: (561)820-2077
**Subject(s):** Business
**Circ:** (Non-paid)16
(Paid)1,852

**The News Observer (7490)**
Dooly Newspapers Inc.
115 E Union St.
PO Box 186
Vienna, GA 31092
Phone: (229)268-2096
Fax: (229)268-1924
**Subject(s):** Paid Community Newspapers
**Circ:** (Free)87
(Paid)1,843

**The Belzoni Banner (16750)**
115 E. Jackson St.
PO Box 610
Belzoni, MS 39038-0610
Phone: (662)247-3373
Fax: (662)247-3372
**Subject(s):** Paid Community Newspapers
**Circ:** ‡1,800

**Pinnacle (11540)**
Berea College
CPO 2216
Berea, KY 40404
Phone: (859)985-3000
Fax: (859)985-3556
**Subject(s):** College Publications
**Circ:** (Free)‡50
(Paid)‡1,800

**The Trimble Banner (11531)**
Landmark Community Newspapers Inc.
PO Box 289
Bedford, KY 40006-0289
Phone: (502)255-3205
Fax: (502)255-7797
**Subject(s):** Paid Community Newspapers
**Circ:** (Paid)‡1,800

**Twin City News (5867)**
Twin City News Inc.
PO Box 505
Chattahoochee, FL 32324
Phone: (850)663-2255
Fax: (850)663-8102
**Subject(s):** Paid Community Newspapers
**Circ:** ‡1,800

**The Graceville News (6058)**
PO Box 187
Graceville, FL 32440
Phone: (904)263-6015
Fax: (904)263-1042
**Subject(s):** Paid Community Newspapers
**Circ:** ‡1750

**The Richton Dispatch (17004)**
PO 429
110 Walnut Street
Richton, MS 39476-1521
Phone: (601)788-6031
Fax: (601)788-6031
**Subject(s):** Paid Community Newspapers
**Circ:** (Free)‡10
(Paid)‡1,750

**Meriwether-Vindicator (7274)**
Star Mercury Publishing Co.
PO Box 426
Manchester, GA 31816
Phone: (706)846-3188
Fax: (706)846-2206
**Subject(s):** Paid Community Newspapers
**Circ:** ‡1,700

**Savannah Jewish News (7397)**
Savannah Jewish Federation
PO Box 23527
Savannah, GA 31403-3527
Phone: (912)355-8111
Fax: (912)355-8116
**Subject(s):** Jewish Publications; Free Newspapers
**Circ:** ‡1,700

**The Headland Observer (192)**
The Dothan Progress
PO Box 1927
Dothan, AL 36302
Phone: (334)793-9586
Fax: (334)702-6043
**Subject(s):** Paid Community Newspapers
**Circ:** (Free)‡67
(Paid)‡1,683

**Gale Directory of Publications & Broadcast Media/140th Ed.**  **Southern States**

**Newspaper Index**

**The Mayo Free Press (5848)**
Mayo Tree Press
PO Box 248
705 North Suwannee Ave
Branford, FL 32008
Phone: (386)294-1210
Fax: (386)294-2666
**Subject(s):** Paid Community Newspapers
**Circ:** ‡1,650

**The Moore County News (28736)**
Moore County News
30 Hiles St.
PO Box 500
Lynchburg, TN 37352
Phone: (931)759-7302
**Subject(s):** Paid Community Newspapers
**Circ:** (Free)‡13
(Paid)‡1,600

**Cedar Key Beacon (5866)**
PO Box 532
Cedar Key, FL 32625-0532
Phone: (352)543-5701
Fax: (352)543-5928
**Subject(s):** Paid Community Newspapers; Travel and Tourism; (Hunting, Fishing, and Game Management)
**Circ:** (Controlled)1,500

**Deer Creek Pilot (17009)**
PO Box 398
Rolling Fork, MS 39159-0398
Phone: (662)873-4354
Fax: (662)873-4355
**Subject(s):** Paid Community Newspapers
**Circ:** ‡1,500

**Glades County Democrat (5883)**
626 W. Sugarland Hwy.
Clewiston, FL 33440
Phone: (863)946-0511
Fax: (863)983-9140
**Subject(s):** Paid Community Newspapers
**Circ:** ‡1,500

**The Sandspur (6750)**
Rollins College
1000 Holt Ave., 2749
Winter Park, FL 32789-4499
Phone: (407)646-2696
Fax: (407)646-1530
**Subject(s):** College Publications
**Circ:** 1,500

**The Santee Striper (27976)**
PO Box 929
Bamberg, SC 29003
Phone: (803)245-5204
Fax: (803)245-3900
**Subject(s):** Paid Community Newspapers
**Circ:** 1,500

**The Whitmire News (28256)**
Hometown News
194 Gilliam St.
PO Box 211
Whitmire, SC 29178
Phone: (803)694-4444
**Subject(s):** Paid Community Newspapers
**Circ:** ‡1,500

**Atkinson County Citizen (7353)**
Atkinson County Citizen Inc.
PO Box 398
Pearson, GA 31642
Phone: (912)422-3824
Fax: (912)422-6050
**Subject(s):** Paid Community Newspapers
**Circ:** (Free)‡53
(Paid)‡1,400

**Bowdon Bulletin (7037)**
PO Box 460
901 Hays Mail Road
Carrollton, GA 30112
Phone: (770)834-6631
Fax: (770)830-9425
**Subject(s):** Paid Community Newspapers
**Circ:** (Paid)1,400

**East Shelby Review (28995)**
Review
PO Box 519
Somerville, TN 38068
Phone: (901)465-4042
Fax: (901)465-5493
**Subject(s):** Free Newspapers
**Circ:** (Free)1,400

**Southern Advocate (16740)**
PO Box 157
Ashland, MS 38603
Phone: (662)224-6681
Fax: (662)224-6681
**Subject(s):** Paid Community Newspapers
**Circ:** 1,400

**Florida Star Times (6093)**
PO Box 40629
Jacksonville, FL 32203-0629
Phone: (904)766-8834
Fax: (904)765-1673
**Subject(s):** Black Publications
**Circ:** (Thurs.)1,399

**The Gulf County Breeze (6731)**
Breeze Publishing Co.
PO Box 1180
Wewahitchka, FL 32465
Phone: (850)639-4848
**Subject(s):** Free Newspapers
**Circ:** (Free)‡200
(Paid)‡1,300

**The Southern Herald (16930)**
Southern Herald
PO Box 674
Liberty, MS 39645
Phone: (601)657-4818
Fax: (601)657-4818
**Subject(s):** Paid Community Newspapers
**Circ:** (Free)‡30
(Paid)‡1,300

**The Fort Meade Leader (5976)**
Frisbie Publishing
25 W. Broadway
PO Box 893
Fort Meade, FL 33841
Phone: (941)285-8625
Fax: (941)285-7634
**Subject(s):** Paid Community Newspapers
**Circ:** ‡1,285

**Highland Echo (28746)**
Maryville College
502 E. Lamar Alexander Pkwy
Maryville, TN 37804
Phone: (865)981-8000
Fax: (865)981-8010
**Subject(s):** College Publications
**Circ:** (Free)1,250

**Patriot-Citizen (7361)**
Star Mercury Publishing Co.
PO Box 250
Richland, GA 31825-0250
Phone: (912)887-3674
**Subject(s):** Paid Community Newspapers
**Circ:** ‡1250

**Small Talk (23471)**
Methodist College
5400 Ramsey St.
Fayetteville, NC 28311
Phone: (910)630-7000
Fax: (910)630-2123
**Subject(s):** College Publications
**Circ:** (Free)‡1,200

**Conservative (17052)**
Montgomery Publishing Inc.
PO Box 151
Winona, MS 38967
Phone: (662)283-1131
Fax: (662)283-5374
**Subject(s):** Paid Community Newspapers
**Circ:** (Paid)‡1,183

**The Hogansville Herald (7272)**
Star Mercury Publishing Co.
PO Box 426
Manchester, GA 31816
Phone: (706)846-3188
Fax: (706)846-2206
**Subject(s):** Paid Community Newspapers
**Circ:** ‡1,150

**The Cannon (28760)**
Christian Brothers University
650 E Pkwy. S
P O Box T12
Memphis, TN 38104-5581
Phone: (901)321-3000
Fax: (901)321-3586
**Subject(s):** College Publications
**Circ:** (Free)‡1,100

**Levy County Journal (5850)**
440 S. Court St.
PO Box 159
Bronson, FL 32621
Phone: (352)486-2312
Fax: (352)486-5042
**Subject(s):** Paid Community Newspapers
**Circ:** (Paid)1,100

**Magnolia Gazette (16940)**
PO Box 152
280 Magnolia St.
Magnolia, MS 39652-0152
Phone: (601)783-2441
Fax: (601)783-2091
**Subject(s):** Paid Community Newspapers
**Circ:** (Paid)‡1,100

**The News & Banner (7163)**
The News & Banner Inc.
210 W Court Squire
PO Box 97
Franklin, GA 30217-0097
Phone: (706)675-3374
Fax: (706)675-3374
**Subject(s):** Paid Community Newspapers
**Circ:** 1,100

**The Wheeler County Eagle (6763)**
PO Box 409
Alamo, GA 30411-0409
Phone: (912)529-6624
Fax: (912)529-5399
**Subject(s):** Paid Community Newspapers
**Circ:** ‡1,081

**Free Press (6633)**
Free Press Publishing Co.
1010 Cass St.
Tampa, FL 33606
Phone: (813)254-5888
Fax: (813)251-0511
**Subject(s):** Paid Community Newspapers
**Circ:** ‡1,040

**The Collegiate (23860)**
Barton College
Box 5000
Wilson, NC 27893
Phone: (252)399-6300
**Subject(s):** College Publications
**Circ:** (Free)‡1,000

**Everglades Echo (5834)**
Tuff Publications Inc.
27200 Riverview Center Blvd., Ste. 107
Bonita Springs, FL 34134-4317
**Subject(s):** Paid Community Newspapers
**Circ:** 1,000

**Talbotton New Era (7443)**
PO Box 248
Talbotton, GA 31827
Phone: (404)846-3188
Fax: (706)846-2206
**Subject(s):** Paid Community Newspapers
**Circ:** ‡1,000

**The Weekly Herald (23839)**
PO Box 387
Williamston, NC 27892
Phone: (252)792-1181
Fax: (252)792-1921
**Subject(s):** Paid Community Newspapers
**Circ:** (Free)⊕21
(Paid)⊕951

**The Profile (7113)**
Agnes Scott College
141 E. College Ave.
Decatur, GA 30030
Phone: (404)471-6000
Fax: (404)471-6298

**Circulation:** ★ = ABC; △ = BPA; ♦ = CAC; • = CCAB; ▢ = VAC; ⊕ = PO Statement; ‡ = Publisher's Report; Boldface figures = sworn; Light figures = estimated.

**Western States**                                              Gale Directory of Publications & Broadcast Media/140th Ed.

Subject(s): College Publications

Circ: (Paid)‡75
      (Free)‡925

**North Trade Journal  (27975)**
Kilgus Publishing Co.
369 McGee St.
PO Box 929
Bamberg, SC 29003
Phone: (803)245-5204
Fax: (803)245-3900
Subject(s): Paid Community Newspapers

Circ: (Non-paid)⊕395
      (Paid)⊕905

**Burroughs Bulletin  (11805)**
Chicago Press Corp.
Burroughs Memorial Collection
University of Louisville Library
Louisville, KY 40292
Phone: (502)852-8729
Fax: (502)852-8734
Subject(s): Literature and Literary Reviews; Science Fiction, Mystery, Adventure, and Romance

Circ: (Paid)‡800

**Crawfordville Advocate-Democrat  (7093)**
The Herald Journal
Rte. 1
PO Box 124
Crawfordville, GA 30631
Phone: (706)453-7988
Fax: (706)453-2311
Subject(s): Paid Community Newspapers

Circ: (Free)10
      (Paid)790

**West Pasco Press  (6323)**
Suncoast News
6214 US Hwy. 19
New Port Richey, FL 34652
Phone: (727)815-1060
Fax: (727)847-2902
Subject(s): Paid Community Newspapers

Circ: (Paid)⊕712

**Advertiser  (28091)**
PO Box 628
Edgefield, SC 29824
Phone: (803)637-3540
Fax: (803)637-0602
Subject(s): Paid Community Newspapers

Circ: 500

**Falcon's Eye  (23641)**
Pfeiffer University
48380 U.S. Hwy. 52 N.
PO Box 960
Misenheimer, NC 28109
Phone: (704)463-1360
Fax: (704)463-1363
Subject(s): College Publications

Circ: 500

**The Dothan Progress  (191)**
PO Box 1927
Dothan, AL 36302
Phone: (334)793-9586
Fax: (334)702-6043
Subject(s): Free Newspapers

Circ: (Paid)361

**McKenzie Banner  (28750)**
Tri County Publishing Company Inc.
3 Banner Row
PO Box 100
Mc Kenzie, TN 38201-0100
Phone: (901)352-3323
Fax: (901)352-3322
Subject(s): Paid Community Newspapers

Circ: (Free)‡200

**The Leon County News  (5901)**
PO Box 307
Crawfordville, FL 32326-0307
Phone: (850)926-7102
Subject(s): Paid Community Newspapers

Circ: ‡100

3820

# Western States

**This Week  (7575)**
Gannett Company Inc.
274 Puuhale Rd., Ste. 200
Honolulu, HI 96819-2234
Phone: (808)843-6000
Fax: (808)843-6090
Subject(s): Free Newspapers

Circ: ‡30,000-44,000

**The Original Pennysaver  (1555)**
The Pennysaver
2830 Orbiter St.
Brea, CA 92821-6224
Phone: (714)996-8900
Fax: (714)993-4711
Subject(s): Shopping Guides

Circ: (Free)‡4,710,500

**USC Today  (4543)**
University of Southern Colorado
Dept. of Mass Communications
2200 Bonforte Blvd.
Pueblo, CO 81001-4901
Phone: (719)549-2100
Fax: (719)549-2120
Subject(s): College Publications

Circ: (Mon.-Thurs.)1,591,629
      (Fri.)2,008,940

**Los Angeles Times  (2260)**
202 W. 1st St.
Los Angeles, CA 90012
Phone: (213)237-7811
Fax: (213)237-7386
Subject(s): Daily Newspapers

Circ: (Mon.-Fri.)★925,135
      (Sat.)★1,006,130
      (Sun.)★1,376,932

**The Denver Post  (4283)**
1560 Broadway
Denver, CO 80202-1577
Phone: (303)820-1010
Subject(s): Daily Newspapers

Circ: (Mon.-Fri.)★275,292
      (Sat.)★595,512
      (Sun.)★750,593

**The Arizona Republic  (746)**
Phoenix Newspapers Inc.
200 E. Van Buren St.
Phoenix, AZ 85004-2238
Phone: (602)444-8000
Fax: (602)444-7363
Subject(s): Daily Newspapers

Circ: (Mon.-Fri.)448,518
      (Sat.)481,937
      (Sun.)562,656

**Rocky Mountain News  (4320)**
Scripps Howard
100 Gene Amole Way
Denver, CO 80204
Phone: (303)892-5000
Subject(s): Daily Newspapers

Circ: (Mon.-Sat.)446,465
      (Sun.)552,085

**San Francisco Chronicle  (3205)**
Hearst Corp.
901 Mission St.
San Francisco, CA 94103
Phone: (415)777-1111
Fax: (415)896-1107
Subject(s): Daily Newspapers

Circ: (Mon.-Fri.)★431,718
      (Sat.)★505,022
      (Sun.)★540,314

**Mundo L.A.  (3953)**
Latin Publications Inc.
7453 Woodley Ave.
Van Nuys, CA 91406
Phone: (818)882-9200
Fax: (818)882-7200
Subject(s): Free Newspapers

Circ: (Free)540,000

**Seattle Times  (32325)**
Knight-Ridder Inc.
1120 John St.
PO Box 70
Seattle, WA 98111
Phone: (206)464-2132
Fax: (206)382-6760
Subject(s): Daily Newspapers

Circ: (Sat.)214,501
      (Mon.-Fri.)225,222
      (Sun.)482,978

**Seattle Post-Intelligencer  (32324)**
101 Elliott Ave. W.
Seattle, WA 98119
Phone: (206)448-8000
Fax: (206)448-8166
Subject(s): Daily Newspapers

Circ: (Sat.)★131,536
      (Mon.-Fri.)★145,964
      (Sun.)★462,920

**The San Diego Union-Tribune  (3054)**
Union-Tribune Publishing Co.
PO Box 120191
San Diego, CA 92112-0191
Phone: (619)299-3131
Fax: (619)260-5081
Subject(s): Daily Newspapers

Circ: (Mon.-Sat.)374,133
      (Sun.)444,649

**Books  (3005)**
San Diego Union-Tribune
PO Box 120191
San Diego, CA 92112
Phone: (619)299-3131
Fax: (619)293-2436
Subject(s): Literature and Literary Reviews

Circ: ‡422,000

**Orange County Register  (3410)**
625 N Grand Ave.
Santa Ana, CA 92701
Subject(s): Daily Newspapers

Circ: (Mon.-Sat.)353,334
      (Sun.)410,207

**The Oregonian  (25970)**
Oregonian Publishing Co.
1320 S.W. Broadway
Portland, OR 97201
Phone: (503)221-8240
Fax: (503)227-5306
Subject(s): Daily Newspapers

Circ: (Sat.)★324,836
      (Mon.-Fri.)★337,707
      (Sun.)★405,295

**Wall Street Journal (Western Edition)  (3234)**
Dow Jones & Company Inc.
201 California St., Ste. 1350
San Francisco, CA 94111
Phone: (415)986-6886
Fax: (415)956-0797
Subject(s): Daily Newspapers; Business

Circ: (Mon.-Fri.)398,205

**Southern California Senior Life (Southern California Edition)  (2337)**
Senior Life
6500 Wilshire Blvd., Ste. 1200
Los Angeles, CA 90048
Phone: (323)782-6005
Fax: (323)651-2099
Subject(s): Senior Citizens' Interests

Circ: (Combined)375,000

**The Sacramento Bee  (2906)**
2100 Q St.
PO Box 15779
Sacramento, CA 95852
Phone: (916)321-1000
Fax: (916)321-1524
Subject(s): Daily Newspapers

Circ: (Mon.-Sat.)296,482
      (Sun.)351,999

**Motorist  (31999)**
AAA Washington
1745-114th Ave. SW
Bellevue, WA 98004
Phone: (425)462-2222
Fax: (425)646-2193

Numbers cited after listings are entry numbers rather than page numbers.

**Subject(s):** Travel and Tourism; Automotive (Consumer)
**Circ:** ‡330,000

**Southern California Senior Life (1789)**
Senior Life
2514 Jamacha Rd., No. 502-42
El Cajon, CA 92019
**Subject(s):** Senior Citizens' Interests
**Circ:** (Combined)‡325,000

**Little Nickel Classifieds (32146)**
3701 148th St. SW
Lynnwood, WA 98037
Phone: (425)742-7244
Fax: (425)743-5330
**Subject(s):** Shopping Guides
**Circ:** (Non-paid)‡320,000

**Investor's Business Daily (2231)**
12655 Beatrice St.
Los Angeles, CA 90066
Phone: (310)448-6700
Fax: (310)577-7301
**Subject(s):** Daily Newspapers; Banking, Finance, and Investments
**Circ:** (Mon.-Fri.)303,581

**San Jose Mercury News (3307)**
750 Ridder Park Dr.
San Jose, CA 95190-0001
Phone: (408)920-5000
Fax: (408)288-8060
**Subject(s):** Daily Newspapers
**Circ:** (Mon.-Sat.)★263,067
(Sun.)★298,067

**Arizona Senior World (901)**
7070 N. Oracle Rd., Ste. 260
Tucson, AZ 85704
Phone: (520)297-1220
Fax: (520)297-0704
**Subject(s):** Senior Citizens' Interests
**Circ:** (Paid)2,500
(Non-paid)297,500

**Charlotte Observer (3284)**
Knight-Ridder Inc.
50 W San Fernando St.
San Jose, CA 95113
Phone: (408)938-7700
**Subject(s):** Daily Newspapers
**Circ:** (Mon.-Sat.)241,071
(Sun.)294,605

**New Tucson Shopper (927)**
Shopper's Guide Inc.
1861 W. Grant Rd.
Tucson, AZ 85745
Phone: (602)622-0101
Fax: (602)622-9651
**Subject(s):** Shopping Guides
**Circ:** (Free)‡293,400

**La Guia Familiar (3952)**
Latin Publications Inc.
7453 Woodley Ave.
Van Nuys, CA 91406
Phone: (818)882-9200
Fax: (818)882-7200
**Subject(s):** Free Newspapers; Spanish; Hispanic Publications
**Circ:** (Free)‡242,375

**Las Vegas CityLife (18688)**
Las Vegas Press
1385 Pama Ln., Ste., 111
Las Vegas, NV 89119-3830
Phone: (702)871-6780
Fax: (702)940-1096
**Subject(s):** Paid Community Newspapers
**Circ:** (Combined)238,000

**Pennysaver (1556)**
Hart-Hanks Communications
2830, Orbiter St.
Brea, CA 92821
Phone: (714)996-8900
Fax: (714)993-4711
**Subject(s):** Shopping Guides
**Circ:** 220,000

**Las Vegas Review-Journal (18690)**
Community Newspaper Holdings Inc.
1111 W. Bonanza Rd.
PO Box 70
Las Vegas, NV 89125
Phone: (702)383-4676
Fax: (702)383-4676
**Subject(s):** Daily Newspapers
**Circ:** (Mon.-Fri.)★159,507
(Sat.)★182,171
(Sun.)★218,624

**Entertainment Today (1572)**
Best Publishing Inc.
2325 W. Victory Blvd.
Burbank, CA 91506
Phone: (818)566-4030
Fax: (818)566-4295
**Subject(s):** Entertainment; Music and Musical Instruments; Motion Pictures
**Circ:** ‡215,000

**San Francisco Independent (3207)**
988 Market St.
San Francisco, CA 94102
Phone: (415)826-1100
Fax: (415)359-2655
**Subject(s):** Free Newspapers
**Circ:** (Wed.)167,252
(Tues.)212,702

**L.A. Weekly (2249)**
6715 Sunset Blvd.
Los Angeles, CA 90028
Phone: (323)465-9909
Fax: (323)465-3220
**Subject(s):** Free Newspapers
**Circ:** (Paid)1,667
(Non-paid)210,240

**Daily News (4056)**
21221 Oxnard St.
PO Box 4200
Woodland Hills, CA 91367
Phone: (818)713-3000
**Subject(s):** Daily Newspapers
**Circ:** (Sat.)164,684
(Mon.-Fri.)190,010
(Sun.)200,419

**Akron Beacon Journal (3279)**
Knight-Ridder Inc.
50 W San Fernando St.
San Jose, CA 95113
Phone: (408)938-7700
**Subject(s):** Daily Newspapers
**Circ:** (Mon.-Sat.)135,002
(Sat.)172,761
(Sun.)193,641

**Contra Costa Times (4019)**
Hills Publications Inc.
2640 Shadelands Dr.
Walnut Creek, CA 94598-2578
Phone: (925)935-2525
**Subject(s):** Daily Newspapers
**Circ:** (Mon.-Sat.)★182,647
(Sun.)★193,640

**The Fresno Bee (1878)**
The McClatchy Co.
1626 E. St.
Fresno, CA 93786-0001
Phone: (559)441-6111
Fax: (559)441-6436
**Subject(s):** Daily Newspapers
**Circ:** (Mon.-Sat.)★158,286
(Sun.)★188,933

**The Arizona Daily Star (896)**
Lee Enterprises Inc.
4850 S. Park Ave.
Tucson, AZ 85714
**Subject(s):** Daily Newspapers
**Circ:** (Mon.-Sat.)102,960
(Sun.)187,003

**The Honolulu Advertiser (7550)**
News Bldg.
605 Kapiolani Blvd.
PO Box 3110
Honolulu, HI 96802
Phone: (808)525-8090
Fax: (808)525-8037

**Subject(s):** Daily Newspapers
**Circ:** (Mon.-Sat.)101,948
(Sun.)185,596

**Coachella Valley Sun (2664)**
Desert Sun Publishing Co.
PO Box 2734
Palm Springs, CA 92263
Phone: (760)322-8889
Fax: (760)778-4513
**Subject(s):** Paid Community Newspapers
**Circ:** 174,000

**Los Angeles Independent (2257)**
Equal Access Media Inc.
4201 Wilshire Blvd., Ste. 600
Los Angeles, CA 90010
Phone: (323)556-5720
Fax: (323)932-8250
**Subject(s):** Free Newspapers
**Circ:** (Paid)68
(Free)162,146

**The San Francisco Bay Guardian (3202)**
135 Mississippi St.
San Francisco, CA 94107-2536
Phone: (415)255-3100
Fax: (415)255-8955
**Subject(s):** Free Newspapers
**Circ:** (Paid)❏143
(Non-paid)160,758

**San Diego Reader (3050)**
1703 India St. (at Date St.)
Little Italy, downtown San Diego
PO Box 85803
San Diego, CA 92186-8580
Phone: (619)235-3000
Fax: (619)231-0489
**Subject(s):** Free Newspapers
**Circ:** (Free)160,000

**Southern California Senior Life (Los Angeles County Edition) (2335)**
Senior Life
6500 Wilshire Blvd., Ste. 1200
Los Angeles, CA 90048
Phone: (323)782-6005
Fax: (323)651-2099
**Subject(s):** Senior Citizens' Interests
**Circ:** (Combined)159,300

**California Legionnaire (1675)**
Concourse Communications
1175 Shaw Ave., Ste. 104
PMB 304
Clovis, CA 93612
Phone: (559)322-2215
Fax: (559)322-2219
**Subject(s):** Veterans
**Circ:** (Free)1,000
(Paid)153,800

**The Salt Lake Tribune (30782)**
Dominic Welch
143 S. Main St.
Salt Lake City, UT 84111
Phone: (801)257-8525
Fax: (801)257-8525
**Subject(s):** Daily Newspapers
**Circ:** (Mon.-Sat.)★133,025
(Sun.)★152,859

**Lexington Herald-Leader (3293)**
Knight-Ridder Inc.
50 W San Fernando St.
San Jose, CA 95113
Phone: (408)938-7700
**Subject(s):** Daily Newspapers
**Circ:** (Mon.-Thurs.)111,168
(Sat.)124,316
(Fri.)134,774
(Sun.)149,614

**The News Tribune (32439)**
The McClatchy Co.
PO Box 11000
Tacoma, WA 98411-0008
Fax: (253)597-8451
**Subject(s):** Daily Newspapers
**Circ:** (Mon.-Sat.)128,000
(Sun.)144,000

---

Circulation: ★ = ABC; △ = BPA; ♦ = CAC; • = CCAB; ❏ = VAC; ⊕ = PO Statement; ‡ = Publisher's Report; Boldface figures = sworn; Light figures = estimated.

# Western States

**Washington State University Hilltopics  (32218)**
Washington State University
PO Box 641040
Pullman, WA 99164-1040
Phone: (509)335-0932
Fax: (509)335-0932
**Subject(s):** College Publications

**Circ:**  ‡140,000

**Phoenix New Times  (770)**
New Times
1201 E. Jefferson
Phoenix, AZ 85034
Phone: (602)271-0040
Fax: (602)340-8806
**Subject(s):** Entertainment

**Circ:**  (Non-paid)130,979

**El Clasificado  (2194)**
1125 Goodrich Boulevard
Los Angeles, CA 90022
Phone: (323)278-5310
Fax: (323)278-5215
**Subject(s):** Free Newspapers; Spanish

**Circ:**  (Non-paid)130,000

**The Spokesman-Review  (32394)**
Cowles Publishing Co.
999 W Riverside Ave.
PO Box 2160
Spokane, WA 99210
Phone: (509)459-5000
Fax: (509)459-5258
**Subject(s):** Daily Newspapers

**Circ:**  (Mon.-Fri.)97,000
(Sat.)109,000
(Sun.)127,000

**La Opinion  (2248)**
Lozano Enterprises
411 W 5th St.
Los Angeles, CA 90013-1028
Phone: (213)622-8332
Fax: (213)896-2151
**Subject(s):** Daily Newspapers; Spanish; Hispanic Publications

**Circ:**  (Sun.)72,601
(Sat.)102,473
(Mon.-Fri.)126,189

**The California Veteran  (2879)**
Veterans of Foreign Wars of the U.S.
1510 J St., Ste. 110
Sacramento, CA 95814-2097
Phone: (916)449-8850
Fax: (916)449-8832
**Subject(s):** Veterans

**Circ:**  120,000

**San Diego Family Magazine  (3047)**
1475 6th Ave., 5th Fl.
San Diego, CA 92101-3200
Phone: (619)685-6970
Fax: (619)685-6978
**Subject(s):** Marriage and Family; Education

**Circ:**  (Paid)‡143
(Free)‡119,862

**The Tribune  (715)**
Thomson Newspapers
120 W. 1st Ave.
Mesa, AZ 85210
Phone: (480)898-6500
Fax: (480)898-6463
**Subject(s):** Daily Newspapers

**Circ:**  (Mon.-Sat.)109,786
(Sun.)110,679

**Press-Telegram  (3304)**
Knight-Ridder Inc.
50 W San Fernando St.
San Jose, CA 95113
Phone: (408)938-7700
**Subject(s):** Daily Newspapers

**Circ:**  (Sat.)87,688
(Mon.-Fri.)99,372
(Sun.)110,033

**South Bay Extra  (3913)**
Daily Breeze
5215 Torrance Blvd.
Torrance, CA 90503-4077
Phone: (310)540-4141
Fax: (310)540-6272

**Subject(s):** Free Newspapers

**Circ:**  (Non-paid)109,515

**The Catholic Sun  (762)**
Roman Catholic Diocese of Phoenix
PO Box 13549
Phoenix, AZ 85002-3549
**Subject(s):** Religious Publications

**Circ:**  (Paid)108,579

**Ventura County Star (Camarillo Edition)  (3978)**
Ventura County Star
PO Box 6711
Ventura, CA 93006
Fax: (805)482-8631
**Subject(s):** Daily Newspapers

**Circ:**  (Mon.-Fri.)94,836
(Sun.)107,441

**San Francisco Examiner  (3206)**
450 Mission St.
San Francisco, CA 94105
Phone: (415)826-1100
Fax: (415)359-2655
**Subject(s):** Daily Newspapers

**Circ:**  (Sat.)78,312
(Mon.-Fri.)107,129

**Miami New Times  (32290)**
New Times
3600 15th Ave. W Ste. 200
Seattle, WA 98119-1330
Phone: (206)320-7788
Fax: (206)320-7717
**Subject(s):** Free Newspapers; Entertainment

**Circ:**  (Paid)33
(Non-paid)106,692

**Ventura County Star  (3977)**
5250 Ralston St.
Ventura, CA 93003
Phone: (805)650-2900
Fax: (805)650-2950
**Subject(s):** Daily Newspapers

**Circ:**  (Tues.)★76,111
(Mon.)★90,695
(Sat.)★98,550
(Sun.)★105,506

**Monterey Park Comet  (1694)**
Eastern Group Publications Inc.
2500 S Atlantic Blvd., Bldg. A
Commerce, CA 90040
Phone: (323)263-5743
Fax: (323)263-9169
**Subject(s):** Free Newspapers; Spanish; Hispanic Publications

**Circ:**  (Paid)23
(Free)104,000

**Chinese L.A. Daily News  (1804)**
9639 Telstar Ave.
El Monte, CA 91731
Phone: (626)453-8800
Fax: (626)453-8822
**Subject(s):** Paid Community Newspapers; Chinese; Ethnic Publications

**Circ:**  (Combined)103,000

**Auto News of America  (31995)**
1075 Bel-Way NE, Ste. 606
Bellevue, WA 98004
Phone: (206)998-1247
Fax: (425)462-1163
**Subject(s):** Automotive (Consumer)

**Circ:**  100,000

**The Classified Flea Market  (2583)**
Classified Flea Market
6001 Telegraph Ave.
Oakland, CA 94609
Phone: (510)420-1972
Fax: (510)420-1919
**Subject(s):** Shopping Guides

**Circ:**  (Combined)100,000

**North County Times  (1830)**
207 E Pennsylvania Ave.
Escondido, CA 92025
Phone: (619)745-6611
Fax: (619)745-8809
**Subject(s):** Daily Newspapers

**Circ:**  (Mon.-Sat.)★93,051
(Sun.)★97,204

**The Modesto Bee  (2480)**
The McClatchy Co.
1325 H St.
Modesto, CA 95354
Phone: (209)578-2028
Fax: (209)578-2207
**Subject(s):** Daily Newspapers

**Circ:**  (Mon.-Sat.)★87,366
(Sun.)★93,259

**Sacramento News & Review  (2912)**
News & Review
1015 20th St.
Sacramento, CA 95814
Phone: (916)498-1234
Fax: (916)498-7910
**Subject(s):** Paid Community Newspapers

**Circ:**  (Combined)93,000

**The Press Democrat  (3498)**
PO Box 910
Santa Rosa, CA 95402
Phone: (707)546-7538
Fax: (800)675-5056
**Subject(s):** Daily Newspapers

**Circ:**  (Mon.-Sat.)★88,836
(Sun.)★92,192

**The North County Times  (2612)**
Howard Publications Inc.
PO Box 90
Oceanside, CA 92049-0090
Phone: (714)433-7333
**Subject(s):** Daily Newspapers

**Circ:**  (Mon.-Sat.)89,754
(Sun.)91,110

**Record Weekly  (3567)**
The Record
530 East Market St.
PO Box 900
Stockton, CA 95201
Phone: (209)546-8238
Fax: (209)547-8180
**Subject(s):** Free Newspapers

**Circ:**  (Free)88,246

**Willamette Week  (25989)**
822 S.W. 10th Ave.
Portland, OR 97205
Phone: (503)243-2122
Fax: (503)243-1115
**Subject(s):** Free Newspapers

**Circ:**  (Paid)124
(Free)87,500

**The Idaho Statesman  (7651)**
Gannett Company Inc.
1200 N. Curtis Rd.
PO Box 40
Boise, ID 83707
Phone: (208)377-6200
Fax: (800)635-8934
**Subject(s):** Daily Newspapers

**Circ:**  (Mon.-Sat.)‡64,526
(Sun.)‡87,188

**Chinese Daily News,Inc  (2510)**
Chinese Daily News Inc.
1588 Corporate Center Dr.
Monterey Park, CA 91754
Phone: (323)268-4982
Fax: (323)265-3476
**Subject(s):** Daily Newspapers; Chinese

**Circ:**  ‡85,000

**Metroactive  (3296)**
Metro Publishing Inc.
550 S 1st St.
San Jose, CA 95113
Phone: (408)298-8000
Fax: (408)298-0602
**Subject(s):** Free Newspapers

**Circ:**  (Free)85,000

**Anchorage Daily News  (496)**
1001 Northway Dr.
Anchorage, AK 99508
Phone: (907)257-4200
Fax: (907)279-8170
**Subject(s):** Daily Newspapers

**Circ:**  (Mon.-Sat.)69,037
(Fri.)79,378
(Sun.)84,275

**Eagle Newspaper  (30666)**
Spectrum Press
1370 S 500 W
Bountiful, UT 84010
Phone: (801)292-1088
Fax: (801)261-5623
**Subject(s):** Paid Community Newspapers

Circ: (Combined)‡83,000

**The Reno Gazette-Journal  (18744)**
Gannett Company Inc.
955 Kuenzli St.
PO Box 22000
Reno, NV 89520
Phone: (775)788-6200
Fax: (702)788-6458
**Subject(s):** Daily Newspapers

Circ: (Mon.-Sat.)★66,409
(Sun.)★82,745

**The Catholic Voice  (2582)**
3014 Lakeshore Ave.
Oakland, CA 94610-3615
Phone: (510)893-5339
Fax: (510)893-4734
**Subject(s):** Religious Publications

Circ: (Free)500
(Paid)82,500

**The Journal—Lynnwood Edition  (32145)**
Journal Newspapers
4610 200th St. SW, Ste. F
Lynnwood, WA 98036-6606
Phone: (425)775-2400
Fax: (425)670-0511
**Subject(s):** Local, State, and Regional Publications; Free Newspapers

Circ: (Free)‡82,000

**The Journal—North Seattle Edition  (32172)**
Journal Newspapers
4610 200th St. SW, Ste. F
Lynnwood, WA 98036-6606
Phone: (425)775-2400
Fax: (425)670-0511
**Subject(s):** Paid Community Newspapers

Circ: (Paid)82,000

**The Journal—Northgate Edition  (32173)**
Journal Newspapers
4610 200th St. SW, Ste. F
Lynnwood, WA 98036-6606
Phone: (425)775-2400
Fax: (425)670-0511
**Subject(s):** Local, State, and Regional Publications; Free Newspapers

Circ: (Combined)‡82,000

**Weekend Balita  (1934)**
Balita Media Inc.
520 E. Wilson Blvd., Ste. 115
Glendale, CA 91206
Phone: (818)552-4503
Fax: (818)552-4592
**Subject(s):** Paid Community Newspapers; Ethnic Publications

Circ: (Combined)80,000

**The San Bernardino County Sun  (2986)**
399 N D St.
San Bernardino, CA 92401-1518
Phone: (909)889-9666
Fax: (909)381-3976
**Subject(s):** Daily Newspapers

Circ: (Sat.)★69,106
(Mon.-Fri.)★71,934
(Sun.)★79,286

**The Register-Guard  (25811)**
Guard Publishing Co.
3500 Chad Dr., 97408
PO Box 10188
Eugene, OR 97440-2188
Phone: (541)485-1234
Fax: (541)984-4699
**Subject(s):** Daily Newspapers

Circ: (Mon.-Fri.)★70,794
(Sun.)★75,460
(Sat.)★79,266

**The Stranger  (32334)**
Loaded-for-Bear Publishing
1535 11th Ave., 3rd Fl.
Seattle, WA 98122
Phone: (206)323-7101
Fax: (206)323-7203
**Subject(s):** Free Newspapers

Circ: (Paid)53
(Non-paid)79,167

**Daily Breeze  (3900)**
5215 Torrance Blvd.
Torrance, CA 90503-4077
Phone: (310)540-4141
Fax: (310)540-6272
**Subject(s):** Daily Newspapers

Circ: (Sun.)76,907
(Mon.-Sat.)78,983

**The Record  (3566)**
530 E. Market St.
Stockton, CA 95202-3009
**Subject(s):** Daily Newspapers

Circ: (Mon.-Thurs.)66,277
(Sat.)70,919
(Fri.)70,919
(Sun.)77,704

**Lovin' Life News  (18694)**
Nevada Senior World
1516 E. Tropicana Ave., Ste. 105
Las Vegas, NV 89119-6526
Phone: (702)367-6709
Fax: (702)367-6883
**Subject(s):** Senior Citizens' Interests; Paid Community Newspapers

Circ: (Combined)75,875

**El Observador  (3286)**
99 North 1st St., Ste. 100
San Jose, CA 95113-1203
Phone: (408)938-1700
Fax: (408)938-1705
**Subject(s):** Free Newspapers; Spanish; Hispanic Publications

Circ: (Paid)451
(Free)75,549

**The Pet Companion  (2601)**
3871 Piedmont Ave.
Oakland, CA 94611
Phone: (510)533-7777
Fax: (510)533-7571
**Subject(s):** Paid Community Newspapers; Pets

Circ: (Controlled)75,200

**Inland Valley Daily Bulletin  (2621)**
California Newspaper Partnership DBA
2041 E. 4th St.
Ontario, CA 91764
Phone: (909)987-6397
Fax: (909)466-0235
**Subject(s):** Daily Newspapers

Circ: (Mon.-Fri.)68,073
(Sat.)69,370
(Sun.)75,143

**The Skanner  (25982)**
Skanner Group Inc.
415 N. Killingsworth St.
Portland, OR 97217
Phone: (503)285-5555
Fax: (503)285-2900
**Subject(s):** Paid Community Newspapers; Black Publications

Circ: (Paid)‡75,000

**The Bakersfield Californian  (1403)**
PO Box BIN 440
Bakersfield, CA 93302
Phone: (661)395-7500
Fax: (661)395-7519
**Subject(s):** Daily Newspapers

Circ: (Mon.-Sat.)★62,278
(Sun.)★74,173

**Deseret News  (30764)**
Deseret News Publishing Co.
30 E. 100 S.
PO Box 1257
Salt Lake City, UT 84110
**Subject(s):** Daily Newspapers

Circ: (Mon.-Sat.)★72,008
(Sun.)★73,601

**Duluth News Tribune  (3285)**
Knight-Ridder Inc.
50 W San Fernando St.
San Jose, CA 95113
Phone: (408)938-7700

**Subject(s):** Daily Newspapers

Circ: (Mon.-Sat.)47,718
(Sun.)71,719

**East Bay Guardian  (3132)**
The San Francisco Bay Guardian
135 Mississippi St.
San Francisco, CA 94107-2536
Phone: (415)255-3100
Fax: (415)255-8955
**Subject(s):** Paid Community Newspapers

Circ: (Paid)2,000
(Non-paid)70,000

**Mean Street  (4042)**
6747-A Greenleaf Ave.
Whittier, CA 90601
Phone: (562)789-9455
Fax: (562)789-9925
**Subject(s):** Free Newspapers

Circ: (Free)70,000

**O.C. Weekly  (3409)**
O.C. Weekly Media Inc.
1666 N. Main St., Ste. 500
Santa Ana, CA 92701-7417
Phone: (714)550-5950
Fax: (714)550-5903
**Subject(s):** Free Newspapers

Circ: (Paid)2
(Non-paid)70,000

**Union Jack  (2044)**
Union Jack Publishing
PO Box 1823
La Mesa, CA 91944-1823
Phone: (619)466-3129
Fax: (619)337-1103
**Subject(s):** Intercultural Interests; Paid Community Newspapers

Circ: (Paid)10,500
(Free)70,000

**The Oakland Tribune  (2600)**
ANG Newspapers
Tribune Tower
401 13th St.
Oakland, CA 94612
Phone: (510)208-6300
**Subject(s):** Daily Newspapers

Circ: (Sat.)★51,994
(Sun.)★65,701
(Mon.-Fri.)★69,135

**Post-Tribune  (3302)**
Knight-Ridder Inc.
50 W San Fernando St.
San Jose, CA 95113
Phone: (408)938-7700
**Subject(s):** Daily Newspapers

Circ: (Mon.-Sat.)61,476
(Sun.)67,343

**Honolulu Star-Bulletin  (7552)**
Midweek Printing Co.
500 Ala Moana Blvd., 7-210
Honolulu, HI 96813
Phone: (808)529-4750
Fax: (808)529-4750
**Subject(s):** Daily Newspapers

Circ: (Mon.-Sun.)66,000

**Newport Beach/Costa Mesa Daily Pilot  (1725)**
California Community News Corp.
330 W Bay St.
PO Box 1560
Costa Mesa, CA 92627
Phone: (714)966-4600
**Subject(s):** Daily Newspapers

Circ: (Paid)381
(Free)65,520

**The Log (Los Angeles/Ventura County Edition)  (3034)**
The Log Newspapers
4918 North Harbor Drive, Ste. 201
San Diego, CA 92106
Phone: (619)226-1608
Fax: (619)226-0573
**Subject(s):** (Boating and Yachting)

Circ: (Combined)⊕65,000

Circulation: ★ = ABC; △ = BPA; ◆ = CAC; ● = CCAB; ▫ = VAC; ⊕ = PO Statement; ‡ = Publisher's Report; Boldface figures = sworn; Light figures = estimated.

**Standard-Examiner (30714)**
Ogden Publishing Corp.
332 Standard Way
PO Box 12790
Ogden, UT 84412-2790
Phone: (801)625-4200
Fax: (801)625-4508
**Subject(s):** Daily Newspapers

**Circ:** (Mon.-Sat.)★60,884
(Sun.)★63,649

**Vida Nueva (2366)**
The Tidings Corp.
3424 Wilshire Blvd., 6th Fl.
Los Angeles, CA 90010
Phone: (213)637-7360
Fax: (213)637-6360
**Subject(s):** Free Newspapers

**Circ:** (Free)❑63,584

**Oakland Post (2599)**
405 14th St., Ste. 400
Oakland, CA 94604
Phone: (510)287-8200
Fax: (510)287-8220
**Subject(s):** Free Newspapers; Black Publications

**Circ:** (Free)‡62,496

**Statesman Journal (26050)**
280 Church St. N.E.
PO Box 13009
Salem, OR 97301
Phone: (503)399-6611
Fax: (503)399-6808
**Subject(s):** Daily Newspapers

**Circ:** (Mon.-Sat.)★53,366
(Sun.)★61,653

**Easy Reader/Redondo Beach Hometown News (1965)**
832 Hermosa Ave.
PO Box 427
Hermosa Beach, CA 90254
Phone: (310)372-4611
Fax: (310)318-6292
**Subject(s):** Paid Community Newspapers

**Circ:** (Combined)61,198

**Classified Gazette (3383)**
The Classified Gazette Inc.
716 4th St.
San Rafael, CA 94901
Phone: (415)457-4888
Fax: (415)457-5731
**Subject(s):** Shopping Guides

**Circ:** (Free)‡60,000

**Compton Metropolitan Gazette (1699)**
First-Line Publishers/L.A. Metro Group
14621 Titus St., Ste. 228
Van Nuys, CA 91402
Phone: (818)782-8695
Fax: (818)782-2924
**Subject(s):** Free Newspapers; Black Publications

**Circ:** (Free)60,000

**El Bohemio News (3135)**
4178 Mission St.
San Francisco, CA 94112
Phone: (415)469-9579
Fax: (415)469-9481
**Subject(s):** Paid Community Newspapers; Hispanic Publications; Spanish

**Circ:** (Free)60,000

**Las Vegas Weekly (18692)**
Radiant City Publications L.L.C.
PO Box 230657
Las Vegas, NV 89123-0011
Phone: (702)990-2416
**Subject(s):** Paid Community Newspapers

**Circ:** (Free)60,000

**Long Beach Express (2094)**
First-Line Publishers/L.A. Metro Group
14621 Titus St., Ste. 228
Van Nuys, CA 91402
Phone: (818)782-8695
Fax: (818)782-2924
**Subject(s):** Free Newspapers; Black Publications

**Circ:** (Free)60,000

**Nifty Nickel (18699)**
909 W Bonanza Rd.
Las Vegas, NV 89106-3528
Phone: (702)224-5555

Fax: (702)224-5501
**Subject(s):** Shopping Guides

**Circ:** (Non-paid)60,000

**Pasadena Gazette (2717)**
First-Line Publishers/L.A. Metro Group
14621 Titus St., Ste. 228
Van Nuys, CA 91402
Phone: (818)782-8695
Fax: (818)782-2924
**Subject(s):** Free Newspapers; Black Publications

**Circ:** (Free)60,000

**San Fernando Gazette Express (2649)**
First-Line Publishers/L.A. Metro Group
14621 Titus St., Ste. 228
Van Nuys, CA 91402
Phone: (818)782-8695
Fax: (818)782-2924
**Subject(s):** Free Newspapers; Black Publications

**Circ:** (Free)60,000

**The Columbian (32461)**
The Columbian Publishing Co.
701 W. 8th St.
PO Box 180
Vancouver, WA 98666
Phone: (360)694-3391
Fax: (360)737-4074
**Subject(s):** Daily Newspapers

**Circ:** (Mon.-Sat.)★49,488
(Sun.)★59,005

**Bradenton Herald (3283)**
Knight-Ridder Inc.
50 W San Fernando St.
San Jose, CA 95113
Phone: (408)938-7700
**Subject(s):** Daily Newspapers

**Circ:** (Mon.-Sat.)48,197
(Sun.)56,930

**The Sun Herald (3311)**
Knight-Ridder Inc.
50 W San Fernando St.
San Jose, CA 95113
Phone: (408)938-7700
**Subject(s):** Daily Newspapers

**Circ:** (Mon.-Sat.)48,844
(Sun.)56,643

**The Herald (32088)**
1213 California St Everett
PO Box 930
Everett, WA 98206
Phone: (425)339-3000
Fax: (425)339-3049
**Subject(s):** Daily Newspapers

**Circ:** (Mon.-Sat.)51,727
(Sun.)56,531

**Ahwatukee Foothills News (736)**
Ahwautkee Foothills News
10631 S. 51st St., Ste. 1
Phoenix, AZ 85044
Phone: (480)898-7900
Fax: (480)893-1684
**Subject(s):** Paid Community Newspapers

**Circ:** (Controlled)56,000

**Precinct Reporter (2982)**
1677 W Baseline St.
San Bernardino, CA 92411
Phone: (909)889-0597
Fax: (909)889-1706
**Subject(s):** Paid Community Newspapers; Black Publications

**Circ:** ‡55,000

**Psychic Reader (1512)**
Deja Vu Publishing
2018 Allston Way
Berkeley, CA 94704
Phone: (510)644-1600
Fax: (510)644-1686
**Subject(s):** Paid Community Newspapers; New Age

**Circ:** (Free)55,000

**Tucson Weekly (941)**
The Tucson Weekly Inc.
PO Box 27087
Tucson, AZ 85726-7087
Phone: (520)792-3630
Fax: (520)792-2096

**Subject(s):** Free Newspapers

**Circ:** (Paid)52
(Free)55,000

**La Oferta Review (3292)**
1376 N Fourth St.
San Jose, CA 95112
Phone: (408)436-7850
Fax: (408)436-7861
**Subject(s):** Paid Community Newspapers; Hispanic Publications; Spanish

**Circ:** 54,915

**Saddleback Valley News (2063)**
The Orange County Register
22481 Aspan St.
Lake Forest, CA 92630
**Subject(s):** Free Newspapers

**Circ:** ‡53,411

**The Pueblo Chieftain (4541)**
PO Box 4040
Pueblo, CO 81003
Phone: (719)544-3520
Fax: (719)546-3235
**Subject(s):** Daily Newspapers

**Circ:** (Mon.-Sat.)★50,779
(Sun.)★53,211

**The Billings Gazette (18066)**
PO Box 36300
Billings, MT 59107-6300
Phone: (406)657-1212
Fax: (406)657-1345
**Subject(s):** Daily Newspapers

**Circ:** (Mon.-Sat.)★47,105
(Sun.)★52,434

**Laughlin Nevada Entertainer (639)**
News West Publishing Co.
PO Box 21209
Bullhead City, AZ 86439
Phone: (928)763-2505
**Subject(s):** Free Newspapers; Local, State, and Regional Publications; Entertainment

**Circ:** (Combined)52,000

**San Gabriel Valley Tribune (4026)**
San Gabriel Newspaper Group
1210 N. Azusa Canyon Rd.
West Covina, CA 91790
**Subject(s):** Daily Newspapers

**Circ:** (Sat.)★48,612
(Mon.-Fri.)★48,920
(Sun.)★51,522

**The Beach Reporter (2432)**
Equal Access Media Inc.
400 S. Sepleveda Blvd., Ste. 247
Manhattan Beach, CA 90266
Phone: (310)372-0388
Fax: (310)372-6605
**Subject(s):** Free Newspapers

**Circ:** (Free)50,915

**AsianWeek (3109)**
Pan Asia Venture Capital Corp.
809 Sacramento St.
San Francisco, CA 94108
Phone: (415)397-0220
Fax: (415)397-7258
**Subject(s):** Ethnic Publications

**Circ:** (Paid)4,066
(Free)‡50,000

**General Aviation News (32130)**
Flyer Media Inc.
5611 76th St. W
PO Box 39099
Lakewood, WA 98439-0099
Phone: (253)471-9888
Fax: (253)471-9911
**Subject(s):** Aviation

**Circ:** (Paid)‡50,000

**The Manila Bulletin USA (3547)**
362 E Grand Ave.
South San Francisco, CA 94080
Phone: (650)876-0410
Fax: (650)873-4335
**Subject(s):** Free Newspapers; Ethnic Publications

**Circ:** (Combined)50,000

## Western States

**Novedades (2290)**
John DiCarlo
1241 Soto St., Ste. 213
Los Angeles, CA 90023
Phone: (323)881-6515
Fax: (323)881-6524
**Subject(s):** Paid Community Newspapers; Spanish; Entertainment; Motion Pictures; Radio, Television, Cable, and Video
**Circ:** (Combined)50,000

**SWEAT Magazine (882)**
SWEAT Marketing
736 E. Loyola Dr.
Tempe, AZ 85282
Phone: (480)968-3555
Fax: (480)968-3555
**Subject(s):** Free Newspapers; (General Sports)
**Circ:** (Paid)100
(Free)50,000

**World Reporter (2378)**
4515 Eagle Rook Bldg.
Los Angeles, CA 90041
Phone: (323)344-3530
Fax: (323)344-3501
**Subject(s):** Free Newspapers; Ethnic Publications
**Circ:** (Combined)50,000

**Sacramento Observer (2913)**
Observer Newspapers
2330 Alhambra Blvd.
Sacramento, CA 95817
Phone: (916)452-4781
Fax: (916)452-7744
**Subject(s):** Paid Community Newspapers; Black Publications
**Circ:** ‡49,090

**Cover Story (2686)**
Antelope Valley Newspapers Inc.
37404 Sierra Hwy.
PO Box 4050
Palmdale, CA 93590-4050
Phone: (661)273-2700
Fax: (661)947-4870
**Subject(s):** Free Newspapers
**Circ:** (Non-paid)48,831

**Salt Lake City Weekly (30780)**
Coppersfield Publishing Inc.
248 S. Main St.
Salt Lake City, UT 84101
Phone: (801)575-7003
Fax: (801)575-6106
**Subject(s):** Entertainment; Local, State, and Regional Publications
**Circ:** (Paid)210
(Non-paid)48,761

**Vecinos del Valle (4070)**
Daily News of Los Angeles
21221 Oxnard St.
Woodland Hills, CA 91367
**Subject(s):** Hispanic Publications; Free Newspapers
**Circ:** (Free)48,371

**The Desert Sun (2666)**
Gannett Company Inc.
750 N. Gene Autry Tr.
PO Box 190
Palm Springs, CA 92263
Phone: (619)332-8889
Fax: (619)778-4654
**Subject(s):** Daily Newspapers
**Circ:** (Mon.-Sat.)46,109
(Sun.)48,234

**Santa Barbara News-Press (3427)**
715 Anacapa St.
Santa Barbara, CA 93101-1359
Phone: (805)564-5200
Fax: (805)966-6258
**Subject(s):** Daily Newspapers
**Circ:** (Mon.-Sat.)44,600
(Sun.)47,902

**Moneysaver (Lewiston) (7723)**
Triad News Publishing Inc.
626 Thain Rd.
PO Box 682
Lewiston, ID 83501
Phone: (208)746-0483
Fax: (208)746-0483
**Subject(s):** Shopping Guides
**Circ:** (Free)47,584

**Diocese of Orange Bulletin (2627)**
Diocese of Orange
Marywood Ctr.
2811 E Villa Real Dr.
Orange, CA 92867-1999
Phone: (714)282-3000
Fax: (714)282-3029
**Subject(s):** Religious Publications
**Circ:** (Free)47,100

**Los Angeles Downtown News (2256)**
1264 W. 1st St.
Los Angeles, CA 90026
Phone: (213)481-1448
Fax: (213)250-4617
**Subject(s):** Free Newspapers
**Circ:** (Free)47,000

**Valley Times (2750)**
Hills Publications Inc.
127 Spring St.
PO Box 607
Pleasanton, CA 94566
Phone: (510)847-2111
Fax: (510)847-2189
**Subject(s):** Daily Newspapers
**Circ:** (Mon.-Sat.)44,354
(Sun.)46,559

**The News-Sentinel (3299)**
Knight-Ridder Inc.
50 W San Fernando St.
San Jose, CA 95113
Phone: (408)938-7700
**Subject(s):** Daily Newspapers
**Circ:** (Mon.-Sat.)46,023

**The Beverly Hills Courier (1529)**
8840 W Olympic Blvd.
Beverly Hills, CA 90211
Phone: (213)278-1322
Fax: (213)271-5118
**Subject(s):** Paid Community Newspapers
**Circ:** (Paid)‡2,930
(Free)‡46,000

**Tri-City Weekly (1835)**
V & P Publishing Company Inc.
PO Box 134
Eureka, CA 95502
Phone: (707)443-5672
Fax: (707)443-5022
**Subject(s):** Shopping Guides
**Circ:** (Combined)❏45,818

**Southern California Senior Life (Orange County Edition) (2336)**
Senior Life
6500 Wilshire Blvd., Ste. 1200
Los Angeles, CA 90048
Phone: (323)782-6005
Fax: (323)651-2099
**Subject(s):** Senior Citizens' Interests
**Circ:** (Combined)45,700

**Inglewood/Hawthorne Wave (2227)**
Wave Newspaper Group
4201 Wilshire Ave., Ste. 600
Los Angeles, CA 90010
Phone: (323)556-5720
Fax: (323)556-5704
**Subject(s):** Free Newspapers; Black Publications
**Circ:** (Non-paid)45,453

**The Olympian (32177)**
Gannett Company Inc.
The Olympian
111 Bethel Street NE
Olympia, WA 98506
**Subject(s):** Daily Newspapers
**Circ:** (Mon.-Sat.)37,968
(Sun.)45,291

**Tri-City Herald (32456)**
PO Box 2608
Tri-Cities, WA 99302-2608
Phone: (509)582-1500
Fax: (509)582-1453
**Subject(s):** Daily Newspapers
**Circ:** (Mon.-Sat.)★41,666
(Sun.)★45,139

**Marinscope Community Newspaper (3509)**
Marin Scope Community Newspapers Inc.
1050 Bridgeway
Sausalito, CA 94965
Phone: (415)332-3778
Fax: (415)332-8714
**Subject(s):** Paid Community Newspapers
**Circ:** (Combined)45,000

**Miniondas (3408)**
Velazquez Publishing Inc.
2025 S. Main St.
Santa Ana, CA 92707
Phone: (714)668-1009
Fax: (714)668-1013
**Subject(s):** Free Newspapers
**Circ:** (Paid)5
(Free)45,000

**Grunion Gazette (2091)**
Gazette Newspapers Inc.
5225 E Second St.
Long Beach, CA 90803
Phone: (562)433-2000
Fax: (562)434-8826
**Subject(s):** Free Newspapers
**Circ:** (Paid)60
(Free)44,500

**Tri-Valley Herald (2749)**
4770 Willow Rd., No. 697
Pleasanton, CA 94588-2762
Phone: (925)416-4822
Fax: (925)416-4850
**Subject(s):** Daily Newspapers
**Circ:** (Sat.)★34,603
(Mon.-Fri.)★43,702
(Sun.)★44,329

**Honolulu Weekly (7553)**
Honolulu Weekly Inc.
1200 College Walk, Ste. 214
Honolulu, HI 96817
Phone: (808)528-1475
Fax: (808)528-3144
**Subject(s):** Free Newspapers
**Circ:** (Paid)48
(Free)43,786

**Daily Camera (Boulder) (4112)**
Scripps Howard Inc.
1048 Pearl
Boulder, CO 80302
Phone: (303)442-1202
Fax: (303)442-1508
**Subject(s):** Daily Newspapers
**Circ:** (Mon.-Sat.)34,927
(Sun.)43,572

**The San Luis Obispo County Telegram Tribune (3340)**
Knight-Ridder Inc.
3825 S. Higuera St.
PO Box 112
San Luis Obispo, CA 93406-0112
Phone: (805)781-7905
Fax: (800)456-8449
**Subject(s):** Daily Newspapers
**Circ:** (Mon.-Sat.)38,048
(Sun.)43,213

**Super Shopper (986)**
The Yuma Daily Sun
2055 S Arizona Ave.
Yuma, AZ 85364
Phone: (928)783-3333
Fax: (928)343-1009
**Subject(s):** Shopping Guides
**Circ:** (Non-paid)♦43,066

**Psychiatric Times (3193)**
CMP Media L.L.C.
600 Harrison St.
San Francisco, CA 94107
Phone: (415)538-8800
Fax: (415)947-6055
**Subject(s):** Psychology and Psychiatry
**Circ:** (Controlled)‡42,583

**South County Journal (32121)**
PO Box 130
Kent, WA 98035
Phone: (253)872-6600
Fax: (253)854-1006

---

Circulation: ★ = ABC; △ = BPA; ♦ = CAC; • = CCAB; ❏ = VAC; ⊕ = PO Statement; ‡ = Publisher's Report; Boldface figures = sworn; Light figures = estimated.

# Western States

**Subject(s):** Daily Newspapers
**Circ:** (Sun.)★41,671
(Mon.-Sat.)★42,042

**The Argonaut (2435)**
The Argonaut Inc.
PO Box 11209
Marina del Rey, CA 90295-7209
Phone: (310)822-1629
Fax: (310)822-2089
**Subject(s):** Free Newspapers
**Circ:** (Free)42,000

**Douglas County News Press/Highlands Ranch Herald (4170)**
Douglas County Publishing
PO Box 1270
Castle Rock, CO 80104
Phone: (303)688-3128
Fax: (303)660-0240
**Subject(s):** Daily Newspapers
**Circ:** (Paid)‡7,245
(Free)‡42,000

**Good News Etc. (4004)**
Good News Publishers Inc.
PO Box 2660
Vista, CA 92085
Phone: (760)724-3075
**Subject(s):** Local, State, and Regional Publications
**Circ:** (Combined)42,000

**Washington State Grange News (32180)**
Washington State Grange
PO Box 1186
Olympia, WA 98507
Phone: (360)357-3548
Fax: (800)854-1635
**Subject(s):** Farm Bureau, Grange, and Cooperative Associations
**Circ:** ‡42,000

**Palo Alto Weekly (2701)**
Embarcadero Publishing Co.
703 High St.
PO Box 1610
Palo Alto, CA 94302
Phone: (650)326-8210
Fax: (650)326-3928
**Subject(s):** Free Newspapers
**Circ:** (Paid)5,501
(Free)41,499

**The Argus (2573)**
ANG Newspapers
PO Box 28884
Oakland, CA 94604-8884
Phone: (510)208-6300
Fax: (510)293-2697
**Subject(s):** Free Newspapers
**Circ:** (Controlled)41,349

**Antelope Valley Press (2685)**
Antelope Valley Newspapers Inc.
37404 Sierra Hwy.
PO Box 4050
Palmdale, CA 93590-4050
Phone: (661)273-2700
Fax: (661)947-4870
**Subject(s):** Daily Newspapers
**Circ:** (Mon.-Sat.)35,326
(Sun.)41,284

**Dollarsaver (1964)**
340 N Jacinto St.
Hemet, CA 92543
Phone: (951)658-3117
Fax: (951)925-0394
**Subject(s):** Shopping Guides
**Circ:** (Free)‡41,000

**Chico News & Review (1650)**
Chico Community Publishing Inc.
353 E. 2nd St.
Chico, CA 95928
Phone: (530)894-2300
Fax: (530)894-0143
**Subject(s):** Free Newspapers
**Circ:** (Paid)52
(Free)40,682

**Farandula USA (3404)**
Velazquez Publishing Inc.
2025 S. Main St.
Santa Ana, CA 92707
Phone: (714)668-1009
Fax: (714)668-1013
**Subject(s):** Free Newspapers
**Circ:** (Free)40,588

**VeloNews (4142)**
Inside Communications Inc.
1830 N 55th St.
Boulder, CO 80301-2700
Phone: (303)440-0601
Fax: (303)444-6788
**Subject(s):** (Bicycling)
**Circ:** (Paid)40,584

**The Tidings (2353)**
The Tidings Corp.
3424 Wilshire Blvd., 6th Fl.
Los Angeles, CA 90010
Phone: (213)637-7360
Fax: (213)637-6360
**Subject(s):** Religious Publications
**Circ:** ‡40,547

**Compton/Carson Wave (2174)**
Wave Newspaper Group
4201 Wilshire Ave., Ste. 600
Los Angeles, CA 90010
Phone: (323)556-5720
Fax: (323)556-5704
**Subject(s):** Free Newspapers; Black Publications
**Circ:** (Non-paid)40,365

**Marin Independent Journal (2558)**
California Newspapers Inc.
150 Alameda Del Prado
Novato, CA 94949
Phone: (415)883-8600
Fax: (415)883-5458
**Subject(s):** Daily Newspapers
**Circ:** (Sat.)38,019
(Sun.)40,071
(Mon.-Fri.)40,140

**South Kitsap Neighbors (32025)**
The Sun
545 Fifth St.
PO Box 259
Bremerton, WA 98337-0053
Phone: (360)377-3711
Fax: (360)377-9237
**Subject(s):** Free Newspapers
**Circ:** (Tues.)◆29,246
(Non-paid)◆40,059

**Yakima Herald-Republic (32508)**
114 N 4th St.
PO Box 9668
Yakima, WA 98909
Phone: (509)248-1251
Fax: (509)577-7767
**Subject(s):** Daily Newspapers
**Circ:** (Mon.-Sat.)★38,104
(Sun.)★40,018

**Coast Weekly (3513)**
668 William Ave.
Seaside, CA 93955
Phone: (831)394-5656
Fax: (831)394-0409
**Subject(s):** Paid Community Newspapers; Entertainment; Local, State, and Regional Publications
**Circ:** 40,000

**Desert Post WEEKLY (1632)**
68-625 Perez Rd., Ste. 6
Cathedral City, CA 92234
Phone: (760)202-3200
Fax: (760)324-2751
**Subject(s):** Paid Community Newspapers
**Circ:** ‡40,000

**Hospitality News (26042)**
Hospitality News Group
PO Box 21027
Salem, OR 97307-1027
Phone: (503)390-8343
Fax: (503)390-8344
**Subject(s):** Hotels, Motels, Restaurants, and Clubs; Food and Grocery Trade
**Circ:** (Non-paid)40,000

**Pasadena Weekly (2719)**
50 S. DeLacey Ave., Ste. 200
Pasadena, CA 91105
Phone: (626)584-1500
Fax: (626)795-0149
**Subject(s):** Free Newspapers
**Circ:** (Paid)29
(Free)35,935
(Combined)40,000

**San Francisco Observer (3210)**
PO Box 15102
San Francisco, CA 94115
Phone: (415)863-6397
Fax: (415)431-2021
**Subject(s):** Free Newspapers
**Circ:** (Paid)121
(Free)40,000

**Santa Barbara Independent (3426)**
122 W. Figueroa St.
Santa Barbara, CA 93101-3106
Phone: (805)965-5205
Fax: (805)965-5518
**Subject(s):** Free Newspapers
**Circ:** (Free)40,000

**Pasadena Star-News (2718)**
San Gabriel Newspaper Group
911 E. Colorado Blvd.
Pasadena, CA 91109
Phone: (818)578-6300
Fax: (818)578-6460
**Subject(s):** Daily Newspapers
**Circ:** (Mon.-Fri.)38,249
(Sun.)38,444
(Sat.)39,738

**Chino Champion (1663)**
Champion Newspapers
13179 9th St.
Chino, CA 91710-4126
Phone: (909)628-5501
Fax: (909)591-6296
**Subject(s):** Paid Community Newspapers
**Circ:** (Combined)39,700

**Chino Hills Champion (1664)**
Champion Newspapers
13179 9th St.
Chino, CA 91710-4126
Phone: (909)628-5501
Fax: (909)591-6296
**Subject(s):** Paid Community Newspapers
**Circ:** (Combined)39,700

**The Record Searchlight Newspaper (2777)**
John P. Scripps Newspapers
1101 Twin View Blvd.
Redding, CA 96003
Phone: (530)243-2424
Fax: (530)225-8212
**Subject(s):** Daily Newspapers
**Circ:** (Mon.-Thurs.)★33,407
(Sat.)★37,226
(Sun.)★39,360

**Capital Press (26037)**
PO Box 2048
Salem, OR 97308
Phone: (503)364-4431
Fax: (503)370-4383
**Subject(s):** Farm Newspapers; General Agriculture
**Circ:** (Paid)38,966

**Southwest News Wave (2339)**
Wave Newspaper Group
4201 Wilshire Ave., Ste. 600
Los Angeles, CA 90010
Phone: (323)556-5720
Fax: (323)556-5704
**Subject(s):** Free Newspapers; Black Publications
**Circ:** 38,932

**Pacific Sun (2470)**
Pacific Sun Publishing Company Inc.
PO Box 5553
Mill Valley, CA 94942
Phone: (415)383-4500
Fax: (415)383-4159
**Subject(s):** Free Newspapers
**Circ:** (Paid)167
(Free)38,707

# Gale Directory of Publications & Broadcast Media/140th Ed.

## Western States

**The Daily Review** (1961)
ANG Newspapers
22533 Foothill Blvd.
Hayward, CA 94541
Phone: (510)783-6111
Fax: (510)293-2341
**Subject(s):** Daily Newspapers
**Circ:** (Sat.)27,125
  (Sun.)38,002
  (Mon.-Fri.)38,218

**The Mail Tribune** (25900)
Medford Mail Tribune Co.
111 N. Fir St.
PO Box 1108
Medford, OR 97501
Phone: (541)776-4411
**Subject(s):** Daily Newspapers
**Circ:** (Mon.-Thurs.)★30,278
  (Sat.)★30,278
  (Sun.)★32,994
  (Fri.)★38,186

**Star-News** (1665)
321 E St.
Chula Vista, CA 91910-2012
Phone: (619)427-3000
Fax: (619)426-6346
**Subject(s):** Paid Community Newspapers
**Circ:** (Mon.-Fri.)35,181
  (Mon.-Sat.)36,400
  (Sun.)38,067

**Des Moines News** (32029)
Northwest Publishing
133 SW 153rd St.
Burien, WA 98166
Phone: (206)444-4873
Fax: (206)444-4877
**Subject(s):** Paid Community Newspapers
**Circ:** (Paid)33,000
  (Free)38,000

**Nickel's Worth** (7686)
107 N. 5th St.
PO Box 2048
Coeur d'Alene, ID 83816
Phone: (208)667-0651
Fax: (208)765-6969
**Subject(s):** Shopping Guides
**Circ:** 38,000

**Sonoran News** (647)
6812 E. Cave Creek Rd.
Cave Creek, AZ 85331
Phone: (480)488-2021
Fax: (480)488-6216
**Subject(s):** Free Newspapers
**Circ:** (Combined)38,000

**New Times** (3338)
505 Higuera St.
San Luis Obispo, CA 93401
Phone: (805)546-8208
Fax: (805)546-8641
**Subject(s):** Free Newspapers
**Circ:** (Paid)28
  (Free)37,981

**The Monterey County Herald** (2501)
Monterey Peninsula Herald Co.
PO Box 271
Monterey, CA 93942
Phone: (831)372-3311
Fax: (831)646-4394
**Subject(s):** Daily Newspapers
**Circ:** (Mon.-Sat.)★33,766
  (Sun.)★37,290

**San Mateo Times** (3375)
1080 S Amphlett Blvd.
San Mateo, CA 94402
Phone: (415)348-4321
Fax: (415)348-4446
**Subject(s):** Daily Newspapers
**Circ:** (Mon.-Fri.)★35,300
  (Sat.)★37,297

**Central Star/Journal Wave** (2162)
Wave Newspaper Group
4201 Wilshire Ave., Ste. 600
Los Angeles, CA 90010
Phone: (323)556-5720
Fax: (323)556-5704
**Subject(s):** Paid Community Newspapers; Black Publications
**Circ:** (Combined)37,210

**Seattle Medium** (32323)
Piloven Publishing
2600 S Jackson St.
Seattle, WA 98144
Phone: (206)323-3070
Fax: (206)322-6518
**Subject(s):** Paid Community Newspapers; Black Publications
**Circ:** 37,000

**The Sun** (32026)
E.W. Scripps Co.
545 5th St.
PO Box 259
Bremerton, WA 98337
Phone: (888)377-3711
Fax: (360)377-9237
**Subject(s):** Daily Newspapers
**Circ:** (Mon.-Sat.)33,552
  (Sun.)36,786

**Great Falls Tribune** (18135)
Gannett Company Inc.
PO Box 5468
Great Falls, MT 59403
Phone: (406)791-1444
Fax: (406)791-1455
**Subject(s):** Daily Newspapers
**Circ:** (Mon.-Sat.)★33,434
  (Sun.)★36,763

**Southern California Senior Life (Southland Edition)** (2338)
Senior Life
6500 Wilshire Blvd., Ste. 1200
Los Angeles, CA 90048
Phone: (323)782-6005
Fax: (323)651-2099
**Subject(s):** Senior Citizens' Interests
**Circ:** (Combined)36,500

**GreatLander Bush Mailer** (500)
3110 Spenard Rd.
Anchorage, AK 99503
Phone: (907)274-0611
Fax: (907)272-2105
**Subject(s):** Shopping Guides
**Circ:** (Free)36,343

**Colorado Springs Independent** (4193)
235 S. Nevada
Colorado Springs, CO 80903
Phone: (719)577-4545
Fax: (719)577-4107
**Subject(s):** Free Newspapers
**Circ:** (Combined)36,300

**West Valley View** (709)
200 W. Wigwam Blvd.
Litchfield Park, AZ 85340-4636
Phone: (623)535-VIEW
Fax: (623)935-2103
**Subject(s):** Paid Community Newspapers
**Circ:** (Controlled)36,228

**Glendale News Press** (1930)
Times Community News
111 W. Wilson Ave., 2nd Fl.
Glendale, CA 91203
Phone: (818)637-3222
Fax: (818)637-3288
**Subject(s):** Daily Newspapers
**Circ:** (Wed.)❏20,966
  (Mon.-Fri.)❏21,766
  (Sat.)❏36,176

**The Daily Sentinel** (4425)
734 S 7th St.
PO Box 668
Grand Junction, CO 81502-0668
Phone: (970)242-5050
Fax: (970)241-6860
**Subject(s):** Daily Newspapers
**Circ:** (Mon.-Sat.)30,340
  (Sun.)35,654

**Eugene Weekly** (25797)
What's Happening Inc.
1251 Lincoln
Eugene, OR 97401
Phone: (541)484-0519
Fax: (541)484-4044
**Subject(s):** Local, State, and Regional Publications; Entertainment
**Circ:** (Free)35,500

**Cycle News** (1719)
CN Publishing
PO Box 5084
Costa Mesa, CA 92628-5084
Phone: (310)427-7433
Fax: (310)427-6685
**Subject(s):** Motorcycles
**Circ:** (Free)1,247
  (Paid)35,496

**Daily Pilot** (1720)
1375 Sunflower Ave.
Costa Mesa, CA 92626
Phone: (716)966-4600
Fax: (714)631-5902
**Subject(s):** Paid Community Newspapers
**Circ:** (Mon.-Fri.)❏22,075
  (Sun.)❏27,538
  (Sat.)❏35,346

**Fort Collins Coloradoan** (4378)
Gannett Company Inc.
PO Box 1577
Fort Collins, CO 80522
Phone: (970)224-7730
Fax: (970)224-7899
**Subject(s):** Daily Newspapers
**Circ:** (Mon.-Sat.)28,859
  (Sun.)35,303

**East Mesa Independent** (629)
Independent Newspapers Inc.
201 W. Apache Trail, Ste. 708
Apache Junction, AZ 85220
Phone: (480)982-7799
Fax: (480)671-0016
**Subject(s):** Free Newspapers
**Circ:** (Combined)‡35,000

**Herald Dispatch** (2222)
4053 Marlton Ave.
PO Box 19027A
Los Angeles, CA 90008
Phone: (323)295-6323
Fax: (323)291-2123
**Subject(s):** Paid Community Newspapers; Black Publications
**Circ:** ‡35,000

**La Jolla Village News** (3032)
San Diego Community Newspaper Group
PO. Box 9550
San Diego, CA 92169-9550
Phone: (858)270-3103
Fax: (858)270-9325
**Subject(s):** Free Newspapers
**Circ:** (Free)35000

**Lake Tahoe Action Magazine** (3541)
Tahoe Daily Tribune
3079 Harrison Ave.
South Lake Tahoe, CA 96150
Phone: (530)541-3880
Fax: (530)541-0373
**Subject(s):** Entertainment
**Circ:** (Paid)‡10,000
  (Free)‡35,000

**Union Hidpana** (3411)
Union Hispana
611 W Civic Center Dr.
Santa Ana, CA 92701
Fax: (714)541-1603
**Subject(s):** Free Newspapers; Hispanic Publications
**Circ:** (Non-paid)35,000

**Grand Forks Herald** (3289)
Knight-Ridder Inc.
50 W San Fernando St.
San Jose, CA 95113
Phone: (408)938-7700
**Subject(s):** Daily Newspapers
**Circ:** (Mon.-Sat.)34,275
  (Sun.)34,885

**Missoulian** (18204)
500 S. Higgins
Missoula, MT 59807
Phone: (406)523-5200
Fax: (406)523-5221

---

Circulation: ★ = ABC; △ = BPA; ♦ = CAC; • = CCAB; ❏ = VAC; ⊕ = PO Statement; ‡ = Publisher's Report; Boldface figures = sworn; Light figures = estimated.

# Western States

**Subject(s):** Daily Newspapers
**Circ:** (Mon.-Sat.)★30,466
(Sun.)★34,855

**Acorn (1329)**
Jbeen NP Publishing
30423 Conwood St., Ste. 108
Agoura Hills, CA 91301
Phone: (818)706-0266
Fax: (805)379-1864
**Subject(s):** Free Newspapers
**Circ:** (Free)❑34,716

**Variety (2365)**
Reed Business Information
5700 Wilshire Blvd., Ste. 120
Los Angeles, CA 90036
Phone: (323)857-6600
Fax: (323)965-2475
**Subject(s):** Motion Pictures; Drama and Theatre; Entertainment; Motion Pictures; Radio, Television, Cable, and Video; Radio, Television, Cable, and Video
**Circ:** (Mon.)34,293

**Daily Press Preview (3989)**
The Daily Press
PO Box 1389
Victorville, CA 92393-1389
Phone: (760)241-7744
Fax: (760)241-7145
**Subject(s):** Free Newspapers
**Circ:** (Tues.)34,000

**RCR Wireless News (4420)**
Crain Communications Inc.
1746 Cole Blvd. Ste. 150
Golden, CO 80401
Phone: (303)733-2500
Fax: (303)733-2244
**Subject(s):** Radio, Television, Cable, and Video
**Circ:** (Paid)9,173
(Free)33,603

**Chico Enterprise-Record (1649)**
Community Newspaper Holdings Inc.
400 E. Park Ave.
Chico, CA 95928
Phone: (916)891-1234
Fax: (916)342-3617
**Subject(s):** Daily Newspapers
**Circ:** (Sun.)★33,401
(Mon.-Sat.)★33,550

**Casper Star-Tribune (33684)**
170 Star Ln.
PO Box 80
Casper, WY 82602
Phone: (307)266-0500
Fax: (307)266-0501
**Subject(s):** Daily Newspapers
**Circ:** (Mon.-Sat.)★30,790
(Sun.)★33,289

**Azteca News (3402)**
810 N. Broadway
Po Box 207
Santa Ana, CA 92702-0207
Phone: (714)972-9912
Fax: (714)973-8117
**Subject(s):** Free Newspapers; Hispanic Publications; Spanish
**Circ:** (Free)‡33,000

**LA Hollywood Independent (2247)**
Los Angeles Independent Newspaper Group
4201 Wilshire Blvd., Ste. 600
Los Angeles, CA 90010
Phone: (323)556-5720
Fax: (323)556-5704
**Subject(s):** Paid Community Newspapers
**Circ:** (Combined)33,000

**Las Vegas Israelite (18689)**
PO Box 14096
Las Vegas, NV 89114
Phone: (702)876-1255
Fax: (702)364-1009
**Subject(s):** Jewish Publications
**Circ:** (Paid)‡10,000
(Free)‡33,000

**Consumers Press (18134)**
Lee Publications
PO Box 2268
Great Falls, MT 59403
Phone: (406)761-2406

Fax: (406)761-8814
**Subject(s):** Shopping Guides
**Circ:** (Combined)32,720

**Tucson Citizen (938)**
4850 S Park Ave.
Tucson, AZ 85714
Phone: (520)573-4561
Fax: (520)573-4569
**Subject(s):** Daily Newspapers
**Circ:** (Mon.-Sat.)32,712

**The Daily Herald (30736)**
Lee Enterprises Inc.
1555 N. Freedom Blvd.
Provo, UT 84603
Phone: (801)375-5103
**Subject(s):** Daily Newspapers
**Circ:** (Mon.-Sat.)30,960
(Sun.)32,578

**The Pacific Northwest Inlander (32391)**
Inland Publications Inc.
1020 W Riverside Ave.
Spokane, WA 99201-1100
Phone: (509)325-0634
Fax: (509)325-0638
**Subject(s):** Free Newspapers
**Circ:** (Paid)45
(Free)32,155

**The Argus (1868)**
ANG Newspapers
39737 Paseo Podue Pkwy.
Fremont, CA 94538
Phone: (510)661-2600
Fax: (510)353-7029
**Subject(s):** Daily Newspapers
**Circ:** (Sat.)★27,375
(Mon.-Fri.)★31,861
(Sun.)★32,124

**The Sun Journal (3512)**
The Sun Newspapers
216 Main St.
PO Box 755
Seal Beach, CA 90740-6318
Phone: (562)430-7555
Fax: (562)430-3469
**Subject(s):** Free Newspapers
**Circ:** (Paid)50
(Free)32,000

**West Hollywood Independent (2369)**
Los Angeles Independent Newspaper Group
4201 Wilshire Blvd., Ste. 600
Los Angeles, CA 90010
Phone: (323)556-5720
Fax: (323)556-5704
**Subject(s):** Free Newspapers
**Circ:** (Paid)9
(Non-paid)31,680

**Mesa Tribune Wave (2272)**
Wave Newspaper Group
4201 Wilshire Ave., Ste. 600
Los Angeles, CA 90010
Phone: (323)556-5720
Fax: (323)556-5704
**Subject(s):** Free Newspapers; Black Publications
**Circ:** 31,609

**Ventura County Reporter (3976)**
1567 Spinnaker Dr., Ste. 202
Ventura, CA 93001
Phone: (805)658-2244
Fax: (805)658-7803
**Subject(s):** Free Newspapers
**Circ:** (Paid)❑5
(Free)❑31,416

**Lighthouse (3905)**
5334 Torrance Blvd.
Torrance, CA 90503
Phone: (310)944-3533
Fax: (310)944-3633
**Subject(s):** Free Newspapers; Japanese; Ethnic Publications
**Circ:** (Combined)31,200

**Hollywood Independent (2224)**
Los Angeles Independent Newspaper Group
4201 Wilshire Blvd., Ste. 600
Los Angeles, CA 90010
Phone: (323)556-5720
Fax: (323)556-5704

**Subject(s):** Paid Community Newspapers
**Circ:** (Controlled)30,460

**News-Enterprise (2111)**
Community Media2
11110 Los Alamitos Blvd., Ste. 101
Los Alamitos, CA 90720
Phone: (714)527-8210
Fax: (562)493-2310
**Subject(s):** Free Newspapers
**Circ:** (Paid)‡350
(Free)‡30,300

**Casper Journal (33683)**
210 S Wolcott St.
Casper, WY 82601-2531
**Subject(s):** Paid Community Newspapers
**Circ:** (Paid)‡4,800
(Combined)30,000

**Christian News Northwest (25919)**
PO Box 974
Newberg, OR 97132
Phone: (503)537-9220
Fax: (503)537-9220
**Subject(s):** Free Newspapers; Religious Publications
**Circ:** (Non-paid)30,000

**The Episcopal News (2197)**
The Episcopal Diocese of Los Angeles
840 Echo Park Ave.
Los Angeles, CA 90026
Phone: (213)482-2040
Fax: (213)240-7670
**Subject(s):** Religious Publications
**Circ:** ‡30,000

**La Prensa San Diego (2526)**
La Prensa Munoz Inc.
101 E. 30th St., Ste. A
National City, CA 91950
Phone: (619)336-0370
Fax: (619)336-0372
**Subject(s):** Paid Community Publications; Hispanic Publications; Spanish
**Circ:** ‡30,000

**Real Change News (32316)**
Real Change
2129 2nd Ave.
Seattle, WA 98121
Phone: (206)441-3247
Fax: (206)441-2455
**Subject(s):** Lifestyle
**Circ:** (Paid)30,000

**The Southern Cross (3060)**
PO Box 81869
San Diego, CA 92138
Phone: (858)490-8266
Fax: (858)490-8355
**Subject(s):** Religious Publications
**Circ:** ‡30,000

**Watts Star Review (2368)**
Herald Dispatch
4053 Marlton Ave.
PO Box 19027A
Los Angeles, CA 90008
Phone: (323)295-6323
Fax: (323)291-2123
**Subject(s):** Paid Community Newspapers; Black Publications
**Circ:** ‡30,000

**White Sheet-The Palm Desert Advertiser (2657)**
Associated Desert Shoppers Inc.
73-400 Hwy. 111
Palm Desert, CA 92260
Phone: (760)346-0601
Fax: (760)346-3597
**Subject(s):** Shopping Guides
**Circ:** (Free)‡30,000

**Facts Newspaper (32268)**
2765 E Cherry St.
PO Box 22015
Seattle, WA 98122
Phone: (206)324-0552
Fax: (206)324-1007
**Subject(s):** Free Newspapers; Black Publications
**Circ:** (Paid)13,000
(Free)29,650

**Metro Santa Cruz (3456)**
Metro Publishing Inc.
115 Cooper St.
Santa Cruz, CA 95060-4526
Fax: (831)457-5828
**Subject(s):** Paid Community Newspapers

**Circ:** (Non-paid)❑29,528

**Downtown Gazette (2090)**
Gazette Newspapers Inc.
5225 E Second St.
Long Beach, CA 90803
Phone: (562)433-2000
Fax: (562)434-8826
**Subject(s):** Free Newspapers

**Circ:** (Free)29,500

**Federal Way Mirror (32091)**
Sound Publishing Inc.
1414 S. 324th St., Ste. B210
Federal Way, WA 98003
Phone: (253)946-2890
Fax: (253)925-5750
**Subject(s):** Paid Community Newspapers

**Circ:** (Paid)904
(Non-paid)29,243

**Vida En El Valle (1883)**
The McClatchy Co.
1626 E St.
Fresno, CA 93786
Phone: (559)441-6111
Fax: (559)441-6436
**Subject(s):** Free Newspapers; Spanish

**Circ:** (Paid)46
(Free)29,190

**Colorado River Weekender (637)**
News West Publishing Co.
PO Box 21209
Bullhead City, AZ 86439
Phone: (928)763-2505
**Subject(s):** Free Newspapers

**Circ:** (Combined)29,146

**Culver City Star (2177)**
Wave Newspaper Group
4201 Wilshire Ave., Ste. 600
Los Angeles, CA 90010
Phone: (323)556-5720
Fax: (323)556-5704
**Subject(s):** Free Newspapers; Black Publications

**Circ:** (Non-paid)29,109

**Bothell-Kenmore Reporter (31996)**
Northwest Media
PO Box 90130
Bellevue, WA 98009-0130
Phone: (425)486-1231
Fax: (425)452-3022
**Subject(s):** Free Newspapers

**Circ:** (Free)29,000

**The Bulletin (25721)**
Western Communications Inc.
1777 SW Chandler Ave.
PO Box 6020
Bend, OR 97702
Phone: (541)382-1811
Fax: (541)383-0372
**Subject(s):** Daily Newspapers

**Circ:** (Mon.-Fri.)27,663
(Sun.)29,007

**CoverStory (2443)**
Appeal Democrat
1530 Ellis Lake Dr.
Marysville, CA 95901
Phone: (530)741-2345
Fax: (530)741-1195
**Subject(s):** Shopping Guides

**Circ:** (Free)‡29,000

**El Latino (3136)**
San Francisco Latino Newspapers
3824 23rd St.
San Francisco, CA 94110
Phone: (415)648-1670
Fax: (415)648-3385
**Subject(s):** Paid Community Newspapers

**Circ:** (Paid)11,500
(Non-paid)28,500

**Coeur d'Alene Press (7684)**
201 North 2nd St.
Coeur d'Alene, ID 83814
Phone: (208)664-8176
Fax: (208)664-0212
**Subject(s):** Daily Newspapers

**Circ:** (Mon.-Sat.)‡14,500
(Sun.)‡28,200

**Antique Journal for the West (1785)**
Krause Publications Inc.
500 Fesler St., Ste. 201
El Cajon, CA 92020
Phone: (619)593-2933
Fax: (619)447-7187
**Subject(s):** Collecting; Antiques

**Circ:** (Combined)28,000

**Northwest Baby & Child (32297)**
Baby Diaper Service
6559 5th Pl. S.
Seattle, WA 98108-3435
Phone: (200)634-BABY
**Subject(s):** Babies; Parenting; Local, State, and Regional Publications

**Circ:** (Paid)1,900
(Free)‡28,000

**Weekly Visalia Times-Daily (4000)**
Visalia Daily
330 N W St.
Visalia, CA 93291-6010
Phone: (559)735-3200
Fax: (559)733-0826
**Subject(s):** Shopping Guides

**Circ:** (Free)28,000

**Lewiston Tribune (7722)**
TPC Holdings, Inc.
PO Box 957
Lewiston, ID 83501
Phone: (208)743-9411
Fax: (208)746-1185
**Subject(s):** Daily Newspapers

**Circ:** (Mon.-Sun.)‡26,330
(Sun.)‡27,608

**The Montclarion (1332)**
Hills Publications
1516 Oak St.
Alameda, CA 94501
Phone: (510)748-1666
Fax: (510)339-7302
**Subject(s):** Paid Community Newspapers

**Circ:** (Paid)❑1,357
(Free)❑27,553

**The Valley Catholic Newspaper (3444)**
Roman Catholic Diocese of San Jose
900 Lafayette St., Ste. 301
Santa Clara, CA 95050-4966
Phone: (408)983-0100
Fax: (408)983-0295
**Subject(s):** Religious Publications

**Circ:** (Free)840
(Paid)27,500

**Visalia Times-Delta (3999)**
Visalia Daily
330 N W St.
Visalia, CA 93291-6010
Phone: (559)735-3200
Fax: (559)733-0826
**Subject(s):** Daily Newspapers

**Circ:** (Mon.-Fri.)21,709
(Sat.)27,454

**Auto Sound & Security (1342)**
McMullen Argus Publishing Inc.
2400 E. Katella Ave., 11th Fl.
Anaheim, CA 92806
Phone: (714)939-2400
Fax: (714)978-6390
**Subject(s):** Automotive (Consumer); Consumer Electronics

**Circ:** (Paid)27,330

**The Wenatchee World (32483)**
World Publishing Co.
14 N. Mission
Wenatchee, WA 98801
Phone: (509)663-5761
Fax: (509)662-5413
**Subject(s):** Daily Newspapers

**Circ:** (Mon.-Fri.)★24,685
(Sun.)★27,037

**Chandler Independent (650)**
Independent Newspapers Inc.
325 E. Elliot, Ste. 21
Chandler, AZ 85225
Phone: (480)497-0048
Fax: (480)926-1019
**Subject(s):** Free Newspapers

**Circ:** (Combined)‡27,000

**The Umpqua Shopper (26027)**
News-Review Publishing Co.
345 NE Winchester
PO Box 1248
Roseburg, OR 97470
Phone: (541)672-3321
Fax: (541)957-4270
**Subject(s):** Shopping Guides

**Circ:** (Free)‡27,000

**Piedmont Press (2736)**
Press Publications
Box 10151, Grand Lake Sta.
Oakland, CA 94610
Phone: (510)428-2000
Fax: (510)595-7676
**Subject(s):** Paid Community Newspapers

**Circ:** (Paid)‡4
(Non-paid)‡26,996

**The Classified Gazette (Sonoma County Edition) (3490)**
The Classified Gazette Inc.
532 College Ave.
Santa Rosa, CA 95404
Phone: (707)526-2434
Fax: (707)527-9251
**Subject(s):** Shopping Guides

**Circ:** (Free)‡26,854

**The Yuma Daily Sun (988)**
2055 S Arizona Ave.
Yuma, AZ 85364
Phone: (928)783-3333
Fax: (928)343-1009
**Subject(s):** Daily Newspapers

**Circ:** (Mon.-Sat.)22,249
(Sun.)26,670

**Santa Cruz County Sentinel (3457)**
Santa Cruz Sentinel Publishers Co.
PO Box 638
Santa Cruz, CA 95061
Phone: (408)423-4242
Fax: (408)423-1154
**Subject(s):** Daily Newspapers

**Circ:** (Mon.-Sat.)★25,305
(Sun.)★26,591

**The Reflector (WA) (31994)**
Case Publishing Inc.
PO Box 2020
Battle Ground, WA 98604
**Subject(s):** Free Newspapers

**Circ:** (Paid)942
(Free)26,160

**La Jolla Light (2039)**
Pacific Sierra Publishing Company Inc.
565 Pearl St., Ste. 300
La Jolla, CA 92037-5051
Phone: (858)459-4201
Fax: (858)459-0977
**Subject(s):** Paid Community Newspapers

**Circ:** ‡26,000

**King County Journal (32120)**
Horvitz Newspapers Inc.
600 Washington Ave. S.
Kent, WA 98032
Phone: (253)437-6040
Fax: (253)437-6043
**Subject(s):** Daily Newspapers

**Circ:** (Sun.)25,166
(Mon.-Sat.)25,408

**The Post-Register (7702)**
333 Northgate Mile
PO BOX 1800
Idaho Falls, ID 83401
Phone: (208)522-1800
Fax: (208)529-3142
**Subject(s):** Daily Newspapers

**Circ:** (Mon.-Sat.)23,746
(Sun.)25,386

**Standard Blade** (4150)
Metrowest Newspapers
139 N. Main St.
PO Box 646
Brighton, CO 80601
Phone: (303)659-2522
Fax: (303)659-2901
**Subject(s):** Paid Community Newspapers

**Circ:** (Paid)6,593
(Non-paid)25,227

**The Adit** (18153)
PO Box 1244
Helena, MT 59624
Phone: (406)443-3690
Fax: (406)449-8170
**Subject(s):** Shopping Guides

**Circ:** (Free)‡25,000

**Antique & Collectables** (1784)
Krause Publications Inc.
500 Fesler St., Ste. 201
El Cajon, CA 92020
Phone: (619)593-2933
Fax: (619)447-1943
**Subject(s):** Antiques; Collecting

**Circ:** (Combined)25,000

**Assistive Technology News** (2865)
1029 J St., Ste 120
Sacramento, CA 95814
Phone: (916)325-1690
Fax: (916)325-1699

**Circ:** 25,000

**Carmel Pine Cone** (1619)
Carmel Communications
PO Box G-1
Carmel, CA 93921
Phone: (831)624-0162
Fax: (831)375-5018
**Subject(s):** Free Newspapers

**Circ:** (Paid)‡25,000

**The City Collegian** (32255)
SCCC Publications
Seattle Central Community College
1701 Broadway, 2SAC 350
Seattle, WA 98122
Phone: (206)587-3800
**Subject(s):** College Publications

**Circ:** (Free)25,000

**El Popular** (1406)
212 Goodman St.
Bakersfield, CA 93305
Phone: (661)398-1000
Fax: (661)325-1351
**Subject(s):** Paid Community Newspapers; Hispanic Publications; Spanish

**Circ:** 25,000

**Gilbert Independent** (682)
Independent Newspapers Inc.
325 E. Elliot Rd., Ste. 21
Chandler, AZ 85225
Phone: (480)497-0048
Fax: (480)926-1019
**Subject(s):** Free Newspapers

**Circ:** (Combined)‡25,000

**India West** (3333)
India West Publications
933 Mac Arthur Blvd.
San Leandro, CA 94577
Phone: (510)383-1140
Fax: (510)383-1155
**Subject(s):** Intercultural Interests; Paid Community Newspapers

**Circ:** 25,000

**Muttmatchers Messenger** (32082)
PO Box 1165
Enumclaw, WA 98022
Phone: (360)825-0741
**Subject(s):** Free Newspapers

**Circ:** 25,000

**Out Front Colorado** (4315)
723 Sherman St.
Denver, CO 80203-3545
Phone: (303)778-7900
Fax: (303)778-7978

**Subject(s):** Paid Community Newspapers; Entertainment

**Circ:** (Free)25,000

**Palo Alto Daily News** (2700)
The Daily News
324 High St.
Palo Alto, CA 94301
Phone: (650)327-9090
Fax: (650)853-0904
**Subject(s):** Daily Newspapers

**Circ:** (Paid)25,000

**Sun Cities Independent** (857)
Independent Newspapers Inc.
10220 W. Bell Rd., Ste. 116
Sun City, AZ 85351
Phone: (623)974-6004
Fax: (623)974-6004
**Subject(s):** Free Newspapers

**Circ:** (Combined)‡25,000

**Trader's Shopper's Guide** (33702)
Graphic Media Inc.
2021 Warren Ave.
Cheyenne, WY 82001-4843
Phone: (307)634-8895
Fax: (307)634-8530
**Subject(s):** Shopping Guides

**Circ:** (Free)‡25,000

**20 de Mayo** (2357)
1824 Sunset Blvd., Ste. 202
Los Angeles, CA 90026
Phone: (213)483-8511
Fax: (213)483-6474
**Subject(s):** Free Newspapers; Hispanic Publications; Spanish

**Circ:** 25,000

**Paramount/Bellflower Herald American** (2298)
Wave Newspaper Group
4201 Wilshire Ave., Ste. 600
Los Angeles, CA 90010
Phone: (323)556-5720
Fax: (323)556-5704
**Subject(s):** Free Newspapers

**Circ:** (Paid)24
(Free)24,800

**The Greenly Tribune** (4442)
Greeley Publishing Co.
501 8th Ave.
PO Box 1690
Greeley, CO 80632
Phone: (970)352-0211
Fax: (970)352-4059
**Subject(s):** Daily Newspapers

**Circ:** (Sun.)24,597
(Mon.-Sat.)24,751

**Daily Times-Call** (4504)
Lehman Communications Corp.
350 Terry St.
PO Box 299
Longmont, CO 80502
Phone: (303)776-2244
Fax: (303)776-0837
**Subject(s):** Daily Newspapers

**Circ:** (Mon.-Sat.)22,085
(Sun.)24,439

**Alhambra Post Advocate** (2125)
Wave Newspaper Group
4201 Wilshire Ave., Ste. 600
Los Angeles, CA 90010
Phone: (323)556-5720
Fax: (323)556-5704
**Subject(s):** Free Newspapers

**Circ:** (Paid)701
(Free)24,210

**South Gate Press** (2330)
Wave Newspaper Group
4201 Wilshire Ave., Ste. 600
Los Angeles, CA 90010
Phone: (323)556-5720
Fax: (323)556-5704
**Subject(s):** Free Newspapers

**Circ:** (Paid)61
(Free)24,076

**Maui News** (7637)
Maui Publishing
100 Mahalani St.
Wailuku, HI 96793
Phone: (808)244-3981

Fax: (808)242-6372
**Subject(s):** Daily Newspapers

**Circ:** (Mon.-Thurs.)17,090
(Fri.)19,286
(Sun.)24,035

**Mesa Legend** (713)
English-Foreign Language Bldg., Rm. EF2N
1833 W. Southern Ave.
Mesa, AZ 85202
Phone: (480)461-7330
Fax: (480)461-7334
**Subject(s):** College Publications

**Circ:** (Free)‡24,000

**Catholic Herald** (2881)
El Heraldo Catolico
5890 Newman Ct.
Sacramento, CA 95819-2608
Phone: (916)452-3691
Fax: (916)452-2945
**Subject(s):** Religious Publications

**Circ:** (Paid)23,500

**Eastside Sun** (1690)
Eastern Group Publications Inc.
2500 S Atlantic Blvd., Bldg. A
Commerce, CA 90040
Phone: (323)263-5743
Fax: (323)263-9169
**Subject(s):** Free Newspapers; Spanish; Hispanic Publications

**Circ:** (Paid)♦112
(Free)♦23,039

**The Daily Californian** (1466)
Independent Berkeley Student Publishing Company Inc.
600 Eshleman Hall
University of California Berkeley
Berkeley, CA 94720
Phone: (510)548-8300
Fax: (510)849-2803
**Subject(s):** College Publications

**Circ:** (Paid)200
(Free)23,000

**Puyallup Herald** (32228)
Olympic Publishing Company Inc.
822 E Main ST.
Puyallup, WA 98371
Phone: (253)841-2481
Fax: (206)840-8249
**Subject(s):** Paid Community Newspapers

**Circ:** (Free)590
(Paid)23,000

**Town of Paradise Valley Independent** (727)
Independent Newspapers Inc.
11000 N. Scottsdale Rd. Ste. 210
Scottsdale, AZ 85254-5269
**Subject(s):** Free Newspapers

**Circ:** (Combined)‡23,000

**Ontario Green Sheet** (2623)
Associated Desert Shoppers Inc.
73-400 Hwy. 111
Palm Desert, CA 92260
Phone: (760)346-0601
Fax: (760)346-3597
**Subject(s):** Shopping Guides

**Circ:** (Free)22,800

**Edicion Bilingue Independent** (2192)
Los Angeles Independent Newspaper Group
4201 Wilshire Blvd., Ste. 600
Los Angeles, CA 90010
Phone: (323)556-5720
Fax: (323)556-5704
**Subject(s):** Free Newspapers

**Circ:** (Paid)7
(Non-paid)22,735

**Missoula Independent** (18203)
Independent Publishing Inc.
PO Box 8275
Missoula, MT 59807
Phone: (406)543-6609
Fax: (406)543-4367
**Subject(s):** Free Newspapers; Alternative and Underground

**Circ:** (Paid)❑31
(Free)❑22,708

**California Advocate** (1872)
1715 E St., No. 108
PO Box 11826
Fresno, CA 93706-1826
Phone: (559)268-0941
Fax: (559)268-0943
**Subject(s):** Paid Community Newspapers; Black Publications

Circ: 22,500

**Random Lengths/Harbor Independent News** (3380)
Random Lengths Inc.
1300 South Pacific Ave.
San Pedro, CA 90731
Phone: (310)519-1016
Fax: (310)832-1000
**Subject(s):** Free Newspapers

Circ: (Free)‡22,500

**San Diego Business Journal** (3043)
4909 Murphy Canyon Rd., No. 200
San Diego, CA 92123
Phone: (858)277-6359
Fax: (858)571-3628
**Subject(s):** Business; Local, State, and Regional Publications

Circ: ‡22,500

**Puget Sound Business Journal (Seattle)** (32310)
American City Business Journals Inc.
801 2nd Ave., No. 210
Seattle, WA 98104-1528
Phone: (206)583-0701
Fax: (206)447-8510
**Subject(s):** Business; Local, State, and Regional Publications

Circ: (Paid)22,221

**Appeal Democrat** (2441)
Freedom Communications Inc.
1530 Ellis Lake Dr.
PO Box 431
Marysville, CA 95901-4269
Phone: (530)741-2345
Fax: (530)741-1195
**Subject(s):** Daily Newspapers

Circ: (Mon.-Sat.)21,969
(Sun.)22,217

**Central Washington Catholic** (32503)
Diocese of Yakima
5301-A Tieton Dr.
Yakima, WA 98908-3493
Phone: (509)965-7117
Fax: (509)966-8334
**Subject(s):** Religious Publications

Circ: (Non-paid)22,000

**Daily Bruin** (2178)
University of California, Los Angeles
118 Kerkhoff Hall
308 Westwood Plaza
Los Angeles, CA 90024
Phone: (310)825-9898
Fax: (310)206-0906
**Subject(s):** College Publications

Circ: (Free)22,000

**Korean Sunday News** (2245)
4950 Wilshire Blvd.
Los Angeles, CA 90010
Phone: (323)954-7500
Fax: (323)954-7503
**Subject(s):** Paid Community Newspapers; Korean; Ethnic Publications

Circ: (Combined)22,000

**The Mountain View News** (849)
Five Star Publishing
PO Box 1119
Sierra Vista, AZ 85635
Phone: (520)458-3340
Fax: (520)458-9338
**Subject(s):** Free Newspapers; Shopping Guides

Circ: (Free)‡22,000

**The Nickel Want Ads** (4427)
Grand Junction Newspapers Inc.
1635 N. First St.
Grand Junction, CO 81501
Phone: (970)242-5555
Fax: (970)245-9250
**Subject(s):** Free Newspapers

Circ: (Combined)22,000

**The Ledger Dispatch** (1379)
Hills Publications Inc.
Crowe/Business
1700 Cavallo Rd.
Antioch, CA 94509
**Subject(s):** Daily Newspapers

Circ: (Mon.-Sat.)20,933
(Sun.)21,903

**Bell/Maywood/Cudahy Industrial Post** (2144)
Wave Newspaper Group
4201 Wilshire Ave., Ste. 600
Los Angeles, CA 90010
Phone: (323)556-5720
Fax: (323)556-5704
**Subject(s):** Paid Community Newspapers

Circ: (Paid)134
(Free)21,662

**The Clovis Independent** (1676)
420 Bullard, No. 105
Clovis, CA 93612
Phone: (559)298-8081
Fax: (559)298-0459
**Subject(s):** Paid Community Newspapers

Circ: (Paid)‡7,400
(Free)‡21,600

**The New Times** (32293)
New Times
3600 15th Ave. W Ste. 200
Seattle, WA 98119-1330
Phone: (206)320-7788
Fax: (206)320-7717
**Subject(s):** New Age; Women's Interests

Circ: (Paid)‡1,500
(Free)‡21,500

**Times-News** (7811)
Howard Publications Inc.
132 3rd St. W
Box 548
Twin Falls, ID 83303
Phone: (208)733-0931
Fax: (208)734-5538
**Subject(s):** Daily Newspapers

Circ: (Mon.-Sat.)★21,440
(Sun.)★21,480

**Fairbanks Daily News-Miner** (541)
200 N. Cushman St.
Fairbanks, AK 99707
Phone: (907)456-6661
Fax: (907)452-5054
**Subject(s):** Daily Newspapers

Circ: (Mon.-Sat.)16,437
(Sun.)21,329

**The Daily News** (32136)
770 11th Ave.
PO Box 189
Longview, WA 98632
Phone: (360)577-2500
Fax: (360)577-2536
**Subject(s):** Daily Newspapers

Circ: (Sun.)★20,895
(Mon.-Sat.)★21,257

**Apache Junction Independent** (628)
Independent Newspapers Inc.
850 S. Ironwood No.112
Apache Junction, AZ 85220
Phone: (480)982-7799
Fax: (480)671-0016
**Subject(s):** Free Newspapers

Circ: (Combined)‡21,000

**Buyer's Guide** (33720)
Buyer Guide
1826 E Sheridan Ave.
Cody, WY 82414
Phone: (307)587-5989
Fax: (307)587-2551
**Subject(s):** Shopping Guides

Circ: (Free)‡21,000

**Daily Republic** (1847)
1250 Texas St.
PO Box 47
Fairfield, CA 94533
Phone: (707)425-4646
Fax: (707)425-5924
**Subject(s):** Daily Newspapers

Circ: (Mon.-Fri.)20,000
(Sat.)21,500

**Mom Guess What Newspaper (MGW)** (2905)
Mom Guess What Newspaper
1103 T St.
Sacramento, CA 95814
Phone: (916)441-6397
Fax: (916)441-6422
**Subject(s):** Gay and Lesbian Interests

Circ: (Paid)‡700
(Free)‡21,000

**The Navajo Times** (979)
Hwy. 264 & Rte. 12
PO Box 310
Window Rock, AZ 86515-0310
Phone: (520)871-6641
Fax: (520)871-6409
**Subject(s):** Paid Community Newspapers; Native American Interests

Circ: 21,000

**The Los Angeles Business Journal** (2254)
5700 Wilshire, No. 170
Los Angeles, CA 90036
Phone: (213)549-5225
Fax: (213)549-5255
**Subject(s):** Business; Local, State, and Regional Publications

Circ: (Paid)20,956

**Times-Standard** (1834)
PO Box 3580
Eureka, CA 95502
Phone: (707)441-0500
Fax: (707)441-0565
**Subject(s):** Daily Newspapers

Circ: (Mon.-Sat.)18,826
(Sun.)20,728

**Idaho Press Tribune** (7760)
1618 N Midland Blvd.
PO Box 9399
Nampa, ID 83652
Phone: (208)467-9251
Fax: (208)467-9562
**Subject(s):** Daily Newspapers

Circ: (Mon.-Sat.)20,488
(Sun.)20,653

**The Westsider** (2371)
Los Angeles Independent Newspaper Group
4201 Wilshire Blvd., Ste. 600
Los Angeles, CA 90010
Phone: (323)556-5720
Fax: (323)556-5704
**Subject(s):** Free Newspapers

Circ: (Paid)11
(Non-paid)20,650

**Daily News-Sun** (856)
News-Sun Inc.
10102 Santa Fe Dr.
PO Box 1779
Sun City, AZ 85372
Phone: (602)977-8351
Fax: (602)876-3698
**Subject(s):** Daily Newspapers

Circ: (Mon.-Sat.)20,516

**Skagit Valley Herald** (32163)
Skagit Valley Publishing Co.
1000 E. College Way
PO Box 578
Mount Vernon, WA 98273-0578
Phone: (360)424-3251
Fax: (360)424-5300
**Subject(s):** Daily Newspapers

Circ: (Mon.-Sat.)19,419
(Sun.)20,441

**Redlands Green Sheet** (2794)
Associated Desert Shoppers Inc.
611 West Redlands Blvd., Ste. C
Redlands, CA 92373
Phone: (909)793-3768
**Subject(s):** Shopping Guides

Circ: (Free)20,400

**News-Times** (25921)
831 NE Avery St.
PO Box 965
Newport, OR 97365
Phone: (541)265-8571
Fax: (541)265-3862
**Subject(s):** Paid Community Newspapers

Circ: ‡20,288

Circulation: ★ = ABC; △ = BPA; ◆ = CAC; • = CCAB; □ = VAC; ⊕ = PO Statement; ‡ = Publisher's Report; Boldface figures = sworn; Light figures = estimated.

# Western States

**Santa Maria Times** (3466)
3200 Skyway Dr.
PO Box 400
Santa Maria, CA 93455-1896
Phone: (805)925-2691
Fax: (805)928-5657
**Subject(s):** Daily Newspapers

**Circ:** (Mon.-Sat.)18,062
(Sun.)20,122

**The Californian** (2961)
Salinas Newspapers Inc.
123 W. Alisal St.
Salinas, CA 93901
Phone: (831)424-2221
Fax: (831)754-4293
**Subject(s):** Daily Newspapers

**Circ:** (Mon.-Fri.)★17,528
(Sat.)★20,090

**The News-Review** (26025)
News-Review Publishing Co.
345 NE Winchester
PO Box 1248
Roseburg, OR 97470
Phone: (541)672-3321
Fax: (541)957-4270
**Subject(s):** Daily Newspapers

**Circ:** (Mon.-Fri.)★19,029
(Sun.)★20,078

**American Spirit Newspaper** (1443)
Sterling Rose Press Inc.
PO Box 14341
Berkeley, CA 94712
Phone: (510)848-ROSE
**Subject(s):** New Age; Alternative and Underground; Free Newspapers

**Circ:** 20,000

**Beach & Bay Press** (3002)
Mannis Communications Inc.
4645 Cass St., Ste. 201
PO Box 9550
San Diego, CA 92169-9550
Phone: (858)270-3103
Fax: (858)713-0095
**Subject(s):** Free Newspapers

**Circ:** (Paid)51
(Free)20,000

**The Central California Catholic Life** (1876)
1550 N Fresno St.
Fresno, CA 93703-3788
Phone: (559)488-7414
Fax: (559)488-7435
**Subject(s):** Religious Publications

**Circ:** (Non-paid)20,000

**Colorado Daily** (4109)
2610 Pearl St.
Boulder, CO 80302
Phone: (303)443-6272
Fax: (303)443-9357
**Subject(s):** Daily Newspapers

**Circ:** (Mon.-Thurs.)17,000
(Fri.)20,000

**El Heraldo Catolico** (2890)
5890 Newman Ct.
Sacramento, CA 95819-2608
Phone: (916)452-3691
Fax: (916)452-2945
**Subject(s):** Religious Publications; Spanish; Hispanic Publications

**Circ:** ‡20,000

**Hilltop Times** (30711)
Standard-Examiner
332 Standard Way
P.O.Box 12790
Ogden, UT 84412-2790
Phone: (801)625-4200
**Subject(s):** Free Newspapers; Military and Navy

**Circ:** (Free)‡20,000

**Mundo Hispano** (30814)
9131 S Monroe St., Ste. C
Sandy, UT 84070
Phone: (801)569-3338
Fax: (801)352-9638
**Subject(s):** Hispanic Publications

**Circ:** (Controlled)20,000

**Nickel Saver** (32156)
715 W. Third Ave.
PO Box 699
Moses Lake, WA 98837
Phone: (509)765-5681
Fax: (509)766-9977
**Subject(s):** Shopping Guides

**Circ:** (Free)‡20,000

**Orange County News** (1920)
7441 Garden Grove Blvd., Ste. G
Garden Grove, CA 92841-4209
Phone: (714)894-2575
Fax: (714)894-0809
**Subject(s):** Paid Community Newspapers

**Circ:** (Paid)‡10,000
(Free)‡20,000

**Saigon Times** (2856)
9234 East Valley Blvd.
Rosemead, CA 91770
Phone: (626)288-2696
Fax: (626)288-2033
**Subject(s):** Free Newspapers; Vietnamese; Ethnic Publications

**Circ:** (Combined)20,000

**The Valley Vantage** (4069)
23009 Ventura Blvd.
Woodland Hills, CA 91364-1107
Phone: (818)223-9545
Fax: (818)223-9552
**Subject(s):** Free Newspapers

**Circ:** (Free)20,000

**West Valley Courier** (25856)
PO Box 588
Hillsboro, OR 97123
Phone: (503)648-1131
Fax: (503)648-9191
**Subject(s):** Shopping Guides

**Circ:** (Free)19,957

**San Francisco Business Times** (3204)
American City Business Journals Inc.
c/o Steve Symanovich
275 Battery St., Ste. 940
San Francisco, CA 94111
Phone: (415)398-2522
Fax: (415)398-2494
**Subject(s):** Local, State, and Regional Publications; Business

**Circ:** (Paid)19,929

**Bajo El Sol** (984)
The Yuma Daily Sun
2055 S Arizona Ave.
Yuma, AZ 85364
Phone: (928)783-3333
Fax: (928)343-1009
**Subject(s):** Shopping Guides; Spanish

**Circ:** (Non-paid)♦19,821

**North San Bernardino Green Sheet** (2981)
Associated Desert Shoppers Inc.
611 West Redlands Blvd., Ste. C
Redlands, CA 92373
Phone: (909)793-3768
**Subject(s):** Shopping Guides

**Circ:** (Free)19,800

**Nisqually Valley Shopper** (32526)
Nisqually Valley News
PO Box 597
Yelm, WA 98597
Phone: (360)458-2681
Fax: (360)458-5741
**Subject(s):** Shopping Guides

**Circ:** (Free)‡19,750

**Boulder Weekly** (4107)
Boulder Weekly Inc.
690 S. Lashley Ln.
Boulder, CO 80303
Phone: (303)494-5511
Fax: (303)494-2585
**Subject(s):** Free Newspapers

**Circ:** (Free)❑19,585

**Valley Shopper-The El Centro Advertiser** (2654)
Associated Desert Shoppers Inc.
73-400 Hwy. 111
Palm Desert, CA 92260
Phone: (760)346-0601
Fax: (760)346-3597

**Subject(s):** Shopping Guides

**Circ:** (Paid)‡19,525

**The Ceres Courier** (1635)
2940 4th St.
PO Box 7
Ceres, CA 95307
Phone: (209)537-5032
Fax: (209)537-0543
**Subject(s):** Free Newspapers

**Circ:** (Free)19,500

**The Prescott Courier** (808)
The Daily Courier
PO Box 312
Prescott, AZ 86302
Phone: (928)445-3333
Fax: (928)775-6718
**Subject(s):** Daily Newspapers

**Circ:** (Mon.-Fri.)17,647
(Sun.)19,500

**San Francisco Bay View** (3203)
4917 Third St.
San Francisco, CA 94124
Phone: (415)671-0789
Fax: (415)671-0316
**Subject(s):** Free Newspapers; Black Publications

**Circ:** (Paid)‡500
(Non-paid)‡19,500

**Pico Rivera/Santa Fe Springs News** (2307)
Wave Newspaper Group
4201 Wilshire Ave., Ste. 600
Los Angeles, CA 90010
Phone: (323)556-5720
Fax: (323)556-5704
**Subject(s):** Free Newspapers

**Circ:** (Free)19,461

**Burbank Leader** (1569)
California Community News Corp.
220 N. Glenoaks Blvd.
Ste. B
Burbank, CA 91502
Phone: (818)843-8700
Fax: (818)954-9439
**Subject(s):** Paid Community Newspapers

**Circ:** (Wed.)❑10,239
(Sat.)❑19,270

**Whittier Independent** (2374)
Wave Newspaper Group
4201 Wilshire Ave., Ste. 600
Los Angeles, CA 90010
Phone: (323)556-5720
Fax: (323)556-5704
**Subject(s):** Free Newspapers

**Circ:** (Free)‡19,115

**California Staats-Zeitung** (2159)
1201 N Alvarado
PO Box 26308
Los Angeles, CA 90026
Phone: (213)413-5500
Fax: (213)413-5469
**Subject(s):** German; Paid Community Newspapers

**Circ:** 18,700

**The Napa Valley Register** (2523)
1615 2nd St.
PO Box 150
Napa, CA 94559
Phone: (707)226-3711
Fax: (707)224-3963
**Subject(s):** Daily Newspapers

**Circ:** (Mon.-Sat.)★17,851
(Sun.)★18,665

**Peninsula Daily News** (32202)
Northwest Media
305 W. 1st St.
P.O. Box 1330
Port Angeles, WA 98362
Phone: (360)452-2345
Fax: (360)417-3521
**Subject(s):** Daily Newspapers

**Circ:** (Mon.-Fri.)★17,167
(Sun.)★18,646

**Gale Directory of Publications & Broadcast Media/140th Ed.**          **Western States**

**The Daily Universe** (30737)
Brigham Young Daily Universe
Brigham Young University
5338 WSC
PO Box 27903
Provo, UT 84602
Phone: (801)422-4757
Fax: (801)422-0177
**Subject(s):** College Publications

Circ: 18,500

**The Thurston-Mason Senior News** (32178)
Thurston County Council on Aging
112 E 4th Ave.
Olympia, WA 98501
Phone: (360)586-3590
Fax: (360)586-3551
**Subject(s):** Senior Citizens' Interests; Free Newspapers

Circ: (Free)18,500

**Wyoming Catholic Register** (33704)
PO Box 1468
2121 Capitol Ave
Cheyenne, WY 82003-1468
Phone: (307)638-1530
Fax: (307)637-7936
**Subject(s):** Religious Publications

Circ: (Paid)18,500

**South Pierce County Dispatch** (32072)
PO Box 248
Eatonville, WA 98328
Phone: (360)832-4411
Fax: (360)832-4972
**Subject(s):** Paid Community Newspapers

Circ: (Paid)5,213
     (Free)18,425

**Brownsville Herald** (1995)
Freedom Communications Inc.
17666 Fitch
Irvine, CA 92614-6022
Phone: (949)253-2300
Fax: (949)474-7675
**Subject(s):** Daily Newspapers

Circ: (Mon.-Fri.)16,632
     (Sun.)18,349

**Western Livestock Journal** (4325)
Crow Publications Inc.
650 S. Lipan
Denver, CO 80233
Phone: (303)722-7600
Fax: (303)722-0155
**Subject(s):** Livestock

Circ: (Paid)18,335

**The Daily Inter Lake** (18173)
Inter Lake Publishing Co.
727 E Idaho
PO Box 7610
Kalispell, MT 59904
Phone: (406)755-7000
Fax: (406)752-6114
**Subject(s):** Daily Newspapers

Circ: (Mon.-Fri.)15,600
     (Sun.)18,300

**West San Bernardino Green Sheet** (2987)
Associated Desert Shoppers Inc.
611 West Redlands Blvd., Ste. C
Redlands, CA 92373
Phone: (909)793-3768
**Subject(s):** Shopping Guides

Circ: (Non-paid)18,300

**Loveland Daily Reporter-Herald** (4510)
Lehman Communications Corp.
PO Box 59
Loveland, CO 80539
Phone: (970)669-5050
Fax: (970)667-1111
**Subject(s):** Daily Newspapers

Circ: (Mon.-Sat.)★17,548
     (Sun.)★18,095

**Firestone Park News/Southeast News Press** (2204)
Herald Dispatch
4053 Marlton Ave.
PO Box 19027A
Los Angeles, CA 90008
Phone: (323)295-6323
Fax: (323)291-2123
**Subject(s):** Paid Community Newspapers; Black Publications

Circ: (Free)‡6,000
     (Paid)‡18,000

**The Omak-Okanogan County Chronicle** (32188)
Omak Chronicle Inc.
618 Okoma Dr.
PO Box 553
Omak, WA 98841
Phone: (509)826-1110
Fax: (509)826-5819
**Subject(s):** Paid Community Newspapers

Circ: (Combined)‡18,000

**Rohnert Park Community Voice** (2019)
The Sonoma Index-Tribune Inc.
10101 Main St. No.112
Kelseyville, CA 95451
Phone: (707)285-3220
Fax: (707)285-3226
**Subject(s):** Paid Community Newspapers

Circ: (Free)18,000

**The Shopper** (32332)
PO Box 16069
Seattle, WA 98116
Phone: (206)932-0300
Fax: (206)937-1223
**Subject(s):** Shopping Guides

Circ: (Free)‡18,000

**South Coast Shopper** (25750)
PO Box 1440
2000 Sherman, N. Bend
Coos Bay, OR 97420
Phone: (541)756-5010
Fax: (541)756-8109
**Subject(s):** Shopping Guides

Circ: (Free)‡18,000

**State Press** (881)
Arizona State University
PO Box 871405
Tempe, AZ 85287
Phone: (480)965-9011
Fax: (480)965-1000
**Subject(s):** College Publications

Circ: (Free)‡18,000

**The Voice of Hawai'i** (7580)
University of Hawaii at Manoa
The Ka Leo Bldg.
1755 Pope Rd. 31-D
Honolulu, HI 96822
Phone: (808)956-7043
Fax: (808)956-9962
**Subject(s):** College Publications

Circ: (Mon.-Fri.)‡18,000

**Laguna Niguel News** (2055)
The Orange County Register
22481 Aspan St.
Lake Forest, CA 92630
Fax: (949)454-7354
**Subject(s):** Free Newspapers

Circ: ‡17,877

**Northeast Sun Commerce Comet** (1695)
Eastern Group Publications Inc.
2500 S Atlantic Blvd., Bldg. A
Commerce, CA 90040
Phone: (323)263-5743
Fax: (323)263-9169
**Subject(s):** Paid Community Newspapers

Circ: (Non-paid)♦15
     (Free)♦17,877

**Herald and News** (25866)
Klamath Publishing
PO Box 788
Klamath Falls, OR 97601-0320
Phone: (541)885-4410
Fax: (541)883-4007
**Subject(s):** Daily Newspapers

Circ: (Mon.-Fri.)17,200
     (Sun.)17,800

**Monterey Park Progress** (2276)
Wave Newspaper Group
4201 Wilshire Ave., Ste. 600
Los Angeles, CA 90010
Phone: (323)556-5720
Fax: (323)556-5704
**Subject(s):** Paid Community Newspapers

Circ: (Free)17,788

**Whittier Daily News** (4044)
San Gabriel Newspaper Group
PO Box 581
Whittier, CA 90608
Phone: (310)698-0955
Fax: (310)698-0450
**Subject(s):** Daily Newspapers

Circ: (Sat.)★17,275
     (Mon.-Fri.)★17,330
     (Sun.)★17,739

**Albany Democrat-Herald** (25686)
Northwest Publishing
600 Lyon St. SW
PO Box 130
Albany, OR 97321-0041
Phone: (541)926-2211
Fax: (541)926-5298
**Subject(s):** Daily Newspapers

Circ: (Sun.)★17,630
     (Mon.-Sat.)★17,702

**Statesman-Examiner** (32058)
220 S Main
PO Box 271
Colville, WA 99114
Phone: (509)684-4567
Fax: (509)684-3849
**Subject(s):** Free Newspapers

Circ: (Paid)‡5,519
     (Free)‡17,629

**The Sun** (32059)
220 S. Main
PO Box 271
Colville, WA 99114
Phone: (509)684-4567
Fax: (509)684-3849
**Subject(s):** Free Newspapers

Circ: (Free)17,629

**The Digger Shopper & News** (2636)
Great Ad-ventures Publishing Inc.
2057 Mitchell Ave.
PO Box 5006
Oroville, CA 95966
Phone: (530)533-2170
Fax: (530)533-2181
**Subject(s):** Shopping Guides

Circ: (Free)‡17,600

**The ADvertiser** (33777)
Edwards Publications
608 E Pershing
Riverton, WY 82501
Phone: (307)857-6114
Fax: (307)856-4356
**Subject(s):** Shopping Guides

Circ: (Free)17,500

**The Almanac** (2449)
Country Almanac
3525 Alameda de las Pulgas
Menlo Park, CA 94025
**Subject(s):** Free Newspapers

Circ: (Free)‡17,500

**Los Gatos Weekly Times** (2412)
Silicon Valley Community Newspapers
245 Almendra Ave.
Los Gatos, CA 95030
Phone: (408)354-3917
Fax: (408)354-3917
**Subject(s):** Free Newspapers

Circ: (Paid)1,667
     (Free)17,506

**The Denver Business Journal** (4280)
American City Business Journals Inc.
1700 Broadway, Ste. 515
Denver, CO 80290-9908
Phone: (303)837-3535
Fax: (303)837-3535
**Subject(s):** Business

Circ: (Paid)17,397

**East Los Angeles Commerce Tribune** (2190)
Wave Newspaper Group
4201 Wilshire Ave., Ste. 600
Los Angeles, CA 90010
Phone: (323)556-5720
Fax: (323)556-5704

Circulation: ★ = ABC; △ = BPA; ♦ = CAC; • = CCAB; ▫ = VAC; ⊕ = PO Statement; ‡ = Publisher's Report; Boldface figures = sworn; Light figures = estimated.

3833

# Western States

**Subject(s):** Free Newspapers
**Circ:** (Paid)1,325
(Free)17,349

**Education California (EDCAL)** (2889)
Education California
1517 L St.
Sacramento, CA 95814
**Phone:** (916)444-3216
**Fax:** (916)444-1085
**Subject(s):** Education
**Circ:** (Controlled)200
(Paid)17,117

**Bozeman Daily Chronicle** (18088)
Pioneer Publishing Co.
PO Box 1190
Bozeman, MT 59771-1190
**Phone:** (406)587-4491
**Fax:** (406)587-7995
**Subject(s):** Daily Newspapers
**Circ:** (Mon.-Sat.)★16,068
(Sun.)★17,057

**Wyoming Tribune-Eagle** (33706)
702 W. Lincolnway
Cheyenne, WY 82001
**Phone:** (307)634-3361
**Fax:** (307)633-3191
**Subject(s):** Daily Newspapers
**Circ:** (Mon.-Sat.)★15,564
(Sun.)★17,054

**Arizona Daily Wildcat** (897)
University of Arizona
615 N Park Ave., No. 101
Tucson, AZ 85721
**Phone:** (520)621-1714
**Fax:** (520)621-3074
**Subject(s):** College Publications
**Circ:** (Free)‡17,000

**The Daily** (32263)
University of Washington
144 Communications Bldg.
PO Box 353720
Seattle, WA 98195
**Phone:** (206)543-7666
**Fax:** (206)543-2345
**Subject(s):** College Publications
**Circ:** 17,000

**El Hispano** (2891)
Elitispano
928 2nd St. 300
PO Box 2856
Sacramento, CA 95812
**Phone:** (916)442-0267
**Fax:** (916)442-2818
**Subject(s):** Paid Community Newspapers; Hispanic Publications; Spanish
**Circ:** (Paid)‡3,250
(Free)‡17,000

**Haleakala Times** (7631)
PO Box 1080
Makawao, HI 96768
**Phone:** (808)579-8028
**Fax:** (808)572-0168
**Subject(s):** Free Newspapers
**Circ:** (Combined)17,000

**Independent News Group** (1592)
1828 El Camino Real, Ste. 508
Burlingame, CA 94010
**Phone:** (650)692-9406
**Fax:** (650)692-7587
**Subject(s):** Paid Community Newspapers
**Circ:** ‡17,000

**Oregon Peaceworker** (26047)
Oregon PeaceWorks
104 Commercial St. NE
Salem, OR 97301
**Phone:** (503)585-2767
**Fax:** (503)588-0088
**Subject(s):** Paid Community Newspapers
**Circ:** (Controlled)17,000

**The Union** (1948)
464 Sutton Way
Grass Valley, CA 95945
**Phone:** (530)273-9561
**Fax:** (530)273-1607

**Subject(s):** Daily Newspapers
**Circ:** (Mon.-Sat.)17,000

**Grants Pass Daily Courier** (25841)
Courier Publishing Co.
409 SE 7th St.
PO Box 1468
Grants Pass, OR 97526
**Phone:** (541)474-3700
**Fax:** (541)474-3814
**Subject(s):** Daily Newspapers
**Circ:** (Mon.-Sat.)16,987

**Lodi News-Sentinel** (2080)
125 N Church St.
Lodi, CA 95240-2102
**Phone:** (209)369-2761
**Fax:** (209)369-1084
**Subject(s):** Daily Newspapers
**Circ:** (Mon.-Sat.)16,869

**Central Kitsap Reporter** (32379)
Sound Publishing Inc.
9989 Silverdale Way NW, Ste. 109
Silverdale, WA 98383
**Phone:** (360)308-9161
**Subject(s):** Paid Community Newspapers
**Circ:** (Paid)422
(Non-paid)16,855

**North Coast Journal** (1387)
North Coast Journal Inc.
145 G St., Ste. A
Arcata, CA 95521
**Phone:** (707)826-2000
**Fax:** (707)826-2060
**Subject(s):** Free Newspapers
**Circ:** (Paid)❑174
(Free)❑16,851

**The Business Journal of Phoenix** (760)
American City Business Journals Inc.
101 N. First Ave., Ste. 2300
Phoenix, AZ 85003
**Phone:** (602)230-0955
**Fax:** (602)230-0955
**Subject(s):** Business; Paid Community Newspapers
**Circ:** (Paid)16,840

**Idaho Catholic Register** (7650)
303 Federal Way
Boise, ID 83705
**Phone:** (208)342-1311
**Fax:** (208)342-0224
**Subject(s):** Religious Publications
**Circ:** ‡16,790

**Los Altos Town Crier** (2114)
The Town Crier Company Inc.
138 Main St.
Los Altos, CA 94022
**Phone:** (650)948-9000
**Fax:** (650)948-6647
**Subject(s):** Paid Community Newspapers
**Circ:** (Combined)16,500

**The Observer** (2503)
PO Box 2079
580 Fremont Street
Monterey, CA 93942
**Phone:** (831)373-2919
**Fax:** (831)373-1175
**Subject(s):** Religious Publications
**Circ:** ‡16,500

**Reedley Exponent** (2805)
Reedley Exponent Inc.
PO Box 432
Reedley, CA 93654-0432
**Phone:** (559)638-2244
**Fax:** (559)638-5021
**Subject(s):** Paid Community Newspapers
**Circ:** (Paid)‡3,650
(Free)‡16,400

**San Clemente Sun-Post News** (2993)
The Orange County Register
95 Avenida Del Mar
San Clemente, CA 92672
**Fax:** (949)492-0401
**Subject(s):** Free Newspapers
**Circ:** ‡16,322

**The Marysville Globe** (32148)
8213A State Ave.
PO Box 145
Marysville, WA 98270
**Phone:** (360)659-1300
**Fax:** (360)658-0350
**Subject(s):** Free Newspapers
**Circ:** (Paid)2,659
(Free)16,081

**Eastside Journal** (2191)
Wave Newspaper Group
4201 Wilshire Ave., Ste. 600
Los Angeles, CA 90010
**Phone:** (323)556-5720
**Fax:** (323)556-5704
**Subject(s):** Free Newspapers
**Circ:** (Controlled)16,075

**Hillsboro Argus** (25854)
Hillsboro Argus Inc.
150 S.E. 3rd Ave.
PO Box 588
Hillsboro, OR 97123
**Phone:** (503)648-1131
**Fax:** (503)648-9191
**Subject(s):** Paid Community Newspapers
**Circ:** ‡16,075

**The Sentinel-Advertiser** (1773)
Sentinel Printing and Publishing
145 S L St.
Dinuba, CA 93618-2324
**Phone:** (559)591-4634
**Fax:** (559)591-1322
**Subject(s):** Shopping Guides
**Circ:** (Free)16,041

**Redmond Sammamish Valley News** (32317)
Pacific Media Group
2314 3rd Ave.
Seattle, WA 98121
**Phone:** (206)461-1300
**Fax:** (206)461-1340
**Subject(s):** Free Newspapers
**Circ:** (Paid)287
(Controlled)16,010

**El Chicano** (2979)
Inland Empire Community Newspapers
PO Box 6247
San Bernardino, CA 92412-6247
**Phone:** (909)381-9898
**Fax:** (909)384-0406
**Subject(s):** Paid Community Newspapers; Spanish; Hispanic Publications
**Circ:** (Free)‡16,000

**San Jose Business Journal** (3306)
American City Business Journals Inc.
c/o Norman Bell
96 N. Third St., Ste. 100
San Jose, CA 95112
**Phone:** (408)295-3800
**Fax:** (408)295-5028
**Subject(s):** Local, State, and Regional Publications; Business
**Circ:** (Paid)16,000

**The Shopper's Weekly** (32376)
611 W Cota St.
Shelton, WA 98584
**Phone:** (360)426-4677
**Fax:** (360)427-1005
**Subject(s):** Shopping Guides
**Circ:** (Non-paid)16,000

**Western Cleaner and Launderer (On line)** (2723)
Wakefield Publishing Co.
3236 Estado St.
Pasadena, CA 91107-2916
**Phone:** (626)793-2911
**Fax:** (626)793-5540
**Subject(s):** Laundry and Dry Cleaning
**Circ:** (Non-paid)⊕16,000

**Hawaii Navy News** (7620)
RFD Publications Inc.
45-525 Luluku Rd.
Kaneohe, HI 96744
**Phone:** (808)235-5881
**Fax:** (808)247-7246
**Subject(s):** Free Newspapers; Military and Navy
**Circ:** (Free)15,873

**Walla Walla Union-Bulletin** (32477)
112 S 1st Ave.
Walla Walla, WA 99362
Phone: (509)525-3300
Fax: (509)525-1232
Subject(s): Daily Newspapers

Circ: (Mon.-Fri.)★14,274
(Sun.)★15,801

**The Daily World** (31976)
Community Newspaper Holdings Inc.
315 S. Michigan
PO Box 269
Aberdeen, WA 98520
Phone: (206)532-4000
Fax: (206)533-1328
Subject(s): Daily Newspapers

Circ: (Mon.-Sat.)15,721
(Sun.)15,795

**The World** (25752)
Southwestern Oregon Publishing Co.
350 Commercial
PO Box 1840
Coos Bay, OR 97420-0147
Phone: (541)269-1222
Fax: (541)267-0294
Subject(s): Daily Newspapers

Circ: (Mon.-Fri.)14,192
(Sat.)15,747

**San Diego Jewish Times** (2043)
Schwarz Publishing Inc.
4731 Palm Ave.
La Mesa, CA 91941
Phone: (619)463-5575
Fax: (619)463-1309
Subject(s): Paid Community Newspapers

Circ: (Non-paid)⊕510
(Paid)⊕15,663

**The Rafu Shimpo** (2317)
259 S Los Angeles St.
Los Angeles, CA 90012
Phone: (213)629-2231
Fax: (213)687-0737
Subject(s): Paid Community Newspapers; Japanese

Circ: (Paid)15,500

**The Record-Gazette** (1436)
Record Inc.
218 N. Murray St.
PO Box 727
Banning, CA 92220
Phone: (951)849-4586
Fax: (951)849-2437
Subject(s): Daily Newspapers

Circ: (Paid)2,962
(Free)15,500

**Victorville Green Sheet** (2655)
Associated Desert Shoppers Inc.
73-400 Hwy. 111
Palm Desert, CA 92260
Phone: (760)346-0601
Fax: (760)346-3597
Subject(s): Shopping Guides

Circ: (Free)15,500

**Pacific Business News** (7564)
American City Business Journals Inc.
1833 Kalakaua Ave., 7th Fl.
Honolulu, HI 96815
Phone: (808)955-8078
Fax: (808)955-8078
Subject(s): Business

Circ: (Paid)15,381

**The Herald Journal** (30687)
75 W. 300 N.
PO Box 487
Logan, UT 84323-0487
Phone: (435)752-2121
Fax: (435)753-6642
Subject(s): Daily Newspapers

Circ: (Mon.-Sat.)★14,874
(Sun.)★15,324

**The Beacon Hill News** (32250)
Pacific Publishing Co.
4000 Aurora Ave. N, Ste. 100
Seattle, WA 98103-7853
Phone: (206)461-3333
Fax: (206)461-1285
Subject(s): Free Newspapers

Circ: (Paid)‡266
(Free)‡15,000

**Milpitas Post** (2473)
59 Marylinn Dr.
Milpitas, CA 95035
Phone: (408)262-2454
Fax: (408)763-9710
Subject(s): Free Newspapers

Circ: (Paid)3,050
(Free)15,300

**Mexican American Sun** (1692)
Eastern Group Publications Inc.
2500 S Atlantic Blvd., Bldg. A
Commerce, CA 90040
Phone: (323)263-5743
Fax: (323)263-9169
Subject(s): Free Newspapers; Spanish; Hispanic Publications

Circ: (Paid)♦19
(Free)♦15,171

**Montebello Comet** (1693)
Eastern Group Publications Inc.
2500 S Atlantic Blvd., Bldg. A
Commerce, CA 90040
Phone: (323)263-5743
Fax: (323)263-9169
Subject(s): Free Newspapers; Spanish; Hispanic Publications

Circ: (Paid)♦10
(Free)♦15,175

**Mount Shasta Herald, Weed Press, Dunsmuir News** (2517)
Siskiyou Newspaper
PO Box 127
Mount Shasta, CA 96067
Phone: (916)926-5214
Fax: (916)926-4166
Subject(s): Paid Community Newspapers

Circ: (Combined)‡15,075

**The Lemoore Advance** (2073)
Central C.A. Weeklies Inc.
The Lemoore Advance
PO Box 547
Lemoore, CA 93245
Phone: (209)924-5361
Fax: (209)924-6220
Subject(s): Paid Community Newspapers

Circ: ‡15,020

**Beirut Times** (2141)
PO Box 93475
Los Angeles, CA 90093
Phone: (323)978-8888
Fax: (323)978-4444
Subject(s): Arabic; Ethnic Publications

Circ: (Non-paid)15,000

**Capitol Hill Times** (32254)
Pacific Publishing Co.
4000 Aurora Ave. N, Ste. 100
Seattle, WA 98103-7853
Phone: (206)461-3333
Fax: (206)461-1285
Subject(s): Paid Community Newspapers

Circ: (Paid)15,000

**The Daily Aztec** (3012)
San Diego State University
BAM-2
San Diego, CA 92182-7800
Phone: (619)594-4199
Fax: (619)594-7277
Subject(s): College Publications

Circ: (Free)15,000

**Daily Utah Chronicle** (30763)
The Daily Utah Chronicle
University of Utah
200 S. Central Campus Dr., No. 236
Salt Lake City, UT 84112
Subject(s): College Publications

Circ: ‡15,000

**El Segundo Herald** (1807)
El Segundo Herald Inc.
PO Box 188
El Segundo, CA 90245
Phone: (310)322-1830
Fax: (310)322-2787

**The Ethiopian Mirror** (1531)
PO Box 6881
Beverly Hills, CA 90212
Phone: (323)939-3059
Fax: (323)939-2636
Subject(s): Black Publications; Ethnic Publications

Circ: (Paid)11,000
(Non-paid)15,000

**Henderson Home News** (18672)
HBC Publications Inc.
2300 Corporate Circle Dr., Ste. 150
Henderson, NV 89074
Phone: (702)435-7700
Fax: (702)434-3527
Subject(s): Paid Community Newspapers

Circ: ‡15,000

**Mountaineer** (4210)
Colorado Publishing Co.
31 E. Platt, Ste. 300
Colorado Springs, CO 80903-3311
Phone: (719)634-5905
Fax: (719)634-5157
Subject(s): Free Newspapers

Circ: (Free)‡15,000

**Nevada Appeal** (18652)
200 Bath St.
PO Box 2288
Carson City, NV 89703-2405
Phone: (702)882-6664
Fax: (702)882-6664
Subject(s): Daily Newspapers

Circ: (Mon.-Fri.)14,481
(Sun.)15,008

**Palos Verdes Peninsula News** (2703)
Equal Access Media Inc.
500 Silver Spur Rd., Ste. 300
Palos Verdes Peninsula, CA 90275
Phone: (310)377-6877
Fax: (310)544-4322
Subject(s): Paid Community Newspapers

Circ: (Sat.)6,200
(Thurs.)15,000

**San Diego Daily Transcript** (3046)
2131 3rd Ave.
PO Box 85469
San Diego, CA 92101
Phone: (619)232-4381
Fax: (619)236-8126
Subject(s): Business; Daily Newspapers; Local, State, and Regional Publications

Circ: (Mon.-Fri.)15,000

**San Ramon Valley Times** (1752)
Hills Publications Inc.
524 Hartz Ave.
PO Box 68
Danville, CA 94526
Phone: (510)837-4267
Fax: (510)837-4334
Subject(s): Daily Newspapers

Circ: ‡15,000

**SLV Midweek** (4516)
Valley Publishing
PO Box 607
Monte Vista, CO 81144-0607
Phone: (719)852-3531
Fax: (719)852-3387
Subject(s): Free Newspapers

Circ: (Free)15,000

**Treasure Valley Reminder** (25931)
Wick Communications
1160 SW 4th St.
PO Box 130
Ontario, OR 97914
Phone: (503)889-5387
Fax: (503)889-3347
Subject(s): Shopping Guides

Circ: (Free)15,000

**Viva** (32454)
Flint Publishing Inc.
PO Box 511
Toppenish, WA 98948
Phone: (509)865-4055

# Western States

Fax: (509)865-2655
**Subject(s):** Hispanic Publications; Free Newspapers
**Circ:** (Non-paid)15,000

**Arizona Daily Sun  (669)**
Lee Enterprises Inc.
1751 S. Thomson
Flagstaff, AZ 86001
Phone: (928)774-4545
**Subject(s):** Daily Newspapers
**Circ:** (Mon.-Sat.)12,382
(Sun.)14,863

**Independent Record  (18156)**
PO Box 4249
317 Cruse Ave.
Helena, MT 59601-5003
Phone: (406)442-7190
**Subject(s):** Daily Newspapers
**Circ:** (Mon.-Sat.)★14,254
(Sun.)★14,788

**Montana Standard  (18100)**
P.O. Box 627
Butte, MT 59703
Phone: (406)496-5500
Fax: (406)496-5551
**Subject(s):** Daily Newspapers
**Circ:** (Mon.-Sat.)14,383
(Sun.)14,760

**Booster Advertiser  (636)**
News West Publishing Co.
PO Box 21209
Bullhead City, AZ 86439
Phone: (928)763-2505
**Subject(s):** Shopping Guides
**Circ:** (Combined)14,751

**Fontana Herald-News  (1854)**
Fontana Herald Publishing
16981, Foothill Blvd. Ste. N.
Fontana, CA 92335
Phone: (909)822-2231
Fax: (909)355-9358
**Subject(s):** Paid Community Newspapers
**Circ:** (Paid)5,263
(Free)14,737

**The Corvallis Gazette-Times  (25763)**
Lee Enterprises
600 Jefferson Ave. S.W.
PO Box 368
Corvallis, OR 97333
Phone: (541)753-2641
Fax: (541)758-9505
**Subject(s):** Daily Newspapers
**Circ:** (Mon.-Sat.)12,245
(Sun.)14,713

**El Mundo  (32481)**
El Mundo Communications Inc.
PO Box 2231
Wenatchee, WA 98807
Phone: (509)663-5737
Fax: (509)663-6957
**Subject(s):** Free Newspapers; Hispanic Publications; Spanish
**Circ:** (Paid)235
(Non-paid)▢14,643

**Aspen Daily News  (4088)**
Ute City Tea Party Ltd.
517 E. Hopkins Ave.
Aspen, CO 81611
Phone: (970)925-2220
Fax: (970)920-2118
**Subject(s):** Daily Newspapers
**Circ:** (Free)14,500

**Central Coast This Week  (3465)**
Santa Maria Times
3200 Skyway Dr.
PO Box 400
Santa Maria, CA 93455-1896
Phone: (805)925-2691
Fax: (805)928-5657
**Subject(s):** Free Newspapers
**Circ:** (Free)14,500

**Coastal Post  (1547)**
Marin county's news monthly-Free press
PO Box 31
Bolinas, CA 94924
Phone: (415)868-1600
Fax: (415)868-0502

**Subject(s):** Paid Community Newspapers
**Circ:** (Combined)14,500

**Rosemead/South San Gabriel Progress  (2324)**
Wave Newspaper Group
4201 Wilshire Ave., Ste. 600
Los Angeles, CA 90010
Phone: (323)556-5720
Fax: (323)556-5704
**Subject(s):** Free Newspapers
**Circ:** (Free)‡14,447

**The Port Orchard Independent  (32205)**
Sound Publishing Inc.
2950 SE Mile Hill Dr.
PO Box 27
Port Orchard, WA 98366
Phone: (360)876-4414
**Subject(s):** Paid Community Newspapers
**Circ:** (Paid)1,346
(Non-paid)14,415

**Blues To Do Monthly  (32252)**
Marlee Walker's Blues To-Do's
PO Box 22950
Seattle, WA 98122-0950
Phone: (206)328-0662
**Subject(s):** Music and Musical Instruments
**Circ:** (Paid)600
(Non-paid)14,400

**The Mountain Democrat  (2742)**
Mountain Democrat
1360 Broadway
PO Box 1088
Placerville, CA 95667
Phone: (530)622-1255
Fax: (530)622-7894
**Subject(s):** Paid Community Newspapers
**Circ:** (Thurs.)11,991
(Mon.)12,566
(Fri.)14,358

**Rancho Bernardo News Journal  (2767)**
Pomerado Publishing
13247 Poway Rd.
Poway, CA 92064-4613
Phone: (619)487-5757
**Subject(s):** Free Newspapers
**Circ:** (Paid)509
(Free)14,182

**The Chronicle  (32034)**
321 N. Pearl St.
PO Box 580
Centralia, WA 98531
Phone: (360)807-8203
Fax: (360)736-4796
**Subject(s):** Daily Newspapers
**Circ:** (Mon.-Sat.)14,126

**Herald Advertiser  (3399)**
Sanger Herald Inc.
740 N St.
Sanger, CA 93657
Phone: (559)875-2511
Fax: (559)875-2521
**Subject(s):** Shopping Guides
**Circ:** (Free)‡14,100

**Intermountain Catholic  (30768)**
Roman Catholic Diocese of Salt Lake City
PO Box 2489
Salt Lake City, UT 84103
**Subject(s):** Religious Publications
**Circ:** ‡14,000

**The Monroe Tribune  (32382)**
Tribune/Marketplace Newspapers Inc.
127 Ave. C
PO Box 499
Snohomish, WA 98291-0499
Phone: (360)568-4121
Fax: (360)568-1484
**Subject(s):** Paid Community Newspapers
**Circ:** (Paid)‡14,000

**Senior Times  (32393)**
Senior Times Inc.
523 N Pines Rd., Ste. B
PO Box 142020
Spokane, WA 99214-2020
Phone: (509)924-2440
Fax: (509)927-1154

**Subject(s):** Senior Citizens' Interests; Free Newspapers
**Circ:** (Combined)14,000

**The Snohomish County Tribune  (32385)**
Tribune Newspapers
127 Ave. C
PO Box 499
Snohomish, WA 98291-0499
Phone: (360)568-4121
Fax: (360)568-1484
**Subject(s):** Paid Community Newspapers
**Circ:** ‡14,000

**The Tri State Trader  (4484)**
Lamar Daily News
310 S 5th St.
PO Box 1217
Lamar, CO 81052
Phone: (719)336-2266
Fax: (719)336-2526
**Subject(s):** Shopping Guides
**Circ:** (Free)‡14,000

**White Sheet-The Lake Havasu  (704)**
Associated Desert Shoppers Inc.
2099 W. Acoma
Lake Havasu City, AZ 86403
Phone: (928)855-7871
Fax: (928)855-8183
**Subject(s):** Shopping Guides
**Circ:** (Free)‡14,000

**The Hanford Sentinel  (1957)**
Lee Enterprises Inc.
PO Box 9
Hanford, CA 93232
Phone: (559)582-0471
Fax: (559)502-8631
**Subject(s):** Daily Newspapers
**Circ:** (Mon.-Fri.)★13,533
(Sun.)★13,965

**Portland Business Journal  (25974)**
American City Business Journals Inc.
c/o Dan Cook
851 SW Sixth Ave., No. 500
Portland, OR 97204
Phone: (503)227-2650
Fax: (503)227-2650
**Subject(s):** Business
**Circ:** (Paid)13,936

**Vail Daily  (4097)**
40780 US Hwy. 6 & 24
Avon, CO 81620
Phone: (970)949-0555
Fax: (970)949-7096
**Subject(s):** Daily Newspapers
**Circ:** (Sun.)11,750
(Mon.-Fri.)13,645

**The Billings Outpost  (18067)**
Wild Raspberry Inc.
1833 Grand Ave.
Billings, MT 59102-2939
Phone: (406)248-1616
Fax: (406)248-2414
**Subject(s):** Free Newspapers
**Circ:** (Free)‡13,500

**The Huachuca Scout  (848)**
Five Star Publishing
PO Box 1119
Sierra Vista, AZ 85635
Phone: (520)458-3340
Fax: (520)458-9338
**Subject(s):** Paid Community Newspapers
**Circ:** 13,500

**Navajo-Hopi Observer  (672)**
Western Newspapers Inc.
2224 E. Cedar Ave.
Flagstaff, AZ 86001
Phone: (928)226-9696
Fax: (928)226-1115
**Subject(s):** Paid Community Newspapers
**Circ:** (Non-paid)13,500

**Santa Ynez Valley News  (3532)**
Valley News
423 2nd St.
PO Box 647
Solvang, CA 93464
Phone: (805)688-5522
Fax: (805)688-7685

**Gale Directory of Publications & Broadcast Media/140th Ed.**  **Western States**

**Subject(s):** Paid Community Newspapers
**Circ:** (Thurs.)7,500
(Tues.)13,500

**The Stanford Daily (3559)**
The Stanford Daily Publishing Corp.
Storke Publication Bldg., Ste. 101
Stanford, CA 94305-2240
Phone: (650)725-2100
Fax: (650)725-1329
**Subject(s):** College Publications
**Circ:** (Free)‡13,500

**Tacoma True Citizen (32441)**
Piloven Publishing
2600 S Jackson St.
Seattle, WA 98144
Phone: (206)323-3070
Fax: (206)322-6518
**Subject(s):** Paid Community Newspapers; Black Publications
**Circ:** 13,500

**Tri-County Shopper (26070)**
West-Lane News
PO Box 188
Veneta, OR 97487
Phone: (541)935-1882
Fax: (541)935-4082
**Subject(s):** Shopping Guides
**Circ:** (Free)13,500

**Hawaii Army Weekly (7618)**
RFD Publications Inc.
45-525 Luluku Rd.
Kaneohe, HI 96744
Phone: (808)235-5881
Fax: (808)247-7246
**Subject(s):** Free Newspapers; Military and Navy
**Circ:** (Free)13,489

**Today's News - Herald (703)**
River City Newspapers
2225 W. Acoma Blvd.
Lake Havasu City, AZ 86403
Phone: (928)453-4237
Fax: (928)855-9892
**Subject(s):** Daily Newspapers
**Circ:** (Mon.-Fri.)11,239
(Sun.)13,484

**Tri-City Weekly (Southern Edition) (1836)**
V & P Publishing Company Inc.
PO Box 134
Eureka, CA 95502
Phone: (707)443-5672
Fax: (707)443-5022
**Subject(s):** Shopping Guides
**Circ:** (Combined)13,438

**Riverside Green Sheet (2836)**
Associated Desert Shoppers Inc.
73-400 Hwy. 111
Palm Desert, CA 92260
Phone: (760)346-0601
Fax: (760)346-3597
**Subject(s):** Shopping Guides
**Circ:** (Free)13,400

**Ute Pass Courier (4615)**
Colorado Community Newspapers
1200 E Hwy. 24
PO Box 340
Woodland Park, CO 80863
Phone: (719)687-3006
Fax: (719)687-3009
**Subject(s):** Paid Community Newspapers
**Circ:** 3,750
13,100

**The California Aggie (1757)**
University of California, Davis
25 Lower Freeborn
One Shields Ave.
Davis, CA 95616
Phone: (530)752-0365
Fax: (530)752-0355
**Subject(s):** College Publications
**Circ:** (Free)‡13,000

**The Jewish Reporter (18683)**
Jewish Federation of Las Vegas
2317 Renaissance Dr.
Las Vegas, NV 89119-6191
Phone: (702)732-0556
Fax: (702)732-3228

**Subject(s):** Jewish Publications; Free Newspapers
**Circ:** (Controlled)13,000

**Kirkland Courier (32124)**
Pacific Publishing Co.
733 7th Ave., Ste. 204
Kirkland, WA 98033-5669
Phone: (425)822-9166
Fax: (425)827-7716
**Subject(s):** Paid Community Newspapers
**Circ:** (Free)‡13,000

**North Scottsdale Independent (832)**
Independent Newspapers Inc.
11000 N. Scottsdale Rd., Ste. 210
Scottsdale, AZ 85254
Phone: (480)483-0977
Fax: (480)948-0496
**Subject(s):** Free Newspapers
**Circ:** (Combined)‡13,000

**The San Diego Voice and Viewpoint (3055)**
PO Box 120095
San Diego, CA 92112-0095
Phone: (619)266-2233
Fax: (619)266-0533
**Subject(s):** Black Publications; Paid Community Newspapers; Hispanic Publications
**Circ:** 13,000

**Vietnam Daily News (3313)**
2350 S 10th St.
San Jose, CA 95112
Phone: (408)292-3422
Fax: (408)293-5153
**Subject(s):** Daily Newspapers; Vietnamese
**Circ:** 13,000

**Huntington Park Bulletin (2225)**
Wave Newspaper Group
4201 Wilshire Ave., Ste. 600
Los Angeles, CA 90010
Phone: (323)556-5720
Fax: (323)556-5704
**Subject(s):** Free Newspapers
**Circ:** (Paid)54
(Free)12,850

**East Bay Business Times (2746)**
American City Business Journals Inc.
6160 Stoneridge Mall Rd., Ste. 300
Pleasanton, CA 94588
Phone: (925)598-1840
Fax: (925)598-1840
**Subject(s):** Business
**Circ:** (Combined)12,817

**Everett News Tribune (32381)**
Tribune Newspapers
127 Ave. C
PO Box 499
Snohomish, WA 98291-0499
Phone: (360)568-4121
Fax: (360)568-1484
**Subject(s):** Paid Community Newspapers
**Circ:** (Non-paid)3,200
(Paid)12,800

**Queen Anne/Magnolia News (32314)**
Pacific Publishing Co.
4000 Aurora Ave. N, Ste. 100
Seattle, WA 98103-7853
Phone: (206)461-3333
Fax: (206)461-1285
**Subject(s):** Paid Community Newspapers
**Circ:** ‡12,800

**Sentinel Plus (1958)**
300 W 6th St.
PO Box 9
Hanford, CA 93232
Phone: (559)582-0471
Fax: (559)587-1876
**Subject(s):** Shopping Guides
**Circ:** (Sun.)12,738
(Mon.-Sat.)12,779

**Laguna Citizen (1917)**
Herburger Publications Inc.
604 N Lincoln Way
PO Box 307
Galt, CA 95632
Phone: (209)745-1551
Fax: (209)745-4492

**Subject(s):** Free Newspapers
**Circ:** (Thurs.)12,700

**The Californian (3597)**
28765 Single Oak Dr., Ste. 100
Temecula, CA 92590
Phone: (951)676-4315
Fax: (951)699-1467
**Subject(s):** Daily Newspapers
**Circ:** (Mon.-Sat.)12,485
(Sun.)12,540

**Sierra Vista Herald (850)**
102 Fab Ave.
Sierra Vista, AZ 85635
Phone: (520)458-9440
Fax: (520)459-0120
**Subject(s):** Daily Newspapers
**Circ:** (Mon.-Fri.)10,978
(Sun.)12,544

**Aging Today (3103)**
American Society on Aging
833 Market St., Ste. 511
San Francisco, CA 94103-1824
Phone: (415)974-9600
Fax: (415)974-0300
**Subject(s):** Gerontology
**Circ:** (Free)‡1,500
(Paid)‡12,500

**Las Vegas Business Press (18687)**
Wick Communications
1385 Pama Ln., No. 111
Las Vegas, NV 89119-3830
**Subject(s):** Paid Community Newspapers
**Circ:** (Controlled)12,500

**Lynwood Press (2267)**
Wave Newspaper Group
4201 Wilshire Ave., Ste. 600
Los Angeles, CA 90010
Phone: (323)556-5720
Fax: (323)556-5704
**Subject(s):** Paid Community Newspapers; Black Publications
**Circ:** 12,500

**Paso Robles Press (2725)**
Paso Robles Communications Group
1636 Spring St.
PO Box 427
Paso Robles, CA 93446
Phone: (805)237-6060
Fax: (805)237-6066
**Subject(s):** Travel and Tourism; Farm Newspapers
**Circ:** (Fri.)5,000
(Wed.)‡12,500

**Sierra Home Advertiser (2566)**
Central Valley Publishing
PO Box 305
Oakhurst, CA 93644-0305
Phone: (559)683-4464
Fax: (559)683-8102
**Subject(s):** Shopping Guides
**Circ:** (Free)‡12,500

**Skagit Weekly (32164)**
Skagit Valley Publishing Co.
1000 E College Way
PO Box 578
Mount Vernon, WA 98273-0578
Phone: (360)424-3251
Fax: (360)424-5300
**Subject(s):** Shopping Guides
**Circ:** (Free)12,500

**White Sheet-The Parker Advertiser (729)**
Associated Desert Shoppers Inc.
2099 W. Acoma
Lake Havasu City, AZ 86403
Phone: (928)855-7871
Fax: (928)855-8183
**Subject(s):** Shopping Guides
**Circ:** (Free)‡12,500

**Calaveras Prospect (Weekly, Citizen & Chronicle) (2974)**
Calaveras First Newspapers
15 N. Main St.
PO Box 1197
San Andreas, CA 95249
Phone: (209)754-3861
Fax: (209)754-1805

Circulation: ★ = ABC; △ = BPA; ♦ = CAC; • = CCAB; ▢ = VAC; ⊕ = PO Statement; ‡ = Publisher's Report; Boldface figures = sworn; Light figures = estimated.

**Subject(s):** Paid Community Newspapers
**Circ:** ‡12,439

**Los Angeles Daily Journal** (2255)
Daily Journal Corp.
915 E. 1st St.
Los Angeles, CA 90012-4050
Phone: (213)229-5300
Fax: (213)680-3682
**Subject(s):** Daily Newspapers; Law
**Circ:** (Free)514
    (Paid)12,433

**The Voice Newspaper** (32337)
Neighborhood House
Jesse Epstein Bldg.
905 Spruce St.
Seattle, WA 98104
Phone: (206)461-8430
Fax: (206)461-3857
**Subject(s):** Free Newspapers
**Circ:** 12,400

**Auburn Journal** (1394)
1030 High St.
PO Box 5910
Auburn, CA 95603-4707
Phone: (530)885-5656
Fax: (530)887-1231
**Subject(s):** Daily Newspapers
**Circ:** (Mon.-Fri.)★11,569
    (Sun.)★12,315

**Central Sun-Press** (7617)
RFD Publications Inc.
45-525 Luluku Rd.
Kaneohe, HI 96744
Phone: (808)235-5881
Fax: (808)247-7246
**Subject(s):** Free Newspapers
**Circ:** (Combined)12,286

**Poway News Chieftain** (2761)
Pomerado Publishing
13247 Poway Rd.
Poway, CA 92064
Phone: (858)748-2311
**Subject(s):** Paid Community Newspapers
**Circ:** (Paid)1,414
    (Free)12,107

**Compton Bulletin** (1698)
American Print Media
800 E. Compton Blvd.
Compton, CA 90221
Phone: (310)635-6776
**Subject(s):** Paid Community Newspapers; Black Publications
**Circ:** (Free)10,000
    (Paid)12,000

**The Daily Evergreen** (32212)
Washington State University
113 Murrow E.
PO Box 642510
Pullman, WA 99164
Phone: (509)335-4573
Fax: (509)335-7401
**Subject(s):** College Publications
**Circ:** (Non-paid)12,000

**Davis County Clipper** (30665)
Clipper Publishing
1370 S 500 W
PO Box 267
Bountiful, UT 84010-0267
Phone: (801)295-2251
Fax: (801)295-3044
**Subject(s):** Free Newspapers
**Circ:** (Free)8,000
    (Paid)12,000

**Hesperia Resorter** (1966)
Valley Wide Newspaper
16925 Main St.
PO Box 400937
Hesperia, CA 92340-0937
Phone: (760)244-3920
Fax: (760)244-6609
**Subject(s):** Free Newspapers
**Circ:** (Paid)‡2,200
    (Free)‡12,000

**Humboldt Beacon & Advance** (1863)
Humboldt Beacon
180 S Fortuna Blvd.
PO Box 310
Fortuna, CA 95540
Phone: (707)725-6166
Fax: (707)725-4981
**Subject(s):** Free Newspapers
**Circ:** (Paid)‡4,750
    (Free)‡12,000

**Idaho Moneysaver** (7747)
Triad News Publishing Inc.
116 S. Jackson, No. 5
Moscow, ID 83843
Phone: (208)883-4420
Fax: (800)278-5051
**Subject(s):** Shopping Guides
**Circ:** (Non-paid)12,000

**International Examiner** (32276)
622 S. Washington St.
Seattle, WA 98104
Phone: (206)624-3925
Fax: (206)624-3046
**Subject(s):** Free Newspapers; Ethnic Publications
**Circ:** (Paid)2,000
    (Free)12,000

**KaMai Forum** (1931)
1108 Vincent Way
Glendale, CA 91205
Phone: (818)956-0551
Fax: (818)956-5322
**Subject(s):** Paid Community Newspapers; Japanese
**Circ:** ‡12,000

**Lake County Advertiser** (18231)
Flathead Publishing Group
PO Box 1090
Polson, MT 59860
Phone: (406)883-4343
Fax: (406)883-4349
**Subject(s):** Shopping Guides
**Circ:** (Non-paid)12,000

**The Malibu Times** (2424)
The Malibu Times Inc.
Las Flores Canyon Rd.
Malibu, CA 90265
Phone: (310)456-5507
Fax: (310)456-8986
**Subject(s):** Paid Community Newspapers
**Circ:** ‡12,000

**The Northern Colorado Business Report** (4381)
141 S. College Ave.
Fort Collins, CO 80524-2810
Phone: (970)221-5400
Fax: (970)221-5432
**Subject(s):** Paid Community Newspapers; Business
**Circ:** (Combined)12,000

**The Peninsula Gateway** (32100)
Peninsula Gateway
3555 Erickson St.
Gig Harbor, WA 98335
Phone: (253)851-9921
Fax: (253)851-3939
**Subject(s):** Paid Community Newspapers
**Circ:** (Combined)‡12,000

**Post Script** (18144)
Ravalli Republic
232 W. Main St.
Hamilton, MT 59840
Phone: (406)363-3300
Fax: (406)363-1767
**Subject(s):** Shopping Guides
**Circ:** (Free)‡12,000

**Record Stockman** (4604)
Record Stockman Inc.
4800 Wadsworth Blvd., Ste. 200
PO Box 1209
Wheat Ridge, CO 80034
**Subject(s):** Livestock; Farm Newspapers
**Circ:** 12,000

**St. Helena Star (online)** (2960)
Krsek Publishing L.P.
1200 Main St., Ste. C
PO Box 346
Saint Helena, CA 94574
Phone: (707)963-2731

Fax: (707)963-8957
**Subject(s):** Paid Community Newspapers
**Circ:** ‡12,000

**TenPercent** (2351)
University of California, Los Angeles
149B Kerckhoff Hall, 308 Westwood Plz.
308 Westwood Plz.
118 Kerckhoff Hall
Los Angeles, CA 90024
Phone: (310)825-2587
Fax: (310)825-2794
**Subject(s):** Gay and Lesbian Interests
**Circ:** 12,000

**UCSD Guardian** (2041)
University of California at San Diego
Mail Code 0316 UCSD
9500 Gilman Dr.
La Jolla, CA 92093-0316
Phone: (619)534-3466
Fax: (619)534-7691
**Subject(s):** College Publications
**Circ:** (Combined)12,000

**Western Livestock Reporter** (18071)
PO Box 30758
Billings, MT 59107
Phone: (406)259-5406
Fax: (406)259-6888
**Subject(s):** Livestock; Farm Newspapers
**Circ:** ‡12,000

**World of Pageantry** (1375)
Harvey Berish
150 S Magnolia Ave.
Anaheim, CA 92804
Phone: (714)952-2263
Fax: (714)535-3552
**Subject(s):** Paid Community Newspapers; Music and Musical Instruments; Music and Musical Instruments
**Circ:** (Paid)⊕12,000

**East Oregonian** (25934)
East Oregonian Publishing Company Inc.
211 SE Byers Ave.
PO Box 1089
Pendleton, OR 97801
Phone: (541)276-2211
Fax: (541)276-8314
**Subject(s):** Daily Newspapers
**Circ:** (Mon.-Sat.)11,107
    (Sun.)11,989

**Bisbee Daily Review** (847)
Sierra Vista Herald
102 Fab Ave.
Sierra Vista, AZ 85635
Phone: (520)458-9440
Fax: (520)459-0120
**Subject(s):** Daily Newspapers
**Circ:** (Mon.-Fri.)10,425
    (Sun.)11,756

**Chronicle/Sentinel-Mist** (26034)
Columbia County Publications
195 S 15th St.
PO Box 1153
Saint Helens, OR 97051
Phone: (503)397-0116
Fax: (503)397-4093
**Subject(s):** Paid Community Newspapers
**Circ:** (Paid)‡6,200
    (Free)11,700

**Bremerton Patriot** (32024)
Sound Publishing Inc.
520 Burwell St.
Bremerton, WA 98337
Phone: (360)782-1581
**Subject(s):** Paid Community Newspapers
**Circ:** (Paid)272
    (Non-paid)11,698

**Desert Mailer News** (2687)
PO Box 4050
Palmdale, CA 93590-4050
Fax: (805)942-6418
**Subject(s):** Paid Community Newspapers
**Circ:** (Tues.)11,677

**Leisure World News (2053)**
The Orange County Register
PO Box 2068
24351 El Toro Rd.
Laguna Woods, CA 92654
Fax: (949)837-0106
**Subject(s):** Paid Community Newspapers
**Circ:** ‡11,555

**Contra Costa Newspapers (4017)**
Hills Publications Inc.
5707 Redwood Rd.
Walnut Creek, CA 94598
Phone: (510)339-4040
Fax: (510)339-4066
**Subject(s):** Free Newspapers
**Circ:** 11,519

**Coronado Journal (1716)**
1224 10th St., Ste. 104
Coronado, CA 92118
Phone: (619)435-3141
Fax: (619)435-3051
**Subject(s):** Paid Community Newspapers
**Circ:** 11,500

**Green Valley News (693)**
Green Valley News & Sun
101-42 S. La Canada
PO Box 567
Green Valley Mall
Green Valley, AZ 85622
Phone: (520)625-5511
Fax: (520)625-8046
**Subject(s):** Paid Community Newspapers
**Circ:** 11,500

**Idaho Mountain Express (7718)**
Express Publishing Inc.
PO Box 1013
Ketchum, ID 83340
Phone: (208)726-8060
Fax: (208)726-2329
**Subject(s):** Free Newspapers
**Circ:** (Paid)‡2,000
    (Free)‡11,500

**Jackson Hole News & Guide (33741)**
PO Box 7445
Jackson, WY 83002
Phone: (307)733-2047
Fax: (307)733-2138
**Subject(s):** Paid Community Newspapers
**Circ:** 11,500

**San Bruno Herald (3373)**
San Mateo County Times
1080 S Amphlett Blvd.
PO Box 5400
San Mateo, CA 94402-1860
Phone: (650)348-4321
Fax: (650)348-4446
**Subject(s):** Paid Community Newspapers
**Circ:** 11,495

**Daily Sun News (32434)**
PO Box 878
Sunnyside, WA 98944
Phone: (509)837-4500
Fax: (509)837-6397
**Subject(s):** Daily Newspapers
**Circ:** (Paid)3,914
    (Free)11,474

**Ahora Spanish News (18736)**
30 Mary St., Ste. 2
PO Box 3582
Reno, NV 89509-3582
Phone: (775)323-6811
Fax: (775)323-6995
**Subject(s):** Paid Community Newspapers; Hispanic Publications; Spanish
**Circ:** (Paid)620
    (Free)11,380

**Market Shopper (1770)**
Reed Print Incorporated Community Newspapers
1231 Jefferson St.
Delano, CA 93215
Phone: (805)725-0600
Fax: (805)725-4373
**Subject(s):** Shopping Guides
**Circ:** (Free)‡11,350

**Sonoma West Exchange (3514)**
Sonoma West Publishers Inc.
PO Box 521
Sebastopol, CA 95473-0521
**Subject(s):** Shopping Guides
**Circ:** (Free)11,300

**Sun-Reporter - Metro Reporter (3221)**
Reporter Publications
1791 Bancroft Ave.
San Francisco, CA 94111
Phone: (415)671-1000
Fax: (415)671-1005
**Subject(s):** Paid Community Newspapers; Black Publications
**Circ:** ‡11,249

**Union-Democrat (3538)**
Union Democrat Inc.
84 S. Washington St.
Sonora, CA 95370
Phone: (209)532-7151
Fax: (209)532-6451
**Subject(s):** Daily Newspapers
**Circ:** (Mon.-Sat.)11,213

**The Springfield News (26059)**
1887 Laura St.
Springfield, OR 97477
Phone: (541)746-1671
Fax: (541)746-0633
**Subject(s):** Paid Community Newspapers
**Circ:** (Paid)11,200

**Arlington Times (31984)**
PO Box 67
Arlington, WA 98223
**Subject(s):** Paid Community Newspapers; Shopping Guides
**Circ:** (Paid)‡2,308
    (Free)‡11,109

**Aspen Times (4090)**
310 E. Main St.
Aspen, CO 81611
Phone: (303)925-3414
Fax: (303)925-6240
**Subject(s):** Daily Newspapers
**Circ:** ‡11,000

**The Courier Express (18127)**
341 3rd Ave. S
PO Box 151
Glasgow, MT 59230
Phone: (406)228-9301
Fax: (406)228-2665
**Subject(s):** Free Newspapers
**Circ:** (Free)‡11,000

**Park Labrea News and Beverly Press (2299)**
PO Box 36036
6720 Melrose Ave.
Los Angeles, CA 90036-6036
Phone: (323)933-5518
**Subject(s):** Free Newspapers
**Circ:** (Free)‡11,000

**The Rocky Mountain Collegian (4383)**
Colorado State University
Lory Student Ctr.
Box 13
Fort Collins, CO 80523
Phone: (970)491-1146
Fax: (970)491-1690
**Subject(s):** College Publications
**Circ:** (Free)‡11,000

**Upper Rogue Independent (25788)**
PO Box 900
Eagle Point, OR 97524
Phone: (541)826-7700
Fax: (541)826-1340
**Subject(s):** Paid Community Newspapers
**Circ:** (Paid)‡2,000
    (Free)‡11,000

**Corridor News (2759)**
Pomerado Publishing
13247 Poway Rd.
Poway, CA 92064
Phone: (858)748-2311
**Subject(s):** Free Newspapers
**Circ:** (Paid)521
    (Free)10,980

**Tracy Press (3915)**
145 W 10th St.
PO Box 419
Tracy, CA 95376-3903
Phone: (209)835-3030
Fax: (209)832-5383
**Subject(s):** Daily Newspapers
**Circ:** (Mon.-Sat.)10,827

**Culver City Chronicle (1733)**
Los Angeles Independent Newspaper Group
4201 Wilshire Blvd., Ste. 600
Los Angeles, CA 90010
Phone: (323)556-5720
Fax: (323)556-5704
**Subject(s):** Free Newspapers
**Circ:** (Paid)7
    (Non-paid)10,770

**The Signal (3944)**
Morris Newspapers Inc.
The Santa Clarita Valley Signal
24000 Creekside Rd.
Valencia, CA 91355
Phone: (661)259-1000
Fax: (661)284-6703
**Subject(s):** Daily Newspapers
**Circ:** (Combined)10,597

**The Sonoma Index-Tribune (3536)**
The Sonoma Index-Tribune Inc.
PO Box C
Sonoma, CA 95476
Phone: (707)938-2111
Fax: (707)938-1600
**Subject(s):** Paid Community Newspapers
**Circ:** (Paid)10,531

**Littleton Independent (4498)**
2329 W Main St., Ste. 103
Littleton, CO 80120
Phone: (303)794-7877
Fax: (303)794-1909
**Subject(s):** Paid Community Newspapers
**Circ:** ‡10,500

**News Pointer (3386)**
Marin Scope Community Newspapers Inc.
PO Box T
San Rafael, CA 94903
**Subject(s):** Paid Community Newspapers
**Circ:** (Combined)‡10,500

**White Sheet-The Tri-State Advertiser (705)**
Associated Desert Shoppers Inc.
2099 W. Acoma
Lake Havasu City, AZ 86403
Phone: (928)855-7871
Fax: (928)855-8183
**Subject(s):** Shopping Guides
**Circ:** (Non-paid)‡10,500

**The Galt Herald (1916)**
Herburger Publications Inc.
No. 604, Lincoln Way
PO Box 307
Galt, CA 95632
Phone: (209)745-1551
**Subject(s):** Paid Community Newspapers
**Circ:** (Wed.)10,400

**Martinez News-Gazette (2440)**
Gibson Publications Inc.
615 Estudillo St.
Martinez, CA 94553
Phone: (925)228-6400
Fax: (925)228-1536
**Subject(s):** Daily Newspapers
**Circ:** (Paid)3,070
    (Free)10,344

**Wood River Journal (7694)**
PO Box 988
Hailey, ID 83333
Phone: (208)788-3444
Fax: (208)788-0083
**Subject(s):** Free Newspapers
**Circ:** (Paid)2,000
    (Free)10,310

**Ag Journal (4474)**
PO Box 500
La Junta, CO 81050
Phone: (719)384-2867
Fax: (800)748-1997

**Subject(s):** Paid Community Newspapers
**Circ:** ‡10,300

**Placer Herald (2847)**
Brehm Inc.
4253 Rocklin Rd.
Rocklin, CA 95677-2831
Phone: (916)624-9713
Fax: (916)624-7469
**Subject(s):** Free Newspapers

**Circ:** (Paid)1,316
(Free)10,277

**Anaheim Hills News (1341)**
The Orange County Register
1771 S. Lewis
Anaheim, CA 92825
Phone: (714)634-1567
Fax: (714)704-3714
**Subject(s):** Free Newspapers

**Circ:** (Paid)25
(Free)10,200

**Arizona Business Gazette (738)**
Phoenix Newspapers Inc.
200 E. Van Buren St.
Phoenix, AZ 85004-2238
Phone: (602)444-8000
Fax: (602)444-7363
**Subject(s):** Business; Law; Local, State, and Regional Publications

**Circ:** (Free)5,744
(Paid)10,208

**Oroville Shopping News (2637)**
Mercury Inc.
PO Box 651
Oroville, CA 95965
Phone: (916)533-3131
Fax: (916)533-3127
**Subject(s):** Shopping Guides

**Circ:** (Free)10,200

**Texas Lawyer (3228)**
The American Lawyer
10 United Nations Plz., 3rd Fl.
San Francisco, CA 94102
Fax: (415)352-0118
**Subject(s):** Paid Community Newspapers

**Circ:** (Paid)10,200

**Davis Enterprise (1760)**
McNaughton Newspapers
315 G St.
Davis, CA 95616
Phone: (530)756-0800
Fax: (530)756-6707
**Subject(s):** Daily Newspapers

**Circ:** (Mon.-Fri.)9,857
(Sun.)10,141

**Hi-Desert Star (4079)**
Hi Desert Publishing
56445 29 Palms Hwy.
PO Box 880
Yucca Valley, CA 92286-2861
Phone: (760)365-3315
Fax: (760)365-8686
**Subject(s):** Paid Community Newspapers

**Circ:** ‡10,100

**Alaska Post (557)**
724 Postal Loop No.5900
Public Affairs Office
Fort Richardson, AK 99505-5900
Phone: (907)384-1539
Fax: (907)384-2060
**Subject(s):** Paid Community Newspapers

**Circ:** (Controlled)10,000

**Ballard News Tribune (32249)**
Robinson Communications
2208 NW Market St., Rm. 202
Seattle, WA 98107
Phone: (206)783-1244
Fax: (206)789-2455
**Subject(s):** Free Newspapers

**Circ:** (Combined)10,000

**Beaverton Valley Times (25949)**
Community Newspapers
1325 SW Custer Dr.
Portland, OR 97219-2750
Phone: (503)684-0360
Fax: (503)620-3433

**Subject(s):** Free Newspapers
**Circ:** (Paid)7,905
(Free)10,000

**The Boulder County Business Report (4106)**
Boulder County Business Report
3180 Sterling Cir., Ste. 201
Boulder, CO 80301-2338
Fax: (303)440-8954
**Subject(s):** Electrical Engineering; Local, State, and Regional Publications

**Circ:** (Paid)10,000

**The Business Examiner (32437)**
Business Examiner Newspaper Group
1517 S. Fawcett St., Ste. 350
Tacoma, WA 98402-1807
Phone: (253)404-0891
Fax: (253)404-0892
**Subject(s):** Business

**Circ:** (Combined)10,000

**The Daily Barometer (25764)**
Oregon State University
118 Memorial Union E.
Corvallis, OR 97331-1614
Phone: (541)737-3374
Fax: (541)737-4999
**Subject(s):** College Publications

**Circ:** (Non-paid)10,000

**Daily Forty-Niner (2089)**
Forty-Niner Advertising
California State University, Long Beach
1250 Bellflower Blvd.
SSPA 010B
Long Beach, CA 90840-4601
Phone: (562)985-8000
Fax: (562)985-1740
**Subject(s):** College Publications

**Circ:** (Free)‡10,000

**Daily Trojan (2180)**
University of Southern California
University Park Campus,
Los Angeles, CA 90089-0895
Phone: (213)740-2707
Fax: (213)740-8829
**Subject(s):** College Publications

**Circ:** ‡10,000

**Deer Park Tribune (32065)**
Tribune Inc.
104 N Main
PO Box 400
Deer Park, WA 99006
Phone: (509)276-5043
Fax: (509)276-2041
**Subject(s):** Paid Community Newspapers

**Circ:** (Paid)‡3,500
(Free)‡10,000

**Freedom Socialist (32270)**
Freedom Socialist Party
5018 Rainier Ave. S
Seattle, WA 98118
Phone: (206)722-2453
Fax: (206)723-7691
**Subject(s):** Politics; Women's Interests

**Circ:** 10,000

**The Glendale Star (683)**
Pueblo Publishers Inc.
7122 N 59th Ave.
Glendale, AZ 85301
Phone: (623)842-6000
Fax: (623)842-6017
**Subject(s):** Paid Community Newspapers

**Circ:** ‡10,000

**Globetrotter (2792)**
Redlands Daily Facts
PO Box 2240
Redlands, CA 92373-0740
Phone: (909)793-3221
Fax: (909)793-9588
**Subject(s):** Free Newspapers; Military and Navy

**Circ:** (Free)10,000

**Golden Gate Xpress (3144)**
San Francisco State University
Dept. of Journalism
1600 Holloway Ave.
San Francisco, CA 94132-1722
Phone: (415)338-3123

Fax: (415)338-3111
**Subject(s):** College Publications

**Circ:** ‡10,000

**The Guardsman (3145)**
City College of San Francisco
50 Phelan Ave., V-67
San Francisco, CA 94112
Phone: (415)239-3446
Fax: (415)239-3884
**Subject(s):** College Publications

**Circ:** ‡10,000

**The Hellenic Calendar (3405)**
2747 N Grand Ave., PMB 250
Santa Ana, CA 92705
Phone: (714)550-9933
Fax: (714)550-9696
**Subject(s):** Paid Community Newspapers; Ethnic Publications

**Circ:** (Combined)10,000

**Highlander (2825)**
University of California, Riverside
Associated Students of the University of California
245 Costo Hall
Riverside, CA 92521
Phone: (951)784-3686
Fax: (951)787-5638
**Subject(s):** College Publications

**Circ:** (Free)‡10,000

**Hokubei Mainichi (3148)**
Hokubei Mainichi Inc.
1746 Post St.
San Francisco, CA 94115
Phone: (415)567-7323
Fax: (415)567-1110
**Subject(s):** Daily Newspapers; Japanese

**Circ:** 10,000

**Kihei Times (7632)**
Haleakala Times
PO Box 1080
Makawao, HI 96768
Phone: (808)579-8028
Fax: (808)572-0168
**Subject(s):** Free Newspapers

**Circ:** (Combined)10,000

**Moscow Moneysaver (7750)**
Triad News Publishing Inc.
116 S. Jackson, No. 5
Moscow, ID 83843
Phone: (208)883-4420
Fax: (800)278-5051
**Subject(s):** Shopping Guides

**Circ:** (Non-paid)10,000

**New University (2006)**
University of California, Irvine
3100 Gateway Commons
Irvine, CA 92697-4250
Phone: (949)824-4286
Fax: (949)824-4287
**Subject(s):** College Publications

**Circ:** (Free)‡10,000

**North Seattle Herald-Outlook (32295)**
Pacific Publishing Co.
4000 Aurora Ave. N, Ste. 100
Seattle, WA 98103-7853
Phone: (206)461-3333
Fax: (206)461-1285
**Subject(s):** Free Newspapers

**Circ:** (Paid)‡10,000

**OCB Tracker (1942)**
657 E. Arrow Hwy., No. M
Glendora, CA 91740
Phone: (626)914-0306
Fax: (626)914-1837
**Subject(s):** Free Newspapers

**Circ:** (Combined)10,000

**Oregon Daily Emerald (25808)**
Oregon Daily Emerald Publishing Co.
Ste. 300, EMU, 13th & University
PO Box 3159
Eugene, OR 97403
Phone: (541)346-4343
Fax: (541)346-5578
**Subject(s):** College Publications

**Circ:** (Free)10,000

# Gale Directory of Publications & Broadcast Media/140th Ed.

# Western States

**The Orion** (1652)
California State University
College of Communication
Chico, CA 95929-0600
Phone: (530)898-4237
Fax: (530)898-4799
**Subject(s):** College Publications
**Circ:** ‡10,000

**Overture** (1974)
Professional Musicians, Local 47
817 N Vine St.
Hollywood, CA 90038
Phone: (323)462-2161
Fax: (323)466-1289
**Subject(s):** Labor; Music and Musical Instruments
**Circ:** (Free)‡450
  (Paid)‡10,000

**The Priest River Times** (7789)
100 McKinley
Priest River, ID 83856
Phone: (208)448-2431
Fax: (208)448-2938
**Subject(s):** Paid Community Newspapers
**Circ:** (Free)‡10,000

**Sedona Excentric** (837)
PO Box 843
Sedona, AZ 86339
Phone: (928)639-4224
Fax: (928)639-4224
**Subject(s):** Paid Community Newspapers; Travel and Tourism; Local, State, and Regional Publications
**Circ:** (Non-paid)‡10,000

**Senior Voice** (504)
Older Persons Action Group Inc.
325 E 3rd Ave., Ste. 300
Anchorage, AK 99501
Phone: (907)276-1059
Fax: (907)278-6724
**Subject(s):** Senior Citizens' Interests; Paid Community Newspapers
**Circ:** (Combined)‡10,000

**Sentinel** (1396)
1226 High St.
Auburn, CA 95603
Phone: (530)823-2463
Fax: (530)823-1309
**Subject(s):** Paid Community Newspapers
**Circ:** (Controlled)10,000

**West Seattle Herald/White Center News** (32342)
West Seattle Hearld/White Center News
3500 SW Alaska St.
Seattle, WA 98126
Phone: (206)932-6456
Fax: (206)937-1223
**Subject(s):** Paid Community Newspapers
**Circ:** ‡10,000

**White Sheet-The Indio Advertiser** (2656)
Associated Desert Shoppers Inc.
73-400 Hwy. 111
Palm Desert, CA 92260
Phone: (760)346-0601
Fax: (760)346-3597
**Subject(s):** Shopping Guides
**Circ:** (Free)‡10,000

**Port Townsend/Jefferson County Leader** (32208)
Port Townsend Publishing Co.
226 Adams St.
PO Box 552
Port Townsend, WA 98368
Phone: (360)385-2900
Fax: (360)385-3422
**Subject(s):** Paid Community Newspapers
**Circ:** ‡9,970

**Steamboat Pilot & Today** (4568)
WorldWest L.L.C.
PO Box 774827
Steamboat Springs, CO 80477
Phone: (970)879-1502
Fax: (970)879-2888
**Subject(s):** Free Newspapers
**Circ:** (Sat.)◻8,076
  (Mon.-Fri.)◻**9,852**

**Daily News** (7744)
Moscow-Pullman Daily News
409 S. Jackson St.
Moscow, ID 83843
Phone: (208)882-5561
Fax: (208)883-8205
**Subject(s):** Daily Newspapers
**Circ:** ‡9,800

**The Gresham Outlook** (25846)
1190 NE Division St.
PO Box 747
Gresham, OR 97030-0747
Phone: (503)665-2181
Fax: (503)665-2187
**Subject(s):** Paid Community Newspapers
**Circ:** (Free)1,050
  (Paid)9,780

**Intermountain Jewish News** (4292)
1275 Sherman St.
Denver, CO 80203-2299
Phone: (303)861-2234
Fax: (303)832-6942
**Subject(s):** Paid Community Newspapers; Jewish Publications
**Circ:** (Free)‡165
  (Paid)‡9,750

**Valley Sun** (622)
Wick Communications Inc.
5751 E Mayflower Ct.
Wasilla, AK 99654-8334
Phone: (907)352-2250
Fax: (907)352-2277
**Subject(s):** Free Newspapers
**Circ:** (Paid)42
  (Free)9,750

**The Prospector** (699)
Western Newspapers Inc.
3015 Stockton Hill Rd.
Kingman, AZ 86401
Phone: (928)753-6397
Fax: (928)753-5661
**Subject(s):** Free Newspapers
**Circ:** (Free)9,749

**Summit Daily** (4403)
Eagle Summit Publishing
PO Box 329
Frisco, CO 80443
Phone: (970)668-3998
Fax: (970)668-3859
**Subject(s):** Free Newspapers
**Circ:** (Sun.)8,821
  (Mon.-Fri.)9,725

**Elk Grove Citizen** (1811)
Herburger Publications Inc.
8970 Elk Grove Blvd.
Elk Grove, CA 95624
Phone: (916)685-3945
**Subject(s):** Free Newspapers
**Circ:** (Wed.)9,700
  (Fri.)9,700

**El Mexicalo** (1405)
931 Niles St.
Bakersfield, CA 93305-4535
Phone: (661)323-9334
Fax: (661)323-6951
**Subject(s):** Paid Community Newspapers; Hispanic Publications; Spanish
**Circ:** (Free)‡5,563
  (Paid)‡9,676

**Casa Grande Dispatch** (643)
Casa Grande Valley Newspapers Inc.
PO Box 15002
Casa Grande, AZ 85230-5002
Phone: (520)836-7461
Fax: (520)836-0343
**Subject(s):** Daily Newspapers
**Circ:** (Mon.-Sat.)9,579

**Durango Herald** (4355)
Durango Herald Inc.
PO Drawer A-0950
Durango, CO 81302-0950
Phone: (970)247-3504
Fax: (970)259-5011
**Subject(s):** Daily Newspapers
**Circ:** (Mon.-Sat.)8,438
  (Sun.)9,545

**Saratoga News** (3309)
Silicon Valley Community Newspapers
1095 Alameda
San Jose, CA 95126
Phone: (408)200-1000
Fax: (408)200-1011
**Subject(s):** Free Newspapers
**Circ:** (Combined)‡9,500

**Shelton-Mason County Journal** (32375)
3rd & Cota Sts.
PO Box 430
Shelton, WA 98584
Phone: (360)426-4412
**Subject(s):** Paid Community Newspapers
**Circ:** ‡9,370

**Mohave Valley Daily News** (640)
2435 Miracle Mile
PO Box 21209
Bullhead City, AZ 86442
Phone: (928)763-2505
Fax: (928)763-7820
**Subject(s):** Paid Community Newspapers
**Circ:** (Mon.-Fri.)7,841
  (Sun.)9,327

**Kingman Daily Miner** (697)
Western Newspapers Inc.
3015 Stockton Hill Rd.
Kingman, AZ 86401
Phone: (928)753-6397
Fax: (928)753-5661
**Subject(s):** Daily Newspapers
**Circ:** (Mon.-Fri.)8,500
  (Sun.)9,200

**Porterville Recorder** (2755)
Freedom Communications Inc.
115 E Oak
PO Box 151
Porterville, CA 93257
Phone: (209)784-5000
Fax: (209)784-1689
**Subject(s):** Daily Newspapers
**Circ:** (Mon.-Sat.)★**9,202**

**The Garden Island** (7626)
Kauai Publishing Co.
3137 Kuhio Hwy.
PO Box 231
Lihue, HI 96766
Phone: (808)245-3681
Fax: (808)245-5286
**Subject(s):** Daily Newspapers
**Circ:** (Mon.-Sat.)★**8,677**
  (Sun.)★**9,130**

**Tahoe Daily Tribune** (3542)
3079 Harrison Ave.
South Lake Tahoe, CA 96150
Phone: (530)541-3880
Fax: (530)541-0373
**Subject(s):** Daily Newspapers
**Circ:** (Paid)‡9,134

**Lincoln Heights Bulletin-News** (2252)
Wave Newspaper Group
4201 Wilshire Ave., Ste. 600
Los Angeles, CA 90010
Phone: (323)556-5720
Fax: (323)556-5704
**Subject(s):** Free Newspapers
**Circ:** (Wed.)9,125
  (Sat.)9,125

**The Valley News Herald** (32395)
523 N Pines Rd.
PO Box 142020
Spokane, WA 99206
Phone: (509)924-2440
Fax: (509)927-1154
**Subject(s):** Paid Community Newspapers
**Circ:** (Paid)‡9,100

**White Mountain Independent** (841)
White Mountain Publishing Co.
3191 S White Mountain Rd., Ste. 4
PO Box 1570
Show Low, AZ 85902-1570
Phone: (928)537-5721
Fax: (928)537-1780
**Subject(s):** Paid Community Newspapers
**Circ:** (Non-paid)⊕17
  (Paid)⊕**9,076**

Circulation: ★ = ABC; △ = BPA; ◆ = CAC; ● = CCAB; ◻ = VAC; ⊕ = PO Statement; ‡ = Publisher's Report; Boldface figures = sworn; Light figures = estimated.

## Western States

**Big Bear Life & the Grizzly (1538)**
Big Bear Grizzly
42007, Fox Farm Rd. Ste. 3B
PO Box 1789
Big Bear Lake, CA 92315
Phone: (909)866-3456
Fax: (909)866-2302
**Subject(s):** Paid Community Newspapers
**Circ:** ‡9,000

**Carson Bulletin (1697)**
American Print Media
800 E. Compton Blvd.
Compton, CA 90221
Phone: (310)635-6776
**Subject(s):** Paid Community Newspapers; Black Publications
**Circ:** (Paid)8,000
(Free)9,000

**Catholic Sentinel (25952)**
Oregon Catholic Press
5536 NE Hassalo
Portland, OR 97213
Phone: (503)281-1191
Fax: (503)282-3486
**Subject(s):** Religious Publications
**Circ:** ‡9,000

**Copper Country News (688)**
247 S Hill St.
Globe, AZ 85501
Phone: (928)425-0355
Fax: (928)425-6535
**Subject(s):** Free Newspapers
**Circ:** (Controlled)‡9,000

**Grant County Journal (32083)**
Journal Publishing
PO Box 998
Ephrata, WA 98823
Phone: (509)754-0996
Fax: (509)754-5112
**Subject(s):** Paid Community Newspapers
**Circ:** (Paid)3,160
(Free)9,000

**Hawaii Marine (7623)**
RFD Publications Inc.
PO Box 63002, Bldg. 216
MCBH
Kaneohe Bay, HI 96863
Phone: (808)257-8836
Fax: (808)257-2511
**Subject(s):** Free Newspapers; Military and Navy
**Circ:** (Free)9,000

**Inglewood Tribune (1988)**
American Print Media
800 E. Compton Blvd.
Compton, CA 90221
Phone: (310)635-6776
**Subject(s):** Free Newspapers; Black Publications
**Circ:** (Paid)1,000
(Free)9,000

**News-Register (25898)**
Oregon Lithoprint
PO Box 727
611 NE 3rd St.
McMinnville, OR 97128
Phone: (503)472-5114
Fax: (503)472-9151
**Subject(s):** Paid Community Newspapers
**Circ:** ‡9,000

**Northwest Asian Weekly (32296)**
412 Maynard Ave. S
Seattle, WA 98104-2917
Phone: (206)223-0623
Fax: (206)223-0626
**Subject(s):** Paid Community Newspapers; Chinese
**Circ:** (Free)‡6,000
(Paid)‡9,000

**Portuguese Journal (1809)**
5404 Valley View Rd.
El Sobrante, CA 94803-3447
Fax: (510)237-3790
**Subject(s):** Portuguese; Ethnic Publications
**Circ:** ‡9,000

**White Sheet-The Morongo Basin Advertiser (2515)**
Associated Desert Shoppers Inc.
73-400 Hwy. 111
Palm Desert, CA 92260
Phone: (760)346-0601
Fax: (760)346-3597
**Subject(s):** Shopping Guides
**Circ:** (Free)‡9,000

**The Weekly Star (3935)**
The Reporter
916 Cotting Ln.
Vacaville, CA 95688
Phone: (707)448-6401
Fax: (707)447-8411
**Subject(s):** Shopping Guides
**Circ:** (Free)‡8,869

**North Kitsap Herald (32211)**
Sound Publishing Inc.
18887 Hwy. 305, Ste. 700
Poulsbo, WA 98370
Phone: (360)779-4464
Fax: (360)779-8276
**Subject(s):** Paid Community Newspapers
**Circ:** (Paid)♦1,650
(Non-paid)♦8,830

**Eastern Arizona Courier (820)**
Wick Communications
301 East Hwy. 70, Ste. A
Safford, AZ 85546
Phone: (928)428-2560
Fax: (928)428-4901
**Subject(s):** Paid Community Newspapers
**Circ:** 8,742

**Denver Herald-Dispatch (4281)**
The Villager Publication Gr.
314 Federal Blvd.
Denver, CO 80219
Phone: (303)936-7778
Fax: (303)936-0994
**Subject(s):** Paid Community Newspapers
**Circ:** 8,600

**Eagle Rock Sentinel (2189)**
Wave Newspaper Group
4201 Wilshire Ave., Ste. 600
Los Angeles, CA 90010
Phone: (323)556-5720
Fax: (323)556-5704
**Subject(s):** Free Newspapers
**Circ:** (Wed.)8,600
(Sat.)8,600

**Lahaina News (7624)**
Hawaii Publications Inc.
PO Box 10427
Lahaina, HI 96761
Phone: (808)667-7866
Fax: (808)667-2726
**Subject(s):** Free Newspapers
**Circ:** (Paid)‡350
(Free)‡8,607

**The Pyramid Shopper (30707)**
Pyramid Publishing
49 W Main
Mount Pleasant, UT 84647
Phone: (435)462-2134
Fax: (435)462-2459
**Subject(s):** Shopping Guides
**Circ:** (Combined)8,600

**Madera Tribune (1788)**
Pacific Sierra Publishing Company Inc.
150 Chambers St. Ste. 9
El Cajon, CA 92020-3366
**Subject(s):** Daily Newspapers
**Circ:** (Mon.-Sat.)8,585

**Five Cities Times Press Recorder (1391)**
South County Publishing Company Inc.
PO Box 460
260 Station Way Ste F (ZIP CODE 93420)
Arroyo Grande, CA 93421
Phone: (805)489-4206
Fax: (805)473-0571
**Subject(s):** Shopping Guides
**Circ:** (Free)‡8,575

**Daily Record (4162)**
Royal Gorge Publishing Corp.
701 S 9th St.
Canon City, CO 81212
Phone: (719)275-7565
Fax: (719)275-1353
**Subject(s):** Daily Newspapers
**Circ:** (Mon.-Sat.)8,523

**Animal People (32051)**
PO Box 960
Clinton, WA 98236-0960
Phone: (360)579-2505
Fax: (360)579-2575
**Subject(s):** Pets; Social and Political Issues
**Circ:** (Paid)6,500
(Controlled)8,500

**Collage (1667)**
The Claremont Colleges
Claremont, CA 91711
Phone: (909)607-3646
**Subject(s):** College Publications
**Circ:** (Controlled)8,500

**Dispatch (579)**
P O Box 3009
150 Trading Bay Rd
Kenai, AK 99611
Phone: (907)283-7551
Fax: (907)283-8144
**Subject(s):** Free Newspapers
**Circ:** (Non-paid)8,500

**Space and Missile Times (2084)**
Lompoc Record
115 North H St
PO Box 578
Lompoc, CA 93436
Phone: (805)736-2313
Fax: (805)736-5654
**Subject(s):** Free Newspapers; Military and Navy
**Circ:** (Free)‡8,500

**The Valley Press (1849)**
Johnson Newspapers Inc.
PO Box V-1
Felton, CA 95018
Phone: (831)335-5321
Fax: (831)335-8102
**Subject(s):** Paid Community Newspapers
**Circ:** (Combined)‡8,500

**Lake Oswego Review (25886)**
Community Newspapers
111 A Ave.
PO Box 548
Lake Oswego, OR 97034
Phone: (503)684-0360
Fax: (503)620-3433
**Subject(s):** Paid Community Newspapers
**Circ:** (Paid)‡8,478

**Press-Tribune (2858)**
Placer Community Newspapers Inc.
188 Cirby Way
Roseville, CA 95678
Phone: (916)786-8746
Fax: (916)786-0332
**Subject(s):** Daily Newspapers
**Circ:** (Combined)8,424

**Lake County Record-Bee (2065)**
Lake County Publishing
PO Box 849
Lakeport, CA 95453
Phone: (707)263-5636
Fax: (707)263-0600
**Subject(s):** Daily Newspapers
**Circ:** (Tues.-Fri.)6,614
(Sun.)8,387

**N.W. Navigator (32380)**
Sound Publishing Inc.
9989 Silverdale Way, Ste. 109
Silverdale, WA 98383
Phone: (360)308-9161
Fax: (360)308-9363
**Subject(s):** Free Newspapers; Military and Navy
**Circ:** (Combined)♦8,382

**Lompoc Record** (2083)
Los Angeles Newspaper Group
115 N. H St.
Lompoc, CA 93436
Phone: (805)736-2313
Fax: (805)737-9038
**Subject(s):** Daily Newspapers

Circ: (Mon.-Fri.)8,098
(Sun.)8,369

**Argus Observer** (25930)
Wick Communications
1160 SW 4th St.
PO Box 130
Ontario, OR 97914-4365
Phone: (541)889-5387
Fax: (541)889-0678
**Subject(s):** Daily Newspapers

Circ: (Mon.-Fri.)7,144
(Sun.)8,292

**The Daily Astorian** (25705)
Astorian Budget Publishing Co.
PO Box 210
Astoria, OR 97103
Phone: (503)325-3211
Fax: (503)325-6573
**Subject(s):** Daily Newspapers

Circ: (Mon.-Fri.)★8,263

**Headlight-Herald** (26066)
Oregon Coast Newspapers
PO Box 444
Tillamook, OR 97141
Phone: (503)842-7535
Fax: (503)842-8842
**Subject(s):** Paid Community Newspapers

Circ: ⊕8,229

**Park Record Newspaper** (30723)
PO Box 3688
1670 Bonanza Drive Ste.202
Park City, UT 84060-3688
Phone: (435)649-9014
Fax: (435)649-4942
**Subject(s):** Free Newspapers

Circ: (Free)‡100
(Paid)‡8,200

**Prescott Valley Tribune** (809)
Western Newspapers Inc.
PO Box 26564
Prescott, AZ 86312
Phone: (928)445-3333
**Subject(s):** Free Newspapers

Circ: (Paid)202
(Free)8,196

**Daily Rocket-Miner** (33783)
Rock Springs Newspapers Inc.
PO Box 98
Rock Springs, WY 82902-0098
Phone: (307)362-3736
Fax: (307)382-2763
**Subject(s):** Daily Newspapers

Circ: (Tues.-Fri.)★8,060

**The Paradise Post** (2706)
PO Drawer 70
Paradise, CA 95967
Phone: (530)877-4413
Fax: (530)877-1326
**Subject(s):** Paid Community Newspapers

Circ: (Sat.)8,040

**Tehachapi News** (3596)
Tehachapi News Publications
411 N Mill St.
PO Box 1840
Tehachapi, CA 93561
Phone: (661)822-6828
Fax: (661)822-4053
**Subject(s):** Paid Community Newspapers

Circ: ‡8,013

**Aztec Press** (904)
Pima County Community College
2202 W Anklam Rd.
Tucson, AZ 85709-0001
Phone: (520)260-6800
Fax: (520)206-6834
**Subject(s):** College Publications

Circ: (Free)‡8,000

**Contra Costa Sun** (4018)
Hills Publications Inc.
2640 Shadelands Dr.
Walnut Creek, CA 94598-2578
Phone: (510)284-4444
Fax: (510)284-1039
**Subject(s):** Free Newspapers

Circ: (Paid)8,000

**Hawaii Hochi** (7546)
917 Kokea St.
Honolulu, HI 96817
Phone: (808)845-2255
Fax: (808)847-7215
**Subject(s):** Paid Community Newspapers; Japanese; Ethnic Publications

Circ: (Combined)8,000

**The Malibu Surfside News** (2423)
PO Box 903
Malibu, CA 90265
Phone: (310)457-2112
Fax: (310)457-9908
**Subject(s):** Free Newspapers

Circ: (Paid)4,000
(Free)8,000

**Mukilteo Tribune** (32383)
Tribune Newspapers
127 Ave. C
PO Box 499
Snohomish, WA 98291-0499
Phone: (360)568-4121
Fax: (360)568-1484
**Subject(s):** Paid Community Newspapers

Circ: (Non-paid)8,000

**Nichi Bei Times** (3180)
2211 Bush Street
San Francisco, CA 94115
Phone: (415)921-6820
Fax: (415)921-0770
**Subject(s):** Daily Newspapers; Japanese; Ethnic Publications

Circ: (Combined)8,000

**North American Post** (32294)
North American Post Publishing Inc.
PO Box 3173
Seattle, WA 98114-3173
Phone: (206)623-0100
Fax: (206)625-1424
**Subject(s):** Japanese; Paid Community Newspapers

Circ: (Fri.)5,000
(Combined)8,000

**Radio & Records** (2316)
Radio and Records Inc.
2049 Century Park E., 41st Fl.
Los Angeles, CA 90067
Phone: (310)553-4330
Fax: (310)203-9763
**Subject(s):** Radio, Television, Cable, and Video

Circ: (Non-paid)500
(Paid)8000

**Manteca Bulletin** (2433)
Manteca Bulletin Daily Newspaper
531 E. Yosemite Ave.
Manteca, CA 95336
Phone: (209)249-3500
Fax: (209)249-3551
**Subject(s):** Daily Newspapers

Circ: (Free)□21
(Paid)□7,911

**The Wave, The Buyer's Guide for the Coastside** (2647)
Pacifica Tribune
PO Box 1189
Pacifica, CA 94044
Phone: (415)359-6666
Fax: (415)359-3821
**Subject(s):** Shopping Guides

Circ: (Free)5,900
(Wed.)7,912

**Northwest Navigator** (31992)
Sound Publishing Inc.
7689 NE Day Rd.
Bainbridge Island, WA 98110
Phone: (206)842-8305
Fax: (206)842-8030
**Subject(s):** Free Newspapers; Paid Community Newspapers

Circ: (Paid)♦4
(Free)♦7,890

**Ukiah Daily Journal** (3929)
Community Newspaper Holdings Inc.
590 S. School St.
PO Box 749
Ukiah, CA 95482-0749
Phone: (707)468-0123
Fax: (707)468-3544
**Subject(s):** Daily Newspapers

Circ: (Mon.-Sat.)★7,677
(Sun.)★7,885

**Tigard Times** (26065)
Community Newspapers
1325 SW Custer Dr.
Portland, OR 97219-2750
Phone: (503)684-0360
Fax: (503)620-3433
**Subject(s):** Free Newspapers

Circ: (Paid)4,937
(Free)7,863

**Wilsonville Spokesman** (26080)
Eagle Newspapers
30250 SW Pkwy. Ave., Ste. No. 10
Wilsonville, OR 97070
Phone: (503)682-3935
Fax: (503)682-6265
**Subject(s):** Free Newspapers

Circ: (Free)‡7,800

**Dana Point News** (1748)
The Orange County Register
22481 Aspan St.
Lake Forest, CA 92630
Fax: (949)454-7354
**Subject(s):** Free Newspapers

Circ: (Controlled)3,605
(Paid)7,783

**Appeal Tribune/Mt. Angel News** (26057)
Silverton Appeal Tribune
399 S. Water St.
PO Box 35
Silverton, OR 97381
Phone: (503)873-8385
Fax: (503)873-8064
**Subject(s):** Paid Community Newspapers

Circ: (Combined)7,700

**The Issaquah Press** (32109)
45 Front St. S.
PO Box 1328
Issaquah, WA 98027
Phone: (425)392-6434
Fax: (425)391-1541
**Subject(s):** Paid Community Newspapers

Circ: ‡7,700

**Uinta County Herald Shoppers Guide** (33729)
Uinta County Herald
PO Box 210
Evanston, WY 82931
Phone: (307)789-6560
Fax: (307)789-2700
**Subject(s):** Shopping Guides

Circ: (Free)‡7,700

**Islands' Weekly** (31990)
Sound Publishing Inc.
7689 NE Day Rd.
Bainbridge Island, WA 98110
Phone: (206)842-8305
Fax: (206)842-8030
**Subject(s):** Free Newspapers

Circ: (Free)♦7,668

**Inyo Register** (1541)
Horizon California Publications Inc.
450 E Line St.
Bishop, CA 93514
Phone: (760)873-3535
**Subject(s):** Paid Community Newspapers

Circ: 7,590

**Academy Spirit** (4583)
Colorado Publishing Co.
Headquarters USAFA, PAI
USAF Academy, CO 80840
Phone: (719)333-4094
Fax: (719)333-4094
**Subject(s):** Free Newspapers; Military and Navy

Circ: (Free)‡7,500

Circulation: ★ = ABC; △ = BPA; ♦ = CAC; • = CCAB; □ = VAC; ⊕ = PO Statement; ‡ = Publisher's Report; Boldface figures = sworn; Light figures = estimated.

## Western States

**The Black Voice News (2816)**
Black Voice News
PO Box 1581
Riverside, CA 92502
Phone: (909)682-6070
**Subject(s):** Paid Community Newspapers; Black Publications
**Circ:** ‡7,500

**Burlington Record & Plains Dealer (4159)**
Burlington Record
PO Box 459
Burlington, CO 80807
Phone: (719)346-5381
Fax: (719)346-5514
**Subject(s):** Paid Community Newspapers
**Circ:** 7,500

**Coalinga Record (1679)**
Central C.A. Weeklies Inc.
227 Coalinga Plaza
PO Box 496
Coalinga, CA 93210
Phone: (209)935-2906
Fax: (209)935-5257
**Subject(s):** Paid Community Newspapers
**Circ:** ‡7,500

**Half Moon Bay Review and Pescadero Pebble (1956)**
Half Bay Review
PO Box 68
Half Moon Bay, CA 94019
Phone: (415)726-4424
Fax: (415)726-7054
**Subject(s):** Paid Community Newspapers
**Circ:** ‡7,500

**Jackson Hole Guide (33740)**
PO Box 7445
Jackson, WY 83002
Phone: (307)733-2047
Fax: (307)733-2138
**Subject(s):** Paid Community Newspapers
**Circ:** 6,000
‡7,500

**The Lynden Tribune (32143)**
Lewis Publishing Company Inc.
113 N. 6th St.
PO Box 153
Lynden, WA 98264
Phone: (360)354-4444
Fax: (360)354-4445
**Subject(s):** Paid Community Newspapers
**Circ:** (Paid)‡7,000
(Free)‡7,500

**Mountain News (2057)**
Brehm Communications Inc.
PO Box 2410
Lake Arrowhead, CA 92352
Phone: (909)336-3555
Fax: (909)337-5275
**Subject(s):** Paid Community Newspapers
**Circ:** ‡7,500

**Orland Press-Register (2635)**
Tri-County Newspapers Inc.
401 Walker St.
Orland, CA 95963
Phone: (530)865-4433
Fax: (530)865-3110
**Subject(s):** Paid Community Newspapers
**Circ:** 7,500

**Sky-Hi News (4422)**
Johnson Media Inc.
PO Box 409
Granby, CO 80446
Phone: (970)726-5721
Fax: (970)726-8789
**Subject(s):** Paid Community Newspapers
**Circ:** (Paid)3,800
(Free)7,500

**Sourdough Sentinel (506)**
Anchorage Publishing Inc.
Public Affairs Office
Elmendorf AFB, AK 99506
Phone: (907)552-2493
Fax: (907)552-5111
**Subject(s):** Free Newspapers; Military and Navy
**Circ:** (Free)7,500

**Space Observer (4217)**
Colorado Publishing Co.
31 E. Platt, Ste. 300
Colorado Springs, CO 80903-3311
Phone: (719)634-5905
Fax: (719)634-5157
**Subject(s):** Free Newspapers; Military and Navy
**Circ:** (Free)‡7,500

**Sun Post News (2995)**
Freedom Communications Inc.
95 Avenida Del Mar
San Clemente, CA 92672
Phone: (949)849-2512
**Subject(s):** Free Newspapers
**Circ:** (Mon.-Fri.)‡7,500

**Tooele Transcript-Bulletin (30820)**
Transcript-Bulletin Publishing Company Inc.
58 N Main St.
PO Box 390
Tooele, UT 84074
Phone: (435)882-0050
Fax: (435)882-6123
**Subject(s):** Paid Community Newspapers
**Circ:** (Free)‡70
(Paid)‡7,500

**Petaluma Argus-Courier (2729)**
The New York Times Co.
1304 Southpoint Blvd.
Petaluma, CA 94953
Phone: (707)762-4541
**Subject(s):** Daily Newspapers
**Circ:** (Combined)7,437

**Coastside Chronicle (3363)**
San Mateo County Times
1080 S Amphlett Blvd.
PO Box 5400
San Mateo, CA 94402-1860
Phone: (650)348-4321
Fax: (650)348-4446
**Subject(s):** Free Newspapers
**Circ:** (Paid)24
(Free)7,401

**El Sereno Star (2195)**
Wave Newspaper Group
4201 Wilshire Ave., Ste. 600
Los Angeles, CA 90010
Phone: (323)556-5720
Fax: (323)556-5704
**Subject(s):** Paid Community Newspapers
**Circ:** (Paid)250
(Free)7,400

**Novato Advance (2559)**
Scripps Marin Publishing Co.
PO Box 8
1068 Machin Ave.
Novato, CA 94948
Phone: (415)892-1516
Fax: (415)897-0940
**Subject(s):** Paid Community Newspapers
**Circ:** (Paid)7,220
(Free)7,400

**White Sheet-The Blythe Advertiser (634)**
Associated Desert Shoppers Inc.
2099 W. Acoma
Lake Havasu City, AZ 86403
Phone: (928)855-7871
Fax: (928)855-8183
**Subject(s):** Shopping Guides
**Circ:** (Free)‡7,400

**Alaska Star (538)**
Alaska Publications
16941 N Eagle River Loop Rd.
Eagle River, AK 99577
Phone: (907)694-2727
Fax: (907)694-1545
**Subject(s):** Paid Community Newspapers
**Circ:** (Free)‡1,200
(Paid)‡7,380

**De Hollandse Krant (32019)**
The J.I. Timmer Publishing Company Ltd.
PO Box 4274
Blaine, WA 98231-4274
**Subject(s):** Dutch
**Circ:** (Paid)•7,364

**The Sequim Gazette (32374)**
Olympic View Publishing Inc.
147 1/2 W Washington St.
PO Box 1750
Sequim, WA 98382
Phone: (360)683-3311
Fax: (360)683-6670
**Subject(s):** Paid Community Newspapers
**Circ:** (Wed.)7,350

**Arizona Silver Belt (687)**
298 N Pine St.
PO Box 31
Globe, AZ 85502
Phone: (928)425-7121
Fax: (928)425-7001
**Subject(s):** Paid Community Newspapers
**Circ:** ‡7,336

**Hawaiian Falcon (7621)**
RFD Publications Inc.
45-525 Luluku Rd.
Kaneohe, HI 96744
Phone: (808)235-5881
Fax: (808)247-7246
**Subject(s):** Free Newspapers; Military and Navy
**Circ:** (Free)7,315

**Delta County Independent (4257)**
Leader Publishing Company Inc.
401 Meeker St.
PO Box 809
Delta, CO 81416-1918
Phone: (970)874-4421
Fax: (970)874-4424
**Subject(s):** Paid Community Newspapers
**Circ:** 7,300

**Los Banos Enterprise (1787)**
Pacific Sierra Publishing Company Inc.
150 Chambers St. Ste. 9
El Cajon, CA 92020-3366
**Subject(s):** Paid Community Newspapers
**Circ:** (Paid)‡4,500
(Free)‡7,300

**Payson Roundup and Advisor (732)**
WorldWest L.L.C.
PO Box 2520
Payson, AZ 85547
Phone: (520)474-5251
Fax: (520)474-1893
**Subject(s):** Paid Community Newspapers
**Circ:** (Paid)7,300

**Daily News (2775)**
Media News Group
545 Diamond Ave.
PO Box 220
Red Bluff, CA 96080
Phone: (530)527-2151
Fax: (530)527-9251
**Subject(s):** Daily Newspapers
**Circ:** (Mon.-Sat.)7,256

**Pacifica Tribune (2646)**
59 Aura Vista
PO Box 1189
Pacifica, CA 94044
Phone: (650)359-6666
Fax: (650)359-3821
**Subject(s):** Paid Community Newspapers
**Circ:** (Wed.)7,248

**Hawaii Kai/East Oahu Sun Press (7619)**
RFD Publications Inc.
45-525 Luluku Rd.
Kaneohe, HI 96744
Phone: (808)235-5881
Fax: (808)247-7246
**Subject(s):** Free Newspapers
**Circ:** (Combined)7,193

**Redland's Daily Facts (2793)**
Donrey Media Group
700 Brookside Ave.
Redlands, CA 92373
Phone: (909)793-3221
Fax: (909)793-9588
**Subject(s):** Daily Newspapers
**Circ:** (Mon.-Fri.)★6,948
(Sun.)★7,190

**Curry Coastal Pilot (25735)**
Western Communications Inc.
PO Box 700
Brookings, OR 97415
Phone: (541)469-3123
Fax: (541)469-4679
**Subject(s):** Paid Community Newspapers
**Circ:** ‡7,150

**Madison Park Times (32287)**
Pacific Publishing Co.
4000 Aurora Ave. N., Ste. 100
Seattle, WA 98103-7853
Phone: (206)461-1346
**Subject(s):** Free Newspapers
**Circ:** ‡7,100

**Juneau Empire (571)**
Morris Communications Corp.
3100 Channel Dr.
Juneau, AK 99801-7814
Phone: (907)586-3740
Fax: (907)586-3028
**Subject(s):** Daily Newspapers
**Circ:** (Free)190
(Paid)7,066

**Whidbey News-Times (32174)**
Sound Publishing Inc.
800 SE Barrington Dr.
PO Box 10
Oak Harbor, WA 98277
Phone: (360)675-6611
**Subject(s):** Paid Community Newspapers
**Circ:** (Free)22
(Paid)7,049

**Cottonwood Journal Extra (656)**
PO Box 2266
830 S. Main, Ste. 1E
Cottonwood, AZ 86326
Phone: (928)634-8551
Fax: (928)634-0823
**Subject(s):** Free Newspapers
**Circ:** (Combined)7,013

**Frontiersman (621)**
Wick Communications Inc.
5751 E Mayflower Ct.
Wasilla, AK 99654-8334
Phone: (907)352-2250
Fax: (907)352-2277
**Subject(s):** Paid Community Newspapers
**Circ:** (Fri.)7,013

**Bell Gardens Sun (1687)**
Eastern Group Publications Inc.
2500 S Atlantic Blvd., Bldg. A
Commerce, CA 90040
Phone: (323)263-5743
Fax: (323)263-9169
**Subject(s):** Paid Community Newspapers
**Circ:** (Paid)♦7,000

**Branding Iron (33752)**
University of Wyoming
PO Box 3625
Laramie, WY 82071
Phone: (307)766-6190
Fax: (307)766-4027
**Subject(s):** College Publications
**Circ:** (Free)7,000

**City on a Hill (3451)**
City on a Hill Press
Student Press Ctr., University of California Santa Cruz
1156 High St.
Santa Cruz, CA 95064
Phone: (831)459-4350
Fax: (831)459-4696
**Subject(s):** College Publications
**Circ:** (Free)‡7,000

**Civic Center NewSource (2169)**
Metropolitan News Co.
210 S. Spring St.
Los Angeles, CA 90012
Phone: (213)346-0033
Fax: (213)687-3886
**Subject(s):** Free Newspapers
**Circ:** (Paid)200
(Non-paid)7,000

**Coastal View (1626)**
4856 Carpinteria Ave.
Carpinteria, CA 93013
Phone: (805)684-4428
Fax: (805)684-4650
**Subject(s):** Free Newspapers
**Circ:** (Paid)250
(Non-paid)7,000

**Cowlitz-Wahkiakum Senior News (32135)**
Lower Columbia Community Action Council
PO Box 2129
Longview, WA 98632-2129
Phone: (360)425-3430
Fax: (360)425-6657
**Subject(s):** Senior Citizens' Interests; Free Newspapers
**Circ:** (Free)‡7,000

**The Exponent (18089)**
ASMSU Exponent
Strand Union Bldg. 330
Bozeman, MT 59717-4200
Phone: (406)994-2224
Fax: (406)994-2253
**Subject(s):** College Publications
**Circ:** (Free)‡7,000

**Grapevine Independent (2768)**
3338 Mather Field Rd.
Rancho Cordova, CA 95670
Phone: (916)361-1234
Fax: (916)361-0491
**Subject(s):** Paid Community Newspapers
**Circ:** (Non-paid)4,000
(Paid)7,000

**Hawaii Catholic Herald (7543)**
1184 Bishop St.
Honolulu, HI 96813
Phone: (808)533-3300
Fax: (808)521-8428
**Subject(s):** Religious Publications
**Circ:** (Non-paid)‡500
(Paid)‡7,000

**Messenger Index (7690)**
PO Box 577
Emmett, ID 83617
Phone: (208)365-6066
Fax: (208)365-6068
**Subject(s):** Paid Community Newspapers
**Circ:** 7,000

**The Mirror (4446)**
Student Media Corp.
823 16th St.
Greeley, CO 80631
Phone: (970)392-9270
Fax: (970)392-9025
**Subject(s):** College Publications
**Circ:** (Free)7,000

**Portland Alliance (25973)**
Northwest Alliance for Alternative Media & Education
2807 SE Stark
Portland, OR 97214
Phone: (503)239-4991
Fax: (503)232-3764
**Subject(s):** Paid Community Newspapers; Environmental and Natural Resources Conservation; Career Development and Employment; Alternative and Underground
**Circ:** (Combined)7,000

**The Shopper News (974)**
Brehm Communications Inc.
180 N Washington
Wickenburg, AZ 85390-1298
Phone: (520)684-3100
Fax: (520)684-3185
**Subject(s):** Shopping Guides
**Circ:** (Free)‡7,000

**Valley Star (3957)**
Los Angeles Valley College
5800 Fulton Ave.
Van Nuys, CA 91401
Phone: (818)781-1200
Fax: (818)947-2610
**Subject(s):** College Publications
**Circ:** (Free)‡7,000

**The Riverton Ranger (33779)**
Riverton Ranger
421 E Main St.
PO Box 993
Riverton, WY 82501
Phone: (307)856-2244
Fax: (307)856-0189
**Subject(s):** Daily Newspapers
**Circ:** (Paid)‡6,970

**The Siuslaw News (25831)**
Central Coast Publishing Co.
PO Box 10
Florence, OR 97439
Phone: (541)997-3441
Fax: (541)997-7979
**Subject(s):** Paid Community Newspapers
**Circ:** 6,913

**The Hermiston Herald (25850)**
Western Communications
Box 46
Hermiston, OR 97838
Phone: (541)567-6457
Fax: (541)567-4125
**Subject(s):** Paid Community Newspapers
**Circ:** (Paid)4,100
(Free)6,900

**Steamboat Pilot (4567)**
1901 Curve Plaza
PO Box 774827
Steamboat Springs, CO 80477
Phone: (970)879-1502
Fax: (970)879-2888
**Subject(s):** Paid Community Newspapers
**Circ:** ‡6,900

**Amador Ledger-Dispatch (1783)**
Pacific Sierra Publishing Company Inc.
150 Chambers St. Ste. 9
El Cajon, CA 92020-3366
**Subject(s):** Paid Community Newspapers
**Circ:** (Combined)‡6,874

**Cody Enterprise (33721)**
Sage Publishing Co.
PO Box 1090
Cody, WY 82414
Phone: (307)587-2231
Fax: (307)587-5208
**Subject(s):** Paid Community Newspapers
**Circ:** (Free)‡288
(Paid)‡6,869

**Arizona Jewish Post (899)**
Jewish Federation of Southern Arizona
3822 E River Rd.
Tucson, AZ 85718
Phone: (520)577-9393
Fax: (520)577-0734
**Subject(s):** Jewish Publications; Paid Community Newspapers
**Circ:** 6,800

**Polk County Itemizer Observer (25780)**
Eagle Newspapers
PO Box 108
Dallas, OR 97338
Phone: (503)623-2373
Fax: (503)623-2395
**Subject(s):** Paid Community Newspapers
**Circ:** ‡6,800

**Shopping News/Penny Pincher (3535)**
The Sonoma Index-Tribune
PO Box C
Sonoma, CA 95476
Phone: (707)938-2111
Fax: (707)938-1600
**Subject(s):** Shopping Guides
**Circ:** (Free)6,800

**Tundra Drums (529)**
PO Box 868
311 Willow St.
Bethel, AK 99559
Phone: (907)543-3500
Fax: (907)543-3312
**Subject(s):** Paid Community Newspapers
**Circ:** ‡6,800

# Western States

**Sedona Red Rock News** (838)
PO Box 619
Sedona, AZ 86339
Phone: (928)282-7795
Fax: (928)282-6011
**Subject(s):** Paid Community Newspapers
**Circ:** (Free)85
(Paid)6,786

**National Masters News** (25805)
PO Box 50098
Eugene, OR 97405
Phone: (541)343-7716
**Subject(s):** (Running)
**Circ:** (Free)‡1,000
(Paid)‡6,775

**The Observer** (25880)
Western Communications Inc.
PO Box 3170
La Grande, OR 97850
Phone: (503)963-3161
Fax: (503)963-7804
**Subject(s):** Daily Newspapers
**Circ:** (Mon.-Sat.)6,768

**The Leisure World Golden Rain News** (3511)
PO Box 2338
Seal Beach, CA 90740
Phone: (562)430-0534
Fax: (562)598-1617
**Subject(s):** Senior Citizens' Interests; Free Newspapers
**Circ:** (Free)2295
(Paid)6705

**Rossmoor News** (4025)
Golden Rain Foundation
PO Box 2190
Walnut Creek, CA 94595
Fax: (510)935-8348
**Subject(s):** Paid Community Newspapers
**Circ:** ‡6700

**Cortez Journal** (4245)
Animas Publishing Inc.
PO Box J
Cortez, CO 81321
Phone: (970)565-8527
Fax: (970)565-8532
**Subject(s):** Paid Community Newspapers
**Circ:** ‡6,685

**Reaper Extra** (30751)
The Richfield Reaper
65 W Ctr.
PO Box 730
Richfield, UT 84701
Phone: (801)896-5476
Fax: (801)896-8123
**Subject(s):** Shopping Guides
**Circ:** (Free)‡6,600

**Mammoth Times** (2430)
New Times Publishing Inc.
Sierra Center Mall
452 Old Mammoth Rd.
PO Box 3929
Mammoth Lakes, CA 93546
Phone: (760)934-3929
Fax: (760)934-3951
**Subject(s):** Free Newspapers
**Circ:** (Free)‡300
(Paid)‡6,520

**Commerce Comet** (1689)
Eastern Group Publications Inc.
2500 S Atlantic Blvd., Bldg. A
Commerce, CA 90040
Phone: (323)263-5743
Fax: (323)263-9169
**Subject(s):** Paid Community Newspapers
**Circ:** (Paid)♦6,500

**Jewish News of Greater Phoenix** (764)
Phoenix Jewish News Inc.
1625 E. Northern Ave.
Ste. 106
Phoenix, AZ 85020
Phone: (602)870-9470
Fax: (602)870-0426
**Subject(s):** Jewish Publications; Paid Community Newspapers
**Circ:** ‡6,500

**The Lumberjack Newspaper** (1386)
Humboldt State University
Nelson Hall E. 6
Arcata, CA 95521
Phone: (707)826-3259
Fax: (707)826-5921
**Subject(s):** College Publications
**Circ:** (Free)‡6,500

**The Poly Post** (2754)
California State Polytechnic University
3801 W Temple Ave., Bldg. 1-210
Pomona, CA 91768-4007
Phone: (909)869-3530
Fax: (909)869-3863
**Subject(s):** College Publications
**Circ:** (Free)‡6,500

**Tiefort Telegraph** (1861)
Aerotech
Public Affairs Office
PO Box 105067
National Training Center
Fort Irwin, CA 92310
Fax: (760)380-3075
**Subject(s):** Military and Navy
**Circ:** (Non-paid)6,500

**Turlock Journal** (3922)
Pacific Sierra Publishing Company Inc.
138 S. Center St.
PO Box 800
Turlock, CA 95380-4508
Phone: (209)634-9141
Fax: (209)664-3680
**Subject(s):** Daily Newspapers
**Circ:** (Mon.-Sat.)6,500

**Viking** (2099)
Long Beach City College
4901 E Carson St.
Room P125
Language Arts Bldg.
Long Beach, CA 90808
Phone: (562)938-4284
Fax: (562)938-4948
**Subject(s):** College Publications
**Circ:** (Free)6,500

**Crosswind** (31989)
Sound Publishing Inc.
7689 NE Day Rd.
Bainbridge Island, WA 98110
Phone: (206)842-8305
Fax: (206)842-8030
**Subject(s):** Free Newspapers
**Circ:** (Non-paid)♦6,481

**Atascadero News** (1393)
PO Box 6068
5660 El Camino Real
Atascadero, CA 93422
Phone: (805)466-2585
Fax: (805)466-2714
**Subject(s):** Paid Community Newspapers
**Circ:** ‡6,450

**River Extra** (702)
River City Newspapers
2225 W. Acoma Blvd.
Lake Havasu City, AZ 86403
Phone: (928)453-4237
Fax: (928)855-9892
**Subject(s):** Free Newspapers
**Circ:** (Free)6,400

**Hungry Horse News** (18112)
Hagadone Corp.
PO Box 189
Columbia Falls, MT 59912
Phone: (406)892-2151
Fax: (406)892-5600
**Subject(s):** Paid Community Newspapers
**Circ:** ‡6,375

**Lakewood Journal** (32471)
Sound Publishing Inc.
PO Box 447
Vashon, WA 98070-0447
Phone: (253)584-8080
Fax: (253)584-6098
**Subject(s):** Paid Community Newspapers
**Circ:** (Paid)1,973
(Non-paid)6,355

**Daily Sparks Tribune** (18761)
1002 C St.
PO Box 887
Sparks, NV 89431-4929
Phone: (775)358-8061
Fax: (775)359-3837
**Subject(s):** Daily Newspapers
**Circ:** ‡6,320

**Lassen County Times** (3589)
Feather Publishing
800 Main St.
Susanville, CA 96130
Phone: (916)257-5321
Fax: (916)257-0408
**Subject(s):** Paid Community Newspapers
**Circ:** (Free)3,705
(Paid)6,252

**The Sheridan Press** (33790)
Sheridan Newspapers Inc.
144 Grinnell St.
PO Box 2006
Sheridan, WY 82801
Phone: (307)672-2431
Fax: (307)672-7950
**Subject(s):** Daily Newspapers
**Circ:** (Mon.-Sat.)6,232

**Baldwinsville Messenger** (26036)
Eagle Newspapers
4901 Indian School Rd. NE
PO Box 12008
Salem, OR 97305
Phone: (503)393-7980
Fax: (503)393-2366
**Subject(s):** Paid Community Newspapers
**Circ:** (Non-paid)433
(Paid)6,200

**The Messenger** (26044)
Eagle Newspapers
4901 Indian School Rd. NE
PO Box 12008
Salem, OR 97305
Phone: (503)393-7980
Fax: (503)393-2366
**Subject(s):** Paid Community Newspapers
**Circ:** ‡6,200

**News-Review** (2808)
PO Box 640
Ridgecrest, CA 93556
**Subject(s):** Free Newspapers
**Circ:** (Paid)2,006
(Free)6,200

**Peoria Times** (685)
Pueblo Publishers Inc.
7122 N 59th Ave.
Glendale, AZ 85301
Phone: (623)842-6000
Fax: (623)842-6017
**Subject(s):** Paid Community Newspapers
**Circ:** ‡6,200

**Rexburg Standard Journal** (7790)
Po Box 10
Rexburg, ID 83440
Phone: (208)356-5441
Fax: (208)356-8312
**Subject(s):** Paid Community Newspapers
**Circ:** ‡6,200

**Foster City Islander** (1864)
1185 Chess Dr., Ste. B
Foster City, CA 94404
Phone: (650)574-5952
Fax: (650)574-1096
**Subject(s):** Free Newspapers
**Circ:** (Free)‡6,175

**Rancho Santa Margarita News** (2772)
The Orange County Register
22481 Aspan Dr.
Lake Forest, CA 92701
**Subject(s):** Free Newspapers
**Circ:** (Free)‡6,177

**Benicia Herald** (1441)
Gibson Publications Inc.
820 1st St.
P.O. Box 65
Benicia, CA 94510-3216
Phone: (707)745-0733

Fax: (707)458-8583
**Subject(s):** Daily Newspapers

Circ: (Paid)4,891
(Free)6,128

**Ramona Sentinel (2765)**
Hansen Publishing L.L.C.
611 Main St.
Ramona, CA 92065
Phone: (760)789-1350
Fax: (760)789-4057
**Subject(s):** Paid Community Newspapers

Circ: (Free)135
(Paid)6,100

**Fayetteville Eagle Bulletin (26039)**
Eagle Newspapers
4901 Indian School Rd. NE
PO Box 12008
Salem, OR 97305
Phone: (503)393-7980
Fax: (503)393-2366
**Subject(s):** Paid Community Newspapers

Circ: (Free)786
(Paid)6,050

**The Arbiter (7643)**
1910 Univ. Dr.
Boise, ID 83725
Phone: (208)345-8204
Fax: (208)345-3198
**Subject(s):** College Publications

Circ: (Free)‡6,000

**The Argonaut (7743)**
Student Media
301 Student Union
Moscow, ID 83844
Phone: (208)885-7845
Fax: (208)885-2222
**Subject(s):** College Publications

Circ: (Paid)250
(Free)6,000

**Campus Press (4108)**
University of Colorado at Boulder
School of Journalism
Campus Box 478
Boulder, CO 80309
Phone: (303)492-4557

Circ: (Controlled)6,000

**Country Gazette (32190)**
208 Corrin Ave. SW
PO Box 1231
Orting, WA 98360
Phone: (360)893-5103
Fax: (360)893-2277
**Subject(s):** Free Newspapers

Circ: (Free)‡6,000

**Daily Titan (1910)**
California State University, Fullerton
College Park Bldg.
2600 E Nutwood Ave., Ste. 670
Fullerton, CA 92831-3110
Phone: (714)278-3373
Fax: (714)278-2702
**Subject(s):** Daily Newspapers; College Publications

Circ: (Free)‡6,000

**Inside Tucson Business (916)**
Territorial Newspapers
3280 E Hemisphere Lp., Ste. 180
PO Box 27087
Tucson, AZ 85706
Phone: (520)294-1200
Fax: (520)294-4040
**Subject(s):** Business

Circ: (Paid)2,000
(Non-paid)6,000

**Lamont Reporter (2067)**
Reed Print Publication
PO Box 548
Lamont, CA 93241
Phone: (661)399-5925
Fax: (661)845-5907
**Subject(s):** Paid Community Newspapers

Circ: 6,000

**The Mojave Desert News (1599)**
MOCAL News Corp.
8046 California City Blvd.
California City, CA 93505
Phone: (760)373-4812
Fax: (760)373-2941
**Subject(s):** Paid Community Newspapers

Circ: (Free)‡200
(Paid)‡6,000

**Montana Kaimin (18207)**
University of Montana
University of Montana, Journalism 206
Missoula, MT 59801
Phone: (406)243-4310
Fax: (406)243-4303
**Subject(s):** College Publications

Circ: (Free)6,000

**The Newport Miner & Gem State Miner (32169)**
PO Box 349
421 South Spokane
Newport, WA 99156-0349
Phone: (509)447-2433
Fax: (509)447-9222
**Subject(s):** Paid Community Newspapers

Circ: ‡6,000

**The Richfield Reaper (30752)**
65 W. Center St.
Richfield, UT 84701
Phone: (435)896-5476
Fax: (435)896-8123
**Subject(s):** Paid Community Newspapers

Circ: 6,000

**Rocky Mountain Baptist (4177)**
Colorado Baptist General Convention
7393 S. Alton Way
Centennial, CO 80112-2302
Phone: (303)771-2480
Fax: (303)771-6272
**Subject(s):** Religious Publications

Circ: ‡6,000

**Sagebrush (18745)**
1262-A N. Sierra St. Ste. A
Reno, NV 89503
Phone: (702)784-4033
Fax: (702)784-1955
**Subject(s):** College Publications

Circ: (Free)‡6,000

**Siskiyou Daily News (4074)**
309 S. Broadway
PO Box 129
Yreka, CA 96097-0129
Phone: (530)842-5777
Fax: (530)842-6787
**Subject(s):** Daily Newspapers

Circ: ‡6,000

**Sonoma West Times & News (3515)**
Sonoma West Publishers Inc.
PO Box 521
Sebastopol, CA 95473-0521
**Subject(s):** Paid Community Newspapers

Circ: 6,000

**Tahoe World (3592)**
395 N. Lake Blvd.
PO Box 138
Tahoe City, CA 96145
Phone: (530)583-3487
Fax: (530)583-7109
**Subject(s):** Paid Community Newspapers

Circ: 6,000

**Dixon's Independent Voice (1776)**
529 N. Adams St., Ste. A
Dixon, CA 95620-2927
Phone: (707)678-8917
Fax: (707)678-4056
**Subject(s):** Paid Community Newspapers

Circ: (Combined)⊕5,980

**Montrose Daily Press (4519)**
535 S 1st
PO Box 850
Montrose, CO 81402
Phone: (970)249-3444
Fax: (970)249-3331

**Subject(s):** Daily Newspapers

Circ: (Sun.)⊐5,676
(Mon.-Fri.)⊐5,953

**Oakdale Leader (2563)**
122 S 3rd Ave.
PO Box 278
Oakdale, CA 95361-0278
Phone: (209)847-3021
Fax: (209)847-9750
**Subject(s):** Paid Community Newspapers

Circ: (Paid)‡4,899
(Free)‡5,911

**Trail-Gazette (4370)**
Estes Park Trail-Gazette
PO Box 1707
Estes Park, CO 80517
Phone: (970)586-3356
Fax: (970)586-9532
**Subject(s):** Paid Community Newspapers

Circ: ‡5,877

**Ketchikan Daily News (584)**
Pioneer Printing Company Inc.
501 Dock St.
PO Box 7900
Ketchikan, AK 99901
Phone: (907)225-3157
Fax: (907)225-1096
**Subject(s):** Daily Newspapers

Circ: ‡5,823

**Box Elder News Journal (30667)**
55 S. 100 W.
PO Box 370
Brigham City, UT 84302
Phone: (435)723-3471
Fax: (435)723-5247
**Subject(s):** Paid Community Newspapers

Circ: (Free)‡5,300
(Paid)‡5,800

**The Calaveras Enterprise (2973)**
Calaveras First Newspapers
15 N. Main St.
PO Box 1197
San Andreas, CA 95249
Phone: (209)754-3861
Fax: (209)754-1805
**Subject(s):** Paid Community Newspapers

Circ: (Paid)5,800

**Vancouver Business Journal (32468)**
2525 E 4TH Plain Blvd.
Vancouver, WA 98661
Phone: (360)695-2442
Fax: (360)695-3056
**Subject(s):** Paid Community Newspapers

Circ: (Controlled)5,793

**The Dispatch (1925)**
6400 Monterey Rd.
PO Box 22365
Gilroy, CA 95020
Phone: (408)842-6400
Fax: (408)842-6411
**Subject(s):** Daily Newspapers

Circ: (Mon.-Fri.)5,786

**Hood River News (25858)**
Eagle Newspapers
419 State Ave.
PO Box 390
Hood River, OR 97031-0900
Phone: (541)386-1234
Fax: (541)386-6796
**Subject(s):** Free Newspapers

Circ: (Free)62
(Paid)5,760

**Peninsula Clarion (580)**
Southeastern Newspapers Inc.
PO Box 3009
Kenai, AK 99611
Phone: (907)283-7551
Fax: (907)283-3299
**Subject(s):** Daily Newspapers

Circ: (Non-paid)⊕339
(Paid)⊕5,710

Circulation: ★ = ABC; △ = BPA; ♦ = CAC; • = CCAB; ▫ = VAC; ⊕ = PO Statement; ‡ = Publisher's Report; Boldface figures = sworn; Light figures = estimated.

# Western States

**Gale Directory of Publications & Broadcast Media/140th Ed.**

**Gardena Valley News  (1922)**
16417 S Western Ave.
PO Box 219
Gardena, CA 90247-0219
Phone: (310)329-6351
Fax: (310)329-7501
**Subject(s):** Paid Community Newspapers
**Circ:**   (Paid)‡5,700

**Post Shopper  (2644)**
839 Via De La Paz
PO Box 725
Pacific Palisades, CA 90272-0725
Phone: (310)454-1321
Fax: (310)454-1078
**Subject(s):** Shopping Guides
**Circ:**   (Free)5,700

**The Canby Herald  (26078)**
Eagle Newspapers
30250 SW Pkwy. Ave., Ste. No. 10
Wilsonville, OR 97070
Phone: (503)682-3935
Fax: (503)682-6265
**Subject(s):** Paid Community Newspapers
**Circ:**   (Paid)‡5,680

**The News Guard  (25892)**
Pacific Coast Newspapers
930 SE Hwy. 101
PO Box 848
Lincoln City, OR 97367
Phone: (503)994-2178
Fax: (503)994-7613
**Subject(s):** Paid Community Newspapers
**Circ:**   (Free)‡173
            (Paid)‡5,648

**Ravalli Republic  (18145)**
232 W. Main St.
Hamilton, MT 59840
Phone: (406)363-3300
Fax: (406)363-1767
**Subject(s):** Daily Newspapers
**Circ:**   ‡5,626

**Journal-Advocate  (4572)**
504 N. 3rd St.
PO Box 1272
Sterling, CO 80751
Phone: (970)522-1990
Fax: (970)522-2320
**Subject(s):** Daily Newspapers
**Circ:**   (Mon.-Sat.)★5,600

**Lake County Leader  (18232)**
Flathead Publishing Group
PO Box 1090
Polson, MT 59860
Phone: (406)883-4343
Fax: (406)883-4349
**Subject(s):** Paid Community Newspapers
**Circ:**   ‡5,600

**News-Times  (25835)**
PO Box 408
2038 Pacific Ave.
Forest Grove, OR 97116
Phone: (503)357-3181
Fax: (503)359-8456
**Subject(s):** Paid Community Newspapers
**Circ:**   (Paid)‡5,600

**Wasco Tribune  (1409)**
Reed Print Inc.
5409 Aldrin Ct.
Bakersfield, CA 93313
Phone: (661)834-0496
Fax: (661)746-5571
**Subject(s):** Paid Community Newspapers
**Circ:**   (Controlled)5,600

**Laramie Daily Boomerang  (33754)**
Laramie Newspapers Inc.
320 E Grand Ave.
Laramie, WY 82070
Phone: (307)742-2176
Fax: (307)721-2973
**Subject(s):** Daily Newspapers
**Circ:**   (Tues.-Fri.)5,511
            (Sun.)5,580

**Daily Record  (32076)**
Pioneer Newspapers
401 N Main Street
Ellensburg, WA 98926
Phone: (509)925-1414
Fax: (509)925-5696
**Subject(s):** Daily Newspapers
**Circ:**   ‡5,525

**Astro News  (1806)**
Aerotech
2420 Vela Way, Ste. 1467
El Segundo, CA 90245-1467
Phone: (310)363-0030
Fax: (310)363-2549
**Subject(s):** Military and Navy; Free Newspapers
**Circ:**   (Non-paid)5,500

**La Canada Valley Sun  (2024)**
No.1061 Valley Sun Ln.
La Canada, CA 91011
Phone: (818)790-8774
Fax: (818)790-5690
**Subject(s):** Paid Community Newspapers
**Circ:**   ‡5,500

**Magna Times & West Valley News  (30702)**
8980 W 2700 S
Magna, UT 84044
Phone: (801)250-5656
Fax: (801)250-5685
**Subject(s):** Paid Community Newspapers
**Circ:**   5,500

**The Newberg Graphic  (25920)**
109 N. School St.
PO Box 700
Newberg, OR 97132
Phone: (503)538-2181
Fax: (503)538-1632
**Subject(s):** Paid Community Newspapers
**Circ:**   ‡5,500

**Seattle Daily Journal of Commerce  (32322)**
Daily Journal of Commerce
83 Columbia St.
Seattle, WA 98104
Phone: (206)622-8272
Fax: (206)622-8416
**Subject(s):** Daily Periodicals; Business; Construction, Contracting, Building, and Excavating
**Circ:**   ‡5,500

**The Valley Courier  (4082)**
Alamosa Newspapers Inc.
401 State Ave.
PO Box 1099
Alamosa, CO 81101
Phone: (719)589-2553
Fax: (719)589-6573
**Subject(s):** Daily Newspapers
**Circ:**   (Non-paid)100
            (Paid)5,500

**Capistrano Valley News  (3330)**
The Orange County Register
22481 Aspan St.
Lake Forest, CA 92630
Fax: (949)454-7354
**Subject(s):** Free Newspapers
**Circ:**   (Paid)3,283
            (Controlled)5,493

**Sun Advocate  (30728)**
845 E Main St.
Price, UT 84501-2708
Phone: (435)637-0732
Fax: (435)637-2716
**Subject(s):** Paid Community Newspapers
**Circ:**   ‡5,450

**Boulder City News  (18649)**
1227 Arizona St.
PO Box 60065
Boulder City, NV 89006
Phone: (702)293-2302
Fax: (702)294-0977
**Subject(s):** Paid Community Newspapers
**Circ:**   ‡5,400

**Fort Bragg Advocate-News  (1857)**
Media News Group
450 N. Franklin St.
PO Box 1188
Fort Bragg, CA 95437
Phone: (707)964-5642
Fax: (707)964-0424
**Subject(s):** Paid Community Newspapers
**Circ:**   (Thurs.)5,400

**The Winslow Mail  (982)**
Western Newspapers Inc.
208 W. 1st St.
Winslow, AZ 86047
Phone: (928)289-2467
Fax: (928)289-4151
**Subject(s):** Free Newspapers
**Circ:**   (Fri.)‡1,700
            (Wed.)‡5,360

**Desert Dispatch  (1438)**
Freedom Communications Inc.
130 Coolwater Ln.
Barstow, CA 92311
Phone: (760)256-8589
Fax: (760)256-0685
**Subject(s):** Daily Newspapers
**Circ:**   (Mon.-Sat.)5,338

**Mariposa Gazette and Miner  (2438)**
Mariposa Gazette
PO Box 38
Mariposa, CA 95338
Phone: (209)966-2500
Fax: (209)966-3384
**Subject(s):** Paid Community Newspapers
**Circ:**   (Paid)‡5,300

**Merced Sunstar  (2530)**
U.S. Media Inc.
PO Box 878
Newman, CA 95360
Phone: (209)854-3787
Fax: (209)854-3851
**Subject(s):** Free Newspapers
**Circ:**   (Free)5,300

**The Mining Record  (4171)**
Howell International Enterprises
P.O. Box 1630
Castle Rock, CO 80104-6130
Phone: (303)663-7820
Fax: (303)663-7823
**Subject(s):** Mining and Minerals; Local, State, and Regional Publications
**Circ:**   ‡5,260

**The Fountain Hills Times  (681)**
Western States Publishers Inc.
PO Box 17869
Fountain Hills, AZ 85269-7869
Phone: (480)837-1925
Fax: (480)837-1951
**Subject(s):** Paid Community Newspapers
**Circ:**   5,200

**Lahontan Valley News/Fallon Eagle Standard  (18666)**
562 N Maine St.
PO Box 1297
Fallon, NV 89406-2813
Phone: (775)423-6041
Fax: (775)423-0474
**Subject(s):** Daily Newspapers
**Circ:**   (Paid)5,200

**Westminster Window  (4593)**
MetroNorth Newspapers Inc.
PO Box 350070
Westminster, CO 80035-0070
Phone: (303)426-6000
Fax: (303)426-4209
**Subject(s):** Paid Community Newspapers
**Circ:**   (Non-paid)109
            (Paid)5,200

**Glenwood Post  (4405)**
2014 Grand Ave.
Glenwood Springs, CO 81601
Phone: (970)945-8515
Fax: (970)945-4487
**Subject(s):** Daily Newspapers
**Circ:**   (Free)‡1,675
            (Paid)⊕5,171

Gale Directory of Publications & Broadcast Media/140th Ed.  Western States

**The Dispatch** (7633)
New Regime Press Inc.
PO Box 96
Maunaloa, HI 96770
Phone: (808)552-2781
Fax: (808)552-2334
**Subject(s):** Paid Community Newspapers
**Circ:** (Controlled)⊕**5,150**

**Parker Pioneer** (728)
Wick Communications Co.
1001-12th St.
PO Box N
Parker, AZ 85344
Phone: (928)669-2275
**Subject(s):** Paid Community Newspapers
**Circ:** 5,149

**Mount Washington Star-Review** (2280)
Wave Newspaper Group
4201 Wilshire Ave., Ste. 600
Los Angeles, CA 90010
Phone: (323)556-5720
Fax: (323)556-5704
**Subject(s):** Free Newspapers
**Circ:** (Controlled)5,135

**Gazette Mountain Life** (2437)
Mariposa Gazette
PO Box 38
Mariposa, CA 95338
Phone: (209)966-2500
Fax: (209)966-3384
**Subject(s):** Shopping Guides
**Circ:** (Paid)‡5,100

**Mercer Island Reporter** (32149)
PO Box 38
7845 SE 30th St.
Mercer Island, WA 98040-0038
Phone: (206)232-1215
Fax: (206)232-1284
**Subject(s):** Paid Community Newspapers
**Circ:** ‡5,100

**The Redmond Spokesman** (26023)
PO Box 788
226 Nw. 6th St.
Redmond, OR 97756
Phone: (541)548-2184
Fax: (541)548-3203
**Subject(s):** Paid Community Newspapers
**Circ:** (Free)‡40
       (Paid)‡5,010

**The Tidings** (25699)
PO Box 7
Ashland, OR 97520
Phone: (503)482-3456
Fax: (503)482-3688
**Subject(s):** Daily Newspapers
**Circ:** (Mon.-Sat.)5,010

**The Bridge** (25950)
Portland Community College
12000 SW 49th Ave.
PO Box 19000
Portland, OR 97280
Phone: (503)977-4184
Fax: (503)977-4956
**Subject(s):** College Publications
**Circ:** (Free)‡5,000

**The Collegian** (1877)
California State University, Fresno
5201 N. Maple Ave., M/S SA42
Fresno, CA 93740-8027
Phone: (559)278-5735
Fax: (559)278-2679
**Subject(s):** Journalism and Publishing; College Publications
**Circ:** (Free)5,000

**The Current** (2886)
American River College
4700 College Oak Dr.
Sacramento, CA 95841
Phone: (916)484-8011
**Subject(s):** College Publications
**Circ:** 5,000

**Daniels County Leader** (18236)
23 Main St.
PO Box 850
Scobey, MT 59263
Phone: (406)487-5303

Fax: (406)487-5304
**Subject(s):** Paid Community Newspapers
**Circ:** ‡5,000

**East West Journal** (7537)
1150 South King Street Suite 103
Honolulu, HI 96814
Phone: (808)596-0099
Fax: (808)596-2292
**Subject(s):** Paid Community Newspapers; Japanese; Ethnic Publications
**Circ:** (Combined)5,000

**The Lance** (2776)
Shasta Community College
11555 N Old Oregon Trl.
PO Box 496006
Redding, CA 96049-6006
Phone: (530)225-4723
Fax: (530)225-4668
**Subject(s):** College Publications
**Circ:** (Non-paid)‡5,000

**Las Vegas Sentinel-Voice** (18691)
Griot Communications Group Inc.
900 E Charleston Blvd.
Las Vegas, NV 89104
Phone: (702)380-8100
Fax: (702)380-8102
**Subject(s):** Paid Community Newspapers; Black Publications
**Circ:** 5,000

**Los Angeles Loyolan** (2259)
Loyola Marymount University
Daum Hall, One LMU Dr. MS-8470
Los Angeles, CA 90045
Phone: (310)338-2879
Fax: (310)338-1901
**Subject(s):** College Publications
**Circ:** (Free)‡5,000

**The Morning News** (7642)
Horizon Publication
34 N. Ash
PO Box 70
Blackfoot, ID 83221
Phone: (208)785-1100
Fax: (208)785-4239
**Subject(s):** Daily Newspapers
**Circ:** ‡5,000

**The Pacifican** (3565)
University of the Pacific
3601 Pacific Ave.
Hand Hall, 3rd Fl.
Stockton, CA 95211
Phone: (209)946-2115
Fax: (209)946-2195
**Subject(s):** College Publications
**Circ:** (Free)5,000

**PCC-Courieronline.com.** (2720)
Pasadena Community College
1570 E. Colorado Blvd., Rm. CC220
Pasadena, CA 91106
Phone: (626)585-7130
Fax: (626)585-7971
**Subject(s):** College Publications
**Circ:** ‡5,000

**The San Bernardino American News** (2984)
The American News
1583 W Baseline St.
San Bernardino, CA 92411-1756
Phone: (909)889-7677
Fax: (909)889-2882
**Subject(s):** Paid Community Newspapers; Black Publications
**Circ:** 5,000

**San Joaquin Farm Bureau News** (3568)
San Joaquin Farm Bureau Federation
PO Box 8444
Stockton, CA 95208
Phone: (209)931-4931
Fax: (209)931-1433
**Subject(s):** Farm Bureau, Grange, and Cooperative Associations
**Circ:** (Paid)‡5,000

**Snoqualmie Valley Record** (32386)
PO Box 300
Snoqualmie, WA 98065
Phone: (425)888-2311
Fax: (425)888-2427

**Subject(s):** Paid Community Newspapers
**Circ:** 5000

**Sonoma Valley News** (3537)
The Sonoma Index-Tribune
PO Box C
Sonoma, CA 95476
Phone: (707)938-2111
Fax: (707)938-1600
**Subject(s):** Shopping Guides
**Circ:** (Free)‡5,000

**Williams-Grand Canyon News** (978)
118 S. 3rd St.
PO Box 667
Williams, AZ 86046-0667
Phone: (928)635-4426
Fax: (928)635-4887
**Subject(s):** Paid Community Newspapers
**Circ:** ‡5,000

**Woodburn Independent** (26082)
Eagle/Webb Press
650 N 1st St.
PO Box 96
Woodburn, OR 97071-0096
Phone: (503)981-3441
Fax: (503)981-1253
**Subject(s):** Paid Community Newspapers
**Circ:** 5,000

**Ojai Valley News** (2618)
Ojai Valley Newspapers L.L.C.
408A Bryant Cir.
PO Box 277
Ojai, CA 93023
Phone: (805)646-1476
Fax: (805)646-4281
**Subject(s):** Paid Community Newspapers
**Circ:** ‡4,940

**Crested Butte Chronicle & Pilot** (4253)
432 Elk Ave
PO Box 369
Crested Butte, CO 81224
Phone: (970)349-0500
Fax: (970)349-9876
**Subject(s):** Paid Community Newspapers
**Circ:** (Free)‡40
       (Paid)‡4,900

**Mountaineer Progress** (2731)
PO Box 290130
Phelan, CA 92329
Phone: (760)868-3245
Fax: (760)868-2700
**Subject(s):** Paid Community Newspapers
**Circ:** ‡4,900

**Vernal Express** (30823)
Vernal Express Publishing Co.
PO Box 1000
Vernal, UT 84078-1000
Phone: (435)789-3511
Fax: (435)789-8690
**Subject(s):** Paid Community Newspapers
**Circ:** (Free)⊕**27**
       (Paid)⊕**4,883**

**Lewistown News-Argus** (18182)
521 W Main St.
PO Box 900
Lewistown, MT 59457-0900
Phone: (406)538-3401
Fax: (406)538-3405
**Subject(s):** Paid Community Newspapers
**Circ:** ‡4,874

**Northend Neighborhood Classifieds** (31991)
Sound Publishing Inc.
7689 NE Day Rd.
Bainbridge Island, WA 98110
Phone: (206)842-8305
Fax: (206)842-8030
**Subject(s):** Free Newspapers
**Circ:** (Ncn-paid)♦**4,821**

**Millard County Gazette** (30674)
Millard County Gazette Inc.
PO Box 609
Delta, UT 84624
Phone: (435)846-2904
Fax: (435)846-2904

**Circulation:** ★ = ABC; △ = BPA; ♦ = CAC; ● = CCAB; ❑ = VAC; ⊕ = PO Statement; ‡ = Publisher's Report; Boldface figures = sworn; Light figures = estimated.

# Western States

Subject(s): Free Newspapers
Circ: (Free)‡4,800

**Acton/Aqua Dulce News** (2853)
Joyce Media Inc.
PO Box 848
Rosamond, CA 93560
Phone: (661)269-2139
Fax: (661)269-2139
Subject(s): Paid Community Newspapers
Circ: (Controlled)4,700

**Escalon Times** (1827)
Morris Newspaper of California
1746 Main St.
PO Box 98
Escalon, CA 95320
Phone: (209)838-7043
Subject(s): Paid Community Newspapers
Circ: 4,700

**South Idaho Press** (7680)
230 E. Main St.
Burley, ID 83318
Phone: (208)678-2201
Fax: (208)678-0412
Subject(s): Daily Newspapers
Circ: (Mon.-Fri.)4,463
(Sun.)4,677

**Delano Record** (1769)
Reed Print Incorporated Community Newspapers
1231 Jefferson St.
Delano, CA 93215
Phone: (805)725-0600
Fax: (805)725-4373
Subject(s): Paid Community Newspapers
Circ: ‡4,650

**Tribune Advertiser** (18120)
Dillon Tribune
22 S Montana
PO Box 911
Dillon, MT 59725-0911
Phone: (406)683-2331
Fax: (406)683-2332
Subject(s): Shopping Guides
Circ: (Free)‡4,600

**The Bainbridge Island Review** (31988)
Sound Publishing Inc.
PO Box 10817
Bainbridge Island, WA 98110
Phone: (206)842-6613
Subject(s): Paid Community Newspapers
Circ: (Non-paid)40
(Paid)4,586

**Palisadian-Post** (2643)
839 Via De La Paz
Pacific Palisades, CA 90272
Phone: (310)454-1321
Fax: (310)454-1078
Subject(s): Paid Community Newspapers
Circ: (Free)145
(Paid)4,564

**Westside Record-Journal** (32096)
Ferndale Record Inc.
2008 Main St.
PO Box 38
Ferndale, WA 98248-0038
Phone: (360)384-1411
Fax: (360)384-1417
Subject(s): Paid Community Newspapers
Circ: (Paid)‡3,000
(Free)4,559

**O & A Marketing News** (1363)
KAL Publications Inc.
559 S Harbor Blvd., Ste. A
Anaheim, CA 92805-4525
Phone: (714)563-9300
Fax: (714)563-9310
Subject(s): Automotive (Trade); Petroleum, Oil, and Gas
Circ: (Free)‡2,732
(Paid)‡4,522

**South Whidbey Record** (32132)
Sound Publishing Inc.
5603 S. Bayview Rd
PO Box 387
Langley, WA 98260
Phone: (360)221-5300

Subject(s): Paid Community Newspapers
Circ: (Non-paid)15
(Paid)4,521

**Bigfork Eagle** (18065)
PO Box 406
Bigfork, MT 59911
Phone: (406)837-5131
Fax: (406)837-1132
Subject(s): Paid Community Newspapers
Circ: (Paid)‡1,600
(Free)‡4,500

**The Free Lance** (1968)
Mainstreet Media Group LLC
350, 6th St.
PO Box 1417
Hollister, CA 95023
Phone: (831)637-5566
Fax: (831)637-4104
Subject(s): Daily Newspapers
Circ: (Mon.-Fri.)4,500

**The Jewish Transcript** (32277)
Jewish Federation
2031 3rd Ave.
Seattle, WA 98121
Phone: (206)443-5400
Fax: (206)443-0303
Subject(s): Jewish Publications; Paid Community Newspapers
Circ: ‡4,500

**Modoc County Record** (1338)
Box 531
Alturas, CA 96101
Phone: (530)233-2632
Fax: (530)233-5113
Subject(s): Paid Community Newspapers
Circ: 4,500

**The Pagosa Springs Sun** (4528)
466 Pagosa St.
PO Box 9
Pagosa Springs, CO 81147
Phone: (970)264-2100
Subject(s): Paid Community Newspapers
Circ: ‡4,500

**The Regal Courier** (25863)
Community Newspapers Inc.
11735 SW Queen Elizabeth, Ste. 106
King City, OR 97224
Phone: (503)639-5414
Fax: (503)968-7397
Subject(s): Senior Citizens' Interests
Circ: 4,500

**St. Mary's Collegian Student News Paper** (2511)
St. Mary's College
PO Box 4407
1928 Saint Marys Rd
Moraga, CA 94575-4407
Phone: (925)631-4279
Fax: (925)631-4675
Subject(s): College Publications
Circ: 4,500

**Synapse** (3223)
University of California, San Francisco
500 Parnassus Ave.
Box 0376
San Francisco, CA 94143-0376
Phone: (415)476-2211
Fax: (415)502-4537
Subject(s): College Publications
Circ: 4,500

**Telluride Daily Planet** (4577)
283 S. Fir St.
PO Box 2315
Telluride, CO 81435
Phone: (970)728-9788
Fax: (970)728-9793
Subject(s): Daily Newspapers
Circ: (Non-paid)4,500

**Uintah Basin Standard** (30753)
268 S 200 E
Roosevelt, UT 84066
Phone: (435)722-5131
Fax: (435)722-4140
Subject(s): Paid Community Newspapers
Circ: (Paid)‡4,500

**The Villager Office Park News** (4455)
The Villager Publishing Co.
8933 E Union Ave., Ste. 230
Greenwood Village, CO 80111
Phone: (303)773-8313
Fax: (303)773-8456
Subject(s): Free Newspapers
Circ: (Non-paid)4,500

**The Western Sun** (1985)
Golden West College
15744 Golden W St.
Huntington Beach, CA 92647
Phone: (714)895-8786
Fax: (714)895-8795
Subject(s): College Publications
Circ: (Free)‡4,500

**Whitman County Gazette** (32052)
211 N Main
PO Box 770
Colfax, WA 99111
Phone: (509)397-4333
Fax: (509)397-4527
Subject(s): Paid Community Newspapers
Circ: 4,450

**The Piedmonter** (1333)
Hills Publications
1516 Oak St.
Alameda, CA 94501
Phone: (510)748-1666
Fax: (510)339-7302
Subject(s): Paid Community Newspapers
Circ: (Paid)❏737
(Free)❏4,412

**The Dixon Tribune** (1775)
Dixon Tribune
145 E A St.
Dixon, CA 95620
Phone: (707)678-5594
Fax: (707)678-5404
Subject(s): Paid Community Newspapers
Circ: (Free)‡1,000
(Paid)‡4,400

**Ft. Lupton Press** (4393)
Metro West Publishing
410 Denver Ave.
PO Box 125
Fort Lupton, CO 80621
Phone: (303)857-4440
Fax: (303)659-2901
Subject(s): Paid Community Newspapers
Circ: (Paid)‡1,100
(Non-paid)‡4,400

**Ranger-Review** (18130)
Livingston Enterprise
119 W Bell St.
PO Box 61
Glendive, MT 59330
Phone: (406)365-3303
Fax: (406)365-5435
Subject(s): Paid Community Newspapers
Circ: ‡4,400

**San Marino Tribune** (3356)
1441 San Marino Ave.
San Marino, CA 91108
Phone: (626)282-5707
Fax: (626)792-4915
Subject(s): Paid Community Newspapers
Circ: (Combined)4,400

**The Fort Morgan Times** (4394)
Eastern Colorado Publishing Co.
329 Main St.
PO Box 4000
Fort Morgan, CO 80701
Phone: (970)867-5651
Fax: (970)867-7448
Subject(s): Daily Newspapers
Circ: (Mon.-Sat.)★4,390

**The South County Spotlight** (26053)
Bridge Publications Inc.
PO Box C
Scappoose, OR 97056
Phone: (503)397-6488
Fax: (503)543-6380
Subject(s): Paid Community Newspapers
Circ: (Paid)4,370

**Buffalo Bulletin (33680)**
PO Box 730
Buffalo, WY 82834
Phone: (307)684-2223
Fax: (307)684-7431
Subject(s): Paid Community Newspapers

Circ: ‡4,350

**Central Oregonian (26019)**
Eagle Newspapers
558 N Main St.
Prineville, OR 97754
Phone: (541)447-6205
Fax: (541)447-1754
Subject(s): Paid Community Newspapers

Circ: ‡4,342

**Havre Daily News (18150)**
PO Box 431
119 Secound St.
Havre, MT 59501
Phone: (406)265-6795
Fax: (406)265-6798
Subject(s): Daily Newspapers

Circ: (Paid)⊕4,348

**The Glasgow Courier (18128)**
341 3rd Ave. S
Glasgow, MT 59230
Phone: (406)228-9301
Fax: (406)228-2665
Subject(s): Free Newspapers; Free Newspapers

Circ: (Paid)‡4,300

**Point Reyes Light (2753)**
PO Box 210
Point Reyes Station, CA 94956
Phone: (415)663-8404
Fax: (415)663-8458
Subject(s): Paid Community Newspapers

Circ: ‡4,300

**Westminister Herald (4039)**
Westminister
PO Box 428
Westminster, CA 92684
Phone: (714)893-4501
Fax: (714)893-4502
Subject(s): Paid Community Newspapers

Circ: ⊕4,300

**Oakdale Advertiser (2562)**
PO Box 278
Oakdale, CA 95361
Phone: (209)847-3021
Fax: (209)847-9750
Subject(s): Shopping Guides

Circ: (Free)4,223

**Borrego Sun (1549)**
Copley Newspapers Inc.
PO Box 249
Borrego Springs, CA 92004
Phone: (760)767-5338
Fax: (760)767-4971
Subject(s): Paid Community Newspapers

Circ: ‡4,200

**Camas-Washougal Post-Record (32031)**
Post Publications
PO Box 03
Camas, WA 98607
Phone: (360)834-2141
Fax: (360)834-3423
Subject(s): Free Newspapers

Circ: (Free)‡3,600
(Paid)‡4,200

**Palo Verde Valley Times (1544)**
231 N Spring St.
PO Box 1159
Blythe, CA 92226
Phone: (760)922-3181
Fax: (760)922-3184
Subject(s): Paid Community Newspapers

Circ: ‡4,200

**The Powell Tribune (33772)**
PO Box 70
128 South Bent
Powell, WY 82435-0070
Phone: (307)754-2221
Fax: (307)754-4873

Subject(s): Paid Community Newspapers
Circ: ‡4,200

**Seattle University Spectator (32327)**
Seattle University
901 12th Avenue
PO Box 222000
Seattle, WA 98122-1090
Phone: (206)296-6000
Fax: (206)296-6477
Subject(s): College Publications

Circ: 4,200

**Western News (18186)**
311 California Ave.
PO Box 1377
Libby, MT 59923
Phone: (406)293-4124
Fax: (406)293-7187
Subject(s): Paid Community Newspapers

Circ: 4,200

**Wallowa County Chieftain (25791)**
Wallowa County Chieftain Inc.
106 NW First St.
PO Box 338
Enterprise, OR 97828
Phone: (541)426-4567
Fax: (541)426-3921
Subject(s): Paid Community Newspapers

Circ: 4,196

**The Cambrian (1610)**
PO Box 67
2442 Main St.
Cambria, CA 93428
Phone: (805)927-8652
Fax: (805)927-4708
Subject(s): Paid Community Newspapers

Circ: 4,100

**The Healdsburg Tribune (1963)**
Sonoma West Publishers Inc.
PO Box 518
Healdsburg, CA 95448
Phone: (707)433-4451
Fax: (707)431-2623
Subject(s): Paid Community Newspapers

Circ: (Free)3,000
‡4,100

**The Lander Wyoming State Journal (33748)**
River Turmain Tournal
332 Main
PO Box 10
Lander, WY 82520
Phone: (307)332-2323
Fax: (307)332-9332
Subject(s): Paid Community Newspapers

Circ: 4,100

**The Anderson Valley Advertiser (1548)**
12451 Anderson Valley Way
Boonville, CA 95415
Phone: (707)895-3016
Fax: (707)895-3355
Subject(s): Paid Community Newspapers

Circ: 4,000

**The Bellingham Business Journal (32005)**
The Bellingham Business Journal L.L.C.
1321 King St. No. 4
Bellingham, WA 98227
Phone: (360)647-8805
Fax: (360)641-0502

Circ: (Paid)‡200
(Non-paid)‡4,000

**Blue Mountain Eagle (25860)**
East Oregonian Publishing Company Inc.
195 N. Canyon Blvd.
John Day, OR 97845
Phone: (541)575-1244
Fax: (541)575-1244
Subject(s): Paid Community Newspapers

Circ: 4,000

**The Clarion (4265)**
University of Denver
Student Media Board
Driscoll University Ctr.
2055 E. Evans
Denver, CO 80210
Phone: (303)871-3131
Fax: (303)871-2568

Subject(s): College Publications
Circ: (Free)‡4,000

**Hilmar Times (4053)**
Mid-Valley Publications
6950 Gerard St.
Winton, CA 95388
Phone: (209)358-5311
Fax: (209)358-7108
Subject(s): Paid Community Newspapers

Circ: ‡4,000

**The Humboldt Sun (18765)**
Winnemucca Publishing
PO Box 3000
Winnemucca, NV 89446
Phone: (775)623-5011
Fax: (775)623-5243
Subject(s): Paid Community Newspapers

Circ: ‡4,000

**Kodiak Daily Mirror (589)**
1419 Selig St.
Kodiak, AK 99615
Phone: (907)486-3227
Fax: (907)486-3088
Subject(s): Daily Newspapers

Circ: (Combined)4,000

**Los Angeles Bulletin (2253)**
Metropolitan News Co.
210 S. Spring St.
Los Angeles, CA 90012
Phone: (213)346-0033
Fax: (213)687-3886
Subject(s): Daily Newspapers

Circ: (Paid)200
(Non-paid)4,000

**The Montanian (18185)**
PO Box 946
Libby, MT 59923
Phone: (406)293-8202
Subject(s): Free Newspapers

Circ: (Combined)4,000

**Mountain Home News (7756)**
Rust Publishing
195 S 3rd E
PO Box 1330
Mountain Home, ID 83647
Phone: (208)587-3331
Fax: (208)587-9205
Subject(s): Paid Community Newspapers

Circ: ‡4,000

**The Mountaineer (4009)**
Mt. San Antonio College
1100 N Grand Ave.
Walnut, CA 91789
Phone: (909)594-5611
Fax: (909)594-7661
Subject(s): College Publications

Circ: (Free)‡4,000

**NIC Sentinel (7685)**
North Idaho College
1000 W. Garden Ave.
Coeur d'Alene, ID 83814
Phone: (208)769-3300
Fax: (208)769-3431
Subject(s): College Publications; Free Newspapers

Circ: (Non-paid)4,000

**Nisqually Valley News (32525)**
PO Box 597
Yelm, WA 98597
Phone: (360)458-2681
Fax: (360)458-5741
Subject(s): Paid Community Newspapers

Circ: ‡4,000

**Norseman (3508)**
West Valley College
14000 Fruitvale
Saratoga, CA 95070-5697
Phone: (408)867-2200
Fax: (408)867-5033
Subject(s): College Publications

Circ: (Free)4,000

---

Circulation: ★ = ABC; △ = BPA; ♦ = CAC; • = CCAB; □ = VAC; ⊕ = PO Statement; ‡ = Publisher's Report; Boldface figures = sworn; Light figures = estimated.

3851

# Western States

**Orem-Geneva Times** (30721)
Utah Valley Publishing
546 S State St.
PO Box 65
Orem, UT 84058
Phone: (801)225-1340
Fax: (801)225-1341
**Subject(s):** Free Newspapers
Circ: (Free)‡1,400
    (Paid)‡4,000

**The Perris Progress** (2728)
240 W 4th St.
PO Box 128
Perris, CA 92572-0128
Fax: (909)657-2182
**Subject(s):** Paid Community Newspapers
Circ: (Paid)‡4,000

**Post Falls Press** (7785)
PO Box 39
318 Spokane St
Post Falls, ID 83877
Phone: (208)773-7502
Fax: (208)773-7002
**Subject(s):** Daily Newspapers
Circ: (Combined)4,000

**Review** (25894)
Eagle Newspapers
4901 Indian School Rd. NE
PO Box 12008
Salem, OR 97305
Phone: (503)393-7980
Fax: (503)393-2366
**Subject(s):** Paid Community Newspapers
Circ: (Free)⊕573
    (Paid)4,005

**The Review** (25893)
Eagle Newspapers
4901 Indian School Rd. NE
PO Box 12008
Salem, OR 97305
Phone: (503)393-7980
Fax: (503)393-2366
**Subject(s):** Paid Community Newspapers
Circ: ‡4,005

**River News Herald & Isleton Journal** (2812)
River News Herald Co.
PO Box 786
Rio Vista, CA 94571
Phone: (707)374-6431
Fax: (707)374-6322
**Subject(s):** Paid Community Newspapers
Circ: ‡4,000

**Shafter Press** (3517)
107 E Lerdo Hwy.
Shafter, CA 93263
Phone: (661)746-4942
Fax: (661)746-5571
**Subject(s):** Paid Community Newspapers
Circ: (Paid)2,300
    (Non-paid)4,000

**Shafter Shopper** (3518)
PO Box 1600
Shafter, CA 93263
Phone: (661)746-4942
Fax: (661)746-5571
**Subject(s):** Shopping Guides
Circ: (Free)‡4,000

**The Star-News** (7736)
Central Idaho Publishing
1000 N 1st St.
McCall, ID 83638-3848
Phone: (208)634-2123
Fax: (208)634-4950
**Subject(s):** Paid Community Newspapers
Circ: ‡4,000

**Sun Star** (542)
University of Alaska
PO Box 756640
Fairbanks, AK 99775
Phone: (907)474-6039
Fax: (907)474-5008
**Subject(s):** College Publications
Circ: (Free)‡4,000

**Talon Marks** (2556)
Cerritos College
11110 Alondra Blvd.
Norwalk, CA 90650-6298
Phone: (562)860-2451
Fax: (562)467-5044
**Subject(s):** College Publications
Circ: (Free)4,000

**Today** (2082)
Loma Linda University
Office of University Relations
24941, Stewart St.
Loma Linda, CA 92350-0001
Phone: (909)558-4526
Fax: (909)558-4181
**Subject(s):** College Publications
Circ: (Non-paid)4,000

**The Torch** (25812)
Lane Community College
Students First! Center
4000 E. 30th Ave.
Student Services Bldg. 1 Lobby
Eugene, OR 97405
Phone: (541)463-3100
Fax: (541)463-3993
**Subject(s):** College Publications
Circ: ‡4,000

**Aliso Viejo News** (2061)
The Orange County Register
22481 Aspan St.
Lake Forest, CA 92630
Fax: (949)454-7354
**Subject(s):** Paid Community Newspapers
Circ: (Paid)2,100
    (Controlled)3,997

**West Linn Tidings** (26076)
Community Newspapers
111 A Ave.
PO Box 548
Lake Oswego, OR 97034
Phone: (503)684-0360
Fax: (503)620-3433
**Subject(s):** Free Newspapers
Circ: (Free)1,075
    (Paid)3,995

**The Record-Courier** (25714)
1718 Main St.
PO Box 70
Baker City, OR 97814-0070
Phone: (541)523-5353
Fax: (541)523-5353
**Subject(s):** Paid Community Newspapers
Circ: ‡3,950

**Leader Garland Times** (30821)
The Leader
119 E Main
Tremonton, UT 84337
Phone: (435)257-5182
Fax: (435)257-6175
**Subject(s):** Paid Community Newspapers
Circ: (Paid)‡3,100
    (Free)‡3,900

**Pioneer Press** (1862)
PO Box 400
Fort Jones, CA 96032
Phone: (530)468-5355
Fax: (530)468-5356
**Subject(s):** Paid Community Newspapers
Circ: 3,900

**Douglas Budget** (33727)
Sage Publishing
Drawer 109
Douglas, WY 82633
Phone: (307)358-2965
Fax: (307)358-2926
**Subject(s):** Paid Community Newspapers
Circ: ‡3,850

**Golden Transcript** (4413)
Jeffco Publishing Inc.
1000 10th St.
Golden, CO 80401
Phone: (303)279-5541
Fax: (303)279-7157
**Subject(s):** Paid Community Newspapers
Circ: (Free)913
    (Paid)3,843

**The Anaconda Leader** (18059)
Leader Printing & Supply Inc.
121 Main St.
Anaconda, MT 59711
Phone: (406)563-5283
Fax: (406)563-5284
**Subject(s):** Paid Community Newspapers
Circ: (Free)60
    (Paid)3,800

**Gunnison Country Times** (4456)
218 N Wisconsin
PO Box 240
Gunnison, CO 81230
Phone: (970)641-1414
Fax: (970)641-6515
**Subject(s):** Paid Community Newspapers
Circ: ‡3,800

**Idyllwild Town Crier** (1986)
54295 Village Center Dr.
PO Box 157
Idyllwild, CA 92549-0157
Phone: (951)659-2145
Fax: (951)659-2071
**Subject(s):** Paid Community Newspapers
Circ: 3,800

**The Madras Pioneer** (25895)
Eagle Newspapers
241 S.E. 6th St.
Madras, OR 97741
Phone: (541)475-2275
Fax: (541)475-3710
**Subject(s):** Paid Community Newspapers
Circ: (Free)75
    (Paid)3,800

**Daily Times** (33774)
Rawlins Newspapers Inc.
522 W.Buffalo St
PO Box 370
Rawlins, WY 82301
Phone: (307)324-3411
Fax: (307)324-2797
**Subject(s):** Daily Newspapers
Circ: ‡3,780

**La Junta Tribune-Democrat** (4475)
La Junta Democrat Publishing Co.
422 Colorado Ave.
PO Box 480
La Junta, CO 81050
Phone: (719)384-4475
Fax: (719)384-4478
**Subject(s):** Daily Newspapers
Circ: ‡3,787

**The Graphic (on line)** (2421)
Pepperdine University
24255 Pacific Coast Hwy.
Malibu, CA 90263
Phone: (310)506-4311
Fax: (310)506-4411
**Subject(s):** College Publications
Circ: (Free)‡3,750

**Stanwood/Camano News** (32432)
Stanwood Camano News and Advertiser
PO Box 999
9005 271 NW Street
Stanwood, WA 98292
Phone: (360)629-2155
Fax: (360)629-4211
**Subject(s):** Paid Community Newspapers
Circ: 3,750

**Brentwood News** (1557)
Brentwood Media Group
1650 Cavallo Rd.
Antioch, CA 94509
Phone: (925)757-2525
Fax: (925)754-9483
**Subject(s):** Paid Community Newspapers
Circ: 3,728

**North Syracuse Star-News** (25928)
Eagle Newspapers
4901 Indian School Rd. NE
PO Box 12008
Salem, OR 97305
Phone: (503)393-7980
Fax: (503)393-2366

**Subject(s):** Paid Community Newspapers
**Circ:** (Non-paid)772
(Paid)3,725

**Agri-Times Northwest (25933)**
Sterling Ag L.L.C.
PO Box 1626
Pendleton, OR 97801-0189
Phone: (541)276-6202
**Subject(s):** Farm Newspapers
**Circ:** (Combined)3,700

**The Carmelite Review (906)**
The Carmelites
1540 E. Glenn St.
Tucson, AZ 85719
Phone: (520)326-4967
Fax: (520)326-7366
**Subject(s):** Religious Publications
**Circ:** (Controlled)‡25
(Paid)‡3,700

**The Chronicle (25777)**
Country Mile Media Inc.
PO Box 428
Creswell, OR 97426
Phone: (541)895-2197
Fax: (541)895-2361
**Subject(s):** Paid Community Newspapers
**Circ:** ‡3,700

**Homer News (563)**
3482 Landings St.
Homer, AK 99603
Phone: (907)235-7767
Fax: (907)235-4199
**Subject(s):** Paid Community Newspapers
**Circ:** (Paid)3,707

**Scotts Valley Banner (3510)**
Johnson Newspapers Inc.
5215 Scotts Valley Dr., Ste. F
Scotts Valley, CA 95066
Phone: (831)438-2500
Fax: (831)438-4114
**Subject(s):** Paid Community Newspapers
**Circ:** (Non-paid)‡2,800
(Paid)‡3,700

**Dinuba Sentinel (1772)**
Sentinel Printing and Publishing
145 S L St.
Dinuba, CA 93618-2324
Phone: (559)591-4634
Fax: (559)591-1322
**Subject(s):** Paid Community Newspapers
**Circ:** (Free)9
(Paid)3,693

**Verde Independent (987)**
Western Newspapers Inc.
1748 S. Arizona Ave.
Yuma, AZ 85364
Phone: (928)783-3311
Fax: (928)783-3313
**Subject(s):** Paid Community Newspapers
**Circ:** (Paid)3,672

**Laurel Outlook (18180)**
Outlook Publishing Inc.
415 E Main
PO Box 278
Laurel, MT 59044
Phone: (406)628-4412
Fax: (406)628-8260
**Subject(s):** Paid Community Newspapers
**Circ:** (Free)‡55
(Paid)‡3,587

**Big Horn County News (18148)**
204 N Center Ave.
PO Box 926
Hardin, MT 59034-1533
Phone: (406)665-1008
Fax: (406)665-1012
**Subject(s):** Paid Community Newspapers
**Circ:** ‡3,550

**Chronicle-News (4580)**
The Shearman Group
200 Church St.
PO Box 763
Trinidad, CO 81082-0763
Phone: (719)846-3311
Fax: (719)846-3612

**Subject(s):** Daily Newspapers
**Circ:** (Mon.-Fri.)3,546

**The Ark (3895)**
The Ark Publishing Co.
Box 1054
Tiburon, CA 94920
Phone: (415)435-2652
Fax: (415)435-0849
**Subject(s):** Paid Community Newspapers
**Circ:** (Free)‡40
(Paid)‡3,500

**Barstow Log (1437)**
Aerotech
Public Affairs Office MCLB
PO Box 110130
Barstow, CA 92311-5050
Phone: (760)577-6430
Fax: (760)577-6350
**Subject(s):** Military and Navy
**Circ:** (Non-paid)3,500

**Illinois Valley News (25744)**
321 S Redwood Hwy.
PO Box 1370
Cave Junction, OR 97523
Phone: (541)592-2541
**Subject(s):** Paid Community Newspapers
**Circ:** ‡3,500

**Livingston Enterprise (18190)**
PO Box 2000
Livingston, MT 59047
Phone: (406)222-2000
Fax: (406)222-8580
**Subject(s):** Daily Newspapers
**Circ:** ‡3,500

**The Panther (2631)**
Chapman University
1 Univ. Dr.
Orange, CA 92866
Fax: (714)744-7021
**Subject(s):** College Publications
**Circ:** (Non-paid)‡3,500

**Park County Republican and The Fairplay Flume (4099)**
Arkansas Valley Publishing Co.
PO Box 460
Bailey, CO 80421-0460
Phone: (303)838-4423
Fax: (303)838-8414
**Subject(s):** Paid Community Newspapers
**Circ:** ‡3,500

**The Santa Clara (3442)**
Santa Clara University
500 El Camino Real
Box 3190
Santa Clara, CA 95053-3190
Phone: (408)554-4445
Fax: (408)554-4673
**Subject(s):** College Publications
**Circ:** (Free)‡3,500

**Shopper's Guide (UT) (30819)**
Transcript-Bulletin Publishing Company Inc.
58 N Main St.
PO Box 390
Tooele, UT 84074
Phone: (435)882-0050
Fax: (435)882-6123
**Subject(s):** Free Newspapers; Military and Navy
**Circ:** (Free)‡3,500

**Valley Roadrunner (3947)**
Palomar Community Newspapers
PO Box 1529
Valley Center, CA 92082
**Subject(s):** Local, State, and Regional Publications
**Circ:** (Combined)3502

**The Villager (4454)**
The Villager Publishing Co.
8933 E Union Ave., Ste. 230
Greenwood Village, CO 80111
Phone: (303)773-8313
Fax: (303)773-8456
**Subject(s):** Free Newspapers
**Circ:** (Free)2,000
(Paid)3,500

**Yellowstone County News, Inc. (18171)**
Yellowstone County Publishing
117 Northern Ave.
PO Box 385
Huntley, MT 59037
Phone: (406)348-2649
Fax: (406)348-2650
**Subject(s):** Paid Community Newspapers
**Circ:** ‡3,500

**The Daily Sitka Sentinel (610)**
112 Barracks
Sitka, AK 99835
Phone: (907)747-3219
Fax: (907)747-8898
**Subject(s):** Daily Newspapers
**Circ:** ‡3,480

**Baker City Herald (25713)**
Western Communications Inc.
1915 1st St.
PO Box 807
Baker City, OR 97814
Phone: (503)523-3673
Fax: (503)523-6426
**Subject(s):** Daily Newspapers
**Circ:** (Mon.-Thurs.)3,173
(Fri.)3,470

**Monroe Monitor/Valley News (32152)**
Monroe Monitor
113 W Main St.
PO Box 399
Monroe, WA 98272
Phone: (360)794-7116
Fax: (360)794-6202
**Subject(s):** Paid Community Newspapers
**Circ:** ‡3,436

**At Your Leisure (32030)**
Post Publications
425 NE 4th Ave.
Camas, WA 98607
Phone: (360)834-2141
Fax: (360)834-3423
**Subject(s):** Shopping Guides
**Circ:** (Free)‡3,400

**The California Tech (2710)**
The California Institute of Technology
Caltech 17-6
1200 E. California Blvd.
Pasadena, CA 91125
Phone: (626)395-6153
**Subject(s):** College Publications
**Circ:** (Free)‡100
(Paid)‡3,400

**Keizertimes (25862)**
Times
142 Chemawa Rd. N
PO Box 20025
Keizer, OR 97303-0025
Phone: (503)390-1051
Fax: (503)390-8023
**Subject(s):** Paid Community Newspapers
**Circ:** 3,400

**Pinedale Roundup (33771)**
Sublette County Newspapers Inc.
PO Box 100
Pinedale, WY 82941
Phone: (307)367-2123
Fax: (307)367-6623
**Subject(s):** Paid Community Newspapers
**Circ:** ‡3,400

**Star Buyer's Guide (32106)**
Star Publishing Inc.
PO Box 150
Grand Coulee, WA 99133
Phone: (509)633-1350
Fax: (509)633-3828
**Subject(s):** Shopping Guides
**Circ:** (Free)‡3400

**Feather River Bulletin (2763)**
Feather Publishing
PO Box B
Quincy, CA 95971
Phone: (530)283-0800
Fax: (530)283-3952
**Subject(s):** Paid Community Newspapers
**Circ:** ‡3,380

## Western States

**Clear Lake Observer-American** (1671)
Lake County Publishing
14913 Lake Shore Dr., Ste. B
PO Box 6200
Clearlake, CA 95422
Phone: (707)994-6444
Fax: (707)994-5335
**Subject(s):** Paid Community Newspapers
**Circ:** ‡3,363

**Star Valley Independent** (33676)
360 Washington
PO Box 129
Afton, WY 83110-0129
Phone: (307)885-5727
Fax: (307)886-5742
**Subject(s):** Paid Community Newspapers
**Circ:** 3,350

**Citizen** (30735)
North County Newspapers
1555 N. Freedom Blvd.
PO Box 717
Provo, UT 84603-0717
Phone: (801)375-5103
Fax: (801)373-5489
**Subject(s):** Paid Community Newspapers
**Circ:** (Paid)‡3,300

**The Goldendale Sentinel** (32103)
Goldendale Publisher
117 W Main St.
Goldendale, WA 98620
Phone: (509)773-3777
Fax: (509)773-4737
**Subject(s):** Paid Community Newspapers
**Circ:** 3,250

**Intermountain News** (1595)
PO Box 1030
Burney, CA 96013-1030
Phone: (530)335-4533
Fax: (530)335-5335
**Subject(s):** Paid Community Newspapers
**Circ:** ‡3,254

**The Journal of the San Juan Islands** (32099)
Sound Publishing Inc.
PO Box 519
Friday Harbor, WA 98250
Phone: (360)378-5696
**Subject(s):** Paid Community Newspapers
**Circ:** (Non-paid)216
(Paid)3,253

**Rocky Ford Daily Gazette** (4556)
912 Elm Ave.
PO Box 430
Rocky Ford, CO 81067-0430
Phone: (719)254-3351
Fax: (719)254-3354
**Subject(s):** Daily Newspapers
**Circ:** ‡3,250

**King City Rustler** (3530)
South Country Newspapers
635 Front St.
Soledad, CA 93960
Phone: (831)385-4880
Fax: (831)385-4799
**Subject(s):** Paid Community Newspapers
**Circ:** ‡3,225

**Arizona Range News** (977)
Wick Communications Co.
122 S. Haskell Ave.
Willcox, AZ 85643
Fax: (520)384-3572
**Subject(s):** Paid Community Newspapers
**Circ:** 3,200

**Bonners Ferry Herald** (7677)
PO Box 539
Bonners Ferry, ID 83805
Phone: (208)267-5521
Fax: (208)267-5523
**Subject(s):** Paid Community Newspapers
**Circ:** ‡3,200

**Carbon County News** (18113)
News Montana Inc.
PO Box 659
Columbus, MT 59019
Phone: (406)322-5212
Fax: (406)322-5391

**Subject(s):** Paid Community Newspapers
**Circ:** 3,200

**Cheney Free Press** (32044)
Journal News Publishing
PO Box 218
Cheney, WA 99004
Phone: (509)299-5678
Fax: (509)235-2887
**Subject(s):** Paid Community Newspapers
**Circ:** ‡3,200

**Green River Star** (33737)
Star Publishing
PO Box 580
Green River, WY 82935
Phone: (307)875-3103
Fax: (307)875-8778
**Subject(s):** Paid Community Newspapers
**Circ:** ‡3,200

**Methow Valley News** (32458)
Methow Valley Publishing Company L.L.C.
101 N Glover
PO Box 97
Twisp, WA 98856
Phone: (509)997-7011
Fax: (509)997-3277
**Subject(s):** Paid Community Newspapers
**Circ:** 3,200

**Musical News** (3174)
Musicians Union Local 6
116 Ninth St.
San Francisco, CA 94103
Phone: (415)575-0777
Fax: (415)863-6173
**Subject(s):** Labor; Music and Musical Instruments
**Circ:** (Free)‡3,200

**San Manuel Miner** (825)
PO Box 60
San Manuel, AZ 85631
Phone: (520)385-2266
Fax: (520)385-4666
**Subject(s):** Paid Community Newspapers
**Circ:** 3,200

**Sanger Herald** (3400)
Sanger Herald Inc.
740 N St.
Sanger, CA 93657
Phone: (559)875-2511
Fax: (559)875-2521
**Subject(s):** Paid Community Newspapers
**Circ:** ‡3,200

**Torrington Telegram** (33799)
Wyoming Newspapers Inc.
2025 Main
Torrington, WY 82240
Phone: (307)532-2184
Fax: (307)532-2283
**Subject(s):** Paid Community Newspapers
**Circ:** ‡3,200

**The Sidney Herald-Leader** (18241)
Wick Communications Co.
310 2nd Ave. NW
Sidney, MT 59270
Phone: (406)482-2403
Fax: (406)482-7802
**Subject(s):** Paid Community Newspapers
**Circ:** (Paid)‡3,136

**The Vashon Beachcomber** (32474)
Sound Publishing Inc.
17502 Vashon Hwy. SW
PO Box 447
Vashon Island, WA 98070
Phone: (206)463-9195
Fax: (206)463-6122
**Subject(s):** Paid Community Newspapers
**Circ:** (Non-paid)155
(Paid)3,126

**The Wray Gazette** (4616)
411 Main St.
PO Box 7
Wray, CO 80758-0007
Phone: (970)332-4846
Fax: (970)332-4065

**Subject(s):** Paid Community Newspapers
**Circ:** (Free)40
(Paid)3,125

**Fernley Leader/Dayton Courier** (18767)
Mason Valley News
207 W Goldfield Ave.
Yerington, NV 89447-2349
Phone: (775)463-2856
Fax: (775)463-5547
**Subject(s):** Paid Community Newspapers
**Circ:** (Paid)3,100

**The Idaho Business Review** (7649)
PO Box 8866
Boise, ID 83707
Phone: (208)336-3768
Fax: (208)336-5534
**Subject(s):** Local, State, and Regional Publications; Business
**Circ:** (Free)450
(Paid)3,100

**Independent Coast Observer** (1954)
Independent Coast Observer Inc.
PO Box 1200
Gualala, CA 95445
Phone: (707)884-3501
Fax: (707)884-1710
**Subject(s):** Paid Community Newspapers
**Circ:** ‡3,100

**Spanish Fork Press** (30816)
J-Mart Publishing Co.
280 N Main St.
Spanish Fork, UT 84660
Phone: (801)798-6816
Fax: (801)798-9770
**Subject(s):** Paid Community Newspapers
**Circ:** ‡3,100

**The Exeter Sun** (1845)
Mineral King Publishing
120 N E St.
PO Box 7
Exeter, CA 93221
Phone: (559)592-3171
Fax: (559)592-4308
**Subject(s):** Paid Community Newspapers
**Circ:** ‡3,099

**Molalla Pioneer** (25916)
217 E. Main St.
PO Box 168
Molalla, OR 97038
Phone: (503)829-2301
Fax: (503)829-2317
**Subject(s):** Free Newspapers
**Circ:** (Free)‡2,950
(Paid)‡3,050

**Northern Kittitas County Tribune** (32050)
PO Box 308
221 Pennsylvania Ave.
Cle Elum, WA 98922
Phone: (509)674-2511
Fax: (509)674-5571
**Subject(s):** Paid Community Newspapers
**Circ:** ‡3,044

**The Argus** (661)
Cochise College
Hwy. 80 W
4190 W. State
Douglas, AZ 85607-6190
Phone: (520)364-7943
Fax: (520)417-4006
**Subject(s):** College Publications
**Circ:** (Controlled)3,000

**Bayou Talk** (2499)
Jo Val
PO Box 1091
Montebello, CA 90640-1091
Phone: (323)864-2036
**Subject(s):** Paid Community Newspapers; Ethnic Publications
**Circ:** (Paid)3,000
(Non-paid)3,000

**The Beacon** (25947)
University of Portland
5000 N Willamette Blvd.
Portland, OR 97203
Phone: (503)943-8000
Fax: (503)283-7399

**Subject(s):** College Publications
**Circ:** (Free)‡3,000

**Burns Times-Herald** (25739)
355 N Broadway Ave.
Burns, OR 97720-1704
Phone: (541)573-2022
Fax: (541)573-3915
**Subject(s):** Paid Community Newspapers
**Circ:** ‡3,000

**Butte Valley Star** (1777)
111 W 3rd St.
PO Box 708
Dorris, CA 96023
Phone: (530)397-2601
**Subject(s):** Paid Community Newspapers
**Circ:** ‡3,000

**Caribou County Sun** (7806)
PO Box 815
Soda Springs, ID 83276
Phone: (208)547-3260
Fax: (208)547-4422
**Subject(s):** Paid Community Newspapers
**Circ:** ‡3,000

**Chaffee County Times** (4558)
Arkansas Valley Publishing Co.
125 E 2nd St.
PO Box 189
Salida, CO 81201-0189
Phone: (719)539-1455
Fax: (719)539-6630
**Subject(s):** Paid Community Newspapers
**Circ:** ‡3,000

**Clearwater Tribune** (7766)
161 Main St.
PO Box 71
Orofino, ID 83544
Phone: (208)476-4571
Fax: (208)476-0765
**Subject(s):** Paid Community Newspapers
**Circ:** ‡3,000

**Communicator** (32389)
Spokane Falls Community College
3410 W Fort George Wright Dr.
MS 3050
Spokane, WA 99224-5288
Phone: (509)533-3602
Fax: (509)533-3651
**Subject(s):** College Publications
**Circ:** (Free)‡3,000

**The Eagle** (30727)
College of Eastern Utah
451 N. 400 E.
Price, UT 84501
Phone: (435)637-2120
**Subject(s):** College Publications
**Circ:** (Free)‡3,000

**East County Journal** (32154)
DeVaul Publishing Inc.
278 W. Main
Morton, WA 98356
Phone: (360)496-5993
Fax: (360)496-5110
**Subject(s):** Paid Community Newspapers
**Circ:** (Paid)‡3,007

**The Fillmore Herald** (1851)
San Cayetano Mountain Investment Corp.
505 Santa Clara St.
Fillmore, CA 93015
Phone: (805)524-0153
Fax: (805)524-0154
**Subject(s):** Paid Community Newspapers
**Circ:** ‡3,000

**Fountain Valley News** (4400)
Shopper Press Inc.
PO Box 400
120 E Ohio
Fountain, CO 80817
Phone: (719)382-5611
Fax: (719)382-5614
**Subject(s):** Paid Community Newspapers
**Circ:** (Paid)3,000

**The Greeter** (18228)
108 N Main
Plentywood, MT 59254
Phone: (406)765-1733
Fax: (406)765-2106
**Subject(s):** Shopping Guides
**Circ:** (Free)‡3,000

**The Independent** (32463)
Clark Community College
1800 E. McLoughlin Blvd.
Vancouver, WA 98663
Phone: (360)992-2159
**Subject(s):** College Publications
**Circ:** (Free)‡3,000

**The Jibsheet** (31998)
Bellevue Community College
3000 Landerholm Cir. SE, C 212
Bellevue, WA 98007
Phone: (425)564-2434
Fax: (425)564-4152
**Subject(s):** College Publications
**Circ:** (Free)3,000

**Kapio** (7556)
Board of Student Publications
Kapiolani Community College
4303 Diamond Head Rd.
Honolulu, HI 96816
Phone: (808)734-9166
**Subject(s):** College Publications
**Circ:** 3,000

**The Kourier** (4046)
PO Box 37
Willow Creek, CA 95573
Phone: (916)629-2811
**Subject(s):** Paid Community Newspapers
**Circ:** ‡3,000

**La Voz** (1742)
De Anza College
21250 Stevens Creek Blvd.
Cupertino, CA 95014
Phone: (408)864-5678
Fax: (408)864-5533
**Subject(s):** College Publications
**Circ:** (Free)‡3,000

**Lake Chelan Mirror** (32042)
315 E Woodin Ave.
PO Box 249
Chelan, WA 98816-0249
Phone: (509)682-2213
Fax: (509)682-4209
**Subject(s):** Paid Community Newspapers
**Circ:** 3,000

**Lebanon Express** (25889)
Lee Enterprises
90 E Grant
PO Box 459
Lebanon, OR 97355
Phone: (541)258-3151
Fax: (541)259-3569
**Subject(s):** Free Newspapers
**Circ:** (Paid)3,000

**Middletown Times Star** (2466)
Middletown Times
21055 Bush Street
PO Box 608
Middletown, CA 95461
Phone: (707)987-3602
Fax: (707)987-3901
**Subject(s):** Paid Community Newspapers
**Circ:** ‡3,000

**Millard County Chronicle Progress** (30673)
P O Box 249
40 N 300 W
Delta, UT 84624-0249
Phone: (435)864-2400
Fax: (775)514-3931
**Subject(s):** Paid Community Newspapers
**Circ:** ‡3,000

**Mines Oredigger** (4417)
Colorado School of Mines Press
Arthur Lakes Library
Golden, CO 80401
Phone: (303)273-3690
Fax: (303)273-3199

**Subject(s):** College Publications
**Circ:** (Paid)‡500
      (Free)‡3,000

**The Montesano Vidette** (32153)
109 W. Marcy Ave.
Po Box 671
Montesano, WA 98563
Phone: (360)249-3311
Fax: (360)249-5636
**Subject(s):** Paid Community Newspapers
**Circ:** (Combined)3,000

**The Mooring Mast** (32438)
Pacific Lutheran University
1010, 122nd St. S
Tacoma, WA 98444
Phone: (253)531-6900
**Subject(s):** College Publications
**Circ:** (Free)‡3,000

**The Mountain Messenger** (1779)
Mountain Messenger
Drawer A
Downieville, CA 95936-0395
Phone: (916)289-3262
Fax: (916)289-3262
**Subject(s):** Paid Community Newspapers
**Circ:** (Paid)‡3,000

**New Era** (26062)
PO Box 39
Sweet Home, OR 97386
Phone: (541)367-2135
Fax: (541)367-2137
**Subject(s):** Paid Community Newspapers
**Circ:** ‡3,000

**The Old Berthoud Recorder** (4100)
120 Bunyan Ave
PO Box J
Berthoud, CO 80513
Phone: (970)532-3715
Fax: (970)532-3918
**Subject(s):** Paid Community Newspapers
**Circ:** (Paid)‡3,000

**The Pioneer Log** (25972)
Lewis & Clark College
0615 SW Palatine Hill Rd.
Mailstop 121
Portland, OR 97219
Phone: (503)768-7146
Fax: (503)768-7130
**Subject(s):** College Publications
**Circ:** (Free)3,000

**Sacramento City College Express** (2908)
Sacramento City College Store
3835 Freeport Blvd.
Sacramento, CA 95822
Phone: (916)558-2561
Fax: (916)558-2282
**Subject(s):** College Publications
**Circ:** (Free)3,000

**San Pedro Valley News-Sun** (630)
Wick Communications Co.
200 S. Ocotillo
Benson, AZ 85602
Phone: (520)586-3382
Fax: (520)586-2382
**Subject(s):** Paid Community Newspapers
**Circ:** 3,000

**Seaside Signal** (26054)
Seaside Signal Publishing
730 Broadway
PO Box 848
Seaside, OR 97138
Phone: (503)738-5561
Fax: (503)738-5672
**Subject(s):** Paid Community Newspapers
**Circ:** ‡3,000

**The Siskiyou** (25698)
Southern Oregon University
Stevenson Union Building Room 121
1250 Siskiyou Blouvard
Ashland, OR 97520
Phone: (541)552-6307
Fax: (541)552-6440
**Subject(s):** College Publications
**Circ:** (Free)‡3,000

# Western States

**The Times Independent** (30704)
The Times Independent Printing Inc.
35 E Ctr.
PO Box 129
Moab, UT 84532
Phone: (435)259-7525
Fax: (435)259-7741
**Subject(s):** Paid Community Newspapers
**Circ:** 3,000

**Umpqua Free Press** (26069)
Douglas County Mail
119 S Main St.
PO Box 729
Myrtle Creek, OR 97457
Phone: (541)863-5233
Fax: (541)863-5234
**Subject(s):** Paid Community Newspapers
**Circ:** 3,000

**The Weekly Calistogan** (1601)
PO Box 385
Calistoga, CA 94515
Phone: (707)942-4035
Fax: (707)942-6757
**Subject(s):** Paid Community Newspapers
**Circ:** ‡3,000

**Western Viking** (32343)
Western Viking Inc.
PO Box 70408
Seattle, WA 98127
Phone: (206)784-4617
Fax: (206)784-4856
**Subject(s):** Paid Community Newspapers; Norwegian
**Circ:** ‡3,000

**Windsor Beacon** (4611)
425 Main St.
Windsor, CO 80550
Phone: (970)686-9646
Fax: (970)686-9647
**Subject(s):** Paid Community Newspapers
**Circ:** (Paid)‡3,000

**Craig Daily Press** (4250)
WorldWest L.L.C.
466 Yampa Ave.
Craig, CO 81625
Phone: (970)824-7031
Fax: (970)824-6810
**Subject(s):** Daily Newspapers
**Circ:** (Free)27
(Paid)2,971

**E.L.A. Brooklyn-Belvedere Comet** (1691)
Eastern Group Publications Inc.
2500 S Atlantic Blvd., Bldg. A
Commerce, CA 90040
Phone: (323)263-5743
Fax: (323)263-9169
**Subject(s):** Free Newspapers; Spanish; Hispanic Publications
**Circ:** (Paid)♦4
(Free)♦2,976

**Huerfano World** (4587)
111 W 7th St.
PO Box 191
Walsenburg, CO 81089
Phone: (719)738-1720
Fax: (719)738-1727
**Subject(s):** Paid Community Newspapers
**Circ:** (Free)‡25
(Paid)‡2,975

**The Recorder-Herald** (7798)
519 Van Dreff St.
PO Box 310
Salmon, ID 83467
Phone: (208)756-2221
Fax: (208)756-2222
**Subject(s):** Paid Community Newspapers
**Circ:** (Non-paid)158
(Paid)2,975

**The Phillips County News** (18192)
Phillips County News
PO Box 850
18 S 1st St. E
Malta, MT 59538-0850
Phone: (406)654-2020
Fax: (406)654-1410
**Subject(s):** Paid Community Newspapers
**Circ:** ‡2,925

**Mineral County Independent-News** (18671)
PO Box 1270
501 D Street
Hawthorne, NV 89415-1270
Phone: (775)945-2414
Fax: (775)945-1270
**Subject(s):** Paid Community Newspapers
**Circ:** (Paid)2,900

**The Mountain Mail** (4559)
Arkansas Valley Publishing Co.
125 E 2nd St.
PO Box 189
Salida, CO 81201-0189
Phone: (719)539-1455
Fax: (719)539-6630
**Subject(s):** Daily Newspapers
**Circ:** (Paid)‡2,900

**Platte County Record Times** (33803)
1007 8th St.
Wheatland, WY 82201-2602
Phone: (307)322-2627
Fax: (307)322-9612
**Subject(s):** Paid Community Newspapers
**Circ:** ‡2,900

**Sanders County Ledger** (18244)
Box 219
Thompson Falls, MT 59873
Phone: (406)827-3421
Fax: (406)827-4375
**Subject(s):** Paid Community Newspapers
**Circ:** ‡2,900

**Winter Park Manifest** (4423)
Johnson Media Inc.
PO Box 409
Granby, CO 80446
Phone: (970)726-5721
Fax: (970)726-8789
**Subject(s):** Paid Community Newspapers
**Circ:** (Free)800
(Paid)2,900

**Springville Herald** (30747)
Art City Publishing
1555 N. Freedom Blvd
P.O. Box 717
Provo, UT 84603-0717
Phone: (801)344-2540
Fax: (801)373-5489
**Subject(s):** Paid Community Newspapers
**Circ:** ‡2,874

**Crestline Courier-News** (2056)
Mountain News
PO Box 2410
Lake Arrowhead, CA 92352
Phone: (909)336-3555
Fax: (909)337-5275
**Subject(s):** Paid Community Newspapers
**Circ:** ‡2,850

**California Real Estate Journal** (2157)
Daily Journal Corp.
915 E. 1st St.
Los Angeles, CA 90012-4050
Phone: (213)229-5300
Fax: (213)680-3682
**Subject(s):** Real Estate
**Circ:** (Non-paid)‡194
(Paid)‡2,842

**Daily Commerce** (2179)
Daily Journal Corp.
915 E. 1st St.
Los Angeles, CA 90012-4050
Phone: (213)229-5300
Fax: (213)680-3682
**Subject(s):** Real Estate; Daily Newspapers
**Circ:** (Free)279
(Paid)2,829

**Wet Mountain Tribune** (4589)
Little Publishing Company Inc.
PO Box 300
Westcliffe, CO 81252
Phone: (719)783-2361
Fax: (719)783-3725
**Subject(s):** Paid Community Newspapers
**Circ:** ‡2,820

**California Courier** (1928)
PO Box 5390
Glendale, CA 91221
Phone: (818)409-0949
Fax: (818)409-9207
**Subject(s):** Paid Community Newspapers; Ethnic Publications
**Circ:** (Free)‡200
(Paid)‡2,800

**The Enterprise** (32491)
Eagle Newspapers
220 E Jewett Blvd.
PO Box 218
White Salmon, WA 98672
Phone: (509)493-2112
Fax: (509)493-2399
**Subject(s):** Paid Community Newspapers
**Circ:** (Free)30
(Paid)2,800

**Franklin County Graphic** (32062)
PO Box 160
Connell, WA 99326
Phone: (509)234-3181
Fax: (509)234-3182
**Subject(s):** Paid Community Newspapers
**Circ:** (Paid)170
(Free)2,808

**The Leavenworth Echo** (32134)
Prairie Media Inc.
215 14th St.
PO Box 39
Leavenworth, WA 98826
Phone: (509)548-5286
Fax: (509)548-5286
**Subject(s):** Paid Community Newspapers
**Circ:** 2,800

**Lehi Free Press** (30682)
North County Newspapers
1555 N. Freedom Blvd.
PO Box 717
Provo, UT 84603-0717
Phone: (801)375-5103
Fax: (801)373-5489
**Subject(s):** Paid Community Newspapers
**Circ:** (Paid)‡2,800

**Roundup Record-Tribune and Winnett Times** (18235)
Roundup Record Tribune Inc.
PO Box 350
Roundup, MT 59072
Phone: (406)323-1105
Fax: (406)323-1761
**Subject(s):** Paid Community Newspapers
**Circ:** ‡2,800

**Dillon Tribune** (18119)
22 S Montana
PO Box 911
Dillon, MT 59725-0911
Phone: (406)683-2331
Fax: (406)683-2332
**Subject(s):** Paid Community Newspapers
**Circ:** (Free)‡20
(Paid)‡2,764

**The Old Lyons Recorder** (4511)
412 High St.
PO Box 1729
Lyons, CO 80540
Phone: (303)823-6625
Fax: (303)823-6633
**Subject(s):** Paid Community Newspapers
**Circ:** (Paid)‡2,750

**Buhl Herald** (7679)
Buhl Herald Inc.
PO Box 312
124 South Broadway
Buhl, ID 83316
Phone: (208)543-4335
Fax: (208)543-6834
**Subject(s):** Paid Community Newspapers
**Circ:** (Free)‡45
(Paid)‡2,700

**Okanogan Valley Gazette-Tribune** (32189)
Oroville Gazette Publishing Ltd.
PO Box 250
Oroville, WA 98844
Phone: (509)476-3602
Fax: (509)476-3054

# Gale Directory of Publications & Broadcast Media/140th Ed. — Western States

**Subject(s):** Paid Community Newspapers
**Circ:** (Paid)2,700

**Chino Valley Review (985)**
Western Newspapers Inc.
1748 S. Arizona Ave.
Yuma, AZ 85364
Phone: (928)783-3311
**Subject(s):** Free Newspapers
**Circ:** (Paid)341
(Free)2,678

**Lamar Daily News and Holly Chieftain (4483)**
Eastern Colorado Publishing Co.
310 S 5th St.
PO Box 1217
Lamar, CO 81052-1217
Phone: (719)336-2266
Fax: (719)336-2526
**Subject(s):** Daily Newspapers
**Circ:** (Mon.-Fri.)★2,638

**Buckeye Valley News (635)**
PO Box 217
Buckeye, AZ 85326
Phone: (623)386-4426
Fax: (623)386-4427
**Subject(s):** Paid Community Newspapers; Farm Newspapers
**Circ:** 2,600

**Clause (1400)**
Azusa Pacific University
Unit 5165
PO Box 9521
Azusa, CA 91702
Phone: (626)815-6000
Fax: (626)812-3017
**Subject(s):** College Publications
**Circ:** (Non-paid)2,600

**Copper Basin News (695)**
Copper Area Publishing
PO Box 579
Kearny, AZ 85237
Phone: (520)363-5554
Fax: (520)363-9663
**Subject(s):** Paid Community Newspapers
**Circ:** ‡2,600

**Glacier Reporter (18099)**
PO Box 349
208 N Peigan
Browning, MT 59417
Phone: (406)338-2090
Fax: (406)338-2410
**Subject(s):** Paid Community Newspapers
**Circ:** ‡2,600

**The Pyramid (30706)**
Pyramid Publishing
49 W Main
Mount Pleasant, UT 84647
Phone: (435)462-2134
Fax: (435)462-2459
**Subject(s):** Paid Community Newspapers
**Circ:** (Paid)2,600

**The Ripon Record (2813)**
130 W Main St.
Ripon, CA 95366
Phone: (209)599-2194
Fax: (209)599-2195
**Subject(s):** Paid Community Newspapers
**Circ:** (Paid)‡2,600

**Skamania County Pioneer (32433)**
Green Leaf Publishing Inc.
198 SW 2nd St.
PO Box 219
Stevenson, WA 98648
Phone: (509)427-8444
Fax: (509)427-4229
**Subject(s):** Paid Community Newspapers
**Circ:** 2,600

**Times Bonanza and Goldfield News (18662)**
PO Box 150820
Ely, NV 89315
Phone: (775)289-4491
Fax: (775)289-4566
**Subject(s):** Paid Community Newspapers
**Circ:** ‡2,600

**City Terrace Comet (1688)**
Eastern Group Publications Inc.
2500 S Atlantic Blvd., Bldg. A
Commerce, CA 90040
Phone: (323)263-5743
Fax: (323)263-9169
**Subject(s):** Free Newspapers; Hispanic Publications; Spanish
**Circ:** (Paid)♦5
(Free)♦2,583

**The Daily Dispatch (663)**
Daily Dispatch
PO Drawer H
Douglas, AZ 85608
Phone: (520)364-3424
Fax: (520)364-6750
**Subject(s):** Daily Newspapers
**Circ:** ‡2,582

**Ely Daily Times (18660)**
Community Newspaper Holdings Inc.
297 Eleventh St. E.
PO Box 150820
Ely, NV 89315-0820
Phone: (775)289-4491
Fax: (775)289-4566
**Subject(s):** Daily Newspapers
**Circ:** ⊕2,585

**Mountain Echo (1848)**
Mountain Echo Inc.
PO Box 224
Fall River Mills, CA 96028
Phone: (530)336-6262
**Subject(s):** Paid Community Newspapers
**Circ:** (Free)‡444
(Paid)‡2,554

**Patterson Irrigator (2726)**
26 N. 3rd St.
Patterson, CA 95363
Phone: (209)892-6187
Fax: (209)892-3761
**Subject(s):** Paid Community Newspapers
**Circ:** (Paid)2,550

**The Akron News-Reporter (4080)**
69 Main St.
Akron, CO 80720
Phone: (970)345-2296
Fax: (970)345-6638
**Subject(s):** Paid Community Newspapers
**Circ:** (Free)‡30
(Paid)‡2,500

**Arvin Tiller (3516)**
Reed Print Inc.
107 E Lerdo Hwy.
Shafter, CA 93263-2701
Phone: (661)746-4942
Fax: (661)746-5571
**Subject(s):** Paid Community Newspapers
**Circ:** (Paid)2,500

**Chinook (33685)**
Casper College
125 College Dr.
Casper, WY 82601-4699
Phone: (307)268-2447
Fax: (307)268-6282
**Subject(s):** College Publications
**Circ:** (Paid)300
(Free)2,500

**The Corcoran Journal (1710)**
1012 Hale
PO Box 487
Corcoran, CA 93212
Phone: (559)992-3115
Fax: (559)992-5543
**Subject(s):** Paid Community Newspapers
**Circ:** (Free)26
(Paid)2,500

**Julian News (2018)**
PO Box 639
Julian, CA 92036-0639
Phone: (760)765-2231
Fax: (760)765-1838
**Subject(s):** Paid Community Newspapers
**Circ:** (Controlled)2,500

**Mendocino County Observer (2071)**
PO Box 490
Laytonville, CA 95454-0490
Phone: (707)984-6223
Fax: (707)984-8118
**Subject(s):** Paid Community Newspapers
**Circ:** (Controlled)2,500

**News Letter Journal (33768)**
Box 40
Newcastle, WY 82701
Phone: (307)746-2777
Fax: (307)746-2660
**Subject(s):** Paid Community Newspapers
**Circ:** (Free)‡40
(Paid)‡2,500

**The Palisade Tribune and Valley Report (4531)**
124 W 3rd
PO Box 8
Palisade, CO 81526
Phone: (970)464-5614
**Subject(s):** Paid Community Newspapers
**Circ:** (Paid)‡1,721
(Free)‡2,500

**Pipelines (3189)**
Plumbers - Steamfitters, U.A. Local 38
1621 Market St.
San Francisco, CA 94103
Phone: (415)626-2000
Fax: (415)626-2009
**Subject(s):** Plumbing and Heating; Labor
**Circ:** (Non-paid)2,500

**Pleasant Grove Review (30725)**
North County Newspapers
1555 N. Freedom Blvd.
PO Box 717
Provo, UT 84603-0717
Phone: (801)375-5103
Fax: (801)373-5489
**Subject(s):** Paid Community Newspapers
**Circ:** (Paid)‡2,500

**Weiser Signal American (7820)**
Signal American Printers Inc.
18 E Idaho
PO Box 709
Weiser, ID 83672
Phone: (208)549-1717
Fax: (208)549-1718
**Subject(s):** Paid Community Newspapers
**Circ:** (Paid)‡2,500

**X-TRA (26020)**
Eagle Newspapers
558 N Main St.
Prineville, OR 97754
Phone: (541)447-6205
Fax: (541)447-1754
**Subject(s):** Shopping Guides
**Circ:** (Free)2,500

**Coquille Valley Sentinel (25760)**
1 Barton's Alley
Coquille, OR 97423-0400
Phone: (541)396-3191
Fax: (541)396-3624
**Subject(s):** Paid Community Newspapers
**Circ:** (Paid)‡2,200
(Free)‡2,495

**Independent Record (33797)**
H-I Inc.
PO Box 31
431 Broadway
Thermopolis, WY 82443-0031
Phone: (307)864-2328
Fax: (307)864-5711
**Subject(s):** Paid Community Newspapers
**Circ:** (Free)19
(Paid)2,495

**Winters Express (4052)**
312 Railroad Ave.
Winters, CA 95694-0608
Phone: (530)795-4551
**Subject(s):** Paid Community Newspapers
**Circ:** ‡2,480

---

Circulation: ★ = ABC; △ = BPA; ♦ = CAC; ● = CCAB; ▫ = VAC; ⊕ = PO Statement; ‡ = Publisher's Report; Boldface figures = sworn; Light figures = estimated.

# Western States

**The Copper Era (653)**
Wick Communications
1 Wards Canyon
P.O. Box 1357
Clifton, AZ 85533
Phone: (520)865-3162
**Subject(s):** Paid Community Newspapers
**Circ:** ‡2,450

**Western World (25717)**
Southwestern Oregon Publishing Co.
PO Box 248
Bandon, OR 97411-0248
Phone: (541)347-2423
Fax: (541)347-2424
**Subject(s):** Paid Community Newspapers
**Circ:** (Free)⊕32
(Paid)⊕**2,414**

**Cloverdale Reveille (1673)**
207 N Cloverdale Blvd.
PO Box 157
Cloverdale, CA 95425-3318
Phone: (707)894-3339
Fax: (707)894-3343
**Subject(s):** Paid Community Newspapers
**Circ:** (Paid)‡2,400

**Estacada County News (25794)**
PO Box 549
Estacada, OR 97023
Phone: (503)630-3241
Fax: (503)630-5840
**Subject(s):** Paid Community Newspapers
**Circ:** ‡2,400

**Chester Progressive (1648)**
Feather Publishing
135 Main St.
PO Box 557
Chester, CA 96020
Phone: (530)258-3115
Fax: (530)258-2365
**Subject(s):** Paid Community Newspapers
**Circ:** 2,390

**The Islands' Sounder (32069)**
Sound Publishing Inc.
c/o Ted grossman, Editor
PO Box 758
Eastsound, WA 98245
Phone: (360)376-4500
Fax: (360)376-4501
**Subject(s):** Paid Community Newspapers
**Circ:** (Non-paid)6
(Paid)2,388

**Coolidge Examiner (655)**
Casa Grande Valley Newspapers
353 W. Central Ave
Coolidge, AZ 85228
Phone: (520)723-5441
Fax: (520)723-7899
**Subject(s):** Paid Community Newspapers
**Circ:** ‡2,364

**Corning Observer (1711)**
Tri-County Newspapers Inc.
1208 Solano St.
Corning, CA 96021
Phone: (530)824-5464
Fax: (530)824-4804
**Subject(s):** Paid Community Newspapers
**Circ:** ‡2,350

**The Independent (32048)**
Chewelah Independent Inc.
PO Box 5
Chewelah, WA 99109
Phone: (509)935-8422
Fax: (509)935-8426
**Subject(s):** Paid Community Newspapers
**Circ:** ‡2,350

**Mendocino Beacon (1858)**
PO Box 1188
Fort Bragg, CA 95437
Phone: (707)964-5642
Fax: (707)964-0424
**Subject(s):** Paid Community Newspapers
**Circ:** (Thurs.)⊕**2,278**

**Inside Passage (570)**
415 6th St.
Juneau, AK 99801
Phone: (907)586-2237
Fax: (907)463-3237
**Subject(s):** Religious Publications
**Circ:** (Paid)2,267

**The Limon Leader (4489)**
1062 Main St.
Box 1300
Limon, CO 80828
Phone: (719)775-2064
Fax: (719)775-9082
**Subject(s):** Paid Community Newspapers
**Circ:** ‡2,225

**The Camillus Advocate (25742)**
Eagle Newspapers
4901 Indian School Rd. NE
PO Box 12008
Salem, OR 97305
Phone: (503)393-7980
Fax: (503)393-2366
**Subject(s):** Paid Community Newspapers
**Circ:** (Free)378
(Paid)‡2,215

**Alpine Sun (1336)**
2144 Alpine Blvd.
PO Box 1089
Alpine, CA 91901
Phone: (619)445-3288
Fax: (619)445-6776
**Subject(s):** Paid Community Newspapers
**Circ:** (Paid)‡2,200

**The Bisbee Observer (631)**
7 Bisbee Rd., Ste. L
Bisbee, AZ 85603
Phone: (520)432-7254
Fax: (520)432-4192
**Subject(s):** Paid Community Newspapers
**Circ:** (Controlled)‡2,200

**Campus Times (2047)**
University of La Verne
1950 3rd St.
La Verne, CA 91750
Phone: (909)392-2712
Fax: (909)392-2706
**Subject(s):** College Publications
**Circ:** (Free)2,200

**The Clear Creek Courant (4467)**
1634 Miner St.
PO Box 2020
Idaho Springs, CO 80452
Phone: (303)567-4491
Fax: (303)567-4492
**Subject(s):** Paid Community Newspapers
**Circ:** (Paid)2,206

**Herald-News (18251)**
408 Main St.
Box 639
Wolf Point, MT 59201
Phone: (406)653-2222
Fax: (406)653-2221
**Subject(s):** Paid Community Newspapers
**Circ:** 2,200

**MotoRacing (2747)**
Kelly Communications
PO Box 1203
Pleasanton, CA 94566-0120
Phone: (925)846-7728
Fax: (925)846-0118
**Subject(s):** (Auto Racing)
**Circ:** (Combined)2,200

**Observer (32301)**
Shoreline Community College
16101 Greenwood Ave. N
Seattle, WA 98133
Phone: (206)546-4101
Fax: (206)546-4599
**Subject(s):** College Publications
**Circ:** (Non-paid)2,200

**The Signal (3448)**
California State University, Stanislaus
24000 Creekside Rd.
Santa Clarita, CA 91355
Phone: (661)259-1234
Fax: (661)254-8068

**Subject(s):** College Publications
**Circ:** (Free)‡2,200

**Southern Utah News (30681)**
Southern Utah Publishing
26 N Main
Kanab, UT 84741
Phone: (435)644-2900
Fax: (435)644-2926
**Subject(s):** Paid Community Newspapers
**Circ:** ‡2,200

**Tobacco Valley News (18124)**
Ten Lakes Publishing
520 Dewey Ave.
PO Box 307
Eureka, MT 59917
Phone: (406)296-2514
Fax: (406)296-2515
**Subject(s):** Paid Community Newspapers
**Circ:** 2,200

**The Tule Times (3549)**
PO Box 692
Springville, CA 93265
Phone: (559)539-3166
Fax: (559)539-2942
**Subject(s):** Free Newspapers
**Circ:** (Free)‡100
(Paid)‡2,200

**Whitworthian (32396)**
Whitworth College
300 W. Hawthorne Rd.
Spokane, WA 99251-4302
**Subject(s):** College Publications
**Circ:** 2,200

**The Arco Advertiser (7641)**
P.O. Box 803
Arco, ID 83213-0803
Phone: (208)527-3038
Fax: (208)527-8210
**Subject(s):** Paid Community Newspapers
**Circ:** ‡2,185

**The Arctic Sounder (594)**
Alaska Newspapers Inc.
301 Calista Ct., Ste. B
Anchorage, AK 99518-3028
Phone: (907)349-6226
Fax: (907)349-6202
**Subject(s):** Paid Community Newspapers
**Circ:** (Paid)2,185

**Choteau Acantha (18110)**
216 1st Ave. NW
PO Box 320
Choteau, MT 59422
Phone: (406)466-2403
Fax: (406)466-2403
**Subject(s):** Paid Community Newspapers
**Circ:** ‡2,150

**The Lovell Chronicle (33765)**
Peck Papers
234 E Main
Box 787
Lovell, WY 82431
Phone: (307)548-2217
Fax: (307)548-2218
**Subject(s):** Paid Community Newspapers
**Circ:** (Free)‡38
(Paid)‡2,138

**The Camp Verde Journal (642)**
PO Box 2048
Camp Verde, AZ 86322
Phone: (928)567-3341
Fax: (928)567-2373
**Subject(s):** Paid Community Newspapers
**Circ:** (Combined)2,126

**Ajo Copper News (627)**
10 Pajaro
PO Box 39
Ajo, AZ 85321
Phone: (520)387-7688
Fax: (520)387-7505
**Subject(s):** Paid Community Newspapers
**Circ:** ‡2,100

**Davenport Times** (32063)
Journal News Publishing
PO Box 66
Davenport, WA 99122
Phone: (509)725-0101
Fax: (509)725-0009
**Subject(s):** Paid Community Newspapers
**Circ:** 2,100

**Emery County Progress** (30676)
410 East Main
Po Box 589
Castle Dale, UT 84513
Phone: (435)381-2431
Fax: (435)381-5431
**Subject(s):** Paid Community Newspapers
**Circ:** (Paid)2,100

**Myrtle Point Herald** (25918)
408 Spruce
PO Box 606
Myrtle Point, OR 97458-0128
Phone: (541)572-2717
Fax: (541)572-2828
**Subject(s):** Paid Community Newspapers
**Circ:** (Free)‡100
(Paid)‡2,100

**News-Ledger** (4030)
816 W Acres Rd.
PO Box 463
West Sacramento, CA 95691-3222
Phone: (916)371-8030
**Subject(s):** Paid Community Newspapers
**Circ:** 2,100

**Stillwater County News** (18114)
News Montana Inc.
PO Box 659
Columbus, MT 59019
Phone: (406)322-5212
Fax: (406)322-5391
**Subject(s):** Paid Community Newspapers
**Circ:** ‡2,100

**The Colorado Leader** (4272)
3480 W 1st Ave.
Denver, CO 80219
Phone: (303)922-0589
Fax: (303)922-2106
**Subject(s):** Paid Community Newspapers
**Circ:** ‡2,065

**The River Press** (18126)
PO Box 69
Fort Benton, MT 59442-0069
Phone: (406)622-3311
Fax: (406)622-5446
**Subject(s):** Paid Community Newspapers
**Circ:** 2,052

**Preston Citizen** (7787)
77 S State St.
PO Box 472
Preston, ID 83263-0472
Phone: (208)852-0155
Fax: (208)852-0158
**Subject(s):** Paid Community Newspapers
**Circ:** (Non-paid)88
(Paid)2,044

**Brewster Quad-City Herald** (32027)
Brewster Quad City Herald Publishing
PO Box 37
525 West Main St
Brewster, WA 98812
Phone: (509)689-2507
Fax: (509)689-2508
**Subject(s):** Paid Community Newspapers
**Circ:** 2,000

**Bulldog Weekly** (2791)
University of Redlands
1200 E. Colton Ave.
PO Box 3080
Redlands, CA 92373-0999
Phone: (909)335-5137
Fax: (909)335-5162
**Subject(s):** College Publications
**Circ:** (Free)‡2,000

**California Hungarians** (2806)
PO Box 370305
Reseda, CA 91337-0305
Phone: (818)996-7685
Fax: (818)996-7685
**Subject(s):** Paid Community Newspapers; Hungarian
**Circ:** ‡2,000

**Channel Town Press** (32128)
306 Morris St
La Conner, WA 98257
Phone: (360)466-3315
Fax: (360)466-1195
**Subject(s):** Paid Community Newspapers
**Circ:** 2,000

**The Chimes** (2045)
Biola University
13800 Biola Ave.
La Mirada, CA 90639-0001
Phone: (562)906-4535
Fax: (310)903-4748
**Subject(s):** College Publications
**Circ:** (Free)2,000

**Clatskanie Chief** (25747)
PO Box 8
Clatskanie, OR 97016
Phone: (503)728-3350
Fax: (503)728-3350
**Subject(s):** Paid Community Newspapers
**Circ:** (Paid)2000

**Clipper** (32087)
Everett Community College
801 Wetmore
Everett, WA 98201
Phone: (206)388-9522
**Subject(s):** College Publications
**Circ:** (Controlled)2,000

**Color Country Shopper** (30680)
Southern Utah Publishing
26 N Main
Kanab, UT 84741
Phone: (435)644-2900
Fax: (435)644-2926
**Subject(s):** Shopping Guides
**Circ:** (Free)‡2,000

**Experience** (2738)
Los Medanos College
2700 E Leland Rd.
Pittsburg, CA 94565
Phone: (925)439-2181
Fax: (925)427-1599
**Subject(s):** College Publications
**Circ:** (Free)2,000

**Garfield County News** (30822)
120 N Main
PO Box 127
Tropic, UT 84776
Phone: (435)679-8730
Fax: (435)679-8847
**Subject(s):** Paid Community Newspapers
**Circ:** (Paid)‡2,000

**Holyoke Enterprise** (4465)
PO Box 297
Holyoke, CO 80734
Phone: (970)854-2811
Fax: (970)854-2232
**Subject(s):** Paid Community Newspapers
**Circ:** (Free)20
(Paid)2,000

**Index** (25834)
Pacific University
2043 College Way
U.C PO Box 586
Forest Grove, OR 97116
Phone: (503)357-6151
Fax: (503)352-3130
**Subject(s):** College Publications
**Circ:** (Free)‡2,000

**Kemmerer Gazette** (33746)
708 J.C. Penny Dr.
PO Box 30
Kemmerer, WY 83101-0300
Phone: (307)877-3347
Fax: (307)877-3736
**Subject(s):** Paid Community Newspapers
**Circ:** (Free)‡50
(Paid)‡2,000

**The Monte Vista Journal** (4515)
Valley Publishing
PO Box 607
Monte Vista, CO 81144-0607
Phone: (719)852-3531
Fax: (719)852-3387
**Subject(s):** Paid Community Newspapers
**Circ:** (Free)33
(Paid)2,000

**The Othello Outlook** (32191)
Basin Publishing Co.
PO Box O
Othello, WA 99344
Phone: (509)488-3342
Fax: (509)488-3345
**Subject(s):** Paid Community Newspapers
**Circ:** ‡2,000

**The Power County Press** (7640)
Crompton Publishing
PO Box 547
174 Idaho St.
American Falls, ID 83211
Phone: (208)226-5294
Fax: (208)226-5295
**Subject(s):** Paid Community Newspapers
**Circ:** ‡2,000

**Rabbit Creek Journal** (1672)
PO Box 309
Clipper Mills, CA 95930
Phone: (530)675-2270
Fax: (530)675-0415
**Subject(s):** Paid Community Newspapers
**Circ:** ‡2,000

**The Retort** (18070)
Association of Students of M.S.U., Billings
1500 Univ. Dr.
Billings, MT 59101-0298
Phone: (406)657-2194
Fax: (406)657-2191
**Subject(s):** College Publications
**Circ:** (Free)2,000

**Rock On** (4480)
Red Rocks Community College
13300 W. 6th Ave.
Lakewood, CO 80228-1255
Phone: (303)914-6600
Fax: (303)914-8154
**Subject(s):** College Publications
**Circ:** (Free)‡2,000

**South Coloradan** (4081)
Adams State College
208 Edgemont Rd.
Alamosa, CO 81102
Phone: (719)587-7904
Fax: (719)587-7656
**Subject(s):** College Publications
**Circ:** (Free)‡2,000

**The Summit** (1790)
Grossmont College
8800 Grossmont College Dr.
El Cajon, CA 92020
Phone: (619)644-7271
Fax: (619)644-7914
**Subject(s):** College Publications
**Circ:** (Free)‡2,000

**Tumbleweed Times** (32157)
Big Bend Community College
7662 Chanute St. NE
Moses Lake, WA 98837
Phone: (509)793-2222
**Subject(s):** College Publications
**Circ:** (Free)2,000

**West-Lane News** (26071)
PO Box 188
Veneta, OR 97487
Phone: (541)935-1882
Fax: (541)935-4082
**Subject(s):** Paid Community Newspapers
**Circ:** ‡2,000

**Wotanin-Wowapi** (18234)
Fort Peck Assiniboine and Sioux Tribes
PO Box 1027
Poplar, MT 59255
Phone: (406)768-5388
Fax: (406)768-5743

# Western States

**Subject(s):** Paid Community Newspapers
**Circ:** (Paid)800
 (Non-paid)2,000

**The Star** (32105)
Star Publishing Inc.
03 Midway Ave. NE
PO Box 150
Grand Coulee, WA 99133-0150
Phone: (509)633-1350
Fax: (509)633-3828
**Subject(s):** Paid Community Newspapers
**Circ:** 1,990

**Eastern Colorado News** (4576)
Eastern Colorado News Inc.
1522 Main St.
PO Box 555
Strasburg, CO 80136
Phone: (303)622-4417
Fax: (303)622-9794
**Subject(s):** Paid Community Newspapers
**Circ:** 1,978

**The News-Examiner** (7740)
Sun News Idaho Inc.
847 Washington
PO Box 278
Montpelier, ID 83254
Phone: (208)847-0552
Fax: (208)847-0553
**Subject(s):** Paid Community Newspapers
**Circ:** (Free)50
 (Paid)1,975

**Independent-Observer** (18115)
Box 966
Conrad, MT 59425
Phone: (406)271-5561
Fax: (406)271-5562
**Subject(s):** Paid Community Newspapers
**Circ:** ‡1,950

**Portola Reporter** (2757)
Feather Publishing
133 W. Sierra Ave.
Portola, CA 96122
Phone: (530)832-4646
Fax: (530)832-5319
**Subject(s):** Paid Community Newspapers
**Circ:** ‡1,950

**Wyvernwood Chronicle** (1696)
Eastern Group Publications Inc.
2500 S Atlantic Blvd., Bldg. A
Commerce, CA 90040
Phone: (323)263-5743
Fax: (323)263-9169
**Subject(s):** Free Newspapers; Spanish; Hispanic Publications
**Circ:** (Paid)♦2
 (Free)♦1,948

**The Big Timber Pioneer** (18064)
Pioneer Newspaper and Commercial Printing
PO Box 830
105 W 2nd Ave.
Big Timber, MT 59011
Phone: (406)932-5298
Fax: (406)932-4931
**Subject(s):** Free Newspapers
**Circ:** (Paid)‡1,900

**The Challis Messenger** (7683)
Custer Publishing Inc.
PO Box 405
Challis, ID 83226
Phone: (208)879-4445
Fax: (208)879-5276
**Subject(s):** Paid Community Newspapers
**Circ:** ‡1,900

**The Independent Enterprise** (18125)
Montpress Inc.
PO Box 106
Forsyth, MT 59327
Phone: (406)356-2149
**Subject(s):** Paid Community Newspapers
**Circ:** 1,900

**New Utah! Lone Peak Edition** (30742)
North County Newspapers
1555 N. Freedom Blvd.
PO Box 717
Provo, UT 84603-0717
Phone: (801)375-5103
Fax: (801)373-5489
**Subject(s):** Paid Community Newspapers
**Circ:** (Paid)1,900

**New Utah! Shopper** (30743)
North County Newspapers
1555 N. Freedom Blvd.
PO Box 717
Provo, UT 84603-0717
Phone: (801)375-5103
Fax: (801)373-5489
**Subject(s):** Shopping Guides
**Circ:** (Paid)1,900

**Quincy Valley Post-Register** (32229)
Quincy Valley Publications, Inc.
PO Box 217
Quincy, WA 98848
Phone: (509)787-4511
Fax: (509)787-2682
**Subject(s):** Paid Community Newspapers
**Circ:** ‡1,900

**Gazette-Times** (25848)
188 W Willow
PO Box 337
Heppner, OR 97836
Phone: (541)676-9228
Fax: (541)676-9211
**Subject(s):** Paid Community Newspapers
**Circ:** ‡1,850

**Independent-Enterprise** (7771)
124 S Main St.
Payette, ID 83661
Phone: (208)642-3357
Fax: (208)642-3560
**Subject(s):** Paid Community Newspapers
**Circ:** (Free)63
 (Paid)1,852

**Julesburg Advocate** (4471)
Eastern Colorado Publishing Co.
108 Cedar
Julesburg, CO 80737
Phone: (970)474-3388
Fax: (970)474-3389
**Subject(s):** Paid Community Newspapers
**Circ:** (Free)30
 (Paid)1,850

**Liberty County Times** (18108)
PO Box 689
Chester, MT 59522
Phone: (406)759-5355
Fax: (406)759-5320
**Subject(s):** Paid Community Newspapers
**Circ:** 1,852

**Saratoga Sun** (33788)
Box 489
Saratoga, WY 82331
**Subject(s):** Paid Community Newspapers
**Circ:** 1,850

**The Shelley Pioneer** (7804)
Pioneer Publications
PO Box P
Shelley, ID 83274
Phone: (208)357-7661
Fax: (208)357-3435
**Subject(s):** Paid Community Newspapers
**Circ:** ‡1,850

**The Sundance Times** (33796)
PO Box 400
Sundance, WY 82729
Phone: (307)283-3411
Fax: (307)283-3332
**Subject(s):** Paid Community Newspapers
**Circ:** ‡1,850

**The West Side Index** (2531)
Mattos Newspapers Inc.
1021 Fresno St.
PO Box 878
Newman, CA 95360
Phone: (209)862-2222
Fax: (209)862-4133
**Subject(s):** Paid Community Newspapers
**Circ:** 1,850

**Brush News-Tribune** (4158)
PO Box 8
Brush, CO 80723
Phone: (970)842-5516
Fax: (970)842-5519
**Subject(s):** Paid Community Newspapers
**Circ:** ⊕1,832

**The Seward Phoenix LOG** (505)
Alaska Newspapers Inc.
301 Calista Ct., Ste. B
Anchorage, AK 99518-3028
Phone: (907)349-6226
Fax: (907)349-6202
**Subject(s):** Paid Community Newspapers
**Circ:** (Free)56
 (Paid)1,838

**Cut Bank Pioneer Press** (18117)
Box 847
517 E Main
Cut Bank, MT 59427
Phone: (406)873-2201
Fax: (406)873-2443
**Subject(s):** Paid Community Newspapers
**Circ:** (Free)‡18
 (Paid)‡1,825

**Arizona Informant** (743)
1746 E Madison, No. 2
Phoenix, AZ 85034
Phone: (602)257-9300
Fax: (602)257-0547
**Subject(s):** Paid Community Newspapers; Black Publications
**Circ:** ‡1,800

**Bridger Valley Pioneer** (33767)
News Media
PO Box 538
Lyman, WY 82937
Phone: (307)787-3229
Fax: (307)787-6795
**Subject(s):** Paid Community Newspapers
**Circ:** (Free)‡123
 (Paid)‡1,800

**The Chinook Opinion** (18109)
The Blaine County Journal News Opinion
217 Indiana
PO Box 279
Chinook, MT 59523-0279
Phone: (406)357-2680
Fax: (406)357-3736
**Subject(s):** Paid Community Newspapers
**Circ:** ‡1,800

**The Cordova Times** (533)
Alaska Newspapers Inc.
PO Box 200
Cordova, AK 99574
Phone: (907)424-7181
Fax: (907)424-5799
**Subject(s):** Paid Community Newspapers
**Circ:** ‡1,800

**Dayton Chronicle** (32064)
358 E Main St.
PO Box 6
Dayton, WA 99328
Phone: (509)382-2221
**Subject(s):** Paid Community Newspapers
**Circ:** ‡1,800

**The Fowler Ensign** (3398)
Mid Valley Publication
740 N St.
Sanger, CA 93657
Phone: (559)875-2511
Fax: (559)875-2521
**Subject(s):** Paid Community Newspapers
**Circ:** ‡1,809

**The Meeker Herald** (4513)
Herald Times
178 Main St.
PO Box 720
Meeker, CO 81641
Phone: (970)878-4017
Fax: (970)878-4016
**Subject(s):** Paid Community Newspapers
**Circ:** (Free)‡20
 (Paid)‡1,800

**The Occidental Weekly** (2291)
Occidental College
1600 Campus Rd.
Box M-40
Los Angeles, CA 90041
Phone: (323)259-2500
Fax: (323)259-2958
**Subject(s):** College Publications

**Circ:** (Paid)‡250
(Free)‡1,800

**Petersburg Pilot** (605)
Pilot Publishing Inc.
PO Box 930
Petersburg, AK 99833
Phone: (907)722-9393
Fax: (907)772-4871
**Subject(s):** Paid Community Newspapers

**Circ:** ‡1,800

**Quaker Campus** (4043)
Whittier College
13406 Philadelphia
PO Box 634
Whittier, CA 90608-0634
Phone: (562)907-4222
Fax: (562)907-4817
**Subject(s):** College Publications

**Circ:** (Free)1,800

**Silver State Post** (18118)
PO Box 111
Deer Lodge, MT 59722
Phone: (406)846-2424
Fax: (406)846-2453
**Subject(s):** Paid Community Newspapers

**Circ:** ‡1,800

**Summit County Bee** (30672)
Wave Publishing
PO Box 7
Coalville, UT 84017
Phone: (435)654-1471
Fax: (435)654-5085
**Subject(s):** Paid Community Newspapers

**Circ:** ‡1,800

**The Times** (32475)
PO Box 97
Waitsburg, WA 99361-0097
Phone: (509)337-6631
Fax: (509)337-6045
**Subject(s):** Paid Community Newspapers

**Circ:** ‡1,800

**Times** (25738)
PO Box 278
219 Millhouse Street
Brownsville, OR 97327
Phone: (541)466-5311
Fax: (541)466-5312
**Subject(s):** Paid Community Newspapers

**Circ:** 1,800

**The Trail** (32442)
University of Puget Sound
1500 N.Warner St.
Tacoma, WA 98416-1095
Phone: (253)879-3197
Fax: (253)879-3661
**Subject(s):** College Publications

**Circ:** (Free)‡1,800

**Valley Press** (18227)
PO Box 667
Plains, MT 59859
Phone: (406)826-3402
Fax: (406)826-5577
**Subject(s):** Paid Community Newspapers

**Circ:** 1,800

**Vestkusten** (2471)
237 Ricardo Rd.
Mill Valley, CA 94941
Phone: (415)381-5149
Fax: (415)381-9664
**Subject(s):** Swedish; Paid Community Newspapers; Ethnic Publications

**Circ:** (Free)‡400
(Paid)‡1,800

**Jefferson Star** (7793)
Pioneer Publications
Box 37
Rigby, ID 83442
Phone: (208)745-8701
Fax: (208)745-8703
**Subject(s):** Paid Community Newspapers

**Circ:** ‡1,750

**The Billings Times** (18068)
2919 Montana Ave.
Billings, MT 59101
Phone: (406)245-4994
Fax: (406)245-5115
**Subject(s):** Paid Community Newspapers

**Circ:** (Free)‡50
(Paid)‡1,700

**Florence Reminder & Blade-Tribune** (679)
Casa Grande Valley Newspapers
PO Box 910
Florence, AZ 85232
Phone: (520)868-5897
**Subject(s):** Paid Community Newspapers

**Circ:** ‡1,700

**Island News** (615)
Island Printing
PO Box 19430
Thorne Bay, AK 99919
Phone: (907)828-3377
Fax: (907)828-3351
**Subject(s):** Paid Community Newspapers

**Circ:** (Free)‡100
(Paid)‡1,700

**Lincoln County Record** (18735)
PO Box 507
Pioche, NV 89043-0507
Phone: (775)726-3333
Fax: (775)726-3331
**Subject(s):** Paid Community Newspapers

**Circ:** ⊕1,700

**Nephi Times-News** (30709)
The Times News Publishing Co.
96 S. Main St.
PO Box 77
Nephi, UT 84648
Phone: (435)623-0525
Fax: (435)623-4735
**Subject(s):** Paid Community Newspapers

**Circ:** ‡1,700

**North Weld Herald** (4361)
208 First St.
Eaton, CO 80615-0235
Phone: (970)454-3466
Fax: (970)454-3466
**Subject(s):** Paid Community Newspapers

**Circ:** 1,700

**Review Independent** (32453)
Flint Publishing Inc.
PO Box 511
Toppenish, WA 98948
Phone: (509)865-4055
Fax: (509)865-2655
**Subject(s):** Paid Community Newspapers

**Circ:** 1,700

**The Tenino Independent & Sun News** (32450)
DeVaul Publishing Inc.
PO Box 4004
Tenino, WA 98589-4004
Phone: (360)264-2500
Fax: (360)264-2955
**Subject(s):** Paid Community Newspapers

**Circ:** (Paid)‡1,700

**Southend Neighborhood Classifieds** (32133)
Sound Publishing Inc.
PO Box 387
Langley, WA 98260
Phone: (360)221-5300
Fax: (360)221-6474
**Subject(s):** Free Newspapers

**Circ:** (Non-paid)♦1,695

**The Times-Journal** (25749)
319 S Main St.
Box 746
Condon, OR 97823
Phone: (541)384-2431
Fax: (541)384-2411

**Subject(s):** Paid Community Newspapers
**Circ:** ‡1,680

**The Wilbur Register** (32492)
Wilbur Register Inc.
110 SE Main
PO Box 186
Wilbur, WA 99185-0186
Phone: (509)647-5551
Fax: (509)647-5552
**Subject(s):** Paid Community Newspapers

**Circ:** ‡1,670

**El Paso County Advertiser & News** (4399)
Shopper Press Inc.
PO Box 400
120 E Ohio
Fountain, CO 80817
Phone: (719)382-5611
Fax: (719)382-5614
**Subject(s):** Paid Community Newspapers

**Circ:** (Paid)1,663

**Fallon County Times** (18060)
PO Box 679
Baker, MT 59313
Phone: (406)778-3344
Fax: (406)778-3347
**Subject(s):** Paid Community Newspapers

**Circ:** 1,650

**The Wahkiakum County Eagle** (32033)
77 Main St.
PO Box 368
Cathlamet, WA 98612-0368
Phone: (360)795-3391
Fax: (360)795-3983
**Subject(s):** Paid Community Newspapers

**Circ:** ‡1,617

**Cashmere Valley Record** (32032)
Prairie Media Inc.
201 Cottage Ave.
PO Box N
Cashmere, WA 98815
Phone: (509)782-3781
Fax: (509)782-9074
**Subject(s):** Paid Community Newspapers

**Circ:** 1,600

**The Clearwater Progress** (7717)
The Clearwater Progress Inc.
417 Main St.
PO Box 428
Kamiah, ID 83536-0428
Phone: (208)935-0838
Fax: (208)935-0973
**Subject(s):** Paid Community Newspapers

**Circ:** ‡1,600

**The Ferndale Enterprise** (1850)
Ferndale Enterprise Inc.
PO Box 1066
250 Francis St.
Ferndale, CA 95536
Phone: (707)786-4611
Fax: (707)786-4311
**Subject(s):** Paid Community Newspapers

**Circ:** 1,600

**Johnstown Breeze** (4470)
PO Box 400
Johnstown, CO 80534
Phone: (970)587-4525
**Subject(s):** Paid Community Newspapers

**Circ:** 1,600

**Metropolitan News-Enterprise** (2273)
Metropolitan News Co.
210 S. Spring St.
Los Angeles, CA 90012
Phone: (213)346-0033
Fax: (213)687-3886
**Subject(s):** Daily Newspapers

**Circ:** (Non-paid)⊕40
(Paid)⊕1,600

**Petroleum News** (502)
Petroleum Newspapers of Alaska L.L.C.
PO Box 231651
Anchorage, AK 99523-1651
Phone: (907)245-5553
Fax: (907)522-9583

# Western States

Subject(s): Mining and Minerals; Petroleum, Oil, and Gas
Circ: (Non-paid)‡800
(Paid)‡1,600

**Greybull Standard  (33739)**
614 Greybull Ave.
Greybull, WY 82426
Phone: (307)765-4485
Fax: (307)765-9486
Subject(s): Paid Community Newspapers
Circ: (Free)‡800
(Paid)‡1,575

**Campbell Express  (1611)**
Hanchett Publishing
334 E Campbell Ave.
Campbell, CA 95008
Phone: (408)374-9700
Fax: (408)374-0813
Subject(s): Paid Community Newspapers
Circ: ‡1,562

**East Washingtonian  (32201)**
742 Main St.
PO Box 70
Pomeroy, WA 99347
Phone: (509)843-1313
Fax: (509)843-3911
Subject(s): Paid Community Newspapers
Circ: ‡1,550

**The Leader  (2415)**
PO Box 299
Lucerne Valley, CA 92356
Phone: (760)248-7878
Fax: (760)248-2042
Subject(s): Paid Community Newspapers
Circ: (Free)‡50
(Paid)‡1,550

**Alarming Cry News  (32131)**
Christian Sons of Liberty
National Headquarters
PO Box 48
Langley, WA 98260
Phone: (360)579-3916
Subject(s): Social and Political Issues; Veterans; Religious Publications
Circ: (Combined)1,500

**The Columbia Press  (26075)**
PO Box 130
Warrenton, OR 97146
Phone: (503)861-3331
Fax: (503)325-1477
Subject(s): Paid Community Newspapers
Circ: ‡1,500

**The Current  (31986)**
Green River Community College
12401 SE 320th St.
Auburn, WA 98092
Phone: (253)833-9111
Fax: (253)288-3457
Subject(s): Journalism and Publishing
Circ: (Controlled)‡1,500

**El Dorado Gazette/Georgetown Gazette and Town Crier  (1802)**
2775 Miners Flat
PO Box 49
Georgetown, CA 95634-0156
Phone: (530)333-4481
Fax: (530)333-0152
Subject(s): Paid Community Newspapers
Circ: ‡1,500

**Florence Citizen  (4375)**
200 S Pikes Peak
Florence, CO 81226
Phone: (719)784-6383
Fax: (719)784-6384
Subject(s): Paid Community Newspapers
Circ: ‡1,500

**The Linfield Review  (25897)**
Linfield College
Unit 4009, 900 SE Baker St.
McMinnville, OR 97128
Phone: (503)472-7715
Fax: (503)472-7854
Subject(s): College Publications; Paid Community Newspapers
Circ: (Combined)1,500

**Loomis News  (2102)**
3550 Taylor Rd.
Loomis, CA 95650
Phone: (916)652-7939
Subject(s): Paid Community Newspapers
Circ: 1,500

**Malad City Idaho Enterprise  (7735)**
Idaho Enterprise
PO Box 205
100 E 90 South
Malad City, ID 83252
Phone: (208)766-4773
Fax: (208)766-4774
Subject(s): Paid Community Newspapers
Circ: ‡1,500

**Middle Park Times  (4473)**
Box 476
Kremmling, CO 80459
Phone: (970)724-3350
Fax: (970)724-0879
Subject(s): Paid Community Newspapers
Circ: (Free)‡20
(Paid)‡1,500

**The Point Weekly  (3042)**
Point Loma Nazarene University
3900 Lomaland Dr.
San Diego, CA 92106-2810
Phone: (619)849-2200
Fax: (619)849-2579
Subject(s): College Publications
Circ: ‡1,500

**San Miguel Basin Forum  (4526)**
PO Box 9
Nucla, CO 81424
Phone: (970)864-7425
Fax: (970)864-7856
Subject(s): Paid Community Newspapers
Circ: ‡1,500

**The Townsend Star  (18246)**
314 Broadway
PO Box 1011
Townsend, MT 59644
Phone: (406)266-3333
Fax: (406)266-5440
Subject(s): Paid Community Newspapers
Circ: ‡1,500

**The Voice  (25881)**
Eastern Oregon University
One University Blvd.
La Grande, OR 97850
Phone: (541)962-3386
Subject(s): College Publications
Circ: (Free)‡1,500

**The Sacramento Gazette  (2909)**
555 University Ave., Ste. 126
Sacramento, CA 95825-6584
Phone: (916)567-9654
Fax: (916)567-9653
Subject(s): Paid Community Newspapers
Circ: (Paid)1,480

**Wrangell Sentinel  (625)**
Jade River Publishing
PO Box 798
Wrangell, AK 99929
Phone: (907)874-2301
Fax: (907)874-2303
Subject(s): Paid Community Newspapers
Circ: (Free)‡25
(Paid)‡1,475

**Marcellus Observer  (26043)**
Eagle Newspapers
4901 Indian School Rd. NE
PO Box 12008
Salem, OR 97305
Phone: (503)393-7980
Fax: (503)393-2366
Subject(s): Paid Community Newspapers
Circ: (Free)‡140
(Paid)‡1,425

**ALKI  (32086)**
Washington Library Association
Everett Public Library
2702 Hoyt Ave.
Everett, WA 98201
Phone: (425)257-7640

Fax: (425)257-8016
Circ: (Paid)1,400

**The Bodega Bay Navigator  (1546)**
1925 Bay Flat Rd.
PO Box 969
Bodega Bay, CA 94923
Phone: (707)875-3574
Subject(s): Paid Community Newspapers
Circ: (Non-paid)400
(Paid)1,400

**Cable Scene  (7697)**
Pioneer Publications
PO Box 3838
Idaho Falls, ID 83403
Phone: (208)523-7777
Fax: (208)745-8703
Subject(s): Radio, Television, Cable, and Video
Circ: (Paid)1,400

**Crusader  (7759)**
Northwest Nazarene University
623 Holly St.
Nampa, ID 83686-5897
Phone: (208)467-8011
Fax: (208)467-8645
Subject(s): College Publications
Circ: (Paid)100
(Non-paid)1,400

**Dolores Star  (4354)**
Animas Publishing
PO Box 660
Durango, CO 81302
Phone: (970)882-4486
Fax: (970)882-4476
Subject(s): Paid Community Newspapers
Circ: (Free)‡10
(Paid)‡1,400

**The Flagler News & Mile Save Shopper  (4374)**
The Flagler News
321 Main Ave.
PO Box 188
Flagler, CO 80815
Phone: (719)765-4468
Fax: (719)765-4517
Subject(s): Paid Community Newspapers
Circ: 1,400

**Fowler Tribune  (4402)**
Tribune
112 E Cranston
Fowler, CO 81039
Phone: (719)263-5311
Fax: (719)263-5100
Subject(s): Paid Community Newspapers
Circ: ‡1,400

**DeWitt Times  (25786)**
Eagle Newspapers
4901 Indian School Rd. NE
PO Box 12008
Salem, OR 97305
Phone: (503)393-7980
Fax: (503)393-2366
Subject(s): Paid Community Newspapers
Circ: (Free)197
(Paid)1,375

**Jackson County Star  (4586)**
PO Box 397
Walden, CO 80480
Phone: (970)723-4404
Fax: (970)723-4474
Subject(s): Paid Community Newspapers
Circ: (Free)‡30
(Paid)‡1,370

**Herald  (18245)**
Jewett Publishing
PO Box 586
17 Main Street
Three Forks, MT 59752
Phone: (406)285-3414
Fax: (406)285-3413
Subject(s): Paid Community Newspapers
Circ: (Paid)1,350

**The Lusk Herald** (33766)
Wyoming Newspapers Inc.
227 S. Main St.
PO Box 30
Lusk, WY 82225
Phone: (307)334-2867
Fax: (307)334-2514
**Subject(s):** Paid Community Newspapers
**Circ:** 1,350

**Eastern Colorado Plainsmen** (4466)
505 3rd Ave.
Box 98
Hugo, CO 80821
Phone: (719)743-2371
**Subject(s):** Paid Community Newspapers
**Circ:** (Free)‡45
(Paid)‡1,315

**The Beaver Press** (30659)
40 E Center St.
PO Box 351
Beaver, UT 84713
Phone: (435)438-2891
Fax: (435)438-8804
**Subject(s):** Paid Community Newspapers
**Circ:** 1,300

**California Publisher** (2876)
California Newspaper Publishers Association
1225 8th St.
No. 260
Sacramento, CA 95814-4809
Phone: (916)449-3687
Fax: (916)443-6447
**Subject(s):** Journalism and Publishing
**Circ:** ‡1,300

**The Drain Enterprise** (25787)
309 1st St.
PO Box 26
Drain, OR 97435
Phone: (541)836-2241
Fax: (541)836-2243
**Subject(s):** Paid Community Newspapers
**Circ:** ‡1,300

**The Dubois Frontier** (33728)
Riverton Ranger
305 South First
PO Box 980
Dubois, WY 82513
Phone: (307)455-2525
Fax: (307)455-3163
**Subject(s):** Paid Community Newspapers
**Circ:** (Free)‡20
(Paid)‡1,300

**North American Pylon** (2748)
Kelly Communications
PO Box 1203
Pleasanton, CA 94566-0120
Phone: (925)846-7728
Fax: (925)846-0118
**Subject(s):** (Auto Racing)
**Circ:** (Free)‡700
(Paid)‡1,300

**The Range-Ledger & Cheyenne Records** (4182)
The Range-Ledger
PO Box 684
Cheyenne Wells, CO 80810
Phone: (719)767-5615
**Subject(s):** Paid Community Newspapers
**Circ:** 1,300

**The Seeley Swan Pathfinder** (18238)
PO Box 702
Seeley Lake, MT 59868
Phone: (406)677-2022
Fax: (406)677-2741
**Subject(s):** Paid Community Newspapers
**Circ:** (Paid)⊕1,300

**Superior Sun** (858)
467 Main St.
Superior, AZ 85273
Phone: (520)689-2436
Fax: (520)363-9663
**Subject(s):** Paid Community Newspapers
**Circ:** ‡1,300

**Times-Clarion** (18149)
111 S Central
PO Box 307
Harlowton, MT 59036-0307
Phone: (406)632-5633
Fax: (406)632-5644
**Subject(s):** Paid Community Newspapers
**Circ:** ‡1,300

**Weekly Register-Call** (4181)
220 Spring St.
PO Box 609
Central City, CO 80427-0609
Phone: (303)582-5333
Fax: (303)582-3932
**Subject(s):** Paid Community Newspapers
**Circ:** (Non-paid)23
(Paid)1,294

**Republican-Rustler** (33679)
409 W C
Box 640
Basin, WY 82410
Phone: (307)568-2458
Fax: (307)568-2459
**Subject(s):** Paid Community Newspapers
**Circ:** ‡1,264

**The Haxtun-Fleming Herald** (4460)
217 S.Colorado Ave.
PO Box 128
Haxtun, CO 80731
Phone: (970)774-6118
Fax: (970)774-7690
**Subject(s):** Paid Community Newspapers
**Circ:** ‡1,250

**The Odessa Record** (32175)
Box 458
Odessa, WA 99159
Phone: (509)982-2632
Fax: (509)982-2651
**Subject(s):** Paid Community Newspapers
**Circ:** ‡1,250

**Port Orford News** (25942)
The Port Orford News
PO Box 5
Port Orford, OR 97465-0005
Phone: (541)332-2361
Fax: (541)332-8101
**Subject(s):** Paid Community Newspapers
**Circ:** ‡1,250

**Rangely Times** (4553)
PO Box 460
Rangely, CO 81648
Phone: (970)675-5033
Fax: (970)675-8709
**Subject(s):** Paid Community Newspapers
**Circ:** 1,250

**Bent County Democrat** (4487)
516 Carson
PO Box 467
Las Animas, CO 81054
Phone: (719)456-1333
Fax: (719)456-1420
**Subject(s):** Paid Community Newspapers
**Circ:** (Non-paid)‡800
(Paid)‡1,200

**Dead Mountain Echo** (25929)
Echo Publishing Inc.
PO Box 900
48013 Highway 58
Oakridge, OR 97463
Phone: (541)782-4241
Fax: (541)782-3323
**Subject(s):** Paid Community Newspapers
**Circ:** ‡1,200

**The Gold Rush** (4614)
ASP Westward/Douglas County Publishing
PO Box 340
Woodland Park, CO 80866
Phone: (719)687-3006
Fax: (719)687-3009
**Subject(s):** Paid Community Newspapers
**Circ:** ‡1,200

**Indian Valley Record** (1951)
Feather Publishing
PO Box 469
Greenville, CA 95947
Phone: (530)284-7800
Fax: (530)284-7800
**Subject(s):** Paid Community Newspapers
**Circ:** 1,205

**The Meagher County News** (18248)
Meagher County News
13 E. Main St.
PO Box 349
White Sulphur Springs, MT 59645
Phone: (406)547-3831
Fax: (406)547-3832
**Subject(s):** Paid Community Newspapers
**Circ:** ‡1,200

**The Ordway New Era** (4527)
Rocky Ford Publishing Co.
223 Main St.
Ordway, CO 81063
Phone: (719)267-3576
Fax: (719)267-4661
**Subject(s):** Paid Community Newspapers
**Circ:** (Free)‡200
(Paid)‡1,200

**Post Falls Tribune** (7786)
PO Box 39
Post Falls, ID 83877
Phone: (208)773-7502
Fax: (208)773-7002
**Subject(s):** Paid Community Newspapers
**Circ:** 1,200

**San Jose Post-Record** (3308)
Daily Journal Corp.
90 N. 1st St., Ste. 100
San Jose, CA 95113
Phone: (408)287-4866
Fax: (408)287-2544
**Subject(s):** Daily Newspapers; Law; Business
**Circ:** 1,200

**The South Seattle Sentinel** (32333)
South Seattle Community College
6000 16th Ave. SW, JMB 119
Seattle, WA 98106-1499
Phone: (206)764-5333
Fax: (206)764-7936
**Subject(s):** College Publications
**Circ:** (Free)1,200

**Sun City News** (2839)
The Press-Enterprise Co.
3512 Fourteenth St.
Riverside, CA 92501
Phone: (909)684-1200
Fax: (909)368-5127
**Subject(s):** Paid Community Newspapers; Senior Citizens' Interests
**Circ:** (Fri.)1,203

**Eloy Enterprise** (644)
Casa Grande Valley Newspapers Inc.
PO Box 15002
Casa Grande, AZ 85230-5002
Phone: (520)836-7461
Fax: (520)836-0343
**Subject(s):** Paid Community Newspapers
**Circ:** ‡1,154

**The Daily Recorder** (2887)
Daily Journal Corp.
901 H St., Ste. 312
PO Box 1048
Sacramento, CA 95812-1048
Phone: (916)444-2355
Fax: (916)444-0636
**Subject(s):** State, Municipal, and County Administration; Law; Daily Newspapers; Real Estate
**Circ:** ‡1,122

**Delta Wind** (535)
TriDelta Inc.
PO Box 986
2887 Alaska Hwy
Delta Junction, AK 99737-0986
Phone: (907)895-5115
Fax: (907)895-5116
**Subject(s):** Paid Community Newspapers
**Circ:** (Free)‡75
(Paid)‡1,125

**Soledad Bee** (3531)
635 Front St.
PO Box 95
Soledad, CA 93960
Phone: (831)678-2660
Fax: (831)385-4799
**Subject(s):** Paid Community Newspapers
**Circ:** 1,125

**The Voice** (4472)
326 1st St.
PO Box 130
Kersey, CO 80644
Phone: (970)356-7176
Fax: (970)356-7176
**Subject(s):** Paid Community Newspapers
**Circ:** 1,125

**Colorado Editor** (4269)
Colorado Press Association
1336 Glenarm Pl.
Denver, CO 80204
Phone: (303)571-5117
Fax: (303)571-1803
**Subject(s):** Journalism and Publishing
**Circ:** ‡1,100

**Dove Creek Press** (4353)
PO Box 598
321 North Main St
Dove Creek, CO 81324
Phone: (970)677-2214
Fax: (970)677-3002
**Subject(s):** Paid Community Newspapers
**Circ:** (Free)‡58
(Paid)‡1,100

**Kiowa County Press** (4360)
1208 Maine St.
PO Box 248
Eads, CO 81036-0248
Phone: (719)438-5800
**Subject(s):** Paid Community Newspapers
**Circ:** (Free)‡50
(Paid)‡1,100

**Port Orford Today** (25943)
The Downtown Fun Zone
832 Hwy. 101
PO Box 49
Port Orford, OR 97465
Phone: (541)332-6565
Fax: (541)332-6565
**Subject(s):** Free Newspapers
**Circ:** 1,100

**Powder River Examiner** (18098)
PO Box 328
Broadus, MT 59317
Phone: (406)436-2244
Fax: (406)436-2244
**Subject(s):** Paid Community Newspapers
**Circ:** 1,100

**Cottonwood Chronicle** (7688)
503 King St.
Box 157
Cottonwood, ID 83522
Phone: (208)962-3851
Fax: (208)962-7131
**Subject(s):** Paid Community Newspapers
**Circ:** ‡1,050

**Lewis County Herald** (7763)
PO Box 159
Nezperce, ID 83543
Phone: (208)937-2671
Fax: (208)962-7131
**Subject(s):** Paid Community Newspapers
**Circ:** ‡1,050

**The Pendleton Record** (25936)
809 SE Ct.
PO Box 69
Pendleton, OR 97801
Phone: (541)276-2853
Fax: (541)278-2916
**Subject(s):** Paid Community Newspapers
**Circ:** ‡1,050

**Upper Country News-Reporter** (7682)
155 N Superior
PO Box 9
Cambridge, ID 83610
Phone: (208)257-3515

**Subject(s):** Paid Community Newspapers
**Circ:** (Free)‡50
(Paid)‡1,056

**Eagle** (18123)
Eagle Publishing Co.
PO Box 66
Ekalaka, MT 59324
Phone: (406)775-6245
Fax: (406)775-8750
**Subject(s):** Paid Community Newspapers
**Circ:** 1,035

**The Inter-City Express** (2591)
Daily Journal Corp.
1939 Harrison St., Ste. 330
Oakland, CA 94612-3532
Phone: (510)272-4747
**Subject(s):** Daily Newspapers; Real Estate; Law
**Circ:** (Non-paid)‡14
(Paid)‡1,023

**Ouray County Plaindealer** (4554)
The Ridgway Sun
PO Box 529
Ridgway, CO 81432
Phone: (970)626-5100
Fax: (970)626-5100
**Subject(s):** Paid Community Newspapers
**Circ:** (Free)‡41
(Paid)‡1,025

**The Aberdeen Times** (7639)
Crompton Publishing
Box 856
Aberdeen, ID 83210
Phone: (208)397-4440
Fax: (208)397-4440
**Subject(s):** Paid Community Newspapers
**Circ:** (Free)⊕18
(Paid)⊕1,000

**The Banner** (2815)
California Baptist College
8432 Magnolia Ave.
Riverside, CA 92504-3297
Phone: (909)689-5771
Fax: (909)351-1808
**Subject(s):** College Publications
**Circ:** (Free)‡1,000

**Boulder Monitor** (18087)
Boulder Monitor Inc.
104 W Centennial
PO Box 66
Boulder, MT 59632
Phone: (406)225-3821
Fax: (406)225-3821
**Subject(s):** Paid Community Newspapers
**Circ:** ‡1,000

**Escondido News-Reporter** (1828)
Metropolitan News Co.
210 S. Spring St.
Los Angeles, CA 90012
Phone: (213)346-0033
Fax: (213)687-3886
**Subject(s):** Free Newspapers
**Circ:** (Paid)200
(Non-paid)1,000

**The Forum** (30766)
Westminster College
1840 S. 1300 E.
Salt Lake City, UT 84105
Phone: (801)832-2680
Fax: (801)832-3104
**Subject(s):** College Publications
**Circ:** (Free)1,000

**Highlander** (4289)
Regis University
3333 Regis Blvd.
Mail Stop I-8
Denver, CO 80221
Phone: (303)964-5391
Fax: (303)964-5530
**Subject(s):** College Publications
**Circ:** 1,000

**Judith Basin Press** (18242)
117 Central Ave.
PO Box 507
Stanford, MT 59479
Phone: (406)566-2471

Fax: (406)566-2312
**Subject(s):** Paid Community Newspapers
**Circ:** 1,000

**Lincoln County Journal** (7805)
Magic Valley Publishing Co.
PO Box 704
Shoshone, ID 83352
Phone: (208)886-2740
Fax: (208)886-2740
**Subject(s):** Paid Community Newspapers
**Circ:** ‡1,000

**Morgan County News** (30705)
The Morgan County News
200 E. 125 N. Ste. B
PO Box 190
Morgan, UT 84050
Phone: (801)829-3451
Fax: (801)829-4073
**Subject(s):** Paid Community Newspapers
**Circ:** (Free)‡100
(Paid)‡1,000

**North County Spectrum** (3041)
Metropolitan News Co.
210 S. Spring St.
Los Angeles, CA 90012
Phone: (213)346-0033
Fax: (213)687-3886
**Subject(s):** Free Newspapers
**Circ:** (Non-paid)1,000

**The Ridgway Sun** (4555)
PO Box 529
Ridgway, CO 81432
Phone: (970)626-5100
Fax: (970)626-5100
**Subject(s):** Paid Community Newspapers
**Circ:** 1,005

**Riverside Bulletin** (2322)
Metropolitan News Co.
210 S. Spring St.
Los Angeles, CA 90012
Phone: (213)346-0033
Fax: (213)687-3886
**Subject(s):** Free Newspapers
**Circ:** (Non-paid)1,000

**Sacramento Bulletin** (2907)
Metropolitan News Co.
530 Bercut Dr., Ste. E
Sacramento, CA 95814
Phone: (916)445-6336
Fax: (916)443-5871
**Subject(s):** Free Newspapers
**Circ:** (Non-paid)1,000

**San Bernardino Bulletin** (2985)
Metropolitan News Co.
215 N. D St., Ste. 101
San Bernardino, CA 92401
Phone: (909)889-6477
Fax: (909)889-3696
**Subject(s):** Free Newspapers
**Circ:** (Non-paid)1,000

**The Searchlight** (18116)
PO Box 496
Culbertson, MT 59218
Phone: (406)787-5821
Fax: (406)787-5271
**Subject(s):** Shopping Guides
**Circ:** (Combined)‡1,000

**Ventura Bulletin** (3975)
Metropolitan News Co.
210 S. Spring St.
Los Angeles, CA 90012
Phone: (213)346-0033
Fax: (213)687-3886
**Subject(s):** Free Newspapers
**Circ:** (Non-paid)1,000

**The Wibaux Pioneer-Gazette** (18250)
120 S Wibaux St.
Wibaux, MT 59353
Phone: (406)796-2218
Fax: (406)796-2218
**Subject(s):** Paid Community Newspapers
**Circ:** ‡1,000

**Gale Directory of Publications & Broadcast Media/140th Ed.**     **Western States**

**The Washington Newspaper** (32339)
Washington Newspaper Publishers Association
3838 Stone Way N
Seattle, WA 98103
Phone: (206)634-3838
Fax: (206)634-3842
**Subject(s):** Journalism and Publishing
**Circ:** ‡970

**The Skagway News** (613)
264 Broadway
PO Box 498
Skagway, AK 99840-0498
Phone: (907)983-2354
Fax: (907)983-2356
**Subject(s):** Paid Community Newspapers
**Circ:** ‡950

**Glenrock Independent** (33736)
207 S 4th St.
PO Box 9
Glenrock, WY 82637
Phone: (307)436-2211
Fax: (307)436-8803
**Subject(s):** Paid Community Newspapers
**Circ:** 944

**McKenzie River Reflections** (25896)
59059 Old McKenzie Hwy.
McKenzie Bridge, OR 97413
Phone: (541)822-3358
Fax: (541)822-3358
**Subject(s):** Paid Community Newspapers
**Circ:** (Paid)922

**Big Sandy Mountaineer** (18063)
Ridick Publishing
123 Main
PO Box 529
Big Sandy, MT 59520
Phone: (406)378-2176
Fax: (406)378-2176
**Subject(s):** Paid Community Newspapers
**Circ:** (Free)‡43
     (Paid)‡912

**The Sun-Tribune** (26026)
News-Review Publishing Co.
345 NE Winchester
PO Box 1248
Roseburg, OR 97470
Phone: (541)672-3321
Fax: (541)957-4270
**Subject(s):** Paid Community Newspapers
**Circ:** (Free)100
     (Paid)900

**Terry Tribune** (18243)
Yellowstone Newspapers
204 Logan Ave.
Box 127
Terry, MT 59349
Phone: (406)635-5513
Fax: (406)635-2149
**Subject(s):** Paid Community Newspapers
**Circ:** ‡900

**The Daily Territorial** (910)
Territorial Newspapers
3280 E Hemisphere Lp., Ste. 180
PO Box 27087
Tucson, AZ 85706
Phone: (520)294-1200
Fax: (520)294-4040
**Subject(s):** Daily Periodicals; Business; Law
**Circ:** (Free)100
     (Paid)892

**Corona-Norco Independent** (2821)
The Press-Enterprise Co.
3512 Fourteenth St.
Riverside, CA 92501
Phone: (909)684-1200
Fax: (909)368-5127
**Subject(s):** Shopping Guides
**Circ:** (Fri.)814

**Weston County Gazette** (33802)
PO Box 526
722 2nd St.
Upton, WY 82730
Phone: (307)468-2642
Fax: (307)468-2397
**Subject(s):** Paid Community Newspapers
**Circ:** 800

**Shoshoni Pioneer** (33795)
Rivertown Ranger
310 W 6th St.
PO Box 420
Shoshoni, WY 82649
Phone: (307)856-2244
Fax: (307)876-2627
**Subject(s):** Paid Community Newspapers
**Circ:** 780

**South Fork Times** (4564)
Valley Publishing
PO Box 158
South Fork, CO 81154-0158
Phone: (719)873-5592
**Subject(s):** Paid Community Newspapers
**Circ:** (Free)7
     (Paid)770

**Guernsey Gazette** (33763)
Lingle Guide
PO Box 278
Lingle, WY 82223
Phone: (307)837-2255
Fax: (307)837-2255
**Subject(s):** Paid Community Newspapers
**Circ:** (Free)‡8
     (Paid)‡720

**Gonzales Tribune** (3529)
South Country Newspapers
635 Front St.
Soledad, CA 93960
Phone: (831)385-4880
Fax: (831)385-4799
**Subject(s):** Paid Community Newspapers
**Circ:** ‡705

**Mukluk News** (616)
PO Box 90
Tok, AK 99780
Phone: (907)883-2571
**Subject(s):** Paid Community Newspapers
**Circ:** (Paid)700

**San Diego Commerce** (3044)
Daily Journal Corp.
c/o Joseph Sorrentino, Managing Editor
2652 4th Ave., 2nd Fl.,
San Diego, CA 92103
Phone: (619)232-3486
Fax: (619)232-1159
**Subject(s):** Business; Real Estate; Paid Community Newspapers
**Circ:** (Free)209
     (Paid)670

**Saguache Crescent** (4557)
316 4th St.
PO Box 195
Saguache, CO 81149
Phone: (719)655-2620
Fax: (719)655-2620
**Subject(s):** Paid Community Newspapers
**Circ:** ‡665

**Reporter** (2097)
Pfanstiel Publishers and Printers Inc.
PO Box 4278
Long Beach, CA 90804
Phone: (562)438-5641
Fax: (562)438-7086
**Subject(s):** Law
**Circ:** ‡650

**Lingle Guide** (33764)
228 Main St.
Lingle, WY 82223
Phone: (307)532-2184
Fax: (307)532-2283
**Subject(s):** Paid Community Newspapers
**Circ:** (Free)‡12
     (Paid)‡640

**The Del Norte Prospector** (4514)
Valley Publishing
PO Box 607
Monte Vista, CO 81144-0607
Phone: (719)852-3531
Fax: (719)852-3387
**Subject(s):** Paid Community Newspapers
**Circ:** (Free)‡5
     (Paid)‡630

**Valley Times** (2513)
The Press-Enterprise Co.
3512 Fourteenth St.
Riverside, CA 92501
Phone: (909)684-1200
Fax: (909)368-5127
**Subject(s):** Paid Community Newspapers
**Circ:** (Combined)634

**Cascade Courier** (18107)
100 1st St. N
Cascade, MT 59421
Phone: (406)468-9231
Fax: (406)468-3030
**Subject(s):** Paid Community Newspapers
**Circ:** (Free)‡15
     (Paid)‡600

**Hayden Valley Press** (4565)
WorldWest L.L.C.
PO Box 4827
Steamboat Springs, CO 80487
Phone: (970)879-1502
**Subject(s):** Paid Community Newspapers
**Circ:** ‡571

**Center Post-Dispatch** (4180)
Valley Publishing
PO Box 1059
Center, CO 81125-1059
Phone: (719)754-3172
**Subject(s):** Paid Community Newspapers
**Circ:** (Free)9
     (Paid)556

**Eureka Sentinel** (18661)
Times Bonanza and Goldfield News
PO Box 150820
Ely, NV 89315
Phone: (775)289-4491
Fax: (775)289-4566
**Subject(s):** Paid Community Newspapers
**Circ:** ‡550

**Eureka Reporter** (1832)
Art City Publishing
513 Second St.
Eureka, CA 95501
Phone: (707)476-8000
**Subject(s):** Paid Community Newspapers
**Circ:** 512

**Campus News** (2509)
East Los Angeles College
Journalism Dept.
1301 Avenida Cesar Chavez
Monterey Park, CA 91754
Phone: (323)265-8819
Fax: (323)265-8975
**Subject(s):** College Publications
**Circ:** (Free)‡500

**Contra Costa News Register** (2439)
820 Main St.
Martinez, CA 94553
Phone: (925)934-2780
Fax: (925)934-2532
**Subject(s):** Law; Business
**Circ:** ‡500

**New Utah! Lindon Edition** (30741)
North County Newspapers
1555 N. Freedom Blvd.
PO Box 717
Provo, UT 84603-0717
Phone: (801)375-5103
Fax: (801)373-5489
**Subject(s):** Paid Community Newspapers
**Circ:** (Paid)500

**The Public Record** (2671)
303 N. Indian Canyon Dr.
PO Box 2724
Palm Springs, CA 92263-2724
Phone: (760)416-9709
Fax: (760)416-9690
**Subject(s):** Business; Free Newspapers
**Circ:** (Paid)‡500
     (Free)‡500

**Lake Elsinore Valley Sun-Tribune** (2832)
The Press-Enterprise Co.
3512 Fourteenth St.
Riverside, CA 92501
Phone: (909)684-1200

3865

Circulation: ★ = ABC; ∆ = BPA; ♦ = CAC; • = CCAB; ▫ = VAC; ⊕ = PO Statement; ‡ = Publisher's Report; Boldface figures = sworn; Light figures = estimated.

## Central Provinces

Fax: (909)368-5127
**Subject(s):** Free Newspapers; Free Newspapers
**Circ:** (Fri.)458

**The Dayton Tribune (25785)**
PO Box 69
Dayton, OR 97114
Phone: (503)864-2310
Fax: (503)864-2310
**Subject(s):** Paid Community Newspapers
**Circ:** ‡424

**Rancho News (3598)**
The Press-Enterprise Co.
3512 Fourteenth St.
Riverside, CA 92501
Phone: (909)684-1200
Fax: (909)368-5127
**Subject(s):** Paid Community Newspapers
**Circ:** (Fri.)412

**Tri-County Tribune (4256)**
PO Box 220
Deer Trail, CO 80105
Phone: (303)769-4646
Fax: (303)769-4650
**Subject(s):** Paid Community Newspapers
**Circ:** ‡400

**The Colorado Tribune (4540)**
Colorado Printing of Pueblo
447 Park Dr.
Pueblo, CO 81005
Phone: (719)561-4008
Fax: (719)561-4007
**Subject(s):** Law
**Circ:** ‡374

**Costilla County Free Press (4561)**
PO Box 306
San Luis, CO 81152
Phone: (719)672-3764
Fax: (719)672-3895
**Subject(s):** Paid Community Newspapers
**Circ:** (Free)‡25
    (Paid)‡275

**Sierra Booster (2414)**
PO Box 8
Loyalton, CA 96118
Phone: (916)993-4379
Fax: (916)993-1732
**Subject(s):** Paid Community Newspapers
**Circ:** (Free)‡930
    (Paid)‡2,26

**Bell Gardens Review (2143)**
Wave Newspaper Group
4201 Wilshire Ave., Ste. 600
Los Angeles, CA 90010
Phone: (323)556-5720
Fax: (323)556-5704
**Subject(s):** Free Newspapers
**Circ:** (Paid)70

## Central Provinces

**The Toronto Star (35828)**
Toronto Star Newspapers Ltd.
1 Yonge St., 5th Fl.
Toronto, ON, Canada M5E 1E6
Phone: (416)367-2000
Fax: (416)869-4834
**Subject(s):** Daily Newspapers
**Circ:** (Sun.)★430,089
    (Mon.-Fri.)★462,985
    (Sat.)★673,663

**The Globe and Mail (35645)**
The Globe & Mail
444 Front St. W.
Toronto, ON, Canada M5V 2S9
Phone: (416)585-5000
Fax: (416)585-5641
**Subject(s):** Daily Newspapers
**Circ:** (Mon.-Fri.)354,574
    (Sat.)416,457

**National Post (35722)**
Business Information Group
12 Concord Plz. 8th Fl.
Toronto, ON, Canada M3C 4J2
Phone: (416)442-5600

Fax: (416)442-2191
**Subject(s):** Daily Newspapers
**Circ:** (Mon.-Fri.)336,150
    (Sat.)399,032

**Anglican Journal/Journal Anglican (35495)**
Board of Trustees of the Anglican Church of Canada
80 Hayden St.
Toronto, ON, Canada M4Y 3G2
Phone: (416)924-9192
Fax: (416)921-4452
**Subject(s):** Religious Publications
**Circ:** (Paid)‡263,000

**The Town Crier (35829)**
Town Crier Inc.
101 Wingold Ave.
Toronto, ON, Canada M6B 1P8
Phone: (416)488-4779
Fax: (416)488-3671
**Subject(s):** Free Newspapers
**Circ:** (Free)‡213,900

**The Classified News (35112)**
Metroland Printing & Publishing
3145 Wolfedale Rd.
Mississauga, ON, Canada L5C 1W1
Phone: (416)273-8111
Fax: (416)273-4991
**Subject(s):** Employment and Human Resources
**Circ:** (Free)174,000

**The Winnipeg Free Press (34517)**
1355 Mountain Ave.
Winnipeg, MB, Canada R2X 3B6
Phone: (204)697-7001
Fax: (204)697-7465
**Subject(s):** Daily Newspapers
**Circ:** (Sun.)★116,616
    (Mon.-Fri.)★117,608
    (Sat.)★167,700

**The Ottawa Citizen (35293)**
Ottawa Citizen Group Inc.
1101 Baxter Rd.
PO Box 5020
Ottawa, ON, Canada K2C 3M4
Phone: (613)829-9100
Fax: (613)726-1198
**Subject(s):** Daily Newspapers
**Circ:** (Sun.)★129,091
    (Mon.-Fri.)★129,175
    (Sat.)★161,246

**The Financial Post (34878)**
CanWest Interactive
300 - 1450 Don Mills Road
Don Mills, ON, Canada M3B 2X7
Phone: (416)422-2222
**Subject(s):** Banking, Finance, and Investments; Daily Newspapers
**Circ:** (Tues.-Fri.)77,757
    (Sat.)155,475

**Share (35795)**
Arnold A. Auguste Associates Ltd.
658 Vaughan Rd.
Toronto, ON, Canada M6E 2Y5
Phone: (416)656-3400
Fax: (416)656-3711
**Subject(s):** Free Newspapers; Ethnic Publications; Black Publications
**Circ:** (Combined)153,000

**The Spectator (34973)**
Joe Tong Inc.
44 Frid St.
PO Box 300
Hamilton, ON, Canada L8N 3G3
Phone: (905)526-3333
Fax: (905)526-6779
**Subject(s):** Daily Newspapers
**Circ:** (Mon.-Fri.)103,915
    (Sat.)129,867

**The Mississauga News (35125)**
3145 Wolfedale Rd.
Mississauga, ON, Canada L5C 3A9
Phone: (905)273-8111
Fax: (905)273-9119
**Subject(s):** Free Newspapers; Free Newspapers
**Circ:** (Thurs.)44,733
    (Sun.)121,390
    (Fri.)121,435
    (Wed.)123,049

**The Scarborough Mirror (35940)**
Metroland
100 Tempo Ave.
Willowdale, ON, Canada M2H 2N8
Phone: (416)493-4400
Fax: (416)493-4703
**Subject(s):** Paid Community Newspapers
**Circ:** (Non-paid)108,216

**The London Free Press (35055)**
369 York St.
PO Box 2280
London, ON, Canada N6A 4G1
Phone: (519)679-6666
Fax: (519)667-4503
**Subject(s):** Daily Newspapers
**Circ:** (Sun.)★65,622
    (Mon.-Fri.)★90,043
    (Sat.)★108,073

**Oshawa-Whitby-Clarington-Port Perry This Week (35199)**
Metroland Printing & Publishing
865 Farewell St.
PO Box 481
Oshawa, ON, Canada L1H 7L5
Fax: (905)579-1809
**Subject(s):** Paid Community Newspapers
**Circ:** (Wed.)84,313
    (Sun.)100,611
    (Fri.)106,550

**Now (35731)**
Now Magazine
189 Church St.
Toronto, ON, Canada M5B 1Y7
Phone: (416)364-1301
Fax: (416)364-1168
**Subject(s):** Entertainment; Alternative and Underground; Free Newspapers
**Circ:** (Paid)55
    (Free)106,103

**Eye Weekly (35631)**
Eye Communications Ltd.
471 Adelaide St. W
70 Peter St.
Toronto, ON, Canada M5V 2G5
Phone: (416)596-4393
**Subject(s):** Free Newspapers
**Circ:** (Paid)3
    (Free)102,484

**Living with Christ (35284)**
Novalis
Saint Paul University
223 Main St.
Ottawa, ON, Canada K1S 1C4
Phone: (613)751-4012
Fax: (613)782-3004
**Subject(s):** Religious Publications
**Circ:** (Paid)100,000

**North York Mirror (35938)**
Metroland
100 Tempo Ave.
Willowdale, ON, Canada M2H 2N8
Phone: (416)493-4400
Fax: (416)493-4703
**Subject(s):** Paid Community Newspapers
**Circ:** (Non-paid)99,028

**Real Estate News (35776)**
1400 Dan Mills Rd.
Toronto, ON, Canada M3B 3N1
Phone: (416)443-8113
Fax: (416)443-9185
**Subject(s):** Real Estate
**Circ:** (Controlled)‡98,720

**The Liberal Newspaper (35377)**
Metroland Printing & Publishing
1550 16th Ave
PO Box 390
Richmond Hill, ON, Canada L4B 3K9
Phone: (905)881-3373
Fax: (905)881-9924
**Subject(s):** Free Newspapers
**Circ:** (Tues.)70,000
    (Thurs.)92,000
    (Sun.)92,000

**Gale Directory of Publications & Broadcast Media/140th Ed.**  **Central Provinces**

**Kitchener-Waterloo Pennysaver (35029)**
Kitchner-Waterloo Pennysaver
685 Wabanaki
Kitchener, ON, Canada N2C 2G3
Phone: (519)894-1400
Fax: (519)894-5401
Subject(s): Shopping Guides
Circ: 90,000

**Kitchener-Waterloo Record (35030)**
225 Fairway Rd., S.
Kitchener, ON, Canada N2G 4E5
Phone: (519)894-2231
Fax: (519)894-3829
Subject(s): Daily Newspapers
Circ: (Mon.-Fri.)66,172
 (Sat.)83,785

**The Windsor Star (35949)**
167 Ferry St.
Windsor, ON, Canada N9A 4M5
Phone: (519)255-5711
Fax: (519)255-5778
Subject(s): Daily Newspapers
Circ: (Mon.-Fri.)★72,435
 (Sat.)★82,129

**The Western Producer (36504)**
2310 Millar Ave.
PO Box 2500
Saskatoon, SK, Canada S7K 2C4
Phone: (306)665-3501
Fax: (306)244-9445
Subject(s): Farm Newspapers
Circ: (Non-paid)275
 (Paid)81,247

**Vaughan Citizen (35379)**
The Liberal
1550 Sixteenth Ave.
PO Box 390
Richmond Hill, ON, Canada L4C 4Y6
Phone: (905)881-3373
Fax: (905)881-9924
Subject(s): Free Newspapers
Circ: (Free)78,000

**The Liberal (35376)**
1550 Sixteenth Ave.
PO Box 390
Richmond Hill, ON, Canada L4C 4Y6
Phone: (905)881-3373
Fax: (905)881-9924
Subject(s): Free Newspapers
Circ: (Thurs.)61,277
 (Tues.)75,312
 (Sun.)75,359

**Peterborough Examiner (35350)**
Hollinger Inc.
730 De King Way
Peterborough, ON, Canada K9J 6W6
Phone: (705)745-4641
Fax: (705)743-4581
Subject(s): Paid Community Newspapers
Circ: (Controlled)71,600

**The Brampton Guardian (34811)**
Brampton Guardian
685 Queen St. W.
Brampton, ON, Canada L6V 1A1
Phone: (905)454-4344
Fax: (905)454-4385
Subject(s): Daily Newspapers
Circ: (Fri.)67,025
 (Sun.)67,063
 (Wed.)67,646

**Mississauga Pennysaver (34813)**
Pennysaver
56 Bramsteele Rd., Unit 1
Brampton, ON, Canada L6W 3M7
Phone: (905)454-0854
Fax: (905)450-5792
Subject(s): Shopping Guides
Circ: (Free)‡65,300

**Leader-Post (36475)**
1964 Park St.
Regina, SK, Canada S4P 3G4
Phone: (306)781-5211
Fax: (306)565-2588

Subject(s): Daily Newspapers
Circ: (Mon.-Thurs.)52,503
 (Sat.)62,634
 (Fri.)65,114

**The Winnipeg Sun (34518)**
1700 Church Ave.
Winnipeg, MB, Canada R2X 3A2
Phone: (204)694-2022
Fax: (204)697-0759
Subject(s): Daily Newspapers
Circ: (Sat.)★44,305
 (Mon.-Fri.)★44,602
 (Sun.)★55,830

**Brampton Pennysaver (34812)**
Pennysaver
56 Bramsteele Rd., Unit 1
Brampton, ON, Canada L6W 3M7
Phone: (905)454-0854
Fax: (905)450-5792
Subject(s): Shopping Guides
Circ: (Free)55,447

**The Community Press (35442)**
February 11th Interactive Publishing Ltd.
PO Box 88
14 Demorest Rd
Stirling, ON, Canada K0K 3E0
Phone: (613)395-3015
Fax: (613)395-2992
Subject(s): Free Newspapers
Circ: (Paid)360
 (Free)54,000

**Ottawa Sun (35296)**
Sun Media Corp.
380 Hunt Club Rd.
PO Box 9729, Sta. T
Ottawa, ON, Canada K1G 5H7
Phone: (613)739-7000
Fax: (613)739-9383
Subject(s): Paid Community Newspapers
Circ: (Sat.)★44,333
 (Mon.-Fri.)★50,757
 (Sun.)★52,406

**Truck News (35833)**
Business Information Group
12 Concorde Place
Suite 800
Toronto, ON, Canada M3C 4J2
Phone: (416)510-6896
Subject(s): Trucks and Trucking
Circ: (Combined)50,952

**The Metro (34496)**
Transcontinental Weeklies
1465 St. James St.
Winnipeg, MB, Canada R3H 0W9
Phone: (204)789-0800
Fax: (204)953-4300
Subject(s): Free Newspapers
Circ: (Free)50,595

**Shopper's Market (34798)**
365 N. Front St. (Bell Tower Plaza)
PO Box 446
Belleville, ON, Canada K8N 5A5
Phone: (613)962-3422
Fax: (613)962-0543
Subject(s): Shopping Guides
Circ: (Free)‡50,000

**Ajax-Pickering News Advertiser (35094)**
Metroland Printing, Publishing & Distributing Ltd.
206-9170 County Rd. 93
Box 77
Mountainview Mall
RR 2
Midland, ON, Canada L4R 4R4
Phone: (705)527-5500
Fax: (705)527-5467
Subject(s): Paid Community Newspapers
Circ: (Sun.)43,090
 (Wed.)44,355
 (Fri.)49,831

**The Lance (34488)**
Transcontinental Weeklies
1465 St. James St.
Winnipeg, MB, Canada R3H 0W9
Phone: (204)789-0800
Fax: (204)953-4300

Subject(s): Free Newspapers
Circ: (Free)48,231

**Thunder Bay Post (35477)**
87 N. Hill St.
Thunder Bay, ON, Canada P7A 5V6
Phone: (807)346-2600
Fax: (807)345-9923
Subject(s): Paid Community Newspapers
Circ: ‡48,000

**Kingston This Week (35012)**
607 Gardiners Rd.
Kingston, ON, Canada K7M 3Y4
Phone: (613)389-7400
Fax: (613)389-7507
Subject(s): Free Newspapers
Circ: (Tues.)47,769
 (Fri.)47,769

**Burlington Post (34825)**
5040 Main Way
Burlington, ON, Canada L7L 7G5
Phone: (905)632-4444
Fax: (905)632-6604
Subject(s): Free Newspapers
Circ: (Wed.)46,635
 (Fri.)47,123
 (Sun.)47,124

**Peterborough This Week (35351)**
Metroland Printing, Publishing & Distributing Ltd.
884 Ford St.
Peterborough, ON, Canada K9J 5V3
Phone: (705)749-3383
Fax: (705)749-0074
Subject(s): Paid Community Newspapers
Circ: (Wed.)45,082
 (Sat.)46,769

**Barrie Advance (34781)**
Metroland Printing, Publishing & Distributing Ltd.
21 Patterson Rd.
Barrie, ON, Canada L4N 7W6
Subject(s): Free Newspapers
Circ: (Tues.)25,962
 (Sun.)45,740
 (Fri.)45,747
 (Wed.)45,754

**Sudbury Northern Life (35456)**
158 Elgin St.
Sudbury, ON, Canada P3E 3N5
Phone: (705)673-5667
Fax: (705)673-4652
Subject(s): Paid Community Newspapers
Circ: (Paid)44,335

**The Canadian Jewish News (35159)**
1500 Don Mills Rd., Ste. 205
North York, ON, Canada M3B 3K4
Phone: (416)391-1836
Fax: (416)391-0949
Subject(s): Jewish Publications; Religious Publications
Circ: (Free)2,995
 (Paid)44,152

**Hamilton Mountain News (35444)**
Brabant Newspapers
333 Arvin Ave.
Stoney Creek, ON, Canada L8E 2M6
Phone: (905)523-5800
Fax: (905)526-1855
Subject(s): Free Newspapers
Circ: (Free)‡43,500

**The Medical Post (35706)**
Rogers Media Publishing
1 Mount Pleasant Rd., 7th Fl.
Toronto, ON, Canada M4Y 2Y5
Phone: (416)596-5523
Fax: (416)764-1765
Subject(s): Medicine and Surgery
Circ: (Combined)43,241

**The Villager (35847)**
Redwood Investments Corp.
2323 Bloor St. W. Ste. 206
Toronto, ON, Canada M6S 4W1
Phone: (416)767-3644
Fax: (416)767-4880
Subject(s): Free Newspapers
Circ: (Paid)‡300
 (Free)‡43,200

Circulation: ★ = ABC; △ = BPA; ♦ = CAC; • = CCAB; ❏ = VAC; ⊕ = PO Statement; ‡ = Publisher's Report; Boldface figures = sworn; Light figures = estimated.

# Central Provinces

**Sarnia Lambton Pennysaver (35410)**
Bowes Publishers Ltd.
1383 Confederation St.
Sarnia, ON, Canada N7S 5P1
Phone: (519)336-1100
Fax: (519)336-1833
**Subject(s):** Paid Community Newspapers
**Circ:** 43,000

**Brantford Pennysaver (35338)**
Pennysaver
59 Grandriver St.
Paris, ON, Canada N3L 2N9
Phone: (519)442-7866
Fax: (519)442-3100
**Subject(s):** Shopping Guides
**Circ:** (Free)42,600

**Computing Canada (35592)**
Transcontinental IT Business Group
25 Sheppard Ave. W, Ste. 100
Toronto, ON, Canada M2N 6S7
Phone: (416)733-7600
Fax: (416)227-8324
**Subject(s):** Computers
**Circ:** 42,113

**The Standard (35403)**
The St. Catharines Standard Ltd.
17 Queen St.
Saint Catharines, ON, Canada L2R 5G5
Phone: (905)684-7251
Fax: (905)684-6032
**Subject(s):** Daily Newspapers
**Circ:** (Mon.-Fri.)33,673
(Sat.)42,010

**Computerworld Canada (35420)**
IT World Canada Inc.
55 Town Center Ct., Ste. 302
Scarborough, ON, Canada M1P 4X4
Phone: (416)290-0240
Fax: (416)290-0238
**Subject(s):** Computers
**Circ:** (Controlled)40,000

**Le Droit (35282)**
P O Box
Ottawa, ON, Canada K1G 3J9
Phone: (613)562-0111
Fax: (613)562-6280
**Subject(s):** Daily Newspapers; French
**Circ:** (Mon.-Fri.)★34,288
(Sat.)★39,123

**CAUT (ACPPU) Bulletin (35251)**
Canadian Association of University Teachers/L'Association Canadienne des Professeures et Professeurs d'Universite
2675 Queensview Dr.
Ottawa, ON, Canada K2B 8K2
Phone: (613)820-2270
Fax: (613)820-7244
**Subject(s):** Education
**Circ:** ‡36,000
39,000

**The Chronicle-Journal (35472)**
75 Cumberland St. S
Thunder Bay, ON, Canada P7B 1A3
Phone: (807)343-6200
Fax: (807)345-5991
**Subject(s):** Daily Newspapers
**Circ:** (Sun.)32,075
(Mon.-Fri.)32,981
(Sat.)38,752

**Oakville Beaver (35177)**
Burlington Post
467 Spears Rd.
Oakville, ON, Canada L6K 3S4
Phone: (416)845-3824
Fax: (416)845-3085
**Subject(s):** Paid Community Newspapers
**Circ:** (Paid)562
(Non-paid)38,750

**The Herald (34484)**
Transcontinental Weeklies
1465 St. James St.
Winnipeg, MB, Canada R3H 0W9
Phone: (204)789-0800
Fax: (204)953-4300
**Subject(s):** Free Newspapers
**Circ:** (Free)‡38,505

**This Week Marketplace (36535)**
Yorkton This Week Ltd.
20 3rd Ave. N
PO Box 1300
Yorkton, SK, Canada S3N 2X3
Phone: (306)782-2465
Fax: (306)786-1898
**Subject(s):** Free Newspapers
**Circ:** (Free)38,000

**XTRA! (35859)**
Pink Triangle Press
45 Charles St.
Toronto, ON, Canada M4Y 1R9
Fax: (416)925-6503
**Subject(s):** Gay and Lesbian Interests
**Circ:** (Paid)❏263
(Free)❏37,810

**Markham Economist & Sun (35087)**
Metroland Community Newspaper
9 Heritage Rd.
Markham, ON, Canada L3P 1M3
Fax: (905)294-1538
**Subject(s):** Paid Community Newspapers
**Circ:** (Tues.)37,137
(Sat.)37,248
(Thurs.)37,333

**The Mississauga Booster (35123)**
Metroland
3145 Wolfedale Rd.
Mississauga, ON, Canada L5C 3A9
Phone: (905)273-8111
Fax: (905)273-9119
**Subject(s):** Free Newspapers
**Circ:** (Free)32,000
(Free)36,000

**Ontario Farmer (35057)**
Bowes Publishers Ltd.
1147 Gainsborough Rd.
PO Box 7400
London, ON, Canada N6H 5L5
Phone: (519)471-8520
Fax: (519)471-1892
**Subject(s):** Farm Newspapers
**Circ:** (Non-paid)1,156
(Paid)34,673

**Whig-Standard (35019)**
Whig - Standard
6 Cataraqui St.
PO Box 2300
Kingston, ON, Canada K7L 4O7
Phone: (613)544-5000
Fax: (613)530-4118
**Subject(s):** Daily Newspapers
**Circ:** (Mon.-Fri.)27,169
(Sat.)34,517

**Sault Ste. Marie This Week (35415)**
2 Towers St.
PO Box 188
Sault Sainte Marie, ON, Canada P6A 5L6
Phone: (705)949-6111
Fax: (705)942-8596
**Subject(s):** Paid Community Newspapers
**Circ:** 34,500

**The Times (34505)**
Transcontinental Weeklies
1465 St. James St.
Winnipeg, MB, Canada R3H 0W9
Phone: (204)789-0800
Fax: (204)953-4300
**Subject(s):** Free Newspapers
**Circ:** (Free)‡32,815

**Corriere Canadese/Canadian Courier (35596)**
Multimedia Nova Corp.
101 Wingold Ave.
Toronto, ON, Canada M6B 1P8
Phone: (416)785-4300
Fax: (416)785-7350
**Subject(s):** Paid Community Newspapers; Italian
**Circ:** (Controlled)‡32,630

**Catholic Register (35579)**
Canadian Register Ltd.
1155 Yonge St., Ste. 401
Toronto, ON, Canada M4T 1W2
Phone: (416)934-3410
Fax: (416)934-3409

**Subject(s):** Religious Publications
**Circ:** ‡32,000

**The Wellington Advertiser (34915)**
W.H.A. Publications Ltd.
POB 252
Fergus, ON, Canada N1M 2W8
Fax: (519)843-7607
**Subject(s):** Shopping Guides
**Circ:** (Free)32,000

**Rural Roots (36465)**
The Prince Albert Daily Herald
PO Box 550
Prince Albert, SK, Canada S6V 5R9
**Subject(s):** Farm Newspapers
**Circ:** (Controlled)31,992

**Cambridge Times (34837)**
1460 Bishop St.
Cambridge, ON, Canada N1R 7N6
Phone: (519)623-7395
Fax: (519)623-9155
**Subject(s):** Free Newspapers
**Circ:** (Free)‡31,400

**Richmond Hill Post (35784)**
Post City Magazines
30 Lesmill Rd.
Toronto, ON, Canada M3B 2T6
Phone: (416)250-7979
Fax: (416)250-1737
**Subject(s):** Free Newspapers
**Circ:** (Free)❏30,591

**Business Executive (35166)**
Advantage Canada Inc.
466 Speers Rd. Ste. 220
Oakville, ON, Canada L6K 3W9
Phone: (905)845-8300
Fax: (905)845-9086
**Subject(s):** Business
**Circ:** (Non-paid)30,000

**Deutsche Presse (German Press) (35608)**
87 Judge Rd
Toronto, ON, Canada M8Z 5B3
Phone: (416)595-9714
Fax: (416)595-9716
**Subject(s):** German; Paid Community Newspapers
**Circ:** ‡30,000

**Niagara Shopping News (35147)**
4949 Victoria Ave.
Niagara Falls, ON, Canada L2E 4C7
Phone: (905)357-2440
Fax: (905)357-1620
**Subject(s):** Shopping Guides
**Circ:** (Free)‡30,000

**The Trailrider (34895)**
14 Hillside Dr. S
Elliot Lake, ON, Canada P5A 1M6
Phone: (705)848-7195
Fax: (705)848-0249
**Subject(s):** (Snowmobiling)
**Circ:** (Controlled)29,500

**Elgin County Market (35407)**
Lambton Sarnia Shopping News
4 Curtis St.
Saint Thomas, ON, Canada N5P 1H4
Phone: (519)631-3782
Fax: (519)631-3759
**Subject(s):** Shopping Guides
**Circ:** (Free)‡29,300

**Pembroke Daily News (35345)**
Osprey Media Group Inc.
186 Alexander St.
PO Box 190
Pembroke, ON, Canada K8A 6X3
Phone: (613)735-3141
Fax: (613)732-2645
**Subject(s):** Daily Newspapers; Free Newspapers
**Circ:** (Wed.)18,794
(Sun.)28,146

**North Toronto Post (35729)**
Post City Magazines
30 Lesmill Rd.
Toronto, ON, Canada M3B 2T6
Phone: (416)250-7979
Fax: (416)250-1737

**Subject(s):** Free Newspapers
**Circ:** (Free)❏28,135

**Investor's Digest of Canada (35667)**
MPL Communications Inc.
133 Richmond St., Ste. 700
Toronto, ON, Canada M5H 3M8
Phone: (416)869-1177
Fax: (416)869-0616
**Subject(s):** Banking, Finance, and Investments
**Circ:** (Paid)25,700
(Non-paid)28,000

**Bayview Post (35503)**
Post City Magazines
30 Lesmill Rd.
Toronto, ON, Canada M3B 2T6
Phone: (416)250-7979
Fax: (416)250-1737
**Subject(s):** Free Newspapers
**Circ:** (Free)❏27,638

**Oxford Shopping News (35960)**
Bowes Publisher Ltd
16 Brock St.
Woodstock, ON, Canada N4S 8A5
Phone: (519)537-6657
Fax: (519)537-8542
**Subject(s):** Shopping Guides
**Circ:** (Free)‡27,580

**Lindsay This Week (35042)**
96 Albert St. S.
Lindsay, ON, Canada K9V 3H7
Phone: (705)324-8600
Fax: (705)324-5694
**Subject(s):** Free Newspapers
**Circ:** (Paid)‡101
(Free)‡27,400

**The Farm Gate and Regional Country News (34910)**
Metroland Printing, Publishing and Distributing Ltd.
424 Main St.
PO Box 850
Exeter, ON, Canada N0M 1S0
Phone: (519)335-1331
**Subject(s):** Farm Newspapers
**Circ:** 25,800

**Thornhill Post (35816)**
Post City Magazines
30 Lesmill Rd.
Toronto, ON, Canada M3B 2T6
Phone: (416)250-7979
Fax: (416)250-1737
**Subject(s):** Free Newspapers
**Circ:** (Free)❏25,806

**Village Post (35846)**
Post City Magazines
30 Lesmill Rd.
Toronto, ON, Canada M3B 2T6
Phone: (416)250-7979
Fax: (416)250-1737
**Subject(s):** Free Newspapers
**Circ:** (Free)❏25,424

**The Sudbury Star (35457)**
33 McKenzie St.
Sudbury, ON, Canada P3C 4Y1
Phone: (705)674-5276
Fax: (705)674-6834
**Subject(s):** Daily Newspapers
**Circ:** (Mon.-Sat.)21,547
(Sun.)25,405

**The Varsity (35844)**
Varsity Publications
University of Toronto
21 Sussex Ave. 2nd Fl.
Toronto, ON, Canada M5S 1J6
Phone: (416)946-7600
Fax: (416)946-7606
**Subject(s):** College Publications
**Circ:** (Free)‡25,000

**Kanata Kourier-Standard (34998)**
Runge Newspapers Inc.
1120 March Rd., Unit C
Kanata, ON, Canada K2K 1X7
Phone: (613)591-3060
Fax: (613)591-8503

**Subject(s):** Free Newspapers
**Circ:** (Paid)50
(Non-paid)24,800

**Waterloo Chronicle (35919)**
Southam (The Fairway Group)
Unit 20-279 Weeber St. N.
Waterloo, ON, Canada N2J 3H8
Phone: (519)886-2830
Fax: (519)886-9383
**Subject(s):** Paid Community Newspapers
**Circ:** 24,500

**Stoney Creek News (35446)**
Brabant Newspapers
333 Arvin Ave.
Stoney Creek, ON, Canada L8E 2M6
Phone: (905)523-5800
Fax: (905)526-1855
**Subject(s):** Free Newspapers
**Circ:** (Free)‡24,000

**The Tribune/Express (34987)**
Compagnie d'edition Andre-Paquette Inc.
299 Main St. E
PO Box 1000
Hawkesbury, ON, Canada K6A 3H1
Phone: (613)632-4155
Fax: (613)632-8601
**Subject(s):** Free Newspapers; French
**Circ:** (Free)23,720

**Plant (35759)**
Rogers Media Publishing
1 Mount Pleasant Rd., 7th Fl.
Toronto, ON, Canada M4Y 2Y5
Phone: (416)596-5523
Fax: (416)764-1765
**Subject(s):** Commerce and Industry
**Circ:** (Paid)●4,596
(Non-paid)●23,681

**The Brantford Expositor (34814)**
The Expositor
53 Dalhousie St.
PO Box 965
Brantford, ON, Canada N3T 5S8
Phone: (519)756-2020
Fax: (519)756-9470
**Subject(s):** Daily Newspapers
**Circ:** (Mon.-Sat.)23,590

**Port Perry Star (35366)**
Chris Hall
188 Mary St.
Port Perry, ON, Canada L9L 1B7
Phone: (905)985-7383
Fax: (905)985-3708
**Subject(s):** Paid Community Newspapers
**Circ:** (Tues.)5,000
(Fri.)23,000

**Sarnia This Week (35412)**
Lambton Sarnia Shopping News
1383 Confederation St.
Sarnia, ON, Canada N7C 5P1
Phone: (519)336-1100
Fax: (519)336-1833
**Subject(s):** Paid Community Newspapers
**Circ:** (Free)6,500
(Paid)23,000

**The Sault Star (35416)**
Osprey Media Group Inc.
145 Old Garden River Rd.
PO Box 460
Sault Sainte Marie, ON, Canada P6A 5M5
Phone: (705)759-3030
Fax: (705)942-8690
**Subject(s):** Daily Newspapers
**Circ:** (Mon.-Sat.)22,525

**Oakville Today (35178)**
871 Equestrian Ct. U-7
Oakville, ON, Canada L6L 6L7
Phone: (905)825-2229
Fax: (905)825-3202
**Subject(s):** Paid Community Newspapers
**Circ:** 22,000

**The Sun Times (35331)**
290, 9th St. E.
Owen Sound, ON, Canada N4K 1N7
Phone: (519)376-2250
Fax: (519)376-7019

**Subject(s):** Daily Newspapers
**Circ:** (Mon.-Thurs.)18,156
(Sat.)18,156
(Fri.)21,951

**The Sarnia Observer (35411)**
140 Front St. S
PO Box 3009
Sarnia, ON, Canada N7T 7M8
Phone: (519)344-3641
Fax: (519)332-2951
**Subject(s):** Daily Newspapers
**Circ:** (Mon.-Sat.)21,917

**Muskoka Advance (34808)**
The Muskoka Sun Ltd.
203-175 Manitoba St.
PO Box 1600
Bracebridge, ON, Canada P1L 1V6
Phone: (705)645-4463
Fax: (705)645-3928
**Subject(s):** Free Newspapers
**Circ:** (Free)21,491

**The Orangeville Banner (35189)**
37 Mill St.
Orangeville, ON, Canada L9W 2M4
Phone: (519)941-1350
Fax: (519)941-9600
**Subject(s):** Paid Community Newspapers
**Circ:** (Paid)●410
(Non-paid)●20,860

**Direction Informatique (35611)**
Transcontinentinal IT Business Group
25 Sheppard Ave. W, Ste. 100
Toronto, ON, Canada M2N 6S7
Phone: (416)733-7600
Fax: (416)227-8324
**Subject(s):** Computers; Communications; French
**Circ:** (Combined)20,585

**Orillia Today (35099)**
Metroland Printing, Publishing & Distributing Ltd.
206-9170 County Rd. 93
Box 77
Mountainview Mall
RR 2
Midland, ON, Canada L4R 4R4
Phone: (705)527-5500
Fax: (705)527-5467
**Subject(s):** Paid Community Newspapers
**Circ:** 20,500

**L'Express (35629)**
17 Carlaw Rd., 2nd Fl.
Toronto, ON, Canada M4M 2R6
Phone: (416)465-2107
Fax: (416)465-3778
**Subject(s):** Paid Community Newspapers; French
**Circ:** (Non-paid)5,000
(Paid)20,000

**The Muskokan (34809)**
16 Manitoba St.
PO Box 1049
Bracebridge, ON, Canada P1L 1V2
Phone: (705)645-8771
Fax: (705)645-1718
**Subject(s):** Travel and Tourism
**Circ:** (Free)20,000

**Polish Canadian Courier/Nowy Kurier (35763)**
Jolanta Cabaj
12 Foch Ave.
Toronto, ON, Canada M5S 2S7
Phone: (416)259-4353
Fax: (416)259-4353
**Subject(s):** Paid Community Newspapers
**Circ:** 20,000

**Chatham This Week (34842)**
Netmar Inc.
930 Richmond St.
Chatham, ON, Canada N7M 5J5
Phone: (519)351-7331
Fax: (519)351-7774
**Subject(s):** Free Newspapers
**Circ:** (Non-paid)19,949

Circulation: ★ = ABC; △ = BPA; ♦ = CAC; ● = CCAB; ❏ = VAC; ⊕ = PO Statement; ‡ = Publisher's Report; Boldface figures = sworn; Light figures = estimated.

## Central Provinces

**The North Bay Nugget**  (35152)
Southam News Inc.
PO Box 570
259 Worthington West
North Bay, ON, Canada P1B 3B5
Phone: (705)472-3200
Fax: (705)472-5128
**Subject(s):** Daily Newspapers

Circ: (Mon.-Thurs.)17,306
(Fri.)19,740
(Sat.)19,740

**The Daily Press, E.M.C.**  (35484)
The Daily Press
187 Cedar St. S.
PO Box 560
Timmins, ON, Canada P4N 7G1
Phone: (705)268-5050
Fax: (705)268-7373
**Subject(s):** Free Newspapers

Circ: (Non-paid)19,663

**Regional Optimist/Advertiser-Post**  (36458)
Battlefords Publishing Ltd.
892 104 St.
PO Box 1029
North Battleford, SK, Canada S9A 3E6
Phone: (306)445-7261
Fax: (306)445-3223
**Subject(s):** Shopping Guides

Circ: (Free)‡19,605

**Moose Jaw This Week**  (36449)
44 Fairford St. W.
Moose Jaw, SK, Canada S6H 1V1
Phone: (306)692-6441
Fax: (306)692-2101
**Subject(s):** Free Newspapers

Circ: (Free)‡19,478

**The Southwest Booster**  (36517)
30 4th Ave. NW
PO Box 1330
Swift Current, SK, Canada S9H 3X4
Phone: (306)773-9321
Fax: (306)773-9136
**Subject(s):** Shopping Guides

Circ: (Free)19,100

**Brandon Sun**  (34412)
501 Rosser Ave.
Brandon, MB, Canada R7A 0K4
Phone: (204)727-2451
Fax: (204)727-0385
**Subject(s):** Daily Newspapers

Circ: (Sun.)★13,007
(Mon.-Fri.)★14,350
(Sat.)★18,926

**The Collingwood Connection**  (35095)
Metroland Printing, Publishing & Distributing Ltd.
206-9170 County Rd. 93
Box 77
Mountainview Mall
RR 2
Midland, ON, Canada L4R 4R4
Phone: (705)527-5500
Fax: (705)527-5467
**Subject(s):** Paid Community Newspapers

Circ: 18,849

**The Timmins Times**  (35486)
815 Pine St. S
Timmins, ON, Canada P4N 8F3
Phone: (705)268-6252
Fax: (705)268-2255
**Subject(s):** Paid Community Newspapers

Circ: (Paid)13
(Non-paid)18,772

**Computer Dealer News**  (35591)
Transcontinental IT Business Group
25 Sheppard Ave. W, Ste. 100
Toronto, ON, Canada M2N 6S7
Phone: (416)733-7600
Fax: (416)227-8324
**Subject(s):** Computers

Circ: 18,729

**The Midland Mirror**  (35098)
Metroland Printing, Publishing & Distributing Ltd.
206-9170 County Rd. 93
Box 77
Mountainview Mall
RR 2
Midland, ON, Canada L4R 4R4
Phone: (705)527-5500
Fax: (705)527-5467
**Subject(s):** Paid Community Newspapers

Circ: (Combined)18,200

**Canadian Flight**  (35216)
Canadian Owners and Pilots Association
75 Albert St., Ste. 207
Ottawa, ON, Canada K1P 5E7
Phone: (613)236-4901
Fax: (613)236-8646
**Subject(s):** Aviation

Circ: ‡18,000

**The Review**  (35148)
PO Box 270
Niagara Falls, ON, Canada L2E 6T6
**Subject(s):** Daily Newspapers

Circ: (Mon.-Sat.)17,788

**Canadian Mennonite**  (35908)
Mennonite Publishing Service
490 Dutton Dr., Unit C5
Waterloo, ON, Canada N2L 6H7
Phone: (519)884-3810
Fax: (519)884-3331
**Subject(s):** Religious Publications

Circ: ‡17,500

**Regional News This Week**  (34836)
Web Craft Ltd.
345 Argyle St. S
Caledonia, ON, Canada N3W 1L8
Phone: (905)765-4210
Fax: (905)765-3563
**Subject(s):** Paid Community Newspapers

Circ: 17,500

**The Selkirk Journal**  (34455)
Interlake Publishing Co.
486 Main St.
PO Box 190
Stonewall, MB, Canada R0C 2Z0
Phone: (204)467-8402
Fax: (204)467-5967
**Subject(s):** Paid Community Newspapers

Circ: (Combined)17,128

**The Intelligencer**  (34797)
45 Bridge St. E
PO Box 5600
Belleville, ON, Canada K8N 1L5
Phone: (613)962-9171
Fax: (613)962-9652
**Subject(s):** Daily Newspapers

Circ: (Sun.)16,235
(Mon.-Fri.)16,825

**Simcoe and Nanticoke Times**  (35432)
395 QueensWay W
PO Box 370
Simcoe, ON, Canada N3R 4L2
Phone: (519)426-5710
Fax: (519)426-9255
**Subject(s):** Free Newspapers

Circ: (Wed.)‡16,680
(Sat.)‡16,680

**Ontario Restaurant News**  (35127)
Ishcom Publications Ltd.
2065 Dundas St. E, Ste. 201
Mississauga, ON, Canada L4X 2W1
Phone: (905)206-0150
Fax: (905)206-9972
**Subject(s):** Hotels, Motels, Restaurants, and Clubs

Circ: 16,500

**Le Carillon**  (34986)
Compagnie d'Edition Andre Paquette Inc.
299 est, rue Principale
C.P. 1000
Hawkesbury, ON, Canada K6A 3H1
Phone: (613)632-4155
Fax: (613)632-8601
**Subject(s):** Paid Community Newspapers; French

Circ: (Paid)‡450
(Free)‡16,300

**Bayside-North Pennysaver**  (35187)
Results Media
205-101 Worthington St. E
N Bay
Ontario, ON, Canada P1B 1G5
Phone: (705)495-1581
Fax: (705)495-8585
**Subject(s):** Shopping Guides

Circ: (Free)‡16,255

**Nipawin N.E. Region Community Booster**  (36455)
Bowes Publishers Ltd.
PO Box 2014
Nipawin, SK, Canada S0E 1E0
Phone: (306)862-4618
Fax: (306)862-4566
**Subject(s):** Paid Community Newspapers

Circ: (Paid)‡16,046

**Creemore Echo**  (34866)
Creemore Echo Communications
176 Mill St.
PO Box 180
Creemore, ON, Canada L0M 1G0
Phone: (705)466-9906
Fax: (705)466-9908
**Subject(s):** Free Newspapers

Circ: (Combined)16,000

**The Gazette**  (35050)
University of Western Ontario
Rm. 267
UCC Bldg. UWO
London, ON, Canada N6A 3K7
Phone: (519)661-3960
Fax: (519)661-3960
**Subject(s):** College Publications

Circ: (Free)‡16,000

**Mainly for Seniors Lambton-Kent**  (35357)
Osprey Media Group
PO Box 40
4182 Petrolia Line
Petrolia, ON, Canada N0N 1R0
Phone: (519)882-1770
Fax: (519)882-3212
**Subject(s):** Senior Citizens' Interests; Free Newspapers

Circ: (Free)16,000

**MSOS Journal**  (34499)
Manitoba Society of Seniors
Ste. 202-232 Portage Ave.
Winnipeg, MB, Canada R3B 2C1
Phone: (204)942-3147
Fax: (204)943-1290
**Subject(s):** Senior Citizens' Interests; Free Newspapers

Circ: (Paid)‡14,000
(Free)‡16,000

**The Parkland Review**  (36519)
Pasquia Publishing
Box 1660
1004-102 Ave.
Tisdale, SK, Canada S0E 1T0
Phone: (306)873-4515
Fax: (306)873-4712
**Subject(s):** Shopping Guides

Circ: (Free)‡15,769

**Crow Wing Warrior**  (34433)
Doug Penner
Box 578
Morris, MB, Canada R0G 1K0
Phone: (204)746-2823
Fax: (204)746-8867
**Subject(s):** Free Newspapers

Circ: (Free)‡15,300

**Georgina Advocate**  (35004)
461 The Queensway S.
Keswick, ON, Canada L4P 2C3
Phone: (905)476-7753
Fax: (905)476-5785
**Subject(s):** Paid Community Newspapers

Circ: (Paid)‡200
(Free)‡15,309

**Standard-Freeholder**  (34863)
44 Pitt St.
Cornwall, ON, Canada K6J 3P3
Phone: (613)933-3160
Fax: (613)933-7521
**Subject(s):** Daily Newspapers

Circ: (Mon.-Sat.)15,100

**Chatham Daily News** (34841)
45 4th St.
PO Box 2007
Chatham, ON, Canada N7M 2G4
Phone: (519)354-2000
Fax: (519)436-0949
Subject(s): Daily Newspapers
Circ: (Mon.-Sat.)14,926

**The Tribune** (35927)
228 E. Main St.
Welland, ON, Canada L3B 5P5
Phone: (905)732-2411
Fax: (905)732-3660
Subject(s): Daily Newspapers
Circ: (Paid)•14,601

**Guelph Mercury** (34946)
8-14 Macdonnell St.
PO Box 3604
Guelph, ON, Canada N1H 6P7
Phone: (519)822-4310
Fax: (519)767-1681
Subject(s): Daily Newspapers
Circ: (Mon.-Sat.)14,500

**The Lawyers Weekly** (35086)
LexisNexis Canada Inc.
Ste. 700, 123 Commerce Valley Dr. E
Markham, ON, Canada L3T 7W8
Phone: (905)479-2665
Fax: (905)479-2826
Subject(s): Law
Circ: (Paid)5,555
 (Controlled)14,357

**The Renfrew Weekend News** (35371)
Runge Publishing Inc.
35 Opeongo Rd.
PO Box 400
Renfrew, ON, Canada K7V 4A8
Phone: (613)432-3655
Fax: (613)432-6689
Subject(s): Free Newspapers
Circ: (Non-paid)14,352

**West-Central Crossroads** (36433)
Jamac Publishing Ltd.
919 Main St.
PO Box 1150
Kindersley, SK, Canada S0L 1S0
Phone: (306)463-4611
Fax: (306)463-6505
Subject(s): Shopping Guides
Circ: (Free)⊕14,300

**The Free Press This Week** (35097)
The Free Press
248 1st St.
PO Box 37
Midland, ON, Canada L4R 4K6
Phone: (705)526-5431
Fax: (705)526-1771
Subject(s): Free Newspapers
Circ: (Non-paid)14,211

**Napanee Beaver** (35139)
Napanee Beaver Publishers
72 Dundas St. E
Napanee, ON, Canada K7R 1H9
Phone: (613)354-6641
Fax: (613)354-2622
Subject(s): Paid Community Newspapers
Circ: (Wed.)3,679
 (Fri.)14,188

**Brighton Independent** (34818)
Conolly Publishing Ltd.
1 Young St.
PO Box 1030
Brighton, ON, Canada K0K 1H0
Phone: (613)475-0255
Fax: (613)475-4546
Subject(s): Paid Community Newspapers
Circ: (Paid)439
 (Controlled)14,091

**University of Toronto Bulletin** (35837)
University of Toronto
21 King's College Cir.
Toronto, ON, Canada M5S 3J3
Phone: (416)978-6981
Fax: (416)978-1632
Subject(s): Education; Free Newspapers
Circ: (Controlled)14,051

**The Brockville Recorder and Times** (34819)
The Recorder and Times Ltd.
1600 California Ave.
Bag 10
Brockville, ON, Canada K6V 5T8
Phone: (613)342-4441
Fax: (613)342-4542
Subject(s): Daily Newspapers
Circ: (Mon.-Sat.)13,479

**Interlake Spectator** (34454)
486 Main St.
PO Box 190
Stonewall, MB, Canada R0C 2V0
Phone: (204)467-2421
Fax: (204)467-5967
Subject(s): Free Newspapers
Circ: (Free)‡13,316

**Chronicle Weekender** (34756)
Chronicle-Guide Newspapers Ltd.
116 John St. N
Arnprior, ON, Canada K7S 2N6
Phone: (613)623-6571
Fax: (613)623-7518
Subject(s): Free Newspapers
Circ: (Non-paid)13,300

**The Manitoba Co-operator** (34489)
Agricore United
PO Box 9800
Winnipeg, MB, Canada R3C 3K7
Phone: (204)954-1400
Fax: (204)954-1422
Subject(s): Farm Newspapers
Circ: (Paid)13,025

**Manitoban** (34493)
The University of Manitoba
105 University Centre
Winnipeg, MB, Canada R3T 2N2
Phone: (204)474-6535
Fax: (204)474-7651
Subject(s): College Publications
Circ: ‡13,000

**East Central Connection** (36526)
East Central Press Ltd.
PO Box 576
Watson, SK, Canada S0K 4V0
Phone: (306)287-4388
Fax: (306)287-3308
Subject(s): Paid Community Newspapers
Circ: ‡12,642

**Booster** (36528)
Weyburn Review
Box 400
904 E. Ave.
Weyburn, SK, Canada S4H 2K4
Phone: (306)842-7487
Fax: (306)842-0282
Subject(s): Shopping Guides
Circ: (Free)‡12,508

**The Beacon Herald** (35449)
The Beacon Herald of Stratford Ltd.
16 Packham Rd
PO Box 430
Stratford, ON, Canada N5A 6T6
Phone: (519)271-1026
Subject(s): Daily Newspapers
Circ: (Mon.-Sat.)12,269

**Flamborough Review** (35085)
Osprey Media Group Inc.
Ste. 110 100 Renfrew Dr.
Markham, ON, Canada L3R 9R6
Phone: (905)752-1132
Subject(s): Paid Community Newspapers
Circ: ‡12,223

**Preeceville Progress** (36409)
Canora Courier Ltd.
Box 746
Canora, SK, Canada S0A 0L0
Phone: (306)563-5131
Fax: (306)563-6144
Subject(s): Paid Community Newspapers
Circ: ‡1,1675

**The Courier Press** (35904)
Lambton Sarnia Shopping News
820 Dufferin Ave.
Wallaceburg, ON, Canada N8A 2V4
Phone: (519)627-1488
Fax: (519)627-0640
Subject(s): Free Newspapers
Circ: (Free)‡11,600

**Orangeville Citizen** (35190)
10 First St.
Orangeville, ON, Canada L9W 2C4
Phone: (519)941-2230
Fax: (519)941-9361
Subject(s): Free Newspapers
Circ: (Free)11,600

**Trader Express** (36417)
Boundry Publishers Ltd.
PO Box 730
Estevan, SK, Canada S4A 2A6
Phone: (306)634-2654
Fax: (306)634-3934
Subject(s): Shopping Guides
Circ: (Free)11,484

**The Barrie Examiner** (34782)
The Barrie Examiner Inc.
571 Bayfield St. N.
Barrie, ON, Canada L4M 4Z9
Phone: (705)726-6537
Fax: (705)726-7245
Subject(s): Daily Newspapers
Circ: (Mon.-Sat.)11,446

**Network Cabling Magazine** (35723)
Kerrwil Publications Ltd.
195, The W. Mall Ste. 500
49 Bather St. Ste.
Toronto, ON, Canada M9C 5K1
Phone: (416)703-7167
Subject(s): Telecommunications
Circ: (Combined)11,237

**The Carillon** (34450)
Derksen Printers Ltd.
377 Main
PO Box 1209
Steinbach, MB, Canada R0A 2A0
Phone: (204)326-3421
Fax: (204)326-4860
Subject(s): Paid Community Newspapers
Circ: (Thurs.)11,004

**Imprint** (35913)
Imprint Publications
University of Waterloo
200 University Ave. W.
Student Life Ctr., Rm. 1116
Waterloo, ON, Canada N2L 3G1
Phone: (519)888-4048
Fax: (519)884-7800
Subject(s): College Publications
Circ: (Paid)50
 (Free)11,000

**Northern Times** (34999)
51 Riverside Dr.
Kapuskasing, ON, Canada P5N 1A7
Phone: (705)335-2283
Fax: (705)337-1222
Subject(s): Paid Community Newspapers
Circ: ‡4,600
 10,829

**Market Connection** (36516)
Last Mountain Times Ltd.
103 1st Ave. W
PO Box 340
Nokomis, SK, Canada S0G 3R0
Phone: (306)528-2020
Fax: (306)528-2090
Subject(s): Free Newspapers
Circ: (Non-paid)⊕10,700

**El Popular** (35616)
2413 Dundas St. W
Toronto, ON, Canada M6P 1X3
Phone: (416)531-2495
Fax: (416)531-7187
Subject(s): Daily Newspapers; Spanish; Hispanic Publications
Circ: ‡10,500

Circulation: ★ = ABC; △ = BPA; ♦ = CAC; • = CCAB; ☐ = VAC; ⊕ = PO Statement; ‡ = Publisher's Report; Boldface figures = sworn; Light figures = estimated.

# Central Provinces

**Herald Leader Press** (34439)
Bowes Publishers Ltd.
1941 Saskatchewan Ave. W
PO Box 130
Portage La Prairie, MB, Canada R1N 3B4
Phone: (204)857-3427
Fax: (204)239-1270
**Subject(s):** Paid Community Newspapers
Circ: ‡10,500

**The Silhouette** (34991)
McMaster Students Union Inc.
McMaster University Student Centre, Room B110
McMaster University
1280 Main St. W
Hmilton, ON, Canada L8S 4S4
Phone: (905)523-0107
**Subject(s):** College Publications
Circ: 10,500

**The Times** (34922)
Southam Inc.
450 Garrison Rd. Unit 1
Fort Erie, ON, Canada I2A 1N2
Phone: (905)871-3100
Fax: (905)871-5243
**Subject(s):** Free Newspapers
Circ: (Paid)‡69
(Free)‡10,500

**The Daily Press** (35483)
187 Cedar St. S.
PO Box 560
Timmins, ON, Canada P4N 7G1
Phone: (705)268-5050
Fax: (705)268-7373
**Subject(s):** Daily Newspapers
Circ: (Mon.-Sat.)10,343
(Sat.)10,457

**PrintAction** (35767)
Youngblood Publishing Ltd.
4580 Dufferin St., Ste. 404
Toronto, ON, Canada M3H 5Y2
Phone: (416)665-7333
Fax: (416)665-7226
**Subject(s):** Printing and Typography
Circ: (Combined)10,287

**Catch da Flava** (35575)
Regent Park Focus Community Coalition
600 Dundas St. E., Rear Basement
Toronto, ON, Canada M5A 2B9
Phone: (416)863-1074
Fax: (416)863-9440
**Subject(s):** Youths' Interests
Circ: (Non-paid)10,000

**The Charlatan** (35252)
Charlatan Publications Inc.
Carleton University
Rm. 531 Unicentre
1125 Colonel By Dr.
Ottawa, ON, Canada K1S 5B6
Phone: (613)520-6680
Fax: (613)520-4051
**Subject(s):** College Publications
Circ: (Free)‡10,000

**The Fulcrum** (35264)
Student Federation of the University of Ottawa
631 King Edward St.
07-85 University Pr.
Ottawa, ON, Canada K1N 6N5
Phone: (613)562-5260
Fax: (613)562-5259
**Subject(s):** College Publications
Circ: 10,000

**Journal Le Voyageur** (35455)
Publications Voyageur Inc.
525 Notre Dame Avenue
Sudbury, ON, Canada P3C 5L1
Phone: (705)673-3377
Fax: (705)673-5854
**Subject(s):** Paid Community Newspapers; French
Circ: 10,000

**Law Times** (34771)
Canada Law Book Inc.
240 Edward St.
Aurora, ON, Canada L4G 3S9
Phone: (905)841-6481
Fax: (905)727-0017
**Subject(s):** Law
Circ: (Non-paid)3,800
(Paid)10,000

**Picton Gazette** (35359)
Napanee Beaver Publishers
267 Main St.
Box 80
Picton, ON, Canada K0K 2T0
Phone: (613)476-3201
Fax: (613)476-3464
**Subject(s):** Paid Community Newspapers
Circ: (Wed.)3,033
(Fri.)10,000

**Queen's Journal** (35017)
272 Earl St.
Kingston, ON, Canada K7L 2H8
Phone: (613)533-2800
Fax: (613)533-6728
**Subject(s):** College Publications
Circ: ‡10,000

**The Sheaf** (36501)
Sheaf Publishing Society
Rm. 108 Memorial Union Bldg.
93 Campus Dr.
Saskatoon, SK, Canada S7N 5B2
Phone: (306)966-8687
Fax: (306)966-8699
**Subject(s):** College Publications
Circ: (Free)‡10,000

**University of Western Ontario Gazette** (35062)
University of Western Ontario
Rm. 263, U.C.C. Bldg.
London, ON, Canada N6A 3K7
Phone: (519)661-3580
Fax: (519)661-3825
**Subject(s):** Free Newspapers
Circ: 10,000

**The Simcoe Reformer** (35433)
105 Donly Dr.
Simcoe, ON, Canada N3Y 4L2
Phone: (519)426-5710
Fax: (519)426-9255
**Subject(s):** Daily Newspapers
Circ: (Mon.-Fri.)9,618

**LaSalle Silhouette** (35037)
Silhouetee Publications
PO Box 20012
LaSalle, ON, Canada N9J 3E5
Phone: (519)250-0816
Fax: (519)250-0189
**Subject(s):** Free Newspapers
Circ: (Non-paid)9,500

**The Daily Sentinel-Review** (35959)
Bowes Publisher Ltd
16-18 Brock St.
PO Box 1000
Woodstock, ON, Canada N4S 3B4
Phone: (519)537-6657
Fax: (519)537-3049
**Subject(s):** Daily Newspapers
Circ: 9,324

**Weyburn This Week** (36530)
A.R. Heath Publishing Ltd.
19-11th St. NE
Weyburn, SK, Canada S4H 1J1
Phone: (306)842-3900
Fax: (306)842-2515
**Subject(s):** Free Newspapers
Circ: (Controlled)‡9,315

**Yorkton This Week** (36537)
Yorkton This Week Ltd.
20 3rd Ave. N
PO Box 1300
Yorkton, SK, Canada S3N 2X3
Phone: (306)782-2465
Fax: (306)786-1898
**Subject(s):** Paid Community Newspapers
Circ: 9,272

**The Canadian Champion** (35102)
Burlington Post
Box 248
Milton, ON, Canada L9T 4N9
Phone: (416)878-2341
Fax: (416)878-4943
**Subject(s):** Paid Community Newspapers
Circ: (Paid)2,139
(Non-paid)9,243

**Ottawa Jewish Bulletin** (35294)
Jewish Community Council of Ottawa
21 Nadolny Sachs Private
Ottawa, ON, Canada K2A 1R9
Phone: (613)798-4696
Fax: (613)798-4730
**Subject(s):** Jewish Publications; Paid Community Newspapers
Circ: (Controlled)9,200

**Wawatay News** (35435)
Wawatay Native Communications Society
16 5th Ave.
PO Box 1180
Sioux Lookout, ON, Canada P8T 1B7
Phone: (807)737-2951
Fax: (807)737-3224
**Subject(s):** Paid Community Newspapers; Native American Interests
Circ: ‡9,200

**The Moose Jaw Times-Herald** (36450)
44 Fairford St. W
Moose Jaw, SK, Canada S6H 1V1
Phone: (306)692-6441
Fax: (306)692-2101
**Subject(s):** Daily Newspapers
Circ: (Paid)9,100

**Golden Words** (35010)
Queen's University Engineering Society
Queen's University
Kingston, ON, Canada K7L 3N6
Phone: (613)533-3051
Fax: (613)533-3233
**Subject(s):** College Publications
Circ: (Paid)‡20
(Free)‡9,000

**PIC Press** (34927)
1000 Islands Publishers Ltd.
79 King St. E
Gananoque, ON, Canada K7G 1E8
Phone: (613)382-2156
Fax: (613)382-3010
**Subject(s):** Free Newspapers
Circ: (Non-paid)9,000

**Uxbridge Times-Journal** (35900)
Metroland Printing, Publishing and Distribution
16 Bascom St.
PO Box 459
Uxbridge, ON, Canada L9P 1M9
Phone: (905)852-9141
Fax: (905)852-9341
**Subject(s):** Paid Community Newspapers
Circ: ‡9,000

**Prince Albert Daily Herald** (36464)
30 10th St. E
PO Box 550
Prince Albert, SK, Canada S6V 0Y5
Phone: (306)764-4276
Fax: (306)763-3331
**Subject(s):** Daily Newspapers
Circ: (Mon.-Sat.)8,675

**St. Thomas Times-Journal** (35409)
Bowes Publishers Ltd.
16 Hincks St.
Saint Thomas, ON, Canada N5R 5Z2
Phone: (519)631-5653
Fax: (800)663-3410
**Subject(s):** Daily Newspapers
Circ: (Mon.-Sat.)8,611

**Daily Packet and Times** (35192)
Orillia Packet and Times
31 Colborne St.E.
PO Box 220
Orillia, ON, Canada L3V 1T4
Phone: (705)325-1355
Fax: (705)329-5926
**Subject(s):** Daily Newspapers
Circ: (Mon.-Sat.)8,583

**Playback** (35761)
Brunico Communications Inc.
366 Adelaide St. W, Ste. 500
Toronto, ON, Canada M5V 1R9
Phone: (416)408-2300

Fax: (416)408-0870
**Subject(s):** Radio, Television, Cable, and Video; Motion Pictures

**Circ:** (Controlled)‡8,500

**Malton Pennysaver** (35072)
Pennysaver
56 Bramsteele Rd., Unit 1
Brampton, ON, Canada L6W 3M7
Phone: (905)454-0854
Fax: (905)450-5792
**Subject(s):** Shopping Guides

**Circ:** (Free)8,360

**The Korea Times Daily** (35687)
The Korea Times
287 Bridgeland Ave.
Toronto, ON, Canada M6H 1X2
Phone: (416)781-7777
Fax: (416)781-7777
**Subject(s):** Daily Newspapers; Korean

**Circ:** (Free)‡1,500
(Paid)‡8,200

**La Rotonde** (35281)
University of Ottawa Students' Federation
85 University (UCU), Rm. 0025
Ottawa, ON, Canada K1N 6N5
Phone: (613)562-5264
Fax: (613)562-5265
**Subject(s):** French; College Publications

**Circ:** ‡8,000

**The Marketplace** (34893)
The Standard
14 Hillside Dr. S
Elliot Lake, ON, Canada P5A 1M6
Phone: (705)848-7195
Fax: (705)848-0249
**Subject(s):** Shopping Guides

**Circ:** (Controlled)8,000

**Restoration** (34859)
2888 Dafoe Rd.
Combermere, ON, Canada K0J 1L0
Phone: (613)756-3713
Fax: (613)756-0211
**Subject(s):** Religious Publications

**Circ:** (Paid)8,000

**Rider** (34754)
1393104 Ontario Ltd.
487 Book Rd. W
Ancaster, ON, Canada L9G 3L1
Phone: (905)648-2035
Fax: (905)648-6977
**Subject(s):** (Horses and Horse Racing)

**Circ:** ‡8,000

**The South Asian Voice** (35180)
Directories International Ltd.
1235 Trapalgar Rd.
P.O. Box 89021
Oakville, ON, Canada L6H 3J0
Phone: (905)337-3030
Fax: (905)338-1364
**Subject(s):** Paid Community Newspapers; Ethnic Publications; Urdu

**Circ:** (Paid)35
(Non-paid)8,000

**The Underground** (35429)
Scarborough College Student Press
University of Toronto
1265 Military Trail.
Rm.207 ( students centre )
Scarborough, ON, Canada M1C 1A4
Phone: (416)287-7054
Fax: (416)287-7055
**Subject(s):** College Publications

**Circ:** (Free)8,000

**Trentonian and Tri-County News** (35886)
Ursbry
41 Quinte St.
PO Box 130
Trenton, ON, Canada K8V 5R3
Phone: (613)392-6501
Fax: (613)392-0505
**Subject(s):** Paid Community Newspapers

**Circ:** 7,958

**The Tillsonburg News** (35482)
25 Townline Rd.
PO Box 190
Tillsonburg, ON, Canada N4G 2R5
Phone: (519)688-6397
Fax: (519)842-3511
**Subject(s):** Paid Community Newspapers

**Circ:** 7,694

**The Herald (Visnyk)** (34485)
Ecclesia Publishing Corp.
9 St. Johns Ave.
Winnipeg, MB, Canada R2W 1G8
Phone: (204)586-3093
Fax: (204)582-5241
**Subject(s):** Ukrainian; Religious Publications

**Circ:** (Non-paid)250
(Paid)‡7,500

**Temiskaming Speaker** (35144)
Temiskaming Printing Company Ltd.
18 Wellington St.
PO Box 580
New Liskeard, ON, Canada P0J 1P0
Phone: (705)647-6791
Fax: (705)647-9669
**Subject(s):** Paid Community Newspapers

**Circ:** (Combined)7,400

**The Winkler Times** (34466)
Bowes Publishers Inc.
324 S. Railway St.
PO Box 1356
Winkler, MB, Canada R6W 4B3
**Subject(s):** Free Newspapers

**Circ:** 7,264

**Carman Valley Leader** (34418)
Interlake Publishing Co.
PO Box 70
Carman, MB, Canada R0G 0J0
Phone: (204)745-2051
Fax: (204)745-3976
**Subject(s):** Paid Community Newspapers

**Circ:** (Combined)‡7,100

**Voice of the Lambton Farmer** (35035)
York Region Printing
254 Main St.
Dresden, ON, Canada N0P 1M0
Phone: (519)683-4485
Fax: (519)683-4355
**Subject(s):** Farm Newspapers; Free Newspapers

**Circ:** (Free)‡7,070

**Catholic New Times** (35578)
80 Sackville St.
Toronto, ON, Canada M5A 3E5
Phone: (416)361-0761
Fax: (416)361-0796
**Subject(s):** Religious Publications

**Circ:** ‡7,000

**Parry Sound North Star** (35425)
IT World Canada Inc.
55 Town Center Ct., Ste. 302
Scarborough, ON, Canada M1P 4X4
Phone: (416)290-0240
Fax: (416)290-0238
**Subject(s):** Paid Community Newspapers

**Circ:** 7,000

**Observer** (35344)
Osprey Media
186 Alexander St.
PO Box 190
Pembroke, ON, Canada K8A 4L9
Phone: (613)732-3691
Fax: (613)732-2645
**Subject(s):** Daily Newspapers

**Circ:** (Mon.-Sat.)6,867

**Thompson Nickel Belt News** (34459)
Precambrian Press Publishers
141 Commercial Pl.
PO Box 887
Thompson, MB, Canada R8N 1N8
Phone: (204)677-4534
Fax: (204)677-3681
**Subject(s):** Paid Community Newspapers

**Circ:** ‡6,721

**The Glengarry News** (34751)
The Glengarry News Ltd.
3 Main St. S.
PO Box 10
Alexandria, ON, Canada K0C 1A0
Phone: (613)525-2020
Fax: (613)525-3824
**Subject(s):** Paid Community Newspapers

**Circ:** (Wed.)6,596

**Huntsville Forester** (34992)
11 Main St., W.
PO Box 940
Huntsville, ON, Canada P1H 2C5
Phone: (705)789-5541
Fax: (705)789-9381
**Subject(s):** Paid Community Newspapers

**Circ:** (Wed.)6,515

**Stouffville Sun** (35447)
34 Civic Ave
PO Box 154
Stouffville, ON, Canada L3P 1M3
Phone: (905)640-2612
Fax: (905)640-8778
**Subject(s):** Paid Community Newspapers

**Circ:** ‡6,500

**The Red River Valley Echo** (34407)
Bowes Publishers Ltd.
Box 700
Altona, MB, Canada R0G 0B0
Phone: (204)324-5001
Fax: (204)324-1402
**Subject(s):** Paid Community Newspapers

**Circ:** ‡6,423

**Voice of the Middlesex Farmer** (35093)
York Region Printing
254 Main St.
Dresden, ON, Canada N0P 1M0
Phone: (519)683-4485
**Subject(s):** Farm Newspapers; Free Newspapers

**Circ:** (Free)‡6,350

**Ancaster News-Journal** (34753)
Brabant Newspapers
47 Cootes Dr.
Ancaster, ON, Canada L9H 1B5
Phone: (905)628-2295
Fax: (905)526-1855
**Subject(s):** Free Newspapers

**Circ:** (Free)6,311

**Dauphin Herald** (34421)
120 1st Ave., NE
PO Box 548
Dauphin, MB, Canada R7N 2V3
Phone: (204)638-4420
Fax: (204)638-8760
**Subject(s):** Paid Community Newspapers

**Circ:** ‡6,300

**West Carleton Review** (34758)
Chronicle-Guide Newspapers Ltd.
116 John St. N
Arnprior, ON, Canada K7S 2N6
Phone: (613)623-6571
Fax: (613)623-7518
**Subject(s):** Free Newspapers

**Circ:** (Non-paid)6,300

**Woodbridge Advertiser** (34793)
PO Box 379
Beeton, ON, Canada L0G 1A0
Phone: (905)729-4501
Fax: (905)729-3961
**Subject(s):** Shopping Guides

**Circ:** ‡6,200

**Ft. Frances Times and Rainy Lake Herald** (34924)
116 1st St.
PO Box 339
Fort Frances, ON, Canada P9A 3M7
Phone: (807)274-5373
Fax: (807)274-7286
**Subject(s):** Paid Community Newspapers

**Circ:** (Wed.)6,114

**The Almaguin News** (34823)
Almaguin Publishing
185 Ontario St.
PO Box 518
Burks Falls, ON, Canada P0A 1C0
Phone: (705)382-3843

Circulation: ★ = ABC; △ = BPA; ♦ = CAC; ● = CCAB; ❑ = VAC; ⊖ = PO Statement; ‡ = Publisher's Report; Boldface figures = sworn; Light figures = estimated.

**Central Provinces**

Fax: (705)382-3440
**Subject(s):** Paid Community Newspapers
**Circ:** 6,000

**The Cord  (35910)**
Wilfrid Laurier University Student Publications
75 University Ave. W.
Waterloo, ON, Canada N2L 3C5
Phone: (519)884-1970
Fax: (519)886-9351
**Subject(s):** College Publications
**Circ:** (Free)‡6,000

**The Eganville Leader  (34892)**
Eganville Leader Publishing Ltd.
150 John St., Box 310
Eganville, ON, Canada K0J 1T0
Phone: (613)628-2332
Fax: (613)628-3291
**Subject(s):** Paid Community Newspapers
**Circ:** 6,000

**La Liberte  (34446)**
Presse-Ouest Ltee.
383, boul. Provencher
PO Box 190
Saint Boniface, MB, Canada R2H 3B4
Phone: (204)237-4823
Fax: (204)231-1998
**Subject(s):** Paid Community Newspapers; French
**Circ:** 6,000

**The Niagara Advance  (35902)**
Box 430
Virgil, ON, Canada L0S 1T0
Phone: (905)468-3283
**Subject(s):** Paid Community Newspapers
**Circ:** ‡6,000

**Parry Sound Beacon-Star  (35424)**
IT World Canada Inc.
55 Town Center Ct., Ste. 302
Scarborough, ON, Canada M1P 4X4
Phone: (416)290-0240
Fax: (416)290-0238
**Subject(s):** Paid Community Newspapers
**Circ:** 6,000

**Heartland Shopper  (34434)**
Sundance Publications Ltd.
423 Mountain Ave.
PO Box 939
Neepawa, MB, Canada R0J 1H0
Phone: (204)476-2309
Fax: (204)476-5802
**Subject(s):** Paid Community Newspapers
**Circ:** ‡5,860

**Barry's Bay This Week  (34788)**
Barry's Bay
41 Bay St.
PO Box 220
Barry's Bay, ON, Canada K0J 1B0
Phone: (613)756-2944
Fax: (613)756-2994
**Subject(s):** Paid Community Newspapers
**Circ:** 5,700

**The Northern Daily News  (35026)**
8 Duncan Ave.
PO Box 1030
Kirkland Lake, ON, Canada P2N 3L4
Phone: (705)567-5321
Fax: (705)567-6162
**Subject(s):** Daily Newspapers
**Circ:** (Mon.-Sat.)5,626

**Cobourg Daily Star  (34852)**
Northumberland Publishers Ltd.
99 King St. W.
PO Box 400
Cobourg, ON, Canada K9A 4L1
Phone: (905)372-0131
Fax: (905)372-4966
**Subject(s):** Daily Newspapers
**Circ:** 5,552

**The Goderich Signal-Star  (34935)**
Box 220, Industrial Park
120 Huckins St.
Goderich, ON, Canada N7A 4B6
Phone: (519)524-2614
Fax: (519)524-5145

**Subject(s):** Paid Community Newspapers
**Circ:** 5,512

**The Dryden Observer  (34887)**
Alex Wilson Coldstream Ltd.
32 Colonization Ave.
PO Box 3009
Dryden, ON, Canada P8N 2Y9
Phone: (807)223-2381
Fax: (807)223-2907
**Subject(s):** Paid Community Newspapers
**Circ:** (Tues.)5,500

**The Age Dispatch  (35452)**
Strathroy Age Dispatch Ltd.
8 Front St. E.
Strathroy, ON, Canada N7G 1Y4
Phone: (519)245-2370
Fax: (519)245-1647
**Subject(s):** Paid Community Newspapers
**Circ:** (Paid)5,400

**Manitoulin Expositor  (35044)**
Manitoulin Publishing Company Ltd.
One Manitowaning Rd.
Box 369
Little Current, ON, Canada P0P 1K0
Phone: (705)368-2744
Fax: (705)368-3822
**Subject(s):** Paid Community Newspapers
**Circ:** (Wed.)5,385

**The Canadian Stamp News  (35392)**
Trajan Publishing Corp.
103 Lakeshore Rd., Ste. 202
Saint Catharines, ON, Canada L2N 2T6
Phone: (905)646-7744
Fax: (905)646-0995
**Subject(s):** Collecting
**Circ:** (Paid)‡5,300

**The Grimsby Independent  (34790)**
Printing & Publishing Ltd.
PO Box 400
4991 King St.
Beansville, ON, Canada L0R 1B0
Phone: (905)945-9264
Fax: (905)563-7977
**Subject(s):** Paid Community Newspapers
**Circ:** ‡5,261

**Weyburn Review  (36529)**
Box 400
904 E. Ave.
Weyburn, SK, Canada S4H 2K4
Phone: (306)842-7487
Fax: (306)842-0282
**Subject(s):** Paid Community Newspapers
**Circ:** ‡5,260

**The Estevan Mercury  (36416)**
Boundry Publishers Ltd.
Box 730
Estevan, SK, Canada S4A 2A6
Phone: (306)634-2654
Fax: (306)634-3934
**Subject(s):** Paid Community Newspapers
**Circ:** 5,059

**The Brock Press  (35387)**
Brock University
500 Glen Ridge Ave.
Saint Catharines, ON, Canada L2S 3A1
Phone: (905)688-5550
Fax: (905)641-7581
**Subject(s):** College Publications
**Circ:** (Free)5,000

**The Carillon  (36472)**
University of Regina Students' Union
Rm. 227 Riddell Centre Univ. of Regina
Regina, SK, Canada S4S 0A2
Phone: (306)586-8867
Fax: (306)586-7422
**Subject(s):** College Publications
**Circ:** (Free)‡5,000

**Haliburton County Echo & Minden Recorder  (34953)**
Algonquin Graphics Ltd.
PO Box 360
Haliburton, ON, Canada K0M 1S0
Phone: (705)457-1037
Fax: (705)457-3275

**Subject(s):** Paid Community Newspapers
**Circ:** ‡5,000

**The Impact  (35937)**
Seneca College Student Federation
1750 Finch Ave. E
Willowdale, ON, Canada M2J 2X5
Phone: (416)491-5050
Fax: (416)756-2765
**Subject(s):** College Publications
**Circ:** (Free)5,000

**Leamington Shopper  (35038)**
Leamington Post & Shopper
27 Princess St.
Leamington, ON, Canada N8H 2X8
Phone: (519)326-4434
Fax: (519)326-2171
**Subject(s):** Paid Community Newspapers
**Circ:** (Paid)5,000

**The Advance Review  (35001)**
Advance Printing Ltd.
Box 669
Kemptville, ON, Canada K0G 1J0
Phone: (613)258-3451
Fax: (613)258-7734
**Subject(s):** Paid Community Newspapers
**Circ:** ‡4,900

**The Standard  (34894)**
Osprey Media Group Inc.
14 Hillside Dr. S.
Elliot Lake, ON, Canada P5A 1M6
Phone: (705)848-7195
Fax: (705)848-0249
**Subject(s):** Free Newspapers
**Circ:** (Paid)4,902

**Times-Advocate  (34913)**
PO Box 850
Exeter, ON, Canada E3B 2T8
Phone: (519)235-1331
Fax: (519)235-0766
**Subject(s):** Paid Community Newspapers
**Circ:** 4,900

**Mercury  (35370)**
Renfrew Newspapers
35 Opeongo Rd., Box 400
Renfrew, ON, Canada K7V 4A8
Phone: (613)432-3655
Fax: (613)432-6689
**Subject(s):** Paid Community Newspapers
**Circ:** (Wed.)4,885

**The Lindsay Daily Post  (35041)**
15 William St. N
Lindsay, ON, Canada K9V 3Z8
Phone: (705)324-2113
Fax: (705)324-0174
**Subject(s):** Daily Newspapers
**Circ:** (Combined)4,793

**Bracebridge Examiner Limited  (34807)**
Bracebridge Examiner
PO Box 1049
Bracebridge, ON, Canada P1L 1V2
Phone: (705)645-8771
Fax: (705)645-1718
**Subject(s):** Paid Community Newspapers
**Circ:** 4,750

**Stonewall Argus & Teulon Times  (34456)**
Interlake Publishing Co.
486 Main St.
PO Box 190
Stonewall, MB, Canada R0C 2Z0
Phone: (204)467-8402
Fax: (204)467-5967
**Subject(s):** Paid Community Newspapers
**Circ:** (Combined)‡4,689

**The Elmira Independent  (34897)**
Metroland Printing, Publishing and Distributing Ltd.
24 Church St. W.
PO Box 128
Elmira, ON, Canada N3B 2Z5
Phone: (519)669-5155
Fax: (519)669-5928
**Subject(s):** Paid Community Newspapers
**Circ:** 4,554

**Gale Directory of Publications & Broadcast Media/140th Ed.**  **Central Provinces**

**The Wiarton Echo** (35934)
Box 220
573 Berford St.
Wiarton, ON, Canada N0H 2T0
Phone: (519)534-1560
Fax: (519)534-4616
**Subject(s):** Paid Community Newspapers
**Circ:** ‡4,542

**The New Pathway** (35724)
The New Pathway Publishers Ltd.
145 Evans Ave.
Toronto, ON, Canada M8Z 5X8
Phone: (416)960-3424
Fax: (416)960-1442
**Subject(s):** Free Newspapers; Ukrainian
**Circ:** (Free)‡110
(Paid)‡4,500

**Star & Times** (34457)
Box 670
Swan River, MB, Canada R0L 1Z0
Phone: (204)734-3858
Fax: (204)734-4935
**Subject(s):** Paid Community Newspapers
**Circ:** 4,500

**Paris Star** (35339)
Bowes Publishing
59 Grand River St. N.
Paris, ON, Canada N3L 2N9
Phone: (519)442-7866
Fax: (519)442-3100
**Subject(s):** Paid Community Newspapers
**Circ:** 4,481

**Fergus-Elora News Express** (34914)
Metroland
390 Tower St. S.
PO Box 130
Fergus, ON, Canada N1M 2W7
Phone: (519)843-1310
Fax: (519)843-1334
**Subject(s):** Free Newspapers
**Circ:** (Paid)4,392

**Voice of the Essex Farmer** (34903)
York Region Printing
254 Main St.
Dresden, ON, Canada N0P 1M0
Phone: (519)683-4485
Fax: (519)683-4355
**Subject(s):** Farm Newspapers; Free Newspapers
**Circ:** (Free)‡4,360

**The Free Press** (35096)
248 1st St.
PO Box 37
Midland, ON, Canada L4R 4K6
Phone: (705)526-5431
Fax: (705)526-1771
**Subject(s):** Paid Community Newspapers
**Circ:** (Tues.)•3,651
(Fri.)•4,344

**The Review** (35901)
996963 Ontario Inc.
41 High St.
PO Box 160
Vankleek Hill, ON, Canada K0B 1R0
Phone: (613)678-3327
Fax: (613)678-2700
**Subject(s):** Paid Community Newspapers
**Circ:** ‡4,338

**The Assiniboia Times** (36403)
PO Box 910
410 1st Ave
Assiniboia, SK, Canada S0H 0B0
Phone: (306)642-5901
Fax: (306)642-4519
**Subject(s):** Paid Community Newspapers
**Circ:** ‡4,300

**Haldimand Press** (34952)
The Haldimand Advocate Ltd.
5 John St.
Hagersville, ON, Canada N0A 1H0
Phone: (905)768-3111
Fax: (905)768-3340
**Subject(s):** Paid Community Newspapers
**Circ:** 4,307

**Port Dover Maple Leaf** (35363)
Maple Leaf
351 Main St.
PO Box 70
Port Dover, ON, Canada N0A 1N0
Phone: (519)583-0112
Fax: (519)583-3200
**Subject(s):** Paid Community Newspapers
**Circ:** (Paid)‡4,250

**New Hamburg Independent** (35143)
The Fairway Group
77 Peel St.
New Hamburg, ON, Canada N3A 1E7
Phone: (519)662-1240
Fax: (519)662-3521
**Subject(s):** Free Newspapers
**Circ:** (Paid)4,200

**The Winchester Press** (35942)
2wo Mor Publications Inc.
Box 399
Winchester, ON, Canada K0C 2K0
**Subject(s):** Paid Community Newspapers
**Circ:** 4,200

**Argus** (35471)
Lakehead University Student Union
955 Oliver Rd.
Thunder Bay, ON, Canada P7B 5E6
Phone: (807)344-6911
Fax: (807)343-8803
**Subject(s):** College Publications
**Circ:** 4,000

**Fortnightly Al-Hilal** (35936)
338 Hollyberry Trl.
Willowdale, ON, Canada M2H 2P6
Phone: (416)493-4374
Fax: (416)493-4374
**Subject(s):** Urdu; Paid Community Newspapers; Ethnic Publications
**Circ:** (Free)‡1,500
(Paid)‡4,000

**Kincardine News** (35006)
719 Queen St.
Kincardine, ON, Canada N2Z 1Z9
Phone: (519)396-2963
Fax: (519)396-6865
**Subject(s):** Paid Community Newspapers
**Circ:** ‡4,003

**Nipawin Journal** (36454)
Bowes Publishers Ltd.
PO Box 2014
Nipawin, SK, Canada S0E 1E0
Phone: (306)862-4618
Fax: (306)862-4566
**Subject(s):** Paid Community Newspapers
**Circ:** 4,000

**The Ryersoniam** (35788)
Ryerson University
80 Gould St.
Toronto, ON, Canada M5B 2M7
Phone: (416)979-5323
Fax: (416)979-5342
**Subject(s):** College Publications
**Circ:** 4,000

**Uniter** (34509)
University of Winnipeg
515 Portage Ave.
Winnipeg, MB, Canada R3D 2E9
Phone: (204)786-7811
Fax: (204)783-7080
**Subject(s):** College Publications
**Circ:** (Free)4,000

**The Aylmer Express** (34777)
The Aylmer Express Ltd.
PO Box 160
390 Talbot St. E
Aylmer, ON, Canada N5H 2R9
Phone: (519)773-3126
Fax: (519)773-3147
**Subject(s):** Paid Community Newspapers
**Circ:** 3,977

**Meadow Lake Progress** (36442)
311 Centre St.
Box 879
Meadow Lake, SK, Canada S9X 1Y6
Phone: (306)236-5265

Fax: (306)236-3130
**Subject(s):** Paid Community Newspapers
**Circ:** 3,933

**Daily Miner & News** (35002)
Bowes Publishers Ltd.
33 Main St. S
PO Box 1620
Kenora, ON, Canada P9N 3X7
Phone: (807)468-5555
Fax: (807)468-4318
**Subject(s):** Daily Newspapers
**Circ:** (Mon.-Fri.)3,825

**The Enterprise-Bulletin** (34857)
77 St. Marie St.
PO. Box 98
Collingwood, ON, Canada L9Y 3Z4
Phone: (705)445-4611
Fax: (705)444-6477
**Subject(s):** Paid Community Newspapers
**Circ:** (Tues.)•3,553
(Fri.)•3,825

**Agricom** (34848)
2474 rue Champlain
Clarence Creek, ON, Canada K0A 1N0
Phone: (613)488-2651
Fax: (613)488-2541
**Subject(s):** Farm Newspapers; General Agriculture
**Circ:** ‡3,800

**The Beeton Record Sentinel** (34792)
Simcoe-York Printing and Publishing Ltd.
34 Main St. W.
Beeton, ON, Canada L0G 1A0
Phone: (905)729-2287
Fax: (905)729-2541
**Subject(s):** Paid Community Newspapers
**Circ:** ‡3,800

**The Dunnville Chronicle** (34891)
131 Lock St. E
Dunnville, ON, Canada N1A 1J6
Phone: (905)774-7632
Fax: (905)774-5744
**Subject(s):** Paid Community Newspapers
**Circ:** 3,800

**The Reminder** (34424)
10 N Ave.
Flin Flon, MB, Canada R8A 0T2
Phone: (204)687-3454
Fax: (204)687-4473
**Subject(s):** Daily Newspapers
**Circ:** (Paid)3,800

**The Tottenham Times** (35884)
Simcoe-York Printing and Publishing Ltd.
34 Main St. W.
Beeton, ON, Canada L0G 1A0
Phone: (905)729-2287
Fax: (905)729-2541
**Subject(s):** Paid Community Newspapers
**Circ:** ‡3,800

**Voxair** (34510)
17 Wing Winnipeg
PO Box 17000 Stn. Forces
Winnipeg, MB, Canada R3J 3Y5
Phone: (204)833-2500
Fax: (204)833-2809
**Subject(s):** Military and Navy; Free Newspapers
**Circ:** (Free)3,800

**The Melfort Journal** (36445)
Box 1300
Melfort, SK, Canada S0E 1A0
Phone: (306)752-5737
Fax: (306)752-5358
**Subject(s):** Paid Community Newspapers
**Circ:** ‡3,760

**Delhi News-Record** (34873)
Bowes Publisher Ltd
237 Main
Delhi, ON, Canada N4B 2M4
Phone: (519)582-2510
Fax: (519)582-0627
**Subject(s):** Paid Community Newspapers
**Circ:** 3,719

Circulation: ★ = ABC; △ = BPA; ♦ = CAC; • = CCAB; ▫ = VAC; ⊕ = PO Statement; ‡ = Publisher's Report; Boldface figures = sworn; Light figures = estimated.

**Borden Citizen** (34805)
CFB Bldg. S-138
Borden, ON, Canada L0M 1C0
Phone: (705)423-2496
Fax: (705)423-3452
**Subject(s):** Free Newspapers; Military and Navy

Circ: (Paid)‡300
(Free)‡3,700

**The Minnedosa Tribune** (34432)
Box 930
Minnedosa, MB, Canada R0J 1E0
Phone: (204)867-3816
Fax: (204)867-5171
**Subject(s):** Paid Community Newspapers

Circ: ‡3,691

**Ayr News** (34779)
Ayr News Ltd.
PO Box 1173
Ayr, ON, Canada N0B 1E0
Phone: (519)632-7432
Fax: (519)632-7743
**Subject(s):** Paid Community Newspapers

Circ: (Paid)3,650

**Opasquia Times** (34435)
New North Ventures
PO Box 750
148 Fisher Ave
The Pas, MB, Canada R9Q 1K8
Phone: (204)623-3435
Fax: (204)623-5601
**Subject(s):** Paid Community Newspapers

Circ: ‡3,637

**The Hanover Post** (34982)
413 18th Ave.
Hanover, ON, Canada N4N 3S5
Phone: (519)364-2001
Fax: (519)364-6950
**Subject(s):** Paid Community Newspapers

Circ: 3,600

**The Stittsville News/The Canada Courier Standard** (35443)
The Stittsville News
1488 Main St.
Box 610
Stittsville, ON, Canada K2S 1A7
Phone: (613)836-1357
Fax: (613)836-5621
**Subject(s):** Paid Community Newspapers

Circ: ‡3,600

**The Daily Graphic** (34438)
Bowes Publishers Ltd.
1941 Saskatchewan Ave. W
PO Box 130
Portage La Prairie, MB, Canada R1N 3B4
Phone: (204)857-3427
Fax: (204)239-1270
**Subject(s):** Daily Newspapers

Circ: (Mon.-Fri.)3,550

**Advance** (36448)
Melville Advance Printing & Publishing Co., (1986) Ltd.
218 3rd Ave., W.
PO Box 1420
Melville, SK, Canada S0A 2P0
Phone: (306)728-5448
Fax: (306)728-4004
**Subject(s):** Paid Community Newspapers

Circ: ‡3,500

**CONTACT** (35885)
PO Box 1000
STN Forces, Ste. 40
Astra, ON, Canada K0K 3W0
Phone: (613)965-7248
Fax: (613)965-7490
**Subject(s):** Free Newspapers; Military and Navy

Circ: (Free)‡3,500

**Daily Commercial News and Construction Record** (35083)
Reed Construction Data
280 Yorkland Blvd.
Markham, ON, Canada L3R 9O3
Phone: (905)752-5408
Fax: (905)752-5545
**Subject(s):** Daily Periodicals; Construction, Contracting, Building, and Excavating

Circ: 3,500

**Dundalk Herald** (34890)
Herald and Advance Newspapers Inc.
PO Box 280
Dundalk, ON, Canada N0C 1B0
Phone: (519)923-2203
Fax: (519)923-2747
**Subject(s):** Paid Community Newspapers

Circ: ‡3,500

**Petrolia Topic** (35358)
4182 Petrolia Line
PO Box 40
Petrolia, ON, Canada M0N 1R0
Phone: (519)882-1770
Fax: (519)882-3212
**Subject(s):** Shopping Guides

Circ: (Paid)3,500

**Clinton News-Record** (34849)
Bowes Publishers Ltd.
53 Albert St. Box 39
Clinton, ON, Canada N0M 1L0
Phone: (519)482-3443
Fax: (519)482-7341
**Subject(s):** Paid Community Newspapers

Circ: (Free)163
(Paid)3,460

**The Reporter** (34928)
1000 Islands Publishers Ltd.
79 King St. E
Gananoque, ON, Canada K7G 1E8
Phone: (613)382-2156
Fax: (613)382-3010
**Subject(s):** Paid Community Newspapers

Circ: (Wed.)3,469

**Le Nord** (34990)
795651 Ontario Inc.
813 rue Georges
C.P. 2320
Hearst, ON, Canada P0L 1N0
Phone: (705)372-1233
Fax: (705)362-5954
**Subject(s):** French; Paid Community Newspapers

Circ: (Free)45
(Paid)3,455

**The Forest Standard** (34918)
Forest Standard
POB 220
Forest, ON, Canada N0N 1J0
Phone: (519)786-5242
Fax: (519)786-4884
**Subject(s):** Paid Community Newspapers

Circ: (Free)‡41
(Paid)‡3,437

**News-Optimist** (36457)
Battlefords Publishing Ltd.
892 104 St.
PO Box 1029
North Battleford, SK, Canada S9A 3E6
Phone: (306)445-7261
Fax: (306)445-3223
**Subject(s):** Paid Community Newspapers

Circ: ‡3,414

**Ingersoll Times** (34995)
Ingersoll Times
19 King St. W
Ingersoll, ON, Canada N5C 2J2
Phone: (519)485-3631
Fax: (519)485-6652
**Subject(s):** Paid Community Newspapers

Circ: 3,400

**Mid-North Monitor** (34901)
15-417 2nd Ave.
Espanola, ON, Canada P5E 1L1
Phone: (705)869-0588
Fax: (705)869-0587
**Subject(s):** Paid Community Newspapers

Circ: 3,400

**Crossroads This Week** (34448)
Nesbitt Publishing Ltd.
353 Station Rd.
Box 160
Shoal Lake, MB, Canada R0J 1Z0
Phone: (204)759-2644
Fax: (204)759-2521
**Subject(s):** Paid Community Newspapers

Circ: (Paid)‡3,385

**Journal** (36427)
PO Box 970
617 Main St.
Humboldt, SK, Canada S0K 2A0
Phone: (306)682-2561
Fax: (306)682-3322
**Subject(s):** Paid Community Newspapers

Circ: 3,343

**Thompson Citizen** (34458)
Precambrian Press Publishers
141 Commercial Pl.
PO Box 887
Thompson, MB, Canada R8N 1N8
Phone: (204)677-4534
Fax: (204)677-3681
**Subject(s):** Paid Community Newspapers

Circ: (Free)‡200
(Paid)‡3,320

**The North Shore Sentinel** (35469)
PO Box 640
155 Main St.
Thessalon, ON, Canada T0R 1L0
Phone: (705)842-2504
Fax: (705)842-2679
**Subject(s):** Paid Community Newspapers

Circ: 3,300

**Journal** (35368)
St. Lawrence Printing Co.
PO Box 549
Prescott, ON, Canada K0E 1T0
Phone: (613)925-4265
Fax: (613)925-3472
**Subject(s):** Paid Community Newspapers

Circ: 3,285

**Gravenhurst Banner** (34937)
PO Box 849
Gravenhurst, ON, Canada P1P 1X2
Phone: (705)687-6674
Fax: (705)687-7213
**Subject(s):** Paid Community Newspapers

Circ: ‡3,250

**Carleton Place Canadian** (34839)
Runge Newspapers
53 Bridge St.
Box 130
Carleton Place, ON, Canada K7C 3P5
Phone: (613)257-1303
Fax: (613)257-7373
**Subject(s):** Paid Community Newspapers

Circ: (Wed.)3,246

**Port Hope Evening Guide** (35365)
NorthUmberland Publishing
97 Walton St.
PO Box 296
Port Hope, ON, Canada L1A 3W4
Phone: (905)885-2471
Fax: (905)885-7442
**Subject(s):** Daily Newspapers

Circ: 3,243

**Wynyard Advance/Gazette** (36534)
Wynyard Advance Ltd.
117 Ave. B E
PO Box 10
Wynyard, SK, Canada S0A 4T0
Phone: (306)554-2224
Fax: (306)554-3226
**Subject(s):** Paid Community Newspapers

Circ: 3,245

**The Wadena News** (36523)
102 1st St. NE
PO Box 100
Wadena, SK, Canada S0A 4J0
Phone: (306)338-2231
Fax: (306)338-3421
**Subject(s):** Paid Community Newspapers

Circ: (Free)53
(Paid)3,232

**The Shoreline News** (35061)
Bowes Publishers Ltd.
1147 Gainsborough Rd.
PO Box 7400
London, ON, Canada N6H 5L5
Phone: (519)471-8520
Fax: (519)471-1892
**Subject(s):** Paid Community Newspapers

Circ: (Combined)3,200

**Sunday Edition News-Optimist (36459)**
Battlefords Publishing Ltd.
892 104 St.
PO Box 1029
North Battleford, SK, Canada S9A 3E6
Phone: (306)445-7261
Fax: (306)445-3223
**Subject(s):** Paid Community Newspapers
**Circ:** 3,143

**Saskatchewan Valley News (36488)**
Kelco Publishers Ltd.
1000 6th St.
Box 10
Rosthern, SK, Canada S0K 3R0
Phone: (306)232-4865
Fax: (306)232-4694
**Subject(s):** Paid Community Newspapers
**Circ:** ‡3,102

**Shaunavon Standard (36512)**
346 Centre
PO Box 729
Shaunavon, SK, Canada S0N 2M0
Phone: (306)297-4144
Fax: (306)297-3357
**Subject(s):** Paid Community Newspapers
**Circ:** 3,100

**Tribune (35453)**
206 King St.
Sturgeon Falls, ON, Canada P2B 1R7
Phone: (705)753-2930
Fax: (705)753-5231
**Subject(s):** Farm Newspapers
**Circ:** (Paid)3,066

**Kindersley Clarion (36431)**
Jamac Publishing Ltd.
919 Main St.
PO Box 1150
Kindersley, SK, Canada S0L 1S0
Phone: (306)463-4611
Fax: (306)463-6505
**Subject(s):** Paid Community Newspapers
**Circ:** 3,039

**The Times (34954)**
Algonquin Graphics Ltd.
PO Box 360
Haliburton, ON, Canada K0M 1S0
Phone: (705)457-1037
Fax: (705)457-3275
**Subject(s):** Paid Community Newspapers
**Circ:** (Free)‡25
  (Paid)‡3,028

**World Spectator (36452)**
PO Box 250
624 Main St.
Moosomin, SK, Canada S0G 3N0
Phone: (306)435-2445
Fax: (306)435-3969
**Subject(s):** Paid Community Newspapers
**Circ:** 3,023

**The Daily Bulletin (34923)**
Ft. Frances Times and Rainy Lake Herald
116 1st St.
PO Box 339
Fort Frances, ON, Canada P9A 3M7
Phone: (807)274-5373
Fax: (807)274-7286
**Subject(s):** Daily Newspapers
**Circ:** (Paid)3,013

**Arthur (35347)**
Trent University
751 George St. N.
Peterborough, ON, Canada
Phone: (705)745-3535
Fax: (705)745-3534
**Subject(s):** College Publications; Paid Community Newspapers
**Circ:** (Free)‡3,000

**Free Press (34902)**
16 Centre St.
Essex, ON, Canada N8M 1N9
Phone: (519)776-8511
Fax: (519)776-4014
**Subject(s):** Paid Community Newspapers
**Circ:** (Free)‡700
  (Paid)‡3,000

**Georgian Bay Today (35639)**
27 St. Clair Ave. E
PO Box 186
Toronto, ON, Canada M4T 2M1
Phone: (416)944-1217
Fax: (416)944-0133
**Subject(s):** Paid Community Newspapers; Travel and Tourism
**Circ:** (Paid)3,000

**Latvija Amerika (35690)**
Amber Printers and Publishers Ltd.
4 Credit Union Dr.
Toronto, ON, Canada M4A 2N8
Phone: (416)466-1514
Fax: (416)465-8168
**Subject(s):** Latvian; Paid Community Newspapers
**Circ:** (Paid)‡3,000

**The Times (34463)**
Broadway St.
PO Box 50
Treherne, MB, Canada R0G 2V0
Phone: (204)723-2542
Fax: (204)723-2754
**Subject(s):** Paid Community Newspapers
**Circ:** 3,000

**Shoreline Beacon Times (35364)**
Bowes Publication
PO Box 580
Port Elgin, ON, Canada N0H 2C0
Phone: (519)832-9001
Fax: (519)389-4793
**Subject(s):** Paid Community Newspapers
**Circ:** ‡2,995

**Herald-Times (35903)**
10 Victoria St. N
Walkerton, ON, Canada N0G 2V0
Phone: (519)881-1600
Fax: (519)881-0276
**Subject(s):** Paid Community Newspapers
**Circ:** ‡2,943

**Virden Empire-Advance (34465)**
Empire Publishing Company Ltd.
Box 250
Virden, MB, Canada R0M 2C0
Phone: (204)748-3931
Fax: (204)748-1816
**Subject(s):** Paid Community Newspapers
**Circ:** ‡2,928

**Blenheim News-Tribune (34802)**
62 Talbot St.
Blenheim, ON, Canada N0P 1A0
Phone: (519)676-3321
Fax: (519)676-3454
**Subject(s):** Paid Community Newspapers
**Circ:** (Wed.)2,917

**Kanadske Listy (Canadian Pages) (35119)**
388 Atwater Ave.
Mississauga, ON, Canada L5G 2A3
Phone: (905)278-4116
**Subject(s):** Czech; Paid Community Newspapers
**Circ:** ‡2,800

**Chronicle-Guide (34755)**
Chronicle-Guide Newspapers Ltd.
116 John St. N
Arnprior, ON, Canada K7S 2N6
Phone: (613)623-6571
Fax: (613)623-7518
**Subject(s):** Paid Community Newspapers
**Circ:** (Wed.)2,756

**Chesterville Record (34847)**
PO Box 368
Chesterville, ON, Canada K0C 1H0
Phone: (613)448-2321
Fax: (613)448-3260
**Subject(s):** Paid Community Newspapers
**Circ:** (Non-paid)300
  (Paid)2,700

**The Record News (35437)**
Performance Printing Ltd.
65 Lorne St.
PO Box 158
Smiths Falls, ON, Canada K7A 4T1
Phone: (613)283-3182
Fax: (613)283-7480

**Subject(s):** Paid Community Newspapers
**Circ:** (Wed.)2,709

**Shellbrook Chronicle (36514)**
Pepperfram
PO Box 10
Shellbrook, SK, Canada S0J 2E0
Phone: (306)747-2442
Fax: (306)747-3000
**Subject(s):** Paid Community Newspapers
**Circ:** ‡2,683

**Tisdale Recorder (36520)**
Pasquia Publishing Ltd.
Box 1660
1004-102 Ave.
Tisdale, SK, Canada S0E 1T0
Phone: (306)873-4515
Fax: (306)873-4712
**Subject(s):** Paid Community Newspapers
**Circ:** ‡2,667

**Huron Expositor (35431)**
Bowes Publishing
11 Main St.
Box 69
Seaforth, ON, Canada N0K 1W0
Phone: (519)527-0240
Fax: (519)527-2858
**Subject(s):** Paid Community Newspapers
**Circ:** (Paid)‡2,658

**Manitoulin Recorder (35073)**
Manitoulin Media Inc.
PO Box 235
Gore Bay, ON, Canada P0P 1H0
Phone: (705)282-2003
Fax: (705)282-2432
**Subject(s):** Paid Community Newspapers
**Circ:** (Fri.)2,650

**The Mount Forest Confederate (35138)**
277 Main St. S
PO Box 130
Mount Forest, ON, Canada N0G 2L0
Phone: (519)323-1550
Fax: (519)323-4548
**Subject(s):** Paid Community Newspapers
**Circ:** ‡2,614

**Signpost (34885)**
15 Bridge St.
Dorchester, ON, Canada N0L 1G2
Phone: (519)268-7337
Fax: (519)268-3260
**Subject(s):** Paid Community Newspapers
**Circ:** ‡2,600

**The Express (35092)**
BREBCO Inc.
68 Sykes St. N
Meaford, ON, Canada N4L 1R2
Phone: (519)538-1421
Fax: (519)538-5028
**Subject(s):** Paid Community Newspapers
**Circ:** (Combined)2,551

**Gazette (34840)**
Runge Newspapers Inc.
53 Bridge St
Carlton Place, ON, Canada K7C 3P5
Phone: (613)256-1311
Fax: (613)257-7373
**Subject(s):** Paid Community Newspapers
**Circ:** (Wed.)2,539

**Maple Creek News (36441)**
Maple Creek
PO Box 1360
Maple Creek, SK, Canada S0N 1N0
Phone: (306)662-2133
Fax: (306)662-3092
**Subject(s):** Paid Community Newspapers
**Circ:** 2,500

**Tekawennake (35185)**
PO Box 130
Ohsweken, ON, Canada N0A 1M0
Phone: (519)753-0077
Fax: (519)753-0011
**Subject(s):** Paid Community Newspapers
**Circ:** 2500

Circulation: ★ = ABC; △ = BPA; ♦ = CAC; ● = CCAB; ❏ = VAC; ⊖ = PO Statement; ‡ = Publisher's Report; Boldface figures = sworn; Light figures = estimated.

**Transcript & Free Press (34932)**
Transcript & Free Press Ltd.
243 Main St.
PO Box 400
Glencoe, ON, Canada N0L 1M0
Phone: (519)287-2615
Fax: (519)287-2408
**Subject(s):** Paid Community Newspapers
**Circ:** (Free)‡56
(Paid)2,500

**The Erin Advocate (34900)**
Erin Advocate Inc.
8 Thompson Crescent
Erin, ON, Canada N0B 1T0
Phone: (519)833-9603
Fax: (519)833-9605
**Subject(s):** Paid Community Newspapers
**Circ:** ‡2,463

**The Grand River Sachem (34835)**
3 Sutherland W
Caledonia, ON, Canada N3W 1C1
Phone: (905)765-4441
Fax: (905)765-3651
**Subject(s):** Paid Community Newspapers
**Circ:** ‡2,400

**The Review Mirror (35930)**
The Rearview Mirror
PO Box 130
Westport, ON, Canada K0G 1X0
Phone: (613)273-8000
Fax: (613)273-8001
**Subject(s):** Paid Community Newspapers
**Circ:** ‡2,400

**Banner (34445)**
Russell Banner
455 Main St. N.
Russell, MB, Canada R0J 1W0
Phone: (204)773-2069
Fax: (204)773-2645
**Subject(s):** Paid Community Newspapers
**Circ:** 2,350

**The Independent (36404)**
The Independent Printers Ltd.
PO Box 40
Biggar, SK, Canada S0K 0M0
Phone: (306)948-3344
Fax: (306)948-2133
**Subject(s):** Paid Community Newspapers
**Circ:** ‡2,347

**Lakeshore News (34794)**
Phoenix Media Group Inc.
419 Notre Dame St., Ste. 100
PO Box 429
Belle River, ON, Canada N0R 1A0
Phone: (519)728-1082
Fax: (519)728-4551
**Subject(s):** Paid Community Newspapers
**Circ:** (Free)‡164
(Paid)‡2,336

**North Renfrew Times (34867)**
Deep River Community Association
21 Champlain St.
PO Box 310
Deep River, ON, Canada K0J 1P0
Phone: (613)584-4161
Fax: (613)584-1062
**Subject(s):** Paid Community Newspapers
**Circ:** ★2,294
2,338

**Canora Courier (36407)**
Canora Courier Ltd.
Box 746
Canora, SK, Canada S0A 0L0
Phone: (306)563-5131
Fax: (306)563-6144
**Subject(s):** Paid Community Newspapers
**Circ:** ‡2,300

**The Jewish Post & News (34487)**
The Jewish Post Ltd.
113 Hutchings St.
Winnipeg, MB, Canada R2X 2V4
Phone: (204)694-3332
Fax: (204)694-3916

**Subject(s):** Paid Community Newspapers; Jewish Publications
**Circ:** (Non-paid)•755
(Paid)•2,306

**The Wingham Advance-Times (35956)**
206 Josephine St.
Wingham, ON, Canada N0G 2W0
Phone: (519)357-2320
Fax: (519)357-2900
**Subject(s):** Free Newspapers
**Circ:** (Paid)‡2,306

**The Enterprise (34997)**
727 Synegogue
PO Box 834
Iroquois Falls, ON, Canada P0K 1G0
Phone: (705)232-4081
Fax: (705)232-4235
**Subject(s):** Paid Community Newspapers
**Circ:** (Wed.)2,296

**Rosetown Eagle (36486)**
Rosetown Publishing Company Ltd.
Box 130
Rosetown, SK, Canada S0L 2V0
Phone: (306)882-4202
Fax: (306)882-4204
**Subject(s):** Paid Community Newspapers
**Circ:** 2,289

**The Kingsville Reporter (35025)**
Sims Publications Inc.
17 Chestnut St.
Kingsville, ON, Canada N9Y 1J9
Phone: (519)733-2211
Fax: (519)733-6464
**Subject(s):** Paid Community Newspapers
**Circ:** ‡2,254

**Carlyle Observer (36410)**
PO. Box 160
Carlyle, SK, Canada S0C 0R0
Phone: (306)453-2525
Fax: (306)453-2938
**Subject(s):** Paid Community Newspapers
**Circ:** ‡2,098

**Guide (34428)**
Struth Publishing Co.
336 Park St. E
Killarney, MB, Canada R0K 1G0
Phone: (204)523-4611
Fax: (204)523-4445
**Subject(s):** Paid Community Newspapers
**Circ:** 2,054

**Roblin Review (34444)**
119 1st Ave. NW
Box 938
Roblin, MB, Canada R0L 1P0
Phone: (204)937-8377
Fax: (204)937-8212
**Subject(s):** Paid Community Newspapers
**Circ:** ‡2,023

**Foam Lake Review (36419)**
324 Main St.
PO Box 550
Foam Lake, SK, Canada S0A 1A0
Phone: (306)272-3262
Fax: (306)272-4521
**Subject(s):** Paid Community Newspapers
**Circ:** 2,000

**The Independent (35005)**
840 Queen St.
PO Box 1240
Kincardine, ON, Canada N2Z 2Z4
Phone: (519)396-3111
Fax: (519)396-3899
**Subject(s):** Paid Community Newspapers
**Circ:** (Paid)‡2,000

**Kerala Express (35683)**
1565 Jane St.
PO Box 34556
Toronto, ON, Canada M9N 2R3
**Subject(s):** Free Newspapers
**Circ:** (Paid)‡120
(Free)‡2,000

**The La Ronge Northerner (36436)**
Timberline Publishing
Box 1350
La Ronge, SK, Canada S0J 1L0
Phone: (306)425-3344
Fax: (306)425-2827
**Subject(s):** Paid Community Newspapers
**Circ:** (Paid)2,000

**The Lakeshore Advance (34936)**
58 Ontario St. N
PO Box 1195
Grand Bend, ON, Canada N0M 1T0
Phone: (519)238-5383
Fax: (519)238-5131
**Subject(s):** Paid Community Newspapers
**Circ:** 2,000

**Marmora Herald (35090)**
Shield Newspaper Group
91 Matthew St.
PO Box 239
Marmora, ON, Canada K0K 2M0
Phone: (613)472-2431
Fax: (613)472-5026
**Subject(s):** Free Newspapers
**Circ:** (Paid)‡14
(Free)‡2,008

**Mildmay Town & Country Crier (35100)**
100 Elora St.
PO Box 190
Mildmay, ON, Canada N0G 2J0
Phone: (519)367-2681
Fax: (519)367-5417
**Subject(s):** Paid Community Newspapers
**Circ:** 2,000

**Nomad (35014)**
St. Lawrence College
100 Portsmouth Ave
Kingston, ON, Canada K7L 5A6
Phone: (613)544-5400
Fax: (613)544-6600
**Subject(s):** College Publications
**Circ:** (Free)2,000

**The Quill (34413)**
BUSU Communications Inc.
270 18th St.
Brandon, MB, Canada R7A 6A9
Phone: (204)727-9667
Fax: (204)727-3498
**Subject(s):** College Publications
**Circ:** (Free)‡2,000

**Recorder (36524)**
Box 9
Wakaw, SK, Canada S0K 4P0
Phone: (306)233-4325
Fax: (306)233-4386
**Subject(s):** Paid Community Newspapers
**Circ:** 2,000

**Nipigon-Red Rock Gazette (35151)**
Lake Shore Community Publishing Ltd.
PO Box 1057
145 Railway St.
Nipigon, ON, Canada P0T 2J0
Phone: (807)887-3583
Fax: (807)887-3720
**Subject(s):** Paid Community Newspapers
**Circ:** (Free)‡55
(Paid)‡1,992

**Northwest Herald (36521)**
Press Herald Publications Ltd.
Main St.
Box 309
Unity, SK, Canada S0K 4L0
Phone: (306)228-2267
Fax: (306)228-2767
**Subject(s):** Paid Community Newspapers
**Circ:** (Free)300
(Paid)1,926

**The Leader (35137)**
The Morrisburg Leader Ltd.
PO Box 891
Morrisburg, ON, Canada K0C 1X0
Phone: (613)543-2987
Fax: (613)543-3643
**Subject(s):** Paid Community Newspapers
**Circ:** (Paid)1,913

**Potashville-Miner Journal** (36415)
Miner Journal
606 2nd Ave.
Box 1000
Esterhazy, SK, Canada S0A 0X0
Phone: (306)745-6669
Fax: (306)745-2699
**Subject(s):** Paid Community Newspapers
**Circ:** ‡1,900

**Hastings Star** (34985)
Shield Newspaper Group
91 Matthew St.
PO Box 239
Marmora, ON, Canada K0K 2M0
Phone: (613)472-2431
Fax: (613)472-5026
**Subject(s):** Free Newspapers
**Circ:** (Paid)6
      (Free)‡1,899

**Ukrainian Voice** (34507)
Trident Press Ltd.
842 Main St.
Winnipeg, MB, Canada R2W 3N8
Phone: (204)589-5871
Fax: (204)586-3618
**Subject(s):** Ukrainian; Paid Community Newspapers
**Circ:** (Free)50
      (Paid)1,880

**The Lucknow Sentinel** (35070)
Box 400
Lucknow, ON, Canada N0G 2H0
Phone: (519)528-2822
Fax: (519)528-3529
**Subject(s):** Paid Community Newspapers
**Circ:** (Paid)1,867

**Rivers Banner** (34443)
Box 70
529 2nd Ave
Rivers, MB, Canada R0K 1X0
Phone: (204)328-7494
**Subject(s):** Paid Community Newspapers
**Circ:** (Paid)‡1,850

**The Western Canadian** (34430)
Bryant Klippenstein
PO Box 190
Manitou, MB, Canada R0G 1G0
Phone: (204)242-2555
Fax: (204)242-3137
**Subject(s):** Paid Community Newspapers
**Circ:** (Free)‡10
      (Paid)‡1,850

**The Citizen** (36435)
South East Press Ltd.
521 Main St.
Kipling, SK, Canada S0G 2S0
**Subject(s):** Paid Community Newspapers
**Circ:** 1,847

**Lac du Bonnet Leader** (34429)
Lana Meiier
PO Box 910
67 Park Avenue
Lac du Bonnet, MB, Canada R0E 1A0
Phone: (204)345-8611
Fax: (204)345-6344
**Subject(s):** Paid Community Newspapers
**Circ:** (Paid)‡1,816

**Craik Weekly News** (36413)
PO Box 360
221 3rd St.
Craik, SK, Canada S0G 0V0
Phone: (306)734-2313
Fax: (306)734-2789
**Subject(s):** Paid Community Newspapers
**Circ:** 1,800

**Hudson Bay Post-Review** (36426)
Post-Review 1990 Ltd.
20 Railway Ave.
PO Box 10
Hudson Bay, SK, Canada S0E 0Y0
Phone: (306)865-2771
Fax: (306)865-2340
**Subject(s):** Paid Community Newspapers
**Circ:** ‡1,800

**Macedonia** (35929)
Box 291
West Hill, ON, Canada M1E 4R5
**Subject(s):** Ethnic Publications; Macedonian
**Circ:** (Free)50
      (Paid)1,800

**Kamsack Times** (36429)
Canora Courier Ltd.
Box 746
Canora, SK, Canada S0A 0L0
Phone: (306)563-5131
Fax: (306)563-6144
**Subject(s):** Paid Community Newspapers
**Circ:** ‡1,790

**Geraldton-Longlac Times-Star** (34930)
4147 Main St.
PO Box 490
Geraldton, ON, Canada D0T 1M0
Phone: (807)854-1919
Fax: (807)854-1682
**Subject(s):** Paid Community Newspapers
**Circ:** ‡1,780

**The Atikokan Progress** (34759)
Atikokan Printing (1994) Ltd.
PO Box 220
Atikokan, ON, Canada P0T 1C0
Phone: (807)597-2731
Fax: (807)597-6103
**Subject(s):** Paid Community Newspapers
**Circ:** (Paid)1,769

**The Parkhill Gazette** (35340)
The Parkhill Gazette Inc.
165 King St.
Box 400
Parkhill, ON, Canada N0M 2K0
Phone: (519)294-6264
Fax: (519)294-6391
**Subject(s):** Paid Community Newspapers
**Circ:** ‡1,765

**The Herald** (36425)
588049 Saskatchewan Ltd.
Box 399
Herbert, SK, Canada S0H 2A0
Phone: (306)784-2422
Fax: (306)784-3246
**Subject(s):** Paid Community Newspapers
**Circ:** 1,700

**Vapaa Sana** (35843)
Vapaa Sana Press Ltd.
191 Eglinton Ave Suite 308
Toronto, ON, Canada M4P 1K1
Phone: (416)321-0808
Fax: (416)321-0811
**Subject(s):** Finnish; Free Newspapers
**Circ:** (Non-paid)107
      (Paid)1,707

**The Four-Town Journal** (36438)
Box 68
Langenburg, SK, Canada S0A 2A0
Phone: (306)743-2617
Fax: (306)743-2299
**Subject(s):** Paid Community Newspapers
**Circ:** (Paid)1,664

**Ft. Qu'Appelle Times** (36421)
141 Broadway St. E
PO Box 940
Fort Qu'Appelle, SK, Canada S0G 1S0
Phone: (306)332-5526
Fax: (306)332-5414
**Subject(s):** Paid Community Newspapers
**Circ:** 1,650

**The Recorder** (34410)
Boissevain Recorder
PO Box 220
Boissevain, MB, Canada R0K 0E0
Phone: (204)534-6479
Fax: (204)534-2977
**Subject(s):** Paid Community Newspapers; Farm Newspapers
**Circ:** ‡1,650

**The Watrous Manitou** (36525)
Saskatchewan Ltd.
PO Box 100
Watrous, SK, Canada S0K 4T0
**Subject(s):** Paid Community Newspapers
**Circ:** (Paid)‡1,632

**Kinistino—Birch Hills Post—Gazette** (36444)
The Melfort Journal
Box 1300
Melfort, SK, Canada S0E 1A0
Phone: (306)752-5737
Fax: (306)752-5358
**Subject(s):** Paid Community Newspapers
**Circ:** ‡1,620

**Brock Citizen** (34791)
Citizens Communication Group Inc.
384 Simcoe St.
PO Box 10
Beaverton, ON, Canada L0K 1A0
**Subject(s):** Paid Community Newspapers
**Circ:** (Paid)1,600

**The Cobden Sun** (34851)
Cobden Sun
36 Crawford St.
PO Box 100
Cobden, ON, Canada K0J 1K0
Phone: (613)646-2380
Fax: (613)646-2700
**Subject(s):** Paid Community Newspapers
**Circ:** ‡1,600

**MANOTICK Messenger** (35074)
1165 Beaverwood Rd.
PO Box 567
Manotick, ON, Canada K4M 1A5
Phone: (613)692-6000
Fax: (613)692-3758
**Subject(s):** Paid Community Newspapers
**Circ:** 1,600

**Melita New Era** (34431)
Box 820
Melita, MB, Canada R0M 1L0
Phone: (204)522-3491
Fax: (204)522-3648
**Subject(s):** Paid Community Newspapers
**Circ:** ‡1,600

**Innisfil Scope** (34996)
Simcoe-York Printing and Publishing Ltd.
34 Main St. W.
Beeton, ON, Canada L0G 1A0
Phone: (705)458-4434
Fax: (905)729-2541
**Subject(s):** Paid Community Newspapers
**Circ:** (Paid)‡1,575

**Gull Lake Advance** (36424)
Peters Printing Ltd.
1462 Conrad Ave.
PO Box 628
Gull Lake, SK, Canada S0N 1A0
Phone: (306)672-3373
Fax: (306)672-3573
**Subject(s):** Paid Community Newspapers
**Circ:** ‡1,514

**Flesherton Advance** (34916)
Herald and Advance Newspapers Inc.
PO Box 280
Dundalk, ON, Canada N0C 1B0
Phone: (519)923-2203
Fax: (519)923-2747
**Subject(s):** Paid Community Newspapers
**Circ:** ‡1,500

**Oxbow Herald** (36462)
PO Box 420
Oxbow, SK, Canada S0C 2B0
Phone: (306)483-2323
Fax: (306)483-5258
**Subject(s):** Paid Community Newspapers
**Circ:** 1,500

**Rainy River Record** (35369)
312, 3rd St.
Box 280
Rainy River, ON, Canada P0W 1L0
Phone: (807)852-3366
Fax: (807)852-4434

## Central Provinces

**Subject(s):** Paid Community Newspapers
**Circ:** ‡1,500

**Satellite 1-416 (35790)**
PO Box 176, Sta. E
Toronto, ON, Canada M6H 4E2
Phone: (416)530-4222
Fax: (416)530-0069
**Subject(s):** Paid Community Newspapers; Ethnic Publications; Czech
**Circ:** (Combined)1,500

**The Harrow News (34984)**
563 Queen St.
PO Box 310
Harrow, ON, Canada N0R 1G0
Phone: (519)738-2542
Fax: (519)738-3874
**Subject(s):** Paid Community Newspapers
**Circ:** ‡1,450

**Lanigan Advisor (36439)**
30 Downing Dr.
PO Box 1029
Lanigan, SK, Canada S0K 2M0
Phone: (306)365-2010
Fax: (306)365-3388
**Subject(s):** Paid Community Newspapers
**Circ:** 1,429

**The Souris Plaindealer (34449)**
PO Box 488
Souris, MB, Canada R0K 2C0
Phone: (204)483-2070
Fax: (204)483-3866
**Subject(s):** Paid Community Newspapers
**Circ:** (Paid)‡1,427

**Algoma News Review (35925)**
37 Ste. Marie St.
PO Box 528
Wawa, ON, Canada P0S 1K0
Phone: (705)856-2267
Fax: (705)856-4952
**Subject(s):** Paid Community Newspapers
**Circ:** (Free)‡50
(Paid)‡1,400

**Mercury (35075)**
Marathan Mercury
10 Peninsula Rd.
Marathon, ON, Canada P0T 2E0
Phone: (807)229-1520
Fax: (807)229-1595
**Subject(s):** Paid Community Newspapers
**Circ:** ‡1403

**Palmerston Observer (35337)**
171 Williams St.
PO Box 757
Palmerston, ON, Canada N0G 2P0
Phone: (519)343-2440
Fax: (519)343-2267
**Subject(s):** Paid Community Newspapers
**Circ:** 1,400

**Tribune (36422)**
Gravel Subscriptions Ltd.
611 Main St.
PO Box 1017
Gravelbourg, SK, Canada S0H 1X0
Phone: (306)648-3479
Fax: (306)648-2520
**Subject(s):** Paid Community Newspapers
**Circ:** (Paid)1,400

**Whitewood Herald (36532)**
Herald Ltd.
708 Railway St.
PO Box 160
Whitewood, SK, Canada S0G 5C0
Phone: (306)735-2230
Fax: (306)735-2899
**Subject(s):** Paid Community Newspapers
**Circ:** 1,400

**The Sentinel Courier (34437)**
13 Railway
PO Box 179
Pilot Mound, MB, Canada R0G 1P0
Phone: (204)825-2772
Fax: (204)825-2439

**Subject(s):** Paid Community Newspapers
**Circ:** (Free)25
(Paid)1,379

**Watford Guide-Advocate (35924)**
5292 Nauvoo Road
PO Box 99
Watford, ON, Canada N0M 2S0
Phone: (519)876-2809
Fax: (519)876-2322
**Subject(s):** Paid Community Newspapers
**Circ:** (Paid)1,373

**The Radville Star (36470)**
129 Main St.
PO Box 370
Radville, SK, Canada S0C 2G0
Phone: (306)869-2202
Fax: (306)869-2533
**Subject(s):** Paid Community Newspapers
**Circ:** 1,350

**Colborne Chronicle (34855)**
Northumberland Publishers
11 King St. E.
PO Box 208
Colborne, ON, Canada K0K 1S0
Phone: (905)355-2843
Fax: (905)355-1639
**Subject(s):** Paid Community Newspapers
**Circ:** 1,300

**The Eston Press Review (36418)**
JAMAC
Po Box 77
112 Mian St.
Eston, SK, Canada S0L 1A0
Phone: (306)962-3221
Fax: (306)962-4445
**Subject(s):** Paid Community Newspapers
**Circ:** ‡1,300

**Gazette-News (34409)**
Gazette Publishing Co.
Box 280
Baldur, MB, Canada R0K 0B0
Phone: (204)535-2127
Fax: (204)535-2350
**Subject(s):** Paid Community Newspapers
**Circ:** 1,300

**Tavistock Gazette (35466)**
119 Woodstock St. S
PO Box 70
Tavistock, ON, Canada N0B 2R0
Phone: (519)655-2341
Fax: (519)655-3070
**Subject(s):** Paid Community Newspapers
**Circ:** 1,300

**Wheatley Journal (35931)**
14 Talbot St. W
PO Box 10
Wheatley, ON, Canada N0P 2P0
Phone: (519)825-4541
Fax: (519)825-4546
**Subject(s):** Paid Community Newspapers
**Circ:** (Paid)1,300

**Grenfell Sun (36423)**
Stone Publications
PO Box 189
Grenfell, SK, Canada S0G 2B0
Phone: (306)697-2722
Fax: (306)697-2689
**Subject(s):** Paid Community Newspapers
**Circ:** ‡1,285

**Carberry News-Express (34417)**
34 Main St.
Box 220
Carberry, MB, Canada R0K 0H0
Phone: (204)834-2153
Fax: (204)834-2714
**Subject(s):** Paid Community Newspapers; Farm Newspapers
**Circ:** ‡1,277

**Tweed News (35887)**
242 Victoria St.
PO Box 550
Tweed, ON, Canada K0K 3J0
Phone: (613)478-2017
Fax: (613)478-2749

**Subject(s):** Paid Community Newspapers
**Circ:** (Paid)‡1,263

**Gazette-Post-News (36411)**
PO Box 220
Carnduff, SK, Canada S0C 0S0
Phone: (306)482-3252
Fax: (306)482-3373
**Subject(s):** Paid Community Newspapers
**Circ:** ‡1,253

**Grandview Exponent (34427)**
416 Main St.
Box 39
Grandview, MB, Canada R0L 0Y0
Phone: (204)546-2555
Fax: (204)546-3081
**Subject(s):** Paid Community Newspapers
**Circ:** ‡1,212

**The Glenboro Gazette (34426)**
Mahatoba Ltd.
702 Railway Ave.
PO Box 10
Glenboro, MB, Canada R0K 0X0
Phone: (204)827-2343
Fax: (204)827-2343
**Subject(s):** Paid Community Newspapers
**Circ:** ‡1,200

**Stayner Sun (35441)**
250 Main St. E
PO Box 80
Stayner, ON, Canada L0M 1S0
Phone: (705)428-2638
Fax: (705)428-6909
**Subject(s):** Paid Community Newspapers
**Circ:** 1,200

**The Reston Recorder (34442)**
Box 10
Reston, MB, Canada R0M 1X0
Phone: (204)877-3321
Fax: (204)877-3115
**Subject(s):** Paid Community Newspapers
**Circ:** (Paid)‡1,131
(Free)‡1,169

**Kelvington Radio (36522)**
The Wadena News
102 1st St. NE
PO Box 100
Wadena, SK, Canada S0A 4J0
Phone: (306)338-2231
Fax: (306)338-3421
**Subject(s):** Paid Community Newspapers
**Circ:** (Paid)1,155

**Millbrook Times (35101)**
28 King St. E
PO Box 230
Millbrook, ON, Canada L0A 1G0
Phone: (705)932-3001
Fax: (705)932-3377
**Subject(s):** Paid Community Newspapers
**Circ:** ‡1,151

**Star and Vidette (35191)**
Claridge Community Newspaper Ltd.
10 First St.
Orangeville, ON, Canada L9W 2C4
Phone: (519)941-2230
Fax: (519)941-9361
**Subject(s):** Paid Community Newspapers
**Circ:** (Free)‡200
(Paid)‡1,150

**Spiritwood Herald (36515)**
Pepperfram
PO Box 10
Shellbrook, SK, Canada S0J 2E0
Phone: (306)747-2442
Fax: (306)747-3000
**Subject(s):** Paid Community Newspapers
**Circ:** ‡1,148

**The Leader News (36432)**
Jamac Publishing Ltd.
919 Main St.
PO Box 1150
Kindersley, SK, Canada S0L 1S0
Phone: (306)463-4611
Fax: (306)463-6505

**Gale Directory of Publications & Broadcast Media/140th Ed.**       **Eastern Provinces**

Subject(s): Paid Community Newspapers
Circ: 1,135

**Times & Star (34423)**
Box 407
Deloraine, MB, Canada R0M 0M0
Phone: (204)747-2249
Fax: (204)747-3999
Subject(s): Paid Community Newspapers
Circ: (Free)50
    (Paid)1,125

**Orono Weekly Times (35198)**
5310 Main St.
PO Box 209
Orono, ON, Canada L0B 1M0
Phone: (905)983-5301
Fax: (905)983-5301
Subject(s): Paid Community Newspapers
Circ: 1,100

**Le Journal de Cornwall (34862)**
Compagnie d'edition Andre-Paquette Inc.
113 Montreal Rd.
Cornwall, ON, Canada K6H 1B2
Phone: (613)938-1433
Fax: (613)938-2798
Subject(s): Paid Community Newspapers; French
Circ: (Paid)‡1,023
    (Free)‡1,077

**Southern Manitoba Review (34419)**
PO Box 249
Cartwright, MB, Canada R0K 0L0
Phone: (204)529-2342
Fax: (204)529-2029
Subject(s): Paid Community Newspapers
Circ: (Free)‡34
    (Paid)‡1,033

**The Markdale Standard (34983)**
The Hanover Post
413 18th Ave.
Hanover, ON, Canada N4N 3S5
Phone: (519)364-2001
Fax: (519)364-6950
Subject(s): Paid Community Newspapers
Circ: (Paid)1,024

**Ituna News (36420)**
Foam Lake Review
324 Main St.
PO Box 550
Foam Lake, SK, Canada S0A 1A0
Phone: (306)272-3262
Fax: (306)272-4521
Subject(s): Paid Community Newspapers
Circ: 1,000

**The Mattawa Recorder (35091)**
341 McConnell St.
Box 67
Mattawa, ON, Canada P0H 1V0
Phone: (705)744-5361
Fax: (705)744-5361
Subject(s): Paid Community Newspapers
Circ: ‡1,000

**Macklin Mirror (36440)**
Holmes Publishing Company Ltd.
Box 100
Macklin, SK, Canada S0L 2O0
Phone: (306)753-2424
Fax: (306)753-2424
Subject(s): Paid Community Newspapers
Circ: ‡970

**Kerrobert Citizen-Dispatch (36430)**
Jamac Publishing Ltd.
919 Main St.
PO Box 1150
Kindersley, SK, Canada S0L 1S0
Phone: (306)463-4611
Fax: (306)463-6505
Subject(s): Paid Community Newspapers
Circ: 950

**Thamesville Herald (35468)**
PO Box 580
Thamesville, ON, Canada N0P 2K0
Phone: (519)692-3825
Fax: (519)692-9515

Subject(s): Paid Community Newspapers
Circ: (Non-paid)‡100
    (Paid)‡900

**Norquay North Star (36408)**
Canora Courier Ltd.
Box 746
Canora, SK, Canada S0A 0L0
Phone: (306)563-5131
Fax: (306)563-6144
Subject(s): Paid Community Newspapers
Circ: ‡860

**The Wilkie Press (36533)**
Press Herald Publications Ltd.
Main St.
Box 309
Unity, SK, Canada S0K 4L0
Phone: (306)228-2267
Fax: (306)228-2767
Subject(s): Paid Community Newspapers
Circ: (Free)150
    (Paid)833

**Broadview Express (36405)**
Stone Publications
PO Box 189
Grenfell, SK, Canada S0G 2B0
Phone: (306)697-2722
Fax: (306)697-2689
Subject(s): Paid Community Newspapers
Circ: 805

**Workplace News (34775)**
CLB Media Inc.
240 Edward St.
Aurora, ON, Canada L4G 3S9
Phone: (905)727-0077
Fax: (905)727-0017
Subject(s): Labor
Circ: (Paid)760

**Ignace Driftwood (34994)**
Driftwood Enterprises
153 Balsam
PO Box 989
Ignace, ON, Canada P0T 1T0
Phone: (807)934-6482
Fax: (807)934-6667
Subject(s): Free Newspapers
Circ: (Paid)720

**The Naicam News (36527)**
East Central Press Ltd.
PO Box 576
Watson, SK, Canada S0K 4V0
Phone: (306)287-4388
Fax: (306)287-3308
Subject(s): Paid Community Newspapers
Circ: (Free)10
    (Paid)702

**Highway 40 Courier (36414)**
PO Box 639
200 Steele Street
Cut Knife, SK, Canada S0M 0N0
Phone: (306)398-4901
Fax: (306)398-4909
Subject(s): Paid Community Newspapers
Circ: (Combined)‡576

**Triangle News (36412)**
Po Box 689
118 Center St.
Coronach, SK, Canada S0H 0Z0
Phone: (306)267-3381
Fax: (306)267-3381
Subject(s): Free Newspapers
Circ: (Free)450
    (Paid)550

**The Prarie Flyer II (36406)**
PO Box 240
Bushell Park, SK, Canada S0H 0N0
Phone: (306)694-2256
Fax: (306)694-2851
Subject(s): Free Newspapers
Circ: (Free)‡500

# Eastern Provinces

**Le Journal de Montreal (36178)**
Journal de Montreal
4545, rue Frontenac
Montreal, QC, Canada H2H 2R7
Phone: (514)521-4545
Fax: (514)521-4416
Subject(s): Daily Newspapers; French
Circ: (Mon.-Fri.)★265,168
    (Sun.)★265,355
    (Sat.)★316,207

**La Presse (36170)**
La Presse Ltee.
7, rue St-Jacques
Montreal, QC, Canada H2Y 1K9
Phone: (514)285-7272
Fax: (514)845-8129
Subject(s): Daily Newspapers; French
Circ: (Mon.-Fri.)170,362
    (Sun.)180,426
    (Sat.)268,420

**The Montreal Gazette (36200)**
CanWest Global Communications Corp.
1010 Sainte-Catherine St. W, Ste. 200
Montreal, QC, Canada H3B 5L1
Phone: (514)987-2222
Subject(s): Daily Newspapers
Circ: (Sun.)★132,383
    (Mon.-Fri.)★135,471
    (Sat.)★157,317

**Le Journal de Quebec (36283)**
Groupe Quebecor Inc.
450, rue Bechard, Vanier
Quebec, QC, Canada G1M 2E9
Phone: (418)683-1573
Fax: (418)683-1027
Subject(s): Daily Newspapers; French
Circ: (Mon.-Fri.)★97,805
    (Sun.)★98,862
    (Sat.)★120,200

**Le Courrier du Sud (The South Shore Courier) (36079)**
Cie Imprimerie & Pub. Rive Sud Ltee.
267 St-Charles Ouest
Longueuil, QC, Canada J4H 1E3
Phone: (450)646-3333
Fax: (450)674-0205
Subject(s): Free Newspapers; French
Circ: (Free)120,000

**Le Soleil (36285)**
925 Chemin St. Louis
PO Box 1547
Quebec, QC, Canada G1K 7J6
Phone: (418)686-3394
Fax: (418)686-3374
Subject(s): Daily Newspapers; French
Circ: (Mon.-Fri.)★76,307
    (Sun.)★82,318
    (Sat.)★108,233

**Courier Laval du Jeudi (36133)**
Les Hebdos Select
625 Blvd. Rene Levesque O. Bureau 800
Montreal, QC, Canada H3B 1R2
Phone: (514)866-3131
Fax: (514)866-3030
Subject(s): Free Newspapers; French
Circ: (Free)106,877

**Le Courrier Laval du Dimanche (36175)**
Le Reseau Select
625 Rene Leuesque W Blvd., Ste. 800
Montreal, QC, Canada H3B 1R2
Phone: (514)866-3131
Fax: (514)866-3030
Subject(s): Free Newspapers; French
Circ: (Controlled)106,877

**The Suburban (36393)**
Michael Publishing Inc.
7575 Transcanada Hwy.
Ville Saint-Laurent, QC, Canada H4T 1V6
Phone: (514)484-1107
Fax: (514)484-9616
Subject(s): Free Newspapers
Circ: (Free)103,962

Circulation: ★ = ABC; △ = BPA; ♦ = CAC; ● = CCAB; ▫ = VAC; ⊖ = PO Statement; ‡ = Publisher's Report; Boldface figures = sworn; Light figures = estimated.

# Eastern Provinces

**The Chronicle Herald (34700)**
The Halifax Herald Ltd.
1650 Argyle St.
Halifax, NS, Canada B3J 2T2
Phone: (902)426-2811
Fax: (902)426-1158
**Subject(s):** Daily Newspapers
**Circ:** (Mon.-Sat.)90,052

**Echos-Vedettes (36138)**
465 McGill Ave 601
Montreal, QC, Canada H2Y 2H1
Phone: (514)528-7111
Fax: (514)528-7115
**Subject(s):** Radio, Television, Cable, and Video; Drama and Theatre; French
**Circ:** (Sat.)76,119

**Montreal Mirror (36201)**
Quebecor Media
465 Mcgill St. 3rd Fl
Montreal, QC, Canada H2Y 4B4
Phone: (514)393-1010
Fax: (514)393-3173
**Subject(s):** Free Newspapers
**Circ:** (Combined)74,188

**La Gazette Populaire (36374)**
942, rue Ste-Genevieve
Trois-Rivieres, QC, Canada G9A 3X6
Phone: (819)375-4012
Fax: (819)375-9670
**Subject(s):** Free Newspapers
**Circ:** (Paid)‡70
       (Free)‡71,000

**The Telegram (34640)**
Columbus Dr.
PO Box 5970
Saint John's, NL, Canada A1C 5X7
Phone: (709)364-2323
Fax: (709)364-1313
**Subject(s):** Daily Newspapers
**Circ:** (Mon.-Fri.)33,065
       (Sun.)33,693
       (Sat.)58,887

**Le Journal de Rosemont et Petite Patrie (36179)**
Le Reseau Select
625 Rene Leuesque W Blvd., Ste. 800
Montreal, QC, Canada H3B 1R2
Phone: (514)866-3131
Fax: (514)866-3030
**Subject(s):** Free Newspapers; French
**Circ:** (Controlled)58,741

**The Halifax Herald (34705)**
The Halifax Herald Ltd.
1650 Argyle St.
Halifax, NS, Canada B3J 2T2
Phone: (902)426-2811
Fax: (902)426-1158
**Subject(s):** Daily Newspapers
**Circ:** (Sun.)54,249

**Longueuil Extra (36081)**
267 rue St. Charles W.
Longueuil, QC, Canada J4H 1E3
Phone: (450)646-3333
Fax: (450)674-0205
**Subject(s):** French; Free Newspapers
**Circ:** (Controlled)54,200

**Le Flambeau de l'Est (36177)**
Le Reseau Select
6424 Jean Talon Est, bur. 202
Montreal, QC, Canada H1S 1M8
**Subject(s):** Free Newspapers; French
**Circ:** (Controlled)50,671

**Express (34635)**
Robinson Blackmore Printing and Publishing
36 Austin St.
Saint John's, NL, Canada A1B 3T7
Phone: (709)579-1312
Fax: (709)579-7745
**Subject(s):** Paid Community Newspapers
**Circ:** (Non-paid)50,515

**The Times-Transcript (34567)**
Moncton Publishing
939 Main St.
PO Box 1001
Moncton, NB, Canada E1C 8P3
Phone: (506)859-4900

Fax: (506)859-4899
**Subject(s):** Daily Newspapers
**Circ:** (Mon.-Fri.)37,286
       (Sat.)49,616

**Le Nord Info (36354)**
Le Reseau Select
50-B rue Turgeon
Sainte-Therese, QC, Canada J7E 3H4
Phone: (514)844-3131
Fax: (514)844-9679
**Subject(s):** Free Newspapers; French
**Circ:** (Controlled)48,775

**Il Cittadino Canadese (36149)**
5960 Jean-Talon E, Ste. 209
Montreal, QC, Canada H1S 1M2
Phone: (514)253-2332
Fax: (514)253-6574
**Subject(s):** Paid Community Newspapers
**Circ:** ‡48,320

**Le Nouvelliste (36375)**
1920 Bellefeuille St.
CP 668
Trois-Rivieres, QC, Canada G9A 3Y2
Phone: (819)376-2501
Fax: (819)691-4356
**Subject(s):** Daily Newspapers; French
**Circ:** (Mon.-Fri.)44,094
       (Sat.)48,256

**L'Artisan (36113)**
Le Reseau Select
625 Rene Leuesque W Blvd., Ste. 800
Montreal, QC, Canada H3B 1R2
Phone: (514)866-3131
Fax: (514)866-3030
**Subject(s):** Free Newspapers; French
**Circ:** (Controlled)‡47,722

**The Telegraph Journal (34585)**
N.B. Publishing Company Ltd.
210 Crown St.
PO Box 2350
Saint John, NB, Canada E2L 3V8
Phone: (506)645-3226
Fax: (506)633-6758
**Subject(s):** Daily Newspapers
**Circ:** (Mon.-Fri.)41,300
       (Sat.)46,500

**L'Action (36044)**
Le Reseau Select
262 boul de l'Industrie
Joliette, QC, Canada J6E 3Z1
**Subject(s):** French; Free Newspapers
**Circ:** (Controlled)45,140

**L'Hebdo Rive-Nord (36147)**
Le Reseau Select
625 Rene Leuesque W Blvd., Ste. 800
Montreal, QC, Canada H3B 1R2
Phone: (514)866-3131
Fax: (514)866-3030
**Subject(s):** Free Newspapers; French
**Circ:** (Controlled)45,118

**La Revue (36370)**
231, Holy-Marie
Terrebonne, QC, Canada J6W 2E4
Phone: (450)964-4444
Fax: (450)471-1023
**Subject(s):** Free Newspapers; French
**Circ:** (Free)‡45,100

**L'Hebdo-Journal (35999)**
Le Reseau Select
525 Barkoff, No. 205
Cap-de-la-Madeleine, QC, Canada G8T 2A5
**Subject(s):** Free Newspapers; French
**Circ:** (Controlled)44,691

**L'Avenir de l'Est (36115)**
Le Reseau Select
625 Rene Leuesque W Blvd., Ste. 800
Montreal, QC, Canada H3B 1R2
Phone: (514)866-3131
Fax: (514)866-3030
**Subject(s):** Free Newspapers; French
**Circ:** (Controlled)‡44,070

**L'Express (36028)**
Le Reseau Select
1050 rue Cormier
Drummondville, QC, Canada J2C 2N6
Phone: (819)478-8171
Fax: (819)478-4306
**Subject(s):** Free Newspapers; French
**Circ:** (Controlled)43,876

**Progres-Dimanche (36009)**
Le Progres du Saguenay
1051, boul. Talbot
Chicoutimi, QC, Canada G7H 5C1
Phone: (418)545-4474
Fax: (418)690-8824
**Subject(s):** French
**Circ:** (Sun.)41,231

**La Terre de Chez Nous (36078)**
Union des Producteurs Agricoles
555, Blvd. Roland Therrien
Longueuil, QC, Canada J4H 3Y9
Phone: (450)679-8483
Fax: (450)670-4788
**Subject(s):** French; Farm Newspapers; Paid Community Newspapers
**Circ:** (Paid)40,400

**La Nouvelle (36389)**
43 est Notre-Dame
PO Box 130
Victoriaville, QC, Canada G6P 3Z4
Phone: (819)758-6211
Fax: (819)758-2759
**Subject(s):** Paid Community Newspapers; French
**Circ:** 40,000

**La Tribune (36361)**
La Tribune Inc.
1950 Roy St.
Sherbrooke, QC, Canada J1K 2X8
Phone: (819)564-5450
Fax: (819)564-8098
**Subject(s):** Daily Newspapers; French
**Circ:** (Mon.-Fri.)30,731
       (Sat.)38,741

**Journal Le Nord (36326)**
Groupe Media Business Inc.
393 des Laurentides
Saint-Jerome, QC, Canada J7Z 4L9
Phone: (450)438-8383
Fax: (450)438-4174
**Subject(s):** Paid Community Newspapers
**Circ:** 38,525

**Beauport Express (35992)**
3333, rue du Carrefour, Ste. 212
Beauport, QC, Canada G1C 5R9
Phone: (418)663-6131
Fax: (418)663-3469
**Subject(s):** Paid Community Newspapers
**Circ:** 38,287

**Le Devoir (36176)**
L'Imprimerie Populaire
2050 De Bleury St., 9th Fl.
Montreal, QC, Canada H3A 3M9
Phone: (514)985-3399
Fax: (514)985-3390
**Subject(s):** Daily Newspapers; French
**Circ:** (Mon.-Fri.)25,080
       (Sat.)38,236

**La Revue de Gatineau (36035)**
Le Reseau Select
430 boul de l'Hopital, Ste. 106
Gatineau, QC, Canada J8T 1T7
Phone: (819)568-7736
Fax: (819)568-7038
**Subject(s):** French; Free Newspapers
**Circ:** (Controlled)‡37,180

**Le Richelieu Dimanche (36325)**
84 rue Richelieu
Saint-Jean, QC, Canada J3B 6X3
Phone: (450)347-0323
Fax: (450)347-4539
**Subject(s):** Free Newspapers; French
**Circ:** (Paid)9
       (Controlled)35,500

# Gale Directory of Publications & Broadcast Media/140th Ed. — Eastern Provinces

## Newspaper Index

**La Parole** (36029)
Le Reseau Select
1050 Cormier
Drummondville, QC, Canada J2C 2N6
**Subject(s):** French; Free Newspapers
**Circ:** (Controlled)‡35,435

**Le Clairon Regional de St. Hyacinthe** (36321)
DBC Communications Inc.
655 Saint-Anne Street
Saint-Hyacinthe, QC, Canada J2S 5G4
Phone: (450)773-6028
Fax: (450)773-3115
**Subject(s):** Paid Community Newspapers; French
**Circ:** 33,926

**Guide de Montreal-Nord** (36146)
Le Reseau Select
6424 Jean-Talon Est, bur. 202
Montreal, QC, Canada H1S 1M8
Phone: (514)899-5888
Fax: (514)899-5984
**Subject(s):** Free Newspapers; French
**Circ:** (Controlled)32,869

**Info Dimanche** (36305)
Le Reseau Select
72 rue Fraser
Riviere-du-Loup, QC, Canada G5R 1C6
Phone: (418)862-1911
Fax: (418)862-6165
**Subject(s):** Free Newspapers; French
**Circ:** (Controlled)30,759

**L'Hebdo du St. Maurice** (36359)
L'Hebdo Du St. Maurice
2102 Champlain Ave.
PO Box 10
Shawinigan, QC, Canada G9N 6T8
Phone: (819)537-5111
Fax: (819)537-5471
**Subject(s):** Free Newspapers
**Circ:** (Combined)30,070

**Progres de St. Leonard** (36224)
Le Reseau Select
6424 rue Jeau-Talon Est, Bureau 202
Montreal, QC, Canada H1S 1M8
Phone: (514)899-5888
Fax: (514)899-5984
**Subject(s):** Free Newspapers; French
**Circ:** (Controlled)30,054

**Progres-Echo** (36300)
Les Editions Belcor
217, Ave. Leonidas
C.P. 3217, Succ. A
Rimouski, QC, Canada G5L 9G6
Phone: (418)723-4800
Fax: (418)723-1855
**Subject(s):** Free Newspapers
**Circ:** (Free)29,868

**Le Journal St. Francois Inc.** (36383)
Journal St. Francois Inc.
55, rue Jacques Cartier
Valleyfield, QC, Canada J6T 4R4
Phone: (450)371-6222
Fax: (450)371-7254
**Subject(s):** Free Newspapers
**Circ:** (Free)‡29,800

**Le Saint Francois** (36384)
Hebdos Monteregiens
55 Jacques-Cartier
Valleyfield, QC, Canada J6T 4R4
Phone: (450)371-6222
Fax: (450)371-7254
**Subject(s):** Free Newspapers
**Circ:** (Free)‡29,800

**Le/The Monitor** (36186)
Le Reseau Select
5925 Monkland
Montreal, QC, Canada H4A 1G7
**Subject(s):** French; Free Newspapers
**Circ:** (Combined)29,500

**L'Oeil Regional** (35993)
Le Reseau Select
393 boul Laurier
Beloeil, QC, Canada J3G 4H6
Phone: (450)467-1821
Fax: (450)467-3087
**Subject(s):** Free Newspapers; French
**Circ:** (Controlled)29,350

**Le Quotidien du Saguenay-Lac-Saint-Jean** (36008)
Le Progres du Saguenay
1051, boul. Talbot
Chicoutimi, QC, Canada G7H 5C1
Phone: (418)545-4474
Fax: (418)690-8824
**Subject(s):** French; Daily Newspapers
**Circ:** (Mon.-Sat.)28,914

**Le Journal de Saint-Hubert** (36320)
5863 blvd. Cousineau
Saint-Hubert, QC, Canada J3Y 7P5
Fax: (514)445-6347
**Subject(s):** Paid Community Newspapers; French
**Circ:** ‡28,800

**La Concorde** (36314)
Le Reseau Select
53 rue Saint-Eustache
Saint-Eustache, QC, Canada J7R 2L2
Phone: (450)472-3440
Fax: (450)473-1629
**Subject(s):** Free Newspapers; French
**Circ:** (Controlled)‡28,650

**La Voix** (36367)
38-A Augusta, 2nd Fl.
Sorel, QC, Canada J3P 1A3
Phone: (514)743-8466
Fax: (514)742-8567
**Subject(s):** Paid Community Newspapers
**Circ:** (Non-paid)28,400

**The Daily Gleaner** (34546)
984 Prospect St. W
PO Box 3370
Fredericton, NB, Canada E3B 2T8
Phone: (506)452-6671
Fax: (506)452-7405
**Subject(s):** Daily Newspapers
**Circ:** (Mon.-Sat.)28,172

**Les Deux Rives** (36368)
77 George St.
Sorel, QC, Canada J3P 1C2
Phone: (450)742-9408
Fax: (450)742-2493
**Subject(s):** Free Newspapers; French
**Circ:** (Free)‡28,000

**The McGill Daily** (36196)
Daily Publication Society/Le Delit Francais
3480 McTavish St. Rm. B-26
Montreal, QC, Canada H3A 1X9
Phone: (514)398-6790
Fax: (514)398-8318
**Subject(s):** College Publications; French
**Circ:** 28,000

**Le Saint Laurent/Portage** (36306)
16 Dudomaine St.
Riviere-du-Loup, QC, Canada G5R 2P5
Phone: (418)867-1465
Fax: (418)862-4387
**Subject(s):** Paid Community Newspapers
**Circ:** (Paid)27,693

**Les Nouvelles de l'Est** (36191)
3829 rue Ontario est
Montreal, QC, Canada H1W 1S5
Fax: (514)526-0515
**Subject(s):** Free Newspapers; French
**Circ:** (Controlled)27,338

**L'Information Regionale** (36005)
Les Hebdos Monteregiens
243, boul. d'Anjou
Chateauguay, QC, Canada J6J 2R3
Fax: (514)691-3883
**Subject(s):** Shopping Guides; French
**Circ:** (Free)‡27,105

**Cape Breton Post** (34736)
255 George St.
PO Box 1500
Sydney, NS, Canada B1P 6K6
Phone: (902)564-5451
Fax: (902)562-7077
**Subject(s):** Daily Newspapers
**Circ:** (Mon.-Sat.)26,500

**Nouvelles Saint-Laurent News** (36333)
685 Decarie, Ste. 304
Saint-Laurent, QC, Canada H4L 5G4
Phone: (514)855-1292
Fax: (514)855-1855
**Subject(s):** Free Newspapers; French
**Circ:** (Free)26,300

**Brossard-Eclair** (35994)
Le Reseau Select
7900 boul Taschereau, No. A-105
Brossard, QC, Canada J4X 1C2
Phone: (450)466-3344
Fax: (450)466-9019
**Subject(s):** Free Newspapers; French
**Circ:** (Controlled)‡26,296

**Le Soleil du St. Laurent** (36385)
Hebdos Monteregiens
184 rue Normandie
Boucherville, QC, Canada J4B 5S7
Phone: (450)655-5556
Fax: (450)655-9951
**Subject(s):** French; Free Newspapers
**Circ:** (Controlled)26,275

**Le Peuple Tribune** (36075)
Publications Le Peuple Inc.
421 Rue. Desjardins
Levis, QC, Canada G6V 5V3
Phone: (418)833-9398
Fax: (418)833-8177
**Subject(s):** French; Free Newspapers
**Circ:** (Free)‡26,033

**L'Eclaireur-Progres/Beauce Nouvelle** (36316)
Hebcor Inc. Division Editions Chaudet
12625 1E Ave. Est
Saint-Georges-de-Beauce, QC, Canada G5Y 2E4
Phone: (418)228-8858
Fax: (418)228-0268
**Subject(s):** Free Newspapers; French
**Circ:** (Paid)1,000
(Free)25,000

**Union** (36391)
Journal L'Union Inc.
43 Notre-Dame Est, C.P. 130
Victoriaville, QC, Canada G6P 3Z4
Phone: (819)758-6211
Fax: (819)758-1632
**Subject(s):** Paid Community Newspapers; French
**Circ:** ‡25,000

**Le Courrier de Portneuf** (36025)
Le Reseau Select
274 Notre Dame
Donnacona, QC, Canada G0A 1T0
**Subject(s):** Free Newspapers
**Circ:** (Controlled)‡23,917

**Le Rimouskois** (36299)
Les Editions Belcor
217, Ave. Leonidas
C.P. 3217, Succ. A
Rimouski, QC, Canada G5L 9G6
Phone: (418)723-4800
Fax: (418)723-1855
**Subject(s):** Free Newspapers; French
**Circ:** (Free)23,463

**L'Information de Ste. Julie** (36351)
Le Reseau Select
566 Jules-Choquet, Local 2
Sainte-Julie, QC, Canada J3E 1W6
**Subject(s):** Free Newspapers; French
**Circ:** (Controlled)22,363

**Lighthouse Log** (34684)
Lighthouse Publishing Ltd.
353 York St.
Bridgewater, NS, Canada B4V 3K2
Phone: (902)543-2457
Fax: (902)543-2228
**Subject(s):** Free Newspapers
**Circ:** (Paid)‡16
(Controlled)‡21,834

**Le Journal de Chambly Inc.** (36002)
Le Reseau Select
1685 rue Bourgogne, CP 175
Chambly, QC, Canada J3L 1V8
Phone: (450)658-6516
Fax: (450)658-3785

---

**Circulation:** ★ = ABC; △ = BPA; ♦ = CAC; • = CCAB; ❏ = VAC; ⊕ = PO Statement; ‡ = Publisher's Report; Boldface figures = sworn; Light figures = estimated.

# Eastern Provinces

**Subject(s):** French; Free Newspapers
**Circ:** (Controlled)‡20,700

**Le Courrier Frontenac** (36371)
Courrier Frontenac Inc.
541 Boul Smith nord
C.P. 789
Thetford Mines, QC, Canada G6G 5V3
Phone: (418)338-5181
Fax: (418)338-5482
**Subject(s):** Free Newspapers; French
**Circ:** (Free)20,572

**The Guardian** (35968)
165 Prince St.
PO Box 760
Charlottetown, PE, Canada C1A 4R7
Phone: (902)629-6000
Fax: (902)566-9030
**Subject(s):** Daily Newspapers
**Circ:** (Mon.-Sat.)20,260

**Le Courrier-Sud** (36258)
Le Reseau Select
3255 rue Marie-Victorin
Nicolet, QC, Canada J3T 1X5
Phone: (514)844-3131
Fax: (514)844-9679
**Subject(s):** Free Newspapers; French
**Circ:** (Controlled)‡20,047

**INSIEME** (36153)
4358, rue Charleroi
Montreal, QC, Canada H1H 1T3
Phone: (514)328-2062
Fax: (514)328-6562
**Subject(s):** Free Newspapers; Italian
**Circ:** (Paid)‡18,000
(Free)‡20,000

**Le Journal St-Louis & Mile End** (36180)
Le Reseau Select
4181, St-Dominique
Montreal, QC, Canada H2W 2A7
Phone: (514)849-9901
Fax: (514)849-9114
**Subject(s):** Free Newspapers; French
**Circ:** (Combined)20,000

**Superintendent's Profile Product-Service Directory** (35978)
525, ave. du Pont
Box 520
Alma, QC, Canada G8B 5W1
Phone: (418)668-4545
Fax: (418)668-8522
**Subject(s):** French; Free Newspapers
**Circ:** (Free)19,957

**La Voix du Sud** (36058)
Le Reseau Select
227-B, No. 2e Ave.
CP 789
Lac Etchemin, QC, Canada G0R 1S0
Phone: (514)844-3131
Fax: (514)844-9679
**Subject(s):** French; Free Newspapers
**Circ:** (Controlled)‡19,144

**La Voix de l'Est** (36039)
76 Dufferin St.
Granby, QC, Canada J2G 9L4
Phone: (450)375-4555
Fax: (450)777-7221
**Subject(s):** French; Daily Newspapers
**Circ:** (Mon.-Fri.)15,281
(Sat.)18,668

**Le Journal de Saint-Bruno** (36312)
1507, rue Roberval
Saint-Bruno, QC, Canada J3V 3P8
Phone: (450)653-3685
Fax: (450)653-6967
**Subject(s):** Paid Community Newspapers; French
**Circ:** 17,573

**Le Placoteux** (36334)
Journal Le Placoteux Enr.
491, 9E Ave. D'Anjou
C.P. 490
Saint-Pascal, QC, Canada G0L 3Y0
Phone: (418)492-2706
Fax: (418)492-9706

**Subject(s):** Free Newspapers; French
**Circ:** (Paid)‡60
(Non-paid)‡17,142

**L'Echo de la Baie** (36257)
140 Boul Perron Ouest
PO Box 129
New Richmond, QC, Canada G0C 2B0
Phone: (418)392-5083
Fax: (418)392-6605
**Subject(s):** Free Newspapers; French
**Circ:** (Paid)‡1,152
(Free)‡16,842

**Le Peuple de la Cote du Sud** (36102)
Peuple Cote Sud
80 Blvd. Tacheast
C.P. 430
Montmagny, QC, Canada G5V 3S7
Phone: (418)248-0415
Fax: (418)248-2377
**Subject(s):** Free Newspapers; French; Free Newspapers
**Circ:** (Free)‡16,250

**L'Express d'Outremont** (36264)
Hebdos Transcontinental
1032, Laurier Ouest
Outremont, QC, Canada H2V 2K8
Phone: (514)276-9615
Fax: (514)274-5564
**Subject(s):** Free Newspapers; French
**Circ:** (Controlled)16,000

**Au Fil des Evenements** (36280)
Universite Laval
3577 Alphonse Desjardins
Quebec, QC, Canada G1K 7P4
Phone: (418)656-7266
Fax: (418)656-2809
**Subject(s):** College Publications; French
**Circ:** (Free)15,000

**L'Echo Abitibien** (35977)
Les Echos Abitibiens
1462 Rue de La Quebecoise, 2o Etage
Val d'Or, QC, Canada J9P 5H4
Phone: (819)825-3755
Fax: (819)825-0361
**Subject(s):** Paid Community Newspapers; French
**Circ:** (Wed.)15,000

**IMPACT CAMPUS** (36345)
Universite Laval
1244, Pavillon Pollack
Sainte-Foy, QC, Canada G1K 7P4
Phone: (418)656-5079
Fax: (418)656-2398
**Subject(s):** College Publications; French
**Circ:** (Free)15,000

**Jacksonville Journal-Courier** (34530)
McLeansboro Times-Leader
355 King Ave.
Bathurst, NB, Canada E2A 1P4
Phone: (506)546-4491
Fax: (506)546-1491
**Subject(s):** Daily Newspapers
**Circ:** (Sun.)14,598
(Mon.-Sat.)14,994

**L'Information de Ste. Agathe** (36100)
Quedecor
1107, rue de Saint-Jouite
Mont-Tremblant, QC, Canada J8E 3J9
Phone: (819)425-8658
Fax: (819)425-7713
**Subject(s):** Free Newspapers; French
**Circ:** (Free)‡14,700

**Le Canada Francais** (36324)
84 Richelieu St.
Saint-Jean, QC, Canada J3B 6X3
Phone: (514)347-0323
Fax: (514)347-4539
**Subject(s):** Paid Community Newspapers; French
**Circ:** (Wed.)14,431

**Le Nord-Est Plus** (36356)
Le Reseau Select
365 boul. Laure
Sept-Iles, QC, Canada G4R 2X1
Phone: (514)844-3131
Fax: (514)844-9679

**Subject(s):** Free Newspapers; French
**Circ:** (Controlled)14,022

**L'Argenteuil** (36060)
La Cie d'Edition Andre Paquette Inc.
52 rue Principale
Lachute, QC, Canada J8H 3A8
Phone: (450)562-2494
Fax: (450)562-1434
**Subject(s):** French; Free Newspapers
**Circ:** (Combined)‡13,500

**La Tribune Canadienne Grecque** (36172)
7835 b Wiseman
Montreal, QC, Canada H3N 2N8
Phone: (514)272-6873
Fax: (514)272-3157
**Subject(s):** Free Newspapers; French; Greek
**Circ:** (Paid)200
(Free)13,500

**Coup d'Oeil** (36254)
Le Reseau Select
350 rue St. Jacques
Napierville, QC, Canada J0J 1L0
Phone: (450)245-3344
Fax: (450)245-7419
**Subject(s):** Free Newspapers; French
**Circ:** (Controlled)‡13,350

**Progres Watchman** (36061)
Compagnie d'edition Andre Paquette Inc.
52, rue Principale
PO Box 220
Lachute, QC, Canada J8H 3A8
Phone: (450)562-8593
Fax: (450)562-1434
**Subject(s):** Paid Community Newspapers
**Circ:** (Combined)‡13,100

**Gulf of Maine Times** (34677)
PO Box 339
Annapolis Royal, NS, Canada B0S 1A0
Phone: (902)532-0200
Fax: (902)532-0250
**Subject(s):** Free Newspapers; Social and Political Issues
**Circ:** (Controlled)13,000

**L'Etoile du Lac** (36309)
Le Reseau Select
1150, boul St. Felicien
Saint-Felicien, QC, Canada G8K 2W5
**Subject(s):** Free Newspapers; French
**Circ:** (Controlled)12,800

**L'Hebdo Mekinac/des Chenaux** (36358)
2102 Champlain
CP 10
Shawinigan, QC, Canada G9N 6T8
Phone: (819)537-5111
Fax: (819)537-5471
**Subject(s):** Free Newspapers; French
**Circ:** (Free)12,716

**The Buzz** (35964)
146 Richmond St.
PO Box 1945
Charlottetown, PE, Canada C1A 7N5
Phone: (902)628-1958
Fax: (902)628-1953
**Subject(s):** Paid Community Newspapers; Entertainment
**Circ:** 12,000

**L'Information** (36098)
L'Information
135 Doucet
Mont-Joli, QC, Canada G5H 1R3
Phone: (418)775-4381
Fax: (418)775-7768
**Subject(s):** French; Free Newspapers
**Circ:** (Free)‡11,920

**Le Peuple de Lotbiniere** (36284)
Publications Le Peuple Inc.
1000, rue St-Joseph
C.P. 130, Laurier Sta.
Quebec, QC, Canada G0S 1N0
Phone: (418)728-2131
Fax: (418)728-4819
**Subject(s):** French; Free Newspapers
**Circ:** (Free)‡11,900

**Gale Directory of Publications & Broadcast Media/140th Ed.**  **Eastern Provinces**

**Le Point (36024)**
Les Editions du Reveil
1570 Boul Wall Bell
Dolbeau, QC, Canada G8L 1H4
Phone: (418)276-5110
Fax: (418)276-5354
**Subject(s):** French; Free Newspapers
**Circ:** 11,466

**L'avenir De L'erable (36268)**
Le Reseau Select
1717 St. Calixte
Plessisville, QC, Canada G6L 1R2
Phone: (819)362-7049
Fax: (819)362-2216
**Subject(s):** Paid Community Newspapers; French
**Circ:** (Tues.)11,093

**The Brunswickan (34545)**
Brunswickan Publishing Inc.
The Brunswickan
21 Pacey Dr.,Ste. 35
Fredericton, NB, Canada E3B 5A3
Phone: (506)453-4983
Fax: (506)453-5073
**Subject(s):** College Publications
**Circ:** ‡11,000

**Le Bulletin (35996)**
Le Reseau Select
435 Principale
Buckingham, QC, Canada J8L 2G8
**Subject(s):** Free Newspapers; French
**Circ:** (Controlled)10,892

**Journal-Pioneer (35973)**
Journal Publishing Company Ltd.
4 Queen St.
PO Box 2480
Summerside, PE, Canada C1N 4K5
Phone: (902)436-2121
Fax: (902)436-3027
**Subject(s):** Daily Newspapers
**Circ:** (Mon.-Sat.)10,226

**The Dalhousie Gazette (34704)**
Dalhousie Gazette Publications Society/Dalhousie University
312-6136 University Ave.
Halifax, NS, Canada B3H 4J2
Phone: (902)494-2507
Fax: (902)494-8890
**Subject(s):** College Publications
**Circ:** 10,000

**The Journal (34706)**
St. Mary's University
Student Centre - Saint Mary's Univ.
923 Robie St.
Halifax, NS, Canada B3H 3C3
Phone: (902)496-8700
Fax: (902)425-4636
**Subject(s):** College Publications
**Circ:** (Free)10,000

**Journal do Emigrante (36161)**
Journal du Emigrante
4276 boul. St. Laurent
Montreal, QC, Canada H2W 1Z3
Phone: (514)843-3863
Fax: (514)843-3863
**Subject(s):** Portuguese; Shopping Guides
**Circ:** (Free)10,000

**TRIDENT (34709)**
Trident Military Newspaper
2740 Barrington St., CFB
PO Box 99000
Halifax, NS, Canada B3K 5X5
Fax: (902)427-4238
**Subject(s):** Military and Navy
**Circ:** (Paid)‡200
(Free)‡10,000

**La Voix du Dimanche (36093)**
305, De La Gare
Matane, QC, Canada J4W 3G2
Phone: (418)562-4040
Fax: (418)562-4607
**Subject(s):** Paid Community Newspapers
**Circ:** 9,800

**The Westmount Examiner (36398)**
The Westmont Examiner
245 Victoria Ave. 10
Westmount, QC, Canada H3Z 2M4
Phone: (514)484-5610
Fax: (514)484-6028
**Subject(s):** Free Newspapers
**Circ:** (Controlled)‡9,800

**Truro Daily News (34743)**
McLeansboro Times-Leader
6 Louise St.
PO Box 220
Truro, NS, Canada B2N 5C3
Phone: (902)893-9405
Fax: (902)893-0518
**Subject(s):** Daily Newspapers
**Circ:** (Mon.-Fri.)7,200
(Sat.)9,200

**La Gatineau (36090)**
114, de la Ferme
Maniwaki, QC, Canada J9E 3J9
Phone: (819)449-1725
Fax: (819)449-5108
**Subject(s):** French; Free Newspapers
**Circ:** (Free)‡9,000

**The Western Star (34599)**
106 W St.
PO Box 460
Corner Brook, NL, Canada A2H 6E7
Phone: (709)634-4348
Fax: (709)634-4675
**Subject(s):** Daily Newspapers
**Circ:** (Mon.-Sat.)8,796

**L'Etincelle (36402)**
193 St. St-George
Windsor, QC, Canada J1S 1J7
Phone: (819)845-2705
Fax: (819)845-5520
**Subject(s):** Paid Community Newspapers; French
**Circ:** (Free)‡8,700

**L'Avant-Poste (35982)**
Les Editions Belcor
59 St-Benoit Ouest
Amqui, QC, Canada G5J 2E4
**Subject(s):** French; Free Newspapers
**Circ:** (Controlled)8,542

**Miramichi Weekend (34564)**
Brunswick News Inc.
175 General Mansion Way
PO Box 500
Miramichi, NB, Canada E1V 3M6
Phone: (506)622-2600
Fax: (506)622-6506
**Subject(s):** Paid Community Newspapers
**Circ:** (Sat.)8,046

**L'Aviron (34534)**
Quebecor Inc.
113 Roseberry St. 406
PO Box 637
Campbellton, NB, Canada E3N 2G6
Phone: (506)753-3628
Fax: (506)759-7738
**Subject(s):** French; Paid Community Newspapers
**Circ:** ‡8,000

**The Casket (34680)**
The Casket Printing and Publishing Co.
88 College St.
PO Box 1300
Antigonish, NS, Canada V2G 2L7
Phone: (902)863-4370
Fax: (902)863-1943
**Subject(s):** Paid Community Newspapers
**Circ:** 8,000

**Hudson Gazette (36040)**
397 Main Rd.
PO Box 70
Hudson, QC, Canada J0P 1H0
Phone: (514)458-5482
Fax: (514)458-3337
**Subject(s):** Paid Community Newspapers
**Circ:** ‡8,000

**Journal Le Madawaska Ltee (34538)**
20, rue St-Francois
Edmundston, NB, Canada E3V 1E3
Phone: (506)735-5575

Fax: (506)735-8086
**Subject(s):** Paid Community Newspapers; French
**Circ:** (Wed.)‡7,724

**Miramichi Leader (34563)**
Brunswick News Inc.
175 General Mansion Way
PO Box 500
Miramichi, NB, Canada E1V 3M6
Phone: (506)622-2600
Fax: (506)622-6506
**Subject(s):** Paid Community Newspapers
**Circ:** (Tues.)★7,688

**Le Progres de Coaticook (36017)**
Le Reseau Select
74 rue Child
Coaticook, QC, Canada J1A 2J9
**Subject(s):** Free Newspapers; French
**Circ:** (Controlled)7,578

**2x4 (All About Wood) (36390)**
Editions C.R. Inc.
PO Box 1010
Victoriaville, QC, Canada G6P 8Y1
Phone: (819)752-4243
Fax: (819)382-2970
**Subject(s):** Wood and Woodworking; Furniture and Furnishings
**Circ:** (Controlled)‡7,569

**L'Information du Nord L'Annonciation (36099)**
Quedecor
1107, rue de Saint-Jouite
Mont-Tremblant, QC, Canada J8E 3J9
Phone: (819)425-8658
Fax: (819)425-7713
**Subject(s):** Paid Community Newspapers; French
**Circ:** (Paid)‡7,500

**Le Havre (36003)**
Le Reseau Select
119 Commerale Ouest
Chandler, QC, Canada G0C 1K0
Phone: (514)844-3131
Fax: (514)844-9679
**Subject(s):** French; Free Newspapers
**Circ:** (Controlled)‡7,493

**The New Freeman (34584)**
New Freeman Ltd.
1 Bayard Dr.
Saint John, NB, Canada E2L 3L5
Phone: (506)653-6806
Fax: (506)653-6818
**Subject(s):** Religious Publications
**Circ:** (Non-paid)‡173
(Paid)‡7,300

**The Northern Light (34531)**
McLeansboro Times-Leader
355 King Ave.
Bathurst, NB, Canada E2A 1P4
Phone: (506)546-4491
Fax: (506)546-1491
**Subject(s):** Paid Community Newspapers
**Circ:** (Wed.)6,786

**Journal des Rivieres (36032)**
322 A. Principal E.
PO Box 960
Farnham, QC, Canada J2N 1L7
Phone: (450)248-3303
Fax: (450)293-2093
**Subject(s):** French; Free Newspapers
**Circ:** (Free)6,650

**The Kentville Advertiser (34730)**
Transcontinental
9185 Commercial St.
New Minas, NS, Canada B4N 3G1
Phone: (902)681-2121
Fax: (902)681-0830
**Subject(s):** Paid Community Newspapers
**Circ:** (Fri.)5,349
(Tues.)6,630

**The Bugle (34592)**
Bugle Observer
110 Carleton St.
Woodstock, NB, Canada E7M 1E4
Phone: (506)328-8863
Fax: (506)328-3208

**Circulation:** ★ = ABC; △ = BPA; ♦ = CAC; ● = CCAB; ▫ = VAC; ⊕ = PO Statement; ‡ = Publisher's Report; Boldface figures = sworn; Light figures = estimated.

3885

## Eastern Provinces

**Subject(s):** Paid Community Newspapers
**Circ:** (Paid)6,310

**Northern Pen (34631)**
PO Box 520
10-12 N St.
Saint Anthony, NL, Canada A0K 4S0
Phone: (709)454-2191
Fax: (709)454-3718
**Subject(s):** Paid Community Newspapers
**Circ:** 6,316

**Yarmouth Vanguard (34746)**
Fundy Group Publications Ltd.
2 2nd St.
PO Box 128
Yarmouth, NS, Canada B5A 4B1
Phone: (902)742-7111
Fax: (902)742-2311
**Subject(s):** Paid Community Newspapers
**Circ:** (Fri.)4,586
(Tues.)6,305

**The Beacon (34606)**
Robinson Blackmore Printing and Publishing
PO Box 420
Gander, NL, Canada A1V 1W8
Phone: (709)256-4371
Fax: (709)256-3826
**Subject(s):** Paid Community Newspapers
**Circ:** (Paid)‡6,200

**Packet (34639)**
Robinson Blackmore Printing and Publishing
36 Austin St.
PO Box 8660, Sta. A
Saint John's, NL, Canada A1B 3T7
Phone: (709)579-1312
Fax: (709)722-2228
**Subject(s):** Free Newspapers
**Circ:** (Free)‡170
(Paid)‡6,022

**Quebec Home & School News (36225)**
Quebec Federation of Home and School Associations
3285 Cavendish Blvd., Ste. 560
Montreal, QC, Canada H4B 2L9
Phone: (514)481-5619
Fax: (514)481-5610
**Subject(s):** Education; Parenting
**Circ:** (Free)1,500
(Paid)5,900

**Le Riverain (36339)**
Sun Media Corp.
21A boul. Ste-Anne Est
CP 1900
Sainte-Anne-des-Monts, QC, Canada G0E 2G0
Phone: (418)763-7777
Fax: (418)763-7778
**Subject(s):** Free Newspapers
**Circ:** (Free)5,894

**Humber Log (34598)**
Robinson Blackmore Printing and Publishing
PO Box 946
Corner Brook, NL, Canada A2H 6G1
Phone: (709)639-9203
Fax: (709)639-1125
**Subject(s):** Paid Community Newspapers
**Circ:** (Free)‡125
(Paid)‡5,835

**Aurora (34694)**
Transcontinental
PO Box 99
Greenwood, NS, Canada B0P 1N0
Phone: (902)765-5441
Fax: (902)765-5833
**Subject(s):** Free Newspapers; Military and Navy
**Circ:** (Free)‡5,800

**The Eastern Graphic (35971)**
Island Press
PO Box 790
567 Main
Montague, PE, Canada C0A 1R0
Phone: (902)838-2515
Fax: (902)838-4392
**Subject(s):** Paid Community Newspapers
**Circ:** (Wed.)5,645

**La Frontiere (36311)**
25 Gamble E
Rouyn-Noranda, QC, Canada J9X 3B6
Phone: (819)762-4361
Fax: (819)797-2450
**Subject(s):** Paid Community Newspapers; French
**Circ:** (Wed.)5,614

**The Coast Guard (34733)**
Fundy Group Publications Ltd.
PO Box 100
Shelburne, NS, Canada B0T 1W0
Phone: (902)875-3244
Fax: (902)875-3454
**Subject(s):** Paid Community Newspapers
**Circ:** 5,600

**L'Echo de Louiseville (36085)**
Le Reseau Select
626, avenue Dalcourt
Louiseville, QC, Canada J3V 2Z6
**Subject(s):** Paid Community Newspapers; French
**Circ:** (Wed.)5,387

**The Record (36362)**
Hollinger Canadian Newspapers L.P.
1195 Galt E.
Sherbrooke, QC, Canada J1G 1Y7
Phone: (819)569-6345
**Subject(s):** Daily Newspapers
**Circ:** (Mon.-Fri.)5,260

**The Tribune (34535)**
The Tribune Publishers Ltd.
6 Shannon St.
PO Box 486
Campbellton, NB, Canada E3N 3G9
Phone: (506)753-4413
Fax: (506)759-9595
**Subject(s):** Paid Community Newspapers
**Circ:** (Wed.)5,238

**The Inverness Oran (34716)**
Inverness Communications Ltd.
PO Box 100
15767 Main St.
Inverness, NS, Canada B0E 1N0
Phone: (902)258-3400
Fax: (902)258-2632
**Subject(s):** Paid Community Newspapers
**Circ:** (Paid)5,073
(Free)5,154

**Advertiser (34615)**
Robinson Blackmore Printing and Publishing
PO Box 129
Grand Falls-Windsor, NL, Canada A2A 2J4
Phone: (709)489-2162
Fax: (709)489-4817
**Subject(s):** Free Newspapers
**Circ:** (Combined)‡5,050

**ADSUM (36109)**
Garnison Valcartier
C.P. 1000
Succ. Forces
Courcelette, QC, Canada G0A 4Z0
Phone: (418)844-5000
Fax: (418)844-6934
**Subject(s):** Military and Navy; Free Newspapers; French
**Circ:** (Free)‡5,000

**Les Enseignants (36062)**
Le Journal Les Enseignants Ltee.
1316 Domaine Du Moulin
L'Ancienne-Lorett, QC, Canada G2E 4N1
Phone: (418)872-6966
Fax: (418)872-6966
**Subject(s):** Education; French
**Circ:** ‡5,000

**La Voix Gaspesienne (36094)**
305 de la Gare St. Bureau 107
Matane, QC, Canada G4W 3J2
Phone: (418)562-4040
Fax: (418)562-4607
**Subject(s):** Paid Community Newspapers; French
**Circ:** (Wed.)4,979

**The Southern Gazette (34621)**
Robinson Blackmore Printing and Publishing
Ville Marie Dr.
PO Box 1116
Marystown, NL, Canada A0G 2M0
Phone: (709)722-8500

Fax: (709)722-2228
**Subject(s):** Paid Community Newspapers
**Circ:** (Free)‡550
(Paid)‡4,850

**The Pilot (34620)**
Robinson Blackmore Printing and Publishing
PO Box 1210
Lewisporte, NL, Canada A0G 3A0
Phone: (709)535-6910
Fax: (709)535-8640
**Subject(s):** Paid Community Newspapers
**Circ:** (Free)‡125
(Paid)‡4,841

**Springhill-Parrsboro Record (34735)**
Advocate Printing and Publishing
72 Main St.
Springhill, NS, Canada V0M 1X0
Phone: (902)597-3731
Fax: (902)667-1402
**Subject(s):** Paid Community Newspapers
**Circ:** ‡4,800

**The Digby Courier (34692)**
PO Box 670
Digby, NS, Canada B0V 1A0
Phone: (902)245-4715
Fax: (902)245-6136
**Subject(s):** Paid Community Newspapers
**Circ:** (Free)‡185
(Paid)‡4,700

**Nor'Wester (34652)**
Robinson Blackmore Printing and Publishing
PO Box 28
Springdale, NL, Canada A0J 1T0
Phone: (709)673-3721
Fax: (709)673-4171
**Subject(s):** Paid Community Newspapers
**Circ:** (Paid)‡3,989
(Free)‡4,700

**L'Echo de Frontenac (36059)**
L'Echo de Frontenac
5040, boul. des Veterans
Lac Megantic, QC, Canada G6B 2G5
Phone: (819)583-1630
Fax: (819)583-1124
**Subject(s):** French; Free Newspapers
**Circ:** (Free)3,992
(Non-paid)4,089
(Paid)4,580

**Saint Croix Courier (34589)**
St. Croix Printing and Publishing Co.
47 Milltown Blvd.
PO Box 250
Saint Stephen, NB, Canada E3L 2X2
Phone: (506)466-3220
Fax: (506)466-9950
**Subject(s):** Paid Community Newspapers
**Circ:** 4,579

**Kings County Record (34590)**
Cadogan Publishing Ltd.
PO Box 40
593 Main St
Sussex, NB, Canada E4E 7H5
Phone: (506)433-1070
Fax: (506)432-3532
**Subject(s):** Free Newspapers
**Circ:** (Tues.)4,524

**The Equity (36360)**
Le Reseau Select
133 rue Centre
Shawville, QC, Canada J0X 2Y0
Phone: (819)647-2204
Fax: (819)647-2206
**Subject(s):** Paid Community Newspapers; French
**Circ:** (Wed.)4,300

**Pictou Advocate (34731)**
Advocate Printing and Publishing
PO Box 1000
Pictou, NS, Canada B0K 1H0
Phone: (902)485-8014
Fax: (902)752-4816
**Subject(s):** Paid Community Newspapers
**Circ:** ‡4,021

**Amherst Daily News  (34675)**
Cumberland Publishing Ltd.
10 Lawrence St.
PO Box 280
Amherst, NS, Canada B4H 3Z2
Phone: (902)667-5102
Fax: (902)667-0419
**Subject(s):** Daily Newspapers

Circ: (Mon.-Fri.)3,956

**The Hants Journal  (34744)**
Optipress Ltd.
Box 550
73 Gerrish St.
Windsor, NS, Canada B0N 2T0
Phone: (902)798-8371
Fax: (902)798-5451
**Subject(s):** Free Newspapers

Circ: (Free)64
     (Paid)3,946

**L'Echo d'Amos  (35980)**
Val D'Or
1462 de la Quebecoise
Quebec, QC, Canada G9P 5H4
Phone: (819)732-6531
Fax: (819)825-0361
**Subject(s):** Paid Community Newspapers; French

Circ: ‡3,921

**Gleaner  (36043)**
Huntingdon Gleaner Inc.
66 Chateauguay St.
Huntingdon, QC, Canada J0S 1H0
Phone: (450)264-5364
Fax: (450)264-9521
**Subject(s):** French; Paid Community Newspapers

Circ: (Wed.)3,534

**Advance  (34720)**
Fundy Group Publications Ltd.
271 Main St.
PO Box 10
Liverpool, NS, Canada B0T 1K0
Phone: (902)354-3441
Fax: (902)354-2455
**Subject(s):** Paid Community Newspapers

Circ: 3,500

**The Aurora  (34619)**
500 Vanier Ave.
Box 423
Labrador City, NL, Canada A2V 2K7
Phone: (709)944-3239
Fax: (709)944-2958
**Subject(s):** Paid Community Newspapers

Circ: ‡3,480

**Journal Constructo  (36331)**
Groupe Constructo
200-1500 boul. Jules-Poitras
Saint-Laurent, QC, Canada H4N 1X7
Phone: (514)745-5720
Fax: (514)339-2267
**Subject(s):** French; Construction, Contracting, Building, and Excavating

Circ: (Combined)3,345

**The Sackville Tribune-Post  (34581)**
110 Main St.
PO Box 6191
Sackville, NB, Canada E4L 1G6
Phone: (506)364-4930
Fax: (506)364-4976
**Subject(s):** Paid Community Newspapers

Circ: (Wed.)3,344

**The Gulf News  (34626)**
Robinson Blackmore Printing and Publishing
Grand Bay Rd.
PO Box 1090
Port-aux-Basques, NL, Canada A0M 1C0
Phone: (709)695-3671
Fax: (709)695-7901
**Subject(s):** Paid Community Newspapers

Circ: ‡3,317

**The Oromocto Post-Gazette  (34577)**
291 Restigouche Rd.
Oromocto, NB, Canada E2V 2H5
Phone: (506)357-9813
Fax: (506)357-5222
**Subject(s):** Military and Navy; Free Newspapers

Circ: (Free)‡540
     (Paid)‡3,240

**L'Echo d'Abitibi Quest  (36053)**
Val D'Or
1462 de la Quebecoise
Quebec, QC, Canada G9P 5H4
Phone: (819)732-6531
Fax: (819)825-0361
**Subject(s):** Paid Community Newspapers; French

Circ: ‡3,212

**Courier Weekend  (34588)**
St. Croix Printing and Publishing Co.
47 Milltown Blvd.
PO Box 250
Saint Stephen, NB, Canada E3L 2X2
Phone: (506)466-3220
Fax: (506)466-9950
**Subject(s):** Paid Community Newspapers

Circ: ‡3,197

**Le Radar  (35997)**
Le Reseau Select
CP 8183
Cap-aux-Meules, QC, Canada G4T 1R3
Phone: (418)986-2345
Fax: (418)986-6358
**Subject(s):** French; Paid Community Newspapers

Circ: (Fri.)3,000

**The Georgian  (34653)**
Robinson Blackmore Printing and Publishing
PO Box 283
Stephenville, NL, Canada A2N 2Z4
Phone: (709)643-4531
Fax: (709)643-5041
**Subject(s):** Paid Community Newspapers

Circ: ‡2,956

**The Register  (34683)**
Transcontinental
227 Commercial St.
Box 640
Berwick, NS, Canada B0P 1E0
Phone: (902)538-3189
Fax: (902)538-8583
**Subject(s):** Paid Community Newspapers

Circ: 2,948

**Gaspe Spec  (36255)**
Sea-Coast Publications Inc.
128 Gerard D. Levesque Boul.
PO Box 99
New Carlisle, QC, Canada G0C 1Z0
Phone: (418)752-5400
Fax: (418)694-1119
**Subject(s):** Paid Community Newspapers

Circ: 2,818

**The Edge  (36328)**
Champlain Regional College Student Association
900 Riverside Dr.
Saint-Lambert, QC, Canada J4P 3P2
Phone: (450)466-4436
Fax: (450)672-9299
**Subject(s):** College Publications

Circ: (Free)2,500

**La Sentinelle  (36007)**
Le Reseau Select
317 3e Rue
Chibougamau, QC, Canada G8P 1N4
Phone: (514)844-3131
Fax: (514)844-9679
**Subject(s):** French; Paid Community Newspapers

Circ: (Tues.)2,394

**West Prince Graphic  (35963)**
Island Press Ltd.
PO Box 339
4 Railway Street
Alberton, PE, Canada C0B 1B0
Phone: (902)853-3320
Fax: (902)853-3071
**Subject(s):** Paid Community Newspapers

Circ: (Wed.)2,155

**The Low Down to Hull & Back News  (36394)**
759 Riverside Rd.
PO Box 99
Wakefield, QC, Canada J0X 3G0
Phone: (819)459-2222
Fax: (819)459-3831
**Subject(s):** Paid Community Newspapers

Circ: 2,000

**L'Uquoi  (36041)**
Universite du Quebec a Hull
283 Alexandre-Tache
C.P. 1250
Hull, QC, Canada J8X 3X7
Phone: (819)595-3900
Fax: (819)773-1835
**Subject(s):** French; College Publications

Circ: (Free)2,000

**La Cataracte  (34561)**
Brunswick News Inc.
229 Broadway Blvd.
PO Box 7363
Grand Falls, NB, Canada E3Z 2K1
Phone: (506)473-3083
Fax: (506)473-3105
**Subject(s):** Paid Community Newspapers; French

Circ: ‡1,963

**The Spectator  (34678)**
Opti Press
52 Victoria St.
PO Box 189
Annapolis Royal, NS, Canada B0S 1A0
Phone: (902)532-2219
Fax: (902)532-2246
**Subject(s):** Paid Community Newspapers

Circ: (Free)‡100
     (Paid)‡1,954

**Quebec Chronicle-Telegraph  (36346)**
3484 chemin Sainte Foy
Sainte-Foy, QC, Canada G1X 1S8
Phone: (418)650-1764
Fax: (418)650-5172
**Subject(s):** Paid Community Newspapers

Circ: (Paid)‡1,816

**Miramichi Headwaters  (34537)**
Brunswick News Inc.
PO Box 40
Doaktown, NB, Canada E0C 1G0
Phone: (506)365-2217
Fax: (506)365-7731
**Subject(s):** Free Newspapers

Circ: (Paid)1,269
     (Free)1,775

**The Advertiser  (34611)**
2 Harris Avenue
PO Box 129
Grand Falls, NL, Canada A2A 1S4
Phone: (709)489-2163
Fax: (709)489-4817
**Subject(s):** Paid Community Newspapers

Circ: (Wed.)1,611

**Northern Reporter  (34617)**
PO Box 310, Sta. B
Happy Valley, NL, Canada A0P 1E0
Phone: (709)896-2595
Fax: (709)896-2812
**Subject(s):** Paid Community Newspapers

Circ: ‡1,500

**The Coaster  (34616)**
Robinson Blackmore Printing and Publishing
PO Box 129
Grand Falls Winser, NL, Canada A2A 2J4
Phone: (709)489-2162
Fax: (709)489-4817
**Subject(s):** Paid Community Newspapers

Circ: ‡1,476

**La Voix Acadienne  (35974)**
La Voix Acadienne Ltee.
5 Ave. Maris Stella
Summerside, PE, Canada C1N 6M9
Phone: (902)436-6005
Fax: (902)888-3976
**Subject(s):** Paid Community Newspapers; French

Circ: (Controlled)1,050

**L'Echo de Malartic  (36089)**
Val D'Or
1462 de la Quebecoise
Quebec, QC, Canada G9P 5H4
Phone: (819)732-6531
Fax: (819)825-0361
**Subject(s):** Paid Community Newspapers; French

Circ: ‡914

Circulation: ★ = ABC; △ = BPA; ♦ = CAC; ● = CCAB; ❏ = VAC; ⊕ = PO Statement; ‡ = Publisher's Report; Boldface figures = sworn; Light figures = estimated.

**Le Courrier de Malartic (36088)**
Le Reseau Select
380 rue Abitibi
CP 4020
Malartic, QC, Canada J0Y 1Z0
Phone: (819)757-4712
Fax: (819)757-4712
**Subject(s):** French

**Circ:** (Controlled)891

**Abaka (36330)**
Tekeyan Armenian Cultural Association
825, rue Manoogian
Saint-Laurent, QC, Canada H4N 1Z5
Phone: (514)747-6680
Fax: (514)747-6162
**Subject(s):** Paid Community Newspapers; Armenian; French

**Circ:** (Free)‡75
(Paid)‡875

**The Townships Sun (36074)**
7 Conley
C.P. 28
Lennoxville, QC, Canada J1M 1Z3
Phone: (819)566-7424
Fax: (819)566-7424
**Subject(s):** Paid Community Newspapers

**Circ:** ‡750

## Northern Provinces

**Nunatsiaq News (34662)**
Nunatext Publishing Corp.
PO Box 8
Iqaluit, NT, Canada X0A 0H0
Phone: (867)979-5357
Fax: (867)979-4763
**Subject(s):** Eskimo Dialects; Paid Community Newspapers

**Circ:** (Combined)‡9,800

**Yukon News (36542)**
211 Wood St.
Whitehorse, YT, Canada Y1A 2E4
Phone: (867)667-6285
Fax: (867)668-3755
**Subject(s):** Paid Community Newspapers

**Circ:** (Mon.)5,740
(Wed.)6,384
(Fri.)7,796

**News/North (34669)**
Northern News Services Ltd.
5108-50th St.
Box 2820
Yellowknife, NT, Canada X1A 2R1
Phone: (867)873-4031
Fax: (867)873-8507
**Subject(s):** Paid Community Newspapers

**Circ:** (Controlled)3,344
(Paid)6,783

**Yellowknifer (34671)**
Northern News Services Ltd.
5108-50th St.
Box 2820
Yellowknife, NT, Canada X1A 2R1
Phone: (867)873-4031
Fax: (867)873-8507
**Subject(s):** Paid Community Newspapers

**Circ:** (Controlled)555
(Paid)4,486

**The Whitehorse Star (36541)**
Whitehorse Star (1977) Ltd.
2149 2nd Ave.
Whitehorse, YT, Canada Y1A 1C5
Fax: (867)668-7130
**Subject(s):** Daily Newspapers

**Circ:** (Mon.-Thurs.)2,621
(Fri.)4,402

**Slave River Journal (34657)**
Cascade Publishing Ltd.
207 McDougal Rd.
PO Box 990
Fort Smith, NT, Canada X0E 0P0
Phone: (867)872-2784
Fax: (867)872-2754
**Subject(s):** Paid Community Newspapers

**Circ:** ‡2,193

**The Hub (34658)**
8-4 Courtoreille St.
Hay River, NT, Canada X0E 1G2
Phone: (867)874-6577
Fax: (867)874-2679
**Subject(s):** Paid Community Newspapers

**Circ:** (Controlled)1,163
(Paid)1,826

**Inuvik Drum (34668)**
Northern News Services Ltd.
5108-50th St.
Box 2820
Yellowknife, NT, Canada X1A 2R1
Phone: (867)873-4031
Fax: (867)873-8507
**Subject(s):** Paid Community Newspapers

**Circ:** (Combined)1,462

**Deh Cho Drum (34666)**
Northern News Services Ltd.
5108-50th St.
Box 2820
Yellowknife, NT, Canada X1A 2R1
Phone: (867)873-4031
Fax: (867)873-8507
**Subject(s):** Paid Community Newspapers

**Circ:** (Combined)1,244

**L'Aquilon (34665)**
PO Box 1325
Yellowknife, NT, Canada X1A 2N9
Phone: (867)873-6603
Fax: (867)873-2158
**Subject(s):** Paid Community Newspapers

**Circ:** ‡1,000

## Western Provinces

**The Vancouver Sun (34343)**
Pacific Newspaper Group Inc.
200 Granville St., Ste. No. 1
Vancouver, BC, Canada V6C 3N3
Phone: (604)605-2000
Fax: (604)605-2720
**Subject(s):** Daily Newspapers

**Circ:** (Mon.-Thurs.)186,665
(Fri.)220,757
(Sat.)249,861

**The Province (34328)**
Pacific Newspaper Group Inc.
200 Granville St., Ste. No. 1
Vancouver, BC, Canada V6C 3N3
Phone: (604)605-2000
Fax: (604)605-2720
**Subject(s):** Daily Newspapers

**Circ:** (Mon.-Fri.)157,485
(Sun.)196,367

**The Edmonton Examiner (33923)**
Bowes Publishers
Ste. 250, 4990 - 92 Ave.
Edmonton, AB, Canada T6B 3A1
Phone: (780)453-9001
Fax: (780)451-1421
**Subject(s):** Free Newspapers

**Circ:** (Paid)162
(Non-paid)172,804

**The Edmonton Journal (33925)**
Southam Publications
PO Box 2421
Edmonton, AB, Canada T5J 0S1
Phone: (780)429-5200
Fax: (780)498-5677
**Subject(s):** Daily Newspapers

**Circ:** (Sun.)139,164
(Sat.)141,193
(Mon.-Thurs.)141,193
(Fri.)168,900

**Calgary Herald (33831)**
CanWest Interactive
215-16 St. SE
Calgary, AB, Canada T2P 0W8
Phone: (403)235-7438
Fax: (403)235-7438
**Subject(s):** Daily Newspapers

**Circ:** (Sun.)★113,167
(Mon.-Thurs.)★114,213
(Sat.)★122,255
(Fri.)★137,047

**The Vancouver Courier (34341)**
Vancouver Courier
1574 W 6th Ave.
Vancouver, BC, Canada V6J 1R2
Phone: (604)738-1411
Fax: (604)738-2154
**Subject(s):** Free Newspapers

**Circ:** (Sun.)106,950
(Wed.)132,650

**The Edmonton Sun (33926)**
Sun Media Corp.
4990 92nd Ave., Ste. 250
Edmonton, AB, Canada T6B 3A1
Phone: (780)468-0100
Fax: (780)468-0319
**Subject(s):** Daily Newspapers

**Circ:** (Mon.-Sat.)74,367
(Sun.)112,133

**The Now Newspaper (34277)**
Lower Mainland Publishing Ltd.
7889 - 132 St., No. 201
Surrey, BC, Canada V3W 4N2
Phone: (604)572-0064
Fax: (604)572-6438
**Subject(s):** Free Newspapers

**Circ:** (Combined)•109,792

**B.C. Bookworld (34288)**
3516 W 13th Ave.
Vancouver, BC, Canada V6R 2S3
Phone: (604)736-4011
Fax: (604)736-4011
**Subject(s):** Literature and Literary Reviews

**Circ:** (Paid)100,000

**Harbor City Star (34200)**
Daily News
2575 McCollough Rd., Ste. B1
Nanaimo, BC, Canada V9E 5W5
Phone: (250)729-4200
Fax: (250)758-4513
**Subject(s):** Free Newspapers

**Circ:** (Paid)‡65
(Free)‡97,381

**The Calgary Sun (33833)**
2615 12th St. NE
Calgary, AB, Canada T2E 7W9
Phone: (403)250-4122
Fax: (403)250-4180
**Subject(s):** Daily Newspapers

**Circ:** (Mon.-Sat.)★64,775
(Sun.)★95,259

**Times Colonist (34390)**
2621 Douglas St.
Victoria, BC, Canada V8T 4M2
Phone: (250)380-5211
Fax: (250)380-5353
**Subject(s):** Daily Newspapers

**Circ:** (Mon.-Sat.)75,072
(Sun.)75,213

**North Shore News (34216)**
North Shore Free Press Ltd.
1139 Lonsdale Ave.
North Vancouver, BC, Canada V7M 2H4
Phone: (604)980-0511
Fax: (604)985-1435
**Subject(s):** Free Newspapers; Free Newspapers

**Circ:** (Paid)557
(Non-paid)65,430

**The Burnaby-New Westminster News Leader (34085)**
Meadow Ridge Publications Ltd.
6569 Kingsway
Burnaby, BC, Canada V5E 1E1
Phone: (604)438-6397
**Subject(s):** Free Newspapers

**Circ:** (Combined)62,034

**Kelowna Capital News (34172)**
Kelowna Capital News Ltd.
2495 Enterprise Way
Kelowna, BC, Canada V1X 7K2
Phone: (250)763-3212
Fax: (250)862-5275
**Subject(s):** Paid Community Newspapers

**Circ:** (Fri.)•50,209
(Sun.)51,535
(Wed.)51,597

# Western Provinces

**Coquitlam Now** (34120)
Lower Mainland Publishing
2700 Barnet Hwy.
Coquitlam, BC, Canada V3E 1K9
Phone: (604)942-4192
Fax: (604)464-4977
**Subject(s):** Free Newspapers
**Circ:** (Non-paid)51,312

**WestCoast Families** (34346)
National Families Network
280 Nelson St., Ste. 224
Vancouver, BC, Canada V6B 2E2
Phone: (604)689-1331
Fax: (604)689-7011
**Subject(s):** Parenting
**Circ:** (Combined)50,000

**Burnaby Now** (34087)
Burnaby NOW
201A-3430 Brighton Ave.
Burnaby, BC, Canada V5A 3H4
Phone: (604)444-3451
Fax: (604)444-3460
**Subject(s):** Free Newspapers
**Circ:** (Non-paid)47,544

**Richmond News** (34249)
Lower Mainland Publishing Group Inc.
5731 No. 3 Rd.
Richmond, BC, Canada V6X 2C9
Phone: (604)270-8031
Fax: (604)270-2248
**Subject(s):** Free Newspapers
**Circ:** (Non-paid)46,937

**The Tri-City News** (34226)
Meadow Ridge Publications Ltd.
1405 Broadway St.
Port Coquitlam, BC, Canada V3C 6L6
**Subject(s):** Free Newspapers
**Circ:** (Non-paid)45,854

**The Richmond Review** (34250)
140-5671 No. 3 Rd.
Richmond, BC, Canada V6X 2C7
Phone: (604)247-3700
Fax: (604)606-8752
**Subject(s):** Free Newspapers
**Circ:** (Thurs.)45,500

**Abbotsford News** (34072)
Hacker Press Ltd.
34375 Gladys Ave.
Abbotsford, BC, Canada V2S 2H5
Phone: (604)853-1144
**Subject(s):** Paid Community Newspapers
**Circ:** (Thurs.)30,862
    (Tues.)42,849
    (Sat.)43,937

**Campbell River/Comox Valley North Islander** (34110)
1040 Cedar St.
PO Box 310
Campbell River, BC, Canada V9W 5B6
Phone: (250)287-7464
Fax: (250)287-8891
**Subject(s):** Free Newspapers
**Circ:** (Non-paid)‡41,506

**Vancouver Buy and Sell Press** (34210)
Buy and Sell Press
350 Columbia St.
New Westminster, BC, Canada V3L 1A6
Phone: (604)540-4455
Fax: (604)540-6451
**Subject(s):** Shopping Guides
**Circ:** (Thurs.)41,052

**Abbotsford Times** (34073)
30887 Peardonville Rd.
Abbotsford, BC, Canada V2T 6K2
Phone: (604)854-5244
Fax: (604)854-1140
**Subject(s):** Free Newspapers
**Circ:** (Non-paid)40,970

**The AdvanceNews** (34186)
Advance Newspaper Ltd.
Ste. 112 - 6375 - 202 St.
Langley, BC, Canada V2Y 1N1
**Subject(s):** Paid Community Newspapers
**Circ:** (Paid)40,400

**Central Alberta Life** (34028)
2950 Bremner Ave., Bag 5200
Red Deer, AB, Canada T4N 5G3
Phone: (403)343-2400
Fax: (403)342-4051
**Subject(s):** Free Newspapers; Farm Newspapers
**Circ:** (Non-paid)37,663

**The Langley Times** (34188)
Tanis Culley
20258 Fraser Hwy.
PO Box 3097
Langley, BC, Canada V3A 4R3
Phone: (604)533-4157
Fax: (604)533-0219
**Subject(s):** Free Newspapers
**Circ:** (Paid)26
    (Non-paid)33,406

**Saanich News** (34389)
818 Broughton St.
Victoria, BC, Canada V8W 1E4
Phone: (250)920-2090
Fax: (250)386-2624
**Subject(s):** Paid Community Newspapers
**Circ:** 32,800

**The Lethbridge Shopper** (34001)
Southern Alberta Newspaper Group
234 12B St. N
Lethbridge, AB, Canada T1H 2K7
Phone: (403)329-8225
Fax: (403)329-8211
**Subject(s):** Shopping Guides
**Circ:** (Free)‡32,500

**The Kootenay Advertiser** (34124)
Kootenay Advertiser 1997 Ltd.
1510 2nd St. N
Cranbrook, BC, Canada V1C 3L2
Phone: (250)489-3455
Fax: (250)489-3743
**Subject(s):** Free Newspapers
**Circ:** (Non-paid)‡31,753

**The Morning Star** (34369)
Caribou Press Ltd.
4407 25th Ave.
Vernon, BC, Canada V1T 1P5
Phone: (250)545-3322
Fax: (250)542-1510
**Subject(s):** Free Newspapers
**Circ:** (Paid)110
    (Non-paid)31,422

**Kamloops This Week** (34162)
Black Press Ltd.
1365 B Dalhousie Dr.
Kamloops, BC, Canada V2C 5P6
Phone: (250)374-7467
Fax: (250)374-1033
**Subject(s):** Free Newspapers
**Circ:** (Non-paid)29,581

**Alberta Sweetgrass** (33913)
Aboriginal Multi Media Society
13245 - 146 St.
Edmonton, AB, Canada T5L 4S8
Phone: (780)455-2700
Fax: (780)455-6777
**Subject(s):** Paid Community Newspapers; Ethnic Publications
**Circ:** (Combined)7,000
    28,000

**Central Alberta Adviser** (34027)
Red Deer Publishing
No. 121, 5301 43 St.
Red Deer, AB, Canada T4N 1C8
Phone: (403)346-3356
Fax: (403)347-6620
**Subject(s):** Free Newspapers
**Circ:** (Free)‡27,865

**The Chilliwack Progress** (34116)
Chilliwack Progress Ltd.
45860 Spadina Ave.
Chilliwack, BC, Canada V2P 6H9
Fax: (604)792-4936
**Subject(s):** Paid Community Newspapers
**Circ:** (Fri.)27,256
    (Tues.)27,451

**Maple Ridge-Pitt Meadows News** (34194)
Meadow Ridge Publications Ltd.
22328 119th Ave.
Maple Ridge, BC, Canada V2X 2Z3
Phone: (604)467-1122
Fax: (604)463-4741
**Subject(s):** Free Newspapers
**Circ:** (Non-paid)27,450

**West Kootenay Weekender** (34206)
Nelson Daily News
266 Baker St.
Nelson, BC, Canada V1L 4H3
Phone: (250)352-3552
Fax: (250)352-2418
**Circ:** 27,000

**Red Deer Life** (34031)
Red Deer Advocate Ltd.
2950 Bremner Ave.
Red Deer, AB, Canada T4N 5G3
Phone: (403)343-2400
Fax: (403)342-4051
**Subject(s):** Free Newspapers
**Circ:** (Non-paid)26,880

**Chilliwack Times** (34117)
Van Net Newspaper
45951 Tretheway Ave.
Chilliwack, BC, Canada V2P 1K4
Phone: (604)792-9117
Fax: (604)792-9300
**Subject(s):** Free Newspapers
**Circ:** (Paid)20
    (Non-paid)26,500

**The Calgary Straight** (34294)
Vancouver Free Press
1770 Burrard St., 2nd Fl.
Vancouver, BC, Canada V6J 3G7
Phone: (604)730-7000
Fax: (604)730-7012
**Subject(s):** Free Newspapers
**Circ:** (Non-paid)26,034

**The Democrat** (34089)
Democrat Publications Ltd.
3110 Boundary Road
Burnaby, BC, Canada V5M 4A2
Phone: (604)430-8600
Fax: (604)432-9517
**Subject(s):** Politics
**Circ:** 25,684

**St. Albert Gazette** (34039)
Gazette Press Ltd.
25 Chisholm Ave.
PO Box 263
Saint Albert, AB, Canada T8N 5A5
Phone: (780)460-5500
Fax: (780)460-8220
**Subject(s):** Paid Community Newspapers
**Circ:** (Sat.)18,893
    (Wed.)25,375

**Community Digest, Alberta Edition** (33842)
Community Digest Multicultural Publications
3545 32nd Ave. NE, Ste. 660
Calgary, AB, Canada T1Y 6M6
Phone: (403)271-8275
**Subject(s):** Ethnic Publications
**Circ:** (Free)25,000

**The Citizen** (34136)
The Cowichan Valley Citizen
469 Whistler St.
Duncan, BC, Canada V9L 4X5
Phone: (250)748-2666
Fax: (250)748-1552
**Subject(s):** Free Newspapers
**Circ:** (Free)‡24,000

**The Lethbridge Herald** (34000)
504 - 7th St. S.
PO Box 670
Lethbridge, AB, Canada T1J 3Z7
Phone: (403)328-4411
Fax: (403)328-4536
**Subject(s):** Daily Newspapers
**Circ:** (Sun.)★18,125
    (Mon.-Thurs.)★19,342
    (Sat.)★21,302
    (Fri.)★23,860

*Circulation: ★ = ABC; △ = BPA; ♦ = CAC; ● = CCAB; □ = VAC; ⊕ = PO Statement; ‡ = Publisher's Report; Boldface figures = sworn; Light figures = estimated.*

**Western Provinces**     Gale Directory of Publications & Broadcast Media/140th Ed.

**The Red Deer Express** (34030)
Red Deer Publishing
No. 121, 5301 43 St.
Red Deer, AB, Canada T4N 1C8
Phone: (403)346-3356
Fax: (403)347-6620
**Subject(s):** Free Newspapers
**Circ:** (Free)‡23,709

**The Medicine Hat Shopper** (34011)
922 Allowance Ave. SE
Medicine Hat, AB, Canada T1A 3G7
Phone: (403)527-5777
Fax: (403)526-7352
**Subject(s):** Shopping Guides
**Circ:** (Free)23,688

**The Pictorial** (34138)
Canadian Forces Base Esquimalt
2742 James St.
Duncan, BC, Canada V9L 2X9
Phone: (604)746-4471
**Subject(s):** Free Newspapers
**Circ:** (Free)‡22,475

**Comox Valley Record** (34121)
PO Box 3729
Courtenay, BC, Canada V9N 7P1
Phone: (250)338-5811
Fax: (250)338-5568
**Subject(s):** Free Newspapers
**Circ:** (Free)22,428

**Red Deer Advocate** (34029)
Red Deer Advocate Ltd.
2950 Bremner Ave.
Red Deer, AB, Canada T4N 5G3
Phone: (403)343-2400
Fax: (403)342-4051
**Subject(s):** Daily Newspapers
**Circ:** (Mon.-Sat.)★17,930
    (Fri.)★21,381

**Penticton Western News** (34220)
2250 Camrose St.
Penticton, BC, Canada V2A 8R1
Phone: (250)492-0444
Fax: (250)492-9843
**Subject(s):** Paid Community Newspapers
**Circ:** (Non-paid)20,062

**Cowichan News Leader** (34137)
Canadian Forces Base Esquimalt
2742 James St.
Duncan, BC, Canada V9L 2X9
Phone: (604)746-4471
Fax: (604)746-8529
**Subject(s):** Free Newspapers
**Circ:** (Free)‡19,576

**The Prince George Citizen** (34231)
The Citizen
150 Brunswick St.
PO Box 5700
Prince George, BC, Canada V2L 5K9
Phone: (250)562-2441
Fax: (250)562-9201
**Subject(s):** Daily Newspapers
**Circ:** (Mon.-Sat.)17,080
    (Fri.)19,192

**Sherwood Park News** (34046)
168 Kaska Rd.
Sherwood Park, AB, Canada T8A 4G7
Phone: (780)464-0033
Fax: (780)464-8512
**Subject(s):** Free Newspapers
**Circ:** (Free)‡18,085

**Windspeaker** (33951)
Aboriginal Multi-Media Society
13245-146 St.
Edmonton, AB, Canada T5L 4S8
Phone: (780)455-2700
Fax: (780)455-7639
**Subject(s):** Paid Community Newspapers; Ethnic Publications; Native American Interests
**Circ:** (Combined)18,000

**The Delta Optimist** (34134)
5485 Ladner Trunk Rd.
Delta, BC, Canada V4K 1X2
Phone: (604)946-4451
Fax: (604)946-5680

**Subject(s):** Free Newspapers
**Circ:** (Non-paid)16,938

**Campbell River Courier-Islander** (34111)
1040 Cedar St.
PO Box 310
Campbell River, BC, Canada V9W 5B5
Phone: (250)287-7464
Fax: (250)287-8891
**Subject(s):** Paid Community Newspapers
**Circ:** (Paid)16,350

**Parksville-Qualicum Beach News** (34219)
Parksville-Qualicum News
No 4-154 Middleton, PO Box 1180
Parksville, BC, Canada V9P 2H2
Phone: (250)248-4341
Fax: (250)248-4655
**Subject(s):** Free Newspapers
**Circ:** (Free)‡16,300

**Crossfield/Irricana Five Village Weekly** (33992)
Tall Taylor Publishing Ltd.
2nd St. & 2nd Ave.
PO Box 40
Irricana, AB, Canada T0M 1B0
Phone: (403)935-4221
Fax: (403)935-4981
**Subject(s):** Free Newspapers
**Circ:** (Free)15,832

**Weekend Advertiser** (34183)
Northern Sentinel Press
626 Enterprise Ave.
Kitimat, BC, Canada V8C 2E4
Phone: (250)632-6144
Fax: (250)639-9373
**Subject(s):** Shopping Guides
**Circ:** (Free)‡15,800

**Akal Guardian** (34273)
Charhdi Kala Weekly Punjabi Newspaper
7743 128th St., Unit 6
Surrey, BC, Canada V3W 4E6
Phone: (604)590-6397
Fax: (604)591-6397
**Subject(s):** Paid Community Newspapers
**Circ:** (Non-paid)15,000

**Charhdi Kala** (34275)
Charhdi Kala Weekly Punjabi Newspaper
7743 128th St., Unit 6
Surrey, BC, Canada V3W 4E6
Phone: (604)590-6397
Fax: (604)591-6397
**Subject(s):** Paid Community Newspapers; Ethnic Publications
**Circ:** 15,000

**Shuswap Market News** (34254)
Box 550
Salmon Arm, BC, Canada V1E 4N7
Phone: (250)679-3554
Fax: (250)679-7677
**Subject(s):** Free Newspapers
**Circ:** (Paid)‡14,900

**Leduc Representative** (33995)
Webco Publishers
4504-61 Ave.
Leduc, AB, Canada T9E 3Z1
Phone: (780)986-2271
Fax: (780)986-6397
**Subject(s):** Free Newspapers; Shopping Guides
**Circ:** (Free)‡13,969

**The Medicine Hat News** (34010)
3257 Dunmore Rd. SE
PO Box 10
Medicine Hat, AB, Canada T1A 7E6
Phone: (403)527-1101
Fax: (403)527-1244
**Subject(s):** Daily Newspapers
**Circ:** (Mon.-Sat.)★13,838

**The Kamloops News** (34161)
Hollinger Inc.
393 Seymour St.
Kamloops, BC, Canada V2C 6P6
Phone: (250)372-2381
Fax: (250)374-3884
**Subject(s):** Daily Newspapers
**Circ:** (Mon.-Sat.)★13,711

**Campbell River Mirror** (34112)
Canadian Forces Base Esquimalt
PO Box 459
Campbell River, BC, Canada V9W 5C1
Phone: (604)287-9227
**Subject(s):** Free Newspapers
**Circ:** (Wed.)‡10,775
    (Fri.)‡13,500

**Camrose Canadian** (33891)
Bowes Publishers Ltd.
4903 49 Ave.
Camrose, AB, Canada T4V 0M9
Phone: (780)672-4421
Fax: (780)672-5323
**Subject(s):** Free Newspapers
**Circ:** ‡13,071

**The Camrose Booster** (33890)
4925 48th St.
Camrose, AB, Canada T4V 1L7
Phone: (780)672-3142
Fax: (780)672-2518
**Subject(s):** Free Newspapers
**Circ:** (Paid)‡26
    (Free)‡12,775

**The Gauntlet** (33851)
Gauntlet Publications Society/University of Calgary
Rm. 319, MacEwan Students' Centre
2500 Univ. Dr. NW
Calgary, AB, Canada T2N 1N4
Phone: (403)220-7750
**Subject(s):** College Publications
**Circ:** (Free)12,000

**The Ubyssey** (34340)
Ubyssey Publications Society
24 Sub UBC
6138 Sub Blvd.
Vancouver, BC, Canada V6T 1Z1
Phone: (604)822-2301
Fax: (604)822-9279
**Subject(s):** College Publications
**Circ:** (Free)‡12,000

**The Windmill Herald** (34191)
VanDerHeide Publishing Company Ltd.
PO Box 3006, Sta. LCD1
Langley, BC, Canada V3A 4R3
Phone: (604)532-1733
Fax: (604)532-1734
**Subject(s):** Ethnic Publications; Paid Community Newspapers; Dutch
**Circ:** ‡11,500

**Wetaskiwin Times Advertiser** (34070)
Bowes Publishers Ltd.
5104 53rd Ave.
Wetaskiwin, AB, Canada T9A 2G5
Phone: (780)352-2231
Fax: (780)352-4333
**Subject(s):** Paid Community Newspapers
**Circ:** ‡11,415

**The Reporter** (34054)
Bowes Publishers Ltd.
5006 50th St.
Stony Plain, AB, Canada T7Z 1T3
Phone: (780)963-2291
Fax: (780)963-9716
**Subject(s):** Paid Community Newspapers
**Circ:** ‡11,320

**Peace Country Extra** (33981)
Bowes Publishers Ltd.
10604 100th St., Bag 3000
Grande Prairie, AB, Canada T8V 6V4
Phone: (780)532-1110
Fax: (780)532-2120
**Subject(s):** Free Newspapers
**Circ:** (Free)11,000

**Airdrie Echo** (33808)
Bowes Publishers Ltd.
114-1 Ave. NE
Airdrie, AB, Canada T4B 2B9
Phone: (403)948-7280
Fax: (403)912-2341
**Subject(s):** Paid Community Newspapers
**Circ:** (Paid)10,780

# Gale Directory of Publications & Broadcast Media/140th Ed.  Western Provinces

**Calgary Country  (33899)**
Bay 8, 206, 5th Ave. W
Cochrane, AB, Canada T4C 1X3
Phone: (403)932-3500
Fax: (403)932-3935
**Subject(s):** Free Newspapers
Circ:  (Free)‡10,400
        (Free)‡10,622

**The Flag & Banner  (34307)**
International Flag & Banner Inc.
1755 W 4th Ave.
Vancouver, BC, Canada V6J 1M2
Phone: (604)736-8161
Fax: (604)736-6439
**Subject(s):** Paid Community Newspapers; Local, State, and Regional Publications
Circ:  (Controlled)⊕**10,000**

**Gateway  (33929)**
University of Alberta
Students Union Bldg., Ste. 3-04
Edmonton, AB, Canada T6G 2J7
Phone: (780)492-5168
Fax: (780)492-6665
**Subject(s):** College Publications
Circ:  10,000

**The Martlet  (34386)**
University of Victoria
Student Union Bldg.
PO Box 3035
Victoria, BC, Canada V8W 3P3
Phone: (250)721-8360
Fax: (250)472-4556
**Subject(s):** College Publications
Circ:  (Free)10,000

**Wainwright Edge  (34062)**
Holmes Publishing Company Ltd.
414 10th St.
Wainwright, AB, Canada T9W 1P5
Phone: (780)842-4465
Fax: (780)842-2760
**Subject(s):** Free Newspapers
Circ:  (Free)9,800

**The Mission City Record  (34197)**
Mission City Record
33047 First Ave.
Mission, BC, Canada V2V 1G2
Phone: (604)826-6221
Fax: (604)826-8266
**Subject(s):** Paid Community Newspapers
Circ:  (Combined)9,734

**Innisfail Booster  (33990)**
Innisfail Publishing Inc.
4932 49th St.
Innisfail, AB, Canada T4G 1N2
Phone: (403)227-3477
Fax: (403)227-3330
**Subject(s):** Shopping Guides
Circ:  (Free)‡9,671

**Quesnel Cariboo Observer  (34243)**
Cariboo Press (1969) Ltd.
188 Carson Ave.
Quesnel, BC, Canada V2J 2Y8
Phone: (250)992-2121
Fax: (250)992-5229
**Subject(s):** Free Newspapers
Circ:  (Paid)5,000
        (Free)9,000

**Aldergrove Star  (34076)**
27106 Fraser Hwy.
Aldergrove, BC, Canada V4W 3P6
Phone: (604)856-8303
Fax: (604)856-5212
**Subject(s):** Paid Community Newspapers
Circ:  8,886

**Nanaimo Daily News  (34201)**
2575 McCullough Rd., Ste. B1
Nanaimo, BC, Canada V9S 5W5
Phone: (250)729-4200
Fax: (250)729-4256
**Subject(s):** Daily Newspapers
Circ:  (Mon.-Sat.)★**8,668**

**Trail/Beaver Valley/Salmo Pennywise  (34171)**
PFW Publications
Box 430
Kaslo, BC, Canada V0G 1M0
Phone: (250)353-2602
Fax: (250)353-7444
**Subject(s):** Shopping Guides
Circ:  (Free)8655

**Okotoks Western Wheel  (34017)**
Western Wheel Publishing
9 McRae St.
Bag 9
Okotoks, AB, Canada T1S 2A2
Phone: (403)938-6397
Fax: (403)938-2518
**Subject(s):** Free Newspapers
Circ:  (Paid)8,600

**The Powell River Peak  (34229)**
Peak Publishing Ltd.
4400 Marine Ave.
Powell River, BC, Canada V8A 2K1
Phone: (604)485-5313
Fax: (604)485-5007
**Subject(s):** Paid Community Newspapers
Circ:  (Paid)‡4,296
        (Non-paid)‡7,975

**Innisfail Province  (33991)**
Innisfail Publishing Inc.
4932 49th St.
Innisfail, AB, Canada T4G 1N2
Phone: (403)227-3477
Fax: (403)227-3330
**Subject(s):** Paid Community Newspapers
Circ:  ‡7,535

**West Side Revue  (34345)**
East Side Revue
1736 E 33rd Ave.
Vancouver, BC, Canada V5N 3E2
Phone: (604)327-1665
**Subject(s):** Free Newspapers
Circ:  (Free)‡7,500

**The Ring  (34388)**
UVic Communications
PO Box 1700
Victoria, BC, Canada
Fax: (250)721-8955
**Subject(s):** College Publications
Circ:  (Combined)7,000

**Cold Lake Sun  (33902)**
Bowes Publishers Ltd.
5217-55 St.
PO Box 268
Cold Lake, AB, Canada T9M 1P1
Phone: (780)594-5881
Fax: (780)594-2120
**Subject(s):** Paid Community Newspapers
Circ:  (Free)‡124
        (Paid)‡6,819

**Ponoka News & Advertiser  (34024)**
Ponoka News
PO Box 4217
5019 A Chipman Ave
Ponoka, AB, Canada T4J 1R6
Phone: (403)783-3311
Fax: (403)783-6300
**Subject(s):** Free Newspapers
Circ:  (Paid)‡25
        (Free)‡6,300

**Fort McMurray Today  (33976)**
Bowes Publishers Ltd.
8550 Franklin Ave.
Fort McMurray, AB, Canada T9H 3G1
Phone: (780)743-8186
Fax: (780)790-1006
**Subject(s):** Daily Newspapers
Circ:  (Mon.-Thurs.)4,398
        (Fri.)6,246

**Castlegar/Slocan Valley Pennywise  (34168)**
PFW Publications
Box 430
Kaslo, BC, Canada V0G 1M0
Phone: (250)353-2602
Fax: (250)353-7444
**Subject(s):** Shopping Guides
Circ:  (Free)6,156

**Williams Lake Tribune  (34404)**
Cariboo Press (1969) Ltd.
188 N 1st Ave.
Williams Lake, BC, Canada V2G 1Y8
Phone: (250)392-2331
Fax: (250)392-1140
**Subject(s):** Paid Community Newspapers
Circ:  ‡6,130

**Alberni Valley Times  (34223)**
4918 Napier St.
Port Alberni, BC, Canada V9Y 7N1
Phone: (250)723-8171
Fax: (250)723-0586
**Subject(s):** Daily Newspapers
Circ:  (Mon.-Fri.)6,121

**The Bowen Island Undercurrent  (34077)**
Metrovalley newspaper group
PO Box 130
Bowen Island, BC, Canada V0N 1G0
Phone: (604)947-2442
Fax: (604)947-0148
**Subject(s):** Paid Community Newspapers
Circ:  ‡6,000

**The 40-Mile County Commentator  (33818)**
Commentator Publishing Company Ltd.
PO Box 580
147 5th Ave W.
Bow Island, AB, Canada T0K 0G0
Phone: (403)545-2258
Fax: (403)545-6886
**Subject(s):** Paid Community Newspapers
Circ:  ‡5,891

**Vegreville Observer  (34060)**
5106 50th St.
PO Box 489
Vegreville, AB, Canada T9C 1R6
Phone: (780)632-2353
Fax: (780)632-3235
**Subject(s):** Free Newspapers
Circ:  (Free)5,700

**The Bulletin  (34270)**
Caribo Press
13226 N Victoria Rd.
PO Box 309
Summerland, BC, Canada V0H 1Z0
Phone: (250)494-5406
Fax: (250)494-5453
**Subject(s):** Free Newspapers
Circ:  (Free)5,500

**Trail Daily Times  (34279)**
Newspaper Ltd.
1163 Cedar Ave.
Trail, BC, Canada V1R 4B8
Phone: (250)368-8551
Fax: (250)368-8550
**Subject(s):** Daily Newspapers
Circ:  (Mon.-Fri.)5,350

**Boundary Bulletin  (34154)**
Hollinger Newspapers Ltd.
7330 2nd St.
PO Box 700
Grand Forks, BC, Canada V0H 1H0
Phone: (250)442-2191
Fax: (250)442-3336
**Subject(s):** Free Newspapers
Circ:  (Free)‡5,270

**Fraser Valley Record  (34196)**
Mission
33047 1st Ave.
Mission, BC, Canada V2V 1G2
Phone: (604)826-6221
Fax: (604)826-8266
**Subject(s):** Paid Community Newspapers
Circ:  (Non-paid)10
        (Paid)5,138

**Drayton Valley Western Review  (33908)**
PO Box 6960
Drayton Valley, AB, Canada T7A 1S3
Phone: (780)542-5380
Fax: (780)542-9200
**Subject(s):** Paid Community Newspapers
Circ:  5,000

Circulation: ★ = ABC; △ = BPA; ♦ = CAC; • = CCAB; ▫ = VAC; ⊕ = PO Statement; ‡ = Publisher's Report; Boldface figures = sworn; Light figures = estimated.

## Western Provinces

**The Lookout (34384)**
Canadian Forces Base Esquimalt
PO Box 17000
STN Forces
Victoria, BC, Canada V9A 7N2
Phone: (250)363-3014
Fax: (250)363-3015
**Subject(s):** Military and Navy; Paid Community Newspapers
**Circ:** ‡5,000

**Olds Gazette (34018)**
Leatherdale Publishing
Box 3870
Olds, AB, Canada T4H 1P6
Phone: (403)556-3351
Fax: (403)556-3464
**Subject(s):** Paid Community Newspapers
**Circ:** 3,990
5,000

**The Other Press (34209)**
Other Publications Society
Rm. 1020-700 Royal Ave.
New Westminster, BC, Canada V3L 5B2
Phone: (604)525-3542
Fax: (604)525-3505
**Subject(s):** Free Newspapers
**Circ:** (Free)5,000

**The Mountaineer (34037)**
The Mountaineer Publishing Co.
4814 49th St.
Rocky Mountain House, AB, Canada T4T 1S8
Phone: (403)845-3334
Fax: (403)845-5570
**Subject(s):** Paid Community Newspapers
**Circ:** (Wed.)4,861

**The Drumheller Mail (33909)**
515 Highway 10 E
PO Box 1629
Drumheller, AB, Canada T0J 0Y0
Phone: (403)823-2580
Fax: (403)823-3864
**Subject(s):** Paid Community Newspapers
**Circ:** ‡4,833

**Salmon Arm Observer (34253)**
51 Hudson Ave.
PO Box 550
Salmon Arm, BC, Canada V1E 4N7
Phone: (250)832-2131
Fax: (250)832-5140
**Subject(s):** Paid Community Newspapers
**Circ:** ‡4,775

**Beaumont Nouvelle (33906)**
La Nouvelle de Beaumont News
17 Athabasca Ave., Ste. 105
Devon, AB, Canada T9G 1G5
Phone: (780)987-3488
Fax: (780)987-4431
**Subject(s):** Paid Community Newspapers
**Circ:** 4,722

**Nelson Pennywise (34170)**
PFW Publications
Box 430
Kaslo, BC, Canada V0G 1M0
Phone: (250)353-2602
Fax: (250)353-7444
**Subject(s):** Shopping Guides
**Circ:** (Free)4,560

**Ukrainian News (33947)**
Edmonton Laser Graphics
12227 107 Ave., Ste. 1
Edmonton, AB, Canada T5M 1Y9
Phone: (780)488-3693
Fax: (780)488-3859
**Subject(s):** Ukrainian; Paid Community Newspapers
**Circ:** (Non-paid)2,000
(Paid)4,487

**Gulf Islands Driftwood (34258)**
Driftwood Publishing Ltd.
328 Lower Ganges Rd.
Salt Spring Island, BC, Canada V8K 2V3
Phone: (250)537-9933
Fax: (250)537-2613
**Subject(s):** Paid Community Newspapers
**Circ:** ‡4,372

**Le Franco-Albertain (33936)**
Le Franco-Albertain Ltee.
8527 82nd Ave., Ste. 201
Edmonton, AB, Canada T6C 3N1
Phone: (780)465-6581
Fax: (780)469-1129
**Subject(s):** French; Paid Community Newspapers
**Circ:** (Free)50
(Paid)4,300

**The Strathmore Standard (34055)**
Westmount Press Ltd.
PO Box 2250
Strathmore, AB, Canada T1P 1K2
Phone: (403)934-3021
Fax: (403)934-5011
**Subject(s):** Paid Community Newspapers
**Circ:** ‡4,241

**Creston Valley Advance (34127)**
1018 Canyon St.
PO Box 1279
Creston, BC, Canada V0B 1G0
Phone: (250)428-2266
Fax: (250)428-3320
**Subject(s):** Paid Community Newspapers
**Circ:** 4,179

**Sunny South News (33898)**
PO Box 30
Coaldale, AB, Canada T1M 1M2
Phone: (403)345-3081
Fax: (403)345-5408
**Subject(s):** Paid Community Newspapers
**Circ:** 4025

**Barrhead Leader (33813)**
PO Box 4520
Barrhead, AB, Canada T7N 1A4
Phone: (780)674-3823
Fax: (780)674-6337
**Subject(s):** Paid Community Newspapers
**Circ:** 4,010

**The MacEwan Journalist (33938)**
Grant MacEwan Community College
10045 156th St.
Center for The Arts Campus
Edmonton, AB, Canada T5J 4S2
Phone: (780)497-5623
Fax: (780)497-4287
**Subject(s):** College Publications
**Circ:** (Controlled)‡4,000

**Onoway Community Voice (34019)**
E.J. Lewchuck & Associates Ltd.
Bag 6000
Spruce Grove, AB, Canada T7X 2Z5
Phone: (780)962-9228
Fax: (780)962-1021
**Subject(s):** Free Newspapers
**Circ:** (Free)‡4,000

**Bonnyville Nouvelle (33817)**
Bonnyville Nouvelle Ltd.
5304 - 50 Ave.
Bonnyville, AB, Canada T9N 1Y4
Phone: (780)826-3876
Fax: (780)826-7062
**Subject(s):** Paid Community Newspapers
**Circ:** ‡3,942

**Canmore Leader (33892)**
50 Lincoln Park, Ste. 100
Canmore, AB, Canada T1W 1N8
Phone: (403)678-2365
Fax: (403)678-2996
**Subject(s):** Paid Community Newspapers
**Circ:** ‡3,845

**The Lacombe Globe (33994)**
5022 - 50 St.
Lacombe, AB, Canada T4L 1W8
Phone: (403)782-3498
Fax: (403)782-5850
**Subject(s):** Paid Community Newspapers
**Circ:** (Free)‡200
(Paid)‡3,800

**Nelson Daily News (34205)**
266 Baker St.
Nelson, BC, Canada V1L 4H3
Phone: (250)352-3552
Fax: (250)352-2418
**Subject(s):** Daily Newspapers
**Circ:** (Mon.-Fri.)3,746

**Capital (34056)**
Shearlaw Publishing
PO Box 158
Three Hills, AB, Canada T0M 2A0
Phone: (403)443-5133
Fax: (403)443-7331
**Subject(s):** Paid Community Newspapers
**Circ:** 3,709

**The Stettler Independent (34052)**
Stettler Independent Management Ltd.
Box 310
Stettler, AB, Canada T0C 2L0
Phone: (403)742-2121
Fax: (403)742-8050
**Subject(s):** Shopping Guides
**Circ:** ‡3,701

**The Valley Echo (34159)**
P.O. Box 70
Invermere, BC, Canada V0A 1K0
Phone: (250)342-9216
Fax: (250)342-3930
**Subject(s):** Paid Community Newspapers
**Circ:** 3400
‡3,580

**Community Press (34044)**
Flagstaff Printing
PO Box 567
Sedgewick, AB, Canada P0B 4C0
Phone: (780)384-2389
Fax: (780)384-3049
**Subject(s):** Paid Community Newspapers
**Circ:** ‡3,577

**Link Newspaper (34098)**
British Columbia Institute of Technology Student Association
3700 Willingdon Ave.
Student Association Campus Centre Bldg.
Burnaby, BC, Canada V5G 3H2
Phone: (604)432-8600
Fax: (604)434-3809
**Subject(s):** College Publications
**Circ:** (Free)‡3,500

**The Star (33894)**
PO Box 2229
36 3rd Ave West
Cardston, AB, Canada T0K 0K0
Phone: (403)653-4664
Fax: (403)653-4006
**Subject(s):** Paid Community Newspapers
**Circ:** 3,500

**Wabamun Community Voice (34050)**
E.J. Lewchuck & Associates Ltd.
Bag 6000
Spruce Grove, AB, Canada T7X 2Z5
Phone: (780)962-9228
Fax: (780)962-1021
**Subject(s):** Free Newspapers
**Circ:** (Free)‡3,500

**The Fairview Post (33973)**
10118-110 St.
Fairview, AB, Canada T0H 1L0
Phone: (780)835-4925
Fax: (780)835-4227
**Subject(s):** Paid Community Newspapers
**Circ:** 3,400

**Parklander (33989)**
Bowes Publishers Ltd.
104 McLeod Ave.
Hinton, AB, Canada T7V 2A9
Phone: (780)865-3115
Fax: (780)865-1252
**Subject(s):** Free Newspapers
**Circ:** (Paid)3,350

**Banff Crag and Canyon (33812)**
Bowes Publishers Ltd.
2nd Fl., 201 Bear St.
Banff, AB, Canada T1L 1H2
Phone: (403)762-2453
Fax: (403)762-5274
**Subject(s):** Paid Community Newspapers
**Circ:** ‡3,323

**The Vulcan Advocate** (34061)
211 Center St.
Box 389
Vulcan, AB, Canada T0L 2B0
Phone: (403)485-2036
Fax: (403)485-6938
**Subject(s):** Paid Community Newspapers

**Circ:** ‡2,408
‡3,317

**Lakeside Leader** (34047)
103 3rd Ave. NE
Slave Lake, AB, Canada T0G 2A0
Phone: (780)849-4380
Fax: (780)849-3903
**Subject(s):** Free Newspapers

**Circ:** (Free)1,020
(Paid)3,291

**The Hanna Herald** (33983)
Box 790
Hanna, AB, Canada T0J 1P0
Phone: (403)854-3366
**Subject(s):** Paid Community Newspapers

**Circ:** 3,200

**Gazette** (34155)
Hollinger Newspapers Ltd.
7330 2nd St.
PO Box 700
Grand Forks, BC, Canada V0H 1H0
Phone: (250)442-2191
Fax: (250)442-3336
**Subject(s):** Paid Community Newspapers

**Circ:** ‡3,198

**North Island Gazette** (34227)
7305 Market St.
Port Hardy, BC, Canada V0N 2P0
Phone: (250)949-6225
Fax: (250)949-7655
**Subject(s):** Paid Community Newspapers

**Circ:** ‡3,167

**Peace River Record Gazette** (34021)
Bowes Publishers Ltd.
PO Box 6870
Peace River, AB, Canada T8S 1S6
Phone: (780)624-2591
Fax: (780)624-8600
**Subject(s):** Paid Community Newspapers

**Circ:** (Paid)3,156

**High River Times** (33987)
618 Center St. S
High River, AB, Canada T1V 1E9
Phone: (403)652-2034
Fax: (403)652-3962
**Subject(s):** Paid Community Newspapers

**Circ:** (Free)199
(Paid)3,130

**Kaslo Pennywise** (34169)
PFW Publications
Box 430
Kaslo, BC, Canada V0G 1M0
Phone: (250)353-2602
Fax: (250)353-7444
**Subject(s):** Shopping Guides

**Circ:** (Free)3,093

**The Daily News** (34238)
Sterling Publishing Company Ltd.
801 2nd Ave. W
Prince Rupert, BC, Canada V8J 1A6
Phone: (250)624-6781
Fax: (250)624-2851
**Subject(s):** Daily Newspapers

**Circ:** (Mon.-Fri.)3,024

**Canadian Forces Base Cold Lake Courier** (33901)
PO Box 6190
Cold Lake, AB, Canada T9M 2C5
Phone: (403)594-5206
Fax: (403)594-2139
**Subject(s):** Military and Navy; Free Newspapers

**Circ:** (Free)‡3,000

**Capilano Courier** (34212)
Capilano Courier Publishing Society
Capilano College
2055 Purcell Way
North Vancouver, BC, Canada V7J 3H5
Phone: (604)986-1911
Fax: (604)984-4985

**Subject(s):** College Publications

**Circ:** (Free)3,000

**Carstairs Courier** (33895)
Tall Taylor Publishing Ltd.
PO Box 114
Carstairs, AB, Canada T0M 0N0
Phone: (403)935-4688
**Subject(s):** Free Newspapers

**Circ:** (Free)3,000

**The Meliorist** (34002)
Meliorist Publishing Society
University of Lethbridge
4401 University Dr., Ste. 166
Lethbridge, AB, Canada T1K 3M4
Phone: (403)329-2334
Fax: (403)329-2333
**Subject(s):** College Publications

**Circ:** (Free)‡3,000

**Sooke News Mirror** (34263)
6595 Sooke Rd.
PO Box 339
Sooke, BC, Canada V0S 1N0
Phone: (250)642-5762
Fax: (604)642-4767
**Subject(s):** Free Newspapers

**Circ:** (Free)3,000

**Wainwright Star Chronicle** (34063)
Holmes Publishing Company Ltd.
414 10th St.
Wainwright, AB, Canada T9W 1P5
Phone: (780)842-4465
Fax: (780)842-2760
**Subject(s):** Free Newspapers

**Circ:** (Paid)‡2,956

**Summerland Review** (34271)
Caribo Press
13226 N Victoria Rd.
PO Box 309
Summerland, BC, Canada V0H 1Z0
Phone: (250)494-5406
Fax: (250)494-5453
**Subject(s):** Paid Community Newspapers

**Circ:** ‡2,854

**The Free Press** (34140)
Sterling Newspapers Ltd.
342 2nd Ave.
Bag 5000
Fernie, BC, Canada V0B 1M0
Phone: (250)423-4666
Fax: (250)423-3110
**Subject(s):** Paid Community Newspapers

**Circ:** (Paid)2,800

**Bridge River-Lillooet News** (34192)
Lillooet News
979 Main St.
PO Box 709
Lillooet, BC, Canada V0K 1V0
Phone: (250)256-4219
Fax: (250)256-4210
**Subject(s):** Paid Community Newspapers

**Circ:** (Combined)2,652

**The Crowsnest Pass Promoter** (33815)
Westmount Press
13343 20th Ave.
PO Box 1019
Blairmore, AB, Canada T0K 0E0
Phone: (403)562-8884
Fax: (403)562-2242
**Subject(s):** Paid Community Newspapers

**Circ:** (Free)‡100
(Paid)‡2,600

**Omineca Express** (34367)
Cariboo Press Ltd.
PO Box 1007
Vanderhoof, BC, Canada V0J 3A0
Phone: (250)567-9258
Fax: (250)567-2070
**Subject(s):** Paid Community Newspapers

**Circ:** ‡2,600

**The Jewish Western Bulletin** (34314)
Western Sky Communications Ltd.
301-68 E 2nd Ave.
Vancouver, BC, Canada V5T 1B1
Phone: (604)689-1520
Fax: (604)689-1525

**Subject(s):** Paid Community Newspapers; Jewish Publications

**Circ:** (Combined)2,587

**Peace River Block News** (34130)
Sterling Newspapers Ltd.
901 100 Ave
Dawson Creek, BC, Canada V1G 1W2
**Subject(s):** Daily Newspapers

**Circ:** ‡2,548

**Ladysmith-Chemainus Chronicle** (34185)
Canadian Forces Base Esquimalt
PO Box 400
Ladysmith, BC, Canada V0R 2E0
Phone: (604)245-2277
**Subject(s):** Paid Community Newspapers

**Circ:** ‡2,533

**Cochrane Times** (33900)
Bay 8 206-5th Ave. W.
Cochrane, AB, Canada T4C 1X3
Phone: (403)932-3500
Fax: (403)932-3935
**Subject(s):** Paid Community Newspapers

**Circ:** ‡2,523

**Fort Nelson News** (34142)
4448 50th Avenue 3
Box 600
Fort Nelson, BC, Canada V0C 1R0
Phone: (250)774-2357
Fax: (250)774-3612
**Subject(s):** Paid Community Newspapers

**Circ:** ‡2,500

**Northern Sentinel** (34182)
Northern Sentinel Press
626 Enterprise Ave.
Kitimat, BC, Canada V8C 2E4
Phone: (250)632-6144
Fax: (250)639-9373
**Subject(s):** Paid Community Newspapers

**Circ:** 2,500

**South Peace News** (33985)
Box 1000
High Prairie, AB, Canada T0G 1E0
Phone: (780)523-4484
Fax: (780)523-3039
**Subject(s):** Paid Community Newspapers

**Circ:** 2,500

**Oliver Chronicle** (34218)
Tydeman Publishing
36083 97th St.
PO Box 880
Oliver, BC, Canada V0H 1T0
Phone: (250)498-4416
Fax: (250)498-3966
**Subject(s):** Paid Community Newspapers

**Circ:** 2,471

**Pincher Creek Echo** (34023)
714 Main St.
PO Box 1000
Pincher Creek, AB, Canada T0K 1W0
Phone: (403)627-3252
Fax: (403)627-3949
**Subject(s):** Paid Community Newspapers

**Circ:** 2,450

**The Daily Bulletin** (34181)
E. Kootenay Newspapers Ltd.
335 Spokane St.
Kimberley, BC, Canada V1A 1Y9
Phone: (250)427-5333
Fax: (250)427-5336
**Subject(s):** Daily Newspapers

**Circ:** (Paid)2,400

**East Side Revue** (34306)
1736 E 33rd Ave.
Vancouver, BC, Canada V5N 3E2
Phone: (604)327-1665
**Subject(s):** Free Newspapers

**Circ:** (Free)‡2,300

**Arrow Lakes News** (34198)
PO Box 189
Nakusp, BC, Canada V0G 1R0
Phone: (250)265-3823
Fax: (250)265-3841

# Western Provinces

Subject(s): Paid Community Newspapers
Circ: ‡2,249

**Smoky River Express (33974)**
South Peace News
PO Box 644
Falher, AB, Canada T0H 1M0
Phone: (780)837-2102
Fax: (780)837-2102
Subject(s): Paid Community Newspapers
Circ: ‡2,244

**The Golden Star (34151)**
413 A 9th Ave. N.
PO Box 149
Golden, BC, Canada V0A 1H0
Phone: (250)344-5251
Fax: (250)344-7344
Subject(s): Paid Community Newspapers
Circ: ‡2,225

**CFB Comox Totem Times (34118)**
Comox, BC, Canada V0R 2K0
Phone: (250)339-2541
Subject(s): Paid Community Newspapers; Military and Navy
Circ: (Combined)2,150

**The Pass Herald (33816)**
The Pass Herald Ltd.
Box 960
Blairmore, AB, Canada T0K 0E0
Phone: (403)562-2248
Fax: (403)562-8379
Subject(s): Paid Community Newspapers
Circ: (Free)110
     (Paid)2,153

**Tofield Mercury (34057)**
PO Box 150
Tofield, AB, Canada T0B 4J0
Phone: (403)662-4046
Fax: (403)662-3735
Subject(s): Paid Community Newspapers
Circ: ‡2,144

**Merritt Herald (34195)**
2090 Granite Ave.
Box 9
Merritt, BC, Canada V1K 1B8
Phone: (250)378-4241
Fax: (250)378-6818
Subject(s): Paid Community Newspapers
Circ: ‡2,094

**Claresholm Local Press (33897)**
EMS Press Ltd.
4913 2 St. W., PO Box 520
Claresholm, AB, Canada T0L 0T0
Phone: (403)625-4474
Fax: (403)625-2828
Subject(s): Paid Community Newspapers
Circ: ‡2,041

**Bricklayer (34026)**
Red Deer College
PO Box 5005
Red Deer, AB, Canada T4N 5H5
Phone: (403)343-1877
Fax: (403)347-8510
Subject(s): College Publications
Circ: ‡2000

**Calmar Community Voice (33889)**
E.J. Lewchuck & Associates Ltd.
Bag 6000
Spruce Grove, AB, Canada T7X 2Z5
Phone: (780)962-9228
Fax: (780)962-1021
Subject(s): Free Newspapers
Circ: (Free)‡2,000

**Lakes District News (34109)**
Cariboo Press Ltd.
Box 309
Burns Lake, BC, Canada V0J 1E0
Phone: (250)692-7526
Fax: (250)692-3685
Subject(s): Paid Community Newspapers
Circ: ‡1,950

**The Provost News (34025)**
Holmes Publishing Company Ltd.
5111-50th St.
PO Box 180
Provost, AB, Canada T0B 3S0
Phone: (780)753-2564
Fax: (780)753-6117
Subject(s): Paid Community Newspapers
Circ: (Free)106
     (Paid)1,941

**The Echo (33984)**
McKenzie Report Inc.
Box 1018
High Level, AB, Canada T0H 1Z0
Phone: (780)926-2000
Fax: (403)926-2001
Subject(s): Paid Community Newspapers
Circ: 1,908

**Queen Charlotte Islands Observer (34242)**
Observer Publishing Company Ltd.
PO Box 205
623 7th Street
Queen Charlotte, BC, Canada V0T 1S0
Phone: (250)559-4680
Fax: (250)559-8433
Subject(s): Paid Community Newspapers
Circ: ‡1,850

**The Weekly Review (34045)**
Flagstaff Printing
PO Box 567
Sedgewick, AB, Canada P0B 4C0
Phone: (780)384-2389
Fax: (780)384-3049
Subject(s): Paid Community Newspapers
Circ: ‡1,856

**Princeton-Similkameen Spotlight (34240)**
The Spotlight
282 Bridge St.
PO Box 340
Princeton, BC, Canada V0X 1W0
Phone: (250)295-3535
Fax: (250)295-7322
Subject(s): Paid Community Newspapers
Circ: 1,800

**Keremeos Review (34180)**
Bennett Publishing Ltd.
PO Box 130
Keremeos, BC, Canada V0X 1N0
Phone: (250)497-2653
Fax: (250)499-2645
Subject(s): Paid Community Newspapers
Circ: (Combined)‡1,735

**Okanagan Falls Review (34217)**
Bennett Publishing Ltd.
PO Box 130
Keremeos, BC, Canada V0X 1N0
Phone: (250)497-2653
Fax: (250)499-2645
Subject(s): Paid Community Newspapers
Circ: ‡1,735

**The Didsbury Review (33907)**
Contemporary Graphics Ltd.
PO Box 760
Didsbury, AB, Canada T0M 0W0
Phone: (403)335-3301
Fax: (403)335-8143
Subject(s): Paid Community Newspapers
Circ: ‡1603

**The Triangle (34041)**
Elk Island Triangle News
Box 170
Saint Michael, AB, Canada T0B 4B0
Phone: (780)896-2223
Fax: (780)896-2281
Subject(s): Paid Community Newspapers
Circ: ‡1,600

**The Macleod Gazette (33975)**
Macleod Gazette Ltd.
Box 720
Fort Macleod, AB, Canada T0L 0Z0
Phone: (403)553-3391
Fax: (403)553-2961
Subject(s): Paid Community Newspapers
Circ: ‡1,544

**Smoky Lake Signal (34049)**
Smoky Lake
4924-50th St.
PO Box 328
Smoky Lake, AB, Canada T0A 3C0
Fax: (403)656-4361
Subject(s): Paid Community Newspapers
Circ: (Free)1,200
     (Paid)1,500

**Valleyview Valley Views (34058)**
Valley Views Publishing Ltd.
4713-50 St.
PO Box 787
Valleyview, AB, Canada T0H 3N0
Phone: (780)524-3490
Fax: (780)524-4545
Subject(s): Paid Community Newspapers
Circ: 1500

**Mayerthorpe Freelancer (34008)**
Bowes Publishers Ltd.
Box 599
Mayerthorpe, AB, Canada T0E 1N0
Phone: (403)786-2602
Fax: (403)786-2663
Subject(s): Paid Community Newspapers
Circ: (Paid)1,455

**The Oyen Echo (34020)**
Holmes Publishing Company Ltd.
PO Box 420
Oyen, AB, Canada T0J 2J0
Phone: (403)664-3622
Fax: (403)664-3622
Subject(s): Paid Community Newspapers
Circ: (Free)‡35
     (Paid)‡1,439

**Edmonton Jewish Life (33924)**
307-10617 105 St. NW
7200 156th Street
Edmonton, AB, Canada T5R 1X3
Phone: (780)488-7276
Fax: (780)484-4978
Subject(s): Jewish Publications
Circ: (Paid)⊕1,415

**The Nanton News (34015)**
Bowes Publishers Ltd.
2129 20th St.
PO Box 429
Nanton, AB, Canada T0L 1R0
Phone: (403)646-2023
Subject(s): Paid Community Newspapers
Circ: 1,353

**Chetwynd Echo (34115)**
B. Sims
PO Box 750
Chetwynd, BC, Canada V0C 1J0
Phone: (250)788-2246
Fax: (250)788-9988
Subject(s): Paid Community Newspapers
Circ: (Paid)‡1,300

**The Record (34149)**
Box 279
Gold River, BC, Canada V0P 1G0
Phone: (250)283-2324
Subject(s): Paid Community Newspapers
Circ: (Combined)1,300

**Consort Enterprise (33903)**
Box 129
Consort, AB, Canada T0C 1B0
Phone: (403)577-3337
Fax: (403)577-3611
Subject(s): Paid Community Newspapers
Circ: ‡1,293

**Houston Today (34158)**
Houston Mall, Hwy. 16
PO Box 899
Houston, BC, Canada V0J 1Z0
Phone: (250)845-2890
Subject(s): Paid Community Newspapers
Circ: 1,257

**Kainai News (34051)**
Blood Tribe Communication News
PO Box 410
Standoff, AB, Canada T0L 1Y0
Phone: (403)737-2121
Fax: (403)737-2336

**Subject(s):** Free Newspapers; Native American Interests

**Circ:** (Free)‡850
(Paid)‡1,250

**Coronation Review (33904)**
Box 70, 4923 Victoria Ave.
Coronation, AB, Canada T0C 1C0
Phone: (403)578-4111
Fax: (403)578-2088
**Subject(s):** Paid Community Newspapers

**Circ:** (Paid)1,220

**Grande Cache Mountaineer (33980)**
Grande Cache Mountaineer Publishing Co.
PO Box 660
Grande Cache, AB, Canada T0E 0Y0
Phone: (780)827-3539
Fax: (780)827-3530
**Subject(s):** Paid Community Newspapers

**Circ:** (Paid)1,217

**Eagle Valley News (34261)**
Cariboo Press (1969) Ltd.
Cariboo Press Ltd.
PO Box 113
Sicamous, BC, Canada V0E 2V0
Phone: (250)836-2570
Fax: (250)836-2661
**Subject(s):** Paid Community Newspapers

**Circ:** ‡1,208

**The Valley Sentinel (34281)**
1012 Commerical Dr.
PO Box 688
Valemount, BC, Canada V0E 2Z0
Phone: (250)566-4425
Fax: (250)566-4528
**Subject(s):** Paid Community Newspapers

**Circ:** (Free)‡12
(Paid)‡1,182

**Castor Advance (33896)**
Stettler Independent Management Ltd.
Box 120
Castor, AB, Canada T0C 0X0
Phone: (403)882-4044
Fax: (403)882-2010
**Subject(s):** Paid Community Newspapers

**Circ:** ‡1,168

**Caledonia Courier (34144)**
PO Box 1298
Fort Saint James, BC, Canada V0J 1P0
Phone: (250)996-8482
Fax: (250)996-8451
**Subject(s):** Paid Community Newspapers

**Circ:** (Paid)‡1,147

**Agassiz Harrison Observer (34074)**
PO Box 129
Agassiz, BC, Canada V0M 1A0
Phone: (604)796-4300
Fax: (604)796-2081
**Subject(s):** Paid Community Newspapers

**Circ:** (Free)469
(Paid)1,011

**Coast Mountain News (34157)**
Box 250
Hagensborg, BC, Canada V0T 1H0
Phone: (250)982-2696
Fax: (250)982-2512
**Subject(s):** Paid Community Newspapers

**Circ:** ‡1,000

**The Times (34193)**
540 MacKenzie Boulvard
PO Box 609
Mackenzie, BC, Canada V0J 2C0
Phone: (250)997-6675
Fax: (250)997-4747
**Subject(s):** Free Newspapers

**Circ:** (Free)1,000

**The Bassano Times (33814)**
Bassano Publishers
402 1st Ave.
PO Box 780
Bassano, AB, Canada T0J 0B0
Phone: (403)641-3636
Fax: (403)641-3952
**Subject(s):** Paid Community Newspapers

**Circ:** 800

**Elk Point Review (33972)**
5022 49th Avenue
PO Box 309
Elk Point, AB, Canada T0A 1A0
Phone: (780)724-4087
Fax: (780)724-4087
**Subject(s):** Paid Community Newspapers

**Circ:** (Paid)‡589

# Periodical Index

Index entries are arranged geographically by region. Within region in this index, citations appear in descending order of circulation. Citations include publication title, entry number (given in parentheses immediately following the title), publisher name, address, phone and fax numbers, publication subject, and circulation figures.

## Great Lakes States

**Taste of Home (33027)**
Reiman Media Group
5400 S. 60th St.
Greendale, WI 53129
Fax: (414)423-3750
Subject(s): Food and Cooking
Circ: (Paid)4,000,000

**Playboy (8379)**
680 N. Lake Shore Dr.
Chicago, IL 60611
Phone: (312)751-8000
Fax: (312)751-8073
Subject(s): Men's Interests
Circ: (Paid)3,014,812

**American Legion Magazine (9813)**
American Legion National Headquarters
700 N Pennsylvania St.
PO Box 1055
Indianapolis, IN 46206
Phone: (317)630-1200
Fax: (317)630-1223
Subject(s): Veterans
Circ: (Paid)2,594,631

**Reminisce (33026)**
Reiman Media Group
5400 S. 60th St.
Greendale, WI 53129
Fax: (414)423-3750
Subject(s): History and Genealogy
Circ: (Paid)⊕1,750,000

**Ebony (8178)**
Johnson Publishing Company Inc.
820 S Michigan Ave.
Chicago, IL 60605-2191
Phone: (312)322-9200
Fax: (312)322-9375
Subject(s): Black Publications; General Editorial
Circ: (Paid)1,728,986

**Our Daily Bread (15344)**
RBC Ministries
PO Box 2222
Grand Rapids, MI 49501-2222
Phone: (616)942-6770
Fax: (616)957-5741
Subject(s): Religious Publications
Circ: (Non-paid)⊕1,600,000

**American Bowler (33021)**
American Bowling Congress
5301 S 76th St.
Greendale, WI 53129
Phone: (414)321-8310
Fax: (414)321-8356
Subject(s): (Bowling)
Circ: 1,500,000

**Endless Vacation (9637)**
Resort Condominiums International Inc.
9998 N. Michigan Rd.
Carmel, IN 46032
Phone: (317)805-9000
Fax: (317)805-9335
Subject(s): Travel and Tourism
Circ: (Paid)1,499,989

**Solidarity (15199)**
International Union, U.A.W.
8000 E. Jefferson Ave.
Detroit, MI 48214
Phone: (313)926-5291
Fax: (313)331-1520
Subject(s): Labor
Circ: (Non-paid)‡1,355,000

**The Elks Magazine (8188)**
425 W Diversey Pkwy.
Chicago, IL 60614-6196
Phone: (773)755-4900
Fax: (773)755-4792
Subject(s): Elks, Benevolent and Protective Order of
Circ: (Paid)1,126,090

**Michigan Living (15154)**
AAA Automobile Club of Michigan
1 Auto Club Dr.
Dearborn, MI 48126
Phone: (313)336-1506
Fax: (313)336-1344
Subject(s): Travel and Tourism
Circ: (Paid)1,037,811

**CONSUMERS DIGEST (9370)**
Consumers Digest Inc.
8001 N Lincoln Ave.
Skokie, IL 60077-3657
Phone: (847)763-9200
Fax: (847)763-0200
Subject(s): Consumerism
Circ: (Paid)1,000,033

**In Motion (9114)**
General Learning Communications
900 Skokie Blvd., Ste. 200
Northbrook, IL 60062
Phone: (847)205-3000
Fax: (847)564-8197
Subject(s): Education
Circ: (Non-paid)1,000,000

**INsider Magazine (9373)**
College Marketing Bureau Inc.
4124 W. Oakton St.
Skokie, IL 60076
Phone: (847)673-3703
Fax: (847)329-0358
Subject(s): College Publications; Youths' Interests
Circ: (Paid)1,000,000

**REQUEST (16387)**
Request Magazine
10400 Yellow Cir. Dr.
Minnetonka, MN 55343
Phone: (952)931-8740
Fax: (952)931-8490
Subject(s): Music and Musical Instruments
Circ: (Paid)1,000,000

**Moose Magazine (8996)**
Moose International
Moose International Inc
Rte 31
Mooseheart, IL 60539
Phone: (630)966-2209
Subject(s): Moose International
Circ: (Controlled)‡950,000

**Jet (8251)**
Johnson Publishing Company Inc.
820 S Michigan Ave.
Chicago, IL 60605-2191
Phone: (312)322-9200
Fax: (312)322-9375
Subject(s): Black Publications; General Editorial
Circ: (Paid)944,073

**Correspondent (32807)**
Aid Association for Lutherans
4321 N Ballard Rd.
Appleton, WI 54919
Phone: (920)734-5721
Fax: (920)730-4765
Subject(s): Religious Publications
Circ: (Controlled)930,000

**GMC Directions (15852)**
Sandy Corp.
1500 W Big Beaver Rd.
Troy, MI 48084
Phone: (248)649-0800
Fax: (248)816-2305
Subject(s): Automotive (Consumer)
Circ: (Non-paid)850,000

**Handy (16382)**
North American Media Group Inc.
12301 Whitewater Dr.
Minnetonka, MN 55343
Phone: (952)936-9333
Fax: (952)936-9169
Subject(s): Home and Garden
Circ: (Paid)850,000

**Pontiac Excitement (15860)**
Sandy Corp.
1500 W Big Beaver Rd.
Troy, MI 48084
Phone: (248)649-0800
Fax: (248)816-2305
Subject(s): Automotive (Consumer)
Circ: (Non-paid)850,000

**Traditional Home (8430)**
Meredith Corp.
333 N. Michigan Ave., Ste. 1500
Chicago, IL 60601
Phone: (312)580-1619
Subject(s): Home and Garden
Circ: (Paid)831,580

Circulation: ★ = ABC; △ = BPA; ♦ = CAC; • = CCAB; ▫ = VAC; ⊕ = PO Statement; ‡ = Publisher's Report; Boldface figures = sworn; Light figures = estimated.

# Great Lakes States

**American Legion Auxiliary's National News (9812)**
American Legion Auxiliary's National News
777 N Meridian, St., 3rd Fl.
Indianapolis, IN 46204-1189
Phone: (317)955-3845
Fax: (317)955-3884
**Subject(s):** Veterans
**Circ:** (Paid)780,000

**North American Hunter (16385)**
North American Media Group Inc.
12301 Whitewater Dr.
Minnetonka, MN 55343
Phone: (952)936-9333
Fax: (952)936-9169
**Subject(s):** (Hunting, Fishing, and Game Management)
**Circ:** (Paid)780,000

**American Girl (33283)**
Pleasant Co.
8400 Fairway Pl.
Middleton, WI 53562
Phone: (608)836-4848
Fax: (608)831-7089
**Subject(s):** Youths' Interests; Children's Interests
**Circ:** (Paid)700,000

**ComputerUser (16288)**
Key Professional Media
220 S. 6th St., 500
Minneapolis, MN 55402
Phone: (612)339-7571
**Subject(s):** Computers
**Circ:** (Paid)1,000
(Non-paid)670,000

**Automobile Magazine (14998)**
Primedia Inc.
120 E. Liberty St.
Ann Arbor, MI 48104-4193
Phone: (734)994-1153
Fax: (734)994-1153
**Subject(s):** Automotive (Consumer)
**Circ:** (Paid)653,574

**Cooking Pleasures (16379)**
North American Media Group Inc.
12301 Whitewater Dr.
Minnetonka, MN 55343
Phone: (952)936-9333
Fax: (952)936-9169
**Subject(s):** Home and Garden
**Circ:** (Paid)600,000

**Home & Away (Ohio Edition) (25194)**
Ohio Auto Club
90 E. Wilson Bridge Rd.
Worthington, OH 43085
Phone: (614)431-7919
Fax: (614)410-0756
**Subject(s):** Travel and Tourism; Local, State, and Regional Publications; Automotive (Consumer)
**Circ:** (Controlled)590,000

**Gardening How-To (16381)**
North American Media Group Inc.
12301 Whitewater Dr.
Minnetonka, MN 55343
Phone: (952)936-9333
Fax: (952)936-9169
**Subject(s):** Home and Garden
**Circ:** (Paid)550,000

**FFA New Horizons (7975)**
The National FFA Organization
191 S. Gary Ave.
Carol Stream, IL 60188
Phone: (630)462-2342
Fax: (630)462-2202
**Subject(s):** General Agriculture; Youths' Interests
**Circ:** (Controlled)‡512,644

**The Lion Magazine (9151)**
Lions Clubs International
300 W 22nd St.
Oak Brook, IL 60523-8815
Phone: (630)571-5466
Fax: (630)571-8890
**Subject(s):** Unclassified Fraternal
**Circ:** (Paid)503,016

**United Hemispheres (8432)**
Pace Communications Inc.
PO Box 66100
Chicago, IL
**Subject(s):** In-Flight Publications
**Circ:** (Non-paid)‡500,771

**Family Safety & Health (8809)**
National Safety Council
1121 Spring Lake Dr.
Itasca, IL 60143-3201
Phone: (630)285-1121
Fax: (630)285-1315
**Subject(s):** Health; Safety
**Circ:** ‡500,000

**North American Fisherman (16384)**
North American Media Group Inc.
12301 Whitewater Dr.
Minnetonka, MN 55343
Phone: (952)936-9333
Fax: (952)936-9169
**Subject(s):** (Hunting, Fishing, and Game Management)
**Circ:** (Paid)500,000

**PGA Tour Partners (16386)**
North American Media Group Inc.
12301 Whitewater Dr.
Minnetonka, MN 55343
Phone: (952)936-9333
Fax: (952)936-9169
**Subject(s):** (Golf)
**Circ:** (Paid)500,000

**The ROTARIAN (8679)**
Rotary International
One Rotary Ctr.
1560 Sherman Ave.
Evanston, IL 60201
Phone: (847)866-3000
Fax: (847)866-9732
**Circ:** (Paid)498,866

**Classic Cookbooks (16284)**
Pillsbury Co.
200 6th St., M.S. 28M7
Minneapolis, MN 55402
Fax: (612)330-4875
**Subject(s):** Food and Cooking
**Circ:** (Paid)450,000

**Country Sampler (9336)**
Country Sampler Group
707 Kautz Rd.
Saint Charles, IL 60174
Phone: (630)377-8000
Fax: (630)377-8914
**Subject(s):** Crafts, Models, Hobbies, and Contests; Home and Garden; Lifestyle
**Circ:** (Paid)434,323

**Ohio Motorist (24783)**
AAA Ohio Motorists Association
5700 Brecksville Rd.
Independence, OH 44131
Phone: (216)606-6194
Fax: (216)606-6710
**Subject(s):** Automotive (Consumer); Travel and Tourism
**Circ:** ‡430,000

**The Lutheran (8320)**
Augsburg Fortress, Publishers
8765 W. Higgins Rd.
Chicago, IL 60631-4183
Phone: (773)380-2540
Fax: (773)380-2751
**Subject(s):** Religious Publications
**Circ:** ‡420,000

**Farm & Ranch Living (33025)**
Reiman Media Group
5925 Country Lane
Greendale, WI 53129
**Subject(s):** General Agriculture; Home and Garden; Lifestyle
**Circ:** 400,000

**Forward Day by Day (24309)**
Forward Movement Publications
300 W 4th St., 2nd Fl.
Cincinnati, OH 45202-2666
Phone: (513)721-6659
Fax: (513)721-0729
**Subject(s):** Religious Publications
**Circ:** 400,000

**The Modern Woodmen Magazine (9293)**
Modern Woodmen of America
1701 1st Ave.
PO Box 2005
Rock Island, IL 61204-2005
Phone: (309)786-6481
Fax: (309)793-5603
**Subject(s):** Modern Woodmen of America
**Circ:** ‡400,000

**The Saturday Evening Post (9910)**
The Saturday Evening Post Society
1100 Waterway Blvd.
Indianapolis, IN 46202
Phone: (317)634-1100
**Subject(s):** Health and Healthcare
**Circ:** (Paid)385,123

**Home & Away (8582)**
AAA Chicago Motor Club
999 E Touhy Ave.
Des Plaines, IL 60018
Phone: (847)390-9000
Fax: (847)390-7060
**Subject(s):** Automotive (Consumer); Travel and Tourism; Local, State, and Regional Publications
**Circ:** 370,000

**JAMA (8250)**
American Medical Association Alliance
515 N. State St.
Chicago, IL 60610
Phone: (312)464-5000
Fax: (312)464-5020
**Subject(s):** Medicine and Surgery
**Circ:** ‡369,826

**AutoWeek (15167)**
Crain Communications Inc.
1155 Gratiot Ave.
Detroit, MI 48207-2997
Phone: (313)446-6000
Fax: (313)446-0347
**Subject(s):** (Auto Racing); Automotive (Consumer)
**Circ:** (Paid)360,000

**Complete Woman (8155)**
Associated Publications Inc.
875 N Michigan Ave., Ste. 3434
Chicago, IL 60611-1901
Phone: (312)266-8680
**Subject(s):** Women's Interests
**Circ:** (Non-paid)5,000
(Paid)350,000

**Home & Family Finance (33188)**
Credit Union National Association Inc.
5710 Mineral Point Rd.
PO Box 431
Madison, WI 53705-0431
Phone: (608)231-4075
Fax: (608)231-4263
**Subject(s):** Business
**Circ:** ‡350,000

**St. Anthony Messenger (24330)**
28 W. Liberty St.
Cincinnati, OH 45202-6498
Phone: (513)241-5615
Fax: (513)241-1197
**Subject(s):** Religious Publications
**Circ:** ‡350,000

**American Medical News (8075)**
American Medical Association Alliance
515 N. State St.
Chicago, IL 60610
Phone: (312)464-5000
Fax: (312)464-5020
**Subject(s):** Medicine and Surgery
**Circ:** (Non-paid)7,685
(Paid)332,331

**Country Extra (33023)**
Reiman Media Group
5400 S. 60th St.
Greendale, WI 53129
Fax: (414)423-3750
**Subject(s):** Lifestyle
**Circ:** (Paid)⊕325,000

**ABA Journal** (8052)
American Bar Association
321 N Clark St.
Chicago, IL 60610
Phone: (312)988-5000
Fax: (312)988-5177
**Subject(s):** Law
**Circ:** (Non-paid)106,251
(Paid)320,100

**This is Indianapolis** (9916)
Indianapolis Convention and Visitors Association
One RCA Dome, Ste. 100
Indianapolis, IN 46225
Phone: (317)639-4282
Fax: (317)684-2598
**Subject(s):** Travel and Tourism; Local, State, and Regional Publications; City, Hotel, Railroad, and Travel Guides
**Circ:** (Controlled)300,000

**ON WISCONSIN** (33208)
Wisconsin Alumni Association
650 N Lake St.
Madison, WI 53706
Phone: (608)262-2551
Fax: (608)265-8771
**Subject(s):** College Publications
**Circ:** ‡294,000

**Home & Away Magazine** (33187)
5401 Excelsior Dr.
Madison, WI 53717
Phone: (608)828-2487
Fax: (608)828-2530
**Subject(s):** Automotive (Consumer)
**Circ:** ‡292,822

**TOPS News** (33338)
TOPS Club Inc.
PO Box 070360
4565 South 5th Street
Milwaukee, WI 53207-0360
Phone: (414)482-4620
Fax: (414)482-1655
**Subject(s):** Health
**Circ:** (Controlled)‡4,803
(Paid)‡292,827

**Country Living (Ohio)** (24545)
Ohio Rural Electric Cooperatives Inc.
6677 Busch Blvd.
PO Box 26036
Columbus, OH 43226-0036
Phone: (614)846-5757
Fax: (614)846-7108
**Subject(s):** Rural Electrification; Local, State, and Regional Publications
**Circ:** (Paid)282,050

**Better Investing** (15563)
National Association of Investors Corp.
711 West Thirteen Mile Rd.
Madison Heights, MI 48071
Phone: (248)583-6242
Fax: (248)583-4880
**Subject(s):** Banking, Finance, and Investments
**Circ:** (Paid)275,000

**Turtle Magazine for Preschool Kids** (9920)
Children's Better Health Institute
1100 Waterway Blvd.
PO Box 567
Indianapolis, IN 46202
Phone: (317)634-1100
Fax: (317)684-8094
**Subject(s):** Children's Interests
**Circ:** (Paid)275,000

**The Hoosier Farmer** (9856)
Indiana Farm Bureau Inc.
225 SE St.
PO Box 1290
Indianapolis, IN 46206
Phone: (317)692-7822
Fax: (317)692-7854
**Subject(s):** Farm Bureau, Grange, and Cooperative Associations
**Circ:** ‡271,000

**Kiwanis Magazine** (9886)
Kiwanis International
3636 Woodview Trace
Indianapolis, IN 46268-3196
Phone: (317)875-8755
Fax: (317)879-0204
**Subject(s):** Unclassified Fraternal
**Circ:** (Paid)258,674

**Today's Christian Woman** (9528)
Christianity Today International
465 Gundersen Dr.
Carol Stream, IL 60188
Phone: (630)260-6200
Fax: (630)260-0114
**Subject(s):** Religious Publications; Women's Interests
**Circ:** (Non-paid)‡6,892
(Paid)‡256,000

**In-Fisherman** (15946)
Primedia Inc.
7819 Highland Scenic Rd.
Baxter, MN 56425
Phone: (218)829-1648
Fax: (218)829-2371
**Subject(s):** (Hunting, Fishing, and Game Management)
**Circ:** (Paid)254,175

**Electric Consumer** (9848)
Indiana Statewide Rural Electric Coop.
PO Box 24517
Indianapolis, IN 46224
Phone: (317)487-2220
Fax: (317)247-5220
**Subject(s):** Rural Electrification; Local, State, and Regional Publications
**Circ:** (Non-paid)172
(Paid)250,000

**Farm Industry News** (16296)
Southwest Farm Press
c/o Karen McMahon
7900 International Drive
Ste. 300
Minneapolis, MN 55425
Phone: (800)722-5334
Fax: (952)851-4601
**Subject(s):** General Agriculture
**Circ:** (Non-paid)‡250,000

**American Motorcyclist** (24999)
American Motorcycle Association
13515 Yarmouth Dr.
Pickerington, OH 43147
Phone: (614)856-1900
Fax: (614)856-1920
**Subject(s):** Motorbikes and Motorcyles
**Circ:** (Paid)245,772

**Travel America** (8680)
World Publishing Co.
990 Grove St.
Evanston, IL 60201-4370
Phone: (847)491-6440
Fax: (847)491-0459
**Subject(s):** Travel and Tourism
**Circ:** (Paid)241,210

**Michigan Country Lines** (15651)
Michigan Electric Cooperative Association
2859 W. Jolly Rd.
Okemos, MI 48864
Phone: (517)351-6322
Fax: (517)351-6396
**Subject(s):** Lifestyle; General Agriculture; Environmental and Natural Resources Conservation
**Circ:** 240,000

**IndustryWeek** (24428)
Penton Media Inc.
1300 E. 9th St.
Cleveland, OH 44114-1530
Phone: (216)696-7000
Fax: (216)696-1752
**Subject(s):** Management and Administration
**Circ:** (Paid)7,229
(Controlled)233,000

**Utne** (16350)
Lens Publishing Company Inc.
1624 Harmon Pl., Ste. 330
Minneapolis, MN 55403
Phone: (612)338-5040
**Subject(s):** General Editorial; Alternative and Underground
**Circ:** (Paid)232,629

**Corvette Quarterly** (15877)
C. E. Publishing
30400 Van Dyke
Warren, MI 48093-2368
Phone: (586)574-9100
Fax: (586)558-5870
**Subject(s):** Automotive (Consumer)
**Circ:** (Non-paid)‡230,000

**Crafts 'N Things** (8577)
Clapper Publishing Company Inc.
2400 Devon, Ste. 375
Des Plaines, IL 60018-4618
Phone: (847)635-5800
Fax: (847)635-6311
**Subject(s):** Crafts, Models, Hobbies, and Contests
**Circ:** (Paid)230,000

**Current Health 2** (9109)
Weekly Reader Corp.
900 Skokie Blvd., Ste. 200
Northbrook, IL 60062-4028
Phone: (847)205-3000
Fax: (847)564-8197
**Subject(s):** Education; Education; Health and Healthcare
**Circ:** (Paid)229,274

**The Artist's Magazine** (24288)
F & W Publications Inc.
4700 E. Galbraith Rd.
Cincinnati, OH 45236
Phone: (513)531-2690
Fax: (513)531-0798
**Subject(s):** Art
**Circ:** (Paid)225,000

**U.S. Kids** (9922)
Children's Better Health Institute
1100 Waterway Blvd.
PO Box 567
Indianapolis, IN 46202
Phone: (317)634-1100
Fax: (317)684-8094
**Subject(s):** Children's Interests
**Circ:** (Non-paid)‡2,000
(Paid)‡225,000

**Woodworker's Journal** (16264)
Rockler Woodworking and Hardware
4365 Willow Dr.
Medina, MN 55340
Phone: (763)478-8306
Fax: (763)478-8396
**Subject(s):** Wood and Woodworking
**Circ:** (Non-paid)‡2,256
(Paid)‡223,758

**Home & Away (Hoosier Edition)** (9854)
Midwest Magazine Network
PO Box 88505
Indianapolis, IN 46208
Phone: (317)923-1500
Fax: (317)924-4669
**Subject(s):** Travel and Tourism; Local, State, and Regional Publications; Automotive (Consumer)
**Circ:** ‡221,977

**Game Informer Magazine** (16299)
Sunrise Publications Inc.
724 N. First St., 4 Fl.
Minneapolis, MN 55401
Phone: (612)486-6100
Fax: (612)486-6101
**Subject(s):** Computers; Games and Puzzles; Radio, Television, Cable, and Video
**Circ:** (Paid)217,653

**Buckeye Farm News** (24534)
Ohio Farm Bureau Federation
Two Nationwide Plz.
PO Box 182383
Columbus, OH 43218-2383
Phone: (614)249-2400
Fax: (614)249-2200
**Subject(s):** General Agriculture
**Circ:** (Non-paid)‡1,106
(Paid)‡215,000

**Writer's Digest** (24346)
F & W Publications Inc.
4700 E. Galbraith Rd.
Cincinnati, OH 45236
Phone: (513)531-2690
Fax: (513)531-0798
**Subject(s):** Book Trade and Author News
**Circ:** 215,000

**Soybean Digest (16346)**
Southwest Farm Press
7900 International Dr., 3rd Fl.
Minneapolis, MN 55425-1510
Phone: (952)851-9329
Fax: (952)851-4601
**Subject(s):** Socialized Farming
**Circ:** (Controlled)‡214,000

**Divine Word Missionaries (9445)**
PO Box 6099
Techny, IL 60082-6099
Phone: (847)272-7600
Fax: (847)272-8572
**Subject(s):** Religious Publications
**Circ:** (Free)210,000

**Good Old Days (9572)**
House of White Birches
306 E Parr Rd.
Berne, IN 46711
Phone: (260)589-4000
Fax: (260)589-8093
**Subject(s):** History and Genealogy
**Circ:** (Paid)‡206,000

**New Equipment Digest (24459)**
Penton Media Inc.
1300 E. 9th St.
Cleveland, OH 44114-1530
Phone: (216)696-7000
Fax: (216)696-1752
**Subject(s):** Machinery and Equipment
**Circ:** (Controlled)206,000

**Shooting Times (9218)**
PRIMEDIA Los Angeles
PO Box 1790
Peoria, IL 61656
Phone: (309)679-5321
Fax: (309)679-5476
**Subject(s):** (Hunting, Fishing, and Game Management); Firearms
**Circ:** (Paid)202,611

**Country Sampler Decorating Ideas (9337)**
Country Sampler Group
707 Kautz Rd.
Saint Charles, IL 60174
Phone: (630)377-8000
Fax: (630)377-8914
**Subject(s):** Home and Garden; Crafts, Models, Hobbies, and Contests
**Circ:** (Paid)200,469

**Home and Away (24312)**
AAA Cincinnati
15 W Central Pkwy.
Cincinnati, OH 45202
Phone: (513)762-3301
**Subject(s):** Travel and Tourism; Automotive (Consumer); Insurance
**Circ:** ‡200,000

**Today's Health & Wellness (16389)**
North American Media Group Inc.
12301 Whitewater Dr.
Minnetonka, MN 55343
Phone: (952)936-9333
Fax: (952)936-9169
**Subject(s):** Health
**Circ:** 200,000

**Tuff Stuff (33100)**
Krause Publications Inc.
700 E. State St.
Iola, WI 54990-0001
Phone: (715)445-2214
Fax: (715)445-4087
**Subject(s):** Collecting; (General Sports)
**Circ:** (Combined)200,000

**Jack And Jill (9877)**
Children's Better Health Institute
1100 Waterway Blvd.
PO Box 567
Indianapolis, IN 46202
Phone: (317)634-1100
Fax: (317)684-8094
**Subject(s):** Children's Interests
**Circ:** (Paid)199,572

**RN (16065)**
Thomson PDR
131 W. 1st St.
Duluth, MN 55802
Phone: (218)723-9200
Fax: (218)723-9308
**Subject(s):** Nursing
**Circ:** (Non-paid)25,557
 (Paid)199,243

**Humpty Dumpty's Magazine (9860)**
Children's Better Health Institute
1100 Waterway Blvd.
PO Box 567
Indianapolis, IN 46202
Phone: (317)634-1100
Fax: (317)684-8094
**Subject(s):** Children's Interests
**Circ:** (Paid)193,923

**Keynoter (9885)**
3636 Woodview Trace
Indianapolis, IN 46268-3196
Phone: (317)875-8755
**Subject(s):** Clubs and Societies; Youths' Interests
**Circ:** (Paid)190,000

**The Royal Neighbor (9295)**
Royal Neighbors of America
230 16th St.
Rock Island, IL 61201-8645
Phone: (309)788-4561
Fax: (309)788-1439
**Subject(s):** Royal Neighbors of America
**Circ:** ‡190,000

**Waifs' Messenger (8442)**
Mission of Our Lady of Mercy Inc.
1140 W Jackson
Chicago, IL 60607
Phone: (312)738-7560
Fax: (312)738-9250
**Subject(s):** Religious Publications
**Circ:** 190,000

**Supertrax International Magazine (15972)**
Supertrax L.L.C.
Dupont Ctr., Ste. 250
9801 Dupont Ave. S
Bloomington, MN 55431-3197
Phone: (952)885-6884
Fax: (952)884-9836
**Subject(s):** (Snowmobiling)
**Circ:** (Paid)‡14,122
 (Non-paid)‡189,908

**Machine Design (24449)**
Penton Media Inc.
1300 E. 9th St.
Cleveland, OH 44114-1530
Phone: (216)696-7000
Fax: (216)696-1752
**Subject(s):** Engineering (Various branches); Machinery and Equipment
**Circ:** (Non-paid)‡186,484

**Football Digest (8671)**
Century Publishing Co.
990 Grove St.
Evanston, IL 60201-4370
Phone: (847)491-6440
Fax: (847)491-0459
**Subject(s):** (Football)
**Circ:** (Paid)185,000

**Chicago Magazine (8130)**
PRIMEDIA Consumer Magazines
435 N. Michigan Ave., Ste. 1100
Chicago, IL 60611
Phone: (312)222-8999
Fax: (312)222-0287
**Subject(s):** Local, State, and Regional Publications; Lifestyle
**Circ:** (Paid)182,140

**PaperWorks (9575)**
House of White Birches
306 E Parr Rd.
Berne, IN 46711
Phone: (260)589-4000
Fax: (260)589-8093
**Subject(s):** Dressmaking, Needlework, and Quilting; Women's Interests
**Circ:** ‡179,650

**Motor Age (8343)**
Adams Business Media
833 W Jackson, 7th Fl.
Chicago, IL 60607
Phone: (312)846-4600
Fax: (312)846-4638
**Subject(s):** Automotive (Trade)
**Circ:** (Controlled)‡175,000

**Christian Reader (7972)**
Christianity Today International
465 Gundersen Dr.
Carol Stream, IL 60188
Phone: (630)260-6200
Fax: (630)260-0114
**Subject(s):** Religious Publications
**Circ:** (Non-paid)3,659
 (Paid)171,990

**Model Railroader (33612)**
Kalmbach Publishing Co.
PO Box 1612
Waukesha, WI 53187-1612
Phone: (262)796-8776
Fax: (262)796-1615
**Subject(s):** Railroad; Crafts, Models, Hobbies, and Contests
**Circ:** (Paid)★171,168

**The Surplus Record (8420)**
Surplus Record Inc.
20 N. Wacker Dr., No. 2500
Chicago, IL 60606
Phone: (312)372-9077
Fax: (312)372-6537
**Subject(s):** Commerce and Industry
**Circ:** (Paid)‡604
 (Non-paid)‡167,907

**EAA Sport Aviation (33450)**
Experimental Aircraft Association Inc.
PO Box 3086
Oshkosh, WI 54903-3086
Phone: (920)426-4800
Fax: (920)426-4828
**Subject(s):** Aviation
**Circ:** (Paid)167,000

**Current Health 1 (9108)**
Weekly Reader Corp.
900 Skokie Blvd.
Northbrook, IL 60062-4028
Phone: (847)205-3000
Fax: (847)564-8197
**Subject(s):** Education; Education; Health and Healthcare
**Circ:** (Paid)165,793

**Cruise Travel Magazine (8667)**
World Publishing Co.
990 Grove St.
Evanston, IL 60201-4370
Phone: (847)491-6440
Fax: (847)491-0459
**Subject(s):** Travel and Tourism
**Circ:** (Paid)165,336

**Eleven (8187)**
WTTW/Chicago
5400 N St. Louis Ave.
Chicago, IL 773509
Phone: (773)583-5000
Fax: (773)509-5305
**Subject(s):** Radio, Television, Cable, and Video
**Circ:** ‡160,000

**MEA Voice (15238)**
Michigan Education Association
1216 Kendale Blvd.
PO Box 2573
East Lansing, MI 48826-2573
Phone: (517)332-6551
Fax: (517)337-5587
**Subject(s):** Education
**Circ:** ‡160,000

**Wisconsin Energy Cooperative News (33219)**
Wisconsin Federation of Co-ops
131 W Wilson St., No. 400
Madison, WI 53703-3269
Phone: (608)258-4400
Fax: (608)258-4407
**Subject(s):** Rural Electrification; Local, State, and Regional Publications
**Circ:** 158,000

**Dental Products Report (9129)**
MEDEC Dental Communications
2 Northfield Plaza, Ste. 300
Northfield, IL 60093-1219
Phone: (847)441-3700
Fax: (847)441-3702
Subject(s): Dentistry

Circ: (Controlled)150,271

**Laboratory Medicine (8303)**
American Society of Clinical Pathologists
2100 W. Harrison St.
Chicago, IL 60612
Phone: (312)738-1336
Fax: (312)738-0101
Subject(s): Laboratory Research (Scientific and Medical)

Circ: (Non-paid)15,583
(Paid)150,205

**Astronomy (33599)**
Kalmbach Publishing Co.
PO Box 1612
Waukesha, WI 53187-1612
Phone: (262)796-8776
Fax: (262)796-1615
Subject(s): Astronomy and Meteorology; Science (General)

Circ: (Paid)★150,132

**AAII Journal (8050)**
American Association of Individual Investors
625 N. Michigan Ave.
Chicago, IL 60611
Phone: (312)280-0170
Fax: (312)280-9883
Subject(s): Banking, Finance, and Investments

Circ: ‡150,000

**Deer and Turkey Show Previews (33278)**
Target Communications Corp.
7626 W Donges Bay Rd.
Mequon, WI 53097
Phone: (262)242-3990
Fax: (262)242-7391
Subject(s): (Hunting, Fishing, and Game Management)

Circ: (Controlled)150,000

**The Family Digest (9715)**
PO Box 40137
Fort Wayne, IN 46804
Subject(s): Religious Publications

Circ: (Non-paid)‡150,000

**Farm Show (16207)**
Farm Show Publishing Inc.
20088 Kenwood Trl., Johnson Bldg.
PO Box 1029
Lakeville, MN 55044-1029
Phone: (952)469-5572
Fax: (952)469-5575
Subject(s): General Agriculture

Circ: ‡150,000

**Notre Dame Magazine (10088)**
University of Notre Dame
538 Grace Hall
Notre Dame, IN 46556
Subject(s): College Publications

Circ: (Controlled)‡150,000

**Your Church (7984)**
Christianity Today International
465 Gundersen Dr.
Carol Stream, IL 60188
Phone: (630)260-6200
Fax: (630)260-0114
Subject(s): Religious Publications; Business

Circ: (Controlled)150,000

**Christianity Today (7973)**
Christianity Today International
465 Gundersen Dr.
Carol Stream, IL 60188
Phone: (630)260-6200
Fax: (630)260-0114
Subject(s): Religious Publications

Circ: (Non-paid)1,572
(Non-paid)2,502
(Paid)‡149,125

**Patient Care (16063)**
Thomson PDR
131 W. 1st St.
Duluth, MN 55802
Phone: (218)723-9200
Fax: (218)723-9308

Subject(s): Medicine and Surgery
Circ: (Controlled)145,000
(Controlled)145,000

**The Sample Case (24602)**
The Order of United Commercial Travelers of America
632 N. Park St.
PO Box 159019
Columbus, OH 43215
Phone: (614)228-3276
Fax: (614)228-1898
Subject(s): Unclassified Fraternal

Circ: (Paid)145,000

**Chilton's Motor Age (8143)**
Advanstar Communications
100 W. Monroe St., Ste. 1100
Chicago, IL 60603
Phone: (312)553-8906
Fax: (312)553-8926
Subject(s): Automotive (Trade)

Circ: (Paid)1,111
(Non-paid)142,036

**Motor Magazine (15856)**
Motor Information Systems
5600 Crooks Rd., Ste. 200
Troy, MI 48098
Subject(s): Automotive (Trade)

Circ: (Paid)3,311
(Non-paid)141,084

**Bead and Button (33600)**
Kalmbach Publishing Co.
PO Box 1612
Waukesha, WI 53187-1612
Phone: (262)796-8776
Fax: (262)796-1615
Subject(s): Crafts, Models, Hobbies, and Contests

Circ: (Paid)★140,878

**Postgraduate Medicine (16336)**
McGraw-Hill Healthcare Information Group
4530 W 77th St.
Minneapolis, MN 55435
Phone: (952)835-3222
Fax: (952)835-3460
Subject(s): Medicine and Surgery

Circ: (Controlled)140,763

**Professional Builder (8590)**
Reed Business Information
1350 E. Touhy Ave.
Des Plaines, IL 60018
Subject(s): Construction, Contracting, Building, and Excavating; Architecture

Circ: 122,000
(Controlled)140,018

**Aldrichimica Acta (33289)**
Aldrich Chemical Company Inc.
1001 W St. Paul Ave.
Milwaukee, WI 53233
Phone: (414)273-3850
Fax: (414)273-4979
Subject(s): Chemistry, Chemicals, and Chemical Engineering

Circ: (Non-paid)140,000

**Glenmary Challenge (24310)**
Glenmary Home Missioners
PO Box 465618
Cincinnati, OH 45246
Phone: (513)874-8900
Fax: (513)874-1690
Subject(s): Religious Publications

Circ: (Non-paid)140,000

**Key to the Door... Illustrated (33563)**
Door County Publishing Co.
Box 130
Sturgeon Bay, WI 54235-0130
Fax: (920)743-5817
Subject(s): Travel and Tourism; City, Hotel, Railroad, and Travel Guides

Circ: (Non-paid)140,000

**Journal of the American Dental Association (8259)**
ADA Publishing
211 E Chicago Ave.
Chicago, IL 60611-2678
Phone: (312)440-2500
Fax: (312)440-3538

Subject(s): Dentistry
Circ: (Non-paid)2,723
(Paid)135,456

**Baseball Digest (8662)**
Century Publishing Co.
990 Grove St.
Evanston, IL 60201-4370
Phone: (847)491-6440
Fax: (847)491-0459
Subject(s): (Baseball)

Circ: (Paid)132,259

**Ladybug (9239)**
The Cricket Magazine Group
Carus Publishing Company
315 Fifth St.
Peru, IL 61354
Subject(s): Children's Interests

Circ: (Paid)‡130,000

**Lutheran Woman Today (16311)**
Augsburg Fortress, Publishers
100 S. Fifth St., Ste. 700
PO Box 1209
Minneapolis, MN 55402-1209
Phone: (612)330-3300
Fax: (800)722-7766
Subject(s): Religious Publications; Women's Interests

Circ: (Paid)130,000

**Ohio Schools (24587)**
Ohio Education Association
225 E Broad St.
Box 2550
Columbus, OH 43216
Phone: (614)227-3014
Fax: (614)224-5659
Subject(s): Education

Circ: ‡128,400

**Wisconsin Natural Resources (33226)**
Department of Natural Resources
101 S. Webster St.
PO Box 7921
Madison, WI 53707-7921
Phone: (608)266-2621
Fax: (608)261-4380
Subject(s): Environmental and Natural Resources Conservation

Circ: (Paid)128,000

**Mayo Clinic Proceedings (16515)**
Dowden Publishing Company Inc.
Mayo Foundation for Medical Education and Research
200 1st St. SW
Rochester, MN 55905
Phone: (507)284-2094
Fax: (507)284-0252
Subject(s): Medicine and Surgery

Circ: (Non-paid)‡127,000

**Family Motor Coaching (24308)**
Family Motor Coaching Inc.
8291 Clough Pke.
Cincinnati, OH 45244-2796
Phone: (513)474-3622
Fax: (513)388-5286
Subject(s): Automotive (Consumer)

Circ: (Paid)⊕125,000

**Minnesota Conservation Volunteer (16595)**
Department of Natural Resources
500 Lafayette Rd.
Saint Paul, MN 55155-4040
Phone: (651)296-6157
Fax: (651)297-3618
Subject(s): Ecology and Conservation; Natural Resources

Circ: 125,000

**Illinois State Magazine (9070)**
Illinois State University
Alumni Services
Campus Box 3100
Normal, IL 61790-3100
Phone: (309)438-2586
Fax: (309)438-8057
Subject(s): College Publications

Circ: (Non-paid)‡124,000

**Drug Topics (16054)**
Thomson PDR
131 W. 1st St.
Duluth, MN 55802
Phone: (218)723-9200

Circulation: ★ = ABC; △ = BPA; ♦ = CAC; • = CCAB; ❏ = VAC; ⊕ = PO Statement; ‡ = Publisher's Report; Boldface figures = sworn; Light figures = estimated.

Fax: (218)723-9308
**Subject(s):** Drugs and Pharmaceuticals
**Circ:** (Paid)1,847
(Controlled)123,113

**Ohio State Alumni Magazine (24588)**
The Ohio State University Alumni Association Inc.
2400 Olentangy River Rd.
Columbus, OH 43210-1061
Phone: (614)292-2970
Fax: (614)292-4998
**Subject(s):** College Publications
**Circ:** ‡121,200

**Anchora (24529)**
Delta Gamma
3250 Riverside Dr.
PO Box 21397
Columbus, OH 43221-0397
Phone: (614)481-8169
Fax: (614)481-0133
**Subject(s):** College Publications
**Circ:** 120,000

**Hoosier Outdoors (9859)**
Recreation Vehicle Indiana Council
3210 Rand Rd.
Indianapolis, IN 46241
Phone: (317)247-6258
Fax: (317)243-9174
**Subject(s):** (General Sports)
**Circ:** (Non-paid)‡120,000

**Loyola Magazine (8317)**
Loyola University of Chicago
6525 N. Sheridan Rd.
Chicago, IL 60626
Phone: (773)274-3000
**Subject(s):** College Publications
**Circ:** (Non-paid)120,000

**Food Management (24411)**
Penton Media Inc.
1300 E. 9th St.
Cleveland, OH 44114-1530
Phone: (216)696-7000
Fax: (216)696-1752
**Subject(s):** Food and Grocery Trade; Hotels, Motels, Restaurants, and Clubs
**Circ:** (Combined)‡117,740

**Restaurant Hospitality (24485)**
Penton Media Inc.
1300 E. 9th St.
Cleveland, OH 44114-1530
Phone: (216)696-7000
Fax: (216)696-1752
**Subject(s):** Hotels, Motels, Restaurants, and Clubs
**Circ:** (Non-paid)‡117,721

**Modern Machine Shop (24326)**
Gardner Publications Inc.
6915 Valley Ave.
Cincinnati, OH 45244-3029
Phone: (513)527-8800
Fax: (513)527-8801
**Subject(s):** Metal, Metallurgy, and Metal Trade
**Circ:** (Free)117,000

**Chicago Parent Magazine (9165)**
Wednesday Journal Inc.
141 S. Oak Park Ave.
Oak Park, IL 60302
Phone: (708)524-8300
Fax: (708)524-0447
**Subject(s):** Parenting
**Circ:** (Paid)608
(Free)115,000

**Journal of Nursing Scholarship (9880)**
Sigma Theta Tau International Honor Society of Nursing
550 W N St.
Indianapolis, IN 46202
Phone: (317)634-8171
Fax: (317)634-8188
**Subject(s):** Nursing; Health and Healthcare
**Circ:** 115,000

**Shotgun News (9220)**
PRIMEDIA Los Angeles
PO Box 1790
Peoria, IL 61656
Phone: (309)679-5321
Fax: (309)679-5476

**Subject(s):** Firearms; Sporting Goods/Retail Sports
**Circ:** (Controlled)115,000

**Deer & Deer Hunting (33073)**
Krause Publications Inc.
700 E. State St.
Iola, WI 54990-0001
Phone: (715)445-2214
Fax: (715)445-4087
**Subject(s):** (Hunting, Fishing, and Game Management)
**Circ:** (Paid)114,010

**DesignMart (24398)**
Penton Media Inc.
1300 E. 9th St.
Cleveland, OH 44114-1530
Phone: (216)696-7000
Fax: (216)696-1752
**Subject(s):** Graphic Arts and Design; Commerce and Industry
**Circ:** (Combined)112,000

**Professional Tool & Equipment News (32981)**
Cygnus Business Media
1233 Janesville Ave.
PO BOX 803
Fort Atkinson, WI 53538-0803
Phone: (920)563-6388
Fax: (920)563-1702
**Subject(s):** Machinery and Equipment; Automotive (Trade)
**Circ:** (Non-paid)‡110,143

**Plant Services (8812)**
Putman Media
555 W Pierce Rd., Ste. 301
Itasca, IL 60143
Phone: (630)467-1300
Fax: (630)467-0197
**Subject(s):** Engineering (Various branches)
**Circ:** (Controlled)‡110,000

**University of Chicago Magazine (8434)**
5801 S.Ellis Ave.
Chicago, IL 60637
Phone: (773)702-2163
Fax: (773)702-0495
**Subject(s):** College Publications
**Circ:** (Non-paid)‡110,000

**Nursing Management (7874)**
Spring House
434 W Downer Pl.
Aurora, IL 60506
**Subject(s):** Nursing
**Circ:** (Controlled)19,337
(Paid)109,492

**Trains (33618)**
Kalmbach Publishing Co.
PO Box 1612
Waukesha, WI 53187-1612
Phone: (262)796-8776
Fax: (262)796-1615
**Subject(s):** Railroad; Crafts, Models, Hobbies, and Contests
**Circ:** (Paid)★109,329

**Designfax (25048)**
Nelson Publishing Inc.
6001 Cochran Rd., Ste. 104
Solon, OH 44139
Phone: (440)248-1125
Fax: (440)248-0187
**Subject(s):** Engineering (Various branches)
**Circ:** (Non-paid)108,919

**FUR-FISH-GAME (24551)**
A.R. Harding Publishing Co.
2878 E Main St.
Columbus, OH 43209
Phone: (614)231-9585
**Subject(s):** (Hunting, Fishing, and Game Management)
**Circ:** 107,313

**The Cross Stitcher (8578)**
Clapper Publishing Company Inc.
2400 Devon, Ste. 375
Des Plaines, IL 60018-4618
Phone: (847)635-5800
Fax: (847)635-6311
**Subject(s):** Crafts, Models, Hobbies, and Contests
**Circ:** (Paid)107,208

**MSI (9154)**
Reed Business Information
MSI Magazine, 2000 Clearwater Dr.
Oak Brook, IL 60523-8809
Phone: (630)288-8101
Fax: (630)288-8764
**Subject(s):** Commerce and Industry
**Circ:** (Non-paid)‡105,500

**Alumnus (7944)**
Southern Illinois University at Carbondale
1247 Communications Bldg.
PO Box 6887
Carbondale, IL 62901
Phone: (618)536-3311
Fax: (618)453-3248
**Subject(s):** College Publications
**Circ:** 105,000

**Automotive Industries (15773)**
Reed Business Information
Publication Headquarters
24901 Northwestern Hwy, Ste. 505
Southfield, MI 48075
Phone: (248)350-8199
Fax: (248)350-2692
**Subject(s):** Automotive (Trade)
**Circ:** (Non-paid)‡105,000

**Pack-O-Fun (8587)**
Clapper Publishing Company Inc.
2400 Devon, Ste. 375
Des Plaines, IL 60018-4618
Phone: (847)635-5800
Fax: (847)635-6311
**Subject(s):** Crafts, Models, Hobbies, and Contests; Children's Interests; Art
**Circ:** (Paid)⊕**105,000**

**Weekly Bible Reader (24345)**
Standard Publishing
8121 Hamilton Ave.
Cincinnati, OH 45231
Phone: (513)931-4050
Fax: (513)931-0950
**Subject(s):** Religious Publications; Education
**Circ:** ‡104,000

**Basketball Digest (8663)**
Century Publishing Co.
990 Grove St.
Evanston, IL 60201-4370
Phone: (847)491-6440
Fax: (847)491-0459
**Subject(s):** (Basketball)
**Circ:** (Paid)‡103,313

**Archives of Internal Medicine (8086)**
American Medical Association Alliance
c/o Philip Greenland,MD
680 N Lake Shore Dr. Ste. 1102
Chicago, IL 60611
Phone: (312)503-5387
Fax: (312)503-5388
**Subject(s):** Medicine and Surgery
**Circ:** (Combined)‡103,271

**Hockey Digest (8672)**
Century Publishing Co.
990 Grove St.
Evanston, IL 60201-4370
Phone: (847)491-6440
Fax: (847)491-0459
**Subject(s):** (Hockey)
**Circ:** (Paid)‡103,003

**BEEF (16275)**
Southwest Farm Press
7900 International Dr., 3rd Fl.
Minneapolis, MN 55425-1510
Phone: (952)851-9329
Fax: (952)851-4601
**Subject(s):** Livestock
**Circ:** (Controlled)‡101,661

**Ward's Auto World (15783)**
Ward's Communications
3000 Town Ctr., Ste. 2750
Southfield, MI 48075-1212
Phone: (248)357-0800
Fax: (248)357-0810
**Subject(s):** Automotive (Trade)
**Circ:** (Controlled)100,541

**Water & Wastes Digest (8595)**
Scranton Gillette Communications Inc.
380 NW Hwy., Ste. 200
Des Plaines, IL 60016-2282
Phone: (847)391-1000
Fax: (847)390-0408
Subject(s): Water Supply and Sewage Disposal
Circ: (Non-paid)‡100,332

**Company (8153)**
American Jesuits
PO Box 60790
Chicago, IL 60660-0790
Phone: (773)761-9432
Fax: (773)761-9443
Subject(s): Religious Publications
Circ: (Controlled)‡100,000

**Industrial Market Place (9372)**
Wineberg Publications
7842 N Lincoln Ave.
Skokie, IL 60077
Phone: (847)676-1900
Fax: (847)676-0063
Subject(s): Machinery and Equipment
Circ: (Controlled)‡100,000

**The Lookout (24325)**
Standard Publishing
8121 Hamilton Ave.
Cincinnati, OH 45231
Phone: (513)931-4050
Fax: (513)931-0950
Subject(s): Religious Publications
Circ: 100,000

**Marquette Magazine (33310)**
Marquette University
PO Box 1881
Milwaukee, WI 53201-1881
Phone: (414)288-7448
Fax: (414)288-5936
Subject(s): Clubs and Societies
Circ: (Non-paid)‡100,000

**Michigan Alumnus (15012)**
Alumni Association of the U-M
200 Fletcher St.
Ann Arbor, MI 48109-1007
Phone: (734)764-0384
Fax: (734)764-4506
Subject(s): College Publications
Circ: 100,000

**Pheasants Forever (16607)**
Pheasants Forever Inc.
1783 Buerkle Cir.
Saint Paul, MN 55110
Phone: (651)773-2070
Subject(s): (Hunting, Fishing, and Game Management)
Circ: (Paid)‡100,000

**Windy City Sports Magazine (8446)**
Windy City Publishing Inc.
1450 W Randolph
Chicago, IL 60607
Phone: (312)421-1551
Fax: (312)421-1454
Subject(s): (General Sports); Local, State, and Regional Publications
Circ: (Controlled)‡100,000

**CWRU (24394)**
Case Western Reserve University
10900 Euclid Ave.
Cleveland, OH 44106
Phone: (216)368-2000
Subject(s): College Publications
Circ: (Controlled)98,000

**Campus Life (7968)**
Christianity Today International
465 Gundersen Dr.
Carol Stream, IL 60188
Phone: (630)260-6200
Fax: (630)260-0114
Subject(s): Youths' Interests; Religious Publications
Circ: (Combined)96,657

**Material Handling Management (24452)**
Penton Media Inc.
1300 E. 9th St.
Cleveland, OH 44114-1530
Phone: (216)696-7000
Fax: (216)696-1752

Subject(s): Materials Handling
Circ: (Non-paid)‡92,836
(Paid)95,497

**(Bowling Green) BGSU Magazine (24200)**
Bowling Green State University
Office of Marketing & Communications
Bowling Green, OH 43403
Phone: (419)372-2531
Subject(s): College Publications
Circ: (Controlled)‡94,000

**Medical Economics (16061)**
Thomson PDR
131 W. 1st St.
Duluth, MN 55802
Phone: (218)723-9200
Fax: (218)723-9308
Subject(s): Medicine and Surgery; Business
Circ: (Controlled)64,000
(Paid)94,000

**Down Beat (8643)**
Maher Publications Inc.
102 N Haven Rd.
Elmhurst, IL 60126
Phone: (630)941-2030
Fax: (630)941-3210
Subject(s): Music and Musical Instruments
Circ: ‡93,797

**Michigan Out-of-Doors (15525)**
Michigan United Conservation Clubs
Box 30235
Lansing, MI 48909
Phone: (517)371-1041
Fax: (517)371-1505
Subject(s): Environmental and Natural Resources Conservation; (Hunting, Fishing, and Game Management)
Circ: (Non-paid)△615
(Paid)△92,226

**Packaging World (8368)**
Summit Publishing Co.
One IBM Plz., Ste. 2401
330 N. Wabash Ave.
Chicago, IL 60611
Phone: (312)222-1010
Fax: (312)222-1310
Subject(s): Packaging
Circ: (Controlled)92,000

**Cleveland Clinic Journal of Medicine (24388)**
Cleveland Clinic Foundation
9500 Euclid Ave., NA 32
Cleveland, OH 44195
Phone: (216)444-2661
Fax: (216)444-9385
Subject(s): Medicine and Surgery
Circ: (Paid)‡509
(Controlled)‡91,879

**Children's Digest (9838)**
Children's Better Health Institute
PO Box 567
Indianapolis, IN 46206
Subject(s): Children's Interests
Circ: (Paid)91,165

**Ohio Magazine (24467)**
1422 Euclid Ave., No. 730
Cleveland, OH 44115
Phone: (216)771-2833
Fax: (216)781-6318
Subject(s): Local, State, and Regional Publications
Circ: (Paid)90,425

**Bird Watcher's Digest (24869)**
Bird Watcher's Digest Press
149 Acme St.
PO Box 110
Marietta, OH 45750
Phone: (740)373-5285
Fax: (740)373-8443
Subject(s): Crafts, Models, Hobbies, and Contests; Ornithology and Oology; Wildlife and Exotic Animals; Natural History and Nature Study
Circ: ‡90,000

**Hay & Forage Grower (16301)**
Southwest Farm Press
7900 International Dr., 3rd Fl.
Minneapolis, MN 55425-1510
Phone: (952)851-9329
Fax: (952)851-4601

Subject(s): Feed and Grain
Circ: (Non-paid)‡90,000

**Illinois Alumni (9471)**
University of Illinois Alumni Association
227 Illini Union
1401 W Green St.
Urbana, IL 61801
Phone: (217)333-1471
Fax: (217)333-7803
Subject(s): College Publications
Circ: (Paid)‡90,000

**University of Dayton Quarterly (24663)**
University of Dayton
300 College Park
Dayton, OH 45469-1659
Phone: (937)229-3241
Fax: (937)229-3063
Subject(s): College Publications
Circ: (Non-paid)‡90,000

**Christian Parenting Today (7971)**
Christianity Today International
465 Gundersen Dr.
Carol Stream, IL 60188
Phone: (630)260-6200
Fax: (630)260-0114
Subject(s): Parenting; Religious Publications
Circ: (Non-paid)‡23,889
(Paid)‡87,194

**Career World (9107)**
Weekly Reader Corp.
900 Skokie Blvd.
Northbrook, IL 60062-4028
Phone: (847)205-3000
Fax: (847)564-8197
Subject(s): Education
Circ: (Paid)87,000

**The Catholic Spirit (16572)**
The Catholic Spirit Publishing Co.
244 Dayton Ave.
Saint Paul, MN 55102
Phone: (651)291-4444
Fax: (651)291-4460
Subject(s): Religious Publications
Circ: (Paid)87,000

**Men of Integrity (7979)**
Christianity Today International
465 Gundersen Dr.
Carol Stream, IL 60188
Phone: (630)260-6200
Fax: (630)260-0114
Subject(s): Religious Publications
Circ: (Paid)86,979

**Decorative Artist's Workbook (24304)**
F & W Publications Inc.
4700 E. Galbraith Rd.
Cincinnati, OH 45236
Phone: (513)531-2690
Fax: (513)531-0798
Subject(s): Art
Circ: ‡86,779

**Bowling Digest (8664)**
Century Publishing Co.
990 Grove St.
Evanston, IL 60201-4370
Phone: (847)491-6440
Fax: (847)491-0459
Subject(s): (Bowling)
Circ: (Paid)86,147

**Bowhunting World (16253)**
Ehlert Publishing Group Inc.
6420 Sycamore Ln., N.
Maple Grove, MN 55369-6355
Phone: (612)476-2200
Fax: (612)476-8065
Subject(s): (Archery)
Circ: ‡85,368

**Children's Playmate Magazine (9839)**
Children's Better Health Institute
1100 Waterway Blvd.
PO Box 567
Indianapolis, IN 46202
Phone: (317)634-1100
Fax: (317)684-8094

# Great Lakes States

**Subject(s):** Children's Interests
**Circ:** (Paid)85,155

**American Trucker—Mid-Atlantic Edition (9825)**
Primedia Business
PO Box 603
Indianapolis, IN 46206
Phone: (317)297-5500
Fax: (317)299-1356
**Subject(s):** Trucks and Trucking
**Circ:** (Combined)85,124

**Extension (8194)**
Catholic Church Extension Society
150 S Wacker Dr., 20th Fl.
Chicago, IL 60606-4103
Phone: (312)236-7240
Fax: (312)236-5276
**Subject(s):** Religious Publications
**Circ:** (Controlled)‡85,000

**Government Product News (24422)**
Penton Media Inc.
1300 E. 9th St.
Cleveland, OH 44114-1530
Phone: (216)696-7000
Fax: (216)696-1752
**Subject(s):** State, Municipal, and County Administration; Congressional and Federal Government Affairs
**Circ:** (Controlled)‡85,000

**Logistics Today (24446)**
Penton Media Inc.
1300 E. 9th St.
Cleveland, OH 44114-1530
Phone: (216)696-7000
Fax: (216)696-1752
**Subject(s):** Computers; Business
**Circ:** (Non-paid)85,000

**Qualified Remodeler Magazine (32982)**
Cygnus Business Media
1233 Janesville Ave.
Fort Atkinson, WI 53538
Phone: (920)563-6388
Fax: (920)563-1702
**Subject(s):** Construction, Contracting, Building, and Excavating
**Circ:** (Controlled)84,500

**Home Cooking (9574)**
House of White Birches
306 E Parr Rd.
Berne, IN 46711
Phone: (260)589-4000
Fax: (260)589-8093
**Subject(s):** Baking
**Circ:** ‡84,266

**Tooling & Production (25052)**
Nelson Publishing Inc.
6001 Cochran Rd., Ste. 104
Solon, OH 44139
Phone: (440)248-1125
Fax: (440)248-0187
**Subject(s):** Commerce and Industry; Metal, Metallurgy, and Metal Trade
**Circ:** (Controlled)‡80,845

**American Machinist (24372)**
Penton Media Inc.
1300 E. 9th St.
Cleveland, OH 44114-1530
Phone: (216)696-7000
Fax: (216)696-1752
**Subject(s):** Metal, Metallurgy, and Metal Trade
**Circ:** (Non-paid)‡80,000

**Chicago Cigar Smoker Magazine (8726)**
Jonathan Scott's Cigar Smoker Magazine
PO Box 2323
Glen Ellyn, IL 60138
Phone: (630)790-3433
Fax: (630)790-3077
**Subject(s):** Men's Interests
**Circ:** (Paid)5,000
(Controlled)80,000

**Equipment Today (32966)**
Cygnus Business Media
1233 Janesville Ave.
Fort Atkinson, WI 53538
Phone: (920)563-6388
Fax: (920)563-1702

**Subject(s):** Construction, Contracting, Building, and Excavating
**Circ:** (Controlled)‡80,000

**Llewellyn's New Worlds of Mind and Spirit (16589)**
Llewellyn Publications
PO Box 64383
Saint Paul, MN 55164-0383
Phone: (651)291-1970
Fax: (651)291-1908
**Subject(s):** Alternative and Underground
**Circ:** (Combined)‡80,000

**On the Mark (9117)**
Corporate Communications
333 Pfingsten Rd.
Northbrook, IL 60062-2096
Phone: (847)272-8800
Fax: (847)272-8129
**Subject(s):** Business
**Circ:** (Non-paid)80,000

**Safe Driver (8813)**
NSC Press
1121 Spring Lake Dr.
Itasca, IL 60143-3201
Phone: (630)285-1121
Fax: (630)285-1319
**Subject(s):** Transportation, Traffic, and Shipping; Trucks and Trucking; Safety
**Circ:** (Paid)80,000

**Spider (9241)**
Carus Publishing
315 5th St.
Peru, IL 61354
Phone: (815)224-5803
Fax: (815)224-6615
**Subject(s):** Children's Interests
**Circ:** (Paid)80,000

**Today's Supervisor (8816)**
NSC Press
1121 Spring Lake Dr.
Itasca, IL 60143-3201
Phone: (630)285-1121
Fax: (630)285-1319
**Subject(s):** Management and Administration; Safety
**Circ:** ‡80,000

**U.S.A. Gymnastics (9921)**
USA Gymnastics
Pan American Plz., Ste. 300
201 S. Capitol Ave.
Indianapolis, IN 46225
Phone: (317)237-5050
Fax: (317)237-5069
**Subject(s):** (General Sports)
**Circ:** ‡80,000

**Automotive News (15166)**
Crain Communications Inc.
1155 Gratiot Ave.
Detroit, MI 48207-2997
Phone: (313)446-6000
Fax: (313)446-0347
**Subject(s):** Automotive (Trade)
**Circ:** (Paid)★79,470

**American Trucker—South Central Edition (9830)**
Primedia Business
PO Box 603
Indianapolis, IN 46206
Phone: (317)297-5500
Fax: (317)299-1356
**Subject(s):** Trucks and Trucking
**Circ:** (Combined)79,058

**Physical Therapy (8376)**
American Physical Therapy Association
Editor in Chief, Department of Physical Therapy
University of Illinois at Chicago
Chicago, IL
**Subject(s):** Medicine and Surgery
**Circ:** (Paid)‡78,000

**Welding Innovation (24497)**
James F. Lincoln Arc Welding Foundation
PO Box 17188
Cleveland, OH 44117
Phone: (216)481-4300
Fax: (216)486-1751
**Subject(s):** Engineering (Various branches); Welding
**Circ:** (Controlled)‡78,000

**Geriatrics (24418)**
Advanstar Communications
7500 Old Oak Blvd.
Cleveland, OH 44130
Phone: (440)243-8100
Fax: (440)891-2735
**Subject(s):** Gerontology
**Circ:** (Controlled)‡77,000

**Modern Healthcare (8338)**
Crain Communications Inc.
360 N. Michigan Ave.
Chicago, IL 60601-3806
Phone: (312)649-5411
Fax: (312)280-3150
**Subject(s):** Health and Healthcare
**Circ:** (Paid)2,828
(Non-paid)76,894

**Cricket Magazine (9238)**
The Cricket Magazine Group
Carus Publishing Company
315 Fifth St.
Peru, IL 61354
**Subject(s):** Children's Interests
**Circ:** (Paid)‡75,000

**Cross Country Skier (32876)**
Country Skier L.L.C.
PO Box 550
Cable, WI 54821
Phone: (715)798-5500
Fax: (715)798-3599
**Subject(s):** (Skiing)
**Circ:** ‡75,000

**Indiana Alumni Magazine (9591)**
Indiana University Alumni Association
1000 E 17th St.
Bloomington, IN 47408-1521
Phone: (812)855-4822
Fax: (812)855-4228
**Subject(s):** College Publications
**Circ:** ‡75,000

**Leaves (15153)**
Mariannhill Mission Society
PO Box 87
Dearborn, MI 48121-0087
Phone: (313)561-2330
**Subject(s):** Religious Publications
**Circ:** (Free)75,000

**Phi Delta Kappan (9609)**
Phi Delta Kappa International
408 N. Union St.
PO Box 789
Bloomington, IN 47402-0789
Phone: (812)339-1156
Fax: (812)339-0018
**Subject(s):** Education
**Circ:** ‡75,000

**Presentations Magazine (16338)**
VNU Business Media
50 S. 9th St.
Minneapolis, MN 55402
Phone: (612)333-0471
Fax: (612)333-6526
**Subject(s):** Business
**Circ:** (Controlled)‡75,000

**Illinois Entertainer (online) (8235)**
Illinois Entertainer
124 W. Polk St., 103
Chicago, IL 60605
**Subject(s):** Entertainment; Music and Musical Instruments
**Circ:** (Combined)74,606

**Leadership (7977)**
Christianity Today International
465 Gundersen Dr.
Carol Stream, IL 60188
Phone: (630)260-6200
Fax: (630)260-0114
**Subject(s):** Religious Publications
**Circ:** (Combined)73,000

**MPLS.ST.PAUL (16327)**
MSP Communications
220 S 6th St., Ste. 500
Minneapolis, MN 55402
Phone: (612)339-7571
Fax: (612)339-5806

Subject(s): Local, State, and Regional Publications; Lifestyle
Circ: (Paid)72,305

**Control** (8807)
Putman Media
555 W Pierce Rd., Ste. 301
Itasca, IL 60143
Phone: (630)467-1300
Fax: (630)467-0197
Subject(s): Computers
Circ: (Non-paid)‡72,217

**Journal of the American Dietetic Association** (8260)
American Dietetic Association
120 S Riverside Plaza, Ste. 2000
Chicago, IL 60606-6995
Phone: (312)899-0040
Fax: (312)899-4817
Subject(s): Health and Healthcare
Circ: (Non-paid)582
(Paid)70,980

**TelephonyOnline** (8425)
Primedia Business Magzenes & Media
330 N.Wabash, Ste. 2300
Chicago, IL 60611
Phone: (312)595-0296
Fax: (800)458-0479
Subject(s): Telecommunications
Circ: (Paid)2,685
(Non-paid)70,065

**Career Directions** (32941)
Directions Publishing Inc.
21 N Henry St.
Edgerton, WI 53534-1821
Phone: (608)884-3367
Fax: (608)884-8187
Subject(s): Education
Circ: (Non-paid)‡70,000

**Concrete Construction** (7821)
Hanley-Wood L.L.C.
426 S. Westgate St.
Addison, IL 60101
Phone: (630)543-0870
Fax: (630)543-3112
Subject(s): Construction, Contracting, Building, and Excavating; Building Materials, Concrete, Brick, and Tile
Circ: (Non-paid)△**12,376**
(Paid)△**70,000**

**Cooking for Profit** (32951)
C P Publishing Inc.
104 S Main St., 7th Fl.
PO Box 267
Fond du Lac, WI 54936-0267
Phone: (920)923-3700
Fax: (920)923-6805
Subject(s): Food and Grocery Trade; Hotels, Motels, Restaurants, and Clubs
Circ: ‡70,000

**Dairy Today** (16396)
Farm Journal Inc.
261 E. Broadway
PO Box 1167
Monticello, MN 55362
Phone: (763)271-3363
Fax: (763)271-3360
Subject(s): Dairying
Circ: (Non-paid)70,000

**Fantasy Sports** (33077)
Krause Publications Inc.
700 E. State St.
Iola, WI 54990-0001
Phone: (715)445-2214
Fax: (715)445-4087
Subject(s): (General Sports)
Circ: (Combined)70,000

**Safety+Health** (8814)
National Safety Council
1121 Spring Lake Dr.
Itasca, IL 60143-3201
Phone: (630)285-1121
Fax: (630)285-1315
Subject(s): Safety; Health and Healthcare
Circ: (Controlled)70,000

**Signal** (15198)
Detroit Educational Television Foundation
7441 Second Ave.
Detroit, MI 48202
Phone: (313)873-7200
Fax: (313)876-8118
Subject(s): Radio, Television, Cable, and Video
Circ: ‡70,000

**Today's Chicago Woman** (8427)
Leigh Communications Inc.
150 E Huron St.
Chicago, IL 60611
Phone: (312)951-7600
Fax: (312)951-9083
Subject(s): Women's Interests; Local, State, and Regional Publications
Circ: (Non-paid)70,000

**Minnesota Golfer** (16100)
TPG Sports Inc.
6550 York Ave., Ste.211
Edina, MN 55435
Subject(s): (Golf)
Circ: (Paid)⊕**69,345**

**Midwest Home & Garden** (16312)
Minnesota Monthly Publications Inc.
600 US Trust Bldg. 730 2nd Ave.S.
Minneapolis, MN 55402
Phone: (612)371-5800
Fax: (612)371-5801
Subject(s): Home and Garden
Circ: (Paid)69,065

**Christian Home & School** (15334)
Christian Schools International
3350 E. Paris Ave. SE
Grand Rapids, MI 49512-3054
Phone: (616)957-1070
Fax: (616)957-5022
Subject(s): Religious Publications; Education; Parenting
Circ: (Paid)‡1,000
(Controlled)‡69,000

**Minnesota Monthly** (16322)
Minnesota Monthly Publications Inc.
600 US Trust Bldg. 730 2nd Ave.S.
Minneapolis, MN 55402
Phone: (612)371-5800
Fax: (612)371-5801
Subject(s): Lifestyle; Local, State, and Regional Publications
Circ: (Paid)68,922

**North Light** (24327)
North Light Book Club
4700 E Galbraith Rd.
Cincinnati, OH 45236
Phone: (513)531-2222
Fax: (513)531-4744
Subject(s): Art and Art History; Art
Circ: (Non-paid)68,635

**Eagle Magazine** (24757)
Fraternal Order of Eagles
1623 Gatewat Cir., S
Grove City, OH 43123-9309
Phone: (614)883-2200
Fax: (614)883-2201
Subject(s): Eagles
Circ: (Paid)68,100

**Crochet World** (9569)
House of White Birches
306 E Parr Rd.
Berne, IN 46711
Phone: (260)589-4000
Fax: (260)589-8093
Subject(s): Dressmaking, Needlework, and Quilting
Circ: ‡68,000

**Massage Therapy Journal** (8678)
American Massage Therapy Association
500 Davis St.
Evanston, IL 60201
Phone: (847)864-0123
Fax: (847)864-1178
Subject(s): Health
Circ: (Paid)68,000

**Walleye In-Sider** (15948)
In-Fisherman
7819 Highland Scenic Rd.
Baxter, MN 56425-8011
Phone: (218)829-1648

Subject(s): (Hunting, Fishing, and Game Management)
Circ: (Paid)67,642

**Metro Parent** (33645)
11111 Plank Ct., Ste. B
PO Box 13491
Wauwatosa, WI 53213
Phone: (414)259-1884
Fax: (414)259-1392
Subject(s): Parenting
Circ: (Paid)154
(Free)67,214

**Public Works** (7823)
Hanley-Wood L.L.C.
426 S Westgate St.
Addison, IL 60101-4546
Phone: (630)543-0870
Fax: (630)543-3112
Subject(s): State, Municipal, and County Administration
Circ: (Paid)458
(Controlled)67,083

**Building Operating Management** (33293)
Trade Press Publishing Corp.
2100 W Florist Ave.
Milwaukee, WI 53209
Phone: (414)228-7701
Fax: (414)228-1134
Subject(s): Construction, Contracting, Building, and Excavating; Building Management and Maintenance
Circ: (Paid)155
(Non-paid)66,966

**Quilt World** (9577)
House of White Birches
306 E Parr Rd.
Berne, IN 46711
Phone: (260)589-4000
Fax: (260)589-8093
Subject(s): Dressmaking, Needlework, and Quilting
Circ: ‡66,042

**Metro Parent Magazine** (15778)
Metro Parent Publishing Group
24567 Northwestern Hwy., Ste. 150
Southfield, MI 48075
Phone: (248)352-0990
Fax: (248)352-5066
Subject(s): Parenting; Local, State, and Regional Publications
Circ: (Controlled)66,000

**Occupational Hazards** (24463)
Penton Media Inc.
1300 E. 9th St.
Cleveland, OH 44114-1530
Phone: (216)696-7000
Fax: (216)696-1752
Subject(s): Safety; Health and Healthcare
Circ: (Controlled)‡65,777

**Forming & Fabricating** (15151)
Society of Manufacturing Engineers
1 SME Dr.
PO Box 930
Dearborn, MI 48121
Phone: (313)271-1500
Fax: (313)425-3401
Subject(s): Metal, Metallurgy, and Metal Trade; Machinery and Equipment; Commerce and Industry
Circ: (Controlled)65,496

**Food Processing** (8810)
Putman Media
555 W Pierce Rd., Ste. 301
Itasca, IL 60143
Phone: (630)467-1300
Fax: (630)467-0197
Subject(s): Food and Grocery Trade
Circ: (Combined)△**65,031**

**Chemical Processing** (8805)
Putman Media
555 W Pierce Rd., Ste. 301
Itasca, IL 60143
Phone: (630)467-1300
Fax: (630)467-0197
Subject(s): Chemistry, Chemicals, and Chemical Engineering
Circ: (Non-paid)‡65,000

**Chemical Product News  (8806)**
Putman Media
555 W Pierce Rd., Ste. 301
Itasca, IL 60143
Phone: (630)467-1300
Fax: (630)467-0197
**Subject(s):** Chemistry, Chemicals, and Chemical Engineering
**Circ:** ‡65,000

**Food & Drug Packaging  (8548)**
Stagnito Communications
155 Pfingston Rd., Ste. 205
Deerfield, IL 60015
Phone: (847)205-5660
Fax: (847)205-5680
**Subject(s):** Packaging
**Circ:** (Combined)65,000

**Graduating Engineer & Computer Careers  (8216)**
Career Recruitment Media
211 W. Wacker Dr., Ste. 900
Chicago, IL 60606
Phone: (312)525-3100
**Subject(s):** Employment and Human Resources; Engineering (Various branches)
**Circ:** (Non-paid)65,000

**Hola Magazine  (33611)**
Spanish Publications Inc.
20975 Swenson Dr., Ste. 125
Waukesha, WI 53186
Phone: (262)798-7956
Fax: (262)798-5260
**Subject(s):** Hispanic Publications
**Circ:** (Free)65,000

**Real Detroit Weekly  (15284)**
Real Detroit Weekly L.L.C.
359 Livernois Ave., 2nd Fl.
Ferndale, MI 48220
Phone: (248)591-7325
Fax: (248)544-9893
**Subject(s):** Music and Musical Instruments; Entertainment
**Circ:** (Free)65,000

**AntiqueWeek (Eastern Edition)  (9962)**
Mayhill Publications
27 N. Jefferson St.
PO Box 90
Knightstown, IN 46148
Fax: (765)345-3398
**Subject(s):** Antiques
**Circ:** 64,959

**AntiqueWeek (Mid-Central Edition)  (9963)**
Mayhill Publications
27 N. Jefferson St.
PO Box 90
Knightstown, IN 46148
Fax: (765)345-3398
**Subject(s):** Antiques
**Circ:** 64,959

**Journal of the American Board of Family Practice  (15183)**
American Board of Family Practice
c/o Nancy Jacobson, Senior Editorial Assistant
Dept. of Family Medicine
Wayne State Univ.
101 E. Alexandrine, Rm. 249
Detroit, MI 48201
**Subject(s):** Health and Healthcare
**Circ:** (Paid)64,644

**Modern Salon  (8881)**
Vance Publishing Corp.
400 Knightsbridge Pkwy.
Lincolnshire, IL 60069
Phone: (847)634-2600
Fax: (847)634-4343
**Subject(s):** Hairstyling; Cosmetics and Toiletries
**Circ:** (Paid)55,126
(Non-paid)64,157

**Country Style Homes Plans and Designs  (16575)**
HomeStyles.com
213 E 4th St., Ste. 400
Saint Paul, MN 55101
Phone: (651)602-5000
Fax: (651)602-5001
**Subject(s):** Home and Garden
**Circ:** (Non-paid)64,000

**Painting  (8588)**
Clapper Publishing Company Inc.
2400 Devon, Suite 375
Des Plaines, IL 60018-4618
Phone: (847)635-6311
Fax: (847)635-6311
**Subject(s):** Crafts, Models, Hobbies, and Contests
**Circ:** (Paid)‡63,238

**Grocery Headquarters  (8218)**
Trend Publishing
One E. Erie, Ste. 401
Chicago, IL 60611
Phone: (312)654-2300
Fax: (312)654-2323
**Subject(s):** Food and Grocery Trade
**Circ:** (Controlled)‡63,207

**Hoard's Dairyman  (32972)**
W.D. Hoard & Sons Co.
28 W Milwaukee Ave.
Fort Atkinson, WI 53538
Phone: (920)563-5551
Fax: (920)563-7298
**Subject(s):** Dairying
**Circ:** (Non-paid)★17,875
(Paid)★63,034

**Fleet Equipment  (7995)**
Transportation Communications
2615 Three Oaks Rd.
Cary, IL 60013
Phone: (847)639-2200
Fax: (847)639-9542
**Subject(s):** Automotive (Trade)
**Circ:** (Controlled)‡63,000

**Funny Times  (24522)**
Funny Times Inc.
PO Box 18530
Cleveland Heights, OH 44118
Phone: (216)371-8600
Fax: (216)371-8696
**Subject(s):** Comics and Comic Technique
**Circ:** ⊕63,000

**Lawn & Landscape Magazine  (24439)**
G.I.E. Media, MC
4012 Bridge Ave.
Cleveland, OH 44113
Phone: (216)961-4130
Fax: (216)961-0364
**Subject(s):** Landscape Architecture
**Circ:** (Combined)‡63,000

**Classic Toy Trains Magazine  (33603)**
Kalmbach Publishing Co.
PO Box 1612
Waukesha, WI 53187-1612
Phone: (262)796-8776
Fax: (262)796-1615
**Subject(s):** Collecting
**Circ:** (Paid)★62,788

**American Trucker—New England Edition  (9828)**
Primedia Business
PO Box 603
Indianapolis, IN 46206
Phone: (317)297-5500
Fax: (317)299-1356
**Subject(s):** Trucks and Trucking
**Circ:** (Combined)62,335

**TRACKS MAGAZINE  (15530)**
Michigan United Conservation Clubs
2101 Wood St.
PO Box 30235
Lansing, MI 48909-7735
Phone: (517)371-1041
Fax: (517)371-1505
**Subject(s):** Ecology and Conservation
**Circ:** 62,000

**American Trucker—Central States Edition  (9818)**
Primedia Business
PO Box 603
Indianapolis, IN 46206
Phone: (317)297-5500
Fax: (317)299-1356
**Subject(s):** Trucks and Trucking
**Circ:** (Combined)61,924

**Birder's World  (33602)**
Kalmbach Publishing Co.
PO Box 1612
Waukesha, WI 53187-1612
Phone: (262)796-8776
Fax: (262)796-1615
**Subject(s):** Biology; Photography; Ecology and Conservation
**Circ:** (Paid)★61,242

**Plastic Canvas Crafts  (9576)**
House of White Birches
306 E Parr Rd.
Berne, IN 46711
Phone: (260)589-4000
Fax: (260)589-8093
**Subject(s):** Crafts, Models, Hobbies, and Contests
**Circ:** ‡60,541

**Automotive Body Repair News  (8092)**
Reed Business Information
100 W. Monroe St., Ste. 1100
Chicago, IL 60603
Phone: (312)553-8900
Fax: (312)553-8926
**Subject(s):** Automotive (Trade)
**Circ:** (Controlled)60,488
(Controlled)60,488

**FineScale Modeler  (33609)**
Kalmbach Publishing Co.
PO Box 1612
Waukesha, WI 53187-1612
Phone: (262)796-8776
Fax: (262)796-1615
**Subject(s):** Crafts, Models, Hobbies, and Contests
**Circ:** (Paid)60,425

**Classic Trains  (33604)**
Kalmbach Publishing Co.
PO Box 1612
Waukesha, WI 53187-1612
Phone: (262)796-8776
Fax: (262)796-1615
**Subject(s):** Crafts, Models, Hobbies, and Contests
**Circ:** (Paid)★60,308

**Do-It-Yourself Retailing  (9846)**
National Retail Hardware Association
5822 W 74th St.
Indianapolis, IN 46278
Phone: (317)290-0338
Fax: (317)328-4354
**Subject(s):** Hardware
**Circ:** (Non-paid)★60,171

**BodyShop Business  (24093)**
Babcox
3550 Embassy Pkwy.
Akron, OH 44333
Phone: (330)670-1234
Fax: (330)670-0874
**Subject(s):** Automotive (Trade)
**Circ:** (Controlled)60,107

**Landscape Management  (24438)**
Advanstar Communications
7500 Old Oak Blvd.
Cleveland, OH 44130-3369
Phone: (440)243-8100
Fax: (440)891-2777
**Subject(s):** Landscape Architecture
**Circ:** (Combined)‡60,014

**American Snowmobiler  (16568)**
2715 Upper Afton Rd., 100
Saint Paul, MN 55119-4774
Phone: (612)738-1953
Fax: (612)738-2302
**Subject(s):** (Snowmobiling)
**Circ:** (Paid)⊕60,000

**Assembly  (15845)**
BNP Media
2401 W Big Beaver Rd., Ste. 700
Troy, MI 48084-3333
Phone: (248)362-3700
Fax: (248)362-0317
**Subject(s):** Electronics Engineering; Engineering (Various branches)
**Circ:** (Controlled)‡60,000

**Automotive Design and Production (15682)**
Gardner Publications Inc.
127 S. Main St., Ste. 4
Plymouth, MI 48170
Phone: (734)416-9705
Fax: (734)416-9707
**Subject(s):** Management and Administration; Metal, Metallurgy, and Metal Trade
**Circ:** (Non-paid)‡60,000

**BMWE Journal (15774)**
Brotherhood of Maintenance of Way Employees
20300 Civic Center Dr., Ste. 320
Southfield, MI 48076-4169
Phone: (248)948-1010
Fax: (248)948-7150
**Subject(s):** Labor; Railroad
**Circ:** ‡60,000

**Catholic Knight Magazine (33296)**
Catholic Knights Insurance
1100 W. Wells St.
PO Box 05900
Milwaukee, WI 53233
Phone: (414)273-6266
Fax: (414)223-3201
**Subject(s):** Unclassified Fraternal; Insurance
**Circ:** (Controlled)‡60,000

**CWB: Custom Woodworking Business (8879)**
Vance Publishing Corp.
PO Box 1400
Lincolnshire, IL 60069
Phone: (847)634-4347
Fax: (847)634-4374
**Subject(s):** Wood and Woodworking
**Circ:** (Controlled)‡60,000

**Embedded Systems Programming (9112)**
CMP Media L.L.C.
Embedded Systems Programming
PO Box 3404
Northbrook, IL 60065-9468
**Subject(s):** Computers
**Circ:** 60,000

**Indy's Child (9875)**
Indy's Child Inc.
1901 Broad Ripple Ave.
Indianapolis, IN 46220
Phone: (317)722-8500
Fax: (317)722-8510
**Subject(s):** Parenting; Children's Interests
**Circ:** (Paid)20
(Free)60,000

**Kappa Delta Pi Record (9884)**
Kappa Delta Pi
3707 Woodview Trace
Indianapolis, IN 46268-1158
Phone: (317)871-4900
Fax: (317)704-2323
**Subject(s):** Education
**Circ:** (Paid)60,000

**Metalforming (24782)**
Precision Metalforming Association
6363 Oak Tree Blvd.
Independence, OH 44131-2500
Phone: (216)901-8800
Fax: (216)901-9669
**Subject(s):** Metal, Metallurgy, and Metal Trade
**Circ:** (Non-paid)60,000

**Roads & Bridges Magazine (8592)**
Scranton Gillette Communications Inc.
380 NW Hwy., Ste. 200
Des Plaines, IL 60016-2282
Phone: (847)391-1000
Fax: (847)390-0408
**Subject(s):** Roads and Streets; Construction, Contracting, Building, and Excavating
**Circ:** (Controlled)‡60,000

**Via Times Newsmagazine (8439)**
PO Box 138155
Chicago, IL 60613
Phone: (773)866-0811
Fax: (773)866-9207
**Subject(s):** Filipino; Ethnic Publications
**Circ:** (Combined)60,000

**American Libraries (8074)**
American Library Association
50 E. Huron St.
Chicago, IL 60611
Phone: (312)280-4216
Fax: (312)440-0901
**Subject(s):** Library and Information Science; Education
**Circ:** (Combined)‡59,300

**Fast & Fun Crochet (9571)**
House of White Birches
306 E Parr Rd.
Berne, IN 46711
Phone: (260)589-4000
Fax: (260)589-8093
**Subject(s):** Dressmaking, Needlework, and Quilting
**Circ:** 59,000

**Marriage Partnership (7978)**
Christianity Today International
465 Gundersen Dr.
Carol Stream, IL 60188
Phone: (630)260-6200
Fax: (630)260-0114
**Subject(s):** Religious Publications
**Circ:** (Non-paid)27,000
(Paid)59,000

**American Fruit Grower (25171)**
Meister Publishing Co.
37733 Euclid Ave.
Willoughby, OH 44094-5992
Phone: (440)942-2000
Fax: (440)942-0662
**Subject(s):** Horticulture
**Circ:** (Paid)‡58,423

**Indianapolis Woman (9874)**
Weiss Communications
6610 N. Shadeland, Ste. 100
Indianapolis, IN 46220
Phone: (317)585-5858
**Subject(s):** Women's Interests; Local, State, and Regional Publications
**Circ:** (Non-paid)58,227

**Hotel & Motel Management (24426)**
Advanstar Communications
7500 Old Oak Blvd.
Cleveland, OH 44130-3369
Phone: (440)243-8100
Fax: (440)891-2777
**Subject(s):** Hotels, Motels, Restaurants, and Clubs
**Circ:** (Paid)1,019
(Controlled)58,144

**Engineered Systems (15850)**
BNP Media
PO Box 4270
Troy, MI 48099
**Subject(s):** Air Conditioning and Refrigeration
**Circ:** (Paid)63
(Controlled)58,000

**Pollution Engineering (15859)**
Reed Business Information
c/o Roy Bigham, Editor
2401 W. Big Beaver, Ste. 7000
Troy, MI 48084
Phone: (248)244-6252
Fax: (248)786-1356
**Subject(s):** Ecology and Conservation; Waste Management and Recycling
**Circ:** (Controlled)‡58,000

**Journal of the American Academy of Physician Assistants (JAAPA) (16058)**
Thomson PDR
131 W. 1st St.
Duluth, MN 55802
Phone: (218)723-9200
Fax: (218)723-9308
**Subject(s):** Medicine and Surgery; Health and Healthcare
**Circ:** (Controlled)57,500

**Pediatrics (8641)**
American Academy of Pediatrics
141 NW Point Blvd.
Elk Grove Village, IL 60007-1098
Phone: (847)434-4000
Fax: (847)228-1281
**Subject(s):** Pediatrics
**Circ:** (Paid)4,000
(Non-paid)57,000

**Sewing Savvy (9578)**
House of White Birches
306 E Parr Rd.
Berne, IN 46711
Phone: (260)589-4000
Fax: (260)589-8093
**Subject(s):** Dressmaking, Needlework, and Quilting; Crafts, Models, Hobbies, and Contests; Women's Interests
**Circ:** (Paid)57,000

**American Trucker—Kentucky/Tennessee Edition (9822)**
Primedia Business
PO Box 603
Indianapolis, IN 46206
Phone: (317)297-5500
Fax: (317)299-1356
**Subject(s):** Automotive (Consumer)
**Circ:** (Combined)56,559

**Heating/Piping/Air Conditioning Engineering (HPAC) (24424)**
Penton Media Inc.
1300 E. 9th St.
Cleveland, OH 44114-1530
Phone: (216)696-7000
Fax: (216)696-1752
**Subject(s):** Air Conditioning and Refrigeration; Plumbing and Heating
**Circ:** (Paid)1,250
(Non-paid)56,308

**Motion System Design (24455)**
Penton Media Inc.
1300 E. 9th St.
Cleveland, OH 44114-1530
Phone: (216)696-7000
Fax: (216)696-1752
**Subject(s):** Engineering (Various branches)
**Circ:** (Controlled)‡56,050

**Crochet! (9568)**
House of White Birches
306 E Parr Rd.
Berne, IN 46711
Phone: (260)589-4000
Fax: (260)589-8093
**Subject(s):** Dressmaking, Needlework, and Quilting; Crafts, Models, Hobbies, and Contests; Women's Interests
**Circ:** (Combined)56,000

**The Sons of Norway Viking (16343)**
Sons of Norway
1455 W. Lake St.
Minneapolis, MN 55408-2666
Phone: (612)827-3611
Fax: (612)827-0658
**Subject(s):** Norwegian; Unclassified Fraternal; Ethnic and Minority Studies
**Circ:** (Combined)‡56,000

**American Trucker—California Edition (9816)**
Primedia Business
PO Box 603
Indianapolis, IN 46206
Phone: (317)297-5500
Fax: (317)299-1356
**Subject(s):** Trucks and Trucking
**Circ:** (Combined)55,429

**Teddy Bear Review (33096)**
Jones Publishing Inc.
N7450 Annstad Rd.
PO Box 5000
Iola, WI 54945-5000
Phone: (715)445-5000
Fax: (715)445-4053
**Subject(s):** Crafts, Models, Hobbies, and Contests
**Circ:** (Paid)‡55,045

**Advanced Imaging (7848)**
Cygnus Business Media Inc.
c/o Larry Adams
3030 Salt Creek Ln.
Arlington Heights, IL 60005
Phone: (847)454-2726
**Subject(s):** Computers; Electronics Engineering
**Circ:** (Controlled)‡55,009

**All About Kids (24280)**
All About Kids Inc.
1077 Celestial St. Ste. 101
Cincinnati, OH 45202
Phone: (513)684-0501
Fax: (513)684-0507

# Great Lakes States

**Subject(s):** Children's Interests; Parenting
**Circ:** (Paid)50
(Free)55,000

**Collectible Automobile (9006)**
Publications International Ltd.
PO Box 482
Dept. ACAT
Mount Morris, IL 61054-0482
**Subject(s):** Automotive (Consumer)
**Circ:** ‡55,000

**The FABRICATOR (9300)**
The Croydon Group Ltd.,
833 Featherstone Rd.
Rockford, IL 61107-6302
Phone: (815)399-8770
Fax: (815)381-1370
**Subject(s):** Metal, Metallurgy, and Metal Trade
**Circ:** (Controlled)55,000

**Forward in Christ (33302)**
Wisconsin Evangelical Lutheran Synod
2929 N Mayfair Rd.
Milwaukee, WI 53222-4398
Phone: (414)256-3888
Fax: (414)256-3899
**Subject(s):** Religious Publications
**Circ:** (Controlled)‡3,000
(Paid)‡55,000

**The Magazine of Sigma Chi (8676)**
Sigma Chi Fraternity
1714 Hinman Ave.
PO Box 469
Evanston, IL 60204-0469
Phone: (847)869-3655
Fax: (847)869-4906
**Subject(s):** Unclassified Fraternal
**Circ:** ‡55,000

**The New American (32810)**
American Opinion Publishing Inc.
PO Box 8040
Appleton, WI 54912
Phone: (920)749-3784
Fax: (920)749-3785
**Subject(s):** General Editorial
**Circ:** ‡55,000

**Purdue Alumnus (10251)**
Purdue Alumni Association Inc.
101 N. Grant St.
PMU 160
West Lafayette, IN 47906-6212
**Subject(s):** College Publications
**Circ:** 55,000

**American Dental Hygienists' Association Access (8066)**
American Dental Hygienists' Association
444 N Michigan Ave., Ste. 3400
Chicago, IL 60611
Phone: (312)440-8904
Fax: (312)467-1406
**Subject(s):** Dentistry; Health and Healthcare
**Circ:** 30,000
(Combined)‡54,299

**DVM Newsmagazine (24401)**
Advanstar Communications
c/o Daniel R. Verdon, Editor
DVM Newsmagazine
7500 Old Oak Blvd.
Cleveland, OH 44130
Fax: (440)891-2675
**Subject(s):** Veterinary Medicine
**Circ:** (Paid)3,000
(Non-paid)54,000

**Locomotive Engineers Journal (24445)**
Brotherhood of Locomotive Engineers
1370 Ontario St., Mezzanine
Cleveland, OH 44113
Phone: (212)241-2630
**Subject(s):** Labor; Railroad
**Circ:** ‡54,000

**Christian Standard (24295)**
Standard Publishing
8121 Hamilton Ave.
Cincinnati, OH 45231
Phone: (513)931-4050
Fax: (513)931-0950

**Subject(s):** Religious Publications
**Circ:** ‡53,080

**Clinical Laboratory Reference (CLR) (16049)**
Thomson PDR
131 W. 1st St.
Duluth, MN 55802
Phone: (218)723-9200
Fax: (218)723-9308
**Subject(s):** Laboratory Research (Scientific and Medical); Medicine and Surgery
**Circ:** (Free)53,000

**HomeStyles Home Plans (16584)**
HomeStyles.com
213 E 4th St., Ste. 400
Saint Paul, MN 55101
Phone: (651)602-5000
Fax: (651)602-5001
**Subject(s):** Home and Garden
**Circ:** (Non-paid)53,000

**New Country Homes (16603)**
HomeStyles.com
213 E 4th St., Ste. 400
Saint Paul, MN 55101
Phone: (651)602-5000
Fax: (651)602-5001
**Subject(s):** Home and Garden
**Circ:** (Non-paid)53,000

**Catechist (24644)**
Peter Li Inc.
2621 Dryden Rd. Ste. 300
Dayton, OH 45439
Phone: (937)298-8965
Fax: (800)370-4450
**Subject(s):** Religious Publications
**Circ:** (Non-paid)‡536
(Paid)‡52,392

**Bridal Crafts (8572)**
Clapper Publishing Company Inc.
2400 Devon, Suite 375
Des Plaines, IL 60018-4618
Phone: (847)635-6311
Fax: (847)635-6311
**Subject(s):** Crafts, Models, Hobbies, and Contests; Brides
**Circ:** (Paid)52,066

**LH (Lodging Hospitality) (24442)**
Penton Media Inc.
1300 E. 9th St.
Cleveland, OH 44114-1530
Phone: (216)696-7000
Fax: (216)696-1752
**Subject(s):** Hotels, Motels, Restaurants, and Clubs
**Circ:** (Controlled)‡51,600

**Wood & Wood Products (8884)**
Vance Publishing Corp.
PO Box 1400
Lincolnshire, IL 60069
Phone: (847)634-4347
Fax: (847)634-4374
**Subject(s):** Wood and Woodworking
**Circ:** (Non-paid)‡51,573

**North Shore Magazine (8740)**
Pioneer Press Newspapers
3701 W. Lake Ave.
Glenview, IL 60025
Phone: (847)486-9200
Fax: (847)486-7416
**Subject(s):** Local, State, and Regional Publications
**Circ:** (Paid)51,340

**American Trucker—Michigan Edition (9824)**
Primedia Business
PO Box 603
Indianapolis, IN 46206
Phone: (317)297-5500
Fax: (317)299-1356
**Subject(s):** Trucks and Trucking
**Circ:** (Combined)51,151

**Cotton Farming (8878)**
Vance Publishing Corp.
400 Knightsbridge Pkwy.
Lincolnshire, IL 60069
Phone: (847)634-2600
**Subject(s):** Socialized Farming
**Circ:** (Non-paid)51,151

**Chicagoland Golf (9537)**
Chicagoland Golf Publishing Co.
6825 Hobson Valley Dr., No. 204
Woodridge, IL 60517
**Subject(s):** (Golf)
**Circ:** (Paid)‡1,375
(Controlled)‡51,125

**Recreation Resources (8396)**
Adams Business Media
833 W Jackson, 7th Fl.
Chicago, IL 60607
Phone: (312)846-4600
Fax: (312)846-4638
**Subject(s):** Landscape Architecture; Travel and Tourism
**Circ:** (Controlled)51,100

**Wood Digest (32986)**
Cygnus Business Media
1233 Janesville Ave.
Fort Atkinson, WI 53538
Phone: (920)563-6388
Fax: (920)563-1702
**Subject(s):** Wood and Woodworking; Furniture and Furnishings
**Circ:** (Controlled)‡51,010

**Journal of AHIMA (8256)**
American Health Information Management Association (AHIMA)
233 N. Michigan Ave., Ste. 2150
Chicago, IL 60601-5800
Phone: (312)233-1100
Fax: (312)233-1090
**Subject(s):** Health and Healthcare; Management and Administration; Library and Information Science
**Circ:** (Non-paid)550
(Paid)50,800

**Counterman (24096)**
Babcox
3550 Embassy Pkwy.
Akron, OH 44333
Phone: (330)670-1234
Fax: (330)670-0874
**Subject(s):** Automotive (Trade); Selling and Salesmanship
**Circ:** (Controlled)50,062

**Wisconsin Trails (32856)**
Trails Media Group Inc.
PO Box 317
1131 Mills St.
Black Earth, WI 53515
Phone: (608)767-8000
Fax: (608)767-5444
**Subject(s):** Local, State, and Regional Publications
**Circ:** 50,050

**Energy User News (8632)**
BNP Media
847S Randall Rd. No.409
Elgin, IL 60123
Phone: (847)622-7263
Fax: (847)622-7264
**Subject(s):** Power and Power Plants; Commerce and Industry
**Circ:** (Paid)894
(Non-paid)50,027

**McKnight's Long-Term Care News (9134)**
Two Northfield Plz., Ste. 300
Northfield, IL 60093-1219
Phone: (847)784-8706
Fax: (847)441-3701
**Subject(s):** Nursing; Hospitals and Healthcare Institutions
**Circ:** (Paid)‡850
(Controlled)‡50,025

**Christian History Magazine (7970)**
Christianity Today International
465 Gundersen Dr.
Carol Stream, IL 60188
Phone: (630)260-6200
Fax: (630)260-0114
**Subject(s):** Religious Publications
**Circ:** ‡50,000

**Cleveland Magazine (24389)**
Great Lakes Publishing Co.
1422 Euclid Ave., Hanna Bldg., Ste. 730
Cleveland, OH 44115
Phone: (216)771-2833
Fax: (216)781-6318
**Subject(s):** Local, State, and Regional Publications
**Circ:** 50,000

**Computer User (16287)**
MSP Communications
220 S 6th St., Ste. 500
Minneapolis, MN 55402
Phone: (612)339-7571
Fax: (612)339-5806
Subject(s): Computers
Circ: (Non-paid)‡50,000

**Conscious Choice (8158)**
Conscious Choice Subscriptions
920 N. Franklin St., Ste. 202
Chicago, IL 60610
Phone: (312)440-4373
Fax: (312)751-3973
Subject(s): Environmental and Natural Resources Conservation; Health
Circ: (Non-paid)50,000

**Contemporary Pediatrics (16051)**
Thomson PDR
131 W. 1st St.
Duluth, MN 55802
Phone: (218)723-9200
Fax: (218)723-9308
Subject(s): Medicine and Surgery; Pediatrics
Circ: (Controlled)48,289
  50,000

**Fine Tuning (33301)**
The Channel 10/36 Friends Inc.
Foundation Hall, 5th Fl.
700 W. State St.
Milwaukee, WI 53233-1443
Phone: (414)297-8000
Fax: (414)297-8007
Subject(s): Radio, Television, Cable, and Video
Circ: 50,000

**Formulary (24413)**
Advanstar Communications
7500 Old Oak Blvd.
Cleveland, OH 44130
Phone: (440)243-8100
Fax: (440)890-2683
Subject(s): Hospitals and Healthcare Institutions; Drugs and Pharmaceuticals
Circ: (Controlled)50,000

**iAm Magazine! (16099)**
iAm Magazine Inc.
5525 Hansen Rd., Apt. 104
Edina, MN 55436-2323
Fax: (952)927-6143
Subject(s): Women's Interests; Lifestyle; Local, State, and Regional Publications
Circ: 50,000

**ISTA Advocate (9876)**
Indiana State Teachers Association
150 W Market St., Ste. 900
Indianapolis, IN 46204-2875
Phone: (317)637-7481
Fax: (317)631-8715
Subject(s): Education; Labor
Circ: (Controlled)‡50,000

**JUF News (8296)**
Jewish Federation of Chicago
1 S.Franklin St.
Ben Gurion Way
Chicago, IL 60606-4594
Phone: (312)346-6700
Subject(s): Jewish Publications
Circ: 50,000

**Protein Science (9978)**
Cambridge University Press
Department of Biochemistry
Purdue University Biochemistry Bldg. W.
Lafayette, IN 47907
Phone: (765)496-3460
Fax: (765)496-3460
Subject(s): Science (General); Biology
Circ: 50,000

**WMU, The Magazine (15482)**
Western Michigan University
1903 W Michigan Ave.
Kalamazoo, MI 49008-5200
Phone: (269)387-8400
Fax: (269)387-8422
Subject(s): College Publications
Circ: (Free)50,000

**Hydraulics & Pneumatics (24427)**
Penton Media Inc.
1300 E. 9th St.
Cleveland, OH 44114-1530
Phone: (216)696-7000
Fax: (216)696-1752
Subject(s): Engineering (Various branches); Machinery and Equipment
Circ: (Controlled)‡49,878

**CE News (8120)**
MERCOR MEDIA Inc.
IBM Plaza, 330 N. Wabash, Ste. 3201
Chicago, IL 60611
Phone: (312)628-5870
Fax: (312)628-5878
Subject(s): Engineering (Various branches); Architecture; Construction, Contracting, Building, and Excavating
Circ: (Controlled)49,610

**Journal of the AVMA (9351)**
American Veterinary Medical Association
1931 N Meacham Rd., Ste. 100
Schaumburg, IL 60173-4360
Phone: (847)925-8070
Fax: (847)925-9329
Subject(s): Veterinary Medicine
Circ: ‡49,600

**American Trucker—Southern Edition (9831)**
Primedia Business
PO Box 603
Indianapolis, IN 46206
Phone: (317)297-5500
Fax: (317)299-1356
Subject(s): Automotive (Consumer)
Circ: (Combined)49,599

**Instant and Small Commercial Printer (8871)**
Innes Publishing Co.
28100 N. Ashley Cir.
PO Box 7280
Libertyville, IL 60048
Phone: (847)816-7900
Fax: (847)247-8855
Subject(s): Printing and Typography
Circ: (Controlled)‡49,289

**Contracting Business (24391)**
Penton Media Inc.
1300 E. 9th St.
Cleveland, OH 44114-1530
Phone: (216)696-7000
Fax: (216)696-1752
Subject(s): Air Conditioning and Refrigeration
Circ: (Controlled)49,001

**Pro (32979)**
Cygnus Business Media
1233 Janesville Ave.
Fort Atkinson, WI 53538
Phone: (920)563-6388
Fax: (920)563-1702
Subject(s): Landscape Architecture; Turf and Turf Maintenance
Circ: (Controlled)‡49,000

**Michigan Farm News (15517)**
Michigan Farm Bureau
7373 W. Saginaw Hwy.
PO Box 30960
Lansing, MI 48909-8460
Phone: (517)323-7000
Fax: (517)323-6541
Subject(s): Farm Newspapers
Circ: (Paid)48,586

**Contractor Magazine (8576)**
Penton Media Inc.
2700 S. River Rd., Ste. 109
Des Plaines, IL 60018
Phone: (847)299-3101
Fax: (847)299-3018
Subject(s): Plumbing and Heating; Commerce and Industry
Circ: (Controlled)48,504
  (Controlled)48,504

**Journal of the American Veterinary Medical Association (9350)**
American Veterinary Medical Association
1931 N Meacham Rd., Ste. 100
Schaumburg, IL 60173-4360
Phone: (847)925-8070
Fax: (847)925-9329
Subject(s): Veterinary Medicine
Circ: (Non-paid)3,198
  (Paid)48,504

**American Trucker—Metro East Edition (9823)**
Primedia Business
PO Box 603
Indianapolis, IN 46206
Phone: (317)297-5500
Fax: (317)299-1356
Subject(s): Trucks and Trucking
Circ: (Combined)48,419

**American Trucker—Illinois Edition (9820)**
Primedia Business
PO Box 603
Indianapolis, IN 46206
Phone: (317)297-5500
Fax: (317)299-1356
Subject(s): Trucks and Trucking
Circ: (Combined)48,387

**Farm Bureau's Rural Route (33177)**
Wisconsin Farm Bureau Federation
PO Box 5550
Madison, WI 53705
Phone: (608)836-5575
Fax: (608)828-5769
Subject(s): Farm Bureau, Grange, and Cooperative Associations
Circ: ‡48,000

**Minnesota (16315)**
University of Minnesota Alumni Association
200 Oak St. SE, Ste. 200
Minneapolis, MN 55455-2040
Phone: (612)624-2323
Fax: (612)626-8167
Subject(s): College Publications
Circ: 48,000

**Today's Catholic Teacher (24662)**
Peter Li Inc.
2621 Dryden Rd. Ste. 300
Dayton, OH 45439
Phone: (937)298-8965
Fax: (800)370-4450
Subject(s): Education; Religious Publications
Circ: (Non-paid)‡2,000
  (Paid)‡48,000

**Business & Health Institute (16047)**
Thomson PDR
131 W. 1st St.
Duluth, MN 55802
Phone: (218)723-9200
Fax: (218)723-9308
Subject(s): Business; Health and Healthcare
Circ: (Paid)3,100
  (Controlled)47,479

**The Big Picture (24291)**
ST Media Group International
407 Gilbert Ave.
Cincinnati, OH 45202
Phone: (513)421-2050
Fax: (513)421-5144
Subject(s): Printing and Typography
Circ: (Paid)762
  (Non-paid)47,420

**Child Life (9837)**
Children's Better Health Institute
1100 Waterway Blvd.
PO Box 567
Indianapolis, IN 46202
Phone: (317)634-1100
Fax: (317)684-8094
Subject(s): Parenting; Health
Circ: (Paid)47,330

**Indianapolis Monthly (9871)**
Emmis Publishing Corp.
1 Emmis Plaza
40 Monument Cir., Ste. 100
Indianapolis, IN 46204
Phone: (317)237-9288
Fax: (317)684-8356
Subject(s): Lifestyle
Circ: (Paid)47,106

---

Circulation: ★ = ABC; △ = BPA; ♦ = CAC; ● = CCAB; ❏ = VAC; ⊕ = PO Statement; ‡ = Publisher's Report; Boldface figures = sworn; Light figures = estimated.

## Great Lakes States

**Babybug** (9237)
The Cricket Magazine Group
Carus Publishing Company
315 Fifth St.
Peru, IL 61354
**Subject(s):** Children's Interests; Literature and Literary Reviews
**Circ:** 47,000

**The DO** (8174)
American Osteopathic Association
142 E Ontario St.
Chicago, IL 60611
Phone: (312)202-8000
Fax: (312)202-8200
**Subject(s):** Osteopathy
**Circ:** (Non-paid)‡47,000

**Futures Magazine** (8209)
833 W. Jackson 7th Fl.
Chicago, IL 60607
Phone: (312)846-4600
Fax: (312)846-4638
**Subject(s):** Banking, Finance, and Investments
**Circ:** (Paid)18,077
(Controlled)46,924

**American Trucker—Mountain America Edition** (9827)
Primedia Business
PO Box 603
Indianapolis, IN 46206
Phone: (317)297-5500
Fax: (317)299-1356
**Subject(s):** Trucks and Trucking
**Circ:** (Combined)46,023

**Good Old Days Specials** (9573)
House of White Birches
306 E Parr Rd.
Berne, IN 46711
Phone: (260)589-4000
Fax: (260)589-8093
**Subject(s):** History and Genealogy
**Circ:** (Paid)46,000

**Products Finishing** (24329)
Gardner Publications Inc.
6915 Valley Ave.
Cincinnati, OH 45244
Phone: (513)527-8800
Fax: (513)527-8801
**Subject(s):** Metal, Metallurgy, and Metal Trade; Plastic and Composition Materials
**Circ:** (Controlled)‡45,677

**Semiconductor International** (9158)
Reed Business Information
2000 Clearwater Dr.
PO Box 5080
Oak Brook, IL 60523
Phone: (630)288-8843
Fax: (630)288-8843
**Subject(s):** Electrical Engineering; Science (General)
**Circ:** (Paid)1,015
(Non-paid)45,541

**BtoB Magazine** (8111)
Crain Communications Inc.
360 N. Michigan Ave.
Chicago, IL 60601-3806
Phone: (312)649-5411
Fax: (312)280-3150
**Subject(s):** Advertising and Marketing
**Circ:** (Controlled)45,000

**Mortar Board Forum** (24568)
Mortar Board
1200 Chambers Rd., No. 201
Columbus, OH 43212-1753
Phone: (614)488-4094
Fax: (614)488-4095
**Subject(s):** Education; Clubs and Societies
**Circ:** 45,000

**Potentials** (16337)
VNU Business Media
50 S. 9th St.
Minneapolis, MN 55402
Phone: (612)333-0471
Fax: (612)333-6526
**Subject(s):** Advertising and Marketing
**Circ:** (Non-paid)★45,000

**Seek** (24333)
Standard Publishing
8121 Hamilton Ave.
Cincinnati, OH 45231
Phone: (513)931-4050
Fax: (513)931-0950
**Subject(s):** Religious Publications
**Circ:** ‡45,000

**American Trucker—Minn/Dakota Truck Edition** (9826)
Primedia Business
PO Box 603
Indianapolis, IN 46206
Phone: (317)297-5500
Fax: (317)299-1356
**Subject(s):** Trucks and Trucking
**Circ:** (Paid)44,773

**American Trucker—Florida Edition** (9819)
Primedia Business
PO Box 603
Indianapolis, IN 46206
Phone: (317)297-5500
Fax: (317)299-1356
**Subject(s):** Automotive (Consumer)
**Circ:** (Combined)44,297

**Turkey and Turkey Hunting Magazine** (33101)
Krause Publications Inc.
700 E. State St.
Iola, WI 54990-0001
Phone: (715)445-2214
Fax: (715)445-4087
**Subject(s):** (Hunting, Fishing, and Game Management)
**Circ:** (Paid)‡44,268

**American Trucker—Cascade Edition** (9817)
Primedia Business
PO Box 603
Indianapolis, IN 46206
Phone: (317)297-5500
Fax: (317)299-1356
**Subject(s):** Trucks and Trucking
**Circ:** (Combined)44,195

**Technical Support** (33428)
NaSPA
7044 S. 13th St.
Oak Creek, WI 53154
Phone: (414)908-4945
Fax: (414)768-8001
**Subject(s):** Computers
**Circ:** (Controlled)44,113

**Fleet Maintenance Supervisor** (32070)
Cygnus Business Media
1233 Janesville Ave.
PO BOX 803
Fort Atkinson, WI 53538-0803
Phone: (920)563-6388
Fax: (920)563-1702
**Subject(s):** Automotive (Trade); Trucks and Trucking
**Circ:** (Controlled)△44,018

**American Trucker—Buckeye Edition** (9815)
Primedia Business
PO Box 603
Indianapolis, IN 46206
Phone: (317)297-5500
Fax: (317)299-1356
**Subject(s):** Trucks and Trucking
**Circ:** (Combined)44,008

**The Catholic Answer** (9804)
Our Sunday Visitor Publishing
200 Noll Plz.
Huntington, IN 46750
Phone: (260)356-8400
Fax: (260)356-8472
**Subject(s):** Religious Publications
**Circ:** (Non-paid)923
(Paid)43,863

**Veterinary Medicine** (16069)
Thomson PDR
131 W. 1st St.
Duluth, MN 55802
Phone: (218)723-9200
Fax: (218)723-9308
**Subject(s):** Veterinary Medicine
**Circ:** △43,648

**Linn's Stamp News** (25041)
911 Vandemark Rd.
PO Box 29
Sidney, OH 45365-0029
Phone: (937)498-0886
Fax: (937)498-0807
**Subject(s):** Collecting
**Circ:** ‡43,000

**The Residential Specialist** (8397)
Council of Residential Specialists
430 N Michigan Ave., 3rd Fl.
Chicago, IL 60611-4092
Phone: (312)321-4400
Fax: (312)329-8551
**Subject(s):** Real Estate
**Circ:** ‡43,000

**Semiconductor Manufacturing Magazine** (9121)
SEMI
PO Box 3417
Northbrook, IL 60065-3417
Phone: (408)943-7047
Fax: (408)943-7965
**Subject(s):** Electronics Engineering; Electrical Engineering; Telecommunications
**Circ:** (Non-paid)43,000

**Contemporary Urology** (16052)
Thomson PDR
131 W. 1st St.
Duluth, MN 55802
Phone: (218)723-9200
Fax: (218)723-9308
**Subject(s):** Medicine and Surgery
**Circ:** (Paid)42742

**Paper, Film & Foil Converter** (8370)
Primedia Business
330 N. Wabash Ave., Ste. 2300
Chicago, IL 60611-3698
Phone: (312)595-1080
Fax: (312)595-8455
**Subject(s):** Packaging
**Circ:** (Non-paid)‡42,548

**CAP Today** (9125)
College of American Pathologists
325 Waukegan Rd.
Northfield, IL 60093-2750
Phone: (847)832-7000
Fax: (847)832-8000
**Subject(s):** Laboratory Research (Scientific and Medical)
**Circ:** (Paid)8,500
(Non-paid)42,200

**Antique Trader Weekly** (33060)
Krause Publications Inc.
700 E. State St.
Iola, WI 54990-0001
Phone: (715)445-2214
Fax: (715)445-4087
**Subject(s):** Art
**Circ:** (Paid)‡42,045

**Health Data Management** (8221)
Thomson Financial
300 South Wacker Dr.
Chicago, IL 60606
Phone: (312)913-1959
Fax: (312)913-1959
**Subject(s):** Health and Healthcare
**Circ:** (Combined)42,020

**Aircraft Maintenance Technology** (32958)
Cygnus Business Media
1233 Janesville Ave.
Fort Atkinson, WI 53538
Phone: (920)563-6388
Fax: (920)563-1702
**Subject(s):** Aviation
**Circ:** (Controlled)△42,000

**Chef** (8123)
Talcott Communications Corp.
20 W. Kinzie, 12th Fl.
Chicago, IL 60610
Phone: (312)849-2220
Fax: (312)849-2174
**Subject(s):** Food and Grocery Trade; Hotels, Motels, Restaurants, and Clubs
**Circ:** (Paid)1,500
(Controlled)42,000

**COMMUNIQUE (24543)**
Business Professionals of America
5454 Cleveland Ave.
Columbus, OH 43231
Phone: (614)895-7277
Fax: (614)895-1165
**Subject(s):** Business
**Circ:** (Controlled)‡1,000
(Paid)‡42,000

**Computerized Investing (8156)**
American Association of Individual Investors
625 N. Michigan Ave.
Chicago, IL 60611
Phone: (312)280-0170
Fax: (312)280-9883
**Subject(s):** Banking, Finance, and Investments
**Circ:** ‡42,000

**Doll Crafter (33076)**
Jones Publishing Inc.
N7450 Annstad Rd.
PO Box 5000
Iola, WI 54945-5000
Phone: (715)445-5000
Fax: (715)445-4053
**Subject(s):** Crafts, Models, Hobbies, and Contests
**Circ:** ‡42,000

**Pharmaceutical Representative (9135)**
McKnight's Long-Term Care News
Two Northfield Plz., Ste. 300
Northfield, IL 60093-1219
Phone: (847)784-8706
Fax: (847)441-3701
**Subject(s):** Drugs and Pharmaceuticals
**Circ:** 42,000

**Athletic Business (33158)**
Athletic Business Publications Inc.
4130 Lien Rd.
Madison, WI 53704
Phone: (608)249-0186
Fax: (608)249-1153
**Subject(s):** Physical Education and Athletics
**Circ:** (Controlled)‡41,400

**Old Cars Price Guide (33089)**
Krause Publications Inc.
700 E. State St.
Iola, WI 54990-0001
Phone: (715)445-2214
Fax: (715)445-4087
**Subject(s):** Automotive (Consumer)
**Circ:** (Paid)41,116

**American Trucker—New York/Pennsylvania Edition (9829)**
Primedia Business
PO Box 603
Indianapolis, IN 46206
Phone: (317)297-5500
Fax: (317)299-1356
**Subject(s):** Trucks and Trucking
**Circ:** (Combined)41,007

**Underhood Service (24107)**
Babcox
3550 Embassy Pkwy.
Akron, OH 44333
Phone: (330)670-1234
Fax: (330)670-0874
**Subject(s):** Automotive (Trade)
**Circ:** (Controlled)40,558

**Wildfowl (15979)**
PRIMEDIA Los Angeles
Wildfowl
2 In-Fisherman Dr.
Brainerd, MN 56425
Phone: (323)782-2563
Fax: (323)782-2477
**Subject(s):** (Hunting, Fishing, and Game Management)
**Circ:** (Paid)40,553

**SECURITY (7905)**
Business News Publishing
1050 Illinois Rte. 83, Ste. 200
Bensenville, IL 60106-1048
Phone: (630)616-0200
Fax: (630)227-0527
**Subject(s):** Building Management and Maintenance; Safety
**Circ:** (Controlled)40,541

**Aftermarket Business (24370)**
Advanstar Communications
c/o Larry Silvey, Editorial Director
7500 Old Oak Blvd.
Cleveland, OH 44130-3343
Phone: (440)891-2612
Fax: (440)891-2675
**Subject(s):** Automotive (Trade)
**Circ:** (Paid)319
(Non-paid)40,129

**P.O.B. (Point of Beginning) (15858)**
BNP Media
755 W. Big Beaver Rd.
Ste. 1000
Troy, MI 48084
Phone: (248)362-5103
Fax: (248)362-5103
**Subject(s):** Engineering (Various branches)
**Circ:** (Controlled)‡40,030

**Batelle Solutions Update (24530)**
Battelle Communications Office
505 King Ave.
Columbus, OH 43201-2693
Phone: (614)424-5336
Fax: (614)424-3889
**Subject(s):** Science (General); Business
**Circ:** (Non-paid)40,000

**CabinetMaker (8573)**
Chartwell Group of Watt Publishing
1350 E Touhy, Ste. 105 W.
Des Plaines, IL 60018
Phone: (847)390-6700
Fax: (847)390-7100
**Subject(s):** Wood and Woodworking
**Circ:** (Controlled)40,000

**Catholic Aid News (16571)**
Catholic Aid Association
3499 Lexington Ave. N.
Saint Paul, MN 55126
Phone: (651)490-0170
Fax: (651)490-0746
**Subject(s):** Religious Publications
**Circ:** 40,000

**Independent Publisher Online (15827)**
Jenkins Group Inc.
400 W Front St., No.4A
Traverse City, MI 49684-2206
Phone: (231)933-0445
Fax: (231)933-0448
**Subject(s):** Book Trade and Author News; Journalism and Publishing
**Circ:** 40,000

**Ivy Leaf (8249)**
Alpha Kappa Alpha Sorority Inc.
5656 S Stony Island Ave.
Chicago, IL 60637-1997
Phone: (773)684-1282
Fax: (773)288-8251
**Subject(s):** Black Publications; Clubs and Societies; Women's Interests
**Circ:** 40,000

**Laminating Design and Technology (32973)**
Cygnus Business Media
1233 Janesville Ave.
Fort Atkinson, WI 53538
Phone: (920)563-6388
Fax: (920)563-1702
**Subject(s):** Furniture and Furnishings
**Circ:** (Controlled)40,000

**Manage (24657)**
National Management Association
2210 Arbor Blvd.
Dayton, OH 45439
Phone: (937)294-0421
Fax: (937)294-2374
**Subject(s):** Management and Administration
**Circ:** (Controlled)40,000

**Modern Metals (8339)**
Trend Publishing
One E. Erie, Ste. 401
Chicago, IL 60611
Phone: (312)654-2300
Fax: (312)654-2323
**Subject(s):** Metal, Metallurgy, and Metal Trade
**Circ:** (Controlled)‡40,000

**Modern Steel Construction (8342)**
American Institute of Steel Construction Inc.
1 E. Wacker Dr., Ste. 3100
Chicago, IL 60601-2001
Phone: (312)670-2400
Fax: (312)670-5403
**Subject(s):** Construction, Contracting, Building, and Excavating
**Circ:** (Controlled)‡40,000

**Practical Welding Today (9303)**
The Croydon Group Ltd.,
833 Featherstone Rd.
Rockford, IL 61107-6302
Phone: (815)399-8770
Fax: (815)381-1370
**Subject(s):** Welding
**Circ:** (Controlled)40,000

**Safeworker (8815)**
NSC Press
1121 Spring Lake Dr.
Itasca, IL 60143-3201
Phone: (630)285-1121
Fax: (630)285-1319
**Subject(s):** Safety
**Circ:** (Paid)40,000

**Transport Technology Today (7997)**
Transportation Communications
2615 Three Oaks Rd.
Cary, IL 60013
Phone: (847)639-2200
Fax: (847)639-9542
**Subject(s):** Transportation, Traffic, and Shipping
**Circ:** (Non-paid)40,000

**U.S. Catholic (8433)**
Claretian Publications
205 W. Monroe St.
Chicago, IL 60606
Phone: (312)236-7782
Fax: (312)236-8207
**Subject(s):** Religious Publications
**Circ:** 40,000

**Welding Design & Fabrication (24496)**
Penton Media Inc.
1300 E. 9th St.
Cleveland, OH 44114-1530
Phone: (216)696-7000
Fax: (216)696-1752
**Subject(s):** Welding; Metal, Metallurgy, and Metal Trade
**Circ:** (Controlled)‡40,000

**Plastics News (24101)**
Crain Communications Inc.
1725 Merriman Rd., Ste. 300
Akron, OH 44313-5283
Phone: (330)836-9180
Fax: (330)836-2831
**Subject(s):** Plastic and Composition Materials; Business
**Circ:** (Paid)21,350
(Non-paid)39,920

**The Courier (16717)**
PO Box 949
Winona, MN 55987-0949
Phone: (507)454-4643
Fax: (507)454-8106
**Subject(s):** Religious Publications
**Circ:** ‡39,700

**The Land (16240)**
Free Press Company Inc.
418 S. 2nd St.
Mankato, MN 56001
Phone: (507)345-4523
**Subject(s):** General Agriculture
**Circ:** (Non-paid)‡39,500

**High Volume Printing (8868)**
Innes Publishing Co.
28100 N. Ashley Cir.
PO Box 7280
Libertyville, IL 60048
Phone: (847)816-7900
Fax: (847)247-8855
**Subject(s):** Printing and Typography
**Circ:** (Controlled)‡39,047

Circulation: ★ = ABC; △ = BPA; ♦ = CAC; ● = CCAB; ▫ = VAC; ⊕ = PO Statement; ‡ = Publisher's Report; Boldface figures = sworn; Light figures = estimated.

**Doll World** (9570)
House of White Birches
306 E Parr Rd.
Berne, IN 46711
Phone: (260)589-4000
Fax: (260)589-8093
**Subject(s):** Crafts, Models, Hobbies, and Contests
**Circ:** ‡39,030

**Credit Union Magazine** (33166)
Credit Union National Association Inc.
5710 Mineral Point Rd.
Madison, WI 53705
Fax: (608)231-4263
**Subject(s):** Banking, Finance, and Investments
**Circ:** (Paid)39,000

**General Dentistry** (8211)
Academy of General Dentistry
211 E. Chicago Ave., Ste. 900
Chicago, IL 60611-1999
Phone: (312)440-4300
Fax: (312)440-0559
**Subject(s):** Dentistry
**Circ:** (Non-paid)‡26,000
(Paid)‡39,000

**Tech Directions** (15023)
Prakken Publications Inc.
3970 Varsity Dr.
PO Box 8623
Ann Arbor, MI 48107-8623
Phone: (734)975-2800
Fax: (734)975-2787
**Subject(s):** Vocational Education
**Circ:** (Paid)500
(Controlled)39,000

**Industrial Paint and Powder** (7896)
Business News Publishing
1050 Illinois Rte. 83, Ste. 200
Bensenville, IL 60106-1048
Phone: (630)616-0200
Fax: (630)227-0527
**Subject(s):** Commerce and Industry
**Circ:** (Controlled)38,300

**The Trapper & Predator Caller** (33099)
Krause Publications Inc.
700 E. State St.
Iola, WI 54990-0001
Phone: (715)445-2214
Fax: (715)445-4087
**Subject(s):** (Hunting, Fishing, and Game Management)
**Circ:** (Paid)‡38,241

**Garden Railways** (33610)
Kalmbach Publishing Co.
PO Box 1612
Waukesha, WI 53187-1612
Phone: (262)796-8776
Fax: (262)796-1615
**Subject(s):** Crafts, Models, Hobbies, and Contests
**Circ:** (Paid)★38,215

**American Trucker—Indiana Edition** (9821)
Primedia Business
PO Box 603
Indianapolis, IN 46206
Phone: (317)297-5500
Fax: (317)299-1356
**Subject(s):** Trucks and Trucking
**Circ:** (Combined)38,045

**The Observer** (9301)
PO Box 7044
Rockford, IL 61125-7044
Phone: (815)399-4300
Fax: (815)399-6225
**Subject(s):** Religious Publications
**Circ:** (Non-paid)‡309
(Paid)‡38,000

**Student Lawyer** (8417)
American Bar Association
c/o Ira Pilchen
American Bar Association
750 N. Lake Shore Dr.
Chicago, IL 60611
Phone: (312)988-6048
Fax: (312)988-6081
**Subject(s):** Law
**Circ:** (Paid)△38,000

**Xavier Magazine** (24347)
Xavier University
Marketing & Printing Services
Alumni Center
1507 Dana Ave.
Cincinnati, OH 45207-7750
Phone: (513)745-3000
Fax: (513)745-2807
**Subject(s):** College Publications
**Circ:** (Non-paid)‡38,000

**Outpatient Care Technology** (9358)
Reilly Communications Group
16 E. Schaumburg Rd.
Schaumburg, IL 60194-3536
Phone: (847)882-6336
Fax: (847)882-0631
**Subject(s):** Hospitals and Healthcare Institutions
**Circ:** △37,700

**Dakota Farmer** (16143)
Farm Progress Cos.
6258 90th Ave. N.
Glyndon, MN 56547
Phone: (218)236-8420
Fax: (218)236-1134
**Subject(s):** General Agriculture
**Circ:** ‡37,530

**The Evangelical Beacon** (16293)
The Evangelical Free Church of America
901 E 78th St.
Minneapolis, MN 55420-1334
Phone: (952)854-1300
**Subject(s):** Religious Publications
**Circ:** 37,500

**AGD Impact** (8056)
Academy of General Dentistry
211 E. Chicago Ave., Ste. 900
Chicago, IL 60611-1999
Phone: (312)440-4300
Fax: (312)440-0559
**Subject(s):** Dentistry
**Circ:** ‡37,000

**FacilityCare** (7853)
Douglas Publications Inc.
350 S. Newbury Pl.
Arlington Heights, IL 60005
Phone: (847)483-9407
Fax: (847)483-9407
**Subject(s):** Health and Healthcare; Management and Administration
**Circ:** (Paid)37,000

**HOW** (24314)
F & W Publications Inc.
4700 E. Galbraith Rd.
Cincinnati, OH 45236
Phone: (513)531-2690
Fax: (513)531-0798
**Subject(s):** Printing and Typography; Graphic Arts and Design
**Circ:** (Paid)37,008

**MSU Alumni Magazine** (15244)
Michigan State University Alumni Association
MSU Union
East Lansing, MI 48824-1029
Phone: (517)355-8314
Fax: (517)432-7769
**Subject(s):** College Publications
**Circ:** 37,000

**MEEN Imaging Technology News** (9354)
Reilly Communications Group
16 E. Schaumburg Rd.
Schaumburg, IL 60194-3536
Phone: (847)882-6336
Fax: (847)882-0631
**Subject(s):** Medicine and Surgery
**Circ:** 36,961

**Contemporary OB/GYN** (16050)
Thomson PDR
131 W. 1st St.
Duluth, MN 55802
Phone: (218)723-9200
Fax: (218)723-9308
**Subject(s):** Medicine and Surgery
**Circ:** (Non-paid)36,901
(Non-paid)36,901

**Journal of the American Osteopathic Association** (8261)
American Osteopathic Association
142 E Ontario St.
Chicago, IL 60611
Phone: (312)202-8000
Fax: (312)202-8200
**Subject(s):** Osteopathy
**Circ:** (Controlled)‡36,615

**The Harmonizer** (33114)
SPEBSQSA Inc.
7930 Sheridan Road
Kenosha, WI 53143-5199
Phone: (262)653-8440
Fax: (262)654-5552
**Subject(s):** Music and Musical Instruments
**Circ:** ‡36,600

**On the Town** (15462)
PO Box 499
Jenison, MI 49429-0499
Phone: (616)669-1366
Fax: (616)662-4060
**Subject(s):** Art; Entertainment
**Circ:** (Paid)□22
(Free)□36,503

**Appliance Design** (25047)
Appliance Manufacturer
5900 Harper Rd., Ste. 105
Solon, OH 44139-1835
Phone: (440)349-3060
Fax: (440)498-9121
**Subject(s):** Appliances
**Circ:** (Non-paid)‡36,040

**Journal of Dental Hygiene** (8270)
American Dental Hygienists' Association
444 N Michigan Ave., Ste. 3400
Chicago, IL 60611
Phone: (312)440-8904
Fax: (312)467-1406
**Subject(s):** Dentistry
**Circ:** (Non-paid)‡2,000
(Paid)‡36,000

**Journal of Explosives Engineering** (24434)
International Society of Explosives Engineers
30325 Bainbridge Rd.
Cleveland, OH 44139-2295
Phone: (440)349-4400
Fax: (440)349-3788
**Subject(s):** Mining and Minerals
**Circ:** (Combined)36,000

**The Zontian** (8450)
Zonta International
557 W Randolph St
Chicago, IL 60661
Phone: (312)930-5848
Fax: (312)930-0951
**Subject(s):** Clubs and Societies; Women's Interests
**Circ:** ‡36,000

**The Writer Magazine** (33620)
Kalmbach Publishing Co.
PO Box 1612
Waukesha, WI 53187-1612
Phone: (262)796-8776
Fax: (262)796-1615
**Subject(s):** Book Trade and Author News
**Circ:** (Paid)★35,627

**Mine & Quarry Trader** (9896)
7355 Woodland Dr.
Indianapolis, IN 46278-1769
Phone: (317)297-5500
Fax: (317)299-1356
**Subject(s):** Mining and Minerals
**Circ:** (Non-paid)35,309

**Managed Healthcare Executive** (24451)
Advanstar Communications
7500 Old Oak Blvd.
Cleveland, OH 44130-3369
Phone: (440)891-2765
Fax: (440)891-2683
**Subject(s):** Health and Healthcare; Hospitals and Healthcare Institutions
**Circ:** (Paid)△2,937
(Controlled)△35,221

**National Hog Farmer** (16328)
Southwest Farm Press
7900 International Dr., 3rd Fl.
Minneapolis, MN 55425-1510
Phone: (952)851-9329
Fax: (952)851-4601
**Subject(s):** Livestock
**Circ:** (Controlled)‡35,169

**Maintenance Solutions** (33309)
Trade Press Publishing Corp.
2100 W Florist Ave.
Milwaukee, WI 53209
Phone: (414)228-7701
Fax: (414)228-1134
**Subject(s):** Building Management and Maintenance
**Circ:** ‡35,050

**Convene** (8160)
Professional Convention Management Association
2301 So. Lake Shore Dr., Ste. 1001
Chicago, IL 60616-1419
Phone: (312)423-7262
Fax: (312)423-7222
**Subject(s):** Hotels, Motels, Restaurants, and Clubs; Conventions, Meetings, and Trade Fairs
**Circ:** (Paid)‡4,000
(Controlled)‡35,010

**Alumnews** (16398)
Moorhead State University
1104 7th Ave. S.
Moorhead, MN 56563-0001
Phone: (218)236-2204
Fax: (218)477-5086
**Subject(s):** College Publications
**Circ:** (Non-paid)‡35,000

**AMA Alliance Today** (8061)
American Medical Association Alliance
515 N. State St.
Chicago, IL 60610
Phone: (312)464-5000
Fax: (312)464-5020
**Subject(s):** Lifestyle; Medicine and Surgery
**Circ:** (Controlled)‡35,000

**Cornerstone** (8161)
Cornerstone Communications Inc.
939 W. Wilson Ave.
Chicago, IL 60640
Phone: (773)561-2450
Fax: (773)989-2076
**Subject(s):** Religious Publications
**Circ:** (Controlled)‡35,000

**Indiana Prairie Farmer** (9751)
Farm Progress Cos.
599N, 100 W. Franklin,
P.O. Box 247
Franklin, IN 46131
Phone: (317)738-0565
Fax: (317)738-5441
**Subject(s):** General Agriculture
**Circ:** ‡35,000

**Key Milwaukee Magazine** (33306)
10800 N. Norway Dr.
Mequon, WI 53092
Phone: (262)242-2077
Fax: (262)242-2745
**Subject(s):** Travel and Tourism; Entertainment; Local, State, and Regional Publications
**Circ:** (Combined)‡35,000

**Lake Union Herald** (15061)
Lake Union Conference of Seventh-day Adventists
PO Box C
Berrien Springs, MI 49103
Phone: (269)473-8200
Fax: (269)473-8209
**Subject(s):** Religious Publications
**Circ:** (Paid)35,000

**Life Without Limits** (33307)
Wisconsin Right to Life Inc.
10625 W. N. Ave., Ste. LL
Milwaukee, WI 53226-2331
Phone: (414)778-5780
Fax: (414)778-5785
**Subject(s):** Marriage and Family; Babies; Abortion; Local, State, and Regional Publications; Politics
**Circ:** (Non-paid)⊕35,000

**Northern Ohio Live** (24461)
Northern Ohio LIVE
11320 Juniper Rd.
Cleveland, OH 44106
Phone: (216)721-1800
Fax: (216)721-2525
**Subject(s):** Entertainment; Local, State, and Regional Publications
**Circ:** (Non-paid)△14,846
(Paid)15,724
(Combined)35,000

**Powder and Bulk Engineering** (16610)
CSC Publishing Inc.
1155 Northland Dr.
Saint Paul, MN 55120-1288
Fax: (651)282-5650
**Subject(s):** Chemistry, Chemicals, and Chemical Engineering; Plastic and Composition Materials; Electronics Engineering
**Circ:** (Free)‡35,005

**Prospect The Magazine of Elmhurst College** (8647)
Elmhurst College
190 Prospect
Elmhurst, IL 60126
Phone: (630)617-3500
Fax: (630)617-3657
**Subject(s):** College Publications
**Circ:** (Controlled)‡35,000

**Referee Magazine** (33493)
Referee Enterprises Inc.
2017 Lathrop Ave.
Racine, WI 53405-3758
**Subject(s):** Physical Education and Athletics
**Circ:** (Non-paid)‡200
(Paid)‡35,000

**Sports Collectors Digest** (33094)
Krause Publications Inc.
700 E. State St.
Iola, WI 54990-0001
Phone: (715)445-2214
Fax: (715)445-4087
**Subject(s):** Collecting; (General Sports)
**Circ:** (Paid)35,000

**Family Times** (16562)
Family Times Inc.
PO Box 16422
Saint Louis Park, MN 55416
Phone: (952)922-6186
**Subject(s):** Parenting
**Circ:** (Combined)34,821

**Farm and Dairy** (25029)
Lyle Printing & Publishing Co.
185-205 E State St.
Box 38
Salem, OH 44460
Phone: (330)337-3419
Fax: (330)337-9550
**Subject(s):** Dairying; General Agriculture; Farm Newspapers
**Circ:** (Non-paid)‡903
(Paid)‡34,783

**Neil Knopf - Editor** (15830)
The Home Shop Machinist
2779 Aero Park Dr.
Traverse City, MI 49684
Phone: (231)946-3712
Fax: (231)946-9588
**Subject(s):** Crafts, Models, Hobbies, and Contests
**Circ:** (Non-paid)‡92
(Paid)‡34,500

**Dramatics Magazine** (24307)
Educational Theatre Association
2343 Auburn Ave.
Cincinnati, OH 45219
Phone: (513)421-3900
Fax: (513)421-7077
**Subject(s):** Drama and Theatre
**Circ:** (Non-paid)‡321
(Paid)‡34,497

**Columbus Monthly** (24542)
CM Media
PO Box 29913
Columbus, OH 43229-7513
Phone: (614)888-4567
Fax: (614)848-3838
**Subject(s):** Local, State, and Regional Publications
**Circ:** (Paid)34,280

**Crain's Detroit Business** (15172)
Crain Communications Inc.
1155 Gratiot Ave.
Detroit, MI 48207-2997
Phone: (313)446-6000
Fax: (313)446-0347
**Subject(s):** Local, State, and Regional Publications; Business
**Circ:** (Paid)★34,224

**Ceramics Monthly** (25155)
The American Ceramic Society
PO Box 6136
Westerville, OH 43086-6136
Phone: (614)895-4213
Fax: (614)891-8960
**Subject(s):** Crafts, Models, Hobbies, and Contests
**Circ:** (Paid)34,000

**Illinois Agri-News** (8848)
Agri-News Publications
420 2nd St.
La Salle, IL 61301
Phone: (815)223-2558
Fax: (815)223-5997
**Subject(s):** General Agriculture
**Circ:** (Paid)‡34,000

**Michigan History** (15521)
Michigan Department of History, Arts & Libraries
Box 30741
Lansing, MI 48909-8241
Phone: (517)373-3703
Fax: (517)241-4909
**Subject(s):** History and Genealogy; Local, State, and Regional Publications
**Circ:** 34,000

**American Trucker—Badger Edition** (9814)
Primedia Business
PO Box 603
Indianapolis, IN 46206
Phone: (317)297-5500
Fax: (317)299-1356
**Subject(s):** Trucks and Trucking
**Circ:** (Combined)33,990

**Coin Prices** (33067)
Krause Publications Inc.
700 E. State St.
Iola, WI 54990-0001
Phone: (715)445-2214
Fax: (715)445-4087
**Subject(s):** Collecting
**Circ:** (Paid)33,582

**Appliance** (9140)
Dana Chase Publications Inc.
1110 Jorie Blvd., CS 9019
Oak Brook, IL 60522-9019
Phone: (630)990-3484
Fax: (630)990-0078
**Subject(s):** Appliances
**Circ:** (Non-paid)△33,500

**Adweek/Midwest** (8055)
VNU Business Publications Inc.
200 W. Jackson Blvd., Ste. 2700
Chicago, IL 60606
Phone: (312)583-5500
Fax: (312)583-5502
**Subject(s):** Advertising and Marketing
**Circ:** (Combined)33,396

**American Tool, Die & Stamping News** (15642)
Eagle Publications Inc.
42400 Grand River, Ste. 103
Novi, MI 48375
Phone: (248)347-3486
Fax: (248)347-3079
**Subject(s):** Metal, Metallurgy, and Metal Trade
**Circ:** (Controlled)33,000

**The Family Friend** (33300)
Catholic Family Life Insurance
PO Box 11563
Milwaukee, WI 53211-0563
Phone: (414)961-0500
Fax: (414)961-0103
**Subject(s):** Insurance; Unclassified Fraternal; Religious Publications
**Circ:** (Non-paid)33,000

Circulation: ★ = ABC; △ = BPA; ♦ = CAC; • = CCAB; ❑ = VAC; ⊕ = PO Statement; ‡ = Publisher's Report; Boldface figures = sworn; Light figures = estimated.

**Healthcare Purchasing News** (8785)
Nelson Publishing Inc.
1282 Old Skokie Rd.
Highland Park, IL 60035
Phone: (847)831-3205
Fax: (847)831-3205
**Subject(s):** Hospitals and Healthcare Institutions
**Circ:** (Paid)80
(Non-paid)33,000

**Middle School Journal** (25159)
National Middle School Association
4151 Executive Pky., Ste. 300
Westerville, OH 43081-3871
Phone: (614)895-4730
Fax: (614)895-4750
**Subject(s):** Education
**Circ:** (Controlled)‡50
(Paid)‡33,000

**Musky Hunter** (33527)
Musky Hunter Magazine
7978 Hwy., 70 E.
Saint Germain, WI 54558
Phone: (715)477-2178
Fax: (715)477-8858
**Subject(s):** (Hunting, Fishing, and Game Management)
**Circ:** 33,000

**Oberlin Alumni Magazine** (24966)
Oberlin College
Daub House
145 W. Lorain St.
Oberlin, OH 44074
Phone: (440)775-8182
Fax: (440)775-6575
**Subject(s):** College Publications
**Circ:** (Non-paid)33,000

**Planning** (8378)
American Planning Association
122 S Michigan Ave., Ste. 1600
Chicago, IL 60603-6107
Phone: (312)431-9100
Fax: (312)431-9985
**Subject(s):** State, Municipal, and County Administration
**Circ:** (Paid)⊕32,136

**Tire Review** (24106)
Babcox
3550 Embassy Pkwy.
Akron, OH 44333
Phone: (330)670-1234
Fax: (330)670-0874
**Subject(s):** Automotive (Trade)
**Circ:** (Controlled)32,050

**AANA Journal** (9199)
AANA Publishing Inc.
222 S Prospect Ave.
Park Ridge, IL 60068
Phone: (847)692-7050
Fax: (847)518-0938
**Subject(s):** Nursing; Medicine and Surgery
**Circ:** (Paid)‡635
(Non-paid)‡32,018

**Banking Strategies** (8095)
Bank Administration Institute
1 N Franklin St., Ste. 1000
Chicago, IL 60606-3421
Phone: (312)683-2464
Fax: (312)683-2373
**Subject(s):** Banking, Finance, and Investments
**Circ:** (Paid)32,000

**Broadcast Engineering** (8109)
Primedia Business Magzenes & Media
330 N.Wabash, Ste. 2300
Chicago, IL 60611
**Subject(s):** Engineering (Various branches); Radio, Television, Cable, and Video
**Circ:** (Controlled)‡32,000

**Lawrence Technological University Magazine** (15777)
Lawrence Technological University
21000 W 10 Mile Rd.
Southfield, MI 48075-1058
Phone: (248)204-2200
Fax: (248)204-2207
**Subject(s):** Education
**Circ:** (Non-paid)32,000

**Milwaukee Magazine** (33319)
417 E Chicago St.
Milwaukee, WI 53202-5828
Phone: (414)273-1101
Fax: (414)273-0016
**Subject(s):** Local, State, and Regional Publications
**Circ:** (Non-paid)8,000
(Paid)32,000

**The Progressive** (33210)
409 E Main St.
Madison, WI 53703
Phone: (608)257-4626
Fax: (608)257-3373
**Subject(s):** Politics; General Editorial
**Circ:** (Non-paid)‡1,000
(Paid)‡32,000

**Senior Life (Northwest Edition)** (10030)
The Papers Inc.
206 S Main St.
PO Box 188
Milford, IN 46542-0188
Phone: (574)658-4111
Fax: (574)658-4701
**Subject(s):** Senior Citizens' Interests
**Circ:** (Free)32,000

**Woman's Life** (15688)
Woman's Life Insurance Society
1338 Military St.
PO Box 5020
Port Huron, MI 48061-5020
Phone: (810)985-5191
Fax: (810)985-6970
**Subject(s):** Insurance; Unclassified Fraternal; Women's Interests
**Circ:** (Non-paid)32,000

**Coins Magazine** (33068)
Krause Publications Inc.
700 E. State St.
Iola, WI 54990-0001
Phone: (715)445-2214
Fax: (715)445-4087
**Subject(s):** Collecting
**Circ:** ‡31,977

**Wall Fashions Magazine** (16618)
Grace McNamara Inc.
4215 White Bear Pkwy., Ste. 100
Saint Paul, MN 55110
Phone: (651)293-1544
Fax: (651)653-4308
**Subject(s):** Paint and Wallcoverings
**Circ:** (Controlled)31,905

**Boat and Motor Dealer** (9057)
Preston Publications
6600 W Touhy Ave.
PO Box 48312
Niles, IL 60714-4588
Phone: (847)647-2900
Fax: (847)647-1155
**Subject(s):** Boats and Marine
**Circ:** (Paid)34
(Controlled)31,706

**Masonry Construction** (7822)
Hanley-Wood L.L.C.
426 S. Westgate St.
Addison, IL 60101
Phone: (630)543-0870
Fax: (630)543-3112
**Subject(s):** Building Materials, Concrete, Brick, and Tile
**Circ:** (Paid)608
(Non-paid)31,639

**Michigan Bar Journal** (15515)
State Bar of Michigan
306 Townsend Street
Lansing, MI 48933-2083
Phone: (517)346-6300
Fax: (517)482-6248
**Subject(s):** Law
**Circ:** ‡31,600

**Filtration News** (15643)
Eagle Publications Inc.
42400 Grand River, Ste. 103
Novi, MI 48375
Phone: (248)347-3486
Fax: (248)347-3079
**Subject(s):** Commerce and Industry
**Circ:** (Controlled)‡31,555

**Metal Architecture** (25187)
Modern Trade Communications Inc.
109 Portage
Woodville, OH 43469
Phone: (419)849-3109
Fax: (419)849-3367
**Subject(s):** Architecture; Construction, Contracting, Building, and Excavating; Engineering (Various branches)
**Circ:** (Controlled)31,483

**The National Gleaner Forum** (14963)
Gleaner Life Insurance Society
PO Box 1894
Adrian, MI 49221-7894
Fax: (517)265-6191
**Subject(s):** Insurance
**Circ:** ⊕31,000

**Outpost Exchange** (33325)
100 E Capitol Dr.
Milwaukee, WI 53212
Phone: (414)964-7789
Fax: (414)431-4214
**Subject(s):** Health and Healthcare; Food and Grocery Trade
**Circ:** (Non-paid)‡31,000

**CNA** (33066)
Krause Publications Inc.
700 E. State St.
Iola, WI 54990-0001
Phone: (715)445-2214
Fax: (715)445-4087
**Subject(s):** Crafts, Models, Hobbies, and Contests
**Circ:** (Combined)△30,791

**Walls & Ceilings** (15868)
BNP Media
2401 W Big Beaver Rd., Ste. 700
Troy, MI 48084-3333
Phone: (248)362-3700
Fax: (248)362-0317
**Subject(s):** Building Materials, Concrete, Brick, and Tile
**Circ:** (Paid)‡243
(Controlled)‡30,600

**Wisconsin Outdoor Journal** (33103)
Krause Publications Inc.
700 E. State St.
Iola, WI 54990-0001
Phone: (715)445-2214
Fax: (715)445-4087
**Subject(s):** (Hunting, Fishing, and Game Management)
**Circ:** (Paid)30,605

**Utillaje** (8437)
Utillaie Inc.
20 N Wacker Dr.
Chicago, IL 60606
Phone: (312)372-9077
Fax: (312)372-6537
**Subject(s):** Machinery and Equipment; Commerce and Industry; Spanish
**Circ:** (Paid)500
(Controlled)30,250

**Contracting Profits** (33298)
Trade Press Publishing Corp.
2100 W Florist Ave.
Milwaukee, WI 53209
Phone: (414)228-7701
Fax: (414)228-1134
**Subject(s):** Business; Service Industries
**Circ:** (Paid)50
(Controlled)30,051

**ActionLINE Magazine** (15772)
Automotive Industry Action Group (AIAG)
26200 Lahser Rd., Ste. 200
Southfield, MI 48034-7100
Phone: (248)358-3570
Fax: (248)358-3253
**Subject(s):** Automotive (Trade)
**Circ:** (Combined)30,000

**Advanced Materials & Processes** (24885)
ASM International
9639 Kinsman Rd.
Materials Park, OH 44073-0002
Phone: (440)338-5151
Fax: (440)338-4634
**Subject(s):** Plastic and Composition Materials; Metal, Metallurgy, and Metal Trade; Ceramics
**Circ:** (Paid)30,000

**The Baffler Magazine** (8094)
The Baffler
PO Box 378293
Chicago, IL 60637
Phone: (773)493-0413
**Subject(s):** Alternative and Underground; Lifestyle

Circ: (Paid)30,000

**The Banner** (15332)
CRC Publications
2850 Kalamazoo Ave. SE
Grand Rapids, MI 49560
Phone: (616)246-0819
Fax: (616)224-0834
**Subject(s):** Religious Publications

Circ: (Controlled)‡255
 (Paid)‡30,000

**Corporate Report Wisconsin** (32855)
Trails Media Group Inc.
PO Box 317
1131 Mills St.
Black Earth, WI 53515
Phone: (608)767-8000
Fax: (608)767-5444
**Subject(s):** Business; Local, State, and Regional Publications

Circ: (Paid)71
 (Controlled)30,000

**Country Business** (9335)
Country Sampler Group
707 Kautz Rd.
Saint Charles, IL 60174
Phone: (630)377-8000
Fax: (630)377-8914
**Subject(s):** Business; Retail; General Merchandise

Circ: (Combined)30,000

**Denison Magazine** (24750)
Denison University
P O Box A
Granville, OH 43023
Phone: (740)587-6267
Fax: (740)587-6364
**Subject(s):** College Publications

Circ: (Controlled)‡30,000

**Exchange Today** (25088)
The National Exchange Club
3050 Central Ave.
Toledo, OH 43606-1700
Phone: (419)535-3232
Fax: (419)535-1989
**Subject(s):** Unclassified Fraternal

Circ: (Controlled)‡750
 (Paid)‡30,000

**Inside Business** (24429)
Great Lakes Publishing Co.
1422 Euclid Ave., Hanna Bldg., Ste. 730
Cleveland, OH 44115
Phone: (216)771-2833
Fax: (216)781-6318
**Subject(s):** Business; Business

Circ: (Non-paid)30,000

**Law Enforcement Technology** (32975)
Cygnus Business Media
1233 Janesville Ave.
Fort Atkinson, WI 53538
Phone: (920)563-6388
Fax: (920)563-1702
**Subject(s):** Police, Penology, and Penal Institutions

Circ: (Non-paid)‡30,000

**The Lion of Alpha Epsilon Pi** (9890)
Alpha Epsilon Pi Fraternity
8815 Wesleyan Rd.
Indianapolis, IN 46268-1171
Phone: (317)876-1913
Fax: (317)876-1057
**Subject(s):** Unclassified Fraternal

Circ: 30,000

**Materials Management in Health Care** (8329)
Health Forum L.L.C.
1 N Franklin, 29th Fl.
Chicago, IL 60606
Phone: (312)893-6800
Fax: (312)422-4506
**Subject(s):** Health and Healthcare; Management and Administration

Circ: (Non-paid)30,000

**The Midwest BEAT Magazine** (9801)
Midwest Beat L.L.P.
2613 41st St.
Highland, IN 46322
Phone: (219)934-9133
**Subject(s):** Music and Musical Instruments; Radio, Television, Cable, and Video; Motion Pictures

Circ: (Non-paid)‡30,000

**Midwest Flyer Magazine** (33445)
Flyer Publications Inc.
PO Box 199
Oregon, WI 53575-0199
Phone: (608)835-7063
**Subject(s):** Aviation

Circ: (Paid)‡7,800
 (Non-paid)‡30,000

**The News in Engineering** (24574)
Ohio State University
Engineering Communications
142 Hitchcock Hall
2070 Neil Ave.
Columbus, OH 43210-1275
Phone: (614)292-2651
**Subject(s):** Engineering (Various branches); College Publications

Circ: (Combined)30,000

**Probate and Property** (8385)
American Bar Association
321 N Clark St.
Chicago, IL 60610
Phone: (312)988-5000
Fax: (312)988-5177
**Subject(s):** Real Estate; Law

Circ: (Controlled)1,391
 (Paid)30,000

**Professional Safety** (8591)
American Society of Safety Engineers
1800 E Oakton Street
Des Plaines, IL 60018
Phone: (847)699-2929
Fax: (847)768-3434
**Subject(s):** Safety

Circ: ‡30,000

**Salon Today Magazine** (8883)
Vance Publishing Corp.
400 Knightsbridge Pkwy.
Lincolnshire, IL 60069
Phone: (847)634-2600
Fax: (847)634-4343
**Subject(s):** Cosmetics and Toiletries; Business; Management and Administration; Education

Circ: ‡30,000

**Silent Advocate** (24336)
St. Rita School for the Deaf
1720 Glendale-Milford Rd.
Cincinnati, OH 45215
Phone: (513)771-7600
Fax: (513)326-8264
**Subject(s):** Handicapped; Hearing and Speech

Circ: (Non-paid)30,000

**TPJ—The Tube & Pipe Journal** (9307)
The Croydon Group Ltd.,
833 Featherstone Rd.
Rockford, IL 61107-6302
Phone: (815)399-8770
Fax: (815)381-1370
**Subject(s):** Metal, Metallurgy, and Metal Trade; Machinery and Equipment

Circ: (Controlled)‡30,000

**Window Fashions** (16620)
Windows Fashions Magazine
4215 White Bear Pkwy., Ste. 100
Saint Paul, MN 55110-7635
Phone: (651)293-1544
Fax: (651)653-4308
**Subject(s):** Interior Design/Decorating

Circ: (Paid)30,000
 (Non-paid)30,000

**Chicago Home and Garden** (8852)
Chicago Home & Garden
825 S Waukegan Rd., No. A8-146
Lake Forest, IL 60045
Phone: (874)604-9590
Fax: (847)604-9593
**Subject(s):** Home and Garden; Local, State, and Regional Publications

Circ: (Non-paid)11,393
 (Paid)29,964

**Fishing Facts Magazine** (7935)
MidWest Outdoors Ltd.
111 Shore Dr.
Burr Ridge, IL 60527
Phone: (630)887-7722
**Subject(s):** (Hunting, Fishing, and Game Management)

Circ: △29,494

**New Beginnings** (9356)
La Leche League International Inc.
1400 N. Meacham Rd.
PO Box 4079
Schaumburg, IL 60173-4808
Phone: (847)519-7730
Fax: (847)519-0035
**Subject(s):** Babies; Parenting; Women's Interests

Circ: (Controlled)⊕300
 (Paid)⊕29,463

**Hunter & Sport Horse** (9717)
Silver Square Tech Inc.
12204 Covington Rd.
Fort Wayne, IN 46814
Phone: (260)625-4030
Fax: (260)625-3480
**Subject(s):** (Horses and Horse Racing)

Circ: (Combined)⊕**29,435**

**My Daily Visitor** (9807)
Our Sunday Visitor Publishing
200 Noll Plz.
Huntington, IN 46750
Phone: (260)356-8400
Fax: (260)356-8472
**Subject(s):** Religious Publications

Circ: ‡29,277

**Food Product Design** (9113)
Weeks Publishing Co.
3400 Dundee Rd., Ste. 360
Northbrook, IL 60062
Phone: (847)559-0385
Fax: (847)559-0389
**Subject(s):** Food and Grocery Trade; Food Production

Circ: (Combined)△29,200

**Import Car** (24099)
Babcox
3550 Embassy Pkwy.
Akron, OH 44333
Phone: (330)670-1234
Fax: (330)670-0874
**Subject(s):** Automotive (Trade)

Circ: (Controlled)29,209

**Farm Chemicals** (25173)
Meister Publishing Co.
37733 Euclid Ave.
Willoughby, OH 44094-5992
Phone: (440)942-2000
Fax: (440)942-0662
**Subject(s):** Fertilizer

Circ: (Paid)△**550**
 (Non-paid)△**29,136**

**MEEN Diagnostic and Invasive Technology** (9353)
Reilly Communications Group
16 E. Schaumburg Rd.
Schaumburg, IL 60194-3536
Phone: (847)882-6336
Fax: (847)882-0631
**Subject(s):** Medicine and Surgery

Circ: (Combined)29,104

**Equipment Solutions** (8190)
Talcott Communications Corp.
20 W. Kinzie, 12th Fl.
Chicago, IL 60610
Phone: (312)849-2220
Fax: (312)849-2174
**Subject(s):** Hotels, Motels, Restaurants, and Clubs; Food Production; Food and Grocery Trade

Circ: (Paid)‡1,265
 (Non-paid)‡29,054

Circulation: ★ = ABC; △ = BPA; ♦ = CAC; • = CCAB; □ = VAC; ⊕ = PO Statement; ‡ = Publisher's Report; Boldface figures = sworn; Light figures = estimated.

**Chip Chats** (24294)
National Wood Carvers Association
7424 Miami Ave.
PO Box 43218
Cincinnati, OH 45243
Phone: (513)561-0627
Subject(s): Crafts, Models, Hobbies, and Contests; Wood and Woodworking
Circ: ‡29,000

**Journal of the American Academy of Orthopaedic Surgeons** (9328)
American Academy of Orthopaedic Surgeons
6300 North River Rd.
Rosemont, IL 60018-4262
Phone: (847)823-7186
Fax: (847)823-8125
Subject(s): Medicine and Surgery
Circ: (Paid)29,000

**Photo Techniques** (9064)
Preston Publications
6600 W Touhy Ave.
PO Box 48312
Niles, IL 60714-4588
Phone: (847)647-2900
Fax: (847)647-1155
Subject(s): Photography
Circ: (Paid)29,000

**Senior Life (South Bend Edition)** (10032)
The Papers Inc.
206 S Main St.
PO Box 188
Milford, IN 46542-0188
Phone: (574)658-4111
Fax: (574)658-4701
Subject(s): Senior Citizens' Interests
Circ: (Paid)35
(Free)28,850

**Scale Auto Magazine** (33616)
Kalmbach Publishing Co.
21027 Crossroads Cir.
PO Box 1612
Waukesha, WI 53187-1612
Phone: (262)796-8776
Fax: (262)796-1615
Subject(s): Crafts, Models, Hobbies, and Contests
Circ: (Paid)★28,788

**Rural Builder** (33092)
Krause Publications Inc.
700 E. State St.
Iola, WI 54990-0001
Phone: (715)445-2214
Fax: (715)445-4087
Subject(s): Construction, Contracting, Building, and Excavating
Circ: ‡28,683

**Cincinnati Magazine** (24299)
Cincinnati Magazine Inc.
One Centennial Plz.
705 Central Ave., Ste. 175
Cincinnati, OH 45202
Phone: (513)421-4300
Fax: (513)562-2746
Subject(s): Local, State, and Regional Publications
Circ: (Non-paid)‡742
(Paid)‡28,576

**EDT** (8183)
American Bar Association
321 N Clark St.
Chicago, IL 60610
Phone: (312)988-5000
Fax: (312)988-5177
Subject(s): Law
Circ: (Paid)28,557

**The Plastics Distributor & Fabricator Magazine** (9281)
One Riverside Rd., Ste.3D
Riverside, IL 60546
Phone: (708)447-0001
Fax: (708)447-0005
Subject(s): Plastic and Composition Materials
Circ: (Non-paid)‡28,142

**Numismatic News** (33088)
Krause Publications Inc.
700 E. State St.
Iola, WI 54990-0001
Phone: (715)445-2214
Fax: (715)445-4087

Subject(s): Collecting
Circ: (Paid)‡28,085

**RadioGraphics** (9156)
Radiological Society of North America
820 Jorie Blvd.
Oak Brook, IL 60523-2251
Phone: (630)571-2670
Fax: (630)571-7837
Subject(s): Medicine and Surgery; Radiology, Ultrasound, and Nuclear Medicine
Circ: 28,000

**Security Distributing & Marketing (SDM)** (7906)
BNP Media
SDM@bnpmedia.com
1050 IL Rte. 83, Ste. 200
Bensenville, IL 60106
Phone: (630)616-0200
Fax: (630)227-0214
Subject(s): Electronics Engineering; Safety
Circ: (Combined)‡28,003

**Senior Life (Allen County Edition)** (10028)
The Papers Inc.
206 S Main St.
PO Box 188
Milford, IN 46542-0188
Phone: (574)658-4111
Fax: (574)658-4701
Subject(s): Senior Citizens' Interests
Circ: (Free)28,000

**Senior Life (St. Joseph Edition)** (10031)
The Papers Inc.
206 S Main St.
PO Box 188
Milford, IN 46542-0188
Phone: (574)658-4111
Fax: (574)658-4701
Subject(s): Senior Citizens' Interests
Circ: (Free)28,000

**Strategic Management Journal** (10255)
John Wiley and Sons Inc.
Krannert Graduate School of Management
Purdue University
West Lafayette, IN 47907
Subject(s): Banking, Finance, and Investments; Business; Management and Administration
Circ: (Paid)28,000

**Vintage Truck** (25204)
Antique Power
PO Box 838
Yellow Springs, OH 45387
Phone: (937)767-1433
Fax: (937)767-2726
Subject(s): Automotive (Consumer)
Circ: (Paid)28,000

**Goldmine** (33080)
Krause Publications Inc.
700 E. State St.
Iola, WI 54990-0001
Phone: (715)445-2214
Fax: (715)445-4087
Subject(s): Collecting; Music and Musical Instruments
Circ: (Paid)‡27,758

**Hospital Pharmacist Report** (16057)
Thomson PDR
131 W. 1st St.
Duluth, MN 55802
Phone: (218)723-9200
Fax: (218)723-9308
Subject(s): Drugs and Pharmaceuticals; Hospitals and Healthcare Institutions
Circ: (Paid)78
(Non-paid)27,706

**Wisconsin Agriculturist** (32864)
Farm Progress Cos.
102 E. Jefferson St.
PO Box 236
Brandon, WI 53919
Phone: (920)346-8333
Fax: (920)346-5732
Subject(s): General Agriculture
Circ: (Paid)3,205
(Non-paid)27,505

**Diesel Progress North American Edition** (33607)
Diesel & Gas Turbine Publications
20855 Watertown Rd., Ste.220
Waukesha, WI 53186
Phone: (262)832-5000
Fax: (262)832-5075
Subject(s): Machinery and Equipment; Engineering (Various branches)
Circ: (Paid)255
(Controlled)27,462

**Modern Baking** (8585)
Donohue-Meehan Publishing Co.
2700 River Rd., Ste. 303
Des Plaines, IL 60018
Phone: (847)299-4430
Fax: (847)296-1968
Subject(s): Baking
Circ: (Controlled)‡27,300

**The American Academy of Orthopaedic Surgeons Bulletin** (9326)
American Academy of Orthopaedic Surgeons
6300 North River Rd.
Rosemont, IL 60018-4262
Phone: (847)823-7186
Fax: (847)823-8125
Subject(s): Medicine and Surgery
Circ: (Combined)27,000

**Health Facilities Management** (8222)
HealthForum
1 N. Franklin St.
Chicago, IL 60606
Phone: (312)422-2806
Fax: (312)433-4650
Subject(s): Hospitals and Healthcare Institutions
Circ: (Paid)1,722
(Controlled)27,000

**Insight (Chicago)** (8240)
Illinois C.P.A. Society
550 W. Jackson, Ste.900
Chicago, IL 60661
Phone: (312)993-0407
Fax: (312)993-9954
Subject(s): Accountants and Accounting
Circ: (Controlled)⊕27,000

**Journal of Economic Perspectives** (16586)
American Economic Association
1600 Grand Ave.
Macalester College
Saint Paul, MN 55105
Phone: (651)696-6822
Fax: (651)696-6825
Subject(s): Economics
Circ: (Paid)27,000

**Journal of Healthcare Management** (8274)
Health Administration Press
1 N. Franklin, Ste. 1700
Chicago, IL 60606-4425
Phone: (312)424-2800
Fax: (312)424-0023
Subject(s): Hospitals and Healthcare Institutions
Circ: (Paid)‡1,500
(Controlled)‡27,000

**Ohio Wesleyan Magazine** (24695)
Ohio Wesleyan University
61 S. Sandusky St.
Delaware, OH 43015
Phone: (740)368-2000
Fax: (614)363-0795
Subject(s): College Publications
Circ: (Non-paid)‡27,000

**Blade Magazine** (33063)
Krause Publications Inc.
700 E. State St.
Iola, WI 54990-0001
Phone: (715)445-2214
Fax: (715)445-4087
Subject(s): Crafts, Models, Hobbies, and Contests
Circ: (Paid)‡26,924

**Indiana Business Magazine** (9864)
1100 Waterway Blvd.
Indianapolis, IN 46202
Phone: (317)692-1200
Fax: (317)692-4250

Subject(s): Business; Local, State, and Regional Publications
Circ: 2,619
(Controlled)3,175
(Non-paid)26,622

**Truck Parts & Service (8555)**
Kona Communications Inc.
707 Lake Cook Rd., Ste. 300
Deerfield, IL 60015
Phone: (847)498-3180
Fax: (847)498-3197
Subject(s): Trucks and Trucking
Circ: (Controlled)‡26,566

**Dollhouse Miniatures Magazine (33608)**
Kalmbach Publishing Co.
PO Box 1612
Waukesha, WI 53187-1612
Phone: (262)796-8776
Fax: (262)796-1615
Subject(s): Crafts, Models, Hobbies, and Contests
Circ: (Paid)★26,545

**Scott Stamp Monthly (25043)**
Scott Publishing Co.
PO Box 828
911 Vandermark Rd.
Sidney, OH 45365-0828
Phone: (937)498-6885
Fax: (937)498-0807
Subject(s): Collecting
Circ: (Non-paid)‡50
(Paid)‡26,500

**Toy Shop (33098)**
Krause Publications Inc.
700 E. State St.
Iola, WI 54990-0001
Phone: (715)445-2214
Fax: (715)445-4087
Subject(s): Crafts, Models, Hobbies, and Contests
Circ: (Paid)‡26,381

**APWA Reporter (8084)**
American Public Works Association
1313 E 60th St.
Chicago, IL 60637-2881
Phone: (312)667-2200
Fax: (312)667-2304
Subject(s): State, Municipal, and County Administration
Circ: (Non-paid)‡497
(Paid)‡26,348

**The Badger Sportsman (32884)**
Calumet Publishing
19 E Main St.
Chilton, WI 53014
Phone: (920)849-4551
Fax: (920)849-4651
Subject(s): (Hunting, Fishing, and Game Management)
Circ: ‡26,200

**AMT Events (9200)**
American Medical Technologists
710 Higgins Rd.
Park Ridge, IL 60068-5765
Phone: (847)823-5169
Fax: (847)823-0458
Subject(s): Medicine and Surgery; Health and Healthcare
Circ: (Controlled)26,000

**Journal of the Coin Laundry and Drycleaning Industry (8604)**
Coin Laundry Association
1315 Butterfield Rd., Ste. 212
Downers Grove, IL 60515
Phone: (630)963-5547
Fax: (630)963-5864
Subject(s): Laundry and Dry Cleaning
Circ: (Controlled)26,000

**LAKE (9990)**
701 State St.
LaPorte, IN 46350
Phone: (219)362-8592
Fax: (219)362-2166
Subject(s): Lifestyle; Local, State, and Regional Publications
Circ: 26,000

**Michigan Snowmobiler (15226)**
PO Box 417
East Jordan, MI 49727
Phone: (231)536-2371
Fax: (231)536-7691

Subject(s): (Snowmobiling)
Circ: ‡26,000

**The SAR Magazine (33334)**
National Society Sons of the American Revolution
PO Box 26595
Milwaukee, WI 53226
Phone: (262)782-9410
Fax: (262)782-6645
Subject(s): History and Genealogy; Unclassified Fraternal
Circ: ‡26,000

**Wooster (25188)**
College of Wooster
Ebert Hall
Wooster, OH 44691
Phone: (330)263-2000
Fax: (330)263-2594
Subject(s): College Publications
Circ: (Controlled)26,000

**Air Conditioning, Heating and Refrigeration News (15843)**
BNP Media
2401 W Big Beaver Rd., Ste. 700
Troy, MI 48084-3333
Phone: (248)362-3700
Fax: (248)362-0317
Subject(s): Air Conditioning and Refrigeration; Plumbing and Heating
Circ: (Non-paid)4,706
(Paid)25,938

**Plumbing Engineer (9119)**
TMB Publishing Inc.
1838 Techny Ct.
Northbrook, IL 60062
Phone: (847)564-1127
Fax: (847)564-1264
Subject(s): Engineering (Various branches); Architecture; Construction, Contracting, Building, and Excavating
Circ: (Free)‡25,600

**In-Plant Printer (8870)**
Innes Publishing Co.
28100 N. Ashley Cir.
PO Box 7280
Libertyville, IL 60048
Phone: (847)816-7900
Fax: (847)247-8855
Subject(s): Printing and Typography
Circ: (Controlled)‡25,502

**Legal Management (8880)**
Association of Legal Administrators
75 Tri-State International, Ste. 222
Lincolnshire, IL 60069-4435
Phone: (847)267-1252
Fax: (847)267-1329
Subject(s): Law; Management and Administration; Business
Circ: (Controlled)‡25,200

**Progressive Railroading (33327)**
Trade Press Publishing Corp.
2100 W Florist Ave.
Milwaukee, WI 53209
Phone: (414)228-7701
Fax: (414)228-1134
Subject(s): Railroad
Circ: (Controlled)△25,052

**Marketing News (8327)**
American Marketing Association
311 S. Wacker Dr., Ste. 5800
Chicago, IL 60606-2266
Phone: (312)542-9000
Fax: (312)542-9001
Subject(s): Advertising and Marketing
Circ: (Non-paid)409
(Paid)25,030

**Art of the West (16378)**
Duerr and Tierney Ltd.
15612 Hwy. 7, Ste. 235
Minnetonka, MN 55345
Phone: (952)935-5850
Fax: (952)935-6546
Subject(s): Art
Circ: (Non-paid)‡5,000
(Paid)‡25,000

**Branches Magazine (9836)**
Apple Press Inc.
PO Box 30348
Indianapolis, IN 46230
Phone: (317)255-5594
Subject(s): Lifestyle; Health; Local, State, and Regional Publications; Alternative and Underground
Circ: (Combined)25,000

**Collector Magazine & Price Guide (33069)**
Krause Publications Inc.
700 E. State St.
Iola, WI 54990-0001
Phone: (715)445-2214
Fax: (715)445-4087
Circ: ‡25,001

**Fox Valley KIDS (33182)**
Erickson Publishing L.L.C.
PO Box 45050
Madison, WI 53744
Phone: (608)831-2131
Fax: (800)722-6461
Subject(s): Parenting
Circ: (Non-paid)25,000

**Green Profit Magazine (7885)**
Ball Publishing
335 N. River St.
PO Box 9
Batavia, IL 60510-0009
Phone: (630)208-9080
Fax: (630)208-9350
Subject(s): Florists and Floriculture
Circ: (Non-paid)25,000

**Illinois CPA Insight (8234)**
Illinois C.P.A. Society
550 W. Jackson, Ste.900
Chicago, IL 60661
Phone: (312)993-0407
Fax: (312)993-9954
Subject(s): Accountants and Accounting
Circ: ‡25,000

**Irish American News (9169)**
7115 W. N. Ave. No. 327
Oak Park, IL 60302
Phone: (708)445-0700
Fax: (708)445-2003
Subject(s): Ethnic Publications
Circ: (Paid)‡25,000

**Made to Measure (8787)**
Halper Publishing Co.
830 Moseley Rd.
Highland Park, IL 60035
Phone: (847)780-2900
Fax: (847)780-2902
Subject(s): Clothing
Circ: (Controlled)⊕25,000

**Motorbooty (15192)**
Clownskull Graphics
PO Box 02007
Detroit, MI 48202
Phone: (313)871-8419
Fax: (313)849-5517
Subject(s): Alternative and Underground; Comics and Comic Technique
Circ: (Paid)25,000

**Out! Resource Guide (8364)**
Lambda Publications Inc.
1115 W Belmont Ave., Ste. 2-D
Chicago, IL 60657
Phone: (773)871-7610
Fax: (773)871-7609
Subject(s): Gay and Lesbian Interests
Circ: (Non-paid)25,000

**PM Engineer (7899)**
BNP Media
1050 IL Rte. 83, Ste. 200
Bensenville, IL 60106-1096
Phone: (630)694-4379
Subject(s): Construction, Contracting, Building, and Excavating
Circ: (Non-paid)25,005

**Rethinking Schools (33331)**
1001 E. Keefe Ave.
Milwaukee, WI 53212
Phone: (414)964-9646
Fax: (414)964-7220

Circulation: ★ = ABC; △ = BPA; ♦ = CAC; ● = CCAB; □ = VAC; ⊕ = PO Statement; ‡ = Publisher's Report; Boldface figures = sworn; Light figures = estimated.

**Subject(s):** Education
**Circ:** (Paid)‡7,000
(Non-paid)‡25,000

**Traffic Safety (8817)**
NSC Press
1121 Spring Lake Dr.
Itasca, IL 60143-3201
Phone: (630)285-1121
Fax: (630)285-1319
**Subject(s):** Safety; Transportation, Traffic, and Shipping
**Circ:** (Non-paid)‡66
(Paid)‡25,000

**Traverse, Northern Michigan's Magazine (15832)**
Prism Publications Inc.
148 E Front St.
Traverse City, MI 49684
Phone: (231)941-8174
Fax: (231)941-8391
**Subject(s):** Lifestyle; Local, State, and Regional Publications
**Circ:** ‡25,000

**Trustee (8431)**
Health Forum L.L.C.
1 N Franklin, 29th Fl.
Chicago, IL 60606
Phone: (312)893-6800
Fax: (312)422-4506
**Subject(s):** Hospitals and Healthcare Institutions
**Circ:** ‡25,000

**Voices Magazine (8905)**
Benedictine University
5700 College Rd.
Lisle, IL 60532-0900
Phone: (630)829-6000
Fax: (630)960-1126
**Subject(s):** College Publications
**Circ:** (Non-paid)‡25,000

**Water Well Journal (25161)**
National Ground Water Association
601 Dempsey Rd.
Westerville, OH 43081-8978
Phone: (614)898-7791
Fax: (614)898-7786
**Subject(s):** Water Supply and Sewage Disposal
**Circ:** (Paid)‡1,500
(Non-paid)‡25,000

**Modern Casting Magazine (9355)**
American Foundry Society
1695 Nory Penny Lane
Schaumburg, IL 60173
Phone: (847)824-0181
Fax: (847)824-7848
**Subject(s):** Metal, Metallurgy, and Metal Trade
**Circ:** (Paid)1,684
(Controlled)24,806

**Cytometry (8168)**
John Wiley and Sons Inc.
C/O Charles L. Goolsby, Department of Pathology
Ward Bldg. 6-204
303 E. Chicago Ave.
Chicago, IL 60611-3008
**Subject(s):** Science (General)
**Circ:** 24,500

**Hardwood Floors (33185)**
Athletic Business Publications Inc.
4130 Lien Rd.
Madison, WI 53704
Phone: (608)249-0186
Fax: (608)249-1153
**Subject(s):** Wood and Woodworking
**Circ:** (Controlled)24,300

**Book Links: Connecting Books, Libraries and Classrooms (8102)**
American Library Association
50 E. Huron St.
Chicago, IL 60611
Phone: (312)944-7298
Fax: (312)280-4380
**Subject(s):** Youths' Interests; Literature and Literary Reviews; Education
**Circ:** (Non-paid)5,735
(Paid)24,265

**Golf Course News (24420)**
United Publications Inc.
4012 Bridge Ave.
Cleveland, OH 44113
Phone: (216)961-4130
Fax: (216)961-0364
**Subject(s):** (Golf); Golf Course Management
**Circ:** (Controlled)‡24,100

**American Music Teacher (24284)**
Music Teachers N.A.
441 Vine St., Ste. 505
Cincinnati, OH 45202-2811
Phone: (513)421-1420
Fax: (513)421-2503
**Subject(s):** Music and Musical Instruments; Education
**Circ:** (Free)‡300
(Paid)‡24,000

**Industrial Heating (15853)**
Business News Publishing Co.
2401 W. Big Beaver Rd., Ste 700
1910 Cochran Rd., Ste. 450
Troy, MI 48084
Phone: (248)244-6498
Fax: (248)244-6439
**Subject(s):** Metal, Metallurgy, and Metal Trade
**Circ:** (Paid)265
(Non-paid)24,000

**N.E.W. Kids (33206)**
Erickson Publishing L.L.C.
PO Box 45050
Madison, WI 53744
Phone: (608)831-2131
Fax: (800)722-6461
**Subject(s):** Parenting
**Circ:** (Non-paid)24,000

**Signatures (9551)**
Anderson University
1100 E 5th St.
Anderson, IN 46012-3495
Phone: (765)641-4100
Fax: (765)641-3888
**Subject(s):** College Publications
**Circ:** (Free)‡24,000

**Booklist (8103)**
American Library Association
50 E. Huron St.
Chicago, IL 60611
Phone: (312)944-7298
Fax: (312)280-4380
**Subject(s):** Library and Information Science; Book Trade and Author News
**Circ:** (Non-paid)‡4,487
(Paid)‡23,713

**American Drycleaner (8067)**
American Trade Magazines
500 N Dearborn St., Ste. 1000
Chicago, IL 60610
Phone: (312)337-7700
Fax: (312)337-8654
**Subject(s):** Laundry and Dry Cleaning
**Circ:** (Controlled)‡23,600

**Pit & Quarry (24478)**
Advanstar Communications
7500 Old Oak Blvd.
Cleveland, OH 44130-3369
Phone: (440)243-8100
Fax: (440)891-2777
**Subject(s):** Mining and Minerals
**Circ:** (Paid)2,437
(Non-paid)23,564

**Roofing Contractor (7904)**
G & M Communications
1050 Illinois Rte. 63, Ste. 200
Bensenville, IL 60106-1096
Phone: (847)588-3333
Fax: (847)647-7055
**Subject(s):** Construction, Contracting, Building, and Excavating; Roofing
**Circ:** (Paid)148
(Non-paid)23,434

**Dane County KIDS (33172)**
Erickson Publishing L.L.C.
PO Box 8457
2001 Fish Hatchery Rd.
Madison, WI 53708-8457
Fax: (608)250-4155

**Subject(s):** Parenting
**Circ:** (Non-paid)23,000

**Goshen College Bulletin (9763)**
Goshen College
1700 S. Main St.
Goshen, IN 46526
Phone: (219)535-7571
Fax: (219)535-7670
**Subject(s):** College Publications
**Circ:** ‡23,000

**Journal of Obstetric, Gynecologic and Neonatal Nursing (JOGNN) (24564)**
Sage Publications Inc.
c/o Nancy K. Lowe
Ohio State University, College of Nursing
1585 Neil Ave.
Columbus, OH 43210-1289
**Subject(s):** Nursing
**Circ:** (Paid)23,000

**Journal of Property Management (8291)**
Institute of Real Estate Management
430 N. Michigan Ave.
Chicago, IL 60611
Phone: (312)329-6000
Fax: (800)338-4736
**Subject(s):** Real Estate; Building Management and Maintenance
**Circ:** ‡23,000

**Process Heating (7902)**
BNP Media
1050 Illinois Rte. 83, Ste. 200
Bensenville, IL 60106-1096
Phone: (630)616-0200
Fax: (630)694-4002
**Subject(s):** Machinery and Equipment; Metal, Metallurgy, and Metal Trade
**Circ:** (Controlled)23,000

**Lake Superior Magazine (16060)**
Lake Superior Port Cities Inc.
325 Lake Ave. S, Ste. 600
PO Box 16417
Duluth, MN 55802-2323
Phone: (218)722-5002
Fax: (218)722-4096
**Subject(s):** Literature and Literary Reviews; Travel and Tourism; History and Genealogy
**Circ:** (Paid)‡22,500

**New Moon (16062)**
New Moon Publishing
34 E Superior St., Ste. 200
Duluth, MN 55802-3003
Phone: (218)728-5507
Fax: (218)728-0314
**Subject(s):** Children's Interests; Youths' Interests
**Circ:** (Paid)22,500

**Journal of Policy Analysis and Management (9605)**
John Wiley and Sons Inc.
Journal of Policy Analysis and Management
Indiana University
School of Public and Environmental Affairs, Spea 241
1315 E. 10th St.
Bloomington, IN 47405-1701
**Subject(s):** State, Municipal, and County Administration
**Circ:** 22,400

**Card Technology (8115)**
Thomson Financial
300 S. Wacker Dr., 18th Fl.
Chicago, IL 60606
Phone: (312)913-1340
Fax: (312)913-1340
**Subject(s):** Automation; Business; Computers
**Circ:** (Combined)‡22,387

**Western Fruit Grower (25179)**
Meister Publishing Co.
37733 Euclid Ave.
Willoughby, OH 44094-5992
Phone: (440)942-2000
Fax: (440)942-0662
**Subject(s):** Horticulture
**Circ:** (Paid)‡3,142
22,377

**Rock Products (8401)**
Primedia Business Magzenes & Media
330 N. Wabash, Ste.2300
Chicago, IL 60611
Phone: (312)726-2574
Fax: (800)621-9907
**Subject(s):** Stone and Rock Products

**Circ:** (Non-paid)△22,172

**Greenhouse Grower (25175)**
Meister Publishing Co.
37733 Euclid Ave.
Willoughby, OH 44094-5992
Phone: (440)942-2000
Fax: (440)942-0662
**Subject(s):** Horticulture

**Circ:** (Controlled)22,060

**Arabian Horse Times (16692)**
1050 NE 8th St. NE
PO Box 1469
Waseca, MN 56093-9803
Phone: (507)835-3204
Fax: (507)835-5138
**Subject(s):** (Horses and Horse Racing)

**Circ:** (Paid)22,000

**The CMA Today (8150)**
American Association of Medical Assistants
20 N Wacker Dr., Ste. 1575
Chicago, IL 60606
Phone: (312)899-1500
Fax: (312)899-1259
**Subject(s):** Health and Healthcare

**Circ:** 22,000

**Contemporary Doll Collector (15620)**
Scott Publications Inc.
801 W Norton Ave., Ste. 200
Muskegon, MI 49441
Phone: (231)733-9382
Fax: (231)733-7635
**Subject(s):** Crafts, Models, Hobbies, and Contests; Collecting

**Circ:** ‡22,000

**Fancy Food & Culinary Products (8197)**
Talcott Communications Corp.
20 W. Kinzie, 12th Fl.
Chicago, IL 60610
Phone: (312)849-2220
Fax: (312)849-2174
**Subject(s):** Food and Grocery Trade

**Circ:** (Paid)3,060
    (Non-paid)22,000

**Living The Word (9361)**
J.S. Paluch Company Inc.
3825 N Willow Rd.
PO Box 2703
Schiller Park, IL 60176
Phone: (847)678-9300
Fax: (847)671-5715
**Subject(s):** Religious Publications

**Circ:** ‡22,000

**Minnesota Law & Politics (16319)**
Law & Politics Media Inc.
220 S. 6th St., Ste. 500
Minneapolis, MN 55402-4402
Phone: (612)335-8808
Fax: (612)335-8809
**Subject(s):** Law; Politics; Local, State, and Regional Publications

**Circ:** (Paid)2,000
    (Controlled)22,000

**Snips Magazine (15863)**
2401 W. Big Beaver., Ste. 700
Troy, MI 48084
Phone: (248)362-3700
Fax: (248)362-0317
**Subject(s):** Air Conditioning and Refrigeration

**Circ:** (Paid)1,151
    (Controlled)22,000

**Wisconsin Lawyer (33223)**
State Bar of Wisconsin
5302 Eastpark Blvd.
PO Box 7158
Madison, WI 53707-7158
Phone: (608)257-3838
Fax: (608)257-5502
**Subject(s):** Law

**Circ:** ‡22,000

**R.S.I. Magazine (24487)**
Advanstar Communications
7500 Old Oak Blvd.
Cleveland, OH 44130-3369
Phone: (440)243-8100
Fax: (440)891-2777
**Subject(s):** Construction, Contracting, Building, and Excavating

**Circ:** (Paid)1,247
    (Non-paid)21,890

**Behavioral Health Management (24379)**
MEDQUEST Communications L.L.C.
3800 Lakeside Ave. E, Ste. 201
Cleveland, OH 44114-3857
Phone: (216)591-9100
Fax: (216)391-9200
**Subject(s):** Business; Management and Administration; Psychology and Psychiatry; Health and Healthcare

**Circ:** 21,802

**Giftware News (8213)**
Talcott Communications Corp.
20 W. Kinzie, 12th Fl.
Chicago, IL 60610
Phone: (312)849-2220
Fax: (312)849-2174
**Subject(s):** Gifts, Toys, and Novelties; Glass and China; Stationery, Office Equipment, and College Store Supplies

**Circ:** (Paid)15,239
    (Non-paid)21,766

**Ag Retailer Magazine (16418)**
AG Retailer
120 W. Main St., P.O. Box 156
New Prague, MN 56071
Phone: (952)758-5812
Fax: (952)758-5813
**Subject(s):** Fertilizer

**Circ:** (Non-paid)21,598

**GeoWorld (8212)**
Adams Business Media
833 W Jackson, 7th Fl.
Chicago, IL 60607
Phone: (312)846-4600
Fax: (312)846-4638
**Subject(s):** Computers

**Circ:** (Paid)21,575

**Outdoor Power Equipment (8365)**
Adams Business Media/Green Media
833 W. Jackson Blvd.
7th Floor
Chicago, IL 60607
Phone: (312)846-4600
Fax: (312)846-4638
**Subject(s):** Landscape Architecture; Home and Garden

**Circ:** (Paid)1,089
    (Controlled)16,930
    (Combined)21,250

**NTEA News (15273)**
National Truck Equipment Association
37400 Hills Tech Dr.
Farmington Hills, MI 48331-3414
Phone: (248)489-7090
Fax: (248)489-8590
**Subject(s):** Trucks and Trucking

**Circ:** (Paid)10,749
    (Controlled)21,062

**Successful Dealer (8554)**
Kona Communications Inc.
707 Lake Cook Rd., Ste. 300
Deerfield, IL 60015
Phone: (847)498-3180
Fax: (847)498-3197
**Subject(s):** Trailers and Accessories; Trucks and Trucking

**Circ:** (Controlled)‡21,049

**Accessory Merchandising (8876)**
Vance Publishing Corp.
400 Knightsbridge Pkwy.
Lincolnshire, IL 60069
Phone: (847)634-2600
**Subject(s):** Furniture and Furnishings; Home Furnishings, Curtains, Draperies

**Circ:** 21,000

**Indiana Agri-News (9861)**
Agri-News Publications
2575 E. 55th Pl., Ste. A
Indianapolis, IN 46220
Phone: (317)726-5391
Fax: (317)726-5390
**Subject(s):** Farm Newspapers; General Agriculture

**Circ:** (Paid)‡8,000
    (Controlled)‡21,000

**Snow Week (16256)**
Ehlert Publishing Group Inc.
6420 Sycamore Ln., N.
Maple Grove, MN 55369-6355
Phone: (612)476-2200
Fax: (612)476-8065
**Subject(s):** (Snowmobiling)

**Circ:** 21,000

**Meat Processing (9011)**
Watt Publishing Co.
122 S. Wesley Ave.
Mount Morris, IL 61054
Phone: (815)734-4171
Fax: (815)734-4201
**Subject(s):** Food and Grocery Trade

**Circ:** (Paid)361
    (Non-paid)20,913

**Healthcare Executive (8224)**
American College of Healthcare Executives
1 N Franklin St. Ste. 1700
Chicago, IL 60606
Phone: (312)424-2800
Fax: (312)424-0023
**Subject(s):** Health and Healthcare

**Circ:** (Non-paid)406
    (Paid)20,832

**Coonhound Bloodlines (15467)**
United Kennel Club Inc.
100 E Kilgore Rd.
Kalamazoo, MI 49002-5584
Phone: (269)343-9020
Fax: (269)343-7037
**Subject(s):** Dogs; (Hunting, Fishing, and Game Management)

**Circ:** (Paid)20,700

**Mass Transit (32976)**
Cygnus Business Media
1233 Janesville Ave.
Fort Atkinson, WI 53538
Phone: (920)563-6388
Fax: (920)563-1702
**Subject(s):** Public Transportation

**Circ:** (Controlled)‡20,506

**Rental Product News (32983)**
Cygnus Business Media
1233 Janesville Ave.
Fort Atkinson, WI 53538
Phone: (920)563-6388
Fax: (920)563-1702
**Subject(s):** Rental Equipment

**Circ:** (Controlled)20,500

**Fine Furnishings International (FFI) (16580)**
Grace McNamara Inc.
4215 White Bear Pkwy., Ste. 100
Saint Paul, MN 55110
Phone: (651)293-1544
Fax: (651)653-4308
**Subject(s):** Interior Design/Decorating; Furniture and Furnishings

**Circ:** (Paid)664
    (Controlled)20,467

**Foundry Management & Technology (24414)**
Penton Media Inc.
1300 E. 9th St.
Cleveland, OH 44114-1530
Phone: (216)696-7000
Fax: (216)696-1752
**Subject(s):** Metal, Metallurgy, and Metal Trade

**Circ:** (Non-paid)‡20,254

**Dairy Foods (7895)**
Reed Business Information
c/o David Phillips, Editor
1050 IL Route 83, Ste. 200
Bensenville, IL 60106
Phone: (630)694-4341
Fax: (630)227-0527
**Subject(s):** Milk and Dairy Products

**Circ:** (Paid)656
    (Controlled)20,230

Circulation: ★ = ABC; △ = BPA; ♦ = CAC; • = CCAB; ❑ = VAC; ⊕ = PO Statement; ‡ = Publisher's Report; Boldface figures = sworn; Light figures = estimated.

**Meat Marketing & Technology** (8331)
Marketing & Technology Group
1415 N Dayton St.
Chicago, IL 60622
Phone: (312)266-3311
Fax: (312)266-3363
**Subject(s):** Food and Grocery Trade; Food Production; Livestock; Poultry and Pigeons
**Circ:** (Combined)20,173

**Visual Merchandising and Store Design** (24344)
ST Media Group International Inc.
407 Gilbert Ave.
Cincinnati, OH 45202
Phone: (513)421-2050
Fax: (513)421-5144
**Subject(s):** Advertising and Marketing
**Circ:** (Paid)7,132
(Non-paid)20,103

**Diesel & Gas Turbine Worldwide** (33605)
Diesel & Gas Turbine Publications
20855 Watertown Rd., Ste.220
Waukesha, WI 53186
Phone: (262)832-5000
Fax: (262)832-5075
**Subject(s):** Machinery and Equipment; Engineering (Various branches)
**Circ:** (Paid)‡675
(Controlled)‡20,050

**Poultry International** (9017)
Watt Publishing Co.
122 S. Wesley Ave.
Mount Morris, IL 61054
Phone: (815)734-4171
Fax: (815)734-4201
**Subject(s):** Poultry and Pigeons; Poultry Products and Supplies
**Circ:** (Controlled)20,059

**Paint & Coatings Industry** (15857)
2401 W Big Beaver Rd., Ste. 700
Troy, MI 48084
Phone: (248)362-3700
Fax: (248)244-3915
**Subject(s):** Paint and Wallcoverings
**Circ:** (Non-paid)‡20,030

**Nuclear Plant Journal** (8732)
799 Roosevelt Rd., Bldg. 6, Ste. 208
Glen Ellyn, IL 60137
Phone: (630)858-6161
Fax: (630)858-8787
**Subject(s):** Power and Power Plants; Nuclear Engineering
**Circ:** (Non-paid)△**20,012**

**AIM Liturgy Resources** (9360)
J.S. Paluch Company Inc.
3825 N Willow Rd.
PO Box 2703
Schiller Park, IL 60176
Phone: (847)678-9300
Fax: (847)671-5715
**Subject(s):** Religious Publications
**Circ:** (Paid)20,000

**ATW's Airport Equipment & Technology** (24375)
Penton Media Inc.
1300 E. 9th St.
Cleveland, OH 44114-1530
Phone: (216)696-7000
Fax: (216)696-1752
**Subject(s):** Aviation
**Circ:** (Combined)20,000

**Billiards Digest** (8100)
Luby Publishing
122 S Michigan Ave., Ste. 1506
Chicago, IL 60603
Phone: (312)341-1110
Fax: (312)341-1469
**Subject(s):** (General Sports)
**Circ:** 20,000

**Bowlers Journal** (8105)
Luby Publishing
122 S Michigan Ave., Ste. 1506
Chicago, IL 60603
Phone: (312)341-1110
Fax: (312)341-1469
**Subject(s):** (Bowling)
**Circ:** 20,000

**Cast On** (25226)
Knitting Guild of America
1100-H Brandywine Blvd.
PO Box 3388
Zanesville, OH 43702-3388
Phone: (740)452-4541
Fax: (740)452-2552
**Subject(s):** Dressmaking, Needlework, and Quilting
**Circ:** (Combined)20,000

**Catalyst: The Leading Edge of Ohio Business** (24701)
Ohio Society of CPAs
535 Metro Pl. S
PO Box 1810
Dublin, OH 43017-1810
Phone: (614)764-2727
Fax: (614)764-5880
**Subject(s):** Accountants and Accounting
**Circ:** ‡20,000

**Catholic Parent** (9805)
Our Sunday Visitor Publishing
200 Noll Plz.
Huntington, IN 46750
Phone: (260)356-8400
Fax: (260)356-8472
**Subject(s):** Parenting; Religious Publications
**Circ:** (Paid)20,000

**Gay Chicago Magazine** (8210)
Gernhardt Publications
3115 N Broadway St.
Chicago, IL 60657-4522
Phone: (312)327-7271
Fax: (312)327-0112
**Subject(s):** Gay and Lesbian Interests
**Circ:** (Paid)‡750
(Free)‡20,000

**Government PROcurement** (24421)
Penton Media Inc.
1300 E. 9th St.
Cleveland, OH 44114-1530
Phone: (216)696-7000
Fax: (216)696-1752
**Subject(s):** Congressional and Federal Government Affairs
**Circ:** (Controlled)20,000

**Hacks 12Sports Magazine** (24311)
9933 Alliance Rd.
Cincinnati, OH 45242
Phone: (513)794-4100
**Subject(s):** (General Sports)
**Circ:** (Combined)20,000

**HomeTown Golf Magazine** (24313)
9933 Alliance Rd.
Cincinnati, OH 45242
Phone: (513)794-4100
**Subject(s):** (Golf)
**Circ:** 20,000

**Language Arts** (9483)
National Council of Teachers of English
1111 W. Kenyon Rd.
Urbana, IL 61801-1096
Phone: (217)328-3870
Fax: (217)328-9645
**Subject(s):** Education
**Circ:** (Paid)20,000

**Light and Life** (9888)
Free Methodist Church of North America
PO Box 535002
770 N Highschool Rd.
Indianapolis, IN 46253-5002
Phone: (317)244-3660
Fax: (317)248-9055
**Subject(s):** Religious Publications
**Circ:** (Controlled)‡200
(Paid)‡20,000

**Lutheran Partners** (8321)
Augsburg Fortress, Publishers
ELCA (DM)
8765 W. Higgins Rd.
Chicago, IL 60631-4195
Phone: (773)380-2884
Fax: (773)380-2829
**Subject(s):** Religious Publications
**Circ:** (Paid)70
(Controlled)20,000

**Miami Valley Fifty Plus** (25114)
TDN Publishing Co.
224 S. Market St.
Troy, OH 45373
Phone: (937)339-9535
Fax: (937)339-8413
**Subject(s):** Senior Citizens' Interests
**Circ:** (Combined)20,000

**Miami Valley Home Finder** (25115)
TDN Publishing Co.
224 S. Market St.
Troy, OH 45373
Phone: (937)339-9535
Fax: (937)339-8413
**Subject(s):** Home and Garden
**Circ:** (Combined)20,000

**Nova Review** (15064)
Nova Media Inc.
1724 N State St.
Big Rapids, MI 49307-9073
Phone: (231)796-4637
Fax: (231)796-4637
**Subject(s):** Art
**Circ:** (Non-paid)20,000

**Pavement** (32978)
Cygnus Business Media
1233 Janesville Ave.
Fort Atkinson, WI 53538
Phone: (920)563-6388
Fax: (920)563-1702
**Subject(s):** Engineering (Various branches); Construction, Contracting, Building, and Excavating
**Circ:** (Controlled)20,000

**Profane Existence** (16339)
PO Box 8722
Minneapolis, MN 55408
Phone: (612)722-1134
Fax: (612)722-1134
**Subject(s):** Alternative and Underground; Music and Musical Instruments
**Circ:** (Combined)20,000

**Small Business Times** (33336)
1123 N. Water St.
Milwaukee, WI 53202
Phone: (414)277-8181
Fax: (414)277-8191
**Subject(s):** Business
**Circ:** (Combined)20,000

**The Tax Lawyer** (8422)
American Bar Association
321 N Clark St.
Chicago, IL 60610
Phone: (312)988-5000
Fax: (312)988-5177
**Subject(s):** Law
**Circ:** (Non-paid)1,800
(Paid)20,000

**Timeline** (24604)
Ohio Historical Society
1982 Velma Ave.
Columbus, OH 43211-2497
Phone: (614)297-2300
Fax: (614)297-2367
**Subject(s):** Art; History and Genealogy
**Circ:** ‡20,000

**Frame Building News** (33079)
Krause Publications Inc.
700 E. State St.
Iola, WI 54990-0001
Phone: (715)445-2214
Fax: (715)445-4087
**Subject(s):** Carpentry; Construction, Contracting, Building, and Excavating
**Circ:** 19,991

**Machinist's Workshop** (15829)
Village Press Publications
2779 Aero Park Dr.
Traverse City, MI 49684
**Subject(s):** Crafts, Models, Hobbies, and Contests; Metal, Metallurgy, and Metal Trade
**Circ:** (Non-paid)‡91
(Paid)‡19,911

**Law and Order** (8550)
Hendon Publishing
130 Waukegan Rd. N., Ste. 202
Deerfield, IL 60015
Phone: (847)444-3300
Fax: (847)444-3333
Subject(s): Police, Penology, and Penal Institutions
Circ: (Paid)11,890
(Controlled)19,888

**American Vegetable Grower** (25172)
Meister Publishing Co.
37733 Euclid Ave.
Willoughby, OH 44094-5992
Phone: (440)942-2000
Fax: (440)942-0662
Subject(s): General Agriculture; Horticulture
Circ: (Paid)9,778
(Non-paid)19,711

**Metal Producing & Processing** (24453)
Penton Media Inc.
1300 E. 9th St.
Cleveland, OH 44114-1530
Phone: (216)696-7000
Fax: (216)696-1752
Subject(s): Metal, Metallurgy, and Metal Trade
Circ: (Controlled)‡19,624

**Messenger** (8633)
Church of the Brethren General Board
1451 Dundee Ave.
Elgin, IL 60120
Phone: (847)742-5100
Fax: (847)742-6103
Subject(s): Religious Publications
Circ: ‡19,500

**P-O-P Times** (9377)
Hoyt Publishing
7400 Skokie Blvd.
Skokie, IL 60077
Phone: (847)675-7400
Fax: (847)675-7494
Subject(s): Advertising and Marketing; Retail
Circ: (Non-paid)△19,379

**Engine Builder** (24097)
Babcox
3550 Embassy Pkwy.
Akron, OH 44333
Phone: (330)670-1234
Fax: (330)670-0874
Subject(s): Automotive (Trade)
Circ: (Controlled)19,064

**Full Cry** (7926)
Gault Publications Inc.
Box 10
Boody, IL 62514
Phone: (217)865-2332
Fax: (217)865-2334
Subject(s): (Hunting, Fishing, and Game Management)
Circ: (Paid)19,029

**Muzzle Blasts** (9756)
National Muzzle Loading Rifle Association
PO Box 67
Friendship, IN 47021
Phone: (812)667-5131
Fax: (812)667-5137
Subject(s): Firearms
Circ: ‡19,000

**The Ryder** (9612)
1316 E. 3rd St.
Bloomington, IN 47401
Phone: (812)339-3460
Subject(s): Entertainment
Circ: (Non-paid)19,000

**The Ohio Farmer** (24823)
Farm Progress Cos.
117 W. Main St., Ste. 202
Lancaster, OH 43130
Phone: (740)654-6500
Fax: (740)654-9367
Subject(s): General Agriculture
Circ: (Paid)15,730
(Non-paid)18,862

**Dental Lab Products** (9127)
MEDEC Dental Communications
2 Northfield Plaza, Ste. 300
Northfield, IL 60093-1219
Phone: (847)441-3700
Fax: (847)441-3702
Subject(s): Dentistry
Circ: (Non-paid)18,827

**American Coin-Op** (8065)
American Trade Magazines
500 N Dearborn St., Ste. 1000
Chicago, IL 60610
Phone: (312)337-7700
Fax: (312)337-8654
Subject(s): Laundry and Dry Cleaning
Circ: (Controlled)18,800

**Utility & Telephone Fleets** (7998)
Practical Communications Inc.
2615 Three Oaks Rd. Ste. 1-B
Cary, IL 60013
Phone: (847)639-2200
Fax: (847)639-9542
Subject(s): Telecommunications; Transportation, Traffic, and Shipping
Circ: (Paid)‡259
(Controlled)‡18,804

**Ophthalmology Times** (24469)
Advanstar Communications
7500 Old Oak Blvd.
Cleveland, OH 44130-3369
Phone: (440)243-8100
Fax: (440)891-2777
Subject(s): Ophthalmology, Optometry, and Optics
Circ: (Controlled)△18,769

**Nude & Natural** (33453)
The Naturist Society
PO Box 132
Oshkosh, WI 54903
Phone: (920)426-5009
Fax: (920)426-5184
Subject(s): Alternative and Underground; Lifestyle
Circ: (Non-paid)6,350
(Paid)18,650

**Detroiter** (15180)
Detroit Regional Chamber
1 Woodward Ave., Ste. 1900
PO Box 33840
Detroit, MI 48232-0840
Phone: (313)596-0384
Fax: (313)964-0183
Subject(s): Business; Local, State, and Regional Publications; Chambers of Commerce and Boards of Trade
Circ: (Controlled)2,000
(Paid)18,535

**Minnesota History** (16598)
Minnesota Historical Society
345 W Kellogg Blvd.
Saint Paul, MN 55102-1906
Phone: (651)296-6126
Fax: (651)297-1345
Subject(s): History and Genealogy
Circ: ‡18,500

**Senior Life (El-Ko Edition)** (10029)
The Papers Inc.
206 S Main St.
PO Box 188
Milford, IN 46542-0188
Phone: (574)658-4111
Fax: (574)658-4701
Subject(s): Senior Citizens' Interests
Circ: (Free)18,500

**Arbor Age** (8085)
Adams Business Media
833 W Jackson, 7th Fl.
Chicago, IL 60607
Phone: (312)846-4600
Fax: (312)846-4638
Subject(s): Landscape Architecture; Seed and Nursery Trade
Circ: (Paid)120
18,469

**Manufactured Home Merchandiser** (8323)
RLD Group Inc.
203 N Wabash, Ste. 800
Chicago, IL 60601-2476
Phone: (312)236-3528
Fax: (312)236-4024

Subject(s): Architecture; Real Estate; Carpentry
Circ: (Controlled)‡18,452

**sportsTURF** (8415)
Adams Business Media
833 W Jackson, 7th Fl.
Chicago, IL 60607
Phone: (312)846-4600
Fax: (312)846-4638
Subject(s): Turf and Turf Maintenance
Circ: (Combined)18,431

**Archives of Ophthalmology** (33155)
American Medical Association Alliance
c/o Editor, Archives of Ophthalmology
2870 University Ave. Ste. 102
Madison, WI 53705
Phone: (608)262-7769
Fax: (608)265-5896
Subject(s): Ophthalmology, Optometry, and Optics
Circ: (Combined)‡18,373

**Outside Plant Magazine** (7996)
Practical Communications Inc.
2615 Three Oaks Rd. Ste. 1-B
Cary, IL 60013
Phone: (847)639-2200
Fax: (847)639-9542
Subject(s): Telecommunications
Circ: (Paid)995
(Controlled)18,211

**The Instrumentalist** (9133)
Instrumentalist Co.
200 Northfield Rd.
Northfield, IL 60093
Phone: (888)446-6888
Fax: (847)446-6263
Subject(s): Music and Musical Instruments
Circ: ‡18,200

**Underground Focus** (33552)
Planet Underground Business Media
PO Box 638
Spooner, WI 54801
Phone: (715)635-7975
Fax: (715)635-7977
Subject(s): Construction, Contracting, Building, and Excavating; Safety
Circ: (Combined)18,200

**Computing Surveys (CSUR)** (9469)
Association for Computing Machinery
c/o Gul A. Agha
Dept. of Computer Science
3121 DCL, MC-258,Univ. of Illinois, Urbana-Champaign
1304 W. Springfield Ave.
Urbana, IL 61801
Phone: (217)244-3087
Fax: (217)244-6869
Subject(s): Computers
Circ: ‡18,036

**American Cooner** (9363)
C & H Publishing
116 E Franklin
Sesser, IL 62884
Phone: (618)625-2711
Fax: (618)625-6221
Subject(s): Dogs
Circ: (Paid)18,000

**The American Historical Review** (9580)
American Historical Association
C/O Michael Grossberg, Editor
914 E. Atwater Ave.
Bloomington, IN 47401
Phone: (812)855-7609
Fax: (812)855-5827
Subject(s): History and Genealogy
Circ: (Controlled)‡18,000

**EAA Experimenter** (33449)
PO Box 3086
Oshkosh, WI 54903-3086
Phone: (920)426-4800
Fax: (920)426-4828
Subject(s): Aviation
Circ: 18,000

**Greenhouse Business** (9190)
Perkins Communications L.L.C.
115 N. Northwest Hwy.
Palatine, IL 60067
Phone: (847)963-9530

Fax: (847)963-9531
**Subject(s):** Florists and Floriculture; Horticulture; Botany
**Circ:** (Non-paid)18,000

**Industria Alimenticia  (8549)**
Stagnito Communications Inc.
155 Pfingsten Rd., Ste. 205
Deerfield, IL 60015
Phone: (847)205-5660
Fax: (847)205-5680
**Subject(s):** Food and Grocery Trade; Food Production; Hispanic Publications; Spanish
**Circ:** △18,000

**The Living Museum  (9406)**
Illinois State Museum
502 S Spring St.
Springfield, IL 62706-5000
Phone: (217)782-7387
Fax: (217)782-1254
**Subject(s):** Anthropology and Ethnology; Museums; Art; Science
**Circ:** (Non-paid)‡18,000

**Madison Magazine  (33199)**
7025 W. Raymond Rd.
Madison, WI 53719
Phone: (608)270-3600
Fax: (608)270-3636
**Subject(s):** Local, State, and Regional Publications
**Circ:** (Combined)18,000

**Michigan Golfer  (15015)**
Great Lakes Sports Publications Inc.
3588 Plymouth Rd., No. 245
Ann Arbor, MI 48105-2603
Phone: (734)507-0241
Fax: (734)434-4765
**Subject(s):** (Golf)
**Circ:** 18,000

**Military Vehicles  (33087)**
Krause Publications Inc.
700 E. State St.
Iola, WI 54990-0001
Phone: (715)445-2214
Fax: (715)445-4087
**Subject(s):** Automotive (Consumer); Crafts, Models, Hobbies, and Contests; Men's Interests
**Circ:** (Paid)‡18,000

**P-O-P Design  (9376)**
Hoyt Publishing
7400 Skokie Blvd.
Skokie, IL 60077
Phone: (847)675-7400
Fax: (847)675-7494
**Subject(s):** Advertising and Marketing; Retail; Graphic Arts and Design
**Circ:** (Non-paid)△18,005

**Wayne State Magazine  (15203)**
Wayne State University
441 Ferry Mall
Detroit, MI 48202-3619
Phone: (313)577-6046
Fax: (313)577-9187
**Subject(s):** Engineering (Various branches)
**Circ:** (Non-paid)18,000

**Supercharger  (15275)**
Society of Automotive Engineers - Detroit Section
28535 Orchard Lake Rd., Ste.200
Farmington Hills, MI 48334
Phone: (248)324-4445
Fax: (248)324-4449
**Subject(s):** Automotive (Trade)
**Circ:** (Paid)17,988

**IGA Grocergram  (8233)**
Pace Communications Inc.
O'Hare Plaza
8725 W. Higgins Rd.
Chicago, IL 60631
Phone: (773)695-2619
Fax: (773)693-7571
**Subject(s):** Food and Grocery Trade
**Circ:** (Paid)‡17,976

**Feed Management  (9008)**
Watt Publishing Co.
122 S. Wesley Ave.
Mount Morris, IL 61054
Phone: (815)734-4171
Fax: (815)734-4201

**Subject(s):** Feed and Grain
**Circ:** (Paid)189
(Non-paid)17,922

**Northern Breezes Sailing Magazine  (16333)**
Northern Breezes Inc.
3949 Winnetka Ave. N.
Minneapolis, MN 55427
Phone: (763)542-9707
Fax: (763)542-8998
**Subject(s):** (Boating and Yachting)
**Circ:** (Paid)‡3,500
(Non-paid)‡17,800

**Pig International  (9016)**
Watt Publishing Co.
122 S. Wesley Ave.
Mount Morris, IL 61054
Phone: (815)734-4171
Fax: (815)734-4201
**Subject(s):** Livestock
**Circ:** (Controlled)17,792

**GPSolo  (8215)**
American Bar Association
321 N Clark St.
Chicago, IL 60610
Phone: (312)988-5000
Fax: (312)988-5177
**Subject(s):** Law
**Circ:** (Non-paid)‡1,877
(Paid)‡17,698

**Ag Consultant  (25170)**
Meister Publishing Co.
37733 Euclid Ave.
Willoughby, OH 44094-5992
Phone: (440)942-2000
Fax: (440)942-0662
**Subject(s):** General Agriculture; Horticulture
**Circ:** (Non-paid)17,623

**Airport Business  (32959)**
Cygnus Business Media
1233 Janesville Ave.
Fort Atkinson, WI 53538
Phone: (920)563-6388
Fax: (920)563-1702
**Subject(s):** Aviation
**Circ:** (Controlled)‡17,500

**Bear Report  (9028)**
Royle Publications Company Inc.
PO Box 571
Mundelein, IL 60060-0571
Phone: (847)462-8041
**Subject(s):** (Football)
**Circ:** (Non-paid)⊕2,000
(Paid)⊕17,500

**Journal of Biomedical Materials Research  (24432)**
John Wiley and Sons Inc.
c/o James M. Anderson
The Institute of Pathology of Case Western Reserve Univ.
1100 Euclid Ave., Rm. 306
Cleveland, OH 44106-2622
**Subject(s):** Biology; Medicine and Surgery
**Circ:** 17,500

**OEM Off-Highway  (32977)**
Cygnus Business Media
1233 Janesville Ave.
Fort Atkinson, WI 53538
Phone: (920)563-6388
Fax: (920)563-1702
**Subject(s):** Commerce and Industry; Farm Implements and Supplies; Construction, Contracting, Building, and Excavating
**Circ:** (Controlled)‡17,500

**Yard and Garden  (32987)**
Cygnus Business Media
1233 Janesville Ave.
Fort Atkinson, WI 53538
Phone: (920)563-6388
Fax: (920)563-1702
**Subject(s):** Home and Garden; Retail
**Circ:** 17,500

**YB News  (25210)**
Nomis Publications Inc.
PO Box 5159
Youngstown, OH 44514
Phone: (330)965-2380
Fax: (800)321-9040

**Subject(s):** Funeral Directors
**Circ:** (Paid)1,555
(Non-paid)17,266

**Marina/Dock Age  (9061)**
Preston Publications
6600 W Touhy Ave.
PO Box 48312
Niles, IL 60714-4588
Phone: (847)647-2900
Fax: (847)647-1155
**Subject(s):** Boats and Marine
**Circ:** (Controlled)‡17,200

**Flora Magazine  (8203)**
Cenflo Inc.
205 W Wacker Dr., Ste. 1040
Chicago, IL 60606-3508
Phone: (312)739-5000
Fax: (312)739-0739
**Subject(s):** Florists and Floriculture
**Circ:** ‡17,100

**Appliance Service News  (9334)**
Gamit Enterprises Inc.
PO Box 809
Saint Charles, IL 60174
**Subject(s):** Appliances
**Circ:** (Combined)‡17,000

**Arborist News Magazine  (8004)**
International Society of Arboriculture
PO Box 3129
Champaign, IL 61826-3129
Phone: (217)355-9411
Fax: (217)355-9516
**Subject(s):** Horticulture
**Circ:** (Controlled)17,000

**The Covenant Companion  (8162)**
Covenant Publications
5101 N Francisco Ave.
Chicago, IL 60625
Phone: (773)784-3000
Fax: (773)784-4366
**Subject(s):** Religious Publications
**Circ:** (Non-paid)500
(Paid)17,000

**Dietary Manager Magazine  (9338)**
Dietary Managers Association (DMA)
406 Surrey Woods Dr.
Saint Charles, IL 60174
Phone: (630)587-6336
Fax: (630)587-6308
**Subject(s):** Health and Healthcare
**Circ:** 17,000

**M  (8322)**
TruServ Corp.
8600 W Bryn Mawr Ave.
Chicago, IL 60631
Phone: (773)695-5224
Fax: (773)695-6785
**Subject(s):** Retail
**Circ:** (Non-paid)17,000

**Michigan Lawyers Weekly  (15645)**
Lawyers Weekly Publications
39500 Orchard Hill Pl., Ste. 155
Novi, MI 48375
Phone: (248)596-2720
Fax: (800)678-5297
**Subject(s):** Law
**Circ:** (Paid)‡4,700
(Controlled)‡17,000

**The National Dipper  (8640)**
1028 W Devon Ave.
Elk Grove Village, IL 60007
Phone: (847)301-8400
Fax: (847)301-8402
**Subject(s):** Milk and Dairy Products
**Circ:** (Non-paid)17,000

**North American Actuarial Journal  (9357)**
Society of Actuaries
475 N Martingale Rd., Ste. 600
Schaumburg, IL 60173-2226
Phone: (847)706-3500
Fax: (847)706-3599
**Subject(s):** Insurance; Banking, Finance, and Investments
**Circ:** (Non-paid)17,000

**Spring Arbor University Journal  (15803)**
Spring Arbor University
106 E. Main St.
Spring Arbor, MI 49283
Phone: (517)750-6458
Fax: (517)750-6620
**Subject(s):** College Publications
**Circ:** (Controlled)17,000

**TRAVELtips  (8610)**
Travel Tips
4901 Forest Ave.
Downers Grove, IL 60515
Phone: (630)964-1431
Fax: (630)852-0414
**Subject(s):** Travel and Tourism
**Circ:** (Controlled)17,000

**Recycling Today  (24483)**
G.I.E. Media, MC
4012 Bridge Ave.
Cleveland, OH 44113
Phone: (216)961-4130
Fax: (216)961-0364
**Subject(s):** Waste Management and Recycling
**Circ:** 16,869

**Clavier  (9126)**
Instrumentalist Co.
200 Northfield Rd.
Northfield, IL 60093
Phone: (888)446-6888
Fax: (847)446-6263
**Subject(s):** Music and Musical Instruments
**Circ:** ‡16,700

**Pest Control  (24472)**
Advanstar Communications
c/o Frank Andorka, Editorial Director
7500 Old Oak Blvd.
Cleveland, OH 44130
Phone: (440)891-2708
Fax: (440)891-2675
**Subject(s):** Building Management and Maintenance
**Circ:** (Paid)‡3,386
       (Controlled)‡16,668

**Feed International  (9007)**
Watt Publishing Co.
122 S. Wesley Ave.
Mount Morris, IL 61054
Phone: (815)734-4171
Fax: (815)734-4201
**Subject(s):** Feed and Grain
**Circ:** (Paid)412
       (Non-paid)16,590

**Feed & Grain  (32968)**
Cygnus Business Media
1233 Janesville Ave.
Fort Atkinson, WI 53538
Phone: (920)563-6388
Fax: (920)563-1702
**Subject(s):** Feed and Grain
**Circ:** (Controlled)‡16,505

**Fired Arts & Crafts  (33078)**
Jones Publishing Inc.
N7450 Annstad Rd.
PO Box 5000
Iola, WI 54945-5000
Phone: (715)445-5000
Fax: (715)445-4053
**Subject(s):** Ceramics
**Circ:** ‡16,500

**Irrigation Journal  (8246)**
Adams Business Media/Green Media
250 S. Wacker Dr., Ste. 1150
Chicago, IL 60606
Phone: (505)293-2000
**Subject(s):** Water Supply and Sewage Disposal
**Circ:** (Controlled)‡16,500

**Lift Equipment  (8311)**
Mercor Media
IBM Plaza, 330 N. Wabash, Ste. 3201
Chicago, IL 60611
Phone: (312)628-5870
Fax: (312)628-5878
**Subject(s):** Machinery and Equipment; Construction, Contracting, Building, and Excavating
**Circ:** (Combined)16,500

**Today's Catholic  (9724)**
150 E. Doan Dr.
PO Box 11169
Fort Wayne, IN 46806
Phone: (260)456-2824
Fax: (219)744-1473
**Subject(s):** Religious Publications
**Circ:** ‡16,500

**ACI Structural Journal  (15267)**
American Concrete Institute
38800 Country Club Dr.
PO BOX 9094
Farmington Hills, MI 48331
Phone: (248)848-3700
Fax: (248)848-3701
**Subject(s):** Building Materials, Concrete, Brick, and Tile
**Circ:** ‡16,400

**Ohio's Country Journal  (24593)**
Agri Communications Inc.
1625 Bethel Rd.
Columbus, OH 43220
Phone: (614)273-0463
Fax: (614)273-0463
**Subject(s):** General Agriculture
**Circ:** (Controlled)‡16,100

**Sanitary Maintenance  (33333)**
Trade Press Publishing Corp.
2100 W Florist Ave.
Milwaukee, WI 53209
Phone: (414)228-7701
Fax: (414)228-1134
**Subject(s):** Building Management and Maintenance; Health and Healthcare
**Circ:** (Paid)521
       (Non-paid)16,071

**Law Practice Management  (8305)**
American Bar Association
321 N Clark St.
Chicago, IL 60610
Phone: (312)988-5000
Fax: (312)988-5177
**Subject(s):** Economics
**Circ:** 16,024

**Case Alumnus  (24383)**
Case Alumni Association
10900 Euclid Ave.
Cleveland, OH 44106
Phone: (216)368-4438
Fax: (216)368-4714
**Subject(s):** College Publications
**Circ:** (Non-paid)‡16,000

**The Church Advocate  (24723)**
Churches of God, General Conference
700 E Melrose Ave.
PO Box 926
Findlay, OH 45840
Phone: (419)424-1961
Fax: (419)424-3433
**Subject(s):** Religious Publications
**Circ:** ‡16,000

**College English  (9467)**
National Council of Teachers of English
1111 W. Kenyon Rd.
Urbana, IL 61801-1096
Phone: (217)328-3870
Fax: (217)328-9645
**Subject(s):** Education
**Circ:** (Paid)16,000

**Dow Theory Forecasts  (9789)**
Horizon Publishing Company L.L.C.
7412 Calumet Ave.
Hammond, IN 46324
Phone: (219)852-3200
Fax: (219)931-6487
**Subject(s):** Banking, Finance, and Investments
**Circ:** (Paid)16,000

**The Historian  (15229)**
Michigan State University Press
c/o History Dept.
Michigan State University
301 Morrill Hall
East Lansing, MI 48824
Phone: (517)432-5040
Fax: (517)432-3629
**Subject(s):** History and Genealogy
**Circ:** (Combined)16,000

**Mouth  (8344)**
Alliance of the American Dental Association
211 E Chicago Ave., Ste. 730
Chicago, IL 60611
Phone: (312)440-2795
Fax: (312)440-2820
**Subject(s):** Dentistry
**Circ:** (Paid)16,000

**Powersports Business  (16255)**
Ehlert Publishing Group Inc.
6420 Sycamore Ln., N.
Maple Grove, MN 55369-6355
Phone: (612)476-2200
Fax: (612)476-8065
**Subject(s):** (Snowmobiling); Sporting Goods/Retail Sports; (Boating and Yachting)
**Circ:** (Controlled)‡16,000

**Quintessence International  (7982)**
Quintessence Publishing Company Inc.
551 Kimberly Dr.
Carol Stream, IL 60188-1881
Phone: (630)682-3223
Fax: (630)682-3288
**Subject(s):** Dentistry
**Circ:** (Paid)‡16,000

**Quirk's Marketing Research Review  (16085)**
Quirk Enterprises Inc.
4662 Slater Rd.
Eagan, MN 55122
Phone: (952)224-1919
Fax: (952)224-1914
**Subject(s):** Advertising and Marketing
**Circ:** (Non-paid)16,000

**TAXPRO Quarterly Journal  (32815)**
National Association of Tax Professionals
720 Association Dr.
PO Box 8002
Appleton, WI 54912-8002
Phone: (920)749-1040
Fax: (800)747-0001
**Subject(s):** Taxation and Tariff; Accountants and Accounting
**Circ:** (Non-paid)1,000
       (Paid)16,000

**Bench & Bar of Minnesota  (16276)**
Minnesota State Bar Association
600 Nicollet Mall, Ste. 380
Minneapolis, MN 55402
Phone: (612)333-1183
Fax: (612)333-4927
**Subject(s):** Law
**Circ:** (Non-paid)‡384
       (Paid)‡15,963

**Signs of the Times & Screen Printing en Espanol  (24335)**
ST Media Group International Inc.
407 Gilbert Ave.
Cincinnati, OH 45202
Phone: (513)421-2050
Fax: (513)421-5144
**Subject(s):** Printing and Typography; Spanish
**Circ:** (Paid)540
       (Non-paid)15,950

**Concrete International  (15270)**
American Concrete Institute
38800 Country Club Dr.
Farmington Hills, MI 48331
Phone: (248)848-3700
Fax: (248)848-3701
**Subject(s):** Building Materials, Concrete, Brick, and Tile; Engineering (Various branches); Construction, Contracting, Building, and Excavating
**Circ:** (Paid)697
       (Controlled)15,625

**LP-Gas  (24448)**
Advanstar Communications
7500 Old Oak Blvd.
Cleveland, OH 44130
Phone: (440)243-8100
Fax: (440)891-2727
**Subject(s):** Petroleum, Oil, and Gas
**Circ:** (Paid)4,178
       (Non-paid)10,756
       15,600

# Great Lakes States

**The American Statistician** (24198)
American Statistical Association
c/o James Albert, Editor
Bowling Green State Univ.
Dept. of Mathematics and Statistics
Bowling Green, OH 43403
Phone: (419)372-7456
**Subject(s):** Statistics
**Circ:** (Controlled)‡13
(Paid)‡15,500

**Environmental Design and Construction** (15851)
BNP Media
2401 W Big Beaver Rd., Ste. 700
Troy, MI 48084-3333
Phone: (248)362-3700
Fax: (248)362-0317
**Subject(s):** Construction, Contracting, Building, and Excavating; Architecture
**Circ:** (Non-paid)△15,500

**Ground Water Monitoring and Remediation** (15469)
National Ground Water Association
Western Michigan University
Department of Chemistry
3442 Wood Hall
Kalamazoo, MI 49008-3805
**Subject(s):** Water Supply and Sewage Disposal
**Circ:** ‡15,500

**Pest Control Technology** (24473)
G.I.E. Media, MC
4012 Bridge Ave.
Cleveland, OH 44113
Phone: (216)961-4130
Fax: (216)961-0364
**Subject(s):** Building Management and Maintenance
**Circ:** (Paid)4,500
(Non-paid)15,500

**Trap & Field** (9919)
Curtis Magazine Group
1000 Waterway Blvd.
Indianapolis, IN 46202
Phone: (317)633-8800
Fax: (317)633-8813
**Subject(s):** (Hunting, Fishing, and Game Management)
**Circ:** (Non-paid)‡500
(Paid)‡15,500

**Key Magazine Cincinnati** (24852)
Key Magazine Inc.
c/o Michael S. Deutsch
598 Weeping Willow Ln.
PO Box 5
Maineville, OH 45039
Phone: (513)300-7386
Fax: (513)697-1902
**Subject(s):** Travel and Tourism; Entertainment; Local, State, and Regional Publications
**Circ:** (Combined)‡15,200

**Electrical Apparatus** (8184)
Barks Publications Inc.
400 N Michigan Ave., Ste. 900
Chicago, IL 60611-4104
Phone: (312)321-9440
Fax: (312)321-1288
**Subject(s):** Electronics Engineering
**Circ:** (Paid)873
(Controlled)15,183

**Medicine and Science in Sports and Exercise** (9894)
Lippincott Williams & Wilkins
C/o Kenneth O. Wilson, Managing Editor
401 W. Michigan St.
Indianapolis, IN 46202-3233
Phone: (317)634-8927
Fax: (317)634-8927
**Subject(s):** Medicine and Surgery
**Circ:** (Non-paid)‡128
(Paid)‡15,160

**American Laundry News** (8072)
American Trade Magazines
500 N Dearborn St., Ste. 1000
Chicago, IL 60610
Phone: (312)337-7700
Fax: (312)337-8654
**Subject(s):** Laundry and Dry Cleaning
**Circ:** ‡15,050

**American Ceramic Society Bulletin** (25151)
The American Ceramic Society
PO Box 6136
Westerville, OH 43086-6136
Phone: (614)890-4700
Fax: (614)891-8960
**Subject(s):** Ceramics
**Circ:** 15,000

**AQUA Magazine** (33153)
Athletic Business Publications Inc.
4130 Lien Rd.
Madison, WI 53704
Phone: (608)249-0186
Fax: (608)249-1153
**Subject(s):** Business
**Circ:** (Controlled)15,000

**Automatic Merchandiser** (32961)
Cygnus Business Media
1233 Janesville Ave.
Fort Atkinson, WI 53538
Phone: (920)563-6388
Fax: (920)563-1702
**Subject(s):** Vending Machines
**Circ:** (Controlled)15,000

**Bee Culture** (24894)
A.I. Root Co.
PO Box 706
Medina, OH 44258
Phone: (330)725-6677
Fax: (330)725-5624
**Subject(s):** Beekeeping
**Circ:** (Non-paid)‡500
(Paid)‡15,000

**The Book Report** (25193)
Linworth Publishing Inc.
480 E Wilson Bridge Rd., Ste. L
Worthington, OH 43085-2372
Phone: (614)436-7107
Fax: (614)436-9490
**Subject(s):** Library and Information Science; Education
**Circ:** ‡15,000

**Cincinnati Wedding** (24301)
Cincinnati Magazine Inc.
One Centennial Plz.
705 Central Ave., Ste. 175
Cincinnati, OH 45202
Phone: (513)421-4300
Fax: (513)562-2746
**Subject(s):** Brides
**Circ:** (Combined)15,000

**Group Tour Magazine Great Lakes Region** (15409)
Shoreline Creations Ltd.
2465 112th Ave.
Holland, MI 49424
Phone: (616)393-2077
Fax: (616)393-0085
**Subject(s):** Travel and Tourism
**Circ:** (Controlled)15,000

**Group Tour Magazine Mid-Atlantic Region** (15410)
Shoreline Creations Ltd.
2465 112th Ave.
Holland, MI 49424
Phone: (616)393-2077
Fax: (616)393-0085
**Subject(s):** Travel and Tourism
**Circ:** (Controlled)15,000

**Group Tour Magazine New England Region** (15411)
Shoreline Creations Ltd.
2465 112th Ave.
Holland, MI 49424
Phone: (616)393-2077
Fax: (616)393-0085
**Subject(s):** Travel and Tourism
**Circ:** (Controlled)15,000

**Group Tour Magazine Southeastern Region** (15412)
Shoreline Creations Ltd.
2465 112th Ave.
Holland, MI 49424
Phone: (616)393-2077
Fax: (616)393-0085
**Subject(s):** Travel and Tourism
**Circ:** (Controlled)15,000

**Group Tour Magazine Western Region** (15413)
Shoreline Creations Ltd.
2465 112th Ave.
Holland, MI 49424
Phone: (616)393-2077
Fax: (616)393-0085
**Subject(s):** Travel and Tourism
**Circ:** (Controlled)15,000

**Kent Alumni** (24808)
Kent Alumni Association
Kent State University
Williamson Alumni Ctr.
PO Box 5190
Kent, OH 44242-0001
Phone: (330)672-5368
**Subject(s):** College Publications
**Circ:** (Controlled)‡15,000

**Marketplace Magazine** (32808)
11 Tri-Park Way
Appleton, WI 54914
Phone: (414)735-5969
Fax: (414)735-5970
**Subject(s):** Business; Advertising and Marketing
**Circ:** (Paid)15,000

**The Mennonite** (9765)
1700 S Main St.
Goshen, IN 46526
Phone: (574)535-6052
Fax: (574)535-6050
**Subject(s):** Religious Publications
**Circ:** ‡15,000

**Northern Lights** (15319)
Otsego County Herald Times Inc.
PO Box 598
Gaylord, MI 49734
Phone: (989)732-1111
Fax: (989)732-3490
**Subject(s):** Travel and Tourism
**Circ:** (Non-paid)15,000

**Over the Back Fence** (24274)
Panther Publishing LLC
PO Box 756
Chillicothe, OH 45601
Phone: (740)772-2165
Fax: (740)773-7626
**Subject(s):** Lifestyle; Local, State, and Regional Publications
**Circ:** (Paid)15,000

**Party & Paper Retailer** (15800)
Great American Publishing Co.
75 Applewood Dr., Ste. A
PO Box 128
Sparta, MI 49345
Phone: (616)887-9008
Fax: (616)887-2666
**Subject(s):** Stationery, Office Equipment, and College Store Supplies; Paper
**Circ:** ‡15,000

**Screen Magazine** (8405)
Screen Enterprises Inc.
222 W. Ontario St., Ste. 500
Chicago, IL 60610
Phone: (312)640-0800
Fax: (312)640-1928
**Subject(s):** Motion Pictures; Radio, Television, Cable, and Video
**Circ:** ‡15,000

**Signalman's Journal** (8708)
Brotherhood of Railroad Signalmen
917 Shenandoah Shores Rd.
Front Royal, IL 22630-6418
**Subject(s):** Railroad
**Circ:** ‡15,000

**Silent Sports** (33623)
Waupaca County Publishing Co.
PO Box 152
717 10th St.
Waupaca, WI 54981-1934
Phone: (715)258-5546
Fax: (715)258-8162
**Subject(s):** (Running); (General Sports); (Bicycling)
**Circ:** (Paid)8,500
(Non-paid)15,000

**SWE, Magazine of the Society of Women Engineers** (8421)
Society of Women Engineers
230 E. Ohio St., Ste. 400
Chicago, IL 60611-3265
Phone: (312)596-5223
Fax: (312)596-5252
**Subject(s):** Women's Interests; Engineering (Various branches)
**Circ:** ‡15,000

**VietNow** (16476)
PO Box 736
Pine Island, MN 55963
**Subject(s):** Veterans
**Circ:** (Combined)15,000

**Benefits Quarterly** (32869)
International Society of Certified Employee Benefit Specialists
18700 W. Bluemound Rd.
PO Box 209
Brookfield, WI 53008-0209
Phone: (262)786-8771
Fax: (262)786-8650
**Subject(s):** Employment and Human Resources
**Circ:** (Paid)‡2,800
(Non-paid)‡14,800

**The Dental Assistant** (8171)
American Dental Assistants Association
35 E Wacker Dr., Ste. 1730
Chicago, IL 60601-2211
Phone: (312)541-1550
Fax: (312)541-1496
**Subject(s):** Dentistry
**Circ:** (Paid)‡14,800

**Hoof Beats** (24554)
U.S. Trotting Association
750 Michigan Ave.
Columbus, OH 43215
Phone: (614)228-1385
Fax: (614)222-6791
**Subject(s):** (Horses and Horse Racing)
**Circ:** (Controlled)‡1,347
(Paid)‡14,803

**Books & Culture** (7967)
Christianity Today International
465 Gundersen Dr.
Carol Stream, IL 60188
Phone: (630)260-6200
Fax: (630)260-0114
**Subject(s):** Religious Publications; Literature and Literary Reviews
**Circ:** (Non-paid)6,009
(Paid)14,743

**Ceramic Source** (25154)
The American Ceramic Society
PO Box 6136
Westerville, OH 43086-6136
Phone: (614)890-4700
Fax: (614)891-8960
**Subject(s):** Ceramics
**Circ:** (Non-paid)6,000
(Paid)14,500

**Tack'n Togs Merchandising** (16388)
Farm Progress Cos.
c/o Paul Wahl, Editor
12400 Whitewater Dr., Ste. 160
Minnetonka, MN 55343-9466
Phone: (952)930-4390
Fax: (952)930-4362
**Subject(s):** Sporting Goods/Retail Sports; General Merchandise; Clothing
**Circ:** (Controlled)‡14,264

**The Fruit Growers News** (15799)
Great American Publishing Co.
75 Applewood Dr., Ste. A
PO Box 128
Sparta, MI 49345
Phone: (616)887-9008
Fax: (616)887-2666
**Subject(s):** General Agriculture; Farm Newspapers
**Circ:** (Paid)‡14,235

**Industria Avicola** (9010)
Watt Publishing Co.
122 S. Wesley Ave.
Mount Morris, IL 61054
Phone: (815)734-4171
Fax: (815)734-4201
**Subject(s):** Poultry and Pigeons; Spanish; Hispanic Publications
**Circ:** (Controlled)14,018

**American Nurseryman** (8077)
American Nurseryman Publishing Co.
223 W Jackson Blvd., Ste. 500
Chicago, IL 60606-6904
Phone: (312)427-7339
Fax: (312)427-7346
**Subject(s):** Horticulture; Seed and Nursery Trade; Landscape Architecture
**Circ:** (Paid)14,000

**Fertility and Sterility** (16512)
The American Society for Productive Medicine
Mayo Clinic
200 1st St. SW, 505 NW
Rochester, MN 55905
Phone: (507)284-3850
Fax: (507)284-0780
**Subject(s):** Medicine and Surgery
**Circ:** ‡14,000

**Government Finance Review** (8214)
Government Finance Officers Association
203 N. LaSalle St., Ste. 2700
Chicago, IL 60601-1210
Phone: (312)977-9700
Fax: (312)977-4806
**Subject(s):** Banking, Finance, and Investments; State, Municipal, and County Administration
**Circ:** 14,000

**International Code Council** (8518)
BOCA International
4051 W Flossmoor Rd.
Country Club Hills, IL 60478
Phone: (708)799-2300
Fax: (888)329-4226
**Subject(s):** Building Management and Maintenance; State, Municipal, and County Administration
**Circ:** ‡14,000

**Journal of Healthcare Information Management** (8273)
Healthcare Information and Management Systems Society
230 E. Ohio St., Ste. 500
Chicago, IL 60611-3269
Phone: (312)664-4467
Fax: (312)664-6143
**Subject(s):** Health and Healthcare; Hospitals and Healthcare Institutions; Management and Administration
**Circ:** 14,000

**Michigan Medicine** (15241)
Michigan State Medical Society
120 W. Saginaw St.
East Lansing, MI 48823
Phone: (517)337-1351
Fax: (517)337-2490
**Subject(s):** Medicine and Surgery
**Circ:** ‡14,000

**Quality Management Journal** (33328)
American Society for Quality
PO Box 3005
Milwaukee, WI 53201-3005
Phone: (414)272-8575
Fax: (414)272-1734
**Subject(s):** Management and Administration
**Circ:** (Paid)14,000

**Vacation Week** (32918)
Eagle River Publications Inc.
346 W Division St.
PO Box 1929
Eagle River, WI 54521
Phone: (715)479-4421
Fax: (715)479-6242
**Subject(s):** Travel and Tourism
**Circ:** (Non-paid)‡14,000

**Geotechnical Fabrics Report (GFR)** (16536)
Industrial Fabrics Association International
1801 County Road B W
Roseville, MN 55113
Phone: (651)222-2508
Fax: (651)631-9334
**Subject(s):** Engineering (Various branches); Textiles
**Circ:** (Paid)2,061
(Controlled)13,939

**Toy Cars & Models** (33097)
Krause Publications Inc.
700 E. State St.
Iola, WI 54990-0001
Phone: (715)445-2214
Fax: (715)445-4087
**Subject(s):** Crafts, Models, Hobbies, and Contests
**Circ:** (Paid)13,838

**Transfusion** (16349)
American Association of Blood Banks
University of Minnesota/Transfusion
Box 198
Rm. D211 MAYO
Minneapolis, MN 55455
Phone: (612)626-3313
Fax: (612)624-5411
**Subject(s):** Medicine and Surgery
**Circ:** (Non-paid)‡158
(Paid)‡13,790

**Stamp Collector** (33095)
Krause Publications Inc.
700 E. State St.
Iola, WI 54990-0001
Phone: (715)445-2214
Fax: (715)445-4087
**Subject(s):** Collecting
**Circ:** (Paid)13,670

**Metal Center News** (9153)
Cahners Publishing
2000 Clearwater Dr.
Oak Brook, IL 60523
Phone: (630)320-7000
**Subject(s):** Metal, Metallurgy, and Metal Trade
**Circ:** (Non-paid)‡13,542

**FloraCulture International Magazine** (7884)
Ball Publishing
335 N. River St.
PO Box 9
Batavia, IL 60510-0009
Phone: (630)208-9080
Fax: (630)208-9350
**Subject(s):** Florists and Floriculture
**Circ:** (Combined)13,500

**Material Handling Network** (8617)
Material Handling Network Inc.
252 E. Washington St.
PO Box 2338
East Peoria, IL 61611-0338
Phone: (309)699-4431
Fax: (309)698-0801
**Subject(s):** Materials Handling
**Circ:** (Paid)155
(Non-paid)13,475

**Discoveries** (33074)
Krause Publications Inc.
700 E. State St.
Iola, WI 54990-0001
Phone: (715)445-2214
Fax: (715)445-4087
**Subject(s):** Music and Musical Instruments; Collecting
**Circ:** (Combined)13,388

**Realty and Building** (8395)
Realty and Building Inc.
111 N Wabash, Ste. 1120
Chicago, IL 60602-2012
Phone: (312)467-1888
Fax: (312)467-0225
**Subject(s):** Banking, Finance, and Investments; Real Estate; Architecture; Construction, Contracting, Building, and Excavating
**Circ:** (Controlled)‡1,130
(Paid)‡13,280

**Archives of Pathology & Laboratory Medicine** (8948)
American Medical Association Alliance
2160 S. First Ave.
Bldg. 102, Office 2649
Maywood, IL 60153
**Subject(s):** Medicine and Surgery; Laboratory Research (Scientific and Medical)
**Circ:** (Paid)3,070
(Controlled)‡13,274

**Diesel Progress International Edition** (33606)
Diesel & Gas Turbine Publications
20855 Watertown Rd., Ste.220
Waukesha, WI 53186
Phone: (262)832-5000

Fax: (262)832-5075
**Subject(s):** Machinery and Equipment; Engineering (Various branches)
Circ: (Paid)‡91
(Controlled)‡13,247

**The Director (32870)**
National Funeral Directors Association
13625 Bishop's Dr.
Brookfield, WI 53005
Phone: (262)789-1880
Fax: (262)789-6977
**Subject(s):** Funeral Directors
Circ: (Non-paid)787
(Paid)13,222

**FFA Advisors Making a Difference (9850)**
The National FFA Organization
6060 FFA Dr.
PO Box 68960
Indianapolis, IN 46268-0960
Phone: (317)802-6060
Fax: (317)802-6061
**Subject(s):** General Agriculture
Circ: (Combined)13,200

**Screen Printing (24332)**
ST Media Group International
407 Gilbert Ave.
Cincinnati, OH 45202
Phone: (513)421-2050
Fax: (513)421-5144
**Subject(s):** Printing and Typography
Circ: (Paid)4,360
(Non-paid)13,101

**Fastener Technology International (25069)**
Initial Publications Inc.
3869 Darrow Rd., Ste. 109
Stow, OH 44224
Phone: (330)686-9544
Fax: (330)686-9563
**Subject(s):** Metal, Metallurgy, and Metal Trade
Circ: (Controlled)‡13,050

**Appliance China Edition (9141)**
Dana Chase Publications Inc.
1110 Jorie Blvd., CS 9019
Oak Brook, IL 60522-9019
Phone: (630)990-3484
Fax: (630)990-0078
**Subject(s):** Appliances
Circ: (Non-paid)13,000

**FATE Magazine (16208)**
PO Box 460
Lakeville, MN 55044
Phone: (952)431-2050
Fax: (952)891-6091
**Subject(s):** Alternative and Underground; New Age
Circ: (Free)300
(Paid)13,000

**Pottery Making Illustrated (25160)**
The American Ceramic Society
c/o Tim Frederich, Editor
PO Box 6136
Westerville, OH 43086-6136
Phone: (614)890-4700
Fax: (614)891-8960
**Subject(s):** Crafts, Models, Hobbies, and Contests
Circ: (Paid)‡13,000

**Ripon Magazine (33517)**
Ripon College
300 Seward St.
PO Box 248
Ripon, WI 54971-0248
Phone: (920)748-8115
Fax: (920)748-9262
**Subject(s):** College Publications
Circ: (Controlled)‡13,000

**Rental Management (8985)**
American Rental Association
1900 19th St.
Moline, IL 61265
Phone: (309)764-2475
Fax: (309)764-1533
**Subject(s):** Rental Equipment
Circ: (Paid)5,491
(Non-paid)12,933

**The Motion Systems Distributor (24456)**
Penton Media Inc.
1300 E. 9th St.
Cleveland, OH 44114-1530
Phone: (216)696-7000
Fax: (216)696-1752
**Subject(s):** Power and Power Plants
Circ: (Controlled)‡12,879

**National Locksmith (9432)**
National Publishing Company Inc.
1533 Burgundy Pkwy.
Streamwood, IL 60107
Phone: (630)837-2044
Fax: (630)837-1210
**Subject(s):** Safety
Circ: (Paid)12,705

**Construction Digest (9841)**
5804 W 74th St.
Indianapolis, IN 46278
Phone: (317)293-6860
Fax: (317)293-7840
**Subject(s):** Construction, Contracting, Building, and Excavating; State, Municipal, and County Administration
Circ: (Paid)496
(Non-paid)12,576

**Floral & Nursery Times (9132)**
XXX Publishing Enterprises Ltd.
436 Frontage Rd., Ste. 100
Northfield, IL 60093
Phone: (847)784-9797
Fax: (847)784-9898
**Subject(s):** Florists and Floriculture
Circ: (Paid)‡4,276
(Controlled)‡12,500

**Learning Disabilities Research and Practice (15010)**
Blackwell Publishers
Educational Studies
School of Education
University of Michigan
610 E. University Ave.
Ann Arbor, MI 48109
Phone: (734)763-3268
Fax: (734)763-3268
**Subject(s):** Education
Circ: 12,500

**The Paper Book (24711)**
National Office of The Delta Theta Phi Law Fraternity, International
38640 Butternut Ridge Rd.
Elyria, OH 44035
Phone: (440)458-4381
Fax: (440)458-4380
**Subject(s):** Law; Unclassified Fraternal
Circ: (Combined)12,500

**Phi Rho Sigma Journal (15591)**
Phi Rho Sigma Medical Society
c/o James L. Jackson, MD, FACS
4011 Orchard Dr., Ste. 2020
Midland, MI 48640
**Subject(s):** Unclassified Fraternal; Medicine and Surgery
Circ: (Non-paid)12,500

**Paperboard Packaging Worldwide (24471)**
Advanstar Communications
7500 Old Oak Blvd.
Cleveland, OH 44130-3369
Phone: (440)243-8100
Fax: (440)891-2777
**Subject(s):** Packaging
Circ: (Paid)1,577
(Controlled)12,478

**Fabric Architecture (16535)**
Industrial Fabrics Association International
1801 County Road B W
Roseville, MN 55113
Phone: (651)222-2508
Fax: (651)631-9334
**Subject(s):** Architecture
Circ: (Paid)621
(Controlled)12,400

**Boxboard Containers (8106)**
Primedia Business Magzenes & Media
29 N. Wacker Dr.
Chicago, IL 60606
Phone: (312)726-2574
Fax: (312)726-2574

**Subject(s):** Packaging
Circ: (Paid)2,356
(Non-paid)12,392

**Sound and Vibration (24161)**
27101 E. Oviatt Rd.
PO Box 40416
Bay Village, OH 44140
Phone: (440)835-0101
Fax: (440)835-9303
**Subject(s):** Engineering (Various branches)
Circ: (Controlled)‡12,356

**The Diabetes Educator (8172)**
American Association of Diabetes Educators
367 W Chicago
Chicago, IL 60610
Phone: (312)654-1710
Fax: (312)654-1216
**Subject(s):** Medicine and Surgery
Circ: (Non-paid)‡200
(Paid)‡12,300

**Journal of Plastic and Reconstructive Surgery (7855)**
American Society of Plastic Surgeons and Plastic Surgery Education Foundation
444 E Algonquin Rd.
Arlington Heights, IL 60005
Phone: (847)228-9900
Fax: (847)228-9131
**Subject(s):** Medicine and Surgery; Health and Healthcare
Circ: 12,300

**College and Research Libraries News (8151)**
Association of College and Research Libraries
50 E. Huron St.
Chicago, IL 60611-2795
Phone: (312)280-2523
Fax: (312)280-2520
**Subject(s):** Library and Information Science
Circ: ‡12,200

**Professional Roofing (9329)**
National Roofing Contractors Association
10255 W Higgins Rd., Ste. 600
Rosemont, IL 60018-5607
Phone: (847)299-9070
Fax: (847)299-1183
**Subject(s):** Roofing
Circ: (Paid)5,945
(Controlled)12,195

**Photo Marketing (15456)**
Photo Marketing Association International
3000 Picture Pl.
Jackson, MI 49201
Phone: (517)788-8100
Fax: (517)788-8371
**Subject(s):** Photography
Circ: (Controlled)12,141

**Archives of Otolaryngology–Head & Neck Surgery (8087)**
American Medical Association Alliance
515 N. State St.
Chicago, IL 60610
Phone: (312)464-5000
Fax: (312)464-5020
**Subject(s):** Medicine and Surgery
Circ: (Combined)‡12,086

**American Woodturner (16569)**
American Association of Woodturners
222 Landmark Ctr.
75 W 5th St.
Saint Paul, MN 55102
Phone: (651)484-9094
Fax: (651)484-1724
**Subject(s):** Wood and Woodworking
Circ: (Paid)12,000

**Building Business & Apartment Management (15268)**
Building Industry Association of Southeastern Michigan
30375 Northwestern Hwy., Ste. 100
Farmington Hills, MI 48334
Phone: (248)737-4477
Fax: (248)862-1055
**Subject(s):** Construction, Contracting, Building, and Excavating; Building Management and Maintenance
Circ: (Controlled)‡100
(Paid)‡12,000

**Dia a Dia** (24305)
Forward Movement Publications
300 W 4th St., 2nd Fl.
Cincinnati, OH 45202-2666
Phone: (513)721-6659
Fax: (513)721-0729
**Subject(s):** Spanish; Religious Publications

**Circ:** (Paid)12,000

**French Review** (7949)
American Association of Teachers of French
Mailcode 4510
Department of Foreign Languages
Southern Illinois University
Carbondale, IL 62901-4510
Phone: (618)453-5731
Fax: (618)453-5733
**Subject(s):** Education

**Circ:** 12,000

**Jam Rag** (15283)
Jam Rag Press
PO Box 20076
Ferndale, MI 48220
Phone: (248)545-4215
**Subject(s):** Music and Musical Instruments

**Circ:** (Non-paid)12,000

**The Journal of American History** (9600)
Organization of American Historians
1215 E. Atwater Ave.
Bloomington, IN 47401
Phone: (812)855-2816
Fax: (812)855-9939
**Subject(s):** History and Genealogy

**Circ:** 12,000

**Law & Social Inquiry** (8306)
University of Chicago Press
1427 E. 60th St.
Chicago, IL 60637
Phone: (773)702-7700
Fax: (773)702-9756
**Subject(s):** Law

**Circ:** 12,000

**Medical Equipment Designer** (25049)
Nelson Publishing Inc.
6001 S. Cochran Rd., Ste. 104
Solon, OH 44139-1855
Phone: (440)248-1125
Fax: (440)248-0187
**Subject(s):** Machinery and Equipment; Medicine and Surgery

**Circ:** (Non-paid)‡12,000

**Orthopaedic Nursing** (8362)
National Association of Orthopaedic Nurses
c/o Mary F. Rodts, MS, MSA, APRN, ONC
Rush University College of Nursing
600 S. Paulina Rm. 1080
Chicago, IL 60612
**Subject(s):** Nursing

**Circ:** (Paid)‡12,000

**PIME World** (15195)
PIME Missionaries
17330 Quincy St.
Detroit, MI 48221-2765
Phone: (313)342-4066
Fax: (313)342-6816
**Subject(s):** Religious Publications

**Circ:** 12,000

**Previews** (9904)
Indianapolis Museum of Art
4000 Michigan Road
4000 Michigan Rd.
Indianapolis, IN 46208-4196
Phone: (317)923-1331
Fax: (317)920-2671
**Subject(s):** Museums; Art

**Circ:** (Controlled)‡12,000

**Shipherd's Record** (15653)
Olivet College
320 S. Main St.
Olivet, MI 49076
Phone: (269)749-7000
**Subject(s):** College Publications

**Circ:** (Non-paid)12,000

**Township Perspective** (9411)
Township Officials of Illinois
408 S. 5th St.
Springfield, IL 62701
Phone: (217)744-2212
Fax: (217)744-7419
**Subject(s):** State, Municipal, and County Administration

**Circ:** (Non-paid)‡200
(Paid)‡12,000

**Let's Play Hockey** (16308)
Let's Play Inc.
2721 E 42nd St.
Minneapolis, MN 55406
Phone: (612)729-0023
Fax: (612)729-0259
**Subject(s):** (Hockey)

**Circ:** (Paid)11,867

**Live Steam** (15828)
Village Press Publications
PO Box 1810
Traverse City, MI 49685-1810
Phone: (800)477-7367
**Subject(s):** Crafts, Models, Hobbies, and Contests

**Circ:** (Non-paid)‡107
(Paid)‡11,764

**ACI Materials Journal** (15266)
American Concrete Institute
38800 Country Club Dr.
PO BOX 9094
Farmington Hills, MI 48331
Phone: (248)848-3700
Fax: (248)848-3701
**Subject(s):** Building Materials, Concrete, Brick, and Tile; Construction, Contracting, Building, and Excavating

**Circ:** 11,700

**WOODALL's Campground Management** (10182)
Woodall Publications Corp.
PO Box 276
Syracuse, IN 46567
Phone: (574)457-3370
Fax: (574)457-8295
**Subject(s):** Parks

**Circ:** (Paid)100
(Non-paid)11,700

**Educational Horizons** (9586)
Pi Lambda Theta
4101 E 3rd St.
PO Box 6626
Bloomington, IN 47401
Phone: (812)339-3411
Fax: (812)339-3462
**Subject(s):** Education

**Circ:** (Paid)⊕**11,553**

**Family Advocate** (8196)
American Bar Association
321 N Clark St.
Chicago, IL 60610
Phone: (312)988-5000
Fax: (312)988-5177
**Subject(s):** Law

**Circ:** (Non-paid)‡1,387
(Paid)‡11,517

**Archives of Physical Medicine and Rehabilitation** (8088)
Elsevier
330 N. Wabash Ave., Ste. 2510
Chicago, IL 60611-3604
Phone: (312)464-9550
Fax: (312)464-9554
**Subject(s):** Medicine and Surgery

**Circ:** 11,500

**College Composition and Communication** (9466)
National Council of Teachers of English
1111 W. Kenyon Rd.
Urbana, IL 61801-1096
Phone: (217)328-3870
Fax: (217)328-9645
**Subject(s):** Education; Communications

**Circ:** (Paid)11,500

**Wisconsin Magazine of History** (33224)
Wisconsin Historical Society Press
816 State St.
Madison, WI 53706-1482
Phone: (608)264-6461
Fax: (608)264-6486

**Subject(s):** History and Genealogy

**Circ:** ‡11,500

**Grand Rapids Magazine** (15338)
Gemini Publications
549 Ottawa Ave. NW, Ste. 201
Grand Rapids, MI 49503-1444
Phone: (616)459-4545
Fax: (616)459-4800
**Subject(s):** Local, State, and Regional Publications

**Circ:** (Non-paid)6,525
(Paid)11,475

**Feedstuffs** (16380)
Miller Publishing Co.
12400 Whitewater Dr., Ste. 160
Minnetonka, MN 55343
Phone: (952)931-0211
Fax: (952)938-1832
**Subject(s):** Feed and Grain

**Circ:** (Non-paid)4,727
(Paid)11,312

**American Fastener Journal** (25013)
293 Hopewell Dr.
Powell, OH 43065
Phone: (614)848-3232
Fax: (614)848-5045
**Subject(s):** Metal, Metallurgy, and Metal Trade

**Circ:** (Paid)844
(Controlled)11,300

**Michigan Municipal Review** (15019)
Michigan Municipal League
1675 Green Road
Ann Arbor, MI 48105
Phone: (734)662-3246
Fax: (734)662-8083
**Subject(s):** State, Municipal, and County Administration

**Circ:** ‡11,300

**CityBusiness** (16283)
527 Marquette Ave. S., Ste. 300
Minneapolis, MN 55402
Phone: (612)288-2100
Fax: (612)288-2121
**Subject(s):** Business; Local, State, and Regional Publications

**Circ:** (Paid)11,278

**Residential Lighting** (8882)
Vance Publishing Corp.
400 Knightsbridge Pkwy.
Lincolnshire, IL 60069
Phone: (847)634-2600
Fax: (847)634-4343
**Subject(s):** Lighting

**Circ:** (Paid)261
(Non-paid)11,057

**American Bee Journal** (8763)
Dadant & Sons Inc.
51 S 2nd St.
Hamilton, IL 62341
Phone: (217)847-3324
Fax: (217)847-3660
**Subject(s):** Beekeeping

**Circ:** (Paid)‡11,000

**Archery Business** (16251)
Ehlert Publishing Group Inc.
6420 Sycamore Ln., N.
Maple Grove, MN 55369-6355
Phone: (612)476-2200
Fax: (612)476-8065
**Subject(s):** Sporting Goods/Retail Sports

**Circ:** (Controlled)11,000

**Commercial Investment Real Estate** (8152)
CCIM Institute
430 N. Michigan Ave., Ste. 800
Chicago, IL 60611-4092
Phone: (312)321-4460
Fax: (312)321-4530
**Subject(s):** Real Estate; Banking, Finance, and Investments

**Circ:** (Paid)‡600
(Controlled)‡11,000

**The Education Digest** (15002)
Prakken Publications Inc.
3970 Varsity Dr.
PO Box 8623
Ann Arbor, MI 48107-8623
Phone: (734)975-2800
Fax: (734)975-2787

**Subject(s):** Education
**Circ:** ‡11,000

**Explorer** (24410)
Cleveland Museum of Natural History
1 Wade Oval Dr.
Cleveland, OH 44106
Phone: (216)231-4600
Fax: (216)231-5919
**Subject(s):** Natural History and Nature Study; Anthropology and Ethnology; Archaeology
**Circ:** ‡11,000

**The Horsemen's Corral** (24937)
211 W Main St.
PO Box 110
New London, OH 44851
Phone: (419)929-8200
Fax: (419)929-3800
**Subject(s):** (Horses and Horse Racing)
**Circ:** 11,000

**Marriage Magazine** (16593)
International Marriage Encounter Inc.
955 Lake Dr.
Saint Paul, MN 55120
Phone: (651)454-6434
Fax: (651)452-0466
**Subject(s):** Marriage and Family
**Circ:** 11,000

**Property/Casualty Insurance Magazine** (9905)
National Association of Mutual Insurance Cos.
3601 Vincennes Rd.
Indianapolis, IN 46268
Phone: (317)875-5250
Fax: (317)879-8408
**Subject(s):** Insurance
**Circ:** (Paid)11,000

**Quill** (9906)
Society of Professional Journalists
Eugene S. Pulliam National Journalism Center
3909 N. Meridian St.
Indianapolis, IN 46208
Phone: (317)927-8000
Fax: (317)920-4789
**Subject(s):** Journalism and Publishing
**Circ:** ‡11,000

**Traces of Indiana and Midwestern History** (9918)
Indiana Historical Society Press
450 W Ohio St.
Indianapolis, IN 46202-3269
Phone: (317)232-1882
Fax: (317)234-0427
**Subject(s):** Local, State, and Regional Publications; History and Genealogy
**Circ:** 11,000

**Chicago Medicine** (8132)
Chicago Medical Society
The Medical Society of Cook County
515 N Dearborn St.
Chicago, IL 60610
Phone: (312)670-2550
Fax: (312)670-3646
**Subject(s):** Medicine and Surgery
**Circ:** (Paid)10,915

**Baking Management** (24378)
Penton Media Inc.
1300 E. 9th St.
Cleveland, OH 44114-1530
Phone: (216)696-7000
Fax: (216)696-1752
**Subject(s):** Baking
**Circ:** (Non-paid)△10,825

**Petfood Industry** (9015)
Watt Publishing Co.
122 S. Wesley Ave.
Mount Morris, IL 61054
Phone: (815)734-4171
Fax: (815)734-4201
**Subject(s):** Pets
**Circ:** (Controlled)‡10,815

**Taxes–The Tax Magazine** (8424)
CCH Inc.
4025 W. Peterson Ave.
Chicago, IL 60646-6085
Phone: (847)267-7000
Fax: (773)866-3895

**Subject(s):** Taxation and Tariff
**Circ:** (Non-paid)‡500
(Paid)‡10,745

**Urology Times** (24492)
Advanstar Communications
7500 Old Oak Blvd.
Cleveland, OH 44130-3369
Phone: (440)243-8100
Fax: (440)891-2777
**Subject(s):** Medicine and Surgery
**Circ:** (Controlled)10,688

**Business First-Columbus** (24535)
Business First
303 W. Nationwide Blvd.
Columbus, OH 43215
Phone: (614)461-4040
Fax: (614)365-2980
**Subject(s):** Business; Local, State, and Regional Publications
**Circ:** (Paid)‡10,612

**Business Communications Review** (9523)
MediaLive BCR Events Inc.
999 Oakmont Plaza Dr.
Westmont, IL 60559
Phone: (630)986-1432
Fax: (630)323-5324
**Subject(s):** Communications
**Circ:** (Non-paid)4,020
(Paid)10,510

**Journal of Applied Polymer Science** (24431)
John Wiley and Sons Inc.
c/o Eric Baer, Dept. of Macromolecular Science
Cleveland, OH 44106
**Subject(s):** Science (General)
**Circ:** 10,500

**The Journal of Infectious Diseases** (8276)
University of Chicago Press
1427 E. 60th St.
Chicago, IL 60637
Phone: (773)702-7700
Fax: (773)702-9756
**Subject(s):** Medicine and Surgery
**Circ:** 10,500

**The Labor Paper** (9214)
400 NE Jefferson, No. 400
Peoria, IL 61603
Phone: (309)674-3148
Fax: (309)674-9714
**Subject(s):** Labor
**Circ:** ‡10,500

**Nuclear News** (8845)
American Nuclear Society
555 N Kensington Ave.
La Grange Park, IL 60526
Phone: (708)352-6611
Fax: (708)352-0499
**Subject(s):** Nuclear Engineering
**Circ:** (Controlled)1,500
(Paid)10,500

**Res Gestae** (9908)
Indiana State Bar Association
230 E. Ohio St., 4th Fl.
Indianapolis, IN 46204-2199
Phone: (317)639-5465
Fax: (317)266-2588
**Subject(s):** Law
**Circ:** (Non-paid)10,500

**Wire & Cable Technology International** (25073)
Initial Publications Inc.
3869 Darrow Rd., Ste. 109
Stow, OH 44224
Phone: (330)686-9544
Fax: (330)686-9563
**Subject(s):** Metal, Metallurgy, and Metal Trade
**Circ:** (Controlled)‡10,500

**Dermatology Times** (24397)
Advanstar Communications
7500 Old Oak Blvd.
Cleveland, OH 44130-3369
Phone: (440)243-8100
Fax: (440)891-2777
**Subject(s):** Medicine and Surgery
**Circ:** (Controlled)10,382

**Rehabilitation Nursing** (8742)
4700 W Lake Ave.
Glenview, IL 60025
Phone: (847)375-4710
Fax: (877)734-9384
**Subject(s):** Nursing
**Circ:** ‡10,300

**Gastrointestinal Endoscopy** (24416)
Mosby Inc.
c/o Michael V. Sivak, Jr., M.D., Editor
Gastrointestinal Endoscopy
University Hospitals of Cleveland
Wearn 11100 Euclid Ave.
Cleveland, OH 44106-5066
Phone: (216)844-7903
Fax: (216)983-0004
**Subject(s):** Medicine and Surgery
**Circ:** (Combined)‡10,250

**Journal of the American Academy of Child and Adolescent Psychiatry** (8257)
Lippincott Williams & Wilkins
Children's Memorial Hospital
2300 Children's Plaza, No.156
Chicago, IL 60614-3394
Phone: (773)327-2920
Fax: (773)327-2927
**Subject(s):** Psychology and Psychiatry
**Circ:** (Controlled)‡479
(Paid)‡10,214

**Seaway Review** (15078)
Harbor House Publishers Inc.
221 Water St.
Boyne City, MI 49712-1244
Phone: (616)582-2814
Fax: (616)582-3392
**Subject(s):** Ships and Shipping
**Circ:** (Non-paid)‡400
(Paid)‡10,200

**The Business Journal Serving Greater Milwaukee** (33294)
600 W. Virginia St., Ste. 500
Milwaukee, WI 53204
Phone: (414)278-7788
Fax: (414)278-7028
**Subject(s):** Local, State, and Regional Publications; Business
**Circ:** (Paid)10,100

**Poultry Magazine** (8383)
Marketing & Technology Group
1415 N Dayton St.
Chicago, IL 60622
Phone: (312)266-3311
Fax: (312)266-3363
**Subject(s):** Poultry and Pigeons
**Circ:** (Controlled)‡10,041

**American Cake Decorating** (16567)
Grace McNamara Inc.
4215 White Bear Pkwy., Ste. 100
Saint Paul, MN 55110
Phone: (651)293-1544
Fax: (651)653-4308
**Subject(s):** Food and Cooking
**Circ:** (Paid)10,000

**Antiques & Collecting Magazine** (8083)
Lightner Publishing Corp.
1006 S Michigan Ave.
Chicago, IL 60605
Phone: (312)939-4767
Fax: (312)939-0053
**Subject(s):** Antiques
**Circ:** (Non-paid)‡6,000
(Paid)‡10,000

**Bear Tracks** (25085)
Good Bears of the World
PO Box 13097
Toledo, OH 43613
Phone: (419)531-5365
Fax: (419)531-5365
**Subject(s):** Clubs and Societies; Crafts, Models, Hobbies, and Contests; Collecting
**Circ:** 10,000

**Boys' Quest** (24193)
Bluffton News
103 N. Main
PO Box 227
Bluffton, OH 45817
Phone: (419)358-4610

**Subject(s):** Children's Interests; Youths' Interests
**Circ:** (Paid)10,000

**Bulletin of the Atomic Scientists (8112)**
Educational Foundation for Nuclear Science
6042 S. Kimbark Ave.
Chicago, IL 60637-2806
Phone: (773)702-2555
Fax: (773)702-0725
**Subject(s):** International Affairs; Peace
**Circ:** ‡10,000

**Culture Wars (10161)**
Ultramontane Associates Inc.
206 Marquette Ave.
South Bend, IN 46617
Phone: (574)289-9786
Fax: (574)289-1461
**Subject(s):** Religious Publications
**Circ:** (Paid)‡10,000

**Engineering Professional (33427)**
Technical Enterprises Inc.
7044 S 13th St.
Oak Creek, WI 53154
Phone: (414)768-8000
Fax: (414)768-8001
**Subject(s):** Engineering (Various branches)
**Circ:** ‡10,000

**Farm Equipment (32967)**
Cygnus Business Media
1233 Janesville Ave.
Fort Atkinson, WI 53538
Phone: (920)563-6388
Fax: (920)563-1702
**Subject(s):** Farm Implements and Supplies
**Circ:** (Controlled)10,000

**Gaming Products and Services (16583)**
WFM Inc.
4215 White Bear Pkwy., Ste. 100
Saint Paul, MN 55110
Phone: (651)762-2046
Fax: (651)762-2035
**Subject(s):** Business
**Circ:** (Paid)10,000

**The Journal of Asian Studies (16303)**
Association for Asian Studies Inc.
Dept. of History
University of Minnesota
614 Social Science Tower
267 19th Ave. S.
Minneapolis, MN 55455
Phone: (612)624-6527
Fax: (612)624-7096
**Subject(s):** Intercultural Interests
**Circ:** ‡10,000

**Journal of Christian Nursing (33190)**
Nurses Christian Fellowship of InterVarsity Christian Fellowship
No.6400 Schroeder Rd.
PO Box 7895
Madison, WI 53707-7895
Phone: (608)274-9001
Fax: (608)274-7882
**Subject(s):** Religious Publications; Nursing
**Circ:** (Controlled)‡150
(Paid)‡10,000

**Library Talk (25195)**
Linworth Publishing Inc.
480 E Wilson Bridge Rd., Ste. L
Worthington, OH 43085-2372
Phone: (614)436-7107
Fax: (614)436-9490
**Subject(s):** Library and Information Science; Education
**Circ:** 10,000

**Materials Evaluation (24567)**
American Society for Nondestructive Testing Inc.
1711 Arlingate Ln.
PO Box 28518
Columbus, OH 43228-0518
Phone: (614)274-6003
Fax: (614)274-6899
**Subject(s):** Commerce and Industry
**Circ:** (Paid)10,000

**Michigan Florist (15393)**
Michigan Floral Association
1152 Haslett Rd.
Haslett, MI 48840-9778
Phone: (517)575-0110
**Subject(s):** Florists and Floriculture
**Circ:** (Controlled)‡10,000

**Michigan Runner & Fitness Sports (15021)**
Great Lakes Sports Publications Inc.
3588 Plymouth Rd., No. 245
Ann Arbor, MI 48105-2603
Phone: (734)507-0241
Fax: (734)434-4765
**Subject(s):** (Running)
**Circ:** ‡10,000

**Miniature Gazette (9639)**
National Association of Miniature Enthusiasts
130 N Rangeline Rd.
PO Box 69
Carmel, IN 46032-0069
Phone: (317)571-8094
Fax: (317)571-8105
**Subject(s):** Collecting; Crafts, Models, Hobbies, and Contests
**Circ:** 10,000

**Ohio Granger (24582)**
Ohio State Grange
1031 E Broad St.
Columbus, OH 43205
Phone: (614)258-9569
Fax: (614)258-3232
**Subject(s):** Farm Bureau, Grange, and Cooperative Associations
**Circ:** ‡10,000

**Ohio Nurses Review (24585)**
Ohio Nurses Association
4000 E Main St.
Columbus, OH 43213-2983
Phone: (614)237-5414
Fax: (614)237-6074
**Subject(s):** Nursing
**Circ:** (Controlled)10,000

**Poetry (8380)**
The Poetry Foundation
1030 N. Clark St., Ste. 420
Chicago, IL 60610
Phone: (312)787-7070
Fax: (312)787-6650
**Subject(s):** Literature and Literary Reviews
**Circ:** (Non-paid)‡90
(Paid)‡10,000

**Productores de Hortalizas (25178)**
Meister Publishing Co.
37733 Euclid Ave.
Willoughby, OH 44094-5992
Phone: (440)942-2000
Fax: (440)942-0662
**Subject(s):** Hispanic Publications; General Agriculture
**Circ:** (Controlled)10,000

**Student Leadership Journal (33213)**
InterVarsity Christian Fellowship
6400 Schroeder Rd.
PO Box 7895
Madison, WI 53707-7895
Phone: (608)274-9001
Fax: (608)274-7882
**Subject(s):** Religious Publications; College Publications
**Circ:** ‡10,000

**This Week in Cleveland Magazine (24490)**
20575 Center Ridge Rd., Ste. 460
Cleveland, OH 44116-3422
Phone: (440)331-8012
Fax: (440)331-1481
**Subject(s):** Local, State, and Regional Publications; City, Hotel, Railroad, and Travel Guides; Travel and Tourism
**Circ:** (Free)10,000

**Up Beat Daily (8648)**
Maher Publications Inc.
102 N Haven Rd.
Elmhurst, IL 60126
Phone: (630)941-2030
Fax: (630)941-3210
**Subject(s):** Music and Musical Instruments
**Circ:** (Non-paid)‡10,000

**Link (8313)**
Yellow Pages Publishers Association
The Merchandise Mart, Ste. 2000
Chicago, IL 60654
Phone: (312)527-7412
Fax: (312)527-7230
**Subject(s):** Advertising and Marketing
**Circ:** (Paid)2,022
(Non-paid)9,971

**American Journal of Hematology (15165)**
John Wiley and Sons Inc.
C/O Ananda S. Prasad, Division of Hematology
Detroit, MI 48201
**Subject(s):** Medicine and Surgery
**Circ:** (Paid)9,800

**Military Trader (33086)**
Krause Publications Inc.
700 E. State St.
Iola, WI 54990-0001
Phone: (715)445-2214
Fax: (715)445-4087
**Subject(s):** Collecting; Military and Navy
**Circ:** (Combined)9,778

**Public Libraries (8388)**
American Library Association
50 E. Huron St.
Chicago, IL 60611
Phone: (312)944-7298
Fax: (312)280-4380
**Subject(s):** Library and Information Science
**Circ:** (Combined)‡9,742

**Bucyrus RFD News (24183)**
Gazette Publishing Company Inc.
PO Box 367
Bellevue, OH 44811
Phone: (419)483-7410
Fax: (419)483-3737
**Subject(s):** General Agriculture
**Circ:** (Paid)300
(Non-paid)9,700

**Agronomy Journal (33149)**
American Society of Agronomy
677 S. Segoe Rd.
Madison, WI 53711-1086
Phone: (608)273-8080
Fax: (608)273-2021
**Subject(s):** Scientific Agricultural Publications
**Circ:** 9,500

**The Municipality (33205)**
League of Wisconsin Municipalities
202 State St., Ste. 300
Madison, WI 53703-2215
Phone: (608)267-2380
Fax: (608)267-0645
**Subject(s):** State, Municipal, and County Administration
**Circ:** ‡9,446

**Farm Chemicals International (25174)**
Meister Publishing Co.
37733 Euclid Ave.
Willoughby, OH 44094-5992
Phone: (440)942-2000
Fax: (440)942-0662
**Subject(s):** Fertilizer
**Circ:** 9,400

**Signs of the Times (24334)**
ST Media Group International Inc.
407 Gilbert Ave.
Cincinnati, OH 45202
**Subject(s):** Advertising and Marketing
**Circ:** (Non-paid)8,358
(Paid)9,299

**Grower Talks (7886)**
Ball Publishing
335 N. River St.
PO Box 9
Batavia, IL 60510-0009
Phone: (630)208-9080
Fax: (630)208-9350
**Subject(s):** Horticulture; Florists and Floriculture; Seed and Nursery Trade
**Circ:** (Paid)9,230

**Classic Boating (33430)**
280 Lac La Belle Dr.
Oconomowoc, WI 53066
Phone: (262)567-4800

## Great Lakes States

Gale Directory of Publications & Broadcast Media/140th Ed.

**Subject(s):** (Boating and Yachting)
**Circ:** (Controlled)9,200

**Meat Business Magazine** (8979)
Record Printing
109 W Washington St.
Millstadt, IL 62260
Phone: (618)233-0145
Fax: (618)476-1616
**Subject(s):** Food and Grocery Trade
**Circ:** (Non-paid)‡9,100

**ALA News** (8877)
Association of Legal Administrators
75 Tri-State International, Ste. 222
Lincolnshire, IL 60069-4435
Phone: (847)267-1252
Fax: (847)267-1329
**Subject(s):** Law
**Circ:** (Controlled)9,000

**Concordia Theological Quarterly** (9714)
Concordia Theological Seminary
6600 N Clinton
Fort Wayne, IN 46825
Phone: (260)452-2249
Fax: (260)452-2227
**Subject(s):** Religious Publications
**Circ:** (Paid)400
(Non-paid)9,000

**Gear Technology** (8639)
Randall Publishing Inc.
1425 Lunt Ave.
Elk Grove Village, IL 60007
Phone: (847)437-6604
Fax: (847)437-6618
**Subject(s):** Engineering (Various branches); Commerce and Industry
**Circ:** (Paid)500
3,000
(Controlled)9,000

**The Indiana Runner** (10158)
PO Box 478
Shelbyville, IN 46176
Phone: (317)392-1195
Fax: (317)398-0194
**Subject(s):** (Running)
**Circ:** (Paid)1,000
(Non-paid)9,000

**Journal of Small Business** (15511)
Small Business Association of Michigan
222 N Washington Sq., Ste. 100
PO Box 16158
Lansing, MI 48933-6158
Phone: (517)482-8788
Fax: (517)482-4205
**Subject(s):** Business; Local, State, and Regional Publications
**Circ:** (Non-paid)9,000

**Leaves Class and Events Magazine** (24818)
Holden Arboretum
9500 Sperry Rd.
Kirtland, OH 44094-5172
Phone: (440)946-4400
Fax: (440)602-8012
**Subject(s):** Botany
**Circ:** ‡9,000

**Michigan Food News** (15518)
Michigan Grocers Association
221 N Walnut
Lansing, MI 48933
Phone: (517)372-6800
Fax: (517)372-3002
**Subject(s):** Food and Grocery Trade
**Circ:** (Controlled)9,000

**Minnesota Medicine** (16321)
Minnesota Medical Association
1300 Godward St. NE, Ste. 2500
Minneapolis, MN 55413
Phone: (612)378-1875
Fax: (612)378-3875
**Subject(s):** Medicine and Surgery
**Circ:** ‡9,000

**PLAYS** (33614)
Kalmbach Publishing Co.
PO Box 1612
Waukesha, WI 53187-1612
Phone: (262)796-8776
Fax: (262)796-1615
**Subject(s):** Drama and Theatre
**Circ:** ‡9,000

**Resource** (15745)
American Society of Agricultural Engineers
2950 Niles Rd.
Saint Joseph, MI 49085-9659
Phone: (269)429-0300
Fax: (269)429-3852
**Subject(s):** Engineering (Various branches); Scientific Agricultural Publications
**Circ:** ‡9,000

**Reunions Magazine** (33332)
PO Box 11727
Milwaukee, WI 53211-0727
Phone: (414)263-4567
Fax: (414)263-6331
**Subject(s):** Conventions, Meetings, and Trade Fairs
**Circ:** (Paid)‡3,000
(Non-paid)‡9,000

**Timeshare Business** (9640)
Resort Condominiums International Inc.
9998 N. Michigan Rd.
Carmel, IN 46032
Phone: (317)805-9000
Fax: (317)805-9335
**Subject(s):** Travel and Tourism
**Circ:** (Controlled)9,000

**Wisconsin Medical Journal** (33225)
Medical Society of Wisconsin
330 E. Lakeside St.
PO Box 1109
Madison, WI 53701-1109
Phone: (608)442-3800
Fax: (608)442-3802
**Subject(s):** Medicine and Surgery
**Circ:** ‡9,000

**The Wisconsin Taxpayer** (33230)
Wisconsin Taxpayers Alliance
401 N. Lawn Ave.
Madison, WI 53704-5033
Phone: (608)241-9789
Fax: (608)241-5807
**Subject(s):** Local, State, and Regional Publications; Taxation and Tariff
**Circ:** (Non-paid)‡700
‡9,000

**Chicago Lawyer** (8129)
Law Bulletin Publishing Co.
415 N. State
Chicago, IL 60610
Phone: (312)644-7800
Fax: (312)644-4255
**Subject(s):** Law
**Circ:** (Paid)1,156
(Non-paid)8,995

**Lithuanian Museum Review** (8314)
Balzekas Museum of Lithuanian Culture
6500 S Pulaski Rd.
Chicago, IL 60629-5136
Phone: (773)582-6500
Fax: (773)582-5133
**Subject(s):** Intercultural Interests
**Circ:** (Paid)‡3500
(Controlled)‡8950

**Music Inc.** (8646)
Maher Publications Inc.
102 N Haven Rd.
Elmhurst, IL 60126
Phone: (630)941-2030
Fax: (630)941-3210
**Subject(s):** Music and Musical Instruments; Music and Musical Instruments
**Circ:** (Controlled)‡8,900

**Economic Trends** (24404)
Federal Reserve Bank of Cleveland
Human Resources
1455 E 6th
PO Box 6387
Cleveland, OH 44101
Phone: (216)579-2000
Fax: (216)579-3050
**Subject(s):** Economics
**Circ:** (Non-paid)8,800

**Living Church** (33308)
Living Church Foundation Inc.
816 E Juneau Ave.
PO Box 514036
Milwaukee, WI 53203-3436
Phone: (414)276-5420
Fax: (414)276-7483
**Subject(s):** Religious Publications
**Circ:** (Non-paid)‡294
(Paid)‡8,738

**Clinical Infectious Diseases** (8149)
University of Chicago Press
1427 E. 60th St.
Chicago, IL 60637
Phone: (773)702-7700
Fax: (773)702-9756
**Subject(s):** Medicine and Surgery
**Circ:** ‡8,700

**Journal of Periodontology** (8287)
The American Academy of Periodontology
737 N. Michigan Ave., Ste. 800
Chicago, IL 60611-2690
Phone: (312)787-5518
Fax: (312)787-3670
**Subject(s):** Dentistry
**Circ:** 8,664

**Business People Magazine** (9712)
Michiana Business Publications Inc.
536 W Cook Rd.
Fort Wayne, IN 46825-6702
Phone: (219)497-0433
Fax: (219)497-0822
**Subject(s):** Business
**Circ:** (Controlled)8,600

**Criminal Justice Magazine** (8165)
American Bar Association
c/o MaryAnn Dadisman
750 N. Lake Shore Dr.
Chicago, IL 60611
Phone: (312)988-6047
Fax: (312)988-6081
**Subject(s):** Law
**Circ:** (Non-paid)1,252
(Paid)8,603

**udm/Upholstery Design and Management** (8594)
Chartwell Group of Watt Publishing
1350 E Touhy, Ste. 105 W.
Des Plaines, IL 60018
Phone: (847)390-6700
Fax: (847)390-7100
**Subject(s):** Furniture and Furnishings
**Circ:** (Non-paid)8,600

**Metro Chicago Real Estate** (8334)
Law Bulletin Publishing Co.
415 N. State
Chicago, IL 60610
Phone: (312)644-7800
Fax: (312)644-4255
**Subject(s):** Real Estate
**Circ:** (Controlled)‡8,582

**CDS Review** (8119)
Chicago Dental Society
401 N Michigan Ave., Ste. 200
Chicago, IL 60611-4272
Phone: (312)836-7305
Fax: (312)836-7337
**Subject(s):** Dentistry
**Circ:** ‡8,500

**The College Store** (24962)
c/o National Association of College Stores
500 E Lorain St.
Oberlin, OH 44074-1294
Phone: (440)775-7777
Fax: (440)775-4769
**Subject(s):** Stationery, Office Equipment, and College Store Supplies
**Circ:** ‡8,500

**Faith and Fellowship** (16120)
Faith & Fellowship Press
704 W. Vernon Ave.
Fergus Falls, MN 56537-2633
Phone: (218)736-7357
Fax: (218)736-2200
**Subject(s):** Religious Publications
**Circ:** (Controlled)‡100
(Paid)‡8,500

**The Hunter's Horn  (9364)**
Hunter's Horn Inc.
PO Box 777
Sesser, IL 62884
Phone: (618)625-2711
Fax: (618)625-6221
**Subject(s):** Dogs

Circ: ‡8,500

**Michigan Christian Advocate  (14962)**
316 Springbrook Ave.
Adrian, MI 49221-2099
Phone: (517)265-2075
Fax: (517)263-7422
**Subject(s):** Religious Publications

Circ: ‡8,500

**Vintage Ford  (9645)**
Model T Ford Club of America
Box 126
Centerville, IN 47330-0126
Phone: (765)855-5248
Fax: (765)588-3428
**Subject(s):** Automotive (Trade)

Circ: (Controlled)8,500

**American Entomologist  (24282)**
Entomological Society of America
c/o Gene Kritsky, Prof. of Biology
College of Mount St. Joseph
5701 Delhi Rd.
Cincinnati, OH 45233-1670
Phone: (513)244-4401
**Subject(s):** Entomology

Circ: (Paid)8300

**Angus Topics  (7963)**
Angus Topics Inc.
PO Box 397
Carmi, IL 62821
Phone: (618)382-8553
Fax: (618)382-3436
**Subject(s):** Livestock

Circ: ‡8,300

**Indiana Beef  (9863)**
Indiana Beef Cattle Association
8770 Guion Rd., Ste. A
Indianapolis, IN 46268
Phone: (317)872-2333
Fax: (317)872-2364
**Subject(s):** Livestock

Circ: ‡8,300

**Interior Construction  (9339)**
Ceilings and Interior Systems Construction Association
1500 Lincoln Hwy, No. 202
Saint Charles, IL 60174
Phone: (630)584-1919
Fax: (630)584-2003
**Subject(s):** Construction, Contracting, Building, and Excavating; Interior Design/Decorating

Circ: (Controlled)‡8,300

**European Rubber Journal  (24098)**
Crain Communications Inc.
1725 Merriman Rd., Ste. 300
Akron, OH 44313-5251
Phone: (330)836-9180
Fax: (330)836-2322
**Subject(s):** Rubber Trade

Circ: (Combined)△8,186

**Kansas City Commerce  (8978)**
Record Printing
109 W Washington St.
Millstadt, IL 62260
Phone: (618)233-0145
Fax: (618)476-1616
**Subject(s):** Business

Circ: (Controlled)⊕8,170

**AFE Facilities Engineering Journal  (24279)**
Association For Facilities Engineering
8160 Corporate Park Dr., Ste. 125
Cincinnati, OH 45242
Phone: (513)489-2473
Fax: (513)247-7422
**Subject(s):** Engineering (Various branches)

Circ: (Non-paid)100
    (Paid)8,000

**American Field  (8068)**
542 S Dearborn St.
Chicago, IL 60605-1598
Phone: (312)663-9797
Fax: (312)663-5557
**Subject(s):** Dogs; (Hunting, Fishing, and Game Management)

Circ: (Non-paid)‡55
    (Paid)‡8,000

**American Record Guide  (24285)**
Record Guide Productions
4412 Braddock St.
Cincinnati, OH 45204
Phone: (513)941-1116
**Subject(s):** Music and Musical Instruments

Circ: (Non-paid)‡140
    (Paid)‡8,000

**Appliance European Edition  (9142)**
Dana Chase Publications Inc.
1110 Jorie Blvd., CS 9019
Oak Brook, IL 60522-9019
Phone: (630)990-3484
Fax: (630)990-0078
**Subject(s):** Appliances

Circ: (Non-paid)8,000

**Appliance Latin America Edition  (9143)**
Dana Chase Publications Inc.
1110 Jorie Blvd., CS 9019
Oak Brook, IL 60522-9019
Phone: (630)990-3484
Fax: (630)990-0078
**Subject(s):** Appliances

Circ: (Non-paid)8,000

**The Bible Friend  (16278)**
Osterhus Publishing House Inc.
4500 W Broadway
Minneapolis, MN 55422
Phone: (763)537-9311
Fax: (763)537-9585
**Subject(s):** Religious Publications

Circ: (Non-paid)3,000
    (Paid)8,000

**Chicago Dental Society News  (8127)**
Chicago Dental Society
401 N Michigan Ave., Ste. 200
Chicago, IL 60611-4272
Phone: (312)836-7305
Fax: (312)836-7337
**Subject(s):** Dentistry

Circ: (Non-paid)8,000

**Chronicles  (9299)**
The Rockford Institute
928 N. Main St.
Rockford, IL 61103
Phone: (815)964-5053
Fax: (815)964-9403
**Subject(s):** Literature and Literary Reviews; Economics; Politics; Intercultural Interests

Circ: ‡8,000

**The Congregationalist  (24856)**
National Association of Congregational Christian Churches
1105 Briarwood Rd.
Mansfield, OH 44907
Phone: (419)756-5526
Fax: (419)756-5526
**Subject(s):** Religious Publications

Circ: (Controlled)8,000

**Indiana Magazine of History  (9595)**
Indiana University Press
Indiana Magazine of History
Ballantine 742
Indiana University
Bloomington, IN 47405
Phone: (812)855-4139
Fax: (812)855-3378
**Subject(s):** History and Genealogy

Circ: 8,000

**Journal for Healthcare Quality  (8738)**
National Association for Healthcare Quality
4700 W. Lake Ave.
Glenview, IL 60025
Phone: (847)375-4720
Fax: (877)218-7939
**Subject(s):** Hospitals and Healthcare Institutions

Circ: (Controlled)500
    (Paid)8,000

**Journal of Nuclear Materials Management  (9116)**
Institute of Nuclear Materials Management
60 Revere Dr., Ste. 500
Northbrook, IL 60062
Phone: (847)480-9573
Fax: (847)480-9282
**Subject(s):** Materials Handling; Nuclear Engineering

Circ: (Paid)‡8,000

**MC Magazine  (9892)**
National Precast Concrete Association
10333 N Meridian St., Ste. 272
Indianapolis, IN 46290
Phone: (317)571-9500
Fax: (317)571-0041
**Subject(s):** Building Materials, Concrete, Brick, and Tile

Circ: (Non-paid)‡8,000

**The North Woods Call  (15106)**
00509 Turkey Run Rd.
Charlevoix, MI 49720
Phone: (231)547-9797
**Subject(s):** Ecology and Conservation; Natural History and Nature Study; Environmental and Natural Resources Conservation

Circ: ‡8,000

**Rosebud  (32879)**
PO Box 459
Cambridge, WI 53523
Phone: (608)423-9609
Fax: (608)423-9690
**Subject(s):** Literature and Literary Reviews; Poetry

Circ: (Paid)‡8000

**TechTrends: for Leaders in Education & Training  (9614)**
Association for Educational Communications and Technology
c/o Elizabeth Boling
Editor-in-Chief, Tech Trends
Education 2276, 201 N. Rose Ave.
Indiana University
Bloomington, IN 47405
Phone: (812)856-8467
Fax: (812)856-8239
**Subject(s):** Education

Circ: ‡8,000

**Live Sound! International  (15639)**
Royle Publishing Company Inc.
Live Sound International
220 Woodruff
Niles, MI 49120
Phone: (269)687-8846
Fax: (269)687-8825
**Subject(s):** Music and Musical Instruments

Circ: (Paid)2,800
    (Non-paid)7,950

**Rubber World  (24104)**
1867 W. Market St.
PO Box 5451
Akron, OH 44313-6901
Phone: (330)864-2122
Fax: (330)864-5298
**Subject(s):** Rubber Trade

Circ: (Paid)2,413
    (Non-paid)7,937

**Illinois School Board Journal  (9397)**
Illinois Association of School Boards
2921 Baker Dr.
Springfield, IL 62703-2236
Phone: (217)528-9688
Fax: (217)528-2831
**Subject(s):** Education

Circ: (Non-paid)‡690
    (Paid)‡7,737

**CarneTec  (8116)**
Marketing & Technology Group
1415 N Dayton St.
Chicago, IL 60622
Phone: (312)266-3311
Fax: (312)266-3363
**Subject(s):** Food and Grocery Trade; Food Production; Livestock; Poultry and Pigeons

Circ: 7,699

**Annals of Surgery  (33152)**
Lippincott Williams & Wilkins
C/o Layton F. Rikkers, MD, Editor-in-Chief
University of Wisconsin Medical School
4/710 Clinical Science Center
600 Highland Ave.
Madison, WI 53792
**Subject(s):** Medicine and Surgery
**Circ:**  (Paid)‡7,619

**Bend of the River Magazine  (24891)**
PO Box 859
Maumee, OH 43537
Phone: (419)893-0022
Fax: (419)893-0022
**Subject(s):** Local, State, and Regional Publications
**Circ:**  (Paid)‡7,500

**Chemical Times & Trends  (25134)**
Chemical Specialties Manufacturers Association (CSMA)
125 Humbolt Ave.
Wadsworth, OH 44281
**Subject(s):** Chemistry, Chemicals, and Chemical Engineering
**Circ:**  ‡7,500

**Illinois Truck News  (9279)**
Illinois Transportation Association
2000 5th Ave.
River Grove, IL 60171
Phone: (847)952-6000
Fax: (847)452-3508
**Subject(s):** Trucks and Trucking
**Circ:**  (Controlled)‡7,500

**NPN International  (8358)**
Adams Business Media
833 W. Jackson Blvd., 7th Fl.
Chicago, IL 60607
Phone: (312)846-4600
Fax: (312)846-4632
**Subject(s):** Food and Grocery Trade; Retail; Petroleum, Oil, and Gas; Advertising and Marketing
**Circ:**  (Controlled)‡7,500

**The Shepherd  (24251)**
Sheep & Farm Life Inc.
POB 97
Cardington, OH 43315-0097
Phone: (419)947-9289
Fax: (419)947-9289
**Subject(s):** Livestock
**Circ:**  ‡7,500

**The Gerontologist  (24419)**
Gerontological Society of America
c/o Linda S.C, Ph.D, Editor-in-Chief
Benjamin Rose, 850 Euclid Ave., Ste. 1100
Cleveland, OH 44114-3301
**Subject(s):** Gerontology
**Circ:**  (Paid)‡7,400

**The Annals of Pharmacotherapy  (24286)**
Harvey Whitney Books Co.
8044 Montgomery Rd., Ste. 415
Box 42696
Cincinnati, OH 45242-0696
Phone: (513)793-3555
Fax: (513)793-3600
**Subject(s):** Drugs and Pharmaceuticals
**Circ:**  ‡7,200

**Contemporary Sociology  (10242)**
American Sociological Association
Purdue University
1365 Stone Hall
West Lafayette, IN 47907-1365
Phone: (765)494-0938
Fax: (765)496-1476
**Subject(s):** Sociology
**Circ:**  ‡7,200

**The Priest  (9810)**
Our Sunday Visitor Publishing
200 Noll Plz.
Huntington, IN 46750
Phone: (260)356-8400
Fax: (260)356-8472
**Subject(s):** Religious Publications
**Circ:**  7,200

**Urethanes Technology  (24108)**
Crain Communications Inc.
1725 Merriman Rd., Ste. 300
Akron, OH 44313-5251
Phone: (330)836-9180
Fax: (330)836-2322
**Subject(s):** Rubber Trade
**Circ:**  (Combined)△7,118

**Journal of Political Economy  (8288)**
University of Chicago Press
1427 E. 60th St.
Chicago, IL 60637
Phone: (773)702-7700
Fax: (773)702-9756
**Subject(s):** Economics
**Circ:**  ‡7,100

**American Farriers Journal  (32868)**
Lessiter Publications Inc.
225 Regency Ct., Ste. 200
Brookfield, WI 53045
Phone: (262)782-4480
Fax: (262)782-1252
**Subject(s):** Livestock; (Horses and Horse Racing)
**Circ:**  (Non-paid)‡200
         (Paid)‡7,000

**EAP Digest  (15849)**
Performance Resource Press Inc.
1270 Rankin Dr., Ste. F
Troy, MI 48083
Phone: (248)588-7733
Fax: (248)588-6633
**Subject(s):** Employment and Human Resources; Health and Healthcare
**Circ:**  (Paid)‡3,000
         (Controlled)‡7,000

**The Quest  (9527)**
Theosophical Society in America
PO Box 270
Wheaton, IL 60189-0270
Phone: (630)668-1571
Fax: (630)668-4976
**Subject(s):** General Editorial
**Circ:**  7,000

**Student Assistance Journal  (15864)**
Performance Resource Press Inc.
1270 Rankin Dr., Ste. F
Troy, MI 48083
Phone: (248)588-7733
Fax: (248)588-6633
**Subject(s):** Education
**Circ:**  (Paid)‡3,000
         (Controlled)‡7,000

**Tribology & Lubrication Technology  (9203)**
Society of Tribologists and Lubrication Engineers
840 Busse Hwy.
Park Ridge, IL 60068-2376
Phone: (847)825-5536
Fax: (847)825-1456
**Subject(s):** Engineering (Various branches)
**Circ:**  (Paid)‡7,000

**Voice  (15378)**
IFCA International
3520 Fairlanes
Box 810
Grandville, MI 49468
Phone: (616)531-1840
Fax: (616)531-1814
**Subject(s):** Religious Publications
**Circ:**  (Non-paid)‡3,000
         (Paid)‡7,000

**The Bible Today  (16018)**
The Liturgical Press
The Bible Today
Liturgical Press
Saint John's Abbey
Collegeville, MN 56321-7500
**Subject(s):** Religious Publications
**Circ:**  (Non-paid)155
         (Paid)6,900

**Leaven  (9352)**
La Leche League International Inc.
1400 N. Meacham Rd.
PO Box 4079
Schaumburg, IL 60173-4808
Phone: (847)519-7730
Fax: (847)519-0035
**Subject(s):** Babies; Parenting; Women's Interests
**Circ:**  (Controlled)⊕225
         (Paid)⊕6,849

**American Journal of Sociology  (8071)**
University of Chicago Press
5835 S. Kimbark Ave.
Chicago, IL 60637-1684
**Subject(s):** Sociology
**Circ:**  ‡6,700

**Camping Magazine  (10016)**
American Camping Association
5000 State Rd. 67 N.
Martinsville, IN 46151-7902
Phone: (765)342-8456
Fax: (765)342-2065
**Subject(s):** (Outdoors)
**Circ:**  (Non-paid)‡350
         (Paid)‡6,550

**Let's Play Softball  (16309)**
Let's Play Inc.
2721 E 42nd St.
Minneapolis, MN 55406
Phone: (612)729-0023
Fax: (612)729-0259
**Subject(s):** (Baseball); (General Sports)
**Circ:**  (Controlled)6,533

**Precision Manufacturing  (16486)**
Synergy Resource Group Inc.
3131 Fernbrook Ln., Ste. 111
Plymouth, MN 55447
Phone: (763)566-5999
Fax: (763)566-5780
**Subject(s):** Commerce and Industry; Machinery and Equipment
**Circ:**  (Non-paid)6,535

**American Journal of Neuroradiology  (9139)**
American Society of Neuroradiology
2210 Midwest Rd., Ste. 205
Oak Brook, IL 60523
Phone: (630)574-0220
Fax: (630)574-0661
**Subject(s):** Radiology, Ultrasound, and Nuclear Medicine
**Circ:**  6,500

**Bank Note Reporter  (33061)**
Krause Publications Inc.
700 E. State St.
Iola, WI 54990-0001
Phone: (715)445-2214
Fax: (715)445-4087
**Subject(s):** Collecting
**Circ:**  (Paid)‡6,509

**Builder Magazine, Uniform Series Edition  (8665)**
Herald Press
2840 Sheridan Rd.
Evanston, IL 60201
**Subject(s):** Religious Publications
**Circ:**  6,500

**CSSR Bulletin  (10209)**
Council of Societies for the Study of Religion
CSSR Executive Office
Valparaiso University
Valparaiso, IN 46383-6493
Phone: (219)464-5515
Fax: (219)464-6714
**Subject(s):** Religious Publications
**Circ:**  ‡6,500

**Dairy Goat Journal  (33671)**
Countryside Publications Ltd.
W11564 Hwy. 64
Withee, WI 54498
Phone: (715)785-7979
Fax: (715)785-7414
**Subject(s):** Livestock
**Circ:**  (Paid)6,500

**Engineering Journal  (8189)**
American Institute of Steel Construction Inc.
1 E. Wacker Dr., Ste. 3100
Chicago, IL 60601-2001
Phone: (312)670-2400
Fax: (312)670-5403
**Subject(s):** Engineering (Various branches)
**Circ:**  ‡6,500

**Evangelical Missions Quarterly (EMQ)** (9525)
EMIS
Wheaton College
500 College Ave.
PO Box 794
Wheaton, IL 60187
Phone: (630)752-7158
Fax: (630)752-7155
**Subject(s):** Religious Publications

**Circ:** ‡6,500

**The Restoration Herald** (24881)
Christian Restoration Association
7133 Central Parke Blvd.
Mason, OH 45040-7451
Phone: (513)229-8000
**Subject(s):** Religious Publications

**Circ:** ‡6,500

**World Coin News** (33104)
Krause Publications Inc.
700 E. State St.
Iola, WI 54990-0001
Phone: (715)445-2214
Fax: (715)445-4087
**Subject(s):** Collecting

**Circ:** (Paid)‡6,434

**American Journal of Veterinary Research** (9348)
American Veterinary Medical Association
1931 N Meacham Rd., Ste. 100
Schaumburg, IL 60173-4360
Phone: (847)925-8070
Fax: (847)925-9329
**Subject(s):** Veterinary Medicine

**Circ:** (Paid)6,400

**Genetic Epidemiology** (16513)
John Wiley and Sons Inc.
C/O Daniel J. Schaid, Section of Biostatistics, Harwick 7
200 First St., SW
Rochester, MN 55905
**Subject(s):** Genetics; Medicine and Surgery

**Circ:** 6,300

**Illinois Dental Journal** (9389)
Illinois State Dental Society
1010 S Second St.
PO Box 376
Springfield, IL 62705
Phone: (217)525-1406
Fax: (217)525-8872
**Subject(s):** Dentistry

**Circ:** (Controlled)‡6,300

**Journal of the Michigan Dental Association** (15510)
Michigan Dental Association
230 N Washington Ave., Ste. 208
Lansing, MI 48933
Phone: (517)372-9070
Fax: (517)372-0008
**Subject(s):** Dentistry

**Circ:** (Paid)6,300

**Applied Occupational & Environmental Hygiene** (24287)
Applied Industrial Hygiene Inc.
1330 Kemper Meadow Dr., Ste. 600
Cincinnati, OH 45240
Phone: (513)742-2020
Fax: (513)742-3355
**Subject(s):** Health and Healthcare; Commerce and Industry

**Circ:** (Non-paid)‡225
(Paid)‡6,278

**Economic Commentary** (24402)
Federal Reserve Bank of Cleveland
Human Resources
1455 E 6th
PO Box 6387
Cleveland, OH 44101
Phone: (216)579-2000
Fax: (216)579-3050
**Subject(s):** Economics

**Circ:** (Non-paid)‡6,200

**Collector** (16286)
ACA International
4040 W 70th St.
PO Box 390106
Minneapolis, MN 55439-0106
Phone: (952)926-6547
Fax: (952)926-1624
**Subject(s):** Business; Banking, Finance, and Investments

**Circ:** ‡6,100

**OAG Air Cargo Guide** (8606)
OAG Worldwide
3025 Highland Pkwy. Ste. 200
Downers Grove, IL 60515-5561
Phone: (630)515-5300
Fax: (630)515-5301
**Subject(s):** Transportation, Traffic, and Shipping

**Circ:** ‡6,029

**Annals of Allergy, Asthma, & Immunology** (16510)
American College of Allergy, Asthma, & Immunology
1948 Westfield Ct. SW
Rochester, MN 55902
Phone: (507)261-8251
**Subject(s):** Medicine and Surgery

**Circ:** (Non-paid)‡200
(Paid)‡6,000

**Business Ethics** (16279)
2845 Harriet Ave., Ste. 207
PO Box 8439
Minneapolis, MN 55408
Phone: (612)879-0695
Fax: (612)879-0699
**Subject(s):** Business

**Circ:** (Paid)5,000
(Non-paid)6,000

**Chamber Way Germany/Midwest** (8121)
German American Chamber of Commerce of the Midwest
401 N Michigan Ave., Ste. 3330
Chicago, IL 60611-4212
Phone: (312)644-2662
Fax: (312)644-0738
**Subject(s):** International Business and Economics; Chambers of Commerce and Boards of Trade

**Circ:** (Controlled)6,000

**The Clergy Journal** (16184)
6160 Carmen Ave. E
Inver Grove Heights, MN 55076
Phone: (651)451-9945
Fax: (651)457-4617
**Subject(s):** Religious Publications

**Circ:** (Paid)‡6,000

**IHRIM.LINK** (8011)
PSP Communications
705 W White St.
Champaign, IL 61820
Phone: (815)838-4591
Fax: (217)359-2744
**Subject(s):** Business

**Circ:** (Paid)5,000
(Non-paid)6,000

**Illinois Issues** (9391)
University of Illinois
PO Box 19243
Springfield, IL 62794-9243
Phone: (217)206-6084
Fax: (217)206-7257
**Subject(s):** State, Municipal, and County Administration

**Circ:** (Non-paid)‡500
(Paid)‡6,000

**The Illinois Manufacturer** (9392)
Illinois Manufacturers' Association
220 E. Adams St.
Springfield, IL 62701
Phone: (630)368-5300
Fax: (630)218-7467
**Subject(s):** Business

**Circ:** (Paid)6,000

**Illinois Parks & Recreation Magazine** (9395)
Illinois Association of Park Districts
211 E Monroe St.
Springfield, IL 62701-1186
Phone: (217)523-4554
Fax: (217)523-4273
**Subject(s):** Ecology and Conservation; Parks; Natural History and Nature Study; Health and Fitness

**Circ:** 6,000

**INFORM (International News on Fats, Oils and Related Materials)** (8013)
AOCS Press
PO Box 3489
Champaign, IL 61826-3489
**Subject(s):** Oils and Fats (Animal & Vegetable)

**Circ:** 6,000

**Microscopy and Microanalysis** (8336)
Microscopy Society of America
230 E Ohio St., Ste. 400
Chicago, IL 60611
Phone: (312)644-1527
Fax: (312)644-8557
**Subject(s):** Science (General); Engineering (Various branches)

**Circ:** 6,000

**Quaker Life** (10129)
Friends United Meeting
101 Quaker Hill Dr.
Richmond, IN 47374-1980
Phone: (765)962-7573
Fax: (765)966-1293
**Subject(s):** Religious Publications

**Circ:** 6,000

**Skin Inc.** (7983)
Allured Publishing Corp.
362 S. Schmale Rd.
Carol Stream, IL 60188-2787
Phone: (630)653-2155
Fax: (630)653-2192
**Subject(s):** Cosmetics and Toiletries; Health and Healthcare

**Circ:** (Controlled)‡3,401
(Paid)‡6,006

**Bioelectromagnetics** (33113)
John Wiley and Sons Inc.
C/O Ben Greenebaum, 900 Wood Rd., Box 2000
Kenosha, WI 53141-2000
**Subject(s):** Medicine and Surgery

**Circ:** (Paid)5,950

**Information Technology and Libraries** (8238)
Library and Information Technology Association
50 E. Huron St.
Chicago, IL 60611-2795
Phone: (312)280-4270
Fax: (312)280-3257
**Subject(s):** Library and Information Science

**Circ:** ‡5,794

**Card Trade** (33065)
Krause Publications Inc.
700 E. State St.
Iola, WI 54990-0001
Phone: (715)445-2214
Fax: (715)445-4087
**Subject(s):** Collecting; Sporting Goods/Retail Sports

**Circ:** (Combined)5,776

**Quarterly Journal of Speech** (16340)
National Communication Association
c/o Karlyn Kohrs Campbell
Department of Speech-Communication
225 Ford Hall, 224 Church St. S.E.
University of Minnesota
Minneapolis, MN 55455-0427
**Subject(s):** Communications; Education

**Circ:** (Non-paid)‡100
(Paid)‡5,695

**The Business to Business Marketer** (8113)
Business Marketing Association
400 N Michigan Ave., No. 1510
Chicago, IL 60611
Phone: (312)822-0005
Fax: (312)822-0054
**Subject(s):** Advertising and Marketing; Telecommunications

**Circ:** (Non-paid)‡5,600

**Molecular Reproduction and Development** (24168)
John Wiley and Sons Inc.
c/o Ralph B.L. Gwatkin, 25460 Bryden Rd.
Beachwood, OH 44122
**Subject(s):** Medicine and Surgery

**Circ:** (Paid)5,600

**Indiana Contractor** (9865)
Indiana Association of Plumbing Heating Cooling Contractors Inc.
9595 Whitley Dr., Ste. 208
Indianapolis, IN 46240
Phone: (317)575-9292
Fax: (317)575-9378
**Subject(s):** Air Conditioning and Refrigeration; Plumbing and Heating

**Circ:** (Controlled)‡5,579

**Bulletin of the Detroit Institute of Arts** (15169)
Detroit Institute of Arts
5200 Woodward Ave.
Detroit, MI 48202
Phone: (313)833-7900
Fax: (313)833-0343
Subject(s): Art and Art History; Museums
Circ: (Combined)5,500

**Journal of Forensic Identification (JFI)** (16267)
International Association for Identification
2535 Pilot Knob Rd., Ste. 117
Mendota Heights, MN 55120-1120
Phone: (651)681-8566
Fax: (651)681-8443
Subject(s): Medicine and Surgery; Police, Penology, and Penal Institutions
Circ: (Combined)5,500

**Midwest Retailer** (15971)
8528 Columbus Ave. S
Bloomington, MN 55420-2460
Phone: (952)854-7610
Fax: (952)854-6460
Subject(s): Flooring and Floor Covering
Circ: (Non-paid)‡5,500

**Ohio Contractor** (24579)
TRIAD
6525 Busch Blvd.
Columbus, OH 43229
Phone: (614)846-8761
Fax: (614)846-8763
Subject(s): Roads and Streets; Construction, Contracting, Building, and Excavating
Circ: (Paid)‡850
(Non-paid)‡5,500

**Ohio Record** (24586)
Ohio Bankers League
37 W Broad St., Ste. 1001
Columbus, OH 43215-4195
Phone: (614)221-5121
Fax: (614)221-3421
Subject(s): Banking, Finance, and Investments
Circ: (Controlled)5,500

**Vision Magazine** (8441)
University of Illinois at Chicago
College of Dentistry
801 S Paulina St.
M/C 621
Chicago, IL 60612-7211
Phone: (312)996-8495
Fax: (312)413-2927
Subject(s): College Publications
Circ: (Non-paid)5,500

**Railway Track & Structures** (8390)
Simmons-Boardman Publishing Corp.
222 S. Riverside Plaza, Ste. 1870
Chicago, IL 60606
Phone: (312)466-1870
Fax: (312)446-1055
Subject(s): Railroad
Circ: (Controlled)3,048
(Paid)5,452

**Current Anthropology** (8167)
University of Chicago Press
1427 E. 60th St.
Chicago, IL 60637
Phone: (773)702-7700
Fax: (773)702-9756
Subject(s): Anthropology and Ethnology
Circ: ‡5,300

**The Joint Commission Journal on Quality Improvement** (9176)
1 Renaissance Blvd.
Oakbrook Terrace, IL 60181
Phone: (630)792-5453
Fax: (630)792-4453
Subject(s): Health and Healthcare
Circ: ‡5,300

**OAG Pocket Flight Guide - Pacific Asia Edition** (8607)
OAG Worldwide
3025 Highland Pkwy. Ste. 200
Downers Grove, IL 60515-5561
Phone: (630)515-5300
Fax: (630)515-5301
Subject(s): Travel and Tourism
Circ: (Non-paid)‡996
(Paid)‡5,303

**The Big Reel** (33062)
Krause Publications Inc.
700 E. State St.
Iola, WI 54990-0001
Phone: (715)445-2214
Fax: (715)445-4087
Subject(s): Motion Pictures
Circ: (Paid)‡5,256

**Library Administration & Management** (8300)
American Library Association
50 E. Huron St.
Chicago, IL 60611
Phone: (312)944-7298
Fax: (312)280-4380
Subject(s): Library and Information Science
Circ: (Paid)‡5,250

**The Urban Lawyer** (8436)
American Bar Association
321 N Clark St.
Chicago, IL 60610
Phone: (312)988-5000
Fax: (312)988-5177
Subject(s): Law
Circ: (Non-paid)150
(Paid)5,250

**Bloodlines** (15464)
United Kennel Club Inc.
100 E Kilgore Rd.
Kalamazoo, MI 49002-5584
Phone: (269)343-9020
Fax: (269)343-7037
Subject(s): Dogs
Circ: (Non-paid)‡190
(Paid)‡5,200

**Cleveland Bar Journal** (24387)
Cleveland Bar Association
1301 E. Ninth St.
Second Level
Cleveland, OH 44144-1253
Phone: (216)696-3525
Fax: (216)696-2413
Subject(s): Law
Circ: (Controlled)5,200

**Illinois Beef** (9388)
Illinois Beef Association
2060 W Iles Ave., Ste. B
Springfield, IL 62704
Phone: (217)787-4280
Fax: (217)793-3605
Subject(s): Livestock
Circ: (Controlled)‡5,200

**Presidents & Prime Ministers** (8733)
President & Prime Ministers
799 Roosevelt Rd., Bldg. 6, Ste. 208
Glen Ellyn, IL 60137
Phone: (630)858-6161
Fax: (630)858-8787
Subject(s): Social and Political Issues
Circ: (Paid)270
(Non-paid)5,200

**The DIAPASON** (8580)
Scranton Gillette Communications Inc.
380 NW Hwy., Ste. 200
Des Plaines, IL 60016-2282
Phone: (847)391-1000
Fax: (847)390-0408
Subject(s): Music and Musical Instruments
Circ: ‡5,100

**Journalism and Mass Communication Quarterly** (24148)
Association for Education in Journalism & Mass Communication
c/o Dan Riffe, Editor
Ohio Univ.
Scripps School of Journalism
Athens, OH 45701
Phone: (740)593-2590
Subject(s): Journalism and Publishing
Circ: ‡5,096

**AALL Spectrum** (8051)
American Association of Law Libraries
53 W Jackson Blvd., Ste. 940
Chicago, IL 60604
Phone: (312)939-4764
Fax: (312)431-1097
Subject(s): Law; Library and Information Science
Circ: 5,000

**AIDS Book Review Journal** (8059)
University of Illinois at Chicago
PO Box 8198
Chicago, IL 60680-8198
Phone: (312)996-2716
Fax: (312)413-0424
Subject(s): Health and Healthcare
Circ: (Non-paid)5,000

**Alamal Magazine** (15708)
Muslim Arab Youth Association
PO Box 1476
Royal Oak, MI 48068
Phone: (248)582-3210
Fax: (248)582-3211
Subject(s): Youths' Interests; Ethnic Publications
Circ: 5,000

**American Experiment Quarterly** (16270)
Center of the American Experiment
c/o Dr. Mitchell B. Pearlstein
1024 Plymouth Bldg.
12 S 6th St.
Minneapolis, MN 55402
Phone: (612)338-3605
Fax: (612)338-3621
Subject(s): Social and Political Issues; Politics
Circ: 5,000

**Automotive Fine Art Journal** (15502)
Bort Productions
PO Box 325
Lake Orion, MI 48361-0325
Phone: (248)814-0627
Fax: (248)814-0627
Subject(s): Automotive (Consumer)
Circ: 5,000

**Biology of Reproduction** (33160)
Society for the Study of Reproduction
1619 Monroe St.
Madison, WI 53711-2063
Phone: (608)256-2777
Fax: (608)256-4610
Subject(s): Biology
Circ: (Controlled)5,000

**Borba** (8104)
Bulgarian National Front
PO Box 46250
Chicago, IL 60646
Phone: (847)692-5460
Fax: (847)692-5460
Subject(s): Ethnic Publications; Bulgarian
Circ: 5,000

**The Bulletin of the Center for Children's Books** (8005)
Graduate School of Library and Information Sciences
University of Illinois, Urbana-Champaign
501 E. Daniel St.
MC-493
Champaign, IL 61820
Phone: (217)244-0324
Fax: (217)333-5603
Subject(s): Book Trade and Author News; Children's Interests
Circ: 5000

**Candy Industry** (8546)
Stagnito Communications Inc.
155 Pfingsten Rd., Ste. 205
Deerfield, IL 60015
Phone: (847)205-5660
Fax: (847)205-5680
Subject(s): Confectionaries and Frozen Dairy Products
Circ: (Paid)1,197
(Non-paid)5,003

**Electronic Distribution Today** (25016)
Custom Media Inc.
PO Box 1676
Powell, OH 43065
Phone: (614)985-4684
Fax: (614)985-4685
Subject(s): Selling and Salesmanship
Circ: 5,000

**Executive Housekeeping Today  (25157)**
International Executive Housekeepers Association Inc.
1001 Eastwind Dr., Ste. 301
Westerville, OH 43081-3361
Phone: (614)895-7166
Fax: (614)895-1248
**Subject(s):** Building Management and Maintenance
**Circ:** (Non-paid)‡168
  (Paid)‡5,000

**Family Relations  (16294)**
National Council on Family Relations
3989 Central Ave. NE, Ste. 550
Minneapolis, MN 55421
Phone: (763)781-9331
Fax: (763)781-9348
**Subject(s):** Sociology; Marriage and Family
**Circ:** ‡5,000

**Fifth Estate  (15282)**
PO Box 201016
Ferndale, MI 48220-1016
Phone: (615)526-5999
**Subject(s):** Environmental and Natural Resources Conservation; Social and Political Issues
**Circ:** (Paid)5,000

**Forensic Quarterly  (9851)**
National Federation of State High School Associations (NFHS)
PO Box 690
Indianapolis, IN 46206
Phone: (317)972-6900
Fax: (317)822-5700
**Subject(s):** Education; Youths' Interests
**Circ:** (Paid)5000

**Forging  (24412)**
Penton Media Inc.
1300 E. 9th St.
Cleveland, OH 44114-1530
Phone: (216)696-7000
Fax: (216)696-1752
**Subject(s):** Metal, Metallurgy, and Metal Trade
**Circ:** (Combined)5,000

**Gases & Welding Distributor  (24415)**
Penton Media Inc.
1300 E. 9th St.
Cleveland, OH 44114-1530
Phone: (216)696-7000
Fax: (216)696-1752
**Subject(s):** Welding
**Circ:** (Paid)668
  (Non-paid)5,000

**The Gun Report  (7825)**
World Wide Gun Report Inc.
110 S College
PO Box 38
Aledo, IL 61231
Phone: (309)582-5311
Fax: (309)582-5555
**Subject(s):** Firearms
**Circ:** ‡5,000

**Hunting Retriever  (15470)**
United Kennel Club Inc.
100 E Kilgore Rd.
Kalamazoo, MI 49002-5584
Phone: (269)343-9020
Fax: (269)343-7037
**Subject(s):** Dogs
**Circ:** (Non-paid)50
  (Paid)5,000

**Journal of the IEST  (9321)**
Institute of Environmental Sciences and Technology
5005 Newport Dr., Ste. 506
Rolling Meadows, IL 60008-3841
Phone: (847)255-1561
Fax: (847)255-1699
**Subject(s):** Electronics Engineering
**Circ:** ‡5,000

**Journal of Irreproducible Results  (8499)**
JIR Publishers
PO Box 234
Chicago Heights, IL 60411
Phone: (650)573-7125
**Subject(s):** Medicine and Surgery; Nursing
**Circ:** ‡5,000

**The Journal for Quality and Participation  (33305)**
American Society for Quality
PO Box 3005
Milwaukee, WI 53201-3005
Phone: (414)272-8575
Fax: (414)272-1734
**Subject(s):** Management and Administration
**Circ:** ‡5,000

**Journal of School Health  (24807)**
American School Health Association
7263 State, Rte. 43
PO Box 708
Kent, OH 44240
Phone: (330)678-1601
Fax: (330)678-4526
**Subject(s):** Health and Healthcare
**Circ:** 5,000

**Management Science  (8677)**
The Institute for Operations Research and the Management Sciences
c/o Prof.Wallace J. Hopp,Editor-In-Chief /
Northwestern Univ.
Dept. Of Industrial Engineering And Management Science
Evanston, IL 60208-3119
Phone: (847)491-4169
Fax: (847)491-8005
**Subject(s):** Business; Management and Administration
**Circ:** (Paid)5,000

**Marine Textiles  (16592)**
RCM Enterprises Inc.
2233 University Ave. W, Ste. 410
Saint Paul, MN 55114-1629
Fax: (612)473-7068
**Subject(s):** Textiles; Boats and Marine
**Circ:** (Paid)‡3,000
  (Non-paid)‡5,000

**The Modern Language Journal  (33202)**
National Federation of Modern Language Teachers Associations
618 Van Hise Hall
1220 Linden Dr.
Madison, WI 53706-1558
Phone: (608)262-5010
Fax: (608)265-4672
**Subject(s):** Philology, Language, and Linguistics
**Circ:** (Controlled)‡74
  (Paid)‡5,000

**Palaestra  (8921)**
Challenge Publications Ltd.
PO Box 508
Macomb, IL 61455
Phone: (309)833-1902
Fax: (309)833-1902
**Subject(s):** Physical Education and Athletics; Handicapped
**Circ:** (Combined)‡5000

**Pension Plan Guide  (8371)**
CCH Inc.
4025 W. Peterson Ave.
Chicago, IL 60646-6085
Phone: (847)267-7000
Fax: (773)866-3895
**Subject(s):** Employment and Human Resources
**Circ:** ‡5,000

**Propeller Magazine  (15255)**
American Power Boat Association
17640 E. 9 Mile Rd.
Eastpointe, MI 48021-0377
Phone: (586)773-9700
Fax: (586)773-6490
**Subject(s):** (Boating and Yachting)
**Circ:** ‡5,000

**Research in the Teaching of English (RTE)  (9488)**
National Council of Teachers of English
1111 W. Kenyon Rd.
Urbana, IL 61801-1096
Phone: (217)328-3870
Fax: (217)328-9645
**Subject(s):** Education
**Circ:** (Paid)5,000

**S Gaugian  (8699)**
Heimburger House Publishing Co.
7236 W Madison St.
Forest Park, IL 60130
Phone: (708)366-1973
Fax: (708)366-1973
**Subject(s):** Crafts, Models, Hobbies, and Contests
**Circ:** ‡5,000

**Upholstery Journal  (16614)**
RCM Enterprises Inc.
2233 University Ave. W, Ste. 410
Saint Paul, MN 55114-1629
Fax: (612)473-7068
**Subject(s):** Furniture and Furnishings
**Circ:** (Paid)3,000
  (Non-paid)5,000

**Ward's Automotive Yearbook  (15786)**
Ward's Communications
3000 Town Ctr., Ste. 2750
Southfield, MI 48075-1212
Phone: (248)357-0800
Fax: (248)357-0810
**Subject(s):** Automotive (Trade)
**Circ:** (Paid)5,000

**Wisconsin West Magazine  (32928)**
Modern Communications Inc.
2905 Seymour Rd.
Eau Claire, WI 54703
Phone: (715)835-3800
Fax: (715)835-3958
**Subject(s):** Local, State, and Regional Publications; Lifestyle
**Circ:** (Combined)5,000

**Worship  (16019)**
The Liturgical Press
St. John's Abbey
PO Box 7500
Collegeville, MN 56321-7500
Phone: (320)363-2213
Fax: (800)445-5899
**Subject(s):** Religious Publications
**Circ:** 5,000

**Zacks Analyst Watch  (8448)**
Zacks Investment Research
155 N. Wacker Dr.
Chicago, IL 60606
Phone: (312)630-9880
Fax: (312)630-9898
**Subject(s):** Business
**Circ:** (Paid)500

**American Association of Neurological Surgeons Bulletin  (9320)**
American Association of Neurological Surgeons
5550 Meadowbrook Dr.
Rolling Meadows, IL 60008
Phone: (847)378-0500
Fax: (847)378-0600
**Subject(s):** Medicine and Surgery; Health and Healthcare
**Circ:** 4,976

**Nursing Outlook  (9900)**
Mosby Inc.
c/o Marion E. Broome, Editor
Professor and University Dean
School of Nursing, Indiana University
1111 Middle Dr., NU 132
Indianapolis, IN 46202-5107
Phone: (317)274-1486
Fax: (317)278-1842
**Subject(s):** Nursing
**Circ:** (Paid)‡4,881

**Milk & Liquid Food Transporter  (32809)**
Glen Street Publications Inc.
W4652 Glen St.
Appleton, WI 54913-9563
Phone: (920)749-4880
Fax: (920)749-4877
**Subject(s):** Milk and Dairy Products; Transportation, Traffic, and Shipping
**Circ:** (Controlled)4,812

**American Musicology Society Journal  (10083)**
American Musicological Society Inc.
c/o Paula Higgins, Editor
University of Notre Dame
Dept. Of Music
Notre Dame, IN 46556
Phone: (219)631-5139
Fax: (219)631-8609
**Subject(s):** Music and Musical Instruments
**Circ:** (Combined)4,800

Circulation: ★ = ABC; △ = BPA; ♦ = CAC; ● = CCAB; ☐ = VAC; ⊕ = PO Statement; ‡ = Publisher's Report; Boldface figures = sworn; Light figures = estimated.

# Great Lakes States

**The Antioch Review** (25203)
Box 148
Yellow Springs, OH 45387
Phone: (937)769-1365
**Subject(s):** Literature and Literary Reviews
**Circ:** ‡4,800

**Dawn** (8169)
Slovenian Women's Union of America/Slovenska Zenska Zveza Ameriki
4851 S. Drexel Blvd.
Chicago, IL 60615
Phone: (773)548-8878
Fax: (773)268-4899
**Subject(s):** Slovene; Ethnic Publications
**Circ:** (Controlled)‡25
(Paid)‡4,800

**Diseases of the Colon and Rectum** (16511)
Lippincott Williams & Wilkins
211 S. Broadway
Ste. Kb-2-21A
Rochester, MN 55904
Phone: (507)284-0713
Fax: (507)284-0713
**Subject(s):** Medicine and Surgery
**Circ:** (Non-paid)730
(Paid)4,809

**Movie Collector's World** (15306)
Arena Publishing Co.
PO Box 309
Fraser, MI 48026
Phone: (586)774-4311
**Subject(s):** Motion Pictures
**Circ:** (Controlled)‡200
(Paid)‡4,800

**RITE** (8400)
Liturgy Training Publications
1800 N Hermitage Ave.
Chicago, IL 60622-1101
Phone: (773)486-8970
Fax: (773)486-7094
**Subject(s):** Religious Publications
**Circ:** (Non-paid)‡2,000
(Paid)‡4,800

**Detroit Labor News** (15177)
Metropolitan Detroit AFL-CIO
600 W Lafayette, Ste. 200
Detroit, MI 48226
Phone: (313)961-0800
**Subject(s):** Labor
**Circ:** (Non-paid)⊕100
(Paid)⊕4,770

**Art Therapy** (9027)
1202 Allanson Rd.
Mundelein, IL 60060-3808
Phone: (847)949-6064
Fax: (847)566-4580
**Subject(s):** Art and Art History
**Circ:** 4,700

**The Elementary School Journal** (8186)
University of Chicago Press
1427 E. 60th St.
Chicago, IL 60637
Phone: (773)702-7700
Fax: (773)702-9756
**Subject(s):** Education
**Circ:** ‡4,700

**Statistical Science** (24171)
Institute of Mathematical Statistics
PO Box 22718
Beachwood, OH 44122
Phone: (216)295-2340
Fax: (216)295-5661
**Subject(s):** Statistics
**Circ:** (Paid)4,700

**Industrial Fabric Products Review** (16537)
Industrial Fabrics Association International
1801 County Road B W
Roseville, MN 55113
Phone: (651)222-2508
Fax: (651)631-9334
**Subject(s):** Textiles
**Circ:** (Controlled)1,911
(Paid)3,437
(Non-paid)4,652

**Credit Union Management** (33167)
Credit Union Executives Society
5510 Research Park Dr.
Madison, WI 53711-5377
Phone: (608)271-2664
Fax: (608)271-2303
**Subject(s):** Banking, Finance, and Investments; Management and Administration
**Circ:** (Non-paid)272
(Paid)4,640

**Gun & Knife Show Calendar** (33081)
Krause Publications Inc.
700 E. State St.
Iola, WI 54990-0001
Phone: (715)445-2214
Fax: (715)445-4087
**Subject(s):** Firearms
**Circ:** (Paid)‡4,648

**The American Archivist** (8063)
Society of American Archivists
527 S Wells St., 5th Fl.
Chicago, IL 60607-3922
Phone: (312)922-0140
Fax: (312)347-1452
**Subject(s):** Library and Information Science; History and Genealogy
**Circ:** 4,634

**Applied Physics Letters** (7845)
American Institute of Physics
c/o Nghi Q. Lam, Editor, Applied Physics Letters
Argonne National Laboratory
Bldg. 203, Rm. R-127, 9700 S. Cass Ave.
PO Box 8296
Argonne, IL 60439-4871
Phone: (630)252-4200
Fax: (630)252-4973
**Subject(s):** Physics
**Circ:** 4,600

**On Premise** (33207)
Tavern League of Wisconsin
2817 Fish Hatchery Rd.
Madison, WI 53713
Phone: (608)270-8591
Fax: (608)270-8595
**Subject(s):** Hotels, Motels, Restaurants, and Clubs
**Circ:** (Controlled)400
(Paid)4,600

**Advances in Wound Care** (7870)
Spring House
434 W Downer Pl.
Aurora, IL 60506
**Subject(s):** Health and Healthcare
**Circ:** (Non-paid)‡2,000
(Paid)‡4,500

**Crop Science** (33170)
Crop Science Society of America
677 S Segoe Rd.
Madison, WI 53711
Phone: (608)273-8080
Fax: (608)273-2021
**Subject(s):** Scientific Agricultural Publications; Science (General)
**Circ:** ‡4,500

**Finer Points Magazine** (24550)
Industrial Diamond Association of America
PO Box 29460
Columbus, OH 43229
Phone: (614)797-2265
Fax: (614)797-2264
**Subject(s):** Commerce and Industry; Machinery and Equipment
**Circ:** (Controlled)4,500

**Fireplug** (15815)
Michigan State Firemen's Association
9001 Miller Rd., Ste. 10
PO Box 405
Swartz Creek, MI 48473-0405
Phone: (810)635-9513
Fax: (810)635-2858
**Subject(s):** Fire Fighting
**Circ:** 4,500

**Journal of the American Academy of Tropical Medicine** (15182)
American Academy of Tropical Medicine
PO Box 24224
Detroit, MI 48224
Phone: (313)882-0641
Fax: (313)882-0979
**Subject(s):** Medicine and Surgery; Health and Healthcare
**Circ:** 4,500

**The Kenyon Review** (24743)
Kenyon College
104 College Dr.
Gambier, OH 43022-9623
Phone: (740)427-5000
Fax: (740)427-5417
**Subject(s):** Literature and Literary Reviews
**Circ:** ‡4,500

**National Bus Trader** (9251)
National Bus Trader Inc.
9698 W Judson Rd.
Polo, IL 61064-9015
Phone: (815)946-2341
Fax: (815)946-2347
**Subject(s):** Travel and Tourism
**Circ:** (Paid)4,500

**Ohio Tavern News** (24591)
The Daily Reporter Inc.
580 S High St., S-316
Columbus, OH 43215
Phone: (614)224-4835
Fax: (614)224-8649
**Subject(s):** Hotels, Motels, Restaurants, and Clubs
**Circ:** (Paid)‡4,000
(Controlled)‡4,500

**The Pope Speaks** (9809)
Our Sunday Visitor Publishing
200 Noll Plz.
Huntington, IN 46750
Phone: (260)356-8400
Fax: (260)356-8472
**Subject(s):** Religious Publications
**Circ:** (Combined)4,500

**Seedstock Edge** (10252)
National Swine Registry
1769 US Hwy. 52 W
PO Box 2417
West Lafayette, IN 47996-2417
Phone: (765)463-3594
Fax: (765)497-2959
**Subject(s):** Livestock
**Circ:** (Non-paid)250
(Paid)4,500

**Soil Science Society of America Journal** (33212)
Soil Science Society of America
677 S Segoe Rd.
Madison, WI 53711-1086
Phone: (608)273-8080
Fax: (608)273-2021
**Subject(s):** Scientific Agricultural Publications; Science (General)
**Circ:** ‡4,500

**CAM Magazine** (15072)
Construction Association of Michigan
43636 Woodward Ave.
PO Box 3204
Bloomfield Hills, MI 48302-3204
Phone: (248)972-1000
Fax: (248)972-1001
**Subject(s):** Construction, Contracting, Building, and Excavating
**Circ:** (Non-paid)389
(Paid)4,461

**Comics & Games Retailer** (33071)
Krause Publications Inc.
700 E. State St.
Iola, WI 54990-0001
Phone: (715)445-2214
Fax: (715)445-4087
**Subject(s):** Selling and Salesmanship; Book Trade and Author News; Comics and Comic Technique
**Circ:** (Non-paid)‡4,434

**The American Journal of Human Genetics** (8070)
University of Chicago Press
1427 E. 60th St.
Chicago, IL 60637
Phone: (773)702-7700

Fax: (773)702-9756
**Subject(s):** Genetics
**Circ:** ‡4,400

**Journal of the Medical Library Association (8281)**
Medical Library Association
65 E Wacker Pl., Ste. 1900
Chicago, IL 60601-7298
Phone: (312)419-9094
Fax: (312)419-8950
**Subject(s):** Library and Information Science; Health and Healthcare; Education
**Circ:** (Paid)‡300
(Non-paid)‡4,400

**Model Retailer (33613)**
Kalmbach Publishing Co.
PO Box 1612
Waukesha, WI 53187-1612
Phone: (262)796-8776
Fax: (262)796-1615
**Subject(s):** Gifts, Toys, and Novelties; Crafts, Models, Hobbies, and Contests; Games and Puzzles
**Circ:** (Paid)★4,320

**The Annals of Statistics (16272)**
Institute of Mathematical Statistics
School of Statistics
Ford 313, 224 Church St. S.E.
Univ. of Minnesota
Minneapolis, MN 55455
**Subject(s):** Statistics
**Circ:** ‡4,300

**Equipment Echoes (24202)**
Historical Construction Equipment Association
16623 Liberty Hi Rd.
Bowling Green, OH 43402
Phone: (419)352-5616
Fax: (419)352-6086
**Subject(s):** History and Genealogy; Construction, Contracting, Building, and Excavating; Mining and Minerals
**Circ:** (Paid)4,300

**Journal of Healthcare Risk Management (8275)**
American Society for Healthcare Risk Management
One N Franklin
Chicago, IL 60606
Phone: (312)422-3980
Fax: (312)422-4580
**Subject(s):** Health and Healthcare; Hospitals and Healthcare Institutions
**Circ:** (Paid)4,300

**The Mississippi Rag (16326)**
The Mississippi Rag Inc.
9448 Lyndale Ave. S, No. 120
Minneapolis, MN 55420
Phone: (952)885-9918
Fax: (952)885-9943
**Subject(s):** Music and Musical Instruments
**Circ:** (Paid)‡4,300

**Cereal Foods World (16573)**
AACC International
3340 Pilot Knob Rd.
Saint Paul, MN 55121
Phone: (651)454-7250
Fax: (651)454-0766
**Subject(s):** Chemistry, Chemicals, and Chemical Engineering; Food and Grocery Trade
**Circ:** (Controlled)‡303
(Paid)‡4,231

**Critical Inquiry (8166)**
University of Chicago Press
University of Chicago
Wieboldt Hall 202
1050 E. 59th St.
Chicago, IL 60637
Phone: (773)702-8477
Fax: (773)702-3397
**Subject(s):** Humanities
**Circ:** ‡4,200

**Lutheran Education Journal (9276)**
7400 Augusta St.
River Forest, IL 60305-1499
Phone: (708)771-8300
Fax: (708)209-3176
**Subject(s):** Religious Publications; Education
**Circ:** ‡4,200

**Triad (15652)**
Michigan Osteopathic Association
2445 Woodlake Cir.
Okemos, MI 48864-5941
Phone: (517)347-1555
Fax: (517)347-1566
**Subject(s):** Medicine and Surgery
**Circ:** (Paid)⊕**4,200**

**Wisconsin Restaurateur (33228)**
Wisconsin Restaurant Association
2801 Fish Hatchery Rd.
Madison, WI 53713-3120
Phone: (608)270-9950
Fax: (608)251-3666
**Subject(s):** Hotels, Motels, Restaurants, and Clubs
**Circ:** ‡4,200

**American Academy of Osteopathy—Quarterly Journal (9811)**
American Academy of Osteopathy
3500 DePauw Blvd., Ste. 1080
Indianapolis, IN 46268
Phone: (317)879-1881
Fax: (317)879-0563
**Subject(s):** Medicine and Surgery; Health and Healthcare
**Circ:** 4,100

**The Battery Man (8098)**
Battery Council International
401 N. Michigan Ave., 24th Fl.
Chicago, IL 60611-4267
Phone: (312)644-6610
Fax: (312)527-6640
**Subject(s):** Electrical Engineering
**Circ:** 4,100

**Catechumenate: A Journal of Christian Initiation (8117)**
Liturgy Training Publications
1800 N Hermitage Ave.
Chicago, IL 60622-1101
Phone: (773)486-8970
Fax: (773)486-7094
**Subject(s):** Religious Publications
**Circ:** (Non-paid)175
(Paid)4,100

**International Journal of Orthodontics (33303)**
International Association for Orthodontics
750 N. Lincoln Memorial Dr., Ste. 422
Milwaukee, WI 53202
Phone: (414)272-2757
Fax: (414)272-2754
**Subject(s):** Dentistry
**Circ:** (Paid)⊕**4,100**

**The Journal of Business (8265)**
University of Chicago Press
1427 E. 60th St.
Chicago, IL 60637
Phone: (773)702-7700
Fax: (773)702-9756
**Subject(s):** Business
**Circ:** ‡4,100

**Sleep (9522)**
American Academy of Sleep Medicine
1 Westbrook Corporate Ctr., Ste. 920
Westchester, IL 60154-5767
Phone: (708)492-0930
Fax: (708)492-0943
**Subject(s):** Health and Healthcare
**Circ:** (Paid)4,051

**Aim–America's Intercultural Magazine (8947)**
Aim Publications
PO Box 1174
Maywood, IL 60153
Phone: (708)344-4414
**Subject(s):** Intercultural Interests; General Editorial
**Circ:** (Controlled)‡3,000
(Paid)‡4,000

**American Journal of Clinical Hypnosis (7912)**
American Society of Clinical Hypnosis
140 N Bloomingdale Rd.
Bloomingdale, IL 60108-1017
Phone: (630)980-4740
Fax: (630)351-8400
**Subject(s):** Psychology and Psychiatry; Health and Healthcare
**Circ:** 4,000

**Architecture Minnesota (16274)**
275 Market St., Ste. 54
Minneapolis, MN 55405-1621
Phone: (612)338-6763
Fax: (612)338-7981
**Subject(s):** Architecture; Local, State, and Regional Publications
**Circ:** (Paid)‡3,000
(Controlled)‡4,000

**The Chicago Reporter (8135)**
Community Renewal Society
332 S. Michigan Ave., Ste. 500
Chicago, IL 60604
Phone: (312)427-4830
Fax: (312)427-6130
**Subject(s):** Social and Political Issues
**Circ:** (Paid)1,500
(Non-paid)4,000

**Clarion (33163)**
Madison Area Technical College
3550 Anderson St.
Madison, WI 53704
Phone: (608)246-6100
Fax: (608)246-6880
**Subject(s):** College Publications
**Circ:** (Non-paid)4,000

**The Columbian (9840)**
The Columbia Club
121 Monument Cir.
Indianapolis, IN 46204
Phone: (317)767-1361
Fax: (317)638-3137
**Subject(s):** Clubs and Societies
**Circ:** ‡4,000

**Computer Listing Service's Machinery & Equipment Guide (9369)**
Wineberg Publications
7842 N Lincoln Ave.
Skokie, IL 60077
Phone: (847)676-1900
Fax: (847)676-0063
**Subject(s):** Commerce and Industry; Machinery and Equipment
**Circ:** (Non-paid)‡4,000

**Construction Equipment Distribution (9145)**
Associated Equipment Distributors
615 W. 22nd St.
Oak Brook, IL 60523
Phone: (630)574-0650
Fax: (630)574-0132
**Subject(s):** Construction, Contracting, Building, and Excavating
**Circ:** ‡4,000

**The Corporate Board (15650)**
Vanguard Publications Inc.
4440 Hagadorn Rd.
Okemos, MI 48864
Phone: (517)336-1700
Fax: (517)336-1705
**Subject(s):** Management and Administration
**Circ:** ‡4,000

**Employee Services Management (8644)**
ESM Association
568 Spring Rd., Ste. D
Elmhurst, IL 60126-3896
Phone: (630)559-0020
Fax: (630)559-0025
**Subject(s):** Health and Healthcare; Employment and Human Resources
**Circ:** (Non-paid)‡600
(Paid)‡4,000

**Energy Journal (24408)**
International Association for Energy Economics
28790 Chagrin Blvd., Ste. 350
Cleveland, OH 44122
Phone: (216)464-5365
Fax: (216)464-2737
**Subject(s):** Ecology and Conservation; Power and Power Plants; Electrical Engineering
**Circ:** (Controlled)4,000

**Engineering Minnesota (16291)**
Meusey Communications
1107 Hazeltine Blvd., Ste. 539
Chaska, MN 55318-1008
Phone: (952)368-4100
Fax: (952)474-7850

**Subject(s):** Engineering (Various branches)
**Circ:** (Non-paid)‡4,000

**Federal Communications Law Journal (9588)**
Federal Communications Bar Association
Federal Communications Law Journal
Indiana University School of Law
211 S. Indiana Ave.
Bloomington, IN 47405-1001
Phone: (812)855-5952
Fax: (812)855-0555
**Subject(s):** Law; Communications
**Circ:** (Paid)‡4,000

**Hoosier Banker (9855)**
Indiana Bankers Association
3135 N Meridian St.
Indianapolis, IN 46208-4717
Phone: (317)921-3135
Fax: (317)921-3131
**Subject(s):** Banking, Finance, and Investments
**Circ:** ‡4,000

**Illinois Technograph (8012)**
Illini Media Co.
57 E. Green St.
Champaign, IL 61820
Phone: (217)333-3733
Fax: (217)244-6616
**Subject(s):** Engineering (Various branches)
**Circ:** (Paid)‡800
(Non-paid)‡4,000

**The Journal of Higher Education (24561)**
The Ohio State University Press
1070 Carmack Rd.
Columbus, OH 43210-1002
Phone: (614)292-6930
Fax: (614)292-2065
**Subject(s):** Education
**Circ:** ‡4,000

**The Journal of Modern History (8282)**
University of Chicago Press
1427 E. 60th St.
Chicago, IL 60637
Phone: (773)702-7700
Fax: (773)702-9756
**Subject(s):** History and Genealogy
**Circ:** ‡4,000

**Journal of Money, Credit, and Banking (24562)**
The Ohio State University Press
1070 Carmack Rd.
Columbus, OH 43210-1002
Phone: (614)292-6930
Fax: (614)292-2065
**Subject(s):** Banking, Finance, and Investments
**Circ:** ‡4,000

**The New Age Citizen (15158)**
New Age Citizen
PO Box 419
Dearborn Heights, MI 48127
Phone: (313)563-3192
Fax: (313)563-3192
**Subject(s):** Social and Political Issues
**Circ:** (Paid)300
(Non-paid)4,000

**New Rules Journal (16330)**
The Institute for Local Self-Reliance
1313 5th St. SE
Minneapolis, MN 55414
Phone: (612)379-3815
Fax: (612)379-3920
**Subject(s):** Social Programs; Politics
**Circ:** (Paid)4,000

**Out Your Backdoor (15898)**
4686 Meridian Rd.
Williamston, MI 48895
Phone: (517)347-1689
Fax: (517)347-7884
**Subject(s):** (Bicycling); (General Sports); (Outdoors); Crafts, Models, Hobbies, and Contests
**Circ:** (Paid)1,000
(Non-paid)4,000

**Plant Disease (16609)**
The American Phytopathological Society
3340 Pilot Knob Rd.
Saint Paul, MN 55121
Phone: (651)454-7250
Fax: (651)454-0766

**Subject(s):** Horticulture; Botany
**Circ:** (Non-paid)‡31
(Paid)‡4,000

**Sheep! Magazine (33672)**
Countryside Publications Ltd.
W11564 Hwy. 64
Withee, WI 54498
Phone: (715)785-7979
Fax: (715)785-7414
**Subject(s):** Livestock
**Circ:** (Paid)4,000

**Spotted News (9221)**
National Spotted Swine Record Inc.
PO Box 9758
Peoria, IL 61612
Phone: (309)691-0151
Fax: (309)691-0168
**Subject(s):** Livestock
**Circ:** (Non-paid)‡3,000
(Paid)‡4,000

**Teaching Theatre (24338)**
Educational Theatre Association
2343 Auburn Ave.
Cincinnati, OH 45219
Phone: (513)421-3900
Fax: (513)421-7077
**Subject(s):** Education; Drama and Theatre
**Circ:** 4,000

**Velocity (8438)**
Strategic Account Management Association (SAMA)
150 N. Wacker Dr., Ste. 2222
Chicago, IL 60606
Phone: (312)251-3131
Fax: (312)251-3132
**Subject(s):** Advertising and Marketing; Selling and Salesmanship
**Circ:** (Controlled)2,500
4,000

**Minnesota Insurance (16007)**
Meusey Communications
1107 Hazeltine Blvd., Ste. 539
Chaska, MN 55318-1008
Phone: (952)368-4100
Fax: (952)474-7850
**Subject(s):** Insurance
**Circ:** (Non-paid)‡3,987

**Michigan Pharmacist (15526)**
Michigan Pharmacists Association
815 N Washington Ave.
Lansing, MI 48906-5198
Phone: (517)484-1466
Fax: (517)484-1893
**Subject(s):** Drugs and Pharmaceuticals
**Circ:** ‡3,900

**The American Naturalist (8076)**
University of Chicago Press
1427 E. 60th St.
Chicago, IL 60637
Phone: (773)702-7700
Fax: (773)702-9756
**Subject(s):** Biology
**Circ:** ‡3,800

**Forest Products Journal (33181)**
Forest Products Society
2801 Marshall Ct.
Madison, WI 53705-2295
Phone: (608)231-1361
Fax: (608)231-2152
**Subject(s):** Wood and Woodworking
**Circ:** 3,800

**Postcard Collector (33091)**
Krause Publications Inc.
700 E. State St.
Iola, WI 54990-0001
Phone: (715)445-2214
Fax: (715)445-4087
**Subject(s):** Crafts, Models, Hobbies, and Contests
**Circ:** (Paid)‡3,800

**Marketing Health Services (8325)**
American Marketing Association
311 S. Wacker Dr., Ste. 5800
Chicago, IL 60606-2266
Phone: (312)542-9000
Fax: (312)542-9001

**Subject(s):** Advertising and Marketing; Health and Healthcare
**Circ:** (Non-paid)‡179
(Paid)‡3781

**Check the Oil! (25015)**
Three Fifty Six Inc.
30 W Olentangy St.
PO Box 937
Powell, OH 43065-0937
Phone: (614)848-5038
Fax: (614)436-4760
**Subject(s):** Collecting; History and Genealogy
**Circ:** (Paid)3,700

**Ethics (8191)**
University of Chicago Press
1427 E. 60th St.
Chicago, IL 60637
Phone: (773)702-7700
Fax: (773)702-9756
**Subject(s):** Philosophy
**Circ:** ‡3,700

**Minnesota Flyer Magazine (16633)**
PO Box 750
Sandstone, MN 55072-0750
Phone: (320)295-2111
Fax: (320)295-2438
**Subject(s):** Aviation
**Circ:** (Non-paid)500
(Paid)3,702

**The Sondheim Review (8410)**
PO Box 11213
Chicago, IL 60611-0213
Phone: (773)275-4254
Fax: (773)275-4254
**Subject(s):** Music and Musical Instruments; Performing Arts
**Circ:** (Controlled)3,700

**Seed World (8593)**
Scranton Gillette Communications Inc.
380 E. Northwest Hwy., Ste. 200
Des Plaines, IL 60016-2282
Phone: (847)390-0408
Fax: (847)390-0408
**Subject(s):** Seed and Nursery Trade
**Circ:** (Paid)1,493
(Non-paid)3,649

**Credit Union Director (33165)**
Credit Union Executives Society
5510 Research Park Dr.
Madison, WI 53711-5377
Phone: (608)271-2664
Fax: (608)271-2303
**Subject(s):** Banking, Finance, and Investments; Management and Administration
**Circ:** 3,616

**Ohio Engineer (24580)**
Ohio Society of Professional Engineers
4795 Evanswood Dr., Ste. 201
Columbus, OH 43229
Phone: (614)846-1144
Fax: (614)846-1131
**Subject(s):** Engineering (Various branches)
**Circ:** (Non-paid)259
(Paid)3,551

**Wisconsin Architect (33217)**
AIA Wisconsin
321 S Hamilton St.
Madison, WI 53703-4000
Phone: (608)257-8477
Fax: (608)257-0242
**Subject(s):** Architecture; Construction, Contracting, Building, and Excavating
**Circ:** ‡3,536

**Voyageur Magazine (33009)**
PO Box 8085
Green Bay, WI 54308-8085
Phone: (920)465-2446
Fax: (920)465-2890
**Subject(s):** History and Genealogy; History and Genealogy
**Circ:** (Paid)3,511

**The Badger Common'Tater (32803)**
Wisconsin Potato and Vegetable Growers Association Inc.
700 5th Ave.
PO Box 327
Antigo, WI 54409
Phone: (715)623-7683
Fax: (715)623-3176

Subject(s): General Agriculture

Circ: (Paid)‡500
(Non-paid)‡3,500

**Banner Sheep Magazine (8527)**
Banner Publications Inc.
350 N 1st
PO Box 500
Cuba, IL 61427-0500
Phone: (309)785-5058
Fax: (309)785-5050
Subject(s): Livestock

Circ: ‡3,500

**Counselor Education and Supervision (24145)**
American Counseling Association
c/o William Kline, CES Editor
Department of Counseling and Higher Education
McCracken Hall 201
Ohio University
Athens, OH 45701-2979
Phone: (740)593-0115
Fax: (740)593-0799
Subject(s): Education; Psychology and Psychiatry

Circ: (Paid)3,500

**Drug Development Research (8177)**
John Wiley and Sons Inc.
c/o Michael Williams
Department of Molecular Pharmacology & Biological Chemistry
Chicago, IL 60611
Subject(s): Drugs and Pharmaceuticals

Circ: 3,500

**Headache Quarterly (8220)**
Diamond Headache Clinic Research & Educational Foundation
467 W Deming Pl., Ste. 500
Chicago, IL 60614-1726
Phone: (773)388-6363
Fax: (773)477-9712
Subject(s): Medicine and Surgery

Circ: (Paid)‡3,500

**Illinois Music Educator (9394)**
Illinois Music Educators Association
72 Marchelle
Springfield, IL 62702
Phone: (217)787-6323
Fax: (217)787-3610
Subject(s): Music and Musical Instruments

Circ: (Controlled)3,500

**Journal of Physical Organic Chemistry (8675)**
John Wiley and Sons Inc.
C/O Prof. Joseph B. Lambert, Dept. of Chemistry
Northwestern Univ.
2145 Sheridan Rd.
Evanston, IL 60208
Subject(s): Chemistry, Chemicals, and Chemical Engineering

Circ: (Paid)3,500

**Journal of Popular Culture (24207)**
Popular Press
Bowling Green University
Popular Culture Ctr.
Bowling Green, OH 43403
Phone: (419)372-7867
Fax: (419)372-8095
Subject(s): Humanities

Circ: ‡3,500

**MHEDA Journal (9494)**
Material Handling Equipment Distributors Association
201 United States Hwy. 45
Vernon Hills, IL 60061-2398
Phone: (847)680-3500
Fax: (847)362-6989
Subject(s): Machinery and Equipment; Commerce and Industry

Circ: 3,500

**Ohio Florists Association Bulletin (24581)**
Ohio Florists' Association
2130 Stella Ct.
Columbus, OH 43215-1033
Phone: (614)487-1117
Fax: (614)487-1216
Subject(s): Florists and Floriculture; Landscape Architecture; Seed and Nursery Trade

Circ: (Paid)3,500

**Railroad History (9487)**
Railway & Locomotive Historical Society
PO Box 517
Urbana, IL 61803-0517
Phone: (217)333-0568
Subject(s): History and Genealogy; Railroad; Clubs and Societies

Circ: (Paid)3,500

**Religious Studies Review (10210)**
Council of Societies for the Study of Religion
CSSR Executive Office
Valparaiso University
Valparaiso, IN 46383-6493
Phone: (219)464-5515
Fax: (219)464-6714
Subject(s): Religious Publications

Circ: ‡3,500

**The Timber Producer (33503)**
PO Box 1278
Rhinelander, WI 54501
Phone: (715)282-5828
Fax: (715)282-4941
Subject(s): Forestry

Circ: (Combined)‡3,500

**Wisconsin Counties (33218)**
Wisconsin Counties Association
22 E Mifflin St., Ste. 900
Madison, WI 53703-4257
Phone: (608)663-7188
Fax: (608)663-7189
Subject(s): State, Municipal, and County Administration

Circ: (Paid)‡3,500
(Non-paid)‡3,500

**Journal of the Society of Architectural Historians (JSAH) (8294)**
Society of Architectural Historians
1365 N. Astor St.
Chicago, IL 60610-2144
Phone: (312)573-1365
Fax: (312)573-1141
Subject(s): Architecture

Circ: (Controlled)‡3,450

**Die Casting Engineer (9530)**
North American Die Casting Association
241 Holbrook Dr.
Wheeling, IL 60090-5809
Phone: (847)279-0001
Fax: (847)279-0002
Subject(s): Engineering (Various branches); Metal, Metallurgy, and Metal Trade

Circ: (Non-paid)‡350
(Paid)‡3,400

**Journal of Consumer Research (8269)**
University of Chicago Press
1427 E. 60th St.
Chicago, IL 60637
Phone: (773)702-7700
Fax: (773)702-9756
Subject(s): Psychology and Psychiatry; Economics

Circ: 3,400

**Journal of Environmental Quality (33191)**
American Society of Agronomy
677 S. Segoe Rd.
Madison, WI 53711-1086
Phone: (608)273-8080
Fax: (608)273-2021
Subject(s): Ecology and Conservation

Circ: 3,400

**The Hearing Professional (15549)**
International Hearing Society
16880 Middlebelt Rd.
Livonia, MI 48154
Phone: (734)522-7200
Fax: (734)522-0200
Subject(s): Hearing and Speech

Circ: (Controlled)‡3,300

**Marketing Research (8328)**
American Marketing Association
311 S. Wacker Dr., Ste. 5800
Chicago, IL 60606-2266
Phone: (312)542-9000
Fax: (312)542-9001
Subject(s): Advertising and Marketing

Circ: (Non-paid)‡59
(Paid)‡3,305

**Cosmetics & Toiletries (7974)**
Allured Publishing Corp.
362 S. Schmale Rd.
Carol Stream, IL 60188-2787
Phone: (630)653-2155
Fax: (630)653-2192
Subject(s): Cosmetics and Toiletries; Chemistry, Chemicals, and Chemical Engineering

Circ: (Paid)3,278

**Illinois Engineer (9390)**
Illinois Society of Professional Engineers Inc.
600 South 2nd Street Suite 403
Springfield, IL 62704
Phone: (217)544-7424
Fax: (217)528-6545
Subject(s): Engineering (Various branches)

Circ: (Non-paid)100
(Paid)3,200

**Phytopathology (16608)**
The American Phytopathological Society
3340 Pilot Knob Rd.
Saint Paul, MN 55121
Phone: (651)454-7250
Fax: (651)454-0766
Subject(s): Botany

Circ: (Non-paid)17
(Paid)3,200

**Northwest Dentistry (16604)**
Minnesota Dental Association
2236 Marshall Ave.
Saint Paul, MN 55104
Phone: (651)647-6673
Fax: (651)646-8246
Subject(s): Dentistry

Circ: (Combined)3,180

**Economic Development and Cultural Change (8179)**
University of Chicago Press
1427 E. 60th St.
Chicago, IL 60637
Phone: (773)702-7700
Fax: (773)702-9756
Subject(s): Economics

Circ: ‡3,150

**Jersey Journal (25020)**
American Jersey Cattle Association
6486 E. Main St.
Reynoldsburg, OH 43068
Phone: (614)861-3636
Fax: (614)861-8040
Subject(s): Dairying

Circ: (Non-paid)1,649
(Paid)3,142

**Signs (8407)**
University of Chicago Press
1427 E. 60th St.
Chicago, IL 60637
Phone: (773)702-7700
Fax: (773)702-9756
Subject(s): Sociology; Women's Interests; Social Sciences; Humanities

Circ: ‡3,149

**Marketing Management (8326)**
American Marketing Association
311 S. Wacker Dr., Ste. 5800
Chicago, IL 60606-2266
Phone: (312)542-9000
Fax: (312)542-9001
Subject(s): Advertising and Marketing

Circ: (Non-paid)‡73
(Paid)‡3,118

**Michigan Master Plumber and Mechanical Contractor (15523)**
Michigan Plumbing and Mechanical Contractors Association (MPMCA)
400 N Walnut St.
Lansing, MI 48933
Phone: (517)484-5500
Fax: (517)484-5225
Subject(s): Plumbing and Heating

Circ: (Controlled)‡3,100

**Teacher Education and Special Education (24337)**
Allen Press Inc.
College of Education
University of Cincinnati
PO Box 210002
Cincinnati, OH 45221-0002
Phone: (513)556-4552
Fax: (513)556-9311
**Subject(s):** Education
**Circ:** (Paid)3,100

**The Journal of Law and Economics (8279)**
University of Chicago Press
c/o Maureen Callahan, Managing Editor
The Univ. of Chicago Law School
1111 E. 60th St.
Chicago, IL 60637
Phone: (773)702-9603
Fax: (773)702-0730
**Subject(s):** Law
**Circ:** (Paid)‡3,050

**The Adcrafter (15163)**
Adcraft Club of Detroit
3011 W Grand Blvd., Ste. 1715
Detroit, MI 48202-3000
Phone: (313)872-7850
Fax: (313)872-7858
**Subject(s):** Advertising and Marketing
**Circ:** ‡3,000

**Annual Review of Communications (8081)**
International Engineering Consortium
300 W Adams, Ste. 1210
Chicago, IL 60606
Phone: (312)559-4100
Fax: (312)559-4111
**Subject(s):** Engineering (Various branches); Electronics Engineering; Communications
**Circ:** 3,000

**The Bar Examiner (33159)**
National Conference of Bar Examiners
402 W Wilson St.
Madison, WI 53703-3614
Phone: (608)280-8550
Fax: (608)280-8552
**Subject(s):** Law
**Circ:** (Non-paid)‡3,000

**The Cadence (16570)**
Northwestern College
3003 N Snelling Ave.
Saint Paul, MN 55113
Phone: (651)631-5100
**Subject(s):** College Publications
**Circ:** (Non-paid)3,000

**The Carousel News & Trader Magazine (24855)**
87 Park Ave. W., No. 206
Mansfield, OH 44902-1612
Phone: (419)529-4999
Fax: (419)529-2321
**Subject(s):** Art and Art History
**Circ:** (Non-paid)200
(Paid)3,000

**Danish Pioneer (8795)**
Bertelsen Publishing Co.
1582 Glen Lake Rd.
Hoffman Estates, IL 60195
Phone: (847)882-2552
Fax: (847)882-7082
**Subject(s):** Danish; Ethnic Publications
**Circ:** (Non-paid)‡250
(Paid)‡3,000

**Emmanuel (24407)**
Congregation of Blessed Sacrament
5384 Wilson Mills Rd.
Cleveland, OH 44143-3092
Phone: (440)449-2103
Fax: (440)449-3862
**Subject(s):** Religious Publications
**Circ:** 3,000

**Format Magazine (16254)**
Decker Publications Inc.
PO Box 2242
Maple Grove, MN 55311
**Subject(s):** Advertising and Marketing; Public Relations; Communications
**Circ:** (Non-paid)3,000

**Illinois Audubon (7878)**
Illinois Audubon Society
6420 Hwy. 4
Ava, IL 62907-2256
**Subject(s):** Wildlife and Exotic Animals; Environmental and Natural Resources Conservation
**Circ:** (Combined)3,000

**Journal of American Folklore (8015)**
University of Illinois Press
1325 S. Oak St.
Champaign, IL 61820-6903
Phone: (217)333-0950
Fax: (217)244-8082
**Subject(s):** History and Genealogy
**Circ:** 3,000

**Journal of the American Oil Chemists' Society (8016)**
AOCS Press
2211 W. Bradley Ave.
Champaign, IL 61821
Phone: (217)359-2344
Fax: (217)351-8091
**Subject(s):** Chemistry, Chemicals, and Chemical Engineering
**Circ:** (Non-paid)‡50
(Paid)‡3,000

**Journal of Multicultural Counseling and Development(JMCD) (7951)**
American Counseling Association
c/o Dr. Patricia B. Elmore, MECD Editor
College of Education
Dean's Office-Mailcode 4624
Southern Illinois University
Carbondale, IL 62901-4624
Phone: (618)453-2415
Fax: (618)453-1646
**Subject(s):** Education; Psychology and Psychiatry
**Circ:** (Paid)‡3,000

**Marquette University Journal (33312)**
Marquette Journal
1131 W. Wisconsin
Johnston hall, Room 009
Milwaukee, WI 53233
Phone: (414)288-7171
Fax: (414)288-1979
**Subject(s):** College Publications
**Circ:** (Non-paid)‡3,000

**Minnesota Technology (16324)**
Minnesota Technology magazine
5 Lind Hall
207 Church St., SE
Minneapolis, MN 55455
Phone: (612)624-9816
Fax: (612)626-0261
**Subject(s):** College Publications
**Circ:** (Non-paid)‡3,000

**MIS Quarterly (16325)**
MIS Research Center
University of Minnesota
Carlson School of Management
321 19th Ave. S., Ste. 3-306
Minneapolis, MN 55455-0413
Phone: (612)624-7803
Fax: (612)626-1316
**Subject(s):** Management and Administration
**Circ:** (Non-paid)100
(Paid)3,000

**Modern Fiction Studies (10248)**
Purdue University
500 Oval Dr.
West Lafayette, IN 47907-2038
Phone: (765)494-4600
Fax: (765)494-3780
**Subject(s):** Literature and Literary Reviews
**Circ:** 3,000

**Ohio Cattleman (24880)**
Ohio Cattlemen's Association/Ohio Beef Council
10600 US Hwy. 42
Marysville, OH 43040
Phone: (614)873-6736
Fax: (614)873-6835
**Subject(s):** Livestock
**Circ:** ‡3,000

**QDT (7981)**
Quintessence Publishing Company Inc.
551 Kimberly Dr.
Carol Stream, IL 60188-1881
Phone: (630)682-3223
Fax: (630)682-3288
**Subject(s):** Dentistry
**Circ:** (Paid)3,000

**Rubber Chemistry and Technology (24102)**
Rubber Division
PO Box 499
Akron, OH 44309-0499
Phone: (330)972-7814
Fax: (330)972-5269
**Subject(s):** Chemistry, Chemicals, and Chemical Engineering; Rubber Trade
**Circ:** ‡3,000

**Tech News (15782)**
Lawrence Technological University
21000 W 10 Mile Rd.
Southfield, MI 48075-1058
Phone: (248)204-2200
Fax: (248)204-2207
**Subject(s):** College Publications
**Circ:** (Non-paid)‡3,000

**Warship International (25095)**
International Naval Research Organization
5905 Reinwood Dr.
Toledo, OH 43613-5605
Phone: (419)472-1331
**Subject(s):** Military and Navy
**Circ:** (Non-paid)62
(Paid)3,000

**Journal of Pediatric Surgery (9881)**
Elsevier
C/o Jay L. Grosfeld, Editor-in-Chief
J.W. Riley Hospital for Children
Department of Surgery
702 Barnhill Dr., Ste. 2500
Indianapolis, IN 46202
**Subject(s):** Pediatrics; Medicine and Surgery
**Circ:** ‡2,900

**New Directions for Evaluation (16329)**
Jossey-Bass Publishers
c/o Jean A. King, Editor-in-Chief
Univ. of Minnesota
330 Wulling Hall
86 Pleasant St., S.E.
Minneapolis, MN 55455
**Subject(s):** Psychology and Psychiatry
**Circ:** (Non-paid)82
(Paid)2,900

**The Hymn (15970)**
The Hymn Society in the U.S. & Canada
c/o Carol A. Pemberton, Editor
Normandale Community College
9700 France Ave. S.
Bloomington, MN 55431
Phone: (612)832-6571
**Subject(s):** Religious Publications; Music and Musical Instruments
**Circ:** (Paid)⊕2,847

**HVAC/R Distribution Today (24555)**
Hardi
1389 Dublin Road
Columbus, OH 43215-1084
Phone: (614)488-1835
Fax: (614)488-0482
**Subject(s):** Air Conditioning and Refrigeration; Plumbing and Heating
**Circ:** (Paid)1,200
(Non-paid)2,800

**Journal of Orofacial Pain (7976)**
Quintessence Publishing Company Inc.
551 Kimberly Dr.
Carol Stream, IL 60188-1881
Phone: (630)682-3223
Fax: (630)682-3288
**Subject(s):** Dentistry
**Circ:** (Paid)⊕2,800

**The Journal of Trace Elements in Experimental Medicine (15186)**
John Wiley and Sons Inc.
c/o Ananda S. Prasad, Editor
Univ. Health Center, Pod 5C
4201 St. Antoine
Detroit, MI 48201
**Subject(s):** Biology; Medicine and Surgery; Toxicology
**Circ:** 2,800

**Social Service Review** (8408)
University of Chicago Press
1427 E. 60th St.
Chicago, IL 60637
Phone: (773)702-7700
Fax: (773)702-9756
**Subject(s):** Sociology
**Circ:** ‡2,800

**Journal of Applied Meteorology** (9477)
American Meteorological Society
c/o Dr. Robert M. Rauber, Chief Editor, Journal of Applied M
Dept. of Atmospheric Sciences
Univ. of Illinois-Urbana/Champaign
105 S. Gregory St.
Urbana, IL 61801
Phone: (217)333-2046
Fax: (217)351-4025
**Subject(s):** Meteorology
**Circ:** ‡2,721

**The Annals of Probability** (8080)
Institute of Mathematical Statistics
5734 Univ.Ave.
Annals of Probability
Dept. of Statistics
Univ. of Chicago
Chicago, IL 60637
**Subject(s):** Mathematics
**Circ:** ‡2,700

**Chicago Review** (8136)
University of Chicago
5801 S. Ellis Ave. Rm. 200
Chicago, IL 60637-1473
Phone: (773)702-8360
Fax: (773)702-8324
**Subject(s):** Literature and Literary Reviews
**Circ:** (Non-paid)‡100
(Paid)‡2,700

**Ecological Restoration** (33174)
University of Wisconsin Press
1930 Monroe St., 3rd Fl.
Madison, WI 53711-2029
Phone: (608)263-1110
Fax: (608)263-1173
**Subject(s):** Ecology and Conservation
**Circ:** (Paid)2,700

**The Wisconsin Jewish Chronicle** (33343)
Wisconsin Jewish Chronicle
1360 N Prospect Ave.
Milwaukee, WI 53202
Phone: (414)390-5888
Fax: (414)271-0487
**Subject(s):** Jewish Publications
**Circ:** (Non-paid)⊕130
(Paid)⊕**2,660**

**Illinois Pharmacist** (9396)
Illinois Pharmacists Association
204 W. Cook St.
Springfield, IL 62704-2526
Phone: (217)522-7300
Fax: (217)522-7349
**Subject(s):** Drugs and Pharmaceuticals
**Circ:** ‡2,610

**Sheltie Pacesetter** (9723)
9428 Blue Mound Dr.
Fort Wayne, IN 46804
Phone: (260)434-1566
Fax: (260)434-1566
**Subject(s):** Pets
**Circ:** (Combined)⊕**2,600**

**Remedial and Special Education (RASE)** (33329)
PRO-ED Inc.
Dept. of Exceptional Education
University of Wisconsin-Milwaukee
679 END Hall
2400 E Hartford Ave.
Milwaukee, WI 53201
Phone: (414)229-4821
Fax: (414)229-5500
**Subject(s):** Education
**Circ:** (Non-paid)97
(Paid)2,587

**Seminars in Thrombosis and Hemostasis** (15197)
Thieme Medical Publishers Inc.
c/o Professor Eberhard F. Mammen, M.D.
Wayne State University
School of Medicine
Detroit, MI 48202
**Subject(s):** Medicine and Surgery
**Circ:** (Paid)2,582

**The Journal of Business Communication** (15289)
Association for Business Communication
c/o Steven M. Ralston, Editor
Dept. of Communication
Univ. of Michigan-Flint
4116 WSW Bldg.
Flint, MI 48507
Phone: (810)766-6679
Fax: (810)766-6834
**Subject(s):** Business; Communications
**Circ:** 2,550

**American Journal of Education** (8069)
University of Chicago Press
1427 E. 60th St.
Chicago, IL 60637
Phone: (773)702-7700
Fax: (773)702-9756
**Subject(s):** Education
**Circ:** ‡2,500

**The Cooperative Accountant** (24648)
National Society of Accountants for Cooperatives
136 S Keowee St.
Dayton, OH 45402
Phone: (937)22-2607
Fax: (937)222-5794
**Subject(s):** Accountants and Accounting
**Circ:** ‡2,500

**Critical Care Nursing Quarterly (CCNQ)** (9781)
Aspen Publishers Inc.
c/o Editor
CCNQ
9383 E. County Rd. 500 S
Greensburg, IN 47240-8138
**Subject(s):** Nursing; Medicine and Surgery
**Circ:** ‡2,500

**Frontiers of Health Services Management** (8208)
Health Administration Press
1 N. Franklin, Ste. 1700
Chicago, IL 60606-4425
Phone: (312)424-2800
Fax: (312)424-0023
**Subject(s):** Health and Healthcare
**Circ:** ‡2,500

**Insurance Insight** (9400)
Professional Independent Insurance Agents of Illinois
4360 Wabash Ave.
Springfield, IL 62711
Phone: (217)793-6660
Fax: (217)793-6744
**Subject(s):** Insurance
**Circ:** (Controlled)2,500

**Journal of Adult Training** (9349)
Evangelical Training Association
1620 Penny Ln.
PO Box 327
Schaumburg, IL 60173
Phone: (630)540-7857
Fax: (847)882-3506
**Subject(s):** Religious Publications; Education; Vocational Education
**Circ:** 2,500

**The Neighborhood Works** (8350)
Center for Neighborhood Technology
2125 W N. Ave.
Chicago, IL 60647
Phone: (312)278-4800
Fax: (312)278-3840
**Subject(s):** Social and Political Issues
**Circ:** (Non-paid)500
(Paid)2,500

**Organic Process Research & Development** (24595)
American Chemical Society
PO Box 3337
Columbus, OH 43210
Phone: (614)447-3671
Fax: (800)333-9511
**Subject(s):** Chemistry, Chemicals, and Chemical Engineering
**Circ:** 2,500

**Special Care in Dentistry** (8414)
Special Care Dentistry
401 N Michigan Ave.
Chicago, IL 60611
Phone: (312)527-6764
Fax: (312)673-6663
**Subject(s):** Dentistry
**Circ:** ‡2,500

**Construction Bulletin Magazine** (16416)
Construction Bulletin
9443 Science Center Dr.
New Hope, MN 55428-3636
Phone: (763)537-1122
Fax: (763)537-1363
**Subject(s):** Construction, Contracting, Building, and Excavating
**Circ:** (Non-paid)722
(Paid)2,496

**Blade Trade** (33064)
Krause Publications Inc.
700 E. State St.
Iola, WI 54990-0001
Phone: (715)445-2214
Fax: (715)445-4087
**Subject(s):** Retail
**Circ:** (Combined)2,410

**Bare Facts for Practicing Doctors** (15168)
Royal College of Physicians and Surgeons of the United States of America
485 Allard Rd.
PO Box 24224
Detroit, MI 48224-0224
Phone: (313)882-0641
Fax: (313)882-0979
**Subject(s):** Medicine and Surgery; Health and Healthcare
**Circ:** 2,400

**Cleveland Physician** (24390)
Academy of Medicine of Cleveland/Northern Ohio Medical Association
6000 Rockside Woods Blvd., Ste. 150
PO Box 901724
Cleveland, OH 44131-2352
Phone: (216)520-1000
Fax: (216)520-0999
**Subject(s):** Medicine and Surgery
**Circ:** (Paid)2,400

**Comparative Education Review** (8154)
University of Chicago Press
1427 E. 60th St.
Chicago, IL 60637
Phone: (773)702-7700
Fax: (773)702-9756
**Subject(s):** Education
**Circ:** ‡2,400

**Health Forum Journal** (8223)
Health Forum L.L.C.
1 N Franklin, 29th Fl.
Chicago, IL 60606
Phone: (312)893-6800
Fax: (312)422-4506
**Subject(s):** Hospitals and Healthcare Institutions
**Circ:** (Paid)‡2,400

**The Journal of Geology** (8271)
University of Chicago Press
1427 E. 60th St.
Chicago, IL 60637
Phone: (773)702-7700
Fax: (773)702-9756
**Subject(s):** Geology
**Circ:** ‡2,400

**Journal of Natural Products** (8284)
American Chemical Society
c/o A. Douglas Kinghorn
Department of Medicinal Chemistry & Pharmacognosy (M/C 781)
College of Pharmacy, University of Illinois
833 S. Wood St.
Chicago, IL 60612
Phone: (312)996-6809
Fax: (312)996-7391
**Subject(s):** Chemistry, Chemicals, and Chemical Engineering
**Circ:** 2,400

Circulation: ★ = ABC; △ = BPA; ♦ = CAC; • = CCAB; ☐ = VAC; ⊕ = PO Statement; ‡ = Publisher's Report; Boldface figures = sworn; Light figures = estimated.

**The Sabbath Recorder** (33107)
SDB Tract and Communication Council
3120 Kennedy Rd.
PO Box 1678
Janesville, WI 53547-1678
Phone: (608)752-5055
Fax: (608)752-7711
**Subject(s):** Religious Publications

**Circ:** (Non-paid)‡2,400

**Teaching Sociology** (10257)
American Sociological Association
c/o Elizabeth Grauerholz, Editor
Department of Sociology and Anthropology
Purdue University Stone Hall
West Lafayette, IN 47907-2059
Phone: (765)494-5874
Fax: (765)494-1476
**Subject(s):** Sociology; Education

**Circ:** ‡2,400

**Consumer Magazine Advertising Source** (8575)
SRDS
1700 Higgins Rd.
Des Plaines, IL 60018-5605
Phone: (847)375-5000
Fax: (847)375-5001
**Subject(s):** Advertising and Marketing

**Circ:** (Paid)2,381

**Skillings Mining Review** (16067)
Skillings Mining Review
11 E. Superior St. Ste. 514
Duluth, MN 55802
Phone: (218)722-2310
Fax: (218)722-0134
**Subject(s):** Mining and Minerals

**Circ:** (Controlled)60
(Paid)2,370

**The Journal of Criminal Justice & Popular Culture** (24320)
University of Albany
c/o Jen Trager, Editor
Division of Criminal Justice
600 Dyer Hall, Univ. of Cincinnati
PO Box 210389
Cincinnati, OH 45221-0389
Phone: (513)556-5936
**Subject(s):** Police, Penology, and Penal Institutions

**Circ:** (Free)2,343

**Journal of Management Accounting Research** (15235)
American Accounting Association
c/o Prof. Joan Luft, Editor
Broad Graduate School of Business
Department of Accounting
East Lansing, MI 48824-1121
**Subject(s):** Accountants and Accounting

**Circ:** (Paid)2,300

**Labor Law Reports** (8301)
CCH Inc.
4025 W. Peterson Ave.
Chicago, IL 60646-6085
Phone: (847)267-7000
Fax: (773)866-3895
**Subject(s):** Labor

**Circ:** ‡2,300

**Movement Disorders** (8345)
John Wiley and Sons Inc.
Rush University Medical Center
1725 W. Harrison St., Ste. 755
Chicago, IL 60612
**Subject(s):** Laboratory Research (Scientific and Medical); Physiology and Anatomy

**Circ:** 2,301

**Personnel Psychology** (24210)
Personnel Psychology Inc.
520 Ordway Ave.
Bowling Green, OH 43402-2756
Phone: (419)352-1562
Fax: (419)352-2645
**Subject(s):** Employment and Human Resources; Psychology and Psychiatry

**Circ:** (Paid)2,300

**Victorian Studies** (9615)
Indiana University Press
c/o Editor, Victorian Studies
Indiana Univ.
Ballatine Hall 338
Bloomington, IN 47405
**Subject(s):** History and Genealogy

**Circ:** 2,300

**Wisconsin Engineer** (33220)
University of Wisconsin
M1066 Engineering Centers Bldg.
Madison, WI 53706
Phone: (608)262-3494
**Subject(s):** Engineering (Various branches)

**Circ:** (Paid)1,300
(Non-paid)2,300

**Medical Care** (9893)
Lippincott Williams & Wilkins
c/o Sue E. Houchin,
Regerstrief Institute for Health Care
RHC/6th Fl.
1050 Wishard Blvd.
Indianapolis, IN 46202
Phone: (317)630-7255
Fax: (317)630-7669
**Subject(s):** Medicine and Surgery; Health and Healthcare

**Circ:** (Paid)2,293

**Eighteenth-Century Studies** (8669)
Johns Hopkins University Press
Eighteenth Century Studies
Department of French & Italian
Northwestern University
Evanston, IL 60208-2204
Phone: (847)491-3877
Fax: (847)491-3877
**Subject(s):** History and Genealogy; Literature

**Circ:** ‡2,278

**Inland Seas** (24124)
Great Lakes Historical Society
413 Oaknoll Dr.
Amherst, OH 44001-1935
Phone: (440)988-3213
Fax: (440)984-2246
**Subject(s):** History and Genealogy

**Circ:** ‡2,250

**The Annals of Applied Probability** (24163)
Institute of Mathematical Statistics
PO Box 22718
Beachwood, OH 44122
Phone: (216)295-2340
Fax: (216)295-5661
**Subject(s):** Mathematics

**Circ:** 2,200

**Christian Magnifier** (16702)
Lutheran Braille Evangelism Association
1740 Eugene St.
White Bear Lake, MN 55110
Phone: (651)426-0469
**Subject(s):** Religious Publications

**Circ:** (Controlled)2,200

**Horizon** (8228)
National Religious Vocation Conference
5420 S Cornell Ave., No. 105
Chicago, IL 60615-5604
Phone: (773)363-5454
Fax: (773)363-5530
**Subject(s):** Religious Publications

**Circ:** (Controlled)72
(Paid)2,200

**Illinois Banker** (9387)
Illinois Bankers Association
133 S. 4th St., Ste. 300
Springfield, IL 62701
Phone: (217)789-9340
Fax: (217)789-5410
**Subject(s):** Banking, Finance, and Investments; Local, State, and Regional Publications

**Circ:** ‡2,200

**The Journal of Religion** (8293)
University of Chicago Press
1427 E. 60th St.
Chicago, IL 60637
Phone: (773)702-7700
Fax: (773)702-9756
**Subject(s):** Religious Publications

**Circ:** ‡2,200

**Lituanus** (8316)
47 W. Polk St., Ste. 100-300
Chicago, IL 60605
Phone: (312)341-9396
**Subject(s):** Intercultural Interests

**Circ:** (Paid)2,200

**Roeper Review** (15073)
Roeper School
41190 Woodward
Bloomfield Hills, MI 48304
**Subject(s):** Education

**Circ:** (Non-paid)200
(Paid)2,200

**Pediatric Critical Care Medicine** (8589)
Lippincott Williams & Wilkins
c/o Patrick M. Kochanek
Society of Critical Care Medicine
701 Lee St., Ste. 200
Des Plaines, IL 60016
Phone: (847)827-6869
**Subject(s):** Medicine and Surgery; Pediatrics

**Circ:** 2,145

**American Journal of Psychology** (8002)
University of Illinois Press
c/o Donelson E.Dulany
Psychology Bldg.
University of Illinois
603 E. Daniel St.
Champaign, IL 61820
Phone: (217)333-5234
Fax: (217)244-5876
**Subject(s):** Psychology and Psychiatry

**Circ:** ‡2,108

**German Studies Review** (16440)
Carleton College
1 N. College St.
Northfield, MN 55057
Phone: (507)646-4000
Fax: (507)646-7900
**Subject(s):** History and Genealogy

**Circ:** (Combined)2,100

**Journal of the American Ceramic Society** (25158)
The American Ceramic Society
PO Box 6136
Westerville, OH 43086-6136
Phone: (614)890-4700
Fax: (614)891-8960
**Subject(s):** Ceramics

**Circ:** (Paid)‡2,100

**Public Budgeting and Finance** (9611)
North-South Center Press at the University of Miami
School of Public and Environmental Affairs
Indiana Univ.
Bloomington, IN
Phone: (812)855-0732
Fax: (812)877-7802
**Subject(s):** Banking, Finance, and Investments; Congressional and Federal Government Affairs

**Circ:** (Paid)‡900
(Non-paid)‡2,100

**Labor Law Journal** (8300)
CCH Inc.
4025 W. Peterson Ave.
Chicago, IL 60646-6085
Phone: (847)267-7000
Fax: (773)866-3895
**Subject(s):** Labor

**Circ:** ‡2,059

**Michigan Law Review** (15017)
Michigan Law Review Association
Hutchins Hall
The University of Michigan Law School
625 S. State St.
Ann Arbor, MI 48109-1215
Phone: (734)764-0542
Fax: (734)647-5817
**Subject(s):** Law

**Circ:** ‡2,040

**American Art** (8064)
University of Chicago Press
1427 E. 60th St.
Chicago, IL 60637
Phone: (773)702-7700
Fax: (773)702-9756
**Subject(s):** Art and Art History; Museums

**Circ:** (Paid)2,000

**Another Chicago Magazine** (8082)
Left Field Press
3709 N. Kenmore
Chicago, IL 60613
**Subject(s):** Literature; Poetry
**Circ:** 2,000

**Catholic Cemetery** (8574)
National Catholic Cemetery Conference
710 N River Rd.
Des Plaines, IL 60016
Phone: (847)824-8131
Fax: (847)824-9608
**Subject(s):** Cemeteries and Monuments
**Circ:** ‡2,000

**Comparative Studies in Society & History** (15000)
Cambridge University Press
c/o Thomas Trautmann, 4418 Modern Languages Bldg.
The University of Michigan
812 E. Washington
Ann Arbor, MI 48109-1275
**Subject(s):** Anthropology and Ethnology; History and Genealogy; Sociology; Political Science
**Circ:** (Paid)‡2000

**Contemporary Literature** (33164)
University of Wisconsin Press
1930 Monroe St., 3rd Fl.
Madison, WI 53711-2029
Phone: (608)263-1110
Fax: (608)263-1173
**Subject(s):** Literature
**Circ:** (Paid)2,000

**Credit Union National Association GAC, Governmental Affairs Conference** (33168)
Credit Union National Association Inc.
5710 Mineral Point Rd.
PO Box 431
Madison, WI 53705-0431
Phone: (608)231-4075
Fax: (608)231-4263
**Subject(s):** Banking, Finance, and Investments
**Circ:** 2,000

**Elysian Fields Quarterly** (16579)
Knothole Publishing
PO Box 14385
Saint Paul, MN 55114-0385
Phone: (651)644-8558
**Subject(s):** (Baseball)
**Circ:** (Non-paid)‡150
(Paid)‡2,000

**Favorite Westerns & Serial World** (16237)
Westerns and Serials Fan Club
527 S Front St.
Mankato, MN 56001-3718
Phone: (507)549-3677
Fax: (507)549-3788
**Subject(s):** Motion Pictures
**Circ:** 2,000

**Illinois Master Plumber** (9393)
Illinois Association of Plumbing-Heating-Cooling Contractors
821 S Grand Ave. W
Springfield, IL 62704
Phone: (217)522-7219
Fax: (217)522-4315
**Subject(s):** Plumbing and Heating; Air Conditioning and Refrigeration
**Circ:** ‡2,000

**Indiana Business Review** (9592)
Indiana Business Research Center
Indiana University
Kelley School of Business
1275 East 10th Street
Bloomington, IN 47405
Phone: (812)855-5507
Fax: (812)855-7763
**Subject(s):** Business; Local, State, and Regional Publications
**Circ:** (Controlled)2,000

**Indiana Musicator** (9719)
Indiana Music Educators Association
C/O Barbara Resch, Editor
3218 Eastbrook Dr.
Fort Wayne, IN 46805
Phone: (260)481-6726
**Subject(s):** Music and Musical Instruments; Education
**Circ:** (Paid)2,000

**Indiana Review** (9596)
Ballantine Hall 465
1020 E Kirkwood Ave.
Bloomington, IN 47405-7103
Phone: (812)855-3439
Fax: (812)855-4253
**Subject(s):** Literature; Poetry
**Circ:** (Combined)2,000

**Journal of Human Resources** (33193)
University of Wisconsin Press
1930 Monroe St., 3rd Fl.
Madison, WI 53711-2029
Phone: (608)263-1110
Fax: (608)263-1173
**Subject(s):** Economics
**Circ:** (Controlled)2,000

**Land Economics** (33196)
University of Wisconsin Press
1930 Monroe St., 3rd Fl.
Madison, WI 53711-2029
Phone: (608)263-1110
Fax: (608)263-1173
**Subject(s):** Economics
**Circ:** 2,000

**The Landscape Contractor** (9149)
Illinois Landscape Contractor Association
2625 Butterfield Rd., Ste. 204-W
Oak Brook, IL 60523-1257
Phone: (630)472-2851
Fax: (630)472-3150
**Subject(s):** Landscape Architecture
**Circ:** (Non-paid)‡760
(Paid)‡2,000

**Library Trends** (8020)
University of Illinois Graduate School of Library & Information Science
501 E Daniel St.
Champaign, IL 61820
Phone: (217)333-1359
Fax: (217)244-7329
**Subject(s):** Library and Information Science
**Circ:** 2,000

**Lightworks** (15071)
Lightworks Magazine Inc.
Box 1202
Birmingham, MI 48012-1202
Phone: (248)626-8026
**Subject(s):** Art and Art History; Art
**Circ:** (Combined)2,000

**Michigan Health and Hospitals** (15520)
Michigan Hospital Association
6215 W. St. Joseph Hwy.
Lansing, MI 48917-4846
Phone: (517)323-3443
Fax: (517)323-0946
**Subject(s):** Hospitals and Healthcare Institutions
**Circ:** ‡2,000

**Moloda Ukraina** (7857)
Association of American Youth of Ukrainian Descent
811 S Roosevelt Ave.
Arlington Heights, IL 60005
**Subject(s):** Ethnic and Minority Studies; Intercultural Interests; Ethnic Publications; Intercultural Interests; Ukrainian
**Circ:** 2,000

**Mushroom the Journal** (8346)
1511 E. 54th St., Garden Apt.
Chicago, IL 60615
Phone: (773)288-2873
**Subject(s):** Natural History and Nature Study
**Circ:** ‡2,000

**Nancy's Magazine** (24569)
N's M Publications
PO Box 82108
Columbus, OH 43202
Phone: (614)267-5060
**Subject(s):** Alternative and Underground
**Circ:** (Combined)2,000

**NARDA Independent Retailer** (8910)
North American Retail Dealers Association
10 E 22nd St., Ste. 310
Lombard, IL 60148
Phone: (630)953-8950
Fax: (630)953-8957
**Subject(s):** Appliances; Furniture and Furnishings; Computers; Consumer Electronics
**Circ:** ‡2,000

**Northwestern Financial Review** (16334)
NFR Communications Inc.
4948 Washburn Ave.S.
Minneapolis, MN 55410
Phone: (612)929-8110
Fax: (612)929-8146
**Subject(s):** Banking, Finance, and Investments
**Circ:** (Paid)2,000

**NSGA Retail Focus** (9021)
National Sporting Goods Association
1601 Feehanville Dr., Ste. 300
Mount Prospect, IL 60056-6035
Phone: (847)296-6742
Fax: (847)391-9827
**Subject(s):** Selling and Salesmanship; Sporting Goods/Retail Sports
**Circ:** (Paid)‡2,000

**NTEA Technical Report** (15274)
National Truck Equipment Association
37400 Hills Tech Dr.
Farmington Hills, MI 48331-3414
Phone: (248)489-7090
Fax: (248)489-8590
**Subject(s):** Trucks and Trucking; Transportation, Traffic, and Shipping
**Circ:** (Paid)2,000

**Old Mill News** (15498)
5667 Leisure S Dr. SE
Kentwood, MI 49548-6851
Phone: (616)455-0609
**Subject(s):** History and Genealogy
**Circ:** ‡2,000

**The Quarterly Review of Economics and Finance** (8029)
Elsevier
University of Illinois
430 Wohlers Hall
1206 S. 6th St.
Champaign, IL 61820
Phone: (217)333-2331
Fax: (217)333-7410
**Subject(s):** Economics; Banking, Finance, and Investments
**Circ:** 2,000

**Review of Politics** (10093)
PO Box B
Notre Dame, IN 46556-0762
Phone: (574)631-6623
Fax: (574)631-3103
**Subject(s):** International Affairs; Politics; Philosophy
**Circ:** 2,000

**Sn3 Modeler** (8700)
Heimburger House Publishing Co.
7236 W Madison St.
Forest Park, IL 60130
Phone: (708)366-1973
Fax: (708)366-1973
**Subject(s):** Crafts, Models, Hobbies, and Contests
**Circ:** (Paid)2,000

**Taproot Reviews Electronic Edition** (24820)
Taproot Reviews
Box 585
Lakewood, OH 44107
**Subject(s):** Poetry
**Circ:** (Paid)500
(Non-paid)2000

**Union Signal** (8681)
National Woman's Christian Temperance Union
1730 Chicago Ave.
Evanston, IL 60201-4585
Fax: (847)864-9497
**Subject(s):** Substance Abuse and Treatment
**Circ:** ‡2,000

**Wisconsin Law Review** (33222)
Economic Justice Institue
975 Bascom Mall
Madison, WI 53706
Phone: (608)262-9143
Fax: (608)263-4128
**Subject(s):** Law
**Circ:** ‡2,000

**World Airshow News** (33447)
Flyer Publications Inc.
PO Box 199
Oregon, WI 53575-0199
Phone: (608)835-7063
**Subject(s):** Aviation; aviation
**Circ:** (Non-paid)‡1,100
(Paid)‡2,000

**The Astronomical Journal** (33157)
University of Chicago Press
c/o John S. Gallagher, III, Space Astronomy Lab
Chamberlin Hall
University of Wisconsin
1150 University Ave.
Madison, WI 53706
Phone: (608)265-6005
Fax: (608)265-6005
**Subject(s):** Astronomy and Meteorology
**Circ:** ‡1,929

**Journal of Near Eastern Studies** (8285)
University of Chicago Press
c/o The Oriental Institute
University of Chicago
1155 E. 58th St.
Chicago, IL 60637
**Subject(s):** Archaeology
**Circ:** ‡1,900

**Operative Dentistry** (9901)
Indiana University
1121 W. Michigan St., Rm. S411
Indianapolis, IN 46202
Phone: (317)278-4800
Fax: (317)278-4900
**Subject(s):** Dentistry
**Circ:** (Controlled)⊕1,890

**Civil War History** (24805)
Kent State University Press
Lowry Hall, Rm. 307
PO Box 5190
Kent, OH 44242-0001
Phone: (330)672-7913
Fax: (330)672-3104
**Subject(s):** History and Genealogy
**Circ:** ‡1,850

**Journal of Labor Economics** (8278)
University of Chicago Press
1427 E. 60th St.
Chicago, IL 60637
Phone: (773)702-7700
Fax: (773)702-9756
**Subject(s):** Labor
**Circ:** ‡1,850

**Africa Today** (9579)
Indiana University Press
221 Woodburn Hall
Indiana University
Bloomington, IN 47405
**Subject(s):** Intercultural Interests
**Circ:** (Controlled)66
(Paid)1,800

**APWS Magazine** (33003)
American Pheasant and Waterfowl Society
W 2270 U.S Hwy. 10
Granton, WI 54436-8854
Phone: (715)238-7291
Fax: (715)238-4623
**Subject(s):** Ornithology and Oology
**Circ:** (Paid)1,800

**CAC Journal** (24381)
Cleveland Athletic Club
1118 Euclid Ave.
Cleveland, OH 44115
Phone: (216)621-8900
Fax: (216)621-3864
**Subject(s):** Clubs and Societies
**Circ:** ‡1,800

**The Duluthian** (16056)
Duluth Chamber of Commerce
5 W 1st St., Ste. 201
Duluth, MN 55802-2115
Phone: (218)722-5501
Fax: (218)722-3183
**Subject(s):** Chambers of Commerce and Boards of Trade; Business; Local, State, and Regional Publications
**Circ:** ‡1,800

**History of Religions** (8226)
University of Chicago Press
1427 E. 60th St.
Chicago, IL 60637
Phone: (773)702-7700
Fax: (773)702-9756
**Subject(s):** Education; Religious Publications
**Circ:** ‡1,800

**The Journal of the Astronautical Sciences** (10243)
American Astronautical Society
Purdue University
Grissom 331
West Lafayette, IN 47907
Phone: (765)494-5786
Fax: (765)494-0307
**Subject(s):** Astronautics
**Circ:** ‡1,800

**Journal of British Studies** (8264)
University of Chicago Press
1427 E. 60th St.
Chicago, IL 60637
Phone: (773)702-7700
Fax: (773)702-9756
**Subject(s):** Intercultural Interests; History and Genealogy
**Circ:** ‡1,800

**Journal of Computer Based Instruction** (24559)
Association for the Development of Computer-Based Instructional Systems
1601 W 5th Ave., Ste. 111
Columbus, OH 43212
**Subject(s):** Computers; Education
**Circ:** 1,800

**Journal of Illinois History** (9402)
Illinois Historic Preservation Agency
1 Old State Capitol Plaza
Springfield, IL 62701-1507
Phone: (217)524-6045
**Subject(s):** History and Genealogy
**Circ:** (Paid)1,800

**Journal of the Pharmacy Society of Wisconsin** (33194)
Pharmacy Society of Wisconsin
701 Heartland Trl.
Madison, WI 53717
Phone: (608)827-9200
Fax: (608)827-9292
**Subject(s):** Drugs and Pharmaceuticals
**Circ:** (Non-paid)150
(Paid)‡1,800

**Journal of Emotional and Behavioral Disorders** (8559)
PRO-ED Inc.
Dept. of Educational Psych., Counseling, & Special Education
Northern Illinois University
Graham Hall
DeKalb, IL 60115-2854
Phone: (815)753-8443
**Subject(s):** Education
**Circ:** (Non-paid)‡94
(Paid)‡1,782

**Perfumer and Flavorist** (7980)
Allured Publishing Corp.
362 S. Schmale Rd.
Carol Stream, IL 60188-2787
Phone: (630)653-2155
Fax: (630)653-2192
**Subject(s):** Chemistry, Chemicals, and Chemical Engineering
**Circ:** ‡1,774

**Education Administration Quarterly** (33299)
Corwin Press
Dept. of Administration Leadership
Univ. of Milwaukee
517 Enderis Hall
2400 E. Hartford Ave.
Milwaukee, WI 53211
**Subject(s):** Education
**Circ:** (Non-paid)81
(Paid)1,751

**Lipids** (8021)
AOCS Press
2211 W. Bradley Ave.
Champaign, IL 61821
Phone: (217)359-2344
Fax: (217)351-8091
**Circ:** (Controlled)50
1,750

**Modern Philology** (8340)
University of Chicago Press
1427 E. 60th St.
Chicago, IL 60637
Phone: (773)702-7700
Fax: (773)702-9756
**Subject(s):** Philology, Language, and Linguistics
**Circ:** ‡1,750

**Studies in Second Language Acquisition** (9613)
Cambridge University Press
CREDLI, Indiana Univ., BH604
1105 E Atwater
Bloomington, IN 47405
**Subject(s):** Philology, Language, and Linguistics
**Circ:** 1750

**International Anesthesiology Clinics** (24318)
Lippincott Williams & Wilkins
C/o William E. Hurford, Editor-in-Chief
Professor and Chair, Department of Anesthesia
University of Cincinnati Medical Center
Cincinnati, OH 45221
**Subject(s):** Medicine and Surgery
**Circ:** (Paid)‡1,700

**Milling Journal** (8537)
Country Journal Publishing Company Inc.
3065 Pershing Ct.
Decatur, IL 62526
Phone: (217)877-9660
Fax: (217)877-6647
**Subject(s):** Commerce and Industry
**Circ:** (Controlled)1,700

**Nonprofit and Voluntary Sector Quarterly** (9898)
Sage Publications Inc.
c/o Janice O'Rourke, Managing Editor
Nonprofit and Voluntary Sector Quarterly
550 W. N. St., Ste. 301
Indianapolis, IN 46202
Phone: (317)278-8981
**Subject(s):** Sociology; Philanthropy and Humanitarianism; Economics
**Circ:** 1,700

**Notre Dame Technical Review** (10089)
357 Cushing Hall
University of Notre Dame
Notre Dame, IN 46556
Phone: (574)631-5531
**Subject(s):** Engineering (Various branches)
**Circ:** 1,700

**Poodle Review** (9485)
2003 E Illini Airport Rd.
Urbana, IL 61801
Phone: (217)328-7375
**Subject(s):** Dogs
**Circ:** (Non-paid)300
(Paid)1,700

**Turf News** (8613)
Turfgrass Producers International
2 E Main St.
East Dundee, IL 60118
Phone: (847)649-5555
Fax: (847)649-5678
**Subject(s):** General Agriculture; Socialized Farming
**Circ:** ‡1,700

**The Review of Higher Education** (15247)
The Johns Hopkins University Press
c/o Dennis Brown, Executive Director, ASHE
Michigan State University
424 Erickson Hall
East Lansing, MI 48824
Phone: (517)432-8805
Fax: (517)432-8806
**Subject(s):** Education
**Circ:** (Combined)1,660

**The Journal of Legal Medicine** (7950)
Taylor & Francis
c/o Marshall B. Kapp, School of Law
Southern Illinois University
Carbondale, IL 62901-6804
Phone: (618)453-8741
Fax: (618)453-3317
**Subject(s):** Medicine and Surgery; Law
**Circ:** (Paid)‡1,622

**Against the Current (15164)**
Center for Changes
7012 Michigan Ave.
Detroit, MI 48210
Phone: (313)841-0160
**Subject(s):** Sociology; Politics
**Circ:** (Paid)‡1,600

**American Music (8003)**
University of Illinois Press
1325 S. Oak St.
Champaign, IL 61820-6903
Phone: (217)333-0950
Fax: (217)244-8082
**Subject(s):** Music and Musical Instruments
**Circ:** ‡1,600

**American Orthoptic Journal (33150)**
University of Wisconsin Press
1930 Monroe St., 3rd Fl.
Madison, WI 53711-2029
Phone: (608)263-1110
Fax: (608)263-1173
**Subject(s):** Medicine and Surgery
**Circ:** (Paid)1,600

**Avanti (16252)**
Avanti Owners Association International
c/o Cornerstone Registration
PO Box 1743
Maple Grove, MN 55311-6743
Phone: (763)420-7829
Fax: (763)420-7849
**Subject(s):** Automotive (Consumer)
**Circ:** 1,600

**The Cremationist of North America (8164)**
Cremation Association of North America
401 N. Michigan Ave.
Chicago, IL 60611
Phone: (312)245-1077
Fax: (312)321-4098
**Subject(s):** Funeral Directors; Cemeteries and Monuments
**Circ:** ‡1,600

**FEDA News and Views (8198)**
Foodservice Equipment Distributors Association
223 W. Jackson Blvd. Ste. 620
Chicago, IL 60606
Phone: (312)427-9605
Fax: (312)427-9607
**Subject(s):** Food and Grocery Trade; Hotels, Motels, Restaurants, and Clubs
**Circ:** (Controlled)1,600

**Financial Manager for the Media Professional (9131)**
Broadcast Cable Financial Management Association
550 Frontage Rd., Ste. 3600
Northfield, IL 60093
Phone: (847)716-7000
Fax: (847)716-7004
**Subject(s):** Radio, Television, Cable, and Video
**Circ:** (Controlled)1,600

**Hypatia (15231)**
Indiana University Press
503 South Kedzie Hall
Michigan State University
Department of Philosophy
East Lansing, MI 48824-1032
Phone: (517)432-8425
Fax: (517)432-1320
**Subject(s):** Women's Interests; Philosophy
**Circ:** 1,600

**IPA Bulletin (9381)**
International Prepress Association
552 W 167th St.
South Holland, IL 60473
Phone: (708)596-5110
Fax: (708)596-5112
**Subject(s):** Graphic Arts and Design; Printing and Typography
**Circ:** ‡1,600

**Mid-American Review (24208)**
Bowling Green State University
Bowling Green, OH 43403
Phone: (419)372-2725
Fax: (419)372-6805
**Subject(s):** Literature; Poetry
**Circ:** (Controlled)1,600

**POA (9903)**
Pony of Americas Club Inc.
5240 Elmwood Ave.
Indianapolis, IN 46203
Phone: (317)788-0107
Fax: (317)788-8974
**Subject(s):** Livestock; (Horses and Horse Racing)
**Circ:** ‡1,600

**REALTORS Land Institute (8394)**
National Association of Realtors
430 N Michigan Ave.
Chicago, IL 60611-4087
Phone: (312)329-8200
Fax: (312)329-8390
**Subject(s):** Real Estate
**Circ:** (Non-paid)‡500
(Paid)‡1,600

**Journal of Chromatographic Science (9059)**
Preston Publications
6600 W Touhy Ave.
PO Box 48312
Niles, IL 60714-4588
Phone: (847)647-2900
Fax: (847)647-1155
**Subject(s):** Chemistry, Chemicals, and Chemical Engineering
**Circ:** (Non-paid)‡63
(Paid)‡1,581

**Journal of Clinical Neurophysiology (8268)**
Lippincott Williams & Wilkins
c/o John S. Ebersole
5841 S. Maryland Ave. MC 2030
The Univ. of Chicago
Chicago, IL 60637-1447
**Subject(s):** Medicine and Surgery; Psychology and Psychiatry
**Circ:** 1,586

**Genetics in Medicine (16300)**
Lippincott Williams & Wilkins
C/o Richard A. King, MD, PhD
Mayo Mail Code 0447, 420 Delaware St. SE
Institute of Human Genetics
University of Minnesota
Minneapolis, MN 55455
Phone: (612)626-4224
Fax: (612)624-6645
**Subject(s):** Medicine and Surgery; Genetics
**Circ:** (Paid)‡1,565

**Toledo Medicine (25093)**
The Academy of Medicine of Toledo and Lucas County
4428 Secor Rd.
Toledo, OH 43623
Phone: (419)473-3200
Fax: (419)475-6744
**Subject(s):** Medicine and Surgery
**Circ:** (Controlled)‡208
(Paid)‡1,568

**Illinois Standardbred & Mid-America Harness News (8603)**
Resource Development Press Ltd.
2235 Durand Dr.
PO Box 399
Downers Grove, IL 60515
Phone: (630)963-0398
Fax: (630)963-2625
**Subject(s):** (Horses and Horse Racing); Livestock
**Circ:** 1,540

**Ceramic Engineering and Science Proceedings (25153)**
The American Ceramic Society
PO Box 6136
Westerville, OH 43086-6136
Phone: (614)890-4700
Fax: (614)891-8960
**Subject(s):** Ceramics
**Circ:** (Non-paid)16
(Paid)1,519

**Art Institute of Chicago Museum Studies (8089)**
Art Institute of Chicago
Publications Department
111 S Michigan Ave.
Chicago, IL 60603-6110
Phone: (312)443-3540
Fax: (312)443-1334
**Subject(s):** Art and Art History
**Circ:** (Paid)1,500

**Bulletin of Concerned Asian Scholars (15104)**
3693 S. Bay Bluffs Dr.
Cedar, MI 49621-9434
Phone: (231)228-7116
Fax: (253)540-2583
**Subject(s):** Intercultural Interests
**Circ:** ‡1,500

**The Cardinal (16716)**
St. Mary's University
700 Terrace Heights, No. 36
Winona, MN 55987
Phone: (507)457-1496
Fax: (507)457-6967
**Subject(s):** College Publications
**Circ:** (Paid)50
(Non-paid)1,500

**Communication Outlook (15228)**
Artificial Language Laboratory
405 Computer Center.
East Lansing, MI 48824-1042
Phone: (517)353-0870
Fax: (517)353-4766
**Subject(s):** Computers; Handicapped
**Circ:** (Paid)1,500

**Field (24963)**
Oberlin College Press
50 N. Professor St.
Oberlin, OH 44074
Phone: (440)775-8408
Fax: (440)775-8124
**Subject(s):** Literature; Poetry
**Circ:** (Non-paid)200
(Paid)1,500

**Heritage of Vermilion County (8529)**
Vermilion County Museum Society
116 N Gilbert St.
Danville, IL 61832
Phone: (217)442-2922
Fax: (217)442-2001
**Subject(s):** History and Genealogy
**Circ:** (Controlled)⊕1,500

**Indiana Pharmacist (9869)**
Indiana Pharmacists Association
729 N Penn St.
Indianapolis, IN 46204
Phone: (317)634-4968
Fax: (317)632-1219
**Subject(s):** Drugs and Pharmaceuticals
**Circ:** ‡1,500

**JMNR (8252)**
E. J. Gossett Publishing Inc.
7145 S Maplewood Ave.
Chicago, IL 60629-2045
Phone: (773)476-5978
Fax: (773)476-3259
**Subject(s):** Nursing; Military and Navy
**Circ:** (Paid)900
(Non-paid)1,500

**Journal of Clinical Ligand Assay (15887)**
Clinical Ligand Assay Society
3139 S Wayne Rd.
Wayne, MI 48184
Phone: (734)722-6290
Fax: (734)722-7006
**Subject(s):** Laboratory Research (Scientific and Medical); Health and Healthcare
**Circ:** 1,500

**Journal of the Lepidopterists' Society (8656)**
Allen Press Inc.
c/o Michael Tolliver, Editor
Department of Biology, Eureka College
300 E. College
Eureka, IL 61530
**Subject(s):** Natural History and Nature Study
**Circ:** (Paid)1,500

**Journal of Manufacturing Systems (15152)**
Society of Manufacturing Engineers
1 SME Dr.
PO Box 930
Dearborn, MI 48121
Phone: (313)271-1500
Fax: (313)425-3401
**Subject(s):** Commerce and Industry
**Circ:** (Paid)1,500

**Journal of Sex & Marital Therapy (24437)**
Taylor & Francis
c/o R. Taylor Segraves, MetroHealth Medical Center
Dept. of Psychology
2500 Metrohealth Dr.
Cleveland, OH 44109-1998
Phone: (216)778-8412
Fax: (216)778-8412
Subject(s): Psychology and Psychiatry
Circ: ‡1,500

**Kaleidoscope (24100)**
United Disability Services
701 S Main St.
Akron, OH 44311-1019
Phone: (330)762-9755
Fax: (330)762-0912
Subject(s): Handicapped; Literature and Literary Reviews
Circ: (Paid)1,500

**The Lebanon Light (24826)**
Lebanon High School
1916 Drake Rd.
Lebanon, OH 45036-1299
Phone: (513)934-5100
Fax: (513)933-2150
Subject(s): Journalism and Publishing
Circ: (Controlled)1,500

**Minnesota Grocer (16597)**
Minnesota Grocers Association
533 St. Clair Ave.
Saint Paul, MN 55102
Phone: (651)228-0973
Fax: (651)228-1949
Subject(s): Food and Grocery Trade
Circ: ‡1,500

**Molecular Plant-Microbe Interactions (MPMI) (16601)**
The American Phytopathological Society
3340 Pilot Knob Rd.
Saint Paul, MN 55121
Phone: (651)454-7250
Fax: (651)454-0766
Subject(s): Scientific Agricultural Publications; Botany
Circ: (Non-paid)7
(Paid)1,500

**The Monist (9240)**
The Hegeler Institute
315 Fifth St.
Peru, IL 61354
Phone: (815)223-4486
Fax: (815)223-4486
Subject(s): Philosophy
Circ: (Non-paid)‡200
(Paid)‡1,500

**Nonprofit Management and Leadership (24460)**
Jossey-Bass Publishers
c/o Roger A. Lohman, Editor
Nonprofit Management & Leadership, Mandel Center for Nonprof
Case Western Reserve Univ.
10900 Euclid Ave.
Cleveland, OH 44106-7167
Subject(s): Management and Administration
Circ: (Paid)1,500

**Northwestern University Law Review (8025)**
University of Illinois Press
1325 S. Oak St.
Champaign, IL 61820-6903
Phone: (217)333-0950
Fax: (217)244-8082
Subject(s): Law
Circ: ‡1,500

**Other Voices (8363)**
University of Illinois at Chicago
601 S Morgan St.
Chicago, IL 60607-7120
Phone: (312)413-2209
Fax: (312)413-1005
Subject(s): Literature and Literary Reviews; Literature
Circ: 1,500

**Properties Magazine (24481)**
PO Box 112167
Cleveland, OH 44111
Phone: (216)251-0035
Fax: (216)251-0064
Subject(s): Building Management and Maintenance
Circ: (Paid)1,500
(Free)1,500

**Shots Magazine (16341)**
Shots
PO Box 27755
Minneapolis, MN 55427-0775
Subject(s): Photography
Circ: (Paid)900
(Non-paid)1,500

**Theory into Practice (24603)**
Ohio State University
The College of Education
341 Ramseyer Hall
29 W Woodruff Ave.
Columbus, OH 43210
Phone: (614)292-3407
Fax: (614)292-7020
Subject(s): Education
Circ: (Non-paid)‡200
(Paid)‡1,500

**Wisconsin Grocer (33221)**
Wisconsin Grocers Association
1 S Pinckney Ste. 504
Madison, WI 53703
Phone: (608)244-7150
Fax: (608)244-9030
Subject(s): Food and Grocery Trade
Circ: ‡1,500

**Witness (15276)**
Oakland Community College
27055 Orchard Lake Rd.
Farmington Hills, MI 48334
Phone: (248)522-3400
Fax: (248)522-3548
Subject(s): Literature and Literary Reviews
Circ: (Paid)‡1,500
(Controlled)‡1,500

**World Order (9533)**
National Spiritual Assembly of the Baha'is of the United States
415 Linden Ave.
Wilmette, IL 60091
Phone: (847)251-1854
Fax: (847)251-3652
Subject(s): Religious Publications
Circ: ‡1,500

**Journal of the Torrey Botanical Society (24147)**
Allen Press
C/O Brian C. McCarthy
Dept. of Environmental and Plant Biology
317 Porter Hall Ohio Univ.
Athens, OH 45701-2979
Phone: (740)593-1615
Fax: (740)593-1130
Subject(s): Botany
Circ: (Combined)‡1,483

**The Basenji (15766)**
Windigo Harbor Media
PO Box 182397
Shelby Township, MI 48318-2397
Phone: (586)612-0279
Subject(s): Dogs
Circ: ‡1,450

**International Journal of American Linguistics (8241)**
University of Chicago Press
1427 E. 60th St.
Chicago, IL 60637
Phone: (773)702-7700
Fax: (773)702-9756
Subject(s): Philology, Language, and Linguistics
Circ: ‡1,450

**The Psychological Record (24744)**
Kenyon College
104 College Dr.
Gambier, OH 43022-9623
Phone: (740)427-5000
Fax: (740)427-5417
Subject(s): Psychology and Psychiatry
Circ: (Non-paid)‡242
(Paid)‡1,450

**International Journal of Plant Sciences (8243)**
University of Chicago Press
1427 E. 60th St.
Chicago, IL 60637
Phone: (773)702-7700
Fax: (773)702-9756
Subject(s): Botany
Circ: ‡1,400

**Journal of English and Germanic Philology (9479)**
University of Illinois Press
107 English Bldg.
608 S. Wright St.
Urbana, IL 61801
Phone: (217)333-4852
Fax: (217)244-3242
Subject(s): Philology, Language, and Linguistics; Literature
Circ: ‡1,400

**The Loon (16310)**
Minnesota Ornithologists' Union
James Ford Bell Museum of Natural History
University of Minnesota
10 Church St. SE
Minneapolis, MN 55455-0104
Subject(s): Ornithology and Oology; Natural History and Nature Study
Circ: (Combined)1,400

**Over the Front (24328)**
League of World War I Aviation Historians
3127 Penrose Pl.
Cincinnati, OH 45211
Phone: (513)481-2209
Fax: (513)481-2209
Subject(s): Aviation; History and Genealogy
Circ: (Paid)1,400

**Pastoral Life (24240)**
Society of St. Paul
P O Box 595
9531 Akron Canfield Rd.
Canfield, OH 44406-0595
Phone: (330)533-5503
Fax: (330)533-1076
Subject(s): Religious Publications
Circ: ‡1,400

**Preaching: Word & Witness (33414)**
Liturgical Publications Inc.
75 Queens Park Cres. E.
New Berlin, WI 53151
Phone: (414)585-4545
Subject(s): Religious Publications
Circ: (Combined)1,400

**Spoon River Poetry Review (9076)**
c/o Dr. Lucia Getsi
Illinois State University
4240 English
Normal, IL 61790-4240
Phone: (309)438-7906
Fax: (309)438-5414
Subject(s): Poetry; Literature and Literary Reviews; Literature
Circ: (Combined)1,400

**Journal of the American Society of Podiatric Medical Assistants (8505)**
American Society of Podiatric Medical Assistants
2124 S Austin Blvd.
Cicero, IL 60804
Phone: (708)863-6303
Fax: (708)863-5375
Subject(s): Podiatry; Health and Healthcare; Medicine and Surgery
Circ: 1,350

**Media Spectrum (15513)**
Michigan Association for Media in Education
1407 Rensen St., Ste. 3
Lansing, MI 48910-3657
Phone: (517)394-2808
Fax: (517)394-2096
Subject(s): Library and Information Science; Education
Circ: 1,350

**Minnesota Law Review (16320)**
University of Minnesota
229 19th Ave. South
Minneapolis, MN 55455-0401
Phone: (612)625-9330
Fax: (612)624-5400
Subject(s): Law
Circ: 1,345

**The Philosopher's Index (24211)**
The Philosopher's Information Center
1616 E Wooster St. 34
Bowling Green, OH 43402
Phone: (419)353-8830
Fax: (419)353-8920

**Subject(s):** Philosophy; Indexes, Abstracts, Reports, Proceedings, and Bibliographies
**Circ:** (Non-paid)‡175
(Paid)‡1,322

**Classical Philology** (8146)
University of Chicago Press
1427 E. 60th St.
Chicago, IL 60637
Phone: (773)702-7700
Fax: (773)702-9756
**Subject(s):** Philology, Language, and Linguistics
**Circ:** ‡1,300

**Economic Development Quarterly** (24403)
Sage Publications Inc.
c/o W. Hill, Editor
Levin College of Urban Affairs
Cleveland State Univ.
Cleveland, OH 44115
**Subject(s):** Economics; International Business and Economics
**Circ:** (Non-paid)‡164
(Paid)‡1,300

**Journal of American Culture** (24204)
Popular Press
Bowling Green University
Popular Culture Ctr.
Bowling Green, OH 43403
Phone: (419)372-7867
Fax: (419)372-8095
**Subject(s):** Sociology
**Circ:** ‡1,300

**The Journal of Legal Studies** (8280)
University of Chicago Press
c/o Maureen Callahan, Managing Editor
The Univ. of Chicago Law School
1111 E. 60th St.
Chicago, IL 60637
Phone: (773)702-9603
Fax: (773)702-0730
**Subject(s):** Law
**Circ:** (Paid)‡1,300

**Journal of Teaching in Physical Education** (10246)
Human Kinetics Publishers Inc.
c/o Bonnie Tjerdsma Blankenship, Ph.D. (Lead Co-Editor)
Dept. of Health and Kinesiology, Purdue Univ.
800 W.
West Lafayette, IN 47907
Phone: (765)494-3188
Fax: (765)496-1239
**Subject(s):** Physical Education and Athletics
**Circ:** (Paid)‡1,300

**Michigan Grange News** (15394)
Michigan State Grange
1730 Chamberlain
Haslett, MI 48840
Phone: (517)339-2171
Fax: (517)339-3636
**Subject(s):** General Agriculture
**Circ:** ‡1,300

**Nuclear Technology** (8847)
American Nuclear Society
555 N Kensington Ave.
La Grange Park, IL 60526
Phone: (708)352-6611
Fax: (708)352-0499
**Subject(s):** Nuclear Engineering
**Circ:** 1,300

**Visible Language** (8440)
c/o Prof. Sharon Helmer Poggenpohl, Editor & Publisher
IIT Institute of Design
350 N. LaSalle St.
Chicago, IL 60610
Phone: (312)595-4921
Fax: (312)595-4901
**Subject(s):** Philology, Language, and Linguistics; Graphic Arts and Design
**Circ:** ‡1,300

**Journal of Analytical Toxicology** (9058)
Preston Publications
6600 W Touhy Ave.
PO Box 48312
Niles, IL 60714-4588
Phone: (847)647-2900
Fax: (847)647-1155
**Subject(s):** Toxicology; Chemistry, Chemicals, and Chemical Engineering
**Circ:** (Non-paid)‡64
(Paid)‡1,250

**The Professional Lawyer** (8386)
Center for Professional Responsibility
321 N. Clark, 15th Fl.
Chicago, IL 60610-4714
Fax: (312)988-5491
**Subject(s):** Law
**Circ:** (Non-paid)250
(Paid)1,250

**The American Book Review** (9066)
The Unit for Contemporary Literature
Illinois State University
Campus Box 4241
Normal, IL 61790-4241
Phone: (309)438-2127
Fax: (309)438-3523
**Subject(s):** Literature and Literary Reviews
**Circ:** (Non-paid)‡1,000
(Paid)‡1,200

**Clockwatch Review** (7913)
Clockwatch Review Press
Dept. of English
Illinois Wesleyan University
PO Box 2900
Bloomington, IL 61702
Phone: (309)556-3352
Fax: (309)556-3411
**Subject(s):** Literature
**Circ:** (Combined)1,200

**Criticism** (15174)
Wayne State University Press
Dept. of English
Wayne State University
Detroit, MI 48202
Phone: (313)577-2450
Fax: (313)577-8618
**Subject(s):** Literature
**Circ:** ‡1,200

**Free Lunch** (8735)
Free Lunch Arts Alliance
PO Box 717
Glenview, IL 60025-0717
Phone: (847)729-3595
**Subject(s):** Poetry
**Circ:** (Combined)‡1,200

**Illinois Journal of Mathematics** (9473)
University of Illinois
1409 W. Green St.
Urbana, IL 61801
Phone: (217)333-3410
Fax: (217)265-0497
**Subject(s):** Mathematics
**Circ:** (Paid)‡1,200

**Journal of the Illinois Optometric Association** (9060)
Illinois Optometric Association
8118 Milwaukee Ave.
Niles, IL 60714-2836
Phone: (847)825-6339
Fax: (847)825-3407
**Subject(s):** Ophthalmology, Optometry, and Optics
**Circ:** 1,200

**The Journal of Pharmacy Technology** (24323)
Harvey Whitney Books Co.
8044 Montgomery Rd., Ste. 415
Box 42696
Cincinnati, OH 45242-0696
Phone: (513)793-3555
Fax: (513)793-3600
**Subject(s):** Drugs and Pharmaceuticals
**Circ:** (Non-paid)‡100
(Paid)‡1,200

**Merrill-Palmer Quarterly** (15187)
Wayne State University Press
Wayne State University
Psychology Dept.
Detroit, MI 48205
Phone: (313)577-0563
**Subject(s):** Psychology and Psychiatry
**Circ:** (Non-paid)‡100
(Paid)‡1,200

**Michigan Christmas Tree Journal** (15434)
Michigan Christmas Tree Association
PO Box 377
Howell, MI 48844
Phone: (517)545-9971
Fax: (517)545-4501
**Subject(s):** Forestry
**Circ:** 1,200

**Michigan Quarterly Review** (15020)
University of Michigan
3574 Rackham Bldg.
Ann Arbor, MI 48109-1070
Phone: (734)764-9265
**Subject(s):** Literature; Literature and Literary Reviews
**Circ:** ‡1,200

**The North American Deer Farmer** (32811)
North American Deer Farmer
1720 W Wisconsin Ave.
Appleton, WI 54914-3254
Phone: (920)734-0934
Fax: (920)734-0955
**Subject(s):** Livestock; General Agriculture
**Circ:** (Combined)1,200

**Nuclear Science and Engineering** (8846)
American Nuclear Society
555 N. Kensington Ave.
La Grange Park, IL 60526
Phone: (708)579-8312
Fax: (708)579-8313
**Subject(s):** Nuclear Engineering
**Circ:** 1,200

**Parish Liturgy** (9382)
American Catholic Press
16565 S State St.
South Holland, IL 60473
Phone: (708)331-5485
Fax: (708)331-5484
**Subject(s):** Religious Publications
**Circ:** (Non-paid)200
(Paid)1,200

**The Sport Psychologist** (8032)
Human Kinetics Publishers Inc.
1607 N. Market St.
PO Box 5076
Champaign, IL 61825-5076
Phone: (217)351-5076
Fax: (217)351-1549
**Subject(s):** Physical Education and Athletics; Psychology and Psychiatry
**Circ:** ‡45
(Paid)‡1,202

**Transactions of the ASAE** (15746)
American Society of Agricultural Engineers
2950 Niles Rd.
Saint Joseph, MI 49085-9659
Phone: (269)429-0300
Fax: (269)429-3852
**Subject(s):** General Agriculture; Engineering (Various branches)
**Circ:** ‡1,200

**Science Fiction Studies** (9774)
SF-TH Inc., EC L-06
DePauw University
Greencastle, IN 46135-0037
Phone: (765)658-4758
Fax: (765)658-4764
**Subject(s):** Literature
**Circ:** (Controlled)1,150

**Ophthalmic Plastic and Reconstructive Surgery** (33324)
Lippincott Williams & Wilkins
c/o Gerald J. Harris
925 N. 87th St.
Medical College of Wisconsin
Milwaukee, WI 53226
**Subject(s):** Laboratory Research (Scientific and Medical)
**Circ:** 1,125

**Sociology of Sport Journal** (8030)
Human Kinetics Publishers Inc.
1607 N. Market St.
PO Box 5076
Champaign, IL 61825-5076
Phone: (217)351-5076
Fax: (217)351-1549
**Subject(s):** Sociology; (General Sports)
**Circ:** (Paid)‡1,119

**Teaching Philosophy  (24983)**
Philosophy Documentation Center
Dept. of Philosophy
Miami University
Oxford, OH 45056
Phone: (513)529-4731
Fax: (513)529-4731
**Subject(s):** Philosophy; Education

Circ: (Non-paid)‡47
     (Paid)‡1,110

**Urban Affairs Review  (8435)**
Sage Publications Inc.
Great Cities Institute
College of Urban Planning and Public Affairs (M/C 107)
University of Illinois at Chicago
412 S. Peoria St., Ste. 400
Chicago, IL 60607-7067
**Subject(s):** Sociology

Circ: (Paid)‡1,110

**American Literary Scholarship  (9581)**
Duke University Press
American Literature Section
Department of English
Indiana University
Bloomington, IN 47405
Phone: (812)855-8224
Fax: (812)855-9535
**Subject(s):** Literature

Circ: (Paid)1,100

**Archival Issues  (33154)**
Midwest Archives Conference
c/o Menzi Behrnd-Klodt
7422 Longmeadow Rd.
Madison, WI 53717
Phone: (608)827-5727
**Subject(s):** History and Genealogy

Circ: 1,100

**Journal of African American Men  (24976)**
Transaction Publishers
Dept. of Physical Education
Miami Univ.
Oxford, OH 45056
Phone: (513)529-2721
**Subject(s):** Men's Interests; Social Sciences; Ethnic and Minority Studies

Circ: (Paid)‡1,100

**Ohioana Quarterly  (24592)**
Ohioana Library Association
274 E First Ave., Ste. 300
Columbus, OH 43201
Phone: (614)466-3831
Fax: (614)728-6974
**Subject(s):** Literature and Literary Reviews

Circ: (Non-paid)†1,000
     (Paid)‡1,100

**Outcomes Management  (15194)**
Lippincott Williams & Wilkins
C/o Marilyn H. Oermann, Ph.D, Editor
Wayne State University
College of Nursing
Detroit, MI
**Subject(s):** Nursing; Health and Healthcare

Circ: (Paid)‡1,100

**Pharmacy in History  (33209)**
American Institute of the History of Pharmacy
777 Highland Ave.
Madison, WI 53705-2222
Phone: (608)262-5378
**Subject(s):** Drugs and Pharmaceuticals; History and Genealogy

Circ: (Non-paid)‡100
     (Paid)‡1,100

**The Short Line  (9219)**
1318 S Johanson Rd.
Peoria, IL 61607-1130
Phone: (309)697-1400
Fax: (309)697-5388
**Subject(s):** Railroad; History and Genealogy

Circ: (Non-paid)20
     (Paid)1,100

**Swedish-American Historical Quarterly  (16632)**
Swedish-American Historical Society
Gustavus Adolphus College
Department of History
Saint Peter, MN 56082
Phone: (507)933-7435

Fax: (507)933-7041
**Subject(s):** Ethnic Publications; History and Genealogy

Circ: (Non-paid)‡52
     (Paid)‡1,050

**Michigan Roads and Construction  (15527)**
2929 Covington Court Ste 100
PO Box 25007
Lansing, MI 48909-5007
Phone: (517)484-7600
Fax: (517)484-4777
**Subject(s):** State, Municipal, and County Administration; Roads and Streets

Circ: (Non-paid)436
     (Paid)1,043

**Philosophy Today  (8375)**
DePaul University
2352 N Clifton Ave.
Chicago, IL 60614-3208
Phone: (773)325-7267
Fax: (773)325-7268
**Subject(s):** Philosophy

Circ: (Non-paid)‡60
     (Paid)‡1,044

**Argumentation and Advocacy  (33520)**
American Forensic Association
PO Box 256
519 East Walnut Street
River Falls, WI 54022
Phone: (715)425-3198
Fax: (715)425-9533
**Subject(s):** Education; Law

Circ: (Paid)1,000

**BCA Journal  (9834)**
Black Coaches Association
Pan American Plz.
201 S Capitol Ave., Ste. 495
Indianapolis, IN 46225
Phone: (317)829-5600
Fax: (317)829-5601
**Subject(s):** Black Publications; Physical Education and Athletics

Circ: 1,000

**Bulletin of the Council for Research in Music Education  (9464)**
School of Music
University of Illinois
1114 W Nevada
Urbana, IL 61801
Phone: (217)333-1027
Fax: (217)244-8136
**Subject(s):** Education; Music and Musical Instruments

Circ: (Non-paid)‡100
     (Paid)‡1,000

**Buoyant Flight  (24095)**
The Lighter Than Air Society
526 S. Main St., Ste. 232
Akron, OH 44311
Phone: (330)535-5827
Fax: (330)668-1105
**Subject(s):** Aviation

Circ: ‡1,000

**Commercial Lending Review  (9285)**
Aspen Publishers Inc.
CCH Incorporated
2700 Lake Cook Rd.
Riverwoods, IL 60015
Phone: (847)267-7000
Fax: (978)371-2961
**Subject(s):** Banking, Finance, and Investments

Circ: (Paid)1,000

**CSS Cable  (16053)**
College of St. Scholastica
1200 Kenwood
Duluth, MN 55811
Phone: (218)723-6187
Fax: (218)723-6290
**Subject(s):** College Publications

Circ: (Controlled)‡1,000

**Current Digest of the Post-Soviet Press  (24547)**
Current Digest of the Soviet Press
3857 N High St.
Columbus, OH 43214-3747
Phone: (614)292-4234
Fax: (614)267-6310
**Subject(s):** International Affairs

Circ: (Paid)1,000

**December  (8784)**
December Press Inc.
1097 Sandwick Ct.
PO Box 302
Highland Park, IL 60035
Phone: (847)940-4122
**Subject(s):** Literature; Poetry

Circ: (Paid)1,000

**Digest of Middle East Studies (DOMES)  (33575)**
Global Information Co.
PO Box 402
Thiensville, WI 53092
Phone: (262)242-9031
**Subject(s):** International Affairs; Intercultural Interests

Circ: (Paid)1,000

**Doing Business in Europe  (8175)**
CCH Inc.
4025 W. Peterson Ave.
Chicago, IL 60646-6085
Phone: (847)267-7000
Fax: (773)866-3895
**Subject(s):** International Business and Economics

Circ: ‡1,000

**Ethics, Law and Aging Review  (24650)**
Springer Publishing Co.
Marshall B. Kapp, Editor
Wright State University School of Medicine
Office of Geriatric Medicine & Gerontology
PO Box 927
Dayton, OH 45401-0927
Phone: (937)775-3392
Fax: (513)775-2581
**Subject(s):** Gerontology; Hospitals and Healthcare Institutions; Law

Circ: (Combined)1,000

**Family and Consumer Sciences Research Journal  (7948)**
Sage Publications Inc.
c/o Jane E. Workman
Fashion Design and Merchandising Program
Southern Illinois University
311 Quigley Hall
Carbondale, IL 62901-4318
**Subject(s):** Home Economics

Circ: (Paid)1,000

**Feminist Periodicals  (33178)**
Women's Studies Librarian
430 Memorial Library
728 State St.
Madison, WI 53706
Phone: (608)263-5754
Fax: (608)265-2754
**Subject(s):** Women's Interests; Indexes, Abstracts, Reports, Proceedings, and Bibliographies

Circ: 1,000

**Fueling Indiana  (9852)**
Indiana Petroleum Marketers and Convenience Store Association (IPCA)
101 W Washington St., Ste. 805 E
Indianapolis, IN 46204
Phone: (317)633-4662
Fax: (317)630-1827
**Subject(s):** Petroleum, Oil, and Gas

Circ: (Controlled)1,000

**The Journal of Aesthetic Education  (9476)**
University of Illinois Press
377 Education Bldg.
University of Illinois
1310 S. Sixth St., MC-708
Urbana, IL 61801
**Subject(s):** Education

Circ: (Non-paid)50
     (Paid)1,000

**Journal of the American Society of Brewing Chemists  (16585)**
American Society of Brewing Chemists
3340 Pilot Knob Rd.
Saint Paul, MN 55121
Phone: (651)454-7250
Fax: (651)454-0766
**Subject(s):** Chemistry, Chemicals, and Chemical Engineering

Circ: (Controlled)1,000

**The Journal of Cognitive Rehabilitation** (9878)
NeuroScience Publishers
6555 Carrollton Ave.
Indianapolis, IN 46220
Phone: (317)257-9672
Fax: (317)257-9674
**Subject(s):** Medicine and Surgery
**Circ:** 1,000

**Journal of Cultural Diversity** (8902)
Tucker Publications Inc.
PO Box 580
Lisle, IL 60532
Phone: (630)969-3809
Fax: (630)969-3895
**Subject(s):** Ethnic and Minority Studies
**Circ:** (Combined)1,000

**Journal of Economics and Management Strategy** (8674)
The MIT Press
c/o Daniel F. Spulber, Kellogg GSM, Leverone Hall
Northwestern University
Evanston, IL 60208-2013
Phone: (847)467-1776
Fax: (847)467-1777
**Subject(s):** Economics; Management and Administration
**Circ:** 1,000

**Journal of Law and Religion** (16587)
Hamline University
1536 Hewitt Ave.
Saint Paul, MN 55104-1284
Phone: (651)523-2800
**Subject(s):** Law; Theology
**Circ:** (Paid)1,000

**Law Enforcement Legal Review** (8730)
Law Enforcement Legal Publications
421 Ridgewood Ave., Ste. 100
Glen Ellyn, IL 60137-4900
Phone: (630)858-6392
Fax: (630)858-6392
**Subject(s):** Law; Safety
**Circ:** (Paid)1,000

**Marquee** (8645)
Theatre Historical Society of America
York Theatre Bldg., 2nd Fl.
152 N York St.
Elmhurst, IL 60126-2806
Phone: (630)782-1800
Fax: (630)782-1802
**Subject(s):** Performing Arts; Architecture
**Circ:** (Controlled)‡1,000

**Midwest Engineer** (8904)
Western Society of Engineers
4513 Lincoln Ave., Ste. 213
Lisle, IL 60532-1290
Phone: (630)724-9770
Fax: (630)241-0142
**Subject(s):** Engineering (Various branches)
**Circ:** ‡1,000

**Monatshefte** (33203)
University of Wisconsin Press
1930 Monroe St., 3rd Fl.
Madison, WI 53711-2029
Phone: (608)263-1110
Fax: (608)263-1173
**Subject(s):** Education; German; Literature
**Circ:** ‡1,000

**Monday Morning Report** (15529)
Alcohol Research Information Service
430 Lathrop St.
Lansing, MI 48912-2410
Phone: (517)485-9900
Fax: (517)485-1928
**Subject(s):** Substance Abuse and Treatment
**Circ:** (Non-paid)‡100
(Paid)‡1,000

**Pig Iron** (25208)
Pig Iron Press
26 N Phelps St.
PO Box 237
Youngstown, OH 44503
Phone: (330)747-6932
Fax: (330)747-0599
**Subject(s):** Poetry; Literature and Literary Reviews
**Circ:** (Paid)1,000

**Poets' Roundtable** (10191)
Poets' Study Club of Terre Haute, Indiana
826 S Center St.
Terre Haute, IN 47807
**Subject(s):** Literature; Poetry
**Circ:** (Controlled)1,000

**Social Philosophy and Policy** (24213)
Cambridge University Press
C/O Ellen Frankel Paul
Social Philosophy and Policy Center
Bowling Green State University
225 Troop St.
Bowling Green, OH 43403-0188
**Subject(s):** Philosophy
**Circ:** 1,000

**Theatre History Studies** (15613)
Mid-America Theatre Association
Central Michigan University
Moore Hall ( Speech and Drama)
Mount Pleasant, MI 48859
Phone: (517)774-9881
Fax: (517)774-2498
**Subject(s):** Drama and Theatre; Performing Arts
**Circ:** (Paid)1,000

**Third Coast** (15480)
Western Michigan Univ.
Dept. of English
Kalamazoo, MI 49008-5331
Phone: (269)387-2675
Fax: (269)387-2562
**Subject(s):** Poetry
**Circ:** (Paid)1,000

**Adapted Physical Activity Quarterly** (24527)
Human Kinetics Publishers Inc.
c/o David L. Porretta
The Ohio State University
202 Pomerene Hall
1760 Neil Ave.
Columbus, OH 43210
Phone: (614)292-0849
Fax: (614)292-7229
**Subject(s):** Health and Healthcare; Handicapped
**Circ:** ‡26
(Paid)‡977

**Journal of Bronchology** (24433)
Lippincott Williams & Wilkins
c/o Atul C. Mehta
The Cleveland Clinic/A90
9500 Euclid Av.
Cleveland, OH 44195
**Subject(s):** Medicine and Surgery
**Circ:** 979

**Journal on Excellence in College Teaching** (24977)
Center for the Enhancement of Learning and Teaching
Miami University
Oxford, OH 45056
Phone: (513)529-9265
Fax: (513)529-9264
**Subject(s):** Education
**Circ:** (Paid)965

**Milton Quarterly** (24149)
Ohio University
Ellis Hall
Athens, OH 45701
Phone: (614)593-2829
Fax: (614)593-2818
**Subject(s):** Literature
**Circ:** ‡950

**Light** (8312)
PO Box 7500
Chicago, IL 60680
Phone: (847)853-1028
Fax: (847)853-1102
**Subject(s):** Literature
**Circ:** (Combined)‡923

**Mammalian Genome** (24450)
Springer-Verlag New York Inc.
Genetics Department
Case Western Reserve University
10900 Euclid Ave.
Cleveland, OH 44106-4955
**Subject(s):** Genetics; Biology
**Circ:** (Combined)925

**ILMDA Advantage** (9399)
Illinois Lumber and Material Dealers Association Inc.
932 S. Spring St.
Springfield, IL 62704
Phone: (217)544-5405
Fax: (217)544-4206
**Subject(s):** Building Materials, Concrete, Brick, and Tile; Wood and Woodworking
**Circ:** (Combined)‡918

**The Bryologist** (7946)
Allen Press Inc.
c/o Dale Vitt, Editor-in-Chief
Dept. of Plant Biology
Southern Illinois Univ.
Carbondale, IL 62901-6509
**Subject(s):** Botany; Biology
**Circ:** (Paid)‡900

**Children's Literature Association Quarterly** (15044)
Children's Literature Association
PO Box 138
Battle Creek, MI 49016-0138
Phone: (269)965-8180
Fax: (269)965-3568
**Subject(s):** Children's Interests
**Circ:** ‡900

**Detroit Society for Genealogical Research Magazine** (15179)
Detroit Society for Genealogical Research Inc.
The Burton Historical Collection
Detroit Public Library
5201 Woodward Ave. & Kirby
Detroit, MI 48202-4093
Phone: (313)833-1480
**Subject(s):** History and Genealogy
**Circ:** ‡900

**Feminist Teacher** (32923)
University of Wisconsin-Eau Claire
405 Hibbard Hall
Eau Claire, WI 54702-4004
Phone: (715)836-2639
Fax: (715)836-5996
**Subject(s):** Women's Interests; Education
**Circ:** (Paid)900

**Hendricks Pioneer** (16167)
PO Box 5
Hendricks, MN 56136-0005
Phone: (507)275-3197
Fax: (507)275-3108
**Subject(s):** Paid Community Newspapers
**Circ:** (Paid)900

**Historic Madison** (33186)
Historic Madison Incorporated of Wisconsin
PO Box 2721
Madison, WI 53701-2721
Phone: (608)233-9394
**Subject(s):** History and Genealogy
**Circ:** (Controlled)900

**Journal of Motor Behavior** (8283)
Heldref Publications
c/o Daniel M. Corcos
University of Illinois
School of Kinesiology (MC 194)
901 W. Roosevelt Rd.
Chicago, IL 60608
**Subject(s):** Medicine and Surgery
**Circ:** (Paid)900

**Journal of Neuro-Ophthalmology** (15009)
Lippincott Williams & Wilkins
c/o Jonathan D. Trobe, Departments of Ophthalmology and Neur
University of Michigan, Kellogg Eye Center
Ann Arbor, MI
**Subject(s):** Laboratory Research (Scientific and Medical)
**Circ:** 906

**Michigan Mathematical Journal** (15018)
University of Michigan
525 E University
Ann Arbor, MI 48109-1109
Phone: (734)647-4462
Fax: (734)763-0938
**Subject(s):** Mathematics
**Circ:** (Paid)900

# Great Lakes States

**The Microscope** (8335)
McCrone Research Institute
2820 S Michigan Ave.
Chicago, IL 60616-3292
Phone: (312)842-7100
Fax: (312)842-1078
**Subject(s):** Ophthalmology, Optometry, and Optics

Circ: (Controlled)‡50
(Paid)‡900

**Rethinking Marxism** (10092)
Taylor and Francis
c/o David F. Ruccio, Editor
Dept. of Economics,Univ.of Notre Dame
Notre Dame, IN 46556
Phone: (574)631-6434
Fax: (574)631-8809
**Subject(s):** Politics

Circ: (Non-paid)‡105
(Paid)‡900

**Canadian Journal of Applied Physiology** (8006)
Human Kinetics Publishers Inc.
1607 N. Market St.
PO Box 5076
Champaign, IL 61825-5076
Phone: (217)351-5076
Fax: (217)351-1549
**Subject(s):** Physical Education and Athletics

Circ: (Non-paid)‡37
(Paid)‡879

**Comparative Drama** (15466)
Western Michigan University
1903 W. Michigan Ave.
Kalamazoo, MI 49008
Fax: (616)387-2562
**Subject(s):** Drama and Theatre; Literature

Circ: (Controlled)‡50
(Paid)‡850

**Indiana Law Review** (9868)
Indiana University School of Law-Indianapolis
Indiana University
530 W New York St.
Indianapolis, IN 46202
Phone: (317)274-4440
Fax: (317)278-3326
**Subject(s):** Law

Circ: (Combined)850

**The Michigan Optometrist** (15524)
Michigan Optometric Association
530 W Ionia St., Ste. A
Lansing, MI 48933-1062
Phone: (517)482-0616
Fax: (517)482-1611
**Subject(s):** Ophthalmology, Optometry, and Optics

Circ: (Controlled)‡99
(Paid)‡856

**Names** (8561)
American Name Society
Northern Illinois University
English Dept.
DeKalb, IL 60115-2863
Phone: (815)753-6627
Fax: (815)753-0606
**Subject(s):** Philology, Language, and Linguistics; Anthropology and Ethnology; Psychology and Psychiatry; Geography

Circ: (Paid)850

**Ohio Northern University Law Review** (24090)
Ohio Northern University
Box 153
Ada, OH 45810
Phone: (419)772-2248
Fax: (419)772-2714
**Subject(s):** Law; College Publications

Circ: (Paid)850

**Xcp: Cross Cultural Poetics** (16353)
College of St. Catherine
601 25th Ave. S.
Minneapolis, MN 55454
Phone: (651)690-7747
Fax: (651)690-7849
**Subject(s):** Poetry; Ethnic and Minority Studies; Intercultural Interests; Politics; Drama and Theatre

Circ: (Combined)850

**The Mennonite Quarterly Review** (9767)
Mennonite Historical Society
1700 S. Main St.
Goshen, IN 46526
Fax: (574)535-7433
**Subject(s):** Religious Publications

Circ: (Controlled)‡180
(Paid)‡820

**New Directions for Adult and Continuing Education** (24573)
Jossey-Bass Publishers
c/o Susan Imel, Editor-in-Chief,ERIC/ACVE,
1900 Kenny Rd.
Columbus, OH 43210-1090
**Subject(s):** Education

Circ: ‡812

**Basta!** (8097)
Chicago Religious Task Force on Central America
59 E Van Buren St., Ste. 1400
Chicago, IL 60605
**Subject(s):** International Affairs

Circ: 800

**Comparative Studies of South Asia, Africa, and the Middle East** (9067)
Duke University Press
Department of History
Illinois State University
Campus Box 4420
Normal, IL 61790-4420
Phone: (309)438-8580
Fax: (309)438-5607
**Subject(s):** Social Sciences; Intercultural Interests; Anthropology and Ethnology

Circ: (Paid)800

**Geographical Analysis** (24552)
The Ohio State University Press
1070 Carmack Rd.
Columbus, OH 43210-1002
Phone: (614)292-6930
Fax: (614)292-2065
**Subject(s):** Geography

Circ: ‡800

**Gobbles** (15990)
Minnesota Turkey Growers Association Inc.
108 Marty Dr.
Buffalo, MN 55313-9338
Phone: (763)682-2171
Fax: (763)682-5546
**Subject(s):** Poultry and Pigeons

Circ: ‡800

**Italian American Chamber of Commerce of Chicago Bulletin** (8248)
Italian American Chamber of Commerce
30 S Michigan Ave., Ste. 504
Chicago, IL 60603
Phone: (312)553-9137
Fax: (312)533-9142
**Subject(s):** Chambers of Commerce and Boards of Trade

Circ: (Paid)800

**Journal of Nursing Law** (32925)
PESI HealthCare L.L.C.
200 Spring St.
PO Box 1000
Eau Claire, WI 54702
Phone: (715)833-5431
Fax: (715)833-5493
**Subject(s):** Nursing; Law

Circ: (Paid)800

**Mathematical Finance** (8330)
Blackwell Publishers
Department of Finance
M/C 168 - University of Illinois
601 S. Morgan Rm. 2431
Chicago, IL 60607-7124
Phone: (312)996-7170
Fax: (312)996-7170
**Subject(s):** Mathematics; Statistics; Economics

Circ: ‡800

**Michigan Botanist** (33451)
Michigan Botanical Club Inc.
C/O Dr. Neil A. Harriman, Editor
Dept. of Biology
University of Wisconsin-Oshkosh
Oshkosh, WI 54901
Phone: (920)424-1002

**Subject(s):** Botany; Local, State, and Regional Publications
Circ: (Combined)⊕800

**New Product News** (8352)
213 W Institute Pl., Ste. 704
Chicago, IL 60610
Phone: (312)932-0600
Fax: (312)932-0474
**Subject(s):** Food and Grocery Trade; Drugs and Pharmaceuticals

Circ: (Paid)‡800

**Ohio State Journal on Dispute Resolution** (24589)
Ohio State University
Ohio State University Moritz College at Law
55W. 12th Ave.
Columbus, OH 43210-1391
Phone: (614)292-7170
Fax: (614)292-3442
**Subject(s):** Law

Circ: (Paid)800

**Research in African Literatures** (24599)
Indiana University Press
Research in African Literatures
Ohio State University
361 Dulles Hall
230 W. 17th Ave.
Columbus, OH 43210
Phone: (614)292-9735
Fax: (614)292-3927
**Subject(s):** Literature

Circ: (Controlled)200
(Paid)800

**Residential Treatment for Children and Youth** (8398)
The Haworth Press Inc.
c/o Richard A. Epstein
Sonya Shankman Orthogenic School, The Univ. of Chicago
1365 E. 60th St.
Chicago, IL 60637
Phone: (773)702-1203
Fax: (773)702-1304
**Subject(s):** Psychology and Psychiatry

Circ: (Paid)799

**Modern Haiku** (8874)
PO Box 68
Lincoln, IL 62656-0068
**Subject(s):** Literature; Poetry

Circ: (Combined)770

**Doody's Health Sciences Book Review Journal** (8176)
Doody's Review Service
Doody Enterprises Inc.
500 N. Michigan Ave., Ste. 1410
Chicago, IL 60611
Phone: (312)644-7640
**Subject(s):** Health and Healthcare; Medicine and Surgery

Circ: (Non-paid)100
(Paid)750

**ECO Communicator** (24950)
East Central Ohio Food Dealers Association Inc.
1200 Rear N Main St.
North Canton, OH 44720
Phone: (330)494-2302
Fax: (330)494-6963
**Subject(s):** Food and Grocery Trade

Circ: ‡750

**Indiana Law Journal** (9594)
Indiana University
211 S Indiana Ave.
Bloomington, IN 47405
Phone: (812)855-7995
Fax: (812)855-6980
**Subject(s):** Law

Circ: (Combined)750

**Journal of the History of Dentistry** (7854)
American Academy of the History of Dentistry
100 S Vail Ave.
Arlington Heights, IL 60005-1866
Phone: (847)670-7561
**Subject(s):** Dentistry

Circ: (Paid)750

**The Music Index** (15879)
Harmonie Park Press
23630 Pinewood
Warren, MI 48091-4759
Phone: (586)755-3080
Fax: (586)755-4213

**Subject(s):** Indexes, Abstracts, Reports, Proceedings, and Bibliographies; Music and Musical Instruments
**Circ:** ‡750

**Rockford Review** (9306)
Rockford Writers' Guild
PO Box 858
Rockford, IL 61105
**Subject(s):** Poetry; Literature
**Circ:** (Paid)750

**Social Cognition** (10253)
Taylor and Francis
Dept. of Psychological Sciences
Purdue Univ.
West Lafayette, IN 47907
Phone: (317)494-6889
Fax: (317)496-1264
**Subject(s):** Psychology and Psychiatry
**Circ:** 756

**The Teacher Educator** (10047)
Ball State University
Teachers College 1008
Muncie, IN 47306-0612
Phone: (765)285-5453
Fax: (765)285-5455
**Subject(s):** Education
**Circ:** (Combined)740

**Communications in Algebra** (33297)
Marcel Dekker Inc.
c/o Mark L. Teply
University of Wisconsin-Milwaukee
Milwaukee, WI 53201
**Subject(s):** Mathematics
**Circ:** 725

**Organization Development Journal** (24272)
Organization Development Institute
11234 Walnut Ridge Rd.
Chesterland, OH 44026-1299
Phone: (440)729-7419
Fax: (440)729-9319
**Subject(s):** Business; Management and Administration
**Circ:** (Combined)720

**Religion and American Culture** (9907)
University of California Press/Journals
c/o Thomas Davis, Managing Editor
Indiana University-Purdue University at Indianapolis
Center for the Study of Religion and American Culture
Cavanaugh Hall 341
Indianapolis, IN 46202-5140
**Subject(s):** History and Genealogy; Theology
**Circ:** 726

**Applied Engineering in Agriculture** (15742)
American Society of Agricultural Engineers
2950 Niles Rd.
Saint Joseph, MI 49085-9659
Phone: (269)429-0300
Fax: (269)429-3852
**Subject(s):** Engineering (Various branches); Scientific Agricultural Publications
**Circ:** (Paid)‡700

**Arctic Anthropology** (33156)
University of Wisconsin Press
1930 Monroe St., 3rd Fl.
Madison, WI 53711-2029
Phone: (608)263-1110
Fax: (608)263-1173
**Subject(s):** Anthropology and Ethnology
**Circ:** (Paid)700

**The Christian Librarian** (24257)
Association of Christian Librarians Inc.
PO Box 4
Cedarville, OH 45314
Phone: (937)766-2255
Fax: (937)766-2337
**Subject(s):** Religious Publications; Library and Information Science
**Circ:** (Non-paid)100
(Paid)700

**Critical Reviews in Environmental Science and Technology** (24546)
CRC Press L.L.C.
Dept. of Natural Resources
Ohio State University
2021 Coffey Rd.
Columbus, OH 43210
Phone: (614)292-9043
Fax: (614)292-7162
**Subject(s):** Ecology and Conservation; Water Supply and Sewage Disposal
**Circ:** (Controlled)700

**Endangered Species UPDATE** (15003)
University of Michigan
430 E. University, Dana Bldg.
Ann Arbor, MI 48109-1115
Phone: (734)763-3243
Fax: (734)936-2195
**Subject(s):** Ecology and Conservation
**Circ:** (Controlled)700

**Fulton County Images** (10137)
Fulton County Historical Society Inc.
37 E 375 N
Rochester, IN 46975-8384
Phone: (574)223-4436
**Subject(s):** History and Genealogy; Local, State, and Regional Publications
**Circ:** (Controlled)700

**Issues in Law & Medicine** (10190)
National Legal Center for the Medically Dependent & Disabled Inc.
3 S 6th St.
Terre Haute, IN 47807-3510
Phone: (812)232-2434
Fax: (812)235-3685
**Subject(s):** Law; Medicine and Surgery; Biology
**Circ:** (Paid)600
(Controlled)700

**Journal of Business and Finance Librarianship** (24557)
The Haworth Press Inc.
Business Library, Raymond E. Mason Hall
Ohio State University
250 W. Woodruff Ave.
Columbus, OH 43210
Phone: (614)292-2136
**Subject(s):** Library and Information Science
**Circ:** 708

**Landscape Journal** (33197)
University of Wisconsin Press
1930 Monroe St., 3rd Fl.
Madison, WI 53711-2029
Phone: (608)263-1110
Fax: (608)263-1173
**Subject(s):** Landscape Architecture
**Circ:** (Paid)700

**Michigan Oil and Gas News** (15610)
600 W Pickard
PO Box 250
Mount Pleasant, MI 48804-0250
Phone: (989)772-5181
Fax: (989)773-2970
**Subject(s):** Petroleum, Oil, and Gas
**Circ:** (Non-paid)‡40
‡700

**Modern Austrian Literature** (24209)
Modern Austrian Literature and Culture Association
GREAL
Bowling Green State University
Bowling Green, OH 43403
Phone: (419)372-7139
Fax: (419)372-2571
**Subject(s):** Literature
**Circ:** ‡700

**Progress in Paper Recycling** (32813)
18 Woodbury Ct.
Appleton, WI 54913-7111
Phone: (920)832-9101
Fax: (920)832-0870
**Subject(s):** Ecology and Conservation; Waste Management and Recycling
**Circ:** (Combined)700

**Quarterly Review of Biophysics** (8389)
Cambridge University Press
Pritzker School of Medicine
5841 S. Maryland Ave., MC 1051 (C-120)
295 Congress Ave
Chicago, IL 60637
**Subject(s):** Biology
**Circ:** 700

**Written Communication** (24810)
Sage Publications Inc.
c/o Kent State University
Department of English
PO Box 5190
Kent, OH 44242
**Subject(s):** Communications
**Circ:** (Paid)‡700

**Journal of Religious Gerontology** (9526)
The Haworth Press Inc.
Wheaton Campus
200 S. Naperville Rd.
Wheaton, IL 60187
Phone: (630)668-3838
Fax: (630)668-5883
**Subject(s):** Gerontology; Religious Publications
**Circ:** 691

**Concrete Abstracts** (15269)
American Concrete Institute
38800 Country Club Dr.
PO BOX 9094
Farmington Hills, MI 48331
Phone: (248)848-3700
Fax: (248)848-3701
**Subject(s):** Building Materials, Concrete, Brick, and Tile; Indexes, Abstracts, Reports, Proceedings, and Bibliographies
**Circ:** ‡676

**Comparative Labor Law & Policy Journal** (8007)
University of Illinois
116 Law Bldg.
504 E Pennsylvania Ave.
Champaign, IL 61820
Phone: (217)333-9852
Fax: (217)244-1478
**Subject(s):** Law; International Business and Economics; Labor
**Circ:** (Combined)650

**Journal of Sociology and Social Welfare** (15473)
Western Michigan University
School of Social Work
Kalamazoo, MI 49008-5354
Phone: (269)387-3205
Fax: (269)387-3217
**Subject(s):** Sociology
**Circ:** ‡650

**Loyola University Chicago Law Journal** (8319)
Loyola University-Chicago/School of Law
1 E Pearson
Chicago, IL 60611
Phone: (312)915 7183
Fax: (312)915-7201
**Subject(s):** College Publications; Law
**Circ:** (Controlled)‡650

**Michigan Banker Magazine** (15514)
PO Box 12236
Lansing, MI 48901-2236
Phone: (517)484-0775
Fax: (517)484-4676
**Subject(s):** Banking, Finance, and Investments
**Circ:** (Paid)‡650

**Renascence** (33330)
Marquette University
Raynor Memorial Libraries, Rm. M164
PO Box 1881
Milwaukee, WI 53201-1881
Phone: (414)288-6725
Fax: (414)288-5433
**Subject(s):** Religious Publications; Literature
**Circ:** (Non-paid)‡25
(Paid)‡650

**Personnel Management Abstracts** (15125)
704 Island Lake Rd.
Chelsea, MI 48118
Phone: (313)475-1979
**Subject(s):** Indexes, Abstracts, Reports, Proceedings, and Bibliographies; Management and Administration
**Circ:** ‡645

**American Journal of Semiotics** (7945)
Semiotic Society of America
Speech Communication Dept.
Southern Illinois University
Carbondale, IL 62901-6605
Phone: (618)453-1894
Fax: (618)453-2812

**Subject(s):** Philology, Language, and Linguistics; Communications; Literature; Philosophy
**Circ:** ‡600

**Fusion Technology** (8844)
American Nuclear Society
c/o Dr. Nermin A. Uckan
American Nuclear Society
555 N. Kensington Ave.
La Grange Park, IL 60526
Phone: (708)579-8312
Fax: (708)579-8313
**Subject(s):** Nuclear Engineering; Science (General)
**Circ:** 600

**Indiana University Mathematics Journal** (9597)
Indiana University
Rawles Hall 115
Bloomington, IN 47405
Phone: (812)855-2252
Fax: (812)855-0046
**Subject(s):** Mathematics
**Circ:** (Non-paid)165
 (Paid)600

**Journal of Interior Design Education and Research** (9879)
Interior Design Educators Council
7150 Winton Dr., No. 300
Indianapolis, IN 46268-4196
Phone: (317)816-6261
Fax: (317)571-5603
**Subject(s):** Interior Design/Decorating
**Circ:** 600

**Journal of Macromolecular Science, Part B, Physics** (9480)
Marcel Dekker Inc.
c/o P. H. Geil
Department of Materials Science and Engineering
University of Illinois
1304 W. Green St.
Urbana, IL 61801
Phone: (217)333-0149
Fax: (217)333-2736
**Subject(s):** Physics
**Circ:** 600

**Karamu** (8045)
Karamu Association English Department
Charleston, IL 61920
Phone: (217)581-6297
**Subject(s):** Literature
**Circ:** (Combined)600

**Kumquat Meringue** (16475)
Penumbra Press
PO Box 736
Pine Island, MN 55963
Phone: (507)367-4430
**Subject(s):** Poetry; Literature and Literary Reviews; Literature
**Circ:** (Paid)600

**Papers on Language & Literature** (8624)
Southern Illinois University Edwardsville
Edwardsville, IL 62026-1434
Phone: (618)650-2119
Fax: (618)650-3509
**Subject(s):** Philology, Language, and Linguistics; Literature
**Circ:** (Non-paid)54
 (Paid)600

**Prayers for Worship** (33413)
Liturgical Publications Inc.
2875 S James Dr.
New Berlin, WI 53151-3662
Phone: (262)785-1188
Fax: (262)785-9567
**Subject(s):** Religious Publications
**Circ:** (Combined)⊕600

**The Steam Automobile Bulletin** (9192)
Steam Automobile Club of America Inc.
150 S. Quentin Rd.
Palatine, IL 60067
Phone: (847)991-3911
**Subject(s):** Automotive (Consumer)
**Circ:** (Paid)600

**Struggle** (15201)
Tim Hall
Box 13261
Detroit, MI 48213-0261
Phone: (313)273-9039
**Subject(s):** Literature; Poetry; Literature and Literary Reviews
**Circ:** (Combined)600

**University of Cincinnati Law Review** (24340)
University of Cincinnati
Rm. 300
Taft Hall
Cincinnati, OH 45221-0040
Phone: (513)556-6000
Fax: (513)556-6265
**Subject(s):** Law
**Circ:** (Combined)600

**Northwestern Journal of International Law & Business** (8357)
Northwestern University School of Law
357 E Chicago Ave.
Chicago, IL 60611
Phone: (312)503-8742
Fax: (312)503-0132
**Subject(s):** Law; Business
**Circ:** (Combined)598

**Journal of Agricultural Lending** (33273)
American Bankers Association
N78 W14573 Appleton Ave., No. 287
Menomonee Falls, WI 53051
Phone: (262)253-6902
Fax: (262)253-6903
**Subject(s):** General Agriculture; Banking, Finance, and Investments
**Circ:** (Paid)580

**Journal of Organizational Behavior-Management** (15185)
The Haworth Press Inc.
c/o Thomas C. Mawhinney
College of Business & Administration, Univ. of Detroit
4001 West McNichols
PO Box 19900
Detroit, MI 48219-0900
Phone: (313)993-1084
**Subject(s):** Management and Administration
**Circ:** (Controlled)‡583

**Marriage and Family Review** (9891)
The Haworth Press Inc.
c/o Suzanne K. Steinmetz
11236 Blackwalnut Pt.
425 University Blvd.
Indianapolis, IN 46236
Phone: (317)274-2516
Fax: (317)278-3654
**Subject(s):** Marriage and Family
**Circ:** (Paid)589

**Numerical Heat Transfer, Part A: Applications** (8360)
Taylor & Francis
c/o W. J. Minkowycz, Dept. of Mechanical Engineering
University of Illinois at Chicago
842 W. Taylor St., Rm 2049
Chicago, IL 60607-7022
**Subject(s):** Chemistry, Chemicals, and Chemical Engineering; Engineering (Various branches); Physics
**Circ:** ‡586

**Journal of Investigative Surgery** (15472)
Taylor & Francis
c/o Luis H. Toledo-Pereyra, Borgess Research Institute
Michigan State University
Kalamazoo, MI
**Subject(s):** Biology; Medicine and Surgery
**Circ:** (Paid)‡571

**Journal of Theory Construction Testing** (8903)
Tucker Publications Inc.
PO Box 580
Lisle, IL 60532
Phone: (630)969-3809
Fax: (630)969-3895
**Subject(s):** Science (General)
**Circ:** (Combined)570

**ABNF Journal** (8901)
Tucker Publications Inc.
PO Box 580
Lisle, IL 60532
Phone: (630)969-3809
Fax: (630)969-3895
**Subject(s):** Health and Healthcare; Nursing; Ethnic and Minority Studies
**Circ:** (Combined)562

**Encounter** (9849)
Christian Theological Seminary
1000 W. 42nd St.
Indianapolis, IN 46208
Phone: (317)924-1331
Fax: (317)923-1961
**Subject(s):** Religious Publications
**Circ:** (Non-paid)‡58
 (Paid)‡568

**Personal Relationships** (9074)
Cambridge University Press
c/o Susan Sprecher
Department of Sociology & Anthropology
Illinois State University
Normal, IL 61790-5378
**Subject(s):** Marriage and Family; Anthropology and Ethnology; Psychology and Psychiatry; Sociology
**Circ:** (Non-paid)‡74
 (Paid)‡567

**Psychoanalytic Social Work** (15196)
The Haworth Press Inc.
Wayne State Univ.
School of Social Work
Detroit, MI 48202
Phone: (313)577-4447
Fax: (313)577-8770
**Subject(s):** Social Programs
**Circ:** (Paid)569

**Church Libraries** (8727)
Evangelical Church Library Association
PO Box 353
Glen Ellyn, IL 60138-0353
Phone: (847)296-3964
Fax: (847)296-0754
**Subject(s):** Library and Information Science
**Circ:** (Controlled)‡100
 (Paid)‡550

**Indiana Audubon Quarterly** (9862)
Indiana Audubon Society Inc.
1005 Buffalo Run Way
Indianapolis, IN 46227
Phone: (317)883-2010
**Subject(s):** Ornithology and Oology
**Circ:** (Combined)556

**Technology and Culture** (15155)
Society for the History of Technology
Henry Ford Museum & Greenfield Village
20900 Oakwood Blvd.
Dearborn, MI 48124
Phone: (313)982-6083
Fax: (313)982-6244
**Subject(s):** History and Genealogy; Automation
**Circ:** 545

**Marketing Education Review** (8324)
American Marketing Association
311 S. Wacker Dr., Ste. 5800
Chicago, IL 60606-2266
Phone: (312)542-9000
Fax: (312)542-9001
**Subject(s):** Education
**Circ:** (Paid)530

**The Classical Bulletin** (9510)
Bolchazy-Carducci Publishers Inc.
1000 Brown St., Unit 101
Wauconda, IL 60084
Phone: (847)526-4344
Fax: (847)526-2867
**Subject(s):** Philology, Language, and Linguistics; History and Genealogy; Literature
**Circ:** (Non-paid)‡480
 (Paid)‡520

**Wisconsin Archeologist** (33342)
Wisconsin Archeological Society
PO Box 1292
Milwaukee, WI 53201
Phone: (414)229-4273
Fax: (414)229-4219
**Subject(s):** Archaeology
**Circ:** ‡527

**Architectural Research Quarterly** (16273)
Cambridge University Press
Univ. of Minnesota
College of Architecture and Landscape Architecture
125 Architecture Bldg, 89 Church St S.E.
Minneapolis, MN 55455
**Subject(s):** Architecture
**Circ:** 500

**Bankruptcy Law Reports** (9284)
CCH Inc.
2700 Lake Cook Rd.
Riverwoods, IL 60015
**Subject(s):** Banking, Finance, and Investments; Law
**Circ:** ‡500

**Computer Science Education** (32921)
University of Wisconsin-Eau Claire
405 Hibbard Hall
Eau Claire, WI 54702-4004
Phone: (715)836-2639
Fax: (715)836-5996
**Subject(s):** Computers; Education
**Circ:** ‡500

**The Emily Dickinson Journal** (24406)
Johns Hopkins University Press
c/o Gary Lee Stonum
English Department
11112 Bellflower Rd.
Case Western Reserve University
Cleveland, OH 44106-7117
Phone: (216)368-3342
Fax: (216)368-4367
**Subject(s):** Literature
**Circ:** (Combined)500

**Journal of the American College of Neuropsychiatrists** (15272)
American College of Neuropsychiatrists
28595 Orchard Lake Rd., Ste. 200
Farmington Hills, MI 48334
Phone: (248)553-0010
Fax: (248)553-0818
**Subject(s):** Psychology and Psychiatry; Medicine and Surgery; Health and Healthcare
**Circ:** 500

**Knowledge, Technology & Policy** (7952)
Transaction Publishers
1309 W. Walnut St.
Carbondale, IL 62901
Phone: (815)331-1290
Fax: (815)331-1290
**Subject(s):** Science (General)
**Circ:** (Paid)‡500

**Luso-Brazilian Review** (33198)
University of Wisconsin Press
1930 Monroe St., 3rd Fl.
Madison, WI 53711-2029
Phone: (608)263-1110
Fax: (608)263-1173
**Subject(s):** Intercultural Interests
**Circ:** (Paid)500

**Magicol** (8745)
Magic Collectors' Association
PO Box 511
Glenwood, IL 60425-0511
Phone: (708)757-4950
**Subject(s):** Crafts, Models, Hobbies, and Contests; Collecting
**Circ:** 500

**NST (Nature, Society and Thought)** (16335)
MEP Publications
University of Minnesota
Physics Bldg.
116 Church St. SE
Minneapolis, MN 55455-0112
Phone: (612)922-7993
**Subject(s):** Humanities; Education; Philosophy; Social Sciences
**Circ:** 500

**Pan-Japan** (9073)
Pan-Japan Journal
Anthropology 4640
338 Schroeder Hall
Illinois State University
Normal, IL 61790
Phone: (309)438-7690
Fax: (309)438-7177
**Subject(s):** Anthropology and Ethnology
**Circ:** ‡500

**Pedagogy** (15345)
Duke University Press
Department of English
Calvin College
3201 Burton St. SE
Grand Rapids, MI 49546
Phone: (616)957-6598
Fax: (616)957-8508
**Subject(s):** Education; Literature
**Circ:** 500

**Philosophy of Music Education Review** (9610)
Indiana University Press
c/o Estelle R. Jorgensen, Editor, Indiana Univ. School of Mu
Music Education Dept.
1201 E. Third St.
Bloomington, IN 47405-7006
Phone: (812)855-2051
Fax: (812)855-4936
**Subject(s):** Music and Musical Instruments; Philosophy
**Circ:** (Paid)500

**Philosophy & Theology** (33326)
Marquette University Press
Memorial Library 116
PO Box 3141
Milwaukee, WI 53201-3141
Phone: (414)288-1564
Fax: (414)288-7813
**Subject(s):** Philosophy; Theology
**Circ:** (Paid)500

**Spring** (14979)
129 Lake Huron Hall
1 Campus Dr.
Grand Valley SU
Allendale, MI 49401-9403
Phone: (616)895-3071
Fax: (616)895-3430
**Subject(s):** Literature; Poetry
**Circ:** (Paid)500

**Substance** (33214)
University of Wisconsin Press
1930 Monroe St., 3rd Fl.
Madison, WI 53711-2029
Phone: (608)263-1110
Fax: (608)263-1173
**Subject(s):** Literature; Social Sciences; Humanities; Philosophy; Mathematics
**Circ:** (Paid)500

**Clinical Neuropharmacology** (15775)
Lippincott Williams & Wilkins
c/o Peter A. LeWitt
Clinical Neuroscience Center
26400 West Twelve Mile Rd, Ste.110
Southfield, MI 48034
**Subject(s):** Laboratory Research (Scientific and Medical); Psychology and Psychiatry
**Circ:** 499

**Notre Dame Journal of Law, Ethics & Public Policy** (10087)
University of Notre Dame
Notre Dame, IN 46556
Phone: (574)631-4888
**Subject(s):** Law; Politics
**Circ:** (Controlled)490

**Journal of Thermal Spray Technology** (24890)
ASM International
9639 Kinsman Rd.
Materials Park, OH 44073-0002
Phone: (440)338-5151
Fax: (440)338-4634
**Subject(s):** Materials Handling; Engineering (Various branches)
**Circ:** (Non-paid)199
(Paid)⊕481

**Journal of Family Psychotherapy** (9791)
The Haworth Press Inc.
c/o Terry S. Trepper
Purdue University Calumet
Family Studies Center
2200 169th St.
Hammond, IN 46323-2094
Phone: (219)989-2541
Fax: (219)989-2777
**Subject(s):** Marriage and Family; Psychology and Psychiatry
**Circ:** 479

**Minas Tirith Evening Star** (15401)
American Tolkien Society
c/o Phil Helms
PO Box 373
Highland, MI 48357-0373
Fax: (248)462-6473
**Subject(s):** Literature and Literary Reviews; Literature
**Circ:** 475

**Religion and Literature** (10091)
University of Notre Dame
1146 Flanner Hall
Notre Dame, IN 46556
Phone: (574)631-5725
Fax: (574)631-8609
**Subject(s):** Literature; Theology
**Circ:** (Paid)450

**Tract Messenger** (16706)
Lutheran Braille Evangelism Association
1740 Eugene St.
White Bear Lake, MN 55110
Phone: (651)426-0469
**Subject(s):** Religious Publications; Blind and Visually Challenged
**Circ:** (Controlled)450

**The Information Society** (9598)
Taylor & Francis
Department of Telecommunications
R-TV Center, 1229 E. 7th St
Indiana University
Bloomington, IN 47405-5501
**Subject(s):** Library and Information Science
**Circ:** ‡417

**The Dandelion** (32900)
PO Box 205
Cornucopia, WI 54827
Phone: (715)742-3940
Fax: (715)742-3940
**Subject(s):** Politics
**Circ:** ‡400

**Fifteenth Century Studies** (15271)
Camden House
29451 Halsted Rd., Apt. 141
Farmington Hills, MI 48331
**Subject(s):** History and Genealogy; Literature
**Circ:** 400

**International Journal of Comparative and Applied Criminal Justice** (15232)
Michigan State University
560 Baker Hall
East Lansing, MI 48824-1118
Phone: (517)355-2197
Fax: (517)432-1787
**Subject(s):** Police, Penology, and Penal Institutions; Safety; Law
**Circ:** (Paid)400

**Israel Studies** (9599)
Indiana University Press
601 N. Morton St.
Bloomington, IN 47404-3797
Phone: (812)855-8817
Fax: (812)855-8507
**Subject(s):** Ethnic and Minority Studies
**Circ:** 400

**Journal of Dispersion Science & Technology** (15905)
Marcel Dekker Inc.
c/o John Texter
Eastern Michigan University
122 Sill Hall
College of Technology
Ypsilanti, MI 48197
Phone: (734)487-3192
Fax: (734)487-7795
**Subject(s):** Science (General)
**Circ:** 400

**New Directions for Child and Adolescent Development** (9484)
Jossey-Bass Publishers
c/o Prof. Reed Larson, Editor-in-chief
Dept. of Human & Community Development
Univ. of Illinois
1105 W. Nevada St.
Urbana, IL 61801
**Subject(s):** Psychology and Psychiatry
**Circ:** (Non-paid)50
(Paid)400

**Western Kentucky Journal** (10070)
Brenda Joyce Jerome
PO Box 325
Newburgh, IN 47629-0325
Phone: (812)853-8092
**Subject(s):** History and Genealogy
**Circ:** (Paid)400

**Journal of Hospitality and Leisure Marketing** (15234)
The Haworth Press Inc.
The School of Hospitality Business
The Eli Broad College of Business/Management
Michigan State Univ.
235 Eppley Ctr.
East Lansing, MI 48824-1121
Phone: (517)353-9211
Fax: (517)484-1170
**Subject(s):** Hotels, Motels, Restaurants, and Clubs; Travel and Tourism
**Circ:** 396

**Electromagnetics** (8185)
Taylor & Francis
c/o H. Y. David Yang, Department of EECS
1120 SEO, M/C 154
University of Illinois at Chicago
Chicago, IL 60607-7053
Phone: (940)565-4415
Fax: (940)565-4415
**Subject(s):** Electronics Engineering
**Circ:** (Combined)‡361

**Advances in Strawberry Production** (15079)
North American Strawberry Growers Association
PMB 326
9864 E Grand River Ave., Ste. 110
Brighton, MI 48116-1999
Phone: (517)548-4990
Fax: (517)548-0813
**Subject(s):** General Agriculture; Fruit, Fruit Products, and Produce Trade
**Circ:** 350

**Aside World** (24227)
World Sidesaddle Federation
Box 1104
Bucyrus, OH 44820
Phone: (419)284-3176
Fax: (419)284-3176
**Subject(s):** (Horses and Horse Racing)
**Circ:** 350

**Food Reviews International** (33180)
Marcel Dekker Inc.
c/o Richard W. Hartel
Department of Food Science
University of Wisconsin Madison
1605 Linden Dr.
Madison, WI 53706
**Subject(s):** Scientific Agricultural Publications; Health and Healthcare; Food and Grocery Trade
**Circ:** 350

**Journal of Germanic Languages** (33192)
Cambridge University Press
University of Wisconsin-Madison
College of letters and science
1220 Linden Dr.
Van Hise Hall 802
Madison, WI 53706
**Subject(s):** Philology, Language, and Linguistics
**Circ:** 350

**Solvent Extraction and Ion Exchange** (7847)
Marcel Dekker Inc.
c/o Renato Chiarizia
Chemistry Division
Argonne National Laboratory
9700 S. Cass Av.
Argonne, IL 60439-4831
**Subject(s):** Science (General); Chemistry, Chemicals, and Chemical Engineering
**Circ:** (Paid)325

**Abraxas** (33148)
Abraxas Press Inc.
PO Box 260113
Madison, WI 53726-0113
Phone: (608)238-0175
**Subject(s):** Literature and Literary Reviews
**Circ:** (Paid)‡250
       (Controlled)‡300

**Crossroads** (8556)
Southeast Asia Publications
Center for SE Asian Studies, Adams Hall 412
Northern Illinois University
DeKalb, IL 60115-2854
Phone: (815)753-1981
Fax: (815)753-1776
**Subject(s):** Anthropology and Ethnology; History and Genealogy; Political Science; Intercultural Interests; Local, State, and Regional Publications
**Circ:** (Paid)300

**George Eliot—George Henry Lewes Studies** (8558)
Northern Illinois University
DeKalb, IL 60115
Phone: (815)753-1857
Fax: (815)753-2003
**Circ:** (Combined)300

**Journal of Agricultural Safety and Health** (15744)
American Society of Agricultural Engineers
2950 Niles Rd.
Saint Joseph, MI 49085-9659
Phone: (269)429-0300
Fax: (269)429-3852
**Subject(s):** Scientific Agricultural Publications; Engineering (Various branches)
**Circ:** 300

**Journal of Philosophical Research** (10086)
Philosophy Documentation Center
Department of Philosophy
University of Notre Dame
100 Malloy Hall
Notre Dame, IN 46556-4619
**Subject(s):** Philosophy
**Circ:** (Paid)300

**Lost and Found Times** (24566)
Luna Bisonte Prods
137 Leland Ave.
Columbus, OH 43214
Phone: (614)846-4126
**Subject(s):** Literature; Poetry
**Circ:** (Combined)300

**Moon Miners' Manifesto** (33321)
Lunar Reclamation Society Inc.
MMM, 1630 N. 32nd St.
Milwaukee, WI 53208-2040
Phone: (414)342-0705
**Subject(s):** Science
**Circ:** (Paid)300

**Rain Crow** (8391)
Rain Crow Publishing
PO Box 11013
Chicago, IL 60611-0013
Phone: (773)562-5786
**Subject(s):** Literature and Literary Reviews
**Circ:** (Paid)300

**World Libraries** (9277)
Dominican University Graduate School of Library and Information Science
7900 W Division
River Forest, IL 60305
Phone: (708)524-6845
Fax: (708)524-6657
**Subject(s):** International Affairs; Library and Information Science
**Circ:** (Controlled)298

**Bible Editions and Versions** (16277)
International Society of Bible Collectors
c/o Carl V. Johnson
PO Box 26654
Minneapolis, MN 55426
**Subject(s):** Religious Publications
**Circ:** 275

**Journal of Ministry in Addiction and Recovery** (16588)
The Haworth Press Inc.
2481 Como Ave
Saint Paul, MN 55108
Phone: (612)641-3584
Fax: (612)641-3584
**Subject(s):** Substance Abuse and Treatment
**Circ:** (Paid)274

**Sport History Review** (8031)
Human Kinetics Publishers Inc.
1607 N. Market St.
PO Box 5076
Champaign, IL 61825-5076
Phone: (217)351-5076
Fax: (217)351-1549
**Subject(s):** History and Genealogy; (General Sports)
**Circ:** (Paid)‡275

**Illinois Classical Studies** (9472)
Stipes Publishing Co.
Department of Classics
4090 Foreign Languages Bldg.
707 S. Matthews Ave.
Urbana, IL 61801-3676
Phone: (217)333-1008
Fax: (217)333-3466
**Subject(s):** Literature; Education
**Circ:** (Controlled)260

**Literary Magazine Review** (33522)
University of Wisconsin–River Falls
English Dept.
410 S 3rd St.
River Falls, WI 54022
Phone: (715)425-3173
Fax: (715)425-0657
**Subject(s):** Literature and Literary Reviews
**Circ:** (Non-paid)‡40
       (Paid)‡265

**Studies in the Linguistic Sciences** (9489)
University of Illinois at Urbana-Champaign
707 S Mathews, 4080 Foreign Language Bldg.
Urbana, IL 61801
Phone: (217)333-3563
Fax: (217)244-8430
**Subject(s):** Hearing and Speech
**Circ:** (Controlled)260

**Alloy Digest** (24886)
ASM International
9639 Kinsman Rd.
Materials Park, OH 44073-0002
Phone: (440)338-5151
Fax: (440)338-4634
**Subject(s):** Engineering (Various branches); Metal, Metallurgy, and Metal Trade; Plastic and Composition Materials
**Circ:** 250

**American Communities Tomorrow** (9500)
Social Sciences Services and Resources
PO Box 153
Wasco, IL 60183
Phone: (630)897-5345
Fax: (630)896-4654
**Subject(s):** Social Sciences; French
**Circ:** 250

**Annals of Behavioral Science & Medical Education** (15084)
Association for the Behavioral Sciences and Medical Education
1460 N Center Rd.
Burton, MI 48509
Phone: (810)715-4365
Fax: (810)715-4371
**Subject(s):** Medicine and Surgery; Health and Healthcare; Psychology and Psychiatry
**Circ:** 250

**Champaign County Genealogical Society Quarterly** (9465)
Champaign County Genealogical Society
c/o Champaign County Historical Archives
201 S Race St.
Urbana, IL 61801-3283
Phone: (217)367-4025
Fax: (217)367-4061
**Subject(s):** History and Genealogy; Local, State, and Regional Publications
**Circ:** (Controlled)250

**Dime Novel Roundup** (16082)
PO Box 226
Dundas, MN 55019-0226
Phone: (507)645-5711
**Subject(s):** Book Trade and Author News
**Circ:** ‡250

**Journal of Cultural Research in Art Education (24560)**
United States Society for Education Through Art
c/o Dr. Christine Ballengee-Morris
Ohio State University
The Union Bldg., 4th Fl, Rm. 442
Columbus, OH 43210
Phone: (614)247-7612
Fax: (740)366-5047
Subject(s): Art and Art History; Education
Circ: 250

**The Listening Eye (24231)**
KSU Geauga Campus
14111 Claridon-Troy Rd.
Burton, OH 44021
Phone: (440)286-3840
Subject(s): Poetry
Circ: (Paid)250

**Michigan Feminist Studies (15014)**
University of Michigan
1122 Ln. Hall
204 S. State St.
Ann Arbor, MI 48109-1290
Phone: (734)615-6610
Fax: (734)647-4943
Subject(s): Women's Interests; College Publications
Circ: (Controlled)250

**Southwest Philosophy Review (9075)**
Southwestern Philosophical Society
Box 4540
Department of Philosophy
Illinois State University
Normal, IL 61790-4540
Phone: (309)438-7666
Fax: (309)438-8028
Subject(s): Philosophy
Circ: (Paid)250

**Thresholds in Education (8564)**
Thresholds in Education Foundation
LEPF Dept.
223 Graham Hall
Northern Illinois University
DeKalb, IL 60115
Phone: (815)753-9359
Fax: (815)753-8750
Subject(s): Education
Circ: ‡250

**Journal of College and University Law (10084)**
National Association of College & University Attorneys (NACUA)
c/o William P. Hoye, Faculty Editor
General Counsel's Office
203 Main Bldg.
Notre Dame, IN 46556
Phone: (574)631-6749
Fax: (574)631-8239
Subject(s): Law
Circ: (Paid)248

**Journal of Marketing for Higher Education (24322)**
The Haworth Press Inc.
c/o Thomas J. Hayes, Ph.D.
Xavier Univ.
3800 Victory Pkwy.
Cincinnati, OH 45207-3214
Phone: (513)745-3059
Subject(s): Advertising and Marketing
Circ: (Controlled)‡248

**Journal of Prevention & Intervention in the Community (8290)**
The Haworth Press Inc.
c/o Joseph R. Ferrari, DePaul Univ.
2219 N. Kenmore Ave.
Chicago, IL 60614-3504
Phone: (773)325-4244
Subject(s): Psychology and Psychiatry
Circ: 237

**Michigan Journal of Gender & Law (15016)**
625 S. State St.
Ann Arbor, MI 48109-1215
Phone: (734)763-7378
Fax: (734)764-6043
Subject(s): Law; Women's Interests; Civil Rights
Circ: (Paid)230

**The Personalist Forum (7953)**
Institute of Liberal Arts
c/o Randy Auxier, Editor
Dept. of Philosophy
Southern Illinois Univ.
Carbondale, IL 62901-4505
Subject(s): Theology; Philosophy
Circ: (Combined)230

**Journal of Psychology and Human Sexuality (16306)**
The Haworth Press Inc.
c/o Eli Coleman
Univ. of Minnesota Medical School
2630 University Ave. S.E
Minneapolis, MN 55414
Subject(s): Psychology and Psychiatry
Circ: 226

**Journal of Toxicology Toxin Reviews (16307)**
Marcel Dekker Inc.
c/o W. T. Shier, College of Pharmacy
University of Minnesota
Minneapolis, MN 55455
Subject(s): Drugs and Pharmaceuticals; Medicine and Surgery
Circ: (Paid)225

**Journal of Agromedicine (33259)**
The Haworth Press Inc.
c/o Steven Kirkhorn, Medical Dir.
National Farm Medicine Center/Occupational Health Dept.
Marshfield Clinic
Marshfield, WI
Subject(s): General Agriculture; Health and Healthcare
Circ: (Paid)218

**ACC Courier (9386)**
American College of Counselors
1124 1/2 South Fifth, Ste. LL-C
Springfield, IL 62704
Phone: (217)726-6220
Fax: (217)726-6220
Subject(s): Psychology and Psychiatry
Circ: 200

**Alarm Clock (15709)**
PO Box 1551
Royal Oak, MI 48068
Phone: (248)442-8634
Fax: (248)478-7241
Subject(s): Music and Musical Instruments; Music and Musical Instruments
Circ: (Non-paid)200

**Dewitt County Genealogical Society Quarterly (8511)**
Dewitt County Genealogical Society
PO Box 632
Warner Public Library 310 N. Quincy
Clinton, IL 61727
Phone: (217)935-3493
Subject(s): History and Genealogy; Local, State, and Regional Publications
Circ: (Controlled)200

**Grasslands Review (24188)**
Box 626
Berea, OH 44017
Phone: (440)826-8071
Subject(s): Literature; Literature and Literary Reviews; Poetry
Circ: (Paid)200

**International Materials Reviews (24888)**
ASM International
9639 Kinsman Rd.
Materials Park, OH 44073-0002
Phone: (440)338-5151
Fax: (440)338-4634
Subject(s): Metal, Metallurgy, and Metal Trade
Circ: (Non-paid)30
(Paid)200

**Journal of Agricultural and Food Information (15233)**
The Haworth Press Inc.
Library Distance Learning Services
Michigan State University
East Lansing, MI 48824-1048
Phone: (517)432-1644
Subject(s): Scientific Agricultural Publications; Food and Grocery Trade
Circ: (Paid)200

**Journal of Family and Consumer Sciences Education (10244)**
National Association of Teacher Educators for Family and Consumer Sciences
c/o Wanda Fox
Department of Curriculum & Instruction
Purdue University
1442 Liberal Arts & Education Bldg.
West Lafayette, IN 47907-1442
Phone: (765)494-7291
Fax: (765)496-1622
Subject(s): Home Economics
Circ: 200

**Journal of Information Ethics (16547)**
International Center for Information Ethics
Learning Resources Services
720 4th Ave. S
St. Cloud State University
Saint Cloud, MN 56301
Phone: (320)308-4822
Fax: (320)308-4778
Subject(s): Political Science
Circ: (Controlled)50
(Paid)200

**Journal of Phase Equilibria and Diffusion (24889)**
ASM International
9639 Kinsman Rd.
Materials Park, OH 44073-0002
Phone: (440)338-5151
Fax: (440)338-4634
Subject(s): Metal, Metallurgy, and Metal Trade
Circ: (Non-paid)‡104
(Paid)‡201

**Military Thought (16313)**
East View Publications
3020 Harbor Lane North
Minneapolis, MN 55447
Phone: (763)550-0961
Fax: (763)559-2931
Subject(s): Military and Navy
Circ: 200

**Oil and Gas (8027)**
Illinois State Geological Survey
615 E Peabody Dr.
Champaign, IL 61820-6964
Phone: (217)333-4747
Fax: (217)333-2830
Subject(s): Petroleum, Oil, and Gas
Circ: (Controlled)‡120
(Paid)‡200

**Hiram Poetry Review (24774)**
Hiram College
PO Box 162
Hiram, OH 44234-0162
Phone: (330)569-5331
Fax: (330)569-5166
Subject(s): Poetry
Circ: (Paid)52
(Non-paid)161

**Immigration and Nationality Law Review (24315)**
William S. Hein & Company Inc.
Immigration and Nationality Law Review
University of Cincinnati College of Law
PO Box 210040
Cincinnati, OH 45221-0040
Subject(s): Law
Circ: 165

**Magazine of Speculative Poetry (32842)**
Box 564
Beloit, WI 53512
Subject(s): Poetry; Science Fiction, Mystery, Adventure, and Romance
Circ: (Combined)150

**Indiana Law Reporter (15142)**
Law Reporter Co.
209 Michigan Ave.
PO Box 270
Crystal Falls, MI 49920
Phone: (906)875-6970
Subject(s): Law
Circ: (Combined)129

# Great Plains States

**American Educational History Journal (24642)**
Midwest History of Education Society
c/o Joseph Watras, Editor
University of Dayton
Dayton, OH 45469-0525
Phone: (937)229-3328
Fax: (937)229-2500
**Subject(s):** History and Genealogy; Education
**Circ:** (Paid)‡110

**Xerolage (33132)**
Rt 1
PO Box 131
La Farge, WI 54639
Phone: (608)625-4619
**Subject(s):** Art and Art History
**Circ:** (Combined)110

**Journal of Nutraceuticals, Functional & Medical Foods (8286)**
The Haworth Press Inc.
c/o Robert E. C. Wildman, Director, Nutrition
Bally Total Fitness Corp.
8700 W Mawr Ave.
Chicago, IL 60631
Phone: (773)399-7610
**Subject(s):** Health and Healthcare; Food Production
**Circ:** (Non-paid)‡23
(Paid)‡97

**Bushong Bulletin (24953)**
Carol Willsey Bell
10460 N Palmyra Rd.
North Jackson, OH 44451-9793
Phone: (330)538-2046
**Subject(s):** History and Genealogy
**Circ:** (Controlled)80

**Dakota Collector (16578)**
Dakota Postal History Society
PO Box 600039
Saint Paul, MN 55106
**Subject(s):** History and Genealogy; Postal and Shipping Supplies
**Circ:** (Combined)70

**Business Outlook for West Michigan (15465)**
W.E. Upjohn Institute for Employment Research
300 S Westnedge Ave.
Kalamazoo, MI 49007-4686
Phone: (269)343-5541
Fax: (269)342-0672
**Subject(s):** Business; Local, State, and Regional Publications
**Circ:** (Controlled)20
(Paid)40

**Agricultural Economics Report (15227)**
Michigan State University
202 Ag Hall
East Lansing, MI 48824-1039
Phone: (517)355-4563
Fax: (517)432-1800
**Subject(s):** Scientific Agricultural Publications
**Circ:** (Non-paid)15

# Great Plains States

**VFW Magazine (17355)**
406 W. 34th St.
Kansas City, MO 64111-2736
Phone: (816)968-1169
Fax: (816)968-1169
**Subject(s):** Veterans
**Circ:** (Paid)18,000,000

**Home & Away (18528)**
AAA Midwest Magazine Network
10703 J St.
Omaha, NE 68127
Phone: (402)592-5000
Fax: (402)331-5194
**Subject(s):** Travel and Tourism; Local, State, and Regional Publications; Automotive (Consumer)
**Circ:** (Paid)3,355,000

**Cosmopolitan (10830)**
Hearst Magazines
PO Box 7162
Red Oak, IA 51591-0162
Phone: (212)649-5000
**Subject(s):** Women's Interests
**Circ:** (Paid)2,592,887

**Daily Word (18014)**
Unity School of Christianity
1901 NW Blue Pkwy.
Unity Village, MO 64065-0001
Phone: (816)524-3550
Fax: (816)251-3554
**Subject(s):** Spanish; Religious Publications; Hispanic Publications
**Circ:** ‡1,500,000

**College Outlook (17321)**
Townsend Outlook Publishing Co.
20 E. Gregory Blvd.
Kansas City, MO 64114
Phone: (816)361-0616
Fax: (816)361-6164
**Subject(s):** Children's Interests; Education
**Circ:** (Non-paid)1,395,153

**Country Home (10463)**
Meredith Corp.
1716 Locust St.
Des Moines, IA 50309-3023
Phone: (515)284-2015
Fax: (515)284-2552
**Subject(s):** Architecture; Home and Garden
**Circ:** (Paid)1,045,729

**Portals of Prayer (17796)**
Concordia Publishing House
3558 S Jefferson Ave.
Saint Louis, MO 63118-3968
Phone: (314)268-1268
Fax: (314)268-1202
**Subject(s):** German; Religious Publications
**Circ:** 950,000

**Living Faith (17225)**
Creative Communications for the Parish
1564 Fencorp Dr.
Fenton, MO 63026
Phone: (636)305-9777
Fax: (636)305-9333
**Subject(s):** Religious Publications
**Circ:** (Paid)725,000

**VFW Auxiliary (17354)**
Ladies Auxiliary to the VFW
406 W. 34th St.
Kansas City, MO 64111
Phone: (816)561-8655
Fax: (816)931-4753
**Subject(s):** Veterans
**Circ:** ‡700,000

**WOOD (10501)**
Meredith Corp.
1912 Grand Ave.
Des Moines, IA 50309-3379
Phone: (515)284-3343
Fax: (515)284-3343
**Subject(s):** Crafts, Models, Hobbies, and Contests; Wood and Woodworking
**Circ:** (Paid)551,121

**WOODMEN Magazine (18542)**
Woodmen of the World/Omaha Woodmen Life Insurance Society
1700 Farnam St.
Omaha, NE 68102
Phone: (402)342-1890
Fax: (402)271-7269
**Subject(s):** Woodmen of the World
**Circ:** ‡485,000

**Truck Paper (18454)**
Sandhills Publishing
120 W. Harvest Dr.
PO Box 85010
Lincoln, NE 68521-4408
Phone: (402)479-2140
Fax: (402)479-2134
**Subject(s):** Trucks and Trucking
**Circ:** (Paid)‡28,577
(Controlled)‡445,186

**Successful Farming (10497)**
Meredith Corp.
1716 Locust St.
Des Moines, IA 50309-3023
Phone: (515)284-3000
Fax: (515)284-3563
**Subject(s):** General Agriculture
**Circ:** (Paid)‡442,000

**Missouri Conservationist (17282)**
Department of Conservation
2901 W. Truman Blvd.
PO Box No. 180
Jefferson City, MO 65109
Phone: (573)751-4115
Fax: (573)751-4467
**Subject(s):** Wildlife and Exotic Animals; Fish and Commercial Fisheries; Ecology and Conservation
**Circ:** (Combined)440,000

**Midwest Traveler (17762)**
AAA Auto Club of Missouri
12901 N 40 Dr.
Saint Louis, MO 63141
Phone: (314)523-7350
Fax: (314)523-6982
**Subject(s):** Clubs and Societies; Travel and Tourism
**Circ:** (Paid)424,296

**Rural Missouri (17290)**
Association of Missouri Electric Cooperatives Inc.
PO Box 1645
2722 E Maccartey St
Jefferson City, MO 65102
Phone: (573)635-6857
Fax: (573)635-2314
**Subject(s):** Rural Electrification; Local, State, and Regional Publications
**Circ:** ‡388,000

**Woodsmith (10502)**
August Home Publishing
2200 Grand Ave.
Des Moines, IA 50312
Phone: (515)282-7000
Fax: (515)283-2003
**Subject(s):** Wood and Woodworking
**Circ:** (Paid)375,000

**Country Gardens (10462)**
Meredith Corp.
1716 Locust St.
Des Moines, IA 50309-3023
Phone: (515)284-3515
Fax: (515)284-2773
**Subject(s):** Home and Garden
**Circ:** (Paid)353,973

**Workbench (10503)**
August Home Publishing
2200 Grand Ave.
Des Moines, IA 50312
Phone: (515)282-7000
Fax: (515)283-2003
**Subject(s):** Crafts, Models, Hobbies, and Contests; Home and Garden
**Circ:** (Paid)352,470

**Voice of the Diabetic (17176)**
National Federation of the Blind
Diabetes Action Network
1412 I-70 Dr. SW, Ste. C
Columbia, MO 65203
Phone: (573)875-8911
Fax: (573)875-8902
**Subject(s):** Health
**Circ:** (Non-paid)‡342,000

**Smart Computing (18449)**
Sandhills Publishing
120 W Harvest Dr.
PO Box 82545
Lincoln, NE 68521
Phone: (402)479-2141
Fax: (402)479-2120
**Subject(s):** Computers
**Circ:** (Non-paid)104,008
(Paid)339,113

**Lutheran Witness (17755)**
Board for Communication Services/The Lutheran Church—Missouri Synod
1333 S Kirkwood Rd.
Saint Louis, MO 63122-7295
Phone: (314)965-9000
Fax: (314)996-1126
**Subject(s):** Religious Publications
**Circ:** ‡275,000

**Today's Pentecostal Evangel (17974)**
General Council of the Assemblies of God
1445 Boonville Ave.
Springfield, MO 65802-1894
Phone: (417)863-1874

Fax: (417)862-0416
**Subject(s):** Religious Publications
**Circ:** (Paid)‡258,000

**American Patchwork and Quilting (10454)**
Mennonite Central Committee
1912 Grand Ave.
Des Moines, IA 50309-3379
Phone: (515)284-2681
Fax: (515)284-3884
**Subject(s):** Crafts, Models, Hobbies, and Contests; Dressmaking, Needlework, and Quilting
**Circ:** (Paid)236,304

**Home & Away (Minnesota Edition) (10322)**
AAA Minnesota/Iowa
2900 AAA Ct.
Bettendorf, IA 52722
Phone: (563)332-7400
Fax: (563)332-1098
**Subject(s):** Automotive (Consumer); Travel and Tourism; Local, State, and Regional Publications
**Circ:** (Controlled)400
(Paid)225,000

**Mountain Movers (17968)**
General Council of the Assemblies of God
1445 Boonville Ave.
Springfield, MO 65802-1894
Phone: (417)863-1874
Fax: (417)862-0416
**Subject(s):** Religious Publications
**Circ:** (Non-paid)‡220,000

**Capper's (11423)**
1503 SW 42nd St.
Topeka, KS 66609-1265
Phone: (785)274-4300
Fax: (785)274-4305
**Subject(s):** General Editorial
**Circ:** (Paid)215,175

**Liguorian (17398)**
Liguori Publications
One Liguori Dr.
Liguori, MO 63057-9999
Phone: (636)464-2500
Fax: (636)464-8449
**Subject(s):** Religious Publications
**Circ:** 200,000

**Beef Today (11038)**
Farm Journal Inc.
RR 1
Box 51
Council Grove, KS 66846
Phone: (316)767-7041
Fax: (316)767-7028
**Subject(s):** Livestock
**Circ:** (Controlled)187,656

**American Family Physician (11193)**
American Academy of Family Physicians
11400 Tomahawk Creek Pky.
Leawood, KS 66211-2672
Phone: (913)906-6000
Fax: (913)906-6010
**Subject(s):** Medicine and Surgery
**Circ:** (Controlled)179,315

**Intro (10474)**
Business Publications Corp.
The Depot at Fourth
100 4th St.
Des Moines, IA 50309
Phone: (515)288-3336
Fax: (515)288-0309
**Subject(s):** Travel and Tourism; Local, State, and Regional Publications
**Circ:** (Controlled)170,000

**Farmland System News (17328)**
Farmland Industries Inc.
PO Box 20111
Kansas City, MO 64195
Fax: (816)713-6979
**Subject(s):** General Agriculture
**Circ:** ‡168,000

**MIZZOU Magazine (17167)**
Alumni Association of the University of Missouri
407 Donald W Reynolds Alumni and Visitor Ctr.
Columbia, MO 65211
Phone: (573)882-7357
Fax: (573)882-7290

**Subject(s):** College Publications
**Circ:** (Non-paid)‡157,500

**EC&M (11304)**
Primedia Business Magzenes & Media
9800 Metcalf Ave.
Overland Park, KS 66212
Phone: (913)341-1300
Fax: (913)967-1898
**Subject(s):** Construction, Contracting, Building, and Excavating; Electrical Engineering; Electronics Engineering
**Circ:** (Paid)1,214
(Controlled)140,064

**Kansas Living (11230)**
Kansas Farm Bureau
2627 KFB Plz.
Manhattan, KS 66503
Phone: (785)587-6000
**Subject(s):** Farm Bureau, Grange, and Cooperative Associations
**Circ:** (Controlled)‡140,000

**Land Line (17242)**
Owner-Operator Independent Drivers Association Inc.
1 NW OOIDA Dr.
PO Box 1000
Grain Valley, MO 64029
Phone: (816)229-5791
Fax: (816)443-2227
**Subject(s):** Trucks and Trucking
**Circ:** (Controlled)‡140,000

**The Lutheran Layman (17754)**
International Lutheran Laymen's League
660 Mason Ridge Center Dr.
Saint Louis, MO 63141-8557
Phone: (314)317-4100
Fax: (314)317-4295
**Subject(s):** Religious Publications
**Circ:** ‡135,000

**Health Perspective (17691)**
Clayton-Davis & Associates
7777 Bonhomme Ave., Ste. 900
Saint Louis, MO 63105
Phone: (314)862-7800
Fax: (314)721-5171
**Subject(s):** Health
**Circ:** (Non-paid)‡125,000

**Columban Mission (18586)**
Society of St. Columban
PO Box 10
Saint Columbans, NE 68056-0010
Phone: (402)291-1920
Fax: (402)291-4984
**Subject(s):** Religious Publications
**Circ:** (Controlled)‡120,000

**The National Catholic Reporter (17339)**
National Catholic Reporter Publishing Company Inc.
115 E. Armour Blvd.
Kansas City, MO 64111-1203
Phone: (816)531-0538
Fax: (816)968-2292
**Subject(s):** Religious Publications
**Circ:** (Paid)‡50,000
120,000

**The Optimist Magazine (17784)**
Optimist International
4494 Lindell Blvd.
Saint Louis, MO 63108
Phone: (314)371-6000
Fax: (314)371-6006
**Subject(s):** Clubs and Societies
**Circ:** ‡118,500

**National Pork Report (10490)**
Pork Publications Inc.
PO Box 9114
1776 Northwest 114th Street
Des Moines, IA 50306-9114
Phone: (515)223-2600
Fax: (515)223-2646
**Subject(s):** Livestock
**Circ:** (Non-paid)‡109,350

**South Dakota Electric Cooperative Connections (28367)**
South Dakota Rural Electric Association
222 W Pleasant Dr.
PO Box 1138
Pierre, SD 57501
Phone: (605)224-8823
Fax: (605)224-4430
**Subject(s):** Lifestyle; Local, State, and Regional Publications
**Circ:** ‡103,000

**Concierge Kansas City (17322)**
Show Me Publishing Inc.
306 E 12th St., Ste. 1014
Kansas City, MO 64106
Fax: (816)474-1111
**Subject(s):** Local, State, and Regional Publications; Travel and Tourism; Business
**Circ:** (Controlled)100,000

**Montana Land Magazine (10420)**
Lee Enterprises Inc.
201 N. Harrison
Davenport, IA 52801
Phone: (563)383-2100
**Subject(s):** Real Estate; Home and Garden
**Circ:** (Controlled)‡100,000

**Moondance (17168)**
University of Missouri-Columbia
Columbia, MO 65211
Phone: (573)882-2121
**Subject(s):** Women's Interests; Literature and Literary Reviews; Art
**Circ:** (Non-paid)100,000

**The Ozarks Mountaineer (17089)**
The Ozarks & Mountaineer Corp.
1335 West Highway 76 Unit 3 Box 3
Branson, MO 65616
Phone: (417)336-2665
Fax: (417)336-2679
**Subject(s):** Local, State, and Regional Publications; History and Genealogy
**Circ:** (Controlled)‡1,500
(Paid)‡10,0000

**Drovers (11200)**
Vance Publishing Corp.
10901 W. 84th Ter.
Lenexa, KS 66214
Phone: (913)438-8700
Fax: (913)438-0697
**Subject(s):** Livestock
**Circ:** (Paid)297
(Controlled)98,000

**Family Practice Management (11194)**
American Academy of Family Physicians
11400 Tomahawk Creek Pky.
Leawood, KS 66211-2672
Phone: (913)906-6000
Fax: (913)906-6010
**Subject(s):** Medicine and Surgery; Health and Healthcare
**Circ:** ‡97,348

**Registered Rep. (18285)**
Primedia Business
2104 Harvell Cir.
Bellevue, NE 68005
Phone: (402)505-7173
Fax: (402)293-0741
**Subject(s):** Business
**Circ:** (Controlled)93,800

**Iowa REC News (10928)**
Iowa Association of Electric Cooperatives
8525 Douglas, No. 48
Urbandale, IA 50322-2992
Phone: (515)276-5350
Fax: (515)276-7946
**Subject(s):** Rural Electrification; Farm Bureau, Grange, and Cooperative Associations; Local, State, and Regional Publications
**Circ:** (Combined)‡93,000

**Northern Iowa Today (10356)**
University of Northern Iowa
University of Marketing and Public Relations
126 E Bartlett Hall
Cedar Falls, IA 50614
Phone: (319)273-2761
Fax: (319)273-2888
**Subject(s):** College Publications
**Circ:** ‡91,000

## Great Plains States

**Show Me Missouri Farm Bureau News (17291)**
Missouri Farm Bureau Federation
701 S. Country Club Dr.
PO Box 658
Jefferson City, MO 65102
Phone: (573)893-1400
Fax: (573)893-1470
**Subject(s):** Farm Bureau, Grange, and Cooperative Associations
**Circ:** (Controlled)‡91,000

**Grit (11428)**
Ogden Publications
1503 SW 42nd St.
Topeka, KS 66609-1265
Phone: (785)274-4300
Fax: (785)274-4305
**Subject(s):** General Editorial
**Circ:** (Paid)90,000

**American Printer (11292)**
Primedia Business Magzenes & Media
9800 Metcalf Ave.
Overland Park, KS 66212
Phone: (913)341-1300
Fax: (913)967-1898
**Subject(s):** Printing and Typography
**Circ:** (Controlled)‡89,755

**High Adventure (17964)**
General Council of the Assemblies of God
1445 Boonville Ave.
Springfield, MO 65802-1894
Phone: (417)863-1874
Fax: (417)862-0416
**Subject(s):** Religious Publications; Youths' Interests
**Circ:** ‡88,000

**Hogs Today (17493)**
Farm Journal Inc.
PO Box 164A
Polo, MO 64671
Phone: (816)586-5641
**Subject(s):** Livestock
**Circ:** (Non-paid)84,547

**Dive Training (17474)**
Dive Training Ltd.
5215 Crooked Rd.
Parkville, MO 64152-3737
Phone: (816)741-5151
Fax: (816)741-6458
**Subject(s):** (Water Sports)
**Circ:** (Paid)18,000
(Non-paid)83,000

**Kansas Country Living (11433)**
Kansas Electric Cooperative Inc.
PO Box 4267
Topeka, KS 66604-0267
Phone: (785)478-4554
Fax: (785)478-4852
**Subject(s):** Rural Electrification; Farm Bureau, Grange, and Cooperative Associations; Local, State, and Regional Publications
**Circ:** ‡80,957

**Research Kansas (17347)**
Show Me Publishing Inc.
306 E 12th St., Ste. 1014
Kansas City, MO 64106
Fax: (816)474-1111
**Subject(s):** Science (General); Laboratory Research (Scientific and Medical); Local, State, and Regional Publications
**Circ:** (Controlled)80,000

**Research Missouri (17348)**
Show Me Publishing Inc.
306 E 12th St., Ste. 1014
Kansas City, MO 64106
Fax: (816)474-1111
**Subject(s):** Science (General); Laboratory Research (Scientific and Medical); Local, State, and Regional Publications
**Circ:** (Controlled)80,000

**Iowa Legionnaire (10480)**
Iowa American Legion
720 Lyon St.
Des Moines, IA 50309-5417
Phone: (515)282-5068
Fax: (515)282-7583
**Subject(s):** Veterans
**Circ:** ‡78,000

**American City and County (18279)**
Primedia Business
2104 Harvell Circle
Bellevue, NE 68005
Phone: (402)505-7173
Fax: (402)293-0741
**Subject(s):** State, Municipal, and County Administration
**Circ:** (Paid)420
(Controlled)74,100

**North Dakota REC Magazine (24027)**
North Dakota Association of Rural Electric Cooperatives
3201 Nygren Dr. NW
PO Box 727
Mandan, ND 58554-0727
Phone: (701)663-6501
Fax: (701)663-3745
**Subject(s):** Rural Electrification; Lifestyle; Local, State, and Regional Publications
**Circ:** ‡71,199

**The Catholic Voice (18522)**
The Catholic Voice Publishing Co.
6060 N.W. Radial Hwy.
Omaha, NE 68104
**Subject(s):** Religious Publications
**Circ:** ‡71,038

**Angus Beef Bulletin (17526)**
Angus Prodcutions Inc.
3201 Frederick Ave.
Saint Joseph, MO 64506-2997
Phone: (816)383-5270
Fax: (816)233-6575
**Subject(s):** Livestock
**Circ:** (Non-paid)‡70,000

**Knitter's (28408)**
XRX Inc.
PO Box 1525
Sioux Falls, SD 57101-1525
Phone: (605)338-2450
Fax: (605)338-2994
**Subject(s):** Dressmaking, Needlework, and Quilting; Crafts, Models, Hobbies, and Contests
**Circ:** ‡70,000

**Rural Electric Nebraskan (18446)**
Nebraska Rural Electric Association
PO Box 82048
800 South 13th Street
Lincoln, NE 68501
Phone: (402)475-4988
Fax: (402)475-0835
**Subject(s):** General Agriculture
**Circ:** ‡66,000

**Grounds Maintenance (11311)**
Primedia Business Magzenes & Media
9800 Metcalf Ave.
Overland Park, KS 66212
Phone: (913)341-1300
Fax: (913)967-1898
**Subject(s):** Landscape Architecture
**Circ:** (Non-paid)‡65,050

**Radiologic Technology (11103)**
American Society of Radiologic Technologists
c/o Michael E. Madden, Director
Medical Diagnostic Imaging Programs
600 Park St.
Hays, KS 67601
Phone: (785)628-5678
**Subject(s):** Radiology, Ultrasound, and Nuclear Medicine
**Circ:** (Paid)‡65,000

**American School & University (11293)**
Primedia Business Magazines & Media
9800 Metcalf Ave.
Overland Park, KS 66212
Phone: (913)967-1960
Fax: (913)514-6960
**Subject(s):** Building Management and Maintenance
**Circ:** (Controlled)63,000

**Affirmative Action Register (17556)**
Affirmative Action Inc.
8356 Olive Blvd.
Saint Louis, MO 63132
Phone: (314)991-1335
Fax: (314)997-1788
**Subject(s):** Employment and Human Resources
**Circ:** (Paid)‡950
(Controlled)‡62,500

**KC Computer User (11318)**
Computer Reporter Inc.
12424 Lamar Ave.
Overland Park, KS 66209-2703
Phone: (913)341-6881
Fax: (913)341-3890
**Subject(s):** Computers
**Circ:** (Paid)60,000

**Motorcycle Events Magazine (28364)**
Motorcycle Events Association Inc.
State Publishing Company
303 E. Sioux Ave.
PO Box 100
Pierre, SD 57501
Phone: (605)224-9999
Fax: (605)224-2063
**Subject(s):** Motorbikes and Motorcycles; Travel and Tourism
**Circ:** (Controlled)60,000

**Buildings (10364)**
Stamats Communications Inc.
615 5th St. SE
PO Box 1888
Cedar Rapids, IA 52406-1888
Phone: (319)364-6167
Fax: (319)365-5421
**Subject(s):** Construction, Contracting, Building, and Excavating
**Circ:** (Non-paid)★57,009

**Wallaces Farmer (10500)**
Farm Progress Cos.
6200 Aurora Ave., Ste. 609E
Ste. 609E
Urbandale, IA 50322-2838
Phone: (515)278-6693
Fax: (515)278-7796
**Subject(s):** General Agriculture
**Circ:** (Paid)12,289
(Non-paid)55,513

**Veterinary Economics (11207)**
Veterinary Healthcare Communications
8033 Flint St.
Lenexa, KS 66214
Phone: (913)492-4300
Fax: (913)492-4157
**Subject(s):** Veterinary Medicine
**Circ:** 54,236

**High Plains Journal (11047)**
High Plains Publishers Inc.
1500 E Wyatt Earp
PO Box 760
Dodge City, KS 67801
Phone: (620)227-7171
Fax: (620)227-7173
**Subject(s):** Farm Newspapers
**Circ:** (Paid)52,886

**Video Systems (11351)**
Primedia Business Magzenes & Media
9800 Metcalf Ave.
Overland Park, KS 66212
Phone: (913)341-1300
Fax: (913)967-1898
**Subject(s):** Radio, Television, Cable, and Video
**Circ:** (Controlled)‡52,000

**Springfield! Magazine (17972)**
Springfield Communications Inc.
PO Box 4749
Springfield, MO 65808
Phone: (417)831-1600
**Subject(s):** Local, State, and Regional Publications
**Circ:** ‡51,600

**Iowa Conservationist (10477)**
Iowa Dept. of Natural Resources
Wallace State Office Bldg.
502 E. 9th St.
Des Moines, IA 50319
Phone: (515)242-5967
**Subject(s):** Ecology and Conservation
**Circ:** (Controlled)4,000
(Paid)50,000

**Utility Business (11350)**
Primedia Business Magzenes & Media
9800 Metcalf Ave.
Overland Park, KS 66212
Phone: (913)341-1300
Fax: (913)967-1898

**Subject(s):** Power and Power Plants
**Circ:** (Combined)50,000

**Women in Business** (17357)
The ABWA Company Inc.
9100 Ward Pkwy.
PO Box 8728
Kansas City, MO 64114-0728
Phone: (816)361-6621
Fax: (816)361-4991
**Subject(s):** Women's Interests; Business
**Circ:** (Paid)50,000

**Farmers Hot Line** (10579)
Heartland Communications Group Inc.
1003 Central Ave.
PO Box 1052
Fort Dodge, IA 50501
Phone: (515)955-1600
**Subject(s):** Farm Implements and Supplies; Machinery and Equipment
**Circ:** (Paid)‡1,660
(Non-paid)‡47,540

**Kansas!** (11430)
Department of Commerce and Housing
1000 SW Jackson St., Ste. 100
Topeka, KS 66612-1354
Phone: (785)296-3479
Fax: (785)296-6988
**Subject(s):** Travel and Tourism
**Circ:** (Combined)46,000

**Today's Farmer** (17175)
MFA Inc.
201 Ray Young Dr.
Columbia, MO 65201
Phone: (573)874-5111
**Subject(s):** General Agriculture
**Circ:** ‡46,000

**World Broadcast Engineering** (11357)
Primedia Business Magzenes & Media
9800 Metcalf Ave.
Overland Park, KS 66212
Phone: (913)341-1300
Fax: (913)967-1898
**Subject(s):** Radio, Television, Cable, and Video
**Circ:** (Combined)45,404

**The American Journal of Anesthesiology** (10640)
Quadrant HealthCom Inc.
200 Hawkins Dr., 6546 JCP
Dept of Anesthesia
Anesthesiology Editorial Office
Univ. of Iowa
Iowa City, IA 52242-1009
Phone: (319)356-4601
Fax: (319)353-6817
**Subject(s):** Medicine and Surgery
**Circ:** ‡45,185

**Expansion Management** (11379)
Penton Media Inc.
1900 W. 75th St., Ste. 100
Prairie Village, KS 66208-3501
Phone: (913)381-8858
Fax: (800)539-7263
**Subject(s):** Economics
**Circ:** (Paid)500
(Non-paid)45,039

**School and Community** (17170)
Missouri State Teachers Association
407 S. Sixth St.
PO Box 458
Columbia, MO 65205
Phone: (573)442-3127
Fax: (573)443-5079
**Subject(s):** Education
**Circ:** ‡43,000

**Waste Age** (18286)
Primedia Business
2104 Harvell Circle
Bellevue, NE 68005
Phone: (402)505-7173
Fax: (402)293-0741
**Subject(s):** Waste Management and Recycling; Water Supply and Sewage Disposal
**Circ:** (Paid)1,000
(Non-paid)43,000

**KETC Guide** (17752)
KETC
3655 Olive St.
Saint Louis, MO 63108
Phone: (314)512-9036
Fax: (314)512-9005
**Subject(s):** Entertainment; Radio, Television, Cable, and Video
**Circ:** (Paid)42,000

**Life Insurance Selling** (17753)
1801 Park 270 Dr., Ste. 550
Saint Louis, MO 63146-4016
Phone: (314)824-5500
Fax: (314)824-5640
**Subject(s):** Insurance
**Circ:** (Paid)41,734

**Undercar Digest** (17977)
M D Publications Inc.
PO Box 2210
3057 East Ciaro
Springfield, MO 65802
Phone: (417)866-3917
Fax: (417)866-2781
**Subject(s):** Automotive (Trade)
**Circ:** (Paid)226
(Controlled)‡40,108

**The Dubuque Area Magazine** (10531)
Julien's Journal
PO Box 801
Dubuque, IA 52004-0801
Phone: (563)557-1914
Fax: (563)557-9635
**Subject(s):** Local, State, and Regional Publications; Entertainment
**Circ:** (Combined)‡40,000

**Farm Collector** (11425)
Ogden Publications
1503 SW 42nd St.
Topeka, KS 66609-1265
Phone: (785)274-4300
Fax: (785)274-4305
**Subject(s):** Collecting; Crafts, Models, Hobbies, and Contests
**Circ:** (Paid)‡40,000

**RF Design** (11338)
Primedia Business Magzenes & Media
9800 Metcalf Ave.
Overland Park, KS 66212
Phone: (913)341-1300
Fax: (913)967-1898
**Subject(s):** Electronics Engineering
**Circ:** (Paid)200
(Non-paid)40,000

**Sickle & Sheaf** (17350)
Alpha Gamma Rho Fraternity
10101 N. Ambassador Dr.
Kansas City, MO 64153-1395
Phone: (816)891-9200
Fax: (816)891-9401
**Subject(s):** Unclassified Fraternal
**Circ:** ‡40,000

**Access Control & Security Systems Integration** (18278)
Primedia Business
2104 Harvell Circle
Bellevue, NE 68005
Phone: (402)505-7173
Fax: (402)293-0741
**Subject(s):** Construction, Contracting, Building, and Excavating
**Circ:** (Paid)‡262
(Controlled)‡39,000

**Transmission and Distribution World** (11349)
Primedia Business Magzenes & Media
9800 Metcalf Ave.
Overland Park, KS 66212
Phone: (913)341-1300
Fax: (913)967-1898
**Subject(s):** Power and Power Plants
**Circ:** (Controlled)‡36,611

**Contractors Hot Line** (10575)
Heartland Communications Group Inc.
1003 Central Ave.
PO Box 1052
Fort Dodge, IA 50501
Phone: (515)955-1600

**Subject(s):** Construction, Contracting, Building, and Excavating; Machinery and Equipment
**Circ:** (Paid)‡3,658
(Non-paid)‡36,342

**Stitches** (11346)
Primedia Business Magazines & Media
9800 Metcalf Ave.
Overland Park, KS 66212
Phone: (913)341-1300
Fax: (913)967-1898
**Subject(s):** Health and Healthcare; Comics and Comic Technique
**Circ:** (Non-paid)•36,336

**PCIM Power Electronic Systems** (11330)
Primedia Business Magazines & Media
9800 Metcalf Ave.
Overland Park, KS 66212
Phone: (913)341-1300
Fax: (913)967-1898
**Subject(s):** Electronics Engineering
**Circ:** 36,000

**Happy Times** (17690)
Concordia Publishing House
3558 S Jefferson Ave.
Saint Louis, MO 63118-3968
Phone: (314)268-1000
Fax: (314)268-1329
**Subject(s):** Religious Publications
**Circ:** ‡35,000

**Luther Alumni Magazine** (10442)
Luther College
700 College Dr.
Decorah, IA 52101-1045
Phone: (563)387-2000
Fax: (563)387-2158
**Subject(s):** Education
**Circ:** (Non-paid)35,000

**NEBRASKAland** (18435)
Nebraska Game and Parks Commission
2200 N 33rd St.
PO Box 30370
Lincoln, NE 68503
Phone: (402)471-0641
Fax: (402)471-5528
**Subject(s):** Environmental and Natural Resources Conservation; Local, State, and Regional Publications
**Circ:** (Non-paid)‡4,100
(Paid)‡35,000

**WHERE St. Louis** (17877)
Miller Publishing Group L.L.C.
1750 S. Brentwood Blvd., Ste. 511
Saint Louis, MO 63144
Phone: (314)968-4940
Fax: (314)968-0813
**Subject(s):** Travel and Tourism
**Circ:** (Controlled)‡34,000

**PC Today** (18440)
Sandhills Publishing
131 W. Grand Dr.
Lincoln, NE 68521
**Subject(s):** Computers
**Circ:** (Paid)33,707

**The Journal of Reproductive Medicine** (17747)
Science Printers and Publishers Inc.
PO Drawer 12425
8342 Olive Blvd.
Saint Louis, MO 63132-2814
Phone: (314)991-4440
Fax: (314)991-4654
**Subject(s):** Medicine and Surgery
**Circ:** (Paid)‡1,514
(Controlled)‡33,659

**Hospital Pharmacy** (17697)
Facts & Comparisons
77 W. Port Plaza, Ste 450
Saint Louis, MO 63125
Phone: (314)216-2100
Fax: (314)878-5563
**Subject(s):** Drugs and Pharmaceuticals
**Circ:** (Paid)‡33,500

**South Dakota Magazine** (28475)
410 E. 3rd
P.O. Box 175
Yankton, SD 57078
Phone: (605)665-6655

# Great Plains States

**Gale Directory of Publications & Broadcast Media/140th Ed.**

**Subject(s):** Local, State, and Regional Publications
**Circ:** (Paid)32,800

**Enrichment Journal** (17961)
General Council of the Assemblies of God
1445 Boonville Ave.
Springfield, MO 65802-1894
Phone: (417)863-1874
Fax: (417)862-0416
**Subject(s):** Religious Publications
**Circ:** ‡32,000

**TED The Electrical Distributor Magazine** (17858)
National Association of Electrical Distributors Inc.
1100 Corporate Sq. Dr., Ste. 100
Saint Louis, MO 63132
Phone: (314)991-9000
Fax: (314)991-3090
**Subject(s):** Electrical Engineering
**Circ:** (Combined)△30,160

**Club Industry's Fitness Business Pro** (18283)
Primedia Business
2104 Harvell Circle
Bellevue, NE 68005
Phone: (402)505-7173
Fax: (402)293-0741
**Subject(s):** Health and Healthcare; Physical Education and Athletics
**Circ:** (Combined)30,107

**Wireless Review** (11356)
Primedia Business Magzenes & Media
9800 Metcalf Ave.
Overland Park, KS 66212
Phone: (913)341-1300
Fax: (913)967-1898
**Subject(s):** Telecommunications
**Circ:** (Paid)1,797
(Controlled)30,028

**Power Quality Assurance** (11332)
Primedia Business Magazines & Media
9800 Metcalf Ave.
Overland Park, KS 66212
Phone: (913)341-1300
Fax: (913)967-1898
**Subject(s):** Power and Power Plants
**Circ:** (Non-paid)30,011

**Aviators Hot Line** (10573)
Heartland Communications Group Inc.
1003 Central Ave.
PO Box 1052
Fort Dodge, IA 50501
Phone: (515)955-1600
**Subject(s):** Aviation
**Circ:** (Combined)‡30,000

**Baking Buyer** (17315)
Sosland Publishing Co.
4800 Main St., Ste. 100
Kansas City, MO 64112
Phone: (816)756-1000
Fax: (816)756-0494
**Subject(s):** Baking
**Circ:** (Non-paid)30,000

**Kansas Alumni** (11177)
University of Kansas Alumni Association
1266 Oread Ave.
Lawrence, KS 66044
Phone: (785)864-4412
Fax: (785)864-5397
**Subject(s):** College Publications
**Circ:** (Non-paid)‡1,500
(Paid)‡30,000

**The National Gardener** (17768)
National Council of State Garden Clubs Inc.
102 S. Elm Ave.
Saint Louis, MO 63119
Phone: (314)968-1664
**Subject(s):** Home and Garden; Horticulture
**Circ:** ‡30,000

**Something Better** (17292)
Missouri NEA
1810 E Elm
Jefferson City, MO 65101-4174
Phone: (573)634-3202
Fax: (573)634-5645

**Subject(s):** Education
**Circ:** (Non-paid)‡1,000
(Paid)‡30,000

**Waste Age Product News** (18287)
Primedia Business
2104 Harvell Circle
Bellevue, NE 68005
Phone: (402)505-7173
Fax: (402)293-0741
**Subject(s):** Waste Management and Recycling
**Circ:** (Combined)30,000

**National Real Estate Investor** (18284)
Primedia Business
2104 Harvell Circle
Bellevue, NE 68005
Phone: (402)505-7173
Fax: (402)293-0741
**Subject(s):** Real Estate
**Circ:** (Paid)‡3,971
(Controlled)‡29,075

**College Review** (24069)
North Dakota State College of Science
800 N. 6th. St.
Wahpeton, ND 58076
Phone: (701)671-2483
Fax: (701)671-2146
**Subject(s):** College Publications
**Circ:** (Controlled)‡29,000

**HC Today** (18367)
Hastings College
Office of Mktg. and Commun.
710 N. Turner Ave
PO Box 269
Hastings, NE 68902-0269
Phone: (402)463-2402
Fax: (402)461-7474
**Subject(s):** College Publications
**Circ:** (Non-paid)‡28,000

**Young & Alive** (18460)
Christian Record Services
PO Box 6097
Lincoln, NE 68506-0097
Phone: (402)488-0981
Fax: (402)488-7582
**Subject(s):** Blind and Visually Challenged
**Circ:** (Non-paid)‡28,000

**The Catholic Advance** (11480)
424 N Broadway St.
Wichita, KS 67202-2310
Phone: (316)269-3965
Fax: (316)269-3902
**Subject(s):** Religious Publications
**Circ:** ‡27,882

**Journal of the Missouri Bar** (17280)
The Missouri Bar
326 Monroe St.
PO Box 119
Jefferson City, MO 65101-3158
Phone: (573)635-4128
Fax: (573)635-2811
**Subject(s):** Law
**Circ:** ‡27,511

**Business Air Today** (10574)
Heartland Communications Group Inc.
1003 Central Ave.
PO Box 1052
Fort Dodge, IA 50501
Phone: (515)955-1600
**Subject(s):** Aviation
**Circ:** (Non-paid)‡27,000

**AGWEEK** (23984)
Grand Forks Herald Inc.
375 2nd Ave. N.
PO Box 6008
Grand Forks, ND 58206-6008
Phone: (701)780-1100
Fax: (701)780-1211
**Subject(s):** Farm Newspapers
**Circ:** (Controlled)517
(Paid)26,831

**Annals of Emergency Medicine** (17573)
Mosby Inc.
11830 Westline Industrial Dr.
Saint Louis, MO 63146
Phone: (800)545-2522

Fax: (800)568-5136
**Subject(s):** Medicine and Surgery
**Circ:** (Non-paid)813
(Paid)26,410

**Pork** (11204)
Vance Publishing Corp.
10901 W. 84th Ter.
Lenexa, KS 66214
Phone: (913)438-8700
Fax: (913)438-0697
**Subject(s):** Livestock
**Circ:** (Controlled)‡26,299

**Paint & Decorating Retailer Magazine** (17227)
Paint and Decorating Retailers Association
403 Axminster Dr.
Fenton, MO 63026-2941
Phone: (636)326-2636
Fax: (636)326-1823
**Subject(s):** Paint and Wallcoverings; Retail
**Circ:** (Combined)‡26,201

**Painting & Wallcovering Contractor** (17791)
Finan Publishing Company Inc.
107 W Pacific Ave.
Saint Louis, MO 63119-3776
Phone: (314)961-6644
Fax: (314)961-4809
**Subject(s):** Paint and Wallcoverings
**Circ:** (Paid)1,926
(Non-paid)26,202

**International Construction** (11314)
Primedia Business Magzenes & Media
9800 Metcalf Ave.
Overland Park, KS 66212
Phone: (913)341-1300
Fax: (913)967-1898
**Subject(s):** Construction, Contracting, Building, and Excavating; International Business and Economics
**Circ:** ‡26,157

**Economic Review** (17325)
Federal Reserve Bank of Kansas City
925 Grand Blvd.
Kansas City, MO 64198-0001
Phone: (816)881-2000
**Subject(s):** Banking, Finance, and Investments
**Circ:** (Free)‡26,000

**Discover Mid-America** (17323)
Discovery Publications Inc.
400 Grand Ave., Ste. B
Kansas City, MO 64106
Phone: (816)474-1516
Fax: (816)474-1427
**Subject(s):** Antiques; General Merchandise
**Circ:** (Non-paid)25,000

**Herald Magazine** (17268)
Herald Publishing House
1001 W. Walnut
PO Box 390
Independence, MO 64051-0390
Phone: (816)521-3015
Fax: (816)521-3066
**Subject(s):** Religious Publications
**Circ:** ‡25,000

**The Iowan** (10613)
Pioneer Communications
PO Box 306
Grundy Center, IA 50638
**Subject(s):** Local, State, and Regional Publications; Travel and Tourism
**Circ:** (Non-paid)‡1,000
(Paid)‡25,000

**Mobile Radio Technology** (11322)
Primedia Business Magzenes & Media
9800 Metcalf Ave.
Overland Park, KS 66212
Phone: (913)341-1300
Fax: (913)967-1898
**Subject(s):** Radio, Television, Cable, and Video; Telecommunications
**Circ:** ‡25,002

**Practical Homeschooling** (17228)
Home Life Inc.
1731 Smizer Mill Rd.
Fenton, MO 63026-2635
Phone: (636)343-6786
Fax: (636)225-0743

**Subject(s):** Education; Parenting
**Circ:** (Paid)25,000

**Ingram's (17332)**
Show Me Publishing Inc.
306 E 12th St., Ste. 1014
Kansas City, MO 64106
Fax: (816)474-1111
**Subject(s):** Business
**Circ:** (Combined)24,944

**Fraternal Herald (10367)**
Western Fraternal Life Association (WFLA)
1900 1st Ave. North East
Cedar Rapids, IA 52402-5372
Phone: (319)363-2653
Fax: (319)363-8806
**Subject(s):** Unclassified Fraternal
**Circ:** (Non-paid)‡24,400

**Vintage Guitar (23909)**
Vintage Guitar Inc.
PO Box 7301
Bismarck, ND 58507
Phone: (701)255-1197
Fax: (701)255-0250
**Subject(s):** Collecting; Music and Musical Instruments
**Circ:** (Non-paid)‡400
(Paid)‡24,300

**DECOR (17645)**
Pfingsten Publishing Company L.L.C.
1801 Park 270 Dr.
Saint Louis, MO 63146
Phone: (314)824-5500
Fax: (314)824-5640
**Subject(s):** Art and Art History; Retail
**Circ:** (Non-paid)785
(Paid)24,245

**Florists' Review Magazine (11426)**
Florist's Review Enterprises Inc.
3300 SW VanBuren
Topeka, KS 66611-2226
Phone: (785)266-0888
Fax: (785)266-0333
**Subject(s):** Florists and Floriculture
**Circ:** (Non-paid)4,008
(Paid)24,054

**Grace Tidings (18526)**
Grace University
1311 S 9th St.
Omaha, NE 68108-3629
Phone: (402)449-2800
Fax: (402)341-9587
**Subject(s):** Religious Publications; College Publications
**Circ:** (Non-paid)24,000

**Nebraska (18423)**
Alumni Association of the University of Nebraska
1520 R St.
Lincoln, NE 68501-0129
Phone: (402)472-4656
**Subject(s):** College Publications
**Circ:** ‡24,000

**North Dakota Outdoors (23903)**
North Dakota Game and Fish Dept.
100 N Bismarck Express Way.
Bismarck, ND 58501-5095
Phone: (701)328-6300
Fax: (701)328-6352
**Subject(s):** (Hunting, Fishing, and Game Management); Local, State, and Regional Publications
**Circ:** (Non-paid)2,000
(Paid)24,000

**Nebraska Farmer (18426)**
Farm Progress Cos.
5625 "O" St., Ste. 5
Lincoln, NE 68510-2133
Phone: (402)489-9331
Fax: (402)489-9335
**Subject(s):** General Agriculture
**Circ:** (Paid)16,436
(Non-paid)23,281

**Angus Journal (17527)**
Angus Prodcutions Inc.
3201 Frederick Ave.
Saint Joseph, MO 64506-2997
Phone: (816)383-5270
Fax: (816)233-6575

**Subject(s):** Livestock
**Circ:** ‡23,000

**Gas Engine Magazine (11427)**
Ogden Publications
1503 SW 42nd St.
Topeka, KS 66609-1265
Phone: (785)274-4300
Fax: (785)274-4305
**Subject(s):** Crafts, Models, Hobbies, and Contests
**Circ:** ‡23,000

**Missouri Wildlife (17288)**
Conservation Federation of Missouri
728 West Main
Jefferson City, MO 65101-1559
Phone: (573)634-2322
Fax: (573)634-8205
**Subject(s):** Environmental and Natural Resources Conservation
**Circ:** (Paid)⊕23,000

**Wheels of Time (17356)**
American Truck Historical Society
PO Box 901611
Kansas City, MO 64190-1611
Phone: (816)891-9900
Fax: (816)891-9903
**Subject(s):** Trucks and Trucking
**Circ:** 22,500

**Daily Devotions for the Deaf (10410)**
Deaf Missions
21199 Greenview Rd.
Council Bluffs, IA 51503
Phone: (712)322-5493
Fax: (712)322-7792
**Subject(s):** Religious Publications; Handicapped
**Circ:** (Non-paid)22,000

**Dealer and Applicator Magazine (11199)**
Vance Publishing Corp.
10901 W. 84th Ter.
Lenexa, KS 66214
Phone: (913)438-8700
Fax: (913)438-0697
**Subject(s):** Scientific Agricultural Publications
**Circ:** (Controlled)‡22,000

**The Draft Horse Journal (10957)**
PO Box 670
Waverly, IA 50677
Phone: (319)352-4046
Fax: (319)352-2232
**Subject(s):** Livestock
**Circ:** (Non-paid)125
(Paid)22,000

**Electrical Wholesaling (11305)**
Primedia Business Magzenes & Media
9800 Metcalf Ave.
Overland Park, KS 66212
Phone: (913)341-1300
Fax: (913)967-1898
**Subject(s):** Electrical Engineering
**Circ:** (Non-paid)12,471
(Paid)‡22,004

**The Grower (11201)**
Vance Publishing Corp.
10901 W. 84th Ter.
Lenexa, KS 66214
Phone: (913)438-8700
Fax: (913)438-0697
**Subject(s):** General Agriculture
**Circ:** (Controlled)‡22,000

**Kansas Farmer (11228)**
Farm Progress Cos.
2507 Sunny Cir.
Manhattan, KS 66502
Phone: (785)532-9010
Fax: (785)532-9135
**Subject(s):** General Agriculture
**Circ:** (Paid)12,656
(Non-paid)21,141

**Optometry (17785)**
American Optometric Association
243 N. Lindbergh Blvd.
Saint Louis, MO 63141
Phone: (314)991-4100
Fax: (314)991-4101

**Subject(s):** Ophthalmology, Optometry, and Optics
**Circ:** (Non-paid)‡6,700
(Paid)‡20,535

**Sound & Video Contractor (11341)**
Primedia Business Magzenes & Media
9800 Metcalf Ave.
Overland Park, KS 66212
Phone: (913)341-1300
Fax: (913)967-1898
**Subject(s):** Radio, Television, Cable, and Video
**Circ:** (Controlled)‡20,536

**Concrete Products (11301)**
Primedia Business Magzenes & Media
9800 Metcalf Ave.
Overland Park, KS 66212
Phone: (913)341-1300
Fax: (913)967-1898
**Subject(s):** Building Materials, Concrete, Brick, and Tile
**Circ:** (Non-paid)20,084

**Christian Education Counselor (17958)**
General Council of the Assemblies of God
1445 Boonville Ave.
Springfield, MO 65802-1894
Phone: (417)863-1874
Fax: (417)862-0416
**Subject(s):** Religious Publications
**Circ:** ‡20,000

**Healing Words (17224)**
Creative Communications for the Parish
1564 Fencorp Dr.
Fenton, MO 63026
Phone: (636)305-9777
Fax: (636)305-9333
**Subject(s):** Religious Publications
**Circ:** ‡20,000

**Jesuit Bulletin (17712)**
The Jesuits of the Missouri Province
3601 Lindell Blvd.
Saint Louis, MO 63108-3393
Phone: (314)977-7363
Fax: (314)977-7362
**Subject(s):** Religious Publications
**Circ:** (Non-paid)20,000

**Military Review (11072)**
USACGSC
290 Grant Ave.
Fort Leavenworth, KS 66027-1254
Phone: (913)684-9327
Fax: (913)684-9328
**Subject(s):** Military and Navy; Portuguese; Spanish
**Circ:** (Paid)‡5,000
(Controlled)‡20,000

**Coal Age (11299)**
Primedia Business Magzenes & Media
9800 Metcalf Ave.
Overland Park, KS 66212
Phone: (913)341-1300
Fax: (913)967-1898
**Subject(s):** Mining and Minerals
**Circ:** (Controlled)‡19,088

**U.S. Water News (11100)**
U.S. Water News Inc.
230 Main St.
Halstead, KS 67056-9983
Phone: (316)835-2222
Fax: (316)835-2223
**Subject(s):** Water Supply and Sewage Disposal
**Circ:** (Paid)‡1,700
(Controlled)‡18,300

**Meat & Poultry (17335)**
Sosland Publishing Co.
4800 Main St., Ste. 100
Kansas City, MO 64112
Phone: (816)756-1000
Fax: (816)756-0494
**Subject(s):** Food and Grocery Trade
**Circ:** (Controlled)‡18,249

**Pocket PC (10562)**
Thaddeus Computing Inc.
110 N. Ct.
Fairfield, IA 52556
Phone: (641)472-6330
Fax: (641)472-1879

Circulation: ★ = ABC; △ = BPA; ♦ = CAC; ♦ = CCAB; ⬜ = VAC; ⊕ = PO Statement; ‡ = Publisher's Report; Boldface figures = sworn; Light figures = estimated.

**Subject(s):** Computers
**Circ:** (Paid)18108

**Buena Vista Today (10898)**
Buena Vista University
610 W Fourth St.
Storm Lake, IA 50588
Phone: (712)749-2120
Fax: (712)749-2037
**Subject(s):** College Publications
**Circ:** (Controlled)‡18,000

**Employment Marketplace (17658)**
12015 Robyn Park Dr.
Saint Louis, MO 63131
Phone: (314)569-3095
Fax: (636)458-4955
**Subject(s):** Employment and Human Resources
**Circ:** (Controlled)18,000

**The Missouri Realtor (17163)**
Missouri Association of Realtors
2601 Bernadette Pl.
PO Box 1327
Columbia, MO 65205
Phone: (573)445-8400
Fax: (573)445-7865
**Subject(s):** Real Estate
**Circ:** ‡18,000

**Missouri Ruralist (17165)**
Farm Progress Cos.
PO Box 6911
Columbia, MO 65205-5012
Phone: (573)875-5445
**Subject(s):** General Agriculture
**Circ:** (Paid)17,087
(Non-paid)17,161

**Transmission Digest (17976)**
MD Publications Inc.
3057 E Cairo
PO Box 2210
Springfield, MO 65801-2210
Phone: (417)866-3917
Fax: (417)866-2781
**Subject(s):** Automotive (Trade)
**Circ:** (Paid)1,360
(Controlled)17,162

**Musicians Hotline (10583)**
Heartland Communications Group Inc.
1003 Central Ave.
PO Box 1052
Fort Dodge, IA 50501
Phone: (515)955-1600
**Subject(s):** Music and Musical Instruments
**Circ:** (Controlled)17,000

**Word and Way (17294)**
3236 Emerald Ln., Ste. 400
Jefferson City, MO 65109
Phone: (573)635-5939
Fax: (573)635-1774
**Subject(s):** Religious Publications
**Circ:** ‡17,000

**South City Journal (17845)**
Pulitzer Publishing
4210 Chippewa
Saint Louis, MO 63116
Phone: (314)664-2700
**Subject(s):** Paid Community Newspapers
**Circ:** (Wed.)16,850

**The Sunflower (23908)**
National Sunflower Association
4023 State St.
Bismarck, ND 58503-0690
Phone: (701)328-5100
Fax: (701)328-5101
**Subject(s):** General Agriculture
**Circ:** 16,667

**Grass & Grain (11225)**
Ag Press Inc.
1531 Yuma St.
Box 1009
Manhattan, KS 66505
Phone: (785)539-7558
Fax: (785)539-2679
**Subject(s):** Farm Newspapers
**Circ:** ‡16,500

**Entertainment Design (11307)**
Primedia Business Magzenes & Media
9800 Metcalf Ave.
Overland Park, KS 66212
Phone: (913)341-1300
Fax: (913)967-1898
**Subject(s):** Graphic Arts and Design; Entertainment
**Circ:** (Combined)16,400

**Iowa Pork Producer (10403)**
Iowa Pork Producers Association
Box 71009
Clive, IA 50325-0009
Phone: (515)225-7675
Fax: (515)225-0563
**Subject(s):** Livestock
**Circ:** (Non-paid)‡16,173

**Land & Water (10581)**
320 A St.
Po Bx 1197
Fort Dodge, IA 50501-1197
Phone: (515)576-3191
Fax: (515)576-2606
**Subject(s):** Ecology and Conservation; Water Supply and Sewage Disposal
**Circ:** (Paid)4,000
(Non-paid)16,000

**Seguridad Latina (11340)**
Primedia Business Magzenes & Media
9800 Metcalf Ave.
Overland Park, KS 66212
Phone: (913)341-1300
Fax: (913)967-1898
**Subject(s):** Safety; Electronics Engineering; Spanish
**Circ:** (Combined)16,000

**Farmer Stockman of the Midwest (11001)**
Telescope Pub. Co.
1817 E U.S 81, Frontage Rd.
Belleville, KS 66935
Phone: (785)527-2224
Fax: (785)527-2225
**Subject(s):** General Agriculture; Livestock
**Circ:** ‡15,057

**Government Video (11409)**
United Entertainment Media
10701 W. 54th St.
Shawnee, KS 66203
Phone: (913)268-5973
Fax: (913)268-0461
**Subject(s):** Radio, Television, Cable, and Video
**Circ:** (Non-paid)15,000

**Iowa Business & Technology Resource Guide (10476)**
Business Publications Corp.
The Depot at Fourth
100 4th St.
Des Moines, IA 50309
Phone: (515)288-3336
Fax: (515)288-0309
**Subject(s):** Business
**Circ:** (Combined)15,000

**Wearables Business (11354)**
Primedia Business Magzenes & Media
9800 Metcalf Ave.
Overland Park, KS 66212
Phone: (913)341-1300
Fax: (913)967-1898
**Subject(s):** Clothing; General Merchandise; Fashion
**Circ:** (Combined)14,723

**North Dakota Horizons (23902)**
Greater North Dakota Association
2000 Schafer St.
PO Box 2639
Bismarck, ND 58502
Phone: (701)222-0929
Fax: (701)222-1611
**Subject(s):** Lifestyle; Local, State, and Regional Publications
**Circ:** (Combined)14,600

**Journal of the American Statistical Association (JASA) (10292)**
American Statistical Association
c/o Mark S. Kaiser
Dept. of Statistics
102E Snedecor Hall
Iowa State University
Ames, IA 50011-1210
Phone: (515)294-8871
**Subject(s):** Statistics
**Circ:** (Controlled)‡195
(Paid)‡14,500

**Ottawa Spirit (11288)**
Ottawa University
1001 S Cedar St.
Box 16
Ottawa, KS 66067-3399
Phone: (785)242-5200
Fax: (785)229-1022
**Subject(s):** College Publications
**Circ:** (Controlled)‡14,500

**MidAmerica Farmer Grower (17475)**
SJS Publishing Company Inc.
19 N Main
Perryville, MO 63775
Phone: (573)547-2244
Fax: (573)547-5663
**Subject(s):** General Agriculture; Local, State, and Regional Publications
**Circ:** (Non-paid)‡10,451
(Paid)‡14,379

**Huskers Illustrated (18411)**
PO Box 83222
Lincoln, NE
Phone: (402)474-4355
Fax: (402)474-5132
**Subject(s):** College Publications; (General Sports)
**Circ:** 14,000

**The American Oil and Gas Reporter (11041)**
PO Box 343
Derby, KS 67037
Phone: (316)788-6271
Fax: (316)788-7568
**Subject(s):** Petroleum, Oil, and Gas
**Circ:** ‡13,540

**Kansas 4-H Journal (11229)**
Kansas 4-H Foundation Inc.
Kansas State University
116 Umberger Hall
Manhattan, KS 66506-3417
Phone: (785)532-5881
Fax: (785)532-6963
**Subject(s):** Clubs and Societies; Youths' Interests; General Agriculture
**Circ:** ‡13,500

**Trucking Times & Sport Utility News (10358)**
Wiesner Publishing L.L.C.
307 Maryhill Dr.
Cedar Falls, IA 50613-5728
Phone: (319)277-8332
Fax: (319)277-8950
**Subject(s):** Automotive (Trade); Trailers and Accessories
**Circ:** (Combined)13,500

**The Journal of Pediatrics (17742)**
Mosby Inc.
11830 Westline Industrial Dr.
Saint Louis, MO 63146
Phone: (800)545-2522
Fax: (800)568-5136
**Subject(s):** Pediatrics
**Circ:** (Free)514
(Paid)13,040

**Bethel College Context (11274)**
Bethel College
300 E 27th St.
North Newton, KS 67117
Phone: (316)283-2500
Fax: (316)284-5286
**Subject(s):** College Publications
**Circ:** (Free)‡13,000

**Kansas City Homes & Gardens (11380)**
Showcase Publishing Inc.
5301 W 75th
Prairie Village, KS 66208
Phone: (913)648-5757
Fax: (913)648-5783
**Subject(s):** Home and Garden; Lifestyle
**Circ:** (Non-paid)‡2,800
(Paid)‡13,000

**Quill & Scroll (10666)**
Quill and Scroll Society
School of Journalism
100 Adler-Journalism Bldg., Rm. E-346
University of Iowa
Iowa City, IA 52242
Phone: (319)335-3457
Fax: (319)335-3989
**Subject(s):** Journalism and Publishing

**Circ:** (Non-paid)‡152
(Paid)‡12,603

**Computer Aided Surgery (17631)**
John Wiley and Sons Inc.
c/o Richard D. Bucholz Editor-in-Chief
Div. of Neurosurgery
St. Louis Univ. Health Sciences Center
1320 S. Grand Blvd.
Saint Louis, MO 63104-1087
Phone: (314)268-5378
Fax: (314)268-5113
**Subject(s):** Medicine and Surgery

**Circ:** (Paid)12,500

**Family Law Quarterly (11424)**
American Bar Association
c/o Linda D. Elrod
Washburn University School of Law
1700 SW College Ave.
Topeka, KS 66621
**Subject(s):** Law

**Circ:** 12,500

**Radio Magazine (11334)**
Primedia Business Magazines & Media
9800 Metcalf Ave.
Overland Park, KS 66212
Phone: (913)341-1300
Fax: (913)967-1898
**Subject(s):** Radio, Television, Cable, and Video

**Circ:** (Controlled)12,500

**American Journal of Obstetrics and Gynecology (17566)**
Mosby Inc.
11830 Westline Industrial Dr.
Saint Louis, MO 63146
Phone: (800)545-2522
Fax: (800)568-5136
**Subject(s):** Medicine and Surgery

**Circ:** (Combined)‡12,245

**Dakota Country (23899)**
Mitzel Outdoor Publications Inc.
PO Box 2714
Bismarck, ND 58502
Phone: (701)255-3031
Fax: (701)255-5038
**Subject(s):** (Hunting, Fishing, and Game Management); Local, State, and Regional Publications

**Circ:** (Non-paid)2,150
(Paid)12,199

**Produce Merchandising (11205)**
Vance Publishing Corp.
c/o Elizabeth Ashby, Editor
10901 W. 84th Terrace
Lenexa, KS 66214
Phone: (913)438-8700
Fax: (913)438-0691
**Subject(s):** Fruit, Fruit Products, and Produce Trade

**Circ:** 12,057

**Conservation Voices (10308)**
Soil and Water Conservation Society
945 SW Ankeny Rd.
Ankeny, IA 50021-9764
Phone: (515)289-2331
Fax: (515)289-1227
**Subject(s):** Ecology and Conservation; Waste Management and Recycling

**Circ:** (Combined)12,032

**Club Connection (17959)**
General Council of the Assemblies of God
1445 Boonville Ave.
Springfield, MO 65802-1894
Phone: (417)863-1874
Fax: (417)862-0416
**Subject(s):** Religious Publications

**Circ:** ‡12,000

**Evangelizing Today's Child (18031)**
Child Evangelism Fellowship Inc.
Box 348
Warrenton, MO 63383
Phone: (636)456-4321
Fax: (636)456-4321
**Subject(s):** Religious Publications; Education

**Circ:** ‡12,000

**Industrial Machine Trader (10580)**
Heartland Communications Group Inc.
1003 Central Ave.
PO Box 1052
Fort Dodge, IA 50501
Phone: (515)955-1600
**Subject(s):** Machinery and Equipment

**Circ:** (Combined)‡12,000

**Small Farm Today (17142)**
Missouri Farm Publishing Inc.
3903 W Ridge Trail Rd.
Clark, MO 65243-9525
Phone: (573)687-3525
Fax: (573)687-3148
**Subject(s):** General Agriculture; Livestock

**Circ:** 12,000

**The Sugarbeet Grower (23956)**
Sugar Publications
503 Broadway
Fargo, ND 58102
Phone: (701)476-2111
Fax: (701)476-2182
**Subject(s):** Sugar and Sugar Beets

**Circ:** (Non-paid)‡12,000

**Valley Potato Grower (23957)**
Red River Valley Potato Growers Association
PO Box 2065
Fargo, ND 58107-2065
Phone: (701)476-2112
Fax: (701)476-2182
**Subject(s):** Food Production

**Circ:** (Paid)200
(Non-paid)11,620

**Farm Equipment Guide (10577)**
Heartland Communications Group Inc.
1003 Central Ave.
PO Box 1052
Fort Dodge, IA 50501
Phone: (515)955-1600
**Subject(s):** Farm Implements and Supplies; Machinery and Equipment

**Circ:** (Non-paid)‡7,500
(Paid)‡11,500

**Baking & Snack (17316)**
Sosland Publishing Co.
4800 Main St., Ste. 100
Kansas City, MO 64112
Phone: (816)756-1000
Fax: (816)756-0494
**Subject(s):** Baking

**Circ:** (Controlled)‡11,379

**The Asphalt Contractor (17262)**
204 W Kansas Ave., Ste. 103
Independence, MO 64050-3700
Phone: (816)343-6462
Fax: (816)254-2128
**Subject(s):** Roads and Streets

**Circ:** 11,152

**Celebration (17318)**
National Catholic Reporter Publishing Company Inc.
115 E. Armour Blvd.
Kansas City, MO 64111-1203
Phone: (816)531-0538
Fax: (816)968-2292
**Subject(s):** Religious Publications

**Circ:** ‡11,000

**Health Progress (17693)**
Catholic Health Association of the United States
4455 Woodson Rd.
Saint Louis, MO 63134-3797
Phone: (314)427-2500
Fax: (314)427-0029
**Subject(s):** Hospitals and Healthcare Institutions

**Circ:** (Controlled)‡9,300
(Paid)‡11,000

**Traders World (17975)**
2508 W. Grayrock St.
Springfield, MO 65810
Phone: (417)882-9697
Fax: (417)885-5180
**Subject(s):** Banking, Finance, and Investments

**Circ:** (Paid)11,000

**Feed-Lot (11045)**
Feed-Lot Magazine
Box 850
Dighton, KS 67839-0850
Phone: (620)397-2838
Fax: (620)397-2839
**Subject(s):** Feed and Grain; Livestock

**Circ:** (Controlled)‡10,777

**Bethany Magazine (11217)**
College Relations
Presser Hall
421 N 1st St.
Lindsborg, KS 67456-1897
Phone: (785)227-3311
Fax: (785)227-2004
**Subject(s):** College Publications

**Circ:** (Controlled)‡10,500

**Catholic Health World (17598)**
Catholic Health Association of the United States
4455 Woodson Rd.
Saint Louis, MO 63134-3797
Phone: (314)427-2500
Fax: (314)427-0029
**Subject(s):** Religious Publications; Medicine and Surgery

**Circ:** (Paid)‡300
(Non-paid)‡10,500

**Iowa County Farmer (10730)**
100 W Main St.
PO Box 208
Marengo, IA 52301
Phone: (319)642-5506
Fax: (319)642-5509
**Subject(s):** Farm Newspapers

**Circ:** (Paid)‡10,140

**AFA Watchbird (17457)**
American Federation of Aviculture
PO Box 7312
North Kansas City, MO 64116-0012
Phone: (816)421-BIRD
Fax: (816)421-3214
**Subject(s):** Ecology and Conservation; Natural History and Nature Study

**Circ:** (Non-paid)100
(Paid)10,000

**Army Motors (17261)**
Military Vehicle Preservation Association
Box 520378
Independence, MO 64052-0378
Phone: (816)833-6872
Fax: (816)833-5115
**Subject(s):** Military and Navy; Automotive (Trade)

**Circ:** (Controlled)10,000

**Collectors News (10611)**
Pioneer Communications Inc.
506 2nd St.
PO Box 306
Grundy Center, IA 50638
Phone: (319)824-6981
Fax: (319)824-3414
**Subject(s):** Crafts, Models, Hobbies, and Contests; Art; Antiques; Collecting

**Circ:** ‡10,000

**Contractors Hot Line Monthly Equipment Guide (10576)**
Heartland Communications Group Inc.
1003 Central Ave.
PO Box 1052
Fort Dodge, IA 50501
Phone: (515)955-1600
**Subject(s):** Construction, Contracting, Building, and Excavating; Machinery and Equipment

**Circ:** (Paid)10,000

**eKC (17326)**
Discovery Publications Inc.
400 Grand Ave., Ste. B
Kansas City, MO 64106
Phone: (816)474-1516
Fax: (816)474-1427

## Great Plains States

**Subject(s):** Local, State, and Regional Publications; Entertainment
**Circ:** (Non-paid)10,000

**Embroidery Professional & Sewing Professional/Round Bobbin (10469)**
Sewing Dealers Trade Association
2724 2nd Ave.
Des Moines, IA 50313-4933
Phone: (515)282-9101
Fax: (515)282-4483
**Subject(s):** Retail; Dressmaking, Needlework, and Quilting
**Circ:** (Non-paid)‡10,000

**Farmer's Digest (10578)**
Heartland Communications Group Inc.
1003 Central Ave.
PO Box 1052
Fort Dodge, IA 50501
Phone: (515)955-1600
**Subject(s):** General Agriculture
**Circ:** 10,000

**Forum (17329)**
Kansas City Artists Coalition
201 Wyandotte
Kansas City, MO 64105
Phone: (816)421-5222
Fax: (816)421-0656
**Subject(s):** Art and Art History
**Circ:** (Paid)600
(Non-paid)10,000

**Hereford World (17331)**
Hereford Publications Inc.
PO Box 014059
1501 Wyandotte
Kansas City, MO 64101-0059
Phone: (816)842-8878
Fax: (816)842-6931
**Subject(s):** Livestock
**Circ:** ‡10,000

**The IAPD Magazine (11195)**
International Association of Plastics Distributors
4707 College Blvd., Ste. 105
Leawood, KS 66211-1667
Phone: (913)345-1005
Fax: (913)345-1006
**Subject(s):** Plastic and Composition Materials
**Circ:** (Paid)10,000
(Non-paid)10,000

**Journal of Gerontological Nursing (10656)**
SLACK Inc.
c/o Kathleen C. Buckwalter, Editor
Univ. of Iowa College of Nursing
Iowa City, IA
**Subject(s):** Gerontology; Nursing
**Circ:** (Paid)‡10,000

**Midwest Entertainment News (10345)**
Country Music Showcase, International Inc.
PO Box 368
Carlisle, IA 50047
Phone: (515)989-3748
Fax: (515)989-0235
**Subject(s):** Music and Musical Instruments; Music and Musical Instruments
**Circ:** 10,000

**Packaging and Converting Hotline (10584)**
IMS L.L.C.
900 Central Ave., Ste. 1
Fort Dodge, IA 50501
Phone: (515)574-2234
Fax: (515)574-2202
**Subject(s):** Business; Packaging
**Circ:** (Combined)10,000

**Voices (17872)**
Women for Faith & Family
PO Box 8326
Saint Louis, MO 63132
Phone: (314)863-8385
Fax: (314)863-5858
**Subject(s):** Women's Interests
**Circ:** (Non-paid)10,000

**Well Nations Magazine (28381)**
Well Nations Inc.
520 Kansas City St., Ste. 308
Rapid City, SD 57701
Phone: (605)348-9283
Fax: (605)348-9284

**Subject(s):** Intercultural Interests; Lifestyle
**Circ:** (Combined)10,000

**Woman's Touch (17978)**
General Council of the Assemblies of God
1445 Boonville Ave.
Springfield, MO 65802-1894
Phone: (417)863-1874
Fax: (417)862-0416
**Subject(s):** Religious Publications; Women's Interests
**Circ:** ‡10,000

**Club Management (17625)**
Finan Publishing Company Inc.
107 W Pacific Ave.
Saint Louis, MO 63119-3776
Phone: (314)961-6644
Fax: (314)961-4809
**Subject(s):** Hotels, Motels, Restaurants, and Clubs
**Circ:** (Controlled)3,355
(Paid)9,957

**Seminars in Oncology (17171)**
Elsevier
C/o John W. Yarbro, Editor
2604 Luan Ct.
Columbia, MO 65203
**Subject(s):** Medicine and Surgery
**Circ:** ‡9,614

**Journal of Soil and Water Conservation (10309)**
Soil and Water Conservation Society
945 SW Ankeny Rd.
Ankeny, IA 50021-9764
Phone: (515)289-2331
Fax: (515)289-1227
**Subject(s):** Ecology and Conservation; Water Supply and Sewage Disposal
**Circ:** 9,358

**The PDA Journal of Pharmaceutical Science & Technology (10662)**
PDA
c/o The University of Iowa
Pharmacy Bldg. S221
Iowa City, IA 52242
Phone: (319)384-4408
Fax: (319)384-4409
**Subject(s):** Drugs and Pharmaceuticals
**Circ:** (Controlled)9,266

**World Grain (17358)**
Sosland Publishing Co.
4800 Main St., Ste. 100
Kansas City, MO 64112
Phone: (816)756-1000
Fax: (816)756-0494
**Subject(s):** Feed and Grain
**Circ:** (Combined)9,017

**INTERMISSION (5439)**
K Communications
135 W Rose Ave.
Saint Louis, MO 63119
Phone: (314)962-0283
Fax: (311)496-2028
**Subject(s):** Performing Arts
**Circ:** (Paid)‡1,000
(Non-paid)‡9,000

**Nebraska Smoke-Eater (18579)**
Smoke-Eater Publications
109 E Main St.
Pierce, NE 68767-0129
Phone: (402)329-4665
Fax: (402)329-6337
**Subject(s):** Fire Fighting
**Circ:** ‡9,000

**Stained Glass Magazine (17509)**
Stained Glass Association of America
10009 E. 62nd St.
Raytown, MO 64133
Phone: (816)737-2090
Fax: (816)737-2801
**Subject(s):** Glass and China
**Circ:** (Non-paid)‡140
(Paid)‡9,000

**St. Louis Construction News & Review (17810)**
Finan Publishing Company Inc.
107 W Pacific Ave.
Saint Louis, MO 63119-3776
Phone: (314)961-6644
Fax: (314)961-4809

**Subject(s):** Construction, Contracting, Building, and Excavating; Architecture
**Circ:** (Paid)‡2,415
(Non-paid)‡8,970

**The Journal of Allergy and Clinical Immunology (17715)**
Mosby Inc.
11830 Westline Industrial Dr.
Saint Louis, MO 63146
Phone: (800)545-2522
Fax: (800)568-5136
**Subject(s):** Medicine and Surgery
**Circ:** (Paid)‡8,800

**The Nebraska Lawyer (18429)**
Nebraska State Bar Association
635 S 14th St., No. 2
PO Box 81809
Lincoln, NE 68501
Phone: (402)475-7091
Fax: (402)475-7098
**Subject(s):** Law
**Circ:** (Combined)8,700

**The CK of A Journal (17603)**
Catholic Knights of America
3525 Hampton Ave.
Saint Louis, MO 63139
Phone: (314)351-1029
**Subject(s):** Religious Publications
**Circ:** 8,500

**Mid-America Commerce and Industry (11440)**
M.A.C.I. Inc.
2432 SW Pepperwood
Topeka, KS 66614
Phone: (785)272-5280
Fax: (785)272-3729
**Subject(s):** Purchasing
**Circ:** (Controlled)‡8,500

**Agri Marketing (17560)**
Doane Agricultural Services
11701 Borman Dr., Ste. 300
Saint Louis, MO 63146-4193
Phone: (314)569-2700
Fax: (314)569-1083
**Subject(s):** General Agriculture; Business
**Circ:** (Paid)212
(Controlled)8,325

**NAEDA Equipment Dealer (17226)**
North American Equipment Dealers Association
1195 Smizer Mill Rd.
Fenton, MO 63026-3480
Phone: (636)340-5000
Fax: (636)349-5443
**Subject(s):** Farm Implements and Supplies
**Circ:** (Non-paid)△2,245
(Paid)△**8,298**

**The Iowa Lawyer (10479)**
The Iowa State Bar Association
521 E Locust, 3rd. Fl.
Des Moines, IA 50309
Phone: (515)243-3179
Fax: (515)243-2511
**Subject(s):** Law
**Circ:** (Controlled)8,250

**Dakota Outdoors (28362)**
Hipple Publishing Company Inc.
333 W Dakota
PO Box 669
Pierre, SD 57501-0669
Phone: (605)224-7301
Fax: (605)224-9210
**Subject(s):** Local, State, and Regional Publications; Boating and Yachting; (Outdoors); (Hunting, Fishing, and Game Management)
**Circ:** (Non-paid)25
(Paid)8,100

**Expo (11308)**
EXPO Magazine Inc.
11600 College Blvd.
Overland Park, KS 66210
Phone: (913)469-1110
Fax: (913)469-0806
**Subject(s):** Conventions, Meetings, and Trade Fairs
**Circ:** (Controlled)7,500

**Jazz Education Journal** (11226)
International Association for Jazz Education
PO Box 724
Manhattan, KS 66505
Phone: (785)776-8744
Fax: (785)776-6190
**Subject(s):** Music and Musical Instruments; Education

Circ: (Non-paid)300
(Paid)7,500

**Original Internist** (17518)
Original Internist Inc.
720 Oak Knoll
Rolla, MO 65401
Phone: (573)341-8448
Fax: (573)341-8494
**Subject(s):** Medicine and Surgery; Health and Healthcare

Circ: 7,500

**Schutzhund USA** (17821)
United Schutzhund Clubs of America
3810 Paule Ave.
Saint Louis, MO 63125-1718
Phone: (314)638-9686
Fax: (314)638-0609
**Subject(s):** Pets

Circ: (Non-paid)500
(Paid)7,500

**Mules and More** (17077)
Mules and More Inc.
PO Box 460
Bland, MO 65014-0460
Phone: (573)646-3934
Fax: (573)646-3407
**Subject(s):** Horses and Horse Racing

Circ: (Combined)⊕7,455

**St. Louis Commerce** (17809)
St. Louis Regional Chamber & Growth Association
(RCGA)
One Metropolitan Sq., Ste. 1300
Saint Louis, MO 63102
Phone: (314)231-5555
Fax: (314)206-3277
**Subject(s):** Chambers of Commerce and Boards of Trade

Circ: (Non-paid)2,826
(Paid)7,154

**Kansas Stockman** (11439)
Kansas Livestock Association
6031 SW 37th
Topeka, KS 66614
Phone: (785)273-5115
Fax: (785)273-3399
**Subject(s):** Livestock

Circ: (Non-paid)‡410
(Paid)‡7,025

**International Social Science Review** (11510)
1001 Millington, Ste. B
Winfield, KS 67156
Phone: (620)221-3128
Fax: (620)221-7124
**Subject(s):** Social Sciences

Circ: (Non-paid)‡150
(Paid)‡7,000

**International Women Pilots/99 News** (11482)
The Ninety-Nines Inc.
807 N. Waco
Suite 22
Wichita, KS 67203
Phone: (316)263-7350
Fax: (316)263-7350
**Subject(s):** Aviation; Women's Interests

Circ: ‡7,000

**The Missouri Review** (17164)
University of Missouri at Columbia
1507 Hillcrest Hall
Columbia, MO 65211
Phone: (573)882-4474
Fax: (573)884-4671
**Subject(s):** Literature and Literary Reviews

Circ: (Non-paid)200
(Paid)6,800

**The Journal of Prosthetic Dentistry** (17745)
Mosby Inc.
11830 Westline Industrial Dr.
Saint Louis, MO 63146
Phone: (800)545-2522
Fax: (800)568-5136
**Subject(s):** Dentistry

Circ: (Paid)‡6,619

**America's Flyways** (17569)
United States Pilots Association
483 S Kirkwood Rd., No. 10
Saint Louis, MO 63122
Phone: (314)849-8772
Fax: (314)849-8772
**Subject(s):** Aviation

Circ: 6,600

**Missouri Medicine** (17284)
Missouri State Medical Association
113 Madison St.
PO Box 1028
Jefferson City, MO 65101-3015
Phone: (573)636-5151
Fax: (573)636-8552
**Subject(s):** Medicine and Surgery

Circ: ‡6,600

**MOUTH** (11442)
MOUTH: Voice of the Disability Nation
4201 SW 30th St.
Topeka, KS 66614
Phone: (785)272-2578
Fax: (785)272-7348
**Subject(s):** Handicapped; Civil Rights

Circ: (Paid)6,540

**Gateway Heritage** (17687)
Missouri Historical Society
PO Box 11940
225 South Skinker
Saint Louis, MO 63112-0040
Phone: (314)746-4599
Fax: (314)746-4548
**Subject(s):** History and Genealogy

Circ: (Controlled)‡500
(Paid)‡6,500

**Steam Traction** (11444)
Ogden Publications
1503 SW 42nd St.
Topeka, KS 66609-1265
Phone: (785)274-4300
Fax: (785)274-4305
**Subject(s):** Crafts, Models, Hobbies, and Contests

Circ: ‡6,500

**Missouri Municipal Review** (17285)
Missouri Municipal League
1727 Southridge Dr.
Jefferson City, MO 65109
Phone: (573)635-9134
Fax: (573)635-9009
**Subject(s):** State, Municipal, and County Administration

Circ: ‡6,200

**Missouri Historical Review** (17160)
State Historical Society of Missouri
1020 Lowry St.
Columbia, MO 65201-7298
Phone: (573)882-7083
Fax: (573)884-4950
**Subject(s):** History and Genealogy

Circ: ‡6,100

**Charolais Journal** (17319)
American-International Charolais Association
PO Box 20247
Kansas City, MO 64195
Phone: (816)464-5977
Fax: (816)464-5759
**Subject(s):** Livestock

Circ: ‡6,000

**Kansas Government Journal** (11434)
League of Kansas Municipalities
300 SW 8th Ave.
Topeka, KS 66603-3912
Phone: (785)354-9565
Fax: (785)354-4186
**Subject(s):** State, Municipal, and County Administration

Circ: ‡6,000

**The Pentecostal Messenger** (17301)
Pentecostal Church of God
4901 Pennsylvania St.
PO Box 850
Joplin, MO 64802-0850
Phone: (417)624-7050
Fax: (417)624-7102
**Subject(s):** Religious Publications

Circ: ‡6,000

**Plastics Hot Line** (10585)
IMS L.L.C.
900 Central Ave., Ste. 1
Fort Dodge, IA 50501
Phone: (515)574-2234
Fax: (515)574-2202
**Subject(s):** Machinery and Equipment

Circ: (Controlled)‡6,000

**Review for Religious** (17799)
3601 Lindell Blvd., Rm. 428
Saint Louis, MO 63108
Phone: (314)977-7363
Fax: (314)977-7362
**Subject(s):** Religious Publications

Circ: (Non-paid)‡242
(Paid)‡6,000

**With** (11270)
Faith & Life Resources
718 Main St.
PO Box 347
Newton, KS 67114-0347
Phone: (620)367-8432
**Subject(s):** Religious Publications; Youths' Interests

Circ: 6,000

**ACTA Cytologica** (17542)
Science Printers and Publishers Inc.
PO Drawer 12425
8342 Olive Blvd.
Saint Louis, MO 63132-2814
Phone: (314)991-4440
Fax: (314)991-4654
**Subject(s):** Medicine and Surgery

Circ: (Controlled)22
(Paid)5,836

**The Auctioneer** (11294)
National Auctioneers Association
8880 Ballentine
Overland Park, KS 66214
Phone: (913)541-8084
Fax: (913)894-5281
**Subject(s):** General Merchandise; Selling and Salesmanship

Circ: ‡5,800

**Bank News** (11412)
Bank News Inc.
5115 Roe Blvd., Ste. 200
PO Box 29156
Shawnee Mission, KS 66201-9156
Phone: (913)261-7000
Fax: (913)261-7010
**Subject(s):** Banking, Finance, and Investments

Circ: (Paid)1,400
(Non-paid)5,800

**Central States Archaeological Journal** (17139)
Central States Archaeological Societies Inc.
PO Box 7145
Chesterfield, MO 63006-7145
Phone: (314)839-2929
Fax: (636)386-2900
**Subject(s):** Archaeology

Circ: ‡5,700

**Career Development Quarterly** (17597)
American Association for Counseling and Development
College of Education
Univ. of Missouri
415 Marillac Hall
One Univ. Blvd.
Saint Louis, MO 63121-4499
Phone: (314)516-7121
Fax: (314)516-5784
**Subject(s):** Education; Employment and Human Resources

Circ: (Non-paid)‡70
(Paid)‡5,500

**Journal of the American Historical Society of Germans from Russia** (18413)
American Historical Society of Germans from Russia
631 D St.
Lincoln, NE 68502-1199
Phone: (402)474-3363
Fax: (402)474-7229
**Subject(s):** History and Genealogy; Intercultural Interests

Circ: 5,500

**Saddle & Bridle Magazine** (17803)
Saddle & Bridle Inc.
375 Jackson Ave.
Saint Louis, MO 63130
Phone: (314)725-9115
Fax: (314)725-6440
**Subject(s):** (Horses and Horse Racing)
**Circ:** (Controlled)‡400
(Paid)‡5,500

**U.S. Roller Skating** (18457)
U.S. Amateur Confederation of Roller Skating
PO Box 6579
Lincoln, NE 68506
Phone: (402)483-7551
Fax: (402)483-1465
**Subject(s):** (Skating)
**Circ:** (Non-paid)200
(Paid)5,500

**Classic Images** (10769)
Muscatine Journal
301 E. 3rd St.
Muscatine, IA 52761
Phone: (563)263-2331
Fax: (563)262-8042
**Subject(s):** Motion Pictures
**Circ:** (Non-paid)500
(Paid)5,400

**Studies in the Spirituality of Jesuits** (17850)
Seminar on Jesuit Spirituality
3601 Lindell Blvd.
Saint Louis, MO 63108
Phone: (314)977-7257
Fax: (314)977-7263
**Subject(s):** Religious Publications
**Circ:** 5,300

**Kanhistique** (11059)
The Ellsworth Reporter
220 N Douglas Ave.
Ellsworth, KS 67439-3216
Phone: (785)472-5085
Fax: (785)472-5087
**Subject(s):** History and Genealogy; Art; Local, State, and Regional Publications
**Circ:** ‡5,215

**Anarchy** (17149)
CAL Press
PO Box 1446
Columbia, MO 65205-1446
Phone: (573)442-4352
**Subject(s):** Alternative and Underground
**Circ:** (Paid)5,200

**Journal of Teacher Education** (10487)
Boston College
Drake University
School of Education
Des Moines, IA 50311
Phone: (515)271-2085
**Subject(s):** Education
**Circ:** (Non-paid)86
(Paid)3,000
(Controlled)5,200

**Missouri Beef Cattleman** (17338)
Missouri Beef Cattleman Inc.
PO Box 025727
Kansas City, MO 64102
Phone: (816)471-0200
Fax: (816)471-0220
**Subject(s):** Livestock
**Circ:** (Controlled)‡5,200

**Nebraska Cattleman** (18424)
The Nebraska Cattlemen Inc.
134 S 13th St., Ste. 900
Lincoln, NE 68508
Phone: (402)475-2333
Fax: (402)475-0822
**Subject(s):** Livestock
**Circ:** (Controlled)‡4,530
(Paid)‡5,067

**Annals of Otology, Rhinology and Laryngology** (17575)
Annals Publishing Co.
4507 Laclede Ave.
Saint Louis, MO 63108
Phone: (314)367-4987
Fax: (314)367-4988
**Subject(s):** Medicine and Surgery
**Circ:** ‡5,006

**Farm & Home Research Quarterly** (28279)
Box 2231
S Dakota State University
Brookings, SD 57007
Phone: (605)688-4018
Fax: (605)688-5683
**Subject(s):** Scientific Agricultural Publications
**Circ:** (Non-paid)‡5,000

**Journal of Pharmaceutical Sciences** (11174)
American Pharmaceutical Association
c/o Dr. Ronald T. Borchardt
Department of Pharmaceutical Chemistry
The University of Kansas
2095 Constant Ave., Rm. 121A
Lawrence, KS 66047
**Subject(s):** Drugs and Pharmaceuticals; Chemistry, Chemicals, and Chemical Engineering
**Circ:** (Non-paid)‡120
(Paid)‡5,000

**Office Technology** (17343)
Business Technology Association
12411 Wornall Rd., Ste. 200
Kansas City, MO 64145
Phone: (816)941-3100
Fax: (816)941-4838
**Subject(s):** Stationery, Office Equipment, and College Store Supplies
**Circ:** ‡5,000

**Steamshovel Press** (17848)
PO Box 210553
Saint Louis, MO 63121
Phone: (314)382-5160
**Subject(s):** Alternative and Underground
**Circ:** (Paid)5,000

**Texas Banking Red Book** (11413)
Texas Bankers Association
PO Box 29156
Shawnee Mission, KS 66201-9156
Phone: (913)261-7000
Fax: (913)261-7010
**Subject(s):** Banking, Finance, and Investments; Local, State, and Regional Publications
**Circ:** (Controlled)‡300
(Paid)‡5,000

**Cherry Diamond** (17599)
Missouri Athletic Club
405 Washington Ave.
Saint Louis, MO 63102
Phone: (314)231-7220
Fax: (314)231-2327
**Subject(s):** Clubs and Societies
**Circ:** 4,900

**Social Justice Review** (17843)
Central Bureau of the Catholic Central Verein of America
3835 Westminster Pl.
Saint Louis, MO 63108
Phone: (314)371-1653
Fax: (314)371-0889
**Subject(s):** Sociology; Theology; Economics; History and Genealogy
**Circ:** (Non-paid)500
(Paid)4,600

**Journal of the West** (11227)
1531 Yuma
Manhattan, KS 66502
Phone: (785)539-1888
Fax: (785)539-2233
**Subject(s):** History and Genealogy
**Circ:** 4,500

**Moila Temple Bulletin** (17530)
Gallatin Publishing Co.
701 N. Noyes Blvd.
Saint Joseph, MO 64506
Phone: (816)232-5129
Fax: (816)232-7739
**Subject(s):** Masons
**Circ:** ‡4,500

**Psychology of Women Quarterly** (17798)
Blackwell Publishers
University of Missouri
Saint Louis, MO 63121
**Subject(s):** Psychology and Psychiatry; Women's Interests
**Circ:** (Non-paid)75
(Paid)4437

**Christmas Trees** (11198)
Tree Publishers Inc.
PO Box 107
Lecompton, KS 66050
Phone: (785)887-6324
Fax: (785)887-6324
**Subject(s):** Socialized Farming; Seed and Nursery Trade
**Circ:** (Controlled)‡41
(Paid)‡4,391

**African American Review** (17557)
Modern Language Association
Saint Louis University
Humanities 317
3800 Lindell Blvd.
Saint Louis, MO 63108-3414
Phone: (314)977-3688
Fax: (314)977-1514
**Subject(s):** Literature; Black Publications
**Circ:** (Non-paid)167
(Paid)4,200

**Milling & Baking News** (17337)
Sosland Publishing Co.
4800 Main St., Ste. 100
Kansas City, MO 64112
Phone: (816)756-1000
Fax: (816)756-0494
**Subject(s):** Baking
**Circ:** (Paid)4,163

**The Student** (18451)
Christian Record Services
PO Box 6097
Lincoln, NE 68506-0097
Phone: (402)488-0981
Fax: (402)488-7582
**Subject(s):** Blind and Visually Challenged
**Circ:** (Non-paid)‡4,103

**The Iowa School Board Dialogue** (10483)
Iowa Association of School Boards
700 2nd Ave., Ste. 100
Des Moines, IA 50309
Phone: (515)288-1991
Fax: (515)243-4992
**Subject(s):** Education
**Circ:** (Non-paid)682
(Paid)4,086

**Implement & Tractor** (10354)
Agra USA
2302 W 1st St.
Cedar Falls, IA 50613-1879
Phone: (319)277-3599
Fax: (319)277-3783
**Subject(s):** Farm Implements and Supplies
**Circ:** (Paid)‡3,000
(Non-paid)‡4,000

**Rare Breeds Journal** (18324)
PO Box 66
Crawford, NE 69339
Phone: (308)665-1431
Fax: (308)665-1931
**Subject(s):** Veterinary Medicine
**Circ:** (Paid)4,000

**Organizational Dynamics** (18439)
American Management Association
C/O F. Luthans, Editor
Dept. of Management
Univ. of Nebraska
Lincoln, NE 68588-0491
**Subject(s):** Management and Administration
**Circ:** (Paid)3,947

**Evolution** (11165)
Allen Press Inc.
810 E 10th
Lawrence, KS 66044
Phone: (785)843-1234
Fax: (785)843-1244
**Subject(s):** Genetics
**Circ:** 3,878

**Geoarchaeology (10647)**
John Wiley and Sons Inc.
C/O E. Arthur Bettis III, Department of Geoscience
121 Trowbridge Hall
Iowa City, IA 52242-1319
**Subject(s):** Archaeology; Anthropology and Ethnology; Geology
**Circ:** 3,850

**Clinical Pharmacology and Therapeutics (17611)**
Mosby Inc.
11830 Westline Industrial Dr.
Saint Louis, MO 63146
Phone: (800)545-2522
Fax: (800)568-5136
**Subject(s):** Drugs and Pharmaceuticals
**Circ:** (Combined)‡3,800

**Kansas History: A Journal of the Central Plains (11435)**
Kansas State Historical Society
6425 SW 6th Ave.
Topeka, KS 66615-1099
Phone: (785)272-8681
Fax: (785)272-8682
**Subject(s):** History and Genealogy
**Circ:** (Non-paid)‡600
(Paid)‡3,800

**Nebraska History (18427)**
Nebraska State Historical Society
POB 82554
Lincoln, NE 68501
Phone: (402)471-3270
Fax: (402)471-3100
**Subject(s):** History and Genealogy
**Circ:** ‡3,800

**Mid-America Transporter (11441)**
Kansas Motor Carriers Association
2900 SW Topeka Blvd.
Topeka, KS 66611
Phone: (785)267-1641
Fax: (785)266-6551
**Subject(s):** Trucks and Trucking
**Circ:** (Non-paid)352
(Paid)3,758

**American Ethnologist (10639)**
American Anthropological Association
c/o Virginia R. Dominguez, Editor
University of Iowa, Department of Anthropology
114 Macbride Hall
Iowa City, IA 52242
Phone: (319)335-1866
Fax: (319)335-0653
**Subject(s):** Anthropology and Ethnology
**Circ:** ‡3,500

**Shorthorn Country (18539)**
American Shorthorn Association
8288 Hascall St.
Omaha, NE 68124
Phone: (402)393-7200
Fax: (402)393-7203
**Subject(s):** Livestock
**Circ:** (Non-paid)‡200
(Paid)‡3,500

**Tradition Magazine (10307)**
National Traditional Country Music Association
650 Main Street
PO Box 492
Anita, IA 50020
Phone: (712)762-4363
**Subject(s):** Music and Musical Instruments
**Circ:** (Paid)‡3,500
(Controlled)‡3,500

**The North American Review (10355)**
University of Northern Iowa
1222 W. 27th St.
Cedar Falls, IA 50614-0516
**Subject(s):** General Editorial; Literature and Literary Reviews
**Circ:** ‡3,400

**North Dakota Stockman (23904)**
North Dakota Stockmen's Association
407 S 2nd St.
Bismarck, ND 58504
Phone: (701)223-2522
Fax: (701)223-2587
**Subject(s):** Livestock
**Circ:** ‡3,400

**Swine Practitioner (11206)**
Vance Publishing Corp.
10901 W. 84th Ter.
Lenexa, KS 66214
Phone: (913)438-8700
Fax: (913)438-0697
**Subject(s):** Livestock; Veterinary Medicine
**Circ:** △3,340

**Iowa Heritage Illustrated (10650)**
State Historical Society of Iowa
402 Iowa Ave.
Iowa City, IA 52240-1806
Phone: (319)335-3916
Fax: (319)335-3935
**Subject(s):** History and Genealogy
**Circ:** ‡3,300

**Cereal Chemistry (11224)**
American Association of Cereal Chemists
3831 Quail Lane
Manhattan, KS 66502-1439
Phone: (785)537-5199
Fax: (785)537-7477
**Subject(s):** Chemistry, Chemicals, and Chemical Engineering; Food and Grocery Trade
**Circ:** (Controlled)‡26
(Paid)‡3,260

**Arteriosclerosis, Thrombosis, and Vascular Biology (10643)**
American Heart Association
University of Iowa
200 Hawkins Dr.
609 MRC
Iowa City, IA 52242-1182
Phone: (319)353-5764
Fax: (319)353-5766
**Subject(s):** Medicine and Surgery
**Circ:** ‡3,242

**Nebraska Municipal Review (18430)**
League of Nebraska Municipalities
1335 L St.
Lincoln, NE 68508-2506
Phone: (402)476-2829
Fax: (402)476-7052
**Subject(s):** State, Municipal, and County Administration
**Circ:** ‡3,200

**Wilson Bulletin (11185)**
Allen Press Inc.
810 E 10th
Lawrence, KS 66044
Phone: (785)843-1234
Fax: (785)843-1244
**Subject(s):** Ornithology and Oology
**Circ:** (Paid)3,200

**Journal of Food Protection (10486)**
International Association for Food Protection
6200 Aurora Ave., Ste. 200W
Des Moines, IA 50322
Phone: (515)276-3344
Fax: (515)276-8655
**Subject(s):** Food and Grocery Trade; Milk and Dairy Products
**Circ:** ‡3,100

**Pro Rege (10866)**
Dordt College
498 4th Ave. NE
Sioux Center, IA 51250
Phone: (712)722-6000
Fax: (712)722-1185
**Subject(s):** Religious Publications; College Publications
**Circ:** (Non-paid)‡3,100

**Analytical and Quantitative Cytology and Histology (17570)**
Science Printers and Publishers Inc.
PO Drawer 12425
8342 Olive Blvd.
Saint Louis, MO 63132-2814
Phone: (314)991-4440
Fax: (314)991-4654
**Subject(s):** Biology; Physiology and Anatomy
**Circ:** (Paid)‡3,090

**Administrative Leadership (17260)**
American Association of Christian Schools
c/o Independence Office
PO Box 1097
Independence, MO 64051-0597
Fax: (816)252-6700
**Subject(s):** Religious Publications; Education
**Circ:** 3,000

**American Journal of Cosmetic Surgery (11164)**
Allen Marketing and Management
PO Box 1897
Lawrence, KS 66044
Phone: (785)843-1235
Fax: (785)843-1274
**Subject(s):** Medicine and Surgery
**Circ:** ‡3,000

**The Business Journal (10739)**
Lee Enterprises Inc.
PO Box 271
Mason City, IA 50402-0271
Phone: (641)424-0818
Fax: (641)424-6786
**Subject(s):** Business
**Circ:** (Non-paid)3,000

**Hawkeye Heritage (10473)**
Iowa Genealogical Society
628 E. Grand Ave.
Des Moines, IA 50309-1924
Phone: (515)276-0287
Fax: (515)727-1824
**Subject(s):** History and Genealogy
**Circ:** (Controlled)3,000

**The Iowa Trucking Lifeliner (10484)**
Iowa Motor Truck Association
717 E Court Ave.
Des Moines, IA 50309
Phone: (515)244-5193
Fax: (515)244-2204
**Subject(s):** Trucks and Trucking
**Circ:** 3,000

**Journal of Geography (18309)**
National Council for Geographic Education
Dept. of Social Sciences and Justice Studies
Chadron State College
1000 Main St.
Chadron, NE 69337
Phone: (308)432-6275
Fax: (308)432-6464
**Subject(s):** Education; Geography
**Circ:** ‡3,000

**Journal of Scientific Exploration (11175)**
810 E. 10th St.
PO Box 1897
Lawrence, KS 66044-8897
Fax: (785)843-1274
**Subject(s):** Science (General)
**Circ:** (Paid)3,000

**Kansas State Engineer (11232)**
K State Engineer
College Of Engineering
133 Ward Hall
Manhattan, KS 66506
Phone: (785)532-6026
Fax: (785)532-6952
**Subject(s):** Engineering (Various branches); College Publications
**Circ:** (Paid)‡100
(Non-paid)‡3,000

**Nebraska Union Farmer (18434)**
Farmers Union of Nebraska
1305 Plum
Box 22667
Lincoln, NE 68542-2667
Phone: (402)476-8815
Fax: (402)476-8859
**Subject(s):** Farm Bureau, Grange, and Cooperative Associations
**Circ:** 3,000

**The Pentagon (11063)**
Kappa Mu Epsilon
Div. of Mathematics and Computer Science
Emporia State University
Emporia, KS 66801-5087
Phone: (620)341-1200
Fax: (620)341-6055
**Subject(s):** Mathematics
**Circ:** (Paid)3,000

**Rolling Along** (23906)
North Dakota Motor Carriers Association Inc.
P.O. Box 874
Bismarck, ND 58502
Phone: (701)223-2700
Fax: (701)223-4324
**Subject(s):** Trucks and Trucking

**Circ:** 3,000

**The St. Louis Journalism Review** (17813)
St. Louis Journalism Review
470 E Lockwood, Rm. 414
Saint Louis, MO 63119
Phone: (314)968-5905
Fax: (314)963-6104
**Subject(s):** Journalism and Publishing; Radio, Television, Cable, and Video

**Circ:** 3,000

**Christian Record** (18405)
Christian Record Services
PO Box 6097
Lincoln, NE 68506-0097
Phone: (402)488-0981
Fax: (402)488-7582
**Subject(s):** Blind and Visually Challenged

**Circ:** (Non-paid)‡2,900

**Medical Directory of Greater Kansas City** (17336)
Metropolitan Medical Society of Greater Kansas City
315 Michold Road ste 250
Kansas City, MO 64112
Phone: (816)531-8432
Fax: (816)531-8438
**Subject(s):** Medicine and Surgery

**Circ:** ‡2,880

**The Journal of Shoulder and Elbow Surgery** (17748)
Mosby Inc.
11830 Westline Industrial Dr.
Saint Louis, MO 63146
Phone: (800)545-2522
Fax: (800)568-5136
**Subject(s):** Medicine and Surgery

**Circ:** (Free)231
(Paid)2,866

**Animal Keepers' Forum** (11421)
American Association of Zoo Keepers Inc.
3601 SW 29th St., Ste. 133
Topeka, KS 66614-2054
Phone: (785)273-9149
Fax: (785)273-1980
**Subject(s):** Zoology

**Circ:** (Controlled)2,850

**Prairie Schooner** (18441)
University of Nebraska
201 Andrews Hall
Lincoln, NE 68588-0334
Phone: (402)472-0911
Fax: (402)472-9771
**Subject(s):** Literature and Literary Reviews

**Circ:** (Non-paid)‡300
(Paid)‡2,800

**The Iowa Review** (10652)
University of Iowa
308 EPB
Iowa City, IA 52242
Phone: (319)335-0462
**Subject(s):** Literature

**Circ:** (Combined)2,700

**The Journal of Laboratory and Clinical Medicine** (17735)
Mosby Inc.
11830 Westline Industrial Dr.
Saint Louis, MO 63146
Phone: (800)545-2522
Fax: (800)568-5136
**Subject(s):** Laboratory Research (Scientific and Medical); Medicine and Surgery

**Circ:** (Non-paid)289
(Paid)2,617

**The Missouri Engineer** (17283)
Missouri Society of Professional Engineers
200 E McCarty St., Ste. 200
Jefferson City, MO 65101
Phone: (573)636-4861
**Subject(s):** Engineering (Various branches)

**Circ:** (Non-paid)900
(Paid)2,600

**The Cleft Palate-Craniofacial Journal** (10644)
Allen Press Inc.
c/o Jerry Moon, Editor
Dept. of Speech Pathology and Audiology
University of Iowa
121 A WJSHC
Iowa City, IA 52242
Phone: (319)335-8722
Fax: (319)335-8851
**Subject(s):** Medicine and Surgery; Laboratory Research (Scientific and Medical); Science (General)

**Circ:** 2,570

**AACS Capitol Comments** (17259)
American Association of Christian Schools
c/o Independence Office
PO Box 1097
Independence, MO 64051-0597
Fax: (816)252-6700
**Subject(s):** Education; Religious Publications

**Circ:** 2,500

**Iowa Grocer** (10478)
Iowa Grocery Industry Association
2540 106th St., Ste. 102
Des Moines, IA 50322-3771
Phone: (515)270-2628
Fax: (515)270-0316
**Subject(s):** Food and Grocery Trade

**Circ:** ‡2,500

**Journal of Paleontology** (10659)
Allen Press Inc.
c/o Editors, Journal of Paleontology
Department of Geology
121 Trowbridge Hall
University of Iowa
Iowa City, IA 52242-1379
Phone: (319)335-1821
**Subject(s):** Geology

**Circ:** ‡2,500

**Kansas Music Review** (11488)
Kansas Music Educators Association
11302 Bekemeyer
Wichita, KS 67212
Phone: (316)978-3103
Fax: (316)729-6785
**Subject(s):** Music and Musical Instruments

**Circ:** 2,500

**The NADE Advocate** (17066)
National Association of Disability Examiners
1117 Sunshine Dr.
Aurora, MO 65605
Phone: (417)888-4152
Fax: (417)888-4069
**Subject(s):** Employment and Human Resources

**Circ:** (Non-paid)‡100
(Paid)‡2,500

**Ventilator-Assisted Living** (17867)
Post-Polio Health International Inc.
4207 Lindell Blvd., No. 110
Saint Louis, MO 63108-2915
Phone: (314)534-0475
Fax: (314)534-5070
**Subject(s):** Health and Healthcare

**Circ:** (Paid)2,500

**Wildlife Harvest** (10603)
Wildlife Harvest Publications
PO Box 96
Goose Lake, IA 52750
Phone: (563)259-4000
Fax: (563)259-4483
**Subject(s):** (Hunting, Fishing, and Game Management)

**Circ:** (Non-paid)‡200
(Paid)‡2,349

**The Journal for Specialists in Group Work** (11371)
Taylor & Francis
Department of Psychology and Counseling
Pittsburg State University
Pittsburg, KS 66762
Phone: (620)235-4530
Fax: (620)235-6102
**Subject(s):** Psychology and Psychiatry

**Circ:** ‡2,300

**Kansas Beverage News** (11486)
2416 E 37th N
Wichita, KS 67219
Phone: (316)838-6700
Fax: (316)838-6795

**Subject(s):** Beverages, Brewing, and Bottling

**Circ:** 2,300

**North Dakota Law Review** (23986)
University of North Dakota
Box 9003
Grand Forks, ND 58202-9003
Phone: (701)777-2941
Fax: (701)777-2217
**Subject(s):** Law

**Circ:** (Controlled)2,300

**Theology Digest** (17860)
St. Louis University
3800 Lindell Blvd.
PO Box 56907
Saint Louis, MO 63108
Phone: (314)977-3410
Fax: (314)977-3704
**Subject(s):** Religious Publications

**Circ:** ‡2,300

**Philosophy of Science** (17345)
University of Chicago Press
222 Cockefair Hall
University of Missouri-Kansas City
Kansas City, MO 64110
Phone: (816)235-2819
Fax: (816)235-2819
**Subject(s):** Science (General); Philosophy

**Circ:** (Non-paid)20
(Paid)2,280

**Focus MDA** (17277)
Missouri Dental Association
3340 American Ave.
Jefferson City, MO 65109-4900
Phone: (573)634-3436
Fax: (573)635-0764
**Subject(s):** Dentistry

**Circ:** ‡2,200

**NLGI Spokesman** (17341)
National Lubricating Grease Institute
4635 Wyandotte St.
Kansas City, MO 64112
Phone: (816)931-9480
Fax: (816)753-5026
**Subject(s):** Petroleum, Oil, and Gas

**Circ:** (Non-paid)‡50
(Paid)‡2,200

**St. Louis Metropolitan Medicine** (17816)
St. Louis Metropolitan Medical Society
3839 Lindell Blvd.
Saint Louis, MO 63108
Phone: (314)371-5225
Fax: (314)533-8601
**Subject(s):** Medicine and Surgery

**Circ:** (Non-paid)190
(Paid)2,066

**Journal of Child Neurology** (18532)
B.C. Decker Inc.
c/o Roger A. Brumback, MD, Editor in Chief
Dept. of Pathology
601 N. 30th St.
Omaha, NE 68131-2197
Phone: (402)280-4854
Fax: (402)280-5247
**Subject(s):** Medicine and Surgery

**Circ:** (Non-paid)60
(Paid)2,041

**Pharmacological Reviews** (18538)
American Society for Pharmacology and Experimental Therapeutics
986260 Nebraska Medical Center
Dept. of Pharmacology
Omaha, NE 68198-6260
Phone: (402)559-7495
Fax: (402)559-7495
**Subject(s):** Drugs and Pharmaceuticals

**Circ:** (Non-paid)‡71
(Paid)‡2,042

**The American Muslim** (17568)
American Muslim Support Group
PO Box 5670
Saint Louis, MO 63121-5670
Phone: (314)291-3711
Fax: (314)291-3711
**Subject(s):** Religious Publications

**Circ:** 2,000

**Chiron Review (11393)**
Chiron Review Press
522 E S Ave.
Saint John, KS 67576-2212
Phone: (620)786-4955
**Subject(s):** Literature
**Circ:** (Combined)2,000

**Creation Research Society Quarterly (17528)**
Creation Research Society
PO Box 8263
Saint Joseph, MO 64508-8263
Phone: (816)279-2312
Fax: (816)279-2312
**Subject(s):** Philosophy; Science (General)
**Circ:** 2,000

**Journal of the Experimental Analysis of Behavior (17730)**
Society for the Experimental Analysis of Behavior
c/o Leonard Green
Department of Psychology
Campus Box 1125
Washington University
Saint Louis, MO 63130
**Subject(s):** Psychology and Psychiatry
**Circ:** (Non-paid)90
(Paid)2,000

**Midwest Modern Language Association Journal (10661)**
Midwest Modern Language Association
302 English-Philosophy Bldg.
University of Iowa
Iowa City, IA 52242-1408
Phone: (319)335-0331
Fax: (319)335-3123
**Subject(s):** Literature; Education
**Circ:** (Paid)2,000

**New Letters (17340)**
University of Missouri at Kansas City
5101 Rockhill Rd.
Kansas City, MO 64110-2445
Phone: (816)235-1168
Fax: (816)235-2611
**Subject(s):** Literature and Literary Reviews
**Circ:** (Non-paid)‡84
(Paid)‡2,000

**O'Lochlaihn's Irish Family Journal (17344)**
Irish Genealogical Foundation
Dept. HPA
PO Box 7575
Kansas City, MO 64116
Phone: (816)454-2410
Fax: (816)454-2410
**Subject(s):** History and Genealogy; Ethnic Publications
**Circ:** (Paid)2,000

**South Dakota Journal of Medicine (28411)**
South Dakota State Medical Association
1323 S Minnesota Ave.
Sioux Falls, SD 57105-0624
Phone: (605)336-1965
Fax: (605)336-0270
**Subject(s):** Medicine and Surgery; Health and Healthcare
**Circ:** (Controlled)2,000

**Wapsipinicon Almanac (10305)**
Route 3 Press
19948 Shooting Star Rd.
Anamosa, IA 52205
Phone: (319)462-4623
**Subject(s):** Local, State, and Regional Publications; Literature and Literary Reviews
**Circ:** (Non-paid)2,000

**Financial Review (17153)**
Eastern Finance Association
Dept. of Finance
College of Business
Univ. of Missouri
Columbia, MO 65211
**Circ:** ‡1,900

**International Flying Farmer (11481)**
International Flying Farmers Inc.
2120 Airport Rd.
PO Box 9124
Wichita, KS 67277
Phone: (316)943-4234
Fax: (316)943-4235
**Subject(s):** General Agriculture; Aviation
**Circ:** (Controlled)‡1,900

**Nebraska Trucker (18433)**
Truck Services Inc.
PO Box 81010
Lincoln, NE 68501
Phone: (402)476-8504
Fax: (402)476-0579
**Subject(s):** Trucks and Trucking
**Circ:** ‡1,900

**Annals of Plastic Surgery (10704)**
Lippincott Williams & Wilkins
C/o William D. Morain, MD, Editor-in-Chief
102 S. Linden
PO Box 10
Lamoni, IA 50140
**Subject(s):** Medicine and Surgery
**Circ:** (Paid)‡1,844

**Human Biology (11167)**
Wayne State University Press
University of Kansas
Dept. of Onthropology
622 Fraser Hall
Lawrence, KS 66045
**Subject(s):** Genetics
**Circ:** 1,800

**Journal of Optometric Vision Development (17738)**
College of Optometrists in Vision Development
243 N Lindbergh Blvd., Ste. 310
Saint Louis, MO 63141
Phone: (314)991-4007
Fax: (314)991-1167
**Subject(s):** Ophthalmology, Optometry, and Optics
**Circ:** (Paid)1,800

**Missouri Grocer (17967)**
Missouri Grocers' Association
315 N Ken Ave.
P O Box 10223
Springfield, MO 65802
Phone: (417)831-6667
Fax: (417)831-3907
**Subject(s):** Food and Grocery Trade
**Circ:** ‡1,750

**Jukebox Collector (10823)**
Jukebox Collector Magazine
2545 SE 60th Ct.
Pleasant Hill, IA 50327-5099
Phone: (515)265-8324
Fax: (515)265-1980
**Subject(s):** Music and Musical Instruments; Crafts, Models, Hobbies, and Contests
**Circ:** ‡1,700

**Kansas Nurse (11437)**
Kansas State Nurses' Association
1208 SW Tyler
Topeka, KS 66612-1735
Phone: (785)233-8638
Fax: (785)233-5222
**Subject(s):** Nursing
**Circ:** (Non-paid)‡100
(Paid)‡1,700

**North Dakota History (23901)**
State Historical Society of North Dakota
N. Dakota Heritage Ctr.
612 E. Blvd. Ave.
Bismarck, ND 58505-0830
Phone: (701)328-2666
Fax: (701)328-3710
**Subject(s):** History and Genealogy
**Circ:** (Combined)1,700

**River Styx (17801)**
Big River Association
634 N Grand Blvd., 12th Fl.
Saint Louis, MO 63103
Phone: (314)533-4541
Fax: (314)533-3345
**Subject(s):** Literature
**Circ:** (Controlled)1,700

**Topics in Early Childhood Special Education (11151)**
PRO-ED Inc.
Juniper Gardens Children's Project
650 Minnesota
Kansas City, KS 66101
Phone: (913)321-3143
Fax: (913)371-8522
**Subject(s):** Education
**Circ:** (Paid)1,700

**Calcified Tissue International (17595)**
Springer-Verlag New York Inc.
Division of Bone and Mineral Diseases
Washington University Medical Center
Barnes-Jewish Hospital
216 S. Kingshighway Blvd.
Saint Louis, MO 63110
Phone: (314)454-8906
Fax: (314)454-5325
**Subject(s):** Medicine and Surgery
**Circ:** (Combined)**1,650**

**Nebraska Music Educator (18300)**
Nebraska Music Educators Association
539 N 6th St.
Broken Bow, NE 68822
Phone: (308)872-6086
Fax: (308)872-2902
**Subject(s):** Education; Music and Musical Instruments
**Circ:** (Paid)1,650

**South Dakota Pharmacist (28369)**
South Dakota Pharmacists Association
215 W Sioux Ave.
PO Box 518
Pierre, SD 57501
Phone: (605)945-0409
Fax: (605)224-1280
**Subject(s):** Drugs and Pharmaceuticals
**Circ:** (Paid)1,650

**American Christmas Tree Journal (17562)**
National Christmas Tree Association
16020 Swingley Ridge Rd. Ste 300
Saint Louis, MO 63141-6372
Phone: (636)449-5050
Fax: (636)449-5051
**Subject(s):** Forestry; Seed and Nursery Trade
**Circ:** ‡1,600

**Focus on Autism and Other Developmental Disabilities (11143)**
PRO-ED Inc.
Dept. of Special Ed.
University of Kansas Medical School
39th & Rainbow Blvd.
Kansas City, KS 66160-7335
Phone: (913)588-5955
Fax: (913)588-5942
**Subject(s):** Health and Healthcare
**Circ:** (Paid)‡1600

**Journal of Computational and Graphical Statistics (10655)**
American Statistical Association
c/o Luke Tierney, Editor
241 Schaeffer Hall
Univ. of Iowa
Iowa City, IA 52242-1409
**Subject(s):** Statistics; Mathematics
**Circ:** (Paid)1,600

**Journal of Neuropathology & Experimental Neurology (11173)**
Allen Press Inc.
810 E 10th
Lawrence, KS 66044
Phone: (785)843-1234
Fax: (785)843-1244
**Circ:** 1,600

**South Dakota History (28368)**
South Dakota State Historical Society
900 Governors Dr.
Pierre, SD 57501-2217
Phone: (605)773-3458
Fax: (605)773-6041
**Subject(s):** History and Genealogy
**Circ:** (Paid)1,600

**Automobile Red Book (11295)**
Primedia Business
PO Box 12901
Overland Park, KS 66212
Phone: (913)967-7453
Fax: (913)967-1901
**Subject(s):** Automotive (Trade)
**Circ:** (Paid)‡1,540

**American Chianina Journal (17485)**
American Chianina Association
1708 N Prairie View Rd.
PO Box 890
Platte City, MO 64079
Phone: (816)431-2808

Fax: (816)431-5381
**Subject(s):** Livestock
**Circ:** ‡1,500

**Coe Review  (10366)**
Coe College
1220 1st Ave. NE
Cedar Rapids, IA 52402
Phone: (319)399-8000
**Subject(s):** Poetry; Literature and Literary Reviews; Literature
**Circ:** (Controlled)1,500

**Iowa Law Review  (10651)**
University of Iowa
College of Law
Boyd Law Bldg., No. 190
Iowa City, IA 52242-1113
Phone: (319)335-9132
Fax: (319)335-9019
**Subject(s):** Law
**Circ:** 1,500

**Uncoverings  (18455)**
American Quilt Study Group
35th & Holdrege, E Campus Loop
PO Box 4737
Lincoln, NE 68504-0737
Phone: (402)472-5361
Fax: (402)472-5428
**Subject(s):** Art and Art History
**Circ:** (Paid)1,500

**U.S. Farm News  (10451)**
U.S. Farmers Association
1407 2nd Ave. S
Denison, IA 51442-2017
Phone: (712)263-2679
**Subject(s):** Peace
**Circ:** ‡1,500

**Journal of Field Ornithology  (11172)**
Association of Field Ornithologists
c/o Allen Press
PO Box 1897
Lawrence, KS 66044-1897
**Subject(s):** Zoology
**Circ:** 1,400

**Marketer  (18421)**
Nebraska Petroleum Marketers & Convenience Store Association
1320 Lincoln Mall
Lincoln, NE 68508
Phone: (402)474-6691
Fax: (402)474-2510
**Subject(s):** Automotive (Trade); Petroleum, Oil, and Gas
**Circ:** (Combined)‡1,400

**The Social Science Journal  (11443)**
Elsevier
Department of Political Science
Washburn University
Topeka, KS 66621
Phone: (785)231-1010
Fax: (785)231-1004
**Subject(s):** Humanities; Social Sciences
**Circ:** ‡1,400

**Oklahoma Beverage News  (25468)**
2416 E 37th N
Wichita, KS 67219
Phone: (316)838-6700
Fax: (316)838-6795
**Subject(s):** Beverages, Brewing, and Bottling
**Circ:** 1,325

**The American Revenuer  (10843)**
American Revenue Association
PO Box 56
Rockford, IA 50468-0056
Phone: (641)756-3542
Fax: (641)756-3352
**Subject(s):** Collecting
**Circ:** (Non-paid)10
    (Paid)1,300

**The Children's Friend  (18404)**
Christian Record Services
PO Box 6097
Lincoln, NE 68506-0097
Phone: (402)488-0981
Fax: (402)488-7582
**Subject(s):** Blind and Visually Challenged
**Circ:** (Non-paid)‡1,300

**Insight  (10648)**
American Society of Ophthalmic Registered Nurses
c/o Sarah Smith, Editor, Dept. of Ophthalmology
University of Iowa
200 Hawkins Dr.
Iowa City, IA 52242-1091
Phone: (319)356-0363
Fax: (319)356-0363
**Subject(s):** Nursing
**Circ:** (Free)210
    (Paid)1,306

**The Journal  (10485)**
Iowa Pharmacy Association
Omega Pl., Ste. 16
8515 Douglas Ave.
Des Moines, IA 50322
Phone: (515)270-0713
Fax: (515)270-2979
**Subject(s):** Drugs and Pharmaceuticals
**Circ:** (Non-paid)50
    (Paid)1,300

**Missouri Pharmacist  (17287)**
Missouri Pharmacy Association
211 E Capital Ave.
Jefferson City, MO 65101
Phone: (573)636-7522
Fax: (573)636-7485
**Subject(s):** Drugs and Pharmaceuticals
**Circ:** (Paid)1,300

**NWSA Journal  (10296)**
Indiana University Press
Iowa State University
255 Ross Hall
Ames, IA 50011
**Subject(s):** Women's Interests
**Circ:** ‡1,300

**South Dakota Stock Grower  (28380)**
South Dakota Stock Growers Association
426 St. Joseph St.
Rapid City, SD 57701-2715
Phone: (605)342-0429
Fax: (605)342-0463
**Subject(s):** Food Production
**Circ:** (Controlled)40
    (Paid)1,309

**Surgical Laparoscopy Endoscopy & Percutaneous Techniques  (10668)**
Lippincott Williams & Wilkins
c/o Carol E. H. Scott-Conner, Dept. of Surgery
200 Hawkins Dr. No.1516 JCP
Iowa City, IA 52242-1086
**Subject(s):** Laboratory Research (Scientific and Medical)
**Circ:** (Paid)1,273

**Journal of Housing for the Elderly  (17158)**
The Haworth Press Inc.
Dept. of Environmental Design
University of Missouri-Columbia
141 Stanley Hall
Columbia, MO 65211-7700
Phone: (573)882-4904
Fax: (573)884-6679
**Subject(s):** Senior Citizens' Interests
**Circ:** 1,250

**Journal of Kansas Pharmacy  (11429)**
Kansas Pharmacists Association
1020 SW Fairlawn Rd.
Topeka, KS 66604
Phone: (785)228-2327
Fax: (785)228-9147
**Subject(s):** Drugs and Pharmaceuticals
**Circ:** (Controlled)147
    (Paid)1,250

**Bulletin of the Menninger Clinic  (11422)**
Guilford Publications
The Menninger Clinic
5800 SW Sixth Ave.
PO Box 829
Topeka, KS 66601-0829
Phone: (785)273-0797
Fax: (785)273-0797
**Subject(s):** Psychology and Psychiatry
**Circ:** (Combined)‡1,220

**Journal of Vascular Nursing  (17751)**
Mosby Inc.
11830 Westline Industrial Dr.
Saint Louis, MO 63146
Phone: (800)545-2522
Fax: (800)568-5136
**Subject(s):** Nursing
**Circ:** (Free)326
    (Paid)1,220

**Advances in Pharmacy  (17552)**
Facts & Comparisons
77 W. Port Plaza, Ste 450
Saint Louis, MO 63125
Phone: (314)216-2100
Fax: (314)878-5563
**Subject(s):** Hospitals and Healthcare Institutions; Drugs and Pharmaceuticals
**Circ:** (Non-paid)78
    (Paid)1,213

**Muse  (17169)**
University of Missouri at Columbia
1 Pickard Hall
Columbia, MO 65211
Phone: (573)882-3591
Fax: (573)884-4039
**Subject(s):** Art and Art History; Archaeology; Museums
**Circ:** (Controlled)660
    (Paid)1,200

**New Directions for Student Services  (10295)**
Jossey-Bass Publishers
c/o John H. Schuh, Editor-in-chief
Professional Studies in Education
N 243 Lagomarcino Hall
Iowa State University
Ames, IA 50011
Phone: (515)294-6393
Fax: (515)294-4942
**Subject(s):** Education
**Circ:** (Controlled)95
    (Paid)1,200

**The Voice  (18458)**
Nebraska Grocery Industry Association
5533 S 27th St., Ste. 104
Lincoln, NE 68512
Phone: (402)423-5533
Fax: (402)423-8686
**Subject(s):** Food and Grocery Trade
**Circ:** ‡1,200

**American Review of Public Administration  (17148)**
Sage Publications Inc.
University of Missouri-Columbia, Truman School of Public Aff
101 Middlebush Hall
101 Middlebush Hall
Columbia, MO 65211-6100
Phone: (573)882-5443
Fax: (573)884-4872
**Subject(s):** State, Municipal, and County Administration
**Circ:** (Paid)‡1,100

**The Kansas Banker  (11432)**
Kansas Bankers Association
610 SW Corporate View
Topeka, KS 66615
Phone: (785)232-3444
Fax: (785)232-3484
**Subject(s):** Banking, Finance, and Investments
**Circ:** ‡1,100

**Latin American Theatre Review  (11178)**
University of Kansas
1440 Jayhawk Blvd., Ste. 320
Lawrence, KS 66045
Phone: (785)864-4213
Fax: (785)864-3800
**Subject(s):** Drama and Theatre; Ethnic and Minority Studies
**Circ:** (Paid)1,100

**Legislative Studies Quarterly  (10660)**
Comparative Legislative Research Center
University of Iowa
334 Schaeffer Hall
Iowa City, IA 52242
Phone: (319)335-2361
Fax: (319)335-3211
**Subject(s):** Politics
**Circ:** (Non-paid)‡40
    (Paid)‡1100

**Southwestern Retailer** (17351)
Western Retail Implement and Hardware Association
638 W. 39th. St.
PO Box 419264
Kansas City, MO 64141-6264
Phone: (816)561-5323
Fax: (816)561-1249
**Subject(s):** Farm Implements and Supplies; Hardware

Circ: (Controlled)‡420
(Paid)‡1,100

**Topeka Genealogical Society Quarterly** (11446)
Topeka Genealogical Society Inc.
PO Box 4048
Topeka, KS 66604-0048
Phone: (785)233-5762
**Subject(s):** History and Genealogy; Local, State, and Regional Publications

Circ: (Controlled)1,095

**Science & Technology Libraries** (18448)
The Haworth Press Inc.
Engineering Library
W 204 Nebraska Hall
University of Nebraska
Lincoln, NE 68588
Phone: (402)472-3412
Fax: (402)472-0663
**Subject(s):** Library and Information Science

Circ: 1,035

**Annals of Iowa** (10642)
State Historical Society of Iowa
402 Iowa Ave.
Iowa City, IA 52240-1806
Phone: (319)335-3916
Fax: (319)335-3935
**Subject(s):** History and Genealogy

Circ: ‡1,000

**Bottles and Extras** (17506)
Federation of Historical Bottle Collectors
c/o June Lowry
401 Johnston Ct.
Raymore, MO 64083
**Subject(s):** Collecting; Crafts, Models, Hobbies, and Contests

Circ: 1,000

**The Collegian** (24005)
Jamestown College
6000 College Ln.
Jamestown, ND 58405
Phone: (701)252-3467
Fax: (701)253-4318
**Subject(s):** College Publications

Circ: (Non-paid)‡1,000

**Grassroots Editor** (17299)
International Society of Weekly Newspaper Editors
c/o Dr. Chad Stebbins
Institute of International Studies
Missouri Southern State College
3950 E. Newman Rd.
Joplin, MO 64801-1595
Phone: (417)625-9736
Fax: (417)659-4445
**Subject(s):** Journalism and Publishing

Circ: ‡1,000

**Journal of Alcohol and Drug Education** (18531)
American Alcohol and Drug Information Foundation
c/o School of HPER
University of Nebraska at Omaha
Omaha, NE 68182-0216
Phone: (402)554-2670
Fax: (402)554-3693
**Subject(s):** Substance Abuse and Treatment; Education

Circ: (Paid)1,000

**Journal of Managerial Issues** (11370)
Pittsburg State University
Dept. of Economics, Finance & Banking
Pittsburg, KS 66762
Phone: (620)235-4547
Fax: (620)235-4572
**Subject(s):** Management and Administration; Business; Advertising and Marketing; Accountants and Accounting

Circ: (Controlled)1,000

**Platte Valley Review** (18388)
University of Nebraska at Kearney
905 W. 25th St.
Kearney, NE 68849
Phone: (308)865-8441
Fax: (308)865-8806

**Subject(s):** Literature

Circ: (Combined)1,000

**Topics in Stroke Rehabilitation** (17862)
Thomas Land Publishers Inc.
255 Jefferson Rd.
Saint Louis, MO 63119-3627
Phone: (314)963-7445
Fax: (314)963-9345
**Subject(s):** Medicine and Surgery; Health and Healthcare

Circ: (Paid)1,000

**Kansas Biology Teacher** (11062)
Emporia State University Printing Service
1200 Commercial
Emporia, KS 66801-5087
**Subject(s):** Education; Biology

Circ: (Combined)980

**Kansas Insurance Agent and Broker** (11436)
Kansas Association of Insurance Agents
815 SW Topeka
Topeka, KS 66612
Phone: (785)232-0561
Fax: (785)232-6817
**Subject(s):** Insurance

Circ: (Non-paid)‡106
(Paid)‡934

**Missouri Law Review** (17161)
University of Missouri at Columbia
School of Law
15 Hulston Hall
Columbia, MO 65211
Phone: (573)882-7055
Fax: (573)882-4984
**Subject(s):** Law

Circ: (Non-paid)‡250
(Paid)‡900

**Missouri Press News** (17162)
Missouri Press Association
802 Locust St.
Columbia, MO 65201-7799
Phone: (573)449-4167
Fax: (573)874-5894
**Subject(s):** Journalism and Publishing

Circ: ‡900

**The Fibonacci Quarterly** (28273)
Fibonacci Association
PO Box 320
Aurora, SD 57002-0320
**Subject(s):** Mathematics

Circ: (Combined)830

**Missouri Archaeologist** (17159)
Missouri Archaeological Society
101A Museum Support Ctr.
Rock Quarry Rd. at Hinkson Creek
Columbia, MO 65211-3170
Phone: (573)882-3544
Fax: (573)882-9410
**Subject(s):** Archaeology; Anthropology and Ethnology

Circ: (Paid)825

**The Midwest Quarterly** (11372)
Pittsburg State University
Pittsburg, KS 66762
Phone: (620)235-4369
Fax: (620)235-4080
**Subject(s):** Education

Circ: (Non-paid)‡150
(Paid)‡800

**Nineteenth Century French Studies** (18437)
University of Nebraska Press
1111 Oldfather Hall
Lincoln, NE 68588-0319
Phone: (402)472-3770
Fax: (402)472-0327
**Subject(s):** Literature

Circ: (Combined)800

**Phreno Cosmian** (28349)
1200 W University Ave.
Dakota Wesleyan University Box 318
Mitchell, SD 57301
Phone: (605)995-2814
Fax: (605)995-2814
**Subject(s):** College Publications

Circ: 800

**South Dakota Bird Notes** (28262)
South Dakota Ornithologist's Union
1200 S Jay St.
Aberdeen, SD 57401-7198
Phone: (605)626-2456
Fax: (605)626-3364
**Subject(s):** Ornithology and Oology

Circ: (Controlled)800

**Chinese American Forum** (17602)
8601 Olive Blvd.
Jefferson Plaza
Saint Louis, MO 63132
Phone: (314)995-3858
Fax: (314)432-1217
**Subject(s):** Chinese; Intercultural Interests

Circ: (Paid)‡500
(Non-paid)‡750

**South Dakota Trucking News** (28412)
South Dakota Trucking Association
3801 S Kiwanis Ave.
Sioux Falls, SD 57105
Phone: (605)334-8871
Fax: (605)334-1938
**Subject(s):** Trucks and Trucking

Circ: ‡750

**Journal of Policy History** (17744)
Penn State University Press
Saint Louis University
3800 Lindell Blvd.
PO Box 56907
Saint Louis, MO 63156-0907
Phone: (314)977-2339
Fax: (314)977-1603
**Subject(s):** History and Genealogy; State, Municipal, and County Administration

Circ: (Paid)700

**Kansas Economic Information** (11487)
Center for Economic Development and Business Research
CEDBR
WSU
1845 Fairmount St.
Wichita, KS 67260
Phone: (316)978-3225
Fax: (316)978-3950
**Subject(s):** Economics

Circ: 700

**Missouri State Genealogical Association Journal** (17166)
Missouri State Genealogical Association
PO Box 833
Columbia, MO 65205
Phone: (573)443-8964
**Subject(s):** History and Genealogy; Local, State, and Regional Publications

Circ: (Paid)705

**North Dakota Quarterly** (23987)
University of North Dakota
PO Box 7209
University Station
Grand Forks, ND 58202
Phone: (701)777-2011
**Subject(s):** Literature and Literary Reviews

Circ: (Controlled)‡200
(Paid)‡700

**Entree** (10470)
Iowa Hospitality Association
8525 Douglas Ave., Ste. 47
Des Moines, IA 50322
Phone: (515)276-1454
Fax: (515)276-3660
**Subject(s):** Hotels, Motels, Restaurants, and Clubs

Circ: (Non-paid)‡650

**Alzheimer Disease and Associated Disorders** (17561)
Lippincott Williams & Wilkins
c/o John C. Morris
Washington Univ. School of Medicine
Washington University-ADRC
4488 Forest Park Av., Ste. 130
Saint Louis, MO 63108
**Subject(s):** Medicine and Surgery; Laboratory Research (Scientific and Medical)

Circ: (Paid)647

# Middle Atlantic States

**The Modern Schoolman** (17767)
St. Louis University
Dept. of Philosophy
3800 Lindell Blvd.
Saint Louis, MO 63156-0907
Phone: (314)977-3155
**Subject(s):** Philosophy
**Circ:** (Non-paid)‡50
(Paid)‡600

**AAFA Action** (17233)
Alford American Family Association
PO Box 1586
Florissant, MO 63031-1586
Phone: (314)831-8648
**Subject(s):** History and Genealogy
**Circ:** 550

**Journal of Social Service Research** (17749)
The Haworth Press Inc.
c/o Curtis McMillen, Comorbidity & Addiction Center
George Warren Brown Schl / Soc Work
Washington University
Campus PO Box 1196
Saint Louis, MO 63130-4899
Phone: (314)935-7517
**Subject(s):** Sociology; Social Programs
**Circ:** 535

**Aeon** (10287)
Aeon: A Journal of Myth and Science
3908 Marigold
Ames, IA 50014
Phone: (515)292-6565
Fax: (515)292-2603
**Subject(s):** Science (General); Archaeology
**Circ:** (Non-paid)100
(Paid)500

**Classical and Modern Literature** (17150)
Department of Classical Studies
420 GCB/University of Missouri
Columbia, MO 65211
Phone: (573)882-3352
**Subject(s):** Literature
**Circ:** 500

**Great Plains Research** (18410)
Center for Great Plains Studies
University of Nebraska-Lincoln
1155 Q St., Hewit Pl.
PO Box 880214
Lincoln, NE 68588-0214
Phone: (402)472-3082
Fax: (402)472-0463
**Subject(s):** Natural History and Nature Study; Social Sciences
**Circ:** (Combined)500

**Manuscripta** (17758)
Brepols Publishers
Vatican Film Library
Pius XII Memorial Library
Saint Louis University
3650 Lindell Blvd.
Saint Louis, MO 63108-3302
Phone: (314)977-3090
Fax: (314)977-3108
**Subject(s):** Literature; History and Genealogy; Humanities; Philology, Language, and Linguistics
**Circ:** (Combined)500

**Quarterly Journal of Business & Economics** (18443)
University of Nebraska
CBA Bldg.
PO Box 880407
Lincoln, NE 68588-0407
Phone: (402)472-7931
Fax: (402)472-5180
**Subject(s):** Banking, Finance, and Investments; Economics
**Circ:** (Non-paid)100
(Paid)500

**Walt Whitman Quarterly Review** (10670)
University of Iowa
308 EPB
Iowa City, IA 52242-1492
Phone: (319)335-0592
Fax: (319)335-2535
**Subject(s):** Literature
**Circ:** (Non-paid)250
(Paid)500

**Forum for Social Economics** (17682)
St. Louis University
3674 Lindell Blvd.
Saint Louis, MO 63108
Phone: (314)977-3814
Fax: (314)977-1478
**Subject(s):** Economics
**Circ:** (Controlled)450

**Journal of Dispute Resolution** (17157)
University of Missouri
206 Hulston Hall
Columbia, MO 65211
Phone: (573)882-9682
Fax: (573)882-3343
**Subject(s):** Law
**Circ:** (Non-paid)14
(Paid)450

**Yellowback Library** (10504)
Yellowback Press
PO Box 36172
Des Moines, IA 50315
Phone: (515)287-0404
**Subject(s):** Science Fiction, Mystery, Adventure, and Romance; Literature and Literary Reviews
**Circ:** ‡450

**Child and Youth Services** (10352)
The Haworth Press Inc.
School of HPELS
203 WRC
Univ. of Northern Iowa
Cedar Falls, IA 50614-0241
**Subject(s):** Social Programs
**Circ:** (Paid)417

**South Dakota Review** (28445)
University of South Dakota
University Exchange
414 E. Clark
Vermillion, SD 57069-2390
Phone: (605)677-5184
Fax: (605)677-5298
**Subject(s):** Literature and Literary Reviews
**Circ:** (Non-paid)‡150
(Paid)‡400

**The Kansas Anthropologist** (11431)
Kansas Anthropological Association
PO Box 750962
Topeka, KS 66675-0962
**Subject(s):** History and Genealogy; Anthropology and Ethnology
**Circ:** (Paid)350

**Explorations in Renaissance Culture** (17962)
Southwest Missouri State University
c/o Tita French Baumlin
Department of English
Southwest Missouri State University
Springfield, MO 65804
Phone: (417)836-4738
Fax: (417)836-4226
**Subject(s):** History and Genealogy; Art and Art History; Literature; Music and Musical Instruments
**Circ:** (Combined)314

**Journal of Database Management** (18414)
Idea Group Publishing
Dept. of Management, 209 CBA
University of Nebraska-Lincoln
Lincoln, NE 68588-0491
Phone: (402)472-5855
Fax: (402)472-5855
**Subject(s):** Computers; Management and Administration
**Circ:** (Controlled)300

**Synthesis and Reactivity in Inorganic and Metal—Organic Chemistry** (17174)
Marcel Dekker Inc.
c/o Kattesh V. Katti
Department of Radiology and Physics
Rm. 106, Alton Bldg., 301 Business loop 70W.
University of Missouri-Columbia
Columbia, MO 65211
**Subject(s):** Chemistry, Chemicals, and Chemical Engineering; Metal, Metallurgy, and Metal Trade
**Circ:** 300

**First Intensity** (11166)
PO Box 665
Lawrence, KS 66044
Phone: (785)749-1501
**Subject(s):** Literature; Poetry
**Circ:** (Paid)‡250

**Somatosensory and Motor Research** (17844)
Taylor & Francis Ltd.
Dept. of Neurology and Neurological Surgery
Washington University School of Medicine
Campus Box 8213
4566 Scott Ave.
Saint Louis, MO 63110
Phone: (314)747-1260
Fax: (314)362-8359
**Subject(s):** Medicine and Surgery
**Circ:** (Paid)250

**Family Records, TODAY** (17327)
American Family Records Association
PO Box 15505
Kansas City, MO 64106
**Subject(s):** History and Genealogy
**Circ:** (Paid)‡210

**Thorny Locust** (17352)
PO Box 32631
Kansas City, MO 64171-5631
**Subject(s):** Literature and Literary Reviews
**Circ:** (Paid)200

**Phelps County Genealogical Society Quarterly** (17519)
Phelps County Genealogical Society
Box 571
Rolla, MO 65402-0571
Phone: (573)364-9597
**Subject(s):** History and Genealogy; Local, State, and Regional Publications
**Circ:** (Paid)190

**Syllecta Classica** (10669)
University of Iowa
Jefferson building 210
Iowa City, IA 52242
Phone: (319)335-2323
Fax: (319)335-2326
**Subject(s):** Literature; Music and Musical Instruments
**Circ:** (Combined)120

# Middle Atlantic States

**USA WEEKEND** (31597)
Gannett Company Inc.
7950 Jones Branch Dr.
Mc Lean, VA 22107
Phone: (800)487-2956
Fax: (703)854-2122
**Subject(s):** General Editorial
**Circ:** 22,700,000

**AARP Bulletin** (5177)
American Association of Retired Persons (AARP)
601 E. St. NW
Washington, DC 20049
Phone: (202)434-2277
Fax: (202)434-6451
**Subject(s):** Senior Citizens' Interests
**Circ:** (Paid)21,068,515

**Modern Maturity** (5549)
American Association of Retired Persons (AARP)
601 E. St. NW
Washington, DC 20049
Phone: (202)434-2277
Fax: (202)434-6451
**Subject(s):** Senior Citizens' Interests
**Circ:** (Paid)20,963,870

**National Geographic** (5564)
National Geographic Society
1145 17th St. NW
Washington, DC 20036-4688
Phone: (202)857-7000
Fax: (202)459-5727
**Subject(s):** Geography; General Editorial; Science
**Circ:** (Paid)7,828,642

**National Geographic Traveler** (5566)
National Geographic Society
1145 17th St. NW
Washington, DC 20036-4688
Phone: (202)857-7000
Fax: (202)459-5727
**Subject(s):** Travel and Tourism
**Circ:** (Paid)5,327,000

**NEA Today (12640)**
National Education Association
PO Box 2035
Annapolis Junction, MD 20701-2035
Fax: (301)206-9789
**Subject(s):** Education
**Circ:** (Paid)2,140,876

**U.S. News & World Report (5729)**
U.S. News & World Report Inc.
1050 Thomas Jefferson St. NW
Washington, DC 20007
Phone: (202)955-2000
Fax: (202)955-2685
**Subject(s):** General Editorial
**Circ:** (Paid)2,070,511

**Smithsonian Magazine (5694)**
750 9th St. NW, Ste. 7100
Washington, DC 20560
Phone: (202)275-2000
Fax: (202)275-1972
**Subject(s):** General Editorial; Museums
**Circ:** (Paid)2,055,887

**The Teamster (5713)**
International Brotherhood of Teamsters
25 Louisiana Ave. NW
Washington, DC 20001-2198
Phone: (202)624-6800
Fax: (202)624-6918
**Subject(s):** Labor
**Circ:** ‡1,760,000

**American Rifleman (31330)**
National Rifle Association of America
11250 Waples Mill Rd.
Fairfax, VA 22030
Phone: (703)267-1200
Fax: (703)267-3989
**Subject(s):** Firearms; (Hunting, Fishing, and Game Management); Firearms
**Circ:** (Paid)1,608,439

**The Public Employee Magazine (5656)**
American Federation of State, County & Municipal Employees
1625 L St. NW
Washington, DC 20036-5687
Phone: (202)429-1000
Fax: (202)429-1293
**Subject(s):** State, Municipal, and County Administration; Employment and Human Resources
**Circ:** ‡1,400,000

**National Geographic WORLD (5567)**
National Geographic Society
1145 17th St. NW
Washington, DC 20036-4688
Phone: (202)857-7000
Fax: (202)459-5727
**Subject(s):** General Editorial; Youths' Interests
**Circ:** (Free)‡13,334
(Paid)‡1,246,210

**American Hunter (31328)**
National Rifle Association of America
11250 Waples Mill Rd.
Fairfax, VA 22030
Phone: (703)267-1200
Fax: (703)267-3989
**Subject(s):** (Hunting, Fishing, and Game Management); Firearms
**Circ:** (Paid)1,203,693

**DAV Magazine (5356)**
Disabled American Veterans
c/o Denvel D. Adams
National Service and Legislative Headquarters
807 Maine Ave. SW
Washington, DC 20024
Phone: (202)554-3501
**Subject(s):** Veterans
**Circ:** ‡1,100,000

**Your Big Backyard (31762)**
National Wildlife Federation
11100 Wildlife Center Dr.
Reston, VA 20190-5362
Phone: (703)438-6000
Fax: (703)438-3570
**Subject(s):** Children's Interests
**Circ:** (Combined)1,100,000

**Kiplinger's Personal Finance Magazine (5525)**
Kiplinger Washington Editors Inc.
1729 H St. N.W.
Washington, DC 20006-3938
Phone: (202)887-6491
Fax: (202)785-3648
**Subject(s):** General Editorial
**Circ:** (Paid)1,019,262

**Working America (5758)**
United Food and Commercial Workers International Union
1775 K St. NW
Washington, DC 20006
Phone: (202)223-3111
Fax: (202)466-1562
**Subject(s):** Labor
**Circ:** (Controlled)‡1,000,000

**Nature Conservancy Magazine (31142)**
The Nature Conservancy
4245 N. Fairfax Dr., Ste. 100
Arlington, VA 22203-1606
Phone: (703)841-5300
Fax: (703)841-9692
**Subject(s):** Environmental and Natural Resources Conservation
**Circ:** ‡830,000

**IBEW Journal (5430)**
International Brotherhood of Electrical Workers
900 Seventh St., NW
Washington, DC 20001
Phone: (202)833-7000
Fax: (202)728-7676
**Subject(s):** Labor
**Circ:** (Paid)800,000

**America's 1st Freedom (31332)**
National Rifle Association of America
11250 Waples Mill Rd.
Fairfax, VA 22030
Phone: (703)267-1200
Fax: (703)267-3989
**Subject(s):** Firearms
**Circ:** (Paid)675,266

**American Educator (5207)**
American Federation of Teachers
555 New Jersey Ave. NW
Washington, DC 20001-2079
Phone: (202)879-4430
Fax: (202)879-2014
**Subject(s):** Education
**Circ:** ‡630,000

**National Wildlife (31745)**
National Wildlife Federation
11100 Wildlife Center Dr.
Reston, VA 20190-5362
Phone: (703)438-6000
Fax: (703)438-3570
**Subject(s):** Environmental and Natural Resources Conservation
**Circ:** (Paid)625,711

**Ranger Rick (31750)**
National Wildlife Federation
11100 Wildlife Center Dr.
Reston, VA 20190-5362
Phone: (703)438-6000
Fax: (703)438-3570
**Subject(s):** Children's Interests
**Circ:** ‡550,000

**BoatU.S. Magazine (30984)**
Boat Owners Association of The United States
880 S. Pickett St.
Alexandria, VA 22304
Phone: (703)823-9550
Fax: (703)461-2847
**Subject(s):** (Boating and Yachting)
**Circ:** (Paid)★542,979

**The Chronicle of Higher Education (5306)**
1255 23rd St. NW, Ste. 700
Washington, DC 20037-1125
Phone: (202)466-1000
Fax: (202)452-1033
**Subject(s):** Education
**Circ:** (Paid)500,000

**Better Nutrition Magazine (31436)**
Sabot Publishing Inc.
301 Concourse Boulevard
Suite 350
Glen Allen, VA 23059
Phone: (804)346-9900
Fax: (804)346-1223
**Subject(s):** Health; Lifestyle
**Circ:** ‡486,500

**The Carpenter (5291)**
United Brotherhood of Carpenters and Joiners of America, AFL-CIO
101 Constitution Ave. NW
Washington, DC 20001
Phone: (202)546-6206
Fax: (202)547-8979
**Subject(s):** Construction, Contracting, Building, and Excavating; Labor
**Circ:** 473,104

**Insight (5436)**
The Washington Times Corp.
3600 New York Ave. NE
Washington, DC 20002-1947
Phone: (202)636-3000
Fax: (202)636-3000
**Subject(s):** General Editorial
**Circ:** 439,687

**Diabetes Forecast (30995)**
American Diabetes Association
1701 N. Beauregard St.
Alexandria, VA 22311
Phone: (703)549-1500
Fax: (703)549-6995
**Subject(s):** Medicine and Surgery
**Circ:** (Paid)434,780

**Greenpeace Magazine (5412)**
Greenpeace USA
702 H St., NW, Ste. 300
Washington, DC 20001
Phone: (202)462-1177
Fax: (202)483-8683
**Subject(s):** Environmental and Natural Resources Conservation
**Circ:** (Paid)‡400,000

**The Scottish Rite Journal (Southern Jurisdiction, USA) (5686)**
Supreme Council of the 33rd Degree
1733 16th St., NW
Washington, DC 20009-3103
Phone: (202)232-3579
Fax: (202)464-0487
**Subject(s):** Masons
**Circ:** (Non-paid)‡400,000

**The Retired Officer Magazine (31064)**
The Retired Officers Association
201 N. Washington St.
Alexandria, VA 22314
Phone: (703)549-2311
**Subject(s):** Military and Navy
**Circ:** (Paid)385,088

**AOPA Pilot (13115)**
421 Aviation Way
Frederick, MD 21701
Phone: (301)695-2000
Fax: (301)695-2375
**Subject(s):** Aviation; Aviation
**Circ:** (Paid)★372,854

**National Parks (5571)**
National Parks & Conservation Association
1776 Massachusetts Ave. N.W.
Washington, DC 20036
Phone: (202)223-6722
**Subject(s):** Parks; Ecology and Conservation
**Circ:** (Paid)348,951

**U.A. Journal (5727)**
United Association of Journeymen & Apprentices of the Plumbing & Pipefitting Industry of the U.S. & Canada
901 Massachusetts Ave.
Washington, DC 20001
Phone: (202)628-5823
Fax: (202)628-5024
**Subject(s):** Labor
**Circ:** (Controlled)330,000

Circulation: ★ = ABC; △ = BPA; ♦ = CAC; ● = CCAB; ☐ = VAC; ⊕ = PO Statement; ‡ = Publisher's Report; Boldface figures = sworn; Light figures = estimated.

**Cooperative Living** (31437)
Virginia, Maryland, and Delaware Association of Electric Cooperatives
4201 Dominion Blvd., Ste. 101
Glen Allen, VA 23060
Phone: (804)346-3344
Fax: (804)346-3448
**Subject(s):** Rural Electrification; Local, State, and Regional Publications
**Circ:** (Paid)325,000

**Vegetarian Times** (31439)
Sabot Publishing Inc.
301 Concourse Blvd.
Ste. 350
Glen Allen, VA 23059
Phone: (804)346-9900
Fax: (804)346-1223
**Subject(s):** Health; Food and Grocery Trade
**Circ:** (Paid)320,954

**Girls' Life (GL)** (12737)
Monarch Services Inc.
4517 Harford Rd.
Baltimore, MD 21214
Phone: (410)254-9200
Fax: (410)254-0991
**Subject(s):** Youths' Interests
**Circ:** (Paid)315,905

**Postal Record** (5625)
National Association of Letter Carriers
100 Indiana Ave. NW
Washington, DC 20001-2144
Phone: (202)393-4695
Fax: (202)737-1540
**Subject(s):** Postal and Shipping Supplies; Labor
**Circ:** 310,000

**The American Postal Worker** (5222)
American Postal Workers Union, AFL-CIO
1300 L St. NW
Washington, DC 20005
Phone: (202)842-4200
Fax: (202)842-4297
**Subject(s):** Postal and Shipping Supplies; Labor
**Circ:** 300,000

**HSUS News** (5426)
Humane Society of the United States
2100 L St. NW
Washington, DC 20037
Phone: (202)452-1100
Fax: (301)258-3080
**Subject(s):** Society for the Prevention of Cruelty to Animals and Anti-Vivisection
**Circ:** (Free)300,000

**Talking Book Topics** (5709)
National Library Service for the Blind and Physically Handicapped
Publications & Media Section NLS/BPH
Washington, DC 20542
Phone: (202)707-9281
Fax: (202)707-0712
**Subject(s):** Handicapped; Blind and Visually Challenged
**Circ:** (Free)‡286,000

**DEFENDERS Magazine** (5357)
Defenders of Wildlife
1130 17th NW
Washington, DC 20036
Phone: (202)682-9400
Fax: (202)682-1331
**Subject(s):** Ecology and Conservation; Natural History and Nature Study
**Circ:** ‡275,000

**Catering Industry Employee** (5293)
Hotel Employees and Restaurant Employees International Union
1219 28th St., NW
Washington, DC 20007-3389
Phone: (202)393-4373
Fax: (202)333-0468
**Subject(s):** Hotels, Motels, Restaurants, and Clubs; Food and Grocery Trade; Labor
**Circ:** ‡215,000

**Teen Times** (31759)
Family, Career and Community Leaders of America
1910 Association Dr.
Reston, VA 20191
Phone: (703)476-4900
Fax: (703)860-2713
**Subject(s):** Youths' Interests; Clubs and Societies
**Circ:** ‡215,000

**USA TODAY Sports Weekly** (31596)
USA TODAY
7950 Jones Branch Dr. 3rd Floor
Mc Lean, VA 22108-9995
Phone: (703)854-6319
**Subject(s):** (Baseball)
**Circ:** (Paid)213,598

**Hearing Loss** (12972)
Self Help for Hard of Hearing People
7910 Woodmont Ave., Ste. 1200
Bethesda, MD 20814
Phone: (301)657-2248
Fax: (301)913-9413
**Subject(s):** Hearing and Speech; Handicapped; Handicapped
**Circ:** (Paid)200,000

**Together** (31468)
Shalom Foundation Inc.
1251 Virginia Ave.
Harrisonburg, VA 22802
Fax: (540)434-0247
**Subject(s):** Religious Publications
**Circ:** (Free)‡200,000

**The Word Among Us** (13216)
The Word Among Us Press
9639 Dr. Perry Rd., Ste. 126 N
Ijamsville, MD 21754
Phone: (301)831-1262
Fax: (301)831-1188
**Subject(s):** Religious Publications
**Circ:** (Paid)200,000

**The Southern States Cooperative Magazine** (31798)
Southern States Cooperative Inc.
PO Box 26234
Richmond, VA 23260-6234
Phone: (804)282-0350
Fax: (804)281-1119
**Subject(s):** Farm Bureau, Grange, and Cooperative Associations
**Circ:** (Paid)‡3,611
(Non-paid)‡198,997

**International Fire Fighter** (5441)
International Association of Fire Fighters
1750 New York Ave. NW
Washington, DC 20006
Phone: (202)737-8484
Fax: (202)737-8418
**Subject(s):** Fire Fighting
**Circ:** (Non-paid)195,000

**Builder** (5282)
Hanley-Wood L.L.C.
1 Thomas Cir., Ste. 600
Washington, DC 20005
Phone: (202)452-0800
Fax: (202)785-1974
**Subject(s):** Architecture
**Circ:** (Controlled)30,000
(Paid)194,000

**DECA Dimensions** (31699)
DECA
1908 Association Dr.
Reston, VA 20191
Phone: (703)860-5000
Fax: (703)860-4013
**Subject(s):** Youths' Interests; Education; Business
**Circ:** (Non-paid)⊕500
(Paid)⊕185,000

**Educational Leadership** (30997)
1703 N. Beauregard St.
Alexandria, VA 22311-1714
Phone: (703)578-9600
Fax: (703)575-5400
**Subject(s):** Education
**Circ:** ‡183,000

**Air Force Magazine** (31105)
Air Force Association
1501 Lee Hwy.
Arlington, VA 22209-1198
Phone: (703)247-5800
**Subject(s):** Aviation; Military and Navy
**Circ:** (Non-paid)6,165
(Paid)182,330

**In Transit** (5432)
Amalgamated Transit Union, AFL-CIO, CLC
5025 Wisconsin Ave. NW
Washington, DC 20016-4139
Phone: (202)537-1645
Fax: (202)244-7824
**Subject(s):** Labor; Transportation, Traffic, and Shipping
**Circ:** (Non-paid)175,000

**A Mind Is...** (31359)
United Negro College Fund
8260 Willow Oak Corp. Dr.
Fairfax, VA 22031
Phone: (703)205-3400
Fax: (703)205-3575
**Subject(s):** Education; Black Publications
**Circ:** 175,000

**The National AMVET** (13227)
AMVETS
4647 Forbes Blvd.
Lanham, MD 20706
Phone: (301)459-9600
Fax: (301)459-7924
**Subject(s):** Veterans
**Circ:** (Controlled)‡4,000
(Paid)‡175,000

**HRMagazine** (31009)
Society for Human Resource Management
1800 Duke St.
Alexandria, VA 22314
Phone: (703)548-3440
Fax: (703)535-6490
**Subject(s):** Employment and Human Resources
**Circ:** 170,705

**B'nai B'rith** (5276)
2020 K St. NW, 7th Fl.
Washington, DC 20006
Phone: (202)857-6600
Fax: (202)296-1092
**Subject(s):** Jewish Publications
**Circ:** (Non-paid)‡2,042
(Paid)‡169,434

**Science News** (5685)
Science Service Inc.
1719 N. St. NW
Washington, DC 20036
Phone: (202)785-2255
Fax: (202)785-1243
**Subject(s):** General Editorial; Science (General)
**Circ:** (Paid)168,621

**Washingtonian Magazine** (5749)
Washington Magazine Inc.
1828 L St. NW, Ste. 200
Washington, DC 20036
Phone: (202)296-1246
**Subject(s):** Local, State, and Regional Publications
**Circ:** (Paid)157,701

**Science** (5682)
American Association for the Advancement of Science
1200 New York Ave. NW
Washington, DC 20005
Phone: (202)326-6400
Fax: (202)289-4950
**Subject(s):** Science (General)
**Circ:** (Paid)155,911

**Social Work** (5696)
National Association of Social Workers
750 1st St. NE, Ste. 700
Washington, DC 20002-4241
Phone: (202)408-8600
Fax: (202)336-8312
**Subject(s):** Sociology
**Circ:** 152,000

**Sigma Phi Epsilon Journal** (31797)
Sigma Phi Epsilon Fraternity Inc.
310 S. Blvd.
PO Box 1901
Richmond, VA 23218-1901
Phone: (804)353-1901
Fax: (804)359-8160
**Subject(s):** Unclassified Fraternal; College Publications
**Circ:** (Controlled)150,500

**AAUW Outlook** (5179)
American Association of University Women
1111 16th St. NW
Washington, DC 20036
Phone: (202)785-7700
Fax: (202)872-1425
Subject(s): Women's Interests
Circ: (Controlled)‡150,000

**LATINA Style** (5531)
1730 Rhode Island Ave., NW, Ste. 1207
Washington, DC 20036
Phone: (202)955-7930
Subject(s): Women's Interests; Hispanic Publications; Fashion; Lifestyle
Circ: (Paid)150,000

**Nation's Building News** (5576)
Nations Building News
1201 15th St. NW
Washington, DC 20005
Phone: (202)822-0525
Fax: (202)861-2131
Subject(s): Construction, Contracting, Building, and Excavating
Circ: 150,000

**Sister 2 Sister** (13360)
Sister 2 Sister Inc.
6930 Carroll Ave., Ste. 200
Takoma Park, MD 20912
Phone: (301)270-5999
Fax: (301)270-0085
Subject(s): Black Publications; Entertainment; Women's Interests
Circ: (Paid)150,000

**Equus** (13163)
Primedia Equine Network
656 Quince Orchard Rd., Ste. 600
Gaithersburg, MD 20878
Phone: (301)977-3900
Fax: (301)990-9015
Subject(s): (Horses and Horse Racing)
Circ: (Paid)148,000

**Old-House Journal** (5603)
DoveTale Publishers
1 Thomas Cir. NW
Washington, DC 20005-5802
Phone: (202)339-0744
Subject(s): Construction, Contracting, Building, and Excavating
Circ: (Paid)146,141

**Naval Affairs** (31046)
Fleet Reserve Association
125 N. West St.
Alexandria, VA 22314-2754
Phone: (703)683-1400
Fax: (703)549-6610
Subject(s): Military and Navy
Circ: (Controlled)‡145,000

**Georgetown Magazine** (5403)
Georgetown University
2115 Wisconsin Ave., Ste. 500
Washington, DC 20007
Phone: (202)687-4317
Fax: (202)687-2311
Subject(s): College Publications
Circ: (Free)‡140,000

**BCTGM News** (13217)
Bakery, Confectionery, Tobacco Workers and Grain Millers International Union (BCTGM)
10401 Connecticut Ave.
Kensington, MD 20895-3961
Phone: (301)933-8600
Fax: (301)946-8452
Subject(s): Confectionaries and Frozen Dairy Products; Baking
Circ: (Controlled)135,000

**Sergeants** (13362)
Air Force Sergeants Association
PO Box 50
Temple Hills, MD 20757-0050
Phone: (301)899-3500
Fax: (301)899-8136
Subject(s): Military and Navy
Circ: (Non-paid)‡131,000

**USBE & Information Technology** (12878)
Career Communications Group Inc.
729 E Pratt St., No. 504
Baltimore, MD 21202
Phone: (410)244-7101
Fax: (410)752-1837
Subject(s): Black Publications; Engineering (Various branches)
Circ: (Non-paid)35,000
(Combined)130,000

**Physics Today** (13058)
American Institute of Physics
One Physics Ellipse
College Park, MD 20740
Phone: (301)209-3040
Fax: (301)209-0842
Subject(s): Physics
Circ: ‡127,000

**Proceedings** (12632)
U.S. Naval Institute
Preble Hall
291 Wood Rd.
Annapolis, MD 21402
Phone: (410)268-6110
Fax: (410)269-7940
Subject(s): Military and Navy
Circ: ‡125,000

**Teacher Magazine** (13011)
Editorial Projects in Education Inc.
6935 Arlington Rd., Ste. 100
Bethesda, MD 20814-5233
Phone: (301)280-3100
Fax: (301)280-3200
Subject(s): Education
Circ: (Non-paid)100,000
(Paid)122,769

**Johns Hopkins Magazine** (12755)
Johns Hopkins University
901 S. Bond St., Ste. 540
Baltimore, MD 21231
Phone: (443)287-9900
Fax: (443)287-9898
Subject(s): Medicine and Surgery; College Publications
Circ: (Controlled)‡121,000

**West Virginia University Alumni Magazine** (32679)
West Virginia University
PO Box 6690
Morgantown, WV 26506-6690
Phone: (304)293-6368
Fax: (304)293-4762
Subject(s): College Publications
Circ: (Controlled)120,000

**Pharmacy Today** (5619)
American Pharmaceutical Association
2215 Constitution Ave., NW
Washington, DC 20037-2985
Phone: (202)628-4410
Fax: (202)783-2351
Subject(s): Drugs and Pharmaceuticals
Circ: 117,000

**Journal of the International Union of Bricklayers & Allied Craftworkers** (5491)
1776 Eye St. NW
Washington, DC 20006
Phone: (202)783-3788
Subject(s): Labor; Construction, Contracting, Building, and Excavating
Circ: (Paid)‡2,000
(Controlled)‡110,000

**Science Illustrated** (31594)
Science Illustrated L.P.
8428 Holly Leaf Dr.
Mc Lean, VA 22102
Phone: (703)356-1688
Fax: (703)356-1688
Subject(s): Science (General); Medicine and Surgery
Circ: (Controlled)‡110,000

**American Psychologist** (5224)
American Psychological Association
750 1st St. NE
Washington, DC 20002-4242
Phone: (202)336-5500
Fax: (202)336-6012
Subject(s): Psychology and Psychiatry
Circ: ‡105,500

**Young Children** (5766)
National Association for the Education of Young Children
1509 16th St. NW
Washington, DC 20036-1426
Phone: (202)232-8777
Fax: (202)328-1846
Subject(s): Education
Circ: ‡104,790

**Aviation Week & Space Technology** (5262)
McGraw-Hill Inc.
1200 G St. NW, Ste. 200
Washington, DC 20005
Phone: (202)383-2350
Fax: (202)383-2438
Subject(s): Aviation; Engineering (Various branches)
Circ: (Paid)104,546

**Monitor on Psychology** (5552)
American Psychological Association
750 1st St. NE
Washington, DC 20002-4242
Phone: (202)336-5500
Fax: (202)336-6012
Subject(s): Psychology and Psychiatry
Circ: ‡102,350

**Internal Medicine News** (13298)
International Medical News Group
c/o Calvin Pierce
12230 Wilkins Ave.
Rockville, MD 20852
Phone: (301)816-8700
Fax: (301)816-8738
Subject(s): Health and Healthcare
Circ: (Paid)101,608

**AAUW in Action** (5178)
American Association of University Women
1111 16th St. NW
Washington, DC 20036
Phone: (202)785-7700
Fax: (202)872-1425
Subject(s): Women's Interests; Education
Circ: (Non-paid)100,000

**Calypso Log** (31451)
The Cousteau Society
710 Sattlers Landing Rd
Hampton, VA 23669
Phone: (757)722-9300
Fax: (757)722-8185
Subject(s): Oceanography and Marine Studies; Ecology and Conservation
Circ: ‡100,000

**The National Rural Letter Carrier** (31045)
National Rural Letter Carriers' Association
1630 Duke St., 4th Fl.
Alexandria, VA 22314-3465
Phone: (703)684-5545
Fax: (703)548-8735
Subject(s): Postal and Shipping Supplies
Circ: (Controlled)‡100,000

**Selling Power** (31412)
Personal Selling Power
1140 International Pkwy.
PO Box 5467
Fredericksburg, VA 22406
Phone: (540)752-7000
Fax: (540)752-7001
Subject(s): Selling and Salesmanship
Circ: (Controlled)90,000
(Paid)100,000

**Washington FAMILIES Magazine** (31496)
FAMILIES Magazines Inc.
485 Spring Park Pl., Ste. 550
Herndon, VA 20170
Phone: (703)318-1385
Fax: (703)318-5509
Subject(s): Parenting
Circ: (Controlled)100,000

**WHERE Washington** (5753)
Miller Publishing Group L.L.C.
1720 Eye Sheet NW, Ste. 600
Washington, DC 20006
Phone: (202)463-4550
Fax: (202)463-4553
Subject(s): Travel and Tourism
Circ: (Controlled)100,000

**The New Republic (5586)**
The New Republic L.L.C.
1331 H St. NW, Ste. 700
Washington, DC 20005
Phone: (202)508-4444
Fax: (202)628-9380
**Subject(s):** General Editorial; Social and Political Issues
**Circ:** (Paid)98,328

**Leatherneck (31673)**
Marine Corps Association
Box 1775
Quantico, VA 22134
Phone: (703)640-6161
Fax: (703)640-0823
**Subject(s):** Military and Navy
**Circ:** 97,600

**Civil Engineering-ASCE (31698)**
American Society of Civil Engineers
1801 Alexander Bell Dr.
Reston, VA 20191-4400
Phone: (703)295-6300
Fax: (703)295-6222
**Subject(s):** Construction, Contracting, Building, and Excavating; Engineering (Various branches)
**Circ:** (Controlled)7,686
     (Paid)95,459

**Air Line Pilot (31486)**
Air Line Pilots Association
535 Herndon Pkwy.
PO Box 1169
Herndon, VA 20170-1169
Phone: (703)689-2270
Fax: (703)689-4370
**Subject(s):** Aviation
**Circ:** ‡95,000

**Finance & Development (5389)**
International Monetary Fund
700 19th St. NW
Washington, DC 20431
Phone: (202)623-7430
Fax: (202)623-7201
**Subject(s):** Banking, Finance, and Investments; International Business and Economics; French; Spanish; Economics; Arabic; Chinese
**Circ:** (Controlled)95,000

**Interchange (Rockville) (13297)**
Transportation Communications International Union
3 Research Pl.
Rockville, MD 20850
Phone: (301)948-4911
Fax: (301)330-7661
**Subject(s):** Labor; Transportation, Traffic, and Shipping
**Circ:** (Controlled)95,000

**Army Times (31882)**
Army Times Publishing Co.
6883 Commercial Dr.
Springfield, VA 22159-0500
Phone: (703)750-9000
Fax: (703)750-8767
**Subject(s):** Military and Navy
**Circ:** (Paid)94,099

**Asha (13286)**
American Speech-Language-Hearing Association
10801 Rockville Pke.
Rockville, MD 20852
Phone: (301)897-5700
Fax: (301)571-0457
**Subject(s):** Hearing and Speech
**Circ:** ‡94,000

**ZooGoer (5768)**
Friends of the National Zoo
3001, National Zoological Park
Connecticut Ave. NW
Washington, DC 20008
Phone: (202)673-4800
**Subject(s):** Zoology; Natural History and Nature Study
**Circ:** (Paid)31,000
     (Combined)90,000

**Advisor Today (31374)**
National Association of Insurance and Financial Advisors
2901 Telestar Ct.
Falls Church, VA 22042
Phone: (703)770-8100
Fax: (703)770-8212
**Subject(s):** Insurance
**Circ:** (Controlled)89,870

**Electrical Contractor (12963)**
National Electrical Contractors Association
3 Bethesda Metro Ctr., Ste. 1100
Bethesda, MD 20814-5372
Phone: (301)215-4502
Fax: (301)215-4501
**Subject(s):** Electrical Engineering
**Circ:** (Non-paid)△87,000

**Family Practice News (13289)**
International Medical News Group
c/o Denise Fulton,
12230 Wilkins Ave.
Rockville, MD 20852
Phone: (301)816-8700
Fax: (301)816-8738
**Subject(s):** Medicine and Surgery
**Circ:** (Controlled)86,077

**ATTENTION (13221)**
Children and Adults With Attention Deficit/Hyperactivity Disorder
8181 Professional Pl., Ste.201
Landover, MD 20785
Phone: (301)306-7070
Fax: (301)306-7090
**Subject(s):** Health
**Circ:** 86,000

**Export Today's Global Business Magazine (5382)**
Trade Communications Inc.
PO Box 28189
Washington, DC 20038
Phone: (240)209-5373
Fax: (202)785-5966
**Subject(s):** International Business and Economics
**Circ:** ‡86,000

**Governing Magazine (5409)**
Times Publishing Co.
1100 Conneticut Ave. NW, Ste. 1300
Washington, DC 20036
Phone: (202)862-8802
Fax: (202)862-0032
**Subject(s):** Congressional and Federal Government Affairs; State, Municipal, and County Administration
**Circ:** (Controlled)86,000

**The Weekly Standard (5752)**
1150 17th St. NW, No. 505
Washington, DC 20036
Phone: (202)293-4900
Fax: (202)293-4901
**Subject(s):** Social and Political Issues
**Circ:** (Combined)⊕85,895

**Almanac of Higher Education (5199)**
National Education Association
1201 16th St. NW
Washington, DC 20036
Phone: (202)833-4000
Fax: (202)822-7974
**Subject(s):** Education
**Circ:** 85,000

**JazzTimes (13345)**
Jazz Times
8737 Colesville Rd., 9th Fl.
Silver Spring, MD 20910-3921
Phone: (301)588-4114
Fax: (301)588-5531
**Subject(s):** Music and Musical Instruments; Music and Musical Instruments
**Circ:** (Non-paid)‡9,000
     (Paid)‡80,898

**British Heritage (31512)**
Primedia
c/o Dana Huntley, Editor
741 Miller Dr., Ste. D-2
Leesburg, VA 20175-8994
Phone: (703)771-9400
Fax: (703)779-8345
**Subject(s):** History and Genealogy; Travel and Tourism
**Circ:** (Paid)80,166

**The Washington Post Magazine (5744)**
The Washington Post
1150 15th St. NW
Washington, DC 20071-2400
Phone: (202)334-6000
Fax: (703)469-2995
**Subject(s):** Local, State, and Regional Publications; General Editorial
**Circ:** (Paid)80,077

**Music Educators Journal (31743)**
MENC: The National Association for Music Education
1806 Robert Fulton Dr.
Reston, VA 20191
Phone: (703)860-4000
Fax: (703)860-1531
**Subject(s):** Music and Musical Instruments; Education
**Circ:** (Paid)‡80,000

**The Officer (5601)**
The Reserve Officers Association
1 Constitution Ave. NE
Washington, DC 20002
Phone: (202)479-2200
Fax: (202)479-0416
**Subject(s):** Military and Navy
**Circ:** 80,000

**Remodeling (5666)**
Hanley-Wood L.L.C.
1 Thomas Cir., Ste. 600
Washington, DC 20005
Phone: (202)452-0800
Fax: (202)785-1974
**Subject(s):** Construction, Contracting, Building, and Excavating
**Circ:** (Paid)1,056
     (Controlled)80,000

**SportsFan Magazine (13009)**
Alan Squire Enterprises
4948 St. Elmo Ave., Ste. 208
Bethesda, MD 20814
Phone: (301)986-7901
Fax: (301)986-9525
**Subject(s):** (General Sports)
**Circ:** ⊕80,000

**Teaching Music (31756)**
MENC: The National Association for Music Education
1806 Robert Fulton Dr.
Reston, VA 20191
Phone: (703)860-4000
Fax: (703)860-1531
**Subject(s):** Music and Musical Instruments; Education
**Circ:** (Paid)80,000

**Thought & Action (5718)**
National Education Association of the United States
1201 16th St. NW
Washington, DC 20036
Phone: (202)822-7207
Fax: (202)822-7206
**Subject(s):** Education
**Circ:** (Paid)80,000

**The Washington Opera Magazine (5742)**
The Washington Opera
2600 Virgina Ave., Ste. 104
Washington, DC 20037
Phone: (202)295-2420
Fax: (202)295-2479
**Subject(s):** Music and Musical Instruments
**Circ:** (Controlled)80,000

**ARMY Magazine (31112)**
Association of the U.S. Army (AUSA)
2425 Wilson Blvd.
Arlington, VA 22201
Phone: (703)841-4300
**Subject(s):** Military and Navy
**Circ:** (Paid)79,091

**Message (13193)**
Review and Herald Publishing Association
55 W Oak Ridge Dr.
Hagerstown, MD 21740
Phone: (301)393-3000
Fax: (301)393-4055
**Subject(s):** Black Publications; Religious Publications
**Circ:** (Non-paid)‡56
     (Paid)‡78,273

**Blue Ridge Country (31833)**
Leisure Publishing Co.
3424 Brambleton Ave.
Roanoke, VA 24018
Phone: (540)989-6138
Fax: (540)989-7603
**Subject(s):** Local, State, and Regional Publications; History and Genealogy
**Circ:** 75,000

**Population Connection (5624)**
1400 16th St. NW, Ste. 320
Washington, DC 20036-2290
Phone: (202)332-2200
Fax: (202)332-2302
**Subject(s):** Environmental and Natural Resources Conservation; Social and Political Issues
**Circ:** (Paid)75,000

**Sea Power (31159)**
Sea Power Magazine
2300 Wilson Blvd.
Arlington, VA 22201-3308
Phone: (703)528-1775
Fax: (703)528-2333
**Subject(s):** Military and Navy
**Circ:** (Controlled)5,919
(Paid)75,000

**The Washington Lawyer (5740)**
The District of Columbia Bar
1250 H St. NW, 6th Fl.
Washington, DC 20005-5937
Phone: (202)737-4700
Fax: (202)626-3471
**Subject(s):** Law
**Circ:** (Non-paid)800
(Paid)75,000

**Human Events (5427)**
Eagle Publishing Inc.
1 Massachusetts Ave. NW
Washington, DC 20001
Phone: (202)216-0600
Fax: (202)216-0611
**Subject(s):** Politics
**Circ:** ‡72,000

**Building Products (5283)**
Hanley-Wood L.L.C.
1 Thomas Cir., Ste. 600
Washington, DC 20005
Phone: (202)785-1974
Fax: (202)785-1974
**Subject(s):** Architecture; Construction, Contracting, Building, and Excavating
**Circ:** (Controlled)‡70,000

**BusinessWoman Magazine (5287)**
Business and Professional Women/USA
1900 M St. NW, Ste. 310
Washington, DC 20036
Phone: (202)293-1100
Fax: (202)861-0298
**Subject(s):** Women's Interests; Business
**Circ:** (Controlled)‡70,000

**Foreign Policy (5392)**
Carnegie Endowment for International Peace
1779 Massachusetts Ave. NW
Washington, DC 20036-2103
Phone: (202)939-2230
Fax: (202)483-4430
**Subject(s):** International Affairs; Peace
**Circ:** (Paid)34,000
(Non-paid)40,000
(Combined)**70,000**

**The Josephite Harvest (12757)**
The Josephites
1130 N. Calvert St.
Baltimore, MD 21202
Phone: (410)727-3386
Fax: (410)727-1006
**Subject(s):** Religious Publications
**Circ:** (Paid)15,000
(Free)70,000

**The National Jurist (31140)**
The National Jurist crittenden magazines
2035 N Lincoln St. No. 205
Arlington, VA 22207
Phone: (703)294-5500
Fax: (703)294-5512
**Subject(s):** Law
**Circ:** (Combined)70,000

**Baltimore's Child (12676)**
11 Dutton Ct.
Baltimore, MD 21228
Phone: (410)367-5883
Fax: (410)719-9342
**Subject(s):** Parenting
**Circ:** (Controlled)‡65,000

**PT, Magazine of Physical Therapy (31062)**
American Physical Therapy Association
1111 N Fairfax St.
Alexandria, VA 22314-1488
Phone: (703)683-6748
Fax: (703)684-7343
**Subject(s):** Health and Healthcare
**Circ:** (Paid)65,000

**Tree Farmer (5723)**
American Forest Foundation
1111 19th St. NW, Ste. 780
Washington, DC 20036
Phone: (202)463-2462
Fax: (202)463-2461
**Subject(s):** Forestry
**Circ:** (Non-paid)8,000
(Paid)8,000
65,000

**Trout (31167)**
Trout Unlimited
1500 Wilson Blvd., Ste. 310
Arlington, VA 22209
Phone: (703)522-0200
Fax: (703)284-9400
**Subject(s):** (Hunting, Fishing, and Game Management)
**Circ:** (Non-paid)1,000
(Paid)65,000

**The Reading Teacher (5151)**
International Reading Association
800 Barksdale Rd.
PO Box 8139
Newark, DE 19714-8139
Phone: (302)731-1600
Fax: (302)731-1057
**Subject(s):** Education
**Circ:** ‡64,000

**Marines Magazine (5540)**
Commandant of the Marine Corps. (PAMCN)
Headquarters - U.S. Marine Corps
Division of Public Affairs, Marine Corps News
Rm. 3134, 2 Navy Annex
Washington, DC 20380-1775
Phone: (703)614-7678
Fax: (703)614-1874
**Subject(s):** Military and Navy
**Circ:** 62,000

**Government Executive (5410)**
National Journal Group Inc.
The Watergate
600 New Hampshire Ave., NW
Washington, DC 20037
Phone: (202)739-8400
Fax: (202)833-8069
**Subject(s):** State, Municipal, and County Administration
**Circ:** (Paid)900
(Controlled)60,450

**Compliance Magazine (31776)**
Douglas Publications Inc.
2807 N Parham Rd.,64 Bldg., Ste. 200
Richmond, VA 23294
Phone: (804)762-9600
Fax: (804)217-8999
**Subject(s):** Safety
**Circ:** (Non-paid)△**60,014**

**American Journal of Speech Language Pathology (13284)**
American Speech-Language-Hearing Association
10801 Rockville Pke.
Rockville, MD 20852
Phone: (301)897-5700
Fax: (301)571-0457
**Subject(s):** Philology, Language, and Linguistics; Hearing and Speech
**Circ:** 60,000

**The American Spectator (5228)**
The American Alternative Foundation
3200 N St. NW (PMB 175)
Washington, DC 20007-2829
Phone: (202)659-7922
Fax: (202)659-7923
**Subject(s):** Politics
**Circ:** (Paid)60,000

**Black Excellence (13343)**
National Association for Equal Opportunity in Higher Education
8701 Georgia Ave., Ste. 200
Silver Spring, MD 20910
Phone: (301)650-2440
Fax: (301)495-3306
**Subject(s):** College Publications; Black Publications
**Circ:** 60,000

**Group Practice Journal (31005)**
American Medical Group Association
1422 Duke St.
Alexandria, VA 22314-3430
Phone: (703)838-0033
Fax: (703)548-1890
**Subject(s):** Medicine and Surgery
**Circ:** (Paid)△**60,000**

**Journal of Child Nutrition & Management (31019)**
American School Food Service Association
700 S Washington St., Ste. 300
Alexandria, VA 22314-4287
Phone: (703)739-3900
Fax: (703)739-3915
**Subject(s):** Education; Food and Grocery Trade
**Circ:** 60,000

**The Wilson Quarterly (5754)**
Woodrow Wilson Center Press
One Woodrow Wilson Plz.
1300 Pennsylvania Ave. NW
Washington, DC 20004-3027
Phone: (202)691-4000
Fax: (202)691-4001
**Subject(s):** General Editorial
**Circ:** (Paid)‡60,000

**Exceptional Children (31124)**
Council for Exceptional Children
1110 N Glebe Rd., Ste. 300
Arlington, VA 22201
Phone: (703)620-3660
Fax: (703)264-9494
**Subject(s):** Education
**Circ:** ‡59,244

**School Foodservice & Nutrition (31067)**
American School Food Service Association
700 S Washington St., Ste. 300
Alexandria, VA 22314-4287
Phone: (703)739-3900
Fax: (703)739-3915
**Subject(s):** Food and Grocery Trade
**Circ:** (Non-paid)5,000
(Paid)58,000

**Virginia Journal of Education (31806)**
Virginia Education Association
116 S 3rd St.
Richmond, VA 23219-3704
Phone: (804)648-5801
Fax: (804)775-8379
**Subject(s):** Education
**Circ:** ‡58,000

**The American Prospect (5223)**
New Prospect Inc.
2000 L Street NW, Ste. 717
Washington, DC 20036
**Subject(s):** Politics
**Circ:** (Combined)55,000

**Hazard Technology (13295)**
EIS International
1401 Rockville Pke., Ste. 500
Rockville, MD 20852
Phone: (301)738-6900
Fax: (301)738-1026
**Subject(s):** Ecology and Conservation
**Circ:** ‡55,000

**Al-Anon Family Group Headquarters—The Forum (31923)**
Al-Anon Family Group Headquarters, World Service Office
1600 Corporate Landing Pkwy.
Virginia Beach, VA 23454-5617
Phone: (757)563-1600
Fax: (757)563-1655
**Subject(s):** Substance Abuse and Treatment
**Circ:** 54,000

Circulation: ★ = ABC; △ = BPA; ♦ = CAC; • = CCAB; ❑ = VAC; ⊕ = PO Statement; ‡ = Publisher's Report; Boldface figures = sworn; Light figures = estimated.

**Nature International Weekly Journal of Science** (5581)
Nature Publishing Group
968 National Press Bldg.
529 14 St. NW
Washington, DC 20045-1938
Phone: (202)737-2355
Fax: (202)628-1609
**Subject(s):** Science (General)

**Circ:** (Non-paid)686
(Paid)53,861

**Lodging Magazine** (5535)
American Hotel & Lodging Association
1201 New York Ave. NW, Ste. 600
Washington, DC 20005-3931
Phone: (202)289-3100
Fax: (202)289-3199
**Subject(s):** Hotels, Motels, Restaurants, and Clubs; Management and Administration

**Circ:** (Paid)4,885
(Non-paid)52,000

**Marine Corps League** (31605)
PO Box 3070
Merrifield, VA 22116
Phone: (703)207-9588
Fax: (703)207-0047
**Subject(s):** Military and Navy

**Circ:** 52,000

**Professional Surveyor** (13142)
Professional Surveyors Publishing Company Inc.
100 Tuscanny Dr., Ste. B1
Frederick, MD 21702
Phone: (301)682-6101
Fax: (301)682-6105
**Subject(s):** Engineering (Various branches); Science (General)

**Circ:** (Controlled)‡52,000

**Virginia** (31268)
University of Virginia Alumni Association
PO Box 3446
Charlottesville, VA 22903
Phone: (434)971-9721
Fax: (434)243-9000
**Subject(s):** College Publications

**Circ:** (Paid)51,500

**Baltimore Magazine** (12673)
1000 Lancaster St., Ste. 400
Baltimore, MD 21202
Phone: (410)752-4200
Fax: (410)625-0280
**Subject(s):** Local, State, and Regional Publications

**Circ:** (Paid)50,186

**Light & Medium Truck** (31036)
TT Publishing
2200 Mill Rd.
Alexandria, VA 22314
Phone: (703)838-1746
Fax: (703)838-6259
**Subject(s):** Trucks and Trucking

**Circ:** ‡50,086

**C.U.A. Magazine** (5347)
The Catholic University of America
620 Michigan Ave. NE
170 Leahy Hall
Washington, DC 20064
Phone: (202)319-5050
Fax: (202)319-4802
**Subject(s):** Education

**Circ:** (Non-paid)50,000

**JJournal of the American Pharmacists Association'** (5455)
American Pharmaceutical Association
2215 Constitution Ave., NW
Washington, DC 20037-2985
Phone: (202)628-4410
Fax: (202)783-2151
**Subject(s):** Drugs and Pharmaceuticals

**Circ:** (Paid)‡50,000

**Language, Speech, and Hearing Services in Schools** (13300)
American Speech-Language-Hearing Association
10801 Rockville Pke.
Rockville, MD 20852
Phone: (301)897-5700
Fax: (301)571-0457
**Subject(s):** Hearing and Speech

**Circ:** ‡49,000

**The Mathematics Teacher** (31741)
National Council of Teachers of Mathematics
1906 Association Dr.
Reston, VA 20191-1502
Phone: (703)620-9840
Fax: (703)476-2970
**Subject(s):** Mathematics; Education

**Circ:** (Paid)49,000

**Emergency Medicine** (13243)
Cadmus Journal Services
940 Elkridge Landing Rd.
Linthicum, MD 21090-2908
Phone: (410)850-0500
Fax: (410)691-6203
**Subject(s):** Medicine and Surgery

**Circ:** (Paid)3,110
(Non-paid)48,258

**Missionhurst** (31136)
Missionhurst C.I.C.M.
4651 N. 25th St.
Arlington, VA 22207-3500
Phone: (703)528-3804
Fax: (703)522-7864
**Subject(s):** Religious Publications

**Circ:** (Controlled)48,000

**Teaching Children Mathematics** (31755)
National Council of Teachers of Mathematics
1906 Association Dr.
Reston, VA 20191-1502
Phone: (703)620-9840
Fax: (703)476-2970
**Subject(s):** Mathematics; Education

**Circ:** 48,000

**Wonderful West Virginia** (32565)
West Virginia Division of Natural Resources
State Capitol Complex
1900 Kanawha Blvd. E.
Bldg. 3, Rm. 662
Charleston, WV 25305-0312
Phone: (304)558-3315
Fax: (304)558-2768
**Subject(s):** Local, State, and Regional Publications

**Circ:** 48,000

**Nursing Spectrum—Washington D.C. & Baltimore** (31384)
Nursing Spectrum Inc.
803 W. Broad St., No. 500
Falls Church, VA 22046
Phone: (703)237-6299
Fax: (703)237-6515
**Subject(s):** Career Development and Employment; Nursing; Career Development and Employment; Nursing

**Circ:** 47,500

**Adventist Review** (13337)
General Conference of Seventh-Day Adventists
12501 Old Columbia Pke.
Silver Spring, MD 20904
Phone: (301)680-6000
Fax: (301)680-6502
**Subject(s):** Religious Publications

**Circ:** ‡47,000

**Academe: Bulletin of the AAUP** (5186)
American Association of University Professors
1012 14th St. NW, Ste. 500
Washington, DC 20005
Phone: (202)737-5900
Fax: (202)737-5526
**Subject(s):** Education

**Circ:** ‡46,000

**American Journal of Psychiatry** (31107)
American Psychiatric Publishing Inc.
1000 Wilson Blvd., Ste. 1825
Arlington, VA 22209-3901
Phone: (703)907-7322
Fax: (703)907-1091
**Subject(s):** Psychology and Psychiatry

**Circ:** (Non-paid)‡700
(Paid)‡45,633

**TRIAL** (5724)
Association of Trial Lawyers of America
1050 31st St. NW
Washington, DC 20007
Phone: (202)965-3500
Fax: (202)965-0030

**Subject(s):** Law

**Circ:** (Non-paid)7,713
(Paid)45,611

**Air Transport World** (5196)
Penton Media Inc.
1350 Connecticut Ave., NW, Ste. 902
Washington, DC 20036
Phone: (202)659-8500
Fax: (202)659-1554
**Subject(s):** Aviation; Management and Administration

**Circ:** (Controlled)‡45,071

**The Chronicle of Philanthropy** (5307)
1255 23rd St. NW, Ste. 700
Washington, DC 20037
Phone: (202)466-1200
Fax: (202)466-2078
**Subject(s):** Philanthropy and Humanitarianism

**Circ:** (Paid)45,063

**American Guidance for Seniors** (31375)
Uniformed Services Almanac Inc.
PO Box 4144
Falls Church, VA 22044
Phone: (703)532-1631
Fax: (703)532-1635
**Subject(s):** Senior Citizens' Interests

**Circ:** (Paid)45,000

**CFA Digest** (31241)
CFA Institute
560 Ray C Hunt Dr.
PO Box 3668
Charlottesville, VA 22903-2981
Phone: (434)951-5346
Fax: (434)951-5350
**Subject(s):** Banking, Finance, and Investments

**Circ:** (Combined)⊕45,000

**FBI Law Enforcement Bulletin** (31672)
U.S. Federal Bureau of Investigation
FBI Academy, Madison Bldg., Rm. 209
Quantico, VA 22135
Phone: (703)632-1952
Fax: (703)632-1968
**Subject(s):** Police, Penology, and Penal Institutions; Law

**Circ:** (Controlled)45,000

**Independent Agent** (31010)
IIAA/MSI Inc.
127 S Peyton St.
Alexandria, VA 22314
Phone: (703)683-4422
Fax: (703)683-7556
**Subject(s):** Insurance

**Circ:** (Controlled)45,000

**The Mariner** (13106)
601 Bridge St.
Elkton, MD 21921
Phone: (410)287-9430
Fax: (410)398-4044
**Subject(s):** (Boating and Yachting)

**Circ:** (Combined)45,000

**Oncology Times** (12835)
Lippincott Williams & Wilkins
351 W. Camden St.
Baltimore, MD 21201
Phone: (410)528-4479
Fax: (410)528-4312
**Subject(s):** Medicine and Surgery

**Circ:** 45,000

**Outdoor America** (13173)
Izaak Walton League
707 Conservation Ln.
Gaithersburg, MD 20878
Phone: (301)548-0150
Fax: (301)548-0146
**Subject(s):** Environmental and Natural Resources Conservation; (Outdoors)

**Circ:** 45,000

**Chesapeake Bay Magazine** (12629)
Chesapeake Bay Communications
1819 Bay Ridge Ave.
Annapolis, MD 21403
Phone: (410)263-2662
Fax: (410)267-6924
**Subject(s):** (Boating and Yachting)

**Circ:** (Paid)44,991

**Provider** (5635)
American Health Care Association
1201 L St. NW
Washington, DC 20005
Phone: (202)842-4444
Fax: (202)842-3860
**Subject(s):** Health and Healthcare

Circ: 44,778

**Morbidity and Mortality Weekly Report** (5554)
Centers for Disease Control and Prevention
Superintendent of Documents
Government Printing Office
Washington, DC 20402-9371
Phone: (202)783-3238
**Subject(s):** Health and Healthcare

Circ: (Combined)44,000

**Aerospace America Magazine** (31689)
American Institute of Aeronautics and Astronautics
1801 Alexander Bell Dr., Ste. 500
Reston, VA 20191-4344
Phone: (703)264-7500
Fax: (703)264-7551
**Subject(s):** Astronautics; Engineering (Various branches)

Circ: (Paid)23,432
(Controlled)43,600

**Seafarers LOG** (13027)
Seafarers Intl. Union
5201 Auth Way
Camp Springs, MD 20746-4275
Phone: (301)899-0675
Fax: (301)899-7355
**Subject(s):** Labor; Ships and Shipping

Circ: (Non-paid)‡43,000

**ASM News** (5257)
ASM Journals
1752 N. St., NW
Washington, DC 20036-2904
Phone: (202)737-3600
Fax: (202)942-9333
**Subject(s):** Biology

Circ: (Non-paid)‡50
(Paid)‡42,684

**Shipmate** (12633)
U.S. Naval Academy Alumni Association
247 King George St.
Annapolis, MD 21402
Phone: (410)295-4000
**Subject(s):** Military and Navy; College Publications

Circ: ‡42,500

**National Guard Magazine** (5568)
1 Massachusetts Ave. NW
Washington, DC 20001
Phone: (202)789-0031
Fax: (202)682-9358
**Subject(s):** Military and Navy

Circ: ‡42,000

**Postmasters Gazette** (31361)
National Association of Postmasters
4016 Williamsburg Crt.
Fairfax, VA 22032
Phone: (703)359-8900
Fax: (703)359-8950
**Subject(s):** Postal and Shipping Supplies

Circ: ‡42,000

**Techniques** (31074)
Association for Career and Technical Education
1410 King St.
Alexandria, VA 22314
Phone: (703)683-3111
Fax: (703)683-7424
**Subject(s):** Vocational Education

Circ: (Paid)‡42,000

**Pediatric News** (13304)
International Medical News Group
c/o Catherine Nellist
12230 Wilkins Ave.
Rockville, MD 20852
Phone: (301)816-8700
Fax: (301)816-8738
**Subject(s):** Pediatrics

Circ: (Controlled)41,690

**The Washington Blade** (5736)
1408 U St. NW, 2nd Fl.
Washington, DC 20009
Phone: (202)797-7000
Fax: (202)797-7040
**Subject(s):** Gay and Lesbian Interests

Circ: (Paid)1,346
(Free)41,446

**CONSTRUCTOR** (30992)
The Associated General Contractors of America
333 John Carlyle St., Ste. 200
Alexandria, VA 22314
Phone: (703)548-3118
Fax: (703)837-5405
**Subject(s):** Construction, Contracting, Building, and Excavating

Circ: (Paid)⊕38,072
(Non-paid)⊕41,026

**Modern Drug Discovery** (5548)
American Chemical Society
1155 Sixteenth St., NW
Washington, DC 20036
Phone: (202)872-4593
Fax: (202)776-8166
**Subject(s):** Chemistry, Chemicals, and Chemical Engineering; Safety; Medicine and Surgery

Circ: 40,100

**AFP Exchange** (12918)
Association for Financial Professionals
7315 Wisconsin Ave., Ste. 600 W.
Bethesda, MD 20814
Phone: (301)907-2862
Fax: (301)907-2864
**Subject(s):** Banking, Finance, and Investments

Circ: (Non-paid)200
(Paid)40,000

**AIIM E-DOC** (13338)
AIIM International
1100 Wayne Ave., Ste. 1100
Silver Spring, MD 20910
Phone: (301)587-8202
Fax: (301)587-2711
**Subject(s):** Business; Computers

Circ: (Non-paid)‡40,000

**The American Journal of Occupational Therapy** (12927)
American Occupational Therapy Association Inc.
4720 Montgomery Ln.
PO Box 31220
Bethesda, MD 20824-1220
Phone: (301)652-2682
Fax: (301)652-7711
**Subject(s):** Medicine and Surgery

Circ: 40,000

**Aviation Maintenance** (13262)
Access Intelligence L.L.C.
1201 Seven Locks Rd., Ste. 300
Potomac, MD 20854
Phone: (301)354-2000
Fax: (301)309-3847
**Subject(s):** Aviation

Circ: (Controlled)‡40,000

**Braille Monitor** (12684)
National Federation of the Blind
1800 Johnson St.
Baltimore, MD 21230
Phone: (410)659-9314
Fax: (410)685-5653
**Subject(s):** Blind and Visually Challenged

Circ: (Non-paid)40,000

**ChemMatters** (5300)
American Chemical Society
1155 16th St., NW
Washington, DC 20036
Phone: (202)872-4600
Fax: (202)872-4615
**Subject(s):** Chemistry, Chemicals, and Chemical Engineering; Education

Circ: (Paid)⊕40,000

**Chesapeake Family** (12630)
Jefferson Communications
1202 W. St., Ste. 100
Annapolis, MD 21401
Phone: (410)263-1641
Fax: (410)280-0255
**Subject(s):** Parenting

Circ: (Controlled)40,000

**Columbia Union Visitor** (13076)
Columbia Union Conference of Seventh-day Adventists
5427 Twin Knolls Rd.
Columbia, MD 21045
Phone: (301)596-0800
Fax: (410)997-7420
**Subject(s):** Religious Publications

Circ: (Controlled)‡40,000

**Custom Home** (5352)
Hanley-Wood L.L.C.
1 Thomas Cir., Ste. 600
Washington, DC 20005
Phone: (202)452-0800
Fax: (202)785-1974
**Subject(s):** Architecture; Construction, Contracting, Building, and Excavating

Circ: ‡40,000

**Daughters of the American Revolution Magazine** (5355)
National Society Daughters of the American Revolution
1776 D St. NW
Washington, DC 20006-5392
Phone: (202)628-1776
Fax: (202)879-3283
**Subject(s):** History and Genealogy; Unclassified Fraternal

Circ: ‡40,000

**France Magazine** (5395)
Maison Francaise
4101 Reservoir Rd. NW
Washington, DC 20007
Phone: (202)944-6195
Fax: (202)944-6148
**Subject(s):** Intercultural Interests

Circ: (Non-paid)40,000

**The Jewish Veteran** (5453)
1811 R. St. NW
Washington, DC 20009
Phone: (202)265-6280
Fax: (202)234-5662
**Subject(s):** Jewish Publications; Veterans

Circ: (Non-paid)5,000
(Paid)40,000

**Professional Pilot** (31059)
Queensmith Communications Corp.
30 S. Quaker Ln. Ste. 300
Alexandria, VA 22314
Phone: (703)370-0606
Fax: (703)370-7082
**Subject(s):** Aviation

Circ: (Controlled)‡40,000

**ProSales** (5634)
Hanley-Wood L.L.C.
1 Thomas Cir., Ste. 600
Washington, DC 20005
Phone: (202)452-0800
Fax: (202)785-1974
**Subject(s):** Construction, Contracting, Building, and Excavating

Circ: (Controlled)40,000

**Towing and Recovery Footnotes** (31634)
Trader Publishing Co.
100 W Plume St.
Norfolk, VA 23510
Phone: (757)640-4000
Fax: (352)377-4129
**Subject(s):** Trucks and Trucking; Transportation, Traffic, and Shipping

Circ: (Controlled)40,000

**Virginia Wildlife** (31813)
Virginia Dept. of Game and Inland Fisheries
4010 W. Broad St.
PO Box 11104
Richmond, VA 23230-1104
Phone: (804)367-1000
Fax: (804)367-0488
**Subject(s):** Local, State, and Regional Publications; Environmental and Natural Resources Conservation

Circ: ‡40,000

**Washington Report on Middle East Affairs** (5746)
American Educational Trust
PO Box 53062
Washington, DC 20009
Phone: (202)939-6050
Fax: (202)265-4574
**Subject(s):** International Affairs

Circ: 40,000

**Washington Technology** (5747)
Post-Newsweek Business Information
10 G St. NE
Washington, DC 20002
Phone: (202)772-2500
Fax: (202)772-2511
**Subject(s):** Business; Computers
**Circ:** (Controlled)40,000

**Style Weekly** (31799)
1707 Summit Ave. 201
Richmond, VA 23230-4500
**Subject(s):** Local, State, and Regional Publications
**Circ:** (Free)39,601

**NASSP Bulletin** (31744)
National Association of Secondary School Principals (NASSP)
1904 Association Dr.
Reston, VA 20191-1537
Phone: (703)860-0200
Fax: (703)476-5432
**Subject(s):** Education
**Circ:** ‡37,500

**Psychiatric News** (31149)
American Psychiatric Publishing Inc.
1000 Wilson Blvd., Ste. 1825
Arlington, VA 22209-3901
Phone: (703)907-7322
Fax: (703)907-1091
**Subject(s):** Psychology and Psychiatry
**Circ:** (Non-paid)‡1,219
(Paid)‡37,436

**Engineering Times** (30998)
National Society of Professional Engineers
1420 King St.
Alexandria, VA 22314
Phone: (703)684-2875
Fax: (703)836-4875
**Subject(s):** Engineering (Various branches)
**Circ:** (Non-paid)8,473
(Paid)36,433

**The American School Board Journal** (30973)
American School Board Journal
1680 Duke St.
Alexandria, VA 22314
Phone: (703)838-6722
Fax: (703)683-7590
**Subject(s):** Education
**Circ:** (Paid)‡36,064

**Cathedral Age** (5294)
Washington National Cathedral
3101 Wisconsin Ave. NW
Washington, DC 20016-5098
Phone: (202)537-5681
Fax: (202)364-6600
**Subject(s):** Local, State, and Regional Publications; Art
**Circ:** ‡36,000

**Mathematics-Teaching in the Middle School** (31742)
National Council of Teachers of Mathematics
1906 Association Dr.
Reston, VA 20191-1502
Phone: (703)620-9840
Fax: (703)476-2970
**Subject(s):** Mathematics; Education
**Circ:** (Paid)36,000

**T+D Magazine** (31073)
American Society for Training & Development
1640 King St.
PO Box 1443
Alexandria, VA 22313-2043
Phone: (703)683-8100
Fax: (703)683-8103
**Subject(s):** Employment and Human Resources
**Circ:** (Non-paid)82
(Paid)35,229

**ACC Docket** (5189)
American Corporate Counsel Association
1025 Connecticut Ave. NW, Ste. 200
Washington, DC 20036
Phone: (202)293-4103
Fax: (202)293-4701
**Subject(s):** Law
**Circ:** (Paid)⊕10,500
(Combined)35,000

**The American Gardener** (30972)
American Horticultural Society
7931 E Blvd. Dr.
Alexandria, VA 22308-1300
Phone: (703)768-5700
Fax: (703)768-7533
**Subject(s):** Horticulture; Ecology and Conservation
**Circ:** 35,000

**Listen** (13192)
The Health Connection
55 W Oak Ridge Dr.
Hagerstown, MD 21740
Phone: (301)393-3267
Fax: (301)393-4055
**Subject(s):** Youths' Interests; Parenting; Substance Abuse and Treatment
**Circ:** ‡35,000

**Music Monthly** (12823)
Maryland Musician Publications
2807 Goodwood Rd.
Baltimore, MD 21214
Phone: (410)426-9000
Fax: (410)426-4100
**Subject(s):** Music and Musical Instruments
**Circ:** (Controlled)35,000

**OfficePRO** (31050)
Stratton Publishing and Marketing Inc.
5285 Shawnee Rd., Ste. 510
Alexandria, VA 22312-2334
Phone: (703)914-9200
Fax: (703)914-6777
**Subject(s):** Business
**Circ:** (Paid)35,000

**The Official Guide to Howard County** (13080)
Patuxent Publishing Co.
10750 Little Patuxent Pkwy.
Columbia, MD 21044
Phone: (410)730-3990
Fax: (410)997-4564
**Subject(s):** Local, State, and Regional Publications
**Circ:** ‡35,000

**TV Technology** (31387)
IMAS Publishing Inc.
5827 Columbia Pike
Falls Church, VA 22041
Phone: (703)998-7600
Fax: (703)671-7409
**Subject(s):** Radio, Television, Cable, and Video
**Circ:** (Controlled)‡35,000

**Armed Forces Journal International** (31881)
Defense News Media Group
6883 Commercial Dr.
Springfield, VA 22159
Phone: (703)750-9000
Fax: (703)848-0480
**Subject(s):** Military and Navy
**Circ:** (Paid)4,000
(Non-paid)34,000

**Parachutist** (31054)
U.S. Parachute Association
1440 Duke St.
Alexandria, VA 22314
Phone: (703)836-3495
Fax: (703)836-2843
**Subject(s):** (General Sports)
**Circ:** (Non-paid)‡500
(Paid)‡34,000

**Rural Electrification Magazine** (31153)
National Rural Electric Cooperative Association
4301 Wilson Blvd.
Arlington, VA 22203-1861
Phone: (703)907-5500
Fax: (703)907-5521
**Subject(s):** Rural Electrification
**Circ:** (Paid)33,119

**American Journal of Public Health** (5215)
American Public Health Association
800 I St. NW
Washington, DC 20001-3710
Phone: (202)777-2742
Fax: (202)777-2534
**Subject(s):** Health and Healthcare
**Circ:** ‡33,000

**ASID ICON** (5256)
The American Society of Interior Designers
608 Massachusetts Ave., NE
Washington, DC 20002
Phone: (202)546-3480
Fax: (202)546-3240
**Subject(s):** Architecture; Interior Design/Decorating; Home Furnishings, Curtains, Draperies
**Circ:** (Controlled)33,000

**Church & State** (5308)
Americans United for Separation of Church & State
518 C St., NE
Washington, DC 20002
Phone: (202)466-3234
Fax: (202)466-2587
**Subject(s):** Religious Publications; Politics; Law
**Circ:** (Controlled)‡2,600
(Paid)‡33,000

**Columbia Magazine** (13075)
Patuxent Publishing Co.
10750 Little Patuxent Pkwy.
Columbia, MD 21044
Phone: (410)730-3990
Fax: (410)997-4564
**Subject(s):** Local, State, and Regional Publications
**Circ:** (Controlled)33,000

**InSights** (31343)
National Rifle Association of America
11250 Waples Mill Rd.
Fairfax, VA 22030
Phone: (703)267-1200
Fax: (703)267-3989
**Subject(s):** (Hunting, Fishing, and Game Management); Youths' Interests; Firearms
**Circ:** (Paid)33,000

**Professional Agent** (31058)
National Association of Professional Insurance Agents
400 N Washington St.
Alexandria, VA 22314
Phone: (703)836-9340
Fax: (703)836-4933
**Subject(s):** Insurance
**Circ:** (Paid)‡33,000

**WHERE Baltimore** (12881)
Abarta Media Group
516 N. Charles St., Ste. 300
Baltimore, MD 21201
Phone: (410)539-4373
Fax: (410)539-4381
**Subject(s):** Travel and Tourism
**Circ:** (Non-paid)33,000

**Clinical Psychiatry News** (13288)
International Medical News Group
12230 Wilkins Ave.
Rockville, MD 20852
Phone: (301)816-8700
Fax: (301)816-8738
**Subject(s):** Psychology and Psychiatry
**Circ:** (Controlled)32,946

**Federal Times** (31885)
Army Times Publishing Co.
6883 Commercial Dr.
Springfield, VA 22159-0500
Phone: (703)750-9000
Fax: (703)750-8767
**Subject(s):** State, Municipal, and County Administration
**Circ:** (Paid)32,589

**Virginia Business** (31803)
Media General Business Communications Inc.
PO Box 85333
Richmond, VA 23293
**Subject(s):** Business; Local, State, and Regional Publications
**Circ:** (Controlled)32,500

**Ob Gyn News** (13302)
International Medical News Group
c/o Kathy Scarbeck
12230 Wilkins Ave.
Rockville, MD 20852
Phone: (301)816-8700
Fax: (301)816-8738
**Subject(s):** Medicine and Surgery
**Circ:** (Controlled)32,131

**Naval History** (12631)
U.S. Naval Institute
Preble Hall
291 Wood Rd.
Annapolis, MD 21402
Phone: (410)268-6110
Fax: (410)269-7940
**Subject(s):** Military and Navy
**Circ:** 32,000

**R.E. Magazine** (31152)
National Rural Electric Cooperative Association
4301 Wilson Blvd.
Arlington, VA 22203-1861
Phone: (703)907-5500
Fax: (703)907-5521
**Subject(s):** Power and Power Plants
**Circ:** (Paid)32,000

**Trusteeship** (5725)
Association of Governing Boards of Universities and Colleges
1 Dupont Cir., Ste. 400
Washington, DC 20036
Phone: (202)296-8400
Fax: (202)223-7053
**Subject(s):** Education
**Circ:** (Paid)32,000

**West Virginia Nurse** (32563)
West Virginia Nurses Association
PO Box 1946
Charleston, WV 25327
Phone: (304)342-1169
Fax: (304)342-6973
**Subject(s):** Nursing; Health and Healthcare
**Circ:** (Paid)⊕32,000

**Stores** (5703)
NRF Enterprises Inc.
325 7th St. NW, Ste. 1100
Washington, DC 20004
Phone: (202)626-8101
**Subject(s):** General Merchandise; Retail
**Circ:** (Paid)15,776
(Non-paid)19,966
(Non-paid)★31,920

**Rotor & Wing** (13271)
Access Intelligence L.L.C.
1201 Seven Locks Rd., Ste. 300
Potomac, MD 20854
Phone: (301)354-2000
Fax: (301)309-3847
**Subject(s):** Aviation
**Circ:** (Paid)7,738
(Non-paid)31,786

**Advances in Pulmonary Hypertension** (13336)
Pulmonary Hypertension Association
850 Sligo Ave., No. 800
Silver Spring, MD 20910
Phone: (800)748-7274
Fax: (301)565-3994
**Subject(s):** Medicine and Surgery; Health and Healthcare
**Circ:** 31,000

**The Futurist** (12969)
World Future Society
7910 Woodmont Ave., Ste. 450
Bethesda, MD 20814
Phone: (301)656-8274
Fax: (301)951-0394
**Subject(s):** Sociology
**Circ:** ‡31,000

**Journal of the National Medical Association** (5494)
National Medical Association
1012 10th St. NW
Washington, DC 20001
Phone: (202)347-1895
Fax: (202)898-2510
**Subject(s):** Medicine and Surgery; Black Publications
**Circ:** (Paid)6,000
(Controlled)31,000

**American Painting Contractor** (31769)
Douglas Publications Inc.
2807 N Parham Rd.,64 Bldg., Ste. 200
Richmond, VA 23294
Phone: (804)762-9600
Fax: (804)217-8999
**Subject(s):** Paint and Wallcoverings; Construction, Contracting, Building, and Excavating
**Circ:** ‡30,736

**Challenge Magazine** (13287)
Disabled Sports, USA
451 Hungerford Dr., Ste. 100
Rockville, MD 20850
Phone: (301)217-0960
Fax: (301)217-0968
**Subject(s):** (General Sports); Handicapped
**Circ:** (Paid)30,000

**Common Ground** (30989)
225 Reinekers Ln., Ste. 300
Alexandria, VA 22314
Phone: (703)548-8600
Fax: (703)684-1581
**Subject(s):** Real Estate
**Circ:** (Paid)‡30,000

**EGA Needle Arts Magazine** (31317)
Embroiderers Guild of America Inc.
Route 1, Box 4510
Dillwyn, VA 23936
Phone: (804)983-3021
Fax: (804)983-1074
**Subject(s):** Clothing; Fashion; Textiles
**Circ:** (Paid)30,000

**Principal** (31056)
National Association of Elementary School Principals
1615 Duke St.
Alexandria, VA 22314-3483
Phone: (703)684-3345
Fax: (703)548-6021
**Subject(s):** Education
**Circ:** ‡30,000

**Profile (Norfolk)** (31631)
DOD High School News Service
9420 Third Ave., Ste. 110
Norfolk, VA 23511-2029
Fax: (757)445-7782
**Subject(s):** Employment and Human Resources; Military and Navy
**Circ:** (Non-paid)30,000

**The Nation's Health** (5578)
American Public Health Association
800 I St. NW
Washington, DC 20001-3710
Phone: (202)777-2742
Fax: (202)777-2534
**Subject(s):** Health and Healthcare
**Circ:** (Non-paid)‡1,000
(Paid)‡29,300

**Association Management** (5259)
American Society of Association Executives
ASAE Bldg.
1575 I St. NW
Washington, DC 20005-1103
Phone: (202)371-0940
Fax: (202)371-8315
**Subject(s):** Management and Administration
**Circ:** (Paid)29,055

**Appalachian Trailway News** (32613)
Appalachian Trail Conservancy
799 Washington St.
PO Box 807
Harpers Ferry, WV 25425-0807
Phone: (304)535-6331
Fax: (304)535-2667
**Subject(s):** (Outdoors); Environmental and Natural Resources Conservation
**Circ:** (Non-paid)‡500
(Paid)‡29,000

**Social Education** (13355)
National Council for the Social Studies
8555 16th St., Ste. 500
Silver Spring, MD 20910
Phone: (301)588-1800
Fax: (301)588-2049
**Subject(s):** Education; Sociology; Social Sciences
**Circ:** (Paid)‡29,000

**American Journal of Health-System Pharmacy** (12925)
American Society of Health-System Pharmacists
7272 Wisconsin Ave.
Bethesda, MD 20814
Phone: (301)657-3000
Fax: (301)657-8857
**Subject(s):** Drugs and Pharmaceuticals
**Circ:** (Non-paid)‡12,655
(Paid)‡28,765

**Marine Corps Gazette** (31674)
Marine Corps Association
Box 1775
Quantico, VA 22134
Phone: (703)640-6161
Fax: (703)640-0823
**Subject(s):** Military and Navy
**Circ:** (Controlled)‡894
(Paid)‡28,718

**Security Management** (31068)
ASIS International
1625 Prince St.
Alexandria, VA 22314-2818
Phone: (703)519-6200
Fax: (703)519-6299
**Subject(s):** Building Management and Maintenance
**Circ:** (Non-paid)356
(Paid)28,697

**The Metropolitan Magazine** (13322)
Pyramid Design Inc.
PO Box 382
Salisbury, MD 21803-0382
Phone: (410)546-6388
Fax: (410)546-6387
**Subject(s):** Local, State, and Regional Publications; Lifestyle
**Circ:** (Free)28,603

**Vibrant Life** (13196)
Review and Herald Publishing Association
55 W Oak Ridge Dr.
Hagerstown, MD 21740
Phone: (301)393-3000
Fax: (301)393-4055
**Subject(s):** Health; Religious Publications
**Circ:** ‡28,000

**Wireless Data News** (13273)
Access Intelligence L.L.C.
1201 Seven Locks Rd., Ste. 300
Potomac, MD 20854
Phone: (301)354-2000
Fax: (301)309-3847
**Subject(s):** Telecommunications; Communications
**Circ:** (Controlled)‡28,000

**USGlass, Metal & Glazing** (31431)
Key Communications Inc.
PO Box 569
Garrisonville, VA 22463
Phone: (540)720-5584
Fax: (540)720-5687
**Subject(s):** Glass and China; Automotive (Trade); Building Materials, Concrete, Brick, and Tile
**Circ:** ∆27,826

**Defense News** (31883)
Army Times Publishing Co.
6883 Commercial Dr.
Springfield, VA 22159-0500
Phone: (703)750-9000
Fax: (703)750-8767
**Subject(s):** Military and Navy
**Circ:** (Paid)11,309
(Controlled)27,177

**Oceana Magazine** (13256)
12505 Coastal Hwy., Ste. 201
Ocean City, MD 21842
Phone: (410)250-5700
Fax: (410)250-9702
**Subject(s):** Local, State, and Regional Publications
**Circ:** (Non-paid)‡27,000

**The Science Teacher** (31158)
National Science Teachers Association
1840 Wilson Blvd.
Arlington, VA 22201-3000
Phone: (703)243-7100
Fax: (703)243-7177
**Subject(s):** Education; Science (General)
**Circ:** ‡27,000

**Aquatics International** (5246)
Hanley-Wood L.L.C.
One Thomas Cir., NW, Ste. 600
Washington, DC 20005
Phone: (202)452-0800
Fax: (202)785-1974
**Subject(s):** Sporting Goods/Retail Sports
**Circ:** (Non-paid)26,500

**SIGNAL** (31363)
Armed Forces Communications & Electronics Association (AFCEA)
4400 Fair Lakes Ct.
Fairfax, VA 22033-3899
Phone: (703)631-6100
Fax: (703)631-6100
**Subject(s):** Computers; Electronics Engineering; Military and Navy; Telecommunications

Circ: (Non-paid)△2,046
(Paid)△26,483

**Electrical Standards and Product Guide** (31859)
National Electrical Manufacturers Association (NEMA)
1300 N. 17th St., Ste. 1847
Rosslyn, VA 22209
Phone: (703)841-3200
Fax: (703)841-5900
**Subject(s):** Electrical Engineering

Circ: (Non-paid)‡26,000

**ElectroIndustry (ei)** (31860)
National Electrical Manufacturers Association (NEMA)
1300 N. 17th St., Ste. 1847
Rosslyn, VA 22209
Phone: (703)841-3200
Fax: (703)841-5900
**Subject(s):** Electrical Engineering

Circ: (Non-paid)26,000

**Science Scope** (31157)
National Science Teachers Association
1840 Wilson Blvd.
Arlington, VA 22201-3000
Phone: (703)243-7100
Fax: (703)243-7177
**Subject(s):** Education; Science (General)

Circ: (Paid)‡15,000
(Non-paid)‡26,000

**Business Credit** (13073)
National Association of Credit Management
8840 Columbia 100 Pkwy.
Columbia, MD 21045
Phone: (410)740-5560
Fax: (410)740-5574
**Subject(s):** Banking, Finance, and Investments

Circ: (Paid)△25,960

**Bluegrass Unlimited** (31935)
Bluegrass Unlimited Inc.
9514 James Madison Hwy.
PO Box 771
Warrenton, VA 20186
Phone: (540)349-8181
Fax: (540)341-0011
**Subject(s):** Music and Musical Instruments

Circ: (Controlled)‡133
(Paid)‡25,951

**Ophthalmology Journal** (12837)
American Academy of Ophthalmology
600 N.Wolfe St.
Jefferson St. Bldg.
Rm. B1-136
Baltimore, MD 21287-8917
Phone: (443)287-2445
Fax: (443)287-2448
**Subject(s):** Medicine and Surgery

Circ: 25,498

**The Religious Herald** (31791)
Religious Herald Publishing Association Inc.
PO Box 8377
Richmond, VA 23226-0377
Phone: (804)672-1973
Fax: (804)672-8323
**Subject(s):** Religious Publications

Circ: 25,040

**The American Enterprise** (5208)
American Enterprise Institute
1150 17th St. NW
Washington, DC 20036-4670
Phone: (202)862-5800
Fax: (202)862-7177
**Subject(s):** Politics

Circ: (Paid)25,000

**American Forests** (5210)
734 15th St. NW, Ste. 800
PO Box 2000
Washington, DC 20013
Phone: (202)955-4500
Fax: (202)955-4588

**Subject(s):** Forestry; Environmental and Natural Resources Conservation

Circ: ‡25,000

**American Journal of Integrated Health Care** (31435)
American College of Managed Care Medicine
4435 Waterfront Dr., Ste. 101
PO Box 4765
Glen Allen, VA 23060
Phone: (804)527-1906
Fax: (804)747-5316
**Subject(s):** Health and Healthcare; Medicine and Surgery; Insurance

Circ: 25,000

**The American Scholar** (5227)
Phi Beta Kappa Society
1606 New Hampshire Ave., NW
Washington, DC 20009
Phone: (202)265-3808
Fax: (202)986-1601
**Subject(s):** Humanities

Circ: ‡25,000

**Clinical Laboratory News** (5312)
American Association for Clinical Chemistry
2101 L St., NW, Ste. 202
Washington, DC 20037-1558
Phone: (202)857-0717
Fax: (202)887-5093
**Subject(s):** Hospitals and Healthcare Institutions; Laboratory Research (Scientific and Medical)

Circ: (Controlled)25,000

**German Life** (13239)
Zeitgeist Publishing Inc.
1068 National Hwy.
LaVale, MD 21502
Phone: (301)729-6190
Fax: (301)729-1720
**Subject(s):** Ethnic Publications

Circ: (Controlled)15,000
(Paid)25,000

**Intercom** (31128)
Society for Technical Communication
901 N. Stuart St., Ste. 904
Arlington, VA 22203
Phone: (703)522-4114
Fax: (703)522-2075
**Subject(s):** Telecommunications

Circ: 25,000

**Richmond Magazine** (31793)
Target Communications Inc.
1427 W. Main St.
Richmond, VA 23220
Phone: (804)355-4500
Fax: (804)355-3110
**Subject(s):** Local, State, and Regional Publications

Circ: (Controlled)‡15,000
(Paid)‡25,000

**Shafer Court Connections** (31796)
Virginia Commonwealth University Alumni Activities
924 W Franklin St.
PO Box 843044
Richmond, VA 23284-3044
Phone: (804)828-2586
Fax: (804)828-8197
**Subject(s):** College Publications

Circ: (Controlled)25,000

**21st Century Science & Technology** (5726)
21st Century Science Associates Inc.
PO Box 16285
Washington, DC 20041-6285
Phone: (703)777-7473
Fax: (703)777-8853
**Subject(s):** Science (General)

Circ: (Paid)25,000

**W & L** (31525)
Washington & Lee University
Publications Office
Mattingly House
Lexington, VA 24450-0303
Phone: (540)463-8957
Fax: (540)458-8024
**Subject(s):** College Publications

Circ: (Controlled)‡25,000

**The War Cry** (31083)
The Salvation Army
615 Slaters Ln.
PO Box 269
Alexandria, VA 22313
**Subject(s):** Philanthropy and Humanitarianism; Religious Publications

Circ: 25,000

**Braille Forum** (5279)
American Council of the Blind
1155 15th St. NW, Ste. 1004
Washington, DC 20005
Phone: (202)467-5081
Fax: (202)467-5085
**Subject(s):** Handicapped

Circ: (Non-paid)24,500

**Momentum** (5551)
National Catholic Educational Association
1077 30th St. NW, Ste. 100
Washington, DC 20007
Phone: (202)337-6232
Fax: (202)333-6706
**Subject(s):** Education; Religious Publications

Circ: (Paid)‡24,500

**AAHPERD Update** (31686)
American Alliance for Health, Physical Education, Recreation & Dance
1900 Association Dr.
Reston, VA 20191-1598
Phone: (703)476-3400
Fax: (703)476-9527
**Subject(s):** Education; Physical Education and Athletics; (General Sports)

Circ: (Paid)24,165

**American Journal of Health Education** (31693)
American Alliance for Health, Physical Education, Recreation & Dance
1900 Association Dr.
Reston, VA 20191-1598
Phone: (703)476-3400
Fax: (703)476-9527
**Subject(s):** Health and Healthcare; Health and Fitness; Physical Education and Athletics

Circ: 24,000

**Journal of Physical Education, Recreation & Dance (JOPERD)** (31727)
American Alliance for Health, Physical Education, Recreation & Dance
1900 Association Dr.
Reston, VA 20191-1598
Phone: (703)476-3400
Fax: (703)476-9527
**Subject(s):** Education; Physical Education and Athletics

Circ: (Paid)24,000

**National Defense Magazine** (31139)
2111 Wilson Blvd., Ste. 400
Arlington, VA 22201-3061
Phone: (703)522-1820
Fax: (703)522-1885
**Subject(s):** Firearms; Military and Navy

Circ: (Non-paid)1,720
(Paid)24,000

**Parks & Recreation Magazine** (31179)
National Recreation and Park Association
22377 Belmont Ridge Rd.
Ashburn, VA 20148
Phone: (703)858-0784
Fax: (703)858-0794
**Subject(s):** Parks

Circ: ‡24,000

**Sojourners** (5699)
2401 15th. St. NW
Washington, DC 20009
Phone: (202)328-8842
Fax: (202)328-8757
**Subject(s):** Religious Publications

Circ: (Non-paid)‡3,000
(Paid)‡24,000

**Vegetarian Journal** (12879)
The Vegetarian Resource Group
PO Box 1463
Baltimore, MD 21203
Phone: (410)366-8343
Fax: (410)366-8804
**Subject(s):** Health; Lifestyle; Food and Cooking

Circ: 24,000

**The Washington Monthly** (5741)
733 15th St. NW, Ste. 520
Washington, DC 20005
Phone: (202)393-5155
Fax: (202)393-2444
**Subject(s):** Politics

Circ: (Non-paid)1,500
       (Paid)24,000

**Floral Management** (31002)
Society of American Florists
1601 Duke St.
Alexandria, VA 22314-3406
Phone: (703)836-8700
Fax: (703)836-8705
**Subject(s):** Florists and Floriculture

Circ: (Non-paid)1,800
       (Paid)23,200

**American Journal of Roentgenology** (31509)
Lippincott Williams & Wilkins
American Roentgen Ray Society
44211 Slatestone Ct.
Leesburg, VA 20176-5109
Phone: (703)729-3353
Fax: (703)729-4839
**Subject(s):** Radiology, Ultrasound, and Nuclear Medicine

Circ: (Non-paid)‡351
       (Paid)‡23,131

**Delaware Today** (5164)
3301 Lancaster Pke., Ste. 5-C
Wilmington, DE 19805-1436
Phone: (302)656-1809
Fax: (302)656-5843
**Subject(s):** Local, State, and Regional Publications

Circ: (Paid)23,138

**AAFCS Action** (30966)
American Association of Family and Consumer Sciences
1555 King St.
Alexandria, VA 22314-2738
Phone: (703)706-4600
Fax: (703)706-4663
**Subject(s):** Home Economics

Circ: (Controlled)100
       (Paid)23,073

**The Crafts Report** (5162)
100 Rogers Rd.
PO Box 1992
Wilmington, DE 19801
Phone: (302)656-2209
Fax: (302)656-4894
**Subject(s):** Crafts, Models, Hobbies, and Contests

Circ: (Paid)⊕23,000

**Journeyman Roofer and Waterproofer** (5522)
United Union of Roofers
1660 L St. NW, Ste. 800
Washington, DC 20036
Phone: (202)463-7663
Fax: (202)463-6906
**Subject(s):** Roofing

Circ: 23,000

**The National Utility Contractor** (31141)
National Utility Contractors Association
4301 N. Fairfax Dr., Ste. 360
Arlington, VA 22203
Phone: (703)358-9300
Fax: (703)358-9307
**Subject(s):** Construction, Contracting, Building, and Excavating

Circ: (Non-paid)△23,000

**Robotics World** (31795)
Douglas Publications Inc.
2807 N Parham Rd.,64 Bldg., Ste. 200
Richmond, VA 23294
Phone: (804)762-9600
Fax: (804)217-8999
**Subject(s):** Automation; Computers

Circ: (Combined)‡22,500

**Utility Fleet Management** (31081)
American Trucking Associations Inc.
2200 Mill Rd.
Alexandria, VA 22314-4677
Phone: (703)838-1700
Fax: (703)683-2292
**Subject(s):** Power and Power Plants; Purchasing; Telecommunications; Water Supply and Sewage Disposal; Automotive (Trade); Trucks and Trucking

Circ: ‡22,014

**Contract Management** (31578)
National Contract Management Association
8260 Greensboro Dr., Ste.200
Mc Lean, VA 22102
Phone: (571)382-0082
Fax: (703)448-0939
**Subject(s):** Purchasing

Circ: (Controlled)22,000

**Food World** (13077)
Best-Met Publishing Company Inc.
5537 Twin Knolls Rd., Ste. 438
Columbia, MD 21045
Phone: (410)730-5013
Fax: (410)740-4680
**Subject(s):** Food and Grocery Trade

Circ: (Non-paid)‡22,000

**Goldenseal** (32554)
West Virginia Division of Culture and History
1900 Kanawha Blvd. E
Charleston, WV 25305-0300
Phone: (304)558-0220
Fax: (304)558-2779
**Subject(s):** History and Genealogy

Circ: (Combined)⊕22,000

**Via Satellite** (13272)
Access Intelligence L.L.C.
1201 Seven Locks Rd., Ste. 300
Potomac, MD 20854
Phone: (301)354-2000
Fax: (301)309-3847
**Subject(s):** Telecommunications

Circ: 22,000

**Black Issues Book Review** (31336)
Cox, Matthews, & Associates Inc.
10520 Warwick Ave., Ste. B-8
Fairfax, VA 22030-3136
Phone: (703)385-2981
Fax: (703)385-1839
**Subject(s):** Ethnic and Minority Studies; Black Publications

Circ: (Paid)★21,943

**NADA's AutoExec Magazine** (31588)
National Automobile Dealers Association
8400 Westpark Dr.
Mc Lean, VA 22102
Phone: (703)821-7000
Fax: (703)821-7234
**Subject(s):** Automotive (Trade)

Circ: (Paid)21,804

**Weatherwise** (5751)
Heldref Publications
1319 18th St., NW
Washington, DC 20036-1802
Phone: (202)296-6267
Fax: (202)296-5149
**Subject(s):** Meteorology

Circ: (Combined)21,800

**The Chronicle of the Horse** (31609)
The Chronicle of the Horse Inc.
PO Box 46
108 De Plains
Middleburg, VA 20118-0046
Phone: (540)687-6341
Fax: (540)687-3937
**Subject(s):** (Horses and Horse Racing)

Circ: (Paid)21,652

**Avionics Magazine** (13263)
Access Intelligence L.L.C.
1201 Seven Locks Rd., Ste. 300
Potomac, MD 20854
Phone: (301)354-2000
Fax: (301)309-3847
**Subject(s):** Aviation; Electronics Engineering

Circ: (Controlled)21,300

**Alam Attijarat (The World of Business)** (5197)
2700 Virginia Ave. NW, Ste. 107
Washington, DC 20037
Phone: (202)337-2413
Fax: (202)337-3383
**Subject(s):** International Business and Economics; Arabic

Circ: (Non-paid)‡20,954

**The Military Engineer** (31039)
The Society of American Military Engineers
607 Prince St.
Alexandria, VA 22314-3117
Phone: (703)549-3800

Fax: (703)684-6153
**Subject(s):** Engineering (Various branches); Military and Navy

Circ: (Paid)20,066

**The World & I** (5762)
The Washington Times Corp.
3600 New York Ave. NE
Washington, DC 20002-1947
Phone: (202)636-3000
Fax: (202)636-3000
**Subject(s):** Philosophy; Art; Politics; Literature and Literary Reviews; Science; Travel and Tourism; Drama and Theatre; Performing Arts; Music and Musical Instruments; Food and Cooking

Circ: (Non-paid)2,781
       (Paid)20,056

**ABC Today** (31104)
Associated Builders & Contractors Inc.
4250 N Fairfax Dr., 9th Fl.
Arlington, VA 22203-1607
Phone: (703)812-2000
Fax: (703)812-8203
**Subject(s):** Construction, Contracting, Building, and Excavating; Labor

Circ: (Non-paid)‡2,000
       (Paid)‡20,000

**American Mathematical Monthly** (5217)
Mathematical Association of America
1529 18th St. NW
Washington, DC 20036-1358
Phone: (202)387-5200
Fax: (202)265-2384
**Subject(s):** Mathematics

Circ: ‡20,000

**Architects' Guide to Glass, Metal & Glazing** (31428)
Key Communications Inc.
PO Box 569
Garrisonville, VA 22463
Phone: (540)720-5584
Fax: (540)720-5687
**Subject(s):** Architecture; Glass and China

Circ: (Controlled)20,000

**Armed Forces Comptroller** (30979)
American Society of Military Comptrollers
415 N. Alfred St.
Alexandria, VA 22314-4650
Phone: (703)549-0360
Fax: (703)549-3181
**Subject(s):** Banking, Finance, and Investments; Military and Navy

Circ: ‡20,000

**Bible Studies** (31378)
Faith at Work
106 E Broad St., Ste. B
Falls Church, VA 22046
Phone: (703)237-3426
Fax: (703)237-0157
**Subject(s):** Religious Publications

Circ: 20,000

**CORRECTIONS TODAY** (13224)
American Correctional Association
4380 Forbes Blvd.
Lanham, MD 20706-4322
Phone: (301)918-1800
Fax: (301)918-1886
**Subject(s):** Police, Penology, and Penal Institutions

Circ: ‡20,000

**Crisis Magazine** (5345)
Morley Publishing Group Inc.
1814 1/2 N St. NW
Washington, DC 20036
Phone: (202)861-7790
Fax: (202)861-7788
**Subject(s):** Religious Publications; Art and Art History

Circ: (Non-paid)3,000
       (Paid)20,000

**Journal of Forestry** (12983)
Society of American Foresters
5400 Grosvenor Ln.
Bethesda, MD 20814
Phone: (301)897-8720
Fax: (301)897-3690
**Subject(s):** Forestry

Circ: 20,000

Circulation: ★ = ABC; △ = BPA; ♦ = CAC; • = CCAB; □ = VAC; ⊕ = PO Statement; ‡ = Publisher's Report; Boldface figures = sworn; Light figures = estimated.

**The National Interest** (5569)
National Interest Inc.
1615 L St. NW, Ste. 1230
Washington, DC 20036-5651
Phone: (202)467-4884
Fax: (202)467-0006
**Subject(s):** International Affairs
**Circ:** (Combined)‡20,000

**NPA Magazine** (31047)
National Society of Accountants
1010 N Fairfax St.
Alexandria, VA 22314-1504
Phone: (703)549-6400
Fax: (703)549-2984
**Subject(s):** Accountants and Accounting
**Circ:** ‡20,000

**The Police Chief** (31055)
International Association of Chiefs of Police
515 N Washington St.
Alexandria, VA 22314
Phone: (703)836-6767
Fax: (703)836-4543
**Subject(s):** Police, Penology, and Penal Institutions
**Circ:** ‡20,000

**American Educational Research Journal** (5206)
American Educational Research Association
1230 17th St. NW
Washington, DC 20036-3078
Phone: (202)223-9485
Fax: (202)775-1824
**Subject(s):** Education
**Circ:** ‡19,800

**The Construction Specifier** (30991)
The Construction Specifications Institute
99 Canal Ctr. Plz., Ste. 300
Alexandria, VA 22314
Phone: (703)684-0300
Fax: (703)684-8436
**Subject(s):** Construction, Contracting, Building, and Excavating
**Circ:** (Paid)19,752

**Glass Magazine** (31580)
National Glass Association
8200 Greensboro Dr., Ste. 302
Mc Lean, VA 22102-3881
Phone: (703)442-4890
Fax: (703)442-0630
**Subject(s):** Glass and China
**Circ:** (Paid)△4,375
(Non-paid)△19,363

**Employee Benefit Plan Review** (13124)
Aspen Publishing Inc
7201 McKinney Cir.
Frederick, MD 21704
Phone: (800)901-9075
Fax: (301)695-7931
**Subject(s):** Employment and Human Resources; Insurance
**Circ:** (Paid)2,624
(Non-paid)19,236

**Sheriff** (31069)
National Sheriffs' Association
1450 Duke St.
Alexandria, VA 22314-3490
Phone: (703)836-7827
Fax: (703)683-6541
**Subject(s):** Police, Penology, and Penal Institutions
**Circ:** ‡19,000

**Skin & Allergy News** (13308)
International Medical News Group
c/o Teresa Lassman
12230 Wilkins Ave.
Rockville, MD 20852
Phone: (301)816-8700
Fax: (301)816-8738
**Subject(s):** Medicine and Surgery
**Circ:** (Controlled)18,782

**AUA Today** (31238)
American Urological Association
Dept. of Urology, Box 422
University of Virginia
Health Science Center
Charlottesville, VA 22908
**Subject(s):** Medicine and Surgery
**Circ:** ‡18,723

**New Homes Register** (12994)
Bartow Communications
7016 Buxton Ter.
Bethesda, MD 20817-4404
Phone: (301)468-7001
Fax: (301)468-7005
**Subject(s):** Real Estate
**Circ:** (Non-paid)18,500

**Electric Perspectives** (5372)
Edison Electric Institute
701 Pennsylvania Ave. NW
Washington, DC 20004-2696
Phone: (202)508-5714
Fax: (202)508-5759
**Subject(s):** Power and Power Plants
**Circ:** (Paid)308
(Controlled)18,200

**American Journalism Review** (13039)
University of Maryland
1117 Journalism Bldg.
College Park, MD 20742-7111
Phone: (301)405-8803
Fax: (301)405-8323
**Subject(s):** Journalism and Publishing
**Circ:** (Paid)8,447
(Controlled)18,033

**Blues Revue** (32742)
Rte. 1
PO Box 75
Salem, WV 26426-9604
Phone: (304)782-1971
Fax: (304)782-1993
**Subject(s):** Music and Musical Instruments
**Circ:** (Paid)18,000

**Easy Reeding** (31778)
Hohner Inc.
PO Box 15035
Richmond, VA 23227-0435
**Subject(s):** Music and Musical Instruments
**Circ:** (Combined)18,000

**FAA Aviation News** (5383)
DOT/FAA
AFS-805, Rm. 832
800 Independence Ave. SW
Washington, DC 20591
Phone: (202)267-8212
Fax: (202)267-9463
**Subject(s):** Aviation
**Circ:** (Controlled)13,000
(Paid)18,000

**GFWC Clubwoman Magazine** (5406)
General Federation of Women's Clubs
1734 N St. NW
Washington, DC 20036-0246
Phone: (202)347-3168
Fax: (202)835-0246
**Subject(s):** Clubs and Societies; Women's Interests
**Circ:** ‡18,000

**Off Our Backs** (5600)
2337 18th St. NW
Washington, DC 20009
Phone: (202)234-8072
Fax: (202)234-8092
**Subject(s):** Women's Interests
**Circ:** (Paid)2,500
(Non-paid)18,000

**Services** (31362)
Building Service Contractors Association Int'l.
10201 Lee Hwy., Ste. 225
Fairfax, VA 22030-2222
Phone: (703)359-7090
Fax: (703)352-0493
**Subject(s):** Building Management and Maintenance
**Circ:** (Paid)4,499
17,916

**Journal of Urology** (12798)
Lippincott Williams & Wilkins
c/o Joy Y. Gillenwater, Editor
1120 N. Charles St.
Baltimore, MD 21201
**Subject(s):** Medicine and Surgery
**Circ:** (Non-paid)‡423
(Combined)‡17,519

**Boma** (5277)
Building Owners & Managers Association International
1201 New York Ave. NW, Ste. 300
Washington, DC 20005
Phone: (202)408-2662
Fax: (202)371-0181
**Subject(s):** Building Management and Maintenance
**Circ:** (Paid)17,500

**Share the Word** (5692)
Paulist National Catholic Evangelization Association
3031 4th St. NE
Washington, DC 20017
Phone: (202)832-5022
Fax: (202)269-0209
**Subject(s):** Religious Publications
**Circ:** (Paid)‡17,500

**Amstat News** (30975)
American Statistical Association
1429 Duke St.
Alexandria, VA 22314-3415
Phone: (703)684-1221
Fax: (703)684-2037
**Subject(s):** Statistics
**Circ:** (Controlled)17,000

**Children and Families** (30987)
National Head Start Association
1651 Prince St.
Alexandria, VA 22314
Phone: (703)739-0875
Fax: (703)739-0878
**Subject(s):** Education
**Circ:** (Paid)17,000

**Goucher College Quarterly** (12738)
Goucher College
1021 Dulaney Valley Rd.
Baltimore, MD 21204
Phone: (410)337-6000
**Subject(s):** College Publications
**Circ:** 17,000

**ROTOR** (31066)
Helicopter Association International
1635 Prince St.
Alexandria, VA 22314
Phone: (703)683-4646
Fax: (703)683-4745
**Subject(s):** Aviation
**Circ:** (Controlled)17,000

**Sea Technology** (31160)
Compass Publications Inc.
1501 Wilson Blvd., Ste. 1001
Arlington, VA 22209-2403
Phone: (703)524-3136
Fax: (703)841-0852
**Subject(s):** Engineering (Various branches); Oceanography and Marine Studies
**Circ:** (Paid)250
(Controlled)17,000

**Lifting & Transportation International** (31783)
Douglas Publications Inc.
2807 N Parham Rd., 64 Bldg., Ste. 200
Richmond, VA 23294
Phone: (804)762-9600
Fax: (804)217-8999
**Subject(s):** Construction, Contracting, Building, and Excavating
**Circ:** (Combined)‡16,854

**Archives of Surgery** (12664)
American Medical Association Alliance
c/o Julie Ann Freischlag, MD
720 Rutland Ave. Ross 759
John Hopkins Medical Institutions
Baltimore, MD 21205
**Subject(s):** Medicine and Surgery
**Circ:** 16,776

**American Political Science Review** (5221)
American Political Science Association
George Washington University
Political Science
2201 G St. NW
Washington, DC 20052
**Subject(s):** Politics
**Circ:** ‡16,000

**Dirty Linen  (12719)**
PO Box 66600
Baltimore, MD 21239-6600
Phone: (410)583-7973
Fax: (410)337-6735
**Subject(s):** Music and Musical Instruments
**Circ:** (Combined)16,000

**Frederick Magazine  (13127)**
Diversions Publications Inc.
6 N. East St., Ste. 301
Frederick, MD 21701-5601
Phone: (301)662-8171
Fax: (301)662-8399
**Subject(s):** Lifestyle; Local, State, and Regional Publications
**Circ:** (Controlled)16,000

**Navy Civil Engineer  (5583)**
Naval Facilities Engineering Command
Washington Navy Yard
1322 Patterson Ave. SE, Ste. 1000
Washington, DC 20374-5065
Phone: (202)685-9008
Fax: (202)685-1484
**Subject(s):** Military and Navy; Engineering (Various branches)
**Circ:** (Paid)‡200
       (Non-paid)‡16,000

**PS  (5636)**
American Political Science Association
1527 New Hampshire Ave. NW
Washington, DC 20036-1206
Phone: (202)483-2512
Fax: (202)483-2657
**Subject(s):** Politics
**Circ:** ‡16,000

**Public Administration Review  (5654)**
American Society for Public Administration
1120 G St. NW, Ste. 700
Washington, DC 20005
Phone: (202)393-7878
Fax: (202)638-4952
**Subject(s):** State, Municipal, and County Administration
**Circ:** ‡16,000

**Presstime  (31916)**
Newspaper Association of America
1921 Gallows Rd., Ste. 600
Vienna, VA 22182-3900
Phone: (703)902-1600
Fax: (703)917-0236
**Subject(s):** Journalism and Publishing
**Circ:** (Non-paid)1,545
       (Paid)15,994

**Business Education Forum  (31697)**
National Business Education Association
1914 Association Dr.
Reston, VA 20191-1596
Phone: (703)860-8300
Fax: (703)620-4483
**Subject(s):** Education; Business
**Circ:** (Paid)12110
       ‡15,873

**Clay Times  (31944)**
15481 Second St.
PO Box 365
Waterford, VA 20197
Phone: (540)882-3576
Fax: (540)882-4196
**Subject(s):** Art and Art History; Ceramics; Crafts, Models, Hobbies, and Contests
**Circ:** (Paid)15,500

**Occupational Outlook Quarterly  (5592)**
U.S. Government Printing Office and Superintendent of Documents
U.S. Department of Labor
2 Massachusetts Ave. NE, RM. 2135
Washington, DC 20212
Phone: (202)691-5745
Fax: (202)691-5745
**Subject(s):** Employment and Human Resources
**Circ:** (Paid)⊕15,500

**Professional School Counseling  (31060)**
American School Counselor Association
1101 King Street Ste 625
Alexandria, VA 22314
Phone: (703)683-2722
Fax: (703)683-1619

**Subject(s):** Education; Psychology and Psychiatry
**Circ:** ‡15,500

**Strange Magazine  (13309)**
11772 Parklawn Dr.
Rockville, MD 20852
Phone: (301)881-3530
Fax: (301)570-7562
**Subject(s):** Alternative and Underground
**Circ:** (Combined)15,500

**America's Pharmicist  (30974)**
National Community Pharmacists Association
205 Daingerfield Rd.
Alexandria, VA 22314-2885
Phone: (703)683-8200
Fax: (703)683-3619
**Subject(s):** Drugs and Pharmaceuticals
**Circ:** (Non-paid)‡8,646
       (Paid)‡15,176

**Medicine  (12813)**
Lippincott Williams & Wilkins
The Johns Hopkins Hospital
Division of Medical Genetics
Blalock 1007
Baltimore, MD 21205
Phone: (410)955-4999
Fax: (410)955-4999
**Subject(s):** Medicine and Surgery
**Circ:** (Non-paid)‡135
       (Paid)‡15,160

**Advance Data from Vital and Health Statistics  (13213)**
U.S. Department of Health and Human Services
National Center for Health Statistics
Division of Data Services
Hyattsville, MD 20782
Phone: (301)458-4000
**Subject(s):** Health and Healthcare; Statistics
**Circ:** (Non-paid)15,000

**American Consulting Engineer  (5204)**
American Consulting Engineers Council
1015 15th St. NW Ste. 802
Washington, DC 20005-2605
Phone: (202)347-7474
Fax: (202)898-0068
**Subject(s):** Engineering (Various branches)
**Circ:** 15,000

**Assisted Living Today  (31333)**
Assisted Living Federation of America
11200 Waples Mill Rd., Ste. 150
Fairfax, VA 22030
Phone: (703)691-8100
Fax: (703)691-8106
**Subject(s):** Health and Healthcare; Gerontology; Senior Citizens' Interests
**Circ:** 15,000

**Braille Book Review  (5278)**
National Library Service for the Blind and Physically Handicapped
1291 Taylor St. NW
Washington, DC 20011
Phone: (202)707-5100
Fax: (202)707-0712
**Subject(s):** Blind and Visually Challenged; Handicapped
**Circ:** (Non-paid)‡15,000

**Change  (5297)**
Heldref Publications
1319 18th St., NW
Washington, DC 20036-1802
Phone: (202)296-6267
Fax: (202)296-5149
**Subject(s):** Education
**Circ:** (Combined)‡15,000

**Children's Voice  (5303)**
Child Welfare League of America Inc.
440 1st St. NW, 3rd Fl.
Washington, DC 20001-2085
Phone: (202)638-2952
Fax: (202)638-4004
**Subject(s):** Children's Interests; Social Programs
**Circ:** 15,000

**Coal Voice  (5317)**
National Mining Association
101 Constitution Ave., NW, Ste. 500 E
Washington, DC 20001-2133
Phone: (202)463-2600
Fax: (202)463-2666

**Subject(s):** Mining and Minerals; Ecology and Conservation
**Circ:** (Combined)‡15,000

**Currents  (5351)**
Council for Advancement and Support of Education
1307 New York Ave. NW, Ste. 1000
Washington, DC 20005-4701
Phone: (202)328-2273
Fax: (202)387-4973
**Subject(s):** Public Relations; Education
**Circ:** ‡15,000

**Engineering Now  (31196)**
Virginia Polytechnic Institute and State University
333 Norris Hall
Blacksburg, VA 24061
Phone: (540)231-6641
Fax: (540)231-3031
**Subject(s):** Engineering (Various branches)
**Circ:** (Controlled)15,000

**The Federal Lawyer  (5386)**
Federal Bar Association
2215 M St. NW
Washington, DC 20037
Phone: (202)785-1614
Fax: (202)785-1568
**Subject(s):** Law
**Circ:** ‡15,000

**Foreign Service Journal  (5393)**
AFSA
2101 E St. NW
Washington, DC 20037
Phone: (202)338-4045
Fax: (202)338-8244
**Subject(s):** International Affairs; International Business and Economics
**Circ:** (Combined)‡15,000

**Hispanic Engineer  (12740)**
Career Communications Group Inc.
729 E Pratt St., No. 504
Baltimore, MD 21202
Phone: (410)244-7101
Fax: (410)752-1837
**Subject(s):** Engineering (Various branches); Hispanic Publications
**Circ:** ‡15,000

**Information Outlook  (31012)**
Special Libraries Association
331 S Patrick St.
Alexandria, VA 22314-3501
Phone: (703)647-4900
Fax: (703)647-4901
**Subject(s):** Library and Information Science
**Circ:** ‡15,000

**Journal of Adolescent & Adult Literacy  (5146)**
International Reading Association
800 Barksdale Rd.
PO Box 8139
Newark, DE 19714-8139
Phone: (302)731-1600
Fax: (302)731-1057
**Subject(s):** Education
**Circ:** ‡15,000

**Journal of Rehabilitation  (31031)**
National Rehabilitation Association
633 S. Washington St.
Alexandria, VA 22314
Phone: (703)836-0850
Fax: (703)836-0848
**Subject(s):** Handicapped
**Circ:** 15,000

**Lacrosse  (12803)**
US Lacrosse Inc.
113 W University Pkwy.
Baltimore, MD 21210
Phone: (410)235-7392
Fax: (410)366-6735
**Subject(s):** (General Sports)
**Circ:** (Non-paid)‡1,000
       (Paid)‡15,000

**Optics & Photonics News  (5606)**
Optical Society of America
2010 Massachusetts Ave., NW
Washington, DC 20036-1023
Phone: (202)223-8130
Fax: (202)223-1096

**Subject(s):** Ophthalmology, Optometry, and Optics; Telecommunications

**Circ:** (Paid)‡15,000

**Plastics Fabricating & Forming  (31429)**
Key Communications Inc.
PO Box 569
Garrisonville, VA 22463
Phone: (540)720-5584
Fax: (540)720-5687
**Subject(s):** Glass and China

**Circ:** (Controlled)‡15,000

**Randolph-Macon Woman's College Alumnae Bulletin  (31541)**
Randolph-Macon Woman's College
2500 Rivermont Ave.
Lynchburg, VA 24503
Phone: (434)947-8000
Fax: (434)947-8148
**Subject(s):** College Publications

**Circ:** (Controlled)‡15,000

**Regulation  (5664)**
Cato Institute
1000 Massachusetts Ave. NW
Washington, DC 20001-5403
Phone: (202)842-0200
Fax: (202)842-3490
**Subject(s):** Congressional and Federal Government Affairs

**Circ:** (Paid)1,500
(Controlled)15,000

**SpeciaList  (31071)**
Special Libraries Association
331 S Patrick St.
Alexandria, VA 22314-3501
Phone: (703)647-4900
Fax: (703)647-4901
**Subject(s):** Library and Information Science

**Circ:** (Combined)15,000

**TESOL Journal  (31076)**
Teachers of English to Speakers of Other Languages Inc.
700 S Washington St., Ste. 200
Alexandria, VA 22314-4287
Phone: (703)836-0774
Fax: (703)836-7864
**Subject(s):** Education; Philology, Language, and Linguistics

**Circ:** (Combined)15,000

**Urban Land Magazine  (5731)**
Urban Land Institute
1025 Thomas Jefferson NW, Ste. 500 W.
Washington, DC 20007
Phone: (202)624-7000
Fax: (202)624-7140
**Subject(s):** Real Estate

**Circ:** (Paid)15,000

**Weekend Adventures Magazine  (13083)**
PO Box 1895
Cumberland, MD 21501-1895
Phone: (301)722-3533
Fax: (301)722-8020
**Subject(s):** Travel and Tourism; (Outdoors)

**Circ:** (Non-paid)15,000

**Winner  (13197)**
The Health Connection
55 W Oak Ridge Dr.
Hagerstown, MD 21740
Phone: (301)393-3267
Fax: (301)393-4055
**Subject(s):** Substance Abuse and Treatment; Education; Youths' Interests

**Circ:** (Paid)15,000

**World Watch  (5764)**
Worldwatch Institute
1776 Massachusetts Ave., NW
Washington, DC 20036-1904
Phone: (202)452-1999
Fax: (202)296-7365
**Subject(s):** Ecology and Conservation; International Affairs; International Business and Economics

**Circ:** (Non-paid)‡1,200
(Paid)‡15,000

**NSBE Magazine  (31048)**
NSBE Publications
1454 Duke St.
Alexandria, VA 22314
Phone: (703)549-2207
Fax: (703)683-5312

**Subject(s):** Employment and Human Resources; Black Publications; Engineering (Various branches)

**Circ:** (Paid)‡8,000
(Non-paid)‡14,934

**National Alliance  (5560)**
National Alliance of Postal and Federal Employees
1628 11th St., NW
Washington, DC 20001
Phone: (202)939-6325
Fax: (202)939-6389
**Subject(s):** Congressional and Federal Government Affairs

**Circ:** ‡14,700

**Public Power  (5659)**
American Public Power Association
2301 M St. NW
Washington, DC 20037-1484
Phone: (202)467-2900
Fax: (202)467-2910
**Subject(s):** Power and Power Plants

**Circ:** (Paid)138
(Controlled)14,700

**AAA Today  (32537)**
Bluefield Automobile Club
622 Commerce St.
Bluefield, WV 24701-3107
Phone: (304)327-8187
Fax: (304)325-5137
**Subject(s):** Travel and Tourism; Automotive (Consumer)

**Circ:** ‡14,695

**The School Administrator  (31156)**
American Association of School Administrators
801 N. Quincy St., Ste. 700
Arlington, VA 22203-1730
Phone: (703)528-0700
Fax: (703)841-1543
**Subject(s):** Education

**Circ:** (Paid)14,500

**Operations Forum  (31053)**
Water Environment Federation
601 Wythe St.
Alexandria, VA 22314-1994
Phone: (703)684-2452
Fax: (703)684-2492
**Subject(s):** Water Supply and Sewage Disposal

**Circ:** (Paid)‡14,451

**Acquisition Review Quarterly  (31403)**
Defense Acquisition University Press
9820 Belvoir Rd.
Fort Belvoir, VA 22060-5565
Phone: (703)805-3801
Fax: (703)805-2917
**Subject(s):** Military and Navy

**Circ:** (Free)14,397

**Science Education  (5154)**
John Wiley and Sons Inc.
School of Education
132F Willard Hall Bldg.
Univ. of Delaware
Newark, DE 19716
**Subject(s):** Science (General)

**Circ:** (Paid)14,350

**The Annals of Dyslexia  (12662)**
The International Dyslexia Association
8600 LaSalle Rd., Chester Bldg., Ste. 382
Chester Bldg.
Ste. 382
Baltimore, MD 21286-2044
Phone: (410)296-0232
Fax: (410)321-5069
**Subject(s):** Health and Healthcare

**Circ:** 14,000

**Ferrum Magazine  (31398)**
Ferrum College
Alumni Office
Ferrum College
Ferrum, VA 24088
**Subject(s):** College Publications

**Circ:** (Controlled)‡14,000

**ITE Journal  (5452)**
Institute of Transportation Engineers
1099 14th St. NW, Ste. 300 W.
Washington, DC 20005-3438
Phone: (202)289-0222
Fax: (202)289-7722

**Subject(s):** Roads and Streets

**Circ:** ‡14,000

**OR/MS Today  (13244)**
The Institute for Operations Research and the Management Sciences
901 Elkridge Landing Rd., Ste. 400
Linthicum, MD 21090-2909
Phone: (410)850-0300
Fax: (410)684-2963
**Subject(s):** Business; Management and Administration

**Circ:** 14,000

**Pallet Enterprise  (31182)**
Industrial Reporting Inc.
10244 Timber Ridge Dr.
Ashland, VA 23005
Phone: (804)550-0323
Fax: (804)550-2181
**Subject(s):** Materials Handling; Wood and Woodworking

**Circ:** (Paid)150
(Controlled)‡14,000

**Sales & Marketing Ideas  (5680)**
National Association of Home Builders
1201 15th St. NW
Washington, DC 20005
Fax: (202)266-8195
**Subject(s):** Construction, Contracting, Building, and Excavating; Advertising and Marketing; Selling and Salesmanship

**Circ:** 14,000

**Worldwatch Paper Series  (5765)**
Worldwatch Institute
1776 Massachusetts Ave., NW
Washington, DC 20036-1904
Phone: (202)452-1999
Fax: (202)296-7365
**Subject(s):** Ecology and Conservation

**Circ:** (Non-paid)‡1,000
(Paid)‡14,000

**Print Solutions  (31057)**
Document Management Industries Association
433 E Monroe Ave.
Alexandria, VA 22301
Phone: (703)836-6232
Fax: (703)836-2241
**Subject(s):** Stationery, Office Equipment, and College Store Supplies

**Circ:** (Non-paid)‡625
(Paid)‡13,800

**Journal of Athletic Training  (31252)**
National Athletic Trainers' Association
Curry School of Education
University of Virginia
405 Emmet St.
Charlottesville, VA 22903
Phone: (804)924-6187
Fax: (804)924-1389
**Subject(s):** (General Sports)

**Circ:** ‡13,500

**O & P Almanac  (31049)**
American Orthotic & Prosthetic Association
330 John Carlyle St., Ste. 200
Alexandria, VA 22314
Phone: (571)431-0876
Fax: (571)431-0899
**Subject(s):** Physiology and Anatomy

**Circ:** ‡13,500

**Psychiatric Services  (13393)**
Association of Partners for Public Lands
2401 Blueridge Ave., Ste. 303
Wheaton, MD 20902-4517
Phone: (301)946-9475
Fax: (301)946-9478
**Subject(s):** Psychology and Psychiatry

**Circ:** (Paid)‡10,000
(Non-paid)‡13,500

**Journal of the American Podiatric Medical Association  (12976)**
American Podiatric Medical Association
9312 Old Georgetown Rd.
Bethesda, MD 20814-1621
Phone: (301)581-9200
Fax: (301)530-2752
**Subject(s):** Podiatry

**Circ:** (Non-paid)‡1,693
(Paid)‡13,397

**Acoustic Output Measurement Standard for Diagnostic Ultrasound Equipment** (13233)
American Institute of Ultrasound in Medicine
14750 Sweitzer Ln., No. 100
Laurel, MD 20707-5906
Phone: (301)498-4100
Fax: (301)498-4450
**Subject(s):** Radiology, Ultrasound, and Nuclear Medicine
**Circ:** 13,000

**Contingencies** (5337)
American Academy of Actuaries
1100 17th St. NW, 7th Fl.
Washington, DC 20036
Phone: (202)223-8196
Fax: (202)872-1948
**Subject(s):** Insurance
**Circ:** (Controlled)‡10,000
(Paid)‡13,000

**Doors and Hardware** (31231)
Door and Hardware Institute
14150 Newbrook Dr., Ste. 200
Chantilly, VA 20151
Phone: (703)222-2010
Fax: (703)222-2410
**Subject(s):** Hardware
**Circ:** (Non-paid)‡200
(Paid)‡13,000

**Foundation News & Commentary** (5394)
Council on Foundations
1828 L St. NW, Ste. 300
Washington, DC 20036
Phone: (202)466-6512
Fax: (202)785-3926
**Subject(s):** Philanthropy and Humanitarianism
**Circ:** ‡13,000

**Future Reflections** (12732)
National Federation of the Blind
1800 Johnson St.
Baltimore, MD 21230
Phone: (410)659-9314
Fax: (410)685-5653
**Subject(s):** Blind and Visually Challenged
**Circ:** (Combined)‡13,000

**Journal of Housing and Community Development** (5486)
National Association of Housing and Redevelopment Officials
630 Eye St. NW
Washington, DC 20001
Phone: (202)289-3500
Fax: (202)289-8181
**Subject(s):** Construction, Contracting, Building, and Excavating
**Circ:** (Non-paid)13,000

**Community Colleges Journal** (5325)
American Association of Community Colleges
1 Dupont Cir. NW, Ste. 410
Washington, DC 20036
Phone: (202)728-0200
Fax: (202)833-2467
**Subject(s):** Education
**Circ:** (Controlled)‡21
(Paid)‡12,800

**Conscience** (5331)
Catholics for a Free Choice
1436 U St. NW, No. 301
Washington, DC 20009-3997
Phone: (202)986-6093
Fax: (202)332-7995
**Subject(s):** Abortion; Religious Publications; Women's Interests
**Circ:** (Combined)12,500

**Journal of Family & Consumer Sciences** (31024)
American Association of Family and Consumer Sciences
400 N. Columbus St., Ste. 202
Alexandria, VA 22314-2752
**Subject(s):** Home Economics
**Circ:** (Non-paid)150
(Paid)12,500

**Military Medicine** (12991)
Association of Military Surgeons of the U.S. (AMSUS)
9320 Old Georgetown Rd.
Bethesda, MD 20814
Phone: (301)897-8800
Fax: (301)503-5446
**Subject(s):** Medicine and Surgery; Military and Navy
**Circ:** (Paid)‡12,500

**APMA News** (12938)
American Podiatric Medical Association
9312 Old Georgetown Rd.
Bethesda, MD 20814-1621
Phone: (301)581-9200
Fax: (301)530-2752
**Subject(s):** Podiatry
**Circ:** (Non-paid)‡125
(Paid)‡12,375

**Journal of Clinical Microbiology** (5466)
ASM Journals
1752 N. St., NW
Washington, DC 20036-2904
Phone: (202)737-3600
Fax: (202)942-9333
**Subject(s):** Biology
**Circ:** (Combined)‡12,253

**American Journal of Audiology** (13283)
American Speech-Language-Hearing Association
10801 Rockville Pke.
Rockville, MD 20852
Phone: (301)897-5700
Fax: (301)571-0457
**Subject(s):** Philology, Language, and Linguistics; Health and Healthcare
**Circ:** 12,000

**Art Calendar** (13317)
PO Box 2675
Salisbury, MD 21802
Phone: (410)749-9625
Fax: (410)749-9626
**Subject(s):** Art and Art History; Advertising and Marketing
**Circ:** (Paid)12,000

**ASEE Prism** (5254)
American Society for Engineering Education
1818 N St., NW, Ste. 600
Washington, DC 20036-2479
Phone: (202)331-3500
Fax: (202)265-8504
**Subject(s):** Education; Engineering (Various branches)
**Circ:** ‡12,000

**Clinical Chemistry** (31242)
American Association for Clinical Chemistry
c/o Dr. David E. Bruns, Editor
PO Box 3757 University Station
Charlottesville, VA 22907-0757
Phone: (804)979-7599
Fax: (804)979-7599
**Subject(s):** Chemistry, Chemicals, and Chemical Engineering; Medicine and Surgery
**Circ:** (Combined)12,000

**CovertAction Quarterly** (5341)
C.A. Publications Inc.
1500 Massachusetts Ave. NW, No. 732
Washington, DC 20005
Phone: (202)331-9763
Fax: (202)331-9751
**Subject(s):** Politics; Congressional and Federal Government Affairs
**Circ:** ‡12,000

**Revista Panamericana de Salud Publica** (5671)
Pan American Health Organization
Publications Program, PAHO
525 23rd St. NW
Washington, DC 20037
Phone: (202)974-3405
**Subject(s):** International Affairs; Health and Healthcare
**Circ:** ‡12,000

**Spiritual Life** (5701)
Washington Province of Discalced Carmelite Friars Inc.
2131 Lincoln Rd. NE
Washington, DC 20002-1199
Fax: (202)832-8967
**Subject(s):** Religious Publications
**Circ:** 12,000

**Virginia United Methodist Advocate** (31440)
United Methodist Communications
10330 Staples Mill Rd.
PO Box 1719
Glen Allen, VA 23060
Phone: (804)521-1100
Fax: (804)521-1173
**Subject(s):** Religious Publications
**Circ:** (Paid)12,000

**Mobility** (5547)
Employee Relocation Council (ERC)
1717 Pennsylvania Ave. NW, Ste. 800
Washington, DC 20006
Phone: (202)857-0857
Fax: (202)659-8631
**Subject(s):** Employment and Human Resources; Real Estate
**Circ:** (Non-paid)‡498
(Paid)‡11,970

**Journal for Research in Mathematics Education** (31730)
National Council of Teachers of Mathematics
1906 Association Dr.
Reston, VA 20191-1502
Phone: (703)620-9840
Fax: (703)476-2970
**Subject(s):** Mathematics; Education
**Circ:** ‡11,844

**AABB News** (12914)
American Association of Blood Banks
8101 Glenbrook Rd.
Bethesda, MD 20814-2749
Phone: (301)907-6977
Fax: (301)951-7150
**Subject(s):** Health and Healthcare
**Circ:** 11,500

**Port of Baltimore** (13378)
Media Two
22 W Pennsylvania Ave., Ste. 305
Towson, MD 21204
Phone: (410)828-0120
Fax: (410)825-1002
**Subject(s):** Ships and Shipping
**Circ:** (Controlled)‡11,500

**School Library Media Activities Monthly** (12858)
LMS Associates
17 E. Henrietta St.
Baltimore, MD 21230
Phone: (410)685-8621
Fax: (410)685-0870
**Subject(s):** Library and Information Science; Education
**Circ:** (Paid)⊕11,500

**The Consultant Pharmacist** (31620)
American Society of Consultant Pharmacists
Insight Therapeutics, LLC
129 W. Virginia Beach Blvd., Ste. 105
Norfolk, VA 23510
**Subject(s):** Drugs and Pharmaceuticals
**Circ:** (Paid)‡11,000
(Controlled)‡11,450

**AAPS Newsmagazine** (31101)
American Association of Pharmaceutical Scientists
2107 Wilson Blvd., No. 700
Arlington, VA 22201-3042
Phone: (703)243-2800
Fax: (703)243-9650
**Subject(s):** Drugs and Pharmaceuticals; Science (General); Medicine and Surgery; Health and Healthcare
**Circ:** 11,000

**Advances in Physiology Education** (12917)
The American Physiological Society
9650 Rockville Pke.
Bethesda, MD 20814-3991
Phone: (301)634-7164
Fax: (301)634-7241
**Subject(s):** Physiology and Anatomy; Education
**Circ:** (Combined)‡11,000

**The American Biology Teacher** (31692)
National Association of Biology Teachers
12030 Sunrise Valley Dr., Ste. 110
Reston, VA 20191
Phone: (703)264-9696
Fax: (703)264-7778
**Subject(s):** Biology; Education
**Circ:** (Controlled)‡100
(Paid)‡11,000

**American String Teacher** (31331)
American String Teachers Association with National School Orchestra Association
4153 Chain Bridge Rd.
Enterprise Hall 3rd Floor
Fairfax, VA 22030-4444
Phone: (703)279-2113

Fax: (703)279-2114
**Subject(s):** Music and Musical Instruments; Performing Arts; Education
**Circ:** 11,000

**Announcer** (13041)
American Association of Physics Teachers
One Physics Ellipse
College Park, MD 20740-3845
Phone: (301)209-3300
Fax: (301)209-0845
**Subject(s):** Physics
**Circ:** (Paid)‡11,000

**Journal of Neurosurgery** (31253)
1224 W Main St., Ste. 450
Charlottesville, VA 22903
Phone: (434)924-5503
Fax: (434)924-2702
**Subject(s):** Medicine and Surgery
**Circ:** ‡11,000

**National Genealogical Society Quarterly** (5563)
Gallaudet Research Institute
Hall Memorial Bldg., HMB S-437
800 Florida Ave. NE
Washington, DC 20002-3695
Phone: (202)651-5575
Fax: (202)651-5746
**Subject(s):** History and Genealogy
**Circ:** ‡11,000

**News in Physiological Sciences (NIPS)** (12995)
The American Physiological Society
9650 Rockville Pke.
Bethesda, MD 20814-3991
Phone: (301)634-7164
Fax: (301)634-7241
**Subject(s):** Physiology and Anatomy
**Circ:** (Paid)‡11,000

**Officer Review** (31051)
Military Order of the World Wars
435 N Lee St.
Alexandria, VA 22314
Phone: (703)683-4911
Fax: (703)683-4501
**Subject(s):** Military and Navy
**Circ:** (Non-paid)‡100
 (Paid)‡11,000

**Applied and Environmental Microbiology** (5244)
ASM Journals
1752 N. St., NW
Washington, DC 20036-2904
Phone: (202)737-3600
Fax: (202)942-9333
**Subject(s):** Biology
**Circ:** (Combined)‡10,880

**American Industrial Hygiene Association Journal** (31329)
American Industrial Hygiene Association
2700 Prosperity Ave., Ste. 250
Fairfax, VA 22031-4319
Phone: (703)849-8888
Fax: (703)207-3561
**Subject(s):** Health and Healthcare
**Circ:** (Paid)‡10,750

**Clinical Microbiology Reviews** (5313)
ASM Journals
1752 N. St., NW
Washington, DC 20036-2904
Phone: (202)737-3600
Fax: (202)942-9333
**Subject(s):** Biology
**Circ:** ‡10,657

**Catholic Woman** (31117)
National Council of Catholic Women
200 N. Glebe Rd., Ste.703
Arlington, VA 22203
Phone: (703)224-0990
Fax: (703)224-0991
**Subject(s):** Religious Publications; Women's Interests
**Circ:** 10,500

**Health Affairs** (12970)
Project HOPE
7500 Old Georgetown Rd., Ste. 600
Bethesda, MD 20814-6133
Phone: (301)656-7401
Fax: (301)654-2845

**Subject(s):** Health and Healthcare
**Circ:** (Paid)‡10,500

**Mid-Atlantic Thoroughbred** (13366)
Maryland Horse Breeders Association
30 E. Padonia Rd., Ste. 303
PO Box 427
Timonium, MD 21093
Phone: (410)252-2100
Fax: (410)560-0503
**Subject(s):** (Horses and Horse Racing)
**Circ:** (Paid)‡10,500

**Antimicrobial Agents and Chemotherapy** (5242)
ASM Journals
1752 N. St., NW
Washington, DC 20036-2904
Phone: (202)737-3600
Fax: (202)942-9333
**Subject(s):** Chemistry, Chemicals, and Chemical Engineering; Medicine and Surgery
**Circ:** (Non-paid)‡30
 (Paid)‡10,314

**Microbiology and Molecular Biology Reviews** (5542)
ASM Journals
1752 N. St., NW
Washington, DC 20036-2904
Phone: (202)737-3600
Fax: (202)942-9333
**Subject(s):** Biology
**Circ:** (Combined)‡10,311

**Franchising World** (5396)
International Franchise Association
1350 New York Ave. NW, Ste. 900
Washington, DC 20005-4709
Phone: (202)628-8000
Fax: (202)628-0812
**Subject(s):** Business; International Business and Economics
**Circ:** (Paid)‡233
 (Controlled)‡10,200

**AGRR** (31427)
AutoGlass Repair and Replacement
PO Box 569
Garrisonville, VA 22463
Phone: (540)720-5584
Fax: (540)720-5687
**Subject(s):** Glass and China
**Circ:** (Non-paid)10,190

**Geotimes** (31003)
American Geological Institute
4220 King St.
Alexandria, VA 22302-1502
Phone: (703)379-2480
Fax: (703)379-7563
**Subject(s):** Geology
**Circ:** (Non-paid)502
 (Paid)10,092

**CQ Weekly** (5343)
Congressional Quarterly
1255, 22nd St. NW
Washington, DC 20037
Phone: (202)419-8500
Fax: (800)380-3810
**Subject(s):** Congressional and Federal Government Affairs
**Circ:** (Paid)6,412
 (Paid)10,083

**ACSM Bulletin** (13155)
American Congress on Surveying and Mapping
6 Montgomery Village Ave., Ste. 403
Gaithersburg, MD 20879-3557
Phone: (240)632-9716
Fax: (240)632-1321
**Subject(s):** Engineering (Various branches); Geography
**Circ:** 10,000

**Albemarle** (31232)
Carden Jennings Publishing
375 Greenbrier Dr., Ste. 100
Charlottesville, VA 22901-1618
Phone: (434)817-2000
Fax: (434)817-2020
**Subject(s):** Lifestyle
**Circ:** (Paid)⊕10,000

**American Hiker** (13339)
American Hiking Society
1422 Fenwick Ln.
Silver Spring, MD 20910-3328
Phone: (301)565-6704

Fax: (301)565-6714
**Subject(s):** (Outdoors)
**Circ:** 10,000

**American Journal on Mental Retardation** (5214)
American Association on Mental Retardation
444 N Capitol St. NW, Ste. 846
Washington, DC 20001-1512
Phone: (202)387-1968
Fax: (202)387-2193
**Subject(s):** Health and Healthcare
**Circ:** (Combined)10,000

**The American Journal of Sports Medicine** (31233)
The American Orthopaedic Society for Sports Medicine
675 Peter Jefferson Pky., Ste. 470
Charlottesville, VA 22911
**Subject(s):** Medicine and Surgery
**Circ:** (Non-paid)‡125
 (Paid)‡10,000

**American Optician** (31488)
Opticians Association of America
441 Carlisle Dr.
Herndon, VA 20170
Phone: (703)437-8780
Fax: (703)437-0727
**Subject(s):** Ophthalmology, Optometry, and Optics
**Circ:** 10,000

**American Whitewater** (13359)
204 B. Philadelphia Ave.
Takoma Park, MD 20912
Phone: (828)252-0728
Fax: (828)252-6482
**Subject(s):** (Outdoors); (Water Sports)
**Circ:** 10,000

**BioScience** (5271)
American Institute of Biological Sciences
1444 I St. NW, Ste. 200
Washington, DC 20005
Phone: (202)628-1500
Fax: (202)628-1509
**Subject(s):** Biology
**Circ:** (Non-paid)‡402
 (Paid)‡10,000

**BYWAYS** (31613)
National Motorcoach Network
PO Box 1088
Mount Jackson, VA 22842-2602
Phone: (703)250-2697
Fax: (703)250-1477
**Subject(s):** Travel and Tourism
**Circ:** (Non-paid)‡10,000

**Defense Transportation Journal** (30994)
National Defense Transportation Association
50 S Pickett St., Ste. 220
Alexandria, VA 22304-7296
Phone: (703)751-5011
Fax: (703)823-8761
**Subject(s):** Military and Navy; Transportation, Traffic, and Shipping
**Circ:** ‡10,000

**EA Journal** (5362)
National Association of Enrolled Agents
1120 Connecticut Ave., NW, Ste. 460
Washington, DC 20036
Phone: (202)822-NAEA
Fax: (202)822-6270
**Subject(s):** Business; Taxation and Tariff
**Circ:** 10,000

**House, Home and Garden** (32663)
Berkley House Direct
809 Virginia Ave.
Martinsburg, WV 25401-2131
Phone: (304)267-2673
Fax: (304)262-4585
**Subject(s):** Home and Garden
**Circ:** ‡10,000

**Journal of Health Education** (31718)
American Alliance for Health, Physical Education, Recreation & Dance
1900 Association Dr.
Reston, VA 20191-1598
Phone: (703)476-3400
Fax: (703)476-9527
**Subject(s):** Health and Healthcare; Education
**Circ:** ‡10,000

**Journal of Ultrasound in Medicine** (13236)
AIUM
14750 Sweitzer Ln., Ste. 100
Laurel, MD 20707-5906
Phone: (301)498-4100
Fax: (301)498-4450
**Subject(s):** Medicine and Surgery
**Circ:** (Paid)10,000

**Lube Report** (31383)
LNG Publishing Company Inc.
6105-G Arlington Blvd.,
Falls Church, VA 22044
Phone: (703)536-0800
Fax: (703)536-0803
**Subject(s):** Petroleum, Oil, and Gas; Oils and Fats (Animal & Vegetable); Automotive (Trade)
**Circ:** (Controlled)10,000

**Multinational Monitor** (5556)
Essential Information Inc.
PO Box 19405
Washington, DC 20036
Phone: (202)387-8030
Fax: (202)234-5176
**Subject(s):** International Affairs
**Circ:** (Non-paid)‡2,000
(Paid)‡10,000

**Public Management (PM)** (5658)
International City/County Management Association
777 N Capitol St. NE, Ste. 500
Washington, DC 20002-4201
Phone: (202)289-4262
Fax: (202)962-3500
**Subject(s):** State, Municipal, and County Administration
**Circ:** (Controlled)‡10,000

**Strategies** (31754)
American Alliance for Health, Physical Education, Recreation & Dance
1900 Association Dr.
Reston, VA 20191-1598
Phone: (703)476-3400
Fax: (703)476-9527
**Subject(s):** Education; Physical Education and Athletics
**Circ:** ‡10,000

**TESOL Quarterly** (31077)
Teachers of English to Speakers of Other Languages Inc.
700 S Washington St., Ste. 200
Alexandria, VA 22314-4287
Phone: (703)836-0774
Fax: (703)836-7864
**Subject(s):** Education; Philology, Language, and Linguistics
**Circ:** ‡10,000

**Vestnik** (12880)
VESTNIK
6100 Park Heights Ave.
Baltimore, MD 21215
Phone: (410)358-0900
**Subject(s):** Soviet Interests; Ethnic Publications; Russian
**Circ:** (Combined)10,000

**Roanoker Magazine** (31840)
Leisure Publishing Co.
3424 Brambleton Ave.
Roanoke, VA 24018
Phone: (540)989-6138
Fax: (540)989-7603
**Subject(s):** Local, State, and Regional Publications
**Circ:** (Non-paid)2,450
(Paid)9,850

**Journal of Bacteriology** (5464)
ASM Journals
1752 N. St., NW
Washington, DC 20036-2904
Phone: (202)737-3600
Fax: (202)942-9333
**Subject(s):** Biology
**Circ:** (Combined)‡9,679

**National Journal** (5570)
National Journal Group Inc.
The Watergate
600 New Hampshire Ave., NW
Washington, DC 20037
Phone: (202)739-8400
Fax: (202)833-8069
**Subject(s):** Politics
**Circ:** (Paid)9,600

**The Mission Helper** (12818)
Mission Helpers of the Sacred Heart
1001 W Joppa Rd.
Baltimore, MD 21204-3787
Phone: (410)823-8585
Fax: (410)825-6355
**Subject(s):** Religious Publications
**Circ:** (Controlled)9,500

**PE & RS Photogrammetric Engineering & Remote Sensing** (13001)
The Imaging and Geospatial Information Society
5410 Grosvenor Ln., Ste. 210
Bethesda, MD 20814-2160
Phone: (301)493-0290
Fax: (301)493-0208
**Subject(s):** Engineering (Various branches)
**Circ:** ‡9,500

**The Sojourner** (31070)
National Sojourners Inc.
8301 E Blvd. Dr.
Alexandria, VA 22308
Phone: (703)765-5000
Fax: (703)765-8390
**Subject(s):** Military and Navy; Masons
**Circ:** (Non-paid)‡200
(Paid)‡9,500

**The Humanist** (5428)
American Humanist Association
National Office
1777 T St. NW
Washington, DC 20009-7125
Phone: (202)238-9088
Fax: (202)238-9003
**Subject(s):** Philosophy
**Circ:** (Non-paid)‡5,664
(Paid)‡9,485

**Molecular and Cellular Biology** (5550)
ASM Journals
1752 N. St., NW
Washington, DC 20036-2904
Phone: (202)737-3600
Fax: (202)942-9333
**Subject(s):** Biology
**Circ:** (Combined)‡9,393

**Fisheries** (12967)
American Fisheries Society
5410 Grosvenor Ln., Ste. 110
Bethesda, MD 20814
Phone: (301)897-8616
Fax: (301)897-8096
**Subject(s):** Fish and Commercial Fisheries
**Circ:** ‡9,300

**Wings of Gold** (31087)
Association of Naval Aviation Inc.
2550 Huntington Ave., No. 201
Alexandria, VA 22303-1400
Phone: (703)960-2490
Fax: (703)960-4490
**Subject(s):** Aviation; Military and Navy
**Circ:** (Non-paid)‡905
(Paid)‡9,200

**Journal of Virology** (5518)
ASM Journals
1752 N. St., NW
Washington, DC 20036-2904
Phone: (202)737-3600
Fax: (202)942-9333
**Subject(s):** Biology
**Circ:** (Non-paid)‡30
(Paid)‡9,195

**JPEN: Journal of Parenteral and Enteral Nutrition** (13348)
American Society for Parenteral and Enteral Nutrition
8630 Fenton St., Ste. 412
Silver Spring, MD 20910
Phone: (301)587-6315
Fax: (301)587-3323
**Subject(s):** Medicine and Surgery
**Circ:** (Non-paid)‡620
(Paid)‡9,129

**National Vanguard** (32616)
National Vanguard Books
PO Box 330
Hillsboro, WV 24946
Fax: (304)653-4690
**Subject(s):** Alternative and Underground
**Circ:** ‡9,100

**Journal of the American Academy of Audiology** (31705)
American Academy of Audiology
11730 Plaza America Dr., Ste. 300
Reston, VA 20190
Phone: (703)790-8466
Fax: (703)790-8631
**Subject(s):** Hearing and Speech; Medicine and Surgery; Health and Healthcare
**Circ:** (Paid)9,065

**Club Director** (5315)
National Club Association
1201 15th St., No. 450
Washington, DC 20005
Phone: (202)822-9822
Fax: (202)822-9808
**Subject(s):** Clubs and Societies
**Circ:** (Controlled)⊕**9,058**

**EH & S Solutions (Environmental Health & Safety Solutions)** (13258)
Weil Communications and Marketing Inc.
PO Box 535
Olney, MD 20830
Phone: (301)924-5490
Fax: (301)924-0265
**Subject(s):** Building Management and Maintenance
**Circ:** (Paid)‡1,600
(Non-paid)9,000

**National Vital Statistics Report** (13214)
National Center for Health Statistics
3311 Toledo Rd.
Hyattsville, MD 20782
Phone: (301)458-4468
Fax: (301)458-4034
**Subject(s):** Statistics
**Circ:** (Non-paid)‡9,000

**Pastoral Music** (13354)
National Association of Pastoral Musicians
962 Wayne Ave., Ste. 210
Silver Spring, MD 20910-4461
Phone: (240)247-3000
Fax: (240)247-3001
**Subject(s):** Music and Musical Instruments
**Circ:** 9000

**UDC Magazine** (31801)
Brannon Publishing Inc.
UDC Business Office
328 North Blvd.
Richmond, VA 23220-4057
Phone: (804)355-1636
Fax: (804)353-1396
**Subject(s):** Clubs and Societies; History and Genealogy
**Circ:** (Paid)9,000

**Infection and Immunity** (5434)
ASM Journals
1752 N. St., NW
Washington, DC 20036-2904
Phone: (202)737-3600
Fax: (202)942-9333
**Subject(s):** Medicine and Surgery
**Circ:** (Combined)‡8,966

**Fabricare** (13234)
International Fabricare Institute
14700 Sweitzer Lane
Laurel, MD 20707
Phone: (301)622-1900
Fax: (301)236-9320
**Subject(s):** Laundry and Dry Cleaning
**Circ:** (Paid)8,800

**Annals of the Association of American Geographers** (5238)
1710 16th St. NW
Washington, DC 20009-3198
Phone: (202)234-1450
Fax: (202)234-2744
**Subject(s):** Geography
**Circ:** ‡8,750

**About Campus** (5184)
American College Personnel Association
1 Dupont Cir. NW, Ste. 300
Washington, DC 20036-1188
Phone: (202)835-2272
Fax: (202)296-3286

**Subject(s):** Education; Management and Administration

Circ: 8,500

**Coal People Magazine** (32553)
PO Box 6247
629 Virginia Street West
Charleston, WV 25362-6247
Phone: (304)342-4129
Fax: (304)343-3124
**Subject(s):** Mining and Minerals

Circ: (Paid)‡3,000
(Non-paid)‡8,500

**Journal of Counseling Psychology** (13053)
American Psychological Association
Department of Psychology
College Park, MD 20742
Phone: (301)314-9202
Fax: (301)314-9202
**Subject(s):** Psychology and Psychiatry

Circ: ‡8,500

**NRB** (31557)
National Religious Broadcasters
9510 Technology Dr.
Manassas, VA 20110
Phone: (703)330-7000
Fax: (703)330-7100
**Subject(s):** Radio, Television, Cable, and Video

Circ: (Controlled)‡8,500

**Surveying and Land Information Science** (13176)
American Congress on Surveying and Mapping
6 Montgomery Village Ave., Ste. 403
Gaithersburg, MD 20879-3557
Phone: (240)632-9716
Fax: (240)632-1321
**Subject(s):** Engineering (Various branches); Geography

Circ: (Paid)8,500

**Vertiflite** (31082)
American Helicopter Society International
217 N. Washington St.
Alexandria, VA 22314-2538
Phone: (703)684-6777
Fax: (703)739-9279
**Subject(s):** Aviation

Circ: ‡8,500

**Virginia Magazine of History and Biography** (31808)
Virginia Historical Society
PO Box 7311
Richmond, VA 23221-0311
Phone: (804)358-4901
Fax: (804)355-2399
**Subject(s):** History and Genealogy

Circ: (Non-paid)‡8,500

**Water Environment Research** (31085)
Water Environment Federation
601 Wythe St.
Alexandria, VA 22314-1994
Phone: (703)684-2452
Fax: (703)684-2492
**Subject(s):** Ecology and Conservation; Water Supply and Sewage Disposal

Circ: ‡8,500

**Distribution Channels** (31341)
American Wholesale Marketers Association
2750 Prosperity Ave., Ste. 530
Fairfax, VA 22031
Phone: (703)208-3358
Fax: (703)573-5738
**Subject(s):** Confectionaries and Frozen Dairy Products

Circ: (Paid)3,754
(Controlled)8,323

**Quotarian** (5662)
Quota International
1420 21st St., NW
Washington, DC 20036
Phone: (202)331-9694
Fax: (202)331-4395
**Subject(s):** Service Industries

Circ: (Controlled)⊕8,322

**Administrative Eyecare** (31326)
American Society of Ophthalmic Administrators
4000 Legato Rd., No. 850
Fairfax, VA 22033
Phone: (703)591-2220
Fax: (703)591-0614

**Subject(s):** Ophthalmology, Optometry, and Optics; Management and Administration

Circ: 8,000

**American Jails** (13188)
American Jail Association
1135 Professional Ct.
Hagerstown, MD 21740-5853
Phone: (301)790-3930
Fax: (301)790-2941
**Subject(s):** Police, Penology, and Penal Institutions

Circ: 8,000

**Composites Manufacturing** (31118)
Composites Fabricators Association
1010 N. Globe Rd., Ste. 450
Arlington, VA 22201
Phone: (703)525-0511
Fax: (703)525-0743
**Subject(s):** Commerce and Industry; Building Materials, Concrete, Brick, and Tile; Automotive (Trade)

Circ: (Combined)8,000

**ICA Review** (31126)
International Chiropractors Association
1110 N Glebe Rd., Ste. 650
Arlington, VA 22201
Phone: (703)528-5000
Fax: (703)528-5023
**Subject(s):** Chiropractic

Circ: (Paid)‡8,000

**Lambda Book Report** (5528)
Lambda Literary Foundation
PO Box 73910
Washington, DC 20056
Phone: (202)682-0952
Fax: (202)682-0955
**Subject(s):** Gay and Lesbian Interests; Literature and Literary Reviews; Women's Interests

Circ: (Non-paid)150
(Paid)8,000

**The Law Forum** (12805)
University of Baltimore
1420 N Charles St.
Baltimore, MD 21202
Phone: (410)837-4459
**Subject(s):** Law; College Publications

Circ: (Controlled)8,000

**Military Retailer** (12992)
Downey Communications Inc.
4800 Montgomery Ln., Ste. 710
Bethesda, MD 20814-3461
Phone: (301)718-7600
Fax: (301)718-7604
**Subject(s):** Military and Navy; Food and Grocery Trade

Circ: (Controlled)8,000

**The Professional Geographer** (5631)
San Diego State University
1710 Sixteenth St., NW
San Diego State University
Washington, DC 20009-3198
Phone: (202)234-1450
Fax: (202)234-2744
**Subject(s):** Geography

Circ: 8,000

**The Public Interest** (5657)
National Affairs Inc.
1112 16th St. NW, Ste. 140
Washington, DC 20036
Phone: (202)785-8555
**Subject(s):** Sociology; Economics; Politics

Circ: 8,000

**Research Quarterly for Exercise and Sport** (31751)
American Alliance for Health, Physical Education, Recreation & Dance
1900 Association Dr.
Reston, VA 20191-1598
Phone: (703)476-3400
Fax: (703)476-9527
**Subject(s):** Education; (Physical Fitness)

Circ: (Paid)8,000

**Rural Cooperatives** (5676)
U.S. Department of Agriculture, Rural Business - Cooperative Service
Mail Stop 0107
1400 Independence Ave. SW
Washington, DC 20250-0107
Phone: (202)720-4581

Fax: (202)720-2080
**Subject(s):** General Agriculture; Food Production

Circ: (Paid)8,000

**The Vintage and Classic Baseball Collector** (13211)
Pretty Panda Publishing
PO Box 1345
Hunt Valley, MD 21030
Phone: (410)560-2298
**Subject(s):** Collecting; (Baseball)

Circ: (Controlled)8,000

**Journal of Abnormal Psychology** (5456)
American Psychological Association
750 1st St. NE
Washington, DC 20002-4242
Phone: (202)336-5500
Fax: (202)336-6012
**Subject(s):** Psychology and Psychiatry

Circ: ‡7,900

**Professional Psychology** (5632)
American Psychological Association
750 1st St. NE
Washington, DC 20002-4242
Phone: (202)336-5500
Fax: (202)336-6012
**Subject(s):** Psychology and Psychiatry

Circ: ‡7,800

**NCP: Nutrition in Clinical Practice** (13353)
American Society for Parenteral and Enteral Nutrition
8630 Fenton St., Ste. 412
Silver Spring, MD 20910
Phone: (301)587-6315
Fax: (301)587-3323
**Subject(s):** Medicine and Surgery

Circ: (Non-paid)‡520
(Paid)‡7,609

**Update (Library of Congress)** (5730)
National Library Service for the Blind and Physically Handicapped
1291 Taylor St. NW
Washington, DC 20011
Phone: (202)707-5100
Fax: (202)707-0712
**Subject(s):** Library and Information Science; Handicapped

Circ: (Non-paid)7,600

**ATA Chronicle** (30980)
American Translators Association
225 Reinekers Ln., Ste. 590
Alexandria, VA 22314
Phone: (703)683-6100
Fax: (703)683-6122
**Subject(s):** Philology, Language, and Linguistics

Circ: 7,500

**Educational Technology Review** (31621)
Association for the Advancement of Computing in Education
PO Box 3728
Norfolk, VA 23514
Phone: (757)623-7588
Fax: (703)997-8760
**Subject(s):** Education

Circ: ‡7,500

**IEEE Circuits and Devices** (13296)
The Institute of Electrical & Electronics Engineers Inc.
c/o Dr. Ronald W. Waynant, FDA/CDRH, HFZ-134
12725 Twinbrook Pkwy, Rm. 267
Rockville, MD 20857
Phone: (301)827-4688
Fax: (301)827-4677
**Subject(s):** Computers; Electronics Engineering

Circ: (Paid)7,500

**Maryland Medicine** (12811)
MedChi
1211 Cathedral St.
Baltimore, MD 21201
Phone: (410)539-0872
Fax: (410)547-0915
**Subject(s):** Medicine and Surgery

Circ: ‡7,500

**Scrap** (5687)
Institute of Scrap Recycling Industries
1325 G. St. NW, Ste. 1000
Washington, DC 20005-3104
Phone: (202)737-1770
Fax: (202)626-0900

**Subject(s):** Metal, Metallurgy, and Metal Trade; Waste Management and Recycling
**Circ:** (Paid)7322

**Miniature Donkey Talk** (13389)
Pheasant Meadow Farm
1338 Hughes Shop Rd.
Westminster, MD 21158
Phone: (410)875-0118
Fax: (410)857-9145
**Subject(s):** Zoology
**Circ:** (Combined)7,300

**ASTRO News** (31334)
American Society for Therapeutic Radiology and Oncology
12500 Fair Lakes Cir., Ste. 375
Fairfax, VA 22033-3882
Phone: (703)502-1550
Fax: (703)502-7852
**Subject(s):** Radiology, Ultrasound, and Nuclear Medicine
**Circ:** 7,200

**Proceedings of the National Academy of Sciences of the United States of America** (5630)
National Academy of Sciences
500 Fifth St., NW
NAS 340
Washington, DC 20001
Phone: (202)334-2348
Fax: (202)334-1346
**Subject(s):** Science (General)
**Circ:** (Non-paid)2,300
(Paid)7,200

**Atlantic Control States Beverage Journal** (32775)
Atlantic Control States Beverage Journal Inc.
2001 Main Street Ste.203
Wheeling, WV 26003
Phone: (304)232-7620
Fax: (304)233-1236
**Subject(s):** Beverages, Brewing, and Bottling
**Circ:** (Paid)3,675
(Controlled)7,159

**Environmental Science & Technology** (5377)
American Chemical Society
1155 16th St. NW
Washington, DC 20036
Phone: (202)872-4600
Fax: (202)872-6067
**Subject(s):** Ecology and Conservation
**Circ:** 7,100

**Independent Banker** (5433)
Independent Community Bankers of America
One Thomas Cir. NW, Ste. 400
Washington, DC 20005-5802
Phone: (202)659-8111
Fax: (202)659-9216
**Subject(s):** Banking, Finance, and Investments
**Circ:** (Non-paid)‡2,329
(Paid)‡7,045

**Environment** (5375)
Heldref Publications
1319 18th St., NW
Washington, DC 20036-1802
Phone: (202)296-6267
Fax: (202)296-5149
**Subject(s):** Ecology and Conservation
**Circ:** (Combined)7,020

**ACCEL** (12915)
American College of Cardiology
9111 Old Georgetown Rd.
Bethesda, MD 20814-1699
Phone: (301)897-5400
Fax: (301)897-9745
**Subject(s):** Medicine and Surgery; Health and Healthcare
**Circ:** 7,000

**Alhambra** (12648)
Order of Alhambra
4200 Leeds Ave.
Baltimore, MD 21229
Phone: (410)242-0660
Fax: (410)536-5729
**Subject(s):** Religious Publications; Handicapped
**Circ:** 7,000

**Animal Sheltering Magazine** (5237)
Humane Society of the United States
2100 L St. NW
Washington, DC 20037
Phone: (202)452-1100
Fax: (301)258-3080
**Subject(s):** Pets
**Circ:** (Paid)7,000

**AutoGlass** (31575)
National Glass Association
8200 Greensboro Dr., Ste. 302
Mc Lean, VA 22102-3881
Phone: (703)442-4890
Fax: (703)442-0630
**Subject(s):** Glass and China; Automotive (Trade)
**Circ:** (Paid)7,000

**Caring** (5289)
National Association for Home Care
228 Seventh St. SE
Washington, DC 20003
Phone: (202)547-7424
Fax: (202)547-3540
**Subject(s):** Health and Healthcare
**Circ:** (Paid)7,000

**Cochran's Corner** (13384)
1003 Tyler Ct.
Waldorf, MD 20602
Phone: (301)870-1664
**Subject(s):** Poetry; Literature
**Circ:** (Combined)7,000

**The Functional Orthodontist** (31961)
AAFO Inc.
106 S Kent St.
Winchester, VA 22601-5052
Phone: (540)662-2200
Fax: (703)665-8910
**Subject(s):** Dentistry
**Circ:** (Controlled)‡7,000

**Housing Policy Debate** (5423)
Fannie Mae Foundation
4000 Wisconsin Ave. NW, N. Tower, Ste. 1
Washington, DC 20016-2804
Phone: (202)274-8000
Fax: (202)274-8100
**Subject(s):** Social Programs; Real Estate
**Circ:** (Non-paid)7,000

**H.S.M.A.I. Marketing Review** (31584)
Hospitality Sales and Marketing Association International
8201 Greensboro Dr., Ste. 300
Mc Lean, VA 22102
Phone: (703)610-9024
Fax: (703)610-9005
**Subject(s):** Hotels, Motels, Restaurants, and Clubs; Advertising and Marketing
**Circ:** (Controlled)7,000

**Interpretation** (31780)
Union-PSCE
3401 Brook Rd.
Richmond, VA 23227
Phone: (804)355-0671
Fax: (804)278-4208
**Subject(s):** Religious Publications
**Circ:** ‡7,000

**Journal of Nuclear Medicine Technology** (31725)
Society of Nuclear Medicine Inc.
1850 Samuel Morse Dr.
Reston, VA 20190-5316
Phone: (703)708-9000
Fax: (703)708-9015
**Subject(s):** Radiology, Ultrasound, and Nuclear Medicine; Medicine and Surgery
**Circ:** ‡7,000

**Legal Times** (5533)
American Lawyer Media L.P.
1730 M St. NW, Ste. 802
Washington, DC 20036
Phone: (202)457-0686
Fax: (202)785-4539
**Subject(s):** Law
**Circ:** (Paid)‡7,000

**Public Personnel Management** (31063)
International Personnel Management Association
1617 Duke St.
Alexandria, VA 22314
Phone: (703)549-7100
Fax: (703)684-0948
**Subject(s):** Employment and Human Resources; State, Municipal, and County Administration
**Circ:** ‡7,000

**Public Utilities Fortnightly** (31917)
Public Utilities Reports Inc.
8229 Boone Blvd., Ste. 400
Vienna, VA 22182-2623
Phone: (703)847-7720
Fax: (703)847-0683
**Subject(s):** Power and Power Plants; Telecommunications
**Circ:** 7,000

**Virginia Medical Quarterly** (31809)
Medical Society of Virginia
4205 Dover Rd.
Richmond, VA 23221
Phone: (804)353-2721
Fax: (804)355-6189
**Subject(s):** Medicine and Surgery
**Circ:** ‡7,000

**The American Journal of Surgical Pathology (AJSP)** (31234)
Lippincott Williams & Wilkins
c/o Stacey E. Mills
Dept. of Pathology
PO Box 800214, OMS Room 3876
Jefferson Park Ave.
Charlottesville, VA 22908
**Subject(s):** Medicine and Surgery
**Circ:** (Paid)6,225
6,865

**Window Film** (31432)
Key Communications Inc.
PO Box 569
Garrisonville, VA 22463
Phone: (540)720-5584
Fax: (540)720-5687
**Subject(s):** Glass and China
**Circ:** (Paid)‡6,831

**American Journal of International Law** (5213)
American Society of International Law
2223 Massachusetts Ave. NW
Washington, DC 20008
Phone: (202)939-6000
Fax: (202)797-7133
**Subject(s):** International Affairs; Law
**Circ:** ‡6,800

**Mortgage Banking Magazine** (5555)
Mortgage Bankers Association of America
1919 Pennsylvania Ave. NW
Washington, DC 20006-3404
Phone: (202)557-2700
Fax: (202)721-0245
**Subject(s):** Banking, Finance, and Investments
**Circ:** ‡6,800

**Psychological Bulletin** (5641)
American Psychological Association
750 1st St. NE
Washington, DC 20002-4242
Phone: (202)336-5500
Fax: (202)336-6012
**Subject(s):** Psychology and Psychiatry
**Circ:** ‡6,800

**Healthplan** (5416)
American Association of Health Plans
1129 20th St. NW, Ste. 600
Washington, DC 20036-3421
Phone: (202)778-3245
Fax: (202)331-7487
**Subject(s):** Health and Healthcare; Management and Administration
**Circ:** (Paid)‡6,700

**Clinical and Diagnostic Laboratory Immunology** (5311)
ASM Journals
1752 N. St., NW
Washington, DC 20036-2904
Phone: (202)737-3600
Fax: (202)942-9333
**Subject(s):** Medicine and Surgery; Laboratory Research (Scientific and Medical)
**Circ:** (Paid)‡6,660

**Gifted Child Quarterly** (5407)
National Association for Gifted Children
1707 L St., NW, Ste. 550
Washington, DC 20036
Phone: (202)785-4268
Fax: (202)785-4248
**Subject(s):** Education
**Circ:** (Paid)6,500

## Middle Atlantic States

**Health & Social Work** (5415)
National Association of Social Workers
750 1st St. NE, Ste. 700
Washington, DC 20002-4241
Phone: (202)408-8600
Fax: (202)336-8312
**Subject(s):** Sociology; Health and Healthcare; Social Sciences
**Circ:** 6,500

**Journal of Dental Research** (31023)
International and American Associations for Dental Research
1619 Duke St.
Alexandria, VA 22314-3406
Phone: (703)548-0066
Fax: (703)548-1883
**Subject(s):** Dentistry
**Circ:** ‡6,500

**Quicks Professional Journal** (12852)
The Engineering Society of Baltimore Inc.
11 West Mount Vernon Place
Baltimore, MD 21201
Phone: (410)539-6914
Fax: (410)783-9372
**Subject(s):** Architecture; Engineering (Various branches); Construction, Contracting, Building, and Excavating
**Circ:** (Non-paid)‡6,500

**The West Virginia Lawyer** (32561)
The West Virginia State Bar
2006 Kanawha Blvd., E.
Charleston, WV 25311-2204
Phone: (304)558-2456
Fax: (304)558-2467
**Subject(s):** Law
**Circ:** (Combined)6,500

**Journal of Endodontics** (13190)
Lippincott Williams & Wilkins
6522 Hunters Green Pkwy.
Hagerstown, MD 21740-2116
Phone: (301)223-2400
Fax: (800)638-3030
**Subject(s):** Dentistry
**Circ:** (Controlled)‡550
 (Paid)‡6,467

**American Antiquity** (5203)
Society for American Archaeology
900 2nd St. NE, No. 12
Washington, DC 20002-3557
Phone: (202)789-8200
Fax: (202)789-0284
**Subject(s):** Archaeology
**Circ:** ‡6,400

**Journal of the American Helicopter Society** (31016)
American Helicopter Society International
217 N. Washington St.
Alexandria, VA 22314-2538
Phone: (703)684-6777
Fax: (703)739-9279
**Subject(s):** Aviation
**Circ:** ‡6,400

**Voice of Youth Advocates** (13229)
Scarecrow Press Inc.
4501 Forbes Blvd., Ste. 200
Lanham, MD 20706
Phone: (301)459-3366
Fax: (301)429-5748
**Subject(s):** Literature; Education
**Circ:** (Combined)6,400

**Seminars in Hematology** (13007)
Elsevier
C/o Neal S. Young, Editor
National Institutes of Health
Bethesda, MD 20892-0002
**Subject(s):** Medicine and Surgery
**Circ:** ‡6,377

**Technometrics** (31075)
American Statistical Association
1429 Duke St.
Alexandria, VA 22314-3415
Phone: (703)684-1221
Fax: (703)684-2037
**Subject(s):** Statistics; Chemistry, Chemicals, and Chemical Engineering; Engineering (Various branches)
**Circ:** (Combined)⊕**6,377**

**American Journal of Epidemiology** (12654)
Oxford University Press
C/O Moyses Szklo, Editor-in-Chief
111 Market Pl., Ste. 840
Baltimore, MD 21202-6709
**Subject(s):** Medicine and Surgery; Science (General)
**Circ:** ‡6,100

**Absolute Magnitude** (31677)
DNA Publications
PO Box 2988
Radford, VA 24143-2988
Phone: (540)763-2925
Fax: (540)763-2924
**Subject(s):** Science Fiction, Mystery, Adventure, and Romance; Poetry; Literature and Literary Reviews
**Circ:** (Non-paid)3,000
 (Paid)6,000

**Agricultural Aviation** (5194)
National Agricultural Aviation Association
1005 E St. SE
Washington, DC 20003
Phone: (202)546-5722
Fax: (202)546-5726
**Subject(s):** Aviation; General Agriculture
**Circ:** (Controlled)6,000

**American Gas** (5211)
American Gas Association
400 N. Capitol St., NW, Ste. 450
Washington, DC 20001
Phone: (202)824-7000
Fax: (202)824-7115
**Subject(s):** Petroleum, Oil, and Gas
**Circ:** (Paid)3,800
 (Non-paid)6,000

**Child Welfare** (5301)
Child Welfare League of America Inc.
440 1st St. NW, 3rd Fl.
Washington, DC 20001-2085
Phone: (202)638-2952
Fax: (202)638-4004
**Subject(s):** Sociology
**Circ:** ‡6,000

**Feminist Studies** (13045)
University of Maryland
0103 Taliaferro
College Park, MD 20742
Phone: (301)405-7415
Fax: (301)405-8395
**Subject(s):** Women's Interests
**Circ:** 6,000

**GAMA International Journal** (31380)
2901 Telestar Ct., Ste. 140
Falls Church, VA 22042-1205
Phone: (703)770-8184
Fax: (703)770-8182
**Subject(s):** Insurance; Banking, Finance, and Investments
**Circ:** (Controlled)6,000

**Journal of Practical Nursing** (31030)
National Association for Practical Nurse Education and Service Inc.
PO Box 25647
Alexandria, VA 22313
Phone: (703)933-1003
Fax: (703)933-1004
**Subject(s):** Nursing
**Circ:** (Paid)‡6,000

**Journal of Rehabilitation Research and Development (JRRD)** (12795)
United States Department of Veterans Affairs
103 S. Gay St., 5th Fl.
Baltimore, MD 21202-7500
Phone: (410)962-1800
Fax: (410)962-9670
**Subject(s):** Laboratory Research (Scientific and Medical)
**Circ:** (Non-paid)6,000

**Academic Medicine** (5187)
Association of American Medical Colleges
2450 N. St., NW
Washington, DC 20037-1126
Phone: (202)828-0400
Fax: (202)828-1125
**Subject(s):** Medicine and Surgery
**Circ:** ‡5,900

**Psychological Review** (5643)
American Psychological Association
750 1st St. NE
Washington, DC 20002-4242
Phone: (202)336-5500
Fax: (202)336-6012
**Subject(s):** Psychology and Psychiatry
**Circ:** ‡5,900

**Textile Rental Magazine** (31078)
Textile Rental Services Association of America
1800 Diagonal Rd., Ste. 200
Alexandria, VA 22314
Phone: (877)770-9274
Fax: (703)519-0026
**Subject(s):** Laundry and Dry Cleaning
**Circ:** ‡5,900

**School Business Affairs** (31753)
The Association of School Business Officials International
11401 N Shore Dr.
Reston, VA 20190-4200
Phone: (703)478-0405
Fax: (703)478-0205
**Subject(s):** Education; Business
**Circ:** ‡5,870

**Science Fiction Chronicle** (31679)
PO Box 2988
Radford, VA 24143-2988
Fax: (540)763-2924
**Subject(s):** Science Fiction, Mystery, Adventure, and Romance; Book Trade and Author News
**Circ:** (Non-paid)200
 (Paid)5,800

**Psychological Assessment** (5640)
American Psychological Association
750 1st St. NE
Washington, DC 20002-4242
Phone: (202)336-5500
Fax: (202)336-6012
**Subject(s):** Psychology and Psychiatry
**Circ:** (Paid)‡5,700

**The China Business Review** (5304)
U.S. China Business Council
1818 N. St. NW, Ste. 200
Washington, DC 20036
Phone: (202)429-0340
Fax: (202)775-2476
**Subject(s):** International Business and Economics; Chinese
**Circ:** (Non-paid)‡100
 (Paid)‡5,600

**Journal of Personality and Social Psychology** (5503)
American Psychological Association
750 1st St. NE
Washington, DC 20002-4242
Phone: (202)336-5500
Fax: (202)336-6012
**Subject(s):** Psychology and Psychiatry
**Circ:** ‡5,600

**Journals of Gerontology** (5521)
Gerontological Society of America
1030 15th St. NW, Ste. 250
Washington, DC 20005
Phone: (202)842-1275
Fax: (202)842-1150
**Subject(s):** Gerontology
**Circ:** (Paid)‡5,600

**American Quarterly** (12658)
Johns Hopkins University Press
2715 N Charles St.
Baltimore, MD 21218-4363
Phone: (410)516-6987
Fax: (410)516-6968
**Subject(s):** Sociology
**Circ:** ‡5,572

**The Tax Executive** (5710)
Tax Executives Institute Inc.
1200 G. St. NW, Ste. 300
Washington, DC 20005-3814
Phone: (202)638-5601
Fax: (202)638-5607
**Subject(s):** Taxation and Tariff; Business
**Circ:** (Combined)5,556

**Journal of Applied Psychology** (5461)
American Psychological Association
750 1st St. NE
Washington, DC 20002-4242
Phone: (202)336-5500
Fax: (202)336-6012
**Subject(s):** Psychology and Psychiatry
**Circ:** ‡5,500

**Transportation Leader** (13218)
Taxicab, Limousine & Paratransit Association
3849 Farragut Ave.
Kensington, MD 20895
Phone: (301)946-5701
Fax: (301)946-4641
**Subject(s):** Transportation, Traffic, and Shipping
**Circ:** ‡5,500

**Developmental Psychology** (5360)
American Psychological Association
750 1st St. NE
Washington, DC 20002-4242
Phone: (202)336-5500
Fax: (202)336-6012
**Subject(s):** Psychology and Psychiatry
**Circ:** ‡5,400

**Journal of College Science Teaching** (31131)
National Science Teachers Association
1840 Wilson Blvd.
Arlington, VA 22201-3000
Phone: (703)243-7100
Fax: (703)243-7177
**Subject(s):** Education
**Circ:** (Non-paid)‡500
(Paid)‡5,200

**Journal of Educational Psychology** (5471)
American Psychological Association
750 1st St. NE
Washington, DC 20002-4242
Phone: (202)336-5500
Fax: (202)336-6012
**Subject(s):** Education; Psychology and Psychiatry
**Circ:** ‡5,100

**AAWM Quarterly News Briefing** (5180)
American Academy of Wound Management
1255 23rd St., NW, No. 200
Washington, DC 20037-1174
Phone: (202)521-0368
Fax: (202)833-3636
**Subject(s):** Health and Healthcare; Public Safety and Emergency Response; Medicine and Surgery
**Circ:** 5,000

**Ambulance Industry Journal** (31571)
American Ambulance Association
8201 Greensboro Dr., Ste. 300
Mc Lean, VA 22102
Phone: (703)610-9000
Fax: (703)610-9005
**Subject(s):** Health and Healthcare; Hospitals and Healthcare Institutions; Medicine and Surgery
**Circ:** 5,000

**AWIS Magazine** (5263)
Association for Women in Science
1200 New York Ave. NW, Ste. 650
Washington, DC 20005
Phone: (202)326-8940
Fax: (202)326-8960
**Subject(s):** Science (General); Women's Interests
**Circ:** 5,000

**Cost Engineering** (32674)
AACE International
209 Prairie Ave., Ste. 100
Morgantown, WV 26501
Phone: (304)296-8444
Fax: (304)291-5728
**Subject(s):** Engineering (Various branches)
**Circ:** ‡5,000

**The CQ Researcher** (5342)
Congressional Quarterly
1255, 22nd St. NW
Washington, DC 20037
Phone: (202)419-8500
Fax: (800)380-3810
**Subject(s):** Politics; Sociology
**Circ:** (Paid)‡5,000

**Innovations** (5435)
National Council on the Aging
300 D St., SW Ste. 801
Washington, DC 20024
Phone: (202)479-1200
Fax: (202)479-0735
**Subject(s):** Gerontology
**Circ:** (Paid)5,000

**The Journal of Biological Chemistry** (12978)
American Society for Biochemistry and Molecular Biology Inc.
9650 Rockville Pke.
Bethesda, MD 20814-3996
Phone: (301)634-7145
Fax: (301)634-7126
**Subject(s):** Biology; Chemistry, Chemicals, and Chemical Engineering
**Circ:** ‡5,000

**Journal of Environmental Engineering** (31715)
American Society of Civil Engineers
1801 Alexander Bell Dr.
Reston, VA 20191-4400
Phone: (703)295-6300
Fax: (703)295-6222
**Subject(s):** Engineering (Various branches)
**Circ:** (Paid)⊕5000

**Journal of Supreme Court History** (5517)
Supreme Court Historical Society
224 E Capitol St. NE
Washington, DC 20003-1036
Phone: (202)543-0400
**Subject(s):** Law; History and Genealogy
**Circ:** 5,000

**Parking Magazine** (5613)
National Parking Association
1112 16th St. NW, Ste. 300
Washington, DC 20036
Phone: (202)296-4336
Fax: (202)331-8523
**Subject(s):** Automotive (Trade)
**Circ:** 5,000

**Population Bulletin** (5623)
Population Reference Bureau
1875 Connecticut Ave. NW, Ste. 520
Washington, DC 20009-5728
Phone: (202)483-1100
Fax: (202)328-3937
**Subject(s):** Statistics; Sociology
**Circ:** ‡5,000

**The Technology Teacher** (31758)
International Technology Education Association
1914 Association Dr., Ste. 201
Reston, VA 20191-1539
Phone: (703)860-2100
Fax: (703)860-0353
**Subject(s):** Education
**Circ:** ‡5,000

**The Textile Museum Journal** (5716)
The Textile Museum
2320 S. St. NW
Washington, DC 20008-4088
Phone: (202)667-0441
Fax: (202)483-0994
**Subject(s):** Art and Art History; Textiles
**Circ:** 400
1,000
5,000

**Today's Engineer** (5720)
IEEE-USA
1828 L St. NW, Ste. 1202
Washington, DC 20036-5104
Phone: (202)785-0017
Fax: (202)785-0835
**Subject(s):** Engineering (Various branches)
**Circ:** (Combined)5,000

**The Journal of Histotechnology** (13019)
Cunningham Associates
4201 Northview Dr., Ste. 502
Bowie, MD 20716-2604
Phone: (301)262-6221
Fax: (301)262-9188
**Subject(s):** Medicine and Surgery
**Circ:** (Controlled)‡250
(Paid)‡4,950

**Ohio Beverage Journal** (32779)
2001 Main St. Ste.203
Wheeling, WV 26003
Phone: (304)232-7620
Fax: (304)233-1236
**Subject(s):** Beverages, Brewing, and Bottling
**Circ:** (Paid)‡2,072
(Controlled)‡4,876

**National Contract Management Journal** (31589)
National Contract Management Association
8260 Greensboro Dr., Ste.200
Mc Lean, VA 22102
Phone: (571)382-0082
Fax: (703)448-0939
**Subject(s):** Purchasing
**Circ:** (Controlled)4,800

**American Rehabilitation** (5225)
Rehabilitation Services Administration
c/o Frank Romano, Editor
Rm. 3212 Mary E. Switzer Bldg.
330 C St., SW
Washington, DC 20202-2531
Phone: (202)205-8296
Fax: (202)205-9874
**Subject(s):** Handicapped
**Circ:** 4,700

**Insulation Outlook** (31013)
National Insulation Association
99 Canal Center Plz., Ste. 222
Alexandria, VA 22314
Phone: (703)683-6480
Fax: (703)549-4838
**Subject(s):** Building Materials, Concrete, Brick, and Tile
**Circ:** (Paid)2,100
(Controlled)4,700

**Journal of Family Psychology** (5480)
American Psychological Association
750 1st St. NE
Washington, DC 20002-4242
Phone: (202)336-5500
Fax: (202)336-6012
**Subject(s):** Psychology and Psychiatry; Marriage and Family
**Circ:** ‡4,700

**JPO: Journal of Prosthetics & Orthotics** (31034)
American Orthotic & Prosthetic Association
330 John Carlyle St., Ste. 200
Alexandria, VA 22314
Phone: (703)836-7116
Fax: (703)836-0838
**Subject(s):** Physiology and Anatomy
**Circ:** (Paid)‡4,600

**Maryland Beverage Journal** (13102)
Beverage Journal Inc.
PO Box 8900
Elkridge, MD 21075-8900
Phone: (410)796-5455
Fax: (410)796-5511
**Subject(s):** Beverages, Brewing, and Bottling
**Circ:** (Controlled)‡1,800
(Paid)‡4,600

**The American Journal of Pathology** (12928)
9650 Rockville Pike
Bethesda, MD 20814-3993
Phone: (301)634-7943
Fax: (301)634-7961
**Subject(s):** Medicine and Surgery; Laboratory Research (Scientific and Medical)
**Circ:** ‡4,500

**Dulcimer Players News** (31960)
Dulcimer Player News
PO Box 2164
Winchester, VA 22604
Phone: (540)678-1305
Fax: (540)678-1151
**Subject(s):** Music and Musical Instruments
**Circ:** (Paid)4,500

**Journal of Democracy** (5467)
Johns Hopkins University Press
Journal of Democracy
1101 15th St., NW, Ste. 800
Washington, DC 20005
Phone: (202)293-0258
Fax: (202)293-0258
**Subject(s):** Political Science
**Circ:** 4,500

Circulation: ★ = ABC; △ = BPA; ♦ = CAC; • = CCAB; ▢ = VAC; ⊕ = PO Statement; ‡ = Publisher's Report; Boldface figures = sworn; Light figures = estimated.

**Journal of Small Business Management** (32677)
Bureau of Business and Economic Research
W. Virginia University
PO Box 6025
Morgantown, WV 26506
Phone: (304)293-7835
**Subject(s):** Management and Administration
**Circ:** ‡4,500

**Maryland Historical Magazine** (12810)
Maryland Historical Society
201 W. Monument St.
Baltimore, MD 21201-4674
Phone: (410)685-3750
Fax: (410)385-2105
**Subject(s):** History and Genealogy
**Circ:** ‡4,500

**The Middle East Journal** (5544)
Middle East Institute
1761 N St. NW
Washington, DC 20036-2882
Phone: (202)785-0191
Fax: (202)452-8876
**Subject(s):** International Affairs; International Business and Economics
**Circ:** ‡4,500

**Science Books & Films** (5684)
American Association for the Advancement of Science
1200 New York Ave. NW
Washington, DC 20005
Phone: (202)326-6400
Fax: (202)289-4950
**Subject(s):** Science (General); Library and Information Science; Education
**Circ:** (Non-paid)‡600
 (Paid)‡4,500

**Virginia Town & City** (31812)
Virginia Municipal League
13 E. Franklin St.
PO Box 12164
Richmond, VA 23241-2164
Phone: (804)649-8471
Fax: (804)343-3758
**Subject(s):** State, Municipal, and County Administration
**Circ:** (Non-paid)‡575
 (Paid)‡4,505

**Journal of Nutrition** (12986)
American Society for Nutrition Sciences
9650 Rockville Pike
Bethesda, MD 20814-3990
Phone: (301)530-7050
Fax: (301)571-1892
**Subject(s):** Medicine and Surgery
**Circ:** (Non-paid)‡204
 (Paid)‡4,420

**The Volta Review** (5734)
Alexander Graham Bell Association for the Deaf
3417 Volta Pl. NW
Washington, DC 20007-2778
Phone: (202)337-5220
Fax: (202)337-8314
**Subject(s):** Hearing and Speech; Education
**Circ:** ‡4,400

**Volta Voices** (5735)
Alexander Graham Bell Association for the Deaf
3417 Volta Pl. NW
Washington, DC 20007-2778
Phone: (202)337-5220
Fax: (202)337-8314
**Subject(s):** Hearing and Speech
**Circ:** (Paid)⊕4,400

**Johns Hopkins APL Technical Digest** (13235)
Johns Hopkins University Applied Physics Laboratory
11100 Johns Hopkins Rd.
Laurel, MD 20723-6099
Phone: (240)228-5625
Fax: (240)228-0343
**Subject(s):** Physics
**Circ:** (Controlled)⊕4,330

**Early Music America** (31119)
905 N. Emerson St.
Arlington, VA 22205
Phone: (703)524-7526
Fax: (703)524-7526
**Subject(s):** Music and Musical Instruments
**Circ:** (Combined)⊕4,252

**Infoline** (31011)
American Society for Training & Development
1640 King St.
PO Box 1443
Alexandria, VA 22313-2043
Phone: (703)683-8100
Fax: (703)683-8103
**Subject(s):** Education
**Circ:** 4,200

**Journal of Chemometrics** (5148)
John Wiley and Sons Inc.
c/o Prof. Steven D. Brown
Dept. of Chemistry, Univ. of Delaware
Newark, DE 19716
**Subject(s):** Chemistry, Chemicals, and Chemical Engineering; Mathematics; Statistics
**Circ:** (Paid)4,200

**Journal of International Business Studies** (5488)
3240 Prospect St. NW
Washington, DC 20007
Phone: (202)944-3755
Fax: (202)944-3762
**Subject(s):** International Business and Economics
**Circ:** (Paid)4,200

**Medical Physics** (13056)
American Institute of Physics
1 Physics Ellipse
College Park, MD 20740-3843
Phone: (301)209-3100
Fax: (301)209-0843
**Subject(s):** Medicine and Surgery; Physiology and Anatomy
**Circ:** ‡4,182

**Journal of Fire Protection Engineering** (12982)
Society of Fire Protection Engineers
7315 Wisconsin Ave., Ste. 1225W
Bethesda, MD 20814-3202
Phone: (301)718-2910
Fax: (301)718-2242
**Subject(s):** Engineering (Various branches); Fire Fighting
**Circ:** 4,150

**AIAA Journal** (31690)
American Institute of Aeronautics and Astronautics
1801 Alexander Bell Dr., Ste. 500
Reston, VA 20191-4344
Phone: (703)264-7500
Fax: (703)264-7551
**Subject(s):** Astronautics; Aviation
**Circ:** ‡4,100

**International Cemetery and Funeral Management** (31702)
International Cemetery and Funeral Association
1895 Preston White Dr., Ste. 220
Reston, VA 20191
Phone: (703)391-8400
Fax: (703)391-8416
**Subject(s):** Cemeteries and Monuments
**Circ:** (Non-paid)2,000
 (Paid)4,100

**Rural Telecommunications** (31154)
National Telecommunications Cooperative Association
4121 Wilson Blvd., 10th Fl.
Arlington, VA 22201
Phone: (703)351-2000
Fax: (703)351-2001
**Subject(s):** Telecommunications
**Circ:** (Non-paid)‡250
 (Paid)‡4,090

**Food Production Management** (13365)
CTI Publications Inc.
2 Oakway Rd.
Timonium, MD 21093-4247
Phone: (410)308-2080
Fax: (410)308-2079
**Subject(s):** Food and Grocery Trade
**Circ:** (Paid)214
 (Non-paid)4,030

**ACTE Quarterly** (30968)
Association of Corporate Travel Executives
515 King St., Ste. 340
Alexandria, VA 22314
Phone: (703)683-5322
Fax: (703)683-2720
**Subject(s):** Travel and Tourism; Business; Travel and Tourism
**Circ:** 4,000

**APF Reporter** (5243)
Alicia Patterson Foundation
1730 Pennsylvania Ave. NW, Ste. 850
Washington, DC 20006
Phone: (202)393-5995
Fax: (301)951-8512
**Subject(s):** Journalism and Publishing
**Circ:** (Controlled)4,000

**ASAE Association Law and Policy** (5253)
American Society of Association Executives
ASAE Bldg.
1575 I St. NW
Washington, DC 20005-1103
Phone: (202)371-0940
Fax: (202)371-8315
**Subject(s):** Law
**Circ:** (Non-paid)4,000

**Aviation, Space, and Environmental Medicine** (30982)
Aerospace Medical Association
320 S Henry St.
Alexandria, VA 22314-3579
Phone: (703)739-2240
Fax: (703)739-9652
**Subject(s):** Medicine and Surgery
**Circ:** ‡4,000

**Journal of Air Traffic Control** (31015)
Air Traffic Control Association (ATCA)
1101 King St., Ste. 300
Alexandria, VA 22314
Phone: (703)299-2430
Fax: (703)299-2437
**Subject(s):** Aviation
**Circ:** ‡4,000

**Journal of Applied Rehabilitation Counseling** (31554)
National Rehabilitation Counseling Association
PO Box 4480
Manassas, VA 20108
Phone: (703)361-2077
Fax: (703)361-2489
**Circ:** (Paid)4,000

**Journal of Competitive Intelligence & Management** (31021)
Society of Competitive Intelligence Professionals
1700 Diagonal Rd., Ste. 600
Alexandria, VA 22314
Phone: (703)739-0696
Fax: (703)739-2524
**Subject(s):** Business; Management and Administration
**Circ:** 4,000

**Journal of Cost Analysis and Management** (31022)
Society of Cost Estimating and Analysis
101 S Whiting St., Ste. 201
Alexandria, VA 22304
Phone: (703)751-8069
Fax: (703)461-7328
**Subject(s):** Economics
**Circ:** (Combined)4,000

**Journal of Criminal Justice Education** (13186)
Academy of Criminal Justice Sciences
7319 Hanover Parkway, Ste. C
Greenbelt, MD 20770
Phone: (301)446-6300
Fax: (301)446-2819
**Subject(s):** Law; Police, Penology, and Penal Institutions; Education
**Circ:** 4,000

**Liberal Education** (5534)
Association of American Colleges & Universities
1818 R St. NW
Washington, DC 20009
Phone: (202)387-3760
Fax: (202)265-9532
**Subject(s):** Education
**Circ:** (Paid)‡900
 (Controlled)‡4,000

**Middle East Research & Information Project** (5545)
1500 Massachusetts Ave. NW, Ste. 119
Washington, DC 20005
Phone: (202)223-3677
Fax: (202)223-3604
**Subject(s):** International Affairs
**Circ:** 4,000

**MOVE Magazine (31137)**
American Association of Motor Vehicle Administrators
4301 Wilson Blvd., Ste. 400
Arlington, VA 22203-1800
Phone: (703)522-4200
Fax: (703)522-1553
**Subject(s):** Automotive (Trade); Automotive (Consumer)
**Circ:** 4,000

**National Trust Forum (5574)**
National Trust for Historic Preservation
1785 Massachusetts Ave. NW
Washington, DC 20036
Phone: (202)588-6000
Fax: (202)588-6223
**Subject(s):** History and Genealogy
**Circ:** (Paid)4,000

**The Public Manager (13270)**
The Bureaucrat Inc.
12007 Titian Way
Potomac, MD 20854
Phone: (301)279-9445
Fax: (301)251-5872
**Subject(s):** Congressional and Federal Government Affairs
**Circ:** ‡4,000

**Topical Time (31919)**
American Topical Association Inc.
2501 Drexel St.
Vienna, VA 22180
Phone: (703)560-2413
**Subject(s):** Collecting
**Circ:** ‡4,000

**The Environmental Forum (5376)**
Environmental Law Institute
2000 L St. NW, Ste. 620
Washington, DC 20036
Phone: (202)939-3800
Fax: (202)939-3868
**Subject(s):** Ecology and Conservation
**Circ:** (Controlled)3,900

**RE:view (5663)**
Heldref Publications
1319 18th St., NW
Washington, DC 20036-1802
Phone: (202)296-6267
Fax: (202)296-5149
**Subject(s):** Education; Handicapped; Blind and Visually Challenged
**Circ:** (Combined)‡3,880

**Free Speech (32615)**
National Vanguard Books
PO Box 330
Hillsboro, WV 24946
Fax: (304)653-4690
**Subject(s):** Alternative and Underground; Social and Political Issues
**Circ:** (Paid)3,800

**Monitor (13021)**
Capital PC User Group
19209 Mt. Airey Rd.
Brookeville, MD 20833
Phone: (301)762-9372
Fax: (301)762-9375
**Subject(s):** Computers; Computers
**Circ:** 3,800

**The Tracker (31800)**
Organ Historical Society
PO Box 26811
Richmond, VA 23261
Phone: (804)353-9226
Fax: (804)353-9266
**Subject(s):** Music and Musical Instruments
**Circ:** ‡3,800

**Annual in Therapeutic Recreation (30977)**
American Therapeutic Recreation Association
1414 Prince St., Ste. 204
Alexandria, VA 22314
Phone: (703)683-9420
Fax: (703)683-9431
**Subject(s):** Health; Handicapped; Health and Healthcare
**Circ:** 3,750

**American Institute for Conservation of Historic and Artistic Works Journal (5212)**
American Institute for Conservation of Historic & Artistic Works
1717 K St. NW, Ste. 200
Washington, DC 20036-5346
Phone: (202)452-9545
Fax: (202)452-9328
**Subject(s):** Art and Art History
**Circ:** (Paid)3,700

**International Journal of Middle East Studies (5446)**
Cambridge University Press
c/o Judith Tucker
Po.Box 571236
Georgetown Univ.
Washington, DC 20057-1236
**Subject(s):** Intercultural Interests
**Circ:** (Non-paid)‡29
 (Paid)‡3650

**BEDTimes (30983)**
International Sleep Products Association
501 Wythe St.
Alexandria, VA 22314-1917
Phone: (703)683-8371
Fax: (703)683-4503
**Subject(s):** Furniture and Furnishings
**Circ:** ‡3,600

**Business Economics (5285)**
National Association for Business Economics
1233 20th St. NW, Ste. 505
Washington, DC 20036
Phone: (202)463-6223
Fax: (202)463-6239
**Subject(s):** Economics
**Circ:** ‡3,600

**HortScience (31007)**
American Society for Horticultural Science
113 SW St., Ste. 200
Alexandria, VA 22314-2851
Phone: (703)836-4606
Fax: (703)836-2024
**Subject(s):** Horticulture
**Circ:** (Paid)3,600

**Journal of the American Institute for Conservation (5460)**
American Institute for Conservation of Historic & Artistic Works
1717 K St. NW, Ste. 200
Washington, DC 20036-5346
Phone: (202)452-9545
Fax: (202)452-9328
**Subject(s):** History and Genealogy
**Circ:** 3,600

**Musical Mainstream (5557)**
National Library Service for the Blind and Physically Handicapped
1291 Taylor St. NW
Washington, DC 20011
Phone: (202)707-5100
Fax: (202)707-0712
**Subject(s):** Blind and Visually Challenged; Music and Musical Instruments; Handicapped
**Circ:** (Non-paid)‡3,600

**Political Money Monitor (5622)**
The National Center for Public Policy Research
501 Capitol Ct. NE
Washington, DC 20002
Phone: (202)543-4110
Fax: (202)543-5975
**Subject(s):** Politics
**Circ:** 3,600

**PsycSCAN (5652)**
American Psychological Association
750 1st St. NE
Washington, DC 20002-4242
Phone: (202)336-5500
Fax: (202)336-6012
**Subject(s):** Psychology and Psychiatry; Indexes, Abstracts, Reports, Proceedings, and Bibliographies
**Circ:** ‡3,600

**William and Mary Quarterly (31955)**
Omohundro Institute of Early American History & Culture
PO Box 8781
Williamsburg, VA 23187-8781
Phone: (757)221-1122
Fax: (757)221-1047
**Subject(s):** History and Genealogy
**Circ:** (Combined)⊖3,600

**American Annals of the Deaf (5202)**
Conference of Educational Administrators Serving the Deaf
Gallaudet University Press
800 Florida Ave. NE
Washington, DC 20002
Phone: (202)651-5488
Fax: (202)651-5489
**Subject(s):** Hearing and Speech
**Circ:** ‡3,500

**Cartography and Geographic Information Science (13157)**
American Congress on Surveying and Mapping
6 Montgomery Village Ave., Ste. 403
Gaithersburg, MD 20879-3557
Phone: (240)632-9716
Fax: (240)632-1321
**Subject(s):** Geography; Engineering (Various branches)
**Circ:** 3,500

**CM News (31491)**
National Concrete Masonry Association
13750 Sunrise Valley Dr.
Herndon, VA 20171-3499
Phone: (703)713-1900
Fax: (703)713-1910
**Subject(s):** Building Materials, Concrete, Brick, and Tile; Construction, Contracting, Building, and Excavating; Landscape Architecture
**Circ:** (Non-paid)‡3,500

**Communicator (5321)**
Radio-Television News Directors Association
1600 K St. NW, No. 700
Washington, DC 20006
Phone: (202)659-6510
Fax: (202)223-4007
**Subject(s):** Radio, Television, Cable, and Video
**Circ:** ‡3,500

**Direction (30996)**
American Moving & Storage Association
1611 Duke St.
Alexandria, VA 22314
Phone: (703)683-7410
Fax: (703)683-7527
**Subject(s):** Transportation, Traffic, and Shipping
**Circ:** ‡3,500

**Family Economics and Nutrition Review (31000)**
U.S. Department of Agriculture
3101 Park Center Dr.
Rm. 1034
Alexandria, VA 22302-1594
Phone: (703)305-7600
Fax: (703)305-3300
**Subject(s):** Health and Healthcare; Economics
**Circ:** (Paid)900
 (Non-paid)3,500

**The FASEB Journal (12966)**
Federation of America Societies for Experimental Biology
Office of Publications
9650 Rockville Pke.
Bethesda, MD 20814-3998
Phone: (301)634-7100
Fax: (301)634-1855
**Subject(s):** Biology
**Circ:** 3,500

**IRIS (31251)**
University of Virginia
Women's Ctr.
PO Box 800588
Charlottesville, VA 22908
Phone: (434)924-4500
Fax: (434)982-2901
**Subject(s):** Women's Interests
**Circ:** (Paid)3,500

**Journal of Health & Social Behavior (31199)**
American Sociological Association
Virginia Tech
540 McBryde Hall
Blacksburg, VA 24061
**Subject(s):** Sociology; Health and Healthcare
**Circ:** ‡3,500

# Middle Atlantic States

**Journal of Healthcare Administrative Management** (31350)
American Association of Healthcare Administrative Management
11240 Waples Mill Rd., Ste. 200
Fairfax, VA 22030
Phone: (703)281-4043
Fax: (703)359-7562
**Subject(s):** Health and Healthcare; Medicine and Surgery; Employment and Human Resources; Hospitals and Healthcare Institutions
**Circ:** 3,500

**The Journal of Molecular Diagnostics** (12984)
9650 Rockville Pike
Bethesda, MD 20814-3993
Phone: (301)634-7943
Fax: (301)634-7961
**Subject(s):** Biology; Medicine and Surgery; Science (General); Laboratory Research (Scientific and Medical)
**Circ:** (Paid)3,500

**Metabolism - Clinical and Experimental** (31456)
Elsevier
C/o James B. Field, Editor-in-Chief
8 Windmill Point Ln.
Hampton, VA 23664-2129
Phone: (757)850-2826
Fax: (757)850-2826
**Subject(s):** Physiology and Anatomy
**Circ:** ‡3,506

**Professional Report** (5633)
Society of Industrial and Office Realtors
1201 New York Ave., NW, Ste. 350
Washington, DC 20005
Phone: (202)449-8200
Fax: (202)449-8201
**Subject(s):** Real Estate
**Circ:** (Paid)3,500

**Radiation Oncology Investigations** (31789)
John Wiley and Sons Inc.
c/o Rupert K. Schmidt-Ullrich, M.D.
Dept. of Radiation Oncology Med. College of Virginia Hospitals
401 College St., Basement B-127
PO Box 980058
Richmond, VA 23298-0058
Phone: (804)828-7238
Fax: (804)828-5510
**Subject(s):** Biology; Medicine and Surgery
**Circ:** 3,500

**Therapeutic Recreation Journal** (31180)
National Recreation and Park Association
22377 Belmont Ridge Rd.
Ashburn, VA 20148
Phone: (703)858-0784
Fax: (703)858-0794
**Subject(s):** Health and Healthcare
**Circ:** (Controlled)‡100
(Paid)‡3,500

**William and Mary Review** (31956)
College of William and Mary
Campus Ctr.
PO Box 8795
Williamsburg, VA 23187
Phone: (757)221-3290
**Subject(s):** Literature
**Circ:** (Combined)3,500

**Destinations** (5359)
American Bus Association
700 13th St. NW, Ste. 575
Washington, DC 20005
Phone: (202)842-1645
Fax: (202)842-0850
**Subject(s):** Travel and Tourism; Public Transportation
**Circ:** (Controlled)‡2,047
(Paid)‡3,449

**American Journal of Physiology: Renal Physiology** (12936)
The American Physiological Society
9650 Rockville Pke.
Bethesda, MD 20814-3991
Phone: (301)634-7164
Fax: (301)634-7241
**Subject(s):** Physiology and Anatomy
**Circ:** (Combined)‡3,421

**Journal of American Hosta Society** (31531)
American Hosta Society
8702 Pinnacle Rock Ct.
Lorton, VA 22079-3029
Phone: (703)690-3021
**Subject(s):** Home and Garden; Botany
**Circ:** 3,422

**Contemporary Psychology** (5336)
American Psychological Association
750 1st St. NE
Washington, DC 20002-4242
Phone: (202)336-5500
Fax: (202)336-6012
**Subject(s):** Psychology and Psychiatry
**Circ:** ‡3,400

**Shakespeare Quarterly** (5691)
The Folger Shakespeare Library
201 East Capitol St., SE
Washington, DC 20003-1094
Phone: (202)675-0349
Fax: (202)544-4623
**Subject(s):** Literature
**Circ:** (Non-paid)‡250
(Paid)‡3,400

**American Journal of Physiology: Lung Cellular and Molecular Physiology** (12934)
The American Physiological Society
9650 Rockville Pke.
Bethesda, MD 20814-3991
Phone: (301)634-7164
Fax: (301)634-7241
**Subject(s):** Physiology and Anatomy
**Circ:** (Combined)‡3,388

**The Journal of Neuroscience** (5496)
Society for Neuroscience
11 Dupont Cir., NW, Ste. 500
Washington, DC 20036
**Subject(s):** Medicine and Surgery
**Circ:** (Non-paid)‡303
(Paid)‡3,341

**American Journal of Physiology: Cell Physiology** (12929)
The American Physiological Society
9650 Rockville Pke.
Bethesda, MD 20814-3991
Phone: (301)634-7164
Fax: (301)634-7241
**Subject(s):** Physiology and Anatomy
**Circ:** (Combined)‡3,310

**Action in Teacher Education** (31687)
Association of Teacher Educators
1900 Association Dr., Ste. ATE
Reston, VA 20191
Phone: (703)620-3110
Fax: (703)620-9530
**Subject(s):** Education
**Circ:** 3,300

**Journal of Experimental Psychology** (5476)
American Psychological Association
750 1st St. NE
Washington, DC 20002-4242
Phone: (202)336-5500
Fax: (202)336-6012
**Subject(s):** Psychology and Psychiatry
**Circ:** ‡3,300

**The Washington Quarterly** (5745)
The MIT Press
Center for Strategic and International Studies
1800 K St., NW, Ste. 400
Washington, DC 20006
Phone: (202)887-0200
Fax: (202)775-3190
**Subject(s):** Politics
**Circ:** (Non-paid)‡250
(Paid)‡3,300

**Clinical Journal of Sport Medicine** (12692)
Lippincott Williams & Wilkins
351 W. Camden St.
Baltimore, MD 21201
Phone: (410)528-4479
Fax: (410)528-4312
**Subject(s):** Laboratory Research (Scientific and Medical)
**Circ:** 3,284

**Virginia Forests** (31805)
Virginia Forestry Association
3808 Augusta Ave
Richmond, VA 23230
Phone: (804)278-8733
Fax: (804)278-8774
**Subject(s):** Forestry; Natural Resources
**Circ:** (Paid)3,250

**Virginia Lawyers Weekly** (31807)
Lawyers Weekly Publications
c/o Paul E. Fletcher, Esq.
801 E. Main St., Ste. 701
Richmond, VA 23219
Phone: (804)788-1932
Fax: (804)788-1932
**Subject(s):** Law
**Circ:** ‡3,250

**American Journal of Physiology: Gastrointestinal and Liver Physiology** (12932)
The American Physiological Society
9650 Rockville Pke.
Bethesda, MD 20814-3991
Phone: (301)634-7164
Fax: (301)634-7241
**Subject(s):** Physiology and Anatomy
**Circ:** (Combined)‡3,241

**American Journal of Physiology: Endocrinology and Metabolism** (12931)
The American Physiological Society
9650 Rockville Pke.
Bethesda, MD 20814-3991
Phone: (301)634-7164
Fax: (301)634-7241
**Subject(s):** Physiology and Anatomy
**Circ:** (Combined)‡3,231

**American Journal of Physiology: Heart and Circulatory Physiology** (12933)
The American Physiological Society
9650 Rockville Pke.
Bethesda, MD 20814-3991
Phone: (301)634-7164
Fax: (301)634-7241
**Subject(s):** Physiology and Anatomy
**Circ:** (Combined)‡3,231

**American Mineralogist** (5218)
Mineralogical Society of America
1015 18th St. NW, Ste. 601
Washington, DC 20036-5212
Phone: (202)775-4344
Fax: (202)775-0018
**Subject(s):** Geology; Science (General)
**Circ:** (Paid)3,200

**Applied Optics** (5245)
Optical Society of America
2010 Massachusetts Ave., NW
Washington, DC 20036-1023
Phone: (202)223-8130
Fax: (202)223-1096
**Subject(s):** Ophthalmology, Optometry, and Optics; Physics
**Circ:** 3,200

**Bottled Water Reporter** (30985)
International Bottled Water Association (IBWA)
1700 Diagonal Rd., Ste. 650
Alexandria, VA 22314
Phone: (703)683-5213
Fax: (703)683-4074
**Subject(s):** Beverages, Brewing, and Bottling
**Circ:** (Non-paid)‡150
(Paid)‡3,200

**The Catholic Spirit** (32776)
1213 Byron St.
PO Box 230
Wheeling, WV 26003
Phone: (304)233-8551
Fax: (304)233-0890
**Subject(s):** Religious Publications
**Circ:** (Paid)‡3,200

**East West Report** (5365)
U.S. Pan Asian American Chamber of Commerce
1329 18th St., NW
Washington, DC 20036
Phone: (202)296-5221
Fax: (202)296-5225
**Circ:** (Paid)‡1,800
(Non-paid)‡3,200

**The Plant Cell (13306)**
American Society of Plant Biologists
15501 Monona Dr.
Rockville, MD 20855-2768
Phone: (301)251-0560
Fax: (301)279-2996
**Subject(s):** Biology
**Circ:** ‡3,200

**Psychology and Aging (5646)**
American Psychological Association
750 1st St. NE
Washington, DC 20002-4242
Phone: (202)336-5500
Fax: (202)336-6012
**Subject(s):** Psychology and Psychiatry
**Circ:** ‡3,200

**SIAM Journal on Applied Mathematics (5155)**
Society for Industrial & Applied Mathematics
c/o L. Pamela Cook
Dept. of Mathematical Sciences
Univ. of Delaware
Newark, DE 19716
**Subject(s):** Mathematics
**Circ:** ‡3,205

**American Journal of Physiology: Regulatory, Integrative and Comparative Physiology (12935)**
The American Physiological Society
9650 Rockville Pke.
Bethesda, MD 20814-3991
Phone: (301)634-7164
Fax: (301)634-7241
**Subject(s):** Physiology and Anatomy
**Circ:** (Combined)‡3,126

**Eye and Contact Lens (12728)**
Lippincott Williams & Wilkins
351 W. Camden St.
Baltimore, MD 21201
Phone: (410)528-4479
Fax: (410)528-4312
**Subject(s):** Ophthalmology, Optometry, and Optics
**Circ:** ‡3,100

**Rocks & Minerals (5673)**
Heldref Publications
1319 18th St., NW
Washington, DC 20036-1802
Phone: (202)296-6267
Fax: (202)296-5149
**Subject(s):** Mining and Minerals; Geology
**Circ:** (Controlled)1,000
(Paid)‡3,100

**The Virginia Engineer (31604)**
7401 Flannigan Mill Rd.
Mechanicsville, VA 23111
Phone: (804)779-3527
Fax: (804)779-3032
**Subject(s):** Engineering (Various branches)
**Circ:** (Controlled)‡753
(Paid)‡3,100

**ABA Bank Marketing (5181)**
American Bankers Association
1120 Connecticut Ave. NW, Ste. 600
Washington, DC 20036
Phone: (202)663-5378
Fax: (202)828-4540
**Subject(s):** Banking, Finance, and Investments; Accountants and Accounting; Advertising and Marketing
**Circ:** (Paid)‡3,091

**ABA Bank Marketing Magazine (5182)**
American Bankers Association
1120 Connecticut Ave. NW, Ste. 600
Washington, DC 20036
Phone: (202)663-5378
Fax: (202)828-4540
**Subject(s):** Advertising and Marketing; Banking, Finance, and Investments
**Circ:** (Paid)‡3,091

**Journal of Applied Physiology (12977)**
The American Physiological Society
9650 Rockville Pke.
Bethesda, MD 20814-3991
Phone: (301)634-7164
Fax: (301)634-7241
**Subject(s):** Physiology and Anatomy
**Circ:** (Combined)‡3,092

**American Journal of Electroneurodiagnostic Technology (32610)**
American Society of Electroneurodiagnostic Technologists Inc.
Rt. 1
Box 59C
Green Bank, WV 24944
Phone: (304)456-4893
Fax: (304)456-3298
**Subject(s):** Health and Healthcare
**Circ:** (Non-paid)‡69
(Paid)‡3,024

**Adult Learning Quarterly (13017)**
American Association for Adult & Continuing Education
10111 Martin L. King Hwy Ste 200-C
Bowie, MD 20720
Phone: (301)459-6261
Fax: (301)459-6241
**Subject(s):** Education
**Circ:** 3,000

**American Brewer (30971)**
PO Box 20268
Alexandria, VA 22320-1268
Phone: (703)567-1962
**Subject(s):** Beverages, Brewing, and Bottling; Business
**Circ:** (Combined)3,000

**American Intelligence Journal (13156)**
National Military Intelligence Association
9200 Centerway Rd.
Gaithersburg, MD 20879
Phone: (301)840-6642
Fax: (301)840-8502
**Subject(s):** Military and Navy
**Circ:** 3,000

**Archives of American Art Journal (5247)**
Archives of American Art
Smithsonian Institution
P.O. Box 37012
The Victor Bldg. 2200
Washington, DC 20013-7012
Phone: (202)275-1961
Fax: (202)275-1955
**Subject(s):** Art and Art History
**Circ:** 3,000

**Bilingual Research Journal (5269)**
National Association for Bilingual Education
1030 15th St. NW, Ste. 470
Washington, DC 20005-1503
Phone: (202)898-1829
Fax: (202)789-2866
**Subject(s):** Philology, Language, and Linguistics
**Circ:** 3,000

**Cast Polymer Connection (31116)**
International Cast Polymer Association
1010 N. Glebe Rd., Ste. 450
Arlington, VA 22201
Phone: (703)525-0320
Fax: (703)525-0743
**Subject(s):** Building Materials, Concrete, Brick, and Tile
**Circ:** (Paid)3,000

**Demography (13344)**
Population Association of America
8630 Fenton St., Ste. 722
Silver Spring, MD 20910-3812
Phone: (301)565-6710
Fax: (301)565-7850
**Subject(s):** Social Sciences; Geography; History and Genealogy
**Circ:** (Paid)3,000

**Mid-Atlantic Builder (12817)**
Home Builders Association of Maryland
1502 Woodlawn Drive
Baltimore, MD 21207-4009
Phone: (410)265-7400
Fax: (410)265-6529
**Subject(s):** Construction, Contracting, Building, and Excavating
**Circ:** ‡3,000

**NABJ Journal (12625)**
National Association of Black Journalists
Univ. of Maryland
8701A Adelphi Rd.
Adelphi, MD 20783-1716
Phone: (301)445-7100
Fax: (301)445-7101
**Subject(s):** Journalism and Publishing; Ethnic and Minority Studies
**Circ:** (Paid)3,000

**Nozzle & Wrench (13228)**
WMDA Service Station & Auto Repair Association
9420 Annapolis Rd., Ste. 307
Lanham, MD 20706-3021
Phone: (301)577-4956
Fax: (301)306-0523
**Subject(s):** Automotive (Trade)
**Circ:** (Controlled)‡3,000

**Sobran's (31918)**
PO Box 1383
Vienna, VA 22183-1383
Phone: (703)255-2211
Fax: (703)281-6617
**Subject(s):** Alternative and Underground; Social and Political Issues
**Circ:** (Combined)‡3,000

**Sociology of Education (5698)**
American Sociological Association
1307 New York Ave. NW, Ste. 700
Washington, DC 20005-4701
Phone: (202)383-9005
Fax: (202)638-0882
**Subject(s):** Sociology; Education
**Circ:** ‡3,000

**World Around You (5760)**
National Deaf Education Center
800 Florida Ave. NE
Washington, DC 20002
Phone: (202)651-5530
Fax: (202)651-5489
**Subject(s):** Handicapped; Youths' Interests
**Circ:** 3,000

**World Climate Report (31502)**
PO Box 455
Ivy, VA 22945
Phone: (804)295-7462
Fax: (804)295-7549
**Subject(s):** Ecology and Conservation; Science (General); Politics
**Circ:** (Combined)3,000

**Journal of American College Health (5459)**
Heldref Publications
1319 18th St., NW
Washington, DC 20036-1802
Phone: (202)296-6267
Fax: (202)296-5149
**Subject(s):** Health and Healthcare
**Circ:** (Combined)‡2,950

**Circulation Research (12690)**
Lippincott Williams & Wilkins
Circulation Research Editorial Office
2700 Lighthouse Point E., Ste. 230
Baltimore, MD 21224
Phone: (410)327-5005
Fax: (410)614-7660
**Subject(s):** Medicine and Surgery
**Circ:** (Paid)‡2,900

**The Journal of Military History (31522)**
Society for Military History
George C. Marshall Library
Virginia Military Institute
Lexington, VA 24450
Phone: (540)464-7468
Fax: (540)464-7330
**Subject(s):** Military and Navy; History and Genealogy
**Circ:** (Non-paid)‡30
(Paid)‡2,900

**Magazine of Virginia Genealogy (31785)**
Virginia Genealogical Society
5001 W Broad St., Ste. 115
Richmond, VA 23230-3023
Phone: (804)285-8954
Fax: (804)285-0394
**Subject(s):** History and Genealogy
**Circ:** (Paid)2,900

**OPASTCO Roundtable (5604)**
Organization for Promotion and Advancement of Small Telecommunications Companies (OPASTCO)
21 Dupont Cir. NW, Ste. 700
Washington, DC 20036
Phone: (202)659-5990
Fax: (202)659-4619

**Subject(s):** Telecommunications
**Circ:** (Non-paid)‡600
(Paid)‡2,900

**Reviews in American History (12855)**
Johns Hopkins University Press
2715 N Charles St.
Baltimore, MD 21218-4363
Phone: (410)516-6987
Fax: (410)516-6968
**Subject(s):** History and Genealogy
**Circ:** ‡2,875

**World Politics (12884)**
Johns Hopkins University Press
2715 N Charles St.
Baltimore, MD 21218-4363
Phone: (410)516-6987
Fax: (410)516-6968
**Subject(s):** Politics; International Affairs
**Circ:** (Non-paid)‡107
(Paid)‡2,830

**Air Traffic Control Quarterly (31106)**
John Wiley and Sons Inc.
Air Traffic Control Association
2300 Clarendon Blvd., Ste. 711
Arlington, VA 22201
Phone: (703)527-7251
Fax: (703)527-7251
**Subject(s):** Engineering (Various branches)
**Circ:** 2,800

**AMSECT Today (31489)**
American Society of Extra-Corporeal Technology
503 Carlisle Dr. No. 125
Herndon, VA 20170-4838
Phone: (703)435-8556
Fax: (703)435-0056
**Circ:** 2,800

**Association for Healthcare Philanthropy—Journal (31377)**
Association for Healthcare Philanthropy
313 Park Ave., Ste. 400
Falls Church, VA 22046
Phone: (703)532-6243
Fax: (703)532-7170
**Subject(s):** Health and Healthcare; Philanthropy and Humanitarianism; Hospitals and Healthcare Institutions; Medicine and Surgery
**Circ:** 2,800

**Developments (5361)**
American Resort Development Association
1201 15th St. NW., Ste. 400
Washington, DC 20005-2842
Phone: (202)371-6700
Fax: (202)289-8544
**Subject(s):** Travel and Tourism; Real Estate
**Circ:** 2,800

**Journal of Extra-Corporeal Technology (31493)**
American Society of Extra-Corporeal Technology
503 Carlisle Dr. No. 125
Herndon, VA 20170-4838
Phone: (703)435-8556
Fax: (703)435-0056
**Subject(s):** Medicine and Surgery; Health and Healthcare
**Circ:** 2,800

**Optometric Education (13303)**
Association of Schools & Colleges of Optometry
6110 Exec. Blvd., No. 510
Rockville, MD 20852
Phone: (301)231-5944
Fax: (301)770-1828
**Subject(s):** Ophthalmology, Optometry, and Optics
**Circ:** ‡2,800

**Spectrum (Greenbelt) (13187)**
National Association of Black Accountants Inc.
7249-A Hanover Pkwy.
Greenbelt, MD 20770
Phone: (301)474-NABA
Fax: (301)474-3114
**Subject(s):** Accountants and Accounting
**Circ:** (Controlled)2,750

**Aviation Mechanics Bulletin (30981)**
Flight Safety Foundation Inc.
601 Madison St., Ste.300
Alexandria, VA 22314-1756
Phone: (703)739-6700
Fax: (703)739-6708

**Subject(s):** Aviation; Safety
**Circ:** 2,700

**Journal of Aircraft (31704)**
American Institute of Aeronautics and Astronautics
1801 Alexander Bell Dr., Ste. 500
Reston, VA 20191-4344
Phone: (703)264-7500
Fax: (703)264-7551
**Subject(s):** Aviation
**Circ:** ‡2,700

**Journal of Guidance, Control, and Dynamics (31717)**
American Institute of Aeronautics and Astronautics
1801 Alexander Bell Dr., Ste. 500
Reston, VA 20191-4344
Phone: (703)264-7500
Fax: (703)264-7551
**Subject(s):** Aviation
**Circ:** ‡2,700

**Journal of Spacecraft and Rockets (31732)**
American Institute of Aeronautics and Astronautics
1801 Alexander Bell Dr., Ste. 500
Reston, VA 20191-4344
Phone: (703)264-7500
Fax: (703)264-7551
**Subject(s):** Astronautics
**Circ:** ‡2,700

**American Journal of Physiology (Consolidated) (12930)**
The American Physiological Society
9650 Rockville Pke.
Bethesda, MD 20814-3991
Phone: (301)634-7164
Fax: (301)634-7241
**Subject(s):** Physiology and Anatomy; Biology; Chemistry, Chemicals, and Chemical Engineering
**Circ:** (Combined)‡2,639

**Cleaning & Restoration (13248)**
ASCR International
8229 Cloverleaf Dr., Ste. 460
Millersville, MD 21108-1538
Phone: (410)729-9900
Fax: (410)729-3603
**Subject(s):** Furniture and Furnishings; Paint and Wallcoverings
**Circ:** ‡2,600

**Hort Technology (31006)**
American Society for Horticultural Science
113 SW St., Ste. 200
Alexandria, VA 22314-2851
Phone: (703)836-4606
Fax: (703)836-2024
**Subject(s):** Horticulture
**Circ:** (Paid)2,600

**Infants and Young Children (13167)**
Aspen Publishers Inc.
c/o James A. Blackman
200 Orchard Ridge Dr.
Gaithersburg, MD 20878
Phone: (301)417-7500
Fax: (301)417-7550
**Subject(s):** Babies
**Circ:** (Paid)2,600

**NAEB Journal (12824)**
National Association of Educational Buyers Inc.
5523 Research Park Dr.
Ste. 340
Baltimore, MD 21228
Phone: (443)543-5540
Fax: (443)543-5550
**Subject(s):** Education
**Circ:** (Paid)2,600

**ITEA Journal of Test and Evaluation (31344)**
International Test and Evaluation Association
4400 Fair Lakes Ct.
Fairfax, VA 22033-3899
Phone: (703)631-6220
Fax: (703)631-6221
**Subject(s):** Statistics
**Circ:** (Combined)2,575

**Stone, Sand & Gravel Review (31072)**
National Stone, Sand & Gravel Association
1605 King St.
Alexandria, VA 22314
Phone: (703)525-8788
Fax: (703)525-7782

**Subject(s):** Stone and Rock Products
**Circ:** (Non-paid)‡1,412
(Paid)‡2,558

**The New Jersey Farmer (13095)**
American Farm Publications Inc.
505 Brookletts Ave.
PO Box 2026
Easton, MD 21601
Phone: (410)822-3965
Fax: (410)822-5068
**Subject(s):** General Agriculture
**Circ:** (Paid)‡2,247
(Controlled)‡2,543

**ACM Transactions on Mathematical Software (TOMS) (13154)**
Association for Computing Machinery
c/o Ronald F.Boisvert
Mathematical and Computational Sciences Division
National Institute of Standards and Technology
100 Bureau Dr., Stop 8910
Gaithersburg, MD 20899-8910
Phone: (301)975-3812
Fax: (301)990-4127
**Subject(s):** Computers
**Circ:** 2,500

**Banking Law Journal (31114)**
A.S. Pratt & Sons
1901 Fort Myer Dr., Ste. 501
Arlington, VA 22209
Phone: (703)528-0145
Fax: (703)528-1736
**Subject(s):** Banking, Finance, and Investments; Law
**Circ:** (Paid)2,500

**Communio-International Catholic Review (5323)**
PO Box 4557
Washington, DC 20017
Phone: (202)526-0251
Fax: (202)526-1934
**Subject(s):** Religious Publications
**Circ:** (Non-paid)‡150
(Paid)‡2,500

**Hopscotch (12742)**
Duke University Press
Project MUSE
2715 N. Charles St.
Baltimore, MD 21218-4319
Phone: (410)516-6989
Fax: (410)516-6968
**Subject(s):** Ethnic and Minority Studies
**Circ:** (Combined)2,500

**Journal of the American Society for Horticultural Science (31018)**
American Society for Horticultural Science
113 SW St., Ste. 200
Alexandria, VA 22314-2851
Phone: (703)836-4606
Fax: (703)836-2024
**Subject(s):** Horticulture
**Circ:** (Paid)2,500

**Journal of Experimental Psychology: Human Perception and Performance (5479)**
American Psychological Association
750 1st St. NE
Washington, DC 20002-4242
Phone: (202)336-5500
Fax: (202)336-6012
**Subject(s):** Psychology and Psychiatry
**Circ:** ‡2,500

**Practice Periodical on Structural Design and Construction (31749)**
American Society of Civil Engineers
1801 Alexander Bell Dr.
Reston, VA 20191-4400
Phone: (703)295-6300
Fax: (703)295-6222
**Subject(s):** Engineering (Various branches); Construction, Contracting, Building, and Excavating
**Circ:** (Paid)2,500

**Review of Metaphysics (5669)**
Philosophy Education Society
The Review of Metaphysics
The Catholic University of America
Washington, DC 20064
Phone: (202)635-8778
Fax: (202)319-4484

Subject(s): Philosophy; Indexes, Abstracts, Reports, Proceedings, and Bibliographies

Circ: ‡2,500

**West Virginia Medical Journal (32562)**
West Virginia State Medical Association
PO Box 4106
Charleston, WV 25364
Phone: (304)925-0342
Fax: (304)925-0345
Subject(s): Medicine and Surgery

Circ: (Controlled)‡100
(Paid)‡2,500

**World Federation for Mental Health Annual Report (12883)**
World Federation for Mental Health
Sheppard & Enoch Pratt Hospital
PO Box 6815
Baltimore, MD 21285-6815
Phone: (410)938-3180
Fax: (410)938-3183
Subject(s): Medicine and Surgery; Health and Healthcare

Circ: (Paid)2500

**Annals of Surgical Oncology (30976)**
Lippincott Williams & Wilkins
Ste. 300, 330 John Carlyle St.
Alexandria, VA 22314
Phone: (703)299-1185
Fax: (703)299-1049
Subject(s): Medicine and Surgery

Circ: 2,424

**Children & Schools (5302)**
National Association of Social Workers
750 1st St. NE, Ste. 700
Washington, DC 20002-4241
Phone: (202)408-8600
Fax: (202)336-8312
Subject(s): Sociology; Education

Circ: 2,400

**Optics Letters (5605)**
Optical Society of America
2010 Massachusetts Ave., NW
Washington, DC 20036-1023
Phone: (202)223-8130
Fax: (202)223-1096
Subject(s): Ophthalmology, Optometry, and Optics; Science (General)

Circ: (Paid)2400

**Prologue (13060)**
National Archives and Records Administration
8601 Adelphi Rd.
College Park, MD 20740-6001
Phone: (301)837-1850
Fax: (301)837-0319
Subject(s): History and Genealogy

Circ: (Combined)2,400

**Bulletin of the History of Medicine (12686)**
Johns Hopkins University Press
2715 N Charles St.
Baltimore, MD 21218-4363
Phone: (410)516-6987
Fax: (410)516-6968
Subject(s): Medicine and Surgery; History and Genealogy

Circ: ‡2,394

**Policy Studies Journal (5621)**
Policy Studies Organization
1527 New Hampshire Ave. NW
Washington, DC 20036
Phone: (202)483-2512
Fax: (202)483-2657
Subject(s): Politics; Sociology

Circ: (Non-paid)‡50
(Paid)‡2,350

**Political Theory (31260)**
Sage Publications Inc.
Political Theory, Department of Politics
University of Virginia
PO Box 400787
Charlottesville, VA 22904
Subject(s): Politics

Circ: (Non-paid)‡95
(Paid)‡2,350

**Journal of Pharmacology & Experimental Therapeutics (12987)**
American Society for Pharmacology and Experimental Therapeutics
9650 Rockville Pke.
Bethesda, MD 20814-3995
Phone: (301)634-7060
Fax: (301)634-7061
Subject(s): Drugs and Pharmaceuticals

Circ: (Non-paid)‡221
(Paid)‡2,320

**Arms Control Today (5250)**
Arms Control Association
1150 Connecticut Ave. NW, Ste. 620
Washington, DC 20036
Phone: (202)463-8270
Fax: (202)463-8273
Subject(s): Peace; International Affairs

Circ: ‡2,300

**Journal of AOAC International (13169)**
AOAC International
481 N Frederick Ave., Ste. 500
Gaithersburg, MD 20877-2417
Phone: (301)924-7077
Fax: (301)924-7089
Subject(s): Chemistry, Chemicals, and Chemical Engineering

Circ: ‡2,300

**Journal of Bridge Engineering (31708)**
American Society of Civil Engineers
1801 Alexander Bell Dr.
Reston, VA 20191-4400
Phone: (703)295-6300
Fax: (703)295-6222
Subject(s): Engineering (Various branches); Public Transportation

Circ: (Paid)2,300

**The Journal of Negro Education (5495)**
Journal of Negro Education
Howard University
PO Box 311
Washington, DC 20059
Phone: (202)806-8120
Fax: (202)806-8434
Subject(s): Education; Black Publications

Circ: (Controlled)‡100
(Paid)‡2,300

**National Civic Review (5561)**
Jossey-Bass Publishers
National Civic League
1319 F St. NW, Ste. 204
Washington, DC 20002
Phone: (202)783-2961
Fax: (202)347-2161
Subject(s): State, Municipal, and County Administration

Circ: ‡2,250

**Journal of Statistics Education (31033)**
American Statistical Association
1429 Duke St.
Alexandria, VA 22314-3415
Phone: (703)684-1221
Fax: (703)684-2037
Subject(s): Statistics; Education

Circ: (Non-paid)2,230

**Journal of Pediatric Orthopaedics (12790)**
Lippincott Williams & Wilkins
351 W. Camden St.
Baltimore, MD 21201
Phone: (410)528-4479
Fax: (410)528-4312
Subject(s): Medicine and Surgery

Circ: 2,222

**The Journal of Educational Research (5472)**
Heldref Publications
1319 18th St., NW
Washington, DC 20036-1802
Phone: (202)296-6267
Fax: (202)296-5149
Subject(s): Education

Circ: (Paid)‡2,200

**Journal of Engineering Mechanics (31714)**
American Society of Civil Engineers
1801 Alexander Bell Dr.
Reston, VA 20191-4400
Phone: (703)295-6300
Fax: (703)295-6222

Subject(s): Engineering (Various branches)

Circ: (Paid)⊕2200

**Journal of the Optical Society of America A: Optics, Image Science, and Vision (5500)**
Optical Society of America
2010 Massachusetts Ave., NW
Washington, DC 20036-1023
Phone: (202)223-8130
Fax: (202)223-1096
Subject(s): Ophthalmology, Optometry, and Optics

Circ: (Paid)2,200

**Social Work Research (5697)**
National Association of Social Workers
750 1st St. NE, Ste. 700
Washington, DC 20002-4241
Phone: (202)408-8600
Fax: (202)336-8312
Subject(s): Sociology; Indexes, Abstracts, Reports, Proceedings, and Bibliographies

Circ: (Paid)2,200

**Undersea & Hyperbaric Medicine (13219)**
Undersea and Hyperbaric Medical Society
10531 Metropolitan Ave.
Kensington, MD 20895
Phone: (301)942-2980
Fax: (301)942-7804
Subject(s): Laboratory Research (Scientific and Medical); Medicine and Surgery

Circ: (Controlled)2,200

**Virginia Law Review (31270)**
Virginia Law Review Association
University of Virginia School of Law
580 Massie Rd.
Charlottesville, VA 22903-1789
Phone: (434)924-3079
Fax: (434)982-2818
Subject(s): Law

Circ: 2,200

**Compoundings (30990)**
Independent Lubricant Manufacturers Association
651 S. Washington St.
Alexandria, VA 22314
Phone: (703)684-5574
Fax: (703)836-8503
Subject(s): Commerce and Industry

Circ: (Paid)2,175

**Journal of Voice (12799)**
Lippincott Williams & Wilkins
351 W. Camden St.
Baltimore, MD 21201
Phone: (410)528-4479
Fax: (410)528-4312
Subject(s): Health and Healthcare

Circ: 2,178

**International Legal Materials (5447)**
American Society of International Law
2223 Massachusetts Ave. NW
Washington, DC 20008
Phone: (202)939-6000
Fax: (202)797-7133
Subject(s): International Affairs

Circ: (Paid)2,111

**Annals of the Entomological Society of America (13223)**
Entomological Society of America
10001 Derekwood Ln., Ste. 100
Lanham, MD 20706-4876
Phone: (301)731-4535
Fax: (301)731-4538
Subject(s): Entomology

Circ: 2,100

**Psychiatry (5637)**
Taylor and Francis
George Washington University Medical Center
2300 Eye St. NW
Washington, DC 20037
Phone: (202)994-2636
Fax: (202)994-4812
Subject(s): Psychology and Psychiatry

Circ: 2,017

Circulation: ★ = ABC; △ = BPA; ◆ = CAC; ● = CCAB; ☐ = VAC; ⊕ = PO Statement; ‡ = Publisher's Report; Boldface figures = sworn; Light figures = estimated.

**Automotive Recycling** (31335)
Automotive Recyclers Association
3975 Fair Ridge Dr., Ste. 20-N.
Fairfax, VA 22033
Phone: (703)385-1001
Fax: (703)385-1494
**Subject(s):** Automotive (Trade)
**Circ:** (Non-paid)‡2,000

**BIA News** (31696)
Brick Industry Association
11490 Commerce Park Dr.
Reston, VA 20191-1525
Phone: (703)620-0010
Fax: (703)620-3928
**Subject(s):** Building Materials, Concrete, Brick, and Tile; Construction, Contracting, Building, and Excavating
**Circ:** 2,000

**Biomacromolecules** (5270)
American Chemical Society
1155 16th St. NW
Washington, DC 20036
Phone: (202)872-4600
Fax: (202)872-6067
**Subject(s):** Biology; Chemistry, Chemicals, and Chemical Engineering
**Circ:** 2000

**The George Washington Law Review** (5400)
2008 G St. NW, 2nd Fl.
Washington, DC 20052
Phone: (202)676-3868
Fax: (202)676-3876
**Subject(s):** Law
**Circ:** ‡2,000

**The International Economy** (5440)
The International Economy Publications Inc.
888 16 Street NW Ste 740
Washington, DC 20006-6805
Phone: (202)861-0791
Fax: (202)861-0790
**Subject(s):** Economics
**Circ:** (Paid)2,000

**Journal of Propulsion and Power** (31729)
American Institute of Aeronautics and Astronautics
1801 Alexander Bell Dr., Ste. 500
Reston, VA 20191-4344
Phone: (703)264-7500
Fax: (703)264-7551
**Subject(s):** Physics; Aviation
**Circ:** ‡2,000

**Journal of Technology Education** (31735)
International Technology Education Association
1914 Association Dr., Ste. 201
Reston, VA 20191-1539
Phone: (703)860-2100
Fax: (703)860-0353
**Subject(s):** Education; Computers
**Circ:** 2,000

**Kennedy Institute of Ethics Journal** (5523)
Johns Hopkins University Press
Joseph & Rose Kennedy Institute of Ethics
Georgetown University
Washington, DC 20057
Phone: (202)687-6790
Fax: (202)687-8089
**Subject(s):** Philosophy; Humanities
**Circ:** 2,000

**Pharmacopeial Forum** (13305)
U.S. Pharmacopeial Convention Inc.
12601 Twinbrook Pkwy.
Rockville, MD 20852
Phone: (301)881-0666
Fax: (301)816-8148
**Subject(s):** Drugs and Pharmaceuticals
**Circ:** (Non-paid)‡200
    (Paid)‡2,000

**The Responsive Community** (5667)
The Reponsive Community
703 Gelman Library
The George Washington University
Washington, DC 20052
Phone: (202)994-8194
Fax: (202)994-1606
**Subject(s):** Political Science; Sociology
**Circ:** (Paid)2,000

**SIAM Journal on Control and Optimization** (13064)
Society for Industrial & Applied Mathematics
c/o Steven I. Marcus
Dept. of Electrical and Computer Engineering
A. V. Williams Bldg.
Univ. of Maryland
College Park, MD 20742
**Subject(s):** Mathematics
**Circ:** ‡2,003

**Topics in Emergency Medicine (TEM)** (13177)
Aspen Publishers Inc.
c/o Carmen Germaine Warner
200 Orchard Ridge Dr.
Gaithersburg, MD 20878
Phone: (301)417-7626
Fax: (301)417-7550
**Subject(s):** Medicine and Surgery
**Circ:** (Paid)2,000

**Journal of Pediatric Gastroenterology & Nutrition** (12789)
Lippincott Williams & Wilkins
351 W. Camden St.
Baltimore, MD 21201
Phone: (410)528-4479
Fax: (410)528-4312
**Subject(s):** Medicine and Surgery
**Circ:** (Paid)1,980

**Journal of Neurophysiology** (12985)
The American Physiological Society
9650 Rockville Pke.
Bethesda, MD 20814-3991
Phone: (301)634-7164
Fax: (301)634-7241
**Subject(s):** Physiology and Anatomy
**Circ:** (Paid)‡1,931

**The Catholic Historical Review** (5295)
CUA Press
620 Michigan Ave., NE, 240 Leahy Hall
Washington, DC 20064
Phone: (202)319-5052
Fax: (202)319-4985
**Subject(s):** History and Genealogy; Religious Publications
**Circ:** (Non-paid)‡166
    (Paid)‡1,926

**Transportation Journal** (31166)
American Society of Transportation and Logistics Inc.
1700 N Moore St., Ste 1900
Arlington, VA 22209
Phone: (703)524-5011
Fax: (703)524-5017
**Subject(s):** Transportation, Traffic, and Shipping
**Circ:** (Controlled)1,913

**Journal of Experimental Psychology: Animal Behavior Processes** (5477)
American Psychological Association
750 1st St. NE
Washington, DC 20002-4242
Phone: (202)336-5500
Fax: (202)336-6012
**Subject(s):** Psychology and Psychiatry
**Circ:** ‡1,900

**Lectura y Vida** (5149)
International Reading Association
800 Barksdale Rd.
PO Box 8139
Newark, DE 19714-8139
Phone: (302)731-1600
Fax: (302)731-1057
**Subject(s):** Hispanic Publications
**Circ:** (Controlled)30
    (Paid)1,900

**Measurement and Evaluation in Counseling and Development** (31038)
American Counseling Association
5999 Stevenson Ave.
Alexandria, VA 22304
Phone: (703)823-6862
Fax: (703)823-0252
**Subject(s):** Education; Psychology and Psychiatry
**Circ:** (Paid)1,900

**Behavioral Neuroscience** (5267)
American Psychological Association
750 1st St. NE
Washington, DC 20002-4242
Phone: (202)336-5500
Fax: (202)336-6012
**Subject(s):** Psychology and Psychiatry
**Circ:** ‡1,850

**Accident Investigation Quarterly** (13383)
Victor T. Craig
PO Box 234
Waldorf, MD 20604-0234
Phone: (301)843-1371
Fax: (301)843-1371
**Subject(s):** Engineering (Various branches); Law
**Circ:** (Combined)1,800

**Delaware Medical Journal** (5141)
Medical Society of Delaware
131 Continental Dr., Ste. 405
Newark, DE 19713-4308
Phone: (302)658-7596
Fax: (302)658-9669
**Subject(s):** Medicine and Surgery
**Circ:** (Free)24
    (Paid)1,800

**Journal of Urban Planning and Development** (31738)
American Society of Civil Engineers
1801 Alexander Bell Dr.
Reston, VA 20191-4400
Phone: (703)295-6300
Fax: (703)295-6222
**Subject(s):** Engineering (Various branches)
**Circ:** (Paid)⊕1,800

**Parliamentary Journal** (5166)
American Institute of Parliamentarians
PO Box 2173
Wilmington, DE 19899-2173
Phone: (302)762-1811
Fax: (302)762-2170
**Subject(s):** Politics
**Circ:** 1,800

**RadTech Report** (13036)
RadTech International North America
6935 Wisconsin Ave., Ste. 207
Chevy Chase, MD 20815
Phone: (240)497-1242
Fax: (240)209-2337
**Subject(s):** Chemistry, Chemicals, and Chemical Engineering
**Circ:** (Non-paid)1,750

**Psychosomatics** (31150)
American Psychiatric Publishing Inc.
1000 Wilson Blvd., Ste. 1825
Arlington, VA 22209-3901
Phone: (703)907-7322
Fax: (703)907-1091
**Subject(s):** Psychology and Psychiatry; Medicine and Surgery
**Circ:** (Non-paid)781
    (Paid)1,747

**Seminars in Speech and Language** (13063)
Thieme Medical Publishers Inc.
c/o Nan Bernstein Ratner, Ph.D.
Chariman, Department of Hearing and Speech Services
University of Maryland
College Park, MD
**Subject(s):** Hearing and Speech
**Circ:** ‡1,733

**American Journal of Islamic Social Sciences** (31487)
PO Box 669
Herndon, VA 20172
Fax: (703)471-3922
**Subject(s):** Social Sciences; Religious Publications
**Circ:** 1,700

**Journal of Neuropsychiatry and Clinical Neurosciences** (31133)
American Psychiatric Publishing Inc.
1000 Wilson Blvd., Ste. 1825
Arlington, VA 22209-3901
Phone: (703)907-7322
Fax: (703)907-1091
**Subject(s):** Psychology and Psychiatry
**Circ:** (Paid)1,700

**Bulletin of the American Astronomical Society** (5284)
American Institute of Physics
C/O Robert W. Milkey
2000 Florida Ave., NW, No. 400
Washington, DC 20009
Phone: (202)328-2010
Fax: (202)234-2560

**Subject(s):** Astronomy and Meteorology; Indexes, Abstracts, Reports, Proceedings, and Bibliographies

**Circ:** ‡1,665

**The German Postal Specialist (12642)**
German Philatelic Society
Box 779
Arnold, MD 21012
Phone: (410)757-2344
Fax: (410)757-6857
**Subject(s):** Collecting

**Circ:** (Controlled)‡30
(Paid)‡1,650

**Journal of Glaucoma (12774)**
Lippincott Williams & Wilkins
351 W. Camden St.
Baltimore, MD 21201
Phone: (410)528-4479
Fax: (410)528-4312
**Subject(s):** Laboratory Research (Scientific and Medical)

**Circ:** 1,618

**Archives of Environmental Health (5248)**
Heldref Publications
1319 18th St., NW
Washington, DC 20036-1802
Phone: (202)296-6267
Fax: (202)296-5149
**Subject(s):** Health and Healthcare

**Circ:** (Paid)‡1,600

**Biotropica (5272)**
Association for Tropical Biology
Botany, MRC-166
U.S. National Herbarium
National Museum of Natural History
Smithsonian Institution
Washington, DC 20560-0166
Phone: (202)633-0920
Fax: (202)786-2563
**Subject(s):** Biology; Science (General); French; Portuguese; Spanish

**Circ:** 1,600

**College Teaching (5320)**
Heldref Publications
1319 18th St., NW
Washington, DC 20036-1802
Phone: (202)296-6267
Fax: (202)296-5149
**Subject(s):** Education

**Circ:** (Paid)‡1,600

**Journal of the History of Philosophy (12778)**
Johns Hopkins University Press
2715 N Charles St.
Baltimore, MD 21218-4363
Phone: (410)516-6987
Fax: (410)516-6968
**Subject(s):** Philosophy; French; German

**Circ:** 1,600

**Journal of Thermophysics and Heat Transfer (31736)**
American Institute of Aeronautics and Astronautics
1801 Alexander Bell Dr., Ste. 500
Reston, VA 20191-4344
Phone: (703)264-7500
Fax: (703)264-7551
**Subject(s):** Aviation; Physics

**Circ:** ‡1,600

**Winterthur Portfolio (5175)**
University of Chicago Press
c/o Lisa L. Lock, Editor
Winterthur Portfolio
Winterthur, DE 19735
Phone: (302)888-4615
Fax: (800)448-3883
**Subject(s):** Art and Art History

**Circ:** (Paid)‡1,600

**Journal of Atmospheric and Oceanic Technology (31455)**
American Meteorological Society
Office of the Chief Editor
Journal Of Atmospheric And Oceanic Technology
Atmospheric Sciences NASA Langley
Research Center MS-401A
Hampton, VA 23681-2199
**Subject(s):** Astronomy and Meteorology; Oceanography and Marine Studies

**Circ:** ‡1,588

**English Literary History (ELH) (12720)**
Johns Hopkins University Press
2715 N Charles St.
Baltimore, MD 21218-4363
Phone: (410)516-6987
Fax: (410)516-6968
**Subject(s):** Literature; History and Genealogy

**Circ:** ‡1,568

**The Journal of General Psychology (5481)**
Heldref Publications
1319 18th St., NW
Washington, DC 20036-1802
Phone: (202)296-6267
Fax: (202)296-5149
**Subject(s):** Psychology and Psychiatry

**Circ:** (Paid)‡1,545

**The Journal of Social Psychology (5514)**
Heldref Publications
1319 18th St., NW
Washington, DC 20036-1802
Phone: (202)296-6267
Fax: (202)296-5149
**Subject(s):** Psychology and Psychiatry; Anthropology and Ethnology

**Circ:** (Paid)‡1,545

**Human Rights Quarterly (12744)**
Johns Hopkins University Press
2715 N Charles St.
Baltimore, MD 21218-4363
Phone: (410)516-6987
Fax: (410)516-6968
**Subject(s):** Philanthropy and Humanitarianism

**Circ:** ‡1,533

**Futures Research Quarterly (12968)**
World Future Society
7910 Woodmont Ave., Ste. 450
Bethesda, MD 20814
Phone: (301)656-8274
Fax: (301)951-0394
**Subject(s):** Sociology

**Circ:** ‡1,500

**Integral Yoga Magazine (31228)**
Integral Yoga Publications
Rte. 1
PO Box 1720
Buckingham, VA 23921-9980
Phone: (434)969-3121
Fax: (434)969-1303
**Subject(s):** Health and Healthcare

**Circ:** 1,500

**Journal of Acquired Immune Deficiency Syndrome (JAIDS) (12758)**
Lippincott Williams & Wilkins
351 W. Camden St.
Baltimore, MD 21201
Phone: (410)528-4479
Fax: (410)528-4312
**Subject(s):** Acquired Immune Deficiency Syndrome

**Circ:** (Non-paid)‡1,505

**Journal of Aquatic Animal Health (32637)**
American Fisheries Society
C/O Dr. Vicki S. Blazer
USGS National Fish Health Research Laboratory
1700 Leetown Rd.
Kearneysville, WV 25430
Phone: (304)724-4434
Fax: (304)724-4435
**Subject(s):** Fish and Commercial Fisheries; Veterinary Medicine

**Circ:** (Paid)1,500

**Journal of Hydraulic Engineering (31719)**
American Society of Civil Engineers
1801 Alexander Bell Dr.
Reston, VA 20191-4400
Phone: (703)295-6300
Fax: (703)295-6222
**Subject(s):** Engineering (Various branches)

**Circ:** (Paid)⊕1,500

**Journal of Water Resources Planning and Management (31739)**
American Society of Civil Engineers
1801 Alexander Bell Dr.
Reston, VA 20191-4400
Phone: (703)295-6300
Fax: (703)295-6222

**Subject(s):** Water Supply and Sewage Disposal; Ecology and Conservation

**Circ:** (Paid)⊕1,500

**Latin American Antiquity (5530)**
Society for American Archaeology
900 2nd St. NE, No. 12
Washington, DC 20002-3557
Phone: (202)789-8200
Fax: (202)789-0284
**Subject(s):** Hispanic Publications; Archaeology

**Circ:** ‡1,500

**Neuropsychology Abstracts (5585)**
American Psychological Association
750 1st St. NE
Washington, DC 20002-4242
Phone: (202)336-5500
Fax: (202)336-6012
**Subject(s):** Psychology and Psychiatry

**Circ:** ‡1,500

**Portal (12847)**
Johns Hopkins University Press
2715 N Charles St.
Baltimore, MD 21218-4363
Phone: (410)516-6987
Fax: (410)516-6968
**Subject(s):** Library and Information Science

**Circ:** (Combined)1,500

**Public Relations Review (13070)**
University of California Press
c/o R.E. Hiebert, Editor
Univ. of Maryland
38091 Beach Rd.
PO BOX 180
Coltons Point, MD 20626-0180
Phone: (301)769-3899
**Subject(s):** Public Relations

**Circ:** (Non-paid)‡55
(Paid)‡1,500

**Quality Matters (5660)**
The American Health Quality Association
1155 21st St. NW Ste.202
Washington, DC 20036
Phone: (202)331-5790
Fax: (202)331-9334
**Subject(s):** Health and Healthcare

**Circ:** (Paid)1,500

**Transportation Quarterly (5722)**
Eno Transportation Foundation Inc.
1634 I St. NW, Ste. 500
Washington, DC 20006-4003
Phone: (202)879-4700
Fax: (202)879-4719
**Subject(s):** Transportation, Traffic, and Shipping

**Circ:** (Controlled)‡1,500

**William & Mary Bill of Rights Journal (31953)**
College of William and Mary School of Law
Box 8795
Williamsburg, VA 23187-8795
Phone: (757)221-3706
Fax: (757)221-3777
**Subject(s):** Law

**Circ:** (Paid)‡1,500

**The Social Studies (5695)**
Heldref Publications
1319 18th St., NW
Washington, DC 20036-1802
Phone: (202)296-6267
Fax: (202)296-5149
**Subject(s):** Education; Sociology

**Circ:** (Paid)1,470

**Journal of Early Christian Studies (12771)**
Johns Hopkins University Press
2715 N Charles St.
Baltimore, MD 21218-4363
Phone: (410)516-6987
Fax: (410)516-6968
**Subject(s):** Theology

**Circ:** (Combined)1,444

**Association Publishing (31574)**
Society of National Association Publications
8405 Greensboro Dr., Ste. 800
Mc Lean, VA 22102
Phone: (703)506-3285
Fax: (703)506-3266

**Subject(s):** Business; Journalism and Publishing

**Circ:** 1,400

**Catholic University Law Review (5296)**
Columbus School of Law
The Catholic University of America
Cardinal Sta.
Washington, DC 20064
Phone: (202)319-5140
**Subject(s):** Law

**Circ:** ‡1,400

**The Clearing House (5310)**
Heldref Publications
1319 18th St., NW
Washington, DC 20036-1802
Phone: (202)296-6267
Fax: (202)296-5149
**Subject(s):** Education

**Circ:** ‡1,400

**Maryland Music Educator (13363)**
Maryland Music Educators Association
c/o Thomas W Fugate
27 Meadow Ln.
Thurmont, MD 21788-1737
Phone: (301)271-7269
Fax: (301)271-7032
**Subject(s):** Music and Musical Instruments; Education

**Circ:** (Combined)1,400

**PsycSCAN (5653)**
American Psychological Association
750 1st St. NE
Washington, DC 20002-4242
Phone: (202)336-5500
Fax: (202)336-6012
**Subject(s):** Psychology and Psychiatry; Indexes, Abstracts, Reports, Proceedings, and Bibliographies

**Circ:** ‡1,400

**Quality Management in Health Care (QMHC) (13175)**
Aspen Publishers Inc.
c/o Jean Carroll
200 Orchard Ridge Dr.
Gaithersburg, MD 20878
Phone: (301)417-7617
Fax: (301)417-7550
**Subject(s):** Health and Healthcare; Management and Administration

**Circ:** (Paid)1,400

**Cornea (12699)**
Lippincott Williams & Wilkins
351 W. Camden St.
Baltimore, MD 21201
Phone: (410)528-4479
Fax: (410)528-4312
**Subject(s):** Laboratory Research (Scientific and Medical); Ophthalmology, Optometry, and Optics

**Circ:** 1,384

**Tax Notes International (31165)**
Tax Analysts
6830 N Fairfax Dr.
Arlington, VA 22213
Phone: (703)533-4400
Fax: (703)533-4444
**Subject(s):** Taxation and Tariff; International Business and Economics

**Circ:** (Paid)1,365

**Microbial Ecology (31763)**
Springer-Verlag New York Inc.
c/o James K. Fredrickson
Biogeochemistry Department
Pacific NW National Laboratory
PO Box 999, P7-50, 902 Battelle Blvd.
Richland, WA 99352
**Subject(s):** Ecology and Conservation

**Circ:** (Combined)1,350

**Family & Community Health (31247)**
Aspen Publishers Inc.
c/o Dean and Professor, School of Nursing
University of Virginia, McLeod Hall
PO Box 800782
202 15th St., SW 22903
Charlottesville, VA 22908-0782
Phone: (434)924-0063
**Subject(s):** Health and Healthcare

**Circ:** (Non-paid)106
(Paid)1,327

**Pathology Case Reviews (12840)**
Lippincott Williams & Wilkins
Dept. of Pathology
N2W50
22 S. Greene St.
Baltimore, MD 21201-1595
Phone: (410)328-5072
Fax: (410)328-0081
**Subject(s):** Medicine and Surgery

**Circ:** (Paid)1,327

**Philosophy and Literature (12842)**
Johns Hopkins University Press
2715 N Charles St.
Baltimore, MD 21218-4363
Phone: (410)516-6987
Fax: (410)516-6968
**Subject(s):** Literature; Philosophy

**Circ:** ‡1,320

**The Collectors Club Philatelist (13281)**
Collectors Club Inc.
PO Box 183
Riva, MD 21140-0183
Phone: (410)974-6380
**Subject(s):** Collecting

**Circ:** ‡1,300

**Current (5349)**
Heldref Publications
1319 18th St., NW
Washington, DC 20036-1802
Phone: (202)296-6267
Fax: (202)296-5149
**Subject(s):** Sociology; Politics; Economics

**Circ:** ‡1,300

**National Honors Report (31678)**
National Collegiate Honors Council
606 Third Ave.
Radford, VA 24141
Phone: (540)831-5004
Fax: (540)831-5004
**Subject(s):** Education

**Circ:** (Paid)1,300

**Physical Disabilities—Education & Related Services (31147)**
Council for Exceptional Children
1110 N Glebe Rd., Ste. 300
Arlington, VA 22201
Phone: (703)620-3660
Fax: (703)264-9494
**Subject(s):** Education; Handicapped

**Circ:** (Non-paid)1,300

**Lotus Remarque (13055)**
Lotus Ltd.
Box L
College Park, MD 20741
Phone: (301)982-4054
**Subject(s):** Automotive (Consumer)

**Circ:** (Non-paid)‡45
(Paid)‡1,250

**Molecular Pharmacology (12993)**
American Society for Pharmacology and Experimental Therapeutics
9650 Rockville Pke.
Bethesda, MD 20814-3995
Phone: (301)634-7060
Fax: (301)634-7061
**Subject(s):** Drugs and Pharmaceuticals

**Circ:** (Non-paid)‡64
(Paid)‡1,218

**AACE Perspective (31685)**
American Association of Code Enforcement
12100 Sunset Hills Rd., Ste. 130
Reston, VA 20190-5202
Phone: (703)234-4073
Fax: (703)435-4390
**Subject(s):** Police, Penology, and Penal Institutions

**Circ:** 1,200

**American Journal of Mathematics (12655)**
Johns Hopkins University Press
c/o Bernard Shiffman
Dept. of Mathematics
Johns Hopkins University
3400 N. Charles St
Baltimore, MD 21218-2680
Phone: (410)516-7411
**Subject(s):** Mathematics

**Circ:** 1,200

**Battler Columns (32712)**
Alderson-Broaddus College
PO Box 2158
Collage Rd.
Philippi, WV 26416
Phone: (304)457-1700
Fax: (304)457-6367
**Subject(s):** College Publications

**Circ:** (Non-paid)‡1,200

**Ethos (31122)**
American Anthropological Association
2200 Wilson Blvd., Ste. 600
Arlington, VA 22201
Phone: (703)528-1902
Fax: (703)528-3546
**Subject(s):** Anthropology and Ethnology; Psychology and Psychiatry

**Circ:** (Paid)‡1,200

**Journal of Labor Research (31352)**
George Mason University
Dept. of Economics
Enterprise Hall - 3rd Floor
4400 University Dr.
Fairfax, VA 22030-4444
Phone: (703)993-1155
Fax: (703)993-1133
**Subject(s):** Labor

**Circ:** ‡1,200

**Journal of Management Systems (31287)**
Maximilian Press Publishers
920 S. Battlefield Blvd., Ste. 100
Chesapeake, VA 23320
Phone: (804)320-5771
Fax: (757)482-0325
**Subject(s):** Management and Administration

**Circ:** 1,200

**Journal of Social History (31355)**
George Mason University
4400 University Dr.
Fairfax, VA 22030-4444
Phone: (703)993-2915
**Subject(s):** Social Sciences; History and Genealogy

**Circ:** (Combined)1,200

**PsycSCAN (5650)**
American Psychological Association
750 1st St. NE
Washington, DC 20002-4242
Phone: (202)336-5500
Fax: (202)336-6012
**Subject(s):** Psychology and Psychiatry

**Circ:** (Paid)1,200

**Shenandoah (31524)**
Mattingly House
2 Lee Ave.
Washington & Lee University
Lexington, VA 24450-0303
Phone: (540)458-8765
Fax: (540)458-8461
**Subject(s):** Literature and Literary Reviews

**Circ:** ‡1,200

**Skyways (31364)**
World War 1 Aeroplanes Inc.
5411 Masser Ln.
Fairfax, VA 22032
Phone: (703)232-6674
**Subject(s):** Aviation; History and Genealogy

**Circ:** (Paid)1,200

**TAMS Journal (13024)**
Token and Medal Society Inc.
PO Box 366
Bryantown, MD 20617-0366
Phone: (301)274-3441
**Subject(s):** Collecting

**Circ:** ‡1,200

**Journal of Applied Biomechanics (5147)**
Human Kinetics Publishers Inc.
c/o Thomas S. Buchanan
Director, Ctr. for Biomed. Engineering Res.
University of Delaware
126 Spencer Lab
Newark, DE 19716
Phone: (302)831-2410
Fax: (302)831-3466
**Subject(s):** Physical Education and Athletics

**Circ:** (Non-paid)‡40
(Paid)‡1,164

**Journal of Cerebral Blood Flow and Metabolism** (12766)
Lippincott Williams & Wilkins
351 W. Camden St.
Baltimore, MD 21201
Phone: (410)528-4479
Fax: (410)528-4312
**Subject(s):** Medicine and Surgery

**Circ:** 1,151

**Journal of Social, Political & Economic Studies** (5513)
Council for Social and Economic Studies Inc.
1133 13 St. NW, Apt. C2
Washington, DC 20005
Phone: (202)371-2700
Fax: (202)371-1523
**Subject(s):** Sociology; Economics; Politics; International Affairs

**Circ:** (Non-paid)‡55
    (Paid)‡1,150

**The Journal of Environmental Education** (5473)
Heldref Publications
1319 18th. St., NW
Washington, DC 20036-1802
Phone: (202)296-6267
Fax: (202)296-5149
**Subject(s):** Ecology and Conservation

**Circ:** (Paid)‡1,140

**West Virginia Construction News** (32559)
Contractors Association of West Virginia
2114 Kanawha Blvd. E
Charleston, WV 25311
Phone: (304)342-1166
Fax: (304)342-1074
**Subject(s):** Construction, Contracting, Building, and Excavating; Engineering (Various branches)

**Circ:** (Paid)‡30
    (Non-paid)‡1,130

**International Journal of Gynecological Pathology** (31250)
Lippincott Williams & Wilkins
c/o Mark H. Stoler
Univ. of Virginia Health System
Jefferson Park Avenue, OMS, Room 3880
Charlottesville, VA
**Subject(s):** Laboratory Research (Scientific and Medical)

**Circ:** 1,120

**Modernism/Modernity** (12820)
Johns Hopkins University Press
2715 N Charles St.
Baltimore, MD 21218-4363
Phone: (410)516-6987
Fax: (410)516-6968
**Subject(s):** Literature; Art and Art History; Music and Musical Instruments; Humanities

**Circ:** (Combined)1,125

**World Affairs** (5759)
Heldref Publications
1319 18th St., NW
Washington, DC 20036-1802
Phone: (202)296-6267
Fax: (202)296-5149
**Subject(s):** International Affairs

**Circ:** (Paid)‡1,110

**Advances in Dental Research** (30969)
International and American Associations for Dental Research
1619 Duke St.
Alexandria, VA 22314-3406
Phone: (703)548-0066
Fax: (703)548-1883
**Subject(s):** Dentistry

**Circ:** (Paid)‡1,100

**ARSC Journal** (12626)
Association for Recorded Sound Collections Inc.
PO Box 543
Annapolis, MD 21404-0543
Phone: (410)757-0488
Fax: (410)349-0175
**Subject(s):** Library and Information Science

**Circ:** 1,100

**Current Antarctic Literature** (5350)
The Library of Congress
Science & Technology Division
101 Independent Ave SE
Washington, DC 20540
Phone: (202)707-5639
Fax: (202)707-1925
**Subject(s):** Science (General); Indexes, Abstracts, Reports, Proceedings, and Bibliographies

**Circ:** (Controlled)‡1,100

**The Journal of Economic Education** (5468)
Heldref Publications
1319 18th St., NW
Washington, DC 20036-1802
Phone: (202)296-6267
Fax: (202)296-5149
**Subject(s):** Economics; Education

**Circ:** (Paid)‡1,100

**Union Seminary Quarterly Review** (31802)
Union-PSCE
3401 Brook Rd.
Richmond, VA 23227
Phone: (804)355-0671
Fax: (804)278-4208
**Subject(s):** Religious Publications; College Publications

**Circ:** (Non-paid)‡100
    (Paid)‡1,100

**West Virginia Dental Journal** (32560)
West Virginia Dental Association
2003 Quarrier St.
Charleston, WV 25311-2212
Phone: (304)344-5246
Fax: (304)344-5316
**Subject(s):** Dentistry

**Circ:** ‡1,100

**Consulting Psychology Journal: Practice and Research** (5335)
Educational Publishing Foundation
750 1st St. NE
Washington, DC 20002-4242
Phone: (202)408-9804
Fax: (202)336-5568
**Subject(s):** Psychology and Psychiatry

**Circ:** (Paid)‡1,050

**Journal of Thoracic Imaging** (12797)
Lippincott Williams & Wilkins
c/o Charles S. White
Dept. of Diagnostic Radiology
Univ. of Maryland Medical Center
Baltimore, MD
**Subject(s):** Radiology, Ultrasound, and Nuclear Medicine

**Circ:** 1,042

**Journal of Clinical Gastroenterology** (12768)
Lippincott Williams & Wilkins
351 W. Camden St.
Baltimore, MD 21201
Phone: (410)528-4479
Fax: (410)528-4312
**Subject(s):** Laboratory Research (Scientific and Medical)

**Circ:** 1,023

**Obstetric Anesthesia Digest** (12834)
Lippincott Williams & Wilkins
351 W. Camden St.
Baltimore, MD 21201
Phone: (410)528-4479
Fax: (410)528-4312
**Subject(s):** Medicine and Surgery

**Circ:** 1,010

**The Americas** (5232)
The Academy of American Franciscan History
The Catholic University of America Press
620 Michigan Ave., NE
Washington, DC 20064
Phone: (202)319-5000
**Subject(s):** Intercultural Interests

**Circ:** ‡1,000

**Business Ethics Quarterly** (5286)
Philosophy Documentation Center
The McDonough School of Business
Georgetown University
37th & O St. NW
Washington, DC 20057-1147
Phone: (202)687-7701
Fax: (202)687-7351
**Subject(s):** Business

**Circ:** (Paid)1,000

**The Exempt Organization Tax Review** (31125)
Tax Analysts
6830 N. Fairfax Dr.
Arlington, VA 22213
Phone: (703)533-4425
Fax: (800)955-3444
**Subject(s):** Taxation and Tariff; Accountants and Accounting; Law

**Circ:** ‡1,000

**Experimental Aging Research** (13164)
Taylor & Francis
c/o Jeffrey W. Elias
P.O. Box 83429
Gaithersburg, MD 20883-3429
**Subject(s):** Biology; Genetics; Gerontology; Laboratory Research (Scientific and Medical)

**Circ:** 1,000

**Greenbrier Historical Society Journal** (32648)
Greenbrier Historical Society
Dept. E, 301 W Washington St.
Lewisburg, WV 24901
Phone: (304)645-3398
Fax: (304)645-5201
**Subject(s):** History and Genealogy

**Circ:** (Controlled)1,000

**Journal of the AHVMA** (12909)
American Holistic Veterinary Medical Association
2218 Old Emmorton Rd.
Bel Air, MD 21015
Phone: (410)569-0795
Fax: (410)569-2346
**Subject(s):** Veterinary Medicine

**Circ:** 1,000

**The Journal of Current Research in Global Business** (5121)
Association for Global Business
c/o Prof.Winston Awadzi, Editor
Delaware State Univ.
Dept. of Economics and Business Administration
Dover, DE 19901
Phone: (302)857-6932

**Circ:** 1,000

**Journal of Educational Multimedia and Hypermedia** (31624)
Association for the Advancement of Computing in Education
PO Box 3728
Norfolk, VA 23514
Phone: (757)623-7588
Fax: (703)997-8760
**Subject(s):** Education; Computers

**Circ:** (Paid)‡1,000

**Journal of Museum Education** (5493)
Museum Education Roundtable
621 Pennsylvania Ave. SE
Washington, DC 20003
Phone: (202)547-8378
Fax: (202)547-8344
**Subject(s):** Museums

**Circ:** 1,000

**Journal of Psychosocial Oncology** (5506)
The Haworth Press Inc.
c/o James R. Zabora
National Catholic School of Social Service
The Catholic Univ. of America
102, Shahan Hall
Washington, DC 20064
Phone: (202)319-5454
Fax: (212)222-1424
**Subject(s):** Medicine and Surgery; Psychology and Psychiatry

**Circ:** (Paid)1,002

**Journal of Religion & Spirituality in Social Work: Social Thought** (5510)
The Haworth Press Inc.
The Catholic University of America
National Catholic School of Social Service
Shahan Hall
Washington, DC 20064
Phone: (202)319-5781
**Subject(s):** Religious Publications; Social Sciences; Social Programs

**Circ:** ‡1,000

Circulation: ★ = ABC; △ = BPA; ♦ = CAC; • = CCAB; ☐ = VAC; ⊕ = PO Statement; ‡ = Publisher's Report; Boldface figures = sworn; Light figures = estimated.

**Journal of Shellfish Research** (13260)
National Shellfisheries Association
National Marine Fisheries Service Laboratory
Oxford, MD 21654
**Subject(s):** Oceanography and Marine Studies
**Circ:** (Controlled)1,000

**Journal of Social and Clinical Psychology** (31354)
Taylor and Francis
Dept. of Psychology
George Mason University
Fairfax, VA 22030
Phone: (703)993-1362
Fax: (703)993-1359
**Subject(s):** Psychology and Psychiatry
**Circ:** 1,000

**The Montage** (12822)
Essex Community College
7201 Rossville Blvd.
Baltimore, MD 21237-3898
Phone: (410)780-6576
Fax: (410)686-9503
**Subject(s):** College Publications
**Circ:** ‡1,000

**Networks** (13057)
John Wiley and Sons Inc.
Van Munching Hall
Univ. of Maryland
College Park, MD 20742
**Subject(s):** Computers
**Circ:** (Paid)1,000

**The News Media & the Law** (31143)
Reporters Committee for Freedom of the Press
1101 Wilson Blvd., Ste. 1100
Arlington, VA 22209
Phone: (703)807-2100
Fax: (703)807-2109
**Subject(s):** Law; Journalism and Publishing; Radio, Television, Cable, and Video
**Circ:** (Paid)‡1,000
    (Non-paid)‡1,000

**The NFIB Foundation Small Business Economic Trends** (5588)
The NFIB Research Foundation
1201 F St. NW Ste. 200
Washington, DC 20004
Phone: (202)554-9000
Fax: (202)554-5572
**Subject(s):** Business
**Circ:** 1,000

**Phoebe** (31360)
George Mason University
4400 University Dr.
Fairfax, VA 22030-4444
Phone: (703)993-2915
**Subject(s):** Literature; Poetry
**Circ:** (Combined)1,000

**Psychological Abstracts** (5639)
American Psychological Association
750 1st St. NE
Washington, DC 20002-4242
Phone: (202)336-5500
Fax: (202)336-6012
**Subject(s):** Psychology and Psychiatry; Indexes, Abstracts, Reports, Proceedings, and Bibliographies
**Circ:** ‡1,000

**Sacred Music** (31421)
Church Music Association of America
134 Christendom Dr.
Front Royal, VA 22630
Phone: (540)636-2900
Fax: (540)636-1655
**Subject(s):** Music and Musical Instruments; Religious Publications; Art and Art History; Humanities
**Circ:** ‡1,000

**Tax Practice Adviser** (5712)
Tax Management Inc.
1250 23rd St. NW
Washington, DC 20037-1166
Phone: (202)785-7195
Fax: (202)833-7297
**Subject(s):** Taxation and Tariff
**Circ:** (Non-paid)279
    (Paid)1,000

**The Thomist** (5717)
Dominican Fathers, Province of St. Joseph
487 Michigan Ave. NE
Washington, DC 20017
Phone: (202)529-5300
Fax: (202)646-4460
**Subject(s):** Religious Publications; Philosophy
**Circ:** (Controlled)50
    (Paid)1000

**Toxicology Pathology** (31760)
Society of Toxicologic Pathologists
1821Michael Faraday Dr., Ste 300
Reston, VA 20190
Phone: (703)438-7508
Fax: (703)438-3113
**Subject(s):** Medicine and Surgery; Veterinary Medicine
**Circ:** (Combined)1,000

**Virginia Journal of International Law** (31269)
Virginia Journal of International Law Association
University of Virginia School of Law
580 Massie Rd.
Charlottesville, VA 22901
Phone: (804)924-3415
Fax: (804)924-3237
**Subject(s):** Law
**Circ:** (Paid)1,000

**Vision** (13222)
National Catholic Office for the Deaf
7202 Buchanan St.
Landover Hills, MD 20784-2236
Phone: (301)577-1684
Fax: (301)577-1690
**Subject(s):** Religious Publications; Handicapped; Hearing and Speech
**Circ:** 1,000

**West Virginia Pharmacists Association** (32564)
2003 Quarrier St.
Charleston, WV 25311
Phone: (304)344-5302
Fax: (304)344-5316
**Subject(s):** Drugs and Pharmaceuticals
**Circ:** ‡1,000

**Delaware Journal of Corporate Law** (5163)
Widener University
Box 7286
Wilmington, DE 19803
Phone: (302)477-2145
Fax: (302)477-2042
**Subject(s):** Law
**Circ:** (Paid)997

**The Mankind Quarterly** (5539)
Scott-Townsend Publishers
1133 13th St. NW, Ste. C-2
Washington, DC 20005
Phone: (202)371-2700
Fax: (202)371-1523
**Subject(s):** Anthropology and Ethnology; Philology, Language, and Linguistics; Sociology
**Circ:** (Non-paid)‡35
    (Paid)‡985

**Washington DC Beverage Journal** (5738)
Beverage Journal Inc.
PO Box 8900
Elkridge, MD 21075-8900
Phone: (410)796-5455
Fax: (410)796-5511
**Subject(s):** Beverages, Brewing, and Bottling
**Circ:** (Paid)‡473
    (Controlled)‡977

**Techniques in Orthopaedics** (12868)
Lippincott Williams & Wilkins
351 W. Camden St.
Baltimore, MD 21201
Phone: (410)528-4479
Fax: (410)528-4312
**Subject(s):** Medicine and Surgery
**Circ:** 964

**Afro-American Historical and Genealogical Society Journal** (5193)
Afro-American Historical and Genealogical Society
PO Box 73067
Washington, DC 20056-3067
Phone: (202)234-5350
Fax: (202)829-8970
**Subject(s):** History and Genealogy; Black Publications
**Circ:** (Paid)910

**Chrysanthemum** (31372)
National Chrysanthemum Society Inc.
10107 Homar Pond Dr.
Fairfax Station, VA 22039-1650
Phone: (703)978-7981
**Subject(s):** Horticulture
**Circ:** (Controlled)900

**Critique** (5346)
Heldref Publications
1319 18th St., NW
Washington, DC 20036-1802
Phone: (202)296-6267
Fax: (202)296-5149
**Subject(s):** Literature
**Circ:** (Paid)905

**Journal** (31837)
History Museum & Historical Society of Western Virginia
Box 1904
Roanoke, VA 24008
Phone: (540)342-5770
Fax: (540)224-1256
**Subject(s):** History and Genealogy
**Circ:** (Paid)900

**The Journal of Experimental Education** (5475)
Heldref Publications
1319 18th St., NW
Washington, DC 20036-1802
Phone: (202)296-6267
Fax: (202)296-5149
**Subject(s):** Education
**Circ:** (Paid)‡900

**PsycSCAN** (5651)
American Psychological Association
750 1st St. NE
Washington, DC 20002-4242
Phone: (202)336-5500
Fax: (202)336-6012
**Subject(s):** Psychology and Psychiatry; Indexes, Abstracts, Reports, Proceedings, and Bibliographies
**Circ:** ‡900

**Techniques in Neurosurgery** (12866)
Lippincott Williams & Wilkins
351 W. Camden St.
Baltimore, MD 21201
Phone: (410)528-4479
Fax: (410)528-4312
**Subject(s):** Medicine and Surgery
**Circ:** (Paid)842
    909

**Journal of Asian American Studies** (12761)
Johns Hopkins University Press
2715 N Charles St.
Baltimore, MD 21218-4363
Phone: (410)516-6987
Fax: (410)516-6968
**Subject(s):** Intercultural Interests
**Circ:** (Combined)895

**Diagnostic Molecular Pathology** (12718)
Lippincott Williams & Wilkins
351 W. Camden St.
Baltimore, MD 21201
Phone: (410)528-4479
Fax: (410)528-4312
**Subject(s):** Laboratory Research (Scientific and Medical); Medicine and Surgery
**Circ:** 868

**Journal of Psychoeducational Assessment** (31950)
c/o Bruce A. Bracken, Ph.D., School of Education
The College of William and Mary
Williamsburg, VA 23187-8795
Phone: (757)221-1712
Fax: (757)221-2975
**Subject(s):** Education; Psychology and Psychiatry
**Circ:** (Controlled)‡74
    (Paid)‡865

**Bogg** (31115)
Bogg Publications
422 N Cleveland St.
Arlington, VA 22201
Phone: (703)243-6019
**Subject(s):** Poetry; Literature
**Circ:** (Controlled)850

**Diacritics** (12717)
Johns Hopkins University Press
2715 N Charles St.
Baltimore, MD 21218-4363
Phone: (410)516-6987
Fax: (410)516-6968
**Subject(s):** Literature
**Circ:** ‡851

**Journal of Colonialism & Colonial History** (13369)
Towson University
c/o Patricia W. Romero
Editor, Towson University
Towson, MD 21252
**Subject(s):** History and Genealogy
**Circ:** (Paid)850

**The Journal of Indo-European Studies** (5487)
Institute for the Study of Man
1133 13th St. NW, Ste. C2
Washington, DC 20005-4298
Phone: (202)371-2700
Fax: (202)371-1523
**Subject(s):** Intercultural Interests; Anthropology and Ethnology; Archaeology; Philology, Language, and Linguistics
**Circ:** (Non-paid)‡56
 (Paid)‡856

**Studies in Conflict and Terrorism** (31162)
Taylor & Francis
c/o Bruce Hoffman
RAND, 1200 S. Hayes
Arlington, VA 22202-5050
**Subject(s):** Sociology; Politics
**Circ:** 850

**The Journal of Group Psychotherapy, Psychodrama, and Sociometry** (5483)
Heldref Publications
1319 18th St., NW
Washington, DC 20036-1802
Phone: (202)296-6267
Fax: (202)296-5149
**Subject(s):** Education; Psychology and Psychiatry
**Circ:** (Combined)848

**Journal of Education for Business** (5469)
Heldref Publications
1319 18th St., NW
Washington, DC 20036-1802
Phone: (202)296-6267
Fax: (202)296-5149
**Subject(s):** Education
**Circ:** (Paid)‡830

**Wide Angle** (12882)
Johns Hopkins University Press
2715 N Charles St.
Baltimore, MD 21218-4363
Phone: (410)516-6987
Fax: (410)516-6968
**Subject(s):** Motion Pictures
**Circ:** ‡828

**American Connemara** (31959)
American Connemara Pony Society
2360 Hunting Ridge Rd.
Winchester, VA 22603
Phone: (540)662-5953
Fax: (540)722-2277
**Subject(s):** Livestock; Wildlife and Exotic Animals
**Circ:** 800

**American Studies International** (5229)
George Washington University
2108 G St. NW
Washington, DC 20052
Phone: (202)994-7368
Fax: (202)994-8651
**Subject(s):** History and Genealogy; Art and Art History; Literature
**Circ:** ‡800

**Environmental & Experimental Botany** (13125)
Aspen Publishing Inc
7201 McKinney Cir.
Frederick, MD 21704
Phone: (800)901-9075
Fax: (301)695-7931
**Subject(s):** Botany
**Circ:** 800

**The Journal of Psychology** (5505)
Heldref Publications
1319 18th St., NW
Washington, DC 20036-1802
Phone: (202)296-6267
Fax: (202)296-5149
**Subject(s):** Psychology and Psychiatry
**Circ:** (Paid)‡800

**Literature Film Quarterly** (13321)
Salisbury University
1101 Camden Ave.
Salisbury, MD 21801-6860
Phone: (410)677-5357
Fax: (410)543-2142
**Subject(s):** Literature; Motion Pictures
**Circ:** ‡800

**Proceedings of the Entomological Society of Washington** (5629)
Entomological Society of Washington
Smithsonian Institution, NMNH, MRC-168
Dept. of Systematic Biology
PO Box 37012
Washington, DC 20013-7012
Phone: (202)382-1786
**Subject(s):** Entomology
**Circ:** ‡800

**Wood & Fiber Science** (31204)
Society of Wood Science and Technology
c/o Geza Ifju, Brooks Forest Products Center
Virginia Tech
Blacksburg, VA 24061-0503
Phone: (540)231-8215
Fax: (540)231-8868
**Subject(s):** Wood and Woodworking; Engineering (Various branches); Science (General)
**Circ:** ‡800

**Anthropological Quarterly (AQ)** (5241)
CUA Press
Catholic University
Washington, DC 20064
Phone: (202)319-4782
Fax: (202)319-4782
**Subject(s):** Anthropology and Ethnology
**Circ:** (Non-paid)‡91
 (Paid)‡794

**Demokratizatsiya** (5358)
Heldref Publications
1319 18th St., NW
Washington, DC 20036-1802
Phone: (202)296-6267
Fax: (202)296-5149
**Subject(s):** International Affairs
**Circ:** (Paid)790

**Journal of Arachnology** (13052)
American Arachnological Society
University of Maryland
College Park, MD 20742-4454
Phone: (301)405-7519
Fax: (301)314-9290
**Subject(s):** Zoology
**Circ:** 790

**ReVision** (5670)
Heldref Publications
1319 18th St., NW
Washington, DC 20036-1802
Phone: (202)296-6267
Fax: (202)296-5149
**Subject(s):** Science (General); Philosophy; Religious Publications
**Circ:** (Paid)‡790

**Configurations** (12697)
Johns Hopkins University Press
2715 N Charles St.
Baltimore, MD 21218-4363
Phone: (410)516-6987
Fax: (410)516-6968
**Subject(s):** Humanities
**Circ:** (Paid)781

**Arethusa** (12665)
Johns Hopkins University Press
2715 N Charles St.
Baltimore, MD 21218-4363
Phone: (410)516-6987
Fax: (410)516-6968
**Subject(s):** Literature
**Circ:** ‡759

**Journal of Appalachian Studies** (32620)
Appalachian Studies Association
ASA Office
Marshall University
One John Marshall Dr.
Huntington, WV 25755
Phone: (304)696-2904
Fax: (304)696-6221
**Subject(s):** Intercultural Interests
**Circ:** 750

**National Environmental Enforcement Journal (NEEJ)** (5562)
National Association of Attorneys General
750 1st St. NE, Ste. 1100
Washington, DC 20002
Phone: (202)326-6000
Fax: (202)408-7014
**Subject(s):** Law; Ecology and Conservation
**Circ:** (Controlled)750

**Science Activities** (5683)
Heldref Publications
1319 18th St., NW
Washington, DC 20036-1802
Phone: (202)296-6267
Fax: (202)296-5149
**Subject(s):** Education; Science (General)
**Circ:** 740

**Journal of Immunotherapy** (12780)
Lippincott Williams & Wilkins
351 W. Camden St.
Baltimore, MD 21201
Phone: (410)528-4479
Fax: (410)528-4312
**Subject(s):** Laboratory Research (Scientific and Medical); Biology
**Circ:** (Paid)732

**Journal of Popular Film and Television** (5504)
Heldref Publications
1319 18th St., NW
Washington, DC 20036-1802
Phone: (202)296-6267
Fax: (202)296-5149
**Subject(s):** Radio, Television, Cable, and Video; Motion Pictures
**Circ:** (Paid)‡735

**American Imago** (12652)
Johns Hopkins University Press
2715 N Charles St.
Baltimore, MD 21218-4363
Phone: (410)516-6987
Fax: (410)516-6968
**Subject(s):** Psychology and Psychiatry
**Circ:** 728

**Psychology of Addictive Behaviors** (5645)
Educational Publishing Foundation
750 1st St. NE
Washington, DC 20002-4242
Phone: (202)408-9804
Fax: (202)336-5568
**Subject(s):** Psychology and Psychiatry
**Circ:** (Paid)‡725

**Administration & Society** (31190)
Sage Publications Inc.
c/o Gary L. Wamsley, Editor
Center for Public Administration and Policy
Virginia Polytechnic Institute and State University
Blacksburg, VA 24061
**Subject(s):** Sociology
**Circ:** (Paid)‡700

**American Politics Research** (13040)
Sage Publications Inc.
c/o James G. Gimpel, Editor
Department of Government and Politics
University of Maryland
3140 Tydings Hall
College Park, MD 20742
**Subject(s):** Politics
**Circ:** (Paid)700

**The American University Law Review** (5231)
Joe Christensen Inc.
4801 Massachusetts Ave. NW, No. 621
Washington, DC 20016
Phone: (202)274-4433
Fax: (202)274-4571

# Middle Atlantic States

**Subject(s):** Law
**Circ:** (Paid)‡570
(Non-paid)‡700

**Arts Education Policy Review** (5252)
Heldref Publications
1319 18th St., NW
Washington, DC 20036-1802
Phone: (202)296-6267
Fax: (202)296-5149
**Subject(s):** Art and Art History; Education
**Circ:** ‡708

**Class Action Reports** (5309)
Class Actions Reports Inc.
4900 Massachusetts Ave. NW, Ste. 230
Washington, DC 20016
Phone: (202)364-1031
Fax: (202)363-6912
**Subject(s):** Law
**Circ:** (Controlled)700

**Comparative Strategy** (31340)
Taylor & Francis
c/o Keith B. Payne, National Institute for Public Policy
3031 Javier Rd, Ste. 300
Fairfax, VA 22031
**Subject(s):** International Affairs
**Circ:** (Paid)700

**Gender Issues** (5398)
Transaction Publishers
School of Public Affairs
Dept. of Justice, Law, and Society
American Univ.
4400 Massachusetts Ave. NW
Washington, DC 20016-8043
Phone: (202)885-2907
Fax: (202)885-2907
**Subject(s):** Sociology; Women's Interests
**Circ:** (Paid)‡700

**The Germanic Review** (5405)
Heldref Publications
1319 18th St., NW
Washington, DC 20036-1802
Phone: (202)296-6267
Fax: (202)296-5149
**Subject(s):** Philology, Language, and Linguistics; Literature
**Circ:** (Paid)‡700

**ICSID Review** (12745)
Johns Hopkins University Press
2715 N Charles St.
Baltimore, MD 21218-4363
Phone: (410)516-6987
Fax: (410)516-6968
**Subject(s):** Law
**Circ:** ‡707

**Journal of the American Institute of Homeopathy** (31017)
American Institute of Homeopathy
801 N Fairfax St., Ste. 306
Alexandria, VA 22314
Phone: (888)445-9988
**Subject(s):** Medicine and Surgery; Health and Healthcare
**Circ:** 700

**Journal of Environmental Horticulture** (5474)
Horticultural Research Institute
1250 I St. NW, Ste. 500
Washington, DC 20005
Phone: (202)789-2900
Fax: (202)789-1893
**Subject(s):** Botany
**Circ:** 700

**Victorian Poetry** (32678)
West Virginia University
West Virginia University Press
PO Box 6295
Morgantown, WV 26506
Phone: (304)293-8400
Fax: (304)293-6585
**Subject(s):** Literature
**Circ:** (Non-paid)86
(Paid)692

**Family Systems** (5384)
Georgetown Family Center
4400 MacArthur Blvd. NW, Ste. 103
Washington, DC 20007
Phone: (202)965-4400
Fax: (202)965-1765

**Subject(s):** Biology
**Circ:** (Combined)680

**The Journal of Genetic Psychology** (5482)
Heldref Publications
1319 18th St., NW
Washington, DC 20036-1802
Phone: (202)296-6267
Fax: (202)296-5149
**Subject(s):** Genetics; Psychology and Psychiatry
**Circ:** (Paid)680

**The Lion and the Unicorn** (12806)
Johns Hopkins University Press
2715 N Charles St.
Baltimore, MD 21218-4363
Phone: (410)516-6987
Fax: (410)516-6968
**Subject(s):** Literature
**Circ:** ‡686

**Nature** (5580)
Nature Publishing Group
968 National Press Bldg.
529 14 St. NW
Washington, DC 20045-1938
Phone: (202)737-2355
Fax: (202)628-1609
**Subject(s):** Laboratory Research (Scientific and Medical); Biology
**Circ:** (Non-paid)681

**Topics in Magnetic Resonance Imaging (TMRI)** (12875)
Lippincott Williams & Wilkins
351 W. Camden St.
Baltimore, MD 21201
Phone: (410)528-4479
Fax: (410)528-4312
**Subject(s):** Medicine and Surgery
**Circ:** 684

**Journal of Community Psychology** (13370)
John Wiley and Sons Inc.
Towson University
8000 York Rd.
Towson, MD 21252-0001
**Subject(s):** Psychology and Psychiatry
**Circ:** (Non-paid)‡49
(Paid)‡678

**Business and Economic History** (31946)
College of William and Mary
PO Box 8795
Williamsburg, VA 23187-8795
Phone: (757)221-4000
**Subject(s):** Business; History and Genealogy
**Circ:** (Combined)650

**Journal of Technology & Teacher Education** (31628)
Association for the Advancement of Computing in Education
PO Box 3728
Norfolk, VA 23514
Phone: (757)623-7588
Fax: (703)997-8760
**Subject(s):** Education
**Circ:** (Paid)‡650

**Mediterranean Quarterly** (5541)
Duke University Press
Mediterranean Affairs, Inc.
National Press Building, Ste. 984
14th and F Sts. NW
Washington, DC 20045
Phone: (202)662-7655
Fax: (202)662-7656
**Subject(s):** Anthropology and Ethnology; Social Sciences
**Circ:** (Paid)650

**Exceptional Child Education Resources** (31123)
Council for Exceptional Children
1110 N Glebe Rd., Ste. 300
Arlington, VA 22201
Phone: (703)620-3660
Fax: (703)264-9494
**Subject(s):** Education
**Circ:** (Non-paid)‡2
(Paid)‡643

**Journal of Women, Politics & Policy** (5520)
The Haworth Press Inc.
American University
Department of Government
4400 Massachusetts Ave., NW
Washington, DC 20016
Phone: (202)885-2903
Fax: (202)885-1305
**Subject(s):** Politics
**Circ:** 635

**Anthropology and Humanism** (31235)
American Anthropological Association
c/o Edith Turner
Editor, Department of Anthropology
Brooks Hall 303
Charlottesville, VA 22903
Phone: (804)924-7044
Fax: (804)924-1350
**Subject(s):** Anthropology and Ethnology
**Circ:** 600

**Arlington Historical Magazine** (31111)
Arlington Historical Society Inc.
c/o W.Karl VanNewkirk
1116 N. Rochester St.
Arlington, VA 22205-1741
Phone: (703)536-5916
**Subject(s):** History and Genealogy
**Circ:** (Controlled)600

**International Journal of Legal Information** (5444)
International Association of Law Libraries
PO Box 5709
Washington, DC 20016-1309
Phone: (804)924-3515
Fax: (804)924-7239
**Subject(s):** Law; International Affairs
**Circ:** (Paid)600

**Literature and Medicine** (12808)
Johns Hopkins University Press
2715 N Charles St.
Baltimore, MD 21218-4363
Phone: (410)516-6987
Fax: (410)516-6968
**Subject(s):** Literature and Literary Reviews; Medicine and Surgery
**Circ:** 606

**Poet Lore** (13003)
The Writer's Center
4508 Walsh St.
Bethesda, MD 20815
Phone: (301)654-8664
Fax: (301)654-8667
**Subject(s):** Literature and Literary Reviews
**Circ:** (Non-paid)‡10
(Paid)‡600

**The Yale Journal of Criticism** (12885)
Johns Hopkins University Press
2715 N Charles St.
Baltimore, MD 21218-4363
Phone: (410)516-6987
Fax: (410)516-6968
**Subject(s):** Literature and Literary Reviews; Art
**Circ:** 606

**Philosophy, Psychiatry & Psychology** (12843)
Johns Hopkins University Press
2715 N Charles St.
Baltimore, MD 21218-4363
Phone: (410)516-6987
Fax: (410)516-6968
**Subject(s):** Philosophy; Psychology and Psychiatry
**Circ:** (Paid)592

**Eighteenth-Century Life** (31947)
Duke University Press
College of William and Mary
Dept. of English
Williamsburg, VA 23187-8795
Phone: (757)221-3906
Fax: (757)221-1844
**Subject(s):** History and Genealogy
**Circ:** 575

**Alternative Press Index** (12649)
PO Box 33109
Baltimore, MD 21218
Phone: (410)243-2471
Fax: (410)235-5325

**Gale Directory of Publications & Broadcast Media/140th Ed.**  **Middle Atlantic States**

**Subject(s):** Indexes, Abstracts, Reports, Proceedings, and Bibliographies; Black Publications; Hispanic Publications; Women's Interests

**Circ:** (Controlled)‡200
(Paid)‡550

**Imprint (31249)**
American Historical Print Collectors Society Inc.
1920 Blue Ridge Rd.
Charlottesville, VA 22903
**Subject(s):** Art and Art History

**Circ:** (Paid)550

**Late Imperial China (12804)**
Johns Hopkins University Press
2715 N Charles St.
Baltimore, MD 21218-4363
Phone: (410)516-6987
Fax: (410)516-6968
**Subject(s):** History and Genealogy

**Circ:** (Combined)553

**SAIS Review (12857)**
Johns Hopkins University Press
2715 N Charles St.
Baltimore, MD 21218-4363
Phone: (410)516-6987
Fax: (410)516-6968
**Subject(s):** International Affairs

**Circ:** (Combined)553

**SPEC Kit (5700)**
ARL
21 Dupont Cir. NW
Washington, DC 20036-1118
Phone: (202)296-2296
Fax: (202)872-0884
**Subject(s):** Library and Information Science

**Circ:** (Non-paid)10
(Paid)550

**Neurosurgery Quarterly (12828)**
Lippincott Williams & Wilkins
c/o Donlin M. Long, Dept. of Neurological Surgery
600 North Wolfe St.
The Johns Hopkins Hospital
Baltimore, MD 21287-0002
**Subject(s):** Laboratory Research (Scientific and Medical)

**Circ:** 547

**Preventing School Failure (5628)**
Heldref Publications
1319 18th St., NW
Washington, DC 20036-1802
Phone: (202)296-6267
Fax: (202)296-5149
**Subject(s):** Parenting; Education; Education

**Circ:** (Paid)540

**Chiropractic History (31764)**
PO Box 1045
Richlands, VA 24641
Phone: (276)963-0395
Fax: (276)964-2225
**Subject(s):** Chiropractic

**Circ:** (Non-paid)‡250
(Paid)‡523

**Historical Methods (5419)**
Heldref Publications
1319 18th St., NW
Washington, DC 20036-1802
Phone: (202)296-6267
Fax: (202)296-5149
**Subject(s):** History and Genealogy

**Circ:** (Paid)511

**AAPS PharmSciTech (31103)**
American Association of Pharmaceutical Scientists
2107 Wilson Blvd., No. 700
Arlington, VA 22201-3042
Phone: (703)243-2800
Fax: (703)243-9650
**Subject(s):** Drugs and Pharmaceuticals; Medicine and Surgery; Health and Healthcare

**Circ:** 500

**Air Media (31922)**
National Air Filtration Association
PO Box 68639
Virginia Beach, VA 23471
Phone: (757)313-7400
Fax: (757)497-1895

**Subject(s):** Air Conditioning and Refrigeration; Plumbing and Heating

**Circ:** 500

**Augusta Historical Bulletin (31892)**
Augusta Historical Society
PO Box 686
Staunton, VA 24402-0686
Phone: (540)248-4151
**Subject(s):** History and Genealogy; Local, State, and Regional Publications

**Circ:** (Controlled)500

**Behavioral Medicine (5266)**
Heldref Publications
1319 18th St., NW
Washington, DC 20036-1802
Phone: (202)296-6267
Fax: (202)296-5149
**Subject(s):** Medicine and Surgery; Psychology and Psychiatry

**Circ:** 505

**The Custom Tailor (5353)**
Custom Tailors and Designers Association of America Inc.
PO Box 53052
Washington, DC 20009-3052
Phone: (202)333-0700
Fax: (202)387-7713
**Subject(s):** Clothing

**Circ:** ‡500

**East Asian Executive Reports (5364)**
International Executive Reports
717 D St. NW, No. 300
Washington, DC 20004-2807
Phone: (202)628-6900
Fax: (202)628-6618
**Subject(s):** International Business and Economics

**Circ:** (Paid)‡400
(Non-paid)500

**Evaluation & the Health Professions (12724)**
Sage Publications Inc.
c/o Barker Bausell, Complemetary Medicine Program
University of Maryland School of Medicine
Kernan Hospital Mansion
2200 Kernan Dr.
Baltimore, MD 21207-6697
**Subject(s):** Health and Healthcare

**Circ:** (Paid)‡500

**Faith & Reason (31420)**
Christendom Press
134 Christendom Dr.
Front Royal, VA 22630
Phone: (540)636-2900
Fax: (540)636-1655
**Subject(s):** Religious Publications

**Circ:** ‡500

**The Hollins Critic (31835)**
Hollins University
Box 9538
Roanoke, VA 24020-1538
Phone: (540)362-6275
Fax: (540)362-6642
**Subject(s):** Literature; Humanities

**Circ:** ‡500

**Hospital Topics (5422)**
Heldref Publications
1319 18th St., NW
Washington, DC 20036-1802
Phone: (202)296-6267
Fax: (202)296-5149
**Subject(s):** Hospitals and Healthcare Institutions

**Circ:** (Paid)500

**International Chinese Snuff Bottle Society Journal (12750)**
International Chinese Snuff Bottle Society
2601 N Charles St.
Baltimore, MD 21218
Phone: (410)467-9400
Fax: (410)243-3451
**Subject(s):** Glass and China

**Circ:** 500

**International Journal of Conflict Management (5145)**
University of Delaware
150 S. College Ave.
Newark, DE 19716
Phone: (302)831-8859
Fax: (302)831-1445

**Subject(s):** Management and Administration

**Circ:** (Paid)500

**Journal of Instruction Delivery Systems (31938)**
Society for Applied Learning Technology
50 Culpeper St.
Warrenton, VA 20186
Phone: (540)347-0055
Fax: (540)349-3169
**Subject(s):** Education

**Circ:** 500

**Middle East Executive Reports (5543)**
International Executive Reports
717 D St. NW, No. 300
Washington, DC 20004-2807
Phone: (202)628-6900
Fax: (202)628-6618
**Subject(s):** International Business and Economics

**Circ:** (Non-paid)‡400
(Paid)‡500

**Minerva (13261)**
The Minerva Center
20 Granada Rd.
Pasadena, MD 21122-2708
Phone: (410)437-5379
Fax: (914)693-2834
**Subject(s):** Women's Interests; Military and Navy; Veterans

**Circ:** (Non-paid)‡20
(Paid)‡500

**Molecular Medicine (12821)**
Johns Hopkins University Press
2715 N Charles St.
Baltimore, MD 21218-4363
Phone: (410)516-6987
Fax: (410)516-6968
**Subject(s):** Biology; Medicine and Surgery; Laboratory Research (Scientific and Medical); Science (General)

**Circ:** (Combined)500

**ANQ (5240)**
Heldref Publications
1319 18th St., NW
Washington, DC 20036-1802
Phone: (202)296-6267
Fax: (202)296-5149
**Subject(s):** Literature

**Circ:** 496

**Journal of Biological Rhythms (12979)**
Sage Publications Inc.
4938 Hampden Lane
PMB 336
2153 N. Campus Dr.
Bethesda, MD 20814-2914
Phone: (301)680-9334
Fax: (301)680-9334
**Subject(s):** Biology

**Circ:** (Non-paid)‡77
(Paid)‡478

**Symposium (5708)**
Heldref Publications
1319 18th St., NW
Washington, DC 20036-1802
Phone: (202)296-6267
Fax: (202)296-5149
**Subject(s):** Literature

**Circ:** (Paid)‡470

**American Currents (12651)**
North American Native Fishes Association
c/o Christopher Scharpf
1107 Argonne Dr.
Baltimore, MD 21218
Phone: (410)243-9050
**Subject(s):** Oceanography and Marine Studies; Fish and Commercial Fisheries

**Circ:** 450

**Commonwealth Novel in English (32540)**
BSC Center for International Understanding
219 Rock St.
Bluefield, WV 24701-2198
Phone: (304)327-4036
Fax: (304)327-4387
**Subject(s):** Literature

**Circ:** (Paid)450

Circulation: ★ = ABC; △ = BPA; ◆ = CAC; • = CCAB; ☐ = VAC; ⊕ = PO Statement; ‡ = Publisher's Report; Boldface figures = sworn; Light figures = estimated.

**Journal of Nonprofit & Public Sector Marketing** (31617)
The Haworth Press Inc.
c/o Walter W. Wymer, Dept. of Management & Marketing
Christopher Newport Univ.
Newport News, VA 23606
Phone: (757)594-7692
Fax: (334)244-3792
**Subject(s):** Advertising and Marketing

**Circ:** 451

**The Poe Messenger** (31787)
Poe Foundation Inc.
1914-16 E. Main St.
Richmond, VA 23223
Phone: (804)648-5523
Fax: (804)648-8729
**Subject(s):** Literature

**Circ:** (Paid)450

**Regent University Law Review** (31925)
Regent University
239 B Robertson Hall
1000 Regent University Dr.
Virginia Beach, VA 23464
Phone: (757)226-4127
Fax: (757)226-4595
**Subject(s):** Law

**Circ:** (Controlled)450

**The Journal of Arts Management, Law, and Society** (5462)
Heldref Publications
1319 18th St., NW
Washington, DC 20036-1802
Phone: (202)296-6267
Fax: (202)296-5149
**Subject(s):** Law; Performing Arts

**Circ:** (Paid)440

**Journal of Modern Greek Studies** (12784)
Johns Hopkins University Press
2715 N Charles St.
Baltimore, MD 21218-4363
Phone: (410)516-6987
Fax: (410)516-6968
**Subject(s):** Literature; Social and Political Issues

**Circ:** ‡446

**Perspectives on Political Science** (5617)
Heldref Publications
1319 18th St., NW
Washington, DC 20036-1802
Phone: (202)296-6267
Fax: (202)296-5149
**Subject(s):** International Affairs; Politics; Philosophy

**Circ:** (Paid)434

**Science Communication** (13062)
Sage Publications Inc.
Philip Merrill College of Journalism
University of Maryland
College Park, MD 20742-7111
Phone: (301)405-2430
Fax: (301)314-9166
**Subject(s):** Education; Social Sciences

**Circ:** (Non-paid)‡12
(Paid)‡418

**The Explicator** (5381)
Heldref Publications
1319 18th St., NW
Washington, DC 20036-1802
Phone: (202)296-6267
Fax: (202)296-5149
**Subject(s):** Literature

**Circ:** (Paid)400

**Gallup Poll Tuesday Briefing** (5397)
Gallup Organization
901 F St. NW
Washington, DC 20004
Phone: (202)715-3030
Fax: (202)715-3042
**Subject(s):** Advertising and Marketing; Indexes, Abstracts, Reports, Proceedings, and Bibliographies

**Circ:** (Paid)400

**Genetic, Social, and General Psychology Monographs** (5399)
Heldref Publications
1319 18th St., NW
Washington, DC 20036-1802
Phone: (202)296-6267
Fax: (202)296-5149
**Subject(s):** Psychology and Psychiatry

**Circ:** (Paid)‡400

**History** (5420)
Heldref Publications
1319 18th St., NW
Washington, DC 20036-1802
Phone: (202)296-6267
Fax: (202)296-5149
**Subject(s):** Literature and Literary Reviews; History and Genealogy

**Circ:** (Paid)‡400

**Inter-American Review of Bibliography** (5438)
Organization of American States
17th St., Ste. 250
Washington, DC 20006
Phone: (202)458-6824
Fax: (202)458-6421
**Subject(s):** Book Trade and Author News; French; Portuguese; Spanish; Hispanic Publications; Indexes, Abstracts, Reports, Proceedings, and Bibliographies

**Circ:** (Paid)‡400
(Non-paid)‡400

**Journal of Social Philosophy** (31255)
North American Society for Social Philosophy
c/o Philosophy Documentation Ctr.
PO Box 7147
Charlottesville, VA 22906-7147
Phone: (434)220-3300
Fax: (434)220-3301
**Subject(s):** Philosophy

**Circ:** 400

**West Virginia University Philological Papers** (32680)
West Virginia University
P.O. Box 6298
205 Chitwood Hall
Morgantown, WV 26506
Phone: (304)293-5121
Fax: (304)293-7655
**Subject(s):** Philology, Language, and Linguistics

**Circ:** 400

**Women and Language** (31369)
George Mason University
4400 University Dr.
Fairfax, VA 22030-4444
Phone: (703)993-1099
Fax: (703)993-1096
**Subject(s):** Women's Interests; Communications; Philology, Language, and Linguistics

**Circ:** (Combined)400

**International Pharmaceutical Abstracts** (12974)
American Society of Health-System Pharmacists
7272 Wisconsin Ave.
Bethesda, MD 20814
Phone: (301)657-3000
Fax: (301)657-8857
**Subject(s):** Drugs and Pharmaceuticals; Indexes, Abstracts, Reports, Proceedings, and Bibliographies

**Circ:** (Non-paid)‡55
(Paid)‡376

**Romance Quarterly** (5675)
Heldref Publications
1319 18th St., NW
Washington, DC 20036-1802
Phone: (202)296-6267
Fax: (202)296-5149
**Subject(s):** Literature

**Circ:** (Paid)365

**Abstracts in Social Gerontology** (5185)
Sage Publications Inc.
National Council on the Aging
409 Third St. SW
Washington, DC 20024
**Subject(s):** Gerontology; Indexes, Abstracts, Reports, Proceedings, and Bibliographies

**Circ:** ‡350

**EBRI Quarterly Pension Investment Report** (5368)
Employee Benefit Research Institute
2121 K St. NW, Ste. 600
Washington, DC 20037-1896
Phone: (202)659-0670
Fax: (202)775-6312
**Subject(s):** Banking, Finance, and Investments; Employment and Human Resources

**Circ:** ‡350

**Immunopharmacology and Immunotoxicology** (13266)
Marcel Dekker Inc.
c/o Michael A. Chirigos, Immunopharmacology Laboratory
National Cancer Institute, National Institutes of Health
4 Cold Spring Ct.
Potomac, MD 20854-2425
**Subject(s):** Drugs and Pharmaceuticals; Medicine and Surgery

**Circ:** (Paid)325

**Journal of Environmental Science and Health, Part B: Pesticides, Food Contaminants, and Agricultural Wastes** (31349)
Marcel Dekker Inc.
c/o Shahamat U. Khan, 4400 University Dr.
Department of Chemistry, MSN 3E2
George Mason University
4400 University Dr.
Fairfax, VA 22030-4444
Phone: (703)993-1072
Fax: (703)993-1055
**Subject(s):** Ecology and Conservation; Science (General)

**Circ:** (Paid)325

**Materials & Manufacturing Processes** (31357)
Marcel Dekker Inc.
c/o T.S. Sudarshan
2721-D Merrilee Dr.
Fairfax, VA 22031
Phone: (703)560-1371
Fax: (703)560-1372
**Subject(s):** Commerce and Industry

**Circ:** (Paid)325

**Polymer-Plastics Technology and Engineering** (31438)
Marcel Dekker Inc.
c/o Munmaya K. Mishra
PO Box 5806
Glen Allen, VA 23058-5806
**Subject(s):** Chemistry, Chemicals, and Chemical Engineering; Plastic and Composition Materials

**Circ:** 325

**Asian Affairs** (5255)
Heldref Publications
1319 18th St., NW
Washington, DC 20036-1802
Phone: (202)296-6267
Fax: (202)296-5149
**Subject(s):** International Affairs; International Business and Economics

**Circ:** 315

**Journal of Environmental Science and Health, Part A: Toxic/Hazardous Substances & Environmental Engineering** (31348)
Marcel Dekker Inc.
c/o Shahamat U. Khan, 4400 University Dr.
Department of Chemistry, MSN 3E2
George Mason University
Fairfax, VA 22030-4444
Phone: (703)993-1072
Fax: (703)993-1055
**Subject(s):** Ecology and Conservation

**Circ:** (Paid)300

**National Apostolate for Inclusion Ministry Quarterly** (13282)
National Apostolate for Inclusion Ministry
PO Box 218
Riverdale, MD 20738-0218
Phone: (301)699-9500
**Subject(s):** Religious Publications; Handicapped

**Circ:** (Paid)300

**Transport Theory and Statistical Physics** (31266)
Marcel Dekker Inc.
c/o John J. Dorning
Thorton Hall (Reactor Facility)
University of Virginia
Charlottesville, VA 22903-2442
**Subject(s):** Physics

**Circ:** 300

**Dieciocho** (31246)
University of Virginia
115 Wilson Hall
PO Box 400777
Charlottesville, VA 22904-4777
Phone: (434)924-7159
Fax: (434)924-7160
**Subject(s):** Ethnic and Minority Studies

**Circ:** (Combined)270

**Romani Studies (13034)**
Gypsy Lore Society Inc.
5607 Greenleaf Rd.
Cheverly, MD 20785
Phone: (301)341-1261
Fax: (301)341-1261
**Subject(s):** Anthropology and Ethnology; Social Sciences
**Circ:** (Paid)272

**Journal of Health and Social Policy (12776)**
The Haworth Press Inc.
c/o Stanley F. Battle
Coppin State Univ.
2500 W. Ave.
Baltimore, MD 21216-3698
Phone: (410)951-3838
Fax: (757)823-2556
**Subject(s):** Health and Healthcare
**Circ:** (Controlled)‡265

**Environmental Carcinogenesis & Ecotoxicology Reviews (31884)**
Marcel Dekker Inc.
c/o Yin-Tak Woo, PO Box 2429
Springfield, VA 22152
**Subject(s):** Ecology and Conservation; Science (General)
**Circ:** (Paid)‡250

**Journal of Environmental Science and Health, Part C: Environmental Carcinogenesis and Ectoxicology Reviews (31886)**
Marcel Dekker Inc.
c/o Yin-Tak Woo
PO Box 2429
Springfield, VA 22152
**Subject(s):** Science (General); Health and Healthcare; Medicine and Surgery
**Circ:** 250

**Machining Science and Technology (13172)**
Marcel Dekker Inc.
c/o Said Jahanmir
Miti Heart Corporation
PO Box 83610
Gaithersburg, MD 20883
**Subject(s):** Engineering (Various branches)
**Circ:** (Paid)250

**Abbey (13071)**
White Urp Publishing
5360 Fallriver Row Ct.
Columbia, MD 21044
Phone: (410)730-4272
**Subject(s):** Literature
**Circ:** (Controlled)200

**Journal of the Alleghenies (13150)**
Council of the Alleghenies Inc.
PO Box 514
Frostburg, MD 21532
Phone: (301)689-8173
**Subject(s):** Local, State, and Regional Publications; History and Genealogy
**Circ:** (Paid)200

**Journal of Relationship Marketing (31663)**
The Haworth Press Inc.
c/o Richard W. Brookes
Virginia State Univ.
1 Hayden Dr.
PO Box 9398
Petersburg, VA 23806-9398
**Subject(s):** Advertising and Marketing
**Circ:** (Paid)148

**Stephen Crane Studies (31202)**
Virginia Polytechnic Institute and State University
Professor Paul Sorrentino, Department Of English
Virginia Tech.
Blacksburg, VA 24061-0112
Phone: (540)231-8650
Fax: (540)231-5692
**Subject(s):** Literature
**Circ:** (Combined)127

**Archaeological Society of Delaware Bulletin (5160)**
Archaeological Society of Delaware
Box 12483
Wilmington, DE 19800
**Subject(s):** Archaeology; Local, State, and Regional Publications
**Circ:** (Paid)100

**Scotia (31632)**
Old Dominion University
Arts and Letters Bldg. 800
Norfolk, VA 23529
Phone: (757)683-3949
Fax: (757)683-5644
**Subject(s):** History and Genealogy; Ethnic and Minority Studies
**Circ:** (Paid)100

## Northeastern States

**Parade (22211)**
Parade Publications
711 3rd Ave.
New York, NY 10017
Phone: (212)450-7000
Fax: (212)450-7087
**Subject(s):** General Editorial
**Circ:** 37,852,000

**The Watchtower (20546)**
Watchtower Bible and Tract Society of New York Inc.
25 Columbia Hts.
Brooklyn, NY 11201-2483
Phone: (718)560-5000
Fax: (718)560-5619
**Subject(s):** Religious Publications; Theology; French; German; Italian; Japanese; Korean; Latvian; Lithuanian; Macedonian; Norwegian; Polish; Portuguese; Romanian; Russian; Serbian; Slovak; Slovene; Swahili; Swedish; Tamil; Turkish; Ukrainian; Vietnamese; Albanian; Arabic; Armenian; Bulgarian; Chinese; Croatian; Czech; Danish; Dutch; Estonian; Finnish; Greek; Hebrew; Hindi; Hungarian; Icelandic; Indonesian
**Circ:** ‡25,618,000

**Awake! (20490)**
Watchtower Bible and Tract Society of New York Inc.
25 Columbia Hts.
Brooklyn, NY 11201-2483
Phone: (718)560-5000
Fax: (718)560-5619
**Subject(s):** Religious Publications; Health and Fitness
**Circ:** ‡22,530,000

**Architectural Designs (5097)**
Architectural Designs Inc.
57 Danbury Rd.
Wilton, CT 06897
Phone: (203)222-1113
Fax: (203)221-9255
**Subject(s):** Home and Garden
**Circ:** ‡20,000,000

**Reader's Digest (22715)**
Reader's Digest Association Inc.
Reader's Digest Rd.
Pleasantville, NY 10570-7000
Phone: (914)238-1000
Fax: (914)238-4559
**Subject(s):** General Editorial
**Circ:** (Paid)12,613,790

**Family Circle (21678)**
G & J USA Publishing
375 Lexington Ave.
New York, NY 10017-5514
Phone: (212)499-2113
Fax: (212)499-2113
**Subject(s):** Women's Interests
**Circ:** (Paid)5,002,042

**Good Housekeeping (21743)**
Hearst Magazines
1790 Broadway
New York, NY 10019
Phone: (212)841-8480
**Subject(s):** Home and Garden; Women's Interests
**Circ:** (Paid)4,558,524

**Woman's Day (22545)**
Hachette Filipacchi Media U.S. Inc.
1633 Broadway
New York, NY 10019
Phone: (212)767-6000
**Subject(s):** Women's Interests
**Circ:** (Paid)4,167,933

**Ladies' Home Journal (22021)**
Meredith Corp.
125 Park Ave.
New York, NY 10017
Phone: (212)455-1313
Fax: (800)374-4545
**Subject(s):** Women's Interests; General Editorial
**Circ:** (Paid)4,101,550

**Time (22455)**
Time Inc.
Time-Life Bldg., Rockefeller Ctr.
1271 Avenue of the Americas
New York, NY 10020
Phone: (212)522-1212
Fax: (212)467-1396
**Subject(s):** General Editorial
**Circ:** (Paid)4,095,935

**Time International (22457)**
Time Inc.
Time-Life Bldg., Rockefeller Ctr.
1271 Avenue of the Americas
New York, NY 10020
Phone: (212)522-1212
Fax: (212)467-1396
**Subject(s):** General Editorial
**Circ:** (Paid)‡4,095,935

**Time for Kids (22458)**
Time Inc.
TIME For Kids
1271 6th Ave., 25th Fl.
New York, NY 10020
**Subject(s):** Children's Interests; General Editorial
**Circ:** (Paid)4,000,000

**Parents Baby (22216)**
G & J USA Publishing
375 Lexington Ave.
New York, NY 10017-5514
Phone: (212)499-2113
Fax: (212)499-2113
**Subject(s):** Parenting; Babies
**Circ:** (Controlled)‡3,700,000

**The People (22228)**
Time Inc.
Time-Life Bldg., Rockefeller Ctr.
1271 Avenue of the Americas
New York, NY 10020
Phone: (212)522-1212
Fax: (212)467-1396
**Subject(s):** General Editorial
**Circ:** (Paid)3,525,250

**Lingo The Journal Of Art (14885)**
Hard Press Inc.
PO Box 184
West Stockbridge, MA 01266
Phone: (413)232-4690
Fax: (413)232-4675
**Subject(s):** Poetry; Literature and Literary Reviews; Music and Musical Instruments; Art and Art History
**Circ:** 3,500,000

**Sports Illustrated (22409)**
Time Inc.
Time-Life Bldg., Rockefeller Ctr.
1271 Avenue of the Americas
New York, NY 10020
Phone: (212)522-1212
Fax: (212)467-1396
**Subject(s):** (General Sports)
**Circ:** (Paid)3,205,241

**Newsweek (22172)**
Newsweek Inc.
251 W 57th St.
New York, NY 10019
Phone: (212)445-4870
Fax: (212)445-5764
**Subject(s):** General Editorial
**Circ:** (Paid)3,138,460

**Prevention (26330)**
Rodale Inc.
33 E. Minor St.
Emmaus, PA 18098-0099
Phone: (610)967-5171
Fax: (610)967-8181
**Subject(s):** Health
**Circ:** (Paid)3,014,859

# Northeastern States

**Highlights for Children (26503)**
Boysville Publishing
803 Church St.
Honesdale, PA 18431
Phone: (717)253-1080
Fax: (717)253-0179
**Subject(s):** Children's Interests
**Circ:** ‡3,000,000

**Touchdown Illustrated (22467)**
PSP Sports
355 Lexington Ave.
New York, NY 10017
Phone: (212)697-1460
Fax: (212)286-8154
**Subject(s):** (Football)
**Circ:** 2,800,000

**Lamaze Parents' Magazine (4677)**
iVillage Parenting Network
9 Old Kings Hwy. S.
Darien, CT 06820
Phone: (203)656-3600
Fax: (203)656-2221
**Subject(s):** Babies; Parenting; Women's Interests
**Circ:** (Non-paid)2,700,000

**Guideposts Magazine (21750)**
Guideposts
16 East 34 St.
New York, NY 10016
Phone: (212)684-0679
Fax: (212)684-0679
**Subject(s):** Religious Publications
**Circ:** (Non-paid)101,785
 (Paid)2,590,323

**Maxim (22066)**
Dennis Publishing
1040 Ave. of the Americas, 12th Fl.
New York, NY 10018
Phone: (212)302-2626
Fax: (212)768-1319
**Subject(s):** Fashion
**Circ:** (Paid)2,458,150

**Martha Stewart Living (22060)**
Martha Stewart Living Omnimedia
11 W. 42nd St., 25th Fl.
New York, NY 10036
Phone: (212)827-8000
Fax: (212)827-8204
**Subject(s):** Home and Garden; Food and Cooking; Crafts, Models, Hobbies, and Contests
**Circ:** (Paid)2,436,422

**Glamour (21738)**
Conde Nast Publications Inc.
4 Times Square, 17th Fl.
New York, NY 10036
Phone: (212)286-3700
Fax: (212)286-5960
**Subject(s):** Fashion; Women's Interests
**Circ:** (Paid)2,361,637

**Advances in Nursing Science (ANS) (26801)**
Lippincott Williams & Wilkins
530 Walnut St.
Philadelphia, PA 19106-3261
Phone: (215)521-8300
Fax: (215)521-8902
**Subject(s):** Nursing
**Circ:** 2,343,169

**Redbook Magazine (22300)**
Hearst Magazines
1790 Broadway
New York, NY 10019
Phone: (212)841-8480
**Subject(s):** General Editorial; Women's Interests
**Circ:** (Paid)2,338,941

**YM (22567)**
G & J USA Publishing
375 Lexington Ave.
New York, NY 10017-5514
Phone: (212)499-2113
Fax: (212)499-2113
**Subject(s):** Youths' Interests; Women's Interests
**Circ:** (Paid)2,202,979

**TV Blueprint (20771)**
Wilen Media Corp.
5 Wellwood Ave.
Farmingdale, NY 11735-1213
Phone: (631)439-5000
Fax: (631)439-4536
**Subject(s):** Radio, Television, Cable, and Video; Radio, Television, Cable, and Video
**Circ:** (Paid)‡2,200,000

**Parents Magazine (22218)**
G & J USA Publishing
375 Lexington Ave.
New York, NY 10017-5514
Phone: (212)499-2113
Fax: (212)499-2113
**Subject(s):** Parenting
**Circ:** (Non-paid)142,708
 (Paid)2,004,929

**New England Review (30900)**
Middlebury College Publications
Middlebury College
Middlebury, VT 05753
Phone: (802)443-5000
Fax: (802)443-2088
**Subject(s):** Literature
**Circ:** ‡2,000,000

**Parents (22215)**
G & J USA Publishing
375 Lexington Ave.
New York, NY 10017-5514
Phone: (212)499-2113
Fax: (212)499-2113
**Subject(s):** Parenting; Babies
**Circ:** (Controlled)‡2,000,000

**Money (22096)**
Time Inc.
Time-Life Bldg., Rockefeller Ctr.
1271 Avenue of the Americas
New York, NY 10020
Phone: (212)522-1212
Fax: (212)467-1396
**Subject(s):** Banking, Finance, and Investments
**Circ:** (Paid)1,906,352

**Baby Talk (21377)**
The Parenting Group
530 5th Ave., 4th Fl.
New York, NY 10036
Phone: (212)522-8989
Fax: (212)522-8699
**Subject(s):** Babies
**Circ:** (Paid)976
 (Controlled)1,801,016

**The WorldPaper (13599)**
World Times Inc.
225 Franklin St., 26th Fl.
Boston, MA 02110
Phone: (617)439-5400
Fax: (617)439-5415
**Subject(s):** International Business and Economics; Sociology
**Circ:** (Paid)1,800,000

**FamilyFun (14323)**
Disney Publishing
244 Main St.
Northampton, MA 01060
Phone: (413)585-0444
Fax: (413)586-5724
**Subject(s):** Parenting
**Circ:** (Non-paid)★128,904
 (Paid)★1,736,719

**Country Living (21562)**
Hearst Magazines
1790 Broadway
New York, NY 10019
Phone: (212)841-8480
**Subject(s):** Home and Garden; Lifestyle
**Circ:** (Combined)★1,734,017

**HEALTH & YOU (27722)**
Health Ink & Vitality Communications
780 Township Line Rd.
Yardley, PA 19067-4200
Phone: (267)585-2800
Fax: (267)685-1228
**Subject(s):** Health
**Circ:** ‡1,700,000

**Men's Health (26327)**
Rodale Inc.
33 E. Minor St.
Emmaus, PA 18098-0099
Phone: (610)967-5171
Fax: (610)967-8181
**Subject(s):** Health; Men's Interests
**Circ:** (Paid)1,659,594

**Woman's World (19076)**
Heinrich Bauer North America Inc.
270 Sylvan Ave.
PO Box 1648
Englewood Cliffs, NJ 07632
Phone: (201)569-0006
Fax: (201)569-3584
**Subject(s):** Women's Interests
**Circ:** (Paid)1,604,003

**Teen People (22442)**
Time Inc.
Teen People Online
Time & Life Bldg., 35th Fl.
Rockefeller Center
New York, NY 10020-1393
Fax: (212)467-0489
**Subject(s):** Lifestyle; Entertainment; Youths' Interests
**Circ:** (Paid)1,600,504

**Columbia (4883)**
Knights of Columbus
1 Columbus Plz.
New Haven, CT 06510-3326
Phone: (203)752-4000
Fax: (203)752-4109
**Subject(s):** Knights of Columbus; Spanish; French
**Circ:** ‡1,600,000

**Life Magazine (22035)**
Time Inc.
Time-Life Bldg., Rockefeller Ctr.
1271 Avenue of the Americas
New York, NY 10020
Phone: (212)522-1212
Fax: (212)467-1396
**Subject(s):** General Editorial
**Circ:** (Paid)1,590,397

**In Style (21812)**
Time Inc.
Time-Life Bldg., Rockefeller Ctr.
1271 Avenue of the Americas
New York, NY 10020
Phone: (212)522-1212
Fax: (212)467-1396
**Subject(s):** Lifestyle; Home and Garden; Entertainment
**Circ:** (Paid)1,584,691

**Popular Science (22253)**
Time4 Media Inc.
2 Park Ave., 9th Fl.
New York, NY 10016-5614
Phone: (212)779-5000
Fax: (212)779-5118
**Subject(s):** General Editorial; Science (General)
**Circ:** (Paid)1,566,817

**Golf Digest (5061)**
Advance Magazine Publishers Inc.
5520 Park Ave.
Trumbull, CT 06611
Phone: (203)373-7176
Fax: (203)371-2132
**Subject(s):** (Golf)
**Circ:** (Paid)1,563,476

**Entertainment Weekly (21653)**
Time Inc.
Time-Life Bldg., Rockefeller Ctr.
1271 Avenue of the Americas
New York, NY 10020
Phone: (212)522-1212
Fax: (212)467-1396
**Subject(s):** Entertainment
**Circ:** (Paid)1,520,463

**Field & Stream (21685)**
Time4 Media Inc.
2 Park Ave., 9th Fl.
New York, NY 10016-5614
Phone: (212)779-5000
Fax: (212)779-5118
**Subject(s):** (Hunting, Fishing, and Game Management)
**Circ:** (Paid)1,500,000

**Parenting Magazine (22214)**
The Parenting Group
530 5th Ave., 4th Fl.
New York, NY 10036
Phone: (212)522-8989
Fax: (212)522-8699
**Subject(s):** Parenting
**Circ:** (Paid)1,415,855

**Golf Magazine (21742)**
Time4 Media Inc.
2 Park Ave., 9th Fl.
New York, NY 10016-5614
Phone: (212)779-5000
Fax: (212)779-5118
**Subject(s):** (Golf); Lifestyle
**Circ:** (Paid)1,405,017

**Car and Driver (21454)**
Hachette Filipacchi Media U.S. Inc.
1633 Broadway
New York, NY 10019
Phone: (212)767-6000
**Subject(s):** Automotive (Consumer)
**Circ:** (Paid)1,402,657

**SELF Magazine (22362)**
Conde Nast Publications Inc.
4 Times Square, 17th Fl.
New York, NY 10036
Phone: (212)286-3700
Fax: (212)286-5960
**Subject(s):** Women's Interests; Health
**Circ:** (Paid)1,360,805

**Take One (18944)**
Connell Communications Inc.
86 Elm St.
Peterborough, NH 03458-1052
Phone: (603)924-7271
Fax: (603)924-7013
**Subject(s):** Motion Pictures; Radio, Television, Cable, and Video
**Circ:** ‡1,325,538

**Parents Expecting (22217)**
G & J USA Publishing
375 Lexington Ave.
New York, NY 10017-5514
Phone: (212)499-2113
Fax: (212)499-2113
**Subject(s):** Babies
**Circ:** (Non-paid)‡1,300,000

**Motor Trend (22108)**
PRIMEDIA Los Angeles
Motor Trend
260 Madison Ave., 8th Fl.
New York, NY 10016
Phone: (212)726-4300
Fax: (917)256-0025
**Subject(s):** Automotive (Consumer)
**Circ:** (Paid)1,285,178

**Rolling Stone (22325)**
Wenner Media
1290 Avenue of the Americas, 2nd Fl.
New York, NY 10104
Phone: (212)484-1794
Fax: (212)767-8209
**Subject(s):** General Editorial; Music and Musical Instruments; Entertainment
**Circ:** (Paid)1,251,520

**Popular Mechanics (22250)**
Hearst Magazines
1790 Broadway
New York, NY 10019
Phone: (212)841-8480
**Subject(s):** Portuguese; Spanish; General Editorial
**Circ:** (Paid)1,224,960

**Real Simple (22297)**
Time Inc.
Time-Life Bldg., Rockefeller Ctr.
1271 Avenue of the Americas
New York, NY 10020
Phone: (212)522-1212
Fax: (212)467-1396
**Subject(s):** Women's Interests; Lifestyle
**Circ:** (Paid)‡1,200,000

**Scholastic Parent & Child (22348)**
Scholastic Library Publishing Inc.
557 Broadway
New York, NY 10012
Phone: (212)343-6100
**Subject(s):** Parenting
**Circ:** (Combined)1,200,000

**Vogue (22522)**
Conde Nast Publications Inc.
4 Times Square, 17th Fl.
New York, NY 10036
Phone: (212)286-3700
Fax: (212)286-5960
**Subject(s):** Fashion
**Circ:** (Paid)1,174,183

**Fitness Magazine (21696)**
G & J USA Publishing
375 Lexington Ave.
New York, NY 10017-5514
Phone: (212)499-2113
Fax: (212)499-2113
**Subject(s):** (Physical Fitness)
**Circ:** (Paid)1,121,229

**Video Event (18945)**
Connell Communications Inc.
86 Elm St.
Peterborough, NH 03458-1052
Phone: (603)924-7271
Fax: (603)924-7013
**Subject(s):** Radio, Television, Cable, and Video; Radio, Television, Cable, and Video
**Circ:** (Paid)‡1,098,659

**Vanity Fair (22514)**
Conde Nast Publications Inc.
4 Times Square, 17th Fl.
New York, NY 10036
Phone: (212)286-3700
Fax: (212)286-5960
**Subject(s):** General Editorial
**Circ:** (Paid)1,050,684

**Best Read Guide (14796)**
900 Route 134
South Dennis, MA 02660
Phone: (508)240-1212
Fax: (508)385-2777
**Subject(s):** Travel and Tourism
**Circ:** (Controlled)‡1,050,000

**PC Magazine (22222)**
Ziff-Davis Publishing Co.
28 E. 28th St.
New York, NY 10016
Phone: (212)503-5100
Fax: (212)503-5000
**Subject(s):** Computers
**Circ:** (Controlled)128,277
(Paid)1,050,000

**TV Guide (27466)**
TV Guide Magazine
100 Matsonford Rd., Bldg. 4
Radnor, PA 19088
Phone: (610)293-8500
Fax: (610)293-6222
**Subject(s):** Radio, Television, Cable, and Video; Radio, Television, Cable, and Video
**Circ:** (Non-paid)209,485
(Paid)1,024,472

**Archie Comics (21091)**
Archie Comic Publications Inc.
325 Fayette Ave.
Mamaroneck, NY 10543
Phone: (914)381-5155
Fax: (914)381-2335
**Subject(s):** Comics and Comic Technique
**Circ:** 1,021,809

**Home Magazine (21773)**
Hachette Filipacchi Media U.S. Inc.
1633 Broadway
New York, NY 10019
Phone: (212)767-6000
**Subject(s):** Home and Garden
**Circ:** (Paid)1,010,623

**Discover (21606)**
Disney Publishing Worldwide
114 Fifth Ave.
New York, NY 10011
Phone: (212)633-4400
Fax: (212)633-4833
**Subject(s):** Science (General); General Editorial
**Circ:** (Paid)1,005,981

**Essence (21659)**
Essence Communications Inc.
1500 Broadway, 6th Fl.
New York, NY 10036
Phone: (212)642-0600
Fax: (212)921-5173
**Subject(s):** Women's Interests; Black Publications
**Circ:** (Paid)1,004,452

**Yahoo! Internet Life (22566)**
Ziff-Davis Inc.
28 E. 28th St.
New York, NY 10016-7930
Phone: (212)503-3500
**Subject(s):** Computers; Computers
**Circ:** (Paid)1,003,771

**The New Yorker (22170)**
Conde Nast Publications Inc.
4 Times Square, 17th Fl.
New York, NY 10036
Phone: (212)286-3700
Fax: (212)286-5960
**Subject(s):** General Editorial
**Circ:** (Paid)1,003,205

**American Homestyle and Gardening (21308)**
The New York Times Co.
229 W 43rd St.
New York, NY 10036-3913
Phone: (212)556-1234
Fax: (212)556-3535
**Subject(s):** Home and Garden
**Circ:** (Non-paid)23,382
(Paid)1,001,530

**Elle (21640)**
Hachette Filipacchi Media U.S. Inc.
1633 Broadway
New York, NY 10019
Phone: (212)767-6000
**Subject(s):** Women's Interests; Fashion
**Circ:** (Paid)1,000,638

**Mission Magazine (22089)**
Society for the Propagation of the Faith
366 5th Ave., 12th Fl.
New York, NY 10001
Phone: (212)563-8700
Fax: (212)563-8725
**Subject(s):** Religious Publications
**Circ:** (Non-paid)1,000,000

**more (22103)**
Meredith Corp.
125 Park Ave.
New York, NY 10017-5529
Phone: (212)557-6600
Fax: (212)551-6918
**Subject(s):** Women's Interests; Fashion
**Circ:** (Paid)850,000
★1,000,000

**Gourmet-The Magazine of Good Living (21744)**
Conde Nast Publications Inc.
4 Times Square, 17th Fl.
New York, NY 10036
Phone: (212)286-3700
Fax: (212)286-5960
**Subject(s):** Lifestyle; Food and Cooking; Travel and Tourism
**Circ:** (Paid)975,216

**Lucky (22046)**
Conde Nast Publications Inc.
4 Times Square, 17th Fl.
New York, NY 10036
Phone: (212)286-3700
Fax: (212)286-5960
**Subject(s):** Fashion; Women's Interests
**Circ:** (Paid)970,672

**Travel Leisure (22480)**
American Express Publishing Corp.
1120 Avenue of the Americas, 10th Fl.
New York, NY 10036
Phone: (212)382-5600

Circulation: ★ = ABC; △ = BPA; ♦ = CAC; • = CCAB; ▫ = VAC; ⊕ = PO Statement; ‡ = Publisher's Report; Boldface figures = sworn; Light figures = estimated

Fax: (212)536-2020
**Subject(s):** Travel and Tourism
**Circ:** (Paid)960,485

**This Old House (22451)**
Time Inc.
1185 Avenue of the Americas, 27th Fl.
New York, NY 10036
Phone: (212)522-9465
Fax: (212)522-9435
**Subject(s):** Home and Garden; Crafts, Models, Hobbies, and Contests
**Circ:** (Paid)950,000

**Business Week (21443)**
McGraw-Hill Inc.
1221 Ave. of The Americas, 43rd Fl.
New York, NY 10020
Phone: (212)512-2511
**Subject(s):** Business; Business
**Circ:** (Paid)949,860

**Marie Claire (22055)**
Hearst Magazines
1790 Broadway
New York, NY 10019
Phone: (212)841-8480
**Subject(s):** Lifestyle
**Circ:** (Paid)948,321

**Child (21483)**
G & J USA Publishing
375 Lexington Ave.
New York, NY 10017-5514
Phone: (212)499-2113
Fax: (212)499-2113
**Subject(s):** Babies; Parenting
**Circ:** (Non-paid)100,185
(Paid)921,332

**GQ (Gentlemen's Quarterly) (21746)**
Conde Nast Publications Inc.
4 Times Square, 17th Fl.
New York, NY 10036
Phone: (212)286-3700
Fax: (212)286-5960
**Subject(s):** Men's Interests; Fashion
**Circ:** (Paid)898,508

**Forbes (21707)**
Forbes Magazine
60 5th Ave.
New York, NY 10011
Phone: (212)620-2200
Fax: (212)206-1873
**Subject(s):** Business
**Circ:** (Paid)884,201

**Allure (21291)**
Conde Nast Publications Inc.
4 Times Square, 17th Fl.
New York, NY 10036
Phone: (212)286-3700
Fax: (212)286-5960
**Subject(s):** Women's Interests; Fashion
**Circ:** (Paid)876,584

**Food & Wine (21702)**
American Express Publishing Corp.
1120 Avenue of the Americas, 10th Fl.
New York, NY 10036
Phone: (212)382-5600
Fax: (212)536-2020
**Subject(s):** Food and Cooking
**Circ:** (Paid)860,254

**House Beautiful (21787)**
Hearst Magazines
1790 Broadway
New York, NY 10019
Phone: (212)841-8480
**Subject(s):** Paint and Wallcoverings; Home and Garden; Construction, Contracting, Building, and Excavating; Architecture
**Circ:** (Paid)853,748

**Fortune (21714)**
Time Inc.
Time-Life Bldg., Rockefeller Ctr.
1271 Avenue of the Americas
New York, NY 10020
Phone: (212)522-1212
Fax: (212)467-1396

**Subject(s):** Business
**Circ:** (Paid)853,267

**Penthouse (22226)**
Penthouse International Ltd.
2 Penn Plaza, Ste. 1125
New York, NY 10121
**Subject(s):** Sex/Erotica
**Circ:** (Paid)851,066

**Us (22511)**
Wenner Media
1290 Avenue of the Americas, 2nd Fl.
New York, NY 10104
Phone: (212)484-1794
Fax: (212)767-8209
**Subject(s):** Entertainment
**Circ:** (Paid)850,434

**Steelabor (27406)**
United Steelworkers of America
5 Gateway Ctr.
Pittsburgh, PA 15222
Phone: (412)562-2442
Fax: (412)562-2445
**Subject(s):** Labor; Metal, Metallurgy, and Metal Trade
**Circ:** ‡840,000

**SmartMoney (22379)**
1755 Broadway, 2nd Fl.
New York, NY 10019
Phone: (212)830-9200
Fax: (212)830-9292
**Subject(s):** Lifestyle; Business
**Circ:** (Paid)824,327

**Midwest Living Magazine (22086)**
Meredith Corp.
125 Park Ave.
New York, NY 10017-5529
Phone: (212)557-6600
Fax: (212)551-6918
**Subject(s):** Lifestyle; Local, State, and Regional Publications; Home and Garden
**Circ:** (Paid)822,148

**Stuff Magazine (22426)**
Dennis Publishing
1040 Ave. of the Americas, 12th Fl.
New York, NY 10018
Phone: (212)302-2626
Fax: (212)768-1319
**Subject(s):** Fashion; Men's Interests; Lifestyle
**Circ:** (Paid)812,079

**Girl Scout Leader (21737)**
Girl Scouts of U.S.A.
420 5th Ave.
New York, NY 10018-2798
Phone: (212)852-8000
Fax: (212)852-6511
**Subject(s):** Parenting
**Circ:** ‡800,000

**Car & Travel Monthly (20806)**
Automobile Club of New York
1415 Kellum Pl.
Garden City, NY 11530
Phone: (516)746-7730
Fax: (516)873-2355
**Subject(s):** Travel and Tourism
**Circ:** ‡797,000

**Conde Nast Traveler (21540)**
Conde Nast Publications Inc.
4 Times Square, 17th Fl.
New York, NY 10036
Phone: (212)286-3700
Fax: (212)286-5960
**Subject(s):** Travel and Tourism
**Circ:** (Paid)785,717

**Careers & Colleges (19443)**
360 Youth L.L.C.
PO Box 22
Keyport, NJ 07735
Phone: (732)264-0460
Fax: (732)264-0460
**Subject(s):** Youths' Interests; Education
**Circ:** (Paid)1,679
(Non-paid)752,000

**Lamaze Para Padres (4676)**
iVillage Parenting Network
9 Old Kings Hwy. S.
Darien, CT 06820
Phone: (203)656-3600
Fax: (203)656-2221
**Subject(s):** Parenting; Babies; Spanish
**Circ:** (Non-paid)△750,000

**Harper's Bazaar (21756)**
Hearst Magazines
1790 Broadway
New York, NY 10019
Phone: (212)841-8480
**Subject(s):** Fashion; Society
**Circ:** (Paid)721,738

**Tennis Magazine (22447)**
Miller Sports Group L.L.C.
79 Madison Ave., 8th Fl.
New York, NY 10016-7802
Phone: (212)636-2700
Fax: (212)636-2730
**Subject(s):** (Racquet Sports)
**Circ:** (Paid)711,855

**Fast Company (13515)**
Fast Company Magazine
77 N Washington St.
Boston, MA 02114
Phone: (617)973-0373
Fax: (617)973-0373
**Subject(s):** Business
**Circ:** (Paid)708,251

**Golf Journal (19085)**
U.S. Golf Association
Golf House
PO Box 708
Far Hills, NJ 07931-0708
Phone: (908)234-2300
Fax: (908)234-2179
**Subject(s):** (Golf)
**Circ:** ‡700,000

**The Sporting News (22407)**
The Sporting News Publishing Co.
475 Park Ave., S., 27th Fl.
New York, NY 10016
Phone: (646)424-2227
Fax: (646)424-2232
**Subject(s):** (General Sports)
**Circ:** (Paid)700,000

**Scientific American (22356)**
Scientific American Magazine
415 Madison Ave.
New York, NY 10017
Phone: (212)754-0550
Fax: (212)755-1976
**Subject(s):** Science (General); French; German; Italian; Japanese; Spanish; General Editorial
**Circ:** (Paid)687,437

**Inside MS (21822)**
National Multiple Sclerosis Society
733 3rd Ave.
New York, NY 10017
Phone: (212)986-3240
Fax: (212)986-7981
**Subject(s):** Health and Healthcare; Medicine and Surgery; Health
**Circ:** 680,000

**Esquire (21657)**
Hearst Magazines
1790 Broadway
New York, NY 10019
Phone: (212)841-8480
**Subject(s):** Fashion; Men's Interests
**Circ:** (Paid)676,052

**Eating Well Magazine (21628)**
Eating Well Inc.
1633 Broadway
New York, NY 10019
Phone: (212)767-6000
**Subject(s):** Food and Cooking; Health
**Circ:** (Paid)676,024

**Inc. (21815)**
Gruner & Jahr USA
375 Lexington Ave.
New York, NY 10017-5514
Phone: (212)499-2000

**Subject(s):** Business
**Circ:** (Paid)665,000

**Marian Helper (14821)**
Association of Marian Helpers
Eden Hill
Stockbridge, MA 01263
Phone: (413)298-3691
**Subject(s):** Religious Publications
**Circ:** (Controlled)650,000

**Angels on Earth (21335)**
Guideposts
C/o Editor
16 E. 34th St.
New York, NY 10016
**Subject(s):** Religious Publications
**Circ:** (Paid)647,478

**Inc. Technology (21816)**
Gruner & Jahr USA
375 Lexington Ave.
New York, NY 10017-5514
Phone: (212)499-2000
**Subject(s):** Business
**Circ:** (Paid)640,000

**Sports Illustrated for Kids (22410)**
Time Inc.
The Home office Si for Kids
135 W., 50th St.
New York, NY 10020-1393
Phone: (212)522-1212
Fax: (212)522-0120
**Subject(s):** (General Sports); Children's Interests
**Circ:** (Non-paid)251,449
(Paid)613,157

**Men's Journal (22074)**
Wenner Media
1290 Avenue of the Americas, 2nd Fl.
New York, NY 10104
Phone: (212)484-1794
Fax: (212)767-8209
**Subject(s):** Men's Interests
**Circ:** (Paid)612,186

**Organic Gardening (26329)**
Rodale Inc.
33 E. Minor St.
Emmaus, PA 18098-0099
Phone: (610)967-5171
Fax: (610)967-8181
**Subject(s):** Horticulture; Home and Garden
**Circ:** (Paid)605,980

**Metropolitan Home (22080)**
Hachette Filipacchi Media U.S. Inc.
1633 Broadway
New York, NY 10019
Phone: (212)767-6000
**Subject(s):** Interior Design/Decorating; Home and Garden
**Circ:** (Paid)604,670

**Let's Find Out (22031)**
Scholastic Library Publishing Inc.
557 Broadway
New York, NY 10012
Phone: (212)343-6100
**Subject(s):** Education; Education
**Circ:** ‡600,000

**Maryknoll Magazine (21132)**
Maryknoll Fathers
PO Box 308
Maryknoll, NY 10545-0308
Phone: (914)941-7636
Fax: (914)945-0670
**Subject(s):** Religious Publications
**Circ:** (Paid)600,000

**Positive Thinking (22690)**
Peale Center for Christian Living
66 E. Main St.
Pawling, NY 12564
Phone: (845)855-5000
Fax: (845)855-1462
**Subject(s):** General Editorial; Religious Publications
**Circ:** (Paid)‡600,000
(Non-paid)‡600,000

**Junior Scholastic (22008)**
Scholastic Library Publishing Inc.
557 Broadway
New York, NY 10012
Phone: (212)343-6100
**Subject(s):** Education; Education
**Circ:** (Paid)591,038

**WHERE New York (22537)**
Miller Publishing Group L.L.C.
79 Madison Ave., 8th Fl.
New York, NY 10016
Phone: (212)636-2700
Fax: (212)636-2710
**Subject(s):** Travel and Tourism
**Circ:** (Non-paid)‡570,619

**SPIN (22403)**
VIBE/SPIN Ventures L.L.C.
205 Liexington Ave., 3rd Fl.
New York, NY 10016
Phone: (212)231-7400
Fax: (212)231-7300
**Subject(s):** Music and Musical Instruments; Entertainment
**Circ:** (Paid)540,063

**Runner's World (26332)**
Rodale Inc.
33 E. Minor St.
Emmaus, PA 18098-0099
Phone: (610)967-5171
Fax: (610)967-8181
**Subject(s):** (Running)
**Circ:** (Paid)530,000

**Arthur Frommer's Budget Travel (21362)**
Newsweek Budget Travel Inc.
530 Seventh Ave.
2nd Fl.
New York, NY 10018
Phone: (646)695-6700
Fax: (646)695-6702
**Subject(s):** Travel and Tourism
**Circ:** (Non-paid)‡38,777
(Paid)‡518,498

**ADVANCE for Nurses (26579)**
Merion Publications Inc.
2900 Horizon Dr.
King of Prussia, PA 19406
Phone: (610)278-1400
Fax: (610)278-1425
**Subject(s):** Medicine and Surgery; Health and Healthcare; Nursing
**Circ:** (Combined)510,000

**Worth Magazine (22564)**
Capital Publishing Co.
575 Lexington Ave.
New York, NY 10022
Phone: (212)223-3100
Fax: (212)223-1598
**Subject(s):** Business; Banking, Finance, and Investments
**Circ:** (Paid)501,071

**Unite! Magazine (22503)**
Union of Needletrades, Industrial & Textile Employees
275 7th Ave., 11th Floor
New York, NY 10001-6708
Phone: (212)265-7000
Fax: (212)582-3175
**Subject(s):** Labor
**Circ:** ‡500,000

**Elle Decor (21642)**
Hachette Filipacchi Media U.S. Inc.
1633 Broadway
New York, NY 10019
Phone: (212)767-6000
**Subject(s):** Home and Garden; Art
**Circ:** (Paid)467,367

**Sports Afield (22408)**
Hearst Magazines
1790 Broadway
New York, NY 10019
Phone: (212)841-8480
**Subject(s):** (General Sports)
**Circ:** (Paid)459,396

**Better Homes and Gardens: Garden, Deck and Landscape (21393)**
Meredith Corp.
125 Park Ave.
New York, NY 10017-5529
Phone: (212)557-6600
Fax: (212)551-6918
**Subject(s):** Home and Garden
**Circ:** (Controlled)459,000

**Popular Photography and Imaging (22252)**
Hachette Filipacchi Media U.S. Inc.
1633 Broadway
New York, NY 10019
Phone: (212)767-6000
**Subject(s):** Photography
**Circ:** (Paid)458,714

**The Atlantic Monthly (13476)**
The Atlantic Monthly Co.
77 N. Washington St.
Boston, MA 02114
Phone: (617)854-7700
Fax: (617)854-7876
**Subject(s):** General Editorial
**Circ:** (Paid)458,667

**Audubon (21374)**
National Audubon Society Inc.
700 Broadway
New York, NY 10003
Phone: (212)979-3000
Fax: (212)979-3188
**Subject(s):** Environmental and Natural Resources Conservation
**Circ:** (Paid)454,885

**The Source (22396)**
Source Publications Inc.
28 W. 23rd St. 10th Fl.
New York, NY 10010
Phone: (212)253-3700
Fax: (212)253-9344
**Subject(s):** Music and Musical Instruments; Alternative and Underground; Entertainment
**Circ:** (Paid)454,726

**W (22525)**
Fairchild Publications Inc.
7 W 34th St.
New York, NY 10001
Phone: (212)630-4000
Fax: (212)630-3555
**Subject(s):** Women's Interests; Lifestyle
**Circ:** (Paid)451,883

**ABS Record (21251)**
American Bible Society
1865 Broadway
New York, NY 10023-7505
Phone: (212)408-1200
Fax: (212)408-1456
**Subject(s):** Religious Publications
**Circ:** 450,000

**Better Homes and Gardens Building Ideas (21391)**
Meredith Corp.
125 Park Ave.
New York, NY 10017-5529
Phone: (212)557-6600
Fax: (212)551-6918
**Subject(s):** Construction, Contracting, Building, and Excavating; Architecture; Home and Garden
**Circ:** (Paid)‡450,000

**Farm Journal (26946)**
Farm Journal Inc.
1818 Market St., 31st Fl.
Philadelphia, PA 19103
Phone: (215)557-8900
Fax: (215)568-4238
**Subject(s):** General Agriculture
**Circ:** (Paid)133,655
(Non-paid)449,384

**Details (21596)**
Conde Nast Publications Inc.
4 Times Square, 17th Fl.
New York, NY 10036
Phone: (212)286-3700
Fax: (212)286-5960
**Subject(s):** Lifestyle; Men's Interests
**Circ:** (Paid)446,223

Circulation: ★ = ABC; △ = BPA; ♦ = CAC; • = CCAB; ☐ = VAC; ⊕ = PO Statement; ‡ = Publisher's Report; Boldface figures = sworn; Light figures = estimated.

**New York Magazine** (22161)
Primedia Inc.
444 Madison Ave., 14th Fl.
New York, NY 10022
Phone: (212)508-0700
**Subject(s):** Local, State, and Regional Publications; Lifestyle
**Circ:** (Paid)440,308

**InformationWEEK** (21109)
CMP Media L.L.C.
600 Community Dri.
Manhasset, NY 11030
Phone: (516)562-5000
**Subject(s):** Computers
**Circ:** (Non-paid)‡440,000

**The Next Step Magazine** (23111)
86 W. Main St.
Victor, NY 14564
Fax: (585)742-1263
**Subject(s):** Education; Career Development and Employment; Youths' Interests
**Circ:** (Non-paid)440,000

**Scholastic Scope Magazine** (22349)
Scholastic Library Publishing Inc.
557 Broadway
New York, NY 10012
Phone: (212)343-6100
**Subject(s):** Education
**Circ:** (Paid)438,662

**Town & Country** (22468)
Hearst Magazines
1790 Broadway
New York, NY 10019
Phone: (212)841-8480
**Subject(s):** Women's Interests; Lifestyle
**Circ:** (Paid)430,367

**Black Enterprise** (21411)
Earl Graves Publishing Co.
130 5th Ave.,10th Fl.
New York, NY 10011-4399
Phone: (212)242-8000
Fax: (212)886-9600
**Subject(s):** Business; Black Publications
**Circ:** (Paid)421,169

**Catholic Digest** (4866)
Bayard Inc.
185 Willow St.
Mystic, CT 06355
**Subject(s):** Religious Publications
**Circ:** (Paid)400,000

**Honey** (21781)
Vanguarde Media Inc.
315 Park Ave. S, 11th Fl.
New York, NY 10010
**Subject(s):** Black Publications; Women's Interests; Fashion
**Circ:** (Combined)★400,000

**Science World Magazine** (22354)
Scholastic Library Publishing Inc.
557 Broadway
New York, NY 10012
Phone: (212)343-6100
**Subject(s):** Education; Education; Science (General)
**Circ:** (Paid)395,228

**Diabetes Self-Management** (21599)
R.A. Rapaport Publishing Inc.
150 W 22nd St., Ste.800
New York, NY 10011
Phone: (212)989-0200
Fax: (212)989-4786
**Subject(s):** Medicine and Surgery
**Circ:** (Non-paid)30,075
 (Paid)374,156

**Bride's Magazine** (21425)
Conde Nast Publications Inc.
4 Times Square, 17th Fl.
New York, NY 10036
Phone: (212)286-3700
Fax: (212)286-5960
**Subject(s):** Brides
**Circ:** (Paid)371,445

**Modern Bride** (22093)
K-III Family Leisure Group
750 Third Ave., 4th Fl.
New York, NY 10017
**Subject(s):** Brides
**Circ:** (Paid)371,160

**Journal of Accountancy** (19430)
The American Institute of Certified Public Accountants
Harborside Financial Center
201 Plaza Three
Jersey City, NJ 07311-3881
Phone: (201)938-3741
Fax: (201)938-3741
**Subject(s):** Accountants and Accounting
**Circ:** (Paid)367,561

**Mother Earth News** (22105)
Sussex Publishers Inc.
49 21st St., 11th Fl.
New York, NY 10010-6213
Phone: (212)260-7210
Fax: (212)260-7566
**Subject(s):** Home and Garden
**Circ:** (Paid)366,793

**Gallery Magazine** (21726)
Montcalm Publishing Corp.
401 Park Ave. S, 3rd Fl.
New York, NY 10016-8802
Phone: (212)779-8900
Fax: (212)725-7215
**Subject(s):** Men's Interests; Sex/Erotica
**Circ:** ‡362,863

**Continental Magazine** (13505)
Pohly & Partners Inc.
27 Melcher St., 2nd Fl.
Boston, MA 02210
Phone: (617)451-1700
Fax: (617)338-7767
**Subject(s):** In-Flight Publications
**Circ:** (Non-paid)360,000

**Country Living Gardener** (21563)
The Hearst Corp.
Editorial Dept.
1790 Broadway, 12th Fl.
New York, NY 10019
Phone: (212)492-1324
Fax: (212)246-3972
**Subject(s):** Home and Garden
**Circ:** (Paid)360,000

**Current Science** (5030)
Weekly Reader Corp.
200 First Stamford Pl.
PO Box 120023
Stamford, CT 06912-0023
Phone: (203)705-3500
Fax: (203)705-1661
**Subject(s):** Education; Science (General)
**Circ:** ‡357,583

**Club Magazine** (4997)
Paragon Publishing Inc.
Box 200
Sandy Hook, CT 06482
Phone: (203)426-6533
Fax: (203)426-9533
**Subject(s):** Sex/Erotica
**Circ:** ‡355,000

**CFO** (13496)
CFO Publishing
253 Summer St.
Boston, MA 02210
Phone: (617)345-9700
Fax: (617)951-9306
**Subject(s):** Management and Administration
**Circ:** (Controlled)‡350,000

**Country Accents** (21558)
Goodman Media Group Inc.
250 W 57th St., Ste. 710
New York, NY 10107-0799
Phone: (212)262-2247
Fax: (212)262-2279
**Subject(s):** Home and Garden; Lifestyle
**Circ:** ‡350,000

**Nursing 96** (26115)
Lippincott Williams & Wilkins
323 Norristown Rd.
Ste. 200
Ambler, PA
Phone: (215)628-7702
Fax: (215)367-2155
**Subject(s):** Nursing
**Circ:** (Paid)350,000

**Playgirl** (22239)
Playgirl Inc.
801 2nd Ave.
New York, NY 10017
Phone: (212)661-7878
Fax: (212)697-6343
**Subject(s):** Women's Interests; Sex/Erotica
**Circ:** 350,000

**American Heritage** (21307)
90 Fifth Ave.
New York, NY 10011
Phone: (212)367-3100
Fax: (212)367-3151
**Subject(s):** History and Genealogy
**Circ:** (Paid)340,000

**IEEE Spectrum** (21805)
Institute of Electrical and Electronics Engineers Inc.
3 Park Ave., 17th Fl.
New York, NY 10016
Phone: (212)705-8900
Fax: (212)705-8999
**Subject(s):** Engineering (Various branches); Science (General)
**Circ:** (Non-paid)30,699
 (Paid)3,39,000

**Journal of Natural History** (27064)
Taylor & Francis
325 Chestnut St., Ste. 800
Philadelphia, PA 19106
Phone: (215)625-8900
Fax: (215)625-8914
**Subject(s):** Biology; Veterinary Medicine; Zoology
**Circ:** (Paid)333,180

**Savoy** (22340)
Vanguarde Media Inc.
315 Park Ave. S, 11th Fl.
New York, NY 10010
**Subject(s):** Black Publications; Lifestyle; Entertainment; Fashion
**Circ:** (Combined)★325,000

**Psychology Today** (22276)
Sussex Publishers Inc.
49 21st St., 11th Fl.
New York, NY 10010-6213
Phone: (212)260-7210
Fax: (212)260-7566
**Subject(s):** Psychology and Psychiatry
**Circ:** (Paid)323,003

**American Journal of Nursing** (26816)
c/o Lippincott, Williams, & Wilkins
530 Walnut St.
Philadelphia, PA 19106-3621
Phone: (215)521-8300
Fax: (215)521-8902
**Subject(s):** Nursing
**Circ:** (Non-paid)20,191
 (Paid)317,111

**Time (Asia)** (22456)
Time Inc.
Time-Life Bldg., Rockefeller Ctr.
1271 Avenue of the Americas
New York, NY 10020
Phone: (212)522-1212
Fax: (212)467-1396
**Subject(s):** Export Consumer Magazines
**Circ:** (Paid)315,753

**Flying** (4774)
Hachette Filipacchi Media U.S. Inc.
500 West Putnam Ave.
Greenwich, CT 06830
Phone: (203)622-2700
Fax: (203)622-2725
**Subject(s):** Aviation; Aviation
**Circ:** (Paid)313,246

**Circus Magazine** (21492)
Circus Enterprises
6 W 18th St., 2nd Fl.
New York, NY 10011
Phone: (212)242-4902
Fax: (212)242-5734
**Subject(s):** Music and Musical Instruments; Entertainment
**Circ:** (Non-paid)7,709
(Paid)307,092

**Reform Judaism** (22301)
Union of American Hebrew Congregations
633 3rd Ave.
New York, NY 10017-6778
Phone: (212)650-4000
**Subject(s):** Jewish Publications
**Circ:** ‡305,000

**Barron's** (21385)
Dow Jones & Company Inc.
200 Liberty St.
New York, NY 10281
Phone: (212)416-2000
Fax: (212)416-2658
**Subject(s):** Banking, Finance, and Investments
**Circ:** (Paid)300,158

**Amnesty Action** (21330)
Amnesty International USA
322 8th Ave.
New York, NY 10001
Phone: (212)807-8400
Fax: (212)627-1451
**Subject(s):** Philanthropy and Humanitarianism; Politics
**Circ:** ‡300,000

**CARGO** (21458)
Conde Nast Publications Inc.
4 Times Square, 17th Fl.
New York, NY 10036
Phone: (212)286-3700
Fax: (212)286-5960
**Subject(s):** Men's Interests; Lifestyle; Fashion
**Circ:** 300,000

**Computer Survival Report** (21538)
Enterprise Publications
400 E 59th St., No. 9-F
New York, NY 10022
Phone: (212)755-4363
**Subject(s):** Computers
**Circ:** (Paid)300,000

**Natural History Magazine** (22133)
American Museum of Natural History
79th St. & Central Park W
New York, NY 10024-5192
Phone: (212)769-5400
Fax: (212)769-5009
**Subject(s):** Natural History and Nature Study; Environmental and Natural Resources Conservation
**Circ:** (Paid)300,000

**Penthouse Variations** (22227)
General Media
2 Penn Plaza 1125
New York, NY 10121
Phone: (212)702-6000
Fax: (212)702-6262
**Subject(s):** Sex/Erotica; Men's Interests
**Circ:** (Combined)300,000

**Stock Guide** (22420)
Standard & Poor's
55 Water St.
New York, NY 10041
Fax: (212)438-3396
**Subject(s):** Banking, Finance, and Investments
**Circ:** (Paid)300,000

**Fine Homebuilding** (4930)
Taunton Press
PO Box 5506
Newtown, CT 06470-5506
Phone: (203)426-8171
Fax: (203)426-3734
**Subject(s):** Architecture; Construction, Contracting, Building, and Excavating
**Circ:** (Paid)296,467

**Wine Spectator** (22539)
M. Shanken Communications Inc.
387 Park Ave. S.
New York, NY 10016
Phone: (212)684-4224
Fax: (212)684-5424
**Subject(s):** Beverages, Brewing, and Bottling; Food and Cooking
**Circ:** (Paid)290,318

**Backpacker Magazine** (26323)
33 E. Minor St.
Emmaus, PA 18098
Phone: (610)967-8296
Fax: (610)967-8963
**Subject(s):** (General Sports)
**Circ:** (Paid)281,566

**Bicycling** (26324)
135 N. Sixth St.
Emmaus, PA 18098-0099
Phone: (610)967-5171
Fax: (610)967-8960
**Subject(s):** (Bicycling)
**Circ:** (Non-paid)6,704
(Paid)280,218

**Cigar Aficionado** (21490)
M. Shanken Communications Inc.
387 Park Ave. S.
New York, NY 10016
Phone: (212)481-8610
Fax: (212)684-5424
**Subject(s):** Men's Interests; Lifestyle
**Circ:** (Paid)280,023

**The Northern Light** (13855)
Supreme Council, Scottish Rite, NMJ, USA
PO Box 519
Lexington, MA 02420
Phone: (781)862-4410
Fax: (781)863-1833
**Subject(s):** Masons
**Circ:** (Paid)‡720
(Non-paid)‡278,000

**The Motorist** (23190)
AAA Automobile Club of Western New York
100 International Dr.
Williamsville, NY 14221-5769
Phone: (716)633-9860
Fax: (716)634-2504
**Subject(s):** Travel and Tourism
**Circ:** (Paid)277,812

**Hadassah Magazine** (21753)
Hadassah, The Women's Zionist Organization of America
50 W 58th St.
New York, NY 10019-2500
**Subject(s):** Jewish Publications; Unclassified Fraternal; Women's Interests
**Circ:** (Paid)272,131

**Starlog** (22416)
Starlog Group Inc.
475 Park Ave. S, 8th Fl.
New York, NY 10016
Phone: (212)689-2830
Fax: (212)889-7933
**Subject(s):** Science Fiction, Mystery, Adventure, and Romance
**Circ:** (Paid)⊕266,855

**Fine Woodworking** (4931)
Taunton Press
191 S. Main St.
Newtown, CT 06470
Phone: (203)270-6751
Fax: (800)283-7252
**Subject(s):** Wood and Woodworking
**Circ:** (Paid)265,029

**Body & Soul Magazine** (14873)
Martha Stewart Living Omnimedia
42 Pleasant St.
Watertown, MA 02472
Phone: (617)926-0200
**Subject(s):** Alternative and Underground; New Age
**Circ:** (Non-paid)14,000
(Paid)261,000

**Connecticut Traveler** (4789)
Connecticut Motor Club AAA
2276 Whitney Ave.
Hamden, CT 06518-3505
Phone: (203)765-4222
Fax: (203)230-0182
**Subject(s):** Travel and Tourism
**Circ:** 258,000

**American Photo** (21322)
Hachette Filipacchi Media U.S. Inc.
1633 Broadway
New York, NY 10019
Phone: (212)767-6000
**Subject(s):** Photography
**Circ:** (Paid)255,971

**U.S.A. Today** (20772)
500 Bi-County Blvd., Ste. 203
Farmingdale, NY 11735
Phone: (631)293-4343
**Subject(s):** General Editorial
**Circ:** ‡254,000

**Forum** (21716)
General Media
2 Penn Plaza 1125
New York, NY 10121
Phone: (212)702-6000
Fax: (212)702-6262
**Subject(s):** Sex/Erotica
**Circ:** 251,795

**Flower & Garden** (19133)
KC Publishing Inc.
Flower & Garden
51 Kings Hwy. W
Haddonfield, NJ 08033
Phone: (856)354-5034
**Subject(s):** Home and Garden
**Circ:** (Paid)250,301

**American Bible Society Record** (21300)
American Bible Society
1865 Broadway
New York, NY 10023
**Subject(s):** Religious Publications
**Circ:** (Controlled)‡250,000

**Coach and Athletic Director** (4659)
Scholastic Library Publishing Inc.
90 Old Sherman Tpke.
Danbury, CT 06816
Phone: (203)797-3500
Fax: (203)797-3657
**Subject(s):** Health and Fitness; Physical Education and Athletics
**Circ:** 2,50,000

**Consumer Reports for Kids** (23203)
Consumers Union of U.S. Inc.
101 Truman Ave.
Yonkers, NY 10703-1057
Phone: (914)378-2740
Fax: (914)378-2985
**Subject(s):** Children's Interests
**Circ:** ‡250,000

**Read** (5038)
Weekly Reader Corp.
200 First Stamford Pl.
PO Box 120023
Stamford, CT 06912-0023
Phone: (203)705-3500
Fax: (203)705-1661
**Subject(s):** Education; Youths' Interests
**Circ:** ‡250,000

**Small Business Opportunities** (22377)
Harris Publications Inc.
1115 Broadway
New York, NY 10010-2803
Phone: (212)807-7100
Fax: (212)924-2352
**Subject(s):** Business
**Circ:** 250,000

**Swank** (19658)
Swank Publications
210 Rte. 4E, Ste. 211
Paramus, NJ 07652
Phone: (201)843-4004
Fax: (201)843-8636
**Subject(s):** Sex/Erotica
**Circ:** (Non-paid)30,000
(Paid)250,000

**Harvard Business Review** (13521)
Harvard Business School Publishing
60 Harvard Way
Boston, MA 02163
Phone: (617)783-7500
Fax: (617)783-7555

# Northeastern States

Subject(s): Management and Administration; Business
Circ: (Paid)249,100

**Hemmings Motor News** (30839)
PO Box 256
Bennington, VT 05201
Phone: (802)447-1561
Fax: (800)227-4373
Subject(s): Automotive (Consumer)
Circ: (Paid)245,287

**Journeys** (5081)
AAA Automobile Club of Hartford
815 Farmington Ave.
West Hartford, CT 06119-1584
Phone: (860)236-3261
Fax: (860)523-1797
Subject(s): Travel and Tourism; Automotive (Consumer)
Circ: 245,000

**Scholastic DynaMath** (4663)
Scholastic Library Publishing Inc.
90 Old Sherman Tpke.
Danbury, CT 06816
Phone: (203)797-3500
Fax: (203)797-3657
Subject(s): Mathematics; Education
Circ: ‡235,000

**True Story** (22492)
Macfadden Communications Group
333 Seventh Ave., Fl. 11
New York, NY 10001-5004
Phone: (212)780-3500
Fax: (212)979-4825
Subject(s): Women's Interests
Circ: (Paid)234,717

**The Housing Authority Journal** (21789)
New York City Housing Authority
250 Broadway, Rm. 917
New York, NY 10007
Phone: (212)776-5000
Fax: (212)306-6482
Subject(s): State, Municipal, and County Administration
Circ: (Non-paid)‡230,000

**The New England Journal of Medicine** (13559)
10 Shattuck St.
Boston, MA 02115-6094
Phone: (617)734-9800
Fax: (617)739-9864
Subject(s): Medicine and Surgery
Circ: (Non-paid)‡10,132
(Paid)‡230,000

**The New York Times Upfront** (4660)
Scholastic Library Publishing Inc.
90 Old Sherman Tpke.
Danbury, CT 06816
Phone: (203)797-3500
Fax: (203)797-3657
Subject(s): Education; Education
Circ: (Paid)230,000

**Scholastic Action** (22343)
Scholastic Library Publishing Inc.
557 Broadway
New York, NY 10012
Phone: (212)343-6100
Subject(s): Education; Education
Circ: 230,000

**Archaeology** (13474)
Archaeological Institute of America
Boston University
656 Beacon St., 4th Fl.
Boston, MA 02215-2006
Phone: (617)353-9361
Subject(s): Archaeology
Circ: (Paid)227,499

**Network Computing** (21112)
CMP Media L.L.C.
600 Community Dr.
Manhasset, NY 11030
Subject(s): Computers
Circ: (Paid)220,000

**True Love** (22490)
Macfadden Communications Group
333 Seventh Ave., Fl. 11
New York, NY 10001-5004
Phone: (212)780-3500
Fax: (212)979-4825
Subject(s): Science Fiction, Mystery, Adventure, and Romance
Circ: (Paid)220,000

**Fly Fishing in Salt Waters** (19800)
Aqua-Field Publishing Company Inc.
39 Avenue of the Common
Shrewsbury, NJ 07702
Phone: (732)935-1222
Subject(s): (Hunting, Fishing, and Game Management)
Circ: (Paid)‡217,000

**The Miraculous Medal** (27149)
Central Association of the Miraculous Medal
475 E Chelten Ave.
Philadelphia, PA 19144-5785
Phone: (215)848-1010
Fax: (215)848-1014
Subject(s): Religious Publications
Circ: (Controlled)2,000
(Paid)215,000

**Harper's Magazine** (21757)
McArthur Foundation
666 Broadway
New York, NY 10012
Phone: (212)614-6500
Fax: (212)228-5889
Subject(s): General Editorial
Circ: (Paid)213,141

**Horticulture** (13526)
F & W Publications
98 N. Washington St.
Boston, MA 02114
Phone: (617)742-5600
Fax: (617)367-6364
Subject(s): Home and Garden; Horticulture
Circ: (Paid)210,000

**Nutrition Health Review** (26475)
Box No. 406
Haverford, PA 19041
Subject(s): Health; Psychology and Psychiatry
Circ: ‡210,000

**Scholastic Instructor** (22346)
Scholastic Library Publishing Inc.
c/o Scholastic Inc.
PO Box 711
New York, NY 10013-0711
Fax: (212)965-7497
Subject(s): Education
Circ: (Paid)208,319

**Industrial Equipment News** (21818)
Thomas Publishing Co.
IENonline.com
5 Penn Plaza
New York, NY 10001
Phone: (212)629-1505
Subject(s): Commerce and Industry
Circ: (Controlled)‡208,174

**NASA Tech Briefs** (22122)
Associated Business Publications Company Ltd.
1466 Broadway, Ste. 910
New York, NY 10036
Phone: (212)490-3999
Fax: (212)986-7864
Subject(s): Astronautics; Science (General)
Circ: (Controlled)‡207,000

**Bridal Guide** (21424)
Globe Communications Corp.
Three E 54th St., 15th Fl.
New York, NY 10022
Phone: (212)838-7733
Subject(s): Brides
Circ: (Paid)205,858

**Pitt Magazine** (27384)
University of Pittsburgh
400 Craig Hall
Pittsburgh, PA 15260
Phone: (412)624-4147
Fax: (412)624-1021
Subject(s): College Publications
Circ: (Non-paid)‡205,000

**Fine Cooking Magazine** (4928)
Taunton Press
PO Box 5506
Newtown, CT 06470-5506
Phone: (203)426-8171
Fax: (203)426-3434
Subject(s): Food and Cooking
Circ: (Paid)202,981

**Boating Magazine** (21414)
Hachette Filipacchi Media U.S. Inc.
1633 Broadway
New York, NY 10019
Phone: (212)767-6000
Subject(s): (Boating and Yachting)
Circ: (Paid)200,783

**Harvard Magazine** (13675)
7 Ware St.
Cambridge, MA 02138
Phone: (617)495-5746
Fax: (617)495-0324
Subject(s): College Publications
Circ: (Paid)‡19,560
(Non-paid)‡200,150

**American Cheerleader** (21302)
Lifestyle Ventures L.L.C.
250 W 57th St., Ste. 420
New York, NY 10107
Phone: (212)265-8890
Fax: (212)265-8908
Subject(s): Youths' Interests; (General Sports)
Circ: (Paid)‡200,000

**BOSTONIA** (13630)
Boston University
10 Lenox St.
Brookline, MA 02446
Phone: (617)353-3180
Fax: (617)353-6488
Subject(s): College Publications
Circ: (Paid)2,000
(Non-paid)200,000

**Business Today (Princeton)** (19711)
Foundation for Student Communication Inc.
48 Univ. Pl.
Princeton Univ.
Princeton, NJ 08544-1011
Phone: (609)258-1111
Fax: (609)258-1222
Subject(s): College Publications; Business
Circ: (Controlled)200,000

**Casting News** (21460)
The John King Network
244 Madison Ave., Ste. 393
New York, NY 10016
Phone: (212)969-8715
Fax: (212)969-8715
Subject(s): Entertainment; Motion Pictures; Radio, Television, Cable, and Video
Circ: (Paid)100,000
(Non-paid)200,000

**CGA World** (26789)
Catholic Golden Age
PO Box 249
Olyphant, PA 18447
Subject(s): Religious Publications; Senior Citizens' Interests
Circ: ‡200,000

**Internet Week** (21110)
CMP Media L.L.C.
600 Community Dr.
Manhasset, NY 11030
Phone: (516)562-5000
Fax: (516)562-5995
Subject(s): Communications; Telecommunications
Circ: (Non-paid)200,000

**Mandate Magazine** (22052)
MMG Inc.
462 Broadway, Ste. 4000
New York, NY 10013
Phone: (212)966-8400
Fax: (212)966-9366
Subject(s): Gay and Lesbian Interests
Circ: 200,000

**Music Gigs & Auditions U.S.A.  (22117)**
The John King Network
244 Madison Ave., Ste. 393
New York, NY 10016
Phone: (212)969-8715
Fax: (212)969-8715
**Subject(s):** Entertainment; Performing Arts
**Circ:** (Paid)‡100,000
(Non-paid)‡200,000

**The Old Farmer's Almanac Gardener's Companion  (18811)**
Yankee Publishing Inc.
PO Box 520
Dublin, NH 03444-0520
Phone: (603)563-8111
Fax: (603)563-8252
**Subject(s):** Home and Garden
**Circ:** (Paid)200,000

**Salute  (20782)**
Military Forces Features Inc.
51 Atlantic Ave., Ste. 200
Floral Park, NY 11001
Fax: (516)616-1936
**Subject(s):** Military and Navy
**Circ:** (Controlled)‡200,000

**Scholastic Choices  (4662)**
Scholastic Library Publishing Inc.
90 Old Sherman Tpke.
Danbury, CT 06816
Phone: (203)797-3500
Fax: (203)797-3657
**Subject(s):** Education; Home Economics
**Circ:** ‡200,000

**Scholastic MATH Magazine  (22347)**
Scholastic Library Publishing Inc.
557 Broadway
New York, NY 10012
Phone: (212)343-6100
**Subject(s):** Mathematics
**Circ:** ‡200,000

**Wizard  (20669)**
Wizard Entertainment
151 Wells Ave.
Congers, NY 10920
Phone: (845)268-2000
Fax: (845)268-6357
**Subject(s):** Comics and Comic Technique; Youths' Interests
**Circ:** (Paid)197,000

**Guitar World  (21751)**
Harris Publications Inc.
1115 Broadway
New York, NY 10010-2803
Phone: (212)807-7100
Fax: (212)924-2352
**Subject(s):** Music and Musical Instruments
**Circ:** (Paid)190,059

**Fine Gardening  (4929)**
Taunton Press
PO Box 5506
Newtown, CT 06470-5506
Phone: (203)426-8171
Fax: (203)426-3734
**Subject(s):** Home and Garden
**Circ:** (Paid)189,009

**Interview  (21847)**
575 Broadway
New York, NY 10012
Phone: (212)941-2800
Fax: (212)941-2885
**Subject(s):** General Editorial
**Circ:** (Paid)185,612

**Better Homes and Gardens Special Interest Publications  (21396)**
Meredith Corp.
125 Park Ave.
New York, NY 10017-5529
Phone: (212)557-6600
Fax: (212)551-6918
**Subject(s):** Food and Cooking; Home and Garden
**Circ:** (Paid)184,500

**Design News  (14855)**
Reed Business Information
225 Wyman St.
Waltham, MA 02451-1216
**Subject(s):** Engineering (Various branches)
**Circ:** (Non-paid)‡182,000

**Art  (21357)**
Scholastic Library Publishing Inc.
557 Broadway
New York, NY 10012
Phone: (212)343-6100
**Subject(s):** Art and Art History
**Circ:** ‡180,000

**Models & Talent Contacts  (22091)**
The John King Network
244 Madison Ave., Ste. 393
New York, NY 10016
Phone: (212)969-8715
Fax: (212)969-8715
**Subject(s):** Entertainment; Drama and Theatre
**Circ:** ‡180,000

**Morbius  (22102)**
Marvel Enterprises
417 5th Ave
New York, NY 10016
Phone: (212)576-4000
Fax: (917)472-2150
**Subject(s):** Comics and Comic Technique
**Circ:** (Paid)180,000

**Playbill  (27234)**
The Philadelphia Spotlite
3401 N I St., 5th Fl.
Philadelphia, PA 19134
Fax: (215)425-1155
**Subject(s):** Drama and Theatre
**Circ:** (Non-paid)180,000

**Temple Review  (27283)**
Temple University
University Services Bldg., Rm. 601
1601 North Broadstreet
Philadelphia, PA 19122
Phone: (215)204-6445
Fax: (215)204-4704
**Subject(s):** College Publications
**Circ:** (Non-paid)‡180,000

**UMASS Magazine  (13423)**
University of Massachusetts
No.103, Munson Hall, Umass
Amherst, MA 01003
Phone: (413)545-2991
Fax: (413)545-3824
**Subject(s):** College Publications
**Circ:** (Free)‡180,000

**Top Producer  (27286)**
Farm Journal Inc.
1818 Market St., 31st Fl.
Philadelphia, PA 19103
Phone: (215)557-8900
Fax: (215)568-4238
**Subject(s):** Business
**Circ:** (Non-paid)178,085

**Diversion  (21612)**
The Hearst Corp.
888 Seventh Ave.
New York, NY 10019
Phone: (212)969-7500
Fax: (212)969-7563
**Subject(s):** Travel and Tourism
**Circ:** (Controlled)177,000

**SAIL  (13584)**
PRIMEDIA Special Interest Publications Inc.
98 N. Washington St.
Boston, MA 02114
Phone: (617)720-8600
Fax: (617)723-0911
**Subject(s):** (Boating and Yachting)
**Circ:** (Paid)★172,344

**SURFER Magazine  (22434)**
Primedia Inc.
745 5th Ave.
New York, NY 10151
Phone: (212)745-0100
Fax: (212)745-0121

**Subject(s):** (Water Sports)
**Circ:** (Paid)170,430

**Chief Executive  (19531)**
110 Summit Ave.
Montvale, NJ 07645
Phone: (201)930-5959
Fax: (201)930-5956
**Subject(s):** Management and Administration
**Circ:** (Controlled)42,000
(Combined)170,000

**Industrial Product Bulletin  (19556)**
Reed Business Information
c/o Anita Lafond, Editor-In-Chief
Reed Business Information In Mfg
301 Gibraltar Dr.
PO Box 650
Morris Plains, NJ 07950
**Subject(s):** Commerce and Industry
**Circ:** (Non-paid)‡170,000

**QST  (4926)**
American Radio Relay League Inc.
225 Main St.
Newington, CT 06111
Phone: (860)594-0200
Fax: (860)594-0259
**Subject(s):** Radio, Television, Cable, and Video
**Circ:** ‡168,975

**Decks & Backyard Projects  (19795)**
Aqua-Field Publishing Company Inc.
39 Avenue of the Common
Shrewsbury, NJ 07702
Phone: (732)935-1222
**Subject(s):** Home and Garden
**Circ:** (Controlled)‡168,830

**True Romance  (22491)**
Macfadden Communications Group
333 Seventh Ave., Fl. 11
New York, NY 10001-5004
Phone: (212)780-3500
Fax: (212)979-4825
**Subject(s):** Science Fiction, Mystery, Adventure, and Romance
**Circ:** 165,723

**Electronic Design  (19653)**
Penton Technology and Lifestyle Media Inc.
45 Eisenhower Dr., 5th Fl.
Paramus, NJ 07652
Phone: (201)843-6511
Fax: (201)845-2482
**Subject(s):** Electronics Engineering
**Circ:** (Non-paid)‡165,000

**Java Developer's Journal  (19536)**
SYS-CON Media
135 Chestnut Ridge Rd.
Montvale, NJ 07645
Phone: (201)802-3000
Fax: (201)782-9601
**Subject(s):** Computers; Telecommunications
**Circ:** 164,000

**Salt Water Sportsman  (22337)**
2 Park Ave.
New York, NY 10016
Phone: (212)779-5179
Fax: (212)779-5999
**Subject(s):** (Hunting, Fishing, and Game Management)
**Circ:** (Paid)163,857

**Mountain Bike Magazine  (26328)**
33 E. Minor St.
Emmaus, PA 18098
Phone: (610)967-5171
Fax: (610)967-7522
**Subject(s):** (Bicycling)
**Circ:** (Paid)162,520

**Wildlife Conservation Magazine  (20482)**
Wildlife Conservation
2300 Southern Blvd.
Bronx, NY 10460
Phone: (718)220-5100
**Subject(s):** Wildlife and Exotic Animals
**Circ:** (Paid)160,652

Circulation: ★ = ABC; △ = BPA; ◆ = CAC; ● = CCAB; ▢ = VAC; ⊕ = PO Statement; ‡ = Publisher's Report; Boldface figures = sworn; Light figures = estimated.

## Northeastern States

**Cruising World** (27865)
Miller Sports Group L.L.C.
5 John Clarke Rd.
PO Box 3400
Newport, RI 02840-0992
Phone: (401)845-5100
Fax: (401)845-5180
Subject(s): (Boating and Yachting)
Circ: (Paid)160,065

**Datamation** (14854)
Reed Business Information
225 Wyman St.
Waltham, MA 02451-1216
Subject(s): Computers
Circ: (Paid)2,168
(Non-paid)160,052

**Action Line** (4669)
Friends of Animals Inc.
777 Post Rd., Ste. 205
Darien, CT 06820
Phone: (203)656-1522
Fax: (203)656-0267
Subject(s): Social and Political Issues
Circ: 160,000

**Internet Shopper** (4675)
Jupitermedia Corporation
23 Old Kings Hwy. S.
Darien, CT 06820
Phone: (203)662-2800
Fax: (203)655-4686
Subject(s): Computers; Consumerism
Circ: (Combined)160,000

**Natural Way Magazine** (23182)
Sportomatic Ltd.
PO Box 392
White Plains, NY 10602
Subject(s): Health
Circ: (Controlled)160,000

**Product Design and Development** (22266)
Reed Business Information
360 Park Avenue South
New York, NY 10010
Phone: (646)746-6400
Subject(s): Commerce and Industry; Engineering (Various branches)
Circ: (Controlled)160,000

**UConn Traditions** (5051)
University of Connecticut
1266 Storrs Rd.
Storrs, CT 06269-4144
Phone: (860)486-3530
Fax: (860)486-4064
Subject(s): College Publications; Education
Circ: (Controlled)160,000

**National Review** (22129)
215 Lexington Ave., 4th Fl.
New York, NY 10016
Phone: (212)679-7330
Fax: (212)849-2835
Subject(s): Politics; Literature
Circ: (Paid)155,664

**Doctor's Shopper** (20505)
Marketing Communications Inc.
1086 Remsen Ave.
Brooklyn, NY 11236
Phone: (718)257-8484
Fax: (718)257-8845
Subject(s): Medicine and Surgery
Circ: (Controlled)‡155,200

**Restaurants & Institutions** (22310)
Reed Business Information
360 Park Ave. S.
New York, NY 10014
Phone: (646)746-6400
Fax: (646)746-6734
Subject(s): Hotels, Motels, Restaurants, and Clubs; Hospitals and Healthcare Institutions
Circ: (Non-paid)154,109

**True Experience** (22489)
Macfadden Communications Group
333 Seventh Ave., Fl. 11
New York, NY 10001-5004
Phone: (212)780-3500
Fax: (212)979-4825

Subject(s): Science Fiction, Mystery, Adventure, and Romance
Circ: (Paid)‡152,344

**Monthly Prescribing Reference** (22100)
Prescribing Reference Inc.
114 W. 26th St., 3rd Fl.
New York, NY 10001-6812
Phone: (646)638-6000
Fax: (646)638-6117
Subject(s): Drugs and Pharmaceuticals
Circ: (Controlled)150,638

**Bloomberg Markets Magazine** (19709)
Bloomberg L.P.
100 Business Park Dr.
PO Box 888
Princeton, NJ 08542-0888
Phone: (609)279-3000
Fax: (609)683-7523
Subject(s): Banking, Finance, and Investments
Circ: (Non-paid)‡150,537

**Chocolatier** (21486)
Haymarket Group Ltd.
45 W 34th St., Ste. 600
New York, NY 10001
Phone: (212)239-0855
Fax: (212)967-4184
Subject(s): Confectionaries and Frozen Dairy Products; Food and Grocery Trade
Circ: (Paid)‡150,000

**CIO Web Business** (13788)
CIO Communications
492 Old Connecticut Path
PO Box 9208
Framingham, MA 01701-9208
Phone: (508)872-8200
Fax: (508)879-7784
Subject(s): Business; Computers
Circ: (Paid)150,000

**Friends of Animals Actionline** (4674)
Friends of Animals Inc.
777 Post Rd., Ste. 205
Darien, CT 06820
Phone: (203)656-1522
Fax: (203)656-0267
Subject(s): Pets
Circ: 150,000

**The Ring** (26191)
London Publishing Co.
6198 Butler Pike Ste. 200
PO Box 910
Blue Bell, PA 19422
Phone: (215)643-6385
Fax: (215)628-3571
Subject(s): (Boxing and Wrestling)
Circ: ‡150,000

**Romantic Times** (20537)
Romantic Times Publishing Group
55 Bergen St.
Brooklyn, NY 11201
Phone: (718)237-1097
Fax: (718)624-4231
Subject(s): Science Fiction, Mystery, Adventure, and Romance
Circ: ‡150,000

**The Secret Place** (27621)
American Baptist Churches, USA
PO Box 851
Valley Forge, PA 19482-0851
Phone: (610)768-2000
Fax: (610)768-2320
Subject(s): Religious Publications
Circ: ‡150,000

**Traveler** (26095)
AAA East Penn
Allentown Store
3300 Lehigh St., S. Mall
Allentown, PA 18103
Phone: (610)434-5141
Fax: (610)778-3381
Subject(s): Automotive (Consumer); Travel and Tourism
Circ: (Controlled)‡150,000

**Fit Magazine** (21694)
Goodman Media Group Inc.
250 W 57th St., Ste. 710
New York, NY 10107-0799
Phone: (212)262-2247
Fax: (212)262-2279
Subject(s): Health and Healthcare; Women's Interests; Lifestyle
Circ: (Paid)149,162

**Bartender Magazine** (19455)
Foley Publishing
PO Box 158
Liberty Corner, NJ 07938
Phone: (908)766-6006
Fax: (908)766-6607
Subject(s): Beverages, Brewing, and Bottling; Hotels, Motels, Restaurants, and Clubs
Circ: (Controlled)‡148,250

**NJEA Review** (19895)
New Jersey Education Association
180 W State St.
PO Box 1211
Trenton, NJ 08607
Phone: (609)599-4561
Fax: (609)392-6321
Subject(s): Education
Circ: (Paid)148,000

**Golf World** (5062)
Advance Magazine Publishers Inc.
5520 Park Ave.
Trumbull, CT 06611
Phone: (203)373-7176
Fax: (203)371-2132
Subject(s): (Golf)
Circ: (Non-paid)9,716
(Paid)147,492

**Literary Cavalcade** (22040)
Scholastic Library Publishing Inc.
557 Broadway
New York, NY 10012
Phone: (212)343-6100
Subject(s): Education
Circ: (Paid)147,480

**Boston Magazine** (13485)
300 Massachusetts Ave.
Boston, MA 02115
Phone: (617)262-9700
Fax: (617)262-4925
Circ: (Paid)146,548

**Penn Lines** (26454)
Pennsylvania Rural Electric Association
PO Box 1266
212 Locust St.
Harrisburg, PA 17108
Phone: (717)233-5704
Fax: (717)234-1309
Subject(s): Rural Electrification; Lifestyle
Circ: (Paid)145,000

**Threads** (4935)
Taunton Press
PO Box 5506
Newtown, CT 06470-5506
Phone: (203)426-8171
Fax: (203)426-3434
Subject(s): Crafts, Models, Hobbies, and Contests; Dressmaking, Needlework, and Quilting
Circ: ‡145,000

**ECN (Electronic Component News)** (21629)
Reed Business Information
360 Park Ave. S
New York, NY 10010
Phone: (646)746-6400
Subject(s): Electronics Engineering
Circ: (Controlled)‡143,050

**Cortlandt Forum** (21555)
Haymarket Media
114 W 26th St.
New York, NY 10001
Phone: (646)638-6117
Fax: (646)638-6150
Subject(s): Medicine and Surgery
Circ: (Non-paid)⊕**141,500**

**Muscular Development** (22934)
Advanced Research Press Inc.
690 Rte. 25A
Setauket, NY 11733-1200
**Subject(s):** (Physical Fitness)
**Circ:** ‡140,000

**Physicians' Travel & Meeting Guide** (19667)
Quadrant HealthCom Inc.
7 Century Dr. Ste 302
Parsippany, NJ 07054
Phone: (973)701-8900
Fax: (973)206-9251
**Subject(s):** Conventions, Meetings, and Trade Fairs; Travel and Tourism
**Circ:** (Paid)6,929
(Non-paid)135,367

**Yachting** (5017)
Time4 Media Inc.
18 Marshall St., Ste. 114
South Norwalk, CT 06854
Phone: (203)299-5900
Fax: (203)299-5901
**Subject(s):** (Boating and Yachting)
**Circ:** (Paid)135,184

**For the Bride by Demetrios** (21706)
DJE Publications Ltd.
222 W 37th St.
New York, NY 10018
Phone: (212)967-0750
Fax: (646)473-0927
**Subject(s):** Brides
**Circ:** (Paid)135,143

**JAX FAX Travel Marketing Magazine** (4853)
Jet Airtransport Exchange Inc.
52 W. Main St.
Milford, CT 06460
Phone: (203)301-0255
Fax: (203)301-0250
**Subject(s):** Travel and Tourism
**Circ:** (Paid)△13,587
(Controlled)△135,000

**Metrokids Magazine** (27142)
Metrokids
4623 S. Broad St.
Philadelphia, PA 19125
Phone: (215)291-5560
Fax: (215)291-5563
**Subject(s):** Children's Interests
**Circ:** (Free)1,35,000

**Catholic New York** (21463)
1011 1st Ave., Ste. 1721
New York, NY 10022-4106
Phone: (212)688-2399
Fax: (212)688-2642
**Subject(s):** Religious Publications
**Circ:** (Paid)★133,917

**American Salon** (21324)
Advanstar Communications
c/o Robbin McClain, Editor-in-Chief
One Park Ave., 2nd Fl.
New York, NY 10016
Phone: (212)951-6640
Fax: (212)951-6624
**Subject(s):** Hairstyling
**Circ:** 133,000

**Dell Horoscope Magazine** (21593)
Dell Magazines
475 Park Ave. S, 11th Fl.
New York, NY 10016
Phone: (212)686-7188
Fax: (212)686-7414
**Subject(s):** Astrology
**Circ:** ‡132,000

**Fly Fisherman** (26440)
Primedia
6405 Flank Dr.
Harrisburg, PA 17112
Phone: (717)657-9526
Fax: (717)657-9526
**Subject(s):** (Hunting, Fishing, and Game Management)
**Circ:** (Paid)130,642

**Bowhunting** (19793)
Aqua-Field Publishing Company Inc.
39 Avenue of the Common
Shrewsbury, NJ 07702
Phone: (732)935-1222
**Subject(s):** (Hunting, Fishing, and Game Management)
**Circ:** (Controlled)‡130,145

**Foreign Affairs** (21713)
Council on Foreign Relations Inc.
Harold Pratt House
58 E 68th St.
New York, NY 10021
Phone: (212)434-9400
Fax: (212)434-9800
**Subject(s):** International Affairs; International Business and Economics
**Circ:** (Paid)130,000

**Wireless Business & Technology** (19547)
SYS-CON Media
135 Chestnut Ridge Rd.
Montvale, NJ 07645
Phone: (201)802-3000
Fax: (201)782-9601
**Subject(s):** Computers; Automation; Business
**Circ:** (Combined)130,000

**SkyGuide** (22374)
American Express Publishing Corp.
1120 Avenue of the Americas, 10th Fl.
New York, NY 10036
Phone: (212)382-5600
Fax: (212)536-2020
**Subject(s):** Travel and Tourism
**Circ:** (Paid)‡129,957

**Restaurant Business** (22309)
VNU Business Publications
770 Broadway
New York, NY 10003-9595
Phone: (646)654-5000
Fax: (646)654-7265
**Subject(s):** Hotels, Motels, Restaurants, and Clubs
**Circ:** (Controlled)129,000

**Motor Boating** (22106)
Time Inc.
18 Marshall St, No. 1145
New York, NY 10019
Phone: (203)299-5950
Fax: (203)299-5951
**Subject(s):** (Boating and Yachting)
**Circ:** (Non-paid)31,612
(Paid)127,664

**Data Centrum** (21588)
21 W 38th St., 4th Fl.
New York, NY 10018-5506
Phone: (212)997-9800
Fax: (212)226-8847
**Subject(s):** Medicine and Surgery
**Circ:** (Non-paid)127,500

**Time Out New York** (22459)
475 10th Ave., 12th Fl.
New York, NY 10018
Phone: (646)432-3000
Fax: (646)432-3010
**Subject(s):** Entertainment; Local, State, and Regional Publications
**Circ:** (Paid)125,580

**Applause** (26831)
WHYY Inc.
150 N Sixth St.
Philadelphia, PA 19106
Phone: (215)351-1200
Fax: (215)351-0398
**Subject(s):** Radio, Television, Cable, and Video
**Circ:** (Controlled)125,000

**CIO Magazine** (13787)
CIO Communications
492 Old Connecticut Path
PO Box 9208
Framingham, MA 01701-9208
Phone: (508)872-8200
Fax: (508)879-7784
**Subject(s):** Business; Management and Administration
**Circ:** (Paid)‡5,052
(Controlled)‡125,000

**Essex County Family** (19575)
Kids Monthly Publications Inc.
1122 Rte. 22 W
Mountainside, NJ 07092
Phone: (908)232-2913
Fax: (908)317-9518
**Subject(s):** Parenting; Children's Interests
**Circ:** (Controlled)125,000

**Middlesex County Family** (19576)
Kids Monthly Publications Inc.
1122 Rte. 22 W
Mountainside, NJ 07092
Phone: (908)232-2913
Fax: (908)317-9518
**Subject(s):** Parenting; Children's Interests
**Circ:** (Controlled)125,000

**Morris County Family** (19577)
Kids Monthly Publications Inc.
1122 Rte. 22 W
Mountainside, NJ 07092
Phone: (908)232-2913
Fax: (908)317-9518
**Subject(s):** Parenting; Children's Interests
**Circ:** (Controlled)125,000

**Union County Family** (19578)
Kids Monthly Publications Inc.
1122 Rte. 22 W
Mountainside, NJ 07092
Phone: (908)232-2913
Fax: (908)317-9518
**Subject(s):** Local, State, and Regional Publications; Parenting
**Circ:** (Controlled)125,000

**Automotive Engineering International** (27643)
S.A.E. International
400 Commonwealth Dr.
Warrendale, PA 15096-0001
Phone: (724)776-4841
Fax: (724)776-4026
**Subject(s):** Automotive (Trade)
**Circ:** (Combined)124,500

**Deer Hunting North America** (19796)
Aqua-Field Publishing Company Inc.
39 Avenue of the Common
Shrewsbury, NJ 07702
Phone: (732)935-1222
**Subject(s):** (Hunting, Fishing, and Game Management)
**Circ:** (Controlled)‡124,500

**Saint Raphael's Better Health** (4901)
St. Raphael's Better Health
1450 Chapel St.
New Haven, CT 06511
Phone: (203)789-3972
Fax: (203)789-4053
**Subject(s):** Health
**Circ:** (Non-paid)124,442

**The New York Review of Books** (22165)
1755 Broadway, 5th Fl.
New York, NY 10019
Phone: (212)757-8070
Fax: (212)333-5374
**Subject(s):** Literature and Literary Reviews
**Circ:** (Paid)★124,030

**The Penn Stater** (27612)
Penn State Alumni Association
Hintz Family Alumni Ctr.
University Park, PA 16802
Phone: (814)865-6516
Fax: (814)865-3325
**Subject(s):** College Publications
**Circ:** 124,000

**Electronic Products** (23084)
Hearst Business Communications/Electronics Group
Electronic Products
50 Charles Lindbergh Blvd., Ste. 100
Uniondale, NY 11553
**Subject(s):** Electronics Engineering
**Circ:** (Controlled)‡123,788

**Fishing Smart!** (19797)
Aqua-Field Publishing Company Inc.
39 Avenue of the Common
Shrewsbury, NJ 07702
Phone: (732)935-1222

## Northeastern States

**Subject(s):** (Hunting, Fishing, and Game Management)
**Circ:** (Controlled)‡122,000

**U.S. Pharmacist (18992)**
Jobson Publishing Corp.
1515 Broad St.
Bloomfield, NJ 07003
Phone: (973)494-5900
Fax: (973)494-5901
**Subject(s):** Drugs and Pharmaceuticals
**Circ:** (Combined)120,874

**Nursing Spectrum—New York & New Jersey Edition (23168)**
Nursing Spectrum Inc.
900 Merchants Concourse
Westbury, NY 11590
Phone: (516)222-0909
Fax: (516)222-0131
**Subject(s):** Career Development and Employment; Nursing
**Circ:** 120,175

**Laboratory Equipment (19558)**
Reed Business Information
301 Gibraltar Dr.
PO Box 650
Morris Plains, NJ 07950-0650
Phone: (973)292-5100
Fax: (973)539-3476
**Subject(s):** Laboratory Research (Scientific and Medical)
**Circ:** (Non-paid)‡120,018

**American History (26433)**
Primedia Enthusiast Publications
6405 Flank Dr.
Harrisburg, PA 17112
Phone: (717)657-9555
Fax: (717)657-9526
**Subject(s):** History and Genealogy
**Circ:** 120,000

**ASME News (21370)**
American Society of Mechanical Engineers
3 Park Ave.
New York, NY 10016-5990
**Subject(s):** Engineering (Various branches)
**Circ:** (Paid)‡120,000

**The Compendium of Continuing Education in Dentistry (19418)**
Dental Learning Systems Company Inc.
Div. of Medical World Communications Inc.
241 Forsgate Dr.
PO Box 505
Jamesburg, NJ 08831-0505
Phone: (732)656-1143
Fax: (732)656-1148
**Subject(s):** Dentistry
**Circ:** (Combined)120,000

**New York State Conservationist (20225)**
New York State Dept. of Environmental Conservation
625 Broadway, 2nd Fl.
Albany, NY 12233-4501
Phone: (518)402-8047
Fax: (518)402-8050
**Subject(s):** Ecology and Conservation
**Circ:** (Non-paid)‡5,000
(Paid)‡120,000

**Old-House Interiors (13802)**
Gloucester Publishers
108 E. Main St.
Gloucester, MA 01930-3846
Phone: (978)283-3200
Fax: (978)283-4629
**Subject(s):** Home and Garden
**Circ:** (Paid)120,000

**Pennsylvania Game News (26457)**
Pennsylvania Game Commission
2001 Elmerton Ave.
Harrisburg, PA 17110-9797
Phone: (717)787-3745
Fax: (717)772-0542
**Subject(s):** Ecology and Conservation; (Hunting, Fishing, and Game Management); Local, State, and Regional Publications
**Circ:** ‡120,000

**Pharmacy Times (19421)**
Romaine Pierson Publishers Inc.
241 Forsgate Dr.
Jamesburg, NJ 08831-1676
Phone: (732)656-1140
Fax: (732)656-1148

**Subject(s):** Drugs and Pharmaceuticals
**Circ:** (Paid)480
(Non-paid)120,000

**Troika (5087)**
Lone Tout Publications Inc.
PO Box 1006
Weston, CT 06883-1006
Phone: (203)319-0873
Fax: (203)222-9332
**Subject(s):** Lifestyle
**Circ:** (Paid)120,000

**UU World (13596)**
Unitarian Universalist Association
25 Beacon St.
Boston, MA 02108-2803
Phone: (617)948-6518
Fax: (617)742-7025
**Subject(s):** Religious Publications
**Circ:** (Paid)‡1,000
(Controlled)‡120,000

**Power and Motoryacht (22258)**
Primedia
260 Madison Ave., 8th Fl.
New York, NY 10016
Fax: (917)256-2282
**Subject(s):** (Boating and Yachting)
**Circ:** (Paid)‡37,746
(Controlled)‡119,424

**Fly Fishing for Trout (19801)**
Aqua-Field Publishing Company Inc.
39 Avenue of the Common
Shrewsbury, NJ 07702
Phone: (732)935-1222
**Subject(s):** (Hunting, Fishing, and Game Management)
**Circ:** (Controlled)‡118,120

**Plant Engineering (22234)**
Reed Business Information
360 Park Ave. S
New York, NY 10010
Phone: (646)746-6400
**Subject(s):** Engineering (Various branches)
**Circ:** (Controlled)‡116,700

**Fly Fishing Made Easy (19798)**
Aqua-Field Publishing Company Inc.
39 Avenue of the Common
Shrewsbury, NJ 07702
Phone: (732)935-1222
**Subject(s):** (Hunting, Fishing, and Game Management)
**Circ:** ‡116,100

**Travel National (20544)**
EWA Publications
2446 E 65th St.
Brooklyn, NY 11234
Phone: (718)763-7034
Fax: (718)763-7035
**Subject(s):** Travel and Tourism
**Circ:** 114,000

**Log Homes Illustrated (22043)**
Goodman Media Group Inc.
250 W 57th St., Ste. 710
New York, NY 10107-0799
Phone: (212)262-2247
Fax: (212)262-2279
**Subject(s):** Home and Garden
**Circ:** (Paid)112,997

**The Moneybook (19823)**
TeeVee Moneysaver Inc., Publications
52 W Main St.
PO Box 954
Somerville, NJ 08876
Phone: (908)722-6270
Fax: (908)722-7303
**Subject(s):** Local, State, and Regional Publications; Entertainment
**Circ:** (Free)112,500

**EE Product News (19652)**
Penton Media Inc.
45 Eisenhower Dr., 5th Fl.
Paramus, NJ 07652
Fax: (201)845-2485
**Subject(s):** Electrical Engineering; Electronics Engineering
**Circ:** 111,968

**Fly Fishing Quarterly (19799)**
Aqua-Field Publishing Company Inc.
39 Avenue of the Common
Shrewsbury, NJ 07702
Phone: (732)935-1222
**Subject(s):** (Hunting, Fishing, and Game Management)
**Circ:** (Controlled)‡111,275

**Pittsburgh Catholic (27387)**
Pittsburgh Catholic Publishing Associates Inc.
135 1st Ave., No. 200
Pittsburgh, PA 15222-1506
Phone: (412)471-1252
Fax: (412)471-4228
**Subject(s):** Religious Publications
**Circ:** ‡110,470

**Tennis Week (22887)**
15 Elm Pl.
Rye, NY 10580
Phone: (914)967-4890
Fax: (914)967-8178
**Subject(s):** (Racquet Sports)
**Circ:** ‡110,470

**The Anthonian (21342)**
St. Anthony's Guild
158 W. 27th St., 6th Fl.
New York, NY 10001-6216
Phone: (212)924-1451
Fax: (212)924-1994
**Subject(s):** Religious Publications
**Circ:** (Controlled)110,000

**Contemporary Bride Magazine (19834)**
North East Publishing Inc.
4475 S. Clinton Ave., Ste. 201
South Plainfield, NJ 07080
Phone: (908)561-6010
Fax: (908)755-7864
**Subject(s):** Brides
**Circ:** (Non-paid)‡110,000

**Playguy Magazine (22240)**
MMG Inc.
462 Broadway, Ste. 4000
New York, NY 10013
Phone: (212)966-8400
Fax: (212)966-9366
**Subject(s):** Gay and Lesbian Interests
**Circ:** 110,000

**Sky & Telescope (13706)**
Sky Publishing Corp.
49 Bay State Rd.
Cambridge, MA 02138
Phone: (617)864-7360
Fax: (617)864-6117
**Subject(s):** Astronomy and Meteorology
**Circ:** (Paid)110,000

**Wine Enthusiast Magazine (20761)**
Wine Enthusiast Co.
103 Fairview Park Dr.
Elmsford, NY 10523
Phone: (914)345-8463
Fax: (914)592-0105
**Subject(s):** Beverages, Brewing, and Bottling
**Circ:** 110,000

**Bookseller (21419)**
VNU Business Media USA
770 Broadway
New York, NY 10003
Phone: (646)654-5000
**Subject(s):** Book Trade and Author News; Journalism and Publishing
**Circ:** 11,050

**Coaching Management (20943)**
Momentum Media
2488 N. Triphammer Rd.
Ithaca, NY 14850
Phone: (607)257-6970
Fax: (607)257-7328
**Subject(s):** Management and Administration; Physical Education and Athletics
**Circ:** (Controlled)‡109,567

**Home Theater (21778)**
PRIMEDIA Los Angeles
Home Theater
110 5th Ave., 5th Fl.
New York, NY 10011
Phone: (212)886-3600

Fax: (212)886-3649
**Subject(s):** Consumer Electronics
**Circ:** (Paid)109,422

**The Metropolitan Museum of Art Bulletin (22081)**
Metropolitan Museum of Art
1000 5th Ave., 82nd St.
New York, NY 10028-0198
Phone: (212)535-7710
Fax: (212)396-5062
**Subject(s):** Art and Art History
**Circ:** (Paid)‡3,000
  (Non-paid)‡108,000

**VARBUSINESS (21120)**
CMP Media L.L.C.
600 Community Dr.
Manhasset, NY 11030
Phone: (516)562-5000
Fax: (516)562-5995
**Subject(s):** Business
**Circ:** (Non-paid)‡107,500

**WoodenBoat (12483)**
WoodenBoat Publications Inc.
Naskeag Rd.
PO Box 78
Brooklin, ME 04616
Phone: (207)359-4651
Fax: (207)359-8920
**Subject(s):** (Boating and Yachting)
**Circ:** (Paid)107,268

**Industrial Maintenance and Plant Operation (19555)**
Reed Business Information
c/o Nancy Syverson
301 Gibraltar Dr.
PO Box 650
Morris Plains, NJ 07950-0650
Phone: (973)292-5100
**Subject(s):** Commerce and Industry; Building Management and Maintenance
**Circ:** (Controlled)107,000

**Modern Materials Handling (14864)**
Reed Business Information
225 Wyman St.
Waltham, MA 02451-1216
**Subject(s):** Commerce and Industry; Materials Handling
**Circ:** (Non-paid)‡105,841

**Inquest Gamer (20667)**
Wizard Entertainment
151 Wells Ave.
Congers, NY 10920
Phone: (845)268-2000
Fax: (845)268-6357
**Subject(s):** Games and Puzzles; Children's Interests; Youths' Interests; Crafts, Models, Hobbies, and Contests
**Circ:** (Paid)105,000

**Architectural Record (21354)**
McGraw-Hill Inc.
Two Penn Plaza
New York, NY 10121-2298
Phone: (212)904-2594
Fax: (212)904-4256
**Subject(s):** Architecture
**Circ:** (Paid)104,301

**The Female Patient (19663)**
Quadrant HealthCom Inc.
7 Century Dr. Ste 302
Parsippany, NJ 07054
Phone: (973)701-8900
Fax: (973)206-9251
**Subject(s):** Medicine and Surgery
**Circ:** (Controlled)104,234

**PM Network (26775)**
Project Management Institute
4 Campus Blvd.
Newtown Square, PA 19073
Phone: (610)356-4600
Fax: (610)356-4647
**Subject(s):** Management and Administration
**Circ:** (Non-paid)‡1,437
  (Paid)‡103,270

**Chemical Equipment (19553)**
Reed Business Information
301 Gibraltar Dr.
PO Box 650
Morris Plains, NJ 07950
Phone: (973)292-5100

Fax: (973)539-3476
**Subject(s):** Chemistry, Chemicals, and Chemical Engineering
**Circ:** (Non-paid)‡1,03,050

**Modern Drummer Magazine (19013)**
Modern Drummer Publications Inc.
12 Old Bridge Rd.
Cedar Grove, NJ 07009-1288
Phone: (973)239-4140
Fax: (973)239-7139
**Subject(s):** Music and Musical Instruments
**Circ:** ‡103,000

**ME—Mobile Entertainment (22067)**
Hachette Filipacchi Media U.S. Inc.
1633 Broadway, 45th Fl.
New York, NY 10019
Phone: (212)767-6000
**Subject(s):** Automotive (Consumer); Consumer Electronics
**Circ:** (Paid)102,992

**Teaching/K-8 (4962)**
40 Richards Ave.
Norwalk, CT 06854-2509
Phone: (203)855-2650
Fax: (203)855-2656
**Subject(s):** Education
**Circ:** (Non-paid)3,736
  (Paid)102,130

**American Artist (21298)**
VNU Business Media USA
770 Broadway
New York, NY 10003
Phone: (646)654-5000
**Subject(s):** Art and Art History; Education; Art
**Circ:** (Paid)102,005

**AV Video & Multimedia Producer (22765)**
PBI Media L.L.C.
2700 Westchester Ave., Ste. 107
Purchase, NY 10577
Phone: (914)251-4705
Fax: (914)251-7107
**Subject(s):** Radio, Television, Cable, and Video
**Circ:** (Paid)‡471
  (Controlled)‡101,420

**Snowboarder (22381)**
Primedia Inc.
745 5th Ave.
New York, NY 10151
Phone: (212)745-0100
Fax: (212)745-0121
**Subject(s):** (Skiing); (General Sports)
**Circ:** (Paid)101,290

**Fleet Owner (5033)**
Primedia Business
11 River Bend Dr. S.
PO Box 4949
Stamford, CT 06907-0949
Phone: (203)358-9900
Fax: (203)358-5811
**Subject(s):** Trucks and Trucking
**Circ:** (Non-paid)‡101,240

**Muscle Mustangs & Fast Fords (19776)**
Primedia
299 Market St.
Saddle Brook, NJ 07663-5312
Phone: (201)712-9300
Fax: (201)712-9899
**Subject(s):** (Auto Racing)
**Circ:** (Paid)101,214

**Opera News (22198)**
Metropolitan Opera Guild Inc.
70 Lincoln Center Plaza
New York, NY 10023
Phone: (212)769-7000
**Subject(s):** Performing Arts; Music and Musical Instruments; Drama and Theatre
**Circ:** (Paid)★101,019

**Packaging Digest (22206)**
Reed Business Information
360 Park Ave. S.
New York, NY 10014
Phone: (646)746-6400
Fax: (646)746-6734
**Subject(s):** Packaging
**Circ:** (Free)100,730

**Internal Medicine World Report (19420)**
Medical World Communications
8 Center Dr.
Monroe Township
Jamesburg, NJ 08831
Phone: (732)656-1140
Fax: (732)656-1323
**Subject(s):** Health and Healthcare
**Circ:** (Controlled)100,423

**Purchasing Magazine (14293)**
Reed Business Information
275 Washington St.
Newton, MA 02458-1630
Fax: (617)558-4327
**Subject(s):** Purchasing
**Circ:** (Non-paid)‡100,203

**Managing Automation (22051)**
Thomas Publishing Co.
5 Penn Plz.
New York, NY 10001
Phone: (212)629-2100
Fax: (212)290-7362
**Subject(s):** Automation
**Circ:** (Non-paid)△100,174

**American Astrology (26109)**
Kappa Publishing Group
7002 W Butler Pl.
Ambler, PA 19002
Phone: (215)643-6385
**Subject(s):** Astrology
**Circ:** 100,000

**Early American Life (26215)**
Celtic Moon Publishing Inc.
PO Box 1264
Camp Hill, PA 17001
Phone: (717)730-6263
Fax: (717)730-7385
**Subject(s):** Art; History and Genealogy; Antiques
**Circ:** (Paid)100,000

**Heavy Metal (22865)**
Metal Mammoth Inc.
N Village Ave., Ste. 12
Rockville Centre, NY 11570
Phone: (516)594-2130
Fax: (516)594-2133
**Subject(s):** Art; Comics and Comic Technique
**Circ:** (Non-paid)1,000
  (Paid)100,000

**Honcho Magazine (21780)**
MMG Inc.
462 Broadway, Ste. 4000
New York, NY 10013
Phone: (212)966-8400
Fax: (212)966-9366
**Subject(s):** Gay and Lesbian Interests
**Circ:** (Paid)100,000

**The Hulk (21791)**
Marvel Enterprises
417 5th Ave
New York, NY 10016
Phone: (212)576-4000
Fax: (917)472-2150
**Subject(s):** Comics and Comic Technique
**Circ:** (Paid)100,000

**Journal America (19146)**
PO Box 459
Hewitt, NJ 07421
Phone: (973)728-8355
Fax: (973)728-7128
**Subject(s):** Lifestyle
**Circ:** (Combined)‡100,000

**NCJW Journal (5090)**
National Council of Jewish Women Inc.
6 Highwood Rd.
Westport, CT 06880-1128
Phone: (203)259-5844
Fax: (203)254-5116
**Subject(s):** Women's Interests; Jewish Publications
**Circ:** (Paid)100,000

**New Living (22983)**
PO Box 1519
Stony Brook, NY 11790
Phone: (631)751-8819
Fax: (631)751-8910

**Subject(s):** Health; (General Sports)

**Circ:** (Free)‡100,000

**Punch in International Travel and Entertainment Magazine (22283)**
Enterprises Publishing
400 E 59th St., Ste. 9F
New York, NY 10022
Phone: (212)755-4363
**Subject(s):** Lifestyle; Travel and Tourism

**Circ:** (Non-paid)100,000

**R & R Shopper's News (23169)**
Executive Business Media Inc.
825 Old Country Rd.
PO Box 1500
Westbury, NY 11590-0812
Phone: (516)334-3030
Fax: (516)334-3059
**Subject(s):** Military and Navy; Lifestyle

**Circ:** (Controlled)‡100,000

**Where & When Pennsylvania's Travel Guide (26745)**
Engle Printing and Publishing Co.
1425 W Main St.
PO Box 500
Mount Joy, PA 17552
Phone: (717)653-1833
Fax: (717)653-6165
**Subject(s):** Travel and Tourism; Local, State, and Regional Publications

**Circ:** (Combined)‡100,000

**Aqua-Field Turkey Hunting Guide (19791)**
Aqua-Field Publishing Company Inc.
39 Avenue of the Common
Shrewsbury, NJ 07702
Phone: (732)935-1222
**Subject(s):** (Hunting, Fishing, and Game Management)

**Circ:** (Controlled)‡99,000

**Railroad Model Craftsman (19632)**
Carstens Publications Inc.
PO Box 700
108 Phil Hardin Rd.
Newton, NJ 07860
Phone: (973)383-3355
Fax: (973)383-4064
**Subject(s):** Crafts, Models, Hobbies, and Contests

**Circ:** (Non-paid)‡500
    (Paid)‡98,000

**Blackpowder Hunter (19792)**
Aqua-Field Publishing Company Inc.
39 Avenue of the Common
Shrewsbury, NJ 07702
Phone: (732)935-1222
**Subject(s):** (Hunting, Fishing, and Game Management)

**Circ:** (Controlled)‡97,100

**CD Review (18934)**
Connell Communications Inc.
86 Elm St.
Peterborough, NH 03458-1052
Phone: (603)924-7271
Fax: (603)924-7013
**Subject(s):** Music and Musical Instruments

**Circ:** (Paid)95,635

**Mechanical Engineering (22068)**
American Society of Mechanical Engineers
3 Park Ave.
New York, NY 10016-5990
**Subject(s):** Engineering (Various branches)

**Circ:** (Non-paid)6,300
    (Paid)95,414

**Back Stage West (21379)**
VNU Business Media USA
770 Broadway
New York, NY 10003
Phone: (646)654-5000
**Subject(s):** Business; Drama and Theatre; Performing Arts

**Circ:** 95,011

**Civil War Times Illustrated (26437)**
Primedia Enthusiast Publications
6405 Flank Dr.
Harrisburg, PA 17112-2753
Phone: (717)540-6694
Fax: (717)657-9552
**Subject(s):** History and Genealogy

**Circ:** 95,000

**Institutional Investor (21824)**
Aspen Publishers
1185 Ave. of the Americas
New York, NY 10036
Phone: (212)730-4002
Fax: (212)597-0338
**Subject(s):** Banking, Finance, and Investments

**Circ:** (Paid)8,000
    (Controlled)95,000

**Kitchen Gardener (4933)**
Taunton Press
PO Box 5506
Newtown, CT 06470-5506
Phone: (203)426-8171
Fax: (203)426-3434
**Subject(s):** Home and Garden; Food and Cooking

**Circ:** ‡95,000

**Women's League Outlook (22553)**
Women's League for Conservative Judaism
475 Riverside Dr., Ste. 820
New York, NY 10115
Phone: (212)870-1260
Fax: (212)870-1261
**Subject(s):** Jewish Publications; Women's Interests

**Circ:** (Controlled)‡95,000

**Family Practice Recertification (19419)**
241 Forsgate Dr.
Jamesburg, NJ 08831
Phone: (732)656-1140
Fax: (732)656-0059
**Subject(s):** Medicine and Surgery

**Circ:** (Controlled)‡94,957

**AMC Outdoors (13468)**
Appalachian Mountain Club
5 Joy St.
Boston, MA 02108
Phone: (617)523-0636
Fax: (617)523-0722
**Subject(s):** Environmental and Natural Resources Conservation; (Outdoors)

**Circ:** (Non-paid)‡1,000
    (Paid)‡94,000

**Empire State Mason (21070)**
Grand Lodge AF & AM
37 Oliver St.
Lockport, NY 14094-4615
Phone: (716)434-4946
Fax: (716)434-4946
**Subject(s):** Masons

**Circ:** (Non-paid)‡3,394
    (Paid)‡94,000

**The Nation (22124)**
The Nation Institute
33 Irving Pl., 8th Fl.
New York, NY 10003
Phone: (212)209-5400
Fax: (212)982-9000
**Subject(s):** General Editorial

**Circ:** (Paid)94,003

**New Jersey Monthly (19570)**
Tomlinson Enterprise
55 Park Pl.
PO Box 920
Morristown, NJ 07963-0920
Phone: (973)539-8230
Fax: (973)538-2953
**Subject(s):** Business; Local, State, and Regional Publications

**Circ:** (Paid)94,000

**American Laboratory News (5003)**
International Scientific Communications Inc.
30 Controls Dr.
PO Box 870
Shelton, CT 06484-0870
Phone: (203)926-9300
Fax: (203)926-9310
**Subject(s):** Science (General)

**Circ:** (Non-paid)92,847

**The Fisherman (22938)**
L.I. Fisherman Publishing Corp.
14 Ramsey Rd.
Shirley, NY 11967
Phone: (631)345-5200
Fax: (631)345-5304
**Subject(s):** (Hunting, Fishing, and Game Management)

**Circ:** (Paid)92,000

**Country Journal (26439)**
Primedia
6405 Flank Dr.
Harrisburg, PA 17112
Phone: (717)540-6700
Fax: (717)657-9552
**Subject(s):** Lifestyle

**Circ:** (Paid)91,456

**Annals of Internal Medicine (26828)**
American College of Physicians
190 N. Independence Mall W.
Philadelphia, PA 19106-1572
Phone: (215)351-2600
Fax: (215)351-2799
**Subject(s):** Physiology and Anatomy; Medicine and Surgery

**Circ:** (Paid)91,224

**Pollution Equipment News (27394)**
Rimbach Publishing Inc.
St. 8650 Babcock Blvd.
Pittsburgh, PA 15237
Phone: (412)364-5366
Fax: (412)369-9720
**Subject(s):** Ecology and Conservation; Waste Management and Recycling; Water Supply and Sewage Disposal

**Circ:** (Controlled)90,600

**R & D Magazine (19562)**
Reed Business Information
301 Gibraltar Dr.
Morris Plains, NJ 07950
Fax: (973)539-3476
**Subject(s):** Engineering (Various branches); Science (General)

**Circ:** (Controlled)90,230

**Radio Control Car Action (4991)**
Air Age Publishing Inc.
100 E Ridge
Ridgefield, CT 06877
Phone: (203)431-9000
Fax: (203)431-3000
**Subject(s):** Crafts, Models, Hobbies, and Contests

**Circ:** (Paid)90,088

**Cheers (4940)**
Adams Business Media
50 Washington St., 10th Fl.
Norwalk, CT 06854
Phone: (203)855-8499
Fax: (203)855-9446
**Subject(s):** Beverages, Brewing, and Bottling; Hotels, Motels, Restaurants, and Clubs

**Circ:** (Controlled)90,000

**Contemporary Record Society News Magazine (26203)**
Contemporary Record Society
724 Winchester Rd.
Broomall, PA 19008
Phone: (610)544-5920
Fax: (432)204-0510
**Subject(s):** Music and Musical Instruments

**Circ:** (Combined)90,000

**CQ Amateur Radio (22724)**
Mainly Marketing
64 Seaview Blvd.
PO Box 748
Port Washington, NY 11050
Fax: (516)621-6209
**Subject(s):** Radio, Television, Cable, and Video

**Circ:** (Non-paid)‡1,700
    (Paid)‡90,000

**Firehouse Magazine (21156)**
Cygnus Business Media Inc.
3 Huntington Quadrangle, Ste. 301 N.
Melville, NY 11747
Phone: (631)845-2700
Fax: (631)845-2798
**Subject(s):** Fire Fighting

**Circ:** (Non-paid)24,743
    (Paid)90,000

**Material Handling Product News (14290)**
Reed Business Information
c/o Joseph Pagnotta, Editor-in-Chief
Material Handling Product News
275 Washington St.
Newton, MA 02458
Phone: (617)558-4389
Fax: (617)928-4389
**Subject(s):** Materials Handling; Storage and Warehousing

**Circ:** (Controlled)90,000

**Gale Directory of Publications & Broadcast Media/140th Ed.**  **Northeastern States**

**ONE** (22194)
Catholic Near East Welfare Association
1011 1st Ave.
New York, NY 10022-4195
Phone: (212)826-1480
Fax: (212)826-8979
**Subject(s):** Religious Publications
**Circ:** (Paid)‡90,000

**Paper Magazine** (22209)
Paper Publishing Co.
365 Broadway
New York, NY 10013
Phone: (212)226-4405
Fax: (212)226-0062
**Subject(s):** Music and Musical Instruments; Lifestyle
**Circ:** (Paid)90,000

**Revista Maryknoll** (21133)
Maryknoll Fathers
PO Box 308
Maryknoll, NY 10545-0308
Phone: (914)941-7636
Fax: (914)945-0670
**Subject(s):** Religious Publications
**Circ:** 90,000

**Printing Impressions** (27241)
North American Publishing Co.
401 N. Broad St., 5th Fl.
Philadelphia, PA 19108
Phone: (215)238-5482
Fax: (215)238-5412
**Subject(s):** Printing and Typography
**Circ:** (Non-paid)88,210

**Newsweek International - Latin America Edition** (22174)
Newsweek Inc.
251 W 57th St.
New York, NY 10019
Phone: (212)445-4870
Fax: (212)445-5764
**Subject(s):** Export Consumer Magazines; General Editorial
**Circ:** (Paid)87,993

**Graphic Arts Monthly Magazine** (21747)
Reed Business Information
c/o. Roger Ynostroza, Editorial Director
360 Park Ave. S.
New York, NY 10010
Phone: (646)746-6400
**Subject(s):** Printing and Typography
**Circ:** (Combined)86,895

**Connecticut Magazine** (5060)
35 Nutmeg Dr.
Trumbull, CT 06611
Phone: (203)380-6600
Fax: (203)380-6610
**Subject(s):** Local, State, and Regional Publications; Lifestyle
**Circ:** (Paid)86,820

**Photonics Spectra** (14739)
Laurin Publishing Company Inc.
Berkshire Common
PO Box 4949
Pittsfield, MA 01202-4949
Phone: (413)499-0514
Fax: (413)442-3180
**Subject(s):** Engineering (Various branches); Science (General)
**Circ:** (Controlled)‡86,500

**Telecommunications Magazine** (14720)
Horizon House Publications Inc.
685 Canton St.
Norwood, MA 02062
Phone: (781)769-9750
Fax: (781)769-9884
**Subject(s):** Telecommunications
**Circ:** (Paid)1,600
 (Controlled)85,068

**AGBU News** (21281)
Armenian General Benevolent Union
55 E 59th St.
New York, NY 10022-1112
Phone: (212)319-6383
Fax: (212)319-6508
**Subject(s):** Ethnic and Minority Studies; Intercultural Interests
**Circ:** 85,000

**Catholic Worker** (21464)
36 E 1st St.
New York, NY 10003
Phone: (212)677-8627
**Subject(s):** Religious Publications
**Circ:** 85,000

**Commercial Carrier Journal** (21521)
Reed Business Information
360 Park Ave. S
New York, NY 10010
Phone: (646)746-6400
**Subject(s):** Trucks and Trucking
**Circ:** (Non-paid)‡85,000

**Project Management Journal** (26776)
Project Management Institute
4 Campus Blvd.
Newtown Square, PA 19073
Phone: (610)356-4600
Fax: (610)356-4647
**Subject(s):** Management and Administration
**Circ:** (Non-paid)‡1,437
 (Paid)‡85,000

**Quiltworks Today** (26738)
Chitra Publications
2 Public Ave.
Montrose, PA 18801
Phone: (570)278-1984
Fax: (570)278-2223
**Subject(s):** Dressmaking, Needlework, and Quilting
**Circ:** ‡85,000

**Logistics Management and Distribution Report** (14863)
Reed Business Information
225 Wyman St.
Waltham, MA 02451-1216
**Subject(s):** Transportation, Traffic, and Shipping
**Circ:** (Non-paid)‡83,285

**Little India** (22041)
Empire State Bldg.
350 Fifth Ave., Ste. 1826
New York, NY 10118
Phone: (212)560-0608
Fax: (212)560-0609
**Subject(s):** Ethnic Publications
**Circ:** (Controlled)‡83,000

**ARTnews Magazine** (21364)
Art News L.L.C.
48 W 38th St.
New York, NY 10018-6238
Phone: (212)398-1690
Fax: (212)819-0394
**Subject(s):** Art
**Circ:** (Paid)82,911

**The Quarterly Review of Wines** (14919)
Q.R.W., Inc.
24 Garfield Ave.
Winchester, MA 01890
Phone: (781)729-7132
Fax: (781)721-0572
**Subject(s):** Beverages, Brewing, and Bottling
**Circ:** (Non-paid)‡53,655
 (Paid)‡82,915

**Wine & Spirits Magazine** (22540)
Wine & Spirits Magazine Inc.
2 W. 32nd St. Ste. 601
New York, NY 10001
Phone: (212)695-4660
Fax: (212)695-2920
**Subject(s):** Beverages, Brewing, and Bottling
**Circ:** ‡82,000

**Creative Woodworks and Crafts** (19626)
All American Crafts Inc.
243 Newton-Sparta Rd.
Newton, NJ 07860
Phone: (973)383-8080
Fax: (973)383-8133
**Subject(s):** Crafts, Models, Hobbies, and Contests
**Circ:** (Combined)⊕81,771

**DOLLS** (19141)
Jones Publishing Inc.
c/o Nayda Rondon, Editor
217 Passaic Ave.
Hasbrouck Heights, NJ 07604
**Subject(s):** Crafts, Models, Hobbies, and Contests
**Circ:** ‡81,724

**Digital Video Magazine** (21102)
CMP Media L.L.C.
600 Community Dr.
Manhasset, NY 11030
Phone: (516)562-5000
Fax: (516)562-5995
**Subject(s):** Telecommunications
**Circ:** (Combined)∆81,326

**Production Technology News** (22267)
Reed Business Information
360 Park Avenue South
New York, NY 10010
Phone: (646)746-6400
**Subject(s):** Metal, Metallurgy, and Metal Trade
**Circ:** (Controlled)‡81,000

**Meetings & Conventions** (19785)
Northstar Travel Media
500 Plaza Dr.
Secaucus, NJ 07094
Phone: (201)902-2000
Fax: (201)902-2045
**Subject(s):** Conventions, Meetings, and Trade Fairs
**Circ:** (Controlled)‡80,511

**Communications of the ACM** (21525)
Association for Computing Machinery
1515 Broadway, 17th Fl.
New York, NY 10036
Phone: (212)626-0500
Fax: (212)944-1318
**Subject(s):** Computers
**Circ:** (Paid)‡80,370

**Model Airplane News** (4988)
Air Age Publishing Inc.
100 E Ridge
Ridgefield, CT 06877
Phone: (203)431-9000
Fax: (203)431-3000
**Subject(s):** Crafts, Models, Hobbies, and Contests
**Circ:** (Paid)80,019

**BackOffice Magazine** (18892)
10 Tara Blvd., 5th Fl.
Nashua, NH 03062-2801
Phone: (603)891-9281
Fax: (603)891-9297
**Subject(s):** Computers
**Circ:** (Combined)‡80,000

**Catalyst** (21462)
Catholic League for Religious and Civil Rights
450 7th Ave.
New York, NY 10123
Phone: (212)371-3191
Fax: (212)371-3394
**Subject(s):** Religious Publications
**Circ:** 80,000

**Chess Life** (21247)
U.S. Chess Federation
3068 US Rt., 9 W. Ste. No. 100
New Windsor, NY 12553
Phone: (914)562-8350
Fax: (914)561-2437
**Subject(s):** Games and Puzzles
**Circ:** ‡80,000

**Electronic House** (13790)
EH Publishing Inc.
111 Speen St., Ste. 200
PO Box 989
Framingham, MA 01701-2000
Phone: (508)663-1500
Fax: (508)663-1599
**Subject(s):** Appliances; Automation; Home Furnishings, Curtains, Draperies; Radio, Television, Cable, and Video
**Circ:** ‡80,000

**Film Bill** (21686)
Film Bill Inc.
250 W 54th St.
New York, NY 10019
Phone: (212)977-4140
Fax: (212)977-4404

*Circulation:* ★ = ABC; ∆ = BPA; ♦ = CAC; • = CCAB; ▫ = VAC; ⊕ = PO Statement; ‡ = Publisher's Report; Boldface figures = sworn; Light figures = estimated.

## Northeastern States

**Subject(s):** Motion Pictures
**Circ:** (Controlled)80,000

**Hand Guns** (21755)
Primedia Special Interest Publication
745 5th Ave.
New York, NY 10151
Phone: (212)745-0100
Fax: (212)745-0121
**Subject(s):** Firearms
**Circ:** ‡80,000

**Sheet Music Magazine** (20361)
Piano Today
333 Adams St.
Bedford Hills, NY 10507
Phone: (914)244-8500
Fax: (914)244-8560
**Subject(s):** Music and Musical Instruments
**Circ:** 80,000

**Vermont Life** (30906)
Vermont Life Magazine
6 Baldwin St.
Montpelier, VT 05602
Phone: (802)828-3241
Fax: (802)828-3366
**Subject(s):** Local, State, and Regional Publications
**Circ:** (Non-paid)‡1,000
  (Paid)‡80,000

**Building Design & Construction** (21430)
Reed Business Information
360 Park Ave. S.
New York, NY 10014
Phone: (646)746-6400
Fax: (646)746-6734
**Subject(s):** Construction, Contracting, Building, and Excavating
**Circ:** (Non-paid)‡78,300

**Brown Alumni Magazine** (27891)
Brown University
71 George St.
Providence, RI 02912
Phone: (401)863-2873
Fax: (401)863-9599
**Subject(s):** College Publications
**Circ:** (Non-paid)78,000

**Right On!** (22318)
Macfadden Communications Group
333 Seventh Ave., Fl. 11
New York, NY 10001-5004
Phone: (212)780-3500
Fax: (212)979-4825
**Subject(s):** Black Publications; Entertainment; Youths' Interests
**Circ:** (Paid)77,247

**Construction Equipment** (21543)
Reed Business Information
360 Park Ave. S.
New York, NY 10014
Phone: (646)746-6400
Fax: (646)746-6734
**Subject(s):** Construction, Contracting, Building, and Excavating
**Circ:** (Free)‡77,013

**NYC/New Youth Connections** (22186)
Youth Communication
224 W 29th St., 2nd Fl.
New York, NY 10001
Phone: (212)279-0708
Fax: (212)279-8856
**Subject(s):** Youths' Interests
**Circ:** (Non-paid)‡77,000

**ACP Observer** (26796)
American College of Physicians
190 N. Independence Mall W.
Philadelphia, PA 19106-1572
Phone: (215)351-2600
Fax: (215)351-2799
**Subject(s):** Medicine and Surgery
**Circ:** (Non-paid)1,551
  (Paid)76,074

**ENR: Engineering News-Record** (21651)
McGraw-Hill Inc.
Two Penn Plaza, 9th Fl.
New York, NY 10121
Phone: (212)904-6428
Fax: (212)904-2820

**Subject(s):** Construction, Contracting, Building, and Excavating; Engineering (Various branches)
**Circ:** (Paid)75,706
  76,000

**Successful Meetings** (22430)
770 Broadway
New York, NY 10003
Phone: (646)654-5000
**Subject(s):** Conventions, Meetings, and Trade Fairs; Travel and Tourism
**Circ:** (Controlled)‡75,296

**ADVANCE for Physical Therapists and PT Assistants** (26581)
Merion Publications Inc.
2900 Horizon Dr.
King of Prussia, PA 19406
Phone: (610)278-1400
Fax: (610)278-1425
**Subject(s):** Health and Healthcare
**Circ:** (Controlled)‡75,000

**BMI Music World** (21413)
Broadcast Music, Inc.
320 W 57th St.
New York, NY 10019
Phone: (212)586-2000
Fax: (212)956-2059
**Subject(s):** Music and Musical Instruments; Music and Musical Instruments
**Circ:** 75,000

**Financial Planning** (21692)
Securities Data Publishing
395 Hudson, 3rd Fl.
40 W. 57th St.
New York, NY 10014
Phone: (212)765-5311
Fax: (646)822-3230
**Subject(s):** Banking, Finance, and Investments
**Circ:** (Paid)25,000
  (Controlled)75,000

**Frontline Solutions** (18938)
Advanstar Communications
c/o Barbara Goode, Group Editorial Director
One Phoenix Mill Ln., Ste. 401
Peterborough, NH 03458
Phone: (603)924-5408
Fax: (603)924-5401
**Subject(s):** Computers
**Circ:** (Paid)83
  (Controlled)75,000

**Investment Advisor Magazine** (19802)
Investment Advisor Group
Revmont Park S.
1161 Broad St.
Ste. 200
Shrewsbury, NJ 07702
Phone: (732)389-8700
Fax: (732)389-6065
**Subject(s):** Banking, Finance, and Investments
**Circ:** (Controlled)‡75,000

**Miniature Quilts** (26737)
Chitra Publications
2 Public Ave.
Montrose, PA 18801
Phone: (570)278-1984
Fax: (570)278-2223
**Circ:** (Paid)‡75,000

**The New Jersey Angler** (26086)
Bill Donovan
1431 Edgehill Rd.
Abington, PA 19001
**Subject(s):** Clubs and Societies; (Hunting, Fishing, and Game Management)
**Circ:** (Combined)75,000

**Show Biz News & Model News** (22370)
The John King Network
244 Madison Ave., Ste. 393
New York, NY 10016
Phone: (212)969-8715
Fax: (212)969-8715
**Subject(s):** Fashion; Drama and Theatre; Entertainment
**Circ:** (Combined)75,000

**Steppin' Out Magazine** (19971)
Lawrence J. Collins
381 Broadway
Westwood, NJ 07675
Phone: (201)358-2929
Fax: (201)358-2824
**Subject(s):** Entertainment
**Circ:** (Non-paid)75,000

**Vice** (20545)
Vice Publishing
75 N 4th St., 3rd Fl.
Brooklyn, NY 11211-3105
**Subject(s):** Alternative and Underground; Dressmaking, Needlework, and Quilting; Fashion
**Circ:** (Non-paid)‡75,000

**Area Auto Racing News** (19888)
PO Box 8547
Trenton, NJ 08650
Phone: (609)888-3618
Fax: (609)888-2538
**Subject(s):** (Auto Racing)
**Circ:** ‡72,000

**Consumer Info News** (20500)
EWA Publications
2446 E 65th St.
Brooklyn, NY 11234
Phone: (718)763-7034
Fax: (718)763-7035
**Subject(s):** Consumerism
**Circ:** 72,000

**Media and Methods Magazine** (27134)
1429 Walnut St.
Philadelphia, PA 19102
Phone: (215)563-6005
Fax: (215)587-9706
**Subject(s):** Education
**Circ:** 72,000

**Swap Meet Magazine** (20633)
Forum Publishing Co.
383 E Main St.
Centerport, NY 11721-1538
Phone: (631)754-5000
Fax: (631)754-0630
**Subject(s):** Retail; General Merchandise
**Circ:** (Non-paid)72,000

**World Industrial Reporter (Reportero Industrial)** (20863)
Keller International Publishing L.L.C.
150 Great Neck Rd.
Great Neck, NY 11021
Phone: (516)829-9210
Fax: (516)829-5414
**Subject(s):** International Business and Economics; Commerce and Industry; Arabic; Spanish
**Circ:** (Non-paid)‡71,101

**American Biotechnology Laboratory** (5001)
International Scientific Communications Inc.
30 Controls Dr.
PO Box 870
Shelton, CT 06484-0870
Phone: (203)926-9300
Fax: (203)926-9310
**Subject(s):** Biology; Laboratory Research (Scientific and Medical)
**Circ:** (Non-paid)‡70,792

**The Magazine Antiques** (22049)
Brant Publications Inc.
575 Broadway
New York, NY 10012
**Subject(s):** Art; Art and Art History; Architecture
**Circ:** (Paid)70,605

**Primary Care & Cancer** (21179)
PRR Inc.
48 S Service Rd.
Melville, NY 11747-2335
Fax: (631)777-8700
**Subject(s):** Medicine and Surgery
**Circ:** (Controlled)70,451

**Home Magazine's Home Plans** (21774)
Hachette Filipacchi Media U.S. Inc.
1633 Broadway
New York, NY 10019
Phone: (212)767-6000

**Subject(s):** Home and Garden
**Circ:** ‡70,013

**Bond Guide (21418)**
Standard & Poor's
55 Water St.
New York, NY 10041
Fax: (212)438-3396
**Subject(s):** Banking, Finance, and Investments
**Circ:** (Paid)70,000

**Chile Pepper Magazine (21485)**
110 William St., 23rd Fl.
New York, NY 10038
Phone: (646)459-4800
Fax: (646)459-4900
**Subject(s):** Food and Cooking; Travel and Tourism
**Circ:** (Controlled)30,000
(Paid)70,000

**Electronic Publishing (18899)**
PennWell Corp.
98 Spit Brook Rd.
Nashua, NH 03062-5737
Phone: (603)891-0123
Fax: (603)891-0574
**Subject(s):** Computers; Graphic Arts and Design
**Circ:** 70,000

**International Figure Skating (13527)**
Madavor Media
420 Boylston St. 5th Fl
Boston, MA 02116
Phone: (617)536-0121
**Subject(s):** (Skating)
**Circ:** (Paid)70,000

**Laser Focus World (18905)**
PennWell Corp.
98 Spit Brook Rd.
Nashua, NH 03062-5737
Phone: (603)891-0123
Fax: (603)891-0574
**Subject(s):** Electronics Engineering
**Circ:** ‡70,000

**Relix Magazine (22304)**
180 Varick St., 4th Fl.
New York, NY 10014
Phone: (646)230-0200
Fax: (646)230-0200
**Subject(s):** Music and Musical Instruments
**Circ:** 70,000

**Retailers Forum Magazine (20632)**
Forum Publishing Co.
383 E Main St.
Centerport, NY 11721
Phone: (631)754-5000
Fax: (631)754-0630
**Subject(s):** Retail
**Circ:** (Non-paid)70,000

**Rutgers Magazine (19692)**
96 Davidson Rd.
Piscataway, NJ 08854
Phone: (732)445-3710
Fax: (732)445-5925
**Subject(s):** College Publications
**Circ:** ‡70,000

**Sales & Marketing Management (22335)**
VNU Business Media
770 Broadway
New York, NY 10003-9595
Phone: (646)654-4500
Fax: (646)654-7473
**Subject(s):** Advertising and Marketing; Selling and Salesmanship
**Circ:** ‡70,000

**Spirit of Change Magazine (14844)**
PO Box 405
Uxbridge, MA 01569
Phone: (508)278-9640
Fax: (508)278-9641
**Subject(s):** Health; New Age
**Circ:** (Combined)70,000

**Western New York Catholic (20584)**
795 Main St.
Buffalo, NY 14203
Phone: (716)847-8727
**Subject(s):** Religious Publications
**Circ:** (Paid)70,000

**Art in America (21358)**
Brant Publications Inc.
575 Broadway
New York, NY 10012-3230
Phone: (212)941-2800
Fax: (212)941-2844
**Subject(s):** Art
**Circ:** (Paid)69,583

**ADVANCE for Imaging and Radiation Therapy Professionals (26574)**
Merion Publications Inc.
2900 Horizon Dr.
King of Prussia, PA 19406
Phone: (610)278-1400
Fax: (610)278-1425
**Subject(s):** Medicine and Surgery; Radiology, Ultrasound, and Nuclear Medicine
**Circ:** (Controlled)‡69,000

**District Administration (4943)**
Professional Media Group L.L.C.
488 Main Ave.
Norwalk, CT 06851
Phone: (203)663-0100
Fax: (203)663-0149
**Subject(s):** Education
**Circ:** (Controlled)△**69,000**

**TURF (30936)**
Moose River Publishing
PO Box 449
Saint Johnsbury, VT 05819
Phone: (802)748-8908
Fax: (802)748-1866
**Subject(s):** Golf Course Management; Turf and Turf Maintenance
**Circ:** (Controlled)‡68,600

**Nursing Spectrum—Philadelphia/Tri-State Edition (26589)**
Nursing Spectrum Inc.
2002 Renaissance Blvd., No. 250
King of Prussia, PA 19406
Phone: (610)292-8000
Fax: (610)292-0179
**Subject(s):** Career Development and Employment; Nursing
**Circ:** 67,925

**Supply Chain Systems Magazine (18943)**
Helmers Publishing Inc.
174 Concord St.
PO Box 874
Peterborough, NH 03458
Phone: (603)924-9631
Fax: (603)924-6746
**Subject(s):** Computers
**Circ:** (Non-paid)67,500

**Running Times (5102)**
Fitness Publishing Inc.
15 River Rd., Ste. 230
Wilton, CT 06897
Phone: (203)761-1113
Fax: (203)761-9933
**Subject(s):** (Physical Fitness)
**Circ:** (Non-paid)15,900
(Paid)67,000

**Nursing Spectrum—New England Edition (13856)**
Nursing Spectrum Inc.
1050 Waltham St., No. 510
Lexington, MA 02421
Phone: (781)863-2300
Fax: (781)863-6277
**Subject(s):** Career Development and Employment; Nursing
**Circ:** 66,500

**Vogue Patterns Magazine (22523)**
Butterick Company Inc.
11 Penn Plaza
New York, NY 10001
**Subject(s):** Dressmaking, Needlework, and Quilting; Fashion
**Circ:** (Paid)66,172

**Interior Design (14860)**
Reed Business Information
225 Wyman St.
Waltham, MA 02451-1216
**Subject(s):** Paint and Wallcoverings; Home Furnishings, Curtains, Draperies; Furniture and Furnishings
**Circ:** (Paid)66,036

**NFPA Journal (14757)**
National Fire Protection Association
1 Batterymarch Pk.
PO Box 9101
Quincy, MA 02169-7471
Phone: (617)770-3000
Fax: (617)770-0700
**Subject(s):** Fire Fighting
**Circ:** ‡66,000

**ADVANCE for Medical Laboratory Professionals (26577)**
Merion Publications Inc.
2900 Horizon Dr.
King of Prussia, PA 19406
Phone: (610)278-1400
Fax: (610)278-1425
**Subject(s):** Medicine and Surgery; Laboratory Research (Scientific and Medical)
**Circ:** (Controlled)‡65,300

**Beverage Dynamics (4939)**
Adams Business Media
50 Washington St., 10th Fl.
Norwalk, CT 06854
Phone: (203)855-8499
Fax: (203)855-9446
**Subject(s):** Beverages, Brewing, and Bottling
**Circ:** (Controlled)△**65,081**

**Electronic Business (14859)**
Reed Business Information
225 Wyman St.
Waltham, MA 02451-1216
**Subject(s):** Electronics Engineering; Purchasing
**Circ:** (Combined)‡65,020

**Bar Journal (20210)**
New York State Bar Association
1 Elk St.
Albany, NY 12207
Phone: (518)463-3200
Fax: (518)487-5517
**Subject(s):** Law
**Circ:** 65,000

**Cardiology Review (19417)**
Medical World Communications
8 Center Dr.
Monroe Township
Jamesburg, NJ 08831
Phone: (732)656-1140
Fax: (732)656-1323
**Subject(s):** Medicine and Surgery
**Circ:** (Controlled)△**65,009**

**Management Accounting Quarterly (19538)**
Institute of Management Accountants
10 Paragon Dr.
Montvale, NJ 07645-1718
Phone: (201)573-9000
Fax: (201)474-1603
**Subject(s):** Accountants and Accounting; Banking, Finance, and Investments; Business
**Circ:** 65,000

**Meeting News (22073)**
VNU Business Media
770 Broadway
New York, NY 10003-9595
Phone: (646)654-4500
Fax: (646)654-7473
**Subject(s):** Conventions, Meetings, and Trade Fairs
**Circ:** (Non-paid)‡65,000

**New Internationalist (22616)**
New Internationalist Publications
PO Box 1062
Niagara Falls, NY 14301
Phone: (905)946-0407
Fax: (905)946-0410
**Subject(s):** Social and Political Issues
**Circ:** (Paid)‡65,000

## Northeastern States

**New Mystery (22146)**
Friends of New Mystery
101 W 23rd St.
New York, NY 10011
Phone: (212)353-3495
Fax: (212)353-3495
**Subject(s):** Science Fiction, Mystery, Adventure, and Romance
**Circ:** (Non-paid)35,000
 (Paid)65,000

**Test & Measurement World (14295)**
Reed Business Information
275 Washington St.
Newton, MA 02458
Phone: (617)964-3030
Fax: (617)558-4470
**Subject(s):** Electronics Engineering
**Circ:** (Controlled)‡65,000

**The WANT ADvertiser (14833)**
WANT AD Publications Inc.
128 Boston Post Rd.
Sudbury, MA 01776-2453
Phone: (978)443-7007
Fax: (978)443-3340
**Subject(s):** Advertising and Marketing
**Circ:** 65,000

**Westchester Magazine (20760)**
100 Clearbrook Rd.
Elmsford, NY 10523-1116
Phone: (914)345-0601
Fax: (914)345-8120
**Subject(s):** Lifestyle; Local, State, and Regional Publications
**Circ:** 65,000

**Speedway Scene (14316)**
Hockomock Publishing
50 Washington St.
PO Box 300
North Easton, MA 02356
Phone: (508)238-7016
Fax: (508)230-2381
**Subject(s):** (Auto Racing)
**Circ:** ‡64,000

**The World at Large (20548)**
The World at Large Inc.
1689-46th St.
Brooklyn, NY 11204
Phone: (718)972-4000
Fax: (718)972-9400
**Subject(s):** General Editorial; Senior Citizens' Interests
**Circ:** ‡64,000

**Strategic Finance (19543)**
Institute of Management Accountants
10 Paragon Dr.
Montvale, NJ 07645-1718
Phone: (201)573-9000
Fax: (201)474-1603
**Subject(s):** Accountants and Accounting
**Circ:** (Paid)63,750

**Fly Rod & Reel (12494)**
Down East Enterprise Inc.
PO Box 370
Camden, ME 04843
Phone: (207)594-9544
Fax: (207)594-7215
**Subject(s):** (Hunting, Fishing, and Game Management)
**Circ:** (Paid)63,420

**Real Estate Software Guide (27917)**
Z-Law Software Inc.
637 Hospital Trust Bldg.
Providence, RI 02903
**Subject(s):** Computers; Real Estate
**Circ:** (Paid)63,000

**Best's Review (19644)**
A.M. Best Co.
Ambest Rd.
Oldwick, NJ 08858
Phone: (908)439-2200
**Subject(s):** Insurance
**Circ:** ‡62,977

**Progressive Grocer (22268)**
VNU Business Media
770 Broadway
New York, NY 10003-9595
Phone: (646)654-4500
Fax: (646)654-7473
**Subject(s):** Food and Grocery Trade
**Circ:** (Controlled)‡62,739

**Surgical Products (19564)**
Reed Business Information
301 Gibraltar Dr.
PO Box 650
Morris Plains, NJ 07950
Phone: (973)292-5100
Fax: (973)539-3476
**Subject(s):** Medicine and Surgery
**Circ:** (Controlled)‡62,600

**American Angler (30836)**
160 Benmont Ave.
PO Box 4100
Bennington, VT 05201-4100
Phone: (802)447-1518
Fax: (802)447-2471
**Subject(s):** (Hunting, Fishing, and Game Management)
**Circ:** (Paid)62,564

**BioTechniques (14893)**
Eaton Publishing
PO Box 1070
Westborough, MA 01581-6070
Phone: (508)614-1414
Fax: (508)616-2930
**Subject(s):** Biology; Laboratory Research (Scientific and Medical)
**Circ:** 62,155

**Industrial Safety and Hygiene News (26524)**
BNP Media
PO Box 178
Huntingdon Valley, PA 19006
Phone: (215)663-9349
Fax: (215)663-9358
**Subject(s):** Health and Healthcare; Safety; Commerce and Industry
**Circ:** (Controlled)‡62,057

**Biomedical Products (19552)**
Reed Business Information
c/o Steve Ernst, Editor
Bioscience Technology
301 Gibraltar Dr.
Morris Plains, NJ 07950
Phone: (973)292-5100
Fax: (973)539-3479
**Subject(s):** Biology; Medicine and Surgery
**Circ:** (Controlled)‡62,020

**Industrial Hygiene News (27358)**
Rimbach Publishing Inc.
St. 8650 Babcock Blvd.
Pittsburgh, PA 15237
Phone: (412)364-5366
Fax: (412)369-9720
**Subject(s):** Health and Healthcare; Safety
**Circ:** (Controlled)62,000

**City Guide Magazine (21495)**
Key Magazine Inc.
c/o Keith Leonard
Empire State Building
350 Fifth Ave., Ste. 2420
New York, NY 10118
Phone: (212)315-0800
**Subject(s):** Travel and Tourism; Entertainment; Local, State, and Regional Publications
**Circ:** (Combined)61,596

**Clinical Laboratory MarketPlace (14716)**
Market Place Publications
89 Access Rd.
Norwood, MA 02062
Phone: (781)762-6600
Fax: (781)762-1300
**Subject(s):** Laboratory Research (Scientific and Medical)
**Circ:** 61,555

**CADALYST (21445)**
Advanstar Communications
1 Park Ave.
New York, NY 10016
Phone: (212)951-6600
Fax: (212)951-6793
**Subject(s):** Computers
**Circ:** (Paid)20,204
 (Non-paid)61,395

**ADVANCE for Speech-Language Pathologists & Audiologists (26585)**
Merion Publications Inc.
2900 Horizon Dr.
King of Prussia, PA 19406
Phone: (610)278-1400
Fax: (610)278-1425
**Subject(s):** Medicine and Surgery
**Circ:** (Controlled)‡61,000

**Employee Benefit News (21647)**
Thomson Financial Securities Data
40 W 57th St. Fl. 11
New York, NY 10019
Phone: (646)822-2000
Fax: (646)822-3230
**Subject(s):** Management and Administration; Employment and Human Resources
**Circ:** (Combined)‡61,000

**Journal of Counseling & Development (20551)**
American Counseling Association
c/o A. Scott McGowan, JCD Editor
Dept. of Counseling and Development
Long Island University, C.W. Post Campus
720 Northern Blvd.
Brookville, NY 11548-1300
Phone: (516)299-2814
Fax: (516)299-3312
**Subject(s):** Philanthropy and Humanitarianism
**Circ:** ‡60,500

**Power (22257)**
McGraw-Hill Inc.
1221 Avenue of the Americas
New York, NY 10020
Phone: (212)337-4062
Fax: (212)627-3811
**Subject(s):** Engineering (Various branches); Power and Power Plants
**Circ:** (Paid)5,977
 (Non-paid)60,463

**Call Center Magazine (21448)**
CMP Media L.L.C.
12 W. 21st St.
New York, NY 10010
Phone: (212)691-8215
Fax: (212)691-1191
**Subject(s):** Communications; Telecommunications
**Circ:** (Non-paid)37,179
 (Paid)60,321

**ADVANCE for Occupational Therapy Practitioners (26580)**
Merion Publications Inc.
2900 Horizon Dr.
King of Prussia, PA 19406
Phone: (610)278-1400
Fax: (610)278-1425
**Subject(s):** Physiology and Anatomy; Education; Handicapped
**Circ:** (Non-paid)‡60,000

**Lasers & Optronics (22025)**
Reed Business Information
360 Park Avenue South
New York, NY 10010
Phone: (646)746-6400
**Subject(s):** Electronics Engineering
**Circ:** (Controlled)50,069
 60,000

**Lehigh Alumni Bulletin (26166)**
Lehigh University
436 Brodhead Ave.
Bethlehem, PA 18015-1690
Phone: (610)758-4180
**Subject(s):** College Publications
**Circ:** (Controlled)‡60,000

**Linux Business Week (19537)**
SYS-CON Media
135 Chestnut Ridge Rd.
Montvale, NJ 07645
Phone: (201)802-3000
Fax: (201)782-9601
**Subject(s):** Computers; Automation; Business
**Circ:** (Combined)60,000

**Managed Care (27723)**
MediMedia USA Inc.
780 Township Line Rd.
Yardley, PA 19067
Phone: (267)685-2788

**MoMA Magazine (22095)**
Museum of Modern Art
11 W 53rd St.
New York, NY 10019
Phone: (212)708-9443
Fax: (212)333-6575
Subject(s): Museums

Circ: (Combined)60,000

**Poets & Writers Magazine (22242)**
Poets & Writers Inc.
72 Spring St., Ste. 301
New York, NY 10012
Phone: (212)226-3586
Fax: (212)226-3963
Subject(s): Book Trade and Author News

Circ: ‡60,000

**Princeton Alumni Weekly (19732)**
194 Nassau St., Ste.38
Princeton, NJ 08542
Phone: (609)258-4885
Fax: (609)258-2247
Subject(s): College Publications

Circ: 60,000

**The Star (22415)**
B'nai B'rith District One
823 United Nations Plz.
New York, NY 10017
Phone: (212)687-2257
Fax: (212)986-7487
Subject(s): Jewish Publications

Circ: ‡60,000

**Tropical Fish Hobbyist (19580)**
T.F.H. Publications Inc.
1 T.F.H. Plz.
3rd & Union Aves.
Neptune, NJ 07753-6497
Phone: (732)988-8400
Fax: (732)988-5466
Subject(s): Pets

Circ: ‡60,000

**Vette (19778)**
Primedia
299 Market St.
Saddle Brook, NJ 07663-5312
Phone: (201)712-9300
Fax: (201)712-9899
Subject(s): Automotive (Consumer)

Circ: (Paid)60,000

**Popular Communications (22730)**
Mainly Marketing
64 Seaview Blvd.
PO Box 748
Port Washington, NY 11050
Fax: (516)621-6209
Subject(s): Telecommunications; Radio, Television, Cable, and Video

Circ: (Non-paid)⊕876
(Paid)⊕59,340

**HOTELS (21786)**
Reed Business Information
360 Park Ave. S.
New York, NY 10014
Phone: (646)746-6400
Fax: (646)746-6734
Subject(s): Hotels, Motels, Restaurants, and Clubs

Circ: (Free)‡59,228

**New York Family (21093)**
New York Family Publications Inc.
141 Halstead Ave., Ste. 302
Mamaroneck, NY 10543-2652
Phone: (914)381-7474
Fax: (914)381-7672
Subject(s): Parenting

Circ: (Paid)266
(Free)59,069

**Westchester Family (21094)**
New York Family Publications Inc.
141 Halstead Ave., Ste. 302
Mamaroneck, NY 10543-2652
Phone: (914)381-7474
Fax: (914)381-7672
Subject(s): Parenting

Circ: (Paid)266
(Free)59,069

**For the Record (27544)**
Great Valley Publishing Co. Inc.
3801 Schuylkill Rd.
Spring City, PA 19475-1529
Phone: (610)948-9500
Fax: (610)948-4202
Subject(s): Medicine and Surgery; Health and Healthcare

Circ: (Controlled)58,000

**Inside (26977)**
The Jewish Federation of Greater Philadelphia
226 S. 16th. St.
Philadelphia, PA 19102
Phone: (215)893-5797
Fax: (215)546-3957
Subject(s): Jewish Publications

Circ: (Paid)200
(Non-paid)58,000

**Kaleidoscope (20429)**
State University of New York College at Brockport
350 New Campus Dr.
Brockport, NY 14420
Fax: (585)395-2451
Subject(s): College Publications

Circ: (Combined)58,000

**Pediatric Annals (19872)**
SLACK Inc.
6900 Grove Rd.
Thorofare, NJ 08086-9447
Phone: (856)848-1000
Fax: (856)848-6091
Subject(s): Pediatrics

Circ: (Controlled)‡58,000

**Sailing World (27873)**
Miller Sports Group L.L.C.
5 John Clarke Rd.
PO Box 3400
Newport, RI 02840-0992
Phone: (401)845-5100
Fax: (401)845-5180
Subject(s): (Boating and Yachting)

Circ: (Paid)57,388

**Plastics World (21178)**
Cygnus Business Media Inc.
3 Huntington Quadrangle, Ste. 301 N.
Melville, NY 11747
Phone: (631)845-2700
Fax: (631)845-2798
Subject(s): Plastic and Composition Materials

Circ: (Controlled)‡57,311

**Electronics Supply and Manufacturing (21104)**
CMP Media L.L.C.
600 Community Dr.
Manhasset, NY 11030
Phone: (516)562-5000
Fax: (516)562-5995
Subject(s): Electronics Engineering; Purchasing

Circ: (Non-paid)‡57,100

**Hotel & Travel Index–International Edition (19784)**
Hotel & Travel Index International Edition
500 Plaza Dr.
Secaucus, NJ 07094
Phone: (201)902-2000
Fax: (201)319-1628
Subject(s): Hotels, Motels, Restaurants, and Clubs; Travel and Tourism

Circ: (Paid)57,000

**Infectious Diseases in Children (19857)**
SLACK Inc.
6900 Grove Rd.
Thorofare, NJ 08086-9447
Phone: (856)848-1000
Fax: (856)848-6091
Subject(s): Medicine and Surgery

Circ: (Controlled)‡57,003

**Movin' Out (27536)**
Pollock Advertising Inc.
118 1/2 Franklin St.
PO Box 97
Slippery Rock, PA 16057
Phone: (724)794-6857
Fax: (724)794-1314

Subject(s): Trucks and Trucking

Circ: (Paid)‡1,000
(Non-paid)‡57,000

**Teaching Exceptional Children (13733)**
Council for Exceptional Children
Champion 108
Boston College
Chestnut Hill, MA 02467
Phone: (617)552-3149
Fax: (617)552-8419
Subject(s): Education

Circ: 56,814

**Unique Homes (19739)**
Unique Homes Magazine Inc.
327 Wall St.
Princeton, NJ 08540
Phone: (609)688-1110
Fax: (609)688-0201
Subject(s): Real Estate; Home and Garden

Circ: (Paid)56,410

**Quick Printing (21184)**
Cygnus Business Media Inc.
3 Huntington Quadrangle, Ste. 301 N.
Melville, NY 11747
Phone: (631)845-2700
Fax: (631)845-2798
Subject(s): Printing and Typography

Circ: (Paid)3,917
(Non-paid)56,133

**The Business Lawyer (21439)**
American Bar Association
c/o Linda C.Hayman
4 Times Sq., 42-200
New York, NY 10036-6522
Phone: (212)735-2637
Fax: (917)777-2637
Subject(s): Law

Circ: (Non-paid)‡5,064
(Paid)‡56,011

**About.Time (22802)**
About.Time Magazine Inc.
283 Genesee St.
Rochester, NY 14611
Phone: (585)235-7150
Fax: (585)235-7195
Subject(s): Black Publications; History and Genealogy

Circ: (Paid)‡56,000

**E (4944)**
Earth Action Network
28 Knight St.
Norwalk, CT 06851
Subject(s): Environmental and Natural Resources Conservation

Circ: 56,000

**The Quilter (19630)**
All American Crafts Inc.
243 Newton-Sparta Rd.
Newton, NJ 07860
Phone: (973)383-8080
Fax: (973)383-8133
Subject(s): Crafts, Models, Hobbies, and Contests

Circ: ⊕56,000

**RailFan & Railroad (19631)**
Carstens Publications Inc.
PO Box 700
108 Phil Hardin Rd.
Newton, NJ 07860
Phone: (973)383-3355
Fax: (973)383-4064
Subject(s): Crafts, Models, Hobbies, and Contests

Circ: ‡56,000

**Kitchen and Bath Design News (21165)**
Cygnus Business Media Inc.
3 Huntington Quadrangle, Ste. 301 N.
Melville, NY 11747
Phone: (631)845-2700
Fax: (631)845-2798
Subject(s): Interior Design/Decorating

Circ: (Non-paid)‡55,837

**Food Arts (21700)**
M. Shanken Communications Inc.
387 Park Ave. S.
New York, NY 10016
Phone: (212)684-4224
Fax: (212)684-5424

**Subject(s):** Food and Grocery Trade; Food and Cooking

**Circ:** (Paid)‡1,513
(Non-paid)‡55,581

**The American Philatelist (26154)**
American Philatelic Society
100 Match Factory Pl.
PO Box 8000
Bellefonte, PA 16823
Phone: (814)933-3803
Fax: (814)933-6128
**Subject(s):** Collecting

**Circ:** ‡55,000

**Dance Magazine (21587)**
333 7th Ave., 11th Fl.
New York, NY 10001-5004
Phone: (646)674-0102
Fax: (646)674-0102
**Subject(s):** Performing Arts

**Circ:** (Non-paid)‡1,082
(Paid)‡55,000

**Game Pro (13517)**
IDG
One Exeter Plz., 15th Fl.
Boston, MA 02116
Phone: (617)534-1200
Fax: (617)262-2300
**Subject(s):** Computers

**Circ:** (Paid)55,000

**Tricycle (22486)**
The Buddhist Ray Inc.
92 Vandam St.
New York, NY 10013
Phone: (212)645-1143
Fax: (212)645-1493
**Subject(s):** Religious Publications

**Circ:** (Paid)55,000

**Computer Graphics World (18897)**
PennWell Corp.
98 Spit Brook Rd.
Nashua, NH 03062-5737
Phone: (603)891-0123
Fax: (603)891-0574
**Subject(s):** Computers; Printing and Typography

**Circ:** (Paid)9,706
(Non-paid)54,961

**Hard Hat News (22682)**
PO Box 121
6113 State Hwy. 5
Palatine Bridge, NY 13428
Phone: (518)673-3237
Fax: (518)673-2381
**Subject(s):** Construction, Contracting, Building, and Excavating

**Circ:** 54,094

**American Journal of Medicine (21314)**
Excerpta Medica Inc.
655 Avenue of the Americas
New York, NY 10010
Phone: (212)989-5800
**Subject(s):** Medicine and Surgery

**Circ:** ‡53,751

**Ithaca College Quarterly (20955)**
Ithaca College
Office of Marketing Communications
Ithaca, NY 14850
Phone: (607)274-3830
Fax: (607)274-1490
**Subject(s):** College Publications

**Circ:** (Free)‡53,000

**Lapidary Journal (26280)**
Primedia Special Interest Publications
60 Chestnut Ave., Ste. 201
Devon, PA 19333-1312
Phone: (610)964-6300
Fax: (610)293-0977
**Subject(s):** Jewelry, Watches, and Clocks

**Circ:** ‡53,000

**Human Resource Executive (26515)**
LRP Publications
747 Dresher Rd., Ste. 500
PO Box 980
Horsham, PA 19044
Phone: (215)784-0860
Fax: (215)784-9639

**Subject(s):** Employment and Human Resources

**Circ:** (Paid)7,049
(Controlled)52,981

**World Press Review (22563)**
700 Broadway
New York, NY 10003
Phone: (212)982-8880
Fax: (212)982-6968
**Subject(s):** General Editorial

**Circ:** (Paid)52,675

**Workforce Diversity (21196)**
Equal Opportunity Publications Inc.
445 Broad Hollow Rd., Ste. 425
Melville, NY 11747
Phone: (631)421-9478
Fax: (631)421-0359
**Subject(s):** Employment and Human Resources

**Circ:** (Non-paid)52,608

**Metal Edge (TV Picture Life) (22076)**
Macfadden Communications Group
333 Seventh Ave., Fl. 11
New York, NY 10001-5004
Phone: (212)780-3500
Fax: (212)979-4825
**Subject(s):** Music and Musical Instruments

**Circ:** (Paid)52,228

**Eyecare Business (26375)**
Boucher Communications Inc.
1300 Virginia Dr., Ste. 400
Fort Washington, PA 19034
Phone: (215)643-8000
Fax: (215)643-8099
**Subject(s):** Ophthalmology, Optometry, and Optics

**Circ:** (Non-paid)52,200

**Practical Diabetology (22260)**
R.A. Rapaport Publishing Inc.
150 W 22nd St., Ste.800
New York, NY 10011
Phone: (212)989-0200
Fax: (212)989-4786
**Subject(s):** Medicine and Surgery

**Circ:** (Controlled)‡52,086

**HealthCare Review New England Edition (18902)**
Healthcare Review Northeast Network
Millyard Technology Park
20 Technology Way
Nashua, NH 03060
Phone: (603)579-8900
Fax: (603)579-8998
**Subject(s):** Health and Healthcare; Medicine and Surgery; Hospitals and Healthcare Institutions

**Circ:** (Paid)❏243
(Combined)❏52,074

**Bentley Observer (14851)**
Bentley College
175 Forest St.
Waltham, MA 02452
Phone: (781)891-2241
Fax: (781)891-3165
**Subject(s):** College Publications

**Circ:** (Controlled)52,000

**Healthstate (19614)**
University of Medicine and Dentistry of New Jersey
30 Bergen St., ADMC 110
Newark, NJ 07107-3000
Phone: (973)972-5521
Fax: (973)972-7261
**Subject(s):** Health and Healthcare

**Circ:** (Non-paid)‡52,000

**Market Watch (22058)**
M. Shanken Communications Inc.
387 Park Ave. S.
New York, NY 10016
Phone: (212)684-4224
Fax: (212)684-5424
**Subject(s):** Beverages, Brewing, and Bottling

**Circ:** ‡51,760

**strategy + business (22422)**
Booz Allen & Hamilton
101 Park Ave.
New York, NY 10178
Phone: (212)551-6222
Fax: (212)551-6008

**Subject(s):** Business

**Circ:** (Paid)38,936
(Non-paid)51,641

**Surgical Rounds (19423)**
Romaine Pierson Publishers Inc.
241 Forsgate Dr.
Jamesburg, NJ 08831-1676
Phone: (732)656-1140
Fax: (732)656-1148
**Subject(s):** Medicine and Surgery

**Circ:** (Controlled)△51,556

**Travel Agent (22478)**
Universal Media Inc.
801 2nd Ave.
New York, NY 10017
Phone: (212)986-5100
Fax: (212)338-9445
**Subject(s):** Travel and Tourism

**Circ:** (Paid)122
(Controlled)51,500

**LCGC (19413)**
Advanstar Communications
Woodbridge Corporate Plaza
485 Rte. 1 S.
Building F, First Fl.
Iselin, NJ 08830
Phone: (732)225-9500
Fax: (732)225-0211
**Subject(s):** Science (General)

**Circ:** (Controlled)‡51,482

**Country Road Chronicles (26283)**
Van Raper Productions Co.
RR2 Box 132
Dingmans Ferry, PA 18328
Phone: (570)828-1778
Fax: (570)828-7959
**Subject(s):** Environmental and Natural Resources Conservation; Intercultural Interests

**Circ:** (Controlled)51,000

**KMWorld (12495)**
Information Today Inc.
18 Bayview St. at Sharp's Wharf
PO Box 1358
Camden, ME 04843
Phone: (207)236-8524
Fax: (207)236-6452
**Subject(s):** Computers

**Circ:** (Non-paid)△51,000

**Inbound Logistics (21813)**
Thomas Publishing Co.
Five Penn Plaza
New York, NY 10001

**Circ:** (Controlled)‡50,500

**Travel Weekly (19787)**
Northstar Travel Media
500 Plaza Dr.
Secaucus, NJ 07094
Phone: (201)902-2000
Fax: (201)902-2045
**Subject(s):** Travel and Tourism

**Circ:** (Paid)50,020

**A/C FLYER (22889)**
The McGraw-Hill Companies Inc.
6 International Dr. Ste. 310
Rye Brook, NY 10573
Phone: (914)933-7620
Fax: (914)939-1184
**Subject(s):** Aviation

**Circ:** 50,000

**Adirondack Life (20995)**
Rte. 86
PO Box 410
Jay, NY 12941
**Subject(s):** Local, State, and Regional Publications

**Circ:** (Non-paid)‡1,000
(Paid)‡50,000

**Catalyst (13655)**
Union of Concerned Scientists
2 Brattle Sq.
Cambridge, MA 02238-9105
Phone: (617)547-5552
Fax: (617)864-9405
**Subject(s):** Science (General); Social and Political Issues

**Circ:** (Paid)50,000

**Christian Science Sentinel  (13500)**
The Christian Science Publishing Society
One Norway St.
Boston, MA 02115
Phone: (617)450-2000
Fax: (617)450-2930
Subject(s): Religious Publications
Circ: (Paid)⊕50,000

**Connecticut Parent Magazine  (4633)**
420 E Main St., Ste. 18
Branford, CT 06405
Phone: (203)483-1700
Subject(s): Parenting
Circ: (Non-paid)‡50,000

**CROSSW'RD Magazine  (21577)**
Crossword Magazine Inc.
PO Box 1503
New York, NY 10021
Phone: (516)535-6811
Subject(s): Crafts, Models, Hobbies, and Contests
Circ: 50,000

**Food Engineering (North American Edition)  (27670)**
Business News Publishing
c/o Joyce Fassl, Editor in Chief,
Food Engineering
901 S. Bolmar St. Ste. P
West Chester, PA 19382
Subject(s): Beverages, Brewing, and Bottling; Food and Grocery Trade
Circ: (Paid)662
(Non-paid)50,000

**IEEE Communications Magazine  (21802)**
Institute of Electrical and Electronics Engineers Inc.
3 Park Ave., 17th Fl.
New York, NY 10016
Phone: (212)705-8900
Fax: (212)705-8999
Subject(s): Telecommunications; Computers
Circ: (Non-paid)1,000
(Paid)50,000

**Microwave Journal  (14719)**
Horizon House Publications Inc.
685 Canton St.
Norwood, MA 02062
Phone: (781)769-9750
Fax: (781)769-9884
Subject(s): Electronics Engineering
Circ: (Combined)50,000

**NJ Good Times  (19878)**
Mature Market Net
1830 Hwy. 9
Toms River, NJ 08755
Phone: (732)505-9700
Subject(s): Senior Citizens' Interests
Circ: (Non-paid)50,000

**The Reporter  (22306)**
Women's American ORT
250 Park Ave. S, Ste. 600
New York, NY 10003
Phone: (212)505-7700
Fax: (212)674-3057
Subject(s): Jewish Publications; Women's Interests
Circ: (Paid)‡50,000

**School Selection Guide  (19000)**
Baker & Taylor
1120 Rte. 22 E
Bridgewater, NJ 08807
Phone: (908)541-7000
Subject(s): Book Trade and Author News; Education
Circ: (Non-paid)50,000

**Today's Facility Manager  (19877)**
Group C Communications Inc.
44 Apple Street
Ste. 3
Tinton Falls, NJ 07724
Phone: (732)842-7433
Fax: (732)758-6634
Subject(s): Architecture; Paint and Wallcoverings
Circ: (Controlled)❏50,000

**New Jersey Realtor Magazine  (19064)**
New Jersey Association of Realtors
295 Pierson Ave.
PO Box 2098
Edison, NJ 08818-3118
Phone: (732)494-5616
Fax: (732)494-4723
Subject(s): Real Estate
Circ: (Non-paid)49,000

**Pittsburgh Magazine  (27390)**
WQED Pittsburgh
4802 5th Ave.
Pittsburgh, PA 15213
Phone: (412)622-1360
Fax: (412)622-7066
Subject(s): Local, State, and Regional Publications
Circ: (Paid)48,575

**Alfred Hitchcock's Mystery Magazine  (21287)**
Dell Magazines
475 Park Ave. S, 11th Fl.
New York, NY 10016
Phone: (212)686-7188
Fax: (212)686-7414
Subject(s): Science Fiction, Mystery, Adventure, and Romance
Circ: (Paid)48,424

**IEEE Potentials  (21804)**
Institute of Electrical and Electronics Engineers Inc.
3 Park Ave., 17th Fl.
New York, NY 10016
Phone: (212)705-8900
Fax: (212)705-8999
Subject(s): Computers; Electrical Engineering
Circ: (Non-paid)866
(Paid)48,252

**Food Manufacturing  (21701)**
Reed Business Information
360 Park Avenue South
New York, NY 10010
Phone: (646)746-6400
Subject(s): Food and Grocery Trade
Circ: (Controlled)‡48,000

**Metropolis Magazine  (22079)**
Bellerophon Publications Inc.
61 W. 23rd St., 4th Fl.
New York, NY 10010
Phone: (212)627-9977
Fax: (212)627-9988
Subject(s): Architecture
Circ: (Combined)48,000

**Military & Aerospace Electronics  (18909)**
PennWell Corp.
98 Spit Brook Rd.
Nashua, NH 00062-5737
Phone: (603)891-0123
Fax: (603)891-0574
Subject(s): Electronics Engineering; Military and Navy
Circ: (Paid)200
(Controlled)48,000

**Columbia College Today  (21510)**
475 Riverside Dr., Ste 917
New York, NY 10115-0998
Phone: (212)870-2752
Fax: (212)870-2747
Subject(s): College Publications
Circ: (Controlled)47,000

**Film Comment  (21687)**
Film Society of Lincoln Center
70 Lincoln Center Plz.
New York, NY 10023
Phone: (212)875-5610
Fax: (212)875-5636
Subject(s): Motion Pictures
Circ: ‡47,000

**High Performance Pontiac  (19775)**
Primedia
299 Market St.
Saddle Brook, NJ 07663-5312
Phone: (201)712-9300
Fax: (201)712-9899
Subject(s): Automotive (Consumer)
Circ: ‡47,000

**Soul Magazine  (19933)**
The Blue Army of Our Lady of Fatima
674 Mountain View Rd.
PO Box 976
Washington, NJ 07882
Phone: (908)213-2223
Fax: (908)213-2263
Subject(s): Religious Publications
Circ: 47,000

**Pharmacy Practice News  (22231)**
The McMahon Publishing Group
545 W 45th St., 8th Fl.
New York, NY 10036
Phone: (212)957-5300
Fax: (212)957-7230
Subject(s): Drugs and Pharmaceuticals
Circ: (Paid)‡189
(Non-paid)‡46,827

**Journal of Speech and Hearing Research  (20817)**
American Speech-Language-Hearing Association
Dale Evan Metz
Department of Communicative Disorders & Sciences
SUNY at Geneseo
1 College Circle
Geneseo, NY 14454
Phone: (716)245-5470
Fax: (716)245-5435
Subject(s): Hearing and Speech; Communications
Circ: ‡46,805

**Plastics Technology  (22238)**
Gardner Publications Inc.
1372 Broadway, Ste. 1403
New York, NY 10018
Phone: (646)827-4859
Fax: (646)827-4859
Subject(s): Machinery and Equipment; Commerce and Industry; Plastic and Composition Materials
Circ: (Non-paid)⊕3,728
(Paid)⊕46,530

**Extended Care Product News  (26658)**
Health Management Publications Inc.
83 General Warren Blvd. Ste. 100
Malvern, PA 19355-1245
Phone: (610)560-0500
Fax: (610)560-0501
Subject(s): Health and Healthcare
Circ: (Controlled)‡46,464

**National Home Channel News  (22125)**
Lebhar-Friedman Inc.
425 Park Ave.
New York, NY 10022
Phone: (212)756-5000
Fax: (212)756-5295
Subject(s): Building Materials, Concrete, Brick, and Tile
Circ: (Paid)5,665
(Non-paid)46,210

**Consulting-Specifying Engineer  (21545)**
Reed Business Information
360 Park Ave. S.
New York, NY 10014
Phone: (646)746-6400
Fax: (646)746-6734
Subject(s): Air Conditioning and Refrigeration; Electrical Engineering; Plumbing and Heating
Circ: (Free)‡46,154

**Bucknell World  (26641)**
Bucknell University
Judd House
Lewisburg, PA 17837
Phone: (570)577-3260
Fax: (570)577-3683
Subject(s): College Publications
Circ: (Non-paid)‡46,000

**Manufacturer's Mart  (27953)**
Manufacturers' Mart Publications
16 High St.
Westerly, RI 02891
Phone: (401)348-0797
Fax: (401)348-0799
Subject(s): Commerce and Industry
Circ: (Non-paid)46,000

**Treasury and Risk Management Magazine  (22482)**
Treasury & Risk Management
475 Park Ave. South 3300
New York, NY 10016
Phone: (212)557-7480
Fax: (212)557-7653
Subject(s): Economics; Banking, Finance, and Investments; Commerce and Industry
Circ: 46,000

**Parents Express** (26381)
Montgomery Newspapers
290 Commerce Dr.
Fort Washington, PA 19034
Phone: (215)628-8330
Fax: (215)648-3630
**Subject(s):** Parenting
**Circ:** (Combined)❏45,155

**Hospital Therapy** (19664)
Quadrant HealthCom Inc.
7 Century Dr. Ste 302
Parsippany, NJ 07054
Phone: (973)701-8900
Fax: (973)206-9251
**Subject(s):** Hospitals and Healthcare Institutions; Health and Healthcare
**Circ:** (Non-paid)‡45,080

**Scientific Computing & Instrumentation** (19563)
Reed Business Information
301 Gibraltar Dr.
PO Box 650
Morris Plains, NJ 07950-0650
Phone: (973)292-5100
Fax: (973)539-3476
**Subject(s):** Computers; Automation
**Circ:** (Non-paid)‡45,027

**Deaf Life** (22814)
MSM Productions Ltd.
1095 Meigs St.
Rochester, NY 14620
Fax: (716)442-6371
**Subject(s):** Handicapped; Hearing and Speech
**Circ:** (Paid)45,000

**Making It! Careers Newsmagazine** (20860)
Workstyles Inc.
5 Rose Ave.
Great Neck, NY 11021
Phone: (516)829-8829
**Subject(s):** Employment and Human Resources; Education
**Circ:** (Paid)5,000
       (Non-paid)45,000

**Midrange Enterprise** (13458)
Manufacturing Publishing
669 Hale St.
Beverly, MA 01915-2166
Phone: (508)922-1075
Fax: (508)921-1255
**Subject(s):** Business; Commerce and Industry
**Circ:** (Combined)45,000

**MuscleCars** (19777)
Primedia
299 Market St.
Saddle Brook, NJ 07663-5312
Phone: (201)712-9300
Fax: (201)712-9899
**Subject(s):** Automotive (Consumer)
**Circ:** ‡45,000

**National Missing Persons Report** (19142)
Search Reports Inc.
345 Blvd.
Hasbrouck Heights, NJ 07604
Phone: (201)288-4445
Fax: (201)288-8055
**Subject(s):** Police, Penology, and Penal Institutions
**Circ:** (Controlled)‡45,000

**Renninger's ANTIQUE GUIDE** (26594)
PO Box 495
Lafayette Hill, PA 19444
Phone: (610)828-4614
Fax: (610)834-1599
**Subject(s):** Antiques; Collecting
**Circ:** (Paid)‡5,000
       (Non-paid)‡45,000

**ADVANCE for Respiratory Care Practitioners** (26584)
Merion Publications Inc.
2900 Horizon Dr.
King of Prussia, PA 19406
Phone: (610)278-1400
Fax: (610)278-1425
**Subject(s):** Medicine and Surgery
**Circ:** (Controlled)44,800

**Fly Tyer** (30838)
Abenaki Publishers Inc.
160 Benmont Ave.
PO Box 4100
Bennington, VT 05201-4100
Phone: (802)447-1518
Fax: (802)447-2471
**Subject(s):** (Hunting, Fishing, and Game Management)
**Circ:** (Paid)44,460

**Converting Magazine** (21551)
Reed Business Information
360 Park Ave. S.
New York, NY 10014
Phone: (646)746-6400
Fax: (646)746-6734
**Subject(s):** Packaging
**Circ:** (Controlled)‡44,414

**Solid State Technology** (18914)
PennWell Corp.
98 Spit Brook Rd.
Nashua, NH 03062-5737
Phone: (603)891-0123
Fax: (603)891-0574
**Subject(s):** Electronics Engineering
**Circ:** (Non-paid)‡44,050

**American Clinical Laboratory** (5002)
International Scientific Communications Inc.
30 Controls Dr.
PO Box 870
Shelton, CT 06484-0870
Phone: (203)926-9300
Fax: (203)926-9310
**Subject(s):** Medicine and Surgery
**Circ:** (Non-paid)‡43,567

**Risk & Insurance** (26517)
LRP Publications
c/o Jack Roberts, Editor-in-Chief
Dept. 635, PO Box 980, Dresher Rd.
Ste. 500
Horsham, PA 19044-0980
Phone: (215)784-0910
Fax: (215)784-0275
**Subject(s):** Insurance
**Circ:** (Paid)3,141
       (Controlled)43,527

**Business Facilities** (19876)
Group C Communications Inc.
44 Apple St.
Ste. 3
Tinton Falls, NJ 07724
Phone: (732)842-7433
Fax: (732)758-6634
**Subject(s):** Commerce and Industry; Real Estate
**Circ:** (Free)43,500

**SC Magazine** (22341)
West Coast Publishing Inc.
114 W. 26th St. 3rd Floor
New York, NY 10001
Phone: (646)638-6006
Fax: (646)638-6110
**Subject(s):** Computers; Automation; Business
**Circ:** (Controlled)43,100

**Wireless Design and Development** (19565)
Reed Business Information
301 Gibraltar Dr.
PO Box 650
Morris Plains, NJ 07950-0650
Phone: (973)292-5100
Fax: (973)539-3476
**Subject(s):** Telecommunications
**Circ:** 43,035

**AudioVideo International** (21373)
275 Madison Ave.
New York, NY 10016
Phone: (212)682-3755
Fax: (212)682-2730
**Subject(s):** Radio, Television, Cable, and Video
**Circ:** (Non-paid)‡43,000

**Ocean Navigator** (12564)
Navigator Publishing L.L.C.
PO Box 569
Portland, ME 04112-0569
Phone: (207)772-2879
Fax: (207)772-2879
**Subject(s):** (Boating and Yachting)
**Circ:** (Non-paid)‡2,000
       (Paid)‡43,000

**Chain Drug Review** (21468)
Racher Press Inc.
220 5th Ave.
New York, NY 10001
Phone: (212)213-6000
Fax: (212)725-3691
**Subject(s):** Drugs and Pharmaceuticals
**Circ:** (Paid)902
       (Non-paid)42,898

**Crain's New York Business** (21566)
Crain Communications Inc.
711 3rd Ave., 3rd Fl.
New York, NY 10017-4036
Phone: (212)210-0100
Fax: (212)210-0244
**Subject(s):** Business; Local, State, and Regional Publications
**Circ:** (Non-paid)★21,574
       (Paid)★42,420

**The Bargain News** (5059)
Bargain News L.L.C.
PO Box 317
Trumbull, CT 06611-0317
Phone: (203)377-3000
**Subject(s):** General Merchandise; Automotive (Consumer)
**Circ:** (Paid)42,000

**Customer Support Management** (5031)
Primedia Business
11 River Bend Dr. S.
PO Box 4949
Stamford, CT 06907-0949
Phone: (203)358-9900
Fax: (203)358-5811
**Subject(s):** Business; Service Industries
**Circ:** (Combined)42,000

**Electronic Packaging & Production** (21638)
Reed Business Information
360 Park Ave. S.
New York, NY 10014
Phone: (646)746-6400
Fax: (646)746-6734
**Subject(s):** Electronics Engineering
**Circ:** (Controlled)‡42,000

**North Shore Homes** (22935)
Times Beacon Record Newspapers
Box 707
Setauket, NY 11733
Phone: (631)751-7744
Fax: (631)751-4165
**Subject(s):** Real Estate; Home and Garden
**Circ:** (Non-paid)‡42,000

**Vermont Magazine** (30901)
PO Box 800
31 A Jon Gram Court
Middlebury, VT 05753-0800
Phone: (802)388-8480
Fax: (802)388-8485
**Subject(s):** Local, State, and Regional Publications
**Circ:** 42,000

**Souvenirs, Gifts, & Novelties Magazine** (26126)
Kane Communications Inc.
10 E Athens Ave., Ste. 208
Ardmore, PA 19003
Phone: (610)645-6940
Fax: (610)645-6943
**Subject(s):** Gifts, Toys, and Novelties
**Circ:** (Controlled)‡41,871

**Convenience Store DECISIONS** (26158)
Penton Media Inc.
Two Greenwood Sq., Ste. 410, 3331 St. Rd.
Bensalem, PA 19020
Phone: (215)245-4555
Fax: (215)245-4060
**Subject(s):** Management and Administration; Food and Grocery Trade
**Circ:** ‡41,716

**American Police Beat** (APB) (13648)
American Police Beat
1 Brattle Sq., 4th Fl.
Cambridge, MA 02138
Phone: (617)491-8878
Fax: (617)354-6515

Subject(s): Police, Penology, and Penal Institutions
Circ: (Paid)★10,976
(Non-paid)★41,564

**Industrial Distribution (14288)**
Reed Business Information
275 Washington St.
Newton, MA 02458
Subject(s): Commerce and Industry
Circ: (Non-paid)‡41,500

**Dartmouth Alumni Magazine (18830)**
Dartmouth College Library
Rm. 115 Baker
Hanover, NH 03755
Phone: (603)646-2560
Fax: (603)646-3702
Subject(s): College Publications
Circ: (Non-paid)‡2,727
(Paid)‡41,251

**ADVANCE for Nurse Practitioners (26578)**
Merion Publications Inc.
2900 Horizon Dr.
King of Prussia, PA 19406
Phone: (610)278-1400
Fax: (610)278-1425
Subject(s): Nursing
Circ: (Controlled)‡41,000

**Berklee Today (13479)**
Berklee College of Music
1140 Boylston St.
Boston, MA 02215-3693
Phone: (617)747-2325
Fax: (617)247-8788
Subject(s): Music and Musical Instruments
Circ: (Non-paid)‡41,000

**Dairy World (14249)**
IBA Inc.
19 River St.
Millbury, MA 01527
Phone: (508)865-2507
Fax: (508)865-5891
Subject(s): Dairying
Circ: (Non-paid)‡40,999

**Chemical Engineering Progress (21478)**
American Institute of Chemical Engineers
3 Park Ave.
New York, NY 10016-5991
Phone: (212)591-8100
Fax: (212)591-8888
Subject(s): Chemistry, Chemicals, and Chemical Engineering; Engineering (Various branches)
Circ: (Paid)40,850

**Adweek Western Edition (21273)**
VNU Business Media USA
770 Broadway
New York, NY 10003
Phone: (646)654-5000
Subject(s): Advertising and Marketing
Circ: (Paid)‡40,441

**Pensions & Investments (22225)**
Crain Communications Inc.
711 3rd Ave., 3rd Fl.
New York, NY 10017-4036
Phone: (212)210-0100
Fax: (212)210-0244
Subject(s): Banking, Finance, and Investments
Circ: (Paid)9,555
(Non-paid)40,231

**Supermarket News (22433)**
Fairchild Publications Inc.
7 W 34th St.
New York, NY 10001
Phone: (212)630-4000
Fax: (212)630-3555
Subject(s): Food and Grocery Trade
Circ: (Paid)40,234

**EQ (22727)**
United Entertainment Media
6 Manhasset Ave.
Port Washington, NY 11050
Phone: (516)944-5940
Fax: (516)767-1745
Subject(s): Electronics Engineering
Circ: (Paid)13,197
(Non-paid)40,095

**Incentive (21814)**
VNU Business Media
770 Broadway
New York, NY 10003-9595
Phone: (646)654-4500
Fax: (646)654-7473
Subject(s): Business
Circ: (Non-paid)40,050

**Food Manufacturing (19554)**
Reed Business Information
301 Gibraltar Dr.
PO Box 650
Morris Plains, NJ 07950
Phone: (973)292-5100
Fax: (973)539-3476
Subject(s): Food and Grocery Trade; Food Production
Circ: 40,043

**Videography (22517)**
United Entertainment Media
460 Park Ave. S., 9th Fl.
New York, NY 10016
Phone: (212)378-0400
Fax: (212)378-2160
Subject(s): Radio, Television, Cable, and Video
Circ: (Controlled)‡40,040

**National Fisherman (12562)**
PO Box 7438
Portland, ME 04112
Phone: (207)842-5608
Fax: (207)842-5609
Subject(s): Fish and Commercial Fisheries; Boats and Marine
Circ: (Paid)40,034

**Powder/ Bulk Solids (19561)**
Reed Business Information
301 Gibraltar Dr.
PO Box 650
Morris Plains, NJ 07950-0650
Phone: (973)292-5100
Fax: (973)539-3476
Subject(s): Chemistry, Chemicals, and Chemical Engineering
Circ: (Non-paid)‡40,020

**American Craft (21304)**
American Craft Council
72 Spring St., 6th Fl.
New York, NY 10012-4019
Phone: (212)274-0630
Fax: (212)274-0650
Subject(s): Art and Art History
Circ: (Paid)40,000

**Antique Automobile (26483)**
Antique Automobile Club of America
501 W Governor Rd.
PO Box 417
Hershey, PA 17033-0417
Phone: (717)534-1910
Fax: (717)534-9101
Subject(s): Art; Automotive (Consumer)
Circ: ‡40,000

**Area Development Magazine (23162)**
Halcyon Business Publications Inc.
400 Post Ave.
Westbury, NY 11590
Phone: (516)338-0900
Fax: (516)338-0100
Subject(s): Commerce and Industry
Circ: (Controlled)‡40,000

**Art Now Gallery Guide–New York Edition (19042)**
Art Now Inc.
97 Grayrock Rd.
PO Box 5541
Clinton, NJ 08809-5541
Phone: (908)638-5255
Fax: (908)638-8737
Subject(s): Art
Circ: (Non-paid)40,000

**The Bond Buyer (21417)**
One State St. Plaza., 27th Fl.
New York, NY 10004
Phone: (212)803-8200
Fax: (212)843-9614
Subject(s): Banking, Finance, and Investments
Circ: 40,000

**Business Solutions (26344)**
Corry Publishing Inc.
5539 Peach St.
Erie, PA 16509
Phone: (814)868-9935
Fax: (814)864-2037
Subject(s): Computers
Circ: (Non-paid)‡40,000

**CPI Purchasing (14853)**
Reed Business Information
225 Wyman St.
Waltham, MA 02451-1216
Subject(s): Chemistry, Chemicals, and Chemical Engineering
Circ: (Non-paid)‡40,007

**ENT (26373)**
101communications L.L.C.
1300 Virginia Dr., Ste. 401
Fort Washington, PA 19034
Phone: (215)643-8050
Fax: (215)643-2143
Subject(s): Computers
Circ: 40,000

**Exceptional Parent (19767)**
Psy-Ed Corp.
65 E. Rte. 4
River Edge, NJ 07661
Phone: (201)489-4111
Fax: (201)489-0074
Subject(s): Handicapped
Circ: (Paid)‡35,000
(Controlled)‡40,000

**EXEC (26188)**
Unisys Corp.
Unisys Way
Blue Bell, PA 19424
Phone: (215)986-6873
Fax: (215)986-2812
Subject(s): Business; Computers
Circ: (Controlled)40,000

**Imprint (20513)**
National Student Nurses' Association Inc.
45 Main St. suite 606
Brooklyn, NY 11201
Phone: (718)210-0705
Fax: (718)210-7010
Subject(s): Nursing
Circ: 40,000

**New York Runner (22166)**
New York Road Runners
9 E 89th St.
New York, NY 10128
Phone: (212)860-4455
Fax: (212)423-0879
Subject(s): (Running)
Circ: ‡40,000

**Parabola (22210)**
Society for the Study of Myth & Tradition
135 E 15th St.
New York, NY 10003
Phone: (212)505-9037
Fax: (212)979-7325
Subject(s): Literature and Literary Reviews
Circ: (Non-paid)520
(Paid)40,000

**The Practical Accountant (22259)**
Thomson Financial
195 Broadway
New York, NY 10007
Phone: (646)822-2000
Fax: (646)822-3230
Subject(s): Accountants and Accounting
Circ: ‡40,000

**RNA (22322)**
Cambridge University Press
40 W. 20th St.
New York, NY 10011-4211
Phone: (212)924-3900
Fax: (212)691-3239
Subject(s): Science (General)
Circ: 40,000

**Russian Life (30904)**
Rich Frontier Pub. Co
PO Box 567
Montpelier, VT 05601-0567
Phone: (802)223-4955

Fax: (802)223-6105
**Subject(s):** General Editorial
**Circ:** 40,000

**Smith Alumnae Quarterly (14325)**
Alumnae Association of Smith College
Smith Alumnae Quarterly
Alumnae House, 33 Elm St.
Northampton, MA 01063
Phone: (413)585-2031
Fax: (413)585-2015
**Subject(s):** College Publications
**Circ:** ‡40,000

**U.S. Tech (27622)**
Mid-Atlantic Tech Publications Inc.
PO Box 957
Rte. 23 & Davis Rd. No.2-215
Valley Forge, PA 19482-0957
Phone: (610)783-6100
Fax: (610)783-0317
**Subject(s):** Electronics Engineering; Engineering (Various branches)
**Circ:** 40,000

**What Is Enlightenment? (13852)**
Moksha Press
PO Box 2360
Lenox, MA 01240
Phone: (413)637-6000
Fax: (413)637-6015
**Subject(s):** Religious Publications
**Circ:** (Paid)40,000

**Zajednicar (27414)**
Croatian Fraternal Union
100 Delaney Dr.
Pittsburgh, PA 15235-5416
Phone: (412)351-3909
**Subject(s):** Croatian; Unclassified Fraternal; Ethnic Publications
**Circ:** (Non-paid)40,000

**Bulletin of the American Physical Society (21151)**
American Institute of Physics
2 Huntington Quadrangle, Ste. 1NO1
Melville, NY 11747-4502
Phone: (516)576-2200
Fax: (516)349-7669
**Subject(s):** Indexes, Abstracts, Reports, Proceedings, and Bibliographies; Physics
**Circ:** ‡39,757

**O Guage Railroading (26754)**
Myron J. Biggar Group Inc.
PO Box 239
65 S Broad St.
Nazareth, PA 18064-0239
Phone: (610)759-0406
Fax: (610)759-0223
**Subject(s):** Crafts, Models, Hobbies, and Contests
**Circ:** (Non-paid)25
(Paid)39,000

**Watercolor (22531)**
VNU Business Media USA
770 Broadway
New York, NY 10003
Phone: (646)654-5000
**Subject(s):** Art and Art History
**Circ:** 38,868

**Travel Trade (22481)**
15 W 44th St.
New York, NY 10036
Phone: (212)730-6600
Fax: (212)730-7137
**Subject(s):** Travel and Tourism
**Circ:** (Non-paid)5,974
(Paid)38,727

**APPAREL Merchandising (21347)**
Lebhar-Friedman Inc.
425 Park Ave.
New York, NY 10022
Phone: (212)756-5000
Fax: (212)756-5295
**Subject(s):** Clothing
**Circ:** (Non-paid)‡38,650

**U.S. Banker (22505)**
Thomson Financial
195 Broadway
New York, NY 10007
Phone: (646)822-2000

Fax: (646)822-3230
**Subject(s):** Banking, Finance, and Investments
**Circ:** (Paid)1,679
(Controlled)38,621

**Kitchen and Bath Business (22013)**
VNU Business Media
770 Broadway
New York, NY 10003
Phone: (646)654-5000
Fax: (646)654-5005
**Subject(s):** Construction, Contracting, Building, and Excavating
**Circ:** (Paid)9,740
(Controlled)38,532

**Films in Review (23117)**
Then and There Media L.L.C.
PO Box 970
Wantagh, NY 11793
**Subject(s):** Motion Pictures
**Circ:** 38,500

**Anesthesiology (26825)**
Lippincott Williams & Wilkins
530 Walnut St.
Philadelphia, PA 19106-3261
Phone: (215)521-8300
Fax: (215)521-8902
**Subject(s):** Medicine and Surgery
**Circ:** (Combined)‡38,453

**CUTIS (19017)**
Quadrant Healthcom
26 Main St., 2nd Fl.
Chatham, NJ 07928
Phone: (973)701-2719
Fax: (973)701-8894
**Subject(s):** Medicine and Surgery; Health and Healthcare
**Circ:** △38,361

**Central PA (26436)**
Central P.A. Magazine
1982 Locust Ln.
PO Box 2954
Harrisburg, PA 17105-2954
Phone: (717)221-2800
Fax: (717)221-2630
**Subject(s):** Local, State, and Regional Publications; Lifestyle
**Circ:** (Paid)38,350

**General Surgery & Laparoscopy News (21731)**
The McMahon Publishing Group
545 W 45th St., 8th Fl.
New York, NY 10036
Phone: (212)957-5300
Fax: (212)957-7230
**Subject(s):** Medicine and Surgery
**Circ:** (Controlled)‡38,303

**Worcester Magazine (14948)**
Worcester Business Journal
172 Shrewsbury St.
Worcester, MA 01604-4636
Phone: (508)755-8004
Fax: (508)755-8860
**Subject(s):** Local, State, and Regional Publications
**Circ:** (Paid)42
(Non-paid)38,182

**School Library Journal (22350)**
Reed Business Information
360 Park Ave. S.
New York, NY 10010
Phone: (646)746-6400
Fax: (646)746-6734
**Subject(s):** Library and Information Science; Education
**Circ:** (Paid)38,021

**International Laboratory (5009)**
International Scientific Communications Inc.
30 Controls Dr.
PO Box 870
Shelton, CT 06484-0870
Phone: (203)926-9300
Fax: (203)926-9310
**Subject(s):** Laboratory Research (Scientific and Medical)
**Circ:** (Paid)86
(Non-paid)37,967

**Physicians News Digest (26753)**
Physicians News Digest Inc.
230 Windsor Ave.
Narberth, PA 19072
Phone: (610)668-1040

Fax: (610)668-9177
**Subject(s):** Medicine and Surgery; Management and Administration
**Circ:** (Paid)‡20
(Controlled)‡37,736

**Agricultura de las Americas (20853)**
Keller International Publishing L.L.C.
150 Great Neck Rd.
Great Neck, NY 11021
Phone: (516)829-9210
Fax: (516)829-5414
**Subject(s):** General Agriculture; Spanish; Hispanic Publications
**Circ:** (Non-paid)37,318

**Genesee Valley Parent Magazine (22702)**
1 Grove St., Ste. 204
Pittsford, NY 14534
Phone: (585)264-9955
Fax: (716)264-0647
**Subject(s):** Parenting; Local, State, and Regional Publications
**Circ:** (Combined)37,060

**American Baptists in Mission (27620)**
American Baptist Churches, USA
PO Box 851
Valley Forge, PA 19482-0851
Phone: (610)768-2000
Fax: (610)768-2320
**Subject(s):** Religious Publications
**Circ:** 37,000

**Communication Systems Design (21099)**
CMP Media L.L.C.
600 Community Dr.
Manhasset, NY 11030
Phone: (516)562-5000
Fax: (516)562-5995
**Subject(s):** Telecommunications
**Circ:** 37,000

**Lightwave (18906)**
PennWell Corp.
98 Spit Brook Rd.
Nashua, NH 03062-5737
Phone: (603)891-0123
Fax: (603)891-0574
**Subject(s):** Electronics Engineering
**Circ:** 37,000

**PowerBuilder Developer's Journal (19542)**
SYS-CON Media
135 Chestnut Ridge Rd.
Montvale, NJ 07645
Phone: (201)802-3000
Fax: (201)782-9601
**Subject(s):** Computers; Automation
**Circ:** (Combined)37,000

**Rider University (19452)**
2083 Lawrenceville Rd.
Lawrenceville, NJ 08648
Phone: (609)896-5000
Fax: (609)895-5440
**Subject(s):** College Publications
**Circ:** (Non-paid)‡37,000

**Cleaning and Maintenance Management Magazine (21047)**
Cleaning Management Institute
13 Century Hill Dr.
Latham, NY 12110-2197
Phone: (518)783-1281
Fax: (518)783-1386
**Subject(s):** Building Management and Maintenance
**Circ:** (Paid)6,472
(Non-paid)36,936

**Corporate Meetings & Incentives (14825)**
Primedia Business Magazines & Media
c/o Barbara Scofidio
132 Great Rd., Ste. 120
Stow, MA 01775-1189
**Subject(s):** Conventions, Meetings, and Trade Fairs; Travel and Tourism
**Circ:** (Controlled)‡36,776

**Direct (5032)**
Primedia Business
11 River Bend Dr. S.
PO Box 4949
Stamford, CT 06907-0949
Phone: (203)358-9900

Fax: (203)358-5811
**Subject(s):** Advertising and Marketing; Business
**Circ:** (Combined)36,582

**Muscle & Nerve (19341)**
John Wiley and Sons Inc.
111 River St.
Hoboken, NJ 07030-5774
Phone: (201)748-6000
Fax: (201)748-6088
**Subject(s):** Medicine and Surgery
**Circ:** 36,400

**Institutional Investor (International Edition) (21825)**
Aspen Publishers
1185 Ave. of the Americas
New York, NY 10036
Phone: (212)730-4002
Fax: (212)597-0338
**Subject(s):** Banking, Finance, and Investments
**Circ:** (Non-paid)36,394

**IE Magazine (5101)**
Cyberactive Media Group Inc.
64 Danbury Rd., Ste. 500
Wilton, CT 06897
Phone: (203)761-6167
Fax: (203)761-6184
**Subject(s):** Computers; Radio, Television, Cable, and Video
**Circ:** (Controlled)‡36,000

**Le Canado-Americain (18870)**
Association Canado-Americaine
52 Concord St.
PO Box 989
Manchester, NH 03101-1806
Phone: (603)625-8577
**Subject(s):** French; Unclassified Fraternal; International Affairs
**Circ:** (Controlled)‡1,333
(Paid)‡36,000

**Religion Teacher's Journal (4868)**
Twenty-Third Publications, Bayard
185 Willow St.
PO Box 180
Mystic, CT 06355
Phone: (860)536-2611
Fax: (800)572-0788
**Subject(s):** Religious Publications
**Circ:** (Paid)36,000

**The Journal of Bone and Joint Surgery (14263)**
20 Pickering St.
Needham, MA 02492
Phone: (781)449-9780
Fax: (781)449-9742
**Subject(s):** Medicine and Surgery
**Circ:** (Non-paid)398
(Paid)‡35,842

**NordicReach (4876)**
Swedish News
PO Box 1710
New Canaan, CT 06840
Phone: (203)299-0380
**Subject(s):** Travel and Tourism; Intercultural Interests
**Circ:** (Paid)35,640

**Amit (21329)**
817 Broadway
New York, NY 10003
Phone: (212)477-4720
Fax: (212)353-2312
**Subject(s):** Jewish Publications; Religious Publications
**Circ:** 35,500

**Target Marketing (27279)**
North American Publishing Co.
401 N. Broad St., 5th Fl.
Philadelphia, PA 19108
Phone: (215)238-5482
Fax: (215)238-5412
**Subject(s):** Advertising and Marketing
**Circ:** (Controlled)‡35,469

**Medical Design Technology (19559)**
Reed Business Information
301 Gibralter Dr.
PO Box 650
Morris Plains, NJ 07950
Phone: (973)292-5100
Fax: (973)539-3476

**Subject(s):** Medicine and Surgery; Business; Engineering (Various branches)
**Circ:** (Non-paid)35,450

**Scholastic Coach & Athletic Director (22345)**
Scholastic Library Publishing Inc.
c/o Bruce Weber, Publisher
557 Broadway
New York, NY 10012
Phone: (212)343-6100
**Subject(s):** Physical Education and Athletics
**Circ:** (Non-paid)14,935
(Paid)35,360

**Ferver (19515)**
Cuizine Enterprises
6 Birchwood Dr.
Medford, NJ 08055
Phone: (609)654-6094
Fax: (609)654-6092
**Subject(s):** Food and Cooking; Local, State, and Regional Publications
**Circ:** (Controlled)35,350

**CleanRooms (18894)**
PennWell Corp.
98 Spit Brook Rd.
Nashua, NH 03062-5737
Phone: (603)891-0123
Fax: (603)891-0574
**Subject(s):** Natural History and Nature Study
**Circ:** (Controlled)△35,156

**Leaders Magazine (22030)**
59 E 54th St.
New York, NY 10022
Phone: (212)758-0740
Fax: (212)593-5194
**Subject(s):** Management and Administration; Business
**Circ:** (Non-paid)‡35,120

**The Antiquer (21343)**
PO Box 2054
New York, NY 10159-2054
Phone: (212)725-1106
Fax: (212)725-1107
**Subject(s):** Antiques; Collecting
**Circ:** (Controlled)35,000

**Fiber Optic Technology (21682)**
Reed Business Information
360 Park Avenue South
New York, NY 10010
Phone: (646)746-6400
**Subject(s):** Telecommunications
**Circ:** (Non-paid)‡35,000

**Flatiron Magazine (21697)**
101 W. 23rd St.
New York, NY 10010
Phone: (212)627-5400
Fax: (212)214-0443
**Subject(s):** Entertainment; Lifestyle
**Circ:** (Controlled)35,000

**IBM Systems Journal (20301)**
IBM Corp.
New Orchard Rd.
Armonk, NY 10504
Phone: (914)499-1900
Fax: (914)945-2018
**Subject(s):** Computers
**Circ:** (Combined)‡35,000

**JCC Circle (21855)**
Jewish Community Centers Association of North America
15 E 26th St.
New York, NY 10010-1579
Phone: (212)532-4949
Fax: (212)481-4174
**Subject(s):** Philanthropy and Humanitarianism; Jewish Publications
**Circ:** ‡35,000

**MAGNET (27124)**
Magnet Magazine Inc.
1218 Chestnut St., Ste. 508
Philadelphia, PA 19107
Phone: (215)413-8570
Fax: (215)413-8569
**Subject(s):** Music and Musical Instruments; Alternative and Underground
**Circ:** 35,000

**Medicina Y Cultura (4987)**
Mundo Medico USA Inc.
158 Danbury Rd., Ste. 8
Ridgefield, CT 06877-3200
Fax: (203)438-1057
**Subject(s):** Health and Healthcare
**Circ:** (Controlled)35,000

**Microwaves & RF Magazine (19654)**
Penton Technology and Lifestyle Media Inc.
45 Eisenhower Dr., 5th Fl.
Paramus, NJ 07652
Phone: (201)843-6511
Fax: (201)845-2482
**Subject(s):** Business
**Circ:** (Controlled)35,000

**New York Sportscene (22878)**
MMB Publishers
2090 Fifth Ave.
Ronkonkoma, NY 11779
Phone: (631)580-7772
Fax: (631)587-3725
**Subject(s):** (General Sports)
**Circ:** (Combined)35,000

**Pharmaceutical Technology (19415)**
Advanstar Communications
485 Rte. 1 S.
Building F, First Fl.
Iselin, NJ 08830
Phone: (732)596-0276
Fax: (732)596-0005
**Subject(s):** Drugs and Pharmaceuticals
**Circ:** (Paid)1,208
(Controlled)35,000

**Plan Sponsor (4777)**
Asset International Inc.
125 Greenwich Ave.
Greenwich, CT 06830
Phone: (203)629-5014
Fax: (203)629-5024
**Subject(s):** Banking, Finance, and Investments
**Circ:** (Non-paid)35,000

**Quarterly Guide (26505)**
The Himalayan Institute Press
630 Main St., Ste. 300
Honesdale, PA 18431
Phone: (570)253-5551
Fax: (570)647-1552
**Subject(s):** Health
**Circ:** (Non-paid)‡35,000

**Retail Merchandiser (22311)**
VNU Business Media USA
770 Broadway
New York, NY 10003
Phone: (646)654-5000
**Subject(s):** Business; Retail
**Circ:** (Controlled)‡35,000

**Simmons Review (13587)**
Simmons College
300 The Fenway
Boston, MA 02115
Phone: (617)521-2363
Fax: (617)521-3193
**Subject(s):** College Publications
**Circ:** (Non-paid)35,000

**TV & Film Extras (22496)**
The John King Network
244 Madison Ave., Ste. 393
New York, NY 10016
Phone: (212)969-8715
Fax: (212)969-8715
**Subject(s):** Entertainment; Drama and Theatre
**Circ:** 35,000

**Whole Earth (19057)**
PO Box 3000
Denville, NJ 07834
**Subject(s):** Literature and Literary Reviews
**Circ:** ‡35,000

**Young Israel Viewpoint (22568)**
National Council of Young Israel
3rd W 16th St.
New York, NY 10011
Phone: (212)929-1525
Fax: (212)727-9526

**Subject(s):** Jewish Publications
**Circ:** ‡35,000

**Anesthesiology News** (21334)
The McMahon Publishing Group
545 W 45th St., 8th Fl.
New York, NY 10036
Phone: (212)957-5300
Fax: (212)957-7230
**Subject(s):** Medicine and Surgery
**Circ:** (Combined)‡34,922

**Clinical Cardiology** (19475)
Clinical Cardiology Publishing Company Inc.
PO Box 832
Mahwah, NJ 07430-0832
Phone: (201)818-1010
Fax: (201)818-0086
**Subject(s):** Medicine and Surgery
**Circ:** (Paid)894
    (Non-paid)34,404

**HX Magazine** (21797)
Two Queens Inc.
230 W. 17th St., 8th Fl.
New York, NY 10011
Phone: (212)352-3535
**Subject(s):** Gay and Lesbian Interests
**Circ:** (Paid)200
    (Free)34,154

**Beverage World** (21398)
VNU Business Publications USA
770 Broadway
New York, NY 10003-9595
Phone: (646)654-7714
Fax: (646)654-7727
**Subject(s):** Beverages, Brewing, and Bottling
**Circ:** (Non-paid)‡34,000

**Circuit Cellar INK** (5064)
Circuit Cellar Inc.
4 Park St.
Vernon, CT 06066
Phone: (860)875-2199
Fax: (860)871-0411
**Subject(s):** Computers
**Circ:** (Non-paid)‡6,800
    (Paid)‡34,000

**Hospitality Product News** (21785)
Advanstar Communications
1 Park Ave.
New York, NY 10016
Phone: (212)951-6600
Fax: (212)951-6793
**Subject(s):** Hotels, Motels, Restaurants, and Clubs
**Circ:** (Non-paid)34,000

**The Nonprofit Times** (19666)
NPT Publishing Group Inc.
120 Littleton Rd., Ste.120
Parsippany, NJ 07054-1803
Phone: (973)394-1800
Fax: (973)394-2888
**Subject(s):** Philanthropy and Humanitarianism
**Circ:** (Paid)2,000
    (Non-paid)34,000

**University Business** (4966)
Professional Media Group L.L.C.
488 Main Ave.
Norwalk, CT 06851
Phone: (203)663-0100
Fax: (203)663-0149
**Subject(s):** Education
**Circ:** (Controlled)34,000

**The CPA Journal** (21565)
New York State Society of CPAs
3 Park Ave., 18th Fl.
New York, NY 10016-5991
**Subject(s):** Accountants and Accounting
**Circ:** (Paid)△33,548

**The Magazine of Fantasy & Science Fiction** (19327)
Spilogale Inc.
PO Box 3447
Hoboken, NJ 07030-1605
Phone: (201)876-2551
Fax: (201)876-2551
**Subject(s):** Science Fiction, Mystery, Adventure, and Romance
**Circ:** ‡33,500

**Optometric Management** (26380)
Boucher Communications Inc.
1300 Virginia Dr., Ste. 400
Fort Washington, PA 19034
Phone: (215)643-8000
Fax: (215)643-8099
**Subject(s):** Ophthalmology, Optometry, and Optics
**Circ:** (Non-paid)33,500

**Radcliffe Quarterly** (13702)
Radcliffe Institute for Advanced Study
10 Garden St.
Cambridge, MA 02138
Phone: (617)495-8601
Fax: (617)495-8422
**Subject(s):** College Publications
**Circ:** (Free)‡33,500

**Adweek/New England** (13464)
Adweek L.P.
100 Boylston St., Ste. 210
Boston, MA 02116
Phone: (617)482-9447
**Subject(s):** Advertising and Marketing
**Circ:** (Paid)‡33,396

**Chain Store Age** (21470)
Lebhar-Friedman Inc.
425 Park Ave.
New York, NY 10022-3556
Phone: (212)756-5209
Fax: (212)756-5209
**Subject(s):** Retail; Drugs and Pharmaceuticals; General Merchandise
**Circ:** (Paid)2,253
    (Non-paid)33,398

**Real Estate Forum** (22292)
Real Estate Media Inc.
520 Eighth Ave., 17th Fl.
New York, NY 10018
Phone: (212)929-6900
Fax: (212)929-7124
**Subject(s):** Real Estate
**Circ:** (Controlled)33,251

**Bullpen** (19889)
Babe Ruth League Inc.
PO Box 5000
Trenton, NJ 08638
Phone: (609)695-1434
Fax: (609)695-2505
**Subject(s):** (Baseball); Youths' Interests
**Circ:** (Controlled)‡33,000

**Hem/Onc Today** (19854)
SLACK Inc.
6900 Grove Rd.
Thorofare, NJ 08086-9447
Phone: (856)848-1000
Fax: (856)848-6091
**Subject(s):** Medicine and Surgery; Health and Healthcare
**Circ:** (Controlled)⊕**33,000**

**Lippincott's Hospital Pharmacy** (22038)
Lippincott Williams & Wilkins
345 Hudson St.
New York, NY 10017
Phone: (212)886-1387
Fax: (212)886-1209
**Subject(s):** Drugs and Pharmaceuticals
**Circ:** 33,000

**Maine Antique Digest** (12611)
911 Main St.
PO Box 1429
Waldoboro, ME 04572-1429
Phone: (207)832-7534
Fax: (207)832-7341
**Subject(s):** Art; Antiques
**Circ:** (Non-paid)‡1,500
    (Paid)‡33,000

**Psychiatric Annals** (19874)
SLACK Inc.
6900 Grove Rd.
Thorofare, NJ 08086-9447
Phone: (856)848-1000
Fax: (856)848-6091
**Subject(s):** Psychology and Psychiatry
**Circ:** (Controlled)‡33,000

**TWICE** (22497)
Reed Business Information
360 Park Ave. S.
New York, NY 10010
Phone: (646)746-6400
Fax: (646)746-6734
**Subject(s):** Radio, Television, Cable, and Video; Telecommunications
**Circ:** (Non-paid)‡33,000

**Flying Models** (19627)
Carstens Publications Inc.
PO Box 700
108 Phil Hardin Rd.
Newton, NJ 07860
Phone: (973)383-3355
Fax: (973)383-4064
**Subject(s):** Crafts, Models, Hobbies, and Contests
**Circ:** ‡32,869

**Publishers Weekly** (22281)
360 Park Ave. S.
New York, NY 10010
Phone: (646)746-6758
Fax: (646)746-6631
**Subject(s):** Book Trade and Author News; Journalism and Publishing
**Circ:** (Paid)32,863

**ComputerTalk for the Pharmacist** (26187)
ComputerTalk Associates Inc.
492 Norristown Rd., Ste. 160
Blue Bell, PA 19422-2355
Phone: (610)825-7686
Fax: (610)825-7641
**Subject(s):** Computers; Drugs and Pharmaceuticals
**Circ:** (Paid)400
    (Non-paid)32,500

**Chemical Engineering** (21477)
Chemical Week Associates
110 Williams St., 11th Fl.
New York, NY 10038
Phone: (212)621-4900
Fax: (212)621-4800
**Subject(s):** Chemistry, Chemicals, and Chemical Engineering; Engineering (Various branches)
**Circ:** (Paid)25,929
    (Non-paid)32,469

**PMLA** (22241)
Modern Language Association of America
26 Broadway, 3rd Fl.
New York, NY 10004-1789
Phone: (646)576-5000
Fax: (646)458-0030
**Subject(s):** Philology, Language, and Linguistics
**Circ:** ‡32,350

**Aerospace Engineering** (27641)
Society of Automotive Engineers Inc.
400 Commonwealth Dr.
Warrendale, PA 15096-0001
Phone: (724)776-4841
Fax: (724)776-4026
**Subject(s):** Aviation; Engineering (Various branches)
**Circ:** 32,238

**Plastics Engineering** (4652)
Society of Plastics Engineers
14 Fairfield Dr.
PO Box 403
Brookfield, CT 06804-0403
Phone: (203)775-0471
Fax: (203)775-8490
**Subject(s):** Engineering (Various branches); Plastic and Composition Materials
**Circ:** 32,035

**Applied Radiology** (19641)
Anderson Publishing Ltd.
1301 W Park Ave.
Ocean, NJ 07712
Phone: (732)695-0600
Fax: (732)695-9501
**Subject(s):** Radiology, Ultrasound, and Nuclear Medicine
**Circ:** (Paid)14
    (Controlled)32,000

**Babson Alumni Magazine** (13442)
Babson College
Nichols Hall
Babson Park, MA 02457
Phone: (781)239-5256
Fax: (781)239-5497

Subject(s): College Publications

Circ: (Controlled)32,000

**A Common Place (26089)**
Mennonite Central Committee
21 S. 12th St.
PO Box 500
Akron, PA 17501
Phone: (717)859-1151
Fax: (717)859-4910
Subject(s): Religious Publications

Circ: 32,000

**Contact Lens Spectrum (26372)**
Boucher Communications Inc.
1300 Virginia Dr., Ste. 400
Fort Washington, PA 19034
Phone: (215)643-8000
Fax: (215)643-8099
Subject(s): Ophthalmology, Optometry, and Optics

Circ: (Non-paid)‡32,000

**FIRST THINGS (21693)**
Institute on Religion & Public Life
156 5th Ave., Ste. 400
New York, NY 10010
Phone: (212)627-1985
Subject(s): Religious Publications; Social and Political Issues

Circ: ‡32,000

**Job Shop Technology (JST) (4980)**
Edwards Publishing Co.
16 Waterbury Rd.
PO Box 7193
Prospect, CT 06712
Phone: (203)758-4474
Fax: (203)758-4475
Subject(s): Commerce and Industry; Machinery and Equipment

Circ: (Controlled)‡32,000

**Soundings Trade Only (4686)**
Soundings Publications L.L.C.
10 Bokum Rd.
Essex, CT 06426
Phone: (860)767-3200
Fax: (860)767-0642
Subject(s): Boats and Marine

Circ: (Paid)1,098
(Free)32,007

**ADVANCE for Physician Assistants (26582)**
Merion Publications Inc.
2900 Horizon Dr.
King of Prussia, PA 19406
Phone: (610)278-1400
Fax: (610)278-1425
Subject(s): Nursing; Health and Healthcare; Medicine and Surgery

Circ: (Non-paid)‡31,900

**Across the Board (21261)**
The Conference Board Inc.
845 3rd Ave.
New York, NY 10022
Phone: (212)339-0345
Fax: (212)836-9740
Subject(s): Management and Administration

Circ: (Non-paid)‡600
(Paid)‡31,600

**Tourist Attractions & Parks Magazine (26127)**
Kane Communications Inc.
10 E Athens Ave., Ste. 208
Ardmore, PA 19003
Phone: (610)645-6940
Fax: (610)645-6943
Subject(s): Parks; Building Management and Maintenance

Circ: (Combined)‡31,388

**ABA Banking Journal (21250)**
Simmons-Boardman Publishing Corp.
345 Hudson St.
New York, NY 10014-4590
Phone: (212)620-7200
Fax: (212)633-1165
Subject(s): Banking, Finance, and Investments

Circ: 31,119

**Bulletin of the National Association of Watch and Clock Collectors (26255)**
National Association of Watch and Clock Collectors Inc.
514 Poplar St.
Columbia, PA 17512-2130
Phone: (717)684-5544

Subject(s): Crafts, Models, Hobbies, and Contests; Jewelry, Watches, and Clocks

Circ: ‡31,000

**Professional Mariner (12567)**
Navigator Publishing L.L.C.
58 Fore St.
Portland, ME 04101
Phone: (207)772-2466
Fax: (207)772-2879
Subject(s): Ships and Shipping

Circ: (Paid)‡31,000

**Maritime Reporter and Engineering News (22057)**
Maritime Activity Reports Inc.
118 E 25th St.
New York, NY 10010
Phone: (212)477-6700
Fax: (212)254-6271
Subject(s): Ships and Shipping

Circ: (Non-paid)‡30,822

**Fraternally Yours, Zenska Jednota (27625)**
First Catholic Slovak Ladies Association
Box 184
Vandergrift, PA 15690
Phone: (724)567-5224
Fax: (724)567-6237
Subject(s): Religious Publications; Slovak

Circ: (Controlled)‡30,800

**Archives of General Psychiatry (13452)**
American Medical Association
c/o Joseph T. Coyle, MD, Editor
McClean Hospital
115 Mill St
Belmont, MA 02478
Phone: (617)855-2170
Fax: (617)855-2579
Subject(s): Psychology and Psychiatry; Medicine and Surgery

Circ: (Combined)‡30,771

**Construction Equipment Guide-Northeast (26371)**
Construction Equipment Guide
470 Maryland Dr.
Fort Washington, PA 19034
Phone: (215)885-2900
Fax: (215)885-2910
Subject(s): Construction, Contracting, Building, and Excavating

Circ: (Paid)‡171
(Non-paid)‡30,585

**Facilities & Event Management (21676)**
Bedrock Communications
650 First Ave., 7th Fl.
New York, NY 10016
Phone: (212)532-4150
Fax: (212)213-6382
Subject(s): Business

Circ: (Controlled)30,582

**Post (22255)**
Post Pro Publishing Inc.
One Park Ave.
New York, NY 10016
Phone: (212)951-6600
Fax: (212)951-6793
Subject(s): Radio, Television, Cable, and Video

Circ: 30,550

**Wireless Systems Design (19659)**
Penton Technology and Lifestyle Media Inc.
45 Eisenhower Dr., 5th Fl.
Paramus, NJ 07652
Phone: (201)843-6511
Fax: (201)845-2482
Subject(s): Computers; Telecommunications

Circ: △30,500

**Williams Alumni Review (14913)**
Alumni Society of Williams College, Hopkins Hall
880 Main St., 4th Fl.
PO Box 676
Williamstown, MA 01267
Phone: (413)597-4278
Fax: (413)597-4158
Subject(s): College Publications

Circ: (Free)‡30,417

**Bulletin (New Series) of the American Mathematical Society (27893)**
American Mathematical Society
201 Charles St.
Providence, RI 02904-2294
Phone: (401)455-4000
Fax: (401)331-3842
Subject(s): Mathematics

Circ: (Paid)30,315

**EMediaLive (5100)**
Online, A Division of Information Today Inc.
88 Danbury Rd.Ste.1D
Wilton, CT 06897
Phone: (203)761-1466
Fax: (203)761-1444
Subject(s): Library and Information Science; Computers

Circ: (Combined)△30,277

**Aviation International News (19522)**
The Convention News Company Inc.
214 Franklin Ave., PO Box 277
Midland Park, NJ 07432
Phone: (201)444-5075
Fax: (201)444-4647
Subject(s): Aviation

Circ: (Non-paid)‡30,256

**Millimeter (22087)**
Primedia Business Magzenes & Media
5 Penn Plaza, 13th Fl.
New York, NY 10001
Phone: (212)563-3028
Fax: (212)563-3028
Subject(s): Radio, Television, Cable, and Video; Motion Pictures

Circ: (Paid)207
(Paid)30,201

**InfoStor (18904)**
PennWell Corp.
98 Spit Brook Rd.
Nashua, NH 03062-5737
Phone: (603)891-0123
Fax: (603)891-0574
Subject(s): Storage and Warehousing

Circ: △30,189

**Giftware Business (21736)**
VNU Business Publications
770 Broadway
New York, NY 10003-9595
Phone: (646)654-5000
Fax: (646)654-7265
Subject(s): Gifts, Toys, and Novelties; Glass and China

Circ: (Paid)4,285
(Controlled)30,114

**Contract (21549)**
VNU eMedia Inc.
770 Broadway, 6th Fl.
New York, NY 10003
Phone: (646)654-5000
Fax: (646)654-7370
Subject(s): Interior Design/Decorating; Architecture

Circ: (Paid)354
(Controlled)30,087

**DigitalTV (21602)**
United Entertainment Media
460 Park Ave. S., 9th Fl.
New York, NY 10016
Phone: (212)378-0400
Fax: (212)378-2160
Subject(s): Radio, Television, Cable, and Video

Circ: (Non-paid)‡30,072

**Pharmaceutical Processing (19560)**
Reed Business Information
c/o Mike Auerbach, Editor
301 Gibraltar Dr.
PO Box 650
Morris Plains, NJ 07950-0650
Phone: (973)292-5100
Fax: (973)539-3476
Subject(s): Drugs and Pharmaceuticals; Cosmetics and Toiletries

Circ: (Non-paid)‡30,025

**Oncology (21113)**
PRR Inc.
CMP Healthcare Media
600 Community Dr.
Manhasset, NY 11030
Phone: (516)562-5114

Fax: (516)562-5141
**Subject(s):** Medicine and Surgery
**Circ:** (Paid)△1,875
(Controlled)△30,016

**Accounting Technology** (21253)
Accountants Media Group
395 Hudson St.
New York, NY 10014
Phone: (212)337-8444
Fax: (212)337-8445
**Subject(s):** Computers; Accountants and Accounting
**Circ:** ‡30,000

**ACHIM Magazine** (21254)
North American Federation of Temple Brotherhoods
633 3rd Ave.
New York, NY 10017
Phone: (212)650-4100
Fax: (212)650-4189
**Subject(s):** Jewish Publications; Religious Publications
**Circ:** 30,000

**Art Now Gallery Guide–West Coast Edition** (19046)
Art Now Inc.
97 Grayrock Rd.
PO Box 5541
Clinton, NJ 08809-5541
Phone: (908)638-5255
Fax: (908)638-8737
**Subject(s):** Art
**Circ:** (Non-paid)30,000

**Clinical Journal of Oncology Nursing** (21503)
Oncology Nursing Society
c/o Joyce P. Griffin-Sobel
749 W. End Ave., Apt. 9B
New York, NY 10025-6229
Phone: (212)866-9774
Fax: (212)866-9774
**Subject(s):** Medicine and Surgery; Health and Healthcare; Nursing
**Circ:** (Combined)‡30,000

**Cobblestone** (18935)
Cobblestone Publishing Co.
30 Grove St., Ste. C
Peterborough, NH 03458
Phone: (603)924-7209
Fax: (603)924-7380
**Subject(s):** Youths' Interests; History and Genealogy
**Circ:** (Paid)30,000

**ColdFusion Developer's Journal (CFDJ)** (19532)
SYS-CON Media
135 Chestnut Ridge Rd.
Montvale, NJ 07645
Phone: (201)802-3000
Fax: (201)782-9601
**Subject(s):** Computers; Automation
**Circ:** (Combined)30,000

**Congress Monthly** (21541)
American Jewish Congress
825 Third Ave., Ste. 1800
New York, NY 10022
Phone: (212)879-4500
**Subject(s):** Jewish Publications
**Circ:** ‡30,000

**Cruise and Vacation Views** (19568)
Orban Communications Inc.
25 Washington St., 4th Fl.
Morristown, NJ 07960
Phone: (973)605-2442
Fax: (973)605-2722
**Subject(s):** Travel and Tourism
**Circ:** (Controlled)30,000

**Energy in the News** (21649)
New York Mercantile Exchange
1 North End Ave.
World Financial Ctr.
New York, NY 10282
Phone: (212)299-2000
Fax: (212)301-4700
**Subject(s):** Banking, Finance, and Investments; Power and Power Plants
**Circ:** (Controlled)30,000

**Free Inquiry** (20256)
Council for Secular Humanism
PO Box 664
Amherst, NY 14226-0664
Phone: (716)636-7571

Fax: (716)636-1733
**Subject(s):** Philosophy
**Circ:** (Non-paid)‡7,000
(Paid)‡30,000

**The Guide** (13520)
Fidelity Publishing
Box 990593
Boston, MA 02115
Phone: (617)266-8557
Fax: (617)266-1125
**Subject(s):** Travel and Tourism; Gay and Lesbian Interests
**Circ:** (Combined)30,000

**Happenings Magazine** (26247)
Happenings Communications Group Inc.
PO Box 61
Clarks Summit, PA 18411-0061
Phone: (570)587-3532
Fax: (570)586-7374
**Subject(s):** Entertainment; Travel and Tourism
**Circ:** (Non-paid)‡30,000

**International Family Planning Perspectives** (21829)
The Alan Guttmacher Institute
120 Wall St.
New York, NY 10005
Phone: (212)248-1111
Fax: (212)248-1951
**Subject(s):** Medicine and Surgery; French; Spanish
**Circ:** (Non-paid)‡1,000
(Paid)‡30,000

**Java Report** (13793)
SIGS Publications & Conferences
600 Worcester Rd., Ste. 301
Framingham, MA 01702-5360
Phone: (508)875-6644
Fax: (508)875-6622
**Subject(s):** Computers
**Circ:** (Paid)30,000

**Literal Latté** (22039)
WordSci Inc.
200 E. 10th St., Ste. 240
New York, NY 10003
Phone: (212)260-5532
Fax: (212)260-5532
**Subject(s):** Literature and Literary Reviews; Poetry
**Circ:** (Paid)‡5,000
(Non-paid)‡30,000

**The Maine Sportsman** (12620)
PO Box 910
Yarmouth, ME 04096
Phone: (207)846-9501
Fax: (207)846-1434
**Subject(s):** (Hunting, Fishing, and Game Management)
**Circ:** ‡30,000

**Multi-Housing News** (22112)
VNU Business Media
770 Broadway
New York, NY 10003
Phone: (646)654-5000
Fax: (646)654-5005
**Subject(s):** Construction, Contracting, Building, and Excavating
**Circ:** (Controlled)‡30,000

**New Jersey Countryside Magazine** (18971)
134 South Finley Avenue
Basking Ridge, NJ 07920-1422
Phone: (908)221-1171
Fax: (908)221-1656
**Subject(s):** Lifestyle
**Circ:** △30,000

**NJW Magazine (New Jersey Woman)** (19100)
177 Main St., Ste. 232
Fort Lee, NJ 07024-6936
Phone: (201)886-2185
**Subject(s):** Women's Interests
**Circ:** (Paid)15,000
(Non-paid)30,000

**The PBA Quarterly** (26453)
The Pennsylvania Bar Association
100 S.St.
PO Box 186
Harrisburg, PA 17108-0186
Phone: (717)238-6715
Fax: (717)238-1204

**Subject(s):** Law
**Circ:** 30,000

**The Pennsylvania Lawyer** (26459)
The Pennsylvania Bar Association
100 S.St.
PO Box 186
Harrisburg, PA 17108-0186
Phone: (717)238-6715
Fax: (717)238-1204
**Subject(s):** Law
**Circ:** 30,000

**SchoolMates** (21249)
U.S. Chess Federation
3068 US Rt., 9 W. Ste. No. 100
New Windsor, NY 12553
Phone: (914)562-8350
Fax: (914)561-2437
**Subject(s):** Games and Puzzles
**Circ:** (Paid)30,000

**Travel World News Magazine** (5016)
Travel Industry Network Inc.
50 Washington St.
South Norwalk, CT 06854
Phone: (203)853-4955
Fax: (203)866-1153
**Subject(s):** Travel and Tourism
**Circ:** (Non-paid)‡30,000

**Vassar Quarterly** (22745)
AAVC
Alumnae House
161 Raymond Ave.
Poughkeepsie, NY 12603
Phone: (845)437-5445
Fax: (845)437-7425
**Subject(s):** College Publications
**Circ:** (Non-paid)‡30,000

**Wesleyan** (4846)
Wesleyan University
229 High St.
Middletown, CT 06459
Phone: (860)685-3699
Fax: (860)685-3601
**Subject(s):** College Publications
**Circ:** (Controlled)30,000

**Worcester Business Journal** (14947)
172 Shrewsbury St.
Worcester, MA 01604-4636
Phone: (508)755-8004
Fax: (508)755-8860
**Subject(s):** Business
**Circ:** 30,000

**The Freeman** (20938)
Foundation for Economic Education Inc.
30 S Broadway
Irvington on Hudson, NY 10533
Phone: (914)591-7230
Fax: (914)591-8910
**Subject(s):** Economics
**Circ:** (Mon.-Fri.)22,451
(Sun.)29,888

**CPCU Journal** (26657)
CPCU Society
720 Providence Rd.
Malvern, PA 19355
Phone: (610)251-2728
Fax: (610)251-2780
**Subject(s):** Insurance
**Circ:** (Paid)29,000

**MHQ** (26449)
Primedia History Group
6405 Flank Dr.
Harrisburg, PA 17112
**Subject(s):** History and Genealogy; Military and Navy
**Circ:** (Paid)‡29,000

**U.S. Frontline News** (22506)
330 Madison Ave., 2nd Fl.
New York, NY 10017
Phone: (212)922-9090
Fax: (212)922-9119
**Subject(s):** Business; Japanese; Ethnic Publications
**Circ:** (Combined)29,000

**Panorama (13572)**
Jerome Press Publications Inc.
332 Congress St.
Boston, MA 02210
Phone: (617)423-3400
Fax: (617)423-7108
**Subject(s):** Travel and Tourism
**Circ:** (Non-paid)‡28,745

**Sporting Goods Business (22405)**
VNU Business Media
770 Broadway
New York, NY 10003
Phone: (646)654-5000
Fax: (646)654-5005
**Subject(s):** Sporting Goods/Retail Sports
**Circ:** (Controlled)‡28,700

**Carnegie Magazine (27330)**
Carnegie Museums of Pittsburgh
4400 Forbes Ave.
Pittsburgh, PA 15213
Phone: (412)622-3314
Fax: (412)578-2465
**Subject(s):** Art and Art History; Natural History and Nature Study; Humanities; Science (General)
**Circ:** (Paid)28,679

**Spectroscopy (19416)**
Advanstar Communications
485 Rte. One S. Bldg. F
Iselin, NJ 08830
Phone: (732)225-9500
Fax: (732)225-0211
**Subject(s):** Science (General)
**Circ:** (Controlled)‡28,612

**The National Law Journal (22127)**
The New York Law Journal
345 Park Ave. S.
New York, NY 10010
Phone: (212)779-9200
Fax: (212)481-8110
**Subject(s):** Law
**Circ:** (Paid)28,540

**Telemarketing & Call Center Solutions (4963)**
Technology Marketing Corp.
1 Technology Plz.
Norwalk, CT 06854
Phone: (203)852-6800
Fax: (203)853-2845
**Subject(s):** Telecommunications; Advertising and Marketing
**Circ:** (Paid)2,170
(Non-paid)28,331

**The American Journal of Orthopedics (19660)**
Quadrant HealthCom Inc.
7 Century Dr. Ste 302
Parsippany, NJ 07054
Phone: (973)701-8900
Fax: (973)206-9251
**Subject(s):** Medicine and Surgery
**Circ:** (Controlled)‡28,313

**Cornell Alumni Magazine (20944)**
Cornell Alumni Federation
c/o Office of Alumni Affairs
626 Thurston Ave.
Ithaca, NY 14853
Phone: (607)255-3517
Fax: (607)272-8532
**Subject(s):** College Publications
**Circ:** ‡28,250

**MMR (22090)**
Racher Press Inc.
220 5th Ave.
New York, NY 10001
Phone: (212)213-6000
Fax: (212)725-3691
**Subject(s):** Retail; General Merchandise
**Circ:** (Paid)6,498
(Non-paid)28,123

**Training and Conditioning (20971)**
Momentum Media
2488 N. Triphammer Rd.
Ithaca, NY 14850
Phone: (607)257-6970
Fax: (607)257-7328
**Subject(s):** (General Sports)
**Circ:** (Controlled)28,126

**Private Label (19101)**
E.W. Williams Publications
2125 Center Ave., Ste. 305
Fort Lee, NJ 07024-5898
Phone: (201)592-7007
Fax: (201)592-7171
**Subject(s):** Food and Grocery Trade; General Merchandise; Drugs and Pharmaceuticals
**Circ:** (Paid)‡961
(Non-paid)‡28,080

**Review of Optometry (26777)**
Jobson Professional Publications Group
11 Campus Blvd., Ste. 100
Newtown Square, PA 19073
Phone: (610)492-1000
Fax: (610)492-1039
**Subject(s):** Ophthalmology, Optometry, and Optics
**Circ:** (Paid)7,045
(Controlled)28,055

**Art Business News (21360)**
Advanstar Communications
1 Park Ave.
New York, NY 10016-5802
Phone: (973)944-7777
Fax: (212)951-6793
**Subject(s):** Art and Art History
**Circ:** 28,000

**The Highlander (13832)**
87 Highland Ave.
Hull, MA 02045
Phone: (781)925-0600
Fax: (781)925-1439
**Subject(s):** Intercultural Interests
**Circ:** 28,000

**Hospitality Design (21784)**
VNU Business Media
770 Broadway
New York, NY 10003-9595
Phone: (646)654-4500
Fax: (646)654-7473
**Subject(s):** Interior Design/Decorating; Hotels, Motels, Restaurants, and Clubs
**Circ:** (Paid)1376
(Controlled)28,000

**Journal of Financial Service Professionals (26774)**
Society of Financial Service Professionals
17 Campus Blvd, Ste. 201
Newtown Square, PA 19073
Phone: (610)526-2500
Fax: (610)527-1499
**Subject(s):** Insurance; Banking, Finance, and Investments
**Circ:** ‡28,000

**Odyssey (18940)**
Cobblestone Publishing Co.
30 Grove St., Ste. C
Peterborough, NH 03458
Phone: (603)924-7209
Fax: (603)924-7380
**Subject(s):** Children's Interests; Astronomy and Meteorology
**Circ:** 28,000

**SDM Dealer/Installer Marketplace (22358)**
Reed Business Information
360 Park Ave. S.
New York, NY 10014
Phone: (646)746-6400
Fax: (646)746-6734
**Subject(s):** Safety
**Circ:** (Combined)28,000

**Transformations (14946)**
Worcester Polytechnic Institute
100 Institute Rd.
Worcester, MA 01609
Phone: (508)831-5464
Fax: (508)831-5721
**Subject(s):** College Publications
**Circ:** (Non-paid)‡28,000

**Auto Merchandising News (4634)**
2370 N Ave., No. 2C
Bridgeport, CT 06604-2326
Phone: (203)335-6181
Fax: (203)579-4082
**Subject(s):** Automotive (Trade)
**Circ:** (Controlled)‡27,917

**Orthopedics (19869)**
SLACK Inc.
6900 Grove Rd.
Thorofare, NJ 08086-9447
Phone: (856)848-1000
Fax: (856)848-6091
**Subject(s):** Medicine and Surgery
**Circ:** (Controlled)‡27,800

**National Underwriter Property and Casualty/Risk and Benefits Management (19343)**
National Underwriter Co.
33-41 Newark St., Second Fl.
Hoboken, NJ 07030
Phone: (201)526-1230
Fax: (201)526-1260
**Subject(s):** Insurance
**Circ:** (Paid)18,564
(Non-paid)27,550

**Professional BoatBuilder (12482)**
WoodenBoat Publications Inc.
Naskeag Rd.
PO Box 78
Brooklin, ME 04616
Phone: (207)359-4651
Fax: (207)359-8920
**Subject(s):** Boats and Marine
**Circ:** (Controlled)27,500

**Seven Days (30860)**
Da Capo Publishing
PO Box 1164, 255 Southern Champlain St.
Burlington, VT 05402-1164
Phone: (802)864-5684
Fax: (802)865-1015
**Subject(s):** Local, State, and Regional Publications; Art; Social and Political Issues
**Circ:** (Paid)❏30
(Free)❏27,406

**The Nurse Practitioner (26114)**
Lippincott Williams & Wilkins
323 Norristown Rd., Ste. 200
Ambler, PA 19002
Fax: (215)367-2147
**Subject(s):** Nursing
**Circ:** (Paid)△27,393

**Journal of Emergency Nursing (27028)**
Mosby
170 S. Independence Mall
Independence Sq. W. 300 E.
Philadelphia, PA 19106-3399
Phone: (215)238-7800
Fax: (215)238-7883
**Subject(s):** Nursing
**Circ:** (Combined)‡27,120

**Adweek (21272)**
VNU Business Media USA
770 Broadway
New York, NY 10003
Phone: (646)654-5000
**Subject(s):** Advertising and Marketing
**Circ:** (Paid)27,003

**American Economic Review (27323)**
American Economic Association
2403 Sidney St. Ste. 260
Pittsburgh, PA 15203
Phone: (412)432-2300
Fax: (412)431-3014
**Subject(s):** Economics
**Circ:** ‡27,000

**Communications Convergence (21526)**
CMP Media L.L.C.
12 W. 21st St.
New York, NY 10010
Phone: (212)691-8215
Fax: (212)691-1191
**Subject(s):** Telecommunications
**Circ:** (Non-paid)46
(Paid)27,000

**Consulting (21544)**
Kennedy Information Inc.
Consulting Magazine
Editorial and Sales Office
29 W. 35th St. - 9th Fl.
New York, NY 10001
Phone: (212)563-1771
**Subject(s):** Business
**Circ:** 27,000

**Journal of Economic Literature (27361)**
American Economic Association
2403 Sidney St. No. 260
Pittsburgh, PA 15203
Phone: (412)432-2300
Fax: (412)432-3014
**Subject(s):** Economics
**Circ:** ‡27,000

**Pastry Art & Design (22221)**
Haymarket Group Ltd.
45 W 34th St., Ste. 600
New York, NY 10001
Phone: (212)239-0855
Fax: (212)967-4184
**Subject(s):** Baking; Food Production
**Circ:** (Combined)27,000

**Smart Business Now Magazine (26590)**
Smart Business Publishing Inc.
20140 Valley Forge Cir.
King of Prussia, PA 19406
Fax: (610)783-1662
**Subject(s):** Business
**Circ:** (Combined)27,000

**Advanced Packaging (18891)**
PennWell Corp.
98 Spit Brook Rd.
Nashua, NH 03062-5737
Phone: (603)891-0123
Fax: (603)891-0574
**Subject(s):** Electronics Engineering
**Circ:** (Controlled)△26,523

**International Biotechnology Laboratory (5008)**
International Scientific Communications Inc.
30 Controls Dr.
PO Box 870
Shelton, CT 06484-0870
Phone: (203)926-9300
Fax: (203)926-9310
**Subject(s):** Laboratory Research (Scientific and Medical)
**Circ:** (Controlled)‡26,432

**Advertising Age (21271)**
Ad Age Group
711 Third Ave.
New York, NY 10017
**Subject(s):** Advertising and Marketing; Statistics
**Circ:** (Paid)26,310

**Embroidery Monogram Business (21645)**
VNU Business Media USA
770 Broadway
New York, NY 10003
Phone: (646)654-5000
**Subject(s):** Textiles; Clothing; Fashion
**Circ:** 26,192

**ART TIMES (21226)**
CSS Publications Inc.
PO Box 730
Mount Marion, NY 12456
Phone: (845)246-6944
Fax: (845)246-6944
**Subject(s):** Literature and Literary Reviews; Art
**Circ:** (Paid)‡1,000
(Non-paid)‡26,000

**Colby (12613)**
Colby College
4000 Mayflower Hill
Waterville, ME 04901-8440
Phone: (207)872-3000
Fax: (207)872-3555
**Subject(s):** College Publications
**Circ:** (Non-paid)‡26,000

**Commentary (21520)**
American Jewish Committee
165 E 56th St.
PO Box 705
New York, NY 10150
Phone: (212)751-4000
Fax: (212)891-1492
**Subject(s):** General Editorial; Jewish Publications
**Circ:** (Non-paid)600
(Paid)26,000

**New Hampshire Magazine (18872)**
150 Dow St.
Manchester, NH 03101
Phone: (603)624-1442
Fax: (603)624-1310

**Subject(s):** Lifestyle; Business; Local, State, and Regional Publications
**Circ:** (Combined)26,000

**The News of New York (21024)**
Medical Society of the State of New York
420 Lakeville Rd.
PO Box 5404
Lake Success, NY 11042-5404
Phone: (516)488-6100
Fax: (516)488-1267
**Subject(s):** Medicine and Surgery
**Circ:** (Controlled)26,000

**Package Printing (27208)**
North American Publishing Co.
401 N. Broad St., 5th Fl.
Philadelphia, PA 19108
Phone: (215)238-5482
Fax: (215)238-5412
**Subject(s):** Printing and Typography
**Circ:** (Non-paid)‡26,000

**Scarlet Street (19118)**
Scarlet Street Inc.
PO Box 604
Glen Rock, NJ 07452
Phone: (201)445-0034
Fax: (201)445-1496
**Subject(s):** Entertainment
**Circ:** (Paid)26,000

**Pro Sound News (22263)**
United Entertainment Media
460 Park Ave. S., 9th Fl.
New York, NY 10016
Phone: (212)378-0400
Fax: (212)378-2160
**Subject(s):** Radio, Television, Cable, and Video; Music and Musical Instruments
**Circ:** (Controlled)‡25,983

**Federal Practitioner (19662)**
Quadrant HealthCom Inc.
7 Century Dr. Ste 302
Parsippany, NJ 07054
Phone: (973)701-8900
Fax: (973)206-9251
**Subject(s):** Medicine and Surgery; Veterans
**Circ:** (Controlled)‡25,853

**Gifts & Decorative Accessories (21735)**
Reed Business Information
360 Park Ave. S.
New York, NY 10010
Phone: (646)746-6400
Fax: (646)746-7431
**Subject(s):** Gifts, Toys, and Novelties
**Circ:** (Paid)25,726

**Lasers in Surgery and Medicine (19317)**
John Wiley and Sons Inc.
111 River St.
Hoboken, NJ 07030-5774
Phone: (201)748-6000
Fax: (201)748-6088
**Subject(s):** Medicine and Surgery
**Circ:** 25,200

**Emergency Medicine News (21646)**
Lippincott Williams & Wilkins
c/o Lisa Hoffman
333 7th Av., 20th Fl.
New York, NY
**Subject(s):** Medicine and Surgery
**Circ:** (Paid)25,036

**Adoptive Families (21267)**
42 W. 38th St., Ste. 901
New York, NY 10018
Phone: (646)366-0830
Fax: (646)366-0842
**Subject(s):** Parenting
**Circ:** (Paid)‡25,000

**American Atheist (19048)**
American Atheist Press
PO Box 5733
225 Cristiani St
Cranford, NJ 07016
Phone: (908)276-7300
Fax: (908)276-7402

**Subject(s):** Atheism
**Circ:** (Non-paid)‡5,000
(Paid)‡25,000

**American Industry (20854)**
Publications for Industry
21 Russell Woods Rd.
Great Neck, NY 11021
Phone: (516)487-0990
Fax: (516)487-0809
**Subject(s):** Commerce and Industry; Purchasing
**Circ:** (Controlled)‡25,000

**American Theatre (21325)**
Theatre Communications Group
520 8th Ave., 24th Fl.
New York, NY 10018-4156
Phone: (212)609-5900
Fax: (212)609-5901
**Subject(s):** Drama and Theatre
**Circ:** ‡25,000

**Architectural Lighting (21353)**
VNU Business Media USA
770 Broadway
New York, NY 10003
Phone: (646)654-5000
**Subject(s):** Architecture; Lighting; Interior Design/Decorating
**Circ:** (Non-paid)25,000

**Beau (23179)**
Sportomatic Ltd.
PO Box 392
White Plains, NY 10602
**Subject(s):** Gay and Lesbian Interests
**Circ:** (Non-paid)25,000

**Blacks in Law Enforcement (20493)**
591 Vanderbilt Ave., Ste. 133
Brooklyn, NY 11238
Phone: (718)455-9059
Fax: (718)574-4236
**Subject(s):** Police, Penology, and Penal Institutions; Black Publications; Ethnic and Minority Studies
**Circ:** 25,000

**Chrysler Power (26665)**
CPO Publishing
PO Box 129
Mansfield, PA 16933
Phone: (570)549-2282
Fax: (570)549-3366
**Subject(s):** Automotive (Consumer)
**Circ:** (Paid)25,000

**Consumer Goods Technology (19756)**
Edgell Communications Inc.
4 Middlebury Blvd.
Randolph, NJ 07869
Phone: (973)252-0100
Fax: (973)252-9020
**Subject(s):** Commerce and Industry
**Circ:** (Controlled)25,000

**Dartmouth Medicine (18854)**
Dartmouth Medical School
One Medical Center Dr., HB 7070
Lebanon, NH 03756
**Subject(s):** Medicine and Surgery; Education
**Circ:** (Non-paid)25,000

**Drew Magazine (19467)**
Drew University
36 Madison Ave. LC25
Madison, NJ 07940
Phone: (973)408-3000
**Subject(s):** College Publications
**Circ:** (Controlled)‡25,000

**Industrial Purchasing Agent (20857)**
Publications for Industry
21 Russell Woods Rd.
Great Neck, NY 11021
Phone: (516)487-0990
Fax: (516)487-0809
**Subject(s):** Purchasing; Commerce and Industry
**Circ:** (Controlled)‡25,000

**Item-Interference Technology Engineers Master (27674)**
Robar Industries Inc.
3 Union Hill Rd.
West Conshohocken, PA 19428-2788
Fax: (610)834-7337

**Subject(s):** Electronics Engineering
**Circ:** (Non-paid)25,000

**Marine Log (22056)**
Simmons-Boardman Publishing Corp.
345 Hudson St.
New York, NY 10014-4590
Phone: (212)620-7200
Fax: (212)633-1165
**Subject(s):** Ships and Shipping
**Circ:** (Paid)500
　　　(Non-paid)25,000

**Metronome Magazine (13462)**
PO Box 921
Billerica, MA 01821
Phone: (978)957-0925
**Subject(s):** Music and Musical Instruments
**Circ:** (Controlled)25,000

**Moravian (26168)**
Moravian Church in America
Interprovincial Board of Communication
PO Box 1245
Bethlehem, PA 18016
Phone: (610)867-0593
Fax: (610)866-9223
**Subject(s):** Religious Publications
**Circ:** ‡25,000

**Natural Life (22615)**
PO Box 112
Niagara Falls, NY 14304
Phone: (716)260-0303
**Subject(s):** Local, State, and Regional Publications; Lifestyle; Alternative and Underground
**Circ:** (Combined)25,000

**oemagazine (18769)**
SPIE - The International Society for Optical Engineering
17 Old Nashua Rd., Ste. 25
Amherst, NH 03031
Phone: (603)672-9850
Fax: (603)672-9851
**Subject(s):** Communications; Engineering (Various branches); Computers
**Circ:** (Controlled)‡25,000

**Progress in Research Overview 2003 (19839)**
Christopher Reeve Paralysis Foundation
500 Morris Ave.
Springfield, NJ 07081
Phone: (973)379-2690
Fax: (973)912-9433
**Subject(s):** Laboratory Research (Scientific and Medical); Handicapped
**Circ:** (Non-paid)25,000

**Public Relations Strategist (22279)**
33 Maiden Ln., 11th Fl.
New York, NY 10038
Phone: (212)460-1459
**Subject(s):** Public Relations
**Circ:** (Paid)‡8,000
　　　(Controlled)‡25,000

**RAC Journal (22871)**
IIT Research Institute
201 Mill St.
Rome, NY 13440-6916
Phone: (315)339-7075
Fax: (315)337-9932
**Subject(s):** Engineering (Various branches)
**Circ:** (Controlled)25,000

**Radio Control Boat Modeler (4990)**
Air Age Publishing Inc.
100 E Ridge
Ridgefield, CT 06877
Phone: (203)431-9000
Fax: (203)431-3000
**Subject(s):** Crafts, Models, Hobbies, and Contests
**Circ:** 25,000

**Research/Penn State (27614)**
Research Publications
304 Old Main
University Park, PA 16802
Phone: (814)863-9580
Fax: (814)863-9659
**Subject(s):** Education
**Circ:** (Controlled)25,000

**Sloan Management Review (13707)**
Massachusetts Institute of Technology
77 Massachusetts Ave., E60-100
Cambridge, MA 02139-4307
Phone: (617)253-7170
Fax: (617)258-9739
**Subject(s):** Management and Administration; Business
**Circ:** ‡25,000

**Spare Change (13710)**
Homeless Empowerment Project Inc.
1151 Massachusetts Ave.
Cambridge, MA 02138
Phone: (617)497-1595
Fax: (617)868-0767
**Subject(s):** Alternative and Underground
**Circ:** (Paid)25,000

**Stratton Magazine (30883)**
Lee A. Romano Associates Inc.
PO Box 358
Dorset, VT 05251
Phone: (802)867-5133
**Subject(s):** Lifestyle; Local, State, and Regional Publications
**Circ:** (Non-paid)25,000

**WebLogic Developers Journal (19545)**
SYS-CON Media
135 Chestnut Ridge Rd.
Montvale, NJ 07645
Phone: (201)802-3000
Fax: (201)782-9601
**Subject(s):** Computers; Automation
**Circ:** (Combined)25,000

**WebSphere Developer's Journal (19546)**
SYS-CON Media
135 Chestnut Ridge Rd.
Montvale, NJ 07645
Phone: (201)802-3000
Fax: (201)782-9601
**Subject(s):** Computers; Automation
**Circ:** (Combined)25,000

**Jewelers' Circular-Keystone (21857)**
Reed Business Information
360 Park Ave. S
New York, NY 10010
Phone: (646)746-6400
**Subject(s):** Jewelry, Watches, and Clocks
**Circ:** (Paid)24,792

**Broadcasting & Cable (21429)**
Reed Business Information
360 Park Ave. S.
New York, NY 10010
Phone: (646)740-0400
Fax: (646)746-6734
**Subject(s):** Radio, Television, Cable, and Video
**Circ:** (Non-paid)10,405
　　　(Paid)24,765

**DVS Guide (13511)**
Descriptive Video Service
WGBH
125 Western Ave.
Boston, MA 02134
Phone: (617)300-3600
Fax: (617)300-1020
**Subject(s):** Blind and Visually Challenged; Radio, Television, Cable, and Video
**Circ:** (Combined)24,688

**Hudson Valley Magazine (22740)**
Suburban Publishing Inc.
22 IBM Rd., Ste. 108
Poughkeepsie, NY 12601-5461
Phone: (845)463-0542
Fax: (845)463-1544
**Subject(s):** Local, State, and Regional Publications
**Circ:** (Paid)24,610

**Collections & Credit Risk (21508)**
SourceMedia Inc.
One State St. Plaza, 27th Fl.
New York, NY 10004
Phone: (212)822-8200
Fax: (212)803-1592
**Subject(s):** Banking, Finance, and Investments
**Circ:** (Controlled)△24,548

**Bay Windows (13477)**
637 Tremont St.
Boston, MA 02118-1201
Phone: (617)266-6670
Fax: (617)266-5973
**Subject(s):** Gay and Lesbian Interests; Literature and Literary Reviews
**Circ:** (Non-paid)24,500

**Yoga International (26507)**
The Himalayan Institute Press
630 Main St., Ste. 300
Honesdale, PA 18431
Phone: (570)253-5551
Fax: (570)647-1552
**Subject(s):** Health
**Circ:** (Combined)24,500

**Business Insurance (21437)**
Crain Communications Inc.
711 3rd Ave., 3rd Fl.
New York, NY 10017-4036
Phone: (212)210-0100
Fax: (212)210-0244
**Subject(s):** Insurance; Banking, Finance, and Investments; Health and Healthcare
**Circ:** (Controlled)21,596
　　　(Paid)24,471

**Antiques and the Arts Weekly (4927)**
Bee Publishing Company Inc.
5 Church Hill Rd.
PO Box 5503
Newtown, CT 06470-5503
Phone: (203)426-8036
Fax: (203)426-1394
**Subject(s):** Art
**Circ:** (Non-paid)‡231
　　　(Paid)‡24,255

**The American Organist (21321)**
American Guild of Organists
475 Riverside Dr., Ste. 1260
New York, NY 10115
Phone: (212)870-2310
Fax: (212)870-2163
**Subject(s):** Music and Musical Instruments
**Circ:** ‡24,000

**ASSEMBLY (23157)**
Association of Graduates
U.S. Military Academy
698 Mills Rd.
West Point, NY 10996
Phone: (845)446-1500
Fax: (845)446-5325
**Subject(s):** Military and Navy
**Circ:** 24,000

**City College Alumnus (21493)**
Alumni Association of City College of New York
PO Box 177
New York, NY 10027
Phone: (212)234-3000
Fax: (212)368-6576
**Subject(s):** College Publications
**Circ:** (Non-paid)24,000

**Pennsylvania Magazine (26217)**
PO Box 755
Camp Hill, PA 17011-0755
Phone: (717)697-4660
**Subject(s):** Local, State, and Regional Publications; Lifestyle
**Circ:** (Non-paid)‡2,000
　　　(Paid)‡24,000

**Picture Framing Magazine (19551)**
Hobby Publications Inc.
207 Commercial Ct.
PO Box 102
Morganville, NJ 07751-0102
Phone: (732)536-5160
Fax: (732)536-5761
**Subject(s):** Art and Art History
**Circ:** (Paid)△24,000

**PrintMedia Magazine (27242)**
North American Publishing Co.
401 N. Broad St., 5th Fl.
Philadelphia, PA 19108
Phone: (215)238-5482
Fax: (215)238-5412
**Subject(s):** Printing and Typography; Journalism and Publishing
**Circ:** (Controlled)‡24,000

## Northeastern States

**Railway Age** (22288)
Simmons-Boardman Publishing Corp.
345 Hudson St.
New York, NY 10014-4590
Phone: (212)620-7200
Fax: (212)633-1165
**Subject(s):** Railroad
**Circ:** (Paid)998
(Non-paid)23,730

**Cabling Installation & Maintenance** (18893)
PennWell Corp.
98 Spit Brook Rd.
Nashua, NH 03062-5737
Phone: (603)891-0123
Fax: (603)891-0574
**Subject(s):** Telecommunications
**Circ:** (Non-paid)23,600

**Barnard Magazine** (21384)
Vagelos Alumnae Center
Barnard College
3009 Broadway
New York, NY 10027-6598
Phone: (212)854-6157
Fax: (212)854-0044
**Subject(s):** College Publications
**Circ:** (Controlled)‡23,500

**Amateur Dancers** (26763)
United States Amateur Ballroom Dancers Association
PO Box 128
New Freedom, PA 17349
Phone: (717)235-6656
Fax: (717)235-4183
**Subject(s):** Performing Arts; Performing Arts
**Circ:** 23,000

**CED** (21465)
Reed Business Information
360 Park Ave. S.
New York, NY 10010
Phone: (646)746-6400
Fax: (646)746-6734
**Subject(s):** Business; Communications
**Circ:** 23,000

**Columbia Journalism Review** (21515)
2950 Broadway, Journalism Bldg.
Columbia Univ.
New York, NY 10027
Phone: (212)854-1881
Fax: (212)854-8580
**Subject(s):** Journalism and Publishing
**Circ:** (Paid)★23,007

**Food Trade News** (26204)
Best-Met Publishing Company Inc.
2200 W. Chester Pike, Ste. A-5
Broomall, PA 19008-3327
Phone: (610)834-3760
Fax: (610)834-3765
**Subject(s):** Food and Grocery Trade
**Circ:** (Controlled)‡23,000

**Foodservice East** (14922)
The Newbury Street Group Inc.
165 New Boston St., No. 236
Woburn, MA 01801
Phone: (781)376-9080
Fax: (781)376-0010
**Subject(s):** Hotels, Motels, Restaurants, and Clubs; Local, State, and Regional Publications
**Circ:** ‡23,000

**Fraternal Leader** (26349)
Loyal Christian Benefit Association
PO Box 13005
Erie, PA 16514-1304
Phone: (814)453-4331
Fax: (814)453-3211
**Subject(s):** Unclassified Fraternal
**Circ:** (Non-paid)23,000

**RGS Magazine** (26266)
Ruffed Grouse Society
451 McCormick Rd.
Coraopolis, PA 15108
Phone: (412)262-4044
Fax: (412)262-9207
**Subject(s):** Environmental and Natural Resources Conservation
**Circ:** 23,000

**Beverage World International** (21400)
Beverage World
VNU Business Publications USA
770 Broadway
New York, NY 10003-9595
Phone: (646)654-7714
Fax: (646)654-7727
**Subject(s):** Beverages, Brewing, and Bottling
**Circ:** ‡22,500

**Swarthmore College Bulletin** (27574)
Swarthmore College
500 College Ave.
Swarthmore, PA 19081-1390
Phone: (610)328-8000
**Subject(s):** College Publications
**Circ:** (Non-paid)‡22,500

**Westminster College Magazine** (26769)
Westminster College
319 S Market St.
New Wilmington, PA 16142
**Subject(s):** College Publications
**Circ:** (Controlled)‡22,500

**Wood Technology** (21123)
CMP Media L.L.C.
600 Community Dr.
Manhasset, NY 11030
Phone: (516)562-5000
Fax: (516)562-5995
**Subject(s):** Lumber; Wood and Woodworking
**Circ:** (Paid)472
(Controlled)22,500

**Business Times** (4881)
Choice Media L.L.C.
PO Box 580
New Haven, CT 06513-0580
Phone: (203)782-1420
**Subject(s):** Business; Local, State, and Regional Publications
**Circ:** (Non-paid)‡22,400

**Forecast** (18997)
Baker & Taylor
1120 Rte. 22 E
Bridgewater, NJ 08807
Phone: (908)541-7000
**Subject(s):** Indexes, Abstracts, Reports, Proceedings, and Bibliographies; Book Trade and Author News
**Circ:** (Non-paid)22,400

**Cardiology Special Edition** (21455)
The McMahon Publishing Group
545 W 45th St., 8th Fl.
New York, NY 10036
Phone: (212)957-5300
Fax: (212)957-7230
**Subject(s):** Medicine and Surgery
**Circ:** (Non-paid)22,343

**Police & Security News** (27465)
Days Communications
1208 Juniper St.
Quakertown, PA 18951-1520
Phone: (215)538-1240
Fax: (215)538-1208
**Subject(s):** Police, Penology, and Penal Institutions; Safety
**Circ:** (Paid)‡449
(Non-paid)‡22,160

**Beverage Aisle** (21397)
Beverage World
VNU Business Publications USA
770 Broadway
New York, NY 10003-9595
Phone: (646)654-7714
Fax: (646)654-7727
**Subject(s):** Beverages, Brewing, and Bottling
**Circ:** (Non-paid)22,012

**Association Meetings** (14824)
Primedia Business Magazines & Media
c/o Regina McGee
132 Great Rd., Ste. 120
Stow, MA 01775-1189
**Subject(s):** Conventions, Meetings, and Trade Fairs
**Circ:** (Controlled)‡22,000

**California Track and Running News** (13738)
Lockwood Publications Inc.
38 Post Oak RD.
Chilmark, MA 02535
Phone: (508)645-2366
Fax: (508)645-2382
**Subject(s):** (Running)
**Circ:** (Combined)22,000

**Computer Living/New York** (20450)
PO Box 1252
Bronx, NY 10471-1252
Phone: (718)601-1326
Fax: (718)601-4165
**Subject(s):** Computers
**Circ:** (Non-paid)‡10,000
(Paid)‡22,000

**The GeDunk: Grove City College Alumni Magazine** (26416)
Grove City College
Public Relations Office
100 Campus Dr.
Grove City, PA 16127-2104
Phone: (724)458-3100
Fax: (724)458-3334
**Subject(s):** College Publications
**Circ:** (Free)‡22,000

**Heron Dance** (30915)
179 Rotax Rd.
North Ferrisburg, VT 05473-9409
**Subject(s):** Poetry; Literature and Literary Reviews; Social and Political Issues; Art
**Circ:** (Paid)22,000

**Log of Mystic Seaport** (4867)
Mystic Seaport Museum Inc.
PO Box 6000
Mystic, CT 06355-0990
Phone: (860)572-0711
Fax: (860)572-5348
**Subject(s):** History and Genealogy; Museums; Boats and Marine
**Circ:** (Controlled)300
(Paid)22,000

**Servicing Management** (5072)
Zackin Publications Inc.
70 Edwin Ave.
PO Box 2180
Waterbury, CT 06722
Phone: (203)755-0158
Fax: (203)755-3480
**Subject(s):** Banking, Finance, and Investments
**Circ:** (Controlled)‡22,000

**UN Chronicle** (22501)
United Nations Publications
2 United Nations Plz., Rm. DC2-853
New York, NY 10017
Phone: (212)963-8302
Fax: (212)963-3489
**Subject(s):** International Affairs; French
**Circ:** (Paid)‡9,000
(Controlled)‡22,000

**ADVANCE for Administrators in Radiation & Radiation Oncology** (26567)
Merion Publications Inc.
2900 Horizon Dr.
King of Prussia, PA 19406
Phone: (610)278-1400
Fax: (610)278-1425
**Subject(s):** Medicine and Surgery; Radiology, Ultrasound, and Nuclear Medicine
**Circ:** (Controlled)‡21,987

**Bedroom** (27889)
Futon Life
301 Friendship St.
Providence, RI 02903-4507
Phone: (401)351-0787
Fax: (401)351-0788
**Subject(s):** Retail; Furniture and Furnishings
**Circ:** (Controlled)21,700

**Futon Life** (27901)
301 Friendship St.
Providence, RI 02903-4507
Phone: (401)351-0787
Fax: (401)351-0788
**Subject(s):** Furniture and Furnishings
**Circ:** (Controlled)21,700

**Journal of Clinical Ultrasound** (19283)
John Wiley and Sons Inc.
111 River St.
Hoboken, NJ 07030-5774
Phone: (201)748-6000
Fax: (201)748-6088

**Subject(s):** Medicine and Surgery
**Circ:** (Paid)21,700

**PROMO (5037)**
Primedia Business
11 River Bend Dr. S.
PO Box 4949
Stamford, CT 06907-0949
Phone: (203)358-9900
Fax: (203)358-5811
**Subject(s):** Advertising and Marketing
**Circ:** (Paid)3,710
   (Non-paid)21,632

**Satellite Broadband (22339)**
VNU Business Media USA
770 Broadway
New York, NY 10003
Phone: (646)654-5000
**Subject(s):** Telecommunications
**Circ:** 21,531

**Library Journal (22032)**
Reed Business Information
360 Park Ave. S.
New York, NY 10010
Phone: (646)746-6400
Fax: (646)746-6734
**Subject(s):** Library and Information Science
**Circ:** (Paid)21,487

**Mortgage Technology (22104)**
Thomson Financial
195 Broadway
New York, NY 10007
Phone: (646)822-2000
Fax: (646)822-3230
**Subject(s):** Banking, Finance, and Investments
**Circ:** (Paid)600
   (Controlled)21,314

**National Jeweler (22126)**
VNU Business Media
770 Broadway
New York, NY 10003
Phone: (646)654-5000
Fax: (646)654-5005
**Subject(s):** Jewelry, Watches, and Clocks
**Circ:** (Paid)9,000
   (Controlled)21,300

**Furniture World Magazine (21239)**
Towse Publishing Co.
1333A N. Ave.
New Rochelle, NY 10804
Phone: (914)235-3095
Fax: (914)235-3278
**Subject(s):** Furniture and Furnishings
**Circ:** (Controlled)21,285

**Wall Street and Technology (21121)**
CMP Media L.L.C.
600 Community Dr.
Manhasset, NY 11030
Phone: (516)562-5000
Fax: (516)562-5995
**Subject(s):** Banking, Finance, and Investments; Business; Computers
**Circ:** (Controlled)‡21,226

**Sys Admin (21119)**
CMP Media L.L.C.
600 Community Dr.
Manhasset, NY 11030
Phone: (516)562-5000
Fax: (516)562-5995
**Subject(s):** Computers
**Circ:** (Paid)‡21,138

**ADVANCE for Managers of Respiratory Care (26576)**
Merion Publications Inc.
2900 Horizon Dr.
King of Prussia, PA 19406
Phone: (610)278-1400
Fax: (610)278-1425
**Subject(s):** Medicine and Surgery; Health and Healthcare
**Circ:** (Controlled)‡21,000

**Art Education (27598)**
National Art Education Association
Art Eduation Program
207 Arts College
The Pennsylvania State University
University Park, PA 16802-2905
Phone: (814)863-8664
Fax: (814)863-8664
**Subject(s):** Art and Art History; Education
**Circ:** (Non-paid)‡63
   (Paid)‡21,000

**BOWDOIN Magazine (12484)**
Bowdoin College
4104 College Station
Brunswick, ME 04011-8432
Phone: (207)725-3136
Fax: (207)725-3003
**Subject(s):** College Publications
**Circ:** (Non-paid)‡21,000

**Current History (26904)**
Current History Inc.
4225 Main St.
Philadelphia, PA 19127
Phone: (215)482-4464
Fax: (215)482-9923
**Subject(s):** International Affairs
**Circ:** ‡21,000

**Geneva Magazine (26145)**
Geneva College
3200 College Ave.
Beaver Falls, PA 15010
Phone: (724)847-6527
**Subject(s):** College Publications
**Circ:** (Controlled)‡21,000

**Man at Arms (27861)**
Andrew Mowbray Publishing Inc.
Box 460
Lincoln, RI 02865
Phone: (401)726-8011
Fax: (401)726-8061
**Subject(s):** Firearms
**Circ:** (Non-paid)‡80
   (Paid)‡21,000

**Proceedings of the IEEE (22264)**
Institute of Electrical and Electronics Engineers Inc.
3 Park Ave., 17th Fl.
New York, NY 10016
Phone: (212)705-8900
Fax: (212)705-8999
**Subject(s):** Engineering (Various branches); Indexes, Abstracts, Reports, Proceedings, and Bibliographies
**Circ:** ‡21,000

**Secondary Marketing Executive (5071)**
Zackin Publications Inc.
70 Edwin Ave.
PO Box 2180
Waterbury, CT 06722
Phone: (800)325-6745
Fax: (203)755-3480
**Subject(s):** Banking, Finance, and Investments
**Circ:** (Controlled)‡21,000

**The Stevens Indicator (19390)**
Stevens Alumni Association
Castle Point
Hoboken, NJ 07030
Phone: (201)216-5531
Fax: (201)216-5374
**Subject(s):** College Publications
**Circ:** (Non-paid)21,000

**The American Journal of Cardiology (21310)**
Excerpta Medica Inc.
655 Avenue of the Americas
New York, NY 10010
Phone: (212)989-5800
**Subject(s):** Medicine and Surgery
**Circ:** ‡20,897

**The Licensing Book (22033)**
Adventure Publishing Group Inc.
1107 Broadway, Ste. 1204
New York, NY 10010-5501
Phone: (212)575-4510
Fax: (212)575-4521
**Subject(s):** Commerce and Industry
**Circ:** ‡20,711

**Advances in Skin & Wound Care (26803)**
Lippincott Williams & Wilkins
530 Walnut St.
Philadelphia, PA 19106-3261
Phone: (215)521-8300
Fax: (215)521-8902
**Subject(s):** Medicine and Surgery; Health and Healthcare
**Circ:** (Controlled)20,558

**Tile & Decorative Surfaces (22454)**
Ashlee Publishing Company Inc.
18 E 41st St.
New York, NY 10017
Phone: (212)376-7722
Fax: (212)376-7723
**Subject(s):** Building Materials, Concrete, Brick, and Tile; Stone and Rock Products
**Circ:** (Paid)1,137
   (Non-paid)20,441

**Orthopedic Special Edition (22200)**
The McMahon Publishing Group
545 W 45th St., 8th Fl.
New York, NY 10036
Phone: (212)957-5300
Fax: (212)957-7230
**Subject(s):** Medicine and Surgery
**Circ:** (Controlled)20,411

**EDN China (14857)**
Reed Business Information
225 Wyman St.
Waltham, MA 02451-1216
**Subject(s):** Electronics Engineering
**Circ:** (Controlled)20,400

**Neurology (27162)**
Lippincott Williams & Wilkins
530 Walnut St.
Philadelphia, PA 19106-3261
Phone: (215)521-8300
Fax: (215)521-8902
**Subject(s):** Medicine and Surgery
**Circ:** (Paid)20,339

**Promotional Marketing (27245)**
North American Publishing Co.
401 N. Broad St., 5th Fl.
Philadelphia, PA 19108
Phone: (215)238-5482
Fax: (215)238-5412
**Subject(s):** Advertising and Marketing
**Circ:** (Combined)‡20,300

**Water Technology (21050)**
National Trade Publications Inc.
13 Century Hill Dr.
Latham, NY 12110-2124
Phone: (518)783-1281
Fax: (518)783-1386
**Subject(s):** Water Supply and Sewage Disposal
**Circ:** (Paid)67
   (Controlled)20,219

**Ostomy/Wound Management (26662)**
Health Management Publications Inc.
83 General Warren Blvd. Ste. 100
Malvern, PA 19355-1245
Phone: (610)560-0500
Fax: (610)560-0501
**Subject(s):** Health and Healthcare
**Circ:** 20,201

**Modern Plastics (22094)**
Chemical Week Associates
110 Williams St., 11th Fl.
New York, NY 10038
Phone: (212)621-4900
Fax: (212)621-4800
**Subject(s):** Plastic and Composition Materials
**Circ:** (Paid)14,750
   (Non-paid)20,197

**Compendium on Continuing Education for the Practicing Veterinarian (27721)**
Veterinary Learning Systems
780 Township Line Rd.
Yardley, PA 19067
Phone: (267)685-2400
Fax: (800)589-0036
**Subject(s):** Veterinary Medicine
**Circ:** (Non-paid)‡11,446
   (Paid)‡20,035

**ABD (21224)**
Air Service Directory Inc.
116 Radio Circle Dr.
Mount Kisco, NY 10549
Phone: (914)242-8700
Fax: (914)242-5422

# Northeastern States

**Subject(s):** Purchasing; Aviation
**Circ:** (Combined)‡20,000

**American Journal of Geriatric Cardiology (4670)**
LeJacq Communications Inc.
3 Parklands Dr.
Darien, CT 06820-3652
Phone: (203)656-1711
Fax: (203)656-1717
**Subject(s):** Medicine and Surgery
**Circ:** (Controlled)20,000

**AudioFile (12553)**
37 Silver St.
PO Box 109
Portland, ME 04112-0109
Phone: (207)774-7563
Fax: (207)775-3744
**Subject(s):** Literature and Literary Reviews
**Circ:** (Combined)20,000

**Bank Insurance Marketing (27655)**
Bank Insurance and Securities Association
303 W Lancaster Ave., Ste. 2C
Wayne, PA 19087
Phone: (610)989-9047
Fax: (610)989-9102
**Subject(s):** Banking, Finance, and Investments; Insurance; Advertising and Marketing
**Circ:** 20,000

**Buffalo Spree (23188)**
Buffalo Spree Magazine
6215 Sheridan Dr.
Williamsville, NY 14221
Phone: (716)634-0820
Fax: (716)810-0075
**Subject(s):** Local, State, and Regional Publications
**Circ:** (Paid)‡5,000
(Non-paid)‡20,000

**Christian Motorsports Illustrated (26664)**
CPO Publishing
PO Box 129
Mansfield, PA 16933
Phone: (570)549-2282
Fax: (570)549-3366
**Subject(s):** Religious Publications; Automotive (Consumer); (Auto Racing)
**Circ:** (Paid)20,000

**Commonwealth (21524)**
Commonweal Foundation
475 Riverside Dr., Rm. 405
New York, NY 10115
Phone: (212)662-4200
Fax: (212)662-4183
**Subject(s):** Religious Publications
**Circ:** ‡20,000

**Congestive Heart Failure (4671)**
LeJacq Communications Inc.
3 Parklands Dr.
Darien, CT 06820-3652
Phone: (203)656-1711
Fax: (203)656-1717
**Subject(s):** Medicine and Surgery
**Circ:** (Controlled)‡20,000

**Couture International Jeweler (21564)**
VNU Business Media USA
770 Broadway
New York, NY 10003
Phone: (646)654-5000
**Subject(s):** Jewelry, Watches, and Clocks; Retail
**Circ:** 20,000

**DAEDALUS (13659)**
American Academy of Arts & Sciences
136 Irving St.
Cambridge, MA 02138
Phone: (617)491-2600
Fax: (617)576-5088
**Subject(s):** Humanities; Social Sciences
**Circ:** ‡20,000

**DJ Times (22725)**
Testa Communications
25 Willowdale Ave.
Port Washington, NY 11050
Phone: (516)767-2500
Fax: (516)767-9335
**Subject(s):** Music and Musical Instruments
**Circ:** 20,000

**Federal Reserve Bank of Boston Regional Review (13516)**
Federal Reserve Bank of Boston
600 Atlantic Ave.
Boston, MA 02210
Phone: (617)973-3000
**Subject(s):** Economics; Business
**Circ:** (Controlled)20,000

**Global Investment Magazine (21739)**
Investment Media Inc.
820 Second Ave., 4th Fl.
New York, NY 10017
Phone: (212)370-3700
Fax: (212)370-4606
**Subject(s):** Banking, Finance, and Investments
**Circ:** (Controlled)△20,000

**Graphis (21748)**
Graphis Inc.
307 5th Ave., 10th Fl.
New York, NY 10016-6517
Phone: (212)532-9387
Fax: (212)213-3229
**Subject(s):** Printing and Typography
**Circ:** (Paid)20,000

**The Horsemen's Yankee Pedlar (14319)**
88 Leicester St.
North Oxford, MA 01537
Phone: (508)987-5886
Fax: (508)987-5887
**Subject(s):** (Horses and Horse Racing)
**Circ:** 20,000

**Inventors' Digest (13530)**
JMH Publishing Co.
30-31 Union Wharf, 3rd Fl.
Boston, MA 02109
Phone: (617)367-4540
Fax: (617)723-6988
**Subject(s):** Patents, Trademarks, and Copyrights
**Circ:** ‡20,000

**Maine Boats & Harbors (12496)**
43 Mechanic St., Ste. 300
PO Box 758
Camden, ME 04843
Phone: (207)236-8622
Fax: (207)236-0811
**Subject(s):** (Boating and Yachting); Local, State, and Regional Publications
**Circ:** (Combined)20,000

**Matilda Ziegler Magazine for the Blind (22065)**
80 8th Ave., Rm. 1304
New York, NY 10011
Phone: (212)242-0263
Fax: (212)633-1601
**Subject(s):** Blind and Visually Challenged
**Circ:** (Non-paid)‡20,000

**NA'AMAT WOMAN (22120)**
NA'AMAT USA
350 5th Ave., Ste. 4700
New York, NY 10118-4700
Phone: (212)563-5222
Fax: (212)563-5710
**Subject(s):** Jewish Publications; Women's Interests
**Circ:** ‡20,000

**New England Ancestors (13556)**
New England Historic Genealogical Society
101 Newbury St.
Boston, MA 02116-3007
Phone: (617)536-5740
Fax: (617)536-7307
**Subject(s):** History and Genealogy
**Circ:** (Paid)20,000

**New Jersey Business (19083)**
New Jersey Business & Industry Association
310 Passaic Ave.
Fairfield, NJ 07004-2519
Phone: (973)882-5004
Fax: (973)882-4648
**Subject(s):** Local, State, and Regional Publications; Business
**Circ:** ‡20,000

**Orion (13805)**
187 Main St.
Great Barrington, MA 01230
Phone: (413)528-4422
Fax: (413)528-0676
**Subject(s):** Environmental and Natural Resources Conservation
**Circ:** (Controlled)‡200
(Paid)‡20,000

**Pennsylvania CPA Journal (27216)**
Pennsylvania Institute of Certified Public Accountants
1650 Arch St., 17th Fl.
Philadelphia, PA 19103
Phone: (215)496-9272
Fax: (215)496-9212
**Subject(s):** Accountants and Accounting
**Circ:** (Non-paid)‡2,500
(Paid)‡20,000

**Piano Today (20360)**
333 Adams St.
Bedford Hills, NY 10507
Phone: (914)244-8500
Fax: (914)244-8560
**Subject(s):** Music and Musical Instruments
**Circ:** ‡20,000

**Refundle Bundle (23205)**
Box 140, Centuck Sta.
Yonkers, NY 10710
Phone: (914)472-2227
Fax: (914)725-1597
**Subject(s):** Consumerism
**Circ:** ‡20,000

**Rhode Island Boating (27844)**
Argosy Communications Ltd.
PO Box 956
East Greenwich, RI 02818-0960
Phone: (401)987-7717
Fax: (401)987-1662
**Subject(s):** Boats and Marine; (Boating and Yachting)
**Circ:** (Paid)50
(Non-paid)20,000

**Stone Magazine (22421)**
Tile and Stone Inc.
18 E 41st St.,
New York, NY 10017
Phone: (212)376-7722
Fax: (212)376-7723
**Subject(s):** Stone and Rock Products
**Circ:** (Paid)1,700
(Non-paid)20,000

**Telecom Asia (22445)**
Advanstar Communications
1 Park Ave.
New York, NY 10016
Phone: (212)951-6600
Fax: (212)951-6793
**Subject(s):** Telecommunications
**Circ:** (Controlled)20,000

**Today's Family (13763)**
Reminder Publications Inc.
280 N. Main St.
East Longmeadow, MA 01028
Phone: (413)525-6661
Fax: (413)525-5882
**Subject(s):** Parenting
**Circ:** (Paid)552
(Free)20,000

**Journal of Research in Science Teaching (19308)**
John Wiley and Sons Inc.
111 River St.
Hoboken, NJ 07030-5774
Phone: (201)748-6000
Fax: (201)748-6088
**Subject(s):** Science (General); Education
**Circ:** 19,950

**The New Gun Week (20575)**
Second Amendment Foundation
PO Box 488
Buffalo, NY 14209-0488
Phone: (716)885-6408
Fax: (716)884-4471
**Subject(s):** Firearms
**Circ:** (Non-paid)390
(Paid)19,641

**LMT (4861)**
LMT Communications Inc.
731 Main St., Ste. A2
Monroe, CT 06468
Phone: (203)459-2888
Fax: (203)459-2889

**The Lancet (North American Edition)** (27115)
Lippincott Williams & Wilkins
530 Walnut St.
Philadelphia, PA 19106-3261
Phone: (215)521-8300
Fax: (215)521-8902
**Subject(s):** Medicine and Surgery
**Circ:** ‡19,614

**Hamilton Alumni Review** (20654)
Hamilton College
College Publications
198 College Hill Rd.
Clinton, NY 13323
Phone: (315)859-4421
Fax: (315)859-4457
**Subject(s):** College Publications
**Circ:** (Non-paid)‡19,500

**Town & Gown** (27553)
Barash Group
403 S. Allen St.
PO Box 77
State College, PA 16804-0077
Phone: (814)238-5051
Fax: (814)238-3415
**Subject(s):** Local, State, and Regional Publications
**Circ:** (Paid)‡500
(Controlled)‡19,500

**Journal of the American Academy of Dermatology** (14941)
Mosby Inc.
University of Massachusetts Medical School
55 Lake Ave.
Worcester, MA 01655
Phone: (508)856-2583
**Subject(s):** Medicine and Surgery
**Circ:** (Paid)‡19,149

**Children's Software Revue (CSR)** (19087)
Children's Software Revue
120 Main St.
Flemington, NJ 08822
Phone: (908)284-0404
Fax: (908)284-0405
**Subject(s):** Education; Computers; Education; Computers; Youths' Interests; Parenting
**Circ:** (Combined)‡19,000

**FLEXO** (22874)
Foundation of Flexographic Technical Association
900 Marconi Ave.
Ronkonkoma, NY 11779-7212
Phone: (631)737-6020
Fax: (631)737-6813
**Subject(s):** Printing and Typography
**Circ:** (Paid)1,963
(Controlled)19,000

**Lawyer's Journal** (13542)
Massachusetts Bar Association
20 W St.
Boston, MA 02111-1204
Phone: (617)338-0500
Fax: (617)338-0650
**Subject(s):** Law
**Circ:** (Controlled)19,000

**P & S Journal** (22205)
Columbia University
630 W 168 St.
New York, NY 10032
Phone: (212)305-7131
Fax: (212)305-4521
**Subject(s):** Medicine and Surgery
**Circ:** (Free)19,000

**Professional Carwashing & Detailing** (21049)
National Trade Publications Inc.
13 Century Hill Dr.
Latham, NY 12110-2124
Phone: (518)783-1281
Fax: (518)783-1386
**Subject(s):** Automotive (Trade)
**Circ:** (Controlled)13,817
19,000

**BioPharm** (19412)
Advanstar Communications
485 Rte. 1 S., Bldg. F, First Fl.
Iselin, NJ 08830
Fax: (541)984-5250
**Subject(s):** Drugs and Pharmaceuticals
**Circ:** (Paid)222
(Non-paid)18,910

**Journal of Pathology** (19303)
John Wiley and Sons Inc.
111 River St.
Hoboken, NJ 07030-5774
Phone: (201)748-6000
Fax: (201)748-6088
**Subject(s):** Medicine and Surgery
**Circ:** (Paid)18,900

**Earth and Mineral Sciences** (27602)
Pennsylvania State University
116 Deike Bldg.
University Park, PA 16802
Phone: (814)865-7931
Fax: (814)865-1379
**Subject(s):** Mining and Minerals; Engineering (Various branches)
**Circ:** (Controlled)‡18,500

**Golf World Business** (5063)
Advance Magazine Publishers Inc.
5520 Park Ave.
Trumbull, CT 06611
Phone: (203)373-7176
Fax: (203)371-2132
**Subject(s):** Golf Course Management
**Circ:** (Controlled)‡18,500

**New England Historical and Genealogical Register** (13558)
New England Historic Genealogical Society
101 Newbury St.
Boston, MA 02116-3007
Phone: (617)536-5740
Fax: (617)536-7307
**Subject(s):** History and Genealogy
**Circ:** ‡18,500

**Retail Info Systems News** (19759)
Edgell Communications Inc.
4 Middlebury Blvd.
Randolph, NJ 07869
Phone: (973)252-0100
Fax: (973)252-9020
**Subject(s):** Retail; Computers
**Circ:** (Controlled)‡18,500

**SYMPHONY** (22437)
American Symphony Orchestra League
33 W 60th St., 5th Fl.
New York, NY 10023-7905
Phone: (212)262-5161
Fax: (212)262-5198
**Subject(s):** Music and Musical Instruments
**Circ:** ‡18,500

**Health Products Business** (21158)
Cygnus Business Media Inc.
3 Huntington Quadrangle, Ste. 301 N.
Melville, NY 11747
Phone: (631)845-2700
Fax: (631)845-2798
**Subject(s):** Food and Grocery Trade; Health and Healthcare
**Circ:** (Paid)12
(Non-paid)18,463

**Saltwater Fly Fishing** (30842)
Abenaki Publishers Inc.
160 Benmont Ave.
PO Box 4100
Bennington, VT 05201-4100
Phone: (802)447-1518
Fax: (802)447-2471
**Subject(s):** (Hunting, Fishing, and Game Management)
**Circ:** (Paid)★18,412

**American Journal of Physical Anthropology** (19160)
John Wiley and Sons Inc.
111 River St.
Hoboken, NJ 07030-5774
Phone: (201)748-6000
Fax: (201)748-6088
**Subject(s):** Anthropology and Ethnology
**Circ:** (Paid)18,200

**Legislative Gazette** (20218)
Rm. 106, Empire State Plaza
Concourse Level
PO Box 7329
Albany, NY 12224
Phone: (518)473-9739
Fax: (518)486-6609
**Subject(s):** Politics; Political Science
**Circ:** (Paid)385
(Non-paid)18,200

**European Clinical Laboratory** (5005)
International Scientific Communications Inc.
30 Controls Dr.
PO Box 870
Shelton, CT 06484-0870
Phone: (203)926-9300
Fax: (203)926-9310
**Subject(s):** Hospitals and Healthcare Institutions
**Circ:** (Non-paid)‡18,072

**Art Now Gallery Guide–Southeast Edition** (19044)
Art Now Inc.
97 Grayrock Rd.
PO Box 5541
Clinton, NJ 08809-5541
Phone: (908)638-5255
Fax: (908)638-8737
**Subject(s):** Art
**Circ:** (Paid)18,000

**Financial Executive** (19092)
Financial Executives Institute
200 Campus Dr.
PO Box 674
Florham Park, NJ 07932-0674
Phone: (973)765-1000
Fax: (973)765-1018
**Subject(s):** Banking, Finance, and Investments; Management and Administration
**Circ:** 18,000

**Lapis** (22023)
New York Open Center
83 Spring St.
New York, NY 10012
Phone: (212)219-2527
**Subject(s):** Philosophy
**Circ:** (Combined)18,000

**Modern Reprographics** (21171)
Cygnus Business Media Inc.
3 Huntington Quadrangle, Ste. 301 N.
Melville, NY 11747
Phone: (631)845-2700
Fax: (631)845-2798
**Subject(s):** Photography; Printing and Typography
**Circ:** 18,000

**The New England Antiques Journal** (14725)
Turley Publications
24 Water St.
Palmer, MA 01069
Phone: (413)283-8393
Fax: (413)283-7107
**Subject(s):** Art; Antiques; Collecting
**Circ:** (Paid)7,000
(Controlled)18,000

**New Jersey Lawyer** (19599)
New Jersey State Bar Association
New Jersey Law Center
1 Constitution Sq.
New Brunswick, NJ 08901-1520
Phone: (732)249-5000
Fax: (732)249-2815
**Subject(s):** Law
**Circ:** 18,000

**Plants & Gardens News** (20532)
Brooklyn Botanic Garden
1000 Washington Ave.
Brooklyn, NY 11225
Phone: (718)623-7200
Fax: (718)622-7839
**Subject(s):** Horticulture; Botany
**Circ:** ‡18,000

**Sign Builder Illustrated** (22372)
345 Hudson St., 12th Fl.
New York, NY 10014
Phone: (212)620-7200
Fax: (212)633-1863
**Subject(s):** Graphic Arts and Design
**Circ:** ‡18,000

**Summer Week/Winter Week (18886)**
Salmon Press
5 Water St.
PO Box 729
Meredith, NH 03253
Phone: (603)279-4516
Fax: (603)279-3331
**Subject(s):** Lifestyle

**Circ:** (Non-paid)18,000

**Transitions Abroad (30843)**
Transitions Abroad Publishing
PO Box 745
Bennington, VT 05201
Phone: (802)442-4827
Fax: (802)442-4827
**Subject(s):** Employment and Human Resources; Travel and Tourism

**Circ:** (Paid)‡18,000

**Women and Guns (20585)**
Second Amendment Foundation
PO Box 488
Buffalo, NY 14209-0488
Phone: (716)885-6408
Fax: (716)884-4471
**Subject(s):** Women's Interests; Firearms

**Circ:** ‡18,000

**The Business Record (22998)**
Liberty Business Development Group
731 James St.
Syracuse, NY 13203
Phone: (315)472-6911
Fax: (315)701-2805
**Subject(s):** Business; Local, State, and Regional Publications

**Circ:** (Controlled)‡17,500

**Precision Shooting (4839)**
Precision Shooting Inc.
222 Mckee St.
Manchester, CT 06040
Phone: (860)645-8776
Fax: (860)643-8215
**Subject(s):** Firearms

**Circ:** 17,500

**Progress in Photovoltaics (19367)**
John Wiley and Sons Inc.
111 River St.
Hoboken, NJ 07030-5774
Phone: (201)748-6000
Fax: (201)748-6088
**Subject(s):** Computers; Electrical Engineering; Nuclear Engineering

**Circ:** (Paid)17,500

**The RMA Journal (27250)**
RMA—The Risk Management Association
1 Liberty Pl.
1650 Market St., Ste. 2300
Philadelphia, PA 19103-7398
Phone: (215)446-4000
Fax: (215)446-4101
**Subject(s):** Banking, Finance, and Investments

**Circ:** (Paid)‡2,500
(Non-paid)‡17,500

**Selling Christmas Decorations (19120)**
Edgell Communications Inc.
3 Oxford Rd.
Goshen, NJ 10924
Phone: (914)291-8723
**Subject(s):** Gifts, Toys, and Novelties

**Circ:** (Controlled)17,500

**Cancer Investigation (21453)**
Marcel Dekker Inc.
c/o Yashar Hirshaut, M.D.
Yeshiva University
2495 Amsterdam Ave.
New York, NY 10033
**Subject(s):** Medicine and Surgery

**Circ:** (Controlled)‡17,420

**HME News (12619)**
United Publications Inc.
106 Lafayette St.
Yarmouth, ME 04096
Phone: (207)846-0600
Fax: (207)846-0657
**Subject(s):** Machinery and Equipment; Medicine and Surgery

**Circ:** (Paid)△17,100

**Aperture (21346)**
547 West 27th St.
New York, NY 10001
Phone: (212)505-5555
Fax: (212)598-4015
**Subject(s):** Photography

**Circ:** ‡17,000

**Applied Clinical Trials (19411)**
Advanstar Communications
485 Rte. 1 S., Bldg. F, First Fl.
Iselin, NJ 08830
Phone: (732)596-0276
Fax: (732)596-0003
**Subject(s):** Health and Healthcare; Laboratory Research (Scientific and Medical)

**Circ:** (Combined)△17,000

**Distribution Sales and Management (20768)**
NPTA Alliance
500 Bi County Blvd., Ste. 200E
Farmingdale, NY 11735
Phone: (631)777-2223
Fax: (631)777-2224
**Subject(s):** Paper; Packaging

**Circ:** (Controlled)17,000

**EXTRA! (21675)**
FAIR
112 W 27 St.
New York, NY 10001
Phone: (212)633-6700
Fax: (212)727-7668
**Subject(s):** Journalism and Publishing

**Circ:** (Non-paid)‡700
6,000
(Paid)‡17,000

**Hearth & Home Magazine (18848)**
Village West Publishing
PO Box 1288
Laconia, NH 03247
Phone: (603)528-4285
Fax: (603)524-0643
**Subject(s):** Furniture and Furnishings; Home Furnishings, Curtains, Draperies

**Circ:** (Non-paid)‡17,000

**Outerwear Magazine (22204)**
Creative Marketing Plus
19 W. 21st St., No. 403
New York, NY 10010
Phone: (212)727-1210
Fax: (212)727-1218
**Subject(s):** Clothing; Shoes, Leather, and Luggage

**Circ:** ‡17,000

**Susquehanna Today (27519)**
Susquehanna University
514 University Ave.
Selinsgrove, PA 17870-1025
Phone: (570)372-4119
Fax: (570)372-4048
**Subject(s):** College Publications

**Circ:** (Non-paid)‡17,000

**Trace: AIGA Journal of Design (22471)**
American Institute of Graphic Arts
164 5th Ave.
New York, NY 10010
Phone: (212)807-1990
Fax: (212)807-1799
**Subject(s):** Graphic Arts and Design

**Circ:** (Controlled)17,000

**Wheels, Etc. (14834)**
WANT AD Publications Inc.
128 Boston Post Rd.
Sudbury, MA 01776-2453
Phone: (978)443-7007
Fax: (978)443-3340
**Subject(s):** Automotive (Consumer)

**Circ:** ‡17,000

**The Journal of Orthopaedic and Sports Physical Therapy (JOSPT) (27077)**
Lippincott Williams & Wilkins
530 Walnut St.
Philadelphia, PA 19106-3261
Phone: (215)521-8300
Fax: (215)521-8902
**Subject(s):** Medicine and Surgery

**Circ:** (Non-paid)‡272
(Paid)‡16,971

**Paper Clips (18999)**
Baker & Taylor
1120 Rte. 22 E
Bridgewater, NJ 08807
Phone: (908)541-7000
**Subject(s):** Indexes, Abstracts, Reports, Proceedings, and Bibliographies; Book Trade and Author News

**Circ:** (Non-paid)16,800

**SAE Off-Highway Engineering (27646)**
S.A.E. International
400 Commonwealth Dr.
Warrendale, PA 15096-0001
Phone: (724)776-4841
Fax: (724)776-4026
**Subject(s):** Automotive (Trade); Engineering (Various branches)

**Circ:** (Controlled)16,772

**Real Estate New York (22293)**
Real Estate Media Inc.
520 Eighth Ave., 17th Fl.
New York, NY 10018
Phone: (212)929-6900
Fax: (212)929-7124
**Subject(s):** Real Estate

**Circ:** (Paid)‡551
(Controlled)‡16,661

**Sound & Communications Magazine (22732)**
Testa Communications
25 Willowdale Ave.
Port Washington, NY 11050
Phone: (516)767-2500
Fax: (516)767-9335
**Subject(s):** Radio, Television, Cable, and Video; Telecommunications

**Circ:** (Paid)458
(Non-paid)16,640

**The Pet Dealer (21173)**
Cygnus Business Media Inc.
PTN Publishing Co.
445 Broad Hollow Rd.
Melville, NY 11747
Phone: (516)845-2700
Fax: (516)845-2797
**Subject(s):** Pets

**Circ:** (Paid)564
(Non-paid)16,597

**Maintenance Supplies (21168)**
Cygnus Business Media Inc.
3 Huntington Quadrangle, Ste. 301 N.
Melville, NY 11747
Phone: (631)845-2700
Fax: (631)845-2798
**Subject(s):** Building Management and Maintenance

**Circ:** (Non-paid)‡16,500

**Style 1900 (19447)**
333 N Main St.
Lambertville, NJ 08530
Phone: (609)397-4104
Fax: (609)397-9377
**Subject(s):** Art and Art History

**Circ:** (Paid)16,500

**Clinical Oncology (26872)**
Elsevier
1600 John F. Kennedy Blvd.
Philadelphia, PA 19103
Phone: (215)239-3900
Fax: (215)239-3990
**Subject(s):** Medicine and Surgery

**Circ:** (Paid)‡16,275

**Auto Laundry News (19098)**
E.W. Williams Publications
2125 Center Ave., Ste. 305
Fort Lee, NJ 07024-5898
Phone: (201)592-7007
Fax: (201)592-7171
**Subject(s):** Automotive (Trade)

**Circ:** (Paid)708
(Non-paid)△15,716
(Controlled)16,269

**Maine Magazine (12539)**
County Wide Communications Inc.
PO Box 497
Machias, ME 04654
Phone: (207)753-0919
**Subject(s):** Local, State, and Regional Publications

**Circ:** (Paid)16,200

**Whole Foods** (19836)
WFC Inc.
4041 G Hadley Rd., Ste.101
South Plainfield, NJ 07080
Phone: (908)769-1160
Fax: (908)769-1171
Subject(s): Food and Grocery Trade; Health and Fitness
Circ: (Paid)303
(Controlled)16,203

**Minority Engineer** (21169)
Equal Opportunity Publications Inc.
445 Broad Hollow Rd., Ste.425
Melville, NY 11747
Phone: (631)421-9421
Fax: (631)421-0359
Subject(s): Engineering (Various branches); Ethnic and Minority Studies
Circ: (Non-paid)‡16,021

**Catalog Age** (5025)
Primedia Business
11 River Bend Dr. S.
PO Box 4949
Stamford, CT 06907-0949
Phone: (203)358-9900
Fax: (203)358-5811
Subject(s): Advertising and Marketing
Circ: (Paid)★486
(Non-paid)★**16,012**

**Hi Class Living** (19075)
M.N.R. Promotions Inc.
120 Sylvan Ave.
Englewood Cliffs, NJ 07632
Phone: (201)363-0200
Fax: (201)363-0204
Subject(s): Lifestyle; Local, State, and Regional Publications; Travel and Tourism
Circ: (Controlled)‡16,000

**The Horn Book Magazine** (13525)
The Horn Book Inc.
56 Roland St., Ste. 200
Boston, MA 02129
Phone: (617)628-0225
Fax: (617)628-0882
Subject(s): Literature and Literary Reviews
Circ: (Combined)16,000

**The Valley** (26120)
Lebanon Valley College
101 North College Ave.
Annville, PA 17003
Subject(s): College Publications
Circ: (Non-paid)‡16,000

**Happi** (19748)
Rodman Publishing Co.
70 Hilltop Rd., 3rd Fl.
Box 555
Ramsey, NJ 07446
Phone: (201)825-2552
Fax: (201)825-0553
Subject(s): Chemistry, Chemicals, and Chemical Engineering
Circ: (Paid)700
(Controlled)15,905

**Soap/Cosmetics/Chemical Specialties** (21188)
Cygnus Business Media Inc.
3 Huntington Quadrangle, Ste. 301 N.
Melville, NY 11747
Phone: (631)845-2700
Fax: (631)845-2798
Subject(s): Chemistry, Chemicals, and Chemical Engineering; Cosmetics and Toiletries
Circ: (Paid)1,187
(Controlled)15,662

**County Lines** (27666)
Valley Del Publications Inc.
893 S Matlack St.
West Chester, PA 19382
Phone: (610)918-9300
Fax: (610)918-1640
Subject(s): Local, State, and Regional Publications
Circ: (Paid)‡400
(Controlled)‡15,600

**Creative** (21567)
Magazines/Creative Inc.
42 W. 38th St.
New York, NY 10018
Phone: (212)840-0160
Fax: (212)819-0945

Subject(s): Advertising and Marketing
Circ: 15,500

**Nephrology Nursing Journal** (19696)
American Nephrology Nurses' Association
E Holly Ave.
Box 56
Pitman, NJ 08071-0056
Phone: (856)256-2320
Fax: (856)589-7463
Subject(s): Nursing
Circ: ‡15,500

**Sons of Italy Times** (27273)
Grand Lodge of Pennsylvania
Curtis Ctr.
601 Walnut St., No. L45
Philadelphia, PA 19106-3323
Phone: (215)592-1713
Fax: (215)592-9152
Subject(s): Italian; Unclassified Fraternal
Circ: ‡15,500

**Dealernews** (21591)
Advanstar Communications
1 Park Ave.
New York, NY 10016
Phone: (212)951-6600
Fax: (212)951-6793
Subject(s): Motorbikes and Motorcycles; (Boating and Yachting)
Circ: (Paid)△105
(Non-paid)△**15,477**

**Stroke** (27276)
Lippincott Williams & Wilkins
530 Walnut St.
Philadelphia, PA 19106-3261
Phone: (215)521-8300
Fax: (215)521-8902
Subject(s): Medicine and Surgery
Circ: (Paid)‡15,300

**Podiatry Management Magazine** (26125)
Kane Communications Inc.
10 E Athens Ave., Ste. 208
Ardmore, PA 19003
Phone: (610)645-6940
Fax: (610)645-6943
Subject(s): Management and Administration
Circ: (Combined)‡15,271

**Journal of Protective Coatings & Linings (JPCL)** (27365)
Technology Publishing Co.
2100 Wharton St., Ste. 310.
Pittsburgh, PA 15203-1951
Phone: (412)431-8300
Fax: (412)431-5428
Subject(s): Paint and Wallcoverings
Circ: (Non-paid)‡5,146
(Paid)‡9,854
(Combined)‡15,260

**Catalog Success Magazine** (26857)
North American Publishing Co.
401 N. Broad St., 5th Fl.
Philadelphia, PA 19108
Phone: (215)238-5482
Fax: (215)238-5412
Subject(s): Business; Retail
Circ: (Combined)15,245

**Podiatry Today** (19541)
Dowden Publishing Company Inc.
110 Summit Ave.
Montvale, NJ 07645
Phone: (201)391-9100
Fax: (201)782-5319
Subject(s): Podiatry; Medicine and Surgery
Circ: (Free)‡15,218

**Nutrition Today** (13566)
Lippincott Williams & Wilkins
C/o Frances Stern Nutrition Center
New England Medical Center
Box 783, 750 Washington St.
Boston, MA 02111
Phone: (617)636-5273
Subject(s): Health and Healthcare
Circ: (Paid)15,200

**The Voice** (19623)
Episcopal Diocese of Newark
31 Mulberry St.
Newark, NJ 07102
Phone: (973)622-4306
Fax: (973)622-3503
Subject(s): Religious Publications
Circ: ‡15,200

**Pulp & Paper International** (21117)
CMP Media L.L.C.
600 Community Dr.
Manhasset, NY 11030
Phone: (516)562-5000
Fax: (516)562-5995
Subject(s): Paper
Circ: (Controlled)15,134

**The Practical Lawyer** (27235)
ALI-ABA Committee on Continuing Professional Education
4025 Chestnut St.
Philadelphia, PA 19104
Phone: (215)243-1604
Fax: (215)243-1664
Subject(s): Law
Circ: (Controlled)15,100

**Ross Reports Television and Film** (22327)
VNU Business Media USA
770 Broadway, 4th Fl.
New York, NY 10003
Phone: (646)654-5741
Fax: (800)745-8922
Subject(s): Performing Arts; Drama and Theatre; Drama and Theatre; Motion Pictures; Entertainment
Circ: (Combined)15,103

**Journal of Electronic Defense** (14717)
Horizon House Publications Inc.
685 Canton St.
Norwood, MA 02062
Phone: (781)769-9750
Fax: (781)769-9884
Subject(s): Military and Navy; Electronics Engineering
Circ: (Paid)‡15,084

**Seafood Business** (12568)
Diversified Business Communications
PO Box 7438
Portland, ME 04112-7438
Phone: (207)842-5603
Fax: (207)842-5603
Subject(s): Fish and Commercial Fisheries; Food and Grocery Trade
Circ: (Paid)1,175
(Controlled)15,087

**New England Bride** (14730)
New England Bride Inc.
215 Newbury St., Ste. 207B
Peabody, MA 01960
Phone: (978)535-4186
Fax: (978)535-3090
Subject(s): Brides
Circ: (Non-paid)‡15,075

**Food Engineering (International Edition)** (27669)
Reed Business Information
c/o Joyce Fassl, 901 S. Bolmar St., Ste. P
West Chester, PA 19382
Phone: (610)436-4220
Subject(s): Food and Grocery Trade; Beverages, Brewing, and Bottling
Circ: (Paid)‡734
(Non-paid)‡15,043

**Workforce Diversity for Engineering and IT Professionals** (21197)
Equal Opportunity Publications Inc.
445 Broad Hollow Rd., Ste.425
Melville, NY 11747
Phone: (631)421-9421
Fax: (631)421-0359
Subject(s): Automation; Computers; Engineering (Various branches)
Circ: (Combined)15,046

**Mediaweek Magazine** (22070)
ADWEEK Magazines
770 Broadway, 6th Fl.
New York, NY 10003
Subject(s): Radio, Television, Cable, and Video
Circ: (Paid)6,989
(Non-paid)15,038

Circulation: ★ = ABC; △ = BPA; ♦ = CAC; ● = CCAB; ❏ = VAC; ⊕ = PO Statement; ‡ = Publisher's Report; Boldface figures = sworn; Light figures = estimated.

# Northeastern States

**Art Now Gallery Guide–Boston/New England Edition** (19039)
Art Now Inc.
97 Grayrock Rd.
PO Box 5541
Clinton, NJ 08809-5541
Phone: (908)638-5255
Fax: (908)638-8737
**Subject(s):** Art
**Circ:** (Non-paid)15,000

**audioXpress** (18932)
Audio Amateur Corporation Inc.
PO Box 876
Peterborough, NH 03458-0876
Phone: (603)924-9464
Fax: (603)924-9467
**Subject(s):** Radio, Television, Cable, and Video; Electronics Engineering
**Circ:** (Paid)15,000

**The Catholic Peace Voice** (26345)
Pax Christi-USA
532 W 8th St.
Erie, PA 16502
Phone: (814)453-4955
Fax: (814)452-4784
**Subject(s):** Religious Publications; Peace
**Circ:** (Non-paid)10,000
(Paid)15,000

**DIY Boat Owner** (22614)
JM Publishing
PO Box 1072
Niagara Falls, NY 14304
Phone: (705)359-2094
Fax: (705)359-2097
**Subject(s):** (Boating and Yachting)
**Circ:** (Controlled)15,000

**J Magazine** (13531)
Genki Publishing Inc.
476 Commonwealth Ave.
Boston, MA 02215-2712
Phone: (617)262-9390
Fax: (617)262-8036
**Subject(s):** Entertainment; Music and Musical Instruments; Japanese; Ethnic Publications
**Circ:** (Combined)15,000

**The Jewish Observer** (21861)
Agudath Israel of America
42 Broadway, 14th Fl.
New York, NY 10004
Phone: (212)797-9000
Fax: (646)254-1600
**Subject(s):** Jewish Publications
**Circ:** ‡15,000

**Mobile Beat** (20729)
Mobile Beat Magazine
PO Box 309
East Rochester, NY 14445-0309
Phone: (585)385-9920
Fax: (585)385-3637
**Subject(s):** Music and Musical Instruments; Entertainment
**Circ:** (Paid)15,000

**Murray Hill News** (22114)
The Murray Hill News Corp.
237 Madison Avenue
New York, NY 10016
Phone: (212)684-6728
**Subject(s):** Entertainment
**Circ:** 15,000

**The Philadelphia Spotlite** (27226)
3401 N I St., 5th Fl.
Philadelphia, PA 19134
Fax: (215)425-1155
**Subject(s):** Local, State, and Regional Publications
**Circ:** (Controlled)15,000

**Retail Systems Reseller** (19760)
Edgell Communications Inc.
4 Middlebury Blvd.
Randolph, NJ 07869
Phone: (973)252-0100
Fax: (973)252-9020
**Subject(s):** Retail
**Circ:** (Controlled)15,000

**South Jersey Parents Express** (26382)
Montgomery Newspapers
290 Commerce Dr.
Fort Washington, PA 19034
Phone: (215)628-8330
Fax: (215)648-3630
**Subject(s):** Parenting
**Circ:** (Combined)14,845

**AAOHN Journal** (19853)
SLACK Inc.
6900 Grove Rd.
Thorofare, NJ 08086-9447
Phone: (856)848-1000
Fax: (856)848-6091
**Subject(s):** Nursing
**Circ:** ‡14,800

**Sensible Sound** (22949)
Sensible Sound Inc.
403 Darwin Dr.
Snyder, NY 14226
Phone: (716)833-0930
Fax: (716)833-0929
**Subject(s):** Music and Musical Instruments
**Circ:** ‡14,700

**The Toy Book** (22470)
Adventure Publishing Group Inc.
1107 Broadway, Ste. 1204
New York, NY 10010-5501
Phone: (212)575-4510
Fax: (212)575-4521
**Subject(s):** Gifts, Toys, and Novelties
**Circ:** (Paid)617
(Non-paid)14,584

**Archives of Dermatology** (18853)
American Medical Association Alliance
Archives of Dermatology
1 Medical Center Dr., Level 2, Bldg 11, Rm 503
Section of Dermatology
Dartmouth-Hitchcock Medical Center
Lebanon, NH 03756-0001
Phone: (603)653-9477
Fax: (603)653-9478
**Subject(s):** Medicine and Surgery
**Circ:** (Combined)‡14,515

**Army Aviation Magazine** (4860)
Army Aviation Publications Inc.
755 Main St. Ste. 4D
Monroe, CT 06468-2830
**Subject(s):** Aviation; Military and Navy
**Circ:** ‡14,500

**Art Culinaire** (19567)
Culinaire Inc.
40 Mills St.
Morristown, NJ 07960
Phone: (973)993-5500
Fax: (973)993-8779
**Subject(s):** Food and Grocery Trade
**Circ:** ‡14,500

**Floor Focus** (22761)
Floor Focus Inc.
28 Old Stone Hill Rd.
Pound Ridge, NY 10576
Phone: (914)764-0556
Fax: (914)764-0560
**Subject(s):** Flooring and Floor Covering
**Circ:** 14,500

**Homiletic and Pastoral Review** (19750)
50 S Franklin Tpke.
PO Box 297
Ramsey, NJ 07446
**Subject(s):** Religious Publications
**Circ:** ‡14,500

**Stamps** (20910)
American Publishing Co.
85 Canisteo St.
Hornell, NY 14843-1544
Phone: (607)324-1425
Fax: (607)324-2317
**Subject(s):** Collecting
**Circ:** ‡14,500

**Entertainment Design** (21652)
Primedia Business Magzenes & Media
32 W. 18th St., 11th Fl.
New York, NY 10011-4612
Phone: (212)229-2084
Fax: (212)229-2084
**Subject(s):** Drama and Theatre
**Circ:** 14,446

**Editor & Publisher** (21633)
Editor & Publisher Magazine
770 Broadway
New York, NY 10003-9595
Fax: (646)654-5370
**Subject(s):** Advertising and Marketing; Journalism and Publishing; Printing and Typography
**Circ:** (Non-paid)3,905
(Paid)14,278

**American Journal of Surgery** (21318)
Excerpta Medica Inc.
655 Avenue of the Americas
New York, NY 10010
Phone: (212)989-5800
**Subject(s):** Medicine and Surgery
**Circ:** 14,241

**East Side Monthly** (27947)
Beacon Communications of Rhode Island
1944 Warwick Ave.
Warwick, RI 02889-5000
Phone: (401)732-3100
Fax: (401)732-3110
**Subject(s):** Free Newspapers
**Circ:** (Free)♦14,247

**Lighting Dimensions** (22036)
Primedia Business Magzenes & Media
32 W. 18th St., 11th Fl.
New York, NY 10011-4612
Phone: (212)229-2084
Fax: (212)229-2084
**Subject(s):** Lighting
**Circ:** ‡14,230

**Books and More for Growing Minds** (18996)
Baker & Taylor
1120 Rte. 22 E
Bridgewater, NJ 08807
Phone: (908)541-7000
**Subject(s):** Indexes, Abstracts, Reports, Proceedings, and Bibliographies; Book Trade and Author News
**Circ:** (Non-paid)14,200

**Children's Business** (21484)
Fairchild Publications Inc.
7 W 34th St.
New York, NY 10001
Phone: (212)630-4000
Fax: (212)630-3555
**Subject(s):** Clothing; Gifts, Toys, and Novelties
**Circ:** (Non-paid)‡14,083

**Critical Care Medicine** (19005)
Society of Critical Care Medicine
C/o Joseph E. Parrillo, M.D. Editor
Robert Wood Johnson Medical School
University of Medicine and Dentistry of New Jersey
Cooper Health System
Camden, NJ 08102
Phone: (847)827-6886
Fax: (847)827-6886
**Subject(s):** Medicine and Surgery
**Circ:** (Non-paid)‡351
(Paid)14,089

**Business NH Magazine** (18868)
Millyard Communication Inc.
670 N Commercial St., Ste. 110
Manchester, NH 03101
Phone: (603)626-6354
Fax: (603)626-6359
**Subject(s):** Business; Local, State, and Regional Publications
**Circ:** (Paid)‡500
(Controlled)‡14,076

**Blood** (26849)
Elsevier
1600 John F. Kennedy Blvd.
Philadelphia, PA 19103
Phone: (215)239-3900
Fax: (215)239-3990
**Subject(s):** Medicine and Surgery
**Circ:** ‡14,043

**Pediatric Nursing** (19698)
Jannetti Publications Inc.
E Holly Ave.
Box 56
Pitman, NJ 08071-0056
Phone: (856)256-2300
Fax: (856)589-7463
**Subject(s):** Nursing; Pediatrics
**Circ:** ‡14,011

**Achshav!** (21255)
United Synagogue Youth
c/o United Synagogue of Conservative Judaism
Department of Youth Activities
155 5th Ave.
New York, NY 10010
Phone: (212)533-7800
Fax: (212)353-9439
**Subject(s):** Jewish Publications; Religious Publications
**Circ:** 14,000

**Complexity** (19204)
John Wiley and Sons Inc.
111 River St.
Hoboken, NJ 07030-5774
Phone: (201)748-6000
Fax: (201)748-6088
**Subject(s):** Biology; Computers; Engineering (Various branches); Mathematics; Physics
**Circ:** 14,000

**Empire State Report** (21228)
25-35 Beechwood Ave.
PO Box 9001
Mount Vernon, NY 10552-9001
Phone: (914)699-2020
Fax: (914)699-2025
**Subject(s):** State, Municipal, and County Administration
**Circ:** (Paid)1,600
(Non-paid)14,000

**Gray Areas** (26205)
Gray Areas Inc.
PO Box 808
Broomall, PA 19008-0808
**Subject(s):** Law; Sociology; Music and Musical Instruments
**Circ:** (Paid)‡14,000

**IBM Journal of Research and Development** (20300)
IBM Corp.
New Orchard Rd.
Armonk, NY 10504
Phone: (914)499-1900
Fax: (914)945-2018
**Subject(s):** Engineering (Various branches); Science (General)
**Circ:** (Combined)‡14,000

**Journal of Cataract and Refractive Surgery** (27017)
American Society of Cataract and Refractive Surgery
Elsevier, Health Sciences Division
The Curtis Center, Ste. 300E
170 S. Independence Mall W.
Philadelphia, PA 19106-3399
Phone: (215)238-7800
Fax: (215)238-7883
**Subject(s):** Medicine and Surgery
**Circ:** ‡14,000

**Medical Advertising** (19964)
Engel Publishing Partners
820 Bear Tavern Rd., Ste. 300
West Trenton, NJ 08628
Fax: (609)530-0207
**Subject(s):** Advertising and Marketing; Drugs and Pharmaceuticals
**Circ:** (Combined)△14,000

**Medical Marketing & Media** (22071)
Haymarket Media
114 W 26th St.
New York, NY 10001
Phone: (646)638-6117
Fax: (646)638-6150
**Subject(s):** Drugs and Pharmaceuticals; Medicine and Surgery; Advertising and Marketing
**Circ:** (Controlled)‡14,000

**New York State Dental Journal** (20226)
New York State Dental Association
121 State St., 4th Fl.
Albany, NY 12207
Phone: (518)465-0044
Fax: (518)427-0461
**Subject(s):** Dentistry
**Circ:** 14,000

**Northern Woodlands** (30880)
Northern Woodlands Magazine
PO Box 471, 1776 Center Rd.
Corinth, VT 05039
Phone: (802)439-6292
Fax: (802)439-6296
**Subject(s):** Environmental and Natural Resources Conservation; (Outdoors)
**Circ:** (Paid)⊕14,000

**Theology Today** (19737)
Princeton Theological Seminary
PO Box 821
Princeton, NJ 08542-0803
Phone: (609)921-8300
**Subject(s):** Religious Publications
**Circ:** ‡14,000

**UK & USA** (22500)
British-America Business Inc.
52 Vanderbilt, 20th Fl.
New York, NY 10017
Phone: (212)661-4060
Fax: (212)661-4074
**Subject(s):** International Business and Economics
**Circ:** (Paid)14,000

**Now Hear This** (18998)
Baker & Taylor
1120 Rte. 22 E
Bridgewater, NJ 08807
Phone: (908)541-7000
**Subject(s):** Indexes, Abstracts, Reports, Proceedings, and Bibliographies; Book Trade and Author News
**Circ:** (Non-paid)13,900

**Journal of Manipulative and Physiological Therapeutics (JMPT)** (27053)
Mosby
170 S. Independence Mall W., Ste. 300 E.
Philadelphia, PA 19106-3399
Phone: (215)238-7869
Fax: (215)238-2239
**Subject(s):** Medicine and Surgery
**Circ:** (Paid)‡13,823

**Ear, Nose & Throat Journal** (26929)
MEDQUEST Communications L.L.C.
1721 Pine St.
Philadelphia, PA 19103-6771
Phone: (215)732-6100
Fax: (215)545-3374
**Subject(s):** Medicine and Surgery
**Circ:** (Combined)△13,784

**Auto Interiors** (21376)
VNU Business Media USA
770 Broadway
New York, NY 10003
Phone: (646)654-5000
**Subject(s):** Automotive (Trade); Transportation, Traffic, and Shipping
**Circ:** 13,642

**Journal of the Audio Engineering Society** (21883)
Audio Engineering Society
60 E. 42nd St., Rm. 2520
New York, NY 10165-2520
Phone: (212)661-8528
Fax: (212)682-0477
**Subject(s):** Engineering (Various branches); Radio, Television, Cable, and Video
**Circ:** ‡13,561

**American Anthropologist** (21297)
American Anthropological Association
c/o Susan H. Lees, Department of Anthropology
Hunter College, 695 Park Ave.
New York, NY 10021
Phone: (212)772-5428
**Subject(s):** Anthropology and Ethnology
**Circ:** ‡13,500

**Connection** (13503)
The New England Board of Higher Education
45 Temple Pl.
Boston, MA 02111
Phone: (617)357-9620
Fax: (617)338-1577
**Subject(s):** Economics; Education
**Circ:** (Controlled)13,500

**Frozen Food Digest Magazine** (21720)
Frozen Food Digest Inc.
271 Madison Ave.
New York, NY 10016
Phone: (212)557-8600
Fax: (212)986-9868
**Subject(s):** Food and Grocery Trade
**Circ:** ‡13,500

**Journal of Solid-State Circuits** (19689)
IEEE Solid-State Circuits Society
c/o IEEE Corporate Office
445 Hoes Ln.
Piscataway, NJ 08855-1331
Phone: (732)981-3400
Fax: (732)981-3401
**Subject(s):** Electrical Engineering; Engineering (Various branches)
**Circ:** 13,500

**Pennsylvania Heritage** (26458)
Pennsylvania Historical and Museum Commission
300 N. St.
Div. of Publications
Commonwealth Keystone Bldg., Plz. Level
300 N. St.
Harrisburg, PA 17120
Phone: (717)787-2407
Fax: (717)787-8312
**Subject(s):** History and Genealogy
**Circ:** ‡13,500

**PSBA Bulletin** (26762)
Pennsylvania School Boards Association
774 Limekiln Rd.
New Cumberland, PA 17070-2398
Phone: (717)774-2331
Fax: (717)774-0718
**Subject(s):** Education
**Circ:** ‡13,400

**Research in Nursing & Health** (22838)
John Wiley and Sons Inc.
c/o Judith Gedney Baggs, School of Nursing
Univ. of Rochester
601 Elmwood Ave., PO Box SON
Rochester, NY 14642
**Subject(s):** Nursing
**Circ:** (Paid)13,300

**Holstein World** (20733)
Dairy Business Communications
6437 Collamer Rd.
East Syracuse, NY 13057-1031
Phone: (315)703-7979
Fax: (315)703-7988
**Subject(s):** Livestock
**Circ:** ‡13,255

**Enterprise Newspapers** (13779)
Falmouth Publishing Co.
50 Depot Ave.
Falmouth, MA 02540
Phone: (508)548-4700
Fax: (508)540-8407
**Subject(s):** Travel and Tourism
**Circ:** (Paid)10,000
(Non-paid)13,241

**Art Now Gallery Guide–Southwest Edition** (19045)
Art Now Inc.
97 Grayrock Rd.
PO Box 5541
Clinton, NJ 08809-5541
Phone: (908)638-5255
Fax: (908)638-8737
**Subject(s):** Art
**Circ:** (Non-paid)‡13,169

**Northern Logger and Timber Processor** (22645)
N.L. Publishing Inc.
PO Box 69
Old Forge, NY 13420
Phone: (315)369-3078
Fax: (315)369-3736
**Subject(s):** Forestry
**Circ:** (Paid)13,052

**Automatic Machining** (23138)
1066 Gravel Rd.
Webster, NY 14580
Phone: (585)787-0820
Fax: (585)787-0868
**Subject(s):** Metal, Metallurgy, and Metal Trade
**Circ:** 13,000

**Dispute Resolution Journal** (21610)
American Arbitration Association
335 Madison Ave., Fl. 10
New York, NY 10017-4605
Phone: (212)716-5800
Fax: (212)716-5905
**Subject(s):** Business
**Circ:** (Paid)‡2,000
(Controlled)‡13,000

**Faces** (18936)
Cobblestone Publishing Co.
30 Grove St., Ste. C
Peterborough, NH 03458
Phone: (603)924-7209
Fax: (603)924-7380
**Subject(s):** Children's Interests; Anthropology and Ethnology; Geography
**Circ:** 13,000

**Latin Mass Magazine** (19753)
50 So. Franklin Turnpike
Ramsey, NJ 07446
Phone: (201)327-5900
**Subject(s):** Religious Publications
**Circ:** (Non-paid)1,500
(Paid)13,000

**Med Ad News** (19963)
Engel Publishing Partners
820 Bear Tavern Rd., Ste. 300
West Trenton, NJ 08628
Fax: (609)530-0207
**Subject(s):** Advertising and Marketing
**Circ:** (Paid)‡3,000
(Controlled)‡13,000

**New York Metro Area Postal Union, Union Mail** (22162)
350 W 31st St., 3rd Fl.
New York, NY 10001
Phone: (212)563-7553
**Subject(s):** Labor; Postal and Shipping Supplies
**Circ:** (Controlled)500
(Paid)13,000

**Operations and Fulfillment** (5036)
Primedia Business
11 River Bend Dr. S.
PO Box 4949
Stamford, CT 06907-0949
Phone: (203)358-9900
Fax: (203)358-5811
**Subject(s):** Materials Handling; Advertising and Marketing
**Circ:** (Paid)‡13,000

**Producers Masterguide** (22205)
60 E. 8th St., 34th Fl.
New York, NY 10003-6514
Phone: (212)777-4002
Fax: (212)777-4101
**Subject(s):** Radio, Television, Cable, and Video
**Circ:** (Paid)‡1,000
(Non-paid)‡13,000

**Sing Out!** (26170)
The Sing Out Corp.
512 E 4th St.
PO Box 5460
Bethlehem, PA 18015-0460
Phone: (610)865-5366
Fax: (610)865-5129
**Subject(s):** Music and Musical Instruments
**Circ:** (Non-paid)‡500
(Paid)‡13,000

**The Village Chronicle** (27839)
56 Freeway Dr.
Cranston, RI 02920
Phone: (401)467-9343
Fax: (401)467-9359
**Subject(s):** Collecting; Crafts, Models, Hobbies, and Contests
**Circ:** (Paid)‡13,000

**Journal of Polymer Science** (27087)
John Wiley and Sons Inc.
c/o Virgil Percec
Roy & Diana Vagelos Laboratories
Dept. of Chemistry, University of Pennsylvania
231 S. 34th St.
Philadelphia, PA 19104-6323
Phone: (215)573-7456
Fax: (215)573-7888
**Subject(s):** Chemistry, Chemicals, and Chemical Engineering; Physics
**Circ:** 12,950

**The Journal of Taxation** (21997)
RIA Group
395 Hudson St., 4th Fl.
New York, NY 10014
Phone: (212)367-6300
Fax: (212)367-6314
**Subject(s):** Taxation and Tariff
**Circ:** (Paid)12,935

**Floor Covering News** (20894)
RO-EL Productions Inc.
550 W. Old Country Rd., Ste. 204
Hicksville, NY 11801
Phone: (516)932-7860
Fax: (516)932-7639
**Subject(s):** Flooring and Floor Covering
**Circ:** (Paid)‡2,855
(Controlled)‡12,906

**PTN (Photographic Trade News)** (21183)
Cygnus Business Media Inc.
3 Huntington Quadrangle, Ste. 301 N.
Melville, NY 11747
Phone: (631)845-2700
Fax: (631)845-2798
**Subject(s):** Photography
**Circ:** (Paid)280
(Non-paid)12,770

**Statistics in Medicine** (13590)
John Wiley and Sons Inc.
C/O Ralph D'Agostino, Department of Mathematics
Boston University
111 Cummington St.
Boston, MA 02215
**Subject(s):** Health and Healthcare; Hospitals and Healthcare Institutions; Laboratory Research (Scientific and Medical); Statistics
**Circ:** (Paid)12,600

**Bulletin of the AMS** (13492)
American Meteorological Society
45 Beacon St.
Boston, MA 02108-3693
Phone: (617)227-2425
Fax: (617)742-8718
**Subject(s):** Astronomy and Meteorology
**Circ:** ‡12,585

**American Sociological Review** (26820)
American Sociological Association
Dept. of Sociology
University of Pennsylvania
3718 Locust Walk
Philadelphia, PA 19104-6299
Fax: (215)898-3371
**Subject(s):** Sociology
**Circ:** ‡12,500

**BioCycle** (26325)
The JG Press Inc.
419 State Ave.
Emmaus, PA 18049
Phone: (610)967-4135
**Subject(s):** Water Supply and Sewage Disposal; Waste Management and Recycling
**Circ:** 12,500

**Industrial Laser Solutions** (18903)
PennWell Corp.
98 Spit Brook Rd.
Nashua, NH 03062-5737
Phone: (603)891-0123
Fax: (603)891-0574
**Subject(s):** Electronics Engineering
**Circ:** (Paid)‡12,503

**Maine Fish and Wildlife** (12447)
Maine Dept. of Inland Fisheries and Wildlife
284 State St., 41SHS
Augusta, ME 04333
Phone: (207)287-8000
Fax: (207)287-6395
**Subject(s):** Ecology and Conservation; Natural History and Nature Study; Local, State, and Regional Publications
**Circ:** (Non-paid)400
(Paid)12,500

**Medical Meetings** (14827)
Primedia Business Magazines & Media
c/o Tamar Hosansky
132 Great Rd., Ste. 120
Stow, MA 01775-1189
**Subject(s):** Conventions, Meetings, and Trade Fairs
**Circ:** (Controlled)‡12,500

**Travel Guide** (19002)
Baker & Taylor
1120 Rte. 22 E
Bridgewater, NJ 08807
Phone: (908)541-7000
**Subject(s):** Book Trade and Author News
**Circ:** (Non-paid)12,500

**W & J Magazine** (27650)
Washington and Jefferson College
60 S Lincoln St.
Washington, PA 15301
Phone: (724)222-4400
Fax: (724)223-5267
**Subject(s):** College Publications
**Circ:** (Free)‡12,500

**AUA News** (26838)
Lippincott Williams & Wilkins
530 Walnut St.
Philadelphia, PA 19106-3261
Phone: (215)521-8300
Fax: (215)521-8902
**Subject(s):** Medicine and Surgery; Health and Healthcare
**Circ:** (Combined)12,405

**IEEE Network** (21803)
Institute of Electrical and Electronics Engineers Inc.
3 Park Ave., 17th Fl.
New York, NY 10016
Phone: (212)705-8900
Fax: (212)705-8999
**Subject(s):** Electrical Engineering; Electronics Engineering
**Circ:** (Non-paid)82
(Paid)12,385

**Bicycle Retailer and Industry News** (21401)
VNU Business Media USA
770 Broadway
New York, NY 10003
Phone: (646)654-5000
**Subject(s):** Retail; (Bicycling)
**Circ:** 12,337

**LDB Interior Textiles** (22029)
E.W. Williams Publications
370 Lexington Ave., Ste. 1409
New York, NY 10017
Phone: (212)661-1516
Fax: (212)661-1713
**Subject(s):** Housewares; Textiles
**Circ:** (Paid)‡146
(Free)‡12,253

**Wire Journal International** (4788)
Wire Association International Inc.
1570 Boston Post Rd.
Guilford, CT 06437
Phone: (203)453-2777
Fax: (203)453-8384
**Subject(s):** Metal, Metallurgy, and Metal Trade
**Circ:** (Controlled)‡12,200

**AISE Steel Technology** (27642)
Association for Iron and Steel Technology
186 Thorn Hill Rd.
Warrendale, PA 15086
Phone: (724)776-6040
Fax: (724)776-1880
**Subject(s):** Metal, Metallurgy, and Metal Trade; Engineering (Various branches)
**Circ:** (Non-paid)‡589
(Paid)‡12,034

**Action!** (26614)
Mobile Air Conditioning Society Worldwide
225 S. Broad St.
PO Box 88
Lansdale, PA 19446
Phone: (215)631-7020
Fax: (215)631-7017
**Subject(s):** Air Conditioning and Refrigeration
**Circ:** 12,000

**The American Poetry Review** (26819)
World Poetry Inc.
117 S 17th St., Ste. 910
Philadelphia, PA 19103
Phone: (215)496-0439
Fax: (215)569-0808
**Subject(s):** Literature and Literary Reviews
**Circ:** (Non-paid)‡1,500
(Paid)‡12,000

**Army-Navy Store and Outdoor Merchandiser** (21150)
Cygnus Business Media Inc.
3 Huntington Quadrangle, Ste. 301 N.
Melville, NY 11747
Phone: (631)845-2700
Fax: (631)845-2798
**Subject(s):** General Merchandise
**Circ:** (Paid)‡12,000

**Art Now Gallery Guide–Chicago/Midwest Edition** (19040)
Art Now Inc.
97 Grayrock Rd.
PO Box 5541
Clinton, NJ 08809-5541
Phone: (908)638-5255
Fax: (908)638-8737
**Subject(s):** Art
**Circ:** (Non-paid)12,000

**The Big Takeover** (21402)
249 Eldridge St., No. 14
New York, NY 10002-1345
Phone: (212)533-6057
**Subject(s):** Music and Musical Instruments
**Circ:** (Paid)12,000

**Bomb** (21416)
New Arts Publications
594 Broadway, Ste. 905
New York, NY 10012
Phone: (212)431-3943
Fax: (212)431-5880
**Subject(s):** Art; Literature and Literary Reviews; Music and Musical Instruments; Motion Pictures
**Circ:** (Non-paid)‡3,000
(Paid)‡12,000

**Cell** (13656)
Cell Press
1100 Massachusetts Ave.
Cambridge, MA 02138
Phone: (617)661-7057
Fax: (617)661-7061
**Subject(s):** Biology
**Circ:** (Combined)‡12,000

**C.F.M.A. Building Profits** (19712)
Construction Financial Management Association
29 Emmons Dr., Ste. F-50
Princeton, NJ 08540
Phone: (609)452-8000
Fax: (609)452-0417
**Subject(s):** Construction, Contracting, Building, and Excavating; Banking, Finance, and Investments
**Circ:** (Paid)7,000
(Combined)12,000

**EContent** (5098)
Online, A Division of Information Today Inc.
88 Danbury Rd.Ste.1D
Wilton, CT 06897
Phone: (203)761-1466
Fax: (203)761-1444
**Subject(s):** Computers
**Circ:** ‡12,000

**Electronic Servicing & Technology** (22726)
Mainly Marketing
PO Box 748
Port Washington, NY 11050
Phone: (516)883-3382
Fax: (516)883-2162
**Subject(s):** Electronics Engineering
**Circ:** 12,000

**Forest Notes** (18784)
Society for the Protection of New Hampshire Forests
54 Portsmouth St.
Concord, NH 03301-5400
Phone: (603)224-9945
Fax: (603)228-0423
**Subject(s):** Environmental and Natural Resources Conservation; Forestry
**Circ:** (Controlled)‡400
(Paid)‡12,000

**Harvard Design Magazine** (13667)
48 Quincy St.
Cambridge, MA 02138
Phone: (617)495-7814
Fax: (617)496-3391
**Subject(s):** Architecture; Landscape Architecture
**Circ:** 12,000

**IEEE Industry Applications Magazine** (19679)
IEEE Inc.
445 Hoes Ln.
PO Box 1331
Piscataway, NJ 08855
Phone: (732)981-0060
**Subject(s):** Electronics Engineering; Electrical Engineering
**Circ:** (Paid)12,000

**IEEE Micro** (23209)
IEEE Computer Society
c/o Pradip Bose, Research Staff Member and Project Leader
IBM T.J. Watson Research Center
PO Box 218
Yorktown Heights, NY 10598
**Subject(s):** Computers
**Circ:** (Paid)12,000

**Modern Grocer** (13756)
GC Publishing Company Inc.
PO Box 2010
Dennis, MA 02638
Phone: (508)385-7700
Fax: (508)385-0089
**Subject(s):** Food and Grocery Trade
**Circ:** (Paid)3,000
(Non-paid)12,000

**Nursing Education Perspectives** (22183)
National League for Nursing
61 Broadway, 33rd Fl.
New York, NY 10006-2701
Phone: (212)363-5555
Fax: (212)812-0391
**Subject(s):** Health and Healthcare; Education
**Circ:** (Paid)3,000
(Controlled)12,000

**Old Sturbridge Visitor** (14830)
Old Sturbridge Inc.
1 Old Sturbridge Village Rd.
Sturbridge, MA 01566-1198
Phone: (508)347-3362
Fax: (508)347-0375
**Subject(s):** Museums
**Circ:** (Combined)12,000

**The Other Side** (27205)
300 W. Apsley
Philadelphia, PA 19144
Phone: (215)849-2178
Fax: (215)849-3755
**Subject(s):** Religious Publications
**Circ:** ‡12,000

**Rug Hooking Magazine** (26638)
1300 Market St., Ste. 202
Lemoyne, PA 17043-1420
Phone: (717)234-5091
Fax: (717)234-1359
**Subject(s):** Dressmaking, Needlework, and Quilting
**Circ:** 12,000

**Today's Parish** (4869)
Twenty-Third Publications, Bayard
185 Willow St.
PO Box 180
Mystic, CT 06355
Phone: (860)536-2611
Fax: (800)572-0788
**Subject(s):** Religious Publications
**Circ:** ‡12,000

**Agribusiness** (19156)
John Wiley and Sons Inc.
111 River St.
Hoboken, NJ 07030-5774
Phone: (201)748-6000
Fax: (201)748-6088
**Subject(s):** Scientific Agricultural Publications
**Circ:** (Paid)11,900

**Biotechnology & Bioengineering** (19180)
John Wiley and Sons Inc.
111 River St.
Hoboken, NJ 07030-5774
Phone: (201)748-6000
Fax: (201)748-6088
**Subject(s):** Biology
**Circ:** (Paid)11,900

**Travelware** (4964)
Business Journals Inc.
50 Day St.
PO Box 5550
Norwalk, CT 06854
Phone: (203)853-6015
Fax: (203)852-8175
**Subject(s):** Shoes, Leather, and Luggage
**Circ:** (Paid)661
(Non-paid)11,778

**Traditional Building** (20542)
Historical Trends Corp.
69A 7th Ave.
Brooklyn, NY 11217
Phone: (718)636-0788
Fax: (718)636-0750
**Subject(s):** Architecture; Construction, Contracting, Building, and Excavating
**Circ:** (Paid)11,240
(Non-paid)11,760

**Northeast Export Magazine** (18874)
Laurentian Business Publishing Inc.
404 Chestnut St., No. 201
Manchester, NH 03101-1831
Phone: (603)626-6354
Fax: (603)626-6359
**Subject(s):** Business; Local, State, and Regional Publications
**Circ:** (Controlled)11,750

**Teratology** (19400)
John Wiley and Sons Inc.
111 River St.
Hoboken, NJ 07030-5774
Phone: (201)748-6000
Fax: (201)748-6088
**Subject(s):** Medicine and Surgery; Biology; Toxicology; Drugs and Pharmaceuticals
**Circ:** (Paid)11,550

**Connecticut Bar Journal** (4797)
Connecticut Bar Associaiton
c/o Peter W. Schroth
Lally School of Management and Technology
Rensselaer Polytechnic Institute
275 Windsor St.
Hartford, CT 06120-2991
Phone: (860)548-7845
Fax: (860)547-0866
**Subject(s):** Law
**Circ:** (Paid)11,500

**Gay and Lesbian Review Worldwide** (13518)
Gay & Lesbian Review Inc.
PO Box 180300
Boston, MA 02118
Phone: (617)421-0082
**Subject(s):** Gay and Lesbian Interests; Literature and Literary Reviews; Literature
**Circ:** (Paid)‡11,500

**IEEE Aerospace and Electronic Systems Magazine** (21801)
Institute of Electrical and Electronics Engineers Inc.
3 Park Ave., 17th Fl.
New York, NY 10016
Phone: (212)705-8900
Fax: (212)705-8999
**Subject(s):** Electronics Engineering; Aviation
**Circ:** (Non-paid)‡500
(Paid)‡11,500

**My Friend** (13553)
Daughters of St. Paul Provincial House
50 Saint Paul's Ave.
Jamaica Plain
Boston, MA 02130-9330
Fax: (617)524-8035
**Subject(s):** Religious Publications; Youths' Interests
**Circ:** ‡11,500

## Northeastern States

**Parameters** (26223)
U.S. Army War College
122 Forbes Ave.
Carlisle, PA 17013-5238
Phone: (717)245-4943
**Subject(s):** Military and Navy; Political Science; International Affairs
**Circ:** (Paid)‡1,500
(Non-paid)‡11,500

**Philadelphia Business Journal** (27219)
400 Market St., Ste. 1200
Philadelphia, PA 19106
Phone: (215)238-1450
Fax: (215)238-9489
**Subject(s):** Business; Local, State, and Regional Publications
**Circ:** (Paid)11,506

**Plastic and Reconstructive Surgery** (13635)
Lippincott Williams & Wilkins
C/o Robert M. Goldwyn, M.D., Editor
1101 Beacon St.
Brookline, MA 02446
Phone: (617)731-8473
Fax: (617)731-9580
**Subject(s):** Medicine and Surgery
**Circ:** (Non-paid)‡315
(Paid)‡11,396

**The Music & Sound Retailer** (22729)
Testa Communications
25 Willowdale Ave.
Port Washington, NY 11050
Phone: (516)767-2500
Fax: (516)767-9335
**Subject(s):** Music and Musical Instruments
**Circ:** (Controlled)11,300

**Otolaryngology–Head and Neck Surgery** (27207)
Mosby
170 S. Independence Mall W., Ste. 300 E.
Philadelphia, PA 19106-3399
Phone: (215)238-7869
Fax: (215)238-2239
**Subject(s):** Medicine and Surgery
**Circ:** (Paid)‡11,300

**Diagnostic Cytopathology** (19210)
John Wiley and Sons Inc.
111 River St.
Hoboken, NJ 07030-5774
Phone: (201)748-6000
Fax: (201)748-6088
**Subject(s):** Medicine and Surgery
**Circ:** 11,200

**Long Island Business News** (22877)
2150 Smithtown Ave.
Ronkonkoma, NY 11779
Phone: (631)737-1700
Fax: (631)737-1890
**Subject(s):** Business; Local, State, and Regional Publications
**Circ:** (Non-paid)3,500
(Paid)8,500
11,200

**Medical and Pediatric Oncology** (27139)
John Wiley and Sons Inc.
Dept. of Radiation Oncology/2 Donner Hospital of the Univ. of Pennsylvania
3400 Spruce St.
Philadelphia, PA 19104
**Subject(s):** Medicine and Surgery; Pediatrics
**Circ:** 11,200

**REVISTA AEREA** (22316)
Strato Publishing Company Inc.
405 E 56th St., Ste. 4E
New York, NY 10022
Phone: (212)223-2707
Fax: (212)371-1224
**Subject(s):** Aviation; Portuguese; Spanish; Hispanic Publications
**Circ:** (Controlled)11,200

**Video Age International** (22516)
TV Trade Media Inc.
216 E 75th St., No. PW
New York, NY 10021
Phone: (212)288-3933
Fax: (212)734-9033
**Subject(s):** Radio, Television, Cable, and Video
**Circ:** (Paid)800
(Non-paid)11,200

**Tea and Coffee Trade Journal** (22439)
Lockwood Trade Journal Co.
26 Broadway, Fl. 9M
New York, NY 10004-1703
Phone: (212)391-2060
Fax: (212)827-0945
**Subject(s):** Food and Grocery Trade
**Circ:** (Combined)11,178

**AJIC (American Journal of Infection Control)** (21285)
Mosby Inc.
c/o Elaine L Larson, Editor
Columbia University School of Nursing
630 W 168th St
New York, NY 10032
**Subject(s):** Health and Healthcare
**Circ:** (Paid)‡11,136

**Beverage World en Espanol** (21399)
Beverage World
VNU Business Publications USA
770 Broadway
New York, NY 10003-9595
Phone: (646)654-7714
Fax: (646)654-7727
**Subject(s):** Beverages, Brewing, and Bottling; Spanish
**Circ:** (Combined)‡11,100

**Nonwovens Industry** (19754)
Rodman Publishing Co.
70 Hilltop Rd., 3rd Fl.
Box 555
Ramsey, NJ 07446
Phone: (201)825-2552
Fax: (201)825-0553
**Subject(s):** Textiles
**Circ:** (Paid)544
(Controlled)11,055

**Accessories** (4937)
Business Journals Inc.
50 Day St.
PO Box 5550
Norwalk, CT 06854
Phone: (203)853-6015
Fax: (203)852-8175
**Subject(s):** Jewelry, Watches, and Clocks; Shoes, Leather, and Luggage; Management and Administration
**Circ:** (Paid)11,000
(Non-paid)11,000

**CBIA News** (4796)
CBIA
350 Church St.
Hartford, CT 06103-1126
Phone: (860)244-1900
Fax: (860)278-8562
**Subject(s):** Management and Administration
**Circ:** ‡11,000

**Cineaste** (21491)
Cineaste Publishers Inc.
304 Hudson St., 6th Fl.
New York, NY 10003-1015
**Subject(s):** Entertainment; Motion Pictures
**Circ:** 11,000

**Current Biography** (20451)
The H.W. Wilson Co.
950 University Ave.
Bronx, NY 10452
Phone: (718)588-8400
Fax: (800)590-1617
**Subject(s):** History and Genealogy
**Circ:** ‡11,000

**Douglass Alumnae Magazine** (19589)
Associate Alumnae of Douglass College
181 Ryders Ln.
New Brunswick, NJ 08901
Phone: (732)932-2880
Fax: (732)932-2883
**Subject(s):** College Publications
**Circ:** ‡11,000

**Eurotec** (21670)
VNU Business Media USA
770 Broadway
New York, NY 10003
Phone: (646)654-5000
**Subject(s):** Engineering (Various branches); Chemistry, Chemicals, and Chemical Engineering
**Circ:** 11,000

**InterfaithFamily.com (IFF)** (14300)
InterfaithFamily.com Inc.
90 Oak St.
PO Box 9129
Newton Upper Falls, MA 02464
Phone: (617)581-6843
Fax: (617)965-7772
**Subject(s):** Jewish Publications; Intercultural Interests; Parenting
**Circ:** 11,000

**Nature Biotechnology** (22134)
Nature Publishing Group
345 Pk. Ave. S, 10th Fl.
New York, NY 10010-1707
Phone: (212)726-9200
Fax: (212)696-9006
**Subject(s):** Biology; Drugs and Pharmaceuticals
**Circ:** (Controlled)5,000
(Paid)11,000

**Vegetarian Voice** (20707)
North American Vegetarian Society
PO Box 72
Dolgeville, NY 13329
Phone: (518)568-7970
Fax: (518)568-7979
**Subject(s):** Environmental and Natural Resources Conservation; Health; Food and Cooking; Lifestyle
**Circ:** (Combined)11,000

**Environmental and Molecular Mutagenesis** (19219)
John Wiley and Sons Inc.
111 River St.
Hoboken, NJ 07030-5774
Phone: (201)748-6000
Fax: (201)748-6088
**Subject(s):** Science (General)
**Circ:** 10,850

**New England Farmer** (26393)
Farm Progress Cos.
c/o John Vogel, Editor
1685 Baltimore Pike
PO Box 4475
Gettysburg, PA 17325-4475
Phone: (717)334-4300
Fax: (717)334-3129
**Subject(s):** Farm Newspapers
**Circ:** (Paid)‡5,402
(Controlled)‡10,783

**Pharmacotherapy** (13575)
Pharmacotherapy Publications Inc.
750 Washington Ave.
NEMC Box 806
Boston, MA 02111
Phone: (617)636-5390
Fax: (617)636-5318
**Subject(s):** Drugs and Pharmaceuticals
**Circ:** ‡10,750

**Down East Magazine** (12493)
Down East Enterprise Inc.
PO Box 679
Camden, ME 04843-0679
Phone: (207)594-9544
Fax: (207)594-7215
**Subject(s):** Local, State, and Regional Publications
**Circ:** (Combined)★107,29

**Digest** (26919)
Philadelphia College of Osteopathic Medicine
4170 City Ave.
Philadelphia, PA 19131
Phone: (215)871-6120
Fax: (215)871-6151
**Subject(s):** Osteopathy; College Publications
**Circ:** (Controlled)‡10,600

**Educational Dealer** (20820)
Fahy-Williams Publishing Inc.
171 Reed St.
PO Box 1080
Geneva, NY 14456
Phone: (315)789-0458
Fax: (315)789-4263
**Subject(s):** Stationery, Office Equipment, and College Store Supplies
**Circ:** (Controlled)‡10,500

**Glass Craftsman** (26198)
Arts & Media Inc.
10 Canal St., Ste 300
Bristol, PA 19007
Phone: (215)826-1799
Fax: (215)860-1812
**Subject(s):** Crafts, Models, Hobbies, and Contests; Collecting
**Circ:** (Combined)10,500

**Government Food Service** (23165)
Executive Business Media Inc.
825 Old Country Rd.
PO Box 1500
Westbury, NY 11590-0812
Phone: (516)334-3030
Fax: (516)334-3059
**Subject(s):** Food and Grocery Trade; Military and Navy
**Circ:** (Controlled)10,500

**Government Recreation and Fitness** (23166)
Executive Business Media Inc.
825 Old Country Rd.
PO Box 1500
Westbury, NY 11590-0812
Phone: (516)334-3030
Fax: (516)334-3059
**Subject(s):** Health and Fitness
**Circ:** (Paid)10,500

**Journal of Coatings Technology** (26189)
Federation of Societies for Coatings Technology
492 Norristown Rd.
Blue Bell, PA 19422-2350
Phone: (610)940-0777
Fax: (610)940-0292
**Subject(s):** Paint and Wallcoverings
**Circ:** ‡10,500

**Slovak Catholic Falcon** (19670)
Slovak Catholic Sokol
205 Madison St.
PO Box 899
Passaic, NJ 07055
Phone: (973)777-2605
Fax: (973)779-8245
**Subject(s):** Religious Publications; Unclassified Fraternal
**Circ:** (Non-paid)‡200
 (Paid)‡10,494

**Calliope** (18933)
Cobblestone Publishing Co.
30 Grove St., Ste. C
Peterborough, NH 03458
Phone: (603)924-7209
Fax: (603)924-7380
**Subject(s):** History and Genealogy; Youths' Interests
**Circ:** (Paid)‡10,400

**The Counselor** (27584)
Advertising Specialty Institute
4800 St. Rd.
Trevose, PA 19053
Phone: (215)942-8600
Fax: (800)546-1399
**Subject(s):** Advertising and Marketing
**Circ:** (Paid)10,400

**MCN, The American Journal of Maternal/Child Nursing** (20931)
Lippincott Williams & Wilkins
100 Bay Dr. E.
Huntington Bay, NY 11743
Phone: (631)424-3747
Fax: (631)547-8943
**Subject(s):** Nursing
**Circ:** (Paid)10,397

**Gastronomica** (14912)
University of California Press/Journals
Williams College
Weston Hall
995 Main St.
Williamstown, MA 01267
**Subject(s):** History and Genealogy; Humanities; Social Sciences
**Circ:** 10,332

**International Railway Journal** (21841)
Simmons-Boardman Publishing Corp.
345 Hudson St.
New York, NY 10014-4590
Phone: (212)620-7200
Fax: (212)633-1165
**Subject(s):** Railroad; French; German; Spanish
**Circ:** (Combined)10,314

**Colored Stone** (26279)
Primedia Special Interest Publications
60 Chestnut Ave., Ste. 201
Devon, PA 19333-1312
Phone: (610)964-6300
Fax: (610)293-0977
**Subject(s):** Jewelry, Watches, and Clocks
**Circ:** (Paid)‡10,230

**Fanfare** (19852)
PO Box 17
Tenafly, NJ 07670
Phone: (201)567-3908
Fax: (201)816-0125
**Subject(s):** Music and Musical Instruments
**Circ:** (Paid)‡9,000
 (Controlled)‡10,200

**Film Journal International** (21688)
Sunshine Group Worldwide Ltd.
770 Broadway, 5th Fl.
New York, NY 10003-9595
Phone: (646)654-7680
Fax: (646)654-7694
**Subject(s):** Motion Pictures
**Circ:** 10,200

**Lab Animal** (22019)
Nature Publishing Group
345 Pk. Ave. S, 10th Fl.
New York, NY 10010-1707
Phone: (212)726-9200
Fax: (212)696-9006
**Subject(s):** Laboratory Research (Scientific and Medical)
**Circ:** (Paid)156
 (Non-paid)10,200

**Communications on Pure and Applied Mathematics** (21527)
John Wiley and Sons Inc.
c/o S.R.S. Varadhan, Courant Inst. of Mathematical Sciences
251 Mercer St.
New York, NY 10012
**Subject(s):** Mathematics
**Circ:** 10,150

**International Journal of Cancer** (19252)
John Wiley and Sons Inc.
111 River St.
Hoboken, NJ 07030-5774
Phone: (201)748-6000
Fax: (201)748-6088
**Subject(s):** Medicine and Surgery
**Circ:** 10,150

**Cancer Research** (26855)
American Association for Cancer Research Inc.
615 Chestnut St., 17th Fl.
Philadelphia, PA 19106-4404
Phone: (215)440-9300
Fax: (215)440-9313
**Subject(s):** Medicine and Surgery; Laboratory Research (Scientific and Medical)
**Circ:** (Paid)‡10,125

**Trusts and Estates** (22493)
Primedia Business
745 Fifth Ave.
New York, NY 10151
Phone: (212)745-0100
Fax: (212)745-0121
**Subject(s):** Banking, Finance, and Investments
**Circ:** (Non-paid)△4,485
 (Paid)△10,035

**Equities Magazine Co.** (22916)
PO Box 130H
Scarsdale, NY 10583
Phone: (914)715-7589
**Subject(s):** Banking, Finance, and Investments
**Circ:** (Non-paid)‡6,595
 (Paid)‡10,017

**Akwesasne Notes** (22882)
Mohawk Nation
PO Box 196
Rooseveltown, NY 13683-0196
Phone: (518)358-9531
Fax: (518)358-5987
**Subject(s):** Native American Interests
**Circ:** ‡10,000

**American Poet** (21323)
The Academy of American Poets
584 Broadway, Ste. 604
New York, NY 10012
Phone: (212)274-0343
Fax: (212)274-9427
**Subject(s):** Literature; Poetry
**Circ:** (Paid)10,000

**Automotive Market Report** (26720)
Automotive Auction Publishing Inc.
607 Laurel Drive
Monroeville, PA 15146
Phone: (412)373-6383
Fax: (412)373-6388
**Subject(s):** Automotive (Trade)
**Circ:** 10,000

**The AV Magazine** (26542)
American Anti-Vivisection Society
801 Old York Rd., Ste. 204
Jenkintown, PA 19046-1685
Phone: (215)887-0816
Fax: (215)887-2088
**Subject(s):** Society for the Prevention of Cruelty to Animals and Anti-Vivisection
**Circ:** (Combined)‡10,000

**Aviation Monthly** (23178)
Peter Katz Productions Inc.
PO Box 831
White Plains, NY 10602-0831
Phone: (914)949-7443
**Subject(s):** Aviation
**Circ:** ‡10,000

**Body Positive** (21415)
19 Fulton St.,
Ste. 308B
New York, NY 10038
Phone: (212)566-7333
Fax: (212)566-4539
**Subject(s):** Acquired Immune Deficiency Syndrome; Health and Healthcare
**Circ:** (Paid)5,000
 (Controlled)10,000

**The Boston Book Review** (13653)
331 Harvard St., Ste. 17
Cambridge, MA 02139
Phone: (617)497-0344
**Subject(s):** Literature; Book Trade and Author News
**Circ:** (Combined)‡10,000

**Business Review** (26853)
Federal Reserve Bank of Philadelphia
10 Independence Mall
Philadelphia, PA 19106-1574
Phone: (215)574-6000
Fax: (215)574-4364
**Subject(s):** Banking, Finance, and Investments
**Circ:** (Non-paid)10,000

**Chamber Music** (21472)
Chamber Music America
305 7th Ave., 5th Fl.
New York, NY 10001
Phone: (212)242-2022
Fax: (212)242-7955
**Subject(s):** Music and Musical Instruments; Music and Musical Instruments
**Circ:** (Non-paid)‡2,000
 (Paid)‡10,000

**Circulation Management** (5026)
Primedia Business
11 River Bend Dr. S.
PO Box 4949
Stamford, CT 06907-0949
Phone: (203)358-9900
Fax: (203)358-5811
**Subject(s):** Journalism and Publishing
**Circ:** (Controlled)‡10,009

**The City Journal** (19056)
Manhattan Institute
PO Box 3000
Denville, NJ 07834-9875
**Subject(s):** Local, State, and Regional Publications
**Circ:** ‡10,000

Circulation: ★ = ABC; △ = BPA; ♦ = CAC; • = CCAB; ▫ = VAC; ⊕ = PO Statement; ‡ = Publisher's Report; Boldface figures = sworn; Light figures = estimated.

# Northeastern States

**Gale Directory of Publications & Broadcast Media/140th Ed.**

**Cultural Survival Quarterly  (13658)**
Cultural Survival Inc.
215 Prospect St.
Cambridge, MA 02139
Phone: (617)441-5400
Fax: (617)441-5417
**Subject(s):** Anthropology and Ethnology
**Circ:** (Paid)10,000

**Dynamic Business  (27344)**
Westinghouse Research and Technology Park
1382 Beulah Road, Bldg. 801
Pittsburgh, PA 15235-5068
Phone: (412)371-1500
Fax: (412)371-0460
**Subject(s):** Business; Local, State, and Regional Publications
**Circ:** (Controlled)‡10,000

**15 Minutes  (13663)**
Harvard Crimson Inc.
14 Plympton St.
Cambridge, MA 02138
Phone: (617)576-6565
Fax: (617)576-7860
**Subject(s):** Entertainment
**Circ:** (Non-paid)‡10,000

**Generation  (20257)**
State University of New York at Buffalo
SUNY at Buffalo
341 Student Union
Amherst, NY 14260
Phone: (716)645-2954
Fax: (716)646-2674
**Subject(s):** College Publications
**Circ:** (Non-paid)‡10,000

**Hair to Stay  (14795)**
Winter Publishing Inc.
PO Box 80667
South Dartmouth, MA 02748-0667
Phone: (508)999-0078
Fax: (508)984-4040
**Subject(s):** Lifestyle
**Circ:** (Paid)10,000

**Harvard Educational Review  (13668)**
Harvard Graduate School of Education
8 Story St., 1st Fl.
Cambridge, MA 02138
Phone: (617)495-3432
Fax: (617)496-3584
**Subject(s):** Education
**Circ:** ‡10,000

**Information Display  (21821)**
Palisades Institute for Research Services
411 Lafayette St., Fl. 2
New York, NY 10003
Phone: (212)460-9700
Fax: (212)460-5460
**Subject(s):** Computers; Electronics Engineering
**Circ:** (Paid)‡3,000
(Non-paid)‡10,000

**Interactions  (21828)**
Association for Computing Machinery
1515 Broadway, 17th Fl.
New York, NY 10036
Phone: (212)626-0500
Fax: (212)944-1318
**Subject(s):** Computers
**Circ:** (Paid)10,000

**Journal of the American Academy of Psychoanalysis  (4627)**
The Guilford Press
PO Box 30
Bloomfield, CT 06002-0030
**Subject(s):** Psychology and Psychiatry
**Circ:** 10,000

**Journal of the Print World  (18884)**
Journal of the Print World Inc.
PO Box 978
Meredith, NH 03253-0978
Phone: (603)279-6479
Fax: (603)279-1337
**Subject(s):** Art
**Circ:** 10,000

**Kashrus Magazine  (20521)**
Yeshiva Birkas Reuven
PO Box 204
Brooklyn, NY 11230
Phone: (718)336-8544
Fax: (718)336-8550
**Subject(s):** Jewish Publications; Food and Cooking
**Circ:** ‡10,000

**Key Magazine Pittsburgh  (27367)**
Key Magazine Inc.
c/o Donald Butler
100 5th Ave., No. 910
Pittsburgh, PA 15222
Phone: (412)281-4490
Fax: (412)281-4491
**Subject(s):** Travel and Tourism; Entertainment; Local, State, and Regional Publications
**Circ:** (Combined)10,000

**LD+A  (22028)**
Illuminating Engineering Society
120 Wall St., 17th Fl.
New York, NY 10005-4001
Phone: (212)248-5000
Fax: (212)248-5017
**Subject(s):** Engineering (Various branches); Lighting
**Circ:** ‡10,000

**Lilith  (22037)**
Lilith Publications
250 W 57th, Ste. 2432
New York, NY 10107
Phone: (212)757-0818
Fax: (212)757-5705
**Subject(s):** Jewish Publications; Women's Interests
**Circ:** ‡10,000

**Long Island  (21166)**
Long Island Association Inc.
300 Broadhollow Rd., Ste. 110W
Melville, NY 11747
Phone: (631)499-4400
Fax: (631)499-2194
**Subject(s):** Business
**Circ:** (Paid)10,000

**Maple Syrup Digest  (30931)**
North American Maple Syrup Council
25 Stowell St.
Saint Albans, VT 05478-2212
**Subject(s):** Food and Grocery Trade; Confectionaries and Frozen Dairy Products; Food Production
**Circ:** 10,000

**Mental Retardation  (23023)**
American Association on Mental Retardation
c/o Steven J. Taylor
Center on Human Policy
805 S. Crouse Ave.,
Syracuse University
Syracuse, NY 13244-2340
Phone: (315)443-3851
**Subject(s):** Handicapped
**Circ:** (Paid)10,000

**Mundo Mercantil  (22113)**
Reed Business Information
360 Park Ave. S.
New York, NY 10014
Phone: (646)746-6400
Fax: (646)746-6734
**Subject(s):** Safety; Spanish
**Circ:** (Combined)10,000

**Naval War College Review  (27867)**
U.S. Naval War College
686 Cushing Rd., Code 32
Newport, RI 02841-1207
Phone: (401)841-2236
Fax: (401)841-1071
**Subject(s):** Military and Navy
**Circ:** (Controlled)‡10,000

**The Northeast  (12563)**
Episcopal Diocese of Maine
143 State St.
Portland, ME 04101
Phone: (207)772-6923
Fax: (207)773-0095
**Subject(s):** Religious Publications
**Circ:** ‡10,000

**The Nouveau Magazine  (26765)**
Nouveau Magazine
5933 Stoney Hill Rd.
New Hope, PA 18938
Phone: (215)794-5996
Fax: (215)794-8305
**Subject(s):** Art
**Circ:** (Non-paid)10,000

**Photograph  (22233)**
Photography in New York International
64 W 89 St.
New York, NY 10024
Phone: (212)787-0401
Fax: (212)799-3054
**Subject(s):** Photography
**Circ:** 10,000

**Photography Quarterly  (23200)**
Center for Photography at Woodstock
59 Tinker St.
Woodstock, NY 12498-9984
Phone: (845)679-9957
Fax: (845)679-6337
**Subject(s):** Photography; Photography
**Circ:** (Paid)10,000

**Portland  (12565)**
578 Congress St.
Portland, ME 04101
**Subject(s):** Local, State, and Regional Publications; Lifestyle
**Circ:** (Paid)‡10,000

**Provincetown Arts  (14753)**
Provincetown Arts Inc.
650 Commercial St.
Provincetown, MA 02657-0035
Phone: (508)487-3167
**Subject(s):** Art and Art History; Literature
**Circ:** (Combined)10,000

**Purpose  (27501)**
Faith & Life Resources
616 Walnut Ave.
Scottdale, PA 15683-1992
Phone: (724)887-8500
Fax: (724)887-3111
**Subject(s):** Religious Publications
**Circ:** 10,000

**Reporter Magazine  (22837)**
37 Lomb Memorial Dr.
Rochester, NY 14623
Phone: (716)475-2212
Fax: (585)475-2214
**Subject(s):** College Publications
**Circ:** (Controlled)‡10,000

**Rugby  (22329)**
The Rugby Press
2350 Broadway
New York, NY 10024
Phone: (212)787-1160
Fax: (212)595-0934
**Subject(s):** (General Sports)
**Circ:** (Paid)10,000

**Satya  (20538)**
Stealth Technologies Inc.
539 First St.
Brooklyn, NY 11215
Phone: (718)832-9557
Fax: (718)832-9558
**Subject(s):** Environmental and Natural Resources Conservation; Social and Political Issues; Pets
**Circ:** (Combined)10,000

**Spirit  (19001)**
Baker & Taylor
1120 Rte. 22 E
Bridgewater, NJ 08807
Phone: (908)541-7000
**Subject(s):** Book Trade and Author News
**Circ:** (Non-paid)10,000

**StateWays  (4961)**
Adams Business Media
50 Washington St., 10th Fl.
Norwalk, CT 06854
Phone: (203)855-8499
Fax: (203)855-9446
**Subject(s):** Beverages, Brewing, and Bottling
**Circ:** (Controlled)‡10,000

**UCWA Quarterly Journal  (13795)**
Quarter Century Wireless Association Inc.
PO Box 3247
Framingham, MA 01705-3247
Phone: (541)683-0987
Fax: (541)683-4181
**Subject(s):** Radio, Television, Cable, and Video
**Circ:** 10,000

**Musical Merchandise Review  (14268)**
Larkin Publications
50 Brook Rd.
Needham, MA 02494
Phone: (781)453-9310
Fax: (781)453-9389
**Subject(s):** Music and Musical Instruments
**Circ:** (Paid)1,338
 (Non-paid)△9,913

**Alternative Energy Retailer  (5067)**
Zackin Publications Inc.
70 Edwin Ave.
PO Box 2180
Waterbury, CT 06722
Phone: (800)325-6745
Fax: (203)755-3480
**Subject(s):** Plumbing and Heating
**Circ:** (Paid)⊕332
 (Controlled)⊕9,837

**American Journal of Medical Genetics  (19159)**
John Wiley and Sons Inc.
111 River St.
Hoboken, NJ 07030-5774
Phone: (201)748-6000
Fax: (201)748-6088
**Subject(s):** Genetics
**Circ:** (Paid)9,800

**Journal of Cellular Physiology  (19279)**
John Wiley and Sons Inc.
111 River St.
Hoboken, NJ 07030-5774
Phone: (201)748-6000
Fax: (201)748-6088
**Subject(s):** Physiology and Anatomy
**Circ:** (Paid)9,800

**Journal of Forecasting  (19290)**
John Wiley and Sons Inc.
111 River St.
Hoboken, NJ 07030-5774
Phone: (201)748-6000
Fax: (201)748-6088
**Subject(s):** Business; Economics; Statistics
**Circ:** (Paid)9,800

**Pediatric Pulmonology  (19353)**
John Wiley and Sons Inc.
111 River St.
Hoboken, NJ 07030-5774
Phone: (201)748-6000
Fax: (201)748-6088
**Subject(s):** Pediatrics
**Circ:** 9,800

**Teacher Librarian  (26192)**
15200 NBN Way
Blue Ridge Summit, PA 17214
Phone: (717)794-3800
Fax: (717)794-3833
**Subject(s):** Library and Information Science; Education
**Circ:** (Combined)9,700

**Lurzer's International Archive  (22048)**
American Showcase Inc.
200 Park Ave. South 1703
New York, NY 10003
Phone: (212)941-2496
Fax: (212)941-5490
**Subject(s):** Advertising and Marketing
**Circ:** (Non-paid)100
 (Paid)9,600

**Health Psychology  (22974)**
American Psychological Association
c/o Arthur A. Stone
Department of Psychiatry
Putnam Hall, S. Campus
State University of New York
Stony Brook, NY 11794-8790
**Subject(s):** Psychology and Psychiatry
**Circ:** 9,500

**Underwater Naturalist  (19147)**
American Littoral Society
Bldg. 18
Sandy Hook
Highlands, NJ 07732
Phone: (732)291-0055
Fax: (732)291-3551
**Subject(s):** Oceanography and Marine Studies
**Circ:** ‡9,500

**Turbomachinery International  (4965)**
Business Journals Inc.
50 Day St.
PO Box 5550
Norwalk, CT 06854
Phone: (203)853-6015
Fax: (203)852-8175
**Subject(s):** Power and Power Plants
**Circ:** (Paid)1,597
 (Non-paid)9,479

**Petroleo Internacional  (20862)**
Keller International Publishing L.L.C.
150 Great Neck Rd.
Great Neck, NY 11021
Phone: (516)829-9210
Fax: (516)829-5414
**Subject(s):** International Business and Economics; Petroleum, Oil, and Gas; Spanish; Hispanic Publications
**Circ:** (Non-paid)9,313

**Outdoors Magazine  (30872)**
Elk Publishing Inc.
531 Main St.
Colchester, VT 05446-7222
Fax: (802)879-2015
**Subject(s):** Local, State, and Regional Publications; (Outdoors); (Hunting, Fishing, and Game Management)
**Circ:** (Controlled)⊕9,300

**Capital District Business Review  (21046)**
American City Business Journals Inc.
40 British American Blvd.
Latham, NY 12110
Phone: (518)640-6801
Fax: (518)640-6801
**Subject(s):** Business; Local, State, and Regional Publications
**Circ:** (Paid)9,273

**Journal of the American Geriatrics Society  (14160)**
Blackwell Publishers
350 Main St.
Malden, MA 02148
Phone: (781)388-8200
Fax: (781)388-8250
**Subject(s):** Gerontology
**Circ:** ‡9,228

**Pennsylvania Township News  (26336)**
Pennsylvania State Association of Township Supervisors
4885, Woodland Dr.
Enola, PA 17025
Phone: (717)763-0930
Fax: (717)763-9732
**Subject(s):** State, Municipal, and County Administration; Local, State, and Regional Publications
**Circ:** (Non-paid)‡1,063
 (Paid)‡9,215

**New Jersey Medicine  (19450)**
Medical Society of New Jersey
2 Princess Rd.
Lawrenceville, NJ 08648
Phone: (609)896-1766
Fax: (609)896-1368
**Subject(s):** Medicine and Surgery; Health and Healthcare
**Circ:** 9,200

**Photographic Video Trade News  (21175)**
Cygnus Business Media Inc.
3 Huntington Quadrangle, Ste. 301 N.
Melville, NY 11747
Phone: (631)845-2700
Fax: (631)845-2798
**Subject(s):** Photography
**Circ:** (Paid)3,755
 (Non-paid)9,204

**SMPTE Journal  (23184)**
Society of Motion Picture and Television Engineers
595 W Hartsdale Ave.
White Plains, NY 10607
Phone: (914)761-1100
Fax: (914)761-3115
**Subject(s):** Motion Pictures; Radio, Television, Cable, and Video
**Circ:** (Paid)‡9,200

**College Store Executive  (23163)**
Executive Business Media Inc.
825 Old Country Rd.
PO Box 1500
Westbury, NY 11590-0812
Phone: (516)334-3030
Fax: (516)334-3059
**Subject(s):** Stationery, Office Equipment, and College Store Supplies
**Circ:** (Paid)185
 (Controlled)9,167

**SIAM News  (27272)**
Society for Industrial & Applied Mathematics
3600 University City Science Ctr.
Philadelphia, PA 19104-2688
Phone: (215)382-9800
Fax: (215)386-7999
**Subject(s):** Mathematics
**Circ:** (Non-paid)‡512
 (Paid)‡9,161

**Military Club & Hospitality  (23167)**
Executive Business Media Inc.
825 Old Country Rd.
PO Box 1500
Westbury, NY 11590-0812
Phone: (516)334-3030
Fax: (516)334-3059
**Subject(s):** Hotels, Motels, Restaurants, and Clubs; Military and Navy
**Circ:** (Paid)‡61
 ‡9,079

**The Art of Eating  (30920)**
Box 242
Peacham, VT 05862
Phone: (802)592-3144
**Subject(s):** Food and Cooking
**Circ:** (Paid)⊕9,000

**Neurosurgery  (27163)**
Lippincott Williams & Wilkins
530 Walnut St.
Philadelphia, PA 19106-3261
Phone: (215)521-8300
Fax: (215)521-8902
**Subject(s):** Medicine and Surgery
**Circ:** (Non-paid)‡365
 (Paid)‡8,950

**Travel Goods Showcase  (19738)**
Travel Goods Association
5 Vaughn Dr., Ste. 105
Princeton, NJ 08540-6515
Phone: (609)720-1200
Fax: (609)720-0620
**Subject(s):** Shoes, Leather, and Luggage
**Circ:** (Non-paid)‡603
 (Paid)‡8,943

**Nantucket Magazine  (14253)**
Nantucket Journal Inc.
2 Greglen Ave., Ste. 408
Nantucket, MA 02554
Phone: (508)228-8700
Fax: (508)228-9063
**Subject(s):** Local, State, and Regional Publications
**Circ:** (Combined)8,864

**Practical Tax Strategies  (22261)**
RIA Group
395 Hudson St., 4th Fl.
New York, NY 10014
Phone: (212)367-6300
Fax: (212)367-6314
**Subject(s):** Accountants and Accounting; Taxation and Tariff
**Circ:** (Non-paid)‡115
 (Paid)‡8831

**Cycling Science  (19062)**
Penner Publishing
9 Debbie Ln.
East Windsor, NJ 08520
Phone: (609)443-0038
Fax: (609)443-4471
**Subject(s):** Science; (Bicycling)
**Circ:** (Non-paid)‡6,500
 (Paid)‡8,800

**Earnshaw's Review (21625)**
Earnshaw Publications Inc.
112 W 34th St. Ste. 1515
New York, NY 10120
Phone: (212)563-2742
Fax: (212)629-3249
**Subject(s):** Clothing
**Circ:** (Paid)3,132
(Non-paid)8,784

**IEEE Engineering in Medicine and Biology Magazine (5045)**
The Institute of Electrical & Electronics Engineers Inc.
c/o Dr. John D. Enderle
University of Connecticut, Rm. 223B
260 Glenbrook Rd., U-2157
Storrs, CT 06269-2157
Phone: (860)486-5521
Fax: (860)486-2500
**Subject(s):** Engineering (Various branches); Electronics Engineering
**Circ:** (Paid)‡8,779

**Journal of Clinical Apheresis (19281)**
John Wiley and Sons Inc.
111 River St.
Hoboken, NJ 07030-5774
Phone: (201)748-6000
Fax: (201)748-6088
**Subject(s):** Medicine and Surgery
**Circ:** (Paid)8,750

**Fellowship (22634)**
Fellowship of Reconciliation
521 N. Broadway
PO Box 271
Nyack, NY 10960
Phone: (845)358-4601
Fax: (845)358-4924
**Subject(s):** Religious Publications
**Circ:** (Paid)‡8,700

**Drycleaners News (5069)**
Zackin Publications Inc.
70 Edwin Ave.
PO Box 2180
Waterbury, CT 06722
Phone: (800)325-6745
Fax: (203)755-3480
**Subject(s):** Laundry and Dry Cleaning
**Circ:** (Paid)41
(Non-paid)8,698

**Risk Management (22321)**
Risk and Insurance Management Society Inc.
1065 Ave. of The Americas, 13th Fl.
New York, NY 10018
Phone: (212)286-9292
**Subject(s):** Insurance; Business
**Circ:** (Non-paid)△6,500
(Paid)△8,672

**Church (21488)**
National Pastoral Life Center
18 Bleecker St.
New York, NY 10012-2404
**Subject(s):** Religious Publications
**Circ:** 8,600

**The Secured Lender (22359)**
Commercial Finance Association
225 W 34th St., Ste. 1815
New York, NY 10122
Phone: (212)594-3490
Fax: (212)564-6053
**Subject(s):** Banking, Finance, and Investments
**Circ:** (Controlled)‡8,600

**Iron & Steel Maker Magazine (27644)**
Iron & Steel Society
186 Thorn Hill Rd.
Warrendale, PA 15086-7528
Phone: (724)776-6040
Fax: (724)776-1880
**Subject(s):** Metal, Metallurgy, and Metal Trade
**Circ:** (Non-paid)1,000
(Paid)8,572

**The Accurate Rifle (4838)**
Precision Shooting Inc.
222 Mckee St.
Manchester, CT 06040
Phone: (860)645-8776
Fax: (860)643-8215

**Subject(s):** Firearms
**Circ:** 8,500

**American Butterflies (19566)**
North American Butterfly Association
4 Delaware Rd.
Morristown, NJ 07960
Phone: (973)285-0907
Fax: (973)285-0936
**Subject(s):** Natural History and Nature Study; Entomology
**Circ:** 8,500

**Barre Life (30828)**
Barre Granite Association
PO Box 481
Barre, VT 05641
Phone: (802)476-4131
Fax: (802)476-4765
**Subject(s):** Stone and Rock Products; Building Materials, Concrete, Brick, and Tile; Mining and Minerals
**Circ:** 8,500

**Commercial Fisheries News (12606)**
Compass Publications Inc. Fisheries Div.
PO Box 37
Stonington, ME 04681
Phone: (207)367-2396
Fax: (207)367-2490
**Subject(s):** Fish and Commercial Fisheries
**Circ:** 8,500

**The Electrochemical Society Interface (19674)**
Electrochemical Society Inc.
65 S. Main St., Bldg. D
Pennington, NJ 08534-2839
Phone: (609)737-1902
Fax: (609)737-2743
**Subject(s):** Electronics Engineering
**Circ:** (Paid)8,500

**Insurance Conference Planner (14826)**
Primedia Business Magazines & Media
c/o Regina Baraban
132 Great Rd., Ste. 200
Stow, MA 01775-1189
**Subject(s):** Insurance
**Circ:** (Controlled)‡8,500

**The Mutual Magazine (26161)**
MBA Inc.
1301 Lancaster Ave., Ste. 102
Berwyn, PA 19312-1290
Phone: (610)722-0253
Fax: (610)722-0256
**Subject(s):** Insurance; Railroad; Unclassified Fraternal
**Circ:** ‡8,500

**Open World for Disability and Mature Travel (22197)**
Society for Accessible Travel and Hospitality
347 5th Ave., No. 610
New York, NY 10016-5010
Phone: (212)447-7284
Fax: (212)725-8253
**Subject(s):** Travel and Tourism; Handicapped
**Circ:** (Paid)1,500
(Non-paid)8,500

**South American Explorer (20969)**
South American Explorers
126 Indian Creek Rd.
Ithaca, NY 14850
Phone: (607)277-0488
Fax: (607)277-6122
**Subject(s):** Travel and Tourism; Science
**Circ:** ‡8,500

**The Winged Foot (22541)**
New York Athletic Club
180 Central Park S, No. 1223
New York, NY 10019
Phone: (212)767-7000
Fax: (212)767-7063
**Subject(s):** Clubs and Societies
**Circ:** (Non-paid)‡400
(Paid)‡8,500

**The Anatomical Record (19162)**
John Wiley and Sons Inc.
111 River St.
Hoboken, NJ 07030-5774
Phone: (201)748-6000
Fax: (201)748-6088
**Subject(s):** Biology
**Circ:** (Paid)8,400

**Dollars & Sense (13510)**
Economic Affairs Bureau
29 Winter St.
Boston, MA 02108
Phone: (617)447-2177
Fax: (617)447-2179
**Subject(s):** Politics; Economics; Ethnic Publications
**Circ:** ‡8,400

**Proteins: Structure, Function, and Genetics (19372)**
John Wiley and Sons Inc.
111 River St.
Hoboken, NJ 07030-5774
Phone: (201)748-6000
Fax: (201)748-6088
**Subject(s):** Genetics; Science (General)
**Circ:** 8,400

**Journal of the American Society of Echocardiography (27010)**
Mosby
170 S. Independence Mall
Independence Sq. W. 300 E.
Philadelphia, PA 19106-3399
Phone: (215)238-7800
Fax: (215)238-7883
**Subject(s):** Medicine and Surgery
**Circ:** ‡8,347

**The Journal of Thoracic and Cardiovascular Surgery (27105)**
Mosby
170 S. Independence Mall W., Ste. 300 E.
Philadelphia, PA 19106-3399
Phone: (215)238-7869
Fax: (215)238-2239
**Subject(s):** Medicine and Surgery
**Circ:** (Combined)‡8,341

**Exchange & Commissary News (23164)**
Executive Business Media Inc.
825 Old Country Rd.
PO Box 1500
Westbury, NY 11590-0812
Phone: (516)334-3030
Fax: (516)334-3059
**Subject(s):** Military and Navy
**Circ:** (Paid)⊕642
8,300

**Gastroenterology and Endoscopy News (21729)**
The McMahon Publishing Group
545 W 45th St., 8th Fl.
New York, NY 10036
Phone: (212)957-5300
Fax: (212)957-7230
**Subject(s):** Medicine and Surgery
**Circ:** (Non-paid)‡8,201

**New Jersey Law Journal (19621)**
238 Mulberry St.
PO Box 20081
Newark, NJ 07101-6081
Phone: (973)642-0075
Fax: (973)642-0920
**Subject(s):** Law
**Circ:** (Mon.)8,245

**Partisan Review (13573)**
Boston University
236 Bay State Rd.
Boston, MA 02215
Phone: (617)353-4260
Fax: (617)353-7444
**Circ:** ‡8,200

**Real Estate Review (22294)**
Warren, Gorham & Lamont R.I.A. Group
395 Hudson St., 4th Fl.
New York, NY 10014-3669
Phone: (212)367-6300
Fax: (212)367-6305
**Subject(s):** Real Estate
**Circ:** 8,200

**Teenpreur (22444)**
Black Enterprise Unlimited
130 5th Ave., 10th Fl.
New York, NY 10011
Phone: (212)242-8000
Fax: (212)886-9509
**Subject(s):** Education
**Circ:** (Combined)8200

**American Journal of Physics** (13400)
American Association of Physics Teachers
Merrill Science Bldg.
Amherst College
Amherst, MA 01002
**Subject(s):** Education; Physics
**Circ:** 8,100

**Friends Journal** (26952)
1216 Arch St., Ste. 2A
Philadelphia, PA 19107-2835
Phone: (215)563-8629
Fax: (215)568-1377
**Subject(s):** Religious Publications
**Circ:** ‡8,100

**Folio** (21699)
Primedia Business
c/o. Geoff Lewis, Editorial Director
249 W. 17th St., 3rd Fl.
New York, NY 10011
Phone: (212)462-3588
**Subject(s):** Journalism and Publishing; Printing and Typography
**Circ:** (Non-paid)661
(Paid)8,063

**American Time** (21326)
VNU Business Media USA
770 Broadway
New York, NY 10003
Phone: (646)654-5000
**Subject(s):** Retail; Jewelry, Watches, and Clocks
**Circ:** (Non-paid)8,000

**Art Now Gallery Guide–Philadelphia Edition** (19043)
Art Now Inc.
97 Grayrock Rd.
PO Box 5541
Clinton, NJ 08809-5541
Phone: (908)638-5255
Fax: (908)638-8737
**Subject(s):** Art
**Circ:** (Non-paid)8,000

**ASDA Today** (21367)
American Society for Dental Aesthetics
635 Madison Ave., 12th Fl.
New York, NY 10022
Phone: (212)751-3263
Fax: (212)308-5182
**Subject(s):** Dentistry; Health and Healthcare; Medicine and Surgery
**Circ:** 8,000

**Balloons & Parties Magazine** (19123)
PartiLife Publications
65 Sussex St.
Hackensack, NJ 07601
Phone: (201)441-4224
Fax: (201)342-8118
**Subject(s):** Entertainment; Interior Design/Decorating
**Circ:** ‡8,000

**Cornell Political Forum** (20950)
118 Eddy St., No.1
Ithaca, NY 14853
Phone: (607)254-5000
Fax: (607)254-5000
**Subject(s):** Economics; Philosophy; Political Science; College Publications
**Circ:** (Non-paid)8,000

**The Dramatist** (21618)
The Dramatists Guild of America Inc.
1501 Broadway, Ste. 701
New York, NY 10036-3988
Phone: (212)398-9366
Fax: (212)944-0420
**Subject(s):** Drama and Theatre; Performing Arts
**Circ:** (Paid)8,000

**IEEE Electrical Insulation Magazine** (19678)
The Institute of Electrical & Electronics Engineers Inc.
445 Hoes Ln.
Piscataway, NJ 08854-1331
Phone: (732)981-0060
Fax: (732)981-1721
**Subject(s):** Electrical Engineering
**Circ:** (Non-paid)1,000
(Paid)8,000

**Journal of Marketing Research** (4896)
American Marketing Association
c/o Dick R. Wittink, Editor
Yale School of Management
PO Box 208200
135 Prospect St.
New Haven, CT 06520-8200
**Subject(s):** Advertising and Marketing
**Circ:** (Paid)‡8,000

**Juris** (27366)
Duquesne School of Law
Duquesne University
900 Locust Street
Pittsburgh, PA 15282
Phone: (412)396-5017
Fax: (412)396-6294
**Subject(s):** Law
**Circ:** (Controlled)8,000

**Kaatskill Life** (20701)
Delaware County Times Inc.
56 Main St.
Delhi, NY 13753
Phone: (607)746-2176
Fax: (607)746-3135
**Subject(s):** Lifestyle; Local, State, and Regional Publications
**Circ:** (Paid)8,000

**Managers Handbook** (5105)
LIMRA International Inc.
300 Day Hill Rd.
Windsor, CT 06095
Phone: (860)688-3358
Fax: (860)298-9555
**Subject(s):** Insurance
**Circ:** ‡8,000

**Midstream** (22085)
Theodor Herzl Foundation Inc.
633 3rd Ave., 21st Fl.
New York, NY 10017-6706
Phone: (212)339-6020
Fax: (212)318-6176
**Subject(s):** Intercultural Interests; Jewish Publications
**Circ:** ‡8,000

**The Morgan Horse** (30940)
American Morgan Horse Association
122 Bostwick Road
Shelburne, VT 05482-0960
Phone: (802)985-4944
Fax: (802)985-8897
**Subject(s):** Livestock; (Horses and Horse Racing)
**Circ:** ‡8,000

**New Jersey Municipalities** (19892)
New Jersey League of Municipalities
407 W. State St.
Trenton, NJ 08618
Phone: (609)695-3481
Fax: (609)695-0151
**Subject(s):** State, Municipal, and County Administration
**Circ:** (Non-paid)‡300
(Paid)‡8,000

**The Nonviolent Activist** (22178)
War Resisters League
339 Lafayette St.
New York, NY 10012
Phone: (212)228-0450
Fax: (212)228-6193
**Subject(s):** Politics; Alternative and Underground
**Circ:** (Non-paid)1,500
(Paid)8,000

**Penn Dental Journal** (27215)
University of Pennsylvania
4001 Spruce St.
Philadelphia, PA 19104
Phone: (215)898-8951
Fax: (215)573-1791
**Subject(s):** Dentistry
**Circ:** (Controlled)8,000

**Political Science Quarterly** (22248)
Academy of Political Science
475 Riverside Dr., Ste. 1274
New York, NY 10115-1274
Phone: (212)870-2500
Fax: (212)870-2202
**Subject(s):** Politics
**Circ:** ‡8,000

**Safety Briefs** (19050)
New Jersey State Safety Council
6 Commerce Dr.
Cranford, NJ 07016
Phone: (908)272-7712
Fax: (908)276-6622
**Subject(s):** Health and Healthcare; Safety
**Circ:** (Non-paid)‡8,000

**Transgender Tapestry** (14867)
International Foundation for Gender Education
PO Box 540229
Waltham, MA 02454-0229
Phone: (781)899-2212
Fax: (781)899-5703
**Subject(s):** Gay and Lesbian Interests; Lifestyle; Alternative and Underground
**Circ:** (Combined)8,000

**The TV Executive** (22494)
TV Trade Media Inc.
216 E 75th St., No. PW
New York, NY 10021
Phone: (212)288-3933
Fax: (212)734-9033
**Subject(s):** Radio, Television, Cable, and Video; Management and Administration
**Circ:** (Paid)100
(Non-paid)8,000

**TV Executive Daily** (22495)
TV Trade Media Inc.
216 E 75th St., No. PW
New York, NY 10021
Phone: (212)288-3933
Fax: (212)734-9033
**Subject(s):** Radio, Television, Cable, and Video; Motion Pictures
**Circ:** (Non-paid)‡8,000

**Video Age Daily** (22515)
TV Trade Media Inc.
216 E 75th St., No. PW
New York, NY 10021
Phone: (212)288-3933
Fax: (212)734-9033
**Subject(s):** Radio, Television, Cable, and Video; Performing Arts
**Circ:** (Non-paid)‡8,000

**VooDoo Magazine** (13716)
MIT
77 Massachusetts Ave., Rm. 50-309
Cambridge, MA 02139
Phone: (617)253-4575
**Subject(s):** Alternative and Underground; College Publications
**Circ:** (Non-paid)8,000

**Wheelings -New England Mechanic** (13799)
Jason Krusa
PO Box M
Franklin, MA 02038-0822
Phone: (508)528-6211
Fax: (508)528-6211
**Subject(s):** Automotive (Trade)
**Circ:** (Controlled)‡1,000
(Paid)‡8,000

**Hounds and Hunting** (26195)
P.O. Box 372
554 Derick Rd.
Bradford, PA 16701
Phone: (814)368-6155
Fax: (814)368-3522
**Subject(s):** Dogs; (Hunting, Fishing, and Game Management)
**Circ:** ‡7,917

**American Window Cleaner Magazine** (20359)
12 Twelve Publishing Corp.
PO Box 98
Bedford, NY 10506
Phone: (914)234-2630
Fax: (914)234-2632
**Subject(s):** Service Industries
**Circ:** (Paid)1,100
(Controlled)7,900

**Collision Magazine** (13798)
Jason Krusa
PO Box M
Franklin, MA 02038-0822
Phone: (508)528-6211
Fax: (508)528-6211

Circulation: ★ = ABC; △ = BPA; ♦ = CAC; • = CCAB; ▫ = VAC; ⊕ = PO Statement; ‡ = Publisher's Report; Boldface figures = sworn; Light figures = estimated.

**Subject(s):** Automotive (Trade)
**Circ:** (Controlled)‡3,000
(Paid)‡7,900

**The Journal of Arthroplasty** (27012)
Elsevier
c/o Richard H. Rothman, Editor-in-Chief
Rothman Institute at Jefferson
925 Chestnut St.
Philadelphia, PA 19107-4216
Phone: (856)795-8409
**Subject(s):** Medicine and Surgery
**Circ:** ‡7,800

**American Journal of Industrial Medicine** (19158)
John Wiley and Sons Inc.
111 River St.
Hoboken, NJ 07030-5774
Phone: (201)748-6000
Fax: (201)748-6088
**Subject(s):** Medicine and Surgery
**Circ:** (Paid)7,700

**Food Industry Advocate** (20215)
Food Industry Alliance of NYS
130 Washington Ave.
Albany, NY 12210
Phone: (518)434-1900
Fax: (212)558-6214
**Subject(s):** Food and Grocery Trade
**Circ:** (Non-paid)‡2,000
(Paid)‡7,700

**The Journal of Futures Markets** (19291)
John Wiley and Sons Inc.
111 River St.
Hoboken, NJ 07030-5774
Phone: (201)748-6000
Fax: (201)748-6088
**Subject(s):** Banking, Finance, and Investments
**Circ:** (Paid)7,700

**Planning Commissioners Journal** (30859)
Champlain Planning Press
PO Box 4295
Burlington, VT 05406
Phone: (802)864-9083
Fax: (802)862-1882
**Subject(s):** State, Municipal, and County Administration
**Circ:** (Non-paid)70
(Paid)7,700

**Rola Boza (God's Field)** (27506)
Polish National Catholic Church
1006 Pittston Ave.
Scranton, PA 18505
Phone: (570)346-9131
Fax: (570)346-2188
**Subject(s):** Religious Publications; Polish
**Circ:** ‡7,700

**Direct Marketing Magazine** (21603)
Hoke Communications Inc.
224 7th St.
New York, NY 10009
Phone: (516)746-6700
Fax: (516)294-8141
**Subject(s):** Advertising and Marketing
**Circ:** (Controlled)932
(Paid)7,660

**Fashion Accessories** (19477)
S.C.M. Publications Inc.
PO Box 859
Mahwah, NJ 07430
Phone: (201)684-9222
Fax: (201)684-9228
**Subject(s):** Jewelry, Watches, and Clocks
**Circ:** (Paid)1,650
(Non-paid)7,651

**Journal of Pediatric Health Care** (27079)
Mosby
170 S. Independence Mall W. 300 E.
Philadelphia, PA 19106-3399
Phone: (215)238-7869
Fax: (215)238-2239
**Subject(s):** Pediatrics
**Circ:** (Combined)‡7,645

**Journal of Vascular Surgery** (27109)
Mosby
170 S. Independence Mall W., Ste. 300 E.
Philadelphia, PA 19106-3399
Phone: (215)238-7869
Fax: (215)238-2239
**Subject(s):** Medicine and Surgery
**Circ:** (Combined)‡7,634

**Martha's Vineyard Magazine** (13770)
34 S Summer St.
PO Box 66
Edgartown, MA 02539
Phone: (508)627-4311
Fax: (508)627-7444
**Subject(s):** Local, State, and Regional Publications; Literature and Literary Reviews; Lifestyle; History and Genealogy; Art
**Circ:** (Non-paid)‡4,400
(Paid)‡7,600

**Automotive Cooling Journal** (19573)
NARSA
15000 Commerce Pkwy., Ste. C
Mount Laurel, NJ 08054
Phone: (856)439-1575
Fax: (856)439-9596
**Subject(s):** Automotive (Trade)
**Circ:** (Paid)‡2,644
(Non-paid)‡7,556

**Human Pathology** (26969)
Elsevier
C/o Fred Gorstein, Editor
Thomas Jefferson University
Dept. of Pathology
225 Jefferson Alumni Hall, 1020 Locust St.
Philadelphia, PA 19107
Phone: (215)955-8703
Fax: (215)955-8703
**Subject(s):** Medicine and Surgery
**Circ:** ‡7,549

**Clinical Leadership and Management Review** (27656)
Clinical Laboratory Management Association
989 Old Eagle School Rd., Ste. 815
Wayne, PA 19087
Phone: (610)995-9580
Fax: (610)995-9568
**Subject(s):** Health and Healthcare
**Circ:** (Non-paid)‡200
(Paid)‡7,500

**Hastings Center Report** (20815)
The Hastings Center
21 Malcolm Gordon Rd.
Garrison, NY 10524
Phone: (845)424-4040
Fax: (845)424-4545
**Subject(s):** Medicine and Surgery
**Circ:** (Controlled)1,000
(Paid)7,500

**Hoosharar Mioutune** (21782)
Armenian General Benevolent Union
55 E 59th St.
New York, NY 10022-1112
Phone: (212)319-6383
Fax: (212)319-6508
**Subject(s):** Philanthropy and Humanitarianism; Armenian; Unclassified Fraternal
**Circ:** ‡7,500

**The Journal of Asian Martial Arts** (26350)
Via Media Publishing Co.
821 W 24th St.
Erie, PA 16502
Phone: (814)455-9517
Fax: (814)455-2726
**Subject(s):** (Martial Arts)
**Circ:** (Paid)1,500
(Non-paid)7,500

**Modernism Magazine** (19446)
David Rago
333 N Main St.
Lambertville, NJ 08530
Phone: (609)397-4104
Fax: (609)397-9377
**Subject(s):** Art and Art History; Graphic Arts and Design
**Circ:** (Paid)‡7,500

**Public Health Reports** (13582)
Oxford University Press
Rm. 1855, JFK Federal Bldg.
Boston, MA 02203
Phone: (617)565-1440
Fax: (617)565-4260
**Subject(s):** Health and Healthcare
**Circ:** 7,500

**Massachusetts Beverage Business** (13547)
New Beverage Publications Inc.
55 Clarendon St.
Boston, MA 02116-6067
Phone: (617)598-1900
Fax: (617)598-1940
**Subject(s):** Beverages, Brewing, and Bottling
**Circ:** (Non-paid)‡560
(Paid)‡7,485

**Spine** (18833)
Lippincott Williams & Wilkins
Dartmouth College
7254 Strasenburgh Hall
Hanover, NH 03755-3863
Phone: (603)650-1122
Fax: (603)650-1500
**Subject(s):** Medicine and Surgery
**Circ:** 7,451

**Annals of Neurology** (19166)
John Wiley and Sons Inc.
111 River St.
Hoboken, NJ 07030-5774
Phone: (201)748-6000
Fax: (201)748-6088
**Subject(s):** Medicine and Surgery
**Circ:** (Paid)7,384

**Urology** (22510)
Excerpta Medica Inc.
655 Avenue of the Americas
New York, NY 10010
Phone: (212)989-5800
**Subject(s):** Medicine and Surgery
**Circ:** (Paid)‡7,228

**Journal of Clinical Psychopharmacology** (13537)
Lippincott Williams & Wilkins
Tufts University
School of Medicine
Dept. of Pharmacology
136 Harrison Ave.
Boston, MA 02111
Phone: (617)636-2178
**Subject(s):** Drugs and Pharmaceuticals; Psychology and Psychiatry
**Circ:** (Non-paid)‡163
(Paid)‡7,214

**Connecticut Medicine** (4884)
Connecticut State Medical Society
160 St. Ronan St.
New Haven, CT 06511
Phone: (203)865-0587
Fax: (203)865-4997
**Subject(s):** Medicine and Surgery
**Circ:** 7,200

**Living City** (20466)
Living City of the Focolare Movement
PO Box 837
Bronx, NY 10465
Phone: (718)828-4559
Fax: (718)892-0419
**Subject(s):** Religious Publications
**Circ:** (Paid)7,200

**The Passionist' Compassion** (19914)
Passionist Missionaries of Union City
526 Monastery Pl.
Union City, NJ 07087
Phone: (201)867-6400
Fax: (201)864-1337
**Subject(s):** Religious Publications
**Circ:** (Controlled)7,200

**Voice: AIGA Journal of Design** (22524)
American Institute of Graphic Arts
164 5th Ave.
New York, NY 10010
Phone: (212)807-1990
Fax: (212)807-1799
**Subject(s):** Graphic Arts and Design
**Circ:** 7,200

**Challenge** (20290)
M.E. Sharpe Inc.
80 Business Park Dr.
Armonk, NY 10504
Phone: (914)273-1800
Fax: (914)273-2106
**Subject(s):** Economics
**Circ:** (Controlled)500
(Paid)‡7,040

**Antique Radio Classified (13722)**
PO Box 2-V75
Carlisle, MA 01741
Phone: (978)371-0512
Fax: (978)371-7129
**Subject(s):** Crafts, Models, Hobbies, and Contests; Collecting; Antiques
**Circ:** (Combined)7,000

**Biopolymers (19179)**
John Wiley and Sons Inc.
111 River St.
Hoboken, NJ 07030-5774
Phone: (201)748-6000
Fax: (201)748-6088
**Subject(s):** Biology; Chemistry, Chemicals, and Chemical Engineering
**Circ:** 7,000

**Clinical Anatomy (19198)**
John Wiley and Sons Inc.
111 River St.
Hoboken, NJ 07030-5774
Phone: (201)748-6000
Fax: (201)748-6088
**Subject(s):** Medicine and Surgery
**Circ:** 7,000

**CNS Focus (20807)**
Cargo Network Services
300 Garden City Plz., Ste. 312
Garden City, NY 11530
Phone: (516)747-3312
Fax: (516)747-3431
**Subject(s):** Ships and Shipping
**Circ:** (Non-paid)7,000

**Econometrica (13660)**
The Econometric Society
NIT, E52-380B
50 Memorial Dr
Cambridge, MA 02142
**Subject(s):** Economics; Statistics; Mathematics
**Circ:** ‡7,000

**The Journal of Comparative Neurology (19286)**
John Wiley and Sons Inc.
111 River St.
Hoboken, NJ 07030-5774
Phone: (201)748-6000
Fax: (201)748-6088
**Subject(s):** Medicine and Surgery
**Circ:** (Paid)7,000

**Journal of Direct and Interactive Marketing (19288)**
John Wiley and Sons Inc.
111 River St.
Hoboken, NJ 07030-5774
Phone: (201)748-6000
Fax: (201)748-6088
**Subject(s):** Advertising and Marketing
**Circ:** 7,000

**Journal of Infusion Nursing (14718)**
Lippincott Williams & Wilkins
Infusion Nurses Society
Publications Department
220 Norwood Park S.
Norwood, MA 02062
Phone: (781)440-9409
Fax: (781)440-9409
**Subject(s):** Nursing; Medicine and Surgery
**Circ:** (Paid)7,000

**Journal of Medical Virology (19298)**
John Wiley and Sons Inc.
111 River St.
Hoboken, NJ 07030-5774
Phone: (201)748-6000
Fax: (201)748-6088
**Subject(s):** Medicine and Surgery
**Circ:** 7,000

**Journal of Surgical Oncology (19312)**
John Wiley and Sons Inc.
111 River St.
Hoboken, NJ 07030-5774
Phone: (201)748-6000
Fax: (201)748-6088
**Subject(s):** Medicine and Surgery
**Circ:** 7,000

**Naval Research Logistics (19346)**
John Wiley and Sons Inc.
111 River St.
Hoboken, NJ 07030-5774
Phone: (201)748-6000
Fax: (201)748-6088
**Subject(s):** Mathematics
**Circ:** (Paid)7,000

**The New Criterion (22142)**
The Foundation for Cultural Review Inc.
900 Broadway 602
New York, NY 10003
Phone: (212)247-6980
Fax: (212)247-3127
**Subject(s):** Drama and Theatre; Art; Literature and Literary Reviews
**Circ:** (Non-paid)1,000
7,000

**New England Economic Indicators (13557)**
Federal Reserve Bank of Boston
600 Atlantic Ave.
Boston, MA 02210
Phone: (617)973-3000
**Subject(s):** Economics
**Circ:** (Free)7000

**New Jersey Jewish News—Central Edition (19972)**
New Jersey Jewish News
901 Rte. 10
Whippany, NJ 07981-1157
Phone: (973)887-8500
Fax: (973)887-5999
**Subject(s):** Paid Community Newspapers; Jewish Publications
**Circ:** (Paid)7,000

**Public Administration and Development (19376)**
John Wiley and Sons Inc.
111 River St.
Hoboken, NJ 07030-5774
Phone: (201)748-6000
Fax: (201)748-6088
**Subject(s):** International Business and Economics; Management and Administration
**Circ:** (Paid)7,000

**Sculpture Review (22357)**
National Sculpture Society
56 Ludlow St., 5th Fl.
New York, NY 10022
Phone: (212)529-1763
Fax: (212)260-1732
**Subject(s):** Art and Art History
**Circ:** 7,000

**System Dynamics Review (19396)**
John Wiley and Sons Inc.
111 River St.
Hoboken, NJ 07030-5774
Phone: (201)748-6000
Fax: (201)748-6088
**Subject(s):** Social Sciences
**Circ:** (Paid)7,000

**Ukrainian Orthodox Word (19827)**
Ukrainian Orthodox Church of the U.S.A.
PO Box 495
South Bound Brook, NJ 08880-1412
Phone: (732)356-0090
Fax: (732)356-5556
**Subject(s):** Religious Publications; Ukrainian
**Circ:** 7,000

**Interfaces (18832)**
The Institute for Operations Research and the Management Sciences
c/o Jeffrey D. Camm, Editor- In-Chief
Univ. Of Cincinnati, Visiting Professor
Tuck School Of Business
Dartmouth College, 100 Tuck Hall
Hanover, NH 03755
Phone: (603)646-4018
**Subject(s):** Management and Administration
**Circ:** ‡6,900

**Library Resources & Technical Services (4844)**
American Library Association
100 Riverview Center
Middletown, CT 06457
Phone: (860)347-6933
Fax: (860)704-0465
**Subject(s):** Library and Information Science
**Circ:** ‡6,756

**Nursing Economics (19697)**
Jannetti Publications Inc.
E Holly Ave.
Box 56
Pitman, NJ 08071-0056
Phone: (856)256-2300
Fax: (856)589-7463
**Subject(s):** Nursing
**Circ:** ‡6,752

**Central N.Y. Business Journal (23000)**
CNY Business Review Inc.
231 Walton St.
Syracuse, NY 13202-1226
Phone: (315)472-3104
Fax: (315)472-3644
**Subject(s):** Local, State, and Regional Publications
**Circ:** (Paid)‡1,300
(Controlled)‡6,700

**Fund Raising Management Magazine (21723)**
Hoke Communications Inc.
224 7th St.
New York, NY 10009
Phone: (516)746-6700
Fax: (516)294-8141
**Subject(s):** Advertising and Marketing
**Circ:** (Controlled)‡1,715
(Paid)‡6,705

**PACE: Pacing and Clinical Electrophysiology (20758)**
Blackwell Publishing/Futura
3 W. Main St.
Elmsford, NY 10523
Phone: (781)388-8372
Fax: (781)388-8265
**Subject(s):** Medicine and Surgery
**Circ:** (Paid)‡6,616

**Drum Business (19011)**
Modern Drummer Publications Inc.
12 Old Bridge Rd.
Cedar Grove, NJ 07009-1288
Phone: (973)239-4140
Fax: (973)239-7139
**Subject(s):** Music and Musical Instruments
**Circ:** (Controlled)6,600

**Oil and Energy (14731)**
New England Fuel Institute
83 Pine St. Ste. 110
Peabody, MA 01960
Phone: (978)535-7606
Fax: (978)535-7826
**Subject(s):** Petroleum, Oil, and Gas
**Circ:** (Paid)‡2,045
(Controlled)‡6,605

**Rhizome Digest (22317)**
Rhizome.org
210 11th Ave., 2nd Fl.
New York, NY 10001
Phone: (212)219-1288
Fax: (212)431-5328
**Subject(s):** Graphic Arts and Design; Computers
**Circ:** (Combined)6,600

**Small World (22378)**
Earnshaw Publications Inc.
112 W 34th St. Ste. 1515
New York, NY 10120
Phone: (212)563-2742
Fax: (212)629-3249
**Subject(s):** Furniture and Furnishings; General Merchandise
**Circ:** (Paid)485
(Non-paid)6,588

**Home Lighting & Accessories (19035)**
Doctorow Communications Inc.
1011 Clifton Ave.
Clifton, NJ 07013
Phone: (973)779-1600
Fax: (973)779-3242
**Subject(s):** Lighting
**Circ:** (Paid)3,465
(Non-paid)6,529

**Academic Questions (19706)**
Transaction Publishers
National Association of Scholars
221 Witherspoon St., 2nd Fl.
Princeton, NJ 08542
Phone: (609)683-0316
Fax: (609)683-0316

*Circulation: ★ = ABC; △ = BPA; ♦ = CAC; • = CCAB; □ = VAC; ⊕ = PO Statement; ‡ = Publisher's Report; Boldface figures = sworn; Light figures = estimated.*

**Subject(s):** Education

**Circ:** (Paid)‡6,500

**Action Sports** (21097)
CMP Media L.L.C.
600 Community Dr.
Manhasset, NY 11030
Phone: (516)562-5000
Fax: (516)562-5995
**Subject(s):** Sporting Goods/Retail Sports

**Circ:** (Controlled)‡1,500
(Paid)‡6,500

**Story Friends** (27502)
Herald Press
616 Walnut Ave.
Scottdale, PA 15683
Phone: (724)887-8500
Fax: (724)887-3111
**Subject(s):** Religious Publications

**Circ:** ‡6,500

**Today Magazine** (12612)
The Association for Work Process Improvement
c/o Dan Bolita
1396 Back Cove Rd.
Waldoboro, ME 04572
Phone: (207)832-6638
Fax: (253)399-8509
**Subject(s):** Service Industries; Retail

**Circ:** 6,500

**Journal of Nuclear Cardiology** (27070)
Mosby
170 S. Independence Mall
Independence Sq. W. 300 E.
Philadelphia, PA 19106-3399
Phone: (215)238-7800
Fax: (215)238-7883
**Subject(s):** Medicine and Surgery; Health and Healthcare

**Circ:** (Combined)‡6,499

**Transactions on Database Systems (TODS)** (22473)
Association for Computing Machinery
1515 Broadway, 17th Fl.
New York, NY 10036
Phone: (212)626-0500
Fax: (212)944-1318
**Subject(s):** Computers

**Circ:** 6,433

**American Writer** (21328)
National Office
113 E. University Place, 6th Fl.
New York, NY 10003
Phone: (212)254-0279
**Subject(s):** Labor; Journalism and Publishing; Literature

**Circ:** (Non-paid)3,500
(Controlled)0,400

**Journal of Occupational and Environmental Medicine** (21964)
Lippincott Williams & Wilkins
c/o Paul W. Brandt-Rauf, M.D. Editor
Columbia University
New York, NY 10032-2698
Phone: (847)818-9266
Fax: (847)818-9266
**Subject(s):** Medicine and Surgery

**Circ:** (Controlled)‡170
(Paid)‡6,389

**Journal of Organizational Behavior** (27364)
John Wiley and Sons Inc.
H. John Heinz III School of Public Policy & Management
Carnegie-Mellon Univ.
Pittsburgh, PA 15213-3890
**Subject(s):** Psychology and Psychiatry

**Circ:** (Paid)6,300

**The Prostate** (19370)
John Wiley and Sons Inc.
111 River St.
Hoboken, NJ 07030-5774
Phone: (201)748-6000
Fax: (201)748-6088
**Subject(s):** Medicine and Surgery

**Circ:** (Paid)6,300

**Sh'ma** (14304)
Jewish Family and Life!
90 Oak St.
PO Box 9129
Newton Upper Falls, MA 02464
Phone: (617)965-7700

Fax: (617)965-7772
**Subject(s):** Jewish Publications

**Circ:** (Non-paid)‡377
(Paid)‡6,287

**Journal of Graph Theory** (30858)
John Wiley and Sons Inc.
Editorial Office of JGT
Dan Archdeacon
Dept. of Mathematics and Statistics, Univ. of Vermont
16 Colchester Ave.
Burlington, VT 05401-1455
Phone: (802)656-0850
Fax: (802)656-2552
**Subject(s):** Mathematics

**Circ:** (Paid)6,230

**ACM Transactions on Graphics (TOG)** (21258)
Association for Computing Machinery
1515 Broadway, 17th Fl.
New York, NY 10036
Phone: (212)626-0500
Fax: (212)944-1318
**Subject(s):** Computers

**Circ:** 6,104

**Nature Genetics** (22135)
345 Park Ave. S., 10th Fl.
New York, NY 10010-1707
Phone: (212)545-8341
Fax: (212)545-8341
**Subject(s):** Biology; Genetics

**Circ:** (Paid)6,100

**Quick Frozen Foods International** (19102)
E.W. Williams Publications
2125 Center Ave., Ste. 305
Fort Lee, NJ 07024-5898
Phone: (201)592-7007
Fax: (201)592-7171
**Subject(s):** Food and Grocery Trade; International Business and Economics; German; French

**Circ:** (Controlled)‡5,528
(Paid)‡6,011

**Amputee Golfer Magazine** (18768)
National Amputee Golf Association
11 Walnut Hill Rd.
Amherst, NH 03031-1713
Phone: (603)672-6444
Fax: (603)672-2987
**Subject(s):** (Golf); Handicapped

**Circ:** 6,000

**Biblical Missions** (26846)
Independent Board for Presbyterian Foreign Missions
246 W. Walnut Ln.
Philadelphia, PA 19144-3299
Phone: (215)438-0511
Fax: (215)438-0560
**Subject(s):** Religious Publications

**Circ:** 6,000

**Boston Review** (13654)
E53-407
MIT
Cambridge, MA 02139-4307
Phone: (617)258-0805
Fax: (617)252-1549
**Subject(s):** Literature and Literary Reviews; Social and Political Issues

**Circ:** (Non-paid)‡4,000
(Paid)‡6,000

**Business People Vermont** (30956)
Mill Publishing Inc.
PO Box 953
Williston, VT 05495-0953
Phone: (802)862-4109
Fax: (802)862-9322
**Subject(s):** Business; Local, State, and Regional Publications

**Circ:** (Controlled)⊕6,000

**Computers in Libraries** (19514)
Information Today Inc.
143 Old Marlton Pike
Medford, NJ 08055-8750
Phone: (609)654-6266
Fax: (609)654-4309
**Subject(s):** Library and Information Science

**Circ:** ‡6,000

**Cornell Law Review** (20949)
Cornell University Law School
137 Myron Taylor Hall
Ithaca, NY 14853
Phone: (607)255-3387
Fax: (607)255-7193
**Subject(s):** Law

**Circ:** ‡6,000

**Cucinazte** (22633)
FIC America
3 S. Broadway
Nyack, NY 10960
Phone: (845)353-8361
Fax: (845)353-2941
**Subject(s):** Food and Grocery Trade; Hotels, Motels, Restaurants, and Clubs

**Circ:** 4,000
6,000

**DDIN International** (14394)
Larson Worldwide Inc.
95 Mt. Blue St.
Norwell, MA 02061-1015
Phone: (781)659-2115
Fax: (781)659-2411
**Subject(s):** Machinery and Equipment

**Circ:** (Combined)6,000

**Field Notes** (21684)
National Audubon Society Inc.
700 Broadway
New York, NY 10003
Phone: (212)979-3000
Fax: (212)979-3188
**Subject(s):** Ornithology and Oology

**Circ:** ‡6,000

**Footsteps** (18937)
Cobblestone Publishing Co.
30 Grove St., Ste. C
Peterborough, NH 03458
Phone: (603)924-7209
Fax: (603)924-7380
**Subject(s):** Black Publications; History and Genealogy; Youths' Interests; Children's Interests

**Circ:** 6,000

**Hobby Merchandiser** (19550)
Hobby Publications Inc.
207 Commercial Ct.
PO Box 102
Morganville, NJ 07751-0102
Phone: (732)536-5160
Fax: (732)536-5761
**Subject(s):** Gifts, Toys, and Novelties; Crafts, Models, Hobbies, and Contests

**Circ:** (Paid)‡2,200
(Non-paid)‡6,000

**Human Life Review** (21794)
Human Life Foundation
215 Lexington Ave., 4th Fl.
New York, NY 10016
Phone: (212)685-5210
Fax: (212)725-9793
**Subject(s):** Social Sciences; Women's Interests

**Circ:** (Paid)6,000

**IEEE Transactions on Industrial Electronics** (21806)
Institute of Electrical and Electronics Engineers Inc.
3 Park Ave., 17th Fl.
New York, NY 10016
Phone: (212)705-8900
Fax: (212)705-8999
**Subject(s):** Electronics Engineering

**Circ:** (Paid)6,000

**International Bulletin of Missionary Research** (4890)
Overseas Ministries Study Center
490 Prospect St.
New Haven, CT 06511-2196
Phone: (203)624-6672
Fax: (203)865-2857
**Subject(s):** Religious Publications

**Circ:** (Non-paid)300
(Paid)6,000

**Journal of Nursing Administration (JONA)** (27072)
Lippincott Williams & Wilkins
530 Walnut St.
Philadelphia, PA 19106-3261
Phone: (215)521-8300
Fax: (215)521-8902

**Subject(s):** Nursing
**Circ:** (Paid)‡6,000

**Journal of Psychosocial Nursing and Mental Health Services (19597)**
SLACK Inc.
c/o Shirley A. Smoyak, Editor
The Bloustein School of Planning and Public Policy
Institute of Health, Health Care Policy & Aging Research
Rutgers-the State University of New Jersey
New Brunswick, NJ
**Subject(s):** Nursing; Psychology and Psychiatry
**Circ:** ‡6,000

**Journal of Sedimentary Research (13691)**
Rutgers University
MIT
Dept. of Earth, Atmospheric & Planetary Sciences
77 Massachusetts Ave.
Cambridge, MA 02139
Phone: (918)493-3361
**Subject(s):** Geology
**Circ:** 6,000

**Link-Up (19517)**
Information Today Inc.
143 Old Marlton Pike
Medford, NJ 08055-8750
Phone: (609)654-6266
Fax: (609)654-4309
**Subject(s):** Computers
**Circ:** (Paid)‡4,000
(Non-paid)‡6,000

**NACLA Report on the Americas (22121)**
38 Greene St., 4th Fl.
New York, NY 10013
Phone: (646)613-1440
Fax: (646)613-1443
**Subject(s):** International Affairs
**Circ:** (Paid)‡6,000

**Nassau Weekly (19728)**
Nassau Inc.
48 Univ. Place, Rm. 002
Armory Bldg., Washington Rd.
Princeton, NJ 08544
Phone: (609)258-1899
Fax: (609)258-7883
**Subject(s):** College Publications
**Circ:** (Non-paid)‡6,000

**Property Digest and Economic Development Magazine (14916)**
Barry Inc.
PO Box 551
Wilmington, MA 01887-0551
Phone: (978)658-0441
Fax: (978)657-8691
**Subject(s):** Real Estate
**Circ:** (Controlled)‡6,000

**Roze Maryi (14822)**
Congregation of Marians
Eden Hill
Stockbridge, MA 01263
Phone: (413)298-3691
Fax: (413)298-3583
**Subject(s):** Religious Publications; Polish
**Circ:** (Controlled)‡1,500
(Paid)‡6,000

**Scandinavian Review (22342)**
American-Scandinavian Foundation
58 Park Ave.
New York, NY 10016
Phone: (212)879-9779
Fax: (212)249-3444
**Subject(s):** Intercultural Interests; Ethnic and Minority Studies
**Circ:** (Paid)6,000

**Speculum, A Journal of Medieval Studies (13711)**
Medieval Academy of America
104 Mt. Auburn St., 5th Fl.
Cambridge, MA 02138
Phone: (617)491-1622
Fax: (617)492-3303
**Subject(s):** History and Genealogy; Literature
**Circ:** ‡6,000

**The Yale Review (4908)**
Blackwell Publishers
Yale University
Box 208243
Yale Sta.
New Haven, CT 06520
Phone: (203)432-0499
Fax: (203)432-0510
**Subject(s):** Literature and Literary Reviews
**Circ:** ‡6,000

**Banks in Insurance Report (19174)**
John Wiley and Sons Inc.
111 River St.
Hoboken, NJ 07030-5774
Phone: (201)748-6000
Fax: (201)748-6088
**Subject(s):** Banking, Finance, and Investments; Insurance
**Circ:** 5,985

**Benefits Law Journal (21389)**
Aspen Publishers
1185 Ave. of the Americas
New York, NY 10036
Phone: (212)597-0200
Fax: (212)597-0338
**Subject(s):** Law; Employment and Human Resources
**Circ:** 5,985

**Employee Relations Law Journal (21648)**
Aspen Publishers
1185 Ave. of the Americas
New York, NY 10036
Phone: (212)597-0200
Fax: (212)597-0338
**Subject(s):** Employment and Human Resources; Management and Administration
**Circ:** 5985

**Employment Relations Today (19217)**
John Wiley and Sons Inc.
111 River St.
Hoboken, NJ 07030-5774
Phone: (201)748-6000
Fax: (201)748-6088
**Subject(s):** Employment and Human Resources
**Circ:** 5,985

**Evolutionary Anthropology (19230)**
John Wiley and Sons Inc.
111 River St.
Hoboken, NJ 07030-5774
Phone: (201)748-6000
Fax: (201)748-6088
**Subject(s):** Anthropology and Ethnology
**Circ:** 5,985

**Federal Facilities Environmental Journal (19231)**
John Wiley and Sons Inc.
111 River St.
Hoboken, NJ 07030-5774
Phone: (201)748-6000
Fax: (201)748-6088
**Subject(s):** Environmental and Natural Resources Conservation
**Circ:** 5,985

**The Journal of Corporate Accounting and Finance (19287)**
John Wiley and Sons Inc.
111 River St.
Hoboken, NJ 07030-5774
Phone: (201)748-6000
Fax: (201)748-6088
**Subject(s):** Accountants and Accounting
**Circ:** 5,985

**Journal of Organizational Excellence (19302)**
John Wiley and Sons Inc.
111 River St.
Hoboken, NJ 07030-5774
Phone: (201)748-6000
Fax: (201)748-6088
**Subject(s):** Employment and Human Resources
**Circ:** (Paid)5,985

**Management Report for Nonunion Organizations (19329)**
John Wiley and Sons Inc.
111 River St.
Hoboken, NJ 07030-5774
Phone: (201)748-6000
Fax: (201)748-6088
**Subject(s):** Law; Management and Administration
**Circ:** 5,985

**Natural Gas (19344)**
John Wiley and Sons Inc.
111 River St.
Hoboken, NJ 07030-5774
Phone: (201)748-6000
Fax: (201)748-6088
**Subject(s):** Natural Resources; Business; Petroleum, Oil, and Gas
**Circ:** 5,985

**Remediation (19382)**
John Wiley and Sons Inc.
111 River St.
Hoboken, NJ 07030-5774
Phone: (201)748-6000
Fax: (201)748-6088
**Subject(s):** Environmental and Natural Resources Conservation; Engineering (Various branches); Law
**Circ:** 5,985

**Genes, Chromosomes and Cancer (19236)**
John Wiley and Sons Inc.
111 River St.
Hoboken, NJ 07030-5774
Phone: (201)748-6000
Fax: (201)748-6088
**Subject(s):** Medicine and Surgery; Laboratory Research (Scientific and Medical)
**Circ:** 5,950

**Human Resource Management (19247)**
John Wiley and Sons Inc.
111 River St.
Hoboken, NJ 07030-5774
Phone: (201)748-6000
Fax: (201)748-6088
**Subject(s):** Employment and Human Resources
**Circ:** 5,950

**International Journal of Quantum Chemistry (19270)**
John Wiley and Sons Inc.
111 River St.
Hoboken, NJ 07030-5774
Phone: (201)748-6000
Fax: (201)748-6088
**Subject(s):** Chemistry, Chemicals, and Chemical Engineering; Science (General)
**Circ:** 5,950

**Journal of Neuroscience Research (19301)**
John Wiley and Sons Inc.
111 River St.
Hoboken, NJ 07030-5774
Phone: (201)748-6000
Fax: (201)748-6088
**Subject(s):** Medicine and Surgery
**Circ:** 5,950

**Surface and Interface Analysis (19395)**
John Wiley and Sons Inc.
111 River St.
Hoboken, NJ 07030-5774
Phone: (201)748-6000
Fax: (201)748-6088
**Subject(s):** Chemistry, Chemicals, and Chemical Engineering
**Circ:** (Paid)5,950

**Thunderbird International Business Review (19401)**
John Wiley and Sons Inc.
111 River St.
Hoboken, NJ 07030-5774
Phone: (201)748-6000
Fax: (201)748-6088
**Subject(s):** Business; Management and Administration
**Circ:** 5,950

**American Heart Journal (26812)**
Mosby
170 S. Independence Mall
Independence Sq. W. 300 E.
Philadelphia, PA 19106-3399
Phone: (215)238-7800
Fax: (215)238-7883
**Subject(s):** Medicine and Surgery
**Circ:** (Combined)‡5,948

**AJNR: American Journal of Neuroradiology (26808)**
Lippincott Williams & Wilkins
530 Walnut St.
Philadelphia, PA 19106-3261
Phone: (215)521-8300
Fax: (215)521-8902
**Subject(s):** Radiology, Ultrasound, and Nuclear Medicine
**Circ:** (Non-paid)‡130
(Paid)‡5,934

**Board Converting News** (18969)
N.V. Business Publishers Corp.
43 Main St.
Avon by the Sea, NJ 07717
Phone: (732)502-0500
Fax: (732)502-9606
**Subject(s):** Packaging
**Circ:** 5,914

**Physical Review Letters** (22791)
American Physical Society
1 Research Rd.
Box 9000
Ridge, NY 11961-9000
Phone: (631)591-4060
Fax: (631)591-4141
**Subject(s):** Physics
**Circ:** 5,900

**The Mass Municipal Directory** (13545)
Massachusetts Municipal Association
60 Temple Pl.
Boston, MA 02111
Phone: (617)426-7272
Fax: (617)695-1314
**Subject(s):** State, Municipal, and County Administration
**Circ:** (Combined)5,884

**Long Island Forum** (23197)
Friends for Long Island's Heritage
PO Box 277
Woodbury, NY 11797
**Subject(s):** History and Genealogy
**Circ:** ‡5,850

**Golf Range Magazine** (4874)
152 Marshal Ridge Rd.
New Canaan, CT 06840-6137
Phone: (203)972-6201
Fax: (203)972-1667
**Subject(s):** Golf Course Management
**Circ:** (Paid)810
(Controlled)5,820

**Nieman Reports** (13696)
Nieman Foundation
1 Francis Ave.
Cambridge, MA 02138
Phone: (617)496-2968
Fax: (617)495-8976
**Subject(s):** Journalism and Publishing
**Circ:** (Combined)5,822

**Infection Control and Hospital Epidemiology** (19855)
SLACK Inc.
6900 Grove Rd.
Thorofare, NJ 08086-9447
Phone: (856)853-5991
Fax: (856)853-5991
**Subject(s):** Medicine and Surgery
**Circ:** 5,810

**Angiology** (20831)
Westminster Publications Inc.
708 Glen Cove Ave.
Glen Head, NY 11545
Phone: (516)759-0025
Fax: (516)759-5524
**Subject(s):** Medicine and Surgery
**Circ:** (Non-paid)‡349
(Paid)‡5,722

**Surface Design Journal** (19073)
Surface Design Association
93 W Ivy Ln.
Englewood, NJ 07631
Phone: (201)568-1084
Fax: (201)567-3709
**Subject(s):** Textiles; Art and Art History
**Circ:** (Combined)5,700

**Pediatric Physical Therapy** (27214)
Lippincott Williams & Wilkins
3307 N. Broad St.
Philadelphia, PA
Phone: (215)204-3378
Fax: (215)204-5600
**Subject(s):** Medicine and Surgery
**Circ:** (Non-paid)‡72
(Paid)‡5,698

**Music Trades** (19071)
Music Trades Corp.
80 W St.
Englewood, NJ 07631
Phone: (201)871-1965
Fax: (201)871-0455
**Subject(s):** Music and Musical Instruments
**Circ:** (Paid)5,668

**Surgery** (27277)
Mosby
170 S. Independence Mall W., Ste. 300 E.
Philadelphia, PA 19106-3399
Phone: (215)238-7869
Fax: (215)238-2239
**Subject(s):** Medicine and Surgery
**Circ:** (Combined)‡5,635

**American Journal of Human Biology** (13647)
John Wiley and Sons Inc.
c/o Peter T. Ellison, Dept. of Anthropology, Harvard Univ.
11 Divinity Ave.
Cambridge, MA 02138
**Subject(s):** Biology
**Circ:** 5,600

**Corporation Records** (21554)
Standard & Poor's
55 Water St.
New York, NY 10041
Fax: (212)438-3396
**Subject(s):** Banking, Finance, and Investments; Daily Periodicals
**Circ:** ‡5,600

**Microscopy Research and Technique** (19337)
John Wiley and Sons Inc.
111 River St.
Hoboken, NJ 07030-5774
Phone: (201)748-6000
Fax: (201)748-6088
**Subject(s):** Physiology and Anatomy; Biology; Chemistry, Chemicals, and Chemical Engineering; Science (General)
**Circ:** 5,600

**Psychology and Marketing** (19374)
John Wiley and Sons Inc.
111 River St.
Hoboken, NJ 07030-5774
Phone: (201)748-6000
Fax: (201)748-6088
**Subject(s):** Psychology and Psychiatry
**Circ:** (Paid)5,600

**World News Digest** (22561)
Facts On File News Services
512, 7th Ave., 22nd Fl.
New York, NY 10018
Phone: (212)290-8090
Fax: (212)967-9051
**Subject(s):** General Editorial; Indexes, Abstracts, Reports, Proceedings, and Bibliographies
**Circ:** (Paid)‡5,600

**Modern Pathology** (27150)
Lippincott Williams & Wilkins
530 Walnut St.
Philadelphia, PA 19106-3261
Phone: (215)521-8300
Fax: (215)521-8902
**Subject(s):** Physiology and Anatomy
**Circ:** (Non-paid)‡87
(Paid)‡5,514

**Seminars in Roentgenology** (27265)
Elsevier
1600 John F. Kennedy Blvd.
Philadelphia, PA 19103
Phone: (215)239-3900
Fax: (215)239-3990
**Subject(s):** Radiology, Ultrasound, and Nuclear Medicine
**Circ:** ‡5,518

**Current Opinion in Rheumatology** (26911)
Lippincott Williams & Wilkins
530 Walnut St.
Philadelphia, PA 19106-3261
Phone: (215)521-8300
Fax: (215)521-8902
**Subject(s):** Medicine and Surgery
**Circ:** (Paid)‡5,500

**FLEXO ESPANOL** (22875)
Foundation of Flexographic Technical Association
900 Marconi Ave.
Ronkonkoma, NY 11779-7212
Phone: (631)737-6020
Fax: (631)737-6813
**Subject(s):** Printing and Typography; Spanish
**Circ:** (Paid)‡2,500
(Non-paid)‡5,500

**Journal of the American Psychoanalytic Association** (21873)
Analytic Press
200 E. 89th St.
New York, NY 10128-4300
Phone: (212)987-5403
Fax: (212)427-0585
**Subject(s):** Psychology and Psychiatry
**Circ:** 5,500

**On the Line** (27500)
Herald Press
616 Walnut Ave.
Scottdale, PA 15683
Phone: (724)887-8500
Fax: (724)887-3111
**Subject(s):** Religious Publications
**Circ:** (Combined)5,500

**Our Preaching** (20280)
Sisters of St. Dominic
555 Albany Ave.
Amityville, NY 11701
Phone: (631)842-6000
Fax: (631)842-0639
**Subject(s):** Religious Publications
**Circ:** 5,500

**The Paris Review** (22219)
62 White St.
New York, NY 10013
Phone: (212)343-1333
Fax: (212)343-1988
**Subject(s):** Literature and Literary Reviews
**Circ:** (Non-paid)‡500
(Paid)‡5,500

**Epilepsia** (14007)
Blackwell Publishers
350 Main St.
Malden, MA 02148
Phone: (781)388-8200
Fax: (781)388-8250
**Subject(s):** Medicine and Surgery
**Circ:** 5471

**The Journal of Invasive Cardiology** (26659)
Health Management Publications Inc.
83 General Warren Blvd. Ste. 100
Malvern, PA 19355-1245
Phone: (610)560-0500
Fax: (610)560-0501
**Subject(s):** Medicine and Surgery
**Circ:** (Non-paid)‡5,000
(Paid)‡5,450

**Mercer Business Magazine** (19891)
2550 Kuser Rd.
PO Box 8307
Trenton, NJ 08650
Phone: (609)586-2056
Fax: (609)586-8052
**Subject(s):** Business; Chambers of Commerce and Boards of Trade
**Circ:** (Non-paid)‡3,169
(Paid)‡5,431

**National Engineer** (13735)
National Association of Power Engineers
One Springfield St.
Chicopee, MA 01013-2624
Phone: (413)592-6273
Fax: (413)592-1998
**Subject(s):** Engineering (Various branches); Power and Power Plants
**Circ:** (Controlled)‡56
(Paid)‡5,422

**The Counseling Psychologist** (21557)
Sage Publications Inc.
Teachers College
Columbia University
525 W 120th St.
PO Box 32
New York, NY 10027
Phone: (212)678-3863
Fax: (212)678-8310
**Subject(s):** Psychology and Psychiatry; Education

**Circ:** (Non-paid)‡128
(Paid)‡5,400

**Professional Insurance Agents** (20839)
PIA Management Services Inc.
25 Chamberlain St.
PO Box 997
Glenmont, NY 12077-0997
Phone: (518)434-3111
Fax: (888)225-6935
**Subject(s):** Insurance

**Circ:** ‡5,400

**Aesthetic Surgery Journal** (26805)
Mosby
170 S. Independence Mall W., Ste. 300 E.
Philadelphia, PA 19106-3399
Phone: (215)238-7869
Fax: (215)238-2239
**Subject(s):** Medicine and Surgery; Health and Healthcare

**Circ:** (Combined)‡5,389

**Cat Fanciers' Almanac** (19505)
Cat Fanciers' Association Inc.
1805 Atlantic
PO Box 1005
Manasquan, NJ 08736-0805
Phone: (732)528-9797
Fax: (732)528-7391
**Subject(s):** Cats

**Circ:** (Free)570
(Paid)5,386

**Clinical Orthopaedics and Related Research** (26873)
Lippincott Williams & Wilkins
c/o University City Science Center
3550 Market St., Ste. 220
Philadelphia, PA 19104
Phone: (215)349-8375
Fax: (215)349-8379
**Subject(s):** Medicine and Surgery

**Circ:** (Paid)5,365

**Journal of Nursing Care Quality (JNCQ)** (21963)
Aspen Publishers Inc.
1185 Ave. of the Americas
New York, NY 10036
Phone: (301)644-3599
Fax: (212)597-0331
**Subject(s):** Nursing

**Circ:** (Non-paid)108
(Paid)5,362

**Monthly Review** (22101)
Monthly Review Press
122 W 27th St.
New York, NY 10001
Phone: (212)691-2555
Fax: (212)727-3676
**Subject(s):** Politics; Economics

**Circ:** (Non-paid)‡97
(Paid)‡5,321

**Emergency Medicine Clinics of North America** (26932)
Harcourt Health Sciences
The Curtis Ctr.
1600 JFK Blvd.
Philadelphia, PA 19103
Phone: (215)238-7800
Fax: (215)238-8772
**Subject(s):** Medicine and Surgery

**Circ:** ‡5,300

**Harvard Law Review** (13674)
1511 Massachusetts Ave.
Cambridge, MA 02138
Phone: (617)495-4650
Fax: (617)495-2748
**Subject(s):** Law

**Circ:** ‡5,275

**Beatles Fan Magazine** (4978)
Good Day Sunshine
315 Derby Ave.
Orange, CT 06477-1345
Phone: (203)891-8131
Fax: (203)891-8433
**Subject(s):** Entertainment

**Circ:** (Non-paid)800
(Paid)5,200

**Genetics** (27353)
Genetics Society of America
4400 5th Ave.
Box I
Pittsburgh, PA 15213
Phone: (412)268-1812
Fax: (412)268-1813
**Subject(s):** Genetics

**Circ:** ‡5,200

**New Hampshire Bar Journal** (18786)
New Hampshire Bar Association
112 Pleasant St.
Concord, NH 03301
Phone: (603)224-6942
Fax: (603)224-2910
**Subject(s):** Law

**Circ:** 5,200

**The Rhode Island Bar Journal** (27919)
Rhose Island Bar Association
115 Cedar St.
Providence, RI 02903
Phone: (401)421-5740
Fax: (401)421-5740
**Subject(s):** Law

**Circ:** (Combined)5,200

**Modern Brewery Age Tabloid Edition** (4956)
Business Journals Inc.
50 Day St.
PO Box 5550
Norwalk, CT 06854
Phone: (203)853-6015
Fax: (203)852-8175
**Subject(s):** Beverages, Brewing, and Bottling

**Circ:** ‡5,181

**Salmagundi** (22907)
Skidmore College
815 N. Broadway
Saratoga Springs, NY 12866
Phone: (518)580-5186
Fax: (518)580-5188
**Subject(s):** Sociology; Literature and Literary Reviews

**Circ:** (Controlled)‡200
(Paid)‡5,100

**Surgical Endoscopy** (22435)
Springer-Verlag New York Inc.
c/o Kenneth A. Forde, M.D.
Columbia University
Department of Surgery
161 Fort Washington Ave.
New York, NY 10032
Phone: (212)305-3849
Fax: (212)305-8679
**Subject(s):** Medicine and Surgery

**Circ:** (Paid)5,090

**ACM Transactions on Programming Languages and Systems** (21260)
Association for Computing Machinery
1515 Broadway, 17th Fl.
New York, NY 10036
Phone: (212)626-0500
Fax: (212)944-1318
**Subject(s):** Computers

**Circ:** -5,000

**The Activist** (21264)
Democratic Socialists of America
198 Broadway, Ste. 700
New York, NY 10038
Phone: (212)727-8610
Fax: (212)608-6955
**Subject(s):** Social and Political Issues; Youths' Interests

**Circ:** (Paid)5,000

**Afterimage** (22803)
Visual Studies Workshop Press
31 Prince St.
Rochester, NY 14607
Phone: (585)442-8676
Fax: (585)442-1992
**Subject(s):** Photography

**Circ:** (Non-paid)‡5,000
(Paid)‡5,000

**Asia & Australasia–Basic Oil Laws & Concession Contracts** (21368)
Barrows Co.
116 E. 66th St.
New York, NY 10021
Phone: (212)772-1199
Fax: (212)288-7242
**Subject(s):** Petroleum, Oil, and Gas

**Circ:** ‡5,000

**Bad Attitude** (13652)
PO Box 390110
Cambridge, MA 02139
**Subject(s):** Women's Interests; Gay and Lesbian Interests

**Circ:** (Paid)‡5,000

**Central American & Caribbean–Basic Oil Laws & Concession Contracts** (21466)
Barrows Co.
116 E. 66th St.
New York, NY 10021
Phone: (212)772-1199
Fax: (212)288-7242
**Subject(s):** Petroleum, Oil, and Gas

**Circ:** ‡5,000

**Chance** (21473)
Springer-Verlag New York Inc.
233 Spring St.
New York, NY 10013
Phone: (212)460-1500
Fax: (212)460-1575
**Subject(s):** Statistics

**Circ:** (Combined)**5,000**

**City Trees** (22939)
Society of Municipal Arborists
4738 Hereendeen Rd.
Shortsville, NY 14548
Phone: (585)289-9763
**Subject(s):** Forestry

**Circ:** (Controlled)5,000

**Dermatology Nursing** (19694)
Jannetti Publications Inc.
E Holly Ave.
Box 56
Pitman, NJ 08071-0056
Phone: (856)256-2300
Fax: (856)589-7463
**Subject(s):** Medicine and Surgery; Nursing

**Circ:** (Paid)‡5,000

**Eire-Ireland** (19569)
Irish American Cultural Institute
1 Lackawanna Pl.
Morristown, NJ 07960
Phone: (973)605-1991
Fax: (973)605-8875
**Subject(s):** Intercultural interests

**Circ:** (Controlled)‡500
(Paid)‡5,000

**Europe–Basic Oil Laws & Concession Contracts** (21665)
Barrows Co.
116 E. 66th St.
New York, NY 10021
Phone: (212)772-1199
Fax: (212)288-7242
**Subject(s):** Petroleum, Oil, and Gas

**Circ:** 5,000

**Hearts Aflame** (19932)
The Blue Army of Our Lady of Fatima
674 Mountain View Rd.
PO Box 976
Washington, NJ 07882
Phone: (908)213-2223
Fax: (908)213-2263
**Subject(s):** Religious Publications; Youths' Interests

**Circ:** ‡5,000

**Information Today** (19516)
Information Today Inc.
143 Old Marlton Pike
Medford, NJ 08055-8750
Phone: (609)654-6266
Fax: (609)654-4309

**Subject(s):** Telecommunications; Computers

Circ: (Paid)‡5,000
(Non-paid)‡5,000

**International Rehabilitation Review (21842)**
Rehabilitation International
25 E. 21 St.
New York, NY 10010
Phone: (212)420-1500
Fax: (212)505-0871
**Subject(s):** Handicapped

Circ: (Paid)5,000

**Journal of Evidence Photography (26504)**
Evidence Photographers International Council
600 Main St.
Honesdale, PA 18431
Phone: (717)253-5450
Fax: (717)253-5011

Circ: (Paid)5,000

**The Journal of Law, Medicine & Ethics (13540)**
American Society of Law, Medicine & Ethics Inc.
765 Commonwealth Ave., Ste. 1634
Boston, MA 02215
Phone: (617)262-4990
Fax: (617)437-7596
**Subject(s):** Law; Medicine and Surgery

Circ: ‡5,000

**The Journal of Psychohistory (21980)**
Association for Psychohistory
140 Riverside Dr., Ste. 14H
New York, NY 10024
Phone: (212)799-2294
Fax: (212)799-1728
**Subject(s):** Psychology and Psychiatry; History and Genealogy

Circ: ‡5,000

**Labor Arbitration in Government (22020)**
American Arbitration Association
335 Madison Ave., Fl. 10
New York, NY 10017-4605
Phone: (212)716-5800
Fax: (212)716-5905
**Subject(s):** Labor

Circ: (Non-paid)‡2,000
(Paid)‡5,000

**Merlyn's Pen: Stories by American Students (27909)**
Merlyn's Pen Publishing
PO Box 2550
Providence, RI 02906
Phone: (401)751-3766
Fax: (401)274-1541
**Subject(s):** Literature and Literary Reviews; Youths' Interests

Circ: (Controlled)‡1,000
(Paid)‡5,000

**Middle East–Basic Oil Laws & Concession Contracts (22084)**
Barrows Co.
116 E. 66th St.
New York, NY 10021
Phone: (212)772-1199
Fax: (212)288-7242
**Subject(s):** Petroleum, Oil, and Gas

Circ: ‡5,000

**MultiCultural Review (20221)**
The Goldman Group
194 Lenox Ave.
Albany, NY 12208
**Subject(s):** Library and Information Science; Book Trade and Author News

Circ: (Paid)‡5,000

**Neuropsychology (27377)**
American Psychological Association
c/o James T. Becker
830 Oxford Bldg.
3501 Forbes Ave.
Pittsburgh, PA 15213-3323
**Subject(s):** Psychology and Psychiatry

Circ: 5,000

**New Jersey Conservation (19086)**
New Jersey Conservation Foundation
Bamboo Brook
170 Longview Rd.
Far Hills, NJ 07931
Phone: (908)234-1225
Fax: (908)234-1189

**Subject(s):** Local, State, and Regional Publications; Environmental and Natural Resources Conservation; (Outdoors)

Circ: (Combined)5,000

**The Noise (13564)**
74 Jamaica St.
Boston, MA 02130
Phone: (617)524-4735
**Subject(s):** Music and Musical Instruments

Circ: (Paid)‡5000

**North Africa–Basic Oil Laws & Concession Contracts (22180)**
Barrows Co.
116 E. 66th St.
New York, NY 10021
Phone: (212)772-1199
Fax: (212)288-7242
**Subject(s):** Petroleum, Oil, and Gas

Circ: ‡5,000

**Nueva Luz (20470)**
En Foco Inc.
32 E. Kingsbridge Rd.
Bronx, NY 10468
Phone: (718)584-7718
Fax: (718)584-7718
**Subject(s):** Photography

Circ: (Combined)5,000

**Oceanus Magazine (14927)**
Woods Hole Oceanographic Institution
Mail Stop 40
Woods Hole, MA 02543
Phone: (508)289-2865
Fax: (508)457-2195
**Subject(s):** Oceanography and Marine Studies; Environmental and Natural Resources Conservation

Circ: (Controlled)5,000

**Perspectives on Sexual and Reproductive Health (22230)**
The Alan Guttmacher Institute
120 Wall St.
New York, NY 10005
Phone: (212)248-1111
Fax: (212)248-1951
**Subject(s):** Medicine and Surgery

Circ: (Non-paid)2,000
(Paid)5,000

**Plymouth County Business Review (14748)**
Plymouth County Development Council
32 Court St., 2nd Fl.
Plymouth, MA 02360
Phone: (508)747-0100
Fax: (508)747-3118
**Subject(s):** Business

Circ: (Non-paid)5,000

**Political Affairs (22246)**
Political Affairs Publishers Inc.
235 W 23rd St., 7th Fl.
New York, NY 10011-2313
Phone: (646)437-5336
Fax: (212)229-1713
**Subject(s):** Politics

Circ: ‡5,000

**Shelterforce (19529)**
National Housing Institute
460 Bloomfield Ave., Ste. 211
Montclair, NJ 07042-3552
Phone: (973)509-2888
Fax: (973)509-8005
**Subject(s):** Construction, Contracting, Building, and Excavating; Politics

Circ: (Combined)⊕5,000

**Socialist Forum (22391)**
Democratic Socialists of America
198 Broadway, Ste. 700
New York, NY 10038
Phone: (212)727-8610
Fax: (212)608-6955
**Subject(s):** Politics

Circ: (Combined)5,000

**South America–Basic Oil Laws & Concession Contracts (22397)**
Barrows Co.
116 E. 66th St.
New York, NY 10021
Phone: (212)772-1199
Fax: (212)288-7242

**Subject(s):** Petroleum, Oil, and Gas; Law

Circ: ‡5,000

**South & Central Africa–Basic Oil Laws & Concession Contracts (22398)**
Barrows Co.
116 E. 66th St.
New York, NY 10021
Phone: (212)772-1199
Fax: (212)288-7242
**Subject(s):** Petroleum, Oil, and Gas

Circ: ‡5,000

**Teaching English in the Two-Year College (TETYC) (13778)**
National Council of Teachers of English
c/o Howard Tinberg, Editor, English Department
Bristol Community College
777 Elsbree St.
Fall River, MA 02720
Fax: (217)328-0977
**Subject(s):** Education

Circ: (Paid)5,000

**Value Retail News (22513)**
International Council of Shopping Centers
1221 Avenue of the Americas, 41st Fl.
New York, NY 10022-1099
Phone: (646)728-3800
Fax: (646)728-3800
**Subject(s):** General Merchandise

Circ: ‡5,000

**Visionaire (22521)**
Visionaire Publishing
11 Mercer St.
New York, NY 10013
Phone: (212)274-8959
Fax: (212)343-2595
**Subject(s):** Fashion; Art

Circ: 5,000

**Working USA (14220)**
Blackwell Publishers
350 Main St.
Malden, MA 02148
Phone: (781)388-8200
Fax: (781)388-8210
**Subject(s):** Labor; Employment and Human Resources

Circ: (Paid)2,143
(Controlled)5,000

**World Journal of Surgery (22559)**
Springer-Verlag New York Inc.
233 Spring St.
New York, NY 10013
Phone: (212)460-1500
Fax: (212)460-1575
**Subject(s):** Medicine and Surgery

Circ: (Combined)5,000

**World Policy Journal (22562)**
World Policy Institute
66 5th Ave., 9th Fl.
New York, NY 10011
Phone: (212)229-5808
Fax: (212)229-5579
**Subject(s):** International Affairs

Circ: 5,000

**New Jersey Beverage Journal (19908)**
Gem Publishers Inc.
2414 Morris Ave.
Union, NJ 07083
Phone: (908)964-5060
Fax: (908)964-1472
**Subject(s):** Beverages, Brewing, and Bottling

Circ: (Non-paid)2,414
(Paid)4,972

**Clinical Pediatrics (20832)**
Westminster Publications Inc.
708 Glen Cove Ave.
Glen Head, NY 11545
Phone: (516)759-0025
Fax: (516)759-5524
**Subject(s):** Medicine and Surgery; Pediatrics

Circ: (Paid)‡4,910

**American Journal of Primatology (19161)**
John Wiley and Sons Inc.
111 River St.
Hoboken, NJ 07030-5774
Phone: (201)748-6000
Fax: (201)748-6088

**Subject(s):** Zoology
**Circ:** (Paid)4,900

**Cell Motility and the Cytoskeleton (19187)**
John Wiley and Sons Inc.
111 River St.
Hoboken, NJ 07030-5774
Phone: (201)748-6000
Fax: (201)748-6088
**Subject(s):** Biology
**Circ:** 4,900

**Human Mutation (19245)**
John Wiley and Sons Inc.
111 River St.
Hoboken, NJ 07030-5774
Phone: (201)748-6000
Fax: (201)748-6088
**Subject(s):** Genetics; Biology
**Circ:** 4,900

**Journal of Labelled Compounds and Radiopharmaceuticals (19295)**
John Wiley and Sons Inc.
111 River St.
Hoboken, NJ 07030-5774
Phone: (201)748-6000
Fax: (201)748-6088
**Subject(s):** Biology; Medicine and Surgery
**Circ:** (Paid)4,900

**Microwave and Optical Technology Letters (19338)**
John Wiley and Sons Inc.
111 River St.
Hoboken, NJ 07030-5774
Phone: (201)748-6000
Fax: (201)748-6088
**Subject(s):** Engineering (Various branches); Science (General)
**Circ:** 4,900

**The Quarterly Journal of Economics (13701)**
The MIT Press
Littauer Center, Rm. 227
Harvard University
1875 Cambridge St.
Cambridge, MA 02138
Phone: (617)495-2142
Fax: (617)495-7730
**Subject(s):** Economics
**Circ:** ‡4,900

**Rapid Communications in Mass Spectrometry (19381)**
John Wiley and Sons Inc.
111 River St.
Hoboken, NJ 07030-5774
Phone: (201)748-6000
Fax: (201)748-6088
**Subject(s):** Chemistry, Chemicals, and Chemical Engineering; Drugs and Pharmaceuticals
**Circ:** (Paid)4,900

**Seminars in Nuclear Medicine (20477)**
Elsevier
C/o Dr Leonard M. Freeman, Editor
Montefiore Medical Center
Department of Nuclear Medicine
111 E. 210 St.
Bronx, NY 10467
**Subject(s):** Radiology, Ultrasound, and Nuclear Medicine
**Circ:** ‡4,897

**Seminars in Ultrasound, CT and MRI (27267)**
Elsevier
1600 John F. Kennedy Blvd.
Philadelphia, PA 19103
Phone: (215)239-3900
Fax: (215)239-3990
**Subject(s):** Radiology, Ultrasound, and Nuclear Medicine
**Circ:** ‡4,880

**Carpet and Rug Industry (19747)**
Rodman Publishing Co.
70 Hilltop Rd., 3rd Fl.
Box 555
Ramsey, NJ 07446
Phone: (201)825-2552
Fax: (201)825-0553
**Subject(s):** Furniture and Furnishings
**Circ:** (Paid)319
(Non-paid)4,807

**Journal for Nurses in Staff Development (JNSD) (27071)**
Lippincott Williams & Wilkins
530 Walnut St.
Philadelphia, PA 19106-3261
Phone: (215)521-8300
Fax: (215)521-8902
**Subject(s):** Nursing
**Circ:** (Paid)4,800

**The Hudson Review (21790)**
The Hudson Review Inc.
684 Park Ave.
New York, NY 10021
Phone: (212)650-0020
Fax: (212)774-1911
**Subject(s):** Literature and Literary Reviews
**Circ:** (Controlled)‡100
(Paid)‡4,700

**Pennsylvania Dental Journal (26456)**
Pennsylvania Dental Association
3501 N. Front St.
Harrisburg, PA 17110
**Subject(s):** Dentistry
**Circ:** (Non-paid)‡200
(Paid)‡4,700

**American Journal of Botany (20942)**
Botanical Society of America
Department of Plant Biology
Cornell Univ.
Ithaca, NY 14853-5908
Phone: (607)254-4708
Fax: (607)254-4695
**Subject(s):** Botany
**Circ:** ‡4,693

**The New York Genealogical and Biographical Record (22158)**
New York Genealogical and Biographical Society
122 E. 58th St.
New York, NY 10022-1939
Phone: (212)755-8532
Fax: (212)754-4218
**Subject(s):** History and Genealogy
**Circ:** ‡4,656

**The Journal of Philosophy (21973)**
Journal of Philosophy Inc.
Columbia University
1150 Amsterdam Ave.
Mail Code 4972
New York, NY 10027
Phone: (212)666-4419
Fax: (212)932-3721
**Subject(s):** Philosophy
**Circ:** ‡4,611

**Administrative Science Quarterly (20940)**
20 Thornwood Dr., Ste. 100
Cornell Univ.
Ithaca, NY 14850-1265
Phone: (607)254-7143
Fax: (607)254-7100
**Subject(s):** Management and Administration
**Circ:** (Paid)‡4,600

**Cornell Focus (20946)**
Cornell University Experiment Station
1150 Comstock Hall
Ithaca, NY 14853-0901
Phone: (607)255-4326
Fax: (607)255-9873
**Subject(s):** Scientific Agricultural Publications
**Circ:** (Non-paid)‡4,600

**International Security (13682)**
The MIT Press
BCSIA (Belfer Center for Science & International Affairs)
John F. Kennedy School of Government
79 JFK St.
Cambridge, MA 02138
Phone: (617)495-1914
Fax: (617)496-4403
**Subject(s):** Military and Navy; Peace; Politics; International Affairs
**Circ:** ‡4,600

**Clinical Neuroscience (19199)**
John Wiley and Sons Inc.
111 River St.
Hoboken, NJ 07030-5774
Phone: (201)748-6000
Fax: (201)748-6088
**Subject(s):** Medicine and Surgery
**Circ:** 4,550

**Hippocampus (13523)**
John Wiley and Sons Inc.
Center for Memory and Brain
Dept. of Psychology
Boston University
2 Cummington St.
Boston, MA 02215
**Subject(s):** Medicine and Surgery
**Circ:** 4,550

**International Journal of Chemical Kinetics (19253)**
John Wiley and Sons Inc.
111 River St.
Hoboken, NJ 07030-5774
Phone: (201)748-6000
Fax: (201)748-6088
**Subject(s):** Chemistry, Chemicals, and Chemical Engineering
**Circ:** 4,550

**Molecular Carcinogenesis (19339)**
John Wiley and Sons Inc.
111 River St.
Hoboken, NJ 07030-5774
Phone: (201)748-6000
Fax: (201)748-6088
**Subject(s):** Medicine and Surgery
**Circ:** 4,550

**Adirondack Forty-Sixer Peaks (20606)**
Adirondack Forty-Sixers
c/o Phil Corell
PO Box 180
Cadyville, NY 12918-0180
Phone: (518)293-6401
**Subject(s):** (Outdoors)
**Circ:** 4,500

**Creative Nonfiction (27333)**
5501 Walnut St., Ste. 202
Pittsburgh, PA 15232
Phone: (412)688-0304
Fax: (412)683-9173
**Subject(s):** Literature and Literary Reviews; Literature
**Circ:** (Paid)4,500

**Experimental Mechanics (4619)**
Society for Experimental Mechanics
7 School St.
Bethel, CT 06801-1405
Phone: (203)790-6373
Fax: (203)790-4472
**Subject(s):** Construction, Contracting, Building, and Excavating; Engineering (Various branches); Plastic and Composition Materials; Building Materials, Concrete, Brick, and Tile
**Circ:** 4,500

**The Harvard Salient (14723)**
Turley Publications
24 Water St.
Palmer, MA 01069
Phone: (413)283-8393
Fax: (413)289-1977
**Subject(s):** College Publications
**Circ:** 4,500

**The Horn Book Guide (13524)**
The Horn Book Inc.
56 Roland St., Ste. 200
Boston, MA 02129
Phone: (617)628-0225
Fax: (617)628-0882
**Subject(s):** Literature and Literary Reviews
**Circ:** (Non-paid)500
(Paid)4,500

**Journal of the New Jersey Dental Association (19634)**
New Jersey Dental Association
1 Dental Plz.
PO Box 6020
North Brunswick, NJ 08902-6020
Phone: (732)821-9400
Fax: (732)821-1082
**Subject(s):** Dentistry
**Circ:** (Non-paid)‡500
(Paid)‡4,500

**The Journal of Portfolio Management (21978)**
Aspen Publishers
1185 Ave. of the Americas
New York, NY 10036
Phone: (212)730-4002
Fax: (212)597-0338

**Subject(s):** Banking, Finance, and Investments
**Circ:** 4,500

**The Mathematical Intelligencer (22062)**
Springer-Verlag New York Inc.
233 Spring St.
New York, NY 10013
Phone: (212)460-1500
Fax: (212)460-1575
**Subject(s):** Mathematics
**Circ:** (Combined)4,500

**Philadelphia Medicine (27223)**
Philadelphia County Medical Society
2100 Spring Garden St.
Philadelphia, PA 19130
Phone: (215)563-5343
Fax: (215)563-3627
**Subject(s):** Medicine and Surgery
**Circ:** (Non-paid)‡4,500

**Trial Lawyers Quarterly (22485)**
New York State Trial Lawyers Association
132 Nassau St., Ste. 200
New York, NY 10038
Phone: (212)349-5890
Fax: (212)608-2310
**Subject(s):** Law
**Circ:** (Controlled)4,500

**Arnoldia (13846)**
Arnold Arboretum
125 Arborway
Jamaica Plain, MA 02130-3500
Phone: (617)524-1718
Fax: (617)524-1418
**Subject(s):** Horticulture; Botany; Landscape Architecture
**Circ:** 4,450

**Vascular and Endovscular Surgery (20836)**
Westminster Publications Inc.
708 Glen Cove Ave.
Glen Head, NY 11545
Phone: (516)759-0025
Fax: (516)759-5524
**Subject(s):** Medicine and Surgery
**Circ:** ‡4,440

**Financial History (21690)**
Museum of American Financial History
26 Broadway, Rm. 947
New York, NY 10004
Phone: (212)908-4110
Fax: (212)908-4601
**Subject(s):** History and Genealogy; Banking, Finance, and Investments
**Circ:** (Paid)†2,100
(Non-paid)‡4,400

**Religious Conference Manager (14828)**
Primedia Business Magazines & Media
c/o Larry Keltto
132 Great Rd., Ste. 120
Stow, MA 01775-1189
**Subject(s):** Business; Religious Publications
**Circ:** 4,407

**Studies in Family Planning (22424)**
Population Council
1 Dag Hammarskjold Plz.
New York, NY 10017
Phone: (212)339-0500
Fax: (212)755-6052
**Subject(s):** Sociology; Health
**Circ:** (Paid)‡1,200
(Non-paid)‡4,400

**Experimental Techniques (4620)**
Society for Experimental Mechanics
7 School St.
Bethel, CT 06801-1405
Phone: (203)790-6373
Fax: (203)790-4472
**Subject(s):** Engineering (Various branches)
**Circ:** ‡4,380

**Ophthalmic Surgery Lasers and Imaging (13569)**
SLACK Inc.
Tufts University School of Medicine
750 Washington St.
Boston, MA 02111
Phone: (617)636-9033
Fax: (617)636-6126

**Subject(s):** Ophthalmology, Optometry, and Optics
**Circ:** ‡4,358

**American Journal of Agricultural Economics (13876)**
Blackwell Publishers
350 Main St.
Malden, MA 02148
Phone: (781)388-8200
Fax: (781)388-8250
**Subject(s):** Scientific Agricultural Publications; Economics
**Circ:** 4,300

**New York Holstein News (20963)**
New York Holstein Association
957 Mitchell St.
Ithaca, NY 14850-4936
Phone: (607)273-7591
Fax: (607)273-7612
**Subject(s):** Livestock
**Circ:** (Controlled)‡4,300

**The Yale Law Journal (4906)**
Yale Law Journal Co.
PO Box 208215
New Haven, CT 06520-8215
Phone: (203)432-1666
Fax: (203)432-7482
**Subject(s):** Law
**Circ:** ‡4,300

**Journal of Career Planning & Employment (26165)**
National Association of Colleges and Employers
62 Highland Ave.
Bethlehem, PA 18017-9085
Phone: (610)868-1421
Fax: (610)868-0208
**Subject(s):** Employment and Human Resources; Education
**Circ:** 4,237

**Chirality (19196)**
John Wiley and Sons Inc.
111 River St.
Hoboken, NJ 07030-5774
Phone: (201)748-6000
Fax: (201)748-6088
**Subject(s):** Medicine and Surgery; Laboratory Research (Scientific and Medical)
**Circ:** (Paid)4,200

**Human Brain Mapping (19244)**
John Wiley and Sons Inc.
111 River St.
Hoboken, NJ 07030-5774
Phone: (201)748-6000
Fax: (201)748-6088
**Subject(s):** Medicine and Surgery; Laboratory Research (Scientific and Medical)
**Circ:** 4,200

**The IMS Bulletin (5053)**
Institute of Mathematical Statistics
Department of Statistics
UCONN
196 Auditorium Rd., U-120
Storrs Mansfield, CT 06269-3120
Phone: (860)486-4113
Fax: (860)486-4113
**Subject(s):** Mathematics; Statistics
**Circ:** (Paid)4,206

**Journal of Advertising Research (21868)**
Advertising Research Foundation
641 Lexington Ave.
New York, NY 10022
Phone: (212)751-5656
Fax: (212)319-5265
**Subject(s):** Advertising and Marketing
**Circ:** (Paid)‡4,200

**Journal of Cosmetic Science (21904)**
Society of Cosmetic Chemists
120 Wall St., Ste. 2400
New York, NY 10005
Phone: (212)668-1500
Fax: (212)668-1504
**Subject(s):** Chemistry, Chemicals, and Chemical Engineering; Cosmetics and Toiletries
**Circ:** 4,200

**Journal of Molecular Recognition (JMR) (19299)**
John Wiley and Sons Inc.
111 River St.
Hoboken, NJ 07030-5774
Phone: (201)748-6000
Fax: (201)748-6088

**Subject(s):** Biology; Chemistry, Chemicals, and Chemical Engineering; Medicine and Surgery
**Circ:** (Paid)4,200

**Journal of Quaternary Science (19306)**
John Wiley and Sons Inc.
111 River St.
Hoboken, NJ 07030-5774
Phone: (201)748-6000
Fax: (201)748-6088
**Subject(s):** Geology; Science (General)
**Circ:** (Paid)4,200

**Numerical Methods for Partial Differential Equations (19350)**
John Wiley and Sons Inc.
111 River St.
Hoboken, NJ 07030-5774
Phone: (201)748-6000
Fax: (201)748-6088
**Subject(s):** Mathematics
**Circ:** (Paid)4,200

**Phytotherapy Research (19360)**
John Wiley and Sons Inc.
111 River St.
Hoboken, NJ 07030-5774
Phone: (201)748-6000
Fax: (201)748-6088
**Subject(s):** Chemistry, Chemicals, and Chemical Engineering; Science (General); Medicine and Surgery; Laboratory Research (Scientific and Medical); Toxicology; Drugs and Pharmaceuticals
**Circ:** 4,200

**Records of New Jersey Birds (18983)**
New Jersey Audubon Society
Box 693
Bernardsville, NJ 07924
Phone: (908)766-5787
Fax: (908)766-7775
**Subject(s):** Natural History and Nature Study
**Circ:** (Controlled)4,200

**Research-Technology Management (22307)**
Industrial Research Institute Inc.
c/o Michael F. Wolff
65 E. 96th St., No. 7B
New York, NY 10128
**Subject(s):** Science (General); Management and Administration
**Circ:** (Non-paid)‡800
(Paid)4,200

**Tobacco International (22460)**
Lockwood Trade Journal Co.
26 Broadway, Fl. 9M
New York, NY 10004-1703
Phone: (212)391-2060
Fax: (212)827-0945
**Subject(s):** Tobacco
**Circ:** (Combined)4,176

**Neuron (13695)**
Cell Press
1100 Massachusetts Ave.
Cambridge, MA 02138
Phone: (617)661-7057
Fax: (617)661-7061
**Subject(s):** Biology
**Circ:** (Combined)‡4,146

**ACM Transactions on Computer Systems (TOCS) (21257)**
Association for Computing Machinery
1515 Broadway, 17th Fl.
New York, NY 10036
Phone: (212)626-0500
Fax: (212)944-1318
**Subject(s):** Computers
**Circ:** 4,100

**Die Unterrichtspraxis/Teaching German (19020)**
American Association of Teachers of German Inc.
112 Haddontowne Ct., No. 104
Cherry Hill, NJ 08034-3668
Phone: (856)795-5553
Fax: (856)795-9398
**Subject(s):** Philology, Language, and Linguistics; Education
**Circ:** (Combined)4,100

**Neutron News** (22141)
Taylor & Francis Group
126 E. 4th St. 10.
New York, NY 10003
Phone: (212)539-1092
**Subject(s):** Science (General); Physics
**Circ:** (Combined)4,100

**American Journal of Physical Medicine and Rehabilitation** (13472)
Lippincott Williams & Wilkins
C/o Walter R. Frontera, MD Editor-In-Chief
Harvard Medical School
Spaulding Rehabilitation Hospital
Boston, MA 02115-6092
Phone: (317)280-9233
Fax: (317)280-9234
**Subject(s):** Medicine and Surgery
**Circ:** (Non-paid)‡216
  (Paid)‡4,091

**Art Now Gallery Guide–International Edition** (19041)
Art Now Inc.
97 Grayrock Rd.
PO Box 5541
Clinton, NJ 08809-5541
Phone: (908)638-5255
Fax: (908)638-8737
**Subject(s):** Art
**Circ:** 4,072

**Ski Area Management** (5108)
Beardsley Publishing Corp.
45 Main St. N.
PO Box 644
Woodbury, CT 06798
Phone: (203)263-0888
Fax: (203)266-0452
**Subject(s):** (Skiing); Sporting Goods/Retail Sports
**Circ:** (Paid)‡4,056

**Journal of the Pennsylvania Osteopathic Medical Association** (26446)
Pennsylvania Osteopathic Medical Association
1330 Eisenhower Blvd.
Harrisburg, PA 17111-2395
Phone: (717)939-9318
Fax: (717)939-7255
**Subject(s):** Osteopathy; Medicine and Surgery
**Circ:** (Combined)⊕4,035

**Vermont Business Magazine** (30873)
Elk Publishing Inc.
531 Main St.
Colchester, VT 05446-7222
Fax: (802)879-2015
**Subject(s):** Business
**Circ:** (Paid)‡1,697
  (Non-paid)‡4,037

**Agricultural News** (22770)
Cornell University Cooperative Extension Association of Saratoga County
36 Queens Ln.
Queensbury, NY 12804
Phone: (518)798-8228
**Subject(s):** General Agriculture
**Circ:** ‡4,000

**Balloon Life** (4833)
Balloon Life Magazine Inc.
PO Box 7
Litchfield, CT 06759
Phone: (860)567-2061
Fax: (206)935-3326
**Subject(s):** (Outdoors)
**Circ:** (Paid)4,000

**Chirurgische Gastroenterologie** (4707)
S. Karger Publishers Inc.
26 W Avon Rd.
PO Box 529
Farmington, CT 06085
Phone: (860)675-7834
Fax: (860)675-7302
**Subject(s):** Medicine and Surgery; German
**Circ:** (Combined)4,000

**Communication Monographs** (26891)
Routledge Journals
325 Chestnut St., 8th Fl.
Philadelphia, PA 19106
Fax: (215)625-8914
**Subject(s):** Communications; Education
**Circ:** ‡4,000

**Cross Currents** (21575)
475 Riverside Dr., Ste. 1945
New York, NY 10115
Phone: (212)870-2544
Fax: (212)870-2539
**Subject(s):** Religious Publications
**Circ:** (Controlled)‡400
  (Paid)‡4,000

**Developmental Medicine and Child Neurology** (21598)
Cambridge University Press
40 W. 20th St.
New York, NY 10011-4211
Phone: (212)924-3900
Fax: (212)691-3239
**Subject(s):** Medicine and Surgery
**Circ:** 4,000

**Doll Castle News** (19931)
Castle Press Publications
PO Box 247
Washington, NJ 07882
Phone: (908)689-7042
Fax: (908)689-6320
**Subject(s):** Crafts, Models, Hobbies, and Contests
**Circ:** 4,000

**Fire Technology** (14756)
National Fire Protection Association
1 Batterymarch Pk.
PO Box 9101
Quincy, MA 02169-7471
Phone: (617)770-3000
Fax: (617)770-0700
**Subject(s):** Fire Fighting; Public Safety and Emergency Response
**Circ:** ‡4,000

**Heritage** (20675)
New York State Historical Association
PO Box 800
Cooperstown, NY 13326
Phone: (607)547-1400
Fax: (607)547-1400
**Subject(s):** History and Genealogy
**Circ:** 4,000

**Indian Artifact Magazine** (27592)
Indian Artifact Magazine Inc.
245 Fairview Rd.
Turbotville, PA 17772-9063
Phone: (570)437-3698
Fax: (570)437-3411
**Subject(s):** Native American Interests
**Circ:** (Non-paid)‡42
  (Paid)‡4,000

**Journal of Nursing Education** (19859)
SLACK Inc.
6900 Grove Rd.
Thorofare, NJ 08086-9447
Phone: (856)848-1000
Fax: (856)848-6091
**Subject(s):** Nursing
**Circ:** (Paid)4,000

**Kirkus Reviews** (22012)
VNU Business Publications
770 Broadway
New York, NY 10003-9595
Phone: (646)654-5000
Fax: (646)654-7265
**Subject(s):** Library and Information Science; Book Trade and Author News
**Circ:** (Paid)‡4,000

**Microlithography World** (18908)
PennWell Corp.
98 Spit Brook Rd.
Nashua, NH 03062-5737
Phone: (603)891-0123
Fax: (603)891-0597
**Subject(s):** Electronics Engineering
**Circ:** (Paid)‡4,000

**Mosaic** (14291)
Educational Development Center Inc.
55 Chapel St.
Newton, MA 02458-1060
Phone: (617)969-7100
Fax: (617)969-5979
**Subject(s):** Education
**Circ:** 4,000

**NAFA Fleet Executive** (19414)
National Association of Fleet Administrators Inc.
100 Wood Ave. S., Ste. 310
Iselin, NJ 08830
Phone: (732)494-8100
Fax: (732)494-6789
**Subject(s):** Automotive (Trade)
**Circ:** (Controlled)3,900
  (Paid)4,000

**New Jersey Lake Survey Fishing Maps Guide** (19803)
New Jersey Sportsmen's Guides
PO Box 100
Somerdale, NJ 08083
Phone: (856)783-1271
Fax: (856)783-1271
**Subject(s):** (Hunting, Fishing, and Game Management)
**Circ:** (Paid)4,000

**The Northeast Square Dancer Magazine** (27879)
E & PJ Enterprises Inc.
145 Stone Dam Rd.
North Scituate, RI 02857
Phone: (401)647-9688
**Subject(s):** Entertainment
**Circ:** ‡4,000

**Peep** (20531)
Peep Magazine
67 Olive St.
Brooklyn, NY 11211
**Subject(s):** Literature and Literary Reviews; Art; Alternative and Underground
**Circ:** (Paid)4,000

**Perspective** (13698)
PO Box 2439
Cambridge, MA 02238
Phone: (617)495-4290
Fax: (617)495-4688
**Subject(s):** Social and Political Issues
**Circ:** (Controlled)4,000

**Philadelphia Museum of Art Bulletin** (27224)
Philadelphia Museum of Art
Publications Dept.
2525 Pennsylvania Ave.
Philadelphia, PA 19130
Phone: (215)684-7250
Fax: (215)235-8715
**Subject(s):** Art and Art History; Art; Museums
**Circ:** (Paid)‡4,000
  (Non-paid)‡4,000

**Psychiatric Rehabilitation Journal** (13580)
940 Commonwealth Ave.
Boston, MA 02215
Phone: (617)353-3549
Fax: (617)353-9209
**Subject(s):** Psychology and Psychiatry
**Circ:** (Paid)4,000

**Radio-TV Interview Report** (26618)
Bradley Communications
135 E. Plumstead Ave.
PO Box 1206
Lansdowne, PA 19050-8206
Phone: (610)259-0707
Fax: (610)284-3704
**Subject(s):** Radio, Television, Cable, and Video
**Circ:** (Non-paid)4,000

**The SandMUtopian Guardian** (22338)
Adam and Gillian's Sensual Whips and Toys Since 1987
Utopian Network
PO Box 1146
New York, NY 10156
Phone: (516)842-7518
Fax: (516)842-7518
**Subject(s):** Sex/Erotica
**Circ:** (Paid)4,000

**Society** (14878)
Transaction Publishers
Dept. of Sociology
Wellesley College
106 Central St.
Wellesley, MA 02481-8203
Phone: (781)283-3662
Fax: (781)283-3662
**Subject(s):** Sociology
**Circ:** (Paid)‡4,000

**Stage Directions** (22412)
Lifestyle Ventures L.L.C.
250 W 57th St., Ste. 420
New York, NY 10107
Phone: (212)265-8890
Fax: (212)265-8908
**Subject(s):** Drama and Theatre

Circ: (Non-paid)‡3,500
(Paid)‡4,000

**Summary of Labor Arbitration Awards** (22431)
American Arbitration Association
335 Madison Ave., Fl. 10
New York, NY 10017-4605
Phone: (212)716-5800
Fax: (212)716-5905
**Subject(s):** Labor

Circ: (Paid)‡750
(Non-paid)‡4,000

**Verhaltenstherapie** (4766)
S. Karger Publishers Inc.
26 W Avon Rd.
PO Box 529
Farmington, CT 06085
Phone: (860)675-7834
Fax: (860)675-7302
**Subject(s):** Medicine and Surgery; German

Circ: ‡4,000

**Viewfinder Journal of Focal Point Gallery** (20481)
Focal Point Press
321 City Island Ave.
Bronx, NY 10464
Phone: (718)885-1403
Fax: (718)885-1451
**Subject(s):** Art and Art History

Circ: 4000

**Voice of Youth** (26526)
Slovene National Benefit Society (SNPJ)
247 W. Allegheny Rd.
Imperial, PA 15126-9774
Phone: (724)695-1100
Fax: (724)695-1555
**Subject(s):** Slovene; Youths' Interests; Unclassified Fraternal; Ethnic Publications

Circ: ‡4,000

**The Whit** (19113)
201 Mullica Hill Rd.
Glassboro, NJ 08028
**Subject(s):** College Publications

Circ: (Non-paid)4,000

**Wire Rope News & Sling Technology** (19031)
VS Enterprises
PO Box 871
Clark, NJ 07066-0871
Phone: (908)486-3221
Fax: (732)396-4215
**Subject(s):** Metal, Metallurgy, and Metal Trade

Circ: (Paid)‡470
(Controlled)‡4,000

**Journal of Cardiovascular Nursing** (21891)
Aspen Publishers Inc.
1185 Ave. of the Americas
New York, NY 10036
Phone: (301)644-3599
Fax: (212)597-0331
**Subject(s):** Nursing

Circ: (Non-paid)4
(Paid)3,970

**Foot & Ankle** (26948)
Lippincott Williams & Wilkins
530 Walnut St.
Philadelphia, PA 19106-3261
Phone: (215)521-8300
Fax: (215)521-8902
**Subject(s):** Medicine and Surgery

Circ: (Non-paid)‡48
(Paid)‡3,941

**Progress in Cardiovascular Diseases** (20472)
Elsevier
C/o Edmund H. Sonnenblick, Editor
Albert Einstein College of Medicine
Division of Cardiology
1300 Morris Park Ave.
Bronx, NY 10461
**Subject(s):** Medicine and Surgery

Circ: ‡3,914

**Bulletin of the New York Academy of Medicine** (21433)
New York Academy of Medicine
1216 Fifth Ave., Rm. 601
New York, NY 10029
Phone: (212)822-7200
Fax: (212)996-7826
**Subject(s):** Medicine and Surgery

Circ: ‡3,900

**Heart and Lung** (26960)
Mosby
170 S. Independence Mall W. 300 E.
Philadelphia, PA 19106-3399
Phone: (215)238-7869
Fax: (215)238-2239
**Subject(s):** Hospitals and Healthcare Institutions

Circ: (Combined)‡3,899

**Advances in Polymer Technology** (19612)
John Wiley and Sons Inc.
c/o Dr. Theodore Davidson, New Jersey Inst. of Technology
Guttenberg Bldg., Ste. 3901
218 Central Ave.
Newark, NJ 07102-1982
Phone: (973)642-4582
Fax: (973)642-4594
**Subject(s):** Chemistry, Chemicals, and Chemical Engineering

Circ: (Paid)3,850

**Aggressive Behavior** (19155)
John Wiley and Sons Inc.
111 River St.
Hoboken, NJ 07030-5774
Phone: (201)748-6000
Fax: (201)748-6088
**Subject(s):** Psychology and Psychiatry

Circ: 3,850

**C++ Scientific Programming** (19184)
John Wiley and Sons Inc.
111 River St.
Hoboken, NJ 07030-5774
Phone: (201)748-6000
Fax: (201)748-6088
**Subject(s):** Computers; Electronics Engineering

Circ: 3,850

**Developmental Genetics** (19208)
John Wiley and Sons Inc.
111 River St.
Hoboken, NJ 07030-5774
Phone: (201)748-6000
Fax: (201)748-6088
**Subject(s):** Genetics

Circ: 3,850

**Journal of Clinical Laboratory Analysis** (19282)
John Wiley and Sons Inc.
111 River St.
Hoboken, NJ 07030-5774
Phone: (201)748-6000
Fax: (201)748-6088
**Subject(s):** Laboratory Research (Scientific and Medical)

Circ: 3,850

**Medicinal Research Reviews** (19333)
John Wiley and Sons Inc.
111 River St.
Hoboken, NJ 07030-5774
Phone: (201)748-6000
Fax: (201)748-6088
**Subject(s):** Medicine and Surgery

Circ: 3,850

**Random Structures & Algorithms** (19380)
John Wiley and Sons Inc.
111 River St.
Hoboken, NJ 07030-5774
Phone: (201)748-6000
Fax: (201)748-6088
**Subject(s):** Mathematics; Computers; Physics

Circ: 3,850

**Seminars in Surgical Oncology** (19385)
John Wiley and Sons Inc.
111 River St.
Hoboken, NJ 07030-5774
Phone: (201)748-6000
Fax: (201)748-6088
**Subject(s):** Medicine and Surgery

Circ: (Paid)3,850

**Teratogenesis, Carcinogenesis and Mutagenesis** (19399)
John Wiley and Sons Inc.
111 River St.
Hoboken, NJ 07030-5774
Phone: (201)748-6000
Fax: (201)748-6088
**Subject(s):** Medicine and Surgery; Hospitals and Healthcare Institutions; Biology

Circ: (Paid)3,850

**Zoo Biology** (19407)
John Wiley and Sons Inc.
111 River St.
Hoboken, NJ 07030-5774
Phone: (201)748-6000
Fax: (201)748-6088
**Subject(s):** Zoology; Biology

Circ: 3,850

**Churchwoman** (21489)
Church Women United
475 Riverside Dr., Ste. 1626
New York, NY 10115
Phone: (212)870-2347
Fax: (212)870-2338
**Subject(s):** Religious Publications; Women's Interests

Circ: (Non-paid)1,978
(Paid)3,831

**Inflammatory Bowel Diseases** (26976)
Lippincott Williams & Wilkins
c/o Molly Sullivan, Editorial Coordinator
Lippincott, Williams & Wilkins
530 Walnut St., 7th Fl.
Philadelphia, PA 19106
Phone: (215)521-8470
Fax: (215)521-8488
**Subject(s):** Medicine and Surgery

Circ: 3,829

**Scanning** (19496)
The Foundation for Advances in Medicine and Science Inc.
PO Box 485
Mahwah, NJ 07430-0485
Phone: (201)818-1010
Fax: (201)818-0086
**Subject(s):** Science (General)

Circ: (Paid)1,870
(Controlled)3,820

**The Lumber Co-Operator** (22779)
Northeastern Retail Lumber Association
585 N. Greenbush Rd.
Rensselaer, NY 12144
Phone: (518)286-1010
Fax: (518)286-1755
**Subject(s):** Forestry

Circ: (Controlled)262
(Paid)3,800

**OCJ (Orthodox Christian Journal)** (26451)
Orthodox Christian Journal
5501 Locust Ln.
Harrisburg, PA 17109
**Subject(s):** Religious Publications

Circ: ‡3,800

**Journalism and Mass Communication Educator** (27609)
Association for Education in Journalism & Mass Communication
c/o Jeremy Cohen, Editor
Office of Undergraduate Education
417 Old Main
Penn State Univ.
University Park, PA 16802-5101
Phone: (814)863-1864
**Subject(s):** Education; Journalism and Publishing

Circ: ‡3,718

**American Journal of Law & Medicine** (13471)
American Society of Law, Medicine & Ethics Inc.
765 Commonwealth Ave., Ste. 1672
Boston, MA 02215
**Subject(s):** Law; Medicine and Surgery

Circ: 3,700

**Antique Bottle and Glass Collector** (26298)
102 Jefferson St.
PO Box 180
East Greenville, PA 18041
Phone: (215)679-5849
Fax: (215)679-3068

**Subject(s):** Glass and China
**Circ:** (Controlled)⊕**3,700**

**Journal of African American History** (21869)
Association for the Study of Afro-American Life and History
Institute for Urban and Minority Education
Teachers College
525 W. 120th St.
PO Box 75
New York, NY 10027
Phone: (212)678-8103
**Subject(s):** Black Publications; History and Genealogy
**Circ:** (Non-paid)‡300
　　　(Paid)‡3,700

**Mission** (26159)
Sisters of the Blessed Sacrament
1663 Bristol Pke.
Bensalem, PA 19020-5796
Phone: (215)244-9900
Fax: (215)639-1154
**Subject(s):** Religious Publications
**Circ:** (Controlled)1,000
　　　(Paid)3,700

**New York Real Estate Journal** (14645)
East Coast Publications
57 Washington St.
Norwell, MA 02061-1715
Phone: (617)871-1853
Fax: (800)654-4993
**Subject(s):** Real Estate
**Circ:** (Paid)3,700

**Journal of Cardiopulmonary Rehabilitation (JCR)** (27015)
Lippincott Williams & Wilkins
530 Walnut St.
Philadelphia, PA 19106-3261
Phone: (215)521-8300
Fax: (215)521-8902
**Subject(s):** Medicine and Surgery
**Circ:** (Paid)3,694

**Bulletin of Allegheny County Medical Society** (27329)
Allegheny County Medical Society
713 Ridge Ave.
Pittsburgh, PA 15212
Phone: (412)321-5030
Fax: (412)321-5323
**Subject(s):** Medicine and Surgery
**Circ:** (Controlled)‡219
　　　(Paid)‡3,687

**International Journal of Intelligent Systems** (19261)
John Wiley and Sons Inc.
111 River St.
Hoboken, NJ 07030-5774
Phone: (201)748-6000
Fax: (201)748-6088
**Subject(s):** Computers
**Circ:** (Combined)3,675

**Journal of Addictive Diseases** (21867)
The Haworth Press Inc.
c/o Barry Stimmel, Mount Sinai School of Medicine
Annenberg 5102G
PO Box 1193
1 Gustave L. Levy Place/Box 1193
New York, NY 10029
Phone: (212)241-6694
Fax: (212)426-7748
**Subject(s):** Substance Abuse and Treatment
**Circ:** (Paid)3,676

**Journal of Applied Mechanics** (21880)
American Society of Mechanical Engineers
3 Park Ave.
New York, NY 10016-5990
Phone: (212)591-7722
Fax: (212)591-7674
**Subject(s):** Engineering (Various branches)
**Circ:** 3,679

**Pi Mu Epsilon Journal** (14942)
Worcester Polytechnic Institute
100 Institute Rd.
Worcester, MA 01609-2280
Phone: (508)831-5241
Fax: (508)831-5824
**Subject(s):** Mathematics
**Circ:** (Controlled)3,600

**John Milton Magazine** (21865)
John Milton Society for the Blind
475 Riverside Dr., Rm. 455
New York, NY 10015
Fax: (212)870-3229
**Subject(s):** Religious Publications; Handicapped
**Circ:** (Non-paid)3,591

**American Jewish History** (21309)
American Jewish Historical Society
15 W 16th St.
New York, NY 10011
Phone: (212)294-6160
Fax: (212)294-6161
**Subject(s):** History and Genealogy; Jewish Publications
**Circ:** ‡3,550

**The Journal of Cell Biology** (21893)
Rockefeller University Press
1114 1st Ave., 3rd Fl.
New York, NY 10021
Phone: (212)327-8575
Fax: (212)327-8511
**Subject(s):** Biology
**Circ:** ‡3,524

**Bible Standard and Herald of Christ's Kingdom** (26238)
Laymen's Home Missionary Movement
1156 St. Matthews Rd.
Chester Springs, PA 19425-2700
Phone: (610)827-7665
**Subject(s):** French; Polish; Religious Publications; German; Malay; Tamil
**Circ:** (Paid)‡3,500

**Choice** (4841)
American Library Association
100 Riverview Ctr.
Middletown, CT 06457
Phone: (860)704-0465
Fax: (860)704-0465
**Subject(s):** Library and Information Science; Education
**Circ:** (Controlled)‡141
　　　(Paid)‡3,500

**The Cornell Hotel and Restaurant Administration Quarterly** (20947)
Cornell University School of Hotel Administration
541 Statler Hall
Ithaca, NY 14853
Phone: (607)255-9780
Fax: (607)254-2922
**Subject(s):** Hotels, Motels, Restaurants, and Clubs
**Circ:** ‡3,500

**Digestive Surgery** (4717)
S. Karger Publishers Inc.
26 W Avon Rd.
PO Box 529
Farmington, CT 06085
Phone: (860)675-7834
Fax: (860)675-7302
**Subject(s):** Medicine and Surgery
**Circ:** 3,500

**Directors & Boards** (26920)
Directors and Boards
1845 Walnut St., Ste. 900
Philadelphia, PA 19103-4709
Phone: (215)567-3200
Fax: (215)405-6078
**Subject(s):** Management and Administration
**Circ:** (Paid)‡1,500
　　　(Non-paid)‡3,500

**Haunts** (27836)
Nightshade Publications
PO Box 8068
Cranston, RI 02920
Phone: (401)781-9438
Fax: (401)943-0980
**Subject(s):** Science Fiction, Mystery, Adventure, and Romance
**Circ:** (Non-paid)150
　　　(Paid)3,500

**Journal of Business Forecasting Methods** (20858)
Graceway Publishing Co.
350 Northern Blvd., Ste. 202
Great Neck, NY 11021
Phone: (516)504-7576
Fax: (516)498-2029
**Subject(s):** Advertising and Marketing; Selling and Salesmanship
**Circ:** (Paid)3,500

**The Journal of Multi-Criteria Decision Analysis** (19300)
John Wiley and Sons Inc.
111 River St.
Hoboken, NJ 07030-5774
Phone: (201)748-6000
Fax: (201)748-6088
**Subject(s):** Management and Administration
**Circ:** (Paid)3,500

**NYSPA Notebook/Psychologist** (20229)
Foundation of the New York State Psychological Association Inc.
6 Executive Park Dr.
Albany, NY 12203
Phone: (518)437-1050
Fax: (518)437-0177
**Subject(s):** Psychology and Psychiatry
**Circ:** ‡3,500

**NYSSA Sphere** (22187)
The New York State Society of Anesthesiologists Inc.
85 Fifth Ave., 8th Fl.
New York, NY 10003
Phone: (212)867-7140
Fax: (212)867-7153
**Subject(s):** Medicine and Surgery
**Circ:** (Combined)3,500

**Organic Letters** (27203)
American Chemical Society
c/o Amos B. Smith, III
Department of Chemistry
University of Pennsylvania
231 S. 34th St.
Philadelphia, PA 19104-6323
Phone: (215)573-6144
Fax: (215)573-8256
**Subject(s):** Chemistry, Chemicals, and Chemical Engineering
**Circ:** 3,500

**Permafrost and Periglacial Processes** (19354)
John Wiley and Sons Inc.
111 River St.
Hoboken, NJ 07030-5774
Phone: (201)748-6000
Fax: (201)748-6088
**Subject(s):** Engineering (Various branches); Geology; Natural Resources
**Circ:** 3,500

**Phytochemical Analysis** (19359)
John Wiley and Sons Inc.
111 River St.
Hoboken, NJ 07030-5774
Phone: (201)748-6000
Fax: (201)748-6088
**Subject(s):** Chemistry, Chemicals, and Chemical Engineering; Drugs and Pharmaceuticals; Science (General); Health and Healthcare
**Circ:** 3,500

**Review of Economics and Statistics** (13705)
The MIT Press
79 JFK St.
Cambridge, MA 02138
Phone: (617)495-2111
Fax: (617)495-5147
**Subject(s):** Economics
**Circ:** 3,500

**Reviews in Medical Virology** (19383)
John Wiley and Sons Inc.
111 River St.
Hoboken, NJ 07030-5774
Phone: (201)748-6000
Fax: (201)748-6088
**Subject(s):** Biology; Science (General); Physiology and Anatomy
**Circ:** (Paid)3,500

**Stress and Health** (19392)
John Wiley and Sons Inc.
111 River St.
Hoboken, NJ 07030-5774
Phone: (201)748-6000
Fax: (201)748-6088
**Subject(s):** Psychology and Psychiatry; Sociology
**Circ:** (Paid)3,500

**Teachers College Record  (22440)**
Teachers College Record Columbia University
Teachers College
Columbia University
525 W. 120th St.
PO Box 103
New York, NY 10027
Phone: (212)678-3774
Fax: (212)678-3790
**Subject(s):** Education
Circ: (Non-paid)‡300
(Paid)‡3,500

**Avotaynu  (18978)**
Avotaynu Inc.
155 N Washington Ave.
Bergenfield, NJ 07621
Phone: (201)387-7200
Fax: (201)387-2855
**Subject(s):** History and Genealogy; Jewish Publications
Circ: (Combined)3,400

**International Journal of Powder Metallurgy  (19721)**
APMI International
105 College Rd. E
Princeton, NJ 08540
Phone: (609)452-7700
Fax: (609)987-8523
**Subject(s):** Metal, Metallurgy, and Metal Trade
Circ: ‡3,400

**Behavior Therapy  (21387)**
Association for Advancement of Behavior Therapy
305 7th Ave., 16th Fl.
New York, NY 10001-6008
Phone: (212)647-1890
Fax: (212)647-1865
**Subject(s):** Psychology and Psychiatry; Medicine and Surgery
Circ: 3,350

**Journal of American Studies  (21875)**
Cambridge University Press
40 W. 20th St.
New York, NY 10011-4211
Phone: (212)924-3900
Fax: (212)691-3239
**Subject(s):** Economics; History and Genealogy; Humanities; Literature; Geography; Politics
Circ: (Paid)‡455
(Non-paid)‡3,346

**Journal of Navigation  (21960)**
Cambridge University Press
40 W. 20th St.
New York, NY 10011-4211
Phone: (212)924-3900
Fax: (212)691-3239
**Subject(s):** Aviation; Boats and Marine; Ships and Shipping
Circ: (Paid)455
(Non-paid)3,346

**Clinical Nurse Specialist  (26438)**
Lippincott Williams & Wilkins
3969 Green St.
Harrisburg, PA 17110
Phone: (717)234-6799
Fax: (717)234-6798
**Subject(s):** Nursing
Circ: (Non-paid)110
(Paid)3,319

**Journal of Prosthodontics  (27090)**
Elsevier
1600 John F. Kennedy Blvd.
Philadelphia, PA 19103
Phone: (215)239-3900
Fax: (215)239-3990
**Subject(s):** Dentistry
Circ: (Paid)3,312

**Journal of the Mississippi State Medical Association  (16939)**
Mississippi State Medical Association
111 Magnolia St.
Magnolia, MS 39652
Phone: (601)783-2374
Fax: (601)783-5126
**Subject(s):** Medicine and Surgery
Circ: (Non-paid)‡100
(Paid)‡3,300

**Topics in Language Disorders (TLD)  (22466)**
Aspen Publishers Inc.
1185 Ave. of the Americas
New York, NY 10036
Phone: (301)644-3599
Fax: (212)597-0331
**Subject(s):** Hearing and Speech
Circ: (Non-paid)78
(Paid)3,278

**Current Opinion in Anesthesiology  (26905)**
Lippincott Williams & Wilkins
530 Walnut St.
Philadelphia, PA 19106-3261
Phone: (215)521-8300
Fax: (215)521-8902
**Subject(s):** Medicine and Surgery
Circ: (Paid)‡3,250

**The Journal of Economic History  (21914)**
Cambridge University Press
40 W. 20th St.
New York, NY 10011-4211
Phone: (212)924-3900
Fax: (212)691-3239
**Subject(s):** Economics; History and Genealogy
Circ: 3,250

**Tracings  (13828)**
Sisters of Providence
5 Gamelin St.
Holyoke, MA 01040
Phone: (413)536-7511
Fax: (413)536-7917
**Subject(s):** Religious Publications
Circ: (Free)‡3,250

**City Limits  (21496)**
City Limits Community Information Service
120 Wall St., 20th Fl.
New York, NY 10005
Phone: (212)479-3344
Fax: (212)344-6457
**Subject(s):** Social and Political Issues
Circ: (Non-paid)1,000
(Paid)3,200

**Early American Industries Association Chronicle  (27866)**
Early American Industries Association Inc.
31 Walnut St
Newport, RI 02840
Phone: (401)846-2542
Fax: (401)846-6615
**Subject(s):** Commerce and Industry
Circ: (Combined)3,200

**German Quarterly  (19022)**
American Association of Teachers of German Inc.
112 Haddontowne Ct., No. 104
Cherry Hill, NJ 08034-3668
Phone: (856)795-5553
Fax: (856)795-9398
**Subject(s):** Literature; Intercultural Interests
Circ: (Combined)3,200

**North American Journal of Fisheries Management  (27863)**
American Fisheries Society
c/o Carolyn A. Griswold
National Marine Fisheries Service
Northeast Fisheries Science Center
28 Tarzwell Dr.
Narragansett, RI 02882
Phone: (401)782-3273
Fax: (401)782-3201
**Subject(s):** Fish and Commercial Fisheries; Management and Administration; Ecology and Conservation
Circ: ‡3,200

**Philosophical Review  (20965)**
Sage School of Philosophy
Cornell University
B7 McGraw Hall
Ithaca, NY 14853-3201
Phone: (607)255-6817
Fax: (607)255-8177
**Subject(s):** Philosophy
Circ: ‡3,200

**Journal of Cardiovascular Electrophysiology  (20756)**
Blackwell Publishing/Futura
3 W. Main St.
Elmsford, NY 10523
Phone: (781)388-8372

Fax: (781)388-8265
**Subject(s):** Medicine and Surgery
Circ: ‡3,164

**Depression and Anxiety  (19207)**
John Wiley and Sons Inc.
111 River St.
Hoboken, NJ 07030-5774
Phone: (201)748-6000
Fax: (201)748-6088
**Subject(s):** Psychology and Psychiatry
Circ: 3,150

**NCGR Journal  (14269)**
National Council for Geocosmic Research Inc.
c/o Lorraine Welsh
42 Gayland Rd.
Needham, MA 02492
Phone: (781)444-4428
Fax: (781)444-4428
**Subject(s):** Astronomy and Meteorology
Circ: (Paid)3,100

**The Quarterly Review of Biology  (22984)**
University of Chicago Press
C-2615 Mellville Library
State Univ. of New York
Stony Brook, NY 11794-3349
Phone: (631)632-6977
Fax: (631)632-9282
**Subject(s):** Biology
Circ: (Non-paid)‡200
(Paid)‡3,100

**Nephron  (4740)**
S. Karger Publishers Inc.
26 W Avon Rd.
PO Box 529
Farmington, CT 06085
Phone: (860)675-7834
Fax: (860)675-7302
**Subject(s):** Medicine and Surgery
Circ: 3,050

**AICHE Journal  (21283)**
American Institute of Chemical Engineers
3 Park Ave.
New York, NY 10016-5991
Phone: (212)591-8100
Fax: (212)591-8888
**Subject(s):** Chemistry, Chemicals, and Chemical Engineering; Engineering (Various branches)
Circ: 3,025

**Aesthetic Plastic Surgery  (21276)**
Springer-Verlag New York Inc.
233 Spring St.
New York, NY 10013
Phone: (212)460-1500
Fax: (212)460-1575
**Subject(s):** Medicine and Surgery
Circ: (Combined)**3,000**

**Allergy and Asthma Proceedings  (27885)**
Ocean Side Publications Inc.
95 Pitman St.
Providence, RI 02906-4311
Phone: (401)331-2510
Fax: (401)331-5138
**Subject(s):** Medicine and Surgery; Health and Healthcare
Circ: (Combined)3,000

**American Journal of Rhinology  (26818)**
Ocean Side Publications
c/o David W. Kennedy, M.D.,
Dept. of Otorhinolaryngology,
Head and Neck Surgery, Univ. of Pennsylvania Medical Center
5 Silverstein, 3400 Spruce St.
Philadelphia, PA 19104
**Subject(s):** Medicine and Surgery
Circ: 3,000

**Card Manufacturing  (19744)**
ICMA
PO Box 727
Princeton Junction, NJ 08550
Phone: (609)799-4900
Fax: (609)799-7032
**Subject(s):** Machinery and Equipment; Commerce and Industry; Intercultural Interests; Banking, Finance, and Investments
Circ: (Paid)3,000

**Catholic Library World** (14738)
Catholic Library Association
100 North St., Ste. 224
Pittsfield, MA 01201-5109
Phone: (413)443-2252
Fax: (413)442-2252
Subject(s): Religious Publications; Library and Information Science
Circ: ‡3,000

**Civil Engineering Practice** (13501)
Boston Society of Civil Engineers Section
Engineering Ctr.
1 Walnut St.
Boston, MA 02108
Phone: (617)227-5551
Fax: (617)227-6783
Subject(s): Engineering (Various branches)
Circ: (Paid)3,000

**The Classical World** (26867)
Classical Association of the Atlantic States
Department of Humanities
University of the Sciences
600 S 43rd St.
Philadelphia, PA 19104-4495
Phone: (434)220-3300
Subject(s): Literature; Art and Art History
Circ: ‡3,000

**Compensation & Benefits Review** (21533)
American Management Association
1601 Broadway
New York, NY 10019
Phone: (212)586-8100
Fax: (212)903-8168
Subject(s): Employment and Human Resources
Circ: (Non-paid)800
(Paid)3000

**Computers in Nursing** (12556)
Lippincott Williams & Wilkins
C/o Leslie H. Nicoll, PhD, Editor-in-Chief
10A Beach St., Ste. 2
Portland, ME 04101
Phone: (207)553-7751
Fax: (207)553-7751
Subject(s): Computers; Nursing
Circ: (Paid)‡3,000

**Cornell Science & Technology Magazine** (20951)
Cornell University
B46 Olin Hall
Ithaca, NY 14853
Phone: (607)255-3312
Fax: (607)255-9606
Subject(s): Engineering (Various branches); Anthropology and Ethnology; Science (General)
Circ: ‡3,000

**Current Opinion in Pediatrics** (26910)
Lippincott Williams & Wilkins
530 Walnut St.
Philadelphia, PA 19106-3261
Phone: (215)521-8300
Fax: (215)521-8902
Subject(s): Medicine and Surgery; Pediatrics
Circ: (Paid)‡3,005

**Editor's Choice** (20982)
The Spirit That Moves Us Press
PO Box 720820
Jackson Heights, NY 11372-0820
Phone: (718)426-8788
Subject(s): Literature; Literature and Literary Reviews; Poetry
Circ: (Paid)3000

**Educational Technology Magazine** (19074)
Educational Technology Publications
700 Palisade Ave.
Englewood Cliffs, NJ 07632-0564
Phone: (201)871-4007
Fax: (201)871-4009
Subject(s): Education
Circ: ‡3,000

**Food Institute Report** (19070)
The Food Institute
1 Broadway, 2nd Fl.
Elmwood Park, NJ 07407
Phone: (201)791-5570
Fax: (201)791-5222
Subject(s): Food and Grocery Trade; Food Production
Circ: (Paid)3,000

**Forum—A Ukrainian Review** (27504)
Ukrainian Fraternal Association
1327 Wyoming Ave.
Scranton, PA 18509
Phone: (570)342-0937
Fax: (570)347-5649
Subject(s): Ethnic Publications; Intercultural Interests
Circ: ‡3,000

**The Gettysburg Review** (26390)
Gettysburg College
300 N. Washington St.
Gettysburg, PA 17325-1491
Phone: (717)337-6770
Fax: (717)337-6775
Subject(s): Literature and Literary Reviews
Circ: (Paid)‡3,000

**Harvard Advocate** (13665)
21 S. St.
Cambridge, MA 02138
Phone: (617)495-0737
Fax: (617)496-9740
Subject(s): Literature and Literary Reviews
Circ: (Paid)‡300
(Non-paid)‡3,000

**HIGHWAY BUILDER** (26443)
TRIAD
800 N. 3rd St.
Harrisburg, PA 17102
Phone: (717)238-2513
Fax: (717)238-5060
Subject(s): Roads and Streets; Transportation, Traffic, and Shipping
Circ: ‡3,000

**The Iconoclast (Mohegan Lake)** (21216)
The Iconoclast
1675 Amazon Rd.
Mohegan Lake, NY 10547-1804
Subject(s): Literature; Poetry
Circ: (Combined)3,000

**Immunity** (13679)
Cell Press
1100 Massachusetts Ave.
Cambridge, MA 02138
Phone: (617)661-7057
Fax: (617)661-7061
Subject(s): Physiology and Anatomy
Circ: 3,000

**International Organization** (13681)
Cambridge University Press
WCFIA/Harvard University
1033 Massachusetts Ave.
Cambridge, MA 02138
Subject(s): International Affairs; International Business and Economics
Circ: ‡3,000

**The Journal of College Radio** (21248)
Intercollegiate Broadcasting System Inc.
367 Windsor Hwy.
New Windsor, NY 12553
Phone: (845)565-0003
Fax: (845)565-7446
Subject(s): Radio, Television, Cable, and Video
Circ: ‡3,000

**Journal of Interactive Learning Research** (26633)
Association for the Advancement of Computing in Education
PO Box 72
Leetsdale, PA 15056-0072
Subject(s): Computers; Education
Circ: (Paid)‡3,000

**Journal of the Society of Pediatric Nurses** (27095)
Nursecom Inc.
1211 Locust St.
Philadelphia, PA 19107-5409
Phone: (215)545-7222
Fax: (215)545-8107
Subject(s): Nursing; Health and Healthcare
Circ: ‡3,000

**Journal of Spinal Cord Medicine** (20984)
American Paraplegia Society
75-20 Astoria Blvd.
Jackson Heights, NY 11372
Phone: (718)803-3782
Fax: (718)803-0414
Subject(s): Medicine and Surgery; Health and Healthcare
Circ: 3,000

**Nashe Zhyttia (Our Life)** (22123)
Ukrainian National Women's League of America Inc.
203 2nd Ave.
New York, NY 10003
Phone: (212)533-4646
Fax: (212)533-5237
Subject(s): Unclassified Fraternal; Ukrainian
Circ: (Non-paid)‡50
(Paid)‡3,000

**New Politics** (22148)
New Politics Associates Inc.
155 W. 72nd St., Rm. 402
New York, NY 10023
Phone: (718)287-2048
Fax: (718)246-9648
Subject(s): Politics; Political Science
Circ: (Paid)3000

**19th Century** (27174)
Victorian Society in America
205 S Camac St.
Philadelphia, PA 19107
Phone: (215)545-8340
Fax: (215)545-8379
Subject(s): History and Genealogy; History and Genealogy
Circ: 3,000

**Northern New Hampshire Magazine** (18780)
Jordan Associates
PO Box 263
Colebrook, NH 03576
Phone: (603)246-8998
Subject(s): Local, State, and Regional Publications
Circ: (Paid)3,000

**Pennsylvania Mennonite Heritage** (26604)
Lancaster Mennonite Historical Society
2215 Millstream Road
Lancaster, PA 17602-1499
Phone: (717)393-9745
Fax: (717)393-9751
Subject(s): History and Genealogy; Religious Publications
Circ: (Combined)3,000

**Physical Review Abstracts** (21176)
American Physical Society
2 Huntington Quadrangle, Ste. 1N01
Melville, NY 11747-4501
Phone: (516)576-2200
Subject(s): Physics
Circ: 3,000

**Press** (26460)
Pennsylvania Newspaper Association
3899 N. Front St.
Harrisburg, PA 17110-1221
Phone: (717)703-3000
Fax: (717)703-3001
Subject(s): Printing and Typography
Circ: 3,000

**Raritan** (19600)
31 Mine St.
New Brunswick, NJ 08903
Phone: (732)932-7887
Fax: (732)932-7855
Subject(s): General Editorial
Circ: (Non-paid)‡500
(Paid)‡3,000

**School Psychology Quarterly** (22351)
Taylor and Francis
72 S Mine St.
New York, NY 10012
Phone: (212)431-9800
Fax: (212)966-6708
Subject(s): Education; Psychology and Psychiatry
Circ: (Paid)3,000

**Searcher** (19519)
Information Today Inc.
143 Old Marlton Pike
Medford, NJ 08055-8750
Phone: (609)654-6266
Fax: (609)654-4309
Subject(s): Computers
Circ: (Non-paid)1,000
(Paid)3,000

**SIECUS Report (22371)**
Sexuality Information and Education Council of the United States
130 W. 42nd St., Ste. 350
New York, NY 10036-7802
Phone: (212)819-9770
Fax: (212)819-9776
**Subject(s):** Health and Healthcare

Circ: (Paid)‡2,700
‏ 3,000

**Social Research (22387)**
New School University
65 5th Ave., Room 344
New York, NY 10003
**Subject(s):** Political Science; Social Sciences

Circ: ‡3,000

**Trendline Current Market Perspectives (22483)**
Standard & Poor's
55 Water St.
New York, NY 10041
Fax: (212)438-3396
**Subject(s):** Banking, Finance, and Investments

Circ: (Paid)3,000

**The Witness (22542)**
The Episcopal Church Publishing Co.
55 W. 116th St., No. 444
New York, NY 10026
Phone: (212)426-9881
**Subject(s):** Religious Publications

Circ: (Non-paid)‡500
‏ (Paid)‡3,000

**Yale Scientific Magazine (4909)**
Yale Sta.
PO Box 209117
New Haven, CT 06520
**Subject(s):** Science (General)

Circ: (Paid)‡1,900
‏ (Non-paid)‡3,000

**Hand Clinics (26959)**
Elsevier
1600 John F. Kennedy Blvd.
Philadelphia, PA 19103
Phone: (215)239-3900
Fax: (215)239-3990
**Subject(s):** Medicine and Surgery

Circ: (Paid)2,986

**The Journal of Pediatric Oncology Nursing (21970)**
Elsevier
c/o Nancy E. Kline, Editor-in-Chief
Director, Nursing Research
Memorial Sloan-Kettering Cancer Center
New York, NY
**Subject(s):** Nursing; Pediatrics

Circ: ‡2,982

**American Journal of Hospice and Palliative Care (14903)**
Prime National Publishing Corp.
470 Boston Post Rd.
Weston, MA 02493
Phone: (781)899-2702
Fax: (781)899-4900
**Subject(s):** Hospitals and Healthcare Institutions

Circ: (Non-paid)‡107
‏ (Paid)‡2,931

**Sewickley Herald (26732)**
Gateway Publications
610 Beatty Rd.
Monroeville, PA 15146
Phone: (412)856-7400
Fax: (412)856-7954
**Subject(s):** Paid Community Newspapers

Circ: (Combined)2,922

**American Journal of Nephrology (4695)**
S. Karger Publishers Inc.
26 W Avon Rd.
PO Box 529
Farmington, CT 06085
Phone: (860)675-7834
Fax: (860)675-7302
**Subject(s):** Laboratory Research (Scientific and Medical); Medicine and Surgery

Circ: 2,900

**Molecular Cancer Research (27151)**
American Association for Cancer Research Inc.
615 Chestnut St., 17th Fl.
Philadelphia, PA 19106-4404
Phone: (215)440-9300
Fax: (215)440-9313
**Subject(s):** Medicine and Surgery; Biology; Laboratory Research (Scientific and Medical)

Circ: (Paid)2,900

**Journal of Emergency Management (14906)**
Prime National Publishing Corp.
470 Boston Post Rd.
Weston, MA 02493
Phone: (781)899-2702
Fax: (781)899-4900
**Subject(s):** Police, Penology, and Penal Institutions; Fire Fighting

Circ: (Paid)‡2,870

**International Journal of Surgical Pathology (20833)**
Westminster Publications Inc.
708 Glen Cove Ave.
Glen Head, NY 11545
Phone: (516)759-0025
Fax: (516)759-5524
**Subject(s):** Health and Healthcare; Medicine and Surgery

Circ: (Combined)2,865

**The Endocrinologist (26933)**
Lippincott Williams & Wilkins
530 Walnut St.
Philadelphia, PA 19106-3261
Phone: (215)521-8300
Fax: (215)521-8902
**Subject(s):** Medicine and Surgery

Circ: (Non-paid)‡85
‏ (Paid)‡2,840

**Journal of Compensation and Benefits (21898)**
RIA Group
395 Hudson St., 4th Fl.
New York, NY 10014
Phone: (212)367-6300
Fax: (212)367-6314
**Subject(s):** Employment and Human Resources

Circ: (Non-paid)1509
‏ (Paid)2816

**ALI-ABA Business Law Course Materials Journal (26809)**
ALI-ABA Committee on Continuing Professional Education
4025 Chestnut St.
Philadelphia, PA 19104
Phone: (215)243-1604
Fax: (215)243-1664
**Subject(s):** Law

Circ: (Non-paid)‡61
‏ (Paid)‡2,802

**Country Airplay Monitor (21559)**
VNU Business Media USA
770 Broadway
New York, NY 10003
Phone: (646)654-5000
**Subject(s):** Radio, Television, Cable, and Video; Music and Musical Instruments

Circ: 2,803

**Current Opinion in Neurology (26906)**
Lippincott Williams & Wilkins
530 Walnut St.
Philadelphia, PA 19106-3261
Phone: (215)521-8300
Fax: (215)521-8902
**Subject(s):** Medicine and Surgery

Circ: (Paid)‡2,809

**Fordham Law Review (21712)**
Fordham University School of Law
140 W 62nd St.
Lincoln Ctr.
New York, NY 10023-7485
Phone: (212)636-6876
Fax: (212)636-6965
**Subject(s):** Law

Circ: 2,800

**Journal of Combinatorial Designs (30857)**
John Wiley and Sons Inc.
c/o Jeffrey H. Dinitz, Editor-in-Chief
Dept. of Mathematics
Univ. of Vermont
Burlington, VT 05405
Phone: (802)656-4292

**Subject(s):** Mathematics

Circ: 2,800

**Journal of Community & Applied Social Psychology (19285)**
John Wiley and Sons Inc.
111 River St.
Hoboken, NJ 07030-5774
Phone: (201)748-6000
Fax: (201)748-6088
**Subject(s):** Psychology and Psychiatry

Circ: (Paid)2,800

**Journal of International Development (19294)**
John Wiley and Sons Inc.
111 River St.
Hoboken, NJ 07030-5774
Phone: (201)748-6000
Fax: (201)748-6088
**Subject(s):** Economics; Politics; Sociology

Circ: (Paid)2,800

**Journal of the New England Water Works Association (13825)**
New England Water Works Association
125 Hopping Brook Rd.
Holliston, MA 01746-1471
Phone: (508)893-7979
Fax: (508)893-9898
**Subject(s):** Water Supply and Sewage Disposal

Circ: (Non-paid)‡243
‏ (Paid)‡2,800

**Linguistic Inquiry (13693)**
The MIT Press
MIT Building E39-352
Cambridge, MA 02139
Phone: (617)253-4059
Fax: (617)253-5017
**Subject(s):** Philology, Language, and Linguistics

Circ: 2,800

**Maine History (12560)**
Maine Historical Society
489 Congress St.
Portland, ME 04101
Phone: (207)774-1822
Fax: (207)775-4301
**Subject(s):** History and Genealogy

Circ: 2,800

**Packaging Technology and Science (19351)**
John Wiley and Sons Inc.
111 River St.
Hoboken, NJ 07030-5774
Phone: (201)748-6000
Fax: (201)748-6088
**Subject(s):** Chemistry, Chemicals, and Chemical Engineering; Engineering (Various branches); Food and Grocery Trade; Science (General); Toxicology

Circ: 2,800

**Pharmacoepidemiology & Drug Safety (19357)**
John Wiley and Sons Inc.
111 River St.
Hoboken, NJ 07030-5774
Phone: (201)748-6000
Fax: (201)748-6088
**Subject(s):** Drugs and Pharmaceuticals; Science (General); Health and Healthcare; Medicine and Surgery; Toxicology

Circ: 2,800

**Rock Airplay Monitor (22324)**
VNU Business Media USA
770 Broadway
New York, NY 10003
Phone: (646)654-5000
**Subject(s):** Music and Musical Instruments; Radio, Television, Cable, and Video

Circ: 2,803

**TDR (The Drama Review) (22438)**
The MIT Press
21 Broadway 6th Fl.
New York, NY
Phone: (212)998-1626
Fax: (212)998-1627
**Subject(s):** Drama and Theatre

Circ: 2,800

**Top 40 Airplay Monitor (22461)**
VNU Business Media USA
770 Broadway
New York, NY 10003
Phone: (646)654-5000

Subject(s): Music and Musical Instruments; Radio, Television, Cable, and Video
Circ: 2,803

**Cancer Epidemiology, Biomarkers & Prevention** (26854)
American Association for Cancer Research Inc.
615 Chestnut St., 17th Fl.
Philadelphia, PA 19106-4404
Phone: (215)440-9300
Fax: (215)440-9313
Subject(s): Health and Healthcare; Medicine and Surgery
Circ: (Controlled)2,741

**Environmental Entomology** (27551)
Entomological Society of America
541 McCormick Ave.
State College, PA 16801-6616
Phone: (814)235-1910
Fax: (814)237-9531
Subject(s): Entomology; Environmental and Natural Resources Conservation
Circ: 2,739

**The Journal of Experimental Medicine** (21920)
Rockefeller University Press
1114 1st Ave., 3rd Fl.
New York, NY 10021
Phone: (212)327-8575
Fax: (212)327-8511
Subject(s): Medicine and Surgery
Circ: ‡2,730

**Journal of Heat Transfer** (21935)
American Society of Mechanical Engineers
3 Park Ave.
New York, NY 10016-5990
Phone: (212)591-7722
Fax: (212)591-7674
Subject(s): Commerce and Industry
Circ: 2,737

**The Mycologist** (22119)
Cambridge University Press
40 W. 20th St.
New York, NY 10011-4211
Phone: (212)924-3900
Fax: (212)691-3239
Subject(s): Botany
Circ: 2,700

**New York State Pharmacist** (20227)
Pharmacists Society of the State of New York
210 Washington Ave., Ext. Ste. 101
Albany, NY 12203
Phone: (518)869-6595
Fax: (518)464-0618
Subject(s): Drugs and Pharmaceuticals
Circ: (Paid)‡2,700

**Philatelic Literature Review** (26156)
American Philatelic Society
100 Match Factory Pl.
PO Box 8000
Bellefonte, PA 16823
Phone: (814)933-3803
Fax: (814)933-6128
Subject(s): Collecting
Circ: ‡2,700

**Ear and Hearing** (26928)
Lippincott Williams & Wilkins
530 Walnut St.
Philadelphia, PA 19106-3261
Phone: (215)521-8300
Fax: (215)521-8902
Subject(s): Medicine and Surgery
Circ: (Controlled)‡250
(Paid)‡2,691

**Journal of Refractive Surgery** (19861)
SLACK Inc.
6900 Grove Rd.
Thorofare, NJ 08086-9447
Phone: (856)848-1000
Fax: (856)848-6091
Subject(s): Medicine and Surgery; Ophthalmology, Optometry, and Optics
Circ: 2,677

**Head & Neck Surgery** (19238)
John Wiley and Sons Inc.
111 River St.
Hoboken, NJ 07030-5774
Phone: (201)748-6000

Fax: (201)748-6088
Subject(s): Medicine and Surgery
Circ: 2,650

**PAJ: A Journal of Performing** (22208)
The MIT Press
PO Box 260
Village Sta.
New York, NY 10014
Phone: (212)243-3885
Subject(s): Performing Arts
Circ: ‡2,640

**Seminars in Anesthesia, Perioperative Medicine and Pain** (27253)
Elsevier
1600 John F. Kennedy Blvd.
Philadelphia, PA 19103
Phone: (215)239-3900
Fax: (215)239-3990
Subject(s): Medicine and Surgery
Circ: ‡2,628

**Physics of Plasmas** (19731)
American Institute of Physics
James Forrestral Campus
MS 20
Princeton, NJ 08543
Phone: (609)243-2424
Fax: (609)243-2427
Subject(s): Physics
Circ: ‡2,611

**Conservative Judaism** (21542)
The Rabbinical Assembly
3080 Broadway
New York, NY 10027
Phone: (212)280-6065
Fax: (212)749-9166
Subject(s): Jewish Publications
Circ: ‡2,600

**Journal for Scientific Study of Religion** (20250)
Society for the Scientific Study of Religion
Div. of Social Sciences, Alfred University
1 Saxon Dr.
1 Saxon Dr.
Alfred, NY 14802
Phone: (607)871-2216
Fax: (607)871-2114
Subject(s): Theology; Religious Publications
Circ: 2,600

**Population and Development Review** (22254)
Population Council
1 Dag Hammarskjold Plz.
New York, NY 10017
Phone: (212)339-0500
Fax: (212)755-6052
Subject(s): Sociology
Circ: (Paid)‡2,400
(Controlled)‡2,600

**Real Estate Finance** (14920)
Aspen Publishers
18 Everett Ave.
Winchester, MA 01890
Subject(s): Real Estate; Banking, Finance, and Investments
Circ: 2,600

**Vermont History** (30830)
Vermont Historical Society Inc.
Vermont History Ctr.
60 Washington St.
Barre, VT 05641-4209
Phone: (802)479-8500
Fax: (802)479-8510
Subject(s): History and Genealogy
Circ: (Controlled)2,600

**AIDS** (26807)
Lippincott Williams & Wilkins
530 Walnut St.
Philadelphia, PA 19106-3261
Phone: (215)521-8300
Fax: (215)521-8902
Subject(s): Acquired Immune Deficiency Syndrome
Circ: (Paid)‡2,585

**The American Journal of Emergency Medicine** (26814)
Elsevier
1600 John F. Kennedy Blvd.
Philadelphia, PA 19103
Phone: (215)239-3900

Fax: (215)239-3990
Subject(s): Medicine and Surgery
Circ: ‡2,561

**Physical Review B** (22787)
American Physical Society
1 Research Rd.
Box 9000
Ridge, NY 11961-9000
Phone: (631)591-4020
Fax: (631)591-4141
Subject(s): Physics
Circ: 2,550

**Academic Exchange Quarterly** (22988)
Rapid Intellect Group Inc.
PO Box 131
Stuyvesant Falls, NY 12174
Phone: (518)372-1347
Subject(s): Education
Circ: (Paid)2,500

**Am Hatorah** (21294)
Zeirei Agudath Israel
42 Broadway 14th Fl.
New York, NY 10004
Phone: (212)797-9000
Fax: (646)254-1600
Subject(s): Jewish Publications; Religious Publications; Intercultural Interests
Circ: 2,500

**ARBA Sicula** (20987)
Arba Sicula
c/o St. John's University
8000 Utopia Pky.
Jamaica, NY 11439
Phone: (718)990-5203
Fax: (718)990-5954
Subject(s): Intercultural Interests
Circ: 2,500

**The Bulletin of Symbolic Logic** (13493)
Association for Symbolic Logic
c/o Akihiro Kanamori
Department of Mathematics
Boston University
Boston, MA 02215
Subject(s): Mathematics; Computers; Philosophy
Circ: ‡2,500

**The Christian Civic League Record** (12444)
Christian Civic League
PO Box 5459
Augusta, ME 04332
Phone: (207)622-7634
Fax: (207)621-0035
Subject(s): Religious Publications; Clubs and Societies
Circ: (Non-paid)‡500
(Paid)‡2,500

**The Exporter** (21674)
Trade Data Reports Inc.
26 Broadway
Ste. 776
New York, NY 10004
Phone: (212)269-2016
Fax: (212)269-2740
Subject(s): International Business and Economics
Circ: (Paid)‡2,500
(Controlled)‡2,500

**Fine Tool Journal** (12581)
Antique and Collectible Tools Inc.
27 Ficket Rd.
Pownal, ME 04069
Phone: (207)688-4962
Fax: (207)688-4831
Subject(s): Machinery and Equipment; Wood and Woodworking
Circ: (Paid)2,500

**The Journal of Aesthetics and Art Criticism** (27008)
Blackwell Publishers
Department of Philosophy
Anderson Hall Rm. 717
Temple University
Philadelphia, PA 19122
Subject(s): Humanities; Art and Art History; Philosophy
Circ: ‡2,500

**Journal of the American Academy of Psychiatry and the Law  (4626)**
American Academy of Psychiatry and the Law
1 Regency Dr.
PO Box 30
Bloomfield, CT 06002-0030
Phone: (860)243-3977
Fax: (860)286-0787
**Subject(s):** Law; Psychology and Psychiatry
**Circ:** 2,500

**Journal of Child and Adolescent Psychiatric Nursing  (27018)**
Nursecom Inc.
1211 Locust St.
Philadelphia, PA 19107-5409
Phone: (215)545-7222
Fax: (215)545-8107
**Subject(s):** Nursing; Psychology and Psychiatry
**Circ:** (Paid)‡2500

**Journal of Cutaneous Medicine & Surgery  (21907)**
Springer-Verlag New York Inc.
233 Spring St.
New York, NY 10013
Phone: (212)460-1500
Fax: (212)460-1575
**Subject(s):** Health and Healthcare; Medicine and Surgery
**Circ:** (Combined)2,500

**Journal of Head Trauma Rehabilitation (JHTR)  (19946)**
Aspen Publishers Inc.
Kessler Medical Rehabilitation Research & Education Corp.
1199 Pleasant Valley Way
West Orange, NJ 07052
Phone: (301)417-7550
Fax: (301)417-7550
**Subject(s):** Medicine and Surgery
**Circ:** (Free)66
         (Paid)2,500

**Journal of Innovative Management  (18956)**
GOAL/QPC
12B Manor Pkwy., Ste. 3
Salem, NH 03079-2862
Phone: (603)890-8800
Fax: (603)870-9122
**Subject(s):** Management and Administration
**Circ:** (Non-paid)1,000
         (Paid)2,500

**Journal of International Taxation  (21941)**
Warren, Gorham & Lamont R.I.A. Group
395 Hudson St., 4th Fl.
New York, NY 10014-3669
Phone: (212)367-6300
Fax: (212)367-6305
**Subject(s):** Taxation and Tariff
**Circ:** (Paid)2,500

**Journal of Perinatal and Neonatal Nursing  (21972)**
Aspen Publishers Inc.
1185 Ave. of the Americas
New York, NY 10036
Phone: (301)644-3599
Fax: (212)597-0331
**Subject(s):** Nursing; Pediatrics
**Circ:** (Non-paid)92
         (Paid)2,500

**Journal of Retailing  (13444)**
University of California Press
c/o Dhruv Grewal, Editor, Prof. of Marketing
Babson College
213 Malloy Hall
Babson Park, MA 02457
Phone: (781)239-3902
Fax: (781)239-5139
**Subject(s):** General Merchandise
**Circ:** (Paid)2,500

**The Journal of Symbolic Logic  (22742)**
Association for Symbolic Logic
Vassar College
124 Raymond Ave.
PO Box 742
Poughkeepsie, NY 12604
Phone: (845)437-7080
Fax: (845)437-7830
**Subject(s):** Mathematics
**Circ:** ‡2,500

**New on the Charts  (21242)**
New On the Charts
70 Laurel Pl.
New Rochelle, NY 10801
Phone: (914)632-3349
Fax: (914)633-7690
**Subject(s):** Music and Musical Instruments
**Circ:** ‡2,500

**Nursing Administration Quarterly (NAQ)  (22182)**
Aspen Publishers Inc.
1185 Ave. of the Americas
New York, NY 10036
Phone: (301)644-3599
Fax: (212)597-0331
**Subject(s):** Nursing
**Circ:** (Non-paid)47
         (Paid)2,500

**Pennsylvania Forests  (26685)**
Pennsylvania Forestry Association
56 E Main St.
Mechanicsburg, PA 17055-3851
Phone: (717)766-5371
Fax: (717)766-5371
**Subject(s):** Forestry; Ecology and Conservation
**Circ:** (Non-paid)‡500
         (Paid)‡2,500

**Penntrux  (26218)**
Pennsylvania Motor Truck Association
910 Linda Ln.
Camp Hill, PA 17011-6401
Phone: (717)761-7122
Fax: (717)761-8434
**Subject(s):** Trucks and Trucking
**Circ:** (Controlled)‡2,500

**Perspectives on Science and Christian Faith  (13845)**
American Scientific Affiliation
PO Box 668
Ipswich, MA 01938
Phone: (978)356-5656
Fax: (978)356-4375
**Subject(s):** Religious Publications
**Circ:** ‡2,500

**Psychoanalytic Dialogues  (19148)**
Analytic Press
101 W St.
Hillsdale, NJ 07642-1422
Phone: (201)358-9477
Fax: (201)358-4700
**Subject(s):** Psychology and Psychiatry
**Circ:** (Paid)2,500

**Queen of All Hearts  (20353)**
Montfort Publications
26 S. Saxon Ave.
Bay Shore, NY 11706
Phone: (631)665-0726
Fax: (631)665-4349
**Subject(s):** Religious Publications
**Circ:** ‡2,500

**The Real Estate Finance Journal  (22291)**
Warren, Gorham & Lamont R.I.A. Group
395 Hudson St., 4th Fl.
New York, NY 10014-3669
Phone: (212)367-6300
Fax: (212)367-6305
**Subject(s):** Real Estate; Banking, Finance, and Investments
**Circ:** 2,500

**SCI Nursing  (20717)**
American Association of Spinal Cord Injury Nurses
Eastern Paralyzed Veterans Association
75-20 Astoria Blvd.
East Elmhurst, NY 11370
Phone: (718)803-3782
Fax: (718)803-0414
**Subject(s):** Nursing
**Circ:** 2,500

**Telos  (22446)**
Telos Press Ltd.
431 E 12th St.
New York, NY 10009
Phone: (212)228-6479
Fax: (212)228-6379
**Subject(s):** Politics
**Circ:** 2,500

**2wice  (20723)**
2wice Arts Foundation Inc.
PO Box 980
East Hampton, NY 11937
Phone: (631)907-8984
Fax: (631)907-8985
**Subject(s):** Art and Art History; Performing Arts; Photography; Drama and Theatre
**Circ:** (Paid)‡2,500

**The Yale Literary Magazine  (4907)**
PO Box 209087, Yale Sta.
New Haven, CT 06520-7394
Phone: (203)432-4771
**Subject(s):** Literature and Literary Reviews
**Circ:** (Paid)130
         (Non-paid)2,500

**Journal of Climate  (13535)**
American Meteorological Society
45 Beacon St.
Boston, MA 02108-3693
Phone: (617)227-2425
Fax: (617)742-8718
**Subject(s):** Astronomy and Meteorology
**Circ:** ‡2,481

**RETINA  (26397)**
Lippincott Williams & Wilkins
c/o Alexander J. Brucker
PO Box 67
Gladwyne, PA 19035
Phone: (610)526-9876
Fax: (610)526-9876
**Subject(s):** Medicine and Surgery
**Circ:** 2,476

**Journal of Fluids Engineering  (21923)**
American Society of Mechanical Engineers
3 Park Ave.
New York, NY 10016-5990
Phone: (212)591-7722
Fax: (212)591-7674
**Subject(s):** Engineering (Various branches)
**Circ:** 2,450

**Maine Motor Transport News  (12448)**
142 Whitten Rd.
PO Box 857
Augusta, ME 04332
Phone: (207)623-4128
Fax: (207)623-4096
**Subject(s):** Trucks and Trucking
**Circ:** (Non-paid)1,500
         (Paid)2,452

**Echocardiography  (20754)**
Blackwell Publishing/Futura
3 W. Main St.
Elmsford, NY 10523
Phone: (781)388-8372
Fax: (781)388-8265
**Subject(s):** Radiology, Ultrasound, and Nuclear Medicine
**Circ:** ‡2,449

**The Manufacturing Confectioner  (19117)**
Manufacturing Confectioner Publishing Co.
175 Rock Rd.
Glen Rock, NJ 07452
Phone: (201)652-2655
Fax: (201)652-3419
**Subject(s):** Confectionaries and Frozen Dairy Products
**Circ:** (Non-paid)2,407
         (Paid)2,446

**Transplantation  (22476)**
Lippincott Williams & Wilkins
C/o Manikkam Suthanthiran, M.D., Editor
Cornell University, Weill Medical College
New York-Presbyterian Hospital
525 E. 68th St., Box 310
New York, NY 10021
Phone: (212)746-4422
Fax: (212)746-8091
**Subject(s):** Medicine and Surgery
**Circ:** (Non-paid)‡401
         (Paid)‡2,449

**Journal of Cardiac Surgery  (20755)**
Blackwell Publishing/Futura
3 W. Main St.
Elmsford, NY 10523
Phone: (781)388-8372
Fax: (781)388-8265

**Subject(s):** Medicine and Surgery

**Circ:** ‡2,417

**Operative Techniques in Otolaryngology (27196)**
Elsevier
1600 John F. Kennedy Blvd.
Philadelphia, PA 19103
Phone: (215)239-3900
Fax: (215)239-3990
**Subject(s):** Medicine and Surgery

**Circ:** (Paid)‡2,419

**CardioVascular and Interventional Radiology (21456)**
Springer-Verlag New York Inc.
233 Spring St.
New York, NY 10013
Phone: (212)460-1500
Fax: (212)460-1575
**Subject(s):** Radiology, Ultrasound, and Nuclear Medicine

**Circ:** (Combined)**2,400**

**Clearwaters (23003)**
New York Water Environment Association Inc.
126 N. Salina St., Ste. 200
Syracuse, NY 13202
Phone: (315)422-7811
Fax: (315)422-3851
**Subject(s):** Water Supply and Sewage Disposal; Ecology and Conservation

**Circ:** (Non-paid)‡300
(Paid)‡2,400

**International Economic Review (26979)**
University of Pennsylvania
3718 Locust Walk
Philadelphia, PA 19104-6297
Phone: (215)898-5841
Fax: (215)573-2072
**Subject(s):** Economics

**Circ:** ‡2,400

**Journal of Rural Health (20573)**
National Rural Health Association
Department of Family Medicine
U. B. Clinical Center
462 Grider St.
Buffalo, NY 14215
**Subject(s):** Health and Healthcare

**Circ:** (Paid)2,400

**Law & Society Review (14213)**
Blackwell Publishing
350 Main St.
Malden, MA 02148
Phone: (781)388-8200
Fax: (781)388-8210
**Subject(s):** Law

**Circ:** ‡2,400

**New Testament Studies (22150)**
Cambridge University Press
40 W. 20th St.
New York, NY 10011-4211
Phone: (212)924-3900
Fax: (212)691-3239
**Subject(s):** Religious Publications

**Circ:** 2,400

**New York State Register (20228)**
New York State Department of State
41 State St.
Albany, NY 12231-0001
Phone: (518)474-0050
Fax: (518)474-4765
**Subject(s):** Law; State, Municipal, and County Administration

**Circ:** 2,400

**Theater (4902)**
Duke University Press
PO Box 208244
New Haven, CT 06520-8244
Phone: (203)432-1568
Fax: (203)432-8336
**Subject(s):** Drama and Theatre; Performing Arts

**Circ:** (Combined)2,400

**Twentieth Century Literature (20235)**
Boyd Printing Co.
49 Sheridan Ave.
Albany, NY 12210
Phone: (518)436-9686
Fax: (518)436-7433

**Subject(s):** Literature

**Circ:** (Non-paid)‡150
(Paid)‡2,400

**Menopause (13550)**
Lippincott Williams & Wilkins
c/o Menopause Managing Editor
55 Fruit St., FH 402
Boston, MA 02114
Phone: (617)724-1372
Fax: (617)724-0988
**Subject(s):** Medicine and Surgery; Women's Interests

**Circ:** (Paid)2,389

**Journal of Conflict Resolution (4891)**
Sage Publications Inc.
c/o Bruce M. Russett, Editor
Dept. of Political Science
Yale Univ.
PO Box 208301
New Haven, CT 06520-8301
**Subject(s):** Peace; Sociology; International Affairs; Political Science

**Circ:** (Non-paid)‡114
(Paid)‡2,363

**Adult Lessons Quarterly (21268)**
John Milton Society for the Blind
475 Riverside Dr., Rm. 455
New York, NY 10015
Fax: (212)870-3229
**Subject(s):** Religious Publications; Handicapped

**Circ:** (Non-paid)2,350

**Business and Society Review (14852)**
Center for Business Ethics
Bentley College
175 Forest St.
Waltham, MA 02452-4705
Phone: (781)891-2981
Fax: (781)891-2988
**Subject(s):** Business

**Circ:** 2,000
‡2,355

**Dermatology (4713)**
S. Karger Publishers Inc.
26 W Avon Rd.
PO Box 529
Farmington, CT 06085
Phone: (860)675-7834
Fax: (860)675-7302
**Subject(s):** Medicine and Surgery

**Circ:** ‡2,350

**Journal of Interventional Cardiology (20757)**
Blackwell Publishing/Futura
3 W. Main St.
Elmsford, NY 10523
Phone: (781)388-8372
Fax: (781)388-8265
**Subject(s):** Medicine and Surgery

**Circ:** 2,333

**Journal of Neurochemistry (14208)**
Blackwell Publishers
350 Main St.
Malden, MA 02148
Phone: (781)388-8200
Fax: (781)388-8250
**Subject(s):** Laboratory Research (Scientific and Medical); Biology

**Circ:** 2333

**Annals of Vascular Surgery (21341)**
Springer-Verlag New York Inc.
233 Spring St.
New York, NY 10013
Phone: (212)460-1500
Fax: (212)460-1575
**Subject(s):** Medicine and Surgery; Health and Healthcare

**Circ:** (Combined)**2,300**

**Harvard Review (13676)**
Lamont Library Level 5
Harvard University
Cambridge, MA 02138
Phone: (617)495-9775
Fax: (617)496-3692
**Subject(s):** Literature; Poetry

**Circ:** (Controlled)2,300

**Journal of Cold War Studies (13686)**
The MIT Press
Davis Ctr.
625 Massachusetts Ave.
Rm. 240A Harvard Univ.
Cambridge, MA 02139
Phone: (617)495-1909
Fax: (617)495-8319
**Subject(s):** History and Genealogy; Military and Navy; International Affairs

**Circ:** (Combined)2,300

**Journal of Materials Research (27645)**
Materials Research Society
506 Keystone Dr.
Warrendale, PA 15086-7573
Phone: (724)779-3003
Fax: (724)779-8313
**Subject(s):** Science (General)

**Circ:** ‡2,300

**Theatre Topics (13422)**
University of Massachusetts
Dept. of Theatre, Fine Arts Center 112
151 Presidents Dr.
Amherst, MA 01003-9331
Phone: (413)584-6812
Fax: (413)577-0025
**Subject(s):** Drama and Theatre

**Circ:** 2,300

**The Tube Council News (19530)**
The Tube Council
26 Park St., Ste. 2031
Montclair, NJ 07042
Phone: (973)744-4551
Fax: (973)744-5568
**Subject(s):** Machinery and Equipment

**Circ:** (Non-paid)2,300

**The Knee (13642)**
Butterworth-Heinemann
30 Corporate Dr., Ste. 400
Burlington, MA 01803
Phone: (781)221-2212
Fax: (781)221-1615
**Subject(s):** Biology; Medicine and Surgery

**Circ:** ‡2,250

**Industrial and Labor Relations Review (20954)**
Cornell University
158 Ives Hall
Ithaca, NY 14853-3901
Phone: (607)255-3295
Fax: (607)255-8016
**Subject(s):** Commerce and Industry; Labor

**Circ:** (Non-paid)‡150
(Paid)‡2,230

**Journal of Engineering for Gas Turbines and Power (21918)**
American Society of Mechanical Engineers
3 Park Ave.
New York, NY 10016-5990
Phone: (212)591-7722
Fax: (212)591-7674
**Subject(s):** Engineering (Various branches); Power and Power Plants

**Circ:** 2,224

**American Journal of Alzheimers Disease (14902)**
Prime National Publishing Corp.
470 Boston Post Rd.
Weston, MA 02493
Phone: (781)899-2702
Fax: (781)899-4900
**Subject(s):** Medicine and Surgery; Health and Healthcare

**Circ:** (Paid)‡2,200

**The Armenian Weekly (14872)**
Hairenik Association Inc.
80 Bigelow Avenue
Watertown, MA 02472
Phone: (617)926-3974
Fax: (617)926-1750
**Subject(s):** Ethnic Publications

**Circ:** (Free)‡300
(Paid)‡2,200

**B&M Bulletin (14790)**
Boston & Maine Railroad Historical Society Inc.
32 Tower St.
Somerville, MA 02143-1427
**Subject(s):** Railroad

**Circ:** ‡2,200

**Chelsea (21475)**
Chelsea Associates Inc.
PO Box 773
Cooper Sta.
New York, NY 10276-0773
Phone: (212)989-3083
Fax: (212)989-3083
**Subject(s):** Literature and Literary Reviews; Poetry; Art
**Circ:** (Non-paid)300
(Paid)2,200

**Curriculum Review (19463)**
PaperClip Communications
125 Paterson Ave.
Little Falls, NJ 07424
Phone: (973)256-1333
Fax: (973)256-8088
**Subject(s):** Education
**Circ:** ‡2,200

**Dysphagia (21622)**
Springer-Verlag New York Inc.
233 Spring St.
New York, NY 10013
Phone: (212)460-1500
Fax: (212)460-1575
**Subject(s):** Medicine and Surgery; Radiology, Ultrasound, and Nuclear Medicine
**Circ:** (Combined)2,200

**Economic Botany (20452)**
New York Botanical Garden Press
200th St. & Southern Blvd.
Bronx, NY 10458-5126
Phone: (718)817-8721
Fax: (718)817-8842
**Subject(s):** Botany
**Circ:** ‡2,200

**The IN-REPORT (27717)**
The Gentle Revolution Press
8801 Stenton Avenue
Wyndmoor, PA 19038
Phone: (215)233-2050
**Subject(s):** Medicine and Surgery; Education
**Circ:** ‡2,200

**Journal of Intensive Care Medicine (14784)**
Sage Publications Inc.
21 N. Quinsiganmond Ave.
Shrewsbury, MA 01545
Phone: (508)754-5098
**Subject(s):** Medicine and Surgery; Hospitals and Healthcare Institutions
**Circ:** ‡2,200

**Journal of Pharmaceutical Finance, Economics & Policy (20395)**
The Haworth Press Inc.
10 Alice St.
Binghamton, NY 13904
Phone: (607)722-5857
Fax: (607)771-0012
**Subject(s):** Drugs and Pharmaceuticals; Medicine and Surgery; Health and Healthcare
**Circ:** (Paid)2,200

**Journal of Physiology (21974)**
Cambridge University Press
40 W. 20th St.
New York, NY 10011-4211
Phone: (212)924-3900
Fax: (212)691-3239
**Subject(s):** Physiology and Anatomy
**Circ:** 2,200

**Managed Care Quarterly (22050)**
Aspen Publishers Inc.
1185 Ave. of the Americas
New York, NY 10036
Phone: (301)644-3599
Fax: (212)597-0331
**Subject(s):** Health and Healthcare; Hospitals and Healthcare Institutions
**Circ:** 2200

**Nursing Forum (27185)**
Nursecom Inc.
1211 Locust St.
Philadelphia, PA 19107-5409
Phone: (215)545-7222
Fax: (215)545-8107
**Subject(s):** Nursing
**Circ:** (Paid)2,200

**Physical Review A (22786)**
American Physical Society
1 Research Rd.
PO Box 9000
Ridge, NY 11961-9000
Phone: (631)591-4010
Fax: (631)591-4141
**Subject(s):** Physics
**Circ:** 2,200

**Theodore Roosevelt Association Journal (22678)**
Theodore Roosevelt Association
PO Box 719
Oyster Bay, NY 11771
Phone: (516)921-6319
Fax: (516)921-6481
**Subject(s):** History and Genealogy
**Circ:** (Paid)2,200

**The Vermont Bar Journal (30905)**
Vermont Bar Association
35-37 Court St.
PO Box 100
Montpelier, VT 05601-0100
Phone: (802)223-2020
Fax: (802)223-1573
**Subject(s):** Law
**Circ:** 2,200

**Computer Music Journal (13657)**
The MIT Press
5 Cambridge Ctr.
Cambridge, MA 02142-1493
Phone: (617)253-5646
Fax: (617)258-6779
**Subject(s):** Computers; Music and Musical Instruments
**Circ:** 2,193

**Columbia Law Review (21516)**
Columbia Law School
435 W 116th St.
New York, NY 10027
Phone: (212)854-1601
Fax: (212)854-7946
**Subject(s):** Law
**Circ:** (Non-paid)20
(Controlled)2,175

**Journal of Pediatric Ophthalmology & Strabismus (19860)**
SLACK Inc.
6900 Grove Rd.
Thorofare, NJ 08086-9447
Phone: (856)848-1000
Fax: (856)848-6091
**Subject(s):** Ophthalmology, Optometry, and Optics; Pediatrics
**Circ:** ‡2,179

**Seminars in Perinatology (27263)**
Elsevier
1600 John F. Kennedy Blvd.
Philadelphia, PA 19103
Phone: (215)239-3900
Fax: (215)239-3990
**Subject(s):** Medicine and Surgery
**Circ:** 2,171

**Journal of the History of Ideas (19594)**
Johns Hopkins University Press
Rutgers University
88 College Ave.
New Brunswick, NJ 08901
Phone: (732)932-1227
Fax: (732)932-8708
**Subject(s):** Philosophy; History and Genealogy; Humanities
**Circ:** (Controlled)‡140
(Paid)‡2,156

**Seminars in Hearing (27398)**
Thieme Medical Publishers Inc.
c/o Catherine V. Palmer, Editor-in-Chief
Dir., Div. of Audiology & Hearing Aids
University of Pittsburgh
4033 Forbes Tower
Pittsburgh, PA 15260
**Subject(s):** Medicine and Surgery
**Circ:** (Non-paid)78
(Paid)2,155

**Philosophy & Public Affairs (19730)**
Princeton University Press
41 William St.
Princeton, NJ 08540
Phone: (609)258-4900
Fax: (609)258-6305
**Subject(s):** Philosophy; Politics
**Circ:** (Non-paid)‡59
(Paid)‡2,127

**Behavioral and Brain Sciences (21388)**
Cambridge University Press
40 W. 20th St.
New York, NY 10011-4211
Phone: (212)924-3900
Fax: (212)691-3239
**Subject(s):** Science (General); Psychology and Psychiatry
**Circ:** 2,100

**The Door Opener (5065)**
An Open Door to the Inner Light Inc.
70 Valley Falls Rd.
Vernon, CT 06066
Phone: (860)875-4101
Fax: (860)875-4101
**Subject(s):** New Age; Health and Healthcare
**Circ:** (Non-paid)400
(Paid)2,100

**Jewish Currents (21859)**
Association for Promotion of Jewish Secularism Inc.
22 E 17th St., Ste. 601
New York, NY 10003-1919
Phone: (212)924-5740
Fax: (212)414-2227
**Subject(s):** Jewish Publications
**Circ:** 2,100

**Journal of Linguistics (21946)**
Cambridge University Press
40 W. 20th St.
New York, NY 10011-4211
Phone: (212)924-3900
Fax: (212)691-3239
**Subject(s):** Philology, Language, and Linguistics
**Circ:** 2,100

**Middle East Quarterly (27146)**
Middle East Forum
Middle East Forum
1500 Walnut St., Ste. 1050
Philadelphia, PA 19102
Phone: (215)546-5406
Fax: (215)546-5409
**Subject(s):** Politics; Intercultural Interests
**Circ:** (Paid)‡2,100

**Montgomery County Law Reporter (26779)**
Montgomery Bar Association
100 W Airy St.
PO Box 268
Norristown, PA 19404-0268
Phone: (610)279-9660
Fax: (610)279-4846
**Subject(s):** Law
**Circ:** ‡2,100

**Rutgers Center of Alcohol Studies (19691)**
Rutgers University
607 Allison Road
Piscataway, NJ 08854-8001
Phone: (732)445-2190
Fax: (732)445-3500
**Subject(s):** Health and Healthcare; Laboratory Research (Scientific and Medical); Drugs and Pharmaceuticals
**Circ:** (Combined)⊕2,100

**Sensations Magazine (19116)**
PO Box 90
Glen Ridge, NJ 07028
**Subject(s):** Literature; Poetry
**Circ:** (Non-paid)2,100

**Facial Plastic Surgery (26485)**
Thieme Medical Publishers Inc.
c/o Fred Fedok, M.D.
Milton S. Hershey Medical Center
Penn State University
500 University Dr.
Hershey, PA 17033
**Subject(s):** Medicine and Surgery
**Circ:** (Paid)2,093

**Journal of Dynamic Systems, Measurement, and Control (21911)**
American Society of Mechanical Engineers
3 Park Ave.
New York, NY 10016-5990
Phone: (212)591-7722
Fax: (212)591-7674

**Subject(s):** Engineering (Various branches)

**Circ:** 2,091

**SIAM Journal on Computing (20968)**
Society for Industrial & Applied Mathematics
c/o Eva Tardos, Editor-in-Chief
Dept. of Computer Science
5144 Upson Hall
Cornell Univ.
Ithaca, NY 14853-5901
**Subject(s):** Mathematics; Computers

**Circ:** ‡2,058

**Journal of Health Care Finance (21934)**
Aspen Publishers Inc.
1185 Ave. of the Americas
New York, NY 10036
Phone: (301)644-3599
Fax: (212)597-0331
**Subject(s):** Health and Healthcare

**Circ:** (Non-paid)73
(Paid)2,034

**Psychosomatic Medicine (27247)**
Lippincott Williams & Wilkins
530 Walnut St.
Philadelphia, PA 19106-3261
Phone: (215)521-8300
Fax: (215)521-8902
**Subject(s):** Psychology and Psychiatry; Medicine and Surgery

**Circ:** (Non-paid)‡117
(Paid)‡2,035

**The Review of Financial Studies (20967)**
Oxford University Press
c/o Maureen O'Hara
Johnson Graduate School of Management
Cornell University
Sage Hall
Ithaca, NY 14853
**Subject(s):** Banking, Finance, and Investments

**Circ:** (Paid)‡2,025

**Seminars in Spine Surgery (27266)**
Elsevier
1600 John F. Kennedy Blvd.
Philadelphia, PA 19103
Phone: (215)239-3900
Fax: (215)239-3990
**Subject(s):** Medicine and Surgery

**Circ:** (Paid)‡2,010

**ADE Bulletin (21266)**
Association of Departments of English
26 Broadway, 3rd Fl.
New York, NY 10004-1789
Phone: (646)576-5130
Fax: (646)458-0033
**Subject(s):** Education

**Circ:** (Controlled)2,000

**Alternatives (21292)**
CPR Institute for Dispute Resolution
366 Madison Ave.
New York, NY 10017
Phone: (212)949-6490
Fax: (212)949-8859
**Subject(s):** Law; Business

**Circ:** 2,000

**American Canadian Genealogist (18866)**
American-Canadian Genealogical Society
PO Box 6478
Manchester, NH 03108-6478
Phone: (603)622-1554
**Subject(s):** History and Genealogy

**Circ:** 2,000

**Annals of Mathematics (19708)**
Princeton University
Washington Rd.
309 Fine Hall
Princeton, NJ 08544
Phone: (609)258-4191
Fax: (609)258-1367
**Subject(s):** Mathematics

**Circ:** ‡2,000

**Ballet Review (21380)**
Dance Research Foundation Inc.
37 W 12th St., No. 7/J
New York, NY 10011
Phone: (212)924-5183
Fax: (212)924-2176

**Subject(s):** Performing Arts

**Circ:** (Paid)2,000

**Business History Review (13494)**
Harvard Business School
Soldiers Field Rd.
Boston, MA 02163
Phone: (617)495-1003
Fax: (617)495-0594
**Subject(s):** Business; Economics; History and Genealogy

**Circ:** (Non-paid)300
(Paid)2,000

**CAPsule (27479)**
Children of Aging Parents
1609 Woodbourne Rd., Ste. 302A
P.O. Box 167
Richboro, PA 18954-0167
**Subject(s):** Gerontology; Health

**Circ:** (Controlled)2,000

**Comparative Politics (21530)**
City University of New York
365 Fifth Ave.
New York, NY 10016-4309
Phone: (212)817-8686
Fax: (212)817-1645
**Subject(s):** Politics

**Circ:** ‡2,000

**Confrontation (20866)**
Long Island University
Greenvale, NY 11548
Phone: (516)299-2720
Fax: (516)299-2735
**Subject(s):** Literature; Poetry

**Circ:** (Combined)2,000

**Current Opinion in Obstetrics & Gynecology (26907)**
Lippincott Williams & Wilkins
530 Walnut St.
Philadelphia, PA 19106-3261
Phone: (215)521-8300
Fax: (215)521-8902
**Subject(s):** Medicine and Surgery

**Circ:** (Paid)‡2,000

**Current Opinion in Orthopaedics (26484)**
Lippincott Williams & Wilkins
Milton S. Hershey Medical Center
H089 Hospital
Hershey, PA 17033-2391
Phone: (717)531-4803
Fax: (717)531-7583
**Subject(s):** Medicine and Surgery

**Circ:** (Paid)‡2,000

**Dickinson Law Review (26221)**
Dickinson School of Law
150 S College St.
Carlisle, PA 17013
Phone: (717)240-5000
Fax: (717)241-3511
**Subject(s):** Law; College Publications

**Circ:** ‡2,000

**Ethnology (27347)**
University of Pittsburgh
Dept. of Anthropology
Room 3310 Bldg WWPH
230 S. Bouquet St.
Pittsburgh, PA 15260
Phone: (412)648-7503
Fax: (412)648-7535
**Subject(s):** Anthropology and Ethnology

**Circ:** ‡2,000

**The Fletcher Forum of World Affairs (14236)**
Fletcher School of Law & Diplomacy
160 Packard Ave.
Medford, MA 02155-7082
Phone: (617)627-3700
**Subject(s):** International Affairs

**Circ:** (Paid)2,000

**Forest Science (19591)**
Society of American Foresters
Cook College, Rutgers University
Department of Ecology, Evolution, and Natural Resources
14 College Farm Rd.
New Brunswick, NJ 08901-8551
Phone: (732)932-9152
Fax: (732)932-8746

**Subject(s):** Forestry

**Circ:** 2,000

**Halana (26123)**
PO Box 502
Ardmore, PA 19003-0502
Fax: (215)781-7542
**Subject(s):** Music and Musical Instruments; Intercultural Interests

**Circ:** (Paid)2,000

**Heaven Bone (20644)**
Heaven Bone Press
1310 Whispering Hills Dr.
PO Box 486
Chester, NY 10918
Fax: (845)469-7880
**Subject(s):** Literature and Literary Reviews

**Circ:** (Paid)‡500
(Controlled)‡2,000

**INQUIRY (22823)**
BlueCross BlueShield-Rochester
165 Court St.
Rochester, NY 14647
Phone: (585)454-1700
Fax: (585)238-4233
**Subject(s):** Medicine and Surgery

**Circ:** ‡2,000

**International Journal of Instructional Media (IJIM) (5056)**
Westwood Press Inc.
149 Goose Ln.
Tolland, CT 06084
Phone: (860)875-5484
**Subject(s):** Education; Telecommunications; Communications

**Circ:** 2,000

**International Migration Review (22963)**
Center for Migration Studies of New York Inc.
209 Flagg Pl.
Staten Island, NY 10304-1199
Phone: (718)351-8800
Fax: (718)667-4598
**Subject(s):** Sociology; International Affairs

**Circ:** ‡2,000

**Jersey Beat (19936)**
418 Gregory Ave.
Weehawken, NJ 07086
Phone: (201)864-9054
**Subject(s):** Alternative and Underground; Music and Musical Instruments

**Circ:** (Combined)2,000

**Jewish Braille Review (21858)**
JBI Intl.
110 E 30th St.
New York, NY 10016
Phone: (212)889-2525
Fax: (212)689-3692
**Subject(s):** Blind and Visually Challenged; Jewish Publications

**Circ:** (Non-paid)‡2,000

**Journal of the American Mosquito Control Association (19063)**
American Mosquito Control Association
PO Box 234
Eatontown, NJ 07724-0234
Phone: (732)544-4645
Fax: (732)542-3267
**Subject(s):** Entomology

**Circ:** 2,000

**Journal of Creative Behavior (13812)**
Creative Education Foundation Inc.
289 Bay Rd.
Hadley, MA 01035-9780
Phone: (413)559-6614
Fax: (413)559-6615
**Subject(s):** Education

**Circ:** 2,000

**Journal of Economic Issues (26642)**
Association for Evolutionary Economics
c/o Office of Sec.-Treas.
Department of Economics
Bucknell University
Coleman Hall 168
Lewisburg, PA 17837
Phone: (570)577-3648
Fax: (570)577-2372

**Subject(s):** Economics

**Circ:** 2,000

**Journal of Graphics Tools (14876)**
A.K. Peters Ltd.
888 Worcester St., Ste. 230
Wellesley, MA 02482
Phone: (781)416-2888
Fax: (781)416-2889
**Subject(s):** Graphic Arts and Design

**Circ:** 2,000

**The Journal of Interdisciplinary History (14306)**
The MIT Press
c/o Ed Freedman, Managing Editor
147 N. St.
Norfolk, MA 02056-1535
Phone: (508)520-0120
Fax: (508)520-0120
**Subject(s):** History and Genealogy

**Circ:** 2,000

**Journal of Personality (4736)**
Blackwell Publishers
Dept. of Psychiatry
University of Connecticut Health Center
263 Farmington Ave.
Farmington, CT 06030
Phone: (860)679-5466
Fax: (860)679-5464
**Subject(s):** Psychology and Psychiatry

**Circ:** ‡2,000

**Journal of Social Policy (21988)**
Cambridge University Press
40 W. 20th St.
New York, NY 10011-4211
Phone: (212)924-3900
Fax: (212)691-3239
**Subject(s):** Social Sciences

**Circ:** 2,000

**The Leather Manufacturer (13435)**
Shoe Trades Publishing Co.
PO Box 1530
Arlington, MA 02474-0023
**Subject(s):** Shoes, Leather, and Luggage

**Circ:** ‡2,000

**The Literary Review (19469)**
Fairleigh Dickinson University
285 Madison Ave.
Madison, NJ 07940
Phone: (973)443-8564
Fax: (973)443-8364
**Subject(s):** Literature

**Circ:** (Controlled)‡200
(Paid)‡2,000

**Medical Anthropology Quarterly (5047)**
American Anthropological Association
c/o Dr. Pamela I. Erickson, Editor
Medical Anthropology Quarterly, Department of Anthropology
354 Mansfield Rd., U-2176
University of Connecticut
Storrs, CT 06269-2176
**Subject(s):** Anthropology and Ethnology

**Circ:** (Paid)2,000

**The Mount Sinai Journal of Medicine (22109)**
Mt. Sinai School of Medicine
1 E 100th St.
P O Box 1094
New York, NY 10029-6574
Phone: (212)241-6108
Fax: (212)722-6386
**Subject(s):** Medicine and Surgery

**Circ:** ‡2,000

**The New England Quarterly (13561)**
Northeastern University
c/o Massachusetts Historical Society
1154 Boylston St.
Boston, MA 02115
Phone: (617)646-0519
Fax: (617)859-0074
**Subject(s):** Literature; History and Genealogy

**Circ:** (Non-paid)‡400
(Paid)‡2,000

**New Jersey History (19620)**
The New Jersey Historical Society
52 Park Pl.
Newark, NJ 07102
Phone: (973)596-8500
Fax: (973)596-6957
**Subject(s):** History and Genealogy

**Circ:** (Paid)2,000

**The New Social Worker (26450)**
White Hat Communications
PO Box 5390
Harrisburg, PA 17110-0390
Phone: (717)238-3787
Fax: (717)238-2090
**Subject(s):** Social Sciences

**Circ:** (Non-paid)1,000
(Paid)2,000

**New York History (20676)**
New York State Historical Association
PO Box 800
Cooperstown, NY 13326
Phone: (607)547-1400
Fax: (607)547-1400
**Subject(s):** History and Genealogy; Local, State, and Regional Publications

**Circ:** (Controlled)69
(Paid)2,000

**Northern Journal of Applied Forestry (18813)**
Society of American Foresters
19 Woodridge Rd.
Durham, NH 03824-2917
Phone: (603)868-5419
Fax: (603)868-7604
**Subject(s):** Forestry

**Circ:** 2,000

**Our Special (13571)**
National Braille Press Inc.
88 Saint Stephen St.
Boston, MA 02115-4302
Phone: (617)266-6160
Fax: (617)437-0456
**Subject(s):** Blind and Visually Challenged; Women's Interests

**Circ:** ‡2,000

**Peacework (13697)**
American Friends Service Committee (AFSC)
2161 Massachusetts Ave.
Cambridge, MA 02140
Phone: (617)661-6130
Fax: (617)354-2832
**Subject(s):** Social and Political Issues

**Circ:** (Combined)2,000

**Pennsylvania Magazine of History and Biography (27218)**
Historical Society of Pennsylvania
1300 Locust St.
Philadelphia, PA 19107-5699
Phone: (215)732-6200
Fax: (215)732-2680
**Subject(s):** History and Genealogy

**Circ:** ‡2000

**The Photo Review (26613)**
140 E Richardson Ave., Ste. 301
Langhorne, PA 19047
Phone: (215)891-0214
**Subject(s):** Photography

**Circ:** (Non-paid)‡250
(Paid)‡2,000

**Porticus (22836)**
Memorial Art Gallery
University of Rochester
500 University Ave.
Rochester, NY 14607
Phone: (585)473-7720
Fax: (585)473-6266
**Subject(s):** Art and Art History

**Circ:** (Controlled)2,000

**Salt Hill (23033)**
Syracuse University
Syracuse, NY 13244
Phone: (315)443-1315
Fax: (315)443-3660
**Subject(s):** Literature

**Circ:** (Combined)2,000

**Spring Journal (4982)**
PO Box 583
Putnam, CT 06260
Phone: (860)974-3195
Fax: (860)974-3195
**Subject(s):** Anthropology and Ethnology

**Circ:** (Paid)‡2000

**Textile Research Journal (19736)**
Textile Research Institute
601 Prospect Ave.
PO Box 625
Princeton, NJ 08540
Phone: (609)430-4843
Fax: (609)683-7836
**Subject(s):** Textiles

**Circ:** ‡2,000

**Timber Framing (30912)**
Timber Framers Guild of North America
c/o Ken Rower
Pine St.
Newbury, VT 05051
Phone: (802)866-5684
Fax: (802)866-5684
**Subject(s):** Construction, Contracting, Building, and Excavating; Wood and Woodworking

**Circ:** (Paid)2,000

**Urologia Internationalis (4765)**
S. Karger Publishers Inc.
26 W Avon Rd.
PO Box 529
Farmington, CT 06085
Phone: (860)675-7834
Fax: (860)675-7302
**Subject(s):** Medicine and Surgery

**Circ:** 2,000

**Human Development (4730)**
S. Karger Publishers Inc.
26 W Avon Rd.
PO Box 529
Farmington, CT 06085
Phone: (860)675-7834
Fax: (860)675-7302
**Subject(s):** Medicine and Surgery

**Circ:** 1,950

**Kidney and Blood Pressure Research (4738)**
S. Karger Publishers Inc.
26 W Avon Rd.
PO Box 529
Farmington, CT 06085
Phone: (860)675-7834
Fax: (860)675-7302
**Subject(s):** Medicine and Surgery

**Circ:** 1,950

**Medical Principles and Practice (1739)**
S. Karger Publishers Inc.
26 W Avon Rd.
PO Box 529
Farmington, CT 06085
Phone: (860)675-7834
Fax: (860)675-7302
**Subject(s):** Medicine and Surgery

**Circ:** 1,950

**Journal of Reconstructive Microsurgery (20464)**
Thieme Medical Publishers Inc.
c/o Berish Strauch, M.D., Professor and Chairman
Dept. of Plastic & Reconstructive Surgery
Montefiore Medical Center
1625 Poplar St., Ste. 200
Bronx, NY 10461
**Subject(s):** Medicine and Surgery

**Circ:** 1,935

**Science & Society (22353)**
The Guilford Press
John Jay College - CUNY, Rm. 4331
445 W. 59th St.
New York, NY 10019
Phone: (212)246-4932
Fax: (212)246-4932
**Subject(s):** Sociology; History and Genealogy; Philosophy

**Circ:** 1,923

**Modern Brewery Age (4955)**
Business Journals Inc.
50 Day St.
PO Box 5550
Norwalk, CT 06854
Phone: (203)853-6015

Fax: (203)852-8175
**Subject(s):** Beverages, Brewing, and Bottling
**Circ:** (Paid)‡1,915

**Biology Digest (19512)**
Plexus Publishing Inc.
143 Old Marlton Pke.
Medford, NJ 08055
Phone: (609)654-6500
Fax: (609)654-4309
**Subject(s):** Biology
**Circ:** 1,900

**Computing Reviews (CR) (21539)**
Association for Computing Machinery
1515 Broadway, 17th Fl.
New York, NY 10036
Phone: (212)626-0500
Fax: (212)944-1318
**Subject(s):** Computers
**Circ:** ‡1,900

**Journal of Health Politics, Policy and Law (4892)**
Duke University Press
C/o Mark Schlesinger, Editor, JHPPL
77 Prospect St.
PO Box 208209
New Haven, CT 06520-8209
Phone: (203)432-3829
**Subject(s):** Health and Healthcare; Politics
**Circ:** ‡1,900

**Journal of Latin American Studies (21945)**
Cambridge University Press
40 W. 20th St.
New York, NY 10011-4211
Phone: (212)924-3900
Fax: (212)691-3239
**Subject(s):** International Affairs
**Circ:** 1,900

**Journal of Studies on Alcohol (19690)**
Rutgers University
607 Allison Rd.
Piscataway, NJ 08854-8001
Phone: (732)445-3510
Fax: (732)445-5944
**Subject(s):** Substance Abuse and Treatment; Medicine and Surgery
**Circ:** (Paid)‡1,900

**Medicine and Health Rhode Island (27908)**
Rhode Island Medical Society
235 Promenade St. 500
Mail Box 20
Providence, RI 02908
Phone: (401)331-3207
Fax: (401)751-8050
**Subject(s):** Medicine and Surgery; Health
**Circ:** (Non-paid)‡175
(Paid)‡1,900

**Physical Review D (22789)**
American Physical Society
1 Research Rd.
Box 9000
Ridge, NY 11961-9000
Phone: (631)591-4040
Fax: (631)591-4141
**Subject(s):** Physics
**Circ:** 1,900

**Physical Review E (22790)**
American Physical Society
1 Research Rd.
Box 9000
Ridge, NY 11961-9000
Phone: (631)591-4050
Fax: (631)591-4141
**Subject(s):** Physics
**Circ:** 1,900

**Pravoslavnaya Zhizn (21004)**
Holy Trinity Monastery
PO Box 36
Jordanville, NY 13361-0036
Phone: (315)858-0940
Fax: (315)858-0505
**Subject(s):** Russian; Religious Publications
**Circ:** ‡1,900

**Transactions and Studies of the College of Physicians of Philadelphia (27289)**
College of Physicians of Philadelphia
19 S 22nd St.
Philadelphia, PA 19103-3097
Phone: (215)563-3737
Fax: (215)569-0356
**Subject(s):** Medicine and Surgery; Indexes, Abstracts, Reports, Proceedings, and Bibliographies
**Circ:** (Combined)1,900

**The Health Care Manager (HCM) (21759)**
Aspen Publishers Inc.
1185 Ave. of the Americas
New York, NY 10036
Phone: (301)644-3599
Fax: (212)597-0331
**Subject(s):** Health and Healthcare; Management and Administration
**Circ:** (Free)66
(Paid)1,899

**Business Communication Quarterly (21434)**
Association for Business Communication
Department of Communication Studies
Baruch College, Box B8-240
One Bernard Baruch Way
New York, NY 10010
Phone: (646)312-3726
Fax: (646)349-5297
**Subject(s):** Business; Communications
**Circ:** (Combined)1,875

**ASAS Journal (14243)**
American Board of Abdominal Surgery
1 E Emerson St.
Melrose, MA 02176
Phone: (617)665-6102
Fax: (617)665-4127
**Subject(s):** Medicine and Surgery; Health and Healthcare
**Circ:** 1,865

**Journal of Pressure Vessel Technology (21979)**
American Society of Mechanical Engineers
3 Park Ave.
New York, NY 10016-5990
Phone: (212)591-7722
Fax: (212)591-7674
**Subject(s):** Commerce and Industry; Engineering (Various branches)
**Circ:** 1,864

**Trends in Amplification (20835)**
Westminster Publications Inc.
708 Glen Cove Ave.
Glen Head, NY 11545
Phone: (516)759-0025
Fax: (516)759-5524
**Subject(s):** Health and Healthcare; Medicine and Surgery; Hearing and Speech
**Circ:** (Combined)1,865

**SIAM Journal on Mathematical Analysis (27922)**
Society for Industrial & Applied Mathematics
c/o Walter Strauss
Dept. of Math, Brown Univ.
151 Thayer St.
PO Box 1917
Providence, RI 02912
**Subject(s):** Mathematics
**Circ:** ‡1,822

**Journal of Radiation Curing (4953)**
Technology Marketing Corp.
1 Technology Plz.
Norwalk, CT 06854
Phone: (203)852-6800
Fax: (203)853-2845
**Subject(s):** Chemistry, Chemicals, and Chemical Engineering
**Circ:** (Paid)690
(Non-paid)1,810

**Ararat (21352)**
Armenian General Benevolent Union
55 E 59th St.
New York, NY 10022-1112
Phone: (212)319-6383
Fax: (212)319-6508
**Subject(s):** Armenian; Unclassified Fraternal
**Circ:** ‡1,800

**The Artilleryman (30946)**
Historical Publications Inc.
234 Monarch Hill Rd.
Tunbridge, VT 05077
Phone: (802)889-3500
Fax: (802)889-5627
**Subject(s):** Firearms; History and Genealogy
**Circ:** 1,800

**The Baker Street Journal (26425)**
PO Box 465
Hanover, PA 17331
Phone: (717)633-8911
**Subject(s):** Science Fiction, Mystery, Adventure, and Romance; Literature
**Circ:** ‡1,800

**The Botanical Review (20444)**
New York Botanical Garden Press
200th St. & Southern Blvd.
Bronx, NY 10458-5126
Phone: (718)817-8721
Fax: (718)817-8842
**Subject(s):** Botany
**Circ:** ‡1,800

**Current Opinion in Oncology (26908)**
Lippincott Williams & Wilkins
530 Walnut St.
Philadelphia, PA 19106-3261
Phone: (215)521-8300
Fax: (215)521-8902
**Subject(s):** Medicine and Surgery
**Circ:** (Paid)‡1,800

**Cytogenetics and Cell Genetics (4710)**
S. Karger Publishers Inc.
26 W Avon Rd.
PO Box 529
Farmington, CT 06085
Phone: (860)675-7834
Fax: (860)675-7302
**Subject(s):** Genetics; Medicine and Surgery; German; French
**Circ:** 1,800

**The Electricity Journal (21636)**
655 Avenue of Americas
New York, NY 10010-1570
Phone: (212)989-5800
Fax: (212)462-1974
**Subject(s):** Power and Power Plants
**Circ:** ‡1,800

**Journal of Cryptology (21906)**
Springer-Verlag New York Inc.
233 Spring St.
New York, NY 10013
Phone: (212)460-1500
Fax: (212)460-1575
**Subject(s):** Science (General); Mathematics
**Circ:** (Combined)**1,800**

**Journal of Vascular Research (4737)**
S. Karger Publishers Inc.
26 W Avon Rd.
PO Box 529
Farmington, CT 06085
Phone: (860)675-7834
Fax: (860)675-7302
**Subject(s):** Medicine and Surgery
**Circ:** 1,800

**Parnassus (22220)**
Poetry in Review Foundation
205 W 89th St., No. 8F
New York, NY 10024
Phone: (212)362-3492
Fax: (212)875-0148
**Subject(s):** Literature; Poetry
**Circ:** (Paid)1,800

**Spaniels in the Field (22401)**
Chiridion Wild Wings Inc.
PO Box 1737
New York, NY 10021
**Subject(s):** Dogs
**Circ:** (Combined)⊕1802

**Studies in Romanticism (13593)**
Boston University
1 Sherborn St.
Boston, MA 02215
Phone: (617)353-2000
Fax: (617)353-6480

**Woman's Art Journal** (26621)
1711 Harris Rd.
Laverock, PA 19038
Phone: (215)233-0639
Fax: (215)233-0639
Subject(s): Women's Interests; Art
Circ: (Combined)‡1,800

**Nurse Practitioner Forum** (27183)
Elsevier
1600 John F. Kennedy Blvd.
Philadelphia, PA 19103
Phone: (215)239-3900
Fax: (215)239-3990
Subject(s): Nursing
Circ: ‡1,785

**Topics in Geriatric Rehabilitation (TGR)** (22464)
Aspen Publishers Inc.
1185 Ave. of the Americas
New York, NY 10036
Phone: (301)644-3599
Fax: (212)597-0331
Subject(s): Gerontology; Medicine and Surgery
Circ: (Non-paid)70
 (Paid)1,768

**Economic Geography** (14935)
Clark University
950 Main St.
Worcester, MA 01610-1477
Phone: (508)793-7311
Fax: (508)793-8881
Subject(s): Geography
Circ: ‡1,750

**English Today** (21650)
Cambridge University Press
40 W. 20th St.
New York, NY 10011-4211
Phone: (212)924-3900
Fax: (212)691-3239
Subject(s): Philology, Language, and Linguistics
Circ: 1750

**Gynaekologisch-geburtshilfliche Rundschau** (4726)
S. Karger Publishers Inc.
26 W Avon Rd.
PO Box 529
Farmington, CT 06085
Phone: (860)675-7834
Fax: (860)675-7302
Subject(s): German; French; Medicine and Surgery
Circ: 1,750

**SIAM Journal on Optimization** (27270)
Society for Industrial & Applied Mathematics
3600 University City Science Ctr.
Philadelphia, PA 19104-2688
Phone: (215)382-9800
Fax: (215)386-7999
Subject(s): Mathematics; Engineering (Various branches); Computers
Circ: ‡1,710

**Analytic Psychology** (4696)
S. Karger Publishers Inc.
26 W Avon Rd.
PO Box 529
Farmington, CT 06085
Phone: (860)675-7834
Fax: (860)675-7302
Subject(s): Psychology and Psychiatry; German; Medicine and Surgery
Circ: 1,700

**APT Bulletin** (20208)
Association for Preservation Technology International
c/o Diana S. Waite, Editor
Mount Ida Press
152 Washington Ave.
Albany, NY 12210
Phone: (518)426-5935
Fax: (518)426-4116
Subject(s): Architecture
Circ: (Paid)1,700

**Armed Forces & Society** (19806)
Transaction Publishers
390 Campus Dr.
Somerset, NJ 08873
Phone: (732)445-1245
Fax: (732)748-9801
Subject(s): Military and Navy; Sociology; Political Science
Circ: (Paid)‡1,700

**Campus Law Enforcement Journal** (5078)
International Association of Campus Law Enforcement Administrators
342 N Main St.
West Hartford, CT 06117-2507
Phone: (860)586-7517
Fax: (860)586-7550
Subject(s): Safety; Police, Penology, and Penal Institutions
Circ: (Paid)1,700

**Color Research and Application** (19202)
John Wiley and Sons Inc.
111 River St.
Hoboken, NJ 07030-5774
Phone: (201)748-6000
Fax: (201)748-6088
Subject(s): Science (General)
Circ: 1,700

**Field Mycology** (21683)
Cambridge University Press
40 W. 20th St.
New York, NY 10011-4211
Phone: (212)924-3900
Fax: (212)691-3239
Subject(s): Botany
Circ: ‡1,700

**Hanging Loose** (20511)
Hanging Loose Press
231 Wyckoff St.
Brooklyn, NY 11217
Phone: (212)206-8465
Fax: (212)243-7499
Subject(s): Literature and Literary Reviews
Circ: (Non-paid)‡300
 (Paid)‡1,700

**Je Me Souviens** (27957)
American-French Genealogical Society
547 Clinton St., Apt. 710
Woonsocket, RI 02895
Phone: (401)356-1276
Subject(s): History and Genealogy
Circ: (Combined)1,700

**Journal of Fluid Mechanics** (21922)
Cambridge University Press
40 W. 20th St.
New York, NY 10011-4211
Phone: (212)924-3900
Fax: (212)001-3239
Subject(s): Chemistry, Chemicals, and Chemical Engineering; Mathematics
Circ: 1,700

**Journal of Humanistic Counseling & Development** (20552)
American Counseling Association
c/o Dr. Mark B. Scholl, JHCEAD Editor
Department of Counseling and Development
720 Northern Blvd.
Long Island University, C.W. Post Campus
Brookville, NY 11548-1326
Phone: (516)299-2815
Fax: (516)299-3312
Subject(s): Education; Psychology and Psychiatry
Circ: (Paid)‡1,700

**Journal of Tribology** (22003)
American Society of Mechanical Engineers
3 Park Ave.
New York, NY 10016-5990
Phone: (212)591-7722
Fax: (212)591-7674
Subject(s): Engineering (Various branches)
Circ: 1,702

**Naturist Life International** (30913)
Naturist Life International Inc.
115 Prospect St.
Newport, VT 05855-2027
Phone: (802)334-5976
Subject(s): Alternative and Underground; Lifestyle
Circ: (Controlled)1,700

**The Opera Quarterly** (22832)
Duke University Press
C/o Dr. E. Thomas Glasgow
Editor, The Opera Quarterly
197 Oaklawn Dr.
Rochester, NY 14617-1813
Subject(s): Music and Musical Instruments
Circ: (Combined)1,700

**Organization Science** (27381)
The Institute for Operations Research and the Management Sciences
c/o Linda Argote, Editor-in-chief
Carnegie Mellon University, Tepper School of Business
Tech and Frew Sts.
Pittsburgh, PA 15213-3890
Phone: (412)268-3683
Fax: (412)268-9525
Subject(s): Management and Administration
Circ: ‡1,700

**The Russian Review** (14217)
Blackwell Publishers
350 Main St.
Malden, MA 02148
Phone: (781)388-8200
Fax: (781)388-8250
Subject(s): Soviet Interests; Intercultural Interests; Art and Art History; Humanities; Literature
Circ: (Non-paid)‡100
 (Paid)‡1,700

**The Biological Bulletin** (14926)
Marine Biological Laboratory
7 MBL St.
Woods Hole, MA 02543
Phone: (508)289-7402
Fax: (508)289-7922
Subject(s): Biology; Oceanography and Marine Studies
Circ: (Controlled)1,690

**Psychology in the Schools** (20576)
John Wiley and Sons Inc.
Dept. of Counseling and Educational Psychology
409 Baldy Hall
State Univ. of New York at Buffalo
Buffalo, NY 14260-1000
Phone: (716)645-6616
Fax: (716)645-6616
Subject(s): Psychology and Psychiatry
Circ: (Non-paid)‡78
 (Paid)‡1,684

**Audiology and Neuro-Otology** (4698)
S. Karger Publishers Inc.
26 W Avon Rd.
PO Box 529
Farmington, CT 06085
Phone: (000)675-7834
Fax: (860)675-7302
Subject(s): Medicine and Surgery; French
Circ: 1,650

**Journal of Child Language** (21895)
Cambridge University Press
40 W. 20th St.
New York, NY 10011-4211
Phone: (212)924-3900
Fax: (212)691-3239
Subject(s): Philology, Language, and Linguistics
Circ: 1,650

**Neuroendocrinology** (4745)
S. Karger Publishers Inc.
26 W Avon Rd.
PO Box 529
Farmington, CT 06085
Phone: (860)675-7834
Fax: (860)675-7302
Subject(s): Medicine and Surgery
Circ: 1,650

**Criminal Law Bulletin** (21570)
West Group
375 Hudson St.
New York, NY 10014
Phone: (212)929-7500
Fax: (212)807-6209
Subject(s): Law
Circ: (Non-paid)397
 (Paid)1,637

**Journal of Spinal Disorders & Techniques** (27096)
Lippincott Williams & Wilkins
Lippincott Williams & Wilkins
530 Walnut St.
Philadelphia, PA 19106-8300
Phone: (215)521-8300
Fax: (215)521-8488
**Subject(s):** Laboratory Research (Scientific and Medical)
Circ: 1,639

**SIAM Journal on Matrix Analysis and Applications** (27269)
Society for Industrial & Applied Mathematics
3600 University City Science Ctr.
Philadelphia, PA 19104-2688
Phone: (215)382-9800
Fax: (215)386-7999
**Subject(s):** Mathematics
Circ: ‡1,623

**Biblical Theology Bulletin** (19828)
Biblical Theology Bulletin Inc.
PO Box 1038
South Orange, NJ 07079
Phone: (973)761-9006
Fax: (973)275-2333
**Subject(s):** Religious Publications
Circ: 1,600

**The British Journal for the History of Science** (21426)
Cambridge University Press
40 W. 20th St.
New York, NY 10011-4211
Phone: (212)924-3900
Fax: (212)691-3239
**Subject(s):** Science (General)
Circ: 1,600

**The Cambridge Law Journal** (21450)
Cambridge University Press
40 W. 20th St.
New York, NY 10011-4211
Phone: (212)924-3900
Fax: (212)691-3239
**Subject(s):** Law
Circ: 1,600

**The Chesterton Review** (19829)
G.K. Chesterton Society
c/o Rev. Ian Boyd, C.S.B
Seton Hall University
400 S Orange Ave.
South Orange, NJ 07079-2687
Phone: (973)275-2430
Fax: (973)275-2594
**Subject(s):** Literature and Literary Reviews
Circ: (Non-paid)30
   (Paid)1,600

**Feedback** (26299)
Broadcast Education Association
Fine Arts Bldg.
East Stroudsburg University
East Stroudsburg, PA 18301
Phone: (570)422-5051
**Subject(s):** Radio, Television, Cable, and Video
Circ: (Non-paid)‡100
   (Paid)‡1,600

**Future Survey** (21014)
World Future Society
5413 Webster Rd.
LaFayette, NY 13084
Phone: (315)677-9278
Fax: (315)677-9248
**Subject(s):** Society; Environmental and Natural Resources Conservation; Business
Circ: (Paid)1,600

**The Journal of African History** (21870)
Cambridge University Press
40 W. 20th St.
New York, NY 10011-4211
Phone: (212)924-3900
Fax: (212)691-3239
**Subject(s):** History and Genealogy
Circ: (Non-paid)‡67
   (Paid)‡1,601

**Journal of the American Society for Psychical Research** (21874)
American Society for Psychical Research Inc.
5 W 73rd St.
New York, NY 10023
Phone: (212)799-5050
Fax: (212)496-2497
**Subject(s):** Psychology and Psychiatry; Science (General)
Circ: 1,600

**Journal of the Marine Biological Association of the United Kingdom** (21952)
Cambridge University Press
40 W. 20th St.
New York, NY 10011-4211
Phone: (212)924-3900
Fax: (212)691-3239
**Subject(s):** Oceanography and Marine Studies
Circ: 1,600

**Journal of Modern African Studies** (21957)
Cambridge University Press
40 W. 20th St.
New York, NY 10011-4211
Phone: (212)924-3900
Fax: (212)691-3239
**Subject(s):** Intercultural Interests; Economics; History and Genealogy; Politics
Circ: 1,600

**Journal of Pediatric Hematology/Oncology** (19596)
Lippincott Williams & Wilkins
Cancer Institute of New Jersey
Robert Wood Johnson Medical School
195 Little Albany St.
New Brunswick, NJ
**Subject(s):** Laboratory Research (Scientific and Medical)
Circ: (Paid)1,600

**Music and Media** (22118)
VNU Business Media USA
770 Broadway
New York, NY 10003
Phone: (646)654-5000
**Subject(s):** Music and Musical Instruments; Performing Arts
Circ: 1,600

**New Hampshire Highways** (18787)
New Hampshire Good Roads Association
261 Sheep Davis Rd., Ste. 5
Concord, NH 03301-5750
Phone: (603)224-1823
**Subject(s):** Roads and Streets
Circ: ‡1,600

**Social Work in Health Care** (22389)
The Haworth Press Inc.
Mount Sinai NYU Health
1 Gustave L. Levy Place
PO Box 1246
New York, NY 10029
Phone: (212)659-9075
Fax: (212)722-2543
**Subject(s):** Psychology and Psychiatry; Health and Healthcare; Sociology
Circ: 1,608

**Westchester Country Club News** (22888)
Westchester Country Club
99 Biltmore Ave.
Rye, NY 10580
Phone: (914)967-6000
Fax: (914)967-3429
**Subject(s):** Clubs and Societies
Circ: ‡1,600

**Cataloging and Classification Quarterly** (27677)
The Haworth Press Inc.
121 Pikemont Dr.
Wexford, PA 15090-8447
Phone: (724)940-4192
**Subject(s):** Library and Information Science
Circ: 1,580

**SIAM Journal on Scientific Computing** (27271)
Society for Industrial & Applied Mathematics
3600 University City Science Ctr.
Philadelphia, PA 19104-2688
Phone: (215)382-9800
Fax: (215)386-7999
**Subject(s):** Mathematics; Computers
Circ: ‡1,585

**Arthritis Care and Research** (19173)
John Wiley and Sons Inc.
111 River St.
Hoboken, NJ 07030-5774
Phone: (201)748-6000
Fax: (201)748-6088
**Subject(s):** Chiropractic
Circ: ‡1,575

**Journal of Nervous and Mental Disease** (27065)
Lippincott Williams & Wilkins
530 Walnut St.
Philadelphia, PA 19106-3261
Phone: (215)521-8300
Fax: (215)521-8902
**Subject(s):** Psychology and Psychiatry; Medicine and Surgery
Circ: (Paid)‡1,577

**American Journal of Otolaryngology** (26817)
Elsevier
1600 John F. Kennedy Blvd.
Philadelphia, PA 19103
Phone: (215)239-3900
Fax: (215)239-3990
**Subject(s):** Medicine and Surgery
Circ: ‡1,565

**The American Neptune** (14774)
Peabody Essex Museum
E.India Sq.
Salem, MA 01970-3783
Fax: (978)744-6776
**Subject(s):** Ships and Shipping; Museums
Circ: ‡1,550

**Current Opinion in Gastroenterology** (13506)
Lippincott Williams & Wilkins
C/O Daniel K. Podolsky, MD
Current Opinion in Gastroenterology
Harvard Medical School
Boston, MA
**Subject(s):** Medicine and Surgery
Circ: (Paid)‡1,540

**Current Surgery** (26912)
Lippincott Williams & Wilkins
530 Walnut St.
Philadelphia, PA 19106-3261
Phone: (215)521-8300
Fax: (215)521-8902
**Subject(s):** Medicine and Surgery
Circ: (Combined)1,542

**Journal of Hypertension** (27040)
Lippincott Williams & Wilkins
530 Walnut St.
Philadelphia, PA 19106-3261
Phone: (215)521-8300
Fax: (215)521-8902
**Subject(s):** Medicine and Surgery
Circ: (Paid)1,549

**Theory of Probability and Its Applications** (27285)
Society for Industrial & Applied Mathematics
3600 University City Science Ctr.
Philadelphia, PA 19104-2688
Phone: (215)382-9800
Fax: (215)386-7999
**Subject(s):** Mathematics
Circ: ‡1,546

**American Journal of Philology** (20652)
Johns Hopkins University Press
Hamilton College
Dept. of Classics
198 College Hill Rd.
Clinton, NY 13323
Phone: (315)856-4677
Fax: (315)856-4677
**Subject(s):** Philology, Language, and Linguistics; History and Genealogy
Circ: ‡1,517

**Activities Directors' Quarterly for Alzheimer's & Other Dementia Patients** (14901)
Prime National Publishing Corp.
470 Boston Post Rd.
Weston, MA 02493
Phone: (781)899-2702
Fax: (781)899-4900
**Subject(s):** Health and Healthcare; Hospitals and Healthcare Institutions
Circ: (Paid)‡1,500

**AGNI** (13465)
Boston University Creative Writing Program
236 Bay State Rd.
Boston, MA 02215
Phone: (617)353-7135
Fax: (617)353-7134
Subject(s): Literature and Literary Reviews; Poetry
Circ: (Non-paid)300
(Paid)1,500

**American Letters & Commentary** (21319)
American Letters & Commentary Inc.
850 Park Ave., Ste. 5B
New York, NY 10021
Phone: (212)734-2233
Fax: (212)327-0706
Subject(s): Literature; Literature and Literary Reviews; Poetry
Circ: (Controlled)1,500

**Bible and Spade** (26088)
Associates for Biblical Research
PO Box 144
Akron, PA 17501-0144
Phone: (717)859-3443
Fax: (717)859-3393
Subject(s): Archaeology; Science
Circ: (Paid)1,500

**Bulletin of the New Jersey Motor Truck Association** (19058)
New Jersey Motor Truck Association
160 Tices Ln.
East Brunswick, NJ 08816
Phone: (732)254-5000
Fax: (732)613-1745
Subject(s): Trucks and Trucking
Circ: ‡1500

**The Chaucer Review** (27599)
Penn State University Press
Dept. of English
Kent State Univ.
PO Box 5190
University Park, PA 16802
Subject(s): Literature
Circ: ‡1,500

**The Citadel** (21208)
Orange County Community College
115 S St.
Middletown, NY 10940-6404
Phone: (845)344-6222
Fax: (845)343-1228
Subject(s): College Publications
Circ: (Non-paid)1,500

**Connecticut Pharmacist** (4996)
Connecticut Pharmacists Association
35 Cold Spring Rd., Ste. 125
Rocky Hill, CT 06067-3167
Phone: (860)563-4619
Fax: (860)257-8241
Subject(s): Drugs and Pharmaceuticals
Circ: (Controlled)1,500

**Digestive Diseases** (4716)
S. Karger Publishers Inc.
26 W Avon Rd.
PO Box 529
Farmington, CT 06085
Phone: (860)675-7834
Fax: (860)675-7302
Subject(s): Medicine and Surgery
Circ: 1,500

**Error Trends Coin Magazine** (22637)
PO Box 158
Oceanside, NY 11572-0158
Phone: (516)764-8063
Subject(s): Collecting
Circ: 1,500

**Harvard Theological Review** (13677)
Harvard Divinity School
45 Francis Avenue
Cambridge, MA 02138-1994
Phone: (617)495-5786
Fax: (617)496-9402
Subject(s): Religious Publications
Circ: 1,500

**The Historical Journal** (21765)
Cambridge University Press
40 W. 20th St.
New York, NY 10011-4211
Phone: (212)924-3900
Fax: (212)691-3239
Subject(s): History and Genealogy
Circ: 1,500

**International Journal of Technology Assessment in Health Care** (21835)
Cambridge University Press
40 W. 20th St.
New York, NY 10011-4211
Phone: (212)924-3900
Fax: (212)691-3239
Subject(s): Hospitals and Healthcare Institutions; Medicine and Surgery
Circ: 1,500

**International Philosophical Quarterly** (20462)
Philosophy Documentation Center
Canisius Hall
Fordham University
Bronx, NY 10458-5154
Subject(s): Philosophy
Circ: (Controlled)‡50
(Paid)‡1,500

**The Journal of Risk and Insurance** (26660)
American Risk and Insurance Association
716 Providence Rd.
PO Box 3028
Malvern, PA 19355-3402
Phone: (610)640-1997
Fax: (610)725-1007
Subject(s): Insurance
Circ: ‡1,500

**Journal of Zoo and Wildlife Medicine** (26689)
American Association of Zoo Veterinarians
6 N. Pennell Rd.
Media, PA 19063
Phone: (610)892-4812
Fax: (610)892-4813
Subject(s): Zoology; Wildlife and Exotic Animals; Veterinary Medicine
Circ: 1,500

**Mathematical Reviews** (27906)
American Mathematical Society
201 Charles St.
Providence, RI 02904-2294
Phone: (401)455-4000
Fax: (401)331-3842
Subject(s): Mathematics; Indexes, Abstracts, Reports, Proceedings, and Bibliographies
Circ: (Paid)‡1,500

**Microform Review** (19610)
K.G. Saur/Reed Reference Publishing
121 Chanlon Rd
New Providence, NJ 07974
Phone: (908)666-3325
Fax: (908)666-8718
Subject(s): Library and Information Science
Circ: 1,500

**MIM Bulletin** (22088)
Society of Turkish-American Architects, Engineers and Scientists
821 United Nations Plz., 2nd Fl.
New York, NY 10017
Phone: (212)682-7688
Fax: (212)687-3026
Subject(s): Architecture; Engineering (Various branches); Science (General); Turkish
Circ: 1,500

**New Jersey Journal of Pharmacy** (19729)
New Jersey Pharmacists Association
760 Alexander Rd.
CN 1
Princeton, NJ 08543-0001
Phone: (609)275-4246
Fax: (609)275-4066
Subject(s): Drugs and Pharmaceuticals
Circ: (Controlled)‡1,500

**Orthodox Life** (21002)
Holy Trinity Monastery
PO Box 36
Jordanville, NY 13361-0036
Phone: (315)858-0940
Fax: (315)858-0505
Subject(s): Religious Publications
Circ: ‡1,500

**Pendle Hill Pamphlets** (27634)
Pendle Hill Publications
338 Plush Mill Rd.
Wallingford, PA 19086
Phone: (610)566-4507
Fax: (610)366-3679
Subject(s): Religious Publications
Circ: (Free)‡100
(Paid)‡1,500

**Physical Review C** (22788)
American Physical Society
1 Research Rd.
Box 9000
Ridge, NY 11961-9000
Phone: (631)591-4030
Fax: (631)591-4141
Subject(s): Physics
Circ: 1,500

**The Pioneer** (27383)
Point Park College
201 Wood St.
Box 627
Pittsburgh, PA 15222
Phone: (412)391-4100
Fax: (412)391-1980
Subject(s): College Publications
Circ: (Non-paid)1,500

**Princeton History** (19733)
Historical Society of Princeton
158 Nassau St.
Princeton, NJ 08542
Phone: (609)921-6748
Fax: (609)921-6939
Subject(s): History and Genealogy; Local, State, and Regional Publications
Circ: 1,500

**Psychoanalytic Inquiry** (19149)
Analytic Press
101 W St.
Hillsdale, NJ 07642-1422
Phone: (201)358-9477
Fax: (201)358-4700
Subject(s): Psychology and Psychiatry
Circ: 1,500

**Radical Teacher** (13703)
Center for Critical Education Inc.
PO Box 382616
Cambridge, MA 02238-2616
Phone: (617)876-7324
Fax: (617)876-7324
Subject(s): Women's Interests; Education
Circ: 1,500

**Social Science History** (27401)
Duke University Press
Department of History
Carnegie Mellon University
Baker Hall 240
Pittsburgh, PA 15213-3890
Phone: (412)268-9111
Fax: (412)268-1019
Subject(s): History and Genealogy
Circ: ‡1,500

**Topics in Health Information Management** (22465)
Aspen Publishers Inc.
1185 Ave. of the Americas
New York, NY 10036
Phone: (301)644-3599
Fax: (212)597-0331
Subject(s): Health and Healthcare
Circ: 1,500

**United Nations Treaty Series** (22504)
United Nations Publications
2 United Nations Plz., Rm. DC2-853
New York, NY 10017
Phone: (212)963-8302
Fax: (212)963-3489
Subject(s): International Affairs
Circ: (Combined)‡1,500

**Women's Studies Quarterly (22554)**
Feminist Press at The City University of New York
The Graduate Ctr.
365 5th Ave., Ste. 5406
New York, NY 10016
Phone: (212)817-7915
Fax: (212)817-1593
Subject(s): Women's Interests; Education; History and Genealogy; Literature and Literary Reviews

Circ: ‡1,500

**Journal of Energy Resources Technology (21917)**
American Society of Mechanical Engineers
3 Park Ave.
New York, NY 10016-5990
Phone: (212)591-7722
Fax: (212)591-7674
Subject(s): Engineering (Various branches)

Circ: 1,493

**New Church Life (26207)**
General Church of the New Jerusalem
PO Box 277
Bryn Athyn, PA 19009
Phone: (215)947-6225
Fax: (215)947-3078
Subject(s): Religious Publications

Circ: (Non-paid)‡130
(Paid)‡1,480

**AJS Review (21286)**
Association for Jewish Studies
15 W 16th St
New York, NY 10011-6301
Phone: (917)606-8249
Fax: (917)606-8222
Subject(s): Intercultural Interests; Hebrew; Yiddish

Circ: 1,450

**Caries Research (4702)**
S. Karger Publishers Inc.
26 W Avon Rd.
PO Box 529
Farmington, CT 06085
Phone: (860)675-7834
Fax: (860)675-7302
Subject(s): Dentistry

Circ: 1,450

**Cellular Physiology and Biochemistry (4704)**
S. Karger Publishers Inc.
26 W Avon Rd.
PO Box 529
Farmington, CT 06085
Phone: (860)675-7834
Fax: (860)675-7302
Subject(s): Medicine and Surgery

Circ: ‡1,450

**English Literary Renaissance (13406)**
Massachusetts Center for Renaissance Studies
PO Box 2300
Amherst, MA 01004
Phone: (413)577-3603
Fax: (413)577-3605
Subject(s): Literature

Circ: (Combined)1,450

**Journal of Cardiovascular Pharmacology (21892)**
Lippincott Williams & Wilkins
c/o Paul M Vanhoutte
Department of Pharmacology
College of Physicians and Surgeons of Columbia Univ.
PH7 West 321, 630 West 168th St.
New York, NY 10032
Subject(s): Drugs and Pharmaceuticals; Laboratory Research (Scientific and Medical)

Circ: 1,451

**Psychological Medicine (22275)**
Cambridge University Press
40 W. 20th St.
New York, NY 10011-4211
Phone: (212)924-3900
Fax: (212)691-3239
Subject(s): Psychology and Psychiatry

Circ: 1,450

**The American Journal of the Medical Sciences (26815)**
Lippincott Williams & Wilkins
530 Walnut St.
Philadelphia, PA 19106-3261
Phone: (215)521-8300
Fax: (215)521-8902
Subject(s): Medicine and Surgery

Circ: 1,430

**Pediatric Emergency Care (27211)**
Lippincott Williams & Wilkins
C/o Stephen Ludwig, MD, Editor
The Children's Hospital of Philadelphia
Rm. 2011, 34th St. & Civic Center Blvd.
Philadelphia, PA 19104
Phone: (215)590-2180
Fax: (215)590-2180
Subject(s): Pediatrics

Circ: (Non-paid)‡292
(Paid)‡1,424

**Abstracts of Papers Presented to the American Mathematical Society (27883)**
American Mathematical Society
201 Charles St.
Providence, RI 02904-2294
Phone: (401)455-4000
Fax: (401)331-3842
Subject(s): Mathematics; Indexes, Abstracts, Reports, Proceedings, and Bibliographies

Circ: (Paid)1,417

**Clinical Nuclear Medicine (27718)**
Lippincott Williams & Wilkins
The Lankenau Hospital
100 Lancaster Ave.
Wynnewood, PA 19096
Phone: (610)526-9331
Fax: (610)526-9331
Subject(s): Radiology, Ultrasound, and Nuclear Medicine; Medicine and Surgery

Circ: (Paid)‡1,407

**Hobby Greenhouse (13449)**
Hobby Greenhouse Association
8 Glen Ter.
Bedford, MA 01730-2048
Phone: (781)275-0377
Subject(s): Horticulture

Circ: (Combined)1,400

**International Archives of Allergy and Immunology (4732)**
S. Karger Publishers Inc.
26 W Avon Rd.
PO Box 529
Farmington, CT 06085
Phone: (860)675-7834
Fax: (860)675-7302
Subject(s): Medicine and Surgery

Circ: 1,400

**International Psychogeriatrics (21840)**
Springer Publishing Co.
11 W. 42nd St. 15th Fl.
New York, NY 10036
Phone: (212)431-4370
Fax: (212)941-7842
Subject(s): Psychology and Psychiatry; Gerontology; Medicine and Surgery

Circ: (Combined)1,400

**The Massachusetts Review (13418)**
University of Massachusetts
South College
Amherst, MA 01003
Phone: (413)545-2689
Fax: (413)577-0740
Subject(s): Humanities

Circ: (Non-paid)‡300
(Paid)‡1,400

**Newport History (27869)**
Newport Historical Society
82 Touro St.
Newport, RI 02840
Phone: (401)846-0813
Fax: (401)846-1853
Subject(s): History and Genealogy

Circ: (Controlled)1,400

**Polymer Engineering and Science (4653)**
Society of Plastics Engineers
14 Fairfield Dr.
PO Box 403
Brookfield, CT 06804-0403
Phone: (203)775-0471
Fax: (203)775-8490
Subject(s): Engineering (Various branches); Plastic and Composition Materials

Circ: 1,400

**The Review of Income and Wealth (22314)**
Blackwell Publishing Ltd.
International Association for Research in Income and Wealth
Dept. of Economics
New York University
269 Mercer St., Rm. 700
New York, NY 10003
Phone: (212)924-4386
Fax: (212)366-5067
Subject(s): Banking, Finance, and Investments

Circ: ‡1,400

**Topics in Clinical Nutrition (TICN) (22463)**
Aspen Publishers Inc.
1185 Ave. of the Americas
New York, NY 10036
Phone: (301)644-3599
Fax: (212)597-0331
Subject(s): Health and Healthcare

Circ: (Non-paid)86
(Paid)1,400

**WW1 Aero (22746)**
World War 1 Aeroplanes Inc.
15 Crescent Rd.
Poughkeepsie, NY 12601
Phone: (845)473-3679
Subject(s): Aviation; History and Genealogy

Circ: (Paid)‡1,400

**Coraopolis Record Star (26723)**
Gateway Publications
610 Beatty Rd.
Monroeville, PA 15146
Phone: (412)856-7400
Fax: (412)856-7954
Subject(s): Paid Community Newspapers

Circ: (Combined)1,389

**Abdominal Imaging (22972)**
Springer-Verlag New York Inc.
c/o Morton A. Meyers
School of Medicine
Health Sciences Center
Stony Brook, NY 11794-8460
Subject(s): Radiology, Ultrasound, and Nuclear Medicine

Circ: (Combined)1,350

**Journal of Biomechanical Engineering (21885)**
American Society of Mechanical Engineers
3 Park Ave.
New York, NY 10016-5990
Phone: (212)591-7722
Fax: (212)591-7674
Subject(s): Engineering (Various branches)

Circ: 1,312

**Journal of Developmental & Behavioral Pediatrics (27022)**
Lippincott Williams & Wilkins
530 Walnut St.
Philadelphia, PA 19106-3261
Phone: (215)521-8300
Fax: (215)521-8902
Subject(s): Pediatrics; Psychology and Psychiatry

Circ: (Free)‡175
(Paid)‡1,317

**Acta Haematologica (4694)**
S. Karger Publishers Inc.
26 W Avon Rd.
PO Box 529
Farmington, CT 06085
Phone: (860)675-7834
Fax: (860)675-7302
Subject(s): Medicine and Surgery; Laboratory Research (Scientific and Medical)

Circ: 1,300

**American Journal of Science (4878)**
210 Whitney Ave.
PO Box 208109
New Haven, CT 06520
Phone: (203)432-3131
Fax: (203)432-5668
Subject(s): Geology

Circ: 1,300

**Chemotherapy (4706)**
S. Karger Publishers Inc.
26 W Avon Rd.
PO Box 529
Farmington, CT 06085
Phone: (860)675-7834

Fax: (860)675-7302
**Subject(s):** Medicine and Surgery
**Circ:** 1,300

**Development and Psychopathology (22816)**
Cambridge University Press
Mount Hope Family Center
c/o Dr Dante Cicchetti, University of Rochester
187 Edinburgh St.
Rochester, NY 14608
**Subject(s):** Psychology and Psychiatry; Pediatrics
**Circ:** 1300

**Industrial Marketing Management (4805)**
Elsevier Science B.V.
Rensselaer Polytechnic Institute
275 Windsor St.
Hartford, CT 06120
**Subject(s):** Advertising and Marketing; Business
**Circ:** 1,304

**Journal of Clinical Monitoring and Computing (14523)**
Kluwer Academic/Plenum Publishing Corp.
101 Philip Dr.
Assinippi Park
Norwell, MA 02061
Phone: (781)871-6600
Fax: (201)348-4505
**Subject(s):** Medicine and Surgery
**Circ:** (Paid)1,300

**Journal of General Education (27607)**
Penn State University Press
820 N University Dr.
USB-1 Ste. C
University Park, PA 16802
Phone: (814)865-1327
Fax: (814)863-1408
**Subject(s):** Education
**Circ:** ‡1300

**Maine Trails (12449)**
Maine Better Transportation Association
146 State St.
Augusta, ME 04330
Phone: (207)622-0526
Fax: (207)623-2928
**Subject(s):** Transportation, Traffic, and Shipping
**Circ:** (Controlled)‡1,300

**Mammoth Trumpet (12474)**
Center for the Study of the First Americans
93 Range Rd.
Blue Hill, ME 04614
Phone: (207)374-5383
Fax: (207)374-5383
**Subject(s):** Anthropology and Ethnology; Archaeology
**Circ:** (Paid)1,300

**News & Food Report (18873)**
New Hampshire Grocers Association
110 Stark St.
Manchester, NH 03101-1934
Phone: (603)669-9333
Fax: (603)623-1137
**Subject(s):** Food and Grocery Trade
**Circ:** ‡1,300

**Pediatric Cardiology (22224)**
Springer-Verlag New York Inc.
233 Spring St.
New York, NY 10013
Phone: (212)460-1500
Fax: (212)460-1575
**Subject(s):** Pediatrics
**Circ:** (Combined)1,300

**Rhode Island Beverage Journal (27920)**
Rhode Island Beverage Journal Inc.
PO Box 185159
Hamden, CT 06518-0157
Phone: (203)288-3375
Fax: (203)288-2693
**Subject(s):** Beverages, Brewing, and Bottling
**Circ:** 1,300

**Medical Reference Services Quarterly (26497)**
The Haworth Press Inc.
George T. Harrell Library
Milton S. Hershey Medical Center
The Pennsylvania State University
PO Box 850
Hershey, PA 17033-0850
Phone: (717)531-8630

**Subject(s):** Library and Information Science; Medicine and Surgery
**Circ:** 1,295

**Journal of AAPOS (American Association for Pediatric Ophthalmology and Strabismus) (27006)**
Mosby
170 S. Independence Mall W., Ste. 300 E.
Philadelphia, PA 19106-3399
Phone: (215)238-7869
Fax: (215)238-2239
**Subject(s):** Medicine and Surgery; Ophthalmology, Optometry, and Optics; Pediatrics
**Circ:** (Combined)‡1,283

**Social Anthropology (22385)**
Cambridge University Press
40 W. 20th St.
New York, NY 10011-4211
Phone: (212)924-3900
Fax: (212)691-3239
**Subject(s):** Anthropology and Ethnology
**Circ:** (Non-paid)‡41
(Paid)‡1263

**Soil Science (19602)**
Lippincott Williams & Wilkins
C/o Dr. Robert L. Tate III, Editor-in-Chief
Rutgers University
Department of Environmental Sciences
14 College Farm Rd.
New Brunswick, NJ 08901-8551
Fax: (800)468-1128
**Subject(s):** Scientific Agricultural Publications; Fertilizer
**Circ:** (Non-paid)‡235
(Combined)‡1,261

**Annals of Nutrition and Metabolism (4697)**
S. Karger Publishers Inc.
26 W Avon Rd.
PO Box 529
Farmington, CT 06085
Phone: (860)675-7834
Fax: (860)675-7302
**Subject(s):** Medicine and Surgery; French; German
**Circ:** 1,250

**Gerontology (4725)**
S. Karger Publishers Inc.
26 W Avon Rd.
PO Box 529
Farmington, CT 06085
Phone: (860)675-7834
Fax: (860)675-7302
**Subject(s):** Gerontology
**Circ:** 1,250

**Hormone Research (4729)**
S. Karger Publishers Inc.
26 W Avon Rd.
PO Box 529
Farmington, CT 06085
Phone: (860)675-7834
Fax: (860)675-7302
**Subject(s):** Medicine and Surgery
**Circ:** 1,250

**Journal of Differential Geometry (13687)**
International Press of Boston Inc.
Department of Mathematics
Harvard University
Cambridge, MA 02138
**Subject(s):** Mathematics; Physics
**Circ:** (Combined)1,250

**The Journal of Ecclesiastical History (21913)**
Cambridge University Press
40 W. 20th St.
New York, NY 10011-4211
Phone: (212)924-3900
Fax: (212)691-3239
**Subject(s):** History and Genealogy
**Circ:** 1,250

**Journal of Roman Archaeology (27881)**
95 Peleg Rd.
Portsmouth, RI 02871
Phone: (401)683-1955
Fax: (401)683-1975
**Subject(s):** Archaeology; History and Genealogy
**Circ:** (Non-paid)1,250

**Latin American Literary Review (27368)**
Latin American Literary Review Press
PO Box 17660
Pittsburgh, PA 15235-0860
Phone: (412)824-7903
Fax: (412)824-7909
**Subject(s):** Literature; Hispanic Publications; Ethnic and Minority Studies
**Circ:** (Combined)1,250

**New Theatre Quarterly (22151)**
Cambridge University Press
40 W. 20th St.
New York, NY 10011-4211
Phone: (212)924-3900
Fax: (212)691-3239
**Subject(s):** Drama and Theatre; Performing Arts
**Circ:** 1,250

**Oncology (4749)**
S. Karger Publishers Inc.
26 W Avon Rd.
PO Box 529
Farmington, CT 06085
Phone: (860)675-7834
Fax: (860)675-7302
**Subject(s):** Medicine and Surgery
**Circ:** 1,250

**Ophthalmologica (4752)**
S. Karger Publishers Inc.
26 W Avon Rd.
PO Box 529
Farmington, CT 06085
Phone: (860)675-7834
Fax: (860)675-7302
**Subject(s):** German; Ophthalmology, Optometry, and Optics; French
**Circ:** 1,250

**The Psychoanalytic Review (22274)**
Guilford Publications
72 Spring St.
New York, NY 10012
Phone: (212)431-9800
Fax: (212)966-6708
**Subject(s):** Psychology and Psychiatry
**Circ:** 1,250

**British Journal of Political Science (21428)**
Cambridge University Press
40 W. 20th St.
New York, NY 10011-4211
Phone: (212)924-3900
Fax: (212)691-3239
**Subject(s):** Political Science
**Circ:** (Non-paid)‡88
(Paid)‡1,231

**AGS Quarterly (13808)**
Association for Gravestone Studies
278 Main St., Ste. 207
Greenfield, MA 01301-3230
Phone: (413)772-0836
**Subject(s):** History and Genealogy
**Circ:** 1,200

**American Go Journal (21306)**
American Go Association
PO Box 397, Old Chelsea Sta.
New York, NY 10113-0397
**Subject(s):** Games and Puzzles; Crafts, Models, Hobbies, and Contests
**Circ:** 1,200

**American Journal of Recreation Therapy (14904)**
Prime National Publishing Corp.
470 Boston Post Rd.
Weston, MA 02493
Phone: (781)899-2702
Fax: (781)899-4900
**Subject(s):** Health and Healthcare
**Circ:** (Paid)‡1,200

**Button (13865)**
PO Box 26
Lunenburg, MA 01462
**Subject(s):** Poetry; Literature and Literary Reviews
**Circ:** (Combined)1,200

**Cells Tissues Organs** (4703)
S. Karger Publishers Inc.
26 W Avon Rd.
PO Box 529
Farmington, CT 06085
Phone: (860)675-7834
Fax: (860)675-7302
**Subject(s):** Medicine and Surgery; Laboratory Research (Scientific and Medical); French; German

Circ: 1,200

**Columbia Journal of Environmental Law** (21514)
Columbia University
Mail Code 3513
New York, NY 10027
Phone: (212)854-1606
Fax: (212)854-7946
**Subject(s):** Law; Ecology and Conservation

Circ: (Paid)‡1,200

**Columbia Law School News** (21517)
Columbia Law School
435 W 116th St.
New York, NY 10027
Phone: (212)854-1601
Fax: (212)854-7946
**Subject(s):** College Publications

Circ: (Controlled)1,200

**The Cord** (22894)
Franciscan Institute
St. Bonaventure University
3261 West State
Saint Bonaventure, NY 14778
Phone: (716)375-2105
Fax: (716)375-2156
**Subject(s):** Religious Publications

Circ: (Non-paid)56
    (Paid)1,200

**Dartmouth College Library Bulletin** (18831)
Dartmouth College Library
Rm. 115 Baker
Hanover, NH 03755
Phone: (603)646-2560
Fax: (603)646-3702
**Subject(s):** Library and Information Science

Circ: (Non-paid)1,200

**Discovery Magazine** (21607)
John Milton Society for the Blind
475 Riverside Dr., Rm. 455
New York, NY 10015
Fax: (212)870-3229
**Subject(s):** Religious Publications; Handicapped

Circ: (Non-paid)1,200

**DNA and Cell Biology** (26923)
Mary Ann Liebert Incorporated Publishers
c/o Mark I. Greene
Dept. of Pathology & Laboratory Medicine
University of Pennsylvania, School of Medicine
Philadelphia, PA 19104-6082
Phone: (215)898-2847
Fax: (215)898-2401
**Subject(s):** Biology

Circ: ‡1,200

**The Hemingway Review** (12552)
University of Idaho Press
c/o Susan F. Beegel
14 Terhune Dr.
Phippsburg, ME 04562
Phone: (207)389-2839
Fax: (207)389-2839
**Subject(s):** Literature

Circ: (Combined)1,200

**International Review of Social History** (21843)
Cambridge University Press
40 W. 20th St.
New York, NY 10011-4211
Phone: (212)924-3900
Fax: (212)691-3239
**Subject(s):** History and Genealogy

Circ: (Non-paid)199
    1,200

**Journal of Andrology** (21877)
American Society of Andrology
1230 York Ave.
New York, NY 10021-6307
Phone: (212)327-8592
Fax: (212)327-8593
**Subject(s):** Biology; Physiology and Anatomy; Laboratory Research (Scientific and Medical); Health and Healthcare

Circ: ‡1,200

**Journal of Armenian Studies** (13456)
National Association for Armenian Studies and Research
395 Concord Ave.
Belmont, MA 02478
Phone: (617)489-1610
Fax: (617)484-1759
**Subject(s):** Intercultural Interests

Circ: 1,200

**Journal of Environmental Systems** (22982)
Baywood Publishing Company Inc.
Department of Technology and Society and Waste Management In
State University of New York at Stony Brook
Stony Brook, NY 11794-2250
**Subject(s):** Ecology and Conservation; Waste Management and Recycling; Water Supply and Sewage Disposal

Circ: (Paid)1,200

**The Journal of Experimental Zoology** (19289)
John Wiley and Sons Inc.
111 River St.
Hoboken, NJ 07030-5774
Phone: (201)748-6000
Fax: (201)748-6088
**Subject(s):** Zoology

Circ: (Paid)1,200

**Journal of Herpetological Medicine and Surgery** (26237)
Association of Reptilian and Amphibian Veterinarians
c/o Wilbur B. Amand
Box 605
Chester Heights, PA 19017
Phone: (610)358-9530
Fax: (610)892-4813
**Subject(s):** Veterinary Medicine

Circ: 1,200

**Journal of Modern Literature** (27061)
Indiana University Press
c/o Editor, Journal of Modern Literature
921 Anderson Hall
Temple University
Philadelphia, PA 19122
**Subject(s):** Literature

Circ: 1,200

**Motor Coach Age** (19655)
Motor Bus Society
PO Box 251
Paramus, NJ 07653-0251
**Subject(s):** Clubs and Societies; Automotive (Consumer)

Circ: 1,200

**Nassau Review** (20812)
Nassau Community College, State University of New York
1 Education Dr.
Garden City, NY 11530
Phone: (516)572-7792
**Subject(s):** Literature; Poetry

Circ: (Non-paid)1,200

**New Jersey Reporter** (19893)
Public Policy Center of New Jersey
36 W. Lafayette St.
Trenton, NJ 08608
Phone: (609)392-2003
Fax: (609)392-6754
**Subject(s):** State, Municipal, and County Administration

Circ: (Controlled)‡600
    (Paid)‡1,200

**North American Shortwave Association (NASWA)—The Journal** (26640)
North American Shortwave Association (NASWA)
45 Wildflower Rd.
Levittown, PA 19057
**Subject(s):** Communications; Radio, Television, Cable, and Video

Circ: (Paid)1,200

**Obesity Research** (13567)
North American Association for the Study of Obesity
Boston Medical Center, Ste.847
650 Albany St.
Boston, MA 02118
Phone: (617)638-7107
Fax: (617)638-6630

**Subject(s):** Medicine and Surgery; Health and Healthcare; Laboratory Research (Scientific and Medical)

Circ: (Paid)1,200

**Proceedings of the American Philosophical Society** (27243)
American Philosophical Society
104 S 5th St.
Philadelphia, PA 19106-3386
Phone: (215)440-3400
Fax: (215)440-3436
**Subject(s):** Humanities; Indexes, Abstracts, Reports, Proceedings, and Bibliographies; History and Genealogy; Science (General)

Circ: (Paid)‡650
    (Non-paid)‡1,200

**Publius: The Journal of Federalism** (26302)
002 Kirby Hall of Civil Rights
Lafayette College
Easton, PA 18042-1785
Phone: (610)330-5808
Fax: (610)330-5648
**Subject(s):** Congressional and Federal Government Affairs; Politics

Circ: (Non-paid)‡100
    (Paid)‡1,200

**Radical History Review** (22287)
Duke University Press
Tamiment Library
New York University
70 Washington Sq. S., 10th Fl.
New York, NY 10012
Phone: (212)998-2632
**Subject(s):** History and Genealogy

Circ: (Paid)1,200

**Religious Studies** (22303)
Cambridge University Press
40 W. 20th St.
New York, NY 10011-4211
Phone: (212)924-3900
Fax: (212)691-3239
**Subject(s):** Religious Publications

Circ: 1,200

**Respiration** (4761)
S. Karger Publishers Inc.
26 W Avon Rd.
PO Box 529
Farmington, CT 06085
Phone: (860)675-7834
Fax: (860)675-7302
**Subject(s):** French; German; Medicine and Surgery

Circ: 1,200

**RILM Abstracts of Music Literature** (22319)
RILM Abstracts
365 5th Ave.
New York, NY 10016
Phone: (212)817-1990
Fax: (212)817-1569
**Subject(s):** Music and Musical Instruments; Indexes, Abstracts, Reports, Proceedings, and Bibliographies

Circ: ‡1,200

**Synthetic Communications** (22691)
Marcel Dekker Inc.
c/o Michael Kolb, Vice President, Chemical Development
Wyeth Research
401 N. Middletown Rd.
Pearl River, NY 10965
**Subject(s):** Chemistry, Chemicals, and Chemical Engineering

Circ: 1,200

**Techniques in Hand and Upper Extremity Surgery** (27281)
Lippincott Williams & Wilkins
C/o Zebulon Spector, Developmental Editor
Lippincott Williams & Wilkins
530 Walnut St.
Philadelphia, PA 19106
**Subject(s):** Medicine and Surgery

Circ: 1,205

**Journal of Elder Abuse and Neglect** (21915)
The Haworth Press Inc.
New York University
246 Green St., 8th Fl.
New York, NY 10003-6677
Phone: (212)998-5303
**Subject(s):** Gerontology; Sociology

Circ: 1,193

**Cognitive and Behavioral Neurology** (26887)
Lippincott Williams & Wilkins
c/o Murray Grossman, M.D., Editor-in-Chief
Univ. of Pennsylvania School of Medicine
Philadelphia, PA 19104
**Subject(s):** Laboratory Research (Scientific and Medical)

**Circ:** 420
1181

**Physical and Occupational Therapy in Pediatrics** (27233)
The Haworth Press Inc.
c/o Robert J Palisano PT, Drexel Univ.
Mailstop 502
245 N 15th St.
Philadelphia, PA 19102-1192
Phone: (215)762-1006
**Subject(s):** Pediatrics; Health and Healthcare

**Circ:** (Controlled)‡1,178

**The American Journal of Bioethics (AJOB)** (20207)
The MIT Press
The American Journal of Bioethics
Albany Medical Center
47 New Scotland Avenue MC-47
Albany, NY 12208
**Subject(s):** Biology; Medicine and Surgery

**Circ:** 1,150

**Biology of the Neonate** (4699)
S. Karger Publishers Inc.
26 W Avon Rd.
PO Box 529
Farmington, CT 06085
Phone: (860)675-7834
Fax: (860)675-7302
**Subject(s):** Medicine and Surgery

**Circ:** 1,150

**Modern Asian Studies** (22092)
Cambridge University Press
40 W. 20th St.
New York, NY 10011-4211
Phone: (212)924-3900
Fax: (212)691-3239
**Subject(s):** Intercultural Interests; Sociology; History and Genealogy; Literature

**Circ:** 1,150

**Pediatric Neurosurgery** (4757)
S. Karger Publishers Inc.
26 W Avon Rd.
PO Box 529
Farmington, CT 06085
Phone: (860)675-7834
Fax: (860)675-7302
**Subject(s):** Pediatrics; Medicine and Surgery

**Circ:** 1,150

**Pharmacology** (4758)
S. Karger Publishers Inc.
26 W Avon Rd.
PO Box 529
Farmington, CT 06085
Phone: (860)675-7834
Fax: (860)675-7302
**Subject(s):** Drugs and Pharmaceuticals

**Circ:** 1,150

**Phonetica** (13420)
S. Karger Publishers Inc.
C/O Prof. John C. Kingston
Linguistics Department
S. College 226
University of Massachusetts
Amherst, MA 01003
**Subject(s):** Medicine and Surgery; French; German

**Circ:** 1,150

**Clinical Techniques in Small Animal Practice** (26877)
Elsevier
1600 John F. Kennedy Blvd.
Philadelphia, PA 19103
Phone: (215)239-3900
Fax: (215)239-3990
**Subject(s):** Veterinary Medicine

**Circ:** ‡1,144

**Afn Shvel** (21277)
League for Yiddish Inc.
200 W 72nd St., Ste. 40
New York, NY 10023
Phone: (212)787-6675
**Subject(s):** Yiddish; Jewish Publications

**Circ:** (Non-paid)100
(Paid)‡1,100

**Ageing and Society** (21282)
Cambridge University Press
40 W. 20th St.
New York, NY 10011-4211
Phone: (212)924-3900
Fax: (212)691-3239
**Subject(s):** Gerontology

**Circ:** (Non-paid)‡102
(Paid)‡1,100

**The Arrow** (22805)
Pierce-Arrow Society
135 Edgerton St.
Rochester, NY 14607-2945
Phone: (585)244-1664
**Subject(s):** Automotive (Consumer)

**Circ:** (Non-paid)‡50
‡1,100

**Criminal Justice and Behavior** (30869)
Sage Publications Inc.
c/o Curt R. Bartol, Ph.D., Editor
Dept. of Psychology
Castleton State College
Castleton, VT 05735
Phone: (802)468-1281
Fax: (802)468-1480
**Subject(s):** Psychology and Psychiatry; Police, Penology, and Penal Institutions

**Circ:** (Paid)‡1,100

**Economics and Philosophy** (21631)
Cambridge University Press
40 W. 20th St.
New York, NY 10011-4211
Phone: (212)924-3900
Fax: (212)691-3239
**Subject(s):** Economics; Philosophy

**Circ:** 1,100

**Fetal Diagnosis and Therapy** (4722)
S. Karger Publishers Inc.
26 W Avon Rd.
PO Box 529
Farmington, CT 06085
Phone: (860)675-7834
Fax: (860)675-7302
**Subject(s):** Medicine and Surgery

**Circ:** 1,100

**Folia Phoniatrica et Logopaedica** (4723)
S. Karger Publishers Inc.
26 W Avon Rd.
PO Box 529
Farmington, CT 06085
Phone: (860)675-7834
Fax: (860)675-7302
**Subject(s):** Medicine and Surgery; French; German

**Circ:** 1,100

**Harvard Journal of Asiatic Studies** (13671)
Harvard-Yenching Institute
2 Divinity Ave.
Cambridge, MA 02138
Phone: (617)495-2758
Fax: (617)495-7798
**Subject(s):** History and Genealogy; Literature

**Circ:** (Paid)1,100

**Healing Ministry** (14905)
Prime National Publishing Corp.
470 Boston Post Rd.
Weston, MA 02493
Phone: (781)899-2702
Fax: (781)899-4900
**Subject(s):** Medicine and Surgery; Health and Healthcare; Religious Publications

**Circ:** 1,100

**IRB** (20816)
The Hastings Center
21 Malcolm Gordon Rd.
Garrison, NY 10524
Phone: (845)424-4040
Fax: (845)424-4545
**Subject(s):** Laboratory Research (Scientific and Medical); Medicine and Surgery

**Circ:** (Paid)1,100

**Journal of Industrial Ecology** (4893)
The MIT Press
c/o Reid Lifset
School of Forestry & Environmental Studies
Yale University
205 Prospect St.
New Haven, CT 06511-2106
Phone: (203)432-6949
Fax: (203)432-5912
**Subject(s):** Ecology and Conservation

**Circ:** (Combined)1,100

**The Long Story** (13850)
18 Eaton St.
Lawrence, MA 01843-1110
Phone: (978)686-7638
**Subject(s):** Literature and Literary Reviews; Poetry

**Circ:** (Combined)1,100

**Minnesota Review** (27372)
Carnegie Mellon University
Baker Hall 259
5000 Forbes Ave.
Pittsburgh, PA 15213
Phone: (412)268-1977
Fax: (412)268-7989
**Subject(s):** Literature

**Circ:** (Combined)1,100

**Present Truth and Herald of Christ's Epiphany** (26239)
Laymen's Home Missionary Movement
1156 St. Matthews Rd.
Chester Springs, PA 19425-2700
Phone: (610)827-7665
**Subject(s):** French; Danish; Polish; Religious Publications; German; Norwegian

**Circ:** (Paid)‡1,100

**Proceedings of the American Mathematical Society** (27911)
American Mathematical Society
201 Charles St.
Providence, RI 02904-2294
Phone: (401)455-4000
Fax: (401)331-3842
**Subject(s):** Mathematics

**Circ:** (Paid)1,100

**Transition** (13715)
Duke University Press
69 Dunster St.
Cambridge, MA 02138
Phone: (617)496-2845
Fax: (617)496-2877
**Subject(s):** Intercultural Interests

**Circ:** (Non-paid)200
(Paid)1,100

**WIN News** (13857)
Women's International Network
187 Grant St.
Lexington, MA 02420-2126
Phone: (781)862-9431
Fax: (781)862-1734
**Subject(s):** Women's Interests

**Circ:** ‡1,100

**Yale Journal of Law and Feminism** (4905)
PO Box 208215
New Haven, CT 06520-8215
Phone: (203)432-4056
Fax: (203)432-2592
**Subject(s):** Women's Interests; Law; Social and Political Issues

**Circ:** (Paid)1,100

**Journal of Progressive Human Services** (12472)
The Haworth Press Inc.
School of Social Work
University of New England
11 Hills Beach Road
Biddeford, ME 04005
Phone: (207)283-0170
Fax: (617)353-5612
**Subject(s):** Social Sciences

**Circ:** (Controlled)‡1,099

**Journal of Experimental and Theoretical Physics (JETP)** (21162)
American Institute of Physics
2 Huntington Quadrangle, Ste. 1NO1
Melville, NY 11747-4502
Phone: (516)576-2200
Fax: (516)349-7669

**Subject(s):** Physics
**Circ:** ‡1,080

**American Antiquarian Society Proceedings (14930)**
American Antiquarian Society
185 Salisbury St.
Worcester, MA 01609-1634
Phone: (508)755-5221
Fax: (508)753-3311
**Subject(s):** History and Genealogy
**Circ:** 1,070

**Securities Regulation Law Journal (22360)**
Warren, Gorham & Lamont R.I.A. Group
395 Hudson St., 4th Fl.
New York, NY 10014-3669
Phone: (212)367-6300
Fax: (212)367-6305
**Subject(s):** Banking, Finance, and Investments; Law
**Circ:** (Non-paid)107
     (Paid)1,074

**Social Work with Groups (22388)**
The Haworth Press Inc.
c/o Roselle Kurland, Hunter College
School of Social Work
129 E. 79th St.
New York, NY 10021
Phone: (212)452-7101
**Subject(s):** Psychology and Psychiatry; Sociology; Social Programs
**Circ:** 1,063

**Cerebrovascular Diseases (4705)**
S. Karger Publishers Inc.
26 W Avon Rd.
PO Box 529
Farmington, CT 06085
Phone: (860)675-7834
Fax: (860)675-7302
**Subject(s):** Medicine and Surgery
**Circ:** ‡1,050

**Dementia and Geriatric Cognitive Disorders (4711)**
S. Karger Publishers Inc.
26 W Avon Rd.
PO Box 529
Farmington, CT 06085
Phone: (860)675-7834
Fax: (860)675-7302
**Subject(s):** Medicine and Surgery
**Circ:** ‡1,050

**European Neurology (4719)**
S. Karger Publishers Inc.
26 W Avon Rd.
PO Box 529
Farmington, CT 06085
Phone: (860)675-7834
Fax: (860)675-7302
**Subject(s):** Medicine and Surgery
**Circ:** 1,050

**Italian Quarterly (19592)**
Rutgers University
84 College Ave.
New Brunswick, NJ 08901-8542
Phone: (732)932-7536
Fax: (732)932-1686
**Subject(s):** Literature; Intercultural Interests
**Circ:** (Paid)1,050

**The Journal of Mind and Behavior (12550)**
Institute of Mind and Behavior
University of Maine
Dept. of Psychology, Rm. 301
5742 Little Hall
Orono, ME 04469-5742
Phone: (207)581-2057
**Subject(s):** Psychology and Psychiatry; Philosophy
**Circ:** (Paid)‡1,058

**Pathobiology (4756)**
S. Karger Publishers Inc.
26 W Avon Rd.
PO Box 529
Farmington, CT 06085
Phone: (860)675-7834
Fax: (860)675-7302
**Subject(s):** Medicine and Surgery; Biology
**Circ:** 1,050

**Stereotactic and Functional Neurosurgery (18855)**
S. Karger Publishers Inc.
C/o David W. Roberts
Section of Neurosurgery
Dartmouth Medical Center
1 Medical Center Dr.
Lebanon, NH 03756-0001
**Subject(s):** Medicine and Surgery
**Circ:** 1,050

**American Baptist Quarterly (27619)**
American Baptist Historical Society
PO Box 851
Valley Forge, PA 19482-0851
Phone: (610)768-2269
Fax: (610)768-2266
**Subject(s):** Religious Publications
**Circ:** (Non-paid)‡56
     (Paid)‡1,030

**New Directions for Institutional Research (27611)**
Jossey-Bass Publishers
c/o J. Fredericks Volkwein, Editor-in-Chief
Center for the Study of Higher Education
Penn State Univ.
403 South Allen St., Suite 104
University Park, PA 16801-5254
**Subject(s):** Education
**Circ:** (Non-paid)70
     (Paid)1,033

**Topics in Clinical Chiropractic Series (22462)**
Aspen Publishers Inc.
1185 Ave. of the Americas
New York, NY 10036
Phone: (301)644-3599
Fax: (212)597-0331
**Subject(s):** Medicine and Surgery; Health and Healthcare
**Circ:** 1,037

**Journal of Ambulatory Care Management (JACM) (21872)**
Aspen Publishers Inc.
1185 Ave. of the Americas
New York, NY 10036
Phone: (301)644-3599
Fax: (212)597-0331
**Subject(s):** Hospitals and Healthcare Institutions; Management and Administration
**Circ:** (Non-paid)123
     (Paid)1,028

**Survey of Anesthesiology (23102)**
Lippincott Williams & Wilkins
C/o Kathryn E. McGoldrick, MD, Editor-in-Chief
New York Medical College
Department of Anesthesiology, Westchester Medical Center
Macy Pavilion W., Rm. 2389
Valhalla, NY 10595
**Subject(s):** Medicine and Surgery
**Circ:** (Non-paid)‡142
     (Paid)‡1,024

**Current Opinion in Ophthalmology (26909)**
Lippincott Williams & Wilkins
530 Walnut St.
Philadelphia, PA 19106-3261
Phone: (215)521-8300
Fax: (215)521-8902
**Subject(s):** Medicine and Surgery; Ophthalmology, Optometry, and Optics
**Circ:** (Paid)‡1,011

**Journal of Gay and Lesbian Psychotherapy (27038)**
The Haworth Press Inc.
4514 Chester Ave.
Philadelphia, PA 19143-3707
Phone: (215)222-2800
Fax: (215)222-3881
**Subject(s):** Psychology and Psychiatry
**Circ:** 1,018

**Seminars in Cutaneous Medicine and Surgery (27257)**
Elsevier
1600 John F. Kennedy Blvd.
Philadelphia, PA 19103
Phone: (215)239-3900
Fax: (215)239-3990
**Subject(s):** Medicine and Surgery
**Circ:** 1,019

**The Allegheny Review (26679)**
Thomson-Shore Inc.
PO Box 32
Allegheny College
Meadville, PA 16335
Phone: (814)332-6553
**Subject(s):** College Publications
**Circ:** (Paid)1,000

**American Journal of Mathematical and Management Sciences (22994)**
American Sciences Press Inc.
20 Cross Rd.
Syracuse, NY 13224-2104
Phone: (315)446-1843
**Subject(s):** Mathematics; Computers; Management and Administration
**Circ:** ‡1,000

**American Journal of Potato Research (12548)**
Potato Association of America
Univ. of Maine
5715 Coburn Hall, Rm. 6
Orono, ME 04469-5715
Phone: (207)581-3042
Fax: (207)581-3015
**Subject(s):** Scientific Agricultural Publications; Spanish
**Circ:** ‡1,000

**Applied Mechanics Reviews (19082)**
American Society of Mechanical Engineers
22 Law Dr.
PO Box 2300
Fairfield, NJ 07007-2300
Phone: (973)882-6381
Fax: (973)882-6381
**Subject(s):** Engineering (Various branches); Science
**Circ:** ‡1,000

**Applied Psycholinguistics (21350)**
Cambridge University Press
40 W. 20th St.
New York, NY 10011-4211
Phone: (212)924-3900
Fax: (212)691-3239
**Subject(s):** Psychology and Psychiatry; Philology, Language, and Linguistics
**Circ:** 1,000

**Automotive History Review (4770)**
Society of Automotive Historians
1102 Long Cove Rd.
Gales Ferry, CT 06335-1812
Phone: (860)464-6466
Fax: (860)464-2614
**Subject(s):** Automotive (Trade); Automotive (Consumer)
**Circ:** 1,000

**Bank Accounting & Finance (13743)**
Aspen Publishers Inc.
129 Everett St.
Concord, MA 01742
Phone: (978)369-6285
Fax: (978)371-2961
**Subject(s):** Banking, Finance, and Investments
**Circ:** (Paid)1,000

**Birth Psychology Bulletin (21410)**
Association for Birth Psychology
444 E 82nd St.
New York, NY 10028
Phone: (212)988-6617
**Subject(s):** Psychology and Psychiatry
**Circ:** 1,000

**Brain, Behavior and Evolution (4701)**
S. Karger Publishers Inc.
26 W Avon Rd.
PO Box 529
Farmington, CT 06085
Phone: (860)675-7834
Fax: (860)675-7302
**Subject(s):** Medicine and Surgery; Biology; Psychology and Psychiatry
**Circ:** 1,000

**Care Management Journals (21457)**
Springer Publishing Co.
Department of Community Medicine
St. Vincent's Hospital - Manhattan
41-51 E. 11th St.
New York, NY 10003
Phone: (212)604-3026
Fax: (212)604-7627

**Subject(s):** Health and Healthcare

**Circ:** (Non-paid)66
(Paid)1000

**Community Genetics** (4708)
S. Karger Publishers Inc.
26 W Avon Rd.
PO Box 529
Farmington, CT 06085
Phone: (860)675-7834
Fax: (860)675-7302
**Subject(s):** Medicine and Surgery; Health and Healthcare

**Circ:** (Combined)1,000

**Comparative Literature Studies** (27600)
Penn State University Press
311 Burrowes Bldg.
Penn State University
University Park, PA 16802
Phone: (814)863-1336
**Subject(s):** Literature

**Circ:** 1,000

**Contemporary Gerontology** (21547)
Springer Publishing Co.
11 W. 42nd St. 15th Fl.
New York, NY 10036
Phone: (212)431-4370
Fax: (212)941-7842
**Subject(s):** Gerontology

**Circ:** (Controlled)1,000

**The Duplex Planet** (22906)
Box 1230
Saratoga Springs, NY 12866
Phone: (518)692-7410
**Subject(s):** Senior Citizens' Interests

**Circ:** (Paid)‡1,000

**Earth's Daughters** (20568)
Box 41, Central Park Sta.
Buffalo, NY 14215
**Subject(s):** Women's Interests; Poetry; Social and Political Issues

**Circ:** (Paid)1,000

**Econometric Theory** (4885)
Cambridge University Press
c/o Peter C. B. Phillips
Cowles Foundation for Research in Economics
Yale University
PO Box 208281
New Haven, CT 06520-8281
**Subject(s):** Economics

**Circ:** 1000

**European Addiction Research** (4718)
S. Karger Publishers Inc.
26 W Avon Rd.
PO Box 529
Farmington, CT 06085
Phone: (860)675-7834
Fax: (860)675-7302
**Subject(s):** Medicine and Surgery

**Circ:** (Combined)1,000

**Fatal Occupational Injuries in Maine** (12445)
Department of Labor
45 State House Sta.
Augusta, ME 04333-0045
Phone: (207)624-6440
Fax: (207)624-6449
**Subject(s):** Safety; Health and Healthcare

**Circ:** (Non-paid)1,000

**Frogpond** (21234)
The Haiku Society of America
PO Box 122
Nassau, NY 12123
Phone: (518)766-2039
**Subject(s):** Literature and Literary Reviews; Poetry

**Circ:** 1,000

**HealthQuest** (26229)
Contact Information
200 Highpoint Dr., Ste. 215
Chalfont, PA 18914
Phone: (215)822-7935
Fax: (215)997-9582
**Subject(s):** Black Publications; Health; Ethnic Publications

**Circ:** (Paid)1,000

**Historical Journal of Massachusetts** (14895)
Westfield State College
P.O. Box 1630
Westfield, MA 01086
Phone: (413)572-5344
Fax: (413)562-3613
**Subject(s):** History and Genealogy; Local, State, and Regional Publications

**Circ:** (Paid)1000

**Hitchcock Annual** (4690)
Sacred Heart University
5151 Park Ave.
Fairfield, CT 06825
Phone: (203)371-7755
**Subject(s):** Motion Pictures

**Circ:** (Combined)1,000

**Human Heredity** (4731)
S. Karger Publishers Inc.
26 W Avon Rd.
PO Box 529
Farmington, CT 06085
Phone: (860)675-7834
Fax: (860)675-7302
**Subject(s):** Medicine and Surgery; Genetics

**Circ:** 1,000

**Inti** (27837)
Onti Publications
Box 20657
Cranston, RI 02920
Phone: (401)865-2690
Fax: (401)865-1112
**Subject(s):** Ethnic and Minority Studies; Literature; Spanish

**Circ:** (Controlled)1,000

**Journal of Accounting, Auditing & Finance** (21866)
Greenwood Publishing Group Inc.
New York University Stern
Henry Kaufman Management Center
44 W. 4th St.
40 West 4th St.
New York, NY 10012
Phone: (212)998-0100
Fax: (212)995-4230
**Subject(s):** Accountants and Accounting

**Circ:** (Paid)1,000

**Journal of the American Apitherapy Society** (22917)
American Apitherapy Society
1209 Post Rd.
Scarsdale, NY 10583-2023
Fax: (914)723-0920
**Subject(s):** Medicine and Surgery; Health and Healthcare

**Circ:** 1,000

**Journal of Black Studies** (27014)
Sage Publications Inc.
c/o Molefi K. Asante, Dept. of African American Studies
Temple Univ.
Gladfelter Hall
Philadelphia, PA 19122
**Subject(s):** Sociology; Black Publications

**Circ:** (Paid)‡1,000

**Journal of Catholic Legal Studies** (22766)
St. Thomas More Institute for Legal Research
St. John's University, School of Law
8000 Utopia Pkwy.
Queens, NY 11439
Phone: (718)990-6655
Fax: (718)990-6649
**Subject(s):** Religious Publications; Law

**Circ:** 1,000

**Journal of Child-Care Administration** (20905)
202 Cirrus Rd.
Holbrook, NY 11741-4407
Phone: (631)472-8009
**Subject(s):** Education; Children's Interests

**Circ:** (Paid)1,000

**Journal of Electrocardiology** (27027)
Elsevier
1600 John F. Kennedy Blvd.
Philadelphia, PA 19103
Phone: (215)239-3900
Fax: (215)239-3990
**Subject(s):** Medicine and Surgery

**Circ:** (Paid)‡1,000

**Journal of Molecular Evolution** (21958)
Springer-Verlag New York Inc.
233 Spring St.
New York, NY 10013
Phone: (212)460-1500
Fax: (212)460-1575
**Subject(s):** Biology

**Circ:** (Combined)1,000

**Journal of Pediatric Orthopaedics, Part B.** (27080)
Lippincott Williams & Wilkins
530 Walnut St.
Philadelphia, PA 19106-3261
Phone: (215)521-8300
Fax: (215)521-8902
**Subject(s):** Medicine and Surgery; Health and Healthcare

**Circ:** (Paid)1,000

**Journal of Terminal Oncology** (14907)
Prime National Publishing Corp.
470 Boston Post Rd.
Weston, MA 02493
Phone: (781)899-2702
Fax: (781)899-4900
**Subject(s):** Medicine and Surgery

**Circ:** (Paid)‡1,000

**Matchbox USA** (4679)
Matchbox U.S.A.
62 Saw Mill Rd.
Durham, CT 06422
Phone: (860)349-1655
Fax: (860)349-1240
**Subject(s):** Collecting; Crafts, Models, Hobbies, and Contests

**Circ:** 1,000

**Mathematics of Computation** (27907)
American Mathematical Society
201 Charles St.
Providence, RI 02904-2294
Phone: (401)455-4000
Fax: (401)331-3842
**Subject(s):** Mathematics

**Circ:** (Paid)1,000

**Media Market Guide** (18862)
SQAD
PO Box 442
Littleton, NH 03561-0442
Phone: (603)869-2418
Fax: (603)869-3135
**Subject(s):** Advertising and Marketing; Radio, Television, Cable, and Video

**Circ:** (Controlled)‡100
(Paid)‡1,000

**Medical Problems of Performing Artists** (26752)
Science & Medicine Inc.
PO Box 313
Narberth, PA 19072
Phone: (610)660-8097
Fax: (610)660-0348
**Subject(s):** Medicine and Surgery

**Circ:** (Paid)‡1,000

**Metabolic Pediatric and Systems Ophthalmology** (22075)
International Society on Metabolic Eye Disease
1125 Park Ave.
New York, NY 10128
Phone: (212)427-1246
Fax: (212)360-7009
**Subject(s):** Ophthalmology, Optometry, and Optics; Pediatrics

**Circ:** ‡1,000

**The Muslim World** (4809)
Blackwell Publishers
Hartford Seminary
77 Sherman St.
Hartford, CT 06105
**Subject(s):** Religious Publications

**Circ:** ‡1,000

**Neuropsychobiology** (4747)
S. Karger Publishers Inc.
26 W Avon Rd.
PO Box 529
Farmington, CT 06085
Phone: (860)675-7834
Fax: (860)675-7302
**Subject(s):** Medicine and Surgery

**Circ:** 1,000

**Oto-Rhino-Laryngologia Nova** (4754)
S. Karger Publishers Inc.
26 W Avon Rd.
PO Box 529
Farmington, CT 06085
Phone: (860)675-7834
Fax: (860)675-7302
**Subject(s):** Medicine and Surgery; French; German
**Circ:** ‡1,000

**Pain Digest** (22207)
Springer-Verlag New York Inc.
233 Spring St.
New York, NY 10013
Phone: (212)460-1500
Fax: (212)460-1575
**Subject(s):** Health and Healthcare; Medicine and Surgery
**Circ:** (Combined)1,000

**Pennsylvania History** (27552)
Pennsylvania Historical Association
108 Weaver Bldg.
Penn State University, PA 16802
Phone: (814)238-4053
Fax: (814)863-7840
**Subject(s):** History and Genealogy
**Circ:** ‡1,000

**Philosophy and Rhetoric** (27613)
Penn State University Press
820 N University Dr.
USB-1 Ste. C
University Park, PA 16802
Phone: (814)865-1327
Fax: (814)863-1408
**Subject(s):** Philosophy
**Circ:** ‡1,000

**POLITY: The Journal of the Northeastern Political Science Association** (13421)
Palgrave Macmillan
426 Thomson Hall
Box 7520
University of Massachusetts
200 Hicks Way
Amherst, MA 01003
**Subject(s):** Politics
**Circ:** (Non-paid)‡100
(Paid)‡1,000

**Presence** (13699)
The MIT Press
Massachusetts Institute of Technology
77 Massachusetts Ave., Rm. 36-709
Cambridge, MA 02139
Phone: (617)253-2534
Fax: (617)258-7003
**Subject(s):** Telecommunications; Computers
**Circ:** (Paid)1000

**Psychoanalysis and Contemporary Thought** (4786)
International Universities Press Inc.
PO Box 389
Guilford, CT 06437
Phone: (203)245-4000
Fax: (203)245-0775
**Subject(s):** Psychology and Psychiatry
**Circ:** 1,000

**Psychotherapy and Psychosomatics** (4760)
S. Karger Publishers Inc.
26 W Avon Rd.
PO Box 529
Farmington, CT 06085
Phone: (860)675-7834
Fax: (860)675-7302
**Subject(s):** Psychology and Psychiatry; Medicine and Surgery
**Circ:** 1,000

**Public Culture** (22278)
Duke University Press
New School University
80 Fifth Ave., Rm. 507
New York, NY 10011
Phone: (212)229-5376
Fax: (212)229-5929
**Subject(s):** Anthropology and Ethnology; Social Sciences
**Circ:** (Combined)1000

**The Quarterly** (20618)
St. Lawrence County Historical Association
3 E Main St.
PO Box 8
Canton, NY 13617-0008
Phone: (315)386-8133
Fax: (315)386-8134
**Subject(s):** History and Genealogy
**Circ:** (Non-paid)75
(Paid)1,000

**Quarterly Journal of Austrian Economics** (22285)
Transaction Publishers
Lubin School of Business
Pace Univ.
1 Pace Plaza
New York, NY 10038
Phone: (212)346-1573
Fax: (212)346-1573
**Subject(s):** Economics
**Circ:** (Combined)1,000

**RCDA** (22289)
Research Center for Religion and Human Rights in Closed Societies Ltd.
475 Riverside Dr., Ste. 1948
New York, NY 10115
Phone: (212)870-2481
Fax: (212)663-6771
**Subject(s):** Religious Publications
**Circ:** (Non-paid)‡500
(Paid)‡1,000

**The Review of Black Political Economy** (19814)
Transaction Publishers
390 Campus Dr.
Somerset, NJ 08873
Phone: (732)445-1245
Fax: (732)748-9801
**Subject(s):** Black Publications; Economics; Ethnic and Minority Studies
**Circ:** (Paid)‡1,000

**Rochester History** (22841)
Office of the City Historian
115 S Ave.
Rochester, NY 14604-1896
Phone: (585)428-8095
Fax: (585)428-8098
**Subject(s):** History and Genealogy
**Circ:** (Paid)1,000

**Seneca Review** (20824)
Hobart and William Smith Colleges
Geneva, NY 14456
Phone: (315)781-3392
Fax: (315)781-3348
**Subject(s):** Literature; Poetry
**Circ:** (Combined)1000

**Shakespeare Studies** (19047)
Associated University Presses
2010 Eastpark Blvd.
Cranbury, NJ 08512
Phone: (609)655-4770
Fax: (609)655-8366
**Subject(s):** Literature
**Circ:** (Paid)1,000

**Skin Pharmacology and Physiology** (4762)
S. Karger Publishers Inc.
26 W Avon Rd.
PO Box 529
Farmington, CT 06085
Phone: (860)675-7834
Fax: (860)675-7302
**Subject(s):** Medicine and Surgery
**Circ:** 1,000

**Spinning Jenny** (22404)
Black Dress Press
PO Box 1373
New York, NY 10276
Phone: (212)504-8222
Fax: (212)504-8222
**Subject(s):** Literature and Literary Reviews; Poetry
**Circ:** (Paid)1,000

**Talisman** (19433)
Talisman House Publishers
PO Box 3157
Jersey City, NJ 07303-3157
Phone: (201)938-0698
Fax: (201)938-1693
**Subject(s):** Poetry; Literature
**Circ:** (Paid)1000

**Taproot Literary Review** (26119)
Taproot Press Publishing Co.
451 Duss Ave.
PO Box 204
Ambridge, PA 15003
Phone: (724)266-8476
**Subject(s):** Literature; Poetry
**Circ:** (Controlled)1,000

**Thoughts for All Seasons** (13447)
Valley Press
86 Leland Rd
Becket, MA 01223
Phone: (413)623-0174
**Subject(s):** Literature and Literary Reviews; Poetry
**Circ:** (Non-paid)1,000

**Transactions of the American Mathematical Society** (27925)
American Mathematical Society
201 Charles St.
Providence, RI 02904-2294
Phone: (401)455-4000
Fax: (401)331-3842
**Subject(s):** Mathematics
**Circ:** (Paid)1,000

**TumorBiology** (4764)
S. Karger Publishers Inc.
26 W Avon Rd.
PO Box 529
Farmington, CT 06085
Phone: (860)675-7834
Fax: (860)675-7302
**Subject(s):** Medicine and Surgery; Biology
**Circ:** 1,000

**Women Studies Abstracts** (19820)
Transaction Publishers
390 Campus Dr.
Somerset, NJ 08873
Phone: (732)445-1245
Fax: (732)748-9801
**Subject(s):** Indexes, Abstracts, Reports, Proceedings, and Bibliographies; Women's Interests
**Circ:** (Paid)‡1,000

**Journal of Gerontological Social Work** (21931)
The Haworth Press Inc.
Brookdale Center on Aging
425 E 25th St., 13th Fl.
New York, NY 10010-2547
Phone: (212)481-4879
**Subject(s):** Gerontology; Sociology
**Circ:** 998

**Proof Texts** (14865)
Johns Hopkins University Press
NEJS Department
Brandeis University
Waltham, MA 02453
Phone: (617)736-2960
Fax: (617)736-2070
**Subject(s):** Sociology
**Circ:** ‡960

**The Reference Librarian** (20231)
The Haworth Press Inc.
c/o Bill Katz PhD
855 Mercer St.
Albany, NY 12208
Phone: (518)442-5118
**Subject(s):** Library and Information Science
**Circ:** (Paid)964

**Blood Purification** (4700)
S. Karger Publishers Inc.
26 W Avon Rd.
PO Box 529
Farmington, CT 06085
Phone: (860)675-7834
Fax: (860)675-7302
**Subject(s):** Medicine and Surgery
**Circ:** 950

**Comparative Economic Studies** (19587)
Rutgers University
New Brunswick, NJ 08901-1248
**Subject(s):** Economics
**Circ:** ‡950

# Northeastern States

**European Journal of Sociology** (21668)
Cambridge University Press
40 W. 20th St.
New York, NY 10011-4211
Phone: (212)924-3900
Fax: (212)691-3239
**Subject(s):** Sociology
**Circ:** 950

**Gynecologic and Obstetric Investigation** (4727)
S. Karger Publishers Inc.
26 W Avon Rd.
PO Box 529
Farmington, CT 06085
Phone: (860)675-7834
Fax: (860)675-7302
**Subject(s):** Medicine and Surgery
**Circ:** 950

**RSO Magazine** (4827)
RSA Publications
19 Pendelton Dr.
PO Box 107
Hebron, CT 06248
Phone: (860)228-0487
Fax: (860)228-4402
**Subject(s):** Nuclear Engineering; Health and Healthcare
**Circ:** (Paid)950

**Seminars in Colon and Rectal Surgery** (13643)
Elsevier
C/o David J. Schoetz, Jr., Associate Editor
The Lahey Clinic
41 Mall Rd.
Burlington, MA 01805
**Subject(s):** Medicine and Surgery
**Circ:** ‡947

**American Journal of Clinical Oncology** (13470)
Lippincott Williams & Wilkins
c/o David E. Wazer, Dept. of Radiation Oncology
Tufts Univ. School of Medicine
750 Washington St.
Boston, MA
**Subject(s):** Laboratory Research (Scientific and Medical)
**Circ:** 713
       (Non-paid)936

**Congregational Library Bulletin** (13502)
Congregational Library
14 Beacon St.
Boston, MA 02108
Phone: (617)523-0470
Fax: (617)523-0491
**Subject(s):** Religious Publications; Library and Information Science
**Circ:** (Paid)925

**the new renaissance** (13437)
Friends of the new renaissance Inc.
26 Heath Rd., No. 11
Arlington, MA 02474-3645
Phone: (781)646-0118
**Subject(s):** Literature; Poetry; Literature and Literary Reviews; Art
**Circ:** (Combined)910

**Historical Footnotes** (5041)
Stonington Historical Society
c/o Betsy Wade
PO Box 288
Stonington, CT 06378
Phone: (860)535-4059
Fax: (860)535-8322
**Subject(s):** History and Genealogy
**Circ:** (Paid)900

**International Labor and Working-Class History** (21838)
Cambridge University Press
c/o Chad Alan Goldberg, Center for Studies of Social Change
New School University, 80 Fifth Ave., Fifth Fl.
New York, NY 10011
**Subject(s):** Labor; History and Genealogy
**Circ:** 900

**Minutia** (19916)
Microcar and Minicar Club
PO Box 43137
Upper Montclair, NJ 07043-0137
**Subject(s):** Automotive (Consumer)
**Circ:** 900

**Occupational Therapy in Mental Health** (22190)
The Haworth Press Inc.
New York University
Dept. of Occupational Therapy
Education Bldg.
35 W. 4th St., 11th Flr.
New York, NY 10012-1172
Phone: (212)998-5832
**Subject(s):** Health and Healthcare; Psychology and Psychiatry
**Circ:** 906

**OTJR** (19871)
SLACK Inc.
6900 Grove Rd.
Thorofare, NJ 08086-9447
Phone: (856)848-1000
Fax: (856)848-6091
**Subject(s):** Laboratory Research (Scientific and Medical); Physiology and Anatomy
**Circ:** (Paid)900

**Parasitology** (22212)
Cambridge University Press
40 W. 20th St.
New York, NY 10011-4211
Phone: (212)924-3900
Fax: (212)691-3239
**Subject(s):** Biology
**Circ:** 900

**The Paterson Literary Review** (19671)
Passaic County Community College
One College Blvd.
Paterson, NJ 07505-1179
Phone: (973)684-6555
Fax: (973)523-5843
**Subject(s):** Literature; Poetry
**Circ:** (Controlled)900

**Romanic Review** (22326)
Columbia University
520 Philosophy Hall
New York, NY 10027-4902
Phone: (212)854-3208
Fax: (212)854-5863
**Subject(s):** Literature; Philology, Language, and Linguistics
**Circ:** (Paid)900

**Thyroid** (22452)
Mary Ann Liebert Incorporated Publishers
c/o Terry F. Davies
Division of Endocrinology, Diabetes & Bone Diseases
Mount Sinai School of Medicine
One Gustave L. Levy Pl., PO Box 1055
New York, NY 10029-6574
Phone: (212)241-4160
Fax: (212)426-8311
**Subject(s):** Medicine and Surgery
**Circ:** 900

**Journal of the London Mathematical Society** (21949)
Cambridge University Press
40 W. 20th St.
New York, NY 10011-4211
Phone: (212)924-3900
Fax: (212)691-3239
**Subject(s):** Mathematics
**Circ:** (Non-paid)‡432
       (Paid)‡894

**Physical & Occupational Therapy in Geriatrics** (20471)
The Haworth Press Inc.
PO Box 630242
Bronx, NY 10463
**Subject(s):** Gerontology
**Circ:** (Combined)890

**Villanova Law Review** (27630)
Villanova University
229 N Spring Mill Rd.
Villanova, PA 19085
Phone: (610)519-4500
Fax: (610)519-6906
**Subject(s):** Law; College Publications
**Circ:** ‡890

**Journal of Sport Rehabilitation** (27098)
Human Kinetics Publishers Inc.
c/o Charles Buz Swanik, Ph.D., ATC, Editor
Temple Univ.
127 Pearson Hall
Philadelphia, PA 19122
Phone: (215)204-9555
**Subject(s):** Physical Education and Athletics
**Circ:** (Paid)‡880

**Folia Primatologica** (4724)
S. Karger Publishers Inc.
26 W Avon Rd.
PO Box 529
Farmington, CT 06085
Phone: (860)675-7834
Fax: (860)675-7302
**Subject(s):** Science (General); Zoology; French; German
**Circ:** 850

**Geological Magazine** (21734)
Cambridge University Press
40 W. 20th St.
New York, NY 10011-4211
Phone: (212)924-3900
Fax: (212)691-3239
**Subject(s):** Geology
**Circ:** 850

**Journal of the American Mathematical Society** (27905)
American Mathematical Society
201 Charles St.
Providence, RI 02904-2294
Phone: (401)455-4000
Fax: (401)331-3842
**Subject(s):** Mathematics
**Circ:** 850

**Journal of the AMIS** (19752)
American Musical Instrument Society
126 Darlington Ave.
Ramsey, NJ 07446
Phone: (201)327-8426
**Subject(s):** Music and Musical Instruments
**Circ:** 850

**Journal of the Catgut Acoustical Society** (22741)
The Violin Society of America
48 Academy Street
Poughkeepsie, NY 12601
Phone: (845)452-7557
Fax: (845)452-7618
**Subject(s):** Music and Musical Instruments; Music and Musical Instruments
**Circ:** 850

**Journal of Toxicology and Environmental Health** (27106)
Taylor & Francis
325 Chestnut St., Ste. 800
Philadelphia, PA 19106
Phone: (215)625-8900
Fax: (215)625-8914
**Subject(s):** Toxicology; Ecology and Conservation; Health and Healthcare
**Circ:** 855

**Language Variation and Change** (22022)
Cambridge University Press
40 W. 20th St.
New York, NY 10011-4211
Phone: (212)924-3900
Fax: (212)691-3239
**Subject(s):** Philology, Language, and Linguistics
**Circ:** 850

**Ophthalmic Research** (4751)
S. Karger Publishers Inc.
26 W Avon Rd.
PO Box 529
Farmington, CT 06085
Phone: (860)675-7834
Fax: (860)675-7302
**Subject(s):** Ophthalmology, Optometry, and Optics
**Circ:** 850

**ORL** (4753)
S. Karger Publishers Inc.
26 W Avon Rd.
PO Box 529
Farmington, CT 06085
Phone: (860)675-7834
Fax: (860)675-7302
**Subject(s):** Medicine and Surgery
**Circ:** 850

**The Trade News** (27287)
Roofing, Metal and Heating Engineers Inc.
PO Box 21187
5525 North American Street
Philadelphia, PA 19120
Phone: (215)927-5262

Fax: (215)224-2690
**Subject(s):** Roofing
**Circ:** (Non-paid)850

**JETP Letters (Journal of Experimental and Theoretical Physics Letters)** (21161)
American Institute of Physics
2 Huntington Quadrangle, Ste. 1NO1
Melville, NY 11747-4502
Phone: (516)576-2200
Fax: (516)349-7669
**Subject(s):** Physics
**Circ:** ‡845

**Journal of the Royal Asiatic Society** (21986)
Cambridge University Press
40 W. 20th St.
New York, NY 10011-4211
Phone: (212)924-3900
Fax: (212)691-3239
**Subject(s):** International Affairs
**Circ:** (Paid)‡544
     (Non-paid)‡839

**Pediatric Pathology & Molecular Medicine** (27213)
Taylor & Francis
325 Chestnut St., Ste. 800
Philadelphia, PA 19106
Phone: (215)625-8900
Fax: (215)625-8914
**Subject(s):** Pediatrics
**Circ:** ‡834

**Seminars in Ophthalmology** (27399)
Elsevier
C/o Thomas R. Friberg, Editor-in-Chief
The Eye and Ear Institute
203 Lothrop St.
Pittsburgh, PA 15213
**Subject(s):** Ophthalmology, Optometry, and Optics
**Circ:** ‡831

**The American Sociologist** (19805)
Transaction Publishers
390 Campus Dr.
Somerset, NJ 08873
Phone: (732)445-1245
Fax: (732)748-9801
**Subject(s):** Sociology
**Circ:** (Paid)‡800

**AOTOS Journal** (21345)
United Seamen's Service
20 Exchange Pl., Ste. 2901
New York, NY 10005
Phone: (212)269-0711
Fax: (212)269-5721
**Subject(s):** Boats and Marine; Fish and Commercial Fisheries
**Circ:** 800

**Boston College Environmental Affairs Law Review** (14285)
Boston College Law School
885 Centre St.
Newton, MA 02459
Phone: (617)552-8550
Fax: (617)552-2615
**Subject(s):** Law; Ecology and Conservation
**Circ:** (Paid)800

**Charioteer** (21474)
Pella Publishing Co.
337 W 36th St.
New York, NY 10018
Phone: (212)279-9586
Fax: (212)594-3602
**Subject(s):** Literature; History and Genealogy; Intercultural Interests
**Circ:** (Paid)800

**Communication Research** (23005)
Sage Publications Inc.
c/o Pamela J. Shoemaker, Co-editor
S.I. Newhouse School of Public Communications
Syracuse Univ.
215 Univ. Pl.
Syracuse, NY 13244-2100
**Subject(s):** Communications
**Circ:** (Paid)800

**Compost Science & Utilization** (26326)
The JG Press Inc.
419 State Ave.
Emmaus, PA 18049
Phone: (610)967-4135
**Subject(s):** Science (General); Ecology and Conservation; Waste Management and Recycling
**Circ:** (Paid)800

**Differences** (27897)
Duke University Press
Pembroke Center
PO Box 1958
Brown University
Providence, RI 02912
Phone: (401)863-1211
Fax: (401)863-1298
**Subject(s):** Women's Interests
**Circ:** 800

**Digestion** (4715)
S. Karger Publishers Inc.
26 W Avon Rd.
PO Box 529
Farmington, CT 06085
Phone: (860)675-7834
Fax: (860)675-7302
**Subject(s):** Medicine and Surgery
**Circ:** ‡800

**European Surgical Research** (4720)
S. Karger Publishers Inc.
26 W Avon Rd.
PO Box 529
Farmington, CT 06085
Phone: (860)675-7834
Fax: (860)675-7302
**Subject(s):** Medicine and Surgery
**Circ:** 800

**Forum Italicum** (22973)
State University of New York at Stony Brook
Stony Brook, NY 11794-3358
Phone: (631)632-7444
Fax: (631)632-7421
**Subject(s):** Ethnic and Minority Studies
**Circ:** (Paid)800

**Genetical Research** (21732)
Cambridge University Press
40 W. 20th St.
New York, NY 10011-4211
Phone: (212)924-3900
Fax: (212)691-3239
**Subject(s):** Biology; Genetics
**Circ:** 800

**Greek Orthodox Theological Review** (13633)
Holy Cross Orthodox Press
50 Goddard Ave.
Brookline, MA 02445
Phone: (617)731-3500
Fax: (617)850-1460
**Subject(s):** Religious Publications
**Circ:** ‡800

**Harvard Journal of Legislation** (13673)
William S. Hein & Company Inc.
Harvard Law School
Publications Center
Hastings Hall
Cambridge, MA 02138
Phone: (617)495-4400
Fax: (617)496-2148
**Subject(s):** Law; Political Science
**Circ:** 800

**Historic Brass Society** (21764)
Historic Brass Society Inc.
148 W. 23rd St., No. 5F
New York, NY 10011
Phone: (212)627-3820
Fax: (212)627-3820
**Subject(s):** Music and Musical Instruments
**Circ:** (Paid)800

**Innovating Magazine** (22780)
The Rensselaerville Institute
63 Huyck Rd.
Rensselaerville, NY 12147
Phone: (518)797-3783
Fax: (518)797-5270
**Subject(s):** Education; Management and Administration; Sociology
**Circ:** (Non-paid)‡27
     (Paid)‡800

**International Journal of the Classical Tradition** (13528)
Transaction Publishers
Institute for the Classical Tradition
Boston Univ.
745 Commonwealth Ave., Ste. B-3
Boston, MA 02215
Phone: (617)353-7369
Fax: (617)353-7369
**Subject(s):** History and Genealogy; Intercultural Interests
**Circ:** (Paid)‡800

**Intervirology** (4733)
S. Karger Publishers Inc.
26 W Avon Rd.
PO Box 529
Farmington, CT 06085
Phone: (860)675-7834
Fax: (860)675-7302
**Subject(s):** Medicine and Surgery
**Circ:** 800

**The Jewish Quarterly Review** (27005)
Center for Advanced Judaic Studies
420 Walnut St.
Philadelphia, PA 19106-3703
Phone: (215)238-1290
Fax: (215)238-1540
**Subject(s):** Jewish Publications
**Circ:** 800

**Journal of Applied School Psychology** (19684)
The Haworth Press Inc.
c/o Charles A. Maher
Rutgers University
152 Frelinghuysen Rd., Ste. A305
Piscataway, NJ 08854
Phone: (732)445-2000
**Subject(s):** Education; Psychology and Psychiatry
**Circ:** 800

**Journal of the Association of Food and Drug Officials** (27727)
Association of Food and Drug Officials
2550 Kingston Rd., Ste. 311
York, PA 17402
Phone: (717)757-2888
Fax: (717)755-8089
**Subject(s):** Drugs and Pharmaceuticals; Health and Healthcare; Food Production
**Circ:** 800

**Journal of the Evangelical Homiletics Society** (14799)
Evangelical Homiletics Society
Gordon-Conwell Theological Seminary
120 Essex St.
South Hamilton, MA 01982-2317
Phone: (978)646-4152
Fax: (978)468-6208
**Subject(s):** Religious Publications; Clubs and Societies
**Circ:** (Paid)800

**Journal of Liquid Chromatography & Related Technologies** (21948)
Marcel Dekker Inc.
270 Madison Ave.
New York, NY 10016-0602
Phone: (212)696-9000
Fax: (212)685-4540
**Subject(s):** Chemistry, Chemicals, and Chemical Engineering
**Circ:** (Paid)800

**Journal of Marine Research** (4895)
Yale University
PO Box 208109
New Haven, CT 06520-8109
Phone: (203)432-3154
Fax: (203)432-3134
**Subject(s):** Laboratory Research (Scientific and Medical); Oceanography and Marine Studies
**Circ:** (Paid)800

**Journal of Membrane Biology** (21956)
Springer-Verlag New York Inc.
233 Spring St.
New York, NY 10013
Phone: (212)460-1500
Fax: (212)460-1575
**Subject(s):** Biology
**Circ:** (Combined)800

**The Journal of Presbyterian History** (27088)
Presbyterian Historical Society
425 Lombard St.
Philadelphia, PA 19147
Phone: (215)627-1852
Fax: (215)627-0509
**Subject(s):** History and Genealogy; Religious Publications
**Circ:** ‡800

**Journal of Public Policy** (21983)
Cambridge University Press
40 W. 20th St.
New York, NY 10011-4211
Phone: (212)924-3900
Fax: (212)691-3239
**Subject(s):** State, Municipal, and County Administration
**Circ:** 800

**Neurosignals** (4748)
S. Karger Publishers Inc.
26 W Avon Rd.
PO Box 529
Farmington, CT 06085
Phone: (860)675-7834
Fax: (860)675-7302
**Subject(s):** Medicine and Surgery
**Circ:** 800

**Onkologie** (4750)
S. Karger Publishers Inc.
26 W Avon Rd.
PO Box 529
Farmington, CT 06085
Phone: (860)675-7834
Fax: (860)675-7302
**Subject(s):** Medicine and Surgery; German
**Circ:** 800

**Polar Record** (22243)
Cambridge University Press
40 W. 20th St.
New York, NY 10011-4211
Phone: (212)924-3900
Fax: (212)691-3239
**Subject(s):** Anthropology and Ethnology; Geology; Geography
**Circ:** 800

**Popular Music** (22251)
Cambridge University Press
40 W. 20th St.
New York, NY 10011-4211
Phone: (212)924-3900
Fax: (212)691-3239
**Subject(s):** Music and Musical Instruments
**Circ:** 800

**Psychopathology** (4759)
S. Karger Publishers Inc.
26 W Avon Rd.
PO Box 529
Farmington, CT 06085
Phone: (860)675-7834
Fax: (860)675-7302
**Subject(s):** Psychology and Psychiatry; Medicine and Surgery
**Circ:** 800

**Publishing Research Quarterly** (22282)
Transaction Publishers
Center for Publishing
NYU School of Continuing Education
11 W. 42nd St., Rm.400
New York, NY 10036-8002
Phone: (212)790-3233
Fax: (212)790-3233
**Subject(s):** Book Trade and Author News; Journalism and Publishing
**Circ:** (Paid)‡800

**Rhodora** (18814)
New England Botanical Club Inc.
Dept. of Plant Biology
University of New Hampshire
Durham, NH 03824-2617
Phone: (603)862-3222
Fax: (603)862-4757
**Subject(s):** Botany
**Circ:** (Non-paid)15
(Paid)800

**Tree Talks** (23046)
Central New York Genealogical Society Inc.
PO Box 104, Colvin Sta.
Syracuse, NY 13205
**Subject(s):** History and Genealogy
**Circ:** (Paid)800

**Berks County Law Journal** (27467)
Berks County Bar Association
PO Box 1058
544-546 Court St.
Reading, PA 19603
Phone: (610)375-4591
Fax: (610)373-0256
**Subject(s):** Law
**Circ:** (Paid)‡796

**Journal of Pharmacy Practice** (27083)
Elsevier
1600 John F. Kennedy Blvd.
Philadelphia, PA 19103
Phone: (215)239-3900
Fax: (215)239-3990
**Subject(s):** Drugs and Pharmaceuticals
**Circ:** ‡781

**Micropaleontology** (22083)
Micropaleontology Press
American Museum of Natural History
256 Fifth Ave.
New York, NY 10001
**Subject(s):** Science (General); Natural History and Nature Study
**Circ:** (Combined)780

**Journal of Sustainable Agriculture** (4691)
The Haworth Press Inc.
Biology Dept.
Fairfield Univ.
Fairfield, CT 06824
Phone: (203)254-4253
Fax: (203)254-4253
**Subject(s):** Scientific Agricultural Publications
**Circ:** (Paid)‡775

**Ultrastructural Pathology** (27293)
Taylor & Francis
325 Chestnut St., Ste. 800
Philadelphia, PA 19106
Phone: (215)625-8900
Fax: (215)625-8914
**Subject(s):** Medicine and Surgery
**Circ:** 779

**Ancient Philosophy** (27325)
Mathesis Publications Inc.
Department of Philosophy
Duquesne University
Pittsburgh, PA 15282
Phone: (412)396-6500
**Subject(s):** History and Genealogy; Philosophy; Science (General)
**Circ:** (Combined)750

**British Journal of Music Education** (21427)
Cambridge University Press
40 W. 20th St.
New York, NY 10011-4211
Phone: (212)924-3900
Fax: (212)691-3239
**Subject(s):** Music and Musical Instruments
**Circ:** 750

**Cambridge Archaeological Journal** (21449)
Cambridge University Press
40 W. 20th St.
New York, NY 10011-4211
Phone: (212)924-3900
Fax: (212)691-3239
**Subject(s):** Archaeology
**Circ:** (Non-paid)99
(Paid)‡750

**Cambridge Opera Journal** (21451)
Cambridge University Press
40 W. 20th St.
New York, NY 10011-4211
Phone: (212)924-3900
Fax: (212)691-3239
**Subject(s):** Music and Musical Instruments
**Circ:** 750

**Entomological News** (19920)
The American Entomological Society
232 Oak Shade Rd.
Tabernacle Twp.
Vincentown, NJ 08088
Phone: (609)268-1734
**Subject(s):** Entomology
**Circ:** ‡750

**The Journal of Agricultural Science** (21871)
Cambridge University Press
40 W. 20th St.
New York, NY 10011-4211
Phone: (212)924-3900
Fax: (212)691-3239
**Subject(s):** Scientific Agricultural Publications
**Circ:** 750

**Journal of Dairy Research** (21908)
Cambridge University Press
40 W. 20th St.
New York, NY 10011-4211
Phone: (212)924-3900
Fax: (212)691-3239
**Subject(s):** Dairying
**Circ:** 750

**The Journal of Knee Surgery** (19858)
SLACK Inc.
6900 Grove Rd.
Thorofare, NJ 08086-9447
Phone: (856)848-1000
Fax: (856)848-6091
**Subject(s):** Medicine and Surgery
**Circ:** (Paid)‡750

**Journal of Water Borne Coatings** (4954)
Technology Marketing Corp.
1 Technology Plz.
Norwalk, CT 06854
Phone: (203)852-6800
Fax: (203)853-2845
**Subject(s):** Paint and Wallcoverings
**Circ:** (Paid)250
(Non-paid)750

**Lancaster Law Review** (26601)
Lancaster Bar Association
28 E Orange St.
Lancaster, PA 17602
Phone: (717)393-0737
Fax: (717)393-0221
**Subject(s):** Law
**Circ:** ‡750

**Radiation Protection Management** (1826)
RSA Publications
19 Pendelton Dr.
PO Box 107
Hebron, CT 06248
Phone: (860)228-0487
Fax: (860)228-4402
**Subject(s):** Nuclear Engineering; Health and Healthcare
**Circ:** (Paid)750

**Stamps Auction News** (20911)
American Publishing Co.
85 Canisteo St.
Hornell, NY 14843-1544
Phone: (607)324-1425
Fax: (607)324-2317
**Subject(s):** Conventions, Meetings, and Trade Fairs
**Circ:** (Non-paid)‡500
(Paid)‡750

**Fordham Intellectual Property, Media & Entertainment Law Journal** (21711)
Lincoln Center
140 W 62nd St.
New York, NY 10023
Phone: (212)636-6948
Fax: (212)636-6582
**Subject(s):** Law
**Circ:** (Combined)745

**Issues in Comprehensive Pediatric Nursing** (19772)
Taylor & Francis
c/o Jane Bliss-Holtz, DNSc, RN
PO Box 619
Rocky Hill, NJ 08553
**Subject(s):** Nursing; Pediatrics
**Circ:** (Combined)740

**Communications in Statistics: Simulation & Computation (21528)**
Marcel Dekker Inc.
270 Madison Ave.
New York, NY 10016-0602
Phone: (212)696-9000
Fax: (212)685-4540
Subject(s): Mathematics
Circ: 725

**Journal of Neurosurgical Anesthesiology (20520)**
Lippincott Williams & Wilkins
c/o James E. Cottrell
SUNY Downstate Medical Center
450 Clarkson Ave., Box 6
Brooklyn, NY 11203-2098
Subject(s): Laboratory Research (Scientific and Medical); Medicine and Surgery
Circ: 728

**Lung (22047)**
Springer-Verlag New York Inc.
233 Spring St.
New York, NY 10013
Phone: (212)460-1500
Fax: (212)460-1575
Subject(s): Medicine and Surgery
Circ: (Combined)725

**Westchester Historian (20759)**
Westchester County Historical Society
2199 Saw Mill River Rd.
Elmsford, NY 10523
Phone: (914)592-4323
Fax: (914)231-1515
Subject(s): History and Genealogy
Circ: (Combined)725

**Algorithmica (21288)**
Springer-Verlag New York Inc.
233 Spring St.
New York, NY 10013
Phone: (212)460-1500
Fax: (212)460-1575
Subject(s): Computers; Mathematics
Circ: (Combined)700

**The Appraisers Standard (30892)**
New England Appraisers Association
5 Gill Ter.
Ludlow, VT 05149
Phone: (802)228-7444
Fax: (802)228-7444
Subject(s): Insurance
Circ: (Combined)700

**Asian American Policy Review (13651)**
Harvard University
79 John F. Kennedy St.
Cambridge, MA 02138
Phone: (617)496-8655
Fax: (617)384-9555
Subject(s): Political Science; Politics; Intercultural Interests
Circ: (Combined)700

**Behavioral Sciences and the Law (20556)**
John Wiley and Sons Inc.
c/o Charles Patrick Ewing, School of Law
John Lord O'Brian Hall
Buffalo, NY 14260-1100
Subject(s): Psychology and Psychiatry
Circ: (Paid)700

**Boundary 2 (27328)**
Duke University Press
c/o Paul A. Bove
Department of English
University of Pittsburgh
526 Cathedral of Learning, 4200 Fifth Ave.
Pittsburgh, PA 15260
Phone: (412)624-6523
Fax: (412)624-6639
Subject(s): Literature; Literature and Literary Reviews
Circ: (Paid)700

**Buffalo Law Journal (20559)**
Business First
465 Main St.
Buffalo, NY 14203-1793
Phone: (716)854-5822
Fax: (716)854-3394
Subject(s): Banking, Finance, and Investments; Law; Real Estate
Circ: (Non-paid)30
      (Paid)700

**College Literature (27665)**
West Chester University
210 E Rosedale Ave.
West Chester, PA 19383
Phone: (610)436-2901
Fax: (610)436-2275
Subject(s): Literature; Education
Circ: (Combined)700

**Competetiveness Review (26530)**
American Society for Competitiveness
Box 1658
Indiana, PA 15705
Fax: (724)357-5743
Subject(s): Business; International Business and Economics
Circ: (Combined)700

**Competetiveness Review (26529)**
American Society for Competitiveness
Box 1658
Indiana, PA 15705
Fax: (724)357-5743
Circ: (Paid)700

**Current Microbiology (21581)**
Springer-Verlag New York Inc.
233 Spring St.
New York, NY 10013
Phone: (212)460-1500
Fax: (212)460-1575
Subject(s): Biology
Circ: (Combined)700

**East Asia (19590)**
Transaction Publishers
Political Science Dept.
Rutgers—The State Univ. of New Jersey
89 George St.
New Brunswick, NJ 08901
Phone: (732)932-7170
Fax: (732)932-7170
Subject(s): Intercultural Interests
Circ: (Paid)‡700

**Educational Policy (13727)**
Corwin Press
Boston College
Campion Hall
Chestnut Hill, MA 02467
Phone: (617)552-4236
Fax: (617)552-8422
Subject(s): Education
Circ: (Non-paid)30
      (Paid)700

**Farming Uncle (20455)**
TORO
Box 427
Bronx, NY 10458
Subject(s): General Agriculture; Social and Political Issues; Alternative and Underground
Circ: (Paid)400
      (Non-paid)700

**Gestalt Review (12558)**
Analytic Press
c/o Joseph Melnick
17 S. St.
Portland, ME 04101
Phone: (207)772-1559
Fax: (207)772-8400
Subject(s): Psychology and Psychiatry
Circ: 707

**Home Planet News (20902)**
Home Planet Publications
P O Box 455
High Falls, NY 12440
Phone: (845)687-4084
Subject(s): Literature and Literary Reviews; Art
Circ: (Non-paid)200
      (Paid)700

**Information Resources Management Journal (26487)**
Idea Group Publishing
701 E. Chocolate Ave., Ste. 200
Hershey, PA 17033-1240
Phone: (717)533-8845
Fax: (717)533-8661
Subject(s): Computers; Business
Circ: (Controlled)700

**International Journal of Commerce and Management (26533)**
International Academy of Business Disciplines
Eberly College of Business Information Technology
Indiana University Of Pennsylvania
PO Box 1658
Indiana, PA 15705
Phone: (724)357-2535
Fax: (724)357-5743
Subject(s): International Business and Economics
Circ: (Paid)700

**International Journal of Short-Term Psychotherapy (19273)**
John Wiley and Sons Inc.
111 River St.
Hoboken, NJ 07030-5774
Phone: (201)748-6000
Fax: (201)748-6088
Subject(s): Psychology and Psychiatry
Circ: 700

**Journal of Business and Economic Studies (22636)**
Dowling College
Idle Hour Blvd.
Oakdale, NY 11769
Phone: (631)244-3214
Subject(s): Business
Circ: (Paid)700

**Journal of Cognitive Psychotherapy (21897)**
Springer Publishing Co.
11 W. 42nd St. 15th Fl.
New York, NY 10036
Phone: (212)431-4370
Fax: (212)941-7842
Subject(s): Psychology and Psychiatry; Social Programs
Circ: (Controlled)80
      (Paid)700

**Journal of New Jersey Poets (19757)**
County College of Morris
214 Center Grove Rd.
Randolph, NJ 07869
Phone: (973)328-5471
Fax: (973)328-5425
Subject(s): Poetry; Literature and Literary Reviews
Circ: (Non-paid)‡300
      (Paid)‡700

**Journal of Nutrition for the Elderly (20708)**
The Haworth Press Inc.
c/o Annette B Natow, Journal Ed.
334 Hollywood Ave.
Douglaston, NY 11363
Phone: (718)229-0606
Fax: (800)HAW-ORTH
Subject(s): Gerontology; Health and Healthcare; Food and Cooking
Circ: (Controlled)‡700

**Journal of Tropical Ecology (22004)**
Cambridge University Press
40 W. 20th St.
New York, NY 10011-4211
Phone: (212)924-3900
Fax: (212)691-3239
Subject(s): Ecology and Conservation
Circ: 700

**Kidney (22010)**
Springer-Verlag New York Inc.
233 Spring St.
New York, NY 10013
Phone: (212)460-1500
Fax: (212)460-1575
Subject(s): Health and Healthcare; Medicine and Surgery
Circ: (Combined)700

**The Lyric (30889)**
PO Box 110
Jericho, VT 05465-0110
Phone: (802)899-3993
Subject(s): Literature and Literary Reviews; Poetry
Circ: (Non-paid)‡28
      (Paid)‡700

**Mid-Atlantic Journal of Business (19830)**
Seton Hall University
Division of Business Research
c/o Mary L. Williams
South Orange, NJ 07079-2692
Phone: (973)761-9000
Fax: (973)761-9217

**Subject(s):** Business
**Circ:** 700

**On the Road (19095)**
Library Outreach Reporter
148 Liberty St.
Fords, NJ 08863
Phone: (718)437-3383
Fax: (732)738-5183
**Subject(s):** Library and Information Science
**Circ:** (Non-paid)‡200
(Paid)‡700

**SMR/Sociological Methods and Research (13708)**
Sage Publications Inc.
Sociological Methods & Research
Department of Sociology, Harvard University
Cambridge, MA 02138
**Subject(s):** Sociology
**Circ:** (Paid)‡700

**Studies in Gender and Sexuality (22425)**
Analytic Press
102 E 22nd ST., Ste. 10H
New York, NY 10010
Phone: (212)982-9359
**Subject(s):** Radio, Television, Cable, and Video; Sociology; Social Sciences
**Circ:** (Combined)700

**Journal of Interlibrary Loan, Document Delivery, and Information Supply (21025)**
The Haworth Press Inc.
54 Northwood Dr.
Lancaster, NY 14043-4551
Phone: (716)686-0906
**Subject(s):** Library and Information Science
**Circ:** 691

**Phonology (22232)**
Cambridge University Press
40 W. 20th St.
New York, NY 10011-4211
Phone: (212)924-3900
Fax: (212)691-3239
**Subject(s):** Philology, Language, and Linguistics
**Circ:** (Non-paid)68
(Paid)‡698

**GLQ (21740)**
Duke University Press
Center for the Study of Gender and Sexuality
New York University
285 Mercer St. 3rd Fl.
New York, NY 10003-6653
Phone: (212)992-9546
Fax: (212)995-4433
**Subject(s):** Gay and Lesbian Interests; Social Sciences
**Circ:** (Combined)675

**Journal of Synagogue Music (21996)**
Cantors Assembly
3080 Broadway, Ste. 613
New York, NY 10027
Phone: (212)678-8834
Fax: (212)662-8989
**Subject(s):** Music and Musical Instruments; Jewish Publications; Religious Publications
**Circ:** 675

**Abstract Bulletin of the Institute of Paper Science and Technology (19151)**
Elsevier Engineering Information
1 Castle Point Ter.
Hoboken, NJ 07030-5996
Fax: (201)356-6801
**Subject(s):** Chemistry, Chemicals, and Chemical Engineering; Paper; Indexes, Abstracts, Reports, Proceedings, and Bibliographies
**Circ:** (Controlled)‡90
(Paid)‡660

**Applied Mathematics and Optimization (27888)**
Springer-Verlag New York Inc.
c/o Paul Dupuis
Division of Applied Mathematics
Brown University
182 George St., PO Box F
Providence, RI 02912
Phone: (401)863-3238
**Subject(s):** Mathematics
**Circ:** (Combined)650

**The Beloit Poetry Journal (12516)**
The Beloit Poetry Journal Foundation Inc.
PO Box 151
Farmington, ME 04938
**Subject(s):** Literature and Literary Reviews
**Circ:** (Non-paid)‡415
(Paid)‡655

**Columbia Human Rights Law Review (21512)**
Columbia Law School
435 W 116th St.
New York, NY 10027
Phone: (212)854-1601
Fax: (212)854-7946
**Subject(s):** Law
**Circ:** (Paid)650

**Contemporary European History (21546)**
Cambridge University Press
40 W. 20th St.
New York, NY 10011-4211
Phone: (212)924-3900
Fax: (212)691-3239
**Subject(s):** History and Genealogy
**Circ:** 650

**Continuity and Change (21548)**
Cambridge University Press
40 W. 20th St.
New York, NY 10011-4211
Phone: (212)924-3900
Fax: (212)691-3239
**Subject(s):** Sociology; History and Genealogy
**Circ:** 650

**Experimental Physiology (21673)**
Cambridge University Press
40 W. 20th St.
New York, NY 10011-4211
Phone: (212)924-3900
Fax: (212)691-3239
**Subject(s):** Physiology and Anatomy
**Circ:** 650

**Film Criticism (26681)**
Allegheny College
520 N Main St.
Meadville, PA 16335
Phone: (814)332-3100
Fax: (814)332-4343
**Subject(s):** Motion Pictures
**Circ:** (Combined)650

**Kingbird (22950)**
Federation of New York State Bird Clubs Inc.
585 Mead Terrace
South Hempstead, NY 11550
Phone: (516)486-5854
**Subject(s):** Ornithology and Oology
**Circ:** (Paid)650

**Pediatric Exercise Science (14805)**
Human Kinetics Publishers Inc.
c/o Thomas W. Rowland, M.D., Editor
Baystate Medical Center
Springfield, MA 01199
Phone: (413)794-7350
Fax: (413)784-5995
**Subject(s):** Physical Education and Athletics
**Circ:** (Non-paid)‡32
(Paid)‡650

**ReCall (22298)**
Cambridge University Press
40 W. 20th St.
New York, NY 10011-4211
Phone: (212)924-3900
Fax: (212)691-3239
**Subject(s):** Science (General)
**Circ:** 650

**Social Text (19601)**
Duke University Press
8 Bishop Pl.
New Brunswick, NJ 08903
Phone: (732)932-1503
Fax: (732)932-8683
**Subject(s):** Social Sciences
**Circ:** (Combined)650

**Substance Use & Misuse (22428)**
Marcel Dekker Inc.
270 Madison Ave.
New York, NY 10016-0602
Phone: (212)696-9000
Fax: (212)685-4540
**Subject(s):** Sociology; Law; Medicine and Surgery; Substance Abuse and Treatment
**Circ:** 650

**Theory of Computing Systems (20582)**
Springer-Verlag New York Inc.
c/o Alan L. Selman
Department of Computer Science and Engineering
The State University of New York
201 Bell Hall
Buffalo, NY 14260
**Subject(s):** Mathematics
**Circ:** (Combined)650

**University of Pennsylvania Journal of International Economic Law (27294)**
University of Pennsylvania
3400 Chestnut St.
Philadelphia, PA 19104-6204
**Subject(s):** Law
**Circ:** (Paid)‡650

**Blueline (Potsdam) (22733)**
Potsdam College
125 Morey Hall
Potsdam, NY 13676
Phone: (315)267-2043
Fax: (315)267-3256
**Subject(s):** Literature; Poetry
**Circ:** (Combined)600

**Courant (23008)**
Syracuse University Library Associates
600 Bird Library
Syracuse, NY 13244-2010
Phone: (315)443-2697
Fax: (315)443-2060
**Subject(s):** Literature; Library and Information Science
**Circ:** (Paid)600

**Discrete and Computational Geometry (21608)**
Springer-Verlag New York Inc.
c/o Jacob E. Goodman
Dept. of Mathematics
City College, C.U.N.Y.
New York, NY 10031
Phone: (212)650-5141
**Subject(s):** Mathematics
**Circ:** (Combined)600

**Ergodic Theory and Dynamical Systems (21656)**
Cambridge University Press
40 W. 20th St.
New York, NY 10011-4211
Phone: (212)924 0000
Fax: (212)691-3239
**Subject(s):** Mathematics
**Circ:** 600

**Free Focus (21717)**
Women's Literary Guild
Box 7415, JFA Sta.
New York, NY 10116-4630
Phone: (212)967-8006
**Subject(s):** Literature; Women's Interests
**Circ:** 600

**The Herb, Spice, and Medicinal Plant Digest (13409)**
The Haworth Press Inc.
Journal of Herbs, Spices, and Medical Plants
12 A Stockbridge Hall
University of Massachusetts
Amherst, MA 01003
Phone: (413)545-2347
Fax: (413)545-3958
**Subject(s):** Botany; Drugs and Pharmaceuticals
**Circ:** 600

**Journal of the Academy of Rehabilitative Audiology (22827)**
Academy of Rehabilitative Audiology
96 Lomb Memorial Dr
Hugh L. Carey Building
Department of Research
National Technical Institute for the Deaf
Rochester, NY 14623-5604
Phone: (585)475-6456
**Subject(s):** Physiology and Anatomy
**Circ:** (Paid)‡600

**Journal of Global Information Management** (26493)
Idea Group Publishing
701 E. Chocolate Ave., Ste. 200
Hershey, PA 17033-1240
Phone: (717)533-8845
Fax: (717)533-8661
**Subject(s):** Computers; Business

Circ: (Controlled)600

**Journal of the Hellenic Diaspora** (21936)
Pella Publishing Co.
337 W 36th St.
New York, NY 10018
Phone: (212)279-9586
Fax: (212)594-3602
**Subject(s):** Intercultural Interests

Circ: (Non-paid)‡100
    (Paid)‡600

**Legal Theory** (4898)
Cambridge University Press
c/o Jules L. Coleman
Yale Law School
127 Wall St.
New Haven, CT 06511
**Subject(s):** Law; Humanities; Social Sciences

Circ: 600

**Meteorological Applications** (22078)
Cambridge University Press
40 W. 20th St.
New York, NY 10011-4211
Phone: (212)924-3900
Fax: (212)691-3239
**Subject(s):** Meteorology

Circ: 600

**Prospects** (22269)
Cambridge University Press
c/o Jack Salzman
180 W. End Ave., No. 20 H
New York, NY 10023
**Subject(s):** Humanities; Social Sciences

Circ: 600

**Research and Theory for Nursing Practice** (22308)
Springer Publishing Co.
11 W. 42nd St. 15th Fl.
New York, NY 10036
Phone: (212)431-4370
Fax: (212)941-7842
**Subject(s):** Nursing; Hospitals and Healthcare Institutions

Circ: (Paid)600

**Robotica** (22323)
Cambridge University Press
40 W. 20th St.
New York, NY 10011-4211
Phone: (212)924-3900
Fax: (212)691-3239
**Subject(s):** Automation; Computers

Circ: 600

**Separation Science and Technology** (23076)
Marcel Dekker Inc.
c/o Steven Cramer,
Isermann Department of Chemical & Biological Engineering
Rensselaer Polytechnic Institute
Troy, NY 12180
**Subject(s):** Science (General); Chemistry, Chemicals, and Chemical Engineering

Circ: (Paid)600

**Stochastic Models** (22419)
Marcel Dekker Inc.
270 Madison Ave.
New York, NY 10016-0602
Phone: (212)696-9000
Fax: (212)685-4540
**Subject(s):** Mathematics; Statistics

Circ: (Paid)**600**

**Wallace Stevens Journal** (22735)
Wallace Stevens Society Inc.
PO Box 5750
Clarkson University
Potsdam, NY 13699-5750
Phone: (315)268-3987
Fax: (315)268-3983
**Subject(s):** Literature; Poetry

Circ: (Non-paid)100
    (Paid)600

**The Yale Journal of Biology & Medicine** (4904)
The Yale Journal of Biology and Medicine Inc.
333 Ceder St.
PO Box 208000
New Haven, CT 06520-8000
Phone: (203)785-4251
Fax: (203)785-4251
**Subject(s):** Medicine and Surgery

Circ: ‡600

**Child and Family Behavior Therapy** (19713)
The Haworth Press Inc.
c/o Cyril M Franks
315 Prospect Ave
Rutgers Univ.
Princeton, NJ 08540-5330
Phone: (609)924-2931
**Subject(s):** Social Sciences

Circ: (Controlled)‡598

**Treasury Bulletin** (27409)
U.S. Government Printing Office and Superintendent of Documents
PO Box 371954
MS4004-MIB
Pittsburgh, PA 15250-7954
Phone: (202)512-1800
Fax: (202)512-2250
**Subject(s):** Congressional and Federal Government Affairs

Circ: 594

**Employment Information in the Mathematical Sciences** (27899)
American Mathematical Society
201 Charles St.
Providence, RI 02904-2294
Phone: (401)455-4000
Fax: (401)331-3842
**Subject(s):** Mathematics; Science (General)

Circ: (Paid)‡580

**Lehigh Law Journal** (26093)
Bar Association of Lehigh County
1114 Walnut St.
Allentown, PA 18102-4734
Phone: (610)433-6204
Fax: (610)770-9826
**Subject(s):** Law

Circ: (Paid)160
    (Controlled)575

**Semiconductors** (21187)
American Institute of Physics
2 Huntington Quadrangle, Ste. 1NO1
Melville, NY 11747-4502
Phone: (516)576-2200
Fax: (516)349-7669
**Subject(s):** Physics

Circ: ‡570

**Journal of College Student Psychotherapy** (26688)
The Haworth Press Inc.
150 Longview Cir.
Media, PA 19086
Phone: (610)359-8132
Fax: (800)342-9678
**Subject(s):** Psychology and Psychiatry

Circ: 565

**Analytical Letters** (21332)
Marcel Dekker Inc.
270 Madison Ave.
New York, NY 10016-0602
Phone: (212)696-9000
Fax: (212)685-4540
**Subject(s):** Chemistry, Chemicals, and Chemical Engineering

Circ: (Paid)550

**Asian Theater Journal** (20489)
University of Hawaii Press
c/o Samuel L. Leiter, Dept. of Theater
Brooklyn College
CUNY
Brooklyn, NY 11210
Phone: (718)780-5764
Fax: (718)951-4606
**Subject(s):** Performing Arts; Drama and Theatre

Circ: (Controlled)40
    (Paid)550

**Cornell Journal of Law and Public Policy** (20948)
Cornell University Law School
Myron Taylor Hall
Ithaca, NY 14853-4901
Phone: (607)255-0526
Fax: (607)255-7193
**Subject(s):** Law; Political Science

Circ: (Paid)550

**Early Music History** (21623)
Cambridge University Press
40 W. 20th St.
New York, NY 10011-4211
Phone: (212)924-3900
Fax: (212)691-3239
**Subject(s):** Music and Musical Instruments; History and Genealogy

Circ: 550

**Financial History Review** (21691)
Cambridge University Press
40 W. 20th St.
New York, NY 10011-4211
Phone: (212)924-3900
Fax: (212)691-3239
**Subject(s):** Banking, Finance, and Investments

Circ: 550

**Journal of Biopharmaceutical Statistics** (13685)
Marcel Dekker Inc.
c/o Shein-Chung Chow, Clinical Biostatistics
Millennium Pharmaceuticals Inc.
Cambridge, MA
**Subject(s):** Laboratory Research (Scientific and Medical)

Circ: 550

**Historical Reflections/Reflexions Historiques** (20249)
Alfred University
Kanakadea Hall
Alfred, NY 14802
Phone: (607)871-2217
Fax: (607)871-3366
**Subject(s):** History and Genealogy

Circ: (Combined)540

**Journal of Clinical Neuromuscular Disease** (22979)
Lippincott Williams & Wilkins
c/o Rahman Pourmand, Dept. of Neurology
State Univ. of New York
HSC T12-020
Stony Brook, NY 11794-8121
**Subject(s):** Medicine and Surgery

Circ: 546

**Journal of Offender Rehabilitation** (19686)
The Haworth Press Inc.
c/o Nathaniel J. Pallone
Rutgers Univ.
215 Smithers Hall, Busch Campus
607 Allison Rd.
Piscataway, NJ 08854-8001
**Subject(s):** Psychology and Psychiatry; Police, Penology, and Penal Institutions

Circ: 540

**Coronary Artery Disease** (30856)
Lippincott Williams & Wilkins
Fletcher Allen Health Care
Fletcher 311/MCHV Campus
111 Colchester Ave.
Burlington, VT
**Subject(s):** Medicine and Surgery

Circ: (Paid)534

**Journal of Vinyl and Additive Technology** (4651)
Society of Plastics Engineers
14 Fairfield Dr.
PO Box 403
Brookfield, CT 06804-0403
Phone: (203)775-0471
Fax: (203)775-8490
**Subject(s):** Plastic and Composition Materials

Circ: ‡535

**Film Literature Index** (20214)
Film and TV Documentation Center
Richardson 390C SUNYA
1400 Washington Ave.
Albany, NY 12222
Phone: (518)442-5745
Fax: (518)442-5367
**Subject(s):** Motion Pictures; Indexes, Abstracts, Reports, Proceedings, and Bibliographies; Radio, Television, Cable, and Video

Circ: ‡525

**The Acquisitions Librarian**  (20204)
The Haworth Press Inc.
School of Information Science Policy
State University of New York at Albany
855 Mercer St.
Albany, NY 12208
Phone: (518)442-5118
**Subject(s):** Library and Information Science
**Circ:** 512

**Journal of Pelvic Medicine & Surgery**  (27082)
Lippincott Williams & Wilkins
530 Walnut St.
Philadelphia, PA 19106-3261
Phone: (215)521-8300
Fax: (215)521-8902
**Subject(s):** Medicine and Surgery
**Circ:** (Paid)519

**Anglo-Saxon England**  (21336)
Cambridge University Press
40 W. 20th St.
New York, NY 10011-4211
Phone: (212)924-3900
Fax: (212)691-3239
**Subject(s):** History and Genealogy
**Circ:** 500

**Annals of the Ukrainian Academy of Arts and Sciences in the U.S.**  (21340)
Ukrainian Academy of Arts and Sciences in the U.S.
206 W 100th St.
New York, NY 10025-5018
Phone: (212)222-1866
Fax: (212)864-3977
**Subject(s):** Intercultural Interests; Ukrainian
**Circ:** 500

**Atomization and Sprays**  (21371)
Begell House Inc.
145 Madison Ave., Ste. 601
New York, NY 10016
Phone: (212)725-1999
Fax: (212)213-8368
**Subject(s):** Engineering (Various branches); Physics
**Circ:** (Paid)500

**Bielaruskaya Dumka**  (19837)
Byelorussian Publishing Association
Box 26
South River, NJ 08882
Phone: (732)613-7171
Fax: (732)257-3994
**Subject(s):** Ethnic and Minority Studies
**Circ:** (Combined)500

**Bird Conservation International**  (21408)
Cambridge University Press
40 W. 20th St.
New York, NY 10011-4211
Phone: (212)924-3900
Fax: (212)691-3239
**Subject(s):** Ecology and Conservation
**Circ:** 500

**Blake/An Illustrated Quarterly**  (22806)
University of Rochester
Department of English
410 Morey Hall
University of Rochester
Rochester, NY 14627-0451
Phone: (585)275-3820
Fax: (585)442-5769
**Subject(s):** Literature
**Circ:** (Paid)‡500

**Bravo**  (19847)
Bravo Editions
1081 Trafalgar St.
Teaneck, NJ 07666
Phone: (201)836-5922
**Subject(s):** Poetry; Literature
**Circ:** (Non-paid)500

**Bus Industry Magazine**  (18867)
Bus History Association Inc.
195 Lancelot Dr.
Manchester, NH 03104-1420
Phone: (603)669-7160
Fax: (603)542-0103
**Subject(s):** Transportation, Traffic, and Shipping
**Circ:** (Combined)500

**The Cafe Review**  (12554)
Yes Books
589 Congress St.
Portland, ME 04101
Phone: (207)775-3233
**Subject(s):** Poetry; Literature
**Circ:** (Controlled)500

**Centre County Heritage**  (27548)
Centre County Historical Society
1001 East College Ave.
State College, PA 16801
Phone: (814)234-4779
**Subject(s):** History and Genealogy
**Circ:** (Controlled)500

**Computer Science Index**  (13842)
EBSCO Publishing Inc.
10 Estes St.
Ipswich, MA 01938
Phone: (978)356-6500
Fax: (978)356-6565
**Subject(s):** Indexes, Abstracts, Reports, Proceedings, and Bibliographies; Computers
**Circ:** (Controlled)500

**Critical Reviews in Therapeutic Drug Carrier Systems**  (21572)
Begell House Inc.
145 Madison Ave., Ste. 601
New York, NY 10016
Phone: (212)725-1999
Fax: (212)213-8368
**Subject(s):** Medicine and Surgery; Drugs and Pharmaceuticals; Engineering (Various branches)
**Circ:** (Paid)500

**Current Psychology**  (19677)
Transaction Publishers
Rutgers—The State University of New Jersey
215 Smithers Hall
607 Allison Rd.
Piscataway, NJ 08854
Phone: (732)445-0794
**Subject(s):** Psychology and Psychiatry
**Circ:** (Paid)‡500

**Dermatologica Helvetica**  (4712)
S. Karger Publishers Inc.
26 W Avon Rd.
PO Box 529
Farmington, CT 06085
Phone: (860)675-7834
Fax: (860)675-7302
**Subject(s):** Medicine and Surgery; German; French
**Circ:** (Combined)500

**Diabetes/Metabolism Reviews**  (19209)
John Wiley and Sons Inc.
111 River St.
Hoboken, NJ 07030-5774
Phone: (201)748-6000
Fax: (201)748-6088
**Subject(s):** Medicine and Surgery
**Circ:** 500

**Diaspora**  (4842)
University of Toronto Press - Journals Div.
c/o Professor Khachig Tololyan
Editor, Diaspora
Wesleyan University
Middletown, CT 06459-0100
**Subject(s):** Ethnic and Minority Studies
**Circ:** 500

**Edinburgh Journal of Botany**  (21632)
Cambridge University Press
40 W. 20th St.
New York, NY 10011-4211
Phone: (212)924-3900
Fax: (212)691-3239
**Subject(s):** Botany
**Circ:** 500

**Experimental Mathematics**  (14875)
A.K. Peters Ltd.
888 Worcester St., Ste. 230
Wellesley, MA 02482
Phone: (781)416-2888
Fax: (781)416-2889
**Subject(s):** Mathematics
**Circ:** (Paid)500

**George Herbert Journal**  (4689)
Sacred Heart University
5151 Park Ave.
Fairfield, CT 06825
Phone: (203)371-7755
**Subject(s):** Literature
**Circ:** (Combined)500

**Germantown Crier**  (26956)
Germantown Historical Society
5501 Germantown Ave.
Philadelphia, PA 19144
Phone: (215)844-0514
Fax: (215)844-2831
**Subject(s):** History and Genealogy
**Circ:** ‡500

**Human & Experimental Toxicology**  (21793)
Nature Publishing Group
345 Park Ave., S
New York, NY 10010-1707
Phone: (212)726-9200
Fax: (212)696-0052
**Subject(s):** Toxicology
**Circ:** (Paid)500

**Indonesia**  (20953)
Southeast Asia Program Publications
The Kahin Center
Cornell University
640 Stewart Ave.
Ithaca, NY 14850
**Subject(s):** Ethnic and Minority Studies; Anthropology and Ethnology
**Circ:** (Combined)500

**Insights for Preachers**  (26263)
King Publications
5697 Applebutter Hill Rd.
Coopersburg, PA 18036-9560
Phone: (610)967-3901
Fax: (610)967-2128
**Subject(s):** Religious Publications
**Circ:** (Controlled)‡50
(Paid)‡500

**Integrative Physiological and Behavioral Science**  (19809)
Transaction Publishers
390 Campus Dr.
Somerset, NJ 08873
Phone: (732)445-1245
Fax: (732)748-9801
**Subject(s):** Physiology and Anatomy; Medicine and Surgery
**Circ:** (Paid)‡500

**International Journal of Human Computer Interaction**  (19480)
Lawrence Erlbaum Associates Inc.
10 Industrial Ave.
Mahwah, NJ 07430-2262
Phone: (201)258-2200
Fax: (201)236-0072
**Subject(s):** Computers
**Circ:** ‡500

**International Journal of Kurdish Studies**  (20514)
Kurdish Library
345 Park Pl.
Brooklyn, NY 11238
Phone: (718)783-7930
Fax: (718)398-4365
**Subject(s):** History and Genealogy; Ethnic and Minority Studies; Intercultural Interests
**Circ:** (Combined)500

**Journal of the American Aging Association**  (26687)
American Aging Association
110 Chesley Dr.
Media, PA 19063
Phone: (610)627-2626
Fax: (610)565-9747
**Subject(s):** Gerontology
**Circ:** 500

**Journal of Architectural Education (JAE)**  (13684)
The MIT Press
5 Cambridge Ctr.
Cambridge, MA 02142-1493
Phone: (617)253-5646
Fax: (617)258-6779
**Subject(s):** Architecture
**Circ:** (Combined)500

**Journal of Foodservice Business Research** (27606)
The Haworth Press Inc.
c/o David A. Cranage
The Pennsylvania State Univ.
School of Hospitality Management
221 Mateer Bldg.
University Park, PA 16802
**Subject(s):** Food and Grocery Trade
**Circ:** (Paid)500

**Journal of Global Competitiveness** (26534)
American Society for Competitiveness
Box 1658
Indiana, PA 15705
Fax: (724)357-5743
**Circ:** (Paid)500

**Journal of Orgonomy** (19725)
American College of Orgonomy
PO Box 490
Princeton, NJ 08542
Phone: (732)821-1144
Fax: (732)821-0174
**Subject(s):** Health and Healthcare; Medicine and Surgery
**Circ:** 500

**Kurdish Life** (20525)
Kurdish Library
345 Park Pl.
Brooklyn, NY 11238
Phone: (718)783-7930
Fax: (718)398-4365
**Subject(s):** Politics; International Affairs
**Circ:** (Paid)500

**Method** (13731)
Lonergan Institute at Boston College
Bapst Library
Boston College
140 Commonwealth Ave
Chestnut Hill, MA 02467
Phone: (617)552-8095
Fax: (617)552-0510
**Subject(s):** Literature; Philosophy
**Circ:** (Combined)500

**Novyj Zhurnal (The New Review)** (22181)
New Review Inc.
611 Broadway, No. 842
New York, NY 10012
Phone: (212)353-1478
Fax: (212)353-1478
**Subject(s):** Russian; Literature
**Circ:** 500

**Rural History** (22331)
Cambridge University Press
40 W. 20th St.
New York, NY 10011-4211
Phone: (212)924-3900
Fax: (212)691-3239
**Subject(s):** History and Genealogy; Literature; Archaeology
**Circ:** 500

**Semigroup Forum** (22363)
Springer-Verlag New York Inc.
233 Spring St.
New York, NY 10013
Phone: (212)460-1500
Fax: (212)460-1575
**Subject(s):** Mathematics; Indexes, Abstracts, Reports, Proceedings, and Bibliographies
**Circ:** (Combined)500

**Slipstream** (22618)
Dept. W-1
PO Box 2071, New Market Sta.
Niagara Falls, NY 14301
Phone: (716)282-2616
**Subject(s):** Literature and Literary Reviews; Poetry
**Circ:** (Non-paid)40
(Paid)500

**Topic (Washington)** (27649)
Washington and Jefferson College
60 S Lincoln St.
Washington, PA 15301
Phone: (724)222-4400
Fax: (724)223-5267
**Subject(s):** Literature; History and Genealogy
**Circ:** (Combined)500

**Transactions of the American Entomological Society** (27288)
The American Entomological Society
The Academy of Natural Sciences
1900 Benjamin Franklin Pkwy.
Philadelphia, PA 19103-1195
Phone: (215)561-3978
Fax: (215)299-1028
**Subject(s):** Entomology
**Circ:** ‡500

**The Trottingbred** (20845)
International Trotting and Pacing Association Inc.
60 Gulf Rd.
Gouverneur, NY 13642
Phone: (315)287-2294
Fax: (315)287-2294
**Subject(s):** Livestock; (Horses and Horse Racing)
**Circ:** ‡500

**The Urban League Review** (22508)
National Urban League
120 Wall St., 7th Fl.
New York, NY 10005
Phone: (212)558-5300
Fax: (212)344-5332
**Subject(s):** Ethnic and Minority Studies; Economics; Sociology
**Circ:** 500

**Voices** (23082)
New York Folklore Society
c/o Fay McMahon, Editor
374 Strong Road
Tully, NY 13159
**Subject(s):** Social Sciences; History and Genealogy
**Circ:** (Controlled)500

**WORD WAYS** (19571)
129 Kitchell.Rd.
Morristown, NJ 07960
Phone: (973)538-4584
**Subject(s):** Philology, Language, and Linguistics
**Circ:** ‡500

**The Clinical Supervisor** (20566)
The Haworth Press Inc.
c/o Lawrence Shulman, Univ. of Buffalo
School of Social Work
686 Baldy Hall
Buffalo, NY 14260-1050
Phone: (716)645-3381
**Subject(s):** Psychology and Psychiatry
**Circ:** (Paid)488

**Journal of Food Products Marketing** (27037)
The Haworth Press Inc.
c/o John L. Stanton, Ph.D., Dept. of Food Marketing
St. Joseph's University
5600 City Ave.
Philadelphia, PA 19131-1395
Phone: (215)660-1607
Fax: (215)660-1604
**Subject(s):** Food and Grocery Trade; Advertising and Marketing
**Circ:** 480

**Russian Social Science Review** (20316)
M.E. Sharpe Inc.
80 Business Park Dr.
Armonk, NY 10504
Phone: (914)273-1800
Fax: (914)273-2106
**Subject(s):** Social Sciences; Soviet Interests
**Circ:** (Paid)⊕487

**Journal of Business-to-Business Marketing** (21889)
The Haworth Press Inc.
c/o J. David Lichtenthal, City Univ. of New York
Zicklin School of Business
1 Bernard Baruch Way
PO Box 12-240
New York, NY 10010-5518
Phone: (646)312-3281
Fax: (646)312-3271
**Subject(s):** Advertising and Marketing
**Circ:** 473

**Journal of Optical Technology** (21163)
American Institute of Physics
2 Huntington Quadrangle, Ste. 1NO1
Melville, NY 11747-4502
Phone: (516)576-2200
Fax: (516)349-7669
**Subject(s):** Ophthalmology, Optometry, and Optics
**Circ:** ‡470

**Santa Clara Computer and High Technology Law Journal** (20579)
Santa Clara University School of Law
c/o William S. Hein & Co., Inc.
1285 Main St.
Buffalo, NY 14209
Fax: (716)883-8100
**Subject(s):** Law
**Circ:** (Paid)463

**Applied Artificial Intelligence** (26832)
Taylor & Francis
325 Chestnut St., Ste. 800
Philadelphia, PA 19106
Phone: (215)625-8900
Fax: (215)625-8914
**Subject(s):** Computers
**Circ:** (Combined)‡453

**Arabic Sciences and Philosophy** (21351)
Cambridge University Press
40 W. 20th St.
New York, NY 10011-4211
Phone: (212)924-3900
Fax: (212)691-3239
**Subject(s):** Science (General); Philosophy
**Circ:** 450

**Current Mathematical Publications** (27896)
American Mathematical Society
201 Charles St.
Providence, RI 02904-2294
Phone: (401)455-4000
Fax: (401)331-3842
**Subject(s):** Mathematics; Indexes, Abstracts, Reports, Proceedings, and Bibliographies
**Circ:** (Paid)450

**Dance Chronicle** (21586)
Marcel Dekker Inc.
270 Madison Ave.
New York, NY 10016-0602
Phone: (212)696-9000
Fax: (212)685-4540
**Subject(s):** Performing Arts
**Circ:** (Paid)450

**International Journal of Public Administration** (26698)
Marcel Dekker Inc.
c/o Jack Rabin ,The Pennsylvania State University-Harrisburg
School of Public Affairs
777 W. Harrisburg Pike
Middletown, PA 17057
**Subject(s):** Politics
**Circ:** ‡450

**Journal of End User Computing** (26492)
Idea Group Publishing
701 E. Chocolate Ave., Ste. 200
Hershey, PA 17033-1240
Phone: (717)533-8845
Fax: (717)533-8661
**Subject(s):** Computers; Business
**Circ:** (Controlled)450

**Journal of Plant Growth Regulation** (21975)
Springer-Verlag New York Inc.
233 Spring St.
New York, NY 10013
Phone: (212)460-1500
Fax: (212)460-1575
**Subject(s):** Science (General); Botany
**Circ:** (Combined)450

**The Pennsylvania Geographer** (26547)
Pennsylvania Geographical Society
Department of Geography
University of Pittsburgh at Johnstown
Johnstown, PA 15904
Phone: (814)269-2994
Fax: (814)269-7255
**Subject(s):** Aviation; Geography; Social Sciences
**Circ:** (Combined)450

**Reflections** (13704)
The MIT Press
c/o Jane Gebhart
Society for Organizational Learning
955 Massachusetts Ave., Ste. 201
Cambridge, MA 02139
Phone: (617)300-9515

# Northeastern States

Fax: (617)354-2093
**Subject(s):** Business
**Circ:** 450

**Science in Context** (22352)
Cambridge University Press
40 W. 20th St.
New York, NY 10011-4211
Phone: (212)924-3900
Fax: (212)691-3239
**Subject(s):** Science (General)
**Circ:** 450

**Studies in American Jewish Literature** (27615)
University of Nebraska Press
116 Burrowes Bldg.
University Park, PA 16802
Phone: (814)237-1609
Fax: (814)863-7285
**Subject(s):** Literature; Jewish Publications
**Circ:** (Combined)450

**Journal of Aging and Social Policy** (13533)
The Haworth Press Inc.
University of Massachusetts-Boston
Gerontology Institute
100 Morrissey Blvd.
Boston, MA 02125-3393
Phone: (617)287-7300
Fax: (617)287-7080
**Subject(s):** Congressional and Federal Government Affairs
**Circ:** 448

**Journal of Global Marketing** (26702)
The Haworth Press Inc.
International Business Press
PO Box 399
Middletown, PA 17057
Phone: (717)566-3054
Fax: (717)566-8589
**Subject(s):** International Business and Economics
**Circ:** 432

**Eastern European Economics** (20297)
M.E. Sharpe Inc.
80 Business Park Dr.
Armonk, NY 10504
Phone: (914)273-1800
Fax: (914)273-2106
**Subject(s):** International Business and Economics
**Circ:** (Paid)⊕422

**Electronics and Communications in Japan** (19215)
John Wiley and Sons Inc.
111 River St.
Hoboken, NJ 07030-5774
Phone: (201)748-6000
Fax: (201)740-0000
**Subject(s):** Electronics Engineering
**Circ:** 425

**Journal of Gay and Lesbian Social Services** (21929)
The Haworth Press Inc.
NYU School of Social Work
1 Washington Square N.211, MC 6112
New York, NY 10003-6654
Phone: (212)992-9711
**Subject(s):** Social Sciences; Gay and Lesbian Interests
**Circ:** (Paid)422

**Journal of Nonlinear Science** (19724)
Springer-Verlag New York Inc.
Princeton University
205 Fine Hall
Princeton, NJ 08544
Phone: (609)258-3008
Fax: (609)258-1735
**Subject(s):** Science (General)
**Circ:** (Combined)425

**Journal of Toxicology, Cutaneous and Ocular Toxicology** (13430)
Marcel Dekker Inc.
c/o Dr. A. Wallace Hayes
Harvard School of Public Health
298 So. Main St.
Andover, MA 01810
Phone: (978)749-3085
**Subject(s):** Drugs and Pharmaceuticals; Medicine and Surgery; Ophthalmology, Optometry, and Optics
**Circ:** (Paid)425

**International Studies of Management & Organization** (21844)
M.E. Sharpe Inc.
Baruch College, CUNY
17 Lexington Ave.
New York, NY 10010
Phone: (212)447-3267
Fax: (212)447-3267
**Subject(s):** Business
**Circ:** (Paid)⊕415

**Journal of Health Care Chaplaincy** (21932)
The Haworth Press Inc.
c/o Larry VandeCreek, Dir. of Pastoral Research
The HealthCare Chaplaincy
New York, NY
**Subject(s):** Social Programs; Health and Healthcare
**Circ:** (Controlled)417

**Plainsong and Medieval Music** (14298)
Cambridge University Press
c/o Professor Joseph Dyer, 73 Wade St
73 Wade St.
Newton Highlands, MA 02461-1714
**Subject(s):** Music and Musical Instruments
**Circ:** (Non-paid)‡47
 (Paid)‡414

**Arms Control Reporter** (13650)
Institute for Defense and Disarmament Studies
675 Massachusetts Ave., 8th Fl.
Cambridge, MA 02139
Phone: (617)354-4337
Fax: (617)354-1450
**Subject(s):** Firearms; Peace
**Circ:** 400

**ATQ** (27857)
University of Rhode Island
English Department
Kingston, RI 02881
Phone: (401)874-2576
Fax: (401)874-2580
**Subject(s):** Literature
**Circ:** (Controlled)‡42
 (Paid)‡404

**Gerontology & Geriatrics Education** (14937)
The Haworth Press Inc.
Consortium Gerontology Studies Program
Colleges of Wooster Consortium Inc.
484 Main St., Ste. 500
Worcester, MA 01608
Phone: (508)797-0069
Fax: (508)797-0069
**Subject(s):** Gerontology
**Circ:** ‡407

**Heat Transfer - Japanese Research** (19241)
John Wiley and Sons Inc.
111 River St.
Hoboken, NJ 07030-5774
Phone: (201)748-6000
Fax: (201)748-6088
**Subject(s):** Engineering (Various branches); Science (General)
**Circ:** 400

**Japanese Journal of Political Science** (21854)
Cambridge University Press
40 W. 20th St.
New York, NY 10011-4211
Phone: (212)924-3900
Fax: (212)691-3239
**Subject(s):** International Affairs; Political Science
**Circ:** ‡400

**Journal of Functional Programming** (21925)
Cambridge University Press
40 W. 20th St.
New York, NY 10011-4211
Phone: (212)924-3900
Fax: (212)691-3239
**Subject(s):** Computers
**Circ:** 400

**Journal of Liposome Research** (21947)
Marcel Dekker Inc.
270 Madison Ave.
New York, NY 10016-0602
Phone: (212)696-9000
Fax: (212)685-4540
**Subject(s):** Medicine and Surgery; Drugs and Pharmaceuticals
**Circ:** (Paid)400

**Journal of Maine Water Utilities Association** (12610)
Maine Water Utilities Association
PO Box P
1419 Old Route 1
Waldoboro, ME 04572
Phone: (207)832-2263
Fax: (207)832-2265
**Subject(s):** Water Supply and Sewage Disposal
**Circ:** 400

**Journal of Plasma Physics** (21976)
Cambridge University Press
40 W. 20th St.
New York, NY 10011-4211
Phone: (212)924-3900
Fax: (212)691-3239
**Subject(s):** Physics
**Circ:** 400

**The Knowledge Engineering Review** (20524)
Cambridge University Press
C/O Dr. Simon Parsons
Dept. of Computer and Information Science
Brooklyn College, City University of New York
2900 Bedford Ave.
Brooklyn, NY 11210
**Subject(s):** Engineering (Various branches)
**Circ:** 400

**Laser and Particle Beams** (22024)
Cambridge University Press
40 W. 20th St.
New York, NY 10011-4211
Phone: (212)924-3900
Fax: (212)691-3239
**Subject(s):** Physics
**Circ:** 400

**The Lit Page** (19094)
Library Outreach Reporter
148 Liberty St.
Fords, NJ 08863
Phone: (718)437-3383
Fax: (732)738-5183
**Subject(s):** Library and Information Science
**Circ:** (Non-paid)‡200
 (Paid)‡400

**Northeastern Geology and Environmental Sciences** (23072)
Northeastern Science Foundation Inc.
PO Box 746
Troy, NY 12181-0746
Phone: (518)273-3247
Fax: (518)273-3249
**Subject(s):** Geology; Natural History and Nature Study
**Circ:** (Paid)400

**Experimental Lung Research** (26944)
Taylor & Francis
325 Chestnut St., Ste. 800
Philadelphia, PA 19106
Phone: (215)625-8900
Fax: (215)625-8914
**Subject(s):** Science (General); Medicine and Surgery
**Circ:** ‡390

**Journal of International Food and Agribusiness Marketing** (26704)
The Haworth Press Inc.
International Business Press (IBP)
PO Box 399
Middletown, PA 17057
Phone: (717)566-3054
Fax: (717)566-8589
**Subject(s):** Food and Grocery Trade
**Circ:** 380

**Women & Criminal Justice** (27533)
The Haworth Press Inc.
c/o Donna Hale, Shippensburg Univ.
Dept. of Criminal Justice
317 Shippen Hall
1871 Old Main Dr.
Shippensburg, PA 17257-2299
Phone: (717)477-1608
Fax: (717)477-4036
**Subject(s):** Police, Penology, and Penal Institutions; Women's Interests
**Circ:** (Controlled)‡382

**Circulatory Shock (19197)**
John Wiley and Sons Inc.
111 River St.
Hoboken, NJ 07030-5774
Phone: (201)748-6000
Fax: (201)748-6088
Subject(s): Medicine and Surgery
Circ: 375

**Immunological Investigations (21809)**
Marcel Dekker Inc.
270 Madison Ave.
New York, NY 10016-0602
Phone: (212)696-9000
Fax: (212)685-4540
Subject(s): Medicine and Surgery
Circ: 375

**Journal of International Consumer Marketing (26703)**
The Haworth Press Inc.
International Business Press
PO Box 399
Middletown, PA 17057
Phone: (717)566-3054
Fax: (717)566-8589
Subject(s): International Business and Economics; Advertising and Marketing
Circ: (Paid)371

**Problems of Economic Transition (20310)**
M.E. Sharpe Inc.
80 Business Park Dr.
Armonk, NY 10504
Phone: (914)273-1800
Fax: (914)273-2106
Subject(s): Economics; Soviet Interests
Circ: (Paid)⊕360

**AI EDAM (14929)**
Cambridge University Press
C/O David C. Brown, Computer Science, WPI
100 Institute Rd.
Worcester, MA 01609-2280
Subject(s): Engineering (Various branches)
Circ: (Non-paid)‡67
(Paid)‡350

**Complementary Health Practice Review (21534)**
Springer Publishing Co.
11 W. 42nd St. 15th Fl.
New York, NY 10036
Phone: (212)431-4370
Fax: (212)941-7842
Subject(s): Health and Healthcare; Medicine and Surgery
Circ: (Controlled)350

**Drying Technology (21621)**
Marcel Dekker Inc.
270 Madison Ave.
New York, NY 10016-0602
Phone: (212)696-9000
Fax: (212)685-4540
Subject(s): Chemistry, Chemicals, and Chemical Engineering
Circ: 350

**Endocrine Research (20569)**
Marcel Dekker Inc.
c/o Dr. Alexander C. Brownie, Department of Biochemistry
140 Farber Hall
University
Buffalo, NY 14214
Subject(s): Medicine and Surgery
Circ: 350

**Hudson Valley Regional Review (20284)**
Bard College
PO Box 5000
Annandale on Hudson, NY 12504-5000
Phone: (845)758-7200
Fax: (845)758-7625
Subject(s): History and Genealogy
Circ: (Paid)350

**Journal of Theoretical Probability (22000)**
Kluwer Academic/Plenum Publishing Corp.
c/o Ms. Ana Bozicevic
233 Spring St.
New York, NY 10013-1578
Phone: (212)620-8015
Fax: (212)463-0742
Subject(s): Mathematics
Circ: (Paid)350

**Mathematical Structures in Computer Science (22064)**
Cambridge University Press
40 W. 20th St.
New York, NY 10011-4211
Phone: (212)924-3900
Fax: (212)691-3239
Subject(s): Computers; Mathematics
Circ: 350

**Meteorological & Geoastrophysical Abstracts (13551)**
Inforonics
American Meteorological Society
45 Beacon St.,
Boston, MA 02108
Subject(s): Astronomy and Meteorology; Indexes, Abstracts, Reports, Proceedings, and Bibliographies
Circ: ‡350

**Molecular Biotechnology (19887)**
Humana Press Inc.
999 Riverview Dr., Ste. 208
Totowa, NJ 07512
Phone: (973)256-1699
Fax: (973)256-8341
Subject(s): Biology; Science (General)
Circ: (Paid)350

**Pediatric Hematology and Oncology (27212)**
Taylor & Francis
325 Chestnut St., Ste. 800
Philadelphia, PA 19106
Phone: (215)625-8900
Fax: (215)625-8914
Subject(s): Medicine and Surgery
Circ: (Paid)‡357

**Works and Days (26536)**
Indiana University of Pennsylvania
110 Leonard Hall
Indiana University of Pennsylvania
Indiana, PA 15705
Phone: (724)357-2261
Fax: (724)357-3056
Subject(s): Literature; Humanities
Circ: 350

**Zygote (19947)**
Cambridge University Press
Institute for Reproductive Medicine & Science
Saint Barnabas Medical Center
101 Old Short Hills Rd. Ste. 501
West Orange, NJ 07052
Subject(s): Biology
Circ: (Non-paid)‡88
(Paid)‡350

**Connecticut Ancestry (5028)**
Connecticut Ancestry Society Inc.
Box 249
Stamford, CT 06904
Subject(s): History and Genealogy
Circ: (Combined)340

**Cybernetics and Systems (26913)**
Taylor & Francis
325 Chestnut St., Ste. 800
Philadelphia, PA 19106
Phone: (215)625-8900
Fax: (215)625-8914
Subject(s): Automation; Mathematics; Computers
Circ: (Combined)‡341

**Journal of Religion and Psychical Research (19023)**
Academy of Religion and Psychical Research
1017 Cardinal Ln.
Cherry Hill, NJ 08003-2943
Phone: (856)795-1360
Fax: (856)795-6357
Subject(s): Theology
Circ: (Controlled)347

**Journal of Religion, Disability & Health (19598)**
The Haworth Press Inc.
Developmental Disabilities UMDNJ
335 Geroge St., 3rd Flr
New Brunswick, NJ 08903-2688
Phone: (732)235-9304
Subject(s): Handicapped; Social Programs; Health and Healthcare; Religious Publications
Circ: (Paid)335

**Anthropology & Archeology of Eurasia (20289)**
M.E. Sharpe Inc.
80 Business Park Dr.
Armonk, NY 10504
Phone: (914)273-1800
Fax: (914)273-2106
Subject(s): Anthropology and Ethnology; Archaeology; Soviet Interests
Circ: (Paid)⊕322

**Artificial Cells, Blood Substitutes and Immobilization Biotechnology (21363)**
Marcel Dekker Inc.
270 Madison Ave.
New York, NY 10016-0602
Phone: (212)696-9000
Fax: (212)685-4540
Subject(s): Biology; Chemistry, Chemicals, and Chemical Engineering; Medicine and Surgery
Circ: 325

**Galilean Electrodynamics (13434)**
141 Rhinecliff St.
Arlington, MA 02476-7331
Phone: (781)643-3155
Fax: (781)646-8114
Subject(s): Physics
Circ: (Combined)‡320

**Hemoglobin (21762)**
Marcel Dekker Inc.
270 Madison Ave.
New York, NY 10016-0602
Phone: (212)696-9000
Fax: (212)685-4540
Subject(s): Medicine and Surgery
Circ: 325

**Hydrobiological Journal (21798)**
Begell House Inc.
145 Madison Ave., Ste. 601
New York, NY 10016
Phone: (212)725-1999
Fax: (212)213-8368
Subject(s): Biology
Circ: 325

**Journal of Teaching in Social Work (21998)**
The Haworth Press Inc.
c/o Florence Vigilante, DSW, Editor
School of Social Work
129 E. 79th St.
Hunter College of CUNY
New York, NY 10021
Phone: (212)452-7037
Fax: (212)650-3527
Subject(s): Education
Circ: (Controlled)327

**Sequential Analysis (5049)**
Marcel Dekker Inc.
c/o Nitis Mukhopadhyay
Department of Statistics
CLAS Bldg, Box 4120
University of Connecticut
Storrs, CT 06269-4120
Phone: (860)486-6144
Fax: (860)486-4113
Subject(s): Mathematics; Statistics
Circ: (Paid)325

**Spectroscopy Letters (5050)**
Marcel Dekker Inc.
c/o Robert G. Michel, 55 N. Eagleville Rd.
Department of Chemistry
University of Connecticut
55 N. Eagleville Rd.
Storrs, CT 06269
Subject(s): Chemistry, Chemicals, and Chemical Engineering
Circ: (Paid)325

**Agricultural Finance Review (20941)**
Cornell University
Department of Applied Economics and Management
357 Warren Hall
Ithaca, NY 14853-7801
Phone: (607)255-4534
Fax: (607)255-1589
Subject(s): General Agriculture
Circ: (Paid)300

**Asian Cinema** (26289)
Asian Cinema Studies Society
669 Ferne Rd.
Drexel Hill, PA 19026
Phone: (610)622-3938
Fax: (610)622-2124
Subject(s): Motion Pictures; Entertainment; Intercultural Interests
Circ: 300

**College & Undergraduate Libraries** (23004)
The Haworth Press Inc.
c/o Inga H. Barnello, Noreen Reale Falcone Library
Le Moyne College
1419 Salt Springs Rd.
Syracuse, NY 13214-1399
Phone: (315)445-4326
Fax: (315)445-4642
Subject(s): Library and Information Science
Circ: 300

**International Journal of Sociology** (20305)
M.E. Sharpe Inc.
80 Business Park Dr.
Armonk, NY 10504
Phone: (914)273-1800
Fax: (914)273-2106
Subject(s): Sociology; Intercultural Interests
Circ: (Paid)⊕302

**Journal of Euromarketing** (26701)
The Haworth Press Inc.
c/o Erdener Kaynak, Ph.D.
PO Box 399
Middletown, PA 17057
Phone: (717)566-3054
Fax: (800)342-9678
Subject(s): International Business and Economics
Circ: (Non-paid)50
(Paid)300

**Journal of NeuroVirology** (26494)
International Society of Neurovirology
c/o Brian Wigdahl, Dept. of Microbiology and Immunology
Penn State College of Medicine
500 University Dr.
PO Box 850
Hershey, PA 17033
Phone: (717)531-8258
Fax: (717)531-5580
Subject(s): Medicine and Surgery; Health and Healthcare; Laboratory Research (Scientific and Medical)
Circ: 300

**Journal of Religious & Theological Information** (26447)
The Haworth Press Inc.
c/o Iren Light Snavely, Temple Univ.
Temple Harrisburg Library
234 Strawberry Sq.
Harrisburg, PA 17101
Phone: (717)232-6400
Subject(s): Library and Information Science
Circ: (Paid)301

**The Journal of Speculative Philosophy** (27608)
Penn State University Press
820 N University Dr.
USB-1 Ste. C
University Park, PA 16802
Phone: (814)865-1327
Fax: (814)863-1408
Subject(s): Philosophy
Circ: ‡300

**Journal of Wood Chemistry and Technology** (23018)
Marcel Dekker Inc.
c/o Leland R. Schroeder
College of Environmental Science and Forestry
State University of New York
Syracuse, NY 13210
Subject(s): Chemistry, Chemicals, and Chemical Engineering; Wood and Woodworking
Circ: 300

**Marine Resource Economics** (27860)
MRE Foundation
Dept. of Environmental & Natural Resource Economics
University of Rhode Island
Kingston, RI 02881-0814
Phone: (401)874-4583
Fax: (401)782-4766
Subject(s): Oceanography and Marine Studies
Circ: ‡300

**MELA Notes** (27141)
Middle East Librarians Association
University of Washington Libraries
3420 Wallnut St.
University of Pennsylvania Libraries
Philadelphia, PA 19104
Phone: (215)898-2196
Fax: (206)685-8782
Subject(s): Library and Information Science
Circ: 300

**Motor Control** (27610)
Human Kinetics Publishers Inc.
c/o Mark Latash, Ph.D.
The Pennsylvania State University
Biomechanics Laboratory
University Park, PA 16802
Phone: (814)863-5374
Fax: (814)865-2440
Subject(s): Medicine and Surgery; Science (General); Physiology and Anatomy
Circ: (Paid)‡307

**Poets at Work** (26655)
PO Box 232
Lyndora, PA 16045
Subject(s): Poetry; Literature and Literary Reviews
Circ: 300

**Puckerbrush Review** (12551)
Puckerbrush Press
76 Main St.
Orono, ME 04473
Phone: (207)866-4868
Subject(s): Literature
Circ: (Paid)300

**ROTA.GENE** (4654)
Print Shack
499 Federal Rd.
Brookfield, CT 06804
Phone: (203)775-4515
Fax: (203)775-0180
Subject(s): History and Genealogy; Rotarians, International Fellowship of
Circ: (Non-paid)‡150
(Paid)‡300

**Studies in the Humanities** (26535)
Indiana University of Pennsylvania
110 Leonard Hall
Indiana University of Pennsylvania
Indiana, PA 15705
Phone: (724)357-2261
Fax: (724)357-3056
Subject(s): Literature; Motion Pictures
Circ: (Paid)300

**Systems and Computers in Japan** (19397)
John Wiley and Sons Inc.
111 River St.
Hoboken, NJ 07030-5774
Phone: (201)748-6000
Fax: (201)748-6088
Subject(s): Mathematics; Computers
Circ: (Paid)‡300

**Technical Physics** (21191)
American Institute of Physics
2 Huntington Quadrangle, Ste. 1NO1
Melville, NY 11747-4502
Phone: (516)576-2200
Fax: (516)349-7669
Subject(s): Physics
Circ: ‡300

**Trends in Organized Crime** (19818)
Transaction Publishers
390 Campus Dr.
Somerset, NJ 08873
Phone: (732)445-1245
Fax: (732)748-9801
Subject(s): Police, Penology, and Penal Institutions
Circ: (Paid)‡300

**Urban Forum** (19819)
Transaction Publishers
390 Campus Dr.
Somerset, NJ 08873
Phone: (732)445-1245
Fax: (732)748-9801
Circ: (Combined)300

**Geomicrobiology Journal** (23069)
Taylor & Francis
c/o Henry Ehrlich, Dept. of Biology
Rensselear Polytechnic Institute
Troy, NY 12180-3590
Subject(s): Biology; Geology
Circ: (Controlled)‡281

**Washington County Reports** (27651)
Washington County Bar Association
30 E Beau, No. 523
Washington, PA 15301
Phone: (724)225-6710
Fax: (724)225-8345
Subject(s): Law
Circ: (Non-paid)25
(Paid)287

**Columbia Journal of Asian Law** (21513)
Columbia University
435 W. 116th St.
New York, NY 10027-7297
Phone: (212)854-2640
Subject(s): Law; Intercultural Interests
Circ: (Paid)‡270

**Current Physics Index** (21153)
American Institute of Physics
2 Huntington Quadrangle, Ste. 1NO1
Melville, NY 11747-4502
Phone: (516)576-2200
Fax: (516)349-7669
Subject(s): Physics; Indexes, Abstracts, Reports, Proceedings, and Bibliographies
Circ: ‡279

**International Journal of Political Economy** (20304)
M.E. Sharpe Inc.
80 Business Park Dr.
Armonk, NY 10504
Phone: (914)273-1800
Fax: (914)273-2106
Subject(s): International Affairs; International Business and Economics
Circ: (Paid)279

**Sociological Research** (20320)
M.E. Sharpe Inc.
80 Business Park Dr.
Armonk, NY 10504
Phone: (914)273-1800
Fax: (914)273-2106
Subject(s): Sociology; Soviet Interests
Circ: (Paid)⊕272

**Latin America Indian Literatures Journal** (26675)
Penn State McKeesport
4000 University Dr.
Mc Keesport, PA 15132-7698
Phone: (412)675-9466
Fax: (412)675-9278
Subject(s): Literature; Anthropology and Ethnology
Circ: (Combined)260

**Anchor** (22692)
Anchor Block Foundation
980 Plymouth St.
Pelham, NY 10803
Subject(s): Collecting; Dutch; German
Circ: 250

**Chinese Studies in History** (20295)
M.E. Sharpe Inc.
80 Business Park Dr.
Armonk, NY 10504
Phone: (914)273-1800
Fax: (914)273-2106
Subject(s): History and Genealogy; Intercultural Interests
Circ: (Paid)⊕252

**Connecticut River Review** (5068)
Connecticut Poetry Society
Joan Ellen Ketreys
PO Box 4053
Waterbury, CT 06704-0053
Phone: (203)753-7815
Fax: (203)753-1703
Subject(s): Poetry
Circ: (Paid)250

**Fullerene Science & Technology** (21722)
Marcel Dekker Inc.
270 Madison Ave.
New York, NY 10016-0602
Phone: (212)696-9000

Fax: (212)685-4540
**Subject(s):** Chemistry, Chemicals, and Chemical Engineering; Physics; Science
**Circ:** (Paid)250

**Huntia (27357)**
Hunt Institute for Botanical Documentation
5000 Forbes Ave.
Pittsburgh, PA 15213-3890
Phone: (412)268-2434
Fax: (412)268-5677
**Subject(s):** Botany
**Circ:** (Combined)250

**International Journal of Electronic Commerce (19929)**
M.E. Sharpe Inc.
PO Box 335
Wanaque, NJ 07465
Phone: (201)839-2417
Fax: (201)839-2417
**Subject(s):** Economics; Computers; Sociology
**Circ:** (Paid)254

**Journal of East-West Business (26700)**
The Haworth Press Inc.
c/o Erdener Kaynak
Pennsylvania State Univ. at Harrisburg
School of Business Administration
777 West Harrisburg Pike
Middletown, PA 17057
**Subject(s):** Business; International Business and Economics
**Circ:** 250

**Journal of Fine and Performing Arts Philately (20859)**
Fine Arts Philatelists
19 Ramsey Rd.
Great Neck, NY 11023
Phone: (516)466-6073
**Subject(s):** Crafts, Models, Hobbies, and Contests; Collecting
**Circ:** 250

**Journal of Hospital Marketing & Public Relations (22964)**
The Haworth Press Inc.
c/o Tony Carter
57 Pembrook Loop
Staten Island, NY 10309
Phone: (718)390-3182
**Subject(s):** Hospitals and Healthcare Institutions
**Circ:** (Controlled)‡250

**Russian Studies in History (20317)**
M.E. Sharpe Inc.
80 Business Park Dr.
Armonk, NY 10504
Phone: (914)273-1800
Fax: (914)273-2106
**Subject(s):** History and Genealogy; Soviet Interests
**Circ:** (Paid)⊕256

**Thinking (19918)**
IAPC
Montclair State University
Upper Montclair, NJ 07043
Phone: (973)655-4277
Fax: (973)655-7834
**Subject(s):** Philosophy
**Circ:** (Non-paid)‡100
 (Paid)‡250

**Transactions of the Moscow Mathematical Society (27926)**
American Mathematical Society
201 Charles St.
Providence, RI 02904-2294
Phone: (401)455-4000
Fax: (401)331-3842
**Subject(s):** Mathematics
**Circ:** (Paid)252

**Fetal and Maternal Medicine Review (21681)**
Cambridge University Press
40 W. 20th St.
New York, NY 10011-4211
Phone: (212)924-3900
Fax: (212)691-3239
**Subject(s):** Medicine and Surgery
**Circ:** (Non-paid)‡58
 (Paid)‡240

**Journal of Teaching in International Business (26705)**
The Haworth Press Inc.
International Business Press
PO Box 399
Middletown, PA 17057
Phone: (717)566-8589
Fax: (717)566-8589
**Subject(s):** International Business and Economics; Education
**Circ:** 245

**Natural Language Engineering (23210)**
Cambridge University Press
c/o Dr Branimir K. Boguraev
IBM Thomas J. Watson Research Center
PO Box 704
Yorktown Heights, NY 10598
**Subject(s):** Philology, Language, and Linguistics; Computers
**Circ:** (Non-paid)‡59
 (Paid)‡245

**Nursing Leadership Forum (22184)**
Springer Publishing Co.
11 W. 42nd St. 15th Fl.
New York, NY 10036
Phone: (212)431-4370
Fax: (212)941-7842
**Subject(s):** Hospitals and Healthcare Institutions; Nursing
**Circ:** (Free)50
 (Paid)240

**Russian Politics and Law (20315)**
M.E. Sharpe Inc.
80 Business Park Dr.
Armonk, NY 10504
Phone: (914)273-1800
Fax: (914)273-2106
**Subject(s):** Soviet Interests; Law
**Circ:** (Paid)⊕248

**Central Asia Monitor (30846)**
Institute for Democratic Development
560 Herrick Rd.
Benson, VT 05743
**Subject(s):** Anthropology and Ethnology; Ethnic and Minority Studies
**Circ:** 235

**The Velikovskian (20790)**
The Velikovskian IVY Press Books
65-35 108th St., Ste. D-15
Forest Hills, NY 11375
Phone: (718)897-2403
**Subject(s):** Science (General)
**Circ:** 235

**Weekly Insiders Turkey Letter (19884)**
Urner Barry Publications Inc.
PO Box 389
Toms River, NJ 08754
Phone: (732)240-5330
Fax: (732)341-0891
**Subject(s):** Poultry and Pigeons
**Circ:** (Paid)230

**The Chinese Economy (20292)**
M.E. Sharpe Inc.
80 Business Park Dr.
Armonk, NY 10504
Phone: (914)273-1800
Fax: (914)273-2106
**Subject(s):** Economics; Intercultural Interests
**Circ:** (Paid)⊕224

**The Japanese Economy (20306)**
M.E. Sharpe Inc.
80 Business Park Dr.
Armonk, NY 10504
Phone: (914)273-1800
Fax: (914)273-2106
**Subject(s):** International Business and Economics
**Circ:** (Paid)⊕225

**Journal of Historical Research in Music Education (20958)**
Ithaca College
3322 Whalen Center for Music
Ithaca, NY 14850
Phone: (607)274-1563
Fax: (607)274-1727
**Subject(s):** Music and Musical Instruments; Education
**Circ:** (Combined)227

**Journal of Trace and Microprobe Techniques (22001)**
Marcel Dekker Inc.
270 Madison Ave.
New York, NY 10016-0602
Phone: (212)696-9000
Fax: (212)685-4540
**Subject(s):** Chemistry, Chemicals, and Chemical Engineering
**Circ:** (Paid)225

**Livingston County Agricultural News (21227)**
Livingston County Extension Service Association
Agricultural Dept.
158 S Main St.
Mount Morris, NY 14510-1594
Phone: (585)658-3250
Fax: (585)658-4707
**Subject(s):** Farm Bureau, Grange, and Cooperative Associations
**Circ:** (Controlled)‡25
 (Paid)‡220

**International Journal of Mental Health (20303)**
M.E. Sharpe Inc.
80 Business Park Dr.
Armonk, NY 10504
Phone: (914)273-1800
Fax: (914)273-2106
**Subject(s):** Psychology and Psychiatry
**Circ:** (Paid)⊕213

**Journal of Agricultural and Environmental Ethics (13821)**
Kluwer Academic Publishers
P.O. Box 358, Accord Sta.
Hingham, MA 02018-0358
**Subject(s):** General Agriculture; Philosophy; Biology
**Circ:** (Non-paid)27
 (Paid)211

**Journal of Russian and East European Psychology (20307)**
M.E. Sharpe Inc.
80 Business Park Dr.
Armonk, NY 10504
Phone: (914)273-1800
Fax: (914)273-2106
**Subject(s):** Psychology and Psychiatry; Soviet Interests
**Circ:** (Paid)⊕217

**Russian Education and Society (20314)**
M.E. Sharpe Inc.
80 Business Park Dr.
Armonk, NY 10504
Phone: (914)273-1800
Fax: (914)273-2106
**Subject(s):** Education; Soviet Interests
**Circ:** (Paid)⊕211

**York Legal Record (27732)**
York County Bar Association
137 E Market St.
York, PA 17401-1221
Phone: (717)854-8755
Fax: (717)843-8766
**Subject(s):** Law
**Circ:** (Non-paid)‡101
 (Paid)‡211

**Annals of Cases on Information Technology (ACIT) (26482)**
Idea Group Publishing
701 E. Chocolate Ave., Ste. 200
Hershey, PA 17033-1240
Phone: (717)533-8845
Fax: (717)533-8661
**Subject(s):** Business; Management and Administration; Automation; Computers
**Circ:** (Paid)200

**Exit 13 Magazine (19084)**
PO Box 423
Fanwood, NJ 07023-1162
Phone: (908)889-5298
**Subject(s):** Poetry; Literature and Literary Reviews
**Circ:** (Non-paid)‡100
 (Paid)‡200

**Fat Tuesday (26400)**
Fat Tuesday Productions
560 Manada Gap Rd.
Grantville, PA 17028
Phone: (717)469-7159
**Subject(s):** Literature
**Circ:** (Paid)200

## Northeastern States

**Gulp** (20370)
21 Main St.
Binghamton, NY 13905
Phone: (607)723-4507
**Subject(s):** Literature and Literary Reviews
**Circ:** (Combined)200

**International Journal of High Speed Electronics and Systems** (23070)
World Scientific Publishing
c/o M S Shur
Center for Integrated Electronics & Electronics Manufacturing
Rm. 9017, CII
Rensselaer Polytechnic Institute, 110 8-th St.
Troy, NY 12180-3590
**Subject(s):** Electrical Engineering
**Circ:** (Non-paid)100
(Paid)200

**Journal of Computing in Higher Education** (13412)
Norris Publishers
PO Box 2593
Amherst, MA 01004-2593
Phone: (413)519-5150
Fax: (413)253-9525
**Subject(s):** Computers; Education
**Circ:** (Paid)200
(Non-paid)200

**Journal of Income Distribution** (19812)
Transaction Publishers
390 Campus Dr.
Somerset, NJ 08873
Phone: (732)445-1245
Fax: (732)748-9801
**Subject(s):** Social and Political Issues; Social Sciences; Economics
**Circ:** (Combined)200

**Journal of Pharmacy Practice** (26599)
Technomic Publishing Company Inc.
851 New Holland Ave.
PO Box 3535
Lancaster, PA 17604
Fax: (717)295-4538
**Subject(s):** Drugs and Pharmaceuticals
**Circ:** (Paid)200

**Markers** (27728)
Association for Gravestone Studies
Penn State York
1031 Edgecomb Ave.
York, PA 17403
Phone: (717)771-4049
Fax: (717)771-4022
**Subject(s):** History and Genealogy; Art and Art History
**Circ:** (Paid)200

**Moksha Journal** (20277)
Santosha.com
42 Merrick Rd.
Amityville, NY 11701
Phone: (516)691-8475
Fax: (516)691-8475
**Subject(s):** Religious Publications; New Age; Alternative and Underground
**Circ:** (Controlled)200

**Structural Chemistry** (18815)
Kluwer Academic/Plenum Publishing Corp.
Dean
University of New Hampshire
Kingsbury Hall
Durham, NH 03824
Phone: (603)862-2486
Fax: (603)862-2486
**Subject(s):** Chemistry, Chemicals, and Chemical Engineering
**Circ:** (Non-paid)‡50
(Paid)‡200

**Chinese Sociology and Anthropology** (20294)
M.E. Sharpe Inc.
80 Business Park Dr.
Armonk, NY 10504
Phone: (914)273-1800
Fax: (914)273-2106
**Subject(s):** Anthropology and Ethnology; Sociology; Intercultural Interests
**Circ:** (Paid)⊕199

**Emerging Markets Finance and Trade** (20298)
M.E. Sharpe Inc.
80 Business Park Dr.
Armonk, NY 10504
Phone: (914)273-1800
Fax: (914)273-2106
**Subject(s):** International Business and Economics; Soviet Interests
**Circ:** (Paid)⊕196

**Horn and Whistle** (26782)
Horn and Whistle Enthusiasts Group
275 Windswept Drive
North East, PA 16428
Phone: (814)725-8150
**Subject(s):** Crafts, Models, Hobbies, and Contests
**Circ:** (Non-paid)10
(Paid)194

**Technical Physics Letters** (21192)
American Institute of Physics
2 Huntington Quadrangle, Ste. 1NO1
Melville, NY 11747-4502
Phone: (516)576-2200
Fax: (516)349-7669
**Subject(s):** Physics
**Circ:** ‡180

**Theory of Probability & Mathematical Statistics** (27924)
American Mathematical Society
201 Charles St.
Providence, RI 02904-2294
Phone: (401)455-4000
Fax: (401)331-3842
**Subject(s):** Mathematics
**Circ:** (Paid)‡189

**Journal of Solid Waste Technology and Management** (26235)
Widener University
1 University Pl.
Chester, PA 19013-5792
Phone: (610)499-4042
Fax: (610)499-1146
**Subject(s):** Engineering (Various branches); Ecology and Conservation
**Circ:** (Combined)175

**European Education** (20299)
M.E. Sharpe Inc.
80 Business Park Dr.
Armonk, NY 10504
Phone: (914)273-1800
Fax: (914)273-2106
**Subject(s):** Education; Intercultural Interests
**Circ:** (Paid)⊕169

**Sugaku Expositions** (27923)
American Mathematical Society
201 Charles St.
Providence, RI 02904-2294
Phone: (401)455-4000
Fax: (401)331-3842
**Subject(s):** Mathematics
**Circ:** (Paid)163

**Chinese Education & Society** (20293)
M.E. Sharpe Inc.
80 Business Park Dr.
Armonk, NY 10504
Phone: (914)273-1800
Fax: (914)273-2106
**Subject(s):** Education; Intercultural Interests
**Circ:** (Paid)⊕151

**Contemporary Chinese Thought** (20296)
M.E. Sharpe Inc.
80 Business Park Dr.
Armonk, NY 10504
Phone: (914)273-1800
Fax: (914)273-2106
**Subject(s):** Philosophy; Intercultural Interests
**Circ:** (Paid)⊕154

**Journal of Culinary Science & Technology** (20380)
The Haworth Press Inc.
10 Alice St.
Binghamton, NY 13904
Phone: (607)722-5857
Fax: (607)771-0012
**Subject(s):** Food and Grocery Trade
**Circ:** (Paid)159

**Journal of Spiritual Bodywork** (27097)
Spiritual Massage Healing Ministry
6907 Sherman St.
Philadelphia, PA 19119
Phone: (215)842-0265
Fax: (215)842-2388
**Subject(s):** Theology; Physical Education and Athletics
**Circ:** (Combined)150

**Low Temperature Physics** (21167)
American Institute of Physics
2 Huntington Quadrangle, Ste. 1NO1
Melville, NY 11747-4502
Phone: (516)576-2200
Fax: (516)349-7669
**Subject(s):** Physics
**Circ:** ‡150

**New York Economic Review** (22658)
New York State Economics Association
Division of Economics and Business
SUNY-Oneonta
Oneonta, NY 13820
Phone: (607)436-3458
Fax: (607)436-2543
**Subject(s):** Business; Economics
**Circ:** (Paid)150

**Northwoods Journal** (12519)
Conservatory of American Letters
30 Bartol Island Rd.
Freeport, ME 04032
**Subject(s):** Literature
**Circ:** (Paid)150

**Particulate Science and Technology** (27209)
Taylor & Francis
325 Chestnut St., Ste. 800
Philadelphia, PA 19106
Phone: (215)625-8900
Fax: (215)625-8914
**Subject(s):** Chemistry, Chemicals, and Chemical Engineering; Engineering (Various branches)
**Circ:** ‡150

**Russian Studies in Literature** (20318)
M.E. Sharpe Inc.
80 Business Park Dr.
Armonk, NY 10504
Phone: (914)273-1800
Fax: (914)273-2106
**Subject(s):** Literature; Soviet Interests
**Circ:** (Paid)⊕157

**Russian Studies in Philosophy** (20319)
M.E. Sharpe Inc.
80 Business Park Dr.
Armonk, NY 10504
Phone: (914)273-1800
Fax: (914)273-2106
**Subject(s):** Philosophy; Soviet Interests
**Circ:** (Paid)⊕158

**Acta Numerica** (21262)
Cambridge University Press
40 W. 20th St.
New York, NY 10011-4211
Phone: (212)924-3900
Fax: (212)691-3239
**Subject(s):** Science (General); Mathematics
**Circ:** (Non-paid)‡5
(Paid)‡148

**Journal of Sustainable Forestry** (4897)
The Haworth Press Inc.
c/o Graeme P. Berlyn,
Yale Univ. School of Forestry, Greeley Mem. Lab
370 Prospect St.
New Haven, CT 06511
Phone: (203)432-5142
Fax: (203)432-3929
**Subject(s):** Forestry
**Circ:** 148

**St. Petersburg Mathematical Journal** (27921)
American Mathematical Society
201 Charles St.
Providence, RI 02904-2294
Phone: (401)455-4000
Fax: (401)331-3842
**Subject(s):** Mathematics
**Circ:** (Paid)‡145

**Statutes and Decisions: The Laws of the USSR and its Successor States** (20321)
M.E. Sharpe Inc.
80 Business Park Dr.
Armonk, NY 10504
Phone: (914)273-1800
Fax: (914)273-2106
**Subject(s):** Law; Soviet Interests
**Circ:** (Paid)⊕145

**American Vedantist** (21327)
Vedanta West Communications
PO Box 237041
New York, NY 10023
Phone: (212)877-4730
Fax: (212)769-4280
**Subject(s):** Religious Publications
**Circ:** (Paid)125
(Non-paid)125

**Treaties and Other International Acts Series** (27410)
U.S. Government Printing Office and Superintendent of Documents
PO Box 371954
MS4004-MIB
Pittsburgh, PA 15250-7954
Phone: (202)512-1800
Fax: (202)512-2250
**Subject(s):** Congressional and Federal Government Affairs; International Affairs
**Circ:** 126

**Heat Exchanger Design Update** (21761)
Begell House Inc.
145 Madison Ave., Ste. 601
New York, NY 10016
Phone: (212)725-1999
Fax: (212)213-8368
**Subject(s):** Engineering (Various branches); Chemistry, Chemicals, and Chemical Engineering
**Circ:** (Paid)100

**Journal of Haitian Studies** (13538)
Haitian Studies Association
c/o University of Massachusetts
100 Morrissey Blvd.
McCormack 2-211
Boston, MA 02125-3393
Phone: (617)287-7138
Fax: (617)287-6797
**Subject(s):** Spanish; Intercultural Interests; French
**Circ:** 103

**Journal of Transnational Management Development** (13541)
The Haworth Press Inc.
c/o Kip Becker, Journal Editor
Dept. of Administrative Sciences
Boston Univ.
808 Commomwealth Ave.
Boston, MA 02215
Phone: (617)353-3016
Fax: (617)353-6840
**Subject(s):** Management and Administration; International Business and Economics
**Circ:** (Paid)107

**Maro Polymer Links/Alerts** (26364)
Maro Publications
327 Huffman Dr.
Exton, PA 19341
Phone: (610)363-9920
Fax: (610)363-9921
**Subject(s):** Science (General)
**Circ:** (Controlled)‡5
(Paid)‡100

**Waterways: Poetry in the Mainstream** (22968)
The Waterways Project
393 St. Pauls Ave.
Staten Island, NY 10304-2127
Phone: (718)442-7429
Fax: (718)442-4978
**Subject(s):** Literature
**Circ:** (Paid)‡50
(Non-paid)‡100

**Journal of Tree Fruit Production** (13415)
The Haworth Press Inc.
c/o Wesley R. Autio
Univ. of Massachusetts
Dept. of Plant and Soil Sciences
205 Bowditch Hall
Amherst, MA 01003
Phone: (413)545-2963
Fax: (413)545-0260

**Subject(s):** Socialized Farming
**Circ:** (Paid)96

**Rhode Island Postal History Journal** (27878)
Rhode Island Postal History Society
c/o Thomas Greene
Box 113822
North Providence, RI 02911
Phone: (401)353-1161
**Subject(s):** Postal and Shipping Supplies; History and Genealogy
**Circ:** 80

**Red Owl** (18951)
35 Hampshire Rd.
Portsmouth, NH 03801-4815
Phone: (603)431-2691
**Subject(s):** Poetry; Literature; Art
**Circ:** (Paid)50
(Non-paid)50

**Abrasive Users News Fax** (26208)
Abrasives Engineering Society
144 Moore Rd.
Butler, PA 16001
Phone: (724)282-6210
Fax: (724)234-2376
**Subject(s):** Engineering (Various branches); Commerce and Industry
**Circ:** (Non-paid)10

**Journal of Pharmacotherapy in Community & Public Health** (4806)
The Haworth Press Inc.
c/o David Nicalau, PharmaD, Hartford Hospital
Div. of Infectious Diseases, 80, Seymour street
Hartford, CT 06102
Phone: (860)545-3941
Fax: (860)545-3992
**Subject(s):** Medicine and Surgery
**Circ:** (Paid)16

# Southern Central States

**Boys' Life** (29978)
Boy Scouts of America
PO Box 152079
Irving, TX 75015-2079
Phone: (972)580-2000
Fax: (972)580-2079
**Subject(s):** Youths' Interests
**Circ:** (Paid)1,259,656

**Scouting** (29981)
Boy Scouts of America
PO Box 152079
Irving, TX 75015-2079
Phone: (972)580-2000
Fax: (972)580-2079
**Subject(s):** Parenting
**Circ:** (Paid)1,000,000

**Texas Co-op Power** (29212)
Texas Electric Cooperatives Inc.
2550 S. IH-35
Austin, TX 78704
Phone: (512)454-0311
Fax: (512)486-6254
**Subject(s):** Local, State, and Regional Publications
**Circ:** (Controlled)△825,000

**Airman** (30349)
Air Force News Service
203 Norton St.
San Antonio, TX 78226-1848
Phone: (210)925-7757
Fax: (210)925-7219
**Subject(s):** Military and Navy
**Circ:** (Controlled)750,000

**Outside** (20165)
Mariah Media Inc.
400 Market St.
Santa Fe, NM 87501
Phone: (505)989-7100
Fax: (505)989-4700
**Subject(s):** (Outdoors); (General Sports)
**Circ:** (Paid)569,224

**TRAVELHOST** (29573)
Travelhost Inc.
10701 Stemmons Fwy.
Dallas, TX 75220
Phone: (972)556-0541
Fax: (972)432-8729
**Subject(s):** Hotels, Motels, Restaurants, and Clubs; Travel and Tourism
**Circ:** (Non-paid)521,215

**Southwest Airlines Spirit** (29727)
American Airlines Publishing
4255 Amon Carter Blvd.
MD 4255
Fort Worth, TX 76155
Phone: (817)967-1804
Fax: (817)931-5782
**Subject(s):** Travel and Tourism; Hotels, Motels, Restaurants, and Clubs
**Circ:** 381,020

**American Way** (29705)
American Airlines Publishing
4255 Amon Carter Blvd.
MD 4255
Fort Worth, TX 76155
Phone: (817)967-1804
Fax: (817)931-5782
**Subject(s):** In-Flight Publications; Travel and Tourism
**Circ:** (Controlled)344,375

**Rural Arkansas** (1180)
Electric Cooperatives of Arkansas
1 Cooperative Way
Little Rock, AR 72209
Phone: (501)570-2200
**Subject(s):** Power and Power Plants
**Circ:** (Paid)312,186

**VACATIONS** (29920)
Vacation Publications Inc.
5851 San Felipe St., Ste. 500
Houston, TX 77057
Phone: (713)974-6903
Fax: (713)974-0445
**Subject(s):** Travel and Tourism
**Circ:** (Paid)305,000

**Ballard Strikes Softball Magazine** (25448)
ASA/USA Softball
2801 NE 50th St.
Oklahoma City, OK 73111
Phone: (405)424-5266
Fax: (405)424-4734
**Subject(s):** (Baseball)
**Circ:** (Controlled)‡302,300

**Texas Monthly** (29231)
PO Box 1569
Austin, TX 78767-1569
Phone: (512)320-6900
Fax: (512)476-9007
**Subject(s):** General Editorial; Local, State, and Regional Publications
**Circ:** (Paid)300,991

**Beckett Anime Collector** (29510)
Beckett Publications
15850 Dallas Pkwy.
Dallas, TX 75248
Phone: (972)991-6657
Fax: (972)991-8930
**Subject(s):** Collecting; Comics and Comic Technique; Crafts, Models, Hobbies, and Contests; Entertainment; Radio, Television, Cable, and Video
**Circ:** (Paid)300,000

**Balls & Strikes Softball Magazine** (25449)
Amateur Softball Association of America
4601 SE 49th St.
Oklahoma City, OK 73135-7203
Phone: (405)672-1601
Fax: (405)672-1601
**Subject(s):** (Baseball)
**Circ:** 27,5000

**Texas Highways** (29218)
Texas Highways Magazine
PO Box 141009
Austin, TX 78714-1009
Phone: (512)486-5823
Fax: (512)486-5879

# Southern Central States

**Subject(s):** Travel and Tourism; Local, State, and Regional Publications

**Circ:** (Controlled)‡25,642
(Paid)‡262,438

**Self-Employed America  (29566)**
National Association for the Self-Employed
DFW Airport
P.O. Box 612067
Dallas, TX 75261-2067
Fax: (800)551-4446
**Subject(s):** Business; Advertising and Marketing; Management and Administration

**Circ:** (Paid)‡250,000

**Oklahoma Living Magazine  (25472)**
PO Box 54309
2325 E I 44 Service Rd.
Oklahoma City, OK 73154
Phone: (405)478-1455
Fax: (405)478-0246
**Subject(s):** Local, State, and Regional Publications; Lifestyle

**Circ:** (Non-paid)1,200
(Paid)240,440

**Private Clubs  (29563)**
ClubCorp Publications Inc.
3030 LBJ Fwy., Ste. 350
Dallas, TX 75234-7395
Phone: (972)888-7547
Fax: (972)888-7338
**Subject(s):** Clubs and Societies

**Circ:** (Paid)239,627

**Saudi Aramco World  (29905)**
Aramco Services Co.
Box 2106
Houston, TX 77252-2106
Phone: (713)432-4000
Fax: (713)432-5536
**Subject(s):** Ethnic Publications; Ethnic and Minority Studies

**Circ:** (Controlled)180,000

**Horse & Rider  (29385)**
Primedia Equine Network
4101 International Pkwy
Carrollton, TX 75007
Phone: (972)309-5688
Fax: (972)309-5670
**Subject(s):** (Horses and Horse Racing)

**Circ:** (Paid)163,144

**Bassin'  (25266)**
NatCom Inc.
15115 S 76th E Ave.
Bixby, OK 74008-4114
Fax: (918)366-6512
**Subject(s):** (Hunting, Fishing, and Game Management)

**Circ:** (Paid)161,447

**Health & Fitness Sports Magazine  (29849)**
Health & Fitness Publishing Inc.
1502 Augusta, Ste. 230
Houston, TX 77057
Phone: (713)552-9991
Fax: (713)552-9997
**Subject(s):** (Physical Fitness); Health

**Circ:** (Non-paid)160,000

**Texas Parks & Wildlife  (29233)**
Texas Parks and Wildlife
4200 Smith School Rd.
Austin, TX 78744
Phone: (512)389-8950
**Subject(s):** (Outdoors)

**Circ:** (Paid)155,964

**Clean Energy Living  (29146)**
Texas Propane Gas Association
8408 N Interegional Hwy.
Austin, TX 78753
Phone: (512)836-8620
Fax: (512)834-0758
**Subject(s):** Petroleum, Oil, and Gas

**Circ:** (Controlled)150,000

**Annie's Plastic Canvas Magazine  (29308)**
The Needlecraft Shop L.L.C.
23 Old Pecan Rd.
Big Sandy, TX 75755
Phone: (903)636-4011
Fax: (800)882-6643
**Subject(s):** Dressmaking, Needlework, and Quilting; Crafts, Models, Hobbies, and Contests

**Circ:** ‡140,000

**Jaycees Magazine  (25609)**
The U.S. Junior Chamber of Commerce
PO Box 7
7447 S.Lewis Ave.
Tulsa, OK 74102
Phone: (918)584-2481
Fax: (918)584-4422
**Subject(s):** Clubs and Societies

**Circ:** ‡135,000

**Louisiana Country  (12080)**
Association of Louisiana Electric Cooperatives Inc.
10725 Airline Hwy.
Baton Rouge, LA 70816
Phone: (225)293-3450
Fax: (225)296-0924
**Subject(s):** General Agriculture; Rural Electrification; Local, State, and Regional Publications

**Circ:** ‡130,000

**The Trident of Delta Delta Delta  (29112)**
Delta Delta Delta
PO Box 5987
Arlington, TX 76005-5987
Phone: (817)633-8001
Fax: (817)652-0212
**Subject(s):** Unclassified Fraternal

**Circ:** ‡129,000

**Oklahoma Country  (25469)**
Oklahoma Farm Bureau Inc.
2501 N. Stiles
Oklahoma City, OK 73105-3126
Phone: (405)523-2300
Fax: (405)523-2362
**Subject(s):** Farm Bureau, Grange, and Cooperative Associations

**Circ:** (Controlled)‡834
(Paid)‡127,247

**Enchantment  (20162)**
New Mexico Rural Electric Cooperatives
614 Don Gaspar Ave.
Santa Fe, NM 87505
Phone: (505)982-4671
Fax: (505)982-0153
**Subject(s):** Rural Electrification; Local, State, and Regional Publications

**Circ:** ‡125,000

**Que Pasa San Antonio  (30376)**
Prime Time Incorporated Newspapers
17400 Judson Rd.
San Antonio, TX 78247
Phone: (210)453-3312
**Subject(s):** Travel and Tourism; Local, State, and Regional Publications

**Circ:** (Combined)125,000

**New Mexico Magazine  (20164)**
PO Box 12002
Santa Fe, NM 87504
Phone: (505)827-7447
Fax: (505)827-6496
**Subject(s):** Local, State, and Regional Publications; Travel and Tourism

**Circ:** (Paid)120,000

**Tierra Grande  (29440)**
Real Estate Center
2115 TAMU
College Station, TX 77843-2115
Phone: (979)845-2031
Fax: (979)845-0460
**Subject(s):** Real Estate

**Circ:** ‡118,000

**Dental Equipment & Materials  (25598)**
PennWell Corp.
1421 S. Sheridan Rd.
Tulsa, OK 74112
Phone: (918)835-3161
Fax: (918)832-9201
**Subject(s):** Dentistry

**Circ:** 109,000

**Cowboys & Indians  (29521)**
USFR Media Group
6688 N. Central Expy., No. 650
Dallas, TX 75206-3914
Phone: (214)750-8222

Fax: (214)750-4522
**Subject(s):** Lifestyle; Local, State, and Regional Publications

**Circ:** (Paid)101,225

**The Baptist Standard  (29507)**
Baptist Standard Publishing Co.
PO Box 660267
Dallas, TX 75266-0267
Phone: (214)630-4571
Fax: (214)638-8535
**Subject(s):** Religious Publications

**Circ:** ‡100,000

**Crappie  (25268)**
NatCom Inc.
15115 S 76th E Ave.
Bixby, OK 74008-4114
Fax: (918)366-6512
**Subject(s):** (Hunting, Fishing, and Game Management)

**Circ:** (Paid)100,000

**Naval Reservist News  (12309)**
Commander Naval Reserve Force
4400 Dauphine St.
New Orleans, LA 70146-5046
Phone: (504)678-6058
Fax: (504)678-5049
**Subject(s):** Military and Navy

**Circ:** (Controlled)‡100,000

**Houston Lifestyle & Homes Magazine  (30455)**
Fort Bend Publishing Group
10707 Corporate Dr., Ste. 170
Stafford, TX 77477
Phone: (281)240-2445
Fax: (281)240-5079
**Subject(s):** Lifestyle; Local, State, and Regional Publications

**Circ:** (Paid)7,000
(Controlled)⊕94,300

**Control Solutions  (25596)**
PennWell Corp.
1421 S. Sheridan Rd.
Tulsa, OK 74112
Phone: (918)835-3161
Fax: (918)832-9201
**Subject(s):** Commerce and Industry; Engineering (Various branches)

**Circ:** (Controlled)‡92,608

**Mothering Magazine  (20163)**
Mothering Magazine Inc.
1611-A Paseo de Peralta
Santa Fe, NM 87501
Phone: (505)984-8116
Fax: (505)986-8335
**Subject(s):** Alternative and Underground; Parenting; Health; Women's Interests

**Circ:** (Non-paid)‡500
(Paid)‡90,000

**ASRT Scanner  (19990)**
American Society of Radiologic Technologists
15000 Central Ave. SE
Albuquerque, NM 87123-3917
Phone: (505)298-4500
Fax: (505)298-5063
**Subject(s):** Radiology, Ultrasound, and Nuclear Medicine; Health and Healthcare; Medicine and Surgery

**Circ:** 85,000

**Hooked on Crochet  (29309)**
The Needlecraft Shop L.L.C.
23 Old Pecan Rd.
Big Sandy, TX 75755
Phone: (903)636-4011
Fax: (800)882-6643
**Subject(s):** Crafts, Models, Hobbies, and Contests

**Circ:** (Paid)85,000

**Occupational Health & Safety  (29560)**
Stevens Publishing Corp.
5151 Beltline Rd., 10th Fl.
Dallas, TX 75254
Phone: (972)687-6700
Fax: (972)687-6799
**Subject(s):** Health and Healthcare; Safety; Public Safety and Emergency Response; Labor

**Circ:** (Combined)△84,103

**Tulanian** (12326)
University Publications
200 Broadway - Ste. 120
New Orleans, LA 70118
**Subject(s):** College Publications
**Circ:** (Controlled)83,000

**Beckett Sports Collectibles and Autographs** (29511)
Statabase Inc.
15850 Dallas Pkwy.
Dallas, TX 75248
Phone: (972)991-6657
Fax: (972)991-8930
**Subject(s):** (General Sports)
**Circ:** (Non-paid)‡345
(Paid)‡81,327

**Texas Bar Journal** (29211)
State Bar of Texas
1414 Colorado St. Ste.312
Austin, TX 78701
Phone: (512)463-1463
Fax: (512)463-3802
**Subject(s):** Law
**Circ:** (Non-paid)‡1,500
(Paid)‡78,000

**Trailblazer** (29743)
Thousand Trails Inc.
3801 Parkwood Blvd., Ste. 100
PO Box 2529
Frisco, TX 75034
Phone: (214)618-7200
Fax: (214)618-7208
**Subject(s):** (Outdoors)
**Circ:** (Paid)‡75,000

**The American Quarter Horse Journal** (29078)
American Quarter Horse Association
1600 Quarter Horse Dr.
PO Box 32470
Amarillo, TX 79104
Phone: (806)376-4811
**Subject(s):** (Horses and Horse Racing); Livestock
**Circ:** (Paid)70,052

**Stroke Connection Magazine** (29569)
American Stroke Association
7272 Greenville Ave.
Dallas, TX 75231-5129
**Subject(s):** Health
**Circ:** (Combined)70,000

**Texas FFA News** (29216)
Texas FFA Association
614 E 12th St.
Austin, TX 78701-1908
Phone: (512)480-8045
Fax: (512)617-8219
**Subject(s):** General Agriculture
**Circ:** (Controlled)68,000

**RDH** (25621)
PennWell Publishing Co.
PO Box 1260
Tulsa, OK 74101-1260
Phone: (918)831-9742
Fax: (918)831-9804
**Subject(s):** Dentistry
**Circ:** (Paid)310
(Non-paid)66,856

**Southwest Art** (29908)
Sabot Publishing Inc.
5444 Westheimer, Ste. 1440
Houston, TX 77056
Phone: (713)296-7900
Fax: (713)850-1314
**Subject(s):** Art
**Circ:** (Paid)65,052

**TSTA Advocate** (29250)
Texas State Teachers Association
316 W 12th St.
Austin, TX 78701
Phone: (512)476-5355
Fax: (512)486-7046
**Subject(s):** Education
**Circ:** 65,000

**WaterWorld** (25634)
PennWell Corp.
c/o James Laughlin
1421 S. Sheridan Rd.
Tulsa, OK 74112
Phone: (918)832-9320
**Subject(s):** Water Supply and Sewage Disposal
**Circ:** (Non-paid)65,000

**D Magazine** (29523)
4311 Oak Lawn Ave., Ste. 100
Dallas, TX 75219
Phone: (214)939-3636
Fax: (214)748-4153
**Subject(s):** Local, State, and Regional Publications
**Circ:** (Paid)60,602

**The Texas Aggie** (29438)
Association of Former Students of Texas A&M University
505 George Bush Dr.
College Station, TX 77840-2918
Phone: (979)845-7514
Fax: (979)845-9263
**Subject(s):** College Publications
**Circ:** 60,000

**U.S. Gospel News** (1148)
603 W Matthews
Jonesboro, AR 72401
Phone: (870)802-0414
Fax: (870)932-6397
**Subject(s):** Religious Publications
**Circ:** (Non-paid)25,000
(Paid)60,000

**Corel** (29149)
Ariel Communications Inc.
PO Box 202380
Austin, TX 78720-3550
Phone: (512)250-1700
Fax: (512)219-3156
**Subject(s):** Computers; Engineering (Various branches)
**Circ:** (Controlled)‡58,000

**Power Engineering** (25618)
PennWell Corp.
1421 S. Sheridan Rd.
Tulsa, OK 74112
Phone: (918)835-3161
Fax: (918)832-9201
**Subject(s):** Engineering (Various branches); Power and Power Plants
**Circ:** (Controlled)58,000

**The Oxford American** (1044)
201 Donaghey Ave.
Main 107
Conway, AR 72035
Phone: (501)450-5376
Fax: (501)450-3490
**Subject(s):** Literature and Literary Reviews
**Circ:** (Paid)56,261

**CPA Technology Advisor** (25547)
Cygnus Publishing Inc.
110 N Bell, Ste. 300
Shawnee, OK 74801
Phone: (405)275-3100
Fax: (405)275-3101
**Subject(s):** Accountants and Accounting; Computers
**Circ:** (Paid)51,411

**Texas Golfer** (29912)
Golfer Magazines Inc.
4920 center St.
Houston, TX 77007
Phone: (877)536-1088
Fax: (877)429-9738
**Subject(s):** (Golf)
**Circ:** (Non-paid)51,377

**Journal of Petroleum Technology** (29873)
Society of Petroleum Engineers
9555 W. Sam Houston Parkway 360
Houston, TX 77036-7840
Phone: (713)779-9595
Fax: (713)779-4216
**Subject(s):** Engineering (Various branches); Petroleum, Oil, and Gas
**Circ:** (Non-paid)4,000
(Paid)51,000

**Book News & Book Business Mart** (29708)
Premier Publishers Inc.
2778 SE Loop 820
PO Box 330309
Fort Worth, TX 76163-0309
Phone: (817)293-7030
Fax: (817)293-3410
**Subject(s):** Book Trade and Author News
**Circ:** (Controlled)50,000

**OffBeat Magazine** (12319)
OffBeat Publications
421 Frenchman St., Ste. 200
New Orleans, LA 70116-2056
Phone: (504)944-4300
Fax: (504)944-4306
**Subject(s):** Music and Musical Instruments
**Circ:** (Combined)50,000

**RIO** (30377)
Paseo del Rio Association
110 Broadway, Ste. 440
San Antonio, TX 78205
Phone: (210)227-4262
Fax: (210)212-7602
**Subject(s):** Local, State, and Regional Publications; Travel and Tourism
**Circ:** (Non-paid)‡50,000

**SMT** (25622)
PennWell Corp.
1421 S. Sheridan Rd.
Tulsa, OK 74112
Phone: (918)835-3161
**Subject(s):** Electronics Engineering
**Circ:** (Controlled)46,017

**Texas Realtor** (29241)
Texas Association of Realtors
1115 San Jacinto, Ste. 200
Austin, TX 78701-1906
Phone: (512)480-8200
Fax: (512)370-2390
**Subject(s):** Real Estate
**Circ:** (Non-paid)‡630
(Paid)‡45,920

**Lost Treasure** (25347)
Lost Treasure Inc.
PO Box 451589
Grove, OK 74345
Phone: (918)786-2182
Fax: (918)786-2192
**Subject(s):** Crafts, Models, Hobbies, and Contests
**Circ:** ‡45,000

**Hart's E&P** (29846)
Hart Energy Publishing
4545 Post Oak Pl., Ste. 210
Houston, TX 77027
Phone: (713)993-9320
Fax: (713)840-0923
**Subject(s):** Natural Resources
**Circ:** (Paid)‡1,145
(Non-paid)‡44,281

**Fire Engineering** (25601)
PennWell Corp.
1421 S. Sheridan Rd.
Tulsa, OK 74112
Phone: (918)835-3161
**Subject(s):** Fire Fighting
**Circ:** (Paid)44,264

**AORN Journal** (30353)
AORN Inc.
c/o Nancy J. Girard
PO Box 291029
San Antonio, TX 78229-1629
Phone: (210)567-5841
Fax: (210)567-1719
**Subject(s):** Nursing
**Circ:** (Paid)44,000

**Oklahoma Today Magazine** (25478)
P.O. Box 1468
Oklahoma City, OK 73102
Phone: (405)521-2496
Fax: (405)522-4588
**Subject(s):** Travel and Tourism; Local, State, and Regional Publications
**Circ:** (Non-paid)‡2,000
(Paid)‡44,000

# Southern Central States

**Key Magazine Houston** (29876)
Key Magazine Inc.
c/o Candy Anderson
1220 Waverly
PO Box 7640
Houston, TX 77270-7640
Phone: (713)880-9200
Fax: (713)861-9543
**Subject(s):** Travel and Tourism; Entertainment; Local, State, and Regional Publications; Spanish
**Circ:** (Combined)‡41,505

**Louisiana Life Magazine** (12246)
111 Veterans Blvd., Ste. 1810
Metairie, LA 70005
Phone: (504)832-3555
Fax: (504)378-0000
**Subject(s):** Local, State, and Regional Publications
**Circ:** ‡40,001

**NOVA Quarterly** (29660)
University of Texas at El Paso
500 W. Univ. Ave.
El Paso, TX 79968
Phone: (915)747-5000
**Subject(s):** College Publications
**Circ:** (Controlled)‡40,000

**State of the Art** (25624)
State Service Systems Inc.
10405-B E 55th Pl.
Tulsa, OK 74146
Phone: (918)627-8000
Fax: (918)627-8660
**Subject(s):** Hairstyling
**Circ:** (Paid)40,000

**Better Roads** (29512)
James Informational Media Inc.
6301 Gaston Ave., Ste. 541
Dallas, TX 75214
Phone: (214)827-4630
**Subject(s):** Roads and Streets; Transportation, Traffic, and Shipping; Engineering (Various branches)
**Circ:** (Non-paid)39,424

**The Oklahoma Mason** (25353)
Grand Lodge A.F. and A.M.
PO Box 1019
102 South Broad
Guthrie, OK 73044-1019
Phone: (405)282-3212
Fax: (405)282-3244
**Subject(s):** Masons
**Circ:** ‡39,000

**Offshore** (29889)
PennWell Publishing Co.
1700 W. Loop S., Ste. 1000
Houston, TX 77027
Phone: (713)621-9720
Fax: (713)963-6296
**Subject(s):** Petroleum, Oil, and Gas
**Circ:** (Paid)841
(Controlled)‡37,289

**World Oil** (29922)
Gulf Publishing Co.
2 Greenway Plz., Ste.1020
Houston, TX 77046
Phone: (713)529-4301
Fax: (713)520-4433
**Subject(s):** Petroleum, Oil, and Gas
**Circ:** 35,947

**Underground Construction** (29918)
Oildom Publishing Company of Texas Inc.
1160 Dairy Ashford St., Ste. 610
PO Box 941669
Houston, TX 77079-8669
Phone: (281)558-6930
Fax: (281)558-7029
**Subject(s):** Construction, Contracting, Building, and Excavating; Building Materials, Concrete, Brick, and Tile
**Circ:** (Paid)35,345

**Paint Horse Journal** (29725)
American Paint Horse Association
PO Box 961023
Fort Worth, TX 76161-0023
Phone: (817)834-2742
Fax: (817)222-8466
**Subject(s):** Livestock; (Horses and Horse Racing)
**Circ:** (Paid)‡35,038

**Connector Specifier** (25595)
PennWell Corp.
1421 S. Sheridan Rd.
Tulsa, OK 74112
Phone: (918)835-3161
**Subject(s):** Electronics Engineering; Electrical Engineering
**Circ:** (Controlled)△35,013

**Creative Kids** (29151)
Prufrock Press
5926 Balcones Dr., Ste.220
Austin, TX 78731
Phone: (512)300-2220
Fax: (512)300-2221
**Subject(s):** Children's Interests; Youths' Interests
**Circ:** 35,000

**Key Magazine Dallas** (29551)
Key Magazine Inc.
c/o Jay Motter
25 Highland Park Village, Ste. 100-750
Dallas, TX 75205
Phone: (214)521-6570
Fax: (214)521-6576
**Subject(s):** Travel and Tourism; Entertainment; Local, State, and Regional Publications
**Circ:** (Controlled)‡35,000

**Our Kids Magazine** (30373)
Trader Publishing Co.
8400 Blanco Rd., Ste. 300
San Antonio, TX 78216
Phone: (210)349-6667
Fax: (210)349-5618
**Subject(s):** Parenting
**Circ:** (Controlled)‡35,000

**Telecom Business** (29910)
Primedia Business Magazines
PO Box 66010
Houston, TX 77266
Phone: (713)523-8124
Fax: (713)523-8384
**Subject(s):** Telecommunications
**Circ:** (Combined)35,000

**Special Interest Autos** (30650)
PO Box 393
Wimberley, TX 78676
Phone: (512)847-9054
Fax: (512)847-9054
**Subject(s):** Automotive (Consumer)
**Circ:** (Non-paid)‡410
(Paid)‡34,434

**The Skeptical Inquirer** (20013)
CSICOP Inc.
944 Deer Dr. NE
Albuquerque, NM 87122
Phone: (505)828-2080
Fax: (505)828-2080
**Subject(s):** Parapsychology; Science (General)
**Circ:** (Non-paid)‡1,598
(Paid)‡34,091

**New Orleans Magazine** (12312)
New Orleans Publishing Group Inc.
111 Veterans Blvd.
Ste. 1440
Metairie, LA 70005
Phone: (504)834-9292
Fax: (504)832-3550
**Subject(s):** Local, State, and Regional Publications
**Circ:** (Paid)14,660
(Non-paid)33,952

**Journal of the American Society for Information Science** (12070)
John Wiley and Sons Inc.
C/O Donald H. Kraft, Department of Computer Science
Baton Rouge, LA 70803
Phone: (504)388-1495
**Subject(s):** Library and Information Science; Communications
**Circ:** 33,600

**AARC Times** (29976)
Daedalus Enterprises Inc.
c/o American Association for Respiratory Care
9425 N. MacArthur Blvd., Ste. 100
Irving, TX 75063-4706
Phone: (972)243-2272
Fax: (972)484-2720
**Subject(s):** Medicine and Surgery
**Circ:** (Non-paid)‡150
(Paid)‡32,500

**The Santa Fean Magazine** (20170)
The Santa Fean L.L.C.
444 Galisteo
Santa Fe, NM 87501
Phone: (505)983-1444
Fax: (505)983-1555
**Subject(s):** Travel and Tourism
**Circ:** (Combined)32,500

**Oil, Gas & Petrochem Equipment** (25613)
PennWell Corp.
PO Box 1260
Tulsa, OK 74101-1260
Phone: (918)832-9201
Fax: (800)331-4463
**Subject(s):** Petroleum, Oil, and Gas
**Circ:** (Combined)‡32,000

**Rehabilitation Technology** (29900)
Oildom Publishing Company of Texas Inc.
1160 Dairy Ashford St., Ste. 610
PO Box 941669
Houston, TX 77079-8669
Phone: (281)558-6930
Fax: (281)558-7029
**Subject(s):** Petroleum, Oil, and Gas; Engineering (Various branches)
**Circ:** (Combined)32,000

**Oil & Gas Journal** (29893)
PennWell Publishing Co.
1700 W. Loop S., Ste. 1000
Houston, TX 77027
Phone: (713)621-9720
Fax: (713)963-6296
**Subject(s):** Petroleum, Oil, and Gas
**Circ:** (Paid)31,354

**Offshore Engineer** (29890)
Atlantic Communications L.L.C.
1635 W. Alabama
Houston, TX 77006
Phone: (713)529-1616
Fax: (713)523-7804
**Subject(s):** Engineering (Various branches); Petroleum, Oil, and Gas
**Circ:** (Combined)△31,269

**Arkansas Wildlife** (1169)
Arkansas Game & Fish Commission
2 Natural Resources Dr.
Little Rock, AR 72205
Phone: (501)223-6300
Fax: (501)223-6447
**Subject(s):** (Hunting, Fishing, and Game Management)
**Circ:** (Paid)31,000

**AAPG Bulletin** (25589)
American Association of Petroleum Geologists
1444 S Boulder
PO Box 979
Tulsa, OK 74101-0979
Phone: (918)584-2555
Fax: (918)560-2632
**Subject(s):** Geology; Petroleum, Oil, and Gas
**Circ:** ‡30,000

**AAPG Explorer** (25590)
American Association of Petroleum Geologists
1444 S Boulder
PO Box 979
Tulsa, OK 74101-0979
Phone: (918)584-2555
Fax: (918)560-2632
**Subject(s):** Geology; Petroleum, Oil, and Gas
**Circ:** (Controlled)‡300
(Paid)‡30,000

**Electric Light & Power** (25600)
PennWell Corp.
1421 S. Sheridan Rd.
Tulsa, OK 74112
Phone: (918)835-3161
Fax: (918)832-9201
**Subject(s):** Power and Power Plants
**Circ:** (Controlled)‡30,000

**Hill Country Sun** (30649)
PO Box 1482
Wimberley, TX 78676
Phone: (512)847-5162
Fax: (512)847-5162
**Subject(s):** Free Newspapers; Local, State, and Regional Publications; Lifestyle
**Circ:** (Non-paid)‡30,000

**Louisiana Engineer & Surveyor Journal (12081)**
Louisiana Engineering Society
9643 Brookline Ave., Ste. 116
Baton Rouge, LA 70809
Phone: (225)924-2021
Fax: (225)924-2049
**Subject(s):** Engineering (Various branches)
**Circ:** (Paid)30,000

**Notices of the American Mathematical Society (25432)**
American Mathematical Society
c/o Andy Magid, Editor
Dept. of Mathematics
601, Elm, PHSC 423
Univ. of Oklahoma
Norman, OK 73019-0001
**Subject(s):** Mathematics
**Circ:** (Paid)29,277

**Drilling Contractor (29840)**
Drilling Contractor Publications Inc.
10370 Richmond Ave., Ste. 760
Houston, TX 77042
Phone: (713)292-1945
Fax: (713)292-1946
**Subject(s):** Construction, Contracting, Building, and Excavating; Petroleum, Oil, and Gas
**Circ:** (Paid)130
(Non-paid)29,000

**Whispering Wind (12160)**
Written Heritage
PO Box 1390
Folsom, LA 70437-1390
Phone: (985)796-5433
Fax: (985)796-9236
**Subject(s):** Native American Interests; Intercultural Interests
**Circ:** ‡28,000

**Texas Medicine (29230)**
Texas Medical Association
401 W 15th St.
Austin, TX 78701
Phone: (512)370-1300
Fax: (512)370-1632
**Subject(s):** Medicine and Surgery
**Circ:** (Paid)‡26,090

**Farmer-Stockman (25519)**
Farm Progress Cos.
107 N. 4th St., Ste. 227
Ponca City, OK 74601-4510
Phone: (405)377-5565
Fax: (405)377-5595
**Subject(s):** General Agriculture
**Circ:** (Paid)15,458
(Non-paid)25,451

**Focus on Members (25459)**
Oklahoma Education Association
323 E Madison
PO Box 18485
Oklahoma City, OK 73154
Phone: (405)528-7785
Fax: (405)524-0350
**Subject(s):** Education
**Circ:** ‡25,000

**New Texas (29188)**
1512 1/2 S Congress Ave., No. 4
Austin, TX 78704-2437
**Subject(s):** Lifestyle
**Circ:** (Non-paid)25,000

**Ride Texas Magazine (29199)**
MotoVenture Inc.
PO Box 90374
Austin, TX 78709-0374
Phone: (512)858-2313
**Subject(s):** Motorbikes and Motorcycles
**Circ:** (Combined)‡25,000

**Texas Gardener (30599)**
Suntex Communications Inc.
PO Box 9005
Waco, TX 76712
Phone: (254)848-9393
Fax: (254)848-9779
**Subject(s):** Home and Garden
**Circ:** ‡25,000

**Utility Automation (25632)**
PennWell Corp.
1421 S. Sheridan Rd.
Tulsa, OK 74112
Phone: (918)835-3161
Fax: (918)832-9201
**Subject(s):** Power and Power Plants; Telecommunications; Automation
**Circ:** (Controlled)‡25,000

**Hydrocarbon Processing (29860)**
Gulf Publishing Co.
2 Greenway Plz., Ste.1020
Houston, TX 77046
Phone: (713)529-4301
Fax: (713)520-4433
**Subject(s):** Petroleum, Oil, and Gas
**Circ:** (Paid)11,099
(Non-paid)24,885

**IAEI News (30305)**
International Association of Electrical Inspectors (IAEI)
901 Waterfall Way, Ste. 602
Richardson, TX 75083
Phone: (972)235-1455
Fax: (972)235-3855
**Subject(s):** Electrical Engineering
**Circ:** ‡24,000

**LSU Magazine (12088)**
LSU Alumni Association
3838 W Lakeshore Dr.
Baton Rouge, LA 70808
Phone: (225)578-3811
Fax: (225)388-3816
**Subject(s):** College Publications
**Circ:** ‡24,000

**School Arts Magazine (29626)**
School Arts Magazine
2223 Parkside Dr.
Denton, TX 76201
Phone: (940)382-8274
**Subject(s):** Education
**Circ:** (Non-paid)441
(Paid)23,829

**Neil Sperry's Gardens Magazine (30143)**
PO Box 864
Mc Kinney, TX 75070
Phone: (972)562-5050
Fax: (214)544-1278
**Subject(s):** Home and Garden
**Circ:** (Non-paid)633
(Paid)23,000

**Southwestern Union Record (29371)**
Southwestern Union Conference of Seventh-Day Adventists
777 S. Burleson Blvd.
PO Box 4000
Burleson, TX 76028
Phone: (817)295-0476
Fax: (817)447-2443
**Subject(s):** Religious Publications
**Circ:** (Controlled)‡400
(Paid)‡23,000

**American Rose (12381)**
American Rose Society
8877 Jefferson Paige Rd.
Shreveport, LA 71119
Phone: (318)938-5402
Fax: (318)938-5405
**Subject(s):** Home and Garden; Horticulture
**Circ:** (Controlled)‡150
(Paid)‡22,109

**Little Rock Family (1179)**
Arkansas Business Publishing Group
122 E. Second St.
Little Rock, AR 72203
Phone: (501)372-1443
Fax: (501)375-7933
**Subject(s):** Parenting
**Circ:** (Free)❏21,334

**Health Sciences at Tulane (12298)**
1430 Tulane Ave., TW 34
New Orleans, LA 70112-2699
Phone: (504)588-5305
Fax: (504)587-2012
**Subject(s):** College Publications; Medicine and Surgery
**Circ:** (Non-paid)21,000

**LAE News (12075)**
Louisiana Association of Educators
PO Box 479
Baton Rouge, LA 70821
**Subject(s):** Education
**Circ:** ‡21,000

**Oklahoma State University Magazine (25567)**
Oklahoma State University
121 Cordell N
Stillwater, OK 74078-2000
Phone: (405)744-6260
Fax: (405)744-8445
**Subject(s):** College Publications
**Circ:** (Controlled)‡500
(Paid)‡21,000

**The Case Manager (1172)**
Mosby Inc.
10801 Executive Center Dr., Ste. 509
Little Rock, AR 72211
Phone: (501)223-0519
Fax: (501)223-0519
**Subject(s):** Insurance; Health and Healthcare; Management and Administration
**Circ:** (Combined)20,000

**Cisco World (29144)**
Publications and Communications LP
11675 Jollyville Rd., Ste. 150
Austin, TX 78759
Phone: (512)250-9023
Fax: (512)331-3900
**Subject(s):** Computers
**Circ:** (Non-paid)‡20,000

**Enterprise Networks & Servers (29155)**
Publications and Communications LP
Enterprise Networks & Servers
11675 Jollyville Rd Ste. 150
Austin, TX 78759
Phone: (512)250-9023
Fax: (512)331-3900
**Subject(s):** Computers
**Circ:** (Controlled)‡20,000

**Frontier Country Key (25548)**
Key Magazine Inc.
c/o Frank Sims
PO Box 3001
Shawnee, OK 74802
Phone: (405)214-9494
Fax: (405)275-1444
**Subject(s):** Travel and Tourism; Entertainment; Local, State, and Regional Publications
**Circ:** (Combined)20,000

**Journal of Marital & Family Therapy (30082)**
American Association for Marriage and Family Therapy
Texas Tech University
MFT Programs, Box 1162
Lubbock, TX 79409-1162
Phone: (806)742-3033
Fax: (806)742-0825
**Subject(s):** Psychology and Psychiatry
**Circ:** (Non-paid)200
(Paid)20,000

**Master Collector (29722)**
Fun Publications Inc.
225 Cattle Baron Park Dr.
Fort Worth, TX 76108
Phone: (817)448-9863
Fax: (817)448-9843
**Subject(s):** Collecting
**Circ:** (Combined)20,000

**101 Fun Things to Do (30130)**
Victory Publishing Ltd.
PO Box 10
Marble Falls, TX 78654
Phone: (830)693-7152
Fax: (830)693-3085
**Subject(s):** Travel and Tourism; Local, State, and Regional Publications
**Circ:** (Non-paid)20,000

**Outdoor Oklahoma (25480)**
Department of Wildlife Conservation
PO Box 53465
1801 North Lincoln Blvd
Oklahoma City, OK 73105
Phone: (405)521-3855
Fax: (405)521-6535

## Southern Central States

**Subject(s):** Environmental and Natural Resources Conservation; Local, State, and Regional Publications
**Circ:** ‡20,000

**Power & Gas Marketing (29898)**
Oildom Publishing Company of Texas Inc.
1160 Dairy Ashford St., Ste. 610
PO Box 941669
Houston, TX 77079-8669
Phone: (281)558-6930
Fax: (281)558-7029
**Subject(s):** Power and Power Plants; Petroleum, Oil, and Gas; Engineering (Various branches)
**Circ:** (Combined)20,000

**Southern Lights (25264)**
Southern Nazarene University
6729 NW 39th Expy.
Bethany, OK 73008-2605
Phone: (405)789-6400
Fax: (405)491-6381
**Subject(s):** College Publications
**Circ:** (Non-paid)‡20,000

**Gulf Coast Fisherman (30292)**
Harold Wells Gulf Coast Fisherman Inc.
211 Oakglen Dr., PO Box 8
Port Lavaca, TX 77979
Phone: (361)552-8864
Fax: (361)552-3139
**Subject(s):** Fish and Commercial Fisheries
**Circ:** (Non-paid)‡200
(Paid)‡19,500

**Houston Business Journal (29850)**
American City Business Journals Inc.
1233 W.t Loop S., Ste. 1300
Houston, TX 77027-9100
Phone: (713)963-0482
Fax: (713)963-0482
**Subject(s):** Business
**Circ:** (Paid)19,214

**Austin Home and Living (29136)**
Publications and Communications LP
11675 Jollyville Rd., Ste. 150
Austin, TX 78759
Phone: (512)250-9023
Fax: (512)331-3900
**Subject(s):** Home and Garden
**Circ:** (Paid)‡1,000
(Controlled)‡19,000

**West Texas Angelus (30338)**
Catholic Diocese of San Angelo
804 Ford St.
PO Box 1829
San Angelo, TX 76902-1829
Phone: (325)651-7500
Fax: (325)651-6688
**Subject(s):** Religious Publications
**Circ:** (Non-paid)‡1,050
(Paid)‡18,950

**The Louisiana Bar Journal (12304)**
Louisiana State Bar Association
601 St. Charles Ave.
New Orleans, LA 70130
Phone: (504)566-1600
Fax: (504)566-0930
**Subject(s):** Law
**Circ:** 18,319

**Arkansas Educator (1164)**
Arkansas Education Association
1500 W 4th Street
Little Rock, AR 72201
Phone: (501)375-4611
Fax: (501)375-4620
**Subject(s):** Education
**Circ:** ‡18,268

**Industrial Fire World (29426)**
589 Graham Rd.
PO Box 9161
College Station, TX 77845
Phone: (979)690-7559
Fax: (979)690-7562
**Subject(s):** Fire Fighting; Safety
**Circ:** (Paid)18,000

**Issues in Science and Technology (30306)**
The Green Center for Science and Society
The University of Texas at Dallas
PO Box 830688, MS JO 30
Richardson, TX 75083-0688
Phone: (972)883-6325
Fax: (972)883-6327
**Subject(s):** Science (General)
**Circ:** ‡18,000

**Skeet Shooting Review (30379)**
National Skeet Shooting Association
5931 Roft Rd.
San Antonio, TX 78253
Phone: (210)688-3371
Fax: (210)688-3014
**Subject(s):** (Hunting, Fishing, and Game Management); Firearms
**Circ:** 17,100

**The Leading Edge (25611)**
Society of Exploration Geophysicists
8801 S Yale Ave., Ste.500
PO Box 702740
Tulsa, OK 74137-2740
Phone: (918)497-5500
Fax: (918)497-5557
**Subject(s):** Science (General)
**Circ:** ⊕16,990

**Geophysics (25603)**
Society of Exploration Geophysicists
8801 S Yale Ave., Ste.500
PO Box 702740
Tulsa, OK 74137-2740
Phone: (918)497-5500
Fax: (918)497-5557
**Subject(s):** Physics; Geology
**Circ:** ‡16,530

**UnderWater Magazine (29919)**
Doyle Publishing Company Inc.
15018 Mintz Ln.
Houston, TX 77014
Phone: (281)440-0278
Fax: (281)440-4867
**Subject(s):** Oceanography and Marine Studies
**Circ:** (Non-paid)16,300

**Cutting Horse Chatter (29713)**
National Cutting Horse Association
260 Bailey Ave.
Fort Worth, TX 76107-1862
Phone: (817)244-6188
Fax: (817)244-2015
**Subject(s):** Livestock; (Horses and Horse Racing)
**Circ:** ‡16,000

**Sooners (25623)**
First Down Publications
4528 S Sheridan, Ste. 216
Tulsa, OK 74145
**Subject(s):** College Publications; (General Sports)
**Circ:** 16,000

**Texas Coach (30417)**
Texas High School Coaches Association
1228 Highway 123
PO Box 1138
San Marcos, TX 78667
Phone: (512)392-3741
Fax: (512)392-3762
**Subject(s):** (General Sports); Education
**Circ:** (Non-paid)‡253
(Paid)‡16,000

**Soaring (20096)**
Soaring Society of America Inc.
PO Box 2100
Hobbs, NM 88241
Phone: (505)392-1177
Fax: (505)392-8154
**Subject(s):** (General Sports); Aviation
**Circ:** 15,911

**Materials Performance (29882)**
NACE International
1440 S Creek Dr.
Houston, TX 77084-4906
Phone: (281)228-6200
Fax: (281)228-6300
**Subject(s):** Metal, Metallurgy, and Metal Trade; Engineering (Various branches); Chemistry, Chemicals, and Chemical Engineering
**Circ:** (Paid)‡15,835

**Greenhouse Management and Production (29717)**
Branch-Smith Inc.
120 St. Louis Ave.
PO Box 1868
Fort Worth, TX 76101
Phone: (817)882-4120
Fax: (817)882-4121
**Subject(s):** Florists and Floriculture
**Circ:** (Combined)‡15,548

**Used Car Dealer (29113)**
National Independent Automobile Dealers Association
2521 Brown Blvd.
Arlington, TX 76006
Phone: (817)640-3838
Fax: (817)649-2377
**Subject(s):** Automotive (Trade); Selling and Salesmanship
**Circ:** (Non-paid)‡358
(Paid)‡15,537

**The Cattleman (29709)**
Texas and Southwestern Cattle Raisers Association Inc.
1301 W. 7th St.
Fort Worth, TX 76102
Phone: (817)332-7064
Fax: (817)332-5446
**Subject(s):** Livestock
**Circ:** (Non-paid)1,590
(Paid)15,415

**Gulf Coast Cattleman (30361)**
Gulf Coast Publishing Corp.
11201 Morning Ct.
San Antonio, TX 78213
Phone: (210)344-8300
Fax: (210)344-4258
**Subject(s):** Livestock
**Circ:** (Controlled)‡15,400

**Nursery Management and Production (29724)**
Branch-Smith Inc.
120 St. Louis Ave.
PO Box 1868
Fort Worth, TX 76101
Phone: (817)882-4120
Fax: (817)882-4121
**Subject(s):** Florists and Floriculture
**Circ:** (Combined)△15,207

**Garden Center Merchandising & Management (29715)**
Branch-Smith Inc.
120 St. Louis Ave.
PO Box 1868
Fort Worth, TX 76101
Phone: (817)882-4120
Fax: (817)882-4121
**Subject(s):** Landscape Architecture
**Circ:** (Combined)‡15,145

**Garden Center Products & Supplies (29716)**
Branch-Smith Inc.
120 St. Louis Ave.
PO Box 1868
Fort Worth, TX 76101
Phone: (817)882-4120
Fax: (817)882-4121
**Subject(s):** Seed and Nursery Trade
**Circ:** 15,000

**Gifted Child Today Magazine (29159)**
Prufrock Press
5926 Balcones Dr., Ste.220
Austin, TX 78731
Phone: (512)300-2220
Fax: (512)300-2221
**Subject(s):** Parenting; Education
**Circ:** (Paid)‡15,000

**HM (30272)**
6307 Cele Rd.
No. 573
Pflugerville, TX 78660
Phone: (512)989-7309
Fax: (512)670-2764
**Subject(s):** Music and Musical Instruments; Religious Publications
**Circ:** (Combined)⊕15,000

**Key Magazine Fort Worth (29719)**
Key Magazine Inc.
c/o Keith Powell
3805 Ivywood Court
Arlington, TX 76016
Phone: (817)654-9760
Fax: (817)654-9740

**Subject(s):** Travel and Tourism; Entertainment; Local, State, and Regional Publications
**Circ:** (Combined)‡15,000

**Persimmon Hill (25481)**
National Cowboy & Western Heritage Museum
1700 NE 63rd St.
Oklahoma City, OK 73111
Phone: (405)478-2250
Fax: (405)478-4714
**Subject(s):** History and Genealogy; Art
**Circ:** ‡15,000

**Perspectiva (20011)**
Educational News Service
600 Central Ave. SE, No. 233
Albuquerque, NM 87102-4640
**Subject(s):** Education; Spanish
**Circ:** 15,000

**Today's Insurance Professionals (25625)**
National Association of Insurance Women (International)
1847 E. 15th St.
Tulsa, OK 74104-4610
Phone: (918)744-5195
Fax: (918)743-1968
**Subject(s):** Insurance; Women's Interests
**Circ:** ‡15,000

**Modern Bulk Transporter (29884)**
Primedia Business Magazines
PO Box 66010
Houston, TX 77266
**Subject(s):** Transportation, Traffic, and Shipping
**Circ:** (Controlled)‡14,772

**Facility Management Journal (29842)**
International Facility Management Association
1 E. Greenway Plz., Ste. 1100
Houston, TX 77046-0194
Phone: (713)623-4362
Fax: (713)623-6124
**Subject(s):** Building Management and Maintenance
**Circ:** 14,600

**The Gamecock (1121)**
Marburger Publishing Company Inc.
PO Box 158
Hartford, AR 72938-0158
Phone: (479)639-2324
**Subject(s):** Poultry and Pigeons; (Hunting, Fishing, and Game Management)
**Circ:** 14,300

**Trailer/Body Builders (29914)**
Primedia Business Magazines
PO Box 66010
Houston, TX 77266
Phone: (713)523-8124
Fax: (713)523-8384
**Subject(s):** Automotive (Trade); Trailers and Accessories
**Circ:** (Controlled)‡14,110

**Sources (29203)**
National Association of Underwater Instructors
Box 49591
Austin, TX 78765
Phone: (512)476-6639
Fax: (512)477-8602
**Subject(s):** (Water Sports)
**Circ:** (Controlled)‡1,000
(Paid)‡14,000

**Texas Public Employee (29240)**
Texas Public Employees Association
512 E 11th St., Ste. 100
Austin, TX 78701
Phone: (512)476-2691
Fax: (512)476-1338
**Subject(s):** Labor
**Circ:** 14,000

**The Oklahoma Bar Journal (25467)**
Oklahoma Bar Association
PO Box 53036
Oklahoma City, OK 73152
Phone: (405)416-7000
Fax: (405)416-7001
**Subject(s):** Law
**Circ:** (Non-paid)⊕164
(Paid)⊕13,656

**AutoInc (29302)**
Automotive Service Association
1901 Airport Frwy.
Bedford, TX 76021
**Subject(s):** Automotive (Trade)
**Circ:** ‡13,000

**Baptist Trumpet (1171)**
Baptist Missionary Association of Arkansas
10712 Interstate 30
PO Box 192208
Little Rock, AR 72219-2208
Phone: (501)565-4601
Fax: (501)565-NEWS
**Subject(s):** Religious Publications
**Circ:** ‡12,700

**New Mexico Farm and Ranch (20104)**
New Mexico Farm & Livestock Bureau
PO Box 20004
Las Cruces, NM 88004-9004
Phone: (505)532-4706
Fax: (505)532-4710
**Subject(s):** General Agriculture
**Circ:** (Controlled)‡175
(Paid)‡12,500

**The Pediatric Infectious Disease Journal (29562)**
Lippincott Williams & Wilkins
C/o John D. Nelson, M.D., Editor-in-Chief
University of Texas
Southwestern Medical Center at Dallas
5323 Harry Hines Blvd., Rm. F3.202
Dallas, TX 75390-9063
Phone: (214)648-2961
Fax: (214)648-2961
**Subject(s):** Pediatrics
**Circ:** (Non-paid)‡302
(Combined)‡12,344

**Piano Guild Notes (29194)**
American College of Musicians
PO Box 1807
Austin, TX 78767-1807
Phone: (512)478-5775
Fax: (512)478-5843
**Subject(s):** Music and Musical Instruments
**Circ:** (Non-paid)‡525
(Paid)‡12,168

**Refrigerated Transporter (29899)**
Primedia Business Magazines
PO Box 66010
Houston, TX 77266
Phone: (713)523-8124
Fax: (713)523-8384
**Subject(s):** Transportation, Traffic, and Shipping
**Circ:** (Controlled)12,022

**Baptist Progress (30615)**
PO Box 2085
Waxahachie, TX 75168
Phone: (972)923-0756
Fax: (972)923-2679
**Subject(s):** Religious Publications
**Circ:** (Non-paid)‡300
(Paid)‡12,000

**MRI Banker's Guide to Foreign Currency (29886)**
Monetary Research Institute
PO Box 3174
Houston, TX 77253-3174
Phone: (713)827-1796
Fax: (713)827-8665
**Subject(s):** Banking, Finance, and Investments
**Circ:** (Non-paid)400
(Paid)12,000

**Promotional Products Business (29980)**
Promotional Products Association International
3125 Skyway Cir. N.
Irving, TX 75038
Phone: (972)258-3104
Fax: (972)258-3012
**Subject(s):** Advertising and Marketing
**Circ:** (Non-paid)384
(Paid)12,000

**View Camera (20068)**
Steve Simmons Photography
PO Box 2328
Corrales, NM 87048-2328
**Subject(s):** Photography
**Circ:** (Controlled)‡225
(Paid)‡11,819

**Bibliotheca Sacra (29513)**
Dallas Theological Seminary
3909 Swiss Ave.
Dallas, TX 75204
Phone: (214)824-3094
Fax: (214)841-3664
**Subject(s):** Religious Publications
**Circ:** ‡11,500

**The Insurance Journal of the West (30029)**
Wells Publishing Inc.
PO Box 940
Kyle, TX 78640-0940
Phone: (512)268-7660
Fax: (512)268-7760
**Subject(s):** Insurance
**Circ:** (Controlled)11,000

**Texas Lone Star (29229)**
Texas Association of School Boards
PO Box 400
Austin, TX 78767-0400
Phone: (512)467-0222
Fax: (512)483-7159
**Subject(s):** Education
**Circ:** (Combined)11,000

**Gas Utility and Pipeline Industries (29539)**
James Informational Media Inc.
6301 Gaston Ave., Ste. 541
Dallas, TX 75214
Phone: (214)827-4630
**Subject(s):** Power and Power Plants; Natural Resources
**Circ:** (Non-paid)10,878

**New Mexico Stockman (20008)**
PO Box 7127
Albuquerque, NM 87194
Phone: (505)243-9515
Fax: (505)243-9598
**Subject(s):** Livestock
**Circ:** ‡10,750

**The Southwestern Musician (29206)**
Texas Music Educators Association
7900 Centre Park Dr.
Austin, TX 78754
Phone: (512)452-0710
Fax: (512)451-9213
**Subject(s):** Music and Musical Instruments; Education
**Circ:** ‡10,500

**Texas Town & City (29247)**
Texas Municipal League
1821 Rutherford Ln., Ste. 400
Austin, TX 78754-5128
Phone: (512)231-7400
Fax: (512)231-7490
**Subject(s):** State, Municipal, and County Administration
**Circ:** (Non-paid)‡750
(Paid)‡10,500

**Gas Industries (29538)**
Gas Industries & E.A. News Inc.
6301 Gaston Ave.
Dallas, TX 75214
Phone: (214)827-4630
**Subject(s):** Petroleum, Oil, and Gas
**Circ:** (Combined)10,338

**Ambush Magazine (12293)**
Ambush Inc.
828-A Bourbon St.
New Orleans, LA 70116-3137
Phone: (504)522-8047
Fax: (504)522-0907
**Subject(s):** Gay and Lesbian Interests
**Circ:** (Combined)10,000

**American Indian Graduate (19988)**
American Indian Graduate Center
4520 Montgomery Blvd. NE, Ste. 1-B
Albuquerque, NM 87109
Phone: (505)881-4584
Fax: (505)884-0427
**Subject(s):** Ethnic Publications; College Publications; Education
**Circ:** 10,000

**Arkansas Cattle Business (1162)**
Arkansas Cattlemen's Association
310 Executive Ct.
Little Rock, AR 72205
Phone: (501)224-2114
Fax: (501)224-5377

**Subject(s):** Livestock

**Circ:** (Controlled)1,000
(Paid)10,000

**Food & Service News (29157)**
Texas Restaurant Association
1400 Lavaca St.
PO Box 1429
Austin, TX 78701
Phone: (512)457-4100
Fax: (512)472-2777
**Subject(s):** Hotels, Motels, Restaurants, and Clubs

**Circ:** ‡10,000

**Inside Texas Running (29863)**
PO Box 19909
Houston, TX 77224
Phone: (281)759-0555
Fax: (281)759-7766
**Subject(s):** (Running)

**Circ:** ‡10,000

**Journal for Minority Medical Students (12302)**
Spectrum Unlimited
3201 General De Gaulle Dr., Ste. 107
New Orleans, LA 70114-4002
Phone: (504)365-7088
Fax: (504)365-0465
**Subject(s):** Medicine and Surgery; Ethnic and Minority Studies; Education

**Circ:** (Non-paid)10,000

**The Keepsake (12303)**
Spectrum Unlimited
3201 General De Gaulle Dr., Ste. 107
New Orleans, LA 70114-4002
Phone: (504)365-7088
Fax: (504)365-0465
**Subject(s):** Ethnic and Minority Studies; Education; Health and Healthcare

**Circ:** (Paid)‡10,000

**Keynotes (29552)**
Associated Locksmiths of America
3500 Easy St.
Dallas, TX 75247
Phone: (214)827-1701
Fax: (214)827-1810
**Subject(s):** Safety

**Circ:** (Controlled)‡10,000

**Lone Star Horse Report (29721)**
316 Bailey Ave., No. 105
Fort Worth, TX 76107
Phone: (817)877-3050
Fax: (817)877-3060
**Subject(s):** Livestock; (Horses and Horse Racing)

**Circ:** (Paid)1,000
(Controlled)10,000

**Maes National Magazine (29881)**
GVR Public Relations Agency
1120 NASA Pkwy., Ste. 405
Houston, TX 77058
Phone: (281)333-1881
Fax: (281)333-1996
**Subject(s):** Science

**Circ:** (Combined)10,000

**New Mexico Woman (20009)**
Duval Publications Inc.
PO Box 12955
Albuquerque, NM 87195
Phone: (505)247-9195
Fax: (505)842-5129
**Subject(s):** Women's Interests

**Circ:** (Paid)‡2,000
(Non-paid)‡10,000

**StarDate (29207)**
StarDate & Universo Productions
2609 University Ave. 3-118
University of Texas
McDonald Observatory
Austin, TX 78712
Phone: (512)471-5285
Fax: (512)471-5060
**Subject(s):** Science; Astronomy and Meteorology

**Circ:** (Paid)10,000

**Texas Law Review Manual on Usage and Style (29226)**
University of Texas School of Law Publications
727 E Dean Keeton St., Ste. 4
Austin, TX 78705
Phone: (512)232-1280
Fax: (512)471-3282
**Subject(s):** Law

**Circ:** 10,000

**Texas Law Review Texas Rules of Form (29227)**
University of Texas School of Law Publications
727 E Dean Keeton St., Ste. 4
Austin, TX 78705
Phone: (512)232-1280
Fax: (512)471-3282
**Subject(s):** Law

**Circ:** 10,000

**Twin Plant News (29662)**
Nibbe, Hernandez & Associates Inc.
725 S. Mesa Hills
Bldg. 1, Ste. 2
El Paso, TX 79912
**Subject(s):** International Business and Economics; Commerce and Industry

**Circ:** (Controlled)9,600

**Blue Bars (29707)**
National Council of Corvette Clubs
Sylvia Hoaldridge
6095 Autumn Hills Dr.
Fort Worth, TX 76140
Phone: (817)561-9314
**Subject(s):** Automotive (Consumer)

**Circ:** 9,500

**The China Painter (25455)**
World Organization of China Painters
2641 NW 10th St.
Oklahoma City, OK 73107-5400
Phone: (405)521-1234
Fax: (405)521-1265
**Subject(s):** Glass and China

**Circ:** ‡9,500

**News Photographer (29189)**
National Press Photographers Association
6677 Whitmarsh Valley Walk
Austin, TX 78746
Phone: (512)328-4788
**Subject(s):** Photography

**Circ:** (Paid)‡9,500

**The Ochsner Journal (12318)**
1514 Jefferson Hwy.
New Orleans, LA 70121
Phone: (504)842-6096
Fax: (504)842-2013
**Subject(s):** Medicine and Surgery; Health and Healthcare

**Circ:** (Combined)9,496

**Hart's Fuel Technology & Management (29847)**
Hart Publications Inc.
4545 Post Oak Pl., Ste. 210
Houston, TX 77027
Phone: (713)993-9320
Fax: (713)840-8585
**Subject(s):** Petroleum, Oil, and Gas

**Circ:** (Paid)1,400
(Non-paid)9,078

**Texas Water Utilities Journal (29249)**
Texas Water Utilities Association
1106 Clayton Ln., Ste. 101E
Austin, TX 78723
Phone: (512)459-3124
Fax: (512)459-7124
**Subject(s):** Water Supply and Sewage Disposal

**Circ:** (Controlled)⊕9,010

**African Violet Magazine (29288)**
African Violet Society of America
2375 North
Beaumont, TX 77702
Phone: (409)839-4725
Fax: (409)839-4329
**Subject(s):** Home and Garden; Botany

**Circ:** 9,000

**Alumni Bulletin (20178)**
Western New Mexico University Alumni Association
PO Box 680
Silver City, NM 88062
Phone: (505)538-6675

**Subject(s):** College Publications

**Circ:** 9,000

**American Red Angus (29613)**
RAAA National Office
4201 N. Interstate 35
Denton, TX 76207
Phone: (940)387-3502
Fax: (940)383-4036
**Subject(s):** Livestock

**Circ:** ‡9,000

**Arkansas Trucking Report (1168)**
Arkansas Trucking Association
1401 W Capitol Ave., Ste. 185
Little Rock, AR 72201
Phone: (501)372-3462
Fax: (501)376-1810
**Subject(s):** Transportation, Traffic, and Shipping

**Circ:** 9,000

**Oklahoma Farmer-Stockman (25520)**
Farm Progress Cos.
107 N. 4th St., Ste. 227
Ponca City, OK 74601-4510
Phone: (405)377-5565
Fax: (405)377-5595
**Subject(s):** General Agriculture

**Circ:** (Non-paid)8,825
(Paid)8,948

**The Quarter Racing Journal (29081)**
American Quarter Horse Association
1600 Quarter Horse Dr.
PO Box 32470
Amarillo, TX 79104
Phone: (806)376-4811
**Subject(s):** Livestock; (Horses and Horse Racing)

**Circ:** (Paid)8,908

**Archives of Neurology (29503)**
American Medical Association Alliance
c/o Roger N. Rosenberg, MD
Department of Neurology
Southwestern Medical Center
University of Texas
Dallas, TX 75390-9108
**Subject(s):** Medicine and Surgery

**Circ:** (Paid)⊕6,095
(Controlled)‡8,874

**Accent West (29076)**
PO Box 1504
320 South Poke Ste 810
Amarillo, TX 79101
Phone: (806)371-8411
Fax: (806)371-7347
**Subject(s):** Lifestyle; Local, State, and Regional Publications

**Circ:** ‡8,500

**Biometrics (29105)**
The International Biometric Society
PO Box 19059
502, Yates St.
Science Hall, Rm. 108
Arlington, TX 76019-0059
Phone: (817)272-7171
Fax: (817)272-7172
**Subject(s):** Statistics

**Circ:** ‡8,500

**Builder Insider (29515)**
Divibest Inc.
PO Box 191125
Dallas, TX 75219-1125
Phone: (214)871-2913
**Subject(s):** Construction, Contracting, Building, and Excavating; Architecture

**Circ:** (Non-paid)8,500

**Journal of Learning Disabilities (29174)**
PRO-ED Inc.
8700 Shoal Creek Blvd.
Austin, TX 78757-6897
Phone: (512)451-3246
Fax: (800)397-7633
**Subject(s):** Education; Psychology and Psychiatry; Handicapped

**Circ:** ‡8,500

**Mandala (20188)**
Foundation for the Preservation of the Mahayana Tradition
125 B La Posta Rd.
PO Box 888
Taos, NM 87571
Phone: (505)758-7766
Fax: (505)758-7765
**Subject(s):** Religious Publications
**Circ:** 8,000

**Texas Dental Journal (29213)**
Texas Dental Association
1946 S IH35, Ste. 400
Austin, TX 78704
Phone: (512)443-3675
Fax: (512)443-3031
**Subject(s):** Dentistry
**Circ:** 7,800

**The American Wanderer (30569)**
American Volkssport Association (AVA)
1001 Pat Booker Rd., Ste. 101
Universal City, TX 78148
Phone: (210)659-2112
Fax: (210)659-1212
**Subject(s):** (Physical Fitness); (General Sports); Health
**Circ:** (Combined)7,500

**Baylor Dental Journal (29509)**
Baylor College of Dentistry
3302 Gaston Ave.
Dallas, TX 75246
Phone: (214)828-8214
Fax: (214)828-8906
**Subject(s):** College Publications; Dentistry
**Circ:** (Controlled)7,500

**National Forum of Applied Educational Research Journal (12213)**
National Forum Journals
PO Box 7400
Lake Charles, LA 70605-7400
Phone: (337)477-0008
Fax: (337)480-3663
**Subject(s):** Education
**Circ:** 7,500

**National Forum of Education Administration and Supervision Journal (12214)**
National Forum Journals
PO Box 7400
Lake Charles, LA 70605-7400
Phone: (337)477-0008
Fax: (337)480-3663
**Subject(s):** Education
**Circ:** 7,500

**National Forum of Special Education Journal (12215)**
National Forum Journals
PO Box 7400
Lake Charles, LA 70605-7400
Phone: (337)477-0008
Fax: (337)480-3663
**Subject(s):** Education
**Circ:** 7,500

**National Forum of Teacher Education Journal (12216)**
National Forum Journals
PO Box 7400
Lake Charles, LA 70605-7400
Phone: (337)477-0008
Fax: (337)480-3663
**Subject(s):** Education
**Circ:** 7,500

**Retailer and Marketing News (29565)**
PO Box 191105
Dallas, TX 75219-1105
Phone: (214)871-2930
**Subject(s):** Selling and Salesmanship; Advertising and Marketing
**Circ:** (Controlled)‡7,500

**Sulphur River Literary Review (29208)**
James Michael Robbins
Box 19228
Austin, TX 78760-9228
Phone: (512)292-9456
**Subject(s):** Literature; Poetry; Literature and Literary Reviews
**Circ:** (Combined)400
 (Paid)450
 (Free)7,500

**Taos Magazine (20189)**
Whitney Publishing Company Inc.
Box 1380
Taos, NM 87571
Phone: (505)758-5404
Fax: (505)758-5404
**Subject(s):** Local, State, and Regional Publications
**Circ:** (Paid)‡300
 (Non-paid)‡7,200

**Texas Architect (29210)**
Texas Society of Architects
816 Congress Ave., Ste. 970
Austin, TX 78701-2443
Phone: (512)478-7386
Fax: (512)478-0528
**Subject(s):** Architecture
**Circ:** (Non-paid)‡4,735
 (Paid)‡7,181

**Field Artillery (25338)**
U.S. Army Field Artillery
PO Box 33311
Fort Sill, OK 73503-0311
Phone: (580)442-5121
Fax: (580)442-7773
**Subject(s):** Military and Navy
**Circ:** (Paid)‡7,000
 (Non-paid)‡7,000

**PRO/E (20167)**
ConnectPress Ltd.
551 W.
701 Cordova Rd.
Santa Fe, NM 87505-4100
Phone: (505)474-5000
Fax: (505)474-5001
**Subject(s):** Computers; Engineering (Various branches)
**Circ:** (Controlled)7,000

**SOLID Solutions Magazine (20171)**
ConnectPress Ltd.
551 W.
701 Cordova Rd.
Santa Fe, NM 87505-4100
Phone: (505)474-5000
Fax: (505)474-5001
**Subject(s):** Computers; Engineering (Various branches)
**Circ:** (Controlled)7,000

**City & Town (1244)**
Arkansas Municipal League
PO Box 38
North Little Rock, AR 72115
Phone: (501)374-3484
Fax: (501)374-0541
**Subject(s):** State, Municipal, and County Administration
**Circ:** ‡6,800

**Gastroenterology Nursing (29107)**
Lippincott Williams & Wilkins
University of Texas at Arlington
School of Nursing
411 S. Nedderman
PO Box 19407
Arlington, TX 76019-0407
Phone: (972)623-2097
Fax: (972)623-2027
**Subject(s):** Medicine and Surgery
**Circ:** (Paid)6,719

**Palomino Horses (25615)**
Palomino Horse Breeders of America
15253 E. Skelly Dr.
Tulsa, OK 74116-2637
Phone: (918)438-1234
Fax: (918)438-1232
**Subject(s):** (Horses and Horse Racing)
**Circ:** ⊕6663

**Arkansas Business (1161)**
Arkansas Business Publishing Group
122 E. Second St.
Little Rock, AR 72203
Phone: (501)372-1443
Fax: (501)375-7933
**Subject(s):** Business; Local, State, and Regional Publications
**Circ:** (Controlled)2,000
 (Paid)6,500

**Aussie Times (29357)**
Australian Shepherd Club of America
PO Box 3790
Bryan, TX 77805-3790
Fax: (979)778-1898

**Subject(s):** Pets; Dogs
**Circ:** 6,500

**Texas Construction (29982)**
McGraw-Hill Inc.
9155 S. Sterling St.
Ste. 160
Irving, TX 75063
Phone: (972)819-1496
Fax: (972)819-1491
**Subject(s):** Construction, Contracting, Building, and Excavating; Architecture; Engineering (Various branches)
**Circ:** (Controlled)‡6,500

**Ranch & Rural Living Magazine (30335)**
PO Box 2678
San Angelo, TX 76902
Phone: (915)655-4434
Fax: (915)658-8250
**Subject(s):** Livestock
**Circ:** (Non-paid)700
 (Paid)6,318

**Reference and User Services Quarterly (25436)**
American Library Association
University of Oklahoma, SLIS
401 W. Brooks St, Rm. 120
Norman, OK 73019-0528
Phone: (405)325-3921
Fax: (405)325-7648
**Subject(s):** Library and Information Science
**Circ:** ‡6,308

**Fort Bend Business Journal (30454)**
Carter Publications Inc.
869 Dulles Ave., Ste. C
Stafford, TX 77477
Phone: (281)499-5600
Fax: (281)499-5002
**Subject(s):** Business
**Circ:** 6,287

**Construction News (1173)**
24 Crownpoint Rd.
Little Rock, AR 72227-2930
**Subject(s):** Construction, Contracting, Building, and Excavating
**Circ:** (Paid)168
 (Controlled)6,279

**Texas Professional Engineer (29238)**
Texas Society of Professional Engineers
3501 Manor Rd.
PO Box 2145
Austin, TX 78768
Phone: (512)472-9286
Fax: (512)472-2934
**Subject(s):** Engineering (Various branches)
**Circ:** (Non-paid)‡500
 (Paid)‡6,200

**Texas Review of Law and Politics (29243)**
The University of Texas School of Law Publications Inc.
The University of Texas School of Law
727 E. Dean Keeton St.
Austin, TX 78705-3299
**Subject(s):** Law; Politics
**Circ:** (Combined)6,200

**The Chronicles of Oklahoma (25457)**
Oklahoma Historical Society
2100 N Lincoln Blvd.
Oklahoma City, OK 73105-4997
Phone: (405)521-2491
**Subject(s):** History and Genealogy
**Circ:** ‡6,100

**The Baptist Challenge (1243)**
The Central Baptist Church of Little Rock
5200 Fairway Ave.
North Little Rock, AR 72116
Phone: (501)771-1125
Fax: (501)771-7729
**Subject(s):** Religious Publications
**Circ:** (Free)6,000

**Cotton Digest International (29834)**
PO Box 820768
Houston, TX 77282-0768
Phone: (713)977-1644
Fax: (713)977-8193
**Subject(s):** Textiles
**Circ:** (Controlled)‡3300
 (Paid)‡6000

# Southern Central States

**Greater Baton Rouge Business Report** (12067)
Louisiana Business Inc.
445 N. Blvd., Ste. 210
PO Box 1949
Baton Rouge, LA 70802
Phone: (225)928-1700
Fax: (225)923-3448
**Subject(s):** Local, State, and Regional Publications; Business
**Circ:** (Paid)‡2,657
(Non-paid)‡6,001

**Play Meter Magazine** (12320)
6600 Fleur De Lis Dr.
PO Box 24170
New Orleans, LA 70124
Phone: (504)488-7003
Fax: (504)488-7083
**Subject(s):** Vending Machines
**Circ:** ‡6,000

**PSA Journal** (25484)
Photographic Society of America
3000 United Founders Blvd., No. 103
Oklahoma City, OK 73112-3940
Phone: (405)843-1437
Fax: (405)843-1438
**Subject(s):** Photography
**Circ:** 6,000

**San Angelo Bridal Guide Magazine** (30336)
Mikeska Inc.
PO Box 5500
San Angelo, TX 76902
Phone: (325)658-8367
Fax: (325)653-9643
**Subject(s):** Brides
**Circ:** (Non-paid)⊕6,000

**Social Studies and the Young Learner** (29202)
National Council for the Social Studies
c/o Sherry L. Field, Editor
Dept. of Curriculum & Instruction
College of Education, SZB 428
University of Texas at Austin
Austin, TX 78712
Phone: (512)471-4611
**Subject(s):** Education; Social Sciences
**Circ:** (Paid)6,000

**Louisiana Agriculture Magazine** (12077)
LSU Agricultural Center
101 Efferson Hall
Baton Rouge, LA 70803
Phone: (225)388-2263
Fax: (225)578-4524
**Subject(s):** Scientific Agricultural Publications
**Circ:** (Controlled)‡5,900

**The Point!** (25483)
Greater Oklahoma City Chamber of Commerce
123 Park Ave.
Oklahoma City, OK 73102
Phone: (405)297-8916
Fax: (405)297-8916
**Subject(s):** Chambers of Commerce and Boards of Trade
**Circ:** ‡5,800

**SPE Drilling and Completion** (30307)
Society of Petroleum Engineers
222 Palisades Creek Dr.
Richardson, TX 75080
Phone: (972)952-9393
Fax: (972)952-9435
**Subject(s):** Engineering (Various branches); Petroleum, Oil, and Gas
**Circ:** ‡5,800

**Forests & People** (12041)
Louisiana Forestry Association
PO Drawer 5067
Alexandria, LA 71307-5067
Phone: (318)443-2558
Fax: (318)443-1713
**Subject(s):** Forestry
**Circ:** (Combined)5,600

**The Insurance Journal of Texas** (30028)
Wells Publishing Inc.
PO Box 940
Kyle, TX 78640-0940
Phone: (512)268-7660
Fax: (512)268-7760
**Subject(s):** Insurance
**Circ:** (Controlled)5,600

**Current Opinion in Lipidology** (29522)
Lippincott Williams & Wilkins
C/O Scott M. Grundy
University of Texas Southwestern Medical Center
Dallas, TX
**Subject(s):** Medicine and Surgery
**Circ:** (Paid)‡5,500

**Environmental Toxicology and Chemistry** (29841)
SETAC
Dept. of Civil & Environmental Engineering, MS31
Rice University
Houston, TX 77005-1892
Phone: (713)348-4701
Fax: (713)348-5948
**Subject(s):** Ecology and Conservation; Chemistry, Chemicals, and Chemical Engineering; Toxicology
**Circ:** 5,500

**Texas Shore Magazine** (29439)
Sea Grant Program
2700 Earl Rudder Fwy. S., Ste. 1800
College Station, TX 77845
Phone: (979)845-3854
Fax: (979)845-7525
**Subject(s):** Environmental and Natural Resources Conservation
**Circ:** (Combined)5,500

**This Week New Orleans** (12323)
Key Magazine Inc.
1401 Holiday Pl.
New Orleans, LA 70114
Phone: (504)227-8069
**Subject(s):** Travel and Tourism; Entertainment; Local, State, and Regional Publications
**Circ:** (Combined)5,500

**Proofs** (25620)
PennWell Corp.
1421 S. Sheridan Rd.
Tulsa, OK 74112
Phone: (918)835-3161
Fax: (918)832-9201
**Subject(s):** Dentistry
**Circ:** ‡5409

**Air Medical Journal** (1159)
Mosby Inc.
34 Barbara Dr.
Little Rock, AR 72204
Phone: (501)223-0183
**Subject(s):** Health and Healthcare; Aviation
**Circ:** (Paid)‡5,250

**Bowling Center Management** (29106)
Bowling Proprietors Association of America
615 Six Flags Dr.
Arlington, TX 76011
Phone: (817)649-5105
Fax: (817)633-2940
**Subject(s):** Business; Management and Administration; Sporting Goods/Retail Sports
**Circ:** 5,200

**County Magazine** (29150)
Texas Association of Counties
PO Box 2131
Austin, TX 78768-2131
Phone: (512)478-8753
Fax: (512)478-0519
**Subject(s):** State, Municipal, and County Administration
**Circ:** (Free)500
(Paid)5,200

**Limousin World** (25352)
2005 Ruhl Dr.
Guthrie, OK 73044
Phone: (405)260-3775
Fax: (405)260-3766
**Subject(s):** Livestock
**Circ:** (Paid)‡4,800
(Non-paid)‡5,200

**Texas Surplus Line Reporter** (12167)
Reporter Publishing Co.
Box 1089
Gretna, LA 70054
Phone: (504)366-8797
Fax: (504)366-1966
**Subject(s):** Insurance
**Circ:** (Paid)‡835
(Non-paid)‡5,110

**Aggies Illustrated** (25591)
First Down Publications
4528 S Sheridan, Ste. 216
Tulsa, OK 74145
**Subject(s):** College Publications; (General Sports)
**Circ:** (Paid)5,000

**American Red Brangus Journal** (29634)
American Red Brangus Association
3995 E Hwy. 290
Dripping Springs, TX 78620-4205
Phone: (512)858-7285
Fax: (512)858-7084
**Subject(s):** Livestock
**Circ:** ‡5,000

**Black Tennis Magazine** (29514)
PO Box 210676
Dallas, TX 75211
**Subject(s):** Black Publications; (Racquet Sports)
**Circ:** ‡5,000

**County Progress** (29038)
500 Chestnut St., Ste. 2000
Abilene, TX 79602
Phone: (325)673-4822
Fax: (325)677-2631
**Subject(s):** State, Municipal, and County Administration
**Circ:** ‡5,000

**Family Medicine** (30360)
Society of Teachers of Family Medicine
7703 Floyd Curl Dr.
San Antonio, TX 78284-7794
Phone: (210)567-4569
Fax: (210)567-4579
**Subject(s):** Medicine and Surgery
**Circ:** (Controlled)‡513
(Paid)‡5,000

**Gilcrease Journal** (25604)
Thomas Gilcrease Museum Association
1400 N. Gilcrease Museum Rd.
Tulsa, OK 74127
Phone: (918)596-2725
Fax: (918)596-2727
**Subject(s):** Art and Art History
**Circ:** (Controlled)5,000

**Journal of Southern History** (29875)
Rice University
PO Box 1892
Houston, TX 77251-1892
Phone: (713)348-6039
Fax: (713)348-4383
**Subject(s):** History and Genealogy
**Circ:** (Controlled)5,000

**Progressive Rentals** (29196)
Association of Progressive Rental Organizations
1504 Robin Hood Trail
Austin, TX 78703
Phone: (512)794-0095
Fax: (512)794-0097
**Subject(s):** Rental Equipment
**Circ:** ‡5,000

**Quote** (12146)
Cheallaigh Shamrock
104 North 3rd St.
PO Box 190
Dodson, LA 71422
Phone: (318)628-8671
Fax: (318)628-8673
**Subject(s):** Public Speaking and Lecturing
**Circ:** ‡5,000

**SAM Advanced Management Journal** (29463)
Society for Advancement of Management
Texas A&M University - Corpus Christi
College of Business
6300 Ocean Dr., FC 111
Corpus Christi, TX 78412
Phone: (361)825-6045
Fax: (361)825-2725
**Subject(s):** Management and Administration
**Circ:** ‡5,000

**SPE Production and Facilities** (30308)
Society of Petroleum Engineers
222 Palisades Creek Dr.
Richardson, TX 75080
Phone: (972)952-9393
Fax: (972)952-9435

Subject(s): Petroleum, Oil, and Gas; Engineering (Various branches)
Circ: ‡5,000

**SPE Reservoir Evaluation & Engineering (30309)**
Society of Petroleum Engineers
222 Palisades Creek Dr.
Richardson, TX 75080
Phone: (972)952-9393
Fax: (972)952-9435
Subject(s): Engineering (Various branches); Petroleum, Oil, and Gas
Circ: ‡5,000

**Clinical Cancer Research (29831)**
American Association for Cancer Research Inc.
c/o Beth Notzon
University of Texas
M. D. Anderson Cancer Center
1515 Holcombe Blvd.
Houston, TX 77030
Phone: (713)792-6015
Fax: (713)792-6016
Subject(s): Medicine and Surgery; Health and Healthcare; Laboratory Research (Scientific and Medical)
Circ: (Combined)⊕4,950

**Volando (29607)**
TWC Publishers
General Delivery
Del Rio, TX 78840-9999
Subject(s): Aviation
Circ: (Paid)‡1,840
(Non-paid)‡4,816

**Journal of Trauma (30367)**
Lippincott Williams & Wilkins
C/o Basil A Pruitt, Jr., Editor
7330 San Pedro, Ste. 654
San Antonio, TX 78216
Phone: (210)342-7903
Fax: (210)342-2966
Subject(s): Medicine and Surgery
Circ: (Non-paid)‡278
(Combined)‡4,799

**Oklahoma COWMAN (25470)**
Oklahoma Cattlemen's Association
PO Box 82395
Oklahoma City, OK 73148
Phone: (405)235-4391
Fax: (405)235-3608
Subject(s): Livestock
Circ: 4,784

**Current Opinion in Psychiatry (29836)**
Lippincott Williams & Wilkins
6550 Fannin SM 677
Houston, TX
Phone: (713)790-4864
Fax: (713)795-4348
Subject(s): Medicine and Surgery; Psychology and Psychiatry
Circ: (Paid)‡4,750

**Dental Economics (25597)**
PennWell Corp.
1421 S. Sheridan Rd.
Tulsa, OK 74112
Phone: (918)835-3161
Fax: (918)832-9201
Subject(s): Dentistry
Circ: (Controlled)‡4,600

**Louisiana Contractor (12079)**
McGraw-Hill Companies Inc./Louisiana Contractor
4000 S Sherwood Forest Blvd., Ste. 202
Baton Rouge, LA 70816
Phone: (225)292-8980
Fax: (225)292-5089
Subject(s): Construction, Contracting, Building, and Excavating
Circ: ⊕4,575

**Endocrinology (29751)**
Endocrine Society
University of Texas Medical Branch
Rm. 111C, Basic Science Bldg.
Galveston, TX 77555-0629
Phone: (301)951-2603
Fax: (301)951-2617
Subject(s): Medicine and Surgery
Circ: (Non-paid)‡453
(Paid)‡4,540

**The Journal of Continuing Education in Nursing (30081)**
SLACK Inc.
c/o Patricia S. Yoder-Wise, RN
Prof., School of Nursing
Texas Tech Univ. Health Sciences Center
Lubbock, TX
Subject(s): Nursing
Circ: ‡4,439

**Endocrine Reviews (29750)**
Endocrine Society
University of Texas Medical Branch
Rm. 111C, Basic Science Building
Galveston, TX 77555-0629
Phone: (409)747-4711
Fax: (409)747-4711
Subject(s): Medicine and Surgery
Circ: (Non-paid)‡378
(Paid)‡4,333

**The Clarinet (29615)**
International Clarinet Association
University of N Texas
College of Music
PO Box 13887
Denton, TX 76203
Phone: (940)565-4096
Fax: (940)565-2002
Subject(s): Music and Musical Instruments
Circ: (Non-paid)‡50
(Paid)‡4,000

**Indigenous Woman (29162)**
Indigenous Women's Network
13621 FM 2769
Austin, TX 78726
Phone: (512)258-3880
Fax: (512)258-1858
Subject(s): Women's Interests; Intercultural Interests; Art; Environmental and Natural Resources Conservation
Circ: (Non-paid)1,000
4,000

**Journal of Medical Licensure and Discipline (29547)**
Federation of State Medical Boards of the United States Inc.
Federation Pl.
PO Box 619850
Dallas, TX 75261-9850
Phone: (817)868-4000
Fax: (817)868-4098
Subject(s): Medicine and Surgery
Circ: (Paid)4,000

**Surplus Line Reporter & Insurance News (12166)**
Reporter Publishing Co.
Box 1089
Gretna, LA 70054
Phone: (504)366-8797
Fax: (504)366-1966
Subject(s): Insurance
Circ: (Non-paid)‡4,008

**Texas Journal of Business Law (29572)**
The University of Texas School of Law Publications Inc.
1700 Pacific
Ste. 3300
Dallas, TX 75201
Subject(s): Law; Business
Circ: (Paid)4,000

**Ultreya Magazine (29574)**
National Ultreya Publications
PO Box 210226
Dallas, TX 75211
Phone: (214)339-6321
Fax: (214)339-6322
Subject(s): Religious Publications
Circ: 4,000

**Human Organization (25460)**
Society for Applied Anthropology
PO Box 2436
Oklahoma City, OK 73101-2436
Phone: (405)843-5113
Fax: (405)843-8553
Subject(s): Sociology; Anthropology and Ethnology
Circ: ‡3,999

**The Beefmaster Cowman (30354)**
Gulf Coast Publishing Corp.
11201 Morning Ct.
San Antonio, TX 78213
Phone: (210)344-8300

Fax: (210)344-4258
Subject(s): Livestock
Circ: (Non-paid)‡210
(Paid)‡3,970

**Sprinkler Age (29568)**
American Fire Sprinkler Association
9696 Skillman St., Ste. 300
Dallas, TX 75243-8264
Phone: (214)349-5965
Fax: (214)343-8898
Subject(s): Fire Fighting
Circ: (Non-paid)‡3,926

**Journal (25461)**
Oklahoma State Medical Association
601 NW Grand Blvd.
Oklahoma City, OK 73118
Phone: (405)843-9571
Fax: (405)842-1834
Subject(s): Medicine and Surgery
Circ: (Non-paid)‡440
(Paid)‡3,900

**Journal of Dental Education (30363)**
American Dental Education Association
Dept. of Periodontics
UTHSC-SA Dental School
7703 Floyd Curl Dr.
San Antonio, TX 78284
Subject(s): Dentistry; Education
Circ: (Controlled)‡195
(Paid)‡3,900

**The Louisiana Cattleman (12366)**
Louisiana Cattlemen's Association
4921 I-10 Frontage Rd. W
Port Allen, LA 70767
Phone: (225)343-3491
Fax: (225)336-0002
Subject(s): Livestock
Circ: (Non-paid)‡800
(Paid)‡3,900

**Pediatric Research (30653)**
Lippincott Williams & Wilkins
Pediatric Research Editorial Office
3400 Research Forest Dr, Ste. B7
The Woodlands, TX 77381
Phone: (281)419-0645
Fax: (281)419-0082
Subject(s): Pediatrics
Circ: (Non-paid)‡23
(Combined)‡3,875

**Miniature Horse World (29071)**
American Miniature Horse Association
5601 South Interstate 35 W
Alvarado, TX 76009
Phone: (817)783-5600
Fax: (817)783-6403
Subject(s): (Horses and Horse Racing)
Circ: 3,800

**Oil and Gas Investor (29892)**
Hart Publications Inc.
4545 Post Oak Pl., Ste. 210
Houston, TX 77027
Phone: (713)993-9320
Fax: (713)840-8585
Subject(s): Banking, Finance, and Investments
Circ: (Non-paid)356
(Paid)3,765

**ByLine (25312)**
PO Box 5240
Edmond, OK 73083-5240
Phone: (405)348-5591
Subject(s): Literature; Journalism and Publishing
Circ: 3,500

**Corrosion (29833)**
NACE International
1440 S Creek Dr.
Houston, TX 77084-4906
Phone: (281)228-6200
Fax: (281)228-6300
Subject(s): Metal, Metallurgy, and Metal Trade; Engineering (Various branches)
Circ: ‡3,500

**JINS** (19998)
Cambridge University Press
c/o Dr. Kathleen Y. Haaland
VA Research Career Scientist
NM VA Healthcare System
1501 San Pedro Dr. SE
Albuquerque, NM 87108
**Subject(s):** Psychology and Psychiatry

**Circ:** 3,500

**Journal for Research in Music Education** (12072)
MENC: The National Association for Music Education
Louisiana State University
School of Music
Baton Rouge, LA 70803-2504
Phone: (225)388-2481
Fax: (225)388-3333
**Subject(s):** Music and Musical Instruments; Education

**Circ:** (Controlled)‡19
(Paid)‡3,500

**Sugar Journal** (12322)
Kriedt Enterprises Ltd.
129 S Cortez St.
New Orleans, LA 70119
Phone: (504)482-3914
Fax: (504)482-4205
**Subject(s):** Socialized Farming; Sugar and Sugar Beets

**Circ:** (Paid)654
(Non-paid)3,319

**Southwestern Historical Quarterly** (29205)
Texas State Historical Association
University of Texas
1 University Sta. D0901
Austin, TX 78712-0332
Phone: (512)471-1525
Fax: (512)471-1551
**Subject(s):** History and Genealogy

**Circ:** ‡3,300

**The Journal of Special Education** (29178)
PRO-ED Inc.
8700 Shoal Creek Blvd.
Austin, TX 78757-6897
Phone: (512)451-3246
Fax: (800)397-7633
**Subject(s):** Education

**Circ:** (Non-paid)‡108
(Paid)‡3,268

**Bass World** (29508)
International Society of Bassists
13140 Coit Rd., Ste. 320
Dallas, TX 75240-5737
Phone: (972)233-9107
Fax: (972)490-4219
**Subject(s):** Music and Musical Instruments

**Circ:** (Paid)3,200

**Counseling and Values** (29618)
American Counseling Association
c/o Dr. Dennis W. Engels, CVJ Editor
Stovall Hall 155
Univ. of North Texas
PO Box 311337
Denton, TX 76203-1337
Phone: (940)565-2918
Fax: (940)565-2905
**Subject(s):** Religious Publications

**Circ:** (Paid)3,200

**Motorcycle Roads** (29885)
Motorcycle Touring Association
11539 Village Place Dr.
Houston, TX 77077
Phone: (281)752-9406
Fax: (281)752-9507
**Subject(s):** Motorbikes and Motorcycles

**Circ:** 3,200

**Texas Hereford** (29729)
Texas Hereford Association
4609 Airport Fwy.
Fort Worth, TX 76117
Phone: (817)831-3161
Fax: (817)831-3162
**Subject(s):** Livestock

**Circ:** ‡3,200

**Physiological Reviews** (29896)
The American Physiological Society
c/o S. L. Hamilton, Editor
Dept. of Molecular Physiology and Biophysics
Baylor College of Medicine
Rm. 410b, One Baylor Plaza
Houston, TX 77030-3498
Phone: (713)798-5704
Fax: (713)798-5441
**Subject(s):** Physiology and Anatomy

**Circ:** (Paid)‡3,187

**Bankers Digest** (29506)
9550 Forest Ln., Ste. 125
Dallas, TX 75243-5928
Phone: (214)221-4544
Fax: (214)221-4546
**Subject(s):** Banking, Finance, and Investments

**Circ:** ‡3,100

**Circulation** (29829)
Lippincott Williams & Wilkins
St. Luke's Episcopal Hospital/Texas Heart Institute
MC1-267 (Rm. B524)
6720 Bertner Ave.
Houston, TX 77030-2697
**Subject(s):** Medicine and Surgery

**Circ:** (Paid)‡3,060

**Bonsai Magazine** (12245)
Bonsai Clubs International
PO Box 8445
Metairie, LA 70011-8445
Phone: (504)832-8071
Fax: (504)834-2298
**Subject(s):** Home and Garden; Botany

**Circ:** 3,000

**Central Oklahoma Home Builder** (25454)
Central Oklahoma Home Builders Association
625 NW Grand Blvd.
Oklahoma City, OK 73118
Phone: (405)843-1508
Fax: (405)843-6714
**Subject(s):** Construction, Contracting, Building, and Excavating

**Circ:** (Controlled)3,000

**Intervention in School and Clinic** (29166)
PRO-ED Inc.
8700 Shoal Creek Blvd.
Austin, TX 78757-6897
Phone: (512)451-3246
Fax: (800)397-7633
**Subject(s):** Education

**Circ:** (Paid)3,000

**The Journal of the Arkansas Medical Society** (1177)
Arkansas Medical Society
PO Box 55088
Little Rock, AR 72215
Phone: (501)224-8967
Fax: (501)224-6489
**Subject(s):** Medicine and Surgery

**Circ:** (Non-paid)‡1,200
(Paid)‡3,000

**Juggle** (29386)
Stagewrite Publishing Inc.
PO Box 112550
Carrollton, TX 75011-2550
Phone: (415)596-3307
Fax: (302)397-2345
**Subject(s):** Performing Arts

**Circ:** 3,000

**Metropolitan Beaumont** (29290)
Beaumont Chamber of Commerce
1110 Park St.
PO Box 3150
Beaumont, TX 77701
Phone: (409)838-6581
Fax: (409)833-6718
**Subject(s):** Local, State, and Regional Publications

**Circ:** ‡3000

**New Orleans Menu** (12313)
New Orleans, Big Bend & Pacific Co., Publishers
PO Box 51831
New Orleans, LA 70151
Phone: (504)524-0348
**Subject(s):** Food and Cooking; Local, State, and Regional Publications

**Circ:** (Combined)3,000

**Psychonomic Bulletin & Review** (29197)
Psychonomic Society Inc.
1710 Fortview Rd.
Austin, TX 78704
Phone: (512)462-2442
Fax: (512)462-1101
**Subject(s):** Psychology and Psychiatry

**Circ:** ‡3,000

**Southern Economic Journal** (25568)
Oklahoma State University
College of Business Administration
Stillwater, OK 74078-4011
Phone: (405)744-7645
Fax: (405)774-5180
**Subject(s):** Economics

**Circ:** 3,000

**Texas Veterinarian** (29248)
Texas Veterinary Medical Association
8104 Exchange Dr.
Austin, TX 78754
Phone: (512)452-4224
Fax: (512)452-6633
**Subject(s):** Veterinary Medicine

**Circ:** (Controlled)‡500
(Paid)‡3,000

**Weather and Forecasting** (25439)
American Meteorological Society
Office of Joint Chief Editors, Weather And Forecasting
NOAA/National Severe Storms Laboratory
1313 Halley Cir.
Norman, OK 73069
**Subject(s):** Astronomy and Meteorology

**Circ:** ‡2,985

**Cinema Journal** (29518)
University of Texas Press
c/o Frank Tomasulo
Department of Cinema-TV
Southern Methodist University
Dallas, TX 75275
Phone: (214)768-3709
Fax: (214)768-2784
**Subject(s):** Motion Pictures; Radio, Television, Cable, and Video

**Circ:** (Combined)⊕2,858

**America's Barrel Racer** (30535)
Go Go Communications Inc.
201 WestMoore, Ste.200
Terrell, TX 75160-4852
Fax: (972)563-7004
**Subject(s):** (Horses and Horse Racing)

**Circ:** (Paid)‡2,800

**Brangus Journal** (30355)
5750 Epsilon
San Antonio, TX 78249
Phone: (210)696-4343
Fax: (210)696-8718
**Subject(s):** Livestock

**Circ:** ‡2,800

**Texas Pharmacy** (29235)
Texas Pharmacy Association
PO Box 14709
Austin, TX 78761-4709
Phone: (512)836-0308
Fax: (800)505-5463
**Subject(s):** Drugs and Pharmaceuticals

**Circ:** ‡2,800

**Gender & Society** (29158)
Sage Publications Inc.
c/o Dr. Christine Williams
Dept. of Sociology, 1 Univ. Station A1700
Univ. of Texas
Austin, TX 78712-0118
Phone: (512)232-6327
Fax: (512)471-1748
**Subject(s):** Sociology; Women's Interests

**Circ:** (Non-paid)‡153
(Paid)‡2,650

**Journal for the Education of the Gifted** (29170)
Prufrock Press
5926 Balcones Dr., Ste.220
Austin, TX 78731
Phone: (512)300-2220
Fax: (512)300-2221
**Subject(s):** Education

**Circ:** (Non-paid)65
(Paid)2,600

**AC Current** (29075)
Amarillo College
PO Box 447
Amarillo, TX 79178-0001
Phone: (806)371-5290
Fax: (806)371-5398
**Subject(s):** College Publications

**Circ:** (Non-paid)2,500

**Facility Manager** (29457)
International Association of Assembly Managers
635 Fritz Dr.
Coppell, TX 75019-4442
Phone: (972)906-7441
Fax: (972)906-7418
**Subject(s):** Entertainment

**Circ:** (Non-paid)‡70
(Paid)‡2,500

**Meat Goat Monthly News** (30333)
Ranch Publishing
PO Box 2678
San Angelo, TX 76902
Phone: (325)655-4434
**Subject(s):** Livestock

**Circ:** 2,500

**Midsouthwest Restaurant** (25465)
Oklahoma Restaurant Association
3800 N Portland
Oklahoma City, OK 73112-2948
Phone: (405)942-8181
Fax: (405)942-0541
**Subject(s):** Hotels, Motels, Restaurants, and Clubs

**Circ:** ‡2,500

**The Southern Review** (12091)
Louisiana State University
43 Allen Hall
Baton Rouge, LA 70803-5005
Phone: (225)578-5108
Fax: (225)578-5098
**Subject(s):** Literature; History and Genealogy

**Circ:** ‡2,500

**The Texas Surveyor** (29246)
Texas Society of Professional Surveyors
2525 Wallingwood Dr., Ste. 300
Austin, TX 78746
Phone: (512)327-7871
Fax: (512)327-7872
**Subject(s):** Engineering (Various branches)

**Circ:** ‡2,500

**Memory & Cognition** (29185)
Psychonomic Society Inc.
1710 Fortview Rd.
Austin, TX 78704
Phone: (512)462-2442
Fax: (512)462-1101
**Subject(s):** Psychology and Psychiatry

**Circ:** ‡2,400

**Communication Disorders Quarterly** (29148)
PRO-ED Inc.
8700 Shoal Creek Blvd.
Austin, TX 78757-6897
Phone: (512)451-3246
Fax: (800)397-7633
**Subject(s):** Philology, Language, and Linguistics

**Circ:** (Paid)2,300

**Paper Money** (29561)
Society of Paper Money Collectors
Box 793941
Dallas, TX 75379-3941
**Subject(s):** Collecting

**Circ:** ‡2,300

**Texas Journal of Chiropractic** (29223)
Texas Chiropractic Association
1122 Colorado, Ste. 307
Austin, TX 78701-2509
Phone: (512)477-9292
Fax: (512)477-9296
**Subject(s):** Chiropractic

**Circ:** (Controlled)‡2,300

**North American Journal of Aquaculture** (25431)
American Fisheries Society
c/o Dr. William L. Shelton
Dept. of Zoology
Univ. of Oklahoma
Norman, OK 73019
Phone: (405)325-1058
Fax: (405)325-0835
**Subject(s):** Fish and Commercial Fisheries; General Agriculture

**Circ:** ‡2,200

**Seminars in Nephrology** (30086)
Elsevier
C/o Neil Kurtzman, Editor
Texas Tech University Health Sciences Center
Dept. of Internal Medicine
Lubbock, TX 79430
**Subject(s):** Medicine and Surgery

**Circ:** ‡2,198

**The Brahman Journal** (29805)
Sagebrush Publishing Company Inc.
1037 Austin St.
Hempstead, TX 77445
Phone: (979)826-4347
Fax: (979)826-2007
**Subject(s):** Livestock

**Circ:** (Non-paid)‡1586
(Paid)‡2183

**Arkansas Banker** (1160)
Arkansas Bankers Association
The Carvill Bldg.
1220 W. 3rd St.
Little Rock, AR 72201
Phone: (501)376-3741
Fax: (501)376-9243
**Subject(s):** Banking, Finance, and Investments

**Circ:** ‡2,000

**The Five Owls** (30128)
PO Box 235
Marathon, TX 79842-0235
Phone: (432)386-4257
Fax: (432)386-9087
**Subject(s):** Education

**Circ:** (Paid)1,500
(Non-paid)2,000

**Journal of Air Law and Commerce** (29543)
Joe Christensen Inc.
School of Law
Southern Methodist University
Dallas, TX 75275
Phone: (214)768-2570
Fax: (214)768-3946
**Subject(s):** Aviation; Law

**Circ:** ‡2,000

**Journal of World Business** (29550)
University of California Press
c/o John W. Slocum, Editor-in-chief
Journal of World Business, Cox School of Business
Southern Methodist University
Dallas, TX 75275
**Subject(s):** International Business and Economics

**Circ:** ‡2,000

**Linden Lane Magazine** (29720)
Linden Lane Press
PO Box 331964
Fort Worth, TX 76163
Phone: (817)731-4657
Fax: (817)738-4435
**Subject(s):** Literature; Spanish

**Circ:** (Paid)2000

**Oklahoma Professional Engineer** (25475)
Oklahoma Society of Professional Engineers
201 NE 27th St., Rm. 125
Oklahoma City, OK 73105
Phone: (405)528-1435
Fax: (405)557-1820
**Subject(s):** Engineering (Various branches)

**Circ:** ‡2,000

**SAC Newsmonthly** (12116)
S.A.C. Newsmonthly
PO Box 159
Bogalusa, LA 70429
Phone: (985)732-5616
Fax: (985)732-3744
**Subject(s):** Crafts, Models, Hobbies, and Contests

**Circ:** (Non-paid)‡30
(Paid)‡2,000

**Social Policy** (12321)
Institute for Social Justice
1024 Elysian Fields Ave.
New Orleans, LA 70117
Phone: (504)943-0044
Fax: (504)944-7078
**Subject(s):** General Editorial

**Circ:** ‡2,000

**World Literature Today** (25440)
630 Parrington Oval. Ste. 110
University of Oklahoma
Norman, OK 73019-4033
Phone: (405)325-4531
Fax: (405)325-7495
**Subject(s):** Literature

**Circ:** (Non-paid)‡200
(Paid)‡1,980

**Individual Psychology** (29163)
University of Wisconsin Press
University of Texas
Educational Psychology
Austin, TX 78712
Phone: (512)471-4531
Fax: (512)320-0668
**Subject(s):** Psychology and Psychiatry

**Circ:** 1,900

**American Catholic Philosophical Quarterly** (29977)
Philosophy Documentation Center
Institute of Philosophical Studies
University of Dallas
1845 E. Northgate Dr.
Irving, TX 75062-4736
Phone: (972)721-4007
Fax: (972)721-4007
**Subject(s):** Philosophy; Religious Publications

**Circ:** ‡1,800

**Perception & Psychophysics** (29193)
Psychonomic Society Inc.
1710 Fortview Rd.
Austin, TX 78704
Phone: (512)462-2442
Fax: (512)462-1101
**Subject(s):** Psychology and Psychiatry

**Circ:** ‡1,800

**Texas Historian** (29220)
Texas State Historical Association
University of Texas
1 University Sta. D0901
Austin, TX 78712-0332
Phone: (512)471-1525
Fax: (512)471-1551
**Subject(s):** History and Genealogy

**Circ:** ‡1,800

**Texas Intellectual Property Law Journal** (29221)
The University of Texas School of Law Publications Inc.
727 E Dean Keeton St.
PO Box 8670
Austin, TX 78705
Phone: (512)232-1395
Fax: (512)475-6741
**Subject(s):** Patents, Trademarks, and Copyrights; Law

**Circ:** (Combined)1,800

**Texas Law Review** (29225)
The University of Texas School of Law Publications Inc.
727 E Dean Keeton St.
PO Box 8670
Austin, TX 78705
Phone: (512)232-1395
Fax: (512)475-6741
**Subject(s):** Law

**Circ:** ‡1,800

**Studies in English Literature, 1500-1900 (SEL)** (29909)
John Hopkins University Press
Studies in English Literature
Rice University
SEL-MS 46, 6100 Main St.
Houston, TX 77005-1892
Phone: (713)348-4697
Fax: (713)348-6245
**Subject(s):** Literature

**Circ:** (Non-paid)‡100
(Paid)‡1,742

**American Fighter Aces and Friends Bulletin** (29126)
American Fighter Aces Association
PO Box 202104
Austin, TX 78720-2104
**Subject(s):** Aviation; Aviation

**Circ:** 1,700

# Southern Central States

**Cotton Gin & Oil Mill Press** (30164)
Haughton Publishing of Texas Inc.
3210 Innovative Way
Mesquite, TX 75149
Phone: (972)288-7511
Fax: (972)285-4881
**Subject(s):** Textiles
**Circ:** (Non-paid)‡200
(Paid)‡1,700

**Journal of Church and State** (30592)
J.M. Dawson Institute of Church-State Studies
Baylor University
One Bear Place
PO Box 97308
Waco, TX 76798-7308
Phone: (254)710-1510
Fax: (254)710-1571
**Subject(s):** Law; Political Science
**Circ:** (Paid)⊕1,700

**The Journal of the Greater Houston Dental Society** (29872)
Greater Houston Dental Society
1 Greenway Plz., Ste. 110
Houston, TX 77046
Phone: (713)961-4337
Fax: (713)961-3617
**Subject(s):** Dentistry
**Circ:** (Non-paid)1,700

**The American Journal of Forensic Medicine and Pathology** (30350)
Lippincott Williams & Wilkins
c/o Vincent J. M. DiMaio
Bexar County Chief Medical Examiner
7337 Louis Pasteur
San Antonio, TX 78229-4565
**Subject(s):** Laboratory Research (Scientific and Medical)
**Circ:** 1,566
1,691

**Arkansas Historical Quarterly** (1070)
Arkansas Historical Association
University of Arkansas
History Dept., 416 Old Main
Fayetteville, AR 72701
Phone: (479)575-5884
Fax: (479)575-2775
**Subject(s):** History and Genealogy
**Circ:** ‡1,600

**ASAIO Journal** (29749)
Lippincott Williams & Wilkins
UTMB School of Medicine
301 University Blvd.
Campus Route 0528
Galveston, TX 77555-0528
Phone: (409)772-8644
Fax: (409)772-1421
**Subject(s):** Medicine and Surgery
**Circ:** 1,026
1,609

**Countermeasures** (20161)
College of Santa Fe
1600 St. Michael's Dr.
Santa Fe, NM 87505
Phone: (505)473-6011
**Subject(s):** Poetry; Literature
**Circ:** (Combined)1,600

**Entrepreneurship Theory and Practice** (30590)
Baylor University
1 Bear Place
Waco, TX 76798
Phone: (254)710-4290
Fax: (254)710-2271
**Subject(s):** Business; Management and Administration
**Circ:** ‡1,600

**Journal of Musculoskeletal Pain** (30366)
The Haworth Press Inc.
c/o I. Jon Russell, M.D.
Dept. of Medicine, MC7868
Health Science Ctr.
7703 Floyd Curl Dr.
San Antonio, TX 78229-3900
Phone: (210)567-4661
Fax: (210)567-6669
**Subject(s):** Health and Healthcare
**Circ:** (Paid)1,588

**Current Opinion in Cardiology** (29835)
Lippincott Williams & Wilkins
6550 Fannin SM 677
Houston, TX 77030
Phone: (713)790-4864
Fax: (713)795-4348
**Subject(s):** Medicine and Surgery
**Circ:** (Paid)‡1,550

**American Dance Circle** (19987)
Lloyd Shaw Foundation
1620 Los Alamos SW
Albuquerque, NM 87104
Phone: (505)247-3921
**Subject(s):** Performing Arts; Performing Arts
**Circ:** 1,500

**Anglican & Episcopal History** (30125)
Historical Society of the Episcopal Church
PO Box 2098
Manchaca, TX 78652
Phone: (512)282-3234
Fax: (512)280-3902
**Subject(s):** History and Genealogy; Religious Publications
**Circ:** ‡1,500

**Art Law & Accounting Reporter** (29825)
Texas Accountants and Lawyers for the Arts (TALA)
1540 Sul Ross
Houston, TX 77006
Phone: (713)526-4876
Fax: (713)526-1299
**Subject(s):** Law; Accountants and Accounting; Art and Art History
**Circ:** (Paid)1,500

**Journal of the American Taxation Association (JATA)** (29168)
American Accounting Association
Department of Accounting
McCombs School of Business
University of Texas
1 University Sta., B6400
Austin, TX 78712-0211
Phone: (512)471-5315
Fax: (512)471-3904
**Subject(s):** Accountants and Accounting
**Circ:** (Paid)1,500

**Louisiana Libraries** (12153)
Louisiana Library Association
421 S 4th St.
Eunice, LA 70535-5301
Phone: (337)550-7890
Fax: (337)550-7846
**Subject(s):** Library and Information Science
**Circ:** (Non-paid)‡50
(Paid)‡1,500

**The Louisiana Pharmacist** (12085)
Louisiana Pharmacists Association
PO Box 14446
Baton Rouge, LA 70898-4446
**Subject(s):** Drugs and Pharmaceuticals
**Circ:** ‡1,500

**James Joyce Quarterly** (25608)
University of Tulsa
600 S College
Tulsa, OK 74104-3189
Phone: (918)631-2501
Fax: (918)631-2065
**Subject(s):** Literature
**Circ:** (Non-paid)‡20
(Paid)‡1,450

**Natural Resources Journal** (20002)
University of New Mexico School of Law
MSCII 6070
1 University of New Mexico
Albuquerque, NM 87131
Phone: (505)277-4910
Fax: (505)277-8342
**Subject(s):** Ecology and Conservation
**Circ:** (Paid)‡1,400

**Oklahoma Pharmacist** (25474)
Oklahoma Pharmaceutical Association
45 NE 52 St.
PO Box 18731
Oklahoma City, OK 73154-0731
Phone: (405)528-3338
Fax: (405)528-1417
**Subject(s):** Drugs and Pharmaceuticals
**Circ:** ‡1,400

**Dallas Journal** (29527)
Dallas Genealogical Society
PO Box 12446
Dallas, TX 75225-0446
Phone: (469)948-1106
**Subject(s):** History and Genealogy
**Circ:** (Paid)⊕1275

**Louisiana Rural Economist** (12087)
Agricultural Economics & Agribusiness
101 Agricultural Administration Bldg.
Louisiana State Univ.
Baton Rouge, LA 70803-5604
Phone: (225)578-3282
Fax: (504)388-2716
**Subject(s):** Economics; General Agriculture
**Circ:** (Controlled)‡1,265

**Dealers' Choice** (29153)
Texas Automobile Dealers Association
PO Box 1028
Austin, TX 78767-1028
Phone: (512)476-2686
Fax: (512)322-0561
**Subject(s):** Automotive (Trade)
**Circ:** (Controlled)550
(Paid)1,250

**Journal of Sport Management** (29179)
Human Kinetics Publishers Inc.
c/o Laurence Chalip
The Univ. of Texas at Austin
Sport Management Program
Bellmont Hall 222, D3700
Austin, TX 78712-1204
Phone: (512)471-1273
Fax: (512)471-8914
**Subject(s):** (General Sports)
**Circ:** (Paid)1,250

**The Annals of the American Society for Adolescent Psychiatry** (29502)
American Society for Adolescent Psychiatry
PO Box 570218
Dallas, TX 75357-0218
Phone: (972)686-6166
Fax: (972)613-5532
**Subject(s):** Psychology and Psychiatry
**Circ:** 1,200

**Journal of Anthropological Research** (19999)
University of New Mexico
Dept. of Anthropology
MSC 01 1040
Albuquerque, NM 87131-0001
Phone: (505)277-4544
Fax: (505)277-0874
**Subject(s):** Anthropology and Ethnology
**Circ:** (Non-paid)‡50
(Paid)1,200

**Learning and Behavior** (29182)
Psychonomic Society Inc.
1710 Fortview Rd.
Austin, TX 78704
Phone: (512)462-2442
Fax: (512)462-1101
**Subject(s):** Psychology and Psychiatry
**Circ:** ‡1,200

**Louisiana History** (12190)
Louisiana Historical Association
PO Box 40831
Lafayette, LA 70504-0831
Phone: (337)482-6027
Fax: (337)482-6028
**Subject(s):** History and Genealogy
**Circ:** ‡1,200

**New Mexico Historical Review** (20004)
University of New Mexico
MSC06 3790, 1013 Mesa Vista Hall
Albuquerque, NM 87131-0001
Phone: (505)277-5839
Fax: (505)277-0992
**Subject(s):** History and Genealogy
**Circ:** (Paid)1,200

**Research Initiative/Treatment Action!** (29901)
The Center for AIDS: Hope & Remembrance Project
PO Box 66306
Houston, TX 77266-6306
Phone: (713)527-8219
Fax: (713)521-3679

**Subject(s):** Health and Healthcare; Medicine and Surgery

**Circ:** 1,200

**The Rural Educator Journal (25437)**
National Rural Education Association
820 Van Vleet Oval, Rm. 227
University of Oklahoma
Norman, OK 73019
Phone: (405)325-7959
Fax: (405)325-7959
**Subject(s):** Education

**Circ:** (Paid)1,200

**Seventeenth-Century News (29435)**
Dept. of English, 4227 TAMU
Texas A&M University
College Station, TX 77843-4227
Phone: (979)845-8340
Fax: (979)862-2292
**Subject(s):** Literature; History and Genealogy

**Circ:** 1,200

**Texas Petroleum and C-Store Journal (29234)**
Texas Petroleum Marketers and Convenience Store Association (TPCA)
701 W 15th St.
Austin, TX 78701
Phone: (512)476-9547
Fax: (512)477-4239
**Subject(s):** Petroleum, Oil, and Gas; Local, State, and Regional Publications

**Circ:** ‡1,200

**Behavior Research Methods (29139)**
Psychonomic Society Inc.
1710 Fortview Rd.
Austin, TX 78704
Phone: (512)462-2442
Fax: (512)462-1101
**Subject(s):** Psychology and Psychiatry

**Circ:** ‡1,150

**Texas Director (29214)**
Texas Funeral Directors Association
314 Highland Mall Blvd., Ste. 510
Austin, TX 78752
Phone: (512)454-5262
Fax: (512)451-9556
**Subject(s):** Funeral Directors

**Circ:** (Non-paid)1,150

**Cognitive, Affective, & Behavioral Neuroscience (29147)**
Psychonomic Society Inc.
1710 Fortview Rd.
Austin, TX 78704
Phone: (512)462-2442
Fax: (512)462-1101
**Subject(s):** Psychology and Psychiatry

**Circ:** ‡1,100

**Texas Propane (29239)**
Texas Propane Gas Association
8408 N Interegional Hwy.
Austin, TX 78753
Phone: (512)836-8620
Fax: (512)834-0758
**Subject(s):** Petroleum, Oil, and Gas

**Circ:** (Controlled)‡1,050

**Tulsa Medicine (25628)**
Tulsa County Medical Society
5315 S Lews Ave.
Tulsa, OK 74105-6539
Phone: (918)743-6184
Fax: (918)743-0336
**Subject(s):** Medicine and Surgery

**Circ:** (Non-paid)‡50
(Paid)‡1,050

**CALICO (30414)**
Computer Assisted Language Instruction
Texas State University
214 Centennial Hall
601 Univ. Dr.
San Marcos, TX 78666
Phone: (512)245-1417
Fax: (512)245-9089
**Subject(s):** Computers; Education

**Circ:** ‡1,020

**Infant Mental Health Journal (12300)**
John Wiley and Sons Inc.
1542 Tulane Ave.
Louisiana State University
New Orleans, LA 70112-2822
Phone: (504)568-6246
Fax: (504)568-6246
**Subject(s):** Psychology and Psychiatry

**Circ:** (Controlled)‡47
(Paid)‡1,010

**AATA Quarterly (29821)**
Animal Transportation Association
AATA International Office
111 E Loop N
Houston, TX 77029
Phone: (713)532-2177
Fax: (713)532-2166
**Subject(s):** Pets; Society for the Prevention of Cruelty to Animals and Anti-Vivisection

**Circ:** 1,000

**American Journal of Pastoral Counseling (25345)**
The Haworth Press Inc.
c/o Richard Dayringer
31990 S. 624th Place, H14
Grove, OK 74344
Phone: (918)786-5274
**Subject(s):** Psychology and Psychiatry; Religious Publications

**Circ:** 1,000

**Emu Today & Tomorrow (25270)**
Emu Today and Tomorrow
11950 W. Highland Ave.
Blackwell, OK 74631-6511
Phone: (580)628-2933
Fax: (580)628-2011
**Subject(s):** Livestock

**Circ:** (Non-paid)⊕100
(Paid)⊕1,000

**Extrapolation (29342)**
University of Texas at Brownsville & Texas Southmost College
80 Fort Brown
Brownsville, TX 78520
Phone: (956)544-8984
Fax: (956)983-7064
**Subject(s):** Literature

**Circ:** ‡1,000

**Film & History (25292)**
Popular Culture Center
RR 3, Box 80
Cleveland, OK 74020
Phone: (918)243-7637
Fax: (918)243-5995
**Subject(s):** Motion Pictures; Radio, Television, Cable, and Video

**Circ:** (Paid)1,000

**Journal of the American Viola Society (29545)**
American Viola Society
c/o AVS National Office
LB 120
13140 Coit Rd., Ste. 320
Dallas, TX 75240-5737
Phone: (972)490-4219
**Subject(s):** Music and Musical Instruments

**Circ:** 1,000

**Journal of Computer Information Systems (25565)**
International Association for Computer Information Systems
c/o Dr. G. Daryl Nord
College of Business Administration
Oklahoma State University
Stillwater, OK 74078
Phone: (405)744-8632
Fax: (405)744-5180
**Subject(s):** Computers

**Circ:** 1,000

**Journal of Electromyography and Kinesiology (12301)**
Lippincott Williams & Wilkins
c/o Mosche Solomonow
Dept. of Orthopaedic Surgery
Louisiana State Univ. Medical Center
New Orleans, LA 70112
**Subject(s):** Laboratory Research (Scientific and Medical)

**Circ:** 1,000

**Journal of the History of Sexuality (29171)**
University of Texas Press
PO Box 7819
Austin, TX 78713-7819
Phone: (512)471-7233
Fax: (512)232-7178
**Subject(s):** Anthropology and Ethnology; History and Genealogy; Sociology; Psychology and Psychiatry

**Circ:** 1,000

**The Louisiana Boardmember (12078)**
Louisiana School Boards Association
7912 Summa Ave.
Baton Rouge, LA 70809
Phone: (225)769-3191
Fax: (225)769-6108
**Subject(s):** Education

**Circ:** ‡1,000

**New Orleans Review (12315)**
Loyola University
Box 195
New Orleans, LA 70118
Phone: (504)865-2295
Fax: (504)865-2294
**Subject(s):** Literature and Literary Reviews

**Circ:** (Non-paid)‡200
(Paid)‡1,000

**Newsreel (30126)**
Newsreel Inc.
PO Box 819
Manchaca, TX 78652-0819
Phone: (512)447-0455
Fax: (512)857-1154
**Subject(s):** Blind and Visually Challenged

**Circ:** (Combined)1000

**Oklahoma Geology Notes (25435)**
Oklahoma Geological Survey
Energy Ctr. University of Oklahoma
100 E Boyd St., Ste. N131
Norman, OK 73019
Phone: (405)325-3031
Fax: (405)325-7069
**Subject(s):** Geology

**Circ:** (Combined)1,000

**Paradoxism (20087)**
Universty of New Mexico
200 College Rd.
Gallup, NM 87301
Phone: (505)863-7500
**Subject(s):** Literature and Literary Reviews; Poetry

**Circ:** (Combined)1000

**Seminars in Pediatric Infectious Diseases (29907)**
Elsevier
C/o Ralph D. Feigin, Editor
College of Medicine
Houston, TX
**Subject(s):** Pediatrics

**Circ:** ‡1,007

**Single Free Press (25543)**
2007 Lona
Seminole, OK 74868
Phone: (405)382-6298
**Subject(s):** Lifestyle

**Circ:** 1,000

**Smarandache Notions Journal (20139)**
American Research Press
Box 141
Rehoboth, NM 87322
**Subject(s):** Mathematics; Physics

**Circ:** (Combined)1,000

**Southwest Review (29567)**
307 Fondren Library W.
PO Box 750374
Dallas, TX 75275-0374
Phone: (214)768-1036
Fax: (214)768-1408
**Subject(s):** Literature and Literary Reviews

**Circ:** (Non-paid)‡400
(Paid)‡1,000

**Texas Studies in Literature and Language (29245)**
University of Texas Press
PO Box 7819
Austin, TX 78713-7819
Phone: (512)471-7233
Fax: (512)232-7178

## Southern Central States

**Subject(s):** Literature
**Circ:** (Controlled)‡50
(Paid)‡1,000

**Tulsa Studies in Women's Literature  (25629)**
Tulsa Studies in Women's Literature, The University of Tulsa
600 S. College Ave.
Tulsa, OK 74104-3189
Phone: (918)631-2503
Fax: (918)584-0623
**Subject(s):** Women's Interests
**Circ:** 1,000

**Louisiana Law Review  (12082)**
Louisiana State University Law Center
Law Ctr.
c/o Paul M. Hebert
Baton Rouge, LA 70803
Phone: (225)578-1683
Fax: (504)578-1685
**Subject(s):** Law
**Circ:** (Paid)⊕982

**American Association of Stratigraphic Palynologists Contributions Series  (29417)**
Texas A & M University
Anthropology Bldg. (TAMU 4352)
College Station, TX 77843-4352
Phone: (979)845-5242
Fax: (979)845-4070
**Subject(s):** Geology; Natural History and Nature Study; Botany; Archaeology
**Circ:** (Combined)952

**Palynology  (29432)**
American Association of Stratigraphic Palynologists Foundation
Anthropology Bldg. (TAMU 4352)
Texas A & M University
College Station, TX 77843-4352
Phone: (979)845-5242
Fax: (979)845-4070
**Subject(s):** Geology; Science (General); Archaeology; Botany; Ecology and Conservation
**Circ:** (Controlled)952

**Arkansas Review  (1291)**
Arkansas State University
Department of English & Philosophy
Box 1890
State University, AR 72467
Phone: (870)972-3043
Fax: (870)972-3045
**Subject(s):** Literature and Literary Reviews
**Circ:** (Paid)900

**Drug Development and Industrial Pharmacy  (29154)**
Marcel Dekker Inc.
c/o Robert O. (Bill) Williams III
University of Texas
Austin, TX 78712-1074
**Subject(s):** Drugs and Pharmaceuticals
**Circ:** 875

**China Clipper  (25425)**
China Stamp Society Inc.
c/o Donald R. Alexander
1021 Valley View Rd.
Norman, OK 73069
Phone: (405)912-5042
**Subject(s):** Collecting; Clubs and Societies
**Circ:** (Controlled)850

**The Coleopterists Bulletin  (12063)**
Coleopterists Society
Louisiana State University
Department of Entomology
Baton Rouge, LA 70803-1710
Phone: (225)578-1634
Fax: (225)578-1643
**Subject(s):** Entomology; Zoology
**Circ:** ‡850

**Flashback  (1073)**
Washington County Historical Society Inc.
118 E Dickson St.
Fayetteville, AR 72701-5612
Phone: (479)521-2970
**Subject(s):** History and Genealogy
**Circ:** (Paid)850

**Archives of Environmental Contamination and Toxicology  (1255)**
Springer-Verlag New York Inc.
c/o Daniel R. Doerge
National Center for Toxicological Research
7719 12th St.
Paron, AR 72122
Phone: (501)821-1147
Fax: (501)821-1146
**Subject(s):** Toxicology; Ecology and Conservation
**Circ:** (Combined)800

**Drug Metabolism Reviews  (1175)**
Marcel Dekker Inc.
c/o Jack A. Hinson, Director of Div. of Toxicology-Slot 638
University of Arkansas for Medical Services
4301 W. Markham St.
Little Rock, AR 72205
Phone: (501)686-7036
Fax: (501)686-8970
**Subject(s):** Medicine and Surgery; Drugs and Pharmaceuticals; Toxicology
**Circ:** 800

**Foreign Policy in Focus  (20179)**
Interhemispheric Resource Center
PO Box 2178
Silver City, NM 88062
Phone: (505)388-0208
Fax: (505)388-0619
**Subject(s):** Political Science
**Circ:** (Non-paid)250
(Paid)800

**Loyola Law Review  (12307)**
Loyola University New Orleans School of Law
7214 St. Charles Ave.
Campus Box 901
ATTN: Business Manager-Law Journals
New Orleans, LA 70118
Phone: (504)861-5558
Fax: (504)861-5559
**Subject(s):** Law
**Circ:** (Paid)800

**Neuroepidemiology  (30372)**
S. Karger Publishers Inc.
c/o Gustavo C. Roman, M.D.
The University of Texas Health Science Center
7703 Floyd Curl Dr.
San Antonio, TX 78229
**Subject(s):** Medicine and Surgery
**Circ:** 800

**The Review of Litigation  (29198)**
The University of Texas School of Law Publications Inc.
727 E. Dean Keeton St.
Austin, TX 78705
Phone: (512)471-4386
**Subject(s):** Law
**Circ:** 800

**American Journal of Contact Dermatitis  (29501)**
Elsevier
C/o Ponciano D. Cruz, Jr., Editor
The Univ. of Texas Southwestern Medical Center
Dept. of Dermatology
5323 Harry Hines Blvd.
Dallas, TX 75390-9069
**Subject(s):** Medicine and Surgery
**Circ:** ‡765

**Arthuriana  (29504)**
International Arthurian Society-North American Branch
Southern Methodist University
Dallas, TX 75275-0432
Phone: (214)768-2959
Fax: (214)768-1234
**Subject(s):** History and Genealogy; Literature
**Circ:** (Paid)‡750

**Journal of Applied Nutrition  (29055)**
International and American Association of Clinical Nutritionists
15280 Addison Rd., Ste. 100, Ste. 130
Addison, TX 75001
Phone: (972)407-9089
Fax: (972)250-0233
**Subject(s):** Health and Healthcare
**Circ:** 750

**Libraries & Culture  (29183)**
University of Texas Press
PO Box 7819
Austin, TX 78713-7819
Phone: (512)471-7233
Fax: (512)232-7178
**Subject(s):** Library and Information Science; History and Genealogy
**Circ:** ‡750

**Texas Press Messenger  (29237)**
Texas Press Association
718 W 5th St., Ste. 100
Austin, TX 78701-2799
Phone: (512)477-6755
Fax: (512)477-6759
**Subject(s):** Journalism and Publishing; Printing and Typography
**Circ:** ‡730

**Conceptions Helpless  (19992)**
University of New Mexico
Marron Hall, Rm. 131
University of New Mexico
Albuquerque, NM 87131
Phone: (505)277-5656
Fax: (505)277-7531
**Subject(s):** Literature; Art and Art History; Architecture
**Circ:** (Controlled)700

**International Journal of Developmental Neuroscience  (29753)**
Aspen Publishing Inc
c/o J.R. Perez-Polo
Gail Borden Bldg.
301 University Blvd.
University of Texas Medical Branch
Galveston, TX 77555-0652
Fax: (409)772-8028
**Subject(s):** Chemistry, Chemicals, and Chemical Engineering; Genetics; Biology
**Circ:** (Non-paid)300
(Paid)700

**Investigative Radiology  (30531)**
Lippincott Williams & Wilkins
C/o Val M. Runge, MD, Editor-in-Chief
Texas A&M University
Scott and White Clinic and Hospital
Health Science Center
Temple, TX
**Subject(s):** Radiology, Ultrasound, and Nuclear Medicine
**Circ:** (Paid)‡709

**The Journal of Personal Selling and Sales Management  (29623)**
Pi Sigma Epsilon
Marketing Department
University of North Texas
PO Box 311396
Denton, TX 76203-3677
Phone: (940)565-3125
Fax: (940)565-3837
**Subject(s):** Selling and Salesmanship; Management and Administration
**Circ:** (Paid)‡700

**New Mexico Law Review  (20007)**
School of Law
MSC11 6070
University of New Mexico
Albuquerque, NM 87131
Phone: (505)277-4910
Fax: (505)277-8342
**Subject(s):** Law
**Circ:** (Combined)700

**Rehabilitation Education  (1076)**
University of Arkansas
West Ave. Annex
Fayetteville, AR 72701
Phone: (501)575-3658
Fax: (501)575-3253
**Subject(s):** Education
**Circ:** (Non-paid)‡50
(Paid)‡700

**The Trumpeter  (29745)**
Croatian Philatelic Society
PO Box 696
Fritch, TX 79036-0696
Phone: (806)857-0129
**Subject(s):** Collecting; Croatian; Serbian; German
**Circ:** (Paid)‡600
(Controlled)‡700

**Youth & Society** (20017)
Sage Publications Inc.
University of New Mexico
Department of Language, Literacy and Sociocultural Studies
MSC 05 3040
Albuquerque, NM 87131-0001
**Subject(s):** Sociology
**Circ:** (Paid)‡700

**Heat Transfer Engineering: An International Quarterly** (25564)
Taylor & Francis
c/o Afshin J. Ghajar
School of Mechanical and Aerospace Engineering
Oklahoma State University
Stillwater, OK 74078-5016
**Subject(s):** Chemistry, Chemicals, and Chemical Engineering; Engineering (Various branches)
**Circ:** ‡688

**Folk Dance Problem Solver** (29156)
Society of Folk Dance Historians
2100 Rio Grande St.
Austin, TX 78705-5578
Phone: (512)478-9676
**Subject(s):** Performing Arts; History and Genealogy
**Circ:** (Combined)650

**Food Additives and Contaminants** (29424)
Taylor & Francis
C/O T. Phillips, Texas A&M University
College of Veterinary Medicine
Department VAPH
College Station, TX 77843-4458
**Subject(s):** Science; Food Production; Safety
**Circ:** 650

**Journal of American Organbuilding** (29870)
American Institute of Organbuilders
Box 130982
Houston, TX 77219-0982
Phone: (713)529-2212
**Subject(s):** Music and Musical Instruments
**Circ:** (Paid)650

**Journal of Family Social Work** (1178)
The Haworth Press Inc.
c/o Howard Moose Turney, School of Social Work
Univ. of Arkansas at Little Rock
2801 S. University
Little Rock, AR 72204
Phone: (501)569-8454
**Subject(s):** Social Programs; Marriage and Family
**Circ:** 654

**New Mexico Geology** (20185)
New Mexico Bureau of Geology and Mineral Resources
801 Leroy Place
Socorro, NM 87801-4796
Phone: (505)835-5410
Fax: (505)835-6333
**Subject(s):** Science (General); Geology
**Circ:** (Combined)650

**The Sabbath Sentinel** (25335)
The Bible Sabbath Association
HC 60, Box 8
Fairview, OK 73737-9504
Phone: (580)227-3200
Fax: (580)227-4495
**Subject(s):** Religious Publications
**Circ:** (Non-paid)‡200
 (Paid)‡650

**The International Trade Journal** (30043)
Taylor & Francis
c/o Antonio J. Rodriguez, Texas A&M International University
5201 University Blvd.
Pellegrino Hall, No. 303
Laredo, TX 78045
**Subject(s):** International Business and Economics
**Circ:** (Paid)‡649

**American Indian Law Review** (25424)
University of Oklahoma College of Law
300 Timberdell Rd.
Norman, OK 73019
Phone: (405)325-2840
Fax: (405)325-6282
**Subject(s):** Law; Ethnic and Minority Studies
**Circ:** (Combined)630

**The American Journal of Criminal Law** (29127)
The University of Texas School of Law Publications Inc.
727 E Dean Keeton St.
PO Box 8670
Austin, TX 78705
Phone: (512)232-1395
Fax: (512)475-6741
**Subject(s):** Law
**Circ:** (Combined)600

**Commercial Recorder** (29712)
PO Box 11038
3032 South Jones Street
Fort Worth, TX 76104-1038
Phone: (817)926-5351
Fax: (817)926-5377
**Subject(s):** Daily Periodicals; Commerce and Industry; Real Estate
**Circ:** ‡600

**Deviant Behavior: An Interdisciplinary Journal** (12189)
Taylor & Francis
Department of Sociology & Anthropology
University of Lafayette Louisiana
PO Box 40198
Lafayette, LA 70504-0198
Phone: (337)482-5694
Fax: (337)482-5694
**Subject(s):** Psychology and Psychiatry; Sociology
**Circ:** 600

**Journal of Aging and Health** (29754)
Sage Publications Inc.
C/O Kyriakos S. Markides, Ph.D., Editor
Center on Ageing, University of Texas Medical Branch
Campus Mail Route 1153
Galveston, TX 77555-1153
**Subject(s):** Gerontology; Health and Healthcare
**Circ:** (Paid)‡600

**Journal of Library Administration** (25426)
The Haworth Press Inc.
Univ. of Oklahoma
Univ. Libraries
401 W. Brooks
Norman, OK 73069
Phone: (405)325-2611
Fax: (405)325-7550
**Subject(s):** Library and Information Science
**Circ:** 600

**Latin American Music Review** (29180)
University of Texas Press
c/o Gerard H. Behague, Editor
University of Texas
School of Music
MRH 3.204
Austin, TX 78712-1208
Phone: (512)471-0373
Fax: (512)471-2333
**Subject(s):** Music and Musical Instruments; Hispanic Publications
**Circ:** (Paid)600

**LOMA Line** (12076)
Louisiana Oil Marketers Association
PO Box 80357
Baton Rouge, LA 70898
Phone: (225)926-8300
Fax: (225)926-7722
**Subject(s):** Petroleum, Oil, and Gas
**Circ:** (Non-paid)600

**Management Communication Quarterly** (29431)
Sage Publications Inc.
Department of Communications
Texas A&M University
Mail Stop 4234
College Station, TX 77843-4234
**Subject(s):** Management and Administration; Communications
**Circ:** (Paid)‡600

**Texas International Law Journal** (29222)
The University of Texas School of Law Publications Inc.
727 E Dean Keeton St.
PO Box 8670
Austin, TX 78705
Phone: (512)232-1395
Fax: (512)475-6741
**Subject(s):** Law; International Affairs
**Circ:** (Paid)600

**Visual Neuroscience** (29921)
Cambridge University Press
C/O Dr Laura J. Frishman, College of Optometry
505 J. Davis Armistead Bldg., Rm. 2195
4901 Calhoun Rd.
Houston, TX 77204-2020
**Subject(s):** Physiology and Anatomy; Laboratory Research (Scientific and Medical)
**Circ:** 600

**Anesthesia File** (30352)
Dannemiller Memorial Educational Foundation
5711 Northwest Parkway, Ste 100
San Antonio, TX 78249
Phone: (210)641-8311
Fax: (210)641-8329
**Subject(s):** Medicine and Surgery; Health and Healthcare
**Circ:** 550

**Military History of the West** (29625)
University of North Texas
Box 310650
Denton, TX 76203-0650
Phone: (940)565-2288
Fax: (940)369-8838
**Subject(s):** History and Genealogy; Military and Navy
**Circ:** (Combined)550

**East Texas Historical Journal** (30201)
East Texas Historical Association
Box 6223, SFA Sta.
Nacogdoches, TX 75962
Phone: (936)468-2407
Fax: (936)468-2190
**Subject(s):** History and Genealogy
**Circ:** (Paid)535

**Memoirs of the American Mathematical Society** (29184)
American Mathematical Society
c/o William Beckner, Editor
Dept. of Mathematics
Univ. of Texas
Austin, TX 78712-1082
**Subject(s):** Mathematics
**Circ:** (Paid)522

**Journal of Technology in Human Services** (29108)
The Haworth Press Inc.
c/o Dick Schoech, Journal Ed.
Univ. of Texas at Arlington
Box 19129
Arlington, TX 76019-0129
Phone: (817)272-3964
**Subject(s):** Computers; Psychology and Psychiatry
**Circ:** (Controlled)‡513

**AnalgesiaFile** (30351)
Dannemiller Memorial Educational Foundation
5711 Northwest Parkway, Ste 100
San Antonio, TX 78249
Phone: (210)641-8311
Fax: (210)641-8329
**Subject(s):** Medicine and Surgery; Health and Healthcare
**Circ:** 500

**Asian Music** (29129)
Society for Asian Music
School of Music
University of Texas at Austin
1 University Station, E3100
Austin, TX 78712-0435
**Subject(s):** Music and Musical Instruments; Intercultural Interests
**Circ:** 500

**Fell Swoop** (12297)
Acre Press
3003 Ponce De Leon St.
New Orleans, LA 70119
Phone: (504)943-5198
**Subject(s):** Literature and Literary Reviews
**Circ:** ‡500

**Journal of Music Theory Pedagogy** (25427)
University of Oklahoma
c/o Dr. Alice Lanning
University of Oklahoma
Carnegie Bldg. Room 100
Norman, OK 73019
Phone: (405)325-3967
Fax: (405)325-7383
**Subject(s):** Music and Musical Instruments; Education
**Circ:** (Paid)500

# Southern Central States

**North Louisiana History (12382)**
North Louisiana Historical Association
Box 6701
Shreveport, LA 71136
Phone: (318)424-4533
Fax: (318)797-5122
**Subject(s):** History and Genealogy; Local, State, and Regional Publications
**Circ:** (Paid)500

**Nova Express (29191)**
PO Box 27231
Austin, TX 78755-2231
**Subject(s):** Science Fiction, Mystery, Adventure, and Romance
**Circ:** (Combined)500

**Oklahoma Business Bulletin (25433)**
Center for Economic and Management Research
307 W. Brooks, Adams Hall, Rm. 4
Norman, OK 73019
Phone: (405)325-2931
Fax: (405)325-7688
**Subject(s):** Business; Local, State, and Regional Publications
**Circ:** ‡500

**Southwestern Mass Communication Journal (1293)**
Southwest Education Council for Journalism and Mass Communication
Arkansas University
PO Box 1930
State University, AR 72467
Phone: (870)972-3075
Fax: (870)972-3856
**Subject(s):** Communications; Journalism and Publishing
**Circ:** (Paid)500

**Southwestern Entomologist (29437)**
Southwestern Entomological Society
c/o Darrel Bay
Texas A&M University
Entomology Dept.
College Station, TX 77843-2475
Phone: (409)845-9731
Fax: (409)845-6305
**Subject(s):** Entomology
**Circ:** (Paid)491

**Houston Journal of Mathematics (29857)**
University of Houston
c/o Robert M. Hardt
Department of Mathematics
Rice University
Houston, TX 77251-1892
**Subject(s):** Mathematics
**Circ:** ‡460

**Cimarron Review (25562)**
Oklahoma State University
205 Morrill Hall
Stillwater, OK 74078-4069
Phone: (405)744-9476
Fax: (405)744-6326
**Subject(s):** Literature; Literature and Literary Reviews
**Circ:** (Non-paid)‡150
(Paid)‡450

**Gulf of Mexico Drilling Report (29844)**
Offshore Data Services Inc.
3200 Wilcrest Dr., Ste. 170
Houston, TX 77042-3366
Phone: (832)463-3000
Fax: (832)463-3100
**Subject(s):** Petroleum, Oil, and Gas
**Circ:** (Paid)450

**Services Marketing Quarterly (12262)**
The Haworth Press Inc.
c/o Robert E. Stevents, Co-Editor
Univ. of Louisiana at Monroe
700 University Ave.
Monroe, LA 71209-0140
Phone: (318)342-1186
**Subject(s):** Advertising and Marketing
**Circ:** (Controlled)‡453

**Texas Journal of Women and the Law (29224)**
The University of Texas School of Law Publications Inc.
727 E Dean Keeton St.
PO Box 8670
Austin, TX 78705
Phone: (512)232-1395
Fax: (512)475-6741
**Subject(s):** Women's Interests; Law
**Circ:** (Combined)450

**Community/Junior College Journal of Research and Practice (29616)**
Taylor & Francis
c/o D. Barry Lumsden, Center for Higher Education
University of North Texas
PO Box 311337
Denton, TX 76203
Phone: (817)565-4415
Fax: (817)565-4415
**Subject(s):** Education
**Circ:** (Non-paid)‡63
(Paid)‡440

**Bulletin of the Oklahoma Ornithological Society (25592)**
Dept. of Biological Sciences
University of Tulsa
Tulsa, OK 74104-3189
Phone: (918)631-3943
Fax: (918)631-2762
**Subject(s):** Ornithology and Oology; Natural History and Nature Study
**Circ:** (Non-paid)‡10
(Paid)‡425

**Clinical and Experimental Hypertension (29832)**
Marcel Dekker Inc.
c/o M. F. Lokhandwala ,Heart and Kidney Institute
453 Science and Research 2
College of Pharmacy
University of Houston
Houston, TX 77204-5041
**Subject(s):** Medicine and Surgery
**Circ:** 425

**Applied Spectroscopy Reviews (12207)**
Marcel Dekker Inc.
c/o Joseph Sneddon , Department of Chemistry
McNeese State University
Lake Charles, LA 70609
**Subject(s):** Chemistry, Chemicals, and Chemical Engineering; Science (General)
**Circ:** (Paid)400

**Colonial Latin America Historical Review (19991)**
Zimmerman Library, Spanish Colonial Research Center
MSC05 3020
1 University of New Mexico
Albuquerque, NM 87131-0001
Phone: (505)277-1370
Fax: (505)277-4603
**Subject(s):** History and Genealogy; Intercultural Interests
**Circ:** (Combined)400

**Global Business and Finance Review (12417)**
413 Holiday Dr., Ste. 101G
Thibodaux, LA 70301
Phone: (985)448-4189
**Subject(s):** International Business and Economics
**Circ:** (Non-paid)150
(Paid)400

**Human Rights Review (12299)**
Transaction Publishers
Dept. of Philosophy
Loyola Univ. of New Orleans
Box 138
6363 St. Charles Ave.
New Orleans, LA 70118
Phone: (504)865-3056
**Subject(s):** Civil Rights
**Circ:** (Paid)‡400

**Journal of American Association of Psychiatric Administrators (29544)**
American Association of Psychiatric Administrators
c/o Frances Roton, Exec. Dir.
PO Box 570218
Dallas, TX 75357-0218
Phone: (972)613-0985
Fax: (972)613-5532
**Subject(s):** Management and Administration; Health and Healthcare; Psychology and Psychiatry; Hospitals and Healthcare Institutions
**Circ:** 400

**Journal of Disability Policy Studies (29169)**
PRO-ED Inc.
8700 Shoal Creek Blvd.
Austin, TX 78757-6897
Phone: (512)451-3246
Fax: (800)397-7633
**Subject(s):** Handicapped
**Circ:** (Paid)400

**Texas Forum on Civil Liberties and Civil Rights (29217)**
The University of Texas School of Law Publications Inc.
727 E Dean Keeton St.
PO Box 8670
Austin, TX 78705
Phone: (512)232-1395
Fax: (512)475-6741
**Subject(s):** Civil Rights; Law
**Circ:** (Combined)400

**Tree Tracers (25387)**
Southwest Oklahoma Genealogical Society
Box 148
Lawton, OK 73502-1048
Phone: (580)581-3450
Fax: (580)248-0243
**Subject(s):** History and Genealogy; Local, State, and Regional Publications
**Circ:** (Combined)400

**White County Heritage (1282)**
White County Historical Society
501 Live Oak Dr.
Searcy, AR 72143
**Subject(s):** History and Genealogy
**Circ:** 400

**Journal of Marketing Channels (29622)**
The Haworth Press Inc.
c/o Lou E. Pelton, College of Business Admin.
Univ. of North Texas
PO Box 311396
Denton, TX 76203-1396
Phone: (940)565-3124
Fax: (940)565-3837
**Subject(s):** Advertising and Marketing
**Circ:** 393

**Louisiana English Journal (12285)**
Northwestern State University
Kyser Hall 316M
Natchitoches, LA 71497
Phone: (318)357-6272
Fax: (318)357-5942
**Subject(s):** Literature
**Circ:** (Paid)‡399

**Utopian Studies (29114)**
Society for Utopian Studies
c/o Ken Roemer
University of Texas at Arlington
English Dept. - Box 19035
Arlington, TX 76013-1908
Phone: (817)272-2729
**Subject(s):** Philosophy; Theology
**Circ:** (Paid)375

**Journal of Police and Criminal Psychology (30415)**
Society of Police and Criminal Psychology
Hines Academy Ctr., Rm. 120
SW Texas State University
San Marcos, TX 78666
Phone: (512)245-2174
Fax: (512)245-8063
**Subject(s):** Police, Penology, and Penal Institutions; Law; Social Sciences
**Circ:** (Controlled)350

**Academic Athletic Journal (29416)**
National Association of Academic Advisors for Athletics
P.O. Box A-7
College Station, TX 77844
Phone: (979)862-4310
Fax: (979)862-2461
**Subject(s):** Physical Education and Athletics; Education
**Circ:** 300

**Journal of Promotion Management (12071)**
The Haworth Press Inc.
c/o Richard Alan Nelson
Manship School of Mass Communication
221 Journalism Bldg.
Louisiana State Univ.
Baton Rouge, LA 70803-7202
Phone: (225)578-6686
Fax: (225)578-2125
**Subject(s):** Advertising and Marketing; Selling and Salesmanship; Management and Administration
**Circ:** 305

**Texas Hispanic Journal of Law and Policy (29219)**
The University of Texas School of Law Publications Inc.
727 E Dean Keeton St.
PO Box 8670
Austin, TX 78705
Phone: (512)232-1395
Fax: (512)475-6741
**Subject(s):** Hispanic Publications; Law
**Circ:** (Combined)300

**Texas Tribune (30547)**
PO Box 446
Tyler, TX 75710-0446
Phone: (903)597-1124
Fax: (903)593-3146
**Subject(s):** Politics
**Circ:** (Paid)‡300

**Thema (12248)**
Box 8747
Metairie, LA 70011-8747
Phone: (504)887-1263
**Subject(s):** Literature and Literary Reviews
**Circ:** (Non-paid)100
(Paid)300

**Whole Notes (20108)**
Whole Notes Press
PO Box 1374
Las Cruces, NM 88004
Phone: (505)541-5744
**Subject(s):** Poetry; Literature
**Circ:** (Controlled)300

**Xavier Review (12328)**
Xavier University of Louisiana
Box 110C
New Orleans, LA 70125-1098
Phone: (504)520-7549
Fax: (504)520-7917
**Subject(s):** Literature
**Circ:** (Combined)300

**Gulf of Mexico Field Development Report (29845)**
Offshore Data Services Inc.
3200 Wilcrest Dr., Ste. 170
Houston, TX 77042-3366
Phone: (832)463-3000
Fax: (832)463-3100
**Subject(s):** Petroleum, Oil, and Gas
**Circ:** (Paid)275

**Nerve Cowboy (29186)**
Liquid Paper Press
PO Box 4973
Austin, TX 78765
**Subject(s):** Literature; Poetry
**Circ:** (Combined)275

**Backtracker (1270)**
Northwest Arkansas Genealogical Society
Box 796
Rogers, AR 72757-0796
Phone: (479)273-3890
**Subject(s):** History and Genealogy; Local, State, and Regional Publications
**Circ:** (Combined)240

**Lucidity (29880)**
Bearhouse Publishing
14781 Memorial Dr., Ste. 10
Houston, TX 77079
Phone: (281)920-1795
**Subject(s):** Literature and Literary Reviews
**Circ:** (Non-paid)‡75
(Paid)‡230

**Small Fruits Review (12090)**
The Haworth Press Inc.
Dept. of Horticulture
Louisiana State University
137 Julian Miller Hall
Baton Rouge, LA 70803-2120
Phone: (225)578-2158
**Subject(s):** Scientific Agricultural Publications
**Circ:** 225

**Arkansas Register (1166)**
Office of the Secretary of State
Rm. 256, State Capitol
Little Rock, AR 72201
Phone: (501)682-1010
Fax: (501)682-3548

**Subject(s):** Politics
**Circ:** (Combined)206

**Both Sides Now (30544)**
Free People Press
10547 State Hwy. 110 N
Tyler, TX 75704-3731
Phone: (903)592-4263
**Subject(s):** Alternative and Underground; Environmental and Natural Resources Conservation; New Age; Politics
**Circ:** ‡200

**Libertas Mathematica (29109)**
University of Texas
Dept. of Mathematics
Box 19408
Arlington, TX 76019
Phone: (817)261-1179
Fax: (817)272-5802
**Subject(s):** Mathematics
**Circ:** 200

**McNeese Review (12211)**
McNeese State University
4205 Ryan St.
PO Box 93465
Lake Charles, LA 70609
Phone: (337)475-5000
Fax: (337)475-5637
**Subject(s):** Literature; Humanities
**Circ:** (Combined)200

**Pottery Southwest (20166)**
Albuquerque Archaeological Society
c/o Eric Blinman
6 Frasco Rd.
Santa Fe, NM 87508-8842
**Subject(s):** Archaeology; Ceramics
**Circ:** (Paid)170

**Q.J.I. (12384)**
Louisiana State University, Shreveport
1 University Pl.
Shreveport, LA 71115-2399
Phone: (318)797-5235
Fax: (318)795-4263
**Subject(s):** Philosophy
**Circ:** (Paid)100

## Southern States

**The Upper Room Daily Devotional Guide/ (28894)**
The Upper Room
1908 Grand Ave.
PO Box 340004
Nashville, TN 37203-0004
Phone: (615)340-7200
Fax: (615)340-7552
**Subject(s):** Religious Publications
**Circ:** 2,750,000

**Southern Living (105)**
Southern Progress
2100 Lakeshore Dr.
Birmingham, AL 35209
Phone: (205)445-6000
Fax: (205)445-6469
**Subject(s):** Home and Garden; Lifestyle
**Circ:** (Paid)2,537,485

**AAA Going Places (6622)**
AAA Auto Club South
1515 N Westshore Blvd.
Tampa, FL 33607
Phone: (813)289-5000
Fax: (813)288-7935
**Subject(s):** Travel and Tourism
**Circ:** (Paid)2,104,400

**COOKING LIGHT (70)**
Southern Progress
2100 Lakeshore Dr.
Birmingham, AL 35209
Phone: (205)445-6000
Fax: (205)445-6600
**Subject(s):** Health and Fitness
**Circ:** (Paid)1,615,023

**Outdoor Life (6647)**
Time4 Media Inc.
Customer Service
PO Box 60001
Tampa, FL 33660-0001
**Subject(s):** (Outdoors)
**Circ:** (Paid)1,369,094

**Health (80)**
Time Health Media Inc.
2100 Lakeshohre Dr.
Birmingham, AL 35209
Phone: (205)445-7005
Fax: (205)445-5123
**Subject(s):** Health
**Circ:** (Paid)1,339,754

**Decision (23340)**
The Billy Graham Evangelistic Association
PO Box 668886
Charlotte, NC 28266-8886
Phone: (704)401-2432
**Subject(s):** Religious Publications
**Circ:** (Paid)350,000
(Non-paid)1,300,000

**Strand Magazine (28180)**
Strand Media Group Inc.
1357-21st Ave. N, Ste. 102
Myrtle Beach, SC 29577
Phone: (843)626-8911
Fax: (843)626-6452
**Subject(s):** Free Newspapers; Travel and Tourism
**Circ:** (Non-paid)‡1,300,000

**WHERE Atlanta (6930)**
Miller Publishing Group L.L.C.
180 Allen Rd.
302 North Bldg.
Atlanta, GA 30328
Phone: (404)843-9800
Fax: (404)843-9070
**Subject(s):** Travel and Tourism; Local, State, and Regional Publications
**Circ:** (Paid)‡300
(Non-paid)1,071,070

**The Flyer (6234)**
Community Newspaper Co.
11900 SW 128th St.
Miami, FL 33186
Phone: (305)232-4115
Fax: (305)251-5141
**Subject(s):** Advertising and Marketing; Spanish; Hispanic Publications
**Circ:** (Non-paid)‡1,018,449

**Vista Magazine (5896)**
Hispanic Publishing Corp.
999 Ponce de Leon, Ste. 600
Coral Gables, FL 33134
Phone: (305)442-2462
Fax: (305)774-3578
**Subject(s):** Hispanic Publications; General Editorial
**Circ:** (Non-paid)960,716

**GO Magazine (23342)**
AAA Carolinas
6600 AAA Dr.
Charlotte, NC 28212
Phone: (704)569-3600
Fax: (843)856-7468
**Subject(s):** Travel and Tourism; Automotive (Trade)
**Circ:** ‡835,000

**Hot Rod Magazine (6168)**
PRIMEDIA Los Angeles
Hot Rod
3816 Industry Blvd.
Lakeland, FL 33811
**Subject(s):** Automotive (Consumer)
**Circ:** (Paid)805,035

**Globe (5819)**
American Media
5401 NW Broken Sound Blvd.
Boca Raton, FL 33487-3587
Phone: (561)994-7210
Fax: (561)241-5689
**Circ:** (Paid)740,425

**Ducks Unlimited (28767)**
1 Waterfowl Way
Memphis, TN 38120
Phone: (901)758-3825

## Southern States

Fax: (901)758-3850
**Subject(s):** (Hunting, Fishing, and Game Management); Environmental and Natural Resources Conservation
**Circ:** (Paid)661,171

**Bassmaster Magazine (346)**
BASS/ESPN
5845 Carmichael Rd.
Montgomery, AL 36117-2329
Phone: (334)272-9530
Fax: (334)279-7148
**Subject(s):** (Hunting, Fishing, and Game Management); (Boating and Yachting)
**Circ:** (Paid)600,000

**SEE Florida Keys (6538)**
Miles Media Group Inc.
6751 Professional Pkwy. W
Sarasota, FL 34240-8443
Phone: (941)342-2300
Fax: (941)907-0300
**Subject(s):** Travel and Tourism
**Circ:** (Non-paid)△600,000

**SEE Emerald Coast (6537)**
Miles Media Group Inc.
6751 Professional Pkwy. W
Sarasota, FL 34240-8443
Phone: (941)342-2300
Fax: (941)907-0300
**Subject(s):** Travel and Tourism
**Circ:** △545,000

**Carolina Country (23693)**
North Carolina Association of Electric Corp.
3400 Sumner Blvd. 27616
PO Box 27306
Raleigh, NC 27616
Phone: (919)872-0800
Fax: (919)878-3970
**Subject(s):** Local, State, and Regional Publications
**Circ:** (Paid)530,000

**Living in South Carolina (27995)**
The Electric Cooperatives of South Carolina
808 Knox Abbott Dr.
Cayce, SC 29033-3311
Phone: (803)796-6060
Fax: (803)796-6064
**Subject(s):** Rural Electrification; Travel and Tourism; Local, State, and Regional Publications
**Circ:** ‡503,000

**Home Life (28856)**
LifeWay Christian Resources
One Lifeway Plz.
Nashville, TN 37234
Phone: (615)251-2000
Fax: (615)277-8272
**Subject(s):** Religious Publications
**Circ:** (Controlled)‡500
    (Paid)‡500,000

**SEE Sarasota, Bradenton, Venice & Gulf Coast Islands Magazine (6539)**
Miles Media Group Inc.
6751 Professional Pkwy. W
Sarasota, FL 34240-8443
Phone: (941)342-2300
Fax: (941)907-0300
**Subject(s):** Travel and Tourism
**Circ:** (Non-paid)500,000

**SKY Magazine—(Delta Air Lines) (23530)**
Pace Communications Inc.
1301 Carolina St.
Greensboro, NC 27401
Phone: (336)378-6065
Fax: (336)273-2864
**Subject(s):** In-Flight Publications; Travel and Tourism
**Circ:** (Controlled)△489,315

**Tennessee Magazine (28888)**
Tennessee Electric Cooperative Association
710 Spence Ln.
PO Box 100912
Nashville, TN 37224
Phone: (615)367-9284
Fax: (615)367-2495
**Subject(s):** Rural Electrification; Local, State, and Regional Publications
**Circ:** (Paid)487,750

**Kentucky Living (11826)**
Kentucky Association of Electric Cooperatives
PO Box 32170
4515 Bishop Lane
Louisville, KY 40218
Phone: (502)451-2430
Fax: (502)459-1611
**Subject(s):** Local, State, and Regional Publications
**Circ:** (Paid)479,791

**Country Weekly (5818)**
1000 American Media Way
Boca Raton, FL 33464-1000
**Subject(s):** Music and Musical Instruments
**Circ:** (Paid)455,086

**GEORGIA Magazine (7471)**
Georgia Electric Membership Corp.
PO Box 1707
Tucker, GA 30085
Phone: (770)270-6950
Fax: (770)270-6995
**Subject(s):** Rural Electrification; Local, State, and Regional Publications
**Circ:** ‡448,000

**Garden Design (6747)**
World Publications Inc.
460 N. Orlando Ave., Ste. 200
Winter Park, FL 32789
Phone: (407)628-4802
Fax: (407)628-7061
**Subject(s):** Landscape Architecture
**Circ:** (Paid)445,805

**Attacheair Magazine (23508)**
Pace Communications Inc.
1301 Carolina St.
Greensboro, NC 27401
Phone: (336)378-6065
Fax: (336)273-2864
**Subject(s):** In-Flight Publications; Travel and Tourism
**Circ:** (Non-paid)‡441,911

**Coastal Living (69)**
Southern Progress
2100 Lakeshore Dr.
Birmingham, AL 35209
Phone: (205)445-6007
Fax: (205)445-8655
**Subject(s):** Lifestyle; Local, State, and Regional Publications
**Circ:** (Paid)435,473

**Veranda (6927)**
Hearst Magazines
455 E. Paces Ferry Rd., Ste. 216
Atlanta, GA 30305
Phone: (404)261-3603
**Subject(s):** Home and Garden
**Circ:** (Paid)419,630

**Southern Accents (103)**
Southern Progress
2100 Lakeshore Dr.
Birmingham, AL 35209
Phone: (205)445-6000
Fax: (205)445-6990
**Subject(s):** Home and Garden
**Circ:** (Paid)400,000

**All Around Kentucky (11803)**
Kentucky Farm Bureau Federation
9201 Bunsen Pkwy.
PO Box 20700
Louisville, KY 40250-0700
Phone: (502)495-5000
Fax: (502)495-5114
**Subject(s):** Farm Bureau, Grange, and Cooperative Associations
**Circ:** (Controlled)‡935
    (Paid)‡387,925

**TODAY in Mississippi (17006)**
Electric Power Association of Mississippi Inc.
PO Box 3300
Ridgeland, MS 39158
Phone: (601)605-8600
Fax: (601)605-8601
**Subject(s):** Rural Electrification; Local, State, and Regional Publications
**Circ:** (Non-paid)‡176
    (Paid)‡386,691

**Alabama Living (343)**
Alabama Rural Electric Association of Cooperatives
340 Technacenter Dr.
Montgomery, AL 36124
Phone: (334)215-2732
Fax: (334)215-2733
**Subject(s):** Rural Electrification
**Circ:** (Paid)360,936

**Progressive Farmer (95)**
Southern Progress
2100 Lakeshore Dr.
Birmingham, AL 35209
**Subject(s):** General Agriculture
**Circ:** (Paid)244,000
    (Non-paid)358,000

**Beta Journal (28228)**
National Beta Club
151 Beta Club Way
Spartanburg, SC 29306-3012
Phone: (864)583-4553
Fax: (864)542-9300
**Subject(s):** Clubs and Societies; Unclassified Fraternal
**Circ:** 350,000

**Buckmasters Whitetail Magazine (347)**
Buckmasters
10350 Hwy. 80 E.
Montgomery, AL 36117
Phone: (334)215-3337
Fax: (334)215-3535
**Subject(s):** (Hunting, Fishing, and Game Management)
**Circ:** (Paid)350,000

**Mature Living (28864)**
Lifeway Christian Resources of the Southern Baptist Convention
One Lifeway Plz.
Nashville, TN 37234-0175
Phone: (615)251-2000
Fax: (615)251-2614
**Subject(s):** Senior Citizens' Interests; Religious Publications
**Circ:** ‡330,000

**Kentucky Travel Guide (11828)**
Editorial Services Co.
812 S 3rd St.
Louisville, KY 40203
Phone: (502)584-2720
Fax: (502)584-2722
**Subject(s):** Travel and Tourism
**Circ:** (Non-paid)300,000

**Links Magazine (28144)**
10 Pope Ave. Executive Park, Ste. 202
Hilton Head Island, SC 29928
Phone: (843)842-6200
Fax: (843)842-6233
**Subject(s):** (Golf); Local, State, and Regional Publications
**Circ:** (Paid)20,791
    (Non-paid)283,806

**Friends & Family (352)**
ALFA/Alabama Farmers Federation
PO Box 11000
Montgomery, AL 36191-0001
Phone: (334)288-3900
Fax: (334)284-3957
**Subject(s):** Health; Farm Bureau, Grange, and Cooperative Associations; General Agriculture
**Circ:** ‡280,000

**Naples Guide (6315)**
847 4th Ave. S
Naples, FL 34102
Phone: (239)262-6524
Fax: (239)262-3468
**Subject(s):** Real Estate; Entertainment; Travel and Tourism; Art
**Circ:** (Controlled)‡270,000

**Fitness Plus Magazine (28986)**
Focus Publishing Ltd.
345 Huskey Dr.
Seymour, TN 37865-4513
**Subject(s):** Health
**Circ:** (Non-paid)250,000

**Road King (28878)**
Parthenon Publishing
28 White Bridge Rd., Ste. 209
Nashville, TN 37205
**Subject(s):** Trucks and Trucking
**Circ:** (Non-paid)250,000

**MicroTimes (7336)**
HPC Inc.
3119 Campus Dr.
Norcross, GA 30071-1402
**Subject(s):** Computers
**Circ:** (Free)230,036

**The Digest (23230)**
The Blue Ridge Digest Publishing Company Inc.
PO Box 1758
Asheville, NC 28802-1758
Phone: (828)667-1607
Fax: (828)667-1607
**Subject(s):** Local, State, and Regional Publications; Travel and Tourism
**Circ:** (Controlled)‡225,000

**Charisma (6152)**
Strang Communications
600 Rineheart Rd.
Lake Mary, FL 32746
Phone: (407)333-0600
Fax: (407)333-7100
**Subject(s):** Religious Publications
**Circ:** (Non-paid)2,000
(Paid)220,000

**Florida Monthly Magazine (5790)**
Florida Media Inc.
801 Douglas Ave., Ste. 100
Altamonte Springs, FL 32714
Phone: (407)816-9596
Fax: (407)801-9373
**Subject(s):** Local, State, and Regional Publications; Lifestyle
**Circ:** (Non-paid)‡5,284
(Paid)‡207,390

**NATSO Truckers News (467)**
Randall Publishing Co.
3200 Rice Mine Rd. North East
Tuscaloosa, AL 35406
Phone: (205)349-2990
Fax: (205)349-4174
**Subject(s):** Trucks and Trucking
**Circ:** (Non-paid)‡206,000

**Trucker's Connection (7342)**
Trucker's Connection Inc.
5960 Crooked Creek Rd., Ste. 15
Norcross, GA 30092
Phone: (770)416-0927
Fax: (770)416-1734
**Subject(s):** Trucks and Trucking
**Circ:** △201,000

**Southern Living Vacations (106)**
Southern Progress
2100 Lakeshore Dr.
Birmingham, AL 35209
Phone: (205)445-6000
Fax: (205)445-6469
**Subject(s):** Travel and Tourism
**Circ:** ‡200,000

**Art & Antiques (6830)**
Billian/Transworld Publishing Inc.
2100 Powers Ferry Rd., Ste. 300
Atlanta, GA 30339
Phone: (770)955-5656
Fax: (770)952-0669
**Subject(s):** Art
**Circ:** (Paid)195,805

**Mississippi Farm Bureau News (16886)**
Mississippi Farm Bureau Federation
6310 Interstate 55 N
PO Box 1972
Jackson, MS 39215-1972
Phone: (601)957-3200
**Subject(s):** Farm Bureau, Grange, and Cooperative Associations; General Agriculture
**Circ:** ‡180,000

**Sport Diver (6752)**
World Publications Inc.
460 N. Orlando Ave., Ste. 200
Winter Park, FL 32789
Phone: (407)628-4802

Fax: (407)628-7061
**Subject(s):** (Water Sports); (General Sports)
**Circ:** (Combined)175,000

**ONSAT (23779)**
Triple D Publishing Inc.
PO Box 167
Shelby, NC 28151
Phone: (704)484-7305
Fax: (704)484-8558
**Subject(s):** Radio, Television, Cable, and Video
**Circ:** (Non-paid)△1,603
(Paid)△158,758

**Sport Fishing (6753)**
World Publications Inc.
460 N. Orlando Ave., Ste. 200
Winter Park, FL 32789
Phone: (407)628-4802
Fax: (407)628-7061
**Subject(s):** (Hunting, Fishing, and Game Management)
**Circ:** (Paid)153,255

**Rodale's SCUBA Diving (7395)**
Rodale Inc.
6600 Abercorn St., Ste. 208
Savannah, GA 31405-5840
Phone: (912)351-0855
Fax: (912)351-0890
**Subject(s):** (Water Sports)
**Circ:** (Non-paid)40,085
(Paid)152,716

**Belize First Magazine (23275)**
Equator Publications
280 Beaverdam Rd.
Candler, NC 28715
Phone: (828)665-4466
Fax: (828)667-1717
**Subject(s):** Travel and Tourism; City, Hotel, Railroad, and Travel Guides
**Circ:** (Paid)5,050
(Non-paid)150,000

**CA (6850)**
Lippincott Williams & Wilkins
c/o American Cancer Society
1599 Clifton Rd., NE
Atlanta, GA 30329
Phone: (404)929-6902
Fax: (404)325-9341
**Subject(s):** Medicine and Surgery
**Circ:** ‡150,000

**Caribbean Travel and Life (6743)**
Caribbean Travel and Life Inc.
460 N Orlando Ave., Ste. 200
Winter Park, FL 32789-2900
Phone: (407)628-4802
Fax: (407)628-7061
**Subject(s):** Travel and Tourism
**Circ:** (Paid)150,000

**Jazziz (5822)**
Jazziz Magazine Inc.
2650 N. Military Trl., Ste. 140
Fountain Sq. II Bldg.
Boca Raton, FL 33431
Phone: (561)893-6868
Fax: (561)893-6867
**Subject(s):** Music and Musical Instruments
**Circ:** (Non-paid)‡65,000
(Paid)‡150,000

**Learning (23522)**
The Education Center Inc.
3515 W Market St., Ste. 200
PO Box 9753
Greensboro, NC 27429-0753
Phone: (877)696-0825
Fax: (336)851-8365
**Subject(s):** Education
**Circ:** (Controlled)150,000

**The Singing News Magazine (23253)**
Singing News Inc.
330 University Hall Dr.
PO Box 2810
Boone, NC 28607-2810
Phone: (828)264-3700
Fax: (828)264-4621
**Subject(s):** Music and Musical Instruments
**Circ:** (Controlled)12,000
(Paid)150,000

**The Florida Catholic (6362)**
498 S. Lake Destiny Rd.
Orlando, FL 32810
Phone: (407)660-9141
Fax: (407)660-2977
**Subject(s):** Religious Publications; Spanish; Hispanic Publications
**Circ:** (Paid)144,250

**Overdrive (468)**
Overdrive Magazine Inc.
3200 Rice Mine Rd., NE
Tuscaloosa, AL 35406
Phone: (205)349-2990
Fax: (205)349-6359
**Subject(s):** Trucks and Trucking
**Circ:** (Paid)6,138
(Controlled)141,969

**Alert Diver (23400)**
Divers Alert Network
Peter B. Bennett Center
6 W Colony Place
Durham, NC 27705
Phone: (919)684-2948
Fax: (919)490-6630
**Subject(s):** (Water Sports)
**Circ:** 140,000

**TV y Novelas (6263)**
Editorial Televisa
6355 NW 36th St.
Miami, FL 33166-7099
Phone: (305)871-6400
Fax: (305)871-4939
**Subject(s):** Spanish; Hispanic Publications; Radio, Television, Cable, and Video
**Circ:** (Paid)136,708

**Art Papers Magazine (6832)**
Art Papers Inc.
PO Box 5748
Atlanta, GA 31107
Phone: (404)588-1837
Fax: (404)588-1836
**Subject(s):** Art and Art History; Photography; Performing Arts
**Circ:** (Paid)135,000

**Elegant Bride (23515)**
Pace Communications Inc.
1301 Carolina St.
Greensboro, NC 27401
Phone: (336)378-6065
Fax: (336)273-2864
**Subject(s):** Brides
**Circ:** (Paid)‡134,177

**Petersen's Circle Track (6172)**
PRIMEDIA Los Angeles
Circle Track
3816 Industry Blvd.
Lakeland, FL 33811
Phone: (863)644-0449
Fax: (863)644-8373
**Subject(s):** (Auto Racing); Automotive (Consumer)
**Circ:** (Paid)130,212

**Above Rubies (28603)**
PO Box 681687
Franklin, TN 37068-1684
Phone: (931)729-9861
Fax: (931)729-1474
**Subject(s):** Marriage and Family
**Circ:** (Non-paid)‡130,000

**Through the Gears Trucking Magazine (15)**
J.B. Scott Publishing
PO Box 2685
Anniston, AL 36202
Phone: (256)237-2801
Fax: (256)237-2802
**Subject(s):** Trucks and Trucking
**Circ:** 130,000

**Rental Guide (6597)**
Rental Guide Magazine
4021 Ardara Dr.
Tallahassee, FL 32309
Phone: (850)894-3278
Fax: (850)894-3271
**Subject(s):** Free Newspapers
**Circ:** (Non-paid)128,926

# Southern States

**North American Whitetail Magazine (7285)**
Primedia Enthusiast Group
2250 Newmarket Pkwy., Ste. 110
Marietta, GA 30067
Phone: (770)953-9222
Fax: (770)933-9510
**Subject(s):** (Hunting, Fishing, and Game Management)
**Circ:** (Paid)‡128,338

**The Baptist Courier (28110)**
Baptist Courier Inc.
100 Manly Street
Greenville, SC 29601
Phone: (864)232-8736
Fax: (864)232-8488
**Subject(s):** Religious Publications
**Circ:** (Non-paid)‡1,000
(Paid)‡125,000

**Pro Trucker (7380)**
Ramp Publishing Group
PO Box 549
Roswell, GA 30077
**Subject(s):** Trucks and Trucking
**Circ:** (Paid)14
(Non-paid)125,000

**Guns&Gear (353)**
BASS/ESPN
PO Box 17900
Montgomery, AL 36141
Phone: (334)396-8230
Fax: (334)396-8230
**Subject(s):** (Hunting, Fishing, and Game Management)
**Circ:** (Paid)123,422

**The Caduceus (11665)**
Kentucky Monthly
213 St. Clair
PO Box 559
Frankfort, KY 40602-0559
Phone: (502)227-0053
**Subject(s):** Unclassified Fraternal
**Circ:** 122,000

**Florida Sportsman (6563)**
Wickstrom Publishers
2700 S. Kanner Hwy.
Stuart, FL 34994
Phone: (772)219-7400
Fax: (772)219-6900
**Subject(s):** (Boating and Yachting); (Outdoors); (Hunting, Fishing, and Game Management)
**Circ:** (Paid)112,873

**American Firearms (5951)**
National Association of Federally Licensed Firearms Dealers
150 SE 12th St. Ste. 200
Fort Lauderdale, FL 33316
Phone: (954)467-9994
Fax: (954)463-2501
**Subject(s):** Firearms
**Circ:** 110,000

**The Baptist Record (16877)**
Mississippi Baptist Convention
POB 530
Jackson, MS 39205
**Subject(s):** Religious Publications
**Circ:** (Controlled)‡500
(Paid)‡108,000

**Boating World (6848)**
Trans World Publishing Inc.
2100 Powers Ferry Rd. 300
Atlanta, GA 30339
Phone: (770)955-5656
Fax: (770)952-0669
**Subject(s):** (Boating and Yachting)
**Circ:** (Non-paid)21,193
(Paid)106,854

**South Florida Parenting (6566)**
South Florida Parenting Inc.
5555 Nob Hill Rd.
Sunrise, FL 33351
Phone: (954)747-3050
Fax: (954)747-3055
**Subject(s):** Free Newspapers
**Circ:** (Free)❑105,902

**The duPont Registry: A Buyer's Gallery of Fine Automobiles (6497)**
duPont Publishing Inc.
3051 Tech Dr.
Saint Petersburg, FL 33716
Phone: (727)573-9339
Fax: (727)489-0255
**Subject(s):** Automotive (Consumer)
**Circ:** (Paid)105,037

**Phi Kappa Phi Forum (45)**
The Honor Society of Phi Kappa Phi
129 Quad Center, Mell St.
Auburn University, AL 36849-5306
Phone: (334)844-5200
Fax: (334)844-5994
**Subject(s):** Education; Clubs and Societies
**Circ:** (Paid)105,000

**Neighbors (357)**
ALFA/Alabama Farmers Federation
PO Box 11000
Montgomery, AL 36191-0001
Phone: (334)288-3900
Fax: (334)284-3957
**Subject(s):** General Agriculture
**Circ:** (Paid)101,159

**Waterski Magazine (6755)**
World Publications Inc.
460 N. Orlando Ave., Ste. 200
Winter Park, FL 32789
Phone: (407)628-4802
Fax: (407)628-7061
**Subject(s):** (Skiing); (Water Sports)
**Circ:** (Paid)100,714

**Aglaia (7470)**
Phi Mu
3558 Habersham at Northlake
Tucker, GA 30084
Phone: (770)496-5582
Fax: (770)496-0833
**Subject(s):** College Publications
**Circ:** 100,000

**Boating Life (6742)**
World Publications Inc.
460 N. Orlando Ave., Ste. 200
Winter Park, FL 32789
Phone: (407)628-4802
Fax: (407)628-7061
**Subject(s):** (Water Sports); (Boating and Yachting)
**Circ:** (Paid)100,000

**Communications News (6329)**
Nelson Publishing Inc.
2500 Tamiami Trail N.
Nokomis, FL 34275
Phone: (941)966-9521
Fax: (941)966-2590
**Subject(s):** Telecommunications
**Circ:** ‡100,000

**Computer Times (11525)**
3206 Kings Ct.
Bardstown, KY 40004
Phone: (502)349-1664
**Subject(s):** Computers
**Circ:** (Combined)100,000

**National Fire & Rescue (23703)**
National Fire and Rescue
5808 Faringdon Pl., Ste. 200
Raleigh, NC 27609-3930
Phone: (919)872-5040
Fax: (919)876-6531
**Subject(s):** Fire Fighting
**Circ:** (Controlled)36,777
100,000

**Our STATE (23526)**
Mann Media Inc.
800 Green Valley Rd., Ste. 106
Greensboro, NC 27408
Phone: (336)286-0600
Fax: (336)286-0100
**Subject(s):** Local, State, and Regional Publications
**Circ:** 98,000

**Pockets Magazine (28876)**
The Upper Room
1908 Grand Ave.
PO Box 340004
Nashville, TN 37203-0004
Phone: (615)340-7200
Fax: (615)340-7552
**Subject(s):** Religious Publications; Children's Interests
**Circ:** (Controlled)‡3,000
(Paid)‡96,000

**Mustang & Fords (6171)**
PRIMEDIA Los Angeles
Mustang & Fords
3816 Industry Blvd.
Lakeland, FL 33811
Phone: (863)644-0449
Fax: (863)644-8373
**Subject(s):** Automotive (Consumer)
**Circ:** (Paid)95,538

**Vanidades Continental (6265)**
Editorial Televisa
6355 NW 36th St.
Miami, FL 33166-7099
Phone: (305)871-6400
Fax: (305)871-4939
**Subject(s):** Women's Interests; Hispanic Publications; Spanish
**Circ:** (Paid)92,777

**The Phi Gamma Delta (11776)**
Phi Gamma Delta Fraternity
PO Box 4599
1201 Red Mile Road
Lexington, KY 40504
Phone: (859)255-1848
Fax: (859)253-0779
**Subject(s):** Unclassified Fraternal
**Circ:** ‡90,000

**Shield & Diamond (28778)**
Pi Kappa Alpha Fraternity
8347 W. Range Cove
Memphis, TN 38125
Phone: (901)748-1868
Fax: (901)748-3100
**Subject(s):** Unclassified Fraternal; College Publications
**Circ:** ‡90,000

**The Bent of Tau Beta Pi (28676)**
Tau Beta Pi Association
508 Dougherty Engineering Bldg.
1512 Middle Dr. - UTK
Knoxville, TN 37996
Phone: (865)546-4578
Fax: (865)546-4579
**Subject(s):** Engineering (Various branches)
**Circ:** (Paid)‡89,138

**Shutterbug (6695)**
Primedia
1419 Chaffee Dr., Ste. 1
Titusville, FL 32780-7315
Phone: (321)269-3212
Fax: (321)225-3149
**Subject(s):** Photography
**Circ:** (Paid)87,000

**Car & Parts Magazine (6167)**
Cars & Parts Magazine
4265PO New Tampa Highway, Ste. 3
Lakeland, FL 33815
**Subject(s):** Automotive (Consumer)
**Circ:** 86,381

**Atlanta Parent (6839)**
Atlanta Parent Inc.
2346 Perimeter Park Dr., Ste. 100
Atlanta, GA 30341
Phone: (770)454-7599
Fax: (770)454-7699
**Subject(s):** Parenting
**Circ:** (Paid)30
(Free)85,000

**Modern Applications News (MAN) (6332)**
Nelson Publishing Inc.
2500 Tamiami Trail N.
Nokomis, FL 34275
Phone: (941)966-9521
Fax: (941)966-2590

# Gale Directory of Publications & Broadcast Media/140th Ed.  Southern States

**Subject(s):** Commerce and Industry; Metal, Metallurgy, and Metal Trade
**Circ:** (Paid)‡17
 (Free)‡118
 (Controlled)‡85,001

**Worldwide Challenge  (6387)**
Campus Crusade for Christ
100 Lake Hart Dr.
Orlando, FL 32832-0100
Phone: (407)826-2390
Fax: (407)826-2374
**Subject(s):** Religious Publications
**Circ:** 85,000

**Equipment World Magazine  (462)**
Randall Publishing Co.
3200 Rice Mine Rd. North East
Tuscaloosa, AL 35406
Phone: (205)349-2990
Fax: (205)349-4174
**Subject(s):** Construction, Contracting, Building, and Excavating
**Circ:** (Controlled)‡84,300

**American Scientist  (23739)**
Sigma Xi, The Scientific Research Society
PO Box 13975
Research Triangle Park, NC 27709-3975
Phone: (919)549-0097
Fax: (919)549-0090
**Subject(s):** Science (General)
**Circ:** (Paid)84,072

**Coping with Cancer  (28607)**
Media America Inc.
PO Box 682268
Franklin, TN 37068-2268
Phone: (615)790-2400
Fax: (615)794-0179
**Subject(s):** Health
**Circ:** ‡80,000

**Dallas/Fort Worth New Homes Guide  (7331)**
HPC Publications
3119 Campus Dr.
Norcross, GA 30071
Phone: (770)446-6580
Fax: (770)448-4822
**Subject(s):** Real Estate; Home and Garden
**Circ:** (Controlled)‡80,000

**Presbyterians Today  (11838)**
Presbyterian Church (U.S.A.)
100 Witherspoon St.
Louisville, KY 40202-1396
Phone: (502)569-5637
Fax: (502)569-8632
**Subject(s):** Religious Publications
**Circ:** ‡80,000

**Sew Beautiful  (147)**
Martha Pullen Company Inc.
149 Old Big Cove Rd.
Brownsboro, AL 35741-9683
Phone: (256)533-9586
Fax: (256)533-9630
**Subject(s):** Dressmaking, Needlework, and Quilting
**Circ:** ‡80,000

**Today's Photographer Magazine  (23619)**
American Image Inc.
PO Box 777
Lewisville, NC 27023
**Subject(s):** Photography
**Circ:** (Controlled)25,000
 (Paid)80,000

**Unique Opportunities  (11845)**
UO Inc.
214 S. 8th St,, Ste. 502
Louisville, KY 40202
Phone: (502)589-8250
Fax: (502)587-0848
**Subject(s):** Medicine and Surgery; Health and Healthcare; Employment and Human Resources
**Circ:** (Controlled)80,000

**World of Fandom  (6659)**
PO Box 9421
Tampa, FL 33604
Phone: (813)933-7424

**Subject(s):** Entertainment; Motion Pictures; Radio, Television, Cable, and Video; Music and Musical Instruments
**Circ:** (Controlled)80,000

**Florida Realtor  (6363)**
Florida Association of Realtors
7025 Augusta Nat'l Dr.
Orlando, FL 32822-5017
Phone: (407)438-1400
Fax: (407)438-1411
**Subject(s):** Real Estate
**Circ:** (Non-paid)△2,495
 (Paid)△78,025

**Emory Magazine  (6869)**
Emory University
1655 N. Decatur Rd.
Atlanta, GA 30322
Phone: (404)727-0162
Fax: (404)727-7259
**Subject(s):** College Publications
**Circ:** (Non-paid)‡78,000

**Aviation History  (6418)**
Primedia History Group
PO Box 420235
Palm Coast, FL 32142-0235
**Subject(s):** History and Genealogy; Aviation
**Circ:** (Controlled)76,102

**EE Evaluation Engineering  (6330)**
Nelson Publishing Inc.
EE-Evaluation Engineering
2500 Tamiami Trail N.
Nokomis, FL 34275
Phone: (941)966-9521
Fax: (941)966-2590
**Subject(s):** Electronics Engineering
**Circ:** (Non-paid)‡76,049

**Althon Sports Insiders' Football News  (5950)**
Insiders Sports Publishing Corp.
PO Box 552200
Fort Lauderdale, FL 33355
**Subject(s):** (Football)
**Circ:** (Non-paid)875
 (Paid)75,000

**Citizen Airman  (7365)**
Air Force Reserve Command
HQ AFRC/PA
255 Richard Ray Blvd., Ste. 137
Robins AFB, GA 31098-1637
Phone: (478)327-1770
Fax: (478)327-0878
**Subject(s):** Military and Navy
**Circ:** (Controlled)75,000

**Our World  (5919)**
Our World Publishing Corp.
1104 N. Nova Rd., Ste. 251
Daytona Beach, FL 32117
Phone: (386)441-5367
Fax: (386)441-5604
**Subject(s):** Gay and Lesbian Interests; Travel and Tourism
**Circ:** ‡75,000

**Over the Road  (7379)**
RAM Publishing Group
PO Box 549
Roswell, GA 30077-0549
**Subject(s):** Trucks and Trucking
**Circ:** (Paid)131
 (Non-paid)74,293

**Imagen  (27802)**
Casiano Communications Inc.
1700 Fernandez Juncos Ave.
San Juan, PR 00909
Phone: (787)728-3000
Fax: (787)268-1001
**Subject(s):** Hispanic Publications; Lifestyle; Women's Interests
**Circ:** ‡70,000

**SBC Life  (28879)**
Southern Baptist Convention Executive Committee
901 Commerce
Nashville, TN 37203
Phone: (615)244-2355
Fax: (615)782-8684
**Subject(s):** Religious Publications
**Circ:** ‡70,000

**The Wine News  (5897)**
T.E. Smith Inc.
PO Box 14-2096
Coral Gables, FL 33114
Phone: (305)740-7170
Fax: (305)740-7153
**Subject(s):** Food and Cooking
**Circ:** (Combined)70,000

**Mopar Muscle  (6170)**
PRIMEDIA Los Angeles
c/o Randy Bolig, Editor
9036 Brittany Way
Lakeland, FL 33811
Phone: (863)644-0449
Fax: (863)644-8373
**Subject(s):** Automotive (Consumer); (Auto Racing)
**Circ:** (Paid)69,621

**Pageantry  (5793)**
Pageantry, Talent & Entertainment Services Inc.
PO Box 160307
Altamonte Springs, FL 32716-0307
Phone: (407)260-2262
Fax: (407)260-5131
**Subject(s):** Fashion; Women's Interests
**Circ:** (Combined)68,000

**Georgia Farm Bureau News  (7245)**
Georgia Farm Bureau Federation
1620 Bass Rd.
PO Box 7068
Macon, GA 31209
Phone: (478)474-8411
**Subject(s):** Farm Bureau, Grange, and Cooperative Associations
**Circ:** ‡66,312

**Wildlife in North Carolina  (23720)**
N.C. Wildlife Resources Commission
512 N Salisbury St., Rm. 315
Raleigh, NC 27604-1188
Phone: (919)733-7123
Fax: (919)715-2381
**Subject(s):** Natural History and Nature Study; Ecology and Conservation; Local, State, and Regional Publications
**Circ:** (Non-paid)‡3,626
 (Paid)‡66,319

**The Florida Bar Journal  (6574)**
The Florida Bar
651 E. Jefferson St.
Tallahassee, FL 32399-2300
Phone: (850)561-5600
Fax: (850)561-5826
**Subject(s):** Law
**Circ:** ‡63,762

**The Christian Index  (6852)**
2930 Flowers Rd. South
Atlanta, GA 30341
Phone: (770)936-5590
Fax: (770)936-5595
**Subject(s):** Religious Publications
**Circ:** (Non-paid)2,000
 (Paid)62,000

**American Quilter  (11930)**
American Quilter's Society
PO Box 3290
5801 Kentucky Dam Rd.
Paducah, KY 42002-3290
Phone: (270)898-7903
Fax: (270)898-1173
**Subject(s):** Dressmaking, Needlework, and Quilting
**Circ:** (Combined)61,000

**Agricultural Review (North Carolina)  (23691)**
North Carolina Dept. of Agriculture
PO Box 27677
Raleigh, NC 27611
Phone: (919)733-5047
Fax: (919)733-5047
**Subject(s):** General Agriculture
**Circ:** (Controlled)‡60,000

**Journal of Minority Employment  (11823)**
National Consortium for Black Professional Development
2210 Goldsmith Office Ctr., Ste. 228-A
Louisville, KY 40218
**Subject(s):** Employment and Human Resources; Ethnic and Minority Studies; Labor
**Circ:** 60,000

*Periodical Index*

Circulation: ★ = ABC; △ = BPA; ◆ = CAC; • = CCAB; ❑ = VAC; ⊕ = PO Statement; ‡ = Publisher's Report; Boldface figures = sworn; Light figures = estimated.

4123

# Southern States

**South Carolina Wildlife** (28065)
South Carolina Department of Natural Resources
1000 Assembly St.
PO Box 167
Columbia, SC 29202-0167
Phone: (803)734-3944
Fax: (803)734-3968
**Subject(s):** (Hunting, Fishing, and Game Management); Environmental and Natural Resources Conservation; Local, State, and Regional Publications
**Circ:** ‡60,000

**Star & Lamp** (23355)
Pi Kappa Phi Fraternity
2102 Cambridge, Beltway Dr., Ste. A
PO Box 240526
Charlotte, NC 28273
Phone: (704)504-0888
Fax: (704)504-0880
**Subject(s):** Unclassified Fraternal
**Circ:** ‡60,000

**Tennessee Alumnus** (28687)
University of Tennessee Alumni Association
91 Communications Bldg.
University of Tennessee
Knoxville, TN 37996-0312
Phone: (865)974-1000
**Subject(s):** College Publications
**Circ:** ‡58,000

**Modern Woodworking** (466)
BNP Media
3200 Rice Mine Rd. NE
Tuscaloosa, AL 35406
Fax: (205)391-2081
**Subject(s):** Wood and Woodworking
**Circ:** 57,000

**Nursing Spectrum—Florida Edition** (5965)
Nursing Spectrum Inc.
1001 W. Cypress Creek Rd., No. 300
Fort Lauderdale, FL 33309-1950
Phone: (954)776-1455
Fax: (954)776-1456
**Subject(s):** Career Development and Employment; Nursing
**Circ:** 57,000

**Net News** (6904)
New South Publishing Inc.
1303 Hightower Trl., Ste. 101
Atlanta, GA 30350
Phone: (770)650-1102
Fax: (770)650-2848
**Subject(s):** (General Sports)
**Circ:** (Paid)56,000

**Recommend** (6289)
Worth International Communications Corp.
5979 NW, 151 St., Ste. 120
Miami Lakes, FL 33014
Phone: (305)828-0123
Fax: (305)826-6950
**Subject(s):** Travel and Tourism
**Circ:** (Non-paid)△55,094

**Biblical Recorder** (23692)
Biblical Recorder Inc.
232 W. Millbrook Rd.
Raleigh, NC 27609
Phone: (919)847-6939
Fax: (919)847-6939
**Subject(s):** Religious Publications
**Circ:** ‡55,000

**Blue & Gold Illustrated—Notre Dame Football** (28496)
Blue & Gold Illustrated
PO Box 1604
Brentwood, TN 37024-1604
Phone: (615)507-1000
**Subject(s):** (Football); College Publications
**Circ:** (Paid)55,000

**Carolina Alumni Review** (23293)
University of North Carolina General Alumni Association
PO Box 660
Chapel Hill, NC 27514
Phone: (919)962-1208
Fax: (919)962-0010
**Subject(s):** College Publications
**Circ:** ‡55,000

**Charlotte Parent** (23337)
Carolina Parenting Inc.
1100 S Mint St., Ste. 201
Charlotte, NC 28203
Phone: (704)344-1980
Fax: (704)344-1983
**Subject(s):** Parenting
**Circ:** (Free)55,000

**Mature Years** (28865)
The United Methodist Publishing House
201 8th Ave. S
PO Box 801
Nashville, TN 37202-0801
Phone: (615)749-6000
Fax: (615)749-6512
**Subject(s):** Religious Publications; Senior Citizens' Interests
**Circ:** ‡55,000

**The Memphis Flyer** (28773)
Contemporary Media Inc.
460 Tennessee St.
Memphis, TN 38103
Phone: (901)521-9000
Fax: (901)521-0129
**Subject(s):** Local, State, and Regional Publications
**Circ:** (Combined)55,000

**The N C Catholic** (23702)
715 Nazareth St.
Raleigh, NC 27606
Phone: (919)821-9730
Fax: (919)821-9705
**Subject(s):** Religious Publications
**Circ:** (Paid)‡55,000

**Young Horizons Indigo** (7114)
PO Box 371595
Decatur, GA 30037
Phone: (404)241-5003
**Subject(s):** Education; Ethnic and Minority Studies; Parenting
**Circ:** (Paid)18,000
54,000

**Auburn Magazine** (34)
Auburn University Alumni Association
317 S College St.
Auburn University
Auburn, AL 36849-5150
Phone: (334)844-2586
Fax: (334)844-1477
**Subject(s):** College Publications
**Circ:** ‡53,000

**Carolina Business** (23670)
Taylor Publications Inc.
PO Box 12006
1430 McCarthy Blvd.
New Bern, NC 28561
Phone: (252)633-5106
Fax: (252)633-2836
**Subject(s):** Business
**Circ:** (Non-paid)20,000
(Combined)53,000

**Medical Laboratory Observer (MLO)** (6331)
Thomson PDR
2500 Tamiami Trail N.
Nokomis, FL 34275
Phone: (941)966-9521
Fax: (941)966-2590
**Subject(s):** Laboratory Research (Scientific and Medical)
**Circ:** (Free)‡53,000

**Florida Trend** (6502)
Trend Magazines Inc.
490 First Ave., S.
Saint Petersburg, FL 33701
Phone: (727)821-5800
Fax: (727)822-5083
**Subject(s):** Banking, Finance, and Investments; Commerce and Industry
**Circ:** (Non-paid)10,371
(Paid)52,969

**Baptist and Reflector** (28495)
Tennessee Baptist Convention, Executive Board
PO Box 728
Brentwood, TN 37024
Phone: (615)371-2255
Fax: (615)371-2014
**Subject(s):** Religious Publications
**Circ:** ‡52,000

**Porsche Panorama** (6909)
Porsche Club of America
912 Lullwater Rd.
Atlanta, GA 30307
Phone: (404)378-9823
Fax: (404)377-7041
**Subject(s):** Automotive (Consumer)
**Circ:** (Non-paid)‡2,000
(Paid)‡51,500

**International Tradequip** (28575)
TAP Publishing Co.
174 Fourth St.
PO Box 3079
Crossville, TN 38555
Phone: (931)484-5137
Fax: (931)484-2532
**Subject(s):** Petroleum, Oil, and Gas
**Circ:** (Combined)51,000

**Internal Auditor** (5792)
Institute of Internal Auditors Inc.
247 Maitland Ave.
Altamonte Springs, FL 32701-4201
Phone: (407)937-1100
Fax: (407)937-1101
**Subject(s):** Business
**Circ:** 50,000

**Ole Miss Alumni Review** (17038)
University of Mississippi Alumni Association
Triplett Alumni Center
Rm. 172
University, MS 38677
Phone: (662)915-7375
Fax: (662)915-7756
**Subject(s):** College Publications
**Circ:** (Paid)20,000
(Controlled)50,000

**Piedmont Triad Newcomer** (23710)
Signature Publishing Inc.
512 Brickhaven Dr.
Raleigh, NC 27606-1492
Fax: (919)850-0873
**Subject(s):** Business; Local, State, and Regional Publications
**Circ:** (Non-paid)50,000

**Quail Unlimited** (28093)
Quail Unlimited Inc.
PO Box 610
Edgefield, SC 29824-0610
Phone: (803)637-5731
Fax: (803)637-0037
**Subject(s):** Environmental and Natural Resources Conservation
**Circ:** (Paid)50,000

**The Sun** (23323)
Sun Publishing Company Inc.
107 N Roberson St.
Chapel Hill, NC 27516
Phone: (919)942-5282
Fax: (919)932-3101
**Subject(s):** Literature and Literary Reviews
**Circ:** (Paid)50,000

**Tabletalk** (6385)
Ligonier Ministries
PO Box 547500
Orlando, FL 32854
Phone: (407)333-4244
Fax: (407)333-4233
**Subject(s):** Religious Publications
**Circ:** (Non-paid)⊕10,000
(Paid)⊕50,000

**Triangle Newcomer** (23718)
Signature Publishing Inc.
512 Brickhaven Dr.
Raleigh, NC 27606-1492
Fax: (919)850-0873
**Subject(s):** Local, State, and Regional Publications
**Circ:** (Non-paid)50,000

**Ultralight Flying!** (28525)
Glider Rider Inc.
1085 Bailey Ave.
Chattanooga, TN 37404
**Subject(s):** Aviation
**Circ:** (Paid)‡50,000

**University of Florida Today Magazine (6048)**
University of Florida Alumni Association
2012 W. University Ave.
Gainesville, FL 32603
Phone: (352)392-1905
Fax: (352)392-8736
**Subject(s):** College Publications
**Circ:** (Controlled)‡50,000

**Wake Boarding (6754)**
World Publications Inc.
460 N. Orlando Ave., Ste. 200
Winter Park, FL 32789
Phone: (407)628-4802
Fax: (407)628-7061
**Subject(s):** (Water Sports); (Boating and Yachting)
**Circ:** (Paid)50,000

**Young Bucks Outdoors (366)**
Buckmasters
10350 Hwy. 80 E.
Montgomery, AL 36117
Phone: (334)215-3337
Fax: (334)215-3535
**Subject(s):** Youths' Interests
**Circ:** (Paid)50,000

**Cosmopolitan en Espanol (6225)**
Editorial Televisa
6355 NW 36th St.
Miami, FL 33166-7099
Phone: (305)871-6400
Fax: (305)871-4939
**Subject(s):** Spanish; Women's Interests; Hispanic Publications
**Circ:** (Paid)49,568

**ASHRAE Journal (6833)**
American Society of Heating, Refrigerating and Air-Conditioning Engineers Inc.
1791 Tullie Cir. NE
Atlanta, GA 30329
Phone: (404)636-8400
Fax: (404)321-5478
**Subject(s):** Air Conditioning and Refrigeration; Plumbing and Heating
**Circ:** (Non-paid)11,157
(Paid)49,200

**KNOW Atlanta Magazine (6898)**
New South Publishing Inc.
1303 Hightower Trl., Ste. 101
Atlanta, GA 30350
Phone: (770)650-1102
Fax: (770)650-2848
**Subject(s):** Lifestyle
**Circ:** (Controlled)⊕**48,000**

**Pedalpoint (28875)**
Lifeway Christian Resources of the Southern Baptist Convention
One Lifeway Plz.
Nashville, TN 37234-0175
Phone: (615)251-2000
Fax: (615)251-2614
**Subject(s):** Music and Musical Instruments; Theology
**Circ:** (Paid)48,000

**Roundel Magazine (28115)**
BMW Car Club of America Inc.
640 S Main St. Ste. 201
Greenville, SC 29601-2564
**Subject(s):** Automotive (Consumer)
**Circ:** (Paid)48,000

**Welding Journal (6267)**
American Welding Society
550 LeJeune Rd. NW
Miami, FL 33126
Phone: (305)443-9353
Fax: (305)443-0559
**Subject(s):** Welding
**Circ:** (Paid)47,719

**Your Health (5828)**
American Media
5401 NW Broken Sound Blvd.
Boca Raton, FL 33487-3587
Phone: (561)994-7210
Fax: (561)241-5689
**Subject(s):** Health and Healthcare
**Circ:** (Paid)47,288

**Today's Woman Magazine (11843)**
Today's Woman
9750 Ormsby Station Rd., Ste. 307
Louisville, KY 40223
Phone: (502)327-8855
Fax: (502)327-8861
**Subject(s):** Women's Interests; Local, State, and Regional Publications; Lifestyle
**Circ:** (Non-paid)‡46,000

**Baseball America (23404)**
Baseball America Inc.
PO Box 2089
Durham, NC 27702
Phone: (919)682-2880
Fax: (800)334-8671
**Subject(s):** (Baseball)
**Circ:** ‡45,000

**Berea College Magazine (11539)**
Berea College
CPO 2216
Berea, KY 40404
Phone: (859)985-3000
Fax: (859)985-3556
**Subject(s):** College Publications
**Circ:** ‡45,000

**Hi-Tech Home (5835)**
BBS Press Service Inc.
PO Box 367209
Bonita Springs, FL 34135
Phone: (239)992-0397
Fax: (239)992-4862
**Subject(s):** Computers
**Circ:** (Controlled)‡45,000

**Journal of the American Disability Association (84)**
American Disability Association
2201 Sixth Ave. S
Birmingham, AL 35233
Phone: (205)328-9090
Fax: (205)251-7417
**Subject(s):** Handicapped; Handicapped
**Circ:** 45,000

**Site Selection Magazine (7339)**
Conway Data Inc.
6625 The Corners Pkwy., Ste. 200
Norcross, GA 30092-2901
Phone: (770)446-6996
Fax: (770)263-8825
**Subject(s):** Commerce and Industry; Real Estate
**Circ:** (Combined)45,000

**Plants Sites & Parks (23528)**
Reed Business Information
7025 Albert Pick Rd., Ste.200
Greensboro, NC 27409
Phone: (336)605-0121
Fax: (336)605-1143
**Subject(s):** Real Estate
**Circ:** (Paid)53
(Controlled)44,500

**Electronic Commerce World (6074)**
2021 Coolidge St.
Hollywood, FL 33020
Fax: (954)925-7533
**Subject(s):** Electronics Engineering; Computers
**Circ:** (Paid)‡44,000

**Folio Weekly (6095)**
Folio Publishing Inc.
9456 Phillips Hwy., Ste. 11
Jacksonville, FL 32256-1351
Phone: (904)260-9770
Fax: (904)260-9773
**Subject(s):** Local, State, and Regional Publications
**Circ:** (Paid)9
(Free)43,401

**Circuits Assembly (6853)**
UP Media Group Inc.
2018 Powers Ferry Rd., Ste. 600
Atlanta, GA 30339
Phone: (678)589-8800
Fax: (678)589-8850
**Subject(s):** Electronics Engineering
**Circ:** (Combined)‡42,371

**Circuit Rider (28849)**
The United Methodist Publishing House
201 8th Ave S.
PO Box 801
Nashville, TN 37202
Phone: (615)749-6488
**Subject(s):** Religious Publications
**Circ:** (Paid)‡500
(Non-paid)‡42,000

**INTECH (23740)**
ISA Services Inc.
67 Alexander Dr.
PO Box 12277
Research Triangle Park, NC 27709-2277
Phone: (919)549-8411
Fax: (919)549-8288
**Subject(s):** Engineering (Various branches)
**Circ:** (Non-paid)8,623
(Paid)41,977

**Georgia Sportsman (7281)**
Primedia Enthusiast Group
2250 Newmarket Pkwy., Ste. 110
Marietta, GA 30067
Phone: (770)953-9222
Fax: (770)933-9510
**Subject(s):** (Hunting, Fishing, and Game Management)
**Circ:** 41,000

**The Ensign (23697)**
THE ENSIGN Magazine
PO Box 31664
Raleigh, NC 27622
Phone: (919)821-0892
Fax: (888)304-0813
**Subject(s):** (Boating and Yachting)
**Circ:** (Paid)40,073

**Corporate & Incentive Travel (5817)**
Coastal Communications Corp.
2650 N Military Trl., Ste. 250
Boca Raton, FL 33431-6390
Phone: (561)989-0600
Fax: (561)989-9509
**Subject(s):** Conventions, Meetings, and Trade Fairs; Travel and Tourism
**Circ:** (Non-paid)40,058

**Barry Magazine (6290)**
University Relations
11300 NE 2nd Ave.
Miami Shores, FL 33161-6695
Phone: (305)899-3188
Fax: (305)899-3186
**Subject(s):** College Publications
**Circ:** (Non-paid)40,000

**Carolina Woman (23279)**
Carolina Woman Inc.
PO Box 3529
Cary, NC 27519
Phone: (919)852-5900
Fax: (919)852-5910
**Subject(s):** Women's Interests; Local, State, and Regional Publications; Lifestyle
**Circ:** ‡40,000

**Good News (12035)**
Forum for Scriptural Christianity Inc.
308 E. Main St.
Wilmore, KY 40390-0150
Phone: (859)858-4661
Fax: (859)858-4972
**Subject(s):** Religious Publications
**Circ:** 40,000

**The Horse (11763)**
Blood-Horse Publications
PO Box 911108
Lexington, KY 40591-1108
Phone: (859)278-2361
Fax: (859)276-4450
**Subject(s):** Veterinary Medicine
**Circ:** (Paid)40,000

**Kentucky Afield (11669)**
Kentucky Afield Magazine
Arnold L. Mitchell Bldg.
No.1 Game Farm Rd.
Frankfort, KY 40601
Phone: (502)564-4336
Fax: (502)564-6508

**Subject(s):** Ecology and Conservation; Local, State, and Regional Publications

**Circ:** (Controlled)‡4,000
(Paid)‡40,000

**Marlin** (6748)
World Publications Inc.
460 N. Orlando Ave., Ste. 200
Winter Park, FL 32789
**Phone:** (407)628-4702
**Fax:** (407)628-7061
**Subject(s):** (Hunting, Fishing, and Game Management)

**Circ:** (Non-paid)10,000
(Paid)40,000

**Sunshine Artist** (6384)
Sunshine Artist Magazine
3210 Dade Ave.
Orlando, FL 32804
**Phone:** (407)228-9772
**Fax:** (407)228-9862
**Subject(s):** Art and Art History

**Circ:** (Combined)⊕**40,000**

**Trucking Co.** (469)
Randall Publishing Co.
3200 Rice Mine Rd. North East
Tuscaloosa, AL 35406
**Phone:** (205)349-2990
**Fax:** (205)349-4174
**Subject(s):** Trucks and Trucking

**Circ:** (Controlled)‡40,000

**The Water Skier** (6459)
USA Water Ski
1251 Holy Cow Rd.
Polk City, FL 33868-8200
**Phone:** (863)324-4341
**Fax:** (863)325-8259
**Subject(s):** (Water Sports)

**Circ:** (Non-paid)‡500
(Paid)‡40,000

**Buena Vida** (27796)
Casiano Communications Inc.
1700 Fernandez Juncos Ave.
San Juan, PR 00909
**Phone:** (787)728-3000
**Fax:** (787)268-1001
**Subject(s):** Health

**Circ:** (Non-paid)‡8,000
(Paid)‡39,500

**Palm Beach Illustrated** (6413)
Palm Beach Media Group
PO Box 3344
Palm Beach, FL 33480
**Phone:** (561)659-0210
**Fax:** (561)659-1736
**Subject(s):** Lifestyle; General Editorial

**Circ:** (Paid)2,428
(Non-paid)39,452

**Brown Gold Magazine** (6519)
NTM Publications
1000 E 1st St.
Sanford, FL 32771-1487
**Phone:** (407)323-3430
**Fax:** (407)330-0376
**Subject(s):** Religious Publications

**Circ:** (Controlled)12,344
(Paid)38,582

**Healthcare Business Month** (28854)
Healthcare Business Media Inc.
210 12th Ave. S
Nashville, TN 37203-4002
**Subject(s):** Medicine and Surgery; Health and Healthcare; Business

**Circ:** (Combined)38,109

**The duPont Registry: A Buyer's Gallery of Fine Boats** (6498)
duPont Publishing Inc.
3051 Tech Dr.
Saint Petersburg, FL 33716
**Phone:** (727)573-9339
**Fax:** (727)489-0255
**Subject(s):** (Boating and Yachting); Boats and Marine

**Circ:** (Paid)16,000
(Controlled)38,000

**Shutterbug's Outdoor & Nature Photography** (6696)
Primedia
1419 Chaffee Dr., Ste. 1
Titusville, FL 32780-7315
**Phone:** (321)269-3212
**Fax:** (321)225-3149
**Subject(s):** Photography

**Circ:** (Combined)37,200

**Glass Patterns Quarterly** (12021)
Glass Patterns Quarterly Inc.
8300 Hidden Valley Rd.
PO Box 69
Westport, KY 40077
**Phone:** (502)222-5631
**Fax:** (502)222-4527
**Subject(s):** Crafts, Models, Hobbies, and Contests; Glass and China

**Circ:** (Paid)⊕**37,000**

**UNCW Magazine** (23845)
The Univ. of N. Carolina at Wilmington
601 S. College Rd.
Wilmington, NC 28403-5993
**Phone:** (910)962-3000
**Subject(s):** College Publications

**Circ:** (Non-paid)37,000

**Georgia Magazine** (6802)
University of Georgia
Public Affairs Office
Stegeman Coliseum/A301
Athens, GA 30602-4370
**Phone:** (706)542-8059
**Fax:** (706)583-0368
**Subject(s):** College Publications

**Circ:** ‡35,000

**Health Management Technology** (6881)
Primedia Business
6151 Powers Ferry Rd.
Atlanta, GA 30339
**Phone:** (770)955-2500
**Fax:** (770)618-0348
**Subject(s):** Computers; Hospitals and Healthcare Institutions

**Circ:** (Paid)3,000
(Non-paid)35,000

**Retail Traffic** (6915)
Primedia Business
6151 Powers Ferry Rd.
Atlanta, GA 30339
**Phone:** (770)955-2500
**Fax:** (770)618-0348
**Subject(s):** Real Estate

**Circ:** (Paid)830
(Controlled)35,000

**WEAVINGS** (28898)
The Upper Room
1908 Grand Ave.
PO Box 340004
Nashville, TN 37203-0004
**Phone:** (615)340-7200
**Fax:** (615)340-7552
**Subject(s):** Religious Publications

**Circ:** (Non-paid)200
(Paid)35,000

**Alabama Alumni Magazine** (455)
University of Alabama
PO Box 861928
Tuscaloosa, AL 35486-0017
**Phone:** (205)348-5963
**Fax:** (205)348-5958
**Subject(s):** College Publications

**Circ:** (Non-paid)34,000

**Mississippi Magazine** (16890)
Downhome Publications Inc.
5 Lakeland Cir.
Jackson, MS 39216-5006
**Phone:** (601)982-8418
**Fax:** (601)982-8447
**Subject(s):** Local, State, and Regional Publications; General Editorial

**Circ:** (Non-paid)‡500
(Paid)‡34,000

**SPORTING CLASSICS** (28066)
Live Oak Press Inc.
9330A Two Notch Rd.
Columbia, SC 29223
**Phone:** (803)736-2424
**Fax:** (803)736-3404

**Subject(s):** (Hunting, Fishing, and Game Management)
**Circ:** ‡34,000

**Structural Engineer** (6921)
Mercor Media Inc.
5605 Glenridge Dr., Ste. 775
Atlanta, GA 30342
**Phone:** (404)497-7890
**Fax:** (404)497-7899
**Subject(s):** Engineering (Various branches)

**Circ:** (Non-paid)34,000

**Atlanta Homes and Lifestyles** (6836)
Wiesner Inc.
1100 Johnson Ferry Rd. NE, Ste. 595
Atlanta, GA 30342
**Phone:** (404)252-6670
**Fax:** (404)252-6673
**Subject(s):** Local, State, and Regional Publications; Real Estate

**Circ:** ‡33,828

**Sewanee** (28983)
University of the South
735 University Ave.
Office of Communications
Sewanee, TN 37383
**Phone:** (931)598-1000
**Fax:** (931)598-1667
**Subject(s):** College Publications

**Circ:** (Free)‡33,500

**Georgia Tech Alumni Magazine** (6879)
Georgia Tech Alumni Association
190 N. Ave. NW
Atlanta, GA 30313
**Phone:** (404)894-2391
**Fax:** (404)894-5113
**Subject(s):** College Publications

**Circ:** (Paid)33,000

**Southern Seminary Magazine** (11840)
Review & Expositor
PO Box 6681
Louisville, KY 40206-0681
**Phone:** (502)327-8347
**Fax:** (502)327-8347
**Subject(s):** Religious Publications; College Publications

**Circ:** (Controlled)33,000

**Aware** (55)
Woman's Missionary Union, SBC
100 Missonary Ridge
Birmingham, AL 35242
**Phone:** (205)991-8100
**Fax:** (205)995-4840
**Subject(s):** Religious Publications

**Circ:** 32,700

**The Brief** (6849)
American Bar Association
c/o Cale Conley, Conley, Sacks & Griggs LLP
4840 Roswell Rd., Ste. E-200
Atlanta, GA 30342
**Phone:** (404)781-9300
**Fax:** (404)781-9304
**Subject(s):** Law

**Circ:** (Non-paid)‡1,741
(Paid)‡32,000

**Hooters Magazine** (6884)
1815 The Exchange
Atlanta, GA 30339
**Phone:** (770)951-2040
**Fax:** (770)618-7049
**Subject(s):** Entertainment

**Circ:** (Paid)32,000

**Vanderbilt Magazine** (28897)
Vanderbilt University
110 21st Ave. S. Ste. 1000
Nashville, TN 37203
**Phone:** (615)322-3988
**Fax:** (615)343-8547
**Subject(s):** College Publications

**Circ:** (Paid)3,000
(Paid)32,000

**Textile World** (6926)
Primedia Business
6151 Powers Ferry Rd.
Atlanta, GA 30339
**Phone:** (770)955-2500
**Fax:** (770)618-0348

**Subject(s):** Textiles
**Circ:** (Paid)617
(Controlled)31,803

**Gray's Sporting Journal (6982)**
Morris Magazines
735 Broad St.
Augusta, GA 30903
Phone: (706)722-5833
Fax: (706)823-3641
**Subject(s):** (Hunting, Fishing, and Game Management)
**Circ:** (Paid)30,689

**Aventura Magazine (5802)**
Discover Magazine Inc.
20533 Biscayne Blvd., Ste. 126
Aventura, FL 33180
Phone: (305)932-2400
Fax: (305)466-9285
**Subject(s):** Local, State, and Regional Publications; Lifestyle
**Circ:** (Combined)30,000

**Bracket Racing USA (6778)**
Primedia
3003 Maple Ln.
Alpharetta, GA 30004-1576
Phone: (404)442-0376
Fax: (404)410-1585
**Subject(s):** (Auto Racing)
**Circ:** (Paid)‡30,000

**The Cluster (7244)**
Mercer University
1400 Coleman Ave.
Macon, GA 31207-0001
Phone: (478)301-5335
Fax: (478)752-4124
**Subject(s):** College Publications
**Circ:** (Paid)‡30,000

**Coping with Allergies and Asthma (28606)**
Media America Inc.
PO Box 682268
Franklin, TN 37068-2268
Phone: (615)790-2400
Fax: (615)794-0179
**Subject(s):** Health
**Circ:** (Paid)‡30,000

**Counselor (5926)**
Health Communications Inc.
3201 SW 15th St.
Deerfield Beach, FL 33442
Phone: (954)360-0909
Fax: (954)360-0034
**Subject(s):** Psychology and Psychiatry; Health and Healthcare
**Circ:** (Paid)30,000

**Digital Output (6463)**
6000A Sawgrass Village Ctr., Ste. 1
Ponte Vedra Beach, FL 32082-5061
**Subject(s):** Graphic Arts and Design; Printing and Typography
**Circ:** 30,000

**Dolphin Digest (6228)**
Curtis Publishing Co.
8033 NW 36th St., No. S-438
Miami, FL 33166
Phone: (305)594-0508
Fax: (305)594-0518
**Subject(s):** (Football)
**Circ:** (Non-paid)500
(Paid)30,000

**Vacation Industry Review (6264)**
Interval International
6262 Sunset Dr.
Miami, FL 33143
**Subject(s):** Travel and Tourism
**Circ:** (Controlled)30,000

**TAPPI JOURNAL (7341)**
Technical Association of Pulp and Paper Industry (TAPPI)
15 Technology Pkwy. S.
Norcross, GA 30092
Phone: (770)446-1400
Fax: (770)446-6947
**Subject(s):** Paper; Packaging
**Circ:** (Non-paid)10,313
(Paid)29,707

**Back Home (23572)**
WordsWorth Communications Inc.
PO Box 70
Hendersonville, NC 28793
Phone: (828)859-9000
Fax: (828)696-0700
**Subject(s):** Lifestyle; Home and Garden
**Circ:** ‡29,414

**The Atlanta Metro (7473)**
4405 Mall Blvd., No. 521
Union City, GA 30291
Phone: (770)969-7711
Fax: (770)969-7811
**Subject(s):** Local, State, and Regional Publications; Ethnic Publications
**Circ:** (Controlled)‡29,000

**Emerging Infectious Diseases (6868)**
U.S. National Center for Infectious Diseases
Centers for Disease Control and Prevention
1600 Clifton Rd., Mailstop C-14
Atlanta, GA 30333
Phone: (404)371-5329
Fax: (404)371-5449
**Subject(s):** Medicine and Surgery; Health and Healthcare
**Circ:** 29,000

**Pizza Today (11837)**
Macfadden Protech
908 S 8th St., Ste. 200
Louisville, KY 40203
Phone: (502)736-9500
Fax: (502)736-9501
**Subject(s):** Food and Grocery Trade; Hotels, Motels, Restaurants, and Clubs
**Circ:** (Paid)11,376
(Non-paid)28,616

**Mississippi State Alumnus (16959)**
Mississippi State Alumni Association
102 George Hall
PO Box 5325
Mississippi State, MS 39762-5325
Phone: (662)325-3442
Fax: (662)325-7455
**Subject(s):** College Publications
**Circ:** (Non-paid)‡28,500

**Journal of Clinical Psychiatry (28768)**
Physicians Postgraduate Press Inc.
PO Box 752870
Memphis, TN 38175
Phone: (901)751-3800
Fax: (901)751-3444
**Subject(s):** Psychology and Psychiatry
**Circ:** (Paid)‡7,100
(Controlled)‡28,400

**The duPont Registry: A Buyer's Gallery of Fine Homes (6499)**
duPont Publishing Inc.
3051 Tech Dr.
Saint Petersburg, FL 33716
Phone: (727)573-9339
Fax: (727)489-0255
**Subject(s):** Lifestyle; Home and Garden; Real Estate
**Circ:** (Paid)22,000
(Controlled)28,000

**Georgia Bar Journal (6877)**
State Bar of Georgia
104 Marietta St., NW, Ste. 100
50 Hurt Plz.
Atlanta, GA 30303
Phone: (404)527-8700
Fax: (404)527-8717
**Subject(s):** Law
**Circ:** 28,000

**Horizons (11816)**
Presbyterian Women in the Presbyterian Church (U.S.A.)
100 Witherspoon St.
Louisville, KY 40202-1396
Phone: (502)569-5368
Fax: (502)569-8085
**Subject(s):** Women's Interests; Religious Publications
**Circ:** (Non-paid)1,000
(Paid)28,000

**LOMA Resource (6899)**
Life Office Management Association
2300 Windy Ridge Pkwy., Ste. 600
Atlanta, GA 30339-8443
Phone: (770)951-1770

Fax: (770)984-0441
**Subject(s):** Insurance
**Circ:** (Non-paid)27,000

**Marine Business Journal (5963)**
Marine Business Journal Inc.
330 N. Andrews Ave., 3rd Fl.
Fort Lauderdale, FL 33301
Phone: (954)522-5515
Fax: (954)522-2260
**Subject(s):** Boats and Marine
**Circ:** (Controlled)1,426
(Paid)27,000

**Resource (6913)**
Life Office Management Association
2300 Windy Ridge Pkwy., Ste. 600
Atlanta, GA 30339-8443
Phone: (770)951-1770
Fax: (770)984-0441
**Subject(s):** Insurance
**Circ:** (Non-paid)27,000

**PhotoPro (6694)**
Primedia
1419 Chaffee Dr., Ste. 1
Titusville, FL 32780-7315
Phone: (321)269-3212
Fax: (321)225-3149
**Subject(s):** Photography
**Circ:** (Non-paid)11,977
(Paid)26,919

**Civitan Magazine (67)**
Civitan International
PO Box 130744
Birmingham, AL 35213-0744
Phone: (205)591-8910
Fax: (205)592-6307
**Subject(s):** Clubs and Societies
**Circ:** ‡26,000

**Professional Photographer Storytellers (6911)**
Professional Photographers of America Inc.
229 Peachtree St. NE, Ste. 2200
Atlanta, GA 30303
Phone: (404)522-8600
Fax: (404)614-6405
**Subject(s):** Photography
**Circ:** (Paid)25,332

**IronWorks (23384)**
Hatton-Brown Publishers
c/o Marilyn Stemp, Managing Editor
PO Box 1696
Clemmons, NC 27012
**Subject(s):** Motorbikes and Motorcyles
**Circ:** (Non-paid)‡7,076
(Paid)‡25,160

**Printed Circuit Design & Manufacture (6910)**
UP Media Group Inc.
PCD&M 2018 Powers Ferry Rd., Ste. 600
Atlanta, GA
Phone: (678)589-8800
Fax: (678)589-8850
**Subject(s):** Electronics Engineering
**Circ:** (Paid)246
(Controlled)25,111

**Automundo Magazine (6220)**
AutoMundo Productions Inc.
2960 SW 8th St., 2nd Fl.
Miami, FL 33135
Phone: (305)541-4198
Fax: (305)541-5138
**Subject(s):** Spanish; Automotive (Consumer); Hispanic Publications
**Circ:** (Paid)25,000
(Non-paid)25,000

**Between the Lines (11921)**
National Softball Association
PO Box 7
Nicholasville, KY 40340
Phone: (859)887-4114
Fax: (606)887-4874
**Subject(s):** (Baseball)
**Circ:** 25,000

# Southern States

**Farmers Exchange (28600)**
Exchange
404 S Main St.
PO Box 490
Fayetteville, TN 37334
Phone: (931)433-9737
Fax: (931)433-0053
**Subject(s):** General Agriculture
**Circ:** (Free)25,000

**Florida Leader for High School Students (6022)**
Oxendine Publishing Inc.
412 NW 16th Ave.
Gainesville, FL 32601
Phone: (352)373-6907
Fax: (352)373-8120
**Subject(s):** Education
**Circ:** 100
(Paid)25,000

**Florida Leader Magazine (6023)**
Oxendine Publishing Inc.
412 NW 16th Ave.
Gainesville, FL 32601
Phone: (352)373-6907
Fax: (352)373-8120
**Subject(s):** College Publications; Youths' Interests; Career Development and Employment
**Circ:** (Controlled)‡25,000

**Key Magazine Nashville (28860)**
U.S. Hospitality Corp.
9 Music Square S. Ste. 224
Nashville, TN 37203
Phone: (615)354-9370
Fax: (615)397-3044
**Subject(s):** Travel and Tourism; Local, State, and Regional Publications
**Circ:** 25,000

**Living Blues (17036)**
Center for the Study of Southern Culture
The University of Mississippi
301 Hill Hall
PO Box 1848
University, MS 38677
Phone: (662)915-5993
Fax: (662)915-7842
**Subject(s):** Music and Musical Instruments; Black Publications
**Circ:** ‡25,000

**Mission Mosaic (89)**
Woman's Missionary Union
100 Missionary Ridge
PO Box 830010
Birmingham, AL 35283-0010
Phone: (205)991-8100
Fax: (205)995-4827
**Subject(s):** Women's Interests; Religious Publications
**Circ:** (Paid)25,000

**Monitoring Times (23261)**
Grove Enterprises Inc.
PO Box 98
Brasstown, NC 28902
Phone: (828)837-9200
Fax: (828)837-2216
**Subject(s):** Radio, Television, Cable, and Video; Crafts, Models, Hobbies, and Contests
**Circ:** 25,000

**North Florida FAMILIES Magazine (6098)**
FAMILIES Magazines Inc.
PO Box 16022
Jacksonville, FL 32245
Phone: (904)727-9290
Fax: (904)727-9652
**Subject(s):** Parenting
**Circ:** (Controlled)25,000

**SPUR MAGAZINE (6985)**
Morris Magazines
735 Broad St.
Augusta, GA 30903
Phone: (706)722-5833
Fax: (706)823-3641
**Subject(s):** Livestock; (Horses and Horse Racing)
**Circ:** 25,000

**This Week of Western North Carolina (23233)**
Mountain Meadows Publications
407 Creekside Dr.
Asheville, NC 28804
**Subject(s):** Travel and Tourism; Local, State, and Regional Publications
**Circ:** (Paid)25,000

**Adhesives Age (6825)**
Primedia Business Magzenes & Media
6151 Powers Ferry Rd., NW
Atlanta, GA 30339
Phone: (770)618-0349
Fax: (770)618-0349
**Subject(s):** Commerce and Industry
**Circ:** (Paid)1,727
(Controlled)24,962

**Artes Graficas (5888)**
B2B Portales
901 Ponce de Leon Blvd., Ste. 601
Coral Gables, FL 33134
Phone: (305)448-6875
Fax: (305)448-9942
**Subject(s):** International Business and Economics; Spanish; Hispanic Publications
**Circ:** 24,112

**The Mountain Spirit (11698)**
Christian Appalachian Project
PO Box 459
6550 U S 321 South
Hagerhill, KY 41222-0459
Phone: (606)789-9791
Fax: (606)789-4865
**Subject(s):** Religious Publications
**Circ:** (Paid)24,000

**Catheterization and Cardiovascular Diagnosis (6340)**
John Wiley and Sons Inc.
c/o Dr. Frank J. Hildner, Editor
Ocala, FL
**Subject(s):** Medicine and Surgery; Biology; Nursing
**Circ:** 23,800

**Bank Director (28494)**
Board Member Inc.
5110 Maryland Way
Ste. 250
Brentwood, TN 37027
Phone: (615)309-3200
Fax: (615)371-0899
**Subject(s):** Banking, Finance, and Investments
**Circ:** (Paid)8,200
(Non-paid)23,780

**Florida Mariner (6703)**
PO Box 1220
Venice, FL 34284
Phone: (941)488-9307
Fax: (941)488-9309
**Subject(s):** (Boating and Yachting); Local, State, and Regional Publications
**Circ:** (Paid)332
(Free)23,500

**Economic Review (6865)**
Federal Reserve Bank of Atlanta
1000 Peachtree St., NE
Atlanta, GA 30309-4470
Phone: (404)745-9068
Fax: (404)521-8050
**Subject(s):** Economics; Banking, Finance, and Investments
**Circ:** (Controlled)‡23,000

**Key Magazine Memphis (28771)**
Key Magazine Inc.
c/o John Rucker
PO Box 111266
Memphis, TN 38111-1266
Phone: (901)458-3912
Fax: (901)458-5723
**Subject(s):** Travel and Tourism; Entertainment; Local, State, and Regional Publications
**Circ:** (Combined)23,000

**Southern Beverage Journal (6260)**
14337 South West 119 Ave.
Miami, FL 33186
Phone: (305)233-7230
Fax: (305)252-2580
**Subject(s):** Beverages, Brewing, and Bottling
**Circ:** ‡23,000

**TechLINKS (6924)**
TechLinks Media Inc.
1055 Spring St.
Atlanta, GA 30309
Phone: (770)436-6789
**Subject(s):** Business; Computers; Automation; Local, State, and Regional Publications
**Circ:** ‡23,000

**Fishing Tackle Retailer (351)**
BASS/ESPN
5776 Carmichael Pkwy.
Montgomery, AL 36117
Phone: (334)272-9530
Fax: (334)279-7148
**Subject(s):** Sporting Goods/Retail Sports
**Circ:** (Controlled)‡22,884

**Davidson Journal (23393)**
Davidson College
Box 7171
431 North Main Street
Davidson, NC 28036-7171
Phone: (704)894-2240
Fax: (704)894-2499
**Subject(s):** College Publications
**Circ:** (Controlled)22,500

**The Peanut Grower (7456)**
Vance Publishing
PO Box 83, 128 1st St., Ste. 223
Tifton, GA 31793
Fax: (912)386-9772
**Subject(s):** General Agriculture
**Circ:** (Controlled)22,500

**Southeast Food Service News (7340)**
Southeast Publishing Company Inc.
5672 Peachtree Pky.
Norcross, GA 30092
Phone: (770)452-1807
Fax: (770)457-3829
**Subject(s):** Food and Grocery Trade
**Circ:** (Paid)‡2,076
(Controlled)‡22,414

**Atlanta Tribune: The Magazine (7377)**
L & L Communications Inc.
875 Old Roswell Rd., Ste. C-100
Roswell, GA 30076
Phone: (770)587-0501
Fax: (770)642-6501
**Subject(s):** Black Publications
**Circ:** (Non-paid)‡10,000
(Paid)‡22,000

**The Blood-Horse (11758)**
Blood Horse Publications
PO Box 911108
Lexington, KY 40591-1108
Phone: (859)278-2361
Fax: (859)276-4450
**Subject(s):** (Horses and Horse Racing)
**Circ:** (Paid)22,000

**Fastline—Bluegrass Truck Edition (11575)**
Fastline
4900 Fox Run Rd.
PO Box 248
Buckner, KY 40010
Phone: (502)222-0146
Fax: (502)222-0615
**Subject(s):** Trucks and Trucking; Local, State, and Regional Publications
**Circ:** (Combined)22,000

**Fastline—Dakota Farm Edition (11576)**
Fastline
4900 Fox Run Rd.
PO Box 248
Buckner, KY 40010
Phone: (502)222-0146
Fax: (502)222-0615
**Subject(s):** Farm Implements and Supplies; General Agriculture; Local, State, and Regional Publications
**Circ:** (Combined)22,000

**Fastline—Dixie Truck Edition (11577)**
Fastline
4900 Fox Run Rd.
PO Box 248
Buckner, KY 40010
Phone: (502)222-0146
Fax: (502)222-0615

**Subject(s):** Local, State, and Regional Publications; Trucks and Trucking
**Circ:** (Combined) 22,000
(Combined) 22,000

**Fastline—Far West Farm Edition (11578)**
Fastline
4900 Fox Run Rd.
PO Box 248
Buckner, KY 40010
Phone: (502) 222-0146
Fax: (502) 222-0615
**Subject(s):** Farm Implements and Supplies; General Agriculture; Local, State, and Regional Publications
**Circ:** (Combined) 22,000

**Fastline—Florida Truck Edition (11579)**
Fastline
4900 Fox Run Rd.
PO Box 248
Buckner, KY 40010
Phone: (502) 222-0146
Fax: (502) 222-0615
**Subject(s):** Trucks and Trucking; Local, State, and Regional Publications
**Circ:** (Combined) 22,000

**Fastline—Georgia Truck Edition (11580)**
Fastline
4900 Fox Run Rd.
PO Box 248
Buckner, KY 40010
Phone: (502) 222-0146
Fax: (502) 222-0615
**Subject(s):** Trucks and Trucking; Local, State, and Regional Publications
**Circ:** (Combined) 22,000

**Fastline—Illinois Farm Edition (11581)**
Fastline
4900 Fox Run Rd.
PO Box 248
Buckner, KY 40010
Phone: (502) 222-0146
Fax: (502) 222-0615
**Subject(s):** General Agriculture; Farm Implements and Supplies; Local, State, and Regional Publications
**Circ:** (Combined) 22,000

**Fastline—Indiana Farm Edition (11582)**
Fastline
4900 Fox Run Rd.
PO Box 248
Buckner, KY 40010
Phone: (502) 222-0146
Fax: (502) 222-0615
**Subject(s):** Farm Implements and Supplies; General Agriculture; Local, State, and Regional Publications
**Circ:** (Combined) 22,000

**Fastline—Iowa Farm Edition (11583)**
Fastline
4900 Fox Run Rd.
PO Box 248
Buckner, KY 40010
Phone: (502) 222-0146
Fax: (502) 222-0615
**Subject(s):** General Agriculture; Farm Implements and Supplies; Local, State, and Regional Publications
**Circ:** (Combined) 22,000

**Fastline—Kansas Farm Edition (11584)**
Fastline
4900 Fox Run Rd.
PO Box 248
Buckner, KY 40010
Phone: (502) 222-0146
Fax: (502) 222-0615
**Subject(s):** Farm Implements and Supplies; General Agriculture; Local, State, and Regional Publications
**Circ:** (Combined) 22,000

**Fastline—Kentucky Farm Edition (11585)**
Fastline
4900 Fox Run Rd.
PO Box 248
Buckner, KY 40010
Phone: (502) 222-0146
Fax: (502) 222-0615
**Subject(s):** General Agriculture; Farm Implements and Supplies; Local, State, and Regional Publications
**Circ:** (Combined) 22,000

**Fastline—Mid-Atlantic Farm Edition (11587)**
Fastline
4900 Fox Run Rd.
PO Box 248
Buckner, KY 40010
Phone: (502) 222-0146
Fax: (502) 222-0615
**Subject(s):** General Agriculture; Farm Implements and Supplies; Local, State, and Regional Publications
**Circ:** (Combined) 22,000

**Fastline—Mid-South Farm Edition (11588)**
Fastline
4900 Fox Run Rd.
PO Box 248
Buckner, KY 40010
Phone: (502) 222-0146
Fax: (502) 222-0615
**Subject(s):** Farm Implements and Supplies; General Agriculture; Local, State, and Regional Publications
**Circ:** (Combined) 22,000

**Fastline—Mid-West Truck Edition (11589)**
Fastline
4900 Fox Run Rd.
PO Box 248
Buckner, KY 40010
Phone: (502) 222-0146
Fax: (502) 222-0615
**Subject(s):** Trucks and Trucking; Local, State, and Regional Publications
**Circ:** (Combined) 22,000

**Fastline—Minnesota Farm Edition (11590)**
Fastline
4900 Fox Run Rd.
PO Box 248
Buckner, KY 40010
Phone: (502) 222-0146
Fax: (502) 222-0615
**Subject(s):** Farm Implements and Supplies; General Agriculture; Local, State, and Regional Publications
**Circ:** (Combined) 22,000

**Fastline Missouri Farm Edition (11591)**
Fastline
4900 Fox Run Rd.
PO Box 248
Buckner, KY 40010
Phone: (502) 222-0146
Fax: (502) 222-0615
**Subject(s):** Farm Implements and Supplies; General Agriculture; Local, State, and Regional Publications
**Circ:** (Combined) 22,000

**Fastline—Nebraska Farm Edition (11592)**
Fastline
4900 Fox Run Rd.
PO Box 248
Buckner, KY 40010
Phone: (502) 222-0146
Fax: (502) 222-0615
**Subject(s):** General Agriculture; Farm Implements and Supplies; Local, State, and Regional Publications
**Circ:** (Combined) 22,000

**Fastline—Northeast Farm Edition (11593)**
Fastline
4900 Fox Run Rd.
PO Box 248
Buckner, KY 40010
Phone: (502) 222-0146
Fax: (502) 222-0615
**Subject(s):** Farm Implements and Supplies; General Agriculture; Local, State, and Regional Publications
**Circ:** (Combined) 22,000

**Fastline—Northland Truck Edition (11594)**
Fastline
4900 Fox Run Rd.
PO Box 248
Buckner, KY 40010
Phone: (502) 222-0146
Fax: (502) 222-0615
**Subject(s):** Trucks and Trucking; Local, State, and Regional Publications
**Circ:** (Combined) 22,000

**Fastline—Northwest Farm Edition (11595)**
Fastline
4900 Fox Run Rd.
PO Box 248
Buckner, KY 40010
Phone: (502) 222-0146
Fax: (502) 222-0615
**Subject(s):** Local, State, and Regional Publications; Farm Implements and Supplies; General Agriculture
**Circ:** (Combined) 22,000

**Fastline Ohio Farm Edition (11596)**
Fastline
4900 Fox Run Rd.
PO Box 248
Buckner, KY 40010
Phone: (502) 222-0146
Fax: (502) 222-0615
**Subject(s):** General Agriculture; Farm Implements and Supplies; Local, State, and Regional Publications
**Circ:** (Combined) 22,000

**Fastline—Oklahoma Farm Edition (11597)**
Fastline
4900 Fox Run Rd.
PO Box 248
Buckner, KY 40010
Phone: (502) 222-0146
Fax: (502) 222-0615
**Subject(s):** General Agriculture; Farm Implements and Supplies; Local, State, and Regional Publications
**Circ:** (Combined) 22,000

**Fastline—Rocky Mountain Farm Edition (11598)**
Fastline
4900 Fox Run Rd.
PO Box 248
Buckner, KY 40010
Phone: (502) 222-0146
Fax: (502) 222-0615
**Subject(s):** Farm Implements and Supplies; General Agriculture; Local, State, and Regional Publications
**Circ:** (Combined) 22,000

**Fastline—South Central Truck Edition (11599)**
Fastline
4900 Fox Run Rd.
PO Box 248
Buckner, KY 40010
Phone: (502) 222-0146
Fax: (502) 222-0615
**Subject(s):** Local, State, and Regional Publications; Trucks and Trucking
**Circ:** (Combined) 22,000

**Fastline—Southeast Farm Edition (11600)**
Fastline
4900 Fox Run Rd.
PO Box 248
Buckner, KY 40010
Phone: (502) 222-0146
Fax: (502) 222-0615
**Subject(s):** General Agriculture; Farm Implements and Supplies; Local, State, and Regional Publications
**Circ:** (Combined) 22,000

**Fastline—Tennessee Farm Edition (11601)**
Fastline
4900 Fox Run Rd.
PO Box 248
Buckner, KY 40010
Phone: (502) 222-0146
Fax: (502) 222-0615
**Subject(s):** Farm Implements and Supplies; General Agriculture; Local, State, and Regional Publications
**Circ:** (Combined) 22,000

**Fastline—Tennessee Truck Edition (11602)**
Fastline
4900 Fox Run Rd.
PO Box 248
Buckner, KY 40010
Phone: (502) 222-0146
Fax: (502) 222-0615
**Subject(s):** Trucks and Trucking; Local, State, and Regional Publications
**Circ:** (Combined) 22,000

**Fastline—Texas Farm Edition (11603)**
Fastline
4900 Fox Run Rd.
PO Box 248
Buckner, KY 40010
Phone: (502) 222-0146
Fax: (502) 222-0615
**Subject(s):** General Agriculture; Farm Implements and Supplies; Local, State, and Regional Publications
**Circ:** (Combined) 22,000

**Fastline—Tri-State Truck Edition  (11604)**
Fastline
4900 Fox Run Rd.
PO Box 248
Buckner, KY 40010
Phone: (502)222-0146
Fax: (502)222-0615
**Subject(s):** Trucks and Trucking; Local, State, and Regional Publications

**Circ:** (Combined)22,000

**Fastline—Wisconsin Farm Edition  (11605)**
Fastline
4900 Fox Run Rd.
PO Box 248
Buckner, KY 40010
Phone: (502)222-0146
Fax: (502)222-0615
**Subject(s):** Farm Implements and Supplies; General Agriculture; Local, State, and Regional Publications

**Circ:** (Combined)22,000

**North Carolina Medical Journal  (23432)**
Woodcroft Professional Ctr.
5501 Fortunes Ridge Dr., Ste. E
Durham, NC 27713
Phone: (919)401-6599
Fax: (919)401-6899
**Subject(s):** Medicine and Surgery

**Circ:** ‡22,000

**Sbusiness  (5982)**
The Association for Services Management International
1342 Colonial Blvd., Ste. 25
Fort Myers, FL 33907
Phone: (239)275-7887
Fax: (239)275-0794
**Subject(s):** Service Industries

**Circ:** (Controlled)22,000

**Carolina Gardener  (23510)**
Carolina Gardener Inc.
PO Box 4504
Greensboro, NC 27404
**Subject(s):** Home and Garden

**Circ:** (Non-paid)‡5,300
       (Paid)‡21,625

**Power Equipment Trade  (361)**
Hatton-Brown Publishers
225 Hanrick St.
PO Box 2268
Montgomery, AL 36102
Phone: (334)834-1170
Fax: (334)834-4525
**Subject(s):** Machinery and Equipment

**Circ:** (Controlled)21,559

**Southern Medical Journal  (28660)**
Southern Medical Association
James H. Quillen College of Medicine
PO Box 70429
Johnson City, TN 37614-0429
Phone: (423)926-1171
Fax: (423)979-3438
**Subject(s):** Medicine and Surgery

**Circ:** ‡21,500

**Markee  (6354)**
HJK Publications Inc.
366 E. Graves Ave., Ste. D
Orange City, FL 32763
Phone: (386)774-8881
Fax: (386)774-8908
**Subject(s):** Radio, Television, Cable, and Video

**Circ:** (Non-paid)⊕21,367

**Nightclub & Bar Magazine  (16982)**
Oxford Publishing Inc.
307 W. Jackson Ave.
Oxford, MS 38655-2154
Phone: (601)236-5510
Fax: (601)236-5541
**Subject(s):** Hotels, Motels, Restaurants, and Clubs

**Circ:** (Paid)2,603
       (Non-paid)21,135

**Thoroughbred Times  (11779)**
Thoroughbred Times Company Inc.
PO Box 8237
Lexington, KY 40533
Phone: (859)260-9800
Fax: (859)260-9812
**Subject(s):** (Horses and Horse Racing)

**Circ:** (Paid)20,836

**Engineering and Mining Journal  (6091)**
Primedia Business Magzenes & Media
c/o Steve Fiscor, Editor-in-Chief
Regency Tower, Ste. 708
9550 Regency Sq. Blvd.
Jacksonville, FL 32225
Phone: (312)595-1080
Fax: (312)595-0296
**Subject(s):** Engineering (Various branches); Mining and Minerals

**Circ:** (Non-paid)‡20,589

**Timber Processing  (365)**
Hatton-Brown Publishers
225 Hanrick St.
PO Box 2268
Montgomery, AL 36102
Phone: (334)834-1170
Fax: (334)834-4525
**Subject(s):** Forestry

**Circ:** (Controlled)20,497

**Timber Harvesting  (364)**
Hatton-Brown Publishers
225 Hanrick St.
PO Box 2268
Montgomery, AL 36102
Phone: (334)834-1170
Fax: (334)834-4525
**Subject(s):** Forestry

**Circ:** (Controlled)20,409

**WATT Poultry USA  (170)**
Watt Publishing Co.
PO Box 950
Cullman, AL 35056
Phone: (256)734-6800
Fax: (256)739-6945
**Subject(s):** Poultry and Pigeons; Poultry Products and Supplies

**Circ:** (Combined)20,126

**Cancer Control  (6624)**
H. Lee Moffitt Cancer Center & Research Institute
12902 Magnolia Dr.
Tampa, FL 33612
Phone: (813)632-1349
Fax: (813)903-4950
**Subject(s):** Medicine and Surgery; Health and Healthcare

**Circ:** 20,023

**aakpRENALIFE  (6623)**
American Association of Kidney Patients
3505 E Frontage Rd., Ste. 315
Tampa, FL 33607-1796
Phone: (813)636-8100
Fax: (813)636-8122
**Subject(s):** Health

**Circ:** (Paid)20,000

**Air and Space Power Journal  (308)**
Cadre/ARJ
401 Chennault Cir.
Maxwell AFB, AL 36112-6428
Phone: (334)953-5322
Fax: (334)953-5811
**Subject(s):** Aviation; Military and Navy

**Circ:** (Paid)‡1,200
       (Controlled)‡20,000

**Draperies and Window Coverings  (6717)**
L.C. Clark Publishing
840 U.S. Highway 1, Ste. 330
West Palm Beach, FL 33406-3878
**Subject(s):** Home Furnishings, Curtains, Draperies

**Circ:** (Paid)5,265
       (Non-paid)20,006

**Florida Market Bulletin  (6579)**
Florida Department of Agriculture & Consumer Services
Mayo Bldg. M9
407 S. Calhoun St.
Tallahassee, FL 32399-0800
Phone: (850)488-4031
Fax: (850)922-2861
**Subject(s):** General Agriculture

**Circ:** (Controlled)‡20,000

**Leisure Scene  (11532)**
Tribune Courier
100 West 11th St.
PO Box 410
Benton, KY 42025
Phone: (270)527-3162
Fax: (270)527-4567
**Subject(s):** Travel and Tourism

**Circ:** (Free)‡20,000

**Today's Christian Doctor  (28498)**
Christian Medical & Dental Society
PO Box 7500
Bristol, TN 37621
Phone: (423)844-1000
Fax: (423)844-1005
**Subject(s):** Medicine and Surgery

**Circ:** (Paid)⊕20,000

**Apparel  (28036)**
Bill Communications Inc.—A VNU Co.
1500 Hampton St., Ste. 150
Columbia, SC 29201
Phone: (803)771-7500
Fax: (803)779-1461
**Subject(s):** Textiles

**Circ:** △19,650

**Memphis Magazine  (28774)**
Contemporary Media Inc.
460 Tennessee St.
Memphis, TN 38103
Phone: (901)521-9000
Fax: (901)521-0129
**Subject(s):** Local, State, and Regional Publications

**Circ:** (Paid)19,500

**Today's Grocer  (6555)**
Florida Grocer Publications Inc.
PO Box 430760
South Miami, FL 33243-0760
Phone: (305)661-0792
Fax: (305)661-6720
**Subject(s):** Spanish; Food and Grocery Trade

**Circ:** (Controlled)‡19,500

**Voice of the Tennessee Walking Horse  (28726)**
Tennessee Walking Horse Breeders and Exhibitors Association
250 N Ellington Pkwy.
Box 286
Lewisburg, TN 37091
Phone: (931)359-1567
Fax: (931)270-8743
**Subject(s):** (Horses and Horse Racing); Livestock

**Circ:** (Non-paid)‡176
       (Paid)‡19,500

**Florida CPA Today  (6575)**
Florida Institute of Certified Public Accountants Inc.
PO Box 5437
Tallahassee, FL 32314
Phone: (850)224-2727
Fax: (850)222-8190
**Subject(s):** Accountants and Accounting

**Circ:** (Controlled)19,400

**UAH (The University of Alabama in Huntsville) Magazine  (272)**
The University of Alabama in Huntsville
118 Alumni House
Huntsville, AL 35899
Phone: (256)824-6120
**Subject(s):** College Publications

**Circ:** ‡19,000

**Welcome to Greater Louisville  (11847)**
Editorial Services Co.
812 S 3rd St.
Louisville, KY 40203
Phone: (502)584-2720
Fax: (502)584-2722
**Subject(s):** Travel and Tourism

**Circ:** (Controlled)19,000

**Paper Industry  (360)**
PO Box 5675
Montgomery, AL 36103-5675
**Subject(s):** Paper

**Circ:** (Controlled)18,880

**Office Dealer  (23655)**
OfficeVision, Inc.
252 N. Main St., Ste. 200
Mt. Airy, NC 27030
Phone: (336)783-0000
**Subject(s):** Stationery, Office Equipment, and College Store Supplies

**Circ:** (Controlled)‡18,500

**Buenhogar** (6222)
Editorial Televisa
6355 NW 36th St.
Miami, FL 33166-7099
Phone: (305)871-6400
Fax: (305)871-4939
**Subject(s):** Spanish; Home and Garden; Hispanic Publications; Women's Interests
**Circ:** ‡18,449

**Centrepiece** (11639)
Centre College
600 W Walnut St.
Danville, KY 40422
Phone: (859)238-5717
Fax: (859)238-5723
**Subject(s):** College Publications
**Circ:** ‡18,000

**Clark Atlanta University Magazine** (6855)
Atlanta University
223 James P. Brawley Dr. SW
Atlanta, GA 30314
Phone: (404)880-8903
**Subject(s):** College Publications
**Circ:** (Controlled)18,000

**Louisville** (11829)
Louisville Magazine Inc.
137 W. Muhammad Ali Blvd.
Louisville, KY 40202
Phone: (502)625-0100
Fax: (502)625-0109
**Subject(s):** Lifestyle
**Circ:** (Paid)18,000

**Mid-South Hunting & Fishing News** (28503)
PO Box 198
42 South Washington Ave
Brownsville, TN 38012
Phone: (731)772-9962
Fax: (731)772-9763
**Subject(s):** (Hunting, Fishing, and Game Management)
**Circ:** (Paid)‡18,000

**Sporting Goods Dealer** (7381)
Bill Communications Inc.
1115 Northmeadow Pkwy.
Roswell, GA 30076
Phone: (770)569-5105
Fax: (770)569-5105
**Subject(s):** Sporting Goods/Retail Sports
**Circ:** (Controlled)‡18,000

**State Government News** (11778)
Council of State Governments
2760 Research Park Dr.
PO Box 11910
Lexington, KY 40578-1910
Phone: (859)244-8000
Fax: (859)244-8001
**Subject(s):** State, Municipal, and County Administration
**Circ:** (Paid)669
(Non-paid)18,000

**Modern Paint and Coatings** (6902)
Argus Business
6151 Powers Ferry Rd.
Atlanta, GA 30339-2941
Phone: (770)955-2500
Fax: (770)618-0348
**Subject(s):** Paint and Wallcoverings
**Circ:** (Paid)397
(Non-paid)17,636

**Pharmaceutical Engineering** (6648)
International Society for Pharmaceutical Engineering Inc.
3109 W Dr. Martin Luther King Jr. Blvd., Ste. 250
Tampa, FL 33607-6260
Phone: (813)960-2105
Fax: (813)264-2816
**Subject(s):** Engineering (Various branches); Drugs and Pharmaceuticals
**Circ:** (Paid)17,500

**Equinews** (12013)
Kentucky Equine Research, Inc.
3910 Delaney Ferry Rd.
Versailles, KY V1T 6Y5
Phone: (859)873-1988
**Subject(s):** (Horses and Horse Racing); Livestock
**Circ:** (Non-paid)‡800
(Paid)‡17,492

**Tampa Bay Magazine** (5878)
Tampa Bay Publications Inc.
2531 Landmark Dr., Ste. 101
Clearwater, FL 33761
Phone: (727)791-4800
Fax: (727)796-0527
**Subject(s):** Local, State, and Regional Publications; Lifestyle
**Circ:** (Controlled)‡15,200
(Paid)‡17,371

**Tallahassee Magazine** (6604)
Rowland Publishing Inc.
PO Box 1837
Tallahassee, FL 32302
Phone: (850)878-0554
Fax: (850)656-1871
**Subject(s):** Lifestyle; Local, State, and Regional Publications
**Circ:** (Controlled)17,300

**The Alabama Cattleman** (341)
Alabama Cattleman's Association
201 S Bainbridge St.
PO Box 2499
Montgomery, AL 36102-2499
Phone: (334)265-1867
Fax: (334)834-5326
**Subject(s):** Livestock
**Circ:** 17,000

**IIE Solutions** (7334)
Institute of Industrial Engineers
3577 Pkwy. Ln., Ste. 200
Norcross, GA 30092
Phone: (770)449-0460
Fax: (770)441-3295
**Subject(s):** Commerce and Industry; Engineering (Various branches)
**Circ:** (Paid)17,000

**Sandlapper** (28166)
Sandlapper Society Inc.
PO Box 1108
Lexington, SC 29071
Phone: (803)359-9954
Fax: (803)359-0629
**Subject(s):** Lifestyle; Local, State, and Regional Publications
**Circ:** 17,000

**The Catholic Week** (309)
356 Government St.
PO Box 349
Mobile, AL 36601
Phone: (251)432-3529
Fax: (251)434-1547
**Subject(s):** Religious Publications
**Circ:** (Non-paid)400
(Paid)16,797

**Boca Raton Magazine** (5816)
JES Publishing Corp.
6413 Congress Ave., Ste. 100
P O Box 820
Boca Raton, FL 33487-0820
Phone: (561)997-8683
Fax: (561)997-8909
**Subject(s):** Local, State, and Regional Publications; Lifestyle
**Circ:** (Non-paid)‡3,993
(Paid)‡16,331

**North Carolina** (23706)
North Carolina Citizens for Business and Industry
225 Hillsborough St., Ste. 460
Raleigh, NC 27603
**Subject(s):** Local, State, and Regional Publications
**Circ:** ‡16,200

**Southern Building** (104)
Southern Building Code Congress International Inc.
900 Montclair Rd.
Birmingham, AL 35213-1206
Phone: (205)591-1853
Fax: (205)599-9891
**Subject(s):** Construction, Contracting, Building, and Excavating
**Circ:** ‡16,200

**Better Crops with Plant Food** (7327)
Potash Phosphate Institute
655 Engineering Dr., Ste. 110
Norcross, GA 30092-2837
Phone: (770)447-0335
Fax: (770)448-0439
**Subject(s):** General Agriculture
**Circ:** (Paid)‡50
(Non-paid)‡16,000

**Home Market Magazine** (16980)
DeSoto County Tribune
8885 Goodman
PO Box 1486
Olive Branch, MS 38654
Phone: (662)895-6220
Fax: (662)895-4377
**Subject(s):** Real Estate
**Circ:** (Free)‡16,000

**Silicon Valley/San Jose Business Journal** (23353)
American City Business Journals Inc.
120 W Morehead St., Ste. 200
Charlotte, NC 28202
Phone: (704)973-1000
Fax: (704)973-1001
**Subject(s):** Business
**Circ:** (Paid)16,000

**Welcome to Miami and the Beaches** (6338)
Welcome Publishing Company Inc.
1751 NE 162nd St.
Box 630-518
North Miami Beach, FL 33162-4757
Phone: (305)944-9444
**Subject(s):** Travel and Tourism
**Circ:** (Non-paid)△16,000

**Workforce Professional** (11680)
International Association of Personnel in Employment Security
1801 Louisville Rd.
Frankfort, KY 40601
Phone: (502)223-4459
Fax: (502)223-4127
**Subject(s):** Business; Management and Administration
**Circ:** (Paid)‡16,000

**Gastroenterology** (23300)
Elsevier
c/o D. A. Brenner
Univ. of North Carolina at Chapel Hill
Chapel Hill, NC
**Subject(s):** Medicine and Surgery
**Circ:** 15,851

**Alamance Magazine** (23267)
PO Box 517
Burlington, NC 27216
Phone: (336)226-8436
Fax: (336)226-8437
**Subject(s):** General Editorial
**Circ:** (Combined)‡15,200

**Tecnologia del Plastico** (5895)
B2B Portales
901 Ponce de Leon Blvd., Ste. 601
Coral Gables, FL 33134
Phone: (305)448-6875
Fax: (305)448-9942
**Subject(s):** Plastic and Composition Materials
**Circ:** (Controlled)15,109

**Actuarial Digest** (6462)
PO Box 1127
Ponte Vedra Beach, FL 32004
Phone: (904)273-1245
**Subject(s):** Insurance
**Circ:** (Controlled)15,000

**Agnes Scott Alumnae Magazine** (7110)
Agnes Scott College
141 E. College Ave.
Decatur, GA 30030
Phone: (404)471-6000
Fax: (404)471-6298
**Subject(s):** College Publications
**Circ:** (Non-paid)15,000

**Alabama Heritage** (457)
University of Alabama
Box 870342
Tuscaloosa, AL 35487-0342
Phone: (205)348-7467
Fax: (205)348-7473
**Subject(s):** History and Genealogy; Local, State, and Regional Publications
**Circ:** ‡15,000

**Business Life Magazine** (23509)
DBA bizlife Magazine
4101A Piedmont Pkwy.
Greensboro, NC 27410-8110
Phone: (336)812-8801
Fax: (336)812-8832

Circulation: ★ = ABC; △ = BPA; ♦ = CAC; • = CCAB; ▫ = VAC; ⊖ = PO Statement; ‡ = Publisher's Report; Boldface figures = sworn; Light figures = estimated.

# Southern States

**Subject(s):** Business
**Circ:** (Combined)‡15,000

**Das Fenster Nach Druben** (6797)
Die Hausfrau Inc.
103 E Meadow Dr.
Athens, GA 30605
Phone: (706)548-4382
Fax: (706)548-8856
**Subject(s):** Ethnic Publications; German
**Circ:** (Free)‡100
(Paid)‡15,000

**Design Cost Data** (6627)
DC & D Technologies Inc.
8602 N. 40th St.
Tampa, FL 33604
Phone: (813)989-9300
Fax: (813)980-3982
**Subject(s):** Architecture; Construction, Contracting, Building, and Excavating
**Circ:** (Controlled)‡15,000
(Controlled)‡15,000

**Hinge Music Magazine** (6367)
The Performing Artist
5005 City St., No. 1326
Orlando, FL 32839
**Subject(s):** Music and Musical Instruments
**Circ:** (Non-paid)15,000

**Key Magazine Atlanta** (6897)
Key Magazine Inc.
Key Atlanta
550 Pharr Rd., Ste. 600
Atlanta, GA 30305
Phone: (404)233-2299
Fax: (770)932-8017
**Subject(s):** Travel and Tourism; Entertainment; Local, State, and Regional Publications
**Circ:** (Combined)15,000

**Parenting for High Potential** (6533)
National Association for Gifted Children
4921 Ringwood Meadow
Sarasota, FL 34235
Phone: (941)342-9928
Fax: (941)342-0064
**Subject(s):** Parenting
**Circ:** (Combined)15,000

**The Pilot Log** (7250)
Pilot International
PO Box 4844
Macon, GA 31208-4844
Phone: (478)743-7403
Fax: (478)743-2173
**Subject(s):** Unclassified Fraternal
**Circ:** (Controlled)‡15,000

**Shuttle Spindle & Dyepot** (7437)
Handweavers Guild of America Inc.
1255 Buford Highway, Ste. 211
Suwanee, GA 30024
Phone: (678)730-0010
Fax: (678)730-0836
**Subject(s):** Crafts, Models, Hobbies, and Contests
**Circ:** 15,000

**Tennessee Conservationist** (28885)
Tennessee Department of Environment & Conservation
401 Church St.
L & C Annex, 8th Fl.
Nashville, TN 37243-0440
Phone: (615)532-0060
Fax: (615)532-8007
**Subject(s):** Environmental and Natural Resources Conservation
**Circ:** (Paid)15,000

**TennisPro** (28145)
Professional Tennis Registry
PO Box 4739
Hilton Head Island, SC 29938
Phone: (843)785-7244
Fax: (843)686-2033
**Subject(s):** Physical Education and Athletics
**Circ:** (Combined)15,000

**Up & Coming Weekly** (23473)
F & B Publications Inc.
208 Rowan St.
PO Box 53461
Fayetteville, NC 28305
Phone: (910)484-6200
Fax: (910)484-9218
**Subject(s):** Free Newspapers; Entertainment; Lifestyle; Local, State, and Regional Publications
**Circ:** (Non-paid)15,000

**Weighing & Measurement** (28631)
WAM Publishing Co.
PO Box 2247
Hendersonville, TN 37077
Phone: (615)824-6920
Fax: (615)824-7092
**Subject(s):** Weights and Measures
**Circ:** ‡15,000

**Mecanica Popular** (6249)
Editorial Televisa
6355 NW 36th St.
Miami, FL 33166-7099
Phone: (305)871-6400
Fax: (305)871-4939
**Subject(s):** Spanish; Crafts, Models, Hobbies, and Contests; Hispanic Publications; Automotive (Trade)
**Circ:** ‡14,977

**Jacksonville Magazine** (6096)
White Publishing Co.
534 Lancaster St.
Jacksonville, FL 32204-4113
Phone: (904)358-8330
Fax: (904)358-8668
**Subject(s):** Lifestyle; Local, State, and Regional Publications
**Circ:** (Free)6,613
(Paid)14,535

**Home Furnishings Retailer** (23588)
3910 Tinsely Dr. Ste. 101
High Point, NC 27265
Phone: (336)886-6100
Fax: (336)801-6102
**Subject(s):** Furniture and Furnishings
**Circ:** (Non-paid)14,500

**The Talon** (16850)
The University of Southern Mississippi Alumni Association
118 College Dr., No. 5013
Hattiesburg, MS 39406-0001
Phone: (601)266-5013
Fax: (601)266-4214
**Subject(s):** College Publications
**Circ:** ‡14,500

**OR/MS Today** (7286)
Lionheart Publishing Inc.
506 Roswell St., Ste. 220
Marietta, GA 30060-4101
Phone: (770)431-0867
Fax: (770)432-6969
**Subject(s):** Computers; Management and Administration; Automation
**Circ:** (Combined)14,268

**Business in Broward** (5954)
PO Box 460669
Fort Lauderdale, FL 33346-0699
**Subject(s):** Business; Local, State, and Regional Publications
**Circ:** (Controlled)‡5,800
(Paid)‡14,200

**Journal of Dental Technology** (6588)
National Association of Dental Laboratories
325 John Knox Blvd., Ste. L103
Tallahassee, FL 32303
Phone: (850)205-5626
Fax: (850)222-0053
**Subject(s):** Dentistry; Laboratory Research (Scientific and Medical)
**Circ:** ‡14,200

**Skydiving** (5934)
1725 N Lexington Ave.
DeLand, FL 32724
Phone: (386)736-4793
Fax: (386)736-9786
**Subject(s):** (General Sports)
**Circ:** ‡14,200

**Air Force Journal of Logistics** (339)
U.S. Air Force Logistics Management Agency
501 Ward St.
Gunter Annex
Montgomery, AL 36114
Phone: (334)953-0887
**Subject(s):** Military and Navy
**Circ:** 14,000

**Asphalt** (11756)
Asphalt Institute
2696 Research Park Dr.
Lexington, KY 40511
Phone: (859)288-4960
Fax: (859)288-4999
**Subject(s):** Roads and Streets; Construction, Contracting, Building, and Excavating; Building Materials, Concrete, Brick, and Tile
**Circ:** 14,000

**Presbyterian College Magazine** (28032)
Presbyterian College
503 S. Broad St.
Clinton, SC 29325
Phone: (864)833-8281
Fax: (864)833-2820
**Subject(s):** College Publications; Education
**Circ:** (Non-paid)14,000

**Public Safety Communications** (5920)
APCO International Inc.
351 N. Williamson Blvd.
Daytona Beach, FL 32114-1112
Phone: (386)322-2500
Fax: (386)322-2501
**Subject(s):** Safety; Communications
**Circ:** (Controlled)‡135
(Paid)‡14,000

**City & Country Club Life** (6292)
Club Publications
665 La Villa Dr.
Miami Springs, FL 33166-6029
Phone: (305)887-1701
Fax: (305)885-1923
**Subject(s):** Clubs and Societies
**Circ:** (Paid)793
(Non-paid)13,903

**Flagpole Magazine** (6798)
112 S Foundry St.
Athens, GA 30601
Phone: (706)549-9523
Fax: (706)548-8981
**Subject(s):** Alternative and Underground; Entertainment; Lifestyle
**Circ:** (Combined)13,803

**Linking Ring** (23428)
International Brotherhood of Magicians
5 Ontario Ct.
Durham, NC 27713-8822
Phone: (919)572-9811
Fax: (919)572-9812
**Subject(s):** Clubs and Societies; Entertainment
**Circ:** (Controlled)13,800

**Dealer Communicator** (6205)
Fichera Publications
441 S. State Rd.7, Ste. 14
Margate, FL 33068
Phone: (954)971-4360
Fax: (954)971-4362
**Subject(s):** Printing and Typography
**Circ:** (Controlled)‡13,633

**SignCraft** (5983)
Signcraft Publishing Company Inc.
PO Box 60031
Fort Myers, FL 33906
Phone: (239)939-4644
Fax: (239)939-0607
**Subject(s):** Advertising and Marketing; Printing and Typography
**Circ:** (Paid)13,476

**Southern Loggin' Times** (363)
Hatton-Brown Publishers
225 Hanrick St.
PO Box 2268
Montgomery, AL 36102
Phone: (334)834-1170
Fax: (334)834-4525
**Subject(s):** Forestry
**Circ:** (Controlled)13,416

**Florida Grower** (6745)
Meister Publishing Co.
1555 Howell Branch Rd., No. C-204
Winter Park, FL 32789
Phone: (407)539-6552
Fax: (407)539-6544
**Subject(s):** General Agriculture
**Circ:** (Controlled)13,396

**Kentucky Bench & Bar Magazine** (11671)
Kentucky Bar Association
514 W Main St.
Frankfort, KY 40601-1883
Phone: (502)564-3795
Fax: (502)564-3225
**Subject(s):** Law
**Circ:** ‡13,322

**Maddux Business Report** (6504)
Maddux Publishing L.C.
PO Box 202
Saint Petersburg, FL 33731
Phone: (727)823-4394
Fax: (727)821-1645
**Subject(s):** Real Estate; Advertising and Marketing; Building Management and Maintenance; Commerce and Industry; Business
**Circ:** (Paid)1,040
(Controlled)13,180

**Ornamental Outlook** (6749)
Meister Publishing Co.
1555 Howell Branch Rd., No. C-204
Winter Park, FL 32789
**Subject(s):** Horticulture; Seed and Nursery Trade
**Circ:** 13,175

**Harper's Bazaar en Espanol** (6236)
Editorial Televisa
6355 NW 36th St.
Miami, FL 33166-7099
Phone: (305)871-6400
Fax: (305)871-4939
**Subject(s):** Hispanic Publications; Women's Interests; Spanish; General Editorial
**Circ:** ‡13,108

**American Journal of Pharmaceutical Education** (6966)
American Association of Colleges of Pharmacy
Clinical Pharmacy Programs
Medical College of Georgia
CJ-1020
Augusta, GA 30912-2452
Phone: (706)721-4450
**Subject(s):** Drugs and Pharmaceuticals
**Circ:** (Paid)‡3,000
(Non-paid)‡13,000

**Farm and Ranch News** (6183)
Farm & Ranch News
PO Box 160
Lithia, FL 33547-0160
Phone: (813)737-6197
**Subject(s):** General Agriculture
**Circ:** (Paid)6,000
(Controlled)13,000

**Fencepost Magazine** (7417)
Dempsey Management Services
2336 Wisteria Dr., Ste. 230
Snellville, GA 30078
Phone: (678)344-6283
Fax: (678)344-6299
**Subject(s):** Building Management and Maintenance
**Circ:** (Non-paid)⊕13,000

**Greenprints** (23467)
PO Box 1355
23 Butterow Cove Rd.
Fairview, NC 28730
Phone: (828)628-1902
Fax: (828)628-1902
**Subject(s):** Home and Garden
**Circ:** (Non-paid)2,000
(Paid)13,000

**Link** (6312)
Distributor's Link Inc.
4297 Corporate Sq. N
Naples, FL 34104
Phone: (239)643-2713
Fax: (239)643-5220
**Subject(s):** Hardware
**Circ:** (Paid)13,000

**The Mississippi Educator** (16885)
Mississippi Association of Educators
775 N State St.
Jackson, MS 39202
Phone: (601)354-4463
Fax: (601)352-7054
**Subject(s):** Education
**Circ:** ‡13,000

**Mississippi United Methodist Advocate** (16894)
Mississippi Conference of the United Methodist Church
321 Mississippi St.
PO Box 1093
Jackson, MS 39201-1002
Phone: (601)354-0515
Fax: (601)948-5982
**Subject(s):** Religious Publications
**Circ:** 13,000

**Physician Executive** (6649)
American College of Physician Executives
4890 W Kennedy Blvd., Ste. 200
Tampa, FL 33609
Phone: (813)287-2000
Fax: (813)287-8993
**Subject(s):** Hospitals and Healthcare Institutions
**Circ:** (Paid)‡300
(Controlled)‡13,000

**Sarasota Magazine** (6536)
Gulfshore Media, Inc.
330 S. Pineapple Ave.
Sarasota, FL 34236
Phone: (941)366-8225
Fax: (941)365-7272
**Subject(s):** Business; Chambers of Commerce and Boards of Trade; Local, State, and Regional Publications
**Circ:** (Combined)‡13,000

**Textiles Panamericanos** (28116)
Billian/Transworld Publishing Inc.
555 N. Pleasantbury Dr., Ste. 132
Greenville, SC 29607
Phone: (864)233-6426
Fax: (864)233-6426
**Subject(s):** Textiles; Spanish; Hispanic Publications
**Circ:** (Controlled)13,000

**The Lane Report** (11772)
Lane Communications Group
201 E. Main St. 14th Fl.
Lexington, KY 40507
Phone: (859)244-3522
Fax: (859)244-3555
**Subject(s):** Business
**Circ:** (Paid)157
(Non-paid)12,763

**Hombre Internacional** (6239)
Editorial Televisa
6355 NW 36th St.
Miami, FL 33166-7099
Phone: (305)871-6400
Fax: (305)871-4939
**Subject(s):** Spanish; Hispanic Publications; Men's Interests; Business
**Circ:** ‡12,749

**Mid-South Horse Review** (16795)
Color Printing
PO Box 5091
Columbus, MS 39704-5091
**Subject(s):** Local, State, and Regional Publications; Pets; (Horses and Horse Racing)
**Circ:** (Free)12,500

**Panel World** (359)
Hatton-Brown Publishers
225 Hanrick St.
PO Box 2268
Montgomery, AL 36102
Phone: (334)834-1170
Fax: (334)834-4525
**Subject(s):** Wood and Woodworking
**Circ:** (Controlled)‡12,192

**Southern PHC Magazine** (23531)
Southern Trade Publications Inc.
Box 7344
Greensboro, NC 27417
Phone: (336)454-3516
Fax: (336)454-3649
**Subject(s):** Air Conditioning and Refrigeration; Plumbing and Heating
**Circ:** (Non-paid)‡12,093

**Citrus and Vegetable Magazine** (6625)
Vance Publishing Corp.
16057 Tampa Palms Blvd. W. No. 416
Tampa, FL 33647-2001
Phone: (813)975-8377
Fax: (813)975-1772
**Subject(s):** Horticulture; Socialized Farming; Fruit, Fruit Products, and Produce Trade
**Circ:** (Controlled)△12,000

**College and Research Libraries** (6792)
Association of College and Research Libraries
50 E. Huron St.
Chicago, IL 60611-2795
Phone: (312)280-2523
Fax: (312)280-2520
**Subject(s):** Library and Information Science
**Circ:** ‡12,000

**Financial Management** (6629)
Financial Management Association International
University of South Florida
College of Business Administration
4202 East Fowler Avenue, BSN 3331
Tampa, FL 33620-5500
Phone: (813)974-2084
Fax: (813)974-3318
**Subject(s):** Banking, Finance, and Investments
**Circ:** ‡12,000

**Gulfshore Life Magazine** (6310)
Gulfshore Media Inc.
9051 Tamiami Trl. N, Ste. 202
Naples, FL 34108-2520
Phone: (239)594-9980
Fax: (239)594-9986
**Subject(s):** Lifestyle; Local, State, and Regional Publications
**Circ:** (Paid)‡12,000
(Non-paid)‡12,000

**Impact** (6368)
Loudmouth Productions Inc.
PMB 361
10151 University Blvd.
Orlando, FL 32817
Phone: (407)263-5504
**Subject(s):** Alternative and Underground; Social and Political Issues
**Circ:** (Non-paid)12,000

**American Shipper** (6089)
PO Box 4728
Jacksonville, FL 32201-4728
Phone: (904)355-2601
Fax: (904)791-8836
**Subject(s):** Transportation, Traffic, and Shipping
**Circ:** (Paid)1,732
(Controlled)‡11,865

**BIOS** (219)
Beta Beta Beta
UNA Box 5079
Florence, AL 35632-0001
Phone: (256)765-6220
Fax: (256)765-6221
**Subject(s):** Clubs and Societies; Biology
**Circ:** 11,500

**Tu Internacional** (6262)
Editorial Televisa
6355 NW 36th St.
Miami, FL 33166-7099
Phone: (305)871-6400
Fax: (305)871-4939
**Subject(s):** Hispanic Publications; Spanish; Women's Interests; Fashion
**Circ:** ‡11,452

**California Builder & Engineer** (7328)
California Builder & Engineer Inc.
30 Technology Prky. S
Norcross, GA 30092
Fax: (800)930-3003
**Subject(s):** Construction, Contracting, Building, and Excavating; Engineering (Various branches)
**Circ:** (Controlled)‡11,281

**Back Home in Kentucky** (28604)
Greysmith Publishing
PO Box 681629
Franklin, TN 37068-1629
Fax: (615)790-6188
**Subject(s):** Local, State, and Regional Publications
**Circ:** ‡11,000

**Casual Living** (23585)
Reed Business Information
PO Box 2754
High Point, NC 27261-2754
Phone: (336)605-0121
Fax: (336)605-3801

**Subject(s):** Furniture and Furnishings
**Circ:** 11,000

**Florida Specifier (6746)**
National Technical Communications Company Inc.
PO Box 2027
Winter Park, FL 32790-2027
Phone: (407)671-7777
Fax: (407)671-7795
**Subject(s):** Waste Management and Recycling; Water Supply and Sewage Disposal; Ecology and Conservation
**Circ:** (Paid)‡1,000
(Controlled)‡11,000

**Information Management Journal (28679)**
Association of Record Managers and Administrators
University of Tennessee-Knoxville
804 Volunteer Blvd.
Knoxville, TN 37996-4330
Phone: (423)974-6509
Fax: (423)974-4967
**Subject(s):** Management and Administration; Computers
**Circ:** 11,000

**Southern Lumberman (28609)**
Hatton-Brown Publishers
PO Box 681629
Franklin, TN 37068
Phone: (615)791-1961
Fax: (615)591-1035
**Subject(s):** Forestry
**Circ:** (Paid)‡4,000
(Controlled)‡11,000

**The Stockman Grass Farmer (17005)**
Mississippi Valley Publishing Corp.
234 W. School St.
Ridgeland, MS 39157
Phone: (601)485-5599
Fax: (601)485-5599
**Subject(s):** General Agriculture; Livestock
**Circ:** (Paid)10,961

**Business Journal - Serving Metropolitan Kansas City (23333)**
American City Business Journals Inc.
120 W Morehead St., Ste. 200
Charlotte, NC 28202
Phone: (704)973-1000
Fax: (704)973-1001
**Subject(s):** Business; Local, State, and Regional Publications
**Circ:** (Paid)10,941

**Rice Journal (23713)**
Specialized Agricultural Publications Inc.
5808 Faringdon Pl., Ste. 200
Raleigh, NC 27609-3930
Phone: (919)872-5040
Fax: (919)876-6531
**Subject(s):** Socialized Farming; Feed and Grain
**Circ:** (Paid)‡177
(Controlled)‡10,876

**Ideas para Su Hogar (Ideas for Your Home) (6240)**
Editorial Televisa
6355 NW 36th St.
Miami, FL 33166-7099
Phone: (305)871-6400
Fax: (305)871-4939
**Subject(s):** Hispanic Publications; Home and Garden; Spanish; Women's Interests
**Circ:** ‡10,848

**Poultry Times (7164)**
Poultry & Egg News Inc.
PO Box 1338
345 Green Street, NW
Gainesville, GA 30501
Phone: (770)536-2476
Fax: (770)532-4894
**Subject(s):** Poultry and Pigeons; Poultry Products and Supplies
**Circ:** (Paid)10,661

**Christian Retailing (6419)**
Strang Communications
P.O. Box 420234
Palm Coast, FL 32142-0234
**Subject(s):** Selling and Salesmanship; Religious Publications
**Circ:** (Controlled)‡10,500

**Forest Landowner (6874)**
Forest Landowners Association
PO Box 450209
Atlanta, GA 31145-0209
Phone: (404)325-2954
Fax: (404)325-2955
**Subject(s):** Forestry
**Circ:** 10,500

**South Carolina Lawyer (28062)**
South Carolina Bar
950 Taylor St.
Columbia, SC 29202
Phone: (803)799-6653
Fax: (803)799-4118
**Subject(s):** Law
**Circ:** (Controlled)10,500

**Infantry (7153)**
U.S. Army Infantry School
PO Box 52005
Fort Benning, GA 31995
Phone: (706)545-2350
Fax: (706)545-4531
**Subject(s):** Military and Navy
**Circ:** (Paid)‡3,700
(Controlled)‡10,360

**MAFES Research Highlights (16957)**
Mississippi Agricultural and Forestry Experiment Station
Box 9625
Mississippi State, MS 39762-9625
Phone: (601)325-1716
Fax: (601)325-1710
**Subject(s):** Scientific Agricultural Publications
**Circ:** (Non-paid)10,300

**Special Warfare (23487)**
John F. Kennedy Special Warfare Center and School
Attn: AOJK-DT-DM
Fort Bragg, NC 28310
Phone: (910)432-5703
Fax: (910)432-3147
**Subject(s):** Military and Navy
**Circ:** (Combined)10,200

**Journal of Oral and Maxillofacial Surgery (11767)**
Elsevier
C/o Dr Leon A. Assael, Editor-in-Chief
Univ. of Kentucky
Office of the Dean, College of Dentistry
800 Rose St.
Lexington, KY 40536-0297
**Subject(s):** Dentistry; Medicine and Surgery
**Circ:** ‡10,037

**ACM Transactions on Networking (TON) (6823)**
Association for Computing Machinery
c/o Simon Lam
College of Computing
Georgia Institute of Technology
Atlanta, GA 30332-0280
Phone: (404)894-6711
Fax: (404)385-0332
**Subject(s):** Computers; Automation
**Circ:** 10000

**Arthritis and Rheumatism (23403)**
John Wiley and Sons Inc.
Box 3806
Durham, NC 27710
Phone: (919)668-0499
Fax: (919)668-0499
**Subject(s):** Medicine and Surgery
**Circ:** ‡10,000

**BioWorld Magazine (6845)**
American Health Consultants Inc.
PO Box 740056
Atlanta, GA 30374
Phone: (404)262-7436
Fax: (404)262-7837
**Subject(s):** Science (General); Biology
**Circ:** (Controlled)‡10,000

**Business Alabama Monthly (65)**
PMT Publishing Company Inc.
529 Beacon Pkwy. W, Ste. 110
Birmingham, AL 35209
Phone: (205)941-1425
**Subject(s):** Business; Local, State, and Regional Publications
**Circ:** (Controlled)8,000
(Paid)10,000

**Marion Military Institute Alumni Bulletin (306)**
Marion Military Institute
PO Box 420
Marion, AL 36756
Phone: (334)683-2347
Fax: (334)683-2380
**Subject(s):** Military and Navy; College Publications
**Circ:** (Controlled)‡10,000

**National Knife Magazine (28521)**
National Knife Collectors Association
PO Box 21070
Chattanooga, TN 37421
Phone: (423)875-6009
Fax: (423)875-6039
**Subject(s):** Crafts, Models, Hobbies, and Contests
**Circ:** (Non-paid)‡350
(Paid)‡10,000

**The Physics Teacher (23252)**
American Association of Physics Teachers
Dept. of Physics & Astronomy
Appalachian State University
Boone, NC 28608-2142
Phone: (828)262-7497
Fax: (828)262-7329
**Subject(s):** Education; Physics
**Circ:** 10,000

**South Carolina United Methodist Advocate (28064)**
The Board of Trustees of the S.C. United Methodist Advocate
4908 Colonial Dr., Ste. 207
Columbia, SC 29203-6070
Phone: (803)786-9486
Fax: (803)735-8168
**Subject(s):** Religious Publications
**Circ:** ‡10,000

**Storytelling Magazine (28665)**
National Storytelling Network
132 Boone St., Ste. 5
Jonesborough, TN 37659
Phone: (423)913-8230
Fax: (423)753-9331
**Subject(s):** Literature and Literary Reviews
**Circ:** ‡10,000

**Truck & SUV Performance (7382)**
Bill Communications Inc.
1115 Northmeadow Pkwy.
Roswell, GA 30076
Phone: (770)569-5105
Fax: (770)569-5105
**Subject(s):** Automotive (Trade); Trucks and Trucking; Trailers and Accessories
**Circ:** (Controlled)‡10,000

**International Fiber Journal (23344)**
International Media Group Inc.
1515 Mockingbird Ln., Ste. 210
Charlotte, NC 28226
**Subject(s):** Materials Handling; International Business and Economics
**Circ:** (Controlled)‡9,843

**The Journal of Consulting and Clinical Psychology (5892)**
American Psychological Association
Journal of Consulting and Clinical Psychology
Department of Psychology
University of Miami
Coral Gables, FL 33124-0751
**Subject(s):** Psychology and Psychiatry; Indexes, Abstracts, Reports, Proceedings, and Bibliographies
**Circ:** ‡9,650

**Kentucky Farmer (11673)**
Farm Progress Cos.
2870 Turfway Dr.
Owensboro, KY 42303
Phone: (502)266-9556
Fax: (502)266-9556
**Subject(s):** General Agriculture
**Circ:** ‡9,535

**WWS/World Wide Shipping (6350)**
World Wide Shipping Guide Inc.
16302 Byrnwyck Ln.
Odessa, FL 33556-2807
Phone: (813)920-4788
Fax: (813)920-8268
**Subject(s):** International Business and Economics; Ships and Shipping
**Circ:** 9,500

**Home Healthcare Nurse** (11815)
Lippincott Williams & Wilkins
3904 Therina Way
Louisville, KY 40241
Phone: (502)339-9005
Fax: (502)339-0087
**Subject(s):** Nursing

**Circ:** (Paid)‡7,833
(Combined)‡9,035

**Journal of Marketing** (28859)
American Marketing Association
c/o Ruth N. Bolton, Editor
W.P. School of Business
Arizona State Univ.
1708 21st Ave.S., Ste.446
Nashville, TN 37212-3704
**Subject(s):** Consumerism

**Circ:** (Free)65
(Paid)‡9028

**Energy Engineering** (7237)
Fairmont Press Inc.
700 Indian Trl.
Lilburn, GA 30047
Phone: (770)925-9388
Fax: (770)381-9865
**Subject(s):** Engineering (Various branches)

**Circ:** (Paid)9,000

**The Journal of Pastoral Care and Counseling** (23274)
Journal of Pastoral Care Publications Inc.
1068 Harbor Dr. SW
Calabash, NC 28467
Phone: (910)579-5084
Fax: (910)579-5084
**Subject(s):** Religious Publications

**Circ:** (Paid)‡9,000

**Port Charleston** (28010)
South Carolina State Ports Authority
176 Concord St.
PO Box 22287
Charleston, SC 29413
Phone: (843)577-8121
**Subject(s):** International Business and Economics; Ships and Shipping

**Circ:** (Combined)9,000

**Vital Speeches of the Day** (28174)
City News Publishing Co.
PO Box 1247
Mount Pleasant, SC 29465-1247
Phone: (843)881-8733
Fax: (843)881-4007
**Subject(s):** General Editorial

**Circ:** ‡9,000

**Mississippi Business Journal** (16884)
Venture Publications Inc.
5120 Galaxie Dr.
Jackson, MS 39206
Phone: (601)364-1000
Fax: (601)364-1007
**Subject(s):** Business; Local, State, and Regional Publications

**Circ:** (Non-paid)‡2,460
(Paid)‡8,620

**Strategic Planning for Energy and the Environment** (7238)
Fairmont Press Inc.
700 Indian Trl.
Lilburn, GA 30047
Phone: (770)925-9388
Fax: (770)381-9865
**Subject(s):** Power and Power Plants; Engineering (Various branches); Ecology and Conservation

**Circ:** (Paid)8,600

**Art Material Trade News** (6831)
Argus Business
6151 Powers Ferry Rd.
Atlanta, GA 30339-2941
Phone: (770)955-2500
Fax: (770)618-0348
**Subject(s):** Art; Crafts, Models, Hobbies, and Contests

**Circ:** (Paid)168
(Non-paid)8,100

**Alliance** (27980)
John W. Yopp Publications Inc.
803 Port Republic St.
Beaufort, SC 29902
Phone: (843)521-0239
Fax: (843)521-1398

**Subject(s):** Funeral Directors; Cemeteries and Monuments

**Circ:** (Controlled)8,000

**Baptist Peacemaker** (23330)
Baptist Peace Fellowship of North America
4800 Wedgewood Dr.
Charlotte, NC 28210
Phone: (704)521-6051
Fax: (704)521-6053
**Subject(s):** Peace; Social and Political Issues

**Circ:** 8,000

**Co-Laborer** (28485)
Women Nationally Active for Christ of the National Association of Free Will Baptists
5233 Mt. View Rd.
PO Box 5002
Antioch, TN 37011-5002
Phone: (615)731-6812
Fax: (615)731-0771
**Subject(s):** Religious Publications

**Circ:** (Controlled)‡1,000
(Paid)‡8,000

**Corporate Real Estate Leader** (6861)
CoreNet Global
600 Embassy Row/Ste. 210
6600 Peachtree Dunwoody Rd.
Atlanta, GA 30328
Phone: (770)395-1573
Fax: (770)395-9744
**Subject(s):** Real Estate

**Circ:** (Controlled)8,000

**Florida Plumbing Prospective** (5791)
R.C. Publications Inc.
PO Box 150278
Altamonte Springs, FL 32715-0278
Phone: (407)265-2947
Fax: (407)265-2948
**Subject(s):** Construction, Contracting, Building, and Excavating

**Circ:** (Combined)8,000

**Journal of the Medical Association of Georgia** (6894)
1330 W Peachtree St., No. 500
Atlanta, GA 30309
Phone: (404)881-5065
Fax: (404)881-5021
**Subject(s):** Medicine and Surgery

**Circ:** 8,000

**Online** (27969)
Online, A Division of Information Today Inc.
303 Holly Creek Dr.
Anderson, SC 29621
Phone: (864)222-9314
Fax: (864)222-9314
**Subject(s):** Computers

**Circ:** (Paid)‡8,000

**Ornamental Miscellaneous Metal Fabricator** (7150)
National Ornamental and Miscellaneous Metals Association
532 Forest Pkwy., Ste. A
Forest Park, GA 30297
Phone: (404)363-4009
Fax: (404)366-1852
**Subject(s):** Metal, Metallurgy, and Metal Trade

**Circ:** (Combined)‡8,000

**Outdoor Alabama** (358)
Alabama Dept. of Conservation and Natural Resources
64 N Union St.
Montgomery, AL 36130-1901
Phone: (334)242-3151
Fax: (334)242-1880
**Subject(s):** Ecology and Conservation; Parks; Zoology

**Circ:** ‡8,000

**Popular Government** (23315)
Institute of Government
University of North Carolina
Knapp-Sanders Bldg., CB 3330
Chapel Hill, NC 27599-3330
Phone: (919)966-4119
Fax: (919)962-2707
**Subject(s):** Politics

**Circ:** (Combined)8,000

**Preaching** (28608)
American Ministry Resources L.L.C.
PO Box 681868
Franklin, TN 37068-1868
Phone: (615)599-9889
Fax: (615)599-8985

**Subject(s):** Religious Publications

**Circ:** ‡8,000

**South Carolina YR and FFA** (28027)
South Carolina Association of Young Farmers and FFA
222 McAdams Hall
Clemson University
Clemson, SC 29634
**Subject(s):** General Agriculture

**Circ:** ‡8,000

**Obstetrical & Gynecological Survey** (28872)
Lippincott Williams & Wilkins
C/o Dr. Howard W. Jones III
Vanderbilt Univ. Med. Center
Div. of Gynecologic Oncology
Dept of Ob/Gyn
Nashville, TN 37232
Phone: (615)343-9933
**Subject(s):** Medicine and Surgery

**Circ:** (Combined)‡7,530

**Homes Magazine** (23553)
Reflector Publishing
1150 Sugg Parkway
PO Box 1967
Greenville, NC 27834
Phone: (252)329-9500
Fax: (252)752-9583
**Subject(s):** Real Estate

**Circ:** (Non-paid)‡7,500

**Horseman and Fair World** (11764)
Horseman Publishing Co.
PO Box 8480
Lexington, KY 40533
Phone: (859)276-4026
Fax: (859)277-8100
**Subject(s):** (Horses and Horse Racing)

**Circ:** ‡7,500

**Relay Magazine** (6596)
Florida Municipal Electric Association Inc.
PO Box 10114
Tallahassee, FL 32302
**Subject(s):** Lighting; Power and Power Plants

**Circ:** (Controlled)7,500

**Robotics & Automation Magazine** (6650)
Institute of Electrical and Electronics Engineers Inc.
c/o Kimon P Valavanis, Univ.of South Florida
Dept. of Computer Science and Engineering
Center for Robot Assisted Search and Rescue
4202 E. Fowler Ave.
Tampa, FL 33620-5399
Phone: (813)974-6564
Fax: (813)974-5456
**Subject(s):** Electronics Engineering

**Circ:** (Paid)‡7,500

**Today's FDA** (6605)
Florida Dental Association
1111 E Tennessee St.
Tallahassee, FL 32308-6914
Phone: (850)681-3629
Fax: (850)561-0504
**Subject(s):** Dentistry

**Circ:** 7,500

**Midwest Contractor** (7337)
Reed Construction Data
30 Technology Pky. S, Ste. 100
Norcross, GA 30092
Phone: (770)209-3664
Fax: (800)444-1059
**Subject(s):** Construction, Contracting, Building, and Excavating

**Circ:** (Paid)283
(Controlled)7,496

**The Cumberland Presbyterian** (28764)
Cumberland Presbyterian Church, Office of General Assembly
1978 Union Avenue
Memphis, TN 38104
Phone: (901)276-4581
Fax: (901)272-3913
**Subject(s):** Religious Publications

**Circ:** ‡7,300

**Wisconsin Perspective** (5794)
R.C. Publications Inc.
PO Box 150278
Altamonte Springs, FL 32715-0278
Phone: (407)265-2947

Fax: (407)265-2948
**Subject(s):** Plumbing and Heating; Air Conditioning and Refrigeration

**Circ:** (Controlled)‡7,200

**Armor** (11661)
U.S. Army Armor Center
Bldg. 1109A 6th Ave., Rm. 371
Fort Knox, KY 40121-5210
Phone: (502)624-2249
**Subject(s):** Military and Navy

**Circ:** (Paid)7,000
   (Non-paid)7,000

**Biomedical Instrumentation & Technology** (6358)
Hanley & Belfus Inc.
6277 Sea Harbor Dr.
Orlando, FL 32887-4800
Phone: (407)345-4000
Fax: (407)363-9661
**Subject(s):** Medicine and Surgery

**Circ:** (Paid)‡7,000

**Developing Alabama** (349)
Alabama Development Office
Alabama Ctr. for Commerce
401 Adams Ave., Ste. 670
6th Fl.
Montgomery, AL 36130
Phone: (334)242-0400
Fax: (334)242-0415
**Subject(s):** Commerce and Industry; Local, State, and Regional Publications

**Circ:** (Non-paid)7,000

**FIU Hospitality Review** (6333)
Florida International University
3000 NE 151st St.
North Miami, FL 33181-3000
Phone: (305)919-4500
Fax: (305)919-4555
**Subject(s):** Hotels, Motels, Restaurants, and Clubs; Management and Administration; Travel and Tourism

**Circ:** (Controlled)7,000

**Macon Magazine** (7246)
Macon Magazine Inc.
2208 Ingleside Ave.
Macon, GA 31204
Phone: (478)746-7779
Fax: (478)743-4608
**Subject(s):** Local, State, and Regional Publications; Lifestyle

**Circ:** (Non-paid)3,000
   (Paid)7,000

**Polo Players Edition** (6714)
Polo Player
3500 Fairlane Farms Rd., No. 9
Wellington, FL 33414-8749
Phone: (561)793-9524
Fax: (561)793-9576
**Subject(s):** (General Sports)

**Circ:** ‡7,000

**Triad Business News** (23532)
100 S Elm St., Ste. 400
Greensboro, NC 27401-2641
**Subject(s):** Business

**Circ:** (Paid)3,117
   (Non-paid)6,917

**Journal of Vacuum Science and Technology A & B** (23741)
American Institute of Physics
Caller Box 13994
Research Triangle Park, NC 27709
Phone: (919)361-2787
Fax: (919)361-1378
**Subject(s):** Science (General)

**Circ:** ‡6,900

**Journal of the American Society of Nephrology** (6030)
Lippincott Williams & Wilkins
4741 NW 8th Ave., Ste. B
Gainesville, FL 32605
Phone: (352)335-1100
Fax: (352)335-8100
**Subject(s):** Medicine and Surgery

**Circ:** (Non-paid)274
   (Paid)6,720

**Microsurgery** (16882)
John Wiley and Sons Inc.
c/o William C. Lineaweaver, MD, FACS, Editor-in-chief
Division of Plastic Surgery
Univ. of Mississippi Medical Center
Jackson, MS
**Subject(s):** Medicine and Surgery

**Circ:** 6,650

**Oral Surgery, Oral Medicine, Oral Pathology, Oral Radiology, and Endodontics** (16896)
Mosby Inc.
c/o James R. Hupp, Editor-in-Chief
School of Dentistry
The Univ. of Mississippi Medical Center
Rm. D216-08, 2500 N. State St.
Jackson, MS 39216-4504
Phone: (601)815-1952
Fax: (601)984-4949
**Subject(s):** Dentistry

**Circ:** (Paid)‡6,529

**Armor Magazine** (11662)
U.S. Armor Association
PO Box 607
Fort Knox, KY 40121-0494
Phone: (502)942-8624
Fax: (502)942-6219
**Subject(s):** Military and Navy

**Circ:** 6,500

**Athens Magazine** (6789)
Morris Communications Corp.
PO Box 912
Athens, GA 30603-0912
Phone: (706)208-2330
Fax: (706)208-2339
**Subject(s):** Local, State, and Regional Publications

**Circ:** 6,500

**Nutrition Reviews** (92)
International Life Sciences Institute
PO Box 830430
Birmingham, AL 35283
Phone: (205)995-1567
Fax: (205)995-1588
**Subject(s):** Health and Healthcare

**Circ:** ‡6,500

**Health Physics** (28006)
Lippincott Williams & Wilkins
C/o Michael T. Ryan, Editor
Charleston Southern University
9200 University Blvd.
PO Box 118087
Charleston, SC 29423-8087
Phone: (843)863-7628
Fax: (843)863-7628
**Subject(s):** Health and Healthcare

**Circ:** (Free)‡273
   (Paid)‡6,472

**Journal of Morphology** (23804)
John Wiley and Sons Inc.
191 Wildwood Dr.
Sylva, NC 28779
**Subject(s):** Biology

**Circ:** 6,300

**Leader's Magazine** (11773)
98 Dennis Dr.
Lexington, KY 40503
Phone: (859)277-6221
Fax: (859)277-8059
**Subject(s):** Insurance

**Circ:** ‡6,249

**Journal of the Kentucky Medical Association** (11822)
Kentucky Medical Association
4965 US Hwy. 42
Louisville, KY 40222-8512
Phone: (502)426-6200
Fax: (502)426-6877
**Subject(s):** Medicine and Surgery

**Circ:** (Controlled)⊕6,234

**Camp Chase Gazette** (28812)
Camp Chase Publishing Company Inc.
PO Box 625
Morristown, TN 37814
Fax: (423)581-8865
**Subject(s):** History and Genealogy; Crafts, Models, Hobbies, and Contests

**Circ:** (Combined)⊕6,200

**Elevator World** (312)
Elevator World Inc.
356 Morgan Ave.
PO Box 6507
Mobile, AL 36606
Phone: (251)479-4514
Fax: (251)479-7043
**Subject(s):** Construction, Contracting, Building, and Excavating; Safety

**Circ:** (Non-paid)‡162
   (Paid)‡6,200

**Business & Economic Review** (28038)
The Moore School of Business
University of S Carolina
Columbia, SC 29208
Phone: (803)777-2510
Fax: (803)777-9344
**Subject(s):** Business; Local, State, and Regional Publications; Economics

**Circ:** ‡6,100

**Oak Ridge National Laboratory Review** (28946)
Department of Energy
Bldg. 4500-N
PO Box 2008
Oak Ridge, TN 37831-6266
Phone: (865)574-7183
Fax: (865)241-6776
**Subject(s):** Science (General); Power and Power Plants

**Circ:** (Non-paid)‡6,100

**American Saddlebred** (11754)
American Saddlebred Horse Association
4093 Iron Works Pkwy.
Lexington, KY 40511
Phone: (859)259-2742
Fax: (859)259-1628
**Subject(s):** (Horses and Horse Racing)

**Circ:** 6,000

**Educational Evaluation and Policy Analysis** (28853)
American Educational Research Association
Vanderbilt Univ.
Dept. of Leadership, Policy and Organizations
210D Payne Hall, Magnolia Cir., Peabody College
PO Box 514
Nashville, TN 37203
Phone: (615)322-8000
**Subject(s):** Education

**Circ:** ‡6,000

**Grit and Steel** (28105)
De Camp Publishing Co.
Drawer 280
Gaffney, SC 29342-0280
Fax: (803)489-2324
**Subject(s):** Poultry and Pigeons; (Hunting, Fishing, and Game Management)

**Circ:** ‡6,000

**Health Science** (6635)
National Health Association
PO Box 30630
Tampa, FL 33630
Phone: (813)855-6607
Fax: (813)855-8052
**Subject(s):** Health and Healthcare

**Circ:** 6,000

**National Drama Service** (28868)
LifeWay Christian Resources
One Lifeway Plz.
Nashville, TN 37234
Phone: (615)251-2000
Fax: (615)277-8272
**Subject(s):** Religious Publications; Drama and Theatre

**Circ:** (Paid)6,000

**Rural Heritage** (28612)
281 Dean Ridge Ln.
Gainesboro, TN 38562-5039
Phone: (931)268-0655
Fax: (931)268-5884
**Subject(s):** Lifestyle; (Horses and Horse Racing); General Agriculture

**Circ:** ‡6,000

**Southern MotoRacing** (23874)
1049 NW Blvd.
PO Box 500
Winston-Salem, NC 27102
Phone: (336)723-5227
Fax: (336)722-3757

**Subject(s):** (Auto Racing)

**Circ:** ‡6,000

**Southern Textile News** (23354)
Mullen Publications Inc.
PO Box 241028
9629 Old Nations Ford Rd.,
Charlotte, NC 28224-1028
Phone: (704)527-5111
Fax: (704)527-5114
**Subject(s):** Textiles

**Circ:** ‡6,000

**Engineering Design and Automation** (11812)
John Wiley and Sons Inc.
C/O Professor and Director
Manufacturing Research Group
Department of Industrial Engineering
Univ. of Louisville
Louisville, KY 40292
**Subject(s):** Engineering (Various branches); Electrical Engineering; Electronics Engineering

**Circ:** 5,985

**Nursery Business Retailer** (5876)
Brantwood Publications Inc.
2410 Northside Dr.
Clearwater, FL 33761
Phone: (727)786-9771
Fax: (727)791-4126
**Subject(s):** Seed and Nursery Trade

**Circ:** (Paid)‡1,806
      (Non-paid)‡5,932

**Florida Fireman** (6460)
Florida State Firemen's Association Inc.
4921 NW 76th Pl.
Pompano Beach, FL 33073
Phone: (954)426-1068
Fax: (954)426-5162
**Subject(s):** Fire Fighting

**Circ:** ‡5,900

**The eJournal of the South Carolina Medical Association** (28043)
Journal of the South Carolina Medical Association
PO Box 11188
Columbia, SC 29211-1188
Phone: (803)798-6207
Fax: (803)772-6783
**Subject(s):** Medicine and Surgery

**Circ:** ‡5,870

**Southern City** (23715)
N.C. League of Municipalities
PO Box 3069
Raleigh, NC 27602
Phone: (919)715-4000
Fax: (919)733-9519
**Subject(s):** State, Municipal, and County Administration

**Circ:** (Controlled)‡500
      (Paid)‡5,700

**Academic Emergency Medicine** (6356)
Hanley & Belfus Inc.
6277 Sea Harbor Dr.
Orlando, FL 32887-4800
Phone: (407)345-4000
Fax: (407)363-9661
**Subject(s):** Medicine and Surgery; Hospitals and Healthcare Institutions

**Circ:** (Paid)5,600

**Developmental Psychobiology** (23514)
John Wiley and Sons Inc.
C/O George F. Michel, Department of Psychology
292 Eberhart Bldg., Walker Ave.
Greensboro, NC 27402-6170
**Subject(s):** Genetics

**Circ:** 5,600

**Kentucky Engineer** (11672)
Kentucky Society of Professional Engineers
160 Democrat Dr.
Frankfort, KY 40601
Phone: (502)695-5680
Fax: (502)695-0738
**Subject(s):** Engineering (Various branches)

**Circ:** (Paid)⊕5,593

**American Wine Society Journal** (23402)
American Wine Society
PO Box 3330
Durham, NC 27702
Phone: (919)403-0022

Fax: (919)403-0392
**Subject(s):** Beverages, Brewing, and Bottling

**Circ:** ‡5,500

**Journal of Quality Health Care** (6321)
American Board of Quality Assurance and Utilization Review Physicians
6640 Congress St.
New Port Richey, FL 34653
Phone: (727)569-0190
Fax: (727)569-0195
**Subject(s):** Medicine and Surgery; Health and Healthcare

**Circ:** 5,500

**Discipliana** (28852)
Disciples of Christ Historical Society
1101 19th Ave. S.
Nashville, TN 37212
Phone: (615)327-1444
Fax: (615)327-1445
**Subject(s):** Religious Publications

**Circ:** (Controlled)‡50
      (Paid)‡5,400

**Journal of Special Education Leadership** (7158)
Council of Administrators of Special Education
c/o Dr. Luann L. Purcell, Exec.Dir.
1005 State University Dr.
Fort Valley, GA 31030
Phone: (478)825-7667
Fax: (478)825-7811
**Subject(s):** Education; Handicapped

**Circ:** 5,300

**History News** (28855)
American Association for State & Local History
1717 Church St.
Nashville, TN 37203-2991
Phone: (615)320-3203
Fax: (615)327-9013
**Subject(s):** History and Genealogy; Museums

**Circ:** (Non-paid)‡828
      (Paid)‡5,100

**Journal of Dairy Science** (6806)
American Dairy Science Association
c/o S.C. Nickerson, Editor-in-Chief
University of Georgia
Animal and Dairy Science Dept.
Athens, GA 30602
Phone: (706)542-6259
Fax: (706)542-2465
**Subject(s):** Dairying

**Circ:** ‡5,062

**Insurance Meetings Management** (5820)
Coastal Communications Corp.
2650 N Military Trl., Ste. 250
Boca Raton, FL 33431-6390
Phone: (561)989-0600
Fax: (561)989-9509
**Subject(s):** Insurance

**Circ:** (Non-paid)5,017

**Advent Christian Witness** (23329)
Advent Christian General Conference
14601 Albemarle Rd.
PO Box 23152
Charlotte, NC 28227
Phone: (704)545-6161
Fax: (704)573-0712
**Subject(s):** Religious Publications

**Circ:** 5,000

**Army Communicator** (7154)
U.S. Army Signal Regiment
USASC & FG,
Bldg. 29808A (Signal Towers)
Rm. 713
Fort Gordon, GA 30905
Phone: (706)791-7204
Fax: (706)791-3917
**Subject(s):** Military and Navy

**Circ:** (Controlled)‡5,000

**ASCnet Quarterly** (5789)
Applied Systems Client Network
801 Douglas Ave., Ste. 205
Altamonte Springs, FL 32714
Phone: (407)869-0404
Fax: (407)869-0418
**Subject(s):** Insurance

**Circ:** 5,000

**babysue** (28547)
PO Box 3360
Cleveland, TN 37320
Phone: (404)320-1178
**Subject(s):** Music and Musical Instruments; Comics and Comic Technique; Alternative and Underground

**Circ:** (Controlled)5,000

**Business Journal of Tri-Cities TN/VA** (28490)
Business Publishers Co.
3010 Hwy. 126
PO Box 643
Blountville, TN 37617-0643
Phone: (423)323-7111
Fax: (423)323-1479
**Subject(s):** Business

**Circ:** (Paid)3,400
      (Controlled)5,000

**The Camellia Journal** (7157)
American Camellia Society
Massee Ln. Gardens
100 Massee Ln.
Fort Valley, GA 31030-9100
Phone: (478)967-2358
Fax: (478)967-2083
**Subject(s):** Horticulture

**Circ:** ‡5,000

**Church & Society** (11806)
National Ministries Division PCUSA
100 Witherspoon St.
Louisville, KY 40202-1396
Phone: (502)569-5810
Fax: (502)569-8116
**Subject(s):** Religious Publications

**Circ:** (Paid)5,000

**Coaching Women's Basketball** (7235)
4646 Lawrenceville Hwy.
Lilburn, GA 30047-3620
Phone: (770)279-8027
Fax: (770)279-8473
**Subject(s):** (Basketball); Education; Women's Interests

**Circ:** (Non-paid)200
      (Paid)5,000

**Florida Engineering Society Journal** (6576)
Florida Engineering Society
PO Box 750
Tallahassee, FL 32302
Phone: (904)224-7121
Fax: (904)222-4349
**Subject(s):** Engineering (Various branches); Local, State, and Regional Publications

**Circ:** (Paid)‡5,000

**The Georgia Review** (6804)
The University of Georgia
Athens, GA 30602-9009
Phone: (706)542-3481
Fax: (706)542-0047
**Subject(s):** Literature

**Circ:** (Combined)‡5,000

**Hogan's Alley** (6883)
PO Box 47684
Atlanta, GA 30362
**Subject(s):** Comics and Comic Technique

**Circ:** (Paid)5000

**Journal of Bone and Mineral Research** (23423)
American Society for Bone and Mineral Research
PO Box 2759
Durham, NC 27715-2759
Phone: (919)620-0681
Fax: (919)620-8465
**Subject(s):** Health and Healthcare

**Circ:** 5,000

**Journal of Communication** (23284)
Oxford University Press
2001 Evans Rd., Ste. 12
Cary, NC 27513
Phone: (919)677-0977
Fax: (919)677-1714
**Subject(s):** Communications; Telecommunications

**Circ:** (Paid)‡5,000

**Letter Arts Review** (23523)
PO Box 9986
1833 Spings Garden St.
Greensboro, NC 27429
Phone: (336)272-6139
Fax: (336)272-9015

## Southern States

**Subject(s):** Art and Art History
**Circ:** (Non-paid)800
(Paid)5,000

**New Writer's Magazine**  (6532)
PO Box 5976
Sarasota, FL 34277
Phone: (941)953-7903
Fax: (941)953-7903
**Subject(s):** Book Trade and Author News
**Circ:** ‡5,000

**Programming Magazine**  (28057)
National Association for Campus Activities
13 Harbison Way
Columbia, SC 29212
Phone: (803)732-6222
Fax: (803)749-1047
**Subject(s):** Education
**Circ:** (Paid)5,000

**South Carolina Historical Magazine**  (28012)
South Carolina Historical Society
Fireproof Bldg.
100 Meeting St.
Charleston, SC 29401
Phone: (843)723-3225
Fax: (843)723-8584
**Subject(s):** History and Genealogy
**Circ:** ‡5,000

**Southern Exposure**  (23441)
Institute for Southern Studies
2009 Chapel Hill Rd.
PO Box 531
Durham, NC 27707
Phone: (919)419-8311
Fax: (919)419-8315
**Subject(s):** General Editorial; History and Genealogy
**Circ:** ‡5,000

**Worship**  (28901)
Lifeway Christian Resources of the Southern Baptist Convention
One Lifeway Plz.
Nashville, TN 37234-0175
Phone: (615)251-2000
Fax: (615)251-2614
**Subject(s):** Music and Musical Instruments; Theology
**Circ:** (Paid)5,000

**Aquaculture Magazine**  (23221)
Achill River Corp.
PO Box 1409
Arden, NC 28704
Phone: (828)687-0011
Fax: (828)681-0601
**Subject(s):** Fish and Commercial Fisheries
**Circ:** (Paid)4,975

**Winston County Journal**  (16933)
Louisville Newspapers Inc.
PO Box 469
Louisville, MS 39339
Fax: (601)773-6242
**Subject(s):** Local, State, and Regional Publications
**Circ:** (Non-paid)‡4,400
(Paid)‡4,900

**AATCC Review**  (23738)
American Association of Textile Chemists and Colorists
1 Davis Dr.
PO Box 12215
Research Triangle Park, NC 27709
Phone: (919)549-8141
Fax: (919)549-8933
**Subject(s):** Textiles
**Circ:** (Non-paid)1,000
(Paid)4,800

**TOPS**  (7152)
Georgia Forestry Association Inc.
PO Box 1217
Forsyth, GA 31029
Phone: (478)992-8110
Fax: (478)992-8109
**Subject(s):** Forestry
**Circ:** (Paid)‡4,800

**Transactions on Information Systems**  (23324)
Association for Computing Machinery
c/o Gary Marchionini
School of Information and Library Science
Univ. of N. Carolina at Chapel Hill
Chapel Hill, NC 27599-3360
Phone: (919)966-3611
Fax: (919)962-8071
**Subject(s):** Computers
**Circ:** 4,573

**Alabama Municipal Journal**  (344)
Alabama League of Municipalities
PO Box 1270
Montgomery, AL 36102
Phone: (334)263-0200
Fax: (334)263-0200
**Subject(s):** State, Municipal, and County Administration; Local, State, and Regional Publications
**Circ:** (Paid)‡200
(Controlled)‡4,500

**Florida Forum**  (6744)
FRSA
4111 Metric Dr.
PO Box 4850
Winter Park, FL 32792-4850
Phone: (407)671-3772
Fax: (407)679-0010
**Subject(s):** Air Conditioning and Refrigeration; Roofing
**Circ:** (Controlled)‡4,500

**Florida Music Director**  (6581)
Florida Music Educators Association
402 Office Plaza Dr.
Tallahassee, FL 32301
Phone: (850)878-6844
Fax: (850)942-1793
**Subject(s):** Music and Musical Instruments
**Circ:** (Paid)‡4,500

**Kentucky Plumbing-Heating-Cooling Index**  (11827)
Kentucky Association of Plumbing-Heating-Cooling Contractors
1501 Durrett Ln.
Louisville, KY 40213
Phone: (502)451-5577
Fax: (502)451-5551
**Subject(s):** Plumbing and Heating
**Circ:** ‡4,500

**Palm Beach Society Magazine**  (6414)
Box 3229
240 Worth Ave.
Palm Beach, FL 33480
Phone: (561)659-5555
Fax: (561)655-6209
**Subject(s):** Society; Local, State, and Regional Publications
**Circ:** (Non-paid)500
(Paid)4,500

**Rug News**  (23222)
Rug News Magazine
9 Willow Ln.
High Vista Estates
Arden, NC 28704
Phone: (828)890-2568
Fax: (828)890-8169
**Subject(s):** Flooring and Floor Covering
**Circ:** (Controlled)4,500

**Southern Reflector**  (7425)
Georgia Southern University
PO Box 8067
Rm. 2022 Williams Center
Georgia Southern University
Statesboro, GA 30460
Phone: (912)681-0069
Fax: (912)486-7113
**Subject(s):** College Publications
**Circ:** (Paid)100
(Controlled)4,500

**Staplreview**  (16831)
Staplcotn
PO Box 547
Greenwood, MS 38935-0547
Phone: (662)453-6231
**Subject(s):** Farm Bureau, Grange, and Cooperative Associations; Textiles; Socialized Farming
**Circ:** ‡4,500

**Tennessee's Business**  (28832)
Middle Tennessee State University
PO Box 102
Murfreesboro, TN 37129
Phone: (615)898-2610
Fax: (615)898-5045
**Subject(s):** Business
**Circ:** (Non-paid)4,500

**Florida Cattleman and Livestock Journal**  (6139)
Florida Cattleman's Association
PO Box 421403
Kissimmee, FL 34742-1403
Phone: (407)846-6221
Fax: (407)933-8209
**Subject(s):** Livestock
**Circ:** (Non-paid)205
(Paid)4,383

**Theatre Design & Technology**  (11841)
U.S. Institute for Theatre Technology
C/O David Rodger, Editor
3001 Springcrest Dr.
Louisville, KY 40241-2755
Phone: (502)426-1211
Fax: (502)423-7467
**Subject(s):** Drama and Theatre
**Circ:** (Non-paid)‡250
(Paid)‡4,250

**American Literature**  (23401)
Duke University Press
c/o Houston A. Baker
Duke Univ.
Campus Box 90020
Durham, NC 27708-0020
Phone: (919)684-3948
Fax: (919)684-4871
**Subject(s):** Literature
**Circ:** ‡4,200

**Studies in Art Education**  (6601)
National Art Education Association
Dept. of Art Ed.
126 MCH-4480
Florida St. Univ.
Tallahassee, FL 32306-4480
Phone: (904)644-1915
Fax: (904)644-5067
**Subject(s):** Art and Art History; Education
**Circ:** (Non-paid)‡30
(Paid)‡4,197

**Business Perspectives**  (28759)
University of Memphis
330 Innovation Dr., Ste. 221
Memphis, TN 38152-3130
Phone: (901)678-2281
Fax: (901)678-4086
**Subject(s):** Business; Economics
**Circ:** (Non-paid)‡4,100

**Seminars in Arthritis and Rheumatism**  (6257)
Elsevier
C/o Roy D. Altman, Editor
PO Box 016960
Miami, FL 33101
**Subject(s):** Medicine and Surgery
**Circ:** ‡4,072

**Advances in Medical Psychotherapy and Psychodiagnosis**  (28838)
American Board of Medical Psychotherapists and Psychodiagnosticians
Park Plaza Medical Bldg.
345 24th Ave. N, Ste 200
Nashville, TN 37203-1520
Phone: (615)327-2984
Fax: (615)327-9235
**Subject(s):** Psychology and Psychiatry
**Circ:** 4,000

**ASCA Magazine**  (5952)
American Swimming Coaches Association
2101 N Andrews Ave., Ste. 107
Fort Lauderdale, FL 33311
Phone: (954)563-4930
Fax: (954)563-9813
**Subject(s):** Physical Education and Athletics; (Water Sports)
**Circ:** 4,000

**Awards Journal (11757)**
Thoroughbred Owners and Breeders Association
PO Box 4367
Lexington, KY 40544
Phone: (859)276-2291
Fax: (859)276-2462
**Subject(s):** (Horses and Horse Racing)
**Circ:** 4,000

**Awards Quarterly (5937)**
American Orchid Society
16700 AOS Ln.
Delray Beach, FL 33446-4351
Phone: (561)404-2000
Fax: (561)404-2100
**Subject(s):** Botany
**Circ:** 4,000

**Communication Education (6793)**
Routledge Journals
Department of Speech Communication
110 Terrel Hall
University of Georgia
Athens, GA 30602
Phone: (706)542-3245
Fax: (706)542-3245
**Subject(s):** Communications; Education
**Circ:** ‡4,000

**Critical Studies in Media Communication (6796)**
Routledge Journals
Department of Speech Communication
110 Terrell Hall
University of Georgia
Athens, GA 30602
Phone: (706)542-3245
Fax: (706)542-3245
**Subject(s):** Communications
**Circ:** ‡4,000

**English Education (6871)**
National Council of Teachers of English
c/o Dana Fox, Editor, Georgia State University
College of Education, MSC 6A0635
33 Gilmer St. SE, Unit 6
Atlanta, GA 30303-3086
Fax: (217)328-0977
**Subject(s):** Education
**Circ:** (Paid)4,000

**The Journal of the Academy of Florida Trial Lawyers (6587)**
218 S. Monroe St.
Tallahassee, FL 32301
Phone: (850)224-9403
Fax: (850)224-4254
**Subject(s):** Law
**Circ:** (Paid)4,000

**MAPS Bulletin (6531)**
Multidisciplinary Association for Psychedelic Studies
2105 Robinson Ave.
Sarasota, FL 34232
Phone: (941)924-6277
Fax: (941)924-6265
**Subject(s):** Drugs and Pharmaceuticals
**Circ:** 4,000

**Spectrum: Journal of State Government (11777)**
Council of State Governments
2760 Research Park Dr.
PO Box 11910
Lexington, KY 40578-1910
Phone: (859)244-8000
Fax: (859)244-8001
**Subject(s):** State, Municipal, and County Administration
**Circ:** 4,000

**Airline, Ship & Catering ONBOARD SERVICES Magazine (6291)**
Club Publications
665 La Villa Dr.
Miami Springs, FL 33166-6029
Phone: (305)887-1701
Fax: (305)885-1923
**Subject(s):** Food and Grocery Trade
**Circ:** (Paid)19
    (Non-paid)3,890

**North Carolina Pharmacist (23314)**
North Carolina Association of Pharmacists
109 Church St.
Chapel Hill, NC 27516
Phone: (919)967-2237
Fax: (919)968-9430

**Subject(s):** Drugs and Pharmaceuticals
**Circ:** (Paid)‡3,819

**Corporate Real Estate Executive (6860)**
CoreNet Global
260 Peachtree St. NW, Ste. 1500
Atlanta, GA 30303-1237
Phone: (404)589-3200
Fax: (404)589-3201
**Subject(s):** Real Estate
**Circ:** (Paid)3,800

**Shekel (6335)**
American Israel Numismatic Association
12555 Biscayne Blvd. No. 733
North Miami, FL 33181
Phone: (305)466-2833
Fax: (305)466-2834
**Subject(s):** Collecting
**Circ:** (Combined)3,800

**Transactions of the American Fisheries Society (40)**
American Fisheries Society
c/o Dr. Dennis R. DeVries
Dept. of Fisheries
Auburn University
Auburn, AL 36849
Phone: (334)844-9322
Fax: (334)844-9208
**Subject(s):** Fish and Commercial Fisheries; Ecology and Conservation; Oceanography and Marine Studies
**Circ:** ‡3,700

**Tequesta (6261)**
Historical Museum of Southern Florida
101 W Flagler St.
Miami, FL 33130
Phone: (305)375-1492
Fax: (305)375-1609
**Subject(s):** History and Genealogy; Law
**Circ:** (Paid)3,600

**The Sewanee Review (28984)**
University of the South
735 University Ave.
Sewanee, TN 37383
Phone: (931)598-1246
**Subject(s):** Literature and Literary Reviews
**Circ:** 3,560

**Alabama Forests (342)**
Alabama Forestry Association
555 Alabama St.
Montgomery, AL 36104-4395
Phone: (334)265-8733
Fax: (334)262-1258
**Subject(s):** Forestry
**Circ:** ‡3,500

**Crossties (251)**
Covey Communications Corp.
PO Box 2267
Gulf Shores, AL 36547
Phone: (251)968-5300
Fax: (251)968-4532
**Subject(s):** Wood and Woodworking
**Circ:** (Controlled)‡3,500

**The Exponent (267)**
The University of Alabama in Huntsville
University of Alabama in Huntsville
104, University Center
Huntsville, AL 35899
Phone: (256)824-6096
Fax: (256)824-6096
**Subject(s):** College Publications
**Circ:** (Non-paid)3,500

**Georgia Historical Quarterly (7394)**
Georgia Historical Society
501 Whitaker St.
Savannah, GA 31401
Phone: (912)651-2125
Fax: (912)651-2831
**Subject(s):** History and Genealogy
**Circ:** ‡3,500

**Higher & Higher (6057)**
PO Box 829
Geneva, FL 32732
Fax: (407)349-5236
**Subject(s):** Music and Musical Instruments; Entertainment
**Circ:** (Combined)3,500

**Hypertension (16879)**
Lippincott Williams & Wilkins
C/O John E. Hall
Department of Physiology and Biophysics
University of Mississippi Medical Center
2500 N. State St.
Jackson, MS 39216-4505
Phone: (601)815-1667
Fax: (601)815-1675
**Subject(s):** Medicine and Surgery
**Circ:** ‡3,500

**Journal of Behavioral Health Services & Research (6636)**
Lippincott Williams & Wilkins
Louis de la Parte Florida Mental Health Institute
University of South Florida
13301 Bruce B. Downs Blvd.
Tampa, FL 33612-3807
Phone: (813)974-6400
Fax: (813)974-6257
**Subject(s):** Health and Healthcare; Psychology and Psychiatry
**Circ:** (Non-paid)100
    (Paid)3,500

**Journal of Developmental Education (23250)**
National Center for Developmental Education
Reich College of Education
Boone, NC 28608
Phone: (828)262-3057
Fax: (828)262-2128
**Subject(s):** Education
**Circ:** (Controlled)3,500

**Shop Talk! (23682)**
Proleptic Inc.
1101 Broad St.
Oriental, NC 28571
Phone: (252)249-3414
Fax: (252)249-3409
**Subject(s):** General Merchandise
**Circ:** (Paid)3,500

**Seminars in Neurology (100)**
Thieme Medical Publishers Inc.
c/o Winfield S. Fisher, Professor, Division of Neurosurgery
Department of Surgery
University of Alabama at Birmingham
514 Medical Education Bldg.
Birmingham, AL 35294
**Subject(s):** Medicine and Surgery
**Circ:** (Paid)3,462

**Human Factors in Ergonomics and Manufacturing (11817)**
John Wiley and Sons Inc.
c/o Waldemar Karwowski, Editor
Center for Industrial Ergonomics
Univ. of Louisville
Louisville, KY 40292
Phone: (502)852-7173
Fax: (502)852-7397
**Subject(s):** Employment and Human Resources; Management and Administration
**Circ:** (Combined)3,325

**Quality Cities (6595)**
Florida League of Cities
301 S Bronough St., Ste. 300
Tallahassee, FL 32301
Phone: (850)222-9684
Fax: (850)222-3806
**Subject(s):** State, Municipal, and County Administration
**Circ:** (Non-paid)‡1,368
    (Paid)‡3,324

**The Chase (11759)**
1150 Industry Rd.
Lexington, KY 40505
Phone: (859)254-4262
Fax: (859)254-3145
**Subject(s):** (Hunting, Fishing, and Game Management)
**Circ:** ‡3,300

**North Carolina Lawyers Weekly (23709)**
Lawyers Weekly Publications
107 Fayetteville Street Mall, Ste. 300
Raleigh, NC 27601
Phone: (919)829-8088
Fax: (800)876-5297
**Subject(s):** Law
**Circ:** (Non-paid)120
    (Paid)3,300

Circulation: ★ = ABC; △ = BPA; ♦ = CAC; ● = CCAB; ❑ = VAC; ⊕ = PO Statement; ‡ = Publisher's Report; Boldface figures = sworn; Light figures = estimated.

**Georgia Music News** (6803)
Georgia Music Educators Association
University of Georgia
School of Music
Athens, GA 30602
Phone: (706)542-3737
Fax: (706)542-2773
**Subject(s):** Music and Musical Instruments
**Circ:** 3,200

**Kentucky Ancestors** (11670)
Kentucky Historical Society
100 W Broadway
Frankfort, KY 40601-1931
Phone: (502)564-1792
Fax: (502)564-4701
**Subject(s):** History and Genealogy
**Circ:** (Paid)3,200

**Laboratory Investigation** (6039)
Lippincott Williams & Wilkins
Laboratory Investigation
Department of Pathology
1600 SW Archer Rd.
Gainesville, FL 32610-0275
**Subject(s):** Laboratory Research (Scientific and Medical)
**Circ:** (Paid)‡3,200

**The Professional Engineer** (23711)
Professional Engineers of North Carolina
111 N Boylan Ave.
Raleigh, NC 27603-1422
Phone: (919)832-7333
Fax: (919)832-7311
**Subject(s):** Engineering (Various branches)
**Circ:** ‡3,200

**Social Forces** (23319)
University of North Carolina Press
IRSS
Manning Hall
University of North Carolina
Chapel Hill, NC 27599
Phone: (919)962-0513
Fax: (919)962-4777
**Subject(s):** Sociology
**Circ:** (Controlled)‡110
 (Paid)‡3,192

**E2SC** (28044)
Institute for Public Service and Policy Research
Univ. of S. Carolina
Carolina Plz., Rm. 1512
Columbia, SC 29208
Phone: (803)777-4565
Fax: (803)777-4575
**Subject(s):** Environmental and Natural Resources Conservation
**Circ:** (Controlled)3,177

**Direct From Midrex** (23341)
Midrex Direct Reduction Corp.
2725 Water Ridge Pkwy., Ste. 100
Charlotte, NC 28217
Phone: (704)373-1600
Fax: (704)373-1611
**Subject(s):** Metal, Metallurgy, and Metal Trade
**Circ:** (Controlled)3,100

**A & T Register** (23507)
North Carolina Agricultural & Technical University
1601 E Market St.
Box E25
Greensboro, NC 27411
Phone: (336)334-7700
Fax: (336)256-2092
**Subject(s):** Black Publications; College Publications
**Circ:** 3,000

**Athletic Therapy Today** (28517)
Human Kinetics Publishers Inc.
c/o Gary B. Wilkerson, Ed.D., ATC, Editor
Dept. No. 6606, Univ. of Tennessee at Chattanooga
615 McCallie Ave.
Chattanooga, TN 37403-2598
Phone: (423)425-5394
Fax: (423)425-5395
**Subject(s):** (General Sports); Medicine and Surgery
**Circ:** 3,000

**Comparative Medicine (CM)** (28763)
American Association for Laboratory Animal Science
9190 Crestwyn Hills Dr.
Memphis, TN 38125-8538
Phone: (901)754-8620

Fax: (901)753-0046
**Subject(s):** Laboratory Research (Scientific and Medical)
**Circ:** ‡3,000

**The Foxfire Magazine** (7321)
The Foxfire Fund Inc.
PO Box 541
Mountain City, GA 30562-0541
Phone: (706)746-5828
Fax: (706)746-5829
**Subject(s):** Ethnic Publications; Intercultural Interests
**Circ:** 3,000

**Journal of the Evangelical Theological Society** (23815)
Evangelical Theological Society
222 N. Wingate St.
Wake Forest, NC 27588
Phone: (919)761-2485
Fax: (919)761-2482
**Subject(s):** Religious Publications
**Circ:** 3,000

**Leader in Christian Education Ministries** (28861)
The United Methodist Publishing House
201 8th Ave. S
PO Box 801
Nashville, TN 37202-0801
Phone: (615)749-6000
Fax: (615)749-6512
**Subject(s):** Religious Publications; Education
**Circ:** (Controlled)1,000
 (Paid)3,000

**Nurse Educator** (5845)
Lippincott Williams & Wilkins
Nurse Educator
Ste. C-12 4301
32nd St. W.
Bradenton, FL 34205-2748
**Subject(s):** Nursing; Education
**Circ:** (Paid)3,000

**The Old-Time Herald** (23433)
Old-Time Music Group Inc.
PO Box 51812
Durham, NC 27717
**Subject(s):** Music and Musical Instruments
**Circ:** (Non-paid)2,000
 (Paid)3,000

**Performance Management Ezine** (6908)
Aubrey Daniels International
3353 Peachtree Rd. NE. Ste. 920
Atlanta, GA 30326
Phone: (678)904-6140
Fax: (678)904-6141
**Subject(s):** Management and Administration
**Circ:** 3,000

**Reach Out Magazine** (6078)
3090 Sheridan St., PMB No. 207
Hollywood, FL 33021-3730
Phone: (954)985-0319
Fax: (954)985-0483
**Subject(s):** Handicapped
**Circ:** (Paid)‡3,000

**Sportsman Pilot** (23226)
PO Box 400
Asheboro, NC 27204-0400
Phone: (336)633-3954
Fax: (336)633-0165
**Subject(s):** Aviation
**Circ:** ‡3,000

**Education** (311)
Project Innovation
PO Box 8508
Spring Hill Station
Mobile, AL 36689-8508
Phone: (251)343-1878
Fax: (251)343-1878
**Subject(s):** Education
**Circ:** ‡2,900

**RFD** (28732)
PO Box 68
Liberty, TN 37095-0068
Phone: (615)536-5176
**Subject(s):** Gay and Lesbian Interests
**Circ:** (Non-paid)‡900
 (Paid)‡2,900

**TVPPA News Magazine** (28524)
TVPPA
PO Box 6189
Chattanooga, TN 37401-6189
Phone: (423)756-6511
Fax: (423)267-2280
**Subject(s):** Power and Power Plants
**Circ:** (Controlled)‡2,855

**Western Builder** (7344)
30 Technology Parkway Ste 100
Norcross, GA 30092
Fax: (404)417-4193
**Subject(s):** Construction, Contracting, Building, and Excavating
**Circ:** (Non-paid)445
 (Paid)2,825

**Cancer Nursing** (6016)
Lippincott Williams & Wilkins
College of Nursing
University of Florida
PO Box 100187
Gainesville, FL 32610-0187
Fax: (352)273-6570
**Subject(s):** Nursing
**Circ:** (Paid)‡2,819

**Palmetto Piper** (28053)
Mechanical Contractor's Association of South Carolina
1504 Morninghill Dr.
PO Box 384
Columbia, SC 29210-6920
Phone: (803)772-7834
Fax: (803)731-0390
**Subject(s):** Air Conditioning and Refrigeration; Plumbing and Heating
**Circ:** ‡2,700

**Register of Kentucky Historical Society** (11678)
Kentucky Historical Society
100 W Broadway
Frankfort, KY 40601-1931
Phone: (502)564-1792
Fax: (502)564-4701
**Subject(s):** History and Genealogy; Local, State, and Regional Publications
**Circ:** (Paid)‡2,700

**Tennessee Historical Quarterly** (28887)
Tennessee Historical Society
Ground Fl., War Memorial Bldg.
Nashville, TN 37243
Phone: (615)741-8934
Fax: (615)741-8937
**Subject(s):** History and Genealogy
**Circ:** (Combined)2,700

**Southern Communication Journal** (16848)
Southern States Communication Association
c/o Dr. John Meyer, Dept. of Speech Comm.
118 College Dr. 5131
University of Southern Mississippi
Hattiesburg, MS 39406
Phone: (601)266-4280
**Subject(s):** Hearing and Speech
**Circ:** (Non-paid)‡50
 (Paid)‡2,650

**Journal of Orthopaedic Trauma** (6642)
Lippincott Williams & Wilkins
c/o Roy Sanders
4 Columbia Dr., Ste.No.710
Tampa, FL 33606
**Subject(s):** Laboratory Research (Scientific and Medical); Physiology and Anatomy
**Circ:** 2543

**Hosiery News** (23343)
The Hosiery Association
3623 Latrobe Dr., Ste. 130
Charlotte, NC 28211
Phone: (704)365-0913
Fax: (704)362-2056
**Subject(s):** Textiles
**Circ:** (Controlled)‡2,500

**InVitro Cellular & Developmental Biology - PLANT** (23345)
Society for In Vitro Biology
13000-F York Rd., Ste. 304
Charlotte, NC 28278
Phone: (704)588-1923
Fax: (704)588-5193

**Subject(s):** Biology
**Circ:** ‡2,500

**Journal of Security Administration** (6245)
BLSS Inc.
Box 164509
Miami, FL 33116-4509
Phone: (305)254-7006
Fax: (305)254-9662
**Subject(s):** Management and Administration
**Circ:** (Paid)2,500

**Journal of Telecommunications in Higher Education** (11768)
ACUTA: The Association for Communications Technology Professionals in Higher Education
152 W Zandale Dr., Ste. 200
Lexington, KY 40503
Phone: (859)278-3338
Fax: (859)278-3268
**Subject(s):** Telecommunications; Education
**Circ:** 2,500

**Reading Improvement** (318)
Project Innovation of Mobile
Spring Hill Sta.
PO Box 8508
Mobile, AL 36689-0508
Phone: (251)343-1878
Fax: (251)343-1878
**Subject(s):** Education
**Circ:** ‡2,500

**Veterans' Bulletin** (6928)
Georgia Dept. of Veterans Service
Floyd Veterans Bldg., 970-E
Atlanta, GA 30334
Phone: (404)656-5933
Fax: (404)656-7006
**Subject(s):** Veterans
**Circ:** (Controlled)‡2,500

**Auditing** (6842)
American Accounting Association
c/o William Messier, Editor
Georgia State University
Scool of Accountancy
College of Business
Atlanta, GA 30302
Phone: (404)651-2611
Fax: (404)651-1033
**Subject(s):** Accountants and Accounting
**Circ:** (Paid)2,400

**Review and Expositor** (11839)
Review & Expositor
PO Box 6681
Louisville, KY 40206-0681
Phone: (502)327-8347
Fax: (502)327-8347
**Subject(s):** Religious Publications
**Circ:** (Paid)‡2,400

**The Tennessee Banker** (28884)
Tennessee Bankers Association
201 Venture Cir.
Nashville, TN 37228
Phone: (615)244-4871
Fax: (615)244-0995
**Subject(s):** Banking, Finance, and Investments
**Circ:** ‡2,350

**Lexington Theological Quarterly** (11775)
Lexington Theological Seminary
631 S Limestone St.
Lexington, KY 40508
Phone: (859)252-0361
Fax: (859)281-6042
**Subject(s):** Religious Publications
**Circ:** (Non-paid)2,300

**Tennessee Dental Association Journal** (28886)
Tennessee Dental Association
2104 Sunset Pl.
Box 120188
Nashville, TN 37212
Phone: (615)383-8962
Fax: (615)383-0214
**Subject(s):** Dentistry
**Circ:** (Combined)2,300

**Tire Retreading/Repair Journal** (11842)
Tire Industry Association
PO Box 37203
Louisville, KY 40233-7203
Phone: (502)968-8900
Fax: (502)964-7859
**Subject(s):** Automotive (Trade)
**Circ:** 2,300

**Cogeneration and Competitive Power Journal** (7236)
Fairmont Press Inc.
700 Indian Trl.
Lilburn, GA 30047
Phone: (770)925-9388
Fax: (770)381-9865
**Subject(s):** Engineering (Various branches)
**Circ:** (Paid)2,200

**Dredging Research** (17040)
United States Army Corps of Engineers
3909 Halls Ferry Rd.
Vicksburg, MS 39180-6199
Phone: (601)634-4261
**Subject(s):** Water Supply and Sewage Disposal; Construction, Contracting, Building, and Excavating; Military and Navy
**Circ:** (Non-paid)2200

**The Hispanic American Historical Review** (23418)
University of Maryland, College Park Campus
Duke University Press
905 W. Main St., Ste. 18 B
Durham, NC 27701
Phone: (919)687-3600
Fax: (919)688-4574
**Subject(s):** History and Genealogy; Hispanic Publications
**Circ:** ‡2,200

**Bluegrass Music News** (11966)
Kentucky Music Educators Association
PO Box 1058
Richmond, KY 40476
Phone: (859)626-5635
Fax: (859)626-1415
**Subject(s):** Education; Music and Musical Instruments
**Circ:** ‡2,100

**History Workshop** (23283)
Oxford University Press
2001 Evans Rd., Ste. 12
Cary, NC 27513
Phone: (919)677-0977
Fax: (919)677-1714
**Subject(s):** History and Genealogy; Social and Political Issues; Women's Interests
**Circ:** (Paid)2,100

**Journal of Physical Oceanography** (6243)
American Meteorological Society
Journal of Physical Oceanography Editor
RSMAS/University of Miami
4600 Rickenbacker Causeway
Miami, FL 33149-1098
**Subject(s):** Oceanography and Marine Studies
**Circ:** ‡2,067

**Against the Grain** (27996)
The Citadel, MSC 98
Charleston, SC 29409
Phone: (843)723-3536
Fax: (843)723-3536
**Subject(s):** Book Trade and Author News; Library and Information Science
**Circ:** (Non-paid)200
(Paid)2,000

**Alabama Counseling Association Journal** (301)
Alabama Counseling Association
217 Darryl St.
Livingston, AL 35470
Phone: (205)652-1712
Fax: (205)652-1576
**Subject(s):** Psychology and Psychiatry; Education
**Circ:** (Non-paid)2000

**Associated Plumbing Heating & Cooling** (53)
PO Box 36972
Birmingham, AL 35236-6972
Phone: (205)985-9488
Fax: (205)733-1006
**Subject(s):** Plumbing and Heating; Air Conditioning and Refrigeration
**Circ:** (Non-paid)‡2,000

**Black Warrior Review** (459)
University of Alabama
PO Box 862936
Tuscaloosa, AL 35486-0027
Phone: (205)348-4518
Fax: (205)348-8036
**Subject(s):** Literature
**Circ:** (Paid)2,000

**Certified Engineering Technician** (7147)
American Society of Certified Engineering Technicians
Box 1348
Flowery Branch, GA 30542-0023
Phone: (770)967-9173
Fax: (770)967-8049
**Subject(s):** Engineering (Various branches)
**Circ:** (Controlled)2,000

**The Christian Observer** (28222)
The Christian Observer Inc.
PO Box 20
Sardinia, SC 29143
Phone: (303)473-3329
**Subject(s):** Religious Publications
**Circ:** (Non-paid)‡20
(Paid)‡2,000

**Cinevue Worldwide Talent Directory and Festival Program Book** (6407)
Steve Postal Productions
108 Carraway St.
Palatka, FL 32177-1150
Phone: (386)328-6656
**Subject(s):** Motion Pictures; Performing Arts; Radio, Television, Cable, and Video
**Circ:** (Paid)‡2,000
(Controlled)‡2,000

**Georgia Business and Economic Conditions** (6800)
University of Georgia
Selig Center Economic Growth, Terry College of Business
Athens, GA 30602
Phone: (706)542-4085
Fax: (706)542-3858
**Subject(s):** Economics; Business; Local, State, and Regional Publications
**Circ:** (Free)‡2,000

**The International Journal of Logistics Management** (6464)
The International Logistics Research Institute Inc.
PO Box 2166
Ponte Vedra Beach, FL 32004-2166
Phone: (941)927-9108
Fax: (941)927-9108
**Subject(s):** Mathematics
**Circ:** 2,000

**Journal of Autism and Developmental Disorders** (23305)
Kluwer Academic/Plenum Publishing Corp.
Department of Psychiatry
CB 7180 Medical School Wing E
Chapel Hill, NC 27599-7180
Phone: (919)966-4127
Fax: (919)966-4127
**Subject(s):** Medicine and Surgery
**Circ:** ‡2,000

**Journal of Civil Defense** (6559)
The American Civil Defense Association
PO Box 1057
PO Box 1057
Starke, FL 32091
Phone: (904)964-5397
Fax: (904)964-9641
**Subject(s):** Public Safety and Emergency Response; Safety
**Circ:** 2,000

**Missiology** (12036)
American Society of Missiology
204 North Lexington Avenue
Wilmore, KY 40390-1199
Phone: (859)858-2216
Fax: (859)858-2375
**Subject(s):** Anthropology and Ethnology; Religious Publications
**Circ:** ‡2,000

**Nuclear Safety** (28945)
Oak Ridge National Laboratory
Bldg. 9201-3, MS No. 8065
PO Box 2008
Oak Ridge, TN 37831
Phone: (865)574-4160

**Subject(s):** Nuclear Engineering

**Circ:** (Controlled)‡1,475
(Paid)‡2,000

**Ohio Valley History** (11836)
Cincinnati Museum Center and The Filson Historical Society
1310 S Third St.
Louisville, KY 40208
Phone: (502)635-5083
Fax: (502)635-5086
**Subject(s):** History and Genealogy

**Circ:** (Controlled)2,000

**Orange Seed Technical Bulletin** (6592)
Florida Department of State
500 S Bronough St.
Tallahassee, FL 32399-0250
Phone: (850)245-6600
Fax: (850)245-6735
**Subject(s):** Library and Information Science

**Circ:** (Non-paid)2000

**Palmetto Pharmacist** (28052)
1350 Browning Rd.
Columbia, SC 29210-6903
Phone: (803)354-9977
Fax: (803)354-9207
**Subject(s):** Drugs and Pharmaceuticals

**Circ:** (Paid)2,000

**Southern Cultures** (23320)
University of North Carolina Press
409 Hamilton Hall, CB 9127
University of North Carolina-Chapel Hill
Chapel Hill, NC 27599-9127
Phone: (919)962-4433
Fax: (919)962-4433
**Subject(s):** History and Genealogy; Social Sciences

**Circ:** (Paid)2,000

**Southern Journal of Applied Forestry** (16961)
Society of American Foresters
Box 9681, Forestry Department
Mississippi State University
Mississippi State, MS 39762
Phone: (662)325-4546
Fax: (662)325-8726
**Subject(s):** Forestry

**Circ:** 2,000

**Trial Advocate Quarterly** (6657)
Florida Defense Lawyers Association
6820 Benjamin Rd., Ste. 3
Tampa, FL 33634
Phone: (813)885-9888
Fax: (813)885-5547
**Subject(s):** Law

**Circ:** (Combined)2,000

**Law and Contemporary Problems** (23427)
Duke University School of Law
PO Box 90364
Durham, NC 27708-0364
Phone: (919)613-7171
Fax: (919)613-7231
**Subject(s):** Law

**Circ:** ‡1,985

**Marketing Science** (6040)
The Institute for Operations Research and the Management Sciences
c/o Prof. Steven M. Shugan, Editor-in-chief
Warrington College of Business Administration
Univ. of Florida
201 Bryan Hall, Campus Box 117155
Gainesville, FL 32611-7155
Phone: (352)392-0161
**Subject(s):** Advertising and Marketing

**Circ:** ‡1,960

**Journal of Insurance Regulation** (7422)
National Association of Insurance Commissioners
c/o Mike Barth, Editor
PO Box 8151
Statesboro, GA 30460-8151
Phone: (912)681-0259
Fax: (608)277-1479
**Subject(s):** Insurance

**Circ:** (Non-paid)15
(Paid)1,950

**The American Genealogist** (7115)
PO Box 398
Demorest, GA 30535-0398
Phone: (706)865-6440
Fax: (706)865-6440
**Subject(s):** History and Genealogy

**Circ:** ‡1,900

**Environmental History** (23413)
Forest History Society
701 William Vickers Ave.
Durham, NC 27701-3162
Phone: (919)682-9319
Fax: (919)682-2349
**Subject(s):** Forestry; Ecology and Conservation; History and Genealogy

**Circ:** ‡1,900

**Information Technology and Disabilities** (11818)
Equal Access to Software and Information
c/o Steve Noble, Editor-in-Chief
Policy Analyst, Kentucky Assistive Technology Service Networ
8412 W.port Rd.
Louisville, KY
Phone: (502)327-0022
Fax: (502)327-9974
**Subject(s):** Handicapped; Computers

**Circ:** (Non-paid)1,900

**Journal of Sport & Exercise Psychology** (6590)
Human Kinetics Publishers Inc.
c/o Robert C. Eklund, Ph.D., Editor
Florida State Univ., Educational Psychology and Learning Sys
307 Stone Bldg
Tallahassee, FL 32306
Phone: (850)645-2909
Fax: (850)644-8776
**Subject(s):** Psychology and Psychiatry; Physical Education and Athletics

**Circ:** (Paid)‡1,891

**Journal of Post Keynesian Economics** (28683)
M.E. Sharpe Inc.
521 Stokely Management Ctr.
Knoxville, TN 37996-0550
Phone: (865)974-1686
Fax: (865)974-1686
**Subject(s):** Economics

**Circ:** (Paid)1,850

**Journal of Computer-Assisted Tomography** (23869)
Lippincott Williams & Wilkins
c/o Allen D. Elster, Division of Radiologic Sciences
Wake Forest University School of Medicine
Winston Salem, NC 27157-1022
**Subject(s):** Radiology, Ultrasound, and Nuclear Medicine

**Circ:** †1,840

**Avian Diseases** (6790)
American Association of Avian Pathologists
953 College Station Rd.
Athens, GA 30602-4875
Phone: (706)542-5645
Fax: (706)542-0249
**Subject(s):** Veterinary Medicine; Ornithology and Oology

**Circ:** 1,800

**Behavioral Research in Accounting** (6524)
American Accounting Association
5717 Bessie Dr.
Sarasota, FL 34233-2399
Phone: (941)921-7747
Fax: (941)923-4093
**Subject(s):** Accountants and Accounting

**Circ:** (Paid)1,800

**Faith and Philosophy** (12034)
Society of Christian Philosophers
Dept. of Philosophy
Asbury College
Wilmore, KY 40390-1198
Phone: (859)858-3511
Fax: (859)858-3921
**Subject(s):** Religious Publications; Philosophy

**Circ:** (Paid)1,800

**Florida Psychologist** (6582)
Florida Psychological Association
408 Office Plaza Dr.
Tallahassee, FL 32301-2757
Phone: (850)656-2222
Fax: (850)942-4586

**Subject(s):** Psychology and Psychiatry

**Circ:** (Controlled)1,800

**The Kentucky Pharmacist** (11675)
Kentucky Pharmacists Association
1228 U.S. 127 South
Frankfort, KY 40601
Phone: (502)227-2303
Fax: (502)227-2258
**Subject(s):** Drugs and Pharmaceuticals

**Circ:** (Non-paid)‡100
(Paid)‡1,800

**Manuscripts** (28050)
The Manuscript Society
Department of History
University of South Carolina
Columbia, SC 29208
Phone: (803)777-4490
Fax: (803)777-4494
**Subject(s):** Literature and Literary Reviews; Collecting

**Circ:** ‡1,800

**SIAM Journal on Numerical Analysis** (6599)
Society for Industrial & Applied Mathematics
c/o Max D. Gunzburger, Editor-In-Chief
School of Computational Science and Information Technology
400 Dirac Science Library
Florida St. Univ.
Tallahassee, FL 32306-4120
**Subject(s):** Mathematics

**Circ:** ‡1,806

**SIAM Journal on Discrete Mathematics** (28060)
Society for Industrial & Applied Mathematics
c/o Jerrold R. Griggs
Dept. of Mathematics
Univ. of S. Carolina
Columbia, SC 29208
**Subject(s):** Mathematics

**Circ:** ‡1,758

**American Songwriter** (28839)
American Songwriter Magazine
50 Music Sq. W., Ste. 604
Nashville, TN 37203
Phone: (615)321-6096
Fax: (615)321-6097
**Subject(s):** Music and Musical Instruments

**Circ:** (Paid)1,728

**Assessment for Effective Information** (27998)
Council for Exceptional Children
AEI
School of Education
The Citadel
171 Moultrie St.
Charleston, SC 29409
Phone: (843)849-9306
Fax: (843)849-9306
**Subject(s):** Education

**Circ:** 1,700

**The Journal of the Bromeliad Society** (6529)
Bromeliad Society Inc.
Marie Selby Botanical Gardens
811 S. Palm Ave.
Sarasota, FL 34236-7726
Phone: (941)365-2080
Fax: (941)365-2080
**Subject(s):** Botany

**Circ:** (Combined)1700

**Soundings** (28686)
Soundings: An Interdisciplinary Journal
216 Aconda Ct.
University of Tennessee
Knoxville, TN 37996-0630
Phone: (865)974-8252
Fax: (865)974-8544
**Subject(s):** Education; Humanities

**Circ:** ‡1,700

**CRANIO** (28519)
Chroma Inc.
PO Box 8887
Chattanooga, TN 37414
Phone: (423)899-1753
Fax: (423)490-0791
**Subject(s):** Medicine and Surgery; Dentistry

**Circ:** (Non-paid)‡308
(Paid)‡1,638

**Epidemiology (23414)**
Lippincott Williams & Wilkins
Snow Bldg., Ste. 606
331 W. Main St.
Durham, NC 27701
Phone: (919)667-1688
**Subject(s):** Medicine and Surgery
**Circ:** (Combined)1,609

**Florida Truck News (6583)**
Florida Trucking Association Inc.
350 E College Ave.
Tallahassee, FL 32301-1565
Phone: (850)222-9900
Fax: (850)222-9363
**Subject(s):** Trucks and Trucking
**Circ:** (Controlled)‡800
(Paid)‡1,600

**Journal of Laser Applications (6372)**
Laser Institute of America
13501 Ingenuity Dr., No. 128
Orlando, FL 32826
Phone: (407)380-1553
Fax: (407)380-5588
**Subject(s):** Science (General); Medicine and Surgery
**Circ:** 1,600

**Kentucky Banker (11825)**
Kentucky Bankers Association
Waterfront Plz., Ste. 1000
325 W Main St.
Louisville, KY 40202
Phone: (502)582-2453
Fax: (502)584-6390
**Subject(s):** Banking, Finance, and Investments
**Circ:** (Combined)1,600

**Merton Seasonal (11834)**
International Thomas Merton Society
Thomas Merton Center
Bellarmine University
2001 Newburg Rd.
Louisville, KY 40205-0671
Phone: (502)452-8187
Fax: (502)452-8452
**Subject(s):** Book Trade and Author News; Literature; Literature and Literary Reviews
**Circ:** 1,600

**Mississippi Pharmacist (16892)**
Mississippi Pharmacists Association
341 Edgewood Terrace Dr.
Jackson, MS 39206-6299
Phone: (601)981-0416
Fax: (601)981-0451
**Subject(s):** Drugs and Pharmaceuticals
**Circ:** 1,600

**Administration in Social Work (28034)**
The Haworth Press Inc.
Univ. of South Carolina
112 Thornwell Annex
Columbia, SC 29208
Phone: (803)777-4210
Fax: (213)740-0789
**Subject(s):** Social Sciences
**Circ:** (Controlled)‡1,577

**Quest (28685)**
Human Kinetics Publishers Inc.
c/o Joy T. DeSensi, Ed.D., Editor
Dept. of Exercise, Sport, and Leisure Studies
College of Education, Health, and Human Sciences
The Univ. of Tennessee, 1914 Andy Holt Ave.
Knoxville, TN 37996-2700
**Subject(s):** Physical Education and Athletics
**Circ:** (Non-paid)44
(Paid)1,562

**Journal of Digital Imaging (6032)**
Elsevier
c/o Janice Honeyman-Buck, Editor-in-Chief
Univ. of Florida
Dept. of Radiology, 1600 SW Archer Rd.
PO Box 100374
Gainesville, FL 32610
**Subject(s):** Radiology, Ultrasound, and Nuclear Medicine
**Circ:** ‡1,527

**American Speech (23291)**
Duke University Press
c/o Connie Eble
Univ. of N. Carolina
Box 90018
Chapel Hill, NC 27599-3250
Phone: (919)687-3670
Fax: (919)688-5595
**Subject(s):** Philology, Language, and Linguistics
**Circ:** 1,500

**CLA Journal (6854)**
College Language Association
Morehouse College
Atlanta, GA 30314
Phone: (404)681-2800
Fax: (404)614-3786
**Subject(s):** Literature; Philology, Language, and Linguistics; Literature
**Circ:** (Controlled)‡10
(Paid)‡1,500

**Journal of Early Southern Decorative Arts (23870)**
Museum of Early Southern Decorative Arts
PO Box 10310
Winston-Salem, NC 27108-0310
Phone: (336)721-7360
Fax: (336)721-7367
**Subject(s):** Art and Art History
**Circ:** (Paid)1,500

**Journal of Health Care for the Poor and Underserved (28858)**
Johns Hopkins University Press
c/o Virginia Brennan, PhD, Editor
Meharry Medical College
1005 D.B. Todd Blvd.
Nashville, TN 37208
Phone: (615)327-6819
Fax: (615)327-6362
**Subject(s):** Health and Healthcare; Ethnic and Minority Studies
**Circ:** ‡1,500

**The Journal of Mississippi History (16881)**
Mississippi Historical Society
Dept. of Archives and History
Box 571
Jackson, MS 39205
Phone: (601)576-6850
Fax: (601)576-6975
**Subject(s):** History and Genealogy
**Circ:** ‡1,500

**Kalliope (6097)**
Florida Community College at Jacksonville
11901 Beach Blvd.
Jacksonville, FL 32246
Phone: (904)646-2081
Fax: (904)646-2081
**Subject(s):** Women's Interests; Literature and Literary Reviews; Art
**Circ:** (Non-paid)100
(Paid)1,500

**The Library Quarterly (6591)**
University of Chicago Press
c/o John Carlo Bertot
School of Information Studies
Florida State University
101 Shores Bldg.
Tallahassee, FL 32306-2100
**Subject(s):** Library and Information Science
**Circ:** (Paid)1,500

**Mississippi Review (16847)**
University of Southern Mississippi
PO Box 5144
Hattiesburg, MS 39406-5144
Phone: (601)266-5600
Fax: (601)266-5757
**Subject(s):** Poetry; Literature; Literature and Literary Reviews
**Circ:** (Combined)1,500

**North Carolina Genealogical Society Journal (23557)**
North Carolina Genealogical Society
PO Box 22
Greenville, NC 27835-0022
Fax: (252)752-0679
**Subject(s):** History and Genealogy; Local, State, and Regional Publications
**Circ:** (Controlled)1,500

**North Carolina Historical Review (23707)**
North Carolina Office of Archives and History
4622 Mail Service Ctr.
Raleigh, NC 27699-4622
Phone: (919)733-7442
Fax: (919)733-1439
**Subject(s):** History and Genealogy
**Circ:** ‡1,500

**Now & Then (28659)**
Center for Appalachian Studies and Services
E Tennessee State Univ.
Box 70556
Johnson City, TN 37614-1707
Phone: (423)439-5348
Fax: (423)439-6340
**Subject(s):**
**Circ:** (Paid)1,500

**River City (28776)**
University of Memphis
101 Wilder Tower
Memphis, TN 38152-3520
Phone: (901)678-4591
Fax: (901)678-2226
**Subject(s):** Literature; College Publications; Poetry
**Circ:** (Controlled)1,500

**South Atlantic Review (6916)**
South Atlantic Modern Language Association
Georgia State University
English Department
GCB 923, Rm. 911
38 Peachtree Center Ave.
Atlanta, GA 30303-3088
Phone: (404)651-2693
Fax: (404)651-2858
**Subject(s):** Literature; Philology, Language, and Linguistics
**Circ:** (Non-paid)‡200
(Paid)‡1,500

**Tennessee Law Review (28688)**
Tennessee Law Review Association
Ste. 337 1505 W. Cumberland Ave.
Knoxville, TN 37996-1810
Phone: (865)974-4464
Fax: (865)974-2576
**Subject(s):** Law
**Circ:** ‡1,500

**Journal of Urban History (23347)**
Sage Publications Inc.
c/o David R. Goldfield, Editor
Department of History
University of North Carolina at Charlotte
Charlotte, NC 28223
**Subject(s):** History and Genealogy
**Circ:** (Non-paid)144
(Paid)1,400

**International Journal of Sport Nutrition & Exercise Metabolism (6586)**
Human Kinetics Publishers Inc.
c/o Emily M. Haymes, Editor
Florida State Univ., Dept. of Nutrition
Food & Exercise Sciences
Tallahassee, FL 32306-1493
Phone: (850)644-4793
Fax: (850)645-5000
**Subject(s):** Physical Education and Athletics
**Circ:** (Paid)‡1,372

**Community College Review (23695)**
North Carolina State University
Dept. of Adult & Community College Education
310 Poe Hall
Box 7801
Raleigh, NC 27695-7801
Phone: (919)515-6248
Fax: (919)515-4039
**Subject(s):** Education
**Circ:** 1,200
1,350

**History of Political Economy (23419)**
Duke University Press
Department of Economics
Duke University
Box 90097
Durham, NC 27708-0097
Phone: (919)684-3936
Fax: (919)681-7869
**Subject(s):** Economics; History and Genealogy
**Circ:** ‡1,350

**Palmetto Poultry Life (28054)**
South Carolina Poultry Federation
1921-A Pickens St.
Columbia, SC 29201
Phone: (803)779-4700
Fax: (803)779-5002
**Subject(s):** Poultry and Pigeons

**Circ:** (Controlled)1,350

**Research on Aging (23437)**
Sage Publications Inc.
c/o Angela M. Rand
Duke University
336 Soc.-Psych. Bldg.
PO Box 90088
Durham, NC 27708
**Subject(s):** Gerontology

**Circ:** (Non-paid)‡84
(Paid)‡1,350

**Journal of Personality Disorders (6242)**
Taylor and Francis
5400 S.W. 99th Terrace
Miami, FL 33156
Phone: (305)284-3361
Fax: (305)661-8888
**Subject(s):** Psychology and Psychiatry

**Circ:** 1,313

**Crystal Growth & Design (460)**
American Chemical Society
c/o Robin D. Rogers
Department of Chemistry
The University of Alabama
Tuscaloosa, AL 35487-0336
Phone: (205)348-0844
Fax: (205)348-0823
**Subject(s):** Biology; Chemistry, Chemicals, and Chemical Engineering

**Circ:** 1,300

**The High School Journal (23301)**
University of North Carolina Press
Campus Box 3500
School of Education, Peabody Hall
University of North Carolina-Chapel Hill
Chapel Hill, NC 27599-3520
Phone: (919)962-1533
Fax: (919)962-1533
**Subject(s):** Education

**Circ:** (Paid)1,300

**Journal of Public Health Dentistry (23309)**
American Association of Public Health Dentistry
University of North Carolina
School of Public Health
1105F McGavran-Greenberg Bldg.
Chapel Hill, NC 27599-7400
Phone: (919)966-7388
Fax: (919)966-0961
**Subject(s):** Dentistry

**Circ:** (Controlled)‡1,300

**The Mississippi Banker (16883)**
Mississippi Bankers Association
640 N State St.
PO Box 37
Jackson, MS 39205
Phone: (601)948-6366
Fax: (601)355-6461
**Subject(s):** Banking, Finance, and Investments

**Circ:** ‡1,300

**North Carolina Insight (23708)**
North Carolina Center for Public Policy Research
PO Box 430
Raleigh, NC 27602
Phone: (919)832-2839
Fax: (919)832-2847
**Subject(s):** Local, State, and Regional Publications; Social and Political Issues

**Circ:** (Paid)‡1,300

**Advances in Anatomic Pathology (6826)**
Lippincott Williams & Wilkins
c/o Mahul B. Amin, Emory Univ. Hospitals
1364 Clifton Rd, N.E., Room No.167
Atlanta, GA
**Subject(s):** Medicine and Surgery

**Circ:** 1,259

**Bow & Swing (5800)**
34 E Main St.
Apopka, FL 32703
Phone: (407)886-7151
Fax: (407)886-8464
**Subject(s):** Performing Arts

**Circ:** (Non-paid)200
(Paid)1,250

**The Chattahoochee Review (7131)**
Georgia Perimeter College
2101 Womack Rd.
Dunwoody, GA 30338-4497
Phone: (770)551-3019
Fax: (770)551-7471
**Subject(s):** Literature and Literary Reviews

**Circ:** (Paid)185
(Non-paid)1,250

**Papers of the Bibliographical Society of America (28055)**
Bibliographical Society of America
University of South Carolina
Thomas Cooper Library
Columbia, SC 29208
Phone: (803)777-7046
Fax: (803)777-7046
**Subject(s):** Book Trade and Author News; Indexes, Abstracts, Reports, Proceedings, and Bibliographies

**Circ:** ‡1,250

**Carolina Christian (23885)**
Carolina Christian Publications Inc.
PO Box 1369
Yadkinville, NC 27055
Phone: (336)374-3199
**Subject(s):** Religious Publications

**Circ:** ‡1,200

**College Student Affairs Journal (28023)**
Clemson University
Clemson, SC 29634
Phone: (864)656-3311
**Subject(s):** Education; College Publications

**Circ:** (Paid)1,200

**Comics Revue (28824)**
Manuscript Press
PO Box 336
Mountain Home, TN 37684
Phone: (423)926-7495
**Subject(s):** Comics and Comic Technique; Collecting

**Circ:** (Non-paid)‡50
(Paid)‡1,200

**Current (16976)**
National Marine Educators Association
PO Box 1470
Ocean Springs, MS 39566-1470
Phone: (601)374-7557
Fax: (601)374-5559
**Subject(s):** Ecology and Conservation

**Circ:** (Non-paid)200
(Paid)1,200

**Focal Point (6584)**
Professional Opticians of Florida
1947 Greenwood Dr.
Tallahassee, FL 32303-4825
Phone: (850)201-2622
Fax: (850)201-2625
**Subject(s):** Ophthalmology, Optometry, and Optics

**Circ:** 1,200

**Health Care Management REVIEW (HCMR) (6086)**
Aspen Publishers Inc.
c/o SueEllen Pinkerton
PO Box 33039
Indialantic, FL 32903
**Subject(s):** Hospitals and Healthcare Institutions

**Circ:** (Paid)‡1,200

**The Hill (11717)**
Henderson Community College
2660 S Green
Henderson, KY 42420-4699
Phone: (270)830-5346
Fax: (270)827-8635
**Subject(s):** College Publications

**Circ:** (Non-paid)‡1,200

**Journal of the Alabama Academy of Science (37)**
10 Cary Hall
Auburn University
Auburn, AL 36830
Phone: (334)844-9262
Fax: (334)844-4065
**Subject(s):** Science (General)

**Circ:** ‡1,200

**Mississippi Libraries Association (16889)**
Mississippi Library Association
PO Box 20448
Jackson, MS 39289-1448
Phone: (601)266-4249
Fax: (601)266-6033
**Subject(s):** Library and Information Science

**Circ:** ‡1,200

**Number One (28614)**
Volunteer State Community College
1480 Nashville Pke.
Gallatin, TN 37066
Phone: (615)452-8600
Fax: (615)230-3228
**Subject(s):** Literature; Poetry

**Circ:** (Controlled)1,200

**The Seed Pod (6508)**
American Hibiscus Society
c/o Rita Hall
3194, 52 Way N
Saint Petersburg, FL 33710
Phone: (727)525-4888
Fax: (727)521-4849
**Subject(s):** Horticulture

**Circ:** (Controlled)1,200

**The Southern Journal of Philosophy (28780)**
University of Memphis
329 Clement Hall
3704 Walker Ave.
Memphis, TN 38152-0001
Phone: (901)678-2669
Fax: (901)678-4365
**Subject(s):** Philosophy

**Circ:** (Non-paid)‡60
(Paid)‡1,200

**Newspaper Research Journal (28775)**
Department of Journalism
University of Memphis
Memphis, TN 38152
Phone: (901)678-4238
Fax: (901)678-4287
**Subject(s):** Journalism and Publishing

**Circ:** ‡1,175

**Seminars in Laparoscopic Surgery (6984)**
Elsevier
C/o Bruce V. MacFadyen, Jr, Editor
Medical College of Georgia
Department of Surgery
1120 15th St.
Augusta, GA 30912-4000
**Subject(s):** Medicine and Surgery

**Circ:** ‡1,172

**Journal of the American Leather Chemists Association (28046)**
American Leather Chemists Association
330 White Falls Dr.
Columbia, SC 29212
**Subject(s):** Chemistry, Chemicals, and Chemical Engineering; Shoes, Leather, and Luggage

**Circ:** 1,150

**Bulletin of Environmental Contamination and Toxicology (6147)**
Springer-Verlag New York Inc.
c/o Herbert N. Nigg, Ph.D.
University of Florida
700 Experiment Sta. Rd.
Lake Alfred, FL 33850
**Subject(s):** Toxicology

**Circ:** (Combined)1,100

**CASTANEA (23335)**
Southern Appalachian Botanical Society
University of N Carolina at Charlotte
Dept. of Biology
Charlotte, NC 28223
Phone: (704)687-4065
**Subject(s):** Botany

**Circ:** (Paid)‡1,100

**Daily Bulletin (23296)**
Institute of Government
University of North Carolina
Knapp-Sanders Bldg., CB 3330
Chapel Hill, NC 27599-3330
Phone: (919)966-4119

Fax: (919)962-2707
**Subject(s):** Politics

**Circ:** (Combined)1,100

**Journal of the History of Medicine and Allied Sciences** (23424)
Oxford University Press
Margaret Humphreys, Department of History
Duke University, Box 90719
Durham, NC 27708
Phone: (919)684-2285
Fax: (919)681-7670
**Subject(s):** History and Genealogy; Medicine and Surgery

**Circ:** 1,100

**Mass Communication and Society** (23311)
Association for Education in Journalism & Mass Communication
c/o Carol Pardun
University of North Carolina
School of Journalism & Mass Communication
CB No. 3365, 397 Carroll Hall
Chapel Hill, NC 27599-3365
Phone: (919)962-0025
**Subject(s):** Communications

**Circ:** (Paid)1,100

**Mississippi Geology** (16887)
Mississippi Department of Environmental Quality
Office of Geology, Box 20307
Jackson, MS 39289
Phone: (601)961-5500
Fax: (601)961-5521
**Subject(s):** Geology; Science (General)

**Circ:** (Non-paid)1,100

**North Carolina Law Review** (23313)
North Carolina Law Review Association
University of North Carolina
Van Hecke-Wettach Hall
Chapel Hill, NC 27599-3380
Phone: (919)962-1526
Fax: (919)962-1527
**Subject(s):** Law

**Circ:** (Controlled)‡500
(Paid)‡1,100

**Studies in Philology** (23322)
University of North Carolina Press
232 Greenlaw Hall, CB 3520
University of North Carolina-Chapel Hill
Chapel Hill, NC 27599-3520
Phone: (919)962-7042
Fax: (919)962-3520
**Subject(s):** Literature; Philology, Language, and Linguistics

**Circ:** (Combined)1,100

**Tennessee Academy of Science Journal** (28632)
Tennessee Academy of Science
2001 Craven Ln.
Hixson, TN 37343
Phone: (865)974-3594
**Subject(s):** Science (General)

**Circ:** ‡1,100

**Oral History Review** (270)
University of California Press/Journals
c/o Andrew J. Dunar, Editor
Univ. of Alabama in Huntsville
Dept. of History
Huntsville, AL 35899
**Subject(s):** History and Genealogy; Humanities

**Circ:** 1,057

**The Journal of ECT** (23871)
Lippincott Williams & Wilkins
c/o Vaughn McCall
Dept. of Psychiatry and Behavioral Medicine
Bowman Gray School of Medicine
Wake Forest Univ., Medical Center Boulevard
Winston Salem, NC 27157-0001
**Subject(s):** Laboratory Research (Scientific and Medical)

**Circ:** (Paid)748
1,017

**ABTA Quarterly Magazine** (5977)
American Bridge Teachers' Association
14840 Crystal Cove Ct.
Fort Myers, FL 33919-7417
Phone: (239)437-4106
**Subject(s):** Games and Puzzles; Crafts, Models, Hobbies, and Contests

**Circ:** 1,000

**Arcana** (27997)
Swedenborg Association
278-A Meeting St.
Charleston, SC 29401
Phone: (843)853-6211
Fax: (843)853-6226
**Subject(s):** Religious Publications; Theology

**Circ:** 1,000

**Best Sellers Collection** (6844)
Drawing Board Atlanta Inc.
PO Box 15556
Atlanta, GA 30333-0556
Phone: (404)681-4601
Fax: (404)624-4063
**Subject(s):** Architecture; Construction, Contracting, Building, and Excavating

**Circ:** (Combined)1,000

**The Chat** (23694)
Carolina Bird Club Inc.
11 W Jones St.
Raleigh, NC 27601-1029
Phone: (919)733-7450
Fax: (919)715-6439
**Subject(s):** Ornithology and Oology

**Circ:** ‡1,000

**Environmental Management** (28942)
Springer-Verlag New York Inc.
c/o Virginia H. Dale
Environmental Sciences Division
Oak Ridge National Laboratory
Oak Ridge, TN 37831-6036
**Subject(s):** Ecology and Conservation

**Circ:** (Combined)**1,000**

**Florida Entomologist** (6082)
Florida Entomological Society
University of Florida, TREC
18905 SW 280 St.
Homestead, FL 33031
Phone: (305)246-7001
Fax: (305)246-7003
**Subject(s):** Entomology; Spanish; Indexes, Abstracts, Reports, Proceedings, and Bibliographies

**Circ:** ‡1,000

**Florida Funeral Director** (6577)
Florida Funeral Directors Services Inc.
PO Box 10727
Tallahassee, FL 32302-2727
Phone: (850)224-1969
Fax: (850)224-7965
**Subject(s):** Funeral Directors

**Circ:** (Non-paid)50
(Paid)1,000

**Florida Review** (6364)
University of Central Florida
PO Box 160000
Orlando, FL 32816-1346
Phone: (407)823-5152
Fax: (407)823-6582
**Subject(s):** Literature; Poetry

**Circ:** (Controlled)1,000

**The Founders Journal** (5859)
PO Box 150931
Cape Coral, FL 33915
Phone: (239)772-1400
Fax: (239)772-1140
**Subject(s):** Religious Publications

**Circ:** (Paid)1,000

**I Am Nation News** (28960)
Mark-Age Inc.
PO Box 10
Pioneer, TN 37847
Phone: (423)784-3269
Fax: (423)784-3269
**Subject(s):**

**Circ:** ‡1,000

**Journal of American Ethnic History** (6888)
Transaction Publishers
School of History, Technology and Society
Georgia Institute of Technology
205 North Ave.
Atlanta, GA 30332
Phone: (404)894-0535
Fax: (404)894-0535
**Subject(s):** History and Genealogy

**Circ:** (Paid)‡1,000

**Journal of Medieval and Early Modern Studies** (23425)
Duke University Press
Duke University
PO Box 90656
Durham, NC 27708-0656
Phone: (919)660-2436
Fax: (919)681-9298
**Subject(s):** History and Genealogy

**Circ:** (Combined)1,000

**Journal of Muscle Shoals History** (222)
Tennessee Valley Historical Society
2815 Alexander St.
Florence, AL 35633
**Subject(s):** History and Genealogy

**Circ:** (Paid)1,000

**Peabody Journal of Education** (28874)
Lawrence Erlbaum Associates Inc.
Box 41
Peabody College of Vanderbilt University
Nashville, TN 37203
Phone: (615)343-7094
Fax: (615)343-7094
**Subject(s):** Education

**Circ:** ‡1,000

**SAQ** (23438)
Duke University Press
09B W. Duke Bldg. Box 90676
Duke University
Durham, NC 27708-0676
Phone: (919)684-2540
Fax: (919)684-3958
**Subject(s):** Literature

**Circ:** ‡1,000

**School Law Bulletin (Chapel Hill)** (23317)
Institute of Government
University of North Carolina
Knapp-Sanders Bldg., CB 3330
Chapel Hill, NC 27599-3330
Phone: (919)966-4119
Fax: (919)962-2707
**Subject(s):** Law

**Circ:** (Combined)1,000

**Social Science Computer Review** (23714)
Sage Publications Inc.
c/o G. David Garson
College of Humanities & Social Science, NCSU
PO Box 8101
Raleigh, NC 27695-8101
**Subject(s):** Computers; Sociology; Economics; Political Science; Psychology and Psychiatry

**Circ:** 1,000

**Southern Poetry Review** (7402)
Armstrong Atlantic State University
11935 Abercorn St.
Savannah, GA 31419
Phone: (912)927-5289
Fax: (912)927-5399
**Subject(s):** Literature; Poetry

**Circ:** (Controlled)1,000

**State and Local Government Review** (6815)
Carl Vinson Institute of Government
201 N. Milledge Ave.
Athens, GA 30602-5482
Phone: (706)542-2736
Fax: (706)542-9301
**Subject(s):** Political Science; Politics

**Circ:** (Controlled)1,000

**Zine World** (28833)
PO Box 330156
Murfreesboro, TN 37133
**Subject(s):** Alternative and Underground; Literature and Literary Reviews

**Circ:** (Paid)1000

**Journal of the National Collegiate Honors Council (JNCHC)** (6494)
Notional Collegiate Honors Council
c/o Ada Long
316 Cook St.
Saint George Island, FL 32328-2453
Phone: (850)927-3776
Fax: (850)927-2337
**Subject(s):** Education

**Circ:** (Non-paid)990

**Copyright Law Reports**  (6496)
CCH Inc.
10100 Ninth St. N.
Saint Petersburg, FL 33716
Phone: (813)576-3189
Fax: (813)577-0301
**Subject(s):** Patents, Trademarks, and Copyrights
**Circ:** ‡950

**The Florida Anthropologist**  (6691)
Florida Anthropological Society Inc.
9907 High Meadow Ave.
Thonotosassa, FL 33592-2458
**Subject(s):** Anthropology and Ethnology; Archaeology
**Circ:** ‡950

**Journal of Crustacean Biology**  (6552)
The Crustacean Society
c/o David Camp, Editor
PO Box 4430
Seminole, FL 33775-4430
Phone: (727)294-0238
Fax: (727)294-0238
**Subject(s):** Biology; Science (General)
**Circ:** (Paid)‡952

**Southern Business & Economic Journal**  (362)
Auburn University at Montgomery
Department of Economics
School of Business, Rm. 324
PO Box 244023
Montgomery, AL 36124-4023
Phone: (334)244-3454
Fax: (334)244-3792
**Subject(s):** Business
**Circ:** (Combined)950

**Southern Quarterly**  (16849)
University of Southern Mississippi
118 College Dr., No. 5053
Hattiesburg, MS 39406-5053
Phone: (601)266-4350
Fax: (601)266-6033
**Subject(s):** Humanities
**Circ:** ‡950

**Duke Mathematical Journal**  (23298)
Duke University Press
Univ. of N. Carolina
Dept. of Mathematics
CB 3250 Phillips Hall
Chapel Hill, NC 27599-3250
Phone: (919)962-8159
Fax: (919)962-8160
**Subject(s):** Mathematics
**Circ:** ‡915

**The Carolina Quarterly**  (20204)
University of North Carolina at Chapel Hill
Greenlaw Hall, CB 3520
Chapel Hill, NC 27599-3520
Phone: (919)962-0244
Fax: (919)962-3520
**Subject(s):** Literature; Poetry; Literature and Literary Reviews
**Circ:** (Combined)900

**English Literature in Transition**  (23516)
ELT Press
English Dept., University of N Carolina
PO Box 26170
Greensboro, NC 27402-6170
Phone: (336)334-5446
Fax: (336)334-3281
**Subject(s):** Literature
**Circ:** ‡900

**Mississippi Law Journal**  (17037)
Box 849
University, MS 38677-0849
Phone: (662)915-6870
Fax: (662)915-7948
**Subject(s):** Law
**Circ:** (Paid)900

**The Mississippi Quarterly**  (16958)
Mississippi State University
Box 5272
Mississippi State, MS 39762
Phone: (662)325-3069
Fax: (662)325-3645
**Subject(s):** Literature
**Circ:** (Combined)900

**Poetics Today**  (23434)
Duke University Press
905 W Main St., Ste. 18 B
PO Box 90660
Durham, NC 27708-0660
Phone: (919)687-3600
Fax: (919)688-4574
**Subject(s):** Literature
**Circ:** (Paid)900

**Southeastern Geographer**  (23559)
Association of American Geographers, Southeastern Div.
East Carolina University
Greenville, NC 27858
Phone: (252)328-6230
Fax: (252)328-6054
**Subject(s):** Geography
**Circ:** (Combined)900

**Theory and Research in Social Education**  (6044)
National Council for the Social Studies
C/O Elizabeth Anne Yeager
School of Teaching and Learning, Univ. of Florida
2423-D Norman Hall
PO Box 117048
Gainesville, FL 32611
Phone: (352)392-9191
Fax: (352)392-9193
**Subject(s):** Social Sciences
**Circ:** 896

**Journal of Pharmaceutical Marketing & Management**  (16981)
The Haworth Press Inc.
Medical Marketing Economics, LLC
1223 Jackson Ave., Ste. 301
Oxford, MS 38655
Phone: (662)281-0502
**Subject(s):** Drugs and Pharmaceuticals
**Circ:** (Paid)886

**Kentucky Law Journal**  (11770)
Univ. of Ky College of Law
University of Kentucky College of Law
148 Law Bldg.
Lexington, KY 40506
Phone: (606)257-8333
Fax: (606)323-1061
**Subject(s):** Law
**Circ:** (Controlled)‡475
(Paid)‡880

**Journal of Parapsychology**  (23426)
Parapsychology Press
2741 Campus Walk Ave., Bldg. 500
Durham, NC 27705
Phone: (919)688-8241
Fax: (919)683-4338
**Subject(s):** Parapsychology; Science (General)
**Circ:** (Non-paid)‡117
(Paid)‡872

**The Mecklenburg Times**  (23349)
400 Clarice Ave., Ste. 100
PO Box 36306
Charlotte, NC 28236-2820
Phone: (704)377-6221
Fax: (704)377-6214
**Subject(s):** Law; Real Estate
**Circ:** (Non-paid)‡81
(Paid)‡857

**NGA News**  (23705)
North Carolina Propane Gas Association
5112 Bur Oak Cir.
Raleigh, NC 27612
Phone: (919)787-8485
Fax: (919)781-7481
**Subject(s):** Petroleum, Oil, and Gas
**Circ:** 850

**Tennessee Trucking News**  (28893)
Tennessee Trucking Association
4531 Trousdale Dr.
Nashville, TN 37204-4513
Phone: (615)777-2882
Fax: (615)777-2024
**Subject(s):** Trucks and Trucking
**Circ:** 853

**Journal of Third World Studies**  (6782)
Association of Third World Studies Inc.
PO Box 1232
Americus, GA 31709
Phone: (229)931-2078

Fax: (229)931-2960
**Subject(s):** International Affairs
**Circ:** (Paid)815

**American Journalism**  (218)
University of North Alabama
Box 5174
Florence, AL 35632
Phone: (256)765-4945
Fax: (256)765-4839
**Subject(s):** History and Genealogy; Communications; Journalism and Publishing
**Circ:** (Paid)800

**Ancient Mesoamerica**  (28841)
Cambridge University Press
C/O William R. Fowler Jr., Vanderbilt University
PO Box 6307-B
Nashville, TN 37235
**Subject(s):** Archaeology
**Circ:** (Non-paid)‡65
(Paid)‡800

**College Student Journal**  (310)
Project Innovation
PO Box 8508
Spring Hill Station
Mobile, AL 36689-8508
Phone: (251)343-1878
Fax: (251)343-1878
**Subject(s):** Education
**Circ:** ‡800

**Communications in Soil Science and Plant Analysis**  (6794)
Marcel Dekker Inc.
c/o Harry A. Mills
183 Paradise Blvd., Ste. 104
Athens, GA 30607
Phone: (706)613-7813
Fax: (706)613-7573
**Subject(s):** Scientific Agricultural Publications
**Circ:** ‡800

**The Greensboro Review**  (23517)
University of North Carolina at Greensboro
134 McIver, UNCG
PO Box 26170
Greensboro, NC 27402-6170
Phone: (336)334-5459
Fax: (336)256-1470
**Subject(s):** Literature
**Circ:** (Combined)800

**Journal of Cancer Education**  (7418)
American Association for Cancer Education
c/o Virginia Krawiec, MPA, Sec.
PO Box 601
Snellville, GA 30078-0601
Phone: (404)329-7612
Fax: (404)321-4669
**Subject(s):** Medicine and Surgery; Health and Healthcare; Health
**Circ:** 800

**Journal of Family Issues**  (6033)
Sage Publications Inc.
c/o Constance Shehan, Editor, Journal of Family Issues
Dept. of Sociology
Univ. of Florida
Gainesville, FL 32611
**Subject(s):** Sociology; Marriage and Family
**Circ:** (Paid)‡800

**Labor Studies Journal**  (11771)
West Virginia University Press
University of Kentucky
Center for Labor Education and Research
235 Business and Economy Building
Lexington, KY 40506
**Subject(s):** Labor
**Circ:** (Paid)‡800

**Poems and Plays**  (28827)
Middle Tennessee State University
English Dept.
Murfreesboro, TN 37132
Phone: (615)898-2712
**Subject(s):** Literature and Literary Reviews; Poetry; Drama and Theatre
**Circ:** (Combined)800

**Social Theory and Practice (6600)**
Florida State University
151 Dodd Hall
Tallahassee, FL 32306-1500
Phone: (850)644-0220
Fax: (850)644-3832
**Subject(s):** Philosophy
**Circ:** (Combined)800

**Southern Literary Journal (23321)**
University of North Carolina Press
Greenlaw Hall, CB 3520
University of North Carolina-Chapel Hill
Chapel Hill, NC 27599-3520
Phone: (919)962-3017
Fax: (919)962-3520
**Subject(s):** Literature
**Circ:** (Paid)800

**Tropical Lepidoptera (6047)**
Association for Tropical Lepidotera
c/o Dr. J. B. Heppner
Florida State Collection of Arthropods
Gainesville, FL
**Subject(s):** Entomology; Zoology
**Circ:** (Combined)805

**Under Western Skies (23830)**
World of Yesterday
104 Chestnut Wood Dr.
Waynesville, NC 28786-6514
Phone: (828)646-6864
**Subject(s):** Motion Pictures; Radio, Television, Cable, and Video
**Circ:** (Paid)800

**Early American Literature (23299)**
University of North Carolina Press
426 Greenlaw Hall, CB 3520
University of North Carolina-Chapel Hill
Chapel Hill, NC 27599-3520
Phone: (919)962-3520
Fax: (919)962-3520
**Subject(s):** Literature
**Circ:** (Paid)750

**Greek, Roman, and Byzantine Studies (23416)**
Duke University
Box 90103
Durham, NC 27708
Phone: (919)684-6456
Fax: (919)681-4262
**Subject(s):** History and Genealogy
**Circ:** (Non-paid)‡20
 (Paid)‡750

**Gulf South Historical Review (313)**
University of South Alabama
Humanities 344
Mobile, AL 36688
Phone: (251)460-6210
Fax: (251)460-6750
**Subject(s):** History and Genealogy
**Circ:** (Combined)750

**Journal of Agricultural and Applied Economics (36)**
C/O Henry W. Kinnucan, Editor
213 Comer Hall
Simmons Dr.
Auburn University
Auburn, AL 36849-5401
Phone: (334)844-5614
Fax: (334)844-5639
**Subject(s):** General Agriculture
**Circ:** (Paid)750

**The Kentucky Press (11676)**
Kentucky Press Association Inc.
101 Consumer Ln.
Frankfort, KY 40601
Phone: (502)223-8821
Fax: (502)226-3867
**Subject(s):** Journalism and Publishing
**Circ:** ‡750

**A Lot of Bunkum (23597)**
Old Buncombe County Geological Society
17 Ravenwood Lne.
Horse Shoe, NC 28742-9704
**Subject(s):** History and Genealogy; Local, State, and Regional Publications
**Circ:** (Controlled)750

**NCLR (23556)**
East Carolina University
Greenville, NC 27858-4353
Phone: (252)328-6046
Fax: (252)328-4889
**Subject(s):** Literature; Poetry
**Circ:** (Paid)750

**Southwest Journal on Aging (23254)**
Partnerships for Aging
C/O W.Edward Folts, Ph.D.
Appalacian State Univ.
209 Chapel Wilson Hall
Boone, NC 28608
Phone: (828)262-2293
**Subject(s):** Gerontology; Health and Healthcare
**Circ:** (Controlled)750

**Smoky Mountain Historical Society Journal (28980)**
Smoky Mountain Historical Society
PO Box 5078
Sevierville, TN 37864-5078
**Subject(s):** History and Genealogy; Local, State, and Regional Publications
**Circ:** (Combined)725

**Appalachian Heritage (11536)**
Berea College
College PO Box 2166
Berea, KY 40404
Phone: (859)985-3000
Fax: (859)985-7300
**Subject(s):** Literature and Literary Reviews; Local, State, and Regional Publications
**Circ:** (Non-paid)200
 (Paid)700

**Birmingham Poetry Review (59)**
UAB (University of Alabama at Birmingham)
1530 3rd Ave. S
HB217
Birmingham, AL 35294-1260
Phone: (205)934-4250
Fax: (205)975-8125
**Subject(s):** Poetry; Literature
**Circ:** (Paid)700

**Buddhist-Christian Studies (12033)**
University of Hawaii Press
204 N. Lexington Ave.
Wilmore, KY 40390
Phone: (859)858-2145
Fax: (859)858-2375
**Subject(s):** Religious Publications; Philology, Language, and Linguistics
**Circ:** (Controlled)60
 (Paid)700

**Business & Professional Ethics Journal (6014)**
Center for Applied Philosophy
Box 118545
Univ. Of Florida
Gainesville, FL 32611
Phone: (352)392-2084
Fax: (352)392-5577
**Subject(s):** Philosophy; Business; Accountants and Accounting
**Circ:** 700

**Cerebral Cortex (23281)**
Oxford University Press
2001 Evans Rd., Ste. 12
Cary, NC 27513
Phone: (919)677-0977
Fax: (919)677-1714
**Subject(s):** Medicine and Surgery; Science (General)
**Circ:** (Paid)700

**Pensacola History Illustrated (6441)**
Pensacola Historical Society
110 E Church St.
Pensacola, FL 32502
Phone: (850)434-5455
Fax: (850)435-1581
**Subject(s):** History and Genealogy; Local, State, and Regional Publications
**Circ:** (Controlled)700

**Politics and Policy (7423)**
Georgia Southern University
Carroll Bldg.
PO Box 8101
Statesboro, GA 30460-8101
Phone: (912)681-5698
Fax: (912)681-5348
**Subject(s):** Political Science
**Circ:** (Paid)700

**Public Finance Review (6912)**
Sage Publications Inc.
Public Finance Review, Georgia State University
Department of Economics
University Plaza
Atlanta, GA 30303-3083
**Subject(s):** Banking, Finance, and Investments
**Circ:** (Paid)‡700

**Snake Nation Review (7474)**
Snake Nation Press
110 W. Force St.
Valdosta, GA 31601
**Subject(s):** Literature and Literary Reviews; Poetry; Literature
**Circ:** (Controlled)700

**Southern Humanities Review (46)**
Auburn University
9088 Haley Ctr.
Auburn University, AL 36849
Phone: (334)844-9088
Fax: (334)844-9027
**Subject(s):** Literature
**Circ:** (Combined)700

**Work and Occupations (28900)**
Sage Publications Inc.
Department of Sociology
Vanderbilt University
PO Box 1811, Sta. B
Nashville, TN 37235
**Subject(s):** Employment and Human Resources; Sociology
**Circ:** (Paid)‡700

**Health Care for Women International (23844)**
Taylor & Francis
c/o Eleanor Krassen Covan
University of North Carolina at Wilmington
601 S. College Rd.
Wilmington, NC 28403-5625
**Subject(s):** Medicine and Surgery; Health and Healthcare; Psychology and Psychiatry; Women's Interests
**Circ:** ‡696

**Geochemistry International (79)**
John Wiley and Sons Inc.
Interperiodica
PO Box 1831
Birmingham, AL 35201-1831
Phone: (205)995-1588
Fax: (800)633-4931
**Subject(s):** Geology; Chemistry, Chemicals, and Chemical Engineering
**Circ:** 675

**Journal of Bank Cost & Management Accounting (6889)**
Association for Management Information in Financial Services
3895 Fairfax Ct.
Atlanta, GA 30339
Phone: (770)444-3557
Fax: (770)444-9084
**Subject(s):** Accountants and Accounting; Banking, Finance, and Investments
**Circ:** 650

**Occupational Therapy in Health Care (23558)**
The Haworth Press Inc.
c/o Anne Elizabeth Dickerson
East Carolina Univ.
Dept. of Occupational Therapy
306 Belk Bldg.
Greenville, NC 27858-4345
Phone: (252)328-4439
Fax: (252)328-4470
**Subject(s):** Health and Healthcare
**Circ:** 650

**Sow's Ear Poetry Review (28089)**
The Word Process
355 Mt. Lebanon Rd.
Donalds, SC 29638
Phone: (864)379-8061
**Subject(s):** Poetry; Literature
**Circ:** (Combined)650

**Tampa Review  (6654)**
University of Tampa Press
401 W Kennedy Blvd.
Box 19F
Tampa, FL 33606-1490
Phone: (813)253-6266
Fax: (813)258-7593
**Subject(s):** Literature; Literature and Literary Reviews

**Circ:** (Paid)650

**Studies in the Literary Imagination  (6922)**
Georgia State University
PO Box 3970
Atlanta, GA 30302-3970
Phone: (404)651-2900
Fax: (404)651-1710
**Subject(s):** Literature

**Circ:** (Paid)624

**American Journal of Semiotics  (6438)**
Semiotic Society of America
Dept. of Anthropology
University of West Florida
Pensacola, FL 32514
Phone: (850)474-2797
Fax: (850)474-6278
**Subject(s):** Education

**Circ:** 600

**Annali D'Italianistica  (23292)**
Annali d'Italianistica Inc.
141 Dey Hall
CB 3170
University of N Carolina
Chapel Hill, NC 27599-3170
Phone: (919)962-1470
Fax: (919)962-5457
**Subject(s):** Literature; Intercultural Interests

**Circ:** 600

**Cliffhanger  (23826)**
World of Yesterday
104 Chestnut Wood Dr.
Waynesville, NC 28786-6514
Phone: (828)646-6864
**Subject(s):** Motion Pictures

**Circ:** (Paid)600

**The Cumberland Flag  (266)**
General Assembly Cumberland Presbyterian Church in America
226 Church St.
Huntsville, AL 35801
Phone: (256)536-7481
Fax: (256)536-7482
**Subject(s):** Religious Publications

**Circ:** (Non-paid)‡25
    (Paid)‡600

**Fish and Wildlife Research Institute Technical Reports  (6500)**
Florida Marine Research Institute
100 8th Ave. SE
Saint Petersburg, FL 33701-5095
Phone: (727)896-8626
Fax: (727)823-0166
**Subject(s):** Oceanography and Marine Studies; Management and Administration

**Circ:** (Non-paid)600

**Florida Marine Research Publications  (6501)**
Florida Marine Research Institute
100 8th Ave. SE
Saint Petersburg, FL 33701-5095
Phone: (727)896-8626
Fax: (727)823-0166
**Subject(s):** Oceanography and Marine Studies

**Circ:** (Non-paid)600

**Henry James Review  (11814)**
Johns Hopkins University Press
University of Louisville
Dept. of English
Louisville, KY 40292
Phone: (502)852-4671
Fax: (502)852-4182
**Subject(s):** Literature

**Circ:** ‡600

**Kentucky English Bulletin  (11558)**
Kentucky Council of Teachers of English-Language Arts
Dept. of English
Bowling Green, KY 42101
Phone: (270)745-5760
Fax: (270)745-2533

**Subject(s):** Education

**Circ:** (Paid)600

**Memoirs of the Hourglass Cruises  (6505)**
Florida Marine Research Institute
100 8th Ave. SE
Saint Petersburg, FL 33701-5095
Phone: (727)896-8626
Fax: (727)823-0166
**Subject(s):** Oceanography and Marine Studies

**Circ:** (Non-paid)600

**Tar River Poetry  (23560)**
East Carolina University
Greenville, NC 27858-4353
Phone: (252)328-6046
Fax: (252)328-4889
**Subject(s):** Poetry; Literature

**Circ:** (Paid)600

**Community & Junior College Libraries  (6456)**
The Haworth Press Inc.
c/o Susan Anderson
St. Petersburg College
7200 66th St. N.
Pinellas Park, FL 33781
Phone: (727)341-3719
Fax: (512)346-1467
**Subject(s):** Library and Information Science

**Circ:** (Paid)587

**Journal of Legal Economics  (221)**
University of North Alabama
PO Box 5077
Florence, AL 35632-0001
Phone: (256)765-4144
Fax: (256)765-4170
**Subject(s):** Economics

**Circ:** (Controlled)35
    (Paid)570

**Aroideana  (6554)**
International Aroid Society
PO Box 43-1853
South Miami, FL 33143
Phone: (772)462-5923
Fax: (305)665-4369
**Subject(s):** Home and Garden; Botany

**Circ:** 550

**Journal of Ethnobiology  (23307)**
Society of Ethnobiology
c/o Margaret Scarry, Sec.-Treas.
Dept. of Anthropology
University of North Carolina
CB 3115, Alumni Bldg.
Chapel Hill, NC 27599-3155
Phone: (919)962-3841
Fax: (919)962-1613
**Subject(s):** Spanish; French; Ethnic and Minority Studies; Biology

**Circ:** 520

**Appalachian Journal  (23249)**
Appalachian State University
Belk Library
PO Box 32026
Boone, NC 28608
Phone: (828)262-4072
Fax: (828)262-2553
**Subject(s):** History and Genealogy

**Circ:** (Paid)500

**Aura Literary/Arts Review  (54)**
University of Alabama - Birmingham
HUC 135
1530 3rd Ave. S
Birmingham, AL 35294-1150
Phone: (205)934-3216
Fax: (205)934-8050
**Subject(s):** Literature and Literary Reviews

**Circ:** (Non-paid)‡500

**Barber Coin Collectors Journal  (28756)**
Barber Coin Collector Society
PO Box 382246
Memphis, TN 38183
**Subject(s):** Collecting; Crafts, Models, Hobbies, and Contests

**Circ:** 500

**Bulletin of the Comediantes  (44)**
Auburn University
6030 Haley Ctr.
Auburn University, AL 36849
Phone: (334)844-4345

Fax: (334)844-6378
**Subject(s):** History and Genealogy; Drama and Theatre; Performing Arts; Intercultural Interests

**Circ:** (Paid)500

**Doklady Earth Sciences  (74)**
John Wiley and Sons Inc.
Interperiodica
PO Box 1831
Birmingham, AL 35201-1831
Fax: (800)633-4931
**Subject(s):** Geology

**Circ:** ‡500

**Eswau Huppeday  (23778)**
Broad River Genealogical Society Inc.
PO Box 2261
Shelby, NC 28151-2261
**Subject(s):** History and Genealogy

**Circ:** (Controlled)500

**Financial Services Review  (6873)**
Cadmus Journal Services
c/o Concrad S. Ciccotello, Editor
Dept. of Risk Management & Insurance
PO Box 4036
Georgia State Univ.
Atlanta, GA 30302-4036
Phone: (404)651-1711
Fax: (404)651-4219
**Subject(s):** Banking, Finance, and Investments

**Circ:** (Paid)500

**Journal of Aquatic Plant Management  (17041)**
Aquatic Plant Management Society
c/o Board of Directors
PO Box 821265
Vicksburg, MS 39182
Phone: (941)694-2174
Fax: (941)694-6959
**Subject(s):** Botany

**Circ:** 500

**Journal of Curriculum Theorizing  (7421)**
Caddo Gap Press
c/o Marla Morris,
Dept. of Curriculum, Foundations, and Research
Georgia Southern Univ.
PO Box 8144
Statesboro, GA 30460-8144
**Subject(s):** Education

**Circ:** (Paid)500

**Journal of Plant Nutrition  (6809)**
Marcel Dekker Inc.
c/o Harry A. Mills
183 Paradise Blvd., Ste.104
Athens, GA 30607
Phone: (706)613-7813
Fax: (706)613-7570
**Subject(s):** Botany

**Circ:** 500

**Pikeville Review  (11948)**
Pikeville College
147 Sycamore St.
Pikeville, KY 41501
Phone: (606)218-5250
Fax: (606)218-5269
**Subject(s):** Literature; Poetry; Literature and Literary Reviews

**Circ:** (Paid)500

**Plating & Surface Finishing  (6383)**
American Electroplaters and Surface Finishers Society
3660 Maguire Blvd., ste.250
Orlando, FL 32803-3075
Phone: (407)281-6441
Fax: (407)281-6446
**Subject(s):** Metal, Metallurgy, and Metal Trade

**Circ:** (Paid)‡508

**Southeastern Geology  (23440)**
Duke University
Box 90233
Durham, NC 27708-0233
Phone: (919)684-5321
Fax: (919)684-5833
**Subject(s):** Geology

**Circ:** ‡500

**Under the Sun  (28566)**
Tennessee Tech University
Box 5053
Cookeville, TN 38505
Phone: (931)372-3778

Fax: (931)372-6363
**Subject(s):** Literature and Literary Reviews
**Circ:** (Paid)500

**James Joyce Literary Supplement** (5891)
University of Miami
PO Box 248145
Coral Gables, FL 33124
Phone: (305)284-3973
Fax: (305)284-5635
**Subject(s):** Literature
**Circ:** (Combined)475

**Journal of Public Policy & Marketing** (6038)
American Marketing Association
c/o Joel B. Cohen, Editor
College of Business Administration
Univ. of Florida
302 Bryan Hall, PO Box117155
Gainesville, FL 32611-7155
Phone: (352)392-0161
Fax: (352)846-0457
**Subject(s):** Advertising and Marketing; Public Relations
**Circ:** (Paid)‡472

**Journal of Women and Aging** (6530)
The Haworth Press Inc.
1348 Cottonwood Tr.
Sarasota, FL 34232
Phone: (941)378-0894
Fax: (305)295-3861
**Subject(s):** Women's Interests; Gerontology
**Circ:** 467

**Archives of Andrology, an International Journal** (28157)
Taylor & Francis
c/o E.S.E. Hafez, Reproductive Health Center
78 Surfsong Rd.
Kiawah Island, SC 29455
**Subject(s):** Medicine and Surgery; Physiology and Anatomy
**Circ:** 453

**Constructive Approximation** (28041)
Springer-Verlag New York Inc.
c/o Ronald A. DeVore
Industrial Mathematics Institute
Department of Mathematics and Statistics
University of South Carolina
Columbia, SC 29208
Phone: (803)777-2632
**Subject(s):** Mathematics; Statistics
**Circ:** (Combined)450

**International Journal of Organizational Analysis** (11557)
Center for Advanced Studies in Management
1574 Mallory Ct.
Bowling Green, KY 42103-1300
Phone: (270)782-2601
Fax: (270)782-2601
**Subject(s):** Management and Administration
**Circ:** (Paid)450

**Journal of Instructional Psychology** (314)
PO Box 8826, Spring Hill Sta.
Mobile, AL 36689-0826
Phone: (251)343-1878
Fax: (251)343-1878
**Subject(s):** Education; Psychology and Psychiatry
**Circ:** ‡450

**Journal of Maintenance in the Addictions** (6373)
The Haworth Press Inc.
Corporate Medical Director
7061 Grand National Dr., Ste. 148
Orlando, FL 32819
Phone: (407)351-7080
**Subject(s):** Psychology and Psychiatry
**Circ:** (Paid)450

**Mark Twain Circular** (28009)
The Citadel
171 Moultrie St.
Charleston, SC 29409
Phone: (843)953-5000
Fax: (843)953-6767
**Subject(s):** Literature
**Circ:** (Paid)450

**Political Communication** (23435)
Taylor & Francis
c/o David L. Paletz, Political Communication
Dept. of Political Science
Box 90204
Duke University
Durham, NC 27708
**Subject(s):** Politics
**Circ:** 450

**Tipularia** (7348)
Georgia Botanical Society
7575 Rico Rd.
Palmetto, GA 30268
Phone: (770)463-4227
**Subject(s):** Botany
**Circ:** (Paid)450

**Entomological Review** (75)
John Wiley and Sons Inc.
Interperiodica
PO Box 1831
Birmingham, AL 35201-1831
Phone: (205)995-1588
Fax: (800)633-4931
**Subject(s):** Entomology
**Circ:** 425

**Holarctic Lepidoptera** (6027)
Association for Tropical Lepidotera
PO Box 141210
Gainesville, FL 32614-1210
Phone: (352)392-5894
Fax: (352)373-3249
**Subject(s):** Entomology; Zoology
**Circ:** (Combined)425

**Paleontological Journal** (94)
John Wiley and Sons Inc.
Interperiodica
PO Box 1831
Birmingham, AL 35201-1831
Phone: (205)995-1588
Fax: (800)995-1588
**Subject(s):** Biology
**Circ:** 425

**Renal Failure** (23316)
Marcel Dekker Inc.
c/o William F. Finn, Department of Medicine
University of N. Carolina
CB 7155, 345 MacNider Bldg.
Chapel Hill, NC 27599
**Subject(s):** Medicine and Surgery
**Circ:** 425

**Resource Sharing & Information Networks** (5967)
The Haworth Press Inc.
c/o Tom W. Sloan, Executive Dir.
Southeast Florida Library Information Network
Northern Illinois University
Fort Lauderdale, FL
**Subject(s):** Library and Information Science
**Circ:** (Paid)424

**The Journal of Craniofacial Surgery** (6638)
Lippincott Williams & Wilkins
Tampa Bay Craniofacial Center Inc.
801 W. Dr. Martin Luther King Jr. Blvd.
Dr. Martin Luther King Jr. Blvd.
Tampa, FL 33603
Phone: (813)238-0400
Fax: (800)783-0409
**Subject(s):** Medicine and Surgery
**Circ:** (Paid)411

**UMI's Banking Information Index** (11844)
Pro Quest Information and Learning
620 S. 3rd St.
Louisville, KY 40205
Phone: (502)583-4111
Fax: (502)589-5572
**Subject(s):** Indexes, Abstracts, Reports, Proceedings, and Bibliographies; Banking, Finance, and Investments
**Circ:** (Non-paid)20
 (Paid)410

**a/b** (23289)
University of North Carolina
CB No.3520
Chapel Hill, NC 27599-3520
Phone: (919)962-8482
Fax: (919)962-3520
**Subject(s):** Literature
**Circ:** (Paid)400

**Ancestry** (6715)
Palm Beach County Genealogical Society Inc.
P.O. Box 1746
West Palm Beach, FL 33402-1746
Phone: (561)832-3279
**Subject(s):** History and Genealogy
**Circ:** (Combined)400

**Argia** (6568)
Dragonfly Society of the Americas
c/o Jerell J. Daigle
2067 Little River Ln.
Tallahassee, FL 32311
**Subject(s):** Entomology; Natural History and Nature Study
**Circ:** 400

**Delos** (6020)
University of Florida
2346 NPB 118440
Gainesville, FL 32611
Phone: (352)377-1560
Fax: (352)392-0524
**Subject(s):** Literature and Literary Reviews
**Circ:** (Controlled)25
 (Paid)400

**Heat Transfer-Recent Contents online Journal** (6026)
American Society of Mechanical Engineers
c/o Jill Peterson, Editor
Dept. of Mechanical Engineering
Univ. of Florida
Gainesville, FL 32611-2050
Phone: (352)392-4514
Fax: (352)392-1071
**Subject(s):** Engineering (Various branches)
**Circ:** (Paid)⊕400

**Independent Republic Quarterly** (28082)
Horry County Historical Society
606 Main St.
Conway, SC 29526-4340
Phone: (843)488-1966
**Subject(s):** History and Genealogy; Local, State, and Regional Publications
**Circ:** (Combined)400

**Jackson County Chronicles** (425)
Jackson County, Alabama Historical Association
435 Barbee Ln.
Scottsboro, AL 35769-3745
Phone: (256)574-3556
**Subject(s):** History and Genealogy
**Circ:** (Paid)400

**Journal of Men's Studies** (28627)
PO Box 32
Harriman, TN 37748-0032
Phone: (423)369-2375
Fax: (423)369-1125
**Subject(s):** Intercultural Interests
**Circ:** (Paid)400

**Journal of Nursing Measurement** (6895)
Springer Publishing Co.
c/o Ora L. Strickland, Ph.D., Editor
Nell Hodgson Woodruff School of Nursing
Emory University
Atlanta, GA 30322
Phone: (404)727-7941
Fax: (404)727-0536
**Subject(s):** Nursing; Hospitals and Healthcare Institutions
**Circ:** (Combined)400

**Nucleosides & Nucleotides & Nucleic Acids** (91)
Marcel Dekker Inc.
c/o John A.Secrist III
Southern Research Institute
PO Box 55305
Birmingham, AL 35255-5305
**Subject(s):** Biology
**Circ:** 400

**Numerical Functional Analysis and Optimization** (6375)
Marcel Dekker Inc.
c/o M. Z. Nashed
Department of Mathematics
PO Box 161364, MAP 209
University of Central Florida
Orlando, FL 32816-1364
**Subject(s):** Mathematics
**Circ:** 400

**The Journal of Deaf Studies and Deaf Education**  (23285)
Oxford University Press
2001 Evans Rd., Ste. 12
Cary, NC 27513
Phone: (919)677-0977
Fax: (919)677-1714
**Subject(s):** Hearing and Speech; Psychology and Psychiatry
**Circ:** (Paid)396

**North Carolina Journal of International Law and Commercial Regulation**  (23312)
University of North Carolina at Chapel Hill
CB 3380
Chapel Hill, NC 27599-3380
Phone: (919)962-4402
Fax: (919)962-4713
**Subject(s):** Law; International Affairs
**Circ:** (Combined)395

**Tennessee Folklore Society Bulletin**  (28831)
Tennessee Folklore Society
Middle Tennessee State University
PO Box 529
Murfreesboro, TN 37132
Phone: (615)898-2663
Fax: (615)898-5098
**Subject(s):** History and Genealogy; Anthropology and Ethnology; Literature
**Circ:** (Non-paid)‡47
     (Paid)‡380

**Electric Machines Components and Systems**  (11761)
Taylor & Francis
c/o Jim Cathey, Editor, ECE Dept.
453C Anderson Hall
Univ. of Kentucky
Lexington, KY 40506-0046
Phone: (859)257-8043
**Subject(s):** Electronics Engineering; Power and Power Plants
**Circ:** (Combined)‡376

**Journal of Immunoassay and Immunochemistry**  (5838)
Marcel Dekker Inc.
c/o Dr. Jack Cazes
PO Box 740295
Boynton Beach, FL 33474-0295
**Subject(s):** Biology
**Circ:** 350

**Art Reference Services Quarterly**  (6013)
The Haworth Press Inc.
University of Florida
201 Fine Arts Bldg. A
Gainesville, FL 32611
Phone: (904)392-0222
**Subject(s):** Architecture; Art and Art History; Library and Information Science
**Circ:** 321

**Instrumentation Science & Technology**  (5837)
Marcel Dekker Inc.
c/o Eleanor Cazes
PO Box 740295
Boynton Beach, FL 33474-0295
**Subject(s):** Science (General); Chemistry, Chemicals, and Chemical Engineering; Ecology and Conservation
**Circ:** 325

**Journal of Child and Adolescent Substance Abuse**  (5959)
The Haworth Press Inc.
c/o Vincent Van Hasselt, Journal Co-Editor
Center for Psychological Studies, Nova Southeastern Univ.
3301 College Ave.
Fort Lauderdale, FL 33314
**Subject(s):** Substance Abuse and Treatment
**Circ:** (Paid)325

**Central Kentucky Researcher**  (11614)
Taylor County Historical Society
Box 14
Campbellsville, KY 42719
Phone: (502)465-7033
**Subject(s):** History and Genealogy; Local, State, and Regional Publications
**Circ:** (Controlled)315

**Leisure Sciences**  (23310)
Taylor & Francis
c/o Karla A. Henderson
Dept. of Recreation and Leisure Studies
CB 3185 Evergreen
Univ. of North Carolina at Chapel Hill
Chapel Hill, NC 27599-3185
Phone: (919)962-1222
Fax: (919)962-1223
**Subject(s):** Sociology
**Circ:** ‡311

**Combinatorics, Probability and Computing**  (28761)
Cambridge University Press
C/O Professor Bela Bollobas
Dept. of Mathematical Sciences
University of Memphis
Memphis, TN 38152
**Subject(s):** Computers
**Circ:** 300

**Gulf of Mexico Science**  (176)
Dauphin Island Sea Lab
101 Bienville Blvd.
Dauphin Island, AL 36528
Phone: (251)861-2141
Fax: (251)861-4646
**Subject(s):** Oceanography and Marine Studies
**Circ:** (Non-paid)114
     (Paid)302

**Journal of Applied Aquaculture**  (11667)
The Haworth Press Inc.
c/o Carl David Webster
Kentucky State Univ.
Aquaculture Research Ctr.
Frankfort, KY 40601
Fax: (502)564-9118
**Subject(s):** Socialized Farming
**Circ:** (Paid)301

**Journal of Mental Health and Aging**  (6640)
Springer Publishing Co.
c/o Donna Cohen, Ph.D., Editor
Univ. of S. Florida
Dept. of Aging and Mental Health
Louis de la Parte Florida Mental Health Institute
Tampa, FL 33612-3899
Phone: (813)974-1952
Fax: (813)974-1968
**Subject(s):** Gerontology; Medicine and Surgery; Health and Healthcare; Psychology and Psychiatry
**Circ:** (Combined)300

**Journal of Thermal Stresses**  (6311)
Taylor & Francis
c/o Richard D. Hetnarski
St. Raphael, Unit 1209
7117 Pelican Bay Blvd.
Naples, FL 34108
**Subject(s):** Physics
**Circ:** ‡308

**Nepantla**  (23429)
Duke University Press
Duke University
Campus Box 90409
2204 Erwin Rd.
Durham, NC 27708-0409
Phone: (919)681-1956
Fax: (919)681-8749
**Subject(s):** Humanities; Social Sciences
**Circ:** 300

**New Vico Studies**  (6905)
Philosophy Documentation Center
c/o Donald Phillip Verene
Dept. of Philosophy
Emory University
Atlanta, GA 30322
Phone: (404)727-4340
Fax: (404)727-4959
**Subject(s):** Philosophy
**Circ:** (Combined)300

**Preparative Biochemistry & Biotechnology**  (5839)
Marcel Dekker Inc.
c/o Eleanor Cazes
PO Box 740295
Boynton Beach, FL 33474-0295
**Subject(s):** Biology
**Circ:** 300

**Southeastern Journal of Music Education**  (6814)
University of Georgia
250 River Rd.
Athens, GA 30602
Phone: (706)542-3737
Fax: (706)542-2773
**Subject(s):** Music and Musical Instruments; Education
**Circ:** (Paid)300

**Oasis**  (6179)
Box 626
Largo, FL 33779-0626
Phone: (727)345-8505
**Subject(s):** Literature
**Circ:** (Combined)290

**Florida Journal of International Law**  (6021)
University of Florida
153 Bruton Geer
Gainesville, FL 32611
Phone: (352)392-4980
Fax: (352)392-3800
**Subject(s):** Law
**Circ:** (Combined)285

**Inhalation Toxicology**  (23699)
Taylor & Francis
c/o Donald E. Gardner, PhD
PO Box 97605
Raleigh, NC 27624-7605
**Subject(s):** Toxicology; Medicine and Surgery
**Circ:** ‡287

**Journal of Pharmacy Teaching**  (17035)
The Haworth Press Inc.
c/o Noel E. Wilkin
The Univ. of Mississippi
School of Pharmacy
Faser Hall, Rm. 219
University, MS 38677-1848
Phone: (662)915-1071
Fax: (662)915-5102
**Subject(s):** Drugs and Pharmaceuticals
**Circ:** (Paid)272

**Bulletin Baudelairien**  (28846)
Vanderbilt University
Box 6325, Sta. B
Nashville, TN 37235
Phone: (615)343-0372
**Subject(s):** Literature
**Circ:** 250

**IMRN**  (23420)
Duke University Press
905 W Main St., Ste. 18 B
PO Box 90660
Durham, NC 27708-0660
Phone: (919)687-3600
Fax: (919)688-4574
**Subject(s):** Mathematics
**Circ:** (Paid)237

**St. Thomas Law Review**  (6256)
St. Thomas University School of Law
16401 NW 37th Ave.
Miami, FL 33054
Phone: (305)623-2380
Fax: (305)474-2410
**Subject(s):** Law
**Circ:** (Paid)‡234

**Journal of Law and Public Policy**  (6036)
153 Bruton-Geer
University of Florida
Gainesville, FL 32611-7636
Phone: (352)392-4980
Fax: (352)392-3800
**Subject(s):** Law
**Circ:** (Paid)225

**Music Reference Services Quarterly**  (28051)
The Haworth Press Inc.
c/o Jennifer Ottervik, Univ. of South Carolina
Music Library - School of Music
Columbia, SC 29208
Phone: (803)777-5425
**Subject(s):** Library and Information Science; Music and Musical Instruments
**Circ:** 213

**Algebras, Groups & Geometries (6422)**
Hadronic Press Inc.
Institute for Basic Research
PO Box 1577
Palm Harbor, FL 34682
Phone: (727)934-9593
Fax: (727)934-9275
**Subject(s):** Mathematics
**Circ:** (Paid)200

**Dreams and Nightmares (461)**
1300 Kicker Rd.
Tuscaloosa, AL 35404-3954
Phone: (205)553-2284
**Subject(s):** Science Fiction, Mystery, Adventure, and Romance
**Circ:** (Combined)200

**Grape Times (6162)**
Florida Grape Growers Association
343 W Central Ave., 1
Lake Wales, FL 33853
Phone: (863)678-0523
Fax: (863)678-0609
**Subject(s):** Beverages, Brewing, and Bottling
**Circ:** 200

**The Journal of Human Performance in Extreme Environments (JHPEE) (6371)**
The Society for Human Performance in Extreme Environments (HPEE)
2652 Corbyton Ct.
Orlando, FL 32828
Phone: (407)381-7762
Fax: (407)381-7762
**Subject(s):** Sociology; Social Sciences; Psychology and Psychiatry; Anthropology and Ethnology; Engineering (Various branches); Medicine and Surgery
**Circ:** (Paid)200

**The Journal of Ideas (6427)**
Institute for Memetic Research Inc.
PO Box 15812
Panama City, FL 32406-5812
**Subject(s):** Philosophy
**Circ:** ‡200

**Professional Educator (39)**
Auburn University
3084 Haley Ctr.
Auburn, AL 36849-5218
Phone: (334)844-5793
Fax: (334)844-5785
**Subject(s):** Education
**Circ:** (Combined)200

**Television News Index and Abstracts (28882)**
Vanderbilt University TV News Archive
110 21st Ave. S., Ste. 704
Nashville, TN 37203
Phone: (615)322-2927
Fax: (615)343-8250
**Subject(s):** Radio, Television, Cable, and Video; Indexes, Abstracts, Reports, Proceedings, and Bibliographies
**Circ:** ‡200

**Bedford Historical Quarterly (28941)**
Bedford County Historical Society
c/o Roy Turrentine
339 Rippy Ridge Rd.
Normandy, TN 37360
Phone: (931)857-9341
**Subject(s):** History and Genealogy
**Circ:** (Combined)196

**Hadronic Journal (6423)**
Hadronic Press Inc.
Institute for Basic Research
PO Box 1577
Palm Harbor, FL 34682
Phone: (727)934-9593
Fax: (727)934-9275
**Subject(s):** Physics
**Circ:** (Paid)150

**Treewell (23356)**
Johnson C. Smith University
100 Beatties Ford Rd.
Charlotte, NC 28216
Phone: (704)378-1000
Fax: (704)378-3556
**Subject(s):** Poetry; College Publications
**Circ:** (Paid)150

**The Matthay News (28640)**
American Matthay Association
2447 Hwy. 45 By-pass
Jackson, TN 38305
**Subject(s):** Music and Musical Instruments
**Circ:** (Paid)142

**Hadronic Journal Supplement (6424)**
Hadronic Press Inc.
Institute for Basic Research
PO Box 1577
Palm Harbor, FL 34682
Phone: (727)934-9593
Fax: (727)934-9275
**Subject(s):** Physics
**Circ:** (Paid)100

## Western States

**Arizona Highways (742)**
2039 W. Lewis Ave.
Phoenix, AZ 85009
Phone: (602)712-2200
Fax: (602)254-4505
**Subject(s):** Travel and Tourism; History and Genealogy
**Circ:** ‡300,000,000

**Friendly Exchange (2212)**
Farmers Insurance Group of Cos.
4680 Wilshire Blvd.
Los Angeles, CA 90010
Phone: (208)239-8400
**Subject(s):** Lifestyle
**Circ:** (Controlled)‡6,100,000

**VIA (3232)**
California State Automobile Association
150 Van Ness Ave.
San Francisco, CA 94102
Phone: (415)565-2451
Fax: (415)863-4726
**Subject(s):** Automotive (Consumer); Travel and Tourism
**Circ:** (Paid)4,000,000

**Toy Tips (1537)**
9663 Santa Monica Blvd.
Beverly Hills, CA 90210
Phone: (310)553-8834
Fax: (310)553-8848
**Subject(s):** Children's Interests; Consumerism; Parenting
**Circ:** (Controlled)3,000,000

**Westways (1727)**
Automobile of S. California
3333 Fairview Rd., A327
Costa Mesa, CA 92626
Phone: (714)885-2376
Fax: (714)885-2335
**Subject(s):** Travel and Tourism
**Circ:** (Paid)2,652,703

**Denver Arts Center Programs (4279)**
The Publishing House Division of Colorado Word Works Inc.
1245 Champa St.
Denver, CO 80204
Phone: (303)893-4000
**Subject(s):** Drama and Theatre; Music and Musical Instruments
**Circ:** 2,600,000

**Focus on the Family Magazine (4197)**
Focus on the Family
8605 Explorer Dr.
Colorado Springs, CO 80920
Phone: (719)531-3400
Fax: (719)531-3484
**Subject(s):** Religious Publications; Marriage and Family
**Circ:** (Free)2,200,000

**Traveling Times (3945)**
Traveling Times Inc.
25061 Ave. Stanford, Ste. 10
Valencia, CA 91355-4551
Phone: (661)295-1250
Fax: (661)295-8558
**Subject(s):** Travel and Tourism
**Circ:** ‡1,650,000

**Shape (4068)**
Weider Publications
21100 Erwin St.
Woodland Hills, CA 91367
**Subject(s):** Health; Women's Interests
**Circ:** (Paid)1,538,192

**Los Angeles Times Magazine (2261)**
Los Angeles Times
202 W. 1st St.
Los Angeles, CA 90012
Phone: (213)237-7811
Fax: (213)237-7386
**Subject(s):** General Editorial
**Circ:** (Sun.)‡1,531,527

**Sunset Magazine (2454)**
Sunset Publishing Corporation
80 Willow Rd.
Menlo Park, CA 94025
Phone: (415)321-3600
Fax: (415)321-0551
**Subject(s):** Home and Garden; Travel and Tourism
**Circ:** (Paid)1,448,007

**Bon Appetit (2151)**
Conde Nast Publications Inc.
6300 Wilshire Blvd.
Los Angeles, CA 90048
Phone: (323)965-3633
**Subject(s):** Food and Cooking; Travel and Tourism
**Circ:** (Paid)1,292,109

**PC WORLD (3188)**
101 Communications
501 2nd St.
San Francisco, CA 94107
Phone: (415)243-0500
Fax: (415)442-1891
**Subject(s):** Computers; Business
**Circ:** (Paid)1,268,016

**Let's Live (2251)**
Franklin Publications
11050 Santa Monica Blvd.
Los Angeles, CA 90025
Phone: (310)445-7500
Fax: (310)445-7583
**Subject(s):** Health
**Circ:** (Combined)‡1,250,000

**ENCORE (32267)**
Encore Publishing Inc.
425 N. 85th St.
Seattle, WA 98103
Phone: (206)443-0445
Fax: (206)443-1246
**Subject(s):** Performing Arts; Drama and Theatre; Entertainment
**Circ:** (Combined)‡1,126,000

**Hustler Magazine (1533)**
L.F.P. Inc.
8484 Wilshire Blvd., Ste. 900
Beverly Hills, CA 90211
Phone: (323)651-5400
**Subject(s):** Sex/Erotica
**Circ:** 1,066,537

**Highways (3966)**
TL Enterprises Inc.
2575 Vista Del Mar
Ventura, CA 93001
Phone: (805)667-4100
Fax: (805)667-4484
**Subject(s):** (Outdoors)
**Circ:** ‡940,000

**Architectural Digest (2135)**
Conde Nast Publications Inc.
6300 Wilshire Blvd.
Los Angeles, CA 90048
Phone: (213)965-3700
Fax: (213)937-1458
**Subject(s):** Home and Garden
**Circ:** (Paid)821,992

**Road & Track (2544)**
Hachette Filipacchi Media U.S. Inc.
1499 Monrovia Ave.
Newport Beach, CA 92663
Phone: (949)631-2757
Fax: (949)631-2757

**Subject(s):** Automotive (Consumer); (Auto Racing)
**Circ:** (Paid)771,024

**Vibe Magazine (4143)**
Time Ventures
PO Box 59580
Boulder, CO 80322
Phone: (303)678-8475
Fax: (303)661-1181
**Subject(s):** Music and Musical Instruments
**Circ:** (Paid)760,152

**Sierra (3214)**
Sierra Club
85 Second St., 2nd Fl.
San Francisco, CA 94105-3441
Phone: (415)977-5500
Fax: (415)977-5799
**Subject(s):** Environmental and Natural Resources Conservation
**Circ:** (Paid)728,000

**Men's Fitness (4063)**
Weider Publications
21100 Erwin St.
Woodland Hills, CA 91367-3712
Phone: (818)884-6800
Fax: (818)595-0463
**Subject(s):** (General Sports)
**Circ:** (Paid)607,738

**Continental Newstime (3010)**
Continental Features/Continental News Service
501 W Broadway, Plz. A
PMB No. 265
San Diego, CA 92101
Phone: (858)492-8696
**Subject(s):** General Editorial
**Circ:** 600,000

**TEEN (2349)**
PRIMEDIA Los Angeles
6420 Wilshire Blvd.
Los Angeles, CA 90048
Phone: (323)782-2000
Fax: (323)782-2223
**Subject(s):** Fashion; Youths' Interests
**Circ:** (Paid)600,000

**Entrepreneur Magazine (1998)**
Entrepreneur Media Inc.
2445 McCabe Way, Ste. 400
Irvine, CA 92614
Phone: (949)261-2325
Fax: (949)261-0234
**Subject(s):** Business
**Circ:** (Paid)563,492

**Wired (3237)**
Wired News
660 3rd St., 1st Fl.
San Francisco, CA 94107
Phone: (415)276-8400
Fax: (415)276-8500
**Subject(s):** Computers
**Circ:** (Paid)507,816

**World Vision Magazine (32093)**
World Vision United States
PO Box 9716
Federal Way, WA 98063-9716
Phone: (253)815-1000
Fax: (253)815-3445
**Subject(s):** Religious Publications
**Circ:** (Controlled)490,000

**This Week Kauai (7577)**
This Week Publications
274 Puuhale Rd., Ste. 200
Honolulu, HI 96819-2234
Phone: (808)843-6000
Fax: (808)843-6090
**Subject(s):** Travel and Tourism
**Circ:** (Non-paid)480,000

**Macworld (3168)**
101 Communications
501 2nd St., Ste. 500
San Francisco, CA 94107-1431
Phone: (415)243-0505
Fax: (415)442-0766
**Subject(s):** Computers
**Circ:** (Non-paid)167,877
(Paid)459,267

**Delicious Living! (4113)**
New Hope Natural Media
1401 Pearl St.
Boulder, CO 80302
Phone: (303)939-8440
Fax: (303)998-9886
**Subject(s):** Health and Fitness; Food and Grocery Trade
**Circ:** (Paid)458,974

**Guns & Ammo (2218)**
PRIMEDIA Los Angeles
6420 Wilshire Blvd.
Los Angeles, CA 90048
Phone: (323)782-2000
Fax: (323)782-2223
**Subject(s):** (Hunting, Fishing, and Game Management); Firearms
**Circ:** (Paid)★454,442

**Muscle & Fitness (4064)**
Weider Publications
21100 Erwin St.
Woodland Hills, CA 91367-3712
Phone: (818)884-6800
Fax: (818)595-0463
**Subject(s):** (Physical Fitness)
**Circ:** (Paid)454,177

**Petersen's 4 Wheel & Off Road (2302)**
PRIMEDIA Los Angeles
6420 Wilshire Blvd.
Los Angeles, CA 90048
Phone: (323)782-2000
Fax: (323)782-2223
**Subject(s):** Automotive (Trade); Trucks and Trucking
**Circ:** (Paid)451,260

**Victoria Ward Centers Magazine (7579)**
This Week Publications
274 Puuhale Rd., Ste. 200
Honolulu, HI 96819-2234
Phone: (808)843-6000
Fax: (808)843-6090
**Subject(s):** Travel and Tourism; Local, State, and Regional Publications; Japanese
**Circ:** 450,000

**Ski (4136)**
Time4 Media Inc.
929 Pearl St., Ste. 200
Boulder, CO 80302
Phone: (303)448-7638
Fax: (888)802-3355
**Subject(s):** (Skiing)
**Circ:** (Paid)428,179

**American Hockey Magazine (4184)**
TPG Sports Inc.
1775 Bob Johnson Rd.
Colorado Springs, CO 80906-4026
Phone: (719)576-8724
Fax: (719)538-1160
**Subject(s):** (Hockey)
**Circ:** (Paid)416,885

**Skiing (4138)**
Time4 Media Inc.
929 Pearl St., Ste. 200
Boulder, CO 80302
Phone: (303)448-7612
Fax: (303)448-7612
**Subject(s):** (Skiing)
**Circ:** (Paid)404,361

**ArcNews (2790)**
Environmental Systems Research Institute
380 New York St.
Redlands, CA 92373-8100
Phone: (909)793-2853
Fax: (909)793-5953
**Subject(s):** Computers; Geography
**Circ:** (Non-paid)400,000

**Grand Times (1800)**
Grand Times Publishing
403 Village Dr.
El Cerrito, CA 94530
Phone: (510)527-4337
**Subject(s):** Senior Citizens' Interests
**Circ:** 400,000

**Petersen's Hunting (2303)**
PRIMEDIA Los Angeles
6420 Wilshire Blvd.
Los Angeles, CA 90048
Phone: (323)782-2000
Fax: (323)782-2223
**Subject(s):** (Hunting, Fishing, and Game Management); Firearms
**Circ:** (Paid)380,798

**Car Craft (2160)**
PRIMEDIA Los Angeles
6420 Wilshire Blvd.
Los Angeles, CA 90048
Phone: (323)782-2000
Fax: (323)782-2223
**Subject(s):** (Auto Racing); Automotive (Consumer)
**Circ:** (Paid)375,186

**InfoWorld (3367)**
155 Bovet Rd., Ste. 800
San Mateo, CA 94402-3115
Phone: (415)572-7341
Fax: (415)358-1269
**Subject(s):** Computers
**Circ:** (Controlled)370,000

**PC Gamer (1563)**
Imagine Media
150 N Hill Dr., Ste. 40
Brisbane, CA 94005
Phone: (415)468-4684
Fax: (415)468-4686
**Subject(s):** Computers; Games and Puzzles
**Circ:** (Paid)357,718

**Paper Crafts Magazine (30663)**
Primedia Special Interest Publication
14850 Pony Express Rd.
Bluffdale, UT 84065-4818
Phone: (801)984-2070
Fax: (801)984-2080
**Subject(s):** Crafts, Models, Hobbies, and Contests
**Circ:** (Paid)350,000

**California Educator (1591)**
California Teachers Association
1705 Murchison Dr.
PO Box 921
Burlingame, CA 94010
Phone: (650)697-1400
Fax: (650)552-5002
**Subject(s):** Education
**Circ:** ‡330,000

**Cycle World (2536)**
Hachette Filipacchi Media U.S. Inc.
c/o New Ideas, 1499 Monrovia Ave.
Newport Beach, CA 92663
Phone: (949)720-5300
Fax: (949)631-0651
**Subject(s):** Motorbikes and Motorcycles
**Circ:** (Paid)326,570

**Four Wheeler Magazine (2208)**
PRIMEDIA Los Angeles
6420 Wilshire Blvd.
Los Angeles, CA 90048
Phone: (323)782-2000
Fax: (323)782-2223
**Subject(s):** Automotive (Consumer)
**Circ:** (Paid)325,441

**MiniTruckin' (1360)**
McMullen Argus Publishing Inc.
2400 E. Katella Ave., 11th Fl.
Anaheim, CA 92806
Phone: (714)939-2400
Fax: (714)978-6390
**Subject(s):** Automotive (Consumer); Trucks and Trucking
**Circ:** ‡325,000

**Movieline (2281)**
Movieline Inc.
10537 Santa Monica Blvd., Ste. 250
Los Angeles, CA 90025-4952
Phone: (310)234-9501
Fax: (310)234-0332
**Subject(s):** Motion Pictures
**Circ:** (Paid)315,873

**Yoga Journal** (1526)
California Yoga Teachers Association
2054 University Ave.
Berkeley, CA 94704
Phone: (510)841-9200
Fax: (510)644-3101
**Subject(s):** Health
**Circ:** (Paid)★310,170

**Diagnostic Imaging** (3125)
CMP Media L.L.C.
C/o John Hayes
600 Harrison St.
San Francisco, CA 94107
Phone: (415)947-6478
Fax: (415)947-6099
**Subject(s):** Radiology, Ultrasound, and Nuclear Medicine
**Circ:** (Non-paid)30,283
(Paid)31.240

**PSM (PlayStation Magazine)** (1564)
Imagine Media
150 N Hill Dr., Ste. 40
Brisbane, CA 94005
Phone: (415)468-4684
Fax: (415)468-4686
**Subject(s):** Computers; Games and Puzzles
**Circ:** (Paid)304,458

**Horizon Air Magazine** (32275)
Paradigm Communications Group
2701 1st Ave., Ste. 250
Seattle, WA 98121
Phone: (206)441-5871
Fax: (206)448-6939
**Subject(s):** In-Flight Publications; Travel and Tourism; Business
**Circ:** ‡300,000

**Maximum PC** (1559)
Imagine Media
150 N Hill Dr., Ste. 40
Brisbane, CA 94005
Phone: (415)468-4684
Fax: (415)468-4686
**Subject(s):** Computers
**Circ:** 3,00,000

**Saludos Hispanos** (2653)
73-121 Fred Waring Dr., Ste. 100
Palm Desert, CA 92260
Phone: (760)776-1206
Fax: (760)776-1214
**Subject(s):** General Editorial; Spanish; Hispanic Publications
**Circ:** 300,000

**Dog Fancy Magazine** (2184)
Fancy Publications
2401 Beverly Boulevard
PO Box 57900
Los Angeles, CA 90057
Phone: (213)385-2222
Fax: (213)385-8565
**Subject(s):** Dogs
**Circ:** (Paid)293,273

**Trailer Life** (3974)
TL Enterprises Inc.
2575 Vista Del Mar
Ventura, CA 93001
Phone: (800)825-6861
Fax: (805)667-4484
**Subject(s):** Travel and Tourism
**Circ:** (Paid)282,976

**Ruralite** (25836)
Ruralite Services Inc.
2040 A St.
PO Box 558
Forest Grove, OR 97116
Phone: (503)357-2105
Fax: (503)357-8615
**Subject(s):** Rural Electrification; Local, State, and Regional Publications
**Circ:** ‡281,400

**The Friend** (30767)
Church of Jesus Christ of Latter-day Saints
50 E N Temple St.
Salt Lake City, UT 84150-3220
Phone: (801)240-2951
Fax: (801)240-2270
**Subject(s):** Religious Publications
**Circ:** 275,000

**Oracle Magazine** (2802)
Oracle Corp.
500 Oracle Pkwy., M/S 10BP1
Redwood City, CA 94065
Phone: (650)506-7000
Fax: (650)633-2424
**Subject(s):** Computers
**Circ:** (Free)‡271,152

**Rocky Mountain Motorist** (4319)
AAA Colorado Inc.
4100 E Arkansas Ave.
Denver, CO 80222
Phone: (303)753-8800
Fax: (303)758-8515
**Subject(s):** Travel and Tourism; Automotive (Consumer)
**Circ:** (Controlled)‡265,000

**Golf Tips** (2215)
Werner Publishing Corp.
12121 Wilshire Blvd., Ste. 1220
12th Fl.
Los Angeles, CA 90025
Phone: (310)820-1500
Fax: (310)826-5008
**Subject(s):** (Golf)
**Circ:** (Paid)262,909

**Cat Fancy Magazine** (2161)
Fancy Publications
2401 Beverly Boulevard
PO Box 57900
Los Angeles, CA 90057
Phone: (213)385-2222
Fax: (213)385-8565
**Subject(s):** Cats
**Circ:** (Paid)261,738

**Motorcyclist** (2279)
PRIMEDIA Los Angeles
6420 Wilshire Blvd.
Los Angeles, CA 90048
Phone: (323)782-2000
Fax: (323)782-2223
**Subject(s):** Motorbikes and Motorcycles
**Circ:** (Paid)255,456

**ComputorEdge** (3009)
The Byte Buyer Inc.
3655 Ruffin Rd., Ste.100
San Diego, CA 92123
Phone: (858)573-0315
Fax: (619)573-0205
**Subject(s):** Computers
**Circ:** (Controlled)250,000

**Preview Theater Magazine** (1577)
Hogan Communications
150 E Olive Ave., Ste. 208
Burbank, CA 91502
Phone: (818)848-4876
Fax: (818)848-4995
**Subject(s):** Radio, Television, Cable, and Video; Music and Musical Instruments
**Circ:** ‡250,000

**PSExtreme** (1866)
1175 Chess Dr., E
Foster City, CA 94404
Phone: (650)372-0942
Fax: (650)372-0753
**Subject(s):** Games and Puzzles
**Circ:** (Paid)125,000
(Non-paid)250,000

**THRASHER** (3229)
High Speed Productions Inc.
1303 Underwood
San Francisco, CA 94124
Phone: (415)822-3083
Fax: (415)822-8359
**Subject(s):** (General Sports); Youths' Interests
**Circ:** ‡250,000

**Veggie Life** (1703)
EGW.com Inc.
1041 Shary Cir.
Concord, CA 94518
Phone: (925)671-9852
Fax: (925)671-0692
**Subject(s):** Health; Food and Cooking
**Circ:** (Paid)250,000

**ZOONOOZ** (3067)
Zoological Society of San Diego Inc.
2920 Zoo Dr.
PO Box 120551
San Diego, CA 92101
Phone: (619)231-1515
Fax: (619)744-3310
**Subject(s):** Zoology
**Circ:** ‡250,000

**New Era** (30777)
Church of Jesus Christ of Latter-day Saints
50 E N Temple St.
Salt Lake City, UT 84150-3220
Phone: (801)240-2951
Fax: (801)240-2270
**Subject(s):** Religious Publications
**Circ:** (Combined)‡230,000

**Resorts & Great Hotels** (1628)
Islands Publishing Co.
6267 Carpinteria Ave., Ste. 200
Carpinteria, CA 93013
Phone: (805)745-7100
Fax: (805)745-7105
**Subject(s):** Travel and Tourism
**Circ:** (Paid)‡230,000

**Easyriders** (1322)
Paisano Publications L.L.C.
PO Box 3000
Agoura, CA 91376
Phone: (818)889-8740
**Subject(s):** Motorbikes and Motorcycles
**Circ:** (Paid)226,948

**Western Horseman** (4220)
3850 N Nevada Ave.
Colorado Springs, CO 80907
Phone: (719)633-5524
Fax: (719)473-0997
**Subject(s):** (Horses and Horse Racing)
**Circ:** (Paid)226,134

**Ironman** (2638)
Ironman Publishing
1701 Ives Ave.
Oxnard, CA 93033
Phone: (805)385-3500
Fax: (805)385-3515
**Subject(s):** Health
**Circ:** (Paid)225,000

**Nurseweek** (3301)
Nurseweek Publishing
6860 Santa Teresa Blvd.
San Jose, CA 95119
Fax: (408)249-3756
**Subject(s):** Nursing
**Circ:** (Controlled)‡225,000

**Money Making Opportunities** (3580)
Success Publishing International
11071 Ventura Blvd.
Studio City, CA 91604
Phone: (818)980-9166
Fax: (818)980-7829
**Subject(s):** Business
**Circ:** (Controlled)⊕220,000

**R/C Modeler** (3527)
R/C Modeler Corp.
144 W. Sierra Madre Blvd.
PO Box 487
Sierra Madre, CA 91025
Phone: (626)355-1476
Fax: (626)355-6415
**Subject(s):** Crafts, Models, Hobbies, and Contests
**Circ:** ‡220,000

**Chevrolet High Performance** (2163)
PRIMEDIA Los Angeles
6420 Wilshire Blvd.
Los Angeles, CA 90048
Phone: (323)782-2000
Fax: (323)782-2223
**Subject(s):** Automotive (Consumer)
**Circ:** (Paid)219,621

**Outdoor Photographer** (2293)
Werner Publishing Corp.
12121 Wilshire Blvd., Ste. 1220
12th Fl.
Los Angeles, CA 90025
Phone: (310)820-1500

Circulation: ★ = ABC; △ = BPA; ♦ = CAC; • = CCAB; ❑ = VAC; ⊕ = PO Statement; ‡ = Publisher's Report; Boldface figures = sworn; Light figures = estimated.

# Western States

Fax: (310)826-5008
**Subject(s):** Photography; Photography
**Circ:** (Paid)215,189

**Puget Sound Computer User (32311)**
KFH Publications
2511 25th Ave. E
Seattle, WA 98112-2259
Phone: (206)547-4950
Fax: (206)545-6591
**Subject(s):** Computers
**Circ:** (Non-paid)208,768

**Horse Illustrated (2476)**
Fancy Publications
PO Box 6050
Mission Viejo, CA 92690
Phone: (949)855-3045
Fax: (949)855-3045
**Subject(s):** (Horses and Horse Racing)
**Circ:** (Paid)206,347

**What's On, The Las Vegas Guide (18703)**
What's On Magazines
4425 Industrial Rd.
Las Vegas, NV 89103
Phone: (702)891-8811
Fax: (702)891-8804
**Subject(s):** Entertainment; Local, State, and Regional Publications
**Circ:** (Paid)2,900
 (Non-paid)205,000

**Petersen's Photographic Magazine (2304)**
PRIMEDIA Los Angeles
6420 Wilshire Blvd.
Los Angeles, CA 90048
Phone: (323)782-2000
Fax: (323)782-2223
**Subject(s):** Photography
**Circ:** (Paid)204,537

**Sport Truck (1367)**
PRIMEDIA Los Angeles
Sport Truck
2400 East Katella Ave., Ste. 1100
Anaheim, CA 92806
Phone: (714)939-2400
Fax: (714)978-6390
**Subject(s):** Trucks and Trucking; Automotive (Consumer)
**Circ:** (Paid)202,635

**Truckin' Magazine (1373)**
McMullen Argus Publishing Inc.
2400 E. Katella Ave., 11th Fl.
Anaheim, CA 92806
Phone: (714)939-2400
Fax: (714)978-6390
**Subject(s):** Automotive (Consumer)
**Circ:** (Paid)2,02,255

**Dirt Rider (2183)**
PRIMEDIA Los Angeles
6420 Wilshire Blvd.
Los Angeles, CA 90048
Phone: (323)782-2000
Fax: (323)782-2223
**Subject(s):** Motorbikes and Motorcycles
**Circ:** (Paid)201,432

**The National Notary (1644)**
National Notary Association
PO Box 2402
Chatsworth, CA 91313-2402
Phone: (818)739-4000
Fax: (818)700-0920
**Subject(s):** Law
**Circ:** ‡200,000

**Signs of the Times (7761)**
Pacific Press Publishing Association
PO Box 5353
Nampa, ID 83653-5353
Phone: (208)465-2500
Fax: (208)465-2531
**Subject(s):** Religious Publications
**Circ:** ‡200,000

**Tinnitus Today (25984)**
American Tinnitus Association (ATA)
PO Box 5
Portland, OR 97207-0005
Phone: (503)248-9985
Fax: (503)248-0024

**Subject(s):** Laboratory Research (Scientific and Medical)
**Circ:** (Paid)200,000

**USC Trojan Family Magazine (2364)**
University of Southern California
Office of University Public Relations
Los Angeles, CA 90089
Phone: (213)740-2684
Fax: (213)821-1100
**Subject(s):** College Publications
**Circ:** (Controlled)‡200,000

**MacAddict (1558)**
150 N. Hill Dr.
Brisbane, CA 94005
Phone: (415)468-2500
**Subject(s):** Computers
**Circ:** (Paid)∆196,000

**Super Chevy (1370)**
McMullen Argus Publishing Inc.
2400 E. Katella Ave., 11th Fl.
Anaheim, CA 92806
Phone: (714)939-2400
Fax: (714)978-6390
**Subject(s):** Automotive (Consumer); (Auto Racing)
**Circ:** (Paid)190,480

**Nevada Events and Shows (18653)**
Nevada Magazine
400 N Carson St., Ste 100
Carson City, NV 89701
Phone: (775)687-5416
Fax: (775)687-6159
**Subject(s):** Travel and Tourism
**Circ:** (Non-paid)‡11,000
 (Paid)‡189,800

**BYU Magazine (30732)**
Brigham Young University
218 UPB
Provo, UT 84602
Phone: (801)378-4900
Fax: (801)378-5669
**Subject(s):** College Publications
**Circ:** (Non-paid)186,000

**Hispanic Business (3417)**
Hispanic Business Inc.
425 Pine Ave.
Santa Barbara, CA 93117-3709
Phone: (805)964-4554
Fax: (805)964-6139
**Subject(s):** Business; Hispanic Publications
**Circ:** (Paid)65,000
 (Controlled)180,000

**TransWorld Snowboarding Magazine (2616)**
TransWorld Media
353 Airport Rd.
Oceanside, CA 92054
Phone: (760)722-7777
Fax: (760)722-0653
**Subject(s):** (General Sports)
**Circ:** (Non-paid)‡109,000
 (Paid)‡180,000

**The Toastmaster (2773)**
Toastmasters International Inc.
23182 Arroyo Vista
Rancho Santa Margarita, CA 92688
Phone: (949)858-8255
Fax: (949)858-1207
**Subject(s):** Public Speaking and Lecturing; Communications
**Circ:** 170,000

**Petersen's Bowhunting (2301)**
PRIMEDIA Los Angeles
c/o Jay Michael Strangis, Editor
6420 Wilshire Boulevard
Los Angeles, CA 90048
Phone: (323)782-2563
Fax: (323)782-2477
**Subject(s):** (Hunting, Fishing, and Game Management)
**Circ:** (Paid)★167,600

**Sew News (4421)**
Primedia Consumer Magazine Group
741 Corporate Cir., Ste. A
Golden, CO 80401
Phone: (303)278-1010
Fax: (303)277-0370
**Subject(s):** Dressmaking, Needlework, and Quilting; Fashion
**Circ:** (Paid)166,734

**High Technology Careers Magazine (3440)**
HTC
4701 Patrick Henry Dr., No. 1901
Santa Clara, CA 95054-1847
Fax: (408)567-0242
**Subject(s):** Employment and Human Resources; Engineering (Various branches)
**Circ:** (Non-paid)‡166,500

**Mother Jones (3171)**
Foundation for National Progress
731 Market St., Ste. 600
San Francisco, CA 94103
Fax: (415)321-1701
**Subject(s):** General Editorial
**Circ:** (Paid)165,663

**Ability Magazine (1718)**
1001 W. 17th St.
Costa Mesa, CA 92627
Phone: (949)854-8700
Fax: (949)548-5966
**Subject(s):** Handicapped
**Circ:** ‡165,000

**Working Money (32345)**
Technical Analysis Inc.
4757 California Ave. SW
Seattle, WA 98116-4499
Phone: (206)938-0570
Fax: (206)938-1307
**Subject(s):** Business; Banking, Finance, and Investments
**Circ:** (Paid)165,000

**Rod & Custom Magazine (2323)**
Rod & Custom
6420 Wilshire Blvd.
Los Angeles, CA 90048
Phone: (323)782-2712
Fax: (323)782-2223
**Subject(s):** Automotive (Consumer)
**Circ:** (Paid)164,221

**The Red Herring (1439)**
Herring Communications Inc.
19 Davis Dr.
Belmont, CA 94002
Phone: (650)428-2900
**Subject(s):** Computers; Telecommunications; Business; Banking, Finance, and Investments
**Circ:** (Non-paid)5,611
 (Paid)162,666

**EDN Magazine Edition (2760)**
Reed Business Information
c/o Maury Wright, 12544 Robison Blvd.
Poway, CA 92064
Phone: (858)748-6785
**Subject(s):** Electronics Engineering
**Circ:** (Paid)3,131
 (Non-paid)161,523

**Colorado Country Life (4268)**
Colorado Rural Electric Association
5400 N. Washington
Denver, CO 80216
Phone: (303)455-4111
Fax: (303)455-4807
**Subject(s):** Rural Electrification; Lifestyle; Local, State, and Regional Publications
**Circ:** 160,000

**Hustler Busty Beauties (1532)**
L.F.P. Inc.
8484 Wilshire Blvd., Ste. 900
Beverly Hills, CA 90211
Phone: (323)651-5400
**Subject(s):** Sex/Erotica
**Circ:** ‡160,000

**Fore Magazine (2549)**
Southern California Golf Association
3740 Cahuenga Blvd.
North Hollywood, CA 91604
Phone: (818)980-3630
Fax: (818)980-1808
**Subject(s):** (Golf)
**Circ:** (Non-paid)3,906
 (Paid)153,443

**Flex Magazines (4059)**
Weider Publications
21100 Erwin St.
Woodland Hills, CA 91367-3712
Phone: (818)884-6800

Fax: (818)595-0463
**Subject(s):** (Physical Fitness)

**Circ:** (Paid)152,588

**Golf Today** (3595)
206 S Mill St.
tehachapi, CA 93561
Phone: (661)823-7842
Fax: (661)823-7942
**Subject(s):** (Golf)

**Circ:** (Free)‡152,000

**Los Angeles Family Magazine** (1823)
Merry Potter
17525 Ventura Blvd., Ste. 312
Encino, CA 91316-5144
Phone: (818)501-2299
Fax: (818)501-8833
**Subject(s):** Parenting

**Circ:** (Non-paid)150,520

**ShowBiz Weekly** (18673)
2290 Corporate Cir. Dr., Ste. 250
Henderson, NV 89074
Phone: (702)383-7185
Fax: (702)383-1089
**Subject(s):** Entertainment; Drama and Theatre

**Circ:** (Non-paid)150,216

**ABBWA Journal** (2434)
American Black Book Writers Association
PO Box 10548
Marina del Rey, CA 90295
**Subject(s):** Book Trade and Author News; Black Publications; Literature

**Circ:** 150,000

**FREEDOM Magazine** (2210)
Church of Scientology International
6331 Hollywood Blvd., Ste. 1200
Los Angeles, CA 90028-6329
Phone: (323)960-3500
Fax: (323)960-3508
**Subject(s):** General Editorial

**Circ:** ‡150,000

**Handloader** (807)
Wolfe Publishing Co.
2625 Stearman Rd., Ste. A
Prescott, AZ 86301-6155
Phone: (928)445-7810
Fax: (928)778-5124
**Subject(s):** Firearms

**Circ:** ‡150,000

**Los Cabos Magazine** (3036)
Promociones Tyson S.A. de C.V.
7770 Regents Rd., No. 113-387
San Diego, CA 92122
Phone: (858)569-0172
Fax: (858)777-3569
**Subject(s):** Travel and Tourism

**Circ:** (Combined)150,000

**Range Magazine** (18654)
PO Box 639
Carson City, NV 89702-0639
Phone: (775)884-2200
Fax: (775)884-2213
**Subject(s):** (Outdoors); Local, State, and Regional Publications

**Circ:** 150,000

**Tips & Tricks** (1536)
L.F.P. Inc.
8484 Wilshire Blvd., Ste. 900
Beverly Hills, CA 90211
Phone: (323)651-5400
**Subject(s):** Youths' Interests; Radio, Television, Cable, and Video; Entertainment; Games and Puzzles; Consumer Electronics

**Circ:** (Paid)★146,566

**MotorHome** (3969)
TL Enterprises Inc.
2575 Vista Del Mar
Ventura, CA 93001
Phone: (805)667-4100
Fax: (805)667-4484
**Subject(s):** (Outdoors); Travel and Tourism

**Circ:** (Paid)142,073

**DRIVE!** (1700)
DRIVE! Magazine
1300 Galaxy Way, Ste. 15
Concord, CA 94520
Phone: (925)682-9900
Fax: (925)682-9907
**Subject(s):** Automotive (Consumer)

**Circ:** (Non-paid)‡135,000

**San Francisco Magazine** (3208)
243 Vallejo St.
San Francisco, CA 94111-1553
Phone: (415)398-2800
Fax: (415)398-6777
**Subject(s):** Local, State, and Regional Publications

**Circ:** (Paid)133,000

**Street Rodder** (2741)
McMullen Argus Publishing Inc.
c/o Brian Brennan 720 Hundley Way
720 Hundley Way
Placentia, CA 92870
**Subject(s):** Automotive (Consumer)

**Circ:** (Paid)132,567

**Business Opportunities Journal(online)** (3006)
Business Service Corp.
PO Box 60762
San Diego, CA 92166-8762
Phone: (619)263-1763
Fax: (619)263-1763
**Subject(s):** Banking, Finance, and Investments; Real Estate

**Circ:** ‡132,000

**SnoWest** (7704)
Harris Publishing Inc.
360 B St.
Idaho Falls, ID 83402
Phone: (208)524-7000
Fax: (208)522-5241
**Subject(s):** (Snowmobiling)

**Circ:** (Paid)18,000
(Non-paid)132,000

**America West Airlines Magazine** (737)
Skyword Marketing Inc.
4636 E Elwood St., Ste. 5
Phoenix, AZ 85040-1963
Phone: (602)997-7200
Fax: (602)997-9875
**Subject(s):** In-Flight Publications

**Circ:** (Controlled)130,000

**Bugle** (18199)
Rocky Mountain Elk Foundation
2291 W. Broadway
Missoula, MT 59808-1813
Phone: (406)523-4500
Fax: (406)523-4550
**Subject(s):** (Outdoors); (Hunting, Fishing, and Game Management); Environmental and Natural Resources Conservation

**Circ:** (Combined)130,000

**California Lawyer** (3117)
Daily Journal Corp.
1145 Market St., 8th Fl.
San Francisco, CA 94103
Phone: (415)252-0500
Fax: (415)252-0288
**Subject(s):** Law

**Circ:** (Controlled)‡130,000

**WildBird Magazine** (2375)
Fancy Publications
2401 Beverly Boulevard
PO Box 57900
Los Angeles, CA 90057
Phone: (213)385-2222
Fax: (213)385-8565
**Subject(s):** Ornithology and Oology

**Circ:** (Paid)127,775

**Stanford Magazine** (3563)
Stanford Alumni Association
326 Galvez St.
Stanford, CA 94305-6105
Phone: (650)725-0672
Fax: (650)725-8676
**Subject(s):** College Publications

**Circ:** (Controlled)127,000

**Adam Film World Guide** (2119)
Holloway House Books Publishing Co.
8060 Melrose Ave.
Los Angeles, CA 90046
Phone: (323)653-8060
Fax: (323)655-9452
**Subject(s):** Motion Pictures; Men's Interests

**Circ:** ‡125,000

**Adam Magazine** (2120)
Players International Publications
8060 Melrose Ave.
Los Angeles, CA 90046
Phone: (323)653-8060
Fax: (323)655-9452
**Subject(s):** Men's Interests

**Circ:** 125,000

**Environmental News Network** (1471)
2020 Milvia St., Ste. 411
Berkeley, CA 94704-1156
**Subject(s):** Ecology and Conservation

**Circ:** (Controlled)125,000

**Gambling Times** (1987)
Gambling Times Inc.
3883 W Century Blvd., Ste. 608
Inglewood, CA 90303-1003
Phone: (310)674-3365
Fax: (310)674-3205
**Subject(s):** Games and Puzzles; Entertainment; (General Sports)

**Circ:** 125,000

**Network Magazine** (3175)
CMP Media L.L.C.
600 Harrison St
San Francisco, CA 94107
**Subject(s):** Computers

**Circ:** (Paid)‡125,000

**New Age Networking Magazine** (18698)
Destiny Productions for Print, Radio & Cable Promotions
3395 S Jones Blvd., No. 217
Las Vegas, NV 89146-6770
Phone: (702)438-1470
Fax: (702)438-2790
**Subject(s):** Business

**Circ:** (Combined)125,000

**Bird Talk** (2147)
Fancy Publications
2401 Beverly Boulevard
PO Box 57900
Los Angeles, CA 90057
Phone: (213)385-2222
Fax: (213)385-8565
**Subject(s):** Pets

**Circ:** (Paid)123,527

**SF Weekly** (3213)
185 Berry, Lobby 4, Ste. 3800
San Francisco, CA 94107
Phone: (415)536-8100
Fax: (415)541-9096
**Subject(s):** Local, State, and Regional Publications; Entertainment; Art

**Circ:** (Non-paid)123,462

**Handguns** (2220)
PRIMEDIA Los Angeles
6420 Wilshire Blvd.
Los Angeles, CA 90048
Phone: (323)782-2000
Fax: (323)782-2223
**Subject(s):** Firearms

**Circ:** (Paid)★120,796

**Dirt Wheels** (3939)
Hi-Torque Publishing Company Inc.
25233 Anza Dr.
Valencia, CA 91355
Phone: (661)295-1910
Fax: (661)295-1278
**Subject(s):** Motorbikes and Motorcycles

**Circ:** (Paid)120,593

**Dr. Dobb's Journal** (3366)
CMP Media L.L.C.
2800 Campus Dr.
San Mateo, CA 94403
Phone: (650)513-4300
Fax: (650)513-4618

**Western States**

Subject(s): Computers
Circ: ∆120,195

**American Handgunner (3000)**
Publishers Development Corp.
12345 World Trade Dr.
San Diego, CA 92128
Subject(s): Firearms
Circ: (Paid)120,092

**Montana Living (18174)**
Montana Living Magazine
14 3rd. St. E.
Kalispell, MT 59901
Phone: (406)756-9777
Fax: (406)756-9778
Subject(s): Travel and Tourism; Lifestyle; Local, State, and Regional Publications
Circ: (Combined)120,000

**Motor World (2277)**
Publishing and Business Consultants
4427 W Slauson Ave.
Los Angeles, CA 90043-2717
Subject(s): Automotive (Consumer)
Circ: (Paid)120,000

**Turbo & High-Tech Performance (1374)**
Illustrated Graphic Communications
2400 E Katella Ave., Ste. 1100
Anaheim, CA 92806
Phone: (714)939-2400
Fax: (714)978-6390
Subject(s): Automotive (Trade)
Circ: ‡120,000

**Quest (929)**
Muscular Dystrophy Association Inc.
3300 E Sunrise Dr.
Tucson, AZ 85718
Phone: (520)529-2000
Fax: (520)529-5383
Subject(s): Handicapped
Circ: (Non-paid)118,000

**Tattoo (1325)**
Paisano Publications L.L.C.
PO Box 3000
Agoura, CA 91376
Phone: (818)889-8740
Subject(s): Motorbikes and Motorcycles; Lifestyle
Circ: (Paid)117,346

**Profit (2803)**
Oracle Corp.
500 Oracle Pkwy., M/S 10BP1
Redwood City, CA 94065
Phone: (650)506-7000
Fax: (650)633-2424
Subject(s): Business; Computers
Circ: (Controlled)‡115,854

**Next Generation (1561)**
Imagine Media
150 N Hill Dr., Ste. 40
Brisbane, CA 94005
Phone: (415)468-4684
Fax: (415)468-4686
Subject(s): Computers; Games and Puzzles
Circ: (Paid)‡115,613

**Discipleship Journal (4195)**
NavPress
PO Box 35004
Colorado Springs, CO 80935
Fax: (719)598-7128
Subject(s): Religious Publications
Circ: (Non-paid)‡3,237
      (Paid)‡115,536

**Focus on the Family Clubhouse (4196)**
Focus on the Family
8605 Explorer Dr.
Colorado Springs, CO 80920
Phone: (719)531-3400
Fax: (719)531-3484
Subject(s): Religious Publications; Youths' Interests; Children's Interests
Circ: (Paid)115,000

**UCLA Magazine (2359)**
University of California, Los Angeles
10920 Wilshire Blvd., Ste. 1500
Los Angeles, CA 90024-6517
Phone: (310)794-6880
Fax: (310)794-6968
Subject(s): College Publications
Circ: 115,000

**POWDER (3331)**
33046 Calle Aviador
San Juan Capistrano, CA 92675
Phone: (949)496-5922
Fax: (949)496-7849
Subject(s): (Skiing)
Circ: ‡112,000

**Surface (3222)**
1663 Mission St., Ste 700
San Francisco, CA 94103
Phone: (415)929-5100
Fax: (415)575-3105
Subject(s): Art; Lifestyle; Fashion; Entertainment
Circ: (Paid)112,000

**The Lesbian News (3904)**
PO Box 55
Torrance, CA 90507
Phone: (310)787-8658
Fax: (310)787-1965
Subject(s): Women's Interests; Gay and Lesbian Interests
Circ: ‡110,000

**Shotgun Sports (1397)**
Shotgun Sports Inc.
PO Box 6810
Auburn, CA 95604
Phone: (530)889-2220
Fax: (530)889-9106
Subject(s): (Hunting, Fishing, and Game Management); Firearms
Circ: ‡108,000

**Black Belt Magazine (3447)**
Ohara
24715 Rockefeller
PO Box 918
Santa Clarita, CA 91355
Phone: (800)288-8671
Fax: (805)257-3028
Subject(s): (Martial Arts)
Circ: ‡105,000

**Not Born Yesterday (2025)**
Osmon Publications
4805 Alta Canyada Rd.
La Canada, CA 91011
Phone: (818)790-0651
Fax: (818)790-2807
Subject(s): Senior Citizens' Interests
Circ: (Paid)‡2,100
      (Controlled)‡104,000

**The Advocate (2121)**
Liberation Publications Inc.
PO Box 4371
Los Angeles, CA 90078
Phone: (323)871-1225
Fax: (323)467-6805
Subject(s): Gay and Lesbian Interests
Circ: (Paid)103,129

**Common Ground (2976)**
305 San Anselmo Ave., Ste. 313
San Anselmo, CA 94960
Phone: (415)459-4900
Fax: (415)459-4974
Subject(s): Religious Publications; Psychology and Psychiatry; Health
Circ: (Paid)‡2,000
      (Non-paid)‡103,000

**Seattle Weekly (32328)**
Seattle Weekly Media Inc.
1008 Western Ave., Ste. 300
Seattle, WA 98104
Phone: (206)623-0500
Fax: (206)467-4338
Subject(s): Lifestyle
Circ: (Paid)85
      (Free)102,464

**Wood Strokes & Woodcrafts (1705)**
EGW.com Inc.
1041 Shary Cir.
Concord, CA 94518
Phone: (925)671-9852
Fax: (925)671-0692
Subject(s): Crafts, Models, Hobbies, and Contests
Circ: (Paid)102,090

**Heavy Duty Trucking (2002)**
Newport Communications
38 Executive Park, Ste. 300
Irvine, CA 92614
Phone: (949)261-1636
Fax: (949)261-2904
Subject(s): Trucks and Trucking
Circ: (Controlled)‡101,976

**Fishing and Hunting News (32269)**
Outdoor Empire Publishing Inc.
PO Box 19000
Seattle, WA 98109
Phone: (206)624-3845
Fax: (206)695-8512
Subject(s): (Hunting, Fishing, and Game Management)
Circ: (Non-paid)7,169
      (Paid)100,186

**Affaire de Coeur (2569)**
Brandywyne Books
3976 Oak Hill Rd.
Oakland, CA 94605
Phone: (510)569-5675
Fax: (510)632-8868
Subject(s): Science Fiction, Mystery, Adventure, and Romance
Circ: (Paid)50,000
      (Non-paid)100,000

**Apogee Photo Magazine (4590)**
Apogee Photo Inc.
11749 Zenobia Loop
Westminster, CO 80031
Phone: (720)920-9695
Subject(s): Photography; Men's Interests
Circ: 100,000

**Femme Fatales (2202)**
Cinefantastique
3740 Overland Ave., Ste. E
Los Angeles, CA 90034
Phone: (310)204-2029
Fax: (310)204-0825
Subject(s): Entertainment; Motion Pictures; Science Fiction, Mystery, Adventure, and Romance; Men's Interests
Circ: ‡100,000

**Mustang Illustrated (1362)**
Primedia Inc.
2400 E Katella Ave., 11th Fl.
Anaheim, CA 92806
Phone: (714)939-2400
Fax: (714)978-6390
Subject(s): Automotive (Consumer)
Circ: ‡100,000

**New Homes Magazine (1724)**
MDM Publications
3151 Airway Ave., Ste. C-3
Costa Mesa, CA 92626
Subject(s): Real Estate
Circ: (Non-paid)‡100,000

**Oregon Quarterly (25809)**
University of Oregon
5228 University of Oregon
Eugene, OR 97403-5228
Phone: (541)346-5047
Fax: (541)346-5571
Subject(s): College Publications
Circ: (Controlled)‡100,000

**Spirit of Aloha (7571)**
Honolulu Publishing Company Ltd.
707 Richards St., No. 525
P.O. Box 80
Honolulu, HI 96813-4623
Phone: (808)524-7400
Fax: (808)531-2306
Subject(s): In-Flight Publications; Travel and Tourism
Circ: 100,000

**TransWorld Skateboarding Magazine (2615)**
TransWorld Media
353 Airport Rd.
Oceanside, CA 92054
Phone: (760)722-7777
Fax: (760)722-0653
**Subject(s):** (General Sports)
**Circ:** 100,000

**Executive Golfer (2000)**
Pazdur Publishing Inc.
2171 Campus Dr., Ste. 330
Irvine, CA 92612
Phone: (949)752-6474
Fax: (949)752-0398
**Subject(s):** (Golf)
**Circ:** (Paid)2,016
(Controlled)99,778

**Custom Classic Trucks (1346)**
PRIMEDIA Anaheim
2100 E Howell Ave., Ste. 209
Anaheim, CA 92806
**Subject(s):** Automotive (Consumer)
**Circ:** (Paid)99,594

**Western Outdoors (2546)**
Western Outdoors Publications
PO Box 2027
Newport Beach, CA 92659-1027
Phone: (714)546-4370
Fax: (714)662-3486
**Subject(s):** (Hunting, Fishing, and Game Management)
**Circ:** (Paid)98,717

**Bow and Arrow Hunting (2626)**
Y-Visionary Publishing L.P.
265 S Anita Dr., Ste. 120
Orange, CA 92868-3310
Phone: (714)939-9991
Fax: (714)939-9909
**Subject(s):** (Archery)
**Circ:** (Non-paid)‡640
(Paid)‡98,500

**Surfing Magazine (1371)**
McMullen Argus Publishing Inc.
2400 E. Katella Ave., 11th Fl.
Anaheim, CA 92806
Phone: (714)939-2400
Fax: (714)978-6390
**Subject(s):** (Water Sports)
**Circ:** (Paid)97,822

**This Week Big Island (7576)**
This Week Publications
274 Puuhale Rd., Ste. 200
Honolulu, HI 96819-2234
Phone: (808)843-6000
Fax: (808)843-6090
**Subject(s):** Travel and Tourism
**Circ:** (Non-paid)97,000

**Critical Care Nurse (1335)**
101 Columbia
Aliso Viejo, CA 92656
Phone: (949)362-2000
Fax: (949)362-2049
**Subject(s):** Nursing
**Circ:** ‡96,000

**Utah State Magazine (30691)**
Utah State University
1420 Old Main Hill
Logan, UT 84322-1420
Phone: (435)797-1353
Fax: (435)797-1364
**Subject(s):** College Publications
**Circ:** (Controlled)96,000

**California Real Estate Magazine (2158)**
California Association of Realtors
525 S. Virgil Ave.
Los Angeles, CA 90020
Phone: (213)739-8200
Fax: (213)351-8478
**Subject(s):** Real Estate
**Circ:** (Non-paid)350
(Paid)95,000

**Foursquare World Advance (2209)**
International Church of the Foursquare Gospel
1910 W Sunset Blvd., Ste. 200
PO Box 26902
Los Angeles, CA 90026-0176
Phone: (213)989-4234
Fax: (213)989-4544
**Subject(s):** Religious Publications
**Circ:** (Controlled)‡95,000

**Rifle (810)**
Wolfe Publishing Co.
2625 Stearman Rd., Ste. A
Prescott, AZ 86301-6155
Phone: (928)445-7810
Fax: (928)778-5124
**Subject(s):** Firearms
**Circ:** ‡95,000

**Youth Runner Magazine (25888)**
PO Box 1156
Lake Oswego, OR 97035
Phone: (503)236-2524
Fax: (503)620-3800
**Subject(s):** (Running); Youths' Interests
**Circ:** (Paid)5,000
(Non-paid)95,000

**Palm Springs Life's Desert Guide (2670)**
Desert Publication Inc.
303 N Indian Canyon Dr.
PO Box 2724
Palm Springs, CA 92262
Phone: (760)325-2333
Fax: (760)325-7008
**Subject(s):** City, Hotel, Railroad, and Travel Guides
**Circ:** (Non-paid)94,218

**Computer (2103)**
IEEE Computer Society
PO Box 3014
PO Box 3014
Los Alamitos, CA 90720-1314
Phone: (714)821-8380
Fax: (714)821-4010
**Subject(s):** Computers
**Circ:** (Combined)94,000

**American Cowboy (33789)**
PO Box 6630
Sheridan, WY 82801
Phone: (307)672-7171
Fax: (307)672-7766
**Subject(s):** Travel and Tourism; Lifestyle
**Circ:** (Paid)92,020

**Elvis International Forum (4034)**
Creative Radio Network
PO Box 7749
Westlake Village, CA 91359-7749
Phone: (818)991-3892
Fax: (818)991-3894
**Subject(s):** Entertainment
**Circ:** (Combined)90,800

**Videomaker Magazine (1654)**
York Publishing
PO Box 4591
Chico, CA 95927
Phone: (530)891-8410
Fax: (530)891-8443
**Subject(s):** Radio, Television, Cable, and Video
**Circ:** (Non-paid)68
(Paid)90,460

**Breakaway Magazine (4188)**
Focus on the Family
8605 Explorer Dr.
Colorado Springs, CO 80920
Phone: (719)531-3400
Fax: (719)531-3484
**Subject(s):** Youths' Interests; Religious Publications
**Circ:** (Paid)90,000

**First Tuesday (2822)**
Realty Publications Inc.
PO Box 20069
Riverside, CA 92516
Phone: (951)781-7300
Fax: (951)781-4721
**Subject(s):** Real Estate
**Circ:** (Paid)5,087
(Non-paid)90,000

**Linux Journal (32286)**
SSC
PO Box 55759
Seattle, WA 98155-0759
Phone: (206)782-7733
Fax: (206)297-7515
**Subject(s):** Computers; Telecommunications
**Circ:** (Combined)90,000

**OC Metro (2542)**
Churm Publishing Inc.
1451 Quail St., Ste. 201
Newport Beach, CA 92660
Phone: (949)757-1404
Fax: (949)757-1996
**Subject(s):** Business; Business
**Circ:** (Combined)90,000

**Tole World (1702)**
EGW.com Inc.
1041 Shary Cir.
Concord, CA 94518
Phone: (925)671-9852
Fax: (925)671-0692
**Subject(s):** Crafts, Models, Hobbies, and Contests
**Circ:** ‡90,000

**Dirt Bike Magazine (3938)**
Hi-Torque Publishing Company Inc.
25233 Anza Dr.
Valencia, CA 91355
Phone: (661)295-1910
Fax: (661)295-1278
**Subject(s):** Motorbikes and Motorcycles
**Circ:** (Paid)88,035

**Clubhouse Jr. (4191)**
Focus on the Family
c/o Clubhouse Jr., Focus on the Family
Colorado Springs, CO 80995
**Subject(s):** Religious Publications; Children's Interests; Youths' Interests
**Circ:** (Controlled)88,000

**Guns Magazine (3016)**
Publishers Development Corp.
12345 World Trade Dr.
San Diego, CA 92128
**Subject(s):** Firearms; (Hunting, Fishing, and Game Management)
**Circ:** (Paid)85,487

**Research (3199)**
Research Magazine Inc.
585 Howard St., 2nd Fl.
San Francisco, CA 94105-3032
Phone: (415)621-4200
Fax: (415)348-0222
**Subject(s):** Banking, Finance, and Investments
**Circ:** (Paid)80
(Non-paid)85,300

**Callback (2493)**
NASA Aviation Safety Reporting System
PO Box 189
Moffett Field, CA 94035-0189
Phone: (650)604-5000
**Subject(s):** Aviation; Safety
**Circ:** (Combined)85,000

**FREEZE (2611)**
TransWorld Media
353 Airport Rd.
Oceanside, CA 92054
Phone: (760)722-7777
Fax: (760)722-0653
**Subject(s):** (Skiing)
**Circ:** (Paid)85,000

**Kit Car Illustrated (1357)**
McMullen Argus Publishing Inc.
2400 E. Katella Ave., 11th Fl.
Anaheim, CA 92806
Phone: (714)939-2400
Fax: (714)978-6390
**Subject(s):** Automotive (Consumer)
**Circ:** 85,000

**Magical Blend Magazine (1651)**
Magical Blend
PO Box 600
Chico, CA 95927-0600
Phone: (530)893-9037
Fax: (530)893-9076

**Subject(s):** Alternative and Underground
**Circ:** (Non-paid)15,000
(Paid)85,000

**Spa Magazine** (1629)
Islands Publishing Co.
6267 Carpinteria Ave., Ste. 200
Carpinteria, CA 93013
Phone: (805)745-7100
Fax: (805)745-7105
**Subject(s):** Travel and Tourism; Health
**Circ:** (Paid)‡85,000

**Closeout News Magazine** (2171)
Closeout News Inc.
5900 Wilshire Blvd., Ste. 510
Los Angeles, CA 90036-5005
Phone: (323)525-2527
**Subject(s):** General Merchandise
**Circ:** (Controlled)‡14,650
(Paid)‡84,000

**Key Magazine Las Vegas** (18686)
Key Magazine Inc.
c/o Nicholas Naff
3626 Pecos McLeod, Ste. 14
Las Vegas, NV 89121
Phone: (702)385-2737
Fax: (702)733-9103
**Subject(s):** Travel and Tourism; Entertainment; Local, State, and Regional Publications
**Circ:** (Combined)‡83,500

**National Dragster** (1941)
National Hot Rod Association
2220 E. Route 66, Ste. 101
Glendora, CA 91740
Phone: (626)963-7695
Fax: (626)335-4307
**Subject(s):** (Auto Racing)
**Circ:** (Non-paid)‡2,627
(Paid)‡82,666

**Motocross Action** (3942)
Hi-Torque Publishing Company Inc.
25233 Anza Dr.
Valencia, CA 91355
Phone: (661)295-1910
Fax: (661)295-1278
**Subject(s):** Motorbikes and Motorcycles
**Circ:** (Paid)82,266

**Pontoon & Deck Boat Magazine** (7701)
Harris Publishing Inc.
360 B St.
Idaho Falls, ID 83402
Phone: (208)524-7000
Fax: (208)522-5241
**Subject(s):** (Boating and Yachting); (Water Sports)
**Circ:** (Combined)82,000

**California Monthly** (1456)
California Alumni Association
Alumni House
Berkeley, CA 94720-7520
Phone: (510)642-5781
Fax: (510)642-6252
**Subject(s):** College Publications
**Circ:** (Non-paid)‡3,400
(Paid)‡81,800

**The East Bay Monthly** (1814)
Klaber Publishing Corp.
1301 59th St.
Emeryville, CA 94608
Phone: (510)658-9811
Fax: (510)658-9902
**Subject(s):** General Editorial
**Circ:** (Paid)‡500
(Controlled)‡80,500

**Children's Ministry Magazine** (4507)
Group Publishing Inc.
PO Box 481
Loveland, CO 80539
Fax: (970)292-4373
**Subject(s):** Religious Publications; Education
**Circ:** (Non-paid)500
(Paid)80,000

**Eligible** (3522)
PO Box 57466
Sherman Oaks, CA 91413
Phone: (818)760-4112
Fax: (818)760-4112

**Subject(s):** Women's Interests
**Circ:** (Non-paid)5,000
(Paid)80,000

**Hawaii** (2221)
Fancy Publications
2401 Beverly Boulevard
PO Box 57900
Los Angeles, CA 90057
Phone: (213)385-2222
Fax: (213)385-8565
**Subject(s):** Travel and Tourism
**Circ:** (Paid)80,000

**Jp** (2243)
PRIMEDIA Los Angeles
c/o John Cappa, Editor
6420 Wilshire Boulevard
Los Angeles, CA 90048
Phone: (323)782-2000
Fax: (323)782-2746
**Subject(s):** Automotive (Consumer); (Auto Racing)
**Circ:** (Combined)80,000

**Mission Frontiers** (2716)
U.S. Center for World Mission
1605 E. Elizabeth St.
Pasadena, CA 91104-2721
Phone: (626)797-1111
Fax: (626)398-2263
**Subject(s):** Religious Publications
**Circ:** ‡80,000

**CADALYST** (3114)
CMP Media L.L.C.
600 Harrison St.
San Francisco, CA 94107
Phone: (415)538-8800
Fax: (415)947-6055
**Subject(s):** Computers
**Circ:** (Paid)21,078
(Controlled)78,943

**Latitudes & Attitudes** (2797)
Latitudes & Attitudes Magazine
PO Box 668
Redondo Beach, CA 90277
Phone: (310)798-3445
Fax: (310)798-3448
**Subject(s):** (Boating and Yachting)
**Circ:** (Paid)‡77,000

**MEN** (2270)
S.L. Inc.
PO Box 4356
Los Angeles, CA 90078-4356
Phone: (323)960-5400
Fax: (323)960-1183
**Subject(s):** Gay and Lesbian Interests
**Circ:** 76,000

**KITPLANES Magazine** (1820)
531 Encinitas Blvd., No. 105
Encinitas, CA 92024
Phone: (760)436-4747
Fax: (760)436-4644
**Subject(s):** Aviation
**Circ:** (Paid)75,984

**Trailer Boats Magazine** (1630)
Poole Publications Inc.
20700 Belshaw Ave.
PO Box 5427
Carson, CA 90749-5427
Phone: (310)537-6322
Fax: (310)537-8735
**Subject(s):** (Boating and Yachting)
**Circ:** (Paid)75,398

**City Sports** (3528)
City Sports Inc.
444 S Cedros Ave., No. 185
Solana Beach, CA 92075
Phone: (858)793-2711
Fax: (858)793-2710
**Subject(s):** (General Sports)
**Circ:** (Non-paid)75,000

**Dragon Magazine** (32232)
Wizards of the Coast Inc.
PO Box 707
Renton, WA 98057
Phone: (425)204-8000

**Subject(s):** Crafts, Models, Hobbies, and Contests; Science Fiction, Mystery, Adventure, and Romance
**Circ:** 75,000

**Home Power** (25696)
PO Box 520
Ashland, OR 97520
Phone: (541)512-0201
Fax: (541)512-0343
**Subject(s):** Home and Garden
**Circ:** 24,600
45,000
75,000

**Music Connection Magazine** (1824)
Music Connection Inc.
16130 Ventura Blvd. Ste. 540
Encino, CA 91436
Phone: (818)995-0101
Fax: (818)995-9235
**Subject(s):** Music and Musical Instruments
**Circ:** ⊕75,000

**Nob Hill Gazette** (3181)
The Hearst Bldg., Ste. 222
5 3rd St.
San Francisco, CA 94103
Phone: (415)227-0190
Fax: (415)974-5103
**Subject(s):** Local, State, and Regional Publications
**Circ:** (Combined)75,000

**Parents' Press** (1510)
1454 6th St.
Berkeley, CA 94710
Phone: (510)524-1602
Fax: (510)524-0912
**Subject(s):** Local, State, and Regional Publications; Parenting
**Circ:** (Combined)75,000

**The Plain Truth (PT)** (2721)
Plain Truth Ministries
Pasadena, CA 91129
**Subject(s):** Religious Publications
**Circ:** (Paid)75,000

**University of San Francisco Magazine** (3231)
University of San Francisco
2130 Fulton St.
San Francisco, CA 94117
Phone: (415)422-2698
Fax: (415)422-2696
**Subject(s):** College Publications
**Circ:** (Controlled)75,000

**Hot Bike** (1353)
McMullen Argus Publishing Inc.
2400 E. Katella Ave., 11th Fl.
Anaheim, CA 92806
Phone: (714)939-2400
Fax: (714)978-6390
**Subject(s):** Motorbikes and Motorcycles
**Circ:** (Paid)74,844

**WEA** (32092)
WEA Board of Directors
PO Box 9100
Federal Way, WA 98063-9100
Phone: (253)765-7027
Fax: (253)946-7612
**Subject(s):** Education; Labor
**Circ:** (Paid)74,000

**Phoenix Home & Garden** (833)
8501 E. Princess Dr., Ste. 190
Scottsdale, AZ 85255
Phone: (480)664-3960
Fax: (480)664-3963
**Subject(s):** Home and Garden
**Circ:** (Paid)73,539

**Car Audio and Electronics** (1344)
McMullen Argus Publishing Inc.
2400 E. Katella Ave., 11th Fl.
Anaheim, CA 92806
Phone: (714)939-2400
Fax: (714)978-6390
**Subject(s):** Automotive (Consumer)
**Circ:** (Paid)72,809

**Computer Technology Review** (1530)
West World Productions
420 N Camden Dr.
Beverly Hills, CA 90210
Phone: (310)276-9500
Fax: (310)246-1405
**Subject(s):** Computers
**Circ:** (Controlled)72,552

**Software Development** (3218)
CMP Media L.L.C.
c/o Alexandra Weber Morales
Software Development, CMP Media LLC
600 Harrison St., 6th Fl.
San Francisco, CA 94107
**Subject(s):** Computers
**Circ:** ‡72,000

**Physician Magazine** (4213)
Focus on the Family
8605 Explorer Dr.
Colorado Springs, CO 80920
Phone: (719)531-3400
Fax: (719)531-3484
**Subject(s):** Health and Healthcare; Religious Publications
**Circ:** ‡71,000

**Communication Arts Magazine** (2450)
Communication Arts
110 Constitution Dr.
Menlo Park, CA 94025-1107
Phone: (650)326-6040
Fax: (650)326-1648
**Subject(s):** Advertising and Marketing; Communications; Graphic Arts and Design
**Circ:** (Paid)‡70,055

**Cinefantastique** (2168)
3740 Overland Ave., Ste. E
Los Angeles, CA 90034
Phone: (310)204-2029
Fax: (310)204-0825
**Subject(s):** Motion Pictures; Science Fiction, Mystery, Adventure, and Romance
**Circ:** ‡70,000

**Inland Empire** (2827)
Sunwest Publishing
3769 Tibbetts St., Ste. A
Riverside, CA 92506-2606
Phone: (909)682-3026
Fax: (909)682-0246
**Subject(s):** Lifestyle; Local, State, and Regional Publications
**Circ:** ‡70,000

**Nevada** (18651)
401 N Carson St., Ste.100
Carson City, NV 89701
Phone: (775)687-5416
Fax: (775)687-6159
**Subject(s):** Local, State, and Regional Publications; Travel and Tourism
**Circ:** (Non-paid)‡10,000
    (Paid)‡70,000

**The Pharos** (2453)
Alpha Omega Alpha Honor Medical Society
525 Middlefield Rd., Ste. 130
Menlo Park, CA 94025
Phone: (415)329-0291
Fax: (415)329-1618
**Subject(s):** Medicine and Surgery
**Circ:** (Controlled)70,000

**Slap** (3215)
High Speed Productions Inc.
1303 Underwood
San Francisco, CA 94124
Phone: (415)822-3083
Fax: (415)822-8359
**Subject(s):** Youths' Interests
**Circ:** (Paid)70,000

**URB** (2362)
6300 Wilshire Blvd Suite 1750
Los Angeles, CA 90048
Phone: (323)315-1700
**Subject(s):** Music and Musical Instruments
**Circ:** (Non-paid)70,000

**FAD Magazine** (2977)
The R.J. Garbosky Co.
29 Bennitt Ave.
San Anselmo, CA 94960
Fax: (415)456-7260

**Subject(s):** Lifestyle
**Circ:** (Paid)‡69,843

**Rifle Shooter Magazine** (2321)
PRIMEDIA Los Angeles
c/o Jerry Lee, Editor
6420 Wilshire Boulevard
Los Angeles, CA 90048
Phone: (323)782-2563
Fax: (323)782-2477
**Subject(s):** (Outdoors); Firearms; (Hunting, Fishing, and Game Management)
**Circ:** (Paid)★69,291

**Curve Magazine** (3124)
Outspoken Enterprises Inc.
1550 Bryant St., Ste. 510
San Francisco, CA 94103
Phone: (415)863-6538
Fax: (415)863-1609
**Subject(s):** Gay and Lesbian Interests; Women's Interests
**Circ:** (Non-paid)305
    (Paid)68,800

**Dune Buggies & Hot VWs** (1721)
2950 Airway, Ste. A7
PO Box 2260
Costa Mesa, CA 92626
Phone: (714)979-2560
Fax: (714)979-3998
**Subject(s):** Automotive (Consumer)
**Circ:** ‡68,324

**Technology & Learning** (3227)
CMP Media L.L.C.
600 Harrison St.
San Francisco, CA 94107
Phone: (415)947-6760
Fax: (415)947-6041
**Subject(s):** Education; Computers
**Circ:** (Paid)12,924
    (Non-paid)68,188

**Dynamic Chiropractic** (1981)
5406 Bolsa Ave.
PO Box 4109
Huntington Beach, CA 92605-4109
Phone: (714)230-3150
Fax: (714)899-4273
**Subject(s):** Chiropractic
**Circ:** (Controlled)68,000

**Personal Watercraft Illustrated** (1726)
Cycle News Inc.
3505-M Cadillac Ave.
Costa Mesa, CA 92626
Phone: (714)751-7433
Fax: (714)751-6685
**Subject(s):** (Boating and Yachting)
**Circ:** (Non-paid)‡2,009
    (Paid)‡66,510

**American Journal of Critical Care** (1334)
American Association of Critical-Care Nurses
101 Columbia
Aliso Viejo, CA 92656-4109
Phone: (949)362-2000
Fax: (949)362-2020
**Subject(s):** Nursing
**Circ:** (Combined)66,500

**Islands Magazine** (1627)
Islands Publishing Co.
6267 Carpinteria Ave., Ste. 200
Carpinteria, CA 93013
Phone: (805)745-7100
Fax: (805)745-7105
**Subject(s):** Travel and Tourism
**Circ:** (Paid)66,000

**Freshmen** (2211)
S.L. Inc.
PO Box 4356
Los Angeles, CA 90078-4356
Phone: (323)960-5400
Fax: (323)960-1183
**Subject(s):** Gay and Lesbian Interests
**Circ:** 65,000

**Heckler** (2893)
1915 21st St.
Sacramento, CA 95814
Phone: (916)456-2300
Fax: (916)737-3920

**Subject(s):** Youths' Interests; (Skiing); (Skating)
**Circ:** (Paid)65,000

**Rock & Gem** (3972)
Miller Magazines Inc.
4880 Market St.
Ventura, CA 93003
Phone: (805)644-3824
Fax: (805)644-3875
**Subject(s):** Mining and Minerals
**Circ:** ‡65,000

**Soaring Spirit** (2427)
Sutphen Services
PO Box 38
Malibu, CA 90265
Phone: (818)706-0963
Fax: (818)706-3606
**Subject(s):** Alternative and Underground
**Circ:** (Controlled)65,000

**Technical Analysis of Stocks & Commodities** (32335)
Technical Analysis Inc.
4757 California Ave. SW
Seattle, WA 98116-4499
Phone: (206)938-0570
Fax: (206)938-1307
**Subject(s):** Banking, Finance, and Investments; Computers; Business
**Circ:** 65,000

**Sybase Magazine** (1782)
Sybase Inc.
1 Sybase Dr.
Dublin, CA 94568
Phone: (925)236-5000
Fax: (925)236-6157
**Subject(s):** Computers
**Circ:** (Controlled)64,672

**National Motorist** (1865)
National Automobile Club
1151 E Hillsdale Blvd.
Foster City, CA 94404
Phone: (650)294-7000
Fax: (650)294-7040
**Subject(s):** Travel and Tourism
**Circ:** ‡64,313

**Total Health** (30755)
Total Health Holdings LCC
165 North 100 East, Ste. 2
Saint George, UT 84770-2505
Phone: (435)673-1789
Fax: (435)634-9336
**Subject(s):** Health; (Physical Fitness)
**Circ:** (Controlled)‡10,000
    (Paid)‡63,000

**Canoe and Kayak Magazine** (32123)
Canoe & Kayak Inc.
10526 NE 68th St., Ste. 3
Kirkland, WA 98083
Phone: (425)827-6363
**Subject(s):** (Outdoors)
**Circ:** ‡62,000

**Vail-Beaver Creek Magazine** (4585)
Mac Media Inc.
PO Box 1414
Vail, CO 81658
Phone: (970)949-9170
Fax: (970)949-9176
**Subject(s):** Local, State, and Regional Publications
**Circ:** (Combined)62,000

**Aloha Festivals Official Magazine** (7527)
This Week Publications
274 Puuhale Rd., Ste. 200
Honolulu, HI 96819-2234
Phone: (808)843-6000
Fax: (808)843-6090
**Subject(s):** Travel and Tourism; Local, State, and Regional Publications
**Circ:** 60,000

**Apartment Management Magazine** (1979)
Apartment News Publications Inc.
15502 Graham St.
Huntington Beach, CA 92649
Phone: (714)893-3971
Fax: (714)893-6484

---

Circulation: ★ = ABC; △ = BPA; ♦ = CAC; ● = CCAB; ▫ = VAC; ⊕ = PO Statement; ‡ = Publisher's Report; Boldface figures = sworn; Light figures = estimated.

# Western States

**Subject(s):** Building Management and Maintenance
**Circ:** (Paid)500
(Non-paid)60,000

**ASU Travel Guide (3382)**
1525 Francisco Blvd. E
San Rafael, CA 94901
Phone: (415)459-0300
Fax: (415)459-0494
**Subject(s):** Travel and Tourism
**Circ:** ‡60,000

**The Black Scholar (2575)**
Black World Foundation
PO Box 22869
Oakland, CA 94618
Phone: (510)547-6633
Fax: (510)547-6679
**Subject(s):** Black Publications; Education
**Circ:** (Paid)10,000
(Non-paid)60,000

**DV Media Group (3130)**
CMP Media L.L.C.
600 Harrison St.
San Francisco, CA 94107
Phone: (415)947-6264
Fax: (415)947-6030
**Subject(s):** Computers; Radio, Television, Cable, and Video
**Circ:** ‡60,000

**E-Business Advisor (3013)**
e-Business Advisor
PO Box 429002
San Diego, CA 92142-9002
Phone: (858)278-5600
Fax: (858)278-0300
**Subject(s):** Computers
**Circ:** (Paid)60,000

**Hispanic Times Magazine (4051)**
PO Box 579
Winchester, CA 92596
Phone: (909)926-2119
**Subject(s):** Business; Spanish; Hispanic Publications; Employment and Human Resources
**Circ:** (Paid)‡628
(Controlled)‡60,000

**Kit Car (1356)**
PRIMEDIA Los Angeles
Kit Car
2400 East Katella Ave., Ste.1100
Anaheim, CA 92806
Phone: (714)939-2400
Fax: (714)978-6390
**Subject(s):** Automotive (Trade)
**Circ:** (Paid)⊕60,000

**Montanan (18208)**
The University of Montana
C/O Joan Melcher, Editor
315 Brantly Hall
Univ. of Montana
Missoula, MT 59812
Phone: (406)243-4842
**Subject(s):** College Publications
**Circ:** (Controlled)60,000

**Parts & People (4316)**
Automotive Counseling & Publishing Company Inc.
450 Lincoln St., Ste. 110
Denver, CO 80203-3459
Phone: (303)765-4664
Fax: (303)765-4650
**Subject(s):** Automotive (Trade)
**Circ:** (Combined)60,000

**Rocky Mountain Golf Magazine (4096)**
Mac Media Inc.
PO Box 1397
Avon, CO 81620
Phone: (970)476-6600
Fax: (970)845-0069
**Subject(s):** (Golf)
**Circ:** (Combined)‡60,000

**Soldier of Fortune (4140)**
Omega Group
5735 Arapahoe Ave., Ste. A-5
Boulder, CO 80303-1340
Phone: (303)444-5617
Fax: (303)444-5617

**Subject(s):** Science Fiction, Mystery, Adventure, and Romance
**Circ:** ‡60,000

**Western & Eastern Treasures (2978)**
People's Publishing Co.
PO Box 219
San Anselmo, CA 94979
Phone: (415)454-3936
Fax: (415)454-4262
**Subject(s):** Crafts, Models, Hobbies, and Contests; Collecting
**Circ:** ‡60,000

**Pacific Union Recorder (4036)**
Pacific Union Conference of Seventh-day Adventists
PO Box 5005
Westlake Village, CA 91359
Phone: (805)497-9457
Fax: (805)495-2644
**Subject(s):** Religious Publications
**Circ:** (Non-paid)‡59,000

**In the Wind (1330)**
Paisano Publications L.L.C.
PO Box 3000
Agoura Hills, CA 91376-3000
Phone: (818)889-1252
Fax: (818)889-1252
**Subject(s):** Motorbikes and Motorcycles; Lifestyle
**Circ:** (Paid)58,771

**Arizona Hunter & Angler (711)**
Allstar Bass Fishing Tournaments Inc.
PO Box 859
Mesa, AZ 85211
Phone: (480)894-2775
Fax: (480)894-2554
**Subject(s):** (Hunting, Fishing, and Game Management)
**Circ:** (Non-paid)‡842
(Paid)‡57,927

**Sea Classics (1646)**
Challenge Publications Inc.
9509 Vassar Ave., Unit A
Chatsworth, CA 91311-0883
Phone: (818)700-6868
Fax: (818)700-6282
**Subject(s):** History and Genealogy; (Boating and Yachting)
**Circ:** (Paid)⊕57,346

**Inn Room Visitors Magazine (1829)**
PO Box 3395
Escondido, CA 92033
**Subject(s):** Travel and Tourism
**Circ:** (Controlled)31,085
(Paid)57,150

**Classic Trucks (1345)**
McMullen Argus Publishing Inc.
2400 E. Katella Ave., 11th Fl.
Anaheim, CA 92806
Phone: (714)939-2400
Fax: (714)978-6390
**Subject(s):** Automotive (Consumer)
**Circ:** (Paid)57,035

**Zoo View (2382)**
Greater Los Angeles Zoo Association
5333 Zoo Dr.
Los Angeles, CA 90027
Phone: (323)644-4200
Fax: (323)644-4720
**Subject(s):** Wildlife and Exotic Animals
**Circ:** (Non-paid)1,000
(Paid)57,000

**Dog World (2185)**
Fancy Publications
2401 Beverly Boulevard
PO Box 57900
Los Angeles, CA 90057
Phone: (213)385-2222
Fax: (213)385-8565
**Subject(s):** Dogs
**Circ:** (Paid)55,771

**Alaska Airlines Magazines (32243)**
Paradigm Communications Group
2701 1st Ave., Ste. 250
Seattle, WA 98121
Phone: (206)441-5871
Fax: (206)448-6939
**Subject(s):** In-Flight Publications; Travel and Tourism
**Circ:** ‡55,000

**Greater Seattle InfoGuide (32498)**
Vernon Publications L.L.C.
12437 NE 173rd Pl.
PO Box 970
Woodinville, WA 98072-7925
Phone: (425)488-3211
Fax: (425)488-0946
**Subject(s):** Travel and Tourism
**Circ:** (Paid)55,000

**Group Magazine (4508)**
Group Publishing Inc.
PO Box 481
Loveland, CO 80539
Fax: (970)292-4373
**Subject(s):** Youths' Interests; Religious Publications
**Circ:** ‡55,000

**RV Life Magazine (32147)**
Business Day Inc.
18717 Avenue 76 W. B
Lynnwood, WA 98037
**Subject(s):** Travel and Tourism
**Circ:** (Controlled)55,000

**Bay Area Parent—East Bay Edition (3360)**
United Advertising Publications
1660 S Amphlett Blvd., Ste 335
San Mateo, CA 94402
Phone: (650)655-7600
Fax: (650)655-7601
**Subject(s):** Parenting
**Circ:** (Paid)401
(Free)54,346

**Juxtapoz (3165)**
High Speed Productions Inc.
1303 Underwood
San Francisco, CA 94124
Phone: (415)822-3083
Fax: (415)822-8359
**Subject(s):** Art
**Circ:** ‡54,000

**Pleasant Hawaii Magazine (7570)**
This Week Publications
274 Puuhale Rd., Ste. 200
Honolulu, HI 96819-2234
Phone: (808)843-6000
Fax: (808)843-6090
**Subject(s):** In-Flight Publications; Travel and Tourism; Local, State, and Regional Publications
**Circ:** 54,000

**4-Wheel Drive & Sport Utility Magazine (1349)**
McMullen Argus Publishing Inc.
2400 E. Katella Ave., 11th Fl.
Anaheim, CA 92806
Phone: (714)939-2400
Fax: (714)978-6390
**Subject(s):** Automotive (Consumer)
**Circ:** (Paid)53,774

**Reptiles (2319)**
Fancy Publications
2401 Beverly Boulevard
PO Box 57900
Los Angeles, CA 90057
Phone: (213)385-2222
Fax: (213)385-8565
**Subject(s):** Pets
**Circ:** (Paid)53,645

**Mix (1817)**
Primedia Business
6400 Hollis St., Ste. 12
Emeryville, CA 94608
Phone: (510)653-3307
Fax: (510)653-5142
**Subject(s):** Radio, Television, Cable, and Video; Music and Musical Instruments
**Circ:** (Paid)2,044
(Controlled)53,597

**Northwest Labor Press (25964)**
Oregon Labor Press Publishing Co.
1827 NE 44th Ave., Ste. 200
PO Box 13150
Portland, OR 97213
Phone: (503)288-3311
Fax: (503)288-3320
**Subject(s):** Labor
**Circ:** ‡53,500

**Emergency Medical Services** (3950)
Summer Communications Inc.
7626 Densmore Ave.
Van Nuys, CA 91406-2042
Phone: (818)786-4367
Fax: (818)786-9246
Subject(s): Medicine and Surgery
Circ: 53,000

**Rocky Mountain Oyster & National Oyster Newspaper** (4606)
Mountaintop Publishing Inc.
3440 Youngfield St., Ste. 267
Wheat Ridge, CO 80033
Phone: (303)985-3034
Fax: (303)986-5664
Subject(s): Sex/Erotica
Circ: (Paid)100
(Non-paid)53,000

**Newport Beach 714(online)** (2541)
Baker Newspaper Group
1901 Westcliff Dr., Ste. 11
Newport Beach, CA 92660
Phone: (949)722-1286
Fax: (949)722-6632
Subject(s): Lifestyle; Local, State, and Regional Publications
Circ: (Free)‡52,000

**Our Animals** (3185)
San Francisco S.P.C.A.
2500 16th St.
San Francisco, CA 94103
Phone: (415)554-3009
Subject(s): Society for the Prevention of Cruelty to Animals and Anti-Vivisection
Circ: (Non-paid)‡52,000

**Police** (3909)
Business Media
3520 Challenger St.
Torrance, CA 90503
Phone: (310)533-2400
Fax: (310)533-2500
Subject(s): Police, Penology, and Penal Institutions
Circ: ‡52,000

**Gentry Magazine** (2451)
18 Media Inc.
618 Santa Cruz Ave.
Menlo Park, CA 94025
Phone: (650)324-1818
Fax: (650)324-1888
Subject(s): Local, State, and Regional Publications; Home and Garden
Circ: (Non-paid)‡32,500
(Non-paid)‡51,500

**America's Network** (3401)
Advanstar Communications
201 E. Sandpointe Ave., Ste. 600
Santa Ana, CA 92707
Phone: (714)513-8664
Fax: (714)513-8693
Subject(s): Telecommunications
Circ: (Paid)1,914
(Non-paid)51,374

**Business Law Today** (18739)
American Bar Association
c/o Rew R. Goodenow
333 Holcomb Ave.
Ste.300
Reno, NV 89502
Phone: (775)323-1601
Fax: (775)348-7250
Subject(s): Law; Business
Circ: (Paid)△50,664

**Climbing Magazine** (4166)
Primedia
0326 Hwy. 133, Ste. 190
Carbondale, CO 81623
Phone: (970)963-9449
Fax: (970)963-9442
Subject(s): (General Sports); (Outdoors)
Circ: (Paid)50,598

**Acoustic Guitar Magazine** (2975)
Acoustic Guitar
PO Box 767
San Anselmo, CA 94979
Phone: (415)485-6946
Fax: (415)485-0831

Subject(s): Music and Musical Instruments; Music and Musical Instruments
Circ: (Paid)50,000

**5280** (4287)
5280 Publishing Inc.
1224 Speer Blvd.
Denver, CO 80204
Phone: (303)832-5280
Fax: (303)832-0470
Subject(s): Local, State, and Regional Publications; Lifestyle; Entertainment
Circ: (Combined)50,000

**Home Education Magazine** (32452)
PO Box 1083
Tonasket, WA 98855
Phone: (509)486-1351
Fax: (509)486-2753
Subject(s): Education; Education; Parenting
Circ: (Non-paid)‡12,400
(Paid)‡12,700
(Combined)50,000

**Journal of Financial Planning** (4302)
Financial Planning Association
4100 E. Mississippi Ave., Ste. 400
Denver, CO 80246-3053
Fax: (303)759-0749
Subject(s): Banking, Finance, and Investments
Circ: (Controlled)‡50,000

**Junior Baseball Magazine** (1612)
2D Publishing
PO Box 9099
Canoga Park, CA 91309
Phone: (818)710-1234
Fax: (818)710-1877
Subject(s): (Baseball); Parenting; Youths' Interests
Circ: (Paid)50,000

**KAET Magazine** (874)
Arizona State University
PO Box 871405
Tempe, AZ 85287
Phone: (480)965-9011
Fax: (480)965-1000
Subject(s): Radio, Television, Cable, and Video
Circ: (Controlled)‡50,000

**Kung Fu/Qigong** (1869)
Pacific Rim Publishing Inc.
40748 Encyclopedia Cr.
Fremont, CA 94538
Phone: (510)656-5100
Fax: (510)656-8844
Subject(s): (Martial Arts)
Circ: (Non-paid)50000

**Latin Beat Magazine** (1923)
15900 Crenshaw Blvd., Ste. 223
Gardena, CA 90249
Phone: (310)516-6767
Fax: (310)516-9916
Subject(s): Music and Musical Instruments
Circ: (Combined)50,000

**Northwest Travel** (25829)
Northwest Regional Magazines
4969 Hwy. 101 N.Ste. 2
Florence, OR 97439
Phone: (541)997-8401
Fax: (541)997-1124
Subject(s): Travel and Tourism
Circ: (Controlled)‡1,950
(Paid)‡50,000

**Oregon Coast** (25830)
Northwest Regional Magazines
4969 Hwy. 101 N.Ste. 2
Florence, OR 97439
Phone: (541)997-8401
Fax: (541)997-1124
Subject(s): Local, State, and Regional Publications
Circ: (Paid)‡50,000

**Pearlridge Magazine** (7568)
This Week Publications
274 Puuhale Rd., Ste. 200
Honolulu, HI 96819-2234
Phone: (808)843-6000
Fax: (808)843-6090

Subject(s): Travel and Tourism; Local, State, and Regional Publications
Circ: 50,000

**Players** (2310)
Players International Publications
8060 Melrose Ave.
Los Angeles, CA 90046
Phone: (323)653-8060
Fax: (323)655-9452
Subject(s): Black Publications; Men's Interests
Circ: 50,000

**The San Juans Beckon** (32071)
Sound Publishing
441 N. Beach Rd.
PO Box 758
Eastsound, WA 98245
Phone: (360)376-4500
Fax: (360)376-4501
Subject(s): Travel and Tourism
Circ: (Free)50,000

**Smart TV & Sound Magazine** (1653)
York Publishing
PO Box 4591
Chico, CA 95927
Phone: (530)891-8410
Fax: (530)891-8443
Subject(s): Computers; Telecommunications; Radio, Television, Cable, and Video
Circ: (Combined)50,000

**Sports Car International** (2860)
Ross Periodicals
PO Box 1529
Ross, CA 94957
Phone: (415)382-0580
Subject(s): Automotive (Consumer)
Circ: (Non-paid)‡1,200
(Paid)‡50,000

**Widescreen Review** (3599)
27645 Commerce Center Dr.
Temecula, CA 92590-2521
Phone: (909)676-4914
Fax: (909)693-2960
Subject(s): Motion Pictures; Entertainment; Radio, Television, Cable, and Video
Circ: (Paid)⊕50,000

**Wine X Magazine** (3501)
4184 Sonoma Mountain Rd.
Santa Rosa, CA 95404
Phone: (707)545-0992
Subject(s): Food and Cooking; Beverages, Brewing, and Bottling; Art and Art History
Circ: (Controlled)50,000

**Woodwork** (2561)
Ross Periodicals
42 Digital Dr., Ste. 5
Novato, CA 94949
Phone: (415)382-0580
Fax: (415)382-0587
Subject(s): Wood and Woodworking
Circ: ‡50,000

**XLR8R** (3239)
1388 Haight St., No. 105
San Francisco, CA 94117
Phone: (415)861-7583
Fax: (415)861-7584
Subject(s): Music and Musical Instruments; Fashion
Circ: (Paid)50,000

**Electronic Musician** (1815)
Primedia Business
6400 Hollis St., Ste. 12
Emeryville, CA 94608
Phone: (510)653-3307
Fax: (510)653-5142
Subject(s): Music and Musical Instruments
Circ: (Non-paid)△17,697
(Paid)△49,775

**BMXer** (649)
American Bicycle Association
PO Box 718
Chandler, AZ 85244
Phone: (480)961-1903
Fax: (480)961-1842
Subject(s): (Bicycling)
Circ: 49,000

**Triathlete** (1821)
Triathlete Group
328 Encinitas Blvd. Ste. 100
Encinitas, CA 92024
Phone: (760)634-4100
Fax: (760)634-4110
**Subject(s):** (General Sports)

Circ: (Paid)49,000

**Biker** (1321)
Paisano Publications L.L.C.
PO Box 3000
Agoura, CA 91376
Phone: (818)889-8740
**Subject(s):** Lifestyle; Motorbikes and Motorcycles

Circ: (Paid)48,033

**Freshwater & Marine Aquarium Magazine** (3526)
R/C Modeler Corp.
144 W. Sierra Madre Blvd.
PO Box 487
Sierra Madre, CA 91025
Phone: (626)355-1476
Fax: (626)355-6415
**Subject(s):** Crafts, Models, Hobbies, and Contests

Circ: ‡48,000

**International Travel News** (2895)
Martin Publications Inc.
2120 28th St.
Sacramento, CA 95818
Phone: (916)457-3643
**Subject(s):** Travel and Tourism

Circ: 48,000

**Latitude 38** (2468)
15 Locust Ave.
Mill Valley, CA 94941
Phone: (415)383-8200
Fax: (415)383-5816
**Subject(s):** (Boating and Yachting)

Circ: (Combined)48,000

**BMX Plus!** (3937)
Hi-Torque Publishing Company Inc.
25233 Anza Dr.
Valencia, CA 91355
Phone: (661)295-1910
Fax: (661)295-1278
**Subject(s):** (Bicycling)

Circ: ‡47,615

**California Nurse** (2581)
California Nurses Association
2000 Franklin St., Ste. 300
Oakland, CA 94612-2908
Phone: (510)273-2200
Fax: (510)663-0629
**Subject(s):** Nursing

Circ: (Controlled)‡500
(Paid)‡47,000

**SuperFord.org** (2346)
PRIMEDIA Los Angeles
6420 Wilshire Blvd.
Los Angeles, CA 90048
Phone: (323)782-2000
Fax: (323)782-2223
**Subject(s):** Automotive (Consumer); (Auto Racing)

Circ: (Paid)46,656

**San Diego Magazine** (3049)
San Diego Magazine Publishing Co.
1450 Front St.
San Diego, CA 92101-7901
Phone: (619)230-9292
Fax: (619)230-0490
**Subject(s):** Local, State, and Regional Publications

Circ: (Paid)46,545

**American Rodder** (1320)
Paisano Publications L.L.C.
PO Box 3000
Agoura, CA 91376
Phone: (818)889-8740
**Subject(s):** Automotive (Consumer)

Circ: (Paid)46,517

**Frontiers** (4027)
Mercury Capital Inc.
8380 Santa Monica Blvd., Ste. 200
West Hollywood, CA 90069
Phone: (323)848-2222
Fax: (323)848-2231
**Subject(s):** Gay and Lesbian Interests

Circ: (Combined)‡46,000

**Coast Magazine** (2535)
240 Newport Center Dr., Ste. 290
Newport Beach, CA 92660
Phone: (949)644-4700
Fax: (949)644-4055
**Subject(s):** Travel and Tourism; Lifestyle; Local, State, and Regional Publications

Circ: (Combined)45,830

**Backwoods Home Magazine** (25839)
Backwoods Home Magazine Inc.
29545 Ellensburg Ave.
PO Box 712
Gold Beach, OR 97444
Phone: (541)247-8900
Fax: (541)247-8600
**Subject(s):** Lifestyle

Circ: ‡45,000

**Bass Player** (3359)
The Music Player Group
2800 Campus Dr.
San Mateo, CA 94403
Phone: (650)513-4400
Fax: (650)513-4642
**Subject(s):** Music and Musical Instruments

Circ: 45,000

**Inside Supply Management** (868)
Institute for Supply Management
PO BOX 22160
PO Box 22160
Tempe, AZ 85285
Phone: (480)752-6276
Fax: (480)752-7890
**Subject(s):** Purchasing; Business

Circ: (Non-paid)‡300
(Paid)‡45,000

**Key Magazine Palm Springs** (830)
Key Magazine Inc.
c/o Steve Vincent
5353 E. Shaw Butte Dr.
Scottsdale, AZ 85254
Phone: (480)596-1470
Fax: (480)922-8882
**Subject(s):** Travel and Tourism; Entertainment; Local, State, and Regional Publications

Circ: (Combined)45,000

**Key Magazine Phoenix/Scottsdale** (684)
Key Magazine Inc.
c/o Michelle Schreck
4914 W. Saddlehorn Rd.
Glendale, AZ 85310
Phone: (623)869-8880
Fax: (623)869-8123
**Subject(s):** Travel and Tourism; Entertainment; Local, State, and Regional Publications

Circ: (Combined)45,000

**Mercy Connections** (4209)
Mission of Mercy
15475 Gleneagle Dr.
PO Box 62600
Colorado Springs, CO 80921
Phone: (719)481-0400
Fax: (719)481-4649
**Subject(s):** Philanthropy and Humanitarianism

Circ: 45,000

**Science of Mind** (1578)
United Church of Religious Science
2600 W. Magnolia Blvd.
Burbank, CA 91505
Phone: (818)526-7757
Fax: (818)556-2253
**Subject(s):** Religious Publications

Circ: (Controlled)‡32,495
(Paid)‡45,000

**Ag Alert** (2861)
California Farm Bureau Federation
2300 River Plaza Dr.
Sacramento, CA 95833
Phone: (916)561-5500
Fax: (916)561-5699
**Subject(s):** Farm Bureau, Grange, and Cooperative Associations

Circ: 44,000

**The Dispatcher** (3129)
International Longshore and Warehouse Union
1188 Franklin St., 4th Fl.
San Francisco, CA 94109
Phone: (415)775-0533
Fax: (415)775-1302
**Subject(s):** Labor

Circ: (Non-paid)‡44,000

**This Week Oahu** (7578)
This Week Publications
274 Puuhale Rd., Ste. 200
Honolulu, HI 96819-2234
Phone: (808)843-6000
Fax: (808)843-6090
**Subject(s):** Travel and Tourism; Local, State, and Regional Publications

Circ: (Non-paid)‡44,000

**Home Media Retailing** (3406)
Advanstar Communications
201 E. Sandpointe Ave.
Ste. 600
Santa Ana, CA 92707
Phone: (714)513-8403
Fax: (714)513-8403
**Subject(s):** Radio, Television, Cable, and Video

Circ: (Paid)422
(Non-paid)43,885

**Colorado Outdoors** (4276)
Colorado Division of Wildlife
6060 Broadway
Denver, CO 80216-1000
Phone: (303)297-1192
Fax: (303)291-7109
**Subject(s):** Environmental and Natural Resources Conservation; (Outdoors); Local, State, and Regional Publications

Circ: (Controlled)‡3,100
(Paid)‡43,576

**Gun Dog** (2217)
PRIMEDIA Los Angeles
6420 Wilshire Blvd.
Los Angeles, CA 90048
Phone: (323)782-2000
Fax: (323)782-2223
**Subject(s):** (Hunting, Fishing, and Game Management)

Circ: (Paid)43,501

**Sun Life Magazine** (686)
Brown & Brown Publishers
PO BOX 10187
Glendale, AZ 85318-0187
Phone: (623)878-2210
**Subject(s):** Lifestyle

Circ: (Free)43,000

**Diablo** (4020)
Diablo Publications
2520 Camino Diablo
Walnut Creek, CA 94597
Phone: (925)943-1111
Fax: (925)943-1045
**Subject(s):** Lifestyle; Local, State, and Regional Publications

Circ: (Paid)402
(Non-paid)42,197

**Montana Magazine** (18161)
PO Box 5630
Helena, MT 59604
Phone: (406)443-2842
Fax: (406)443-5480
**Subject(s):** Local, State, and Regional Publications

Circ: ‡42,000

**Spotlight Big Island** (7572)
Spotlight Hawaii Publishing
532 Cummins St.
Honolulu, HI 96814
Phone: (808)593-9404
Fax: (808)593-9494
**Subject(s):** Travel and Tourism; Local, State, and Regional Publications

Circ: (Non-paid)42,000

**Spotlight Kauai** (7573)
Spotlight Hawaii Publishing
532 Cummins St.
Honolulu, HI 96814
Phone: (808)593-9404
Fax: (808)593-9494
**Subject(s):** Travel and Tourism; Local, State, and Regional Publications

Circ: (Non-paid)42,000

**Ala Moana Shopping Center Magazine (7526)**
This Week Publications
274 Puuhale Rd., Ste. 200
Honolulu, HI 96819-2234
Phone: (808)843-6000
Fax: (808)843-6090
**Subject(s):** Travel and Tourism; Local, State, and Regional Publications; Japanese
**Circ:** 41,600

**Nuevo Mundo (3300)**
San Jose Mercury News
750 Ridder Park Dr.
San Jose, CA 95190
Phone: (408)920-5000
Fax: (408)271-3790
**Subject(s):** General Editorial
**Circ:** (Free)❏41,416

**Tailgate (1324)**
Paisano Publications L.L.C.
PO Box 3000
Agoura, CA 91376
Phone: (818)889-8740
**Subject(s):** Automotive (Consumer); (Auto Racing); Lifestyle
**Circ:** (Paid)‡41,250

**ACE FitnessMatters (2997)**
American Council on Exercise
4851 Paramont Dr.
San Diego, CA 92123
Phone: (858)279-8227
Fax: (858)279-8064
**Subject(s):** Health; (Physical Fitness)
**Circ:** (Paid)41,000

**Electrical News (1383)**
135 E. La Porte St.
PO Box 660760
Arcadia, CA 91066-0760
Phone: (626)446-8652
Fax: (626)447-6047
**Subject(s):** Lighting; Electrical Engineering
**Circ:** (Paid)‡1,100
(Free)‡41,000

**The RangeFinder (3484)**
The RangeFinder Publishing Company Inc.
1312 Lincoln Blvd.
PO Box 1703
Santa Monica, CA 90406
Phone: (310)451-8506
Fax: (310)395-9058
**Subject(s):** Photography
**Circ:** (Paid)8,412
(Controlled)40,959

**Adventure Cyclist (18198)**
Adventure Cycling Association
150 E Pine St.
PO Box 8308
Missoula, MT 59807
Phone: (406)721-1776
Fax: (406)721-8754
**Subject(s):** (Bicycling)
**Circ:** 40,000

**Association News (2136)**
Schneider Publishing Company Inc.
11835 W Olympic Blvd., 12th Fl.
Los Angeles, CA 90064
Phone: (310)577-3700
Fax: (310)577-3715
**Subject(s):** Conventions, Meetings, and Trade Fairs; Management and Administration
**Circ:** (Controlled)‡40,000

**The Bloomsbury Review (4262)**
1553 Platte St., Ste. 206
Denver, CO 80202-1167
**Subject(s):** Literature and Literary Reviews
**Circ:** (Paid)‡10,000
(Controlled)‡40,000

**Chiropractic Products (2167)**
Novicom Inc.
6100 Center Dr., Ste. 1000
Los Angeles, CA 90045
Phone: (310)642-4400
Fax: (310)641-4444
**Subject(s):** Chiropractic
**Circ:** (Controlled)40,000

**Gleaner (32462)**
North Pacific Union Conference of Seventh-Day Adventists
PO Box 871150
Vancouver, WA 98687-1150
Phone: (360)816-1483
**Subject(s):** Religious Publications
**Circ:** ‡40,000

**KEY Magazine, Carmel and Monterey Peninsula (1622)**
Key Magazine - Carmel/Monterey
PO Box 223859
Carmel, CA 93922
Phone: (831)648-1460
Fax: (831)648-1977
**Subject(s):** Local, State, and Regional Publications; Travel and Tourism
**Circ:** (Non-paid)**40,000**

**Minority Business Entrepreneur (3907)**
3528 Torrance Blvd., Ste. 101
Torrance, CA 90503
Phone: (310)540-9398
Fax: (310)792-8263
**Subject(s):** Business; Black Publications; Hispanic Publications; Women's Interests
**Circ:** 40,000

**Physical Therapy Products (2306)**
Novicom Inc.
6100 Center Dr., Ste. 1000
Los Angeles, CA 90045
Phone: (310)642-4400
Fax: (310)641-4444
**Subject(s):** Health and Healthcare
**Circ:** (Controlled)40,000

**Powerboat Magazine (3971)**
1691 Spinnaker Dr., Ste. 206
Ventura, CA 93001-4378
Phone: (805)639-2222
Fax: (805)639-2220
**Subject(s):** (Boating and Yachting)
**Circ:** 40,000

**Pulp and Paper (3195)**
Pulp & Paper
55 Hawthorne, Ste. 510
San Francisco, CA 94105
Phone: (415)947-3600
Fax: (415)947-3700
**Subject(s):** Paper
**Circ:** (Paid)2,000
(Controlled)40,000

**RACQUETBALL Magazine (4216)**
United States Racquetball Association
1685 W. Uintah
Colorado Springs, CO 80904-2906
Phone: (719)635-5396
Fax: (719)635-0685
**Circ:** (Paid)40,000

**Skeptic (1337)**
Skeptic Magazine
PO Box 338
Altadena, CA 91001
Phone: (626)794-3119
Fax: (626)794-1301
**Subject(s):** Parapsychology; Science
**Circ:** (Controlled)40,000

**WHERE Seattle (32344)**
Miller Publishing Group L.L.C.
1904 3rd Ave., Ste. 623
Seattle, WA 98101
Phone: (206)826-2665
**Subject(s):** Travel and Tourism
**Circ:** (Controlled)40,000

**WOODALL'S Camperways (3979)**
Woodall Publications Corp.
2575 Vista Del Mar Dr.
Ventura, CA 93001
Phone: (805)667-4100
Fax: (303)728-7306
**Subject(s):** Lifestyle; (Outdoors)
**Circ:** 40,000

**WOODALL's Midwest RV Traveler (3980)**
Woodall Publications Corp.
2575 Vista Del Mar Dr.
Ventura, CA 93001
Phone: (805)667-4100
Fax: (303)728-7306

**Subject(s):** Lifestyle; (Outdoors)
**Circ:** 40,000

**Journal of the American Water Works Association (4295)**
American Water Works Association
6666 W. Quincy Ave.
Denver, CO 80235
Phone: (303)794-7711
Fax: (303)347-0804
**Subject(s):** Water Supply and Sewage Disposal
**Circ:** (Controlled)‡3,993
(Paid)‡39,040

**Safari Magazine (934)**
Safari Club Intl.
4800 W Gates Pass Rd.
Tucson, AZ 85745
Phone: (520)620-1220
Fax: (520)622-1205
**Subject(s):** (Hunting, Fishing, and Game Management)
**Circ:** (Controlled)‡39,000

**Contemporary Long Term Care (2175)**
Leisure Publications
4160 Wilshire Blvd.
Los Angeles, CA 90010
Phone: (323)801-0160
Fax: (323)417-4860
**Subject(s):** Health and Healthcare; Hospitals and Healthcare Institutions
**Circ:** (Paid)2,529
(Non-paid)38,337

**GPS World (25798)**
Advanstar Communications
PO Box 10488
Eugene, OR 97440
Phone: (541)343-1200
Fax: (541)984-5333
**Subject(s):** Transportation, Traffic, and Shipping; Aviation
**Circ:** 38,000

**Key Magazine Colorado (4497)**
Key Magazine Inc.
PO Box 270246
Littleton, CO 80127
Phone: (303)971-0993
**Subject(s):** Travel and Tourism; Entertainment; Local, State, and Regional Publications
**Circ:** (Combined)**38,000**

**Prorodeo Sports News (4215)**
Professional Rodeo Cowboys Association Inc.
101 Pro Rodeo Dr.
Colorado Springs, CO 80919-2301
Phone: (719)593-8840
Fax: (719)548-4876
**Subject(s):** (Horses and Horse Racing)
**Circ:** ‡37,972

**Nailpro (3954)**
Creative Age Publications Inc.
7628 Densmore Ave.
Van Nuys, CA 91406-2042
Phone: (818)782-7328
Fax: (818)782-7450
**Subject(s):** Cosmetics and Toiletries
**Circ:** (Paid)△19,041
(Non-paid)△37,604

**Injection Molding Magazine (4290)**
Canon Communications L.L.C.
55 Madison St., Ste. 770
Denver, CO 80206
Phone: (303)321-2322
Fax: (303)321-3552
**Subject(s):** Plastic and Composition Materials
**Circ:** (Combined)‡37,500

**Washington CEO (32338)**
Washington CEO Inc.
12201 Tukwila International Blvd., Ste. 150
Seattle, WA 98168
Phone: (206)441-8415
Fax: (206)441-8325
**Subject(s):** Business; Local, State, and Regional Publications
**Circ:** (Controlled)37,000

**4-Wheel ATV Action (3940)**
Hi-Torque Publishing Company Inc.
25233 Anza Dr.
Valencia, CA 91355
Phone: (661)295-1910
Fax: (661)295-1278

# Western States

**Subject(s):** Motorbikes and Motorcyles
**Circ:** (Paid)36,826

**Flyfishing & Tying Journal (25956)**
Frank Amato Publications Inc.
PO Box 82112
Portland, OR 97282
Phone: (503)653-8108
Fax: (503)653-2766
**Subject(s):** (Hunting, Fishing, and Game Management)
**Circ:** ‡36,056

**Cinefex (2819)**
PO Box 20027
Riverside, CA 92516
Phone: (909)781-1917
Fax: (909)788-1793
**Subject(s):** Motion Pictures
**Circ:** (Non-paid)1,000
 (Paid)36,000

**Scope (2081)**
Loma Linda University
Office of University Relations
24941, Stewart St.
Loma Linda, CA 92350-0001
Phone: (909)558-4526
Fax: (909)558-4181
**Subject(s):** College Publications
**Circ:** (Free)‡36,000

**Fire-Rescue Magazine (3015)**
Jems Communications
525 B St., Ste. 1900
San Diego, CA 92101
Phone: (619)687-3272
Fax: (619)699-6396
**Subject(s):** Safety; Medicine and Surgery
**Circ:** (Paid)9,709
 (Non-paid)35,991

**The WREN Magazine (33732)**
PO Box 549
Gillette, WY 82717
Phone: (307)682-7527
Fax: (307)682-7528
**Subject(s):** Rural Electrification; Local, State, and Regional Publications
**Circ:** (Combined)35,483

**Boxing USA (4187)**
United States of America Boxing
1 Olympic Plz.
Colorado Springs, CO 80909
Phone: (719)866-4506
Fax: (719)652-3426
**Subject(s):** (Boxing and Wrestling)
**Circ:** 35,000

**Bridge U.S.A. (3897)**
20300 S Vermont Ave., Ste. 200
Torrance, CA 90502
Phone: (310)532-5921
Fax: (310)532-1184
**Subject(s):** Japanese; Ethnic Publications
**Circ:** (Combined)35,000

**Computer Bits (25853)**
4660 NE Belknap Ct., Ste. 101N
Hillsboro, OR 97124
Phone: (503)924-5786
**Subject(s):** Computers
**Circ:** (Non-paid)35,000

**Flowers (2206)**
Teleflora
11444 W Olympic Blvd.
Los Angeles, CA 90064
Phone: (310)966-3518
Fax: (310)966-3610
**Subject(s):** Florists and Floriculture
**Circ:** (Combined)△**35,000**

**National Cattlemen Magazine (4175)**
National Cattlemen's Beef Association
9110 E. Nichols Ave.
Centennial, CO 80112
**Subject(s):** Livestock
**Circ:** (Paid)35,000

**Oregon Teamster (25969)**
Joint Council of Teamsters, No. 37
1872 NE 162nd Ave.
Portland, OR 97230-5642
Phone: (503)251-2339
Fax: (503)251-2303
**Subject(s):** Labor
**Circ:** (Non-paid)35,000

**Route 66 Magazine (18730)**
PO Box 66
Laughlin, NV 89028
Phone: (702)299-0856
Fax: (702)299-0896
**Subject(s):** Travel and Tourism; History and Genealogy
**Circ:** (Paid)5,000
 (Non-paid)35,000

**Soccer America (2605)**
Berling Communications Inc.
PO Box 23704
Oakland, CA 94623
Phone: (510)420-3640
Fax: (510)420-3655
**Subject(s):** (Soccer)
**Circ:** (Paid)‡35,000

**Spotlight Oahu (7574)**
Spotlight Hawaii Publishing
532 Cummins St.
Honolulu, HI 96814
Phone: (808)593-9404
Fax: (808)593-9494
**Subject(s):** Travel and Tourism; Local, State, and Regional Publications
**Circ:** (Non-paid)35,000

**Tacoma Reporter (32440)**
YodaMedia Inc.
PO Box 1743
Tacoma, WA 98401-1743
Fax: (253)272-8824
**Subject(s):** Free Newspapers
**Circ:** 35,000

**Wyoming Wildlife (33707)**
Wyoming Game and Fish Dept.
5400 Bishop Blvd.
Cheyenne, WY 82006
Phone: (307)777-4600
Fax: (307)777-4610
**Subject(s):** Ecology and Conservation; (Hunting, Fishing, and Game Management); Natural History and Nature Study; Local, State, and Regional Publications
**Circ:** (Controlled)‡1,100
 (Paid)‡35,000

**American Fitness (3519)**
15250 Ventura Blvd., Ste. 200
Sherman Oaks, CA 91403
Phone: (818)905-0040
Fax: (818)990-5468
**Subject(s):** (Physical Fitness)
**Circ:** (Non-paid)‡7,292
 (Paid)‡34,708

**Community Pharmacist (4477)**
ELF Publications Inc.
5285 W Louisiana Ave.
Lakewood, CO 80232-5976
Phone: (303)975-0075
**Subject(s):** Drugs and Pharmaceuticals
**Circ:** (Controlled)‡34,000

**Everton's Genealogical Helper & Geneology Online (30685)**
Everton Publishers Inc.
PO Box 368
Logan, UT 84323-0368
Phone: (435)752-6022
Fax: (435)752-1541
**Subject(s):** History and Genealogy
**Circ:** ‡34,000

**TravelAge West (2355)**
Northstar Travel Media
11400 W.Olympic Blvd. Suite 325
Los Angeles, CA 90064
Fax: (310)954-2520
**Subject(s):** Travel and Tourism
**Circ:** (Controlled)‡34,001

**Sacramento Magazine (2911)**
Sacramento Magazines Corp.
706 56th St., Ste. 210
Sacramento, CA 95819
Phone: (916)452-6200
Fax: (916)414-6060
**Subject(s):** Local, State, and Regional Publications; Lifestyle
**Circ:** (Non-paid)△4,107
 (Paid)△**33,132**

**Before & After (2857)**
JMS Publishing L.L.C.
2007 Opportunity Dr., Ste. 10
Roseville, CA 95678-3007
Phone: (916)784-3880
Fax: (916)784-3995
**Subject(s):** Graphic Arts and Design
**Circ:** (Paid)‡33,000

**Cable Yellow Pages (3898)**
Teton Media Inc.
20917 Higgins Ct.
Torrance, CA 90501
Phone: (310)212-0772
Fax: (310)212-5942
**Subject(s):** Radio, Television, Cable, and Video
**Circ:** (Non-paid)‡33,000

**Midwest Airlines Magazine (32291)**
Paradigm Communications Group
2701 1st Ave., Ste. 250
Seattle, WA 98121
Phone: (206)441-5871
Fax: (206)448-6939
**Subject(s):** Business; Travel and Tourism
**Circ:** (Non-paid)33,000

**MOTION (18650)**
Motion Corp.
PO Box 21730
Carson City, NV 89721-1730
Phone: (775)246-9292
Fax: (775)246-9222
**Subject(s):** Electronics Engineering; Safety
**Circ:** (Non-paid)33,000

**Weekend Woodcrafts (1704)**
EGW.com Inc.
1041 Shary Cir.
Concord, CA 94518
Phone: (925)671-9852
Fax: (925)671-0692
**Subject(s):** Crafts, Models, Hobbies, and Contests
**Circ:** (Paid)33,000

**Dayspa (3948)**
Creative Age Publications Inc.
7628 Densmore Ave.
Van Nuys, CA 91406-2042
Phone: (818)782-7328
Fax: (818)782-7450
**Subject(s):** Hairstyling; Health and Healthcare; Business
**Circ:** (Controlled)32,564

**Rock & Ice (4167)**
Big Stone Publishers
1101 Village Rd., UL-4D
Carbondale, CO 81623
Phone: (970)704-1442
Fax: (970)963-4965
**Subject(s):** (General Sports)
**Circ:** (Paid)32,500

**Ministry & Liturgy (3297)**
Resource Publications Inc.
160 E. Virginia St., No. 290
San Jose, CA 95112-5876
Phone: (408)286-8505
Fax: (408)287-8748
**Subject(s):** Religious Publications
**Circ:** (Paid)7,000
 (Non-paid)32,000

**Workforce (2013)**
Crain Communications, Inc.
4 Executive Circle, Ste. 185
Irvine, CA 92614
Phone: (949)255-5340
**Subject(s):** Employment and Human Resources
**Circ:** ‡32,000

**Imaging Magazine (3153)**
CMP Media L.L.C.
C/O John Hayes
600 Harrison St.
San Francisco, CA
**Subject(s):** Computers
**Circ:** 31,240

**Oncology Nursing Forum (3943)**
Oncology Nursing Society
c/o Rose Mary Carroll-Johnson
25319 Via Saludo
Valencia, CA 91355
Phone: (661)255-3805
Fax: (661)255-3805
**Subject(s):** Nursing
**Circ:** ‡31,225

**English Journal (4377)**
National Council of Teachers of English
359 Eddy Hall
1773 Campus Delivery
English Dept.
Colorado State University
Fort Collins, CO 80523-1773
Phone: (970)491-6417
Fax: (970)491-3097
**Subject(s):** Education
**Circ:** (Paid)31,000

**Washington Magazine (32000)**
Fivash Publishing Group
1500 114th Ave. SE, Ste. 101
Bellevue, WA 98004-6902
Phone: (206)441-8415
Fax: (206)441-8325
**Subject(s):** Lifestyle; Home and Garden; Travel and Tourism
**Circ:** (Paid)23,000
(Non-paid)31,000

**Import Automotive Parts & Accessories (1602)**
Meyers Publishing
799 Camarillo Springs Rd.
Camarillo, CA 93012-8111
Phone: (805)445-8881
Fax: (805)445-8882
**Subject(s):** Automotive (Trade)
**Circ:** (Paid)△30
(Controlled)△30,981

**Worldradio (2921)**
Worldradio Inc.
2224 Beaumont St., Ste. D
Sacramento, CA 95815
Phone: (877)472-8643
Fax: (916)457-7339
**Subject(s):** Radio, Television, Cable, and Video; Crafts, Models, Hobbies, and Contests
**Circ:** ‡30,700

**Sea Magazine (2011)**
Duncan McIntosh Company Inc.
17782 Cowan, Ste. A
Irvine, CA 92614
Phone: (949)660-6150
Fax: (949)660-6172
**Subject(s):** (Boating and Yachting)
**Circ:** (Paid)18,693
(Non-paid)30,693

**Archives of Pediatrics & Adolescent Medicine (32247)**
American Medical Association Alliance
c/o Frederick P. Rivara, MD, MPH
6200 NE 74th St, Ste. 210
Department of Pediatrics
University of Washington
Seattle, WA 98115-8160
Phone: (206)685-3573
Fax: (206)685-3572
**Subject(s):** Pediatrics; Medicine and Surgery
**Circ:** (Combined)‡30,334

**After Five Magazine (1594)**
PO Box 492905
37095 Mian St. Ste.c
Burney, CA 96013
Phone: (530)335-5360
Fax: (530)335-5335
**Subject(s):** Lifestyle
**Circ:** (Non-paid)‡30,122

**Animal Issues (2863)**
Animal Protection Institute
1122 S. St.
Sacramento, CA 95814
Phone: (916)447-3085
Fax: (916)447-3070
**Subject(s):** Wildlife and Exotic Animals; Environmental and Natural Resources Conservation; Pets
**Circ:** (Non-paid)‡1,000
(Paid)‡30,000

**Appaloosa Journal (7742)**
Appaloosa Horse Club
2720 W. Pullman Rd.
Moscow, ID 83843
Phone: (208)882-5578
Fax: (208)882-8150
**Subject(s):** (Horses and Horse Racing); Livestock
**Circ:** 30,000

**Barter News (2475)**
PO Box 3024
Mission Viejo, CA 92690
Phone: (949)831-0607
Fax: (949)831-9378
**Subject(s):** Banking, Finance, and Investments
**Circ:** (Controlled)30,000

**Bay and Delta Yachtsman (18738)**
Recreation Publications Inc.
4090 S. McCarran Blvd., Ste. E
Reno, NV 89502-7529
Phone: (775)353-5100
Fax: (775)353-5111
**Subject(s):** (Boating and Yachting)
**Circ:** ‡30,000

**Contemporary Orthopaedics (3899)**
Business Media
3520 Challenger St.
Torrance, CA 90503
Phone: (310)533-2400
Fax: (310)533-2500
**Subject(s):** Medicine and Surgery
**Circ:** (Non-paid)30,000

**International Arabian Horse (4094)**
International Arabian Horse Association
10805 E Bethany Dr.
Aurora, CO 80014
Phone: (303)696-4500
Fax: (303)696-4599
**Subject(s):** Livestock; (Horses and Horse Racing)
**Circ:** ‡30,000

**KOCE Viewers Guide (1984)**
KOCE-TV Foundation
1571, Gothard St.
Huntington Beach, CA 92647
Phone: (714)895-5623
Fax: (714)895-0852
**Subject(s):** Radio, Television, Cable, and Video
**Circ:** ‡30,000

**Mountainwest Golf (7700)**
Harris Publishing Inc.
360 B St.
Idaho Falls, ID 83402
Phone: (208)524-7000
Fax: (208)522-5241
**Subject(s):** (Golf)
**Circ:** (Combined)30,000

**Ostomy Quarterly (2008)**
United Ostomy Association Inc.
19772 MacArthur Blvd., Ste. 200
Irvine, CA 92612-2405
Phone: (714)660-8624
Fax: (714)660-9262
**Subject(s):** Medicine and Surgery
**Circ:** ‡30,000

**Plastics Auxiliaries & Machinery (4317)**
Canon Communications L.L.C.
55 Madison St., Ste. 770
Denver, CO 80206
Phone: (303)321-2322
Fax: (303)321-3552
**Subject(s):** Plastic and Composition Materials
**Circ:** (Controlled)30,000

**Puget Sound Parent (32313)**
Northwest Parent Publishing
123 NW 36th St., Ste. 215
Seattle, WA 98107-4959
Phone: (206)441-0191
Fax: (206)441-4919
**Subject(s):** Parenting; Local, State, and Regional Publications
**Circ:** (Combined)30,000

**Respiratory Therapy Products (2320)**
CurAnt Communications Inc.
6701 Center Dr. W, Ste. 450
Los Angeles, CA 90045
Phone: (310)642-4400
Fax: (310)641-4444
**Subject(s):** Health and Healthcare; Machinery and Equipment
**Circ:** (Controlled)30,000

**St. Patrick Hospital Health Update (18211)**
St. Patrick Hospital
500 W. Broadway
PO Box 4587
Missoula, MT 59802
Phone: (406)543-7271
Fax: (406)329-5875
**Subject(s):** Health and Healthcare; Medicine and Surgery
**Circ:** (Controlled)30,000

**San Diego This Week (3053)**
Key Magazine Inc.
c/o Harriet King
438 Camino Del Rio South, No. 118
San Diego, CA 92108
Phone: (619)299-6121
Fax: (619)299-6125
**Subject(s):** Travel and Tourism; Entertainment; Local, State, and Regional Publications
**Circ:** (Combined)**30,000**

**Sea Kayaker Magazine (32321)**
Sea Kayaker Inc.
PO Box 17029
Seattle, WA 98107-0729
Phone: (206)789-9536
Fax: (206)781-1141
**Subject(s):** (Boating and Yachting)
**Circ:** (Paid)30,000

**The Star (4481)**
1235 Pierce St.
Lakewood, CO 80214
Phone: (303)235-0116
Fax: (303)237-6080
**Subject(s):** Automotive (Consumer)
**Circ:** (Non-paid)‡2,000
(Paid)‡30,000

**WOODALL'S Southern RV (3982)**
Woodall Publications Corp.
2575 Vista Del Mar Dr.
Ventura, CA 93001
Phone: (805)667-4100
Fax: (805)728-7306
**Subject(s):** Trailers and Accessories
**Circ:** (Paid)30,000

**Arizona Gourmet (898)**
Oser Communications Group Inc.
1350 N Kolb Rd., Ste. 130
Tucson, AZ 85715
Phone: (520)721-1300
Fax: (520)721-6300
**Subject(s):** Food and Cooking
**Circ:** (Combined)29,353

**Orange Coast (2543)**
3701 Birch St., Ste. 100
Newport Beach, CA 92660
Phone: (949)862-1133
Fax: (949)862-0133
**Subject(s):** Local, State, and Regional Publications; Travel and Tourism
**Circ:** (Paid)29,118

**Apartment Age Magazine (2131)**
621 S Westmoreland Ave.
Los Angeles, CA 90005
Phone: (213)384-4131
Fax: (213)382-3970
**Subject(s):** Real Estate
**Circ:** (Paid)‡12,000
(Controlled)‡29,000

---

Circulation: ★ = ABC; △ = BPA; ♦ = CAC; • = CCAB; ▫ = VAC; ⊕ = PO Statement; ‡ = Publisher's Report; Boldface figures = sworn; Light figures = estimated.

# Western States

**California CPA**  (2801)
The California Society of Certified Public Accountants
1235 Radio Rd.
Redwood City, CA 94065
Phone: (650)802-2600
Fax: (650)802-2230
**Subject(s):** Accountants and Accounting
**Circ:** (Controlled)‡500
‡29,000

**Emergency**  (3901)
Business Media
3520 Challenger St.
Torrance, CA 90503
Phone: (310)533-2400
Fax: (310)533-2500
**Subject(s):** Hospitals and Healthcare Institutions; Medicine and Surgery
**Circ:** 29,000

**Wireless Week**  (4464)
PO Box 266008
Highlands Ranch, CO 80163-6008
Phone: (303)470-4800
Fax: (303)470-4892
**Subject(s):** Radio, Television, Cable, and Video; Telecommunications
**Circ:** (Controlled)‡28,809

**Honolulu Magazine**  (7551)
Pacific Basin Communications
1000 Bishop St., Ste. 405
Honolulu, HI 96813
Phone: (808)537-9500
Fax: (808)537-6455
**Subject(s):** Local, State, and Regional Publications; Lifestyle
**Circ:** (Paid)28,672

**JEMS**  (3020)
Jems Communications
525 B St., Ste. 1900
San Diego, CA 92101
Phone: (619)687-3272
Fax: (619)699-6396
**Subject(s):** Medicine and Surgery; Safety; Health and Healthcare
**Circ:** (Controlled)12,000
(Paid)28,000

**Miata Magazine**  (4005)
Media Source Publishing Group
770 Sycamore Ave., Ste. J-445
Vista, CA 92083
Phone: (760)631-1202
Fax: (760)631-1206
**Subject(s):** Automotive (Consumer)
**Circ:** (Non-paid)10,000
(Paid)28,000

**Strength and Conditioning Journal**  (4218)
National Strength & Conditioning Association (NSCA)
1885 Bob Johnson Dr.
Colorado Springs, CO 80906-4000
Phone: (719)632-6722
Fax: (719)632-6367
**Subject(s):** Physical Education and Athletics; Health and Fitness
**Circ:** (Paid)28,000

**Tucson Lifestyle Magazine**  (939)
Conley Publishing Co.
7000 E Tanque Verde
Tucson, AZ 85715
Phone: (520)721-2929
Fax: (520)721-8665
**Subject(s):** Local, State, and Regional Publications; Lifestyle
**Circ:** (Paid)‡6,000
(Controlled)‡28,000

**Landscape Architect and Specifier News**  (3925)
Landscape Communications Inc.
14771 Plaza Dr., Ste. M
Tustin, CA 92780
Phone: (714)979-5276
Fax: (714)979-3543
**Subject(s):** Landscape Architecture
**Circ:** (Controlled)‡27,487

**The Numismatist**  (4212)
American Numismatic Association
818 N Cascade Ave.
Colorado Springs, CO 80903-3279
Phone: (719)632-2646
Fax: (719)634-4085
**Subject(s):** Collecting
**Circ:** (Controlled)27,300

**Asia-Pacific Defense Forum**  (7514)
U.S. Pacific Command
Box 64013
Camp H M Smith, HI 96861-4013
Phone: (808)477-2813
Fax: (808)477-1471
**Subject(s):** Military and Navy
**Circ:** (Non-paid)27,000

**The Food & Beverage Journal**  (3492)
Journal Publications Inc.
4343 Sonoma Hwy.
Santa Rosa, CA 95409
Phone: (707)568-5960
Fax: (707)568-5980
**Subject(s):** Food and Grocery Trade; Food Production; Beverages, Brewing, and Bottling
**Circ:** (Combined)27,000

**ICS Cleaning Specialist**  (4061)
Business News Publishing Company II L.L.C.
22801 Ventura Blvd., No. 115
Woodland Hills, CA 91364
Phone: (818)224-8035
Fax: (818)224-8042
**Subject(s):** Furniture and Furnishings; Building Management and Maintenance
**Circ:** 27,000

**Java Magazine**  (869)
414 S Mill Ave., Ste. 201
Tempe, AZ 85281
Phone: (480)966-6352
Fax: (480)967-0168
**Subject(s):** Alternative and Underground; Art; Music and Musical Instruments; Fashion; Motion Pictures
**Circ:** (Controlled)27,000

**National Floor Trends Magazine**  (4066)
Business News Publishing Company II L.L.C.
22801 Ventura Blvd., No. 115
Woodland Hills, CA 91364
Phone: (818)224-8035
Fax: (818)224-8042
**Subject(s):** Furniture and Furnishings
**Circ:** 27,000

**Permanent Buildings & Foundations**  (30744)
R.W. Nielsen Co.
350 E Center St.
Ste. 201
Provo, UT 84606
Phone: (801)373-0013
Fax: (801)373-0015
**Subject(s):** Construction, Contracting, Building, and Excavating
**Circ:** (Paid)‡2,824
(Non-paid)‡26,653

**Law Enforcement Product News**  (4306)
General Communications Inc.
100 Garfield St.
Denver, CO 80206
Phone: (303)322-6400
Fax: (303)322-0627
**Subject(s):** Police, Penology, and Penal Institutions; Safety
**Circ:** (Non-paid)26,417

**California Fire Service**  (2870)
California State Firefighters Association
2701 K St., Ste. 201
Sacramento, CA 95816-5113
Fax: (916)446-9889
**Subject(s):** Fire Fighting
**Circ:** (Paid)‡26,000

**Critical Care International**  (1971)
GLOBETECH Publishing Inc.
450 North Park Road
Hollywood, CA 33021
Phone: (954)893-0003
Fax: (954)893-0038
**Subject(s):** Medicine and Surgery; Health and Healthcare; French; German; Italian; Spanish
**Circ:** (Controlled)‡26,000

**Fitness Management Magazine**  (2205)
Leisure Publications
4160 Wilshire Blvd.
Los Angeles, CA 90010
Phone: (323)801-0160
Fax: (323)417-4860
**Subject(s):** Health and Healthcare; Management and Administration
**Circ:** (Paid)243
(Controlled)26,000

**Labmedica**  (1973)
GLOBETECH Publishing Inc.
450 North Park Road
Hollywood, CA 33021
Phone: (954)893-0003
Fax: (954)893-0038
**Subject(s):** Laboratory Research (Scientific and Medical)
**Circ:** (Non-paid)‡26,000

**Military**  (2903)
MHR Publishing Corp.
2122 28th St.
Sacramento, CA 95818
Phone: (916)457-8990
**Subject(s):** Veterans; Military and Navy
**Circ:** ‡26,000

**Twins Magazine**  (4178)
The Business Word
11211 E., Arapahoe Rd., Ste. 101
Centennial, CO 80112-3851
Phone: (303)290-8500
Fax: (303)290-9025
**Subject(s):** Parenting; Babies
**Circ:** (Non-paid)22,080
(Paid)25,624

**India Currents**  (3290)
PO Box 21285
San Jose, CA 95151
Phone: (408)274-6966
Fax: (408)274-2733
**Subject(s):** Ethnic Publications
**Circ:** (Non-paid)‡25,600
(Non-paid)‡25,600

**Intelligent Enterprise**  (3368)
CMP Media L.L.C.
2800 Campus Dr.
San Mateo, CA 94403
Phone: (650)513-4300
Fax: (650)513-4613
**Subject(s):** Computers
**Circ:** (Non-paid)1,683
(Paid)25,427

**Security Sales**  (3912)
Business Media
3520 Challenger St.
Torrance, CA 90503
Phone: (310)533-2400
Fax: (310)533-2500
**Subject(s):** Safety
**Circ:** 25,140

**Truck Fleet Management**  (2674)
Adams Business Media
420 S. Palm Canyon Dr.
Palm Springs, CA 92262
Phone: (760)318-7000
Fax: (760)323-4877
**Subject(s):** Trucks and Trucking
**Circ:** (Paid)383
(Non-paid)25,058

**The Beat (Los Angeles)**  (2140)
Bongo Productions
5900 Wilshire Blvd., Ste. 1900
PO Box 1710
Los Angeles, CA 90036
Phone: (323)634-1800
Fax: (323)931-4710
**Subject(s):** Music and Musical Instruments
**Circ:** (Non-paid)25,000

**BETA (Bulletin of Experimental Treatments for AIDS)**  (3111)
San Francisco AIDS Foundation
PO Box 426182
San Francisco, CA 94142-6182
Phone: (415)487-8060
Fax: (415)487-8069
**Subject(s):** Health and Healthcare; Acquired Immune Deficiency Syndrome
**Circ:** (Non-paid)25,000

**California Broker** (1570)
McGee Publishers
217 E Alameda Ave., Ste. 301
Burbank, CA 91502-1500
Phone: (818)848-2957
Fax: (818)843-3489
**Subject(s):** Insurance
**Circ:** ‡25,000

**Cocktails Magazine** (18680)
Destiny Productions for Print, Radio & Cable Promotions
3395 S Jones Blvd., No. 217
Las Vegas, NV 89146-6770
Phone: (702)438-1470
Fax: (702)438-2790
**Subject(s):** Beverages, Brewing, and Bottling
**Circ:** (Paid)25,000

**Composites Technology** (4597)
Ray Publishing Inc.
4891 Independence St., Ste. 270
Wheat Ridge, CO 80033
Phone: (303)467-1776
Fax: (303)467-1777
**Subject(s):** Chemistry, Chemicals, and Chemical Engineering; Plastic and Composition Materials
**Circ:** (Controlled)‡25,000

**East Bay Labor Journal** (2586)
Alameda County Central Labor Council
7992 Capwell Dr.
Oakland, CA 94621
Phone: (510)632-4242
Fax: (510)632-3993
**Subject(s):** Labor
**Circ:** (Controlled)25,000

**Home Business** (1983)
United Marketing and Research Company Inc.
9582 Hamilton Ave., PMB 368
Huntington Beach, CA 92646
Phone: (714)968-0331
Fax: (714)962-7722
**Subject(s):** Business; Business
**Circ:** (Paid)25,000

**NEXUS Magazine** (4312)
2940 E. Colfax, No. 131
Denver, CO 80206
Phone: (303)321-5006
Fax: (603)754-4744
**Subject(s):** Health; Lifestyle; Politics
**Circ:** (Non-paid)200
(Paid)25,000

**Salt Lake Magazine** (30781)
JES Publishing L.P.
240 E Morris Ave., Ste. 350
Salt Lake City, UT 84119
Phone: (801)485-5100
Fax: (801)485-5133
**Subject(s):** Lifestyle
**Circ:** (Combined)25,000

**Self-Realization** (2328)
Self-Realization Fellowship, Publishers
3208 Humboldt St.
Los Angeles, CA 90031
Phone: (323)276-6002
Fax: (323)276-6003
**Subject(s):** Religious Publications
**Circ:** 25,000

**Small Farmer's Journal** (26058)
PO Box 1627
Sisters, OR 97759
Phone: (541)549-2064
Fax: (541)549-4403
**Subject(s):** General Agriculture; Livestock
**Circ:** 25,000

**Spokane Coeur d'Alene Living** (32431)
Northwest Best Direct, Inc.
5805 E Shorp Ave., Ste. 1
Spokane Valley, WA 99212
Phone: (509)533-5350
Fax: (509)535-3542
**Subject(s):** Local, State, and Regional Publications
**Circ:** (Paid)1,900
(Non-paid)25,000

**The Union Register** (25987)
Western Council of Industrial Workers, AFL-CIO
12788 SE Stark St.
Portland, OR 97233-1539
Phone: (503)228-0235
Fax: (503)228-0245
**Subject(s):** Labor
**Circ:** ‡25,000

**Specialty Automotive Magazine** (1604)
Meyers Publishing
799 Camarillo Springs Rd.
Camarillo, CA 93012-8111
Phone: (805)445-8881
Fax: (805)445-8882
**Subject(s):** Automotive (Trade)
**Circ:** (Paid)‡22
(Controlled)‡24,947

**Automated Builder** (3961)
CMN Associates Inc.
1445 Donlon St., Ste. 16
Ventura, CA 93003-5640
Phone: (805)642-9735
Fax: (805)642-8820
**Subject(s):** Construction, Contracting, Building, and Excavating
**Circ:** (Controlled)24,739

**Recording** (4133)
Music Maker Publications Inc.
5412 Idylwild Trl., Ste. 100
Boulder, CO 80301
Phone: (303)516-9118
Fax: (303)516-9119
**Subject(s):** Music and Musical Instruments; Music and Musical Instruments
**Circ:** (Non-paid)‡2,857
(Paid)‡24,679

**Special Events** (2428)
Miramar Communications Inc.
23805 Stuart Ranch Rd., Ste. 235
PO Box 8987
Malibu, CA 90265-8987
Phone: (310)317-4522
Fax: (310)317-9644
**Subject(s):** Management and Administration
**Circ:** (Paid)1,557
(Controlled)24,408

**Houseboat Magazine** (7698)
Harris Publishing Inc.
c/o Brady L Kay, Houseboat
360 B St.
Idaho Falls, ID 83402
**Subject(s):** (Boating and Yachting); Home and Garden
**Circ:** (Paid)7,785
(Non-paid)24,172

**Black & White Magazine** (1390)
Black & White
PO Box 700
Arroyo Grande, CA 93421
Phone: (805)474-6633
**Circ:** 24,000

**Command Magazine** (3336)
XTR Corp.
PO Box 4017
San Luis Obispo, CA 93403
Phone: (805)546-9596
Fax: (805)546-0570
**Subject(s):** Firearms; Military and Navy; History and Genealogy
**Circ:** (Non-paid)‡100
‡24,000

**Plus Magazine** (3339)
San Luis Obispo, CA 93401-7164
Phone: (805)544-8711
**Subject(s):** Senior Citizens' Interests
**Circ:** (Controlled)‡24,000

**School Bus Fleet** (3911)
Business Media
3520 Challenger St.
Torrance, CA 90503
Phone: (310)533-2400
Fax: (310)533-2500
**Subject(s):** Public Transportation
**Circ:** (Paid)231
(Controlled)24,000

**Stanford Business** (3558)
Stanford Graduate School of Business
News & Publications Office
Stanford, CA 94305-5015
Phone: (650)723-3157
Fax: (650)725-6750
**Subject(s):** College Publications
**Circ:** (Controlled)4,000
(Paid)24,000

**Track & Field News** (2521)
2570 El Camino Real, Ste. 606
Mountain View, CA 94040
Phone: (650)948-8188
Fax: (650)948-9445
**Subject(s):** (Running); Sports
**Circ:** (Non-paid)2,309
(Paid)24,000

**Update Magazine** (3956)
Production Update Magazine
7021 Hayvenhurst Ave., Ste. 205
Van Nuys, CA 91406
Phone: (818)785-6362
Fax: (818)785-8092
**Subject(s):** Motion Pictures
**Circ:** 24,000

**Educational Researcher** (865)
American Educational Research Association
C/O Kathy Nakagawa
Book Review Section
Arizona State Univ.
Division of Psychology in Education
Tempe, AZ 85287-0611
Phone: (480)965-0582
**Subject(s):** Education
**Circ:** ‡23,800

**Filipinas Magazine** (3545)
Filipinas Publishing Inc.
1486 Huntington Ave., Ste. 300
South San Francisco, CA 94080
Phone: (650)872-8650
Fax: (650)872-8651
**Subject(s):** Ethnic Publications
**Circ:** (Non-paid)973
(Paid)23,697

**Salmon Trout Steelheader** (25978)
Frank Amato Publications Inc.
PO Box 82112
Portland, OR 97282
Phone: (503)653-8108
Fax: (503)653-2766
**Subject(s):** (Hunting, Fishing, and Game Management)
**Circ:** (Non-paid)‡198
(Paid)‡23,604

**True West** (648)
True West Magazine
6702 E. Cave Creek Rd.
PO Box 8008
Cave Creek, AZ 85327
Phone: (480)575-1881
Fax: (480)575-1903
**Subject(s):** History and Genealogy; Local, State, and Regional Publications
**Circ:** (Non-paid)‡273
(Paid)‡23,267

**Print-Equip News** (1933)
P-EN Publications Inc.
POB 5540
Glendale, CA 91221
**Subject(s):** Printing and Typography
**Circ:** (Controlled)23,258

**Windows Developer's Journal** (3236)
CMP Media L.L.C.
Windows Developer Network
600 Harrison St.
San Francisco, CA 94107
Phone: (415)947-6000
Fax: (415)947-6027
**Subject(s):** Computers
**Circ:** (Non-paid)‡263
(Paid)‡23,057

**Micro** (2274)
Canon Communications L.L.C.
11444 W. Olympic Blvd., Ste. 900
Los Angeles, CA 90064
Phone: (310)445-3746
Fax: (310)445-4200

**Subject(s):** Electronics Engineering

**Circ:** (Controlled)23,000

**Pet Product News** (2300)
Fancy Publications
2401 Beverly Boulevard
PO Box 57900
Los Angeles, CA 90057
Phone: (213)385-2222
Fax: (213)385-8565
**Subject(s):** Pets

**Circ:** (Controlled)‡23,000

**Wildlife Art** (2766)
Pothole Publications Inc.
PO Box 219
Ramona, CA 92065
Phone: (760)788-WILD
Fax: (952)736-1030
**Subject(s):** Art and Art History; Art

**Circ:** ‡23,000

**DirectGuide** (32264)
Vogel Communications Inc.
701 5th Ave. 36th Fl.
Seattle, WA 98104
Phone: (206)262-8183
Fax: (206)262-8187
**Subject(s):** Entertainment; Radio, Television, Cable, and Video

**Circ:** (Paid)22,973

**THE PRESS Magazine** (4453)
Primedia Business
5680 Greenwood Plaza Blvd., Ste.100
Greenwood Village, CO 80111
Phone: (303)741-2901
Fax: (720)489-3101
**Subject(s):** Textiles

**Circ:** (Controlled)‡22,979

**Dialysis & Transplantation** (3949)
Creative Age Publications Inc.
7628 Densmore Ave.
Van Nuys, CA 91406-2042
Phone: (818)782-7328
Fax: (818)782-7450
**Subject(s):** Medicine and Surgery

**Circ:** (Non-paid)△22,701

**Mobile Electronics Magazine** (3908)
Business Media
3520 Challenger St.
Torrance, CA 90503
Phone: (310)533-2400
Fax: (310)533-2500
**Subject(s):** Automotive (Trade)

**Circ:** (Paid)76
(Non-paid)22,576

**Los Angeles Lawyer** (2258)
Los Angeles County Bar Association
261 S. Figueroa St., Ste. 300
Los Angeles, CA 90012
Phone: (213)627-2727
**Subject(s):** Law

**Circ:** (Non-paid)2,723
(Paid)22,536

**CED (Communications Engineering & Design)** (4462)
Communications Engineering & Design
PO Box 266007
Highlands Ranch, CO 80163-6007
Phone: (303)470-4800
Fax: (303)470-4890
**Subject(s):** Electronics Engineering

**Circ:** (Non-paid)‡22,500

**Delphi Informant** (2888)
Informant Communications Group
5105 Florin Perkins Road
Sacramento, CA 95826
Phone: (916)379-0609
Fax: (916)379-0610
**Subject(s):** Computers

**Circ:** (Non-paid)‡500
(Paid)‡22,500

**High Country News** (4532)
119 Grand Ave.
PO Box 1090
Paonia, CO 81428
Phone: (970)527-4898
Fax: (970)527-4897
**Subject(s):** Ecology and Conservation

**Circ:** (Combined)22,500

**Light of Consciousness** (924)
Truth Consciousness at Desert Ashram
3403 W Sweetwater Dr.
Tucson, AZ 85745-9301
Phone: (520)743-8821
Fax: (520)743-3394
**Subject(s):** New Age

**Circ:** (Paid)22,500

**Today's Liturgy** (25985)
Oregon Catholic Press
5536 NE Hassalo
Portland, OR 97213
Phone: (503)281-1191
Fax: (503)282-3486
**Subject(s):** Religious Publications

**Circ:** ‡22,500

**Inside Triathlon** (4119)
Inside Communications Inc.
1830 N 55th St.
Boulder, CO 80301-2700
Phone: (303)440-0601
Fax: (303)444-6788
**Subject(s):** (Triathlons and Biathlons)

**Circ:** (Paid)22,374

**iSeries News Magazine** (4509)
Penton Media
221 E 29th St.
Loveland, CO 80538
Phone: (970)663-4700
Fax: (970)667-2321
**Subject(s):** Computers

**Circ:** (Paid)22,285

**Anesthesia & Analgesia** (3106)
Lippincott Williams & Wilkins
The Hearst Bldg.
5 Third St., Ste. 1216
San Francisco, CA 94103
Phone: (415)777-2750
Fax: (415)777-2803
**Subject(s):** Medicine and Surgery

**Circ:** ‡22,084

**The Bicycle Paper** (32251)
Seattle Publishing
68 S. Washington St.
Seattle, WA 98104
Phone: (206)903-1333
Fax: (206)903-8565
**Subject(s):** (Bicycling)

**Circ:** (Paid)1,000
(Non-paid)22,000

**Birding** (4186)
American Birding Association Inc.
720 W Monument St.
PO Box 6599
Colorado Springs, CO 80904
Phone: (719)578-0607
Fax: (719)578-9705
**Subject(s):** (Outdoors)

**Circ:** (Paid)22,000

**Poetry Flash** (1511)
Poetry Flash Inc.
1450 4th St., Ste. 4
Berkeley, CA 94710
Phone: (510)525-5476
Fax: (510)525-6752
**Subject(s):** Literature and Literary Reviews

**Circ:** (Paid)‡3,000
(Controlled)‡22,000

**Tribal College Journal** (4512)
Tribal College Journal of American Indian Higher Education
PO Box 720
Mancos, CO 81328
Phone: (970)533-9170
Fax: (970)533-9145
**Subject(s):** Education; Ethnic and Minority Studies

**Circ:** 22,000

**Automotive Fleet** (3896)
Business Media
3520 Challenger St.
Torrance, CA 90503
Phone: (310)533-2400
Fax: (310)533-2500
**Subject(s):** Automotive (Trade); Transportation, Traffic, and Shipping

**Circ:** (Paid)252
(Non-paid)21,706

**AWHONN Lifelines** (3619)
Sage Publications Inc.
2455 Teller Rd.
Thousand Oaks, CA 91320
**Subject(s):** Medicine and Surgery; Health and Healthcare; Nursing

**Circ:** (Paid)21,500

**Medical Imaging** (2269)
Medical World Communications
6100 Center Dr., Ste. 1000
Los Angeles, CA 90045
**Subject(s):** Health and Healthcare; Medicine and Surgery

**Circ:** (Controlled)21,195

**Dallas Apparel News** (2181)
Apparel News Group
110 E 9th St., Ste. A-777
Los Angeles, CA 90079-1777
Phone: (213)627-3737
Fax: (213)627-5707
**Subject(s):** Clothing

**Circ:** 21,023

**Northwest Yachting** (32299)
7342 15th Ave. NW
Seattle, WA 98117-5401
Phone: (206)789-8116
Fax: (206)781-1554
**Subject(s):** (Boating and Yachting)

**Circ:** (Paid)1000
(Non-paid)21,000

**RV Business** (3973)
TL Enterprises Inc.
2575 Vista Del Mar
Ventura, CA 93001
Phone: (805)667-4100
Fax: (805)667-4484
**Subject(s):** Trailers and Accessories

**Circ:** (Combined)21,000

**The Fish Sniffer** (1812)
Northern California Angler Publications
10535-H E. Stockton Blvd
PO Box 994
Elk Grove, CA 95759
Phone: (916)685-2245
Fax: (916)685-1498
**Subject(s):** (Hunting, Fishing, and Game Management)

**Circ:** (Controlled)‡1,150
(Paid)‡20,500

**Metro Magazine** (3906)
Business Media
3520 Challenger St.
Torrance, CA 90503
Phone: (310)533-2400
Fax: (310)533-2500
**Subject(s):** Public Transportation

**Circ:** (Controlled)20,500

**Western Roofing/Insulation/Siding** (18746)
Dodson Publications Inc.
546 Court St.
Reno, NV 89501
Phone: (775)333-1080
Fax: (775)333-1081
**Subject(s):** Roofing; Building Materials, Concrete, Brick, and Tile

**Circ:** (Paid)‡3,973
(Controlled)‡20,410

**School Transportation News** (2799)
STN Media Company Inc.
700 Torrance Blvd., Ste. C
PO Box 789
Redondo Beach, CA 90277
Phone: (310)792-2226
Fax: (310)792-2231
**Subject(s):** Transportation, Traffic, and Shipping; Education

**Circ:** (Paid)★1,192
(Non-paid)★20,244

**Architectural West** (18737)
Dodson Publications Inc.
546 Court St.
Reno, NV 89501
Phone: (775)333-1080
Fax: (775)333-1081

**Gale Directory of Publications & Broadcast Media/140th Ed.**  **Western States**

**Subject(s):** Architecture; Construction, Contracting, Building, and Excavating; Building Materials, Concrete, Brick, and Tile
**Circ:** (Controlled)20,200

**Motorcycle Industry Magazine (18669)**
Industry Shopper Publishing Inc.
PO Box 160
Gardnerville, NV 89410
Phone: (775)782-0222
Fax: (775)782-0266
**Subject(s):** Motorcycles
**Circ:** (Non-paid)20,202

**Printwear (4155)**
National Business Media Inc.
PO Box 1416
Broomfield, CO 80038
Phone: (303)469-0424
Fax: (303)469-5730
**Subject(s):** Textiles; Printing and Typography
**Circ:** (Combined)△20,046

**Access VB- SQL Advisor (2996)**
Advisor Media Inc.
4849 Viewridge Ave.
PO Box 429002
San Diego, CA 92123
Phone: (858)278-5600
Fax: (858)278-0300
**Subject(s):** Computers; Business
**Circ:** (Paid)20,000

**Al Talib (2124)**
U.C.L.A.
118 Kerckhoff Hall
308 Westwood Plz.
University of California, Los Angeles
Los Angeles, CA 90024-1641
Phone: (310)825-2787
Fax: (310)206-0906
**Subject(s):** College Publications; Ethnic Publications
**Circ:** (Controlled)20,000

**Ancient Wisdom for Modern Living (2130)**
Philosophical Research Society Inc.
3910 Los Feliz Blvd.
Los Angeles, CA 90027
Phone: (323)663-2167
Fax: (323)663-9443
**Subject(s):** Philosophy; Psychology and Psychiatry; Religious Publications
**Circ:** (Free)20,000

**Archery (2789)**
National Field Archery Association
31407 Outer I-10
Redlands, CA 92373
Phone: (909)794-2133
Fax: (909)794-8512
**Subject(s):** (Archery)
**Circ:** 20,000

**Book Dealers World (25774)**
North American Bookdealers Exchange
PO Box 606
Cottage Grove, OR 97424
Phone: (541)942-7455
**Subject(s):** Book Trade and Author News
**Circ:** ‡20,000

**Cancer Victors Journal (2744)**
International Association of Cancer Victors and Friends
7740 W Manchester Ave., Ste. 203
Playa del Rey, CA 90293
Phone: (310)822-5032
Fax: (310)822-4193
**Subject(s):** Medicine and Surgery; Education
**Circ:** (Paid)‡20,000

**Comstock's Business Magazine (2884)**
Comstock Publishing Inc.
3090 Fite Cir., Ste. 101
Sacramento, CA 95827
Phone: (916)364-1000
Fax: (916)364-0280
**Subject(s):** Business
**Circ:** (Controlled)20,000

**Electronic Green Journal (EGJ) (7745)**
University of Idaho Library
Moscow, ID 83844-2360
Phone: (208)885-6631
Fax: (208)885-6817

**Subject(s):** Ecology and Conservation
**Circ:** (Non-paid)20,000

**Gauntlet (4198)**
5307 Arroyo St.
Colorado Springs, CO 80922-3625
**Subject(s):** Literature and Literary Reviews; Social and Political Issues
**Circ:** (Paid)20,000

**The Growing Edge (25765)**
New Moon Publishing Inc.
PO Box 1027
Corvallis, OR 97339-1027
Phone: (541)757-8477
Fax: (541)757-0028
**Subject(s):** Horticulture; General Agriculture
**Circ:** (Non-paid)1,000
       (Paid)20,000

**Guest Life Monterey Bay (1620)**
Pacific/Guest Life Inc.
2 NW Lincoln on 7th
PO Box 7540
Carmel, CA 93921-7540
Phone: (831)626-5740
Fax: (831)626-5744
**Subject(s):** General Editorial
**Circ:** (Controlled)20,000

**High-Performance Composites (4600)**
Ray Publishing Inc.
4891 Independence St., Ste. 270
Wheat Ridge, CO 80033
Phone: (303)467-1776
Fax: (303)467-1777
**Subject(s):** Engineering (Various branches); Plastic and Composition Materials; Chemistry, Chemicals, and Chemical Engineering
**Circ:** (Controlled)‡20,000

**Journal of Environmental Health (4301)**
National Environmental Health Association
720 S. Colorado Blvd., Ste. 970-S
Denver, CO 80246-1925
Phone: (303)756-9090
Fax: (303)691-9490
**Subject(s):** Ecology and Conservation
**Circ:** (Controlled)20,000

**Journal Francais (3158)**
France Press Inc.
944 Market St., Ste. 210
San Francisco, CA 94102
Phone: (415)981-9088
Fax: (415)981-9177
**Subject(s):** French; Ethnic Publications
**Circ:** ‡20,000

**La Gente de Aztlan (2246)**
University of California, Los Angeles
118 Kerkhoff Hall
308 Westwood Plaza
Los Angeles, CA 90024
Phone: (310)825-9898
Fax: (310)206-0906
**Subject(s):** College Publications; Hispanic Publications; Native American Interests
**Circ:** (Non-paid)20,000

**Loud (2699)**
Loud Magazine
625 Emerson St., Suite 300
Palo Alto, CA 94301
Phone: (650)322-7004
Fax: (650)322-7009
**Subject(s):** Music and Musical Instruments
**Circ:** 20,000

**MindFreedom Journal (25804)**
Support Coalition
454 Willamette, Ste. 216
PO Box 11284
Eugene, OR 97440-3484
Phone: (541)345-9106
Fax: (541)345-3737
**Subject(s):** Politics; Health and Healthcare
**Circ:** (Paid)20,000

**Mines Magazine (4416)**
Colorado School of Mines Alumni Association
1600 Arapahoe St.
PO Box 1410
Golden, CO 80401-1851
Phone: (303)273-3295

Fax: (303)273-3583
**Subject(s):** Engineering (Various branches); Mining and Minerals
**Circ:** ‡20,000

**Mobile Business Advisor (3038)**
Advisor Media Inc.
4849 Viewridge Ave.
PO Box 429002
San Diego, CA 92123
Phone: (858)278-5600
Fax: (858)278-0300
**Subject(s):** Business; Computers
**Circ:** (Paid)20,000

**North Tahoe/Truckee Week (1625)**
PO Box 67
Carnelian Bay, CA 96140
Phone: (530)546-5995
Fax: (530)546-8113
**Subject(s):** Travel and Tourism
**Circ:** (Controlled)‡20,000

**OrthoKineticReview (2292)**
Novicom Inc.
6100 Center Dr., Ste. 1000
Los Angeles, CA 90045
Phone: (310)642-4400
Fax: (310)641-4444
**Subject(s):** Podiatry
**Circ:** (Controlled)20,000

**Outlook (32302)**
Program for Appropriate Technology in Health
1455 NW Leary Way
Seattle, WA 98107-5136
Phone: (206)285-3500
Fax: (206)285-6619
**Subject(s):** Health and Healthcare; Women's Interests; Medicine and Surgery; Chinese; French; Portuguese; Russian; Spanish
**Circ:** (Non-paid)20,000

**Roadracing World & Motorcycle Technology (2059)**
581 Birch St., Unit C
Lake Elsinore, CA 92530
Phone: (951)245-6411
Fax: (951)245-6417
**Subject(s):** (Auto Racing); Automotive (Consumer); Motorbikes and Motorcycles
**Circ:** (Paid)‡20,000

**Rosicrucian Digest (3305)**
Rosicrucian Order, AMORC
Rosicrucian Park
1342 Naglee Ave.
San Jose, CA 95191
Phone: (408)947-3600
Fax: (408)947-3677
**Subject(s):** Philosophy
**Circ:** (Combined)‡20,000

**SageWoman Magazine (2752)**
SageWoman
PO Box 641
Point Arena, CA 95468
Phone: (707)882-2052
Fax: (707)882-2793
**Subject(s):** Women's Interests; Religious Publications
**Circ:** (Non-paid)‡100
       (Paid)‡20,000

**Ski Racing (4137)**
1830 N. 55th St.
Boulder, CO 80301-2700
Phone: (303)440-0601
**Subject(s):** (Skiing)
**Circ:** ‡20,000

**Stone Soup (3458)**
Children's Art Foundation Inc.
PO Box 83
Santa Cruz, CA 95063
Phone: (831)426-5557
Fax: (831)426-1161
**Subject(s):** Children's Interests; Youths' Interests
**Circ:** (Combined)20,000

**Tikkun Magazine (1522)**
2342 Shattuck Ave., No. 1200
Berkeley, CA 94704-1517
Phone: (415)575-1200
Fax: (415)575-1255

**Circulation:** ★ = ABC; △ = BPA; ♦ = CAC; ● = CCAB; □ = VAC; ⊕ = PO Statement; ‡ = Publisher's Report; Boldface figures = sworn; Light figures = estimated.

## Western States

**Subject(s):** Politics; Jewish Publications
**Circ:** (Combined)20,000

**Truck Sales & Leasing Magazine** (2012)
Newport Communications East
38 Executive Park, Ste. 300
Irvine, CA 92614
Phone: (949)261-1636
**Subject(s):** Trucks and Trucking
**Circ:** (Controlled)‡20,000

**Truth Seeker** (3064)
Truth Seeker Company Inc.
PO Box 28550
San Diego, CA 92198-0550
Phone: (760)489-5211
Fax: (760)489-5311
**Subject(s):** Agnostic and Free Thought
**Circ:** (Non-paid)20,000

**Yes! A Journal of Positive Futures** (31993)
Positive Futures Networks
284 Madrona Way NE Ste. 116
PO Box 10818
Bainbridge Island, WA 98110-0818
Phone: (206)842-0216
Fax: (206)842-5208
**Subject(s):** Lifestyle
**Circ:** (Non-paid)3,000
  (Paid)‡20,000

**Water Conditioning & Purification** (942)
Publicom Inc.
2800 E. Ft. Lowell Rd.
Tucson, AZ 85716
Phone: (520)323-6144
Fax: (520)323-7412
**Subject(s):** Water Supply and Sewage Disposal
**Circ:** (Paid)1,071
  (Controlled)19,824

**Mountain Living** (4174)
Wiesner Publishing L.L.C.
7009 S Potomac St., Ste. 200
Centennial, CO 80112
Phone: (303)397-7600
Fax: (303)397-7619
**Subject(s):** Local, State, and Regional Publications; Home and Garden
**Circ:** (Non-paid)11,300
  (Paid)19,700

**Palm Springs Life** (2669)
Desert Publication Inc.
303 N Indian Canyon Dr.
PO Box 2724
Palm Springs, CA 92262
Phone: (760)325-2333
Fax: (760)325-7008
**Subject(s):** Local, State, and Regional Publications
**Circ:** (Paid)19,250

**Apparel News South** (2132)
Apparel News Group
110 E 9th St., Ste. A-777
Los Angeles, CA 90079-1777
Phone: (213)627-3737
Fax: (213)627-5707
**Subject(s):** Clothing
**Circ:** 19,248

**BlueRibbon Magazine** (7773)
BlueRibbon Coalition
4555 Burley Dr.
PO Box 5449
Pocatello, ID 83202
Phone: (208)237-1008
Fax: (208)237-9424
**Subject(s):** Travel and Tourism; (Outdoors); Automotive (Consumer)
**Circ:** 19,000

**California Agriculture** (2578)
DANR-University of California
1111 Franklin St., 6th Fl.
Oakland, CA 94607-5200
Phone: (510)987-0044
Fax: (510)465-2659
**Subject(s):** General Agriculture; Scientific Agricultural Publications
**Circ:** (Paid)850
  (Controlled)19,000

**Legal Assistant Today** (1723)
James Publishing Inc.
3505 Cadillac Ave., Ste. H
Costa Mesa, CA 92626
Phone: (714)755-5450
Fax: (714)751-2709
**Subject(s):** Law
**Circ:** ‡19,000

**MGMA Connexion** (4364)
Medical Group Management Association
104 Inverness Ter. E
Englewood, CO 80112-5306
Phone: (303)799-1111
Fax: (303)643-4439
**Subject(s):** Medicine and Surgery; Banking, Finance, and Investments; Management and Administration
**Circ:** (Controlled)19,000

**Nor'westing** (32300)
Nor'westing Publications Inc.
PO Box 17002
Seattle, WA 98107-0702
Phone: (206)216-0023
Fax: (206)216-0026
**Subject(s):** (Boating and Yachting)
**Circ:** 19,000

**Flooring Magazine** (4505)
Douglas Publications Inc.
1133 Frontier Dr.
Longmont, CO 80501
**Subject(s):** Construction, Contracting, Building, and Excavating; Flooring and Floor Covering
**Circ:** (Combined)18,800

**UEA Action** (30708)
Utah Education Association
875 E. 5180 S.
Murray, UT 84107-5299
Phone: (801)266-4461
Fax: (801)265-2249
**Subject(s):** Education
**Circ:** (Controlled)‡917
  (Paid)‡18,800

**Rental Equipment Register** (2426)
Miramar Communications Inc.
c/o Michael Roth
23805 Stuart Rand Rd. No. 235
Malibu, CA 90265
**Subject(s):** Rental Equipment
**Circ:** (Non-paid)‡18,532

**Digital Graphics** (4153)
National Business Media Inc.
PO Box 1416
Broomfield, CO 80038
Phone: (303)469-0424
Fax: (303)469-5730
**Subject(s):** Computers; Telecommunications; Automation
**Circ:** (Paid)△72
  (Non-paid)△18,513

**The Bear Deluxe Magazine** (25948)
Orlo
PO Box 10342
Portland, OR 97296
Phone: (503)242-1047
**Subject(s):** Environmental and Natural Resources Conservation; Literature and Literary Reviews
**Circ:** (Paid)500
  (Non-paid)18,500

**TradeShow & Exhibit Manager** (3485)
Goldstein & Associates
1150 Yale St., Ste. 12
Santa Monica, CA 90403
Phone: (310)828-1309
Fax: (310)829-1169
**Subject(s):** Conventions, Meetings, and Trade Fairs
**Circ:** 18,500

**Review of Educational Research** (4134)
American Educational Research Association
c/o Margaret D. LeCompte
School of Education
UCB 249, Education 124
University of Colorado
Boulder, CO 80309-0249
Phone: (303)492-7951
**Subject(s):** Education
**Circ:** ‡18,400

**State Legislatures** (4323)
National Conference of State Legislatures
7700 E. First Pl.
Denver, CO 80230
Phone: (303)364-7700
Fax: (303)364-7800
**Subject(s):** Politics; State, Municipal, and County Administration
**Circ:** (Paid)‡18,385

**Stitches Magazine** (4452)
Intertec Publishing Corp.
5680 Greenwood Plz. Blvd., Ste. 100
Greenwood Village, CO 80111
Phone: (303)741-2901
Fax: (720)489-3101
**Subject(s):** Textiles; Clothing
**Circ:** (Combined)18,302

**Arts & Activities** (3001)
12345 World Trade Dr.
San Diego, CA 92128
Phone: (858)605-0200
Fax: (858)605-0247
**Subject(s):** Education
**Circ:** (Combined)18,268

**Boise Family Magazine** (7644)
13191 W. Scotfield St.
Boise, ID 83713-0899
Phone: (208)938-2119
Fax: (208)938-2117
**Subject(s):** Parenting; Local, State, and Regional Publications
**Circ:** (Controlled)18,000

**Earth Island Journal** (3131)
Earth Island Institute
300 Broadway, Ste. 28
San Francisco, CA 94133
Phone: (415)788-3666
Fax: (415)788-7324
**Subject(s):** Environmental and Natural Resources Conservation
**Circ:** (Combined)18,000

**Journal of the California Dental Association** (2897)
California Dental Association
1201 K St.
PO Box 13749
Sacramento, CA 95814
Phone: (916)443-3382
Fax: (916)443-2943
**Subject(s):** Dentistry
**Circ:** (Non-paid)‡1,200
  (Paid)‡18,000

**Journal of Dermatologic Surgery** (2592)
American College of Phlebology
100 Webster St., Ste. 101
Oakland, CA 94607-3724
Phone: (510)834-6500
Fax: (510)832-7300
**Subject(s):** Medicine and Surgery; Health and Healthcare
**Circ:** 18,000

**Trail Blazer Horseback Trail Riding** (815)
4241 Covina Cir.
Prescott Valley, AZ 86314
Phone: (928)772-9233
Fax: (928)772-9558
**Subject(s):** (Horses and Horse Racing)
**Circ:** (Non-paid)4,000
  (Paid)18,000

**Newspapers & Technology** (4311)
Mary L. Van Meter
1623 Blake St., Ste. 250
Denver, CO 80202
Phone: (303)575-9595
Fax: (303)575-9555
**Subject(s):** Journalism and Publishing; Communications
**Circ:** (Non-paid)‡17,822

**Western Dairy Business** (3917)
Dairy Business Communications
Ste. 218
S. Laspina
Tulare, CA 93274
**Subject(s):** Dairying
**Circ:** ‡17,500

**Fresh Cut** (32504)
Columbia Publishing
417 N 20th Ave.
Yakima, WA 98902-7008
Phone: (509)248-2452
Fax: (509)248-4056
**Circ:** (Combined)17,497

**CDA Update** (2883)
California Dental Association
1201 K St.
PO Box 13749
Sacramento, CA 95814
Phone: (916)443-3382
Fax: (916)443-2943
**Subject(s):** Dentistry
**Circ:** (Non-paid)‡104
(Paid)‡17,447

**Furniture Today** (2550)
Reed Business Information
PO Box 16327
North Hollywood, CA 91615-6327
Phone: (336)605-0121
Fax: (336)605-1143
**Subject(s):** Furniture and Furnishings
**Circ:** (Non-paid)4,708
(Paid)17,326

**HomeCare Magazine** (2422)
Miramar Communications Inc.
23805 Stuart Ranch Rd., Ste. 235
PO Box 8987
Malibu, CA 90265-8987
Phone: (310)317-4522
Fax: (310)317-9644
**Subject(s):** Health and Healthcare
**Circ:** (Controlled)‡17,069

**Mining Engineering** (4500)
Society for Mining, Metallurgy, and Exploration Inc.
8307 Shaffer Pky.
PO Box 277002
Littleton, CO 80127-4102
Phone: (303)973-9550
Fax: (303)973-3845
**Subject(s):** Engineering (Various branches); Metal, Metallurgy, and Metal Trade; Mining and Minerals
**Circ:** (Paid)17,057

**Human Resource Development Quarterly** (3151)
Jossey-Bass Publishers
989 Market St.
San Francisco, CA 94103-1741
Phone: (415)433-1740
Fax: (415)951-8553
**Subject(s):** Employment and Human Resources
**Circ:** 17,000

**Loggers World** (32040)
Loggers World Publications
4206 Jackson Hwy.
Chehalis, WA 98532-8425
Phone: (360)262-3376
Fax: (360)262-3337
**Subject(s):** Forestry
**Circ:** 17,000

**Steamboat Magazine** (4566)
Mac Media L.L.C.
Ski Town Publications, Inc.
100 Park Ave., Ste. 209
PO Box 881659
Steamboat Springs, CO 80488
Phone: (970)871-9413
Fax: (970)871-1922
**Subject(s):** Local, State, and Regional Publications; Lifestyle
**Circ:** (Paid)‡3,000
(Controlled)‡17,000

**IEEE Software** (2109)
IEEE Computer Society
PO Box 3014
PO Box 3014
Los Alamitos, CA 90720-1314
Phone: (714)821-8380
Fax: (714)821-4010
**Subject(s):** Computers
**Circ:** (Paid)16,982

**Mortgage Originator Magazine** (3039)
Pfingsten Publishing L.L.C.
3990 Old Town Ave., Ste. A203
San Diego, CA 92110
Phone: (619)223-9989
Fax: (619)223-9943
**Subject(s):** Banking, Finance, and Investments; Real Estate
**Circ:** (Combined)16,522

**Shooting Industry** (3057)
Publishers Development Corp.
12345 World Trade Dr.
San Diego, CA 92128
**Subject(s):** Firearms
**Circ:** (Paid)‡893
(Non-paid)‡16,462

**Narrow Gauge and Short Line Gazette** (2115)
Benchmark Publications Ltd.
PO Box 26
800 West El Camino Real Ste 180
Los Altos, CA 94023-0026
Phone: (650)941-3823
Fax: (650)941-3845
**Subject(s):** Crafts, Models, Hobbies, and Contests
**Circ:** (Non-paid)‡219
(Paid)‡16,300

**Leadership Magazine** (2899)
Association of California School Administrators
1517 L St.
Sacramento, CA 95814
Phone: (916)444-3216
Fax: (916)444-3245
**Subject(s):** Education
**Circ:** (Non-paid)294
(Paid)16,205

**TelevisionWeek** (2350)
Crain Communications Inc.
6500 Wilshire Blvd., Ste. 2300
Los Angeles, CA 90048
Phone: (323)370-2432
Fax: (323)653-4425
**Subject(s):** Radio, Television, Cable, and Video
**Circ:** (Paid)‡10,708
(Non-paid)‡16,124

**Bus Ride** (759)
Power Trade Media L.L.C.
4742 N. 24th St., Ste. 340
Phoenix, AZ 85016-4884
Phone: (602)265-7600
Fax: (602)227-7588
**Subject(s):** Public Transportation
**Circ:** (Non-paid)‡6,500
(Paid)‡7,200
(Combined)16,000

**Heritage Quest Magazine** (30710)
Heritage Quest
669 W. 900 N.
PO Box 540670
North Salt Lake, UT 84054
Phone: (801)298-5358
Fax: (801)298-5468
**Subject(s):** History and Genealogy
**Circ:** (Paid)‡16,000

**Potato Grower** (7703)
Harris Publishing Inc.
360 B St.
Idaho Falls, ID 83402
Phone: (208)524-7000
Fax: (208)522-5241
**Subject(s):** Socialized Farming
**Circ:** (Combined)16,000

**The Sugar Producer** (7705)
Harris Publishing Inc.
360 B St.
Idaho Falls, ID 83402
Phone: (208)524-7000
Fax: (208)522-5241
**Subject(s):** Socialized Farming; Sugar and Sugar Beets
**Circ:** (Controlled)‡16,000

**TRENDS Magazine** (4482)
American Animal Hospital Association
12575 W. Bayaud Ave.
Lakewood, CO 80228
Phone: (303)986-2800
Fax: (303)986-1700
**Subject(s):** Veterinary Medicine
**Circ:** 16,000

**California Apparel News** (2156)
Apparel News Group
110 E 9th St., Ste. A-777
Los Angeles, CA 90079-1777
Phone: (213)627-3737
Fax: (213)627-5707
**Subject(s):** Clothing
**Circ:** (Non-paid)6,000
15,872

**24x7** (2356)
Medical World Communications
6100 Center Dr., Ste. 1000
Los Angeles, CA 90045
**Subject(s):** Health and Healthcare; Medicine and Surgery
**Circ:** (Controlled)15,766

**Exhibit Builder** (4057)
Exhibit Builder Inc.
PO Box 4144
Woodland Hills, CA 91364
Phone: (818)225-0100
Fax: (818)225-0138
**Subject(s):** Conventions, Meetings, and Trade Fairs; Museums
**Circ:** 15,585

**Colorado Episcopalian** (4270)
Diocese of Colorado
1300 Washington St.
Denver, CO 80203-2008
Phone: (303)837-1173
Fax: (303)837-1311
**Subject(s):** Religious Publications
**Circ:** (Non-paid)‡15,500

**Engineering & Science** (2711)
The California Institute of Technology
Caltech 17-6
1200 E. California Blvd.
Pasadena, CA 91125
Phone: (626)395-6153
**Subject(s):** Science (General); College Publications
**Circ:** (Paid)200
(Non-paid)15,500

**MacTech Magazine** (4035)
PO Box 5200
Westlake Village, CA 91359-5200
Phone: (805)494-9797
Fax: (805)494-9798
**Subject(s):** Computers
**Circ:** (Combined)‡15,488

**American Journal of Orthodontics and Dentofacial Orthopedics** (32246)
Mosby Inc.
c/o David L. Turpin, DDS, Editor-in-Chief
University of Washington, Department of Orthodontics
D-569, HSC Box 357446
Seattle, WA 98195-7446
Phone: (206)221-5413
Fax: (206)221-5467
**Subject(s):** Dentistry
**Circ:** (Paid)‡15,309

**Adventure Travel Business** (18675)
Adventure Media Inc.
PO Box 3210
Incline Village, NV 89450
Phone: (775)832-3700
Fax: (775)832-3775
**Subject(s):** Travel and Tourism
**Circ:** (Non-paid)15,000

**Aerotech News & Review** (2068)
Aerotech
456 E Ave. K4, Ste. 8
Lancaster, CA 93535
Phone: (661)945-5634
Fax: (661)723-7757
**Subject(s):** Military and Navy; Astronautics
**Circ:** (Non-paid)15,000

**AFCI Locations** (18155)
Association of Film Commissioners International
PO Box 1419
Helena, MT 59624
Phone: (406)495-8045
Fax: (406)495-8039
**Subject(s):** Motion Pictures; Local, State, and Regional Publications
**Circ:** 15,000

## Western States

**Assisted Living Success** (756)
Virgo Publishing Inc.
3300 N Central Ave., Ste. 2500
Phoenix, AZ 85067-0079
Phone: (480)990-1101
Fax: (480)990-0819
**Subject(s):** Hospitals and Healthcare Institutions
**Circ:** (Combined)15,000

**Autograph Collector** (1713)
Odyssey Publications Inc.
510-A S. Corona Mall
Corona, CA 92879
Phone: (951)734-9636
Fax: (951)371-7139
**Subject(s):** Crafts, Models, Hobbies, and Contests
**Circ:** (Paid)3,000
(Non-paid)15,000

**California-Arizona Texas Cotton** (1873)
Western Agricultural Publishing Company Inc.
4969 E Clinton Way, No. 104
Fresno, CA 93727-1549
Phone: (559)252-7000
Fax: (559)252-7387
**Subject(s):** Socialized Farming
**Circ:** ‡15,000

**Cattle Guard** (4087)
The Ag Journal
8833 Ralston Rd.
Arvada, CO 80002
Phone: (303)431-6446
Fax: (303)431-6446
**Subject(s):** Livestock
**Circ:** ‡15,000

**European Medical Device Manufacturer** (2199)
Canon Communications L.L.C.
11444 W. Olympic Blvd., Ste. 900
Los Angeles, CA 90064
Phone: (310)445-3746
Fax: (310)445-4200
**Subject(s):** Machinery and Equipment
**Circ:** (Non-paid)15,000

**France Today** (3140)
France Press Inc.
944 Market St., Ste. 210
San Francisco, CA 94102
Phone: (415)981-9088
Fax: (415)981-9177
**Subject(s):** Intercultural Interests
**Circ:** ‡15,000

**Grocers Report** (3385)
Super Markets Productions Ltd.
PO Box 6124
San Rafael, CA 94903
Phone: (415)479-0211
Fax: (415)479-0211
**Subject(s):** Food and Grocery Trade
**Circ:** (Controlled)‡15,000

**The Lightbulb/Invent! Journal** (3423)
Inventors Workshop International
1029 Castillo St.
Santa Barbara, CA 93101-3736
Phone: (805)962-5722
Fax: (805)899-4927
**Subject(s):** Patents, Trademarks, and Copyrights
**Circ:** (Combined)15,000

**Lotus Advisor Magazine** (3037)
Advisor Media Inc.
4849 Viewridge Ave.
PO Box 429002
San Diego, CA 92123
Phone: (858)278-5600
Fax: (858)278-0300
**Subject(s):** Computers; Telecommunications
**Circ:** (Combined)15,000

**MediaFile** (3169)
Media Alliance
942 Market St., Ste. 503
San Francisco, CA 94103
Phone: (415)546-6334
Fax: (415)546-6218
**Subject(s):** Communications
**Circ:** 15,000

**MultiMedia Internetscholarshipools** (32464)
Information Today Inc.
10000 NE 7th Ave., Ste. 100
Vancouver, WA 98685
Phone: (360)882-0988
**Subject(s):** Computers; Education
**Circ:** 15,000

**Natural Foods Merchandiser** (4130)
New Hope Natural Media
1401 Pearl St.
Boulder, CO 80302
Phone: (303)939-8440
Fax: (303)998-9886
**Subject(s):** Food and Grocery Trade
**Circ:** (Paid)△15,003

**Northwest Palate Magazine** (25965)
Pacifica Publishing Inc.
PO Box 10860
Portland, OR 97296-0860
Phone: (503)224-6039
Fax: (503)222-5312
**Subject(s):** Food and Cooking; Travel and Tourism
**Circ:** (Paid)15,000

**Outburn** (3865)
PO Box 3187
Thousand Oaks, CA 91359-0187
Phone: (805)493-5861
**Subject(s):** Music and Musical Instruments; Alternative and Underground
**Circ:** 15,000

**Pilot Getaways** (503)
Frostbite Publications L.L.C.
PO Box 220168
Anchorage, AK 99522
Phone: (907)258-6898
Fax: (907)258-4354
**Subject(s):** Aviation
**Circ:** (Paid)15,000

**Powerlifting USA Magazine** (1603)
Powerlifting USA
PO Box 467
Camarillo, CA 93011-0467
Phone: (805)482-2378
Fax: (805)987-4275
**Subject(s):** (Physical Fitness)
**Circ:** (Non-paid)‡100
(Paid)‡15,000

**RAND Review** (3483)
RAND
1776 Main St.
PO Box 2138
Santa Monica, CA 90407-2138
Phone: (310)393-0411
Fax: (310)393-4818
**Subject(s):** Education; Science (General); Health and Healthcare; International Affairs; Social Programs; Transportation, Traffic, and Shipping
**Circ:** (Controlled)15,000

**SCP Journal** (1517)
PO Box 4308
Berkeley, CA 94704
Phone: (510)540-0300
Fax: (510)540-1107
**Subject(s):** Alternative and Underground; New Age
**Circ:** (Paid)15,000

**Stanford Lawyer** (3562)
Stanford Law School
559 Nathan Abbott Way
Crown Quadrangle
559 Nathan Abbott Way
Stanford, CA 94305-8610
Phone: (650)725-9301
Fax: (650)725-9786
**Subject(s):** College Publications; Law
**Circ:** (Controlled)15,000

**Strings** (3387)
STRINGS
255 W. End Ave.
San Rafael, CA 94901
Phone: (415)485-6946
Fax: (415)485-0831
**Subject(s):** Music and Musical Instruments
**Circ:** ‡15,000

**Written By Magazine** (2380)
Writers Guild America, West
7000 W. 3rd St.
Los Angeles, CA 90048-4329
Phone: (323)951-4000
Fax: (323)782-4800
**Subject(s):** Entertainment; Radio, Television, Cable, and Video
**Circ:** 15,000

**Wing & Shot** (2376)
PRIMEDIA Los Angeles
6420 Wilshire Blvd.
Los Angeles, CA 90048
Phone: (323)782-2000
Fax: (323)782-2223
**Subject(s):** (Hunting, Fishing, and Game Management)
**Circ:** (Paid)14,809

**New Oxford Review** (1505)
New Oxford Review Inc.
1069 Kains Ave.
Berkeley, CA 94706
Phone: (510)526-5374
Fax: (510)526-3492
**Subject(s):** Religious Publications
**Circ:** ‡14,635

**IABC Communication World** (3152)
1 Hallidie Plz., Ste. 600
San Francisco, CA 94102
Phone: (415)544-4700
Fax: (415)544-4747
**Subject(s):** Communications
**Circ:** (Non-paid)657
(Paid)14,506

**IEEE Internet Computing** (2108)
IEEE Computer Society
PO Box 3014
PO Box 3014
Los Alamitos, CA 90720-1314
Phone: (714)821-8380
Fax: (714)821-4010
**Subject(s):** Computers; Telecommunications
**Circ:** (Paid)14,455

**Resource Recycling** (25977)
PO Box 42270
Portland, OR 97242-0270
Phone: (503)233-1305
Fax: (503)233-1356
**Subject(s):** Waste Management and Recycling
**Circ:** (Paid)2,697
(Controlled)14,350

**Generations, Journal of the American Society on Aging** (3142)
American Society on Aging
833 Market St., Ste. 511
San Francisco, CA 94103-1824
Phone: (415)974-9600
Fax: (415)974-0300
**Subject(s):** Gerontology
**Circ:** (Controlled)300
(Paid)14,200

**Wheat Life** (32238)
Washington Association of Wheat Growers
109 E 1st Ave.
Ritzville, WA 99169
Phone: (509)659-0610
Fax: (509)659-4302
**Subject(s):** Socialized Farming
**Circ:** 14,065

**Alternative Therapies in Health and Medicine** (1819)
InnoVision Communications L.L.C.
169 Saxony Rd., Ste. 103
Encinitas, CA 92024
Phone: (760)633-3910
Fax: (760)633-3918
**Subject(s):** Medicine and Surgery; Health and Healthcare
**Circ:** (Paid)14,000

**The Colorado Lawyer** (4271)
Colorado Bar Association
1900 Grant St., Ste. 900
Denver, CO 80203
Phone: (303)860-1115
Fax: (303)894-0821
**Subject(s):** Law
**Circ:** (Paid)14,000

**The Journal of Diagnostic Medical Sonography (JDMS) (3773)**
Sage Publications Inc.
2455 Teller Rd.
Thousand Oaks, CA 91320
**Subject(s):** Medicine and Surgery; Physics
**Circ:** (Paid)14,000

**SSM (4322)**
AORN Inc.
2170 S. Parker Rd., Ste. 300
Denver, CO 80231
Phone: (303)755-6304
Fax: (303)750-3441
**Subject(s):** Medicine and Surgery; Health and Healthcare
**Circ:** (Combined)14,000

**Oregon State Bar Bulletin (25887)**
Oregon State Bar
5200 SW Meadows Rd.
Lake Oswego, OR 97035-0889
Phone: (503)620-0222
Fax: (503)684-1366
**Subject(s):** Law
**Circ:** (Paid)‡13,988

**Journal of the American Animal Hospital Association (4294)**
American Animal Hospital Association
PO Box 15089
Denver, CO 80215-0899
Phone: (303)986-2800
**Subject(s):** Veterinary Medicine
**Circ:** 13,500

**Reeves Journal (2054)**
Business News Publishing Co.
23421 S. Pointe Dr., Ste. 280
PO Box 30700
Laguna Hills, CA 92653
Phone: (949)830-0881
Fax: (949)859-7845
**Subject(s):** Air Conditioning and Refrigeration; Plumbing and Heating
**Circ:** (Controlled)‡13,500

**Orange County Business Journal (2007)**
2600 Michelson Dr., No. 170
Irvine, CA 92612
Phone: (949)833-8373
**Subject(s):** Business; Local, State, and Regional Publications
**Circ:** (Non-paid)599
(Paid)13,456

**Alaska Fisherman's Journal (32244)**
Diversified Business Publications
4055 21st Ave. W.
Seattle, WA 98199
Phone: (206)283-1150
Fax: (206)286-8594
**Subject(s):** Fish and Commercial Fisheries
**Circ:** (Paid)△1,865
(Non-paid)△7,589
△13,401

**Mainline Modeler (32168)**
Hundman Publishing
13110 Beverly Park Rd.
Mukilteo, WA 98275
Phone: (425)743-2607
Fax: (425)787-9269
**Subject(s):** Crafts, Models, Hobbies, and Contests
**Circ:** 13,405

**Correctional News (3384)**
1241 Andersen Dr., Ste. N
San Rafael, CA 94901
Phone: (415)460-6185
Fax: (415)460-6288
**Subject(s):** Construction, Contracting, Building, and Excavating; Police, Penology, and Penal Institutions
**Circ:** (Combined)13,218

**Liberty (32207)**
Liberty Foundation
PO Box 1181
Port Townsend, WA 98368
Phone: (360)379-0242
**Subject(s):** Social and Political Issues
**Circ:** (Non-paid)⊕100
(Paid)⊕13,000

**9-1-1 Magazine (3926)**
Official Publications Inc.
18201 Weston Pl.
Tustin, CA 92780
Phone: (714)544-7776
Fax: (714)838-9233
**Subject(s):** Public Safety and Emergency Response
**Circ:** (Paid)13,000

**Senior Messenger (32467)**
City of Vancouver
PO Box 1995
Vancouver, WA 98668-1995
Phone: (360)696-8077
Fax: (360)696-8942
**Subject(s):** Senior Citizens' Interests
**Circ:** (Non-paid)13,000

**Model Railroading (4095)**
Highlands Station Inc.
2600 S Parker Rd., Ste. 1-211
Aurora, CO 80014
Phone: (303)338-1700
Fax: (303)338-1949
**Subject(s):** Crafts, Models, Hobbies, and Contests
**Circ:** (Combined)⊕**12,860**

**Emmy (2548)**
Academy of Television Arts and Sciences
5220 Lankershim Blvd.
North Hollywood, CA 91601-3109
Phone: (818)754-2800
Fax: (818)761-2827
**Subject(s):** Entertainment
**Circ:** (Non-paid)‡2,331
(Paid)‡12,788

**Building Products Digest (2534)**
Cutler Publishing Inc.
4500 Campus Dr., Ste. 480
Newport Beach, CA 92660-1872
Phone: (949)852-1990
Fax: (949)852-0231
**Subject(s):** Wood and Woodworking; Building Materials, Concrete, Brick, and Tile
**Circ:** (Controlled)‡12,750

**RadioResource International (4176)**
Pandata Corp.
7108 S Alton Way, Bldg. H
Centennial, CO 80112-2129
Phone: (303)792-2390
Fax: (303)792-2391
**Subject(s):** Radio, Television, Cable, and Video; Telecommunications
**Circ:** (Non-paid)12,730

**The Business Journal (2866)**
1400 X St
Sacramento, CA 95814-5221
Phone: (916)447-7661
Fax: (916)444-7779
**Subject(s):** Business; Local, State, and Regional Publications
**Circ:** (Paid)12,727

**The Hook (3017)**
Tailhook Association
9696 Business Park Ave.
San Diego, CA 92131
Phone: (858)689-9223
Fax: (858)578-8839
**Subject(s):** Military and Navy; Aviation; History and Genealogy
**Circ:** (Non-paid)‡244
(Paid)‡12,636

**Pharmaceutical Executive (25810)**
Advanstar Communications
859 Willamette St.
Eugene, OR 97401
Phone: (541)343-1200
Fax: (541)984-5250
**Subject(s):** Drugs and Pharmaceuticals
**Circ:** (Paid)1,920
(Controlled)12,502

**Watch & Clock Review (4324)**
Golden Bell Press
2403 Champa St.
Denver, CO 80205
Phone: (303)296-1600
Fax: (303)295-2159
**Subject(s):** Jewelry, Watches, and Clocks
**Circ:** (Paid)‡3,000
(Non-paid)‡12,500

**Pacific Builder & Engineer (32125)**
10504 NE 37th Cir., No. 7
Kirkland, WA 98033-7920
Phone: (425)486-8553
Fax: (425)488-0946
**Subject(s):** Construction, Contracting, Building, and Excavating; Engineering (Various branches); Petroleum, Oil, and Gas
**Circ:** (Paid)251
(Controlled)12,274

**Bible Advocate (4261)**
Church of God (Seventh Day)
PO Box 33677
Denver, CO 80233
Phone: (303)452-7973
Fax: (303)452-0657
**Subject(s):** Religious Publications
**Circ:** (Controlled)‡12,200

**ARTWEEK (3280)**
PO Box 26340
San Jose, CA 95159-6340
Phone: (408)441-7065
Fax: (408)441-9519
**Subject(s):** Art; Photography
**Circ:** (Non-paid)‡3,000
(Paid)‡12,000

**Brazzil (2155)**
PO Box 50536
Los Angeles, CA 90050-0536
Phone: (323)255-8062
Fax: (323)257-3487
**Subject(s):** Intercultural Interests
**Circ:** 12,000

**HealthCare Distributor (4478)**
ELF Publications Inc.
5285 W Louisiana Ave.
Lakewood, CO 80232-5976
Phone: (303)975-0075
**Subject(s):** Drugs and Pharmaceuticals
**Circ:** ‡12,000

**ICG Magazine (2226)**
International Cinematographers Guild
7755 Sunset Blvd.
Los Angeles, CA 90046
Phone: (323)876-0160
Fax: (323)876-6383
**Subject(s):** Motion Pictures; Radio, Television, Cable, and Video
**Circ:** (Combined)⊕**12,000**

**International Documentary (2228)**
International Documentary Association
1201 W 5th St., Ste. M320
Los Angeles, CA 90017
Phone: (213)534-3600
Fax: (213)534-3610
**Subject(s):** Motion Pictures
**Circ:** 12,000

**Log Trucker (32039)**
Loggers World Publications
4206 Jackson Hwy.
Chehalis, WA 98532-8425
Phone: (360)262-3376
Fax: (360)262-3337
**Subject(s):** Transportation, Traffic, and Shipping; Forestry
**Circ:** (Combined)‡12,000

**Loving More (4125)**
Pep Publishing
PO Box 4358
Boulder, CO 80306-4358
Phone: (303)543-7540
**Subject(s):** Lifestyle; Sex/Erotica
**Circ:** ‡12,000

**Plastic Surgery Products (2309)**
Novicom Inc.
6100 Center Dr., Ste. 1000
Los Angeles, CA 90045
Phone: (310)642-4400
Fax: (310)641-4444
**Subject(s):** Medicine and Surgery
**Circ:** (Controlled)12,000

**Racing WHEELS Newspaper (32466)**
Racing Wheels
3617 NE 51st St., Apt. 4
PO Box 1555
Vancouver, WA 98661-2355
Phone: (360)892-5590

---

**Circulation:** ★ = ABC; △ = BPA; ♦ = CAC; ◆ = CCAB; ❏ = VAC; ⊕ = PO Statement; ‡ = Publisher's Report; Boldface figures = sworn; Light figures = estimated.

# Western States

Fax: (360)892-8021
**Subject(s):** (Auto Racing)
**Circ:** (Paid)8,000
(Non-paid)12,000

**Shaman's Drum (26077)**
Cross-Cultural Shamanism Network
PO Box 270
Williams, OR 97544
Phone: (541)846-1313
Fax: (541)846-1204
**Subject(s):** Theology
**Circ:** (Combined)12,000

**SIAM Review (4135)**
Society for Industrial & Applied Mathematics
c/o Robert Schnabel, Editor-In-Chief
University of Colorado-Boulder
Academic Affairs, Regent Hall 303-I
Campus Box 40
Boulder, CO 80309
**Subject(s):** Mathematics
**Circ:** ‡11,669

**American Trapper (33778)**
National Trappers Association
PO Box 513
Riverton, WY 82501
Phone: (307)856-3830
Fax: (307)857-2993
**Subject(s):** Fur Trade and Fur Farming
**Circ:** ‡11,500

**IEA Reporter (7652)**
Idaho Education Association
PO Box 2638
Boise, ID 83701
Phone: (208)344-1732
Fax: (208)336-6967
**Subject(s):** Education
**Circ:** (Non-paid)‡600
(Paid)‡11,500

**Northwest Motor (4313)**
Automotive Counseling & Publishing Co.
450 Lincoln St., Ste. 110
PO Box 300804
Denver, CO 80203
Phone: (303)765-4664
Fax: (303)765-4650
**Subject(s):** Automotive (Trade)
**Circ:** ‡11,500

**Journal of the ACM (JACM) (3587)**
Association for Computing Machinery
c/o Prabhakar Raghavan
894 Ross Dr.
Sunnyvale, CA 94089
Phone: (408)542-2229
Fax: (408)541-1600
**Subject(s):** Computers
**Circ:** ‡11,400

**Journal of the American Planning Association (JAPA) (25960)**
American Planning Association
PO Box 751
Portland State University
Portland, OR 97207-0751
Phone: (503)725-4087
Fax: (503)725-9515
**Subject(s):** Architecture
**Circ:** (Paid)⊕**11,400**

**Beverage Industry News (2745)**
Industry Publications Inc.
171 Mayhew Way, Ste. 202
Pleasant Hill, CA 94523
Phone: (925)932-4999
Fax: (925)932-4966
**Subject(s):** Beverages, Brewing, and Bottling
**Circ:** (Non-paid)‡5,618
(Paid)‡11,250

**Turning the Tide (1738)**
Anti-Racist Action/People Against Racist Terror
PO Box 1055
Culver City, CA 90232
Phone: (310)495-0299
**Subject(s):** Politics; Civil Rights
**Circ:** (Paid)‡750
(Non-paid)‡11,250

**Clinical Obstetrics Gynecology (30762)**
Lippincott Williams & Wilkins
C/o James R. Scott, MD, Editor
University of Utah School of Medicine
Department of Obstetrics and Gynecology
Salt Lake City, UT
**Subject(s):** Medicine and Surgery
**Circ:** ‡11,170

**Computer Fair Show Program (2514)**
National Productions
17660 Monterey Rd., Ste. G
Morgan Hill, CA 95037
Phone: (408)465-2300
Fax: (408)465-2700
**Subject(s):** Computers
**Circ:** (Non-paid)‡11,000

**Journal of the American Academy of Religion (4041)**
Oxford University Press
Department of Religious Studies
Whittier College
Whittier, CA 90609
Phone: (562)907-4200
Fax: (562)907-4910
**Subject(s):** Religious Publications
**Circ:** 11,000

**The Keeper's Log (3166)**
U.S. Lighthouse Society
244 Kearny St., 5th Fl.
San Francisco, CA 94108-4507
Phone: (415)362-7255
**Subject(s):** Oceanography and Marine Studies; Lighting
**Circ:** (Non-paid)‡200
(Paid)‡11,000

**Neonatal Network (3496)**
2270 Northpoint Pwy.
Santa Rosa, CA 95407-7398
Phone: (707)569-1415
Fax: (707)569-0786
**Subject(s):** Nursing
**Circ:** (Controlled)11,000

**New Perspectives Quarterly (2284)**
Blackwell Publishers
Center for the Study of Democracy
10951 W. Pico Blvd., 3rd Fl.
Los Angeles, CA 90064
Phone: (310)474-0011
Fax: (310)474-8061
**Subject(s):** Politics
**Circ:** (Non-paid)559
(Paid)11,002

**Reading Research Quarterly (18700)**
International Reading Association
University of Nevada
College of Education
4505 Maryland Pkwy
Las Vegas, NV 89154-3042
Phone: (702)895-4217
Fax: (702)895-4353
**Subject(s):** Education
**Circ:** ‡11,000

**The People (2520)**
Socialist Labor Party of America
PO Box 218
Mountain View, CA 94042-0218
Phone: (408)280-7266
Fax: (408)280-6964
**Subject(s):** Labor; Politics
**Circ:** 10,900

**Ag Equipment Power (32387)**
Clintron Publishers
5817 S. Magnolia St.
PO Box 30998
Spokane, WA 99223-3016
Phone: (509)458-3924
Fax: (509)458-3947
**Subject(s):** Farm Implements and Supplies
**Circ:** 10,600
(Non-paid)‡10,800

**Chicago Apparel News (2164)**
Apparel News Group
110 E 9th St., Ste. A-777
Los Angeles, CA 90079-1777
Phone: (213)627-3737
Fax: (213)627-5707
**Subject(s):** Clothing
**Circ:** 10,764

**ACSM's Health & Fitness Journal (18677)**
Lippincott Williams & Wilkins
C/o Lawrence A. Golding Ph.D., Editor-in-Chief
University of Nevada
Las Vegas, NV
**Subject(s):** Physical Education and Athletics; Health and Fitness
**Circ:** ‡10,700

**IEEE Computer Graphics and Applications (2106)**
IEEE Computer Society
PO Box 3014
PO Box 3014
Los Alamitos, CA 90720-1314
Phone: (714)821-8380
Fax: (714)821-4010
**Subject(s):** Computers
**Circ:** (Non-paid)77
(Paid)10,519

**Aspen Magazine (4089)**
Ridge Publications
720 E. Durant Ave. Ste. E8
Aspen, CO 81611
Phone: (970)920-4040
Fax: (970)920-4044
**Subject(s):** Lifestyle; Local, State, and Regional Publications
**Circ:** (Paid)5,500
(Non-paid)10,500

**Magic (18695)**
Stagewrite Publishing Inc.
6220 Stevenson Way
Las Vegas, NV 89120
Phone: (702)798-0099
Fax: (702)798-0220
**Subject(s):** Performing Arts; Drama and Theatre; Entertainment
**Circ:** (Controlled)10,500

**Timber West (32074)**
Timber West Publications
300 Admiral Way, Ste. 208
PO Box 610
Edmonds, WA 98020-0610
Phone: (425)778-3388
Fax: (425)771-3623
**Subject(s):** Forestry
**Circ:** (Paid)135
(Controlled)10,500

**Western City (2920)**
League of California Cities
1400 K St.
Sacramento, CA 95816
Phone: (916)658-8289
Fax: (800)262-1801
**Subject(s):** State, Municipal, and County Administration
**Circ:** (Paid)‡10,500

**Journal of Clinical Orthodontics (4121)**
JCO Inc.
1828 Pearl St.
Boulder, CO 80302
Phone: (303)443-1720
Fax: (303)443-9356
**Subject(s):** Dentistry
**Circ:** (Paid)‡10,445

**IEEE Antennas & Propogation (2035)**
IEEE Inc.
1446 Vista Claridad
La Jolla, CA 92037
Phone: (858)459-8305
Fax: (858)459-7140
**Subject(s):** Electrical Engineering; Telecommunications
**Circ:** (Controlled)10,400

**The Oregon Episcopal Church News (25966)**
Episcopal Diocese of Oregon
11800 SW Military Ln.
Portland, OR 97219-8436
Phone: (503)636-5613
Fax: (503)636-5616
**Subject(s):** Religious Publications
**Circ:** (Combined)10,350

**Sign Business (4157)**
National Business Media Inc.
PO Box 1416
Broomfield, CO 80038
Phone: (303)469-0424
Fax: (303)469-5730

**Subject(s):** Printing and Typography

**Circ:** (Paid)△7,732
(Non-paid)△10,319

**Hawaii Business** (7542)
PacificBasin Communications
PO Box 913
Honolulu, HI 96808-0913
Phone: (808)537-9500
Fax: (808)537-6455
**Subject(s):** Management and Administration; Local, State, and Regional Publications; Business

**Circ:** (Paid)‡3,057
(Non-paid)‡10,197

**LACMA Physician** (2629)
Los Angeles County Medical Association
300 S. Flower St.,
Orange, CA 92868
Phone: (714)978-1100
Fax: (714)978-6039
**Subject(s):** Medicine and Surgery

**Circ:** (Non-paid)‡651
(Paid)‡10,154

**New York Apparel News** (2285)
Apparel News Group
110 E 9th St., Ste. A-777
Los Angeles, CA 90079-1777
Phone: (213)627-3737
Fax: (213)627-5707
**Subject(s):** Clothing

**Circ:** 10,049

**Accounting Review** (32242)
American Accounting Association
c/o Prof. Terry Shevlin, Dept. of Accounting
University of Washington
Box 353200
Seattle, WA 98195-3200
**Subject(s):** Accountants and Accounting

**Circ:** 10,000

**Alumni Report** (3358)
Junior Statesmen Foundation
400 S El Camino Real, Ste. 300
San Mateo, CA 94402
Phone: (650)347-1600
Fax: (650)347-7200
**Subject(s):** College Publications; Education; Youths' Interests

**Circ:** 10,000

**American Fencing** (4183)
United States Fencing Association
1 Olympic Plz.
Colorado Springs, CO 80909-5744
Phone: (719)866-4511
Fax: (719)632-5737
**Subject(s):** (General Sports)

**Circ:** 10,000

**American Journal of Orthopsychiatry** (860)
American Orthopsychiatric Association
Dept. of Psychology
Arizona State Univ.
Box 871104
Tempe, AZ 85287-1104
Phone: (480)727-5718
Fax: (212)564-6180
**Subject(s):** Psychology and Psychiatry

**Circ:** ‡10,000

**Arabian Horse World** (1609)
1316 Tamson Dr., Ste. 101
Cambria, CA 93428
Phone: (805)771-2300
Fax: (805)927-6522
**Subject(s):** Livestock; (Horses and Horse Racing)

**Circ:** 10,000

**arcCa** (2864)
AIACC
1303 J St., Ste. 200
Sacramento, CA 95814
Phone: (916)448-9082
Fax: (916)442-5346
**Subject(s):** Architecture

**Circ:** 10,000

**Bus Conversions** (4037)
7246 Garden Grove Blvd.
Westminster, CA 92683-2225
Phone: (714)799-0062
Fax: (714)799-0042

**Subject(s):** Automotive (Consumer)

**Circ:** (Paid)10,000

**California Coast & Ocean** (2580)
California State Coastal Conservancy
1330 Broadway, Ste. 1100
Oakland, CA 94612-2530
Phone: (510)286-1015
Fax: (510)286-0470
**Subject(s):** Art and Art History; Environmental and Natural Resources Conservation; Wildlife and Exotic Animals

**Circ:** (Combined)10,000

**California Engineer** (1453)
California Engineer Publishing Co.
University of California, Berkeley
221 Bechtel Engineering Ctr.
Berkeley, CA 94720-0001
Phone: (510)642-8679
**Subject(s):** Engineering (Various branches); College Publications

**Circ:** (Controlled)‡10,000

**California Manufacturer** (2873)
California Manufacturers Association
1040 45th St., Ste. 2200
Sacramento, CA 95819
Phone: (916)441-5420
Fax: (916)447-9401
**Subject(s):** Business

**Circ:** ‡10,000

**The California Southern Baptist** (1875)
California Southern Baptist Convention
678 E Shaw Ave.
Fresno, CA 93710-7704
Phone: (559)229-9533
Fax: (559)229-2824
**Subject(s):** Religious Publications

**Circ:** ‡10,000

**Cascade Horseman** (25865)
Cascade Magazine
PO Box 1390
Klamath Falls, OR 97601-1390
Phone: (541)885-4460
Fax: (541)885-4447
**Subject(s):** Livestock

**Circ:** 10,000

**College & Career Guide News for College Students** (908)
Corporate Marketing & Publishing
6506 E Calle Bellatrix, Ste. 100
Tucson, AZ 85710
Phone: (520)790-4044
**Subject(s):** Education; Career Development and Employment

**Circ:** (Non-paid)10,000

**The Comics Journal** (32259)
Fantagraphics Books
7563 Lake City Wy NE
Seattle, WA 98115
Phone: (206)524-1967
Fax: (206)524-2104
**Subject(s):** Comics and Comic Technique; Book Trade and Author News

**Circ:** (Paid)‡10,000

**Electrifying Times** (25722)
63600 Deschutes Market Rd.
Bend, OR 97701
Phone: (541)388-1908
Fax: (541)388-2750
**Subject(s):** Automotive (Consumer)

**Circ:** 10,000

**Fem** (2201)
University of California, Los Angeles
149B Kerckhoff Hall, 308 Westwood Plz.
308 Westwood Plz.
118 Kerckhoff Hall
Los Angeles, CA 90024
Phone: (310)825-2587
Fax: (310)825-2794
**Subject(s):** Women's Interests

**Circ:** (Non-paid)‡10,000

**Frank Lloyd Wright Quarterly** (828)
Wright Foundation
PO Box 4430
Cactus Rd. & 114th St.
Scottsdale, AZ 85260
Phone: (480)860-2700
Fax: (480)860-4872

**Subject(s):** Architecture

**Circ:** (Controlled)10,000

**Gems & Gemology** (1614)
Gemological Institute of America
Robert Mouawad Campus
5345 Armada Dr.
Carlsbad, CA 92008
Phone: (760)603-4504
Fax: (760)603-4595
**Subject(s):** Jewelry, Watches, and Clocks; Mining and Minerals

**Circ:** 10,000

**Handball** (914)
U.S. Handball Association
2333 N. Tucson Blvd.
Tucson, AZ 85716
Phone: (520)795-0434
Fax: (520)795-0465
**Subject(s):** (General Sports)

**Circ:** ‡10,000

**IDEA Personal Trainer** (3019)
IDEA Inc.
10455 Pacific Center Court
San Diego, CA 92121-3773
Phone: (858)535-8979
Fax: (858)535-8234
**Subject(s):** Physical Education and Athletics; Business

**Circ:** (Combined)10,000

**International California Mining Journal** (1380)
PO Box 2260
Aptos, CA 95001
Phone: (831)479-1500
Fax: (831)479-4385
**Subject(s):** Mining and Minerals

**Circ:** ‡10,000

**Journal of the American Association for Medical Transcription** (2479)
American Association for Medical Transcription
100 Sycamore Ave.
Modesto, CA 95354-0550
Phone: (209)527-9620
Fax: (209)527-9633
**Subject(s):** Medicine and Surgery; Health and Healthcare

**Circ:** 10,000

**Kit Builders Magazine** (2739)
Monsters in Motion
181 W. Orangethorpe Ave., Ste. E
Placentia, CA 92870
Phone: (714)577-8863
Fax: (714)577-8865
**Subject(s):** Crafts, Models, Hobbies, and Contests

**Circ:** (Controlled)10,000

**LCT** (3903)
Business Media
3520 Challenger St.
Torrance, CA 90503
Phone: (310)533-2400
Fax: (310)533-2500
**Subject(s):** Automotive (Trade)

**Circ:** (Non-paid)‡200
(Paid)‡10,000

**Locus** (2595)
Locus Publications
PO Box 13305
Oakland, CA 94661
Phone: (510)339-9196
Fax: (510)339-8144
**Subject(s):** Book Trade and Author News

**Circ:** ‡10,000

**Montana** (18157)
Montana Historical Society
225 N. Roberts
PO Box 201201
Helena, MT 59620-1201
Phone: (406)444-2694
Fax: (406)444-2696
**Subject(s):** History and Genealogy

**Circ:** ‡10,000

**NAPRA Review** (32070)
Networking Alternatives for Publishers, Retailers, & Artists Inc.
109 N. Beach Rd.
PO Box 9
Eastsound, WA 98245-0009
Phone: (360)376-2702

## Western States

Fax: (360)376-2704
**Subject(s):** Music and Musical Instruments; Book Trade and Author News; New Age
**Circ:** (Non-paid)10,000

**New Age Retailer (32009)**
Continuity Publishing Inc.
1300 N. State St., Ste. 105
Bellingham, WA 98225
Phone: (360)676-0789
Fax: (360)676-0932
**Subject(s):** Book Trade and Author News; New Age; Retail
**Circ:** (Non-paid)10,000

**NOMMO (2289)**
University of California, Los Angeles
118 Kerkhoff Hall
308 Westwood Plaza
Los Angeles, CA 90024
Phone: (310)825-9898
Fax: (310)206-0906
**Subject(s):** Law; Black Publications
**Circ:** (Non-paid)10,000

**Optical Engineering (32010)**
International Society for Optical Engineering
1000 20th St.
PO Box 10
Bellingham, WA 98225
Phone: (360)676-3290
Fax: (360)647-1445
**Subject(s):** Computers; Ophthalmology, Optometry, and Optics
**Circ:** (Paid)10,000

**PC AI Online (768)**
Knowledge Technology Inc.
PO Box 30130
Phoenix, AZ 85046
Phone: (602)971-1869
Fax: (602)971-2321
**Subject(s):** Computers
**Circ:** (Combined)10,000

**Philae (4363)**
Pleiades Magazine
PO Box 140213
Edgewater, CO 80214-9998
Phone: (303)237-1019
**Subject(s):** Literature; Poetry; Literature and Literary Reviews
**Circ:** (Non-paid)10,000

**San Francisco Attorney Magazine (3201)**
Bar Association of San Francisco
465 California St., Ste. 1100
San Francisco, CA 94104-1826
Phone: (415)982-1600
Fax: (415)477-2388
**Subject(s):** Law; Local, State, and Regional Publications
**Circ:** (Paid)10,000

**Single Again Magazine (2859)**
1237 Crescendo Dr.
Roseville, CA 95678
**Subject(s):** Lifestyle
**Circ:** (Paid)10,000

**Snohomish County Seniors (32384)**
127 Ave. C
PO Box 499
Snohomish, WA 98291-0499
Phone: (360)568-4121
Fax: (360)568-1484
**Subject(s):** Home and Garden
**Circ:** (Non-paid)‡10,000

**Song Manh Magazine (3310)**
Song Sao Cho Manh Inc.
PO Box 21245
San Jose, CA 95151-1245
Phone: (408)605-0605
Fax: (408)729-5595
**Subject(s):** Vietnamese; Health
**Circ:** 10,000

**Spirit & Life (936)**
Benedictine Sisters of Perpetual Adoration
800 N Country Club Rd.
Tucson, AZ 85716-4583
Phone: (520)325-6401
**Subject(s):** Religious Publications
**Circ:** ‡10,000

**Sun Diamond Grower (3569)**
Sun Diamond Growers of California
1050 Diamond St.
Stockton, CA 95205
Phone: (209)467-6000
Fax: (209)467-6714
**Subject(s):** Socialized Farming
**Circ:** (Controlled)‡10,000

**WOODALL's Northeast Outdoors (3981)**
Woodall Publications Corp.
2575 Vista Del Mar Dr.
Ventura, CA 93001
Phone: (805)667-4100
Fax: (303)728-7306
**Subject(s):** Travel and Tourism
**Circ:** (Paid)10,000
(Non-paid)10,000

**Woodworkers West (2377)**
PO Box 452058
Los Angeles, CA 90045
Phone: (310)216-9265
Fax: (310)216-9274
**Subject(s):** Wood and Woodworking
**Circ:** (Combined)10,000

**The Fence Post (4610)**
Greeley Publishing Co.
423 Main St.
Windsor, CO 80550
Phone: (970)686-5898
Fax: (970)686-5694
**Subject(s):** General Agriculture
**Circ:** (Non-paid)‡400
(Paid)‡9,700

**California Journal (2871)**
Information for Public Affairs Inc.
2101 K St.
Sacramento, CA 95816
Phone: (916)444-0840
Fax: (916)446-5369
**Subject(s):** Politics
**Circ:** (Non-paid)225
(Paid)9,500

**Solar Today (4139)**
American Solar Energy Society Inc.
2400 Central Ave., Ste. A
Boulder, CO 80301
Phone: (303)443-3130
Fax: (303)443-3212
**Subject(s):** Power and Power Plants
**Circ:** (Paid)9,500

**Northeast Outdoors (3970)**
Woodall Publishing Corp.
2575 Vista Del Mar Dr.
Ventura, CA 93001
**Subject(s):** (Outdoors)
**Circ:** (Non-paid)⊕1,365
(Paid)⊕9,394

**The Montana Catholic (18158)**
Roman Catholic Diocese of Helena
515 N. Ewing
PO Box 1729
Helena, MT 59624-1729
Phone: (406)442-5820
Fax: (406)442-5191
**Subject(s):** Religious Publications
**Circ:** ‡9,200

**Tradeshow Week (2354)**
Tradeshow Week Inc.
5700 Wilshire Blvd., Ste. 120
Los Angeles, CA 90036
Phone: (323)965-5300
Fax: (323)965-5330
**Subject(s):** Business; Conventions, Meetings, and Trade Fairs
**Circ:** (Paid)2,394
(Combined)9,097

**Agency Sales Magazine (2060)**
Manufacturers' Agents National Association
One Spectrum Pointe, Ste. 150
Lake Forest, CA 92630-2283
Phone: (949)859-4040
Fax: (949)855-2973
**Subject(s):** Selling and Salesmanship
**Circ:** ‡9,000

**American Suzuki Journal (4104)**
Suzuki Association of Americas
PO Box 17310
Boulder, CO 80308-7310
Phone: (303)444-0948
Fax: (303)444-0984
**Subject(s):** Education; Music and Musical Instruments
**Circ:** ‡9,000

**Black Lace (2148)**
BLK Publishing Co.
Box 83912
Los Angeles, CA 90083-0912
Phone: (310)410-0808
Fax: (310)410-9250
**Subject(s):** Women's Interests; Gay and Lesbian Interests; Ethnic Publications
**Circ:** (Non-paid)200
(Paid)9,000

**Montana Farm Bureau Spokesman (18090)**
Montana Farm Bureau Federation
502 S. 19th Ave., No. 104
Bozeman, MT 59718
Phone: (406)587-3153
Fax: (406)587-0319
**Subject(s):** General Agriculture
**Circ:** ‡9,000

**Nevada Business Journal (18696)**
A Division of Business Link L.L.C.
2127 Paradise Rd.
Las Vegas, NV 89104-2515
Phone: (702)735-7003
Fax: (702)733-5953
**Subject(s):** Business; Local, State, and Regional Publications
**Circ:** (Paid)‡6,000
(Controlled)‡9,000

**Release Print (3198)**
Film Arts Foundation
145 9th St. No. 101
San Francisco, CA 94103
Phone: (415)552-8760
Fax: (415)552-0882
**Subject(s):** Motion Pictures; Radio, Television, Cable, and Video
**Circ:** (Combined)9,000

**Right of Way (3910)**
International Right of Way Association
19750 S Vermont Ave., Ste. 220
Torrance, CA 90502-1144
Phone: (310)538-0233
Fax: (310)538-1471
**Subject(s):** Construction, Contracting, Building, and Excavating; Engineering (Various branches); Real Estate; Environmental and Natural Resources Conservation; Law
**Circ:** ‡9,000

**Seattle's Child (Snohomish County Edition) (32330)**
Northwest Parent Publishing
123 NW 36th St., Ste. 215
Seattle, WA 98107-4959
Phone: (206)441-0191
Fax: (206)441-4919
**Subject(s):** Parenting
**Circ:** (Combined)8,850

**TEST Engineering & Management (2606)**
The Mattingley Publishing Company Inc.
3756 Grand Ave., Ste. 205
Oakland, CA 94610-1545
Phone: (510)839-0909
Fax: (510)839-2950
**Subject(s):** Engineering (Various branches)
**Circ:** (Non-paid)‡8,772

**Developmental Dynamics (30765)**
John Wiley and Sons Inc.
C/O Gary C. Schoenwolf
Dept. of Neurobiology & Anatomy & Children's Health Research
University of Utah School of Medicine
20 N. 1900 E., Rm. 401 MREB (Bldg. 531)
Salt Lake City, UT 84132-3401
**Subject(s):** Biology; Physiology and Anatomy
**Circ:** 8,750

**Rice Farming (2481)**
Vance Publishing Corp.
2800 Braden Ave., No. 25
Modesto, CA 95356
Phone: (209)571-0419
Fax: (209)571-0419

**Subject(s):** General Agriculture
**Circ:** ‡8,753

**Genealogical Computing** (30738)
MyFamily.com Inc.
360 W. 4800 N
Provo, UT 84604
Phone: (801)705-7000
Fax: (801)705-7001
**Subject(s):** Computers; History and Genealogy
**Circ:** (Controlled)‡50
(Paid)‡8,700

**IT Professional** (2110)
IEEE Computer Society
PO Box 3014
PO Box 3014
Los Alamitos, CA 90720-1314
Phone: (714)821-8380
Fax: (714)821-4010
**Subject(s):** Computers; Automation
**Circ:** (Combined)‡8,557

**CBA Marketplace** (4190)
CBA Service Corporation Inc.
CBA International
PO Box 62000
Colorado Springs, CO 80962-2000
Phone: (719)265-9895
Fax: (719)272-3510
**Subject(s):** Religious Publications; Book Trade and Author News; Retail
**Circ:** (Non-paid)‡567
(Paid)‡8,514

**North Bay Biz** (3497)
Gammon L.L.C.
3565 Airway Dr.
Santa Rosa, CA 95403-1605
Phone: (707)575-8282
Fax: (707)546-7268
**Subject(s):** Business
**Circ:** (Non-paid)⊕5,485
(Paid)⊕8,515

**InSite** (4200)
Christian Camping International/USA
405 W. Rockrimmon Blvd.
Colorado Springs, CO 80919
**Subject(s):** (Outdoors); Religious Publications
**Circ:** ‡8,500

**Journal of Asthma** (4297)
Marcel Dekker Inc.
c/o David G. Tinkelman
National Jewish Medical and Research Center
Denver, CO
**Subject(s):** Medicine and Surgery
**Circ:** (Paid)8,500

**Mortuary Management** (2502)
Abbott & Hast Publications
761 Lighthouse Ave., Ste. A
Monterey, CA 93940-1033
Phone: (831)657-9403
Fax: (831)657-9137
**Subject(s):** Funeral Directors
**Circ:** (Paid)⊕8,500

**The National Tombstone Epitaph** (889)
Tombstone Epitaph Corp.
Box 1880
Tombstone, AZ 85638
Phone: (602)457-2211
**Subject(s):** History and Genealogy
**Circ:** ‡8,500

**International Journal of Eating Disorders** (2229)
John Wiley and Sons Inc.
C/O Michael Strober, Department of Psychiatry
760 Westwood Plaza
Los Angeles, CA 90024
**Subject(s):** Psychology and Psychiatry
**Circ:** 8,400

**Journal of Computational Chemistry** (2037)
John Wiley and Sons Inc.
c/o Charles L. Brooks
Department of Molecular Biology (TPC6)
10550 N. Torrey Pines Rd.
La Jolla, CA 92037-1000
**Subject(s):** Chemistry, Chemicals, and Chemical Engineering
**Circ:** (Paid)8,400

**California Odd Fellow and Rebekah** (2076)
Linden Publications
19033 E Main St.
PO Box 129
Linden, CA 95236-0129
Phone: (209)887-3829
Fax: (209)887-3829
**Subject(s):** Odd Fellows, Independent Order of
**Circ:** ‡8,125

**Almond Facts** (2862)
Blue Diamond Growers
1802 C St.
PO Box 1768
Sacramento, CA 95814
Phone: (916)442-0771
**Subject(s):** Socialized Farming
**Circ:** (Controlled)8,000

**The Business Journal** (1871)
1315 Van Ness, Ste.200
Fresno, CA 93721
Phone: (559)490-3400
Fax: (559)490-3532
**Subject(s):** Business
**Circ:** ‡8,000

**Pool & Spa News** (2312)
Leisure Publications
4160 Wilshire Blvd.
Los Angeles, CA 90010
Phone: (323)801-0160
Fax: (323)417-4860
**Subject(s):** Sporting Goods/Retail Sports
**Circ:** (Paid)7,800
(Non-paid)8,000

**Readings** (880)
American Orthopsychiatric Association
Dept. of Psychology
Arizona State Univ.
Box 871104
Tempe, AZ 85287-1104
Phone: (480)727-5718
Fax: (212)564-6180
**Subject(s):** Psychology and Psychiatry
**Circ:** 8,000

**Resource Library Magazine** (2632)
Traditional Fine Arts Online Inc.
PMB 392
8502 E. Chapman
Orange, CA 92869-2461
Phone: (714)997-8500
**Subject(s):** Art
**Circ:** (Non-paid)8,000

**S.D.T.A. Teacher Advocate** (3056)
San Diego Teachers Association
10393 San Diego Mission Rd., No. 100
San Diego, CA 92108
Phone: (619)283-4411
Fax: (619)282-7659
**Subject(s):** Education
**Circ:** (Non-paid)‡8,000

**The Sunflower** (3429)
Nuclear Age Peace Foundation
PMB 121
1187 Coast Village Rd., Ste. 1
Santa Barbara, CA 93108-2794
Phone: (805)965-3443
Fax: (805)568-0466
**Subject(s):** Peace
**Circ:** (Non-paid)8,000

**The Threepenny Review** (1521)
PO Box 9131
Berkeley, CA 94709
Phone: (510)849-4545
Fax: (510)849-4551
**Subject(s):** Literature and Literary Reviews
**Circ:** (Non-paid)‡2,000
(Paid)‡8,000

**American Journal of Clinical Nutrition** (1753)
The American Society for Clinical Nutrition
Univ. of California
3247 Meyer Hall
One Shields Ave.
Davis, CA 95616-8790
Phone: (530)752-8363
Fax: (530)752-8371
**Subject(s):** Medicine and Surgery
**Circ:** ‡7,934

**California Schools Magazine** (4029)
California School Boards Association
3100 Beacon Blvd.
PO Box 1660
West Sacramento, CA 95691
Phone: (916)371-4691
Fax: (916)372-3369
**Subject(s):** Education
**Circ:** (Non-paid)‡465
(Paid)‡7,840

**Interact** (3586)
International Association of Hewlett-Packard Computer Users
1192 Borregas Ave.
Sunnyvale, CA 94089
Phone: (408)747-0227
Fax: (408)747-0947
**Subject(s):** Computers
**Circ:** (Controlled)‡4,000
(Paid)‡7,615

**EDUCAUSE Quarterly** (4115)
EDUCAUSE
4772 Walnut St., Ste. 206
Boulder, CO 80301-2538
Phone: (303)449-4430
Fax: (303)440-0461
**Subject(s):** Education; Library and Information Science
**Circ:** (Free)⊕170
(Paid)7,600

**The Washington Nurse** (32340)
Washington State Nurses Association
575 Andover Park W, No. 101
Seattle, WA 98188-3348
Phone: (206)575-7979
Fax: (206)575-1908
**Subject(s):** Health and Healthcare; Nursing
**Circ:** (Controlled)7,600

**Potato Country** (32506)
Columbia Publishing
417 N 20th Ave.
Yakima, WA 98902-7008
Phone: (509)248-2452
Fax: (509)248-4056
**Subject(s):** Socialized Farming; Fruit, Fruit Products, and Produce Trade
**Circ:** (Controlled)‡7,544

**Alternative Medicine Review** (7689)
Thorne Research Inc.
25820 Highway 2 West
P.O. Box 25
Dover, ID 83825
Phone: (208)263-1337
Fax: (208)365-2488
**Subject(s):** Medicine and Surgery; Health and Healthcare; Health
**Circ:** (Paid)⊕7,500

**Collegiate Baseball Newspaper** (909)
Collegiate Baseball Newspaper Inc.
2515 N. Stone Ave.
Tucson, AZ 85705
Phone: (520)623-4530
Fax: (520)624-5501
**Subject(s):** (Baseball)
**Circ:** ‡7,500

**Education and Training in Developmental Disabilities** (864)
Council for Exceptional Children
Arizona State University
Special Education Program
Tempe, AZ 85287-2011
Phone: (480)965-1449
Fax: (480)965-4942
**Subject(s):** Education
**Circ:** ‡7,500

**Journal of Marriage and Family** (25767)
National Council on Family Relations
c/o Alexis Walker
18 Milam Hall
Oregon State University
Corvallis, OR 97331
Phone: (541)737-1092
Fax: (541)737-8997
**Subject(s):** Marriage and Family
**Circ:** ‡7,500

**Skinned Knuckles (2498)**
SK Publications
175 May Ave.
Monrovia, CA 91016
Phone: (626)358-6255
**Subject(s):** Automotive (Consumer)
**Circ:** (Paid)7,500

**Jurimetrics (873)**
American Bar Association
c/o Gail K Geer, Jurimetrics Journal
College of Law
Arizona State University
PO Box 877906
Tempe, AZ 85287-7906
Phone: (480)727-6523
Fax: (480)965-2427
**Subject(s):** Law
**Circ:** 7,400

**Computing in Science & Engineering (2104)**
IEEE Computer Society
PO Box 3014
PO Box 3014
Los Alamitos, CA 90720-1314
Phone: (714)821-8380
Fax: (714)821-4010
**Subject(s):** Engineering (Various branches); Computers; Automation
**Circ:** (Paid)‡7,293

**MARINE DIGEST (32288)**
Marine Publishing Inc.
1710 S Norman St.
Seattle, WA 98144
Phone: (206)709-1840
Fax: (206)682-4023
**Subject(s):** Ships and Shipping
**Circ:** (Controlled)‡7,200

**AI Magazine (2448)**
American Association for Artificial Intelligence
445 Burgess Dr.
Menlo Park, CA 94025-3442
Phone: (650)328-3123
Fax: (650)321-4457
**Subject(s):** Computers
**Circ:** 7,000

**Alaska Business Monthly (494)**
Alaska Business Publishing Company Inc.
PO Box 241288
Anchorage, AK 99524-1288
Phone: (907)276-4373
Fax: (907)279-2900
**Subject(s):** Business
**Circ:** (Paid)‡3,000
 (Non-paid)‡7,000

**California Family Physician (3116)**
California Academy of Family Physicians
1520 Pacific Ave.
San Francisco, CA 94109
Phone: (415)345-8667
Fax: (415)345-8668
**Subject(s):** Medicine and Surgery
**Circ:** ‡7,000

**California State Association of Counties California County (2878)**
California State Association of Counties
1100 K St., Ste. 101
Sacramento, CA 95814
Phone: (916)327-7500
Fax: (916)441-5507
**Subject(s):** Politics; Local, State, and Regional Publications
**Circ:** (Non-paid)7,000

**CLAIMS (32073)**
Claims
15112 64th Ave. W
Edmonds, WA 98026
Phone: (425)745-6394
**Subject(s):** Insurance
**Circ:** (Non-paid)‡3,000
 (Paid)‡7,000

**Exclusive Reports online (2634)**
Tradeline Inc.
PO Box 1568
Orinda, CA 94563
Phone: (925)254-1744
Fax: (925)254-1093
**Subject(s):** Architecture; Engineering (Various branches)
**Circ:** 7,000

**Film Score Magazine (1735)**
Film Score Monthly
8503 Washington Blvd.
Culver City, CA 90232
Phone: (310)253-9595
Fax: (310)253-9588
**Subject(s):** Motion Pictures; Music and Musical Instruments; Radio, Television, Cable, and Video
**Circ:** (Combined)7,000

**Glass Art (4463)**
Travin Inc.
Glass Art Magazine
PO Box 260377
Highlands Ranch, CO 80163
Phone: (303)791-8998
Fax: (303)791-7739
**Subject(s):** Glass and China
**Circ:** ‡7,000

**MultiLingual Computing & Technology (7803)**
Multilingual Computing Inc.
319 N First Ave.
Sandpoint, ID 83864
Phone: (208)263-8178
Fax: (208)263-6310
**Subject(s):** Computers; Business
**Circ:** (Combined)7,000

**Northwest Runner (32298)**
4831 NE 44th St.
Seattle, WA 98105
Phone: (206)527-5301
Fax: (206)527-1223
**Subject(s):** (Running)
**Circ:** (Paid)7,000

**Oregon Historical Quarterly (25968)**
Oregon Historical Society
1200 SW Park Ave.
Portland, OR 97205-2483
Phone: (503)222-1741
Fax: (503)221-2035
**Subject(s):** History and Genealogy
**Circ:** (Non-paid)250
 (Paid)7,000

**USA Table Tennis Magazine (4219)**
USA Table Tennis
One Olympic Plaza
Colorado Springs, CO 80909-5769
Phone: (719)866-4583
Fax: (719)632-6071
**Subject(s):** (General Sports); (Racquet Sports)
**Circ:** (Non-paid)800
 (Paid)7,000

**Pacific Coast Nurseryman and Garden Supply Dealer (1943)**
Cox Publishing Company Inc.
105 N. Vermont Ave.
PO Box 1477
Glendora, CA 91740
Phone: (626)914-3916
**Subject(s):** Horticulture; Landscape Architecture; Seed and Nursery Trade
**Circ:** (Non-paid)‡3,624
 (Paid)‡6,840

**The Tomato Magazine (32507)**
Columbia Publishing
417 N 20th Ave.
Yakima, WA 98902-7008
Phone: (509)248-2452
Fax: (509)248-4056
**Subject(s):** Socialized Farming; Fruit, Fruit Products, and Produce Trade
**Circ:** (Controlled)‡6,742

**Seaways' Ships in Scale (30818)**
Seaways Publishing Inc.
Four Winds Publishing
1750 W. Stardust Dr.
Taylorsville, UT 84118
Phone: (801)964-2077
Fax: (801)964-2077
**Subject(s):** Crafts, Models, Hobbies, and Contests
**Circ:** (Paid)⊕6,700

**Colorado Farmer-Stockman (32460)**
Farm Progress Cos.
12309 NE, 21st St.
Vancouver, WA 98684
Phone: (360)546-2977
Fax: (360)546-2977

**Subject(s):** General Agriculture
**Circ:** (Paid)3,421
 (Non-paid)6,690

**Journal of the American Medical Directors Association (JAMDA) (3745)**
Lippincott Williams & Wilkins
c/o Dan Osterweil
1685 Sweet Briar Pl.
Thousand Oaks, CA 91362
Phone: (805)241-1163
Fax: (805)241-1163
**Subject(s):** Medicine and Surgery
**Circ:** (Paid)6,546

**Art Access (32248)**
PO Box 4163
Seattle, WA 98194
Phone: (206)855-9668
Fax: (206)855-7854
**Subject(s):** Art
**Circ:** (Combined)6,500

**Contact Point (3123)**
University of the Pacific School of Dentistry
2155 Webster St.
San Francisco, CA 94115
Phone: (415)929-6550
Fax: (415)929-6654
**Subject(s):** Dentistry; College Publications
**Circ:** (Non-paid)‡6,500

**EarthLight Magazine (2585)**
111 Fairmount Ave.
Oakland, CA 94611
Phone: (510)451-4926
Fax: (510)451-3505
**Subject(s):** Environmental and Natural Resources Conservation; Alternative and Underground
**Circ:** (Non-paid)500
 (Paid)6,500

**Geology (4118)**
Geological Society of America Inc.
PO Box 9140
PO Box 9140
Boulder, CO 80301-9140
Phone: (303)447-2020
Fax: (303)357-1070
**Subject(s):** Geology
**Circ:** (Paid)‡6,500

**San Francisco Art Institute Magazine (3200)**
San Francisco Art Institute
800 Chestnut St.
San Francisco, CA 94133
Phone: (415)771-7020
Fax: (415)749-4590
**Subject(s):** Art and Art History
**Circ:** (Combined)6,500

**Pacific Fishing (32303)**
Pacific Fishing Magazine
1710 S. Norman St.
Seattle, WA 98144
Phone: (206)709-1840
Fax: (206)324-8939
**Subject(s):** Fish and Commercial Fisheries
**Circ:** (Paid)6,413

**Journal of Foot and Ankle Surgery (3157)**
Lippincott Williams & Wilkins
c/o John M. Schuberth, DPM Editor
PO Box 590595
San Francisco, CA 94159-0595
Fax: (847)292-2022
**Subject(s):** Podiatry
**Circ:** (Non-paid)‡200
 (Paid)6,400

**Human Factors (3479)**
Human Factors and Ergonomics Society
PO Box 1369
Santa Monica, CA 90406-1369
Phone: (310)394-1811
Fax: (310)394-2410
**Subject(s):** Science (General); Engineering (Various branches)
**Circ:** (Combined)6,300

**Northwest Public Power Association Bulletin (32465)**
Northwest Public Power Association (NWPPA)
9817 NE 54th St.
Vancouver, WA 98662-6064
Phone: (360)254-0109

Fax: (360)254-5781
**Subject(s):** Power and Power Plants
**Circ:** (Paid)‡6,300

**Journal of Interpersonal Violence** (32280)
Sage Publications Inc.
c/o Jon R. Conte
School of Social Work JH-30
University of Washington
4101 15th Ave. NE
Seattle, WA 98195
**Subject(s):** Psychology and Psychiatry
**Circ:** (Non-paid)‡157
(Paid)‡6,250

**Bowls** (2152)
United States Lawn Bowls Association
1764 N Fairfax
Los Angeles, CA 90046
**Subject(s):** (Bowling)
**Circ:** 6,200

**Worm Digest** (25843)
PO Box 2654
Grants Pass, OR 97528
Phone: (541)476-9626
Fax: (541)476-4555
**Subject(s):** Environmental and Natural Resources Conservation; Fertilizer; Ecology and Conservation
**Circ:** (Non-paid)‡800
(Paid)‡6,200

**Geriatric Nursing** (2991)
Mosby Inc.
c/o Priscilla R. Ebersole, Editor
2790 Rollingwood Dr.
San Bruno, CA 94066
Fax: (650)952-3155
**Subject(s):** Gerontology; Nursing
**Circ:** (Paid)‡6,050

**Abstracts with Programs** (4101)
Geological Society of America Inc.
PO Box 9140
PO Box 9140
Boulder, CO 80301-9140
Phone: (303)447-2020
Fax: (303)357-1070
**Subject(s):** Geology
**Circ:** 6,000

**American Pit Bull Terrier Gazette** (30760)
American Dog Breeders Association
c/o Kate Greenwood
PO Box 1771
Salt Lake City, UT 84110
Phone: (801)936-7513
Fax: (801)936-4229
**Subject(s):** Dogs; Pets
**Circ:** 6,000

**Ark Today** (32388)
Genesis Institute
10220 N Nevada, Ste. 280
Spokane, WA 99218
Phone: (509)467-7913
Fax: (509)467-0344
**Subject(s):** Religious Publications; Theology
**Circ:** 6,000

**Birth of Tragedy Magazine** (3551)
C.F.Y.
PO Box 19271
Stanford, CA 94309
Phone: (650)714-4891
**Subject(s):** Alternative and Underground; Social and Political Issues
**Circ:** (Combined)6,000

**CALF News Magazine** (4189)
CALF News Magazine Ltd.
10720 Black Forest Dr. S
Colorado Springs, CO 80906
Phone: (719)495-0303
Fax: (719)495-9204
**Subject(s):** Livestock
**Circ:** 6,000

**California Pharmacist** (2874)
California Pharmacists Association
4030 Lennane Dr.
Sacramento, CA 95834
Phone: (916)779-1400
Fax: (916)779-1401

**Subject(s):** Drugs and Pharmaceuticals
**Circ:** ‡6,000

**Chalcedon Report** (3946)
Chalcedon Inc.
PO Box 158
Vallecito, CA 95251
Phone: (209)736-4365
Fax: (209)736-0536
**Subject(s):** Religious Publications
**Circ:** (Non-paid)‡6,000

**Epic Journal** (4362)
Pleiades Magazine
PO Box 140213
Edgewater, CO 80214-9998
Phone: (303)237-1019
**Subject(s):** Literature; Poetry; Literature and Literary Reviews
**Circ:** (Non-paid)6,000

**Habibi** (2518)
PO Box 4081
Mountain View, CA 94040
Phone: (415)841-2721
**Subject(s):** Entertainment; Intercultural Interests
**Circ:** ‡6,000

**Journal of the American Rhododendron Society** (32162)
American Rhododendron Society
12781 Josh Wilson Rd.
Mount Vernon, WA 98273
**Subject(s):** Horticulture
**Circ:** (Controlled)6,000

**Mercury** (3170)
Astronomical Society of the Pacific
390 Ashton Ave.
San Francisco, CA 94112
Phone: (415)337-1100
Fax: (415)337-5205
**Subject(s):** Astronomy and Meteorology; Science; Education
**Circ:** (Non-paid)‡200
(Paid)‡6,000

**The Mini-Storage Messenger** (767)
Mini-Storage Messenger
2531 W. Dunlap Ave.
Phoenix, AZ 85021
Phone: (602)678-3579
Fax: (602)678-3511
**Subject(s):** Storage and Warehousing
**Circ:** (Non-paid)500
(Paid)6,000

**NETA World** (4525)
InterNational Electrical Testing Association
106 Stone St.
PO Box 687
Morrison, CO 80465
Phone: (303)697-8441
Fax: (303)697-8431
**Subject(s):** Electrical Engineering; Lighting
**Circ:** (Controlled)6,000

**Southwest Contractor** (774)
McGraw-Hill Inc.
3110 N Central, Ste. 155
Phoenix, AZ 85012
Phone: (602)631-3068
Fax: (602)631-3080
**Subject(s):** Construction, Contracting, Building, and Excavating; Mining and Minerals; Roads and Streets; State, Municipal, and County Administration; Local, State, and Regional Publications; Architecture
**Circ:** (Combined)6,000

**Townsend Letter for Doctors & Patients** (32209)
911 Tyler St.
Port Townsend, WA 98368-6541
Phone: (360)385-6021
Fax: (360)385-0699
**Subject(s):** Medicine and Surgery; Health and Healthcare
**Circ:** (Controlled)6,000

**Utah Science** (30690)
Utah State University
4845 University Blvd., Rm. 225
Logan, UT 84322-4845
Phone: (435)797-2206
**Subject(s):** Scientific Agricultural Publications
**Circ:** (Non-paid)6,000

**Journal of Microcolumn Separations** (30739)
John Wiley and Sons Inc.
c/o Milton L. Lee
Dept. of Chemistry and Biochemistry
Brigham Young Univ.
Provo, UT 84602-5700
**Subject(s):** Chemistry, Chemicals, and Chemical Engineering
**Circ:** 5,985

**Journal of Cellular Biochemistry** (2236)
John Wiley and Sons Inc.
c/o C. Fred Fox
Department of Microbiology and Molecular Genetics
609 CE Young Dr. E., 1602 MSB
Los Angeles, CA 90095-1489
**Subject(s):** Biology
**Circ:** (Paid)5,950

**BOXOFFICE Magazine** (2709)
RLD Communications Inc.
155 S. El Molino Ave., Ste. 100
Pasadena, CA 91101
Phone: (626)396-0250
Fax: (626)396-0248
**Subject(s):** Motion Pictures
**Circ:** (Paid)5,940

**Nevada Lawyer** (18697)
State Bar of Nevada
3444 Golden Pedal St.
Las Vegas, NV 89129
Phone: (702)254-8997
Fax: (702)804-5304
**Subject(s):** Law
**Circ:** (Controlled)5,900

**Oregon Wheat** (25935)
Oregon Wheat Growers League
115 SE 8th St.
Pendleton, OR 97801-2319
Phone: (541)276-7330
Fax: (541)276-1723
**Subject(s):** Socialized Farming
**Circ:** ‡5,800

**Crone Chronicles** (18179)
Crone Corp.
PO Box 457
Laurel, MT 59044
Phone: (406)628-6243
Fax: (406)628-6243
**Subject(s):** Women's Interests
**Circ:** (Combined)5,540

**California Management Review (CMR)** (1455)
University of California, Berkeley
F501 Haas School of Business, No. 1900
Berkeley, CA 94720-1900
Phone: (510)642-7159
Fax: (510)642-1318
**Subject(s):** Management and Administration; Business
**Circ:** ‡5,500

**California Thoroughbred** (1382)
California Thoroughbred Breeders Association
201 Colorado Pl.
PO Box 60018
Arcadia, CA 91066-6018
Phone: (626)445-7800
Fax: (626)574-0852
**Subject(s):** Livestock; (Horses and Horse Racing)
**Circ:** 5,500

**Cascade Cattleman** (25864)
Cascade Magazine
PO Box 1390
Klamath Falls, OR 97601-1390
Phone: (541)885-4460
Fax: (541)885-4447
**Subject(s):** Livestock
**Circ:** 5,500

**Colorado Medicine** (4273)
Colorado Medical Society
7351 Lowry Blvd.
Denver, CO 80230
Phone: (720)859-1001
**Subject(s):** Medicine and Surgery
**Circ:** 5,500

# Western States

**Judaism** (3454)
American Jewish Congress
Kresge College
University of California
Santa Cruz, CA 95064
Phone: (831)459-3882
Fax: (831)459-3535
**Subject(s):** Jewish Publications

**Circ:** ‡5,500

**Wings** (25990)
Xerces Society
4828 SE Hawthorne Blvd.
Portland, OR 97215
Phone: (503)232-6639
Fax: (503)233-6794
**Subject(s):** Ecology and Conservation; Entomology

**Circ:** (Paid)5,500

**Hawaii Bar Journal** (7540)
Grass Shack Productions
1132 Bishop St., No. 906
Honolulu, HI 96813-2814
Phone: (808)537-1868
Fax: (808)521-7936
**Subject(s):** Law

**Circ:** (Non-paid)500
(Paid)5,400

**Light Metal Age** (3546)
Fellom Publishing Co.
170 S Spruce Ave., Ste. 120
South San Francisco, CA 94080
Phone: (650)588-8832
Fax: (650)588-0901
**Subject(s):** Metal, Metallurgy, and Metal Trade

**Circ:** (Paid)5,380

**The Bear Laker** (7739)
Sun News Idaho Inc.
847 Washington
PO Box 278
Montpelier, ID 83254
Phone: (208)847-0552
Fax: (208)847-0553
**Subject(s):** Travel and Tourism

**Circ:** ‡5,300

**Ergonomics in Design** (3478)
Human Factors and Ergonomics Society
PO Box 1369
Santa Monica, CA 90406-1369
Phone: (310)394-1811
Fax: (310)394-2410
**Subject(s):** Commerce and Industry

**Circ:** (Paid)5,300

**Operations Research** (0555)
The Institute for Operations Research and the Management Sciences
c/o Lawrence M. Wein
Prof. of Operations, Information and Technology
Stanford Univ.
Stanford, CA 94305-5015
Phone: (650)724-1676
Fax: (650)725-0468
**Subject(s):** Business

**Circ:** (Paid)‡5,300

**Journal of Neurobiology** (3029)
John Wiley and Sons Inc.
c/o Eduardo Macagno
University of California
San Diego, CA 92103
**Subject(s):** Medicine and Surgery

**Circ:** 5,250

**Ex-CBI Roundup** (2537)
Dwight King Publishing
PO Box 11688
Newport Beach, CA 92658-5038
Phone: (949)759-3553
**Subject(s):** Military and Navy

**Circ:** ‡5,247

**Strategy & Tactics** (1408)
Decision Games
PO Box 21598
Bakersfield, CA 93390
Phone: (661)587-9633
Fax: (661)587-5031
**Subject(s):** Military and Navy; History and Genealogy

**Circ:** (Paid)⊕5,200

**Pacific Shipper** (2095)
Commonwealth Business Media
110 W. Ocean Blvd., Ste. 906
Long Beach, CA 90802-4631
Phone: (562)495-2989
Fax: (800)221-8633
**Subject(s):** Ships and Shipping

**Circ:** (Paid)5,083

**AGAIN Magazine** (1440)
Conciliar Press
10090 A Hwy. 9
Ben Lomond, CA 95005
Phone: (831)336-5118
Fax: (831)336-8882
**Subject(s):** Religious Publications

**Circ:** (Free)50
(Paid)5,000

**Arab-American Affairs** (1927)
The News Circle Publishing House
PO Box 3684
Glendale, CA 91201-0684
Phone: (818)507-0333
Fax: (818)246-1936
**Subject(s):** Ethnic Publications

**Circ:** (Combined)‡5,000

**AZ Med** (757)
Arizona Medical Association Inc.
810 W Bethany Home Rd.
Phoenix, AZ 85013
Phone: (602)347-6900
Fax: (602)242-6283
**Subject(s):** Medicine and Surgery

**Circ:** (Controlled)5,000

**Bulletin of the King County Medical Society** (32253)
Winslow Communications L.L.C.
317 S. Bennett St.
Seattle, WA 98108
Phone: (206)682-7813
Fax: (206)782-7778
**Subject(s):** Medicine and Surgery

**Circ:** ‡5,000

**California Community Care News** (2868)
PO Box 163270
Sacramento, CA 95816-9270
Phone: (916)455-0723
Fax: (916)455-7201
**Subject(s):** Health and Healthcare

**Circ:** (Paid)5,000

**The California Surveyor** (3489)
California Land Surveyors Association
PO Box 9098
Santa Rosa, CA 95405-9990
Phone: (707)578-0018
Fax: (707)578-4406
**Subject(s):** Engineering (Various branches)

**Circ:** (Non-paid)‡5,000

**Cartoonist and Comic Artist Magazine** (3403)
2747 N Grand Ave., PMB 250
Santa Ana, CA 92705
Phone: (714)550-9933
Fax: (714)550-9696
**Subject(s):** Comics and Comic Technique

**Circ:** (Paid)5,000

**Colorado Engineer** (4110)
University of Colorado
Campus Box 422
Boulder, CO 80309-0422
Phone: (303)492-8635
Fax: (303)492-2199
**Subject(s):** Engineering (Various branches)

**Circ:** (Non-paid)‡5,000
(Non-paid)‡5,000

**Digger** (26079)
Oregon Association of Nurseries
29751 SW Town Ctr. Loop W
Wilsonville, OR 97070
Phone: (503)682-5089
Fax: (503)682-5099
**Subject(s):** Seed and Nursery Trade; Landscape Architecture

**Circ:** (Controlled)‡5,000

**Ecology Terrain** (1470)
Ecology Center
2530 San Pablo Ave.
Berkeley, CA 94702
Phone: (510)548-2220

Fax: (510)548-2240
**Subject(s):** Ecology and Conservation

**Circ:** (Paid)5,000

**Economic Geology** (4492)
Economic Geology Publishing Company Inc.
7811 Shaffer Pkwy.
Littleton, CO 80127
Phone: (720)981-7882
Fax: (720)981-7874
**Subject(s):** Geology; Mining and Minerals

**Circ:** 5,000

**Geological Society of America Bulletin** (4117)
Geological Society of America Inc.
PO Box 9140
PO Box 9140
Boulder, CO 80301-9140
Phone: (303)447-2020
Fax: (303)357-1070
**Subject(s):** Geology

**Circ:** ‡5,000

**Horseless Carriage Gazette** (2565)
Horseless Carriage Club of America
40631 Hwy. 41
Oakhurst, CA 93644
Phone: (559)658-8800
**Subject(s):** Crafts, Models, Hobbies, and Contests

**Circ:** 5,000

**Journal of Forensic Sciences** (4202)
American Academy of Forensic Sciences
PO Box 669
Colorado Springs, CO 80901
Phone: (719)636-1100
Fax: (719)636-1993
**Subject(s):** Science (General); Literature; Medicine and Surgery

**Circ:** 5,000

**La Red—The Net** (2519)
Floricanto Press
650 Castro St., Ste. 120-331
Mountain View, CA 94041-2055
Phone: (415)552-1879
Fax: (702)995-1410
**Subject(s):** Literature; Ethnic and Minority Studies

**Circ:** (Combined)5,000

**Library Mosaics** (1736)
Yenor Inc.
Box 5171
Culver City, CA 90231
Phone: (310)645-4998
Fax: (310)910-1386
**Subject(s):** Library and Information Science

**Circ:** 5,000

**Mercury** (2271)
The Los Angeles Athletic Club
431 W 7th St.
Los Angeles, CA 90014
Phone: (213)625-2211
Fax: (213)689-1194
**Subject(s):** (General Sports); Clubs and Societies

**Circ:** ‡5,000

**News from Native California** (1506)
Heyday Books
PO Box 9145
Berkeley, CA 94709-0145
Phone: (510)549-3564
Fax: (510)549-1889
**Subject(s):** Local, State, and Regional Publications; Native American Interests

**Circ:** (Controlled)500
(Paid)5,000

**Official Magazine** (2622)
IAPMO
5001 E Philadelphia St.
Ontario, CA 91761-2816
Phone: (909)472-4100
Fax: (909)472-4244
**Subject(s):** Plumbing and Heating

**Circ:** (Paid)‡5,000

**Pacific Ties** (2296)
U.C.L.A.
118 Kerckhoff Hall
308 Westwood Plz.
University of California, Los Angeles
Los Angeles, CA 90024-1641
Phone: (310)825-2787

Fax: (310)206-0906
**Subject(s):** College Publications

**Circ:** (Controlled)‡5,000

**Plant Physiology** (2835)
American Society of Plant Biologists
c/o Natasha V. Raikhel
Department of Botany and Plant Sciences
University of California, 2109 Batchelor Hall
Riverside, CA 92521-0124
Phone: (909)787-4401
Fax: (909)787-4437
**Subject(s):** Botany

**Circ:** ‡5,000

**Pool Dust** (876)
PO Box 419
Tempe, AZ 85280-0419
**Subject(s):** (General Sports); Music and Musical Instruments

**Circ:** (Non-paid)‡5,000

**Recharger Magazine** (18701)
2800 W Sahara Ave., Ste. 5C
Las Vegas, NV 89102-4384
Phone: (702)438-5557
Fax: (702)438-4025
**Subject(s):** Waste Management and Recycling

**Circ:** (Non-paid)‡750
(Paid)‡5,000

**Washington Trails** (32341)
Washington Trails Association
2019 3rd Ave, Ste. 100
Seattle, WA 98121
Phone: (206)625-1367
Fax: (206)625-9249
**Subject(s):** (Outdoors)

**Circ:** ‡5,000

**The Way of St. Francis** (2918)
Franciscan Friars of California Inc.
c/o David Elliott, Editor
1112 26th St.
Sacramento, CA 95816-5610
Phone: (916)443-5717
Fax: (916)443-2019
**Subject(s):** Religious Publications

**Circ:** (Controlled)5,000

**Colorado Municipalities** (4275)
Colorado Municipal League
1144 Sherman St.
Denver, CO 80203-2207
Phone: (303)831-6411
Fax: (303)860-8175
**Subject(s):** State, Municipal, and County Administration

**Circ:** (Controlled)350
(Paid)4,950

**California Dairy** (1674)
California Dairy Herd Improvement Association
150 Clovis Ave., Ste. 102
Clovis, CA 93612
Phone: (559)323-2600
Fax: (559)323-2603
**Subject(s):** Dairying

**Circ:** 4,835

**Seattle's Child** (32329)
Northwest Parent Publishing
123 NW 36th St., Ste. 215
Seattle, WA 98107-4959
Phone: (206)441-0191
Fax: (206)441-4919
**Subject(s):** Parenting

**Circ:** (Non-paid)‡4,050
(Paid)‡4,800

**The Automotive Booster of California** (1343)
KAL Publications Inc.
559 S Harbor Blvd., Ste. A
Anaheim, CA 92805-4525
Phone: (714)563-9300
Fax: (714)563-9310
**Subject(s):** Automotive (Trade)

**Circ:** (Non-paid)‡4,700

**Building Management Hawaii** (7532)
Trade Publishing Co.
287 Mokauea St.
Honolulu, HI 96819
Phone: (808)848-0711
Fax: (808)841-3053
**Subject(s):** Building Management and Maintenance

**Circ:** (Non-paid)4,700

**Autograph Times** (859)
12213 W Bell Rd., Ste. 212
Surprise, AZ 85374
Phone: (623)544-4037
Fax: (623)214-5419
**Subject(s):** Collecting

**Circ:** (Non-paid)1,800
(Paid)4,600

**Peninsula Business Journal** (32373)
Olympic View Publishing Inc.
147 1/2 W Washington St.
PO Box 1750
Sequim, WA 98382
Phone: (360)683-3311
Fax: (360)683-6670
**Subject(s):** Business

**Circ:** (Paid)200
(Non-paid)4,600

**The Anvil's Ring** (1924)
Artist-Blacksmith's Association of North America
6690 Wentworth Spring Rd.
PO Box 1849
Georgetown, CA 95634
Phone: (530)333-2687
Fax: (530)333-2689
**Subject(s):** Metal, Metallurgy, and Metal Trade

**Circ:** (Paid)4,574

**Computer Applications in Engineering Education** (7534)
John Wiley and Sons Inc.
C/O Director, Hawaii Center for Advanced Communications
College of Engineering, Univ. of Hawaii at Manoa
2540 Dole St., Holmes Hall 483
Honolulu, HI 96822
**Subject(s):** Engineering (Various branches); Education

**Circ:** 4,550

**Applied Language Learning** (2500)
Foreign Language Center
Presidio
Monterey, CA 93944-5006
Phone: (831)242-5638
Fax: (831)242-5850
**Subject(s):** Education; Philology, Language, and Linguistics

**Circ:** (Non-paid)4,500

**CALYX** (25762)
Calyx Books
PO Box B
Corvallis, OR 97339-0539
Phone: (541)753-9384
Fax: (541)753-0515
**Subject(s):** Literature; Art and Art History; Women's Interests

**Circ:** (Non-paid)500
(Paid)4,500

**Ecological Applications** (4114)
Ecological Society of America
c/o David Schimel, Ecological Applications
National Center for Atmospheric Research
1850 Table Mesa Dr.
Boulder, CO
Phone: (303)497-1610
Fax: (303)497-1695
**Subject(s):** Ecology and Conservation

**Circ:** ‡4,500

**Journal of the American Association of Gynecologic Laparoscopists** (3463)
American Association of Gynecologic Laparoscopists
13021 E Florence Ave.
Santa Fe Springs, CA 90670-4505
Phone: (562)946-8774
Fax: (562)946-0073
**Subject(s):** Medicine and Surgery; Health and Healthcare

**Circ:** 4,500

**Journal of Hand Therapy** (3159)
Hanley & Belfus Inc.
875 La Playa, No. 278
San Francisco, CA 94121
**Subject(s):** Medicine and Surgery

**Circ:** ‡4,500

**Arizona Beverage Analyst** (4258)
Bell Publications
2403 Champa St.
Denver, CO 80205
Phone: (303)296-1600
Fax: (303)295-2159
**Subject(s):** Beverages, Brewing, and Bottling

**Circ:** (Paid)‡135
(Controlled)‡4,417

**California Veterinarian** (2880)
California Veterinary Medical Association
1400 River Park Dr., Ste. 100
Sacramento, CA 95815-4505
Phone: (916)649-0599
Fax: (916)646-9156
**Subject(s):** Veterinary Medicine

**Circ:** (Non-paid)‡3,000
(Paid)‡4,300

**Reviews of Modern Physics** (32319)
American Institute of Physics
c/o George F. Bertsch, University of Washington
Dept. of Physics
Physics/Astronomy Bldg., B434
PO Box 351560
Seattle, WA 98195-1560
Phone: (206)685-2391
Fax: (206)543-6782
**Subject(s):** Physics

**Circ:** (Paid)4,300

**Film Quarterly** (1474)
University of California Press/Journals
2120 Berkeley Way
Berkeley, CA 94704-1012
Phone: (510)642-4247
Fax: (510)643-7127
**Subject(s):** Motion Pictures

**Circ:** ‡4,226

**Glia** (32273)
John Wiley and Sons Inc.
Dept. of Neurology, Rm. No.RR650
Univ. of Washington School of Medicine
1959 NE Pacific,
Box 356465
Seattle, WA 98195-6465
**Subject(s):** Biology; Chemistry, Chemicals, and Chemical Engineering; Physiology and Anatomy

**Circ:** 4,200

**Professional Speaker** (877)
National Speakers Association
1500 S Priest Dr.
Tempe, AZ 85281
Phone: (480)968-2552
Fax: (480)968-0911
**Subject(s):** Public Speaking and Lecturing

**Circ:** (Controlled)⊕4,200

**Wines & Vines** (3388)
The Hiaring Co.
1800 Lincoln Ave.
San Rafael, CA 94901-1298
Phone: (415)453-9700
Fax: (415)453-2517
**Subject(s):** Beverages, Brewing, and Bottling

**Circ:** ‡4,185

**NARHA Strides** (4308)
North American Riding for the Handicapped Association Inc.
PO Box 33150
Denver, CO 80233
Phone: (303)452-1212
Fax: (303)252-4610
**Subject(s):** Handicapped; (Horses and Horse Racing)

**Circ:** 4,100

**Home Energy** (1481)
Home Energy Magazine
2124 Kittredge St., No. 95
Berkeley, CA 94704
Phone: (510)524-5405
Fax: (510)486-4673
**Subject(s):** Building Materials, Concrete, Brick, and Tile; Ecology and Conservation

**Circ:** (Combined)‡4,091

# Western States

**IEEE Design and Test of Computers  (2036)**
IEEE Computer Society
c/o Rajesh K. Gupta
University of California, San Diego
AP&M 3111 9500 Gilman Dr.
La Jolla, CA 92093
Phone: (858)822-4391
Fax: (858)534-7029
**Subject(s):** Computers

Circ:  (Non-paid)45
       (Paid)4,051

**African Arts  (2122)**
African Studies Center
PO Box 951310
University of California
Los Angeles, CA 90095-1310
Phone: (310)825-1218
Fax: (310)206-2250
**Subject(s):** Art and Art History

Circ:  4,000

**Alaska Geographic  (25944)**
Alaska Geographic Society
3019 NW Yeon
Portland, OR 97210
Phone: (503)226-2402
Fax: (800)355-9685
**Subject(s):** Geography

Circ:  (Paid)4,001

**The Annals of the American Academy of Political and Social Science  (3609)**
Sage Publications Inc.
2455 Teller Rd.
Thousand Oaks, CA 91320
**Subject(s):** Sociology; Politics

Circ:  (Paid)‡4,000

**ASHE-ERIC  (3108)**
Jossey-Bass Publishers
989 Market St.
San Francisco, CA 94103-1741
Phone: (415)433-1740
Fax: (415)951-8553
**Subject(s):** Education

Circ:  ‡4,000

**Authorship  (4535)**
The National Writers Association
10940 S. Parker Rd., No. 508
Parker, CO 80134
Phone: (303)841-0246
Fax: (303)841-2607
**Subject(s):** Book Trade and Author News

Circ:  ‡4,000

**BYU Studies  (30733)**
Brigham Young University
Brigham Young University
403 CB
Provo, UT 84602
Phone: (801)422-6691
Fax: (801)422-0232
**Subject(s):** Literature and Literary Reviews

Circ:  (Non-paid)250
       (Paid)4,000

**Classical Singer Magazine  (30675)**
Classical Singer
PO Box 1710
Draper, UT 84020
Phone: (801)254-1025
Fax: (801)254-3139
**Subject(s):** Music and Musical Instruments; Employment and Human Resources

Circ:  (Combined)4000

**ECS State Education Leader  (4286)**
Education Commission of the States
700 Broadway, No. 1200
Denver, CO 80203-3460
Phone: (303)299-3600
Fax: (303)296-8332
**Subject(s):** Education

Circ:  (Paid)1,000
       (Controlled)4,000

**Film/Tape World  (3139)**
Planet Communications
670 5th St.
San Francisco, CA 94107-1517
Phone: (415)543-6100
Fax: (415)546-7556
**Subject(s):** Motion Pictures; Radio, Television, Cable, and Video

Circ:  (Controlled)4,000

**German Shepherd Dog Review  (692)**
German Shepherd Dog Club of America
1902C N Abrego Dr.
Green Valley, AZ 85614
Phone: (520)625-9528
Fax: (520)625-4789
**Subject(s):** Dogs

Circ:  ‡4,000

**Journal of Behavioral Optometry  (3407)**
Optometric Extension Program Foundation
1921 E Carnegie Ave., Ste. 3-L
Santa Ana, CA 92705-5510
Phone: (949)250-8070
Fax: (949)250-8157
**Subject(s):** Ophthalmology, Optometry, and Optics

Circ:  4,000

**Meadmaker's Journal  (4426)**
American Mead Association
PO Box 4666
Grand Junction, CO 81502
**Subject(s):** Beverages, Brewing, and Bottling; Food and Cooking

Circ:  4,000

**Medical Acupuncture  (2268)**
American Academy of Medical Acupuncture
4929 Wilshire Blvd., Ste. 428
Los Angeles, CA 90010
Phone: (323)937-5514
Fax: (323)937-0959
**Subject(s):** Medicine and Surgery; Health and Healthcare

Circ:  4,000

**New Moon Rising  (25842)**
1630 Williams Hwy.
No. 148
Grants Pass, OR 97527-5660
Phone: (503)961-0772
Fax: (503)961-0772
**Subject(s):** Theology; New Age; Alternative and Underground

Circ:  4,000

**Prison Legal News  (32309)**
2400 NW 80th St., No. 148
Seattle, WA 98117
Phone: (206)246-1022
Fax: (206)505-9449
**Subject(s):** Law; Politics; Civil Rights

Circ:  (Non-paid)230
       (Paid)4,000

**Public Works Management & Policy  (3880)**
Sage Publications Inc.
2455 Teller Rd.
Thousand Oaks, CA 91320
**Subject(s):** Engineering (Various branches); Management and Administration

Circ:  (Paid)4,000

**RePlay Magazine  (3594)**
PO Box 7004
Tarzana, CA 91357
Phone: (818)776-2880
Fax: (818)776-2888
**Subject(s):** Machinery and Equipment; Gifts, Toys, and Novelties

Circ:  (Combined)4,000

**Language Learning and Technology  (7558)**
University of Hawaii
1859 E.-W. Rd., No. 106
Honolulu, HI 96822-2322
Phone: (808)956-9424
Fax: (808)956-5983
**Subject(s):** Education; Computers

Circ:  (Non-paid)3,944

**Journal for Vascular Ultrasound  (25867)**
Allen Press Inc.
Journal for Vascular Ultrasound Vascular Laboratory
Merle West Medical Center
2865 Daggett Ave.
Klamath Falls, OR 97601
Phone: (541)885-2697
Fax: (541)885-6726
**Subject(s):** Medicine and Surgery; Laboratory Research (Scientific and Medical)

Circ:  (Combined)3,900

**The Daily Journal  (4278)**
McGraw-Hill Inc.
2000 S Colorado Blvd., Ste. 2000
Denver, CO 80222
Phone: (303)756-9995
Fax: (303)756-4465
**Subject(s):** Daily Periodicals; Construction, Contracting, Building, and Excavating; Real Estate

Circ:  (Paid)‡1,206
       (Controlled)‡3,859

**Jonathan  (2233)**
Jonathan Club
545 S Figueroa St.
Los Angeles, CA 90071
Phone: (213)624-0881
Fax: (213)488-1425
**Subject(s):** Clubs and Societies

Circ:  (Controlled)‡3,800

**National Horseman  (831)**
The National Horseman
16101 N 82nd St., Ste. 10
Scottsdale, AZ 85260-1830
Phone: (480)922-5202
Fax: (480)922-5212
**Subject(s):** Livestock; (Horses and Horse Racing)

Circ:  (Non-paid)1,000
       (Paid)3,800

**Serb World U.S.A.  (935)**
Serb World U.S.A. Inc.
415 E Mabel St.
Tucson, AZ 85705
Phone: (520)624-4887
**Subject(s):** Ethnic Publications

Circ:  ‡3,800

**Simulation  (3058)**
The Society for Modeling & Simulation International
4838 Ronson Ct., Ste. L
PO Box 17900
San Diego, CA 92177-7900
Phone: (858)277-3888
Fax: (858)277-3930
**Subject(s):** Computers

Circ:  ‡3,800

**The Merchant Magazine  (2540)**
Cutler Publishing Inc.
4500 Campus Dr., Ste. 480
Newport Beach, CA 92660-1872
Phone: (949)852-1990
Fax: (949)852-0231
**Subject(s):** Wood and Woodworking; Building Materials, Concrete, Brick, and Tile

Circ:  (Controlled)269
       (Paid)‡3,798

**The Royal Spaniels  (2467)**
Premiere Publications
14531 Jefferson St.
Midway City, CA 92655
Phone: (714)893-0053
Fax: (714)893-5085
**Subject(s):** Dogs; Pets

Circ:  (Combined)3,745

**Social Problems  (1519)**
University of California Press/Journals
2120 Berkeley Way
Berkeley, CA 94704-1012
Phone: (510)642-4247
Fax: (510)643-7127
**Subject(s):** Sociology

Circ:  3,747

**Apartment News  (1919)**
Orange County Multi-Housing Service Corp.
12822 Garden Grove Blvd., Ste. D
Garden Grove, CA 92843
Phone: (714)638-5550
Fax: (714)638-6042
**Subject(s):** Building Management and Maintenance

Circ:  ‡3700

**Juco Review  (4205)**
National Junior College Athletic Association
1755 Telstar Dr., Ste. 103
Colorado Springs, CO 80920
Phone: (719)590-9788
Fax: (719)590-7324
**Subject(s):** (General Sports)

Circ:  (Non-paid)200
       (Paid)3,650

**IEEE Intelligent Systems** (2107)
IEEE Computer Society
PO Box 3014
PO Box 3014
Los Alamitos, CA 90720-1314
Phone: (714)821-8380
Fax: (714)821-4010
**Subject(s):** Computers

Circ: ‡3,612

**American Breweriana** (4538)
American Breweriana Association Inc.
4603 Castor Dr.
Pueblo, CO 81001
**Subject(s):** Collecting; Beverages, Brewing, and Bottling

Circ: (Controlled)3,600

**The Crafts Fair Guide** (1717)
Crafts Fair Guide
PO Box 688
Corte Madera, CA 94976-0688
Phone: (415)924-3259
**Subject(s):** Crafts, Models, Hobbies, and Contests

Circ: 3,500

**Highway 17 Almanack & Gazetteer** (3452)
PO Box 3602
Santa Cruz, CA 95063-3602
Phone: (831)479-3675
Fax: (408)924-3229
**Subject(s):** Alternative and Underground

Circ: (Non-paid)1,500
(Paid)3,500

**International Journal of Imaging Systems and Technology** (2003)
John Wiley and Sons Inc.
Univ. of California
Dept. of Radiological Sciences
Irvine, CA 92697
**Subject(s):** Engineering (Various branches); Computers

Circ: 3,500

**Iron Feather Journal** (4120)
Phun Inc.
PO Box 1905
Boulder, CO 80306
**Subject(s):** Music and Musical Instruments; Computers; Alternative and Underground

Circ: (Combined)3,500

**Journal of Palestine Studies** (1492)
Institute for Palestine Studies
University of California Press
2000 Center St., Ste. 303
Berkeley, CA 94704-1223
Phone: (510)643-7154
Fax: (510)642-9917
**Subject(s):** Intercultural Interests; Politics

Circ: (Paid)3,500

**Journal of San Diego History** (3031)
San Diego Historical Society
PO Box 81825
San Diego, CA 92138
Phone: (619)232-6203
**Subject(s):** History and Genealogy; Local, State, and Regional Publications

Circ: (Combined)3,500

**Pay Dirt Magazine** (632)
Copper Queen Publishing Company Inc.
Drawer 48
Bisbee, AZ 85603
Phone: (520)432-2244
Fax: (520)432-2247
**Subject(s):** Mining and Minerals; Local, State, and Regional Publications

Circ: ‡3,500

**Restoration** (930)
International Society for Vehicle Preservation
PO Box 50046
Tucson, AZ 85703-1046
Phone: (520)622-2201
Fax: (520)792-8501
**Subject(s):** Automotive (Consumer)

Circ: (Paid)‡1,500
(Controlled)‡3,500

**Wild Duck Review** (2528)
PO Box 335
Nevada City, CA 95959
Phone: (831)471-9246
Fax: (831)471-9246
**Subject(s):** Literature and Literary Reviews; Ecology and Conservation; Politics

Circ: (Paid)‡3,500

**Journal of Range Management** (4479)
Society for Range Management
445 Union Blvd., Ste. 230
Lakewood, CO 80228-1259
Phone: (303)986-3309
Fax: (303)986-3892
**Subject(s):** Scientific Agricultural Publications; Ecology and Conservation

Circ: 3,400

**World Dredging, Mining & Construction** (2014)
World Dredging Magazine
17951-C Skypark Cir.
Irvine, CA 92614
Phone: (949)553-0836
Fax: (949)863-9261
**Subject(s):** Ships and Shipping; Mining and Minerals

Circ: ‡3,400

**The Agencies** (1969)
Acting World Books
PO Box 3899
Hollywood, CA 90078
Phone: (818)905-1345
Fax: (818)905-1345
**Subject(s):** Motion Pictures; Radio, Television, Cable, and Video; Performing Arts

Circ: (Paid)487
(Combined)3,390

**Daily Journal of Commerce** (25953)
2840 N.W. 35th Ave. 97210
PO Box 10127
Portland, OR 97296
Phone: (503)226-1311
Fax: (503)224-7140
**Subject(s):** Daily Periodicals; Business; Local, State, and Regional Publications

Circ: (Controlled)809
(Paid)3,341

**Advertising & Marketing Review** (4408)
CSC Publishing
622 Gardenia Ct.
Golden, CO 80401
Phone: (303)277-9840
Fax: (303)278-9909
**Subject(s):** Advertising and Marketing

Circ: (Combined)3,300

**American Journal of Enology and Viticulture** (1754)
American Society for Enology and Viticulture
PO Box 1855
Davis, CA 95617
Phone: (530)753-3142
Fax: (530)753-3318
**Subject(s):** Beverages, Brewing, and Bottling; General Agriculture; Horticulture; Botany

Circ: 3,300

**Economic Inquiry** (1982)
Western Economic Association Intl.
7400 Center Ave., Ste. 109
Huntington Beach, CA 92647-3039
Phone: (714)898-3222
Fax: (714)891-6715
**Subject(s):** Economics

Circ: (Non-paid)25
(Paid)3,300

**Wyoming Trucker** (33687)
Wyoming Trucking Association
PO Box 1909
Casper, WY 82601
Phone: (307)234-1579
Fax: (307)234-7082
**Subject(s):** Trucks and Trucking

Circ: (Non-paid)‡3,300

**Coaching Volleyball** (4192)
American Volleyball Coaches Association
1227 Lake Plaza Dr., Ste. B
Colorado Springs, CO 80906
Phone: (719)576-7777
Fax: (719)576-7778
**Subject(s):** (General Sports); Education

Circ: (Paid)3,250

**Social Psychology Quarterly** (3557)
American Sociological Association
Stanford University
Department of Sociology
Bldg. 120, Rm. 160
450 Serra Mall
Stanford, CA 94305-2047
Phone: (650)725-6793
Fax: (650)725-6471
**Subject(s):** Sociology; Psychology and Psychiatry

Circ: ‡3,250

**Contemporary Economic Policy** (2087)
Western Economic Association Intl.
c/o Darwin C. Hall, Department of Economics
California State University
1250 Bellflower Blvd
Long Beach, CA 90840-4607
Phone: (562)985-5069
Fax: (562)985-5804
**Subject(s):** Sociology; Economics

Circ: (Non-paid)‡75
(Paid)‡3,200

**Journal of Financial and Quantitative Analysis** (32279)
Journal of Financial & Quantitative Analysis
University of Washington
School of Business Administration
115 Lewis Hall
PO Box 353200
Seattle, WA 98195-3200
Phone: (206)543-4598
Fax: (206)616-1894
**Subject(s):** Banking, Finance, and Investments; Statistics

Circ: ‡3,200

**The Psychoanalytic Quarterly** (2116)
670 Berry Ave.
Los Altos, CA 94024
Phone: (650)941-5420
Fax: (650)941-5420
**Subject(s):** Psychology and Psychiatry; Indexes, Abstracts, Reports, Proceedings, and Bibliographies

Circ: ‡3,200

**Timbertimes** (25855)
Box 219
Hillsboro, OR 97123
Phone: (503)293-6658
Fax: (503)615-8557
**Subject(s):** Crafts, Models, Hobbies, and Contests; History and Genealogy; Local, State, and Regional Publications

Circ: 3,200

**AAWCC Quarterly** (735)
American Association for Women in Community Colleges
1202 W Thomas Rd.
Phoenix, AZ 85013
Phone: (602)285-7449
Fax: (602)285-7832
**Subject(s):** Women's Interests; Education

Circ: 3,000

**Alameda-Contra Medical Association** (2570)
Alameda-Contra Costa Medical Association
6230 Claremont Ave.
Oakland, CA 94618
Phone: (510)654-5383
Fax: (510)654-8959
**Subject(s):** Medicine and Surgery

Circ: (Non-paid)3,000

**American Breweriana Journal** (4539)
American Breweriana Association Inc.
PO Box 11157
Pueblo, CO 81001
Phone: (719)544-9267
Fax: (719)544-4289
**Subject(s):** Beverages, Brewing, and Bottling; Collecting

Circ: 3,000

**Annals of Behavioral Medicine** (2030)
Society of Behavioral Medicine
Dept. of Family and Preventitve Medicine
UCSD/SOM
9500 Gilman Dr., No. 0628
La Jolla, CA 92092-0628
**Subject(s):** Medicine and Surgery; Psychology and Psychiatry

Circ: ‡3,000

# Western States

**Arizona Food Industry Journal (740)**
Arizona Grocers Publishing Company Inc.
120 E Pierce St.
Phoenix, AZ 85004
Phone: (602)252-9761
Fax: (602)252-9021
**Subject(s):** Food and Grocery Trade
**Circ:** ‡3,000

**Bet-Nahrain Magazine (2478)**
Bet Nahrain
c/o Third Branch
PO Box 4116
Modesto, CA 95352
Phone: (209)538-4130
Fax: (209)538-2795
**Subject(s):** Ethnic and Minority Studies; Arabic; Ethnic Publications
**Circ:** 3,000

**The Braille Mirror (2153)**
Braille Institute Press
741 N. Vermont Ave.
Los Angeles, CA 90029
Phone: (323)663-1111
Fax: (323)663-0867
**Subject(s):** Blind and Visually Challenged
**Circ:** (Controlled)3,000

**California Territorial Quarterly (2704)**
6848U Skyway
Paradise, CA 95969
Phone: (530)872-3363
**Subject(s):** History and Genealogy; Local, State, and Regional Publications
**Circ:** (Controlled)‡3,000

**Geocosmic Magazine (3548)**
National Council for Geocosmic Research Inc.
c/o Terry Lamb
8810-C Jamacha Blvd., PMB 183
Spring Valley, CA 91977-5633
Phone: (619)303-9236
Fax: (619)303-9236
**Subject(s):** Astronomy and Meteorology
**Circ:** (Paid)3,000

**Gesar (1479)**
2425 Hillside Ave.
Berkeley, CA 94704
Fax: (510)845-7540
**Subject(s):** Religious Publications
**Circ:** ‡3,000

**Impact! (2590)**
The World Institute on Disability
510 16th St., Ste. 100
Oakland, CA 94612
Phone: (510)763-4100
Fax: (510)763-4109
**Subject(s):** Handicapped
**Circ:** (Non-paid)3,000

**Journal of the ASFMRA (4296)**
American Society of Farm Managers and Rural Appraisers
950 S. Cherry St., Ste. 508
Denver, CO 80246-2664
Phone: (303)758-3513
Fax: (303)758-0190
**Subject(s):** General Agriculture
**Circ:** (Combined)3,000

**Journal of the Association of Nurses in AIDS Care (3751)**
Sage Publications
2455 Teller Rd.
Thousand Oaks, CA 91320
Phone: (805)499-0721
Fax: (805)499-0871
**Subject(s):** Acquired Immune Deficiency Syndrome; Medicine and Surgery; Health and Healthcare; Nursing
**Circ:** (Paid)‡3,000

**Journal of Pain and Palliative Care Pharmacotherapy (30772)**
The Haworth Press Inc.
c/o Arthur G. Lipman
Univ. of Utah Health Sciences Ctr.
30 S. 2000 E., Rm 258
Salt Lake City, UT 84112-5820
Phone: (801)581-5986
Fax: (801)585-6160
**Subject(s):** Drugs and Pharmaceuticals
**Circ:** (Paid)3,000

**Jump Cut (1495)**
Jump Cut Associates
PO Box 865
Berkeley, CA 94701
Phone: (510)658-7721
Fax: (510)658-7769
**Subject(s):** Radio, Television, Cable, and Video; Motion Pictures; Photography
**Circ:** (Paid)3,000

**New Thought (714)**
International New Thought Alliance
5003 E Broadway Rd.
Mesa, AZ 85206
Phone: (480)830-2461
Fax: (480)830-2561
**Subject(s):** Religious Publications; Alternative and Underground
**Circ:** ‡3,000

**The Rottweiler Quarterly (1926)**
GRQ Publications
1405 Villa Real Ct.
Gilroy, CA 95020-9218
Phone: (408)848-1313
**Subject(s):** Dogs
**Circ:** (Non-paid)250
3,000

**San Diego County Physician (3045)**
San Diego County Medical Society
3702 Ruffin Rd., Ste. 206
San Diego, CA 92123-1842
Phone: (858)565-8888
Fax: (858)565-1334
**Subject(s):** Medicine and Surgery; Health and Healthcare
**Circ:** (Paid)3,000

**The Scribe (25980)**
Medical Society of Metropolitan Portland
1325 SW Custer Dr.
Portland, OR 97219-2750
**Subject(s):** Medicine and Surgery
**Circ:** ‡3,000

**Sharing Ideas News Magazine (1944)**
Royal Publishing Inc.
PO Box 398
Glendora, CA 91740
Phone: (626)335-8069
Fax: (626)335-6127
**Subject(s):** Public Speaking and Lecturing
**Circ:** (Controlled)‡1,000
(Paid)‡3,000

**Sinister Wisdom (1518)**
Sinister Wisdom Inc.
PO Box 3252
Berkeley, CA 94703-0252
**Subject(s):** Gay and Lesbian Interests; Women's Interests
**Circ:** (Non-paid)‡500
(Paid)‡3,000

**Social Justice (3217)**
Global Options
PO Box 40601
San Francisco, CA 94140-0601
Phone: (415)550-1703
Fax: (510)620-0668
**Subject(s):** Sociology
**Circ:** (Non-paid)‡50
(Paid)‡3,000

**Texas Longhorn Journal (4502)**
Texas Longhorn Journal Inc.
PMB 210-110
40 W Littleton Blvd.
Littleton, CO 80120-2478
Phone: (303)730-3006
Fax: (303)797-0276
**Subject(s):** Livestock
**Circ:** ‡3,000

**Tribal: The Magazine of Tribal Art (3230)**
Tribarts Inc.
2261 Market St., PMB Ste. 644
San Francisco, CA 94114
Phone: (415)970-0220
Fax: (415)431-8321
**Circ:** (Paid)3,000

**Young Voices Magazine (32181)**
Young Voices
PO Box 2321
Olympia, WA 98507
Fax: (360)705-9669
**Subject(s):** Poetry; Literature and Literary Reviews; Art; Youths' Interests; Children's Interests
**Circ:** 3,000

**Monthly Weather Review (4128)**
American Meteorological Society
Office of the Co-Chief Editors
NCAR, FL-3, Rm. 3075, PO Box 3000
Boulder, CO 80307-3000
Phone: (303)497-8936
**Subject(s):** Astronomy and Meteorology
**Circ:** ‡2,972

**ACTEC Journal (2118)**
American College of Trust and Estate Counsel
3415 S Sepulveda Blvd., Ste. 330
Los Angeles, CA 90034
Phone: (310)398-1888
Fax: (310)572-7280
**Subject(s):** Law
**Circ:** 2,800

**Alameda County Bar Association Bulletin (2571)**
Alameda County Bar Association
610 16th St., Ste. 426
Oakland, CA 94612
Phone: (510)893-7160
Fax: (510)893-3119
**Subject(s):** Law
**Circ:** (Controlled)2,800

**Mathematics of Operations Research (3294)**
The Institute for Operations Research and the Management Sciences
c/o Nimrod Megiddo, Editor-In-Chief
Ibm Almaden Research Center
650 Harry Rd., K53-B2
San Jose, CA 95120
**Subject(s):** Management and Administration; Mathematics
**Circ:** ‡2,800

**San Bernardino County Museum Association Quarterly (2795)**
San Bernardino County Museum Association
2024 Orange Tree Ln.
Redlands, CA 92374
Phone: (909)307-2669
Fax: (909)307-0539
**Subject(s):** History and Genealogy
**Circ:** (Non-paid)200
(Paid)2,800

**Small Press Review (2707)**
Dustbooks
PO Box 100
Paradise, CA 95967
Phone: (530)877-6110
Fax: (530)877-0222
**Subject(s):** Literature and Literary Reviews
**Circ:** (Paid)2,800

**The Orthodox Word (2743)**
St. Herman of Alaska Brotherhood
10 Beegum George Rd.
PO Box 70
Platina, CA 96076
Phone: (530)352-4430
Fax: (530)352-4432
**Subject(s):** Religious Publications
**Circ:** (Controlled)‡400
(Paid)‡2,790

**Seminars in Respiratory and Critical Care Medicine (2329)**
Thieme Medical Publishers Inc.
c/o Joseph P. Lynch MD., Assistant Chief
Div. of Pulmonary, Critical Care, & Hospitals
David Geffen School of Medicine at UCLA
10833 Le Conte Ave., Rm. 37-131 CHS
Los Angeles, CA 90095-1690
**Subject(s):** Medicine and Surgery
**Circ:** (Paid)2,785

**Journal of Pediatric Nursing** (2242)
Elsevier
C/o Cecily Lynn Betz, Editor
University of Southern California
Department of Nursing
Univ. Affiliated Program at Childrens Hospital Los Angeles
Los Angeles, CA
**Subject(s):** Nursing

Circ: (Paid)2,752

**Bulletin** (1799)
Seismological Society of America
201 Plz. Professional Bldg.
El Cerrito, CA 94530-4003
Phone: (510)525-5474
Fax: (510)525-7204
**Subject(s):** Seismology; Geology

Circ: (Paid)‡2,737

**Journal of Geoscience Education** (32008)
National Association of Geoscience Teachers
c/o Dr. Robert Christman
Department of Geology - 9080
Western Washington University
PO Box 5443
Bellingham, WA 98227-5443
Phone: (360)650-3587
Fax: (360)650-7302
**Subject(s):** Geology; Education

Circ: 2,700

**Carrot Country** (32502)
Columbia Publishing
417 N 20th Ave.
Yakima, WA 98902-7008
Phone: (509)248-2452
Fax: (509)248-4056
**Subject(s):** Fruit, Fruit Products, and Produce Trade; Packaging

Circ: (Controlled)‡2,650

**Journal of Combinatorial Chemistry** (18741)
American Chemical Society
c/o Anthony W. Czarnik
Department of Chemistry/216
University of Nevada
1664 North Virginia St.
Reno, NV 89557-0020
Phone: (775)853-1111
Fax: (775)853-1124
**Subject(s):** Chemistry, Chemicals, and Chemical Engineering

Circ: 2,650

**Nebraska Beverage Analyst** (4309)
Bell Publications
2403 Champa St.
Denver, CO 80205
Phone: (303)296-1600
Fax: (303)295-2159
**Subject(s):** Beverages, Brewing, and Bottling

Circ: (Paid)‡141
(Non-paid)‡2,634

**Intermountain Contractor** (30769)
McGraw-Hill Inc.
1743 W. Alexander St.
Salt Lake City, UT 84119
Phone: (801)972-4400
Fax: (801)972-8975
**Subject(s):** Construction, Contracting, Building, and Excavating

Circ: (Paid)‡2,600

**Agroborealis** (539)
University of Alaska Fairbanks
PO Box 757140
Fairbanks, AK 99775
Phone: (907)474-5042
Fax: (907)474-6184
**Subject(s):** General Agriculture; Scientific Agricultural Publications

Circ: (Non-paid)2,500

**AIE Perspectives Newsmagazine** (1808)
American Institute of Engineers
4630 Appian Way, Ste. 206
El Sobrante, CA 94803-1875
Phone: (510)758-6240
Fax: (510)758-6240
**Subject(s):** Engineering (Various branches)

Circ: 2,500

**The Broadside** (25720)
Central Oregon Community College
2600 College Way
Bend, OR 97701
Phone: (541)383-7252
Fax: (541)383-7284
**Subject(s):** College Publications

Circ: (Non-paid)‡2,500

**IIE Transactions on Design & Manufacturing** (1483)
IIE Transactions
c/o. Candace A. Yano
Univ. of California at Berkeley
Dept. of Industrial Engineering and Operations Research
4135 Etcheverry Hall
Berkeley, CA 94720-1777
Phone: (510)642-4992
Fax: (510)642-1403
**Subject(s):** Engineering (Various branches)

Circ: (Paid)2,500

**IIE Transactions on Scheduling & Logistics** (1485)
IIE Transactions
c/o. Candace A. Yano, University of California at Berkeley
Dept. of Industrial Engineering and Operations Research
4135 Etcheverry Hall
Tech D237, 2145 Sheridan Rd.
Berkeley, CA 94720-1777
Phone: (510)642-4992
Fax: (510)642-1403
**Subject(s):** Engineering (Various branches)

Circ: (Paid)2,500

**JRTE Journal of Research on Computing in Education** (30775)
International Society for Technology in Education
c/o Lynne Schrum, Editor, University of Utah
Department of Teaching and Learning
1705 E. Campus Center Rd., 142A
Salt Lake City, UT 84117
Phone: (801)587-7800
Fax: (801)581-3609
**Subject(s):** Computers; Education

Circ: 2,500

**Oregon Beef Producer** (26045)
3415 Commercial St., Ste. 217
Salem, OR 97302-4668
Phone: (503)361-8941
Fax: (503)361-8947
**Subject(s):** Livestock

Circ: 2,500

**Pacific Telecommunications Review** (7567)
Pacific Telecommunications Council
2454 S. Beretania St., 3rd Fl.
Honolulu, HI 96826-1596
Phone: (808)941-3789
Fax: (808)944-4874
**Subject(s):** Telecommunications; Radio, Television, Cable, and Video

Circ: (Controlled)2,500

**Publication of the Astronomical Society of the Pacific** (879)
University of Chicago Press
c/o Anne P. Cowley
Department of Physics and Astronomy
Arizona State University
PO Box 871504
Tempe, AZ 85287-1504
Phone: (480)965-8011
Fax: (480)965-8011
**Subject(s):** Astronomy and Meteorology

Circ: ‡2,500

**San Francisco Medicine** (3209)
San Francisco Medical Society
1409 Satter St.
San Francisco, CA 94109
Phone: (415)561-0850
Fax: (415)561-0833
**Subject(s):** Medicine and Surgery

Circ: 2,500

**Violence and Victims** (32336)
Springer Publishing Co.
Dept. of Psychiatry and Behavioral Sciences
University of Washington School of Medicine
325 9th Ave.
Box 359896
Seattle, WA 98104
Phone: (206)731-3425
Fax: (206)731-8615
**Subject(s):** Psychology and Psychiatry; Law; Sociology

Circ: (Non-paid)100
(Paid)2,500

**Western Historical Quarterly** (30693)
Western History Association
Utah State University
0740 Old Main Hill
Logan, UT 84322-0740
Phone: (435)797-1301
Fax: (435)797-3899
**Subject(s):** History and Genealogy

Circ: (Paid)⊕2,500

**The Wyoming Lawyer** (33705)
Wyoming State Bar
PO Box 109
Cheyenne, WY 82003-0109
Phone: (307)632-9061
Fax: (307)632-3737
**Subject(s):** Law

Circ: (Paid)2,500

**ZYZZYVA** (3241)
PO Box 590069
San Francisco, CA 94159-0069
Phone: (415)752-4393
Fax: (415)752-4391
**Subject(s):** Literature and Literary Reviews

Circ: (Non-paid)‡1,000
(Paid)‡2,500

**The Griffith Observer** (2216)
Griffith Observatory
2800 E Observatory Rd.
Los Angeles, CA 90027
Phone: (323)664-1181
Fax: (323)663-4323
**Subject(s):** Astronomy and Meteorology

Circ: (Controlled)80
(Paid)2,400

**Midwifery Today** (25803)
PO Box 2672
Eugene, OR 97402-0223
Phone: (541)344-7438
Fax: (541)344-1422
**Subject(s):** Babies

Circ: (Combined)‡2,400

**Adolescence** (2998)
Libra Publishers Inc.
3089C Clairemont Dr., PMB 383
San Diego, CA 92117
Phone: (858)571-1414
Fax: (858)571-1414
**Subject(s):** Psychology and Psychiatry

Circ: (Non-paid)‡55
(Paid)‡2,300

**American Weather Observer** (827)
American Weather Observers Supplemental Observation Network
9595 E Thunderbird Rd., Apt. 1016
Scottsdale, AZ 85260-3742
**Subject(s):** Meteorology

Circ: 2,300

**FPC/Fire Protection Contractor** (1395)
Haden B. Brumbeloe and Associates Inc.
550 High St., Ste 220
Auburn, CA 95603
Phone: (530)823-0706
Fax: (530)823-6937
**Subject(s):** Safety; Fire Fighting

Circ: (Controlled)2,300

**Journal of Arizona History** (918)
Arizona Historical Society
949 E 2nd St.
Tucson, AZ 85719
Phone: (520)628-5774
Fax: (520)628-5695
**Subject(s):** History and Genealogy

Circ: (Controlled)2,300

**Journal of Psychology and Christianity** (1401)
Christian Association for Psychological Studies
Brian E. Eck
Azusa Pacific University
Dept. of Psychology
Azusa, CA 91702-7000
Phone: (626)815-6000
Fax: (626)812-3072

Subject(s): Religious Publications; Psychology and Psychiatry
Circ: (Non-paid)‡200
(Paid)‡2,300

**Juvenile and Family Court Journal** (18743)
National Council of Juvenile and Family Court Judges
PO Box 8970
Reno, NV 89507
Phone: (775)784-6012
Fax: (775)784-6628
Subject(s): Law
Circ: (Combined)⊕2,300

**Mountain Geologist** (4307)
Rocky Mountain Association of Geologists
820 16th St., No. 505
Denver, CO 80202-3218
Phone: (303)573-8621
Fax: (303)628-0546
Subject(s): Geology
Circ: (Paid)2,300

**Wenatchee Business Journal** (32482)
The Wenatchee Business Journal Inc.
304 S Mission St.
Wenatchee, WA 98801
Phone: (509)663-6730
Fax: (509)663-4399
Subject(s): Local, State, and Regional Publications; Business
Circ: (Paid)‡1,900
(Non-paid)‡2,300

**Natural Areas Journal** (25723)
Natural Areas Association
PO Box 1504
Bend, OR 97709
Phone: (541)317-0199
Fax: (541)317-0140
Subject(s): Ecology and Conservation; Natural Resources
Circ: (Combined)2,250

**Always Jukin' Magazine** (32245)
Always Jukin'
404 E Howell, Ste. 100
Seattle, WA 98122
Phone: (206)652-4005
Fax: (206)652-4007
Subject(s): Crafts, Models, Hobbies, and Contests
Circ: (Non-paid)250
(Paid)2,200

**Desert Call** (4255)
Spiritual Life Institute of America
PO Box 219
Crestone, CO 81131
Phone: (719)256-4778
Fax: (719)256-4719
Subject(s): Religious Publications
Circ: (Non-paid)200
(Paid)2,200

**Fair Dealer** (2892)
Western Fairs Association
1776 Tribute, Ste. 210
Sacramento, CA 95815-4495
Phone: (916)927-3100
Fax: (916)927-6397
Subject(s): Service Industries
Circ: (Controlled)2,200

**La Verne Magazine** (2048)
University of La Verne
1950 3rd St.
La Verne, CA 91750
Phone: (909)392-2712
Fax: (909)392-2706
Subject(s): Local, State, and Regional Publications
Circ: (Combined)2,200

**McIlvainea** (25837)
North American Mycological Association
6615 Tudor Ct.
Gladstone, OR 97027-1032
Phone: (503)657-7358
Subject(s): Botany
Circ: 2,200

**Veterinary Surgery** (1766)
Elsevier
C/o Dean's Office
Univ. of California
School of Veterinary Medicine
Davis, CA 95616-8734
Subject(s): Veterinary Medicine
Circ: ‡2,195

**Stanford Law Review** (3561)
Stanford Law School
559 Nathan Abbott Way
Crown Quadrangle
559 Nathan Abbott Way
Stanford, CA 94305-8610
Phone: (650)725-9301
Fax: (650)725-9786
Subject(s): Law
Circ: (Combined)2,167

**Bellingham Review** (32006)
Western Washington University
Mail Stop 9053
Bellingham, WA 98225
Phone: (360)650-4863
Subject(s): Literature
Circ: (Controlled)2,100

**California Garden** (3007)
San Diego Floral Association
1650 El Prado, Rm. 105
San Diego, CA 92101-1622
Phone: (619)232-5762
Fax: (619)232-5762
Subject(s): Florists and Floriculture; Horticulture
Circ: 2,100

**Conflict Resolution & Mediation** (3122)
Jossey-Bass Publishers
989 Market St.
San Francisco, CA 94103-1741
Phone: (415)433-1740
Fax: (415)951-8553
Subject(s): Psychology and Psychiatry
Circ: (Non-paid)‡98
(Paid)‡2,108

**Bison World** (4591)
National Bison Association
1400 W 122nd Ave., Ste. 106
Westminster, CO 80234-3440
Phone: (303)292-2833
Fax: (303)292-2564
Subject(s): Livestock
Circ: ‡2,000

**The Commentator** (2173)
Southwestern University
675 S Westmoreland
Los Angeles, CA 90005
Phone: (213)738-6700
Fax: (213)383-1688
Subject(s): College Publications
Circ: (Non-paid)2,000

**Elepaio** (7538)
Hawaii Audubon Society
850 Richards St., Ste. 505
Honolulu, HI 96813-4709
Phone: (808)528-1432
Fax: (808)537-5294
Subject(s): Ornithology and Oology; Zoology
Circ: ‡2,000

**Hawaii Beverage Guide** (7541)
PO Box 853
Honolulu, HI 96808
Subject(s): Beverages, Brewing, and Bottling
Circ: ‡2,000

**International Journal of Humanities and Peace** (670)
Vasant V. Merchant
1436 N Evergreen Dr.
Flagstaff, AZ 86001
Phone: (928)774-4793
Fax: (928)774-4793
Subject(s): Humanities; Peace
Circ: (Paid)2000

**Journal of Direct Instruction** (25800)
Association for Direct Instruction
PO Box 10252
Eugene, OR 97440
Phone: (541)485-1293
Fax: (541)683-7543

Subject(s): Education
Circ: 2,000

**Journal of the International Association of Jazz Record Collectors** (1803)
International Association of Jazz Record Collectors
5300 Bantry Pl.
El Dorado Hills, CA 95762
Phone: (916)941-8505
Fax: (916)941-8507
Subject(s): Music and Musical Instruments
Circ: ‡2,000

**The Journal of the Seattle-King County Dental Society** (32284)
Winslow Communications L.L.C.
317 S. Bennett St.
Seattle, WA 98108
Phone: (206)682-7813
Fax: (206)782-7778
Subject(s): Dentistry
Circ: ‡2,000

**Kosmon Voice 2** (698)
Kosmon Publishing Inc.
2330 Suffock Ave.
Kingman, AZ 86401-1204
Phone: (928)757-4150
Subject(s): New Age
Circ: (Paid)2,000

**Left Curve** (2594)
Left Curve Publications
410 Webster St.
Oakland, CA 94607
Phone: (510)763-7193
Subject(s): Alternative and Underground; Art; Social and Political Issues
Circ: (Paid)1850
2000

**Maledicta** (3495)
Maledicta Press
PO Box 14123
Santa Rosa, CA 95402-6123
Phone: (707)795-8178
Subject(s): Philology, Language, and Linguistics; Alternative and Underground
Circ: (Paid)2,000

**The Mirage** (664)
Cochise College
Hwy. 80 W
4190 W. State
Douglas, AZ 85607-6190
Phone: (520)364-7943
Fax: (520)417-4006
Subject(s): Art; Literature and Literary Reviews
Circ: (Non-paid)2,000

**Mystery Readers Journal** (1502)
Mystery Readers International
Box 8116
Berkeley, CA 94707-8116
Phone: (510)845-3600
Fax: (510)845-1975
Subject(s): Literature; Science Fiction, Mystery, Adventure, and Romance
Circ: (Controlled)2,000

**Perceptual and Motor Skills** (18209)
Ammons Scientific Ltd.
Box 9229
Missoula, MT 59807-9229
Phone: (406)728-1710
Subject(s): Psychology and Psychiatry
Circ: ‡2,000

**Psychological Perspectives** (2315)
C. G. Jung Institute of Los Angeles
10349 W. Pico Blvd.
Los Angeles, CA 90064
Phone: (310)556-1193
Fax: (310)556-2290
Subject(s): Psychology and Psychiatry
Circ: (Paid)2,000
(Non-paid)2,000

**Psychological Reports** (18210)
Ammons Scientific Ltd.
Box 9229
Missoula, MT 59807-9229
Phone: (406)728-1710

**Subject(s):** Psychology and Psychiatry
**Circ:** ‡2,000

**Pulse of the Planet  (25697)**
Orgone Biophysical Research Laboratory
Greensprings Center
PO Box 1148
Ashland, OR 97520
Phone: (541)552-0118
Fax: (541)552-0118
**Subject(s):** Ecology and Conservation
**Circ:** (Paid)2,000

**RAND Journal of Economics  (3482)**
RAND
1776 Main St.
PO Box 2138
Santa Monica, CA 90407-2138
Phone: (310)393-0411
Fax: (310)393-4818
**Subject(s):** Economics
**Circ:** (Non-paid)‡80
    (Paid)‡2,000

**Raven Chronicles  (32315)**
Richard Hugo House
1634 11th Ave.
Seattle, WA 98122-2419
**Subject(s):** Literature; Poetry
**Circ:** (Paid)2,000

**RMRScience  (4382)**
U.S. Forest Service
2150 Centre Ave. Bldg. A
Fort Collins, CO 80526
Phone: (970)498-1100
Fax: (970)295-5927
**Subject(s):** Forestry; Natural Resources
**Circ:** (Controlled)2,000

**School Science and Mathematics  (25770)**
School Science and Mathematics Association
Oregpon State Univesity
239 Weniger Hall
Corvallis, OR 97331-6508
Phone: (541)737-2545
Fax: (541)737-1817
**Subject(s):** Education; Mathematics; Science (General)
**Circ:** ‡2,000

**Seminars in Vascular Surgery  (4562)**
Elsevier
C/o Robert B. Rutherford, Editor
0146 Springbeauty Dr., Mesa Cortina
PO Box 23159
Silverthorne, CO 80498
**Subject(s):** Medicine and Surgery
**Circ:** ‡2,006

**Sierra Sacramento Valley Medicine  (2915)**
Media Marketing
5380 Elvas Ave., No. 100
Sacramento, CA 95819
Phone: (916)452-2671
Fax: (916)452-2690
**Subject(s):** Medicine and Surgery; Health and Healthcare
**Circ:** (Controlled)2,000

**Sonoran Quarterly  (773)**
Desert Botanical Garden
1201 N Galvin Pkwy.
Phoenix, AZ 85008
Phone: (480)941-1225
Fax: (480)481-8124
**Subject(s):** Botany
**Circ:** (Paid)2,000

**Technical Communication Quarterly  (30689)**
Lawrence Erlbaum Associates Inc.
Department of English
Utah State University
3200 Old Main Hill
Logan, UT 84322-3200
**Subject(s):** Book Trade and Author News; Education
**Circ:** (Combined)2,000

**Unsearchable Riches  (3449)**
Concordant Publishing Concern Inc.
15570 Knochaven Rd.
Santa Clarita, CA 91387
Phone: (661)252-2112
Fax: (661)252-2112
**Subject(s):** Religious Publications
**Circ:** ‡2,000

**Video Librarian  (32241)**
8705 Honeycomb Ct. NW
Seabeck, WA 98380
Phone: (360)830-9345
Fax: (360)830-9346
**Subject(s):** Library and Information Science; Education
**Circ:** (Non-paid)100
    (Paid)2,000

**Capitalism, Nature, Socialism  (3450)**
Taylor and Francis
c/o James O'Connor, Ph.D.
PO Box 8467
Santa Cruz, CA 95062
Phone: (831)459-4541
Fax: (831)459-3518
**Subject(s):** Politics
**Circ:** (Combined)‡1,983

**Western Journal of Nursing Research  (3892)**
Sage Publications Inc.
2455 Teller Rd.
Thousand Oaks, CA 91320
**Subject(s):** Nursing
**Circ:** (Non-paid)‡110
    (Paid)‡1,950

**New Directions for Higher Education  (1504)**
Jossey-Bass Publishers
c/o Martin Kramer, Editor-in-chief
2807 Shasta Road
Berkeley, CA 94708-2011
**Subject(s):** Education
**Circ:** (Non-paid)63
    (Paid)1,927

**Nineteenth-Century Literature  (2287)**
University of California Press/Journals
Nineteenth-Century Literature
Dept. of English
Univ. of California
405 Hilgard Ave.
Los Angeles, CA 90024-1530
**Subject(s):** Literature
**Circ:** ‡1,913

**Journal of Japanese Studies  (32281)**
University of Washington
Box 353650
Seattle, WA 98195-3650
Phone: (206)543-9302
Fax: (206)685-0668
**Subject(s):** Intercultural Interests
**Circ:** (Paid)1,900

**Journal of Phycology  (25768)**
Blackwell Publishing Ltd.
Oregon State University
104 Ocean Administration Bldg.
Corvallis, OR 97331
Phone: (541)737-9176
Fax: (541)737-8269
**Subject(s):** Botany
**Circ:** ‡1,900

**Language in Society  (922)**
Cambridge University Press
c/o Jane Hill, University of Arizona
Dept. of Anthropology, Rm. 310
Tucson, AZ
**Subject(s):** Philology, Language, and Linguistics; Sociology
**Circ:** 1,900

**Linguistics Analysis  (32473)**
Linguistic Analysis
PO Box 2418
Vashon Island, WA 98070
Phone: (206)567-4373
Fax: (206)567-5711
**Subject(s):** Philology, Language, and Linguistics
**Circ:** (Controlled)1,900

**Sociological Abstracts  (3059)**
Cambridge Scientific Abstracts
Sociological Abstracts
PO Box 22206
San Diego, CA 92192
Phone: (858)695-8803
Fax: (858)695-0416
**Subject(s):** Sociology; Indexes, Abstracts, Reports, Proceedings, and Bibliographies
**Circ:** ‡1,900

**Terrier Type  (2027)**
Dan Kiedrowski Co,
PO Drawer A
La Honda, CA 94020
Phone: (650)747-0549
Fax: (650)747-0549
**Subject(s):** Pets
**Circ:** (Combined)‡1,900

**Seminars in Reproductive Endocrinology  (25981)**
Thieme Medical Publishers Inc.
Leon Speroff, M.D.
Oregon Health Sciences University
Portland, OR 97201
Phone: (503)494-4469
Fax: (503)494-5083
**Subject(s):** Medicine and Surgery
**Circ:** (Non-paid)97
    (Paid)1,811

**American Journal of Bariatric Medicine  (4093)**
American Society of Bariatric Physicians
2821 S. Parker Rd., Ste. 625
Aurora, CO 80014
Phone: (303)770-2526
Fax: (303)779-4834
**Subject(s):** Medicine and Surgery; Health and Healthcare
**Circ:** (Controlled)1,800

**Astrophysical Journal Supplement Series  (903)**
The Astrophysical Journal
Steward Observatory
933 N Cherry Ave.
Tucson, AZ 85721
Phone: (520)621-5145
Fax: (520)621-5153
**Subject(s):** Astronomy and Meteorology
**Circ:** (Paid)‡1,800

**Cumulative Index to Nursing & Allied Health Literature (Print Index)  (1929)**
Cinahl Information Systems
1509 Wilson Ter.
Glendale, CA 91206
Phone: (818)409-8005
Fax: (818)546-5679
**Subject(s):** Indexes, Abstracts, Reports, Proceedings, and Bibliographies; Nursing
**Circ:** ‡1,800

**ECA Magazine  (1778)**
Engineering Contractors Association
8310 Florence Ave.
Downey, CA 90240
Phone: (562)861-0929
Fax: (562)923-6179
**Subject(s):** Construction, Contracting, Building, and Excavating; Engineering (Various branches)
**Circ:** (Non-paid)‡1,800

**Hawaii Medical Journal  (7548)**
1345 S Beretania St., No. 301
Honolulu, HI 96814-1821
**Subject(s):** Medicine and Surgery
**Circ:** ‡1800

**Hawaiian Journal of History  (7549)**
Hawaiian Historical Society
560 Kawaiahao St.
Honolulu, HI 96813-5023
Phone: (808)537-6271
Fax: (808)537-6271
**Subject(s):** History and Genealogy; Local, State, and Regional Publications
**Circ:** (Combined)⊕1,800

**Journal of Economic Entomology  (2828)**
Entomological Society of America
c/o John T. Trumble, University of California
Department of Entomology UCR
Riverside, CA 92521-0001
Phone: (909)787-5624
Fax: (909)787-5624
**Subject(s):** Entomology; Economics; General Agriculture
**Circ:** 1,800

**Journal of Pesticide Reform  (25801)**
Northwest Coalition for Alternatives to Pesticides
PO Box 1393
Eugene, OR 97440-1393
Phone: (541)344-5044
Fax: (541)344-6923
**Subject(s):** Environmental and Natural Resources Conservation; Social and Political Issues
**Circ:** 1,800

# Western States

**The Journal of Supply Chain Management  (872)**
Institute for Supply Management
PO BOX 22160
PO Box 22160
Tempe, AZ 85285
Phone: (480)752-6276
Fax: (480)752-7890
**Subject(s):** Purchasing
**Circ:** ‡1,800

**The Labrador Quarterly  (4602)**
Hoflin Publishing Inc.
4401 Zephyr St.
Wheat Ridge, CO 80033-3299
Phone: (303)420-2222
Fax: (303)422-7000
**Subject(s):** Dogs
**Circ:** (Non-paid)‡200
    (Paid)‡1,800

**Many Mountains Moving  (4126)**
420 22nd Street
Boulder, CO 80302
Phone: (303)545-9942
Fax: (303)444-6510
**Subject(s):** Intercultural Interests; Literature
**Circ:** (Non-paid)200
    (Paid)1,800

**Representations  (1515)**
University of California Press/Journals
2120 Berkeley Way
Berkeley, CA 94704-1012
Phone: (510)642-4247
Fax: (510)643-7127
**Subject(s):** State, Municipal, and County Administration
**Circ:** ‡1,800

**Transactional Analysis Journal  (2607)**
International Transactional Analysis Association Inc.
436 14th St., Ste. 1301
Oakland, CA 94612-2710
Phone: (510)625-7720
Fax: (510)625-7725
**Subject(s):** Psychology and Psychiatry
**Circ:** (Paid)1,800

**The Match!  (925)**
PO Box 3012
Tucson, AZ 85702
**Subject(s):** Alternative and Underground; Society
**Circ:** 1,750

**Colorado Beverage Analyst  (4207)**
Bell Publications
2403 Champa St.
Denver, CO 80205
Phone: (303)296-1600
Fax: (303)295-2159
**Subject(s):** Beverages, Brewing, and Bottling
**Circ:** (Paid)‡345
    (Controlled)‡1,743

**Sociological Perspectives  (3354)**
University of California Press
c/o Donald C. Barrett, Editor
California State Univ.
San Marcos, CA 92096-0001
Phone: (760)750-4117
**Subject(s):** Sociology
**Circ:** ‡1,736

**American Salers  (4534)**
American Salers Association
19590 E Main St., Ste. 202
Parker, CO 80138-7371
Phone: (303)770-9292
Fax: (303)770-9302
**Subject(s):** Livestock
**Circ:** (Paid)‡1,720

**China Report  (3629)**
Sage Publications Inc.
2455 Teller Rd.
Thousand Oaks, CA 91320
**Subject(s):** International Affairs
**Circ:** (Paid)1,700

**Journal of Special Education Technology  (18685)**
Boyd Printing Co.
Dept. of Special Education, UNLV
4505 Maryland Pkwy.
PO Box 453014
4505 Maryland Pkwy.
Las Vegas, NV 89154-3014
Phone: (702)895-1102
Fax: (702)895-2669
**Subject(s):** Education
**Circ:** (Paid)1,700

**Research on Social Work Practice  (3883)**
Sage Publications Inc.
2455 Teller Rd.
Thousand Oaks, CA 91320
**Subject(s):** Sociology
**Circ:** (Paid)‡1,700

**School Intervention Report  (32320)**
Safe Schools Coalition Inc.
10501 Meridian Ave. N.
Seattle, WA 98133
**Subject(s):** Education
**Circ:** (Non-paid)‡1,000
    (Paid)‡1,700

**Otology & Neurotology  (3556)**
Lippincott Williams & Wilkins
Robert K. Jackler
300 Pasteur Dr., Edwards Bldg. R135
Stanford, CA 94305-5328
Phone: (415)209-9738
Fax: (415)209-6719
**Subject(s):** Medicine and Surgery
**Circ:** (Paid)1,694

**French Historical Studies  (1761)**
Duke University Press
c/o Jo Burr Margadant and Ted W. Margadant
Department of History
University of California, Davis
One Shields Ave.
Davis, CA 95616-8611
Phone: (530)752-9142
Fax: (530)752-5301
**Subject(s):** History and Genealogy
**Circ:** (Paid)1,650

**Environment and Behavior  (913)**
Sage Publications Inc.
c/o Robert Bechtel, Editor, Environment and Behavior
Environmental Psychology Program
Univ. of Arizona
Tucson, AZ 85721
**Subject(s):** Psychology and Psychiatry; Architecture
**Circ:** (Non-paid)‡152
    (Paid)‡1,600

**Evaluation Review  (2200)**
Sage Publications Inc.
c/o Richard A. Berk, Editor
Department of Statistics
8130 Mathmatical Science Bldg., UCLA
Los Angeles, CA 90095-1554
**Subject(s):** Psychology and Psychiatry; Sociology
**Circ:** (Non-paid)‡208
    (Paid)‡1,600

**Law Enforcement Journal  (2630)**
The Law Enforcement Legal Reporter Inc.
PO Box 4608
Orange, CA 92863-4608
Phone: (714)637-7237
Fax: (714)637-7130
**Subject(s):** Police, Penology, and Penal Institutions
**Circ:** (Controlled)1,600

**Learning and Leading with Technology  (25802)**
ISTE (International Society for Technology in Education)
480 Charnelton St.
Eugene, OR 97401-2626
Phone: (541)302-3777
Fax: (541)302-3778
**Subject(s):** Computers; Education
**Circ:** (Paid)‡1,600
    (Free)‡1,600

**Medical Decision Making  (25961)**
Hanley & Belfus Inc.
3181 SW Sam Jackson Park Rd.
Mailcode: BICC
Portland, OR 97239
Phone: (503)494-6058

**Subject(s):** Medicine and Surgery
**Circ:** ‡1,600

**The Public Historian  (1513)**
University of California Press/Journals
2120 Berkeley Way
Berkeley, CA 94704-1012
Phone: (510)642-4247
Fax: (510)643-7127
**Subject(s):** History and Genealogy
**Circ:** 1,600

**Science, Technology & Human Values  (3888)**
Sage Publications Inc.
2455 Teller Rd.
Thousand Oaks, CA 91320
**Subject(s):** Science (General); Philosophy
**Circ:** (Paid)1,600

**Journal of World History  (7555)**
University of Hawaii Press
c/o Jerry H. Bentley, 2530 Dole St.
Dept. of History
Univ. of Hawaii
Honolulu, HI 96822
Phone: (808)956-8505
Fax: (808)956-9600
**Subject(s):** History and Genealogy
**Circ:** (Controlled)50
    (Paid)1,575

**Austin-Healey Magazine  (3584)**
Austin-Healey Club
1160-B La Rochelle Terr.
Sunnyvale, CA 94089
Phone: (408)541-9608
Fax: (408)541-9320
**Subject(s):** Automotive (Consumer)
**Circ:** (Non-paid)‡100
    (Paid)‡1,550

**Group & Organization Management  (3699)**
Sage Publications Inc.
2455 Teller Rd.
Thousand Oaks, CA 91320
**Subject(s):** Psychology and Psychiatry
**Circ:** (Non-paid)‡146
    (Paid)‡1,550

**Latin American Perspectives  (2833)**
Sage Publications Inc.
PO Box 5703
Riverside, CA 92517-5703
**Subject(s):** International Affairs; Hispanic Publications
**Circ:** (Non-paid)‡83
    (Paid)‡1,550

**The American Journal of Dermatopathology  (3105)**
Lippincott Williams & Wilkins
c/o Philip E. LeBoit
Univ. of California
1701 Divisadero St., Rm. 350
San Francisco, CA 94115-3011
**Subject(s):** Laboratory Research (Scientific and Medical)
**Circ:** (Paid)1,512

**Skull Base  (772)**
Thieme Medical Publishers Inc.
c/o Robert Spetzler, M.D.
Division of Neurosurgery
Barrow Neurosurgical Associates
Phoenix, AZ 85013
**Subject(s):** Medicine and Surgery
**Circ:** (Paid)‡1,517

**Amerasia Journal  (2127)**
UCLA Asian American Studies Center Publications
3230 Campbell Hall
Box 951546
Los Angeles, CA 90095-1546
Phone: (310)825-2974
Fax: (310)206-9844
**Subject(s):** Intercultural Interests
**Circ:** (Non-paid)45
    (Paid)1,500

**American Board of Neurological and Orthopedic Medicine and Surgery Journal**  (18678)
American Board of Neurological and Orthopaedic Medicine and Surgery
c/o Bartholomew A. Sinatra
522 Rossmore Dr.
Las Vegas, NV 89110-4123
**Subject(s):** Medicine and Surgery; Health and Healthcare
**Circ:** 1,500

**Anthropology and Education Quarterly**  (894)
American Anthropological Association
c/o Dr. Teresa McCarty, Editor
University of Arizona, 1430 E. 2nd St., PO Box 210069
Department of Language, Reading, and Culture
College of Education Bldg., Rm. 512
Tucson, AZ 85721-0069
Phone: (520)621-1311
Fax: (520)621-1853
**Subject(s):** Anthropology and Ethnology
**Circ:** ‡1,500

**Biodynamics**  (25861)
Biodynamic Farming & Gardening Association
25844 Butler Rd.
Junction City, OR 97448
Phone: (541)998-0105
Fax: (541)998-0106
**Subject(s):** Ecology and Conservation; Scientific Agricultural Publications
**Circ:** ‡1,500

**California Law Review**  (1454)
Joe Christensen Inc.
School of Law
592 Simon Hall, University of California
Berkeley, CA 94720
Phone: (510)642-7562
Fax: (510)642-3476
**Subject(s):** Law
**Circ:** ‡1,500

**Crime & Delinquency**  (2088)
Sage Publications Inc.
c/o Elizabeth Piper Deschenes, Editor-Elect
Department of Criminal Justice
California State University
1250 Bellflower Blvd.
Long Beach, CA 90840
**Subject(s):** Police, Penology, and Penal Institutions
**Circ:** (Paid)1,500

**Dialogue**  (26038)
Blindskills Inc.
PO Box 5181
Salem, OR 97304-0181
Phone: (503)581-4224
Fax: (503)581-0178
**Subject(s):** Blind and Visually Challenged
**Circ:** (Paid)‡1,500

**The Fourth R**  (3494)
Polebridge Press
PO Box 6144
Santa Rosa, CA 95406
Phone: (707)523-1323
Fax: (707)523-1350
**Subject(s):** Religious Publications
**Circ:** (Paid)1,500

**International Dredging Review**  (4380)
PO Box 1487
Fort Collins, CO 80522
Phone: (970)568-0833
Fax: (970)568-0834
**Subject(s):** Water Supply and Sewage Disposal
**Circ:** (Controlled)1,450
(Paid)1,500

**Journal of the Academy of Marketing Science**  (3743)
Sage Publications Inc.
2455 Teller Rd.
Thousand Oaks, CA 91320
**Subject(s):** Advertising and Marketing
**Circ:** ‡1,500

**Journal of Applied Behavioral Science**  (3748)
Sage Publications Inc.
2455 Teller Rd.
Thousand Oaks, CA 91320
**Subject(s):** Sociology
**Circ:** (Paid)1,500

**Journal of Cross-Cultural Psychology**  (3771)
Sage Publications Inc.
2455 Teller Rd.
Thousand Oaks, CA 91320
**Subject(s):** Psychology and Psychiatry
**Circ:** (Paid)‡1,500

**The Journal of Historical Review**  (2539)
Institute for Historical Review
PO Box 2739
Newport Beach, CA 92659
Phone: (949)631-1490
Fax: (949)631-0981
**Subject(s):** History and Genealogy
**Circ:** 1,500

**Journal of Humanistic Psychology**  (2239)
Sage Publications Inc.
c/o Thomas C. Greening, Ph.D., Editor
1314 Westwood Blvd.
Los Angeles, CA 90024
**Subject(s):** Psychology and Psychiatry
**Circ:** (Paid)‡1,500

**Korean Culture**  (2244)
Korean Cultural Center
5505 Wilshire Blvd.
Los Angeles, CA 90036
Phone: (323)936-7141
Fax: (323)936-5712
**Subject(s):** Intercultural Interests; Korean
**Circ:** (Non-paid)200
(Paid)1,500

**The Line Rider**  (7653)
Idaho Cattle Association
PO Box 15397
Boise, ID 83715
Phone: (208)343-1615
Fax: (208)344-6695
**Subject(s):** Livestock
**Circ:** ‡1,500

**Neural Computation**  (3040)
The MIT Press
c/o Dr. Terrence Sejnowski
The Salk Institute
San Diego, CA 92186-5800
Phone: (619)453-4100
Fax: (619)587-0417
**Subject(s):** Medicine and Surgery; Laboratory Research (Scientific and Medical)
**Circ:** ‡1,500
‡1,500

**The North American Technocrat**  (32095)
Technocracy Inc.
2475 Harksell Rd.
Ferndale, WA 98248
Phone: (360)366-1012
Fax: (360)366-1409
**Subject(s):** Political Science; Science (General); Economics; Social Sciences
**Circ:** 1,500

**Poetry USA**  (3190)
National Poetry Association Inc.
SOMAR
934 Brannan St., 2nd Fl.
San Francisco, CA 94103
Phone: (415)552-9261
Fax: (415)552-9271
**Subject(s):** Poetry
**Circ:** (Paid)1,500

**Voice of Washington Music Educators**  (32075)
Washington Music Educator's Association
PO Box 1117
Edmonds, WA 98020-1117
Phone: (425)771-7859
Fax: (425)776-1795
**Subject(s):** Education; Music and Musical Instruments
**Circ:** (Controlled)1,500

**Bonsai Journal**  (18172)
American Bonsai Society Inc.
PO Box 460328
Huson, MT 59846
Phone: (406)626-4176
Fax: (406)626-1971
**Subject(s):** Horticulture
**Circ:** (Paid)1,450

**Music Perception**  (1501)
University of California Press/Journals
2120 Berkeley Way
Berkeley, CA 94704-1012
Phone: (510)642-4247
Fax: (510)643-7127
**Subject(s):** Music and Musical Instruments
**Circ:** ‡1,450

**Pacific Historical Review**  (25971)
University of California Press/Journals
Pacific Historical Review
Portland State Univ.
487 Cramer Hall
Portland, OR 97207-0751
Phone: (503)725-8230
Fax: (503)725-8235
**Subject(s):** History and Genealogy
**Circ:** ‡1,448

**Cultural Anthropology**  (32262)
American Anthropological Association
c/o Ann Anagnost, Editor, Cultural Anthropology
Department of Anthropology Department of Anthropology
Box 353100, University of Washington
Seattle, WA 98195-3100
Phone: (206)543-7693
Fax: (206)543-3285
**Subject(s):** Anthropology and Ethnology
**Circ:** ‡1,400

**The Duckburg Times**  (2187)
The Duckburg News
3010 Wilshire Blvd., Ste. 362
Los Angeles, CA 90010-1146
Phone: (213)388-2364
**Subject(s):** Entertainment; Children's Interests; Youths' Interests
**Circ:** ‡1,400

**International Journal of Offshore and Polar Engineering**  (1741)
International Society of Offshore & Polar Engineers
PO Box 189
PO Box 189
Cupertino, CA 95015-0189
Phone: (650)254-1871
Fax: (650)254-2038
**Subject(s):** Engineering (Various branches)
**Circ:** (Combined)1400

**Journal of Film and Video**  (2238)
University of Illinois Press
3800 Barham Blvd., Ste. 305
Los Angeles, CA 90068
Phone: (323)851-6199
Fax: (323)851-6748
**Subject(s):** Radio, Television, Cable, and Video; Motion Pictures
**Circ:** 1,400

**Mexican Studies-Estudios Mexicanos**  (1500)
University of California Press/Journals
2120 Berkeley Way
Berkeley, CA 94704-1012
Phone: (510)642-4247
Fax: (510)643-7127
**Subject(s):** Ethnic and Minority Studies; Intercultural Interests; Humanities
**Circ:** (Paid)❑1,400

**Philosophy East & West**  (7569)
University of Hawaii Press
c/o Roger T. Ames
2530 Dole St.
Honolulu, HI 96822
Phone: (808)956-7288
Fax: (808)956-9228
**Subject(s):** Philosophy
**Circ:** (Controlled)‡50
(Paid)‡1,400

**Sports Medicine and Arthroscopy Review**  (3219)
Lippincott Williams & Wilkins
c/o W. Dilworth Cannon
Dept. of Orthopaedic Surgery, Univ. of California
1701 Divisadero St., No.240
San Francisco Medical Center
San Francisco, CA 94115-1351
**Subject(s):** Medicine and Surgery
**Circ:** 834
1,404

# Western States

**Journal of Psychology and Theology** (2046)
Rosemead School of Psychology and Theology
Biola University
13800 Biola Ave.
La Mirada, CA 90639-0001
Phone: (562)944-0351
Fax: (562)906-4547
**Subject(s):** Psychology and Psychiatry; Religious Publications; Philosophy; Humanities
Circ: ‡1,350

**Mexican Studies/Estudios Mexicanos** (2005)
University of California Press/Journals
University of California, Irvine
240 Krieger Hall
Irvine, CA 92697-3275
Phone: (949)824-6632
Fax: (949)824-2865
**Subject(s):** Ethnic and Minority Studies; International Affairs; Hispanic Publications; Spanish
Circ: 1,350

**Modern Language Quarterly** (32292)
Duke University Press
Department of English
University of Washington
PO Box 354330
Seattle, WA 98195-4330
Phone: (206)543-6827
Fax: (206)685-2673
**Subject(s):** Literature; Philology, Language, and Linguistics
Circ: (Non-paid)‡75
      (Paid)‡1,350

**Oregon Geology** (25967)
Department of Geology & Mineral Industries
800 NE Oregon St., Ste. 965
Portland, OR 97232
Phone: (503)731-4100
Fax: (503)731-4066
**Subject(s):** Geology
Circ: (Controlled)‡1,350

**Philosophy of the Social Sciences** (3869)
Sage Publications Inc.
2455 Teller Rd.
Thousand Oaks, CA 91320
**Subject(s):** Philosophy; Sociology
Circ: (Non-paid)‡114
      (Paid)‡1,350

**Alcoholism: Clinical and Experimental Research** (1813)
Lippincott Williams & Wilkins
c/o Ivan Diamond, M.D Editor
Ernest Gallo Clinic and Research Center
5858 Horton St., Suite 200
Emeryville, CA 94608-2007
**Subject(s):** Substance Abuse and Treatment
Circ: (Non-paid)‡408
      (Paid)‡1,333

**Cow Country** (33700)
Wyoming Stock Growers Association
113 E 20th St.
PO Box 206
Cheyenne, WY 82003
Phone: (307)638-3942
Fax: (307)634-1210
**Subject(s):** Livestock
Circ: (Non-paid)‡207
      (Paid)‡1,335

**19th-Century Music** (1507)
University of California Press/Journals
2120 Berkeley Way
Berkeley, CA 94704-1012
Phone: (510)642-4247
Fax: (510)643-7127
**Subject(s):** Music and Musical Instruments
Circ: 1,326

**Cardiology** (905)
S. Karger Publishers Inc.
c/o Janet S. Frank, Editorial Assistant
4214 North Rillito Creek Pl.
Tucson, AZ 85719
**Subject(s):** Medicine and Surgery
Circ: 1,300

**Colorado Review** (4376)
Colorado State University
Fort Collins, CO 80523
Phone: (970)491-5449
Fax: (970)491-0283

**Subject(s):** Literature; Poetry
Circ: (Paid)1,300

**Latin American Politics and Society** (4124)
School of International Studies
1800 30th St., Ste. 314
Boulder, CO 80301-1026
Phone: (303)444-6684
Fax: (303)444-0824
**Subject(s):** International Affairs; Political Science
Circ: (Controlled)202
      (Paid)1,300

**The Montana Business Quarterly** (18205)
Bureau of Business and Economic Research
Univ. of Montana
BBER-Univ. of Montana
32 Campus Dr. No. 6840
Missoula, MT 59812-6840
Phone: (406)243-5113
Fax: (406)243-2086
**Subject(s):** Economics; Local, State, and Regional Publications
Circ: (Non-paid)‡200
      (Paid)‡1,300

**New Directions for Mental Health Services** (3178)
Jossey-Bass Publishers
989 Market St.
San Francisco, CA 94103-1741
Phone: (415)433-1740
Fax: (415)951-8553
**Subject(s):** Psychology and Psychiatry
Circ: (Non-paid)70
      (Paid)1,303

**Pacific Northwest Quarterly** (32304)
University of Washington
Box 353587
Seattle, WA 98195-3587
Phone: (206)543-2992
**Subject(s):** History and Genealogy; Local, State, and Regional Publications
Circ: 1,300

**Ultrasound Quarterly** (2361)
Lippincott Williams & Wilkins
c/o Philip W. Ralls
PO Box 631, 1200 N. State St.
Keck School of Medicine,Univ. of Southern California
1000 Montauk Hwy.
Los Angeles, CA 90033
Phone: (323)226-7207
Fax: (323)226-7325
**Subject(s):** Laboratory Research (Scientific and Medical)
Circ: 1307

**Journal of Homosexuality** (3160)
The Haworth Press Inc.
Harrington Park Press
PO Box 411077
San Francisco, CA 94141-1077
Phone: (415)826-3052
**Subject(s):** Psychology and Psychiatry; Gay and Lesbian Interests
Circ: 1,298

**Educational and Psychological Measurement** (3667)
Sage Publications Inc.
2455 Teller Rd.
Thousand Oaks, CA 91320
**Subject(s):** Education; Psychology and Psychiatry
Circ: (Paid)‡1,250

**Northwest Review** (25806)
369 PLC
University of Oregon
Eugene, OR 97403
Phone: (541)346-3957
Fax: (541)346-1509
**Subject(s):** Literature; Literature and Literary Reviews
Circ: (Controlled)1,250

**ProTooner** (1746)
PO Box 2270
Daly City, CA 94017-2270
Phone: (650)755-4827
Fax: (650)755-4827
**Subject(s):** Comics and Comic Technique
Circ: (Paid)1,230

**Sexually Transmitted Diseases** (3212)
Lippincott Williams & Wilkins
Department of Lab Medicine
San Francisco General Hospital
Bldg. 30, Rm. 416
1001 Potrero Ave.
San Francisco, CA 94110
**Subject(s):** Medicine and Surgery; Physiology and Anatomy
Circ: 1,227

**American Indian Culture and Research Journal** (2128)
American Indian Studies Center Publications at UCLA
3220 Campbell Hall
Box 951548
Los Angeles, CA 90095-1548
Phone: (310)206-7508
Fax: (310)206-7060
**Subject(s):** Ethnic and Minority Studies
Circ: (Combined)1,200

**The Beethoven Journal** (3282)
American Beethoven Society
San Jose State University
1 Washington Sq.
San Jose, CA 95192-0171
Phone: (408)808-2058
Fax: (408)808-2060
**Subject(s):** Music and Musical Instruments
Circ: 1,200

**The Intermountain Retailer** (30770)
Utah Food Industry Association
1578 W 1700 S.
Ste 100
Salt Lake City, UT 84104
Phone: (801)973-9517
Fax: (801)972-8712
**Subject(s):** Food and Grocery Trade
Circ: ‡1,200

**Journal of Black Psychology** (3756)
Sage Publications Inc.
2455 Teller Rd.
Thousand Oaks, CA 91320
**Subject(s):** Black Publications; Psychology and Psychiatry
Circ: (Paid)1,200

**Journal of Mormon History** (30720)
Mormon History Association
581 South 630 E
Orem, UT 84097
Phone: (801)224-0241
Fax: (801)224-5684
**Subject(s):** Religious Publications; History and Genealogy
Circ: 1,200

**Meteoritics and Planetary Science** (7562)
Meteoritical Society
c/o Ed Scott
Hawaii Institute Geophysics & Planetary
University of Hawaii
Honolulu, HI 96822
Fax: (808)956-6322
**Subject(s):** Science (General); Astronomy and Meteorology
Circ: 1,200

**PARA DOXA** (32472)
Delta Productions
PO Box 2237
Vashon, WA 98070-2237
Phone: (206)567-4373
Fax: (206)567-5711
**Subject(s):** Literature and Literary Reviews; Science Fiction, Mystery, Adventure, and Romance
Circ: (Non-paid)500
      (Paid)1,200

**Processed World** (3191)
1095 Market St., No. 210
San Francisco, CA 94103
**Subject(s):** Commerce and Industry
Circ: (Non-paid)800
      (Paid)1,200

**Southern California Anthology** (2331)
University of Southern California
WPH 404
Los Angeles, CA 90089-4034
Phone: (213)740-3252
Fax: (213)740-5775
**Subject(s):** Literature
Circ: (Paid)1,200

**Southern California Quarterly** (2334)
Historical Society of Southern California
200 E Ave., 43
Los Angeles, CA 90031-1304
Phone: (323)222-0546
Fax: (323)222-0771
**Subject(s):** History and Genealogy; Local, State, and Regional Publications
**Circ:** (Paid)1,200

**Western American Literature** (30692)
Western Literature Association
3200 Old Main Hill
Utah State University
Logan, UT 84322-3200
Phone: (435)797-1603
Fax: (435)797-4099
**Subject(s):** Literature
**Circ:** (Non-paid)‡50
  (Paid)‡1,200

**Western States Jewish History** (4071)
Western States Jewish History Association
22711 Cass Ave.
Woodland Hills, CA 91364
Phone: (818)225-9631
Fax: (818)225-9631
**Circ:** (Paid)1,200

**The Clinical Journal of Pain** (32256)
Lippincott Williams & Wilkins
c/o Dennis C. Turk
Univ. of Washington
Seattle, WA 98195
**Subject(s):** Laboratory Research (Scientific and Medical)
**Circ:** 1,140

**Christian Monthly** (26085)
Apostolic Lutheran Church of America
PO Box 220
Yamhill, OR 97148
Phone: (503)662-4465
Fax: (503)662-4465
**Subject(s):** Religious Publications
**Circ:** (Non-paid)‡500
  ‡1,100

**Christianity and Literature** (2420)
Pepperdine University
Humanities Division
Malibu, CA 90263
Phone: (310)506-7232
Fax: (310)506-4206
**Subject(s):** Literature; Religious Publications
**Circ:** (Paid)1,100

**English Language Notes** (4116)
University of Colorado
CB 226
Boulder, CO 80309
Phone: (303)492-7176
Fax: (303)492-3521
**Subject(s):** Literature
**Circ:** (Non-paid)‡150
  (Paid)‡1,100

**Family Therapy** (3014)
Libra Publishers Inc.
3089C Clairemont Dr., PMB 383
San Diego, CA 92117
Phone: (858)571-1414
Fax: (858)571-1414
**Subject(s):** Psychology and Psychiatry
**Circ:** (Non-paid)‡50
  (Paid)‡1,100

**Hawaii Dental Journal** (7545)
Hawaii Medical Journal
1345 S Beretania St., No. 301
Honolulu, HI 96814-1821
**Subject(s):** Dentistry
**Circ:** (Paid)1,100

**The Journal of Borderland Research** (1833)
Borderland Sciences Research Foundation
PO Box 6250
Eureka, CA 95502
Phone: (707)445-2247
Fax: (707)445-1401
**Subject(s):** Science (General)
**Circ:** (Non-paid)‡100
  (Paid)‡1,100

**Journal of Medical Entomology** (1762)
Entomological Society of America
c/o John D. Edman
Center for Vector-Borne Disease Research
School of Veterinary Medicine, One Shields Ave.
University of California
Davis, CA 95616
Phone: (530)754-6087
Fax: (530)752-3349
**Subject(s):** Entomology
**Circ:** 1,100

**Journal of Neuroimaging** (3808)
Sage Publications Inc.
2455 Teller Rd.
Thousand Oaks, CA 91320
**Subject(s):** Medicine and Surgery
**Circ:** (Paid)1,100

**Journal of Research in Crime and Delinquency** (3818)
Sage Publications Inc.
2455 Teller Rd.
Thousand Oaks, CA 91320
**Subject(s):** Police, Penology, and Penal Institutions; Psychology and Psychiatry
**Circ:** (Paid)‡1,100

**Legal Reference Services Quarterly** (923)
The Haworth Press Inc.
James E. Rogers College of Law
University of Arizona
Tucson, AZ 85721
Phone: (520)621-5477
**Subject(s):** Library and Information Science; Law
**Circ:** 1,101

**Neurohabilitation and Neural Repair** (3857)
Sage Publications Inc.
2455 Teller Rd.
Thousand Oaks, CA 91320
**Subject(s):** Medicine and Surgery; Physiology and Anatomy
**Circ:** (Non-paid)50
  (Paid)1,100

**Qualitative Health Research** (3882)
Sage Publications Inc.
2455 Teller Rd.
Thousand Oaks, CA 91320
**Subject(s):** Health and Healthcare
**Circ:** (Non-paid)118
  (Paid)1,100

**Swedish American Genealogist** (32137)
Swenson Swedish Immigration Research Center,
c/o Harold L. Bern
2341 E Lynnwood Dr.
Longview, WA 98632
**Subject(s):** History and Genealogy; Ethnic and Minority Studies
**Circ:** (Controlled)1,100

**Western Birds** (2648)
Western Field Ornithologists
1359 Solano Dr.
Pacifica, CA 94044-4258
Phone: (650)359-2068
**Subject(s):** Ornithology and Oology
**Circ:** (Paid)1,100

**Pulse** (2735)
Southern California Veterinary Medical Association
8338 Rosemead Blvd.
Pico Rivera, CA 90660
Phone: (562)948-4979
Fax: (562)942-2977
**Subject(s):** Veterinary Medicine
**Circ:** (Non-paid)‡78
  (Paid)‡1,060

**Rhetorica** (1516)
University of California Press/Journals
2120 Berkeley Way
Berkeley, CA 94704-1012
Phone: (510)642-4247
Fax: (510)643-7127
**Subject(s):** Philosophy
**Circ:** 1,062

**Agricultural History** (1442)
University of California Press/Journals
2120 Berkeley Way
Berkeley, CA 94704-1012
Phone: (510)642-4247
Fax: (510)643-7127
**Subject(s):** General Agriculture; History and Genealogy
**Circ:** ‡1,050

**Contexts** (1463)
University of California Press/Journals
2120 Berkeley Way
Berkeley, CA 94704-1012
Phone: (510)642-4247
Fax: (510)643-7127
**Subject(s):** Sociology; Social Sciences
**Circ:** (Paid)⊐1,040

**The Dutch Harbor Fisherman** (537)
Alaska Newspapers Inc.
PO Box 920472
Dutch Harbor, AK 99692
Phone: (907)581-2092
Fax: (907)581-2090
**Subject(s):** Paid Community Newspapers
**Circ:** (Paid)⊕1,002
  (Controlled)1,046

**Southern California Law Review** (2333)
University of Southern California
University Park Campus
Los Angeles, CA 90089
Phone: (213)740-2311
Fax: (213)740-5502
**Subject(s):** Law
**Circ:** (Non-paid)‡100
  (Paid)‡1,033

**Western Humanities Review** (30785)
University of Utah
255 S Central Campus Dr., Rm. 3500
Salt Lake City, UT 84112-0494
Phone: (801)581-6070
Fax: (801)585-5167
**Subject(s):** Humanities
**Circ:** ‡1,033

**Women and Health** (1767)
The Haworth Press Inc.
c/o Ellen B. Gold, Professor and Chief
Division of Epidemiology
Dept. of Public Health Sciences
University of California
Davis, CA 95616-8638
**Subject(s):** Health and Healthcare; Women's Interests
**Circ:** (Controlled)‡1,010

**Akita World** (4595)
Hoflin Publishing Inc.
4401 Zephyr St.
Wheat Ridge, CO 80033-3299
Phone: (303)420-2222
Fax: (303)422-7000
**Subject(s):** Dogs
**Circ:** (Non-paid)100
  (Paid)1,000

**Albanian Catholic Bulletin** (3104)
Albanian Catholic Institute
University of San Francisco
650 Parker Ave.
San Francisco, CA 94118
Phone: (415)422-6966
Fax: (415)387-1867
**Subject(s):** Religious Publications
**Circ:** 1,000

**ALCOR** (826)
Alcor Life Extension Foundation
7895 E Acoma Dr., Ste. 110
Scottsdale, AZ 85260-6916
Phone: (480)905-1906
Fax: (480)922-9027
**Subject(s):** Alternative and Underground; Health
**Circ:** 1,000

**American Journal of Forensic Psychiatry** (2532)
American College of Forensic Psychiatry
Box 5870, Balboa Island
Newport Beach, CA 92662
Phone: (949)673-7773
Fax: (949)673-7710
**Subject(s):** Psychology and Psychiatry
**Circ:** ‡1,000

**And The Music Plays On** (32436)
Del Shannon Appreciation Society
PO Box 44201
Tacoma, WA 98444-0201
Phone: (253)537-1248

**Subject(s):** Music and Musical Instruments
**Circ:** 1,000

**ASA Bulletin** (1712)
Avicultural Society of America
c/o Joe Krader
2910 Alps Rd.
Corona, CA 92881-3996
**Subject(s):** Zoology
**Circ:** 1,000

**CutBank** (18200)
University of Montana
32 Campus Dr.
Missoula, MT 59812
Phone: (406)243-0211
**Subject(s):** Literature; Poetry
**Circ:** (Controlled)1000

**Desert Plants** (911)
2120 E Allen Rd.
Tucson, AZ 85719
Phone: (520)318-7046
Fax: (520)318-7272
**Subject(s):** Botany
**Circ:** (Combined)1,000

**Five Fingers Review** (1475)
Five Fingers Press
1341 7th St.
Berkeley, CA 94710
Phone: (510)524-0852
Fax: (510)524-0852
**Subject(s):** Literature; Literature and Literary Reviews; Poetry
**Circ:** (Paid)1,000

**Harmony** (3146)
Sea Fog Press
447 20th Ave.
San Francisco, CA 94121
Phone: (415)221-8527
**Subject(s):** Philanthropy and Humanitarianism; Sociology
**Circ:** (Non-paid)‡100
(Paid)‡1,000

**Hastings Communications and Entertainment Law Journal (COMM/ENT)** (3147)
University of California, Hastings College of the Law
200 McAllister St.
San Francisco, CA 94102-4978
Phone: (415)565-4600
**Subject(s):** Law
**Circ:** (Non-paid)150
(Paid)1,000

**Healthcare Advertising Review** (4173)
The Business Word
11211 E., Arapahoe Rd., Ste. 101
Centennial, CO 80112-3851
Phone: (303)290-8500
Fax: (303)290-9025
**Subject(s):** Advertising and Marketing; Hospitals and Healthcare Institutions
**Circ:** (Paid)‡1,000

**Home Health Care Management and Practice** (3710)
Sage Publications Inc.
2455 Teller Rd.
Thousand Oaks, CA 91320
**Subject(s):** Nursing
**Circ:** 1,000

**H2SO4** (3150)
PO Box 423354
San Francisco, CA 94142
Phone: (415)431-2135
Fax: (415)431-2135
**Subject(s):** Literature; Alternative and Underground
**Circ:** (Combined)‡1000

**IIE Transactions** (1482)
c/o. Candace A. Yano, University of California at Berkeley
Dept. of Industrial Engineering and Operations Research
4135 Etcheverry Hall
Berkeley, CA 94720-1777
Phone: (510)642-4992
Fax: (510)642-1403
**Subject(s):** Engineering (Various branches)
**Circ:** (Paid)1,000

**The Institutional Real Estate Letter** (4022)
Institutional Real Estate Inc.
1475 N. Broadway, Ste. 300
Walnut Creek, CA 94596
Phone: (925)933-4040
Fax: (925)934-4099
**Subject(s):** Real Estate
**Circ:** (Paid)500
(Non-paid)1,000

**Journal of Craniomandibular Orthopedics** (32278)
International College of Cranio-Mandibular Orthopedics
c/o Hallie Truswell
619 N 35th St., Ste. 307
Seattle, WA 98103
Phone: (206)633-4355
Fax: (206)633-4352
**Subject(s):** Medicine and Surgery; Health and Healthcare
**Circ:** 1,000

**Journal of Energy and Development** (4122)
International Research Center for Energy & Economic Development
850 Willowbrook Rd.
Boulder, CO 80302
Phone: (303)442-4014
Fax: (303)442-5042
**Subject(s):** Ecology and Conservation; Power and Power Plants
**Circ:** (Combined)1,000

**Journal of Experiential Education** (4123)
Association for Experiential Education
2305 Canyon Blvd., Ste. 100
Boulder, CO 80302-5651
Phone: (303)440-8844
Fax: (303)440-9581
**Subject(s):** Education
**Circ:** 1,000

**Journal of Interdisciplinary Studies** (2714)
Institute for Interdisciplinary Research
1065 Pine Bluff Dr.
Pasadena, CA 91107-1751
Phone: (626)351-0419
**Subject(s):** Humanities; Social Sciences
**Circ:** (Non-paid)1,000

**Journal of Intravenous Therapy** (2240)
PO Box 67159
Los Angeles, CA 90067-7159
Phone: (310)475-5339
Fax: (310)475-5339
**Subject(s):** Nursing; Drugs and Pharmaceuticals
**Circ:** ‡1,000

**Journal of Management Education** (3803)
Sage Publications Inc.
2455 Teller Rd.
Thousand Oaks, CA 91320
**Subject(s):** Education; Management and Administration
**Circ:** (Paid)1,000

**Journal of the Southwest** (921)
University of Arizona
1052 N Highland Ave.
Tucson, AZ 85721
Phone: (520)621-2484
Fax: (520)621-9922
**Subject(s):** History and Genealogy
**Circ:** (Paid)1,000

**Manoa** (7559)
University of Hawaii Press
Dept. of English
Univ. of Hawaii
1733 Donaghho Rd.
Honolulu, HI 96822
Phone: (808)956-3070
Fax: (808)956-3083
**Subject(s):** Poetry; Literature and Literary Reviews
**Circ:** (Controlled)65
(Paid)1,000

**The Montana Food Distributor** (18160)
Montana Food Distributors Association
25 Neill Ave., Ste. 101
PO Box 5775
Helena, MT 59604
Phone: (406)449-6394
Fax: (406)449-0647
**Subject(s):** Food and Grocery Trade
**Circ:** (Non-paid)‡100
(Paid)‡1,000

**Montana Journalism Review** (18206)
The University of Montana
Missoula, MT 59812
Phone: (406)243-4001
**Subject(s):** Journalism and Publishing
**Circ:** (Non-paid)1,000

**One to One** (1880)
Cree Yadio Services
Box 9787
Fresno, CA 93794
Phone: (559)448-0700
Fax: (559)448-0761
**Subject(s):** Radio, Television, Cable, and Video
**Circ:** (Paid)1,000

**The Posthorn** (4131)
Scandinavian Collectors Club
c/o Paul Albright
4615 Hampshire St.
Boulder, CO 80301-4210
Phone: (303)530-0498
**Subject(s):** Crafts, Models, Hobbies, and Contests
**Circ:** 1,000

**Rocky Mountain Review of Language and Literature** (32217)
Rocky Mountain Modern Language Association
Secretariat at Washington State University
PO Box 642610
Pullman, WA 99164-2610
Phone: (509)335-4198
Fax: (509)335-3708
**Subject(s):** Philology, Language, and Linguistics; Literature; Local, State, and Regional Publications
**Circ:** (Controlled)1,000

**Scandinavian Studies** (30746)
Society for the Advancement of Scandinavian Study
Brigham Young University
3003 JKHB
P.O. Box 26118
Provo, UT 84602-6118
Phone: (801)378-4636
Fax: (801)422-0307
**Subject(s):** Philology, Language, and Linguistics
**Circ:** ‡1,000

**Schnauzer Shorts** (2026)
Dan Kiedrowski Co.
PO Drawer A
La Honda, CA 94020
Phone: (650)747-0549
Fax: (650)747-0549
**Subject(s):** Pets
**Circ:** (Combined)⊕1,000

**Sexuality & Culture** (2098)
Transaction Publishers
Dept. of Sociology
California State Univ.
Long Beach, CA 90840
Phone: (562)985-4602
Fax: (562)985-4602
**Subject(s):** Social Sciences
**Circ:** 1,000

**Sonoma Medicine** (3500)
Sonoma County Medical Association
3033 Cleveland Ave.
Santa Rosa, CA 95403
Phone: (707)525-4265
Fax: (707)525-4328
**Subject(s):** Medicine and Surgery
**Circ:** (Combined)1,000

**Weber Studies** (30715)
Weber State University
1214 University Cir.
Ogden, UT 84408-1214
**Subject(s):** Literature; Poetry; Humanities
**Circ:** (Combined)1,000

**Western Journal of Applied Forestry** (3341)
Society of American Foresters
California Polytechnic State University
Department of Natural Resources Management
San Luis Obispo, CA 93407
Phone: (805)756-1402
Fax: (805)756-2021
**Subject(s):** Forestry
**Circ:** 1,000

**Wingspan** (33703)
Laramie County Community College
1400 E College Dr.
Cheyenne, WY 82007
Phone: (307)778-1304
Fax: (307)778-1177
**Subject(s):** College Publications
**Circ:** (Non-paid)‡1,000

**Cambridge Quarterly of Healthcare Ethics** (1458)
Cambridge University Press
c/o Dr. Thomasine Kushner, University Hall
University of California, Berkeley
Berkeley, CA 94720
**Subject(s):** Health and Healthcare
**Circ:** 950

**SAFE Journal** (25778)
SAFE Association
300 North Mill St., Unit B
Creswell, OR 97426
Phone: (541)895-3012
Fax: (541)895-3014
**Subject(s):** Safety
**Circ:** (Combined)950

**Applied Immunohistochemistry & Molecular Morphology** (2133)
Lippincott Williams & Wilkins
c/o Clive R. Taylor,Dept. of Pathology
2011 Zonal Avenue, HMR 204
The Keck School of Medicine
Univ. of Southern California
Los Angeles, CA 90089
**Subject(s):** Medicine and Surgery
**Circ:** 933

**American Indian Quarterly** (667)
University of Nebraska Press
Northern Arizona University
Dept. of AIS
PO Box 15020
Flagstaff, AZ 86011-5020
Phone: (520)523-5159
Fax: (520)523-1080
**Subject(s):** Native American Interests; Literature and Literary Reviews
**Circ:** 900

**Anales de la Literatura Espanola Contemporanea** (4105)
Society of Spanish and Spanish-American Studies
Department of Spanish & Portuguese, University of Colorado
134 McKenna Languages Bldg., 278 UCB
Boulder, CO 80309-0278
Phone: (303)492-5900
Fax: (303)492-3699
**Subject(s):** Literature; Intercultural Interests; Spanish
**Circ:** 900

**Comparative Political Studies (CPS)** (32260)
Sage Publications Inc.
c/o James A. Caporaso, Editor
Dept. of Political Science
353530, Univ. of Washington
Seattle, WA 98195
**Subject(s):** Politics
**Circ:** (Paid)‡900

**Journal of Linguistic Anthropology (JLA)** (3422)
American Anthropological Association
c/o Mary Bucholtz, Department of Linguistics
University of California
3607 S. Hall
Santa Barbara, CA 93106-3100
Phone: (805)893-5415
Fax: (805)893-7769
**Subject(s):** Anthropology and Ethnology
**Circ:** (Paid)900

**Linguistics and Language Behavior Abstracts** (3033)
Cambridge Scientific Abstracts
Sociological Abstracts
PO Box 22206
San Diego, CA 92192
Phone: (858)695-8803
Fax: (858)695-0416
**Subject(s):** Philology, Language, and Linguistics; Indexes, Abstracts, Reports, Proceedings, and Bibliographies
**Circ:** ‡900

**Multicultural Education** (3173)
Caddo Gap Press
3145 Geary Blvd., No. 275
San Francisco, CA 94118
Phone: (415)666-3012
Fax: (415)666-3552
**Subject(s):** Education
**Circ:** (Paid)900

**Natural Business** (4154)
Natural Business Communications
360 Interlocken Blvd., Ste. 350
Broomfield, CO 80021
Phone: (303)222-8283
Fax: (303)222-8250
**Subject(s):** Food and Grocery Trade; Health and Healthcare; Cosmetics and Toiletries
**Circ:** (Paid)900

**Office Manager** (25807)
Oregon Law Review
School of Law
1221 University of Oregon
Eugene, OR 97403-1221
Phone: (541)346-3844
Fax: (541)346-1564
**Subject(s):** Law
**Circ:** ‡900

**Rhetoric Society Quarterly** (30745)
Rhetoric Society of America
c/o English Department
Brigham Young University
3146 JKHB
Box 26280
Provo, UT 84602-6280
**Subject(s):** Literature; Communications
**Circ:** (Paid)900

**San Diego Law Review** (3048)
San Diego Law Review Association
5998 University of San Diego, School of Law
5998 Alcala Park
San Diego, CA 92110
Phone: (619)260-4531
Fax: (619)260-7497
**Subject(s):** Law
**Circ:** 900

**Teacher Education Quarterly** (3225)
Caddo Gap Press
3145 Geary Blvd., No. 275
San Francisco, CA 94118
Phone: (415)666-3012
Fax: (415)666-3552
**Subject(s):** Education
**Circ:** 900

**Review of Public Personnel Administration** (3884)
Sage Publications Inc.
2455 Teller Rd.
Thousand Oaks, CA 91320
**Subject(s):** Employment and Human Resources
**Circ:** (Non-paid)60
 (Paid)863

**Urban Education** (3890)
Corwin Press
2455 Teller Rd.
Thousand Oaks, CA 91320
Phone: (805)499-4224
Fax: (805)499-5323
**Subject(s):** Education
**Circ:** (Non-paid)‡111
 (Paid)‡862

**Masonry Society Journal** (4127)
The Masonry Society
3970 Broadway, Ste. 201-D
Boulder, CO 80304-1135
Phone: (303)939-9700
Fax: (303)541-9215
**Subject(s):** Construction, Contracting, Building, and Excavating; Architecture
**Circ:** (Controlled)850

**The Nugget and CGS News** (2597)
California Genealogical Society
1611 Telegraph Ave., Ste. 100
Oakland, CA 94612-2154
Phone: (510)663-1358
Fax: (510)663-1358
**Subject(s):** History and Genealogy
**Circ:** 850

**Southwestern Lore** (4321)
Colorado Archaeological Society Inc.
2077 S. Vrain St.
Denver, CO 80219
Phone: (303)866-4671
Fax: (303)866-2711
**Subject(s):** Archaeology
**Circ:** ‡850

**Environmental Law (Portland)** (25954)
Northwestern School of Law
10015 SW Terwilliger Blvd.
Portland, OR 97219
Phone: (503)768-6700
Fax: (503)768-6671
**Subject(s):** Law; Ecology and Conservation; Natural Resources
**Circ:** (Combined)849

**The American Journal of Drug and Alcohol Abuse** (1992)
Marcel Dekker Inc.
c/o Edward Kaufman, Clinical Professor
Department of Psychiatry & Human Behavior
College of Medicine
University of California
Irvine, CA
**Subject(s):** Psychology and Psychiatry; Substance Abuse and Treatment
**Circ:** 825

**New Directions for Community Colleges** (2283)
Jossey-Bass Publishers
c/o Arthur M. Cohen, Editor-in-Chief
Univ. of California, Los Angeles
3051 Moore Hall, PO Box 951521
Los Angeles, CA 90095-1521
**Subject(s):** Education
**Circ:** (Non-paid)178
 (Paid)827

**Women & Therapy** (3314)
The Haworth Press Inc.
c/o Ellyn Kaschak
San Jose State University
San Jose, CA 95192
Phone: (408)924-5630
**Subject(s):** Psychology and Psychiatry; Women's Interests
**Circ:** (Paid)823

**American Journal of Forensic Psychology** (2533)
American College of Forensic Psychiatry
Box 5870, Balboa Island
Newport Beach, CA 92662
Phone: (949)673-7773
Fax: (949)673-7710
**Subject(s):** Psychology and Psychiatry
**Circ:** ‡800

**Annual of Champions** (2547)
Rhodesian Ridgeback Club of the U.S.
PO Box 27
Nipomo, CA 93444
**Subject(s):** Dogs; Pets
**Circ:** 800

**Binocular Vision & Strabismus Quarterly** (4352)
Binoculus Publishing
740 Piney Acres Cir.
PO Box 3727
Dillon, CO 80435-3727
Phone: (970)262-0753
Fax: (970)262-0753
**Subject(s):** Medicine and Surgery; Ophthalmology, Optometry, and Optics
**Circ:** (Combined)800

**Criminal Justice Abstracts** (3644)
Sage Publications Inc.
2455 Teller Rd.
Thousand Oaks, CA 91320
**Subject(s):** Law; Sociology; Indexes, Abstracts, Reports, Proceedings, and Bibliographies
**Circ:** ‡800

**Developmental Neuroscience** (2182)
S. Karger Publishers Inc.
C/o Prof. A.T. Campagnoni
Mental Retardation Research Center
UCLA School of Medicine
760 Westwood Plaza
Los Angeles, CA 90024
**Subject(s):** Medicine and Surgery
**Circ:** 800

**Educational Foundations (3133)**
Caddo Gap Press
3145 Geary Blvd., No. 275
San Francisco, CA 94118
Phone: (415)666-3012
Fax: (415)666-3552
**Subject(s):** Education
**Circ:** 800

**Feminist Bookstore News (3138)**
PO Box 882554
San Francisco, CA 94188
Phone: (415)642-9993
Fax: (415)642-9995
**Subject(s):** Women's Interests; Book Trade and Author News
**Circ:** (Non-paid)‡50
     (Paid)‡800

**Forum (3493)**
Polebridge Press
PO Box 6144
Santa Rosa, CA 95406
Phone: (707)523-1323
Fax: (707)523-1350
**Subject(s):** Religious Publications
**Circ:** (Paid)805

**Journal of Psychoactive Drugs (3163)**
Haight-Ashbury Publications
612 Clayton St.
San Francisco, CA 94117-2958
Phone: (415)565-1904
Fax: (415)864-6162
**Subject(s):** Drugs and Pharmaceuticals
**Circ:** ‡800

**Journal of Regression Therapy (2830)**
International Association for Regression Research and Therapies
PO Box 20151
Riverside, CA 92516
Phone: (909)784-1570
Fax: (909)784-8440
**Subject(s):** Psychology and Psychiatry
**Circ:** 800

**Politics & Society (3874)**
Sage Publications Inc.
2455 Teller Rd.
Thousand Oaks, CA 91320
**Subject(s):** Social Sciences; Sociology; Politics; Economics
**Circ:** (Paid)800

**Summer Academe (3220)**
Caddo Gap Press
3145 Geary Blvd., No. 275
San Francisco, CA 94118
Phone: (415)666-3012
Fax: (415)666-3552
**Subject(s):** Education
**Circ:** (Paid)800

**Theosophy (2352)**
The Theosophy Co.
245 W. 33rd St.
Los Angeles, CA 90007
Phone: (213)748-7244
Fax: (213)748-0634
**Subject(s):** Philosophy
**Circ:** (Paid)800

**World Scanner Report (660)**
Commtronics Engineering
10718 Manzanita Trl.
Dewey, AZ 86327-5304
**Subject(s):** Electrical Engineering; Radio, Television, Cable, and Video
**Circ:** (Non-paid)50
     (Paid)800

**Arizona Archaeologist (895)**
Arizona Archaeological Society Inc.
Arizona State Museum
University of Arizona
Tucson, AZ 85721-0026
Phone: (520)621-2970
**Subject(s):** Archaeology
**Circ:** (Controlled)780

**The Radiologist (2602)**
Lippincott Williams & Wilkins
C/o Ronald L. Eisenberg, M.D., Editor-in-Chief
Highland General Hospital
Department of Radiology
1411 E. 31st St.
Oakland, CA 94602
Phone: (510)437-4205
Fax: (510)437-5176
**Subject(s):** Radiology, Ultrasound, and Nuclear Medicine
**Circ:** 767

**Technical Services Quarterly (4447)**
The Haworth Press Inc.
James A. Michener Library
University of Northern Colorado
Greeley, CO 80639
Phone: (970)351-2601
**Subject(s):** Library and Information Science
**Circ:** 768

**Alaska Fishery Research Bulletin (569)**
Alaska Department of Fish and Game
Publications Section,
PO Box 25526
Juneau, AK 99802-5526
Phone: (907)465-4210
Fax: (907)465-2604
**Subject(s):** Fish and Commercial Fisheries
**Circ:** (Controlled)750

**Comitatus (2172)**
University of California at Los Angeles
302 Royce Hall
Los Angeles, CA 90095-1485
Phone: (310)825-1537
Fax: (310)825-0655
**Subject(s):** History and Genealogy
**Circ:** (Paid)750

**Hawaii Orchid Journal (7636)**
Honolulu Orchid Society/Pacific Orchid Society
c/o B. Brunson
86-560 W Kolia Pl.
Waianae, HI 96792
**Subject(s):** Botany; Socialized Farming; Horticulture
**Circ:** ‡750

**Powder Diffraction (3303)**
JCPDS-International Centre for Diffraction Data
c/o Ting C. Huang, Editor-in-Chief
6584 Radko Dr.
San Jose, CA 95119-1924
**Subject(s):** Commerce and Industry
**Circ:** (Non-paid)57
     (Paid)750

**Urban History (2363)**
Cambridge University Press
c/o Philip J.Ethington
Univ. of Southern California
Dept. of History, 3520 Trousdale Pkwy, SOS 254
Los Angeles, CA 90089-0034
**Subject(s):** History and Genealogy
**Circ:** 750

**Activities, Adaptation & Aging (4490)**
The Haworth Press Inc.
8714 W. Swarthmore Pl.
Littleton, CO 80123
Phone: (303)933-1269
**Subject(s):** Hospitals and Healthcare Institutions
**Circ:** 737

**Entertainment Law Reporter; Movies Music Broadcasting Theater Publishing Multimedia Sports (3477)**
Entertainment Law Reporter Publishing Co.
2118 Wilshire Blvd., No. 311
Santa Monica, CA 90403-5784
Phone: (310)829-9335
**Subject(s):** Radio, Television, Cable, and Video
**Circ:** (Paid)730

**Journal of Ethnic & Cultural Diversity in Social Work (2237)**
The Haworth Press Inc.
c/o Diane de Anda, Dept. of Social Welfare
UCLA School of Public Policy & Social Research
405 N. Hilgard Ave.
PO Box 951656
Los Angeles, CA 90095-1656
Phone: (310)397-4613
**Subject(s):** Ethnic and Minority Studies; Sociology; Social Programs
**Circ:** 732

**AFFILIA: Journal of Women and Social Work (3605)**
Sage Publications Inc.
2455 Teller Rd.
Thousand Oaks, CA 91320
**Subject(s):** Women's Interests; Sociology; Social Programs
**Circ:** (Paid)‡700

**Behavior Modification (25833)**
Sage Publications Inc.
Michel Hersen, Ph.D., ABPP, Behavior Modification
School of Professional Psychology
Pacific Univ.
2004 Pacific Ave.
Forest Grove, OR 97116-2328
**Subject(s):** Psychology and Psychiatry
**Circ:** (Paid)700

**Clinical Nursing Research (3632)**
Sage Publications Inc.
2455 Teller Rd.
Thousand Oaks, CA 91320
**Subject(s):** Nursing
**Circ:** (Paid)‡700

**Denver Quarterly (4284)**
University of Denver
Dept. of English
2000 E. Asbury
Denver, CO 80208
Phone: (303)871-2892
Fax: (303)871-2853
**Subject(s):** Literature
**Circ:** (Non-paid)‡200
     (Paid)‡700

**Journal of Contemporary Ethnography (JCE) (3769)**
Sage Publications Inc.
2455 Teller Rd.
Thousand Oaks, CA 91320
**Subject(s):** Anthropology and Ethnology
**Circ:** (Paid)‡700

**The Journal of Early Adolescence (3774)**
Sage Publications Inc.
2455 Teller Rd.
Thousand Oaks, CA 91320
**Subject(s):** Psychology and Psychiatry; Pediatrics
**Circ:** (Paid)700

**MCOA Journal (4208)**
Mastiff Club of America
PO Box 14067
Colorado Springs, CO 80914-0067
Phone: (719)683-7101
**Subject(s):** Dogs; Pets
**Circ:** 700

**Modern China (2275)**
Sage Publications Inc.
Modern China, Department of History
University of California
Los Angeles, CA 90095-1473
**Subject(s):** International Affairs
**Circ:** (Paid)‡700

**New Mexico Beverage Analyst (4310)**
Bell Publications
2403 Champa St.
Denver, CO 80205
Phone: (303)296-1600
Fax: (303)295-2159
**Subject(s):** Beverages, Brewing, and Bottling
**Circ:** (Non-paid)‡154
     (Paid)‡704

**Planetarian (2308)**
International Planetarium Society
2800 E Observatory Rd.
Los Angeles, CA 90027
Phone: (319)466-3192
Fax: (319)351-6772
**Subject(s):** Astronomy and Meteorology
**Circ:** (Paid)700

**The Siberian Quarterly (4608)**
Hoflin Publishing Inc.
4401 Zephyr St.
Wheat Ridge, CO 80033-3299
Phone: (303)420-2222
Fax: (303)422-7000
**Subject(s):** Dogs
**Circ:** (Paid)700

**Tundra (32240)**
22230 NE 28th Pl.
Sammamish, WA 98074-6408
Phone: (425)836-8875
**Subject(s):** Poetry; Literature

Circ: (Combined)700

**Northwest Science (32046)**
Washington State University Press
c/o Suzanne Schwab, Editor
Dept. of Biology
Eastern Washington Univ.
Cheney, WA 99004
**Subject(s):** Science (General)

Circ: (Non-paid)‡70
      (Paid)‡687

**Pacific Science (7566)**
University of Hawaii Press
c/o Curtis C. Daehler, Department of Botany
St. John 406
Honolulu, HI 96822
Phone: (808)956-3930
Fax: (808)956-3923
**Subject(s):** Biology; Physics

Circ: (Controlled)‡30
      (Paid)‡680

**positions (32308)**
Duke University Press
University of Washington
PO Box 353650
Jackson School of International Studies
Lewis Annex No. 2
Seattle, WA 98195-3650
Phone: (206)616-1566
Fax: (206)616-2427
**Subject(s):** Intercultural Interests

Circ: (Combined)660

**Chinese Language Teachers Association Journal (1946)**
Chinese Language Teachers Association
391-C Cannon Green Dr.
Goleta, CA 93117
Phone: (805)968-4422
**Subject(s):** Education; Ethnic and Minority Studies; Literature

Circ: 650

**Journal of Parametrics (651)**
International Society of Parametric Analysts
PO Box 3185
Chandler, AZ 85244
Phone: (480)917-4747
Fax: (480)792-6930
**Subject(s):** Mathematics

Circ: 650

**Rays from the Rose Cross (2613)**
Rosicrucian Fellowship
2222 Mission Ave
PO Box 713
Oceanside, CA 92054-2399
Phone: (760)757-6600
Fax: (760)721-3806
**Subject(s):** Religious Publications; New Age

Circ: (Combined)‡650

**UAS Explorations (572)**
c/o Art Petersen, Editor
University of Alaska SE
11120 Glacier Hwy.
Juneau, AK 99801-8671
Phone: (907)465-6528
Fax: (907)465-6543
**Subject(s):** Literature; Poetry

Circ: 650

**Ancestors West (1945)**
Santa Barbara County Genealogical Society
Box 1303
Goleta, CA 93116
Phone: (805)884-9909
**Subject(s):** History and Genealogy

Circ: (Combined)640

**The Veliger (3430)**
California Malacozoological Society Inc.
Santa Barbara Museum Of Natural History
2559 Puesta Del Sol Rd.
Santa Barbara, CA 93105
Phone: (805)682-4711
Fax: (805)963-9679

**Subject(s):** Natural History and Nature Study

Circ: (Non-paid)‡10
      (Paid)‡640

**AERO Sun-Times (18154)**
432 N Last Chance Gulch St.
Helena, MT 59601-5014
Phone: (406)443-7272
Fax: (406)442-9120
**Subject(s):** General Agriculture; Ecology and Conservation

Circ: (Controlled)50
      (Paid)630

**Public Library Quarterly (657)**
The Haworth Press Inc.
488 Mill Dr., Second Flr.
Cottonwood, AZ 86326-5340
Phone: (928)639-2798
Fax: (928)639-4352
**Subject(s):** Library and Information Science

Circ: 630

**Communications in Partial Differential Equations (3552)**
Marcel Dekker Inc.
c/o R. Mazzeo
Department of Mathematics
Stanford University
Stanford, CA 94305
**Subject(s):** Mathematics

Circ: 625

**SNEWS (25869)**
12119 Lupine Ln.
Klamath Falls, OR 97603-9637
Phone: (541)882-5196
**Subject(s):** Plumbing and Heating

Circ: (Paid)625

**Aztlan (2139)**
UCLA Chicano Studies Research Center Press
193 Haines Hall
Los Angeles, CA 90095-1544
Phone: (310)825-2642
Fax: (310)206-1784
**Subject(s):** Ethnic and Minority Studies

Circ: (Paid)‡600

**The Boston Quarterly (4596)**
Hoflin Publishing Inc.
4401 Zephyr St.
Wheat Ridge, CO 80033-3299
Phone: (303)420-2222
Fax: (303)422-7000
**Subject(s):** Dogs

Circ: (Paid)600

**China Review International (7533)**
University of Hawaii Press
c/o Daniel Cole, Center for Chinese Studies
University of Hawaii
1890 East-West Rd., Moore Hall 417
Honolulu, HI 96822
Phone: (808)956-8891
Fax: (808)956-2682
**Subject(s):** Literature; Chinese

Circ: (Controlled)45
      (Paid)600

**Communication Abstracts (3633)**
Sage Publications Inc.
2455 Teller Rd.
Thousand Oaks, CA 91320
**Subject(s):** Communications; Indexes, Abstracts, Reports, Proceedings, and Bibliographies

Circ: (Paid)600

**Denver University Law Review (4285)**
Denver University College of Law
University of Denver College of Law
7039 E. 18th Ave. Ste. P212
Denver, CO 80208
Phone: (303)871-6140
Fax: (303)871-6847
**Subject(s):** Law

Circ: ‡600

**The German Shepherd Quarterly (4599)**
Hoflin Publishing Inc.
4401 Zephyr St.
Wheat Ridge, CO 80033-3299
Phone: (303)420-2222
Fax: (303)422-7000

**Subject(s):** Dogs

Circ: (Paid)‡600

**Index to Foreign Legal Periodicals (1486)**
University of California Press/Journals
The Law Library
Boalt Hall School of Law
Univ. of California
Berkeley, CA 94720
**Subject(s):** Law

Circ: 600

**The Irish Wolfhound Quarterly (4601)**
Hoflin Publishing Inc.
4401 Zephyr St.
Wheat Ridge, CO 80033-3299
Phone: (303)420-2222
Fax: (303)422-7000
**Subject(s):** Dogs

Circ: (Paid)‡600

**Jewish Social Studies (3553)**
Indiana University Press
c/o Aron Rodrigue,Editor, Jewish Studies Program
Bldg. 240, Rm 103
Stanford University
Stanford, CA 94305-2190
**Subject(s):** History and Genealogy; Jewish Publications

Circ: 600

**Journal of Adolescent Research (3744)**
Sage Publications Inc.
2455 Teller Rd.
Thousand Oaks, CA 91320
**Subject(s):** Health and Healthcare; Psychology and Psychiatry

Circ: (Paid)‡600

**Journal of Applied Business Research (4494)**
Western Academic Press
PO Box 620760
Littleton, CO 80162
Phone: (303)904-4750
Fax: (303)978-0413
**Subject(s):** Business

Circ: (Controlled)‡50
      (Paid)‡600

**Journal of French Language Studies (3420)**
Cambridge University Press
c/o Prof. William J. Ashby
Department of French and Italian
University of California
Santa Barbara, CA 93106-4140
**Subject(s):** French; Philology, Language, and Linguistics

Circ: 600

**Journal of Social Behavior and Personality (2557)**
Select Press
40 Philip Terrace
Novato, CA 94945
Phone: (415)209-9838
**Subject(s):** Psychology and Psychiatry; Sociology

Circ: (Paid)‡600

**Journal of Sport & Social Issues (3827)**
Sage Publications Inc.
2455 Teller Rd.
Thousand Oaks, CA 91320
**Subject(s):** (General Sports); Sociology

Circ: (Paid)600

**Simulation & Gaming (3889)**
Sage Publications Inc.
2455 Teller Rd.
Thousand Oaks, CA 91320
**Subject(s):** Computers; Mathematics

Circ: (Paid)600

**Classical Antiquity (1461)**
University of California Press/Journals
Univ. of California
Dept. of Classics
7303 Dwinelle Hall, No. 2520
Berkeley, CA 94720-2520
**Subject(s):** History and Genealogy; Archaeology; Literature; Philosophy; Anthropology and Ethnology

Circ: 592

## Western States

**Berkeley Journal of Employment and Labor Law** (1449)
University of California Press/Journals
2120 Berkeley Way
Berkeley, CA 94704-1012
Phone: (510)642-4247
Fax: (510)643-7127
**Subject(s):** Law
**Circ:** 582

**ESQ** (32213)
Washington State University
Pullman, WA 99164-5020
Phone: (509)335-4816
Fax: (509)335-2582
**Subject(s):** Literature and Literary Reviews
**Circ:** (Non-paid)‡43
(Paid)‡588

**Minerals and Metallurgical Processing** (4499)
Society for Mining, Metallurgy, and Exploration Inc.
8307 Shaffer Pky.
PO Box 277002
Littleton, CO 80127-4102
Phone: (303)973-9550
Fax: (303)973-3845
**Subject(s):** Mining and Minerals
**Circ:** ‡587

**Society & Natural Resources** (30688)
Taylor & Francis
Institute for Social Science Research on Natural Resources,
Utah State University
0730 Old Main Hill
Logan, UT 84322-0730
Phone: (435)797-1241
Fax: (435)797-1240
**Subject(s):** Ecology and Conservation; Forestry; (Hunting, Fishing, and Game Management)
**Circ:** (Paid)‡576

**The Contemporary Pacific** (7535)
University of Hawaii Press
1890 East-West Road, 215 Moore Hall
Center for Pacific Island Studies
University of Hawaii at Manoa
Honolulu, HI 96822
Phone: (808)956-7700
Fax: (808)956-7053
**Subject(s):** Intercultural Interests
**Circ:** (Controlled)15
(Paid)560

**Historical Studies in the Physical and Biological Sciences** (1480)
University of California Press/Journals
Univ. of California
Office for History of Science and Technology
543 Stephens Hall, No. 2350
Berkeley, CA 94720-2350
**Subject(s):** Science (General); History and Genealogy; Biology
**Circ:** 566

**Asian Perspectives** (7529)
University of Hawaii Press
c/o Miriam T. Stark, Dept. of Anthropology
2424 Maile Way, 346 Saunders Bldg.
University of Hawaii at Manoa
Honolulu, HI 96822
Phone: (808)956-7552
Fax: (808)956-9541
**Subject(s):** Archaeology
**Circ:** (Controlled)25
(Paid)550

**Journal of Carbohydrate Chemistry** (18202)
Marcel Dekker Inc.
Shafizadeh Rocky Mountain Center
University of Montana
Missoula, MT 59812
**Subject(s):** Chemistry, Chemicals, and Chemical Engineering
**Circ:** 550

**Journal of Employee Ownership Law and Finance** (2593)
National Center for Employee Ownership
1736 Franklin St., 8th Fl.
Oakland, CA 94612
Phone: (510)208-1300
Fax: (510)272-9510
**Subject(s):** Labor; Business
**Circ:** (Combined)550

**Pearl** (2096)
Pearl Editions
3030 E Second St.
Long Beach, CA 90803
Phone: (562)434-4523
Fax: (562)434-4523
**Subject(s):** Poetry; Literature and Literary Reviews; Literature
**Circ:** (Combined)550

**Clinical Gerontologist** (2112)
The Haworth Press Inc.
Stanford University School of Medicine
PO Box 3926
Los Altos, CA 94024-0926
Phone: (650)400-8171
**Subject(s):** Gerontology
**Circ:** (Paid)540

**Computers in the Schools** (18740)
The Haworth Press Inc.
Dept. of Educational Counseling and Educational Psychology
College of Education
University of Nevada-Reno
Reno, NV 89557
Phone: (775)784-6327
Fax: (775)784-6298
**Subject(s):** Computers
**Circ:** (Paid)542

**Journal of Materials Engineering and Performance** (2241)
ASM International
Loyola Marymount University
1 LMU Dr.
Los Angeles, CA 90045-2659
Phone: (310)338-2700
Fax: (310)338-5896
**Subject(s):** Metal, Metallurgy, and Metal Trade; Engineering (Various branches)
**Circ:** (Non-paid)⊕141
(Paid)⊕**541**

**Alaska History** (495)
Alaska Historical Society
PO Box 100299
Anchorage, AK 99510-0299
Phone: (907)276-1596
Fax: (907)276-1596
**Subject(s):** History and Genealogy; Local, State, and Regional Publications
**Circ:** (Paid)500

**Bamboo Ridge** (7530)
Bamboo Ridge Press
PO Box 61781
Honolulu, HI 96839-1781
Phone: (808)626-1481
Fax: (808)626-1481
**Subject(s):** Literature and Literary Reviews
**Circ:** ‡500

**Cross-Cultural Research** (3648)
Sage Publications Inc.
2455 Teller Rd.
Thousand Oaks, CA 91320
**Subject(s):** Anthropology and Ethnology; Social Sciences
**Circ:** (Paid)‡500

**Hispanic Journal of Behavioral Sciences** (3707)
Sage Publications Inc.
2455 Teller Rd.
Thousand Oaks, CA 91320
**Subject(s):** Hispanic Publications; Psychology and Psychiatry
**Circ:** (Paid)500

**Human Resources Abstracts** (3714)
Sage Publications Inc.
2455 Teller Rd.
Thousand Oaks, CA 91320
**Subject(s):** Employment and Human Resources; Indexes, Abstracts, Reports, Proceedings, and Bibliographies
**Circ:** (Paid)‡500

**Journal of Business and Technical Communication** (3758)
Sage Publications Inc.
2455 Teller Rd.
Thousand Oaks, CA 91320
**Subject(s):** Communications
**Circ:** (Paid)500

**Journal of Communication and Religion** (30712)
Religious Communication Association
1605 University Cir.
Weber State University
Ogden, UT 84408
Phone: (801)626-7455
Fax: (801)626-7975
**Subject(s):** Theology; Religious Publications; Communications
**Circ:** 500

**Journal of Family Nursing** (3784)
Sage Publications Inc.
2455 Teller Rd.
Thousand Oaks, CA 91320
**Subject(s):** Nursing
**Circ:** (Paid)500

**Journal of the Idaho Academy of Science** (7774)
Idaho Academy of Science
909 Lucille Ave.
Pocatello, ID 83201-2542
Phone: (208)234-7001
**Subject(s):** Science (General)
**Circ:** (Paid)500

**Journal of Planning Literature** (3814)
Sage Publications Inc.
2455 Teller Rd.
Thousand Oaks, CA 91320
**Subject(s):** Indexes, Abstracts, Reports, Proceedings, and Bibliographies; State, Municipal, and County Administration
**Circ:** (Paid)‡500

**Journal of Pyrotechnics** (4609)
Journal of Pyrotechnics Inc.
1775 Blair Rd.
Whitewater, CO 81527-9553
Phone: (970)245-0692
Fax: (970)245-0692
**Subject(s):** Science (General)
**Circ:** (Combined)500

**Making Scents** (766)
International Aromatherapy and Herb Association
c/o Jeffrey Schiller
3541 W Acapulco Ln.
Phoenix, AZ 85053-4625
Phone: (602)938-4439
**Subject(s):** Alternative and Underground; Health
**Circ:** 500

**Mormon Historical Studies** (30679)
433 E 300 S
Hyrum, UT 84319
Phone: (435)245-3507
**Subject(s):** Religious Publications
**Circ:** (Non-paid)‡15
(Paid)‡500

**Nurse Author and Editor** (1932)
Cinahl Information Systems
1509 Wilson Ter.
Glendale, CA 91206
Phone: (818)409-8005
Fax: (818)546-5679
**Subject(s):** Nursing
**Circ:** (Paid)‡500

**Pangolin Papers** (32171)
Turtle Press
Box 241
Nordland, WA 98358
Phone: (360)385-3626
**Subject(s):** Literature; Literature and Literary Reviews
**Circ:** (Paid)500

**Poe Studies/Dark Romanticism** (32216)
Washington State University
Pullman, WA 99164-5020
Phone: (509)335-4816
Fax: (509)335-2582
**Subject(s):** Literature
**Circ:** (Combined)500

**Red Wheelbarrow** (1743)
De Anza College
21250 Stevens Creek Blvd.
Cupertino, CA 95014
Phone: (408)864-5678
Fax: (408)864-5533
**Subject(s):** Literature
**Circ:** 500

**A Shepherd in Arcadia** (834)
Universal Life Trust
2765 N Scottsdale Rd., Ste. 104 B
Scottsdale, AZ 85257
Phone: (602)990-7061
Fax: (602)990-8237
Subject(s): Religious Publications
Circ: 500

**Studies in Comparative International Development** (1520)
Transaction Publishers
Dept. of Political Science
210 Barrows Hall
Univ. of California
Berkeley, CA 94720-1950
Phone: (510)642-9515
Fax: (510)642-9515
Subject(s): Politics; International Affairs
Circ: (Paid)‡500

**Women's Studies** (1669)
Taylor & Francis
Department of English
Claremont Graduate University
Blaisdell House
143 E. Tenth St.
Claremont, CA 91711
Phone: (909)607-7938
Fax: (909)607-7938
Subject(s): Women's Interests; History and Genealogy; Literature; Art and Art History; Poetry
Circ: (Paid)500

**Blue Unicorn** (2020)
Blue Unicorn Inc.
22 Avon Rd.
Kensington, CA 94707
Phone: (510)526-8439
Subject(s): Literature; Poetry
Circ: (Combined)475

**Almanac** (2572)
Society for Pacific Coast Native Iris
4333 Oak Hill Rd.
Oakland, CA 94605
Subject(s): Horticulture; Botany; Clubs and Societies
Circ: (Paid)450

**Bellowing Ark** (32378)
Bellowing Ark Press
PO Box 55564
Shoreline, WA 98155
Phone: (206)440-0791
Subject(s): Literature and Literary Reviews
Circ: (Non-paid)‡100
 (Paid)‡450

**Biography** (7531)
University of Hawaii Press
University of Hawaii
Honolulu, HI 96822
Phone: (808)956-3774
Fax: (808)956-3774
Subject(s): Literature
Circ: (Controlled)‡50
 (Paid)‡450

**Contributions** (1759)
Water Resources Center
Centers for Water & Wildland Resources
University of California
1 Shields Ave.
Davis, CA 95616
Subject(s): Water Supply and Sewage Disposal; Ecology and Conservation
Circ: (Non-paid)450

**Historic Kern** (1407)
Kern County Historical Society
PO Box 141
Bakersfield, CA 93302
Phone: (661)322-4962
Subject(s): History and Genealogy; Local, State, and Regional Publications
Circ: (Controlled)450

**Fiber and Integrated Optics** (1613)
Taylor & Francis
c/o Henri Hodara, L-3 PHOTONICS
5957 Landau Court
Carlsbad, CA 92008
Phone: (760)431-6800
Subject(s): Electronics Engineering; Ophthalmology, Optometry, and Optics
Circ: ‡443

**The Four Seasons** (1476)
Regional Parks Botanic Garden
Tilden Regional Park
Berkeley, CA 94708-2396
Phone: (510)841-8732
Fax: (510)848-6025
Subject(s): Botany; Natural History and Nature Study; Ecology and Conservation
Circ: (Combined)431

**Pancreas** (2297)
Lippincott Williams & Wilkins
c/o Vay Liang W. Go
900 Veteran Av.
Los Angeles, CA 90095
Subject(s): Laboratory Research (Scientific and Medical)
Circ: 414

**Rogue Digger** (25941)
Rogue Valley Genealogical Society Inc.
95 Houston Rd.
PO Box 1468
Phoenix, OR 97535-1468
Phone: (541)512-2340
Subject(s): History and Genealogy
Circ: (Paid)413

**Advances in Astronautical Sciences** (2999)
Univelt Inc.
PO Box 28130
San Diego, CA 92198-0130
Phone: (760)746-4005
Fax: (760)746-3139
Subject(s): Astronautics
Circ: 400

**American Academy of Gnathologic Orthopedics—Journal** (4016)
American Academy of Gnathologic Orthopedics
2651 Oak Grove Rd.
Walnut Creek, CA 94598
Fax: (925)676-7678
Subject(s): Dentistry; Health and Healthcare; Medicine and Surgery
Circ: 400

**American Music Research Center Journal** (4103)
University of Colorado at Boulder
288 UCB
Boulder, CO 80309
Phone: (303)735-3645
Fax: (303)492-5619
Subject(s): Music and Musical Instruments
Circ: (Combined)400

**Journal of the American Society of Church Growth** (2713)
American Society for Church Growth
Center for Lifelong Learning
135 N Oakland Ave.
Pasadena, CA 91182
Phone: (626)584-5290
Fax: (626)584-5313
Subject(s): Religious Publications
Circ: 400

**Journal of the Los Angeles International Fern Society** (2715)
Los Angeles International Fern Society
1404 La Loma Rd.
Pasadena, CA 91105
Phone: (626)441-3148
Subject(s): Horticulture; Home and Garden
Circ: (Combined)400

**Journal of Thought** (3164)
Caddo Gap Press
3145 Geary Blvd., No. 275
San Francisco, CA 94118
Phone: (415)666-3012
Fax: (415)666-3552
Subject(s): Education
Circ: ‡400

**The Malamute Quarterly** (4603)
Hoflin Publishing Inc.
4401 Zephyr St.
Wheat Ridge, CO 80033-3299
Phone: (303)420-2222
Fax: (303)422-7000
Subject(s): Dogs
Circ: (Paid)‡400

**Nocturnal Lyric** (25707)
PO Box 542
Astoria, OR 97103
Phone: (503)325-2340
Subject(s): Poetry; Literature and Literary Reviews; Alternative and Underground
Circ: (Paid)400

**Oceanic Linguistics** (7563)
University of Hawaii Press
c/o Byron W. Bender, Dept. of Linguistics
1890 East-West Rd.
Univ. of Hawaii
Honolulu, HI 96822
Phone: (808)956-8374
Fax: (808)956-9166
Subject(s): Intercultural Interests; Philology, Language, and Linguistics
Circ: (Controlled)30
 (Paid)400

**Rapa Nui Journal** (2413)
Easter Island Foundation
PO Box 6774
Los Osos, CA 93412-6774
Phone: (805)528-8558
Fax: (805)534-9301
Subject(s): Anthropology and Ethnology; Archaeology
Circ: 400

**The Rhodesian Ridgeback Quarterly** (4605)
Hoflin Publishing Inc.
4401 Zephyr St.
Wheat Ridge, CO 80033-3299
Phone: (303)420-2222
Fax: (303)422-7000
Subject(s): Dogs
Circ: (Paid)400

**The Samoyed Quarterly** (4607)
Hoflin Publishing Inc.
4401 Zephyr St.
Wheat Ridge, CO 80033-3299
Phone: (303)420-2222
Fax: (303)422-7000
Subject(s): Dogs
Circ: (Paid)400

**Shemp!** (7609)
Larry Yoshida
593 Waikala St.
Kahului, HI 96732-1736
Phone: (808)877-5198
Subject(s): Entertainment
Circ: (Combined)400

**Studies in American Political Development** (2344)
Cambridge University Press
Political Science Dept.
Univ. of California
405 Hilgard Ave.
Los Angeles, CA 90024-1472
Subject(s): Political Science
Circ: 400

**Wyoming Archeologist** (33686)
Wyoming Archeological Society Inc.
1617 Westridge Ter.
Casper, WY 82604-3305
Phone: (307)268-2212
Fax: (307)268-2224
Subject(s): Archaeology
Circ: (Combined)400

**Western Lumber Facts** (25988)
Western Wood Products Association
522 SW 5th Ave., Ste. 500
Portland, OR 97204-2122
Phone: (503)224-3930
Fax: (503)224-3934
Subject(s): Forestry; Statistics
Circ: 380

**Golden Gate University Law Review** (3143)
Golden Gate University School of Law
536 Mission St.
San Francisco, CA 94105
Phone: (415)442-6680
Fax: (415)442-6609
Subject(s): Law
Circ: (Paid)375

Circulation: ★ = ABC; △ = BPA; ♦ = CAC; ● = CCAB; □ = VAC; ⊖ = P.O. Statement; ‡ = Publisher's Report; Boldface figures = sworn; Light figures = estimated.

# Western States

**Behavioral & Social Sciences Librarian  (3003)**
The Haworth Press Inc.
c/o Mark Stover, San Diego State Univ.
5500 Campanile Dr.
San Diego, CA 92182-8050
Phone: (619)594-2131
**Subject(s):** Library and Information Science

Circ: 367

**Arizona Quarterly  (900)**
University of Arizona
1731 E. 2nd St.
Tucson, AZ 85705-0014
**Subject(s):** Literature; Humanities

Circ: (Non-paid)‡300
    (Paid)‡350

**Early China  (1467)**
Institute of East Asian Studies
2223 Fulton St., 6th Fl.
Berkeley, CA 94720-2318
Phone: (510)643-2809
Fax: (510)643-7062
**Subject(s):** History and Genealogy; Intercultural Interests

Circ: (Controlled)350

**Hubbub  (25958)**
5344 SE 38th St.
Portland, OR 97202
Phone: (503)775-0370
**Subject(s):** Literature; Poetry

Circ: (Combined)350

**Northwest Anthropological Research Notes  (7751)**
625 N Garfield
Moscow, ID 83843-3624
Phone: (208)882-0413
Fax: (208)882-3393
**Subject(s):** Anthropology and Ethnology; Archaeology

Circ: (Paid)350

**Probability in the Engineering and Informational Sciences  (2314)**
Cambridge University Press
c/o Prof. Sheldon M. Ross
Epstein Department of Industrial and Systems Engineering
3715 McClintock Ave.
Los Angeles, CA 90089-0193
**Subject(s):** Engineering (Various branches); Mathematics; Physics

Circ: 350

**The Trail  (18247)**
Lost Trail Publishing
Box 486
Trego, MT 59934
Phone: (406)882-4737
**Subject(s):** History and Genealogy; Local, State, and Regional Publications

Circ: (Non-paid)250
    (Paid)350

**Chicano-Latin Law Review  (2165)**
University of California, Los Angeles
School of Law, P.O. Box 951476
405 Hilgard Ave.
405 Hilgard Ave.
Los Angeles, CA 90095-1476
Phone: (310)206-9103
Fax: (310)206-6489
**Subject(s):** Law; Ethnic and Minority Studies

Circ: 340

**Energy Sources  (33753)**
Taylor & Francis
c/o James Speight
2476 Overland Rd.
Laramie, WY 82070-4808
**Subject(s):** Petroleum, Oil, and Gas; International Affairs; Power and Power Plants; Nuclear Engineering; Electrical Engineering; Chemistry, Chemicals, and Chemical Engineering

Circ: (Controlled)‡345

**Umpqua Trapper  (26028)**
Douglas County Historical Society
733 W Ballf St.
Roseburg, OR 97470
**Subject(s):** History and Genealogy; Local, State, and Regional Publications

Circ: (Paid)340

**Colorado School of Mines Quarterly  (4410)**
Colorado School of Mines
Golden, CO 80401
Phone: (303)273-3690
Fax: (303)384-2075
**Subject(s):** Mining and Minerals

Circ: ‡300

**The Dalmatian Quarterly  (4598)**
Hoflin Publishing Inc.
4401 Zephyr St.
Wheat Ridge, CO 80033-3299
Phone: (303)420-2222
Fax: (303)422-7000
**Subject(s):** Dogs

Circ: (Paid)300

**Educational Administration Abstracts  (3662)**
Corwin Press
2455 Teller Rd.
Thousand Oaks, CA 91320
Phone: (805)499-0721
Fax: (805)499-0871
**Subject(s):** Education; Indexes, Abstracts, Reports, Proceedings, and Bibliographies

Circ: (Paid)300

**Genealogical Journal of Oneida County, New York  (7648)**
The Family Tree
PO Box 4311
Boise, ID 83711
Phone: (208)853-1624
**Subject(s):** History and Genealogy

Circ: (Paid)300

**International Business & Economics Research Journal  (4493)**
Western Academic Press
PO Box 620760
Littleton, CO 80162
Phone: (303)904-4750
Fax: (303)978-0413
**Subject(s):** Business

Circ: (Controlled)‡200
    (Paid)‡300

**Journal of Business & Economic Research  (4495)**
Western Academic Press
PO Box 620760
Littleton, CO 80162
Phone: (303)904-4750
Fax: (303)978-0413
**Subject(s):** Business; Economics

Circ: (Controlled)‡50
    (Paid)‡300

**Journal of College Teaching & Learning  (4496)**
Western Academic Press
PO Box 620760
Littleton, CO 80162
Phone: (303)904-4750
Fax: (303)978-0413
**Subject(s):** Education

Circ: (Controlled)‡50
    (Paid)‡300

**Journal of Language and Social Psychology  (3800)**
Sage Publications Inc.
2455 Teller Rd.
Thousand Oaks, CA 91320
**Subject(s):** Psychology and Psychiatry; Communications; Sociology

Circ: (Paid)300

**Leading Edge Magazine  (30740)**
4198 JFSB
Provo, UT 84604
Phone: (801)422-3553
**Subject(s):** Science Fiction, Mystery, Adventure, and Romance

Circ: (Paid)‡300

**Monthly F.O.B. Price Summary, Past Sales (Inland Mills)  (25963)**
Western Wood Products Association
522 SW 5th Ave., Ste. 500
Portland, OR 97204-2122
Phone: (503)224-3930
Fax: (503)224-3934
**Subject(s):** Forestry; Statistics

Circ: 300

**North American Journal of Economics and Finance  (1668)**
Elsevier Science B.V.
Lowe Institute of Political Economy
Claremont McKenna College
850 Columbia Ave.
Claremont, CA 91711-6420
Phone: (909)621-8012
Fax: (909)607-8008
**Subject(s):** Economics; Banking, Finance, and Investments

Circ: (Non-paid)50
    (Paid)300

**One to One II  (1881)**
Cree Yadio Services
Box 9787
Fresno, CA 93794
Phone: (559)448-0700
Fax: (559)448-0761
**Subject(s):** Radio, Television, Cable, and Video

Circ: (Paid)300

**PoetsWest Online  (32307)**
PoetsWest
1011 Boren Ave.
PMB 155
Seattle, WA 98104
Phone: (206)682-1268
**Subject(s):** Literature; Poetry; Literature and Literary Reviews

Circ: (Free)300

**Review of Business Information Systems  (4501)**
Western Academic Press
PO Box 620760
Littleton, CO 80162
Phone: (303)904-4750
Fax: (303)978-0413
**Subject(s):** Business

Circ: (Controlled)‡50
    (Paid)‡300

**Sage Family Studies Abstracts  (3885)**
Sage Publications Inc.
2455 Teller Rd.
Thousand Oaks, CA 91320
**Subject(s):** Sociology; Indexes, Abstracts, Reports, Proceedings, and Bibliographies

Circ: (Paid)‡300

**Sage Public Administration Abstracts  (3886)**
Sage Publications Inc.
2455 Teller Rd.
Thousand Oaks, CA 91320
**Subject(s):** State, Municipal, and County Administration; Indexes, Abstracts, Reports, Proceedings, and Bibliographies

Circ: (Paid)‡300

**Sage Urban Studies Abstracts  (3887)**
Sage Publications Inc.
2455 Teller Rd.
Thousand Oaks, CA 91320
**Subject(s):** Sociology; Indexes, Abstracts, Reports, Proceedings, and Bibliographies

Circ: (Paid)‡300

**Silver Wings  (1677)**
Poetry on Wings
PO Box 2340
Clovis, CA 93613-2340
Phone: (559)347-0194
**Subject(s):** Poetry; Religious Publications

Circ: (Paid)300

**Synapse  (2804)**
John Wiley and Sons Inc.
c/o John E. Johnson, Jr., Editor-in-Chief
165 Cervantes Rd.
Redwood City, CA 94062
Phone: (650)366-1644
Fax: (650)367-9630
**Subject(s):** Medicine and Surgery

Circ: (Paid)290

**Monthly F.O.B. Price Summary, Past Sales (Coast Mills)  (25962)**
Western Wood Products Association
522 SW 5th Ave., Ste. 500
Portland, OR 97204-2122
Phone: (503)224-3930
Fax: (503)224-3934
**Subject(s):** Forestry; Statistics

Circ: 280

**Thomas Jefferson Law Review (3063)**
2121 San Diego Ave.
San Diego, CA 92110
Phone: (619)298-3111
Fax: (619)692-8149
**Subject(s):** Law
**Circ:** (Combined)280

**Export Report (25955)**
Western Wood Products Association
522 SW 5th Ave., Ste. 500
Portland, OR 97204-2122
Phone: (503)224-3930
Fax: (503)224-3934
**Subject(s):** Forestry; Statistics
**Circ:** 275

**Injury and Illness Incidence (25959)**
Western Wood Products Association
522 SW 5th Ave., Ste. 500
Portland, OR 97204-2122
Phone: (503)224-3930
Fax: (503)224-3934
**Subject(s):** Forestry; Statistics
**Circ:** 275

**The Kerf (1730)**
College of the Redwoods
883 W Washington Blvd.
Crescent City, CA 95531
Phone: (707)465-2300
**Subject(s):** Poetry; Environmental and Natural Resources Conservation
**Circ:** (Non-paid)275

**Experimental Heat Transfer (1472)**
Taylor & Francis
c/o Per F. Peterson, Department of Nuclear Engineering
University of California
4155 Etcheverry Hall
Berkeley, CA 94720-1730
Phone: (510)643-7749
Fax: (510)643-9685
**Subject(s):** Engineering (Various branches); Chemistry, Chemicals, and Chemical Engineering; Nuclear Engineering
**Circ:** (Paid)‡267

**Issues in Applied Linguistics (IAL) (2232)**
UCLA Applied Linguistics/TESL
3300 Rolfe Hall
PO Box 951531
Los Angeles, CA 90095-1531
Phone: (310)206-1327
Fax: (310)206-4118
**Subject(s):** Philology, Language, and Linguistics
**Circ:** (Non-paid)50
(Paid)250

**Mathematical Research Letters (2040)**
International Press of Boston Inc.
c/o M. Salah Baouendi
Univ. of Mathematics 0112
Univ. of California, San Diego
La Jolla, CA 92093-0112
Fax: (619)534-5273
**Subject(s):** Mathematics
**Circ:** (Combined)250

**Smith-Kettlewell Technical File (3216)**
Smith-Kettlewell Eye Research Institute
2318 Fillmore St.
San Francisco, CA 94115
Phone: (415)345-2124
Fax: (415)345-8455
**Subject(s):** Blind and Visually Challenged
**Circ:** (Paid)250

**Ufahamu (2360)**
University of California at Los Angeles
10244 Bunche Hall
Box 951310
Los Angeles, CA 90095-1310
Phone: (310)825-6059
**Subject(s):** Intercultural Interests
**Circ:** (Combined)250

**Women in Sport and Physical Activity Journal (18705)**
Women of Diversity Productions
5790 N Park St.
Las Vegas, NV 89149-2304
Phone: (702)341-9807
Fax: (702)341-9828
**Subject(s):** Physical Education and Athletics; Women's Interests
**Circ:** (Paid)250

**Shaw Historical Library Journal (25868)**
Oregon Institute of Technology
3201 Campus Dr.
Klamath Falls, OR 97601-8801
Phone: (541)885-1772
Fax: (541)885-1777
**Subject(s):** History and Genealogy
**Circ:** (Combined)240

**Chinese Law and Government (2166)**
M.E. Sharpe Inc.
UCLA
C/O James Tong, Dept. of Political Science, Bunche Hall
Los Angeles, CA 90024
**Subject(s):** Law; Intercultural Interests
**Circ:** (Paid)⊕227

**Western North American Naturalist (30748)**
Brigham Young University
290 Life Science Museum
Provo, UT 84602-0200
Phone: (801)422-4636
**Subject(s):** Biology; Natural History and Nature Study
**Circ:** (Paid)225

**Animation Journal (3446)**
AJ Press
20124 Zimmerman Pl.
Santa Clarita, CA 91390-3102
**Subject(s):** Motion Pictures; Radio, Television, Cable, and Video
**Circ:** (Paid)200

**Armenian Numismatic Journal (2733)**
Armenian Numismatic Society
8511 Beverly Park Pl.
Pico Rivera, CA 90660-1920
Phone: (562)695-0380
**Subject(s):** Metal, Metallurgy, and Metal Trade
**Circ:** (Paid)200

**Genealogical Goldmine (2705)**
Paradise Genealogical Society Inc.
PO Box 460
Paradise, CA 95967-0460
Phone: (530)877-2330
**Subject(s):** History and Genealogy
**Circ:** (Combined)200

**Genealogical Journal of Jefferson County, New York (7647)**
The Family Tree
PO Box 4311
Boise, ID 83711
Phone: (208)853-1624
**Subject(s):** History and Genealogy
**Circ:** (Paid)‡200

**Journal of Acoustic Emission (1822)**
Acoustic Emission Group
PMB 409
4924 Balboa Blvd.
Encino, CA 91316
Phone: (310)825-5233
Fax: (818)990-1686
**Subject(s):** Engineering (Various branches)
**Circ:** (Paid)200

**Marine Geodesy (7560)**
Taylor & Francis
c/o Dr. Narendra Saxena
School of Ocean & Earth Science & Technology
Univ. of Hawaii at Manoa
2525 Correa Rd., HIG 440
Honolulu, HI 96822
Phone: (808)956-2580
Fax: (808)956-2580
**Subject(s):** Oceanography and Marine Studies
**Circ:** (Paid)‡200

**Morgan Pony Express (18101)**
National Morgan Pony Registry
920 Antimony, Ste. 100
Butte, MT 59701
Phone: (406)723-6983
**Subject(s):** (Horses and Horse Racing)
**Circ:** 200

**Olympia Genealogical Society Quarterly (32176)**
Olympia Genealogical Society
Box 1313
Olympia, WA 98507-1313
**Subject(s):** History and Genealogy; Local, State, and Regional Publications
**Circ:** (Controlled)200

**Peace Research Abstracts Journal (3867)**
Sage Publications Inc.
2455 Teller Rd.
Thousand Oaks, CA 91320
**Subject(s):** Indexes, Abstracts, Reports, Proceedings, and Bibliographies; Peace
**Circ:** (Paid)200

**Quartz Hill Journal of Theology (2762)**
43543 51st St. W
Quartz Hill, CA 93536
Phone: (661)722-0891
Fax: (661)943-3484
**Subject(s):** Religious Publications; Theology
**Circ:** 200

**Skinner Kinsmen Update (2770)**
Brandywine Press
Box 2594
Rancho Cucamonga, CA 91729
**Subject(s):** History and Genealogy
**Circ:** (Combined)200

**Theosophical History (4073)**
20733 Via Sonrisa
Yorba Linda, CA 92886
Phone: (714)278-3727
Fax: (714)693-0142
**Subject(s):** History and Genealogy
**Circ:** (Combined)205

**Journal of Aquatic Food Product Technology (25706)**
The Haworth Press Inc.
OSU Seafoods Laboratory
Oregon State Univ.
2001 Marine Dr., Rm. 253
Astoria, OR 97103-3427
Phone: (503)325-4531
**Subject(s):** Oceanography and Marine Studies; Food Production; Laboratory Research (Scientific and Medical)
**Circ:** 170

**Korean Studies (7557)**
University of Hawaii Press
1881 East-West Rd.
Center for Korean Studies
Honolulu, HI 96822
Phone: (808)956-7041
Fax: (808)956-2213
**Subject(s):** Ethnic and Minority Studies; Korean
**Circ:** (Controlled)60
(Paid)160

**Topicator (26064)**
TOPICATOR Inc.
PO Box 757
Terrebonne, OR 97760
Phone: (541)923-7334
**Subject(s):** Advertising and Marketing; Indexes, Abstracts, Reports, Proceedings, and Bibliographies
**Circ:** ‡160

**Journal of the Flagstaff Institute (671)**
The Flagstaff Institute
PO Box 986
Flagstaff, AZ 86002-0986
Phone: (928)779-0052
Fax: (928)774-8589
**Subject(s):** Commerce and Industry; International Business and Economics
**Circ:** (Combined)150

**Slavic & East European Information Resources (3376)**
The Haworth Press Inc.
112 S Delaware St.
San Mateo, CA 94402-2142
Phone: (650)725-1052
Fax: (650)725-1068
**Subject(s):** Library and Information Science; Intercultural Interests
**Circ:** 150

**Educational Leadership and Administration (3134)**
Caddo Gap Press
3145 Geary Blvd., No. 275
San Francisco, CA 94118
Phone: (415)666-3012

**Central Provinces**　　　　　　　　　　　　　　　Gale Directory of Publications & Broadcast Media/140th Ed.

Fax: (415)666-3552
**Subject(s):** Education
**Circ:** (Paid)125

**Journal of Nanoscience and Nanotechnology (3941)**
American Scientific Publishers
25650 , The Old Rd., Ste. 208
Valencia, CA 91381-0751
Phone: (661)799-7200
Fax: (661)799-7230
**Subject(s):** Science (General)
**Circ:** (Paid)120

**Notes and Abstracts in American and International Education (3182)**
Caddo Gap Press
3145 Geary Blvd., No. 275
San Francisco, CA 94118
Phone: (415)666-3012
Fax: (415)666-3552
**Subject(s):** Education
**Circ:** (Paid)125

**Taboo (3224)**
Caddo Gap Press
3145 Geary Blvd., No. 275
San Francisco, CA 94118
Phone: (415)666-3012
Fax: (415)666-3552
**Subject(s):** Education
**Circ:** (Paid)125

**Vitae Schololasticae (3233)**
Caddo Gap Press
3145 Geary Blvd., No. 275
San Francisco, CA 94118
Phone: (415)666-3012
Fax: (415)666-3552
**Subject(s):** Education
**Circ:** (Paid)125

**Art (18679)**
Art: Mag
PO Box 70896
Las Vegas, NV 89170
Phone: (702)734-8121
**Subject(s):** Literature; Art; Literature and Literary Reviews; Alternative and Underground
**Circ:** 100

**Journal of Container-Transport (2497)**
Society of Freight Car Historians
PO Box 2480
Monrovia, CA 91017
**Subject(s):** History and Genealogy; Railroad
**Circ:** 100

**Journal of Neuro-AIDS (3162)**
The Haworth Press Inc.
c/o Richard W. Price, San Francisco General Hospital
Dept. of Neurology, Rm. 4M62
1001 Potrero Ave.
San Francisco, CA 94110
Phone: (415)476-5582
Fax: (415)476-5582
**Subject(s):** Acquired Immune Deficiency Syndrome
**Circ:** (Paid)74

**Journal of Emotional Abuse (3027)**
The Haworth Press Inc.
c/o Robert A. Geffner, Calif. Schl. Of Prof. Pshchology
Alliant International Univ.
6160 Cornerstone Ct. E.
San Diego, CA 92121
Phone: (858)623-2777
Fax: (717)459-5934
**Subject(s):** Psychology and Psychiatry; Social Sciences
**Circ:** (Non-paid)‡4
　　　(Paid)‡25

## Central Provinces

**What's Cooking Magazine (34884)**
Redwood Custom Communications Inc.
Kraft Canada Inc.
PO Box 1200
Don Mills, ON, Canada M3B 3L6
**Subject(s):** Food and Cooking
**Circ:** (Non-paid)1,300,000

**Starweek Magazine (35805)**
Toronto Star Newspapers Ltd.
1 Yonge St., 5th Fl.
Toronto, ON, Canada M5E 1E6
Phone: (416)367-2000
Fax: (416)869-4834
**Subject(s):** Radio, Television, Cable, and Video
**Circ:** ‡750,000

**Chatelaine (35583)**
Rogers Media Publishing
1 Mount Pleasant Rd., 7th Fl.
Toronto, ON, Canada M4Y 2Y5
Phone: (416)596-5523
Fax: (416)764-1765
**Subject(s):** Women's Interests
**Circ:** (Paid)716,727

**Elm Street The Look (35619)**
St. Joseph Media
111 Queen St. E.
Toronto, ON, Canada M5C 1S2
Phone: (416)595-9944
Fax: (416)595-7217
**Subject(s):** Women's Interests; Lifestyle; Local, State, and Regional Publications
**Circ:** (Paid)44,842
　　　(Non-paid)597,736

**Homemaker's Magazine (Madame au Foyer) (35658)**
Transcontinental Publications Inc.
25 Sheppard Ave. W, Ste. 100
Toronto, ON, Canada M2N 6S7
Phone: (416)733-7600
Fax: (416)218-3632
**Subject(s):** Women's Interests; French
**Circ:** (Non-paid)270,349
　　　(Paid)550,000

**Maclean's (35699)**
Rogers Media Publishing
1 Mount Pleasant Rd., 7th Fl.
Toronto, ON, Canada M4Y 2Y5
Phone: (416)596-5523
Fax: (416)764-1765
**Subject(s):** General Editorial
**Circ:** (Paid)506,428

**TV Guide Canada (35835)**
Transcontinental Publications Inc.
25 Sheppard Ave. W, Ste. 100
Toronto, ON, Canada M2N 6S7
Phone: (416)733-7600
Fax: (416)218-3632
**Subject(s):** Radio, Television, Cable, and Video
**Circ:** (Paid)500,629

**The Fatima Crusader (34920)**
National Committee for National Pilgrim Virgin of Canada
452 Kraft Rd.
Fort Erie, ON, Canada L2A 4M7
Phone: (905)871-8041
Fax: (905)871-3646
**Subject(s):** Religious Publications
**Circ:** (Non-paid)‡500,000

**Food & Drink (35637)**
Liquor Control Board of Ontario
55 Lakeshore Blvd. E
Toronto, ON, Canada M5E 1A4
Phone: (416)864-6770
Fax: (416)365-5935
**Subject(s):** Food and Cooking
**Circ:** (Combined)500,000

**Legion Magazine (35283)**
Canvet Publications Ltd.
359 Kent St., Ste. 407
Ottawa, ON, Canada K2P 0R6
Phone: (613)235-8741
Fax: (613)233-7159
**Subject(s):** Veterans; Senior Citizens' Interests
**Circ:** (Paid)346,127

**Carguide Magazine (Le Magazine Carguide) (35172)**
Formula Publications
447 Speers Rd., Ste. 4
Oakville, ON, Canada L6K 3S7
Phone: (905)842-6591
Fax: (905)842-6843
**Subject(s):** Automotive (Consumer)
**Circ:** (Combined)333,043

**The Globe and Mail Report on Business Magazine (35646)**
The Globe & Mail
444 Front St. W.
Toronto, ON, Canada M5V 2S9
Phone: (416)585-5000
Fax: (416)585-5641
**Subject(s):** Business
**Circ:** (Controlled)‡320,000

**Marquee Magazine (35121)**
Marquee Media Inc.
1325 Burnhamthorpe Rd. E
Mississauga, ON, Canada L4Y 3V8
Phone: (905)274-7174
Fax: (905)274-9799
**Subject(s):** Motion Pictures
**Circ:** (Controlled)‡312,000

**Teen Tribune (34883)**
Tribute Publishing Inc.
71 Barber Greene Rd.
Don Mills, ON, Canada M3C 2A2
Phone: (416)445-0544
Fax: (416)445-2894
**Subject(s):** Youths' Interests; Entertainment; Motion Pictures
**Circ:** (Non-paid)•299,500

**Rob Magazine (35785)**
The Globe & Mail
444 Front St. W.
Toronto, ON, Canada M5V 2S9
Phone: (416)585-5000
Fax: (416)585-5641
**Subject(s):** Business
**Circ:** (Paid)276,000

**City Parent (35173)**
467 Speers Rd.
Oakville, ON, Canada L6K 3S4
Phone: (905)815-0017
Fax: (905)337-5571
**Subject(s):** Parenting; Children's Interests
**Circ:** 260,000

**What! A Magazine (34515)**
M2 Communications Inc.
108-93 Lombard Ave.
Winnipeg, MB, Canada R3B 3B1
Phone: (204)985-8160
Fax: (204)943-8991
**Subject(s):** Youths' Interests
**Circ:** (Non-paid)247,249

**University of Toronto Magazine (35840)**
University of Toronto
21 King's College Cir.
Toronto, ON, Canada M5S 3J3
Phone: (416)978-6981
Fax: (416)978-1632
**Subject(s):** Education
**Circ:** (Controlled)240,441

**Canadian Geographic (35219)**
Canadian Geographic Enterprises
39 McArthur Ave.
Ottawa, ON, Canada K1L 8L7
Phone: (613)745-4629
Fax: (613)744-0947
**Subject(s):** History and Genealogy; Travel and Tourism; Environmental and Natural Resources Conservation
**Circ:** (Paid)229,180

**Time (Canada) (35817)**
Time Canada Ltd.
175 Bloor St. E, Ste. 602
N Twr.
Toronto, ON, Canada M4W 3R8
Phone: (416)929-1115
Fax: (416)929-0019
**Subject(s):** Export Consumer Magazines
**Circ:** (Paid)225,000

**CARPNews Fifty Plus (35574)**
CARP
27 Queen St. E., Ste. 300
Toronto, ON, Canada M5C 2M6
Phone: (416)363-8748
Fax: (416)363-8747
**Subject(s):** Senior Citizens' Interests
**Circ:** (Combined)210,244

**Style at Home (35809)**
Transcontinental Publications Inc.
25 Sheppard Ave. W, Ste. 100
Toronto, ON, Canada M2N 6S7
Phone: (416)733-7600
Fax: (416)218-3632
**Subject(s):** Home and Garden
**Circ:** (Paid)210,000

**Today's Parent Pregnancy & Birth (35823)**
Today's Parent Group
1 Mount Pleasant Rd., 8th Fl.
Toronto, ON, Canada M4Y 2Y5
Fax: (416)764-2801
**Subject(s):** Babies; Parenting
**Circ:** (Non-paid)199,575

**Canadian House & Home Magazine (35536)**
Canadian Home Publishers Inc.
511 King St. W. Ste. 120
Toronto, ON, Canada M5V 2Z4
Phone: (905)946-1021
**Subject(s):** Home and Garden
**Circ:** (Paid)191,420

**Professionally Speaking/Pour Parler Profession (35768)**
Ontario College of Teachers
121 Bloor St. E., 6th Fl.
Toronto, ON, Canada M4W 3M5
Phone: (416)961-8800
Fax: (416)961-8822
**Subject(s):** Education
**Circ:** 10,000
  (Combined)170,000

**FLARE (35635)**
Rogers Media Publishing
One Mount Pleasant Rd.
8th Fl.
Toronto, ON, Canada M4Y 2Y5
Phone: (416)764-2863
Fax: (416)764-2866
**Subject(s):** Women's Interests; Fashion
**Circ:** (Paid)160,220

**Thunder Bay Guest Magazine (35474)**
T.Bay Post Inc.
87 N. Hill St.
Thunder Bay, ON, Canada P7A 5V6
Phone: (807)346-2600
Fax: (807)345-9923
**Subject(s):** Travel and Tourism
**Circ:** (Controlled)‡160,000

**Today's Parent Newborn (35822)**
Today's Parent Group
1 Mount Pleasant Rd., 8th Fl.
Toronto, ON, Canada M4Y 2Y5
Fax: (416)764-2801
**Subject(s):** Health and Healthcare; Pediatrics; Parenting
**Circ:** (Non-paid)154,755

**Owl Canadian Family (35748)**
St. Joseph Media
111 Queen St. E, Ste. 450
Toronto, ON, Canada M5C 1S2
Phone: (416)595-9944
Fax: (416)595-7217
**Subject(s):** Education; Parenting
**Circ:** (Non-paid)154,519

**Best Wishes Magazine (35507)**
Family Communications Inc.
65 The E. Mall
Toronto, ON, Canada M8Z 5W3
Phone: (416)537-2604
Fax: (416)538-1794
**Subject(s):** Parenting
**Circ:** (Non-paid)153,239

**Canadian Gardening (35079)**
Avid Media Inc.
210-340 Ferrier St.
Markham, ON, Canada L3R 2Z5
Phone: (905)475-8440
Fax: (905)475-9246
**Subject(s):** Home and Garden
**Circ:** (Paid)152,733

**Shift (35797)**
Shift Multimedia
111 Queen St. East, Ste. 450
Toronto, ON, Canada M5C 1S2
Phone: (416)595-9944

Fax: (416)595-7217
**Subject(s):** Entertainment; Lifestyle
**Circ:** (Paid)‡150,000

**Score (35791)**
Canadian Controlled Media Communications
5397 Eglinton Ave. W, Ste. 101
Toronto, ON, Canada M9C 5K6
Phone: (416)928-2909
Fax: (416)966-1181
**Subject(s):** (Golf)
**Circ:** (Paid)•4,846
  (Non-paid)•145,423

**Expecting (35627)**
Family Communications Inc.
65 The E. Mall
Toronto, ON, Canada M8Z 5W3
Phone: (416)537-2604
Fax: (416)538-1794
**Subject(s):** Babies; Parenting
**Circ:** (Non-paid)143,041

**SIMNOW (35428)**
SIM Canada
10 Huntingdale Blvd.
Scarborough, ON, Canada M1W 2S5
Phone: (416)497-2424
Fax: (416)497-2444
**Subject(s):** Religious Publications
**Circ:** (Controlled)‡132,000

**OTF (FEO) Interaction (35744)**
Ontario Teachers' Federation
1300 Yonge St., Ste. 200
Toronto, ON, Canada M4T 1X3
Phone: (416)966-3424
Fax: (416)966-5450
**Subject(s):** Education; French
**Circ:** (Non-paid)‡130,000

**Canadian Home Workshop (35081)**
Avid Media Inc.
210-340 Ferrier St.
Markham, ON, Canada L3R 2Z5
Phone: (905)475-8440
Fax: (905)475-9246
**Subject(s):** Home and Garden
**Circ:** (Paid)128,328

**Profiles (35769)**
York University
4700 Keele St.
Toronto, ON, Canada M3J 1P3
Phone: (416)736-2100
Fax: (416)650-2979
**Subject(s):** College Publications
**Circ:** (Non-paid)123,850

**Today's Parent (35821)**
Today's Parent Group
1 Mount Pleasant Rd., 8th Fl.
Toronto, ON, Canada M4Y 2Y5
Fax: (416)764-2801
**Subject(s):** Parenting
**Circ:** (Non-paid)52,000
  (Paid)121,000

**Toronto Life Fashion Magazine (35827)**
Key Media Ltd.
Urban Group
St. Joseph Media Corp
Queen Richmond Centre
Toronto, ON, Canada M5C1S2
**Subject(s):** Fashion
**Circ:** (Non-paid)39,224
  (Paid)118,023

**On Manitoba (34501)**
University of Manitoba
180 Dafoe Rd.
Winnipeg, MB, Canada R3T 2N2
Phone: (204)474-9946
Fax: (204)474-7531
**Subject(s):** College Publications
**Circ:** ‡118,000

**Canadian Nurse (L'Infirmiere Canadienne) (35241)**
Canadian Nurses Association
50 Driveway
Ottawa, ON, Canada K2P 1E2
Phone: (613)237-2133
Fax: (613)237-3520

**Subject(s):** Nursing; French
**Circ:** (Combined)111,563

**Canadian Home Workshop (35535)**
25 Sheppard Ave., W.
Toronto, ON, Canada M2N 6S7
**Subject(s):** Crafts, Models, Hobbies, and Contests
**Circ:** (Paid)110,743

**Snow Goer (35089)**
Avid Media Inc.
210-340 Ferrier St.
Markham, ON, Canada L3R 2Z5
Phone: (905)475-8440
Fax: (905)475-9246
**Subject(s):** (Snowmobiling)
**Circ:** (Paid)35,328
  (Non-paid)105,613

**Gardening Life (35638)**
Gardening Life Publishing
511 King St. W, Ste. 120
Toronto, ON, Canada M5V 2Z4
Phone: (416)593-0204
Fax: (416)591-1630
**Subject(s):** Home and Garden
**Circ:** (Combined)105,290

**Exclaim! (35623)**
1059434 Ontario Inc.
7B Pleasant Blvd., Unit No. 966
Toronto, ON, Canada M4T 1K2
Phone: (416)535-9735
Fax: (416)535-0566
**Subject(s):** Music and Musical Instruments; Entertainment; Youths' Interests
**Circ:** (Non-paid)102,302

**Canadian Home and Country (35080)**
Avid Media Inc.
210-340 Ferrier St.
Markham, ON, Canada L3R 2Z5
Phone: (905)475-8440
Fax: (905)475-9246
**Subject(s):** Home and Garden
**Circ:** (Paid)‡100,981

**Homes Magazine (35890)**
Homes Publishing Group
178 Main St.
Unionville, ON, Canada L3R 2G9
Phone: (905)479-4663
Fax: (905)479-4482
**Subject(s):** Real Estate; Home and Garden
**Circ:** 100,000

**Living Safety Magazine (35285)**
Canada Safety Council
1020 Thomas Spratt Pl.
Ottawa, ON, Canada K1G 5L5
Phone: (613)739-1535
Fax: (613)739-1566
**Subject(s):** Safety; Health; French
**Circ:** ‡100,000

**The Student Traveller (35807)**
Canadian Federation of Students-Services
45 Charles St., E, Ste. 200
Toronto, ON, Canada M4Y 1S2
Phone: (416)966-2887
Fax: (416)966-4043
**Subject(s):** Travel and Tourism
**Circ:** (Non-paid)‡100,000

**The United Church Observer (35836)**
Observer Publications Inc.
478 Huron St.
Toronto, ON, Canada M5R 2R3
Phone: (416)960-8500
Fax: (416)960-8477
**Subject(s):** Religious Publications
**Circ:** ‡95,000

**Toronto Life (35826)**
Key Media Ltd.
Urban Group
St. Joseph Media Corp
Queen Richmond Centre
Toronto, ON, Canada M5C1S2
**Subject(s):** Local, State, and Regional Publications; Lifestyle
**Circ:** (Paid)92,574

Circulation: ★ = ABC; △ = BPA; ♦ = CAC; • = CCAB; □ = VAC; ⊕ = PO Statement; ‡ = Publisher's Report; Boldface figures = sworn; Light figures = estimated.

## Central Provinces

**Queen's Alumni Review (35016)**
Queen's University
Office of Advancement
Kingston, ON, Canada K7L 3N6
Phone: (613)533-2060
Fax: (613)533-6828
**Subject(s):** College Publications

Circ: (Paid)‡100
(Controlled)‡89,000

**The Green and White (36495)**
University of Saskatchewan Alumni Association
Rm. 223 Kirk Hall
117 Science Pl.
Univ. of Saskatchewan
Saskatoon, SK, Canada S7N 5C8
Phone: (306)966-5186
Fax: (306)966-5571
**Subject(s):** College Publications

Circ: (Controlled)88,807

**Tabaret (35307)**
University of Ottawa
550 Cumberland St., Rm. 281
178 Laurier E
Ottawa, ON, Canada K1N 6N5
Phone: (613)562-5708
Fax: (613)562-5117
**Subject(s):** French

Circ: (Non-paid)‡88,000

**Ontario Out of Doors (35739)**
Rogers Media Publishing
1 Mount Pleasant Rd., 7th Fl.
Toronto, ON, Canada M4Y 2Y5
Phone: (416)596-5523
Fax: (416)764-1765
**Subject(s):** (Outdoors); (Hunting, Fishing, and Game Management)

Circ: (Non-paid)•1,000
(Paid)•85,704

**Ontario Snowmobiler (35146)**
Ontario Snowmobiler Publishing Ltd.
78 Main St. S
Newmarket, ON, Canada L3Y 3Y6
Phone: (905)898-8585
Fax: (905)848-8071
**Subject(s):** (Snowmobiling)

Circ: (Paid)85,000

**Outdoor Canada (35745)**
Outdoor Canada Publishing Ltd.
25 Sheppard Ave. W.
Toronto, ON, Canada M2N 6S7
Phone: (416)733-7600
**Subject(s):** (General Sports); (Hunting, Fishing, and Game Management); (Outdoors)

Circ: (Paid)82,422

**Canadian Business (35525)**
CB Media Ltd.
One Mount Pleasant Rd., 11th Fl.
Toronto, ON, Canada M4Y 2Y5
Phone: (416)596-5999
Fax: (416)764-1255
**Subject(s):** Business; Banking, Finance, and Investments

Circ: (Paid)81,377

**WeddingBells Magazine (35852)**
Wedding Bells Inc.
34 King St. E, Ste. 800
Toronto, ON, Canada M5E 2X8
**Subject(s):** Brides

Circ: (Paid)26,369
(Non-paid)80,114

**Our Ontario (35163)**
Ontario Public Service Employees Union
100 Lesmill Rd.
North York, ON, Canada M3B 3P8
Phone: (416)443-8888
Fax: (416)443-1762
**Subject(s):** Labor

Circ: (Controlled)80,000

**WHERE Toronto (35854)**
Miller Publishing Group L.L.C.
6 Church St., 2nd Fl.
Toronto, ON, Canada M5E 1M1
Phone: (416)364-3336
Fax: (416)594-3375
**Subject(s):** Local, State, and Regional Publications; Travel and Tourism

Circ: (Non-paid)‡77,000

**Renovation & Decor (35899)**
Homes Publishing Group
178 Main St.
Unionville, ON, Canada L3R 2G9
Phone: (905)479-4663
Fax: (905)479-4482
**Subject(s):** Home and Garden

Circ: (Controlled)75,000

**Today's Bride Magazine (35819)**
Family Communications Inc.
Family Communications
1-37 Hanna Ave.
Toronto, ON, Canada M6K 1W9
**Subject(s):** Brides

Circ: (Paid)27,395
(Non-paid)72,890

**CA Magazine (35516)**
Canadian Institute of Chartered Accountants
277 Wellington St. W
Toronto, ON, Canada M5V 3H2
Phone: (416)977-3222
Fax: (416)204-3409
**Subject(s):** Accountants and Accounting; French

Circ: (Non-paid)3,386
(Paid)71,448

**Homes & Cottages (35118)**
The In-Home Show
4-2650 Meadowvale Blvd.
Mississauga, ON, Canada L5N 6M5
Phone: (905)567-1440
Fax: (905)567-1442
**Subject(s):** Building Management and Maintenance

Circ: (Non-paid)67,000

**Wood Lebois (35316)**
Janam Publications
Canadian Wood Council
1400 Blair Pl. Ste. 210
Ottawa, ON, Canada K1J 9B8
Phone: (819)778-5040
Fax: (819)595-8553
**Subject(s):** Architecture; Construction, Contracting, Building, and Excavating; Wood and Woodworking

Circ: (Combined)67,000

**Chickadee (35584)**
Bayard Press
49 Front St. E., No. 200
Toronto, ON, Canada M5E 1B3
Phone: (416)340-2700
Fax: (416)340-9769
**Subject(s):** Children's Interests

Circ: (Paid)370
(Paid)66,645

**CMA News (35254)**
Canadian Medical Association
1867 Alta Vista Dr.
Ottawa, ON, Canada K1G 6R7
Phone: (613)731-4552
Fax: (800)267-4022
**Subject(s):** Medicine and Surgery; Health and Healthcare

Circ: ‡66,413

**Canadian Medical Association Journal (35240)**
Canadian Medical Association
1867 Alta Vista Dr.
Ottawa, ON, Canada K1G 6R7
Phone: (613)731-4552
Fax: (800)267-4022
**Subject(s):** Medicine and Surgery; Biology; Chemistry, Chemicals, and Chemical Engineering; French

Circ: (Combined)•66,024

**Engineering Dimensions (35620)**
Professional Engineers Ontario
25 Sheppard Ave. W, Ste. 1000
Toronto, ON, Canada M2N 6S9
Phone: (416)224-1100
Fax: (416)224-8168
**Subject(s):** Engineering (Various branches)

Circ: (Combined)•65,246

**View (35947)**
University of Windsor
Windsor, ON, Canada N9B 3P4
Phone: (519)253-3000
Fax: (519)973-7067
**Subject(s):** College Publications

Circ: ⊕65,000

**OWL (35747)**
Bayard Press
49 Front St. E., No. 200
Toronto, ON, Canada M5E 1B3
Phone: (416)340-2700
Fax: (416)340-9769
**Subject(s):** Children's Interests

Circ: (Non-paid)352
(Paid)63,059

**Diabetes Dialogue (35609)**
Canadian Diabetes Association
15 Toronto St.
Toronto, ON, Canada M5C 2E3
Phone: (416)363-3393
Fax: (416)363-3393
**Subject(s):** Medicine and Surgery

Circ: (Controlled)‡60,928

**Cottage Life (35598)**
Quarto Communications
54 St. Patrick St.
Toronto, ON, Canada M5T 1V1
Phone: (416)599-2000
Fax: (416)599-0800
**Subject(s):** Home and Garden; Lifestyle

Circ: (Non-paid)9,876
(Paid)60,258

**Hi-Rise (34880)**
VAL Publications Ltd.
95 Leeward Glenway, No. 121
Don Mills, ON, Canada M3C 2Z6
Phone: (416)424-1393
Fax: (416)467-8262
**Subject(s):** Lifestyle

Circ: (Controlled)‡60,000

**Scoregolf for Women (35792)**
Canadian Controlled Media Communications
5397 Eglinton Ave. W, Ste. 101
Toronto, ON, Canada M9C 5K6
Phone: (416)928-2909
Fax: (416)966-1181
**Subject(s):** Women's Interests; (Golf)

Circ: (Paid)1,000
(Non-paid)59,000

**Chirp (35585)**
St. Joseph Media
111 Queen St. E, Ste. 450
Toronto, ON, Canada M5C 1S2
Phone: (416)595-9944
Fax: (416)595-7217
**Subject(s):** Education; Parenting

Circ: (Combined)58,070

**Camping Canada's RV Lifestyle Magazine (35107)**
Taylor Publishing Group
1020 Brevik Pl., Ste. 5
Mississauga, ON, Canada L4W 4N7
Phone: (905)624-8218
Fax: (905)624-6764
**Subject(s):** (Outdoors)

Circ: (Combined)‡52,000

**The Beaver (34471)**
Canada's National History Society
No. 478-167 Lombard Ave.
Winnipeg, MB, Canada R3B 0T6
Phone: (204)988-9300
Fax: (204)988-9309
**Subject(s):** History and Genealogy

Circ: (Paid)51,000

**Journal of Esthetic and Restorative Dentistry (34968)**
B.C. Decker Inc.
20 Hughson St. S., 10th Fl.
PO Box 620, LCD 1
Hamilton, ON, Canada L8N 3K7
Phone: (905)522-7017
Fax: (905)522-7839
**Subject(s):** Dentistry

Circ: 50,000

**Vitality Magazine (35848)**
356 Dupont St.
Vitality Magazine
Toronto, ON, Canada M5R 1V9
Phone: (416)964-0528
**Subject(s):** Health and Healthcare; Local, State, and Regional Publications

Circ: (Paid)50,000

**Education Forum** (35614)
Ontario Secondary School Teachers' Federation
60 Mobile Dr.
Toronto, ON, Canada M4A 2P3
Phone: (416)751-8300
Fax: (416)751-3875
**Subject(s):** Education
**Circ:** (Combined)49,800

**Investment Executive** (35666)
25 Sheppard Ave. W, Ste. 100
Toronto, ON, Canada M2N 6S7
Phone: (416)733-7600
Fax: (416)218-3544
**Subject(s):** Banking, Finance, and Investments; Management and Administration
**Circ:** (Controlled)45,600

**Mere Nouvelle** (35709)
Today's Parent Group
1 Mount Pleasant Rd., 8th Fl.
Toronto, ON, Canada M4Y 2Y5
Fax: (416)764-2801
**Subject(s):** Health and Healthcare; Pediatrics; Parenting
**Circ:** (Non-paid)45,025

**Performing Arts and Entertainment in Canada** (35752)
Performing Arts in Canada
104 Glenrose Ave.
Toronto, ON, Canada M4T 1K8
Fax: (416)484-6214
**Subject(s):** Performing Arts; Drama and Theatre
**Circ:** (Paid)44,630

**Info-Link** (34907)
I-L Focus Inc.
3044 Bloor St. W, No. 270
Etobicoke, ON, Canada M8X 2Y8
Phone: (416)604-7552
Fax: (416)604-2545
**Subject(s):** Architecture; Construction, Contracting, Building, and Excavating; Interior Design/Decorating
**Circ:** (Combined)•44,168

**Physician's Management Manuals** (35757)
Rogers Media Publishing
1 Mount Pleasant Rd., 7th Fl.
Toronto, ON, Canada M4Y 2Y5
Phone: (416)596-5523
Fax: (416)764-1765
**Subject(s):** Medicine and Surgery; Management and Administration
**Circ:** (Combined)41,101

**The Barrie Examiner This Week** (34783)
The Barrie Examiner Inc.
571 Bayfield St. N.
Barrie, ON, Canada L4M 4Z9
Phone: (705)726-6537
Fax: (705)726-7245
**Subject(s):** Free Newspapers
**Circ:** (Tues.)39,728
 (Thurs.)40,981

**Canadian Guider** (35532)
Girl Guides of Canada
50 Merton St.
Toronto, ON, Canada M4S 1A3
Phone: (416)487-5281
Fax: (416)487-5570
**Subject(s):** Youths' Interests
**Circ:** (Paid)‡300
 (Controlled)‡40,000

**Chart Magazine** (35582)
Chart Communications
41 Britain St., Ste. 200
Toronto, ON, Canada M5A 1R7
Phone: (416)363-3101
Fax: (416)363-3109
**Subject(s):** Music and Musical Instruments
**Circ:** (Combined)40,000

**Klublife** (35685)
Klublife Publishing Inc.
439 King St. W. 4th Fl.
Toronto, ON, Canada M5V 1K1
Phone: (416)644-8681
Fax: (416)644-8684
**Subject(s):** Music and Musical Instruments; Lifestyle; Youths' Interests
**Circ:** (Combined)40,000

**KnitNet** (35686)
eob Inc.
2938 Dundas St. W, Ste. 688
Toronto, ON, Canada M6P 4E7
Phone: (416)410-9880
Fax: (416)410-9880
**Subject(s):** Dressmaking, Needlework, and Quilting
**Circ:** (Non-paid)40,000

**Presbyterian Record** (35765)
Presbyterian Record Inc.
50 Wynford Dr.
Toronto, ON, Canada M3C 1J7
Phone: (416)441-1111
Fax: (416)441-2825
**Subject(s):** Religious Publications
**Circ:** ‡40,000

**The Canadian Bar Review (La Revue du Barreau Canadien)** (35211)
The Canadian Bar Foundation
Dow's Lake Ct.
865 Carling Ave., Ste. 500
Ottawa, ON, Canada K1S 5S8
Phone: (613)237-2925
Fax: (613)237-0185
**Subject(s):** Law; French
**Circ:** (Non-paid)‡2
 (Paid)‡38,128

**Hamilton Magazine** (34966)
Town Publishing
875 Main St. W
Hamilton, ON, Canada L8S 4P9
Phone: (905)522-6117
Fax: (905)529-2242
**Subject(s):** Lifestyle; Local, State, and Regional Publications
**Circ:** (Paid)1,000
 (Non-paid)38,000

**Hospital News Canada** (35659)
Trader Media Corp.
15 Apex Rd.
Toronto, ON, Canada M6A 2V6
Phone: (416)781-5516
Fax: (416)781-5499
**Subject(s):** Hospitals and Healthcare Institutions
**Circ:** (Non-paid)38,000

**Ski Canada** (35798)
Solstice Publishing Inc.
117 Indian Rd.
Toronto, ON, Canada M6R 2V5
Phone: (416)538-2293
Fax: (416)538-2475
**Subject(s):** (Skiing)
**Circ:** (Controlled)•10,106
 (Paid)•37,668

**PETS Magazine** (35378)
Kenilworth Media Inc.
15 Wertheim Ct., Ste. 710
Richmond Hill, ON, Canada L4B 3H7
Phone: (905)771-7333
Fax: (905)771-7336
**Subject(s):** Pets
**Circ:** (Non-paid)•2,476
 (Paid)•37,179

**Nickel** (35727)
Nickel Institute
53 Univ. Ave. Ste. 1801
Toronto, ON, Canada M5J 2H7
Phone: (416)591-7999
Fax: (416)591-7987
**Subject(s):** Mining and Minerals
**Circ:** (Non-paid)37,000

**Grainews** (34483)
Agricore United
2800-201 Portage Ave.
PO Box 6600
Winnipeg, MB, Canada R3C 3A7
Phone: (204)944-5511
Fax: (204)944-5454
**Subject(s):** General Agriculture; Farm Newspapers
**Circ:** (Non-paid)8,276
 (Paid)36,977

**Dogs in Canada** (34905)
Apex Publishing Ltd.
89 Skyway Ave., Ste. 100
Etobicoke, ON, Canada M9W 6R4
Phone: (416)798-9778
Fax: (416)798-9671
**Subject(s):** Dogs
**Circ:** (Non-paid)2,855
 (Paid)36,207

**The Port Hole (Le Hublot)** (35426)
Canadian Power & Sail Squadrons
26 Golden Gate Ct.
Scarborough, ON, Canada M1P 3A5
Phone: (416)293-2438
Fax: (416)293-2445
**Subject(s):** French; (Boating and Yachting)
**Circ:** (Controlled)‡35,000

**Automotive Parts & Technology** (34904)
Cardiff Communications Ltd.
130 Belfield Rd.
Etobicoke, ON, Canada M9W 1G1
Phone: (416)614-0955
Fax: (416)614-2781
**Subject(s):** Automotive (Trade)
**Circ:** (Combined)•34,605

**Canadian Family Physician** (35108)
The College of Family Physicians of Canada
2630 Skymark Ave.
Mississauga, ON, Canada L4W 5A4
Phone: (905)629-0900
Fax: (905)629-0893
**Subject(s):** Medicine and Surgery; French
**Circ:** (Combined)33,908

**NATIONAL** (35290)
The Canadian Bar Foundation
Dow's Lake Ct.
865 Carling Ave., Ste. 500
Ottawa, ON, Canada K1S 5S8
Phone: (613)237-2925
Fax: (613)237-0185
**Subject(s):** Law
**Circ:** (Non-paid)835
 (Paid)33,131

**World of Wheels** (35134)
Annex Publishing & Printing Inc.
6200 Dixie Rd., Ste. 220
Mississauga, ON, Canada L5T 2E1
Phone: (905)795-0110
Fax: (905)795-2967
**Subject(s):** Automotive (Consumer)
**Circ:** (Paid)32,761

**Country Guide** (34479)
Farm Business Communications
2500-201 Portage Ave.
Winnipeg, MB, Canada R3C 3A7
Phone: (204)942-8463
Fax: (204)942-8463
**Subject(s):** General Agriculture
**Circ:** (Non-paid)16,980
 (Paid)31,910

**The Canadian Leader** (35239)
Canyouth Publications Ltd.
1345 Baseline Rd.
Ottawa, ON, Canada K2C 0A7
Phone: (613)224-5131
Fax: (613)224-3571
**Subject(s):** Youths' Interests
**Circ:** •31,785

**Nature Canada** (35291)
Canadian Nature Federation
1 Nicholas St., Ste. 606
Ottawa, ON, Canada K1N 7B7
Phone: (613)562-3447
Fax: (613)562-3371
**Subject(s):** Natural History and Nature Study; Ecology and Conservation
**Circ:** 31,400

**Service Station and Garage Management** (35794)
Business Information Group
12 Concorde Pl., Ste. 800
Toronto, ON, Canada M3C 4J2
Phone: (416)442-2122
Fax: (416)442-2191
**Subject(s):** Automotive (Trade)
**Circ:** (Combined)•30,360

**Today's Trucking** (35824)
New Communications Group Inc.
451 Attwell Dr.
Toronto, ON, Canada M9W 5C4
Phone: (416)614-2200
Fax: (416)614-8861

**Central Provinces** — **Gale Directory of Publications & Broadcast Media/140th Ed.**

**Subject(s):** Trucks and Trucking
**Circ:** (Combined)•29,945

**Canadian Musician (35390)**
Norris-Whitney Communications
23 Hannover Dr., No. 7
Saint Catharines, ON, Canada L2W 1A3
Phone: (905)641-3471
Fax: (905)641-1648
**Subject(s):** Music and Musical Instruments
**Circ:** ‡29,500

**Canadian Lawyer (34762)**
Canadian Lawyer Magazine Ltd.
240 Edward St.
Aurora, ON, Canada L4G 3S9
Phone: (905)841-6480
Fax: (905)727-0017
**Subject(s):** Law
**Circ:** (Controlled)27,506

**Heavy Construction News (35654)**
Rogers Media Publishing
1 Mount Pleasant Rd., 7th Fl.
Toronto, ON, Canada M4Y 2Y5
Phone: (416)596-5523
Fax: (416)764-1765
**Subject(s):** Construction, Contracting, Building, and Excavating
**Circ:** (Combined)26,981

**Manufacturing Automation (35700)**
Kerrwil Publications Ltd.
195, The W. Mall Ste. 500
49 Bather St. Ste.
Toronto, ON, Canada M9C 5K1
Phone: (416)703-7167
**Subject(s):** Machinery and Equipment; Engineering (Various branches)
**Circ:** (Combined)26,348

**The Guardian (35945)**
C.A.W. Locals
1855 Turner Rd.
Windsor, ON, Canada N8W 3K2
Phone: (519)258-6400
Fax: (519)258-0424
**Subject(s):** Labor
**Circ:** ‡26,000

**Cattlemen (34477)**
Farm Business Communications
2500-201 Portage Ave
Winnipeg, MB, Canada R3C 3A7
Phone: (204)942-8463
Fax: (204)942-8463
**Subject(s):** Livestock
**Circ:** (Paid)25,759

**Foodservice and Hospitality Magazine (34879)**
Kostuch Publications Ltd.
23 Lesmill Rd., Ste. 101
Don Mills, ON, Canada M3B 3P6
Phone: (416)447-0888
Fax: (416)447-5333
**Subject(s):** Hotels, Motels, Restaurants, and Clubs
**Circ:** (Controlled)25,051

**Canadian Process Equipment & Control News (35372)**
Canadian Process Equipment & Control News Ltd.
29-588 Edward Ave.
Richmond Hill, ON, Canada L4C 9Y6
Phone: (905)770-8077
Fax: (905)770-8075
**Subject(s):** Chemistry, Chemicals, and Chemical Engineering
**Circ:** (Combined)25,000

**Del Condominium Life (35603)**
Del Property Management Inc.
4800 Dufferin St.
Toronto, ON, Canada M3H 5S9
Phone: (416)661-3151
**Subject(s):** Lifestyle; Local, State, and Regional Publications
**Circ:** (Controlled)25,000

**Family Chronicle (35373)**
Moorshead Magazines Ltd.
505 Consumers Rd., No. 500
Richmond Hill, ON, Canada M2J 4V8
Phone: (416)491-3699
Fax: (416)491-3966
**Subject(s):** History and Genealogy
**Circ:** (Paid)25,000

**Rotunda (35786)**
Royal Ontario Museum
100 Queen's Park
Toronto, ON, Canada M5S 2C6
Phone: (416)586-5585
Fax: (416)586-5649
**Subject(s):** Museums; Natural History and Nature Study; Art
**Circ:** 25,000

**Salon Magazine (35789)**
Salon Communications Inc.
365 Bloor St. E., Ste. 1902
Toronto, ON, Canada M4W 3L4
Phone: (416)869-3131
Fax: (416)869-3008
**Subject(s):** Hairstyling
**Circ:** (Controlled)25,000

**Scope Camping News (34993)**
Merton Publications Ltd.
1070 Gainsborough Rd. W
PO Box 39
Hyde Park, ON, Canada N6H 5M8
**Subject(s):** (Outdoors)
**Circ:** (Controlled)‡25,000

**Wood Design & Building (35315)**
Janam Publications
26 St. Raymond Blvd. Ste. 206
Gatineau, QC, Canada J8Y 1R4
Phone: (800)520-6281
Fax: (819)595-8553
**Subject(s):** Architecture; Construction, Contracting, Building, and Excavating; Wood and Woodworking
**Circ:** (Paid)8,000
(Non-paid)25,000

**explore (35628)**
Quarto Communications
54 St. Patrick St.
Toronto, ON, Canada M5T 1V1
Phone: (416)599-2000
Fax: (416)599-0800
**Subject(s):** (General Sports); Travel and Tourism
**Circ:** (Paid)•24,575

**University Affairs (Affaires Universitaires) (35311)**
Association of Universities and Colleges of Canada
350 Albert St., Ste. 600
Ottawa, ON, Canada K1R 1B1
Phone: (613)563-1236
Fax: (613)563-9745
**Subject(s):** Education; French
**Circ:** (Combined)24,500

**EP&T (Electronic Products and Technology) (35114)**
LVP Media Inc.
27-1200 Aerowood Dr.
Mississauga, ON, Canada L4W 2S7
Phone: (905)624-8100
Fax: (905)624-1760
**Subject(s):** Electronics Engineering
**Circ:** (Controlled)•24,108

**Ontario Medical Review (35737)**
Ontario Medical Association
525 University Ave., Ste. 300
Toronto, ON, Canada M5G 2K7
Phone: (416)599-2580
Fax: (416)340-2232
**Subject(s):** Medicine and Surgery
**Circ:** (Combined)•24,029

**IPP&T (Industrial Process Products and Technology) (35176)**
Swan Erickson Publishing Inc.
1011 Upper Middle Rd. E.
Ste. 1235
Oakville, ON, Canada L6H 5Z9
Phone: (905)475-4231
Fax: (905)475-3512
**Subject(s):** Commerce and Industry
**Circ:** (Combined)23,775

**Big Buck (36489)**
Big Buck Enterprises Corp.
243 Adilman Dr.
Saskatoon, SK, Canada S7K 7R6
Phone: (306)382-2723
Fax: (306)931-2394
**Subject(s):** (Hunting, Fishing, and Game Management)
**Circ:** (Paid)23,094

**Canadian Flight Annual (35217)**
Canadian Owners and Pilots Association
75 Albert St., Ste. 207
Ottawa, ON, Canada K1P 5E7
Phone: (613)236-4901
Fax: (613)236-8646
**Subject(s):** Aviation
**Circ:** ‡23,000

**Canadian Sportfishing (35905)**
Canadian Sportfishing Productions Inc.
937 Centre Rd., Dept. 2020
Waterdown, ON, Canada L0R 2H0
Phone: (905)689-1112
Fax: (905)689-2065
**Subject(s):** (Hunting, Fishing, and Game Management); (Outdoors)
**Circ:** (Combined)22,533

**Mariage Quebec (35701)**
Wedding Bells
111 Queen St. Ste. 200
Toronto, ON, Canada M5E 1C8
Phone: (416)862-8479
**Subject(s):** Brides
**Circ:** (Combined)22,413

**Canadian Industrial Equipment News (35538)**
Business Information Group
12 Concorde Pl., Ste. 800
Toronto, ON, Canada M3C 4J2
Phone: (416)442-2122
Fax: (416)442-2191
**Subject(s):** Commerce and Industry
**Circ:** (Combined)22,363

**Canadian Electronics (34761)**
CLB Media Inc.
240 Edward St.
Aurora, ON, Canada L4G 3S9
Phone: (905)727-0077
Fax: (905)727-0017
**Subject(s):** Electronics Engineering
**Circ:** (Combined)•22,120

**Ovation (34502)**
Manitoba Theatre Centre
174 Market Ave.
Winnipeg, MB, Canada R3B 0P8
Phone: (204)956-1340
Fax: (204)947-3741
**Subject(s):** Drama and Theatre
**Circ:** 22,000

**Teach Magazine (35811)**
TEACH Magazine
206-258 Wallace Ave.
Toronto, ON, Canada M6P 3M9
Phone: (416)537-2103
Fax: (416)537-3491
**Subject(s):** Education
**Circ:** (Paid)1,100
(Controlled)22,000

**The Ontario Technologist (35740)**
Ontario Association of Certified Engineering Technicians and Technologists
10 Four Seasons Pl., Ste. 404
Toronto, ON, Canada M9B 6H7
Phone: (416)621-9621
Fax: (416)621-8694
**Subject(s):** Engineering (Various branches)
**Circ:** (Paid)‡21,800

**Truck West (35834)**
Business Information Group
12 Concorde Pl., Ste. 800
Toronto, ON, Canada M3C 4J2
Phone: (416)442-2122
Fax: (416)442-2191
**Subject(s):** Trucks and Trucking
**Circ:** (Combined)21,417

**CAD Systems (35519)**
Kerrwil Publications Ltd.
195, The W. Mall Ste. 500
49 Bather St. Ste.
Toronto, ON, Canada M9C 5K1
Phone: (416)703-7167
**Subject(s):** Architecture; Automation; Computers
**Circ:** (Combined)21,211

# Gale Directory of Publications & Broadcast Media/140th Ed.  Central Provinces

**Motor Truck (35718)**
Business Information Group
12 Concorde Pl., Ste. 800
Toronto, ON, Canada M3C 4J2
Phone: (416)442-2122
Fax: (416)442-2191
**Subject(s):** Trucks and Trucking
**Circ:** (Combined)•21,194

**Laboratory Product News (35688)**
Business Information Group
12 Concorde Pl., Ste. 800
Toronto, ON, Canada M3C 4J2
Phone: (416)442-2122
Fax: (416)442-2191
**Subject(s):** Laboratory Research (Scientific and Medical)
**Circ:** (Combined)•20,359

**Metalworking Production and Purchasing (34772)**
CLB Media Inc.
240 Edward St.
Aurora, ON, Canada L4G 3S9
Phone: (905)727-0077
Fax: (905)727-0017
**Subject(s):** Metal, Metallurgy, and Metal Trade
**Circ:** (Combined)•20,234

**Benefits and Pensions Monitor (35506)**
Powershift Communications Inc.
245 Fairview Mall Dr., Ste. 501
5th Floor, Toronto
Toronto, ON, Canada M2J 4T1
Phone: (416)494-1066
Fax: (416)494-2536
**Subject(s):** Banking, Finance, and Investments; Health and Healthcare
**Circ:** (Combined)20,108

**Pharmacy Practice (35755)**
Rogers Media Publishing
1 Mount Pleasant Rd., 7th Fl.
Toronto, ON, Canada M4Y 2Y5
Phone: (416)596-5523
Fax: (416)764-1765
**Subject(s):** Drugs and Pharmaceuticals
**Circ:** (Combined)20,077

**Canadian Shareowner (35564)**
121 Richmond St. W. 7th Fl.
Toronto, ON, Canada M5H 2K1
Phone: (416)595-9600
Fax: (416)595-0400
**Subject(s):** Education; Banking, Finance, and Investments
**Circ:** (Non-paid)‡200
(Paid)‡20,000

**Horse-Canada.com Magazine (34769)**
Canadian Horse Publications
PO Box 670
Aurora, ON, Canada L4G 4J9
Phone: (905)727-0107
Fax: (905)841-1530
**Subject(s):** (Horses and Horse Racing)
**Circ:** (Paid)20,000

**IT Magazine (35669)**
Rogers Media Publishing
1 Mount Pleasant Rd., 7th Fl.
Toronto, ON, Canada M4Y 2Y5
Phone: (416)596-5523
Fax: (416)764-1765
**Subject(s):** Computers; Machinery and Equipment
**Circ:** 20,000

**Ottawa Business Journal (35292)**
InBusiness Media Network Inc.
1686 Woodward Dr.
Ottawa, ON, Canada K2C 3R8
Phone: (613)230-8699
Fax: (613)230-9606
**Subject(s):** Business; Local, State, and Regional Publications
**Circ:** (Combined)•20,000

**Performing Arts in Canada (35751)**
104 Glenrose Ave.
Toronto, ON, Canada M4T 1K8
Phone: (416)484-4534
Fax: (416)484-6214
**Subject(s):** Performing Arts; Entertainment
**Circ:** ‡20,000

**Trot (35130)**
Canadian Trotting Association
2150 Meadowvale Blvd.
Mississauga, ON, Canada L5N 6R6
Phone: (905)858-3060
Fax: (905)858-3111
**Subject(s):** French; (Horses and Horse Racing)
**Circ:** (Non-paid)‡2,000
(Paid)‡20,000

**Journal of the Canadian Dental Association (Journal de l'Association Dentaire Canadienne) (35275)**
Canadian Dental Association
1815, Alta Vista Dr.
Ottawa, ON, Canada K1G 3Y6
Phone: (613)523-1770
Fax: (613)565-7488
**Subject(s):** Dentistry; French
**Circ:** (Combined)•19,897

**Focus Newsmagazine (34934)**
Signal Star Publishing
Box 220
Goderich, ON, Canada N7A 4B6
**Subject(s):** Local, State, and Regional Publications
**Circ:** (Non-paid)19,600

**Mississauga Business Times (35124)**
Metroland News
3145 Wolfedale Rd.
Mississauga, ON, Canada L5C 3A9
Phone: (905)273-8285
**Subject(s):** Business; Local, State, and Regional Publications
**Circ:** (Controlled)‡19,500

**Design Product News (34767)**
CLB Media Inc.
240 Edward St.
Aurora, ON, Canada L4G 3S9
Phone: (905)727-0077
Fax: (905)727-0017
**Subject(s):** Engineering (Various branches)
**Circ:** (Combined)19,416

**Materials Management & Distribution (35705)**
Rogers Media Publishing
One Mount Pleasant Rd., 7th Fl.
Toronto, ON, Canada M4Y 2Y5
Phone: (416)764-2000
Fax: (416)764-1746
**Subject(s):** Materials Handling; Transportation, Traffic, and Shipping; Purchasing
**Circ:** (Combined)19,226

**Design Engineering (35607)**
Rogers Media Publishing
1 Mount Pleasant Rd., 7th Fl.
Toronto, ON, Canada M4Y 2Y5
Phone: (416)596-5523
Fax: (416)764-1765
**Subject(s):** Engineering (Various branches)
**Circ:** (Combined)•19,190

**Canadian Machinery and Metalworking (35548)**
Rogers Media Publishing
1 Mount Pleasant Rd., 7th Fl.
Toronto, ON, Canada M4Y 2Y5
Phone: (416)596-5523
Fax: (416)764-1765
**Subject(s):** Machinery and Equipment; Metal, Metallurgy, and Metal Trade
**Circ:** (Paid)•306
(Non-paid)•19,120

**Canadian MoneySaver (34789)**
PO Box 370
Bath, ON, Canada K0H 1G0
Phone: (613)352-7448
Fax: (613)352-7700
**Subject(s):** Business; Consumerism; Banking, Finance, and Investments
**Circ:** ‡19,100

**Environmental Science & Engineering (34768)**
Environmental Science & Engineering Publications Inc.
220 Industrial Pkwy. S., Unit 30
Aurora, ON, Canada L4G 3V6
Phone: (905)727-4666
Fax: (905)841-7271
**Subject(s):** Waste Management and Recycling; Water Supply and Sewage Disposal; Ecology and Conservation; Engineering (Various branches)
**Circ:** (Combined)19,095

**Pentecostal Testimony (35128)**
Pentecostal Assemblies of Canada
2450 Milltower Ct.
Mississauga, ON, Canada L5N 5Z6
Phone: (905)542-7400
Fax: (905)542-7313
**Subject(s):** Religious Publications
**Circ:** ‡19,000

**The Registered Nurse Journal (35778)**
Registered Nurses Association of Ontario
438 University Ave., Ste. 1600
Toronto, ON, Canada M5G 2K8
Phone: (416)599-1925
Fax: (416)599-1926
**Subject(s):** Nursing
**Circ:** (Controlled)‡19,000

**Machinery & Equipment MRO (35698)**
Business Information Group
12 Concorde Pl., Ste. 800
Toronto, ON, Canada M3C 4J2
Phone: (416)442-2122
Fax: (416)442-2191
**Subject(s):** Machinery and Equipment
**Circ:** (Combined)18,828

**Dairy Update-Demographic Section of Country Guide Magazine (34480)**
Farm Business Communications
Box 9800, Stn. Main
8th Fl., 220 Portage Ave.
Winnipeg, MB, Canada R3C 3A7
Phone: (204)954-1400
Fax: (204)942-8463
**Subject(s):** Dairying
**Circ:** ‡18,653

**Pharmacy Post (35754)**
Rogers Publishing
1 Mt. Pleasant Rd.
12th Floor
Toronto, ON, Canada M4Y 2Y5
Phone: (416)764-2000
Fax: (416)764-3931
**Subject(s):** Drugs and Pharmaceuticals; French
**Circ:** (Combined)18,529

**Electrical Business (35617)**
Kerrwil Publications Ltd.
195, The W. Mall Ste. 500
49 Bather St. Ste.
Toronto, ON, Canada M9C 5K1
Phone: (416)703-7167
**Subject(s):** Electrical Engineering
**Circ:** (Combined)•18,429

**Canadian Transportation & Logistics (35566)**
Business Information Group
12 Concorde Pl., Ste. 800
Toronto, ON, Canada M3C 4J2
Phone: (416)442-2122
Fax: (416)442-2191
**Subject(s):** Transportation, Traffic, and Shipping
**Circ:** (Combined)‡18,382

**Modern Purchasing (35712)**
Rogers Media Publishing
1 Mount Pleasant Rd., 7th Fl.
Toronto, ON, Canada M4Y 2Y5
Phone: (416)596-5523
Fax: (416)764-1765
**Subject(s):** Purchasing
**Circ:** (Combined)18,313

**Technology in Government (35812)**
Transcontinental IT Business Group
25 Sheppard Ave. W, Ste. 100
Toronto, ON, Canada M2N 6S7
Phone: (416)733-7600
Fax: (416)227-8324
**Subject(s):** Computers; Automation; Politics
**Circ:** (Combined)18,318

**PEM Plant Engineering and Maintenance (34832)**
Clifford/Elliot Ltd.
209-3228 S Service Rd.
Burlington, ON, Canada L7N 3H8
Phone: (905)634-2100
Fax: (800)268-7977
**Subject(s):** Building Management and Maintenance; Engineering (Various branches)
**Circ:** (Combined)18,089

*Periodical Index*

Circulation: ★ = ABC; △ = BPA; ♦ = CAC; • = CCAB; □ = VAC; ⊕ = PO Statement; ‡ = Publisher's Report; Boldface figures = sworn; Light figures = estimated.

## Central Provinces

**Canadian Grocer** (35531)
Rogers Media Publishing
1 Mount Pleasant Rd., 7th Fl.
Toronto, ON, Canada M4Y 2Y5
Phone: (416)596-5523
Fax: (416)764-1765
**Subject(s):** Food and Grocery Trade
**Circ:** (Paid)•2,341
(Non-paid)•18,054

**Plumbing & HVAC Product News** (34908)
Nytek Publishing Inc.
451 Attwell Dr.
Etobicoke, ON, Canada M9W 5C4
Phone: (416)242-8088
Fax: (416)242-8085
**Subject(s):** Plumbing and Heating
**Circ:** (Combined)•18,031

**Advocif** (35494)
Financial Advisors Association of Canada
350 Bloor St. E, 2nd Fl.
Toronto, ON, Canada M4W 3W8
Phone: (416)444-5251
Fax: (416)444-8031
**Subject(s):** Insurance; French
**Circ:** (Paid)‡1,500
(Controlled)‡18,000

**Charolais Connection** (36474)
Charolais Banner Ltd.
1933 8th Ave., No. 200
Regina, SK, Canada S4R 1E9
Phone: (306)546-3940
Fax: (306)546-3942
**Subject(s):** Livestock
**Circ:** (Non-paid)‡300
(Paid)‡18,000

**Commerce & Industry** (34478)
Mercury Publications Ltd.
1839 Inkster Blvd.
Winnipeg, MB, Canada R2X 1R3
Phone: (204)954-2085
Fax: (204)954-2057
**Subject(s):** Commerce and Industry
**Circ:** (Combined)•18,000

**Dental Practice Management** (35605)
Business Information Group
12 Concorde Pl., Ste. 800
Toronto, ON, Canada M3C 4J2
Phone: (416)442-2122
Fax: (416)442-2191
**Subject(s):** Dentistry
**Circ:** ‡18,000

**Geriatrics Today** (35641)
FD Communications Inc.
5863 Leslie St., Box 1002
Toronto, ON, Canada M2H 1J8
Phone: (416)224-5055
Fax: (416)224-5455
**Subject(s):** Health and Healthcare; Gerontology
**Circ:** (Combined)18,000

**Key to Kingston** (35011)
Kingston Publications
Box 1352
Kingston, ON, Canada K7L 5C6
Phone: (613)549-8442
Fax: (613)549-4333
**Subject(s):** Travel and Tourism
**Circ:** (Non-paid)‡18,000

**Oral Health** (35742)
Business Information Group
12 Concorde Pl., Ste. 800
Toronto, ON, Canada M3C 4J2
Phone: (416)442-2122
Fax: (416)442-2191
**Subject(s):** Dentistry
**Circ:** (Controlled)•18,000

**Canadian Industrial Machinery** (34827)
Canadian Industrial Publishing Inc.
5100 S. Service Rd., Unit 36
Burlington, ON, Canada L7L 6A5
Phone: (905)637-2317
Fax: (905)634-2776
**Subject(s):** Metal, Metallurgy, and Metal Trade
**Circ:** (Combined)17,464

**Benefits Canada** (35505)
Rogers Media Publishing
1 Mount Pleasant Rd., 7th Fl.
Toronto, ON, Canada M4Y 2Y5
Phone: (416)596-5523
Fax: (416)764-1765
**Subject(s):** Employment and Human Resources
**Circ:** (Combined)•17,212

**Ontario Medicine** (35738)
Rogers Media Publishing
1 Mount Pleasant Rd., 7th Fl.
Toronto, ON, Canada M4Y 2Y5
Phone: (416)596-5523
Fax: (416)764-1765
**Subject(s):** Medicine and Surgery
**Circ:** (Combined)17,087

**Canadian Cooperative Wool Growers Magazine** (34861)
Canadian Co-Operative Wool Growers Ltd.
c/o Ontario Stockyards Inc.
RR 1, Hwy. 89
Box 1051
Cookstown, ON, Canada L0L 1L0
Phone: (705)458-4800
Fax: (705)458-0186
**Subject(s):** Livestock
**Circ:** 5,000
⊕12,000
(Non-paid)17,000

**Mennonite Brethren Herald** (34494)
Canadian Conference of Mennonite Brethren Churches
3-169 Riverton Ave.
Winnipeg, MB, Canada R2L 2E5
Phone: (204)654-5760
Fax: (204)654-1865
**Subject(s):** Religious Publications
**Circ:** ‡17,000

**Strategy** (35806)
Brunico Communications Inc.
366 Adelaide St. W, Ste. 500
Toronto, ON, Canada M5V 1R9
Phone: (416)408-2300
Fax: (416)408-0870
**Subject(s):** Advertising and Marketing
**Circ:** (Combined)16,700

**Indian Life** (34486)
Intertribal Christian Communications
188 Henderson Hwy.
Winnipeg, MB, Canada R2L 1L6
Phone: (204)661-3982
Fax: (204)661-3982
**Subject(s):** Native American Interests; Religious Publications
**Circ:** (Non-paid)‡3,175
(Paid)‡16,530

**HPAC (Heating-Plumbing-Air Conditioning Magazine)** (35661)
Rogers Media Publishing
One Mount Pleasant Rd., 7th Fl.
Toronto, ON, Canada M4Y 2Y5
Phone: (416)764-2000
Fax: (416)764-1746
**Subject(s):** Air Conditioning and Refrigeration; Plumbing and Heating
**Circ:** (Combined)16,528

**Government Purchasing Guide** (35374)
Kenilworth Media Inc.
15 Wertheim Ct., Ste. 710
Richmond Hill, ON, Canada L4B 3H7
Phone: (905)771-7333
Fax: (905)771-7336
**Subject(s):** Purchasing; State, Municipal, and County Administration
**Circ:** (Combined)•16,401

**EDGE** (35612)
Transcontinential IT Business Group
25 Sheppard Ave. W, Ste. 100
Toronto, ON, Canada M2N 6S7
Phone: (416)733-7600
Fax: (416)227-8324
**Subject(s):** Business; Automation; Computers
**Circ:** (Combined)16,361

**Western Grocer** (34512)
Mercury Publications Ltd.
1839 Inkster Blvd.
Winnipeg, MB, Canada R2X 1R3
Phone: (204)954-2085

Fax: (204)954-2057
**Subject(s):** Food and Grocery Trade
**Circ:** (Combined)•16,200

**Channel Business** (35581)
Rogers Media Publishing
1 Mount Pleasant Rd., 7th Fl.
Toronto, ON, Canada M4Y 2Y5
Phone: (416)596-5523
Fax: (416)764-1765
**Subject(s):** Computers
**Circ:** (Controlled)•16,150

**Bar & Beverage Business Magazine** (34470)
Mercury Publications Ltd.
1839 Inkster Blvd.
Winnipeg, MB, Canada R2X 1R3
Phone: (204)954-2085
Fax: (204)954-2057
**Subject(s):** Hotels, Motels, Restaurants, and Clubs; Beverages, Brewing, and Bottling
**Circ:** (Combined)16,077

**Profile Kingston** (35015)
Riverview Publishing Inc.
PO Box 91
Kingston, ON, Canada K7L 4V6
Phone: (613)546-6723
Fax: (613)546-0707
**Subject(s):** Lifestyle; Local, State, and Regional Publications
**Circ:** (Controlled)16,000

**Canadian Art** (35523)
Canadian Art Foundation
51 Front St. E, Ste. 210
Toronto, ON, Canada M5E 1B3
Phone: (416)368-8854
Fax: (416)368-6135
**Subject(s):** Art
**Circ:** (Non-paid)‡4,864
(Paid)‡15,828

**Hardware & Home Centre Magazine** (35650)
Business Information Group
12 Concorde Pl., Ste. 800
Toronto, ON, Canada M3C 4J2
Phone: (416)442-2122
Fax: (416)442-2191
**Subject(s):** Wood and Woodworking; Building Materials, Concrete, Brick, and Tile
**Circ:** (Controlled)15,749

**Heating, Plumbing, Air Conditioning Buyers' Guide** (35653)
Rogers Media Publishing
One Mount Pleasant Rd., 7th Fl.
Toronto, ON, Canada M4Y 2Y5
Phone: (416)764-2000
Fax: (416)764-1746
**Subject(s):** Air Conditioning and Refrigeration; Plumbing and Heating
**Circ:** (Controlled)15,528

**The Canadian Journal of Cardiology (Journal Canadien de Cardiologie)** (35167)
Pulsus Group Inc.
2902 S Sheridan Way
Oakville, ON, Canada L6J 7L6
Phone: (905)829-4770
Fax: (905)829-4799
**Subject(s):** Medicine and Surgery
**Circ:** (Combined)15,500

**The Canadian Journal of Gastroenterology** (35169)
Pulsus Group Inc.
2902 S Sheridan Way
Oakville, ON, Canada L6J 7L6
Phone: (905)829-4770
Fax: (905)829-4799
**Subject(s):** Medicine and Surgery
**Circ:** (Paid)‡200
(Controlled)‡15,500

**Canadian Respiratory Journal** (35171)
Pulsus Group Inc.
2902 S Sheridan Way
Oakville, ON, Canada L6J 7L6
Phone: (905)829-4770
Fax: (905)829-4799
**Subject(s):** Medicine and Surgery; Health and Healthcare
**Circ:** (Controlled)15,500

# Gale Directory of Publications & Broadcast Media/140th Ed.

## Central Provinces

**Home Improvement Retailing** (35657)
Powershift Communications Inc.
245 Fairview Mall Dr., Ste. 501
5th Floor, Toronto
Toronto, ON, Canada M2J 4T1
Phone: (416)494-1066
Fax: (416)494-2536
**Subject(s):** Hardware; Building Materials, Concrete, Brick, and Tile; Construction, Contracting, Building, and Excavating
**Circ:** (Combined)15,356

**Hardware Merchandising** (35651)
Rogers Media Publishing
1 Mount Pleasant Rd., 7th Fl.
Toronto, ON, Canada M4Y 2Y5
Phone: (416)596-5523
Fax: (416)764-1765
**Subject(s):** Hardware; Building Materials, Concrete, Brick, and Tile
**Circ:** (Combined)•15,136

**Produits Pour L'Industrie Quebecoise** (34773)
CLB Media Inc.
240 Edward St.
Aurora, ON, Canada L4G 3S9
Phone: (905)727-0077
Fax: (905)727-0017
**Subject(s):** Commerce and Industry; French
**Circ:** (Combined)15,074

**Association** (35497)
Naylor Communications Ltd.
10 King St. E., Ste. 1100
Toronto, ON, Canada M5C 1C3
Phone: (519)794-3430
**Subject(s):** Business; Management and Administration
**Circ:** (Combined)15,000

**Exodus Magazine** (35626)
Jewish Russian Community Centre of Toronto
5987 Bathurst St., Ste. 3
Toronto, ON, Canada M2R 1Z3
Phone: (416)222-7105
Fax: (416)222-7812
**Subject(s):** Jewish Publications; Russian
**Circ:** (Non-paid)3,000
       (Paid)15,000

**Turf & Recreation** (34877)
Turf and Recreation Publishing Inc.
275 James St.
Delhi, ON, Canada N4B 2B2
Phone: (519)582-8873
Fax: (519)582-8877
**Subject(s):** Parks; Cemeteries and Monuments; Golf Course Management
**Circ:** (Combined)15,000

**Western Restaurant News** (34514)
Mercury Publications Ltd.
1839 Inkster Blvd.
Winnipeg, MB, Canada R2X 1R3
Phone: (204)954-2085
Fax: (204)954-2057
**Subject(s):** Food and Grocery Trade
**Circ:** 14,723

**Network World Canada** (35422)
IT World Canada Inc.
55 Town Center Ct., Ste. 302
Scarborough, ON, Canada M1P 4X4
Phone: (416)290-0240
Fax: (416)290-0238
**Subject(s):** Computers
**Circ:** (Controlled)14,538

**Electricity Today** (34749)
Hurst Communications Group Inc.
204-15 Harwood Ave. S
Ajax, ON, Canada L1S 2B9
Phone: (905)686-1040
Fax: (905)686-1078
**Subject(s):** Electrical Engineering
**Circ:** (Paid)37
       (Non-paid)14,500

**Seasons** (34882)
Federation of Ontario Naturalists
355 Lesmill Rd.
Don Mills, ON, Canada M3B 2W8
Phone: (416)444-8419
Fax: (416)444-9866
**Subject(s):** Environmental and Natural Resources Conservation
**Circ:** (Combined)‡14,500

**Ontario Dairy Farmer** (35056)
Bowes Publishers Ltd.
1147 Gainsborough Rd.
PO Box 7400
London, ON, Canada N6H 5L5
Phone: (519)471-8520
Fax: (519)471-1892
**Subject(s):** Dairying; General Agriculture
**Circ:** 14,411

**Canadian Journal of Medical Laboratory Science (CJLMS)** (34960)
Canadian Society for Medical Laboratory Science
PO Box 2830, LCD 1
Hamilton, ON, Canada L8N 3N8
Phone: (905)528-8642
Fax: (905)528-4968
**Subject(s):** Laboratory Research (Scientific and Medical); French
**Circ:** (Controlled)451
       (Paid)14,326

**Gifts & Tablewares** (35643)
Business Information Group
12 Concorde Pl., Ste. 800
Toronto, ON, Canada M3C 4J2
Phone: (416)442-2122
Fax: (416)442-2191
**Subject(s):** Gifts, Toys, and Novelties; Stationery, Office Equipment, and College Store Supplies
**Circ:** (Paid)1,796
       (Non-paid)14,065

**Ballet-Hoo** (34469)
Royal Winnipeg Ballet
380 Graham Ave.
Winnipeg, MB, Canada R3C 4K2
Phone: (204)956-0183
Fax: (204)943-1994
**Subject(s):** Performing Arts
**Circ:** (Paid)‡100
       (Non-paid)‡14,000

**Canadian Occupational Safety** (34828)
Clifford/Elliot Ltd.
209-3228 S Service Rd.
Burlington, ON, Canada L7N 3H8.
Phone: (905)634-2100
Fax: (800)268-7977
**Subject(s):** Safety; Health and Healthcare
**Circ:** (Combined)14,000

**Housewares Canada** (35660)
Business Information Group
12 Concorde Pl., Ste. 800
Toronto, ON, Canada M3C 4J2
Phone: (416)442-2122
Fax: (416)442-2191
**Subject(s):** Appliances
**Circ:** ‡14,000

**Press Review** (35766)
1 Yonge St. 1801
Toronto, ON, Canada M5E 1W7
Phone: (416)368-0512
Fax: (416)366-0104
**Subject(s):** Journalism and Publishing
**Circ:** ‡14,000

**CANADIAN SECURITY** (34763)
CLB Media Inc.
240 Edward St.
Aurora, ON, Canada L4G 3S9
Phone: (905)727-0077
Fax: (905)727-0017
**Subject(s):** Safety; Communications
**Circ:** ‡13,771

**Travelweek** (35832)
Concepts Travel Media Ltd.
282 Richmond St. E., Ste. 100
Toronto, ON, Canada M5A 1P4
Phone: (416)365-1500
Fax: (416)365-1504
**Subject(s):** Travel and Tourism
**Circ:** (Combined)13,563

**Canadian Travel Press** (35567)
Baxter Publishing Co.
310 Dupont St.
Toronto, ON, Canada M5R 1V9
Phone: (416)968-7252
Fax: (416)968-2377
**Subject(s):** Travel and Tourism
**Circ:** (Controlled)13,551

**London Business Monthly Magazine** (35054)
PO Box 7400
London, ON, Canada N5Y 4X3
Phone: (519)472-7601
Fax: (519)473-2256
**Subject(s):** Business
**Circ:** (Paid)‡1,020
       (Non-paid)‡13,467

**Azure Magazine** (35501)
Azure Publishing Inc.
460 Richmond St. W, Ste. 601
Toronto, ON, Canada M5V 1Y1
Phone: (416)203-9674
Fax: (416)203-9842
**Subject(s):** Architecture
**Circ:** (Combined)•13,230

**Airforce** (35203)
Airforce Productions Ltd.
PO Box 2460, Sta. D
Ottawa, ON, Canada K1P 5W6
Phone: (613)992-5184
Fax: (613)995-2196
**Subject(s):** Military and Navy
**Circ:** (Non-paid)3,299
       (Paid)13,227

**Canadian Packaging** (35556)
Rogers Media Publishing
1 Mount Pleasant Rd., 7th Fl.
Toronto, ON, Canada M4Y 2Y5
Phone: (416)596-5523
Fax: (416)764-1765
**Subject(s):** Packaging
**Circ:** (Combined)13,188

**The Packet & Times This Week** (35195)
Orillia Packet and Times
31 Colborne St.E.
PO Box 220
Orillia, ON, Canada L3V 1T4
Phone: (705)325-1355
Fax: (705)329-5926
**Subject(s):** Free Newspapers
**Circ:** (Non-paid)13,113

**Civic Public Works** (35588)
Rogers Media Publishing
1 Mount Pleasant Rd., 7th Fl.
Toronto, ON, Canada M4Y 2Y5
Phone: (416)596-5523
Fax: (416)764-1765
**Subject(s):** State, Municipal, and County Administration
**Circ:** (Combined)13,085

**Canadian Messenger** (35550)
Apostleship of Prayer
661 Greenwood Ave.
Toronto, ON, Canada M4J 4B3
Phone: (416)466-1195
**Subject(s):** Religious Publications
**Circ:** ‡13,000

**Messenger of the Sacred Heart** (35710)
Apostleship of Prayer
661 Greenwood Ave.
Toronto, ON, Canada M4J 4B3
Phone: (416)466-1195
**Subject(s):** Religious Publications
**Circ:** (Controlled)70
       (Paid)13,000

**RCMP Veterans' Association Quarterly/Association des anciens de la GRC Trimestrialle** (35306)
Royal Canadian Mounted Police Veterans' Association
Attn: The Quarterly
1200 Vanier Pkwy.
Ottawa, ON, Canada K1A 0R2
Phone: (613)993-3738
Fax: (613)993-4353
**Subject(s):** History and Genealogy; Police, Penology, and Penal Institutions
**Circ:** 13,000

**Steel Marketplace** (35445)
PO Box 10099, Sta. Winona
Stoney Creek, ON, Canada L8E 5R1
Phone: (905)643-7321
Fax: (905)643-2684
**Subject(s):** Metal, Metallurgy, and Metal Trade
**Circ:** 13,000

Circulation: ★ = ABC; ∆ = BPA; ♦ = CAC; • = CCAB; ☐ = VAC; ⊖ = PO Statement; ‡ = Publisher's Report; Boldface figures = sworn; Light figures = estimated.

**Central Provinces**                                                                 Gale Directory of Publications & Broadcast Media/140th Ed.

**Cosmetics** (35597)
Rogers Media Publishing
1 Mount Pleasant Rd., 7th Fl.
Toronto, ON, Canada M4Y 2Y5
Phone: (416)596-5523
Fax: (416)764-1765
**Subject(s):** Cosmetics and Toiletries
**Circ:** (Controlled)‡12,850

**Wings Magazine** (35133)
Annex Publishing & Printing Inc.
6200 Dixie Rd., Ste. 220
Mississauga, ON, Canada L5T 2E1
Phone: (905)795-0110
Fax: (905)795-2967
**Subject(s):** Aviation
**Circ:** (Combined)•12,832

**L'Epicier** (35621)
Rogers Media Publishing
1 Mount Pleasant Rd., 7th Fl.
Toronto, ON, Canada M4Y 2Y5
Phone: (416)596-5523
Fax: (416)764-1765
**Subject(s):** Food and Grocery Trade; French
**Circ:** (Controlled)12,806

**Marketing Magazine** (35703)
Rogers Media Publishing
One Mount Pleasant Rd., 7th Fl.
Toronto, ON, Canada M4Y 2Y5
Phone: (416)764-2000
Fax: (416)764-1519
**Subject(s):** Advertising and Marketing
**Circ:** (Paid)12,761

**Pharmacy Connection** (35753)
Ontario College of Pharmacists
483 Huron Street
Toronto, ON, Canada M5R 2R4
Phone: (416)962-4861
Fax: (416)847-8200
**Subject(s):** Drugs and Pharmaceuticals
**Circ:** 12,200

**L'Automobile** (35500)
Business Information Group
12 Concorde Pl., Ste. 800
Toronto, ON, Canada M3C 4J2
Phone: (416)442-2122
Fax: (416)442-2191
**Subject(s):** Automotive (Trade); French
**Circ:** (Combined)•12,087

**Transport Routier** (35830)
New Communications Group Inc.
451 Attwell Dr.
Toronto, ON, Canada M9W 5C4
Phone: (416)614-2200
Fax: (416)614-8861
**Subject(s):** Trucks and Trucking; French
**Circ:** (Combined)•12,022

**Blue Line Magazine** (35077)
4981 Hwy. 7 E, Ste. 254
Markham, ON, Canada L3R 1N1
Phone: (905)640-3048
Fax: (905)640-7547
**Subject(s):** Police, Penology, and Penal Institutions
**Circ:** (Combined)⊕12,000

**Cerebus** (35028)
Aardvark-Vanaheim Inc.
PO Box 1674, Sta. C
Kitchener, ON, Canada N2G 4R2
Phone: (519)576-0610
Fax: (519)576-0955
**Subject(s):** Comics and Comic Technique
**Circ:** 12,000

**Model Aviation Canada** (34831)
Model Aeronautics Association of Canada
5100 S Service Rd., Unit 9
Burlington, ON, Canada L7L 6A5
Phone: (905)632-9808
Fax: (905)632-3304
**Subject(s):** Crafts, Models, Hobbies, and Contests
**Circ:** (Non-paid)⊕12,000

**Bodyshop** (35509)
Business Information Group
12 Concorde Pl., Ste. 800
Toronto, ON, Canada M3C 4J2
Phone: (416)442-2122
Fax: (416)442-2191
**Subject(s):** Automotive (Trade)
**Circ:** (Combined)•11,834

**Applied Arts Magazine** (35156)
Applied Arts Inc.
18 Wynford Dr., Ste. 411
North York, ON, Canada M3C 3S2
Phone: (416)510-0909
Fax: (416)510-0913
**Subject(s):** Photography; Art and Art History; Printing and Typography
**Circ:** (Combined)11,500

**TV This Week** (36536)
Yorkton This Week Ltd.
20 3rd Ave. N
PO Box 1300
Yorkton, SK, Canada S3N 2X3
Phone: (306)782-2465
Fax: (306)786-1898
**Subject(s):** Radio, Television, Cable, and Video
**Circ:** (Paid)‡11,316

**Canadian Printer Magazine** (35560)
Rogers Media Publishing
1 Mount Pleasant Rd., 7th Fl.
Toronto, ON, Canada M4Y 2Y5
Phone: (416)596-5523
Fax: (416)764-1765
**Subject(s):** Printing and Typography
**Circ:** (Paid)143
   (Non-paid)11,302

**Market News** (35702)
Marketnews and Beaumont Publishing
701 Evans Aven, Ste. 102
Toronto, ON, Canada M9C 1A3
Phone: (416)667-9945
Fax: (416)667-0609
**Subject(s):** Computers
**Circ:** (Combined)11,200

**Accident Prevention** (35491)
Industrial Accident Prevention Association
207 Queens Quay W, Ste. 550
Toronto, ON, Canada M5J 2Y3
Phone: (416)506-8888
Fax: (416)506-8880
**Subject(s):** Safety; Ecology and Conservation
**Circ:** (Combined)11,173

**Woodworking** (34774)
CLB Media Inc.
240 Edward St.
Aurora, ON, Canada L4G 3S9
Phone: (905)727-0077
Fax: (905)727-0017
**Subject(s):** Wood and Woodworking
**Circ:** (Combined)•11,171

**Jobber News** (35671)
Business Information Group
12 Concorde Pl., Ste. 800
Toronto, ON, Canada M3C 4J2
Phone: (416)442-2122
Fax: (416)442-2191
**Subject(s):** Automotive (Trade)
**Circ:** (Combined)11,127

**Cabling Networking Systems** (35518)
Business Information Group
12 Concorde Pl., Ste. 800
Toronto, ON, Canada M3C 4J2
Phone: (416)442-2122
Fax: (416)442-2191
**Subject(s):** Telecommunications; Engineering (Various branches)
**Circ:** (Combined)11,000

**Zwiazkowiec (Alliancer)** (35860)
Polish Alliance Press Ltd.
1586 Bloor Street West
Toronto, ON, Canada M6P 1A7
Phone: (416)531-2491
Fax: (416)531-5153
**Subject(s):** Polish; Unclassified Fraternal
**Circ:** (Fri.)11,000

**Windsport Magazine** (35855)
Windsport Publishing
2255 B. Queen, Ste. 3266 E
Toronto, ON, Canada M4E 1G3
Phone: (416)406-2400
Fax: (416)406-0656
**Subject(s):** (Water Sports)
**Circ:** (Non-paid)‡4,800
   (Paid)‡10,700

**Plastics in Canada** (35760)
Rogers Media Publishing
1 Mount Pleasant Rd., 7th Fl.
Toronto, ON, Canada M4Y 2Y5
Phone: (416)596-5523
Fax: (416)764-1765
**Subject(s):** Plastic and Composition Materials
**Circ:** (Combined)10,550

**Marketnews** (35704)
Marketnews Magazine
701 Evans Ave., Ste. 102
Toronto, ON, Canada M9C 1A3
Phone: (416)667-9945
Fax: (416)667-0609
**Subject(s):** Electronics Engineering; Radio, Television, Cable, and Video
**Circ:** (Combined)•10,538

**Northern Ontario Business** (35423)
IT World Canada Inc.
55 Town Center Ct., Ste. 302
Scarborough, ON, Canada M1P 4X4
Phone: (416)290-0240
Fax: (416)290-0238
**Subject(s):** Business; Local, State, and Regional Publications
**Circ:** (Controlled)‡10,500

**Meetings & Incentive Travel** (35707)
Rogers Media Publishing
1 Mount Pleasant Rd., 7th Fl.
Toronto, ON, Canada M4Y 2Y5
Phone: (416)596-5523
Fax: (416)764-1765
**Subject(s):** Travel and Tourism; Conventions, Meetings, and Trade Fairs
**Circ:** (Combined)•10,422

**The Graphic Monthly** (35116)
North Island Publishing
1606 Sedlescomb Dr., Unit 8
Mississauga, ON, Canada L4X 1M6
Phone: (905)625-7070
Fax: (905)625-4856
**Subject(s):** Printing and Typography
**Circ:** (Controlled)10,413

**Canadian Plastics** (35558)
Business Information Group
12 Concorde Pl., Ste. 800
Toronto, ON, Canada M3C 4J2
Phone: (416)442-2122
Fax: (416)442-2191
**Subject(s):** Plastic and Composition Materials
**Circ:** (Combined)10,244

**Canadian Mining Journal** (35551)
Business Information Group
12 Concorde Pl., Ste. 800
Toronto, ON, Canada M3C 4J2
Phone: (416)442-2122
Fax: (416)442-2191
**Subject(s):** Mining and Minerals
**Circ:** (Combined)•10,158

**Taxi News** (35810)
Chedmount Investments Ltd.
38 Fairmount Crescent
Toronto, ON, Canada M4L 2H4
Phone: (416)466-2328
Fax: (416)466-4220
**Subject(s):** Public Transportation
**Circ:** (Free)10,100

**Travel Courier** (35831)
Baxter Publishing Co.
310 Dupont St.
Toronto, ON, Canada M5R 1V9
Phone: (416)968-7252
Fax: (416)968-2377
**Subject(s):** Travel and Tourism
**Circ:** (Controlled)10,034

**The Canadian Manager** (35549)
The Canadian Institute of Management
250 Consumers Rd., Ste. 301
Toronto, ON, Canada M2J 4V6
Phone: (416)493-0155
Fax: (416)495-8723

**Subject(s):** Management and Administration
**Circ:** (Paid)‡5,000
(Controlled)‡10,000

**Canadian Pizza Magazine** (34869)
Annex Publishing & Printing Inc.
222 Argyle Ave.
Delhi, ON, Canada N4B 2Y2
Phone: (519)582-2513
Fax: (519)582-4040
**Subject(s):** Food and Grocery Trade
**Circ:** 10,000

**Curriculum Inquiry** (35602)
Blackwell Publishers
Ontario Institute for Studies in Education
252 Bloor St. W., Ste. 10-150
Toronto, ON, Canada M5S 1V6
Phone: (416)926-4754
Fax: (416)926-4754
**Subject(s):** Education
**Circ:** 10,000

**The Hockey Talk** (35656)
Scarborough Mirror
100 Tempo Avenue
Toronto, ON, Canada M2H 3S5
Phone: (416)493-4400
Fax: (416)495-0629
**Subject(s):** (Hockey)
**Circ:** ‡10,000

**Ontario Milk Producer** (35126)
Ontario Milk Marketing Board
6780 Campobello Rd.
Mississauga, ON, Canada L5N 2L8
Phone: (905)821-8970
Fax: (905)821-3160
**Subject(s):** Dairying
**Circ:** (Non-paid)‡1,200
(Paid)‡10,000

**Specialty & Performance Magazine** (35803)
Business Information Group
12 Concorde Pl., Ste. 800
Toronto, ON, Canada M3C 4J2
Phone: (416)442-2122
Fax: (416)442-2191
**Subject(s):** Automotive (Trade)
**Circ:** (Controlled)10,000

**Word** (35857)
Mercury Press
22 Prince Rupert Ave.
Toronto, ON, Canada M6P 2A7
Phone: (416)767-4352
Fax: (416)767-4631
**Subject(s):** Literature and Literary Reviews
**Circ:** (Combined)10,000

**The Rural Voice** (34804)
PO Box 429
Blyth, ON, Canada N0M 1H0
Phone: (519)523-4311
Fax: (519)523-9140
**Subject(s):** General Agriculture
**Circ:** (Non-paid)‡3,669
(Paid)‡9,831

**Canadian Journal of Medical Radiation Technology** (35225)
Canadian Association of Medical Radiation Technologists
1095 Carling Ave, Ste 500
Ottawa, ON, Canada K1Y 4P6
Phone: (613)234-0012
Fax: (613)234-1097
**Subject(s):** Radiology, Ultrasound, and Nuclear Medicine; French; Medicine and Surgery
**Circ:** (Non-paid)‡89
(Paid)‡9,798

**Trade and Commerce** (34506)
The Winnipeg Sun
1700 Church Ave.
Winnipeg, MB, Canada R2X 3A2
Phone: (204)694-2022
Fax: (204)697-0759
**Subject(s):** Banking, Finance, and Investments; Commerce and Industry
**Circ:** (Paid)221
(Non-paid)9,745

**Canadian Pharmaceutical Journal** (35243)
Canadian Pharmacists Association
1785 Alta Vista Dr.
Ottawa, ON, Canada K1G 3Y6
Phone: (613)523-7877
Fax: (613)523-2332
**Subject(s):** Drugs and Pharmaceuticals
**Circ:** (Non-paid)8,298
(Paid)9,600

**Solid Waste & Recycling** (35800)
Business Information Group
12 Concorde Pl., Ste. 800
Toronto, ON, Canada M3C 4J2
Phone: (416)442-2122
Fax: (416)442-2191
**Subject(s):** Waste Management and Recycling
**Circ:** (Combined)•9,600

**The Canadian Postmaster (Le Maitre de Poste Canadien)** (35245)
Canadian Postmasters and Assistants Association
281 Queen Mary
Ottawa, ON, Canada K1K 1X1
Phone: (613)745-2095
Fax: (613)745-5559
**Subject(s):** Postal and Shipping Supplies; French; Labor
**Circ:** ‡9,500

**Antique & Collectibles Showcase** (35384)
Trajan Publishing Corp.
103 Lakeshore Rd., Ste. 202
Saint Catharines, ON, Canada L2N 2T6
Phone: (905)646-7744
Fax: (905)646-0995
**Subject(s):** Art; Antiques
**Circ:** (Paid)9,400

**Food in Canada** (35636)
Rogers Media Publishing
1 Mount Pleasant Rd., 7th Fl.
Toronto, ON, Canada M4Y 2Y5
Phone: (416)596-5523
Fax: (416)764-1765
**Subject(s):** Beverages, Brewing, and Bottling; Food and Grocery Trade
**Circ:** (Combined)9,065

**Hotelier** (34881)
Kostuch Publications Ltd.
23 Lesmill Rd., Ste. 101
Don Mills, ON, Canada M3B 3P6
Phone: (416)447-0888
Fax: (416)447-5333
**Subject(s):** Hotels, Motels, Restaurants, and Clubs
**Circ:** (Controlled)9,044

**ARTFOCUS** (35496)
Fleisher Fine Arts Inc.
PO Box 1063 Sta. F
Toronto, ON, Canada M4Y 2T7
**Subject(s):** Art
**Circ:** 9,000

**Canadian Consulting Engineer** (35527)
Business Information Group
12 Concorde Pl., Ste. 800
Toronto, ON, Canada M3C 4J2
Phone: (416)442-2122
Fax: (416)442-2191
**Subject(s):** Engineering (Various branches)
**Circ:** (Combined)•9,000

**Canadian Poultry Magazine/La Revue Canadienne D'Aviculture** (34870)
Annex Publishing & Printing Inc.
222 Argyle Ave.
Delhi, ON, Canada N4B 2Y2
Phone: (519)582-2513
Fax: (519)582-3412
**Subject(s):** Poultry and Pigeons
**Circ:** 9,000

**The Renal Family** (35105)
Multimed Inc.
66 Martin St.
Milton, ON, Canada L9T 2R2
Phone: (905)875-2456
Fax: (905)875-2864
**Subject(s):** Medicine and Surgery
**Circ:** (Non-paid)‡9,000

**Spiritan Missionary News** (35804)
Spiritans, The Congregation of the Holy Ghost
121 Victoria Park Ave.
Toronto, ON, Canada M4E 3S2
Phone: (416)698-2003
Fax: (416)691-8760
**Subject(s):** Religious Publications
**Circ:** (Controlled)9,000

**The Grower** (34945)
Ontario Fruit & Vegetable Growers' Association
355 Elmira Rd., N Ste.105
Guelph, ON, Canada N1K 1S5
Phone: (519)763-8728
Fax: (519)763-6604
**Subject(s):** Socialized Farming
**Circ:** (Combined)‡8939

**Ontario Hog Farmer** (35058)
Bowes Publishers Ltd.
1147 Gainsborough Rd.
PO Box 7400
London, ON, Canada N6H 5L5
Phone: (519)471-8520
Fax: (519)471-1892
**Subject(s):** Livestock
**Circ:** (Paid)26
(Non-paid)8,614

**Canadian Tax Journal (Revue fiscale canadienne)** (35565)
Canadian Tax Foundation
595 Bay St., Ste. 1200
Toronto, ON, Canada M5G 2N5
Phone: (416)599-0283
Fax: (416)599-9283
**Subject(s):** Banking, Finance, and Investments; Taxation and Tariff
**Circ:** ‡8,300

**Landscape Trades** (35104)
Landscape Ontario Horticultural Trades Association
7856 Fifth Line S, RR4
Milton, ON, Canada L9T 2X8
Phone: (905)875-1805
Fax: (905)875-0183
**Subject(s):** Landscape Architecture; Seed and Nursery Trade
**Circ:** (Combined)•8,272

**OH&S Canada** (35733)
Business Information Group
12 Concorde Pl., Ste. 800
Toronto, ON, Canada M3C 4J2
Phone: (416)442-2122
Fax: (416)442-2191
**Subject(s):** Health and Healthcare; Safety
**Circ:** (Non-paid)2,405
(Paid)8,271

**Canadian Journal of Clinical Pharmacology** (35168)
Pulsus Group Inc.
2902 S Sheridan Way
Oakville, ON, Canada L6J 7L6
Phone: (905)829-4770
Fax: (905)829-4799
**Subject(s):** Laboratory Research (Scientific and Medical); Drugs and Pharmaceuticals
**Circ:** (Controlled)8,000

**CIO Canada** (35419)
IT World Canada Inc.
55 Town Center Ct., Ste. 302
Scarborough, ON, Canada M1P 4X4
Phone: (416)290-0240
Fax: (416)290-0238
**Subject(s):** Computers
**Circ:** (Controlled)•8,000

**Horsepower, Magazine for Young Horse Lovers** (34770)
Horse Publications Group
225 Industrial Pkwy. S
PO Box 670
Aurora, ON, Canada L4G 4J9
Phone: (905)727-0107
Fax: (905)841-1530
**Subject(s):** (Horses and Horse Racing); Children's Interests
**Circ:** (Non-paid)‡500
(Paid)‡8,000

# Central Provinces

**Pakeeza International** (35179)
Directories International Ltd.
1235 Trapalgar Rd.
P.O. Box 89021
Oakville, ON, Canada L6H 3J0
Phone: (905)337-3030
Fax: (905)338-1364
**Subject(s):** Urdu; Intercultural Interests
**Circ:** (Paid)‡35
(Non-paid)‡8,000

**Pool & Spa Marketing** (35088)
Hubbard Marketing & Publishing Ltd.
270 Esna Park Dr., Unit 12
Markham, ON, Canada L3R 1H3
Phone: (905)513-0090
Fax: (905)513-1377
**Subject(s):** Sporting Goods/Retail Sports; Advertising and Marketing
**Circ:** (Paid)‡2,000
(Non-paid)‡7,000
8,000

**Scarboro Missions** (35427)
Scarboro Foreign Mission Society
2685 Kingston Rd.
Scarborough, ON, Canada M1M 1M4
Phone: (416)261-7135
Fax: (416)261-0820
**Subject(s):** Religious Publications
**Circ:** (Non-paid)5,000
(Paid)8,000

**Wireless Telecom** (35314)
Canadian Wireless Telecommunications Association
130 Albert St., Ste. 1110
Ottawa, ON, Canada K1P 5G4
Phone: (613)233-4888
Fax: (613)233-2032
**Circ:** (Non-paid)8,000

**Canada & Arab World** (35520)
602 Millwood Rd.
Toronto, ON, Canada M4S 1K8
Phone: (416)362-0304
Fax: (416)816-0238
**Subject(s):** Arabic; International Affairs; International Business and Economics
**Circ:** (Non-paid)‡5,300
(Paid)‡7,900

**Broadcaster** (35511)
Business Information Group
12 Concorde Pl., Ste. 800
Toronto, ON, Canada M3C 4J2
Phone: (416)442-2122
Fax: (416)442-2191
**Subject(s):** Radio, Television, Cable, and Video
**Circ:** (Controlled)7,697

**Canadian Insurance X Canadian Insurance Magazine** (35539)
Stone & Cox Ltd.
111 Peter St., Ste. 500
Toronto, ON, Canada M5V 2H1
Phone: (416)599-0772
Fax: (416)599-0867
**Subject(s):** Insurance
**Circ:** (Paid)•4,058
(Non-paid)•7,569

**Agri-Food Research in Ontario/Recherche Agro-alimentaire en Ontario** (34939)
Ministry of Agriculture, Food & Rural Affairs
1 Stone Rd. W.
Guelph, ON, Canada N1G 4Y2
Phone: (519)826-4191
Fax: (519)826-4211
**Subject(s):** Scientific Agricultural Publications; General Agriculture; Food Production
**Circ:** (Combined)7,500

**Canadian Coin News** (35388)
Trajan Publishing Corp.
103 Lakeshore Rd., Ste. 202
Saint Catharines, ON, Canada L2N 2T6
Phone: (905)646-7744
Fax: (905)646-0995
**Subject(s):** Collecting
**Circ:** (Paid)7,500

**The Canadian Journal of Psychiatry** (35232)
Canadian Psychiatric Association
141 Laurier Ave., W., Ste. 701
Ottawa, ON, Canada K1P 5J3
Phone: (613)234-2815
Fax: (613)234-9857
**Subject(s):** Psychology and Psychiatry
**Circ:** 7,500

**Municipal World** (35408)
Municipal World Inc.
PO Box 399
Station Main
Saint Thomas, ON, Canada N5P 3V3
Phone: (519)633-0031
Fax: (519)633-1001
**Subject(s):** State, Municipal, and County Administration
**Circ:** (Combined)7,500

**Thunder Bay Business** (35473)
North Superior Publishing Inc.
1145 Barton St.
Thunder Bay, ON, Canada P7B 5N3
Phone: (807)623-2348
Fax: (807)623-7515
**Subject(s):** Business
**Circ:** (Controlled)‡7,500

**Green Teacher** (35649)
95 Robert St.
Toronto, ON, Canada M5S 2K5
Phone: (416)960-1244
Fax: (416)925-3474
**Subject(s):** Education; Ecology and Conservation
**Circ:** (Controlled)7,400

**Journal of Psychiatry and Neuroscience** (35278)
Canadian Medical Association
1867 Alta Vista Dr.
Ottawa, ON, Canada K1G 6R7
Phone: (613)731-4552
Fax: (800)267-4022
**Subject(s):** Psychology and Psychiatry
**Circ:** (Paid)7,300

**Prairie Messenger** (36453)
Order of St. Benedict
100 College Dr.
Box 190
Muenster, SK, Canada S0K 2Y0
Phone: (306)682-1772
Fax: (306)682-5285
**Subject(s):** Religious Publications
**Circ:** (Paid)‡7,300

**Canadian Association of Radiologists Journal** (34957)
Canadian Medical Association
c/o Craig Coblentz
Department of Radiology
HHSC - MUMC Site
1200 Main St. W.
Hamilton, ON, Canada L8N 3Z5
Phone: (905)521-1390
Fax: (905)521-2100
**Subject(s):** Biology; Chemistry, Chemicals, and Chemical Engineering; Laboratory Research (Scientific and Medical); Medicine and Surgery
**Circ:** 7,200

**CME Magazine** (35113)
Canadian Manufacturers & Exporters
5995 Avebury Rd., Ste. 900
Mississauga, ON, Canada L5R 3P9
Phone: (905)568-8300
Fax: (905)568-3598
**Subject(s):** Commerce and Industry
**Circ:** (Paid)823
(Non-paid)7,171

**The Canadian Journal of Occupational Therapy (Revue Canadienne d'Ergotherapie)** (35227)
Canadian Association of Occupational Therapists
Carleton Technology & Training Centre Bldg. Ste. 3400
1125 Colonel By Dr.
Ottawa, ON, Canada K1S 5R1
Phone: (613)523-2268
Fax: (613)523-2552
**Subject(s):** Medicine and Surgery
**Circ:** (Non-paid)‡76
(Paid)‡7,000

**Ploughshares Monitor** (35918)
Project Ploughshares
57 Erb St. W
Waterloo, ON, Canada N2L 6C2
Phone: (519)888-6541
Fax: (519)888-0018
**Subject(s):** Peace; Politics
**Circ:** (Paid)7,000

**Ontario Dentist** (35735)
The Ontario Dental Association
4 New St.
Toronto, ON, Canada M5R 1P6
Phone: (416)922-3900
Fax: (416)922-9005
**Subject(s):** Dentistry
**Circ:** (Non-paid)400
(Paid)6,800

**Adnews** (35492)
Bale Communications Inc.
80 Park Lawn Rd., Ste. 212
Toronto, ON, Canada M8Y 3H8
Phone: (416)252-9400
Fax: (416)252-8002
**Subject(s):** Advertising and Marketing
**Circ:** (Combined)6,625

**Canadian Veterinary Journal** (35248)
Canadian Veterinary Medical Association
339 Booth St.
Ottawa, ON, Canada K1R 7K1
Phone: (613)236-1162
Fax: (613)236-9681
**Subject(s):** Veterinary Medicine
**Circ:** 5,500
‡6,600

**Border Crossings Magazine** (34473)
500-70 Arthur St.
Winnipeg, MB, Canada R3B 1G7
Phone: (204)942-5778
Fax: (204)949-0793
**Subject(s):** Art and Art History; Art
**Circ:** 6,500

**The Corinthian Horse Sport** (34765)
Horse Publications Group
225 Industrial Pkwy. S.
PO Box 670
Aurora, ON, Canada L4G 4J9
Phone: (905)727-0107
Fax: (905)841-1530
**Subject(s):** (Horses and Horse Racing)
**Circ:** (Non-paid)‡200
(Paid)6,500

**Bakers Journal** (34868)
Annex Publishing & Printing Inc.
222 Argyle Ave.
Delhi, ON, Canada N4B 2Y2
Phone: (519)582-2513
Fax: (519)582-4040
**Subject(s):** Baking; Confectionaries and Frozen Dairy Products
**Circ:** (Controlled)•6,433

**Canadian Journal of Rural Medicine** (35236)
Canadian Medical Association
1867 Alta Vista Dr.
Ottawa, ON, Canada K1G 6R7
Phone: (613)731-4552
Fax: (800)267-4022
**Subject(s):** Medicine and Surgery; Health and Healthcare; Health; French
**Circ:** 6,300

**Fabricare Canada** (35174)
Box 968
Oakville, ON, Canada L6J 5E8
Phone: (905)337-0516
Fax: (905)337-0525
**Subject(s):** Laundry and Dry Cleaning
**Circ:** (Controlled)6,300

**Coatings Magazine** (35589)
Rogers Media Publishing
One Mount Pleasant Rd., 7th Fl.
Toronto, ON, Canada M4Y 2Y5
Phone: (416)764-2000
Fax: (416)764-1746
**Subject(s):** Paint and Wallcoverings
**Circ:** (Paid)•114
(Non-paid)•6,148

**Canadian Architect** (35522)
Business Information Group
12 Concorde Pl., Ste. 800
Toronto, ON, Canada M3C 4J2
Phone: (416)442-2122
Fax: (416)442-2191
**Subject(s):** Architecture

Circ: (Paid)4,127
(Non-paid)6,117

**Western Hotelier** (34513)
Mercury Publications Ltd.
1839 Inkster Blvd.
Winnipeg, MB, Canada R2X 1R3
Phone: (204)954-2085
Fax: (204)954-2057
**Subject(s):** Hotels, Motels, Restaurants, and Clubs

Circ: (Combined)6,115

**Cablecaster** (35517)
Business Information Group
12 Concorde Pl., Ste. 800
Toronto, ON, Canada M3C 4J2
Phone: (416)442-2122
Fax: (416)442-2191
**Subject(s):** Radio, Television, Cable, and Video

Circ: (Controlled)6,075

**Camping Canada Dealer News** (35106)
Taylor Publishing Group
1020 Brevik Pl., Ste. 5
Mississauga, ON, Canada L4W 4N7
Phone: (905)624-8218
Fax: (905)624-6764
**Subject(s):** Trailers and Accessories

Circ: (Non-paid)‡6,000

**The Canadian Appraiser** (34475)
Appraisal Institute of Canada
3C-2020 Portage Ave.
Winnipeg, MB, Canada R3J 0K4
Phone: (204)985-9780
Fax: (204)985-9795
**Subject(s):** Real Estate

Circ: 6,000

**Canadian Journal of Dietetic Practice and Research** (35082)
Dietitians of Canada
pg(e)tools
500 Cochrane Dr., No. 5
Markham, ON, Canada L3R 8E2
Phone: (905)940-0200
Fax: (905)940-0204
**Subject(s):** Health and Healthcare

Circ: (Combined)6,000

**Quill & Quire** (35775)
111 Queen St. East, Ste. 320
Toronto, ON, Canada M5C 1S2
Phone: (416)364-3333
Fax: (416)595-5415
**Subject(s):** Book Trade and Author News

Circ: (Combined)6,000

**Helicopters Magazine** (35117)
Annex Publishing & Printing Inc.
6200 Dixie Rd., Ste. 220
Mississauga, ON, Canada L5T 2E1
Phone: (905)795-0110
Fax: (905)795-2967
**Subject(s):** Aviation

Circ: (Controlled)5,846

**Canadian Auto World** (34826)
Annex Publishing & Printing Inc.
5040 Mainway, No. 1
Burlington, ON, Canada L7L 7G5
Phone: (905)632-7986
Fax: (905)632-7087
**Subject(s):** Automotive (Trade)

Circ: (Combined)‡5,763

**Canadian Journal of Allergy & Clinical Immunology** (34959)
B.C. Decker Inc.
20 Hughson St. S., 10th Fl.
Hamilton, ON, Canada L8N 3K7
Phone: (905)522-7017
**Subject(s):** Health and Healthcare

Circ: 5,730

**Long Term Care** (34757)
Ontario Long Term Care Association
51 Ottawa St.
Arnprior, ON, Canada K7S 1W9
Phone: (613)623-6975
Fax: (613)623-5179
**Subject(s):** Health and Healthcare; Medicine and Surgery

Circ: (Controlled)**5,600**

**Canadian Yachting Magazine** (35571)
Kerrwil Publications Ltd.
195, The W. Mall Ste. 500
49 Bather St. Ste.
Toronto, ON, Canada M9C 5K1
Phone: (416)703-7167
**Subject(s):** (Boating and Yachting); Travel and Tourism

Circ: (Non-paid)806
(Paid)5,597

**Canadian Jeweller** (35541)
Style Communications
555 Richmond St. W, Ste. 701
Toronto, ON, Canada M5V 3B1
Phone: (416)203-6737
Fax: (416)203-1057
**Subject(s):** Jewelry, Watches, and Clocks

Circ: (Combined)5,500

**The Register** (35777)
Ontario Principals' Council
180 Dundas St. W, 25th Fl.
Toronto, ON, Canada M5G 1Z8
Phone: (416)322-6600
Fax: (416)322-6618
**Subject(s):** Education

Circ: (Combined)5,500

**Union Farmer** (36503)
National Farmers Union
2717 Wentz Ave.
Saskatoon, SK, Canada S7K 4B6
Phone: (306)652-9465
Fax: (306)664-6226
**Subject(s):** Farm Bureau, Grange, and Cooperative Associations

Circ: ‡5,500

**The Ottawa Construction News** (35141)
Asset Beam Publishing Ltd.
1 Cleopatra Dr., Ste. 202
Nepean, ON, Canada K2G 3M9
Phone: (613)224-3460
Fax: (613)224-1076
**Subject(s):** Construction, Contracting, Building, and Excavating

Circ: (Non-paid)5,393

**Die Mennonitische Post** (34451)
Publishing Board
383 Main St.
Steinbach, MB, Canada R5G 1Z4
Phone: (204)326-6790
Fax: (204)326-6302
**Subject(s):** German; Religious Publications

Circ: ‡5,200

**Glass Canada** (34911)
AIS Communications Ltd.
145 Thames Rd. W
Exeter, ON, Canada N0M 1S3
Phone: (519)235-2400
Fax: (519)235-0798
**Subject(s):** Glass and China

Circ: (Non-paid)‡5,200

**Families** (35632)
Ontario Genealogical Society
40 Orchard View Blvd., Ste. 102
Toronto, ON, Canada M4R 1B9
Phone: (416)489-0734
Fax: (416)489-9803
**Subject(s):** History and Genealogy

Circ: (Combined)5,150

**Canadian Underwriter** (35569)
Business Information Group
12 Concord Plz. 8th Fl.
Toronto, ON, Canada M3C 4J2
Phone: (416)442-5600
Fax: (416)442-2191
**Subject(s):** Insurance

Circ: (Non-paid)4,709
(Paid)5,126

**Canadian Journal of Anesthesia (Journal canadien d'anesthesie)** (35543)
Canadian Anesthesiologists' Society
1 Eglinton Ave. E., Ste. 208
Toronto, ON, Canada M4P 3A1
Phone: (416)480-0602
Fax: (416)480-0320
**Subject(s):** Medicine and Surgery

Circ: 5,100

**Fire Fighting in Canada** (34874)
Annex Publishing & Printing Inc.
222 Argyle Ave.
Delhi, ON, Canada N4B 2Y2
Phone: (519)582-2513
Fax: (519)582-4040
**Subject(s):** Fire Fighting

Circ: (Controlled)•**5,083**

**Canadian Treasurer** (35568)
Treasury Management Association of Canada
8 King St. E, Ste. 1010
Toronto, ON, Canada M5C 1B5
Phone: (416)367-8501
Fax: (416)367-3240
**Subject(s):** Business

Circ: (Controlled)**5,000**

**Feliciter** (35260)
Canadian Library Association
328 Frank St.
Ottawa, ON, Canada K2P 0X8
Phone: (613)232-9625
Fax: (613)563-9895
**Subject(s):** Library and Information Science

Circ: (Controlled)‡5,000

**Motorsport Dealer & Trade** (35719)
Turbopress Inc.
411 Richmond St. E, Ste. 301
Toronto, ON, Canada M5A 3S5
Phone: (416)362-7966
Fax: (416)362-3950
**Subject(s):** Motorbikes and Motorcycles

Circ: (Controlled)‡5,000

**The Mystery Review** (34856)
PO Box 233
Colborne, ON, Canada K0K 1S0
Fax: (613)475-3400
**Subject(s):** Science Fiction, Mystery, Adventure, and Romance

Circ: (Paid)‡5,000

**Pedal Magazine** (35750)
317 Adelaide St. W, Ste. 703
Toronto, ON, Canada M5V 1P9
Phone: (416)977-2100
Fax: (416)977-9200
**Subject(s):** (Bicycling); (General Sports)

Circ: (Paid)‡5,000

**The Spill Magazine** (35129)
Spill Magazine
3055 Harold Sheard Dr.
Mississauga, ON, Canada L4T 1V4
Phone: (905)677-8337
Fax: (905)677-9705
**Subject(s):** Music and Musical Instruments

Circ: (Free)5,000

**Toys & Games** (35164)
Chelsie Communications Inc.
61 Alness St., Ste. 216
North York, ON, Canada M3J 2H2
Phone: (416)663-9229
Fax: (416)663-2353
**Subject(s):** Children's Interests; Gifts, Toys, and Novelties

Circ: (Combined)5,000

**Holstein Journal** (35375)
30 East Beaver Creek Rd., Ste. 210
Richmond Hill, ON, Canada L4B 1J2
Phone: (905)886-4222
Fax: (905)886-0037
**Subject(s):** Dairying; Livestock

Circ: (Non-paid)77
(Paid)4,877

**Canadian HR Reporter** (35537)
Thomson Carswell
2075 Kennedy Rd.
Toronto, ON, Canada M1T 3V4
Phone: (416)609-8000
Fax: (416)298-5094

Circulation: ★ = ABC; △ = BPA; ♦ = CAC; • = CCAB; ❑ = VAC; ⊕ = PO Statement; ‡ = Publisher's Report; Boldface figures = sworn; Light figures = estimated.

**Subject(s):** Employment and Human Resources
**Circ:** (Non-paid)•4,686
(Paid)•4,859

**Alternatives Journal (35906)**
Alternatives Inc.
University of Waterloo
c/o Faculty of Environmental Studies
Waterloo, ON, Canada N2L 3G1
Phone: (519)888-4442
Fax: (519)746-0292
**Subject(s):** Ecology and Conservation
**Circ:** 4,500

**Canadian Thoroughbred (34764)**
Canadian Horse Publications Inc.
225 Industrial Pkwy. S.
PO Box 670
Aurora, ON, Canada L4G 4J9
Phone: (905)727-0107
Fax: (905)841-1530
**Subject(s):** (Horses and Horse Racing); Livestock
**Circ:** ‡4,500

**Glad Tidings (35644)**
Women's Missionary Society
50 Wynford Dr.
Toronto, ON, Canada M3C 1J7
Phone: (416)441-1111
Fax: (416)441-2825
**Subject(s):** Religious Publications
**Circ:** (Non-paid)‡200
(Paid)‡4,500

**Masthead (35122)**
Masthead Publishing Ltd.
1606 Sedlescomb Dr., Unit 8
Mississauga, ON, Canada L4X 1M6
Phone: (905)625-7070
Fax: (905)625-4856
**Subject(s):** Journalism and Publishing
**Circ:** (Controlled)4,445

**Christian Courier (35394)**
Reformed Faith Witness
1 Hiscott St.
Saint Catharines, ON, Canada L2R 1C7
Phone: (905)682-8311
Fax: (905)682-8313
**Subject(s):** Dutch; Religious Publications
**Circ:** (Non-paid)‡100
(Paid)‡4,400

**Country Music News (35258)**
PO Box 7323
Vanier Terminal
Ottawa, ON, Canada K1L 8E4
Phone: (613)745-6006
Fax: (613)745-0576
**Subject(s):** Music and Musical Instruments
**Circ:** (Controlled)‡1,800
(Paid)‡4,200

**Greenhouse Canada (34876)**
Annex Publishing & Printing Inc.
222 Argyle Ave.
Delhi, ON, Canada N4B 2Y2
Phone: (519)582-2513
Fax: (519)582-4040
**Subject(s):** Horticulture
**Circ:** (Paid)‡4,200

**Canadian Chemical News (L'Actualite Chimique Canadienne) (35212)**
The Chemical Institute of Canada
130 Slater St., Ste. 550
Ottawa, ON, Canada K1P 6E2
Phone: (613)232-6252
Fax: (613)232-5862
**Subject(s):** Chemistry, Chemicals, and Chemical Engineering; French
**Circ:** (Non-paid)814
(Paid)4,171

**The Canadian Sportsman (35448)**
25 Old Plank Rd.
PO Box 129
Straffordville, ON, Canada N0J 1Y0
Phone: (519)866-5558
Fax: (519)866-5596
**Subject(s):** (Horses and Horse Racing)
**Circ:** (Combined)•4,076

**Canadian Camera (35928)**
Canadian Association for Photographic Art/L'Association canadienne d'art photographique
4 Quaker Ct.
Wellington, ON, Canada K0K 3L0
Phone: (613)399-5855
Fax: (613)399-5855
**Subject(s):** Photography
**Circ:** ‡4,000

**Link & Visitor (35694)**
Baptist Women of Ontario & Quebec
1-315 Lonsdale Rd.
Toronto, ON, Canada M4V 1X3
Phone: (416)544-8550
**Subject(s):** Religious Publications; Women's Interests
**Circ:** (Combined)4,000

**Peritoneal Dialysis International (35060)**
Multimed Inc.
C/O Peter G. Blake
Division of Nephrology, Rm. 2937F
London Health Sciences Centre, Victoria Campus
Westminister Site, 800 Commissioners Rd. E.
London, ON, Canada N6A 4G5
Phone: (519)685-8326
Fax: (519)685-8395
**Subject(s):** Health and Healthcare
**Circ:** (Paid)‡4,000

**Western Canada Highway News (34511)**
Craig Kelman and Associates Ltd.
3C-2020 Portage Ave.
Winnipeg, MB, Canada R3J 0K4
Phone: (204)985-9780
Fax: (204)985-9795
**Subject(s):** Trucks and Trucking; Transportation, Traffic, and Shipping
**Circ:** (Non-paid)‡4,000

**Ground Water Canada (34912)**
AIS Communications Ltd.
145 Thames Rd. W
Exeter, ON, Canada N0M 1S3
Phone: (519)235-2400
Fax: (519)235-0798
**Subject(s):** Water Supply and Sewage Disposal
**Circ:** (Controlled)‡3,920

**ISIS (35668)**
University of Chicago Press
304 Bethune College
York University
4700 Keele St.
Toronto, ON, Canada M3J 1P3
Phone: (416)650-8289
Fax: (416)650-8289
**Subject(s):** Science (General)
**Circ:** ‡3,836

**Canadian Rental Service (34909)**
AIS Communications Ltd.
145 Thames Rd. W
Exeter, ON, Canada N0M 1S3
Phone: (519)235-2400
Fax: (519)235-0798
**Subject(s):** Rental Equipment
**Circ:** (Controlled)‡3,762

**Queen's Quarterly (35018)**
144 Barrie St.
Kingston, ON, Canada K7L 3N6
**Subject(s):** General Editorial; Humanities
**Circ:** ‡3,750

**Canadian Economic Observer (35213)**
Statistics Canada
18-K R.H. Coats Bldg.
Ottawa, ON, Canada K1A 0T6
Phone: (613)951-3634
Fax: (613)951-1584
**Subject(s):** Economics
**Circ:** ‡3,600

**Athletics Magazine (35498)**
1185 Eglinton Ave. E, Ste. 302
Toronto, ON, Canada M3C 3C6
Phone: (416)426-7215
Fax: (416)426-7358
**Subject(s):** (Physical Fitness)
**Circ:** ‡3,500

**Canadian Music Trade (35389)**
Norris-Whitney Communications
23 Hannover Dr., No. 7
Saint Catharines, ON, Canada L2W 1A3
Phone: (905)641-3471
Fax: (905)641-1648
**Subject(s):** Music and Musical Instruments
**Circ:** (Controlled)‡3,500

**Chem 13 News (35909)**
University of Waterloo
Dept. of Chemistry
Waterloo, ON, Canada N2L 3G1
Phone: (519)888-4567
Fax: (519)888-9168
**Subject(s):** Chemistry, Chemicals, and Chemical Engineering; Education
**Circ:** (Paid)3,500

**The Journal of Rheumatology (35680)**
The Journal of Rheumatology Publishing Company Ltd.
365 Bloor St. E, Ste. 901
Toronto, ON, Canada M4W 3L4
Phone: (416)967-5155
Fax: (416)967-7556
**Subject(s):** Medicine and Surgery
**Circ:** (Non-paid)‡60
(Paid)‡3,500

**Public Sector Management/Management et Secteur Public (35772)**
Institute of Public Administration of Canada
1075 Bay St., Ste. 401
Toronto, ON, Canada M5S 2B1
Phone: (416)924-8787
Fax: (416)924-4992
**Subject(s):** Politics
**Circ:** (Paid)3,500

**Canadian Public Administration (Administration publique du Canada) (35561)**
Institute of Public Administration of Canada
1075 Bay St., Ste. 401
Toronto, ON, Canada M5S 2B1
Phone: (416)924-8787
Fax: (416)924-4992
**Subject(s):** State, Municipal, and County Administration; French
**Circ:** 3,400

**Canadian Social Trends (35247)**
Statistics Canada
R.H. Coats Bldg., Lobby
Holland Ave.
Tunney's Pasture
Ottawa, ON, Canada K1A 0T6
**Subject(s):** Statistics; Social Sciences
**Circ:** (Paid)3,300

**Catholic Insight (35576)**
31 Adelaide St., E
PO Box 625, Adelaide State
Toronto, ON, Canada M5C 2J8
Phone: (416)204-9601
Fax: (416)204-1027
**Subject(s):** Religious Publications; Theology
**Circ:** (Non-paid)400
(Paid)3,300

**The Manitoba Museum Annual Report (34492)**
The Manitoba Museum
190 Rupert Ave.
Winnipeg, MB, Canada R3B 0N2
Phone: (204)956-2830
Fax: (204)942-3679
**Subject(s):** Museums
**Circ:** (Non-paid)3,200

**The Bread of Life (34933)**
C.C.S.O. Bread of Life Renewal Centre
23-837 Eastvale Dr.
Gloucester, ON, Canada K1J 7T5
Phone: (613)748-0054
Fax: (905)761-9489
**Subject(s):** Religious Publications
**Circ:** 3,000

**Brick (35510)**
PO Box 537, Sta. Q
Toronto, ON, Canada M4T 2M5
Phone: (416)593-9684
**Subject(s):** Literature
**Circ:** (Paid)3,000

**Broken Pencil (35512)**
PO Box 203, Sta. P
Toronto, ON, Canada M5S 2S7
Phone: (416)531-2813
Subject(s): Alternative and Underground; Literature and Literary Reviews
Circ: (Combined)3,000

**C International Contemporary Art (35514)**
C The Visual Arts Foundation
PO Box 5, Sta. B
Toronto, ON, Canada M5T 2T2
Phone: (416)539-9495
Fax: (416)539-9903
Subject(s): Art
Circ: 3,000

**Canadian Journal of Political Science (Revue canadienne de science politique) (35230)**
Canadian Political Science Association
NO. 204 - 260, rue Dalhousie, Ste. 204
Ottawa, ON, Canada K1N 7E4
Phone: (613)562-1202
Fax: (613)241-0019
Subject(s): Politics; French
Circ: 3,000

**Canadian Journal of Public Health (35233)**
Canadian Public Health Association
1565 Carling Ave., Ste. 400
K1Z8R1
Ottawa, ON, Canada K1Z 8R1
Phone: (613)725-3769
Fax: (613)725-9826
Subject(s): Health and Healthcare
Circ: ‡3000

**Canadian Woman Studies (Les Cahiers de la Femme) (35570)**
Inanna Publications Inc.
York University
212 Founders College
4700 Keele St.
Toronto, ON, Canada M3J 1P3
Phone: (416)736-5356
Fax: (416)736-5765
Subject(s): Women's Interests; French
Circ: (Non-paid)‡120
(Paid)‡3,000

**Coda Magazine (35590)**
Warwick Publishing Inc.
161 Frederick St., Ste. 200
Toronto, ON, Canada M5A 4P3
Phone: (416)596-1555
Fax: (416)596-1520
Subject(s): Music and Musical Instruments
Circ: (Non-paid)‡100
(Paid)‡3,000

**The Forestry Chronicle (35261)**
Canadian Institute of Forestry/Institut Forestier du Canada
151 Slater St., Ste. 606
Ottawa, ON, Canada K1P 5H3
Phone: (613)234-2242
Fax: (613)234-6181
Subject(s): Forestry
Circ: ‡3,000

**Fruit and Vegetable Magazine (34875)**
Annex Publishing & Printing Inc.
222 Argyle Ave.
Delhi, ON, Canada N4B 2Y2
Phone: (519)582-2513
Fax: (519)582-4040
Subject(s): Socialized Farming; Fruit, Fruit Products, and Produce Trade
Circ: (Paid)‡3,000

**Thunder Bay Life (35476)**
North Superior Publishing Inc.
1145 Barton St.
Thunder Bay, ON, Canada P7B 5N3
Phone: (807)623-2348
Fax: (807)623-7515
Subject(s): Entertainment; Lifestyle; Local, State, and Regional Publications
Circ: ‡3,000

**Canadian Journal of Respiratory Therapy (35235)**
Canadian Society of Respiratory Therapists
1785 Alta Vista Dr., Ste. 102
Ottawa, ON, Canada K1G 3Y6
Phone: (613)731-3164
Fax: (613)521-4314

Subject(s): Health and Healthcare
Circ: 2,900

**Canadian Journal of Civil Engineering (Revue Canadienne de Genie Civil) (35221)**
National Research Council Canada, NRC Research Press
1200 Montreal Rd.
Bldg. M-58
Ottawa, ON, Canada K1A 0R6
Phone: (613)993-9101
Fax: (613)952-9907
Subject(s): Engineering (Various branches); French
Circ: ‡2,885

**Gujarat Vartman (34886)**
250 Norfinch Dr.
Downsview, ON, Canada M3N 1Y4
Phone: (416)736-1640
Fax: (416)736-0848
Subject(s): Ethnic Publications
Circ: (Non-paid)2,874

**Canadian Journal of Surgery (35237)**
Canadian Medical Association
1867 Alta Vista Dr.
Ottawa, ON, Canada K1G 6R7
Phone: (613)731-4552
Fax: (800)267-4022
Subject(s): Medicine and Surgery; French
Circ: (Combined)2,800

**Education Canada (35613)**
Canadian Education Association
317 Adelaide St. W, Ste. 300
Toronto, ON, Canada M5V 1P9
Phone: (416)591-6300
Fax: (416)591-5345
Subject(s): Education
Circ: (Controlled)‡800
(Paid)‡2,800

**Journal of Continuing Education in the Health Professions (34967)**
B.C. Decker Inc.
20 Hughson St. S., 10th Fl.
PO Box 620, LCD 1
Hamilton, ON, Canada L8N 3K7
Phone: (905)522-7017
Fax: (905)522-7839
Subject(s): Medicine and Surgery; Health and Healthcare
Circ: (Paid)2,790

**Canadian Geotechnical Journal (Revue Canadienne de Geotechnique) (35109)**
National Research Council Canada, NRC Research Press
2180 Meadowvale Boul.
Mississauga, ON, Canada L5N 5S3
Phone: (905)567-4444
Fax: (905)567-6561
Subject(s): Geology; French
Circ: ‡2,700

**Canadian Vending Magazine (34872)**
Annex Publishing & Printing Inc.
222 Argyle Ave.
Delhi, ON, Canada N4B 2Y2
Phone: (519)582-2513
Fax: (519)582-4040
Subject(s): Vending Machines
Circ: (Paid)‡600
(Non-paid)‡2,600

**Monthly Crop and Livestock Report (34948)**
Ontario Ministry of Agriculture, Food and Rural Affairs
PO Box 3650
Guelph, ON, Canada N1H 8T7
Subject(s): Livestock; General Agriculture
Circ: (Non-paid)2,600

**Obesity Surgery (35732)**
FD Communications Inc.
c/o Mervyn Deitel, MD, Editor
3100 Bayview Ave., Unit 4
Toronto, ON, Canada M2N 5L3
Phone: (416)224-5455
Fax: (416)224-5455
Subject(s): Medicine and Surgery
Circ: 2,600

**Horticulture Review (35103)**
Landscape Ontario Horticultural Trades Association
7856 Fifth Line S, RR4
Milton, ON, Canada L9T 2X8
Phone: (905)875-1805
Fax: (905)875-0183

Subject(s): Horticulture
Circ: (Paid)2,558

**Journal of Systemic Therapies (35053)**
Taylor and Francis
c/o Don Efron
Box 2484, Sta. B
London, ON, Canada N6A 4G7
Subject(s): Psychology and Psychiatry; Education
Circ: (Paid)‡2,500

**German American Trade (35642)**
Ruland Communications Inc.
12 Lawton Blvd.
Toronto, ON, Canada M4V 1Z4
Fax: (416)927-9118
Subject(s): Chambers of Commerce and Boards of Trade
Circ: 2,400

**Journal of Travel Medicine (34969)**
B.C. Decker Inc.
20 Hughson St. S., 10th Fl.
PO Box 620, LCD 1
Hamilton, ON, Canada L8N 3K7
Phone: (905)522-7017
Fax: (905)522-7839
Subject(s): Medicine and Surgery; Health and Healthcare
Circ: (Paid)‡2,406

**Canadian Association of Radiologists Journal (35210)**
Canadian Medical Association
1867 Alta Vista Dr.
Ottawa, ON, Canada K1G 6R7
Phone: (613)731-4552
Fax: (800)267-4022
Subject(s): Radiology, Ultrasound, and Nuclear Medicine; French
Circ: ‡2,250

**The Sentinel (35941)**
British America Publishing Company Ltd.
Canadian Orange Headquarters
94 Sheppard Ave. W
Willowdale, ON, Canada M2N 1M5
Phone: (416)223-1690
Fax: (416)223-1324
Subject(s): Unclassified Fraternal
Circ: (Paid)‡2,229

**Modern Drama (35711)**
University of Toronto Press - Journals Div.
c/o Graduate Center for Study of Drama
214 College St., 3rd Floor
University of Toronto
Toronto, ON, Canada M5T 2Z9
Subject(s): Drama and Theatre
Circ: 2,177

**Canadian Historical Review (35534)**
University of Toronto Press - Journals Div.
c/o University of Toronto Press Inc.
5201 Dufferin St.
Toronto, ON, Canada M3H 5T8
Subject(s): History and Genealogy; French
Circ: 2,100

**Charolais Banner (36473)**
Charolais Banner Ltd.
1933 8th Ave., No. 200
Regina, SK, Canada S4R 1E9
Phone: (306)546-3940
Fax: (306)546-3942
Subject(s): Livestock
Circ: ‡2,100

**Physics in Canada (35299)**
Canadian Association of Physicists
150 Louis Pasteur Ave., Ste. 112
McDonald Bldg.
Ottawa, ON, Canada K1N 6N5
Phone: (613)562-5614
Fax: (613)562-5615
Subject(s): Physics
Circ: ‡2,050

**Canadian Journal of Fisheries & Aquatic Science (35224)**
National Research Council Canada, NRC Research Press
1200 Montreal Rd.
Bldg. M-58
Ottawa, ON, Canada K1A 0R6
Phone: (613)993-9101
Fax: (613)952-9907

**Central Provinces**

**Subject(s):** Fish and Commercial Fisheries
**Circ:** 2,000

**Canadian Journal of Veterinary Research (35238)**
Canadian Veterinary Medical Association
339 Booth St.
Ottawa, ON, Canada K1R 7K1
Phone: (613)236-1162
Fax: (613)236-9681
**Subject(s):** Veterinary Medicine
**Circ:** ‡2,000

**Canadian Parliamentary Review (35242)**
151 Sparks St., Rm. 1200
Ottawa, ON, Canada K1A 0A6
Phone: (613)996-1662
Fax: (613)995-5357
**Subject(s):** Politics; French
**Circ:** 500
2,000

**The Canadian Tobacco Grower (34871)**
Annex Publishing & Printing Inc.
222 Argyle Ave.
Delhi, ON, Canada N4B 2Y2
Phone: (519)582-2513
Fax: (519)582-4040
**Subject(s):** Socialized Farming; Tobacco
**Circ:** (Paid)‡2,000

**Loyalist Gazette (34926)**
United Empire Loyalists' Association of Canada
c/o Peter Johnson UE
751 Will Johnson Rd., R.R. No. 1
Frankford, ON, Canada K0K 1C0
**Subject(s):** History and Genealogy
**Circ:** (Paid)2,000

**Monarchy Canada (35713)**
Fealty Enterprises
3050 Yonge St., Ste. 206-A
Toronto, ON, Canada M4N 2K4
Phone: (416)482-4909
Fax: (416)544-8082
**Subject(s):** General Editorial
**Circ:** ‡2,000

**Resources for Feminist Research (Documentation sur la Recherche Feministe) (35783)**
Ontario Institute for Studies in Education/UT
252 Bloor St. W
Toronto, ON, Canada M5S 1V6
Phone: (416)923-6641
Fax: (416)926-4725
**Subject(s):** Women's Interests; French
**Circ:** ‡2,000

**Socialist Worker (35799)**
International Socialists
PO Box 339
Sta. E
Toronto, ON, Canada M6H 4E3
Phone: (416)972-6391
Fax: (416)972-6319
**Subject(s):** Politics; Alternative and Underground
**Circ:** ‡2,000

**Women & Environments (35856)**
WEED Foundation
IWSGS, New College, U of T
40 Willcocks St.
Toronto, ON, Canada M5S 1C6
Phone: (416)978-5259
Fax: (416)946-5561
**Subject(s):** Women's Interests; Environmental and Natural Resources Conservation
**Circ:** 2,000

**Canadian Journal on Aging (La Revue Canadienne du vieillissement) (34958)**
McMaster Centre for Gerontological Studies
1280 Main St. W
Rm. 226, Kenneth Taylor Hall
Hamilton, ON, Canada L8S 4M4
Phone: (905)525-9140
Fax: (905)525-4198
**Subject(s):** Gerontology
**Circ:** (Non-paid)27
(Paid)1,935

**Canadian Advertising Rates & Data (35521)**
Rogers Media Publishing
1 Mount Pleasant Rd., 7th Fl.
Toronto, ON, Canada M4Y 2Y5
Phone: (416)596-5523

Fax: (416)764-1765
**Subject(s):** Advertising and Marketing
**Circ:** (Combined)•1,901

**Canadian Field-Naturalist (35215)**
Ottawa Field-Naturalists Club
PO Box 35069, Westgate PO
Ottawa, ON, Canada K1Z 1A2
Phone: (613)722-3050
**Subject(s):** Natural History and Nature Study
**Circ:** (Controlled)‡1,900

**Journal of Scholarly Publishing (35681)**
University of Toronto Press - Journals Div.
5201 Dufferin St.
Toronto, ON, Canada M3H 5T8
Phone: (416)667-7810
Fax: (416)667-7881
**Subject(s):** Journalism and Publishing
**Circ:** 1,800

**Lang Van (35689)**
VBC—Vietnamese Broadcasting Corp.
PO Box 218, Sta. U
Toronto, ON, Canada M8Z 5P1
Phone: (905)607-8012
Fax: (905)607-8011
**Subject(s):** Literature; Vietnamese
**Circ:** (Controlled)1,800

**Canadian Journal of Microbiology (Revue Canadienne de Microbiologie) (35226)**
National Research Council Canada, NRC Research Press
1200 Montreal Rd.
Bldg. M-58
Ottawa, ON, Canada K1A 0R6
Phone: (613)993-9101
Fax: (613)952-9907
**Subject(s):** Biology; French
**Circ:** ‡1,725

**Canadian Journal of Chemistry (Revue Canadienne de Chimie) (35046)**
National Research Council Canada, NRC Research Press
c/o Dr. R.J. Puddephatt
Canadian Journal of Chemistry, Department of Chemistry
University of Western Ontario
1151 Richmond St.
London, ON, Canada N6A 5B7
Phone: (519)661-2111
Fax: (519)850-2371
**Subject(s):** Chemistry, Chemicals, and Chemical Engineering; French
**Circ:** ‡1,700

**Ontario History (35939)**
The Ontario Historical Society
34 Parkview Ave.
Willowdale, ON, Canada M2N 3Y2
Phone: (416)226-9011
Fax: (416)226-2740
**Subject(s):** History and Genealogy
**Circ:** ‡1,700

**The Ontario Land Surveyor (35736)**
Association of Ontario Land Surveyors
1043 McNicoll Ave.
Toronto, ON, Canada M1W 3W6
Phone: (416)491-9020
Fax: (416)491-2576
**Subject(s):** Engineering (Various branches)
**Circ:** ‡1,650

**WRLA Yardstick (34519)**
Craig Kelman and Associates Ltd.
3C-2020 Portage Ave.
Winnipeg, MB, Canada R3J 0K4
Phone: (204)985-9780
Fax: (204)985-9795
**Subject(s):** Lumber; Hardware
**Circ:** (Controlled)1,650

**Promin (34972)**
Ukrainian Women's Association of Canada
202-450 Main St.
Box 57268
Jackson Station
Hamilton, ON, Canada L8P 4X1
Phone: (905)572-9626
Fax: (905)524-5362
**Subject(s):** Ethnic Publications; Ukrainian
**Circ:** ‡1,637

**Inuit Art Quarterly (35272)**
Inuit Art Foundation
2081 Merivale Rd.
Ottawa, ON, Canada K2G 1G9
Phone: (613)224-8189
Fax: (613)224-2907
**Subject(s):** Art and Art History
**Circ:** (Controlled)1,500
(Paid)1,600

**Saskatchewan Genealogical Society Bulletin (36476)**
Saskatchewan Genealogical Society
1870 Lorne St., Rm. 201
Regina, SK, Canada S4P 3E1
Phone: (306)780-9207
Fax: (306)781-6021
**Subject(s):** History and Genealogy
**Circ:** (Controlled)1,550

**Canadian Journal of Program Evaluation/Revue Canadienne D'evaluation de Programme (35454)**
University of Calgary Press
Department of Political Science
Sudbury, ON, Canada P3E 2C6
Phone: (705)675-1151
Fax: (705)675-4852
**Subject(s):** Health and Healthcare; Social Sciences
**Circ:** 1,525

**Bratstvo (Fraternity) (35158)**
1 Secroft Crescent
North York, ON, Canada M3N 1R5
Phone: (416)663-3409
Fax: (416)665-3564
**Subject(s):** Serbian; Social and Political Issues; Ethnic Publications
**Circ:** (Controlled)700
(Paid)1,500

**crosscurrents (35601)**
Centre for Addiction and Mental Health
33 Russell St.
Toronto, ON, Canada M5S 2S1
Phone: (416)595-6714
Fax: (416)595-6892
**Subject(s):** Substance Abuse and Treatment; Psychology and Psychiatry
**Circ:** (Paid)‡1,100
(Controlled)‡1,500

**Human Rights Tribune (35269)**
Human Rights Internet
One Nicholas St., Ste. 300
Ottawa, ON, Canada K1N 7B7
Phone: (613)789-7407
Fax: (613)789-7414
**Subject(s):** Civil Rights; Sociology
**Circ:** (Controlled)1,500

**The LBMAO Reporter (35120)**
Perks Publications Inc.
5155 Spectrum Way, No. 27
Mississauga, ON, Canada L4W 5A1
Phone: (905)625-3006
Fax: (888)365-2626
**Subject(s):** Wood and Woodworking
**Circ:** (Non-paid)‡1,500

**Prairie Fire (34503)**
Prairie Fire Press Inc.
423-100 Arthur St.
Winnipeg, MB, Canada R3B 1H3
Phone: (204)943-9066
Fax: (204)942-1555
**Subject(s):** Literature and Literary Reviews
**Circ:** ‡1,500

**Municipal Leader (34440)**
Association of Manitoba Municipalities
1910 Saskatchewan W.
Portage La Prairie, MB, Canada R1N 0P1
Phone: (204)857-8666
Fax: (204)856-2370
**Subject(s):** State, Municipal, and County Administration
**Circ:** (Paid)1,450

**Atlantic Trucking (35499)**
Atlantic Provinces Trucking Association
920 Yonge St., Ste. 600
Toronto, ON, Canada M4W 3C7
Phone: (416)961-1028
Fax: (416)924-4408
**Subject(s):** Trucks and Trucking
**Circ:** (Non-paid)‡100
(Paid)‡1,400

**Genome (35162)**
National Research Council Canada, NRC Research Press
Dept. of Biology
York University
4700 Keele St.
North York, ON, Canada M3J 1P3
Phone: (416)736-5731
Fax: (416)736-5731
Subject(s): Genetics; French
Circ: ‡1,400

**Journal of Canadian Studies (Revue d'Etudes Canadiennes) (35349)**
Trent University
1600 W. Bank Dr.
Peterborough, ON, Canada K9H 3N6
Phone: (705)748-1011
Fax: (705)748-1110
Subject(s): Humanities; French
Circ: ‡1,350

**Canadian Journal of Ophthalmology (Journal Canadien d'Ophtalmologie) (35228)**
Canadian Ophthalmological Society/Societe Canadienne d'Ophtalmologie
1525 Carling Ave., Ste. 610
Ottawa, ON, Canada K1Z 8R9
Phone: (613)729-6779
Fax: (613)729-7209
Subject(s): Ophthalmology, Optometry, and Optics
Circ: (Paid)‡1,300

**Canadian Journal of Zoology (Revue Canadienne de Zoologie) (35161)**
National Research Council Canada, NRC Research Press
Dept of Biology
York University
4700 Keele St.
North York, ON, Canada M3J 1P3
Phone: (416)650-8016
Fax: (416)650-8016
Subject(s): Zoology; French
Circ: ‡1,300

**Canadian Theatre Review (34941)**
University of Toronto Press - Journals Div.
c/o Phyllis Reynen, Editor
School of Literatures and Performance Studies in English
Massey Hall
University of Guelph
Guelph, ON, Canada N1G 2W1
Phone: (519)824-4120
Fax: (519)824-0560
Subject(s): Entertainment; Drama and Theatre
Circ: 1,300

**International Journal (35664)**
Canadian Institute of International Affairs
205 Richmond St. W.
Toronto, ON, Canada M5V 1V3
Phone: (416)977-9000
Fax: (416)977-7521
Subject(s): International Affairs
Circ: ‡1,300

**Briarpatch (36471)**
Briarpatch Inc.
2138 McIntyre St.
Regina, SK, Canada S4P 2R7
Phone: (306)525-2949
Subject(s): General Editorial; Politics
Circ: (Controlled)‡350
(Paid)‡1,250

**Biochemistry and Cell Biology (Biochimie et Biologie Cellulaire) (34472)**
National Research Council Canada, NRC Research Press
Rm. T251 - 770 Bannatyne Ave.
University of Manitoba
Winnipeg, MB, Canada R3E 0W3
Phone: (204)977-5695
Fax: (204)977-5697
Subject(s): Biology; French
Circ: ‡1,225

**Contemporary Accounting Research (35595)**
Canadian Academic Accounting Association
Joseph Rotman School of Management
Univ of Toronto
105 St. George St.
Toronto, ON, Canada M5J 3E6
Phone: (416)946-8601
Fax: (416)971-3048
Subject(s): Accountants and Accounting
Circ: (Controlled)1,225

**Behind the Headlines (35504)**
Canadian Institute of International Affairs
205 Richmond St. W, Ste, 302
Toronto, ON, Canada M5V 1V3
Phone: (416)977-9000
Fax: (416)977-7521
Subject(s): International Affairs; Congressional and Federal Government Affairs; Politics
Circ: (Paid)1,200

**Canadian Ceramics Quarterly (35935)**
Canadian Ceramic Society
2175 Sheppard Ave. E, Ste. 310
Willowdale, ON, Canada M2J 1W8
Phone: (416)491-2886
Fax: (416)491-1670
Subject(s): Ceramics
Circ: ‡1,200

**The Canadian Modern Language Review/La Revue canadienne des langues vivantes (35552)**
University of Toronto Press - Journals Div.
c/o University of Toronto Press - Journals Division
5201 Dufferin St.
Toronto, ON, Canada M3H 5T8
Subject(s): Philology, Language, and Linguistics; French
Circ: (Combined)1,200

**Ontario Mathematics Gazette (35059)**
Ontario Association for Mathematics Education
70 Chestnut Ct.
London, ON, Canada N6K 4J5
Phone: (519)471-6234
Fax: (519)471-6324
Subject(s): Education; Mathematics
Circ: (Paid)1,200

**Phoenix (35756)**
Trinity College
Toronto, ON, Canada M5S 1H8
Phone: (416)978-3037
Fax: (416)978-4949
Subject(s): Literature and Literary Reviews; History and Genealogy
Circ: (Paid)1,200

**Writer's Lifeline (34864)**
Vesta Publications Ltd.
Po Box 1641
Cornwall, ON, Canada K6H 5V6
Phone: (613)932-2135
Fax: (613)932-7735
Subject(s): Book Trade and Author News; Journalism and Publishing
Circ: (Non-paid)‡300
(Paid)‡1,200

**Canadian Journal of Criminology/Revue Canadienne de Criminologie (35223)**
Canadian Criminal Justice Association
1750 Courtwood Cres., Ste. 308
Ottawa, ON, Canada K2C 2B5
Phone: (613)725-3715
Fax: (613)725-3720
Subject(s): Police, Penology, and Penal Institutions
Circ: (Controlled)1,100

**Canadian Occupational Health and Safety News (COHSN) (35554)**
Business Information Group
12 Concorde Pl., Ste. 800
Toronto, ON, Canada M3C 4J2
Phone: (416)442-2122
Fax: (416)442-2191
Subject(s): Safety; Health and Healthcare
Circ: ‡1,100

**Geomatica (35265)**
Canadian Institute of Geomatics
1390 Prince of Wales Dr., Ste. 400
Ottawa, ON, Canada K2C 3N6
Phone: (613)224-9851
Fax: (613)224-9577
Subject(s): Engineering (Various branches)
Circ: (Controlled)‡43
(Paid)‡1,046

**Descant (35606)**
Descant Arts and Letters Foundation
PO Box 314, Sta. P
Toronto, ON, Canada M5S 2S8
Phone: (416)593-2557
Fax: (416)593-9362

Subject(s): Literature and Literary Reviews; Photography
Circ: (Non-paid)‡75
(Paid)‡1,025

**Beads (35207)**
Society of Bead Researchers
1600 Liverpool Ct.
Ottawa, ON, Canada K1A 0M5
Phone: (613)990-4814
Fax: (613)952-1756
Subject(s): Anthropology and Ethnology; Archaeology
Circ: (Controlled)50
(Paid)1,000

**Biotechnology Advances (35907)**
Elsevier Science B.V.
University of Waterloo
Waterloo, ON, Canada N2L 3G1
Phone: (519)746-4979
Fax: (519)746-4979
Subject(s): Biology; Chemistry, Chemicals, and Chemical Engineering; Genetics
Circ: 1,000

**The Canadian (34795)**
The Sir James Whitney School
350 Dundas St. W
Belleville, ON, Canada K8T 1B2
Phone: (613)967-2823
Fax: (613)967-2857
Subject(s): Education
Circ: ‡1,000

**The Canadian Entomologist (35214)**
Entomological Society of Canada
393 Winston Ave.
Ottawa, ON, Canada K2A 1Y8
Phone: (613)725-2619
Fax: (613)725-9349
Subject(s): Entomology
Circ: ‡1,000

**Canadian Journal of Agricultural Economics (36492)**
Agricultural Institute of Canada
Dept. of Agricultural Economics
Univ. of Saskatchewan
Saskatoon, SK, Canada S7N 5A8
Phone: (306)966-2041
Fax: (306)966-8413
Subject(s): Economics
Circ: (Paid)1,000

**Canadian Journal of Physiology and Pharmacology (Revue Canadienne de Physiologie et Pharmacologie) (35229)**
National Research Council Canada, NRC Research Press
Rm. 398, M-55, 1200 Montreal Rd.
Ottawa, ON, Canada K1A 0R6
Phone: (613)998-9432
Fax: (613)991-1183
Subject(s): Physiology and Anatomy; French; Drugs and Pharmaceuticals
Circ: ‡1,000

**Canadian Oncology Nursing Journal (35555)**
Pappin Communications
61 Glenvale Blvd.
Toronto, ON, Canada M4G 2V5
Phone: (416)480-5942
Fax: (416)480-6002
Subject(s): Nursing; Medicine and Surgery
Circ: 1,000

**Canadian Vocational Journal (35249)**
Canadian Vocational Association
PO Box 3435 Sta. D
Ottawa, ON, Canada K1P 6L4
Phone: (613)838-6012
Fax: (613)838-6012
Subject(s): Vocational Education
Circ: ‡1,000

**Caravan (35250)**
Canadian Conference of Catholic Bishops
2500 Don Reid Dr.
Ottawa, ON, Canada K1H 2J2
Phone: (613)241-7538
Fax: (613)241-5090
Subject(s): Religious Publications; Education
Circ: (Non-paid)‡100
(Paid)‡1,000

**CCL Canadian Children's Literature (Litterature Canadienne pour la Jeunesse)** (34943)
CCL Canadian Children's Literature
University of Guelph
4th Fl., MacKinnon Bldg.
Guelph, ON, Canada N1G 2W1
Phone: (519)824-4120
Fax: (519)837-1315
Subject(s): Literature; French; Children's Interests
Circ: ‡1,000

**Journal of Orthomolecular Medicine** (35679)
International Schizophrenia Foundation
16 Florence Ave.
Toronto, ON, Canada M2N 1E9
Phone: (416)733-2117
Fax: (416)733-2352
Subject(s): Medicine and Surgery; Psychology and Psychiatry
Circ: 1,000

**Megadrilogica** (35031)
Oligochaetology Laboratory
18 Broadview Ct.
Kitchener, ON, Canada N2A 2X8
Phone: (519)896-4728
Subject(s): Zoology
Circ: (Paid)1,000

**Mennonite Review** (34495)
Canadian Conference of Mennonite Brethren Churches
3-169 Riverton Ave.
Winnipeg, MB, Canada R2L 2E5
Phone: (204)654-5760
Fax: (204)654-1865
Subject(s): Religious Publications; German
Circ: (Paid)‡900
    (Non-paid)‡1,000

**The Oil Can** (34500)
Naylor Communications Ltd.
100 Sutherland Ave.
Winnipeg, MB, Canada R2W 3C7
Phone: (204)947-0222
Fax: (204)947-2047
Subject(s): Petroleum, Oil, and Gas
Circ: (Controlled)‡1,000

**The Structurist** (36502)
Box 378
RPO University
University of Saskatchewan
Saskatoon, SK, Canada S7N 4J8
Phone: (306)966-4198
Fax: (306)966-4197
Subject(s): Art and Art History; Architecture
Circ: (Paid)1,000

**University of Toronto Law Journal** (35839)
University of Toronto Press - Journals Div.
Faculty of Law
University of Toronto
Toronto, ON, Canada M5S 2C5
Phone: (416)978-4414
Fax: (416)978-2648
Subject(s): Law
Circ: 1,000

**University of Toronto Quarterly** (35841)
University of Toronto Press - Journals Div.
University of Toronto Quarterly
Editorial Department
10 St. Mary St. Ste. 700
Toronto, ON, Canada M4Y 2W8
Subject(s): Literature; Philosophy
Circ: 945

**Osgoode Hall Law Journal** (35743)
4700 Keele St., Rm. 312
Toronto, ON, Canada M3J 1P3
Phone: (416)736-5354
Fax: (416)736-5869
Subject(s): Law
Circ: 465
    900

**Communications in Statistics: Theory & Methods** (34963)
Marcel Dekker Inc.
c/o N. Balakrishnan
Department of Mathematics and Statistics
McMaster Univ.
Hamilton, ON, Canada L8S 4K1
Subject(s): Mathematics
Circ: 800

**Mouseion** (34498)
University of Calgary Press
c/o Dr. Mark Joyal, Department of Classics
University of Manitoba
Dept. of Classics
Winnipeg, MB, Canada R3T 2M8
Subject(s): Archaeology
Circ: (Paid)800

**Thunder Bay Historical Museum Society, Papers and Records** (35475)
Thunder Bay Historical Museum Society
425 Donald St. E
Thunder Bay, ON, Canada P7E 5V1
Phone: (807)623-0801
Fax: (807)622-6880
Subject(s): History and Genealogy
Circ: (Controlled)800

**Victorian Periodicals Review** (35845)
University of Toronto Press - Journals Div.
5201 Dufferin St.
Toronto, ON, Canada M3H 5T8
Phone: (416)667-7810
Fax: (416)667-7881
Subject(s): Journalism and Publishing; Library and Information Science
Circ: (Combined)800

**Canadian Mathematical Bulletin** (34961)
University of Toronto Press - Journals Div.
c/o Maung Min-Oo ,Editor-in chief
Dept. of Mathematics and Statistics
McMaster University
Hamilton, ON, Canada L8S 4K1
Subject(s): Mathematics
Circ: (Paid)775

**Mosaic** (34497)
208 Tier Bldg.
The University of Manitoba
Winnipeg, MB, Canada R3T 2N2
Phone: (204)474-9763
Fax: (204)474-7584
Subject(s): Literature
Circ: (Non-paid)‡150
    (Paid)‡750

**Adoption Helper** (35439)
Family Helper Publishing
Box 1353
Southampton, ON, Canada N0H 2L0
Subject(s): Parenting; Babies
Circ: (Paid)700

**Clinical and Investigative Medicine** (35253)
Canadian Medical Association
1867 Alta Vista Dr.
Ottawa, ON, Canada K1G 6R7
Phone: (613)731-4552
Fax: (800)267-4022
Subject(s): Medicine and Surgery; Laboratory Research (Scientific and Medical); French
Circ: ‡700

**Listening In** (35695)
Ontario DX Association
155 Main St. N., Apt. 313
Toronto, ON, Canada L3Y 8C2
Subject(s): Radio, Television, Cable, and Video
Circ: (Non-paid)200
    (Paid)700

**Ontario Archaeology** (35734)
Ontario Archaeological Society
1444 Queen St. E.
Toronto, ON, Canada M4L 1E1
Phone: (416)406-5959
Fax: (416)406-5959
Subject(s): Archaeology
Circ: (Paid)700

**Renaissance and Reformation/Renaissance et Reforme** (35781)
Centre for Reformation and Renaissance Studies
71 Queen's Park Crescent E
Toronto, ON, Canada M5S 1K7
Phone: (416)585-4465
Fax: (416)585-4430
Subject(s): History and Genealogy; Literature
Circ: (Combined)700

**Canadian Journal of History/Annales canadiennes d'histoire** (36493)
University of Saskatchewan
707 Arts Bldg.
9 Campus Dr.
Saskatoon, SK, Canada S7N 5A5
Phone: (306)966-5794
Fax: (306)966-5852
Subject(s): History and Genealogy
Circ: (Combined)690

**Canadian Gemmologist** (35218)
Canadian Gemmological Association
525 Fielding Dr.
Ottawa, ON, Canada K1V 7G7
Phone: (613)526-4868
Subject(s): Jewelry, Watches, and Clocks
Circ: (Paid)650

**Therapeutic Drug Monitoring** (35814)
Lippincott Williams & Wilkins
c/o Gideon Koren
Division of Clinical Pharmacology/Toxicology
555 University Ave.
Hospital for Sick Children
Toronto, ON, Canada M5G 1X8
Subject(s): Toxicology; Drugs and Pharmaceuticals
Circ: 635

**The New Quarterly** (35917)
The New Quarterly Literary Society Inc.
c/o St. Jerome's University
290 Westmount Rd., N
Waterloo, ON, Canada N2L 3G3
Phone: (519)884-8111
Fax: (519)884-5759
Subject(s): Literature and Literary Reviews
Circ: (Non-paid)100
    (Paid)600

**Biological Therapies in Dentistry** (34956)
B.C. Decker Inc.
20 Hughson St. S., 10th Fl.
PO Box 620, LCD 1
Hamilton, ON, Canada L8N 3K7
Phone: (905)522-7017
Fax: (905)522-7839
Subject(s): Dentistry
Circ: (Paid)⊕500

**Canadian Journal of Latin American and Caribbean Studies** (35048)
Canadian Association for Latin American and Caribbean Studies
Dept. of Sociology
University of Western Ontario
London, ON, Canada N6A 5C2
Phone: (519)661-3600
Fax: (519)661-3200
Subject(s): Ethnic and Minority Studies; Intercultural Interests
Circ: (Controlled)500

**Canadian Journal of Law & Jurisprudence** (35049)
University of Western Ontario
London, ON, Canada N6A 3K7
Phone: (519)661-2111
Fax: (519)661-3790
Subject(s): Law; Philosophy
Circ: (Combined)500

**The Canadian Locksmith Magazine** (35547)
The Canadian Locksmith Press
137 Vaughan Rd.
Toronto, ON, Canada M6C 2L9
Phone: (416)653-2199
Fax: (416)656-3068
Subject(s): Safety
Circ: 500

**Canadian Plant Disease Survey** (35244)
Agriculture and Agri-Food Canada
Publishing and Depository Services
Public Works and Government Services Canada
Ottawa, ON, Canada K1A 0S9
Phone: (613)941-5995
Fax: (519)954-5779
Subject(s): Botany; Statistics
Circ: (Controlled)500

**Journal of Canadian Poetry** (35276)
Borealis Press Ltd.
Department of English
University of Ottawa
Ottawa, ON, Canada K1N 6N5
Phone: (613)562-5875

Fax: (613)562-5770
**Subject(s):** Poetry; Literature and Literary Reviews; Literature
**Circ:** (Combined)500

**Manitoba Law Journal (34491)**
University of Manitoba
104 Robson Hall
Winnipeg, MB, Canada R3T 2N2
Phone: (204)474-6159
Fax: (204)474-7580
**Subject(s):** Law
**Circ:** (Combined)500

**Post-adoption Helper (35440)**
Family Helper Publishing
Box 1353
Southampton, ON, Canada N0H 2L0
**Subject(s):** Parenting
**Circ:** (Paid)500

**The Tocqueville Review/La Revue Tocqueville (35818)**
University of Toronto Press - Journals Div.
5201 Dufferin St.
Toronto, ON, Canada M3H 5T8
Phone: (416)667-7810
Fax: (416)667-7881
**Subject(s):** Social Sciences; French; Politics
**Circ:** (Combined)500

**English Quarterly (34481)**
Canadian Council of Teachers of English Language Arts
10-730 River Rd.
Winnipeg, MB, Canada R2M 5A4
Phone: (204)255-1676
Fax: (204)253-2562
**Subject(s):** Education
**Circ:** (Paid)450

**Thalia (35308)**
Association for the Study of Humor
Department of English
University of Ottawa
Ottawa, ON, Canada K1N 6N5
**Subject(s):** Literature; Humanities
**Circ:** 450

**Body Cast (35157)**
Pappin Communications
c/o CSOT
18 Wynford Dr., Ste. 715A
North York, ON, Canada M3C 3S2
Phone: (416)445-4516
**Subject(s):** Nursing
**Circ:** 400

**Environments (35911)**
University of Waterloo
Waterloo, ON, Canada N2L 3G1
Phone: (519)888-4567
Fax: (519)725-2827
**Subject(s):** Ecology and Conservation; Geography
**Circ:** (Combined)400

**Saskatoon History Review (36499)**
Saskatoon Heritage Society
831 Temperance St.
Saskatoon, SK, Canada S7N 0M8
**Subject(s):** History and Genealogy; Local, State, and Regional Publications
**Circ:** (Combined)400

**Urban History Review (35842)**
Becker Associates
PO Box 507, Sta. Q
Toronto, ON, Canada M4T 2M5
Phone: (416)483-7282
Fax: (426)489-1713
**Subject(s):** History and Genealogy; Social Sciences
**Circ:** (Paid)400

**Ultimate Reality and Meaning (34508)**
University of Toronto Press - Journals Div.
C/o John F. Perry, St. Paul's College
University of Manitoba
70 Dysart Rd.
Winnipeg, MB, Canada R3T 2M6
Phone: (204)474-7186
Fax: (204)474-7163
**Subject(s):** Philosophy
**Circ:** 370

**Essays in Theatre/Etudes Theatrales (34944)**
University of Guelph
Guelph, ON, Canada N1G 2W1
Phone: (519)824-4120
Fax: (519)766-0844
**Subject(s):** Literature; Drama and Theatre; Performing Arts
**Circ:** (Combined)350

**Leisure/Loisir (35916)**
Wilfrid Laurier University Press
Faculty of Physical Education and Recreation Studies
University of Manitoba
Winnipeg, MB, Canada R3T 2N2
Phone: (204)474-8643
Fax: (204)474-7634
**Subject(s):** Physical Education and Athletics
**Circ:** (Non-paid)‡50
(Paid)‡350

**Canadian Review of Comparative Literature (35562)**
University of Toronto Press - Journals Div.
5201 Dufferin St.
Toronto, ON, Canada M3H 5T8
Phone: (416)667-7810
Fax: (416)667-7881
**Subject(s):** Literature
**Circ:** (Combined)300

**Lumen (36497)**
Academic Printing and Publishing
University of Saskatchewan
Department of Languages Linguistics
9, Campus Dr.
Saskatoon, SK, Canada S7N 5A5
Phone: (306)966-5633
**Subject(s):** History and Genealogy; Literature; Philosophy
**Circ:** (Paid)300

**Water Quality Research Journal of Canada (34833)**
Canadian Association on Water Quality
867 Lakeshore Rd.
Burlington, ON, Canada L7R 4L7
Phone: (905)336-4513
Fax: (905)336-4420
**Subject(s):** Water Supply and Sewage Disposal; Ecology and Conservation; Waste Management and Recycling
**Circ:** (Paid)300

**Wascana Review of Contemporary Poetry and Short Fiction (36477)**
University of Regina
Dept. of English
Regina, SK, Canada S4S 0A2
Fax: (306)585-5429
**Subject(s):** Literature; Poetry
**Circ:** (Controlled)278

**Canadian Biosystems Engineering (36491)**
Canadian Society of Agricultural Engineering
c/o Agricultural & Bioresource Engineering
57 Campus Dr.
Saskatoon, SK, Canada S7N 5A9
Phone: (306)966-5319
Fax: (306)966-5334
**Subject(s):** Scientific Agricultural Publications
**Circ:** (Controlled)250

**Dreams and Visions (35193)**
Skysong Press
35 Peter St. S.
Orillia, ON, Canada L3V 5A8
Fax: (705)329-1770
**Subject(s):** Science Fiction, Mystery, Adventure, and Romance; Religious Publications
**Circ:** (Paid)200

**Germano-Slavica (35912)**
University of Waterloo
200 university avenue west
Waterloo, ON, Canada N2L 3G1
Phone: (519)888-4567
Fax: (519)746-5243
**Subject(s):** Philology, Language, and Linguistics; Intercultural Interests
**Circ:** (Paid)‡200

**Saskatchewan Archaeology (36498)**
Saskatchewan Archaeological Society
1730 Quebec Ave., Ste. 1
Saskatoon, SK, Canada S7K 1V9
Phone: (306)664-4124
Fax: (306)665-1128
**Subject(s):** Archaeology
**Circ:** (Paid)200

**Text Technology (34974)**
Wright State University, Lake Campus
c/o Joanne Buckley, Editor
Togo Salmon Hall, Rm. 205A
McMaster Univ.
1280 Main St. W.
Hamilton, ON, Canada L8S 4M2
**Subject(s):** Computers
**Circ:** (Paid)200

**Physics Essays (35300)**
Physics Essays Publication
2012 Woodglen Crescent
Ottawa, ON, Canada K1J 6G4
Phone: (819)457-1020
Fax: (819)457-1020
**Subject(s):** Physics; Mathematics; Chemistry, Chemicals, and Chemical Engineering; Science (General)
**Circ:** ‡171

**Bulletin on Current Research in Soviet and East European Law (35513)**
CREES, MCIS, University of Toronto
1 Devonshire Pl.
Toronto, ON, Canada M5S 3K7
Phone: (416)946-8938
Fax: (416)946-8939
**Subject(s):** Law; International Affairs
**Circ:** (Paid)130
150

**Exports of Canadian Grain and Wheat Flour (34482)**
600-303 Main St.
Winnipeg, MB, Canada R3C 3G8
Phone: (204)983-2770
Fax: (204)983-2751
**Subject(s):** Feed and Grain; Local, State, and Regional Publications
**Circ:** (Paid)150

**Epoch (34806)**
Clarington Museums
37 Silver St.
PO Box 188
Bowmanville, ON, Canada L1C 3K9
Phone: (905)623-2734
Fax: (905)623-5684
**Subject(s):** History and Genealogy
**Circ:** (Non-paid)‡100
(Paid)‡125

**Inroads (35142)**
280 Huron St.
New Hamburg, ON, Canada N3A 1J5
Phone: (519)662-3390
Fax: (519)662-3594
**Subject(s):** Politics
**Circ:** (Non-paid)100
(Paid)120

# Eastern Provinces

**Reader's Digest Canada (36228)**
Reader's Digest
1125 Stanley St.
Montreal, QC, Canada H3B 5H5
Phone: (514)940-0751
Fax: (514)940-3637
**Subject(s):** General Editorial; French
**Circ:** (Paid)1,025,256

**MovieEntertainment Feature (36205)**
Feature Publishing Ltd.
2100 St. Catherine St. W, 2nd Fl.
Montreal, QC, Canada H3H 2T3
Phone: (514)939-5024
Fax: (514)939-8027
**Subject(s):** Radio, Television, Cable, and Video
**Circ:** (Combined)•900,000

**Documentation et Bibliotheques (36137)**
ASTED Inc.
3414, Ave. du Parc Ste. 202
Montreal, QC, Canada H2X 2H5
Phone: (514)281-5012
Fax: (514)281-8219
**Subject(s):** Library and Information Science; French
**Circ:** 800,000

**Touring** (36072)
Consultants CGEI Inc.
3281 Jean-Beraud Ave.
Laval, QC, Canada H7T 2L2
Phone: (514)334-5912
Fax: (450)688-6269
Subject(s): Travel and Tourism
Circ: (Paid)540,672

**Primeurs** (36221)
Feature Publishing Ltd.
2100 St. Catherine St. W, 2nd Fl.
Montreal, QC, Canada H3H 2T3
Phone: (514)939-5024
Fax: (514)939-8027
Subject(s): Radio, Television, Cable, and Video; French
Circ: (Combined)450,000

**Reader's Digest Magazine, Canadian Edition** (36229)
Reader's Digest
1125 Stanley St.
Montreal, QC, Canada H3B 5H5
Phone: (514)940-0751
Fax: (514)940-3637
Subject(s): General Editorial; French
Circ: (Paid)225,000

**Virage** (36244)
Editador (9012-3993 Quebec Inc.)
4545 Pierre-De Coubertin Ave.
C.P. 1000, Succursale M.
Montreal, QC, Canada H1V 3R2
Phone: (514)252-3017
Fax: (514)252-3154
Subject(s): Senior Citizens' Interests
Circ: (Combined)218,636

**L'actualite** (36106)
Rogers Media
1001 boul. De Maisonneuve Ouest, Ste. 800
1200 McGill College
Montreal, QC, Canada H3B 4G7
Phone: (514)845-5141
Fax: (514)845-3879
Subject(s): General Editorial; French
Circ: (Paid)190,745

**Chatelaine** (36127)
Rogers Media
1001 boul. De Maisonneuve Ouest, Ste. 800
1200 McGill College
Montreal, QC, Canada H3B 4G7
Phone: (514)845-5141
Fax: (514)845-3879
Subject(s): French; Women's Interests
Circ: (Paid)182,099

**Coup de Pouce** (36132)
2001 rue University, bureau 900
Montreal, QC, Canada H3A 2A6
Phone: (514)499-0491
Subject(s): Women's Interests; Lifestyle; French
Circ: (Paid)172,413

**ARCHIE** (36327)
Les Editions Heritage Inc.
300, rue Arran
Saint-Lambert, QC, Canada J4R 1K5
Phone: (514)875-0327
Fax: (514)672-5448
Subject(s): Comics and Comic Technique; French
Circ: (Combined)‡165,000

**Les Diplomes** (36190)
Les Diplomes de l'Universite de Montreal
CP 6128, succursale Centre-ville
Montreal, QC, Canada H3C 3J7
Phone: (514)343-6230
Fax: (514)343-5798
Subject(s): College Publications
Circ: (Controlled)165,000

**Ski Presse** (36097)
Ski Press Media Inc.
850 Bernard Pilon
McMasterville, QC, Canada J3G 5X7
Subject(s): (Skiing)
Circ: (Paid)423
(Non-paid)150,577

**Le Bel Age** (36173)
Transcontinental Media
1100 Rene-Levesque Blvd. W, 24th Fl.
Montreal, QC, Canada H3B 4X9
Phone: (514)392-9000
Fax: (514)392-4726
Subject(s): French; Senior Citizens' Interests
Circ: (Paid)149,754

**Pensez-Y Bien!** (36056)
Editions E.J.S.
13 chemin Pied-de-Roi
Lac Beaufort, QC, Canada G0A 2C0
Phone: (418)841-0972
Fax: (418)686-1942
Subject(s): Local, State, and Regional Publications
Circ: (Non-paid)134,609

**Harrowsmith Country Life** (36267)
Malcolm Publishing Inc.
3650 Blvd. Pitfield
Pierrefonds, QC, Canada H8Y 3L4
Phone: (514)327-4464
Fax: (514)327-0514
Subject(s): Lifestyle
Circ: (Paid)125,138

**McGill News** (36198)
The McGill Alumni Association
3640 de la Montagne
Montreal, QC, Canada H3G 2A8
Phone: (514)398-3549
Fax: (514)398-5293
Subject(s): College Publications
Circ: (Controlled)‡115,000

**Le Journal Voir** (36181)
Communication Voir Inc.
355 Ste-Catherine St. W
Montreal, QC, Canada H3B 1A5
Phone: (514)848-0805
Fax: (514)848-9004
Subject(s): Lifestyle
Circ: (Paid)⎕174
(Free)⎕107,652

**Nouvelles CEQ** (36209)
Centrale de l'enseignement du Quebec
9405, rue Sherbrooke Est
Montreal, QC, Canada H1L 6P3
Phone: (514)356-8888
Fax: (514)356-9999
Subject(s): Education; Labor
Circ: (Non-paid)95,498

**RND (Revue Notre-Dame)** (36366)
Revue Notre-Dame
2215 Marie-Victorin
Sillery, QC, Canada G1T 1J6
Phone: (418)681-3581
Fax: (418)681-1139
Subject(s): Religious Publications; French
Circ: ‡93,000

**Le Magazine Affaires Plus** (36182)
Transcontinental Media
1100 Rene-Levesque Blvd. W, 24th Fl.
Montreal, QC, Canada H3B 4X9
Phone: (514)392-9000
Fax: (514)392-4726
Subject(s): French; Business
Circ: (Paid)92,887

**VOILA QUEBEC** (36087)
Les Publications Vacances (Quebec) Inc.
1255 Avenue Maguire
Maguire Sillery, QC, Canada J1T 1Z2
Phone: (418)694-1272
Fax: (418)694-1119
Subject(s): Travel and Tourism; French
Circ: (Controlled)88,766

**Le Magazine Enfants Quebec** (36329)
Les Editions Heritage Inc.
300, rue Arran
Saint-Lambert, QC, Canada J4R 1K5
Phone: (514)875-0327
Fax: (514)672-5448
Subject(s): Parenting; Children's Interests; Youths' Interests; Education
Circ: (Combined)72,102

**Perspective Infirmiere** (36218)
Ordre des infirmieres et infirmiers du Quebec
4200, boul. Dorchester Ouest
Montreal, QC, Canada H3Z 1V4
Phone: (514)935-2501
Fax: (514)935-2055
Subject(s): Nursing
Circ: (Combined)65,853

**Decoration Chez-Soi** (36263)
TVA Publications Inc.
7 Chemin Bates
Outremont, QC, Canada H2V 4V7
Phone: (514)333-4488
Fax: (514)333-9795
Subject(s): Home and Garden; French
Circ: (Paid)65,386

**Revue Notre-Dame du Cap** (36000)
626 Notre-Dame
Cap-de-la-Madeleine, QC, Canada G8T 4G9
Phone: (819)374-2441
Fax: (819)374-2441
Subject(s): French; Religious Publications
Circ: ‡65,000

**The ICAO Journal** (36148)
International Civil Aviation Organization
999 University St., 12th Fl.
Montreal, QC, Canada H3C 5H7
Subject(s): Aviation; French; Spanish; Russian
Circ: 58,482

**Le Messager de St. Antoine** (36057)
250
Lac Bouchette, QC, Canada G0W 1V0
Phone: (418)348-6344
Fax: (418)348-9960
Subject(s): Religious Publications; French
Circ: ⊕51,000

**Plan** (36219)
Ordre des Ingenieurs du Quebec
Windsor Station, Office 350
1100 Delagauchetiere W.
Montreal, QC, Canada H3B 2F2
Phone: (514)845-1833
Subject(s): Engineering (Various branches); French
Circ: (Combined)48,000

**Dalhousie Alumni Magazine** (34703)
Dalhousie University
Macdonald Bldg., Rm. 100
Halifax, NS, Canada B3H 3J5
Phone: (902)494-2071
Fax: (902)494-1141
Subject(s): Education
Circ: (Controlled)46,000

**Sentier Chasse-Peche** (36237)
Le Groupe Polygone Editeurs Inc.
11450, Albert-Hudon
Montreal, QC, Canada H1G 3J9
Phone: (514)327-4464
Fax: (514)327-0602
Subject(s): (Hunting, Fishing, and Game Management); Environmental and Natural Resources Conservation; French
Circ: (Non-paid)1,260
(Paid)45,091

**C'est Pour Quand?** (36064)
Communications Famille Inc.
Family Communications Inc.
2260 des Patriotes
Laval, QC, Canada H7L 3K8
Phone: (450)622-0091
Fax: (450)622-0099
Subject(s): Nursing; Parenting
Circ: (Non-paid)44,000

**Revue Commerce** (36231)
Transcontinental Media
1100 Rene-Levesque Blvd. W, 24th Fl.
Montreal, QC, Canada H3B 4X9
Phone: (514)392-9000
Fax: (514)392-4726
Subject(s): French; Business; Economics
Circ: (Paid)43,111

**Mon Bebe** (36071)
Communications Famille Inc.
Family Communications Inc.
2260 des Patriotes
Laval, QC, Canada H7L 3K8
Phone: (450)622-0091
Fax: (450)622-0099
Subject(s): Parenting
Circ: (Non-paid)43,000

**Gale Directory of Publications & Broadcast Media/140th Ed.**   **Eastern Provinces**

**Magazine Finance  (36192)**
Editions du Journal de l'Assurance Inc.
321, Rue de la Commune W, Ste. 100
Montreal, QC, Canada H2Y 2E1
Phone: (514)289-9595
Fax: (514)289-9527
**Subject(s):** Banking, Finance, and Investments
**Circ:** (Combined)40,000

**L'Oratoire  (36213)**
Oratoire St. Joseph Du-Mont-Royal
3800 Queen Mary Rd.
Montreal, QC, Canada H3V 1H6
Phone: (514)733-8211
Fax: (514)733-9735
**Subject(s):** Religious Publications; French
**Circ:** (Non-paid)‡2,000
  (Paid)‡40,000

**Le Magazine PME  (36183)**
Transcontinental Media
1100 Rene-Levesque Blvd. W, 24th Fl.
Montreal, QC, Canada H3B 4X9
Phone: (514)392-9000
Fax: (514)392-4726
**Subject(s):** Business; French
**Circ:** (Combined)•**39,764**

**Doctor's Review  (36136)**
Parkhurst Publishing Ltd.
400 McGill St., 3rd Fl.
Montreal, QC, Canada H2Y 2G1
Phone: (514)397-8833
Fax: (514)397-0228
**Subject(s):** Medicine and Surgery; Travel and Tourism
**Circ:** (Combined)38,500

**Parkhurst Exchange  (36217)**
Parkhurst Publishing Ltd.
400 McGill St., 3rd Fl.
Montreal, QC, Canada H2Y 2G1
Phone: (514)397-8833
Fax: (514)397-0228
**Subject(s):** Medicine and Surgery
**Circ:** (Combined)38,500

**Les Debrouillards  (36189)**
Publications BLD
4388 rue Saint-Denis, Bureau 304
Montreal, QC, Canada H2J 2L1
Phone: (514)844-4388
Fax: (514)844-8407
**Subject(s):** Education; Science (General); French
**Circ:** (Controlled)37,500

**Montreal Scope  (36202)**
Plaza Metro Ltd.
1253 McGill College, bureau 232
Montreal, QC, Canada H3B 2Y5
Phone: (514)933-3333
Fax: (514)931-9581
**Subject(s):** Local, State, and Regional Publications
**Circ:** (Non-paid)•**36,636**

**The Canadian Journal of CME (Continuing Medical Education)  (36271)**
STA Communications Inc.
955 St. Jean Blvd., Ste. 306
Pointe-Claire, QC, Canada H9R 5K3
Phone: (514)695-7623
Fax: (514)695-8554
**Subject(s):** Medicine and Surgery
**Circ:** (Controlled)35,886

**The Canadian Journal of Diagnosis  (36272)**
STA Communications Inc.
955 St. Jean Blvd., Ste. 306
Pointe-Claire, QC, Canada H9R 5K3
Phone: (514)695-7623
Fax: (514)695-8554
**Subject(s):** Medicine and Surgery
**Circ:** (Combined)35,733

**Renovation Bricolage  (36265)**
TVA Publications Inc.
7 Chemin Bates
Outremont, QC, Canada H2V 4V7
Phone: (514)333-4488
Fax: (514)333-9795
**Subject(s):** Home and Garden; French
**Circ:** (Paid)35,576

**The Annals of Saint Anne de Beaupre  (36338)**
Redemptorist Fathers
PO Box 1000
Sainte-Anne-de-Beaupre, QC, Canada G0A 3C0
Phone: (418)827-4538
Fax: (418)827-4530
**Subject(s):** Religious Publications
**Circ:** (Paid)35,000

**Adorable  (36278)**
Magazine Adorable Inc.
410, boul. Charest est
Bureau 540
Quebec, QC, Canada G1K 8G3
Phone: (418)266-6166
Fax: (418)263-0247
**Subject(s):** Youths' Interests
**Circ:** (Combined)33,598

**Atlantic Business Journal  (34579)**
Southeast Publishing Inc.
30 Trider Ct., Ste. 100
Riverview, NB, Canada E1B 3R6
Phone: (506)386-2645
Fax: (416)946-1891
**Subject(s):** Business; Local, State, and Regional Publications
**Circ:** 33,000

**Quebec Habitation  (35984)**
A.P.C.H.Q.
5930, boul. Louis H. Lafontaine
Anjou, QC, Canada H1M 1S7
Phone: (514)353-9960
Fax: (514)353-0835
**Subject(s):** Construction, Contracting, Building, and Excavating; Business
**Circ:** (Combined)32,000

**Spa Management  (36239)**
Publicom Inc.
CP 365 Pl. D'Armes
Montreal, QC, Canada H2Y 3H1
Phone: (514)274-0004
Fax: (514)274-5884
**Subject(s):** Health and Fitness; Cosmetics and Toiletries
**Circ:** (Paid)‡30,712

**Atlantic Business Magazine  (34633)**
Communications Ten Ltd.
197 Water St. 2nd Floor
PO Box 2356, Sta. C
Saint John's, NL, Canada A1C 6E7
Phone: (709)726-9300
Fax: (709)726-3013
**Subject(s):** Business
**Circ:** (Non-paid)30,500

**In Montreal  (36150)**
Federation CJA
1 Carre Cummings Sq.
Montreal, QC, Canada H3W 1M6
Phone: (514)345-2645
Fax: (514)345-2655
**Subject(s):** Jewish Publications; Youths' Interests; Lifestyle; Local, State, and Regional Publications
**Circ:** (Paid)30,000

**Le Monde de L'Auto  (36332)**
St. Laurent
7575, Transcanadienne, Ste. 401
Saint-Laurent, QC, Canada H4T 1V6
Phone: (514)956-1461
**Subject(s):** Automotive (Consumer)
**Circ:** (Controlled)30,000

**Movin'  (36206)**
Canadian National Railways
Public Affairs & Advertising
PO Box 8100
Montreal, QC, Canada H3C 3N4
Phone: (514)399-5430
Fax: (514)399-5344
**Subject(s):** Railroad
**Circ:** (Non-paid)‡30,000

**The Torch  (34691)**
Nationwide Promotion Ltd.
12 Dawn Dr.
Dartmouth, NS, Canada B3B 1H9
Phone: (902)468-5141
Fax: (902)468-4843
**Subject(s):** Unclassified Fraternal; Clubs and Societies
**Circ:** (Non-paid)30,000

**Construire  (36131)**
Association de la construction du Quebec
7400, Blvd. les Galeries d'Anjou, Bureau 205
Montreal, QC, Canada H1M 3M2
Phone: (514)354-8249
Fax: (514)354-4258
**Subject(s):** French; Construction, Contracting, Building, and Excavating
**Circ:** (Combined)27,400

**The Newfoundland Herald  (34637)**
Sunday Herald Ltd.
458 Logy Bay Rd.
PO Box 2015
Saint John's, NL, Canada A1C 5R7
Phone: (709)726-7060
Fax: (709)726-6971
**Subject(s):** Entertainment; Radio, Television, Cable, and Video
**Circ:** (Non-paid)544
  (Paid)27,383

**Cycle Canada  (35995)**
Turbopress Inc.
C/O Bruce Reeve, Editor
4105 Matte Blvd, Ste. G
Brossard, QC, Canada J4Y 2P4
**Subject(s):** Motorbikes and Motorcycles
**Circ:** (Non-paid)8,000
  (Paid)26,000

**Journal de l'Assurance  (36164)**
Editions du Journal de l'Assurance Inc.
321, Rue de la Commune W, Ste. 100
Montreal, QC, Canada H2Y 2E1
Phone: (514)289-9595
Fax: (514)289-9527
**Subject(s):** Insurance; Business; French
**Circ:** (Controlled)26,000

**Missions Etrangeres  (36070)**
Societe des Missions-Etrangeres
160 Pl. Juge Desnoyers
Laval, QC, Canada H7G 1A5
Phone: (450)667-4190
Fax: (450)667-3006
**Subject(s):** Religious Publications; French
**Circ:** ‡25,000

**WHERE Halifax  (34710)**
Metro Guide publishing
1300 Hollis St.
Halifax, NS, Canada B3J 1T6
Phone: (902)420-9943
Fax: (902)429-9058
**Subject(s):** Travel and Tourism
**Circ:** (Non-paid)25,000

**Camping Caravaning  (36118)**
Communications Camping Caravaning Inc.
4545 Pierre-De Coubertin Ave.
C.P. 1000, Succursale M.
Montreal, QC, Canada H1V 3R2
Phone: (514)252-3003
Fax: (514)254-0694
**Subject(s):** (Outdoors); French
**Circ:** (Paid)4,046
  (Non-paid)23,176

**Quebec Science  (36227)**
Quebec Science Inc.
4388 Saint-Denis St., office 300
Montreal, QC, Canada H2J 2L1
Phone: (514)843-6888
Fax: (514)843-4897
**Subject(s):** Science (General); French
**Circ:** (Paid)22,601

**Logistics Magazine  (36337)**
Logistics Publishing Inc.
916, Ste-Adele bvd, Office 115
Sainte-Adele, QC, Canada J8B 2N2
Phone: (450)229-7777
Fax: (450)229-3233
**Subject(s):** Materials Handling
**Circ:** (Combined)21,919

**Le Bulletin des Agriculteurs  (36174)**
1200, Ave. McGill College, Bureau 800
Montreal, QC, Canada H3B 4G7
Phone: (514)845-5141
Fax: (514)843-2180
**Subject(s):** General Agriculture; French
**Circ:** (Paid)21,291

Circulation: ★ = ABC; △ = BPA; ♦ = CAC; • = CCAB; ❑ = VAC; ⊕ = PO Statement; ‡ = Publisher's Report; Boldface figures = sworn; Light figures = estimated.

# Eastern Provinces

**The Atlantic Co-operator (34566)**
Atlantic Co-operative Publishers
123 Halifax St.
Moncton, NB, Canada E1C 8N5
Phone: (506)858-6614
Fax: (506)858-6615
**Subject(s):** Business; General Merchandise
**Circ:** (Combined)21,000

**Le Chef du Service Alimentaire (36313)**
Le Chef D.S.A. Inc.
C.P. 1010
Saint-Etienne-de-Lauzon, QC, Canada G6J 1S2
Phone: (418)831-5317
Fax: (418)831-5372
**Subject(s):** Food and Grocery Trade; Hotels, Motels, Restaurants, and Clubs; French; Hospitals and Healthcare Institutions
**Circ:** (Controlled)•20,629

**Spa Destinations (36238)**
Publicom Inc.
CP 365 Pl. D'Armes
Montreal, QC, Canada H2Y 3H1
Phone: (514)274-0004
Fax: (514)274-5884
**Subject(s):** Travel and Tourism
**Circ:** (Non-paid)20,500

**Journal Industriel du Quebec (36068)**
Info-Industriel Inc.
1254 Jilles
Laval, QC, Canada H7P 4V2
Phone: (450)628-6269
Fax: (450)628-6167
**Subject(s):** Automation; French
**Circ:** (Combined)20,431

**Journal L'Itineraire (36163)**
2103, Ste-Catherine Is, 3rd Stage
Montreal, QC, Canada H2K 2H9
Phone: (514)597-0238
Fax: (514)597-1544
**Subject(s):** Social and Political Issues
**Circ:** (Paid)20,000

**Le Journal Industriel du Quebec (36069)**
Info-Industriel Inc.
1254 Jilles
Laval, QC, Canada H7P 4V2
Phone: (450)628-6269
Fax: (450)628-6167
**Subject(s):** Commerce and Industry; French
**Circ:** (Combined)19,652

**Wine Tidings (36245)**
Kylix Media Inc
5165 Sherbrooke St. W, No. 414
Montreal, QC, Canada H4A 1T6
Phone: (514)481-5892
Fax: (514)481-9699
**Subject(s):** Beverages, Brewing, and Bottling
**Circ:** (Combined)19,300

**The Coast (34701)**
Coast Publishing Ltd.
5435 Portland Pl.
Halifax, NS, Canada B3K 6R7
Phone: (902)422-6278
Fax: (902)425-0013
**Subject(s):** Local, State, and Regional Publications; Entertainment
**Circ:** (Paid)11
(Free)19,276

**L'Echo du Transport (36065)**
Les Editions Bomart Ltee.
3380, Francis-Hugues
Laval, QC, Canada H7L 5A7
Phone: (450)975-7667
Fax: (450)975-4847
**Subject(s):** Trucks and Trucking; French
**Circ:** (Controlled)18,625

**Mount Allison Record (34580)**
Mount Allison University
82 York St.
Sackville, NB, Canada E4L 1G2
Phone: (506)364-2345
Fax: (506)364-2623
**Subject(s):** College Publications
**Circ:** (Controlled)18,500

**Le Medecin du Quebec (36184)**
Federation of General Practitioners of Quebec
1440 Ste-Catherine St. W, Ste. 1000
Montreal, QC, Canada H3G 1R8
Phone: (514)878-1911
Fax: (514)878-2659
**Subject(s):** Medicine and Surgery; French
**Circ:** (Combined)18,200

**Atlantic Snowmobiler (34544)**
Atlantic Snowmobiler Publishing Inc.
527 Beaverbrook Ct., Ste. 510
Fredericton, NB, Canada E3B 1X6
Phone: (506)444-6489
Fax: (506)444-6453
**Subject(s):** (Snowmobiling)
**Circ:** (Combined)18,193

**The Insurance Journal (36154)**
Editions du Journal de l'Assurance Inc.
321, Rue de la Commune W, Ste. 100
Montreal, QC, Canada H2Y 2E1
Phone: (514)289-9595
Fax: (514)289-9527
**Subject(s):** Banking, Finance, and Investments; Insurance
**Circ:** (Combined)18,000

**Magazine Circuit Industriel (36286)**
P.A.P. Communication Inc.
1627, boul. St-Joseph
Quebec, QC, Canada G2K 1H1
Phone: (418)623-3383
Fax: (418)623-5033
**Subject(s):** Commerce and Industry; French
**Circ:** (Controlled)17,652

**L'Actualite Medicale (36107)**
Rogers Media
1001 boul. De Maisonneure Ouest, Ste. 800
1200 McGill College
Montreal, QC, Canada H3B 4G7
Phone: (514)845-5141
Fax: (514)845-3879
**Subject(s):** Medicine and Surgery
**Circ:** (Combined)17,157

**Le Journal des Pays d'En Haut (36336)**
1012 rue Valiquette
PO Box 1890
Sainte-Adele, QC, Canada J8B 2M3
Phone: (450)229-6664
Fax: (450)229-6063
**Subject(s):** French
**Circ:** 17,000

**Le Garagiste (00000)**
Publications Rousseau & Associe
2938, Terrasse Abenaquis
Longueuil, QC, Canada J4M 2B3
Phone: (450)448-2220
Fax: (450)448-1041
**Subject(s):** Automotive (Trade); French
**Circ:** (Combined)16,363

**Le Lingot (36045)**
Alcan
PO Box 1370
Jonquiere, QC, Canada G7S 4K9
Phone: (418)699-4010
Fax: (418)699-4100
**Subject(s):** French; Commerce and Industry; Metal, Metallurgy, and Metal Trade
**Circ:** ‡16,000

**Perspectives in Cardiology (36275)**
STA Communications Inc.
955 St. Jean Blvd., Ste. 306
Pointe-Claire, QC, Canada H9R 5K3
Phone: (514)695-7623
Fax: (514)695-8554
**Subject(s):** Medicine and Surgery
**Circ:** (Controlled)15,269

**Apostolat International (36110)**
Oblates of Mary Immaculate
8844 Notre-Dame, Est
Montreal, QC, Canada H1L 3M4
Phone: (514)351-9310
Fax: (514)351-1314
**Subject(s):** Religious Publications; French
**Circ:** ‡15,000

**Magnificat (36101)**
The Apostles of Infinite Love
Editions Magnificat
PO Box 4478
Mont-Tremblant, QC, Canada J8E 1A1
Phone: (819)688-5225
Fax: (819)688-6548
**Subject(s):** Religious Publications; French
**Circ:** 15,000

**Canadian Forest Industries (35988)**
JCFT Forest Communications
90 Morgan, Unit 14
Baie D'urfe', QC, Canada H9X 3A8
Phone: (514)457-2211
Fax: (514)457-2558
**Subject(s):** Forestry
**Circ:** (Combined)14,218

**Nos Animaux (36208)**
Les Productions L'Animal Inc.
4930 Cote des Neiges
Montreal, QC, Canada H3V 1H2
**Subject(s):** Veterinary Medicine; French
**Circ:** (Non-paid)11,000
(Paid)14,000

**Journal of Pulp & Paper Science (36166)**
Pulp and Paper Technical Association of Canada
740 Notre Dame W., Ste. 1070
Montreal, QC, Canada H3C 3X6
Phone: (514)392-0265
Fax: (514)392-0369
**Subject(s):** Paper; Chemistry, Chemicals, and Chemical Engineering
**Circ:** (Combined)13,150

**Orah Magazine (36212)**
Hadassah-Wizo Organization of Canada
1310 Greene Ave., Rm. 900
Montreal, QC, Canada H3Z 2B8
Phone: (514)937-9431
Fax: (514)933-6483
**Subject(s):** Jewish Publications
**Circ:** 12,582

**Le Clinicien (36273)**
STA Communications Inc.
955 St. Jean Blvd., Ste. 306
Pointe-Claire, QC, Canada H9R 5K3
Phone: (514)695-7623
Fax: (514)695-8554
**Subject(s):** Medicine and Surgery
**Circ:** (Controlled)12,416

**Geo Plein Air (36144)**
Les Editions Tricycle Inc.
1251 Rachel St. E.
Montreal, QC, Canada H2J 2J9
Phone: (514)521-8356
Fax: (514)521-5711
**Subject(s):** (Outdoors)
**Circ:** (Non-paid)8,959
(Paid)12,333

**Aggregates & Roadbuilding Magazine (36396)**
Franmore Communications Inc.
4999 St. Catherine St. W, Ste. 315
Westmount, QC, Canada H3Z 1T3
Phone: (514)487-9868
Fax: (514)487-9276
**Subject(s):** Stone and Rock Products; Building Materials, Concrete, Brick, and Tile
**Circ:** (Combined)•11,988

**Group Travel (Voyage en Groupe) (36063)**
590 Chemin St-Jean
Laprairie, QC, Canada J5R 2L1
Phone: (450)444-5870
**Subject(s):** Travel and Tourism; French
**Circ:** (Paid)415
(Controlled)11,750

**Fibre Expression (36344)**
Quebec Forest Industry Council
Pl. Iberville II
1175 Ave. Lavigerie, Ste. 200
Sainte-Foy, QC, Canada G1V 4P1
Phone: (418)651-9352
Fax: (418)657-7971
**Subject(s):** Paper
**Circ:** 11,500

**Gale Directory of Publications & Broadcast Media/140th Ed.**     **Eastern Provinces**

**RG (36234)**
C.P. 915 Succursale C
Montreal, QC, Canada H2L 4V2
Phone: (514)523-9463
Fax: (514)523-2214
**Subject(s):** Gay and Lesbian Interests
**Circ:** (Non-paid)‡11,500

**Eastern Woods and Waters (34686)**
Land & Sea Events
40 Aldeiney Dr., Ste. 303
Dartmouth, NS, Canada B2Y 2N5
Phone: (902)464-3757
Fax: (902)464-3755
**Subject(s):** (Hunting, Fishing, and Game Management); Environmental and Natural Resources Conservation
**Circ:** (Non-paid)5,647
    (Paid)11,208

**Moto Journal (36204)**
Turbopress Inc.
5000 rue Buchan No. 600A
Montreal, QC, Canada H4P 1T2
Phone: (514)738-4929
Fax: (514)738-4929
**Subject(s):** Motorbikes and Motorcycles; French
**Circ:** (Non-paid)2,000
    (Paid)11,000

**Atlantic Salmon Journal (34583)**
Atlantic Salmon Federation
PO Box 5200
Saint Andrews, NB, Canada E5B 3S8
Phone: (506)529-1033
Fax: (506)529-4438
**Subject(s):** (Hunting, Fishing, and Game Management); Environmental and Natural Resources Conservation
**Circ:** (Paid)‡416
    (Non-paid)‡10,584

**Canadian Mining & Metallurgical Bulletin (36125)**
Canadian Institute of Mining, Metallurgy, and Petroleum
1210-3400 de Maisonneuve Blvd. W.
Montreal, QC, Canada H3Z 3B8
**Subject(s):** Metal, Metallurgy, and Metal Trade; Mining and Minerals
**Circ:** ‡10,140

**Pulp & Paper Canada (36276)**
Business Information Group
1 Holiday St., E. Twr., Ste. 705
Pointe-Claire, QC, Canada H9R 5N3
Phone: (514)630-5955
Fax: (514)630-5980
**Subject(s):** Paper
**Circ:** (Combined)•10,131

**Gestion Logistique (36066)**
Les Editions Bomart Ltee.
3380, Francis-Hugues
Laval, QC, Canada H7L 5A7
Phone: (450)975-7667
Fax: (450)975-4847
**Subject(s):** Transportation, Traffic, and Shipping; French
**Circ:** 10,104

**Ascent Magazine (36114)**
Yasodhara Ashram Society
837 rue Gilford
Montreal, QC, Canada H2J 1P1
Phone: (514)499-3999
Fax: (514)499-3904
**Subject(s):** Health and Healthcare; Theology; Physical Education and Athletics
**Circ:** (Controlled)10,000

**Celtic Heritage (34699)**
Clansman Publishing Ltd.
PO Box 8805, Sta. A
Halifax, NS, Canada B3K 5M4
Phone: (902)835-6244
Fax: (902)835-0080
**Subject(s):** Ethnic Publications
**Circ:** (Paid)‡7,091
    (Non-paid)‡10,000

**Kateri (36050)**
Vice Postulation for the Cause of Canonization of Blessed Kateri Tekakwitha
PO Box 70
Kahnawake, QC, Canada J0L 1B0
Phone: (450)638-1546
Fax: (450)632-6031
**Subject(s):** Religious Publications; French
**Circ:** 10,000

**L'Ancai, La Voix du Vrac (36279)**
L'Association Nationale des Camionneurs Artisans Inc.
670 Bouvier St., Ste. 235
Quebec, QC, Canada G2K 1A7
Phone: (418)623-7923
Fax: (418)623-0448
**Circ:** (Controlled)9,849

**Electricite Quebec (36140)**
Corporation of Master Electricians of Quebec
5925, Blvd. Decarie, Ste. 100
Montreal, QC, Canada H3W 3C9
Phone: (514)738-2184
Fax: (514)738-2192
**Subject(s):** French; Electrical Engineering
**Circ:** (Controlled)9,670

**La Revue du Barreau (36171)**
Barreau du Quebec
445 St. Lawrence Blvd.
Montreal, QC, Canada H2Y 3T8
Phone: (514)954-3400
Fax: (514)954-3477
**Subject(s):** Law; French
**Circ:** ‡9,662

**Tourisme Plus (36241)**
Le Magazine Voyager Inc.
11800 5th Ave., Ste. 301
Montreal, QC, Canada H1E 7C1
Phone: (514)881-8583
Fax: (514)881-8292
**Subject(s):** Travel and Tourism; French
**Circ:** (Combined)9,341

**Electronique Industrielle et Commerciale (EIC) (36141)**
SERPRO Communication Inc.
8403 Rue Oscar-Roland
Montreal, QC, Canada H2M 2T4
Phone: (514)383-7700
Fax: (514)383-7691
**Subject(s):** Electronics Engineering; French
**Circ:** (Controlled)9,202

**La Flute (36169)**
Montreal Policemen's Brotherhood Inc.—Fraternite des Policiers et Policieres de Montreal Inc.
480 Gilford St.
Montreal, QC, Canada H2J 1N3
Phone: (514)527-4161
Fax: (514)527-7830
**Subject(s):** Labor; Police, Penology, and Penal Institutions
**Circ:** (Controlled)8,500

**Rural Delivery (34724)**
DvL Publishing Inc.
PO Box 1509
Liverpool, NS, Canada B0T 1K0
Phone: (902)354-5411
**Subject(s):** Farm Newspapers
**Circ:** (Non-paid)500
    (Paid)8,500

**CIM Reporter (36128)**
Canadian Institute of Mining, Metallurgy, and Petroleum
3400 de Maisonneuve Blvd. W., Ste. 1210
Montreal, QC, Canada H3Z 3B8
Phone: (514)939-2710
Fax: (514)939-2714
**Subject(s):** Mining and Minerals
**Circ:** (Controlled)**8,106**

**Italian Commerce of Commerce of Canada (36158)**
Italian Chamber of Commerce of Canada
550 Sherbrooke St. W, Ste. 1150
Montreal, QC, Canada G1K 7P4
Phone: (514)844-4249
Fax: (514)844-4875
**Subject(s):** Chambers of Commerce and Boards of Trade; French; Italian; Economics
**Circ:** (Non-paid)‡8,000

**Kids Creations (36167)**
Children's Apparel Manufacturers' Association
6900 Decarie, Ste. 3110
Montreal, QC, Canada H3X 2T8
Phone: (514)731-7774
Fax: (514)731-7459
**Subject(s):** Clothing; French
**Circ:** (Non-paid)7,571

**The Oratory (36214)**
Oratoire St. Joseph Du-Mont-Royal
3800 Queen Mary Rd.
Montreal, QC, Canada H3V 1H6
Phone: (514)733-8211
Fax: (514)733-9735
**Subject(s):** Religious Publications
**Circ:** (Paid)7,500

**Quebec Pharmacie (36226)**
Les Publications Codex
4378 Pierre de Coubertin
Montreal, QC, Canada H1V 1A6
Phone: (514)254-0346
Fax: (514)254-5010
**Subject(s):** Drugs and Pharmaceuticals; French
**Circ:** (Controlled)7,422

**Canadian Wood Products (35989)**
JCFT Forest Communications
90 Morgan, Unit 14
Baie D'urfe', QC, Canada H9X 3A8
Phone: (514)457-2211
Fax: (514)457-2558
**Subject(s):** Wood and Woodworking
**Circ:** (Combined)7,358

**Inter-Mecanique du Batiment (36155)**
CMMTQ
8175 Saint-Laurent Blvd.
Montreal, QC, Canada H2P 2M1
Phone: (514)382-2668
Fax: (514)382-1566
**Subject(s):** Construction, Contracting, Building, and Excavating; Building Management and Maintenance; Plumbing and Heating; French
**Circ:** (Combined)•6,750

**Artere (36111)**
Editions 2000 Neuf
606 Cathcart, Ste. 330
Montreal, QC, Canada H3B 1K9
Phone: (514)282-4252
Fax: (514)868-0608
**Subject(s):** Health and Healthcare; Hospitals and Healthcare Institutions
**Circ:** (Paid)‡6,661

**L'Actualite Pharmaceutique (36108)**
Rogers Media
1001 boul. De Maisonneuve Ouest, Ste. 800
1200 McGill College
Montreal, QC, Canada H3B 4G7
Phone: (514)845-5141
Fax: (514)845-3879
**Subject(s):** Drugs and Pharmaceuticals
**Circ:** (Paid)381
    (Non-paid)6,311

**Orient (36215)**
Missions des Peres de Sainte-Croix
4901, rue Piedmont
Montreal, QC, Canada H3V 1E3
Phone: (514)731-6231
Fax: (514)731-7820
**Subject(s):** Religious Publications; French
**Circ:** (Non-paid)‡50
    (Paid)‡6,000

**Operations Forestieres et de Scierie (35990)**
JCFT Forest Communications
90 Morgan, Unit 14
Baie D'urfe', QC, Canada H9X 3A8
Phone: (514)457-2211
Fax: (514)457-2558
**Subject(s):** Forestry; French
**Circ:** (Non-paid)•5,615

**Gestion (36145)**
Ecole des Haules Etudes Commerciales
3000 Chemin Cote-Sainte-Catherine
Montreal, QC, Canada H3T 2A7
Phone: (514)340-6677
Fax: (514)340-6975
**Subject(s):** Management and Administration; French
**Circ:** (Paid)5,500

**Info Presse Communications (36151)**
Editions Info Presse Inc.
4310, boul. Saint-Laurent
Montreal, QC, Canada H2W 1Z3
Phone: (514)842-5873
Fax: (514)842-2422

*Circulation:* ★ = ABC; △ = BPA; ♦ = CAC; • = CCAB; ❑ = VAC; ⊕ = PO Statement; ‡ = Publisher's Report; Boldface figures = sworn; Light figures = estimated.

**Subject(s):** Advertising and Marketing; Radio, Television, Cable, and Video
**Circ:** (Controlled)2,500
(Paid)5,500

**Journal Dentaire du Quebec (JDQ) (36160)**
Ordre des Dentistes du Quebec
625, Rene-Levesque Blvd. W., 15th Fl.
Montreal, QC, Canada H3B 1R2
Phone: (514)875-8511
Fax: (514)393-9248
**Subject(s):** Dentistry; French
**Circ:** ‡5,300

**Master Guide (36287)**
Apex Publications Inc.
185 St. Paul
Quebec, QC, Canada G1K 3W2
Phone: (418)692-2110
Fax: (418)692-3392
**Subject(s):** Photography
**Circ:** (Combined)5,250

**Continuite (36281)**
Editions Continuite Inc.
82, Grande Allee Ouest
Quebec, QC, Canada G1R 2G6
Phone: (418)647-4525
Fax: (418)647-6483
**Subject(s):** History and Genealogy; French; Ethnic and Minority Studies
**Circ:** ⊕3,920
⊕5,000

**L'Optometriste (36211)**
Association des Optometristes du Quebec
1265 Berri St., Ste. 740
Montreal, QC, Canada H2L 4X4
Phone: (514)288-6272
Fax: (514)288-7071
**Subject(s):** Ophthalmology, Optometry, and Optics; French
**Circ:** (Controlled)‡4,400

**Les Papetieres du Quebec (36274)**
Business Information Group
1 Holiday St., E, Twr., Ste. 705
Pointe-Claire, QC, Canada H9R 5N3
Phone: (514)630-5955
Fax: (514)630-5980
**Subject(s):** Paper; French
**Circ:** (Combined)‡4,348

**Vie Des Arts (36243)**
La Vie des Arts
486, Sainte-Catherine Ouest, Ste. 400
Montreal, QC, Canada H3B 1A6
Phone: (514)282-0205
Fax: (514)282-0235
**Subject(s):** French; Art
**Circ:** (Non-paid)•1,728
(Paid)•4,072

**Le Technologue (36185)**
1265 Berri, Office 720
Montreal, QC, Canada H2L 4X4
Phone: (514)845-3247
Fax: (514)845-3459
**Subject(s):** Scientific Agricultural Publications; Construction, Contracting, Building, and Excavating; Engineering (Various branches); Forestry; Science (General); French
**Circ:** (Combined)4,000

**Relations (36230)**
Centre Justice et Foi
25, Jarry Ouest
Montreal, QC, Canada H2P 1S6
Phone: (514)387-2541
Fax: (514)387-0206
**Subject(s):** General Editorial; French
**Circ:** ‡4,000

**Vecteur Environnement (36242)**
Riseau Envirnement
133 Sir G.-E. Cartier
Montreal, QC, Canada H4C 3A1
Phone: (514)846-8085
Fax: (514)846-8094
**Subject(s):** Water Supply and Sewage Disposal; French
**Circ:** (Combined)4,000

**Quebec Vert (36289)**
Trans Continental Media
1320, boul. St-Joseph
Quebec, QC, Canada G2K 1G2
Phone: (418)628-8690

Fax: (418)628-0524
**Subject(s):** Landscape Architecture; Seed and Nursery Trade; French
**Circ:** ‡3,760

**Atlantic Forestry Review (34722)**
DvL Publishing Inc.
PO Box 1509
Liverpool, NS, Canada B0T 1K0
Phone: (902)354-5411
**Subject(s):** Forestry
**Circ:** (Paid)3,500
(Controlled)3,500

**Canadian Operating Room Nursing Journal (34698)**
Clockwork Communications, Inc.
PO Box 33145
Halifax, NS, Canada B3L 4T6
Phone: (902)497-1598
Fax: (902)444-0694
**Subject(s):** Nursing
**Circ:** ‡3,500

**ARQ, La revue d'architecture (36335)**
Art et architecture Quebec
86, Rue Morin
Sainte-Adele, QC, Canada J8B 2P7
Phone: (450)229-0551
**Subject(s):** Architecture; French
**Circ:** (Controlled)3,485

**Policy Options (36220)**
Institute for Research on Public Policy
1470 Peel St., Ste. 200
Montreal, QC, Canada H3A 1T1
Phone: (514)985-2461
Fax: (514)985-2559
**Subject(s):** Economics; French
**Circ:** (Paid)3,100
(Non-paid)3,100

**L'Action Nationale (36105)**
La Ligue d'Action Nationale
425 bd de Naisonneuve O., No. 1002
Montreal, QC, Canada H3A 3G5
Phone: (514)845-8533
Fax: (514)845-8529
**Subject(s):** Politics; French
**Circ:** (Paid)‡3,000

**Atlantic Horse & Pony (34723)**
DvL Publishing Inc.
PO Box 1509
Liverpool, NS, Canada B0T 1K0
Phone: (902)354-5411
**Subject(s):** (Horses and Horse Racing)
**Circ:** (Controlled)‡1,000
(Paid)‡3,000

**Canadian Nursing Home Journal (34697)**
Clockwork Communications, Inc.
PO Box 33145
Halifax, NS, Canada B3L 4T6
Phone: (902)497-1598
Fax: (902)444-0694
**Subject(s):** Hospitals and Healthcare Institutions; Health and Healthcare
**Circ:** (Paid)1,730
3,000

**Guide du Transport par Camion (36067)**
Les Editions Bomart Ltee.
3380, Francis-Hugues
Laval, QC, Canada H7L 5A7
Phone: (450)975-7667
Fax: (450)975-4847
**Subject(s):** Transportation, Traffic, and Shipping
**Circ:** 3,000

**Quart de Rond (36083)**
The Building Materials Retailers Association of Quebec
474, Trans-Canada
Longueuil, QC, Canada J4G 1N8
Phone: (514)646-5842
Fax: (514)646-6171
**Subject(s):** French; Building Materials, Concrete, Brick, and Tile; Hardware
**Circ:** (Combined)3,000

**Porc Quebec (36082)**
La Federation des producteurs de porcs du Quebec
555 boul. Roland-Therrien
Longueuil, QC, Canada J4H 3Y9
Phone: (450)679-0530
Fax: (450)670-4788

**Subject(s):** General Agriculture
**Circ:** (Combined)2,905

**Le Trait d'Union (36187)**
Cegep de Maisonneuve
3800, rue Sherbrooke Est
Montreal, QC, Canada H1X 2A2
Phone: (514)256-6891
Fax: (514)259-2105
**Subject(s):** College Publications; French
**Circ:** (Non-paid)2,800

**Le Medecin Veterinaire du Quebec (36322)**
Ordre des Medecins Veterinaires du Quebec
800, ave. Sainte-Anne, bureau 200
Saint-Hyacinthe, QC, Canada J2S 5G7
Phone: (450)774-1427
Fax: (450)774-7635
**Subject(s):** Veterinary Medicine; French
**Circ:** (Non-paid)‡2,700

**Folk-Lore (36142)**
Association Quebecoise des Loisirs Folkloriques
4545, Ave. Pierre-De Coubertin
Case postale 1000, succ. M
Montreal, QC, Canada H1V 3R2
Phone: (514)252-3022
Fax: (514)251-8038
**Subject(s):** History and Genealogy
**Circ:** (Controlled)2,500

**Nuit Blanche (36288)**
1026 rue St-Jean, Bureau 403
Quebec, QC, Canada G1R 1R7
Phone: (418)692-1354
Fax: (418)692-1355
**Subject(s):** Literature; French
**Circ:** (Controlled)2,500

**Phare/Beacon (35979)**
B.F.C. Bagotville
CP 369
Alouette, QC, Canada G0V 1A0
Phone: (418)677-8160
**Subject(s):** Aviation; Military and Navy; French
**Circ:** (Controlled)2,500

**Arts Atlantic (34696)**
Arts Atlantic Inc.
PO Box 36007
RPO Spring Garden
Halifax, NS, Canada B3J 3S9
Phone: (902)420-5045
Fax: (902)491-8624
**Subject(s):** Art and Art History
**Circ:** (Combined)2,200

**Atlantic Beef Quarterly (34721)**
DVL Publishing Inc.
190 Main St.
PO Box 1509
Liverpool, NS, Canada B0T 1K0
Phone: (902)354-5411
**Subject(s):** Livestock
**Circ:** (Paid)2000
(Non-paid)2000

**Caper Times (34737)**
University College of Cape Breton
1250 Grand Lake Rd.
PO Box 5300
Sydney, NS, Canada B1P 6L2
Phone: (902)539-5300
Fax: (902)562-0119
**Subject(s):** College Publications
**Circ:** (Free)2,000

**Pottersfield Portfolio (34732)**
9879 Kempt Head Rd.
Ross Ferry, NS, Canada B1X 1N3
**Subject(s):** Poetry; Literature and Literary Reviews
**Circ:** (Combined)2000

**The Textile Journal (La Revue du Textile) (36323)**
Textile Technology Centre
3000 Boulle St.
Saint-Hyacinthe, QC, Canada J2S 1H9
Phone: (514)778-1870
Fax: (514)778-9016
**Subject(s):** Textiles
**Circ:** (Controlled)2,000

**Kindred Spirit** (35970)
Kindred Spirits
Box 491
Kensington, PE, Canada C0B 1M0
Phone: (902)836-5502
Fax: (902)836-5509
**Subject(s):** New Age; Alternative and Underground; Health
**Circ:** (Paid)1,800

**Meta** (36199)
Les Presses de L'Universite de Montreal
M. Andre Clas, Dept. Linquistique
Universite Montreal
C.P. 6128, Succ. Centre-ville
Montreal, QC, Canada H3C 3J7
Phone: (514)343-7047
Fax: (514)343-2284
**Subject(s):** Philology, Language, and Linguistics; French
**Circ:** ‡1,800

**Circuit** (36129)
Les Presses de L'Universite de Montreal
CP 6128
Succ. Downtown Area
Montreal, QC, Canada H3C 3J7
Phone: (514)343-6933
Fax: (514)343-2232
**Subject(s):** Music and Musical Instruments; French
**Circ:** (Combined)1,500

**The Image News** (36397)
Promotional Products Association of Canada Inc.
4920 Ouest de Maisonneuve W., Ste. 305
Westmount, QC, Canada H3Z 1N1
Phone: (514)489-5359
Fax: (514)489-7760
**Subject(s):** Advertising and Marketing
**Circ:** 1,500

**McGill Law Journal/Revue de Droit de McGill** (36197)
3644 Peel St.
Montreal, QC, Canada H3A 1W9
Phone: (514)398-7397
Fax: (514)398-7360
**Subject(s):** Law
**Circ:** (Combined)1,500

**Revue Relations Industrielles/Industrial Relations** (36290)
Depart des Industrielles
Local 3129, J.-A.-DeSeve
Universite Laval
Quebec, QC, Canada G1K 7P4
Phone: (418)656-2468
Fax: (418)656-3175
**Subject(s):** Employment and Human Resources; French; Labor
**Circ:** (Non-paid)150
(Paid)1,500

**Canadian Journal of Soil Science** (35965)
Agricultural Institute of Canada
c/o Dr. M. R. Carter
Agriculture and Agri-Food Canada
Crops and Livestock Research Centre
440 University Ave.
Charlottetown, PE, Canada C1A 4N6
Phone: (902)566-6869
Fax: (902)566-6821
**Subject(s):** Scientific Agricultural Publications
**Circ:** (Paid)1,250

**Canadian Journal of Mathematics** (36124)
Canadian Mathematical Society
C/O Henri Darmon and Niky Kamran, Editors-in-Chief
Dept. of Mathematics and statistics
McGill University
Montreal, QC, Canada H3A 2K6
**Subject(s):** Mathematics; French
**Circ:** 1,226

**Journal of Palliative Care** (36165)
Centre for Bioethics
Clinical Research Institute of Montreal
110 Pine Ave. W
Montreal, QC, Canada H2W 1R7
Phone: (514)987-5617
Fax: (514)987-5695
**Subject(s):** Medicine and Surgery
**Circ:** (Non-paid)‡79
(Paid)‡1,200

**Infor** (36152)
University of Toronto Press - Journals Div.
C.P. 6128 Succ. Centre-ville
Montreal, QC, Canada H3C 3J7
**Subject(s):** Library and Information Science; French
**Circ:** 1,125

**Canadian Journal of Plant Science** (34742)
Agricultural Institute of Canada
c/o Dr. Yousef A. Papadopoulos
Agriculture and Agri-Food Canada
Crops and Livestock Research Centre
14 Fundy Dr.
Truro, NS, Canada B2N 5Z3
Phone: (902)896-0400
Fax: (902)896-0200
**Subject(s):** Scientific Agricultural Publications; Botany
**Circ:** ‡1,100

**Revue d'histoire de l'Amerique francaise** (36232)
Institut d'histoire de l'Amerique francaise
261 Ave. Bloomfield
Montreal, QC, Canada H2V 3R6
Phone: (514)278-2232
Fax: (514)271-6369
**Subject(s):** History and Genealogy; Intercultural Interests
**Circ:** (Controlled)1,100

**Canadian Journal of Chemical Engineering** (36121)
The Chemical Institute of Canada
Ecole Polytechnique
Dept. Of Chemical Engineering
C.P. 6079
Succ. Centre-Ville
Montreal, QC, Canada H3C 3A7
Phone: (514)340-4711
Fax: (514)340-2994
**Subject(s):** Chemistry, Chemicals, and Chemical Engineering; Engineering (Various branches)
**Circ:** ‡1,050

**The Fiddlehead** (34548)
Campus House
University of New Brunswick
PO Box 4400
Fredericton, NB, Canada E3B 5A3
Phone: (506)453-3501
Fax: (506)453-5069
**Subject(s):** Literature and Literary Reviews
**Circ:** (Non-paid)‡50
(Paid)‡900

**Labour/Le Travail** (34636)
Canadian Committee on Labour History
Memorial University of Newfoundland
Faculty of Arts Publications, FM 2005
Saint John's, NL, Canada A1C 5S7
Phone: (709)737-2144
Fax: (709)737-4342
**Subject(s):** Labor; International Affairs
**Circ:** 900

**Acadiensis** (34542)
University of New Brunswick
Department of History
Fredericton, NB, Canada E3B 5A3
Phone: (506)453-4978
Fax: (506)453-5068
**Subject(s):** History and Genealogy
**Circ:** (Controlled)850

**Aujourd'hui Credo** (36077)
Eglise Unie Du Canada
1332, Victoria
Longueuil, QC, Canada J4V 1L8
Phone: (514)466-7733
Fax: (514)466-2664
**Subject(s):** Religious Publications
**Circ:** 800

**Sante Mentale au Quebec** (36235)
Revue Sante Mentale au Quebec, C.P.
548, Succ. Pl. d'Armes
Montreal, QC, Canada H2Y 3H3
Phone: (514)523-0607
Fax: (514)523-0797
**Subject(s):** Psychology and Psychiatry; Laboratory Research (Scientific and Medical)
**Circ:** (Paid)750

**The Antigonish Review** (34679)
St. Francis Xavier University
PO Box 5000
Antigonish, NS, Canada B2G 2W5
Phone: (902)867-3962

Fax: (902)867-5563
**Subject(s):** Literature and Literary Reviews
**Circ:** (Non-paid)200
(Paid)700

**Canadian Review of Studies in Nationalism** (35966)
Canadian Review of Studies in Nationalism Inc.
c/o University of Prince Edward Island
Charlottetown, PE, Canada C1A 4P3
Phone: (902)894-4409
Fax: (902)628-4323
**Subject(s):** Ethnic and Minority Studies; Social Sciences
**Circ:** (Controlled)600

**ellipse** (34547)
471 Smythe, No. 27009
Fredericton, NB, Canada E3B 3E3
Phone: (506)451-0408
Fax: (506)455-9980
**Subject(s):** Poetry; Literature; French
**Circ:** (Combined)560

**Agenda** (36341)
Quebec Dans Le Monde
C P 8503
Sainte-Foy, QC, Canada G1V 4N5
Phone: (418)659-5540
Fax: (418)659-4143
**Subject(s):** Travel and Tourism; French
**Circ:** 500

**Scrivener** (36236)
McGill University
Arts Bldg., Office 305
853 Sherbrooke St. W
Montreal, QC, Canada H3A 2T6
Phone: (514)398-6588
**Subject(s):** Literature; Art and Art History; Photography
**Circ:** (Combined)500

**Education Libraries Concordia University** (36139)
Special Library Association
Concordia University
1455 de Maisonneuve St., Rm. 583-1
LB-583-1
Montreal, QC, Canada H3G 1M8
Phone: (514)848-2424
Fax: (514)848-4520
**Subject(s):** Library and Information Science; Education
**Circ:** (Combined)400

**Kodaly Society of Canada, Alla Breve** (34688)
Kodaly Society of Canada
8 Royalvue Ct.
Dartmouth, NS, Canada B2Y 4L6
**Subject(s):** Music and Musical Instruments; Education
**Circ:** (Paid)400

**APLA Bulletin** (34695)
Atlantic Provinces Library Association (APLA)
Dalhousie University
School of Library and Information Studies
Acadia University
Halifax, NS, Canada B3H 4H8
Phone: (902)494-3656
Fax: (902)494-2451
**Subject(s):** Library and Information Science
**Circ:** (Paid)350

**Canadian Jewish Studies/Etudes Juives Canadiennes** (36120)
Association for Canadian Jewish Studies
Dept. of Religion
Concordia University
1455 de Maisonneuve Blvd. W
Montreal, QC, Canada H3G 1M8
Phone: (514)848-2424
Fax: (514)848-4541
**Subject(s):** Jewish Publications; Intercultural Interests; French
**Circ:** (Paid)354

**Island Sport Scene** (35969)
Sport Prince Edward Island Inc.
PO Box 302
Charlottetown, PE, Canada C1A 7K7
Phone: (902)368-4110
Fax: (902)368-4548
**Subject(s):** Physical Education and Athletics
**Circ:** (Non-paid)350

## Northern Provinces

**KOLA** (36168)
PO Box 44595
Barclay
Montreal, QC, Canada H3S 2W6
Phone: (514)887-9060
Fax: (514)483-7213
Subject(s): Black Publications; Literature
Circ: (Combined)325

**Emploi Plus** (35985)
DGR Publication
1256 Principale N St., Ste. 203
L'Annonciation, QC, Canada J0T 1T0
Phone: (819)275-3293
Fax: (819)275-3293
Subject(s): Literature; Science (General); French
Circ: (Combined)300

**Newfoundland Studies** (34638)
Memorial University
FM 2005
Saint John's, NL, Canada A1C 5S7
Phone: (709)737-2144
Fax: (709)737-4342
Subject(s): Education; Local, State, and Regional Publications
Circ: (Controlled)300

**Onomastica Canadiana** (36036)
Canadian Society for the Study of Names
c/o Helen Kerfoot
Canadian Society for the Study of Names
C.P. 2164, Succursale Hull
Gatineau, QC, Canada J8X 3Z4
Phone: (613)992-3405
Fax: (613)943-8282
Subject(s): Philology, Language, and Linguistics; History and Genealogy
Circ: (Paid)250

## Northern Provinces

**Up Here** (34670)
Outcrop Ltd.
4920-52nd St., Ste.200
PO Box 1350
Yellowknife, NT, Canada X1A 3T1
Phone: (867)766-6710
Fax: (867)873-9876
Subject(s): Lifestyle; Local, State, and Regional Publications
Circ: (Non-paid)6,019
(Paid)18,953

## Western Provinces

**Westworld** (34104)
Canada Wide Magazines & Communications Ltd.
4180 Lougheed Hwy., 4th Fl.
Burnaby, BC, Canada V5C 6A7
Phone: (604)299-7311
Fax: (604)299-9188
Subject(s): Travel and Tourism; Automotive (Consumer)
Circ: (Controlled)‡2,387
(Paid)‡503,226

**Westworld British Columbia** (34106)
Canada Wide Magazines & Communications Ltd.
4180 Lougheed Hwy., 4th Fl.
Burnaby, BC, Canada V5C 6A7
Phone: (604)299-7311
Fax: (604)299-9188
Subject(s): Automotive (Trade)
Circ: (Paid)503,226

**Westworld Alberta** (34105)
Canada Wide Magazines & Communications Ltd.
4180 Lougheed Hwy., 4th Fl.
Burnaby, BC, Canada V5C 6A7
Phone: (604)299-7311
Fax: (604)299-9188
Subject(s): Automotive (Consumer); Travel and Tourism
Circ: (Paid)439,599

**WHERE Canadian Rockies** (33874)
RMV Publications Ltd.
One Palliser Sq., Ste. 250
125 Ninth Ave. SE
Calgary, AB, Canada T2G 0P6
Phone: (403)299-1885
Fax: (403)299-1899
Subject(s): Travel and Tourism
Circ: (Non-paid)375,000

**Island Visitor** (34382)
Visitor Publications
818 Broughton St.
Victoria, BC, Canada V8W 1E4
Phone: (250)388-3676
Fax: (250)386-2624
Subject(s): Travel and Tourism
Circ: (Non-paid)350,000

**WHERE Victoria** (34393)
Pacific Island Publishers
818 Broughton St.
Victoria, BC, Canada V8W 1E4
Phone: (250)383-3633
Fax: (250)480-3233
Subject(s): Travel and Tourism
Circ: (Controlled)‡281,000

**alive** (34079)
ALIVE Magazine
7432 Fraser Pk. Dr.
Burnaby, BC, Canada V5J 5B9
Phone: (604)435-1919
Fax: (604)435-4888
Subject(s): Health and Healthcare; Health and Fitness
Circ: ‡240,000

**WHERE Edmonton** (33950)
Tanner Publishing Ltd.
9343 50th St., No. 4
Edmonton, AB, Canada T6B 2L5
Phone: (780)465-3362
Fax: (780)448-0424
Subject(s): Travel and Tourism
Circ: (Controlled)240,000

**Western Living** (33949)
Transcontinental Publishing
10301 108th St., Ste. 201
Edmonton, AB, Canada T5J 1L7
Phone: (403)424-7171
Fax: (403)425-6488
Subject(s): Local, State, and Regional Publications; Lifestyle
Circ: (Paid)•1,921
(Non-paid)•208,058

**REALM Magazine** (34100)
Yes Canada - BC Publishing Div.
5172 Kingsway, Ste. 310
Burnaby, BC, Canada V5H 2E8
Fax: (604)412-4144
Subject(s): Career Development and Employment
Circ: (Combined)185,000

**Sphere Magazine** (34101)
Yes Canada - BC Publishing Div.
5172 Kingsway, Ste. 310
Burnaby, BC, Canada V5H 2E8
Fax: (604)412-4144
Subject(s): Career Development and Employment; French
Circ: (Combined)185,000

**Trek Magazine** (34338)
University of British Columbia Alumni Association
6251 Cecil Green Park Rd.
Vancouver, BC, Canada V6T 1Z1
Phone: (604)822-3313
Fax: (604)822-8928
Subject(s): College Publications
Circ: (Combined)‡130,000

**British Columbia Magazine** (34375)
3939 Quadna St., Ste. 302
Victoria, BC, Canada V8X 1J5
Phone: (250)380-7611
Fax: (250)384-9926
Subject(s): Travel and Tourism; Local, State, and Regional Publications; (Outdoors)
Circ: (Non-paid)1,000
(Paid)125,000

**Georgia Straight** (34311)
Vancouver Free Press
2nd Fl., 1770 Burrard St
Vancouver, BC, Canada V6J 3G7
Phone: (604)730-7010
Fax: (604)730-7010
Subject(s): Entertainment; Lifestyle
Circ: (Free)122,000

**Westworld Saskatchewan** (34107)
Canada Wide Magazines & Communications Ltd.
4180 Lougheed Hwy., 4th Fl.
Burnaby, BC, Canada V5C 6A7
Phone: (604)299-7311
Fax: (604)299-9188
Subject(s): Automotive (Consumer)
Circ: (Paid)108,042

**Going Places** (34092)
Canada Wide Magazines & Communications Ltd.
4180 Lougheed Hwy., 4th Fl.
Burnaby, BC, Canada V5C 6A7
Phone: (604)299-7311
Fax: (604)299-9188
Subject(s): Automotive (Consumer); Travel and Tourism
Circ: (Paid)106,654

**TV Week Magazine** (34102)
Canada Wide Magazines & Communications Ltd.
4180 Lougheed Hwy., 4th Fl.
Burnaby, BC, Canada V5C 6A7
Phone: (604)299-7311
Fax: (604)299-9188
Subject(s): Radio, Television, Cable, and Video
Circ: (Non-paid)1,457
(Paid)67,816

**CGA Magazine** (34301)
Certified General Accountants Association of Canada
800-1188 W. Georgia St.
Vancouver, BC, Canada V6E 4A2
Phone: (604)669-3555
Fax: (604)689-5845
Subject(s): Accountants and Accounting
Circ: (Combined)60,000

**UVic Torch** (34392)
UVic Communications
PO Box 1700
Stn. CSC
Victoria, BC, Canada
Fax: (250)721-8955
Subject(s): College Publications
Circ: (Free)54,000

**Where Vancouver Magazine** (34350)
Where Vancouver Inc.
2208 Spruce St.
Vancouver, BC, Canada V6H 2P3
Phone: (604)736-5586
Fax: (604)736-3465
Subject(s): Entertainment; Travel and Tourism; Local, State, and Regional Publications
Circ: (Non-paid)‡52,000

**Vancouver Magazine** (34342)
Transcontinental Publishing
2608 Granville St., Ste. 500
Vancouver, BC, Canada V6H 3V3
Phone: (604)877-7732
Fax: (604)877-4823
Subject(s): Local, State, and Regional Publications
Circ: (Paid)5,627
(Non-paid)49,125

**The Outdoor Edge** (34322)
OP Publishing Ltd.
1080 Howe St., Ste. 900
Vancouver, BC, Canada V6Z 2T1
Phone: (604)606-4644
Fax: (604)687-1925
Subject(s): (Hunting, Fishing, and Game Management)
Circ: (Paid)48,915

**SOHO Business Report** (34119)
HB Communications Group
439 A. Marmont St.
Coquit Lam, BC, Canada V3K 4S4
Phone: (604)936-5815
Fax: (604)854-5805
Subject(s): Business
Circ: (Paid)1,881
(Non-paid)43,346

**The ATA Magazine** (33915)
Alberta Teachers' Association (ATA)
11010 142nd St. NW
Edmonton, AB, Canada T5N 2R1
Phone: (780)447-9400
Fax: (780)455-6481
Subject(s): Education
Circ: ‡42,000

**Gale Directory of Publications & Broadcast Media/140th Ed.**  **Western Provinces**

**Gardens West (34309)**
Cornwall Publishing Company Ltd.
PO Box 2680, STN Terminal
Vancouver, BC, Canada V6B 3W8
Phone: (604)879-4991
Fax: (604)879-5110
**Subject(s):** Home and Garden
**Circ:** (Paid)39,301

**Commerce News (33921)**
Edmonton Chamber of Commerce
No. 700 - 9990 Jasper Ave.
Edmonton, AB, Canada T5J 1P7
Phone: (780)409-2131
Fax: (780)424-7946
**Subject(s):** Chambers of Commerce and Boards of Trade; Business; Local, State, and Regional Publications
**Circ:** (Non-paid)36,000

**WHERE Ottawa (33875)**
St. Joseph Media Ltd.
Ste. 250, 1 Palliser Sq.
125 9th Ave. SE
Calgary, AB, Canada T2G 0P6
Phone: (403)299-1888
Fax: (403)299-1899
**Subject(s):** Travel and Tourism
**Circ:** 35,000

**Nursing BC (34318)**
Registered Nurses Association of British Columbia
2855 Arbutus St.
Vancouver, BC, Canada V6J 3Y8
Phone: (604)736-7331
Fax: (604)738-2272
**Subject(s):** Nursing
**Circ:** (Combined)34,454

**The PEGG (33943)**
Association of Professional Engineers, Geologists, and Geophysicists of Alberta
1500 Scotia One
10060 Jasper Ave. NW
Edmonton, AB, Canada T5J 4A2
Phone: (780)426-3990
Fax: (780)426-1877
**Subject(s):** Engineering (Various branches); Geology
**Circ:** (Controlled)31,647

**Heavy Equipment Guide (34312)**
Baum Publications Ltd.
201 - 2323 Boundary Rd.
Vancouver, BC, Canada V5M 4V8
Phone: (604)291-9900
Fax: (604)291-1906
**Subject(s):** Machinery and Equipment
**Circ:** (Combined)30,978

**Business in Calgary (33830)**
Business in Calgary magazine
101 - 6th Ave. S.W., Ste. 1025
Calgary, AB, Canada T2P 3P4
Phone: (403)264-3270
Fax: (403)264-3276
**Subject(s):** Business
**Circ:** (Combined)30,368

**Alberta Golf (34078)**
Canada Wide Magazines & Communications Ltd.
4180 Lougheed Hwy., 4th Fl.
Burnaby, BC, Canada V5C 6A7
Phone: (604)299-7311
Fax: (604)299-9188
**Subject(s):** (Golf)
**Circ:** (Paid)30,000

**Pacific Golf (34099)**
Canada Wide Magazines & Communications Ltd.
4180 Lougheed Hwy., 4th Fl.
Burnaby, BC, Canada V5C 6A7
Phone: (604)299-7311
Fax: (604)299-9188
**Subject(s):** (Golf)
**Circ:** (Paid)30,000

**The Northern Horizon (34129)**
B. Sims
901 100th Ave
Dawson Creek, BC, Canada V1G 1W2
Phone: (250)782-4888
Fax: (250)782-6300
**Subject(s):** Farm Newspapers
**Circ:** (Paid)‡2,648
 (Non-paid)‡29,040

**VU Magazine (33948)**
Vogel Satellite T.V. Publishing Inc.
1109 Toronto Dominion Twr., Edmonton Centre
10088 - 102 Ave.
Edmonton, AB, Canada T5J 2Z1
Phone: (780)424-6222
Fax: (780)425-8392
**Subject(s):** Radio, Television, Cable, and Video; Entertainment
**Circ:** (Paid)28,637

**Network (33861)**
Business in Calgary magazine
101 - 6th Ave. S.W., Ste. 1025
Calgary, AB, Canada T2P 3P4
Phone: (403)264-3270
Fax: (403)264-3276
**Subject(s):** Cemeteries and Monuments
**Circ:** (Controlled)2,200
 (Paid)28,096

**WHERE Calgary (33873)**
St. Joseph Media Ltd.
Ste. 250, 1 Palliser Sq.
125 9th Ave. SE
Calgary, AB, Canada T2G 0P6
Phone: (403)299-1888
Fax: (403)299-1899
**Subject(s):** Entertainment; Travel and Tourism; Local, State, and Regional Publications
**Circ:** (Non-paid)28,000

**B. C. Business (34082)**
Canada Wide Magazines & Communications Ltd.
4180 Lougheed Hwy., 4th Fl.
Burnaby, BC, Canada V5C 6A7
Phone: (604)299-7311
Fax: (604)299-9188
**Subject(s):** Business; International Business and Economics; Economics
**Circ:** ‡26,000

**Community Digest, BC Edition (34303)**
Community Digest Multicultural Publications
661A Market Hill
Vancouver, BC, Canada V5Z 4B5
Phone: (604)875-8313
Fax: (604)875-0336
**Subject(s):** Ethnic Publications
**Circ:** (Free)‡25,000

**Western Sportsman (34347)**
OP Publishing Ltd.
1080 Howe St., Ste. 900
Vancouver, BC, Canada V6Z 2T1
Phone: (604)606-4644
Fax: (604)687-1925
**Subject(s):** (Hunting, Fishing, and Game Management)
**Circ:** (Paid)23,666

**Canadian Environmental Protection (34296)**
Baum Publications Ltd.
201 - 2323 Boundary Rd.
Vancouver, BC, Canada V5M 4V8
Phone: (604)291-9900
Fax: (604)291-1906
**Subject(s):** Water Supply and Sewage Disposal; Waste Management and Recycling
**Circ:** (Combined)21,304

**WaveLength Magazine (34148)**
2735 N. Rd.
Gabriola Island, BC, Canada V0R 1X7
Phone: (250)247-8858
Fax: (250)247-9789
**Subject(s):** (Water Sports); (Outdoors)
**Circ:** (Paid)•319
 (Non-paid)•21,054

**Adbusters (34283)**
Media Foundation
1243 W. 7th Ave.
Vancouver, BC, Canada V6H 1B7
Phone: (604)736-9401
Fax: (604)737-6021
**Subject(s):** Radio, Television, Cable, and Video
**Circ:** (Non-paid)‡5,000
 (Paid)‡20,000

**Innovation (34095)**
The Association of Professional Engineers and Geoscientists of British Columbia
200-4010 Regent St.
Burnaby, BC, Canada V5C 6N2
Phone: (604)430-8035
Fax: (604)430-8085
**Subject(s):** Engineering (Various branches)
**Circ:** (Combined)•19,500

**Gardenwise Magazine (34091)**
4180 Lougheed Hwy., 4th Fl.
Burnaby, BC, Canada V5C 6A7
Phone: (604)299-7311
Fax: (604)299-9188
**Subject(s):** Home and Garden
**Circ:** (Non-paid)16,962
 (Paid)18,038

**The Supply Post (34190)**
Ken Kenward Enterprises Ltd.
26730 56th Ave., No. 105
Langley, BC, Canada V4W 3X5
Phone: (604)607-5577
Fax: (604)607-0533
**Subject(s):** Forestry; Ecology and Conservation
**Circ:** (Combined)‡18,000

**YES Mag (34394)**
Peter Piper Publishing Inc.
3968 Long Gun Pl.
Victoria, BC, Canada V8N 3A9
Phone: (250)477-5543
Fax: (250)477-5390
**Subject(s):** Mathematics; Science (General); Youths' Interests; Children's Interests
**Circ:** (Paid)18,000

**Oil & Gas Product News (34320)**
Baum Publications Ltd.
201 - 2323 Boundary Rd.
Vancouver, BC, Canada V5M 4V8
Phone: (604)291-9900
Fax: (604)291-1906
**Subject(s):** Petroleum, Oil, and Gas
**Circ:** (Combined)17,511

**Landscaping & Groundskeeping Journal (34316)**
Baum Publications Ltd.
201 - 2323 Boundary Rd.
Vancouver, BC, Canada V5M 4V8
Phone: (604)291-9900
Fax: (604)291-1906
**Subject(s):** Landscape Architecture
**Circ:** (Combined)16,664

**Recycling Product News (34331)**
Baum Publications Ltd.
201 - 2323 Boundary Rd.
Vancouver, BC, Canada V5M 4V8
Phone: (604)291-9900
Fax: (604)291-1906
**Subject(s):** Ecology and Conservation
**Circ:** (Combined)16,631

**Pacific Yachting (34325)**
OP Publishing Ltd.
1080 Howe St., Ste. 900
Vancouver, BC, Canada V6Z 2T1
Phone: (604)606-4644
Fax: (604)687-1925
**Subject(s):** (Boating and Yachting)
**Circ:** (Non-paid)4,887
 (Paid)16,466

**Logging & Sawmilling Journal (34215)**
Box 86670
North Vancouver, BC, Canada V7L 4L2
Phone: (604)990-9970
Fax: (604)990-9971
**Subject(s):** Forestry
**Circ:** (Combined)•16,203

**Grocer Today Magazine (34093)**
Canada Wide Magazines & Communications Ltd.
4180 Lougheed Hwy., 4th Fl.
Burnaby, BC, Canada V5C 6A7
Phone: (604)299-7311
Fax: (604)299-9188
**Subject(s):** Food and Grocery Trade
**Circ:** (Combined)16,000

**naturalSCIENCE (34387)**
Heron Publishing
202 - 3994 Shelbourne St.
Victoria, BC, Canada V8N 3E2
Phone: (250)721-9921
Fax: (250)721-9924
**Subject(s):** Science (General)
**Circ:** 16,000

Circulation: ★ = ABC; △ = BPA; ♦ = CAC; • = CCAB; ▫ = VAC; ⊖ = PO Statement; ‡ = Publisher's Report; Boldface figures = sworn; Light figures = estimated.

# Western Provinces

**Canadian Traveller (34300)**
ACT Communications, Inc.
104-1260 Hornby St.
Vancouver, BC, Canada V6Z 1W2
Phone: (604)699-9990
Fax: (604)699-9993
Subject(s): Travel and Tourism
Circ: (Combined)‡14,954

**BC Business Magazine (34083)**
Canada Wide Magazines & Communications Ltd.
4180 Lougheed Hwy., 4th Fl.
Burnaby, BC, Canada V5C 6A7
Phone: (604)299-7311
Fax: (604)299-9188
Subject(s): Business
Circ: (Paid)•9,150
(Non-paid)•11,866

**The Alberta Game Warden (34038)**
Gazette Press Ltd.
25 Chisholm Ave.
PO Box 263
Saint Albert, AB, Canada T8N 5A5
Phone: (780)460-5500
Fax: (780)460-8220
Subject(s): Environmental and Natural Resources Conservation; Local, State, and Regional Publications
Circ: ‡11,000

**The Advocate (34285)**
Vancouver Bar Association
1600 Cathedral Pl.
925 W. Georgia St.
Vancouver, BC, Canada V6C 3L2
Phone: (604)631-9112
Fax: (604)631-9190
Subject(s): Law
Circ: (Non-paid)‡500
(Paid)‡10,500

**Alberta Beef Magazine (33821)**
Creative Motion Publishing
2915 19th St. NE, Ste. 202
Calgary, AB, Canada T2E 7A2
Phone: (403)250-1090
Fax: (403)291-9546
Subject(s): Livestock
Circ: (Paid)2,700
(Controlled)10,200

**Business in Vancouver Media Group (34293)**
BIV Publications Ltd.
500-1155 W. Pender St.
Vancouver, BC, Canada V6E 2P4
Phone: (604)688-2398
Fax: (604)688-1963
Subject(s): Business; Local, State, and Regional Publications
Circ: (Paid)10,000

**The Reflector (33870)**
Reflector Publications Society
4825 Mount Royal Gate SW
Calgary, AB, Canada T3E 6K6
Phone: (403)440-6268
Fax: (403)440-6762
Subject(s): College Publications
Circ: (Non-paid)‡10,000

**Specialty Wood Journal (34335)**
Baum Publications Ltd.
201 - 2323 Boundary Rd.
Vancouver, BC, Canada V5M 4V8
Phone: (604)291-9900
Fax: (604)291-1906
Subject(s): Wood and Woodworking; Forestry
Circ: (Combined)9,942

**Energy Processing/Canada (33846)**
Northern Star Communications Ltd.
900-6 Ave. SW, 5th Fl.
Calgary, AB, Canada T2P 3K2
Phone: (403)263-6881
Fax: (403)263-6886
Subject(s): Chemistry, Chemicals, and Chemical Engineering; Petroleum, Oil, and Gas
Circ: (Combined)9,800

**BCMJ (The British Columbia Medical Journal) (34291)**
British Columbia Medical Association
115-1665 W Broadway
Vancouver, BC, Canada V6J 5A4
Phone: (604)736-5551
Fax: (604)733-7317

Subject(s): Medicine and Surgery
Circ: (Controlled)‡9,600

**Beyond Numbers (34292)**
Institute of Chartered Accountants of B.C.
One Bentall Centre, Ste. 500
505 Burrard St.
PO Box 22
Vancouver, BC, Canada V7X 1M4
Phone: (604)681-3264
Fax: (604)681-1523
Subject(s): Accountants and Accounting; Business
Circ: (Controlled)‡9,200

**Diver Magazine (34214)**
Seagraphics Publications Ltd.
241 E First St.
North Vancouver, BC, Canada V7L 1B4
Phone: (604)940-6262
Fax: (604)980-6236
Subject(s): (Water Sports)
Circ: ‡8,000

**Award Magazine (34081)**
Canada Wide Magazines & Communications Ltd.
4180 Lougheed Hwy., 4th Fl.
Burnaby, BC, Canada V5C 6A7
Phone: (604)299-7311
Fax: (604)299-9188
Subject(s): Architecture; Construction, Contracting, Building, and Excavating; Interior Design/Decorating
Circ: (Combined)7,657

**BC Home (34084)**
Canada Wide Magazines & Communications Ltd.
4180 Lougheed Hwy., 4th Fl.
Burnaby, BC, Canada V5C 6A7
Phone: (604)299-7311
Fax: (604)299-9188
Subject(s): Home and Garden
Circ: (Non-paid)6,900

**Canadian Biker (34378)**
Canadian Biker Publication Ltd.
735 Market St.
PO Box 4122
Victoria, BC, Canada V8T 2E2
Phone: (250)384-0333
Fax: (250)384-1832
Subject(s): Motorbikes and Motorcycles
Circ: (Non-paid)4,600
(Paid)6,900

**Hospitality Today (34094)**
Canada Wide Magazines & Communications Ltd.
4180 Lougheed Hwy., 4th Fl.
Burnaby, BC, Canada V5C 6A7
Phone: (604)299-7311
Fax: (604)299-9188
Subject(s): Hotels, Motels, Restaurants, and Clubs
Circ: (Combined)6,814

**Occupational Therapy NOW (34403)**
Canadian Association of Occupational Therapists
c/o Westprint Communications
1454 129A St.
White Rock, BC, Canada V4A 3Y7
Phone: (604)536-4570
Fax: (604)536-4570
Subject(s): Health and Healthcare; Medicine and Surgery
Circ: (Combined)6,500

**Collision Quarterly (34088)**
Automotive Retailers' Publishing Company Ltd.
8980 Fraserwood Ct., Unit 1
Burnaby, BC, Canada V5J 5H7
Phone: (604)432-7987
Fax: (604)432-1756
Subject(s): Automotive (Trade)
Circ: (Controlled)6,179

**The Alberta Doctors' Digest (33911)**
Alberta Medical Association
12230 106 Ave. NW
Edmonton, AB, Canada T5N 3Z1
Phone: (780)482-2626
Fax: (780)482-5445
Subject(s): Medicine and Surgery
Circ: (Non-paid)6,000

**Geist (34310)**
1014 Homer St., No. 103
Vancouver, BC, Canada V6B 2W9
Phone: (604)681-9161
Fax: (604)669-8250

Subject(s): Literature and Literary Reviews
Circ: (Paid)6,000

**Ralph (34330)**
PO Box 93627
Vancouver, BC, Canada V6E 4L7
Phone: (604)654-2929
Fax: (604)654-1993
Subject(s): Poetry; Music and Musical Instruments
Circ: (Controlled)6,000

**Propane/Canada (33869)**
Northern Star Communications Ltd.
900-6 Ave. SW, 5th Fl.
Calgary, AB, Canada T2P 3K2
Phone: (403)263-6881
Fax: (403)263-6886
Subject(s): Petroleum, Oil, and Gas
Circ: (Combined)‡5,200

**Prairie Hog Country (33996)**
MSA Publishing Inc.
Box 3326
Leduc, AB, Canada T9E 6M1
Fax: (780)980-5303
Subject(s): Livestock
Circ: (Controlled)‡4,775

**Simmental Country (33871)**
Simmental Country (1997) Ltd.
4101 19th St. NE, Ste. 13
Calgary, AB, Canada T2E 7C4
Phone: (403)250-5255
Fax: (403)250-5121
Subject(s): Livestock
Circ: (Non-paid)‡350
(Paid)‡4,500

**Dance International (34305)**
Vancouver Ballet Society
Scotiabank Dance Centre
677 Davie St., Level 6
Vancouver, BC, Canada V6B 2G6
Phone: (604)681-1525
Fax: (604)681-7732
Subject(s): Performing Arts; Drama and Theatre
Circ: (Paid)4,000

**RicePaper (34332)**
Ricepaper Magazine
12-2414 Main St.
Vancouver, BC, Canada V5T 3E3
Phone: (604)879-5962
Fax: (604)879-5962
Subject(s): Social and Political Issues; Ethnic Publications
Circ: (Combined)4,000

**Swedish Press (34337)**
Swedish Press Inc.
1294 W. 7th Ave.
Vancouver, BC, Canada V6H 1B6
Phone: (604)731-6381
Fax: (604)731-2292
Subject(s): Swedish; Ethnic Publications
Circ: (Non-paid)1,000
(Paid)4,000

**Watershed Sentinel (34401)**
PO Box 39
Whaletown, BC, Canada V0P 1Z0
Phone: (250)935-6992
Fax: (250)935-6992
Subject(s): Lifestyle; Local, State, and Regional Publications
Circ: (Combined)4,000

**BC Pharmacy (34289)**
British Columbia Pharmacy Association
1530-1200 W 73rd Ave.
Vancouver, BC, Canada V6P 6G5
Phone: (604)261-2092
Fax: (604)261-2097
Subject(s): Drugs and Pharmaceuticals
Circ: (Non-paid)3,800

**Canadian Rodeo News (33839)**
Canadian Rodeo News Ltd.
223, 2116 27th Ave. NE
Calgary, AB, Canada T2E 7A6
Phone: (403)250-7292
Fax: (403)250-6926
Subject(s): (Horses and Horse Racing); Livestock
Circ: (Non-paid)‡942
‡3,058

# Gale Directory of Publications & Broadcast Media/140th Ed.  Western Provinces

**Canadian Hereford Digest** (33835)
Gilmore Publications Ltd.
5160 Skyline Way NE
Calgary, AB, Canada T2E 6V1
Phone: (403)274-1734
Fax: (403)275-4999
**Subject(s):** Livestock
**Circ:** 3,000

**Northern Aquaculture Magazine** (34122)
Capamara Communications Inc.
5001 Forbidden Plateau Rd.
Courtenay, BC, Canada V9J 1R3
Phone: (250)338-2455
Fax: (250)338-2466
**Subject(s):** Fish and Commercial Fisheries
**Circ:** ‡3,000

**Journal of Commerce** (34097)
Journal of Commerce Ltd.
101 - 4299 Canada Way
Burnaby, BC, Canada V5G 1H3
Phone: (604)433-8164
Fax: (604)433-9549
**Subject(s):** Construction, Contracting, Building, and Excavating; Commerce and Industry
**Circ:** (Combined)2,537

**Pacific Affairs** (34324)
The University of British Columbia
Pacific Affairs
No. 164-1855 W. Mall
Vancouver, BC, Canada V6T 1Z2
Phone: (604)822-6508
Fax: (604)822-9452
**Subject(s):** International Affairs; International Business and Economics
**Circ:** ‡2,500

**Canadian Journal of Earth Sciences (Revue Canadienne des Sciences de la Terre)** (33918)
National Research Council Canada, NRC Research Press
Dept. of Earth and Atmospheric Sciences
University of Alberta
Edmonton, AB, Canada T6G 2E3
Phone: (780)492-8594
Fax: (780)492-8594
**Subject(s):** Geology; French
**Circ:** ‡2,200

**Harbour & Shipping** (34400)
Progress Publishing Company Ltd.
Suite 200
1865 Marine Dr.
West Vancouver, BC, Canada V7V 1J7
Phone: (604)922-6717
Fax: (604)922-1739
**Subject(s):** International Business and Economics; Ships and Shipping
**Circ:** 2,000

**MPH** (34189)
Vincent Owners Club
105-26730 56th Ave.
Langley, BC, Canada V4W 3X5
**Subject(s):** Motorcycles; Motorbikes and Motorcyles
**Circ:** 2,000

**Outlook** (34323)
Canadian Jewish Outlook Society
6184 Ash St., No. 3
Vancouver, BC, Canada V5Z 3G9
Phone: (604)324-5101
Fax: (604)325-2570
**Subject(s):** Jewish Publications; Politics
**Circ:** 2,000

**On Spec** (33940)
Copper Pig Writers' Society
Box 4727
Edmonton, AB, Canada T6E 5G6
Phone: (780)413-0215
Fax: (780)413-1538
**Subject(s):** Science Fiction, Mystery, Adventure, and Romance
**Circ:** (Combined)1,700

**Canadian Journal of Neurological Sciences** (33837)
7015 Macleod Trail S.W., Ste. 709
Calgary, AB, Canada T2H 1K7
Phone: (403)229-9575
Fax: (403)229-1661
**Subject(s):** Medicine and Surgery
**Circ:** 1,600

**Global Governance** (33930)
Lynne Rienner Publishers
Department of Political Science
University of Alberta
Edmonton, AB, Canada T6G 2H4
Phone: (780)492-9970
**Subject(s):** Politics; International Affairs
**Circ:** (Paid)1,600

**Artichoke** (34286)
Artichoke Publishing
901 Jervis St., No. 208
Vancouver, BC, Canada V6E 2B6
Phone: (604)683-1941
Fax: (604)683-1941
**Subject(s):** Art
**Circ:** (Paid)1,500

**Canadian Literature** (34299)
University of British Columbia
Buchanan E158
1866 Main Mall
Vancouver, BC, Canada V6T 1Z1
Phone: (604)822-2780
Fax: (604)822-5504
**Subject(s):** Literature and Literary Reviews; French
**Circ:** (Non-paid)‡150
(Paid)‡1,500

**Journal of Employment Counseling** (34315)
American Association for Counseling and Development
Dept. of Educational and Counselling Psychology
2125 Main Mall
Vancouver, BC, Canada V6T 1Z4
Phone: (604)822-6757
Fax: (604)822-2328
**Subject(s):** Employment and Human Resources
**Circ:** (Non-paid)‡60
(Paid)‡1,400

**Event** (34208)
Douglas College
PO Box 2503
New Westminster, BC, Canada V3L 5B2
Phone: (604)527-5293
Fax: (604)527-5095
**Subject(s):** Literature
**Circ:** (Combined)1,300

**BSDA News Magazine** (34274)
No. 2, 19299-94 Ave.
Surrey, BC, Canada V4N 4E6
Phone: (604)513-2205
Fax: (604)513-2206
**Subject(s):** Building Materials, Concrete, Brick, and Tile
**Circ:** (Non-paid)‡1,200

**Dynamics** (33845)
Pappin Communications
c/o Paula Price
Mount Royal College
Advanced Specialty Health Studies
4825 Richard Rd. SW
Calgary, AB, Canada T3E 6K6
Phone: (403)440-6553
Fax: (403)440-6555
**Subject(s):** Nursing
**Circ:** ‡1,200

**PRISM International** (34327)
Creative Writing Program
University of British Columbia (UBC)
Buch.
E. 462 - Main Mall
Vancouver, BC, Canada V6T 1Z1
Phone: (604)822-2514
Fax: (604)822-3616
**Subject(s):** Literature and Literary Reviews
**Circ:** (Non-paid)‡100
(Paid)‡1,200

**Canadian Public Policy–Analyse de Politiques** (33838)
University of Toronto Press - Journals Div.
c/o Kenneth J. McKenzie, Dept. of Economics
Univ. of Calgary
2500 Univ. Dr. N.W.
Calgary, AB, Canada T2N 1N4
**Subject(s):** French; State, Municipal, and County Administration
**Circ:** (Non-paid)‡32
(Paid)‡1,100

**British Columbia Genealogist** (34248)
British Columbia Genealogical Society
PO Box 88054, Lansdowne Mall
PO Box 88054
Richmond, BC, Canada V6X 3T6
Phone: (604)502-9119
Fax: (604)502-9119
**Subject(s):** History and Genealogy; Local, State, and Regional Publications
**Circ:** (Paid)1,000

**Canadian Journal of Animal Science** (33917)
Agricultural Institute of Canada
c/o Dr. M.A. Price
Dept. of Agricultural Food and Nutritional Science
Univ. of Alberta
Edmonton, AB, Canada T6G 2P5
Phone: (780)492-3235
Fax: (780)492-4265
**Subject(s):** Livestock
**Circ:** (Paid)1,000

**Canadian Journal of Sociology/Cahiers canadiens de sociologie** (33919)
University of Toronto Press - Journals Div.
The Editor, Canadian Journal of Sociology
Department of Sociology
University of Alberta
Edmonton, AB, Canada T6G 2H4
**Subject(s):** Social Sciences
**Circ:** (Combined)1000

**The Malahat Review** (34385)
University of Victoria
PO Box 1700
STN CSC
Victoria, BC, Canada V8W 2Y2
Phone: (250)721-8524
Fax: (250)472-5051
**Subject(s):** Literature and Literary Reviews
**Circ:** (Controlled)250
(Paid)1,000

**Room of One's Own** (34333)
Growing Room Collective
PO Box 46160, Sta. D
Vancouver, BC, Canada V6J 5G5
Phone: (604)654-4634
Fax: (604)654-4662
**Subject(s):** Women's Interests; Literature and Literary Reviews
**Circ:** (Non-paid)‡200
(Paid)‡1,000

**Tree Physiology** (34391)
Heron Publishing
202 - 3994 Shelbourne St.
Victoria, BC, Canada V8N 3E2
Phone: (250)721-9921
Fax: (250)721-9924
**Subject(s):** Botany; Ecology and Conservation; Forestry
**Circ:** (Controlled)1,000

**Canadian Journal of Philosophy** (33998)
University of Calgary Press
University of Lethbridge
4401 University Dr.
Lethbridge, AB, Canada T1K 3M4
Phone: (403)329-2545
Fax: (403)329-5109
**Subject(s):** Philosophy; French
**Circ:** 950

**Cartographica** (34379)
University of Toronto Press - Journals Div.
c/o Department of Geography
University of Victoria
PO Box 3050
Victoria, BC, Canada V8W 3P5
Phone: (250)721-7333
**Subject(s):** Geography
**Circ:** 950

**Ageing International** (34187)
Transaction Publishers
Graduate Program in Psychology
Trinity Western University
Langley, BC, Canada V2Y 1Y1
**Subject(s):** Gerontology; Senior Citizens' Interests
**Circ:** (Paid)‡900

**The Capilano Review** (34213)
2055 Purcell Way
North Vancouver, BC, Canada V7J 3H5
Phone: (604)984-1712

Circulation: ★ = ABC; △ = BPA; ♦ = CAC; • = CCAB; ☐ = VAC; ⊕ = PO Statement; ‡ = Publisher's Report; Boldface figures = sworn; Light figures = estimated.

Fax: (604)990-7837
**Subject(s):** Literature
**Circ:** (Combined)900

**International History Review (34096)**
EAA 2010, Simon Fraser University
Burnaby, BC, Canada V5A 1S6
Phone: (604)291-3561
Fax: (604)291-3429
**Subject(s):** Political Science; History and Genealogy
**Circ:** (Controlled)900

**ARIEL (33827)**
University of Calgary
SS 1152
2500 University Dr. NW
Calgary, AB, Canada T2N 1N4
Phone: (403)220-4657
Fax: (403)289-1123
**Subject(s):** Literature
**Circ:** (Combined)850

**Seminar (33946)**
University of Toronto Press - Journals Div.
c/o Prof. Raleigh Whitinger, Editor
MLCS B 200 Arts Bldg.
Univ. of Alberta
Edmonton, AB, Canada T6G 2E6
Phone: (780)492-4110
Fax: (780)492-9106
**Subject(s):** Intercultural Interests
**Circ:** 825

**The Canadian Journal of Linguistics/Revue canadienne de linguistique (34297)**
University of Toronto Press - Journals Div.
C/o Rose-Marie Dechaine
Department of Linguistics
University of British Columbia
1866 Main Mall, Buchanan E270
Vancouver, BC, Canada V6T 1Z1
Phone: (604)822-6466
**Subject(s):** Philology, Language, and Linguistics; French
**Circ:** (Combined)800

**Crux Mathematicorum with Mathematical Mayhem (34160)**
Canadian Mathematical Society
c/o James Totten
Dept. of Mathematics & Statistics
Univ. College of the Cariboo
PO Box 3010
kamloops, BC, Canada V2C 5N3
**Subject(s):** Mathematics; French; Education
**Circ:** 800

**Canadian Slavonic Papers/Revue Canadienne des Slavistes (33920)**
Canadian Slavonic Papers
200 Arts Bldg.
University of Alberta
Edmonton, AB, Canada T6G 2E6
Phone: (780)492-2566
Fax: (780)492-9106
**Subject(s):** Intercultural Interests
**Circ:** (Non-paid)50
 (Paid)750

**Journal of Distance Education (33934)**
Canadian Association for Distance Education
Faculty of Education
845 Education South
University of Alberta
Edmonton, AB, Canada T6G 2G5
Phone: (780)492-7941
Fax: (780)492-0236
**Subject(s):** Education
**Circ:** (Controlled)700

**Sub-TERRAIN Magazine (34336)**
175 E. Broadway, No. 204-A
PO Box 3008, MPO
Vancouver, BC, Canada V6B 3X5
Phone: (604)876-8710
Fax: (604)879-2667
**Subject(s):** Literature and Literary Reviews
**Circ:** (Paid)⊕700

**Filling Station (33849)**
PO Box 22135 Bankers Hall
Calgary, AB, Canada T2P 4J5
**Subject(s):** Literature and Literary Reviews; Poetry
**Circ:** (Non-paid)75
 (Paid)625

**BC Studies (34290)**
The University of British Columbia
1866 Main Mall
Buchanan E, Rm. 162
Vancouver, BC, Canada V6T 1Z1
Phone: (604)822-3727
Fax: (604)822-0606
**Subject(s):** History and Genealogy
**Circ:** (Controlled)‡50
 (Paid)‡600

**The Claremont Review (34380)**
Claremont Review Publishers
4980 Wesley Rd.
Victoria, BC, Canada V8Y 1Y9
Phone: (250)658-5221
Fax: (250)658-5387
**Subject(s):** Literature and Literary Reviews; Youths' Interests
**Circ:** (Combined)600

**The Prairie Journal of Canadian Literature (33867)**
Prairie Journal Trust
Brentwood PO
PO Box 61203
Calgary, AB, Canada T2L 2K6
**Subject(s):** Literature; Poetry
**Circ:** (Paid)600

**The Trumpeter (33810)**
c/o Athabasca Univ.
1 Univ. Dr.
Athabasca, AB, Canada T9S 3A3
Phone: (780)675-6143
Fax: (780)675-6186
**Subject(s):** Ecology and Conservation; Philosophy
**Circ:** (Non-paid)‡200
 (Paid)‡600

**West Coast Line (34103)**
West Coast Review Publishing Society
2027 E Academic Annex
Simon Fraser University
Burnaby, BC, Canada V5A 1S6
Phone: (604)291-4287
Fax: (604)291-4622
**Subject(s):** Literature
**Circ:** (Paid)550

**Archaea (34372)**
Heron Publishing
202 - 3994 Shelbourne St.
Victoria, BC, Canada V8N 3E2
Phone: (250)721-9921
Fax: (250)721-9924
**Subject(s):** Biology; Science (General)
**Circ:** (Paid)500
 (Non-paid)500

**Onsite Review (33864)**
Association for Nonprofit Architectural Fieldwork
1326 11th Ave. SE
Calgary, AB, Canada T2G 0Z5
Phone: (403)266-5827
**Subject(s):** Architecture
**Circ:** (Paid)500

**The Alberta Journal of Educational Research (33912)**
Dean of Education
University of Alberta
Faculty of Education
845 Education South
Edmonton, AB, Canada T6G 2G5
Phone: (780)492-7941
Fax: (780)492-0236
**Subject(s):** Education
**Circ:** ‡450

**Canadian Journal of Communication (33836)**
Simon Fraser University
Graduate Program in Communications and Culture
University of Calgary
Calgary, AB, Canada T2N 1N4
Phone: (403)210-8170
Fax: (403)210-8170
**Subject(s):** Communications
**Circ:** (Controlled)40
 (Paid)405

**Journal of Advanced Transportation (33857)**
Institute for Transportation Inc.
4625 Varsity Dr. NW, No. 305, Ste. 68
Calgary, AB, Canada T3A 0Z9
Phone: (403)286-7676
Fax: (403)286-9638
**Subject(s):** Transportation, Traffic, and Shipping; Engineering (Various branches)
**Circ:** (Combined)355

**Avicultural Journal (34114)**
Avicultural Advancement Council of Canada
PO Box 123
Chemainus, BC, Canada V0R 1K0
Phone: (250)246-4803
Fax: (250)246-4912
**Subject(s):** Ornithology and Oology
**Circ:** (Paid)300

**Canadian Bulletin of Medical History/Bulletin Canadien D'historie de la Medecine (34199)**
Malaspina University College
c/o Dr. Cheryl Krasnick Warsh
Department of History
Malaspina University College
900 5th St.
Nanaimo, BC, Canada V9R 5S5
Phone: (250)753-3245
Fax: (250)741-2667
**Subject(s):** History and Genealogy; Medicine and Surgery
**Circ:** (Paid)300

**Philosophy in Review/Comptes rendus Philosophiques (34173)**
Academic Printing and Publishing
OKANAGAN University College
Department of Philosophy
3333 College Way
Kelowna, BC, Canada V1V 1V7
Phone: (250)762-5445
Fax: (250)764-6428
**Subject(s):** Philosophy
**Circ:** (Combined)260

**Past Imperfect (33942)**
University of Alberta
c/o History Dept.
2-28 Tory Bldg.
Edmonton, AB, Canada T6G 2H4
Phone: (780)492-4568
Fax: (780)492-4568
**Subject(s):** History and Genealogy; Education
**Circ:** (Paid)75

# Cable Index

Index entries are arranged geographically by region. Within region in this index, citations appear in descending order of number of subscribing households. Citations include cable company name, entry number (given in parentheses immediately following the title), address, phone and fax numbers, cities served, and number of subscribing households.

## Great Lakes States

**Comcast Cable  (8649)**
688 Industrial Dr.
Elmhurst, IL 60126
Phone: (630)716-2000
Fax: (630)716-2424
**Cities Served:** Elmhurst, Rolling Meadows, Romeoville, IL
**Subscribing Households:** 365,000

**Comcast  (15684)**
14909 Beck Rd.
PO Box 8009C
Plymouth, MI 48170
Phone: (248)855-6971
Fax: (734)254-1780
**Cities Served:** Cleveland, Dayton, OH
**Subscribing Households:** 354,000

**Comcast  (16621)**
10 River Park Plz.
Saint Paul, MN 55107-1219
Phone: (651)222-3333
Fax: (651)312-5288
**Subscribing Households:** 330,000

**Time Warner Communications  (24609)**
1266 Dublin Rd.
Columbus, OH 43215
Phone: (614)481-5000
Fax: (614)481-5328
**Subscribing Households:** 207,000

**Time Warner Cable  (33347)**
1320 N. Doctor Martin Luther King Jr. Dr.
Milwaukee, WI 53212
Phone: (414)277-4000
**Cities Served:** Adell, Belgium, Cascade, Cedar Grove, Elkhart, Glenbeulah, Hingham, Oostburg, Plymouth, Random Lake, Waldo, WI
**Subscribing Households:** 200,000

**Time Warner Cable  (24348)**
11252 Cornell Park Dr.
Cincinnati, OH 45242
Phone: (513)489-2337
Fax: (513)489-5070
**Cities Served:** Arlington Heights, Deer Park, Goshen, Lebanon, Loveland, Maineville, Montgomery, Reading, Springdale, Woodlawn, Wyoming, OH
**Subscribing Households:** 185,000

**Booth American Co.  (15204)**
333 W. Fort St., Ste. 1230
Detroit, MI 48226
Phone: (313)202-3360
Fax: (313)965-1160
**Cities Served:** Kernville, CA; Madeira, FL; Bingham Farms, Birmingham, Bloomfield Hill, Jackson, MI; Boone, NC; Andersonville, SC; Watertown, SD; Blacksburg, Salem, VA
**Subscribing Households:** 141,761

**Buckeye Cablevision  (25096)**
5566 Southwyck Blvd.
Toledo, OH 43614
Phone: (419)724-9802
Fax: (419)724-7074
**Cities Served:** Harbor View, Holland, Maumee, Middleton Township, Monclova Township, Northwood, Oregon, Ottawa Hills, Perrysburg, Perrysburg Township, Rossford, Spencer Township, Springfield Township, Sylvania, Sylvania Township, Toledo, Washington Township, Waterville, Waterville Township, OH
**Subscribing Households:** 130,000

**Comcast  (15349)**
3500 Patterson Ave. SE, Ste. A
Grand Rapids, MI 49512-5699
**Subscribing Households:** 125,000

**Bright House Networks  (9925)**
3030 Roosevelt Ave.
Indianapolis, IN 46218
Phone: (317)632-9077
Fax: (317)632-5311
**Subscribing Households:** 118,000

**Charter Communications  (33108)**
1348 Plainfield Ave.
Box 1127
Janesville, WI 53547
Phone: (262)736-4297
Fax: (608)849-5083
**Cities Served:** Arlington, Black Earth, Dane, Lodi, Mazomonie, Mount Horeb, New Glarus, Poynette, Prairie Du Sac, Verona, Waunakee, WI
**Subscribing Households:** 102,000

**Warner Cable of Canton  (24951)**
5520 Whipple Ave. NW
North Canton, OH 44720
Phone: (330)494-9200
Fax: (330)497-6397
**Subscribing Households:** 78,000

**Comcast Cable TV  (15821)**
24744 Eureka Rd.
Taylor, MI 48180
Phone: (734)946-6000
Fax: (734)946-1924
**Cities Served:** Allen Park, Berlin, Brownstown, Ecorse, Flat Rock, Garden City, Grosse Ile, Inkster, Melvindale, River Rouge, Rockwood, South Rockwood, Southgate, Taylor, MI
**Subscribing Households:** 70,000

**Insight Communications  (9309)**
810 20th Street
Rockford, IL 61104
Phone: (815)987-4510
Fax: (815)962-9643
**Cities Served:** Cherry Valley, Loves Park, Machesney Park, New Milford, Rockford, IL
**Subscribing Households:** 65,000

**Cox Cable Quad Cities  (8986)**
3900 26th Ave.
Moline, IL 61265
Phone: (309)762-4166
Fax: (309)797-2414
**Cities Served:** Bettendorf, Davenport, Eldridge, Long Grove, Mount Joy, Panorama Park, Pleasant Valley, Riverdale, IA; East Moline, Hampton, Silvis, IL
**Subscribing Households:** 60,162

**Time Warner Cable  (33646)**
2767 N. Mayfair Rd.
Wauwatosa, WI 53222
Phone: (414)259-1445
Fax: (414)259-3227
**Subscribing Households:** 60,000

**AT&T Broadband & Internet Service  (9223)**
3517 N. Dries Ln.
Peoria, IL 61604
Phone: (309)686-2600
Fax: (309)688-9828
**Subscribing Households:** 55,383

**Charter Communications  (8939)**
210 W. Division St.
Maryville, IL 62062
Phone: (618)345-8121
Fax: (618)345-6234
**Cities Served:** Caseyville, Collinsville, Columbia, Dupo, Edwardsville, Glen Carbon, Granite City, Highland, Madison, Madison County, Marine, Maryville, Millstadt, Monroe County, Pontoon Beach, Saint Jacob, St. Clair County, St. Jacob, Troy, Venice, Waterloo, IL
**Subscribing Households:** 49,000

**Insight Communications  (9412)**
711 S. Dirksen Pkwy.
Box 3066
Springfield, IL 62708
Phone: (217)788-5656
Fax: (217)788-8093
**Cities Served:** Ball Township, Bissell Township, Curran Township, Curran-Gardner Township, Gardner Township, Grandview, Jerome, Leland Grove, Rochester, Southern View, Spaulding, Springfield, Springfield Township, Woodside Township, IL
**Subscribing Households:** 47,905

**Time Warner Cable  (33117)**
Box 309
1320 N. Dr. Martin Luther King
Kenosha, WI 53141-0309
Phone: (262)656-8460
Fax: (262)656-8490
**Subscribing Households:** 46,000

**Insight Communications, Inc.  (10076)**
15229 Stoney Creek Way
Noblesville, IN 46060
Phone: (317)776-0660
Fax: (317)773-5439
**Subscribing Households:** 43,924

## Great Lakes States

**Armstrong Cable Services (24954)**
9328 Woodworth Rd.
North Lima, OH 44452
Phone: (330)758-6411
Fax: (330)726-0117
**Cities Served:** Austintown, Boardman, Campbell, Canfield, McDonald, Poland, OH
**Subscribing Households:** 43,000

**Charter Communications (33440)**
PO Box 279
Onalaska, WI 54650
Phone: (608)783-5255
Fax: (608)783-7033
**Cities Served:** Brockway, Holmen, La Crosse, Leon, Melrose, Mindoro, Onalaska, Sparta, Tomah, WI
**Subscribing Households:** 42,000

**Comcast (15625)**
Box 978
Muskegon, MI 49443
Phone: (616)392-2800
Fax: (616)733-0426
**Subscribing Households:** 41,590

**Insight Media Advertising (9979)**
325 S. Creasy Ln.
Box 4609
Lafayette, IN 47905
Phone: (765)447-6886
Fax: (765)447-7622
**Cities Served:** Battle Ground, Dayton, Lafayette, Mullberry, Shadeland, West Lafayette, IN
**Subscribing Households:** 39,000

**Comcast Communications (10211)**
17 N. Washington St.
Valparaiso, IN 46383
Phone: (219)462-9990
Fax: (219)462-2413
**Subscribing Households:** 34,564

**Massillon Cable TV Inc. (24883)**
814 Cable Ct. NW
PO Box 1000
Massillon, OH 44648-0814
Phone: (330)833-4134
Fax: (330)833-7522
**Cities Served:** Brewster, Canal Fulton, Jackson, Massillon, Navarre, OH
**Subscribing Households:** 31,000

**Charter Communications (15384)**
1202 W. Benton
Greenville, MI 48838-0187
Phone: (616)754-0530
Fax: (616)754-5344
**Cities Served:** Grant, Newaygo, MI
**Subscribing Households:** 30,000

**Adelphia (24123)**
3416 State Rte. 132
Amelia, OH 45102
Phone: (513)797-4400
Fax: (513)797-8625
**Subscribing Households:** 29,954

**Time Warner Cable (24860)**
Box 576
Mansfield, OH 44901
Phone: (419)756-3333
Fax: (419)756-5319
**Subscribing Households:** 29,000

**Insight Communications (9955)**
3408 Industrial Pkwy.
Jeffersonville, IN 47130
Phone: (812)288-6471
Fax: (812)288-7818
**Cities Served:** Crestwood, La Grange, KY
**Subscribing Households:** 28,000

**AT & T Cable Services (8834)**
6 Dearborn Sq.
Kankakee, IL 60901
Phone: (815)937-2700
Fax: (815)937-2714
**Subscribing Households:** 26,000

**Time Warner Cable (10195)**
1605 Wabash Ave.
Terre Haute, IN 47807-3701
Phone: (812)232-5013
Fax: (812)232-7453
**Subscribing Households:** 26,000

**TCI Cablevision of West Oakland County (15876)**
3166 Martin Rd.
Walled Lake, MI 48390
Phone: (248)669-3901
Fax: (248)669-8260
**Cities Served:** Commerce Township, Highland Township, Lyon Township, Milford, New Hudson, Northville, Walled Lake, White Lake, Wixom, MI
**Subscribing Households:** 22,000

**Erie County Cablevision Inc. (25035)**
409 E. Market St.
PO Box 5800
Sandusky, OH 44870
Phone: (419)627-1371
Fax: (419)627-0180
**Cities Served:** Bay View, Castalia, Huron, Sandusky, Townsend Twp., OH
**Subscribing Households:** 20,810

**Cablevision Associates of Gary (9760)**
925 Kentucky
Box M 869
Gary, IN 46402
Phone: (219)882-9701
Fax: (219)882-6946
**Subscribing Households:** 18,000

**Charter Communications (10223)**
PO Box 557
Vincennes, IN 47591
Phone: (812)882-8501
Fax: (812)886-5916
**Cities Served:** Bridgeport, Lawrenceville, IL; Bicknell, Bruceville, Edwardsport, Freelandville, Vincennes, Washington, IN
**Subscribing Households:** 17,100

**Cass Communications (9497)**
PO Box 200
Virginia, IL 62691
Phone: (217)452-7725
Fax: (217)452-7030
**Cities Served:** Ashland, Baylis, Chandlerville, Chatham, Divernon, Easton, Glenarm, Havana, Kampsville, Manito, Milton, Mt. Sterling, Pawnee, Pleasant Plains, Rushville, Tallula, Versailles, Virginia, IL; Palmyra, MO
**Subscribing Households:** 16,521

**River Raisin Cable (15601)**
1145 S. Telegraph Rd.
Monroe, MI 48161
Phone: (325)243-9350
Fax: (325)243-2366
**Subscribing Households:** 16,451

**Bright House Networks (10011)**
2923 S. Western Ave.
Marion, IN 46953-3569
Phone: (765)662-0071
Fax: (765)668-5463
**Cities Served:** Gas City, Jonesboro, Marion, IN
**Subscribing Households:** 16,100

**Insight Communications (8530)**
806 1/2 E. Main St
Danville, IL 61832
Phone: (217)443-2941
Fax: (217)443-3907
**Subscribing Households:** 16,000

**Bright House Networks (9641)**
516 E. Carmel Dr.
Carmel, IN 46032
Phone: (317)844-8877
Fax: (317)843-2047
**Cities Served:** Carmel, Fortyville, Zionsville, IN
**Subscribing Households:** 15,564

**Adelphia Cable Communications (24843)**
1801 Elyria Ave.
Lorain, OH 44052
Phone: (440)245-3535
Fax: (440)245-6094
**Subscribing Households:** 15,000

**Tekstar Cablevision Inc, dba Arvig Communication Systems (16471)**
150 2nd Ave. SW
Perham, MN 56573
Phone: (218)346-5500
Fax: (218)346-8829
**Subscribing Households:** 15,000

**Clear Picture Inc. (25189)**
444 W. Miltown Rd.
PO Box 917
Wooster, OH 44691
Phone: (330)345-8114
Fax: (330)345-5265
**Subscribing Households:** 14,300

**Charter Media (33668)**
310 E. Jackson St.
Wisconsin Rapids, WI 54494-4864
Phone: (715)423-4605
Fax: (715)423-1885
**Cities Served:** Biron, Grand Rapids, Grant, Nekoosa, Port Edwards, Rudolph, Saratoga, Seneca, Wisconsin Rapids, WI
**Subscribing Households:** 13,000

**Comcast (15038)**
PO Box 305
Bad Axe, MI 48413-0305
Phone: (989)269-8927
Fax: (989)269-9125
**Subscribing Households:** 12,000

**Wyandotte Municipal Services (15899)**
3005 Biddle Ave.
Wyandotte, MI 48192
Phone: (734)324-7100
Fax: (734)324-7119
**Cities Served:** Wyandotte, MI
**Subscribing Households:** 10,069

**Wood CableComm (24215)**
118 N. Main St.
Bowling Green, OH 43402
Phone: (419)352-8424
Fax: (419)354-0651
**Cities Served:** Fort Seneca, Fostoria, Fremont, Gibsonburg, Kansas, Lindsey, Oak Harbor, Old Fort, Rising Sun, Tiffin, West Mills Grove, OH
**Subscribing Households:** 9,000

**Time Warner Cable (25031)**
427 E. State St.
Salem, OH 44460
Phone: (330)332-0332
Fax: (330)747-5003
**Subscribing Households:** 8,800

**Charter Communications (9632)**
604 E. National Ave.
Box 485
Brazil, IN 47834-2696
Phone: (812)448-8308
Fax: (812)443-0808
**Cities Served:** Brazil, Carbon, Eastern Terre Haute, Harmony, Knightsville, Seelyville, Staunton, Vigo County, IN
**Subscribing Households:** 7,502

**Charter Communications (7891)**
4336 E. Rt. 161
Belleville, IL 62221
Phone: (618)566-2218
Fax: (618)566-4624
**Subscribing Households:** 7,423

**TCI of Indiana (10063)**
Box 610
New Castle, IN 47362
Phone: (765)352-0675
Fax: (765)521-8654
**Subscribing Households:** 7,250

**Charter Communications (15146)**
7372 Davison Rd.
Davison, MI 48423-2012
Phone: (810)653-0966
Fax: (810)653-8287
**Cities Served:** Almont, Atlas, Davison, Dryden, Goodrich, Grand Blanc, Imlay City, Mount Morris, North Branch, Otisville, Richfield, MI
**Subscribing Households:** 7,215

**Sjoberg's Inc. (16666)**
315 N. Main
Thief River Falls, MN 56701
Phone: (218)681-3044
Fax: (218)681-6801
**Subscribing Households:** 7,000

**Western Wisconsin Communications Cooperative (33058)**
23451 Whitehall Rd.
PO Box 727
Independence, WI 54747
Phone: (715)985-3004
Fax: (715)985-3261
**Subscribing Households:** 6,900

**Charter Communications (16722)**
127 W. 4th St.
Winona, MN 55987
Fax: (507)452-5549
**Cities Served:** Altura, Goodview, Homer, Lewiston, MN City, Rollingstone, Stockton, Winona, MN; Fountain City, WI
**Subscribing Households:** 6,000

**Nelsonville TV Cable, Inc. (24928)**
1 W. Columbus St.
Nelsonville, OH 45764
Phone: (740)753-2686
Fax: (740)753-4965
**Subscribing Households:** 6,000

**Adelphia (24088)**
110 Chestnut St.
Aberdeen, OH 45101
Phone: (513)941-5153
Fax: (513)941-1704
**Cities Served:** Aberdeen, Bentonville, Georgetown, Higginsport, Manchester, Ripley, Russellville, Sardina, OH
**Subscribing Households:** 5,500

**Triax Cablevision (16154)**
1105 N.W. 4th St.
Grand Rapids, MN 55744
Phone: (218)326-0900
Fax: (218)326-6705
**Cities Served:** Grand Rapids, Keewatin, Nashwauk, MN
**Subscribing Households:** 5,300

**Bresnan Communications (16260)**
1104 E. College Dr.
Marshall, MN 56258
Phone: (507)532-5747
Fax: (507)537-1572
**Cities Served:** Marshall, MN
**Subscribing Households:** 5,200

**Frankfort Cable Communications, Inc. (9745)**
Box 9
Frankfort, IN 46041
Phone: (765)659-4622
Fax: (765)654-7031
**Subscribing Households:** 5,033

**Time Warner Cable (24771)**
131 Catherine St.
Hillsboro, OH 45133-1011
Fax: (513)382-6419
**Subscribing Households:** 4,320

**Clinton Cable TV Co. Inc. (10194)**
Box 665
Terre Haute, IN 47808
Phone: (812)235-8174
Fax: (812)235-8174
**Cities Served:** Clinton, Fairview, Parke, Rosedale, Universal, Vermillion, Vigo, IN
**Subscribing Households:** 4,150

**Comcast Cablevision (15205)**
12775 Lyndon Ave.
Detroit, MI 48227
Fax: (313)934-9490
**Subscribing Households:** 4,100

**Charter Communications (33504)**
8121 Lincoln
24 W. Rives
Rhinelander, WI 54501
Phone: (715)369-3942
Fax: (715)362-4441
**Cities Served:** Rhinelander, WI
**Subscribing Households:** 3,600

**CenturyTel Telview (33496)**
201 Stark St.
Randolph, WI 53956
Phone: (920)326-5808
Fax: (920)326-4125
**Cities Served:** Cambria, Fairwater, Fall River, Friesland, Pacific Township, Pardeeville, Randolph, Rio, Saddle Ridge Estates, Town of Fox Lake, Wyocena, WI
**Subscribing Households:** 3,425

**CenturyTel TeleVideo (33469)**
135 N. Bonson St.
PO Box 638
Platteville, WI 53818
Phone: (608)348-3048
Fax: (608)837-2330
**Cities Served:** Platteville, WI
**Subscribing Households:** 3,100

**Insight Communications (10155)**
998 N. O'Brien St.
Seymour, IN 47274-1859
Phone: (812)522-8791
Fax: (812)522-8828
**Subscribing Households:** 2,500

**Lowell Cable TV (15558)**
127 N. Broadway
PO Box 229
Lowell, MI 49331-0229
Phone: (616)897-8405
Fax: (616)897-4082
**Cities Served:** Lowell, MI
**Subscribing Households:** 2,360

**Kas Cable TV Inc. (24667)**
40003 Kauffman
PO Box 31706
Dayton, OH 45437
Phone: (937)256-5057
Fax: (937)256-0682
**Cities Served:** WPAFB, OH
**Subscribing Households:** 2,311

**Harmon Cable Communications (16669)**
125 3rd St.
Tracy, MN 56175
Fax: (507)629-3208
**Cities Served:** Tracy, MN
**Subscribing Households:** 2,225

**New Paris Telephone Quality Cablevision (10068)**
PO Box 7
New Paris, IN 46553
Phone: (574)831-2225
Fax: (574)831-7125
**Cities Served:** Goshen, Millersburg, New Paris, IN
**Subscribing Households:** 2,210

**Adams Telcom Inc. (8748)**
PO Box 248
Golden, IL 62339
Phone: (217)696-2701
Fax: (217)696-4811
**Cities Served:** Bowen, Coatsburg, Fowler, Lima, Loraine, Marcelline, Mendon, Paloma, Plymouth, Ursa, IL
**Subscribing Households:** 2,065

**CenturyTel TeleVideo (32881)**
PO Box 126
Casco, WI 54205
Phone: (920)837-7474
Fax: (920)837-2330
**Cities Served:** Casco, Forestville, New Franken, WI
**Subscribing Households:** 1980

**GLW Broadband (24749)**
PO Box 67
PO Box 67
Grafton, OH 44044
Phone: (440)926-3230
Fax: (440)926-2889
**Subscribing Households:** 1,935

**Windom Cable Communications (16715)**
444 9th St.
Box 38
Windom, MN 56101
Phone: (507)831-6129
Fax: (507)831-6127
**Cities Served:** Windom, MN
**Subscribing Households:** 1,600

**Community Antenna System Inc. (33053)**
1010 Lake St.
Hillsboro, WI 54634
Phone: (608)489-2321
Fax: (612)330-2578
**Cities Served:** Cazenovia, Elroy, Hillsboro, Kendall, WI
**Subscribing Households:** 1,553

**Jackson Municipal TV System (16189)**
80 W. Ashley
Jackson, MN 56143
Phone: (507)847-3225
Fax: (507)847-5586
**Cities Served:** Jackson, MN
**Subscribing Households:** 1,557

**Charter Communications (16142)**
2104 E. 10th St.
Box 7
Glencoe, MN 55336
Phone: (612)864-5612
Fax: (612)864-5612
**Cities Served:** Glencoe, MN
**Subscribing Households:** 1,500

**Pine Island Telephone Co. (16477)**
Box 588
Pine Island, MN 55963
Phone: (507)356-8302
Fax: (507)356-4001
**Subscribing Households:** 1,350

**GLW Broadband Inc. (25146)**
PO Box 238
Wellington, OH 44090
Phone: (440)647-6445
Fax: (440)926-2889
**Cities Served:** Wellington, OH
**Subscribing Households:** 1,220

**County Marshall Cable (24243)**
PO Box 21300
Canton, OH 44701
Phone: (330)430-3517
Fax: (330)430-3508
**Cities Served:** Morristown, OH; Glendale, Sherrard, West Liberty, WV
**Subscribing Households:** 1200

**Oconto Falls Cable TV (33439)**
PO Box 70
Oconto Falls, WI 54154
Phone: (920)846-4504
Fax: (920)846-4348
**Cities Served:** Oconto Falls, WI
**Subscribing Households:** 1036

**NET Cable (33490)**
122 S. Saint Augustine St.
PO Box 860
Pulaski, WI 54162
Phone: (920)822-8121
Fax: (920)822-8665
**Cities Served:** Pulaski, WI
**Subscribing Households:** 950

## Great Lakes States

**Channel Communication** (33010)
2121 Woodale Ave.
Green Bay, WI 54313-8907
Phone: (414)452-5058
Fax: (414)451-6814
**Cities Served:** Carlton, Cooperstown, Francis Creek, Gibson, Kossath, Maribel, Michicot, WI
**Subscribing Households:** 860

**HLM Cable Corp.** (33590)
PO Box 930067
Verona, WI 53593-0067
Phone: (608)848-9922
Fax: (608)848-9924
**Cities Served:** Arpin, Auburndale, Bluffview Acres, Hewitt, Junction City, Marshfield, Pittsville, Rudolph, Vesper, WI
**Subscribing Households:** 817

**OTEC Communication Co.** (24972)
245 W. 3rd
PO Box 427
Ottoville, OH 45876-0427
Phone: (419)453-3324
Fax: (419)453-2468
**Subscribing Households:** 801

**United Data-Vision** (16643)
308 Frontage Rd.
Sebeka, MN 56477
Phone: (218)837-5155
Fax: (218)837-5001
**Subscribing Households:** 772

**WarrenCable** (10233)
426 N. Wayne
PO Box 330
Warren, IN 46792
Phone: (260)375-2115
Fax: (260)375-2244
**Cities Served:** Warren, IN
**Subscribing Households:** 728

**Nova Cablevision Inc.** (8714)
1345 No Seminary
Box 1412
Galesburg, IL 61401
Phone: (309)342-9681
Fax: (309)342-4408
**Cities Served:** Cameron, Gladstone, Little York, Norris, Trivoli, IL
**Subscribing Households:** 698

**Manawa Telecom** (33245)
131 2nd St.
PO Box 130
Manawa, WI 54949
Phone: (920)596-2700
Fax: (920)596-3775
**Cities Served:** Manawa, WI
**Subscribing Households:** 664

**Sunman Telecommunications Corp.** (10179)
Box 145
Sunman, IN 47041
Phone: (812)623-2123
Fax: (812)623-4159
**Cities Served:** Napolean, New Point, St. Leon, Sunman, IN
**Subscribing Households:** 625

**City of Fosston Cable TV** (16133)
220 E. 1st St.
Fosston, MN 56542
Phone: (218)435-1737
Fax: (218)435-1961
**Subscribing Households:** 605

**Crystal Cable TV** (15141)
122 Lake St.
Box 365
Crystal, MI 48818
Phone: (989)235-6100
Fax: (989)235-6247
**Cities Served:** Crystal, MI
**Subscribing Households:** 600

**Data Video Systems Inc.** (16464)
222 Clayborn Ave. S
PO Box 45
Parkers Prairie, MN 56361
Phone: (218)338-4000
Fax: (218)338-3297
**Cities Served:** Eagle Bend, Miltona, Parkers Prairie, Urbank, MN
**Subscribing Households:** 606

**Bagley Public Utilities** (15940)
18 Main Ave. S.
PO Box M
Bagley, MN 56621
Phone: (218)694-2300
Fax: (218)694-6632
**Subscribing Households:** 534

**Centurytel Televideo** (33577)
PO Box 307
Thorp, WI 54771-0307
Phone: (715)669-5304
Fax: (715)669-5501
**Cities Served:** Thorp, WI
**Subscribing Households:** 526

**Moultrie Telecommunications, Inc.** (8915)
111 State & Broadway
Box 350
Lovington, IL 61937
Phone: (217)873-5215
Fax: (217)873-4990
**Cities Served:** Lovington, IL
**Subscribing Households:** 474

**Merrimac Area Cable** (33282)
327 Palisade St.
PO Box 40
Merrimac, WI 53561
Phone: (608)493-9470
Fax: (608)493-9902
**Cities Served:** Merrimac, WI
**Subscribing Households:** 468

**Becks Cable Systems** (9270)
Box 300A, RR2
Ramsey, IL 62080
Phone: (618)423-2844
Fax: (618)423-2377
**Cities Served:** Dix, Donnellson, Kell, Ohlman, Panama, Rosamond, IL
**Subscribing Households:** 410

**Blackduck Cablevision Inc.** (15967)
50 Margaret Ave. NE
PO Box 325
Blackduck, MN 56630-0325
Phone: (218)835-7890
Fax: (218)835-3299
**Cities Served:** Blackduck, MN
**Subscribing Households:** 400

**Harmony Cable Inc.** (16160)
35 1st Ave. NE
PO Box 308
Harmony, MN 55939
Phone: (507)886-2525
Fax: (507)886-2500
**Subscribing Households:** 385

**Coleraine Cable Communications System** (16017)
302 Roosevelt Ave.
PO Box 670
Coleraine, MN 55722
Phone: (218)245-2112
Fax: (218)245-2123
**Cities Served:** Coleraine, MN
**Subscribing Households:** 379

**Heritage Lake Cable** (9775)
502 N. Jackson St.
Greencastle, IN 46135
Phone: (765)653-6541
Fax: (765)653-6532
**Subscribing Households:** 360

**Hadland Communications Inc.** (32834)
Box 1286
Bayfield, WI 54814
Phone: (715)779-5840
Fax: (715)779-5840
**Subscribing Households:** 310

**Hickory Tech** (16243)
PO Box 3248
Mankato, MN 56002
Phone: (507)387-1151
Fax: (507)387-6776
**Subscribing Households:** 288

**Dodge County Cablevision** (33589)
PO Box 930067
Verona, WI 53593-0067
Phone: (608)848-9922
Fax: (608)848-9924
**Cities Served:** Brownsville, Farmersville, Kekoskee, Knowles, Leroy, South Byron, WI
**Subscribing Households:** 265

**Hidden Valley TV** (16723)
458 W. 8th St.
Winona, MN 55987
Phone: (507)452-2666
**Cities Served:** Hidden Valley, MN
**Subscribing Households:** 250

**Nicollet Cable TV** (16505)
PO Box 109
Redwood Falls, MN 56283
Phone: (507)637-8351
Fax: (507)637-8351
**Cities Served:** Nicollet, MN
**Subscribing Households:** 205

**City of Taconite Cable TV** (16659)
PO Box 137
Taconite, MN 55786
Phone: (218)245-1831
Fax: (218)245-1831
**Cities Served:** Taconite, MN
**Subscribing Households:** 110

**Hanska Cable TV** (16502)
PO Box 109
Redwood Falls, MN 56283
Phone: (507)637-8351
**Cities Served:** Hanska, MN
**Subscribing Households:** 100

**McNabb Cable & Satellite, Inc.** (8952)
302 W. Main St.
PO Box 218
McNabb, IL 61335
Phone: (815)882-2202
Fax: (815)882-2141
**Cities Served:** McNabb, IL
**Subscribing Households:** 90

**Wood Lake Cable TV** (16506)
PO Box 109
Redwood Falls, MN 56283
Phone: (507)637-8351
Fax: (507)637-8351
**Cities Served:** Wood Lake, MN
**Subscribing Households:** 90

**Comfrey Cable TV** (16500)
PO Box 109
Redwood Falls, MN 56283
Phone: (507)637-8351
Fax: (507)637-8351
**Cities Served:** Comfrey, MN
**Subscribing Households:** 80

**Echo Cable TV** (16501)
PO Box 109
Redwood Falls, MN 56283
Phone: (507)637-8351
Fax: (507)637-8351
**Subscribing Households:** 50

**Richland-Grant Telephone Cooperative (32862)**
Box 67
Box 67
Blue River, WI 53518
Phone: (608)537-2461
Fax: (608)537-2222
**Subscribing Households:** 31

# Great Plains States

**Cox Communications, Inc. (11495)**
701 E. Douglas
Wichita, KS 67202
Phone: (316)262-4270
Fax: (316)262-2309
**Cities Served:** Andover, Arkansas City, Augusta, Buhler, Derby, El Dorado, Goddard, Great Bend, Halstead, Harper, Haven, Haysville, Herington, Hesston, Hoisington, Hutchinson, Inman, Junction City, LaCrosse, Larned, Lyons, Maize, Medicine Lodge, Mulvane, Newton, Nickerson, Peabody, Pratt, Rose Hill, Sedgwick, Sharon, Towanda, Valley Center, Wichita, Winfield, KS
**Subscribing Households:** 315,778

**Cox Communications, Omaha, LLC (18543)**
11505 W. Dodge Rd.
Omaha, NE 68154
Phone: (402)933-2000
Fax: (402)933-0010
**Cities Served:** Carter Lake, IA
**Subscribing Households:** 91,000

**TCI Cablevision of Missouri (17187)**
901 N. College Ave.
Columbia, MO 65201
Phone: (573)443-1535
Fax: (573)499-0317
**Cities Served:** Columbia, Fulton, Jefferson City, Mexico, Moberly, MO
**Subscribing Households:** 55,000

**Media Com (10376)**
6300 Council St., NE, Ste. A
Cedar Rapids, IA 52402
Phone: (319)395-9699
Fax: (319)393-7017
**Cities Served:** Bertram, Cedar Rapids, Fairfax, Hiawatha, Marion, Toddville, IA
**Subscribing Households:** 48,000

**Sioux Falls Cable TV (28432)**
5001 W. 41 St.
Sioux Falls, SD 57105
Phone: (605)339-3339
Fax: (605)330-4309
**Cities Served:** Baltic, Crooks, Renner, Sioux Falls, SD
**Subscribing Households:** 36,000

**Sunflower Broadband (11188)**
644 New Hampshire
PO Box 808
Lawrence, KS 66044-0808
Phone: (785)832-6376
Fax: (785)832-6363
**Cities Served:** Eudora, Lawrence, KS
**Subscribing Households:** 29,084

**CableONE (10874)**
900 Steuben St.
Sioux City, IA 51101
Phone: (712)233-2000
Fax: (712)233-2235
**Cities Served:** Sergeant Bluff, Sioux City, IA; North Sioux City, ND; Dakota City, South Sioux City, NE
**Subscribing Households:** 29,000

**St. Joseph Cablevision (17538)**
102 N. Woodbine
PO Box 8069
Saint Joseph, MO 64508
Phone: (816)279-1234
Fax: (816)279-8773
**Subscribing Households:** 29,000

**Media Com (10676)**
546 Southgate Ave.
Iowa City, IA 52240
Phone: (319)351-0408
Fax: (319)351-3839
**Cities Served:** Coralville, Johnston County, University Heights, IA
**Subscribing Households:** 24,000

**Midcontinent Communications (23920)**
719 Memorial Hwy.
Bismarck, ND 58504-5330
Phone: (701)221-0778
Fax: (701)255-0806
**Subscribing Households:** 24,000

**AT&T Broadband (10299)**
225 S. Dayton Ave.
Ames, IA 50010
Phone: (515)233-4646
Fax: (515)233-1422
**Cities Served:** Ames, Boone, Granger, Guthrie Center, Huxley, Jefferson, Madrid, Nevada, Perry, Polk City, Randall, Sheldahl, Slater, Story City, Woodward, IA
**Subscribing Households:** 20,171

**CableOne (17302)**
PO Box 2525
112 E. 32nd St.
Joplin, MO 64804
Phone: (417)624-6340
Fax: (417)623-5413
**Cities Served:** Carterville, Joplin, Redings Mill, Saginaw, Shoal Creek, Webb City, MO
**Subscribing Households:** 17,000

**Time Warner Cable (11192)**
541 McDonald Rd.
PO Box 577
Leavenworth, KS 66048
Phone: (913)682-2113
Fax: (913)682-8705
**Cities Served:** Fort Leavenworth B.V.A., Lansing, Leavenworth, Platte City, Tracy, Weston, KS
**Subscribing Households:** 14,000

**Eagle Cable TV & Internet of Hays (11105)**
2300 Hall St.
Hays, KS 67601
Phone: (785)726-3291
Fax: (785)625-8030
**Cities Served:** Ellis, Goodland, Hays, Hoxie, Russell, Wakeeney, KS
**Subscribing Households:** 13,000

**Cox Communications (17128)**
231 E 4th St.
PO Box 696
Carthage, MO 64836
Phone: (417)358-3002
Fax: (417)359-5373
**Subscribing Households:** 11,370

**Mediacom (28481)**
PO Box 178
Yankton, SD 57078
Phone: (605)665-8030
Fax: (605)665-0683
**Cities Served:** Alton, Orange City, IA; Luverne, Worthington, MN; Canton, Vermillion, Yankton, SD
**Subscribing Households:** 11,122

**Mediacom LLC of Minnesota (28287)**
746 22nd Ave
Brookings, SD 57006
Phone: (605)692-5508
Fax: (914)695-2699
**Subscribing Households:** 9,000

**Midcontinent Communications (28463)**
635 Eighth Ave. South
Box 1023
Watertown, SD 57201
Phone: (605)886-7990
Fax: (605)886-9327
**Subscribing Households:** 7,600

**Cox Communications (17090)**
310 Walnut
Branson, MO 65616
Phone: (417)334-7897
Fax: (417)334-7897
**Cities Served:** Branson, Hollister, MO
**Subscribing Households:** 7,025

**Cable One (17377)**
402 N. Main
Box D
Kirksville, MO 63501
Phone: (660)665-7066
Fax: (660)627-2603
**Cities Served:** Kirksville, MO
**Subscribing Households:** 6,600

**U.S. Cable (17250)**
647 Clinic Rd.
Hannibal, MO 63401-3607
Phone: (573)221-0060
Fax: (573)221-0128
**Cities Served:** Hannibal, MO
**Subscribing Households:** 6,588

**Time Warner Cable (17370)**
717 Rte. VV
West South Bypass
Kennett, MO 63857
Phone: (573)888-4686
Fax: (573)888-1846
**Subscribing Households:** 5,100

**Cox Communications (11246)**
322 N. Main
Box 887
McPherson, KS 67460
Phone: (620)241-6880
Fax: (620)241-3187
**Cities Served:** McPherson, KS
**Subscribing Households:** 4,905

**Time Warner Cable (17412)**
117 E. Arrow
Marshall, MO 65340
Phone: (660)886-9618
**Cities Served:** Marshall, MO
**Subscribing Households:** 4,500

**Sumner Cable TV, Inc. (11469)**
117 W. Harvey
Wellington, KS 67152
Phone: (620)326-8989
Fax: (620)326-5332
**Cities Served:** Wellington, KS
**Subscribing Households:** 3,225

**Golden West Cablevision (28383)**
2727 N. Plaza Dr.
Rapid City, SD 57702
Phone: (605)348-6529
Fax: (605)342-1160
**Cities Served:** Buffalo Gap, Evergreen, Kadoka, Kyle, Manderson, Martin, Midland, New Underwood, Oelrich, Philip, Springfield, Wall, Wamblee, White River, SD
**Subscribing Households:** 3003

**Time Warner Cable (18341)**
506 C St.
Fairbury, NE 68352
Phone: (402)421-0330
Fax: (402)421-0310
**Cities Served:** Fairbury, Superior, NE
**Subscribing Households:** 2,874

**Alliance Communications Cooperative, Inc. (28315)**
612 3rd St.
PO Box 349
Garretson, SD 57030
Phone: (605)594-3411
Fax: (605)594-6776
**Cities Served:** Brandon, Garretson, SD
**Subscribing Households:** 2,565

**Shellsburg Cablevision Corp.** (10858)
124 Main St.
PO Box 390
Shellsburg, IA 52332
Phone: (319)436-2224
Fax: (319)436-2228
**Subscribing Households:** 2,546

**Winnebago Co-op Cablevision** (10702)
704 E. Main St.
Lake Mills, IA 50450
Phone: (641)592-1000
**Cities Served:** Buffalo Center, Forest City, Lake Mills, Thompson, IA
**Subscribing Households:** 2,360

**Time Warner Cable** (11031)
PO Box 345
Colby, KS 67701-0345
**Cities Served:** Colby, KS; Trenton, NE
**Subscribing Households:** 2,092

**Panora Cooperative Cablevision Assoc. Inc.** (10815)
114 E. Main
PO Box 217
Panora, IA 50216
Phone: (641)755-2200
Fax: (641)755-2425
**Cities Served:** Bagley, Jamaica, Linden, Panora, Yale, IA
**Subscribing Households:** 1,948

**Eagle Cable** (11391)
336 E. Wichita
Russell, KS 67665
Phone: (785)483-3244
Fax: (785)483-2569
**Cities Served:** Russell, KS
**Subscribing Households:** 1,800

**City of Baxter Springs** (10997)
City Hall
PO Box 577
Baxter Springs, KS 66713
Phone: (620)856-2114
Fax: (620)856-2460
**Cities Served:** Baxter Springs, KS
**Subscribing Households:** 1,682

**Allegiance Communications, Inc.** (11253)
108 N. Main St.
Box 176
Medicine Lodge, KS 67104
Phone: (620)886-3731
**Cities Served:** Harper, Medicine Lodge, Sharon, KS
**Subscribing Households:** 1,600

**Sky Scan Cable Co.** (18326)
PO Box 604
Creighton, NE 68729-0604
**Cities Served:** Fairfax, Geddes, Pickstown, SD
**Subscribing Households:** 1,587

**Great Plains Cable TV Inc.** (18295)
1635 Front St.
Box 500
Blair, NE 68008
Phone: (402)426-9511
Fax: (402)426-6475
**Subscribing Households:** 1,500

**Charter Media** (17944)
210 W. 7th St.
Sedalia, MO 65301
Phone: (660)827-2344
Fax: (660)826-4583
**Cities Served:** Eldorado Springs, MO
**Subscribing Households:** 1,121

**EPIC Touch Co.** (11055)
610 S. Cosmos
Elkhart, KS 67950
Phone: (620)697-2111
Fax: (620)697-9997
**Cities Served:** Elkhart, Rolla, KS; Keyes, OK
**Subscribing Households:** 1,062

**City of Unionville CATV** (18013)
1611 Grant
PO Box 255
Unionville, MO 63565
Phone: (660)947-3818
Fax: (660)947-7756
**Cities Served:** Unionville, MO
**Subscribing Households:** 962

**Modern Communications** (10841)
115 1st Ave.-West
Rock Rapids, IA 51246-1501
Phone: (712)472-2519
Fax: (712)472-3604
**Cities Served:** Rock Rapids, IA
**Subscribing Households:** 965

**Eagle Cable TV Co.** (11462)
529 Russell
Box 426
Wa Keeney, KS 67672
Phone: (785)743-5616
Fax: (785)625-8030
**Cities Served:** Wakeeney, KS
**Subscribing Households:** 900

**Valley Cablevision of South Dakota Inc.** (28299)
Box 98
Dell Rapids, SD 57022
Phone: (605)428-5421
Fax: (605)428-3132
**Subscribing Households:** 900

**Dickey Rural Services Inc.** (23949)
9628 Hwy 281
PO Box 69
Ellendale, ND 58436
Phone: (701)349-3687
Fax: (701)344-4300
**Cities Served:** Forman, Gwinner, Litchville, Marion, Milnor, Wyndemere, ND
**Subscribing Households:** 878

**Northeast Iowa Telephone Co./CATV** (10754)
113 N. Page
PO Box 835
Monona, IA 52159
Phone: (563)539-2122
Fax: (563)539-2003
**Cities Served:** Farmersburg, Luana, Monona, St. Olaf, IA
**Subscribing Households:** 850

**Kahoka Communications Cable** (17311)
250 N. Morgan
Kahoka, MO 63445
Phone: (816)727-3711
Fax: (816)727-3750
**Cities Served:** Kahoka, MO
**Subscribing Households:** 775

**James Valley Co-op Telephone Co.** (28319)
Box 260
Groton, SD 57445
Phone: (605)397-2323
Fax: (605)397-2350
**Cities Served:** Andover, Claremont, Columbia, Groton, Hecla, Stratford, Turton, SD
**Subscribing Households:** 750

**Hartley Municipal Cable TV** (10626)
11 S. Central Ave.
Hartley, IA 51346
Phone: (712)728-3051
Fax: (712)728-2878
**Cities Served:** Hartley, IA
**Subscribing Households:** 704

**Communication1 Cablevision Inc.** (10689)
105 S. Main
PO Box 20
Kanawha, IA 50447
Phone: (641)762-3772
Fax: (641)762-8201
**Subscribing Households:** 622

**Heck's TV & Cable** (10312)
Box 517
Box 517
Armstrong, IA 50514
Phone: (712)864-3431
**Cities Served:** Crystal Lake, Lakota, Renwick, Woden, IA; Emmons, MN
**Subscribing Households:** 550

**Curtis Cable TV Co., Inc.** (18331)
Box 8
Curtis, NE 69025
Phone: (308)367-8600
**Cities Served:** Curtis, Maywood, NE
**Subscribing Households:** 500

**Mid-Kansas Cable Services, Inc.** (11261)
109 N. Christian
Moundridge, KS 67107
Phone: (620)345-2832
Fax: (620)345-6106
**Subscribing Households:** 465

**Coon Rapids Municipal Cable** (10407)
123 3rd Ave.
PO Box 207
Coon Rapids, IA 50058
Phone: (712)999-5514
Fax: (712)684-5148
**Cities Served:** Coon Rapids, IA
**Subscribing Households:** 454

**Mediapolis Cablevision Co.** (10751)
652 Main St.
PO Box 398
Mediapolis, IA 52637
Phone: (319)394-3996
Fax: (319)394-9155
**Subscribing Households:** 450

**Atwood Cable Systems Inc.** (10994)
423 State St.
Atwood, KS 67730
Phone: (785)626-3261
Fax: (785)626-9005
**Cities Served:** Atwood, KS
**Subscribing Households:** 434

**Dumont Cablevision** (10541)
506 Pine St.
Dumont, IA 50625
Phone: (641)857-3213
Fax: (641)857-3300
**Cities Served:** Bristow, Dumont, Geneva, IA
**Subscribing Households:** 425

**Mechanicsville Telephone Co.** (10749)
107 N. John
Mechanicsville, IA 52306
Phone: (563)432-7221
Fax: (563)432-7721
**Cities Served:** Mechanicsville, IA
**Subscribing Households:** 419

**Siebring Cable** (10598)
301 S. Main St.
PO Box 36
George, IA 51237-0036
Phone: (712)475-3747
Fax: (712)475-2517
**Cities Served:** George, IA
**Subscribing Households:** 400

**South Benton Cablevision, Inc.** (10695)
86 Main St.
Keystone, IA 52249-0277
Phone: (319)442-3243
Fax: (319)442-3210
**Subscribing Households:** 363

**Goldfield Communication Services Corp.** (10602)
PO Box 67
Goldfield, IA 50542
Phone: (515)825-3888
Fax: (515)825-3801
**Cities Served:** Badger, Goldfield, Woolstock, IA
**Subscribing Households:** 340

**SRT Telephone (24042)**
617 Arbor Ave.
Minot, ND 58703
Phone: (701)852-8288
**Cities Served:** Velva, ND
**Subscribing Households:** 310

**Midcontinent Communications (28431)**
5001 W. 41 St.
Sioux Falls, SD 57105
Fax: (605)330-4309
**Subscribing Households:** 300

**Wall Lake Cable TV System (10935)**
108 Main St.
Wall Lake, IA 51466
**Cities Served:** Wall Lake, IA
**Subscribing Households:** 295

**Readlyn Telephone Co. (10829)**
121 Main St.
Readlyn, IA 50668
Phone: (319)279-3375
Fax: (319)279-7575
**Cities Served:** Readlyn, IA
**Subscribing Households:** 282

**Van Horne Cablevision and Television (10931)**
204 Main St.
Box 96
Van Horne, IA 52346
Phone: (319)228-8791
Fax: (319)228-8784
**Cities Served:** Van Horne, IA
**Subscribing Households:** 248

**Wheat State Telecable Inc. (11456)**
106 W. 1st St.
Box 320
Udall, KS 67146
Phone: (620)782-3341
Fax: (620)782-3302
**Cities Served:** Udall, KS
**Subscribing Households:** 240

**Scranton Community Antenna Television (10850)**
1200 Main St.
Box 8
Scranton, IA 51462
Phone: (712)652-3355
Fax: (712)652-3777
**Cities Served:** Scranton, IA
**Subscribing Households:** 224

**Templeton Telephone Co. (10919)**
115 Main
Box 77
Templeton, IA 51463
Phone: (712)669-3311
Fax: (712)669-3312
**Cities Served:** Dedham, Templeton, IA
**Subscribing Households:** 214

**WinDBreak Cable (18350)**
760 M St.
Gering, NE 69341
Phone: (308)436-4650
Fax: (308)436-4779
**Cities Served:** Harrison, Lyman, NE
**Subscribing Households:** 120

**Kennebec Telephone Co. Inc. (28331)**
PO Box 158
Kennebec, SD 57544
Phone: (605)869-2229
Fax: (605)869-2221
**Cities Served:** Kennebec, SD
**Subscribing Households:** 106

**PEC Cable (10677)**
Eastdale Plaza
1700 1st Ave., No. 1
Iowa City, IA 52240
Phone: (319)351-2297
Fax: (319)358-5810
**Cities Served:** Nichols, IA
**Subscribing Households:** 95

**City of Cawker Cable TV (11018)**
804 Locust St.
PO Box 2
Cawker City, KS 67430
Phone: (785)781-4713
Fax: (785)781-4436
**Cities Served:** Cawker City, KS
**Subscribing Households:** 27

## Middle Atlantic States

**Cox Communications (31497)**
3080 Centerville Rd.
PO Box 10800
Herndon, VA 20171
Phone: (703)378-8400
Fax: (703)480-4990
**Subscribing Households:** 202,000

**Comcast (31815)**
918 North Blvd.
Richmond, VA 23230-4687
Phone: (804)355-6565
Fax: (804)915-0707
**Subscribing Households:** 148,000

**Comcast (5138)**
4008 N. DuPont Hwy.
New Castle, DE 19720-6325
Phone: (302)656-3370
Fax: (302)661-8108
**Cities Served:** Arden, Ardencroft, Ardentown, Bellefonte, Elsmere, New Castle, Neward, Newport, DE
**Subscribing Households:** 144,000

**Comcast (13230)**
9609 Anapolis Rd.
Lanham, MD 20706
Phone: (301)306-5700
Fax: (301)731-7822
**Subscribing Households:** 81,000

**Comcast (5769)**
900 Michigan Ave. NE
Washington, DC 20017
Phone: (202)635-5100
Fax: (202)462-4064
**Cities Served:** Washington, DC
**Subscribing Households:** 79,000

**Comcast Cablevision of Harford County (12623)**
30 N. Parke St.
Aberdeen, MD 21001
Phone: (410)272-7500
Fax: (410)272-6203
**Subscribing Households:** 56,400

**Cox Communications Roanoke (31841)**
5400 Fallowater Ln.
Roanoke, VA 24014
Phone: (540)776-3848
Fax: (540)776-3847
**Cities Served:** Roanoke City, Vinton, VA
**Subscribing Households:** 56,000

**Millennium Digital Medium (13249)**
406 Headquarters Dr., Ste. 201
Millersville, MD 21108
Phone: (410)987-8400
Fax: (410)987-4890
**Subscribing Households:** 50,000

**Columbia Cable of Virginia (31969)**
4391 Dale Blvd.
Woodbridge, VA 22193
Phone: (703)221-3536
Fax: (703)670-5479
**Cities Served:** Dale City, Dumfries, Ft. Belvoir, Lake Ridge, Occoquan, Quantico, Quantico Town, Triangle, Woodbridge, VA
**Subscribing Households:** 47,500

**Newport News Cablevision (31619)**
179 Louise Dr.
Newport News, VA 23601
Phone: (757)596-6032
Fax: (757)595-2396
**Cities Served:** Fort Eustis, Newport News, VA
**Subscribing Households:** 47,000

**Adelphia (32723)**
302 N. Mildred St.
Ranson, WV 25438
Phone: (304)725-9185
Fax: (304)725-0930
**Cities Served:** Baker Heights, Bakerton, BoLivar, Charles Town, Harpers Ferry, Hedgesville, Hodgesville, Inwood, Kearneysville, Martins Berg, Martinsburg, Middleway, Ranson, Shenandoah Jct., Sheperds Town, Summit Point, WV
**Subscribing Households:** 28,995

**Antietam Cable TV (13198)**
1000 Willow Circle
Hagerstown, MD 21740
Phone: (301)797-6226
Fax: (301)797-4829
**Subscribing Households:** 28,000

**American Cable TV (5135)**
PO Box 440
Millsboro, DE 19966
Phone: (302)732-6600
Fax: (302)732-6616
**Subscribing Households:** 23,138

**Adelphia Cable Communications (31566)**
390 Commonwealth Blvd.
Martinsville, VA 24112
Phone: (800)835-4949
Fax: (703)666-2577
**Cities Served:** Henry County, Martinsville, VA
**Subscribing Households:** 21,700

**Adelphia (32621)**
51 W. 6th Ave.
Huntington, WV 25701
Phone: (304)522-8226
Fax: (304)523-5493
**Cities Served:** Barboursville, Huntington, WV
**Subscribing Households:** 21,500

**GMP Cable TV (13210)**
44150 Airport View Dr.
Hollywood, MD 20636
Phone: (301)373-3201
Fax: (301)373-3757
**Subscribing Households:** 20,000

**Comcast Cable (13386)**
336 Post Office Rd.
Waldorf, MD 20602
Phone: (301)843-3520
Fax: (301)843-7212
**Subscribing Households:** 19,600

**Cox Communications (31413)**
1310 Belman Rd.
Fredericksburg, VA 22401
Phone: (540)373-6343
Fax: (540)371-2391
**Cities Served:** Fredericksburg, VA
**Subscribing Households:** 16,700

**Clearview Partners (13111)**
109 E. Jarrettsville Rd.
Forest Hill, MD 21050
Phone: (410)838-7600
Fax: (410)838-8546
**Cities Served:** Harford County, MD; Chanceford Twp., Crossroads Boro, Delta, East Hopewell Twp., Fawn Grove, Fawn Twp., Hopewell Twp., Lower Chanceford Twp., North Hopewell Twp., Peach Bottom Twp., Shrewsbury Twp., Stewartstown, Winterstown Boro, PA
**Subscribing Households:** 10,379

**Charter Communications (31406)**
200 Main St.
PO Box 994
Franklin, VA 23851
Phone: (757)569-9122
Fax: (757)569-8621
**Cities Served:** Franklin, Isle of Wight County, Ivor, Smithfield, Southampton County, Wakefield, Waverly, Windsor, VA
**Subscribing Households:** 9,200

# Northeastern States

**First Commonwealth Cablevision, Ltd. (31871)**
PO Box 1147
126 Urbanna St.
Saluda, VA 23149
Phone: (804)758-5870
Fax: (804)758-4714

Subscribing Households: 5,200

**Nesbe (32690)**
216 Howard Ave.
Mullens, WV 25882
Phone: (304)732-6114
Fax: (304)294-4717

Cities Served: Rockview, WV

Subscribing Households: 5,000

**Adelphia Cable Communications (31666)**
25225 Harwell Dr.
Petersburg, VA 23803
Phone: (804)725-3412

Subscribing Households: 2000

**Washington Cable (5772)**
700 7th St. SW
Washington, DC 20024-2484
Phone: (202)646-1600
Fax: (202)479-4396

Cities Served: Washington, DC; Fairfax, VA

Subscribing Households: 2,000

**Telemedia (31301)**
PO Box 85
Colonial Beach, VA 22443
Phone: (804)224-7101
Fax: (804)224-9616

Subscribing Households: 1,660

**Philippi Communications System (32713)**
108 N. Main St.
Box 460
Philippi, WV 26416
Phone: (304)457-3700
Fax: (304)457-2703

Cities Served: Philippi, WV

Subscribing Households: 1,350

**Moorefield CableVision (32673)**
741 N. Main St.
Box 659
Moorefield, WV 26836
Fax: (304)538-6175

Cities Served: Duregon, Moorefield, WV

Subscribing Households: 1,202

**Bath CATV Inc. (31500)**
Rte. 220 N
Box 568
Hot Springs, VA 24445

Cities Served: Bavoca, Hot Springs, Warm Springs, VA

Subscribing Households: 991

**BASCO Electronics Inc. (32773)**
420 W. 2nd St.
Weston, WV 26452
Phone: (304)269-7530
Fax: (304)269-6581

Cities Served: Alum Bridge, Broad Run, Elk City, Ireland, Walkersville, WV

Subscribing Households: 700

**Rural Retreat Cable TV Inc. (31861)**
228 Sage Rd.
Rural Retreat, VA 24368
Phone: (276)686-5242
Fax: (276)686-5242

Cities Served: Rural Retreat, VA

Subscribing Households: 600

## Northeastern States

**Comcast Cable Communications Inc. (27303)**
1500 Market St.
Philadelphia, PA 19102
Phone: (215)665-1700
Fax: (215)981-7790

Subscribing Households: 2,900,000

**Adelphia Communications Corp. (26271)**
1 North Main St.
Coudersport, PA 16915
Phone: (814)274-9830
Fax: (814)274-8631

Subscribing Households: 1,100,000

**Comcast Cable (27415)**
300 Corliss St.
Pittsburgh, PA 15220-4815
Phone: (412)875-1100
Fax: (412)331-7452

Subscribing Households: 925,558

**Queens Inner Unity Cable Systems (22785)**
133-19 Atlantic Ave.
Richmond Hill, NY 11418
Phone: (718)739-7498
Fax: (718)739-6124

Cities Served: Brooklyn, Manhattan, Queens, NY

Subscribing Households: 700,000

**Tele-Media Corp. (26157)**
PO Box 39
Bellefonte, PA 16823
Phone: (814)353-2025
Fax: (814)353-2072

Subscribing Households: 475,000

**Cablevision of New York City (20483)**
930 Soundview Ave.
Bronx, NY 10473
Phone: (718)991-6000
Fax: (718)378-2625

Cities Served: Bronx, Brooklyn, NY

Subscribing Households: 460,000

**Chapter & Verse TV (27927)**
PO Box 41000
Providence, RI 02940-1000
Phone: (401)785-1685

Subscribing Households: 350,800

**Comcast (4829)**
222 New Park Dr.
PO Box 4222
Kensington, CT 06037
Phone: (860)505-6248
Fax: (860)505-3352

Cities Served: Branford, Hartford, Lakeville, Plainville, Vernon, CT

Subscribing Households: 247,000

**US Cable Corp. (19549)**
28 W. Grand Ave.
Montvale, NJ 07645
Phone: (201)930-9000
Fax: (201)930-9232

Subscribing Households: 220,099

**Cablevision (19640)**
40 Potash Rd.
Oakland, NJ 07436-1870
Phone: (201)337-1550
Fax: (201)337-9126

Subscribing Households: 214,000

**Cablevision of Connecticut LP (4970)**
28 Cross St.
Norwalk, CT 06851
Phone: (203)750-5600
Fax: (203)846-9412

Cities Served: Darien, Easton, Fairfield County, Greenwich, New Canaan, Norwalk, Redding, Stamford, Weston, Westport, Wilton, CT

Subscribing Households: 203,000

**Armstrong Group of Companies (26210)**
1 Armstrong Pl.
Butler, PA 16001
Phone: (724)283-0925
Fax: (724)283-9655

Subscribing Households: 172,000

**Cablevision of Monmouth (18975)**
Box 58
Belmar, NJ 07719-0058
Phone: (732)922-1800
Fax: (732)922-1783

Subscribing Households: 170,000

**Cablevision of Monmouth (19928)**
1501 18th Ave.
Wall, NJ 07719
Phone: (732)922-1800
Fax: (732)681-5458

Subscribing Households: 120,000

**Charter Communications (14949)**
95 Higgins St.
Worcester, MA 01606-1913
Phone: (508)853-1515
Fax: (508)854-5042

Cities Served: Central, MA

Subscribing Households: 120,000

**Time Warner Cable (22969)**
100 Cable Way
Staten Island, NY 10303
Phone: (718)447-7000
Fax: (718)816-8433

Subscribing Households: 111,000

**Comcast (18877)**
751 E. Industrial Park Dr.
Manchester, NH 03109
Phone: (603)626-9900
Fax: (603)641-2996

Cities Served: Antrim, Auburn, Bedford, Boscawen, Bow, Bridgewater, Bristol, Candia, Canterbury, Chichester, Concord, NH

Subscribing Households: 104,000

**Cablevision of Southern Connecticut (4638)**
122 River St.
Bridgeport, CT 06604
Phone: (203)336-2225
Fax: (203)333-5883

Subscribing Households: 93,000

**Cox Communication (27952)**
9 J.P. Murphy Hwy.
West Warwick, RI 02893-2381
Phone: (401)383-2000
Fax: (401)828-3835

Subscribing Households: 86,000

**Susquehanna Communications (27735)**
1050 E. King St.
York, PA 17403
Phone: (717)846-4551
Fax: (717)843-5400

Cities Served: York, PA

Subscribing Households: 86,000

**Comcast Cable Co. (26606)**
1131 S. Duke St.
Lancaster, PA 17602-4660
Phone: (717)291-3000
Fax: (717)239-3801

Subscribing Households: 85,000

**Time Warner Cable (13785)**
85 E. Belcher Rd.
Foxboro, MA 02035
Fax: (508)698-0601

Subscribing Households: 72,600

**Comcast (14281)**
630 Mt. Pleasant St.
New Bedford, MA 02740
Phone: (508)998-9000

Subscribing Households: 66,000

**Time Warner Cable (12570)**
118 Johnson Rd.
Box 8180
Portland, ME 04102
Phone: (207)253-2400
Fax: (207)775-6422

Cities Served: Cape Elizabeth, Cumberland, Falmouth, Gorham, New Gloucester, North Yarmouth, Portland, Scarborough, South Portland, Westbrook, Yarmouth, ME

Subscribing Households: 61,000

**Gale Directory of Publications & Broadcast Media/140th Ed.**  **Northeastern States**

**Eastern Connecticut Cable Television, Inc.  (5075)**
61 Myrock Ave.
PO Box 6001
Waterford, CT 06385
Phone: (203)442-8525
Fax: (203)443-6031
**Cities Served:** Newport, RI
**Subscribing Households:** 55,337

**Cablevision of New Jersey, Inc.  (19053)**
5 Legion Dr.
Cresskill, NJ 07626
Phone: (201)569-3720
Fax: (201)569-3082
**Subscribing Households:** 55,000

**Cablevision of Rockland  (23156)**
235 W. Nyack Rd.
West Nyack, NY 10994
Phone: (845)623-9497
Fax: (845)623-5619
**Cities Served:** Montvale, NJ; Rockland County, NY
**Subscribing Households:** 55,000

**Twin County Trans Video Inc.  (26173)**
2124 Avenue C
Bethlehem, PA 18017-2120
Fax: (215)261-5099
**Subscribing Households:** 54,016

**Cablevision  (19408)**
360 1st St.
Hoboken, NJ 07030
Phone: (201)798-6060
Fax: (201)798-4163
**Subscribing Households:** 47,520

**Cable Holdings  (22569)**
445 Park Ave., Ste. 1401
New York, NY 10022-2606
Phone: (212)421-9870
Fax: (212)688-3043
**Subscribing Households:** 46,000

**Tele-Media Company of Western Connecticut  (4998)**
80 Great Hill Rd.
Seymour, CT 06483
Phone: (203)735-9504
Fax: (203)734-3425
**Subscribing Households:** 43,600

**Charter Communications  (26103)**
2200 Beale Ave.
Altoona, PA 16601
Phone: (814)946-5491
Fax: (814)943-1721
**Cities Served:** Blair County, PA
**Subscribing Households:** 43,000

**Adelphia Cable Communications of Niagara  (22619)**
2604 Seneca Ave.
Niagara Falls, NY 14305
Fax: (716)297-0616
**Cities Served:** Lewiston, Lockport, Niagara, Sanborn, NY
**Subscribing Households:** 42,000

**Adelphia Cable Communications  (26270)**
1 North Main St.
Coudersport, PA 16915
Phone: (814)274-9830
Fax: (814)274-8631
**Cities Served:** Onondaga County, NY
**Subscribing Households:** 39,000

**Comcast Cablevision  (27714)**
29 York Rd.
Willow Grove, PA 19090
Phone: (215)657-6990
Fax: (215)961-3875
**Cities Served:** Abington, Bryn Athyn, Cheltenham, Jenkentown, Lower Moreland, Rockledge, Upper Moreland, PA
**Subscribing Households:** 38,500

**Comcast  (18965)**
901 W. Leeds Ave.
Absecon, NJ 08201
Phone: (609)641-6700
Fax: (609)272-0455

**Subscribing Households:** 37,731

**Suscom  (27704)**
330 Basin St.
Williamsport, PA 17701
Phone: (570)326-3384
Fax: (570)326-7833
**Cities Served:** Avis, Hughesville, Jersey Shore, Montgomery, Muncy, Renovo, Williamsport, PA
**Subscribing Households:** 37,000

**Comcast Cable  (13627)**
4 Main St.
Brockton, MA 02301
Phone: (508)588-2434
Fax: (508)588-5168
**Subscribing Households:** 34,500

**Jones Intercable Inc.  (19907)**
Black Horse Pike & Cable TV Ln.
PO Box 775
Turnersville, NJ 08012
Phone: (856)582-9335
Fax: (856)875-1390
**Cities Served:** Buena Vista Township, Chesilhurst, Folsom, Monroe Township, Washington Township, Waterford Township, Winslow Township, NJ
**Subscribing Households:** 34,245

**Cablevision of Hamilton  (19898)**
2137 Hamilton Ave.
Trenton, NJ 08619
Phone: (609)586-2291
Fax: (609)586-2478
**Cities Served:** Allentown, Hamilton Twp., Washington Twp., NJ
**Subscribing Households:** 32,500

**Armstrong Utilities Inc.  (27742)**
521 Perry Way
Zelienople, PA 16063
Phone: (724)776-4200
Fax: (724)452-8008
**Subscribing Households:** 32,000

**Blue Ridge CATV Inc.  (26340)**
804 Academy Heights Ave.
Box 150
Ephrata, PA 17522
Phone: (717)733-4111
Fax: (717)733-3245
**Cities Served:** Akron, Denver, Ephrata, Lititz, Manheim, PA
**Subscribing Households:** 32,000

**Adelphia Cable Communications  (26180)**
1 Adelphia Dr.
Blairsville, PA 15717
Phone: (724)459-5400
Fax: (724)459-0648
**Cities Served:** Blairsville, Delmont, Export, Indiana, Latrobe, Ligonier, Murrysville, PA
**Subscribing Households:** 30,000

**Service Electric Cablevision  (26178)**
6400 Perkiomen Ave.
Birdsboro, PA 19508
Phone: (610)582-5317
Fax: (610)582-3094
**Subscribing Households:** 30,000

**Cablevision Systems  (23213)**
2013 Crompond Rd.
Yorktown Heights, NY 10598
Phone: (914)962-5311
Fax: (914)962-9489
**Cities Served:** Bedford, Mt. Kisco, North Castle, Putnam Valley, Somers, Yorktown, NY
**Subscribing Households:** 25,300

**Comcast  (18921)**
460 Amherst St.
Nashua, NH 03063
Phone: (603)889-1363
Fax: (603)882-4415
**Subscribing Households:** 25,000

**Time Warner Cable Ithaca  (20973)**
519 W. State St.
Ithaca, NY 14850
Phone: (607)272-3456
Fax: (607)277-5404
**Subscribing Households:** 25,000

**Cablevision of Elizabeth  (19068)**
536 N. Broad St.
Elizabeth, NJ 07208
Phone: (908)353-0404
Fax: (908)289-5895
**Subscribing Households:** 23,808

**Auburn Cablevision Inc.  (20327)**
32 Owasco St.
Auburn, NY 13021
Phone: (315)252-7563
Fax: (315)252-9514
**Cities Served:** Auburn, Fleming, Hammonds Port, Mottville, Owasco, Pennyan, Sennett, Skaneateles, Skaneateles Falls, Spafford, Throop, NY
**Subscribing Households:** 22,000

**The Community Voice Channel  (4631)**
200 Boston Tpke.
PO Box 9171
Bolton, CT 06043
Phone: (860)645-1454
Fax: (860)645-1635
**Subscribing Households:** 21,000

**Adams CATV Inc.  (26220)**
19 N. Main St.
Carbondale, PA 18407
Phone: (570)282-6121
Fax: (570)282-3787
**Cities Served:** Carbondale, Clifford, Hamlin, Jermyn, Lake Ariel, Lenoxville, Mayfield, Simpson, Susquehanna, Waymart, PA
**Subscribing Households:** 18,500

**Comcast  (27456)**
2323 W. End Ave.
Pottsville, PA 17901
Phone: (610)323-4742
Fax: (717)622-3099
**Subscribing Households:** 18,250

**Cablevision  (23124)**
19 South St.
Warwick, NY 10990
Phone: (973)728-0302
Fax: (845)986-0031
**Cities Served:** Chester, Florida, Greenwood Lake, Pine Island, Warwick, West Milford, NY
**Subscribing Households:** 18,000

**Falcon Cable TV  (22709)**
68 Bridge St.
PO Box 570
Plattsburgh, NY 12901
Fax: (518)563-2696
**Subscribing Households:** 17,000

**Comcast  (13796)**
14 Burr St.
Framingham, MA 01701-4617
Phone: (508)872-6300
Fax: (508)875-1846
**Subscribing Households:** 16,000

**New England Cablevision  (18955)**
PO Box 1450
22 Farmington Rd.
Rochester, NH 03867
Phone: (603)332-5466
Fax: (603)335-4106
**Cities Served:** Lebanon, ME; Barrington, East Rochester, Farmington, Gonic, Milton, Rochester, Strafford, NH
**Subscribing Households:** 15,700

**Comcast  (14770)**
41 Marble St.
Revere, MA 02151
Phone: (781)284-6833
Fax: (781)286-1542
**Cities Served:** Revere, MA
**Subscribing Households:** 14,500

*Cable Index*

Circulation: ★ = ABC; △ = BPA; ◆ = CAC; ● = CCAB; ❑ = VAC; ⊕ = PO Statement; ‡ = Publisher's Report; Boldface figures = sworn; Light figures = estimated.

# Northeastern States

**Adelphia Cable** (30844)
107 McKinley St.
Bennington, VT 05201-1024
Phone: (802)447-1534
Fax: (802)442-2063
**Cities Served:** Hoosick, Hoosick Falls, North Hoosick, Rensselaer County, NY; Arlington, Bennington, Manchester, North Bennington, Old Bennington, Pownal, Shaftsbury, Sunderland, Woodford, VT
**Subscribing Households:** 14,322

**New England Cablevision Inc.** (13803)
38 Blackburn Center
Gloucester, MA 01930
Phone: (508)332-5466
Fax: (508)281-8679
**Subscribing Households:** 12,500

**Shrewsbury's Community Cablevision** (14785)
100 Maple Ave.
Shrewsbury, MA 01545
Phone: (508)841-8500
Fax: (508)842-9419
**Cities Served:** Shrewsbury, MA
**Subscribing Households:** 11,508

**Comcast** (13623)
197 Quincy Ave.
Braintree, MA 02184
Phone: (781)848-2350
Fax: (781)848-9719
**Subscribing Households:** 10,448

**Cablevision of Dutchess** (23195)
Rte. 22, RR 1
Box 133
Wingdale, NY 12594
Phone: (845)832-3350
Fax: (845)832-3129
**Cities Served:** Amenia, Clinton, Dover, Millbrook, Millerton, Pine Plains, Stanford, Union Vale, Washington, Wassaic, Wingdale, NY
**Subscribing Households:** 9,450

**Adelphia Cable of MV** (14846)
Box 2109
Vineyard Haven, MA 02568
Phone: (508)693-6644
Fax: (508)693-3669
**Cities Served:** Aquinnah, Chilmark, Edgartown, Oak Bluffs, Vineyard Haven, West Tisbury, MA
**Subscribing Households:** 9,000

**Time Warner Cable of Maine** (12584)
67 Industrial Dr
Presque Isle, ME 04769-1249
Phone: (207)764-1349
Fax: (207)764-1299
**Cities Served:** Caribou, Caswell, Connor, Fort Fairfield AFB, Limestone, New Sweden, Presque Isle, Westfield, Woodland, ME
**Subscribing Households:** 9,000

**Warner Cable Communications** (18771)
219 Main St.
Berlin, NH 03570
Phone: (603)752-4330
Fax: (603)752-3940
**Subscribing Households:** 7,747

**TKR Cable Company of Maple Shade** (19507)
30 W. Main St.
Maple Shade, NJ 08052
Phone: (856)779-0771
Fax: (856)456-9430
**Subscribing Households:** 6,500

**Coudersport TV Cable Co.** (26272)
14 S. Main St.
Coudersport, PA 16915
Phone: (814)274-9830
Fax: (814)274-6593
**Cities Served:** Austin, Coudersport, Port Allegany, Roulette, PA
**Subscribing Households:** 6,200

**Phoenix Cable, Inc.** (19755)
17 S. Franklin Tpk
Ramsey, NJ 07446
Phone: (201)825-9090
Fax: (201)825-8794
**Subscribing Households:** 5458

**Amrac Clearview** (13451)
40 Daniel Shays Hwy.
Belchertown, MA 01007
Fax: (413)323-7466
**Cities Served:** Belchertown, Hadley, MA
**Subscribing Households:** 4,827

**Coaxial Cable Corp.** (26314)
105 Walker Dr.
Edinboro, PA 16412
Phone: (814)734-1424
Fax: (814)734-8898
**Cities Served:** Cambridge Springs, Cambridge Twp., Edinboro, Franklin Twp., Townville Boro, Venago, Venango Twp., Washington Twp., Woodcock Boro, PA
**Subscribing Households:** 4,800

**Comcast Cable** (26712)
804 Plum St.
PO Box 66
Millersburg, PA 17061
Phone: (717)692-4772
Fax: (717)692-5654
**Subscribing Households:** 4,620

**Time Warner Cable** (20912)
156 Main St.
Hornell, NY 14843-0089
**Cities Served:** Dansville, Grousklard, Sparta, Springwater, Wayland, West Sparta, NY
**Subscribing Households:** 4,300

**Casco Cable TV** (12487)
336 Bath Rd.
Brunswick, ME 04011-2635
Phone: (207)729-6663
**Subscribing Households:** 3,600

**Polaris Cable** (12524)
72 Main St.
Box 610
Houlton, ME 04730
Phone: (207)532-2579
Fax: (207)532-4025
**Cities Served:** Bridgewater, Danforth, Enfield, Hodgdon, Houlton, Howland, Island Falls, Littleton, Medway, Monticello, Oakfield, Passadumkeag, Patten, Smyrna, ME
**Subscribing Households:** 2,990

**MCT Cable** (18794)
11 Kearsarge Ave.
PO Box 340
Contoocook, NH 03229
Phone: (603)746-3000
Fax: (603)746-3566
**Cities Served:** Bradford, Newbury, Sutton, Warner, NH
**Subscribing Households:** 2,204

**Bucktail Broadcasting Corp.** (26333)
19 E. 4th St.
PO Box 331
Emporium, PA 15834
Phone: (800)892-7300
Fax: (814)486-3661
**Cities Served:** Emporium, PA
**Subscribing Households:** 2,115

**Barry Electronics Inc.** (26256)
Box 144
Commodore, PA 15729-1044
Phone: (724)254-1440
**Cities Served:** Bell Township, Mahaffey, PA
**Subscribing Households:** 2000

**Newport Cable TV Inc.** (5076)
61 Myrock Ave.
Box 6001
Waterford, CT 06385
Phone: (203)442-8525
Fax: (203)443-6031
**Subscribing Households:** 2,000

**Kearsarge Cable Communications Inc.** (18924)
173 Main St.
New London, NH 03257
Phone: (603)526-2211
Fax: (603)526-9910
**Cities Served:** New London, Wilmot, NH
**Subscribing Households:** 1,743

**Johnsonburg Community TV Co. Inc.** (26545)
Market Box 248
Johnsonburg, PA 15845
Phone: (814)965-4888
**Subscribing Households:** 1,621

**Trans-Video Inc.** (30918)
56 Depot Sq.
Northfield, VT 05663
Phone: (802)485-3811
Fax: (802)485-8451
**Cities Served:** Northfield, Northfield Falls, Riverton, VT
**Subscribing Households:** 1,600

**White Mountain Cablevision** (18781)
PO Box 66
Colebrook, NH 03576
Phone: (603)237-5573
Fax: (603)237-8256
**Cities Served:** Beecher Falls, Canaan, Lemington, VT
**Subscribing Households:** 1,584

**Southern Vermont Cable Co.** (30847)
PO Box 166
Bondville, VT 05340
Fax: (802)297-3714
**Cities Served:** Dummerston, Newfane, Putney, Townshed, VT
**Subscribing Households:** 1,262

**Youngsville TV Corp.** (27741)
3 W. Main St.
Youngsville, PA 16371
Phone: (814)563-3336
Fax: (814)563-7299
**Subscribing Households:** 1,230

**Duncan Cable TV** (30958)
Box 685
Wilmington, VT 05363
Phone: (802)464-2233
Fax: (802)464-3232
**Subscribing Households:** 1,100

**Millheim TV Transmission Co.** (26715)
PO Box 365
Millheim, PA 16854
Phone: (814)349-4837
Fax: (814)349-4416
**Cities Served:** Aaronsburg, Coburn, Millheim, Springmills, PA
**Subscribing Households:** 900

**Country Cable** (27450)
196 S. Main St.
Pleasant Gap, PA 16823
Phone: (814)359-3161
Fax: (814)359-2145
**Cities Served:** Huston Township, Union Township, Unionville, PA
**Subscribing Households:** 880

**SkiSat** (18960)
Box 465
Waterville Valley, NH 03215
Phone: (603)236-4850
Fax: (603)236-3661
**Subscribing Households:** 834

**Lincolnville Communications** (12535)
Box 200
Lincolnville, ME 04849
Phone: (207)763-9900
Fax: (207)763-9902
**Subscribing Households:** 800

**Somerfield Cable TV Co.** (26087)
6511 National Pike
Addison, PA 15411-9343
Phone: (814)395-3084
**Cities Served:** Addison, PA

**Subscribing Households:** 673

**Block Island Cable TV Inc. (27829)**
Drawer A-2
Block Island, RI 02807
Phone: (401)466-2479
Fax: (401)596-7366

**Subscribing Households:** 550

**Russell Municipal Cable TV (14773)**
Town Hall, 65 Main St.
Box 408
Russell, MA 01071
Phone: (413)862-4707
Fax: (413)862-3103

**Cities Served:** Russell, MA

**Subscribing Households:** 470

**Cable Communications of Willsboro (23192)**
6 Essex Rd.
PO Box 625
Willsboro, NY 12996
Phone: (518)963-4116
Fax: (518)963-7405

**Cities Served:** Essex, Willsboro, NY

**Subscribing Households:** 453

**Empire Access (22762)**
c/o N. Penn Telephone Co.
PO Box 349
Prattsburgh, NY 14873
Phone: (607)522-3712
Fax: (607)522-4228

**Cities Served:** East Smithfield, PA

**Subscribing Households:** 135

**C-Tec Cable Systems of PA, Inc. (26171)**
2124 Avenue C
Bethlehem, PA 18017-2120
Phone: (610)262-6100
Fax: (610)261-5099

**Subscribing Households:** 80

**Valley Cable Systems (26284)**
PO Box 78
Doylesburg, PA 17219
Phone: (717)349-7711

**Cities Served:** Allensville, PA

**Subscribing Households:** 88

**Barrett's TV Cable System (27587)**
RD 1, Box 197
Troy, PA 16947
Phone: (570)297-3607

**Cities Served:** Big Pond, Colxroads, Little Pond, West Burlington, PA

**Subscribing Households:** 70

## Southern Central States

**TCI Cablevision of Dallas, Inc. (29602)**
1565 Chenault St.
Dallas, TX 75228-5499
Phone: (214)828-9323
Fax: (214)320-7336

**Subscribing Households:** 136,000

**Time Warner Communications (29681)**
7010 Airport Rd.
El Paso, TX 79906-4943
Phone: (915)775-7441
Fax: (915)772-4605

**Cities Served:** Canutillo, El Paso, Socorro, TX

**Subscribing Households:** 120,000

**Cox Communications Oklahoma City (25486)**
2312 NW 10th St.
Oklahoma City, OK 73107
Phone: (405)600-8282
Fax: (405)600-9268

**Subscribing Households:** 118,000

**Jones Intercable Inc. (20018)**
4611 Montbel Pl., NE
Albuquerque, NM 87107
Fax: (505)761-6273

**Subscribing Households:** 115,000

**Time Warner Cable (30612)**
215 Factory Dr.
Box 7852
Waco, TX 76714-7852
Phone: (254)776-2996
Fax: (254)339-2023

**Cities Served:** Killeen, Temple, Waco, TX

**Subscribing Households:** 115,000

**Paragon Cable (29987)**
2951 Kinwest Pkwy.
Irving, TX 75063
Phone: (972)501-7000
Fax: (972)501-7070

**Subscribing Households:** 80,000

**Cox Cable Lubbock (30090)**
6710 Hartford Ave.
Lubbock, TX 79413
Phone: (806)698-8010
Fax: (806)793-7818

**Cities Served:** Lubbock, Midland, TX

**Subscribing Households:** 76,000

**Comcast (29115)**
2421 Matlock Rd.
Arlington, TX 76015
Phone: (972)647-5730
Fax: (817)548-7420

**Cities Served:** Dalworthington Gardens, Pantego, TX

**Subscribing Households:** 63,000

**Etan Industries, Inc. (29579)**
PO Box 802068
Dallas, TX 75380
Phone: (972)385-9601
Fax: (972)701-8332

**Subscribing Households:** 55,000

**Charter Communications (12171)**
701 Westin Oaks Dr.
Hammond, LA 70403
Phone: (504)549-1783
Fax: (504)543-0867

**Subscribing Households:** 43,000

**US Cable (30429)**
611 W. Avenue A
Seminole, TX 79360
Phone: (432)498-8420
Fax: (432)759-3379

**Cities Served:** Artesia, Carlsbad, Chama, Dexter, Dixon, Espanola, Eunice, Hagerman, Hobbs, Jal, Loving, Penasco, Tierra Amarilla, NM; Alpine, Comstock, Denver City, Fort Stockton, Iraan, Lajitas, McCamey, Rankin, Sanderson, Seagraves, Seminole, Van Horn, West Odessa, TX

**Subscribing Households:** 40,000

**Cox Communications (1097)**
314 S. 17th
Fort Smith, AR 72901-3408
Phone: (479)782-8941
Fax: (479)783-7892

**Cities Served:** Alma, Barling, Cedarville, Dyer, Ft. Smith, Greenwood, Hartford, Lavaca, Mansfield, Midland, Mount Burg, Mulberry, Rudy, Van Buren, AR; Muldrow, Roland, OK

**Subscribing Households:** 38,000

**Cox Communications (30172)**
PO Box 4247
Midland, TX 79704
Phone: (432)694-7721
Fax: (915)694-3267

**Subscribing Households:** 30,600

**Time Warner Cable (30646)**
3225 Maurine St.
Wichita Falls, TX 76305
Phone: (940)855-5700
Fax: (940)855-0465

**Subscribing Households:** 26,000

**Resort TV Cable Co., Inc. (1140)**
410 Airport Rd., Ste. H
Box 2770
Hot Springs National Park, AR 71914
Phone: (501)624-5781
Fax: (501)624-0502

**Cities Served:** Hot Springs, Mt. Pine, AR

**Subscribing Households:** 22,595

**Charter Communications (12419)**
1306 Ridgefield Rd.
PO Box 5178
Thibodaux, LA 70301
Phone: (888)821-4559
Fax: (985)447-9541

**Cities Served:** Labadieville, Napoleonvile, Paulina, Raceland, Thibodaux, Vacherie, LA

**Subscribing Households:** 22,467

**Lawton Cablevision Inc. (25395)**
Box 708A
Lawton, OK 73502
Phone: (580)353-2250
Fax: (580)355-7531

**Subscribing Households:** 22,057

**Cox Communications (1077)**
3390 N. Futrall Dr.
Fayetteville, AR 72703
Phone: (479)751-2000
Fax: (479)521-3825

**Subscribing Households:** 20,500

**Cox Communications (25573)**
802 E. 6th Ave.
Stillwater, OK 74074
Phone: (405)377-7785
Fax: (405)372-3980

**Cities Served:** Cushing, Perkins, Perry, Stillwater, OK

**Subscribing Households:** 16,000

**Cebridge Connections (30024)**
4103 W. Lake Houston Pkwy.
Kingwood, TX 77339
Phone: (281)360-2576
Fax: (281)360-1320

**Cities Served:** Forest Cove, Kingwood, Porter, TX

**Subscribing Households:** 15,000

**Cox Communications (25325)**
131 E. Main
Enid, OK 73701-5741
Phone: (580)363-1870
Fax: (580)242-4801

**Subscribing Households:** 15,000

**Cox Communications (20059)**
1106 Main St.
Box 1330
Clovis, NM 88101
Phone: (505)763-4411

**Cities Served:** Cannon AFB, Clovis, Texico, NM; Farwell, TX

**Subscribing Households:** 11,800

**Charter Communications (12123)**
4506 Country Drive
Bourg, LA 70343
Phone: (888)821-4559
Fax: (985)594-7953

**Subscribing Households:** 11,581

**East Arkansas Video, Inc. (1092)**
521 N. Washington
Forrest City, AR 72335
Phone: (870)238-3530
Fax: (970)633-8898

**Subscribing Households:** 11,000

**Cable One (25252)**
811 W. Broadway
Ardmore, OK 73401
Phone: (580)657-3312
Fax: (580)226-4472

**Subscribing Households:** 10,200

**CE Bridge Connections (12423)**
1000 W. LaSalle St.
Ville Platte, LA 70586
Phone: (337)363-0621
Fax: (337)363-9171

**Cities Served:** Iberia, Lydia, Mamou, Parish, Ville Platte, LA

**Subscribing Households:** 9,304

## Southern Central States

**Allen's TV Cable Service Inc.** (12278)
PO Box 2643
Morgan City, LA 70381
Phone: (504)384-8335
Fax: (504)384-5243
**Cities Served:** Bayou L'Ourse, Belle River, Berwick, Morgan City, Pierre Part, Stephensville, LA
**Subscribing Households:** 9,200

**Friendship Cable** (30554)
PO Box 139400
Tyler, TX 75713-9400
Phone: (903)833-5003
Fax: (903)859-4151
**Cities Served:** Boyce, Cheneyville, Clayton, Colfax, Cotton Port, Kolin, Krotz Springs, Lecompte, Montgomery, Moreauville, Natchez, Newellton, Simmersport, St. Joseph, Water Proof, Woodworth, LA
**Subscribing Households:** 8,700

**SWC Cable** (30059)
PO Box 1151
Lewisville, TX 75067
Phone: (972)353-9320
Fax: (817)627-8303
**Subscribing Households:** 8,100

**Cable One** (25235)
1610 Arlington, Bldg. 1
Ada, OK 74820
Phone: (405)332-8333
Fax: (405)332-4005
**Cities Served:** Ada, Byng, Francis, Pickett, OK
**Subscribing Households:** 7,000

**Williamson County Cablevision Co., Inc.** (29763)
111 N. College
Box 839
Georgetown, TX 78626
Phone: (512)869-2571
Fax: (512)869-2962
**Cities Served:** Georgetown, Jarrell, Leander, Pflugeville, TX
**Subscribing Households:** 7,000

**Guadalupe Valley Communications Systems Inc.** (29317)
1221 S. Main St.
Boerne, TX 78006
Phone: (830)249-8181
Fax: (830)249-8107
**Cities Served:** Boerne, Fair Oaks Ranch, South Canyon Lake, TX
**Subscribing Households:** 6,500

**CMA Communications** (12113)
PO Box 760
Belle Chasse, LA 70037
Phone: (504)392-4060
Fax: (504)393-7193
**Subscribing Households:** 6,000

**Comcast Cable** (20125)
PO Box 3290
Los Lunas, NM 87031
Phone: (505)865-2288
Fax: (505)865-5197
**Cities Served:** Belen, Los Lunas, NM
**Subscribing Households:** 5,700

**Cam-Tel Co.** (1031)
113 Madison Ave.
Box 835
Camden, AR 71701
Phone: (870)836-8111
Fax: (870)836-2109
**Subscribing Households:** 5,577

**Cabletel** (1024)
Box 127
Blytheville, AR 72316
Phone: (870)763-6688
Fax: (870)763-7683
**Cities Served:** Blytheville, Dell, AR
**Subscribing Households:** 5,300

**Time Warner Cable** (30436)
205 E. Ave. J
Silsbee, TX 77656
Phone: (409)385-4694
Fax: (409)385-2473
**Subscribing Households:** 5,173

**Time Warner Cable** (30573)
340 N. Getty St.
Uvalde, TX 78801
Phone: (830)278-2525
Fax: (830)278-2726
**Cities Served:** Uvalde, TX
**Subscribing Households:** 4,985

**TCA Cable TV** (30445)
2211 Ave. R
Box 366
Snyder, TX 79549
Phone: (915)573-3536
Fax: (915)573-6360
**Cities Served:** Snyder, TX
**Subscribing Households:** 4,700

**Crown Cable** (29996)
122 N. Austin
Jasper, TX 75951
Phone: (409)384-6862
Fax: (409)384-7817
**Subscribing Households:** 4,580

**Cable One** (25319)
210 N. Oklahoma
Box 863
Elk City, OK 73644
Phone: (580)225-3244
Fax: (580)225-5011
**Cities Served:** Elk City, OK
**Subscribing Households:** 4,300

**Cox Communications** (999)
2505 Pine St.
Box 1185
Arkadelphia, AR 71923
Phone: (870)246-7611
**Subscribing Households:** 4278

**Longview Kilgore Cable TV Co.** (30017)
910 N. Kilgore
Box 150
Kilgore, TX 75662
Phone: (903)984-8584
Fax: (903)983-1172
**Cities Served:** Kilgore, TX
**Subscribing Households:** 4,000

**Hereford Cablevision Co.** (29811)
119 E. 4th
PO Box 1656
Hereford, TX 79045
Phone: (806)364-3912
Fax: (806)364-7147
**Cities Served:** Hereford, TX
**Subscribing Households:** 3,960

**Comcast** (29771)
616 Oak St.
Box 958
Graham, TX 76450
Phone: (940)549-3737
**Cities Served:** Graham, TX
**Subscribing Households:** 3,526

**Cable One** (25294)
PO Box 367
Clinton, OK 73601-0367
Phone: (580)323-2225
Fax: (580)323-5869
**Cities Served:** Clinton, OK
**Subscribing Households:** 3,300

**Willow Park Cable T.V.** (29060)
Box 595
Aledo, TX 76008
Fax: (817)441-6464
**Subscribing Households:** 3,175

**Cox Communications** (12183)
208 Hudson Ave.
Jonesboro, LA 71251
Phone: (318)259-4447
Fax: (318)259-4446
**Cities Served:** East Hodge, Hodge, Jonesboro, North Hodge, Quitman, LA
**Subscribing Households:** 2,700

**Classic Cable** (30039)
403 E. 3rd St.
Box 71
Lampasas, TX 76550
Phone: (512)556-6112
Fax: (512)556-8244
**Cities Served:** Lampasas, TX
**Subscribing Households:** 2,350

**Gilmer Cable Television Co. Inc.** (29765)
PO Box 1600
Gilmer, TX 75644
Phone: (903)843-5597
Fax: (903)843-2045
**Subscribing Households:** 2,100

**Cable One** (25365)
315 S. Washington
PO Box 720
Hobart, OK 73651
Phone: (580)726-2523
Fax: (580)726-5818
**Cities Served:** Hobart, OK
**Subscribing Households:** 1,531

**Circle Bar Cable Television, Inc.** (30238)
PO Box 777
Ozona, TX 76943
Phone: (915)392-3323
Fax: (915)392-5878
**Subscribing Households:** 1,350

**Carlyss Cablevision, Inc.** (12411)
Box 2447
Sulphur, LA 70664-2447
Phone: (337)583-4973
Fax: (337)583-9854
**Subscribing Households:** 1,333

**Mountain Zone TV Systems** (29069)
PO Box 1377
Alpine, TX 79831-1377
Phone: (432)837-2300
Fax: (432)837-5423
**Cities Served:** Balmorhea, Fort Davis, Marathon, Marfa, Presidio, Valentine, TX
**Subscribing Households:** 1,300

**Comcast Cable** (20109)
110 E. Idaho Ave., A
Las Cruces, NM 88005-3253
Phone: (505)678-3440
Fax: (505)678-0328
**Subscribing Households:** 1040

**Classic Cable** (30552)
6151 Paluxy Dr.
Tyler, TX 75703
Phone: (903)833-5003
Fax: (409)246-3715
**Cities Served:** Grapeland, Latexo, TX
**Subscribing Households:** 642

**Cebridge Connections** (30551)
PO Box 139400
Tyler, TX 75713-9400
Fax: (903)561-6419
**Cities Served:** Hooker, OK
**Subscribing Households:** 633

**Mission Cable** (25683)
1904 Main St.
Woodward, OK 73801-2943
Phone: (580)254-2394
Fax: (580)938-2768
**Cities Served:** Shattuck, OK
**Subscribing Households:** 577

**Creekside Communications L.L.C.** (29373)
PO Box 1309
Burnet, TX 78611
**Subscribing Households:** 375

**Vi-Tel Inc. (25299)**
Box 789
Davenport, OK 74026
Phone: (918)377-2347
Fax: (918)377-2506
**Cities Served:** Davenport, OK
**Subscribing Households:** 282

**Mid-Coast Cable TV (29657)**
PO Box 1269
El Campo, TX 77437
Phone: (361)782-2993
Fax: (979)543-9501
**Cities Served:** Blessing, TX
**Subscribing Households:** 273

**Fort Davis TV Cable (29067)**
Box 1377
Alpine, TX 79831
Phone: (432)837-2300
Fax: (432)837-5423
**Cities Served:** Fort Davis, TX
**Subscribing Households:** 190

## Southern States

**Time Warner Cable (28784)**
6555 Quince Rd., No. 400
Memphis, TN 38119
Phone: (901)365-1770
Fax: (901)369-4515
**Cities Served:** Como, Robinsonville, Sardis Lake, MS
**Subscribing Households:** 220,000

**Viacom Cable (28903)**
660 Mainstream Dr.
Box 80570, Metro Center
Nashville, TN 37228-0570
Phone: (615)244-7462
Fax: (615)255-6528
**Cities Served:** Brentwood, TN
**Subscribing Households:** 139,000

**TCI of South Florida (6270)**
18601 NW 2nd Ave.
Miami, FL 33169
Phone: (305)620-8715
Fax: (305)614-6718
**Subscribing Households:** 125,000

**Time Warner Cable (23360)**
316 E. Morehead
Charlotte, NC 28202
Phone: (704)377-9600
Fax: (704)332-4550
**Cities Served:** Matthews, NC
**Subscribing Households:** 108,000

**Comcast Communications, Inc. (5973)**
644 S. Andrews Ave.
Fort Lauderdale, FL 33301
Phone: (954)527-6620
Fax: (954)523-4247
**Cities Served:** Aventura, Hallandale, Lauderdale-by-the-Sea, Oakland Park, Sea Ranch Lakes, FL
**Subscribing Households:** 105,000

**Media Partners (6415)**
A Division of Adelphia
1400 North Pt. Parkway
West Palm Beach, FL 33407
Phone: (561)844-3211
Fax: (561)844-6733
**Cities Served:** Palm Beach Gardens, FL
**Subscribing Households:** 100,000

**Scripps Howard Cable (28690)**
614 N. Central St.
Knoxville, TN 37917-7389
Phone: (615)971-1544
Fax: (615)637-8805
**Cities Served:** Knoxville, KY
**Subscribing Households:** 94,000

**Time Warner Cable (23533)**
1813 Spring Garden St.
Greensboro, NC 27403
Phone: (336)379-0200
Fax: (336)274-9609
**Cities Served:** Greensboro, NC
**Subscribing Households:** 94,000

**Adelphia (7042)**
156 Morningside Dr.
Box 785
Cartersville, GA 30120
Phone: (404)382-0531
Fax: (404)386-2540
**Cities Served:** Canton, Cartersville, GA; Mooresville, NC; Fredericksburg, Garrisonville, Warrenton, VA
**Subscribing Households:** 93,887

**Media One of South Florida (6070)**
2151 W. 62nd St.
Hialeah, FL 33016-2624
Phone: (305)456-4200
Fax: (305)819-5218
**Cities Served:** Coral Gables, Doral, Fountainbleau, Hialeah, Hialeah Gardens, Medley, Miami Lakes West, Miami Springs, Sweetwater, Virginia Gardens, West Miami, FL
**Subscribing Households:** 90,000

**Time Warner Cable (23877)**
1410 Trade Mart Blvd.
Winston-Salem, NC 27127
Phone: (336)785-3390
Fax: (336)785-9899
**Cities Served:** Bermuda Run, Clemmons, Davie County, Forsyth County, Kernersville, Lewisville, Rural Hall, Walkertown, Winston-Salem, NC
**Subscribing Households:** 85,141

**Time Warner Cable (28181)**
1901 Oak St.
Myrtle Beach, SC 29577
Fax: (843)913-7980
**Cities Served:** Andrews, Briarcliffe Acres, Carolina Forest, Conway, Forestbrook, Garden City, Georgetown, Horry County, Murrells Inlet, Myrtle Beach, North Myrtle Beach, Pawleys Island, Surfside Beach, SC
**Subscribing Households:** 85,000

**Insight Communications/ICN6 (11631)**
717 Madison Ave.
Covington, KY 41012
Phone: (859)431-7766
Fax: (859)491-6397
**Subscribing Households:** 82,000

**Time Warner Cable (16899)**
5375 Executive Pl.
Box 9426
Jackson, MS 39286
Phone: (601)982-1187
Fax: (601)321-3888
**Cities Served:** Bolton, Cleary Heights, Clinton, Edwards, Florence, Jackson, Madison, Pearl River Valley Water Dist., Raymond, Richland, Ridgeland, MS
**Subscribing Households:** 80,000

**Advance-Newhouse—Birmingham Division (110)**
6429 1st Ave. S.
Birmingham, AL 35212
Phone: (205)290-1300
Fax: (205)599-5657
**Subscribing Households:** 78,000

**Insight Cable (11780)**
2544 Palumbo Dr.
Lexington, KY 40509
Phone: (859)514-1400
Fax: (859)269-6990
**Subscribing Households:** 69,000

**Comcast (7403)**
5515 Abercorn St.
Box 22907
Savannah, GA 31405
Phone: (912)354-2813
Fax: (912)353-6045
**Cities Served:** Bloomingdale, Garden City, Midway, Pooler, Port Wentworth, Rincon, Springfield, Thunderbolt, Vernonburg, GA; Brunson, Varnville, SC
**Subscribing Households:** 66,000

**Comcast (6269)**
1306 NW 7th Ave.
Miami, FL 33136
Phone: (305)324-1194
Fax: (305)325-8741
**Cities Served:** Miami, Opa-Locka, FL
**Subscribing Households:** 65,000

**Cox Communications (6006)**
784 N. Beal Pkwy.
Drawer 2827
Fort Walton Beach, FL 32549
Phone: (850)862-0175
Fax: (850)862-1708
**Subscribing Households:** 58,300

**Comcast (6181)**
8130 County Rd. 44, Leg A
Leesburg, FL 34788-3704
Phone: (352)787-7875
Fax: (352)365-6279
**Cities Served:** Eustis, Fruitland Park, Howey-in-the-Hills, Lady Lake, Lake County, Montverde, Mount Dora, Mount Plymouth, Sorrento, Tavares, Umatilla, FL
**Subscribing Households:** 57,000

**Adelphia Cable (6720)**
500 Australian Ave. S, No. 1000
West Palm Beach, FL 33401
Phone: (561)833-8244
Fax: (561)833-6023
**Subscribing Households:** 48,500

**Charter Communications (6818)**
495 Hawthorne Ave., Ste. 102
Athens, GA 30606
Phone: (706)543-6585
Fax: (706)354-8027
**Subscribing Households:** 47,164

**Comcast Cablevision (273)**
2047 Max Luther Dr.
Huntsville, AL 35810
Phone: (256)859-7800
Fax: (256)852-5599
**Subscribing Households:** 45,000

**Wometco Cable (7217)**
6435 Tara Blvd., Ste. 22
Jonesboro, GA 30236
Phone: (404)340-0030
Fax: (404)471-6639
**Subscribing Households:** 45,000

**Comcast Cablevision of Tuscaloosa (471)**
700 14th St.
Parkview Center
Tuscaloosa, AL 35402
Phone: (205)345-0424
Fax: (205)345-8223
**Cities Served:** Northport, AL
**Subscribing Households:** 41,000

**Charter Communications (23578)**
1121 Lenoir-Rhyne Blvd.
PO Box 2989
Hickory, NC 28603
Phone: (828)322-3875
Fax: (828)322-5492
**Cities Served:** Catawba, Claremont, Denver, Granite Falls, Hickory, Hildebran, Longview, Maiden, Rhodhiss, Sherrills Ford, NC
**Subscribing Households:** 36,500

**Charter Communications, Inc. (28667)**
PO Box 3608
Kingsport, TN 37664
Phone: (423)247-7631
Fax: (423)247-1807
**Cities Served:** Kingsport, TN
**Subscribing Households:** 35,282

**Time Warner Cable (28096)**
3232 Bryson Dr.
Florence, SC 29501
Phone: (843)662-8191
Fax: (843)665-5483

# Southern States

**Subscribing Households:** 33,065

**Advanced Cable Communications (5900)**
12409 NW 35th St.
Coral Springs, FL 33065
Phone: (954)753-0100
Fax: (954)345-8164
**Cities Served:** Coral Springs, FL
**Subscribing Households:** 32,500

**Cox Communications (6344)**
Box 2318
Ocala, FL 34478
Phone: (352)237-1111
Fax: (352)237-6706
**Cities Served:** Ocala, Silver Springs, FL
**Subscribing Households:** 31,000

**Charter Communications (7431)**
PO Box 1470
Stockbridge, GA 30281
Phone: (770)320-8580
Fax: (770)389-0166
**Cities Served:** Stockbridge, GA
**Subscribing Households:** 28,000

**ParCable Inc. (16898)**
Box 260
Jackson, MS 39205
Phone: (601)354-5300
Fax: (601)354-4609
**Subscribing Households:** 25,000

**SusCom (16991)**
5193 Old Brandon Rd.
Pearl, MS 39208
Phone: (601)939-6240
Fax: (601)939-2912
**Cities Served:** Brandon, Florence, Flowood, Johns, Pearl, Pelahatchie, Puckett, Star, MS
**Subscribing Households:** 24,213

**Adelphia Cable Communication (28146)**
12 Pope Ave.
PO Box 5625
Hilton Head Island, SC 29928
Phone: (843)785-5175
Fax: (561)882-4338
**Subscribing Households:** 24,000

**Charter Communications (23256)**
220 Postal St.
Box 1219
Boone, NC 28607
Phone: (828)264-9411
Fax: (828)262-5703
**Cities Served:** Ashe County, Avery County, Watauga County, NC; Carter County, Johnson County, Unicol County, TN
**Subscribing Households:** 23,500

**Insight Communications (11560)**
515 Double Springs Rd.
Bowling Green, KY 42101
Phone: (270)782-0903
Fax: (270)782-8355
**Cities Served:** Alvaton, Bowling Green, Oakland, Richpond, Rockfield, Smiths Grove, Woodburn, KY
**Subscribing Households:** 23,000

**Catawba Services Inc. (28215)**
PO Box 11703
Rock Hill, SC 29731-1703
Phone: (803)326-2721
Fax: (803)324-2600
**Cities Served:** Rock Hill, SC
**Subscribing Households:** 22,487

**Inter Mountain Cable Inc. (11705)**
Box 159
Harold, KY 41635
Phone: (606)478-9406
Fax: (606)478-2280
**Subscribing Households:** 20,500

**Time Warner Cable (23769)**
1216 Lincolnton Rd.
Salisbury, NC 28147
Phone: (704)633-5484
Fax: (704)637-6978

**Cities Served:** Cleveland, East Spencer, Faith, Gold Hill, Granite Quarry, Rockwell, Salisbury, Spencer, Woodleaf, NC
**Subscribing Households:** 20,424

**Enstar Cable (23786)**
PO Box 1996
Snow Hill, NC 28580
Phone: (252)747-5682
Fax: (919)441-1581
**Subscribing Households:** 20,000

**Horry Telephone Cablevision (28084)**
3480 Hwy. 701 N.
PO Box 1820
Conway, SC 29526
Phone: (843)369-7873
Fax: (843)365-1111
**Cities Served:** Aynor, Bucksport, Conway, Little River, Longs, Loris, Wampee, SC
**Subscribing Households:** 20,000

**Sanmans Communications (28814)**
PO Box 1620
Morristown, TN 37816
Phone: (423)586-8700
Fax: (423)586-9065
**Subscribing Households:** 19,000

**Mediacom (6066)**
4435 Gulf Breeze Pkwy.
Gulf Breeze, FL 32561
Phone: (904)932-9233
Fax: (904)932-9237
**Subscribing Households:** 18,916

**Phenix City CATV (406)**
PO Box 130
Phenix City, AL 36868
Phone: (334)297-0310
Fax: (334)298-0833
**Cities Served:** Crawford, Fort Mitchell, Hatchechubee, Hurtsboro, Phenix City, Salem, Seale, Smiths, AL
**Subscribing Households:** 17,000

**Charter Communications, L.P. (7)**
1232 Cherokee Rd.
PO Box 687
Alexander City, AL 35010
Phone: (256)234-3456
Fax: (256)329-0716
**Cities Served:** Alexander City, Camp Hill, Goodwater, Jackson's Gap, New Site, Rockford, AL
**Subscribing Households:** 16,000

**Otar Cable TV Co. (23395)**
651 S. Main St.
PO Box 950
Dobson, NC 27017
Phone: (336)386-4461
Fax: (540)864-5656
**Cities Served:** Carrol, Craig, Floyd, VA
**Subscribing Households:** 14,200

**United Cable Systems Inc. (11724)**
Box 1410
Hindman, KY 41822
Phone: (606)785-3450
Fax: (606)785-3110
**Subscribing Households:** 12,784

**Comcast (7179)**
1150 Everee Inn Rd.
Griffin, GA 30224
Phone: (770)228-3333
Fax: (770)228-1982
**Subscribing Households:** 12,200

**Adelphia (16832)**
PO Box 1119
Greenwood, MS 38935-1119
Phone: (662)453-1168
Fax: (662)453-3084
**Subscribing Households:** 12,146

**Century Cullman Corp. (171)**
256 US Hwy. 278 E.
Cullman, AL 35055-8691
Phone: (205)739-4451
Fax: (205)734-8463

**Cities Served:** Blountsville, Cullman, Hanceville, Warrior, AL
**Subscribing Households:** 12,000

**Adelphia (27823)**
Sabana Seca Ave.
Box 51508
Toa Baja, PR 00950-2296
Phone: (787)261-0525
Fax: (787)784-2735
**Cities Served:** Baja, Catano, Toa, Toa Alta, PR
**Subscribing Households:** 11,500

**TV Service Inc. (11723)**
Box 1410
Hindman, KY 41822
Phone: (606)785-3450
Fax: (606)785-3110
**Subscribing Households:** 10,300

**Adelphia (28142)**
1920 W. Bobo Newsome Hwy.
Box 1069
Hartsville, SC 29550
Phone: (843)332-0195
Fax: (843)383-6253
**Cities Served:** Cheraw, Hartsville, SC
**Subscribing Households:** 10,000

**CableONE, Inc. (28590)**
416 W. Court
Box 888
Dyersburg, TN 38024
Phone: (901)285-4174
Fax: (901)287-8040
**Cities Served:** Dyersburg, Friendship, TN
**Subscribing Households:** 9,745

**Comcast (6429)**
1316 Harrison Ave.
Panama City, FL 32401-2435
Phone: (850)769-0392
Fax: (850)769-8074
**Cities Served:** Panama City Beach, FL
**Subscribing Households:** 8,500

**Northland Cable TV (7427)**
32 E. Vine St.
PO Box 407
Statesboro, GA 30458
Phone: (912)489-8715
Fax: (912)489-5479
**Cities Served:** Brooklet, Statesboro, GA
**Subscribing Households:** 8,500

**Charter Communications (28163)**
PO Box 850
Laurens, SC 29360
Phone: (864)682-2222
Fax: (864)682-4576
**Subscribing Households:** 8,000

**Charter Communications (11869)**
30 Oakdale Ave.
Madisonville, KY 42431-3237
Phone: (270)821-6777
Fax: (270)821-6152
**Subscribing Households:** 7,300

**Comporium Communications (28102)**
PO Box 1299
Fort Mill, SC 29716
Phone: (803)548-6000
Fax: (803)547-6655
**Cities Served:** Fort Mill, Regent Park, Tega Cay, SC
**Subscribing Households:** 7,299

**Comcast (6099)**
5805 S. Point Pkwy.
Jacksonville, FL 32211-7028
Phone: (904)261-3624
Fax: (904)374-8472
**Cities Served:** Amelia Island, Callghan, Fernandina, Folkston, Hilliard, Kings Bay, Nahunta, Plantation, GA
**Subscribing Households:** 7,200

**Northland Cable Television (17016)**
PO Box 1447
Starkville, MS 39759
Phone: (662)323-1615
Fax: (662)323-1682
**Subscribing Households:** 7,000

**Sylvan Valley CATV Co. (23262)**
Box 1177
Brevard, NC 28712
Phone: (828)884-2671
Fax: (828)885-2300
**Cities Served:** Brevard, Rosman, NC
**Subscribing Households:** 6,990

**Communicomm Services (6072)**
17774 NW US Hwy. 441
PO Box 905
High Springs, FL 32655
Phone: (386)454-2299
Fax: (386)454-3705
**Subscribing Households:** 6,800

**West Alabama TV Cable Co. (215)**
Box 660
Fayette, AL 35555
Phone: (205)932-4700
Fax: (205)932-3585
**Cities Served:** Belk, Brilliant, Detroit, Fayette, Hamilton, Winfield, AL
**Subscribing Households:** 6,775

**Riviera Utilities Cable TV (228)**
413 E. Laurel Ave.
PO Box 2050
Foley, AL 36536
Phone: (251)943-5001
Fax: (251)943-5275
**Subscribing Households:** 6,675

**Charter Communications (11646)**
Box 9001736
Douglas, KY 41560
Phone: (912)384-4675
Fax: (912)384-4132
**Subscribing Households:** 6,200

**Better Vision Cable Co. (414)**
Box 900
Roanoke, AL 36274
Phone: (334)863-8112
Fax: (334)863-2027
**Subscribing Households:** 5,700

**Charter Communications (7477)**
4020 US Hwy. 41 S
Valdosta, GA 31601-2164
**Subscribing Households:** 5,100

**TWC of North Carolina (23737)**
PO Box 1886
Reidsville, NC 27323-1886
Phone: (910)627-5161
Fax: (910)627-9780
**Cities Served:** Eden, Madison, Mayodan, NC
**Subscribing Households:** 4,981

**Northland Cable (16815)**
Box 1538
Forest, MS 39074
Phone: (601)469-3712
Fax: (601)469-4203
**Subscribing Households:** 4,250

**Northland Cable (16919)**
Box 1667
Kosciusko, MS 39090
Phone: (662)289-3281
Fax: (662)289-2910
**Subscribing Households:** 4,000

**American Cablevision Services Inc. (6144)**
4100 Pleasant Hill Rd.
Kissimmee, FL 34746-2940
Phone: (407)933-5308
Fax: (407)343-8021
**Cities Served:** Kissimmee, Poinciana, FL
**Subscribing Households:** 3,800

**Kings Bay Communications, Inc. (7220)**
PO Box 1267
Kingsland, GA 31548
Phone: (912)729-3153
**Cities Served:** Camden County, Kingsland, GA
**Subscribing Households:** 3,650

**Ripley Video Cable Co. (17008)**
115 N. Main St.
Ripley, MS 38663
Phone: (662)837-4881
Fax: (662)837-9332
**Cities Served:** Blue Mountain, Falkner, Pine Grove, Ripley, MS
**Subscribing Households:** 3,654

**Charter Communications (7184)**
PO Box 329
536 E. Robinson Ave.
Grovetown, GA 30813-0329
Phone: (706)860-1580
Fax: (864)254-7373
**Subscribing Households:** 3,480

**Tri-County Cable (249)**
Box 886
Guin, AL 35563
Phone: (205)468-3601
Fax: (205)468-2200
**Subscribing Households:** 3,400

**Twin County Cablevision (17045)**
917 Robinson
PO Box 61
Waynesboro, MS 39367-0061
Phone: (601)776-3426
Fax: (601)735-0249
**Subscribing Households:** 3,400

**Galaxy Cable (16774)**
PO Box 570
Canton, MS 39046
Fax: (601)859-1821
**Subscribing Households:** 3,315

**Harlan Community Television Inc. (11701)**
124 S. 1st St.
Box 592
Harlan, KY 40831
Phone: (606)573-2945
Fax: (606)573-6959
**Subscribing Households:** 3,250

**Charter Communications (11958)**
3004 S. Lake Dr.
PO Box 699
Prestonsburg, KY 41653
Phone: (606)886-2291
Fax: (606)886-1075
**Subscribing Households:** 3,100

**Charter Communications (485)**
204C S. Elm St.
Tuskegee, AL 36083
Phone: (205)727-4484
Fax: (205)727-4554
**Cities Served:** Tuskegee, AL
**Subscribing Households:** 3000

**Southern Cable Communications (28108)**
PO Box 1998
2101 S Frasier
Georgetown, SC 29442
Phone: (843)546-2200
Fax: (843)527-2374
**Cities Served:** Plantation, NC; Bald Head, Brick Landing, Holden Beach, Lakeview, Nicoles, Sunset Harbor, SC
**Subscribing Households:** 3,000

**Big Sandy TV Cable, Inc. (12020)**
PO Box 586
West Van Lear, KY 41268
Phone: (606)789-3455
Fax: (606)789-5352
**Subscribing Households:** 2,750

**Trenton TV Cable Co. (29016)**
PO Box 345
Trenton, TN 38382
Phone: (731)855-2808

Fax: (731)855-9512
**Cities Served:** Trenton, TN
**Subscribing Households:** 2,400

**Northland Cable Television (23596)**
479 South St.
PO Box 1087
PO Box 1087
Highlands, NC 28741
Phone: (828)526-5675
Fax: (828)526-9266
**Subscribing Households:** 2,384

**Charter Communications (27961)**
306 S. Main St.
Abbeville, SC 29620
Phone: (864)459-9646
Fax: (864)254-7373
**Subscribing Households:** 2,289

**Century Communication (7023)**
Box 1336
Brunswick, GA 31521
Phone: (912)264-1569
Fax: (912)264-4618
**Subscribing Households:** 1,970

**Belhaven Cable TV (23240)**
235 Pamolico St.
PO Box 8
Belhaven, NC 27810
Phone: (252)943-3736
Fax: (252)943-3738
**Subscribing Households:** 1600

**Luverne TV Cable Service (303)**
514 Forest Ave.
Luverne, AL 36049
Phone: (334)335-5059
**Cities Served:** Brantley, Crenshaw County, Glenwood, Luverne, Rutledge, AL
**Subscribing Households:** 1,550

**Kennedy Cablevision, Inc. (7357)**
Hwy. 280 W
PO Box 2059
Reidsville, GA 30453
Phone: (912)557-6133
Fax: (912)557-6515
**Cities Served:** Cobbtown, Reidsville, GA
**Subscribing Households:** 1400

**Adelphia (12008)**
323 Lexington Ave.
Vanceburg, KY 41179
Phone: (606)796-3490
**Cities Served:** Blackoak, Green Valley, Vanceburg, KY
**Subscribing Households:** 1,150

**Galaxy Cablevision (16965)**
PO Box 308
Monticello, MS 39654
Phone: (601)587-7861
Fax: (601)587-7410
**Subscribing Households:** 1,025

**Valley Cable TV Inc. (7160)**
PO Box 508
Fort Valley, GA 31030
Phone: (478)825-3626
Fax: (478)825-1639
**Subscribing Households:** 650

**Farmers Telephone Cooperative Inc. (28159)**
1101 E. Main St.
PO Box 588
Kingstree, SC 29556
Phone: (843)382-1387
Fax: (843)382-3909
**Cities Served:** Olanta, Turbeville, SC
**Subscribing Households:** 609

**Piedmont Cable Corp. (7358)**
PO Box 2059
228 W. Brazell
Reidsville, GA 30453
Phone: (912)557-6133
Fax: (912)557-6545
**Cities Served:** Byron, Fort Valley, Lizella, GA

**Subscribing Households:** 600

**Black Mountain Television (11866)**
PO Box 698
Lynch, KY 40855
Phone: (606)848-2977
Fax: (606)848-7379
**Cities Served:** Lynch, KY
**Subscribing Households:** 390

**Time Warner Cable (23788)**
390 W Pennsylvania
Southern Pines, NC 28387
Phone: (910)692-6684
**Cities Served:** Pinehurst, NC
**Subscribing Households:** 340

**Leesburg Lakeshore Mobile Home Park (6182)**
1208 N. Lee St.
Leesburg, FL 34748
Phone: (352)787-5683
Fax: (352)787-1561
**Subscribing Households:** 184

## Western States

**Cox Enterprises (2015)**
9451 Toledo Way
Irvine, CA 92618-1805
Phone: (949)660-0500
Fax: (949)546-2000
**Subscribing Households:** 1,300,000

**Comcast Spotlight (25992)**
2000 SW 1st Ave., Ste. 200
Portland, OR 97201
Phone: (503)295-0123
Fax: (503)295-1006
**Cities Served:** Corvallis, Eugene, Portland, Salem, OR; Vancouver, WA
**Subscribing Households:** 572,000

**Comcast Cable (4366)**
6850 S. Tucson Way
Englewood, CO 80112
Phone: (303)444-7331
Fax: (303)778-2912
**Subscribing Households:** 397,000

**CableRep Las Vegas (18706)**
1433 Mineral Ave.
Las Vegas, NV 89106-4342
**Subscribing Households:** 390,000

**Cox Communications (3068)**
5159 Federal Blvd.
San Diego, CA 92105
Phone: (619)263-9251
Fax: (619)266-5555
**Cities Served:** Alpine, Chula Vista, City of San Diego, El Cajon, Imperial Beach, La Mesa, Lemon Grove, National City, Pine Valley, Poway, Santee, CA
**Subscribing Households:** 326,000

**Oceanic Cablevision, Inc. (7634)**
200 Akamainui St.
Mililani, HI 96789
Phone: (808)625-8100
Fax: (808)625-5888
**Subscribing Households:** 245,000

**Cox Communications (2774)**
29947 Avenida de las Bandera
Rancho Santa Margarita, CA 92688-2113
Phone: (949)546-2000
Fax: (714)661-7297
**Cities Served:** Dana Point, Irvine, Laguna Beach, Laguna Hills, Laguna Nigel, Lake Forest, Mission Viejo, Newport Beach, Orange, San Clemente, Tustin, CA
**Subscribing Households:** 227,000

**Comcast Cablevision (3412)**
1830 E. Warner Ave.
Santa Ana, CA 92705-5505
Phone: (714)338-2027
Fax: (714)871-8136

**Cities Served:** Buena Park, Fullerton, Newport Beach, Placentia, Santa Ana, Seal Beach, CA
**Subscribing Households:** 225,000

**Comcast (2922)**
4350 Pell Dr.
Sacramento, CA 95838
Phone: (916)927-2225
Fax: (916)927-0605
**Subscribing Households:** 210,000

**Time Warner Cable - San Diego (3097)**
8949 Ware Ct.
San Diego, CA 92121
Fax: (858)566-6248
**Cities Served:** Clairemont, Del Mar Heights, La Jolla, Linda Vista, Mira Mesa, Mission Beach, North Poway, Pacific Beach, San Diego County, Tierrasanta, University City, CA
**Subscribing Households:** 205,000

**Comcast (3315)**
1900 South 10 St.
San Jose, CA 95112
Phone: (408)918-3200
Fax: (408)294-7280
**Cities Served:** Campbell, San Jose, Santa Clara West County, CA
**Subscribing Households:** 196,000

**Northland Communications Corp. (32372)**
101 Stewart, No. 700
Seattle, WA 98101
Phone: (206)621-1351
Fax: (206)623-9015
**Subscribing Households:** 176,420

**Comcast (32443)**
2316 S. State St.
Tacoma, WA 98405
Phone: (253)503-8000
Fax: (253)503-8100
**Subscribing Households:** 153,000

**Adelphia Communications (4221)**
213 N. Union Blvd.
Colorado Springs, CO 80909-5705
Phone: (719)457-4501
Fax: (719)457-4503
**Subscribing Households:** 136,000

**Time Warner Communications (1921)**
1199 Valley View
Garden Grove, CA 92845
Phone: (714)903-8200
Fax: (714)898-1524
**Cities Served:** Fountain Valley, Garden Grove, Huntington Beach, Los Alamitos, Orange, Rossmoor, Stanton, Westminster, CA
**Subscribing Households:** 130,000

**Comcast (25991)**
3075 NE Sandy Blvd.
Portland, OR 97232
Phone: (503)605-6000
Fax: (503)230-2218
**Subscribing Households:** 128,000

**Charter Communications (18747)**
9335 Prototype Dr.
Reno, NV 89511
Phone: (775)850-1200
Fax: (775)850-1229
**Subscribing Households:** 117,000

**Comcast Cablevision of California, Inc. (2624)**
1260 DuPont St.
Ontario, CA 91761
Phone: (909)475-5600
Fax: (909)988-8432
**Subscribing Households:** 100,000

**Comcast Cable (32397)**
1717 E. Buckeye
Box Hay C-1
Spokane, WA 99207
Phone: (509)484-4931
Fax: (509)483-9261
**Cities Served:** Millwood, Spokane, WA
**Subscribing Households:** 91,000

**Bright House Networks (1410)**
3701 N. Sillect Ave.
Bakersfield, CA 93308
Phone: (661)323-4892
Fax: (661)634-2255
**Subscribing Households:** 90,022

**Mission Cable Co. (4351)**
1873 S. Bellaire St., No. 1550
Denver, CO 80222-4348
Fax: (303)756-5774
**Subscribing Households:** 80,000

**TCI Oakland (2610)**
4215 Foothill Blvd.
Oakland, CA 94601
Phone: (510)534-3364
Fax: (510)436-7531
**Cities Served:** Emeryville, Oakland, Piedmont, CA
**Subscribing Households:** 72,000

**Adelphia (2529)**
2323 Teller Rd.
Newbury Park, CA 91320
Phone: (805)375-3121
Fax: (805)375-3176
**Cities Served:** Agoura, Calabasas, Camarillo, Fillmore, Moorpark, Newbury Park, Ojai, Piru, Santa Paula, Thousand Oaks, Westlake Village, CA
**Subscribing Households:** 70,000

**Adelphia (1376)**
3041 E. Miraloma Ave.
Anaheim, CA 92806
Phone: (714)632-9222
Fax: (714)630-4353
**Subscribing Households:** 66,000

**Adelphia (1616)**
5720 El Camino Real
Carlsbad, CA 92008
Phone: (760)438-7741
Fax: (760)438-8461
**Cities Served:** Carlsbad, Del Mar, Encinitas, Fallbrook, Lake San Marcos, Solana Beach, Vista, CA
**Subscribing Households:** 65,000

**Comcast Cablevision (25814)**
2897 Chad Dr.
Eugene, OR 97408
Phone: (541)484-3000
Fax: (541)343-5025
**Cities Served:** Avadore, Eugene, Glenwood, Harrisburg, Junction City, Santa Clara, Springfield, OR
**Subscribing Households:** 60,000

**Time Warner Cable (3914)**
1511 Cravens Ave.
Torrance, CA 90501
Phone: (310)618-9496
Fax: (310)618-1049
**Subscribing Households:** 60,000

**Charter Communications (3342)**
PO Box 1205
San Luis Obispo, CA 93406
Phone: (805)238-1397
Fax: (805)541-6042
**Cities Served:** Arroyo Grande, Avila Beach, Cayucos, Grover Beach, Heritage Ranch, Morro Bay, Nipomo, Paso Robles, Pismo Beach, San Luis Obispo, San Miguel, CA
**Subscribing Households:** 47,000

**Comcast Communications (4506)**
434 Kimbark St.
Longmont, CO 80501
Phone: (303)776-6600
Fax: (303)678-5302
**Cities Served:** Battlement Mesa, Berthoud, Ft. Lupton, Lafayette, Longmont, Louisville, Lovebud, Parachute, Superior, CO
**Subscribing Households:** 45,000

**TCI Hawaiian Islands (7614)**
350 Hoohana
Kahului, HI 96732
Fax: (808)877-3534
**Cities Served:** Hawaii Kai (Honolulu), Ka'u District, Lanai, Maui, Molokai, HI

Subscribing Households: 39,521

**Charter Communications (3990)**
12490 Business Center Dr., Ste. 2
Victorville, CA 92392
Phone: (760)843-3000
Fax: (760)241-7659
Cities Served: Apple Valley, Hesperia, Spring Valley Lake, Victorville, CA
Subscribing Households: 35,000

**Comcast (1745)**
5595 Corporate Dr.
Cypress, CA 90630
Phone: (714)816-0569
Fax: (714)220-3921
Cities Served: Cypress, LaPalma, Lakewood, CA
Subscribing Households: 25,000

**Wave Broadband (32206)**
4519 S. E. Mile Hill Dr.
Port Orchard, WA 98366
Phone: (360)871-4043
Fax: (360)871-5418
Subscribing Households: 24,000

**Cox Cable Bakersfield (1411)**
820 22nd St.
Bakersfield, CA 93301
Phone: (661)327-0821
Fax: (661)327-7921
Cities Served: Bakersfield, CA
Subscribing Households: 22,600

**Oceanic Time Warner (7630)**
3022 Peleke St., Ste. 8
Lihue, HI 96766
Phone: (808)245-7720
Fax: (808)245-5221
Cities Served: Barking Sands Naval Base, Kauai County, HI
Subscribing Households: 20,000

**Adelphia (4015)**
20965 Lycoming St.
Walnut, CA 91789
Phone: (909)594-2729
Fax: (909)598-0235
Cities Served: Diamond Bar, Rowland Heights, CA
Subscribing Households: 19,500

**Cable One (7812)**
261 Eastland Dr.
Box 1946
Twin Falls, ID 83301
Phone: (208)733-6230
Fax: (208)733-6296
Cities Served: Burley, Filer, Gooding, Hansen, Heyburn, Jerome, Kimberly, Oakley, Paul, Rupert, Twin Falls, Wendell, ID
Subscribing Households: 18,462

**Oceanic Time Warner (7625)**
910 Honoapiilani Hwy., Ste. 6
910 Honoapiilani Hwy., Ste. 6
Lahaina, HI 96761
Phone: (808)661-4607
Fax: (808)661-8865
Subscribing Households: 17,500

**AT&T Broadband (30694)**
1350 North 200 West
Logan, UT 84321
Phone: (435)752-9731
Fax: (435)753-6099
Cities Served: Bear Lake, Preston, ID; Tremonton, UT
Subscribing Households: 17,185

**Hawaiian Cablevision (7519)**
1257 Kilauea Ave.
Hilo, HI 96720-4205
Phone: (808)961-0443
Fax: (808)961-2518
Subscribing Households: 17,000

**Wireless Broadcasting Systems of Sacramento, Inc. (2959)**
1513 Sports Dr., No. 9
Sacramento, CA 95834
Fax: (916)928-0825

Cities Served: Arden-Arcade, Sacramento, CA
Subscribing Households: 17,000

**Bresnan Communications (33688)**
451 S. Durbin
Casper, WY 82601
Phone: (307)265-3130
Fax: (307)266-6821
Cities Served: Bar Nunn, Evansville, Mills, Mountain View, Natrona County, Paradise Valley, WY
Subscribing Households: 16,500

**Cablevision of Lake Havasu City (706)**
730 N. Acoma
Lake Havasu City, AZ 86403
Phone: (928)855-7815
Fax: (928)855-1979
Cities Served: Desert Hills, Lake Havasu City, AZ
Subscribing Households: 16000

**Cable One (7775)**
204 W. Alameda Rd.
Pocatello, ID 83201
Phone: (208)232-1784
Fax: (208)234-4756
Subscribing Households: 15,000

**Charter Communications (32478)**
126 W. Poplar
Walla Walla, WA 99362
Phone: (509)529-9500
Fax: (509)522-1719
Cities Served: Milton-Freewater, OR; College Place, Dixie, Prescott, Starbuck, Waitsburg, Walla Walla, Washtucna, WA
Subscribing Households: 14,500

**Independent Cable Systems of Idaho (7807)**
Box 858
Soda Springs, ID 83276
Phone: (208)547-4341
Fax: (208)547-4833
Subscribing Households: 14,000

**Pullman TV Cable Co., Inc. (7755)**
PO Box 8336
Moscow, ID 83843
Fax: (208)882-9106
Cities Served: Genesse, Julietta, Kendrick, Onaway, Potlatch, ID; Albion, Colton, Moscow, Palouse, Pullman, Uniontown, WA
Subscribing Households: 14,000

**Charter Communications (1539)**
41490 Big Bear Blvd.
Box 1771
Big Bear Lake, CA 92315
Phone: (909)866-0475
Fax: (909)866-9519
Subscribing Households: 13,000

**San Bruno Municipal Cable TV (2992)**
398 El Camino Real
San Bruno, CA 94066
Phone: (650)616-3100
Fax: (650)871-5526
Subscribing Households: 12,049

**Eagle West, L. L. C. (716)**
9333 E. Apache, No. 3C
Mesa, AZ 85207
Phone: (800)558-5564
Fax: (602)380-5877
Cities Served: Alpine, Bagdad, Black Canyon City, Casa Grande, Christopher Creek, Coucho Valley, Eagar, East Mesa, Florence Gardens, Kohl's Ranch, Springerville, St. Johns, Tonto Village, Williams, Yarnell, AZ; Glenwood, Reserve, NM
Subscribing Households: 12,000

**TCI Cable (3916)**
305 W. 11th St.
PO Box 530
Tracy, CA 95376
Fax: (209)832-1148
Subscribing Households: 12,000

**Wave Broadband (32204)**
725 E. 1st St.
Port Angeles, WA 98362
Phone: (360)452-8466
Fax: (360)457-5901
Cities Served: Clallam Bay, Port Angeles, Sekiu, Sequim, WA
Subscribing Households: 11,500

**Sweetwater Cable Television Co. (33787)**
602 Broadway
Rock Springs, WY 82901
Phone: (307)362-3773
Fax: (307)382-2781
Cities Served: Green River, Rock Springs, WY
Subscribing Households: 10,696

**Avenue TV Cable Service Inc. (3983)**
1954 E. Main St.
PO Box 1458
Ventura, CA 93002
Fax: (805)643-1284
Cities Served: New Cuyama, Ventura, CA
Subscribing Households: 10,500

**Comcast Cable (4091)**
201 Aspen Airport Bus. Ctr.
Aspen, CO 81611
Phone: (970)925-4098
Fax: (970)925-4106
Subscribing Households: 10,289

**Desert Hot Springs Cablevision (1771)**
11855 Palm Dr.
Desert Hot Springs, CA 92240
Phone: (760)251-6539
Fax: (760)329-0792
Cities Served: Desert Hot Springs, CA
Subscribing Households: 10,000

**GCI (543)**
505 Old Steve Hwy., Ste. 101
Fairbanks, AK 99701
Phone: (907)452-7191
Fax: (907)456-3163
Cities Served: Eielson, Fairbanks, Fort Greely, Fort Wainwright, North Pole, North Star Bourough, AK
Subscribing Households: 10,000

**Crestview Cable TV (26021)**
350 N. E. Dunham
Prineville, OR 97754
Phone: (541)447-4342
Fax: (541)447-5987
Cities Served: Culver, Enterprise, Joseph, La Pine, Lostines, Madras, Metolius, Prineville, Wallowa, Wallowa Lake, OR
Subscribing Households: 9,600

**Volcano Vision, Inc. (2737)**
Box 890
Pine Grove, CA 95665
Phone: (209)296-2288
Fax: (209)296-2230
Cities Served: Comancha, Jackson, Kirkwood, Pine Grove, Pioneer, Volcano, West Point, CA
Subscribing Households: 8,900

**Mediacom Az, LLc (722)**
PO Box 400
Nogales, AZ 85628-0400
Phone: (520)287-3123
Fax: (520)287-4010
Cities Served: Ajo, Amado, Arivaca Jct., Nogales, Rio Rico, AZ
Subscribing Households: 8,500

**Knology Broadband of California (1637)**
13100 Alondra Blvd., Ste. 104
Cerritos, CA 90703
Phone: (562)802-2253
Fax: (562)926-8017
Cities Served: Cerritos, CA
Subscribing Households: 8,100

**American Cablevision of South Pasadena (3544)**
1024 Mission St. Frnt.
South Pasadena, CA 91030-5215
Cities Served: San Marino, South Pasadena, CA

# Western States

Subscribing Households: 7,800

**Charter Communications (32077)**
1105 E. 10th Ave.
Box 674
Ellensburg, WA 98926
Phone: (509)925-9210
Fax: (509)962-2034

Cities Served: Ellensburg, Kittitas, WA

Subscribing Households: 7,628

**Adelphia (2383)**
912 N. Eastern Ave.
Los Angeles, CA 90063
Phone: (323)269-0391
Fax: (323)269-8257

Subscribing Households: 6,250

**Sedona Cablevision (840)**
65 Coffee Pot Dr.
Sedona, AZ 86336
Fax: (928)282-6336

Cities Served: Sedona, Village of Oak Creek, AZ

Subscribing Households: 5,671

**GCI (623)**
Box 873107
501 N. Main Street
Wasilla, AK 99654
Phone: (907)373-2288
Fax: (907)376-8888

Cities Served: Palmer, Wasilla, AK

Subscribing Households: 5,600

**Tri-Lakes Cable (4524)**
47 3rd St.
Box 1929
Monument, CO 80132
Fax: (719)481-2211

Cities Served: Gleneagle, Monument, CO

Subscribing Households: 5,100

**Eagle West LLC (696)**
PO Box 567
Kearny, AZ 85237
Phone: (602)363-5525
Fax: (602)363-5191

Subscribing Households: 5,000

**British-American Communications (3582)**
7469 Foothill Blvd.
Sunland, CA 91040-2958
Phone: (818)951-3900
Fax: (818)951-2951

Cities Served: Century City, Marina Del Ray, Studio City, West Los Angeles, CA

Subscribing Households: 4,800

**Telepro Communications (32004)**
1200 112th Ave. NE, Ste. C115
Bellevue, WA 98004-3745
Phone: (425)957-4730
Fax: (425)957-0119

Cities Served: Costa Mesa, Culver City, Marina del Rey, Mira Loma, Ontario, Rialto, Riverside, CA; Bellevue, WA

Subscribing Households: 4,200

**Cable One (689)**
727 Paxton Ave.
PO Box 69
Globe, AZ 85502
Phone: (928)425-3161
Fax: (928)425-5404

Cities Served: Central Heights, Globe, Miami, Wheatfield, AZ

Subscribing Households: 4000

**Bresnan Communications (18212)**
924 S. 3rd St. W.
Missoula, MT 59801
Phone: (406)728-4200
Fax: (406)542-3914

Cities Served: Alberton, Arlee, Big Flat, Bonner, Clinton, Florence, Frenchtown, Grant Creek, Huson, Lolo, Milltown, Polson, Seeley Lake, Superior, Victor, MT

Subscribing Households: 3,681

**Charter Communications (2758)**
Box 1210
Portola, CA 96122
Fax: (916)832-4465

Cities Served: Blairsden, Crescent Mills, Graeagle, Greenville, Loyalton, Portola, Quincy, CA

Subscribing Households: 3,650

**Green River Cable TV Co. (33738)**
151 E. Flaming Gorge Way
Green River, WY 82935
Phone: (307)875-2506
Fax: (307)382-2781

Cities Served: Green River, WY

Subscribing Households: 3,554

**Comcast (4503)**
7580 S. Pierce St., Unit 7
Littleton, CO 80123
Phone: (303)930-2000
Fax: (303)972-9417

Cities Served: Evergreen, Idledale, Kittredge, CO

Subscribing Households: 3,500

**Adelphia (18187)**
Box 1378
Libby, MT 59923
Phone: (406)293-8788
Fax: (406)293-3630

Cities Served: Bonners Ferry, ID; Libby, Troy, MT

Subscribing Households: 3,240

**Adelphia Communications (33730)**
1020 Main St.
Evanston, WY 82930
Phone: (307)789-7042
Fax: (307)789-7754

Cities Served: Evanston, WY

Subscribing Households: 3200

**Cable One (633)**
99 Bisbee Rd.
Bisbee, AZ 85603
Phone: (520)432-4807
Fax: (520)432-7981

Subscribing Households: 3,000

**Kodiak Cablevision (591)**
2011 Mill Bay Rd.
Kodiak, AK 99615
Phone: (907)486-3334
Fax: (907)486-5160

Cities Served: Kodiak, AK

Subscribing Households: 2,900

**CMA Cablevision (18731)**
3030 Needle Hwy., Ste. 1400
Laughlin, NV 89029
Phone: (702)298-3214
Fax: (702)298-3075

Subscribing Households: 2,700

**Frazier Park Cable TV (1867)**
PO Box 2169
Frazier Park, CA 93225
Phone: (661)245-3946

Cities Served: Frazier Park, Lake of the Woods, Lebec, Pine Mountain, CA

Subscribing Households: 2,600

**Stuck Electric Inc. (26056)**
147 W. Main St.
Sheridan, OR 97378
Phone: (503)843-2322
Fax: (503)843-2321

Subscribing Households: 2,475

**Horizon Cable TV, Inc. (1846)**
Box 937
Fairfax, CA 94978
Phone: (415)883-9251
Fax: (415)382-0814

Cities Served: Dillon Beach, Inverness, Novato, Olema, Pt. Keyes, Stinson Beach, CA

Subscribing Households: 2300

**Hood Canal Communications (32459)**
PO Box 249
Union, WA 98592-0249
Phone: (360)898-2481
Fax: (360)898-2244

Cities Served: Hoodsport, Lilliwaup, Potlatch, Shelton, Union, WA

Subscribing Households: 2,200

**Cable One (724)**
155 5th Ave.
PO Box 666
Page, AZ 86040
Phone: (520)645-2132

Subscribing Households: 2000

**Indevideo Co. Inc. (778)**
Box 56339
Phoenix, AZ 85079
Phone: (602)248-8333
Fax: (602)248-0690

Cities Served: Gisela, Grand Canyon, Leupp, Spring Valley, Tuba City, Tusayan, AZ

Subscribing Households: 2000

**Central Valley Cable (1884)**
2441 N Grove Industrial Dr.
Fresno, CA 93727-1535

Subscribing Households: 1,800

**Milestone Communications (4523)**
1850 Woodmoor Dr., Ste. 200
PO Box 7000
Monument, CO 80132-9072
Phone: (719)488-2916

Subscribing Households: 1,750

**Sun Country Cable (1953)**
18638 Main St.
Box 435
Groveland, CA 95321
Phone: (209)962-6373
Fax: (209)962-4923

Cities Served: Big Oak Flat, Groveland, CA

Subscribing Households: 1700

**Tongue River Cable TV (33773)**
PO Box 759
Ranchester, WY 82839
Phone: (307)655-9011
Fax: (307)655-9021

Cities Served: Dayton, Edgerton, Hulett, Midwest, Osage, Pine Haven, Ranchester, Story, Sundance, Wyodak, WY

Subscribing Households: 1660

**Telluride Cablevision (4579)**
220 S. Pine
Box 979
Telluride, CO 81435
Phone: (970)728-4436
Fax: (970)728-3687

Cities Served: Ophir, Telluride, CO

Subscribing Households: 1,500

**Catalina Cable TV Co. (1399)**
Box 2143
Avalon, CA 90704
Phone: (310)510-0255
Fax: (310)510-2565

Cities Served: Avalon, CA

Subscribing Households: 1,380

**Central Valley Cable TV (1955)**
PO Box 429
Gualala, CA 95445-0429
Phone: (707)884-4111
Fax: (707)884-4116

Subscribing Households: 1,350

**Blue Mountain TV Cable Co. (25917)**
PO Box 267
Mount Vernon, OR 97865
Phone: (541)932-4613

Subscribing Households: 1,150

**Alsea River Cable TV (26072)**
220 Spring, No. 2
PO Box 386
Waldport, OR 97394
Phone: (541)563-4807
Fax: (541)563-7341
**Cities Served:** Tidewater, Waldport, OR
**Subscribing Households:** 980

**Siskiyou Cablevision Inc. (1831)**
Box 700
Etna, CA 96027
Phone: (530)467-5666
Fax: (530)467-6401
**Subscribing Households:** 978

**Colfax Highline Cable (32053)**
300 N. Mill St., Ste. 2
Colfax, WA 99111-1867
Phone: (509)397-2211
Fax: (509)397-3951
**Cities Served:** Colfax, Steptoe, WA
**Subscribing Households:** 950

**Cable and Communications Corp. (18111)**
Box 280
Circle, MT 59215
Phone: (406)485-3301
Fax: (406)485-2924
**Cities Served:** Circle, Ekalaka, Jordan, Richey, Savage, Wibaux, MT
**Subscribing Households:** 935

**Copper Mountain Metropolitan District (4244)**
513 Copper Rd.
PO Box 3002
Copper Mountain, CO 80443
Phone: (970)968-2537
Fax: (970)968-2932
**Cities Served:** Copper Mountain, CO
**Subscribing Households:** 920

**Champion Cable (33770)**
PO Box 518
Pine Bluffs, WY 82082
Phone: (307)245-3392
Fax: (307)245-3280
**Cities Served:** Fort Laramie, Guernsey, Pine Bluffs, WY
**Subscribing Households:** 900

**HFU TV (1680)**
26 HFU Circle
Coleville, CA 96107
Phone: (530)495-2224
Fax: (530)495-2500
**Cities Served:** Coleville, Walker, CA; Holbrook Junction, Topaz Lake, Topaz Ranch Estates, NV
**Subscribing Households:** 880

**R & R Cable Co. (32239)**
Box 610
Roslyn, WA 98941
Phone: (509)649-2212
Fax: (509)649-3200
**Cities Served:** Lake Cleelum, Ronald, Roslyn, WA
**Subscribing Households:** 739

**Elgin Television Association (25790)**
830 Alder
PO Box 246
Elgin, OR 97827
Phone: (541)437-4575
**Subscribing Households:** 687

**Colton Cable TV (25748)**
PO Box 68
Colton, OR 97017
Phone: (503)824-3211
Fax: (503)824-9944
**Cities Served:** Colton, OR
**Subscribing Households:** 650

**U.S. Cable TV of Jekyll Island (3351)**
PO Box 4017
San Luis Obispo, CA 93407
Phone: (805)546-9596
Fax: (805)546-0570
**Subscribing Households:** 650

**Lone Pine Television (2085)**
Box 867
Lone Pine, CA 93545
Phone: (760)876-5461
Fax: (760)876-9101
**Cities Served:** Lone Pine, CA
**Subscribing Households:** 625

**Heppner TV Inc. (25849)**
162 N. Main St.
PO Box 587
Heppner, OR 97836
Phone: (541)676-9663
Fax: (541)676-9655
**Subscribing Households:** 610

**Television Association of Republic - Television (32234)**
N. 147 Clark
PO Box 555
Republic, WA 99166-0555
Phone: (509)775-3822
Fax: (509)775-3822
**Cities Served:** Republic, WA
**Subscribing Households:** 585

**Rural Route Video (4469)**
PO Box 640
Ignacio, CO 81137-0640
Phone: (970)563-9593
Fax: (970)563-9381
**Subscribing Households:** 400

**Haines Cable TV (560)**
PO Box 454
Haines, AK 99827
Phone: (907)766-2137
Fax: (907)766-2345
**Cities Served:** Haines, Skagway, AK
**Subscribing Households:** 380

**Mullan Television Co. (7758)**
Box 615
Mullan, ID 83846
Phone: (208)744-1625
**Cities Served:** Mullan, ID
**Subscribing Households:** 377

**City of Cascade Locks (25743)**
140 Wanapa
PO Box 308
Cascade Locks, OR 97014
Phone: (541)374-8484
Fax: (541)374-8752
**Subscribing Households:** 360

**Glide Cablevision (25838)**
19181 N. Umpqua
PO Box 609
Glide, OR 97443
Phone: (541)496-0515
Fax: (541)496-0515
**Cities Served:** Glide, Idleyld Park, OR
**Subscribing Households:** 300

**Philipsburg Cable TV (18225)**
Box 40
Philipsburg, MT 59858
**Subscribing Households:** 300

**WSS Cable TV Inc. (18226)**
PO Box 40
Philipsburg, MT 59858
Phone: (406)859-3645
**Cities Served:** White Sulphur Springs, MT
**Subscribing Households:** 256

**Chinook Progressive Club TV (32049)**
Box 15
Chinook, WA 98614
Phone: (360)777-8412
Fax: (360)777-8255
**Subscribing Households:** 245

**Downieville TV (1780)**
PO Box 393
Downieville, CA 95936
Phone: (530)289-0216
**Cities Served:** Downieville, CA
**Subscribing Households:** 225

**Whitehall Cable TV (18249)**
509 1st St. E.
Whitehall, MT 59759
Phone: (406)287-3913
**Cities Served:** Whitehall, MT
**Subscribing Households:** 226

**Deary Television Co-op Inc. (7810)**
PO Box 154
Troy, ID 83871-0154
Phone: (208)877-1582
**Cities Served:** deary, ID
**Subscribing Households:** 202

**Idaho City Cable TV (7695)**
PO Box 70
Idaho City, ID 83631
Phone: (208)392-4290
Fax: (208)392-4505
**Cities Served:** Idaho City, ID
**Subscribing Households:** 200

**Lake Hughes Television Cable Service (3987)**
1399 Arundell Ave.
Ventura, CA 93003
Phone: (805)642-0241
Fax: (805)650-1869
**Cities Served:** Lake Hughes, CA
**Subscribing Households:** 200

**Skagway Cable TV (562)**
PO Box 454
Haines, AK 99827
Phone: (907)983-2205
Fax: (907)766-2345
**Cities Served:** Skagway, AK
**Subscribing Households:** 140

**Mt. Dutton Cable Corp. (588)**
Box 38
King Cove, AK 99612
Phone: (907)497-2346
Fax: (907)497-2444
**Subscribing Households:** 125

**Capp's TV Electronics Inc. (3984)**
1399 Arundell Ave.
Ventura, CA 93003
Phone: (805)642-0241
Fax: (805)650-1869
**Cities Served:** Lake Hughes, CA
**Subscribing Households:** 114

**Bovill TV Cable Co. (7678)**
PO Box 617
Bovill, ID 83806-0617
Phone: (208)826-3234
**Cities Served:** Bovill, ID
**Subscribing Households:** 37

# Central Provinces

**Rogers Cable (35380)**
244 Newkirk Rd.
Richmond Hill, ON, Canada L4C 3S5
Phone: (905)884-8111
Fax: (905)884-8151
**Cities Served:** King Township, Markham, Richmond Hill, Stouffville, Vaughn, Whitchurch, ON, Canada
**Subscribing Households:** 101,246

**Northern Cable Holdings Ltd. (35465)**
500 Barrydowne Rd., No. 15
PO Box 4500
Sudbury, ON, Canada P3A 5W1
Phone: (705)560-1560
Fax: (705)560-4752
**Cities Served:** Elliot Lake, Kapuskasing, New Liskeard, Sturgeon Falls, Sudbury, Timmins, ON, Canada
**Subscribing Households:** 99,288

# Eastern Provinces

**Rogers Cable (34787)**
1 Sperling Dr.
PO Box 8500
Barrie, ON, Canada L4M 6B8
Phone: (705)737-4660
Fax: (705)737-3840
Subscribing Households: 94,589

**Shaw Cablesystems (36511)**
2326 Hanselman Ave.
Box 1950
Saskatoon, SK, Canada S7L 5Z3
Phone: (306)665-3796
Fax: (306)665-3738
Subscribing Households: 60,467

**Shaw Cable (36510)**
2326 Hanselman Ave.
Saskatoon, SK, Canada S7L 5Z3
Phone: (306)693-8585
Fax: (306)244-0105
Subscribing Households: 31,000

**Aurora Cable TV, Ltd. (34776)**
PO Box 547
Aurora, ON, Canada L4G 3H3
Phone: (905)727-1981
Fax: (905)727-7407
Cities Served: Aurora, Oakrides, ON, Canada
Subscribing Households: 12,500

**Amtelecom Communications (34778)**
18 Sydenham St. E.
PO Box 1800
Aylmer, ON, Canada N5H 3E7
Phone: (519)773-8441
Fax: (519)765-3265
Cities Served: Alvinston, Aylmer, Bothwell, Brownsville, Courtland, Embro, Glencoe, Langton, Lyons, Mt. Brydges, Port Bruce/Copenhagen, Port Burwell, Port Rowan, Pt. Burwell, Simcoe, Springfield, St. Williams, Staffordville, Wardsville, ON, Canada
Subscribing Households: 9,950

**Access Communications (36460)**
1192 99th St.
North Battleford, SK, Canada S9A 0P3
Phone: (306)445-7545
Fax: (306)445-0755
Subscribing Households: 9,500

**Access Communication (36538)**
22 6th Ave. N.
PO Box 550
Yorkton, SK, Canada S3N 2W7
Phone: (306)783-1566
Fax: (306)782-1952
Subscribing Households: 9,300

**Cogeco Cable Inc. (34989)**
1444 Aberdeen St.
Hawkesbury, ON, Canada K6A 1K7
Fax: (613)632-8531
Cities Served: Chute a Blondeau, Hawkesbury, L'Orignal, Vankleek Hill, ON, Canada
Subscribing Households: 6,500

**Shaw Cable TV (35467)**
Box 580
Terrace Bay, ON, Canada P0T 2W0
Fax: (807)825-9497
Subscribing Households: 6,500

**Compton Cable TV Ltd. (35367)**
Box 73
Port Perry, ON, Canada L9L 1A2
Phone: (905)985-8171
Fax: (905)985-0010
Cities Served: Coppins Corners, Epsom, Goodwood, Oak Hills, Port Perry, Prince Albert, Utica, Uxbridge, ON, Canada
Subscribing Households: 4,900

**Shaw Cable (34462)**
50 Selkirk Ave.
Thompson Plaza
Thompson, MB, Canada R8N 0M7
Phone: (204)778-7321
Fax: (204)677-9953
Cities Served: Thompson, MB, Canada

Subscribing Households: 4,030

**Nor-Del Cablevision Ltd. (35165)**
PO Box 340
Norwich, ON, Canada N0J 1P0
Phone: (519)879-6527
Fax: (519)879-6387
Cities Served: Delhi, Norwich, Otterville, Port Douer, Waterford, ON, Canada
Subscribing Households: 3,450

**Mitchell Seaforth Cable TV Ltd. (34889)**
123 Ontario St.
Dublin, ON, Canada N0K 1E0
Phone: (519)345-2341
Fax: (519)345-2873
Cities Served: Dublin, Mitchell, ON, Canada
Subscribing Households: 2,404

**Astrocom Cablevision Inc. (34931)**
Box 910
Geraldton, ON, Canada P0T 1M0
Phone: (807)854-1569
Fax: (807)854-2169
Cities Served: Geraldton, Longlac, ON, Canada
Subscribing Households: 1,621

**Shilo Cablevision (34447)**
PO Box 40
Shilo, MB, Canada R0K 2A0
Phone: (204)765-2586
Fax: (204)765-3014
Cities Served: Manitoba, Shilo, MB, Canada
Subscribing Households: 561

**Hasting's Cable Vision Ltd. (35071)**
Box 459
Madoc, ON, Canada K0K 2K0
Phone: (613)473-2839
Fax: (613)473-4853
Cities Served: Madoc, ON, Canada
Subscribing Households: 500

**Ponteix TV Club (36463)**
Box 330
Ponteix, SK, Canada S0N 1Z0
Phone: (306)625-3222
Fax: (306)625-3204
Cities Served: Ponteix, SK, Canada
Subscribing Households: 230

# Eastern Provinces

**Persona Communications (34648)**
Sta. A.
PO Box 12155
Saint John's, NL, Canada A1B 4L1
Phone: (709)754-3775
Fax: (709)754-3883
Subscribing Households: 75,000

**COGECO Cable, Inc. (36378)**
1630 6th St.
Trois-Rivieres, QC, Canada G8Y 5B8
Phone: (819)379-2443
Fax: (819)379-9174
Subscribing Households: 53,059

**Cable 2000 Inc. (34532)**
PO Box 2000
Bathurst, NB, Canada E2A 4W4
Phone: (506)547-8877
Fax: (506)546-8208
Cities Served: Bathurst, Campbellton, Dalhousie, Shediac, Tracadie, Woodstock, NB, Canada
Subscribing Households: 47,000

**Seaside Communications (34693)**
1318 Grand Lake Rd.
PO Box 4558
Glace Bay, NS, Canada B1A 5V4
Phone: (902)539-6250
Fax: (902)539-2597
Cities Served: Baddeck, Dominion, Glace Bay, L'Ardoise, Louisbourg, Main-a-dieu/Catalone, Marion Bridge/Albert Bridge, New Waterford, River Bourgeois, St. Peters, NS, Canada

Subscribing Households: 14,217

**Eastlink Cable Systems (34729)**
PO Box 157
New Glasgow, NS, Canada B2H 5E2
Phone: (902)695-2323
Fax: (902)755-2236
Subscribing Households: 12,150

**Video Dery Ltee. (36392)**
1013 Rue Bagot
Box 1154
Ville de la Baie, QC, Canada G7B 3P3
Phone: (418)544-3358
Fax: (418)544-0187
Subscribing Households: 11,500

**Telecable Charlevoix Inc. (36052)**
88 11th Ave.
La Pocatiere, QC, Canada G0R 1Z0
Phone: (418)856-2253
Fax: (418)856-4772
Subscribing Households: 10,551

**Cogeco (36357)**
410 Evangeline
Sept-Iles, QC, Canada G4R 2N5
Phone: (418)962-3508
Fax: (418)962-3531
Cities Served: Port Cartier, Sept-Iles, QC, Canada
Subscribing Households: 10,000

**Cogeco Cable (35987)**
323 boul LaSalle
Baie-Comeau, QC, Canada G4Z 2L5
Phone: (418)296-9505
Fax: (418)296-6733
Subscribing Households: 8,800

**Cooperative de Cablodistribution de l'Arriere-Pays (36004)**
860, ave. Notre-Dame
Charlesbourg, QC, Canada G2N 1P7
Phone: (418)849-7125
Fax: (418)849-7128
Cities Served: Bon-Pasteur, Lac Beauport, Lac Delage, Lac-St-Charles, Notre-Dame-Des-Laurentides, Ste-Brigitte-de-Laval, Stoneham, QC, Canada
Subscribing Households: 8300

**Fundy Cablevision Ltd. (34576)**
454 King George Hwy.
Newcastle, NB, Canada E1V 1M1
Fax: (506)622-3712
Subscribing Households: 8,050

**Le Cable de Riviere-du-Loup Ltee. (36308)**
279-A LaFontaine C.P. 1390
Riviere-du-Loup, QC, Canada G5R 4L9
Phone: (418)867-1478
Fax: (418)867-2829
Cities Served: Environs, Riviere-Du-Loup, QC, Canada
Subscribing Households: 7,757

**Prince County Cable (35976)**
Box 4
Summerside, PE, Canada C1N 4P6
Phone: (902)892-6445
Fax: (902)436-5799
Cities Served: Kensington, Miscouche, Saint Eleanors, Summerside, Wilmot, PE, Canada
Subscribing Households: 5,400

**Electro-Vision (La Tuque) Inc. (36055)**
333 St. Joseph
La Tuque, QC, Canada G9X 1L3
Phone: (819)523-3737
Fax: (819)523-3506
Subscribing Households: 4,800

**Video Tron (36315)**
1258 Blvd. Sacrecoeur
Saint-Felicien, QC, Canada G8K 2P8
Phone: (418)679-0953
Fax: (418)679-2520
Subscribing Households: 4,198

**Video Derv Ltee  (35991)**
79 boul. Fafard
Baie Saint-Paul, QC, Canada G3Z 2J8
Phone: (418)435-3220
Fax: (418)435-4060
**Cities Served:** Baie St. Paul, St. Francois, St. Urbain, QC, Canada
**Subscribing Households:** 2,545

**Cablevision Warwick Inc.  (36395)**
14 boul. Beaumier
C.P. 999
Warwick, QC, Canada J0A 1M0
Phone: (819)358-5858
Fax: (819)358-5592
**Subscribing Households:** 1,600

**Club TV de Matagami/Matagami TV Club  (36092)**
Box 517
Matagami, QC, Canada J0Y 2A0
Phone: (819)739-2148
Fax: (819)739-2612
**Subscribing Households:** 882

**Cable Axion Digitel Inc.  (36086)**
250 Axion Rd.
Magog, QC, Canada J1X 6J2
Phone: (819)843-0611
Fax: (819)868-4249
**Subscribing Households:** 175

## Northern Provinces

**Northwestel Cable Inc.  (34674)**
5120 49th St.
PO Box 1469
Yellowknife, NT, Canada X1A 2P1
Phone: (867)920-3690
Fax: (867)920-2331
**Cities Served:** Fort Good Hope, Nanisivik, Norman Wells, Pangnirtung, Tuktoyaktuk, Yellowknife, NT, Canada; Watson Lake, YT, Canada
**Subscribing Households:** 5,000

## Western Provinces

**Delta Cable Communications Ltd.  (34135)**
5381 48th Ave.
Delta, BC, Canada V4K 1W7
Phone: (604)946-1144
Fax: (604)946-5627
**Cities Served:** Point Roberts, WA; Delta, BC, Canada
**Subscribing Households:** 29,500

**Shaw Cable  (34035)**
6123 48th Ave.
Red Deer, AB, Canada T4N 5Z9
Phone: (403)346-6633
Fax: (403)346-3962
**Cities Served:** Black Falls, Penhold, Red Deer, Sylvan, AB, Canada
**Subscribing Households:** 20,000

**Shaw Community 4  (34139)**
35 Queens Rd.
Duncan, BC, Canada V9L 2W1
Phone: (250)701-4077
Fax: (250)701-4090
**Subscribing Households:** 20,000

**Coast Cable Communications Ltd.  (34259)**
PO Box 218
5555 Wharf Rd.
Sechelt, BC, Canada V0N 3A0
Phone: (604)885-3224
Fax: (604)946-1144
**Cities Served:** Gibsons, Langdale, Pander Harbour, Roberts Creek, Sechelt, Secret Cove, BC, Canada
**Subscribing Households:** 8,900

**Shaw Cablesystems Inc.  (34179)**
2350 Hunter Rd.
Kelowna, BC, Canada V1X 7H6
Phone: (250)378-2568
Fax: (250)712-2310
**Cities Served:** Merritt, BC, Canada

**Subscribing Households:** 4,038

**Revelstoke Cable TV Ltd.  (34247)**
416 2nd St. W.
Revelstoke, BC, Canada V0E 2S0
Phone: (250)837-5246
Fax: (250)837-2900
**Cities Served:** Revelstoke, BC, Canada
**Subscribing Households:** 2,720

**Cable TV Slave Lake Ltd.  (34048)**
Box 1008
Slave Lake, AB, Canada T0G 2A0
Phone: (780)849-5188
Fax: (780)849-6809
**Cities Served:** Slave Lake, AB, Canada
**Subscribing Households:** 1,900

**Saltspring Cablevision (1981) Ltd.  (34257)**
PO Box 300
Salt Spring, BC, Canada V8K 2V9
Phone: (250)537-5550
Fax: (250)537-5550
**Cities Served:** Ganges-Fulford Harbour, BC, Canada
**Subscribing Households:** 1541

**Taxada Community TV Assn.  (34282)**
Box 158
Vananda, BC, Canada V0N 3K0
Phone: (604)486-4420
**Cities Served:** Vananda, BC, Canada
**Subscribing Households:** 135

**Riondel Community Cable Video Society  (34252)**
Box 59
Riondel, BC, Canada V0B 2B0
Phone: (250)225-3433
Fax: (250)225-3433
**Cities Served:** Riondel, BC, Canada
**Subscribing Households:** 105

# Radio Index

Index entries are arranged geographically first by region and then by Area of Dominant Influence (ADI). Within ADI in this index, citations appear alphabetically by station call letters. Citations include station call letters and channel, entry number (given in parentheses immediately following the title), address, phone and fax numbers, and format.

## Great Lakes States

### Alpena, MI

**WATZ-AM - 1450  (14990)**
123 Prentiss St.
PO Box 536
Alpena, MI 49707
Phone: (989)354-8400
Fax: (989)354-3436
**Format:** News; Talk; Sports

**WATZ-FM - 99.3  (14991)**
123 Prentiss St.
PO Box 536
Alpena, MI 49707
Phone: (989)354-8400
Fax: (989)354-3436
**Format:** Contemporary Country

**WCML-FM - 91.7  (14992)**
Central Michigan University
Public Broadcasting Center
1999 E. Campus Dr.
Mount Pleasant, MI 48859
Phone: (989)774-3105
Fax: (989)774-4427
**Format:** Jazz; News; Classical

**WHSB-FM - 107.7  (14994)**
1491 M-32 W.
Alpena, MI 49707
Phone: (517)354-4611
Fax: (517)354-4014
**Format:** Adult Contemporary

### Cedar Rapids-Waterloo-Dubuque, IA

**WPVL-AM - 1590  (33470)**
PO Box 1
Platteville, WI 53818
Phone: (608)348-2775
Fax: (608)348-2780
**Format:** Middle-of-the-Road (MOR)

**WPVL-FM - 107.1  (33471)**
1245 N. 4th St
PO Box 1
Platteville, WI 53818
Phone: (608)348-2775
Fax: (608)348-2780
**Format:** Oldies

**WQPC-FM - 94.3  (33489)**
640 N. Villa Louis Rd.
PO Box 90
Prairie du Chien, WI 53821
Phone: (608)326-2411
Fax: (608)326-2412
**Format:** Country

### Charleston-Huntington, WV

**WPAY-FM - 104.1  (25012)**
1009 Gallia St
Portsmouth, OH 45662
Phone: (740)353-5176
Fax: (740)353-1715
**Format:** Country

### Chicago (LaSalle), IL

**WAIT-AM - 850  (8525)**
8800 Rte. 14
Crystal Lake, IL 60012
Phone: (815)459-7000
Fax: (815)459-7027
**Format:** Adult Contemporary

**WAJK-FM - 99.3  (8850)**
PO Box 215
La Salle, IL 61301
Phone: (815)223-3100
Fax: (815)223-3095
**Format:** Adult Contemporary

**WBBM-AM - 780  (8451)**
630 N. McClurg Ct.
Chicago, IL 60611
Phone: (312)202-3248
Fax: (312)951-3674
**Format:** News

**WBBM-FM - 96.3  (8452)**
630 N. McClurg Ct.
Chicago, IL 60611-3074
Phone: (312)202-3248
Fax: (312)951-3674
**Format:** Contemporary Hit Radio (CHR)

**WBGX-AM - 1570  (8772)**
15700 Campbell Ave.
Harvey, IL 60426
Phone: (708)331-7840
Fax: (708)333-7840
**Format:** Gospel

**WBIG-AM - 1280  (7875)**
620 Eola Rd.
Aurora, IL 60504
Phone: (630)851-5200
Fax: (630)851-5286
**Format:** News; Talk; Sports

**WCKG-FM - 105.9  (8455)**
2 Prudential Plaza, Ste. 1059
Chicago, IL 60601
Phone: (312)240-7900
Fax: (312)565-3181
**Format:** Talk

**WCRX-FM - 88.1  (8456)**
600 S. Michigan
Chicago, IL 60605
Phone: (312)663-1693
Fax: (312)663-5204
**Format:** Alternative/New Music/Progressive

**WEJM-FM - 106.3  (8457)**
800 S. Wells, Ste.250
Chicago, IL 60607
Phone: (312)360-9000
Fax: (312)306-9070
**Format:** Adult Contemporary; Urban Contemporary

**WERV-FM - 95.9  (7876)**
1884 Plain Ave.
Aurora, IL 60504-8560
**Format:** Oldies; Classic Rock

**WESL-AM - 1490  (8619)**
149 S. 8th St.
East Saint Louis, IL 62201
Phone: (618)271-7687
Fax: (618)875-4315
**Format:** Blues

**WGCI-AM - 1390  (8459)**
233 N. Michigan Ave., Ste. 2800
Chicago, IL 60601
Phone: (312)540-2000
Fax: (312)987-4453
**Format:** Oldies; Blues

**WGCI-FM - 107.5  (8460)**
233 N. Michigan Ave., Ste. 600
Chicago, IL 60604
Phone: (312)986-6900
Fax: (312)427-7410
**Format:** Urban Contemporary

**WGRB-AM - 1390  (8463)**
233 N Michigan Ave., Fl. 28
Chicago, IL 60601
Phone: (312)540-2000
Fax: (312)322-3032
**Format:** Gospel

**WIIL-FM - 95.1  (33473)**
8500 Green Bay Rd.
Pleasant Prairie, WI 53158
Phone: (262)694-7800
Fax: (414)694-7767
**Format:** Album-Oriented Rock (AOR)

**WIND-AM - 560  (8466)**
625 N. Michigan Ave., Ste. 300
Chicago, IL 60611-3110
Phone: (312)981-1800
Fax: (312)981-1840
**Format:** Hispanic

**WJCG-FM - 89.9  (8467)**
820 N. LaSalle Blvd.
Chicago, IL 60610
Phone: (312)329-4000
Fax: (312)329-8980
**Format:** Religious

**WJJG-AM - 1530  (7910)**
5629 St. Charles Rd. No. 208
Berkeley, IL 60163
Phone: (708)493-1530

# Cincinnati, OH

Format: Talk

**WKAN-AM - 1320  (8835)**
2 Dearborn Sq.
Kankakee, IL 60901
Phone: (815)935-9555
Fax: (815)935-9593
Format: Adult Contemporary

**WKAN-FM - 1320  (8836)**
2 Dearborn Sq.
Kankakee, IL 60901-3933
Phone: (815)935-9555
Fax: (815)935-9593
Format: Country

**WKKC-FM - 89.3  (8470)**
6800 S. Wentworth Ave.
Chicago, IL 60621
Phone: (773)602-5313
Fax: (773)602-5532
Format: Full Service

**WKKD-AM - 1580  (7877)**
1884 Plain Ave.
Aurora, IL 60504-8560
Format: News; Sports; Classic Rock

**WKRS-AM - 1220  (9514)**
3250 Belvidere Rd.
Waukegan, IL 60085
Phone: (847)336-7900
Fax: (847)336-1523
Format: News; Sports; Information; Information

**WLPO-AM - 1220  (8851)**
PO Box 215
La Salle, IL 61301
Phone: (815)223-3100
Fax: (815)223-3095
Format: Oldies

**WLS-AM - 890  (8475)**
190 N. State, 9th Fl.
Chicago, IL 60601
Phone: (312)984-0891
Fax: (312)984-5305
Format: News; Talk; Talk

**WLUP-FM - 97.9  (8476)**
875 N. Michigan Ave., Ste. 3750
Chicago, IL 60611
Phone: (312)440-5270
Fax: (312)440-9896
Format: Album-Oriented Rock (AOR)

**WMBI-AM - 1110  (8479)**
820 N. LaSalle Dr.
Chicago, IL 60610
Phone: (312)329-4300
Fax: (312)329-4468
Format: Religious

**WNUA-FM - 95.5  (8481)**
233 N. Michigan Ave., Ste. 2800
Chicago, IL 60601
Phone: (312)540-2000
Fax: (312)938-7334
Format: Jazz

**WOJO-FM - 105.1  (8482)**
625 N. Michigan Ave., 3rd Fl.
Chicago, IL 60611-3110
Phone: (312)649-0105
Fax: (312)664-2472
Format: Hispanic

**WRRG-FM - 88.9  (9280)**
2000 5th Ave.
River Grove, IL 60171
Phone: (708)456-0300
Fax: (708)583-3120
Format: Alternative/New Music/Progressive

**WRZA-FM - 99.9  (8484)**
6012 S. Pulaski Rd.
Chicago, IL 60629
Fax: (312)733-2214
Format: Hispanic

**WSPY-FM - 107.1  (9250)**
1 Broadcast Center
Plano, IL 60545
Phone: (708)552-1000
Fax: (708)552-9300

Format: Talk; Adult Contemporary; News

**WUBT-FM - 103.5  (8488)**
875 N. Michigan Ave., Ste. 4000
Chicago, IL 60611-1901
Phone: (312)440-5270
Fax: (312)440-9143
Format: Oldies; Blues

**WUSN-FM - 99.5  (8489)**
2 Prudential Plaza, Ste. 1310
Chicago, IL 60601
Phone: (312)649-0099
Fax: (312)664-3999
Format: Country

**WVAZ-FM - 102.7  (8490)**
233 N Michigan Ave., Ste. 2800
Chicago, IL 60601-5704
Phone: (312)360-9000
Fax: (312)360-9070
Format: Adult Contemporary; Urban Contemporary; Information

**WVON-AM - 1450  (8491)**
3350 S. Kedzie Ave.
Chicago, IL 60623
Phone: (773)247-6200
Fax: (773)247-5336
Format: Talk

**WWJY-FM - 103.9  (9796)**
6405 Olcott St.
Hammond, IN 46320-2835
Format: Adult Contemporary

**WXEX-FM - 107.9  (8493)**
150 N. Michigan Ave., No. 1040
Chicago, IL 60601
Phone: (312)920-9500
Fax: (312)920-9515
Format: Public Radio

**WYCA-FM - 92.3  (9797)**
6336 Calumet Ave.
PO Box 3003
Hammond, IN 46324
Phone: (219)933-4455
Fax: (219)933-0233
Format: Religious

**WZZN-FM - 94.7  (8497)**
190 N State St.
Chicago, IL 60601
Phone: (312)984-9923
Fax: (312)984-5357
Format: Classic Rock

## Cincinnati, OH

**WAKW-FM - 93.3  (24349)**
6275 Collegevue Pl.
Cincinnati, OH 45224-1959
Phone: (513)542-9393
Fax: (513)542-9333
Format: Contemporary Christian

**WCKY-AM - 1360  (24352)**
8044 Montgomery Rd., Suite 650
Cincinnati, OH 45202
Phone: (513)686-8300
Fax: (513)655-9700
Format: Sports; Talk

**WHSS-FM - 89.5  (24761)**
Hamilton High School
1111 Eaton Ave.
Hamilton, OH 45013
Phone: (513)887-4818
Fax: (513)887-4879
Format: Alternative/New Music/Progressive

**WJVS-FM - 88.3  (24356)**
3254 E. Kemper Rd.
Cincinnati, OH 45241-1581
Phone: (513)771-8810
Format: Public Radio; Educational

**WKRC-AM - 550  (24358)**
8044 Montgomery St.
Cincinnati, OH 45236
Phone: (513)686-8300
Fax: (513)723-9221

Format: Talk; News

**WOBO-FM - 88.7  (24973)**
PO Box 338
Owensville, OH 45160
Phone: (513)724-3939
Fax: (513)724-6042

**WOXY-FM - 97.7  (24363)**
700 W. Pete Rose Way
Cincinnati, OH 45203
Phone: (513)621-0012
Fax: (513)523-1412
Format: Alternative/New Music/Progressive

**WPFB-AM - 910  (24904)**
4505 Central Ave.
Middletown, OH 45044
Phone: (513)422-3625
Fax: (513)424-9732
Format: News; Talk

**WPFB-FM - 105.9  (24905)**
4505 Central Ave.
Middletown, OH 45044-5240
Phone: (513)422-3625
Fax: (513)424-9732
Format: Country

**WTSJ-AM - 1050  (24365)**
635 W. 7th St., Ste. 400
Cincinnati, OH 45203
Phone: (513)533-2500
Fax: (513)533-2527
Format: Religious; Talk; News; Eclectic; Public Radio; Public Radio

**WVMX-FM - 101.9  (24366)**
8044 Montgomery Rd., Suite 650
Cincinnati, OH 45219-3161
Phone: (513)686-8300
Fax: (513)763-5541
Format: Contemporary Christian

**WVXU-FM - 91.7  (24367)**
3800 Victory Pkwy.
Cincinnati, OH 45207-7211
Phone: (513)731-9898
Fax: (513)745-3483
Format: News; Eclectic; Public Radio; Public Radio

## Cleveland (Akron, Canton, & Sandusky), OH

**WABQ-AM - 1540  (24498)**
8000 Euclid Ave.
Cleveland, OH 44103-4229
Phone: (216)231-8005
Format: Gospel

**WAKR-AM - 1590  (24111)**
1795 W. Market St.
Akron, OH 44313-7001
Fax: (216)864-6799
Format: Middle-of-the-Road (MOR); Full Service

**WBKC-AM - 1460  (24986)**
1 Radio Pl.
Painesville, OH 44077
Phone: (440)951-1460
Fax: (440)352-8194
Format: News; Talk; Classical

**WCPZ-FM - 102.7  (25036)**
1640 Cleveland Rd.
Sandusky, OH 44870
Phone: (419)625-1010
Fax: (419)625-1348
Format: Adult Contemporary

**WCRF-FM - 103.3  (24502)**
9756 Barr Rd.
Cleveland, OH 44141
Phone: (440)526-1111
Fax: (440)526-1319

**WCUE-AM - 1150  (24994)**
4075 Bellaire Ln.
Peninsula, OH 44264
Phone: (330)920-1150
Format: Religious

**WEOL-AM - 930  (24712)**
538 Broad St.
Box 4006
Elyria, OH 44036
Phone: (440)322-3761

Fax: (440)284-3189
**Format:** News; Sports

**WFXN-FM - 102.3 (24133)**
2435 Mansfield Rd.
Ashland, OH 44805
Phone: (419)289-2605
Fax: (419)289-0304
**Format:** Classic Rock

**WGAR-FM - 99.5 (24505)**
6200 Oak Tree Blvd., Ste. 4
Cleveland, OH 44131-6933
**Format:** Country

**WGGN-FM - 97.7 (24255)**
3809 Maple Ave.
Castalia, OH 44824-9731
Phone: (419)684-5370
Fax: (419)684-5378
**Format:** Religious; Contemporary Christian; Adult Contemporary

**WHBC-AM - 1480 (24244)**
550 Market Ave. S.
PO Box 9917
Canton, OH 44711
Phone: (216)456-7166
Fax: (216)456-7199
**Format:** Full Service

**WHBC-FM - 94.1 (24245)**
550 Market Ave. S.
PO Box 9917
Canton, OH 44711
Phone: (330)456-7166
Fax: (330)456-7199
**Format:** Adult Contemporary

**WINW-AM - 1520 (24246)**
237 Tuscarawas St. W
Canton, OH 44702-2201
**Format:** Music of Your Life

**WJCU-FM - 88.7 (24506)**
John Carroll University Radio
20700 N. Park Blvd.
Cleveland, OH 44118
Phone: (216)397-4437
Fax: (216)397-4439
**Format:** Full Service

**WJMO-AM - 1490 (24507)**
2510 St. Clair Ave.
Cleveland, OH 44114
Phone: (216)621-9300
Fax: (216)771-4164
**Format:** Oldies

**WJMP-AM - 1520 (24113)**
PO Box 2170
Akron, OH 44309-2170
Phone: (216)673-2323
Fax: (216)673-0301
**Format:** Oldies

**WKFM-FM - 96.1 (24906)**
10327 Milan Rd., US Rte. 250
Milan, OH 44846
Phone: (419)609-5961
Fax: (419)609-2679
**Format:** Country

**WKNR-AM - 850 (24508)**
9446 Broadview Rd.
Cleveland, OH 44147
Phone: (440)838-1220
Fax: (440)526-1993
**Format:** Sports

**WLEC-AM - 1450 (25037)**
1640 Cleveland Rd.
Sandusky, OH 44870
Phone: (419)626-2000
Fax: (419)625-1348

**WLKR-FM - 95.3 (24907)**
10327 Milan Rd.
U.S. Rte. 250
Milan, OH 44846
Phone: (419)668-8151
Fax: (419)609-2679
**Format:** Adult Contemporary

**WOBL-AM - 1320 (24969)**
PO Box 277
Oberlin, OH 44074-0277
Phone: (440)774-1320
Fax: (440)774-1336

**Format:** Country

**WQAL-FM - 104.1 (24513)**
1 Radio Ln.
Cleveland, OH 44114-4016
Phone: (216)696-0123
Fax: (216)363-7104
**Format:** Adult Contemporary

**WRCW-AM - 1060 (24248)**
4601 Hills & Dales Rd. NW
Canton, OH 44708
Phone: (330)477-8585
**Format:** Adult Contemporary; Talk

**WRDL-FM - 88.9 (24136)**
401 College Ave.
Ashland, OH 44805
Phone: (419)289-5139
Fax: (419)289-5329
**Format:** Alternative/New Music/Progressive

**WRUW-FM - 91.1 (24514)**
11220 Bellflower Rd.
Cleveland, OH 44106
Phone: (216)368-2208
Fax: (216)368-5414
**Format:** Full Service

**WTAM-AM - 1100 (24515)**
6200 Oak Tree Blvd., No. 4
Cleveland, OH 44131-2510
Phone: (216)520-2600
Fax: (216)901-8152
**Format:** News; Sports; Talk

**WTUZ-FM - 99.9 (24940)**
2424 East High Ave.
New Philadelphia, OH 44663
Phone: (330)339-2222
Fax: (330)339-5930
**Format:** Contemporary Country

**WZIP-FM - 88.1 (24117)**
302 E. Buchtel Ave.
Akron, OH 44325-1004
Phone: (330)972-7105
Fax: (330)972-5521

## Columbus (Chillicothe), OH

**WBEX-AM - 1490 (24276)**
Box 94
Chillicothe, OH 45601
Fax: (614)773-0933
**Format:** Oldies; News; Full Service

**WBNS-AM - 1460 (24610)**
605 S Front St.
Columbus, OH 43215-5134
Phone: (614)460-3850
Fax: (614)460-3757
**Format:** Sports

**WBNS-FM - 97.1 (24611)**
605 S Front St.
Columbus, OH 43215
Phone: (614)460-3850
Fax: (614)460-3757
**Format:** Oldies

**WBZX-FM - 99.7 (24613)**
1458 Dublin Rd.
Columbus, OH 43215
Phone: (614)481-7800
Fax: (614)481-8070
**Format:** Album-Oriented Rock (AOR)

**WCHO-AM - 1250 (25140)**
1535 N. North St.
Washington Court House, OH 43160
Phone: (740)335-0941
Fax: (740)335-6869

**WCHO-FM - 105.5 (25141)**
1535 N. North St.
Washington Court House, OH 43160
Phone: (740)335-0941
Fax: (740)335-6869
**Format:** Country; Contemporary Country; Contemporary Country

**WCOL-FM - 92.3 (24615)**
2323 W. Fifth Ave.
Columbus, OH 43215
Phone: (614)486-6101
Fax: (614)487-2554

**Format:** Country

**WDIF-FM - 94.3 (24875)**
1330 North Main St.
Marion, OH 43302
Phone: (740)383-1131
Fax: (740)387-3697
**Format:** Adult Contemporary; News; Sports; Sports

**WFII-AM - 1230 (24616)**
1301 Dublin Rd.
Columbus, OH 43215
Phone: (614)273-9344
Fax: (614)487-2559
**Format:** News; Talk

**WFJX-FM - 105.7 (24617)**
6172 Busch Blvd., Ste. 2000
Columbus, OH 43229
Phone: (614)430-9624
Fax: (614)847-9593
**Format:** Classic Rock

**WFXJ-FM - 107.5 (24140)**
3226 Jefferson Rd.
Ashtabula, OH 44004
Phone: (440)993-2126
Fax: (440)992-2658
**Format:** Sports

**WHOK-FM - 95.5 (24824)**
280 N High St., 10th Fl.
Lancaster, OH 43130-3149
Phone: (614)225-9465
Fax: (614)677-0116
**Format:** Country

**WJAW-FM - 100.9 (24872)**
PO Box 708
Marietta, OH 45750
Fax: (740)373-1717
**Format:** Adult Contemporary; Soft Rock; Sports

**WKKJ-FM - 93.3 (24277)**
Box 94
Chillicothe, OH 45601
Phone: (614)773-2244
Fax: (614)773-0933
**Format:** Country

**WLGN-AM - 98.3 (24840)**
1 Radio Ln.
PO Box 429
Logan, OH 43138-0429
Phone: (740)385-2151
Fax: (740)385-4022
**Format:** Country

**WLGN-FM - 98.3 (24841)**
1 Radio Ln.
PO Box 429
Logan, OH 43138
Phone: (740)385-2151
Fax: (740)385-4022
**Format:** Hot Country

**WLOH-AM - 1320 (24825)**
724 S. Columbus St.
Lancaster, OH 43130
Phone: (740)653-4373
Fax: (740)653-0702

**WLVQ-FM - 96.3 (24619)**
280 North High St.
Columbus, OH 43215-7000
Phone: (614)488-9696
Fax: (614)821-9630
**Format:** Album-Oriented Rock (AOR)

**WMNI-AM - 920 (24620)**
1458 Dublin Rd.
Columbus, OH 43215
Phone: (614)481-7800
Fax: (614)481-8070
**Format:** Big Band/Nostalgia

**WMRN-AM - 1490 (24876)**
1330 N. Main St.
Marion, OH 43302
Phone: (740)383-1131
Fax: (740)387-3697
**Format:** Adult Contemporary; Oldies; Talk; News; Sports; Agricultural; News; Sports; Agricultural

**WOSU-FM - 89.7 (24622)**
2400 Olentangy River Rd.
Columbus, OH 43210
Phone: (614)292-9678
Fax: (614)292-0513

Format: Classical

**WSNY-FM - 94.7  (24624)**
4401 Carriage Hill Ln.
Columbus, OH 43220-3800
Phone: (614)451-2191
Fax: (614)451-1831
Format: Adult Contemporary

**WTVN-AM - 610  (24626)**
1301 Dublin
Columbus, OH 43215-7009
Phone: (614)486-6101
Fax: (614)487-2559
Format: News; Talk

**WXIC-AM - 660  (25144)**
PO Box 227
Waverly, OH 45690
Phone: (614)947-7660
Fax: (614)947-4600
Format: Southern Gospel; Country

**WXIZ-FM - 100.9  (25145)**
PO Box 227
Waverly, OH 45690
Phone: (614)947-2166
Fax: (614)947-4600
Format: Country

## Daveport,IA-Rock Island, Moline,IL

**WDLM-AM - 960  (8614)**
PO Box 149
East Moline, IL 61244
Phone: (309)762-9887
Fax: (309)234-5114
Format: Religious

**WDLM-FM - 89.3  (8615)**
PO Box 149
East Moline, IL 61244
Phone: (309)762-9887
Format: Religious

**WGEN-AM - 1500  (8718)**
PO Box 222
Galva, IL 61434
Phone: (309)932-2288
Fax: (309)932-2248
Format: Full Service; Agricultural; Sports; Adult Contemporary

**WJBD-AM - 1350  (9343)**
310 W. McMackin
PO Box 70
Salem, IL 62881
Phone: (618)548-2000
Fax: (618)548-2079
Format: Adult Contemporary; Full Service; Full Service

**WSDR-AM - 1240  (9429)**
3101 Freeport Rd.
Sterling, IL 61081
Phone: (815)622-3156
Fax: (815)625-6940
Format: Talk; News; Sports; Agricultural; Sports; Agricultural

**WSSQ-FM - 94.3  (9430)**
3101 Freeport Rd.
Sterling, IL 61081
Phone: (815)625-3400
Fax: (815)625-6940
Format: Adult Contemporary; Top 40; Top 40

## Dayton, OH (Richmond, IN)

**WCDR-FM - 90.3  (24258)**
PO Box 601
Cedarville, OH 45314-0601
Phone: (937)766-5595
Fax: (937)766-7927
Format: Religious

**WCSM-AM - 1350  (24262)**
PO Box 492
Celina, OH 45822-0492
Phone: (419)586-5134
Fax: (419)586-3814

**WCSM-FM - 96.7  (24263)**
PO Box 492
Celina, OH 45822-0492
Phone: (419)586-5134
Fax: (419)586-3814

Format: Adult Contemporary

**WDKF-FM - 94.5  (24669)**
101 Pine St.
Dayton, OH 45402
Phone: (937)224-1137
Fax: (937)224-3667
Format: Contemporary Hit Radio (CHR)

**WDPR-FM - 88.1  (24670)**
126 N. Main St., Ste. 110
Dayton, OH 45402
Phone: (937)496-3850
Fax: (937)496-3852
Format: Classical

**WDPS-FM - 89.5  (24671)**
441 River Corridor Dr.
Dayton, OH 45402
Fax: (513)262-3744
Format: Eclectic

**WDSJ-FM - 106.5  (24672)**
101 Pine St.
Dayton, OH 45402
Phone: (937)224-1137
Fax: (937)224-3667
Format: Jazz

**WECI-FM - 91.5  (10130)**
Earlham College
801 National Rd. West
Drawer 45
Richmond, IN 47374
Phone: (765)983-1246
Fax: (765)983-1641
Format: Eclectic

**WFMG-FM - 101.3  (10131)**
2301 W. Main St.
PO Box 1646
Richmond, IN 47374
Phone: (765)962-6533
Fax: (765)966-1499
Format: Adult Contemporary

**WGXM-FM - 98.1  (24676)**
2251 Timber Ln.
Dayton, OH 45414
Phone: (937)275-8434
Fax: (937)278-5888
Format: Country; Soft Rock; Alternative/New Music/Progressive

**WHIO-AM - 1210  (24677)**
1414 Wilmington Ave
PO Box 1206
Dayton, OH 45401-1206
Phone: (937)259-2111
Fax: (937)259-2168
Format: Oldies; News

**WHKO-FM - 99.1  (24678)**
1414 Wilmington Ave.
Box 1206
Dayton, OH 45401
Phone: (937)259-2111
Fax: (937)259-2168
Format: Contemporary Country

**WHON-AM - 930  (10132)**
Box 1647
Richmond, IN 47375
Phone: (765)966-9393
Fax: (765)966-4824
Format: News; Talk

**WING-AM - 1410  (24679)**
717 E. David Rd.
Dayton, OH 45429
Phone: (937)294-5858
Fax: (937)297-5233
Format: News; Talk

**WIZE-AM - 1340  (24681)**
101 Pine St.
Dayton, OH 45402
Phone: (937)224-1137
Fax: (937)224-3667
Format: Adult Contemporary; Oldies

**WKBV-AM - 1490  (10133)**
2301 W. Main St., Box 1646
Richmond, IN 47374
Phone: (765)962-6533
Fax: (765)966-1499

Format: News; Sports; Talk

**WMMX-FM - 107.7  (24683)**
101 Pine St.
Ste. 200
Dayton, OH 45402
Fax: (513)224-3667
Format: Adult Contemporary

**WMUB-FM - 88.5  (24985)**
Miami University
Oxford, OH 45056-1618
Phone: (513)529-5885
Fax: (513)529-6048
Format: Public Radio; Jazz; Talk

**WMVR-AM - 1080  (25045)**
2929 W Russell Rd.
Sidney, OH 45365-8686
Phone: (937)498-1055
Fax: (937)498-2277
Format: Adult Contemporary

**WMVR-FM - 105.5  (25046)**
2929 W Russell Rd.
Sidney, OH 45365-8686
Phone: (937)498-1055
Fax: (937)498-2277
Format: Adult Contemporary

**WONE-AM - 980  (24684)**
101 Pine St., Ste. 200
Dayton, OH 45402
Phone: (937)224-1137
Fax: (937)224-3667
Format: Adult Contemporary

**WQLK-FM - 96.1  (10134)**
Box 1647
Richmond, IN 47375
Phone: (765)962-1595
Fax: (765)966-4824
Format: Hot Country

**WYSO-FM - 91.3  (25206)**
Antioch University
795 Livermore St.
Yellow Springs, OH 45387
Phone: (937)767-6422
Fax: (937)767-6461
Format: Public Radio; Eclectic

**WZLR-FM - 95.7  (24689)**
1414 Wilmington Ave.
PO Box 1206
Dayton, OH 45401-1206
Phone: (937)259-2111
Fax: (937)259-2168
Format: Oldies

## Detroit, MI

**CIDR-FM - 93.9  (15069)**
30100 Telegraph Rd., Ste. 460
Bingham Farms, MI 48025
Phone: (313)961-9811
Fax: (313)961-1603
Format: Adult Contemporary

**WAAM-AM - 1600  (15027)**
4230 Packard Rd.
Ann Arbor, MI 48108
Phone: (734)971-1600
Fax: (734)973-2916
Format: Talk; News

**WAHS-FM - 89.5  (15035)**
2800 Waukegan
Auburn Hills, MI 48326
Phone: (248)852-9427
Fax: (248)852-0595
Format: Educational

**WCAR-AM - 1090  (15317)**
32500 Park Ln.
Garden City, MI 48135
Phone: (734)525-1111
Fax: (734)525-3608
Format: Eclectic

**WDET-FM - 101.9  (15207)**
4600 Cass Avenue
Detroit, MI 48201
Phone: (313)577-4146
Fax: (313)577-1300

Format: Alternative/New Music/Progressive; Jazz; News;
Folk; Blues

**WDTR-FM - 90.9 (15210)**
9345 Lawton Ave.
Detroit, MI 48206
Phone: (313)596-3507
Fax: (313)596-3517
Format: Information; Educational

**WDTW AM - 1310 (15279)**
27675 Halsted Rd.
PO Box 1310
Farmington Hills, MI 48331
Phone: (248)324-5800
Fax: (248)848-0313
Format: Talk; News

**WDTW-FM - 106.7 (15211)**
2930 E Jefferson Ave.
Detroit, MI 48207
Phone: (313)259-4323
Fax: (313)259-9817
Format: Classic Rock

**WGPR-FM - 107.5 (15213)**
3146 E. Jefferson Ave.
Detroit, MI 48207
Phone: (313)259-8862
Fax: (313)259-6662
Format: Urban Contemporary

**WHLS-AM - 1450 (15691)**
808 Huron Ave.
PO Box 807
Port Huron, MI 48061-0807
Phone: (810)982-9000
Fax: (810)987-9380

**WHMI-FM - 93.5 (15436)**
1277 Parkway Dr.
PO Box 935
Howell, MI 48844
Phone: (517)546-0860
Fax: (517)546-1758

**WJLB-FM - 97.9 (15215)**
645 Griswold St., Ste. 633
Detroit, MI 48226-4177
Phone: (313)965-2000
Fax: (313)965-9970
Format: Urban Contemporary

**WKRK-FM - 97.1 (15790)**
15600 W. Twelve Mile Rd.
Southfield, MI 48076
Phone: (248)395-9797
Fax: (248)423-7725
Format: Talk

**WLEN-FM - 103.9 (14965)**
242 W. Maumee St.
PO Box 687
Adrian, MI 49221
Phone: (517)263-1039
Fax: (517)265-5362
Format: Adult Contemporary

**WLQV-AM - 1500 (15556)**
29200 Vassar Dr., Ste. 150
Livonia, MI 48152
Phone: (248)477-4600
Fax: (248)477-6911
Format: Religious

**WLSP-AM - 1530 (15544)**
G-3338 E Bristol Rd.
Burton, MI 48529
Phone: (810)743-1080
Format: Big Band/Nostalgia

**WMKM-AM - 1440 (15217)**
2994 E Grand Blvd.
Detroit, MI 48202
Phone: (313)871-1440
Fax: (313)871-6088
Format: Gospel

**WMUZ-FM - 103.5 (15218)**
12300 Radio Pl.
Detroit, MI 48228
Phone: (313)272-3434
Fax: (313)272-5045
Format: Religious; Contemporary Christian; Talk

**WMXD-FM - 92.3 (15219)**
645 Griswold
Detroit, MI 48226
Phone: (313)965-2000

Fax: (313)965-3965
Format: Adult Contemporary; Urban Contemporary; Urban Contemporary

**WOMC-FM - 104.3 (15285)**
2201 Woodward Heights Blvd.
Ferndale, MI 48220
Phone: (248)546-9600
Fax: (248)546-5446
Format: Oldies

**WRIF-FM - 101.1 (15286)**
One Radio Plz.
Ferndale, MI 48220
Phone: (248)547-0101
Fax: (248)542-8800
Format: Album-Oriented Rock (AOR)

## Duluth, MN-Superior, WI

**KDAL-AM - 610 (16070)**
715 E. Central Entrance
Duluth, MN 55811
Phone: (218)722-4321
Fax: (218)722-5423
Format: Adult Contemporary; News; Information; Information

**KDNW-FM - 97.3 (16072)**
1101 E. Central Entrance
Duluth, MN 55811
Phone: (218)722-6700
Fax: (218)722-1092
Format: Religious

**KGHS-AM - 1230 (16182)**
519 Third St.
International Falls, MN 56649
Phone: (218)283-3481
Fax: (218)283-3087
Format: Adult Contemporary; News

**KKCB-FM - 105.1 (16073)**
14 E. Central Entrance
Duluth, MN 55811
Phone: (218)727-4500
Fax: (218)727-9356
Format: Country

**KKIM-FM - 94.3 (15916)**
PO Box 140
Aitkin, MN 56431
Phone: (218)927-2344
Fax: (218)927-2100
Format: Country

**KKIN-AM - 930 (15917)**
PO Box 140
Aitkin, MN 56431
Phone: (218)927-2100
Fax: (218)927-4090
Format: Music of Your Life

**KLDJ-FM - 101.7 (16074)**
14 E Central Entrance
Duluth, MN 55811
Phone: (218)727-4500
Fax: (218)727-9356
Format: Oldies

**KOZY-AM - 1320 (16153)**
Box 597
Grand Rapids, MN 55744
Phone: (218)326-3446
Fax: (218)326-3448
Format: Oldies; News

**KQDS-FM - 94.9 (16075)**
2001 London Rd.
Duluth, MN 55812
Phone: (218)728-1622
Fax: (218)728-5809
Format: Classic Rock

**KRBT-AM - 1340 (16110)**
Box 650
Eveleth, MN 55734
Phone: (218)741-5922
Fax: (218)741-7302
Format: Talk

**KSDM-FM - 104.1 (16183)**
519 Third St.
International Falls, MN 56649
Phone: (218)283-2622
Fax: (218)283-3087

Format: Country

**KUMD-FM - 103.3 (16076)**
130 Humanities Bldg.
Duluth, MN 55812
Phone: (218)726-7181
Fax: (218)726-6571
Format: Public Radio; Alternative/New Music/Progressive; News; Information

**KUWS-FM - 91.3 (33573)**
1800 Grand Ave.
Superior, WI 54880-2898
Phone: (715)394-8530
Fax: (715)394-8404
Format: Public Radio; News; Jazz; Urban Contemporary; Alternative/New Music/Progressive; Talk

**WEVE-FM - 97.9 (16111)**
PO Box 650
Eveleth, MN 55734
Phone: (218)741-5922
Fax: (218)741-7302
Format: Adult Contemporary

**WHSM-AM - 910 (33048)**
16880 W. US Hwy. 63
Hayward, WI 54843
Phone: (715)634-4836
Fax: (715)634-8256
Format: Music of Your Life

**WHSM-FM - 101.1 (33049)**
16880 W. US Hwy. 63
Hayward, WI 54843
Phone: (715)634-4836
Fax: (715)634-8256
Format: Adult Contemporary

**WMFG-AM - 1240 (16175)**
807 W. 37th St.
Hibbing, MN 55746
Phone: (218)263-7531
Fax: (218)263-6112
Format: Sports

**WNCB-FM - 89.5 (16079)**
425 W. Superior St., Ste. 300
Duluth, MN 55802
Phone: (218)722-3017
Fax: (218)722-1650
Format: Contemporary Christian

**WRLS-FM - 92.3 (33051)**
PO Box 1008
Hayward, WI 54843
Phone: (715)634-4871
Fax: (715)634-3025
Format: Adult Contemporary; Sports

**WWJC-AM - 850 (16081)**
1120 E McCuen St
Duluth, MN 55808-2199
Phone: (218)626-2738
Format: Religious

## Erie, PA

**WREO-FM - 97.1 (24141)**
3226 Jefferson Rd.
Ashtabula, OH 44004
Phone: (216)993-2126
Fax: (216)992-2658
Format: Adult Contemporary

## Evansville, IN (Madisonville, KY)

**WBDC-FM - 100.9 (9950)**
PO Box 1009
Jasper, IN 47547-1009
Phone: (812)683-4144
Fax: (812)683-5891
Format: Country

**WBTO-FM - 102.3 (10225)**
PO Box 242
Vincennes, IN 47591
Phone: (812)882-6060
Fax: (812)885-2604
Format: Classic Rock

**WDKS-FM - 106.1 (9693)**
1133 Lincoln Ave
PO Box 78
Evansville, IN 47701-4078
Phone: (812)425-4226

Fax: (812)421-0005
**Format:** Adult Contemporary; Contemporary Hit Radio (CHR)

**WFIW-AM - 1390  (8689)**
Box 310
Fairfield, IL 62837
Phone: (618)842-2159
Fax: (618)847-5907
**Format:** News; Talk

**WFIW-FM - 104.9  (8690)**
Box 310
Fairfield, IL 62837
Phone: (618)842-2159
Fax: (618)847-5907
**Format:** Adult Contemporary

**WGAB-AM - 1180  (10071)**
1180 Maple Ln.
Newburgh, IN 47630
Phone: (812)853-9422

**WGBF-AM - 1280  (9696)**
1133 Lincoln Ave
Evansville, IN 47714
Phone: (812)425-4226
Fax: (812)421-0005
**Format:** News; Talk; Sports

**WGBF-FM - 103.1  (9697)**
113 Lincoln Ave.
PO Box 78
Evansville, IN 47711
Phone: (812)425-4226
Fax: (812)421-0005
**Format:** Album-Oriented Rock (AOR)

**WITZ-AM - 990  (9951)**
Old U.S. 231 S.
Box 167
Jasper, IN 47546
Phone: (812)482-2131
Fax: (812)482-9609
**Format:** Adult Contemporary; Top 40; Easy Listening

**WITZ-FM - 104.7  (9952)**
Old U.S. 231 S.
Box 167
Jasper, IN 47546
Phone: (812)482-2131
Fax: (812)482-9609
**Format:** Adult Contemporary; Top 40; Easy Listening

**WJPS-AM - 1400  (9699)**
1162 Mt. Auburn Rd.
PO Box 3848
Evansville, IN 47736
**Format:** Oldies

**WNIN-FM - 88.3  (9701)**
405 Carpenter St.
Evansville, IN 47708
Phone: (812)423-2973
Fax: (812)428-7548
**Format:** Public Radio; Classical; Blues; News; Folk; News; Folk

**WOKZ-FM - 105.9  (8691)**
Box 310
Fairfield, IL 62837
Phone: (618)842-2159
Fax: (618)847-5907
**Format:** Country

**WPSR-FM - 90.7  (9702)**
5400 1st Ave.
Evansville, IN 47710
Phone: (812)435-8241
Fax: (812)435-8241
**Format:** Full Service

**WQKZ-FM - 98.5  (9953)**
1978 S. Witz Rd.
Jasper, IN 47546
Phone: (812)367-1884
Fax: (812)482-9609

**WRAY-AM - 1250  (10121)**
PO Box 8
Princeton, IN 47670
Phone: (812)386-1250
Fax: (812)386-6249
**Format:** Hot Country

**WRAY-FM - 98.1  (10122)**
PO Box 8
Princeton, IN 47670
Phone: (812)386-1250
Fax: (812)386-6249

**Format:** Hot Country

**WROY-AM - 1460  (7965)**
101 N. Church
PO Box 400
Carmi, IL 62821
Phone: (618)382-4161
Fax: (618)382-4162
**Format:** Oldies; News; Sports

**WRUL-FM - 97.3  (7966)**
101 N. Church
PO Box 400
Carmi, IL 62821
Phone: (618)382-4161
Fax: (618)382-4162
**Format:** Country; News; Sports

**WSWI-AM - 820  (9703)**
Radio Center
8600 University Blvd.
Evansville, IN 47712
Phone: (812)465-1665
Fax: (812)461-5261
**Format:** Alternative/New Music/Progressive

**WTCJ-AM - 1230  (10187)**
Hwy. 66
PO Box 397
Tell City, IN 47586
Phone: (812)547-2345
Fax: (812)547-2346
**Format:** Adult Contemporary; Soft Rock

**WVHI-AM - 1330  (9705)**
114 NW Martin Luther King Blvd
Evansville, IN 47708
Phone: (812)425-2221
Fax: (812)425-2078
**Format:** Religious

**WVJC-FM - 89.1  (9003)**
2200 College Dr.
Mount Carmel, IL 62863
Phone: (618)262-8989
Fax: (618)262-7317
**Format:** Alternative/New Music/Progressive

**WYFX-FM - 106.7  (10043)**
7109 Upton Rd
Mount Vernon, IN 47620
Phone: (812)838-1590
Fax: (812)838-6434
**Format:** Middle-of-the-Road (MOR)

## Fargo, ND

**KBOT-FM - 104.1  (16044)**
PO Box 746
Detroit Lakes, MN 56502
Phone: (218)847-5624
Fax: (218)847-7657
**Format:** Hot Country

**KBRF-AM - 1250  (16124)**
728 Western Ave. N.
Fergus Falls, MN 56537
Phone: (218)736-7596
Fax: (218)736-2836
**Format:** Contemporary Country; Talk; Agricultural; News; Information

**KDLM-AM - 1340  (16045)**
1340 Richwood Rd.
PO Box 746
Detroit Lakes, MN 56502
Phone: (218)847-5624
Fax: (218)847-7657
**Format:** Adult Contemporary; News; Information; Sports

**KJJK-AM - 1020  (16125)**
PO Box 495
Fergus Falls, MN 56538
Phone: (218)736-5408
Fax: (218)736-2836
**Format:** Oldies

**KJJK-FM - 96.5  (16126)**
PO Box 495
Fergus Falls, MN 56538-0495
Phone: (218)736-7596
Fax: (218)736-2836
**Format:** Hot Country

**KKAQ-AM - 1460  (16663)**
PO Box 40
Thief River Falls, MN 56701-0040
Phone: (218)681-4900

Fax: (218)681-3717
**Format:** Contemporary Country

**KRJB-FM - 106.3  (15912)**
312 W. Main St.
Ada, MN 56510
Phone: (218)784-2844
Fax: (218)784-3749
**Format:** Full Service

**KRJM-FM - 101.5  (16236)**
213 N Main St.
PO Box 420
Mahnomen, MN 56557
Phone: (218)935-5355
Fax: (218)959-9020
**Format:** Oldies

**KTRF-AM - 1230  (16665)**
Hwy. 32 N.
PO Box 40
Thief River Falls, MN 56701
Phone: (218)681-1230
Fax: (218)681-3717
**Format:** Full Service

**KZCR-FM - 103.3  (16127)**
728 Western Ave. N.
PO Box 495
Fergus Falls, MN 56538
Phone: (218)736-5553
Fax: (218)736-2836

## Flint-Saginaw-Bay City, MI

**WCEN-AM - 1150  (15726)**
1705 Tittabawassee Rd.
Saginaw, MI 48604-9431
Fax: (517)772-9420
**Format:** Big Band/Nostalgia; Talk; News

**WCEN-FM - 94.5  (15727)**
1795 Tittabawassee Rd.
Saginaw, MI 48604-9431
Fax: (517)772-9420
**Format:** Country

**WCHW-FM - 91.3  (15054)**
1624 Columbus Ave.
Bay City, MI 48706
Phone: (989)892-1741
Fax: (989)892-7946
**Format:** Album-Oriented Rock (AOR)

**WCMU-FM - 89.5  (15614)**
Public Broadcasting Center
Central Michigan University
1999 E. Campus Dr.
Mount Pleasant, MI 48859
Phone: (989)774-3105
Fax: (989)774-4427
**Format:** Jazz; Blues; News; Classical; Public Radio

**WFBE-FM - 95.1  (15294)**
G 4511 Miller Rd.
Flint, MI 48507
Phone: (810)720-9510
Fax: (810)720-9513
**Format:** Public Radio; Full Service; Eclectic; Eclectic

**WFDF-AM - 910  (15295)**
6317 Taylor Dr.
Flint, MI 48507-4683
Phone: (810)238-7300
Fax: (810)238-7310
**Format:** Talk; News; Sports

**WFLT-AM - 1420  (15296)**
317 S. Averill
Flint, MI 48506
Phone: (810)239-5733
Fax: (810)239-7134
**Format:** Religious; Gospel; Gospel

**WFYC-AM - 1280  (14985)**
PO Box 669
Alma, MI 48801-0669
Phone: (517)463-3175
Fax: (517)463-6674
**Format:** Sports

**WGDN-FM - 103.1  (15327)**
3601 W. Woods Rd.
Gladwin, MI 48624
Phone: (989)426-1031
Fax: (989)426-9436

**Format:** Country

**WHNN-FM - 96.1 (15728)**
1740 Champagne Dr. N.
Saginaw, MI 48604-9239
Phone: (989)776-2100
Fax: (989)776-2121
**Format:** Oldies

**WIOS-AM - 1480 (15818)**
PO Box 549
Tawas City, MI 48764-0549
Fax: (517)362-4544
**Format:** Easy Listening; Talk; Sports

**WKCQ-FM - 98.1 (15731)**
Box 1776
Saginaw, MI 48605
Phone: (989)752-8161
Fax: (989)752-8102
**Format:** Country

**WKJC-FM - 104.7 (15819)**
523 Meadow Rd.
PO Box 549
Tawas City, MI 48764-0549
Phone: (989)362-3417
Fax: (989)362-4544
**Format:** Country; Sports

**WLEW-AM - 1340 (15039)**
935 S. Van Dyke Rd.
Bad Axe, MI 48413
Phone: (989)269-9931
Fax: (989)269-7702
**Format:** Contemporary Country

**WLEW-FM - 102.1 (15040)**
935 S. Van Dyke Rd.
Bad Axe, MI 48413
Phone: (989)269-9931
Fax: (989)269-7702
**Format:** Adult Contemporary; Classic Rock

**WMIC-AM - 660 (15755)**
19 S. Elk
Sandusky, MI 48471
Phone: (810)648-2700
Fax: (810)648-3242
**Format:** Full Service

**WMLM-AM - 1520 AM (14986)**
4170 N. State Rd.
Alma, MI 48801
Phone: (989)463-4013
**Format:** Country

**WOAP-AM - 1090 (15664)**
2301 N. Shiawassee St.
PO Box 128
Owosso, MI 48867
Phone: (989)725-8196
Fax: (989)725-6626
**Format:** Big Band/Nostalgia; Religious

**WPRJ-FM - 101.7 (15138)**
227 Jackson Rd.
PO Box 236
Coleman, MI 48618
Phone: (517)465-9775
Fax: (517)465-1060
**Format:** Contemporary Christian

**WSAM-AM - 1400 (15734)**
Box 1776
Saginaw, MI 48605
Phone: (989)752-8161
Fax: (989)752-8102
**Format:** Middle-of-the-Road (MOR)

**WSGW-AM - 790 (15735)**
1795 Tittabawassee
Saginaw, MI 48605
Phone: (517)752-3456
Fax: (517)754-5046
**Format:** News; Talk

**WTGV-FM - 97.7 (15756)**
19 S. Elk
Sandusky, MI 48471
Phone: (810)648-2700
Fax: (810)648-3242

**Format:** Middle-of-the-Road (MOR)

**WTLZ-FM - 107.1 (15736)**
1795 Tittabawassee
Saginaw, MI 48604-9431
**Format:** Jazz; Ethnic; Religious; Urban Contemporary; Religious; Urban Contemporary

**WVXH-FM - 92.1 (15389)**
560 E. Larch Rd.
Harrison, MI 48625
Phone: (989)539-0069
Fax: (989)539-0060
**Format:** Educational; Eclectic; Public Radio

**WWBN-FM - 101.5 (15085)**
G 3338 E. Bristol Rd.
Burton, MI 48529
Phone: (810)742-1470
Fax: (810)742-5170
**Format:** Album-Oriented Rock (AOR)

**WWCK-AM - 105.5 (15300)**
6317 Taylor Dr.
Flint, MI 48507-4683
Phone: (810)744-1570
Fax: (810)743-2500
**Format:** Contemporary Hit Radio (CHR)

## Fort Wayne (Angola), IN

**WAJI-FM - 95.1 (9727)**
347 W. Berry St., Ste. 417
Fort Wayne, IN 46802
Phone: (219)423-3676
Fax: (219)422-5266
**Format:** Adult Contemporary

**WBNI-FM - 91.3 (9730)**
3204 Clairmont Ct.
Fort Wayne, IN 46808
Phone: (260)452-1189
Fax: (260)452-1188
**Format:** Public Radio; News; Information; Classical; Jazz

**WERT-AM - 1220 (25130)**
9070 Menden
PO Box 487
Van Wert, OH 45891
Phone: (419)238-1220
Fax: (419)238-2578
**Format:** Adult Contemporary; News; Agricultural; Sports; Agricultural; Sports

**WFCV-AM - 1090 (9733)**
3737 Lake Ave.
Fort Wayne, IN 46805
Phone: (219)423-2337
Fax: (219)423-6355
**Format:** Religious

**WGL-FM - 102 (9736)**
2000 Lower Huntington Rd.
Fort Wayne, IN 46819
Phone: (219)747-1511
Fax: (219)747-3999
**Format:** Adult Contemporary

**WGLL-AM - 1570 (9554)**
5446 CR 29
Auburn, IN 46706
Fax: (219)925-1345
**Format:** Talk

**WMEE-FM - 97.3 (9738)**
2915 Maples Rd.
Fort Wayne, IN 46816
Phone: (260)447-5511
Fax: (260)447-7546
**Format:** Contemporary Hit Radio (CHR)

**WNUY-FM - 100.1 (9627)**
118 S. Main
PO Box 321
Bluffton, IN 46714
Phone: (260)824-2804
Fax: (260)824-2805
**Format:** Adult Contemporary

**WQHK-AM - 1380 (9740)**
2915 Maples Rd.
Fort Wayne, IN 46816
Phone: (260)447-5105
Fax: (812)332-0129

**Format:** Country

**WXKE-FM - 103.9 (9741)**
2541 Goshen Rd.
Fort Wayne, IN 46808
Fax: (219)482-5151
**Format:** Album-Oriented Rock (AOR); Classic Rock; Alternative/New Music/Progressive

**WYSR-FM - 94.1 (9742)**
2000 Lower Huntington Rd.
Fort Wayne, IN 46819
Phone: (219)747-1511
Fax: (219)747-3999
**Format:** Oldies

## Grand Rapids-Kalamazoo-Battle Creek, MI

**WBBL-AM - 1340 (15350)**
60 Monroe Center
Grand Rapids, MI 49503
Phone: (616)456-5461
Fax: (616)451-3299
**Format:** Sports

**WBCH-AM - 1220 (15399)**
119 W. State St.
PO Box 88
Hastings, MI 49058
Phone: (269)945-3414
Fax: (269)945-3470
**Format:** Hot Country

**WBMX-AM - 640 (15352)**
1345 Thomas St. SE
Grand Rapids, MI 49506-2651
**Format:** Adult Contemporary; Middle-of-the-Road (MOR); News; News

**WBXX-FM - 95.3 (15046)**
390 Golden Ave.
Battle Creek, MI 49015
Phone: (616)963-5555
Fax: (616)963-5185
**Format:** Adult Contemporary

**WCSG-FM - 91.3 (15353)**
1159 E. Beltline Ave. NE
Grand Rapids, MI 49525
Phone: (616)942-1500
Fax: (616)942-7078
**Format:** Religious

**WEFG-FM - 97.5 (15311)**
517 Beebe St.
Fremont, MI 49412-1301
**Format:** Classic Rock

**WFAT-FM - 96.5 (15483)**
6021 S. Westnedge Ave.
Kalamazoo, MI 49002-2811
Phone: (269)327-7600
Fax: (269)327-0726
**Format:** Adult Contemporary

**WFUR-AM - 1570 (15354)**
PO Box 1808
Grand Rapids, MI 49501
Phone: (616)451-9387
Fax: (616)451-8460
**Format:** Religious

**WGHN-AM - 1370 (15329)**
1 South Harbor
Grand Haven, MI 49417
Phone: (616)842-8110
Fax: (616)842-4350
**Format:** Adult Contemporary

**WGHN-FM - 92.1 (15330)**
1 South Harbor
Grand Haven, MI 49417
Phone: (616)842-8110
**Format:** Adult Contemporary

**WGNB-FM - 89.3 (15909)**
3764 84th Ave.
PO Box 40
Zeeland, MI 49464
Phone: (616)772-7300
Fax: (616)772-9663

**Format:** Religious

**WGVU-AM - 1480  (15357)**
301 W. Fulton
Grand Rapids, MI 49504-6492
Phone: (616)331-6666
Fax: (616)336-7204
**Format:** News; Information

**WGVU-FM - 88.5  (15358)**
301 W. Fulton
Grand Rapids, MI 49504-6492
Phone: (616)331-6666
Fax: (616)336-7204
**Format:** Public Radio; Jazz; News; Information

**WHTC-AM - 1450  (15417)**
87 Central
Holland, MI 49423
Phone: (616)392-3121
Fax: (616)392-8066
**Format:** Full Service

**WJNZ-AM - 1680  (15499)**
3777 44th St. SE
Kentwood, MI 49512-3945
Phone: (616)656-0586
Fax: (616)656-9326
**Format:** Urban Contemporary

**WJQK-FM - 99.3  (15910)**
425 Centerstone Ct.
Zeeland, MI 49464
Phone: (616)931-9930
Fax: (616)931-1280
**Format:** Religious; Contemporary Christian

**WKPR-AM - 1420  (15488)**
2244 Ravine Rd.
PO Box 50867
Kalamazoo, MI 49004
Phone: (269)381-1420
Fax: (269)381-1420
**Format:** Middle-of-the-Road (MOR); Religious

**WLCS-FM - 98.3  (15312)**
517 Beebe St.
Fremont, MI 49412-1301
Phone: (231)759-0544
Fax: (231)759-3410
**Format:** Oldies

**WLHT-FM - 95.7  (15362)**
PO Box 96
Grand Rapids, MI 49501
Phone: (616)451-4800
Fax: (616)451-0113
**Format:** Adult Contemporary

**WLKM-AM - 1520  (15825)**
59750 Constantine Rd.
Three Rivers, MI 49093
Phone: (269)278-1815
Fax: (269)273-7975
**Format:** Country

**WLKM-FM - 95.9  (15826)**
59750 Constantine Rd.
Three Rivers, MI 49093
Phone: (269)278-1815
Fax: (269)273-7975
**Format:** Soft Rock; News; Agricultural

**WMFN-AM - 640  (15363)**
2422 Burton St. S.E.
Grand Rapids, MI 49546-4806
Phone: (616)940-8600
Fax: (616)949-9262
**Format:** Talk

**WMHG-AM - 1600  (15626)**
3565 Green St.
Muskegon, MI 49444
Phone: (231)733-2600
Fax: (231)739-9037
**Format:** Middle-of-the-Road (MOR)

**WMRR-FM - 101.7  (15627)**
3565 Green St.
Muskegon, MI 49444
Phone: (231)733-2600
Fax: (231)733-7461
**Format:** Album-Oriented Rock (AOR)

**WMSH-AM - 1230  (15812)**
70808 S. Nottawa
PO Box 7080
Sturgis, MI 49091
Phone: (269)651-2383

Fax: (269)659-1111
**Format:** Oldies

**WMUK-FM - 102.1  (15490)**
Western Michigan University
Kalamazoo, MI 49008
Fax: (616)387-4630
**Format:** Classical; News; Jazz; Public Radio; Bluegrass

**WMUS-FM - 106.9  (15629)**
3565 Green St.
Muskegon, MI 49442
Phone: (231)733-2600
Fax: (231)733-7461
**Format:** Contemporary Country

**WNWN-FM - 98.5  (15047)**
25 W. Michigan Ave., 4th Fl.
Battle Creek, MI 49017
Phone: (269)968-1991
Fax: (269)968-1881
**Format:** Contemporary Country

**WODJ-FM - 107.3  (15365)**
60 Monroe Center St. NW, 10th Fl.
Grand Rapids, MI 49503
Phone: (616)956-3323
Fax: (616)956-3424
**Format:** Oldies

**WOLY-AM - 1500  (15048)**
15074 6 1/2 Mile Rd.
Battle Creek, MI 49017
Fax: (616)965-1315
**Format:** Religious

**WOOD-AM - 1300  (15366)**
77 Monroe Center St. N.W., No. 1000
Grand Rapids, MI 49503-2903
Phone: (616)459-1919
Fax: (616)242-6599
**Format:** News; Talk

**WOOD-FM - 105.7  (15367)**
77 Monroe Center, Ste. 1000
Grand Rapids, MI 49503
Phone: (616)459-1919
Fax: (616)242-6599
**Format:** Adult Contemporary

**WPNW AM - 1260  (15418)**
5658 143rd Ave.
Holland, MI 49423
Phone: (616)394-1260
Fax: (616)394-9008
**Format:** Religious; Talk

**WQSN-AM - 1660  (15492)**
4200 W. Main St.
Kalamazoo, MI 49006
Phone: (616)345-7121
Fax: (616)345-1436
**Format:** Sports

**WQXC-FM - 100.9  (15662)**
PO Box 80
Otsego, MI 49078-0080
Fax: (616)692-6861
**Format:** Oldies

**WRCC-AM - 1400  (15050)**
390 Golden Ave.
Battle Creek, MI 49015
Phone: (616)963-5555
Fax: (616)963-5185

**WSHN-AM - 1550  (15313)**
PO Box 190
Fremont, MI 49412
Phone: (231)924-4700
Fax: (231)924-9746
**Format:** Talk; News; Sports

**WSHN-FM - 100.1  (15314)**
PO Box 190
Fremont, MI 49412
Phone: (231)924-4700
Fax: (231)924-9746
**Format:** Country

**WSHZ-FM - 107.9  (15630)**
3565 Green St.
Muskegon, MI 49444
Phone: (231)733-2600
Fax: (231)733-7461

**Format:** Adult Contemporary

**WTKG-AM - 1230  (15370)**
77 Monroe Center, Ste. 1000
Grand Rapids, MI 49503
Phone: (616)459-1919
Fax: (616)732-3330
**Format:** Talk

**WYGR-AM - 1530  (15901)**
PO Box 9591
Wyoming, MI 49509
Phone: (616)452-8589
Fax: (616)248-0176
**Format:** Hispanic

# Green Bay-Appleton (Suring), WI

**KFIZ-AM - 1450  (32954)**
254 Winnebago Dr.
Fond du Lac, WI 54935
Phone: (414)921-1071
Fax: (414)921-0757
**Format:** Talk; News; Adult Contemporary; Sports

**WAGN-AM - 1340  (33252)**
N2880 Roosevelt Rd.
Marinette, WI 54143-9717
Phone: (715)735-6631
Fax: (715)732-0125
**Format:** Adult Contemporary

**WCUB-AM - 980  (33247)**
1915 Mirro Dr.
PO Box 1990
Manitowoc, WI 54221-1990
Phone: (920)683-6800
Fax: (920)683-6807
**Format:** Country

**WDOR-FM - 93.9  (33566)**
PO Box 549
800 S. 15th Ave.
Sturgeon Bay, WI 54235
Phone: (920)743-4411
Fax: (920)743-2334
**Format:** Sports; Soft Rock

**WECB-FM - 104.3  (32817)**
PO Box 1573
Appleton, WI 54913-1573
Phone: (920)833-9999
Fax: (920)833-1329
**Format:** Oldies

**WEMI-FM - 91.9  (32818)**
1909 W. 2nd St.
Appleton, WI 54914
Phone: (920)749-9456
Fax: (920)749-0474
**Format:** Adult Contemporary; Religious

**WFCL-AM - 1380  (33533)**
1456 E Green Bay St.
Shawano, WI 54166
Phone: (715)524-2194
Fax: (715)524-9980
**Format:** Adult Album Alternative

**WHYB-FM - 103.7  (33253)**
N2880 Roosevelt Rd.
Marinette, WI 54143-9717
Phone: (715)735-6631
Fax: (715)732-0125
**Format:** Country

**WKSZ-FM - 95.9  (33015)**
1263 Main St.
Green Bay, WI 54302
Phone: (414)431-0959
Fax: (414)431-8490
**Format:** Adult Contemporary

**WLTU-FM - 92.1  (33248)**
1915 Mirro Dr.
PO Box 1990
Manitowoc, WI 54221-1990
Phone: (920)683-6800
Fax: (920)683-6807
**Format:** Oldies

**WMAM-AM - 570  (33255)**
N2880 Roosevelt Rd.
Marinette, WI 54143-9717
Phone: (715)735-6631
Fax: (715)732-0125

**Format:** Sports; Sports

**WNAM-AM - 1280  (33389)**
1427 S. Commercial St.
Neenah, WI 54956-4637
Phone: (920)727-2045
Fax: (920)722-0211
**Format:** Big Band/Nostalgia

**WNFL-AM - 1440  (33017)**
115 S. Jefferson St.
Green Bay, WI 54301
Phone: (920)435-3771
Fax: (920)455-1155
**Format:** Talk

**WOBE-FM - 101.5  (15444)**
212 W J St.
Iron Mountain, MI 49801
Phone: (906)774-5731
Fax: (906)774-4542
**Format:** Oldies

**WOZZ-FM - 93.5  (32819)**
1500 N. Casloma Dr., Ste. 307
Appleton, WI 54915-8220
Phone: (920)733-4996
Fax: (920)733-5507
**Format:** Classic Rock

**WPCK-FM - 104.9  (33455)**
PO Box 3450
Oshkosh, WI 54903-3450
Phone: (920)236-4242
Fax: (920)236-4240
**Format:** Country

**WQLH-FM - 98.5  (33019)**
810 Victoria St.
Box 310
Green Bay, WI 54305-0310
Fax: (414)468-0250
**Format:** Contemporary Hit Radio (CHR)

**WRJQ-AM - 1570  (32820)**
PO Box 1519
Appleton, WI 54912-1519
**Format:** Big Band/Nostalgia; Ethnic; Ethnic

**WRVM-FM - 102.7  (33574)**
Hwy. 32 W.
Box 212
Suring, WI 54174
Phone: (920)842-2839
**Format:** Religious

**WTCH-AM - 960  (33536)**
1456 E. Green Bay St.
Shawano, WI 54166
Phone: (715)524-2194
Fax: (715)524-9980
**Format:** Country; News; Sports

**WTRW-AM - 1590  (33586)**
1414 16th St.
Two Rivers, WI 54241-3031
Phone: (920)794-1800
Fax: (920)794-8791
**Format:** Oldies

**WZOR-FM - 94.7  (33020)**
1263 Main St., Ste. 225
Green Bay, WI 54302
Fax: (920)739-0494

## Indianapolis (Marion), IN

**WBAT-AM - 1400  (10012)**
PO Box 839
Marion, IN 46952-0839
**Format:** Oldies

**WBDG-FM (Giant 90.9) - 90.9  (9927)**
1200 N. Girls School Rd.
Indianapolis, IN 46214
Phone: (317)244-9234
Fax: (317)243-5506
**Format:** Contemporary Hit Radio (CHR)

**WBRI-AM - 1500  (9928)**
4802 E. 62nd St.
Indianapolis, IN 46220
Phone: (317)255-5484
Fax: (317)255-8592
**Format:** Information

**WBWB-FM - 96.7  (9618)**
304 State Rd. 446
PO Box 7797
Bloomington, IN 47407
Phone: (812)336-8000
Fax: (812)336-7000
**Format:** Adult Contemporary

**WCJC-FM - 99.3  (10013)**
PO Box 839
Marion, IN 46952-0839
**Format:** Contemporary Country

**WCKN-AM - 1260  (9929)**
6161 Fall Creek Rd.
Indianapolis, IN 46220
Phone: (317)257-7565
Fax: (317)253-6501
**Format:** Country

**WEDM-FM - 91.1  (9930)**
Walker Career Ctr.
9651 E. 21st St.
Indianapolis, IN 46229
Phone: (317)532-6301
Fax: (317)532-6199
**Format:** Contemporary Hit Radio (CHR)

**WFBQ-FM - 94.7  (9931)**
6161 Fall Creek Rd.
Indianapolis, IN 46220
Phone: (317)257-7565
Fax: (317)475-7484
**Format:** Album-Oriented Rock (AOR)

**WFCI-FM - 89.5  (9753)**
Franklin College of Indiana
Shirk Hall
Franklin, IN 46131
Phone: (317)738-8205
Fax: (317)738-8233
**Format:** Top 40

**WFYI-FM - 90.1  (9933)**
1401 N. Meridian St.
Indianapolis, IN 46202
Phone: (317)636-2020
Fax: (317)633-7418
**Format:** Public Radio; Talk; Classical; News; News

**WGCL-AM - 1370  (9620)**
400 One City Centre
Bloomington, IN 47404
Phone: (812)332-3366
Fax: (812)331-4570
**Format:** News; Talk

**WGOM-AM - 860  (10014)**
820 S. Pennsylvania St.
PO Box 1538
Marion, IN 46952
Phone: (765)664-7396
Fax: (765)668-6767
**Format:** Talk; News; Sports

**WHBU-AM - 1240  (9677)**
9821 S. County Rd. 800 W
Daleville, IN 47334-9421
Phone: (765)644-7791
Fax: (765)641-2383
**Format:** Talk; News; Sports; Sports

**WHHH-FM - 96.3  (9935)**
21 E Saint Joseph St.
Indianapolis, IN 46204-1025
**Format:** Contemporary Hit Radio (CHR)

**WHUT-AM - 1470  (9936)**
36 S. Pennsylvania St., Ste. 200
Indianapolis, IN 46204-3627
Phone: (317)974-0267
Fax: (317)644-1775
**Format:** Big Band/Nostalgia

**WICR-FM - 88.7  (9937)**
1400 E. Hanna Ave.
Indianapolis, IN 46227
Phone: (317)788-3280
Fax: (317)788-3490
**Format:** Classical; Jazz

**WIFE-FM - 100.3  (9664)**
406 1/2 Central Ave.
PO Box 619
Connersville, IN 47331
Phone: (765)825-6411
Fax: (765)825-2411

**Format:** Country

**WIJY-FM - 95.9  (9754)**
645 Industrial Dr.
Franklin, IN 46131-9617
Phone: (317)736-4040
Fax: (317)736-7998
**Format:** Urban Contemporary

**WIOU-AM - 1350  (9971)**
PO Box 2208
Kokomo, IN 46904-2208
Phone: (765)453-1212
Fax: (765)455-3882
**Format:** Sports; Oldies

**WIRE-FM - 100.9  (9938)**
PO Box 68920
Indianapolis, IN 46268-0920
Phone: (317)239-9473
**Format:** Country

**WLBC-FM - 104.1  (10051)**
800 E. 29th St.
Muncie, IN 47302
Phone: (765)288-4403
Fax: (765)288-0429
**Format:** Adult Contemporary

**WMDH-FM - 102.5  (10065)**
1134 West State Road 38
PO Box 690
New Castle, IN 47362
Phone: (765)282-7539
Fax: (765)529-1688
**Format:** Country

**WMRI-FM - 106.9  (10015)**
820 S. Pennsylvania St., Box 1538
Marion, IN 46952
Phone: (765)664-7396
Fax: (765)668-6767
**Format:** Adult Contemporary

**WNTS-AM - 1590  (9942)**
4800 E. Raymond St.
Indianapolis, IN 46203
Phone: (317)359-5591
**Format:** Religious

**WQME-FM - 98.7 FM  (9552)**
1100 E. 5th St.
Anderson, IN 46012-3495
Phone: (765)641-4349
Fax: (765)641-3825
**Format:** Adult Contemporary; Contemporary Christian

**WRDZ-FM - 98.3  (9643)**
630 W Carmel Dr., Ste. 160
Carmel, IN 46032
Phone: (317)574-2000
Fax: (317)581-1985
**Format:** Contemporary Hit Radio (CHR)

**WRFT-FM - 91.5  (9943)**
6141 S. Franklin Rd.
Indianapolis, IN 46259
Phone: (317)862-6649
Fax: (317)862-7262
**Format:** Eclectic

**WSAL-AM - 1230  (10002)**
PO Box 719
Logansport, IN 46947
Phone: (574)722-4000
Fax: (574)722-4010
**Format:** Full Service

**WSKT-FM - 92.7  (10175)**
201 N. Vandalia
Spencer, IN 47460
Phone: (812)829-9393
Fax: (812)829-9747
**Format:** Country

**WSYW-AM - 810  (9946)**
1800 N. Meridian St., Ste. 605
Indianapolis, IN 46202-1433
Fax: (317)273-1507
**Format:** Classical; Urban Contemporary

**WSYW-FM - 107.1  (9947)**
1800 N. Meridian St., Ste. 605
Indianapolis, IN 46202-1433
Fax: (317)273-1507

La Crosse-Eau Claire, WI  
GALE Directory of Publications & Broadcast Media/140th Ed.

**Format:** Classical

**WTTS-FM - 92.3 (9623)**
400 1 City Centre
PO Box 62
Bloomington, IN 47404
Phone: (812)332-3366
Fax: (812)331-4570
**Format:** Blues; Alternative/New Music/Progressive; Classic Rock; Classic Rock

**WWWY-FM - 104.9 (9660)**
PO Box 1789
Columbus, IN 47202-1789
**Format:** Adult Contemporary

**WXFN-AM - 1340 (10052)**
800 E. 29th St.
Muncie, IN 47302
Phone: (765)288-4403
Fax: (765)288-0429
**Format:** Sports

**WZWZ-FM - 92.5 (9974)**
PO Box 2208
Kokomo, IN 46904-2208
Phone: (765)453-1212
Fax: (765)455-3882
**Format:** Adult Contemporary

## La Crosse-Eau Claire, WI

**KAGE-FM - 95.3 (16725)**
752 Bluffview Circle
PO Box 767
Winona, MN 55987-0767
Phone: (507)452-4000
Fax: (507)452-9494
**Format:** Adult Contemporary

**KWNO-FM - 99.3 (16728)**
PO Box 767
Winona, MN 55987-0767
Phone: (507)452-4000
Fax: (507)452-9494
**Format:** Hot Country

**WATQ-FM - 106.7 (32929)**
619 Cameron St.
Eau Claire, WI 54703
Phone: (715)830-4000
Fax: (715)835-9680
**Format:** Country

**WAXX-FM - 104.5 (32930)**
Box 6000
Eau Claire, WI 54702
Phone: (715)832-1530
Fax: (715)832-5329
**Format:** Country

**WAYY-AM - 790 (32796)**
944 Harlem Ave.
Altoona, WI 54720
Phone: (715)832-1530
Fax: (715)832-5329
**Format:** News; Talk

**WBIZ-AM - 1400 (32931)**
619 Cameron St.
PO Box 45
Eau Claire, WI 54702
Phone: (715)835-5111
Fax: (715)835-9680
**Format:** Sports

**WBIZ-FM - 100.7 (32932)**
619 Cameron St.
PO Box 45
Eau Claire, WI 54703
Phone: (715)830-4000
Fax: (715)835-9680
**Format:** Contemporary Hit Radio (CHR)

**WCFW-FM - 105.7 (32890)**
318 Well St.
Chippewa Falls, WI 54729
Phone: (715)723-2257
Fax: (715)723-8276
**Format:** Middle-of-the-Road (MOR)

**WEAQ-AM - 1150 (32933)**
PO Box 1
Eau Claire, WI 54702
Phone: (715)832-1530
Fax: (715)832-5329

**Format:** Sports

**WECL-FM - 92.9 (32797)**
944 Harlem St.
Altoona, WI 54720
Phone: (715)832-1530
Fax: (715)832-5329
**Format:** Classic Rock

**WEIO-AM - 1050 (32935)**
1819 Mitchell Ave.
Eau Claire, WI 54701
Phone: (715)836-9476
Fax: (715)836-9788

**WFBZ-FM - 105.5 (33125)**
PO Box 1624
La Crosse, WI 54602-1624
Phone: (608)784-9524
Fax: (608)526-6813
**Format:** Alternative/New Music/Progressive

**WIAL-FM - 94.1 (32798)**
944 Harlem St.
PO Box 2
Altoona, WI 54720
Phone: (715)832-1530
Fax: (715)832-5329
**Format:** Contemporary Hit Radio (CHR); Contemporary Hit Radio (CHR)

**WISM-FM - 98.1 (32936)**
1819 Mitchell Ave.
Eau Claire, WI 54701
Phone: (715)836-9476
Fax: (715)836-9788
**Format:** Classic Rock; Album-Oriented Rock (AOR)

**WLFN-AM - 1490 (33441)**
1407 2nd Ave. N
PO Box 2017
Onalaska, WI 54650
Phone: (608)782-8335
Fax: (608)782-8340
**Format:** Oldies

**WLSU-FM - 88.9 (33128)**
1725 State St.
La Crosse, WI 54601
Phone: (608)785-8380
Fax: (608)785-5005
**Format:** Public Radio; Classical; Jazz

**WLXR-FM - 104.9 (33442)**
1407 2nd Ave. N
PO Box 2017
Onalaska, WI 54650
Phone: (608)782-8335
Fax: (608)782-8340
**Format:** Contemporary Hit Radio (CHR)

**WUEC-FM - 89.7 (32939)**
University of Wisconsin-Eau Claire
Eau Claire, WI 54701
Phone: (715)836-4170
Fax: (715)836-4647
**Format:** Classical; News; Jazz; Information; Blues; Folk

**WVCF-FM - 90.5 (33368)**
3434 W. Kilbourn Ave.
Milwaukee, WI 53208
Phone: (414)935-3000
**Format:** Religious

**WVRQ-AM - 1360 (33592)**
E7601A County Rd. SS
Viroqua, WI 54665
Phone: (608)637-7200
Fax: (608)637-7299
**Format:** Oldies

**WVRQ-FM - 102.3 (33593)**
E7601A County Rd. SS
Viroqua, WI 54665
Phone: (608)637-7200
Fax: (608)637-7299
**Format:** Contemporary Country

## Lafayette, IN

**WAZY-AM - 1410 (9980)**
3824 S 18th St
Lafayette, IN 47909-1410
Phone: (765)474-1410
Fax: (765)474-3442

**WJEF-FM - 91.9 (9982)**
1801 S. 18th St.
Lafayette, IN 47905
Phone: (765)772-4700
**Format:** Oldies

**WKHY-FM - 93.5 (9983)**
711 N. Earl Ave.
PO Box 7093
Lafayette, IN 47904
Phone: (765)448-1566
Fax: (765)448-1348
**Format:** Classic Rock; Album-Oriented Rock (AOR)

**WKOA-FM - 105.3 (9984)**
3575 McCarty Lane
Lafayette, IN 47905
Phone: (765)447-2186
Fax: (765)447-5058
**Format:** Country

**WXXB-FM - 102.9 (9986)**
PO Box 7093
Lafayette, IN 47903
Phone: (765)448-1566
Fax: (765)448-1348
**Format:** Contemporary Hit Radio (CHR)

## Lansing (Ann Arbor), MI

**WCSR-AM - 1340 (15407)**
170 N. West St.
PO Box 273
Hillsdale, MI 49242
Phone: (517)437-4444
Fax: (517)437-7461
**Format:** Adult Contemporary

**WCSR-FM - 92.1 (15408)**
170 N. West St.
PO Box 273
Hillsdale, MI 49242
Phone: (517)437-4444
Fax: (517)437-7461
**Format:** Adult Contemporary

**WHZZ-FM - 101.7 (15531)**
600 W. Cavanaugh
Lansing, MI 48919
Phone: (517)393-1320
Fax: (517)393-0882
**Format:** Contemporary Hit Radio (CHR)

**WILS-AM - 1320 (15532)**
600 W. Cavanaugh Rd.
PO Box 25008
Lansing, MI 48910-5008
Phone: (517)393-1320
Fax: (517)393-0882
**Format:** Adult Contemporary

**WJIM-AM - 1240 (15533)**
3420 Pine Tree Rd.
Lansing, MI 48911
Phone: (517)394-7272
Fax: (517)394-3391
**Format:** News; Talk

**WJIM-FM - 97.5 (15534)**
3420 Pine Tree Rd.
Lansing, MI 48911
Phone: (517)394-7272
Fax: (517)394-3391
**Format:** Oldies

**WKAR-AM - 870 (15251)**
Michigan State University
283 Communications Arts Bldg.
East Lansing, MI 48824
Phone: (517)355-6540
Fax: (517)353-7124
**Format:** Talk; News; Information; Information

**WKHM-AM - 970 (15458)**
1700 Glenshire Dr.
Jackson, MI 49201
Phone: (517)787-9546
Fax: (517)787-7517
**Format:** News; Talk; Sports

**WLCM-AM - 1390 (15118)**
PO Box 338
Charlotte, MI 48813
Phone: (517)543-8200
Fax: (517)543-7779

**Format:** Religious

**WMMQ-FM - 94.9 (15537)**
3200 Pine Tree
Lansing, MI 48911
Phone: (517)393-1010
Fax: (517)393-4041
**Format:** Classic Rock

**WQHH-FM - 96.5 (15147)**
101 Northcrest Rd., Ste. 4
Lansing, MI 48906-1262
Phone: (517)484-9600
Fax: (517)484-9699
**Format:** Urban Contemporary

**WVFN-AM - 730 (15538)**
3420 Pine Tree
Lansing, MI 48911
Phone: (517)394-7272
Fax: (517)394-3391
**Format:** Sports; Talk

**WVIC-FM - 94.1 (15420)**
2495 N. Cedar St
Holt, MI 48842
Phone: (517)699-0111
Fax: (517)699-1880
**Format:** Classic Rock

**WXLA-AM - 1180 (15539)**
101 Northcrest Rd., Ste. 4
Lansing, MI 48906-1262
Phone: (517)484-9600
Fax: (517)484-9699
**Format:** Adult Contemporary; Urban Contemporary

## Lima, OH

**WDOH-FM - 107.1 (24697)**
PO Box 100
Delphos, OH 45833-0100
Phone: (419)692-3963
Fax: (419)692-5896
**Format:** Country

**WIMT-FM - 102.1 (24833)**
667 W Market St.
Lima, OH 45801
Phone: (419)223-2060
Fax: (419)229-3888
**Format:** Contemporary Country

**WKKI-FM - 94.3 (24264)**
PO Box 322
Celina, OH 45822-0322
Phone: (419)586-7715
Fax: (419)586-1074
**Format:** Adult Contemporary

**WTGN-FM - 97.7 (24835)**
1600 Elida Rd.
Lima, OH 45805-1597
Phone: (419)227-2525
Fax: (419)222-5438
**Format:** Religious

**WZOQ-FM - 92.1 (24836)**
1301 N. Cable Rd.
Lima, OH 45805
Phone: (419)331-1600
Fax: (419)228-5085
**Format:** Adult Contemporary

## Louisville, KY

**WAVG-AM - 1450 (9956)**
213 Magnolia Ave.
PO Box 726
Jeffersonville, IN 47130
Phone: (812)283-3577
Fax: (812)285-5060
**Format:** Country

**WBIW-AM - 1340 (9564)**
424 Heltonville Rd.
PO Box 1307
Bedford, IN 47421
Phone: (812)275-7555
Fax: (812)279-8046

**Format:** Oldies

**WIKI-FM - 95.3 (10081)**
2470 N State Hwy. 7
North Vernon, IN 47265-7184
**Format:** Contemporary Country

**WMPI-FM - 105.3 (10152)**
Box 270
Scottsburg, IN 47170
Phone: (812)752-3688
Fax: (812)752-2345
**Format:** Contemporary Country

**WSLM-AM - 1220 (10148)**
Radio Ridge
Hwy. 56 E.
PO Box 385
Salem, IN 47167
Phone: (812)883-5750
Fax: (812)883-2797
**Format:** Contemporary Country; Agricultural; Agricultural

**WSLM-FM - 97.9 (10149)**
PO Box 385
Salem, IN 47167-0385
Phone: (812)883-5750
Fax: (812)883-2797
**Format:** Gospel; Sports; Talk; Agricultural; Talk

**WXLM-FM - 105.7 (10059)**
PO Box 655
New Albany, IN 47151
**Format:** Bluegrass

**WXLN-AM - 1570 (10060)**
PO Box 655
New Albany, IN 47151-0655
**Format:** Religious; Talk; Talk

## Madison, WI

**WCLO-AM - 1230 (33109)**
PO Box 5001
Janesville, WI 53547-5001
Phone: (608)752-7895
Fax: (608)752-4438
**Format:** Talk; News

**WDDC-FM - 100.1 (33482)**
PO Box 448
Portage, WI 53901-0448
Phone: (608)742-1001
Fax: (608)742-1688
**Format:** Contemporary Country

**WDMP-AM - 810 (32913)**
PO Box 9
Dodgeville, WI 53533
Phone: (608)935-2302
Fax: (608)935-3464
**Format:** Country; Agricultural

**WDMP-FM - 99.3 (32914)**
PO Box 9
Dodgeville, WI 53533
Phone: (608)935-2302
Fax: (608)935-3464
**Format:** Country; Agricultural

**WFAW-AM - 940 (32988)**
PO Box 94
Fort Atkinson, WI 53538
Phone: (920)563-9329
Fax: (920)563-0315
**Format:** News; Talk

**WGEZ-AM - 1490 (32847)**
622 Public Ave.
Beloit, WI 53511
Phone: (608)365-8865
Fax: (608)365-8867
**Format:** Oldies

**WHIT-AM - 1550 (33234)**
PO Box 44408
Madison, WI 53744
Phone: (608)273-1000
Fax: (608)281-0005
**Format:** Talk; Sports

**WIBA-AM - 1310 (33235)**
PO Box 99
Madison, WI 53701
Phone: (608)281-1070
Fax: (608)276-9422

**Format:** Information; News; Sports; Sports

**WIBA-FM - 101.5 (33236)**
PO Box 99
Madison, WI 53701
Phone: (608)274-5450
Fax: (608)274-5521
**Format:** Classic Rock

**WIBU-AM - 900 (33484)**
N2349 Wibu Rd
Poynette, WI 53955
Phone: (608)635-7341
Fax: (608)635-7343
**Format:** Music of Your Life; Easy Listening

**WKCH-FM - 106.5 (32989)**
PO Box 94
Fort Atkinson, WI 53538
Phone: (262)473-9524
Fax: (920)563-0315
**Format:** Oldies

**WOLX-FM - 94.9 (33241)**
7601 Ganserway
Madison, WI 53719
Phone: (608)826-0077
Fax: (608)826-1244
**Format:** Oldies

**WPDR-AM - 1350 (33483)**
PO Box 448
Portage, WI 53901-0448
Phone: (608)742-8833
Fax: (608)742-1688
**Format:** Adult Contemporary; Talk

**WRJC-AM - 1270 (33266)**
Fairway Ln.
PO Box 200
Mauston, WI 53948-0200
Phone: (608)847-6565
Fax: (608)847-6249

**WRPQ-AM - 740 (32832)**
Box 456
Baraboo, WI 53913
Phone: (608)356-3974
Fax: (608)355-9952
**Format:** Easy Listening

**WWQM-FM - 106.3 (33244)**
PO Box 2058
Madison, WI 53701
Phone: (608)273-1000
Fax: (608)321-0005
**Format:** Country

## Mankato, MN

**KDOG-FM - 96.7 (16244)**
Hwy. 14 E.
Box 1420
Mankato, MN 56001
Phone: (507)345-4537
**Format:** Contemporary Hit Radio (CHR)

**KEEZ-FM - 99.1 (16245)**
54934 210th Ln.
Mankato, MN 56001-2100
Phone: (507)345-4646
Fax: (507)345-3299
**Format:** Adult Contemporary; Sports; News

**KMSU-FM - 89.7 (16247)**
AF 205
Mankato, MN 56001
Phone: (507)389-5678
Fax: (507)389-1705
**Format:** Public Radio; Eclectic; Eclectic

**KTOE-AM - 1420 (16250)**
Box 1420
Mankato, MN 56001
Phone: (507)345-4537
**Format:** Adult Contemporary; News; Talk

## Marquette, MI

**WCCY-AM - 1400 (15425)**
313 Montezuma Ave.
Houghton, MI 49931
Phone: (906)482-7700
Fax: (906)482-7751

# Marquette, MI

**Format:** Contemporary Country

**WDMJ-AM - 1320 (15576)**
1009 W Ridge St., Ste. A
Marquette, MI 49855
Phone: (906)225-1313
Fax: (906)225-1324
**Format:** News; Talk; Sports

**WEUL-FM - 98.1 (15500)**
130 Carmen Dr.
Marquette, MI 49855
Phone: (906)249-1423
**Format:** Religious

**WHWL-FM - 95.7 (15579)**
130 Carmen Dr.
Marquette, MI 49855
Phone: (906)249-1423
Fax: (906)249-4042
**Format:** Religious

**WIAN-AM - 1240 (15452)**
845 W. Washington St.
PO Box 700
Marquette, MI 49855
Phone: (906)225-1313
Fax: (906)225-1324
**Format:** News; Talk; Sports

**WMQT-FM - 107.7 (15581)**
121 N. Front St., Ste. A
Marquette, MI 49855
Phone: (906)225-9100
Fax: (906)225-5577
**Format:** Adult Contemporary

**WOLV-FM - 97.7 (15427)**
313 E. Montezuma Ave.
Houghton, MI 49931
Phone: (906)482-7700
Fax: (906)486-7751
**Format:** Adult Contemporary

## Milwaukee (Kenosha & Racine), WI

**WBEV-AM - 1430 (32837)**
100 Stoddart St.
PO Box 902
Beaver Dam, WI 53916
Phone: (920)885-4442
Fax: (920)885-2152
**Format:** News; Talk; Sports; Agricultural; Oldies; Agricultural; Oldies

**WBFM-FM - 93.7 (33539)**
2100 Washington Ave.
PO Box 27
Sheboygan, WI 53082
Phone: (920)458-2107
Fax: (920)458-9775
**Format:** Country

**WBSD-FM - 89.1 (32875)**
400 McCanna Pkwy.
Burlington, WI 53105
Phone: (262)763-0195
Fax: (262)763-0207
**Format:** Adult Album Alternative

**WEMP-AM - 1250 (33034)**
11800 W. Grange Ave.
Hales Corners, WI 53130
Phone: (414)529-1250
Fax: (414)529-2122
**Format:** Oldies

**WEZY-FM - 92.1 (33494)**
4201 Victory Ave.
Racine, WI 53405
Phone: (262)634-3311
Fax: (262)634-6515
**Format:** Adult Contemporary

**WFMR-FM - 106.9 (33350)**
5407 W. Mckinley Ave.
Milwaukee, WI 53208
Phone: (414)978-9000
Fax: (414)978-9001
**Format:** Classical

**WGLB-AM - 1560 (33352)**
5181 N 35th St.
Milwaukee, WI 53209
Phone: (414)527-4365
Fax: (414)527-4367
**Format:** Gospel

**WGLB-FM - 100.1 (33476)**
900 E. Green Bay Rd.
Port Washington, WI 53074
Phone: (262)284-2666
Fax: (262)284-2667
**Format:** Oldies

**WHBL-AM - 1330 (33540)**
2100 Washington Ave.
PO Box 27
Sheboygan, WI 53082
Phone: (920)458-2107
Fax: (920)458-9775
**Format:** News; Talk; Sports; Sports

**WISN-AM - 1130 (33353)**
PO Box 402
Milwaukee, WI 53201-0402
Phone: (414)342-8812
Fax: (414)344-1870
**Format:** Talk

**WJYI-AM - 1340 (33356)**
5407 W. McKinley Ave.
Milwaukee, WI 53208
Phone: (414)978-9000
Fax: (414)978-9001
**Format:** Contemporary Christian

**WLTQ-FM - 97.3 (33358)**
PO Box 402
Milwaukee, WI 53201
Phone: (414)342-1111
Fax: (414)344-1870
**Format:** Adult Contemporary

**WLZR-FM - 102.9 (33359)**
5407 W. McKinley Ave.
Milwaukee, WI 53208
Phone: (414)978-9000
Fax: (414)978-9001
**Format:** Album-Oriented Rock (AOR)

**WMDC-FM - 98.7 (33268)**
132 N main st
Mayville, WI 53050
Phone: (920)387-0000
Fax: (920)387-2222
**Format:** Oldies

**WMIL-FM - 106.1 (33361)**
12100 W. Howard Ave.
PO Box 20920
Milwaukee, WI 53220-0920
Phone: (414)545-8900
Fax: (414)545-4069
**Format:** Contemporary Country

**WMSE-FM - 91.7 (33362)**
1025 N. Broadway
Milwaukee, WI 53202
Phone: (414)277-7247
Fax: (414)277-7149
**Format:** Alternative/New Music/Progressive

**WNOV-AM - 860 (33364)**
3815 N. Teutonia Ave.
PO Box 06348
Milwaukee, WI 53206
Phone: (414)449-9668
Fax: (414)449-9945
**Format:** Gospel; Blues

**WOKY-AM - 920 (33030)**
12100 W. Howard Ave.
PO Box 20920
Greenfield, WI 53228-0920
Phone: (414)545-5920
Fax: (414)545-4069
**Format:** Middle-of-the-Road (MOR)

**WRJN-AM - 1400 (33495)**
4201 Victory Ave.
Racine, WI 53405
Phone: (262)634-3311
Fax: (262)634-6515
**Format:** Talk; News; News

**WTMJ-AM - 620 (33365)**
720 E. Capitol Dr.
Milwaukee, WI 53212
Phone: (414)332-9611
Fax: (414)967-5298
**Format:** News; Talk; Sports

**WUWM-FM - 89.7 (33367)**
University of Wisconsin
PO Box 413
Milwaukee, WI 53201
Phone: (414)227-3355
Fax: (414)229-5749
**Format:** Public Radio; News; Adult Album Alternative; Adult Album Alternative

**WVCY-FM - 107.7 (33371)**
3434 W. Kilbourn Ave.
Milwaukee, WI 53208
Phone: (414)935-3000
Fax: (414)935-3015
**Format:** Religious

**WXRO-FM - 95.3 (32838)**
100 Stoddart St.
PO Box 902
Beaver Dam, WI 53916
Phone: (920)885-4442
Fax: (920)885-2152
**Format:** News; Contemporary Country; Agricultural; Agricultural

## Minneapolis-St. Paul, MN

**KASM-AM - 1150 (15919)**
Box 390
Albany, MN 56307
Phone: (320)845-2184
Fax: (320)845-2187
**Format:** Talk; Ethnic; Country; Polka; Agricultural; Big Band/Nostalgia

**KBHP-FM - 101.1 (15955)**
502 Beltrami Ave., NW
Bemidji, MN 56601
Phone: (218)751-4120
Fax: (218)751-8091
**Format:** Country; Contemporary Country

**KBUN-AM - 1450 (15957)**
502 Beltrami Ave., NW
PO Box 1656
Bemidji, MN 56619-1656
Phone: (218)444-1500
Fax: (218)751-8091
**Format:** Sports; Talk

**KCLD-FM - 104.7 (16553)**
PO Box 1458
Saint Cloud, MN 56302
Phone: (320)251-1450
Fax: (320)251-8952
**Format:** Contemporary Hit Radio (CHR)

**KDIZ-AM - 1440 (16357)**
2000 Elm St. SE
Minneapolis, MN 55414
Phone: (612)617-4000
Fax: (612)676-8214

**KDWA-AM - 1460 (16162)**
514 Vermillion St.
PO Box 215
Hastings, MN 55033
Phone: (612)437-1460
Fax: (612)438-3042
**Format:** Oldies; News; Sports; Talk

**KDWB-FM - 101.3 (16564)**
1600 Utica Ave. S., Suite 400
Saint Louis Park, MN 55416
Phone: (952)417-3000
Fax: (952)417-3001
**Format:** Contemporary Hit Radio (CHR)

**KEYL-AM - 1400 (16222)**
PO Box 187
221 Central Ave.
Long Prairie, MN 56347
Phone: (612)732-2164
Fax: (612)732-2284
**Format:** Country; Full Service

**KFAI-FM - 90.3 & 106.7 (16359)**
1808 Riverside Ave.
Minneapolis, MN 55407
Phone: (612)341-3144
Fax: (612)341-4281

**Format:** Full Service; Eclectic; Ethnic

**KFXN-AM - 690**  (16360)
1600 Utica Ave. S, Ste. 400
Minneapolis, MN 55416
Phone: (952)820-4200
Fax: (952)820-4227
**Format:** Sports

**KJZI-FM - 100.3**  (16361)
1600 Utica Ave. S, Ste. 400
Minneapolis, MN 55416
Phone: (612)330-0100
Fax: (612)333-1616
**Format:** Jazz

**KKEQ-FM - 107.1**  (16136)
Hwy. 2 E.
PO Box 606
Fosston, MN 56542-0606
Phone: (218)435-1919
Fax: (218)435-1480
**Format:** Religious

**KLBB-AM - 1400**  (16102)
4930 West 77th St., Suite 364
Edina, MN 55435
Phone: (952)820-8520
Fax: (952)820-8502
**Format:** Big Band/Nostalgia

**KLFD-AM - 1410**  (16217)
234 N. Sibley Ave.
Litchfield, MN 55355
Phone: (320)693-3281
Fax: (320)693-3283
**Format:** Full Service

**KLIZ-AM - 1380**  (15981)
602 Laurel St.
PO Box 980
Brainerd, MN 56401
Phone: (218)829-2853
Fax: (218)829-6983
**Format:** Talk; News

**KLTF-AM - 960**  (16220)
16405 Haven Rd.
Little Falls, MN 56345
Phone: (320)632-5414
Fax: (320)632-2571
**Format:** Adult Contemporary; Country; Talk

**KNOF-FM - 95.3**  (16623)
1347 Selby Ave.
Saint Paul, MN 55104
Phone: (651)645-8271
Fax: (651)645-4593
**Format:** Religious

**KNSI-AM - 1450**  (16554)
Box 1458
Saint Cloud, MN 56302
Phone: (320)251-1450
Fax: (320)251-8952
**Format:** News; Talk

**KQQL-FM - 107.9**  (16363)
60 S. 6th St., Ste. 930
Minneapolis, MN 55402-4409
Phone: (612)333-8118
Fax: (612)333-1616
**Format:** Oldies

**KRBI-AM - 1310**  (16248)
54934 210th Lane
Mankato, MN 56001-2100
Phone: (507)345-4646
Fax: (507)931-4740
**Format:** Talk; Country; News; Sports

**KRBI-FM - 105.5**  (16249)
54934 210th Lane
Mankato, MN 56001
Phone: (507)345-4646
Fax: (507)345-3299

**KSTP-FM - 94.5**  (16364)
3415 University Ave.
Minneapolis, MN 55414
Phone: (612)642-4141
Fax: (612)642-4142
**Format:** Adult Contemporary

**KSUM-AM - 1370**  (16117)
1371 W. Lair Rd.
PO Box 491
Fairmont, MN 56031
Phone: (507)235-5595
Fax: (507)235-3299

**Format:** Agricultural; News; Sports; Contemporary Country; Sports; Contemporary Country

**KTCZ-FM - 97.1**  (16365)
Butler Sq., Ste. 306C
Minneapolis, MN 55403
Phone: (612)339-0000
Fax: (612)349-6854
**Format:** Album-Oriented Rock (AOR)

**KTIS-AM - 900**  (16625)
3003 N. Snelling Ave.
Saint Paul, MN 55113-1598
Phone: (651)631-5000
Fax: (651)631-5010
**Format:** Religious

**KTIS-FM - 98.5**  (16539)
3003 N. Snelling Ave.
Roseville, MN 55113
Phone: (651)631-5000
Fax: (651)631-5084

**KXDL-FM - 99.7**  (16223)
PO Box 187
221 Central Ave.
Long Prairie, MN 56347
Phone: (320)732-2164
Fax: (320)732-2284
**Format:** Oldies

**WCTS-AM - 1030**  (16488)
900 Forestview Ln. N.
Plymouth, MN 55441-5934
Phone: (763)417-8270
Fax: (763)417-8278
**Format:** Religious

**WDGY-AM - 630**  (16371)
2619 East Lake St.
Minneapolis, MN 55406
Phone: (612)729-3776
Fax: (651)436-6770
**Format:** Talk; Sports

**WFMP-FM - 107.1**  (16628)
3415 University Ave.
Saint Paul, MN 55114
Phone: (651)642-4107
**Format:** Country; News; News

**WIXK-AM - 1590**  (33425)
125 E. 3rd St.
PO Box 8
New Richmond, WI 54017
Phone: (715)246-2254
Fax: (715)246-7090
**Format:** Country; News; News

**WJON-AM - 1240**  (16556)
640 Lincoln Ave. SE
Saint Cloud, MN 56304-1024
Phone: (320)251-4422
Fax: (320)251-1855
**Format:** News; Talk; Sports; Full Service; Sports; Full Service

**WLKX-FM - 95.9**  (16131)
15226 W. Freeway Dr.
Forest Lake, MN 55025
Phone: (651)464-6796
Fax: (651)464-3638
**Format:** Talk; News; Sports; Country; Contemporary Christian

**WLOL-FM - 100.3**  (16373)
60 S. 6th St., Ste. 930
Minneapolis, MN 55402-4409
Phone: (612)330-0100
Fax: (612)330-0897
**Format:** Classic Rock

**WLTE-FM - 102.9**  (16374)
625 2nd Ave. S., Ste. 550
Minneapolis, MN 55402-1912
Phone: (612)339-1029
Fax: (612)339-5653
**Format:** Adult Contemporary

**WMCN-FM - 91.7**  (16629)
1600 Grand Ave.
Saint Paul, MN 55105
Phone: (651)696-6082
Fax: (651)696-6685
**Format:** Eclectic

**WMIN-AM - 740**  (16630)
PO Box 25130
Saint Paul, MN 55125
Phone: (651)436-4000
Fax: (651)436-5018

**WQPM-FM - 106.1**  (16492)
PO Box 106
Princeton, MN 55371
Phone: (763)389-1300
Fax: (763)389-1359
**Format:** Contemporary Country

**WRDN-AM - 1430**  (33277)
313 Main St.
Menomonie, WI 54751
Phone: (715)231-9500
Fax: (715)231-9505
**Format:** Contemporary Country

**WWJO-FM - 98.1**  (16557)
640 Lincoln Ave. SE
PO Box 220
Saint Cloud, MN 56304-0824
Phone: (320)251-4422
Fax: (320)251-1855
**Format:** Contemporary Country

## Paducah, KY-Cape Girardeau, MO-Marion, IL

**WDDD-AM - 810**  (8934)
1 Broadcast Center
Marion, IL 62959-0127
Phone: (618)997-8121
Fax: (618)993-2319
**Format:** News; Sports; Talk; Talk

**WDDD-FM - 107.3**  (8935)
1922 N. Court
Marion, IL 62959
Phone: (618)997-8121
Fax: (618)993-2319
**Format:** Country

**WEBQ-AM - 1240**  (8768)
701 S. Commercial St.
Harrisburg, IL 62946
Phone: (618)253-7282
Fax: (618)252-2366
**Format:** Country; Agricultural; Agricultural

**WGGH-AM - 1150**  (8937)
PO Box 340
Marion, IL 62959
Phone: (618)993-8102
Fax: (618)997-2307
**Format:** Southern Gospel

**WMOK-AM - 920**  (8962)
339 Fairground Rd
PO Box 720
Metropolis, IL 62960-0720
Phone: (618)524-4400
Fax: (618)524-3133
**Format:** Country

**WNTX-AM - 750**  (8963)
6120 Waldo Church Rd.
Metropolis, IL 62960-4903
Phone: (618)564-2171
Fax: (618)564-3202
**Format:** Talk; News

## Parkersburg, WV

**WMOA-AM - 1490**  (24873)
PO Box 708
Marietta, OH 45750
Phone: (614)373-1490
Fax: (614)373-1717
**Format:** Adult Contemporary; Sports

## Peoria-Bloomington, IL

**WBYS-FM - 1560**  (7943)
1000 E. Linn St.
PO Box 600
Canton, IL 61520
Phone: (309)647-1560
Fax: (309)647-1563
**Format:** Adult Contemporary

**WIHN-FM - 96.7**  (9078)
108 Boeykens Place
Normal, IL 61761-6185
Phone: (309)888-4496
Fax: (309)452-9677

## Quincy, IL-Hannibal, MO

**Format:** Classic Rock

**WOAM-AM - 1350 (9228)**
PO Box 180
Peoria, IL 61650-0180
Phone: (309)685-1350
Fax: (309)685-7150

**WPBG-FM - 93.3 (9229)**
331 Fulton St., Ste. 1200
Peoria, IL 61602
Phone: (309)688-3131
Fax: (309)673-9562
**Format:** Oldies

**WQEZ-FM - 94.3 (9231)**
335 E. High Point Rd.
Peoria, IL 61614-3011
Fax: (309)688-9346
**Format:** Adult Contemporary; Soft Rock

**WWSS-AM - 1290 (9234)**
331 Fulton St., Ste. 1200
Peoria, IL 61602-1499
Phone: (309)637-3700
Fax: (309)686-8655
**Format:** Sports; Sports

**WXCL-FM - 104.9 (9235)**
4234 N. Brandywine Dr., Suite D
PO Box 180
Peoria, IL 61650-0810
Phone: (309)686-0101
Fax: (309)686-0111
**Format:** Country

## Quincy, IL-Hannibal, MO

**KGRC-FM - 92.9 (9261)**
329 Maine
Quincy, IL 62301
Phone: (217)224-4102
Fax: (217)224-4133
**Format:** Adult Contemporary

**WBBA-AM - 1580 (9247)**
PO Box 150
Pittsfield, IL 62363
Phone: (217)285-9750
Fax: (217)285-4006
**Format:** Talk; News; News

**WBBA-FM - 97.5 (9248)**
PO Box 150
Pittsfield, IL 62363
Phone: (217)285-9750
Fax: (217)285-4006
**Format:** Contemporary Country

**WKXQ-FM - 92.5 (9332)**
109 N. Liberty
PO Box 196
Rushville, IL 62681
Phone: (217)322-9200
Fax: (217)322-4925
**Format:** Adult Contemporary

**WTAD-AM - 930 (9268)**
329 Maine St.
Quincy, IL 62301
Phone: (217)224-4102
Fax: (217)224-4133
**Format:** News; Talk

## Rochester, MN-Mason City, IA-Austin, MN

**KATE-AM - 1450 (15921)**
305 S. 1st Ave.
Albert Lea, MN 56007
Phone: (507)373-2338
Fax: (507)373-4736
**Format:** News; Talk; Information; Middle-of-the-Road (MOR)

**KCPI-FM - 94.9 (15923)**
305 S. 1st Ave.
Albert Lea, MN 56007
Phone: (507)373-2338
Fax: (507)373-4736
**Format:** Adult Contemporary; Classic Rock

**KMFX-FM - 102.5 (16520)**
1530 Greenview Dr. SW, Ste. 200
Rochester, MN 55902
Phone: (507)288-3888
Fax: (507)288-7815

**Format:** Country

**KROC-FM - 106.9 (16525)**
122 SW 4th St.
Rochester, MN 55902
Phone: (507)286-1010
Fax: (507)286-9370
**Format:** Contemporary Hit Radio (CHR)

**KWEB-AM - 1270 (16527)**
1530 Greenview Dr. SW, Ste. 200
Rochester, MN 55902
Phone: (507)288-3888
Fax: (507)288-7815
**Format:** Sports

**KYBA-FM - 105.3 (16531)**
122 4th St. SW
Rochester, MN 55902
Phone: (507)286-1010
Fax: (507)286-9370
**Format:** Soft Rock

## Rockford, IL

**WFPS-FM - 92.1 (8706)**
834 N. Tower Rd.
PO Box 747
Freeport, IL 61032
Phone: (815)235-7191
Fax: (815)235-4318
**Format:** Country

**WFRL-AM - 1570 (8707)**
834 N Tower Rd.
PO Box 747
Freeport, IL 61032-0747
Phone: (815)235-7191
Fax: (815)235-4318
**Format:** Adult Contemporary

**WFRX-AM - 1300 (8936)**
1822 No. Ct.
Marion, IL 62959
Phone: (618)997-8123
Fax: (618)997-2319
**Format:** Middle-of-the-Road (MOR)

**WGSL-FM - 91.1 (8913)**
5375 Pebble Creek Trail
PO Box 2730
Loves Park, IL 61111
Phone: (815)654-1200
Fax: (815)282-7779
**Format:** Religious

**WJVL-FM - 99.9 (33110)**
1 S. Parker Dr.
Janesville, WI 53545
Phone: (608)752-7895
Fax: (608)752-4438
**Format:** Country

**WNIJ-FM - 90.5 (8567)**
NIU Broadcast Center
801 N. 1st St.
DeKalb, IL 60115-2854
Phone: (815)753-9000
Fax: (815)753-9938
**Format:** Public Radio; Jazz; News; News

**WNIU-FM - 89.5 (8568)**
NIU Broadcast Center
801 N. 1st St.
DeKalb, IL 60115-2854
Phone: (815)753-9000
Fax: (815)753-9938
**Format:** Public Radio; Classical; Classical

**WQFL-FM - 100.9 (8914)**
5375 Pebble Creek Tr.
Loves Park, IL 61111-4326
Phone: (815)654-1200
Fax: (815)282-7779
**Format:** Religious; Contemporary Christian

**WROK-AM - 1440 (9314)**
3901 Brendenwood
PO Box 136
Rockford, IL 61107
Phone: (815)399-2233
Fax: (815)399-8148
**Format:** News; Talk

**WXRX-FM - 104.9 (9316)**
2830 Sandy Hollow Rd.
Rockford, IL 61109-2369
Phone: (815)874-7861

Fax: (815)874-2202
**Format:** Album-Oriented Rock (AOR)

**WYHY-FM - 95.3 (9317)**
2830 Sandy Hollow Rd.
Rockford, IL 61109
Phone: (815)874-7861
Fax: (815)874-2202

**WZOK-FM - 97.5 (9318)**
3901 Brendenwood
Rockford, IL 61107
Phone: (815)399-2233
Fax: (815)399-8148
**Format:** Contemporary Hit Radio (CHR)

## St. Louis, MO (Mt. Vernon, IL)

**WAOX-FM - 105.3 (8907)**
Box 10
Litchfield, IL 62056
Phone: (217)532-2085
Fax: (217)532-2431
**Format:** Adult Contemporary

**WBGZ-AM - 1570 (7836)**
PO Box 615
Alton, IL 62002
Phone: (618)465-3535
Fax: (618)465-3546
**Format:** Talk; News; Sports; Sports

**WCBW-AM - 880 (8783)**
13063 Winu Dr.
PO Box 303
Highland, IL 62249
Phone: (618)654-7521
Fax: (618)654-6333
**Format:** Talk; News; Agricultural; Full Service; Sports; Religious

**WIBI-FM - 91.1 (7961)**
PO Box 140
Carlinville, IL 62626
Phone: (217)854-4800
Fax: (217)854-4810
**Format:** Contemporary Christian

**WJBD-FM - 100.1 (9344)**
PO Box 70
Salem, IL 62881
Phone: (618)548-2000
Fax: (618)548-2079
**Format:** Adult Contemporary; News; Sports; Sports

**WJBM-AM - 1480 (8824)**
1010 Shipman Rd.
Jerseyville, IL 62052-2826
**Format:** News; Talk; Sports

**WLCA-FM - 89.9 (8746)**
5800 Godfrey Rd.
Godfrey, IL 62035
Phone: (618)466-8936
Fax: (618)466-7458

**WSIE-FM - 88.7 (8625)**
Southern Illinois University
PO Box 1773
Edwardsville, IL 62026
Phone: (618)650-2228
Fax: (618)650-2233
**Format:** Public Radio; Jazz; News; News

## Sioux Falls-Mitchell, SD

**KARZ-FM - 107.5 (16261)**
1414 E. College Dr.
PO Box 61
Marshall, MN 56258
Phone: (507)532-2282
Fax: (507)532-3739
**Format:** Classical

**KLQL-FM - 101.1 (16227)**
PO Box 599
Hwy. 16 E
Luverne, MN 56156
Phone: (507)283-4444
Fax: (507)283-4445

Format: Country; Agricultural

**KQAD-AM - 800 (16228)**
Cty. Rd. 4 E.
PO Box 599
Luverne, MN 56156
Phone: (507)283-4444
Fax: (507)283-4445
Format: Adult Contemporary; News; Sports; Agricultural; Sports; Agricultural

**KWOA-AM - 730 (16734)**
28779 County Hwy. 35
Worthington, MN 56187-6387
Format: News; Talk; Information; Information

## South Bend-Elkhart, IN

**WAOR-FM - 95.3 (10034)**
237 W. Edison Rd., Ste. 200
Mishawaka, IN 46545-3103
Format: Classic Rock

**WAUS-FM - 90.7 (15062)**
Andrews University
Berrien Springs, MI 49104
Phone: (269)471-3400
Fax: (269)471-3804
Format: News; Classical

**WAWC-FM - 103.5 (10183)**
10129 N. 800 E.
Syracuse, IN 46567
Phone: (219)457-8181
Fax: (219)457-4488

**WBYT-FM - 100.7 (10035)**
1 Edison Ctr., Ste. 200
237 Edison Rd.
Mishawaka, IN 46545
Phone: (219)258-5483
Fax: (219)258-0930
Format: Country

**WDOW-AM - 1440 (15223)**
Marcellus Hwy.
PO Box 150
Dowagiac, MI 49047
Fax: (616)782-5107
Format: Sports; Talk

**WETL-FM - 91.7 (10165)**
635 S. Main St.
South Bend, IN 46601
Phone: (574)283-7566
Fax: (574)283-7562
Format: Talk; Information; Eclectic

**WFRN-AM - 1270 (9682)**
PO Box 307
Elkhart, IN 46515
Phone: (219)875-5166
Fax: (219)875-6662
Format: Gospel; Talk

**WHLY-AM - 1620 (10166)**
3371 Cleveland Rd., Ste. 300
South Bend, IN 46628
Phone: (574)273-9300
Fax: (574)273-9090
Format: Middle-of-the-Road (MOR)

**WHME-FM - 103.1 (10167)**
61300 S. Ironwood Rd.
South Bend, IN 46614
Phone: (574)291-8200
Fax: (574)291-9043
Format: Religious; Contemporary Christian

**WIRX-FM - 107.1 (15747)**
PO Box 107
Saint Joseph, MI 49085
Phone: (616)925-1111
Fax: (616)925-1011
Format: Album-Oriented Rock (AOR)

**WNIL-AM - 1290 (10036)**
237 W. Edison Rd., Ste. 200
Mishawaka, IN 46545-3103
Format: Oldies

**WNSN-FM - 101.5 (10169)**
300 W. Jefferson Blvd.
South Bend, IN 46601
Phone: (574)233-3141
Fax: (574)239-4231

Format: Adult Contemporary

**WRSW-AM - 1480 (10237)**
216 W. Market St.
Warsaw, IN 46580
Phone: (574)372-3064
Fax: (574)267-2230
Format: Contemporary Hit Radio (CHR); Full Service

**WSBT-AM - 960 (10170)**
202 S. Michigan St., Ste. 1100
South Bend, IN 46601
Phone: (574)233-3141
Fax: (574)239-4231
Format: News; Talk

**WSJM-AM - 1400 (15748)**
PO Box 107
Saint Joseph, MI 49085
Phone: (616)925-1111
Fax: (616)925-1011
Format: News; Talk

**WTRC-AM - 1340 (9686)**
58096 C.R. 7 S.
Elkhart, IN 46517
Fax: (219)295-2FAX
Format: Oldies; News; Sports

## Springfield-Decatur-Champaign, IL

**WBCP-AM - 1580 (9490)**
904 N. 4th St., Unit D.
PO Box 1023
Champaign, IL 61820
Phone: (217)359-1580
Fax: (217)359-1583
Format: Urban Contemporary; Adult Contemporary

**WCVS-FM - 96.7 (9413)**
3055 S 4th St.
Springfield, IL 62703
Phone: (217)528-3033
Fax: (217)528-5348
Format: Classic Rock

**WCZQ-FM - 105.5 (8995)**
PO Box 105
Monticello, IL 61856
Phone: (217)762-2588
Fax: (217)762-2589
Format: Country

**WDAN-AM - 1490 (8531)**
1501 N. Washington
Danville, IL 61832-2463
Phone: (217)442-1700
Fax: (217)431-1489
Format: Talk; News; Sports; Sports

**WDZ-AM - 1050 (8541)**
337 N. Water St.
Decatur, IL 62523
Phone: (217)423-9744
Fax: (217)423-9764
Format: News; Talk; Sports; Sports

**WDZQ-FM - 95.1 (8542)**
337 N. Water St.
Decatur, IL 62523
Phone: (217)429-9595
Fax: (217)423-9764
Format: Contemporary Country

**WEIU-FM - 88.9 (8047)**
Eastern Illinois University
Charleston, IL 61920
Phone: (217)581-7371
Fax: (217)581-6650
Format: Full Service

**WEVX-FM - 95.3 (8037)**
4108 Fieldstone, Ste. C
Champaign, IL 61822
Phone: (217)367-1195
Fax: (217)367-3291
Format: Album-Oriented Rock (AOR)

**WFMB-AM - 1450 (9414)**
3055 S. 4th St.
Springfield, IL 62703
Phone: (217)528-3033
Fax: (217)528-5348

Format: Sports; Sports

**WFMB-FM - 104.5 (9415)**
3055 S. 4th
Springfield, IL 62703
Phone: (217)528-3033
Fax: (217)528-5348
Format: Contemporary Country

**WIAI-FM - 99.1 (8533)**
PO Box 970
Danville, IL 61832
Phone: (217)443-5500
Fax: (217)443-6308
Format: Country

**WITY-AM - 980 (8534)**
PO Box 142
Danville, IL 61834
Phone: (217)446-1312
Fax: (217)446-1314
Format: Adult Contemporary

**WJVO-FM - 105.5 (8822)**
1251 E. Morton Rd
PO Box 1055
Jacksonville, IL 62651
Phone: (217)245-5119
Fax: (217)245-1596
Format: Country; Country

**WKIO-FM - 92.5 (8040)**
2603 W. Bradley Ave.
Champaign, IL 61821-1823
Phone: (217)352-1040
Fax: (217)356-3330
Format: Oldies

**WLBH-AM - 1170 (8945)**
N. Rte. 45
PO Box 1848
Mattoon, IL 61938
Phone: (217)234-6464
Fax: (217)234-6019

**WLBH-FM - 96.9 (8946)**
N. Rte. 45
PO Box 1848
Mattoon, IL 61938
Phone: (217)234-6464
Fax: (217)234-6019
Format: Adult Contemporary; Adult Contemporary

**WLRW-FM - 94.5 (8041)**
2603 W. Bradley Ave.
Champaign, IL 61821-1823
Phone: (217)352-4141
Fax: (217)352-1256
Format: Adult Contemporary; Contemporary Hit Radio (CHR); Contemporary Hit Radio (CHR)

**WMHX-FM - 93.9 (9418)**
3501 E. Sangamon Ave.
Springfield, IL 62707
Phone: (217)753-5400
Fax: (217)753-7902
Format: Contemporary Country

**WPCD-FM - 88.7 (8042)**
2400 W. Bradley Ave.
Champaign, IL 61821
Phone: (217)351-2450
Fax: (217)373-3899
Format: Classic Rock; Urban Contemporary

**WPGU-FM - 107.1 (8043)**
24 E. Green St., Ste. 107
Champaign, IL 61820
Phone: (217)244-3000
Fax: (217)244-3001
Format: Alternative/New Music/Progressive

**WQNA-FM - 88.3 (9421)**
2201 Toronto Rd.
Springfield, IL 62707
Phone: (217)529-5431
Fax: (217)529-7861
Format: Eclectic; Educational

**WRAN-FM - 98.3 (9367)**
PO Box 169
Taylorville, IL 62568-0169
Phone: (217)824-3395
Fax: (217)824-3301

Terre Haute, IN

**Format:** Easy Listening

**WSOY-AM - 1340  (8544)**
1100 E. Pershing Rd.
Decatur, IL 62526
Phone: (217)877-5371
Fax: (217)877-8777
**Format:** Information; News; Talk; Talk

**WSOY-FM - 102.9  (8545)**
1100 E. Pershing Rd.
Decatur, IL 62526
Phone: (217)877-5371
Fax: (217)877-8777
**Format:** Adult Contemporary

**WUIS-FM - 91.9  (9424)**
University of Illinois at Springfield
Springfield, IL 62794-9243
Phone: (217)206-6516
Fax: (217)206-6527
**Format:** Public Radio; News; Classical

**WXFM-FM - 99.3  (9026)**
120 Wildwood
Mount Zion, IL 62549
Phone: (217)864-4141
Fax: (217)864-4727
**Format:** Adult Contemporary

**WYMG-FM - 100.5  (9425)**
3501 E. Sangamon Ave.
Springfield, IL 62707-9777
Phone: (217)753-5400
Fax: (217)753-7902
**Format:** Classic Rock

## Terre Haute, IN

**WACF-FM - 98.5  (9196)**
PO Box 277
Paris, IL 61944
Phone: (217)465-6336
Fax: (217)466-1408
**Format:** Country

**WBGL-FM - 91.7  (8034)**
2108 W. Springfield
Champaign, IL 61821
Phone: (217)359-8232
Fax: (217)359-7374
**Format:** Religious

**WBOW-AM - 1300  (10197)**
1301 Ohio St.
Terre Haute, IN 47807
Phone: (812)234-9770
Fax: (812)238-1576
**Format:** Sports; Talk

**WCBH-FM - 104.3  (8627)**
208 W. Jefferson
Effingham, IL 62401
Phone: (217)342-4141
Fax: (217)342-4143
**Format:** Adult Contemporary

**WIKK-FM - 103.5  (9180)**
4667 Radio Tower Rd.
PO Box L
Olney, IL 62450
Phone: (618)393-2156
Fax: (618)392-4536
**Format:** Classic Rock

**WISU-FM - 89.7  (10198)**
Indiana State University
217 N. 6th St.
Terre Haute, IN 47809
Phone: (812)237-3252
Fax: (812)237-3241
**Format:** Jazz; Blues

**WLEZ-FM - 102.7  (10199)**
1072 Windsor Rd.
Terre Haute, IN 47802
Phone: (812)299-4343
Fax: (812)299-4608
**Format:** Adult Contemporary; Soft Rock

**WMGI-FM - 100.7  (10200)**
824 S. 3rd St.
Terre Haute, IN 47807-4609
Phone: (812)232-4161
Fax: (812)234-9999

**Format:** Contemporary Christian

**WNDI-FM - 95.3  (10178)**
RR 5, 19 B
Sullivan, IN 47882-9805
Phone: (812)268-6322
Fax: (812)268-6652
**Format:** Contemporary Country; Contemporary Country

**WPRS-AM - 1440  (9197)**
12861 Illinois Hwy. 133 W
Paris, IL 61944
Phone: (217)465-6336
Fax: (217)466-1408
**Format:** Middle-of-the-Road (MOR)

**WSDM-FM - 97.7  (10202)**
1301 Ohio St.
Terre Haute, IN 47807
Phone: (812)234-9770
Fax: (812)238-1576
**Format:** Oldies

**WSDX-AM - 1130  (10203)**
1301 Ohio St.
Terre Haute, IN 47807
Phone: (812)234-9770
Fax: (812)238-1576
**Format:** Talk; Sports

**WTHI-AM - 1480  (10204)**
PO Box 1486
Terre Haute, IN 47808
Phone: (812)232-9481
Fax: (812)234-0089
**Format:** News; Talk; Talk

**WTHI-FM - 99.9  (10205)**
918 Ohio St
PO Box 1486
Terre Haute, IN 47807
Phone: (812)232-9481
Fax: (812)234-0089
**Format:** Contemporary Country

**WVLN-AM - 740  (9181)**
4667 Radio Tower Rd.
PO Box L
Olney, IL 62450
Phone: (618)393-2156
Fax: (618)392-4536
**Format:** Talk; Sports

**WWBL-FM - 106.5  (10241)**
PO Box 616
Washington, IN 47501
Phone: (812)254-4300
Fax: (812)885-2604
**Format:** Country

**WZDM-FM - 92.1  (10227)**
522 Busseron St.
PO Box 242
Vincennes, IN 47591
Phone: (812)882-6060
Fax: (812)885-2604
**Format:** Adult Contemporary

## Toledo, OH

**WCKY-FM - 103.7  (24726)**
1624 Tiffin Ave.
PO Box 338
Findlay, OH 45840
Phone: (419)425-1077
Fax: (419)422-4329
**Format:** Country

**WGBE-FM - 90.9  (25098)**
PO Box 30
Toledo, OH 43614
Phone: (419)380-4600
Fax: (419)380-4710
**Format:** Classical; News; Public Radio

**WGTE-FM - 91.3  (25099)**
PO Box 30
Toledo, OH 43614
Phone: (419)380-4600
Fax: (419)380-4710
**Format:** Public Radio; News; Information; Classical

**WKKO-FM - 99.9  (25102)**
3225 Arlington Ave.
Toledo, OH 43614
Phone: (419)240-1000
Fax: (419)385-2902

**Format:** Contemporary Country

**WKXA-FM - 100.5  (24728)**
551 Lake Cascades Pkwy.
Findlay, OH 45840
Phone: (419)422-4545
Fax: (419)422-6736
**Format:** Adult Contemporary

**WOTL-FM - 90.3  (25105)**
716 N. Westwood
Toledo, OH 43607
Phone: (419)537-1505
**Format:** Religious

**WPFX-FM - 107.7  (24949)**
1624 Tiffin Ave.
Findlay, OH 45840
Phone: (419)425-1077
Fax: (419)422-2954
**Format:** Oldies

**WSPD-AM - 1370  (25107)**
125 S. Superior St.
Toledo, OH 43602
Phone: (419)244-8321
Fax: (419)244-7631
**Format:** News; Sports; Talk

**WTOD-AM - 1560  (25108)**
3225 Arlington Ave.
Toledo, OH 43614
Phone: (419)725-5700
Fax: (419)385-2902
**Format:** Country

**WTTF-AM - 1600  (25082)**
112 S. Washington St.
Tiffin, OH 44883-0338
Phone: (419)447-2212
Fax: (419)447-1709
**Format:** Adult Contemporary

**WXTS-FM - 88.3  (25112)**
2400 Collingwood
Toledo, OH 43620
Phone: (419)244-6875
Fax: (419)249-8248
**Format:** Jazz

## Traverse City-Cadillac, MI

**WAIR-FM - 92.5  (15833)**
1020 Hastings St.
Traverse City, MI 49686-3457
Fax: (616)348-2092
**Format:** Oldies

**WATT-AM - 1240  (15088)**
PO Box 520
Cadillac, MI 49601
Phone: (231)775-1263
Fax: (231)779-2844
**Format:** Talk; News

**WBCM-FM - 93.5  (15834)**
314 E. Front St.
Traverse City, MI 49684
Fax: (616)929-3988
**Format:** Country

**WBNZ-FM - 99.3  (15305)**
1532 Forrester Rd.
Frankfort, MI 49635
Phone: (231)352-9603
Fax: (231)352-7877
**Format:** Adult Contemporary; News; Sports

**WCCW-FM - 107.5  (15835)**
300 E. Front St.
Traverse City, MI 49684
Phone: (616)946-6211
Fax: (616)946-1914
**Format:** Oldies

**WGRY-AM - 1230  (15380)**
6514 Old Lake Rd.
Grayling, MI 49738
Phone: (989)348-6171
Fax: (989)348-6181

**WGRY-FM - 100.3  (15381)**
6514 Old Lake Rd.
Grayling, MI 49738
Phone: (989)348-6171
Fax: (989)348-6181

**Format:** Country

**WIDG-AM - 940 (15123)**
1356 Mackinaw Ave.
Cheboygan, MI 49721-1003
Phone: (231)627-2341
Fax: (231)627-7000
**Format:** Sports

**WJML-AM - 1110 (15674)**
2175 Click Rd.
Petoskey, MI 49770
Phone: (231)348-5000
**Format:** News; Talk

**WKLA-FM - 106.3 (15561)**
5941 W. U.S. 10
Ludington, MI 49431-2447
Phone: (231)843-3438
Fax: (231)843-1886
**Format:** Adult Contemporary

**WKNW-AM - 1400 (15761)**
1402 Ashmun St.
Sault Sainte Marie, MI 49783
Phone: (906)635-0995
Fax: (906)635-1216
**Format:** Talk; News; Sports

**WLDR-FM - 101.9 (15836)**
13999 S West Bay Shore Dr.
Traverse City, MI 49684
Phone: (231)947-3220
Fax: (231)947-7201
**Format:** Country

**WLJN-AM - 1400 (15837)**
Box 1400
Traverse City, MI 49685
Phone: (231)946-1400
Fax: (231)946-3959
**Format:** Religious; Talk

**WLJN-FM - 89.9 (15838)**
Box 1400
Traverse City, MI 49685
Phone: (231)946-1400
Fax: (231)946-3959
**Format:** Religious

**WNMC-FM - 90.7 (15839)**
1701 E. Front St.
Traverse City, MI 49686
Phone: (231)995-1090
Fax: (231)922-8963
**Format:** Jazz; Blues; Ethnic; Urban Contemporary; Alternative/New Music/Progressive; Talk; Folk

**WOLW-FM - 91.1 (15321)**
Box 695
Gaylord, MI 49734-0695
Phone: (989)732-6274
Fax: (989)732-8171
**Format:** Religious

**WTCM-AM - 580 (15841)**
314 E. Front St.
Traverse City, MI 49684
Fax: (616)929-3988
**Format:** Talk; News

**WWKK-AM - 750 (15678)**
2175 Click Rd.
Petoskey, MI 49770
Phone: (231)348-5000
**Format:** News; Talk

**WYSS-FM - 99.5 (15764)**
1402 Ashmun
Sault Sainte Marie, MI 49783
Phone: (906)635-0995
Fax: (906)635-1216
**Format:** Adult Contemporary

## Wausau-Rhinelander, WI

**WDLB-AM - 1450 (33262)**
1710 North Central Ave.
PO Box 630
Marshfield, WI 54449
Phone: (715)384-2191
Fax: (715)387-3588

**Format:** Talk; News; Sports; Agricultural; Oldies; Agricultural; Oldies

**WGLX-FM - 103.3 (33670)**
645 25th Ave. N.
Box 8022
Wisconsin Rapids, WI 54494
Phone: (715)424-1300
Fax: (715)424-1347
**Format:** Classic Rock

**WIFC-FM - 95.5 (33637)**
PO Box 2048
Wausau, WI 54402-2048
Phone: (715)842-1672
Fax: (715)848-3158
**Format:** Public Radio

**WIGM-AM - 1490 (33270)**
630 S. 8th
PO Box 59
Medford, WI 54451
Phone: (715)748-2566
**Format:** Talk; Sports

**WJMT-AM - 730 (33281)**
120 S. Mill St.
Merrill, WI 54452
Phone: (715)536-6262
Fax: (715)536-6208
**Format:** Adult Contemporary; Talk

**WKEB-FM - 99.3 (33271)**
630 S. 8th
PO Box 59
Medford, WI 54451
Phone: (715)748-2566
**Format:** Adult Contemporary

**WLJY-FM - 106.5 (33263)**
PO Box 630
Marshfield, WI 54449
Phone: (715)384-2191
Fax: (715)387-3588
**Format:** Easy Listening

**WOBT-AM - 1240 (33506)**
3616 Hwy. 47 N.
Rhinelander, WI 54501
Phone: (715)362-6140
Fax: (715)362-1973
**Format:** Sports; Sports

**WOSQ-FM - 92.3 (33264)**
1710 North Central Ave.
PO Box 630
Marshfield, WI 54449-0630
Phone: (715)384-2191
Fax: (715)387-3588
**Format:** Country

**WRHN-FM - 100.1 (33507)**
3616 Hwy. 47 N.
Rhinelander, WI 54501
Phone: (715)362-6140
Fax: (715)362-1973
**Format:** Adult Contemporary; Soft Rock; Soft Rock

**WSPT-AM - 1010 (33557)**
500 Division St.
Stevens Point, WI 54481-0247
Phone: (715)341-9800
Fax: (715)341-0000
**Format:** News; Talk; Talk

**WSPT-FM - 97.9 (33558)**
500 Division St.
Stevens Point, WI 54481
Phone: (715)341-9800
Fax: (715)341-0000
**Format:** Adult Contemporary

## Wheeling, WV-Steubenville, OH

**WCMJ-FM - 96.7 (24237)**
4988 Skyline Dr.
PO Box 338
Cambridge, OH 43725
Phone: (740)432-5605
Fax: (740)432-1991
**Format:** Adult Contemporary

**WDIG-AM - 950 (25063)**
4039 Sunset Blvd.
Steubenville, OH 43952
Phone: (740)264-1760
Fax: (740)264-5035

**Format:** Gospel

**WILE-AM - 1270 (24238)**
4988 Skyline Dr.
PO Box 338
Cambridge, OH 43725
Phone: (740)432-5605
Fax: (740)432-1991
**Format:** Middle-of-the-Road (MOR)

**WOGH-FM - 103.5 (25064)**
320 Market
Steubenville, OH 43952
Phone: (614)283-4747
Fax: (614)283-3655
**Format:** Country

**WOMP-AM - 1290 (24178)**
PO Box 448
Bellaire, OH 43906
Phone: (740)676-5661
Fax: (740)676-2742
**Format:** News; Talk; Sports

**WOMP-FM - 100.5 (24179)**
PO Box 448
Bellaire, OH 43906
Phone: (740)676-5661
Fax: (740)676-2742
**Format:** Adult Contemporary

**WSTV-AM - 1340 (25065)**
PO Box 320
Steubenville, OH 43952
Phone: (740)283-4747
Fax: (740)283-3655
**Format:** News; Talk; Sports

**WWKC-FM - 104.9 (24239)**
4988 Skyline Dr.
PO Box 338
Cambridge, OH 43725
Phone: (740)732-5777
**Format:** Country

## Youngstown, OH

**WAKZ-FM - 95.9 (24195)**
7461 South Ave.
Boardman, OH 44512
Phone: (330)965-0057
Fax: (330)729-9991
**Format:** Contemporary Hit Radio (CHR)

**WBBG-FM - 93.3 (25212)**
7461 South Ave.
PO Box 9248
Youngstown, OH 44512
Phone: (330)965-0057
Fax: (330)729-9991
**Format:** Oldies

**WBBW-AM - 1240 (25213)**
4040 Simon Rd.
Youngstown, OH 44512
Phone: (330)783-1000
Fax: (330)783-0060
**Format:** Sports; Talk; Talk

**WGFT-FM - 101.1 (25215)**
34 Federal Plaza W.
Youngstown, OH 44503
Phone: (330)744-5115
Fax: (330)744-4020
**Format:** Talk; Gospel

**WKBN-AM - 570 (24196)**
7461 S. Ave
PO Box 9248
Boardman, OH 44512
Phone: (330)965-0057
Fax: (330)965-8277
**Format:** Talk; News; News

**WRTK-AM - 1390 (25221)**
7461 South Ave.
Youngstown, OH 44512
Phone: (330)740-9300
Fax: (330)740-9303
**Format:** Big Band/Nostalgia

**WWSY-FM - 95.9 (24218)**
6874 Strimbu Dr. SE
Brookfield, OH 44403
Phone: (330)448-5050
Fax: (330)448-5055

Zanesville, OH

**Format:** Easy Listening

**WYSU-FM - 88.5 (25224)**
Youngstown State University
Youngstown, OH 44555
Phone: (330)941-3363
Fax: (330)941-1501
**Format:** Classical; News; Jazz

## Zanesville, OH

**WCVZ-FM - 92.7 (25229)**
2477 E. Pike
Zanesville, OH 43701-4626
Phone: (740)455-3181
Fax: (740)455-6195
**Format:** Adult Contemporary

**WHIZ-AM - 1240 (25230)**
629 Downard Rd.
Zanesville, OH 43701
Phone: (740)452-5431
Fax: (740)452-6553
**Format:** Full Service

**WHIZ-FM - 102.5 (25231)**
629 Downard Rd.
Zanesville, OH 43701
Phone: (740)452-5431
Fax: (740)452-6553
**Format:** Adult Contemporary

**WWJM-FM - 105.9 (25233)**
247 Market St.
Zanesville, OH 43701
Phone: (740)455-3961
Fax: (740)455-2306

## Great Plains States

### Cedar Rapids-Waterloo-Dubuque, IA

**KATF-FM - 92.9 (10534)**
PO Box 659
Dubuque, IA 52004-0659
**Format:** Adult Contemporary

**KBBG-FM - 88.1 (10942)**
918 Newell St.
Waterloo, IA 50703
Phone: (319)235-1515
Fax: (319)234-6182
**Format:** Blues; Gospel; Jazz; Educational; Jazz; Educational

**KCII-AM - 106.1 (10938)**
PO Box 524
Washington, IA 52353
Phone: (319)653-2113
Fax: (319)653-3500
**Format:** Adult Contemporary; Sports

**KCII-FM - 106.1 (10939)**
110 E. Main St.
PO Box 524
Washington, IA 52353
Phone: (319)653-2113
Fax: (319)653-3500
**Format:** Adult Contemporary; Sports; News

**KCNZ-AM - 1250 (10359)**
721 Shirley St.
PO Box 248
Cedar Falls, IA 50613
Phone: (319)277-1918
Fax: (319)277-5202
**Format:** News; Talk; Sports

**KDEC-AM - 1240 (10444)**
110 Highland Dr.
PO Box 27
Decorah, IA 52101
Phone: (563)382-4252
Fax: (563)382-9540
**Format:** News

**KDEC-FM - 100.5 (10445)**
110 Highland Dr.
PO Box 27
Decorah, IA 52101
Phone: (563)382-4251
Fax: (563)382-9540

**Format:** Adult Contemporary

**KDTH-AM - 1370 (10535)**
PO Box 659
Dubuque, IA 52004-0659
Phone: (563)690-0800
Fax: (563)690-0858
**Format:** Talk; Adult Contemporary; News; Agricultural

**KFMW-FM - 107.9 (10944)**
514 Jefferson St.
Waterloo, IA 50701
Phone: (319)234-2200
Fax: (319)233-4946
**Format:** Album-Oriented Rock (AOR); Classic Rock; Contemporary Hit Radio (CHR)

**KHAK-FM - 98.1 (10372)**
425 2nd St. SE, 4th Fl.
Cedar Rapids, IA 52401
Phone: (319)365-9431
Fax: (319)363-8062
**Format:** Country

**KHKE-FM - 89.5 (10361)**
University of Northern Iowa
Cedar Falls, IA 50614-0359
Phone: (319)273-6400
Fax: (319)273-2682
**Format:** Public Radio; Jazz; Classical

**KLYV-FM - 105.3 (10538)**
5490 Saratoga
PO Box 1280
Dubuque, IA 52004-1280
Phone: (319)557-1040
Fax: (319)583-4535
**Format:** Top 40; Adult Contemporary

**KMJM-AM - 1360 (10373)**
600 Old Marion Rd. NE
Cedar Rapids, IA 52402
Phone: (319)395-0530
Fax: (319)393-9527
**Format:** Sports

**KMRY-AM - 1450 (10374)**
1957 Blairsferry Rd. NE
Cedar Rapids, IA 52402
Phone: (319)393-1450
Fax: (319)393-1407
**Format:** Big Band/Nostalgia; Easy Listening

**KNWS-AM - 101.9 (10945)**
4880 Texas
Waterloo, IA 50702-4742
Phone: (319)296-1975
Fax: (319)296-1977
**Format:** Religious

**KNWS-FM - 101.9 (10946)**
4880 Texas
Waterloo, IA 50702-4742
Phone: (319)296-1975
Fax: (319)296-1977
**Format:** Religious

**KOEL-AM - 950 (10791)**
2502 S Frederick Ave.
Oelwein, IA 50662-3116
**Format:** News

**KOKZ-FM - 105.7 (10947)**
PO Box 1540
Waterloo, IA 50704
Phone: (319)234-2200
Fax: (319)233-7430
**Format:** Contemporary Hit Radio (CHR)

**KUNI-FM - 90.9 (10362)**
University of Northern Iowa
Cedar Falls, IA 50614-0359
Phone: (319)273-6400
Fax: (319)273-2682
**Format:** Public Radio; Adult Contemporary; Ethnic; Eclectic; Urban Contemporary; Classical

**KWLO-AM - 1330 (10948)**
514 Jefferson St
PO Box 1540
Waterloo, IA 50704
Phone: (319)234-2200
Fax: (319)234-9999

**Format:** Big Band/Nostalgia

**KXEL-AM - 1540 (10952)**
514 Jefferson St.
Box 1540
Waterloo, IA 50704
Phone: (319)233-3371
Fax: (319)233-4946
**Format:** News; Talk

**KZIA-FM - 102.9 (10375)**
1110 26th Ave. SW
Cedar Rapids, IA 52404-3430
Phone: (319)363-2061
Fax: (319)363-2948
**Format:** Top 40

**WDBQ-AM - 1490 (10539)**
5490 Saratoga Rd.
PO Box 1280
Dubuque, IA 52004-1280
Phone: (319)583-6471
Fax: (319)583-4535
**Format:** News; Talk

**WDBQ-FM - 107.5 (10540)**
5490 Saratoga Rd.
Dubuque, IA 52002
Phone: (319)557-1040
Fax: (319)583-4535
**Format:** Oldies

**WFXN-AM - 1230 (10432)**
3535 E Kimberly Rd.
Davenport, IA 52807
Phone: (563)344-7140
Fax: (563)344-7065
**Format:** Sports

### Cheyenne, WY-Scottsbluff, NE (Sterling, CO)

**KAAQ-FM - 105.9 (18257)**
1210 W. 10th St.
PO Box 600
Alliance, NE 69301
Phone: (308)762-1400
Fax: (308)762-7804
**Format:** Country

**KCMI-FM - 96.9 (18597)**
209 East 15th St.
PO Box 1888
Scottsbluff, NE 69363-1888
Phone: (308)632-5264
Fax: (308)635-0104
**Format:** Religious

**KNEB-AM - 960 (18600)**
PO Box 239
Scottsbluff, NE 69363-0239
Phone: (308)632-7121
Fax: (308)635-1079
**Format:** Country; Agricultural

**KNEB-FM - 94.1 (18601)**
PO Box 239
Scottsbluff, NE 69363-0239
Phone: (308)632-7121
Fax: (308)635-1079
**Format:** Contemporary Country; Agricultural

### Chicago (LaSalle), IL

**KHMO-AM - 1070 (17248)**
119 N. 3rd St.
PO Box 711
Hannibal, MO 63401
Phone: (573)221-3450
Fax: (573)221-5331
**Format:** Talk; News

### Columbia-Jefferson City, MO

**KBIA-FM - 91.3 (17177)**
409 Jesse Hall
University of Missouri-Columbia
Columbia, MO 65211
Phone: (573)882-3431
Fax: (573)882-2636

Format: Public Radio; News; Classical

**KFRU-AM - 1400 (17180)**
503 Old 63 N.
Columbia, MO 65201-6387
Phone: (573)449-4141
Fax: (573)449-7770
Format: News; Talk; Sports

**KJMO-FM - 100.1 (17296)**
3605 Country Club Dr.
Jefferson City, MO 65109
Phone: (573)893-5100
Fax: (573)893-8330
Format: Classic Rock

**KLOZ-FM - 92.7 (17312)**
160 Hwy. 42
Kaiser, MO 65047-2011
Phone: (573)348-1958
Fax: (573)348-1923
Format: Adult Contemporary

**KPLA-FM - 101.5 (17184)**
503 Old 63 N.
Columbia, MO 65201
Phone: (573)449-4141
Fax: (573)449-7770
Format: Adult Contemporary

**KWWC-FM - 90.5 (17186)**
Stephens College
Box 2114
Columbia, MO 65215
Phone: (314)876-7297
Fax: (314)876-7248
Format: Jazz

**KWWR-FM - 95.7 (17427)**
1705 E. Liberty St.
PO Box 475
Mexico, MO 65265-0475
Phone: (573)581-5500
Fax: (573)581-1801
Format: Country; News; Agricultural

**KZZT-FM - 105.5 (17432)**
Jct. of Hwy. 63 & Rte. EE.
PO Box 128
Moberly, MO 65270
Phone: (660)263-9390
Fax: (660)263-8800
Format: Oldies

## Daveport,IA-Rock Island, Moline,IL

**KBOB-FM - 99.7 (10425)**
1229 Brady St.
Davenport, IA 52803-4616
Phone: (563)326-2541
Fax: (563)326-1819
Format: Country

**KBUR-AM - 1490 (10336)**
1411 N. Roosevelt Ave.
PO Box 70
Burlington, IA 52601
Phone: (319)752-2701
Fax: (319)752-5287
Format: Adult Contemporary; Full Service; Full Service

**KCQQ-FM - 106.5 (10426)**
3535 E Kimberly Rd.
Davenport, IA 52807
Phone: (319)344-7000
Fax: (319)359-8524
Format: Classic Rock

**KDMG-FM - 103.1 (10338)**
2850 Mt. Pleasant St.
Burlington, IA 52601
Phone: (319)752-5402
Fax: (319)752-4715
Format: Country

**KGRS-FM - 107.3 (10339)**
1411 N. Roosevelt Ave.
PO Box 70
Burlington, IA 52601
Phone: (319)752-2701
Fax: (319)752-5287

Format: Adult Contemporary

**KJOC-AM - 1170 (10427)**
1229 Brady St.
Davenport, IA 52803
Phone: (563)326-2541
Fax: (563)326-1819
Format: Sports

**KKMI-FM - 93.5 (10340)**
2850 Mt. Pleasant St.
Burlington, IA 52601
Phone: (319)752-5402
Fax: (319)752-4715
Format: Adult Contemporary; Oldies; Oldies

**KMXG-FM - 96.1 (10429)**
3535 E. Kimberly Rd.
Davenport, IA 52807
Phone: (563)344-7000
Fax: (563)344-7065
Format: Adult Contemporary

**KUUL-FM - 103.7 (10430)**
3535 E. Kimberly Rd.
Davenport, IA 52807
Phone: (563)344-7000
Fax: (563)344-7065
Format: Oldies

**WKBF-AM - 1270 (10434)**
3535 E. Kimberly Rd.
Davenport, IA 52807
Phone: (563)344-7000
Fax: (563)344-7087
Format: Big Band/Nostalgia

**WLLR-AM - 1230 (10435)**
3535 E. Kimberly Rd.
Davenport, IA 52807
Phone: (563)344-7000
Fax: (563)359-8524
Format: Country; Sports

**WLLR-FM - 103.7-FM (10436)**
3535 E. Kimberly Rd.
Davenport, IA 52807
Phone: (563)344-7000
Fax: (563)359-8524
Format: Contemporary Country

**WOC-AM - 1420 (10437)**
3535 E. Kimberly Rd.
Davenport, IA 52807
Phone: (563)344-7000
Fax: (563)344-7007
Format: Talk; News

**WXLP-FM - 96.9 (10438)**
1229 Brady St.
Davenport, IA 52803
Phone: (563)326-2541
Fax: (563)326-1819
Format: Album-Oriented Rock (AOR)

## Denver (Steamboat Springs), CO

**KCSR-AM - 610 (18310)**
226 Bordeaux
Chadron, NE 69337
Phone: (308)432-5545
Fax: (308)432-5601
Format: Country

## Des Moines, IA

**KBGG-AM - 1390 (10929)**
4143 109th St.
Urbandale, IA 50322
Phone: (515)331-9200
Fax: (515)331-9292

**KBOE-AM - 740 (10803)**
2172 230th St.
Hwy. 63 N.
PO Box 380
Oskaloosa, IA 52577-0380
Phone: (641)673-3493
Fax: (641)673-3495
Format: Contemporary Country

**KCOB-AM - 1280 (10782)**
PO Box 66
Newton, IA 50208-0066
Phone: (515)792-5262
Fax: (515)792-8403

Format: Country

**KCOB-FM - 95.9 (10783)**
PO Box 66
Newton, IA 50208-0066
Phone: (515)792-5262
Fax: (515)792-8403
Format: Country

**KDFR-FM - 91.3 (10507)**
PO Box 57023
Des Moines, IA 50317
Phone: (515)262-0449
Format: Religious

**KDPS-FM - 88.1 (10509)**
1800 Grand Ave.
Des Moines, IA 50307
Phone: (515)242-7723
Fax: (515)242-7598
Format: Eclectic

**KDRB-FM - 106.3 (10510)**
1801 Grand Ave.
Des Moines, IA 50309
Phone: (515)242-3500
Fax: (515)242-3798
Format: Contemporary Hit Radio (CHR)

**KFJB-AM - 1230 (10737)**
123 W. Main St.
Marshalltown, IA 50158
Phone: (641)753-3361
Fax: (641)752-7201
Format: News; Talk

**KGRA-FM - 98.9 (10910)**
204 S Division St.
Stuart, IA 50250
Phone: (515)523-1817
Fax: (515)386-2215
Format: Country

**KGRN-AM - 1410 (10609)**
Box 660
Grinnell, IA 50112
Fax: (515)236-8896
Format: Full Service; Middle-of-the-Road (MOR); Country; Adult Contemporary

**KHBT-FM - 97.7 (10632)**
2196 Montana Ave.
PO Box 217
Humboldt, IA 50548
Phone: (515)332-4100
Fax: (515)332-2723
Format: Classic Rock

**KIAQ-FM - 96.9 (10586)**
1014 Central Ave.
Fort Dodge, IA 50501
Phone: (515)573-5748
Fax: (515)573-3376
Format: Country; Hot Country

**KIOA-FM - 93.3 (10513)**
1416 Locust St.
Des Moines, IA 50309-3014
Phone: (515)280-1350
Fax: (515)280-3011
Format: Oldies

**KKDM-FM - 107.5 (10514)**
1801 Grand Ave.
Des Moines, IA 50309
Phone: (515)242-3500
Fax: (515)242-3798
Format: Contemporary Hit Radio (CHR)

**KKEZ-FM - 94.5 (10588)**
540 A St.
PO Box 578
Fort Dodge, IA 50501
Phone: (515)576-7333
Fax: (515)955-4250
Format: Album-Oriented Rock (AOR)

**KQWC-AM - 1570 (10964)**
PO Box 550
Webster City, IA 50595
Phone: (515)832-1570
Fax: (515)832-2079

# Fargo, ND

**Format:** Talk; Agricultural; News; Agricultural; News; Agricultural

**KQWC-FM - 95.7  (10965)**
1020 E. 2nd St.
PO Box 550
Webster City, IA 50595
Phone: (515)832-1570
Fax: (515)832-2079
**Format:** Talk; News; News; News

**KRKN-FM - 104.3  (10811)**
416 E. Main St.
Ottumwa, IA 52501
**Format:** Contemporary Country

**KRKQ-FM - 98.3  (10930)**
4143 109th St.
Urbandale, IA 50322
Phone: (515)331-9200
Fax: (515)331-9292

**KRNT-AM - 1350  (10519)**
1416 Locust St.
Des Moines, IA 50309
Phone: (515)280-1350
Fax: (515)280-3011
**Format:** Big Band/Nostalgia; Sports

**KWDM-FM - 88.7  (10971)**
1140 35th St.
West Des Moines, IA 50266
Phone: (515)226-2660
Fax: (515)226-2609
**Format:** Alternative/New Music/Progressive; Alternative/New Music/Progressive

**KWKY-AM - 1150  (10521)**
PO Box 662
Des Moines, IA 50303
Phone: (515)981-0981
Fax: (515)981-0840
**Format:** Talk; Religious; Sports

**KWMT-AM - 540  (10593)**
540 A St.
Fort Dodge, IA 50501-0578
Phone: (515)576-7333
Fax: (515)955-4250
**Format:** Country

**KXIA-FM - 101.1  (10738)**
PO Box 698
Marshalltown, IA 50158
**Format:** Contemporary Country; Sports

**KXTX-AM - 940  (10523)**
1416 Locust St.
Des Moines, IA 50309-3014
Phone: (515)244-1350
Fax: (515)280-3011
**Format:** Oldies

**WHO-AM - 1040  (10525)**
1801 Grand Ave.
Des Moines, IA 50309
Phone: (515)242-3500
Fax: (515)242-3798
**Format:** News; Talk; Sports

**WOI-AM - 640  (10303)**
Iowa State University
Communications Bldg.
Ames, IA 50011
Phone: (515)294-2025
Fax: (515)294-1544
**Format:** Public Radio; News

**WOI-FM - 90.1  (10304)**
Iowa State University
Communications Bldg.
Ames, IA 50011
Phone: (515)294-2025
Fax: (515)294-1544
**Format:** Public Radio; Classical

# Fargo, ND

**KBMW-AM - 107.1  (24071)**
605 Dakota Ave
Wahpeton, ND 58074
Phone: (701)642-8747
Fax: (701)642-9501

**Format:** Oldies

**KBMW-AM - 1450  (24072)**
PO Box 1115
Wahpeton, ND 58074
Phone: (701)642-8747
Fax: (701)642-9501
**Format:** Country

**KFAB-FM - 92.7  (23959)**
1020 25th St. S
Fargo, ND 58103
Phone: (701)237-5346
Fax: (701)235-4042
**Format:** Country

**KFNW-AM - 1200  (23963)**
5702 52nd Ave. South
Fargo, ND 58104
Phone: (701)282-5910
Fax: (701)282-5781
**Format:** Religious

**KFNW-FM - 97.9  (23964)**
5702 52nd Ave. South
Fargo, ND 58104
Phone: (701)282-5910
Fax: (701)282-5781
**Format:** Religious

**KKBX-FM - 101.9  (23965)**
1020 25th St. S
Fargo, ND 58103
Phone: (701)237-5346
Fax: (701)235-4042
**Format:** Classic Rock

**KLTA-FM - 105.1  (23966)**
2720 7th Ave. SW
Fargo, ND 58103-8710
Phone: (701)239-4500
Fax: (701)235-9082
**Format:** Adult Contemporary

**KOVC-AM - 1490  (24065)**
232 3rd St. NE
PO Box 994
Valley City, ND 58072
Phone: (701)845-1490
Fax: (701)845-1245
**Format:** Country

**KQDJ-AM - 1400  (24009)**
Box 1170
Jamestown, ND 58402
Phone: (701)252-1400
Fax: (701)252-1402
**Format:** Adult Contemporary; Talk; Information

**KQDJ-FM - 101.1  (24066)**
136 Central Ave. N.
PO Box 994
Valley City, ND 58072
Phone: (701)845-1490
Fax: (701)845-1245
**Format:** Adult Contemporary

**KQWB-AM - 1660  (23967)**
2720 7th Ave.S
PO Box 9919
Fargo, ND 58103
Phone: (701)237-4500
Fax: (701)235-9082

**KQWB-FM - 98.7  (23968)**
2720 7th Ave.
PO Box 9919
Fargo, ND 58103
Phone: (701)237-4500
Fax: (701)237-5400
**Format:** Classic Rock; Album-Oriented Rock (AOR)

**KSNR-FM - 100.3  (23993)**
505 University Ave.
PO Box 40
Grand Forks, ND 58203
Phone: (701)746-1417
Fax: (701)746-1410
**Format:** Oldies

**KVOX-AM - 1280  (23971)**
PO Box 2966
Fargo, ND 58108-2966
Phone: (701)237-5346
Fax: (701)235-4042

**Format:** Sports; News; Talk

**KVOX-FM - 99.9  (23972)**
2720 27th Ave. S.
PO Box 2966
Fargo, ND 58103
Phone: (701)241-99FM
**Format:** Contemporary Country

**KXGT-FM - 95.5  (24012)**
Box 1170
Jamestown, ND 58402-1170
Phone: (701)252-1400
Fax: (701)252-1402
**Format:** Oldies

**KZLT-FM - 104.3  (23995)**
PO Box 13638
Grand Forks, ND 58208
Phone: (701)775-4611
Fax: (701)772-0540
**Format:** Talk; News; Agricultural; Sports; Adult Contemporary; Sports; Adult Contemporary

**WDAY-FM - 93.7  (23976)**
1020 25th St. S
Fargo, ND 58103
Phone: (701)237-5346
Fax: (701)235-4042
**Format:** Contemporary Hit Radio (CHR)

# Joplin, MO-Pittsburg, KS

**KBTN-AM - 1420  (17445)**
216 W. Spring
PO Box K
Neosho, MO 64850
Phone: (417)451-1420
Fax: (417)451-2526
**Format:** Country

**KKOW-AM - 860  (11373)**
1162 E. Hwy. 126
Pittsburg, KS 66762
Phone: (620)231-7200
Fax: (620)231-3321
**Format:** Country; Agricultural

**KKOW-FM - 96.9  (11374)**
1162 E. Hwy. 126
Pittsburg, KS 66762
Phone: (620)231-7200
Fax: (620)231-3321
**Format:** Contemporary Country

**KLKC-AM - 1540  (11364)**
RR 4
PO Box 853
Parsons, KS 67357
Phone: (620)421-6400
**Format:** Talk; Adult Contemporary; Oldies

**KNEM-AM - 1240  (17448)**
Box 447
Nevada, MO 64772
Phone: (417)667-3113
Fax: (417)667-9797
**Format:** Country

**KNMO-FM - 97.5  (17449)**
Box 447
Nevada, MO 64772
Phone: (417)667-3113
Fax: (417)667-9797
**Format:** Country

**KOBC-FM - 90.7  (17304)**
2711 Peace Church Rd.
Joplin, MO 64801
Phone: (417)781-6401
Fax: (417)782-1841
**Format:** Contemporary Christian; Adult Contemporary; Adult Contemporary

**KOCR-AM - 1310  (17305)**
1111 N Main St.
Joplin, MO 64801
Phone: (417)781-6401
Fax: (417)782-1841
**Format:** Religious

**KQYX-AM - 1450  (17307)**
2510 W 20th St.
Joplin, MO 64804
Phone: (417)781-1313
Fax: (417)781-1316

**Format:** News; Talk; Talk

**KSEK-AM - 1340 (11376)**
1604 E. Quincy
Pittsburg, KS 66762
Phone: (620)232-1340
Fax: (620)232-5550

## Kansas City, MO (Lawrence, KS)

**KAIR-FM - 93.7 (10992)**
PO Box G
Atchison, KS 66002
Phone: (913)367-1470
Fax: (913)367-7021
**Format:** Country

**KAOL-AM - 1430 (17124)**
102 N. Mason
Carrollton, MO 64633
Fax: (816)542-0420
**Format:** Country; Agricultural

**KCCV-AM - 760 (11358)**
10550 Barkley
Overland Park, KS 66212
Phone: (913)642-7600
Fax: (913)642-2424
**Format:** Religious; News; Information; Talk; Information; Talk

**KCCV-FM - 92.3 (11359)**
10550 Barkley, Ste. 108
Overland Park, KS 66212
Phone: (913)642-7600
Fax: (913)642-2424
**Format:** Religious; Talk

**KCTE-AM - 1510 (17272)**
10841 E. 28th St.
Independence, MO 64052
Fax: (816)254-6929
**Format:** Sports

**KCUR-FM - 89.3 (17359)**
4825 Troost Ave., Ste. 202
Kansas City, MO 64110
Phone: (816)235-1551
Fax: (816)235-2864
**Format:** Public Radio; Talk; Jazz; News; Jazz; News

**KCXL-AM - 1140 (17395)**
310 S. La Frenz
Liberty, MO 64068
Phone: (816)792-1140
Fax: (816)792-8258
**Format:** Talk

**KEXS-AM - 1090 (17217)**
201 Industrial Park Rd.
Excelsior Springs, MO 64024
Phone: (816)630-1090
Fax: (816)630-6063
**Format:** Southern Gospel

**KGOZ-FM - 101.7 (18009)**
804 Main
Trenton, MO 64683
Phone: (660)359-2727
Fax: (660)359-4126
**Format:** Hot Country

**KKFI-FM - 90.1 (17360)**
PO Box 32250
Kansas City, MO 64171-5250
Phone: (816)931-3122
**Format:** Public Radio; Full Service; Eclectic

**KLWN-AM - 1320 (11186)**
3125 W. 6th St.
Lawrence, KS 66049-3101
Phone: (785)843-1320
Fax: (785)841-5924
**Format:** News; Talk; Sports; Talk

**KPRT-AM - 1590 (17363)**
11131 Colorado
Kansas City, MO 64137-2546
Phone: (816)576-7400
Fax: (816)966-1055
**Format:** Gospel

**KSIS-AM - 1050 (17947)**
2209 S Limit Ave.
Sedalia, MO 65301-6950
Phone: (660)826-1050
Fax: (660)827-5072

**Format:** News; Talk

**KTTN-AM - 1600 (18010)**
PO Box 307
Trenton, MO 64683
Phone: (660)359-2261
Fax: (660)359-4126
**Format:** Soft Rock

**KTTN-FM - 92.3 (18011)**
PO Box 307
Trenton, MO 64683
Phone: (660)359-2261
Fax: (660)359-4126
**Format:** Country; Information; Religious; Gospel

## Lincoln-Hastings-Kearney, NE

**KAMI-AM - 1580 (18321)**
PO Box 15
Cozad, NE 69130-0015
Phone: (308)784-1580
Fax: (308)784-1583
**Format:** Talk

**KAMI-FM - 104.5 (18322)**
PO Box 15
Cozad, NE 69130-0015
Phone: (308)784-1580
Fax: (308)784-1583
**Format:** Country

**KAWL-AM - 1370 (18647)**
1309 Rd. 11
York, NE 68467-9804
Phone: (402)362-4433
Fax: (402)362-6501
**Format:** Oldies; Full Service

**KBBK-FM - 107.3 (18461)**
4343 O St.
Lincoln, NE 68503
Phone: (402)475-4567
Fax: (402)479-1411
**Format:** Adult Contemporary

**KCNT-FM - 88.1 (18368)**
PO Box 1024
Hastings, NE 68902
Phone: (402)461-2580
Fax: (402)461-2507
**Format:** Contemporary Hit Radio (CHR); Educational

**KFGE-FM - 98.1 (18463)**
4343 O St.
Lincoln, NE 68510
Fax: (402)479-1411
**Format:** Hot Country

**KFOR-AM - 1240 (18464)**
3800 Cornhusker Hwy.
Lincoln, NE 68504-1533
Phone: (402)466-1234
Fax: (402)483-4095
**Format:** News; Talk; Adult Contemporary

**KGFW-AM - 1340 (18389)**
PO Box 669
Kearney, NE 68848
Phone: (308)237-2131
Fax: (308)237-0312
**Format:** Talk; News

**KGMT-AM - 1310 (18339)**
414 4th St.
Fairbury, NE 68352-2514
Phone: (402)729-3382
Fax: (402)729-3446
**Format:** Adult Contemporary

**KHAS-AM - 1230 (18369)**
500 E. J St.
PO Box 726
Hastings, NE 68902
Phone: (402)462-5101
Fax: (402)461-3866
**Format:** Adult Contemporary; Information; Sports; Agricultural

**KIBZ-FM - 106.3 (18465)**
4630 Antelope Creek Rd., Ste. 200
Lincoln, NE 68506
Phone: (402)484-8000
Fax: (402)483-9138

**Format:** Album-Oriented Rock (AOR)

**KIOD-FM - 105.3 (18485)**
106 W. 8th St.
Box 939
McCook, NE 69001
Phone: (308)345-1981
Fax: (308)345-7202
**Format:** Contemporary Country

**KKAN-AM - 1490 (11367)**
205 F St.
PO Box 548
Phillipsburg, KS 67661
Phone: (785)543-2151
Fax: (785)543-2152
**Format:** Full Service; Eclectic; Hot Country; Adult Contemporary; Hot Country; Adult Contemporary

**KKPR-FM - 98.9 (18390)**
PO Box 130
Kearney, NE 68848
Phone: (308)236-9900
Fax: (308)234-6781
**Format:** Oldies

**KLCV-FM - 88.5 (18466)**
100 N. 56th St., Ste. 110
Lincoln, NE 68504
Phone: (402)465-8850
Fax: (402)465-8852
**Format:** Religious; News; Talk

**KLIN-AM - 1400 (18467)**
4343 O St.
Lincoln, NE 68510
Phone: (402)475-4567
Fax: (402)479-1411
**Format:** News; Talk

**KLMY-FM - 104.1 (18469)**
4630 Antelope Creek Rd. Ste. 200
Lincoln, NE 68506
Phone: (402)484-8000
Fax: (402)489-9989
**Format:** Contemporary Hit Radio (CHR)

**KLNE-FM - 88.7 (18399)**
PO Box 83111
Lincoln, NE 68503
Phone: (402)472-3611
Fax: (402)472-2403
**Format:** Public Radio; Jazz; Classical; News; News

**KLPR-FM - 91.3 (18391)**
University of Nebraska at Kearney
Kearney, NE 68849
Phone: (308)234-8250
**Format:** Jazz; Blues; Alternative/New Music/Progressive

**KQKY-FM - 105.9 (18392)**
Waitt Radio
PO Box 669
Kearney, NE 68848
Phone: (308)237-2131
Fax: (308)237-0312
**Format:** Top 40

**KQMA-FM - 92.5 (11368)**
205 F St.
PO Box 548
Phillipsburg, KS 67661
Phone: (785)543-2151
Fax: (785)543-2152
**Format:** Eclectic; Hot Country; Adult Contemporary

**KRVN-AM - 880 (18401)**
PO Box 880
Lexington, NE 68850-0880
Phone: (308)324-2371
Fax: (308)324-5786
**Format:** Country; Agricultural; News; Sports

**KRVN-FM - 93.1 (18402)**
PO Box 880
Lexington, NE 68850-0880
Phone: (308)324-2371
Fax: (308)324-5786
**Format:** News; Sports

**KSWN-FM - 93.9 (18488)**
PO Box 939
McCook, NE 69001
Phone: (308)345-1100
Fax: (308)345-7202

## Mankato, MN

**Format:** Talk; News

**KSYZ-FM - 107.7  (18361)**
3532 West Capital Ave.
Grand Island, NE 68803
Phone: (308)381-1077
Fax: (308)384-8900
**Format:** Adult Contemporary

**KTMX-FM - 104.9  (18648)**
1309 Rd. 11
York, NE 68467-9804
Phone: (402)362-4433
Fax: (402)362-6501
**Format:** Adult Contemporary

**KUTT-FM - 99.5  (18340)**
414 4th St.
Fairbury, NE 68352
Phone: (402)729-3382
Fax: (402)729-3446
**Format:** Contemporary Country

**KXNE-FM - 89.3  (18501)**
1800 N. 33rd St.
PO Box 83111
Lincoln, NE 68501
Phone: (402)472-3611
Fax: (402)472-2403
**Format:** Public Radio; Classical; News; Jazz

**KXPN - 1460  (18393)**
403 E. 25th St
PO Box 130
Kearney, NE 68848
Phone: (308)236-9900
Fax: (308)234-6781
**Format:** Sports

**KZEN-FM - 100.3  (18319)**
1418 25th St.
Columbus, NE 68601-2820
Phone: (402)564-2866
Fax: (402)564-2967
**Format:** Country

**KZUM-FM - 89.3  (18478)**
941 O St., Ste. 1025
Lincoln, NE 68508-3608
Phone: (402)474-5086
Fax: (402)474-5091
**Format:** Eclectic; News; News

## Mankato, MN

**KILR-FM - 95.9  (10560)**
Hwy. 4 N.
PO Box 453
Estherville, IA 51334
Phone: (712)362-2644
Fax: (712)362-5951
**Format:** Country

## Memphis, TN

**KCRV-FM - 105.1  (17368)**
1303 Southwest Dr.
PO Box 509
Kennett, MO 63857
Phone: (573)888-4616
Fax: (573)888-4991
**Format:** Oldies

## Minneapolis-St. Paul, MN

**KDIO-AM - 1350  (28343)**
Box 1005
Milbank, SD 57252
Phone: (605)839-2581
**Format:** Talk; News; Sports; Agricultural

## Minot-Bismarck-Dickinson, ND-Glendive, MT

**KBMR-AM - 1130  (23910)**
3500 E. Rosser Ave.
PO Box 1256
Bismarck, ND 58502
Phone: (701)255-1234
Fax: (701)222-1131

**Format:** Country

**KBYZ-FM - 96.5  (23912)**
1830 N. 11th St.
PO Box 1377
Bismarck, ND 58502
Phone: (701)663-6411
Fax: (701)663-8790
**Format:** Classic Rock

**KCND-FM - 90.5  (23913)**
c/o North Dakota Public Radio
207 N. 5th St.
Fargo, ND 58102
Phone: (701)241-6900
Fax: (701)239-7650
**Format:** Public Radio; News; Classical; Jazz

**KDPR-FM - 89.9  (23941)**
c/o North Dakota Public Radio
207 N. 5th St.
Fargo, ND 58102
Phone: (701)241-6900
Fax: (701)239-7650
**Format:** Public Radio; Classical; Jazz

**KFYR-AM - 550  (23914)**
206 N 4th St.
Bismarck, ND 58501
Phone: (701)258-5555
Fax: (701)255-8155
**Format:** Full Service

**KLXX-AM - 1270  (23915)**
PO Box 1377
Bismarck, ND 58502-1377
Phone: (701)663-6411
Fax: (701)663-8790
**Format:** Big Band/Nostalgia; Sports; Sports

**KMPR-FM - 88.9  (24036)**
c/o North Dakota Public Radio
207 N. 5th St.
Fargo, ND 58102
Phone: (701)241-6900
Fax: (701)239-7650
**Format:** Public Radio; News; Classical; Jazz

**KPOK-AM - 1340  (23926)**
11 1/2 N Maine
PO Box 829
Bowman, ND 58623
Phone: (701)523-3883
Fax: (701)523-3885
**Format:** Country; Agricultural; Agricultural

**KPPR-FM - 90.5  (24083)**
c/o North Dakota Public Radio
207 N. 5th St.
Fargo, ND 58102
Phone: (701)241-6900
Fax: (701)239-7650
**Format:** Public Radio; News; Classical; Jazz

**KQDY-FM - 94.5  (23916)**
3500 E. Rosser Ave.
PO Box 94
Bismarck, ND 58501
Phone: (701)258-9400
Fax: (701)222-1131
**Format:** Contemporary Country

**KSSS-FM - 101.5  (23917)**
PO Box 2156
Bismarck, ND 58502
Phone: (701)344-5000
Fax: (701)222-1131
**Format:** Country

**KXMR-AM - 710  (23918)**
3500 E Rosser Ave.
Bismarck, ND 58501
Phone: (701)255-1234
Fax: (701)222-1131
**Format:** Sports

**KYYY-FM - 92.9  (23919)**
3500 E. Rosser Ave.
Bismarck, ND 58501-3376
**Format:** Contemporary Hit Radio (CHR); News; News

**KZRX-FM - 92.1  (23944)**
11291 39th St. SW
Dickinson, ND 58602
Phone: (701)227-1876
Fax: (701)483-1959

**Format:** Adult Contemporary

## North Platte, NE

**KELN-FM - 97.1  (18507)**
PO Box 248
North Platte, NE 69103
Phone: (308)532-1120
Fax: (308)532-0458
**Format:** Adult Contemporary

**KODY-AM - 1240  (18511)**
305 E. 4th
PO Box 1085
North Platte, NE 69103
Phone: (308)532-3344
Fax: (308)534-6651
**Format:** Talk; News

**KOOQ-AM - 1410  (18512)**
PO Box 248
North Platte, NE 69103
Phone: (308)532-1120
Fax: (308)532-0458
**Format:** Oldies; Agricultural; News

**KXNP-FM - 103.5  (18514)**
305 E. 4th St.
PO Box 1085
North Platte, NE 69103
Phone: (308)532-3344
Fax: (308)534-6651
**Format:** Contemporary Country

## Omaha, NE

**KAZP-AM - 1620  (18544)**
5011 Capitol Ave.
Omaha, NE 68132-2921
Phone: (402)342-2000
Fax: (402)346-5748
**Format:** Sports

**KCRO-AM - 660  (18545)**
11717 Burt St., Ste. 202
Omaha, NE 68154-1500
Phone: (402)422-1600
Fax: (402)422-1602
**Format:** Religious

**KDSN-AM - 1530  (10452)**
1530 Ridge Rd.
PO Box 670
Denison, IA 51442
Phone: (712)263-3141
Fax: (712)263-2088
**Format:** Country

**KDSN-FM - 107.1  (10453)**
1530 Ridge Rd.
PO Box 670
Denison, IA 51442
Phone: (712)263-3141
Fax: (712)263-2088
**Format:** Adult Contemporary

**KFAB-AM - 1110  (18549)**
5010 Underwood Ave.
Omaha, NE 68132
Phone: (402)561-2000
Fax: (402)556-8937
**Format:** News; Talk

**KHUS-FM - 93.3  (18552)**
5010 Underwood Ave.
Omaha, NE 68132
Phone: (402)561-2000
Fax: (402)556-8937
**Format:** Album-Oriented Rock (AOR)

**KIWR-FM - 89.7  (10412)**
1700 College Rd.
Council Bluffs, IA 51503
Phone: (712)325-3254
Fax: (712)325-3391
**Format:** Public Radio; Alternative/New Music/Progressive

**KKCD-FM - 92.3 KEZO, 105.9 KKLD, 104.5 KRSZ, 97.7 KQLH, 94.1 KMXM,KBBX  (18555)**
11128 John Galt Blvd.
Omaha, NE 68137
Fax: (402)598-6605

**Format:** Album-Oriented Rock (AOR); Adult Contemporary

**KKOT-FM - 93.5 (18316)**
1418 25th St.
Columbus, NE 68601-2820
Phone: (402)564-2866
Fax: (402)564-2867
**Format:** Classic Rock

**KOIL-AM - 1020 (18557)**
5011 Capitol Ave.
Omaha, NE 68132-2921
Phone: (402)342-2000
Fax: (402)345-3652

**KSRZ-FM - 104.5 (18560)**
11128 John Galt Blvd., Ste. 192
Omaha, NE 68137-2321
Phone: (402)592-5300
Fax: (402)331-1348
**Format:** Adult Contemporary

**KTIC-AM - 840 (18640)**
1011 N. Lincoln St.
Box 84
West Point, NE 68788
Phone: (402)372-5423
Fax: (402)372-5425
**Format:** Full Service; Agricultural

**KTNC-AM - 1230 (18342)**
1602 Stone St.
PO Box 589
Falls City, NE 68355-0589
Phone: (402)245-2453
Fax: (402)245-5862
**Format:** Oldies; News; Sports

**KWPN-FM - 107.9 (18641)**
1011 N Lincoln
Box 84
West Point, NE 68788-0084
Phone: (402)372-5423
Fax: (402)372-5425
**Format:** Full Service

**KXKT-FM - 103.7 (10316)**
5010 Underwood Ave.
Omaha, NE 68132
Phone: (402)561-2000
Fax: (402)556-8937
**Format:** Contemporary Hit Radio (CHR)

## Ottumwa, IA-Kirksville, MO (Wapello, IA)

**KBIZ-AM - 1240 (10808)**
Broadcast Center
209 S. Market
Ottumwa, IA 52501
Phone: (515)682-4535
Fax: (515)684-5892
**Format:** News; Sports; Oldies; Agricultural

**KIIK-FM - 95.9 (10564)**
57 1/2 S. Court
Fairfield, IA 52556
Phone: (641)472-4191
Fax: (641)472-2071
**Format:** Oldies

**KIRX-AM - 1450 (17378)**
1308 N. Baltimore
PO Box 130
Kirksville, MO 63501
Phone: (816)665-3781
Fax: (816)665-0711
**Format:** Full Service; Oldies; Talk; News; Sports; Information

**KLEE-AM - 1480 (10809)**
601 W. 2nd St.
Ottumwa, IA 52501
Phone: (641)682-8711
Fax: (641)682-8482
**Format:** Country; News; Talk

**KOTM-FM - 97.7 (10810)**
601 W. 2nd St.
Ottumwa, IA 52501
Phone: (641)682-8711
Fax: (641)682-8482

**Format:** Contemporary Hit Radio (CHR)

**KRXL-FM - 94.5 (17379)**
1308 N. Baltimore
PO Box 130
Kirksville, MO 63501
Phone: (816)665-9828
Fax: (816)665-0711
**Format:** Classic Rock

**KTWA-FM - 92.7 (10812)**
Broadcast Center
PO Box 190
Ottumwa, IA 52501
Phone: (515)682-4535
Fax: (515)684-5892
**Format:** Adult Contemporary

## Paducah,KY-Cape Girardeau,MO-Marion,IL

**KAPE-AM - 1550 (17115)**
901 S. Kings Hwy
PO Box 558
Cape Girardeau, MO 63703
Phone: (573)339-7000
Fax: (573)651-4100

**KCGQ-FM - 99.3 (17117)**
PO Box 1610
Cape Girardeau, MO 63702-1610
Phone: (573)334-9936
Fax: (573)335-4806
**Format:** Album-Oriented Rock (AOR)

**KDEX-AM - 1590 (17196)**
20487 State Hwy. 114
PO Box 249
Dexter, MO 63841-0249
Phone: (573)624-3591
Fax: (573)624-9926
**Format:** Contemporary Country

**KDEX-FM - 102.3 (17197)**
20487 State Hwy. 114
PO Box 249
Dexter, MO 63841
Phone: (573)624-3591
Fax: (573)624-9926
**Format:** Contemporary Country

**KEZS-FM - 102.9 (17118)**
PO Box 1610
Cape Girardeau, MO 63701
Phone: (314)335-8291
Fax: (314)335-4806
**Format:** Country

**KGIR-AM - 1220 (17120)**
324 Broadway
PO Box 1610
Cape Girardeau, MO 63702-1610
Phone: (573)335-8291
Fax: (573)335-4806
**Format:** Sports; Sports

**KLID-AM - 1340 (17497)**
KLID Bldg.
102 N. 11th
Poplar Bluff, MO 63901
Phone: (573)686-1600
Fax: (573)686-2560
**Format:** Oldies; Alternative/New Music/Progressive

**KRCU-FM - 90.9 (17121)**
1 University Plaza
Cape Girardeau, MO 63701
Phone: (573)651-5070
Fax: (573)651-5071
**Format:** Public Radio; Full Service; Full Service

**KSIM-AM - 1400 (17955)**
519 Greer Ave.
PO Box 69
Sikeston, MO 63801
Phone: (573)471-1400
Fax: (573)471-1402
**Format:** News; Talk; Talk

**KZIM-AM - 960 (17122)**
PO Box 1610
Cape Girardeau, MO 63702
Phone: (573)335-5512
Fax: (573)335-4806

**Format:** News; Sports; Agricultural; Talk; Agricultural; Talk

## Rapid City, SD

**KBFS-AM - 1450 (28274)**
PO Box 787
Belle Fourche, SD 57717
Phone: (605)892-2571
Fax: (605)892-2573
**Format:** Country; Sports; Agricultural

**KBHU-FM - 89.1 (28436)**
Black Hills State University
Spearfish, SD 57799
Phone: (605)642-6265
Fax: (605)642-6762
**Format:** Alternative/New Music/Progressive

**KFXS-FM - 100.3 (28384)**
660 Flormann, Ste. 100
Rapid City, SD 57701
Phone: (605)343-6161
Fax: (605)343-9012
**Format:** Classic Rock

**KIMM-AM - 1150 (28385)**
PO Box 2480
Rapid City, SD 57709
Phone: (605)343-6161
Fax: (605)343-9012
**Format:** Country

**KIQK-FM - 104.1 (28386)**
306 E. St. Joseph St.
PO Box 1680
Rapid City, SD 57701
Phone: (605)343-0888
Fax: (605)342-3075
**Format:** Country

**KKLS-AM - 920 (28388)**
660 Flormann St.
Rapid City, SD 57701
Phone: (605)343-6161
Fax: (605)343-9012
**Format:** Oldies

**KLMP-FM - 97.9 (28390)**
PO Box 168
Rapid City, SD 57709-0168
Phone: (605)342-6822
Fax: (605)348-0854
**Format:** Religious; Talk

**KRCS-FM - 93.1 (28393)**
PO Box 2480
Rapid City, SD 57709
Phone: (605)343-6161
Fax: (605)343-9012
**Format:** Contemporary Hit Radio (CHR)

**KSDZ-FM - 95.5 (18353)**
Box 390
Gordon, NE 69343
Phone: (308)282-2500
Fax: (308)282-0061
**Format:** Hot Country; Oldies

**KSLT-FM - 107.3 (28394)**
1853 Fountain Plaza Dr
PO Box 168
Rapid City, SD 57702
Phone: (605)342-6822
Fax: (605)342-0854
**Format:** Religious; Contemporary Christian

**KTOQ-AM - 1340 (28395)**
306 1/2 E. St. Joseph
PO Box 1680
Rapid City, SD 57709-1680
Phone: (605)342-3075
Fax: (605)342-3075
**Format:** Adult Contemporary

## Rochester, MN-Mason City, IA-Austin, MN

**KCMR-FM - 97.9 (10743)**
Will F Muse Center
600 First Street N.W., Suite 101
PO Box 979
Mason City, IA 50401
Phone: (641)424-9300
Fax: (641)423-2221

**Format:** Easy Listening; Religious; Religious

**KCZQ-FM - 102.3  (10415)**
116 1st Ave. W.
Cresco, IA 52136-1514
Phone: (563)547-1000
Fax: (563)547-2200
**Format:** Adult Contemporary

**KIAI-FM - 93.9  (10745)**
PO Box 1300
Mason City, IA 50402
Phone: (641)423-1300
Fax: (641)423-2906
**Format:** Country

**KIOW-FM - 107.3  (10571)**
18643 360th St.
Box 308
Forest City, IA 50436
Phone: (641)585-1073
Fax: (641)585-2990
**Format:** Contemporary Country; Adult Contemporary; Full Service

**KRNI-AM - 1010  (10746)**
c/o KUNI-FM
University of Northern Iowa
Cedar Falls, IA 50614-0359
Phone: (319)273-6400
Fax: (319)273-2682
**Format:** Public Radio; Eclectic

**KUNY-FM - 91.5  (10747)**
c/o KUNI
University of Northern Iowa
Cedar Falls, IA 50614-0359
Phone: (319)273-6400
Fax: (319)273-2682
**Format:** Public Radio; Eclectic

## Rochester, NY

**KCHA-FM - 95.9  (10390)**
207 N. Main St.
Charles City, IA 50616
Phone: (641)228-1000
Fax: (641)228-1200
**Format:** Adult Contemporary

## St. Joseph, MO

**KAAN-AM - 870  (17075)**
Hwy. 69 S.
PO Box 447
Bethany, MO 64424
Phone: (660)425-6380
Fax: (660)425-8148
**Format:** Country

**KAAN-FM - 95.5  (17076)**
Hwy. 69 S.
PO Box 447
Bethany, MO 64424
Phone: (660)425-6380
Fax: (660)425-8148
**Format:** Country

**KGNM-AM - 1270  (17534)**
2414 S. Leonard Rd.
Saint Joseph, MO 64503-1899
Phone: (816)233-2577
Fax: (816)233-2374
**Format:** Adult Contemporary; Contemporary Christian; Contemporary Christian

**KKJO-FM - 105.5  (17535)**
PO Box 8550
Saint Joseph, MO 64508-8550
Phone: (816)233-8881
Fax: (816)279-8280
**Format:** Adult Contemporary

**KSFT-AM - 1550  (17537)**
PO Box 8550
Saint Joseph, MO 64508-8550
Phone: (816)233-8881
Fax: (816)279-8280

**Format:** Oldies

## St. Louis, MO (Mt. Vernon, IL)

**KATZ-FM - 100.3  (17907)**
10155 Corporate Sq. Dr.
Saint Louis, MO 63132
Phone: (314)969-1600
Fax: (314)692-5127
**Format:** Jazz

**KCLC-FM - 89.1  (17524)**
Lindenwood College
Saint Charles, MO 63301
**Format:** News; Adult Contemporary; Bluegrass; Religious; Public Radio

**KEZK-FM - 98.1  (17912)**
3100 Market St.
Saint Louis, MO 63103-2526
Phone: (314)531-0000
Fax: (314)531-9855
**Format:** Talk

**KJFF-AM - 1400  (17230)**
1026 Scenic Dr.
Festus, MO 63028
Fax: (314)937-3636
**Format:** Talk; News

**KJFM-FM - 102.1  (17401)**
615 Georgia St.
PO Box 438
Louisiana, MO 63353
Phone: (573)754-5102
Fax: (573)754-5544
**Format:** Contemporary Country

**KMJM-FM - 104.9  (17915)**
1001 Highland Plaza Drive W.
Saint Louis, MO 63110
Phone: (314)333-8000
Fax: (314)692-5127
**Format:** Urban Contemporary

**KPNT-FM - 105.7  (17919)**
1215 Cole St.
Saint Louis, MO 63103
Phone: (314)231-1057
Fax: (314)621-3000
**Format:** Alternative/New Music/Progressive

**KSD-FM - 93.7  (17920)**
1910 Pine St., Ste. 225
Saint Louis, MO 63103
Phone: (314)436-9370
Fax: (014)425-0937
**Format:** Country

**KSHE-FM - 94.7  (17922)**
700 St. Louis Union Sta.
The Annex No. 101
Saint Louis, MO 63103
Phone: (314)621-0095
Fax: (314)621-3428
**Format:** Album-Oriented Rock (AOR)

**KSIV-AM - 1320  (17923)**
1750 S. Brentwood Blvd., Ste. 811
Saint Louis, MO 63144
Phone: (314)961-1320
Fax: (314)961-7562
**Format:** Talk; Religious

**KSLZ-FM - 107.7  (17924)**
10155 Corporate Square Dr.
Saint Louis, MO 63132
Phone: (314)692-5108
Fax: (314)692-5123
**Format:** Contemporary Hit Radio (CHR)

**KTUI-AM - 1560  (18000)**
PO Box 99
Sullivan, MO 63080
Phone: (573)468-5101
Fax: (573)468-5884
**Format:** News; Talk

**KTUI-FM - 100.9  (18001)**
PO Box 99
Sullivan, MO 63080
Phone: (573)468-5101
Fax: (573)468-5884

**Format:** Country; Sports; Sports

**KWMU-FM - 90.7  (17926)**
University of Missouri-St. Louis
One University Blvd.
Saint Louis, MO 63121
Phone: (314)516-5968
Fax: (314)516-5993
**Format:** Public Radio; News; Jazz

**KWRE-AM - 730  (18044)**
PO Box 220
Warrenton, MO 63383
Phone: (636)456-3311
Fax: (636)456-8767
**Format:** Country

**WIL-AM - 1430  (17191)**
11647 Olive Blvd.
Creve Coeur, MO 63141-7001
**Format:** Middle-of-the-Road (MOR)

**WRYT-AM - 1080  (17931)**
3515 Hampton Ave.
Saint Louis, MO 63139
Phone: (314)752-7000
Fax: (877)305-1234
**Format:** Religious

**WVRV-FM - 101.1  (17933)**
11647 Olive Blvd.
Saint Louis, MO 63141
Phone: (314)983-6000
Fax: (314)994-9447
**Format:** Album-Oriented Rock (AOR)

## Sioux City, IA

**KAYL-AM - 990  (10901)**
604 1/2 Lake Ave.
Storm Lake, IA 50588
Phone: (712)732-3520
Fax: (712)732-1746
**Format:** Big Band/Nostalgia

**KEXL-FM - 106.7  (18500)**
PO Box 789
Norfolk, NE 68702
Phone: (402)371-0780
Fax: (402)371-6303
**Format:** Adult Contemporary; News; Sports

**KGLI-FM - 95.5  (10875)**
1113 Nebraska St.
Sioux City, IA 51105
Phone: (712)258-5595
Fax: (712)252-2120
**Format:** Adult Contemporary; Adult Contemporary

**KICD-FM - 107.7  (10890)**
2600 Highway Blvd.
PO Box 260
Spencer, IA 51301
Phone: (712)262-1240
Fax: (712)262-2076
**Format:** Country

**KIWA-AM - 1550  (10856)**
411 9th St.
Sheldon, IA 51201
Phone: (712)324-2597
Fax: (712)324-2340
**Format:** Country; Talk; Talk

**KIWA-FM - 105.3  (10857)**
411 9th St.
Sheldon, IA 51201
Phone: (712)324-2597
Fax: (712)324-2340
**Format:** Country; Talk

**KKIA-FM - 92.9  (10904)**
145 Old Creek Rd.
PO Box 108
Storm Lake, IA 50588
Phone: (712)732-9200
Fax: (712)732-3095
**Format:** Hot Country

**KKMA-FM - 99.5  (10876)**
2000 Indian Hills Dr.
Sioux City, IA 51104
Phone: (712)239-2100
Fax: (712)239-3346

**Format:** Oldies

**KLEM-AM - 1410 (10708)**
37 2nd Ave.
Le Mars, IA 51031-1410
Phone: (712)546-4121
Fax: (712)546-9672
**Format:** Full Service

**KSCJ-AM - 1360 (10879)**
2000 Indian Hills Dr.
Sioux City, IA 51104
Phone: (712)239-2100
Fax: (712)239-3346
**Format:** Talk; News; Sports; Sports

**KSOU-AM - 1090 (10870)**
128 20th St. SE
PO Box 298
Sioux Center, IA 51250-0298
Phone: (712)722-1090
Fax: (712)722-1102
**Format:** Contemporary Christian

**KSOU-FM - 93.9 (10871)**
PO Box 298
Sioux Center, IA 51250-0288
Phone: (712)722-1090
Fax: (712)722-1102
**Format:** Adult Contemporary

**KSUX-FM - 105.7 (10882)**
2000 Indian Hills Dr.
Sioux City, IA 51104-1699
Phone: (712)239-2100
Fax: (712)239-3346
**Format:** Country

**KTCH-AM - 1590 (18635)**
PO Box 413
Wayne, NE 68787-0413
Phone: (402)375-3700
Fax: (402)375-5402
**Format:** Country

**KTCH-FM - 104.9 (18636)**
PO Box 413
Wayne, NE 68787
Phone: (402)375-3700
Fax: (402)375-5402
**Format:** Oldies

**KTFC-FM - 103.3 (10883)**
1534 Buchanan Ave.
Sioux City, IA 51106
Phone: (712)252-4621
Fax: (712)255-6300
**Format:** Gospel

**KUOO-FM - 103.9 (10894)**
Box 528
Hwy. 9 W.
Spirit Lake, IA 51360
Phone: (712)336-5800
Fax: (712)336-1634
**Format:** Adult Contemporary

**KWIT-FM - 90.3 (10885)**
4647 Stone Ave.
Sioux City, IA 51106
Phone: (712)274-6406
Fax: (712)274-6411
**Format:** Public Radio; Jazz; News; Classical; Hispanic; Classical; Hispanic

**KWSL-AM - 1470 (10886)**
1113 Nebraska St.
Sioux City, IA 51105
Phone: (712)255-1470
Fax: (712)252-2430
**Format:** News; Talk

## Sioux Falls-Mitchell, SD

**KCFS-FM - 94.5 (28414)**
1101 W. 22nd St.
Sioux Falls, SD 57105-1699
Phone: (605)331-6691
Fax: (605)331-6615
**Format:** Alternative/New Music/Progressive; Religious

**KDSD-FM - 90.9 (28361)**
c/o South Dakota Public Broadcasting
555 N. Dakota St.
PO Box 5000
Vermillion, SD 57069
Phone: (605)677-5861
Fax: (605)677-5010
**Format:** Classical; News; Jazz

**KELO-AM - 1320 (28417)**
500 S. Phillips
Sioux Falls, SD 57104
Phone: (605)331-5350
Fax: (605)336-0415
**Format:** News; Talk

**KELO-FM - 92.5 (28418)**
500 S. Phillips
Sioux Falls, SD 57104
Phone: (605)331-5350
Fax: (605)336-0415
**Format:** Adult Contemporary

**KESD-FM/South Dakota Public Broadcasting - 88.3 (28282)**
555 N Dakota St.
PO Box 5000
Vermillion, SD 57069
Phone: (605)677-5861
Fax: (605)677-5010
**Format:** News; Jazz; Classical

**KGIM-AM - 1420 (28265)**
349 Berkshire Plaza
PO Box 306
Aberdeen, SD 57401
Phone: (605)229-3636
Fax: (605)229-4849
**Format:** Country; Full Service; Agricultural; Adult Contemporary; Adult Contemporary

**KJJQ-AM - 910 (28284)**
111 Main Ave
PO Box 790
Brookings, SD 57006
Phone: (605)692-9125
Fax: (605)692-6434
**Format:** Oldies

**KKAA-AM - 1560 (28266)**
PO Box 1930
Aberdeen, SD 57402-1930
Phone: (605)225-1560
Fax: (605)225-8290
**Format:** News; Agricultural; Talk

**KKLS-FM - 104.7 (28419)**
3205 S. Meadow
Sioux Falls, SD 57106
Phone: (605)361-0300
Fax: (605)361-5410
**Format:** Contemporary Hit Radio (CHR)

**KKQQ-FM - 102.3 (28285)**
111 Main Ave.
PO Box 790
Brookings, SD 57006
Phone: (605)692-9125
Fax: (605)692-6434
**Format:** Classic Rock

**KMIT-FM - 105.9 (28350)**
501 S. Ohlman
Mitchell, SD 57301
Phone: (605)996-9667
Fax: (605)996-0013
**Format:** Country; Agricultural; News; Sports; News; Sports

**KMXC-FM - 97.3 (28420)**
2600 S. Spring Ave.
Sioux Falls, SD 57105
Phone: (605)331-6499
Fax: (605)339-2735
**Format:** Contemporary Hit Radio (CHR)

**KNWC-AM - 1270 (28421)**
26908 Marion Rd.
Sioux Falls, SD 57106
Phone: (605)339-1270
Fax: (605)339-1271
**Format:** Gospel; Religious

**KNWC-FM - 96.5 (28422)**
26908 Marion Rd.
Sioux Falls, SD 57106
Phone: (605)339-1270
Fax: (605)339-1271
**Format:** Gospel; Religious

**KOLY-AM - 1300 (28355)**
118 E. 3rd St.
PO Box 400
Mobridge, SD 57601
Phone: (605)845-3654
Fax: (605)845-3656

**KOLY-FM - 99.5 (28356)**
118 E. 3rd St.
PO Box 400
Mobridge, SD 57601
Phone: (605)845-3654
Fax: (605)845-3656
**Format:** Hot Country

**KORN-AM - 1490 (28351)**
PO Box 921
Mitchell, SD 57301
Phone: (605)996-1490
Fax: (605)996-6680
**Format:** Talk; News

**KQKD-AM - 1380 (28398)**
726 W 3rd St., Ste. A
Redfield, SD 57469-1209
Phone: (605)472-1380
Fax: (605)472-1382
**Format:** Country

**KQRN-FM - 107.3 (28352)**
PO Box 921
Mitchell, SD 57301
Phone: (605)996-1073
Fax: (605)996-6680
**Format:** Adult Contemporary

**KRRO-FM - 103.7 (28423)**
500 S. Phillips Ave.
Sioux Falls, SD 57104
Phone: (605)331-5350
Fax: (605)336-0415
**Format:** Classic Rock; Alternative/New Music/Progressive

**KRSD-FM - 88.1 (28424)**
Augustana College
PO Box 737
Sioux Falls, SD 57197
Phone: (605)335-6666
Fax: (605)335-1259
**Format:** Public Radio; Classical; News; Eclectic; News; Eclectic

**KSOO-AM - 1140 (28426)**
2600 S. Spring Ave.
Sioux Falls, SD 57105
Phone: (605)339-1140
Fax: (605)339-2735
**Format:** Full Service

**KTSD-FM - 91.1 (28400)**
c/o South Dakota Public Broadcasting
555 N. Dakota St.
PO Box 5000
Vermillion, SD 57069
Phone: (605)677-5861
Fax: (605)677-5010
**Format:** Classical; News; Jazz

**KTWB-FM - 101.9 (28428)**
500 S. Phillips Ave.
Sioux Falls, SD 57104
Phone: (605)331-5350
Fax: (605)336-0415
**Format:** Country

**KUSD-FM - 89.7 (28449)**
555 N. Dakota Sts.
PO Box 5000
Vermillion, SD 57069
Phone: (605)677-5861
Fax: (605)677-5010
**Format:** Classical; Jazz; News

**KWSN-AM - 1230 (28429)**
500 S. Phillips Ave.
Sioux Falls, SD 57104
Phone: (605)331-5350
Fax: (605)336-0415
**Format:** News; Talk

**KWYR-FM - 93.7 (28470)**
346 Main St.
Box 491
Winner, SD 57580
Phone: (605)842-3333
Fax: (605)842-3875
**Format:** Adult Contemporary; Top 40; News; Sports

**KXRB-AM - 1000 (28430)**
3205 S. Meadow
Sioux Falls, SD 57106
Phone: (605)361-0300
Fax: (605)361-5410

# Springfield, MO

**Format:** Country

**WNAX-AM - 570 (28482)**
1609 Hwy. 50 E.
Yankton, SD 57078
Phone: (605)665-7442
Fax: (605)665-8788
**Format:** Country; News; Agricultural; Sports; Agricultural; Sports

## Springfield, MO

**KAMS-FM - 95.1 (18006)**
Mammoth Spring
PO Box 15
Thayer, MO 65791
Phone: (417)264-7211
Fax: (417)264-7212
**Format:** Country; Contemporary Country; News; Sports

**KAYQ-FM - 97.1 (18046)**
PO Box 1420
Warsaw, MO 65355
Phone: (660)438-7343
Fax: (660)438-7159
**Format:** Country

**KBNN-AM - 750 (17386)**
PO Box 1112
Lebanon, MO 65536
Phone: (417)532-9111
Fax: (417)588-4191
**Format:** Talk; News

**KELE-AM - 1360 (17440)**
800 N. Hubbard
Mountain Grove, MO 65711
Phone: (417)926-4650
Fax: (417)926-7604
**Format:** Contemporary Christian; Talk

**KESM-AM - 1580 (17206)**
200 Radio Ln.
El Dorado Springs, MO 64744
Phone: (417)876-2741
Fax: (417)876-2743
**Format:** Country; Adult Contemporary

**KESM-FM - 105.5 (17207)**
200 Radio Ln.
El Dorado Springs, MO 64744
Phone: (417)876-2741
Fax: (417)876-2743
**Format:** Country; Adult Contemporary

**KGBX-FM - 105.9 (17980)**
1856 S. Glenstone Ave.
Springfield, MO 65804-2303
Phone: (417)890-5555
Fax: (417)869-1000
**Format:** Adult Contemporary

**KGMY-AM - 1400 (17981)**
1856 S. Glenstone Ave.
Springfield, MO 65804-2303
Phone: (417)577-7005
Fax: (417)890-5050
**Format:** Music of Your Life

**KKBL-FM - 95.9 (17434)**
1569 N. Central
Monett, MO 65708
Phone: (417)235-6041
Fax: (417)235-6388
**Format:** Adult Contemporary

**KRMO-AM - 990 (17435)**
1569 N. Central
Monett, MO 65708
Phone: (417)235-6041
Fax: (417)235-6388
**Format:** Country; News

**KSMU-FM - 91.1 (17986)**
901 S. National Ave.
Springfield, MO 65804
Phone: (417)836-5878
Fax: (417)836-5889
**Format:** Public Radio

**KTOZ-AM - 1060 (17988)**
610 W. College
Springfield, MO 65806
Phone: (417)832-1060
Fax: (417)864-4111

**Format:** Jazz; Big Band/Nostalgia; Blues

**KTTS-FM - 94.7 (17989)**
2330 W. Grand
Springfield, MO 65801
Phone: (417)865-6614
Fax: (417)865-9643
**Format:** Contemporary Country; Agricultural

**KWTO-AM - 560 (17992)**
3000 E. Chestnut Expy.
Springfield, MO 65802
Phone: (417)862-5600
Fax: (417)869-7675
**Format:** Talk; News

**KXUS-FM - 97.3 (17994)**
1856 S Glenstone Ave.
Springfield, MO 65804
Phone: (417)890-5555
Fax: (417)890-5050
**Format:** Classic Rock

**KZRQ-FM - 104.1 (17995)**
322 E. Walnut St., Ste. 2000
Springfield, MO 65806-2302
**Format:** Album-Oriented Rock (AOR)

## Terre Haute, IN

**WBOW-AM - 640 (17086)**
PO Box 430
Bowling Green, MO 63334-0430
**Format:** Full Service

## Topeka, KS

**KJCK-AM - 1420 (11138)**
Box 789
Junction City, KS 66441
Phone: (785)762-5525
Fax: (785)762-5387
**Format:** News; Talk

**KJCK-FM - 97.5 (11139)**
Box 789
Junction City, KS 66441
Phone: (785)762-5525
Fax: (785)762-5387
**Format:** Contemporary Hit Radio (CHR)

**KJTY-FM - 88.1 (11447)**
1005 SW 10th St.
Topeka, KS 66604-1103
Phone: (785)357-8888
Fax: (785)357-0100
**Format:** Religious; Educational

**KMAJ-AM - 1440 (11448)**
5315 SW 7th St.
Topeka, KS 66606-2371
Fax: (913)272-6219
**Format:** Talk

**KMAJ-FM - 107.7 (11449)**
5315 SW 7th St.
Topeka, KS 66606-2371
Fax: (913)272-6219
**Format:** Adult Contemporary

**KMAN-AM - 1350 (11237)**
2414 Casement Rd.
PO Box 1350
Manhattan, KS 66502-0011
Phone: (913)776-1350
Fax: (913)539-1000
**Format:** Talk; News; Sports

**KQLA-FM - 103.5 (11140)**
PO Box 789
Junction City, KS 66441-0789
Phone: (785)762-5525
Fax: (785)762-5387
**Format:** Adult Contemporary; Adult Contemporary

**KTPK-FM - 106.9 (11451)**
2121 SW Chelsea
Topeka, KS 66614
Phone: (785)273-1069
Fax: (785)273-0123
**Format:** Country

**WIBW-FM - 97.3 (11452)**
PO Box 1818
Topeka, KS 66601
Phone: (913)272-3456

Fax: (913)272-3536
**Format:** Contemporary Country

## Tulsa (Bartlesville), OK

**KIND-AM - 1010 (11129)**
122 W. Myrtle St.
Independence, KS 67301-3317
Phone: (620)331-3000
Fax: (620)331-8008
**Format:** Adult Contemporary

## Wichita-Hutchinson, KS

**KBUF-AM - 1030 (11081)**
1402 E. Kansas
PO Box 759
Garden City, KS 67846
Fax: (316)276-3568
**Format:** Country; Agricultural; Talk

**KCVW-FM - 94.3 (11122)**
100 N. Main St., Ste. 402
Hutchinson, KS 67501
Fax: (316)529-0943
**Format:** Religious

**KFDI-FM - 101.3 (11497)**
4200 N. Old Lawrence Rd.
PO Box 1402
Wichita, KS 67219
Phone: (316)838-9141
Fax: (316)838-3607
**Format:** Country

**KFH-AM - 1330 (11498)**
2120 N. Woodlawn, Ste.352
Wichita, KS 67208
Phone: (316)436-1480
Fax: (316)685-3314
**Format:** Sports; Sports

**KGGG-FM - 94.7 (11123)**
106 N. Main
Hutchinson, KS 67501
Phone: (316)665-5758
Fax: (316)665-6655
**Format:** Oldies

**KGNO-AM - 1370 (11050)**
2601 Central
Village Plz., Ste. C
Dodge City, KS 67801
Phone: (620)225-4455
Fax: (620)225-6655
**Format:** Full Service; Oldies

**KGTR-FM - 96.7 (11093)**
5501 W. 10th
Great Bend, KS 67530
Phone: (316)285-2127
Fax: (316)285-2102
**Format:** Oldies

**KHAZ-FM - 99.5 (11108)**
2300 Hall St.
PO Box 6
Hays, KS 67601-0006
Phone: (785)625-2578
Fax: (785)625-3632
**Format:** Country

**KHMY-FM - 93.1 (11383)**
1700 W. 17th
Hutchinson, KS 67501
Phone: (620)662-5900
Fax: (620)662-5357
**Format:** Classic Rock

**KHOK-FM - 100.7 (11094)**
1200 Baker Rd.
PO Box 609
Great Bend, KS 67530
Phone: (316)792-3647
Fax: (316)792-3649
**Format:** Hot Country

**KHUT-FM - 102.9 (11125)**
17th & Harding St., Box 1036
Hutchinson, KS 67504-1036
Fax: (316)662-5357

Format: Country

**KLKC-FM - 93.5 (11365)**
RR 4
PO Box 853
Parsons, KS 67357
Phone: (620)421-6400
Fax: (316)421-5570
Format: Talk; Adult Contemporary; Oldies

**KMUW-FM - 89.1 (11500)**
3317 E. 17th St.
Wichita, KS 67208
Phone: (316)978-6789
Fax: (316)978-3946
Format: Classical; Jazz; News

**KNNS-AM - 1510 (11095)**
5501 W. 10th
Great Bend, KS 67530
Fax: (316)285-2102
Format: Middle-of-the-Road (MOR)

**KOLS-FM - 95.5 (11051)**
2601 Central
Village Plz., Ste. C
Dodge City, KS 67801
Phone: (620)227-9555
Fax: (620)225-6655
Format: Adult Contemporary

**KRZZ-FM - 96.3 (11503)**
9323 E. 37th St. N.
Wichita, KS 67226-2000
Phone: (316)494-6600
Fax: (316)494-6730
Format: Classic Rock; Album-Oriented Rock (AOR)

**KSGL-AM - 900 (11504)**
3337 W. Central
Wichita, KS 67203
Phone: (316)942-3231
Fax: (316)942-9314
Format: Religious

**KSKG-FM - 99.9 (11403)**
1825 South Ohio
Salina, KS 67401
Phone: (785)825-4631
Fax: (785)825-4600
Format: Country

**KSLS-FM - 101.5 (11215)**
224 N. Kansas Ave.
Liberal, KS 67901-3326
Phone: (620)624-8156
Fax: (620)624-4606
Format: Contemporary Country

**KTHR-FM - 107.3 (11506)**
2402 E 37th St. N
Wichita, KS 67219
Phone: (316)832-9600
Fax: (316)832-0112
Format: Classic Rock

**KXKU-FM - 97.1 (11126)**
106 N. Main
Hutchinson, KS 67501
Fax: (316)665-6655
Format: Country

**KXXX-AM - 790 (11030)**
1065 South Range
Colby, KS 67701
Phone: (913)462-3305
Fax: (913)462-3307
Format: Contemporary Country

**KYEZ-FM - 93.7 (11404)**
131 N. Santa Fe
Box 0080
Salina, KS 67402-0080
Phone: (785)823-1111
Fax: (785)823-2034
Format: Contemporary Country

**KYUU-AM - 1470 (11216)**
224 N. Kansas Ave.
Liberal, KS 67901-3326
Phone: (620)624-8156
Fax: (620)624-4606
Format: Contemporary Country

**KZCH-FM - 96.3 (11508)**
2402 E 37th St. N
Wichita, KS 67219
Phone: (316)832-9600
Fax: (316)832-0112

Format: Contemporary Hit Radio (CHR)

# Middle Atlantic States

## Baltimore, MD

**WAMD-AM - 970 (12624)**
400 Hiob Ln.
PO Box 970
Aberdeen, MD 21001
Phone: (410)272-4400
Fax: (410)575-6890
Format: Oldies

**WBIS-AM - 1190 (12634)**
1610 West St.
Annapolis, MD 21401
Phone: (410)269-0700
Fax: (410)269-0692
Format: News; Talk

**WBJC-FM - 91.5 (12889)**
2901 Liberty Heights Ave.
Baltimore, MD 21215-7893
Phone: (410)462-8444
Format: Classical; Public Radio; Public Radio

**WBMD-AM - 750 (13381)**
305 Washington Ave., 4th Fl.
Towson, MD 21204-4715
Phone: (410)821-9000
Fax: (410)483-2314
Format: Religious

**WCAO-AM - 600 (12890)**
711 W. 40th Street, Suite 350
Baltimore, MD 21211
Phone: (410)366-7600
Fax: (410)235-3899
Format: Gospel

**WCTR-AM - 1530 (13033)**
PO Box 700
Chestertown, MD 21620-0700
Phone: (410)778-1530
Fax: (410)778-4800
Format: Talk; News; Sports; Adult Contemporary; Agricultural; Adult Contemporary; Agricultural

**WERQ-AM - 1010 (12892)**
100 St. Paul St., 4th Fl.
Baltimore, MD 21202
Phone: (410)332-8200
Fax: (410)593-4550

**WERQ-FM - 92.3 (12893)**
100 St. Paul St., 4th Fl.
Baltimore, MD 21202
Phone: (410)332-8200
Fax: (410)539-4550
Format: Contemporary Hit Radio (CHR)

**WIYY-FM - 97.9 (12895)**
3800 Hooper Ave.
Baltimore, MD 21211-1313
Phone: (410)889-0098
Fax: (410)675-7946
Format: Album-Oriented Rock (AOR)

**WPOC-FM - 93.1 (12901)**
711 W. 40th St.
Baltimore, MD 21211
Phone: (410)366-7600
Fax: (410)235-3899
Format: Country

**WRBS-FM - 95.1 (12902)**
3600 Georgetown Rd.
Baltimore, MD 21227-1698
Phone: (410)247-4100
Fax: (410)247-4533
Format: Religious

**WTTR-AM - 1470 (13392)**
101 WTTR Ln.
Westminster, MD 21158
Phone: (410)848-5511
Fax: (410)876-5095
Format: Full Service; Sports; Agricultural; Oldies

**WWIN-AM - 1400 (12905)**
100 St. Paul St.
Baltimore, MD 21202
Phone: (410)332-8200
Fax: (410)783-4791

Format: Gospel; Religious

**WWIN-FM - 95.9 (12906)**
100 St. Paul St.
Baltimore, MD 21202
Phone: (410)332-8200
Fax: (410)752-2252
Format: Urban Contemporary

## Bluefield-Beckley-Oak Hill, WV

**WAMN-AM - 1050 (31206)**
PO Box 889
Blacksburg, VA 24063
Phone: (540)327-9266
Format: Religious

**WELC-AM - 1150 (32768)**
US Rte. 52 Premier Mt.
PO Box 949
Welch, WV 24801
Phone: (304)436-2131
Fax: (304)436-2132
Format: Adult Contemporary; Religious; Religious

**WHAJ-FM - 104.5 (32542)**
900 Bluefield Ave.
Bluefield, WV 24701
Phone: (304)327-7114
Fax: (304)325-7850
Format: Contemporary Hit Radio (CHR)

**WHIS-AM - 1440 (32543)**
900 Bluefield Ave.
Bluefield, WV 24701
Phone: (304)327-7114
Fax: (304)325-7850
Format: News; Talk; Information; Information

**WJLS-AM - 560 (32529)**
102 N. Kanawa St
PO Box 5499
Beckley, WV 25802
Phone: (304)253-7311
Fax: (304)253-3466
Format: Religious; Southern Gospel

**WJLS-FM - 99.5 (32530)**
102 N Kanawha St.
PO Box 25801
Beckley, WV 25801
Phone: (304)253-7311
Fax: (304)253-3466
Format: Country

**WKOY-FM - 100.9 (32722)**
900 Bluefield Ave.
Bluefield, WV 24701
Phone: (304)324-2665
Fax: (304)325-7850
Format: Oldies

**WOAY-AM - 860 (32699)**
240 Central Ave.
PO Box 140
Oak Hill, WV 25901
Phone: (304)465-0534
Fax: (304)465-1486
Format: Religious

**WPIB-FM - 90.9 (32545)**
PO Box 889
Blacksburg, VA 24063
Phone: (540)951-9791
Fax: (540)237-1025
Format: Religious

## Bristol,VA-Kingsport-Johnson Cty-Greenville,TN

**WAXM-FM - 93.5 (31647)**
724 Park Ave.
Norton, VA 24273
Fax: (540)679-1198
Format: Country

**WGAT-AM - 1050 (31434)**
117 E. Jackson St., Ste. 2
Gate City, VA 24251
Phone: (276)386-7025
Fax: (276)386-3600

# Charleston-Huntington, WV

**Format:** Sports; Talk

**WXBQ-AM - 980 (31221)**
901 E. Valley Dr.
PO Box 1389
Bristol, VA 24201
Phone: (276)669-8112
Fax: (276)669-0541
**Format:** News; Talk; Talk

**WXBQ-FM - 96.9 (31222)**
PO Box 1389
Bristol, VA 24203
Phone: (276)669-8112
Fax: (276)669-0541
**Format:** Country; Contemporary Country; Contemporary Country

**WZAP-AM - 690 (31223)**
11373 Wallace Pike
PO Box 369
Bristol, VA 24203
Phone: (276)669-6950
Fax: (276)669-0794
**Format:** Religious

## Charleston-Huntington, WV

**WAMX-FM - 106.3 (32622)**
134 4th Ave.
Huntington, WV 25701
Phone: (304)525-7788
Fax: (304)525-6281
**Format:** Alternative/New Music/Progressive

**WBKS-FM - 107.1 (32623)**
134 4th Ave.
Huntington, WV 25701
Phone: (304)525-7788
Fax: (304)525-6281
**Format:** Contemporary Hit Radio (CHR)

**WBVB-FM - 97.1 (32624)**
134 4th Ave.
Huntington, WV 25701
Phone: (304)525-7788
Fax: (304)525-6281
**Format:** Oldies

**WCHS-AM - 580 (32566)**
1111 Virginia St. E.
Charleston, WV 25301
Phone: (304)342-8131
Fax: (304)344-4745
**Format:** Talk; News; Sports

**WCWV-FM - 92.9 (32751)**
713 Main St.
Summersville, WV 26651
Phone: (304)872-5202
Fax: (304)872-6904
**Format:** Adult Contemporary; Soft Rock; Religious

**WDBS-FM - 97.1 (32754)**
180 Main St.
Sutton, WV 26601
Phone: (304)765-7373
Fax: (304)765-7836
**Format:** Country

**WDGG-FM - 93.7 (32625)**
401 11th St., Ste. 200
Huntington, WV 25713
Phone: (304)523-8401
Fax: (304)523-4848
**Format:** Country

**WEMM-FM - 107.9 (32626)**
703 3rd Ave.
Huntington, WV 25701
Phone: (304)525-5141
Fax: (304)525-0748
**Format:** Southern Gospel

**WFGH-FM - 90.7 (32600)**
Tolsia High School
PO Box 410
Fort Gay, WV 25514
Phone: (304)648-5752
Fax: (304)648-5447
**Format:** Eclectic

**WMEJ-FM - 91.9 (32628)**
PO Box 7575
Huntington, WV 25777
Phone: (304)867-5333

**Format:** Religious; Easy Listening; Easy Listening

**WMUL-FM - 88.1 (32629)**
Marshall University
One John Marshall Dr.
Huntington, WV 25755-2635
Phone: (304)696-6640
Fax: (304)696-3232
**Format:** Eclectic

**WOKU-AM - 1080 (32635)**
3006 Mt. Vernon Rd. Ste 1080
Hurricane, WV 25526
Phone: (304)757-9661
Fax: (304)757-9620
**Format:** Religious

**WQBE-AM - 97.5 (32567)**
PO Box 871
Charleston, WV 25323
Phone: (304)744-9691
Fax: (304)744-8562
**Format:** News; Sports; Talk; Talk

**WQBE-FM - 97.5 (32568)**
PO Box 871
Charleston, WV 25323
Phone: (304)744-9691
Fax: (304)744-8562
**Format:** Country

**WRVC-AM - 930 (32630)**
PO Box 1150
Huntington, WV 25713
Phone: (304)523-8401
Fax: (304)523-4848
**Format:** Talk; News; News

**WRVC-FM - 92.7 (32631)**
401 11th St., No. 200
Huntington, WV 25701
Phone: (304)523-8401
Fax: (304)523-4848
**Format:** Oldies

**WVAF-FM - 99.9, repeater 95.3 (32569)**
1111 Virginia St. East
Charleston, WV 25301
Phone: (304)342-8131
Fax: (304)344-4745
**Format:** Adult Contemporary

**WVHU-AM - 800 (32633)**
134 4th Ave
Huntington, WV 25701
Phone: (304)525-7788
Fax: (304)525-6281
**Format:** Oldies

**WVOW-AM - 1290 (32656)**
PO Box 1776
Logan, WV 25601
Phone: (304)752-5080
Fax: (304)752-5080
**Format:** Adult Contemporary

**WVOW-FM - 101.9 (32657)**
PO Box 1776
Logan, WV 25601
Phone: (304)752-5080
Fax: (304)752-5080
**Format:** Adult Contemporary

**WVPN-FM - 88.5 (32572)**
600 Capitol St.
Charleston, WV 25301
Phone: (304)556-4900
Fax: (304)556-4981
**Format:** Classical; News; Jazz

**WVSR-AM - 1240 (32573)**
817 Suncrest Pl.
PO Box 1389
Charleston, WV 25303
Phone: (304)342-3136
Fax: (304)342-3118
**Format:** Sports

**WVSR-FM - 102.7 (32574)**
817 Suncrest Pl.
Charleston, WV 25303
Phone: (304)342-3136
Fax: (304)342-3118

**Format:** Adult Contemporary

**WXCC-FM - 96.5 (32788)**
5 1/2 E. 2nd Ave.
PO Box 1409
Williamson, WV 25661
Phone: (304)235-3600
Fax: (304)235-8118
**Format:** Country

## Charlotte (Hickory), NC

**WBZK-AM - 980 (31208)**
PO Box 889
Blacksburg, VA 24063-0889
**Format:** Oldies

## Charlottesville, VA

**WCHV-AM - 1260 (31273)**
1150 Pepsi Place, Suite 300
Charlottesville, VA 22901
Phone: (434)978-4408
Fax: (434)978-0723
**Format:** Oldies; Urban Contemporary

**WCYK-AM - 810 (31274)**
PO Box 7703
Charlottesville, VA 22906-7703
Phone: (434)978-4408
Fax: (434)978-0723
**Format:** Country

**WHTE-FM - 101.9 (31276)**
1150 Pepsi Place, Ste. 300
Charlottesville, VA 22901
Phone: (434)978-4408
Fax: (434)978-0723
**Format:** Contemporary Hit Radio (CHR)

**WKAV-AM - 1400 (31278)**
1150 Pepsi Place, Suite 300
Charlottesville, VA 22901
Phone: (434)978-4408
Fax: (434)978-0723
**Format:** Big Band/Nostalgia

**WKTR-AM - 840 (31676)**
PO Box 309
Quinque, VA 22965
Phone: (757)357-9546
Fax: (757)365-0412
**Format:** Religious

**WQMZ-FM - 95.1 (31279)**
1140 Rose Hill Dr.
Charlottesville, VA 22903-5128
Phone: (434)220-2300
Fax: (434)220-2304
**Format:** Adult Contemporary

**WVTU-FM - 89.3 (31282)**
3520 Kingsbury Ln.
Roanoke, VA 24014
Phone: (540)989-8900
Fax: (540)767-2727
**Format:** Talk; News; Classical

**WWWV-FM - 97.5 (31283)**
1140 Rose Hill Dr.
Charlottesville, VA 22903
Phone: (434)220-2300
Fax: (434)220-2304
**Format:** Classic Rock

## Clarksburg-Weston, WV

**WBTQ-FM - 93.5 (32588)**
228 Randolph Ave.
Elkins, WV 26241
Phone: (304)472-1400
Fax: (304)472-1740
**Format:** Oldies

**WELK-FM - 94.7 (32592)**
228 Randolph Ave.
Elkins, WV 26241
Phone: (304)636-8800
Fax: (304)636-8801
**Format:** Top 40

**WGYE-FM - 102.7 (32595)**
1489 Locust Ave.
Fairmont, WV 26554
Phone: (304)624-1400

Fax: (304)624-1402
**Format:** Adult Contemporary

**WHAW-AM - 980 (32774)**
300 Harrison Ave.
Weston, WV 26452
Phone: (304)269-5555
Fax: (304)269-4800
**Format:** Folk; Bluegrass; Country; Classic Rock

**WKMM-FM - 96.7 (32647)**
106 E. Main St.
Kingwood, WV 26537
Phone: (304)329-0967
Fax: (304)329-2131
**Format:** Country

**WOTR-FM - 96.3 (32658)**
PO Box 505
Lost Creek, WV 26385
Phone: (304)745-4243
**Format:** Gospel

**WXKX-AM - 1340 (32579)**
PO Box 2208
Clarksburg, WV 26302
Fax: (304)624-5526
**Format:** Sports

## Greensboro-Winston Salem-High Point, NC

**WBRF-FM - 98.1 (31425)**
325 Poplar Knob Rd.
PO Box 838
Galax, VA 24333
Phone: (276)236-9273
Fax: (276)236-7198
**Format:** Full Service; Country; Religious; Bluegrass

**WTJY-FM - 89.5 (31212)**
PO Box 889
Blacksburg, VA 24063
Phone: (540)961-2377
**Format:** Alternative/New Music/Progressive

**WXRI-FM - 91.3 (31214)**
PO Box 889
Blacksburg, VA 24063
Phone: (336)773-0869
**Format:** Southern Gospel

## Hagerstown, MD

**WARK-AM - 1490 (13199)**
880 Commonwealth Ave.
Hagerstown, MD 21740-6881
Phone: (301)733-4500
Fax: (301)733-0040
**Format:** Talk; Oldies

**WARX-FM - 106.9 (13200)**
880 Commonwealth Ave.
Hagerstown, MD 21740
Phone: (301)733-4500
Fax: (301)733-0040
**Format:** Oldies

**WCBC-AM - 1270 (13084)**
35 Baltimore St.
PO Box 1290
Cumberland, MD 21501
Phone: (301)724-5000
Fax: (301)722-8336
**Format:** Talk; Adult Contemporary; News; Sports; Oldies; Sports; Oldies

**WCRH-FM - 90.5 (13395)**
PO Box 439
Williamsport, MD 21795
Phone: (301)582-0285
Fax: (301)582-2707
**Format:** Religious

**WDIH-FM - 90.3 (13325)**
7754 Jersey Rd.
PO Box 186
Salisbury, MD 21801
Phone: (410)546-7772
**Format:** Adult Contemporary

**WJEJ-AM - 1240 (13203)**
1135 Haven Rd.
Hagerstown, MD 21742
Phone: (301)739-2323
Fax: (301)797-7408

**Format:** Full Service; Easy Listening; Oldies

**WQHQ-FM - 104.7 (13330)**
351 Tilghman Rd.
Salisbury, MD 21804-1920
Phone: (410)742-1923
Fax: (410)742-2329
**Format:** Adult Contemporary

**WWFG-FM - 99.9 (13333)**
Gateway Crossing
351 Tilghman Rd.
Salisbury, MD 21804
Phone: (410)742-1923
Fax: (410)742-2329
**Format:** Country

## Harrisonburg, VA

**WACL-FM - 98.5 (31469)**
207 University Blvd.
Harrisonburg, VA 22801
Phone: (540)434-1777
Fax: (540)432-9968
**Format:** Classic Rock

**WBTX-AM - 1470 (31224)**
PO Box 337
Broadway, VA 22815
Phone: (540)896-8933
Fax: (540)896-1448
**Format:** Gospel; News; Sports

**WHBG-AM - 1360 (31472)**
4850 Connecticut Ave. NW
PO Box 752
Harrisonburg, VA 22801-0752
Phone: (540)434-0331
Fax: (540)434-7087
**Format:** News; Talk

**WKCY-AM - 1300 (31474)**
207 University Blvd., Ste. 200-202
PO Box 1107
Harrisonburg, VA 22801
Phone: (540)434-1777
Fax: (540)432-9968
**Format:** Talk; Talk

**WKCY-FM - 104.3 (31475)**
207 University Blvd., Ste. 200-202
PO Box 1107
Harrisonburg, VA 22801
Phone: (540)434-1777
Fax: (540)432-9968
**Format:** Country

**WKDW-AM - 900 (31476)**
PO Box 2189
PO Box 1107
Harrisonburg, VA 22801
Phone: (540)434-1777
Fax: (540)434-9968
**Format:** Country

**WLTK-FM - 103.3 (31225)**
166 Main St.
PO Box 337
Broadway, VA 22815
Phone: (540)896-9585
Fax: (540)896-1448
**Format:** Religious; Contemporary Christian

**WMRA-FM - 90.7 (31477)**
PO Box 1292
Harrisonburg, VA 22801
Phone: (540)568-6221
Fax: (540)568-3814
**Format:** Classical; Folk; Public Radio; News; Public Radio; News

**WQPO-FM - 100.7 (31481)**
PO Box 752
Harrisonburg, VA 22801
Phone: (540)434-0331
Fax: (540)434-7087
**Format:** Adult Contemporary

**WSVA-AM - 550 (31482)**
4850 Connecticut Ave. NW
PO Box 752
Harrisonburg, VA 22801
Phone: (540)434-0331
Fax: (540)434-7087

**Format:** News; Talk; Talk

**WSVO-FM - 93.1 (31897)**
74 Orchard Hill Cir.
PO Box 2189
Staunton, VA 24402-2189
Phone: (540)886-2376
Fax: (540)885-8662
**Format:** Oldies

**WTON-AM - 1240 (31898)**
304 W. Beverley St.
Staunton, VA 24401
Phone: (540)885-5188
Fax: (540)885-1240
**Format:** Country; Sports; Sports

**WTON-FM - 94.3 (31899)**
304 W. Beverly St.
PO Box 1085
Staunton, VA 24401
Phone: (540)885-5188
Fax: (540)885-1240
**Format:** Classic Rock

**WXJM-FM - 88.7 (31485)**
James Madison
Anthony Seeger
800 S. Main St.
Harrisonburg, VA 22807
Phone: (540)568-6878
Fax: (540)568-7907
**Format:** Alternative/New Music/Progressive

## Norfolk-Portsmouth-Newport News-Hampton, VA

**WARR-AM - 1520 (31459)**
PO Box 610
Hampton, VA 23669-0610
**Format:** Religious; Blues; Jazz; Urban Contemporary; Jazz; Urban Contemporary

**WCDG-FM - 92.1 (31636)**
1003 Norfolk Sq.
Norfolk, VA 23502
Phone: (757)466-0009
Fax: (757)466-0082
**Format:** Urban Contemporary

**WHOV-FM - 88.1 (31461)**
Hampton University
Hampton, VA 23668
Phone: (757)727-5670
Fax: (757)727-5084
**Format:** Jazz; Urban Contemporary; Gospel; Eclectic

**WKGM-AM - 940 (31873)**
Box 339
Smithfield, VA 23430
Phone: (757)357-9546
Fax: (757)365-0412
**Format:** Religious

**WLQM-AM - 1250 (31407)**
320 N Franklin St.
PO Box 735
Franklin, VA 23851
Phone: (757)562-3135
Fax: (757)562-2345
**Format:** Country; Gospel

**WLQM-FM - 101.7 (31408)**
PO Box 735
Franklin, VA 23851
Phone: (757)562-3135
Fax: (757)562-2345
**Format:** Country; Sports

**WMBG-AM - 740 (31958)**
1005 Richmond Rd.
Williamsburg, VA 23185
Phone: (757)229-7400
**Format:** Adult Contemporary

**WPTE-FM - 94.9 (31932)**
236 Clearfield Ave., Ste. 206
Virginia Beach, VA 23462-1816
Phone: (757)497-2000
Fax: (757)456-0100

**Parkersburg, WV**

Format: Adult Contemporary

**WTJZ-AM - 1270 (31462)**
PO Box 610
Hampton, VA 23669-0610
Format: Gospel; Religious

**WWDE-FM - 101.3 (31933)**
236 Clearfield Ave., Ste. 206
Virginia Beach, VA 23462
Phone: (757)499-9290
Fax: (757)471-1100
Format: Easy Listening; Soft Rock; Adult Contemporary; Adult Contemporary

## Parkersburg, WV

**WADC-AM - 1050 (32703)**
PO Box 4739
Parkersburg, WV 26104-4739
Format: Middle-of-the-Road (MOR)

**WHBR-FM - 103.1 (32704)**
5 Rosemar Cir.
Parkersburg, WV 26104
Phone: (304)485-4565
Fax: (304)485-7365

**WLTP-AM - 1450 (32757)**
6006 Grand Central Ave.
PO Box 5559
Vienna, WV 26105
Phone: (304)295-6077
Fax: (304)295-4389
Format: News; Talk; Sports

**WRRR-FM - 93.9 (32741)**
PO Box 374
Saint Marys, WV 26170
Phone: (304)684-3400
Fax: (304)684-9241
Format: Adult Contemporary

**WXCR-FM - 92.3 (32696)**
PO Box 564
New Martinsville, WV 26155
Phone: (304)684-3400
Fax: (304)684-9241
Format: Classic Rock

## Philadelphia, PA

**WDOV-AM - 1410 (5123)**
1575 Mckee Rd., Ste. 206
Dover, DE 19904
Phone: (302)674-1410
Fax: (302)674-5978

**WJBR-AM - 1290 (5111)**
3001 Philadelphia Pike
Claymont, DE 19703
Fax: (302)529-9536
Format: Big Band/Nostalgia

**WJBR-FM - 99.5 (5171)**
812 Philadelphia Pike
Wilmington, DE 19809
Phone: (302)765-1160
Fax: (302)765-1192
Format: Adult Contemporary

**WSTW-FM - 93.7 (5174)**
2727 Shipley Rd.
PO Box 7492
Wilmington, DE 19803
Phone: (302)478-2700
Fax: (302)478-0100
Format: Adult Contemporary; Contemporary Hit Radio (CHR)

## Pittsburgh, PA

**WAJR-AM - 1440 (32681)**
Greer Bldg.
1251 Earl Core Rd.
Morgantown, WV 26505
Phone: (304)296-0029
Fax: (304)296-3876
Format: Talk; News; Country; Country

**WKHJ-FM - 104.5 (13251)**
PO Box 2337
Mountain Lake Park, MD 21550
Phone: (301)334-4272
Fax: (301)334-2152

Format: Adult Contemporary

**WVAQ-FM - 101.9 (32685)**
1251 Earl Core Rd.
Morgantown, WV 26505
Phone: (304)296-0029
Fax: (304)296-3876
Format: Contemporary Hit Radio (CHR)

## Richmond, VA

**WBBC-FM - 93.5 (31216)**
950 Kenbridge Rd.
PO Box 300
Blackstone, VA 23824
Phone: (804)292-4146
Fax: (804)292-7669
Format: Hot Country

**WBTJ-FM - 106.5 (31817)**
3245 Basie Rd.
Richmond, VA 23228
Phone: (804)474-0000
Fax: (804)474-0096
Format: Urban Contemporary

**WCDX-FM - 92.1 (31818)**
2809 Emerywood Pkwy., Ste. 300
Richmond, VA 23294
Phone: (804)672-9299
Fax: (804)672-9314
Format: Urban Contemporary; Top 40

**WCVE-FM - 88.9 (31819)**
23 Sesame St.
Richmond, VA 23235
Phone: (804)320-1301
Fax: (804)320-8729
Format: Public Radio; Jazz; News; Classical

**WFTH-AM - 1590 (31822)**
227 E. Belt Blvd.
Richmond, VA 23224
Phone: (804)233-0765
Fax: (804)233-3725
Format: Gospel

**WGGN-AM - 820 (31290)**
4301 W. Hundred Rd.
Chester, VA 23831
Phone: (804)717-2000
Fax: (804)717-2009
Format: Religious

**WJMO-FM - 105.7 (31823)**
2809 Emerywood Pkwy., No. 300
Richmond, VA 23294
Phone: (804)672-9299
Fax: (804)672-9314

**WLSA-FM - 105.5 (31534)**
PO Box 277
Louisa, VA 23093-0277
Phone: (540)967-1150
Format: Country

**WMXB-FM - 103.7 (31824)**
812 Moorefield Park Dr., Ste. 300
Richmond, VA 23236
Phone: (804)330-5700
Fax: (804)330-3244
Format: Adult Contemporary

**WNDJ-FM - 104.9 (31912)**
PO Box 896
Urbanna, VA 23175
Phone: (804)758-9635
Fax: (804)758-5835
Format: Big Band/Nostalgia

**WRNL-AM - 910 (31826)**
3245 Basie Rd.
PO Box 659512
Richmond, VA 23228-3404
Phone: (804)780-3400
Fax: (804)780-3427
Format: Sports

**WROU-AM - 1240 (31291)**
4301 W. Hundred Rd
Chester, VA 23831
Phone: (804)717-2000
Fax: (804)717-2009

Format: Gospel

**WRVQ-FM - 94.5 (31827)**
3245 Basie Rd.
Richmond, VA 23228
Phone: (804)345-9436
Fax: (804)576-3222
Format: Contemporary Hit Radio (CHR)

## Roanoke-Lynchburg, VA

**SPIRIT-FM - 90.9 (31205)**
PO Box 889
Blacksburg, VA 24060
Phone: (540)200-3213
Fax: (540)200-3215
Format: Religious; Contemporary Christian

**WAKG-FM - 103.3 (31313)**
PO Box 1629
Danville, VA 24543
Phone: (434)797-4290
Fax: (434)797-3918
Format: Contemporary Country

**WAMV-AM - 1420 (31095)**
1 School Rd.
PO Box 1420
Amherst, VA 24521
Fax: (804)946-2201
Format: Full Service

**WBRG-AM - 1050 (31543)**
PO Box 1079
Lynchburg, VA 24505
Phone: (804)845-5916
Format: News; Talk; Sports

**WBTM-AM - 1330 (31314)**
PO Box 1629
Danville, VA 24543
Phone: (434)793-4411
Fax: (434)797-3918
Format: News; Full Service

**WFIR-AM - 960 (31842)**
3934 Electric Rd.
Roanoke, VA 24018
Phone: (540)345-1511
Fax: (540)342-2270
Format: News; Talk; Talk

**WFNR-AM - 710 (31682)**
7080 Lee Hwy.
Radford, VA 24141-8416
Phone: (540)382-6106
Fax: (540)381-2932
Format: News; Talk; Sports

**WGMN-AM - 1240 (31844)**
3807 Brandon Ave. SW, Ste. 2350
Roanoke, VA 24018
Phone: (540)725-1220
Fax: (540)725-1245
Format: Sports

**WHHV-AM - 1400 (31499)**
343 Virginia St.
PO Box 648
Hillsville, VA 24343
Phone: (540)728-9114
Fax: (540)728-9968
Format: Full Service

**WILA-AM - 1580 (31315)**
865 Industrial Ave.
PO Box 3444
Danville, VA 24543
Fax: (804)792-2134
Format: Gospel

**WIQO-FM - 100.9 (31304)**
PO Box 710
Covington, VA 24426
Phone: (540)962-1133
Fax: (540)962-4401
Format: Country

**WKBA-AM - 1550 (31846)**
2043 10th St. NE
PO Box 1092
Roanoke, VA 24012
Phone: (540)343-5597
Fax: (540)345-4064

**Format:** Full Service

**WKDE-AM - 1000 (31090)**
PO Box 390
Altavista, VA 24517
Phone: (434)369-5588
Fax: (434)369-1632

**WKDE-FM - 105.5 (31091)**
PO Box 390
Altavista, VA 24517
Phone: (434)369-5588
Fax: (434)369-1632
**Format:** Country

**WKEY-AM - 1340 (31305)**
PO Box 710
Covington, VA 24426
Phone: (540)912-1133
Fax: (540)962-4401
**Format:** Oldies

**WLLL-AM - 930 (31545)**
105 Whitehall Rd.
Lynchburg, VA 24501
Phone: (434)385-9555
Fax: (434)385-6073
**Format:** Talk

**WLVA-AM - 590 (31546)**
19 Wadsworth St., No. C
Lynchburg, VA 24501-3547
Phone: (434)847-7590
Fax: (434)845-5520

**WLYK-FM - 100.1 (31547)**
3831 Old Forest Rd., Ste. 6
Lynchburg, VA 24501
Phone: (540)774-9200
Fax: (540)774-5667
**Format:** Contemporary Hit Radio (CHR)

**WPAR-FM - 91.3 (31868)**
PO Box 889
Blacksburg, VA 24063
Phone: (540)961-2377
**Format:** Religious

**WPVR-FM - 94.9 (31847)**
PO Box 92
Roanoke, VA 24022-0092
Phone: (540)345-3841
Fax: (540)342-2270
**Format:** Classic Rock

**WREL-AM - 1450 (31528)**
PO Drawer 902
Lexington, VA 24450
Phone: (540)463-2161
Fax: (540)463-9524
**Format:** News; Talk; Sports

**WREL-FM - 96.7 (31529)**
PO Drawer 902
Lexington, VA 24450
Phone: (540)463-2161
Fax: (540)463-9524
**Format:** Country

**WRIS-AM - 1410 (31849)**
219 Luckett St.
Box 6099
Roanoke, VA 24017
Phone: (540)342-1410
Fax: (540)345-5952
**Format:** Religious

**WROV-AM - 1240 (31850)**
3807 Brandon Ave. SW, No. 2350
Roanoke, VA 24018-1477
Phone: (540)343-4444
Fax: (540)343-0616
**Format:** Album-Oriented Rock (AOR)

**WSBV-AM - 1560 (31877)**
Hwy. 879 E., Box 778
South Boston, VA 24592
Phone: (434)572-4418
Fax: (434)572-9245
**Format:** Talk; News; Religious; Bluegrass

**WSLC-AM - 610 (31869)**
1002 Newman Dr.
Salem, VA 24153
Fax: (703)389-0837

**Format:** Country; Sports

**WSLQ-FM - 99.1 (31870)**
1002 Newman Dr.
Salem, VA 24153
Phone: (540)387-0234
Fax: (540)389-0837
**Format:** Adult Contemporary

**WTOY-AM - 1480 (31852)**
504 23rd St. NW
Roanoke, VA 24017
Phone: (540)344-9689
Fax: (540)344-0976
**Format:** Adult Contemporary

**WXLK-FM - 92.3 (31856)**
3934 Electric Rd. SW
Roanoke, VA 24018
Phone: (540)774-9236
Fax: (540)774-5667
**Format:** Contemporary Hit Radio (CHR)

## Salisbury, MD

**WOCM-FM - 98.1 (5158)**
PO Box 379
Selbyville, DE 19975
Phone: (302)436-9725
Fax: (302)436-9726
**Format:** Adult Album Alternative

**WOCQ-FM - 103.9 (5129)**
20200 Dupont Blvd.
Georgetown, DE 19947-3105
**Format:** Contemporary Hit Radio (CHR)

**WSCL-FM - 89.5 (13331)**
PO Box 2596
Salisbury, MD 21802-2596
Phone: (410)543-6895
Fax: (410)548-3000
**Format:** Classical; News; News

## Washington, DC

**WASH-FM - 97.1 (5771)**
3400 Idaho Ave. NW
Washington, DC 20016
Fax: (202)895-5103
**Format:** Adult Contemporary

**WBQB-FM - 101.5 (31414)**
1914 Mimosa
PO Box 269
Fredericksburg, VA 22405
Phone: (540)373-7721
Fax: (540)899-3879
**Format:** Adult Contemporary

**WFLS-FM - 93.3 (31415)**
616 Amelia St.
Fredericksburg, VA 22401
Phone: (540)374-1500
Fax: (540)374-5525
**Format:** Country

**WFRB-AM - 560 (13151)**
242 Finzel Rd.
Frostburg, MD 21532
Phone: (301)689-8871
Fax: (301)689-8880
**Format:** Talk; Sports; Religious

**WFTR-AM - 1450 (31422)**
1106 Elm St.
PO Box 192
Front Royal, VA 22630-0192
Phone: (540)635-4121
Fax: (540)635-9387

**WFVA-AM - 1230 (31416)**
1914 Mimosa
PO Box 290
Fredericksburg, VA 22405
Phone: (540)373-7721
Fax: (540)899-3879
**Format:** Full Service

**WHAG-AM - 1410 (13201)**
1250 Maryland Ave.
Hagerstown, MD 21740-7244
Phone: (301)797-7300
Fax: (301)797-2659

**Format:** Talk; Sports; News

**WHUR-FM - 96.3 (5774)**
529 Bryant St. NW
Washington, DC 20059
Phone: (202)806-3500
Fax: (202)806-3522
**Format:** Urban Contemporary; Adult Contemporary

**WINC-AM - 1400 (31963)**
520 N. Pleasant Valley Rd.
Box 3300
Winchester, VA 22604
Phone: (703)667-2224
Fax: (703)722-3295
**Format:** Talk; News

**WINX-FM - 94.3 (31939)**
6546 Lovers Ln.
Warrenton, VA 20186-8752
Phone: (540)347-9430
Fax: (540)349-1148
**Format:** Oldies

**WJYJ-FM - 90.5 (31878)**
830 Gunnery Hill Rd.
PO Box 42179
Spotsylvania, VA 22553
Phone: (540)786-5960
Fax: (540)786-0001
**Format:** Contemporary Christian; Information

**WKGO-FM - 106.1 (13085)**
350 Byrd Ave.
Cumberland, MD 21502
Phone: (301)722-6666
Fax: (301)722-0945
**Format:** Adult Contemporary

**WKLP-AM - 1390 (32642)**
PO Box F
Keyser, WV 26726-0180
Phone: (304)788-1662
Fax: (304)788-1662
**Format:** Music of Your Life

**WKMZ-FM - 95.9 (32666)**
1606 W. King St.
PO Box 909
Martinsburg, WV 25401
Phone: (304)263-8868
Fax: (304)263-8906
**Format:** Contemporary Hit Radio (CHR)

**WKYS-FM - 93.9 (13231)**
5900 Princess Garden Pkwy.
Lanham, MD 20706
Phone: (202)432-9597
Fax: (202)432-5477
**Format:** Adult Contemporary; Contemporary Hit Radio (CHR)

**WMAL-AM - 630 (5778)**
4400 Jenifer St. NW
Washington, DC 20015-2113
Phone: (202)686-3100
Fax: (202)537-0009
**Format:** Full Service

**WPFW-FM - 89.3 (5779)**
2390 Champlain St., NW, 2nd Fl.
Washington, DC 20009
Phone: (202)588-0893
Fax: (202)588-0561
**Format:** Jazz; Ethnic; News

**WPLC-FM - 94.3 (31558)**
7450 Donset Ct.
Manassas, VA 20109-3046
Phone: (703)369-1080
Fax: (703)369-6901
**Format:** Adult Contemporary

**WQWV-FM - 103.7 (32710)**
PO Box 55
Petersburg, WV 26847
Phone: (304)257-4432
Fax: (304)257-9733
**Format:** Adult Contemporary

**WQZK-FM - 94.1 (32643)**
Drawer F
Keyser, WV 26726-0180
Phone: (301)786-4661
Fax: (301)788-1662

## Wheeling, WV-Steubenville, OH

**Format:** Classic Rock

**WRAA-AM - 1330 (31536)**
130 University Blvd., Ste. B
Luray, VA 22835
Phone: (540)743-5167
Fax: (540)743-9522
**Format:** Country

**WRNR-AM - 740 (32667)**
1762 Eagle School Rd
PO Box 709
Martinsburg, WV 25401
Phone: (304)263-6586
Fax: (304)263-3082
**Format:** News; Talk; Sports; Sports

**WRQX-FM - 107.3 (5783)**
4400 Jenifer St. NW, 4th Fl.
Washington, DC 20015-2113
Phone: (202)686-3100
Fax: (202)364-9668
**Format:** Adult Contemporary

**WTBO-AM - 1450 (13087)**
350 Byrd Ave.
PO Box 1644
Cumberland, MD 21502
Phone: (301)722-6666
Fax: (301)722-0945
**Format:** Adult Album Alternative; Adult Album Alternative

**WTOP-AM - 1500 (5784)**
3400 Idaho Ave. NW
Washington, DC 20016-3046
Phone: (202)895-5000
Fax: (202)895-5140
**Format:** News; Sports; Sports

**WWZZ-FM - 104.1 (31173)**
2000 15th St. N., Ste. 200
Arlington, VA 22201
Phone: (703)522-1041
Fax: (703)526-0250
**Format:** Contemporary Hit Radio (CHR)

**WYSK-AM - 1350 (31418)**
616 Amelia St.
Fredericksburg, VA 22401
Phone: (540)374-5500
Fax: (540)374-5525
**Format:** Hispanic

**WZRV-FM - 95.3 (31423)**
1106 Elm St.
PO Box 192
Front Royal, VA 22630-0192
Phone: (540)635-4121
Fax: (540)635-9387
**Format:** Oldies

## Wheeling, WV-Steubenville, OH

**WBBD-AM - 1400 (32780)**
1015 Main St.
Wheeling, WV 26003
Phone: (304)232-1170
Fax: (304)234-0041
**Format:** Middle-of-the-Road (MOR); Big Band/Nostalgia

**WCDK-FM - 106.3 (32765)**
2307 Pennsylvania Ave.
Weirton, WV 26062-3603
Phone: (304)723-1444
Fax: (304)723-1688
**Format:** Classic Rock

**WEIR-AM - 1430 (32766)**
2307 Pennsylvania Ave.
Weirton, WV 26062
Phone: (304)723-1444
Fax: (304)723-1688
**Format:** Sports

**WPHP-FM - 91.9 (32781)**
Parkview Rd.
2203 National Rd.
Wheeling, WV 26003
Phone: (304)243-0410
Fax: (304)243-0449
**Format:** Top 40

**WVBC-FM - 88.1 (32536)**
Bethany College
Bethany, WV 26032
Phone: (304)829-7853
Fax: (304)829-7855

**Format:** Eclectic; Educational

**WWVA-AM - 1170 (32783)**
1015 Main St.
Wheeling, WV 26003-2782
Phone: (304)232-1170
Fax: (304)234-0041
**Format:** Talk; Talk

## Wilmington, NC

**WCCA-FM - 106.3 (31544)**
PO Box 11798
Lynchburg, VA 24506-1798
Phone: (919)754-9840
Fax: (919)754-2456
**Format:** Country

## Northeastern States

### Albany-Schenectady-Troy, NY

**WAMC-FM - 90.3 (20237)**
318 Central Ave.
Albany, NY 12206
Phone: (518)465-5233
Fax: (518)432-6974
**Format:** Public Radio; Folk; News; Jazz

**WBEC-AM - 1420 (14741)**
211 Jason St.
Pittsfield, MA 01201
Phone: (413)499-3333
Fax: (413)442-1590
**Format:** Full Service; News; Talk

**WBEC-FM - 105.5 (14742)**
211 Jason St.
Pittsfield, MA 01201-5907
Phone: (413)499-3333
Fax: (413)442-1590
**Format:** Contemporary Hit Radio (CHR)

**WBKK-FM - 97.7 (22921)**
108 Erie Blvd.
PO Box 972
Schenectady, NY 12305
Phone: (518)388-9255
Fax: (518)374-6851
**Format:** Classical

**WBTN-AM - 1370 (30845)**
407 Harwood Hill Rd.
Bennington, VT 05201
Phone: (802)442-6321
Fax: (802)442-3112
**Format:** News; Talk; Sports; Full Service

**WBUG-AM - 1570 (23092)**
PO Box 4490
Utica, NY 13504-4490
**Format:** Country

**WBUG-FM - 101.1 (23093)**
PO Box 4490
Utica, NY 13504-4490
Phone: (315)734-9245
Fax: (315)624-9245
**Format:** Country

**WCAN-FM - 93.3 (20610)**
c/o WAMC-FM
318 Central Ave.
Albany, NY 12206
Phone: (518)465-5233
Fax: (518)432-6974
**Format:** Public Radio; News; Jazz; Folk

**WCDB-FM - 90.9 (20238)**
Campus Center 316
1400 Washington Ave.
Albany, NY 12222
Phone: (518)442-4242
**Format:** Alternative/New Music/Progressive

**WCKL-AM - 560 (20923)**
5620 Rte. 9G
Hudson, NY 12534
Phone: (518)828-5006
Fax: (518)828-1080

**WCSS-AM - 1490 (20282)**
120 Genesee Ln.
Amsterdam, NY 12010
Phone: (518)843-2500
Fax: (518)842-0315
**Format:** Full Service; Middle-of-the-Road (MOR); Middle-of-the-Road (MOR)

**WCTW-FM - 98.5 (20924)**
5620 RT9G
Hudson, NY 12534
Phone: (518)828-5006
Fax: (518)828-1080
**Format:** Adult Contemporary

**WEGB-FM - 93.7 (22922)**
11Dennis Terrace
Schenectady, NY 12303
Phone: (518)456-6101
Fax: (518)456-6377

**WENU-AM - 1410 (22771)**
89 Everts Ave.
Queensbury, NY 12804
Phone: (518)793-7733
Fax: (518)793-0838

**WENU-FM - 101.7 (22772)**
89 Everts Ave.
Queensbury, NY 12804
Phone: (518)793-7733
Fax: (518)793-0838

**WFLY-FM - 92.3 (21051)**
6 Johnson Rd.
Latham, NY 12110
Phone: (518)786-6600
Fax: (518)786-6696
**Format:** Urban Contemporary

**WGY-AM - 810 (20239)**
1 Washington Sq.
Albany, NY 12205
Phone: (518)452-4800
Fax: (518)452-4855
**Format:** News; Talk

**WHAZ-AM - 1330 (20661)**
30 Park Ave.
Cohoes, NY 12047-3330
Phone: (518)237-1330
Fax: (518)235-4468
**Format:** Religious

**WHRL-FM - 103.1 (20240)**
One Washington Sq.
Albany, NY 12205
Phone: (518)452-4000
Fax: (518)452-4855
**Format:** Alternative/New Music/Progressive

**WHUC-AM - 1230 (20925)**
5620 Rt 96
Hudson, NY 12534
Phone: (518)828-5006
Fax: (518)828-1080
**Format:** Music of Your Life

**WIZR-AM - 930 (21000)**
105 S Comrie Ave.
Johnstown, NY 12095-3149
Phone: (518)762-4631
Fax: (518)762-0105
**Format:** Big Band/Nostalgia

**WKKF-FM - 102.3 (20241)**
1 Washington Sq.
Albany, NY 12205-5512
Phone: (518)452-4800
Fax: (518)452-4855
**Format:** Contemporary Hit Radio (CHR)

**WMHT-FM - 89.1 (22925)**
PO Box 17
Schenectady, NY 12301
Phone: (518)357-1700
Fax: (518)357-1709
**Format:** Public Radio; Classical; Classical

**WQAR-FM - 101.3 (22971)**
21 Malta Commons
Malta, NY 12020
Phone: (518)899-3000
Fax: (518)899-3057

**Format:** Adult Contemporary

**WRCZ-FM - 94.5 (22927)**
11 Dennis Terrace
Schenectady, NY 12303-2805
Phone: (518)456-6101
Fax: (518)456-6377
**Format:** Classic Rock

**WRPI-FM - 91.5 (23077)**
1 WRPI Plaza
Troy, NY 12180-3590
Phone: (518)276-6271
Fax: (518)276-6920
**Format:** Public Radio; Alternative/New Music/Progressive; Alternative/New Music/Progressive

**WRVE-FM - 99.5 (20243)**
1 Washington Sq.
Albany, NY 12205
Phone: (518)452-4800
Fax: (518)452-4855
**Format:** Adult Contemporary

**WSRD-FM - 104.9 (21001)**
105 S Comrie Ave.
Johnstown, NY 12095-3149
**Format:** Oldies

**WWSC-AM - 1450 (20841)**
128 Glen St.
Glens Falls, NY 12801
Phone: (518)761-9890
Fax: (518)792-3374
**Format:** Adult Contemporary; Full Service; Full Service

**WZCR-FM - 93.5 (20926)**
5620 Rt 96
Hudson, NY 12534
Phone: (518)828-5006
Fax: (518)828-1080
**Format:** Oldies

## Bangor, ME

**WBFB-FM - 104.7 (12477)**
12 Acme Rd., Ste. 207
Brewer, ME 04412-1546
Fax: (207)989-8321
**Format:** Contemporary Country

**WFZX-FM - 101.7 (12511)**
24 Buttermilk Rd.
Ellsworth, ME 04605
Phone: (207)368-1021
Fax: (207)368-1021
**Format:** Classic Rock

**WGUY-FM - 102.1 (12543)**
162 Elm St., Ste. 3
Newport, ME 04953
Phone: (207)368-1021
Fax: (207)368-3299
**Format:** Oldies

**WHSN-FM - 89.3 (12461)**
1 College Circle
Bangor, ME 04401
Phone: (207)941-7116
Fax: (207)947-3987
**Format:** Alternative/New Music/Progressive

**WJCX-FM - 99.5 (12462)**
2881 Ohio St., Ste. 8
Bangor, ME 04401
Phone: (207)884-6052
Fax: (207)884-6052
**Format:** Contemporary Christian; Talk

**WKSQ-FM - 94.5 (12463)**
184 Target Ind Cir
Bangor, ME 04401
Phone: (207)947-9100
Fax: (207)948-0392
**Format:** Adult Contemporary

**WLKE-FM - 99.1 (12512)**
24 Buttermilk Rd.
Ellsworth, ME 04605
Phone: (207)667-7573
Fax: (207)667-9494
**Format:** Country

**WSKW-AM - 1160 (12597)**
PO Box 159
Skowhegan, ME 04976-0159
Phone: (207)474-5171
Fax: (207)474-3299

**Format:** Sports; Talk

**WZON-AM - 620 (12466)**
PO Box 1929
Bangor, ME 04402-1929
Phone: (207)990-2800
Fax: (207)942-4657
**Format:** Talk; News; News

## Binghamton, NY

**WATS-AM - 960 (27491)**
204 Desmond St.
Sayre, PA 18840
Phone: (570)888-7745
Fax: (570)888-9005
**Format:** Adult Contemporary

**WAVR-FM - 102.1 (27492)**
204 Desmond St.
Sayre, PA 18840
Phone: (570)888-7745
Fax: (570)888-9005
**Format:** Adult Contemporary

**WCDO-AM - 1490 (22941)**
75 Main St.
Sidney, NY 13838
Phone: (607)563-3588
Fax: (607)563-7805
**Format:** Adult Contemporary; Oldies; News; News

**WCDO-FM - 100.9 (22942)**
75 Main St.
Sidney, NY 13838
Phone: (607)563-3588
Fax: (607)563-7805
**Format:** Adult Contemporary; News; Oldies; Oldies

**WCDW-FM - 100.5 (20405)**
495 Court St., 2nd Fl.
Binghamton, NY 13904
Phone: (607)772-1005
Fax: (607)772-2945
**Format:** Oldies

**WEBO-AM - 1330 (22675)**
PO Box 604
212 Main St.
Owego, NY 13827
Phone: (607)687-9605
Fax: (607)687-4184
**Format:** News; Sports

**WENE-AM - 1430 (23105)**
320 N Jensen Rd.
Vestal, NY 13850
Phone: (607)584-5800
Fax: (607)584-5900
**Format:** Talk; Sports; Sports

**WHRW-FM - 90.5 (20406)**
Binghamton University
PO Box 6000
Binghamton, NY 13902
Phone: (607)777-2137
Fax: (607)777-4958
**Format:** Alternative/New Music/Progressive; Alternative/New Music/Progressive

**WHWK-FM - 98.1 (20407)**
PO Box 414
Binghamton, NY 13901
Phone: (607)772-9801
Fax: (607)772-9806
**Format:** Contemporary Country

**WINR-AM - 680 (20762)**
3646 George F. Hwy.
Endwell, NY 13760-5947
Fax: (607)775-4246
**Format:** Middle-of-the-Road (MOR)

**WKOP-AM - 1360 (20408)**
PO Box 414
Binghamton, NY 13902-0414
Phone: (607)722-3437
Fax: (607)722-3438
**Format:** Music of Your Life

**WKXZ-FM - 93.9 (22631)**
43 Hale St.
Norwich, NY 13815-2038
Phone: (607)334-2218
Fax: (607)334-9867

**Format:** Adult Contemporary

**WLTB-FM - 101.7 (23108)**
1808 vestal Parkway E.
PO Box 7
Vestal, NY 13851
Phone: (607)748-9131
Fax: (607)748-0061
**Format:** Adult Contemporary

**WMRV-FM - 105.7 (23109)**
320 Jensen Rd.
Vestal, NY 13850
Phone: (607)584-5800
Fax: (607)584-5900
**Format:** Contemporary Hit Radio (CHR); Top 40

**WNBF-AM - 1290 (20409)**
PO Box 414
Binghamton, NY 13902
Phone: (607)772-8400
Fax: (607)772-9806
**Format:** News; Talk; Talk

**WRIV-AM - 1390 (22801)**
40 W. Main St.
PO Box 1390
Riverhead, NY 11901
Phone: (631)727-1390
Fax: (631)369-9748
**Format:** Middle-of-the-Road (MOR)

**WSQG-FM - 89.3 (20413)**
PO Box 3000
Binghamton, NY 13902
Phone: (607)729-0100
Fax: (607)729-7328
**Format:** Classical; Jazz; Folk; News; Folk; News

## Boston-Worcester,MA-Derry-Manchester,NH

**WBCN-FM - 104.1 (13602)**
83 Leo M. Birmingham Parkway
Boston, MA 02215-3480
Phone: (617)746-1000
Fax: (617)247-2266
**Format:** Alternative/New Music/Progressive

**WBET-AM - 1460 (13628)**
60 Main St.
Brockton, MA 02301
Phone: (508)587-2400
Fax: (508)587-4786
**Format:** News; Talk

**WBUR-FM - 90.9 (13603)**
890 Commonwealth Ave.
Boston, MA 02215
Phone: (617)353-0909
Fax: (617)353-4747
**Format:** News; Information; Eclectic; Eclectic

**WBYY-FM - 98.7 (18804)**
PO Box 400
Dover, NH 03820
Phone: (603)742-0987
Fax: (603)742-0448
**Format:** Adult Contemporary

**WBZ-AM - 1030 (13604)**
1170 Soldiers Field Rd.
Boston, MA 02134-1092
Phone: (617)787-7000
Fax: (617)787-7060
**Format:** News; Talk; Talk

**WCAT-FM - 99.9 (14722)**
660 E. Main St.
PO Box 90
Orange, MA 01364
Phone: (978)544-2321
**Format:** Adult Contemporary

**WCCM-AM - 1490 (14245)**
462 Merriman St.
Methuen, MA 01844
Phone: (978)683-7171
Fax: (978)687-1180
**Format:** News; Talk; Sports

**WCIB-FM - 101.9 (13836)**
154 Barnstable Rd.
Hyannis, MA 02601
Phone: (508)778-2888
Fax: (508)778-9651

**Format:** Classic Rock

**WCOD-FM - 106.1 (14886)**
278 S. Sea Ave.
West Yarmouth, MA 02673-5633
Phone: (508)760-5252
Fax: (508)760-5353
**Format:** Adult Contemporary

**WCRB-FM - 102.5 (14870)**
750 South St.
Waltham, MA 02453
Phone: (781)893-7080
Fax: (781)893-0038
**Format:** Classical

**WCUW-FM - 91.3 (14951)**
910 Main St.
Worcester, MA 01610
Phone: (508)753-1012
**Format:** Ethnic; News; Eclectic

**WEEI-AM - 850 (13606)**
20 Guest St.
Boston, MA 02135-2040
Phone: (617)779-3500
Fax: (617)779-3557
**Format:** Sports

**WEIM-AM - 1280 (13782)**
762 Water St.
Fitchburg, MA 01420
Phone: (978)343-3766
Fax: (978)345-6397
**Format:** Sports; Adult Contemporary; News; Talk

**WERS-FM - 88.9 (13607)**
120 Boylston St.
Boston, MA 02116
Phone: (617)824-8891
Fax: (617)824-8804
**Format:** Eclectic

**WFEA-AM - 1370 (18878)**
500 Commercial St.
Manchester, NH 03101
Phone: (603)669-5777
Fax: (603)669-4641

**WGFP-AM - 940 (14952)**
19 Norwich St.
Worcester, MA 01608
Phone: (508)791-2111
Fax: (508)752-6897
**Format:** News; Talk; Talk

**WGXL-FM - 92.3 (18858)**
31 Hanover St., Ste. 4
Lebanon, NH 03766
Phone: (603)488-1400
Fax: (603)488-1755
**Format:** Adult Contemporary

**WHDQ-FM - 106.1 (18777)**
PO Box 1230
Claremont, NH 03743-1230
Phone: (603)542-7735
Fax: (603)542-8721
**Format:** Adult Contemporary

**WICN-FM - 90.5 (14953)**
50 Portland St.
Worcester, MA 01608
Phone: (508)752-0700
Fax: (508)752-7518
**Format:** Jazz; Folk; Bluegrass; News

**WJIB-AM - 740 (13719)**
443 Concord Ave.
Cambridge, MA 02138
Phone: (617)868-7400
**Format:** Adult Contemporary

**WKBK-AM - 1290 (18962)**
69 Stanhope Ave.
Keene, NH 03431
Phone: (603)352-9230
Fax: (603)357-3926
**Format:** News; Talk

**WKOX-AM - 1200 (14239)**
99 Revere Beach Pkwy.
Medford, MA 02155-5124

**WKXL-AM - 1450 (18790)**
37 Redington Rd.
Concord, NH 03301
Phone: (603)225-5521
Fax: (603)224-6404

**Format:** News; Talk; Sports; Sports

**WOCN-FM - 103.9 (13837)**
737 Main St.
Hyannis, MA 02601
Phone: (508)771-1224
Fax: (508)775-2605
**Format:** Adult Contemporary

**WOKQ-FM - 97.5 (18806)**
PO Box 576
Dover, NH 03821-0576
Phone: (603)749-9750
Fax: (603)749-1459
**Format:** Country

**WOKQ-FM - 105.3 (18805)**
PO Box 576
Dover, NH 03821-0576
Phone: (603)749-9750
Fax: (603)749-1459
**Format:** Classic Rock

**WPLM-AM - 1390 (14751)**
PO Box 1390
Plymouth, MA 02362
Phone: (508)746-1390
Fax: (508)830-1128
**Format:** News

**WPLM-FM - 99.1 (14752)**
PO Box 1390
Plymouth, MA 02362
Phone: (508)746-1390
Fax: (508)830-1128
**Format:** Easy Listening

**WPXC-FM - 102.9 (13838)**
154 Barnstable Rd.
Hyannis, MA 02601-2930
Phone: (508)778-2888
Fax: (508)790-4967
**Format:** Album-Oriented Rock (AOR); Classic Rock

**WQLL-FM - 96.5 (13614)**
500 Commercial St.
Manchester, NH 03101
Phone: (603)669-7979
Fax: (603)669-4641
**Format:** Oldies; Full Service

**WQRC-FM - 99.9 (13839)**
737 W. Main St.
Hyannis, MA 02601-3499
Phone: (508)771-1224
Fax: (508)775-2605
**Format:** Full Service; Adult Contemporary

**WRKO-AM - 680 (13616)**
20 Guest St.
Boston, MA 02135-2040
Fax: (617)236-6889
**Format:** Talk

**WSRS-FM - 96.1 (14728)**
96 Stereo Ln.
Paxton, MA 01612
Phone: (508)757-9696
Fax: (508)757-7279
**Format:** Adult Contemporary

**WTAG-AM - 580 (14729)**
58 Stereo Ln.
Paxton, MA 01612
Phone: (508)795-0580
Fax: (508)757-1779
**Format:** Talk; Sports; Sports

**WTPL-FM - 107.7 (18793)**
37 Redington Rd.
Box 875
Concord, NH 03302-0875
Phone: (603)225-5521
Fax: (603)224-6404
**Format:** News; Talk; Sports

**WTSA-AM - 1450 (30853)**
PO Box 819
Brattleboro, VT 05302
Phone: (802)254-4577
Fax: (802)257-4644
**Format:** Sports

**WUMB-FM - 91.9 (13619)**
University of Massachusetts at Boston
Boston, MA 02125-3393
Phone: (617)287-6900
Fax: (617)287-6916

**Format:** Folk

**WUNR-AM - 1600 (13620)**
160 N. Washington St.
Boston, MA 02114-2142
Phone: (617)367-9003
Fax: (617)367-2265
**Format:** Ethnic

**WXKS-FM - 107.9 (14242)**
Box 128
Medford, MA 02155
Fax: (617)391-3064
**Format:** Contemporary Hit Radio (CHR)

**WZLX-FM - 100.7 (13621)**
The Prudential Tower, Ste. 2450
Boston, MA 02199
Phone: (617)267-0123
Fax: (617)421-9305
**Format:** Classic Rock

## Buffalo (Jamestown), NY

**WBKX-FM - 96.5 (20796)**
3561 Willow Rd.
PO Box 209
Dunkirk, NY 14048
Phone: (716)366-8580
Fax: (716)366-1416
**Format:** Adult Contemporary; News; News

**WBRR-FM - 100.1 (26196)**
PO Box 545
Bradford, PA 16701
Phone: (814)368-4141
**Format:** Contemporary Hit Radio (CHR)

**WBTA-AM - 1490 (20339)**
438 E. Main St.
Batavia, NY 14020
Phone: (585)344-1490
Fax: (585)344-1441
**Format:** Full Service; Soft Rock; News; Talk

**WDCX-FM - 99.5 (20588)**
625 Delaware Ave.
Buffalo, NY 14202
Phone: (716)883-3010
Fax: (716)883-3606
**Format:** Religious

**WDOE-AM - 1410 (20713)**
Willow Rd.
Box 209
Dunkirk, NY 14048
Phone: (716)366-1410
Fax: (716)366-1416
**Format:** Full Service

**WESB-AM - 1490 (26197)**
PO Box 545
Bradford, PA 16701
Phone: (814)368-4141
**Format:** Adult Contemporary

**WGCC-FM - 90.7 (20340)**
1 College Rd.
Batavia, NY 14020
Phone: (585)343-0055
Fax: (585)345-6806
**Format:** Album-Oriented Rock (AOR); Alternative/New Music/Progressive

**WGRF-FM - 96.9 (20590)**
50 James E Casey Dr.
Buffalo, NY 14206-2367
Phone: (716)881-4555
Fax: (716)884-2931
**Format:** Classic Rock

**WHDL-AM - 1450 (22649)**
3163 NY ST Rte. 417
Olean, NY 14760
Phone: (716)372-0161
Fax: (716)372-0164
**Format:** Oldies

**WHLD-AM - 1270 (20592)**
225 Delaware Ave., Ste. 1A
Buffalo, NY 14202
Phone: (716)855-1270
Fax: (716)855-4681

**Gale Directory of Publications & Broadcast Media/140th Ed.**  Erie, PA

Format: Ethnic; Religious; Talk

**WJQZ-FM - 103.5  (23147)**
82 Railroad Ave.
Wellsville, NY 14895
Phone: (585)593-6070
Fax: (585)593-6212
Format: Adult Contemporary

**WJYE-FM - 96.1  (20595)**
14 Lafayette Square
Buffalo, NY 14203
Phone: (716)856-3550
Fax: (716)852-0537
Format: Adult Contemporary

**WKSE-FM - 98.5  (20597)**
500 Corporate Pkwy., Ste. 200
Buffalo, NY 14226-1263
Fax: (716)882-2048
Format: Contemporary Hit Radio (CHR)

**WMNY-AM - 1120  (20598)**
225 Delaware Ave., Ste. 1A
Buffalo, NY 14202-2108
Phone: (716)848-1120
Fax: (716)848-9518
Format: Gospel

**WMXO-FM - 101.5  (22650)**
231 N. Union St.
Olean, NY 14760
Phone: (716)375-1015
Fax: (716)375-7705
Format: Adult Contemporary; Talk; Talk

**WNED-AM - 970  (20599)**
PO Box 1263
Buffalo, NY 14240-1263
Phone: (716)845-7000
Fax: (716)845-7043
Format: Public Radio; News; News

**WPIG-FM - 95.7  (22651)**
3219 W. State Rd.
Olean, NY 14760
Phone: (716)372-0161
Fax: (716)372-0164
Format: Contemporary Country

**WUFO-AM - 1080  (20603)**
89 LaSalle Ave.
Buffalo, NY 14214
Phone: (716)834-1080
Fax: (716)837-1438
Format: Adult Contemporary; Gospel; Gospel

**WUFX-FM - 103.3  (20604)**
225 Delaware Ave., Ste. 1A
Buffalo, NY 14202-2108
Phone: (716)885-1400
Fax: (716)882-8810
Format: Classic Rock

**WYRK-FM - 106.5  (20605)**
1200 Rand Bldg.
Buffalo, NY 14203
Phone: (716)852-7444
Fax: (716)852-5683
Format: Country

## Burlington-Hartford, VT-Plattsburgh, NY

**WANC-FM - 103.9  (23065)**
c/o WAMC-FM
318 Central Ave.
Albany, NY 12206
Phone: (518)465-5233
Fax: (518)432-6974
Format: Public Radio; News; Classical; Folk

**WCVR-FM - 102.1; 102.3  (30923)**
PO Box 249
Randolph Center, VT 05060
Phone: (802)728-4411
Fax: (802)728-4013
Format: Classic Rock

**WEZF-FM - 92.9  (30864)**
63 Bay State Rd.
PO Box 1093
Burlington, VT 05402-1093
Phone: (802)655-0093
Fax: (802)655-0478

Format: Adult Contemporary

**WGLY-FM - 93.5  (30886)**
PO Box 8310
Essex, VT 05451-8260
Phone: (802)878-8885
Fax: (802)879-6835
Format: Religious; Contemporary Christian

**WICY-AM - 1490  (21089)**
86 Porter Rd.
Malone, NY 12953
Phone: (518)483-1100
Fax: (518)483-1382
Format: Oldies

**WIRD-AM - 920  (21020)**
17 Wilmington Rd.
PO Box 861
Lake Placid, NY 12946
Phone: (518)523-3341
Fax: (518)523-1349
Format: Sports

**WIRY-AM - 1340  (22711)**
301 Cornelia St.
Plattsburgh, NY 12901
Phone: (518)563-1340
Fax: (518)563-1343
Format: Adult Contemporary

**WJJR-FM - 98.1  (30928)**
67 Merchant Row
PO Box 30
Rutland, VT 05701
Phone: (802)775-7500
Fax: (802)775-7555
Format: Adult Contemporary

**WJOY-AM - 1230  (30865)**
PO Box 4489
Burlington, VT 05406
Phone: (802)658-1230
Fax: (802)862-0786
Format: Big Band/Nostalgia

**WLPW-FM - 105.5  (21021)**
17 Wilmington Rd.
PO Box 861
Lake Placid, NY 12946
Phone: (518)523-3341
Fax: (518)523-1349
Format: Adult Contemporary

**WMXR-FM - 93.9  (18859)**
31 Hanover St., No. 4
Lebanon, NH 03766-1312
Phone: (603)298-9494
Format: Oldies

**WOKO-FM - 98.9  (30866)**
70 Joy Drive
PO Box 4489
Burlington, VT 05406
Phone: (802)658-1230
Fax: (802)862-0786
Format: Country

**WPLT-FM - 93.9  (22712)**
Office of Campus Life
110 Angell College Ctr.
Plattsburgh, NY 12901
Phone: (518)564-2727
Fax: (518)564-3994
Format: Eclectic

**WSNO-AM - 1450  (30833)**
41 Jacques St.
Barre, VT 05641
Phone: (802)476-4168
Fax: (802)479-5893
Format: Country; News; Talk

**WVMT-AM - 620  (30876)**
118 Malletts Bay Ave.
PO Box 620
Colchester, VT 05446
Phone: (802)655-1620
Fax: (802)655-1329
Format: News; Talk; Sports

**WXXX-FM - 95.5  (30879)**
PO Box 620
Colchester, VT 05446
Phone: (802)655-9550
Fax: (802)655-1329

Format: Contemporary Hit Radio (CHR)

## Denver (Steamboat Springs), CO

**KVLE-FM - 102.3  (26132)**
12 E. Newfield Way
Bala Cynwyd, PA 19004-2322
Format: Country; Oldies; Oldies

## Elmira, NY

**WABH-AM - 1380  (20343)**
E. Washington St.
PO Box 72
Bath, NY 14810
Phone: (607)776-3326
Fax: (607)776-6161
Format: Oldies

**WCBA-AM - 1350  (20680)**
Box 1047
Corning, NY 14830
Phone: (607)962-4646
Fax: (607)962-1138
Format: Oldies; Big Band/Nostalgia

**WCBA-FM - 98.7  (20681)**
PO Box 1047
Corning, NY 14830
Phone: (607)962-4646
Fax: (607)962-1138
Format: Adult Contemporary

**WCLI-AM - 1450  (20683)**
PO Box 1047
Corning, NY 14830-0847
Phone: (607)962-4646
Fax: (607)962-1138
Format: Talk

**WECW-FM - 107.7  (20746)**
Elmira College
Elmira, NY 14901
Phone: (607)735-1885
Fax: (607)735-1701
Format: Eclectic

**WLNL-AM - 1000  (20919)**
3134 Lake Rd.
Horseheads, NY 14845
Phone: (607)737-9208
Fax: (607)737-9210
Format: Religious

**WMKB-FM - 96.9  (20920)**
3134 Lake Rd.
Horseheads, NY 14845
Phone: (607)737-9208
Fax: (607)737-9210
Format: Religious

**WNBT-AM - 1490  (27663)**
PO Box 98
Wellsboro, PA 16901
Phone: (570)724-1490
Fax: (570)724-6971
Format: Adult Contemporary

**WPGI-FM - 100.9  (20749)**
2205 College Ave.
Elmira, NY 14903
Phone: (607)732-9744
Format: Contemporary Country

**WQIX-AM - 820  (20750)**
2205 College Ave.
Elmira, NY 14903
Format: Country; Talk; News

## Erie, PA

**WPSE-AM - 1450  (26356)**
Penn State-Behrend
5091 Station Rd.
Erie, PA 16563-1450
Phone: (814)898-6495
Format: News; Sports; Sports

**WRIE-AM - 1260  (26359)**
471 Robison Rd.
Erie, PA 16509
Phone: (814)868-5355
Fax: (814)868-1876

Circulation: ★ = ABC;  △ = BPA;  ♦ = CAC;  • = CCAB;  □ = VAC;  ⊕ = PO Statement;  ‡ = Publisher's Report;  Boldface figures = sworn;  Light figures = estimated.

**Format:** Big Band/Nostalgia

**WRKT-FM - 100.9  (26784)**
1 Broadcast Park
North East, PA 16428
Phone: (814)725-4000
Fax: (814)725-5401
**Format:** Album-Oriented Rock (AOR); Classic Rock

**WRTS-FM - 103.7  (26785)**
1 Broadcast Park
North East, PA 16428
Phone: (814)725-4000
Fax: (814)725-5401
**Format:** Top 40

**WTIV-AM - 1230  (27580)**
PO Box 6066
Titusville, PA 16354-0184
Phone: (814)827-3651
Fax: (814)827-1679
**Format:** Middle-of-the-Road (MOR)

**WXKC-FM - 99.9  (26360)**
471 Robison Rd.
Erie, PA 16509
Phone: (814)868-5355
Fax: (814)868-1876
**Format:** Adult Contemporary

**WXTA-FM - 97.9  (26315)**
471 Robison Rd.
Erie, PA 16509-5425
Phone: (814)868-5355
Fax: (814)868-1876
**Format:** Country

## Harrisburg-York-Lancaster-Lebanon, PA

**WADV-AM - 940  (26629)**
720 E. Kercher Ave.
Lebanon, PA 17046
Phone: (717)273-2611
Fax: (717)273-7293
**Format:** Southern Gospel; Country; Bluegrass

**WARM-FM - 103.3  (27736)**
PO Box 910
York, PA 17405
Phone: (717)764-1155
Fax: (717)252-4708
**Format:** Soft Rock

**WAVL-AM - 910  (26121)**
826 Radio Station Ln.
PO Box 277
Apollo, PA 15613
Phone: (724)478-4020
Fax: (724)478-4028
**Format:** Religious

**WDAC-FM - 94.5  (26607)**
683 Lancaster Pike
PO Box 3022
Lancaster, PA 17604
Phone: (717)284-4123
Fax: (717)284-2300
**Format:** Religious

**WGCB-FM - 96.1  (27476)**
Windsor Rd.
PO Box 88
Red Lion, PA 17356
Phone: (717)244-5360
Fax: (717)246-8473
**Format:** Religious

**WGET-AM - 1320  (26394)**
1560 Fairfield Rd.
PO Box 3179
Gettysburg, PA 17325-0179
Phone: (717)334-3101
Fax: (717)334-5822
**Format:** Adult Contemporary; News

**WGTY-FM - 107.7  (26395)**
1560 Fairfield Rd.
PO Box 3179
Gettysburg, PA 17325
Phone: (717)334-3101
Fax: (717)334-5822
**Format:** Contemporary Country

**WHBO-FM - 92.7  (26663)**
1996 Auction Rd.
Manheim, PA 17545
Phone: (717)653-0800
Fax: (717)653-0122
**Format:** Oldies

**WHKF-FM - 99.3  (26462)**
600 Corporate Cir.
Harrisburg, PA 17110
Phone: (717)540-8800
Fax: (717)540-8814
**Format:** Contemporary Hit Radio (CHR)

**WHP-AM - 580  (26463)**
600 Corporate Cir.
Harrisburg, PA 17110
Phone: (717)540-8800
Fax: (717)541-0094
**Format:** Talk; News

**WIEZ-AM - 670  (26648)**
12 1/2 E. Market St.
Lewistown, PA 17044-2123
Phone: (717)248-6757
Fax: (717)248-6759
**Format:** Oldies

**WIOV-FM - 105.1  (26342)**
44 Bethany Rd
Ephrata, PA 17522
Phone: (717)626-1700
Fax: (717)738-1661
**Format:** Country

**WJTL-FM - 90.3  (26609)**
PO Box 1614
Lancaster, PA 17608-4792
Phone: (717)392-3690
Fax: (717)390-2892
**Format:** Contemporary Hit Radio (CHR); Religious

**WJUN-AM - 1220  (26693)**
Old Rte. 22 E.
Mexico, PA 17056
Phone: (717)436-2135
Fax: (717)436-8155
**Format:** Sports

**WKBO-AM - 1230  (26467)**
600 Corporate Cir.
Harrisburg, PA 17110-9787
Phone: (717)540-8800
Fax: (717)540-9271
**Format:** Oldies; Big Band/Nostalgia; Music of Your Life

**WLBR-AM - 1270  (26630)**
PO Box 1270
Lebanon, PA 17042
Phone: (717)272-7651
Fax: (717)274-0161
**Format:** Adult Contemporary

**WLCH-FM - 91.3  (26610)**
30 N. Ann St., 1st Fl.
Lancaster, PA 17602
Phone: (717)295-7760
Fax: (717)295-7759
**Format:** Talk; Hispanic; News; Eclectic; Religious; Eclectic; Religious

**WLPA-AM - 1490  (26611)**
PO Box 4368
Lancaster, PA 17604-4368
Phone: (717)653-0800
Fax: (717)653-0122
**Format:** Sports

**WMRF-FM - 95.9  (26650)**
12 1/2 E. Market St.
PO Box 667
Lewistown, PA 17044-2123
Phone: (717)248-6757
Fax: (717)248-6759
**Format:** Contemporary Hit Radio (CHR)

**WMSS-FM - 91.1  (26707)**
214 Race St.
Middletown, PA 17057
Phone: (717)948-9136
**Format:** Contemporary Hit Radio (CHR); Alternative/New Music/Progressive

**WNCE-FM - 92.1  (26469)**
3400 N. 6th St.
Harrisburg, PA 17110-1423
Phone: (717)697-1141
Fax: (717)697-1149
**Format:** Easy Listening

**WOYK-AM - 1350  (27737)**
PO Box 20249
York, PA 17402
Phone: (717)840-0355
Fax: (717)840-0355
**Format:** Sports

**WQIC-FM - 100.1  (26631)**
Rte. 72 N.
PO Box 1270
Lebanon, PA 17042
Phone: (717)272-7651
Fax: (717)274-0161
**Format:** Soft Rock

**WQLV-FM - 98.9  (26713)**
309 Peachtree Dr.
PO Box 158
Millersburg, PA 17061
Phone: (717)692-2193
Fax: (717)692-2080
**Format:** Adult Contemporary

**WRKZ-FM - 106.7  (26498)**
PO Box Z
Hershey, PA 17033-0450
Phone: (717)367-7700
Fax: (717)367-9322
**Format:** Contemporary Country

**WROZ-FM - 101.3  (26612)**
PO Box 4368
Lancaster, PA 17604-4368
Phone: (717)653-0800
Fax: (717)653-0122
**Format:** Soft Rock

**WRVV-FM - 97.3  (26471)**
600 Corporate Circle
Harrisburg, PA 17110
Phone: (717)540-8800
Fax: (717)540-9271
**Format:** Adult Contemporary

**WSBA-AM - 910  (27739)**
5989 Susquehanna Plaza Dr.
PO Box 910
York, PA 17402
Phone: (717)764-1155
Fax: (717)252-4708
**Format:** News; Talk

**WWII-AM - 720  (27534)**
8 W. Main St.
Shiremanstown, PA 17011
Phone: (717)731-9944
Fax: (717)731-4002
**Format:** Religious; Polka; Talk; Talk

## Hartford-New Haven (New London), CT

**WATR-AM - 1320  (5073)**
1 Broadcast Ln.
Waterbury, CT 06706
Phone: (203)755-1121
Fax: (203)574-3025
**Format:** News; Talk; Music of Your Life; Music of Your Life

**WAVZ-AM - 1300  (4791)**
Radio Towers Park
495 Benham St.
Hamden, CT 06514-2009
Phone: (203)248-8814
Fax: (203)281-2795
**Format:** Album-Oriented Rock (AOR)

**WCNI-FM - 91.1  (4917)**
Box 4972, Connecticut College
270 Mohegan Ave.
New London, CT 06320
Phone: (860)439-2853
Fax: (860)439-2850
**Format:** Eclectic

**WDRC-AM - 1360  (4628)**
869 Blue Hills Ave.
Bloomfield, CT 06002
Phone: (860)243-1115
Fax: (860)286-8257

**Format:** News; Talk; Sports

**WDRC-FM - 102.9 (4629)**
869 Blue Hills Ave.
Bloomfield, CT 06002
Phone: (860)243-1115
Fax: (860)286-8257
**Format:** Oldies

**WELI-AM - 960 (4792)**
495 Benham St.
Hamden, CT 06514
Phone: (203)281-9600
Fax: (203)407-4652
**Format:** News; Talk

**WHCN-FM - 105.9 (4814)**
10 Columbus Blvd.
Hartford, CT 06106
Phone: (860)723-6000
Fax: (860)723-6106
**Format:** Classic Rock

**WILI-AM - 1400 (5095)**
720 Main St.
Willimantic, CT 06226
Phone: (860)456-1111
Fax: (860)456-9501
**Format:** Full Service; Adult Contemporary

**WILI-FM - 98.3 (5096)**
720 Main St.
Willimantic, CT 06226
Phone: (860)456-1111
Fax: (860)456-9501
**Format:** Adult Contemporary; Contemporary Hit Radio (CHR)

**WKSS-FM - 95.7 (4815)**
10 Columbus Blvd.
Hartford, CT 06106-1944
Phone: (860)723-6160
Fax: (860)723-6198
**Format:** Contemporary Hit Radio (CHR)

**WLAT-AM - 910 (4816)**
330 Main St.
Hartford, CT 06106
Phone: (860)524-0001
Fax: (860)548-1922
**Format:** Hispanic

**WPOP-AM - 1410 (4818)**
10 Columbus Blvd.
Hartford, CT 06106
Phone: (860)723-6000
Fax: (860)723-6079
**Format:** Sports

**WQTQ-FM - 89.9 (4820)**
Weaver High School
415 Granby St.
Hartford, CT 06112
Phone: (860)695-1900
Fax: (860)286-9908
**Format:** Urban Contemporary; Educational; Oldies; Gospel; Jazz; Rap; Reggae; Hip Hop; Blues

**WQUN-AM - 1220 (4795)**
Quinnipiac College
275 Mount Carmel Ave.
Hamden, CT 06518
Phone: (203)582-8984
Fax: (203)582-5372
**Format:** News; Information

**WRCH-FM - 100.5 (4768)**
10 Executive Dr.
Farmington, CT 06032-2841
Phone: (203)677-6700
Fax: (203)677-5483
**Format:** Adult Contemporary

**WRTC-FM - 89.3 (4822)**
Trinity College
300 Summit St.
Hartford, CT 06106
Phone: (203)297-2439
Fax: (203)297-5201
**Format:** Eclectic; Jazz; Religious; Alternative/New Music/Progressive

**WRYM-AM - 840 (5082)**
5 Acadia St.
West Hartford, CT 06119
Phone: (860)232-3325
Fax: (860)666-5647

**Format:** Hispanic

**WSCS-FM - 90.9 (18927)**
100 Main St.
New London, NH 03257
Phone: (603)526-3493
Fax: (603)526-3452
**Format:** Educational

**WWYZ-FM - 92.5 (4825)**
10 Columbus Blvd.
Hartford, CT 06106
Phone: (860)723-6000
Fax: (860)723-6159
**Format:** Country

## Johnstown-Altoona, PA

**WALY-FM - 103.9 (26500)**
1 Forever Dr.
Hollidaysburg, PA 16648-3029
Phone: (814)941-9800
Fax: (814)943-2754
**Format:** Oldies

**WAYC-FM - 100.9 (26150)**
134 E. Pitt St.
PO Box 1
Bedford, PA 15522-0001
Phone: (814)623-1000
Fax: (814)623-9692
**Format:** Adult Contemporary

**WBFD-AM - 1310 (26151)**
134 E. Pitt St.
PO Box 1
Bedford, PA 15522-0001
Phone: (814)623-1000
Fax: (814)623-9692
**Format:** Oldies

**WBHV-FM - 103.1 (27556)**
2551 Park Center Blvd.
State College, PA 16801-3007
Phone: (814)237-4959
Fax: (814)234-1659
**Format:** Contemporary Hit Radio (CHR)

**WBVE-FM - 107.5 (26152)**
134 E. Pitt St.
PO Box 1
Bedford, PA 15522-0001
Phone: (814)623-1000
Fax: (814)623-9692
**Format:** Classic Rock

**WECZ-AM - 1540 (27463)**
904 North Main St.
Punxsutawney, PA 15767
Phone: (814)938-6000
Fax: (814)938-4237
**Format:** Information; News

**WFRJ-FM - 88.9 FM (27715)**
1322 Seanor Rd.
Windber, PA 15963
Phone: (814)322-3144
**Format:** Religious

**WGLU-FM - 92.1 (26550)**
Geistown Cloverleaf Complex
2447 Bedford St., Ste. 101
Johnstown, PA 15904
Phone: (814)266-9458
Fax: (814)266-9212
**Format:** Contemporary Hit Radio (CHR)

**WHJB-AM - 1600 (26153)**
PO Box 672
Bedford, PA 15522
Phone: (814)624-0016
Fax: (814)623-9692

**WHUN-AM - 1150 (26522)**
RR 4 Box 160-A
Huntingdon, PA 16652
Phone: (814)643-9620
Fax: (814)643-9625
**Format:** Country

**WJSM-AM - 1110 (26669)**
Rte. 2 Box 87
Martinsburg, PA 16662-9130
Phone: (814)793-2188

**WJSM-FM - 92.7 (26670)**
Rte. 2, Box 87
Martinsburg, PA 16662-9130
Phone: (814)793-2188
Fax: (814)793-9727
**Format:** Southern Gospel

**WKMC-AM - 1370 (27484)**
1345 S. Main St.
Roaring Spring, PA 16673
Phone: (814)224-7501
Fax: (814)224-7504
**Format:** Country

**WKYE-FM - 95.5 (26553)**
109 Plaza Dr.
Johnstown, PA 15905-1212
Phone: (814)255-4186
Fax: (814)255-1477
**Format:** Adult Contemporary

**WKYE-FM - 850 (26552)**
109 Plaza Dr.
Johnstown, PA 15905-1212
Phone: (814)255-4186
Fax: (814)255-6145
**Format:** Oldies; Country

**WLEM-AM - 1250 (26334)**
145 E. 4th St.
Emporium, PA 15834
Phone: (814)486-3712
Fax: (814)486-1772
**Format:** Adult Contemporary; Oldies; Contemporary Country; Contemporary Country

**WMKX-FM - 105.5 (26202)**
51 Pickering St.
Brookville, PA 15825
Phone: (814)849-8100
Fax: (814)849-4585

**WNTJ-AM - 96.5 (26555)**
970 Tripoli
PO Box 370
Johnstown, PA 15902
Phone: (814)535-8554
Fax: (814)535-8557
**Format:** Talk; News; News

**WPRR-FM - 100.1 (26501)**
One Forever Dr.
Hollidaysburg, PA 16648
**Format:** Contemporary Hit Radio (CHR)

**WPXZ-FM - 104.1 (27464)**
904 North Main St.
Punxsutawney, PA 15767
Phone: (814)938-6000
Fax: (814)938-4237
**Format:** Adult Contemporary; News; Sports

**WQYX-FM - 93.1 (26252)**
110 Healy Ave.
Clearfield, PA 16830-5032
Phone: (814)765-5541
Fax: (814)765-6333
**Format:** Adult Contemporary

**WRSC-AM - 1390 (27562)**
160 Clearview Ave.
State College, PA 16801
Phone: (814)238-5085
Fax: (814)238-8993
**Format:** News; Talk; Sports; Sports

**WRTA-AM - 1240 (26106)**
1417 12th Ave.
PO Box 272
Altoona, PA 16603
Phone: (814)943-6112
Fax: (814)944-9782
**Format:** Talk; News

**WVAM-AM - 1430 (26502)**
One Forever Dr.
Hollidaysburg, PA 16648
Phone: (814)944-9456
Fax: (814)944-0250

New York, NY

**Format:** News; Talk

**WVSC-AM - 990  (26558)**
109 Plaza Dr., Ste. 2
Johnstown, PA 15905-1212
**Format:** Oldies

**WYSN-AM - 1330  (26560)**
858 Olim St.
Johnstown, PA 15904-2522

## New York, NY

**WALK-AM - 1370  (22685)**
66 Colonial Dr.
Patchogue, NY 11772
Fax: (516)475-9016
**Format:** Adult Contemporary

**WALK-FM - 97.5  (22686)**
66 Colonial Dr.
Patchogue, NY 11772
Fax: (516)475-9016
**Format:** Adult Contemporary

**WAMK-FM - 90.9  (21008)**
c/o WAMC-FM
318 Central Ave.
Albany, NY 12206
Phone: (518)465-5233
Fax: (518)432-6974
**Format:** Public Radio; News; Eclectic

**WAWZ-FM - 99.1  (19979)**
Weston Canal Rd.
PO Box 9058
Zarephath, NJ 08890
Phone: (732)469-0991
Fax: (732)469-2115
**Format:** Contemporary Christian

**WBLI-FM - 106.1  (23152)**
555 Sunrise Hwy.
West Babylon, NY 11704-6009
Phone: (631)699-9254
Fax: (631)376-0812
**Format:** Contemporary Hit Radio (CHR)

**WBPM-FM - 94.3  (22748)**
20 Tucker Drive
Poughkeepsie, NY 12601
Phone: (845)471-2300
Fax: (845)471-2683
**Format:** Oldies

**WCBS-AM - 880  (22575)**
524 W 57th St.
New York, NY 10019
Phone: (212)975-2127
Fax: (212)975-4674
**Format:** News

**WCBS-FM - 101.1  (22576)**
1515 Broadway, 40th Fl.
New York, NY 10036-8900
Phone: (212)846-5100
**Format:** Oldies

**WCTC-AM - 1450  (19604)**
PO Box 100
New Brunswick, NJ 08903
Fax: (908)249-9010
**Format:** News; Talk

**WCUM-AM - 1450  (4639)**
PO Box 3975
Bridgeport, CT 06605-2247
Phone: (203)335-1450
Fax: (203)337-1220
**Format:** Hispanic

**WCZX-FM - 97.7  (22750)**
PO Box 416
Poughkeepsie, NY 12602
Fax: (914)454-1204
**Format:** Adult Contemporary; Oldies

**WEOK-AM - 1390  (22752)**
PO Box 416
Poughkeepsie, NY 12602
Phone: (845)471-1500
Fax: (845)454-1204
**Format:** Hispanic; Contemporary Hit Radio (CHR)

**WFAS-FM - 103.9  (20880)**
365 Secor Rd.
Hartsdale, NY 10530-1229
Phone: (914)693-2400

Fax: (914)693-4489
**Format:** Adult Contemporary

**WFDU-FM - 89.1  (19851)**
1000 River Rd.
Teaneck, NJ 07666
Phone: (201)692-2806
Fax: (201)692-2807
**Format:** Jazz; Alternative/New Music/Progressive; Country; Folk; Ethnic; Blues

**WFIT-AM - 530  (22578)**
230 W. 27th St.
New York, NY 10001
Phone: (212)760-7876
**Format:** Alternative/New Music/Progressive

**WFKP-FM - 99.3  (22753)**
20 Tucker Dr.
Poughkeepsie, NY 12603
Phone: (845)471-2300
Fax: (845)471-2683
**Format:** Adult Contemporary

**WFNP-FM - 88.7  (21238)**
State University of New York
SUB, Rm. 309
New Paltz, NY 12561
Phone: (914)257-3084
Fax: (914)257-3099
**Format:** Public Radio; Eclectic

**WFUV-FM - 90.7  (20484)**
Fordham University
Bronx, NY 10458
Phone: (718)817-4550
Fax: (718)365-9815
**Format:** Public Radio; Folk; Ethnic; Ethnic

**WGHQ-AM - 920  (22754)**
20 Tucker Dr.
Poughkeepsie, NY 12603
**Format:** News; Talk

**WGNY-FM - 103.1  (22611)**
PO Box 2307
Newburgh, NY 12550
Phone: (845)561-2131
Fax: (845)561-2138
**Format:** Adult Contemporary

**WHCR-FM - 90.3  (22579)**
City College of New York
138th & Convent Ave.
Nac Bldg., Rm. 1515
New York, NY 10031
Phone: (212)650-7481
Fax: (212)650-5736
**Format:** Public Radio; Urban Contemporary; News; Hispanic; Hip Hop

**WHUD-FM - 100.7  (20356)**
PO Box 310
Beacon, NY 12508
Phone: (914)838-6000
Fax: (914)838-2109
**Format:** Adult Contemporary

**WICC-AM - 600  (4641)**
2 Lafayette Sq., 7th Fl.
Bridgeport, CT 06604-6000
Phone: (203)366-6000
Fax: (203)384-0600
**Format:** Adult Contemporary

**WINS-AM - 1010  (22580)**
888 7th Ave.
New York, NY 10106
Phone: (212)397-1010
Fax: (212)247-7918
**Format:** News

**WJRZ-FM - 100.1  (19885)**
22 W. Water St.
PO Box 100
Toms River, NJ 08754
Phone: (732)349-1100
Fax: (732)505-8700
**Format:** Country; Oldies

**WKCR-FM - 89.9  (22581)**
2920 Broadway
New York, NY 10027
Phone: (212)854-9920
Fax: (212)854-9296

**Format:** Jazz; Ethnic; News; Bluegrass; Classical; Alternative/New Music/Progressive

**WKDM-AM - 1380  (22582)**
449 Boardway, 2nd Fl.
New York, NY 10013
Phone: (212)966-1059
Fax: (212)704-4097
**Format:** Hispanic; Contemporary Hit Radio (CHR)

**WKIP-AM - 1450  (22755)**
20 Tucker Dr.
Poughkeepsie, NY 12603
Phone: (845)471-2300
Fax: (845)471-2683
**Format:** Music of Your Life

**WKNY-AM - 1490  (21009)**
718 Broadway
Kingston, NY 12401
Phone: (845)331-1790
Fax: (914)331-9569
**Format:** Adult Contemporary; Soft Rock

**WLAD-AM - 800  (4666)**
198 Main St.
Danbury, CT 06810
Phone: (203)744-4800
Fax: (203)778-4655
**Format:** Full Service

**WLNA-AM - 1420  (20357)**
PO Box 310
Beacon, NY 12508
Phone: (845)838-6000
Fax: (845)838-2109

**WMCA-AM - 570  (22583)**
777 Terrace Ave, 6th Floor
Hasbrouck Heights, NJ 07604-3100
Phone: (201)298-5700
Fax: (201)298-5797
**Format:** Religious

**WMNR-FM - 88.1  (4864)**
PO Box 920
Monroe, CT 06468-1981
Phone: (203)268-9667
**Format:** Classical; Big Band/Nostalgia; Classical; Big Band/Nostalgia

**WNEW-FM - 102.7  (22585)**
888 7th Ave. 10th Fl.
New York, NY 10106
Phone: (212)489-1027
Fax: (212)489-1623
**Format:** Album-Oriented Rock (AOR)

**WNWK-FM - 105.9  (22587)**
449 Broadway, 2nd Fl.
New York, NY 10013
Phone: (212)966-1059
Fax: (212)966-9580
**Format:** Talk; Ethnic; News; Religious; News; Religious

**WNYC-AM - 820  (22588)**
1 Centre St.
New York, NY 10007
Phone: (212)669-7800
Fax: (212)609-3312
**Format:** Public Radio; Information; News; Talk; Talk

**WNYC-FM - 93.9  (22589)**
1 Centre St., 24th Floor
New York, NY 10007
Phone: (212)669-7800
**Format:** Public Radio; Classical; Classical

**WNYE-FM - 91.5  (20549)**
112 Tillary St.
Brooklyn, NY 11201
Phone: (718)250-5800
Fax: (718)855-8863
**Format:** Educational

**WNYU-FM - 89.1  (22590)**
721 Broadway, 11th Fl.
New York, NY 10003
Phone: (212)998-1660
Fax: (212)998-1652
**Format:** Alternative/New Music/Progressive

**WOBM-AM - 1160  (18973)**
1015 Atlantic City Blvd.
Bayville, NJ 08721-3541
Fax: (908)364-2462

Gale Directory of Publications & Broadcast Media/140th Ed.    Philadelphia, PA

**Format:** Big Band/Nostalgia

**WPDH-FM - 101.5 (22756)**
PO Box 416
Poughkeepsie, NY 12602
Phone: (845)471-1500
Fax: (845)454-1204
**Format:** Classic Rock

**WPKF-FM - 96.1 (22757)**
20 Tucker Dr.
Poughkeepsie, NY 12603
Phone: (845)471-2300
Fax: (845)471-2683
**Format:** Contemporary Hit Radio (CHR); Urban Contemporary

**WPKN-FM - 89.5 (4642)**
244 University Ave.
Bridgeport, CT 06601
**Format:** Eclectic

**WPLJ-FM - 95.5 (22595)**
2 Penn Plaza, 17th Fl.
New York, NY 10121
Phone: (212)613-8900
Fax: (212)947-1340
**Format:** Top 40

**WPSC-FM - 88.7 (19935)**
300 Pompton Rd.
Wayne, NJ 07470
Phone: (973)720-3331
Fax: (973)720-2483
**Format:** Alternative/New Music/Progressive

**WPUB-AM - 640 (22596)**
41 Park Row
New York, NY 10038
Phone: (212)346-1270
Fax: (212)346-1563
**Format:** Alternative/New Music/Progressive; Blues; Hip Hop

**WQCD-FM - 101.9 (22597)**
395 Hudson St.
New York, NY 10014
Phone: (212)352-1019
Fax: (212)929-8559
**Format:** Jazz

**WQHT-FM - 97.1 (22598)**
395 Hudson St.
New York, NY 10014
Phone: (212)229-9797
Fax: (212)929-8559
**Format:** Contemporary Hit Radio (CHR)

**WQQQ-FM - 103.3 (4832)**
PO Box 446
Lakeville, CT 06039
Phone: (860)435-3333
Fax: (860)435-3334
**Format:** Adult Contemporary

**WRCN-FM - 103.9 (21144)**
3241 Rte. 112, Bldg. 7
Medford, NY 11763
Phone: (631)451-1039
Fax: (631)451-0891

**WRKL-AM - 910 (22716)**
Rt. 202
Pomona, NY 10970
Phone: (845)354-2000
Fax: (845)354-4796
**Format:** Talk; Full Service; News

**WRKS-FM - 98.7 (22600)**
395 Hudson St., 7th Fl.
New York, NY 10014
Phone: (212)242-9870
Fax: (212)929-8559
**Format:** Urban Contemporary

**WRNQ-FM - 92.1 (22758)**
20 Tucker Dr.
Poughkeepsie, NY 12603
Phone: (845)471-2300
Fax: (845)471-2683
**Format:** Adult Contemporary

**WRWD-FM - 107.3 (20658)**
1153 Route 44 55
Clintondale, NY 12515-5119
Phone: (914)454-2800
Fax: (914)471-0793

**Format:** Country; Contemporary Country

**WRXC-FM - 90.1 (4865)**
1014 Monroe Tpke.
Monroe, CT 06468
**Format:** Jazz; Classical; Big Band/Nostalgia

**WSKQ-FM - 97.9 (22601)**
26 W. 56th St.
New York, NY 10018
Phone: (212)541-6700
Fax: (212)977-4024
**Format:** Hispanic; Hispanic; Hispanic

**WSOU-FM - 89.5 (19833)**
400 S. Orange Ave.
South Orange, NJ 07079
Phone: (973)761-9768
Fax: (973)761-7593
**Format:** Album-Oriented Rock (AOR)

**WTHE-AM - 1520 (21215)**
260 E. 2nd St.
Mineola, NY 11501
Phone: (516)742-1520
Fax: (516)742-2878
**Format:** Religious; Gospel

**WWDJ-AM - 970 (19144)**
777 Terrace Ave.
Hasbrouck Heights, NJ 07604
Phone: (201)298-9700
Fax: (201)298-5797
**Format:** Religious

**WWPR-FM - 105.1 (22602)**
1120 6th Ave.
New York, NY 10036
Phone: (212)704-1051
Fax: (212)398-3299
**Format:** Adult Contemporary

## Philadelphia, PA

**KYW-AM - 1060 (27305)**
Independence Mall E.
Philadelphia, PA 19106-4657
Phone: (215)238-4700
Fax: (215)238-4545
**Format:** News

**WBUD-AM - 1260 (19899)**
109 Walters Ave.
Trenton, NJ 08638
Phone: (609)882-4600
Fax: (609)883-6684

**WBYO-FM - 88.9 (27524)**
PO Box 186
Sellersville, PA 18960
Phone: (215)721-2141
Fax: (215)721-9811
**Format:** Contemporary Christian; Religious; Religious

**WEST-AM - 1400 (26303)**
436 Northampton St.
Easton, PA 18042-3516
Phone: (610)258-9378
Fax: (610)250-9675
**Format:** Big Band/Nostalgia

**WFMZ-FM - 100.7 (26096)**
300 E. Rock Rd.
Allentown, PA 18103
Phone: (610)797-4530
Fax: (610)797-7289
**Format:** Adult Contemporary

**WGLS-FM - 89.7 (19114)**
Rowan University
Glassboro, NJ 08028
Phone: (856)863-9457
Fax: (856)256-4704
**Format:** Classic Rock; Talk

**WGPA-AM - 1100 (26176)**
528 N. New St.
Bethlehem, PA 18018
Phone: (610)866-8074
Fax: (610)866-9381
**Format:** News; Information; Oldies; Polka

**WHAT-AM - 1340 (27308)**
10 Shurs Ln., Ste. 204
Philadelphia, PA 19127
Phone: (267)285-5161
Fax: (267)285-5185

**Format:** Talk; Gospel

**WHOL-AM - 1600 (26098)**
1125 Colorado St.
Allentown, PA 18103
Phone: (610)434-4801
Fax: (215)663-9765
**Format:** Religious; Hispanic; Talk

**WIP-AM - 610 (27310)**
441 N. 5th St.
Philadelphia, PA 19123
Phone: (215)922-5000
Fax: (215)922-2434
**Format:** Sports

**WJJZ-FM - 106.1 (27311)**
440 Domino Ln.
Philadelphia, PA 19128
Phone: (215)508-1200
Fax: (215)509-1083
**Format:** Jazz

**WKAP-AM - 1470 (27685)**
1541 Alta Dr., Ste. 400
Whitehall, PA 18052
Phone: (610)434-1742
Fax: (610)434-6288
**Format:** Big Band/Nostalgia

**WKDU-FM - 91.7 (27312)**
3210 Chestnut St.
Philadelphia, PA 19104
Phone: (215)895-5920
Fax: (215)895-1414
**Format:** Jazz; Ethnic; Religious; Urban Contemporary; Alternative/New Music/Progressive; Urban Contemporary; Alternative/New Music/Progressive

**WLEV-FM - 96.1 (26634)**
PO Box 25096
Lehigh Valley, PA 18002
Phone: (610)266-7600
Fax: (610)250-9674
**Format:** Adult Contemporary

**WMUH-FM - 91.7 (26099)**
Muhlenberg College
2400 Chew St.
Allentown, PA 18104
Phone: (484)664-3239
Fax: (484)664-3539
**Format:** Eclectic; Educational; Ethnic

**WPAZ-AM - 1370 (27455)**
Broadcast Lodge
224 Maugers Mill Rd.
Pottstown, PA 19464
Phone: (610)326-4000
Fax: (610)326-7984
**Format:** News; Talk; Sports

**WPHE-AM - 690 (27313)**
PO Box 46325
Philadelphia, PA 19160-6327
Phone: (215)739-3083
Fax: (215)739-1337
**Format:** Talk; News; Religious

**WPHI-FM - 103.9 (26261)**
1000 River Rd., Ste. 400
Conshohocken, PA 19428
Phone: (610)276-1100
Fax: (610)276-1139
**Format:** Urban Contemporary

**WPHT-AM - 1210 (26140)**
10 Monument Rd.
Bala Cynwyd, PA 19004
Phone: (610)668-5800
Fax: (610)668-5888
**Format:** Talk

**WRAW-AM - 1340 (27471)**
1265 Perkiomen Ave.
Reading, PA 19602-1366
Phone: (610)376-6671
Fax: (610)376-1270

**WRFY-FM - 102.5 (27472)**
1265 Perkiomen Ave.
Reading, PA 19602
Phone: (610)376-6671
Fax: (610)376-1270

# PITTSBURGH, PA

**Format:** Contemporary Hit Radio (CHR)

**WRNJ-AM - 1510 (19132)**
PO Box 1000
Hackettstown, NJ 07840-1000
Phone: (908)850-1000
Fax: (908)852-8000
**Format:** Full Service; Talk; Oldies

**WSSJ-AM - 1310 (19008)**
6th & Market St.
Camden, NJ 08101
Fax: (609)365-5602
**Format:** Adult Contemporary; Top 40; Oldies

**WTKU-FM - 98.3 (19461)**
1601 New Rd.
Linwood, NJ 08221-1116
Phone: (609)601-1100
Fax: (609)601-0450
**Format:** Oldies; Adult Contemporary

**WTTH-FM - 96.1 (19700)**
8025 Black Horse Pike
Pleasantville, NJ 08232
Phone: (609)348-4040
Fax: (609)348-1303
**Format:** Urban Contemporary

**WUSL-FM - 98.9 (27319)**
440 Domino Ln.
Philadelphia, PA 19128
Phone: (215)483-8900
Fax: (800)669-9936
**Format:** Urban Contemporary

**WUSS-AM - 1490 (19462)**
1601 New Rd.
Linwood, NJ 08221
Phone: (609)601-1100
Fax: (609)601-0450
**Format:** Gospel

**WVCH-AM - 740 (26199)**
308 Dutton Mill Rd.
Brookhaven, PA 19015
Phone: (610)872-8861
Fax: (610)872-8865
**Format:** Religious; Contemporary Christian

**WWDB-FM - 96.5 (26142)**
555 E City Ave., Ste. 330
Bala Cynwyd, PA 19004-1137
**Format:** Talk

**WXPN-FM - 88.5 (27320)**
3905 Spruce St.
Philadelphia, PA 19104
Phone: (215)898-6677
Fax: (215)898-0707
**Format:** Public Radio; Alternative/New Music/Progressive; Blues; Blues

**WYSP-FM - 94.1 (27321)**
101 S. Independence Mall E.
Philadelphia, PA 19106
Phone: (215)625-9460
Fax: (215)625-6560

**WZZO-FM - 95.1 (27686)**
1541 Alta Dr., Ste. 400
Whitehall, PA 18052-5632
Phone: (610)434-1742
Fax: (610)434-9511
**Format:** Album-Oriented Rock (AOR)

# Pittsburgh, PA

**KQV-AM - 1410 (27418)**
650 Smithfield St.
Pittsburgh, PA 15222
Phone: (412)562-5900
Fax: (412)562-5936
**Format:** News

**WBGG-AM - 970 (27419)**
200 Fleet St., Ste. 4
Pittsburgh, PA 15220
Phone: (412)937-1441
Fax: (412)937-0323
**Format:** Sports

**WBZY-AM - 1280 (26759)**
219 Savannah Gardner Rd.
New Castle, PA 16101
Phone: (724)654-5501
Fax: (724)654-3101

**Format:** Music of Your Life

**WBZZ-FM - 93.7 (27420)**
Foster Plz. Five
Pittsburgh, PA 15220
Phone: (412)920-9400
Fax: (412)920-9444
**Format:** Contemporary Hit Radio (CHR)

**WCCS-AM - 1160 (26537)**
PO Box 1020
Indiana, PA 15701
Phone: (724)349-1160
Fax: (724)479-3500
**Format:** Full Service; Adult Contemporary

**WDDH-FM - 97.5 (27483)**
PO Box O
Ridgway, PA 15853-0250
Phone: (814)772-9700
Fax: (814)772-9750
**Format:** Country

**WDSY-FM - 107.9 (27421)**
Foster Plz. Five
651 Holiday Dr., Ste. 310
Pittsburgh, PA 15220
Phone: (412)920-9400
Fax: (412)920-9444
**Format:** Country

**WDUQ-FM - 90.5 (27422)**
Duquesne University
Pittsburgh, PA 15282-0001
Phone: (412)396-6030
Fax: (412)396-5061
**Format:** Public Radio; Jazz; News

**WFRA-AM - 1450 (26386)**
1411 Liberty St.
Franklin, PA 16323
Phone: (814)432-2188
Fax: (814)437-9372

**WISR-AM - 680 (26212)**
112 Hollywood Dr., Ste. 203
PO Box 151
Butler, PA 16003
Phone: (724)283-1500
Fax: (724)283-3005
**Format:** News; Talk

**WJPA-AM - 1450 (27652)**
98 S. Main St.
Washington, PA 15301
Phone: (724)222-2110
Fax: (724)228-2299
**Format:** News; Sports; Oldies

**WJPA-FM - 95.3 (27653)**
98 S. Main St.
Washington, PA 15301
Phone: (724)222-2110
Fax: (724)228-2299
**Format:** Oldies; News; Sports

**WKHB-AM - 620 (26786)**
1918 Lincoln Hwy.
North Versailles, PA 15137
Phone: (412)823-7000
**Format:** Talk; Full Service

**WLSW-FM - 103.9 (26259)**
PO Box 763
Connellsville, PA 15425
Phone: (724)628-2800
Fax: (724)628-7380
**Format:** Adult Contemporary

**WLTJ-FM - 92.9 (27424)**
650 Smithfield St.
Pittsburgh, PA 15222
Phone: (412)316-3342
Fax: (412)316-3387
**Format:** Adult Contemporary

**WOGG-FM - 94.9 (26206)**
123 Blaine Rd.
Brownsville, PA 15417-9330
Phone: (724)938-2000
Fax: (724)938-7824
**Format:** Hot Country

**WOXX-FM - 99.3 (26387)**
PO Box 908
Franklin, PA 16323-0908
Phone: (814)432-2188
Fax: (814)437-9372

**Format:** Adult Contemporary

**WRRK-FM - 96.9 (27434)**
650 Smithfield St, No. 2200
Pittsburgh, PA 15222-3900
Phone: (412)922-9290
Fax: (412)928-9290
**Format:** Album-Oriented Rock (AOR)

**WWCH-AM - 1300 (26245)**
PO Box 688
1168 Greenville Pike
Clarion, PA 16214
Phone: (814)226-4500
Fax: (814)226-5898
**Format:** Country

**WWSW-AM - 970 (27436)**
200 Fleet St., 4th Fl.
Pittsburgh, PA 15220-2908
Fax: (412)323-5313
**Format:** Oldies

**WWSW-FM - 94.5 (27437)**
200 Fleet St., Ste. 4th Fl.
Pittsburgh, PA 15220-2908
Fax: (412)323-5313
**Format:** Oldies

**WXDX-FM - 105.9 (27438)**
200 Fleet St.
Pittsburgh, PA 15220-2908
Phone: (412)937-1441
Fax: (412)937-0323
**Format:** Alternative/New Music/Progressive

**WZPT-FM - 100.7 (27439)**
Foster Plz. Five
651 Holiday Dr., Ste. 310
Pittsburgh, PA 15220
Phone: (412)920-9400
Fax: (412)920-9444
**Format:** Adult Contemporary

# Portland-Poland Spring, ME

**WBLM-FM - 102.9 (12571)**
1 City Center
Portland, ME 04101
Phone: (207)774-6364
Fax: (207)774-8707
**Format:** Album-Oriented Rock (AOR); Classic Rock

**WCYY-FM - 94.3 (12574)**
One City Center
Portland, ME 04101
Phone: (207)774-6364
Fax: (207)774-8707
**Format:** Alternative/New Music/Progressive

**WGAN-AM - 560 (12599)**
420 Western Ave.
South Portland, ME 04106
Phone: (207)774-4561
Fax: (207)774-3788
**Format:** Talk; News; News

**WIGY-FM - 97.5 (12453)**
150 Whitten Rd.
Augusta, ME 04330
Phone: (207)629-9000
Fax: (207)629-9007
**Format:** Adult Contemporary; Sports

**WJBQ-FM - 97.9 (12575)**
1 City Ctr.
Portland, ME 04101-4004
**Format:** Contemporary Hit Radio (CHR)

**WJTO-AM - 730 (12469)**
PO Box 308
Bath, ME 04530-0308
Phone: (207)443-6671

**WLAM-AM - 870 (12439)**
PO Box 8
Auburn, ME 04212-0008
Phone: (207)797-0780
Fax: (207)797-0368

**Format:** Big Band/Nostalgia

**WLAM-FM-1470 - 106.7 (12440)**
PO Box 8
Auburn, ME 04212-0008
**Format:** News

**WLOB-AM - 1310 (12576)**
779 Warren Ave.
Portland, ME 04103-1007
Phone: (207)773-9695
Fax: (207)761-4406
**Format:** News; Talk

**WLOB-FM - 96.3 (12577)**
779 Warren Ave.
Portland, ME 04103-1007
Phone: (207)773-9695
Fax: (207)761-4406
**Format:** News; Talk

**WSJB-FM - 91.5 (12603)**
St. Joseph's College
278 Whites Bridge Rd.
Standish, ME 04084
Phone: (207)892-6766
**Format:** Contemporary Hit Radio (CHR); Eclectic

**WTME-AM - 780 (12547)**
243 Main St.
PO Box 72
Norway, ME 04268-0072
Phone: (207)743-5911
Fax: (207)743-5913
**Format:** Talk; Sports; Sports

**WZAN-AM - 970 (12602)**
420 Western Ave.
South Portland, ME 04106-1704
Phone: (207)774-4561
Fax: (207)774-3788
**Format:** Talk

## Presque Isle, ME

**WBPW-FM - 96.9 (12585)**
PO Box 312
Presque Isle, ME 04769
Phone: (207)769-6600
Fax: (207)764-5274
**Format:** Hot Country

**WCXU-FM - 97.7 (12499)**
152 E. Green Ridge Rd.
Caribou, ME 04736
Phone: (207)473-7513
Fax: (207)472-3221
**Format:** Adult Contemporary

**WCXX-FM - 102.3 (12500)**
152 E. Green Ridge Rd.
Caribou, ME 04736
Phone: (207)473-7513
Fax: (207)472-3221
**Format:** Adult Contemporary

**WQHR-FM - 96.1 (12587)**
427 Caribou Rd.
PO Box 312
Presque Isle, ME 04769
Phone: (207)769-6600
Fax: (207)764-5274
**Format:** Adult Contemporary

**WUPI-FM - 92.1 (12588)**
c/o University of Maine
181 Main St.
Presque Isle, ME 04769
Phone: (207)768-9742
**Format:** Alternative/New Music/Progressive

## Providence, RI-New Bedford, MA

**WADK-AM - 1540 (27875)**
15 Dr. Marcus Wheatland Blvd.
PO Box 367
Newport, RI 02840
Phone: (401)846-1540
Fax: (401)846-1598
**Format:** Talk; News

**WALE-AM - 990 (27928)**
1185 N. Main St.
Providence, RI 02904
Phone: (401)521-0990
Fax: (401)521-5077

**Format:** Talk

**WBOT-FM - 97.7 (13629)**
60 Main St.
90 Warren St.
Brockton, MA 02301
Phone: (508)587-9898
**Format:** Urban Contemporary

**WHJJ-AM - 920 (27931)**
75 Oxford St., Ste. 301
Providence, RI 02905
Phone: (401)781-9979
Fax: (401)781-9329
**Format:** Talk; News; News

**WHJY-FM - 94.1 (27932)**
75 Oxford St.
Providence, RI 02905
Phone: (401)781-9979
Fax: (401)781-9329
**Format:** Album-Oriented Rock (AOR)

**WHTB-AM - 1400 (14787)**
1 Home St.
PO Box 927
Somerset, MA 02725
Phone: (508)678-9727
Fax: (508)673-0310
**Format:** Ethnic; Talk; Talk

**WINY-AM - 1350 (4983)**
45 Pomfret St.
PO Box 231
Putnam, CT 06260
Phone: (203)928-1350
Fax: (203)928-7878
**Format:** Adult Contemporary

**WJJF-AM - 1180 (27955)**
19 Railroad Ave.
Westerly, RI 02891
Phone: (401)596-6795
Fax: (401)596-6782
**Format:** Country

**WNRI-AM - 1380 (27958)**
786 Diamond Hill Rd.
Woonsocket, RI 02895
Phone: (401)769-6925
Fax: (401)762-0442
**Format:** Talk; Adult Contemporary; News

**WOTB-FM - 100.3 (27876)**
140 Thames St.
Newport, RI 02840
Phone: (401)846-6900
Fax: (401)846-1548
**Format:** Jazz

**WPEP-AM - 1570 (14838)**
41 Taunton Green
Taunton, MA 02780-3213
Phone: (508)822-1570
**Format:** News; Talk; Talk

**WPRO-AM - 630 (27848)**
1502 Wampanoag Trail
East Providence, RI 02915
Phone: (401)433-4200
Fax: (401)433-5967
**Format:** Talk; News

**WPRO-FM - 92.3 (27849)**
1502 Wampanoag Trail
East Providence, RI 02915
Phone: (401)433-4200
Fax: (401)433-5967
**Format:** Top 40

**WSNE-FM - 93.3 (27935)**
75 Oxford St.
Providence, RI 02905-4722
Phone: (401)438-9300
Fax: (401)467-2329
**Format:** Adult Contemporary

**WWRX-FM - 103.7 (27937)**
150 Chestnut St.
Providence, RI 02903
Phone: (401)273-6397
Fax: (401)272-8712

**Format:** Alternative/New Music/Progressive

## Rochester, NY

**WBBF-FM - 98.9 (22843)**
500 B Forman Bldg.
Rochester, NY 14604-1727
Fax: (716)325-5139
**Format:** Oldies

**WBSU-FM - 89.1 (20433)**
Seymour Union
Brockport, NY 14420
Phone: (585)395-2580
Fax: (585)395-5334
**Format:** Contemporary Hit Radio (CHR); Sports; News; Album-Oriented Rock (AOR); Alternative/New Music/Progressive

**WEZO-AM - 950 (22846)**
500 Forman Bldg.
Rochester, NY 14604
Fax: (716)325-5139
**Format:** Big Band/Nostalgia

**WFLK-FM - 101.7 (20826)**
481 Hamilton St.
Geneva, NY 14456-3047
Phone: (315)781-1101
Fax: (315)781-6600
**Format:** Hot Country

**WFLR-AM - 1570 (20710)**
30 Main St.
Dundee, NY 14837
Phone: (607)243-7158
Fax: (607)243-7662
**Format:** Country

**WFLR-FM - 95.9 (20711)**
30 Main St.
Dundee, NY 14837
Phone: (607)243-7158
Fax: (607)243-7662
**Format:** Adult Contemporary

**WFXF-FM - 95.1 (22847)**
207 Midtown Plz.
Rochester, NY 14604
Phone: (585)246-0440
Fax: (585)454-7065
**Format:** Classic Rock

**WGVA-AM - 1240 (20827)**
3568 Lenox Rd.
Geneva, NY 14456
Phone: (315)781-1240
Fax: (315)781-7700
**Format:** Full Service

**WHAM-AM - 1180 (22848)**
PO Box 40400
Rochester, NY 14604
Phone: (585)454-3942
Fax: (585)454-5081
**Format:** News; Talk

**WHTK-AM - 1280 (22850)**
207 Midtown Plz.
Rochester, NY 14604
Phone: (585)246-0440
Fax: (585)454-5081
**Format:** Sports; Talk

**WIRQ-FM - 94.3 (22851)**
260 Cooper Rd.
Rochester, NY 14617
Phone: (585)336-3065
Fax: (585)336-2929
**Format:** Alternative/New Music/Progressive

**WISY-FM - 102.3 (22852)**
207 Midtown Plz.
Rochester, NY 14604
Phone: (585)246-0440
Fax: (585)454-5081
**Format:** Adult Contemporary; Soft Rock

**WRMM-FM - 101.3 (22856)**
1700 HSBC Plaza
Rochester, NY 14604-2414
Phone: (585)222-1013
Fax: (716)399-5750

Springfield, MA

Format: Soft Rock

**WVOR-FM - 100.5 (22860)**
PO Box 40400
Rochester, NY 14604
Fax: (716)454-5081
**Format:** Adult Contemporary

## Springfield, MA

**WAIC-FM - 91.9 (14810)**
1000 State St.
Springfield, MA 01109
Phone: (413)736-7662
Fax: (413)737-2803
**Format:** Adult Contemporary; Jazz; Religious; Urban Contemporary

**WFCR-FM - 88.5 (13426)**
Hampshire House
University of Massachusetts
Amherst, MA 01003-9257
Phone: (413)545-0100
Fax: (413)545-2546
**Format:** Classical; Jazz; News; Folk; Public Radio

**WHMP-AM - 1400 (14327)**
15 Hampton Ave.
PO Box 268
Northampton, MA 01060
Phone: (413)586-7400
Fax: (413)585-0927
**Format:** News; Talk

**WHYN-AM - 560 (14812)**
1331 Main St.
Springfield, MA 01103
Phone: (413)781-1011
Fax: (413)734-4434
**Format:** News; Talk

**WMAS-AM - 1450 (14813)**
PO Box 9500
Springfield, MA 01102
Phone: (413)737-1414
Fax: (413)737-1488
**Format:** Music of Your Life; Middle-of-the-Road (MOR)

**WMAS-FM - 94.7 (14814)**
PO Box 9500
Springfield, MA 01102
Phone: (413)737-1414
Fax: (413)737-1488
**Format:** Adult Contemporary

**WNEK-FM - 105.1 (14815)**
Western New England College
1215 Wibraham Rd.
Springfield, MA 01119
Phone: (413)782-1582
Fax: (413)796-2111
**Format:** Full Service; Educational

**WNNZ-AM - 640 (14816)**
1331 Main St., Ste. 5
Springfield, MA 01103-1621
Phone: (413)781-1011
Fax: (413)734-4434
**Format:** Talk

**WSCB-FM - 89.9 (14817)**
263 Alden St.
Springfield, MA 01109
Phone: (413)748-3131
Fax: (413)748-3153
**Format:** Eclectic

## Syracuse, NY

**WAER-FM - 88.3 (23048)**
215 University Pl.
Syracuse, NY 13244-2110
Phone: (315)443-4021
Fax: (315)443-2148
**Format:** Public Radio; Jazz; News; Sports; News; Sports

**WBXL-FM - 90.5 (20333)**
E. Oneida St. Complex
Baker High School
Baldwinsville, NY 13027
Phone: (315)635-6010
Fax: (315)638-6150

**Format:** Adult Contemporary; Contemporary Hit Radio (CHR)

**WDWN-FM - 89.1 (20328)**
197 Franklin St.
Auburn, NY 13021
Phone: (315)255-1743
Fax: (315)255-2690
**Format:** Alternative/New Music/Progressive

**WFBL-AM - 1050 (20334)**
PO Box 1050
Baldwinsville, NY 13027
Phone: (315)635-3971
Fax: (315)635-3490
**Format:** Big Band/Nostalgia

**WITC-FM - 88.9 (20629)**
Cazenovia College Seminary St.
Cazenovia, NY 13035
Phone: (315)655-7154
Fax: (315)655-2190
**Format:** Album-Oriented Rock (AOR); Alternative/New Music/Progressive; Alternative/New Music/Progressive

**WMHR-FM - 102.9 (23055)**
4044 Makyes Rd.
Syracuse, NY 13215
Phone: (315)469-5051
Fax: (315)469-4066
**Format:** Religious

**WNTQ-FM - 93.1 (23056)**
1064 James St.
Syracuse, NY 13203-2704
Phone: (315)421-9393
Fax: (315)446-1614
**Format:** Contemporary Hit Radio (CHR)

**WOLF-AM - 1490 (23057)**
401 W. Kirkpatrick St.
Syracuse, NY 13204-1305
Phone: (315)472-0222
Fax: (315)478-7745
**Format:** Public Radio

**WPIE-AM - 1160 (23081)**
Box 1160
Trumansburg, NY 14886
**Format:** Talk; Sports

**WSCP-FM - 101.7 (22764)**
5090 Rte. 11
PO Box 640
Pulaski, NY 13142-0590
Phone: (315)298-3185
Fax: (315)298-6181
**Format:** Country; Bluegrass; Bluegrass

**WYYY-FM - 94.5 (23062)**
500 Plum St., No. 100
Syracuse, NY 13201-1127
Phone: (315)472-9797
Fax: (315)472-2323
**Format:** Adult Contemporary

**WZUN-FM - 102.1 (23063)**
235 Walton St.
Syracuse, NY 13202
Phone: (315)472-9111
Fax: (315)472-1888
**Format:** Adult Contemporary

**WZZZ-AM - 1300 (20805)**
PO Box 295
Fulton, NY 13069
Phone: (315)593-1300
Fax: (315)598-5158
**Format:** Information; Talk; Oldies

## Utica, NY

**WIBX-AM - 950 (21129)**
9418 River Rd.
Marcy, NY 13403
Phone: (315)768-9500
Fax: (315)736-0720

**WLZW-FM - 98.7 (21130)**
9418 River Rd.
Marcy, NY 13403
Phone: (315)768-9500
Fax: (315)768-1987
**Format:** Adult Contemporary

**WOUR-FM - 96.9 (23095)**
239 Genesee St.
Utica, NY 13501-3496
Phone: (315)797-0803

Fax: (315)797-7813
**Format:** Public Radio

**WOWB-FM - 105.5 (23096)**
PO Box 4490
Utica, NY 13504-4490
Phone: (315)797-9797
Fax: (315)724-8094
**Format:** Contemporary Hit Radio (CHR)

**WRNY-AM - 1350 (23098)**
239 Genesee St., No. 500
Utica, NY 13501-3412
Phone: (315)721-7827
Fax: (315)797-7813
**Format:** Big Band/Nostalgia

**WSKS-FM - 102.5 (23099)**
239 Genesee St., Suite 500
Utica, NY 13501
Phone: (315)797-0803
Fax: (315)797-7813
**Format:** Contemporary Hit Radio (CHR)

**WTLB-AM - 1310 (23126)**
39 Kellogg Rd.
Washington Mills, NY 13479
Phone: (315)797-1330
Fax: (315)738-1073

**WUTQ-AM - 1550 (23100)**
239 Genesee St.
Utica, NY 13501-3496
Phone: (315)721-7827
Fax: (315)797-7813
**Format:** Big Band/Nostalgia

## Washington, DC

**WCHA-AM - 800 (26232)**
25 Penncraft Ave., 4th Fl.
Chambersburg, PA 17201-5600
Phone: (717)264-7121
Fax: (717)263-9649
**Format:** Country

**WIKZ-FM - 95.1 (26233)**
25 Penncraft Ave.
Chambersburg, PA 17201
Phone: (717)263-0813
Fax: (717)263-9649
**Format:** Adult Contemporary

**WQCM-FM - 96.7 (26420)**
25 Penncraft Ave
Chambersburg, PA 17201
**Format:** Classic Rock

## Watertown-Carthage, NY

**WATN-AM - 1240 (23129)**
199 Wealtha Ave.
Watertown, NY 13601
Phone: (315)782-1240
Fax: (315)782-0312
**Format:** News; Talk

**WBDR-FM - 102.7 (23130)**
199 Wealtha Ave.
Watertown, NY 13601
Phone: (315)782-1240
Fax: (315)782-0312
**Format:** Country

**WMHI-FM - 102.9 (23054)**
4044 Makyes Rd.
Syracuse, NY 13215
Phone: (315)469-5051
**Format:** Religious

**WOTT-FM - 100.7 (23133)**
199 Wealtha Ave.
Watertown, NY 13601
Phone: (315)782-0103
Fax: (315)782-0312
**Format:** Classic Rock

**WPDM-AM - 1470 (22736)**
Potsdam-Canton Rd.
PO Box 348
Potsdam, NY 13676
Phone: (315)265-5510
Fax: (315)265-4040

**Format:** Oldies; Adult Contemporary

**WSNN-FM - 99.3  (22737)**
Potsdam-Canton Rd.
PO Box 348
Potsdam, NY 13676
Phone: (315)265-5510
Fax: (315)265-4040
**Format:** Adult Contemporary; Oldies

**WTOJ-FM - 103.1  (23134)**
199 Wealtha Ave.
Watertown, NY 13601
Phone: (315)782-1240
Fax: (315)782-0312
**Format:** Adult Contemporary

**WYBG-AM - 1050  (21138)**
24 Andrews St.
PO Box 298
Massena, NY 13662
Phone: (315)764-0554
Fax: (315)764-0118
**Format:** Adult Contemporary; Talk; News; Sports; Oldies

## Wilkes Barre-Scranton, PA

**WARM-AM - 590  (27694)**
600 Baltimore Dr.
Wilkes Barre, PA 18702
Phone: (570)824-9000
Fax: (570)820-0520
**Format:** Music of Your Life

**WEJL-AM - 630  (27510)**
149 Penn Ave.
Scranton, PA 18503
Phone: (717)346-6555
Fax: (717)346-6038
**Format:** Sports

**WEZX-FM - 106.9  (27511)**
149 Penn Ave.
Scranton, PA 18503
Phone: (717)961-1842
Fax: (717)346-6038
**Format:** Classic Rock

**WFBS-AM - 1280  (26160)**
114 Market St.
Berwick, PA 18603-4639
Phone: (570)752-8012
Fax: (570)752-1131
**Format:** Oldies; Sports

**WGGY-FM - 101.3  (27444)**
305 Highway 315
Pittston, PA 18640
Phone: (570)883-1111
Fax: (570)883-1360
**Format:** Country

**WGRC-FM - 91.3  (26646)**
101 Armory Blvd.
Lewisburg, PA 17837-0279
Phone: (570)523-1190
Fax: (570)523-1114
**Format:** Religious; Contemporary Christian

**WHGL-FM - 100.3  (27588)**
170 Redington Ave.
Troy, PA 16947
Phone: (570)297-0100
Fax: (570)297-3193
**Format:** Country

**WICK-AM - 1400  (27512)**
1049 N. Sekol Rd.
Scranton, PA 18504
Phone: (570)344-1221
Fax: (570)344-0996
**Format:** Oldies

**WISL-AM - 1590  (27708)**
PO Box 3638
Williamsport, PA 17701-8638
**Format:** Adult Contemporary

**WLGL-FM - 92.3  (27520)**
PO Box 90
Selinsgrove, PA 17870
Phone: (570)374-8819
Fax: (570)374-7444

**Format:** Contemporary Country

**WMLP-AM - 1380  (26716)**
Box 334
Milton, PA 17847
Phone: (570)568-1380
Fax: (570)568-1300
**Format:** Talk

**WPAM-AM - 1450  (27457)**
PO Box 732
Pottsville, PA 17901
Phone: (570)622-1450
Fax: (570)622-4690
**Format:** Classic Rock

**WPEL-AM - 1250  (26740)**
9 Locust St.
PO Box 248
Montrose, PA 18801
Phone: (570)278-2811
Fax: (570)278-1442
**Format:** Southern Gospel

**WPEL-FM - 96.5  (26741)**
9 Locust St.
PO Box 248
Montrose, PA 18801
Phone: (570)278-2811
Fax: (570)278-1442
**Format:** Religious; Easy Listening

**WPPA-AM - 1360  (27458)**
Box 540
Pottsville, PA 17901
Phone: (570)622-1360
Fax: (570)622-2822
**Format:** Adult Contemporary; News; Sports

**WQFM-FM - 92.1  (27513)**
149 Penn Ave.
Scranton, PA 18503
Phone: (570)346-6555
Fax: (570)346-6038
**Format:** Oldies

**WQFN-FM - 100.1  (27514)**
149 Penn Ave.
Scranton, PA 18503
Phone: (570)346-6555
Fax: (570)346-6038
**Format:** Oldies

**WRKC-FM - 88.5  (27701)**
133 N. Franklin St.
Wilkes Barre, PA 18711-0801
Phone: (570)208-5931
Fax: (570)825-9049
**Format:** Eclectic

**WTTC-AM - 1550  (27493)**
204 Deswand St.
Sayre, PA 18840
Phone: (570)888-7745
Fax: (570)888-9005
**Format:** Oldies

**WTTC-FM - 95.3  (27494)**
204 Desmond St.
Sayre, PA 18840-2041
Phone: (570)888-7745
Fax: (570)888-9005
**Format:** Oldies

**WVLY-FM - 100.9  (26717)**
Box 334
Milton, PA 17847
Phone: (570)568-1380
Fax: (570)568-1300
**Format:** Soft Rock

**WVMW-FM - 91.5  (27516)**
Marywood University
Scranton, PA 18509
Phone: (570)348-6202
Fax: (570)384-1817
**Format:** Eclectic

**WWDL-FM - 104.9  (27517)**
1049 N. Sekol Rd.
Scranton, PA 18504
Phone: (570)344-1221
Fax: (570)344-0996
**Format:** Adult Contemporary

**WYCK-AM - 1340  (27518)**
1049 N. Sekol Rd.
Scranton, PA 18504
Phone: (570)344-1221

Fax: (570)344-0996
**Format:** Oldies

**WYGL-AM - 1240  (27522)**
PO Box 90
Selinsgrove, PA 17870
Phone: (570)374-8819
Fax: (570)374-7444
**Format:** Contemporary Country

**WYGL-FM - 100.5  (27523)**
PO Box 90
Selinsgrove, PA 17870
Phone: (570)374-8819
Fax: (570)374-7444
**Format:** Contemporary Country

**WZYY-FM - 106.9  (27478)**
240 11th St.
PO Box 30
Renovo, PA 17764-0030
Phone: (570)923-9106
Fax: (570)923-3291
**Format:** Adult Contemporary

## Youngstown, OH

**WJST-FM - 92.1  (26760)**
219 Savannah-Gardner Rd.
New Castle, PA 16101
Phone: (724)654-5501
Fax: (724)654-3101
**Format:** Adult Contemporary; Sports

# Southern Central States

## Abilene-Sweetwater, TX

**KACU-FM - 89.7  (29040)**
1201 E Ambler St.
Abilene, TX 79699
Phone: (325)674-2441
Fax: (325)674-2417
**Format:** Public Radio; Classical; News

**KATX-FM - 97.7  (29646)**
611 W. Commerce
Eastland, TX 76448
Phone: (254)629-2621
Fax: (254)629-8520
**Format:** Country

**KBCY-FM - 99.7  (29041)**
2525 S. Danville Dr.
Abilene, TX 79606
Phone: (915)793-9700
Fax: (915)692-1576
**Format:** Full Service; Country; Country

**KEAN-AM - 1280  (29042)**
3911 S. 1st Ave.
Abilene, TX 79605
Phone: (915)676-7711
Fax: (915)676-3851
**Format:** Contemporary Country

**KEAS-AM - 1590  (29647)**
611 W. Commerce
Eastland, TX 76448
Phone: (254)629-2621
Fax: (254)619-8520
**Format:** Country

**KGNZ-FM - 88.1  (29045)**
542 Butternut
Abilene, TX 79602
Phone: (325)673-3045
Fax: (325)672-7938
**Format:** Religious; Contemporary Christian

**KORQ-FM - 96.1  (29046)**
1740 N. 1st St.
Abilene, TX 79603-7401
Phone: (915)437-9596
Fax: (915)673-1819
**Format:** Contemporary Hit Radio (CHR)

**KPSM-FM - 99.3  (29354)**
PO Box 1549
Brownwood, TX 76804
Phone: (915)646-5993
Fax: (915)643-9772

# Albuquerque (Santa Fe & Hobbs), NM

**Format:** Adult Contemporary; Religious

**KSLI-AM - 1280  (29048)**
3911 S 1st St.
Abilene, TX 79605
Phone: (915)676-7711
Fax: (915)676-3851
**Format:** Talk

**KULL-FM - 92.5  (29049)**
3911 S 1st St.
Abilene, TX 79605
Phone: (915)676-7711
Fax: (915)676-3851
**Format:** Oldies

**KVMX-FM - 96.7  (29639)**
PO Box 380789
Duncanville, TX 75138-0789
**Format:** Country

**KWKC-AM - 1340  (29050)**
1749 North 2nd
Abilene, TX 79603
Phone: (915)673-1455
Fax: (915)673-3485
**Format:** Sports; Talk

**KYYW-AM - 1470  (29051)**
3911 S 1st St.
Abilene, TX 79605
Phone: (915)676-7711
Fax: (915)676-3851
**Format:** Country

**KZQQ-AM - 1560  (29052)**
1749 N. Second
Abilene, TX 79603
Phone: (915)673-1455
Fax: (915)673-3485
**Format:** Music of Your Life; Easy Listening

## Albuquerque (Santa Fe & Hobbs), NM

**KABQ-AM - 1350  (20019)**
2700 San Pedro Dr. NE, Ste. 104
Albuquerque, NM 87110
Phone: (505)265-8331
Fax: (505)266-3836
**Format:** Hispanic

**KARS-AM - 860  (20049)**
208 N 2nd St
Belen, NM 87002
Phone: (505)864-7447
Fax: (505)864-2719
**Format:** Hispanic; Country; Hispanic; Country

**KBOM-FM - 106.7  (20173)**
2600-A Camino Entrada
Santa Fe, NM 87505
Phone: (505)471-1067
Fax: (505)473-2667
**Format:** Oldies

**KDAZ-AM - 730  (20025)**
5010 4th St. NW
PO Box 4338
Albuquerque, NM 87196
Phone: (505)345-7373
Fax: (505)345-5669
**Format:** Talk; Talk

**KEXT-FM - 104.7  (20026)**
6320 Zuni Rd. SE
Albuquerque, NM 87108
Fax: (505)266-3836
**Format:** Hispanic

**KGLX-FM - 99.1  (20090)**
1632 S. 2nd St.
Gallup, NM 87301
Phone: (505)863-9391
Fax: (505)863-9393
**Format:** Country

**KHFM-FM - 96.3  (20027)**
Radio Center
4125 Carlisle NE
Albuquerque, NM 87107
Phone: (505)889-8161
Fax: (505)878-0980

**Format:** Classical

**KHOB-AM - 1390  (20097)**
1304 W. Broadway Pl.
Hobbs, NM 88240-5508
Phone: (505)392-9292
Fax: (505)392-7579
**Format:** Oldies; Talk; Talk

**KINN-AM - 1270  (19981)**
PO Box 1848
Alamogordo, NM 88311
Phone: (505)434-1414
Fax: (505)434-2213
**Format:** News; Talk

**KKOB-AM - 770  (20028)**
500 4th St. NW
Albuquerque, NM 87102
Phone: (505)767-6700
Fax: (505)767-6767
**Format:** New Age

**KKOR-FM - 94.5  (20091)**
300 W. Aztec Ave., Ste. 200
Gallup, NM 87301
Phone: (505)863-6851
Fax: (505)863-2429
**Format:** Contemporary Hit Radio (CHR)

**KLEA-AM - 630  (20128)**
Country Club Rd.
PO Box 877
Lovington, NM 88260
Phone: (505)396-2244
Fax: (505)396-3355
**Format:** Adult Contemporary

**KLEA-FM - 101.7  (20129)**
1 Country Club Rd.
PO Box 877
Lovington, NM 88260
Phone: (505)396-2244
Fax: (505)396-3355
**Format:** Oldies

**KLMA-FM - 96.5  (20098)**
108 S. Willow
Hobbs, NM 88240-0457
Phone: (505)391-9650
Fax: (505)397-9373
**Format:** Hispanic

**KPER-FM - 95.7  (20099)**
PO Box 5967
Hobbs, NM 88241-5967
Phone: (505)393-1551
Fax: (505)007-0000
**Format:** Country

**KPZA-FM - 103.7  (20100)**
1 Radio Sq.
619 N. Turner
Hobbs, NM 88240
Phone: (505)397-4969
Fax: (505)393-4310
**Format:** Hispanic

**KRST-FM - 92.3  (20038)**
500 4th St. N.W.
Albuquerque, NM 87102-2183
Phone: (505)767-6700
Fax: (505)767-6767
**Format:** Country

**KSEL-AM - 1450  (20135)**
42437 US 70
Portales, NM 88130
Phone: (505)359-1759
Fax: (505)359-0724

**KSEL-FM - 95.3  (20136)**
42437 Clovis Hwy.
PO Box 886
Portales, NM 88130
Phone: (505)359-1759
Fax: (505)359-0724
**Format:** Country; Country

**KSVP-AM - 990  (20046)**
317 W. Quay
Artesia, NM 88210
Phone: (505)746-2751
Fax: (505)748-3748

**Format:** News; Talk; Talk

**KSWV-AM - 810  (20176)**
PO Box 1088
Santa Fe, NM 87501
Phone: (505)989-7441
Fax: (505)989-7607
**Format:** Oldies; Hispanic; Ethnic

**KTZA-FM - 92.9  (20047)**
317 W. Quay
Artesia, NM 88210
Phone: (505)746-2751
Fax: (505)748-3748
**Format:** Country

**KXXI-FM - 93.7  (20093)**
300 W. Aztec Ave., Ste. 200
Gallup, NM 87301
Phone: (505)863-6851
Fax: (505)863-2429
**Format:** Classic Rock

**KZOR-FM - 94.1  (20101)**
1 Radio Sq.
619 N. Turner
Hobbs, NM 88240
Phone: (505)397-4969
Fax: (505)393-4310
**Format:** Adult Contemporary

## Alexandria, LA

**KAPB-FM - 97.7  (12243)**
520 Chester
Box 7
Marksville, LA 71351
Phone: (318)253-9331
Fax: (318)253-5262
**Format:** Country

**KKST-FM - 98.7  (12047)**
1515 Jackson St
Alexandria, LA 71301
Phone: (318)443-7454
Fax: (318)442-2747
**Format:** Adult Contemporary

**KRRV-FM - 100.3  (12049)**
1515 Jackson St.
Alexandria, LA 71301
Phone: (318)443-7454
Fax: (318)442-2747
**Format:** Country

**KSYL-AM - 970  (12050)**
1115 Texas Ave.
PO Box 7057
Alexandria, LA 71301
Phone: (318)445-1234
Fax: (318)445-7321
**Format:** Adult Contemporary

**KZMZ-FM - 96.9  (12051)**
1515 Jackson St.
Alexandria, LA 71301
Phone: (318)443-7454
Fax: (318)443-7306
**Format:** Classic Rock; Classic Rock

## Amarillo, TX

**KACV-FM - 89.9  (29085)**
2408 S. Jackson
PO Box 447
Amarillo, TX 79178
Phone: (806)371-5222
Fax: (806)371-5258
**Format:** Jazz; Blues; Album-Oriented Rock (AOR); Classical; Alternative/New Music/Progressive; Classical; Alternative/New Music/Progressive

**KATP-FM - 101.9  (29087)**
6204 W 34th Ave.
Amarillo, TX 79109
**Format:** Country

**KBZD-FM - 99.7  (29088)**
3639 Wolflin Ave.
Amarillo, TX 79102-2119
Phone: (806)372-6543
Fax: (806)379-7993

**Format:** Blues

**KDDD-AM - 800 (29636)**
408 N. Dumas Ave.
PO Box 555
Dumas, TX 79029
Phone: (806)934-9203
Fax: (806)935-3836
**Format:** Hispanic

**KDDD-FM - 95.3 (29637)**
408 N. Dumas Ave.
PO Box 555
Dumas, TX 79029
Phone: (806)935-4141
Fax: (806)935-3836
**Format:** Country

**KDJW-AM - 1360 (29090)**
1721 Avondale St.
Amarillo, TX 79106
Phone: (806)331-2826
Fax: (806)358-9285

**KGNC-AM - 710 (29091)**
3505 Olsen Blvd.
Amarillo, TX 79109
Phone: (806)355-9801
Fax: (806)354-9450
**Format:** Talk; News; Sports; Agricultural

**KGNC-FM - 97.9 (29092)**
3505 Olsen Blvd.
Amarillo, TX 79109
Phone: (806)355-9801
Fax: (806)354-8779
**Format:** Country

**KLSR-FM - 105.3 (30161)**
114 N 7th
PO Box 400
Memphis, TX 79245
Phone: (806)259-3511
**Format:** Adult Contemporary; Contemporary Country; Contemporary Country

**KOJW-AM - 1360 (29095)**
1721 Avondale St.
Amarillo, TX 79106
Phone: (806)353-4448
Fax: (806)353-8911
**Format:** Country

**KQTY-AM - 1490 (29324)**
2112 Thornton
PO Box 165
Borger, TX 79008-0165
Phone: (806)273-7533
Fax: (806)273-3727
**Format:** Country; Classic Rock

**KSRW-FM - 96.1 (29399)**
1511 Ave. F NW
Childress, TX 79201
Phone: (940)937-6316
Fax: (940)937-6551
**Format:** Contemporary Country

**KTQM-FM - 99.9 (20065)**
PO Box 869
Clovis, NM 88102-0869
Phone: (505)762-4411
Fax: (505)769-0197
**Format:** Adult Contemporary

**KWKA-AM - 680 (20066)**
PO Box 869
Clovis, NM 88102
Phone: (505)762-4411
Fax: (505)769-0197
**Format:** Full Service; Oldies; News

## Ardmore-Ada, OK

**KADA-AM - 1230 (25236)**
1019 N. Broadway
PO Box 609
Ada, OK 74820
Phone: (580)332-1212
Fax: (580)332-0128
**Format:** News; Contemporary Country; Sports; Religious; Religious

**KALV-AM - 1430 (25247)**
Rte. 1, Box 53
Alva, OK 73717
Phone: (580)327-1430
Fax: (580)327-1433

**Format:** Talk; News; Sports; Religious; Agricultural; Country; Religious; Agricultural; Country

**KIXD-FM - 106.1 (25402)**
1101 Hwy. 81 N.
Marlow, OK 73055
Phone: (580)658-9292
**Format:** Country

**KKAJ-FM - 95.7 (25254)**
1205 Northglen
PO Box 429
Ardmore, OK 73401-0429
Phone: (405)226-0421
Fax: (405)226-0464
**Format:** Country

**KLBC-FM - 106.3 (25309)**
PO Box 190
Durant, OK 74702
Phone: (580)924-3100
Fax: (580)920-1426
**Format:** Country

**KLCU-FM - 90.3 (25391)**
2800 W. Gore Blvd.
Lawton, OK 73505
Phone: (580)581-2472
Fax: (580)581-5511
**Format:** Classical

**KVSO-AM - 1240 (25255)**
1205 Northglen
Box 429
Ardmore, OK 73402-0429
Phone: (405)226-0421
Fax: (405)226-0464
**Format:** Talk; Sports

## Austin, TX

**KASE-FM - 100.7 (29256)**
3601 S. Congress Ave., Bldg. F
Austin, TX 78704
Phone: (512)684-7300
Fax: (512)684-7441
**Format:** Country

**KAZI-FM - 88.7 (29257)**
8906 Wall St., Ste. 202
Austin, TX 78754-4542
Phone: (512)836-2887
Fax: (512)836-1146
**Format:** Urban Contemporary; Jazz; Gospel; Rap; Hip Hop; Reggae; Rap; Hip Hop; Reggae

**KELG-AM - 1440 (29258)**
7524 N. Lamar Blvd., Ste. 200
Austin, TX 78752
Phone: (512)453-1491
Fax: (512)453-6809
**Format:** Hispanic

**KHHL-FM - 98.9 (29261)**
12710 Research Blvd., Ste. 390
Austin, TX 78759
Phone: (512)331-9191
Fax: (512)331-9933
**Format:** Adult Contemporary

**KKMJ-FM - 95.5 (29264)**
4301 Westbank Dr., Bldg. B, Ste. 350
Austin, TX 78746
Phone: (512)327-9595
Fax: (512)329-6252
**Format:** Adult Contemporary

**KLBJ-AM - 590 (29265)**
8309 I H 35 North
Austin, TX 78753
Phone: (512)832-4051
Fax: (512)832-4063
**Format:** Talk; News; Sports; Sports

**KVET-AM - 1300 (29272)**
3601 S. Congress Ave., Bldg. F
Building F
Austin, TX 78704
Phone: (512)495-1300
Fax: (512)495-9423
**Format:** Country

**KVET-FM - 98.1 (29273)**
705 N. Lamar Blvd.
Austin, TX 78703
Phone: (512)495-1300
Fax: (512)499-0249

**Format:** Country

## Baton Rouge, LA

**KKAY-AM - 1590 (12149)**
706 Railroad Ave.
Donaldsonville, LA 70346-3338
Phone: (225)473-6397
Fax: (225)473-6397
**Format:** Cajun; Zydeco

**KLSU-FM - 91.1 (12093)**
Louisiana State University
39 Hodges Hall
Baton Rouge, LA 70803
Phone: (225)578-8688
Fax: (225)578-0579
**Format:** Alternative/New Music/Progressive

**WBRH-FM - 90.3 (12098)**
2825 Government St.
Baton Rouge, LA 70806
Phone: (225)383-3243
Fax: (225)379-7685
**Format:** Public Radio; Jazz

**WDGL-FM - 98.1 (12100)**
PO Box 2231
Baton Rouge, LA 70801-2231
Phone: (225)388-9898
Fax: (225)499-9800
**Format:** Classic Rock

**WFMF-FM - 102.5 (12102)**
5555 Hilton Ave., Ste. 500
Baton Rouge, LA 70808
Phone: (225)231-1860
Fax: (225)231-1879
**Format:** Contemporary Hit Radio (CHR)

**WJBO-AM - 1150 (12103)**
5555 Hilton Ave., 5th Fl.
Baton Rouge, LA 70809
Phone: (504)231-1860
Fax: (504)231-1869
**Format:** Talk; News

**WKAY-AM - 1590 (12150)**
706 Railroad
Donaldsonville, LA 70346
Phone: (225)473-6397
Fax: (225)474-0073
**Format:** Cajun; Zydeco

**WLSS-FM - 102.5 (12105)**
5555 Hilton Ave. 5th Fl.
Baton Rouge, LA 70806
Phone: (504)231-1860
Fax: (504)231-1869
**Format:** Contemporary Hit Radio (CHR)

**WNDC-AM - 910 (12106)**
PO Box 52951
Baton Rouge, LA 70892-2951
**Format:** Gospel

**WQCK-FM - 92.7 (12056)**
13567 Plank Rd.
Baker, LA 70714
Phone: (225)775-5557
Fax: (225)774-7785
**Format:** Adult Contemporary; Religious

**WSKR-AM - 1210 (12108)**
5555 Hilton Ave., Ste. 500
Baton Rouge, LA 70808
Phone: (225)231-1860
Fax: (225)231-1869
**Format:** Sports

**WYNK-AM - 1380 (12110)**
5555 Hilton Ave., No. 500
Baton Rouge, LA 70808-2597
Phone: (225)231-1860
Fax: (225)231-1869

## Beaumont-Port Arthur, TX

**KAYC-AM - 1450 (30210)**
117 Nederland Ave.
PO Box 870
Nederland, TX 77627
Phone: (409)724-1292
Fax: (409)724-7055

# Beaumont-Port Arthur, TX

**Format:** Sports

**KCOL-FM - 92.5  (29294)**
27 Sawyer St.
PO Box 22257
Beaumont, TX 77720-2257
Phone: (409)832-9250
Fax: (409)832-5686
**Format:** Oldies

**KQHN-AM - 1510  (29297)**
755 S. 11th St., Ste. 102
Beaumont, TX 77701
Phone: (409)833-9421
Fax: (409)833-9296
**Format:** Gospel

**KTXB-FM - 89.7  (30141)**
PO Box 1358
Mauriceville, TX 77626
Phone: (409)745-1737
**Format:** Religious; Gospel

**KTXJ-AM - 1350  (29998)**
Hwy. 190 E.
PO Box 2008
Jasper, TX 75951
Phone: (409)384-6801
Fax: (409)384-3866
**Format:** News

**KWYX-FM - 102.7  (29999)**
Hwy. 190 E.
PO Box 2008
Jasper, TX 75951
Phone: (409)384-6801
Fax: (409)384-3866
**Format:** Country

**KZZB-AM - 990  (29300)**
2531 Calder St.
Beaumont, TX 77702
Phone: (409)833-0990
Fax: (409)833-0995
**Format:** Contemporary Hit Radio (CHR)

## Corpus Christi, TX

**KBNJ-FM - 91.7  (29465)**
3766 Saturn Rd.
PO Box 3765
Corpus Christi, TX 78413
Phone: (361)561-0231
Fax: (361)855-0977
**Format:** Religious; Ethnic

**KCCT-AM - 1150  (29466)**
Box 5278
Corpus Christi, TX 78405
Phone: (361)289-0000
Fax: (361)289-6215
**Format:** Hispanic

**KEYS-AM - 1440  (29468)**
PO Box 9757
Corpus Christi, TX 78469-9757
Phone: (361)882-7411
Fax: (361)882-9767
**Format:** News; Talk; Sports

**KKTX-AM - 1360  (29472)**
Radio Plaza
501 Tupper Lane
Corpus Christi, TX 78417
Phone: (361)289-0111
Fax: (361)289-5035
**Format:** Talk; News

**KLTG-FM - 96.5  (29473)**
1300 Antelope
PO Box 898
Corpus Christi, TX 78403
Phone: (316)883-1600
Fax: (361)888-5685
**Format:** Oldies

**KOUL-FM - 103.7  (29477)**
1300 Antelope
PO Box 898
Corpus Christi, TX 78403
Fax: (512)883-9303
**Format:** Country

**KSIX-AM - 1230  (29481)**
710 Buffalo St., Ste. 608
Box TV-10
Corpus Christi, TX 78401
Phone: (361)882-5749

Fax: (361)884-1240
**Format:** News

**KZFM-FM - 95.5  (29482)**
PO Box 9757
Corpus Christi, TX 78469-9757
Phone: (361)560-5595
Fax: (361)882-9767
**Format:** Contemporary Hit Radio (CHR)

## Dallas-Fort Worth, TX

**KAAM-AM - 1310  (29580)**
15851 Dallas Pkwy., Ste. 1200
Dallas, TX 75248
Phone: (214)770-7777
Fax: (214)770-7747
**Format:** Big Band/Nostalgia

**KBFB-FM - 97.9  (29581)**
13331 Preston Rd., Ste. 1180
Dallas, TX 75240
Phone: (972)331-5400
Fax: (972)331-5560
**Format:** Soft Rock

**KCBI-FM - 90.9  (29116)**
411 Ryan Plaza Drive
Arlington, TX 76011
Phone: (817)792-3800
Fax: (817)277-9929

**KCOM-AM - 1550  (29449)**
PO Box 9
Comanche, TX 76442
Phone: (915)356-2558
Fax: (915)356-5757
**Format:** Country; Religious; Hispanic; Hispanic

**KDFT-AM - 540  (29584)**
PO Box 411540
Dallas, TX 75241-8540
Phone: (214)337-5994
Fax: (214)337-6076
**Format:** Southern Gospel

**KDMX-FM - 102.9  (29586)**
14001 Dallas Pkwy., No. 300
Dallas, TX 75240-4346
Phone: (972)991-1029
Fax: (972)448-1029
**Format:** Adult Contemporary

**KERA-FM - 90.1  (29589)**
3000 Harry Hines Blvd.
Dallas, TX 75201
Phone: (214)740-9248
Fax: (214)740-9009
**Format:** Full Service; Public Radio; News; Information; Adult Album Alternative

**KESS-AM - 1270  (29591)**
7700 John W. Carpenter Fwy.
Dallas, TX 75247
Phone: (214)630-9202
Fax: (214)920-2570
**Format:** Hispanic

**KFJZ-AM - 870  (29732)**
4240 Brair Creek
PO Box 6158
Fort Worth, TX 76115-0158
Phone: (817)336-7175
Fax: (817)338-1205
**Format:** Hispanic

**KFXR-AM - 1190  (29056)**
15851 N Dallas Pkwy., Ste. 1200
Addison, TX 75001
Phone: (972)770-7777
Fax: (972)770-7737
**Format:** Sports

**KGVL-AM - 1400  (29783)**
PO Box 1015
Greenville, TX 75403
Phone: (903)455-1400
Fax: (903)455-5485
**Format:** Country

**KHKS-FM - 106.1  (29592)**
14001 Dallas Pkwy., Ste. 300
Dallas, TX 75240-1358
Phone: (214)866-8000
Fax: (214)866-8501

**Format:** Top 40

**KHVN-AM - 970  (29593)**
5787 S Hampton Rd., Ste. 285
Dallas, TX 75232
Phone: (214)331-5486
Fax: (214)331-1908
**Format:** Gospel

**KHYI-FM - 95.3  (30286)**
PO Box 940670
Plano, TX 75094
Phone: (972)396-1640
Fax: (972)396-1643
**Format:** Country; Sports

**KIKT-FM - 93.5  (29784)**
PO Box 1015
Greenville, TX 75403
Phone: (903)455-1400
Fax: (903)455-5485
**Format:** Country

**KLUV-FM - 98.7  (29595)**
4131 N. Central Expy., No. 700
Dallas, TX 75204
Phone: (214)526-9870
Fax: (214)443-1570
**Format:** Oldies

**KNES-FM - 99.1  (29688)**
627 W. Commerce
PO Box 347
Fairfield, TX 75840
Phone: (903)389-5637
Fax: (903)389-7172
**Format:** Country; Gospel

**KNIN-FM - 92.9  (30643)**
2525 Kell Blvd., Suite 200
Wichita Falls, TX 76308
Phone: (940)763-1111
Fax: (940)322-3166
**Format:** Contemporary Hit Radio (CHR)

**KPLX-FM - 99.5  (29597)**
3500 Maple at Turtle Creek, Ste. 1600
Dallas, TX 75219
Phone: (214)526-2400
Fax: (214)520-4343
**Format:** Contemporary Country

**KPYK-AM - 1570  (30536)**
1412-C West Moore Ave.
PO Box 157
Terrell, TX 75160
Phone: (972)524-5795
Fax: (972)524-5795
**Format:** Big Band/Nostalgia; Easy Listening; Talk

**KTCU-FM - 88.7  (29733)**
TCU Box 298020
Fort Worth, TX 76129
Phone: (817)921-7634
Fax: (817)921-7703
**Format:** Full Service

**KTCY-FM - 104.9  (30144)**
5307 E. Mockingbird Ln., Ste. 500
Dallas, TX 75206-5118
Phone: (214)887-9107
Fax: (214)841-4215
**Format:** Hispanic

**KTNO-AM - 1540  (29119)**
3105 Arkansas Ln.
Arlington, TX 76016
Phone: (817)469-1540
Fax: (817)261-2137
**Format:** Hispanic; Religious

**KXEB-AM - 910  (29599)**
5307 E. Mockingbird Ln., Ste. 500
Dallas, TX 75206-5118
Phone: (214)528-1600
Fax: (214)528-4667
**Format:** Hispanic

**KXVI-FM - 95.9  (29758)**
PO Box 497933
Garland, TX 75049
Fax: (972)675-8652
**Format:** News; Talk; Contemporary Christian

**KYNG-FM - 105.3  (29601)**
12201 Merit Dr., No. 930
Dallas, TX 75251
Phone: (972)716-7800
Fax: (972)716-7835

Gale Directory of Publications & Broadcast Media/140th Ed.  Houston, TX

**Format:** Country

## El Paso, TX (Las Cruces, NM)

**KBNA-AM - 920 (29664)**
2211 E. Missouri Ave., No. 300
El Paso, TX 79903-3813
Phone: (915)544-9797
Fax: (915)544-1247
**Format:** Hispanic

**KBNA-FM - 97.5 (29665)**
2211 E. Missouri Ave., Ste. 300
El Paso, TX 79903-3813
Phone: (915)544-9797
Fax: (915)544-1247
**Format:** Hispanic

**KDEM-FM - 94.3 (20070)**
Box 470
Deming, NM 88030
Phone: (505)546-9011
Fax: (505)546-9342
**Format:** Adult Contemporary

**KELP-AM - 1590 (29667)**
6900 Commerce Ave.
El Paso, TX 79915-1102
Phone: (915)779-0016
Fax: (915)779-6641
**Format:** Religious; Talk

**KGRT-FM - 103.9 (20110)**
PO Box 968
1355 E. California
Las Cruces, NM 88004
Phone: (505)525-9298
Fax: (505)525-9419
**Format:** Country

**KHEY-AM - 1380 (29669)**
4045 N. Mesa
El Paso, TX 79902
Phone: (915)351-5400
Fax: (915)351-3102
**Format:** Sports

**KHEY-FM - 96.3 (29670)**
4045 N. Mesa St.
El Paso, TX 79902
Phone: (915)351-5400
Fax: (915)351-3102
**Format:** Country

**KHQT-FM - 103.1 (20111)**
PO Box 968
1355 E. California
Las Cruces, NM 88004
Phone: (505)525-9298
Fax: (505)525-9419
**Format:** Contemporary Hit Radio (CHR)

**KINT-FM - 93.9 (29671)**
5426 N Mesa St.
El Paso, TX 79912
Phone: (915)581-1126
Fax: (915)585-4611
**Format:** Ethnic; Hispanic

**KKVS-FM - 98.7 (20112)**
PO Box 968
1355 E. California
Las Cruces, NM 88004
Phone: (505)525-9298
Fax: (505)525-9419
**Format:** Hispanic

**KMVR-FM - 104.9 (20113)**
PO Drawer 1838
Las Cruces, NM 88004-1838
Phone: (505)526-2496
Fax: (505)523-3918
**Format:** Adult Contemporary

**KOBE-AM - 1450 (20114)**
PO Drawer 1838
Las Cruces, NM 88004
Phone: (505)526-2496
Fax: (505)523-3918
**Format:** News; Talk; Sports

**KOTS-AM - 1230 (20071)**
Box 470
Deming, NM 88031-0470
Phone: (505)546-9011
Fax: (505)546-9342

**Format:** Country; Hispanic

**KPRR-FM - 102.1 (29675)**
4045 N. Mesa St.
El Paso, TX 79902-1526
Fax: (915)566-0928
**Format:** Contemporary Hit Radio (CHR)

**KRSY-AM - 1230 (19982)**
PO Box 2710
Alamogordo, NM 88311
Phone: (505)437-1505
Fax: (505)437-5566
**Format:** Sports; Talk; News

**KRSY-FM - 92.7 (19983)**
PO Box 2710
Alamogordo, NM 88311-2710
Phone: (505)437-1505
Fax: (505)437-5566
**Format:** Country

**KRWG-FM - 90.7 (20115)**
PO Box 3000
Las Cruces, NM 88003
Phone: (505)646-4525
Fax: (505)646-1974
**Format:** Public Radio; Classical; Jazz; News; Jazz; News

**KSNM-AM - 570 (20117)**
1355 E. California
PO Box 968
Las Cruces, NM 88004
Phone: (505)525-9298
Fax: (505)525-9419
**Format:** Middle-of-the-Road (MOR)

**KSVE-AM - 1150 (29678)**
5426 N Mesa St.
El Paso, TX 79912-5421
Phone: (915)581-1126
Fax: (915)585-4611
**Format:** Talk; Talk

**KVER-FM - 91.1 FM (29680)**
PO Box 12008
El Paso, TX 79913-0008
Phone: (915)544-9190
**Format:** Hispanic; Religious

## Fort Smith, AR

**KAYR-AM - 1060 (1304)**
4608 Radio Tower Rd.
Van Buren, AR 72956-8696
Phone: (501)474-3422
Fax: (501)474-2649
**Format:** Hispanic

**KBBQ-FM - 100.7 (1098)**
323 N. Greenwood
PO Box 303 72902
Fort Smith, AR 72901
Phone: (501)783-5379
Fax: (501)785-2638
**Format:** Oldies

**KERX-FM - 95.3 (1006)**
1912 Church St.
Barling, AR 72923-2305
Phone: (479)484-7285
Fax: (479)484-7290
**Format:** Adult Album Alternative

**KFPW-AM - 1230 (1099)**
323 N. Greenwood
PO Box 303 72902
Fort Smith, AR 72901
Phone: (501)783-5379
Fax: (501)785-2638
**Format:** Easy Listening

**KFSA-AM - 950 (1100)**
6420 S. Zero St.
PO Box 6210
Fort Smith, AR 72901
Phone: (479)646-6700
Fax: (479)646-1373
**Format:** News; Southern Gospel

**KHGG-AM - 1580 (1103)**
PO Box 573
Fort Smith, AR 72902-0573
Phone: (501)288-1047
Fax: (501)288-0942

**Format:** Sports; Talk

**KKBD-FM - 95.9 (1104)**
423 Garrison Ave.
Fort Smith, AR 72901-1931
Phone: (479)782-8888
Fax: (479)785-5946
**Format:** Classic Rock

**KKEG-FM - 92.1 (1084)**
24 E. Meadow St., No. 1
Fayetteville, AR 72701-5320
Phone: (479)587-9921
Fax: (479)587-9920
**Format:** News; Sports; Album-Oriented Rock (AOR); Classic Rock

**KLSZ-FM - 102.7 (1305)**
4608 Radio Tower Rd.
Van Buren, AR 72956-8696
Phone: (501)474-3422
Fax: (501)474-2649
**Format:** Classic Rock

**KMAG-FM - 99.1 (1105)**
311 Lexington Ave.
Fort Smith, AR 72901-1931
Phone: (479)782-8888
Fax: (479)785-5946
**Format:** Country

**KTCS-AM - 1410 (1106)**
Box 180188
Fort Smith, AR 72918-0188
Phone: (479)646-6151
Fax: (479)646-3509
**Format:** Contemporary Country

**KTCS-FM - 99.9 (1107)**
Box 180188
Fort Smith, AR 72918-0188
Phone: (479)646-6151
Fax: (479)646-3509
**Format:** Hot Country

**KUOA-AM - TER0 (1288)**
2000 W University
Siloam Springs, AR 72761
Phone: (479)524-7360
Fax: (479)524-7451
**Format:** Talk

**KWHN-AM - 1650 (1108)**
311 Lexington Ave.
Fort Smith, AR 72901-1931
Phone: (479)782-8888
Fax: (479)785-5946
**Format:** News; Talk; Sports

**KYHN-AM - 1320 (1109)**
423 Garrison Ave.
Fort Smith, AR 72901-1931
Phone: (479)782-8888
Fax: (479)785-5946
**Format:** News; Talk; Sports

**KZBB-FM - 97.9 (1110)**
311 Lexington Ave.
Fort Smith, AR 72901-1931
Phone: (479)782-8888
Fax: (479)785-5946
**Format:** Contemporary Hit Radio (CHR)

**KZKZ-FM - 106.3 (1111)**
PO Box 6210
Fort Smith, AR 72906
Phone: (479)646-6700
Fax: (479)646-1373
**Format:** Contemporary Christian

## Houston, TX

**KANI-AM - 1500 (30632)**
215 Milam
Wharton, TX 77488
Phone: (979)532-3800
Fax: (979)532-8510
**Format:** Country; Talk; Religious

**KBME-AM - 790 (29924)**
2000 W. Loop S.
Houston, TX 77027
Phone: (713)212-8000
Fax: (713)212-8963

Circulation: ★ = ABC; △ = BPA; ♦ = CAC; • = CCAB; ▢ = VAC; ⊕ = PO Statement; ‡ = Publisher's Report; Boldface figures = sworn; Light figures = estimated.    4297

**Jonesboro, AR**

Format: Sports

**KCOH-AM - 1430 AM (29925)**
5011 Almeda Rd.
Houston, TX 77004
Phone: (713)522-1001
Fax: (713)521-0769
Format: Talk; Urban Contemporary

**KHCB-FM - 105.7 (29927)**
2424 South Blvd.
Houston, TX 77098
Phone: (713)520-5200
Format: Religious

**KIKK-AM - 650 (29933)**
24 E Greenway Plz., Ste. 1900
Houston, TX 77046-2419
Phone: (713)881-5100
Fax: (713)881-5271
Format: Country

**KIKK-FM - 95.7 (29934)**
24 Greenway Plz., Ste. 1900
Houston, TX 77046-2419
Phone: (713)881-5100
Fax: (713)881-5271
Format: Country

**KILT-AM - 610 (29935)**
24 Greenway Plz., Ste. 1900
Houston, TX 77046-2419
Format: Sports

**KILT-FM - 100.3 (29936)**
24 Greenway Plaza., Ste. 1900
Houston, TX 77046-2419
Phone: (713)881-5100
Fax: (713)881-5271
Format: Country

**KIOX-AM - 1270 (29283)**
Box 2340
Bay City, TX 77404-2340
Fax: (979)245-6463
Format: Country

**KJOJ-FM - 103.3 (29937)**
3000 Bering Dr.
Houston, TX 77057
Phone: (713)315-3400
Fax: (713)315-3565
Format: Hispanic

**KLDE-FM - 107.5 (29940)**
1990 Post Oak Blvd., Ste. 2300
Houston, TX 77056-3847
Phone: (713)390-5533
Fax: (713)622-7479
Format: Oldies

**KMIC-AM - 1590 (29944)**
3050 Post Oak Blvd., No. 220
Houston, TX 77056-6515
Phone: (713)552-1590
Fax: (713)552-1588

**KMJQ-FM - 102.1 (29945)**
24 Greenway Plaza, No. 1508
Houston, TX 77046
Phone: (713)390-5102
Fax: (713)623-0106
Format: Urban Contemporary

**KODA-FM - 99.1 (29946)**
3050 Post Oak Blvd., 12th Fl.
Houston, TX 77056
Phone: (713)390-5991
Fax: (713)830-8099
Format: Adult Contemporary

**KPFT-FM - 90.1 (29947)**
419 Lovett Blvd.
Houston, TX 77006
Phone: (713)526-4000
Fax: (713)526-5750
Format: Adult Contemporary

**KRBE-FM - 104 (29949)**
9801 Westheimer, No. 700
PO Box 1432
Houston, TX 77042
Phone: (713)266-1000
Fax: (713)954-2344

Format: Contemporary Hit Radio (CHR)

**KSBJ-FM - 89.3 (29966)**
327 Wilson Rd.
Humble, TX 77338
Phone: (281)446-5725
Fax: (281)540-2198
Format: Religious; Contemporary Christian

**KSEV-AM - 700 (29951)**
11451 Katy Fwy., Ste. 215
Houston, TX 77079
Phone: (281)558-5738
Fax: (281)588-4800
Format: News; Talk; Sports

**KTBZ-FM - 94.5 (29952)**
2000 West Loop S., Suite 300
Houston, TX 77027
Phone: (713)212-8000
Fax: (713)212-8945
Format: Alternative/New Music/Progressive

**KTEK-AM - 1110 (29953)**
6161 Savoy, Ste. 1200
Houston, TX 77036
Phone: (713)260-3600
Fax: (713)260-3628
Format: Religious; Talk; Ethnic

**KTSU-FM - 90.9 (29959)**
3100 Cleburne Ave.
Houston, TX 77004
Phone: (713)313-7591
Fax: (713)313-7479
Format: Jazz; Religious; Oldies; Oldies

**KWHI-AM - 1280 (29334)**
Box 1280
Brenham, TX 77833
Phone: (979)836-3655
Fax: (979)830-8141
Format: Country

**KWWJ-AM - 1360 (29287)**
4638 Decker Dr.
Baytown, TX 77520
Phone: (281)837-8777
Fax: (281)424-7588
Format: Religious

**KYND-AM - 1520 (29962)**
PO Box 19886
Houston, TX 77224
Phone: (281)373-1520
Format: Public Radio

**Jonesboro, AR**

**KBTM-AM - 1230 (1151)**
PO Box 1737
Jonesboro, AR 72403
Phone: (870)932-1079
Fax: (870)932-3814
Format: News; Talk

**KFCM-FM - 98.3 (1039)**
PO Box 909
Cherokee Village, AR 72525
Phone: (870)856-3630
Fax: (870)856-4088
Format: Oldies

**KPOC-AM - 1420 (1262)**
No. 1 Radio Dr.
Pocahontas, AR 72455
Phone: (870)892-5234
Fax: (870)892-5235
Format: News; Sports

**KPOC-FM - 103.9 (1263)**
No. 1 Radio Dr.
Pocahontas, AR 72455
Phone: (870)892-5234
Fax: (870)892-5235
Format: Adult Contemporary

**KRLW-AM - 1320 (1264)**
PO Box 508
Pocahontas, AR 72455
Phone: (870)892-5234
Fax: (870)892-5235
Format: Oldies

**KRLW-FM - 106.3 (1265)**
PO Box 508
Pocahontas, AR 72455
Phone: (870)892-5234

Fax: (870)892-5235
Format: Country

**KWHF-FM - 95.9 (1156)**
PO Box 1737
Jonesboro, AR 72403
Phone: (870)932-8400
Fax: (870)932-3814
Format: Country

**Lafayette, LA**

**KAJN-FM - 102.9 (12139)**
110 W. 3rd St.
Crowley, LA 70526
Phone: (318)783-1560
Fax: (318)783-1674
Format: Religious

**KDYS-AM - 1520 (12196)**
202 Galbert Rd
Lafayette, LA 70506
Phone: (337)232-1311
Fax: (337)233-3779
Format: Educational

**KEUN-AM - 1490 (12154)**
330 W. Laurel Ave.
Eunice, LA 70535
Phone: (318)457-3041
Fax: (318)457-3081
Format: Country; Sports; News; Cajun

**KFXZ-FM - 106.3 (12197)**
3225 Ambassador Caffery Pkwy.
Lafayette, LA 70506-7214
Fax: (318)988-0443
Format: Urban Contemporary

**KJCB-AM - 770 (12198)**
413 Jefferson St.
Lafayette, LA 70501-7057
Phone: (318)233-4262
Format: Jazz; Religious; Urban Contemporary; Oldies; Urban Contemporary; Oldies

**KJJB-FM - 105.5 (12155)**
330 W. Laurel Ave.
Eunice, LA 70535-3306
Phone: (318)457-3041
Fax: (318)457-3081
Format: Country

**KNIR-AM - 1360 (12292)**
PO Box 12948
New Iberia, LA 70562-2948
Fax: (318)365-6314

**KOGM-FM - 107.1 (12360)**
PO Box 1150
Opelousas, LA 70570
Phone: (337)942-2633
Fax: (337)942-2635
Format: Oldies

**KPEL-FM - 105.1 (12201)**
1749 Bertrand Dr.
PO Box 3706
Lafayette, LA 70506
Phone: (337)233-7003
Fax: (337)234-7360
Format: Talk

**KSLO-AM - 1230 (12361)**
216 N Ct.
PO Box 1150
Opelousas, LA 70571-1150
Phone: (337)942-2633
Fax: (337)942-2635
Format: News; Information; Country; Contemporary Country; Agricultural; French

**KSMB-FM - 94.5 (12203)**
PO Box 3345
Lafayette, LA 70502
Phone: (337)232-1311
Fax: (337)233-3779
Format: Top 40

**KVOL-AM - 1330 (12204)**
202 Galbert Rd.
PO Box 3345
Lafayette, LA 70506-1806
Phone: (337)233-1330
Fax: (337)237-7733

**Format:** Sports; Talk

**KVOL-FM - 105.9 (12205)**
202 Galbert Rd.
PO Box 3345
Lafayette, LA 70502
Phone: (337)233-1330
Fax: (337)233-3779
**Format:** Talk; Sports

**KVPI-AM - 1050 (12424)**
809 W. LaSalle St.
PO Drawer J
Ville Platte, LA 70586
Phone: (337)363-2124
Fax: (337)363-3574
**Format:** News

**KVPI-FM - 92.5 (12425)**
809 W. LaSalle St.
PO Drawer J
Ville Platte, LA 70586
Phone: (337)363-2124
Fax: (337)363-3574
**Format:** Oldies

**KXKC-FM - 99.1 (12206)**
202 Galbert Road
PO Box 3345
Lafayette, LA 70502
Phone: (337)232-1311
**Format:** Contemporary Country

## Lake Charles, LA

**KEZM-AM - 1310 (12412)**
101 W. Napoleon St.
Sulphur, LA 70663-3343
Phone: (337)527-3611
Fax: (337)527-0213
**Format:** Sports

**KHLA-FM - 99.5 (12218)**
900 N Lakeshore Dr.
PO Box 3067
Lake Charles, LA 70601
Phone: (337)433-1641
Fax: (337)433-2999
**Format:** Adult Contemporary

**KLCL-AM - 1470 (12219)**
900 N Lakeshore Dr.
PO Box 3067
Lake Charles, LA 70601-3067
Phone: (337)433-1641
Fax: (337)433-2999
**Format:** Cajun; Country

**KYKZ-FM - 96.1 (12223)**
425 Broad St.
Lake Charles, LA 70601
Phone: (337)439-3300
Fax: (337)433-7701
**Format:** Contemporary Country

## Laredo, TX

**KLAR-AM - 1300 (30049)**
PO Box 2517
Laredo, TX 78044-2517
Phone: (210)723-7459
Fax: (210)723-4471
**Format:** News; Talk

**KRRG-FM - 98.1 (30050)**
902 E. Calton St.
Laredo, TX 78042-6117
Fax: (512)724-9813
**Format:** Adult Contemporary; Contemporary Hit Radio (CHR)

## Little Rock, AR

**KAAY-AM - 1090 (1182)**
700 Wellington Hills Rd.
Little Rock, AR 72211
Phone: (501)401-0200
Fax: (501)401-0387
**Format:** Religious

**KAMD-FM - 97.1 (1032)**
133 W. Washington St., Ste. A
PO Box 957
Camden, AR 71711-0957
Phone: (870)836-9567
Fax: (870)836-9567

**Format:** Contemporary Country

**KARN-AM - 920 (1184)**
700 Wellington Hills Rd.
Little Rock, AR 72211-2026
Fax: (501)401-0367
**Format:** Talk; News

**KBOK-AM - 1310 (1210)**
302 S Main St.
Malvern, AR 72104-3737
Phone: (501)332-6981
Fax: (501)332-6984
**Format:** News; Country

**KDJE-FM - 100.3 (1187)**
10800 Colonel Glenn Rd.
Little Rock, AR 72204
Phone: (501)217-5000
Fax: (501)372-7787
**Format:** Contemporary Hit Radio (CHR)

**KELD-AM - 1400 (1064)**
2525 Northwest Ave.
El Dorado, AR 71730
Phone: (870)863-1400
Fax: (870)863-4555
**Format:** News; Talk; Talk

**KFFB-FM - 106.1 (1068)**
PO Box 1050
Fairfield Bay, AR 72088
Phone: (501)356-5106
Fax: (501)723-4861

**KHKN-FM - 106.7 (1188)**
10800 Colonel Glenn Rd.
Little Rock, AR 72204
Phone: (501)217-5000
Fax: (501)228-9547
**Format:** Country

**KIPR-FM - 92.3 (1189)**
700 Wellington Hills Rd.
Little Rock, AR 72211-2026
Phone: (501)401-0200
Fax: (501)664-9201
**Format:** Urban Contemporary

**KISI-FM - 101.5 (1211)**
302 S Main St.
Malvern, AR 72104-3737
**Format:** Oldies

**KITA-AM - 1440 (1190)**
723 W. 14th St.
Little Rock, AR 72202-3721
Phone: (501)375-1440
Fax: (501)375-0947
**Format:** Talk; Ethnic; Religious; Religious

**KLAZ-AM - 1420 (1134)**
PO Box 21430
Hot Springs, AR 71903-1430
Phone: (501)525-1301
Fax: (501)525-4344
**Format:** Easy Listening

**KLAZ-FM - 105.9 (1135)**
208 Buena Vista Rd.
PO Box 21430
Hot Springs, AR 71913-1430
Phone: (501)525-4600
Fax: (501)525-4344
**Format:** Contemporary Hit Radio (CHR)

**KMSX-FM - 94.9 (1195)**
10800 Colonel Glenn Rd.
Little Rock, AR 72204
Phone: (501)217-5000
Fax: (501)228-9547
**Format:** Adult Contemporary

**KQUS-FM - 97.5 (1136)**
125 Corporate Terrace
Hot Springs, AR 71913
Phone: (501)525-9700
Fax: (501)525-9739
**Format:** Country

**KUAR-FM - 89.1 (1200)**
2801 S. University Ave.
Little Rock, AR 72204
Phone: (501)569-8485
Fax: (501)569-8488

**Format:** News; Information

**KWXI-AM - 670 (1113)**
PO Box 740
Glenwood, AR 71943
Phone: (501)356-2151
Fax: (501)356-4684
**Format:** Country

**KZLE-FM - 93.1 (1010)**
PO Box 2037
Batesville, AR 72503-2077
Phone: (870)793-4196
Fax: (870)793-4437
**Format:** Adult Contemporary

**KZNG-AM - 1340 (1139)**
125 Corporate Terrace
Hot Springs, AR 71913
Phone: (501)525-9700
Fax: (501)525-9739
**Format:** Talk; News

## Lubbock, TX

**KCLV-AM - 1240 (20060)**
2112 Thornton
PO Box 1907
Clovis, NM 88101
Phone: (505)763-4401
Fax: (505)769-2564
**Format:** Country

**KCLV-FM - 99.1 (20061)**
2112 Thornton
PO Box 1907
Clovis, NM 88101
Phone: (505)763-4401
Fax: (505)769-2564
**Format:** Country

**KFMX-FM - 94.5 (30094)**
4413 82nd St., Ste. 300
Lubbock, TX 79424
Phone: (806)798-7078
Fax: (806)798-7052
**Format:** Album-Oriented Rock (AOR)

**KFYO-AM - 790 (30095)**
4413 82nd St., Suite 300
Lubbock, TX 79424
Phone: (806)798-7078
Fax: (806)798-7052
**Format:** News; Talk; Country

**KJAK-FM - 92.7 (30096)**
PO Box 6490
Lubbock, TX 79493
Phone: (806)745-6677
Fax: (806)745-8140
**Format:** Religious

**KJTV-AM - 950 (30097)**
PO Box 3757
Lubbock, TX 79452-3757
Phone: (806)745-3434
Fax: (806)748-2470
**Format:** News; Talk

**KKAM-AM - 1340 (30098)**
4413 82nd St., Ste. 300
Lubbock, TX 79424
Phone: (806)798-7078
Fax: (806)798-7052
**Format:** Sports

**KLFB-AM - 1420 (30099)**
2700 Marshall St
Lubbock, TX 79415-1100
Phone: (806)765-8114
Fax: (806)791-0527
**Format:** Hispanic

**KLLL-AM - 1590 (30100)**
33 Briercroft Office Pk.
Lubbock, TX 79412-3020
Phone: (806)770-5555
Fax: (806)770-5363
**Format:** Contemporary Country

**KLLL-FM - 96.3 (30101)**
33 Briercroft Office Pk.
Lubbock, TX 79412-3020
Phone: (806)763-1911
Fax: (806)770-5363

# McAllen-Brownsville, TX

**Format:** Contemporary Country

**KLVT-AM - 1230  (30055)**
PO Box 967
Levelland, TX 79336
Phone: (806)894-3134
Fax: (806)894-3135
**Format:** Gospel

**KMMX-FM - 100.3  (30102)**
33 Briercroft Office Park
Lubbock, TX 79412-3020
Phone: (806)762-3000
Fax: (806)770-5363
**Format:** Adult Contemporary

**KONE-FM - 101.1  (30104)**
33 Briercroft Office Park
Lubbock, TX 79412-3020
Phone: (806)762-3000
Fax: (806)770-5363
**Format:** Classic Rock

**KTXT-FM - 88.1  (30105)**
Texas Tech University
PO Box 43081
Lubbock, TX 79409
Phone: (806)742-3916
Fax: (806)742-3906
**Format:** Alternative/New Music/Progressive

**KVOP-AM - 1090  (30280)**
3218 N. Quincy
PO Box 1420
Plainview, TX 79072
Phone: (806)296-2771
Fax: (806)293-5732
**Format:** Hispanic

**KVOP-FM - 106.9  (30281)**
3218 N. Quincy
PO Box 1420
Plainview, TX 79072
Phone: (806)296-2771
Fax: (806)293-5732
**Format:** Adult Contemporary

**KXTQ-FM - 93.7  (30108)**
9800 University
PO Box 3757
Lubbock, TX 79452-3757
Phone: (806)745-3434
Fax: (806)748-2470
**Format:** Tejano

## McAllen-Brownsville, TX

**KBFM-FM - 104.1  (30623)**
910 E. Pike St.
Weslaco, TX 78596
Phone: (866)973-1041
Fax: (956)973-9355
**Format:** Contemporary Hit Radio (CHR); Contemporary Hit Radio (CHR)

**KBNR-FM - 88.3  (29343)**
PO Box 5480
Brownsville, TX 78523-5480
Phone: (956)542-6933
Fax: (956)542-0523
**Format:** Religious; Hispanic

**KBOR-AM - 1700  (29344)**
1050 McIntosh Dr
Brownsville, TX 78521-2484
Phone: (956)544-1600
Fax: (956)544-0311
**Format:** Hispanic

**KBRN-AM - 1500  (30149)**
PO Box 252
McAllen, TX 78505-0252
Phone: (512)249-9336
Fax: (512)249-2783
**Format:** Middle-of-the-Road (MOR)

**KCZO-FM - 92.1  (30150)**
PO Box 252
McAllen, TX 78502
Fax: (210)781-2730
**Format:** Hispanic; Religious

**KHKZ-FM - 106.3  (29345)**
1050 Macintosh
Brownsville, TX 78521
Phone: (956)544-1600
Fax: (956)544-0311
**Format:** Adult Contemporary

**KIRT-AM - 1580  (30154)**
608 S. 10th St.
McAllen, TX 78501
Phone: (956)686-2111
Fax: (956)668-0307
**Format:** Hispanic

**KJAV-FM - 104.9  (29057)**
PO Box 252
McAllen, TX 78502
Phone: (210)781-5528
Fax: (210)781-2730
**Format:** Hispanic; Religious

**KQXX-AM - 1600  (29346)**
1050 Macintosh
Brownsville, TX 78521
Phone: (956)544-1600
Fax: (956)544-0311
**Format:** Oldies

**KQXX-FM - 98.5  (30624)**
901 E. Pike St.
Weslaco, TX 78596-4937
Phone: (866)973-1041
Fax: (956)973-9355
**Format:** Hispanic

**KTEX-FM - 100.3  (30626)**
910 E. Pike St.
Weslaco, TX 78596
Phone: (956)702-7070
Fax: (956)702-7700
**Format:** Country

**KTJN-FM - 106  (30627)**
901 E. Pike Blvd.
Weslaco, TX 78596-4937
**Format:** Hispanic

**KURV-AM - 710  (29653)**
2921 N. Closner
Edinburg, TX 78539
Phone: (956)383-2777
Fax: (956)383-2570
**Format:** Talk; News; Sports; Agricultural

**KVJY-AM - 840  (29797)**
3301 S. EXPWY 83
Harlingen, TX 78550
Fax: (512)421-2582
**Format:** Talk

**KVNS-AM - 1700  (29348)**
1050 Macintosh
Brownsville, TX 78521
Phone: (956)544-1600
Fax: (956)544-0311
**Format:** News; Talk

## Memphis, TN

**KFIN-FM - 107.9  (1152)**
403 W. Parker Rd.
Drawer 1737
Jonesboro, AR 72403
Phone: (870)932-1079
Fax: (870)932-3814
**Format:** Contemporary Country

**KKLV-FM - 94.7  (1313)**
102 N. 5th St.
West Memphis, AR 72301
Phone: (870)735-6622
Fax: (870)735-6646
**Format:** Religious

**KSUD-AM - 730  (1314)**
102 N. 5th St.
West Memphis, AR 72301
Phone: (870)735-6622
Fax: (870)735-6646
**Format:** Contemporary Christian; Talk; Sports

**KWYN-AM - 1400  (1317)**
Hwy. 64 W.
Wynne, AR 72396
Phone: (501)238-8141
Fax: (501)238-5997
**Format:** Country; Talk; Information

**KWYN-FM - 92.5  (1318)**
PO Box 789
Wynne, AR 72396
Phone: (501)238-8141
Fax: (501)238-5997

**Format:** Country

## Monroe, LA-El Dorado, AR

**KIXB-FM - 103.3  (1065)**
2525 Northwest Ave.
El Dorado, AR 71730
Fax: (501)863-4555
**Format:** Country

**KJLO-FM - 104.1  (12265)**
PO Box 4808
Monroe, LA 71211-4808
Phone: (318)388-2323
Fax: (318)388-0569
**Format:** Country

**KLBQ-FM - 99.3  (1066)**
1904 W. Hillsboro
El Dorado, AR 71730
Phone: (870)862-0099
Fax: (870)863-6221
**Format:** Adult Contemporary; Top 40

**KMLB-AM - 1440  (12267)**
PO Box 4808
Monroe, LA 71211
Phone: (318)361-0786
Fax: (318)388-0569
**Format:** News; Talk

**KNOE-AM - 101.9  (12268)**
PO Box 4067
Monroe, LA 71201
Phone: (318)388-8888
Fax: (318)322-8774
**Format:** Adult Contemporary

**KNOE-FM - 101.9  (12269)**
1400 Oliver Rd.
PO Box 4067
Monroe, LA 71201
Phone: (318)388-8888
Fax: (318)322-8774
**Format:** Adult Contemporary; Adult Contemporary

**KPCH-FM - 97.7  (12375)**
1319 N. Vienna
PO Box 430
Ruston, LA 71273-0977
Phone: (318)255-5000
Fax: (318)255-5084
**Format:** Oldies; Sports

**KRUS-AM - 1490  (12376)**
500N Monroe St.
PO Box 430
Ruston, LA 71270
Phone: (318)255-2530
Fax: (318)225-2100
**Format:** Blues

**KRVV-FM - 100.1  (12271)**
PO Box 4808
Monroe, LA 71211-4808
Phone: (318)388-2323
Fax: (318)388-0569
**Format:** Urban Contemporary; Soft Rock

**KXKZ-FM - 107.5  (12377)**
PO Box 430
Ruston, LA 71273
Phone: (318)255-5000
Fax: (318)255-5084
**Format:** Country

**KYEA-FM - 98.3  (12273)**
1200 N. 18th St., Ste. D
Monroe, LA 71201-5449
Phone: (318)387-3922
Fax: (318)325-7203
**Format:** Urban Contemporary

## New Orleans, LA

**KCIL-FM - 107.5  (12178)**
120 Prevost
Houma, LA 70364
Phone: (985)851-1020
Fax: (985)872-4403
**Format:** Contemporary Country

**KJIN-AM - 1490  (12179)**
120 Prevost
Houma, LA 70364
Phone: (985)851-1020

Fax: (985)872-4403
**Format:** Big Band/Nostalgia

**KMEZ-FM - 102.9  (12114)**
1450 Poydras St.
New Orleans, LA 70112
Phone: (504)593-2171
Fax: (504)593-1865
**Format:** Urban Contemporary

**KTIB-AM - 640  (12421)**
108 Green St.
Thibodaux, LA 70301
Phone: (985)447-9006
Fax: (985)446-2338
**Format:** Oldies; News

**WABL-AM - 1570  (12249)**
PO Box 8888
Metairie, LA 70011
Phone: (504)309-7260
Fax: (504)309-7262
**Format:** Full Service

**WBOK-AM - 1230  (12333)**
1639 Gentilly Blvd.
New Orleans, LA 70119-2100
Phone: (504)943-4600
Fax: (504)944-4662
**Format:** Religious

**WNOE-FM - 101.1  (12339)**
929 Howard Ave.
New Orleans, LA 70113
Phone: (504)679-7300
Fax: (504)679-7345
**Format:** Contemporary Country

**WODT-FM - 1280  (12341)**
929 Howard Ave.
New Orleans, LA 70113-1148
Phone: (504)827-6000
Fax: (504)827-6048
**Format:** Blues

**WQUE-FM - 93.3  (12342)**
2228 Gravier
New Orleans, LA 70119
Fax: (504)827-6045
**Format:** Urban Contemporary

**WSLA-AM - 1560  (12405)**
38230 Coast Blvd.
PO Box 1175
Slidell, LA 70459
**Format:** News; Talk; Sports

**WSMB-AM - 1350  (12345)**
1450 Poydras St., Ste. 500
New Orleans, LA 70112
Phone: (504)593-2100
Fax: (504)593-1850
**Format:** Talk; News; News

**WTUL-FM - 91.5  (12346)**
Tulane University Center
New Orleans, LA 70118
Phone: (504)865-5887
Fax: (504)862-3072
**Format:** Full Service; Public Radio; Public Radio

**WWL-AM - 870  (12348)**
1450 Poydras, Ste. 500
New Orleans, LA 70112-6010
Phone: (504)593-6376
Fax: (504)593-1850
**Format:** News; Talk; Sports; Sports

**WWNO-FM - 89.9  (12350)**
University of New Orleans
New Orleans, LA 70148
Phone: (504)280-7000
Fax: (504)280-6061
**Format:** Classical; Jazz; News; Public Radio

**WYLD-AM - 940  (12353)**
2228 Gravier St.
New Orleans, LA 70119
Fax: (504)827-6048
**Format:** Religious; Gospel

**WYLD-FM - 98.5  (12354)**
2228 Gravier St.
New Orleans, LA 70119
Phone: (504)827-6000
Fax: (504)827-6045

**Format:** Urban Contemporary

## Odessa-Midland, TX

**KCRS-AM - 550  (30222)**
1330 E 8th St., Ste. 207
Odessa, TX 79761
Phone: (915)520-5277
Fax: (915)520-6761
**Format:** News; Talk

**KCRS-FM - 103.3  (30223)**
1330 E. Eighth Street, Suite 207
Odessa, TX 79760-4716
Phone: (432)563-9102
**Format:** Adult Contemporary

**KFST-AM - 860  (29703)**
PO Box 165, RR. 2
Fort Stockton, TX 79735
Phone: (915)336-2228
Fax: (915)336-5834
**Format:** Adult Contemporary

**KFST-FM - 94.3  (29704)**
954 S. Hwy. 385
Fort Stockton, TX 79735
Phone: (915)336-2228
Fax: (915)336-5834
**Format:** Country; Hispanic; Hispanic

**KFZX-FM - 102.1  (30224)**
1330 E. 8th St., Ste. 207
Odessa, TX 79761
Phone: (915)563-9102
Fax: (915)580-9102
**Format:** Classic Rock; Album-Oriented Rock (AOR)

**KIKZ-AM - 1250  (30427)**
105 11th St. NW
Seminole, TX 79360
Phone: (915)758-5878
Fax: (915)758-5474
**Format:** Full Service; Country; Religious; Hispanic; Religious; Hispanic

**KIUN-AM - 1400  (30267)**
316 S. Cedar
PO Box 469
Pecos, TX 79772
Phone: (915)445-2497
Fax: (432)445-4092
**Format:** Hispanic; Country; Country

**KJBC-AM - 1150  (30173)**
1903 S. Lamesa Rd.
Midland, TX 79701
**Format:** Gospel; News; Information; Talk; Southern Gospel

**KKKK-FM - 101.3  (30225)**
12200 N Service Rd. Interstate 20 E
PO Box 60375
Odessa, TX 79765
Phone: (915)563-2266
Fax: (915)563-2288
**Format:** Religious

**KMND-AM - 1510  (30177)**
11300 State Hwy. 191, Ste. 2
Midland, TX 79707-1367
**Format:** News; Talk

**KMRK-FM - 96.1  (30226)**
1330 E 8th St., Ste. 207
Odessa, TX 79761
Phone: (915)563-9102
Fax: (915)580-9102
**Format:** Hip Hop; Contemporary Hit Radio (CHR)

**KNDA-AM - 1000  (30227)**
1100 S Grant Ave.
Odessa, TX 79761-6614
Phone: (915)381-2077
**Format:** Hispanic

**KODM-FM - 97.9  (30178)**
PO Box 61147
Midland, TX 79711-1147
Phone: (915)561-9809
Fax: (915)563-5530
**Format:** Adult Contemporary

**KOZA-AM - 1230  (30228)**
1100 S. Grant
Odessa, TX 79760
Phone: (915)333-1227
Fax: (926)333-3044

**Format:** Hispanic

**KQLM-FM - 107.9  (30230)**
1319 S Crane Street
Odessa, TX 79761
Phone: (915)333-1227
Fax: (915)333-3044
**Format:** Ethnic

**KRIL-AM - 1410  (30231)**
1410 Crane Hwy.
PO Box 4312
Odessa, TX 79760
**Format:** News; Classical

**KSEM-FM - 106.3  (30428)**
105 11th St. NW
Seminole, TX 79360
Phone: (915)758-3798
Fax: (915)758-5474
**Format:** Country; Religious

**KTXC-FM - 104.7  (30179)**
PO Box 60403
Midland, TX 79711-0403
Phone: (915)362-0401
**Format:** Country

## Oklahoma City, OK

**KATT-FM - 100.5  (25487)**
4045 NW 64th, Ste. 600
Oklahoma City, OK 73116-1684
Phone: (405)848-0100
Fax: (405)843-5288
**Format:** Album-Oriented Rock (AOR)

**KCDL-FM - 99.3  (25669)**
PO Box 587
Weatherford, OK 73096-0587
**Format:** Country

**KCLI-AM - 1320  (25295)**
700 Frisco
Clinton, OK 73601
Phone: (580)323-0617
Fax: (580)323-0717
**Format:** Oldies

**KEBC-AM - 1340  (25489)**
PO Box 1000
Oklahoma City, OK 73101-1000
Phone: (405)822-2828
**Format:** Eclectic

**KGOU-FM - 106.3  (25441)**
780 Van Vleet Oval
Norman, OK 73019
Phone: (405)325-5468
Fax: (405)325-7129
**Format:** News; Talk; Blues

**KHBZ-FM - 94.7  (25492)**
50 Penn Pl., Ste. 1000
Oklahoma City, OK 73118
Phone: (405)840-5271
Fax: (405)858-1449
**Format:** Alternative/New Music/Progressive

**KIRC-FM - 105.9  (25553)**
2 E. Main St.
Shawnee, OK 74801
Phone: (405)878-1803
Fax: (405)878-0162
**Format:** Country

**KIXR-FM - 104.7  (25522)**
PO Box 2631
Ponca City, OK 74602
Phone: (580)765-5491
Fax: (580)762-8329

**KJYO-FM - 102.7  (25493)**
PO Box 1000
Oklahoma City, OK 73101
Phone: (405)840-5271
Fax: (405)848-5318
**Format:** Top 40

**KKMG-FM - 93.3  (25494)**
5105 S. Shields Blvd.
Oklahoma City, OK 73129
Phone: (405)616-5500
Fax: (405)616-5505

Roswell, NM

**Format:** Southern Gospel

**KMZE-FM - 92.1  (25681)**
2730 Williams Ave.
Box D
Woodward, OK 73801
Phone: (405)256-3692
Fax: (405)256-3825
**Format:** Adult Contemporary

**KOKF-FM - 90.9  (25499)**
7700 N. Council Rd.
Oklahoma City, OK 73132
Phone: (405)460-9136
Fax: (405)728-7521
**Format:** Urban Contemporary; Contemporary Hit Radio (CHR); Alternative/New Music/Progressive; Alternative/New Music/Progressive

**KQCV-AM - 800  (25501)**
1919 N. Broadway
Oklahoma City, OK 73103
Phone: (405)521-1414
Fax: (405)521-1391
**Format:** Religious; Talk

**KROU-FM - 105.7  (25442)**
780 Van Vleet Oval
Norman, OK 73019
Phone: (405)325-3388
Fax: (405)325-7129
**Format:** News; Talk; Jazz; Blues

**KSPI-AM - 780  (25575)**
PO Box 1269
Stillwater, OK 74076-2288
Phone: (405)372-7800
Fax: (405)372-6969
**Format:** News; Talk; Talk

**KTLV-AM - 1220  (25415)**
3336 SE 67th St.
Oklahoma City, OK 73135
Phone: (405)672-1220
Fax: (405)672-5858
**Format:** Religious

**KTOK-AM - 1000  (25505)**
50 Penn Pl., Ste. 1000
PO Box 1000
Oklahoma City, OK 73101
Phone: (405)840-5271
Fax: (405)840-4025
**Format:** Talk; News

**KTST-FM - 101.9  (25506)**
50 Penn Place, Suite 1000
Oklahoma City, OK 70110
Phone: (405)840-5271
Fax: (405)858-1106
**Format:** Country

**KVSP-AM - 1140  (25507)**
1528 NE 23rd St.
Oklahoma City, OK 73111
Phone: (405)460-5877
Fax: (405)424-6708
**Format:** Urban Contemporary

**KWCO-AM - 105.5  (25288)**
500 W. Country Club
PO Box 1268
Chickasha, OK 73023-1268
Phone: (405)224-1560
Fax: (405)602-1229
**Format:** Talk

**KWEY-AM - 1590  (25670)**
PO Box 587
Weatherford, OK 73096
Fax: (405)772-1590
**Format:** Country; Agricultural

**KWEY-FM - 97.3  (25671)**
PO Box 587
Weatherford, OK 73096
Phone: (580)772-5939
**Format:** Country

**KWOX-FM - 101.1  (25682)**
101 Centre
Box K-101
Woodward, OK 73801
Fax: (405)256-3825

**Format:** Contemporary Country

**KWSH-AM - 1260  (25555)**
2 E. Main St.
Shawnee, OK 74801-6904
Phone: (405)382-0105
Fax: (405)878-1803
**Format:** Contemporary Country

**KWSH-FM - 104.7  (25556)**
2 E. Main St.
Shawnee, OK 74801-6904
Phone: (405)257-5441
Fax: (405)878-0162
**Format:** Country

**KXOO-FM - 94.3  (25321)**
PO Box 945
Elk City, OK 73648
Phone: (580)225-9696
Fax: (580)225-9699
**Format:** Contemporary Christian

**KXXY-FM - 96.1  (25508)**
50 Penn Pl., Ste. 1000
PO Box 1000
Oklahoma City, OK 73118
Phone: (405)858-1400
Fax: (405)858-1106
**Format:** Country

**KYIS-FM - 98.9  (25509)**
4045 NW 64th St., Ste. 600
Oklahoma City, OK 73116-1684
Phone: (405)848-0100
Fax: (405)848-5288
**Format:** Contemporary Hit Radio (CHR)

**WBBZ-AM - 1230  (25527)**
PO Box 588
Ponca City, OK 74602
Phone: (580)765-6607
Fax: (580)765-6611
**Format:** Adult Contemporary; Sports; News

## Roswell, NM

**KBIM-AM - 910  (20142)**
PO Box 2308
Roswell, NM 88202
Phone: (505)623-9100
Fax: (505)623-4775
**Format:** News; Talk

**KBIM-FM - 94.9  (20143)**
PO Box 2308
Roswell, NM 88202
Phone: (505)623-9100
Fax: (505)623-4775
**Format:** Adult Contemporary

**KEND-FM - 106.5  (20146)**
1405 W 2nd St.
Roswell, NM 88201
Phone: (505)625-2098
Fax: (505)622-3877
**Format:** Contemporary Country

**KPSA-AM - 1230  (20150)**
PO Box 670
Roswell, NM 88202-1981
Phone: (505)622-0290
Fax: (505)622-9041
**Format:** Hispanic

**KRDD-AM - 1320  (20152)**
PO Box 1615
Roswell, NM 88201
Fax: (505)623-8111

## San Angelo, TX

**KCRN-AM - 1340  (30339)**
17 S. Chadbourne, Suite 500
PO Box 32
San Angelo, TX 76902-0032
Phone: (325)655-6917
Fax: (325)665-7806
**Format:** Religious

**KCRN-FM - 93.9  (30340)**
17 S. Chadbourne, Suite 500
PO Box 32
San Angelo, TX 76902
Phone: (325)655-6917
Fax: (325)655-7806

**Format:** Religious

**KELI-FM - 98.7  (30341)**
1301 S. Bryant Blvd.
PO Box 1878
San Angelo, TX 76902
Phone: (915)655-5483
Fax: (915)658-7377
**Format:** Oldies

**KGKL-AM - 960  (30342)**
1301 S. Bryant Blvd.
San Angelo, TX 76901
Phone: (915)655-7161
Fax: (915)658-7377
**Format:** Classical; Country

**KGKL-FM - 97.5  (30343)**
1301 S. Bryant
San Angelo, TX 76901
Phone: (915)655-7161
Fax: (915)658-7377
**Format:** Country

**KKSA-AM - 1260  (30345)**
2824 Sherwood Way
San Angelo, TX 76901
Phone: (325)949-2112
Fax: (325)944-0851
**Format:** News; Sports; Talk

**KMBL-AM - 1450  (30007)**
214 Pecan St.
Junction, TX 76849
Phone: (915)446-3371
Fax: (915)446-4101
**Format:** Country

**KNEL-AM - 1490  (29328)**
117 S. Blackburn
PO Box 630
Brady, TX 76825
Phone: (915)597-2119
Fax: (915)597-1925
**Format:** Oldies

**KNEL-FM - 95.3  (29329)**
117 S. Blackburn
PO Box 630
Brady, TX 76825
Phone: (915)597-2119
Fax: (915)597-1925
**Format:** Country

**KSJT-FM - 107.5  (30346)**
209 W. Beauregard Ave.
San Angelo, TX 76903-5823
Phone: (915)655-1717
Fax: (915)657-0601
**Format:** Hispanic; News; News

## San Antonio (Kerrville), TX

**KAJA-FM - 97.3  (30382)**
6222 NW Interstate 10
San Antonio, TX 78201
Phone: (210)736-9700
Fax: (210)735-8811
**Format:** Contemporary Country

**KCJZ-FM - 106.7  (30383)**
8122 Datapoint Dr., Ste. 500
San Antonio, TX 78229
Phone: (210)615-5400
Fax: (210)615-5300
**Format:** Oldies; Blues

**KEDA-AM - 1540  (30387)**
510 S. Flores St.
San Antonio, TX 78204
Phone: (512)226-5254
Fax: (512)227-7937
**Format:** Hispanic; Tejano

**KGNB-AM - 1420  (30214)**
1540 Loop 337 N.
New Braunfels, TX 78130
Phone: (830)625-7311
Fax: (830)625-7336
**Format:** Full Service

**KLUP-AM - 930  (30393)**
9601 Mcallister Fwy. Ste. 1200
San Antonio, TX 78216-4686
Phone: (210)344-8481
Fax: (210)340-1213

**Gale Directory of Publications & Broadcast Media/140th Ed.**  Springfield, MO

**Format:** Big Band/Nostalgia; Middle-of-the-Road (MOR)

**KNBT-FM - 92.1 (30215)**
1540 Loop 337 N.
New Braunfels, TX 78130
Phone: (830)625-7311
**Format:** Country

**KSAQ-FM - 96.1 (30399)**
217 Alamo Plaza, Ste. 200
San Antonio, TX 78205
Phone: (210)271-9600
Fax: (210)271-0489
**Format:** Album-Oriented Rock (AOR)

**KSJL-AM - 760 (30401)**
217 Alamo Plaza, Ste. 200
San Antonio, TX 78205
Phone: (210)271-9600
Fax: (210)271-0489
**Format:** Adult Contemporary; Urban Contemporary

**KSMG-FM - 105.3 (30403)**
8930 Fourwinds Dr., No. 500
San Antonio, TX 78239
Phone: (210)646-0105
Fax: (210)646-9711
**Format:** Adult Contemporary; Adult Contemporary

**KTDR-FM - 96.3 (29609)**
307 E. 8th
Del Rio, TX 78840
Phone: (830)775-6291
Fax: (830)775-6545

**KTFM-FM - 102.7 (30405)**
4050 Eisenhower Rd.
San Antonio, TX 78218
Phone: (512)599-5500
Fax: (512)599-5588
**Format:** Contemporary Hit Radio (CHR)

**KTJK-AM - 1230 (29610)**
PO Box 1489
Del Rio, TX 78841-1489
Phone: (830)775-9583
Fax: (830)774-4009
**Format:** Tejano; News; Sports

**KVOU-AM - 1400 (30571)**
1400 Batesville Rd.
PO Box 758
Uvalde, TX 78801
Phone: (830)278-2555
Fax: (830)278-9461
**Format:** News; Big Band/Nostalgia; Agricultural; Agricultural

**KVWG-AM - 1280 (30263)**
1581 Oilfield Rd.
PO Box K
Pearsall, TX 78061
Phone: (210)334-3664
Fax: (210)334-3665
**Format:** Country; Hispanic; Hispanic

**KVWG-FM - 95.3 (30264)**
Oil Field Rd.
Box K
Pearsall, TX 78061
Phone: (210)334-3664
Fax: (210)334-3664
**Format:** Country; Hispanic

**KXXM-FM - 96.1 (30409)**
6222 W IH 10
San Antonio, TX 78201
Phone: (210)736-9700
Fax: (210)735-8811
**Format:** Contemporary Hit Radio (CHR)

**KYUF-FM - 104.9 (30572)**
1400 Batesville Rd.
Uvalde, TX 78802
Phone: (210)278-2555
Fax: (210)278-9461
**Format:** Sports; Contemporary Country

## Shreveport, LA-Texarkana, TX

**KBCL-AM - 1070 (12387)**
316B Gregg St.
Shreveport, LA 71104
Phone: (318)861-1070
Fax: (318)868-0990

**Format:** Religious; News; Talk; Talk

**KBEL-FM - 96.7 (25376)**
PO Box 418
Idabel, OK 74745
Phone: (580)286-6642
Fax: (580)286-6643
**Format:** Country

**KCIJ-FM - 106.5 (12287)**
213 Renee St.
Natchitoches, LA 71457
Phone: (318)354-4000
Fax: (318)352-9598
**Format:** Classic Rock

**KDAQ-FM - 89.9 (12388)**
PO Box 5250
Shreveport, LA 71135-2301
Phone: (318)797-5150
Fax: (318)797-5265
**Format:** Public Radio; Jazz; Eclectic; Classical; Eclectic; Classical

**KEWL-AM - 1400 (30538)**
1323 College Dr.
Texarkana, TX 75503-3531
Phone: (903)793-1100
Fax: (903)794-4717
**Format:** Oldies; Talk

**KFYX-FM - 107.1 (30540)**
615 Olive St.
Texarkana, TX 75501
Phone: (903)793-4671
Fax: (903)792-4261
**Format:** Country

**KIMP-AM - 960 (30193)**
Hwy. 67 W., Box 990
Mount Pleasant, TX 75456
Phone: (903)572-8726
Fax: (903)572-7232
**Format:** News; Talk

**KIOU-AM - 1480 (12390)**
4149 Geroge Rd
Shreveport, LA 71107
Phone: (318)222-0272
Fax: (318)222-0482
**Format:** Gospel

**KJVC-FM - 92.7 (12233)**
1549 Greenbridge
PO Box 700
Logansport, LA 71049
Phone: (318)697-4000
Fax: (318)697-4004
**Format:** Country

**KKBI-FM - 106.1 (25279)**
617 S. Park Dr.
PO Box 1016
Broken Bow, OK 74728
Phone: (580)584-3388
Fax: (580)584-3341
**Format:** Contemporary Country

**KLSA-FM - 90.7 (12391)**
1 University Plaza
Shreveport, LA 71105
Phone: (318)797-5150
Fax: (318)797-5154
**Format:** Classical; Jazz; News; News

**KMJI-FM - 93.3 (1300)**
2324 Arkansas Blvd.
Texarkana, AR 71854
Phone: (903)334-9336
Fax: (903)334-9310
**Format:** Adult Contemporary

**KORI-FM - 104.7 (12234)**
222 Main St
PO Box 700
Logansport, LA 71049
Phone: (318)697-4000
Fax: (318)697-4004
**Format:** Country

**KOSY-AM - 790 (1301)**
2324 Arkansas Blvd.
Texarkana, AR 71854
Phone: (870)772-3771
Fax: (870)772-0364

**Format:** Middle-of-the-Road (MOR)

**KPWW-FM - 95.9 (1302)**
2324 Arkansas Blvd.
Texarkana, AR 71854
Phone: (870)772-3771
Fax: (870)772-0364
**Format:** Contemporary Hit Radio (CHR)

**KRMD-AM - 1340 (12121)**
270 Plaza Loop
Bossier City, LA 71111
Phone: (318)549-8500
Fax: (318)549-8505
**Format:** Sports

**KRMD-FM - 101.1 (12122)**
270 Plaza Loop
Bossier City, LA 71111
Phone: (318)549-8500
Fax: (318)549-8505
**Format:** Contemporary Country

**KRRP-AM - 950 (12133)**
Rte. 4, Box 197
Coushatta, LA 71019
Phone: (318)932-6704
Fax: (318)932-9700
**Format:** Classical

**KSCL-FM - 91.3 (12394)**
2911 Centenary Blvd.
Shreveport, LA 71104
Phone: (318)869-5297
Fax: (318)869-5294
**Format:** Alternative/New Music/Progressive; Jazz; Ethnic; Urban Contemporary; Ethnic; Urban Contemporary

**KSYB-AM - 1300 (12396)**
PO Box 7685
Shreveport, LA 71137-7277
Phone: (318)222-2744
Fax: (318)425-7507
**Format:** Sports

**KTAL-FM - 98.1 (12398)**
208 N. Thomas Dr.
Shreveport, LA 71107
Phone: (318)222-3122
Fax: (318)459-1493
**Format:** Album-Oriented Rock (AOR)

**KTFS-AM - 940 (30541)**
615 Olive St.
Texarkana, TX 75501
Phone: (903)793-4671
Fax: (903)792-4261
**Format:** News; Talk

**KYGL-FM - 106.3 (1303)**
2324 Arkansas Blvd.
Texarkana, AR 71854
Phone: (870)772-3771
Fax: (870)772-0364
**Format:** Classic Rock

**KZBL-FM - 100.7 (12241)**
605 San Antonio Ave.
Many, LA 71449
Phone: (318)357-1007
Fax: (318)256-0950
**Format:** Oldies

## Springfield, MO

**KCWD-FM - 96.7 (1118)**
600 S. Pine St., Box 850
Harrison, AR 72601
Phone: (501)741-1402
Fax: (501)741-9702
**Format:** Classic Rock

**KKTZ-FM - 93.5 (1231)**
2352 Hwy. 62 B
Mountain Home, AR 72653-6847
Phone: (870)492-6022
Fax: (870)492-2137
**Format:** Adult Contemporary

**KSAR-FM - 92.3 (1280)**
PO Box 458
Salem, AR 72576
Phone: (870)856-3630
Fax: (870)856-4408

4303

**Format:** Country; News

**KTHS-AM - 1480 (1019)**
PO Box 191
Berryville, AR 72616
Phone: (501)423-2147
Fax: (501)423-2146
**Format:** Country; Religious

**KTHS-FM - 107.1 (1020)**
PO Box 191
Berryville, AR 72616
Phone: (870)423-2147
Fax: (870)423-2146
**Format:** Country; Sports

**KTLO-AM - 1240 (1233)**
620 Hwy. 5 N.
PO Box 2010
Mountain Home, AR 72654-2010
Phone: (870)425-3101
Fax: (870)424-4314
**Format:** Country

**KTLO-FM - 97.9 (1234)**
PO Box 2010
Mountain Home, AR 72654-2010
Phone: (870)425-3101
Fax: (870)424-4314
**Format:** Middle-of-the-Road (MOR)

## Tulsa (Bartlesville), OK

**KCFO-AM - 970 (25636)**
3737 S. 37th W. Ave.
Tulsa, OK 74107-5136
Phone: (918)445-1186
Fax: (918)446-7508
**Format:** Religious

**KEOK-FM - 101.7 (25584)**
PO Box 676
Tahlequah, OK 74465-0676
Phone: (918)456-2511
Fax: (918)456-3231
**Format:** Country

**KGND-AM - 1470 (25349)**
PO Box 451750
Grove, OK 74345-1750
**Format:** Country

**KGND-FM - 107.5 (25350)**
PO Box 451750
Grove, OK 74345
Phone: (918)786-6161
Fax: (918)786-2284
**Format:** Adult Contemporary; Soft Rock

**KGTO-AM - 1050 (25638)**
7136 S. Yale, Ste. 500
Tulsa, OK 74133
Phone: (918)491-9691
Fax: (918)493-2376
**Format:** Adult Contemporary

**KGVE-FM - 99.3 (25351)**
Mailing: PO Box 451749
Grove, OK 74345
Phone: (918)786-2211
Fax: (918)786-2284
**Format:** Contemporary Country

**KHTT-FM - 106.9 (25639)**
7030 S. Yale, Ste. 711
Tulsa, OK 74136
Phone: (918)492-2020
Fax: (918)496-2681
**Format:** Contemporary Hit Radio (CHR); News; News

**KJSR-FM - 103.3 (25640)**
7136 S. Yale Ave., Ste. 500
Tulsa, OK 74136-6358
**Format:** Classic Rock

**KMCO-FM - 101.3 (25406)**
PO Box 1068
McAlester, OK 74502-1068
Phone: (918)426-1050
Fax: (918)423-7119
**Format:** Contemporary Country

**KMMY-FM - 97.1 (25418)**
215 State St., Ste. 910
Muskogee, OK 74401-6650
Phone: (918)687-3697
Fax: (918)682-6775

**Format:** Country

**KMYZ-AM - 1570 (25643)**
5810 E. Skelly Dr., Ste. 810
PO Box 1270
Tulsa, OK 74101-1270
Phone: (918)665-3131
Fax: (918)663-6622
**Format:** Contemporary Hit Radio (CHR)

**KNED-AM - 1150 (25407)**
PO Box 1068
McAlester, OK 74502-1068
Phone: (918)423-1460
Fax: (918)423-7119
**Format:** Country

**KQLL-AM - 1430 (25648)**
2625 S Memorial Dr.
PO Box 659512
Tulsa, OK 74129-2600
**Format:** Talk; Sports; Sports

**KQLL-FM - 106.1 (25649)**
2625 S Memorial Dr.
PO Box 659512
Tulsa, OK 74129-2600
**Format:** Oldies

**KRMG-AM - 740 (25651)**
7136 S. Yale, Ste. 500
Tulsa, OK 74136
Phone: (918)493-7400
Fax: (918)493-5345
**Format:** Talk; News; Sports; Sports

**KTBT-FM - 101.5 (25652)**
2625 S Memorial Dr.
Tulsa, OK 74129
Phone: (918)388-5100
Fax: (918)388-5400
**Format:** Contemporary Hit Radio (CHR)

**KTBZ-AM - 1430 (25653)**
2625 S Memorial Dr.
Tulsa, OK 74129
Phone: (918)388-5100
Fax: (918)388-5400
**Format:** Sports

**KTLQ-AM - 1350 (25585)**
5686 S Muskogee Ave.
PO Box 676
Tahlequah, OK 74465-0676
Phone: (918)456-2511
Fax: (918)456-3231
**Format:** Southern Gospel

**KTMC-AM - 1400 (25408)**
PO Box 1068
McAlester, OK 74502
Phone: (918)423-1460
Fax: (918)423-7119
**Format:** Music of Your Life

**KTSO-FM - 94.1 (25654)**
5810 E. Skelly Dr., Ste. 801
Tulsa, OK 74135
Phone: (918)660-0301
Fax: (918)663-6622
**Format:** Oldies

**KWEN-FM - 95.5 (25658)**
7136 S. Yale, Ste. 500
Tulsa, OK 74136
Phone: (918)494-9500
Fax: (918)493-2376
**Format:** Contemporary Country

**KWON-AM - 1400 (25260)**
Box 1100
Bartlesville, OK 74005
Phone: (918)336-1001
Fax: (918)336-6939
**Format:** News; Sports; Talk

**KYAL-AM - 1550 (25660)**
2448 E. 81st St., Ste. 5500
Tulsa, OK 74137
Phone: (918)492-2660
Fax: (918)492-8840
**Format:** Urban Contemporary

**KYFM-FM - 100.1 (25261)**
1200 SE Frank Phillips Blvd.
PO Box 1100
Bartlesville, OK 74003
Phone: (918)336-1001
Fax: (918)336-6939

**Format:** Adult Contemporary

## Tyler-Longview-Jacksonville, TX

**KBGE-AM - 1240 (30555)**
3810 Brookside Dr.
Tyler, TX 75701
Phone: (903)581-0606
Fax: (903)581-2011
**Format:** Classic Rock

**KCKL-FM - 95.9 (30124)**
PO Box 489
Malakoff, TX 75148
Phone: (903)489-1238
Fax: (903)489-2671
**Format:** Country

**KCUL-AM - 1410 (30137)**
PO Box AA
Marshall, TX 75671
Phone: (903)935-2500
Fax: (903)938-9730
**Format:** Talk; News; Religious

**KCUL-FM - 92.3 (30138)**
200 I20 W.
PO Box AA
Marshall, TX 75670
Phone: (903)935-2500
Fax: (903)938-9730
**Format:** Oldies

**KDOK-FM - 92.1 (30556)**
1001 E SE Loop 323, Ste. 455
PO Box 92
Tyler, TX 75701
Phone: (903)593-2519
Fax: (903)597-8378
**Format:** Middle-of-the-Road (MOR)

**KEBE-AM - 1400 (29992)**
PO Box 1648
Jacksonville, TX 75766
Phone: (903)586-2527
Fax: (903)589-0677
**Format:** News; Talk; Information

**KEES-AM - 1430 (30557)**
1001 E SE Loop 323, Ste. 455
Tyler, TX 75701-2001
Phone: (903)593-2519
Fax: (903)593-4918
**Format:** Talk

**KGLD-AM - 1330 (30558)**
PO Box 1330
Tyler, TX 75710
Phone: (903)593-2519
Fax: (903)597-8378
**Format:** Oldies

**KKTX-AM - 1240 (30560)**
3810 Brookside Dr.
Tyler, TX 75701-9420
Phone: (903)297-3696
**Format:** Classic Rock

**KLVQ-AM - 1410 (29123)**
Hwy. 31 E., Box 489
Malakoff, TX 75148
Phone: (903)489-1238
Fax: (903)489-2671
**Format:** Southern Gospel

**KMOO-FM - 99.9 (30185)**
Greenville Hwy.
PO Box 628
Mineola, TX 75773
Phone: (903)569-3823
Fax: (903)569-6641
**Format:** Country

**KNUE-FM - 101.5 (30562)**
3810 Brookside Dr.
Tyler, TX 75701
Phone: (903)581-0606
Fax: (903)581-2011
**Format:** Contemporary Country

**KOOI-FM - 106.5 (29993)**
Radio Center
PO Box 1648
Jacksonville, TX 75766
Phone: (903)586-2527
Fax: (903)586-1394

**Format:** Adult Contemporary; Soft Rock; Full Service; Full Service

**KRBA-AM - 1340 (30112)**
121 Cotton Sq.
PO Box 1345
Lufkin, TX 75901
Phone: (936)634-6661
Fax: (936)632-5722
**Format:** Ethnic; Country; Religious

**KSFA-AM - 860 (30113)**
PO Box 2209
Lufkin, TX 75902-2209
Phone: (936)639-4455
Fax: (936)639-5540
**Format:** News; Talk; Sports; Sports

**KTBB-AM - 600 (30563)**
PO Box 6
Tyler, TX 75710
Phone: (903)593-2519
Fax: (903)593-4918
**Format:** Talk; News; Sports; Sports

**KTYL-FM - 93.1 (30564)**
3810 Brookside Dr.
Tyler, TX 75701-9420
Phone: (903)581-8197
Fax: (903)581-2011
**Format:** Adult Contemporary

**KUEZ-FM - 100.1 (30116)**
121 Calder Sq.
PO Box 1345
Lufkin, TX 75901
Phone: (409)634-6661
Fax: (409)632-5722
**Format:** Adult Contemporary; Soft Rock; Oldies

**KVNE-FM - 89.5 (30565)**
2721 E. Erwin St.
PO Box 8525
Tyler, TX 75711
Phone: (903)593-5863
Fax: (903)593-2663
**Format:** Adult Contemporary

**KYKX-FM - 105.7 (30074)**
481 E Loop 281
Longview, TX 75605
Phone: (903)663-9458
Fax: (903)663-1022
**Format:** Country

**KYZS-AM - 1490 (30566)**
PO Box 6
Tyler, TX 75710-1490
Phone: (903)593-1490
Fax: (903)597-8378
**Format:** Talk

**KZEY-AM - 690 (30567)**
PO Box 4248
Tyler, TX 75712
Phone: (903)593-1744
Fax: (903)593-2666
**Format:** Urban Contemporary

## Victoria, TX

**KLUB-FM - 106.9 (30585)**
107 North Star Dr.
Victoria, TX 77901
Phone: (361)573-0777
Fax: (361)578-0059
**Format:** Classic Rock

**KQVT-FM - 92.3 (30586)**
107 North Star Dr.
Victoria, TX 77901
Phone: (361)573-0777
Fax: (361)578-0059
**Format:** Adult Contemporary

**KVCQ-FM - 97.7 (29496)**
Victoria Hwy.
Cuero, TX 77954
Phone: (361)275-3420

**Format:** Oldies

## Waco-Temple-Bryan, TX

**KAGC-AM - 1510 (29359)**
Box 4066
Bryan, TX 77805
Phone: (409)779-1510
Fax: (409)779-1587
**Format:** Religious; Contemporary Christian

**KBGO-FM - 95.7 (30604)**
314 West State, Hwy. 6
Waco, TX 76712
**Format:** Oldies

**KBRQ-FM - 102.5 (30605)**
314 West State, Hwy 6
Waco, TX 76712
Phone: (254)776-3900
Fax: (254)776-3917
**Format:** Classic Rock

**KEYR-FM - 92.9 (30606)**
1018 N. Valley Mills Dr.
Waco, TX 76710
Phone: (254)772-0930
Fax: (254)772-1580
**Format:** Adult Contemporary

**KNFX-FM - 99.5 (29364)**
1730 Briarcrest Dr.
Bryan, TX 77802
Phone: (979)846-5597
Fax: (979)268-9090
**Format:** Classic Rock

**KORA-FM - 98.3 (29365)**
PO Box 3069
Bryan, TX 77805
Phone: (979)776-1240
Fax: (979)776-4700
**Format:** Country

**KQRL-AM - 1580 (30607)**
PO Box 8093
Waco, TX 76714
Phone: (254)772-0930
Fax: (254)772-1580
**Format:** News; Talk; Gospel; Hispanic; Hispanic

**KTAM-AM - 1240 (29366)**
1240 E. Villa Maria Rd.
PO Box 3069
Bryan, TX 77802
Phone: (979)776-1240
Fax: (979)776-4700
**Format:** Hispanic

**KTON-AM - 940 (29305)**
PO Box 1387
Belton, TX 76513
Phone: (254)939-9377
Fax: (254)939-9458
**Format:** Religious

**KTSR-FM - 92.1 (29444)**
2700 E. BYP, No. 5000
College Station, TX 77845-5010
**Format:** Classic Rock

**KVJM-FM - 103.1 (29367)**
219 N. Main, Ste. 600
Bryan, TX 77803
Phone: (979)779-3337
Fax: (979)779-3444
**Format:** Adult Contemporary

**KYCX-FM - 104.9 (30169)**
Box 1590
Mexia, TX 76667
Phone: (817)562-5328
Fax: (817)562-6729
**Format:** Contemporary Country

## Wichita Falls, TX-Lawton, OK

**KBZQ-FM - 99.5 (25388)**
1006 NW 47th St., No. B
Lawton, OK 73505
Phone: (580)357-9950
Fax: (580)357-9995

**Format:** Adult Contemporary

**KBZS-FM - 106.3 (30641)**
2525 Kell Blvd., Ste. 200
Wichita Falls, TX 76308
Phone: (940)763-1111
Fax: (940)322-3166
**Format:** Adult Contemporary

**KCCU-FM - 89.3 (25389)**
Administration Bldg.
2800 West Gore Blvd.
Lawton, OK 73505
Phone: (580)581-2425
Fax: (580)581-5571
**Format:** Jazz; Easy Listening; Classical; News

**KEYB-FM - 107.9 (25241)**
808 N. Main
Altus, OK 73522
Phone: (580)482-1555
Fax: (580)482-8353
**Format:** Country

**KFXI-FM - 92.1 (25401)**
1101 Hwy. 81
Marlow, OK 73055
Phone: (580)658-9292
**Format:** Contemporary Country

**KMOC-FM - 89.5 (30642)**
1040 W Wenonah
PO Box 41
Wichita Falls, TX 76307
Phone: (940)767-3303
Fax: (940)723-5807
**Format:** Religious; Contemporary Christian

**KNTX-AM - 1410 (29326)**
PO Box 1080
Bowie, TX 76230-1080
Phone: (940)872-2288
Fax: (940)872-1228
**Format:** Oldies

**KWFS-AM - 1290 (30644)**
2525 Kell Blvd., Suite 200
Wichita Falls, TX 76308
Phone: (940)763-1111
Fax: (940)763-8181
**Format:** News; Hispanic; Country; Country

# Southern States

## Aguadilla-Mayaguez, Puerto Rico

**WAEL-FM - 96.1 (27774)**
PO Box 1370
Mayaguez, PR 00681-1370
Phone: (809)832-4560
Fax: (809)792-3140
**Format:** Contemporary Hit Radio (CHR); Hispanic; Hispanic

**WIOB-FM - 97.5 (27776)**
Darlington Bldg.
PO Box 43
Mayaguez, PR 00681
Phone: (809)832-1150
**Format:** Easy Listening; Hispanic; Hispanic

**WKJB-AM - 710 (27777)**
637 S. Post St.
PO Box 1293
Mayaguez, PR 00680
Phone: (809)834-6666
Fax: (809)831-6925
**Format:** News; Talk

**WKJB-FM - 99.1 (27778)**
637 S. Post St.
PO Box 1293
Mayaguez, PR 00680
Phone: (809)834-6666
Fax: (809)834-8380
**Format:** News; Soft Rock; Easy Listening; Oldies; Easy Listening; Oldies

**WORA-AM - 760 (27779)**
3822 Marine Sta.
Mayaguez, PR 00680
Phone: (809)832-1150
Fax: (809)834-0488

Albany (Valdosta & Cordele), GA

**Format:** Top 40; Hispanic; Hispanic

**WPRA-AM - 990 (27781)**
PO Box 1869
Mayaguez, PR 00680
**Format:** Top 40; Hispanic; Hispanic

**WTIL-AM - 1300 (27782)**
Box 1360
Post & Bosque Sts.
Mayaguez, PR 00681
**Format:** Adult Contemporary; Big Band/Nostalgia; News; Hispanic

**WTPM-FM - 92.9 (27783)**
Sector Cuba, No.1060
Mayaguez, PR 00680
Phone: (787)831-9200
Fax: (787)265-4044
**Format:** Religious; Classical; Easy Listening; News; Talk; Hispanic; News; Talk; Hispanic

**WVID-FM - 90.3 (27824)**
PO Box 1020
Trujillo Alto, PR 00977-1020
Phone: (787)832-9090
Fax: (787)761-8018
**Format:** Jazz; Educational

## Albany (Valdosta & Cordele), GA

**WAFT-FM - 101.1 (7479)**
215 Waft Hill Ln.
Valdosta, GA 31602-6512
Phone: (229)244-5180
Fax: (229)242-8808
**Format:** Religious

**WALG-AM - 1590 (6770)**
1104 W. Broad Ave.
Albany, GA 31707-4340
**Format:** Talk

**WANL-AM - 1250 (6771)**
2804 N. Jefferson St.
PO Box 90
Albany, GA 31701
Phone: (912)432-1250
Fax: (912)432-1927
**Format:** Religious

**WGPC-FM - 104.5 (6773)**
2011 Gillionville Rd.
Albany, GA 31707
Phone: (229)883-6500
Fax: (229)883-1450
**Format:** Full Service

**WJEM-AM - 1150 (7482)**
PO Box 368
Valdosta, GA 31603-0368
Phone: (229)241-9797
Fax: (229)253-1133
**Format:** Talk; News; Country

**WJYF-FM - 95.3 (7461)**
PO Box 968
Tifton, GA 31793-0968
Phone: (229)382-1340
Fax: (229)386-8658
**Format:** Adult Contemporary

**WKAA-FM - 97.7 (7462)**
PO Box 7
Tifton, GA 31793-0007
Fax: (912)423-8313
**Format:** Oldies

**WMGR-FM - 97.3 (7003)**
PO Drawer 930
Bainbridge, GA 39818
Phone: (229)246-1650
Fax: (229)246-1403
**Format:** Contemporary Hit Radio (CHR)

**WQPW-FM - 95.7 (7317)**
10181 Adel Hwy.
Morven, GA 31638-3726
Phone: (912)244-8642
Fax: (912)242-7620

**Format:** Adult Contemporary; Adult Contemporary

**WQVE-FM - 105.5 (6775)**
1104 W Broad Ave.
Albany, GA 31707-4340
**Format:** Adult Contemporary

**WSTI-FM - 105.3 (7483)**
2612 Madison Hwy., Ste. C
Valdosta, GA 31601-6900
Phone: (229)249-8200
Fax: (229)249-9948
**Format:** Adult Contemporary

**WTIF-AM - 1340 (7464)**
PO Box 968
Tifton, GA 31794
Phone: (229)382-1340
Fax: (229)386-8658
**Format:** Country

**WVVS-FM - 90.9 (7484)**
University Union, 2nd Fl.
Valdosta State University
Valdosta, GA 31698-0002
Phone: (229)259-2015
**Format:** Alternative/New Music/Progressive; Urban Contemporary

**WWRQ-FM - 107.7 (7485)**
5A A1 Brooks Dr.
Valdosta, GA 31601
Phone: (912)244-1009
Fax: (912)247-4722
**Format:** Album-Oriented Rock (AOR)

## Anniston, AL

**WANA-AM - 1490 (16)**
PO Box 1965
Anniston, AL 36202
Phone: (256)237-1627
Fax: (256)237-1628
**Format:** Gospel

**WDNG-AM - 1450 (17)**
PO Box 1450
Anniston, AL 36202
Phone: (256)236-8291
Fax: (256)236-2892
**Format:** Adult Contemporary

**WLJS-FM - 91.9 (292)**
Jacksonville State University
700 Pelham Rd.
Jacksonville, AL 36265
Phone: (256)782-5572
Fax: (256)782-5645
**Format:** Alternative/New Music/Progressive; Jazz; Classic Rock

## Atlanta (Athens & Rome), GA

**WAEC-AM - 860 (6934)**
1465 Northside Dr., Ste. 218
Atlanta, GA 30318
Phone: (404)355-8699
Fax: (404)355-4156
**Format:** Religious

**WAFS-AM - 920 (6935)**
1827 Powers Ferry Rd., Ste. 200
Atlanta, GA 30339
Phone: (770)226-0920
Fax: (770)226-0927
**Format:** Religious

**WAZX-AM - 1550 (7416)**
2460 Atlanta Rd.
Smyrna, GA 30080
Phone: (770)436-6171
Fax: (770)436-0100
**Format:** Hispanic; Public Radio

**WBCX-FM - 89.1 (7169)**
Brenau University
500 Washington St. SE
Gainesville, GA 30501
Phone: (770)538-4708
Fax: (770)538-4558
**Format:** Classical; Jazz

**WBKZ-AM - 880 (6819)**
1186 W Broad St
Athens, GA 30606
Phone: (706)548-8800

Fax: (706)549-8800
**Format:** Urban Contemporary; Gospel; Hispanic

**WBTR-FM - 92.1 (7039)**
102 Parkwood Cir.
PO Box 569
Carrollton, GA 30117
Phone: (770)832-9685
Fax: (770)830-1027
**Format:** Country

**WBZY-FM - 96.7 (6940)**
1819 Peachtree Rd. NE, Ste. 700
Atlanta, GA 30309
Phone: (404)367-0640
Fax: (404)367-1055
**Format:** Alternative/New Music/Progressive

**WCOH-AM - 1400 (7325)**
154 Boone Dr.
Newnan, GA 30263
Phone: (770)253-4636
Fax: (770)251-8260
**Format:** Country

**WEBS-AM - 1030 (7031)**
PO Box 1299
Calhoun, GA 30703
Phone: (706)629-2238
Fax: (706)629-7092
**Format:** News; Oldies; News; Oldies

**WFTD-AM - 1080 (7297)**
774 Roswell St.
Marietta, GA 30060
Fax: (404)424-9853
**Format:** Contemporary Christian; Talk

**WGAU-AM - 1340 (6820)**
850 Bobbin Mill Rd.
Athens, GA 30606
Phone: (706)549-1340
Fax: (706)546-0441
**Format:** News; Talk; Sports

**WGTA-AM - 950 (7436)**
339 Hwy 100
PO Box 200
Summerville, GA 30747
Phone: (770)857-2466
Fax: (706)857-3652
**Format:** Country; Gospel

**WGUN-AM - 1010 (7472)**
2901 Mountain Industrial Blvd.
Tucker, GA 30084-3073
Phone: (404)491-1010
Fax: (404)491-3019
**Format:** Information

**WJJC-AM - 1270 (7081)**
220 Little St.
PO Box 379
Commerce, GA 30529
Phone: (706)335-3155
Fax: (706)335-7622
**Format:** Country; Southern Gospel; Sports

**WJTH-AM - 900 (7032)**
329 Richardson Rd., SE
PO Box 1119
Calhoun, GA 30703-1119
Phone: (706)629-6397
Fax: (706)629-8463
**Format:** Country

**WKCX-FM - 97.7 (7369)**
710 Turner McCall Blvd.
PO Box 1546
Rome, GA 30165
Phone: (706)291-9766
Fax: (706)291-9706
**Format:** Adult Contemporary

**WKEU-AM - 1450 (7182)**
1000 Memorial Dr.
PO Box 997
Griffin, GA 30224
Phone: (404)227-5507
Fax: (404)229-2291
**Format:** Middle-of-the-Road (MOR)

**WKKP-AM - 1410 (7301)**
12 N. Cedar St.
PO Box 351
McDonough, GA 30253
Phone: (770)775-3151
Fax: (770)775-3153

**Format:** Middle-of-the-Road (MOR); Adult Contemporary; Oldies; News

**WKUN-AM - 1580 (7315)**
PO Box 649
Monroe, GA 30655
Phone: (770)267-6558
Fax: (770)267-0341
**Format:** Gospel

**WLAQ-AM - 1410 (7370)**
2 Mt. Alto Rd.
Rome, GA 30165
Phone: (706)232-7767
Fax: (706)295-9225
**Format:** News; Talk; Sports

**WLKQ-FM - 102.3 (7027)**
6259 Woodlakle Dr.
Buford, GA 30518-3558
Phone: (770)932-1102
Fax: (770)932-0988
**Format:** Oldies

**WMKJ-FM - 96.7 (7351)**
PO Box 2547
Peachtree City, GA 30269
Phone: (404)577-4850
Fax: (404)251-8260
**Format:** Adult Contemporary

**WNGC-FM - 106.1 (6821)**
850 Bobbin Mill Rd.
Athens, GA 30606
Phone: (706)549-5500
Fax: (706)546-0441
**Format:** Country

**WQTU-FM - 102.3 (7371)**
20 Davenport Dr.
Rome, GA 30165
Phone: (706)291-9496
Fax: (706)291-7107
**Format:** Adult Contemporary

**WQUL-FM - 97.7 (7183)**
PO Box 997
1000 Memorial Dr.
Griffin, GA 30224
Fax: (404)229-2291
**Format:** Oldies

**WRAS-FM - 88.5 (6953)**
Georgia State University
33 Gilmer St.
Atlanta, GA 30303
Phone: (404)463-9021
Fax: (404)463-9164
**Format:** Alternative/New Music/Progressive

**WRBN-FM - 104.1 (7056)**
PO Box 1149
Clayton, GA 30525
Phone: (706)782-1041
Fax: (706)782-4252
**Format:** Adult Contemporary; Adult Contemporary

**WROM-AM - 710 (7373)**
1105 Calhoun Ave.
PO Box 5031
Rome, GA 30162-5031
Phone: (706)234-7171
Fax: (706)234-8043
**Format:** Religious; Southern Gospel

**WRWH-AM - 1350 (7059)**
PO Box 181
Cleveland, GA 30528
Phone: (706)865-3181
Fax: (706)865-0421
**Format:** Country; Talk; Talk

**WSB-FM - 98.5 (6957)**
1601 W. Peachtree St. NE
Atlanta, GA 30309
Phone: (404)897-7500
Fax: (404)897-7363
**Format:** Adult Contemporary

**WSSA-AM - 1570 (7142)**
2424 Old Rex Morrow Rd.
Ellenwood, GA 30294
Phone: (404)361-8843
Fax: (404)366-9772

**Format:** Religious; Southern Gospel; Religious; Southern Gospel

**WSTR-FM - 94.1 (6959)**
3350 Peachtree Rd., Penthouse Ste.
Atlanta, GA 30326
Phone: (404)261-2970
Fax: (404)365-9026
**Format:** Contemporary Hit Radio (CHR)

**WTRP-AM - 620 (7228)**
806 Franklin Rd.
PO Box 1203
Lagrange, GA 30241
Phone: (706)884-8611
Fax: (706)884-8612
**Format:** Adult Contemporary; Sports; News; Talk

**WTSH-AM - 1360 (7374)**
PO Box 6008
Rome, GA 30162
Phone: (706)291-9496
Fax: (706)235-7107
**Format:** News; Sports

**WTSH-FM - 107.1 (7375)**
PO Box 6008
Rome, GA 30162
Fax: (706)235-7107
**Format:** Country

**WWEV-FM - 91.5 (7096)**
1705 Sawnee Dr.
PO Box 248
Cumming, GA 30040
Phone: (770)781-9150
Fax: (770)781-5003
**Format:** Religious; Contemporary Christian

**WYXC-AM - 1270 (7044)**
1410 Hwy. 411 NE
Cartersville, GA 30121
Phone: (770)382-1270
Fax: (770)936-1967
**Format:** News; Talk

## Augusta, GA

**WACG-FM - 90.7 (6986)**
2500 Walton Way
Augusta, GA 30904-2200
Phone: (706)737-1661
**Format:** News; Classical; Public Radio; Jazz

**WAKB-FM - 96.9 (6988)**
PO Box 10003
Augusta, GA 30903
Phone: (803)279-2330
Fax: (803)854-1055
**Format:** Urban Contemporary

**WEKL-FM - 102.3 (6989)**
2743 Perimeter Pkwy., Ste. 100-200
Augusta, GA 30909-6415
Phone: (706)396-6000
Fax: (706)396-6010
**Format:** Classic Rock

**WFAM-AM - 1050 (6990)**
552 Laney-Walker Extension
Augusta, GA 30901
Phone: (706)722-6077
Fax: (706)722-7066
**Format:** Religious; Talk; Gospel

**WGUS-AM - 1380 (28194)**
500 Carolina Springs Rd.
North Augusta, SC 29841-9437
Phone: (803)279-1977
Fax: (803)396-6010
**Format:** News; Talk

**WKZK-AM - 1600 (6994)**
PO Box 1454
Augusta, GA 30903
Phone: (706)738-9191
Fax: (706)481-8442
**Format:** Gospel

**WPEH-AM - 1420 (7241)**
5442 Middleground Rd.
PO Box 425
Louisville, GA 30434
Phone: (478)625-7248
Fax: (478)625-7249

**Format:** Country; Oldies

**WPEH-FM - 92.1 (7242)**
5442 Middleground Rd.
PO Box 425
Louisville, GA 30434
Phone: (478)625-7248
Fax: (478)625-7249
**Format:** Country; Oldies

**WRDW-AM - 1480 (6995)**
PO Box 211045
Augusta, GA 30917-1045
Fax: (706)481-0092
**Format:** Sports

**WRXR-FM - 96.3 (28196)**
500 Carolina Springs Rd.
Lamar Bldg., 14th Fl.
North Augusta, SC 29841
Phone: (803)279-1977
Fax: (803)279-1175
**Format:** Album-Oriented Rock (AOR)

**WSLT-FM - 98.3 (27972)**
PO Box 211045
Augusta, SC 30917
**Format:** Adult Contemporary

**WTHB-AM - 1550 (6997)**
PO Box 1584
Augusta, GA 30903-1584
Phone: (803)279-2330
Fax: (803)279-8149
**Format:** Gospel

**WTHO-FM - 101.7 (7454)**
788 Cedar Rock Rd
PO Drawer 900
Thomson, GA 30824
Phone: (706)595-5122
Fax: (706)595-3021
**Format:** Country; News; Sports; Sports

**WTWA-AM - 1240 (7455)**
788 Cedar Rock Rd.
Thomson, GA 30824
Phone: (706)595-1561
Fax: (706)595-3021
**Format:** Middle-of-the-Road (MOR)

**WXKT-FM - 100.1 (7496)**
823 Berkshire Dr.
Washington, GA 30673
Phone: (706)678-7100
Fax: (706)678-1925
**Format:** Adult Contemporary; Sports

## Biloxi-Gulfport-Pascagoula, MS

**WBUV-FM - 104.9 (16755)**
286 Debuys Rd.
Biloxi, MS 39531
Phone: (228)388-2323
Fax: (228)388-2362
**Format:** Urban Contemporary

**WGCM-FM - 102.3 (16842)**
PO Box 2639
Gulfport, MS 39501-2639
Fax: (601)863-7516
**Format:** Oldies

**WGUD-AM - 1490 (16988)**
PO Box 307
Pascagoula, MS 39568
Phone: (601)475-2111
Fax: (601)474-2236
**Format:** News; Sports

**WKNN-FM - 99.1 (16756)**
286 DeBuys Rd.
Biloxi, MS 39531
Phone: (228)388-2323
Fax: (228)388-2362
**Format:** Country

**WMAH-FM - 90.3 (16758)**
c/o Mississippi Public Broadcasting
3825 Ridgewood Rd.
Jackson, MS 39211-6463
Phone: (601)432-6565
Fax: (601)432-6806

# Birmingham (Gadsden), AL

**Format:** Classical; News; Information; Public Radio

**WOSM-FM - 103.1 (16977)**
4720 Radio Rd.
Ocean Springs, MS 39564
Phone: (228)875-9031
Fax: (228)875-6461
**Format:** Southern Gospel

**WROA-AM - 1390 (16843)**
PO Box 2639
Gulfport, MS 39503
Phone: (228)896-5500
Fax: (228)896-0458
**Format:** Middle-of-the-Road (MOR); News; Sports

**WZKX-FM - 107.9 (16845)**
PO Box 2639
Gulfport, MS 39505
Phone: (601)832-5111
Fax: (601)832-7699
**Format:** Contemporary Hit Radio (CHR); News; News

**WZZJ-AM - 1580 (16989)**
5115 Telephone Rd.
Pascagoula, MS 39567
Phone: (228)762-5683
Fax: (228)762-1222
**Format:** Contemporary Christian; Contemporary Christian

## Birmingham (Gadsden), AL

**WATV-AM - 900 (114)**
3025 Ensley Ave.
PO Box 39054
Birmingham, AL 35208
Phone: (205)780-2014
Fax: (205)780-4034
**Format:** Full Service

**WBFR-FM - 89.5 (115)**
244 Goodwin Crest Dr., Ste. 118
Birmingham, AL 35209-3711
Phone: (205)942-3530
Fax: (205)942-6618
**Format:** Religious; Eclectic; Eclectic

**WBHK-FM - 98.7 (116)**
950 22nd St. N, Ste. 1000
Birmingham, AL 35203-5301
Phone: (205)322-2987
**Format:** Urban Contemporary

**WDJC-FM - 93.7 (122)**
Box 59621
Birmingham, AL 35259-9621
Phone: (205)879-3324
Fax: (205)802-4555
**Format:** Religious

**WDXB-FM - 102.5 (123)**
530 Beacon Pkwy. W, Ste. 600
Birmingham, AL 35209
Phone: (205)439-9600
Fax: (205)439-8390
**Format:** Country

**WEIS-AM - 990 (158)**
PO Box 297
Centre, AL 35960
Phone: (256)927-5152
Fax: (256)927-6503
**Format:** Country; Southern Gospel

**WFEB-AM - 1340 (440)**
1209 Millerville Hwy.
PO Box 358
Sylacauga, AL 35150
Phone: (256)245-3281
Fax: (256)245-3050
**Format:** News; Talk; Sports

**WFMH-AM - 1460 (172)**
1707 Warnke Rd. NW
Cullman, AL 35055
Phone: (256)734-3271
Fax: (256)734-3622
**Format:** Southern Gospel; Gospel; Gospel

**WFMH-FM - 95.5 (173)**
1707 Warnke Rd. NW
Cullman, AL 35055-2231
Phone: (256)734-3271
Fax: (256)734-3622

**Format:** Country; Country

**WHMA-AM - 1390 (19)**
PO Box 278
PO Box 278
Anniston, AL 36202
Phone: (256)237-8741
Fax: (256)231-9414
**Format:** Sports; Talk

**WHMA-FM - 100.5 (20)**
Williamson Commerce Center, 8th Fl.
801 Noble St.
Anniston, AL 36201
Phone: (256)237-8741
Fax: (256)231-9414
**Format:** Country; Hot Country

**WJBB-AM - 1230 (259)**
PO Drawer 370
Haleyville, AL 35565-0370
Phone: (205)486-2277
Fax: (205)486-3905
**Format:** News; Southern Gospel; Southern Gospel

**WJBY-AM - 930 (236)**
2725 Rainbow Dr.
Gadsden, AL 35901
Phone: (205)442-1222
Fax: (205)442-1229
**Format:** Religious

**WJLD-AM - 1400 (127)**
1449 Spaulding Ishkooda Rd.
Birmingham, AL 35211
Phone: (205)942-1776
Fax: (205)942-4814
**Format:** Blues; Talk; Gospel

**WLPH-AM - 1480 (132)**
PO Box 100067
Birmingham, AL 35210
Phone: (205)956-5470
Fax: (205)956-5471
**Format:** Religious

**WRFS-AM - 1050 (9)**
PO Box 1640
Columbus, GA 31994
Phone: (334)821-0744
Fax: (334)821-0744
**Format:** Middle-of-the-Road (MOR)

**WSGN-FM - 91.5 (237)**
PO Box 227
Gadsden, AL 35902-0227
Phone: (205)549-8439
Fax: (205)549-8404
**Format:** Educational; Classical; Information

**WTRB-FM - 98.3 (22)**
PO Box 26
Ashland, AL 36251
Phone: (256)354-4601
Fax: (256)354-7224
**Format:** Adult Contemporary

**WVSU-FM - 91.1 (139)**
800 Lakeshore Dr.
Birmingham, AL 35229
Phone: (205)726-2877
Fax: (205)726-4032
**Format:** Jazz

**WZZK-AM - 610 (142)**
530 Beacon Pkwy. W., No. 300
Birmingham, AL 35209-3175
Fax: (205)916-1150
**Format:** Contemporary Country

**WZZK-FM - 104.7 (143)**
530 Beacon Pkwy. W., No. 300
Birmingham, AL 35209-3175
Phone: (205)942-7800
Fax: (205)916-1151
**Format:** Contemporary Country

**WZZX-AM - 780 (23)**
PO Box 26
Ashland, AL 36251
Fax: (256)354-7224

**Format:** Country; Gospel; Talk

## Bowling Green (Campbellsville), KY

**WAIN-AM - 1270 (11622)**
PO Box 69
Columbia, KY 42728-0069
Phone: (270)384-2134
Fax: (270)384-6722
**Format:** News; Talk

**WAIN-FM - 93.5 (11623)**
PO Box 69
Columbia, KY 42728
Phone: (270)384-2134
Fax: (270)384-6722
**Format:** Country

**WBVR-FM - 96.7 (11561)**
2465 Russellville Rd.
Bowling Green, KY 42101
Phone: (502)843-3333
Fax: (502)843-0454
**Format:** Country

**WCVK-FM - 90.7 (11562)**
PO Box 539
Bowling Green, KY 42102
Phone: (270)781-7326
Fax: (270)781-8005
**Format:** Religious

**WDCL-FM - 89.7 (11563)**
Western Kentucky University
1 Big Red Way
Bowling Green, KY 42101
Phone: (502)745-5489
Fax: (502)745-2084
**Format:** Public Radio

**WKYU-FM - 88.9 (11567)**
Western Kentucky University
1 Big Red Way
Bowling Green, KY 42101
Phone: (270)745-6272
Fax: (502)745-2084
**Format:** Public Radio

**WUHU-FM - 107.1 (11569)**
901 Lehman Ave., Ste. 1
Box 900
Bowling Green, KY 42101
Phone: (502)843-0107
Fax: (502)782-0767
**Format:** Adult Contemporary

## Bristol,VA-Kingsport-Johnson Cty-Greenville,TN

**WCSK-FM - 90.3 (28670)**
1800 Legion Dr.
Kingsport, TN 37660
**Format:** Eclectic

**WETB-AM - 790 (28661)**
PO Box 4127
Johnson City, TN 37602
Phone: (423)928-7131
Fax: (423)928-8392
**Format:** Southern Gospel

**WGRV-AM - 1340 (28624)**
PO Box 278
Greeneville, TN 37744
Phone: (423)638-4147
Fax: (423)638-1979
**Format:** Country

**WHCB-FM - 91.5 (28491)**
4045 Weaver Pike
PO Box 2061
Bluff City, TN 37618
Phone: (423)878-6279
Fax: (423)878-6520
**Format:** Talk; Eclectic; Religious; Religious

**WIKQ-FM - 103.1 (28625)**
PO Box 278
Greeneville, TN 37744
Phone: (423)639-1831
Fax: (423)639-1979

**Format:** Country; Contemporary Country

**WOPI-AM - 1490 (28500)**
288 Delaney St.
Bristol, TN 37620
Phone: (423)764-5131
Fax: (423)246-6261
**Format:** Country; Bluegrass

**WSMG-AM - 1450 (28626)**
1004 Armour Rd.
PO Box 278
Greeneville, TN 37744
Phone: (423)638-3188
Fax: (423)638-1979
**Format:** Soft Rock

## Charleston-Huntington, WV

**WLGC-AM - 1520 (11519)**
1401 Winchester Ave, 1st. Fl.
Ashland, KY 41101
Fax: (606)920-9523
**Format:** Sports

**WLGC-FM - 105.7 (11520)**
1401 Winchester Ave, 1st. Fl.
Ashland, KY 41101
Fax: (606)920-9523
**Format:** Country

## Charleston, SC

**WDKD-AM - 1310 (28239)**
PO Box 1296
Sumter, SC 29151-1269
**Format:** Country

**WPAL-AM - 730 (28197)**
2045 Spaulding Dr.
PO Box 30999
North Charleston, SC 29406-4960
**Format:** Blues

**WSSB-FM - 90.3 (28208)**
South Carolina State University
PO Box 7619
Orangeburg, SC 29117
Phone: (803)536-8196
Fax: (803)533-3652
**Format:** Educational; Information; Jazz; Jazz

**WSSX-FM - 95.1 (28017)**
PO Box 30909
Charleston, SC 29417
**Format:** Adult Contemporary

**WTMZ-AM - 910 (28200)**
4230 Faber Place Dr., Ste. 100
North Charleston, SC 29405
Phone: (843)277-1200
Fax: (843)277-1212
**Format:** Talk; Big Band/Nostalgia

**WXLY-FM - 102.5 (28177)**
950 Houston-Northcutt Blvd., Ste. 201
Mount Pleasant, SC 29464
Phone: (843)881-9591
Fax: (843)884-1218
**Format:** Oldies

## Charlotte (Hickory), NC

**WAIZ-AM - 630 (23579)**
PO Box 938
Hickory, NC 28603
Phone: (828)322-9472
Fax: (828)464-9662
**Format:** Oldies

**WAVO-AM - 1150 (23361)**
5732 N. Tryon St.
Charlotte, NC 28213
Phone: (704)596-4900
Fax: (704)596-6939
**Format:** Religious

**WAYN-AM - 900 (23756)**
1223 Rockingham Rd.
PO Box 519
Rockingham, NC 28379
Phone: (910)895-4041
Fax: (910)895-4993

**Format:** Adult Contemporary; News; Sports

**WBAV-AM - 1600 (23362)**
1520 South Blvd., Ste. 300
Charlotte, NC 28203-3701
Phone: (704)342-2644
**Format:** Gospel; Gospel

**WBT-AM - 1110 (23363)**
1 Julian Price Pl.
Charlotte, NC 28208
Phone: (704)374-3500
Fax: (704)374-3885
**Format:** News; Talk; Talk

**WCGC-AM - 1270 (23242)**
PO Box 1360
Belmont, NC 28012
Phone: (704)825-2812
Fax: (704)825-2127
**Format:** Talk; News; Sports

**WGAS-AM - 1420 (23368)**
PO Box 16408
Charlotte, NC 28297-6408
Phone: (704)865-5796
**Format:** Middle-of-the-Road (MOR); Religious; Contemporary Christian; Contemporary Christian

**WGWG-FM - 88.3 (23369)**
Box 876
Boiling Springs, NC 28017
Phone: (704)406-3525
Fax: (704)406-4338
**Format:** Adult Album Alternative; Contemporary Christian

**WHKY-AM - 1290 (23581)**
PO Box 1059
Hickory, NC 28603
Phone: (828)322-5115
Fax: (828)322-8256
**Format:** Talk

**WIBT-FM - 96.1 (23370)**
801 E Morehead St., Ste. 200
Charlotte, NC 28202
Phone: (704)338-9600
Fax: (704)334-9525
**Format:** Contemporary Hit Radio (CHR)

**WKSK-AM - 580 (23834)**
240 Radio Rd.
PO Box 729
West Jefferson, NC 28694
Phone: (336)246-6001
**Format:** Country

**WLNK-FM - 107.9 (23372)**
1 Julian Price Pl.
Charlotte, NC 28208
Phone: (704)374-3500
Fax: (704)374-3885
**Format:** Adult Contemporary

**WLWL-AM - 770 (23757)**
PO Box 1536
Rockingham, NC 28379
Phone: (910)997-2526
Fax: (910)997-2527
**Format:** Full Service

**WMNC-FM - 92.1 (23653)**
1103 N. Green St.
PO Box 969
Morganton, NC 28680-0969
Phone: (828)437-0521
Fax: (828)433-8855
**Format:** Hot Country

**WNMX-FM - 1240 (23374)**
920 Ursuline St.
PO Box 18614
Charlotte, NC 28218
Phone: (704)596-1240
Fax: (704)596-6939
**Format:** Religious; Religious

**WOGR-AM - 1540 (23376)**
1501 N. I-85 Service Rd.
PO Box 16408
Charlotte, NC 28216
Phone: (704)393-1540
Fax: (704)393-1527
**Format:** Religious

**WRCM-FM - 91.9 (23377)**
PO Box 17069
Charlotte, NC 28227
Phone: (704)821-9293

Fax: (704)821-9285
**Format:** Contemporary Christian; Adult Contemporary

**WRNA-AM - 1140 (23604)**
PO Box 8146
Kannapolis, NC 28083-8146
Phone: (704)857-1101
Fax: (704)857-0680
**Format:** Southern Gospel; Religious

**WSAT-AM - 1280 (23770)**
1525 Jake Alexander Blvd. W.
Drawer 99
Salisbury, NC 28145
Phone: (704)633-0621
Fax: (704)636-2955
**Format:** Oldies; Sports; News; Full Service; News

**WSGE-FM - 91.7 (23391)**
201 Hwy. 321 S.
Dallas, NC 28034-1499
Phone: (704)922-6334
Fax: (704)922-6514
**Format:** Classic Rock; Big Band/Nostalgia; Blues; Hispanic; Country; Contemporary Christian

**WSTP-AM - 1490 (23771)**
PO Box 4157
Salisbury, NC 28145-4157
Phone: (704)636-3811
Fax: (704)637-1490
**Format:** Talk; News

## Chattanooga (Cleveland), TN

**WAWL-FM - 91.5 (28527)**
4501 Amnicola Hwy.
Chattanooga, TN 37406
Phone: (423)697-4437
Fax: (423)697-2596
**Format:** Album-Oriented Rock (AOR); Alternative/New Music/Progressive

**WBLJ-AM - 1230 (7102)**
PO Box 1284
Dalton, GA 30722-1284
Phone: (706)278-5511
Fax: (706)278-9917
**Format:** Full Service; News; Talk

**WDAL-AM - 1430 (7103)**
PO Box 1284
Dalton, GA 30721
Phone: (706)278-5511
Fax: (706)278-9917
**Format:** News; Talk; Talk

**WDEF-AM - 1370 (28528)**
2615 S. Broad St.
Chattanooga, TN 37408
Phone: (423)321-6200
Fax: (423)321-6264
**Format:** Adult Contemporary

**WDEF-FM - 92.3 (28529)**
2615 S. Broad St.
PO Box 11008
Chattanooga, TN 37408
Phone: (423)321-6200
Fax: (423)321-6264
**Format:** Adult Contemporary

**WDYN-FM - 89.7 (28531)**
1815 Union Ave.
Chattanooga, TN 37404
Phone: (423)493-4383
Fax: (423)493-4526
**Format:** Religious

**WFLI-AM - 1070 (28532)**
621 O'Grady Dr.
Chattanooga, TN 37409
Phone: (423)821-3555
Fax: (423)821-3557
**Format:** Gospel

**WLMR-AM - 1450 (28536)**
PO Box 72725
Chattanooga, TN 37407
Phone: (423)624-4200
Fax: (423)624-4722
**Format:** Adult Contemporary

**WQCH-AM - 1590 (7225)**
PO Box 746
La Fayette, GA 30728
Phone: (706)638-3276
Fax: (706)638-3896

4309

## Chicago (LaSalle), IL

**Format:** Country

**WQMT-FM - 98.9 (7104)**
PO Box 1284
Dalton, GA 30722-1284
Phone: (706)278-5511
Fax: (706)287-9917
**Format:** Country

**WSKZ-FM - 106.5 (28538)**
PO Box 11202
Chattanooga, TN 37401
Phone: (423)756-6141
Fax: (423)266-1652
**Format:** Adult Contemporary

**WWIC-AM - 1050 (429)**
815 W. Willow St.
PO Box 759
Scottsboro, AL 35768
Phone: (256)259-1050
Fax: (256)575-2411
**Format:** Country

**WYXI-AM - 1390 (28489)**
112 E. Madison Ave.
PO Box 1390
Athens, TN 37371-1390
Phone: (423)745-1390
**Format:** Oldies; News; Talk

## Chicago (LaSalle), IL

**WSOF-FM - 89.9 (11873)**
1415 Island Ford Rd.
PO Box 1246
Madisonville, KY 42431-9419
Phone: (270)825-3004
Fax: (270)825-3005
**Format:** Religious

## Cincinnati, OH

**WCVG-AM - 1320 (11747)**
PO Box 15034
Latonia, KY 41015
Phone: (859)291-2255
Fax: (859)655-4345
**Format:** Gospel

**WFTM-AM - 1240 (11886)**
626 Forest Ave.
PO Box 100
Maysville, KY 41056
Phone: (606)564-3361
Fax: (606)564-4291

**WFTM-FM - 95.9 (11887)**
626 Forest Ave.
PO Box 100
Maysville, KY 41056
Phone: (606)564-3361
Fax: (606)564-4291
**Format:** Adult Contemporary

## Columbia, SC

**WCAM-AM - 1590 (27993)**
5 The Commons Ward Rd
PO Box 753
Camden, SC 29020
Phone: (803)438-9002
Fax: (803)408-2288
**Format:** Middle-of-the-Road (MOR); Big Band/Nostalgia; Big Band/Nostalgia

**WCOS-FM - 97.5 (28069)**
316 Greystone Blvd.
Columbia, SC 29210-8007
Phone: (803)343-1100
Fax: (803)748-9267
**Format:** Country

**WDXY-AM - 1240 (28240)**
PO Box 1269
Sumter, SC 29151
Phone: (803)775-2321
Fax: (803)773-4856

**Format:** News; Talk; Sports

**WIBZ-FM - 95.5 (28241)**
PO Box 1269
Sumter, SC 29151
**Format:** Oldies

**WIGL-FM - 102.9 (28242)**
PO Box 1269
Sumter, SC 29151-1269
Phone: (803)536-1710
Fax: (803)531-1089
**Format:** Contemporary Country

**WISW-AM - 1320 (28072)**
1801 Trostan Hwy
PO Box 5106
Columbia, SC 29250
Phone: (803)796-7600
Fax: (803)796-5502
**Format:** News

**WKHT-FM - 93.7 (28243)**
PO Box 1269
Sumter, SC 29151
Phone: (803)775-0753
Fax: (803)773-4856
**Format:** Oldies

**WPUB-FM - 94.3 (27994)**
PO Box 753
Camden, SC 29020
Phone: (803)438-9002
**Format:** Adult Contemporary

**WQXL-AM - 1470 (28077)**
PO Box 3277
Columbia, SC 29230-3277
Phone: (803)742-1470
Fax: (803)252-2158
**Format:** Religious

**WRJA-FM - 88.1 (28245)**
1101 George Rogers Blvd.
Columbia, SC 29201-4761
Phone: (803)737-3420
Fax: (803)737-3552
**Format:** Public Radio; News; Jazz

**WVOC-AM - 560 (28079)**
316 Greystone Blvd.
Columbia, SC 29210-8007
Phone: (803)343-1100
Fax: (803)256-5255
**Format:** News; Talk; Talk

## Columbus, GA (Opelika, AL)

**WAGH FM 00.0 (7007)**
1501 13th Ave.
Columbus, GA 31901
Phone: (706)576-3000
Fax: (706)576-3005
**Format:** Urban Contemporary

**WAUD-AM - 1230 (42)**
2514 S. College St.
Auburn, AL 36830
Phone: (334)887-3401
Fax: (334)826-9599
**Format:** Sports; Easy Listening; News

**WBFA-FM - 101.3 (7068)**
1501 13th Ave.
Columbus, GA 31901
Phone: (706)576-3000
Fax: (706)576-3005
**Format:** Urban Contemporary

**WCGQ-FM - 107.3 (7069)**
18 9th St., Ste. 104
Columbus, GA 31901-2761
Phone: (706)327-1217
Fax: (706)596-4600
**Format:** Adult Contemporary

**WDAK-AM - 540 (7070)**
1501 13th Ave.
Columbus, GA 31904-2847
Phone: (706)596-3000
**Format:** Sports; Talk

**WDEC-FM - 94.7 (6783)**
1028 Adderton St.
PO Box 727
Americus, GA 31709
Phone: (229)924-1390
Fax: (229)928-2337

**Format:** Adult Contemporary

**WEAM-AM - 1580 (7071)**
PO Box 1998
Columbus, GA 31902-1998
Phone: (706)298-1590
Fax: (706)298-7800
**Format:** Gospel

**WGSY-FM - 100.1 (7072)**
PO Box 687
Columbus, GA 31902-0687
Phone: (706)576-3000
Fax: (706)576-3010
**Format:** Adult Contemporary

**WISK-AM - 1390 (6784)**
Hwy. 30 W.
PO Box 727
Americus, GA 31709
Fax: (912)928-2337
**Format:** Talk; News

**WISK-FM - 98.7 (6785)**
Hwy. 30 W.
PO Box 727
Americus, GA 31709
Phone: (912)924-6500
Fax: (912)928-2337
**Format:** Country

**WPNX-AM - 1460 (7074)**
PO Box 687
Columbus, GA 31902-0687
Phone: (706)576-3000
Fax: (706)576-3010
**Format:** Southern Gospel

**WSTH-FM - 106.1 (7077)**
1501 13th Ave.
PO Box 687
Columbus, GA 31901
Phone: (706)576-3000
Fax: (706)576-3010
**Format:** Country

## Columbus-Tupelo (West Point), MS

**WACR-AM - 1050 (16797)**
1910 14th Ave. N.
PO Box 1078
Columbus, MS 39703
Fax: (601)328-1054
**Format:** Religious; Urban Contemporary

**WACR-FM - 103.9 (16798)**
1910 14th Ave. N.
PO Box 1078
Columbus, MS 39703
Phone: (601)328-1050
Fax: (601)328-1054
**Format:** Urban Contemporary

**WELO-AM - 580 (17021)**
PO Box 410
Tupelo, MS 38802
Phone: (662)842-7658
Fax: (662)842-0197
**Format:** Oldies; News; Talk

**WESE-FM - 92.5 (17022)**
PO Box 3300
Tupelo, MS 38803
Phone: (662)842-1067
Fax: (662)842-0725
**Format:** Urban Contemporary

**WFTA-FM - 101.9 (17023)**
PO Box 2116
Tupelo, MS 38803
Phone: (662)842-2101
Fax: (662)842-9568
**Format:** Adult Contemporary

**WJWF-AM - 1400 (16800)**
702 2nd Ave. N.
PO Box 707
Columbus, MS 39703
Phone: (601)328-1400
Fax: (601)328-1421

**Format:** Religious; Contemporary Christian

**WKOR-AM - 980 (16801)**
PO Box 1076
Columbus, MS 39703-1076
**Format:** Information; News; Talk; Talk

**WMAV-FM - 90.3 (16984)**
c/o Mississippi Public Broadcasting
3825 Ridgewood Rd.
Jackson, MS 39211
Phone: (601)432-6565
Fax: (601)432-6806
**Format:** Classical; Information; News; Public Radio

**WMBC-FM - 103.1 (16802)**
702 2nd Ave. N.
PO Box 707
Columbus, MS 39703
Fax: (601)328-1421
**Format:** Country

**WMXU-FM - 106.1 (16803)**
PO Box 1076
Columbus, MS 39703
Fax: (601)328-1122
**Format:** Urban Contemporary

**WSSO-AM - 1230 (16804)**
601 2nd Ave. N.
Columbus, MS 39701-3929
Fax: (601)323-0573
**Format:** Sports

**WSYE-FM - 93.3 (17026)**
PO Box 1623
Tupelo, MS 38802
Fax: (601)844-7400
**Format:** Adult Contemporary

**WTUP-AM - 1490 (17027)**
PO Box 3300
Tupelo, MS 38803-3300
Phone: (662)844-1490
Fax: (601)842-0725
**Format:** Sports

**WWKZ-FM - 105.3 (17029)**
PO Box 3300
Tupelo, MS 38803-3300
**Format:** Contemporary Hit Radio (CHR)

**WWMS-FM - 97.5 (17030)**
PO Box 410
Tupelo, MS 38802
Phone: (601)234-6881
Fax: (601)236-5014
**Format:** Contemporary Country; News; Agricultural

**WZLQ-FM - 98.5 (17031)**
PO Box 410
Tupelo, MS 38802
Phone: (662)842-7658
Fax: (662)842-0197
**Format:** Hot Country

## Dothan, AL

**WDJR-FM - 96.9 (196)**
PO Box 9663
Dothan, AL 36303
Phone: (334)712-9233
Fax: (334)712-0374
**Format:** Country

**WGTF-FM - 89.5 (197)**
107 Wanda Ct.
Dothan, AL 36303-2963
Phone: (334)794-4770
Fax: (334)794-4770
**Format:** Religious

**WKMX-FM - 106.7 (206)**
100 N. Main
Enterprise, AL 36330
Phone: (334)347-2278
Fax: (334)393-2141
**Format:** Adult Contemporary

**WTBF-AM - 970 (447)**
POB 619
Thomasville, AL 36784
Phone: (334)636-4438
Fax: (334)636-4439

**Format:** Sports; Talk

**WTBF-FM - 94.7 (451)**
67 Court Sq.
Troy, AL 36081
Phone: (334)566-0300
Fax: (334)566-5689
**Format:** News

**WTYS-AM - 1340 (6211)**
PO Box 777
2725 Jefferson St.
Marianna, FL 32447-0777
Fax: (904)526-3687
**Format:** News; Talk

**WULA-AM - 1240 (208)**
Hwy. 431 S.
Eufaula, AL 36027
Phone: (334)688-2121
Fax: (334)688-2112
**Format:** News; Talk

**WULA-FM - 92.7 (209)**
Hwy. 431 S.
Eufaula, AL 36027
**Format:** Adult Contemporary

**WVOB-FM - 91.3 (199)**
PO Box 1944
Dothan, AL 36302
Phone: (334)671-9862
Fax: (334)793-4344
**Format:** Religious; Educational

## Evansville, IN (Madisonville, KY)

**WFMW-AM - 730 (11870)**
2380 N. Main St.
PO Box 338
Madisonville, KY 42431
Phone: (502)821-4096
Fax: (502)821-5954
**Format:** Country

**WHRZ-FM - 97.7 (11871)**
265 S. Main St.
PO Box 1310
Madisonville, KY 42431
Phone: (270)825-9779
Fax: (270)825-3260
**Format:** Country

**WKTG-FM - 93.9 (11872)**
PO Box 338
Madisonville, KY 42431
Phone: (502)821-1156
Fax: (502)821-5954
**Format:** Classic Rock

**WOMI-AM - 1490 (11925)**
3301 Frederica St.
Owensboro, KY 42301
Phone: (270)683-1558
Fax: (270)685-2500
**Format:** News; Talk; Talk

**WSNR-AM - 1600 (11708)**
Box 106
Hartford, KY 42347-0106
Fax: (502)298-9326
**Format:** News; Sports

## Florence-Myrtle Beach, SC

**WCRE-AM - 1420 (28021)**
541 Hwy No. 1 S.
PO Box 160
Cheraw, SC 29520
Phone: (843)537-7887
Fax: (843)537-7307

**WJXY-AM - 1050 (28178)**
11640 Hwy. 17 Byp.
Murrells Inlet, SC 29576-9332
Phone: (803)397-1050
Fax: (803)397-3668

**Format:** Music of Your Life

**WKZQ-FM - 101.7 (28183)**
PO Box 2389
Myrtle Beach, SC 29578
**Format:** Soft Rock

**WMXT-FM - 102.1 (28211)**
2014 N. Irby St.
Florence, SC 29501-1504
Phone: (843)661-5000
Fax: (843)661-0888
**Format:** Adult Contemporary

**WOLS-AM - 1230 (28100)**
338 E. McIver Rd.
Florence, SC 29506-6918
Phone: (843)665-1230
Fax: (843)665-8786
**Format:** Religious

**WSYN-FM - 106.5 (28179)**
11640 Hwy. 17 Byp.
Murrells Inlet, SC 29576-9332
Phone: (843)651-7869
Fax: (843)651-3197
**Format:** Oldies

**WVCO-FM - 94.9 (28185)**
1114 Third Ave. S.
Myrtle Beach, SC 29577
Phone: (843)445-9491
Fax: (843)445-9490
**Format:** Oldies

**WYAK-FM - 103.1 (28188)**
1571 Trade St.
Myrtle Beach, SC 29577-6536
Phone: (843)626-9103
Fax: (843)651-6840
**Format:** Contemporary Country

**WYAV-FM - 104.1 (28189)**
1116 Ocala St.
Myrtle Beach, SC 29577
Phone: (843)448-1041
Fax: (843)626-5988
**Format:** Adult Contemporary

## Fort Myers-Naples, FL

**WARO-FM - 94.5 (5984)**
2824 Palm Beach Blvd.
Fort Myers, FL 33916
Phone: (239)337-2346
Fax: (239)332-0767
**Format:** Classic Rock

**WAVV-FM - 101.1 (6318)**
11800 Tamiami Trail E.
Naples, FL 34113-7985
Phone: (941)775-9288
Fax: (941)793-7000
**Format:** Easy Listening; Jazz

**WBTT-FM - 105.5 (5986)**
13320 Metro Pkwy., Ste. 1
Fort Myers, FL 33912
Phone: (239)225-4300
Fax: (239)225-4410
**Format:** Urban Contemporary

**WCKT-FM - 100.1 (5987)**
13320 Metro Pkwy., Ste. 1
Fort Myers, FL 33912
Phone: (239)225-4300
Fax: (239)225-4410
**Format:** Country

**WCRM-AM - 1350 (5988)**
3448 Canal St.
Fort Myers, FL 33916-6513
Phone: (239)332-1350
Fax: (239)332-8890
**Format:** Gospel; Ethnic

**WGCU-FM - 90.1 (5990)**
Florida Gulf Coast University
10501 FGCU Blvd. S.
Fort Myers, FL 33965-6565
Fax: (941)590-2511
**Format:** Jazz; News; Classical; Public Radio

**WIKX-FM - 92.9 (6482)**
4810 Deltona Dr.
Punta Gorda, FL 33950
Phone: (941)639-1188
Fax: (941)639-6742

# Gainesville (Ocala), FL

**Format:** Country

**WINK-AM - 1240 (5991)**
2824 Palm Beach Rd.
Fort Myers, FL 33916-1590
Phone: (239)337-2346
Fax: (941)332-0767
**Format:** Talk; News

**WINK-FM - 96.9 (5992)**
2824 Palm Beach Blvd.
Fort Myers, FL 33916-1590
Fax: (941)332-0767
**Format:** Adult Contemporary

**WJST-FM - 106.3 (5945)**
PO Box 307
Estero, FL 33928-0307
Phone: (813)275-9980
Fax: (813)275-5611

**WKII-AM - 1070 (6483)**
3151 Cooper St., Ste. 56
Punta Gorda, FL 33950
Phone: (941)639-1112
Fax: (941)637-6187
**Format:** Middle-of-the-Road (MOR)

**WMYR-AM - 1410 (5993)**
2835 Hanson St.
Fort Myers, FL 33916
Phone: (239)332-2102
Fax: (239)332-3135

**WNOG-AM - 1270 (5994)**
2824 Palm Beach Blvd.
Fort Myers, FL 33916
Phone: (239)337-2346
Fax: (239)332-0767
**Format:** Talk; News

**WPJS-AM - 1330 (6319)**
3033 Riviera Dr., Ste. 200
Naples, FL 34103-2748
Phone: (239)403-3906
**Format:** Urban Contemporary

**WSGL-FM - 103.1 (6320)**
2640 Golden Gate Pkwy, Ste. 316
Naples, FL 34105-3203
Phone: (239)435-9100
Fax: (239)793-7329
**Format:** Adult Contemporary

**WSOR-FM - 90.9 (5996)**
940 Tarpon St.
Fort Myers, FL 33916
Fax: (239)334-0596
**Format:** Religious

**WTLQ-AM - 1240 (5997)**
2824 Palm Beach Blvd.
Fort Myers, FL 33916
Phone: (239)479-5558
Fax: (239)332-0767
**Format:** Talk

**WTLT-FM - 93.5 (5998)**
2824 Palm Beach Blvd.
Fort Myers, FL 33916
Phone: (941)337-2346
Fax: (941)332-0767
**Format:** Adult Contemporary

**WWGR-FM - 101.9 (5836)**
10915 K-Nine Dr.
Bonita Springs, FL 34135-6802
Phone: (239)485-8383
Fax: (239)495-6543
**Format:** Country

# Gainesville (Ocala), FL

**WKTK-FM - 98.5 (6050)**
3600 NW 43rd St.
Gainesville, FL 32606-8127
Phone: (352)377-0985
Fax: (352)377-1884
**Format:** Adult Contemporary

**WLUS-AM - 980 (6051)**
3135 SE 27th St.
Gainesville, FL 32641
Phone: (352)372-2528
Fax: (352)372-0851

**Format:** Middle-of-the-Road (MOR); Talk

**WMFQ-FM - 92.9 (6345)**
3357 SW 7th St.
Ocala, FL 34474
Phone: (352)732-9877
Fax: (352)622-6675
**Format:** Adult Contemporary; Soft Rock

**WOGK-FM - 93.7 (6348)**
3602 NE 20th Pl.
Ocala, FL 34470-4957
Phone: (352)622-5600
Fax: (352)622-7822
**Format:** Country

**WRZN-AM - 720 (6069)**
3988 N. Roscoe Rd.
Hernando, FL 34442
Phone: (352)726-7221
Fax: (352)726-3172
**Format:** Big Band/Nostalgia; Middle-of-the-Road (MOR)

**WSKY-FM - 97.3 (6054)**
3600-B NW 43rd St.
Gainesville, FL 32606-8127
Phone: (904)376-1230
Fax: (904)376-2666
**Format:** News; Talk

**WTRS-FM - 102.3 (6349)**
3357 SW 7th St.
Ocala, FL 34474
Phone: (352)732-9877
Fax: (352)622-6675
**Format:** Contemporary Country; Country; Country

# Greensboro-Winston Salem-High Point, NC

**WBAG-AM - 1150 (23268)**
PO Box 2450
Burlington, NC 27216
Phone: (336)226-1150
Fax: (336)226-1180
**Format:** News; Talk; Sports

**WBFJ-AM - 1550 (23878)**
1249 Trade St.
Winston-Salem, NC 27101
Phone: (336)777-1893
Fax: (336)777-1032
**Format:** Adult Contemporary; Religious

**WBFJ-FM - 89.3 (23879)**
1249 Trade St.
Winston-Salem, NC 27101
Phone: (336)721-1560
Fax: (336)777-1032
**Format:** Adult Contemporary; Contemporary Christian

**WFDD-FM - 88.5 (23880)**
PO Box 8850
Winston-Salem, NC 27109-8805
Phone: (336)758-8850
Fax: (336)758-5193
**Format:** Public Radio; Full Service; Classical; News

**WGBT-FM - 94.5 (23535)**
2 Pai Pk., Ste. B
Greensboro, NC 27409
Phone: (336)333-2100
Fax: (336)887-0104
**Format:** Contemporary Hit Radio (CHR)

**WGOS-AM - 1070 (23590)**
6223 Old Mendenhall Rd.
High Point, NC 27263-7624
Phone: (910)434-5024
Fax: (336)434-6018
**Format:** Talk; Hispanic

**WIFM-AM - 100.9 (23462)**
815 N Bridge ST
PO Box 1038
Elkin, NC 28621
Phone: (336)835-2511
Fax: (336)835-5248
**Format:** News; Talk

**WIFM-FM - 100.9 (23463)**
813 N. Bridge St.
PO Box 1038
Elkin, NC 28621
Phone: (336)835-2511
Fax: (336)835-5248

**Format:** Adult Contemporary

**WIST-FM - 98.3 (23592)**
1607 Country Club Dr.
PO Box 5663
High Point, NC 27262
Phone: (336)887-0983
Fax: (336)887-3055
**Format:** Adult Contemporary

**WKRR-FM - 92.3 (23538)**
192 E. Lewis St.
Greensboro, NC 27406
Phone: (336)274-8042
Fax: (336)274-1629
**Format:** Classic Rock

**WKSI-FM - 98.7 (23539)**
7819 National Service Rd., Ste. 401
Greensboro, NC 27409-9401
Fax: (919)275-6236
**Format:** Adult Contemporary

**WKZL-FM - 107.5 (23540)**
192 E. Lewis St.
Greensboro, NC 27406
Phone: (336)274-8042
Fax: (336)274-1629
**Format:** Contemporary Hit Radio (CHR)

**WLXN-AM - 1440 (23621)**
200 Radio Dr.
Lexington, NC 27292
Phone: (336)248-2716
Fax: (336)248-2800
**Format:** Talk; News; Sports; Sports

**WMFR-AM - 1230 (23593)**
PO Box 5525
High Point, NC 27262-5525
Fax: (910)887-0104
**Format:** News; Talk

**WMQX-FM - 93.1 (23542)**
7819 National Service Rd., No. 401
Greensboro, NC 27409-9401
Phone: (336)605-5200
Fax: (336)605-0138
**Format:** Oldies

**WPET-AM - 950 (23544)**
7819 National Service Rd., Ste. 401
Greensboro, NC 27409
Phone: (336)605-5200
Fax: (336)387-7206
**Format:** Southern Gospel; Sports

**WQFS-FM - 90.9 (23545)**
PO Box 17714
Greensboro, NC 27410
Phone: (336)316-2352
Fax: (336)316-2949
**Format:** Alternative/New Music/Progressive

**WQMG-FM - 97.1 (23546)**
7819 National Service Rd., Ste. 401
Greensboro, NC 27409
Phone: (336)605-5200
Fax: (336)605-0138
**Format:** Adult Contemporary

**WSJS-AM - 600 (23881)**
875 W. Fifth St.
Winston-Salem, NC 27101-2505
Phone: (910)727-8826
Fax: (910)777-3915
**Format:** News; Talk

**WTCK-AM - 1320 (23547)**
2 Pai Park, No. B
Greensboro, NC 27409-9428
Phone: (910)378-WTCK
Fax: (910)887-0104
**Format:** Sports; Talk

**WTOB-AM - 1380 (23882)**
4405 Providence Ln., Ste. D
Winston-Salem, NC 27106
Phone: (336)759-0363
Fax: (336)759-0366
**Format:** Religious; Talk

**WUAG-FM - 103.1 (23549)**
Taylor Bldg.
UNCG Campus
Greensboro, NC 27413
Phone: (336)334-5470

Format: Alternative/New Music/Progressive

## Greenville-New Bern-Washington, NC

**WCZI-FM - 98.3 (23561)**
211 Commerce St.
Greenville, NC 27834
Phone: (919)756-9898
Fax: (919)355-2234
Format: News; Talk

**WEED-AM - 1390 (23759)**
1 Weed Rd.
PO Box 2666
Rocky Mount, NC 27802-2267
Fax: (919)443-5977
Format: Full Service

**WERO-FM - 93.3 (23825)**
PO Box 1707
Washington, NC 27889
Phone: (252)946-2162
Fax: (252)946-0330
Format: Classic Rock; Oldies

**WERX-FM - 102.5 (23451)**
PO Box 1408
Edenton, NC 27932-0950
Phone: (252)449-8331
Fax: (919)482-5591
Format: Album-Oriented Rock (AOR)

**WGHB-AM - 1250 (23469)**
Hwy. 121 N.
PO Box 229
Farmville, NC 27828
Phone: (919)753-4121
Fax: (919)753-4123
Format: Gospel; Sports

**WJCV-AM - 1290 (23599)**
123 A Arnold Rd. Extension
PO Box 1216
Jacksonville, NC 28546
Phone: (910)347-6141
Fax: (910)347-1290
Format: Gospel

**WNBR-FM - 94.1 (23802)**
702 Hartness Rd.
Statesville, NC 28677
Phone: (252)247-2002
Fax: (252)726-3188
Format: Country

**WNCT-AM - 1070 (23562)**
408 West Arlington Blvd., Suite 101-B
Greenville, NC 27834
Phone: (252)355-8822
Fax: (252)757-0286
Format: News; Agricultural; Country

**WNCT-FM - 107.9 (23563)**
2929 Radio Station Rd.
Greenville, NC 27835-7167
Phone: (252)757-0011
Fax: (252)757-0286
Format: Adult Contemporary; Oldies

**WOOW-AM - 1340 (23565)**
310 Evans St. Mall
Greenville, NC 27834
Fax: (919)757-1793
Format: Talk; Jazz; Gospel; Blues

**WTEB-FM - 89.3 (23675)**
Craven Community College
800 College Court
New Bern, NC 28562
Phone: (252)638-3434
Fax: (252)638-3538
Format: News; Classical; Public Radio

**WZMB-FM - 91.3 (23566)**
East Carolina University
Mendenhall Student Center
Greenville, NC 27858-4353
Phone: (919)328-4751
Fax: (919)328-4773

Format: Full Service; Eclectic; Alternative/New Music/Progressive; Alternative/New Music/Progressive

## Greenville-Spartanburg, SC-Asheville, NC

**WBCU-AM - 1460 (28249)**
210 E. Main St.
Union, SC 29379
Phone: (864)427-2411
Fax: (864)429-2975
Format: Contemporary Country; Information; News

**WBRM-AM - 1250 (23634)**
147 N. Garden St.
Marion, NC 28752
Phone: (704)652-9500
Fax: (828)652-9700
Format: Country

**WBZT-FM - 96.7 (28117)**
7 N Laurens St.
Greenville, SC 29601
Phone: (864)242-1005
Fax: (864)239-3553
Format: Album-Oriented Rock (AOR)

**WCQS-FM - 88.1 (23234)**
73 Broadway
Asheville, NC 28801
Phone: (828)253-6875
Fax: (828)253-6700
Format: Classical

**WESC-FM - 92.5 (28118)**
7 N. Laurens St., Ste. 700
Greenville, SC 29601
Phone: (864)242-4660
Fax: (864)242-8813
Format: Country

**WFIS-AM - 1600 (28103)**
PO Box 156
Fountain Inn, SC 29644
Phone: (864)963-5991
Fax: (864)963-5992
Format: News; Talk; Sports

**WFQS-FM - 91.3 (23235)**
73 Broadway
Asheville, NC 28801
Phone: (704)253-6875
Fax: (704)253-6700
Format: Classical; Public Radio; Folk; News; Folk; News

**WFSC-AM - 1050 (23490)**
180 Radio Hill Rd.
PO Box 470
Franklin, NC 28734
Phone: (828)524-4418
Fax: (828)524-2788
Format: Oldies

**WGVL-AM - 1440 (28121)**
7 N. Laurens St., Ste. 700
Greenville, SC 29601
Phone: (864)467-1440
Fax: (864)271-3830
Format: Gospel

**WKDK-AM - 1240 (28190)**
PO Box 753
Newberry, SC 29108
Phone: (803)276-2957
Fax: (803)276-3337
Format: Adult Contemporary; News; Sports; Oldies

**WKSF-FM - 99.9 (23237)**
Summerlin Rd.
Asheville, NC 28806
Phone: (828)257-2700
Fax: (828)255-7850
Format: Contemporary Country

**WKYK-AM - 940 (23272)**
401 Sawmill Rd.
PO Box 744
Burnsville, NC 28714
Phone: (828)682-3798
Fax: (828)682-6227
Format: Country

**WNCC-FM - 96.7 (23491)**
180 Radio Hill Rd.
PO Box 470
Franklin, NC 28734
Phone: (828)524-4418
Fax: (828)524-2788
Format: Country

**WNEG-AM - 630 (7466)**
121 W. Doyle St.
PO Box 1159
Toccoa, GA 30577
Phone: (706)886-2191
Fax: (706)282-0189

**WPFJ-AM - 1480 (23492)**
185 Franklin Plz.
PO Box 1335
Franklin, NC 28734-3028
Phone: (828)369-5033
Fax: (828)369-3197
Format: Contemporary Christian

**WPTL-AM - 920 (23277)**
PO Box 909
Canton, NC 28716
Phone: (828)648-3576
Fax: (828)648-3577
Format: Country; Religious

**WSPA-AM - 950 (28231)**
250 International Dr.
Spartanburg, SC 29303
Phone: (864)576-7777
Format: News; Talk

**WTPT-FM - 93.3 (28130)**
223 S. Pleasantburg Dr. Ste. B-3
Greenville, SC 29607-2521
Phone: (864)467-9330
Fax: (864)271-5029

**WWNC-AM - 570 (23239)**
Summerlin Rd.
Asheville, NC 28806
Phone: (828)253-3835
Fax: (828)255-7850
Format: Full Service; Country

**WZLA-FM - 92.9 (27962)**
112 N. Main St.
PO Box 548
Abbeville, SC 29620
Phone: (864)366-5785
Fax: (864)366-9391
Format: Oldies

**WZOO-AM - 710 (23228)**
Box 460
Asheboro, NC 27204-0460
Phone: (336)672-0985
Format: Gospel

## Greenwood-Greenville, MS

**KUUZ-FM - 95.9 (16820)**
PO Box 1794
Greenville, MS 38702-1794
Phone: (601)332-0025
Fax: (601)332-0038
Format: Contemporary Country

**WABG-AM - 960 (16833)**
PO Box 408
Greenwood, MS 38930
Phone: (601)453-7822
Fax: (601)455-3311
Format: Country; Talk

**WBAD-FM - 94.3 (16823)**
PO Box 4426
Greenville, MS 38704-4426
Phone: (662)335-9265
Fax: (662)335-5538
Format: Urban Contemporary

**WBAQ-FM - 97.9 (16824)**
PO Box 656
Greenville, MS 38702-0656
Phone: (601)335-3383
Fax: (601)335-3383
Format: Easy Listening

**WCLD-AM - 1490 (16784)**
Drawer 780
Drawar 780
Cleveland, MS 38732
Phone: (662)843-4091
Fax: (662)843-9805

**Format:** Sports

**WCLD-FM - 103.9 (16785)**
Drawer 780
Cleveland, MS 38732
Phone: (662)843-4091
Fax: (662)843-9805
**Format:** Urban Contemporary

**WDMS-FM - 100.7 (16825)**
1383 Pickett St.
Greenville, MS 38701
Phone: (662)334-4559
Fax: (662)332-1315
**Format:** Contemporary Country

**WDSK-AM - 1410 (16786)**
PO Box 1438
Cleveland, MS 38732
Phone: (662)846-0929
Fax: (662)843-1410
**Format:** News; Talk

**WDTL-FM - 92.9 (16787)**
PO Box 1438
Cleveland, MS 38732
Phone: (662)846-0929
Fax: (662)843-1410
**Format:** Country

**WELZ-AM - 1460 (16752)**
PO Box 299
Belzoni, MS 39038
Phone: (601)247-1744
Fax: (601)247-1744
**Format:** Religious; Talk

**WESY-AM - 1580 (16826)**
7 Oaks Rd.
PO Box 5804
Greenville, MS 38704-5804
Phone: (662)378-9405
Fax: (662)335-5538
**Format:** Religious; Urban Contemporary

**WGRM-AM - 1240 (16834)**
1110 Wright St.
Greenwood, MS 38930
Phone: (662)453-1240
Fax: (662)453-1241
**Format:** Gospel

**WGRM-FM - 93.9 (16835)**
1110 Wright St.
Greenwood, MS 38930
Phone: (662)453-1240
Fax: (662)453-1241
**Format:** Gospel

**WGVM-AM - 1260 (16827)**
1383 Pickett St.
Greenville, MS 38701
Phone: (662)334-4550
Fax: (662)332-1315
**Format:** Sports; Talk

**WIQQ-FM - 102.3 (16828)**
Unit 39, Delta Plaza Mall
Hwy. 1 S.
Greenville, MS 38701
Phone: (662)378-2617
Fax: (662)378-8341
**Format:** Contemporary Hit Radio (CHR)

**WKXG-AM - 1540 (16836)**
Browning Rd.
PO Box 1686
Greenwood, MS 38930
Phone: (601)455-5733
**Format:** Urban Contemporary; Blues; Gospel

**WMAO-FM - 90.9 (16837)**
c/o Mississippi Public Broadcasting
3825 Ridgewood Rd.
Jackson, MS 39211-6463
Phone: (601)432-6565
Fax: (601)432-6806
**Format:** Classical; News; Information; Public Radio

**WMJW-FM - 107.5 (16788)**
PO Box 780
Cleveland, MS 38732
Phone: (662)843-9091
Fax: (662)843-9805

**Format:** Adult Contemporary

**WNIX-AM - 1330 (16829)**
Delta Plaza Mall, Unit 39
Hwy. 1 S.
Greenville, MS 38701
Phone: (662)378-2617
Fax: (662)378-8341

**WRKG-FM - 95.3 (16789)**
PO Box 1438
Cleveland, MS 38732
Phone: (662)846-0929
Fax: (662)843-1410
**Format:** Classic Rock

## Huntsville-Decatur-Florence, AL

**WAFN-FM - 92.7 (275)**
PO Box 4184
Huntsville, AL 35815
Phone: (256)586-9300
Fax: (256)586-9301
**Format:** Oldies

**WAHR-FM - 99.1 (276)**
1900 Memorial Pkwy. SW
Huntsville, AL 35801-5002
Phone: (256)534-9900
Fax: (256)536-4416
**Format:** Adult Contemporary; Soft Rock

**WAJF-AM - 1490 (178)**
PO Box 1501
Decatur, AL 35602-1501
Phone: (256)350-1754
Fax: (256)350-3474
**Format:** Urban Contemporary

**WBCF-AM - 1240 (223)**
525 E. Tennessee St.
Box 1316
Florence, AL 35631-1316
Phone: (205)764-8170
Fax: (205)764-8340
**Format:** News; Talk

**WBHP-AM - 1230 (179)**
401 14th St.
Decatur, AL 35601
Phone: (256)353-1750
Fax: (256)353-2470
**Format:** Talk; News

**WBXR-AM - 1140 (28601)**
2926-D Huntsville Hwy
Fayetteville, TN 37334
Phone: (931)433-7017
Fax: (931)433-8282
**Format:** Religious

**WDJL-AM - 1000 (277)**
7200 Stringfield Rd.
Huntsville, AL 35806
Phone: (256)852-1223
Fax: (256)852-1900
**Format:** Urban Contemporary; Gospel

**WEUP-AM - 1600 (278)**
PO Box 11398
Huntsville, AL 35814
Phone: (205)837-9387
Fax: (205)837-9404
**Format:** Urban Contemporary

**WHIY-AM - 1190 (279)**
2609 Jordan Lane
PO Box 37
Huntsville, AL 35816
Phone: (256)837-9387
Fax: (256)827-9404
**Format:** Country

**WHOS-AM - 800 (181)**
401 14th St.
Decatur, AL 35601
Phone: (256)353-1750
Fax: (256)353-2470
**Format:** News; Talk

**WJRA-AM - 1310 (182)**
303 2nd Ave. SE, Ste. F
Decatur, AL 35601-2325
Phone: (205)351-1081

**Format:** Gospel; Religious; Religious

**WKAX-AM - 1500 (423)**
113 Washington Ave.
Russellville, AL 35653
Phone: (256)332-6103
Fax: (256)332-7430
**Format:** Gospel; Southern Gospel; Hispanic

**WKEA-FM - 98.3 (427)**
John T. Reid Pkwy.
Rte. 4
PO Box 966
Scottsboro, AL 35768-0966
Phone: (256)259-2341
Fax: (205)574-2156
**Format:** Contemporary Country

**WKGL-FM - 97.7 (481)**
509 N Main St.
Tuscumbia, AL 35674-2048
**Format:** Oldies

**WLRH-FM - 89.3 (281)**
University of Alabama-Huntsville
John Wright Dr.
Huntsville, AL 35899
Phone: (256)895-9574
Fax: (256)830-4577
**Format:** Classical; Jazz; News; Public Radio

**WMXN-AM - 98.3 (428)**
PO Box 966
Scottsboro, AL 35768
Phone: (256)259-2341
Fax: (256)574-2156
**Format:** Adult Contemporary

**WOCG-FM - 90.1 (282)**
Oakwood Rd. NW
Huntsville, AL 35896
Phone: (205)726-7418
Fax: (205)726-7417
**Format:** Religious

**WRSA-FM - 96.9 (283)**
PO Box 4144
Huntsville, AL 35802
Fax: (205)498-2791
**Format:** Easy Listening

**WSLV-AM - 1110 (28486)**
500 Stateline Rd. W.
PO Box 96
Ardmore, TN 38449
Phone: (931)427-2178
Fax: (931)427-2179
**Format:** Country; Country

**WYAM-AM - 890 (184)**
1301 Central Parkway S.W.
Decatur, AL 35601
Phone: (256)355-4567
Fax: (256)351-1234
**Format:** Talk

**WYFD-FM - 91.7 (285)**
8415 Whitesburg Dr., Ste. A
Huntsville, AL 35802-3009
Phone: (256)650-0917
Fax: (256)650-0917
**Format:** Religious; Educational

**WZCT-AM - 1330 (430)**
2002 E.Willow
Scottsboro, AL 35768
Phone: (256)574-1330
Fax: (256)218-3013
**Format:** Southern Gospel

**WZZA-AM - 1410 (482)**
1570 Woodmont Dr.
Tuscumbia, AL 35674
Phone: (256)381-1862
Fax: (256)381-6006
**Format:** Blues; Talk; News; Gospel

## Jackson, MS

**WAKH-FM - 105.7 (16943)**
PO Box 1649
McComb, MS 39648-1649
Phone: (601)684-4654
Fax: (601)684-4658

**Format:** Country

**WBKN-FM - 92.1  (16768)**
PO Box 711
Brookhaven, MS 39602-0711
Phone: (601)833-6221
Fax: (601)833-6221
**Format:** Contemporary Country; Southern Gospel

**WCHJ-AM - 1470  (16769)**
983 Sawmill
PO Box 177
Brookhaven, MS 39601
Phone: (601)823-9006
Fax: (601)823-0503
**Format:** Gospel

**WHLH-FM - 95.5  (16902)**
1375 Beasley Rd.
Jackson, MS 39206
Phone: (601)982-1062
Fax: (601)362-1905
**Format:** Contemporary Hit Radio (CHR)

**WMAB-FM - 89.9  (16962)**
c/o Mississippi Public Broadcasting
3825 Ridgewood Rd.
Jackson, MS 39211-6463
Phone: (601)432-6565
Fax: (601)432-6806
**Format:** Classical; News; Information; Public Radio

**WMAE-FM - 89.5  (16765)**
c/o Mississippi Public Broadcasting
3825 Ridgewood Rd.
Jackson, MS 39211
Phone: (601)432-6565
Fax: (601)432-6806
**Format:** News; Bluegrass; Classical; Information; Public Radio

**WMAU-FM - 88.9  (16771)**
c/o Mississippi Public Broadcasting
3825 Ridgewood Rd.
Jackson, MS 39211-6463
Phone: (601)432-6565
Fax: (601)432-6806
**Format:** Classical; News; Information; Public Radio

**WMLC-AM - 1270  (16966)**
PO Box 444
Monticello, MS 39654-0444
Fax: (601)587-7524
**Format:** Talk; Sports; Sports

**WMPN-FM - 91.3  (16909)**
c/o Mississippi Public Broadcasting
3825 Ridgewood Rd.
Jackson, MS 39211
Phone: (601)432-6565
Fax: (601)432-6806
**Format:** News; Information; Public Radio

**WMPR-FM - 90.1  (16911)**
1018 Pecan Park
Jackson, MS 39209
Phone: (601)948-5835
Fax: (601)948-6162
**Format:** Public Radio; Alternative/New Music/Progressive; Gospel; Jazz; Blues

**WMSI-FM - 102.9  (16912)**
PO Box 31999
Jackson, MS 39286
Phone: (601)982-1062
Fax: (601)362-1905
**Format:** Country

**WRTM-AM - 1490  (17043)**
PO Box 820583
Vicksburg, MS 39182
Phone: (601)636-7944
Fax: (601)373-1243
**Format:** Gospel

**WTWZ-AM - 1120  (16915)**
4611-C Terry Rd.
Jackson, MS 39212-5646
Phone: (601)346-0074
Fax: (601)346-0896
**Format:** Religious; Bluegrass

**WZRX-AM - 1590  (16917)**
2980 Forest Ave. Ext.
PO Box 9734
Jackson, MS 39286
Phone: (601)981-9080
Fax: (601)981-9093

**Format:** Gospel

## Jackson, TN

**WDXI-AM - 1310  (28643)**
One Radio Park Dr.
PO Box 3845
Jackson, TN 38303-3845
Phone: (901)427-9611
Fax: (901)424-1321
**Format:** News; Information; Sports; Talk

**WFKX-FM - 95.7  (28644)**
111 W. Main St.
Jackson, TN 38301
Phone: (901)427-9616
Fax: (901)427-9302
**Format:** Adult Contemporary; Urban Contemporary

**WHHM-FM - 107.7  (28645)**
111 W. Main St.
Jackson, TN 38301
Phone: (731)427-9616
Fax: (731)427-9302
**Format:** Adult Contemporary

**WKNP-FM - 90.1  (16906)**
c/o WKNO-FM
900 Getwell Rd.
Memphis, TN 38111
Phone: (901)325-6544
Fax: (901)325-6506
**Format:** Public Radio; Classical; News; News

**WLSZ-FM - 105.3  (28637)**
PO Box 488
Humboldt, TN 38343
Phone: (901)784-1053
Fax: (901)784-4033
**Format:** Contemporary Hit Radio (CHR); Top 40; Contemporary Christian

**WMXX-FM - 103.1  (28646)**
One Radio Park Dr.
PO Box 3845
Jackson, TN 38303-3845
Phone: (901)427-9611
Fax: (901)424-1321
**Format:** Adult Contemporary; Oldies

**WWYN-FM - 106.9  (28649)**
111 W. Main St.
Jackson, TN 38301
Phone: (731)427-9616
Fax: (731)427-9302
**Format:** Country; News; Talk

**WYNU-FM - 92.3  (28650)**
122 Radio Rd.
Jackson, TN 38301
Phone: (731)427-3316
Fax: (731)427-4576
**Format:** Classic Rock

## Jacksonville (Brunswick), FL

**WAOC-AM - 1420  (6491)**
PO Box 3847
Saint Augustine, FL 32085
Phone: (904)829-3416
Fax: (904)826-8051
**Format:** Country

**WAPE-FM - 95.1  (6100)**
8000 Belfort Pkwy.
Jacksonville, FL 32256
Phone: (904)245-8500
Fax: (904)245-8501
**Format:** Contemporary Hit Radio (CHR)

**WAYR-AM - 550  (6059)**
2500 Russell Rd.
Green Cove Springs, FL 32043-9492
Phone: (904)272-1111
Fax: (904)284-2501
**Format:** Religious

**WEJZ-FM - 96.1  (6101)**
6440 Atlantic Blvd
Jacksonville, FL 32211
Phone: (904)727-9696
Fax: (904)721-9322

**Format:** Adult Contemporary

**WFKS-FM - 97.9  (6102)**
11700 Central Pkwy.
Jacksonville, FL 32224
Phone: (904)636-0507
Fax: (904)636-7971
**Format:** Contemporary Hit Radio (CHR)

**WFOY-AM - 1240  (6492)**
PO Box 3847
Saint Augustine, FL 32085
Phone: (904)829-3416
Fax: (904)829-8051
**Format:** Talk; Sports; News

**WFXJ-AM - 930  (6103)**
11700 Central Pkwy.
Jacksonville, FL 32224
Phone: (904)636-0507
Fax: (904)636-7971
**Format:** Sports

**WFYV-FM - 104.5  (6104)**
8000 Belfort Pkwy.
Jacksonville, FL 32256-6971
Phone: (904)642-1055
Fax: (904)641-3297
**Format:** Classic Rock

**WJAQ-FM - 100.9  (6208)**
4376 W. Lafayette St., Ste. A
PO Box 569
Marianna, FL 32446
Phone: (850)482-3046
Fax: (850)482-3049

**WJBT-FM - 92.7  (6060)**
10592 E. Balmoral Cir., Ste. 1
Jacksonville, FL 32218
Phone: (904)696-1015
Fax: (904)696-1011

**WJFR-FM - 88.7  (6108)**
2611 WERD Radio Dr.
Jacksonville, FL 32204
Phone: (904)389-9088
**Format:** Religious

**WJXR-FM - 92.1  (6110)**
PO Box 1
Jacksonville, FL 32234
Phone: (904)259-2292
Fax: (904)358-2265

**WKBX-FM - 106.3  (7222)**
111 N. Grove Blvd.
PO Box 2525
Kingsland, GA 31548
Phone: (912)729-6106
Fax: (912)729-4106
**Format:** Country; News

**WNZS-AM - 930  (6114)**
11700 Central Pkwy.
Jacksonville, FL 32224
Phone: (904)448-0930
Fax: (904)997-7713
**Format:** Sports

**WPLK-AM - 800  (6411)**
PO Box 335
Palatka, FL 32178-0335
Phone: (386)325-5800
Fax: (904)328-8725
**Format:** Oldies

**WSOL-FM - 101.5  (6119)**
10592 E. Balmoral Cir., Ste. 1
Jacksonville, FL 32218
Phone: (904)696-1015
Fax: (904)696-1011
**Format:** Adult Contemporary

**WSVE-AM - 1280  (6120)**
4343 Spring Grove St.
Jacksonville, FL 32209-3629
Phone: (904)768-1211
Fax: (904)768-5115
**Format:** Religious

**WTOT-AM - 980  (6210)**
4376 Lafayette St.
PO Box 569
Marianna, FL 32446
Phone: (850)482-3046
Fax: (850)482-3049

## Knoxville (Crossville), TN

**Format:** Country

**WVOJ-AM - 970 (6122)**
2427 University Blvd. N.
Jacksonville, FL 32211
Phone: (904)743-6234
Fax: (904)745-0331
**Format:** Sports; Talk

**WWUF-FM - 97.7 (6962)**
1350 Paces Forest Dr.
Atlanta, GA 30301
Phone: (912)283-2229
Fax: (912)285-9797
**Format:** Classic Rock

**WZAZ-AM - 1400 (6123)**
11700 Central Pkwy.
Jacksonville, FL 32224
Phone: (904)997-1880
Fax: (904)997-7740
**Format:** Gospel

## Knoxville (Crossville), TN

**WAEW-AM - 1330 (28577)**
196 10th St.
PO Box 1110
Crossville, TN 38557
Phone: (615)484-5115
Fax: (615)456-1195
**Format:** News; Talk; Gospel; Gospel

**WCPM-AM - 1280 (11633)**
101 Keller St.
Cumberland, KY 40823
Phone: (606)589-4623
**Format:** Religious; Country

**WECO-AM - 940 (29024)**
PO Box 100
Wartburg, TN 37887
Phone: (423)346-3900
Fax: (423)346-7686
**Format:** Gospel

**WECO-FM - 101.3 (29025)**
PO Box 100
Wartburg, TN 37887
Phone: (423)346-3900
Fax: (423)346-7686
**Format:** Country

**WFXY-AM - 1490 (11891)**
PO Box 999
Middlesboro, KY 40965
Phone: (606)248-1574
Fax: (606)248-6397
**Format:** Adult Contemporary; News; News

**WGLH-AM - 960 (28711)**
PO Box 1530
La Follette, TN 37766-1530
Fax: (865)457-5900
**Format:** Religious

**WHLN-AM - 1410 (11703)**
PO Box 898
Harlan, KY 40831
Phone: (606)573-2540
Fax: (606)573-7557
**Format:** Oldies

**WIMZ-AM - 1240 (28694)**
1100 Sharps Ridge Rd.
Knoxville, TN 37917
Phone: (865)525-6000
Fax: (865)637-3350
**Format:** Sports

**WIMZ-FM - 103.5 (28695)**
1100 Sharps Ridge Rd.
Knoxville, TN 37917
Phone: (865)525-6000
Fax: (865)525-2000
**Format:** Album-Oriented Rock (AOR)

**WJFC-AM - 1480 (28655)**
PO Box 430
Jefferson City, TN 37760
Phone: (423)475-3825
Fax: (423)475-3800

**Format:** Country; Bluegrass

**WJXB-FM - 97.5 (28698)**
1100 Sharps Ridge Rd.
PO Box 27100
Knoxville, TN 37917
Phone: (865)525-6000
Fax: (865)525-2000
**Format:** Adult Contemporary

**WKCS-FM - 91.1 (28699)**
2509 Broadway NE
Knoxville, TN 37917
Phone: (865)594-1259
**Format:** Adult Contemporary; Soft Rock; Soft Rock

**WLIL-AM - 730 (28724)**
Box 340
Lenoir City, TN 37771
Fax: (423)986-1716
**Format:** Contemporary Country

**WLOD-AM - 1140 (28735)**
Box 465
Loudon, TN 37774
Fax: (615)458-4621
**Format:** Gospel; Bluegrass

**WMIK-AM - 560 (11892)**
PO Box 608
Middlesboro, KY 40965
Phone: (606)248-5842
Fax: (606)248-7660
**Format:** Southern Gospel

**WMIK-FM - 92.7 (11893)**
PO Box 608
Middlesboro, KY 40965
Phone: (606)248-5842
Fax: (606)248-7660
**Format:** Religious; Contemporary Christian

**WMTN-AM - 1300 (28818)**
510 W. Economy Rd.
Morristown, TN 37814-3223
Phone: (615)586-7993
Fax: (423)581-4290
**Format:** Oldies; News

**WOFE-AM - 580 (28970)**
807 S. Gateway Ave.
PO Box 387
Rockwood, TN 37854
Fax: (865)354-9658
**Format:** Gospel

**WQBB-AM - 1040 (28701)**
8419 Kingston Pike
Knoxville, TN 37919-5352
Fax: (423)673-0408
**Format:** Adult Contemporary

**WQLA-FM - 104.9 (28713)**
PO Box 1530
La Follette, TN 37766
Fax: (865)457-5900
**Format:** Country

**WRJZ-AM - 620 (28702)**
1621 East Magnolia Ave.
Knoxville, TN 37917
Phone: (865)525-0620
Fax: (865)521-8923
**Format:** Religious; Contemporary Christian; Middle-of-the-Road (MOR)

**WUOT-FM - 91.9 (28705)**
University of Tennessee
209 Communications Bldg.
Knoxville, TN 37996-0322
Phone: (865)974-5375
Fax: (865)974-3941
**Format:** Public Radio; Jazz; Classical; Classical

**WUTK-AM - 850 (28706)**
University of Tennessee
P103 Andy Holt Tower
Knoxville, TN 37996-0115
Phone: (615)974-6897
Fax: (615)974-2814
**Format:** News

**WVOZ-AM - 1180 (28709)**
802 S. Central
Knoxville, TN 37902
Phone: (865)546-4653
Fax: (865)637-7133

**Format:** Music of Your Life

**WXVL-FM - 99.3 (28578)**
196 10th St.
PO Box 1110
Crossville, TN 38557
Phone: (931)484-5115
Fax: (931)456-1195
**Format:** Contemporary Hit Radio (CHR); Contemporary Hit Radio (CHR)

## Laurel-Hattiesburg, MS

**WAML-AM - 1340 (16852)**
1 Commerce Dr., No. 106
Hattiesburg, MS 39402-1450
Phone: (601)425-4285
**Format:** Gospel

**WBBN-FM - 95.9 (16925)**
PO Box 6408
Laurel, MS 39441-6408
Phone: (601)649-0095
Fax: (601)649-8199
**Format:** Country

**WEEZ-AM - 890 (16854)**
1 Commerce Dr., Ste. 106
Hattiesburg, MS 39402
Phone: (601)649-3641
Fax: (601)426-8255
**Format:** Gospel

**WEEZ-FM - 99.3 (16855)**
1 Commerce Dr., No. 106
Hattiesburg, MS 39402-1499
Phone: (601)425-4486
**Format:** Gospel; Religious

**WFFF-AM - 1360 (16792)**
PO Box 550
Columbia, MS 39429
Phone: (601)736-1360
Fax: (601)736-1361
**Format:** Country

**WFFF-FM - 96.7 (16793)**
Garner Shopping Centerr
PO Box 550
Columbia, MS 39429
Phone: (601)736-1360
Fax: (601)736-1361
**Format:** Adult Contemporary

**WFOR-AM - 1400 (16856)**
2414 W. 7th
Hattiesburg, MS 39401
Phone: (601)544-1400
Fax: (601)582-5481
**Format:** Southern Gospel

**WHER-FM - 103.7 (16857)**
2414 W. 7th St.
Hattiesburg, MS 39401
Phone: (601)544-3232
Fax: (601)582-5481
**Format:** Oldies

**WJDR-FM - 98.3 (17001)**
Columbia Ave
37 S. High School Ave.
Prentiss, MS 39474
Phone: (601)792-2056
Fax: (601)792-2057
**Format:** Contemporary Country

**WJMG-FM - 92.1 (16858)**
1204 Gravel Line St.
Hattiesburg, MS 39401
Phone: (601)544-1941
Fax: (601)544-1947
**Format:** Urban Contemporary; Adult Contemporary; Adult Contemporary

**WKNZ-FM - 107.1 (16859)**
PO Box 15935
Hattiesburg, MS 39404-5216
Phone: (601)264-0443
Fax: (601)264-5733
**Format:** Country

**WORV-AM - 1580 (16860)**
1204 Graveline
Hattiesburg, MS 39401
Fax: (601)544-1947

**Format:** Urban Contemporary; Gospel; Blues

## Lexington, KY

**WBUL-FM - 98.1** (11781)
2601 Nicholasville Rd.
Lexington, KY 40503
Phone: (859)422-1000
Fax: (859)422-1038
**Format:** Country

**WCGW-AM - 770** (11782)
3270 Blazer Pkwy., No. 102
Lexington, KY 40509
Phone: (859)264-9700
Fax: (859)264-9705
**Format:** Southern Gospel

**WCYO-FM - 100.7** (11971)
128 Big Hill Ave.
Richmond, KY 40475
Phone: (859)623-1340
Fax: (859)623-1341
**Format:** Contemporary Country

**WDFB-AM - 1170** (11641)
3596 Alum Springs Rd.
Danville, KY 40422-9607
Phone: (859)236-9333
Fax: (859)236-3348
**Format:** Religious

**WEZJ-FM - 104.3** (12030)
522 Main St.
Williamsburg, KY 40769
Phone: (606)549-2285
Fax: (606)549-5565
**Format:** Contemporary Country

**WFKY-AM - 1490** (11682)
306 W. Main St., Ste. 509
Frankfort, KY 40601
Phone: (502)223-8281
Fax: (502)875-1225
**Format:** Oldies

**WFLE-AM - 1060, FM 95.1** (11659)
Fleming County Industrial Park
RR 3, No.1 Radio Dr.
Flemingsburg, KY 41041
Phone: (606)849-4433
Fax: (606)845-9353
**Format:** Country

**WFLE-FM - 95.1** (11783)
RR.3, No. 1 Radio Dr.
Fleming County Industrial Park
Flemingsburg, KY 41041
Phone: (606)849-4433
Fax: (606)845-9353
**Format:** Country

**WFLW-AM - 1360** (11897)
Worsham Ln.
PO Box 696
Monticello, KY 42633
Phone: (606)348-8427
Fax: (606)348-3867
**Format:** Southern Gospel

**WFTG-AM - 1400** (11798)
534 Tobacco Rd.
London, KY 40741
Phone: (606)864-2148
Fax: (606)864-0645
**Format:** News; Talk

**WGKS-FM - 96.9** (11784)
1500 Greendale Rd.
PO Box 111788
Lexington, KY 40578
Phone: (859)233-1515
Fax: (859)223-4248
**Format:** Adult Contemporary

**WHBN-AM - 1420** (11643)
2063 Shakertown Rd.
Danville, KY 40422
Phone: (859)236-2711
Fax: (859)236-1461
**Format:** Country

**WHIR-AM - 1230** (11644)
2063 Shakertown Rd.
Danville, KY 40422
Phone: (859)236-2711
Fax: (859)236-1461
**Format:** News; Sports; Talk

**WHMJ-FM - 102.3** (11994)
PO Box 740
Somerset, KY 42502
Phone: (606)678-5151
Fax: (606)678-2026
**Format:** Oldies

**WIFX-FM - 94.3** (12024)
PO Box 729
Whitesburg, KY 41858
Phone: (606)633-9439
Fax: (606)633-3314
**Format:** Adult Contemporary; Top 40

**WIRV-AM - 1550** (11737)
1030 Winchester Rd.
PO Box 281
Irvine, KY 40336
Phone: (606)723-5138
Fax: (606)723-5180
**Format:** Oldies

**WJMD-FM - 104.7** (11713)
PO Box 7001
Hazard, KY 41702
Phone: (606)439-3358
Fax: (606)439-3118
**Format:** Religious; Southern Gospel

**WKCA-FM - 107.7** (11929)
PO Box 1010
Owingsville, KY 40360
Phone: (606)674-2266
Fax: (606)674-6700
**Format:** Contemporary Country

**WKDP-FM - 99.5** (11628)
821 Adams Rd.
Corbin, KY 40701-4708
Phone: (606)528-6617
Fax: (606)523-0427
**Format:** Country

**WKED-AM - 1130** (11683)
306 W. Main St., Ste. 509
Frankfort, KY 40601
Phone: (502)875-1130
Fax: (502)875-1225

**WKED-FM - 103.7** (11684)
115 W Main St.
Frankfort, KY 40601
Phone: (502)875-1130
Fax: (502)875-1225
**Format:** Adult Contemporary

**WKIC-AM - 1390** (11714)
PO Box 7428
Hazard, KY 41702-7898
Phone: (606)436-2121
Fax: (606)436-4172
**Format:** Contemporary Hit Radio (CHR)

**WKLB-AM - 1290** (11875)
PO Box 448
Manchester, KY 40962
Phone: (606)598-2445
Fax: (606)598-2653
**Format:** Country

**WKYM-FM - 101.7** (11898)
150 Worsham Ln.
PO Box 696
Monticello, KY 42633
Phone: (606)348-7083
Fax: (606)348-3867
**Format:** Oldies; Classic Rock

**WLXG-AM - 1300** (11788)
401 W. Main St.
Lexington, KY 40507
Phone: (859)233-1515
Fax: (859)233-4248
**Format:** Sports

**WMST-AM - 1150** (11909)
34 Broadway
PO Box 381
Mount Sterling, KY 40353
Phone: (859)498-1150
Fax: (606)498-7930
**Format:** Classic Rock

**WRSL-AM - 1520** (12001)
PO Box 300
Stanford, KY 40484
Phone: (606)365-0959

Fax: (606)365-3247
**Format:** Southern Gospel

**WSGS-FM - 101.1** (11715)
PO Box 7898
Hazard, KY 41702
Phone: (606)436-2121
**Format:** Country

**WSIP-FM - 98.9** (11943)
124 Main St.
PO Box 597
Paintsville, KY 41240
Phone: (606)789-5311
Fax: (606)789-7200
**Format:** Country

**WTKT-FM - 103.3** (11790)
2601 Nicholasville Rd.
Lexington, KY 40503-3307
**Format:** Oldies

**WTLO-AM - 1480** (11997)
290 WTLO Rd.
PO Drawer 1480
Somerset, KY 42501
Phone: (606)678-8151
Fax: (606)678-8152
**Format:** Oldies; News; Talk

**WUKY-FM - 91.3** (11791)
University of Kentucky
340 McVey Hall
Lexington, KY 40506
Phone: (859)257-3221
Fax: (859)257-6291
**Format:** News; Adult Album Alternative

**WVLK-FM - 92.9** (11793)
300 W Vine, 3rd Fl.
Lexington, KY 40507
Phone: (859)253-5900
Fax: (859)253-5940
**Format:** Country

**WWEL-FM - 103.9** (11799)
534 Tobacco Rd.
London, KY 40741
Phone: (606)864-2148
Fax: (606)864-0645
**Format:** Country

## Louisville, KY

**WASE-FM - 103.5** (11651)
519 N. Miles
PO Box 2087
Elizabethtown, KY 42702
Phone: (270)766-1035
Fax: (270)769-1052
**Format:** Oldies

**WBRT-AM - 1320** (11528)
106 S. 3rd St.
Bardstown, KY 40004
Phone: (502)348-3943
Fax: (502)348-4043
**Format:** Country

**WCKQ-FM - 104.1** (11615)
PO Box 1053
Campbellsville, KY 42719-1053
Phone: (270)789-2401
Fax: (270)789-1450
**Format:** Adult Contemporary

**WCND-AM - 940** (11681)
115 W Main
Frankfort, KY 40601
Phone: (502)875-1130
Fax: (502)875-1225
**Format:** Oldies

**WFPK-FM - 91.9** (11851)
619 S. 4th St.
Louisville, KY 40202-2403
Phone: (502)574-1640
Fax: (502)574-1671
**Format:** Adult Album Alternative; Adult Album Alternative

**WFPL-FM - 89.3** (11852)
619 S. 4th St.
Louisville, KY 40202-2403
Phone: (502)814-6500
Fax: (502)814-6599

Macon, GA

**Format:** Public Radio; News; Talk

**WHAS-AM - 840  (11853)**
4000 Radio Drive
Louisville, KY 40218
Phone: (502)479-2222
Fax: (502)479-2224
**Format:** News; Talk

**WIEL-AM - 1400  (11652)**
406 S. Mulberry
PO Box L
Elizabethtown, KY 42701
Phone: (270)769-1400
**Format:** Sports

**WLBN-AM - 1590  (11750)**
Box 680
Lebanon, KY 40033
Phone: (270)692-3126
Fax: (270)692-6003
**Format:** Music of Your Life

**WLLV-AM - 1240  (11859)**
2001 W. Broadway, Ste. 13
Louisville, KY 40203-3551
Phone: (502)571-1240
Fax: (502)776-1250
**Format:** Gospel

**WLSK-FM - 100.9  (11751)**
Radio Station Rd., Box 680
Lebanon, KY 40033
Phone: (270)692-3126
Fax: (270)692-6003
**Format:** Classic Rock

**WMTL-AM - 870  (11753)**
2160 Brandenburg Rd.
Leitchfield, KY 42754
Phone: (270)259-3165
Fax: (270)259-5693
**Format:** Bluegrass

**WOKH-FM - 96.7  (11529)**
106 S. 3rd St.
Bardstown, KY 40004
Phone: (502)348-3943
Fax: (502)348-4043
**Format:** Adult Contemporary

**WQMF-FM - 95.7  (11860)**
4000 Radio Dr. Ste 1
Louisville, KY 40218
Fax: (502)896-1496
**Format:** Classic Rock

**WQXE-FM - 98.3  (11653)**
Box 517
Elizabethtown, KY 42702
Phone: (502)737-8000
Fax: (502)737-7229
**Format:** Adult Contemporary

**WTCO-AM - 1450  (11616)**
PO Box 1053
Campbellsville, KY 42719
Phone: (270)469-9826
Fax: (270)789-1450
**Format:** Sports

**WTFX-FM - 100.5  (11863)**
4000 Radio Dr., No. 1
Louisville, KY 40218
Phone: (502)571-1005
Fax: (502)479-2234
**Format:** Album-Oriented Rock (AOR)

**WTMT-AM - 620  (11864)**
300 Distillery Commons, Ste. 200
Louisville, KY 40206-1913
**Format:** Sports

## Macon, GA

**WAYS-FM - 99.1  (7252)**
PO Box 900
Macon, GA 31202-0900
Phone: (478)646-1055
Fax: (912)752-1339
**Format:** Oldies

**WBML-AM - 900  (7253)**
PO Box 6298
Macon, GA 31208
Phone: (912)743-5453
Fax: (912)743-9265

**Format:** Religious; Gospel

**WDDO-AM - 1240  (7254)**
544 Mulberry St., Ste. 500
Macon, GA 31202
Phone: (478)746-6286
Fax: (478)742-8061
**Format:** Gospel

**WDEN-AM - 1500  (7255)**
544 Mulberry, 5th Fl., No. 500
Macon, GA 31201
Phone: (478)745-3383
Fax: (478)745-9693
**Format:** Country

**WDEN-FM - 99.1  (7256)**
544 Mulberry St., Ste. 500
Macon, GA 31201-8258
Phone: (478)745-3383
Fax: (478)745-9693
**Format:** Contemporary Country

**WEBL-FM - 102.5  (7257)**
7080 Industrial Hwy.
Macon, GA 31216
Phone: (478)781-1063
Fax: (478)781-6711
**Format:** Country

**WGUR-FM - 88.9  (7309)**
Box 3124
Milledgeville, GA 31061-1000
Phone: (912)445-4102
Fax: (912)454-1483
**Format:** Top 40; Alternative/New Music/Progressive

**WIBB-FM - 97.9  (7260)**
7080 Industrial Hwy.
Macon, GA 31216
Phone: (478)781-1063
Fax: (478)781-6711
**Format:** Urban Contemporary

**WKTM-FM - 106.1  (7186)**
2278 Wortham Ln.
Grovetown, GA 30813
Phone: (706)309-9610
Fax: (706)309-9669
**Format:** Hispanic

**WKXK-FM - 97.9  (245)**
563 Manningham Rd.
PO Box 1150
Greenville, AL 36037
Phone: (334)382-6555
Fax: (334)382-7770
**Format:** Country

**WMAC-AM - 940  (7262)**
PO Box 900
Macon, GA 31202
Phone: (478)746-6286
Fax: (478)741-8811
**Format:** News; Talk; Sports

**WMCG-FM - 104.9  (7126)**
PO Box 130
Dublin, GA 31040-0130
Phone: (912)365-7788
Fax: (912)365-7799
**Format:** Country

**WMGB-FM - 93.7  (7264)**
544 Mulberry St., Ste. 500
Macon, GA 31201-8258
Phone: (478)746-6286
Fax: (478)742-8061
**Format:** Contemporary Hit Radio (CHR)

**WPEZ-FM - 93.7  (7266)**
544 Mulberry St., Ste. 500
Macon, GA 31201-8258
Phone: (478)746-6286
Fax: (478)742-8061
**Format:** Adult Contemporary

**WQBZ-FM - 106.3  (7268)**
7080 Industrial Hwy.
Macon, GA 31206-7538
Phone: (912)781-1063
Fax: (478)781-6711
**Format:** Album-Oriented Rock (AOR)

**WQSY-FM - 103.9  (7190)**
Eastman Hwy., PO Box 1398
Hawkinsville, GA 31036-0489
Fax: (912)892-9063

**Format:** Soft Rock

**WQZY-FM - 95.9  (7128)**
807 Bellevue Ave.
PO Box 130
Dublin, GA 31021
Phone: (478)272-4422
Fax: (478)275-4657
**Format:** Country

**WSNT-AM - 1490  (7390)**
PO Box 150
Sandersville, GA 31082
Phone: (478)552-5182
Fax: (478)553-0800
**Format:** Gospel

**WSNT-FM - 99.9  (7391)**
PO Box 150
Sandersville, GA 31082
Phone: (478)552-5182
Fax: (478)553-0800
**Format:** Country

**WVKX-FM - 103.7  (7201)**
104 High Hill St.
PO Box 569
Irwinton, GA 31042
Phone: (912)946-3445
Fax: (912)946-2406
**Format:** Urban Contemporary; Blues

**WXKO-AM - 1150  (7162)**
Hwy. 341 N.
PO Box 1150
Fort Valley, GA 31030-1150
Phone: (478)825-1150
Fax: (478)827-1273
**Format:** Religious; Ethnic

## Memphis, TN

**WCRV-AM - 640  (28786)**
555 Perkins Rd
Memphis, TN 38117-4410
Phone: (901)763-4640
Fax: (901)763-4920
**Format:** Religious; Talk

**WEVL-FM - 89.9  (28789)**
518 S. Main St.
PO Box 40952
Memphis, TN 38103-4443
Phone: (901)528-1990
**Format:** Full Service

**WGSF-AM - 1210  (28790)**
6080 Mt. Moriah
Memphis, TN 38115
**Format:** News; Hispanic

**WHAL-FM - 95.7  (28791)**
2650 Thousand Oaks Blvd., Ste. 4100
Memphis, TN 38118
Phone: (901)259-1300
Fax: (901)259-6451
**Format:** Contemporary Christian; Gospel

**WJBI-AM - 1290  (16743)**
Hwy. 6 W.
PO Box 1440
Batesville, MS 38606
Fax: (601)563-9002
**Format:** Country; Southern Gospel

**WKNA-FM - 88.9  (17013)**
900 Getwell Rd.
Memphis, TN 38111
Phone: (901)325-6544
Fax: (901)325-6506
**Format:** Talk; Public Radio; News; News

**WKNO-FM - 91.1  (28795)**
900 Getwell Rd.
Memphis, TN 38111
Phone: (901)325-6544
Fax: (901)325-6506
**Format:** Classical; Public Radio; News; News

**WKRA-AM - 1110  (16866)**
1400 HW 4 East-C
PO Box 398
Holly Springs, MS 38635
Phone: (662)252-1110
Fax: (662)252-2739

**Format:** Gospel; Southern Gospel

**WKRA-FM - 92.7  (16867)**
Hwy. 4 East-C
PO Box 398
Holly Springs, MS 38635
Phone: (662)252-6692
Fax: (662)252-2739
**Format:** Urban Contemporary

**WMC-AM - 790  (28798)**
One Bockhead Plaza
1960 Union Ave.
Memphis, TN 38104
Phone: (901)726-0496
Fax: (901)726-5847
**Format:** News; Talk; Talk

**WMOD-FM - 96.7  (28493)**
100 E. Market St.
PO Box 438
Bolivar, TN 38008-0438
Phone: (731)658-4320
Fax: (731)658-7328
**Format:** Country

**WNAU-AM - 1470  (16974)**
PO Box 808
New Albany, MS 38652
Phone: (601)534-8133
Fax: (601)538-4183
**Format:** Oldies; Sports

**WNWS-AM - 1520  (28504)**
Box 198
Brownsville, TN 38012
Phone: (731)772-3700
Fax: (731)772-9763
**Format:** Hispanic

**WODZ-AM - 680  (28801)**
5904 Ridgeway Center Pkwy.
Memphis, TN 38120
Phone: (901)767-0104
Fax: (901)767-0582
**Format:** Oldies

**WQOX-FM - 88.5  (28803)**
3333 Covington Pike
Memphis, TN 38128
Phone: (901)385-4317
Fax: (901)385-4304
**Format:** Adult Contemporary

**WRVR-FM - 104.5  (28806)**
5904 Ridgeway Center Pkwy.
Memphis, TN 38120
Phone: (901)767-0104
Fax: (901)767-0582
**Format:** Adult Contemporary

**WTBG-FM - 95.3  (28505)**
Box 198
Brownsville, TN 38012
Phone: (731)772-3700
Fax: (731)772-9763
**Format:** Country

**WTNE-AM - 1500  (28506)**
42 S. Washington Ave.
PO Box 198
Brownsville, TN 38012
Phone: (731)855-0098
Fax: (731)855-1600
**Format:** Adult Contemporary

**WUMR-FM - 91.7  (28807)**
University of Memphis Department of Communication
Memphis, TN 38152
Phone: (901)678-3176
Fax: (901)678-4899
**Format:** Jazz

## Meridian, MS

**WALT-AM - 910  (16947)**
3436 Hwy. 45 N.
Box 5797
Meridian, MS 39302
Phone: (601)693-2661
Fax: (601)483-0826
**Format:** Talk

**WFFX-AM - 1450  (16948)**
4307 Highway 39 N.
Meridian, MS 39301
Phone: (601)693-2381
Fax: (601)485-2972
**Format:** Sports; Talk

**WJDQ-FM - 101.3  (16949)**
4307 Hwy. 39 N.
Meridian, MS 39301
Phone: (601)693-2381
Fax: (601)485-2972
**Format:** Adult Contemporary

**WKZB-FM - 93.5  (16950)**
116 Skyland Dr.
Meridian, MS 39301
Phone: (601)483-9393
Fax: (601)483-9310
**Format:** Classic Rock

**WNBN-AM - 1290  (16953)**
1290 266-23rd St.
Meridian, MS 39301
Phone: (601)483-7930
Fax: (601)483-3411
**Format:** Religious; Gospel; Urban Contemporary

**WSLY-FM - 104.9  (492)**
11474 U.S. Hwy. 11
York, AL 36925
Phone: (205)392-5234
Fax: (205)392-5536
**Format:** Blues; Urban Contemporary; Urban Contemporary

**WWSL-FM - 102.3  (16993)**
PO Box 26
Philadelphia, MS 39350
Phone: (601)656-7102
Fax: (601)656-1491
**Format:** Soft Rock

**WYYW-FM - 95.1  (16956)**
4307 Hwy 39N
Meridian, MS 39302
Phone: (601)693-2381
Fax: (601)485-2972
**Format:** Country

## Miami (Ft. Lauderdale), FL

**WAVS-AM - 1170  (5915)**
6360 SW 41st Place
Davie, FL 33314
Phone: (954)584-1170
Fax: (954)581-6441
**Format:** Ethnic

**WAXY-AM - 709  (6271)**
4000 Hollywood Blvd.
Miami, FL 33169
Phone: (305)521-5100
Fax: (305)652-5385
**Format:** Adult Contemporary; Oldies; Oldies

**WEDR-FM - 99.1  (6080)**
2741 N. 29th Ave
Hollywood, FL 33020
Phone: (305)623-7711
Fax: (305)847-3215
**Format:** Urban Contemporary

**WEXY-AM - 1520  (5974)**
412 W. Oakland Park Blvd.
Fort Lauderdale, FL 33311-1712
Fax: (305)561-9830
**Format:** Religious; Urban Contemporary

**WFKZ-FM - 103.1  (6689)**
93351 Overseas Hwy.
Tavernier, FL 33070
Phone: (305)852-9085
Fax: (305)852-5586
**Format:** Classic Rock

**WFLC-FM - 97.3  (6081)**
2741 N. 29th Ave.
Hollywood, FL 33020
Phone: (954)584-7117
Fax: (954)847-3230
**Format:** Adult Contemporary

**WLQY-AM - 1320  (6336)**
10800 Biscayne Blvd., Ste. 810
North Miami, FL 33161
Phone: (305)891-1729
Fax: (305)891-1583
**Format:** Religious; Hispanic; Ethnic; Ethnic

**WLRN-FM - 91.3  (6276)**
172 NE 15th St.
Miami, FL 33132-1348
Phone: (305)995-1717

Fax: (305)995-2299
**Format:** Public Radio; News; Talk

**WMRZ-AM - 790  (6280)**
20450 NW 2nd Ave.
Miami, FL 33169
Phone: (305)653-8811
Fax: (305)652-5385
**Format:** News; Talk

**WMXJ-FM - 102.7  (6281)**
20450 NW 2nd Ave.
Miami, FL 33169
Phone: (305)550-9695
Fax: (305)652-3032
**Format:** Oldies

**WOCN-AM - 1450  (6282)**
350 NE 71st St.
Miami, FL 33138
Phone: (305)759-7280
Fax: (305)759-2276
**Format:** Hispanic

**WPLL-FM - 103.5  (6302)**
7601 Riviera Blvd.
Miramar, FL 33023-6574
**Format:** Adult Contemporary

**WPOW-FM - 96.5  (6284)**
20295 NW 2nd Ave.
Miami, FL 33169
Phone: (305)653-6796
Fax: (305)770-1456
**Format:** Top 40

**WRMS-FM - 97.9  (6729)**
2406 S. Congress Ave.
West Palm Beach, FL 33406-7610
Phone: (561)432-5100
Fax: (561)432-5111
**Format:** Big Band/Nostalgia

**WWNN-AM - 980  (5830)**
6699 N. Federal Highway
Boca Raton, FL 33487
Phone: (561)997-0074
Fax: (561)997-0476
**Format:** News

## Mobile, AL-Pensacola, FL

**WABB-AM - 1480  (322)**
1551 Springhill Ave.
PO Box 2148
Mobile, AL 36652
Phone: (334)432-5572
Fax: (334)438-4044
**Format:** Sports; Information; Talk; News

**WABB-FM - 97.5  (323)**
1551 Springhill Ave.
PO Box 2148
Mobile, AL 36652
Fax: (334)438-4044
**Format:** Contemporary Hit Radio (CHR)

**WABF-AM - 1220  (213)**
460 S. Section St., Box 1220
PO Drawer 1220
Fairhope, AL 36533-1220
Phone: (334)928-2384
Fax: (205)928-9229

**WASG-AM - 550  (31)**
1318 S. Main St.
Atmore, AL 36502-2899
Phone: (205)368-2511
Fax: (205)368-4227
**Format:** Country; Agricultural; News; Talk

**WBHY-AM - 840  (324)**
PO Box 1328
Mobile, AL 36633-1328
Phone: (251)473-8488
**Format:** Talk

**WBHY-FM - 88.5  (325)**
PO Box 1328
Mobile, AL 36633-1328
Phone: (251)473-8488
**Format:** Contemporary Christian

**WBLX-FM - 92.9  (326)**
1204 Dauphin St.
Mobile, AL 36604
Phone: (334)432-7609
Fax: (334)434-6596

**Format:** Urban Contemporary

**WHEP-AM - 1310 (229)**
PO Box 1747
Foley, AL 36536
Phone: (251)943-7131
Fax: (251)943-7031
**Format:** News; Sports; Talk

**WHOD-AM - 1230 (289)**
4428 Hwy. 43 N.
PO Box 518
Jackson, AL 36545-0518
Fax: (334)246-1980
**Format:** News; Talk; Sports

**WHOD-FM - 94.5 (290)**
4428 Hwy. 43 N.
PO Box 518
Jackson, AL 36545-0518
Phone: (334)246-4431
Fax: (334)246-1980
**Format:** Adult Contemporary

**WJLQ-FM - 100.7 (6447)**
6565 N. W St.
Pensacola, FL 32505
Phone: (850)478-6011
Fax: (850)478-3971
**Format:** Contemporary Hit Radio (CHR)

**WKSJ-FM - 94.9 (330)**
PO Box 161489
Mobile, AL 36616-2489
Phone: (334)450-0100
Fax: (334)344-3525
**Format:** Contemporary Country

**WLPR-AM - 960 (331)**
PO Box 1328
Mobile, AL 36633-1328
Phone: (251)473-8488
**Format:** Southern Gospel

**WMFC-FM - 99.3 (337)**
820 Pineville Rd.
PO Box 645
Monroeville, AL 36461-0645
Phone: (334)575-3281
Fax: (334)575-3280
**Format:** Oldies

## Montgomery-Selma, AL

**WDXX-FM - 100.1 (432)**
505 Lauderdale St.
PO Box 1055
Selma, AL 36701
Phone: (334)875-3350
Fax: (334)874-6759
**Format:** Contemporary Country

**WHBB-AM - 1490 (433)**
505 Lauderdale St.
PO Box 1055
Selma, AL 36701
Phone: (334)875-3350
Fax: (334)874-6959
**Format:** News; Talk

**WVAS-FM - 90.7 (378)**
915 S. Jackson St.
Montgomery, AL 36101-0271
Phone: (334)229-4708
Fax: (334)269-4995
**Format:** Jazz

## Nashville (Cookeville), TN

**WAMB-AM - 1160 (28904)**
1617 Lebanon Rd.
Nashville, TN 37210
Phone: (615)889-1960
**Format:** Big Band/Nostalgia; Sports

**WAMB-FM - 98.7 (28585)**
1617 Lebanon Rd.
Nashville, TN 37210
Phone: (615)889-1960
Fax: (615)889-1973
**Format:** Middle-of-the-Road (MOR); Big Band/Nostalgia

**WATX-AM - 1590 (28567)**
259 S. Willow Ave.
Cookeville, TN 38501
Phone: (931)528-6064

Fax: (931)520-1590
**Format:** Talk; News

**WBUZ-FM - 102.9 (28905)**
1824 Murfreesboro Rd.
PO Box 290099
Nashville, TN 37229-0099
Phone: (615)399-1029
Fax: (615)399-1023
**Format:** Country

**WDBL-AM - 1590 (29007)**
Box 606
Springfield, TN 37172
Fax: (615)384-9325
**Format:** Contemporary Country; Urban Contemporary

**WDBL-FM - 94.3 (29008)**
PO Box 606
Springfield, TN 37172-0606
Fax: (615)384-9325
**Format:** Alternative/New Music/Progressive

**WENO-AM - 760 (28907)**
333 Murfreesboro Rd.
Nashville, TN 37210
Phone: (615)248-1689
Fax: (615)248-7786
**Format:** Talk; Religious

**WFGZ-FM - 94.5 (28583)**
500 E. College St.
Dickson, TN 37055
Phone: (615)446-3764
Fax: (615)446-1781
**Format:** Contemporary Christian

**WGIC-FM - 98.5 (28568)**
698 S. Willow Ave.
Cookeville, TN 38501
Phone: (931)526-2131
Fax: (931)528-8400
**Format:** Adult Contemporary

**WGSQ-FM - 94.7 (28569)**
698 S Willow Ave.
Cookeville, TN 38501
Phone: (931)526-7144
Fax: (931)528-8400
**Format:** Country

**WHOP-AM - 1230 (11728)**
PO Box 709
Hopkinsville, KY 42240
Fax: (270)885-2688
**Format:** Adult Contemporary; News

**WHOP-FM - 98.7 (11729)**
PO Box 709
Hopkinsville, KY 42240
Phone: (502)885-5331
Fax: (502)885-2688
**Format:** Country

**WKDA-AM - 1200 (28912)**
1617 Lebanon Rd.
PO Box 399
Nashville, TN 37210
Phone: (615)889-1960
Fax: (615)902-9102
**Format:** Talk; News; Hispanic

**WKDZ-FM - 106.5 (11611)**
PO Box 1900
Cadiz, KY 42211-0316
Phone: (270)522-3232
Fax: (270)522-1110
**Format:** Country

**WKSR-AM - 1420 (28966)**
104 S. 2nd St.
PO Box 738
Pulaski, TN 38478
Fax: (615)424-3157
**Format:** Country

**WKSR-FM - 98.3 (28967)**
104 S. 2nd St.
PO Box 738
Pulaski, TN 38478
Phone: (615)363-2505
Fax: (615)424-3157
**Format:** Country

**WKYR-FM - 107.9 (11608)**
Box 340
Burkesville, KY 42717-0340
Fax: (502)433-7195

**Format:** Contemporary Country

**WLCK-AM - 1250 (11981)**
104 1/2 Public Sq.
PO Box 158
Scottsville, KY 42164
Fax: (502)237-3533
**Format:** Religious

**WLZK-FM - 94.1 (28954)**
110 India Rd.
PO Box 1239
Paris, TN 38242
Phone: (731)644-9455
Fax: (731)644-9970
**Format:** Adult Contemporary

**WMCP-AM - 1280 (28562)**
816 S. Garden St., Ste. 306
Columbia, TN 38401
Fax: (615)381-2510
**Format:** Country

**WMDB-AM - 880 (28917)**
3051 Stokers Ln.
Nashville, TN 37218
Phone: (615)255-2876
**Format:** Top 40; Gospel; Urban Contemporary; Jazz

**WNAH-AM - 1360 (28919)**
44 Music Sq. E.
Nashville, TN 37203
Phone: (615)254-7611
Fax: (615)254-4565
**Format:** Gospel

**WNAZ-FM - 89.1 (28920)**
333 Murfreesboro Rd.
Nashville, TN 37210
Phone: (615)248-1689
Fax: (615)248-7786
**Format:** Religious; Music of Your Life; Contemporary Christian; Adult Contemporary

**WNRZ-FM - 91.5 (28922)**
333 Murfreesboro Rd.
Nashville, TN 37210
Phone: (615)248-1689
Fax: (615)248-7786
**Format:** Religious; Music of Your Life; Contemporary Christian; Adult Contemporary

**WQDQ-AM - 1200 (28924)**
PO Box 40333
Nashville, TN 37204
**Format:** Middle-of-the-Road (MOR)

**WQQK-FM - 92.1 (28925)**
10 Music Cir. E
Nashville, TN 37203-4338
**Format:** Urban Contemporary; Urban Contemporary

**WQZQ-FM - 102.5 (28584)**
1824 Murfreesboro Rd.
Nashville, TN 37217
Phone: (615)399-1029
Fax: (615)399-1023
**Format:** Top 40

**WRKK-FM - 105.5 (29002)**
520 N. Spring St.
Sparta, TN 38583-1305
Phone: (931)836-1055
Fax: (931)836-2320
**Format:** Album-Oriented Rock (AOR)

**WSM-FM - 95.5 (28932)**
2804 Opryland Drive
Nashville, TN 37214
Phone: (615)889-6595
Fax: (615)458-2445
**Format:** Contemporary Country

**WSMT-AM - 1050 (29003)**
520 N. Spring St.
Sparta, TN 38583-1396
Phone: (931)836-1055
Fax: (931)836-2320
**Format:** Southern Gospel

**WTTU-FM - 88.5 (28570)**
Box 5113
Cookeville, TN 38505
Phone: (615)372-3169

**Format:** Alternative/New Music/Progressive

**WTZX-AM - 860 (29004)**
520 N. Spring St.
Sparta, TN 38583-1305
Phone: (931)836-1055
Fax: (931)836-2320
**Format:** Oldies

**WVCP-FM - 88.5 (28616)**
1480 Nashville Pike
Ramer Bldg., Ste. 101
Gallatin, TN 37066-3188
Phone: (615)230-3618
Fax: (615)230-4803
**Format:** Eclectic

**WWTN-FM - 99.7 (28936)**
2644 McGavock Pike
Nashville, TN 37214
Phone: (615)889-6595
Fax: (615)885-9900
**Format:** News; Talk; Sports

**WZYX-AM - 1440 (28573)**
540 W. Cumberland St.
PO Box 398
Cowan, TN 37318-0398
Phone: (931)967-7471
Fax: (931)962-1440
**Format:** Gospel; Country; News; News

## Norfolk-Portsmouth-Newport News-Hampton, VA

**WGAI-AM - 560 (23455)**
Box 1408
Elizabeth City, NC 27909
Fax: (919)335-2496
**Format:** News; Talk; Sports; Gospel

## Orlando-Daytona Beach-Melbourne, FL

**WAOA-FM - 107.1 (6215)**
1775 W. Hibiscus Blvd., Ste. 301
Melbourne, FL 32901
Fax: (407)724-1565
**Format:** Contemporary Hit Radio (CHR)

**WAPN-FM - 91.5 (5922)**
1508 State Ave.
PO Box 250311
Daytona Beach, FL 32125
Phone: (386)677-4272
Fax: (386)673-3715
**Format:** Religious

**WBVD-FM - 95.1 (6216)**
1388 S Babcock St.
Melbourne, FL 32901
Phone: (321)733-1000
Fax: (321)733-0904
**Format:** Urban Contemporary

**WCFB-FM - 94.5 (6390)**
4192 John Young Pkwy.
Orlando, FL 32804
Phone: (407)294-2945
Fax: (407)291-4879
**Format:** Adult Contemporary

**WCIF-FM - 106.3 (6217)**
3301 Dairy Rd.
Box 32902
Melbourne, FL 32902
Phone: (321)725-9243
**Format:** Religious

**WDBO-AM - 580 (6391)**
4192 John Young Pkwy.
Orlando, FL 32804
Phone: (407)295-5858
Fax: (407)291-4879
**Format:** Talk; News; Sports; News; Sports

**WEBG-FM - 100.3 (6196)**
2500 Maitland Center Pkwy., Ste. 401
Maitland, FL 32751
Phone: (407)916-7800
Fax: (407)916-7400
**Format:** Oldies

**WFLF-AM - 540 (6197)**
2500 Maitland Center Pkwy., Ste. 401
Maitland, FL 32751
Phone: (407)916-7800
Fax: (407)916-7400
**Format:** News; Talk

**WHOO-AM - 990 (6393)**
4192 N John Young Pkwy.
Orlando, FL 32804-2620
**Format:** Big Band/Nostalgia

**WOCL-FM - 105.9 (6397)**
1800 Pembrook Dr. Ste. 400
Orlando, FL 32810
Phone: (407)919-1000
**Format:** Alternative/New Music/Progressive; Alternative/New Music/Progressive

**WOMX-FM - 105.1 (6398)**
1800 Pembrook Dr., Ste. 400
Orlando, FL 32810
Phone: (407)919-1000
Fax: (407)919-1136
**Format:** Adult Contemporary

**WONQ-AM - 1030 (5864)**
1033 Semoran Blvd., No. 253
Casselberry, FL 32707-5758
Phone: (407)830-0800
Fax: (407)260-6100
**Format:** Hispanic

**WRMQ-AM - 1140 (5865)**
1033 E. Semoran Blvd., Ste. 253
Casselberry, FL 32707
Phone: (407)830-0800
Fax: (407)260-6100
**Format:** Hispanic

**WROD-AM - 1340 (5925)**
PO Box 991
Daytona Beach, FL 32115
Phone: (386)253-0000
Fax: (386)255-3178
**Format:** Music of Your Life

**WSDO-AM - 1400 (6520)**
PO Box 1448
Sanford, FL 32772-1448
Phone: (407)322-1400
**Format:** News; Talk; Hispanic

**WWKA-FM - 92.3 (6402)**
4192 John Young Pkwy.
Orlando, FL 32804
Phone: (407)298-9292
Fax: (407)291-4879
**Format:** Contemporary Country

**WXTO-AM - 1600 (6403)**
PO Box 680889
Orlando, FL 32868
Phone: (407)291-1395
Fax: (407)578-1734
**Format:** Hispanic

## Paducah,KY-Cape Girardeau,MO-Marion,IL

**WAVJ-FM - 104.9 (11962)**
PO Box 270
Princeton, KY 42445
Fax: (502)365-2073
**Format:** Soft Rock

**WCBL-FM - 99.1 (11535)**
PO Box 387
Benton, KY 42025
Phone: (270)527-3102
Fax: (270)527-5606
**Format:** Oldies

**WDXR-AM - 1450 (11935)**
No. 1 Executive Blvd.
Paducah, KY 42001
Phone: (502)443-1000
Fax: (502)442-1000
**Format:** Sports

**WDXR-FM - 94.3 (11936)**
No. 1 Executive Blvd.
PO Box 2250
Paducah, KY 42001
Phone: (270)443-1000
Fax: (270)442-1000
**Format:** Adult Contemporary

**WGKY-FM - 95.9 (12028)**
930 Wickliffe
PO Box 500
Wickliffe, KY 42087-0500
Phone: (270)335-3696
Fax: (270)335-3698
**Format:** Country

**WKJM-AM - 1320 (11881)**
PO Box 679
Mayfield, KY 42066-0679
Phone: (270)247-5122
Fax: (270)247-4207
**Format:** Sports

**WKYQ-FM - 93.3 (11937)**
6000 WKYQ Rd.
Paducah, KY 42003
Phone: (502)554-0093
Fax: (502)554-5468
**Format:** Contemporary Country; Agricultural; News

**WKYX-AM - 570 (11938)**
Box 2397
Paducah, KY 42002-2397
Phone: (270)554-8255
Fax: (502)554-5468
**Format:** Talk; News; Sports; Oldies

**WLLE-FM - 94.7 (11882)**
U.S. Hwy. 45 N.
Mayfield, KY 42066
Phone: (502)247-5122
Fax: (502)247-4207
**Format:** Country

**WYMC-AM - 1430 (11883)**
197 WYMC Rd.
PO Box V
Mayfield, KY 42066
Phone: (270)247-1430
Fax: (270)247-1825
**Format:** Middle-of-the-Road (MOR)

## Panama City, FL

**WDIZ-AM - 590 (6430)**
1834 Lisenby Ave.
Panama City, FL 32405
Phone: (850)769-1408
Fax: (850)769-0659
**Format:** Sports

**WEBZ-FM - 93.5 (6431)**
1834 Lisenby Ave.
Panama City, FL 32405
Phone: (850)769-1408
Fax: (850)769-0659
**Format:** Urban Contemporary

**WFBX-FM - 94.5 (6432)**
1834 Lisenby Ave.
Panama City, FL 32405
Phone: (850)769-1408
Fax: (850)769-0659
**Format:** Album-Oriented Rock (AOR)

**WFSY-FM - 98.5 (6433)**
PO Box 759
Panama City, FL 32402-0759
Phone: (850)769-1408
Fax: (850)769-6620
**Format:** Contemporary Hit Radio (CHR)

**WILN-FM - 105.9 (6434)**
7106 Laird St., Ste. 102
Panama City, FL 32408-7622
Phone: (904)233-6606
Fax: (904)233-1541
**Format:** Contemporary Hit Radio (CHR)

**WPHK-FM - 102.7 (5814)**
20872 Kelly Ave.
Blountstown, FL 32424
Phone: (850)674-5101
Fax: (904)674-2965
**Format:** Country

**WTBB-FM - 97.7 (6436)**
7106 Laird St., Ste. 102
Panama City, FL 32408-7622
Phone: (904)233-6606
Fax: (904)233-1541

**Format:** Album-Oriented Rock (AOR)

**WYBT-AM - 5000  (5815)**
20872 Kelly Ave.
Blountstown, FL 32424
Phone: (850)674-5101
Fax: (904)674-2965
**Format:** Oldies

**WZEP-AM - 1460  (5932)**
PO Box 627
DeFuniak Springs, FL 32435
Phone: (850)892-3158
Fax: (850)892-9675
**Format:** Full Service; News; Country; Oldies

## Ponce, Puerto Rico

**WIOC-FM - 105.1  (27787)**
PO Box 7302, Ponce Bypass
Ponce, PR 00732
Phone: (787)842-1287
Fax: (787)842-2941
**Format:** Adult Contemporary

**WLEO-AM - 1170  (27788)**
PO Box 7213
Ponce, PR 00732
Phone: (787)842-0048
Fax: (809)840-0049
**Format:** Full Service; Hispanic

**WOQI-FM - 93.3  (27789)**
PO Box 7243
PO Box 7243
Ponce, PR 00732-7243
Phone: (787)840-5550
Fax: (787)840-7077
**Format:** Hispanic

**WPAB-AM - 550  (27790)**
PO Box 7243
Ponce, PR 00732-7243
Phone: (787)840-5550
Fax: (787)840-7077
**Format:** Hispanic; News; Talk; Talk

**WPPC-AM - 1570  (27791)**
1896 Las Americas Ave.
PO Box 9064
Ponce, PR 00728-1818
Phone: (787)848-4670
Fax: (787)848-4670
**Format:** Religious

**WPRP-AM - 910  (27792)**
Box 7302, Ponce Bypass
Ponce, PR 00732
Fax: (809)841-6121
**Format:** Top 40; Hispanic

**WZAR-FM - 101.9  (27793)**
PO Box 7213
Ponce, PR 00732
Phone: (809)723-4195
Fax: (809)840-0049
**Format:** Top 40; Hispanic; Hispanic

## Raleigh-Durham, NC

**WAZZ-AM - 1490  (23474)**
508 Person St.
Fayetteville, NC 28301-4202
Phone: (910)484-1490
Fax: (910)323-5635
**Format:** Big Band/Nostalgia; Adult Contemporary; Adult Contemporary

**WEEB-AM - 990  (23789)**
1650 Mitland Rd
PO Box 1855
Southern Pines, NC 28388
Phone: (910)692-7440
Fax: (910)692-7372
**Format:** Talk; News; Sports; Sports

**WFMC-AM - 730  (23502)**
2581 US 71 W.
Goldsboro, NC 27530
Phone: (919)734-4211
Fax: (919)736-3876

**Format:** Gospel; Urban Contemporary

**WFNC-AM - 640  (23476)**
1009 Drayton Rd.
PO Box 35297
Fayetteville, NC 28303
Phone: (910)864-5222
Fax: (910)864-3065
**Format:** News; Talk; Sports

**WIOZ-AM - 550  (23790)**
200 Short Rd.
Southern Pines, NC 28387
Phone: (910)692-2107
Fax: (919)692-6849
**Format:** Big Band/Nostalgia

**WJTX-LP - 107.5 Mhz, Channel 298  (23722)**
804 E. Millbrook Rd.
Raleigh, NC 27609-5352
Phone: (919)787-8782
Fax: (919)787-8782
**Format:** Jazz; Contemporary Hit Radio (CHR)

**WKIX-FM - 96.1  (23503)**
2581 US Highway 70 West
Goldsboro, NC 27530
**Format:** Country

**WKRX-FM - 96.7  (23763)**
2070 Hurdle Mills Rd.
PO Box 1176
Roxboro, NC 27573
Phone: (336)599-0266
Fax: (336)599-9411
**Format:** Country

**WPJL-AM - 1240  (23725)**
515 Bart St.
Raleigh, NC 27610
Phone: (919)834-6401
**Format:** Religious

**WPTM-FM - 102.3  (23750)**
PO Box 910
Roanoke Rapids, NC 27870
Phone: (252)536-3115
Fax: (252)536-3045
**Format:** Talk; Country; Contemporary Country; Religious; Agricultural; Bluegrass

**WQNX-AM - 1350  (23215)**
PO Box 1350
Aberdeen, NC 28315-1350
Phone: (910)944-1350
Fax: (910)994-8182
**Format:** Talk; News

**WQOK-FM - 97.5  (23727)**
8001-101 Creedmoor Rd.
Raleigh, NC 27613
Phone: (919)848-9736
Fax: (919)848-4724
**Format:** Urban Contemporary

**WRBZ-AM - 850  (23729)**
5000 Falls of Neuse Rd., No. 308
Raleigh, NC 27609
Phone: (919)875-9100
Fax: (919)875-9080
**Format:** Talk; Sports

**WRDU-FM - 106.1  (23731)**
3100 Smoketree Ct., Ste. 700
Raleigh, NC 27604-1050
Phone: (919)876-1061
Fax: (919)876-2929
**Format:** Classic Rock; Album-Oriented Rock (AOR)

**WRTP-AM - 1530, 1060, 1000  (23445)**
3013 Guess Rd.
Durham, NC 27705
Phone: (919)477-7222
Fax: (919)477-4424
**Format:** Contemporary Christian

**WRVA-FM - 100.7  (23733)**
3100 Smoketree Ct., Ste. 700
Raleigh, NC 27604
Phone: (919)878-1500
Fax: (919)876-8578
**Format:** Oldies

**WRXO-AM - 1430  (23764)**
2070 Hurdle Mills Rd.
PO Box 1176
Roxboro, NC 27573
Phone: (336)599-0266
Fax: (336)599-9411

**WSMY-AM - 1400  (23751)**
PO Box 910
Roanoke Rapids, NC 27870
Phone: (252)536-3115
Fax: (252)536-3045
**Format:** Gospel; Urban Contemporary

**WSRC-AM - 1410  (23446)**
3202 Guess Rd.
Durham, NC 27705-2647
Phone: (919)477-7999
Fax: (919)477-9811
**Format:** Sports; Religious; News; News

**WTIK-AM - 1310  (23447)**
707 Leon St.
Durham, NC 27704
Phone: (919)220-3226
Fax: (919)220-0006
**Format:** Talk; Ethnic; Ethnic

**WUNC-FM - 91.5  (23327)**
CB 0915 Swain Hall
University of North Carolina
Chapel Hill, NC 27599-0915
Phone: (919)966-5454
Fax: (919)966-5955
**Format:** Talk; Classical; Folk; News

## San Juan-Caguas, Puerto Rico

**WBMJ-AM - 1190  (27804)**
PO Box 367000
San Juan, PR 00936-7000
Phone: (787)724-1190
Fax: (787)722-5395
**Format:** Religious; Educational

**WBRQ-FM - 97.7  (27760)**
PO Box 364701
San Juan, PR 00936-4701
Phone: (809)720-7797
Fax: (809)746-6162
**Format:** Hispanic; Top 40

**WCAD-FM - 105.7  (27805)**
Arquidiocesis de San Juan, Apartado 1967
San Juan, PR 00913
**Format:** Classic Rock; Oldies; Hispanic

**WERR-FM - 104  (27806)**
PO Box 29404
San Juan, PR 00929
Phone: (787)751-1310
Fax: (787)751-6854
**Format:** Religious

**WIPR-FM - 91.3  (27807)**
PO Box 190909
San Juan, PR 00919
Phone: (809)766-0505
Fax: (787)250-8258
**Format:** Hispanic

**WNEL-AM - 1430  (27755)**
PO Box 487
Caguas, PR 00726
Phone: (787)744-3131
Fax: (787)743-0253
**Format:** Big Band/Nostalgia

**WQII-AM - 1140  (27813)**
PO Box 9066590
San Juan, PR 00906-6590
Phone: (787)723-4848
Fax: (787)723-4035
**Format:** Middle-of-the-Road (MOR); Hispanic; Talk; Talk

**WRSJ-AM - 1560  (27814)**
Box 193419
San Juan, PR 00919-3419
Fax: (809)781-7416
**Format:** Easy Listening; Religious; Hispanic

**WRTU-FM - 89.7  (27815)**
Ponce De Leon & Pastrana Sts.
PO Box 21305
San Juan, PR 00931-1305
Phone: (787)763-4699
Fax: (787)763-5205
**Format:** Jazz; News; Classical; Easy Listening; Folk; Easy Listening; Folk

**WSKN-AM - 630  (27816)**
Eleanor Roosevelt, 117
San Juan, PR 00918
Fax: (809)764-3460

**Format:** Talk; News

**WUNO-AM - 1320  (27817)**
PO Box 3222
San Juan, PR 00936
Phone: (809)758-1300
**Format:** News; Hispanic; Hispanic

**WVIS-FM - 106.1  (27818)**
PO Box 6556, Loiza Sta.
San Juan, PR 00914-6556
Phone: (787)725-4164
Fax: (787)721-2086
**Format:** Oldies

**WVJP-AM - 1110  (27756)**
Box 207
Caguas, PR 00726
Phone: (809)743-5791
Fax: (809)746-6996
**Format:** Adult Contemporary; Easy Listening; Hispanic

**WVJP-FM - 103.3  (27757)**
PO Box 207
Caguas, PR 00726
Phone: (787)743-5790
Fax: (787)746-6996
**Format:** Hispanic

**WZNT-FM - 93.7  (27819)**
PO Box 949
Guaynabo, PR 00970
Phone: (809)720-5001
Fax: (809)720-2126
**Format:** Top 40; Hispanic; Hispanic

## Savannah, GA

**WAEV-FM - 97.3  (7404)**
245 Alfred St.
Savannah, GA 31408
Phone: (912)964-7794
Fax: (912)964-9414
**Format:** Top 40; Adult Contemporary

**WCLA-AM - 1470  (7053)**
316 N. River St.
Claxton, GA 30417
Phone: (912)739-3035
Fax: (912)739-0050
**Format:** Gospel

**WDMG-AM - 860  (7121)**
620 E. Ward St.
Douglas, GA 31533-3915
Phone: (912)389-0995
Fax: (912)383-8552
**Format:** News; Talk; Sports; Classic Rock

**WDMG-FM - 99.5  (7122)**
620 E. Ward St.
Douglas, GA 31533-3915
Phone: (912)389-0995
Fax: (912)383-8552
**Format:** News; Talk; Sports; Classic Rock

**WGCO-FM - 98.3  (7405)**
401 Mall Blvd., Ste. 101 D
Savannah, GA 31406
Phone: (912)351-9830
Fax: (912)352-4821
**Format:** Oldies

**WHCJ-FM - 90.3  (7407)**
PO Box 20484
Savannah, GA 31402-9716
Phone: (912)356-2399
Fax: (912)356-2041
**Format:** Jazz; Gospel; Blues

**WIFO-FM - 105.5  (7213)**
PO Box 647
Jesup, GA 31598-0647
Phone: (912)427-3712
Fax: (912)530-7717
**Format:** Country

**WJWJ-FM - 89.9  (27983)**
PO Box 1165
PO Box 1165
Beaufort, SC 29901
Phone: (843)524-0808
Fax: (843)524-1016

**Format:** Public Radio; Classical

**WKUB-FM - 105.1  (7503)**
Box 1472
Waycross, GA 31502
Phone: (912)449-3391
Fax: (912)449-6284
**Format:** Country

**WLOP-AM - 1370  (7214)**
PO Box 647
Jesup, GA 31598-0647
Phone: (912)427-3711
Fax: (912)530-7717
**Format:** Country

**WLOW-FM - 107.9  (28148)**
1 St. Augustine Pl.
Hilton Head Island, SC 29928
Phone: (843)785-9569
Fax: (843)842-3369
**Format:** Big Band/Nostalgia

**WMCD-FM - 100.1  (7428)**
569 E Olive
Statesboro, GA 30459
Phone: (912)764-5446
Fax: (912)764-8827
**Format:** Adult Contemporary; Adult Contemporary

**WNMT-AM - 1520  (7409)**
217 E. 65th St.
Savannah, GA 31405-5308
Phone: (912)354-4601
**Format:** Country

**WSGA-FM - 104.7  (7199)**
120 Liberty St./CD-104
Hinesville, GA 31313
Phone: (912)369-1047
Fax: (912)876-6920
**Format:** News; Talk

**WSVH-FM - 91.1  (7410)**
12 Ocean Science Circle
Savannah, GA 31411
Phone: (912)598-3300
Fax: (912)598-3306
**Format:** Public Radio; Classical; Jazz; News; Information; News; Information

**WTCQ-FM - 97.7  (7488)**
1501 Mount Vernon Rd.
PO Box 900
Vidalia, GA 30474
Phone: (912)537-9202
Fax: (912)537-4477
**Format:** Adult Contemporary

**WUFE-AM - 1260  (7010)**
PO Box 390
Baxley, GA 31515
Phone: (912)367-3000
Fax: (912)367-9779
**Format:** Gospel

**WVOP-AM - 970  (7489)**
1501 Mt. Vernon Rd.
PO Box 900
Vidalia, GA 30474
Phone: (912)537-9202
Fax: (912)537-4477
**Format:** Oldies

## Tallahassee, FL-Thomasville (Bainbridge), GA

**WAIB-FM - 103.1  (6606)**
3000 Olson Rd.
PO Box 13909.
Tallahassee, FL 32317
Phone: (850)386-8004
Fax: (850)422-1897
**Format:** Country

**WBWT-FM - 100.7  (6607)**
325 John Knox Rd., Bldg. G
Tallahassee, FL 32303
Phone: (850)422-3107
Fax: (850)383-0750
**Format:** Urban Contemporary

**WCVC-AM - 1330  (6610)**
117 1/2 Henderson Rd.
Tallahassee, FL 32312-2337
Phone: (850)386-1330
Fax: (850)386-2138

**Format:** Religious; Southern Gospel

**WGOV-AM - 950  (7481)**
2973 U.S. 84 W.
Valdosta, GA 31601
Phone: (229)242-4513
Fax: (229)247-7676
**Format:** Urban Contemporary

**WHBT-AM - 1410  (6615)**
3411 W Tharpe St.
PO Box 316
Tallahassee, FL 32303
Phone: (850)201-3000
Fax: (850)201-2329
**Format:** Religious; Gospel

**WHBX-FM - 96.1  (6616)**
3411 W Tharpe St.
Tallahassee, FL 32303
Phone: (850)201-3000
Fax: (850)201-2329
**Format:** Urban Contemporary

**WHGH-AM - 840  (7449)**
PO Box 2218
Thomasville, GA 31799
Phone: (229)228-4124
Fax: (229)225-9508
**Format:** Urban Contemporary

**WJEP-AM - 1020  (7450)**
Hwy. 3
PO Box 90
Thomasville, GA 31799-0090
Phone: (912)228-5683
Fax: (912)436-0544
**Format:** Religious; Contemporary Christian

**WMGR-AM - 930  (7002)**
203 W. Shotwell St.
Bainbridge, GA 39819-3903
Phone: (229)246-1650
Fax: (229)246-1403
**Format:** Oldies

**WNLS-AM - 1270  (6617)**
Bldg. G
325 John Knox Rd.
Tallahassee, FL 32303
Phone: (850)422-3107
Fax: (850)514-4441
**Format:** Sports; News; Talk

**WPAX-AM - 1240  (7451)**
117 Remington Ave.
Thomasville, GA 31792
Phone: (912)226-1240
Fax: (912)226-1361

**WQHL-AM - 1250  (6188)**
1305 Helvenston St.
Live Oak, FL 32064
Phone: (386)362-1250
Fax: (386)364-3504

**WTNT-FM - 94.9  (6618)**
325 John Knox Rd.
Bldg. G
Tallahassee, FL 32303
Phone: (850)385-9868
Fax: (850)383-0747
**Format:** Contemporary Country

## Tampa-St. Petersburg (Lakeland, Sarasota), FL

**WAMA-AM - 1550  (6660)**
PO Box 151300
Tampa, FL 33684-1300
**Format:** Hispanic

**WAVP-AM - 1390  (5803)**
PO Box 29
Avon Park, FL 33826-0029
Phone: (941)452-6162
Fax: (941)452-1006
**Format:** Hispanic

**WBVM-FM - 90.5  (6662)**
3816 Morrison Ave.
PO Box 18081
Tampa, FL 33629
Phone: (813)289-8040
Fax: (813)282-3580

## Tuscaloosa, AL

Format: Religious; Classical; Classical

**WCTQ-FM - 106.5  (6543)**
1779 Independence Blvd.
Sarasota, FL 34234
Phone: (941)552-4800
Fax: (941)552-4900
Format: Country

**WDAE-AM - 620  (6663)**
4002 Gandy Blvd.
Tampa, FL 33611
Phone: (813)839-9393
Fax: (813)831-3299
Format: Sports

**WDUV-FM - 105.5  (6664)**
4002 W. Gandy Blvd., No. A
Tampa, FL 33611-3410
Format: Easy Listening

**WGWD-FM - 93.3  (6061)**
100A N. Madison
PO Box 919
Quincy, FL 32351
Phone: (904)627-7086
Fax: (904)627-3422
Format: Country

**WHPT-FM - 102.5  (6510)**
11300 4th St. N., Ste. 300
11300 4th St. N., Ste. 318
Saint Petersburg, FL 33716
Phone: (727)577-7131
Fax: (727)579-2662
Format: Adult Contemporary; Album-Oriented Rock (AOR)

**WJIS-FM - 88.1  (5846)**
6469 Parkland Dr.
Sarasota, FL 34243
Phone: (941)753-0401
Fax: (941)753-2963
Format: Contemporary Christian

**WLSS AM - 930  (6544)**
533A S. Washington Blvd.
Sarasota, FL 34236
Phone: (941)363-0930
Fax: (941)362-4434

**WMMG-AM - 820  (6670)**
1915 N. Dale Mabary Hwy., Ste. 200
Tampa, FL 33607
Phone: (813)871-1819
Fax: (813)871-1155

**WONN-AM - 1230  (6175)**
404 W. Lime St.
PO Box 2038
Lakeland, FL 33801
Phone: (863)682-8184
Fax: (863)683-2409
Format: Easy Listening

**WQBN-AM - 1300  (6674)**
PO Box 151300
Tampa, FL 33684-1300
Phone: (813)871-1333
Fax: (813)876-1333

**WQYK-AM - 1010  (6675)**
5510 W. Gray St., Ste. 130
Tampa, FL 33609-1088
Phone: (813)287-0995
Fax: (813)636-0995
Format: Talk

**WQYK-FM - 99.5  (6676)**
5510 W. Gray St., Ste. 130
Tampa, FL 33609-1088
Phone: (813)287-0995
Fax: (813)636-0995
Format: Contemporary Country

**WRBQ-FM - 104.7  (6511)**
9721 Executive Center Dr N., Suite 200
Saint Petersburg, FL 33702
Phone: (813)287-1047
Fax: (813)287-1833
Format: Country

**WRXB-AM - 1590  (6512)**
2060 1st Ave. N.
Saint Petersburg, FL 33713-8802
Phone: (727)327-9792
Fax: (727)321-3025

Format: Urban Contemporary

**WSIR-AM - 1490  (6741)**
665 Lake Howard Dr. SW
Winter Haven, FL 33880-2577
Phone: (863)295-9411
Fax: (863)452-1006
Format: Adult Contemporary; Hispanic

**WSJT-FM - 94.1  (6513)**
9721 Executive Center Dr. N, Ste. 200
Saint Petersburg, FL 33702
Phone: (727)568-0941
Fax: (727)568-9758

**WSUN-AM - 620  (6514)**
11300 4th St. N, No. 300
Saint Petersburg, FL 33716
Phone: (727)576-1073
Fax: (727)578-9797
Format: Talk; Sports

**WTAN-AM - 1340  (5880)**
706 North Mrytle Ave
Clearwater, FL 33755
Phone: (727)441-3311
Fax: (813)447-7709
Format: Talk

**WTIS-AM - 1110  (6515)**
311 112th Ave. NE
Saint Petersburg, FL 33716
Phone: (727)576-2234
Fax: (727)577-3814
Format: Religious

**WTMP-AM - 1150  (6677)**
5207 Washington Blvd.
Tampa, FL 33619
Phone: (813)620-1300
Fax: (813)628-0713
Format: Urban Contemporary

**WTWB-AM - 1570  (6177)**
777 Carpenters Way
Lakeland, FL 33809
Phone: (863)815-1570
Fax: (863)853-5532
Format: Contemporary Christian; Talk

**WUTZ-AM - 1080  (6682)**
University of Tampa
401 W. Kennedy Blvd.
Tampa, FL 33606
Phone: (813)253-3333
Format: Alternative/New Music/Progressive

**WWAB-AM - 1330  (6178)**
1203 West Chase St.
PO Box 65
Lakeland, FL 33802-0065
Phone: (863)682-2998
Fax: (863)687-4000
Format: Urban Contemporary; Blues

**WWBF-AM - 1130  (5807)**
1130 Radio Rd.
Bartow, FL 33830
Phone: (863)533-0744
Fax: (863)533-8546
Format: Oldies

**WWOJ-FM - 99.1  (6550)**
3750 U.S. 27 N., Ste. 1
Sebring, FL 33870
Phone: (863)382-9999
Fax: (863)382-1982
Format: Country

**WWRM-FM - 94.9  (6518)**
11300 4th Street N., Ste. 300
Saint Petersburg, FL 33702-8444
Phone: (727)579-2000
Fax: (727)576-8098
Format: Adult Contemporary

**WWTK-AM - 730  (6551)**
3750 U.S. 27 N., Ste. 1
Sebring, FL 33870
Phone: (863)382-9999
Fax: (863)382-1982
Format: Talk

**WXTB-FM - 97.8  (6684)**
4002 W. Gandy Blvd.
Tampa, FL 33611
Phone: (813)832-1000
Fax: (813)832-1098

Format: Album-Oriented Rock (AOR)

**WYUU-FM - 92.5  (6685)**
5510 Gray St, Suite 130
Tampa, FL 33609
Phone: (813)287-1047
Fax: (813)282-3299
Format: Oldies

## Tuscaloosa, AL

**WLAY-FM - 100.3  (382)**
520 E. 2nd St.
Muscle Shoals, AL 35661
Phone: (205)383-2525
Fax: (205)381-1450
Format: Country

**WRTR-FM - 105.5  (474)**
3900 11th Ave. S.
PO Box 20126
Tuscaloosa, AL 35402-0126
Phone: (205)344-4589
Fax: (205)752-9269
Format: Classic Rock

**WYLS-AM - 670  (493)**
11474 U.S. Hwy. 11
York, AL 36925
Phone: (205)392-5234
Fax: (205)392-5536
Format: Middle-of-the-Road (MOR); Big Band/Nostalgia; Big Band/Nostalgia

## West Palm Beach-Ft. Pierce-Vero Beach, FL

**WAVW-FM - 101.7  (6002)**
PO Box 39
Fort Pierce, FL 34954
Phone: (772)335-9300
Fax: (561)335-3291
Format: Country

**WCNO-FM - 89.9  (6417)**
2960 S.W. Mapp Rd.
Palm City, FL 34990
Phone: (772)221-1100
Fax: (772)221-8716
Format: Religious

**WEAT-AM - 850  (6721)**
2406 S. Congress Ave.
West Palm Beach, FL 33406
Fax: (561)965-1102
Format: News; Sports

**WEAT-FM - 104.3  (6722)**
701 Northpoint Pkwy., Ste. 500
West Palm Beach, FL 33407
Phone: (561)686-9505
Format: Adult Contemporary; Soft Rock

**WLVJ-AM - 640  (6724)**
2406 S Congress Ave.
West Palm Beach, FL 33406-7619
Format: Religious; News; News

**WMBX-FM - 102.3  (6725)**
701 Northpoint Pkwy., Ste. 500
West Palm Beach, FL 33407
Phone: (772)930-1023
Fax: (772)640-9065
Format: Adult Contemporary

**WQCS-FM - 88.9  (6003)**
3209 Virginia Ave.
Fort Pierce, FL 34981
Phone: (772)462-4744
Fax: (772)462-4743
Format: Public Radio; Classical

**WQOL-FM - 103.7  (6476)**
PO Box 0093
Port Saint Lucie, FL 34985
Phone: (561)335-9300
Fax: (561)335-3291
Format: Oldies

**WTTB-AM - 1490  (6710)**
1235 16th St.
Vero Beach, FL 32960
Phone: (772)567-0937
Fax: (772)562-4747

**Format:** News; Talk; Sports

**WWRF-AM - 1380 (6730)**
2326 S Congress Dr., Ste. 2A
West Palm Beach, FL 33406
Phone: (561)721-9950
Fax: (561)721-9973
**Format:** Hispanic

**WXEL-FM - 90.7 (5841)**
3401 S. Congress Ave.
PO Box 6607
Boynton Beach, FL 33426
Phone: (561)737-8000
Fax: (561)369-3067
**Format:** Public Radio; News; Classical; Classical

## Wilmington, NC

**WAAV-FM - 94.1 (23848)**
PO Box 626
Wilmington, NC 28402
Phone: (910)763-9977
Fax: (910)763-0201
**Format:** News; Sports; Talk

**WENC-AM - 1220 (23835)**
108 Radio Station Rd.
Whiteville, NC 28472
Phone: (910)642-2133
Fax: (910)642-5981
**Format:** Gospel

**WGNI-FM - 102.7 (23849)**
3233 Burnt Mill Rd.
Wilmington, NC 28403-2359
Phone: (919)763-9977
Fax: (919)763-0201
**Format:** Adult Contemporary

**WHQR-FM - 91.3 (23850)**
254 N. Front St.
Wilmington, NC 28401-3920
Phone: (910)343-1640
Fax: (910)251-8693
**Format:** Public Radio; News; Eclectic

**WLNC-AM - 1300 (23614)**
1300 Lila Dr.
PO Box 1748
Laurinburg, NC 28352-1748
Phone: (910)276-1300
Fax: (910)277-0013
**Format:** Adult Contemporary; Soft Rock; Oldies; Oldies

**WLTT-FM - 103.7 (23777)**
PO Box 1550
Shallotte, NC 28459-1550
Phone: (910)754-9840
Fax: (910)754-2456
**Format:** Adult Contemporary

**WMFD-AM - 630 (23852)**
25 N. Kerr Ave.
Wilmington, NC 28405-3403
Phone: (910)791-3088
Fax: (910)791-0112
**Format:** News; Talk

**WRQR-AM - 104.5 (23853)**
25 N. Kerr Ave.
Wilmington, NC 28405-3403
Phone: (910)791-3088
Fax: (910)791-0112
**Format:** Educational

**WTXY-AM - 1540 (23836)**
501 W. Virgil St.
PO Box 1038
Whiteville, NC 28472
Phone: (910)642-8214
Fax: (910)640-1540
**Format:** News; Talk; Sports; Oldies

**WWIL-AM - 1490 (23856)**
PO Box 957
Wilmington, NC 28402-0957
Phone: (910)763-2452
Fax: (910)763-6578
**Format:** Gospel

**WWIL-FM - 90.5 (23857)**
PO Box 957
Wilmington, NC 28402-0957
Phone: (910)763-2452
Fax: (910)763-6578

**Format:** Contemporary Christian

# Western States

## Alaska

**KFBX-AM - 970 (548)**
546 9th Ave.
Fairbanks, AK 99701
Phone: (907)457-1921
Fax: (907)457-2128
**Format:** News; Talk

**KIYU-AM - 910 (558)**
PO Box 165
Galena, AK 99741
Phone: (907)656-1488
Fax: (907)656-1734
**Format:** Public Radio; Eclectic; Eclectic

**KKED-FM - 104.7 (551)**
546 9th Ave.
Fairbanks, AK 99701
Phone: (907)457-1921
Fax: (907)457-2128
**Format:** Album-Oriented Rock (AOR)

**KLEF-FM - 98.1 (518)**
3601 C St., Ste. 290
Anchorage, AK 99503
Phone: (907)561-5556
Fax: (907)562-4219
**Format:** Classical

**KRSA-AM - 580 (607)**
12th & H St.
PO Box 650
Petersburg, AK 99833
Phone: (907)772-3891
Fax: (907)772-4538
**Format:** Full Service; Contemporary Christian

**KVAK-AM - 1230 (620)**
PO Box 367
Valdez, AK 99686
Phone: (907)835-5825
Fax: (907)835-5158
**Format:** Country

## Albuquerque (Santa Fe & Hobbs), NM

**KISZ-FM - 97.9 (4246)**
Box 1299
Cortez, CO 81321
Phone: (970)565-3409
Fax: (970)565-8567
**Format:** Country

**KIUP-AM - 930 (4357)**
PO Box P
Durango, CO 81302-3030
Phone: (940)259-4444
Fax: (940)247-1005
**Format:** Middle-of-the-Road (MOR)

**KRSJ-FM - 100.5 (4359)**
PO Drawer P
Durango, CO 81302
Phone: (970)259-4444
Fax: (970)247-1005
**Format:** Country

## Anchorage, AK

**KABN-AM - 840 (507)**
2509 Eide St., Ste. 6
Anchorage, AK 99503
Phone: (907)277-5652
Fax: (907)344-5728
**Format:** Talk

**KADX-FM - 94.7 (508)**
2509 Eide St., Ste. 6
Anchorage, AK 99503
Phone: (907)277-5652
Fax: (907)344-5728

**KATB-FM - 89.3 (510)**
6401 E. Northern Lights Blvd.
Anchorage, AK 99504
Phone: (907)333-5282

Fax: (907)333-9851
**Format:** Religious

**KAXX-AM - 1020 (511)**
2509 Eide St., Ste. 6
Anchorage, AK 99503
Phone: (907)277-5652
Fax: (907)344-5728
**Format:** Sports

**KBRJ-FM - 104.1 (512)**
11259 Tower Rd.
Anchorage, AK 99515
Fax: (907)349-3299
**Format:** Hot Country

**KBYR-AM - 700 (513)**
1399 W 34th Ave., Ste. 202
Anchorage, AK 99503
Phone: (907)278-5297
Fax: (907)272-5797
**Format:** News; Talk

**KENI-AM - 650 (514)**
800 E. Diamond Blvd., Ste. 3-370
Anchorage, AK 99515
Phone: (907)522-1515
Fax: (907)349-6801
**Format:** Talk; News

**KHAR-AM - 590 (516)**
301 Arctic Slope
Anchorage, AK 99518
Phone: (907)344-9622
Fax: (907)349-3299
**Format:** Big Band/Nostalgia

**KMBQ-FM - 99.7 (624)**
2200 E Parks Hwy.
Wasilla, AK 99654
Phone: (907)373-0222
Fax: (907)376-1575
**Format:** Adult Contemporary

**KMXS-FM - 103.1 (519)**
301 Arctic Slope
Anchorage, AK 99518
Phone: (907)344-9622
Fax: (907)349-7326
**Format:** Adult Contemporary

**KTZN-AM - 550 (523)**
800 E Dimond Blvd., Ste. 3-370
Anchorage, AK 99515
Phone: (907)522-1515
Fax: (907)349-6801
**Format:** Sports

**KWHL-FM - 106.5 (524)**
9200 Lake Otis Pkwy.
Anchorage, AK 99507
Phone: (907)344-9622
Fax: (907)349-7326
**Format:** Album-Oriented Rock (AOR)

## Bakersfield, CA

**KBKO-FM - 96.5 (1414)**
1100 Mohawk St., Ste. 280
Bakersfield, CA 93309
Phone: (661)322-9929
Fax: (661)322-7239
**Format:** Country

**KCNQ-FM - 102.5 (2021)**
PO Box 2008
Kernville, CA 93238-2008
Phone: (760)379-5636
Fax: (760)376-3119
**Format:** Country

**KDFO-AM - 800 (1417)**
1100 Mohawk St., Ste. 280
Bakersfield, CA 93309
Phone: (661)322-9929
Fax: (661)322-7239
**Format:** Hispanic

**KDFO-FM - 98.5 (1418)**
1100 Mohawk St., Ste. 280
Bakersfield, CA 93309
Phone: (661)322-9929
Fax: (661)322-7239

## Bend, OR

Format: Classic Rock

**KERI-AM - 1180  (1419)**
1400 Easton Dr., Suite 144
Ste. 205
Bakersfield, CA 93309
Phone: (661)328-1410
Fax: (661)328-0873
Format: Religious; Talk

**KERN-AM - 1410  (1420)**
1400 Easton Drive
Bakersfield, CA 93312
Phone: (805)328-1410
Fax: (805)328-0873
Format: Talk; News

**KGEO-AM - 1230  (1422)**
1400 Sastun Dr., No. 134
Box 260
Bakersfield, CA 93309
Phone: (661)328-1410
Fax: (661)328-0873
Format: News; Talk

**KGET-AM - 970  (1423)**
1100 Mohawk St., Ste. 280
Bakersfield, CA 93309
Phone: (661)322-9929
Fax: (661)322-7239
Format: News; Talk

**KGFM-FM - 101.5  (1424)**
1400 Easton Dr., Ste.144
PO Box 2700
Bakersfield, CA 93303-2700
Phone: (661)328-1410
Fax: (661)328-0873
Format: Soft Rock

**KGZO-FM - 90.9  (1607)**
2310 Ponderosa Dr., Ste. 28
Camarillo, CA 93010
Phone: (805)482-4797
Fax: (805)388-5202
Format: Hispanic; Religious

**KHIS-AM - 800  (1425)**
1100 Mohawk St., Ste. 280
Bakersfield, CA 93309-7416
Phone: (661)322-9929
Fax: (661)322-9239
Format: Religious

**KLLY-FM - 95.3  (1428)**
3651 Pegasus
Bakersfield, CA 93308
Phone: (661)393-1900
Fax: (661)393-1915
Format: Adult Contemporary

**KNZR-AM - 1560  (1429)**
3651 Pegasus Dr., Suite 107
PO Box 80658
Bakersfield, CA 93380
Phone: (661)399-1560
Fax: (805)393-1915
Format: Talk; News

**KRAB-FM - 106.1  (1430)**
1100 Mohawk St., Ste 280
Bakersfield, CA 93309
Phone: (661)322-9929
Fax: (661)322-7239
Format: Alternative/New Music/Progressive; Album-Oriented Rock (AOR)

**KUZZ-AM - 550  (1433)**
3223 Sillect Ave.
Bakersfield, CA 93308
Phone: (661)326-1011
Fax: (661)328-7503
Format: Country

**KUZZ-FM - 107.9  (1434)**
3223 Sillect Ave.
Bakersfield, CA 93308
Phone: (661)326-1011
Fax: (661)328-7503
Format: Contemporary Country

## Bend, OR

**KLRR-FM - 01.75  (25725)**
711 NE Butler Market Rd.
PO Box 5037
Bend, OR 97708
Phone: (541)382-5263
Fax: (541)388-0456
Format: Adult Contemporary

**KMGX-FM - 100.7  (25726)**
969 SW Colorado Ave.
Bend, OR 97702-3120
Format: Soft Rock

**KMJZ-FM - 95.1  (25727)**
854 NE 4th St.
Bend, OR 97701-4711
Phone: (541)383-3825
Fax: (541)383-3403
Format: Jazz

**KNLR-FM - 97.5  (25728)**
PO Box 7408
Bend, OR 97708
Phone: (541)389-8873
Fax: (541)389-5291
Format: Religious; Contemporary Christian

**KQAK-FM - 105.7  (25729)**
854 NE 4th St.
Bend, OR 97701-4711
Phone: (541)383-3825
Fax: (541)383-3403
Format: Oldies

**KSJJ-FM - 102.9  (25730)**
969 SW Colorado Ave.
Bend, OR 97702-3120
Format: Country

**KXIX-FM - 94.1  (25734)**
969 SW Colorado Ave.
Bend, OR 97702
Phone: (541)382-5611
Fax: (541)389-7885
Format: Top 40

## Bethel, AK

**KYKD-FM - 100.1  (530)**
406 Ptarim Rd.
PO Box 2428
Bethel, AK 99559-0820
Phone: (907)543-5953
Fax: (907)543-5952
Format: Easy Listening; Religious; Religious

**KYUK-AM - 640  (531)**
640 Radio St.
PO Box 468
Bethel, AK 99559
Phone: (907)543-3131
Fax: (907)543-3130
Format: Eclectic; Adult Contemporary; Country; Oldies; Blues; Talk; News; Sports; Jazz; Classical; Talk; News; Sports; Jazz; Classical

## Billings-Hardin, MT

**KATL-AM - 770  (18195)**
810 S. Haynes Ave.
PO Box 700
Miles City, MT 59301-0700
Phone: (406)232-7700
Fax: (406)232-2231
Format: Adult Contemporary

**KBUL-AM - 970  (18075)**
27 N. 27th Penthouse
Billings, MT 59101
Phone: (406)248-7827
Fax: (406)252-9577
Format: News

**KCTR-FM - 102.9  (18076)**
27 N. 27th, Penthouse Ste.
PO Box 1276
Billings, MT 59101
Phone: (406)248-7827
Fax: (406)252-9577
Format: Contemporary Country

**KMHK-FM - 95.5  (18078)**
27 N. 27th, 23rd Fl.
Billings, MT 59101
Phone: (406)248-7827
Fax: (406)252-9577
Format: Classic Rock

**KMTA-AM - 1050  (18197)**
508 Main St.
Box 1426
Miles City, MT 59301
Phone: (406)232-5626
Fax: (406)232-7000

**KPRK-AM - 1340  (18191)**
PO Box 1340
Livingston, MT 59047
Phone: (406)222-2841
Fax: (406)222-1341
Format: Contemporary Country

**KRKX-FM - 94.1  (18079)**
2075 Central Ave.
Billings, MT 59102-4956
Phone: (406)652-8400
Fax: (406)652-4899
Format: Classic Rock

**KYYA-FM - 93.3  (18084)**
2075 Central Ave.
Billings, MT 59102-4596
Phone: (406)652-8400
Fax: (406)652-4899
Format: Adult Contemporary; Top 40

**KZMQ-AM - 1140  (33725)**
1949 Mountain View Dr.
PO Box 1210
Cody, WY 82414-1210
Phone: (307)578-5000
Fax: (307)527-5045
Format: Country; Oldies

**KZMQ-FM - 100.3  (33726)**
1949 Mountain View Dr.
PO Box 1210
Cody, WY 82414-1210
Phone: (307)587-5000
Fax: (307)527-5045
Format: Country; Hot Country

## Boise, ID

**KBGN-AM - 1060  (7681)**
3303 E. Chicago
Caldwell, ID 83605
Phone: (208)459-3635
Format: Religious

**KBKR-AM - 1490  (25715)**
PO Box 907
La Grande, OR 97850-0907
Phone: (541)963-4121
Fax: (541)963-3117
Format: News; Talk

**KBOI-AM - 670  (7657)**
1419 W. Bannock
PO Box 1280
Boise, ID 83702
Phone: (208)336-3670
Fax: (208)336-3734
Format: Full Service; Adult Contemporary

**KBSM-FM - 91.7  (7737)**
c/o KBSU-FM
Boise State University
1910 University Dr.
Boise, ID 83725
Phone: (208)426-3663
Fax: (208)344-6631
Format: Public Radio; Classical; News

**KBSU-FM - 90.3  (7658)**
Boise State University
1910 University Dr.
Boise, ID 83725
Phone: (208)426-3663
Fax: (208)344-6631
Format: Public Radio; Classical; News; News

**KBSW-FM - 91.7  (7813)**
315 Falls Ave.
Twin Falls, ID 83301
Phone: (208)736-3046
Fax: (208)736-2188
Format: Public Radio; Classical; News; News

**KBXL-FM - 94.1  (7660)**
1440 S Weideman
Boise, ID 83709-1308
Phone: (208)377-3790
Fax: (208)377-3792

**Format:** Contemporary Christian; Talk

**KCIX-FM - 105.9   (7661)**
827 Park Blvd., No. 201
Boise, ID 83712-7782
Phone: (208)344-6363
Fax: (208)275-8858
**Format:** Adult Contemporary

**KIDO-AM - 580   (7663)**
827 E. Park Blvd., Ste. 201
Boise, ID 83712
Phone: (208)344-6363
Fax: (208)385-7385
**Format:** Talk; News; News

**KIOV-AM - 1450   (7772)**
401 S. 9th St.
Boise, ID 83702-7004
Phone: (208)881-1450
**Format:** Top 40; Country; Country

**KKBC-FM - 95.3   (25716)**
PO Box 907
La Grande, OR 97850-0907
Phone: (541)963-4121
Fax: (541)963-3117
**Format:** Classical

**KKIC-AM - 950   (7666)**
PO Box 4489
Boise, ID 83711
Phone: (208)322-3437
**Format:** Country; Agricultural; Agricultural

**KLTB-FM - 104.3   (7667)**
827 E. Park Blvd., Ste. 201
Boise, ID 83712
Phone: (208)344-6363
Fax: (208)342-0444
**Format:** Oldies

**KQFC-FM - 97.9   (7669)**
1419 W. Bannock
PO Box 1280
Boise, ID 83701
Phone: (208)336-3670
Fax: (208)336-3734
**Format:** Classic Rock

**KSAS-FM - 103.3   (7670)**
827 E Park Blvd., Ste. 201
Boise, ID 83712
Phone: (208)344-6363
Fax: (208)385-9064
**Format:** Contemporary Hit Radio (CHR)

**KSPD-AM - 790   (7671)**
1440 S Weideman Dr.
Boise, ID 83709-1308
Phone: (208)377-3790
Fax: (208)377-3792
**Format:** Religious; Talk

**KWEI-AM - 1260   (7673)**
1156 N. Orchard St.
Boise, ID 83706
Phone: (208)367-1859
Fax: (208)383-9170
**Format:** News; Talk; News; Talk; Hispanic; News; Talk

**KWEI-FM - 99.5   (7674)**
1156 N. Orchard St.
PO Box 5234
Boise, ID 83704
Phone: (208)367-1859
Fax: (208)383-9170
**Format:** Hispanic

## Butte, MT

**KMBR-FM - 95.5   (18102)**
PO Box 3788
Butte, MT 59702-3788
Phone: (406)494-4442
Fax: (406)494-6020
**Format:** Classic Rock; Album-Oriented Rock (AOR); Album-Oriented Rock (AOR)

**KOPR-FM - 94.1   (18103)**
660 Dewey Blvd.
Butte, MT 59701
Phone: (406)494-7777
Fax: (406)494-5534

**Format:** Adult Contemporary

**KXTL-AM - 1370   (18106)**
PO Box 3788
Butte, MT 59702-3788
Phone: (406)494-4442
Fax: (406)494-6020
**Format:** Oldies; Sports; News

## Casper-Riverton, WY

**KCSP-FM - 90.3   (33689)**
1400 Kati Ln.
Casper, WY 82601
Phone: (307)265-5414
**Format:** Contemporary Christian

**KCWC-FM - 88.1   (33780)**
2660 Peck Ave.
Riverton, WY 82501
Phone: (307)855-2268
Fax: (307)856-3893
**Format:** Jazz

**KKTL-AM - 1400   (33692)**
150 Nichols Ave.
Casper, WY 82601
Phone: (307)266-5252
Fax: (307)235-9143
**Format:** Talk

**KMGW-FM - 94.5   (33693)**
150 N Nichols
Casper, WY 82601
Phone: (307)266-5252
Fax: (307)235-9143
**Format:** Adult Contemporary

**KRVK-FM - 107.9   (33694)**
150 Nichols Ave.
Casper, WY 82601
Phone: (307)266-5252
Fax: (307)237-5836
**Format:** Classic Rock

**KTRS-FM - 104.7   (33695)**
251 W. 1st St.
Casper, WY 82601
Phone: (307)235-7000
Fax: (307)237-5836
**Format:** Contemporary Hit Radio (CHR)

**KTRZ-FM - 93.1   (33782)**
PO Box 808
Riverton, WY 82501
Phone: (307)856-2922
Fax: (307)856-7552
**Format:** Classic Rock

**KTWO-AM - 1030   (33696)**
150 N. Nichols
Casper, WY 82601
Phone: (307)266-5252
Fax: (307)235-9143
**Format:** Country

**KUWR-FM - 95.1   (33762)**
PO Box 3984
Laramie, WY 82071-3984
Phone: (307)766-4240
Fax: (307)766-6184
**Format:** News; Adult Album Alternative; Classical

**KUYO-AM - 830   (33698)**
PO Box 50607
Casper, WY 82605-0607
Phone: (307)577-5896
**Format:** Religious

**KWYY-FM - 95.5   (33699)**
150 Nichols Ave.
Casper, WY 82601
Phone: (307)266-5252
Fax: (307)237-5836
**Format:** Country

## Cheyenne, WY-Scottsbluff, NE (Sterling, CO)

**KFBC-AM - 1240   (33709)**
1806 Capitol Ave.
Cheyenne, WY 82001-4597
Phone: (307)634-4461
Fax: (307)632-8586

**Format:** News; Talk; Sports; Sports

**KGAB-AM - 650   (33710)**
1912 Capitol Ave., Ste. 300
Cheyenne, WY 82001
Phone: (307)632-4400
Fax: (307)632-1818
**Format:** Talk

**KGHL-AM - 790   (18077)**
222 N. 32nd St., 10th Fl.
Billings, MT 59101-1911
Phone: (406)656-1410
Fax: (406)656-0110
**Format:** Country

**KIGN-FM - 101.9   (33712)**
1912 Capitol Ave., Ste. 300
Cheyenne, WY 82001
Phone: (307)632-4400
Fax: (307)632-1818
**Format:** Classic Rock

**KIMX-FM - 105.5   (33760)**
302 S. 2nd St., Ste. 202
Laramie, WY 82070
Phone: (307)745-5208
Fax: (307)745-8570
**Format:** Adult Contemporary

**KLEN-FM - 106.3   (33715)**
1912 Capitol Ave., Ste. 300
Cheyenne, WY 82001
Phone: (307)632-4400
Fax: (307)632-1818
**Format:** Adult Contemporary

**KMTN-FM - 1290   (33743)**
645 S. Cache
PO Box 927
Jackson, WY 83001
Phone: (307)733-4500
Fax: (307)733-7773
**Format:** Album-Oriented Rock (AOR); Classic Rock; Classic Rock

**KOWB-AM - 1290   (33761)**
Box 1290
Laramie, WY 82070
Phone: (307)745-4888
Fax: (307)742-4576
**Format:** News; Talk; Sports

**KRAE-AM - 1480   (33717)**
2109 E. 10th St.
PO Box 189
Cheyenne, WY 82003
Phone: (307)638-8921
Fax: (307)638-8922
**Format:** Oldies

**KSTC-AM - 1230   (4575)**
803 W. Main
PO Box 830
Sterling, CO 80751
Phone: (970)522-1607
Fax: (970)522-1322
**Format:** Oldies

## Chico-Redding, CA

**KFMF-FM - 93.9   (1655)**
1459 Humboldt Rd., Ste. D
Chico, CA 95928
Phone: (530)899-3600
Fax: (530)343-0243
**Format:** Soft Rock

**KHSL-FM - 103.5   (1656)**
2654 Cramer Ln.
Chico, CA 95928
Phone: (530)345-0021
Fax: (530)893-2121
**Format:** Country; Contemporary Country; Contemporary Country

**KNCQ-FM - 97.3   (2780)**
1588 Charles Dr.
Redding, CA 96003
Phone: (530)244-9700
Fax: (530)244-9707
**Format:** Contemporary Country

**KNNN-FM - 99.3   (2781)**
3660 Alta Mesa Dr.
Redding, CA 96002
Phone: (530)226-9500
Fax: (530)221-4940

**Colorado Springs-Pueblo, CO**

**Format:** Adult Contemporary

**KNRO-AM - 1670 (2782)**
3360 Alta Mesa Dr.
Redding, CA 96002
Phone: (530)226-9500
Fax: (530)221-4940
**Format:** Contemporary Country

**KPPL-FM - 107.5 (1660)**
1459 Humboldt Rd., Ste. D
Chico, CA 95928
Phone: (530)342-5775
Fax: (530)343-0243
**Format:** Soft Rock; Soft Rock

**KQMS-AM - 1400 (2783)**
3360 Alta Mesa Dr.
Redding, CA 96002
Phone: (530)221-1400
Fax: (530)221-4940
**Format:** Talk; News; News

**KRDG-FM - 105.3 (2784)**
3360 Alta Mesa Dr.
Redding, CA 96002
Phone: (530)226-9500
Fax: (530)221-4940
**Format:** Oldies

**KRRX-FM - 106.1 (2785)**
3360 Alta Mesa
Redding, CA 96002
Phone: (530)226-9500
Fax: (530)221-4940
**Format:** Album-Oriented Rock (AOR)

**KSHA-FM - 104.3 (2786)**
3360 Alta Mesa Dr.
Redding, CA 96002
Phone: (530)226-8200
Fax: (530)221-6653
**Format:** Soft Rock

**KVIP-AM - 540 (2787)**
1139 Hartnell Ave.
PO Box 492727
Redding, CA 96049-2727
Phone: (530)222-4455
Fax: (530)222-4484
**Format:** Religious

**KVIP-FM - 98.1 (2788)**
1139 Hartnell Ave.
PO Box 492727
Redding, CA 96049-2727
Phone: (530)222-4455
Fax: (530)222-4484
**Format:** Religious

## Colorado Springs-Pueblo, CO

**KAFA-FM - 104.5 (4584)**
PO Box 6066
USAF Academy, CO 80841
Phone: (719)333-5232
Fax: (719)333-6376
**Format:** Alternative/New Music/Progressive

**KBZC-AM - 1300 (4222)**
6805 Corporate Dr., Ste. 130
Colorado Springs, CO 80919
Phone: (719)593-2700
Fax: (719)593-2727
**Format:** Contemporary Country

**KCCY-FM - 96.9 (4223)**
2864 S Circle, Ste. 150
Colorado Springs, CO 80906
Phone: (719)540-9200
Fax: (719)579-0882
**Format:** Country

**KCMN-AM - 1530 (4224)**
5050 Edison, Ste. 218
Colorado Springs, CO 80915
Phone: (719)570-1530
Fax: (719)570-1007
**Format:** Big Band/Nostalgia

**KDZA-FM - 107.9 (4546)**
106 W 24th St.
Pueblo, CO 81003
Phone: (719)545-2080
Fax: (719)543-9898

**Format:** Oldies

**KFEL-AM - 970 (4547)**
PO Box 8055
Pueblo, CO 81008-8055
Phone: (719)543-7506
Fax: (719)543-0432
**Format:** Contemporary Christian

**KGFT-FM - 100.7 (4226)**
7150 Campus Dr
Colorado Springs, CO 80920
Phone: (719)531-5438
Fax: (719)531-5588
**Format:** Religious

**KIBT-FM - 96.1 (4227)**
2864 S Circle Dr., Ste. 150
Colorado Springs, CO 80906
Phone: (719)540-9200
Fax: (719)457-0109
**Format:** Classic Rock

**KNKN-FM - 107.1 (4549)**
30 N Electronic Dr.
Pueblo, CO 81007
Phone: (719)547-0411
Fax: (719)547-9301
**Format:** Contemporary Christian

**KRDO-AM - 1240 (4235)**
PO Box 1457
Colorado Springs, CO 80901-1457
Phone: (719)632-1515
Fax: (719)635-8455
**Format:** Talk; Sports

**KRDO-FM - 95.1 (4236)**
3 S 7th St.
Colorado Springs, CO 80905
Phone: (719)632-1515
Fax: (719)635-8455
**Format:** Adult Contemporary

**KRMX-AM - 107.1 (4550)**
30 N. Electronic Dr.
Pueblo, CO 81007-1444
Phone: (719)545-2883
Fax: (719)545-2931
**Format:** Hispanic

**KSKX-FM - 105.5 (4238)**
3 S 7th St.
PO Box 1457
Colorado Springs, CO 80901
Phone: (719)578-1055
Fax: (719)520-9374
**Format:** Jazz

**KSLV-AM - 1240 (4517)**
109 Adams St.
PO Box 631
Monte Vista, CO 81144
Phone: (719)852-3581
Fax: (719)852-3583
**Format:** Country

**KSLV-FM - 95.3 (4518)**
109 Adams St.
PO Box 631
Monte Vista, CO 81144
Phone: (719)852-3581
Fax: (719)852-3583
**Format:** Adult Contemporary

**KSPK-FM - 102.3, 103.5 (4588)**
516 Main St.
Walsenburg, CO 81089
Phone: (719)738-3636
Fax: (719)738-2010
**Format:** Country

**KSPZ-FM - 92.9 (4239)**
6805 Corporate Dr., Ste. 130
Colorado Springs, CO 80919
Phone: (719)540-9200
Fax: (719)579-0882
**Format:** Oldies

**KTLF-FM - 90.5 (4240)**
1665 Briargate Blvd., Ste. 100
Colorado Springs, CO 80920
Phone: (719)593-0600
Fax: (719)593-2399

**Format:** Religious

**KTSC-FM - 89.5 (4551)**
2200 Bonforte Blvd.
Pueblo, CO 81001-4901
Phone: (719)549-2192
Fax: (719)549-2120
**Format:** Album-Oriented Rock (AOR)

**KVUU-FM - 99.9 (4552)**
2864 S. Circle Dr., Ste. 150
Colorado Springs, CO 80906
Phone: (719)540-9200
Fax: (719)579-0884
**Format:** Adult Contemporary; Adult Contemporary

**KYZX-FM - 103.9 (4243)**
1805 E. Cheyenne Rd.
Colorado Springs, CO 80906
Phone: (719)520-9000
Fax: (719)634-5837
**Format:** Classic Rock

## Denver (Steamboat Springs), CO

**KALC-FM - 105.9 (4326)**
4700 S. Syracuse, Ste. 1050
Denver, CO 80237
Phone: (303)572-7000
Fax: (303)615-5393
**Format:** Adult Contemporary; Classic Rock

**KBCO-AM - 1190 (4327)**
8975 E. Kenyon Ave.
Denver, CO 80237
Fax: (303)694-4919
**Format:** Talk

**KBCR-AM - 1230 (4569)**
PO Box 774050
Steamboat Springs, CO 80477
Phone: (303)879-2270
Fax: (303)879-1404
**Format:** Oldies; Sports

**KBCR-FM - 96.9 (4570)**
Box 4050
Steamboat Springs, CO 80477
Phone: (303)879-2270
Fax: (303)879-1404
**Format:** Country

**KBNO-AM - 1280 (4328)**
600 Grant, Ste. 600
Denver, CO 80203
Phone: (303)733-5266
Fax: (303)733-5242
**Format:** Hispanic

**KCOL-AM - 600 (4387)**
1612 Laporte Ave.
Fort Collins, CO 80522
Phone: (970)482-5991
Fax: (970)482-5994
**Format:** News; Talk

**KCSU-FM - 90.5 (4388)**
Lory Student Center
Colorado State University
Fort Collins, CO 80523
Fax: (303)491-7612
**Format:** Alternative/New Music/Progressive; Educational

**KEZW-AM - 1430 (4330)**
4700 S Syracuse St., Ste. 1050
Denver, CO 80237-2713
Phone: (303)967-2000
Fax: (303)696-0522
**Format:** Big Band/Nostalgia

**KFMD-FM - 95.7 (4331)**
4695 S Monaco St.
Denver, CO 80237
Phone: (303)713-8000
Fax: (303)713-8742
**Format:** Contemporary Hit Radio (CHR)

**KGWY-FM - 100.7 (33734)**
PO Box 1179
Gillette, WY 82717
Phone: (307)686-2242
Fax: (307)686-7736
**Format:** Country

**KHOW-AM - 630 (4332)**
8975 E. Kenyon Ave.
Denver, CO 80237-1836
Phone: (303)713-8000

Fax: (303)694-4919
**Format:** Talk

**KJME-AM - 1390 (4334)**
930 W 7th Ave
Denver, CO 80204-4345
Phone: (303)623-1390
**Format:** Hispanic; Ethnic

**KJQY-FM - 95.5 (4335)**
4695 S Monaco St.
Denver, CO 80237
Phone: (719)545-2080
Fax: (719)543-9898
**Format:** Contemporary Hit Radio (CHR)

**KKZN-AM - 760 (4337)**
4695 S Monaco St.
Denver, CO 80237
Phone: (303)713-8000
Fax: (303)713-8736
**Format:** Sports

**KLTT-AM - 670 (4151)**
2150 W. 29th Ave., Ste. 300
Denver, CO 80211
Phone: (303)477-1217
Fax: (303)433-7257
**Format:** Religious

**KLZ-AM - 560 (4338)**
2150 W. 29th Ave., Ste. 300
Denver, CO 80211
Phone: (303)433-5500
Fax: (303)433-1555
**Format:** Contemporary Christian

**KNNG-FM - 104.7 (4573)**
803 W. Main
PO Box 830
Sterling, CO 80751
Phone: (970)522-1607
Fax: (970)522-1322
**Format:** Country

**KOSI-FM - 101.1 (4340)**
4700 S Syracuse St., Ste. 1050
Denver, CO 80237-2713
Phone: (303)696-1714
Fax: (303)696-0522
**Format:** Adult Contemporary

**KPMX-FM - 105.7 (4574)**
117 Main St.
Sterling, CO 80751
Phone: (970)522-4800
Fax: (970)522-3997
**Format:** Adult Contemporary

**KQMT-FM - 99.5 (4342)**
4700 S Syracuse St., Ste. 1050
Denver, CO 80237-2713
Phone: (303)967-2700
Fax: (303)696-0522
**Format:** Classic Rock; Classic Rock; Classic Rock

**KRAI-AM - 550 (4251)**
1111 W. Victory Way
Craig, CO 81625
Phone: (970)824-6574
Fax: (970)826-4581
**Format:** Country

**KRAI-FM - 93.7 (4252)**
1111 W. Victory Way
PO Box 65
Craig, CO 81626-0065
Phone: (970)824-6574
Fax: (970)826-4581

**KRFX-FM - 103.5 (4343)**
4695 S. Monaco St.
Denver, CO 80237-3403
Phone: (303)713-8000
Fax: (303)892-4700
**Format:** Classic Rock

**KTCL-FM - 93.3 (4344)**
4695 S Monaco
Denver, CO 80237
Phone: (303)713-8000
**Format:** Eclectic; Alternative/New Music/Progressive; Alternative/New Music/Progressive

**KUAD-FM - 99.1 (4612)**
600 Main St.
Windsor, CO 80550
Fax: (303)686-7491

**Format:** Country

**KVOD-FM - 92.5 (4347)**
1560 Broadway, Ste. 1100
Denver, CO 80202
Phone: (303)839-1649
Fax: (303)832-0964
**Format:** Classical

## El Centro, CA-Yuma, AZ

**KAWC-FM - 88.9 (990)**
Arizona Western College Campus
Business Administration Bldg.
Box 929
Yuma, AZ 85366-0929
Fax: (520)344-7740
**Format:** Classical; Jazz; News

**KBLU-AM - 560 (991)**
755 W. 28th St.
Yuma, AZ 85364
Phone: (928)344-4980
Fax: (928)344-4983
**Format:** Oldies

**KEKA-FM - 101.5 (1839)**
1101 Marsh Rd.
Eureka, CA 95501-1574
Phone: (707)442-5744
**Format:** Contemporary Country

**KGBA-FM - 100.1 (1794)**
605 State St.
El Centro, CA 92243
Phone: (760)352-9860
Fax: (760)352-1883
**Format:** Adult Contemporary; Religious; Religious

**KINS-AM - 980 (1842)**
1101 Marsh Rd.
Eureka, CA 95501
Phone: (707)442-5744
Fax: (707)444-3899
**Format:** Talk; News; Sports; Sports

**KJOK-AM - 1400 (993)**
949 S. Ave. B
Yuma, AZ 85364
Phone: (928)782-4321
Fax: (928)343-1710
**Format:** Oldies

**KLJZ-FM - 93.1 (994)**
949 S. Ave. B
Yuma, AZ 85364
Phone: (928)782-4321
Fax: (928)343-1710

**KMXX-FM - 99.3 (1552)**
1603 N Imperial Dr.
El Centro, CA 92243-1333
**Format:** Hispanic

**KROP-AM - 1300 (1553)**
120 S. Plaza
PO Box 238
Brawley, CA 92227
Phone: (619)344-1300
Fax: (619)344-1763
**Format:** Country

**KSIQ-FM - 96.1 (1554)**
120 S. Plaza
PO Box 238
Brawley, CA 92227
Phone: (760)344-1300
Fax: (760)344-1763
**Format:** Top 40

**KWST-AM - 1430 (1796)**
1803 N Imperial Ave
El Centro, CA 92243
Phone: (760)482-7777
Fax: (760)352-1430

**KXO-AM - 1230 (1797)**
420 Main St.
El Centro, CA 92243
Phone: (760)352-1230
**Format:** Oldies; News; Sports; Agricultural

**KXO-FM - 107.5 (1798)**
420 Main St.
El Centro, CA 92243
Phone: (760)352-1230

**Format:** Adult Contemporary

**KYJT-FM - 100.9 (996)**
755 W 28th St.
Yuma, AZ 85364
Phone: (520)344-4980
Fax: (520)344-4983
**Format:** Classic Rock

**XEMBC-AM - 1190 (3392)**
PO Box 430155
San Ysidro, CA 92143
Phone: (619)230-0203
**Format:** Hispanic; Talk

**XEWV-AM - 940 (3393)**
PO Box 430155
San Ysidro, CA 92143
Phone: (619)230-0203
**Format:** Hispanic

**XEWV-FM - 106.7 (3394)**
2630 E. Beyer Blvd., Ste. 265
PO Box 430155
San Ysidro, CA 92143
Phone: (619)230-0203
**Format:** Hispanic

## Eugene, OR

**KDCQ-FM - 93.5 (25755)**
PO Box 478
Coos Bay, OR 97420
Phone: (541)269-0935
Fax: (541)269-9376
**Format:** Oldies

**KDUK-FM - 104.7 (25815)**
1345 Olive St.
PO Box 1120
Eugene, OR 97440
Phone: (541)485-1120
Fax: (541)484-5769
**Format:** Contemporary Hit Radio (CHR)

**KKNU-FM - 93.1 (25819)**
925 Country Club Rd., Ste. 200
Eugene, OR 97401-2297
Phone: (541)484-9400
Fax: (541)344-9424
**Format:** Contemporary Country

**KKXO-AM - 1450 (25820)**
925 Country Club Rd., Ste. 200
Eugene, OR 97401-2297
Phone: (541)484-1450
Fax: (541)344-9424
**Format:** Big Band/Nostalgia

**KLOO-AM - 1340 (25689)**
2840 Marion St. SE
Albany, OR 97322
Phone: (541)926-8628
Fax: (541)928-1261
**Format:** Talk

**KLOO-FM - 106.3 (25690)**
2840 Marion St. SE
Albany, OR 97321
Phone: (541)926-8628
Fax: (541)928-1261
**Format:** Classic Rock

**KNND-AM - 1400 (25776)**
321 Main St.
Cottage Grove, OR 97424
Phone: (541)942-2468
Fax: (503)942-5797
**Format:** News; Country

**KODZ-FM - 99.1 (25823)**
1345 Olive St.
PO Box 1120
Eugene, OR 97440
Phone: (541)485-1120
Fax: (541)484-5769
**Format:** Oldies

**KPNW-AM - 1120 (25824)**
1345 Olive St.
PO Box 1120
Eugene, OR 97440
Phone: (541)485-1120
Fax: (541)484-5769

## Eureka, CA

**Format:** News; Sports; Talk

**KQEN-AM - 1240 (26029)**
1445 W. Harvard Ave.
Roseburg, OR 97470
Phone: (503)672-6641
Fax: (503)673-7598
**Format:** Adult Contemporary; News; Talk

**KRSB-FM - 103.1 (26031)**
1445 W Harvard Ave.
Roseburg, OR 97470
Phone: (503)672-6641
Fax: (503)673-7598
**Format:** Contemporary Country

**KSHR-FM - 97.3 (25757)**
PO Box 180
Coos Bay, OR 97420-0021
Phone: (541)267-2121
Fax: (541)267-5229
**Format:** Hot Country; Hot Country; Hot Country

**KTHH-AM - 990 (25693)**
2840 Marion St. SE
Albany, OR 97321
Phone: (541)926-8628
Fax: (541)928-1261
**Format:** Country

**KUGN-AM - 590 (25826)**
1200 Executive Pwky., Ste. 440
Eugene, OR 97401
Phone: (541)485-5846
Fax: (541)485-0969
**Format:** News; Talk; Talk

**KUGN-FM - 97.9 (25827)**
1200 Executive Pwky., Ste. 440
Eugene, OR 97401
Phone: (541)485-5846
Fax: (541)485-0969
**Format:** Country

## Eureka, CA

**KGOE-AM - 1480 (1841)**
5640 S. Broadway
Eureka, CA 95501
Phone: (707)443-1621
Fax: (707)443-6848
**Format:** News; Talk

**KPOD-FM - 97.9 (1732)**
1345 Northcrest Dr.
PO Box 1089
Crescent City, CA 95531
Phone: (707)464-3183
Fax: (707)464-4303
**Format:** Country

**KRED-FM - 92.3 (1843)**
5640 S. Broadway
Eureka, CA 95503
Phone: (707)443-1621
Fax: (707)443-6848
**Format:** Country

**KXGO-FM - 93.1 (1844)**
603 F St.
Eureka, CA 95501
Phone: (707)445-8105
Fax: (707)445-3906
**Format:** Classic Rock

## Fairbanks (North Pole), AK

**KFAR-AM - 660 (547)**
1060 Aspen St.
Fairbanks, AK 99709-5501
Phone: (907)451-5910
Fax: (907)451-5999
**Format:** Talk; News; Public Radio

**KIAK-AM - 970 (549)**
546 9th Ave.
Fairbanks, AK 99701-4902
Phone: (907)457-1921
Fax: (907)457-2128
**Format:** Contemporary Country

**KIAK-FM - 102.5 (550)**
546 9th Ave.
Fairbanks, AK 99701-4902
Phone: (907)457-1921

**Format:** Country

**KWLF-FM - 98.1 (556)**
1060 Aspen St.
Fairbanks, AK 99709-5501
Phone: (907)451-5910
Fax: (907)451-5999
**Format:** Contemporary Hit Radio (CHR); Adult Contemporary

## Flagstaff, AZ

**KAZM-AM - 780 (839)**
PO Box 1525
Sedona, AZ 86339
Phone: (928)282-4154
Fax: (928)282-2230
**Format:** Talk; News; Sports; Contemporary Hit Radio (CHR)

**KSED-FM - 107.5 (675)**
112 East Route. 66, Ste. 105
Flagstaff, AZ 86001
Phone: (520)779-1177
Fax: (520)774-5179
**Format:** Country

**KVNA-FM - 97.5 (677)**
2690 Huntington Dr.
Flagstaff, AZ 86004
Phone: (602)526-2700
Fax: (602)774-5852
**Format:** Adult Contemporary

## Fresno-Visalia (Hanford), CA

**KAAT-FM - 103.1 & translators 104.3 (2567)**
PO Box 2020
40356 Oak Parkway
Oakhurst, CA 93644
Phone: (559)683-1031
Fax: (559)683-5488
**Format:** Adult Contemporary; Soft Rock; Big Band/Nostalgia

**KABX-FM - 97.5 (2457)**
1020 Main St.
Merced, CA 95341
Phone: (209)723-2191
Fax: (209)383-2950
**Format:** Oldies

**KARM-FM - 89.7 (4001)**
1300 S. Woodland Dr.
Visalia, CA 93277
Phone: (559)627-5276
Fax: (559)627-5288
**Format:** Religious

**KCBL-AM - 1340 (1886)**
83 E Shaw Ave., Ste. 150
Fresno, CA 93710
Phone: (559)243-4300
Fax: (559)243-4301
**Format:** Sports

**KEYQ-AM - 980 (1606)**
2310 Ponderosa Dr., No. 28
Camarillo, CA 93010
Phone: (805)482-4797
Fax: (805)388-5202
**Format:** Hispanic; Religious

**KEZL-FM - 96.7 (1887)**
83 E. Shaw Ave., Ste. 150
Fresno, CA 93710-7616
Phone: (559)230-4300
Fax: (559)243-4301
**Format:** Jazz

**KFCF-FM - 88.1 (1888)**
PO Box 4364
Fresno, CA 93744
Phone: (559)233-2221
Fax: (559)233-5776
**Format:** Eclectic

**KFSO-FM - 92.9 (1890)**
83 E. Shaw Ave., Ste. 150
Fresno, CA 93710-7616
Phone: (559)230-4300
Fax: (559)230-4301

**Format:** Oldies

**KFSR-FM - 90.7 (1891)**
California State University Fresno
5201 N. Maple Ave
Mail Stop No. 119
Fresno, CA 93740
Phone: (559)278-2598
Fax: (559)278-6985
**Format:** Eclectic; Adult Album Alternative; Jazz; Blues; Hip Hop; Reggae; Soft Rock

**KHOT-AM - 1250 (1894)**
1742 E. Griffith Way
PO Box 112
Fresno, CA 93726
Fax: (509)229-2229
**Format:** Hispanic

**KIGS-AM - 620 (1959)**
6165 East Lacey Blvd.
Hanford, CA 93230
Phone: (559)582-0361
Fax: (559)582-3981
**Format:** Hispanic; Top 40

**KJFX-FM - 95.7 (1896)**
1066 E Shaw Ave.
Fresno, CA 93710-7807
**Format:** Classic Rock

**KMJ-AM - 580 (1897)**
1071 W. Shaw Ave.
Fresno, CA 93711
Phone: (559)490-5800
Fax: (559)490-5838
**Format:** Talk; News; News

**KOQO-FM - 101.9 (1900)**
1071 W Shaw Ave.
Fresno, CA 93711-3702
Phone: (559)247-2102
**Format:** Hispanic

**KQEQ-AM - 1210 (1901)**
139 W. Olive Ave.
Fresno, CA 93728
Phone: (209)233-8803
Fax: (209)233-8871
**Format:** Hispanic

**KRDU-AM - 1130 (1774)**
597 N. Alta Ave.
Dinuba, CA 93618
Phone: (559)486-1130
Fax: (559)591-4822
**Format:** Religious

**KSEQ-FM - 97.1 (4002)**
617 W. Tulare Ave.
Visalia, CA 93277-2552
Phone: (209)627-9710
Fax: (209)627-1590
**Format:** Adult Contemporary

**KSKS-FM - 93.7 (1903)**
1071 W Shaw Ave.
Fresno, CA 93711-3702
**Format:** Country

**KVBL-AM - 1400 (1906)**
83 E Shaw Ave., Ste. 150
Fresno, CA 93710
Phone: (559)243-4300
Fax: (559)243-4301
**Format:** Sports

**KXEX-AM - 1550 (1909)**
139 W. Olive Ave.
Fresno, CA 93728
Phone: (559)233-8803
Fax: (559)233-8871
**Format:** Public Radio

**KYOS-AM - 1480 (2464)**
1020 W. Main St.
Merced, CA 95340
Phone: (209)723-2191
Fax: (209)383-2950
**Format:** News; Talk; Talk

## Grand Junction-Durango, CO

**KCIC-FM - 88.5 (4428)**
3102 E Rd.
Grand Junction, CO 81504
Phone: (970)434-8391

**Format:** Religious

**KEXO-AM - 1230 (4430)**
315 Kennedy Ave.
Grand Junction, CO 81501
Phone: (970)242-7788
Fax: (970)245-5858
**Format:** Contemporary Christian; Contemporary Christian

**KIQX-FM - 101.3 (4356)**
PO Box X
Durango, CO 81302
Phone: (970)259-4444
Fax: (970)247-1005
**Format:** Adult Contemporary

**KJOL-FM - 90.3 (4432)**
1360 E. Sherwood Ave.
Grand Junction, CO 81501-7546
Fax: (303)242-1309
**Format:** Contemporary Christian

**KJYE-FM - 92.3 (4433)**
1360 E. Sherwood Dr.
Grand Junction, CO 81501
Phone: (970)254-2100
Fax: (970)245-7551
**Format:** Easy Listening

**KKNN-FM - 95.1 (4434)**
315 Kennedy Ave.
Grand Junction, CO 81501-7552
Phone: (970)241-9595
Fax: (970)245-5858
**Format:** Classic Rock

**KMGJ-FM - 93.1 (4435)**
1360 E. Sherwood Dr.
Grand Junction, CO 81501-7546
Phone: (970)254-2100
Fax: (970)245-7551
**Format:** Adult Contemporary

**KMSA-FM - 91.3 (4436)**
1175 Texas Ave.
Grand Junction, CO 81502
Phone: (970)248-1240
Fax: (970)248-1708
**Format:** Alternative/New Music/Progressive

**KPRN-FM - 89.5 (4437)**
414 Main St.
Grand Junction, CO 81501-2512
Phone: (303)241-5776
Fax: (303)245-8176
**Format:** News; Classical; Public Radio

**KTMM-AM - 1340 (4441)**
1360 E. Sherwood Dr.
Grand Junction, CO 81501-7548
Phone: (970)254-2100
Fax: (970)245-7551
**Format:** Sports; Talk; Talk

## Great Falls, MT

**KLCM-FM - 95.9 (18183)**
PO Box 620
Lewistown, MT 59457
Phone: (406)538-3495
Fax: (406)538-3495
**Format:** Adult Contemporary

**KSEN-AM - 1150 (18239)**
830 Oilfield Ave.
Shelby, MT 59474
Phone: (406)434-5241
Fax: (406)434-2122
**Format:** Adult Contemporary

**KXLO-AM - 1230 (18184)**
PO Box 620
Lewistown, MT 59457
Phone: (406)538-3441
Fax: (406)538-3495
**Format:** Country; Full Service

**KZIN-FM - 96.3 (18240)**
830 Oilfield Ave.
Shelby, MT 59474
Phone: (406)434-5241
Fax: (406)434-2122

**Format:** Country

## Helena, MT

**KBLL-AM - 1240 (18164)**
1400 11th Ave.
Helena, MT 59601
Phone: (406)442-6620
Fax: (406)442-6161
**Format:** News; Talk

**KBLL-FM - 99.5 (18165)**
1400 11th Ave.
Helena, MT 59601
Phone: (406)442-6620
Fax: (406)442-6161
**Format:** Country

**KGVW-AM - 640 (18062)**
2050 Amsterdam Rd.
Belgrade, MT 59714
Phone: (406)388-4281
Fax: (406)388-1700
**Format:** Adult Contemporary; Religious; Religious

**KHKR-AM - (18167)**
Box 4111
Helena, MT 59604
Phone: (406)442-4490
Fax: (406)442-7356
**Format:** Country

**KMTX-FM - 105.3 (18169)**
PO Box 1183-59624
Helena, MT 59624
Phone: (406)442-0400
Fax: (406)442-0491
**Format:** Adult Contemporary

**KZMT-FM - 101.1 (18170)**
110 E. Broadway St.
Helena, MT 59601-4232
Phone: (406)442-4490
Fax: (406)442-7356
**Format:** Classic Rock; Classic Rock

## Honolulu, HI

**KAIM-AM - 870 (7581)**
560 N. Nimitz Hwy., Ste. 109
Honolulu, HI 96817-5330
Phone: (808)533-0065
Fax: (808)524-2104
**Format:** Talk

**KAIM-FM - 95.5 (7582)**
560 N. Nimitz Hwy., Ste. 109
Honolulu, HI 96817-5330
Phone: (808)533-0065
**Format:** Contemporary Christian

**KDNN-FM - 98.5 (7585)**
650 Iwilei Rd., Ste. 400
Honolulu, HI 96817
Phone: (808)550-9200
Fax: (808)550-9510
**Format:** Hawaiian

**KHBZ-AM - 990 (7588)**
650 Iwilei Rd., Ste. 400
Honolulu, HI 96817
Phone: (808)550-9200
Fax: (808)550-9510
**Format:** News; Talk

**KHPR-FM - 88.1 (7590)**
738 Kaheka St.
Honolulu, HI 96814
Phone: (808)955-8821
Fax: (808)942-5477
**Format:** Information; Classical

**KIKI-AM - 990 (7591)**
650 Iwilei Rd., Ste. 400
Honolulu, HI 96817-5319
Fax: (808)531-4606
**Format:** Contemporary Hit Radio (CHR)

**KIKI-FM - 93.9 (7592)**
650 Iwilei Rd., Ste. 400
Honolulu, HI 96817-5319
Phone: (808)550-9200
Fax: (808)550-9504

**Format:** Contemporary Hit Radio (CHR)

**KIPO-FM - 89.3 (7594)**
738 Kaheka St.
Honolulu, HI 96814
Phone: (808)955-8821
Fax: (808)942-5477
**Format:** Classical; Information; Jazz

**KKEA-AM - 1420 (7595)**
1088 Bishop St., LL2
Honolulu, HI 96813
Phone: (808)536-3624
Fax: (808)536-0608
**Format:** Sports; Talk

**KKUA-FM - 90.7 (7596)**
738 Kaheka St.
Honolulu, HI 96814
Phone: (808)955-8821
Fax: (808)942-5477
**Format:** Public Radio; Classical; News

**KLHT-AM - 1040 (7513)**
98-1016 Komo Mai Dr.
Aiea, HI 96701
Phone: (808)524-1040
Fax: (808)487-1040
**Format:** Religious

**KNDI-AM - 1270 (7597)**
1734 S. King St.
Honolulu, HI 96826
Phone: (808)946-2844
Fax: (808)947-3531
**Format:** Ethnic; Religious

**KORL-AM - 690 (7598)**
1833 Kalakaua Ave, Ste. 500
Honolulu, HI 96815
Phone: (808)591-9369
Fax: (808)591-9349
**Format:** Public Radio

**KUMU-FM - 94.7 (7605)**
765 Amana St., Ste. 206
Honolulu, HI 96814-3248
Phone: (808)947-1500
Fax: (808)947-1506
**Format:** Easy Listening

**KWAI-AM - 1080 (7606)**
100 N Beretania St., Ste. 401
Honolulu, HI 96817-4712
Phone: (808)523-3868
Fax: (808)531-6532
**Format:** Talk; Sports

**KZOO-AM - 1210 (7608)**
2752 Woodlawn Dr., Ste. 5-204A
Honolulu, HI 96822
Phone: (808)593-2880
Fax: (808)596-0083
**Format:** Talk; Ethnic; News; Eclectic; Religious; Big Band/Nostalgia; Easy Listening; Religious; Big Band/Nostalgia; Easy Listening

## Idaho Falls-Pocatello, ID

**KBRV-AM - 790 (7776)**
PO Box Z
Pocatello, ID 83206-1394
Phone: (208)232-7177
**Format:** Talk; Sports

**KFTZ-FM - 103.3 (7708)**
1190 E Lincoln Rd.
Idaho Falls, ID 83401-2122
**Format:** Contemporary Hit Radio (CHR)

**KID-AM - 590 (7709)**
1406 Commerce Way
Idaho Falls, ID 83401
Phone: (208)524-5900
Fax: (208)522-9696
**Format:** Full Service; News; Talk; Sports; Talk; Sports

**KID-FM - 96.1 (7710)**
1406 Commerce Way
Idaho Falls, ID 83404
Phone: (208)524-5900
Fax: (208)522-9696
**Format:** Hot Country

**KMGI-FM - 102.5 (7778)**
544 N. Arthur Ave., Box 40
Pocatello, ID 83204
Phone: (208)233-2121

Juneau, AK

Fax: (208)233-7682
**Format:** Classic Rock

**KPKY-FM - 94.9 (7779)**
259 E. Center
Pocatello, ID 83204-0998
Phone: (208)233-1133
Fax: (208)232-1240
**Format:** Oldies; News; News

**KSEI-AM - 930 (7781)**
544 N. Arthur Ave.,
PO Box 40
Pocatello, ID 83204
Phone: (208)233-2121
Fax: (208)234-0105
**Format:** Sports; Talk; Talk

**KUPI-AM - 980 (7712)**
854 Lindsay Blvd.
Idaho Falls, ID 83401
Phone: (208)522-1101
Fax: (208)522-6110
**Format:** Big Band/Nostalgia; Sports

**KUPI-FM - 99.1 (7713)**
854 Lindsay Blvd.
Idaho Falls, ID 83401
Phone: (208)522-1101
Fax: (208)522-6110
**Format:** Country

**KWIK-AM - 1240 (7782)**
259 E Center
Pocatello, ID 83204-0998
Phone: (208)233-4891
Fax: (208)232-1240
**Format:** News; Sports; Sports

**KZBQ-AM - 1290 (7783)**
PO Box 97
Pocatello, ID 83204-0097
**Format:** Contemporary Country

**KZBQ-FM - 93.7 (7784)**
PO Box 97
Pocatello, ID 83204-0097
**Format:** Contemporary Country

## Juneau, AK

**KJNO-AM - 630 (574)**
3161 Channel Dr., Ste. 2
Juneau, AK 99801
Phone: (907)586-3630
Fax: (907)463-3685
**Format:** Talk; Sports

**KTKU-FM - 105.1 (577)**
3161 Channel Dr., Ste. 2
Juneau, AK 99801
Phone: (907)586-3630
Fax: (907)463-3685
**Format:** Hot Country

**KTOO-FM - 104.3 (578)**
360 Egan Dr.
Juneau, AK 99801-1748
Phone: (907)586-1670
Fax: (907)586-3612
**Format:** Public Radio; News; Classical; Jazz; Classical; Jazz

## Ketchikan, AK

**KGTW-FM - 106.7 (585)**
526 Stedman St.
Ketchikan, AK 99901
Phone: (907)225-2193
Fax: (907)225-0444
**Format:** Country

**KRBD-FM - 105.9 (586)**
123 Stedman
Ketchikan, AK 99901
Phone: (907)225-9655
Fax: (907)247-0808
**Format:** Eclectic; Public Radio; Public Radio

**KTKN-AM - 930 (587)**
526 Stedman St.
Ketchikan, AK 99901
Phone: (907)225-2193
Fax: (907)225-0444

**Format:** News; Sports; Sports

## Las Vegas, NV

**KBAD-AM - 920 (18707)**
6755 W Flamingo Rd.
Las Vegas, NV 89147-8667
**Format:** Sports

**KCEP-FM - 88.1 (18709)**
330 W. Washington St.
Las Vegas, NV 89106-3327
Phone: (702)648-0104
Fax: (702)647-0803
**Format:** Blues; Urban Contemporary

**KDOX-AM - 1280 (18710)**
740 N. Eastern Ave., Ste. 100
Las Vegas, NV 89101-2886
Phone: (702)732-1664
Fax: (702)732-3060
**Format:** Hispanic; Adult Contemporary

**KDWN-AM - 720 (18711)**
1 Main St.
PO Box 760
Las Vegas, NV 89125-0760
Phone: (702)385-7212
Fax: (702)385-7990
**Format:** Talk; News; Sports

**KENO-AM - 1460 (18712)**
8755 W Flamingo Rd.
Las Vegas, NV 89147-8667
Phone: (702)461-8225
**Format:** News

**KIWD FM - 101.9 (18713)**
1130 E. Desert Inn Rd.
Las Vegas, NV 89109-2812
Phone: (702)732-7753
Fax: (702)732-4890
**Format:** Country

**KJUL-FM - 104.3 (18714)**
1455 E. Tropicana Ave., Ste. 800
Las Vegas, NV 89119-6522
Phone: (702)730-0300
Fax: (702)730-8447

**KKVV-AM - 1060 AM (18715)**
3185 S. Highland Dr., Ste. 13
Las Vegas, NV 89109
Phone: (702)731-5588
Fax: (702)731-5851
**Format:** Contemporary Christian; Talk

**KNUU-AM - 970 (18719)**
1455 E. Tropicana Ave., Ste. 550
Las Vegas, NV 89119
Phone: (702)735-8644
Fax: (702)735-8184
**Format:** Talk; News

**KOMP-FM - 92.3 (18720)**
8755 W Flamingo Rd.
Las Vegas, NV 89147-8667
**Format:** Album-Oriented Rock (AOR)

**KQOL-FM - 93.1 (18721)**
1130 E Desert Inn Rd.
Las Vegas, NV 89109
Phone: (702)732-7753
Fax: (702)732-4890
**Format:** Oldies

**KTPH-FM - 91.7 (18764)**
1289 S. Torrey Pines
Las Vegas, NV 89146
Phone: (702)258-9895
Fax: (702)258-5646
**Format:** Classical; News

**KUNV-FM - 91.5 (18725)**
University of Nevada at Las Vegas
4505 S. Maryland Pkwy.
Las Vegas, NV 89154
Phone: (702)895-3877
Fax: (702)895-4857
**Format:** Eclectic; Jazz

**KWID-FM - 101.9 (18726)**
1130 E Desert Inn Rd.
Las Vegas, NV 89109
Phone: (702)892-0727
Fax: (702)732-4890

**Format:** Hispanic

**KWNR-FM - 95.5 (18727)**
2880 Meade Avenue, Suite 250
Las Vegas, NV 89102
Phone: (702)238-7300
Fax: (702)732-4890
**Format:** Contemporary Country

**KXPT-FM - 97.1 (18729)**
8755 W Flamingo Rd.
Las Vegas, NV 89147-8667

## Los Angeles (Corona & San Bernardino), CA

**KABC-AM - 790 (2384)**
3321 S. La Cienega Blvd.
Los Angeles, CA 90016-3114
Phone: (310)840-4900
Fax: (310)840-4977
**Format:** Talk

**KCXX-FM - 103.9 (2988)**
242 E. Airport Dr., Suite 106
San Bernardino, CA 92408
Phone: (909)384-1039
Fax: (909)888-7302
**Format:** Alternative/New Music/Progressive

**KDIF-AM - 1440 (2840)**
1465 Spruce St., Ste. A
Riverside, CA 92507
Phone: (909)784-4210
Fax: (909)784-4213
**Format:** Hispanic

**KDIS-AM - 1110 (2389)**
3321 S. La Cienega Blvd.
Los Angeles, CA 90016
Phone: (310)840-2800
Fax: (310)840-2806
**Format:** Educational

**KFI-AM - 640 (1579)**
3400 W Olive Ave., Suite 550
Burbank, CA 91505
Phone: (818)559-2252
Fax: (213)385-7076
**Format:** Talk

**KFI-AM - 640 (2390)**
610 S Ardmore Ave.
Los Angeles, CA 90005
Phone: (213)385-0101
Fax: (213)380-8364
**Format:** Talk; News

**KFRG-FM - 95.1 (1684)**
900 E. Washington, Ste. 315
Colton, CA 92324
Phone: (909)825-9525
Fax: (909)514-0951
**Format:** Country

**KFWB-AM - 980 (2392)**
6230 Yucca St.
Los Angeles, CA 90028
Phone: (323)462-5392
Fax: (323)871-4670
**Format:** News

**KGGI-FM - 99.1 (2841)**
2001 Iowa Ave., Ste. 200
Riverside, CA 92507
Phone: (909)684-1991
Fax: (909)274-4949
**Format:** Contemporary Hit Radio (CHR)

**KHHT-FM - 92.3 (1580)**
3400 Riverside Dr., Ste. 800
Burbank, CA 91505
Phone: (818)845-1027
Fax: (818)295-6466
**Format:** Urban Contemporary

**KHJ-AM - 930 (1581)**
1845 W. Empire Ave.
Burbank, CA 91504-3402
Phone: (818)729-5300
Fax: (818)729-5678

**KJLH-FM - 102.3 (1989)**
161 N. La Brea Ave.
Inglewood, CA 90301
Phone: (310)330-2200
Fax: (310)330-5555

**Format:** Urban Contemporary

**KKBE-FM - 105.5 (3986)**
2284 Victoria Ave., Ste. 2G
Ventura, CA 93003
Phone: (805)289-1400
Fax: (805)644-4257
**Format:** Country

**KLAC-AM - 570 (1584)**
3400 W. Olive
Burbank, CA 91505
Phone: (818)559-2252
Fax: (818)637-2267
**Format:** Sports

**KLOS-FM - 95.5 (2395)**
3321 S. La Cienega Blvd.
Los Angeles, CA 90016
Phone: (310)840-4800
Fax: (310)840-4846
**Format:** Album-Oriented Rock (AOR)

**KLRD-FM - 90.1 (4078)**
35225 Ave. A, Ste. 105
Yucaipa, CA 92399-4359
Phone: (909)790-1848
Fax: (909)790-0228
**Format:** Religious; Contemporary Hit Radio (CHR)

**KMZT-FM - 105.1 (2399)**
1500 Cotner Ave.
PO Box 250028
Los Angeles, CA 90025-3303
Phone: (310)478-5540
Fax: (310)445-1439
**Format:** Jazz; Classical; Classical

**KNX-AM - 1070 (2400)**
6121 Sunset Blvd.
Los Angeles, CA 90028-6455
Phone: (323)460-3000
Fax: (323)460-3275
**Format:** News

**KOST-FM - 103.5 (1586)**
3400 W. Olice
Burbank, CA 91505
Phone: (818)559-2252
Fax: (213)385-0281
**Format:** Adult Contemporary

**KRLA-AM - 1110 (2401)**
3580 Wilshire Blvd.
Los Angeles, CA 90010
Phone: (213)383-4222
Fax: (213)386-3679
**Format:** Oldies

**KRTH-FM - 101.1 (2402)**
5670 Wilshire Blvd
Los Angeles, CA 90036
Phone: (323)936-5784
Fax: (323)936-3427
**Format:** Oldies

**KSCA-FM - 101.9 (1939)**
655 N Central Ave., Ste. 2500
Glendale, CA 91203-1422
Phone: (818)500-4500
Fax: (818)500-4329

**KSGN-FM - 89.7 (2843)**
11498 Pierce St.
Riverside, CA 92505
Phone: (909)687-5746
Fax: (909)785-2288
**Format:** Religious

**KTNQ-AM - 1020 (1940)**
655 N Central Ave., Ste. 2500
Glendale, CA 91203-1422
Phone: (818)500-4500
Fax: (818)500-4329
**Format:** Hispanic; News; Talk

**KUSC-FM - 91.5 (2405)**
Box 77913
Los Angeles, CA 90007-0913
Phone: (213)225-7400
Fax: (213)225-7410
**Format:** Public Radio; Classical

**KVCR-FM - 91.9 (2989)**
701 S. Mt. Vernon Ave.
San Bernardino, CA 92410
Phone: (909)384-4444
Fax: (909)885-2116

**Format:** Public Radio; Talk; News

**KWRM-AM - 1370 (1715)**
210 Radio Rd.
PO Box 100
Corona, CA 92879
Phone: (909)737-1370
Fax: (909)735-9572
**Format:** Hispanic

**KWRN-AM - 1550 (3996)**
15165 7th St., Ste. D
PO Box 1283
Victorville, CA 92392
Phone: (760)955-8722
Fax: (760)955-5751
**Format:** Middle-of-the-Road (MOR); Hispanic

**KXLU-FM - 88.9 (2407)**
One LMU Dr.
Los Angeles, CA 90045
Phone: (310)338-2866
Fax: (310)338-5959
**Format:** Classical; Jazz; Alternative/New Music/Progressive; News; Public Radio; Ethnic; News; Public Radio; Ethnic

**KXTA-AM - 1150 (2409)**
610 S Ardmore
Los Angeles, CA 90005
Phone: (213)385-0101
Fax: (213)380-8364
**Format:** Sports

## Medford, OR

**KAGO-FM - 99.5 (25872)**
PO Box 339
Klamath Falls, OR 97601-0350
Phone: (541)882-8833
Fax: (541)882-8836

**KFLS-AM - 1450 (25874)**
PO Box 1450
Klamath Falls, OR 97601
Phone: (541)882-4656
Fax: (541)884-2845
**Format:** News; Sports

**KKRB-FM - 106.9 (25876)**
PO Box 1450
Klamath Falls, OR 97601
Phone: (541)882-4656
Fax: (541)884-2845
**Format:** Adult Contemporary

**KMED-AM - 1440 (25908)**
3624 Avion Dr.
Medford, OR 97504
Phone: (541)773-1440
Fax: (541)858-5416
**Format:** News; Talk

**KROG-FM - 96.9 (25845)**
511 Rossanley Dr.
Medford, OR 97501-1771
**Format:** Adult Contemporary

**KSYC-FM - 103.9 (4076)**
316 Lawrence Ln.
Yreka, CA 96097
Phone: (530)842-4158
Fax: (530)842-7635
**Format:** Country

**KTMT-FM - 93.7 (25914)**
1438 Rossanley Dr.
PO Box 159
Medford, OR 97501-1751
Phone: (541)779-1550
Fax: (541)776-2360
**Format:** Contemporary Hit Radio (CHR)

## Missoula, MT

**KERR-AM - 750 (18233)**
581 N. Reservoir Rd.
Polson, MT 59860-9730
Phone: (406)883-5255
Fax: (406)883-4441
**Format:** Country

**KGRZ-AM - 1450 (18215)**
N. 1212 Washington, Ste. 307
PO Box 4106
Missoula, MT 59806
Phone: (406)728-1450

Fax: (406)721-3020
**Format:** Sports; Talk; Talk

**KGVO-AM - 1290 (18216)**
400 N Ryman
Missoula, MT 59802
Phone: (406)728-9300
Fax: (406)542-2329
**Format:** Talk; News

**KLCY-AM - 930 (18217)**
3250 S. Reserve St., Ste. 200
PO Box 5417
Missoula, MT 59801
Phone: (406)728-9300
Fax: (406)542-2329
**Format:** Big Band/Nostalgia

**KLTC-FM - 107.5 (18218)**
400 N Ryman
Missoula, MT 59802
Phone: (406)728-9300
Fax: (406)542-2329
**Format:** Adult Contemporary

**KMSO-FM - 102.5 (18219)**
725 Strand Ave.
PO Box 309
Missoula, MT 59806
Phone: (406)542-1025
Fax: (406)721-1036
**Format:** Adult Contemporary

**KYLT-AM - 1340 (18221)**
1600 North Ave. W.
Missoula, MT 59801-5500
Phone: (406)728-5000
Fax: (406)721-3020
**Format:** Oldies

**KYSS-FM - 94.9 (18222)**
400 Ryman
PO Box 1547
Missoula, MT 59806
Phone: (406)728-9300
Fax: (406)542-2329
**Format:** Contemporary Country

**KZOQ-FM - 100.1 (18223)**
1600 North Ave. W.
Missoula, MT 59801-5500
Phone: (406)728-5000
Fax: (406)721-3020
**Format:** Classic Rock

## Palm Springs, CA

**KCDZ-FM - 107.7 (2017)**
6448 Hallee Rd., Ste. 5
Joshua Tree, CA 92252-1908
Phone: (760)366-8471
Fax: (760)366-2976

**KCMJ-AM - 1140 (2677)**
490 S. Farrell Dr.
Palm Springs, CA 92262
Phone: (760)320-6818
Fax: (760)320-1493
**Format:** Oldies; Big Band/Nostalgia

**KDES-AM - 920 (2678)**
2100 E Tahquitz Canyon Way
Palm Springs, CA 92262
Phone: (760)325-2582
Fax: (760)322-3562
**Format:** News; Talk

**KESQ-AM - 1400 (2658)**
42650 Melanie Pl.
Palm Desert, CA 92211-5170
Phone: (619)568-6830
Fax: (619)568-3984
**Format:** Hispanic; Religious

**KMRJ-FM - 99.5 (2680)**
1061 S Palm Canyon Dr.
Palm Springs, CA 92264
Phone: (760)778-6995
Fax: (760)778-1249
**Format:** Alternative/New Music/Progressive

**KPLM-FM - 106.1 (2681)**
PO Box 1825
Palm Springs, CA 92262-7543
Fax: (619)320-3037

Phoenix (Kingman, Prescott), AZ

**Format:** Country

**KPSI-AM - 920 (2683)**
2100 E. Tahquitz Canyon Way
Palm Springs, CA 92262
Phone: (619)325-2582
Fax: (619)322-3562
**Format:** News; Talk

**KPSI-FM - 100.5 (2684)**
2100 E. Tahquitz Canyon Way
Palm Springs, CA 92262
Phone: (619)325-2582
Fax: (619)322-3562
**Format:** Adult Contemporary

**KUNA-FM - 96.7 (2661)**
42650 Melanie Pl.
Palm Desert, CA 92211-5170
Phone: (760)568-6830
Fax: (760)568-3984
**Format:** Ethnic; Hispanic

**KWXY-AM - 1340 (1633)**
68700 Dinah Shore Dr.
Cathedral City, CA 92234-5705
Phone: (619)328-1104
Fax: (619)328-7814
**Format:** Easy Listening

## Phoenix (Kingman, Prescott), AZ

**KAAA-AM - 1230 (700)**
2534 Hualapai Mountain Rd.
Kingman, AZ 86401
Phone: (928)753-1551
Fax: (928)753-1551
**Format:** News; Talk

**KASA-AM - 1540 (779)**
1445 W. Baseline Rd.
Phoenix, AZ 85041
Phone: (602)276-5272
Fax: (602)276-8119
**Format:** Religious

**KBAQ-FM - 89.5 (717)**
1435 S. Dobson Rd.
Mesa, AZ 85202
Fax: (602)835-5925
**Format:** Classical

**KFLG-FM - 94.7 (641)**
1531 Jill Way, Ste. 5
Bullhead City, AZ 86442
Fax: (520)763-3775
**Format:** Country; News

**KFNN-AM - 1510 (782)**
4800 N. Central Ave.
Phoenix, AZ 85012-1722
Phone: (602)241-1510
Fax: (602)241-1540
**Format:** Talk; News

**KFYI-AM - 910 (783)**
645 E. Missouri Ave., Ste. 119
Phoenix, AZ 85012-1370
Fax: (602)817-1199
**Format:** News; Talk

**KGME-AM - 1360 (784)**
4745 N 7, Ste. 410
Phoenix, AZ 85014
Phone: (602)266-1360
Fax: (602)263-4820
**Format:** Sports

**KGMN-FM - 99.9 (701)**
812 E. Beale St.
Kingman, AZ 86401
Phone: (928)753-9100
Fax: (928)753-1978
**Format:** Country

**KIKO-AM - 1340 (720)**
4501 Broadway
Miami, AZ 85539
Phone: (520)425-4472
Fax: (520)425-9393
**Format:** Oldies; News; Sports

**KISO-AM - 1230 (786)**
840 N. Central Ave.
Phoenix, AZ 85004
Phone: (602)258-8181
Fax: (602)420-9916

**Format:** Urban Contemporary

**KKFR-FM - 92.3 (787)**
5300 N. Central Ave.
Phoenix, AZ 85012-1410
Phone: (602)258-6161
Fax: (602)817-1199

**KKLT-FM - 98.7 (788)**
5300 N. Central Ave.
Phoenix, AZ 85012-1410
Phone: (602)274-6200
Fax: (602)266-3858
**Format:** Adult Contemporary

**KMXP-FM - 96.9 (789)**
645 E. Missouri Ave., No. 360
Phoenix, AZ 85012-1369
Phone: (602)279-5577
Fax: (602)230-2781

**KNOT-AM - 1450 (812)**
116 S. Alto St.
PO Box 151
Prescott, AZ 86302
Phone: (928)445-6880
Fax: (928)445-6852
**Format:** Country

**KOY-AM - 101.5 (793)**
840 N. Central Ave.
Phoenix, AZ 85004
Phone: (602)258-8181
Fax: (602)420-9916
**Format:** Big Band/Nostalgia

**KPHX-AM - 1480 (796)**
824 E. Washington St.
Phoenix, AZ 85034
Phone: (602)257-1351
Fax: (602)256-0741
**Format:** Hispanic; Adult Contemporary; News; Eclectic; Sports; Top 40; Religious; Sports; Top 40; Religious

**KPPV-FM - 106.7 (816)**
PO Box 26523
Prescott Valley, AZ 86312
Phone: (928)445-8289
Fax: (928)442-0448
**Format:** Adult Contemporary

**KRDS-FM - 1190 (799)**
8611 N. Black Canyon Hwy., Ste. 206
Phoenix, AZ 85021-4188
Phone: (602)995-9555
Fax: (602)995-3390
**Format:** Contemporary Christian

**KSUN-AM - 1400 (801)**
714 N. 3rd St.
Phoenix, AZ 85004-2018
Phone: (602)252-0030
Fax: (602)252-4211
**Format:** Adult Contemporary; Hispanic; Hispanic

**KTAR-AM - 620 (802)**
5300 N. Central Ave.
Phoenix, AZ 85012-1410
Phone: (602)274-6200
Fax: (602)266-3858
**Format:** News; Talk; Sports

**KTMG-FM - 99.1 (813)**
116 S. Alto St.
PO Box 151
Prescott, AZ 86302
Phone: (928)445-6880
Fax: (928)445-6852
**Format:** Soft Rock

**KWCY-FM - 103.5 (804)**
5555 N. 7th Ave., No. A-100
Phoenix, AZ 85013
**Format:** Contemporary Country

**KXAM-AM - 1310 (719)**
4725 N. Scottsdale Rd., Ste. 234
Scottsdale, AZ 85251
Phone: (480)423-1310
Fax: (480)423-3867
**Format:** Talk

**KYCA-AM - 1490 (814)**
600 6th St., Box 1631
PO Box 86302
Prescott, AZ 86301
Phone: (602)445-1700

**Format:** News; Sports; Talk; Talk

**KYOT-FM - 95.5 (805)**
840 N. Central Ave.
Phoenix, AZ 85004
Phone: (602)260-9555
Fax: (602)420-9916
**Format:** Jazz

**KZON-FM - 101.5 (806)**
840 N. Central Ave.
Phoenix, AZ 85004
Phone: (602)258-8181
Fax: (602)420-9916
**Format:** Alternative/New Music/Progressive; Top 40

## Portland, OR

**KBAM-AM - 1270 (32138)**
1323 14th Ave.
Longview, WA 98632
Fax: (206)423-1378
**Format:** Country

**KBCH-AM - 1400 (25922)**
PO Box 1430
Newport, OR 97365-0136
Phone: (503)265-2266
Fax: (503)265-6397
**Format:** Full Service

**KBPS-FM - 89.9 (25995)**
515 NE 15th
Portland, OR 97232
Phone: (503)916-5828
Fax: (503)916-2642
**Format:** Classical

**KBVM-FM - 88.3 (25996)**
PO Box 5888
Portland, OR 97228
Phone: (503)285-5200
Fax: (503)285-3322
**Format:** News; Talk

**KCBZ-FM - 96.5 (25710)**
5421 Bay Creek Dr.
PO Box 1258
Astoria, OR 97103
Phone: (503)717-0812
Fax: (503)717-9578
**Format:** Adult Contemporary

**KCRF-FM - 96.7 (25923)**
906 SW Alder St
PO Box 1430
Newport, OR 97365-0156
Phone: (541)265-2266
Fax: (541)265-6397
**Format:** Classic Rock

**KEDO-AM - 1400 (32139)**
1130 14th Ave.
Longview, WA 98632
Phone: (360)425-1500
Fax: (360)423-1554
**Format:** Oldies; News; Information

**KEX-AM - 1190 (25998)**
4949 SW Macadam Ave.
Portland, OR 97201
Phone: (503)225-1190
Fax: (503)227-5873
**Format:** News; Talk

**KFLY-FM - 101.5 (25817)**
1345 Olive St.
Eugene, OR 97440
Phone: (541)393-0088
Fax: (541)484-5769
**Format:** Adult Contemporary

**KGAL-AM - 1580 (25890)**
36991 KGAL Dr.
Lebanon, OR 97355
Phone: (541)451-5425
Fax: (541)451-5429
**Format:** News; Talk; Sports

**KKGT-AM - 1150 (25746)**
15240 SE 82nd Dr.
Clackamas, OR 97015-9606
Phone: (503)222-1150
Fax: (503)722-9111

**Format:** Talk

**KKRZ-FM - 100.3 (26001)**
4949 SW Macadam Ave.
Portland, OR 97239
Phone: (503)323-6400
Fax: (503)323-6660
**Format:** Contemporary Hit Radio (CHR)

**KKSL-AM - 1290 (26002)**
4700 SW Macadam Ave., No. 102
Portland, OR 97201
Phone: (503)242-1950
Fax: (503)242-0155
**Format:** Religious; Talk

**KLBM-AM - 1450 (25883)**
PO Box 907
La Grande, OR 97850
Phone: (541)963-4121
Fax: (541)963-3117
**Format:** News; Talk

**KLCK-AM - 1400 (32104)**
514 S. Columbus
PO Box 305
Goldendale, WA 98620
Phone: (509)773-3300
Fax: (509)773-3301
**Format:** Oldies

**KLOG-AM - 1490 (32112)**
506 Cowlitz Way W.
PO Box 90
Kelso, WA 98626
Phone: (360)636-0110
Fax: (360)577-6949
**Format:** Adult Contemporary; Sports

**KLYK-FM - 105.5 (32141)**
1130 14th Ave.
Longview, WA 98632
Phone: (360)425-1500
Fax: (360)423-1554
**Format:** Contemporary Hit Radio (CHR)

**KMUZ-AM - 1230 (26004)**
5110 SE Stark St.
Portland, OR 97215
Phone: (503)234-5550
Fax: (503)234-5583
**Format:** Ethnic

**KNPT-AM - 1310 (25924)**
906 SW Alder
PO Box 1430
Newport, OR 97365
Phone: (503)265-2266
Fax: (503)265-6397
**Format:** News; Talk; Sports; Sports

**KOTK-AM - 1080 (26007)**
700 SW Bancroft St.
Portland, OR 97239
Phone: (503)223-1441
Fax: (503)245-8865
**Format:** Talk

**KPOJ-AM - 620 (26010)**
4949 SW Macadam Ave.
Portland, OR 97201
Phone: (503)225-1190
Fax: (503)227-5873
**Format:** Talk; News

**KPSU-AM - 1450 (26011)**
PO Box 751-SD
Portland, OR 97207
Phone: (503)725-5669
Fax: (503)725-4079
**Format:** Eclectic

**KRKT-AM - 990 (25691)**
2840 Marion St. SE
Albany, OR 97322
Phone: (503)926-8628
Fax: (503)928-1261
**Format:** Country

**KRKT-FM - 99.9 (25692)**
2840 Marion St. SE
Albany, OR 97321-3978
Phone: (503)588-0222
Fax: (503)928-1261

**Format:** Contemporary Country

**KRRC-FM - 104.1 (26012)**
Reed College
3203 SE Woodstock Blvd.
Portland, OR 97202
**Format:** Alternative/New Music/Progressive

**KRVO-FM - 105.9 (26013)**
4949 SW Macadam Ave.
Portland, OR 97201
Phone: (503)802-1600
Fax: (503)802-1659
**Format:** Classic Rock

**KSHO-AM - 920 (25891)**
36991 KGAL Dr.
Lebanon, OR 97355
Phone: (541)451-5425
Fax: (541)451-5429
**Format:** Middle-of-the-Road (MOR)

**KUBQ-FM - 98.7 (25884)**
PO Box 907
La Grande, OR 97850
Phone: (541)963-4121
Fax: (541)963-3117
**Format:** Contemporary Hit Radio (CHR)

**KUFO-FM - 101.1 (26015)**
2040 SW 1st Ave.
Portland, OR 97201
Phone: (503)222-1011
Fax: (503)222-2047
**Format:** Album-Oriented Rock (AOR)

**KUIK-AM - 1360 (25857)**
PO Box 566
Hillsboro, OR 97123
Phone: (503)640-1360
Fax: (503)640-6108
**Format:** News; Talk; Information; Sports; Information; Sports

**KUKN-FM - 105.5 (32113)**
506 Cowlitz Way W.
PO Box 90
Kelso, WA 98626
Phone: (360)636-0110
Fax: (360)577-6949
**Format:** Country

**KUPL-AM - 970 (26016)**
222 SW Columbia, Ste. 350
Portland, OR 97201-5302
Phone: (503)223-0300
**Format:** Country

**KUPL-FM - 98.7 (26017)**
222 SW Columbia, Ste. 350
Portland, OR 97201
Phone: (503)223-0300
Fax: (503)223-6542
**Format:** Country

**KVAS-AM - 1230 (25712)**
1006 W. Marine Dr.
Astoria, OR 97103-5826
Phone: (503)325-2911
Fax: (503)325-5570
**Format:** Country

**KWJJ-FM - 99.5 (26018)**
0700 SW Bancroft St.
Portland, OR 97239
Phone: (503)223-1441
Fax: (503)223-6909
**Format:** Country

**KXPC-FM - 103.7 (25695)**
1207 9th Ave. SE
Albany, OR 97321-4811
Phone: (541)928-1926
**Format:** Contemporary Country

**KYTE-FM - 102.7 (25927)**
906 SW Alder
PO Box 1430
Newport, OR 97365
Phone: (503)265-2266
Fax: (503)265-6397
**Format:** Adult Contemporary

**KYYT-FM - 102.3 (25784)**
PO Box 1023
The Dalles, OR 97058
Phone: (541)296-9102
Fax: (541)298-7775

**Format:** Country; Agricultural

**KZOE-FM - 90.3 (32142)**
3609 Columbia Heights Rd.
Longview, WA 98632
Phone: (360)578-1929
**Format:** Religious

## Reno, NV

**KDOT-FM - 104.5 (18749)**
2900 Sutro St.
Reno, NV 89512
Fax: (702)323-1450
**Format:** Alternative/New Music/Progressive

**KHIT-AM - 1450 (18750)**
2900 Sutro St.
Reno, NV 89512
Phone: (775)329-9261
Fax: (775)323-1450
**Format:** Country

**KHWK-FM - 92.7 (18763)**
PO Box 1669
Tonopah, NV 89049
Phone: (775)482-5724
Fax: (775)482-3238
**Format:** Adult Contemporary; Album-Oriented Rock (AOR); Contemporary Hit Radio (CHR); Contemporary Hit Radio (CHR)

**KJDX-FM - 93.3 (3590)**
3015 Johnstonville Rd.
Susanville, CA 96130-8739
Phone: (530)257-2121
Fax: (530)257-6955
**Format:** Country

**KNIS-FM - 91.3 (18655)**
6363 Hwy. 50 E.
Carson City, NV 89701
**Format:** Religious; Contemporary Christian

**KODS-FM - 103.7 (18752)**
300 E. 2nd St., 14th Fl.
Reno, NV 89501-1500
Phone: (702)829-1964
Fax: (702)825-3183

**KPLY-AM - 1230 (18755)**
300 E. 2nd St., 14th Fl.
Reno, NV 89501-1500
Phone: (702)829-1964
Fax: (702)825-3183
**Format:** Sports; News; News

**KRNV-FM - 102.1 (18722)**
1500 Foremaster Lane 2
Las Vegas, NV 89101
Phone: (775)333-1017
Fax: (775)333-9047

**KSUE-AM - 1240 (3591)**
3015 Johnstonville Rd.
Susanville, CA 96130-8739
Phone: (916)257-2121
Fax: (916)257-6955
**Format:** Full Service; Talk; Oldies; News

**KWNZ-FM - 97.3 (18759)**
300 E. 2nd St., 14th Flr.
Reno, NV 89501
Phone: (775)829-1964
Fax: (775)825-3183
**Format:** Contemporary Hit Radio (CHR)

**KXEQ-AM - 1340 (18760)**
225 Linden St.
Reno, NV 89502
Phone: (775)827-1111
Fax: (775)827-2082
**Format:** Hispanic

## Sacramento-Stockton, CA

**KATM-FM - 103.3 (2482)**
1581 Cummins Dr., Ste. 135
Modesto, CA 95358-6402
Phone: (209)766-5000
Fax: (209)522-2061

# Sacramento-Stockton, CA

**Format:** Country

**KBEE-AM - 970 (2483)**
1581 Cummins Dr., Ste. 135
Modesto, CA 95358
Phone: (209)523-7756
Fax: (209)522-2061
**Format:** Big Band/Nostalgia

**KCTC-AM - 1320 (2923)**
280 Commerce Dr.
Sacramento, CA 95815-4212
Phone: (916)441-5282
Fax: (916)446-4142
**Format:** Middle-of-the-Road (MOR); Sports; Sports

**KDND-FM - 107.9 (2924)**
5345 Madison Ave.
Sacramento, CA 95841
Phone: (916)334-7777
Fax: (916)339-4290

**KEBR-AM - 88.1 (2925)**
4135 Northgate Blvd., Ste.1
Sacramento, CA 95834
Phone: (916)641-8191
Fax: (916)641-8238
**Format:** Religious

**KFBK-AM - 1530 (2927)**
1440 Ethan Way, Ste. 200
Sacramento, CA 95825
Phone: (916)929-5325
Fax: (916)564-6731
**Format:** News; Talk; Talk

**KFIV-AM - 1360 (2484)**
2121 Lancey Dr.
Modesto, CA 95351
Phone: (209)551-1306
Fax: (209)551-1359
**Format:** Talk; News

**KHTK-AM - 1140 (2930)**
5244 Madison Ave.
Sacramento, CA 95841
Phone: (916)338-9200
Fax: (916)338-9202
**Format:** Talk; Sports

**KJSN-FM - 102.3 (2487)**
2121 Lancey Dr.
Modesto, CA 95351
Phone: (209)551-1306
Fax: (209)551-1359
**Format:** Adult Contemporary

**KMIX-AM - 1390 (3573)**
6820 Pacific Ave.
Stockton, CA 95207
Phone: (209)474-0154
Fax: (209)474-0150
**Format:** Hispanic

**KMIX-FM - 100.9 (3574)**
6820 Pacific Ave., Ste. 3A
Stockton, CA 95207-2631
Phone: (209)474-0154
Fax: (209)474-0316

**KMRQ-FM - 96.7 (2488)**
2121 Lancey Dr., 1
Modesto, CA 95355
Phone: (209)551-1306
Fax: (209)551-1359
**Format:** Alternative/New Music/Progressive

**KNCO-AM - 830 (1949)**
1255 E. Main St., Ste. A
Grass Valley, CA 95945
Phone: (530)272-3424
Fax: (530)272-2872
**Format:** News; Talk; Talk

**KNCO-FM - 94.1 (1950)**
1255 E. Main St., Ste. A
Grass Valley, CA 95945
Phone: (530)272-3424
Fax: (530)272-2872
**Format:** Country

**KQOD-FM - 100.1 (3575)**
1 Atherton IS
Stockton, CA 95204-3806
Phone: (209)462-5367
Fax: (209)462-7959

**Format:** Oldies

**KRAK-FM - 98.5 (2942)**
5244 Madison Ave.
Sacramento, CA 95841
Phone: (916)766-1937
Fax: (916)338-9202
**Format:** Country

**KRXQ-FM - 93.7 (2943)**
5345 Madison, Ste. 100
Sacramento, CA 95841-3109
Phone: (916)766-5000
Fax: (916)339-4292
**Format:** Album-Oriented Rock (AOR)

**KSFM-FM - 102.5 (2944)**
1750 Howe Ave., Ste. 500
Sacramento, CA 95825-3370
Phone: (916)920-1025
Fax: (916)929-5341
**Format:** Contemporary Hit Radio (CHR)

**KSMJ-AM - 1380 (2945)**
5345 Madison Ave.
Sacramento, CA 95841
Phone: (916)334-7777
Fax: (916)339-4293
**Format:** Oldies

**KSSU-AM - 1580 (2947)**
California State University
c/o ASI Business Office
6000 J St.
Sacramento, CA 95819-6011
Phone: (916)278-5882
Fax: (916)278-5897
**Format:** Alternative/New Music/Progressive

**KSTN-AM - 1420 (3576)**
2171 Ralph Ave.
Stockton, CA 95206
Phone: (209)948-5786
**Format:** Oldies

**KSTN-FM - 107.3 (3577)**
2171 Ralph Ave.
Stockton, CA 95206
Phone: (209)948-5786

**KTRB-AM - 860 (1905)**
5111 E McKinley Ave.
Fresno, CA 93727
Phone: (209)526-8600
Fax: (209)578-3568
**Format:** Ethnic; Hispanic

**KUBA-AM - 1600 (4077)**
P.O. Drawer 232
Yuba City, CA 95992
Phone: (530)673-1600
Fax: (530)673-4768
**Format:** News; Talk; Agricultural

**KUOP-FM - 91.3 (3578)**
3601 Pacific Ave.
Stockton, CA 95211
Phone: (209)946-2582
**Format:** Public Radio; Eclectic; Eclectic

**KUYL-AM - 1280 (2491)**
2121 Lancey Dr.
Modesto, CA 95355
Phone: (209)551-1306
Fax: (209)551-1359
**Format:** Religious

**KWOD-FM - 106.5 (2951)**
5345 Madison Ave.
Sacramento, CA 95814
Phone: (916)448-1065
Fax: (916)448-1655
**Format:** Alternative/New Music/Progressive

**KXCL-FM - 103.9 (2952)**
298 Commerce Cir.
Sacramento, CA 95815
**Format:** Adult Contemporary

**KXPR-FM - 90.9 (2953)**
705 Folsom Blvd.
Sacramento, CA 95826
Phone: (916)278-8900
Fax: (916)278-8989

**Format:** Public Radio; News; Classical; Classical

**KYCC-FM - 90.1 (3579)**
9019 N. West Ln.
Stockton, CA 95210
Phone: (209)477-3690
**Format:** Religious

**KYDS-FM - 91.5 (2954)**
4300 El Camino Ave.
Sacramento, CA 95821
Phone: (916)971-7453
Fax: (916)971-7429
**Format:** Contemporary Hit Radio (CHR); Eclectic; Eclectic

**KYMX-FM - 96.1 (2955)**
280 Commerce Circle
Sacramento, CA 95815
Phone: (916)923-6800
Fax: (916)646-3418
**Format:** Adult Contemporary

**KZZO-FM - 100.5 (2958)**
280 Commerce Circle
Sacramento, CA 95815-4212
Phone: (916)923-6800
Fax: (916)927-6468
**Format:** Oldies

# Salinas-Monterey, CA

**KBOQ-FM - 95.5 (2505)**
2511 Garden Rd., Ste. C-150
Monterey, CA 93940
Phone: (831)656-9550
Fax: (831)656-9551
**Format:** Classical

**KDBV-AM - 980 (2962)**
517 S. Main St., Ste. 201
PO Box 1939
Salinas, CA 93901
Phone: (831)757-5911
Fax: (831)757-8015
**Format:** Hispanic

**KDON-FM - 102.5 (2963)**
55 Plaza Circle
Salinas, CA 93901
Phone: (831)649-5366
Fax: (831)758-1890
**Format:** Contemporary Hit Radio (CHR)

**KHDC-FM - 90.9 (2964)**
161 Main St., Ste. 4
Salinas, CA 93901
Phone: (831)757-8039
Fax: (831)757-9854
**Format:** Ethnic; Educational

**KPRC-FM - 100.7 (2967)**
903 N Main St.
Salinas, CA 93906
Phone: (831)755-8181
Fax: (831)755-8193
**Format:** Hispanic

**KRAY-FM - 103.5 (2968)**
517 S. Main St., Ste. 201
PO Box 1939
Salinas, CA 93902-1939
Phone: (831)757-5911
Fax: (831)757-8015
**Format:** Hispanic; Adult Contemporary

**KRML-AM - 1410 (1623)**
The Eastwood Building
PO Box 7300
Carmel, CA 93921
Phone: (831)624-6432
Fax: (831)625-5598
**Format:** Jazz

**KWAV-FM - 96.9 (2507)**
PO Box 1391
Monterey, CA 93942
Phone: (831)649-0969
Fax: (831)649-3335
**Format:** Adult Contemporary

**KXDC-FM - 101.7 (33719)**
6807 Fozglove Dr.
Cheyenne, WY 82009
Fax: (408)643-1100

Format: Public Radio

**KZFX-AM - 1380 (2972)**
903 N. Main St.
Salinas, CA 93906
Phone: (831)755-8181
Fax: (831)755-8193
Format: Sports

## Salt Lake City (Cedar City), UT

**KBLQ-FM - 92.9 (30695)**
PO Box 3369
Logan, UT 84321
Phone: (801)752-1390
Fax: (801)752-1392
Format: Hot Country

**KBRE-AM - 940 (30668)**
PO Box 819
Cedar City, UT 84720
Phone: (801)586-5273
Fax: (801)586-0458
Format: Oldies

**KDYL-AM - 1060 (30790)**
PO Box 57760
Salt Lake City, UT 84157
Phone: (801)262-5624
Fax: (801)266-1510
Format: Adult Contemporary

**KELK-AM - 1240 (18657)**
1800 Idaho St.
Elko, NV 89801
Phone: (775)738-1240
Fax: (775)753-5556

**KGNT-FM - 103.9 (30696)**
810 West 200 North
PO Box 3369
Logan, UT 84323-3369
Phone: (435)752-1390
Fax: (435)752-1392
Format: Oldies

**KJMY-FM - 99.5 (30795)**
2801 S. Decker Lake Dr.
Salt Lake City, UT 84119
Phone: (801)908-1300
Fax: (801)908-1449
Format: Adult Album Alternative

**KLCY-FM - 105.9 (30824)**
2425 N. Vernal Ave.
Box 307
Vernal, UT 84078
Fax: (801)789-6977
Format: Contemporary Country

**KLGN-AM - 1390 (30697)**
PO Box 3369
Logan, UT 84321
Phone: (801)752-1390
Fax: (801)752-1392
Format: Urban Contemporary; Big Band/Nostalgia

**KLKO-FM - 93.7 (18658)**
1800 Idaho St.
Elko, NV 89801
Phone: (775)738-1240
Fax: (775)753-5556
Format: Classic Rock

**KNRS-AM - 570 (30798)**
2801 S. Decker Lake Dr.
Salt Lake City, UT 84119
Phone: (801)908-1300
Fax: (801)908-1499
Format: Talk; News

**KODJ-FM - 94.1 (30799)**
2801 S Decker Lake Dr.
Salt Lake City, UT 84119
Phone: (801)908-1300
Fax: (801)908-1429
Format: Oldies

**KOSY-FM - 106.5 (30800)**
2801 S Decker Lake Dr.
Salt Lake City, UT 84101
Phone: (801)303-4100
Fax: (801)303-4110

Format: Soft Rock

**KSOP-FM - 104.3 (30804)**
PO Box 25548
Salt Lake City, UT 84125
Phone: (801)972-1043
Fax: (801)974-0868
Format: Country; Contemporary Country

**KSSD-FM - 92.5 (30669)**
6200 W. Hwy. 16
PO Box 819
Cedar City, UT 84720
Phone: (435)586-5900
Fax: (435)586-4444
Format: Contemporary Country

**KSUB-AM - 590 (30670)**
1105 N Iron Springs Rd.
PO Box 819
Cedar City, UT 84720
Phone: (435)586-5341
Fax: (435)586-0437
Format: Talk; News; Sports

**KUBL-FM - 93.3 (30807)**
434 Bearcat Dr.
Salt Lake City, UT 84115
Phone: (801)485-6700
Fax: (801)487-5369
Format: Country

**KUSU-FM - 89.5, 91.5 (30699)**
8505 Old Main Hill
Logan, UT 84322-8505
Phone: (435)797-3138
Fax: (435)797-3150
Format: News; Information; Public Radio; Classical; Folk

**KUTA-AM - 790 (30660)**
2575 N. Radio Hill Rd.
Blanding, UT 84511
Phone: (435)678-2261
Format: Sports; News; Talk; Oldies

**KVEL-AM - 920 (30825)**
2425 N. Vernal Ave.
Box 307
Vernal, UT 84078
Fax: (801)789-6977
Format: News; Talk; Sports

**KXRV-FM - 105.7 (30811)**
2801 S. Decker Lake Dr.
Salt Lake City, UT 84101
Phone: (801)303-4100
Fax: (801)303-4110
Format: Soft Rock

**KZHT-FM - 94.9 (30812)**
2801 Decker Lake Dr.
Salt Lake City, UT 84119-2330
Fax: (801)264-8978
Format: Contemporary Hit Radio (CHR)

## San Diego, CA

**KBZT-FM - 94.9 (3070)**
1615 Murray Canyon Rd., Ste. 710
San Diego, CA 92108
Phone: (619)291-9797
Fax: (619)543-1353
Format: Oldies

**KCEO-AM - 1000 (1617)**
1835 Aston Ave.
Carlsbad, CA 92008
Phone: (760)729-1000
Fax: (760)434-2367
Format: Talk; News; News

**KFSD-AM - 1450 (1618)**
1835 Aston Ave.
Carlsbad, CA 92008-7310
Phone: (760)729-1000
Fax: (760)476-9604
Format: Classical

**KHTS-FM - 93.3 (3078)**
9660 Granite Ridge Dr.
San Diego, CA 92123
Phone: (619)291-9191
Fax: (619)294-2916

Format: Contemporary Hit Radio (CHR)

**KLSD-AM - 1360 (3080)**
9660 Granite Ridge Dr.
San Diego, CA 92123
Phone: (858)278-1130
Fax: (858)715-3303
Format: Talk

**KMYI-FM - 94.1 (3081)**
9660 Granite Ridge Dr.
San Diego, CA 92123
Phone: (619)291-9191
Fax: (619)294-2916
Format: Adult Contemporary

**KMYT-FM - 94.5 (3082)**
9660 Granite Ridge Dr.
San Diego, CA 92123
Phone: (909)929-5088
Fax: (909)658-8822
Format: Talk; News

**KPBS-FM - 89.5 (3085)**
5200 Campanile Dr.
San Diego, CA 92182-5400
Phone: (619)594-8100
Fax: (619)594-3787
Format: News; Public Radio

**KPLN-FM - 103.7 (3087)**
8033 Linda Vista Rd
San Diego, CA 92111
Phone: (858)560-1037
Fax: (858)571-0326
Format: Classic Rock

**KTMQ-FM - 103.3 (3093)**
9660 Granite Ridge Dr.
San Diego, CA 92123
Phone: (858)292-2000
Fax: (858)277-1015
Format: Classic Rock

**KUSS-FM - 95.7 (3095)**
9660 Granite Ridge Dr.
San Diego, CA 92123
Phone: (858)565-6006
Fax: (858)279-9553
Format: Country

**XEBG-AM - 1550 (3391)**
PO Box 430155
San Ysidro, CA 92143
Phone: (619)230-0203
Format: Hispanic; Sports; News; Contemporary Hit Radio (CHR)

**XTRA-FM - 91.1 (3099)**
9660 Granite Ridge Dr.
San Diego, CA 92123
Phone: (858)292-2000
Fax: (858)560-8090

## San Francisco-Oakland-San Jose

**KARA-FM - 105.7 (3316)**
750 Story Rd.
San Jose, CA 95122
Phone: (408)293-8030
Fax: (408)293-6124
Format: Adult Contemporary

**KAZA-AM - 1290 (3317)**
765 Story Rd.
PO Box 1290
San Jose, CA 95108
Phone: (408)881-1290
Fax: (408)881-1292
Format: Hispanic

**KBLX-FM - 1400 (3245)**
55 Hawthorne, Ste. 900
San Francisco, CA 94105
Phone: (415)284-1029
Fax: (415)764-1029
Format: Ethnic

**KCBC-AM - 770 (2564)**
10948 Cleveland Ave.
Oakdale, CA 95361-0077
Phone: (209)847-7700
Fax: (209)847-1769

**KCBS-AM - 740 (3248)**
865 Battery St.
San Francisco, CA 94111-1503
**Format:** News; Information; Information

**KCNL-FM - 104.9 (3319)**
1420 Koll Cir., Ste. A
San Jose, CA 95112
Phone: (408)453-5400
Fax: (408)452-1330
**Format:** Adult Album Alternative

**KCSM-FM - 91.1 (3377)**
1700 W. Hillsdale Blvd.
San Mateo, CA 94402
Phone: (650)341-7721
Fax: (650)574-6675
**Format:** Public Radio; Jazz; News

**KDAC-AM - 1230 (3930)**
1400 Kuki Ln.
Ukiah, CA 95482
Phone: (707)964-3250
Fax: (707)466-5852
**Format:** News; Talk

**KDFC-FM - 102.1 (3251)**
201 Third St.
San Francisco, CA 94103
Phone: (415)764-1021
Fax: (415)777-4611
**Format:** Classical

**KEAR-FM - 106.9 (2608)**
290 Hegenberger Rd.
Oakland, CA 94621-1436
Phone: (510)568-6200
Fax: (510)568-6190
**Format:** Religious; Educational

**KEST-AM - 1450 (3254)**
145 Natoma, Suite 101
San Francisco, CA 94105
Phone: (415)978-5378
Fax: (415)978-5380
**Format:** New Age; Talk; Ethnic; Ethnic

**KGO-AM - 810 (3258)**
900 Front St.
San Francisco, CA 94111-1450
Phone: (415)954-8100
Fax: (415)362-5827
**Format:** News; Talk

**KIQI-AM - 1010 (3260)**
730 Harrison, Ste. 300
San Francisco, CA 94107
Phone: (415)695-1010
Fax: (415)695-1015
**Format:** Hispanic

**KLIV-AM - 1590 (3321)**
750 Story Rd.
PO Box 995
San Jose, CA 95122
Phone: (408)293-8030
Fax: (408)293-6124
**Format:** News

**KLLC-FM - 97.3 (3264)**
865 Battery St.
San Francisco, CA 94111-1503
Phone: (415)765-4097
Fax: (415)765-4084
**Format:** Adult Album Alternative; Adult Contemporary

**KMFB-FM - 92.7 (2447)**
14200 Prairie Way
Mendocino, CA 95460-9720
Phone: (707)964-4653
Fax: (707)964-3299
**Format:** Oldies; Eclectic

**KMKY-AM - 1310 (3266)**
900 Front St.
San Francisco, CA 94111
Phone: (415)788-1310
Fax: (415)788-1212

**KOIT-AM - 1260 (3268)**
201 3rd Streer, Suite 200
San Francisco, CA 94103
Phone: (415)777-0965
Fax: (415)896-0965

**Format:** Adult Contemporary

**KOIT-FM - 96.5 (3269)**
201 3rd Streer, Suite 200
San Francisco, CA 94103
Phone: (415)777-0965
Fax: (415)896-0965
**Format:** Adult Contemporary

**KPOO-FM - 89.5 (3271)**
1329 Divisadero St.
PO Box 423030
San Francisco, CA 94115
Phone: (415)346-5373
Fax: (415)346-5173
**Format:** Full Service

**KRRS-AM - 1460 (3504)**
PO Box 2277
Santa Rosa, CA 95405
Phone: (707)545-1460
Fax: (707)545-0112
**Format:** Hispanic

**KRTY-FM - 95.3 (3323)**
750 Story Rd.
PO Box 995
San Jose, CA 95122-9510
Phone: (408)293-8030
Fax: (408)293-6124
**Format:** Country

**KSAY-FM - 98.5 (1860)**
684-C S. Main St.
PO Box 2269
Fort Bragg, CA 95437
Phone: (707)964-KSAY
Fax: (707)964-2722
**Format:** Adult Contemporary; News

**KSFO-AM - 560 (3274)**
900 Front St.
San Francisco, CA 94111-1450
Phone: (415)398-5600
Fax: (415)954-2795
**Format:** Oldies; Sports; Sports

**KSJS-FM - 90.5 (3325)**
HGH 126
San Jose, CA 95192-0094
Phone: (408)924-4548
Fax: (408)924-4583
**Format:** Eclectic

**KSRO-AM - 1350 (3505)**
1410 Neotomas Ave., Suite 200
PO Box 2158
Santa Rosa, CA 95405-0158
Phone: (707)543-0151
Fax: (707)571-1077
**Format:** Talk; News; News

**KUKI-AM - 1400 (3931)**
1400 Kuki Ln.
Ukiah, CA 95482
Phone: (707)466-5868
Fax: (707)466-5852
**Format:** News; Talk; Tejano; Hispanic

**KUKI-FM - 103.3 (3932)**
1400 Kuki Ln.
Ukiah, CA 95482
Phone: (707)466-5868
Fax: (707)466-5852
**Format:** Country

**KXFX-FM - 101.7 (3506)**
1410 Neotomas Ave., Ste. 200
PO Box 2158
Santa Rosa, CA 95405
Phone: (707)543-0100
Fax: (707)571-1097
**Format:** Album-Oriented Rock (AOR)

**KZST-FM - 100.1 (3507)**
3392 Mendecino Ave.
PO Box 100
Santa Rosa, CA 95403
Phone: (707)528-4434
Fax: (707)527-8216

**Format:** Adult Contemporary

# Santa Barbara-Santa Maria-San Luis Obispo, CA

**KBKO-AM - 1490 (3431)**
414 E Cota St.
Santa Barbara, CA 93101
Phone: (870)879-8300
Fax: (870)879-8430
**Format:** Hispanic

**KBOX-FM - 104.1 (3467)**
2325 Skyway Dr., Ste. J
Santa Maria, CA 93455
Phone: (805)922-1041
Fax: (805)928-3069
**Format:** Adult Contemporary

**KIST-FM - 107.7 (3435)**
414 E Cota St.
Santa Barbara, CA 93101
Phone: (805)879-8300
Fax: (805)879-8430
**Format:** Contemporary Hit Radio (CHR)

**KKJL-AM - 1400 (3344)**
PO Box 1400
San Luis Obispo, CA 93406
Phone: (805)543-9400
Fax: (805)543-0787
**Format:** Adult Contemporary

**KLEI-AM - 1130 (7615)**
4120 Marina Dr.
Santa Barbara, CA 93110
**Format:** Easy Listening

**KOXR-AM - 910 (2641)**
200 S.A. St
Oxnard, CA 93030-5710
Phone: (805)487-0444
Fax: (805)487-2117
**Format:** Hispanic

**KRKC-FM - 102.1 (2023)**
1134 San Antonio Dr.
King City, CA 93930-3317
Phone: (831)385-5421
Fax: (831)385-0635
**Format:** Adult Contemporary

**KSMA-AM - 1240 (3470)**
Box 1240
Santa Maria, CA 93456
Phone: (805)925-2582
Fax: (805)928-1544
**Format:** News; Talk

**KSMY-FM - 106.7 (3471)**
2215 Skyway Dr.
Santa Maria, CA 93455
Phone: (805)545-0101
Fax: (805)541-5303
**Format:** Adult Contemporary

**KSTT-FM - 101.3 (3347)**
51 Zaca Ln., Ste. 110
San Luis Obispo, CA 93401
Phone: (805)545-0101
Fax: (805)541-5303
**Format:** Adult Contemporary

**KSYV-FM - 96.7 (3533)**
1693 Mission Dr.
Solvang, CA 93463
Phone: (805)688-5798
Fax: (805)688-2271
**Format:** Adult Contemporary; News; Sports; Sports

**KTAP-AM - 1600 (3473)**
104 W. Chapel St.
Santa Maria, CA 93458
Phone: (805)928-4334
Fax: (805)349-2765
**Format:** Hispanic

**KTLK AM - 1340 (3437)**
414 E. Cota St.
Santa Barbara, CA 93101
Phone: (805)879-8300
Fax: (805)879-8430

**Format:** Oldies

**KURQ-FM - 107.3  (3348)**
51 Zaca Ln., Ste. 110
San Luis Obispo, CA 93401
Phone: (805)545-0101
Fax: (805)541-5303
**Format:** Alternative/New Music/Progressive

**KXFM-FM - 99.1  (3476)**
PO Box 1240
Santa Maria, CA 93456
Phone: (805)925-0101
Fax: (805)928-1554
**Format:** Oldies

**KZOZ-FM - 93.3  (3350)**
3620 Sacremento Dr., Ste. 204
San Luis Obispo, CA 93401
Phone: (805)781-2750
Fax: (805)781-2758
**Format:** Album-Oriented Rock (AOR)

## Seattle-Tacoma (Bellingham), WA

**KAPS-AM - 660  (32165)**
Box 70
Mount Vernon, WA 98273
Phone: (206)424-7676
Fax: (206)424-1660
**Format:** Country; News

**KARR-AM - 1460  (32126)**
PO Box 883
Kirkland, WA 98083
Phone: (425)828-6738
**Format:** Religious

**KAYO-FM - 99.3  (32183)**
PO Box 7489
Olympia, WA 98507
Phone: (360)704-3143
**Format:** Hot Country; Hot Country

**KBKW-AM - 1450  (31977)**
1520 Simpson Ave.
PO Box 1198
Aberdeen, WA 98520
Phone: (360)533-3000
Fax: (360)532-1456
**Format:** News; Talk; Information; Hispanic

**KBSG-FM - 97.3  (32346)**
1820 Eastlake Ave. E.
Seattle, WA 98102-3711
Phone: (206)343-9700
Fax: (206)623-7677
**Format:** Oldies

**KCIS-AM - 630  (32347)**
19303 Fremont Ave. N.
Seattle, WA 98133
Phone: (206)546-7350
Fax: (206)546-7372
**Format:** Religious

**KCMS-FM - 105.3  (32348)**
19303 Fremont Ave. N.
Seattle, WA 98133
Phone: (206)546-7350
Fax: (206)546-7372
**Format:** Religious; Contemporary Christian

**KELA-AM - 1470  (32036)**
1635 S. Gold St.
Centralia, WA 98531
Phone: (360)736-3321
Fax: (360)736-0150
**Format:** Talk; News; Sports

**KFNK-FM - 104.9  (32350)**
351 Elliott Ave. W, Ste. 300
Seattle, WA 98119
Phone: (253)671-0195
Fax: (671)383-1221
**Format:** Alternative/New Music/Progressive

**KGHP-FM - 89.9  (32102)**
14105 Purdy Dr. NW
Gig Harbor, WA 98332
Phone: (253)857-3513
Fax: (253)853-5841
**Format:** Eclectic

**KGMI-AM - 790  (32014)**
2219 Yew Street Rd.
Bellingham, WA 98229
Phone: (360)734-9790
Fax: (360)733-4551
**Format:** Talk; News; Full Service; Full Service

**KHHO-AM - 850  (32352)**
351 Elliott Ave. W, Ste. 300
Seattle, WA 98119
Phone: (206)494-2000
Fax: (206)286-2376
**Format:** Sports

**KIRO-AM - 710  (32355)**
2807 3rd Ave.
Seattle, WA 98121
Phone: (206)728-7777
Fax: (206)441-4180
**Format:** News; Sports; Talk; Talk

**KISM-FM - 92.9  (32015)**
2219 Yew Street Rd.
Bellingham, WA 98226
Phone: (360)734-9790
Fax: (360)733-4551
**Format:** Classic Rock

**KIXT-AM - 930  (32016)**
2219 Yew Street Rd.
Bellingham, WA 98226
Phone: (360)734-8555
Fax: (360)733-4551
**Format:** Country; Hot Country

**KJET-FM - 105.7  (31979)**
1520 Simpson Ave.
PO Box 1198
Aberdeen, WA 98520
Phone: (360)533-3000
Fax: (360)532-1456
**Format:** Adult Contemporary

**KJR-AM - 950  (32356)**
351 Elliott Ave. W., Ste. 300
Seattle, WA 98119
Phone: (206)494-2000
Fax: (206)286-2376
**Format:** Sports

**KJR-FM - 95.7  (32357)**
351 Elliott Ave. W., Ste. 300
Seattle, WA 98119
Phone: (206)285-2295
Fax: (206)286-2376
**Format:** Classic Rock

**KMAS-AM - 1030  (32377)**
PO Box 760
Shelton, WA 98584
Phone: (206)426-1030
**Format:** Adult Contemporary; News; News

**KNDD-FM - 107.7  (32362)**
1100 Olive Way, Ste. 1550
Seattle, WA 98101
Phone: (206)622-3251
Fax: (206)682-8349
**Format:** Alternative/New Music/Progressive

**KNWX-AM - 1210  (32364)**
1820 Eastlake Ave. E.
Seattle, WA 98102-3711
Phone: (206)726-7000
Fax: (206)726-6936
**Format:** News

**KPLU-FM - 88.5  (32446)**
121st & Park
Tacoma, WA 98447
Phone: (253)535-7587
Fax: (253)535-8332
**Format:** Public Radio; News; Jazz; Jazz

**KRIZ-AM - 1420  (32367)**
2600 S. Jackson St.
Seattle, WA 98144
Phone: (206)329-7880
Fax: (206)322-6518
**Format:** Urban Contemporary

**KSWW-FM - 102.1  (31980)**
1520 Simpson Ave.
PO Box 1198
Aberdeen, WA 98520
Phone: (360)533-3000
Fax: (360)532-1456
**Format:** Adult Contemporary

**KUGS-FM - 89.3  (32017)**
200 Viking Union MS 1106
Western Washington University
Bellingham, WA 98225
Phone: (360)676-5847
Fax: (360)650-6507
**Format:** Alternative/New Music/Progressive; Eclectic

**KUOW-FM - 94.9  (32369)**
4518 University WY. NE., Ste. 310
Seattle, WA 98105-4535
Phone: (206)543-2710
Fax: (206)543-2720
**Format:** Public Radio; Information; News

**KVTI-FM - 90.9  (32448)**
4500 Steilacoom Blvd. SW
Tacoma, WA 98499-4098
Phone: (253)589-5884
Fax: (253)589-5797
**Format:** Top 40

**KXPH-AM - 1540  (32371)**
114 Lakeside Ave.
Seattle, WA 98122-1827
Phone: (206)292-7800
Fax: (206)292-2140
**Format:** Ethnic; Ethnic

**KZIZ-AM - 1420  (32449)**
c/o KRIZ-AM
2600 S. Jackson St.
Seattle, WA 98144
Fax: (206)322-6518
**Format:** Urban Contemporary

## Sitka, AK

**KCAW-FM - 104.7  (611)**
2B Lincoln St.
Sitka, AK 99835
Phone: (907)747-5877
Fax: (907)747-5977
**Format:** Public Radio

**KSBZ-FM - 103.1  (612)**
611 Lake St.
Sitka, AK 99835
Phone: (907)747-6626
Fax: (907)747-8455
**Format:** Country

## Spokane, WA

**KAAR-FM - 95.3  (32399)**
1212 Washington, Ste. 124
Spokane, WA 99201
Fax: (509)326-1560
**Format:** Religious; Contemporary Christian

**KAGU-FM - 88.7  (32401)**
E. 502 Boone Ave.
Spokane, WA 99258
Phone: (509)484-2820
Fax: (509)484-2804
**Format:** Alternative/New Music/Progressive

**KAQQ-AM - 1280  (32402)**
808 E Sprague
Spokane, WA 99202
Phone: (509)459-9800
Fax: (509)459-9850
**Format:** Middle-of-the-Road (MOR)

**KATW-FM - 101.5  (7724)**
403 C St.
Lewiston, ID 83501
Phone: (208)743-6564
Fax: (208)798-0110
**Format:** Adult Contemporary

**KCLK-AM - 1430  (7725)**
403 C St.
Lewiston, ID 83501
Phone: (208)743-6564
Fax: (208)798-0110
**Format:** Sports; Talk

**KCLK-FM - 94.1  (7726)**
403 C St.
Lewiston, ID 83501
Phone: (208)743-6564
Fax: (208)798-0110

Format: Country

**KCRK-FM - 92.1 (32060)**
Box 111
Colville, WA 99114
Phone: (509)684-5032
Fax: (509)684-5034
**Format:** Adult Contemporary

**KCVL-AM - 1240 (32061)**
Mantz & Rickey Rds.
Box 111
Colville, WA 99114
Phone: (509)684-5032
Fax: (509)684-5034
**Format:** Country

**KEYF-AM - 1050 (32405)**
751 B St., Ste. 1920
PO Box 30013
Spokane, WA 99223-3026
Phone: (509)448-1111
Fax: (509)448-6523

**KEYF-FM - 101.1 (32406)**
PO Box 30013
Spokane, WA 99223-3026
Phone: (509)232-1011
Fax: (509)448-6523
**Format:** Oldies

**KEYG-AM - 1490 (32107)**
PO Box K
Grand Coulee, WA 99133
Phone: (509)633-2020
Fax: (509)633-1014
**Format:** Country; Classic Rock

**KEZE-FM - 105.7 (32407)**
PO Box 30013
500 W. Boone
Spokane, WA 99201
Phone: (509)323-9396
Fax: (509)448-4549
**Format:** Album-Oriented Rock (AOR)

**KGA-AM - 1510 (32408)**
PO Box 30013
Spokane, WA 99223
Phone: (509)448-7000
Fax: (509)448-7015
**Format:** Country

**KHTR-FM - 104.3 (32221)**
1101 Old Wawawai Rd.
PO Box 1
Pullman, WA 99163
Phone: (509)332-6551
Fax: (509)332-5151
**Format:** Contemporary Hit Radio (CHR)

**KISC-FM - 98.1 (32411)**
808 E.Sprague
Spokane, WA 99202
Phone: (509)242-2400
Fax: (509)242-1160
**Format:** Adult Contemporary

**KIXZ-FM - 96.1 (32412)**
808 E Sprague Ave.
Spokane, WA 99202
Phone: (509)242-2400
Fax: (509)459-9850
**Format:** Country

**KKZX-FM - 98.9 (32413)**
808 E Sprague Ave.
Spokane, WA 99202-2126
Phone: (509)242-2400
Fax: (509)242-1160
**Format:** Classic Rock

**KMBI-AM - 1330 (32414)**
5408 S. Freya
Spokane, WA 99223
Phone: (509)448-2555
Fax: (509)448-6855
**Format:** Religious

**KMBI-FM - 107.9 (32415)**
5408 S. Freya
Spokane, WA 99223
Phone: (509)448-2555
Fax: (509)448-6855

**Format:** Religious

**KMJY-FM - 104.5 (7765)**
282 Memory Ln.
PO Box 17400
Oldtown, ID 83822
Phone: (208)437-5700
Fax: (208)437-5887
**Format:** Contemporary Country

**KQNT-AM - 590 (32418)**
808 E Sprague Ave.
Spokane, WA 99202
Phone: (509)242-2400
Fax: (509)459-9850
**Format:** Talk

**KSFC-FM - 91.9 (32420)**
3410 W. Ft. George Wright Dr.
Spokane, WA 99204
Phone: (509)533-3830
Fax: (509)533-3433
**Format:** Album-Oriented Rock (AOR)

**KULE-AM - 730 (32084)**
910 Basin SW
Ephrata, WA 98823
Phone: (509)754-4661
Fax: (509)754-4110
**Format:** Talk; News; Sports

**KULE-FM - 92.3 (32085)**
910 Basin SW
Ephrata, WA 98823
Phone: (509)754-4661
Fax: (509)754-4110
**Format:** Contemporary Country

**KVAB-FM - 102.9 (7733)**
403 C St.
Lewiston, ID 83501
Phone: (208)743-6564
Fax: (208)798-0110
**Format:** Classic Rock

**KVNI-AM - 1080 (7687)**
504 E. Sherman
Coeur d'Alene, ID 83814-2731
Phone: (208)664-9271
Fax: (208)667-0945
**Format:** News; Country; Country

**KXLY-AM - 920 (32427)**
W. 500 Boone Ave.
Spokane, WA 99201-2457
Phone: (509)328-6292
Fax: (509)327-3605
**Format:** News; Information; Talk; Sports

**KXLY-FM - 99.9 (32428)**
W. 500 Boone Ave.
Spokane, WA 99201
Phone: (509)328-6292
Fax: (509)325-0676
**Format:** Contemporary Hit Radio (CHR)

**KZFN-FM - 106.1 (7754)**
1114 N. Almon
PO Box 8849
Moscow, ID 83843
Phone: (208)882-2551
Fax: (208)883-3571
**Format:** Contemporary Hit Radio (CHR)

**KZZL-FM - 99.5 (32056)**
840 Westfairview
PO Box 710
Colfax, WA 99111
Phone: (509)397-3441
Fax: (509)397-4752
**Format:** Country

## Tucson, AZ

**KAPR-AM - 930 (665)**
3434 N. Washington Ave.
Douglas, AZ 85607
Fax: (520)364-5277
**Format:** Hispanic

**KCUB-AM - 1290 (947)**
575 W. Roger Rd.
Tucson, AZ 85705
Phone: (520)887-1000
Fax: (520)887-6397

**Format:** Country

**KFFN-AM - 1490 (948)**
3438 N. Country Club
Tucson, AZ 85716
Phone: (520)795-1490
Fax: (520)327-2260
**Format:** Sports; Talk

**KFLT-AM - 830 (949)**
7355 N. Orade, No. 102
PO Box 36868
Tucson, AZ 85740
Phone: (520)797-3700
Fax: (520)797-3375
**Format:** Talk; News; Middle-of-the-Road (MOR); Religious; Middle-of-the-Road (MOR); Religious

**KGVY-AM - 1080 (694)**
PO Box 767
Green Valley, AZ 85622
Phone: (520)399-1000
Fax: (520)399-9300
**Format:** Music of Your Life; Full Service

**KIIM-FM - 99.5 (951)**
575 W. Roger Rd.
Tucson, AZ 85705
Phone: (520)887-1000
Fax: (520)887-6397
**Format:** Contemporary Country

**KLPX-FM - 96.1 (952)**
3871 N. Commerce Drive
Tucson, AZ 85705
Phone: (520)407-4500
Fax: (520)407-4600
**Format:** Album-Oriented Rock (AOR)

**KRQ-FM - 93.7 (958)**
3202 N. Oracle Rd.
Tucson, AZ 85705
Phone: (520)618-2100
Fax: (520)618-2135
**Format:** Big Band/Nostalgia

**KTAN-AM - 1420 (851)**
PO Box 2770
Sierra Vista, AZ 85636-2770
Phone: (520)458-4313
Fax: (520)458-4317
**Format:** News; Talk; Sports

**KTKT-AM - 990 (960)**
1920 W. Copper
Tucson, AZ 85745
Phone: (520)622-6711
Fax: (520)624-3226
**Format:** News

**KTZR-FM - 97.1 (962)**
3202 N Oracle Rd.
Tucson, AZ 85705
Phone: (520)618-2100
Fax: (520)618-2170
**Format:** Hispanic

**KVOI-AM - 690 (723)**
3222 S. Richey Blvd.
Tucson, AZ 85713-5453
Phone: (520)790-2440
Fax: (520)790-2937
**Format:** Talk

**KWFM-AM - 1450 (967)**
3202 N Oracle Rd.
Tucson, AZ 85705
Phone: (520)618-2100
Fax: (520)622-2680
**Format:** Oldies

**KWMT-FM - 92.9 (969)**
3202 N Oracle Rd.
Tucson, AZ 85705
Phone: (520)618-2100
Fax: (520)618-2200
**Format:** Adult Album Alternative

**KXCI-FM - 91.3 (970)**
220 S. 4th Ave.
Tucson, AZ 85701-2104
Phone: (520)623-1000
Fax: (520)882-5820
**Format:** Full Service; Eclectic

**KXEW-AM - 1600 (971)**
3202 N. Oracle Rd.
Tucson, AZ 85705
Phone: (520)618-2100

Fax: (520)618-2170
**Format:** Tejano

**KXKQ-FM - 94.1 (824)**
Drawer L
Safford, AZ 85546
Phone: (928)428-4994
Fax: (928)428-6818
**Format:** Contemporary Country

## Twin Falls, ID

**KEZJ-AM - 1450 (7815)**
415 Park Ave.
PO Box 1259
Twin Falls, ID 83301
Phone: (208)733-7512
Fax: (208)733-7525
**Format:** Talk; Contemporary Country; Contemporary Country

**KEZJ-FM - 95.7 (7816)**
415 Park Ave.
PO Box 1259
Twin Falls, ID 83301
Phone: (208)733-7512
Fax: (208)733-7525
**Format:** Country

**KLIX-AM - 1310 (7817)**
415 Park Ave.
PO Box 1259
Twin Falls, ID 83303-1259
Phone: (208)733-7512
Fax: (208)733-7525
**Format:** Talk; News

**KLIX-FM - 96.5 (7818)**
Box 1259
415 Park Ave.
Twin Falls, ID 83303
Phone: (208)733-1310
Fax: (208)733-7525
**Format:** Oldies

## Yakima, WA

**KALE-AM - 960 (32115)**
Symphony Towers
830 N. Columbia Center Blvd., Ste. B-2
Kennewick, WA 99336
Phone: (509)783-0783
Fax: (509)735-8627
**Format:** Music of Your Life

**KATS-FM - 94.5 (32510)**
4010 Summitview Ave., Ste. 200
Yakima, WA 98908-2966
**Format:** Classic Rock

**KBBO-AM - 1390 (32511)**
1200 Chesterly Dr., Ste. 160
PO Box 127
Yakima, WA 98902-7345
Phone: (509)248-1390
Fax: (509)453-6530
**Format:** Religious

**KDBL-FM - 92.9 (32512)**
4010 Summit View
Yakima, WA 98908
Phone: (509)972-3461
Fax: (509)972-3542
**Format:** Adult Contemporary

**KEYW-FM - 98.3 (32193)**
2621 W. A St.
Pasco, WA 99301-4702
Phone: (509)547-9791
Fax: (509)547-8509
**Format:** Adult Contemporary

**KFFM-FM - 107.3 (32514)**
4010 Summitview Ave., Ste. 200
Yakima, WA 98908-2966
**Format:** Contemporary Hit Radio (CHR)

**KIT-AM - 1280 (32516)**
4010 Summitview Ave., Ste. 200
Yakima, WA 98908-2966
**Format:** News; Talk; Sports; Sports

**KJOX-AM - 980 (32517)**
1200 Chesterly Dr.
PO Box 160
Yakima, WA 98902
Phone: (509)248-2900
Fax: (509)452-9661
**Format:** Classic Rock

**KMWX-AM - 1460 (32518)**
4010 Summitview Ave., Ste. 200
Yakima, WA 98908-2966
**Format:** Oldies

**KQBE-FM - 103.1 (32079)**
Davidson Bldg., Ste. 209
PO Box 1032
Ellensburg, WA 98926
Phone: (509)962-2823
Fax: (509)962-5105
**Format:** Adult Contemporary

**KQSN-FM - 92.9 (32519)**
4010 Summitview Ave., Ste. 200
Yakima, WA 98908-2966
**Format:** Adult Contemporary; Adult Contemporary

**KRSE-FM - 105.7 (32520)**
1200 Chesterly Dr., Ste. 160
Yakima, WA 98902-7345
Phone: (509)248-1390
Fax: (509)452-9661
**Format:** Adult Contemporary

**KUTI-AM - 1460 (32521)**
4010 Summit View
Yakima, WA 98908
Phone: (509)972-3461
Fax: (509)972-3542
**Format:** Country

**KWHT-FM - 103.5 (25940)**
2003 NW 56th St.
Pendleton, OR 97801-4593
Phone: (503)278-2500
Fax: (503)276-6842
**Format:** Country

**KXLE-AM - 1240 (32080)**
1311 Vantage Hwy.
Ellensburg, WA 98926
Phone: (509)925-1488
Fax: (509)962-7882
**Format:** News; Talk; Sports

**KXRX-FM - 97.1 (32200)**
2621 W. A St.
Pasco, WA 99301
Phone: (509)547-9791
Fax: (509)547-8509
**Format:** Album-Oriented Rock (AOR)

# Central Provinces

## Detroit, MI

**CKLW-AM - 800 (35955)**
1640 Ouellette Ave.
Windsor, ON, Canada N8X 1L1
Phone: (519)258-8888
Fax: (519)258-0182
**Format:** Talk; News

# Television Index

Index entries are arranged geographically first by region and then by Area of Dominant Influence (ADI). Within ADI in this index, citations appear alphabetically by station call letters. Citations include station call letters and channel, entry number (given in parentheses immediately following the title), address, phone and fax numbers, and format.

## Great Lakes States

### Alpena, MI

**WCML-TV - 6 (14993)**
c/o WCMU-TV
Central Michigan University
1999 E. Campus Dr.
Mount Pleasant, MI 48859
Phone: (989)774-3105
Fax: (989)774-4427
**Format:** Public TV

### Chicago (LaSalle), IL

**WBBM-TV - 2 (8453)**
630 N. McClurg Ct.
Chicago, IL 60611
Phone: (312)202-3248
Fax: (312)202-3878
**Format:** Commercial TV

**WCIU-TV - 26 (8454)**
26 N. Halsted
Chicago, IL 60661
Phone: (312)705-2600
Fax: (312)705-2656
**Format:** Commercial TV

**WFLD-TV - 32 (8458)**
205 N. Michigan Ave.
Chicago, IL 60601
Phone: (312)565-5532
Fax: (312)819-1332
**Format:** Commercial TV

**WGN-TV - 9 (8462)**
2501 W. Bradley Pl.
Chicago, IL 60618-4718
Phone: (773)528-2311
Fax: (773)528-6857
**Format:** Commercial TV

**WMAQ-TV - 5 (8478)**
NBC Tower
454 N. Columbus Dr.
Chicago, IL 60611-5555
Phone: (312)836-5555
Fax: (312)836-5520
**Format:** Commercial TV

**WPWR-TV - 50 (8483)**
2151 N. Elston Ave.
Chicago, IL 60614
Fax: (773)276-6477
**Format:** Commercial TV

**WSNS-TV - 44 (8487)**
454 N. Columbus
Chicago, IL 60633
Phone: (312)836-3000
Fax: (312)836-3232
**Format:** Commercial TV

**WYCC-TV - 20 (8495)**
7500 S. Pulaski Rd.
Chicago, IL 60652
Phone: (773)838-7878
Fax: (773)581-2071
**Format:** Public TV

**WYIN-TV - 56 (10022)**
8625 Indiana Pl.
Merrillville, IN 46410
Phone: (219)756-5656
Fax: (219)755-4312
**Format:** Public TV

### Cincinnati, OH

**WCPO-TV - 9 (24353)**
1720 Gilbert Avenue
Cincinnati, OH 45202
Phone: (513)721-9900
Fax: (513)721-6032
**Format:** Commercial TV

### Cleveland (Akron, Canton, & Sandusky), OH

**WBNX-TV - 55 (24640)**
2690 State Rd.
Cuyahoga Falls, OH 44223
Phone: (440)843-5555
Fax: (440)842-5597
**Format:** Commercial TV

**WDLI-TV - 17 (24846)**
6600 Atlantic Blvd.
Louisville, OH 44641
Phone: (330)875-5542
Fax: (330)875-9986
**Format:** Commercial TV

**WEWS-TV - 5 (24504)**
3001 Euclid Ave.
Cleveland, OH 44115
Phone: (216)431-5555
Fax: (216)361-1762
**Format:** Commercial TV

**WGGN-TV - 52 (24256)**
3809 Maple Ave.
Castalia, OH 44824
Phone: (419)684-5379
Fax: (419)684-5378
**Format:** Commercial TV

**WQHS-TV - 61 (24990)**
2861 W. Ridgewood Dr.
Parma, OH 44134
Phone: (440)888-0061
Fax: (440)888-7023
**Format:** Commercial TV

**WVIZ-TV - 25 (24517)**
4300 Brookpark Rd.
Cleveland, OH 44134
Phone: (216)398-2800
Fax: (216)749-2560
**Format:** Public TV

**WVPX-TV - 23 (24520)**
1333 Lakeside Ave.
Cleveland, OH 44114
Phone: (216)344-7465
Fax: (216)344-7430
**Format:** Commercial TV

### Columbus (Chillicothe), OH

**WBNS-TV - 10 (24612)**
770 Twin Rivers Dr.
PO Box 1010
Columbus, OH 43215
Phone: (614)460-3700
Fax: (614)460-2891
**Format:** Commercial TV

**WSFJ-TV - 51 (24623)**
3948 Townsfairway
Columbus, OH 43219
Phone: (614)416-6080
Fax: (740)323-3242
**Format:** Commercial TV

**WSYX-TV - 6 (24625)**
1261 Dublin Rd.
Box 718
Columbus, OH 43215
Phone: (614)481-6666
Fax: (614)481-6624
**Format:** Commercial TV

### Daveport, IA-Rock Island, Moline, IL

**WHBF-TV - 4 (9297)**
231 18th St.
Rock Island, IL 61201
Phone: (309)786-5441
Fax: (309)788-3642
**Format:** Commercial TV

### Dayton, OH (Richmond, IN)

**WDTN-TV - 2 (24673)**
4595 S. Dixie Ave.
PO Box 741
Dayton, OH 45439
Phone: (937)293-2101
Fax: (937)294-6542
**Format:** Commercial TV

**WKEF-TV - 22 (24682)**
1731 Soldiers Home Rd.
Dayton, OH 45418
Phone: (937)263-2662
Fax: (937)268-2332
**Format:** Commercial TV

**WRGT-TV - 45 (24685)**
45 Broadcast Plaza
Dayton, OH 45408
Phone: (937)263-4500

**Detroit, MI**

Fax: (937)268-5265
**Format:** Commercial TV

### Detroit, MI

**WGPR-TV - 62  (15214)**
3140-3146 E. Jefferson Ave.
Detroit, MI 48207
Phone: (313)259-8862
Fax: (313)259-6662
**Format:** Commercial TV

**WKBD-TV - 50  (15789)**
26905 W. 11 Mile Rd., Box 50
Southfield, MI 48037-0050
Phone: (248)350-5050
Fax: (810)355-2692
**Format:** Sports

### Duluth, MN-Superior, WI

**KDLH-TV - 3  (16071)**
425 Superior St. W.
Duluth, MN 55802
Phone: (218)733-0303
Fax: (218)727-7515
**Format:** Commercial TV

**WDIO-TV - 10  (16077)**
10 Observation Rd.
PO Box 16897
Duluth, MN 55811-0897
Phone: (218)727-6864
Fax: (218)727-4415
**Format:** Commercial TV

**WIRT-TV - 10  (16174)**
c/o WDIO-TV
10 Observation Rd.
Duluth, MN 55811
Phone: (218)727-6864
Fax: (218)727-4415
**Format:** Commercial TV

### Evansville, IN (Madisonville, KY)

**WEHT-TV - 25  (9694)**
PO Box 25
Evansville, IN 47701
Fax: (812)826-6823
**Format:** Commercial TV

**WFIE-TV - 14  (9695)**
1115 Mt. Auburn Rd.
Evansville, IN 47720
Phone: (812)426-1414
Fax: (812)426-1945
**Format:** Commercial TV

### Flint-Saginaw-Bay City, MI

**WAQP-TV - 49  (15725)**
2865 Trautner Dr.
Saginaw, MI 48604
Phone: (989)249-5969
**Format:** Commercial TV; Religious

**WEYI-TV - 25  (15134)**
2225 W. Willard Rd., Box 250
Clio, MI 48420
Phone: (810)687-1000
Fax: (810)687-4925
**Format:** Commercial TV

**WJRT-TV - 12  (15298)**
2302 Lapeer Rd.
Flint, MI 48503
Phone: (810)233-3130
Fax: (810)257-2834
**Format:** Commercial TV

### Fort Wayne (Angola), IN

**WANE-TV - 15  (9728)**
2915 W. State Blvd.
Box 1515
Fort Wayne, IN 46808
Phone: (260)424-1515
Fax: (260)424-1428

**Format:** Commercial TV

**WFFT-TV - 55  (9734)**
3707 Hillegas Rd.
Fort Wayne, IN 46808
Phone: (260)471-5555
Fax: (260)484-4331
**Format:** Commercial TV

**WFWA-TV - 39  (9735)**
2501 E. Coliseum Blvd.
Fort Wayne, IN 46805
Phone: (260)484-8839
Fax: (260)482-3632
**Format:** Public TV

### Grand Rapids-Kalamazoo-Battle Creek, MI

**WGVK-TV - 52  (15356)**
301 W. Fulton
Grand Rapids, MI 49504-6492
Phone: (616)331-6666
Fax: (616)331-6625
**Format:** Public TV

**WGVU-TV - 35  (15359)**
301 W. Fulton
Grand Rapids, MI 49504-6492
Phone: (616)331-6666
Fax: (616)331-6625
**Format:** Public TV

**WOOD-TV - 8  (15368)**
120 College Ave., SE
Grand Rapids, MI 49503
Phone: (616)456-8888
Fax: (616)456-9169
**Format:** Commercial TV

**WOTV-TV - 41  (15049)**
5200 W. Dickman Rd., Box 1616
Battle Creek, MI 49016
Phone: (616)968-9341
Fax: (616)966-6837
**Format:** Commercial TV

**WTLJ-TV - 54  (14980)**
10290 48th Ave.
Allendale, MI 49401
Phone: (616)895-4154
Fax: (616)892-4401
**Format:** Religious

**WXMI-TV - 17  (15374)**
3117 Plaza Dr. NE
Grand Rapids, MI 49525
Phone: (616)364-8722
Fax: (616)364-8506
**Format:** Commercial TV

**WZZM-TV - 13  (15376)**
PO Box Z
Grand Rapids, MI 49501
Phone: (616)785-1313
Fax: (616)785-1301
**Format:** Commercial TV

### Green Bay-Appleton (Suring), WI

**WACY-TV - 32  (33011)**
1391 North Rd.
PO Box 12328
Green Bay, WI 54307-2328
Phone: (920)490-0320
Fax: (920)494-7071
**Format:** Commercial TV

**WGBA-TV - 26  (33013)**
1391 North Rd.
PO Box 19099
Green Bay, WI 54307-9099
Phone: (920)494-2626
Fax: (920)494-9550
**Format:** Commercial TV

**WIWB-TV - 14  (33014)**
975 Parkview Rd., Ste. 4
Green Bay, WI 54304
Phone: (920)983-9014
Fax: (920)983-9424

**Format:** Commercial TV; Religious

**WPNE-TV - 38  (33018)**
821 University Avenue
Madison, WI 53706
Phone: (920)465-2500
**Format:** Public TV

### Indianapolis (Marion), IN

**WHMB-TV - 40  (10077)**
10511 Greenfield Ave.
Noblesville, IN 46060
Phone: (317)773-5050
Fax: (317)776-4051
**Format:** Religious

**WIPB-TV - 49  (10050)**
Edmund F. Ball Bldg.
Ball State University
BC 207
Muncie, IN 47306
Phone: (765)285-1249
Fax: (765)285-5548
**Format:** Public TV

**WISH-TV - 8  (9939)**
PO Box 7088
Indianapolis, IN 46207
Phone: (317)923-8888
Fax: (317)926-1144
**Format:** Commercial TV

**WTIU-TV - 30  (9622)**
Indiana University
Radio-TV Bldg.
Bloomington, IN 47405
Phone: (812)855-8000
Fax: (812)855-0729
**Format:** Public TV

### La Crosse-Eau Claire, WI

**KQEG-TV - 23  (33124)**
505 King St., Ste. 221
La Crosse, WI 54601
Phone: (608)784-0876
Fax: (608)784-1138
**Format:** Commercial TV

**WEAU-TV - 13  (32934)**
1907 S. Hastings Way
Eau Claire, WI 54701
Phone: (715)835-1313
Fax: (715)832-0246
**Format:** Commercial TV

**WLAX-TV - 25  (33127)**
1305 Interchange Pl.
La Crosse, WI 54603
Phone: (608)781-0025
Fax: (608)781-1456
**Format:** Commercial TV

**WQOW-TV - 18  (32938)**
5545 Hwy. 93
Eau Claire, WI 54701
Phone: (715)835-1881
Fax: (715)835-8009
**Format:** Commercial TV

**WXOW-TV - 19  (16201)**
3705 Hwy. 25
La Crescent, MN 55947
Phone: (507)895-9969
Fax: (507)895-8124
**Format:** Commercial TV

### Lansing (Ann Arbor), MI

**WKAR-TV - 23  (15252)**
283 Communication Arts Bldg.
East Lansing, MI 48824-1212
Phone: (517)432-9527
Fax: (517)353-7124
**Format:** Public TV

**WLNS-TV - 6  (15535)**
2820 E. Saginaw
Lansing, MI 48912
Phone: (517)372-8282
Fax: (517)374-7610

Format: Commercial TV

## Lima, OH

**WLIO-TV - 35  (24834)**
1424 Rice Ave.
PO Box 1689
Lima, OH 45805
Phone: (419)228-8835
Fax: (419)229-7091
Format: Commercial TV

## Madison, WI

**Charter Communications - 27  (33232)**
5727 Tokay Blvd.
Madison, WI 53719
Phone: (608)274-1234
Fax: (608)274-9514
Format: Commercial TV

**WHA-TV - 21  (33233)**
821 University Ave.
Madison, WI 53706
Phone: (608)263-2121
Fax: (608)263-9763
Format: Public TV

**WHRM-TV - 20  (33636)**
821 University Ave.
Madison, WI 53706
Phone: (608)263-2121
Format: Public TV

## Mankato, MN

**KEYC-TV - 12  (16246)**
1570 Lookout Dr.
PO Box 128
Mankato, MN 56001
Phone: (507)625-7905
Fax: (507)625-5745
Format: Commercial TV

## Marquette, MI

**WJMN-TV - 3  (15263)**
c/o WFRV CBSS, Inc.
PO Box 19055
Green Bay, WI 54307-9055
Phone: (414)437-5411
Fax: (414)437-4576
Format: Commercial TV

**WNMU-TV - 13  (15583)**
Northern Michigan University
Marquette, MI 49855
Phone: (906)227-1300
Fax: (906)227-2905
Format: Public TV

## Milwaukee (Kenosha & Racine), WI

**WCGV-TV - 24  (33348)**
4041 N. 35th St.
Milwaukee, WI 53216-1705
Phone: (414)442-7050
Fax: (414)874-1899
Format: Commercial TV

**WDJT-TV - 58  (33349)**
809 S. 60th St.
Milwaukee, WI 53214
Phone: (414)777-5800
Fax: (414)607-8103
Format: Commercial TV

**W46AR-TV - 46  (33351)**
809 S. 60th St.
Milwaukee, WI 53214
Phone: (414)607-8146
Fax: (414)607-8103
Format: Hispanic

**WITI-TV - 6  (33355)**
9001 N. Green Bay Rd.
Milwaukee, WI 53209
Phone: (414)355-6666

Format: Commercial TV

**WJJA-TV - 49  (33429)**
4311 E. Oakwood Rd.
Oak Creek, WI 53154
Phone: (414)764-4953
Format: Commercial TV

**WTMJ-TV - 4  (33366)**
720 E. Capitol Dr.
Milwaukee, WI 53212
Phone: (414)332-9611
Fax: (414)967-5400
Format: Commercial TV

**WVCY-TV - 30  (33372)**
3434 W. Kilbourn Ave.
Milwaukee, WI 53208
Phone: (414)935-3000
Fax: (414)935-3015
Format: Religious

**WVTV-TV - 18  (33373)**
4041 N. 35th St.
Milwaukee, WI 53216
Phone: (414)442-7050
Fax: (414)874-1899
Format: Commercial TV

## Minneapolis-St. Paul, MN

**KARE-TV - 11  (16354)**
8811 Olson Memorial Hwy.
Minneapolis, MN 55427
Phone: (763)546-1111
Fax: (763)546-8590
Format: Commercial TV

**KCCO-TV - 7  (16356)**
90 S. 11th St.
Minneapolis, MN 55403
Phone: (612)339-4444
Fax: (320)763-4991
Format: Commercial TV

**KMSP-TV - 9  (16096)**
11358 Viking Dr.
Eden Prairie, MN 55344-7258
Phone: (952)944-9999
Fax: (952)995-9999
Format: Commercial TV

**KMWB-TV - 23  (16622)**
1640 Como Ave.
Saint Paul, MN 55108-0125
Phone: (651)646-2300
Fax: (651)646-1220
Format: Commercial TV

**KSAX-TV - 42  (15930)**
415 Filmore Ave.
Box 189
Alexandria, MN 56308
Phone: (320)763-5729
Fax: (320)763-4627
Format: Commercial TV

**WCCO-TV - 4  (16370)**
90 S. 11th St.
Minneapolis, MN 55403
Phone: (612)339-4444
Fax: (612)330-2603
Format: Commercial TV

## Paducah,KY-Cape Girardeau,MO-Marion,IL

**KPOB-TV - 15  (17500)**
c/o WSIL-TV
1416 Country Air Dr.
Carterville, IL 62918
Phone: (618)985-2333
Fax: (618)985-3709
Format: Commercial TV

**WSIL-TV - 3  (7991)**
1416 Country Air Dr.
Carterville, IL 62918
Phone: (618)985-2333
Fax: (618)985-3709

Format: Commercial TV

## Peoria-Bloomington, IL

**WEEK-TV - 25  (9226)**
2907 Springfield Rd.
Peoria, IL 61611
Phone: (309)698-2525
Fax: (309)829-4083
Format: Commercial TV

**WHOI-TV - 19  (8522)**
500 N. Stewart St.
Creve Coeur, IL 61610-3284
Phone: (309)698-1919
Fax: (309)698-4819
Format: Commercial TV

**WTVP-TV - 47  (9233)**
101 State St.
Peoria, IL 61602-1547
Phone: (309)677-4747
Fax: (309)677-4730
Format: Public TV

**WYZZ-TV - 43  (7920)**
2714 E. Lincoln
Bloomington, IL 61704
Phone: (309)661-4343
Fax: (309)663-6943
Format: Commercial TV

## Quincy, IL-Hannibal, MO

**KHQA-TV - 7  (9262)**
301 S. 36th St.
Quincy, IL 62301
Phone: (217)222-6200
Fax: (217)228-3164
Format: Commercial TV

**WQEC-TV - 27  (9266)**
PO Box 6248
Springfield, IL 62708
Phone: (217)483-7887
Fax: (217)483-1112
Format: Public TV

## Rochester, MN-Mason City, IA-Austin, MN

**KXLT-TV - 47  (16530)**
6301 Bandel Rd. NW
Rochester, MN 55901-8758
Phone: (507)252-4747
Fax: (507)252-5050
Format: Commercial TV

## Rockford, IL

**WQRF-TV - 39  (9312)**
401 S. Main St.
Rockford, IL 61101
Phone: (815)987-3950
Fax: (815)964-9974
Format: Commercial TV

**WTVO-TV - 17  (9315)**
Box 470
Rockford, IL 61105
Phone: (815)963-0029
Fax: (815)963-0201
Format: Commercial TV

## South Bend-Elkhart, IN

**WNIT-TV - 34  (9684)**
PO Box 3434, 2300 Charger Blvd.
Elkhart, IN 46515
Phone: (219)674-5961
Fax: (219)262-8497
Format: Public TV

**WSJV-TV - 28  (9685)**
58096 County Rd. 7 S.
Elkhart, IN 46517
Phone: (574)679-4545
Fax: (574)294-1324

Springfield-Decatur-Champaign, IL

**Format:** Commercial TV

## Springfield-Decatur-Champaign, IL

**WB23 - 23 (8540)**
2510 Parkway Ct.
Decatur, IL 62526
Phone: (217)428-2323
Fax: (217)428-6455
**Format:** Commercial TV; Religious

**WEIU-TV - 51 (8048)**
Radio & TV Center
Eastern Illinois University, 1521 Buzzard
Charleston, IL 61920
Phone: (217)581-5956
Fax: (217)581-6650
**Format:** Public TV

**WICD-TV - 15 (8039)**
250 S. Country Fair Dr.
Champaign, IL 61821
Phone: (217)351-8500
Fax: (217)351-6056
**Format:** Commercial TV

**WICS-TV - 20 (9416)**
2680 E. Cook St.
Springfield, IL 62703
Phone: (217)753-5620
Fax: (217)753-8177
**Format:** Commercial TV

**WRSP-TV - 55 (9422)**
3003 Old Rochester Rd.
Springfield, IL 62703
Phone: (217)523-8855
Fax: (217)523-4410
**Format:** Commercial TV

**WSEC-TV - 8 (9423)**
PO Box 6248
Springfield, IL 62708
Phone: (217)483-7887
Fax: (217)483-1112
**Format:** Public TV

## Terre Haute, IN

**WTWO-TV - 2 (10206)**
PO Box 299
Terre Haute, IN 47808
Phone: (812)696-2121
Fax: (812)696-2755
**Format:** Commercial TV

**WVUT-TV - 22 (10226)**
1200 N. 2nd St.
Vincennes, IN 47591
Fax: (812)882-2237
**Format:** Public TV

## Toledo, OH

**WTOL-TV - 11 (25109)**
730 N. Summit St.
PO Box 1111
Toledo, OH 43699-1111
Phone: (419)248-1111
Fax: (419)248-1177
**Format:** Commercial TV

**WTVG-TV - 13 (25110)**
4247 Dorr St.
Toledo, OH 43607
Phone: (419)531-1313
Fax: (419)531-1399
**Format:** Commercial TV

## Traverse City-Cadillac, MI

**WCMV-TV - 27 (15089)**
c/o WCMU-TV
Central Michigan University
1999 E. Campus Dr.
Mount Pleasant, MI 48859
Phone: (989)774-3105
Fax: (989)774-4427
**Format:** Public TV

**WCMW-TV - 21 (15567)**
c/o WCMU-TV
Central Michigan University
1999 E. Campus Dr.
Mount Pleasant, MI 48859
Phone: (989)774-3105
Fax: (989)774-4427
**Format:** Public TV

**WFVX-TV - 45 (15090)**
7669 S. 45 Rd.
Cadillac, MI 49601
Phone: (616)775-9813
Fax: (616)775-1898
**Format:** Commercial TV

**WPBN-TV - 7 (15840)**
8581 M-72 W.
PO Box 546
Traverse City, MI 49685
Phone: (231)947-7770
Fax: (231)947-0354
**Format:** Commercial TV

**WTOM-TV - 4 (15842)**
8518 M-72 W.
PO Box 546
Traverse City, MI 49684
Phone: (231)947-7770
Fax: (231)947-0354
**Format:** Commercial TV

## Wausau-Rhinelander, WI

**WAOW-TV - 9 (33634)**
1908 Grand Ave.
Wausau, WI 54403
Phone: (715)842-2251
Fax: (715)848-0195
**Format:** Commercial TV

## Wheeling, WV-Steubenville, OH

**WTOV-TV - 9 (25066)**
Box 9999
Steubenville, OH 43952
Phone: (740)282-9999
Fax: (740)282-0350
**Format:** Commercial TV

## Youngstown, OH

**WFMJ-TV - 21 (25214)**
101 W. Boardman St.
Youngstown, OH 44503
Phone: (330)744-8611
Fax: (330)744-3402
**Format:** Commercial TV

**WYTV-TV - 33 (25225)**
3800 Shady Run Rd.
Youngstown, OH 44502
Phone: (330)783-2930
Fax: (330)782-8154
**Format:** Commercial TV

## Zanesville, OH

**WHIZ-TV - 18 (25232)**
629 Downard Rd.
Zanesville, OH 43701
Phone: (740)452-5431
Fax: (740)452-6553
**Format:** Commercial TV

# Great Plains States

## Cedar Rapids-Waterloo-Dubuque, IA

**KFXA-TV - 40 (10536)**
744 Main St.
PO Box 1090
Dubuque, IA 52001
Phone: (563)556-4040
Fax: (563)557-7101

**Format:** Commercial TV

**KIIN-TV - 12 (10512)**
Iowa Public Television
PO Box 6450
Johnston, IA 50131
Phone: (515)242-3100
Fax: (515)242-4150
**Format:** Public TV

**KRIN-TV - 32 (10686)**
Iowa Public Television
PO Box 6450
Johnston, IA 50131
Phone: (515)242-3100
Fax: (515)242-4150
**Format:** Public TV

**KWWL-TV - 7 (10951)**
500 E. 4th St.
Waterloo, IA 50703
Phone: (319)291-1200
Fax: (319)291-1233
**Format:** Commercial TV

## Cheyenne, WY-Scottsbluff, NE (Sterling, CO)

**KDUH-TV - 4 (18598)**
PO Box 1529
Scottsbluff, NE 69363
Phone: (308)632-3071
Fax: (308)632-3596
**Format:** Commercial TV

**KSTF-TV - 10 (18349)**
3385 N. 10th Ave.
Gering, NE 69341
Phone: (308)632-6107
Fax: (308)632-3470
**Format:** Commercial TV

**KTNE-TV - 13 (18261)**
c/o KUON-TV
PO Box 83111
Lincoln, NE 68501
Phone: (402)472-3611
Fax: (402)472-1785
**Format:** Public TV

## Columbia-Jefferson City, MO

**KMOS-TV - 6 (18023)**
Central Missouri State University
Warrensburg, MO 64093
Phone: (660)543-4155
Fax: (660)543-8863
**Format:** Public TV

**KNLJ-TV - 25 (17451)**
PO Box 2525
New Bloomfield, MO 65063-2525
Phone: (573)896-5105
Fax: (573)896-4376
**Format:** Commercial TV; Religious

## Daveport, IA-Rock Island, Moline, IL

**KLJB-TV - 18 (10428)**
937 E 53rd St., Ste. D
Davenport, IA 52807
Phone: (563)386-1818
Fax: (563)386-8543
**Format:** Commercial TV

## Des Moines, IA

**KDIN-TV - 11 (10508)**
Iowa Public Television
PO Box 6450
Johnston, IA 50131
Phone: (515)242-3100
Fax: (515)242-4150
**Format:** Public TV

**KDSM-TV - 17 (10511)**
4023 Fleur Dr.
Des Moines, IA 50321
Phone: (515)287-1717
Fax: (515)287-0064

**KTIN-TV - 21 (10589)**
Iowa Public Television
PO Box 6450
Johnston, IA 50131
Phone: (515)242-3100
Fax: (515)242-4150
**Format:** Public TV

**WOI-TV - 5 (10972)**
3903 Westown Parkway
West Des Moines, IA 50266
Phone: (515)457-9645
Fax: (515)457-1034
**Format:** Commercial TV

## Fargo, ND

**KBRR-TV - 10 (16662)**
c/o KVRR-TV
4015 9th Ave. SW
PO Box 9115
Fargo, ND 58103
Phone: (701)277-1515
Fax: (701)277-1830
**Format:** Commercial TV

**KJRR-TV - 7 (24008)**
c/o KVRR-TV
4015 9th Ave. SW
PO Box 9115
Fargo, ND 58103
Phone: (701)277-1515
Fax: (701)277-1830
**Format:** Commercial TV

**KNRR-TV - 12 (24053)**
c/o KVRR-TV
4015 9th Ave. SW
PO Box 9115
Fargo, ND 58106
Phone: (701)277-1515
Fax: (701)277-1830
**Format:** Commercial TV

**KVLY-TV - 11 (23970)**
PO Box 1878
Fargo, ND 58107
Phone: (701)237-5211
Fax: (701)232-0493
**Format:** Commercial TV

**KVRR-TV - 15 (23973)**
4015 9th Ave. SW
PO Box 9115
PO Box 9115
Fargo, ND 58103
Phone: (701)277-1515
Fax: (701)277-1830
**Format:** Commercial TV

**KXJB-TV - 4 (23974)**
1350 21st Ave. S
Fargo, ND 58103-3313
Phone: (701)282-0444
Fax: (701)232-0493
**Format:** Commercial TV

**WDAY-TV - 6 (23977)**
301 S. 8th St.
Fargo, ND 58103
Phone: (701)237-6500
Fax: (701)241-5368
**Format:** Commercial TV

**WDAZ-TV - 8 (23997)**
2220 S. Washington
PO Box 12639
Grand Forks, ND 58208-2639
Phone: (701)775-2511
Fax: (701)746-8565
**Format:** Commercial TV

## Joplin, MO-Pittsburg, KS

**KOAM-TV - 7 (11375)**
PO Box 659
Pittsburg, KS 66762
Phone: (620)231-0400
Fax: (417)624-3158
**Format:** Commercial TV

**KODE-TV - 12 (17306)**
1928 W. 13th St.
Joplin, MO 64801
Phone: (417)623-7260
Fax: (417)623-3736
**Format:** Commercial TV

## Kansas City, MO (Lawrence, KS)

**KSMO-TV - 62 (11155)**
10 E. Cambridge Circle Dr., Ste. 300
Kansas City, KS 66103-1342
Phone: (913)621-6262
Fax: (913)621-4703
**Format:** Commercial TV

**WDAF-TV - 4 (17364)**
3030 Summit, Signal Hill
Kansas City, MO 64108
Phone: (816)753-4567
Fax: (816)561-4181
**Format:** Commercial TV

## Lincoln-Hastings-Kearney, NE

**KGIN-TV - 11 (18358)**
123 N. Locust
Grand Island, NE 68801
Phone: (308)563-2200
Fax: (308)382-3216
**Format:** Commercial TV

**KHAS-TV - 5 (18370)**
6475 N. Osborn Dr.
N. Hwy. 281
PO Box 578
Hastings, NE 68901
Phone: (402)463-1321
Fax: (402)463-6551
**Format:** Commercial TV

**KHGI-TV - 13/6 (18269)**
PO Box 220
PO Box 220
Axtell, NE 68924
Phone: (308)743-2494
Fax: (308)743-2644
**Format:** Commercial TV

**KHNE-TV - 29 (18372)**
c/o KUON-TV
PO Box 83111
Lincoln, NE 68501
Phone: (402)472-3611
Fax: (402)472-1785
**Format:** Public TV

**KLKN-TV - 8 (18468)**
3240 S. 10th St.
Lincoln, NE 68502
Phone: (402)434-8000
Fax: (402)436-2236
**Format:** Commercial TV

**KLNE-TV - 3 (18400)**
c/o KUON-TV
PO Box 83111
Lincoln, NE 68501
Phone: (402)472-3611
Fax: (402)472-1785
**Format:** Public TV

**KMNE-TV - 7 (18272)**
c/o KUON-TV
PO Box 83111
Lincoln, NE 68501
Phone: (402)472-3611
Fax: (402)472-1785
**Format:** Public TV

**KOLN-TV - 10 (18471)**
Box 30350
Lincoln, NE 68503
Phone: (402)467-4321
Fax: (402)467-9210
**Format:** Commercial TV

**KSNB-TV - 4 (18270)**
KHGI-TV
PO Box 220
Axtell, NE 68924
Phone: (308)743-2494
Fax: (308)743-2644

**Format:** Commercial TV

**KUON-TV - 12 (18477)**
PO Box 83111
Lincoln, NE 68501
Phone: (402)472-3611
Fax: (402)472-1785
**Format:** Public TV

**KWNB-TV - 6 (18374)**
c/o KHGI-TV
PO Box 220
PO Box 220
Axtell, NE 68924
Phone: (308)743-2494
Fax: (308)743-2644
**Format:** Commercial TV

## Minot-Bismarck-Dickinson, ND-Glendive, MT

**KBMY-TV - 17 (23911)**
3128 E. Broadway
Bismarck, ND 58501
Phone: (701)223-1700
Fax: (701)258-0886
**Format:** Commercial TV

**KQCD-TV - 7 (23942)**
373 21st St. East
Dickinson, ND 58601
Phone: (701)483-7777
Fax: (701)483-8231
**Format:** Commercial TV

**KUMV-TV - 8 (24084)**
602 Main St.
PO Box 1287
Williston, ND 58801
Phone: (701)572-4676
Fax: (701)572-0118
**Format:** Commercial TV

**KXMA-TV - 2 (23943)**
Drawer B
Dickinson, ND 58602
Phone: (701)483-1400
Fax: (701)227-8896
**Format:** Commercial TV

**KXMD-TV - 11 (24085)**
1802 13th Ave. W
PO Box 790
Williston, ND 58801
Phone: (701)572-2345
Fax: (701)572-0658
**Format:** Commercial TV

## North Platte, NE

**KNOP-TV - 2 (18510)**
Box 749
North Platte, NE 69103
Phone: (308)532-2222
Fax: (308)532-9579
**Format:** Commercial TV

**KPNE-TV - 9 (18513)**
c/o KUON-TV
PO Box 38111
Lincoln, NE 68501
Phone: (402)472-3611
Fax: (402)472-1785
**Format:** Public TV

## Omaha, NE

**KETV-TV - 7 (18548)**
2665 Douglas St.
Omaha, NE 68131-2699
Phone: (402)345-7777
Fax: (402)978-8931
**Format:** Commercial TV

**KHIN-TV - 36 (10833)**
Iowa Public Television
PO Box 6450
Johnston, IA 50131
Phone: (515)242-3100
Fax: (515)242-4150

Format: Public TV

**KMTV-TV - 3 (18556)**
10714 Mockingbird Dr.
Omaha, NE 68127
Phone: (402)592-3333
Fax: (402)597-7698
Format: Commercial TV

**KPTM-TV - 42 (18558)**
4625 Farnam St.
Omaha, NE 68132
Phone: (402)558-4200
Fax: (402)554-4290
Format: Commercial TV

## Ottumwa, IA-Kirksville, MO (Wapello, IA)

**KYOU-TV - 15 (10813)**
820 W. 2nd St.
Ottumwa, IA 52501
Phone: (515)684-5415
Fax: (515)682-5173
Format: Commercial TV

## Paducah, KY-Cape Girardeau, MO-Marion, IL

**KFVS-TV - 12 (17119)**
310 Broadway
PO Box 100
Cape Girardeau, MO 63702
Phone: (573)335-1212
Fax: (573)335-6303
Format: Commercial TV

## Rapid City, SD

**KBHE-TV - 9 (28448)**
c/o South Dakota Public Broadcasting
555 N. Dakota St.
PO Box 5000
Vermillion, SD 57069-5000
Phone: (605)677-5861
Fax: (605)677-5010
Format: Public TV

**KIVV-TV - 5 (28387)**
PO Box 677
Rapid City, SD 57709
Phone: (605)394-7777
Fax: (605)348-9128
Format: Commercial TV

**KOTA-TV - 3 (28392)**
Box 1760
Rapid City, SD 57709
Phone: (605)342-2000
Fax: (605)342-7305
Format: Commercial TV

**KRNE-TV - 12 (18490)**
c/o KUON-TV
PO Box 83111
Lincoln, NE 68501
Phone: (402)472-3611
Fax: (402)472-1785
Format: Public TV

**KZSD-TV - 8 (28340)**
c/o KUSD-TV
555 N. Dakota St.
PO Box 5000
Vermillion, SD 57069-5000
Phone: (605)677-5861
Fax: (605)677-5010
Format: Public TV

## Rochester, MN-Mason City, IA-Austin, MN

**KYIN-TV - 24 (10748)**
Iowa Public Television
PO Box 6450
Johnston, IA 50131
Phone: (515)242-3100
Fax: (515)242-4150

## St. Joseph, MO

**KQTV-TV - 2 (17536)**
40th & Faraon Sts.
PO Box 8369
Saint Joseph, MO 64508
Phone: (816)364-2222
Fax: (816)364-3787
Format: Commercial TV

## St. Louis, MO (Mt. Vernon, IL)

**KDNL-TV - 30 (17910)**
1215 Cole St.
Saint Louis, MO 63106
Phone: (314)436-3030
Fax: (314)259-5538
Format: Commercial TV

**KETC-TV - 9 (17911)**
3655 Olive St.
Saint Louis, MO 63108-3601
Phone: (314)512-9000
Fax: (314)512-9005
Format: Public TV

**KMOV-TV - 4 (17916)**
1 Memorial Dr.
Saint Louis, MO 63102
Phone: (314)621-4444
Fax: (314)621-4775
Format: Commercial TV

**KNLC-TV - 24 (17918)**
1411 Locust St.
Saint Louis, MO 63106
Phone: (314)436-2424
Fax: (314)436-2434
Format: Religious

**KSDK-TV - 5 (17921)**
1000 Market St.
Saint Louis, MO 63101
Phone: (314)421-5055
Fax: (314)444-5289
Format: Commercial TV

## Sioux City, IA

**KSIN-TV - 27 (10881)**
Iowa Public Television
PO Box 6450
Johnston, IA 50131
Phone: (515)242-3100
Fax: (515)242-4150
Format: Public TV

**KXNE-TV - 19 (18502)**
c/o KUON-TV
PO Box 83111
Lincoln, NE 68501
Phone: (402)472-3611
Fax: (402)472-1785
Format: Public TV

## Sioux Falls-Mitchell, SD

**KDLO-TV - 3 (28312)**
c/o KELO-LAND Television
501 S. Phillips Ave.
Sioux Falls, SD 57104
Phone: (605)336-1100
Fax: (605)334-3447
Format: Commercial TV

**KDLT-TV - 46 (28416)**
3600 S. Westport Ave.
Sioux Falls, SD 57106
Phone: (605)361-5555
Fax: (605)361-7017
Format: Commercial TV

**KDSD-TV - 16 (28264)**
c/o South Dakota Public Broadcasting
555 N Dakota St.
PO Box 5000
Vermillion, SD 57069-5000
Phone: (605)677-5861
Fax: (605)677-5010

Format: Public TV

**KESD-TV - 8 (28283)**
c/o South Dakota Public Broadcasting
555 N. Dakota St.
PO Box 5000
Vermillion, SD 57069-5000
Phone: (605)677-5861
Fax: (605)677-5010
Format: Public TV

**KPLO-TV - 6 (28399)**
c/o KELO-TV
501 S. Phillips Ave.
Sioux Falls, SD 57104
Phone: (605)336-1100
Fax: (605)334-3447
Format: Commercial TV

**KPSD-TV - 13 (28304)**
c/o South Dakota Public Broadcasting
555 N. Dakota St.
PO Box 5000
Vermillion, SD 57069-5000
Phone: (605)677-5861
Fax: (605)677-5010
Format: Public TV

**KSFY-TV - 13 (28425)**
300 N. Dakota Ave., Ste. 100
Sioux Falls, SD 57104-6020
Phone: (605)336-1300
Fax: (605)336-7936
Format: Commercial TV

**KTSD-TV - 10 (28401)**
c/o South Dakota Public Broadcasting
555 N. Dakota St.
PO Box 5000
Vermillion, SD 57069-5000
Phone: (605)677-5861
Fax: (605)677-5010
Format: Public TV

**KTTW-TV - 17 (28427)**
PO Box 5103
Sioux Falls, SD 57117-5103
Phone: (605)338-0017
Fax: (605)338-7173
Format: Commercial TV

**KUSD-TV - 2 (28450)**
c/o South Dakota Public Broadcasting
555 N. Dakota St.
PO Box 5000
Vermillion, SD 57069-5000
Phone: (605)677-5861
Fax: (605)677-5010
Format: Public TV

## Springfield, MO

**KOZK-TV - 21 (17985)**
901 S National Ave.
Springfield, MO 65804-0027
Phone: (417)836-3500
Format: Public TV

**KSPR-TV - 33 (17987)**
PO Box 6030
Springfield, MO 65801-6030
Phone: (417)831-1333
Fax: (417)831-4125
Format: Commercial TV

## Topeka, KS

**KTKA-TV - 49 (11450)**
2121 Chelsea
Topeka, KS 66614
Phone: (785)273-4949
Fax: (785)273-7811
Format: Commercial TV

## Wichita-Hutchinson, KS

**KBSD-TV - 6 (11049)**
Box 157
Dodge City, KS 67801
Phone: (620)227-3121
Fax: (620)225-1675

Format: Commercial TV

**KBSH-TV - 7 (11107)**
2300 Hall St.
Hays, KS 67601
Phone: (785)625-5277
Fax: (785)625-1161
Format: Commercial TV

**KLBY-TV - 4 (11028)**
990 S. Range
Colby, KS 67701
Phone: (785)462-8644
Fax: (785)462-3522
Format: Commercial TV

**KOOD-TV - 9 (11010)**
Box 9
Bunker Hill, KS 67626
Phone: (785)483-6990
Fax: (785)483-4605
Format: Public TV

**KPTS-TV - 8 (11502)**
320 W. 21st St.
Wichita, KS 67203
Phone: (316)838-3090
Fax: (316)838-8586
Format: Public TV

**KSNG-TV - 11 (11084)**
204 Fulton Terr.
Garden City, KS 67846
Phone: (620)276-2311
Fax: (620)275-0576
Format: Commercial TV

**KSNK-TV - 8 (11280)**
West Hwy. 36
PO Box 238
Oberlin, KS 67749
Phone: (785)475-2248
Fax: (785)475-3944
Format: Commercial TV

**KSNW-TV - 3 (11505)**
833 N. Main
Box 333
Wichita, KS 67201
Phone: (316)265-3333
Fax: (316)292-1197
Format: Commercial TV

**KSWK-TV - 3 (11162)**
Box 9, 6th & Elm St.
Bunker Hill, KS 67626
Phone: (913)483-6990
Fax: (913)483-4605
Format: Public TV

**KWCH-TV - 12 (11507)**
2815 E. 37th St. N.
Wichita, KS 67201
Phone: (316)838-1212
Fax: (316)831-6198
Format: Commercial TV

# Middle Atlantic States

## Baltimore, MD

**WBAL-TV - 11 (12887)**
3800 Hooper Ave.
Baltimore, MD 21211
Phone: (410)467-1929
Fax: (410)338-6460
Format: Commercial TV

**WJZ-TV - 13 (12896)**
3725 Maldden Ave.
TV Hill
Baltimore, MD 21211
Phone: (410)578-7513
Fax: (410)578-7502
Format: Commercial TV

**WMAR-TV - 2 (12898)**
6400 York Rd.
Baltimore, MD 21212
Phone: (410)377-2222
Fax: (410)377-0493

Format: Commercial TV

**WUTB-TV - 24 (12904)**
4820 Seton Dr., Ste. M-N
Baltimore, MD 21215
Phone: (410)358-2400
Fax: (410)764-7232
Format: Commercial TV

## Bluefield-Beckley-Oak Hill, WV

**WOAY-TV - 4 (32700)**
Rte. 16 S.
PO Box 3001
Oak Hill, WV 25901
Phone: (304)469-3361
Fax: (304)465-1420
Format: Commercial TV

**WVSX-TV - 59 (32602)**
141 Old Cline Rd.
Ghent, WV 25843-9343
Phone: (304)787-5959
Fax: (304)787-2440
Format: Commercial TV

**WVVA-TV - 6 (32547)**
Rte. 460 Bypass
PO Box 1930
Bluefield, WV 24701
Phone: (304)325-5487
Fax: (304)327-5586
Format: Commercial TV

## Charlottesville, VA

**WVIR-TV - 29 (31281)**
503 E. Market St.
Charlottesville, VA 22902
Phone: (434)220-2900
Fax: (434)220-2905
Format: Commercial TV

## Clarksburg-Weston, WV

**WBOY-TV - 12 (32578)**
904 W. Pike St.
Clarksburg, WV 26301-2555
Phone: (304)623-3311
Fax: (304)624-6152
Format: Commercial TV

## Hagerstown, MD

**WHAG-TV - 25 (13202)**
13 E. Washington St.
Hagerstown, MD 21740
Phone: (301)797-4400
Fax: (301)733-1735
Format: Commercial TV

## Harrisonburg, VA

**WHSV-TV - 3 (31473)**
80 N. Main St.
PO Box TV 3
Harrisonburg, VA 22801
Phone: (540)433-9191
Fax: (540)433-2700
Format: Commercial TV

## Norfolk-Portsmouth-Newport News-Hampton, VA

**Lockwood Broadcasting - 49 (31458)**
220 Salter Creek Rd.
Hampton, VA 23666
Phone: (757)722-9736
Fax: (757)726-0196
Format: Commercial TV

**WAVY-TV - 10 (31668)**
300 Wavy St.
Portsmouth, VA 23704
Phone: (757)393-1010
Fax: (757)399-7628

Format: Commercial TV

**WTKR-TV - 3 (31643)**
720 Boush St.
Norfolk, VA 23510
Phone: (757)446-1000
Fax: (757)640-0164
Format: Commercial TV

**WTVZ-TV - 33 (31644)**
900 Granby St.
Norfolk, VA 23510
Phone: (757)622-3333
Fax: (757)623-1541
Format: Commercial TV

## Richmond, VA

**WCVW-TV - 57 (31821)**
23 Sesame St.
Richmond, VA 23235
Phone: (804)320-1301
Fax: (804)320-8729
Format: Public TV

**WRIC-TV - 8 (31825)**
Arboretum Pl.
Richmond, VA 23236-4364
Phone: (804)330-8888
Fax: (804)330-8883
Format: Commercial TV

**WTVR-TV - 6 (31829)**
3301 W. Broad St.
Richmond, VA 23230
Phone: (804)254-3600
Fax: (804)254-3699
Format: Public TV

**WWBT-TV - 12 (31831)**
5710 Midlothian Tpke.
Richmond, VA 23225
Phone: (804)230-1212
Fax: (804)230-2793
Format: Commercial TV

## Roanoke-Lynchburg, VA

**WFXR-TV - 27 (31843)**
PO Box 2127
Roanoke, VA 24009-2127
Phone: (540)344-2127
Fax: (540)345-1912
Format: Commercial TV

**WJPR-TV - 21 (31845)**
PO Box 2127
Roanoke, VA 24009-2127
Phone: (540)344-2127
Fax: (540)345-1912
Format: Commercial TV

**WSLS-TV - 10 (31851)**
PO Box 10
401 3rd. St. SW
Roanoke, VA 24022-0010
Phone: (540)981-9110
Fax: (540)343-3157
Format: Commercial TV

## Salisbury, MD

**WBOC-TV - 16 (13323)**
WBOC Box 2057
Salisbury, MD 21802
Phone: (410)749-1111
Fax: (410)749-2361
Format: Commercial TV

**WMDT-TV - 47 (13329)**
202 Downtown Plaza
Salisbury, MD 21801
Phone: (410)742-4747
Fax: (410)742-5767
Format: Commercial TV

## Washington, DC

**WETA-TV - 26 (31170)**
2775 S. Quincy St.
Arlington, VA 22206-2236
Phone: (703)998-2600
Fax: (703)998-9401

---

Circulation: ★ = ABC; △ = BPA; ♦ = CAC; • = CCAB; ❑ = VAC; ⊖ = PO Statement; ‡ = Publisher's Report; Boldface figures = sworn; Light figures = estimated.

## Washington, DC

**Format:** Public TV

**WHUT-TV - 32  (5775)**
2222 4th St. NW
Washington, DC 20059
Phone: (202)806-3012
Fax: (202)806-3300
**Format:** Public TV

**WRC-TV - 4  (5782)**
4001 Nebraska Ave. NW
Washington, DC 20016
Phone: (202)885-4111
Fax: (202)885-4104
**Format:** Commercial TV

**WUSA-TV - 9  (5787)**
4100 Wisconsin Ave. NW
Washington, DC 20016
Phone: (202)895-5500
Fax: (202)364-6163
**Format:** Commercial TV

## Wheeling, WV-Steubenville, OH

**WTRF-TV - 7  (32782)**
96 16th St.
Wheeling, WV 26003
Phone: (304)232-7777
Fax: (304)232-4975
**Format:** Commercial TV

# Northeastern States

## Albany-Schenectady-Troy, NY

**WMHT-TV - 17  (22926)**
17 Fern Ave.
PO Box 17
Schenectady, NY 12301
Phone: (518)357-1700
Fax: (518)357-1709
**Format:** Public TV

**WNYT-TV - 13  (21199)**
News Channel 13
15 N. Pearl St.
PO Box 4035
Menands, NY 12204
Phone: (518)436-4791
Fax: (518)434-0659
**Format:** Commercial TV

**WRGB-TV - 6  (22928)**
1400 Balltown Rd.
Schenectady, NY 12309
Phone: (518)346-6666
Fax: (518)346-6249
**Format:** Commercial TV

**WTEN-TV - 10  (20244)**
341 Northern Blvd.
341 Northern Blvd.
Albany, NY 12204
Phone: (518)436-4822
Fax: (518)462-6065
**Format:** Commercial TV

## Bangor, ME

**WLBZ-TV - 2  (12464)**
PO Box 415
329 Mt. Hope Ave
Bangor, ME 04402-0415
Phone: (207)942-4821
Fax: (207)945-6816
**Format:** Commercial TV

**WVII-TV - 7  (12465)**
371 Target Industrial Circle
P.O. Box 1101
Bangor, ME 04401
Phone: (207)945-6457
Fax: (207)942-0511

**Format:** Commercial TV

## Binghamton, NY

**WBNG-TV - 12  (20999)**
560 Columbia Dr.
PO Box 12
Johnson City, NY 13790
Phone: (607)729-8812
Fax: (607)797-6211
**Format:** Commercial TV

**WICZ-TV - 40  (23106)**
4600 Vestal Pkwy E
Vestal, NY 13850-3674
Phone: (607)770-4040
Fax: (607)798-7950
**Format:** Commercial TV

**WSKG-TV - 46  (20411)**
PO Box 3000
Binghamton, NY 13902
Phone: (607)729-0100
Fax: (607)729-7328
**Format:** Public TV

## Boston-Worcester,MA-Derry-Manchester,NH

**WBZ-TV - 4  (13605)**
1170 Soldiers Field Rd.
Boston, MA 02134
Phone: (617)787-7000
Fax: (617)787-5969
**Format:** Commercial TV

**WFXT-TV - 25  (13753)**
25 Fox Dr.
PO Box 9125
Dedham, MA 02027-9125
Phone: (781)467-1300
Fax: (781)467-7213
**Format:** Commercial TV

**WGBH-TV - 2  (13610)**
125 Western Ave.
Boston, MA 02134
Phone: (617)300-2000
Fax: (617)787-0714
**Format:** Public TV

**WLVI-TV - 56  (13612)**
75 Morrissey Blvd.
Boston, MA 02125
Phone: (617)265-5656
Fax: (617)265-2538
**Format:** Commercial TV

**WMFP-TV - 62  (13613)**
One Beacon St. 35th Fl.
Boston, MA 02108
Phone: (617)720-1062
**Format:** Public TV

**WMUR-TV -   (18881)**
PO Box 9
Manchester, NH 03105
Phone: (603)669-9999
Fax: (603)641-9044
**Format:** Commercial TV

**WNDS-TV - 50  (18802)**
50 Television Pl.
Derry, NH 03038-1451
Phone: (603)434-8850
Fax: (603)434-8627
**Format:** Commercial TV

**WSBK-TV - 38  (13617)**
1170 Soldiers Field Rd
Boston, MA 02134
Phone: (617)783-3838
Fax: (617)254-6303
**Format:** Commercial TV

**WUTF-TV - 66  (13831)**
71 Parmenter Rd.
Hudson, MA 01749
Phone: (978)562-0660
Fax: (978)562-1166

## Buffalo (Jamestown), NY

**WGRZ-TV - 2  (20591)**
259 Delaware Ave.
Buffalo, NY 14202
Phone: (716)849-2200
Fax: (716)849-7602
**Format:** Commercial TV

**WIVB-TV - 4  (20594)**
2077 Elmwood Ave.
Buffalo, NY 14207
Phone: (716)874-4410
Fax: (716)879-4896
**Format:** Commercial TV

**WNED-TV - 17  (20600)**
Horizon Plaza
PO Box 1263
Buffalo, NY 14240
Phone: (716)845-7000
Fax: (716)845-7036
**Format:** Public TV

**WNYB-TV - 26  (22668)**
5775 Big Tree Rd.
Orchard Park, NY 14127-2208
Phone: (716)662-2659
Fax: (716)667-2499
**Format:** Religious

## Burlington-Hartford, VT-Plattsburgh, NY

**Mountain Lake PBS - 57  (22710)**
1 Sesame St.
Plattsburgh, NY 12901
Phone: (518)563-9770
Fax: (518)561-1928
**Format:** Public TV

**WCAX-TV - 3  (30862)**
PO Box 608
Burlington, VT 05402
Phone: (802)658-6300
Fax: (802)652-6399
**Format:** Commercial TV

**WVNY-TV - 22  (30868)**
530 Shelburne Rd.
Box 22
Burlington, VT 05401
Phone: (802)860-2222
Fax: (802)865-9976
**Format:** Commercial TV

## Erie, PA

**WICU-TV - 66  (26354)**
3514 State ST
Erie, PA 16508
Phone: (814)454-5201
Fax: (814)455-0703
**Format:** Commercial TV

**WICU-TV - 12  (26355)**
3514 State St.
Erie, PA 16508
Phone: (814)453-2211
Fax: (814)455-0703
**Format:** Commercial TV

## Harrisburg-York-Lancaster-Lebanon, PA

**WGCB-TV - 49  (27477)**
2900 Windsor Rd.
PO Box 88
Red Lion, PA 17356
Phone: (717)246-1681
Fax: (717)244-9316
**Format:** Commercial TV

**WITF-TV - 33  (26466)**
1982 Locust Ln.
Harrisburg, PA 17109
Phone: (717)236-6000
Fax: (717)236-4628

**Format:** Public TV

**WPMT-TV - 43 (27738)**
2005 S. Queen St.
York, PA 17403
Phone: (717)843-0043
Fax: (717)843-9741
**Format:** Commercial TV

## Hartford-New Haven (New London), CT

**WEDH-TV - 24 (4812)**
1049 Asylum Ave.
Hartford, CT 06105-2432
**Format:** Public TV

**WEDN-TV - 53 (4973)**
1049 Asylum Ave.
Hartford, CT 06105-2411
**Format:** Public TV

**WEDY-TV - 65 (4910)**
240 New Britain Ave.
Box 6240
Box 6240
Hartford, CT 06106-3185
Phone: (860)278-5310
Fax: (860)278-2157
**Format:** Public TV

**WRDM TV - 13 (4821)**
886 Maple Ave.
Hartford, CT 06114
Phone: (860)956-1303
Fax: (860)956-6834
**Format:** Hispanic

**WTXX-TV - 20 (4824)**
One Corporate Center
Hartford, CT 06103
Phone: (860)527-6161
Fax: (860)520-6576
**Format:** Commercial TV

**WVIT-TV - 30 (5083)**
1422 New Britain Ave.
West Hartford, CT 06110
Phone: (860)521-3030
Fax: (860)521-4860
**Format:** Commercial TV

## Johnstown-Altoona, PA

**WATM-TV - 23 (26549)**
1450 Scalp Ave
Johnstown, PA 15904
Phone: (814)266-8088
Fax: (814)266-7749
**Format:** Commercial TV

**WJAC-TV - 6 (26551)**
49 Old Hickory Ln.
Johnstown, PA 15905
Phone: (814)255-7600
Fax: (814)255-3958
**Format:** Commercial TV

**WKBS-TV - 47 (27632)**
1 Signal Hill Dr.
Wall, PA 15148-1499
**Format:** Commercial TV

**WWCP-TV - 8 (26559)**
1450 Scalp Ave.
Johnstown, PA 15904
Phone: (814)266-8088
Fax: (814)266-7749
**Format:** Commercial TV

## New York, NY

**WABC-TV - 7 (22572)**
7 Lincoln Sq.
New York, NY 10023
Phone: (212)456-7777
Fax: (212)456-2381
**Format:** Commercial TV

**WCBS-TV - 2 (22577)**
51 W. 52nd St.
524 W. 57th St.
New York, NY 10019
Phone: (212)975-2127

Fax: (212)975-1907
**Format:** Commercial TV

**WLIG-TV - 55 (21198)**
270 S. Service Rd.
Melville, NY 11747
Phone: (973)644-3164
Fax: (973)777-8180
**Format:** Commercial TV

**WNJB-TV - 58 (19606)**
New Jersey Network
PO Box 777
Trenton, NJ 08625-0777
Phone: (609)777-5000
Fax: (609)633-2927
**Format:** Public TV

**WNJT-TV - 52 (19903)**
New Jersey Network
25 S Stocton St.
Trenton, NJ 08611
Phone: (609)777-5000
Fax: (609)633-2927
**Format:** Public TV

**WNJU-TV - 47 (19103)**
2200 Fletcher Ave 6th Fl
Fort Lee, NJ 07024
Phone: (201)969-4247
Fax: (201)969-4111
**Format:** Commercial TV

**WNYW-TV - 5 (22591)**
205 E. 67th St.
New York, NY 10021
Phone: (212)452-5555
Fax: (212)879-1152
**Format:** Commercial TV

**WPIX-TV - 11 (22594)**
220 E. 42nd St.
New York, NY 10017
Phone: (212)949-1100
Fax: (212)986-1032
**Format:** Commercial TV

**WTBY-TV - 54 (20777)**
PO Box 534
Fishkill, NY 12524
Phone: (845)596-4610
**Format:** Commercial TV

**WWOR-TV - 9 (19788)**
9 Broadcast Plaza
Secaucus, NJ 07096
Phone: (201)348-0009
**Format:** Commercial TV

## Philadelphia, PA

**KYW-TV - 3 (27306)**
Independence Mall E.
Philadelphia, PA 19106
Phone: (215)233-3333
Fax: (215)238-4783
**Format:** Commercial TV

**WFMZ-TV - 69 (26097)**
300 E. Rock Rd.
Allentown, PA 18103
Phone: (610)797-4530
Fax: (610)798-4089
**Format:** Commercial TV

**WMGM-TV - 40 (19459)**
1601 New Rd.
Linwood, NJ 08221
Phone: (609)927-4440
Fax: (609)927-7014
**Format:** Commercial TV

**WNJS-TV - 23 (19007)**
New Jersey Network
PO Box 777
PO Box 777
Trenton, NJ 08625-0777
Phone: (609)777-5000
Fax: (609)633-2927
**Format:** Public TV

**WPHL-TV - 17 (27314)**
5001 Wynnefield Ave.
Philadelphia, PA 19131
Phone: (215)878-1700
Fax: (215)879-3665

**Format:** Commercial TV

**WPVI-TV - 6 (27315)**
4100 City Line Ave.
Philadelphia, PA 19131
Phone: (215)878-9700
Fax: (215)581-4530
**Format:** Commercial TV

**WTVE-TV - 51 (27473)**
1729 N. 11th St.
Reading, PA 19604
Phone: (610)921-9181
Fax: (610)921-9139
**Format:** Commercial TV

**WUVP-TV - 65 (19625)**
4449 N. Delsea Dr.
Newfield, NJ 08344
Phone: (856)691-6565
Fax: (856)691-2483
**Format:** Commercial TV

## Pittsburgh, PA

**KDKA-TV - 2 (27417)**
1 Gateway Center
Pittsburgh, PA 15222
Phone: (412)575-2200
Fax: (412)575-2399
**Format:** Commercial TV

**WPCB-TV - 40 (27633)**
Rte. 48, Signal Hill Dr.
Wall, PA 15148-1499
Phone: (412)824-3930
Fax: (412)824-5442
**Format:** Commercial TV

**WPGH-TV - 53 (27426)**
750 Ivory Ave.
Pittsburgh, PA 15214
Phone: (412)931-5300
Fax: (412)931-8135
**Format:** Commercial TV

**WPXI-TV - 11 (27429)**
11 Television Hill
Pittsburgh, PA 15214
Phone: (412)237-1100
Fax: (412)323-8097
**Format:** Commercial TV

**WQED-TV - 16 (27431)**
4802 5th Ave.
Pittsburgh, PA 15213
Phone: (412)622-1550
Fax: (412)622-1488
**Format:** Public TV

**WTAE-TV - 4 (27435)**
400 Ardmore Blvd.
Pittsburgh, PA 15221
Phone: (412)242-4300
Fax: (412)244-4512
**Format:** Commercial TV

## Portland-Poland Spring, ME

**WMTW-TV - 8 (12441)**
99 Danville Corner Rd.
PO Box 8
Auburn, ME 04210
Phone: (207)782-1800
Fax: (207)782-2165
**Format:** Commercial TV

## Providence, RI-New Bedford, MA

**WPRI-TV - 12 (27846)**
25 Catamore Blvd.
East Providence, RI 02914-1203
Phone: (401)438-3310
Fax: (401)431-1012
**Format:** Commercial TV

## Rochester, NY

**WUHF-TV - 31 (22859)**
360 East Ave.
Rochester, NY 14604
Phone: (585)232-3700
Fax: (585)546-4774

Circulation: ★ = ABC; △ = BPA; ♦ = CAC; ● = CCAB; ☐ = VAC; ⊕ = PO Statement; ‡ = Publisher's Report; Boldface figures = sworn; Light figures = estimated.

Rochester, NY

## Springfield, MA

**ABC-40 - 40 (14808)**
1300 Liberty St.
Box 40
Springfield, MA 01104
Phone: (413)733-4040
Fax: (413)781-1363
**Format:** Commercial TV

**WGBY-TV - 57 (14811)**
44 Hampden St.
Springfield, MA 01103
Phone: (413)781-2801
Fax: (413)731-5093
**Format:** Public TV

**WWLP-TV - 22 (14820)**
PO Box 2210
Springfield, MA 01102
Phone: (413)786-2200
Fax: (413)786-2261
**Format:** Commercial TV

## Syracuse, NY

**WCNY-TV - 24 (23051)**
506 Old Liverpool Rd.
PO Box 2400
Syracuse, NY 13220-2400
Phone: (315)453-2424
Fax: (315)451-8824
**Format:** Public TV

**WIXT-TV - 9 (20735)**
5904 Bridge St.
East Syracuse, NY 13057
Phone: (315)446-9999
Fax: (315)251-1567
**Format:** Commercial TV

**WSTM-TV - 3 (23058)**
1030 James St.
Syracuse, NY 13203
Phone: (315)477-9400
Fax: (315)474-5082
**Format:** Commercial TV

**WSYT-TV - 68 (23060)**
1000 James St.
Syracuse, NY 13203
Phone: (315)472-6800
Fax: (315)471-8889
**Format:** Commercial TV

## Watertown-Carthage, NY

**WNPE-TV - 16 (23132)**
1056 Arsenal St.
1056 Arsenal St.
Watertown, NY 13601
Phone: (315)782-3142
Fax: (315)782-2491
**Format:** Public TV

**WNPI-TV - 18 (22632)**
c/o WNPE-TV
1056 Arsenal St.
Watertown, NY 13601
Phone: (315)782-3142
Fax: (315)782-2491
**Format:** Public TV

## Wilkes Barre-Scranton, PA

**WNEP-TV - 16 (26743)**
16 Montage Mountain Rd.
Moosic, PA 18507
Phone: (570)346-7474
Fax: (570)347-0359
**Format:** Commercial TV

**WOLF-TV - 56/53 (27700)**
1181 Hwy. 315
Wilkes Barre, PA 18702-6928
Phone: (570)970-5600
Fax: (570)970-5601

**Format:** Commercial TV

**WVIA-TV - 44 (27449)**
100 WVIA Way
Pittston, PA 18640
Phone: (570)826-6144
Fax: (570)655-1180
**Format:** Public TV

**WWLF-TV - 56 (27702)**
1181 Hwy. 315
Wilkes Barre, PA 18702-6928
Phone: (570)970-5600
Fax: (570)970-5601
**Format:** Commercial TV

# Southern Central States

## Abilene-Sweetwater, TX

**KRBC-TV - 9 (29047)**
4510 S. 14th
Abilene, TX 79605
Phone: (915)692-4242
Fax: (915)692-8265
**Format:** Commercial TV

## Albuquerque (Santa Fe & Hobbs), NM

**KASA-TV - 2 (20022)**
1377 University Blvd.
Albuquerque, NM 87102
Phone: (505)246-2222
Fax: (505)766-7705
**Format:** Commercial TV

**KCHF-TV - 11 (20174)**
216-TV E. Frontage Rd.
Santa Fe, NM 87505
Phone: (505)473-1111
Fax: (505)345-5669
**Format:** Commercial TV

**KLUZ-TV - 41 (20031)**
2725-F Broadbent Pkwy. NE
Albuquerque, NM 87107
Phone: (505)342-4141
Fax: (505)344-8714
**Format:** Commercial TV; Hispanic

**KNAT-TV - 23 (20033)**
1510 Coors Rd. NW
Albuquerque, NM 87121
Phone: (505)836-6585
Fax: (505)831-8725
**Format:** Contemporary Christian

**KOAT-TV - 7 (20035)**
3801 Carlisle Blvd. NE
PO Box 25982
Albuquerque, NM 87125
Phone: (505)884-7777
Fax: (505)884-6282
**Format:** Commercial TV

**KOB-TV - 4 (20036)**
4 Broadcast Plaza SW
Box 1351
Albuquerque, NM 87103
Phone: (505)243-4411
Fax: (505)764-2522
**Format:** Commercial TV

**KRPV-TV - 27 (20153)**
2606 S. Main
Roswell, NM 88201
Phone: (505)622-5778
Fax: (505)622-3424
**Format:** Religious

## Alexandria, LA

**KALB-TV - 5 (12043)**
605 Washington St.
Alexandria, LA 71301
Phone: (318)445-2456
Fax: (318)442-7427

**Format:** Commercial TV

## Amarillo, TX

**KACV-TV - 2 (29086)**
2408 S. Jackson
Box 477
Amarillo, TX 79109
Phone: (806)371-5222
Fax: (806)371-5258
**Format:** Public TV

**KCIT-TV - 14 (29089)**
1015 S. Fillmore
Amarillo, TX 79101
Phone: (806)374-1414
Fax: (806)381-2943
**Format:** Commercial TV

## Austin, TX

**KLRU-TV - 18 (29267)**
2504-B Whitis
Austin, TX 78712
Phone: (512)471-4811
Fax: (512)475-9090
**Format:** Public TV

## Baton Rouge, LA

**KWBJ-TV - 39 (12283)**
608 Michigan St.
Morgan City, LA 70380
Phone: (985)384-6960
Fax: (985)385-1916
**Format:** Commercial TV

**WAFB-TV - 9 (12096)**
844 Government St.
Baton Rouge, LA 70802-6090
Phone: (225)383-9999
Fax: (225)379-7891
**Format:** Commercial TV

**WBRZ-TV - 2 (12099)**
1650 Highland Rd. (70802)
Box 2906
Baton Rouge, LA 70821
Phone: (225)387-2222
Fax: (225)336-2246
**Format:** Commercial TV

**WVLA-TV - 33 (12109)**
10000 Perkins Rd.
Baton Rouge, LA 70810
Phone: (225)766-3233
Fax: (225)768-9191
**Format:** Commercial TV

## Beaumont-Port Arthur, TX

**KBTV-TV - 4 (29293)**
6155 Eastern Freeway, Ste. 300
Beaumont, TX 77706
Phone: (409)840-4444
Fax: (409)899-4539
**Format:** Commercial TV

## Corpus Christi, TX

**KIII-TV - 3 (29471)**
PO Box 6669
Corpus Christi, TX 78466
Phone: (361)814-9463
Fax: (361)855-8419
**Format:** Commercial TV

**KORO-TV - 28 (29476)**
PO Box 2667
Corpus Christi, TX 78403-2667
**Format:** Commercial TV

**KRIS-TV - 6 (29478)**
409 S. Staples
Corpus Christi, TX 78401
Phone: (361)886-6100
Fax: (361)886-6175

Format: Commercial TV

## Dallas-Fort Worth, TX

**KDFI-TV - 27 (29583)**
400 N. Griffin St.
Dallas, TX 75202-1952
Phone: (214)720-4444
Fax: (214)720-3355
**Format:** Commercial TV

**KDFW-TV - 4 (29585)**
400 N. Griffin
Dallas, TX 75202
Phone: (214)720-4444
Fax: (214)720-3112
**Format:** Commercial TV

**KDTN-TV - 2 (29587)**
PO Box 612066
Dallas, TX 75261
**Format:** Public TV

**KDTX-TV - 58 (29985)**
2823 W. Irving Blvd.
Irving, TX 75061
Phone: (972)313-1333
Fax: (972)790-5853
**Format:** Religious

**KERA-TV - 13 (29590)**
3000 Harry Hines Blvd.
Dallas, TX 75201
Phone: (972)263-3151
Fax: (214)754-0635
**Format:** Public TV

**KUVN-TV - 23 (29598)**
2323 Bryan St., Ste. 1900
Dallas, TX 75201-2646
Phone: (214)758-2300
Fax: (214)758-2324
**Format:** Commercial TV

**KXTX-TV - 39 (29600)**
3900 Harry Hines Blvd.
PO Box 190307
Dallas, TX 75219
Phone: (214)521-3900
Fax: (214)523-5946
**Format:** Commercial TV

**WFAA-TV - 8 (29603)**
606 Young St.
Dallas, TX 75202-4810
Phone: (214)748-9631
Fax: (214)977-6585
**Format:** Commercial TV

## El Paso, TX (Las Cruces, NM)

**ICEP, Inc. - 44 (29663)**
5925 Cromo Dr.
El Paso, TX 79912-5537
Phone: (915)585-6344
Fax: (915)585-6333
**Format:** Commercial TV

**KDBC-TV - 4 (29666)**
2201 Wyoming
El Paso, TX 79903
Phone: (915)496-4444
Fax: (915)496-4591
**Format:** Commercial TV

**KFOX-TV - 14 (29668)**
6004 N. Mesa
El Paso, TX 79912
Phone: (915)833-8585
Fax: (915)833-8973
**Format:** Commercial TV

**KINT-TV - 26 (29672)**
5426 N. Mesa
El Paso, TX 79912
Phone: (915)581-1126
Fax: (915)581-1393
**Format:** Commercial TV

**KRWG-TV - 22 (20116)**
Box 30001, MSC:TV 22
NMSU
Las Cruces, NM 88003
Phone: (505)646-2222
Fax: (505)646-1924

**Format:** Public TV

**KSCE-TV - 38 (29677)**
6400 Escondido Dr.
El Paso, TX 79912-2939
Phone: (915)585-8838
Fax: (915)585-8841
**Format:** Religious; Educational

**KTSM-TV - 9 (29679)**
801 N. Oregon St.
El Paso, TX 79902
Phone: (915)532-5421
Fax: (915)532-6793
**Format:** Commercial TV

## Fort Smith, AR

**KFSM-TV - 5 (1101)**
PO Box 369
Fort Smith, AR 72902
Phone: (479)783-3131
Fax: (479)783-2912
**Format:** Commercial TV

**KFTA-TV - 24 (1081)**
15 S. Block St.
Ste. 101
Fayetteville, AR 72701
Phone: (479)571-5100
Fax: (479)571-8914
**Format:** Commercial TV

**KHOG-TV - 29 (1082)**
15 N. Church St.
Fayetteville, AR 72701
**Format:** Commercial TV

## Houston, TX

**KHTV-TV - 39 (29932)**
7700 Westpark Dr.
Houston, TX 77063
Phone: (713)390-5103
Fax: (713)781-3441
**Format:** Commercial TV

**KLTJ-TV - 22 (29942)**
1050 Gemini St.
Houston, TX 77058-2706
Phone: (281)212-1077
Fax: (281)212-1022
**Format:** Religious

**KTFH-TV - 49 & 33 (29954)**
256 N. Sam Houston Pkwy. E., Ste. 49
Houston, TX 77060
Phone: (281)820-4900
Fax: (281)820-4048
**Format:** Religious

**KTRK-TV - 13 (29957)**
3310 Bissonnett
Houston, TX 77005
Phone: (713)666-0713
Fax: (713)644-0013
**Format:** Commercial TV

**KXLN-TV - 45 (29961)**
9440 Kirby Dr.
Houston, TX 77054
Phone: (713)662-4545
Fax: (713)668-9054
**Format:** Commercial TV

## Lafayette, LA

**KADN-TV - 15 (12194)**
1500 Eraste Landry Rd.
Lafayette, LA 70506
Phone: (337)237-1500
Fax: (337)237-2237
**Format:** Commercial TV

**KATC-TV - 3 (12195)**
PO Box 63333
Lafayette, LA 70596
Phone: (337)235-3333
Fax: (337)235-9363

**Format:** Commercial TV

## Lake Charles, LA

**KPLC-TV - 7 (12220)**
320 Division St.
PO Box 1490
Lake Charles, LA 70601
Phone: (337)439-9071
Fax: (337)437-7600
**Format:** Commercial TV

**KVHP-TV2 - 29 (12222)**
129 W. Prien Lake Rd.
Lake Charles, LA 70601
Phone: (337)474-1316
Fax: (337)474-9028
**Format:** Commercial TV

## Laredo, TX

**KGNS-TV - 8 (30047)**
120 W. Delmar
PO Box 2829
Laredo, TX 78044
Phone: (956)727-8888
Fax: (956)727-5336
**Format:** Commercial TV

**KVTV-TV - 13 (30051)**
Box 2039
Laredo, TX 78044
Phone: (956)723-2923
Fax: (956)223-0474
**Format:** Commercial TV

## Little Rock, AR

**KARK-TV - 4 (1183)**
1401 W. Capital, Ste. 104
Little Rock, AR 72201
Phone: (501)376-4444
Fax: (501)376-1852
**Format:** Commercial TV

**KASN-TV - 38 (1185)**
10800 Colonel Glenn Rd.
Little Rock, AR 72204-8017
Phone: (501)225-0038
Fax: (501)225-0428
**Format:** Commercial TV

**KATV-TV - 7 (1186)**
PO Box 77
Little Rock, AR 72203
Phone: (501)372-7777
Fax: (501)324-7852
**Format:** Commercial TV

**KTHV-TV - 11 (1199)**
720 Izard St.
PO Box 269
Little Rock, AR 72203
Phone: (501)376-1111
Fax: (501)376-3719
**Format:** Commercial TV

**KVTN-TV - 25 (1202)**
PO Box 22007
Little Rock, AR 72221
Phone: (501)223-2525
Fax: (501)221-3837
**Format:** Religious

## Lubbock, TX

**KBZO-TV - 51 (30092)**
1220 Broadway
Lubbock, TX 79401
Phone: (806)763-6051
Fax: (806)744-8363
**Format:** Hispanic

**KCBD-TV - 11 (30093)**
5600 Avenue A
Lubbock, TX 79404
Phone: (806)744-1414
Fax: (806)744-0449

**Format:** Commercial TV

KTXT-TV - 5; 39  (30106)
Tech Sta.
Box 42161
Lubbock, TX 79409-2161
Phone: (806)742-2209
Fax: (806)742-1274
**Format:** Public TV

KUPT-TV - 22  (30107)
Box 3757
Lubbock, TX 79452
Phone: (806)745-3434
Fax: (806)748-1949
**Format:** Commercial TV

## McAllen-Brownsville, TX

KLUJ-TV - 44  (29794)
1920 Albert Coneway Dr., Ste. 117
1920 Albert Coneway Dr., Ste. 117
Harlingen, TX 78550
Phone: (956)425-4225
Fax: (956)412-1740
**Format:** Public TV

KMBH-TV - 60  (29796)
Box 2147
Harlingen, TX 78551
Phone: (956)421-4111
Fax: (956)421-4150
**Format:** Public TV

KVEO-TV - 23  (29347)
394 N. Expressway
Brownsville, TX 78521
Phone: (956)544-2323
Fax: (956)544-4636
**Format:** Commercial TV

## Monroe, LA-El Dorado, AR

KMCT-TV - 39  (12432)
701 Parkwood
West Monroe, LA 71291-5435
Phone: (318)322-1399
Fax: (318)323-3783
**Format:** Commercial TV

KNOE-TV - 8  (12270)
1400 Oliver Rd.
PO Box 4067
Monroe, LA 71201
Phone: (318)388-8888
Fax: (318)322-8774
**Format:** Commercial TV

## New Orleans, LA

WGNO-TV - 26  (12336)
World Trade Center, Ste. 2800
2 Canal St.
New Orleans, LA 70130
Phone: (504)260-2600
Fax: (504)619-6332
**Format:** Commercial TV

WVUE-TV - 8  (12347)
1025 S. Jefferson Davis Pkwy.
New Orleans, LA 70125
Phone: (504)486-6161
Fax: (504)483-1543
**Format:** Commercial TV

WYES-TV - 12  (12352)
916 Navarre Ave.
New Orleans, LA 70124
Phone: (504)486-5511
Fax: (504)483-8408
**Format:** Public TV

## Odessa-Midland, TX

KMID-TV - 2  (30175)
3200 LaForce Blvd.
Drawer 60230
Midland, TX 79711
Phone: (432)563-2222
Fax: (432)563-5819

**Format:** Commercial TV

KMLM-TV - 42  (30176)
PO Box 7708
Midland, TX 79708-7708
Fax: (915)561-8236
**Format:** Religious

KPEJ-TV - 24  (30229)
1550 W. I 20
PO Box 11009
Odessa, TX 79760
Phone: (432)580-0024
Fax: (432)337-6306
**Format:** Commercial TV

KWES-TV - 9  (30180)
PO Box 60150
Midland, TX 79711
Phone: (432)567-9999
Fax: (432)567-9992
**Format:** Commercial TV

## Oklahoma City, OK

KAUT-TV - 43  (25488)
11901 N. Eastern Ave.
PO Box 14190
Oklahoma City, OK 73131
Phone: (405)478-4300
Fax: (405)516-4329
**Format:** Commercial TV

KETA-TV - 13  (25490)
7403 N. Kelly Ave.
Box 14190
Oklahoma City, OK 73113
Phone: (405)848-8501
Fax: (405)841-9216
**Format:** Public TV

KFOR-TV - 4  (25491)
444 E. Britton Rd.
Oklahoma City, OK 73114-7515
Phone: (405)424-4444
Fax: (405)478-6206
**Format:** Commercial TV

KOCO-TV - 5  (25497)
1300 E. Britton Rd.
Oklahoma City, OK 73131
Phone: (405)478-3000
Fax: (405)478-6697
**Format:** Commercial TV

KOKH-TV - 25  (25500)
1228 E. Wilshire Blvd.
Oklahoma City, OK 73111
Phone: (405)460-5025
Fax: (405)478-4343
**Format:** Commercial TV

KTBO-TV - 14  (25504)
1600 E Hefner Rd.
Oklahoma City, OK 73131-1610
Phone: (405)848-1414
**Format:** Commercial TV

## Roswell, NM

KBIM-TV - 10  (20144)
214 N. Main St.
PO Box 910
Roswell, NM 88201
Phone: (505)622-2120
Fax: (505)623-6606
**Format:** Commercial TV

KOBR-TV - 8  (20149)
124 E. 4th St.
Roswell, NM 88201
Phone: (505)625-8888
Fax: (505)625-8866
**Format:** Commercial TV

## San Antonio (Kerrville), TX

KABB-TV - 29  (30381)
4335 NW Loop 410
San Antonio, TX 78229-5168
Phone: (210)366-1129
Fax: (210)377-4758

**Format:** Commercial TV

KENS-TV - 5  (30388)
5400 Fredericksburg Rd.
PO Box TV5
San Antonio, TX 78229
Phone: (210)366-5000
Fax: (210)377-0740
**Format:** Commercial TV

KHCE-TV - 23  (30389)
PO Box 691246
San Antonio, TX 78269-1246
Phone: (210)479-0123
Fax: (210)492-5679
**Format:** Religious; Educational

KSAT-TV - 12  (30400)
1408 N. St. Mary's St.
San Antonio, TX 78215
Phone: (210)351-1200
Fax: (210)351-1297
**Format:** Commercial TV

KWEX-TV - 41  (30408)
411 E. Durango
San Antonio, TX 78204
Phone: (210)227-4141
Fax: (210)227-0469
**Format:** Commercial TV

## Shreveport, LA-Texarkana, TX

KMSS-TV - 33  (12392)
PO Box 30033
Shreveport, LA 71130
Phone: (318)631-5677
Fax: (318)631-4195
**Format:** Commercial TV

KSLA-TV - 12  (12395)
1812 Fairfield
Shreveport, LA 71101
Phone: (318)222-1212
Fax: (318)677-6703
**Format:** Commercial TV

## Tulsa (Bartlesville), OK

KDOR-TV - 17  (25277)
2120 N. Yellowood
Broken Arrow, OK 74012
Phone: (918)250-0777
Fax: (918)461-8817
**Format:** Commercial TV

KTUL-TV - 8  (25655)
Box 8
Tulsa, OK 74101
Phone: (918)460-8000
Fax: (918)445-8888
**Format:** Commercial TV

## Tyler-Longview-Jacksonville, TX

KLTV-TV - 7  (30561)
PO Box 957
Tyler, TX 75710
Phone: (903)597-5588
Fax: (903)510-7847
**Format:** Commercial TV

## Victoria, TX

KAVU-TV - 25  (30583)
3808 N. Navarro
Victoria, TX 77901
Phone: (361)575-2500
Fax: (361)575-2255
**Format:** Commercial TV

## Waco-Temple-Bryan, TX

KBTX-TV - 3  (29361)
4141 E. 29th St.
Bryan, TX 77802
Phone: (979)846-7777
Fax: (979)846-1490

Format: Commercial TV

**KCEN-TV - 6 (30533)**
PO Box 6103
Temple, TX 76503
Phone: (817)773-6868
Fax: (817)859-4004
Format: News

**KNCT-TV - 46 (30020)**
PO Box 1800
Killeen, TX 76540
Phone: (817)526-1176
Fax: (817)526-1850
Format: Public TV

**KWTX-TV - 10 (30611)**
6700 American Plaza
PO Box 2636
Waco, TX 76702-2636
Phone: (254)778-0116
Fax: (254)751-1088
Format: Commercial TV

## Wichita Falls, TX-Lawton, OK

**KAUZ-TV - 6 (30640)**
PO Box 2130
Wichita Falls, TX 76307
Phone: (940)322-6957
Fax: (940)761-3331
Format: Commercial TV

**KSWO-TV - 7 (25393)**
Hwy. 7 E.
PO Box 708
Lawton, OK 73501
Phone: (580)795-2345
Fax: (580)357-5623
Format: Commercial TV

# Southern States

## Aguadilla-Mayaguez, Puerto Rico

**WCCV-TV - 54 (27758)**
PO Box 949
Camuy, PR 00627-0949
Phone: (787)898-5120
Fax: (787)898-0529
Format: Commercial TV

**WOLE-TV - 12 (27743)**
Bo. Palmar
PO Box 415
Aguadilla, PR 00605
Phone: (787)891-0390
Fax: (787)891-3380
Format: Commercial TV

**WORA-TV - 5 (27780)**
Ave. Gonzalez Clemente, No. 449
PO Box 43
Mayaguez, PR 00681
Phone: (787)831-5555
Fax: (787)833-0075
Format: Commercial TV

## Albany (Valdosta & Cordele), GA

**WALB-TV - 10 (6769)**
PO Box 3130
Albany, GA 31706-3130
Phone: (229)446-1010
Fax: (229)446-4000
Format: Commercial TV

**WSST-TV - 55 (7087)**
PO Box 917
Cordele, GA 31015
Phone: (229)273-0001
Fax: (229)273-8894
Format: Commercial TV

## Atlanta (Athens & Rome), GA

**WATC-TV - 57 (7345)**
1862 Enterprise Dr.
Norcross, GA 30093
Phone: (770)300-9828
Fax: (770)300-9838

Format: Educational

**WGCL-TV - 46 (6944)**
425 14th St. NW
Atlanta, GA 30318
Phone: (404)253-2788
Fax: (404)327-3003
Format: Commercial TV

**WSB-TV - 2 (6958)**
1601 W. Peachtree St. NE 30309
Atlanta, GA 30309
Phone: (404)897-7000
Fax: (404)897-7370
Format: Commercial TV

**WUPA-TV - 69 (6961)**
2700 NE Expy., BLDG. A
Atlanta, GA 30345
Phone: (404)325-6929
Fax: (404)633-4567
Format: Commercial TV

**WXIA-TV - 11 (6963)**
1611 W. Peachtree St. NE
Atlanta, GA 30309
Phone: (404)892-1611
Format: Commercial TV

## Augusta, GA

**WAGT-TV - 26 (6987)**
905 Broad St.
PO Box 1526
Augusta, GA 30903-1526
Phone: (706)826-0026
Fax: (706)261-0162
Format: Commercial TV

**WJBF-TV - 6 (6992)**
1001 Reynolds St.
PO Box 1404
Augusta, GA 30903
Phone: (706)722-6664
Fax: (706)722-0022
Format: Commercial TV

## Biloxi-Gulfport-Pascagoula, MS

**WLOX-TV - 13 (16757)**
208 Debuys Rd.
Biloxi, MS 39531
Phone: (228)896-1313
Fax: (228)896-0749
Format: Commercial TV

**WMAH-TV - 19 (16759)**
c/o WMPN-TV
3825 Ridgewood Rd.
Jackson, MS 39211
Phone: (601)432-6565
Fax: (601)982-6746
Format: Public TV

**WXXV-TV - 25 (16844)**
PO Box 2500
Gulfport, MS 39505
Phone: (228)832-2525
Fax: (228)832-4442
Format: Commercial TV

## Birmingham (Gadsden), AL

**WABM-TV - 68 (112)**
651 Beacon Parkway W, Ste. 105
Birmingham, AL 35209
Phone: (205)943-2168
Fax: (205)290-2114
Format: Commercial TV

**WIAT-TV - 42 (126)**
2075 Golden Crest Dr.
Birmingham, AL 35209
Phone: (205)322-4200
Fax: (205)320-2713
Format: Commercial TV

**WPXH-TV - 44 (135)**
2085 Golden Crest Dr.
Birmingham, AL 35209
Phone: (205)870-4404
Fax: (205)870-0544

Format: Commercial TV

**WTJP-TV - 60 (238)**
313 Rosedale Ave.
Gadsden, AL 35901-5361
Phone: (256)546-8860
Fax: (256)543-8623
Format: Religious; Public Radio

**WTTO-TV - 21 (138)**
651 Beacon Parkway W., Ste. 105
PO Box 832100
Birmingham, AL 35209
Phone: (205)943-2168
Fax: (205)290-2115
Format: Commercial TV

**WVTM-TV - 13 (140)**
1732 Valley View Dr
Birmingham, AL 35209
Phone: (205)933-1313
Fax: (205)933-7516
Format: Commercial TV

## Bristol,VA-Kingsport-Johnson Cty-Greenville,TN

**WJHL-TV - 11 (28663)**
PO Box 1130
PO Box 1130
Johnson City, TN 37605-1130
Phone: (423)926-2151
Fax: (423)434-4537
Format: Commercial TV

## Charleston, SC

**WITV-TV - 7 (28016)**
c/o South Carolina Educational Television
PO Box 11000
1101 George Rogers Blvd.
Columbia, SC 29211
Phone: (803)737-3200
Fax: (803)737-3476
Format: Public TV

**WTAT-TV - 24 (28199)**
4301 Arco Ln.
North Charleston, SC 29418
Phone: (843)744-2424
Fax: (843)554-9649
Format: Commercial TV

## Charlotte (Hickory), NC

**WCCB-TV - 18 (23365)**
1 Television Pl.
Charlotte, NC 28205
Phone: (704)372-1800
Fax: (704)376-3415
Format: Commercial TV

**WHKY-TV - 14 (23582)**
526 Main Ave. SE
PO Box 1059
Hickory, NC 28603
Phone: (828)322-5115
Fax: (828)322-8256
Format: Commercial TV

**WUNE-TV - 17 (23627)**
10 T.W. Alexander Dr.
PO Box 14900
Research Triangle Park, NC 27709-4900
Phone: (919)549-7000
Fax: (919)549-7201
Format: Public TV

**WUNG-TV - 58 (23746)**
c/o UNC-TV
10 T.W. Alexander Dr.
PO Box 14900
Research Triangle Park, NC 27709-4900
Phone: (919)549-7000
Fax: (919)549-7201
Format: Public TV

## Chattanooga (Cleveland), TN

**WDEF-TV - 12 (28530)**
3300 Broad St.
Chattanooga, TN 37408
Phone: (423)785-1200

## Chattanooga (Cleveland), TN

Fax: (423)785-1271
**Format:** Commercial TV

**WFLI-TV - 53 (28533)**
6024 Shallowford Rd., Ste. 100
Chattanooga, TN 37421
Phone: (423)893-9553
Fax: (423)893-9853
**Format:** Commercial TV

**WRCB-TV - 03 (28537)**
900 Whitehall Rd.
Chattanooga, TN 37405-3249
Phone: (423)267-5412
Fax: (423)267-6840
**Format:** Commercial TV

**WTCI-TV - 45 (28539)**
4411 Amnicola Hwy.
Chattanooga, TN 37406
Phone: (423)629-0045
Fax: (423)698-8557
**Format:** Public TV

**WTVC-TV - 9 (28540)**
4279 Benton Dr.
PO Box 60028
Chattanooga, TN 37406-0028
Phone: (615)756-5500
Fax: (615)757-7401
**Format:** Commercial TV

## Columbia, SC

**WIS-TV - 10 (28071)**
1111 Bull St.
Columbia, SC 29201
Phone: (803)758-1010
Fax: (803)758-1155
**Format:** Commercial TV

**WOLO-TV - 25 (28075)**
5807 Shakespeare Rd.
PO Box 4217
Columbia, SC 29240
Phone: (803)754-7525
Fax: (803)754-6147
**Format:** Commercial TV

**WRJA-TV - 27 (28246)**
18 N. Harvin St.
Sumter, SC 29150
Phone: (803)773-5546
Fax: (803)775-1059
**Format:** Public TV

## Columbus, GA (Opelika, AL)

**WACS-TV - 25 (7108)**
Rte. 1, Box 75A
Parrott, GA 39877-9620
Phone: (404)685-2400
Fax: (404)685-2591
**Format:** Public TV

**WLTZ-TV - 38 (7073)**
PO Box 12289
Columbus, GA 31917-2289
Phone: (706)561-3838
Fax: (706)563-8467
**Format:** Commercial TV

**WRBL-TV - 3 (7075)**
1350 13th Ave., No. 31902
PO Box 270
Columbus, GA 31902-0270
Phone: (706)323-3333
Fax: (706)327-6655
**Format:** Commercial TV

**WTVM-TV - 9 (7078)**
1909 Wynnton Rd
Columbus, GA 31906
Phone: (706)324-6471
Fax: (706)327-0179
**Format:** Commercial TV

**WXTX-TV - 54 (7079)**
PO Box 1848
Columbus, GA 31902
Phone: (706)561-5400
Fax: (706)322-7527

**Format:** Commercial TV

## Columbus-Tupelo (West Point), MS

**WCBI-TV - 4 (16799)**
PO Box 271
Columbus, MS 39703
Phone: (662)327-4444
Fax: (662)328-5222
**Format:** Commercial TV

**WLOV-TV - 27 (17025)**
PO Box 350
Beech Springs Rd.
Tupelo, MS 38802
Phone: (662)842-7620
Fax: (662)844-7061
**Format:** Commercial TV

**WMAB-TV - 2 (16963)**
c/o WMPN-TV
3825 Ridgewood
Jackson, MS 39211
Phone: (601)432-6565
Fax: (601)982-6746
**Format:** Public TV

**WMAE-TV - 12 (16908)**
3825 Ridgewood Dr.
Jackson, MS 39211
Phone: (601)432-6565
Fax: (601)982-6746
**Format:** Public TV

**WTVA-TV - 9 (17028)**
Box 350
Tupelo, MS 38801
Phone: (601)842-7620
Fax: (601)844-7061
**Format:** Commercial TV

## Dothan, AL

**WDFX-TV - 34 (194)**
2221 Ross Clark Dr.
Dothan, AL 36301
Phone: (334)794-3434
Fax: (334)794-0034
**Format:** Commercial TV

**WDHN-TV - 18 (195)**
Hwy. 52 E.
PO Box 6237
Dothan, AL 36302
Phone: (334)793-1818
Fax: (004)700-0623
**Format:** Commercial TV

## Florence-Myrtle Beach, SC

**WBTW-TV - 13 (28097)**
3430 TV Rd.
Florence, SC 29501
Phone: (843)317-1302
Fax: (843)317-1410
**Format:** Commercial TV

**WHMC-TV - 23 (28085)**
c/o South Carolina Educational Television
PO Box 11000
1101 George Rogers Blvd.
Columbia, SC 29211
Phone: (803)737-3200
Fax: (803)737-3476
**Format:** Public TV

**WJPM-TV - 33 (28099)**
c/o South Carolina Educational Television
1101 George Rogers Blvd.
Columbia, SC 29201
Phone: (803)737-3200
**Format:** Public TV

## Fort Myers-Naples, FL

**WFTX-TV - 36/4 (5862)**
621 SW Pine Island Rd.
Cape Coral, FL 33991
Phone: (239)574-3636
Fax: (239)574-4803

**Format:** Commercial TV

## Gainesville (Ocala), FL

**WOGX-TV - 51 (6160)**
35 Skyline Dr.
Lake Mary, FL 32746
Phone: (352)873-6951
Fax: (407)333-0234
**Format:** Commercial TV

## Greensboro-Winston Salem-High Point, NC

**WFMY-TV - 2 (23534)**
PO Box TV2
1615 Phillips Ave.
Greensboro, NC 27420
Phone: (336)379-9369
Fax: (336)273-9433
**Format:** Commercial TV

**WGHP-TV - 8 (23589)**
HP-8
2005 Francis St.
High Point, NC 27261
Phone: (336)275-1850
Fax: (336)841-8051
**Format:** Commercial TV

**WGPX-TV - 16 (23536)**
1114 N. O'Henry Blvd.
Greensboro, NC 27405
Phone: (336)272-9227
Fax: (336)272-9298
**Format:** Commercial TV

**WLXI-TV - 61 (23541)**
2109 Patterson St.
Greensboro, NC 27407
Phone: (336)855-5610
Fax: (336)855-3645
**Format:** Commercial TV

**WTWB-TV - 20 (23548)**
622-G Guilford College Rd.
Greensboro, NC 27409
Phone: (336)510-2020
Fax: (336)517-2020
**Format:** Commercial TV

**WUPN-TV - 48 (23883)**
3500 Myer Lee Drive
Winston-Salem, NC 27101
Phone: (336)274-4848
Fax: (336)723-8217
**Format:** Commercial TV

## Greenville-New Bern-Washington, NC

**WCTI-TV - 12 (23672)**
PO Box 12325
225 Glenburnie Dr.
New Bern, NC 28561
Phone: (252)638-1212
Fax: (252)637-4141
**Format:** Commercial TV

**WNCT-TV - 9 (23564)**
3321 S. Evans St.
PO Box 898
Greenville, NC 27835-0898
Phone: (252)355-8500
Fax: (252)355-8568
**Format:** Commercial TV

**WUNF-TV - 33 (23745)**
PO Box 14900
Research Triangle Park, NC 27709-4900
Phone: (919)549-7000
Fax: (919)549-7201
**Format:** Public TV

**WUNK-TV - 25 (23747)**
c/o UNC-TV
10 T.W. Alexander Dr.
PO Box 14900
Research Triangle Park, NC 27709-4900
Phone: (919)549-7000
Fax: (919)549-7201

**Format:** Public TV

**WUNM-TV - 19 (23749)**
c/o UNC-TV
10 T.W. Alexander Dr.
PO Box 14900
Research Triangle Park, NC 27709-4900
Phone: (919)549-7000
Fax: (919)549-7043
**Format:** Public TV

## Greenville-Spartanburg, SC-Asheville, NC

**WGGS-TV - 16 (28120)**
3409 Rutherford Rd. Ext.
PO Box 1616
Greenville, SC 29602
Phone: (864)244-1616
Fax: (864)292-8481
**Format:** Commercial TV; Religious

**WHNS-TV - 21 (28122)**
21 Interstate Ct.
Greenville, SC 29615
Phone: (864)288-2100
Fax: (864)297-0728
**Format:** Commercial TV

**WLOS-TV - 13 (23238)**
110 Technology Dr.
Asheville, NC 28803-3477
Phone: (704)651-4567
Fax: (828)255-4612
**Format:** Commercial TV

**WNTV-TV - 29 (28126)**
c/o South Carolina Educational Television
PO Box 11000
1101 George Rogers Blvd.
Columbia, SC 29211
Phone: (803)737-3200
Fax: (803)737-3476
**Format:** Public TV

**WRET-TV - 49/29 (28230)**
Box 4069
800 University Way
Media Building USCS
Spartanburg, SC 29305
Phone: (864)503-9371
Fax: (864)503-3615
**Format:** Public TV

**WSPA-TV - 7 (28233)**
Box 1717
Spartanburg, SC 29304
Phone: (864)576-7777
Fax: (864)587-4480
**Format:** Commercial TV

## Greenwood-Greenville, MS

**WMAO-TV - 23 (16838)**
c/o WMPN-TV
3825 Ridgewood Rd.
Jackson, MS 39211
Phone: (601)432-6565
Fax: (601)982-6746
**Format:** Public TV

## Huntsville-Decatur-Florence, AL

**WAFF-TV - 48 (274)**
1414 N. Memorial Pkwy.
Huntsville, AL 35810
Phone: (205)533-4848
Fax: (205)533-1337
**Format:** Commercial TV

**WHNT-TV - 19 (280)**
200 Holmes Ave.
Huntsville, AL 35801
Phone: (256)533-1919
Fax: (256)536-9468
**Format:** Commercial TV

**WZDX-TV - 54 (286)**
PO Box 3889
Huntsville, AL 35810
Phone: (256)533-5454
Fax: (256)533-5315

**Format:** Commercial TV

## Jackson, MS

**WDBD-TV - 40 (16900)**
1 Great Place
PO Box 10888
Jackson, MS 39209
Phone: (601)922-1234
Fax: (601)922-6752
**Format:** Commercial TV

**WJTV-TV - 12 (16905)**
1820 TV Rd.
Jackson, MS 39204
Phone: (601)372-6311
Fax: (601)371-8256
**Format:** Commercial TV

**WLBT-TV - 3 (16907)**
715 S. Jefferson St.
Jackson, MS 39201
Phone: (601)948-3333
Fax: (601)960-4435
**Format:** Commercial TV

**WMPN-TV - 29 (16910)**
3825 Ridgewood Rd.
Jackson, MS 39211
Phone: (601)432-6565
Fax: (601)982-6746
**Format:** Public TV

## Jacksonville (Brunswick), FL

**WJWB-TV - 17 (6109)**
9117 Hogan Rd.
Jacksonville, FL 32216
Phone: (904)641-1700
Fax: (904)641-0306
**Format:** Commercial TV

**WTLV-TV - 12 (6121)**
1070 E. Adams St.
Jacksonville, FL 32202
Phone: (904)354-1212
Fax: (904)354-3299
**Format:** Commercial TV

## Knoxville (Crossville), TN

**WATE-TV - 6 (28691)**
1306 Broadway NE
Knoxville, TN 37917
Phone: (615)637-6666
Fax: (615)525-4091
**Format:** Commercial TV

**WBIR-TV - 10 (28693)**
1513 Hutchison Ave.
Knoxville, TN 37917
Phone: (865)637-1010
Fax: (865)637-6380
**Format:** Commercial TV

**WSJK-TV - 2 (28703)**
1611 E. Magnolia
Knoxville, TN 37917-0321
Phone: (865)595-0220
Fax: (865)595-0300
**Format:** Public TV

## Laurel-Hattiesburg, MS

**WDAM-TV - 7 (16853)**
Hwy. 11 N
PO Box 16269
Hattiesburg, MS 39404-6269
Phone: (601)544-4730
Fax: (601)584-9302
**Format:** Commercial TV

## Lexington, KY

**WKYT-TV - 27 (11785)**
2851 Winchester Rd. 40509
PO Box 55037
Lexington, KY 40555
Phone: (859)299-0411
Fax: (859)299-5531

**Format:** Commercial TV

**WLEX-TV - 18 (11786)**
1065 Russell Cave Rd.
PO Box 1457
Lexington, KY 40591
Phone: (859)259-1818
Fax: (859)255-2418
**Format:** Commercial TV

**WLJC-TV - 65 (11530)**
PO Box Y
Beattyville, KY 41311
Phone: (606)464-3600
Fax: (606)464-5021
**Format:** Commercial TV

**WYMT-TV - 57 (11716)**
199 Black Gold Blvd.
PO Box 1299
Hazard, KY 41702
Phone: (606)436-5757
Fax: (606)439-3760
**Format:** Commercial TV

## Louisville, KY

**WAVE-TV - 3 (11848)**
725 S. Floyd St.
Louisville, KY 40203
Phone: (502)585-2201
Fax: (502)561-4115
**Format:** Commercial TV

**WBNA-TV - 21 (11849)**
3701 Fern Valley Rd.
Louisville, KY 40219
Phone: (502)964-2121
Fax: (502)966-9692
**Format:** Commercial TV

**WLKY-TV - 32 (11858)**
1918 Mellwood Ave.
PO Box 6205
Louisville, KY 40206
Phone: (502)893-3671
Fax: (502)897-2384
**Format:** Commercial TV

## Macon, GA

**WGNM-TV - 64 (7258)**
PO Box 2637
Macon, GA 31203
Phone: (478)746-6464
Fax: (478)745-2367
**Format:** Commercial TV

**WMAZ-TV - 13 (7263)**
1314 Gray Hwy.
PO Box 5008
Macon, GA 31208-5008
Phone: (912)752-1313
Fax: (912)752-1331
**Format:** Commercial TV

**WMGT-TV - 41 (7265)**
PO Box 4328
Macon, GA 31208-4328
Phone: (478)745-4141
Fax: (478)742-2626
**Format:** Commercial TV

## Memphis, TN

**WHBQ-TV - 13 (28793)**
485 S. Highland St.
Memphis, TN 38111
Phone: (901)320-1313
Fax: (901)320-1366
**Format:** Commercial TV

**WMAV-TV - 18 (16985)**
c/o WMPN-TV
3825 Ridgewood Rd.
Jackson, MS 39211
Phone: (601)432-6565
Fax: (601)982-6746
**Format:** Public TV

**WREG-TV - 3 (28805)**
803 Channel 3 Dr.
Memphis, TN 38103
Phone: (901)543-2333
Fax: (901)543-2198

## Meridian, MS

**WMAW-TV - 14 (16952)**
c/o WMPN-TV
3825 Ridgewood Rd.
Jackson, MS 39211
Phone: (601)432-6565
Fax: (601)982-6746
**Format:** Public TV

## Miami (Ft. Lauderdale), FL

**WBFS-TV - 33 (6272)**
16550 NW 52nd Ave.
Miami, FL 33014
Phone: (305)621-3333
Fax: (305)628-3448
**Format:** Commercial TV

**WHFT-TV - 45 (6437)**
3324 Pembroke Rd.
Pembroke Park, FL 33021
Phone: (954)962-1700
Fax: (954)962-2817
**Format:** Religious

**WLTV-TV - 23 (6277)**
9405 NW 41st
Miami, FL 33178
Phone: (305)470-2323
Fax: (305)471-4236
**Format:** Commercial TV

**WPLG-TV - 10 (6283)**
3900 Biscayne Blvd.
Miami, FL 33137
Phone: (305)576-1010
Fax: (305)325-2480
**Format:** Commercial TV

**WSCV-TV - 51 (6303)**
15000 SW 27th St.
Miramar, FL 33027
Phone: (305)888-5151
Fax: (305)888-9270
**Format:** Commercial TV

## Mobile, AL-Pensacola, FL

**WHBR-TV - 33 (420)**
22080 County Rd. 64
Robertsdale, AL 36567
Phone: (251)960-1191
Fax: (251)960-1192
**Format:** Religious

**WKRG-TV - 5 (329)**
555 Broadcast Dr.
Mobile, AL 36606
Phone: (251)479-5555
Fax: (251)473-8130
**Format:** Commercial TV

**WSRE-TV - 23 (6448)**
1000 College Blvd.
Pensacola, FL 32504-8998
Phone: (850)484-1200
Fax: (850)484-1255
**Format:** Public TV

## Montgomery-Selma, AL

**WAIQ-TV - 26 (367)**
1255 Madison Ave.
Montgomery, AL 36107
Phone: (334)264-9900
Fax: (334)264-7045
**Format:** Public TV

**WNCF-TV - 32 (376)**
3251 Harrison Rd.
Montgomery, AL 36109
Phone: (334)270-3200
Fax: (334)271-6348
**Format:** Commercial TV

**WSFA-TV - 12 (377)**
PO Box 251200
Montgomery, AL 36125-1200
Phone: (334)288-1212
Fax: (334)613-8302
**Format:** Commercial TV

## Nashville (Cookeville), TN

**WHTN-TV - 39 (28821)**
9582 Lebanon Rd.
Mount Juliet, TN 37122
Phone: (615)754-0039
Fax: (615)754-0047
**Format:** Religious

**WKRN-TV - 2 (28914)**
441 Murfreesboro Rd.
Nashville, TN 37210
Phone: (615)248-7200
Fax: (615)369-7329
**Format:** Commercial TV

**WNAB-TV - 58 (28918)**
631 Mainstream Dr.
Nashville, TN 37228
**Format:** Commercial TV

**WSMV-TV - 4 (28933)**
5700 Knob Rd.
Nashville, TN 37209
Phone: (615)353-4444
Fax: (615)353-2348
**Format:** Commercial TV

## Norfolk-Portsmouth-Newport News-Hampton, VA

**WUND-TV - 2 (23744)**
c/o UNC-TV
10 T.W. Alexander Dr.
PO Box 14900
Research Triangle Park, NC 27709-4900
Phone: (919)549-7000
Fax: (919)549-7201
**Format:** Public TV

## Orlando-Daytona Beach-Melbourne, FL

**WACX-TV - 55 (6389)**
4520 Parkbreeze Ct.
Orlando, FL 32808
Phone: (407)298-5555
**Format:** Commercial TV

**WBCC-TV - 60 (5885)**
1519 Clearlake Rd.
Cocoa, FL 32922
Phone: (321)433-7111
Fax: (321)433-7154
**Format:** Educational

**WCEU-TV - 15 (5923)**
PO Box 9245
Daytona Beach, FL 32120-9245
Phone: (386)254-4415
Fax: (386)254-4427

**WESH-TV - 2 (6392)**
PO Box 547697
Orlando, FL 32854
Phone: (407)645-2222
Fax: (407)539-7823
**Format:** Commercial TV

**WTGL-TV - 52 (6304)**
15000 SW 27th St.
Miramar, FL 33027-4147
Phone: (407)423-5200
Fax: (954)622-6107

## Paducah, KY-Cape Girardeau, MO-Marion, IL

**WPSD-TV - 6 (11939)**
PO Box 1197
Paducah, KY 42002-1197
Phone: (502)415-1900
Fax: (502)415-1995

## Panama City, FL

**WMBB-TV - 13 (6435)**
613 Harrison Ave.
Box 1340
Panama City, FL 32402
Phone: (850)769-2313
Fax: (850)769-8231
**Format:** Commercial TV

## Ponce, Puerto Rico

**WMTJ-TV - 40 & 26 (27794)**
PO Box 21345
Rio Piedras, PR 00928
Phone: (787)766-2600
Fax: (787)250-8546
**Format:** Public TV

## Raleigh-Durham, NC

**WLFL-TV - 22 (23724)**
3012 Highwoods Blvd.
Raleigh, NC 27604
Phone: (919)872-9535
Fax: (919)878-3341
**Format:** Commercial TV

**WRDC-TV - 28 (23730)**
3012 Highwoods Blvd., Ste. 101
Raleigh, NC 27604
Fax: (919)878-3697
**Format:** Commercial TV

**WTVD-TV - 11 (23448)**
411 Liberty St.
Durham, NC 27702-2009
Phone: (919)683-1111
Fax: (919)682-7225
**Format:** Commercial TV

**WUNC-TV - 4 (23743)**
PO Box 14900
Research Triangle Park, NC 27709-4900
Phone: (919)549-7000
Fax: (919)549-7201
**Format:** Public TV

**WUVC-TV - 40 (23481)**
230 Donaldson St.
Fayetteville, NC 28301
Phone: (910)323-4040
Fax: (910)323-3924
**Format:** Commercial TV

## Savannah, GA

**WGSA-TV - 34 (7406)**
401 Mall Blvd., Ste. 202-A
Savannah, GA 31406-4867
Phone: (912)692-8000
Fax: (912)692-0400
**Format:** Commercial TV

**WJWJ-TV - 16 (27984)**
925 Ribaut Rd.
Beaufort, SC 29901-1165
Phone: (843)524-0808
Fax: (843)524-1016
**Format:** Public TV

**WTOC-TV - 11 (7412)**
PO Box 8086
Savannah, GA 31412
Phone: (912)234-1111
Fax: (912)238-5133
**Format:** Commercial TV

## Tallahassee, FL-Thomasville (Bainbridge), GA

**WCTV-TV - 6 (6609)**
4000 County Rd. 12
Tallahassee, FL 32312
Phone: (850)893-6666
Fax: (850)893-5193

**Gale Directory of Publications & Broadcast Media/140th Ed.**  **Butte, MT**

Format: Commercial TV

**WFSU-TV - 11 (6613)**
1600 Red Barber Plaza
Tallahassee, FL 32310
Phone: (904)487-3170
Fax: (904)487-3093
Format: Public TV

**WTLH-TV - 49 (6293)**
PO Box 949
Midway, FL 32343-0949
Phone: (850)576-4990
Fax: (850)942-0062
Format: Commercial TV

**WTWC-TV - 40 (6619)**
8440 Deerlake Rd.
Tallahassee, FL 32312
Phone: (850)893-4140
Fax: (850)893-6974
Format: Commercial TV

**WTXL-TV - 27 (6620)**
8927 Thomasville Rd.
Tallahassee, FL 32312
Phone: (850)668-1460
Format: Commercial TV

## Tampa-St. Petersburg (Lakeland, Sarasota), FL

**WCLF-TV - 22 (5879)**
PO Box 6922
Clearwater, FL 33758-6928
Phone: (727)535-5622
Fax: (727)531-2497

**WEDU-TV - 3 (6665)**
1300 North Blvd.
Tampa, FL 33607
Phone: (813)254-9338
Fax: (813)253-0826
Format: Public TV

**WFTS-TV - 28 (6668)**
4045 N Himes Ave.
Tampa, FL 33607-6607
Phone: (813)354-2828
Fax: (813)870-2828
Format: Commercial TV

**WMOR-TV - 32 (6672)**
7201 E. Hillsborough Ave.
Tampa, FL 33610
Phone: (813)626-3232
Fax: (813)622-7732
Format: Commercial TV

**WTOG-TV - 44 (6516)**
365 105th Terr. NE
Saint Petersburg, FL 33716
Phone: (727)576-4444
Fax: (727)577-1806
Format: Commercial TV

**WTTA-TV - 38 (6678)**
7622 Bald Cypress Pl.
Tampa, FL 33614-2417
Phone: (813)886-9882
Fax: (813)880-8100
Format: Commercial TV

**WUSF-TV - 16 (6681)**
University of South Florida
4202 Fowler Ave., TVB100
Tampa, FL 33620-6902
Phone: (813)974-8700
Fax: (813)974-4806
Format: Public TV

**WVEA-TV - 62 (6683)**
2610 W. Hillsborough Ave.
Tampa, FL 33614
Phone: (813)872-6262
Fax: (813)998-3600
Format: Commercial TV

## West Palm Beach-Ft. Pierce-Vero Beach, FL

**WPBF-TV - 25 (6416)**
3970 RCA Blvd., Ste. 7007
Palm Beach Gardens, FL 33410
Phone: (561)694-2525

Fax: (561)624-1089
Format: Commercial TV

**WPEC-TV - 12 (6728)**
PO Box 198512
West Palm Beach, FL 33419-8512
Phone: (561)844-1212
Fax: (561)842-1212
Format: Commercial TV

**WXEL-TV - 42 (5842)**
3401 S. Congress Ave.
Boynton Beach, FL 33426
Phone: (561)737-8000
Fax: (561)369-3067
Format: Public TV

## Wilmington, NC

**WSFX-TV - 26 (23854)**
322 Shipyard Blvd.
Wilmington, NC 28412-1835
Phone: (910)343-8826
Fax: (910)202-0493
Format: Commercial TV

**WUNJ-TV - 39 (23866)**
PO Box 210
10 T.W. Alexander Dr.
Winnabow, NC 28479
Phone: (910)253-4191
Fax: (919)549-7239
Format: Public TV

# Western States

## Albuquerque (Santa Fe & Hobbs), NM

**KREZ-TV - 6 (4358)**
158 Bodo Dr.
PO Box 2508
Durango, CO 81301
Phone: (970)259-6666
Fax: (970)247-8472
Format: Commercial TV

## Anchorage, AK

**KTVA-TV - 11 (522)**
1007 W. 32nd Ave.
Anchorage, AK 99503
Phone: (907)273-3192
Fax: (907)273-3189
Format: Commercial TV

**KYES-TV - 5 (525)**
3700 Woodland Dr., Ste. 800
Anchorage, AK 99517
Phone: (907)248-5937
Fax: (907)339-3889
Format: Commercial TV

## Bakersfield, CA

**KBAK-TV - 29 (1413)**
1901 Westwind
Bakersfield, CA 93301
Phone: (661)325-6397
Fax: (661)327-5603
Format: Commercial TV

**KERO-TV - 23 (1421)**
321 21st St.
Bakersfield, CA 93301
Phone: (661)637-2320
Fax: (661)323-5538
Format: Commercial TV

**KUVI-TV - 45 (1432)**
5801 Truxtun Ave.
Bakersfield, CA 93309-0609
Phone: (805)328-7545
Fax: (805)328-7576

Format: Commercial TV

## Bend, OR

**KTVZ-TV - 21 (25731)**
PO Box 6038
Bend, OR 97708-6038
Phone: (541)383-2121
Fax: (541)382-1616
Format: Commercial TV

## Bethel, AK

**KYUK-TV - 4 (532)**
PO Box 468
Bethel, AK 99559
Phone: (907)543-3131
Fax: (907)543-3130
Format: Public TV

## Billings-Hardin, MT

**KSVI-TV - 6 (18080)**
445 S. 24th St. W.
Billings, MT 59102-6265
Phone: (406)652-4743
Fax: (406)652-6963
Format: Commercial TV

**KTVQ-TV - 2 (18081)**
3203 3rd Ave. N.
Billings, MT 59101
Phone: (406)252-5611
Fax: (406)252-9938
Format: Commercial TV

**KULR-TV - 8 (18082)**
2045 Overland Ave.
PO Box 80810
Billings, MT 59108-0810
Phone: (406)656-8000
Fax: (406)652-8207
Format: Commercial TV

## Boise, ID

**KAID-TV - 4 (7656)**
1455 N. Orchard
Boise, ID 83706
Phone: (208)373-7220
Fax: (208)373-7245
Format: Public TV

**KIVI-TV - 6 (7762)**
1866 E. Chisholm Dr.
Nampa, ID 83687
Phone: (208)467-3301
Fax: (208)381-6680
Format: Commercial TV

**KTVB-TV - 7 (7672)**
5407 Fairview Ave.
PO Box 7
83707
Boise, ID 83706
Phone: (208)375-7277
Fax: (208)378-1762
Format: Commercial TV

## Butte, MT

**KBZK-TV - 7 (18093)**
1128 E. Main St.
Bozeman, MT 59715
Phone: (406)586-3280
Fax: (406)586-4135
Format: Commercial TV

**KTVM-TV - 6 (18104)**
750 Dewey Blvd., Ste. 1
Box 3118
Butte, MT 59701
Phone: (406)494-7603
Fax: (406)494-2572
Format: Commercial TV

**KXLF-TV - 4 (18105)**
1003 S. Montana St.
PO Box 3500
Butte, MT 59701
Phone: (406)496-8400
Fax: (406)782-8906

## Casper-Riverton, WY

**KCWC-TV - 4 (33781)**
2660 Peck Ave.
Riverton, WY 82501
Phone: (307)856-6994
Fax: (307)856-3893
Format: Public TV

**KFNB-TV - 20, 25 (33690)**
1856 Skyview Dr.
Casper, WY 82601
Phone: (307)577-5923
Fax: (307)234-4005
Format: Commercial TV

**KGWC-TV - 14 (33691)**
1856 Skyview Dr.
Casper, WY 82601
Phone: (307)577-5923
Fax: (307)234-4005
Format: Commercial TV

**KGWL-TV - 5 (33750)**
c/o KGWN-TV
1856 Skyview Dr.
Casper, WY 82601
Phone: (307)577-5923
Fax: (307)234-4005
Format: Commercial TV

**KGWR-TV - 13 (33784)**
c/o KGWN-TV
1856 Skyview Dr.
Casper, WY 82601
Phone: (307)577-5923
Fax: (307)577-4005
Format: Commercial TV

**KTWO-TV - 2 (33697)**
1896 Skyview Dr.
Casper, WY 82601-9638
Format: Commercial TV

## Colorado Springs-Pueblo, CO

**KRDO-TV - 13 (4237)**
399 S. 8th St.
PO Box 1457
Colorado Springs, CO 80905
Phone: (719)632-1515
Fax: (719)520-9374
Format: Commercial TV

**KXRM-TV - 21 (4242)**
560 Wooten Rd.
Colorado Springs, CO 80915-3524
Phone: (719)596-2100
Fax: (719)591-4180
Format: Commercial TV

## Denver (Steamboat Springs), CO

**KTVD-TV - 20 (4179)**
11203 E. Peakview Ave.
PO Box 6522
Centennial, CO 80111
Phone: (303)792-2020
Fax: (303)790-4633
Format: Commercial TV

**KWGN-TV - 2 (4368)**
6160 S. Wabash Way
Englewood, CO 80111
Phone: (303)740-2222
Fax: (303)740-2847
Format: Commercial TV

## El Centro, CA-Yuma, AZ

**KECY-TV - 9 (1793)**
646 Main St.
El Centro, CA 92243
Phone: (619)353-9990
Fax: (619)352-5471
Format: Commercial TV

**KSWT-TV - 13 (995)**
1301 S. 3rd Ave.
Yuma, AZ 85364
Phone: (928)782-5113
Fax: (928)782-0320
Format: Commercial TV

## Eugene, OR

**KEZI-TV - 9 (25816)**
2295 Coburg Road, Ste. 200
PO Box 7009
Eugene, OR 97401-0009
Phone: (541)485-5611
Fax: (541)342-1568
Format: Commercial TV

## Fairbanks (North Pole), AK

**KATN-TV - 2 (545)**
516 2nd Ave.
Suite 400
Fairbanks, AK 99701
Phone: (907)452-2125
Fax: (907)456-8225
Format: Commercial TV

**KJNP-TV - 4 (604)**
Box 56359
North Pole, AK 99705
Phone: (907)488-2216
Fax: (907)488-5246
Format: Commercial TV; Religious

**KTVF-TV - 11 (554)**
3528 International Way
Fairbanks, AK 99701
Phone: (907)458-1800
Fax: (907)458-1820
Format: Commercial TV

## Fresno-Visalia (Hanford), CA

**KAIL-TV - 53 (1678)**
1590 Alluvial Ave.
Clovis, CA 93612
Phone: (209)299-9753
Fax: (209)299-1523
Format: Commercial TV

**KFTV-TV - 21 (1892)**
3239 W. Ashlan
Fresno, CA 93722
Phone: (559)222-2121
Fax: (559)222-0917
Format: Commercial TV

**KGMC-TV - 43 (1893)**
706 W. Herndon Ave.
Fresno, CA 93650
Phone: (559)435-7000
Fax: (559)435-3201
Format: Commercial TV

**KMSG-TV - 55 (1898)**
2144 Fine St.
Fresno, CA 93727
Phone: (559)455-5511
Fax: (559)455-0551
Format: Commercial TV

**KSEE-TV - 24 (1902)**
5035 E. McKinley
Fresno, CA 93727
Phone: (559)454-2424
Fax: (559)454-2485
Format: Commercial TV

## Grand Junction-Durango, CO

**KREX-TV - 5 (4438)**
345 Hillcrest Manor
Grand Junction, CO 81501
Phone: (970)242-5000
Fax: (970)242-0886
Format: Commercial TV

## Great Falls, MT

**KFBB-TV - 5 (18138)**
Box 1139, Harve Hwy.
Great Falls, MT 59403
Phone: (406)453-4377
Fax: (406)727-9703
Format: Commercial TV

**KRTV-TV - 3 (18142)**
PO Box 2989
Great Falls, MT 59403
Phone: (406)791-5400
Fax: (406)791-5479
Format: Commercial TV

**KTGF-TV - 16 (18143)**
118 6th St. S.
Great Falls, MT 59401-3688
Phone: (406)761-8816
Fax: (406)454-3484
Format: Commercial TV

## Honolulu, HI

**KBFD-TV - 32 (7583)**
1188 Bishop St.
Penthouse 1
Honolulu, HI 96813
Phone: (808)521-8066
Fax: (808)521-5233
Format: Commercial TV

**KGMD-TV - 9 (7586)**
1534 Kapiolani Blvd.
Honolulu, HI 96814
Phone: (808)973-5462
Fax: (808)944-5252
Format: Commercial TV

**KHON-TV - 2 (7589)**
88 Piikoi St.
Honolulu, HI 96814-4245
Phone: (808)591-2222
Fax: (808)593-8479
Format: Commercial TV

**KIKU-TV - 20 (7593)**
737 Bishop St., Ste. 1430
Honolulu, HI 96813-3204
Phone: (808)847-2021
Fax: (808)841-3326
Format: Commercial TV

## Idaho Falls-Pocatello, ID

**KIDK-TV - 3 (7711)**
1255 E. 17th St.
Idaho Falls, ID 83404
Phone: (208)522-5100
Fax: (208)522-5103
Format: Commercial TV

**KPVI-TV - 6 (7780)**
902 E. Sherman
Pocatello, ID 83201
Phone: (208)232-6666
Fax: (208)233-6678
Format: Commercial TV

## Juneau, AK

**KJUD-TV - 8 (575)**
175 S. Franklin St.
Juneau, AK 99801
Phone: (907)586-3145
Fax: (907)463-3041
Format: Commercial TV

## Las Vegas, NV

**KLAS-TV - 8 (18716)**
3228 Channel Lake Dr.
Box 15047
Las Vegas, NV 89114
Phone: (702)792-8888
Fax: (702)734-7437
Format: Commercial TV

**KLVX-TV - 10 (18718)**
4210 Channel 10 Dr.
Las Vegas, NV 89119
Phone: (702)799-1010
Fax: (702)799-2806
Format: Public TV

**KTNV-TV - 13 (18724)**
3355 South Valley View Blvd.
Las Vegas, NV 89102
Phone: (702)876-1313

Fax: (702)871-1961
**Format:** Commercial TV

**KVVU-TV - 5  (18674)**
25 TV-5 Dr.
Henderson, NV 89014
Phone: (702)435-5555
Fax: (702)451-4220
**Format:** Commercial TV

## Los Angeles (Corona & San Bernardino), CA

**KCOP-TV - 13  (2388)**
1999 S. Bundy
Los Angeles, CA 90025
Phone: (310)584-2000
Fax: (310)584-2024
**Format:** Commercial TV

**KHSC-TV - 46  (2625)**
3833 Ebony St.
Ontario, CA 91761
Phone: (909)390-8846
Fax: (909)390-8857
**Format:** Commercial TV

**KLCS-TV - 58  (2394)**
1061 W. Temple St.
Los Angeles, CA 90012
Phone: (213)625-6958
Fax: (213)481-1019
**Format:** Public TV

**KMEX-TV - 34  (2398)**
5999 Center Dr.
Los Angeles, CA 90045
Phone: (310)216-3434
Fax: (310)348-3493
**Format:** Hispanic

**KNBC-TV - 4  (1585)**
3000 W. Alameda Ave.
Burbank, CA 91523
Phone: (818)840-4444
Fax: (818)840-4271
**Format:** Commercial TV

**KTBN-TV - 40  (3413)**
Box A
Santa Ana, CA 92711
Phone: (714)832-2950
Fax: (714)665-2165
**Format:** Religious

**KTLA-TV - 5  (1975)**
5800 Sunset Blvd.
Hollywood, CA 90028
Phone: (323)460-5500
Fax: (323)460-5952
**Format:** Commercial TV

**KVCR-TV - 24  (2990)**
701 S. Mt. Vernon Ave.
San Bernardino, CA 92410-2798
Phone: (909)888-6511
**Format:** Public TV

## Medford, OR

**KDKF-TV - 31  (25873)**
231 E. Main St.
Klamath Falls, OR 97601-3231
Phone: (503)882-5648
Fax: (541)883-8931
**Format:** Commercial TV

**KOBI-TV - 5  (25909)**
125 S. Fir
PO Box 1489
Medford, OR 97501
Phone: (541)779-5555
Fax: (541)779-5564
**Format:** Commercial TV

**KOTI-TV - 2  (25878)**
222 S. 7th St.
PO Box 2K
Klamath Falls, OR 97601
Phone: (541)882-2222
Fax: (541)883-7664

**Format:** Commercial TV

**KSYS-TV - 8  (25912)**
34 S. Fir
Medford, OR 97501
Phone: (541)779-0808
Fax: (541)779-2178
**Format:** Public TV

## Palm Springs, CA

**KMIR-TV - 36  (2660)**
72920 Parkview Dr.
Palm Desert, CA 92260
Phone: (760)568-3636
Fax: (760)568-1176
**Format:** Commercial TV

## Phoenix (Kingman, Prescott), AZ

**KAET-TV - 8  (884)**
Arizona State University
Tempe, AZ 85287-1405
Phone: (480)965-3506
Fax: (480)965-1000
**Format:** Public TV

**KPAZ-TV - 21  (794)**
3551 E. McDowell
Phoenix, AZ 85008
Phone: (602)273-1477
Fax: (602)267-9427
**Format:** Commercial TV

**KPHO-TV - 5  (795)**
4016 N. Black Canyon
Phoenix, AZ 85017
Phone: (602)264-1000
Fax: (602)263-8818
**Format:** Commercial TV

**KPNX-TV - 12  (797)**
1101 N. Central Ave.
PO Box 711
Phoenix, AZ 85004
Phone: (602)257-1212
Fax: (602)258-8186
**Format:** Commercial TV

**KSAZ-TV - 10  (800)**
511 W. Adams St.
Phoenix, AZ 85003
Phone: (602)257-1234
Fax: (602)262-0177
**Format:** Commercial TV

## Portland, OR

**KATU-TV - 2  (25993)**
PO Box 2
Portland, OR 97207
Phone: (503)231-4222
Fax: (503)231-4263
**Format:** Commercial TV

**KOIN-TV - 6  (26005)**
222 SW Columbia St.
Portland, OR 97201
Phone: (503)464-0600
Fax: (503)464-0717
**Format:** Commercial TV

**KOPB-TV - 10  (26006)**
Oregon Public Broadcasting
7140 S.W. Macadam Ave.
Portland, OR 97219
Phone: (503)244-9900
**Format:** Public TV

**KPDX-TV - 49  (25718)**
14975 NW Greenbrier Pkwy.
Beaverton, OR 97006
Phone: (503)906-1249
Fax: (503)548-6910
**Format:** Commercial TV

**KPTV-TV - 12  (25719)**
14975 N. W. Greenbriar Pkwy.
Beaverton, OR 97006
Phone: (503)906-1249
Fax: (503)736-1290

**Format:** Commercial TV

## Reno, NV

**KAME-TV - 21  (18748)**
4920 Brookside Ct.
Reno, NV 89502
Phone: (775)856-2121
Fax: (775)856-9146
**Format:** Commercial TV

**KOLO-TV - 8  (18753)**
4850 Ampere Dr.
PO Box 10000
Reno, NV 89502-0005
Phone: (775)858-8888
Fax: (775)858-8855
**Format:** Commercial TV

**KREN-TV - 27  (18756)**
940 Matley Ln., Ste. 15
Reno, NV 89502-2139
Phone: (775)333-2727
Fax: (775)327-6827
**Format:** Commercial TV

**KRNV-TV - 4  (18757)**
1790 Vassar
Reno, NV 89502
Phone: (775)322-4444
Fax: (775)785-1200
**Format:** Commercial TV

## Sacramento-Stockton, CA

**KMAX-TV - 31  (2941)**
500 Media Pl.
Sacramento, CA 95815
Phone: (916)925-3100
Fax: (916)920-1078
**Format:** Commercial TV

**KOVR-TV - 13  (4033)**
2713 KOVR Dr.
West Sacramento, CA 95605
Phone: (916)374-1313
Fax: (916)374-1459
**Format:** Commercial TV

**KSPX-TV - 29  (2946)**
29 Television Circle
Sacramento, CA 95814
Phone: (916)443-2929
Fax: (916)443-2914
**Format:** Commercial TV

**KTXL-TV - 40  (2949)**
4655 Fruitridge Rd.
Sacramento, CA 95820
Phone: (916)454-4422
Fax: (916)739-1079
**Format:** Commercial TV

**KUVS-TV - 19  (2950)**
1710 Arden Way
Sacramento, CA 95815
Phone: (916)927-1900
Fax: (916)614-1904
**Format:** Commercial TV

## Salinas-Monterey, CA

**KSMS-TV - 67  (2506)**
67 Garden Ct.
Monterey, CA 93940
Phone: (831)757-6711
Fax: (831)373-6700
**Format:** Commercial TV

## Salt Lake City (Cedar City), UT

**KSTU-TV - 13  (30805)**
5020 W. Amelia Earhart Dr.
Salt Lake City, UT 84116
Phone: (801)536-1325
Fax: (801)536-1313
**Format:** Commercial TV

**KUTV-TV - 2  (30809)**
299 South Main St. Suite 150
Salt Lake City, UT 84119
Phone: (801)973-3000
Fax: (801)973-3349

**Format:** Commercial TV

## San Diego, CA

**KBNT-TV - 19 (3069)**
5770 Ruffin Rd.
San Diego, CA 92123-1013
Phone: (858)576-1919
Fax: (858)715-1919

**KFMB-TV - 8 (3075)**
7677 Enigeer Rd.
San Diego, CA 92111
Phone: (858)292-7600
Fax: (858)495-9363
**Format:** Commercial TV

**KGTV-TV - 10 (3077)**
Box 85347
San Diego, CA 92186
Phone: (619)237-1010
Fax: (619)262-1302
**Format:** Commercial TV

**KPBS-TV - 15 (3086)**
5200 Campanile Dr.
San Diego, CA 92182
Phone: (619)594-1515
Fax: (619)594-3812
**Format:** Public TV

**KUSI-TV - 51 (3094)**
PO Box 719051
San Diego, CA 92171
Phone: (858)571-5151
Fax: (858)571-4852
**Format:** News; Talk

## San Francisco-Oakland-San Jose

**KBWB-TV - 20 (3247)**
2500 Marin St.
San Francisco, CA 94124
Phone: (415)821-2020
Fax: (415)641-1163
**Format:** Commercial TV

**KCNS-TV - 38 (3249)**
1550 Bryant St., Ste. 740
San Francisco, CA 94103
Phone: (415)863-3800
Fax: (415)863-3998
**Format:** Commercial TV; Ethnic

**KDTV-TV - 14 (3253)**
50 Freemont St., 41st Fl.
San Francisco, CA 94105
Phone: (415)538-8000
Fax: (415)538-8053
**Format:** Commercial TV; Hispanic

**KGO-TV - 7 (3259)**
900 Front St.
San Francisco, CA 94111
Phone: (415)954-7926
Fax: (415)936-6402
**Format:** Commercial TV

**KICU-TV - 36 (3320)**
2102 Commerce Dr.
San Jose, CA 95131
Phone: (408)953-3636
Fax: (408)953-3610
**Format:** Commercial TV

**KPIX-TV - 5 (3270)**
855 Battery St.
San Francisco, CA 94111-1597
Phone: (415)362-5550
Fax: (415)765-8844
**Format:** Commercial TV

**KRON-TV - 4 (3273)**
1001 Van Ness Ave.
San Francisco, CA 94109
Phone: (415)441-4444
Fax: (415)561-8759
**Format:** Commercial TV

**KSTS-TV - 48 (3327)**
2349 Bering Dr.
San Jose, CA 95131
Phone: (408)435-8848
Fax: (408)433-5921

**Format:** Commercial TV; Hispanic

**KTNC-TV - 42 (1708)**
5101 Port Chicago Hwy.
Concord, CA 94520
Phone: (925)686-4242
Fax: (925)825-4242
**Format:** Commercial TV

**KTSF-TV - 26 (1565)**
100 Valley Dr.
Brisbane, CA 94005
Phone: (415)468-2626
Fax: (415)467-7559
**Format:** Commercial TV

**KTVU-TV - 2 (2609)**
2 Jack Lyndon Sq.
Oakland, CA 94607
Phone: (510)834-1212
Fax: (510)272-9957
**Format:** Commercial TV

## Santa Barbara-Santa Maria-San Luis Obispo, CA

**KADY-TV - 63 (1605)**
950 Flynn Rd.
Camarillo, CA 93012
Phone: (805)388-0081
Fax: (805)388-9693
**Format:** Commercial TV

**KCOY-TV - 12 (3468)**
1211 W. McCoy Ln.
Santa Maria, CA 93455
Phone: (805)925-1200
Fax: (805)922-9830
**Format:** Commercial TV

**KEYT-TV - 3 (3434)**
730 Miramonte Dr.
Santa Barbara, CA 93102
Phone: (805)882-3933
Fax: (805)882-3934
**Format:** Commercial TV

**K07TA-TV - 7 (3469)**
1138 W. Church
Santa Maria, CA 93458-4228
Phone: (805)928-7700
Fax: (805)928-8606
**Format:** Commercial TV

**KTAS-TV - 33 (3474)**
PO Box 172
Santa Maria, CA 93456-0172
Phone: (805)928-7700
Fax: (805)928-8606
**Format:** Commercial TV; Hispanic

## Seattle-Tacoma (Bellingham), WA

**KBCB-TV - 24 (32013)**
4164 Meridian St., Ste. 102
Bellingham, WA 98226
Phone: (360)647-8842
Fax: (360)647-9204
**Format:** Commercial TV

**KBTC-TV - 28 (32444)**
2320 S. 19th Street
Tacoma, WA 98405
Phone: (253)680-7700
Fax: (253)680-7725
**Format:** Commercial TV

**KCTS-TV - 9 (32349)**
401 Mercer St.
Seattle, WA 98109
Phone: (206)728-6463
Fax: (206)443-6691
**Format:** Public TV

**KING-TV - 5 (32354)**
333 Dexter Ave. N.
Seattle, WA 98109
Phone: (206)448-3166
Fax: (206)448-4525
**Format:** Commercial TV

**KTBW-TV - 20 (32094)**
1909 S. 341st Pl.
Federal Way, WA 98003
Phone: (253)927-7720
Fax: (253)874-7432

**Format:** Commercial TV; Religious

**KVOS-TV - 12 (32018)**
1151 Ellis St.
Bellingham, WA 98225
Phone: (360)671-1212
Fax: (360)647-0824
**Format:** Commercial TV

## Sitka, AK

**KTNL-TV - 13 (553)**
717 Farmers Loop Rd.
Fairbanks, AK 99712-1410
Fax: (907)457-3672
**Format:** Commercial TV

## Spokane, WA

**KAYU-TV - 28 (32403)**
4600 S. Regal
Spokane, WA 99223
Phone: (509)448-2828
Fax: (509)448-0926
**Format:** Commercial TV

**KHQ-TV - 6 (32410)**
PO Box 600
Spokane, WA 99210-0600
Phone: (509)448-4655
Fax: (509)448-4644
**Format:** Commercial TV

**KLEW-TV - 3 (7727)**
2626 17th St., Box 615
Lewiston, ID 83501
Phone: (208)746-2636
Fax: (208)746-4819
**Format:** Commercial TV

**KREM-TV - 2 (32419)**
Box 8037
4103 S. Regal St.
Spokane, WA 99223
Phone: (509)448-2000
Fax: (509)448-2090
**Format:** Commercial TV

**KXLY-TV - 4 (32429)**
W. 500 Boone Ave.
Spokane, WA 99201
Phone: (509)324-4000
Fax: (509)328-5274
**Format:** Commercial TV

## Tucson, AZ

**KGUN-TV - 9 (950)**
7280 E. Rosewood St.
Tucson, AZ 85710-1350
Phone: (520)722-5486
Fax: (520)290-7738
**Format:** Commercial TV

**KMSB-TV - 11 (953)**
1855 N. 6th Ave.
Tucson, AZ 85705
Phone: (520)770-1123
Fax: (520)629-7185
**Format:** Commercial TV

**KTTU-TV - 18 (961)**
1855 N. 6th Ave.
Tucson, AZ 85705
Phone: (520)624-0180
Fax: (520)629-7185
**Format:** Commercial TV

**KUAT-TV - 6 (963)**
University of Arizona
MLB Rm. 223
PO Box 210067
Tucson, AZ 85721
Phone: (520)621-5828
Fax: (520)621-9105
**Format:** Public TV

**KVOA-TV - 4 (966)**
Box 5188
Tucson, AZ 85703
Phone: (520)792-2270
Fax: (520)620-1309

Format: Commercial TV

## Twin Falls, ID

**KMVT-TV - 11 (7819)**
1100 Blue Lake Blvd. N.
Twin Falls, ID 83301
Phone: (208)733-1100
Fax: (208)733-4649
**Format:** Commercial TV

## Yakima, WA

**KAPP-TV - 35 (32509)**
PO Box 10208
Yakima, WA 98909-1208
Phone: (509)453-0351
Fax: (509)453-3623
**Format:** Commercial TV

**KEPR-TV - 19 (32192)**
c/o KIMA-TV
2801 Terrace Heights Dr.
Yakima, WA 98901
Phone: (509)575-0029
Fax: (509)248-1218
**Format:** Commercial TV

**KIMA-TV - 29 (32515)**
2801 Terrace Heights Dr.
2801 Terrace Heights Dr.
Yakima, WA 98901
Phone: (509)575-0029
Fax: (509)248-1218
**Format:** Commercial TV

**KNDU-TV - 25 (32235)**
3312 W. Kennewick Ave.
Kennewick, WA 99336-2916
Phone: (509)737-6700
Fax: (509)737-6767
**Format:** Commercial TV

**KYVE-TV - 47 (32522)**
1105 S. 15th Ave.
Yakima, WA 98902
Phone: (509)452-4700
Fax: (509)452-4704
**Format:** Public TV

# Central Provinces

## Detroit, MI

**CBET-TV - 9 (35953)**
825 Riverside Dr. W.
Windsor, ON, Canada N9A 5K9
Phone: (519)255-3411
Fax: (519)255-3412
**Format:** Commercial TV